PRESENTED TO

_____

_____

BY

_____

_____

ON

_____

_____

YOUR WORD IS A LAMP TO MY FEET AND
A LIGHT FOR MY PATH. PSALM 119:105

THIS CERTIFIES THAT

_____

AND

_____

WERE UNITED IN

*H*OLY *M*ATRIMONY

ON _____ THE _____

DAY OF _____ A.D. _____

AT _____

IN ACCORDANCE WITH THE LAWS OF _____

OFFICIATING _____

WITNESS _____

WITNESS _____

A MAN WILL . . . BE UNITED TO HIS WIFE
AND THEY WILL BECOME ONE FLESH. GENESIS 2:24

MARRIAGES

HUSBAND

WIFE

PLACE   DATE

HUSBAND

WIFE

PLACE   DATE

HUSBAND

WIFE

PLACE   DATE

HUSBAND

WIFE

PLACE   DATE

HUSBAND

WIFE

PLACE   DATE

HUSBAND

WIFE

PLACE   DATE

LOVE IS PATIENT, LOVE IS KIND . . .
LOVE NEVER FAILS. 1 CORINTHIANS 13:4,8

BIRTHS

NAME
_____

BORN TO _____ DATE

NAME
_____

BORN TO _____ DATE

NAME
_____

BORN TO _____ DATE

NAME
_____

BORN TO _____ DATE

NAME
_____

BORN TO _____ DATE

NAME
_____

BORN TO _____ DATE

NAME
_____

BORN TO _____ DATE

NAME
_____

BORN TO _____ DATE

YOU KNIT ME TOGETHER IN MY
MOTHER'S WOMB. PSALM 139:13

BAPTISMS

NAME

MINISTER

PLACE   DATE

NAME

MINISTER

PLACE   DATE

NAME

MINISTER

PLACE   DATE

NAME

MINISTER

PLACE   DATE

NAME

MINISTER

PLACE   DATE

NAME

MINISTER

PLACE   DATE

MAKE DISCIPLES OF ALL NATIONS,
BAPTIZING THEM. MATTHEW 28:19

SPECIAL EVENTS

EVENT
_____

PLACE _____ DATE _____

EVENT
_____

PLACE _____ DATE _____

EVENT
_____

PLACE _____ DATE _____

EVENT
_____

PLACE _____ DATE _____

EVENT
_____

PLACE _____ DATE _____

EVENT
_____

PLACE _____ DATE _____

THE LORD REIGNS,
LET THE EARTH BE GLAD. PSALM 97:1

CHURCH RECORD

EVENT

MINISTER

CHURCH   DATE

EVENT

MINISTER

CHURCH   DATE

EVENT

MINISTER

CHURCH   DATE

EVENT

MINISTER

CHURCH   DATE

EVENT

MINISTER

CHURCH   DATE

EVENT

MINISTER

CHURCH   DATE

You ARE . . . MEMBERS OF
GOD'S HOUSEHOLD. EPHESIANS 2:19

Deaths

NAME

DATE

NAME

DATE

NAME

DATE

NAME

DATE

NAME

DATE

NAME

DATE

NAME

DATE

NAME

DATE

FOR TO ME, TO LIVE IS CHRIST
AND TO DIE IS GAIN. PHILIPPIANS 1:21

The Quest
Study Bible

*F*or the LORD gives wisdom,
and from his mouth come
knowledge and understanding.

PROVERBS 2:6

The Quest Study Bible

*F*or the LORD gives wisdom,
and from his mouth come
knowledge and understanding.

PROVERBS 2:6

NEW INTERNATIONAL VERSION

Zondervan Publishing House
Grand Rapids, Michigan

You will be pleased to know that a portion of the purchase price of your new NIV Bible has been provided to International Bible Society to help spread the gospel of Jesus Christ around the world!

CONTENTS

WELCOME to The Quest Study Bible!

If you've ever read the Bible and found yourself asking the tough questions—why did that happen? what could this possibly mean? does this make any difference in my life right now?—then this Bible is just for you.

Thanks to the combined efforts of the editors of *Leadership* and *Christianity Today* and scores of contributors, the study helps in this Bible tackle difficult questions that you've always wanted answered but never had a chance to ask.

The Quest Study Bible was conceived in 1989 when representatives from two publishing companies, Zondervan Publishing House and Christianity Today, Inc., began discussing the possibilities of again working together on a landmark Bible edition (they had earlier collaborated on *The Student Bible*). As editors and researchers explored options, they agreed that Bible readers were routinely seeking answers to provocative questions that arose as they read the Bible. Comprehensive research was carried out on two primary levels. Focus groups from around the country evaluated the usefulness of potential study Bible features and helped select the features that would be included in this Bible. Finally, more than a thousand people received portions of Scripture (all 66 Bible books were represented in the survey) and were asked, "What questions do you have about this portion of the Bible?" Their responses helped determine what kinds of questions the notes would answer. Yes, they wanted explanations of puzzling terms and phrases, but most of all they wanted to understand the reasons behind the actions and instructions of Scripture. Overwhelmingly, people asked "how" and "why" questions.

What Makes this Bible Distinctive?

The Quest Study Bible is like a press conference. There's a prepared statement—the text of the Bible. In this case, it's the highly respected New International Version, today's most accurate and readable modern English translation.

After the text is presented, readers—like reporters at a press conference—address their most pressing questions to the spokesperson. In this Bible edition, the answers come from respected resource people—Bible scholars, pastors and writers—who provide interesting answers in an engaging style.

Here are some of the specific features you'll find in this Bible:

BOOK INTRODUCTIONS

At the beginning of each Bible book, you'll find direct answers to specific questions about the book: Who wrote it? Why? What should I look for as I read it? You'll begin to gain understanding of some of the themes covered in each Bible book.

TIME LINES AND MAPS

The time lines included in the introductions to many Bible books and the two-color maps strategically located throughout the Bible will help you locate when and where the action being described took place.

SIDE-COLUMN NOTES

This Bible is designed for maximum ease of use. The majority of the study helps are located right alongside the Bible text. Here you will find notes, many of which are formatted as questions and answers, which clarify the meaning of the Bible text. These notes deal with such issues as:

- **Perplexing words and phrases.**
- **The cultural context.** When reading the Bible, it is important to understand what was going on in the culture of the day—to grasp something of the way life was experienced by the people of Bible times.
- **"Reasonable cause" for God's mysterious action.** Why did God do the things he did—like punish a nation for its king's decision to take a census? We cannot completely know God's mind, but we can venture some plausible explanations.
- **Fair summations of controversial passages.** While recognizing that portions of the Bible have been debated for centuries, these study notes try to offer balanced summaries of the various interpretations.
- **Explanations of peculiar types of writing.** Why take the time to read a list of names? How should Biblical poetry be interpreted? Or ancient laws? The notes help explain the significance of these kinds of literature.
- **Other passages that cover the same or similar events or topics.** "Scripture Links" point you to other places in the Bible where a related event or topic is mentioned. These cross references typically indicate why the verse or passage to which you are directed is relevant.

You may find that some pages of *The Quest Study Bible* contain fewer study helps than other pages. Certain sections of the Scripture text do not lend themselves to the kinds of questions raised and explanations offered in *The Quest Study Bible.*

ARTICLES

On many pages of this Bible you will find special articles of pressing interest. These articles take on some of the most popular and provocative questions asked by contemporary readers of the Bible.

DICTIONARY

The dictionary found in the back of this Bible contains definitions of some of the names, words, phrases and place names found in the Scripture text of the New International Version. As you read the Bible, you will find these dictionary words marked in the Scripture text with a small "D"—alerting you that a definition of that word or phrase can be found in the dictionary. Only the first occurrence of the word or phrase on each Scripture page will be tagged with a "D."

SUBJECT INDEX

The Subject Index at the back of this Bible lists major subjects that may be of interest and gives you the Scripture verses and page numbers where notes or articles related to those subjects may be found.

INDEXES TO MAPS AND CHARTS

In the back of *The Quest Study Bible* you will find indexes to the in-text maps and the in-text charts. These indexes list all the titles of the two-color maps and the charts, as well as the page numbers where they are located.

CONCORDANCE

A concordance is included in the back of *The Quest Study Bible* to help you find Bible verses quickly and easily. Key words in a Bible verse will help you find a verse for which you remember a word or two but not a location.

READING PLAN

A carefully designed, multi-level reading plan is included in the back of this Bible. You choose from three "courses." Course 1 features two-week reading plans that take you quickly into passages every Christian should know. Course 2 lists 186 chapters to be read over six months; taken together, these selections provide a good foundation of Bible understanding. Course 3 takes you completely through the Bible in three years, alternating between Old Testament and New Testament readings.

THE WORD OF GOD

Far more important than any of the tools we've provided, however, is the text itself, the Word of God. The Bible is a supernaturally powerful book, one that can be explained simply to preschoolers and at the same time studied inexhaustively by scholars. Whatever your situation, whatever your need, we offer this new Bible edition with the hope and the prayer that the power of God's Word may penetrate and transform your heart.

ACKNOWLEDGMENTS

Many people worked very hard to make *The Quest Study Bible* a reality. In addition to those listed on the Contributors page, several others deserve our expressions of gratitude: Bruce Ryskamp, Jeannette Taylor, Linda Peterson and Doris Rikkers of Zondervan, together with Paul Robbins, Terry Muck and Roy Coffman of Christianity Today, Inc., were key players in early discussions of this new study Bible concept. Philip Yancey and Tim Stafford, authors of the notes in *The Student Bible*, offered helpful insights for this project as well. John LaRue, Hope Grant and Virginia Vagt helped design focus groups and surveys and tabulated the results. Richard Doebler played a huge role in overseeing hundreds of writing assignments and reviewing thousands of notes and articles. Bonnie Rice hosted countless lunches for editors and contributors as they refined questions and answers. Anne McGuinness managed the publication as a whole, coordinating the many people and projects involved in development and composition. June Gunden and her staff at Peachtree Proofreading Services provided an expert editorial eye. The monumental feat of typesetting was in the capable hands of Charles Hewitt and his expert team at Auto-Graphics, Inc. Sharon Wright applied her years of Bible design experience to create an appealing interior layout as well as charts and time lines. Production and printing were expertly handled by Randy VanderWel. Sarah Hupp along with Connie and Christina Van Dyke sorted through thousands of study notes to compile a comprehensive Subject Index. Denise Lyons, with the help of Ruth DeJager, Anne Berens, Sarah Hupp, Leslie Hoffman, Jesslyn De-Boer and Laura Weller, oversaw the coding and proofing of all study material through every stage of the project. Ryan Knutzen devoted many hours of research to development of time lines. It has been a great privilege to be involved in the making of this special Bible edition. The effect on me has been life-changing, and I would like nothing better than that reading *The Quest Study Bible* would have the same effect on you.

—Marshall Shelley
Editorial vice-president
Christianity Today, Inc.

EDITORIAL STAFF

GENERAL EDITOR:
Marshall Shelley

ASSOCIATE EDITORS:
Richard Doebler
Paul Woods

COPY EDITOR:
June Gunden

CONTRIBUTORS

Contributing Editors:
Jeanette D. Gardner
David L. Goetz
Kevin A. Miller
Kevin D. Miller
Stephen M. Miller
Bob Moeller
Elizabeth Cody Newenhuyse
Douglas C. Schmidt
Patricia H. Picardi
Jane M. Vogel
Gary Wilde

Editorial Assistant:
Cynthia Thomas

Contributors include:
Jim Abrahamson
Benjamin C. Aker
Robert Alden
Leslie Allen
Max E. Anders
Leith Anderson
Gleason L. Archer, Jr.
Greg Asimakoupoulos
Mark Bailey
Donald N. Bastian
Craig L. Blomberg
Darrell L. Bock
Greg Boyd
Stuart Briscoe
C. S. Burdan
Gary Burge
David Burnham
Lloyd Carr
John Castelein
Robert Chisholm
Rodney Clapp
Mark Coppenger
Raymond Dillard
Richard Doebler
John Duckworth
Jim Edlin
Lee Eclov
Mark Fackler
David Faust
Paul D. Feinberg
Jeron Ashford Frame
Mark J. Galli
Jeanette D. Gardner
William L. Gartner
George Gianoulis
Susan M. Gilliland
David L. Goetz
Reg Grant
Dietrich Gruen
Victor P. Hamilton
Janis Long Harris
Warren Heard
Gordon Hugenberger
Fisher Humphreys
Darrell W. Johnson
Jan Johnson
Robert K. Johnston
Walter C. Kaiser, Jr.
Dennis F. Kinlaw
Martin I. Klauber
John R. Kohlenberger III

Paul E. Koptak
Craig Brian Larson
Gary Larson
Douglas L. LeBlanc
Raymond Levang
Larry R. Libby
Tremper Longman III
Robert Lowery
Dennis Magary
William Marty
Steve Mathewson
Stephen M. Miller
Bob Moeller
Douglas J. Moo
Joe Morgado
Terry C. Muck
Michael D. Nelson
Phillip D. Nelson
Jeffrey Niehaus
Carolyn Nystrom
David O'Brien
J. Randall Petersen
Patricia H. Picardi
Timothy M. Powell
Steve Rabey
James W. Reapsome
Martha G. Reapsome
Deborah J. Rotman
Robert Saucy
Joel Scandrett
Douglas C. Schmidt
David Scholer
Samuel J. Schultz
Harry E. Shields
Ray C. Stedman
Richard Strauss
Douglas Stuart
Tim Sutherland
Daniel Taylor
Alden Thompson
Rick Thompson
Jim A. Townsend
Wil Triggs
Jane M. Vogel
Bruce Waltke
Gaylyn R. Whalin
W. Terry Whalin
Rob Wilkins
Will Willimon
Sherwood E. Wirt
J. Isamu Yamamoto
Robert Yarbrough

ABBREVIATIONS

GENESIS	Gen.	NAHUM	Nahum
EXODUS	Exodus	HABAKKUK	Hab.
LEVITICUS	Lev.	ZEPHANIAH	Zeph.
NUMBERS	Num.	HAGGAI	Haggai
DEUTERONOMY	Deut.	ZECHARIAH	Zech.
JOSHUA	Joshua	MALACHI	Mal.
JUDGES	Judges	MATTHEW	Matt.
RUTH	Ruth	MARK	Mark
1 SAMUEL	1 Samuel	LUKE	Luke
2 SAMUEL	2 Samuel	JOHN	John
1 KINGS	1 Kings	ACTS	Acts
2 KINGS	2 Kings	ROMANS	Romans
1 CHRONICLES	1 Chron.	1 CORINTHIANS	1 Cor.
2 CHRONICLES	2 Chron.	2 CORINTHIANS	2 Cor.
EZRA	Ezra	GALATIANS	Gal.
NEHEMIAH	Neh.	EPHESIANS	Eph.
ESTHER	Esther	PHILIPPIANS	Phil.
JOB	Job	COLOSSIANS	Col.
PSALMS	Psalm	1 THESSALONIANS	1 Thes.
PROVERBS	Prov.	2 THESSALONIANS	2 Thes.
ECCLESIASTES	Eccl.	1 TIMOTHY	1 Tim.
SONG OF SONGS	Song	2 TIMOTHY	2 Tim.
ISAIAH	Isaiah	TITUS	Titus
JEREMIAH	Jer.	PHILEMON	Philem.
LAMENTATIONS	Lam.	HEBREWS	Heb.
EZEKIEL	Ezek.	JAMES	James
DANIEL	Daniel	1 PETER	1 Peter
HOSEA	Hosea	2 PETER	2 Peter
JOEL	Joel	1 JOHN	1 John
AMOS	Amos	2 JOHN	2 John
OBADIAH	Obad.	3 JOHN	3 John
JONAH	Jonah	JUDE	Jude
MICAH	Micah	REVELATION	Rev.

THE NEW INTERNATIONAL VERSION is a completely new translation of the Holy Bible made by over a hundred scholars working directly from the best available Hebrew, Aramaic and Greek texts. It had its beginning in 1965 when, after several years of exploratory study by committees from the Christian Reformed Church and the National Association of Evangelicals, a group of scholars met at Palos Heights, Illinois, and concurred in the need for a new translation of the Bible in contemporary English. This group, though not made up of official church representatives, was transdenominational. Its conclusion was endorsed by a large number of leaders from many denominations who met in Chicago in 1966.

Responsibility for the new version was delegated by the Palos Heights group to a self-governing body of fifteen, the Committee on Bible Translation, composed for the most part of biblical scholars from colleges, universities and seminaries. In 1967 the New York Bible Society (now the International Bible Society) generously undertook the financial sponsorship of the project—a sponsorship that made it possible to enlist the help of many distinguished scholars. The fact that participants from the United States, Great Britain, Canada, Australia and New Zealand worked together gave the project its international scope. That they were from many denominations—including Anglican, Assemblies of God, Baptist, Brethren, Christian Reformed, Church of Christ, Evangelical Free, Lutheran, Mennonite, Methodist, Nazarene, Presbyterian, Wesleyan and other churches—helped to safeguard the translation from sectarian bias.

How it was made helps to give the New International Version its distinctiveness. The translation of each book was assigned to a team of scholars. Next, one of the Intermediate Editorial Committees revised the initial translation, with constant reference to the Hebrew, Aramaic or Greek. Their work then went to one of the General Editorial Committees, which checked it in detail and made another thorough revision. This revision in turn was carefully reviewed by the Committee on Bible Translation, which made further changes and then released the final version for publication. In this way the entire Bible underwent three revisions, during each of which the translation was examined for its faithfulness to the original languages and for its English style.

All this involved many thousands of hours of research and discussion regarding the meaning of the texts and the precise way of putting them into English. It may well be that no other translation has been made by a more thorough process of review and revision from committee to committee than this one.

From the beginning of the project, the Committee on Bible Translation held to certain goals for the New International Version: that it would be an accurate translation and one that would have clarity and literary quality and so prove suitable for public and private reading, teaching, preaching, memorizing and liturgical use. The Committee also sought to preserve some measure of continuity with the long tradition of translating the Scriptures into English.

In working toward these goals, the translators were united in their commitment to the authority and infallibility of the Bible as God's Word in written form. They believe that it contains the divine answer to the deepest needs of humanity, that it sheds unique light on our path in a dark world, and that it sets forth the way to our eternal well-being.

The first concern of the translators has been the accuracy of the translation and its fidelity to the thought of the biblical writers. They have weighed the significance of the lexical and grammatical details of the Hebrew, Aramaic and Greek texts. At the same time, they have striven for more than a word-for-word translation. Because thought patterns and syntax differ from language to language, faithful communication of the meaning of the writers of the Bible demands frequent modifications in sentence structure and constant regard for the contextual meanings of words.

A sensitive feeling for style does not always accompany scholarship. Accordingly the Committee on Bible Translation submitted the developing version to a number of stylistic consultants. Two of them read every book of both Old and New Testaments twice—once before and once after the last major revision—and made invaluable suggestions. Samples of the translation were tested for clarity and ease of reading by various kinds of people—young and old, highly educated and less well educated, ministers and laymen.

Concern for clear and natural English—that the New International Version should be idiomatic but not idiosyncratic, contemporary but not dated—motivated the translators and consultants. At the same time, they tried to reflect the differing styles of the biblical writers. In view of the international use of English, the translators sought to avoid obvious Americanisms on the one hand and obvious Anglicisms on the other. A British edition reflects the comparatively few differences of significant idiom and of spelling.

As for the traditional pronouns "thou," "thee" and "thine" in reference to the Deity, the translators judged that to use these archaisms (along with the old verb forms such as "doest," "wouldest" and "hadst") would violate accuracy in translation. Neither Hebrew, Aramaic nor Greek uses special pronouns for the persons of the Godhead. A present-day translation is not enhanced by forms that in the time of the King James Version were used in everyday speech, whether referring to God or man.

For the Old Testament the standard Hebrew text, the Masoretic Text as published in the latest editions of *Biblia Hebraica,* was used throughout. The Dead Sea Scrolls contain material bearing on an earlier stage of the Hebrew text. They were consulted, as were the Samaritan Pentateuch and the ancient scribal traditions relating to textual changes. Sometimes a variant Hebrew reading in the margin of the Masoretic Text was followed instead of the text itself. Such instances, being variants within the Masoretic tradition, are not specified by footnotes. In rare cases, words in the consonantal text were divided differently from the way they appear in the Masoretic Text. Footnotes indicate this. The translators also consulted the more important early versions—the Septuagint; Aquila, Symmachus and Theodotion; the Vulgate; the Syriac Peshitta; the Targums; and for the Psalms the *Juxta Hebraica* of Jerome. Readings from these versions were occasionally followed where the Masoretic Text seemed doubtful and where accepted principles of textual criticism showed that one or more of these textual witnesses appeared to provide the correct reading. Such instances are footnoted. Sometimes vowel letters and vowel signs did not, in the judgment of the translators, represent the correct vowels for the original consonantal text. Accordingly some words were read with a different set of vowels. These instances are usually not indicated by footnotes.

The Greek text used in translating the New Testament was an eclectic one. No other piece of ancient literature has such an abundance of manuscript witnesses as does the New Testament. Where existing manuscripts differ, the translators made their choice of readings according to accepted principles of New Testament textual criticism. Footnotes call attention to places where there was uncertainty about what the original text was. The best current printed texts of the Greek New Testament were used.

There is a sense in which the work of translation is never wholly finished. This applies to all great literature and uniquely so to the Bible. In 1973 the New Testament in the New International Version was published. Since then, suggestions for corrections and revisions have been received from various sources. The Committee on Bible Translation carefully considered the suggestions and adopted a number of them. These were incorporated in the first printing of the entire Bible in 1978. Additional revisions were made by the Committee on Bible Translation in 1983 and appear in printings after that date.

As in other ancient documents, the precise meaning of the biblical texts is sometimes uncertain. This is more often the case with the Hebrew and Aramaic texts than with the Greek text. Although archaeological and linguistic discoveries in this century aid in understanding difficult passages, some uncertainties remain. The more significant of these have been called to the reader's attention in the footnotes.

In regard to the divine name *YHWH*, commonly referred to as the *Tetragrammaton*, the translators adopted the device used in most English versions of rendering that name as "Lord" in capital letters to distinguish it from *Adonai*, another Hebrew word rendered "Lord," for which small letters are used. Wherever the two names stand together in the Old Testament as a compound name of God, they are rendered "Sovereign Lord."

Because for most readers today the phrases "the Lord of hosts" and "God of hosts" have little meaning, this version renders them "the Lord Almighty" and "God Almighty." These renderings convey the sense of the Hebrew, namely, "he who is sovereign over all the 'hosts' (powers) in heaven and on earth, especially over the 'hosts' (armies) of Israel." For readers unacquainted with Hebrew this does not make clear the distinction between *Sabaoth* ("hosts" or "Almighty") and *Shaddai* (which can also be translated "Almighty"), but the latter occurs infrequently and is always footnoted. When *Adonai* and *YHWH Sabaoth* occur together, they are rendered "the Lord, the Lord Almighty."

As for other proper nouns, the familiar spellings of the King James Version are generally retained. Names traditionally spelled with "ch," except where it is final, are usually spelled in this translation with "k" or "c," since the biblical languages do not have the sound that "ch" frequently indicates in English—for example, in *chant.* For well-known names such as Zechariah, however, the traditional spelling has been retained. Variation in the spelling of names in the original languages has usually not been indicated. Where a person or place has two or more different names in the Hebrew, Aramaic or Greek texts, the more familiar one has generally been used, with footnotes where needed.

To achieve clarity the translators sometimes supplied words not in the original texts but required by the context. If there was uncertainty about such material, it is enclosed in brackets. Also for the sake of clarity or style, nouns, including some proper nouns, are sometimes substituted for pronouns, and vice versa. And though the Hebrew writers often shifted back and forth between first, second and third personal pronouns without change of antecedent, this translation often makes them uniform, in accordance with English style and without the use of footnotes.

Poetical passages are printed as poetry, that is, with indentation of lines with separate stanzas. These are generally designed to reflect the structure of Hebrew poetry. This poetry is normally characterized by parallelism in balanced lines. Most of the poetry in the Bible is in the Old Testament, and scholars differ regarding the scansion of Hebrew lines. The translators determined the stanza divisions for the most part by analysis of the subject matter. The stanzas therefore serve as poetic paragraphs.

As an aid to the reader, italicized sectional headings are inserted in most of the books. They are not to be regarded as part of the NIV text, are not for oral reading, and are not intended to dictate the interpretation of the sections they head.

The footnotes in this version are of several kinds, most of which need no explanation. Those giving alternative translations begin with "Or" and generally introduce the alternative with the last word preceding it in the text, except when it is a single-word alternative; in poetry quoted in a footnote a slant mark indicates a line division. Footnotes introduced by "Or" do not have uniform significance. In some cases two possible translations were considered to have about equal validity. In other cases, though the translators were convinced that the translation in the text was correct, they judged that another interpretation was possible and of sufficient importance to be represented in a footnote.

In the New Testament, footnotes that refer to uncertainty regarding the original text are introduced by "Some manuscripts" or similar expressions. In the Old Testament, evidence for the reading chosen is given first and evidence for the alternative is added after a semicolon (for example: Septuagint; Hebrew *father*). In such notes the term "Hebrew" refers to the Masoretic Text.

It should be noted that minerals, flora and fauna, architectural details, articles of clothing and jewelry, musical instruments and other articles cannot always be identified with precision. Also measures of capacity in the biblical period are particularly uncertain (see the table of weights and measures following the text).

Like all translations of the Bible, made as they are by imperfect man, this one undoubtedly falls short of its goals. Yet we are grateful to God for the extent to which he has enabled us to realize these goals and for the strength he has given us and our colleagues to complete our task. We offer this version of the Bible to him in whose name and for whose glory it has been made. We pray that it will lead many into a better understanding of the Holy Scriptures and a fuller knowledge of Jesus Christ the incarnate Word, of whom the Scriptures so faithfully testify.

The Committee on Bible Translation

June 1978
(Revised August 1983)

Names of the translators and editors may be secured
from the International Bible Society,
translation sponsors of the New International Version,
1820 Jet Stream Drive, Colorado Springs, Colorado
80921-3696 U.S.A.

THE **OLD** TESTAMENT

GENESIS

Why read this book?

If you're like most people, you've wondered about the deep questions of life: *Why are we here? What is life all about?* Genesis takes you back to the beginning of time to find the answers. It tells about many beginnings: the first plants and animals; the first man and woman; the first sin; the first news of God's salvation. It also shows God's dealings with Noah, Abraham and others, demonstrating his desire to fellowship with his people.

Who wrote this book and when?

Moses probably wrote it around 1440 B.C. But since he was not an eyewitness to the creation, he relied on revelation from God and, perhaps, earlier oral or written records.

What period of history does it cover?

From the time of the creation (a date that can only be speculated) to the time when the Israelites arrived in Egypt and grew into a nation (about 1800 B.C.).

Why was it written?

To show that when God made the creation, it was good. But Genesis goes on to say that when sin entered the world, it corrupted the creation, and caused God to initiate his plan for salvation. Genesis provides the framework upon which the rest of the Bible builds.

To whom was it written?

Since this book announces that *all peoples on earth will be blessed* through Abraham (12:3), it seems fair to conclude that all people can benefit from the account of this patriarch and his descendants.

What to look for in Genesis:

Notice the focus Genesis places on the relationship between God and humanity—broken in the garden and restored through sacrifices and personal encounters with God. Through the stories of history Genesis illustrates cycles of sin and repentance.

When did these things happen?

TIME LINE	2200 BC	2100	2000	1900	1800	1700	1600	1500	1400
Creation, Fall									
The Flood									
The Tower of Babel									
Abraham's life (c.2166-1991 B.C.)									
Isaac's life (c.2066-1886 B.C.)									
Jacob's life (c.2006-1859 B.C.)									
Joseph's life (c.1915-1805 B.C.)									
Book of Genesis written (c.1446-1406 B.C.)									

Why did God's Spirit hover over the dark waters of the earth? (1:2)

To preserve that which had been created up to this point and to prepare it for the further activity of God. The Holy Spirit was just as much a participant in the creation as the other two persons of the Godhead. This verse celebrates the Spirit's role in that process.

Were these literal 24-hour days? (1:5–31)

See article: *How technical is this description of creation?* (chs. 1–2).

Evening . . . morning (1:5)

The Hebrew calendar calculates dates from sunset to sunset.

How was there light before God created the sun and the moon? (1:14–16)

Some say that the earlier *light* created by God (v. 3) was from some source other than the sun. They speculate about a chemical, electrical, radioactive or some other type of iridescence. Others say that the phrase *the heavens and the earth* (v. 1) means the universe—all the heavenly bodies including sun, moon and stars. According to this view God created the sources of light (v. 1) but did not reveal them until later (v. 3)—perhaps by removing some sort of cloud of darkness (v. 2). Finally he brought the process to completion and established the rhythm and order of the solar system that give us days, nights and seasons (v. 14). In this view, the sun and moon were in existence already when in v. 14 God assigned their place and purpose.

The Beginning

1 In the beginning God created the heavens and the earth. ²Now the earth was*ᵃ* formless and empty, darkness was over the surface of the deep, and the Spirit of God was hovering over the waters.

³And God said, "Let there be light," and there was light. ⁴God saw that the light was good, and he separated the light from the darkness. ⁵God called the light "day," and the darkness he called "night." And there was evening, and there was morning—the first day.
⁶And God said, "Let there be an expanse between the waters to separate water from water." ⁷So God made the expanse and separated the water under the expanse from the water above it. And it was so. ⁸God called the expanse "sky." And there was evening, and there was morning—the second day.
⁹And God said, "Let the water under the sky be gathered to one place, and let dry ground appear." And it was so. ¹⁰God called the dry ground "land," and the gathered waters he called "seas." And God saw that it was good.
¹¹Then God said, "Let the land produce vegetation: seed-bearing plants and trees on the land that bear fruit with seed in it, according to their various kinds." And it was so. ¹²The land produced vegetation: plants bearing seed according to their kinds and trees bearing fruit with seed in it according to their kinds. And God saw that it was good. ¹³And there was evening, and there was morning—the third day.
¹⁴And God said, "Let there be lights in the expanse of the sky to separate the day from the night, and let them serve as signs to mark seasons and days and years, ¹⁵and let them be lights in the expanse of the sky to give light on the earth." And it was so. ¹⁶God made two great lights—the greater light to govern the day and the lesser light to govern the night. He also made

ᵃ2 Or possibly become

How technical is this description of creation? (chs. 1–2)

While the "days" of creation could be either a figure of speech or literal 24-hour periods, this passage is nevertheless an orderly narration of what took place. It tells us that there is intelligence, meaning and purpose behind all existence. In other words, the word of God is seen in the *method* of creation as well as the *source* of creation (Psalm 33:6,9; Heb. 11:3). Yet human beings have been given the privilege to explore, through scientific investigation, how God may have engineered these events, and how long he took. Most understand the six days of creation to represent long periods of time, simply because 24-hour days were not created until the fourth day. Actually, the word *day* is used in chs. 1–2 in three distinct ways: (1) as approximately 12 hours of *daylight* (1:5); (2) as 24 hours (1:14) and (3) as a period of time involving, at the very minimum, the whole creative activity from day one to day seven (see 2:4, where the word that is translated *when* is the same word that is elsewhere translated *day*). The *light* (v. 3) did not come from the earth's sun if it was not created until the fourth day. It could have come from other sources that God provided in the universe prior to the sun. We can only speculate about what the atmospheric conditions might have been at that time.

the stars. **17**God set them in the expanse of the sky to give light on the earth, **18**to govern the day and the night, and to separate light from darkness. And God saw that it was good. **19**And there was evening, and there was morning—the fourth day.

20And God said, "Let the water teem with living creatures, and let birds fly above the earth across the expanse of the sky." **21**So God created the great creatures of the sea and every living and moving thing with which the water teems, according to their kinds, and every winged bird according to its kind. And God saw that it was good. **22**God blessed them and said, "Be fruitful and increase in number and fill the water in the seas, and let the birds increase on the earth." **23**And there was evening, and there was morning—the fifth day.

24And God said, "Let the land produce living creatures according to their kinds: livestock, creatures that move along the ground, and wild animals, each according to its kind." And it was so. **25**God made the wild animals according to their kinds, the livestock according to their kinds, and all the creatures that move along the ground according to their kinds. And God saw that it was good.

26Then God said, "Let us make man in our image, in our likeness, and let them rule over the fish of the sea and the birds of the air, over the livestock, over all the earth,*a* and over all the creatures that move along the ground."

27So God created man in his own image,
in the image of God he created him;

a26 Hebrew; Syriac all the wild animals

Why did God say, *Let us* [plural] *make man in our image?* (1:26)

Often kings refer to themselves in this way. The word for God in Hebrew (*Elohim*) is plural, so the statement likely indicates that God was taking counsel with himself. This may also hint at the mystery of the Trinity—in the unity of God there is plurality. Some think this describes God speaking to his heavenly court of angels.

What is *the image of God?* (1:27)

God's image does not refer to anything physical but rather to something spiritual. Most point to the human spirit by which individuals can communicate with God and have a relationship with their Maker. Some expressions of the human spirit may be the conscience, personality and will—aspects also seen in God's character. The Bible later speaks of other characteristics that we can have in common with God such as *righteousness and holiness* (Eph. 4:24).

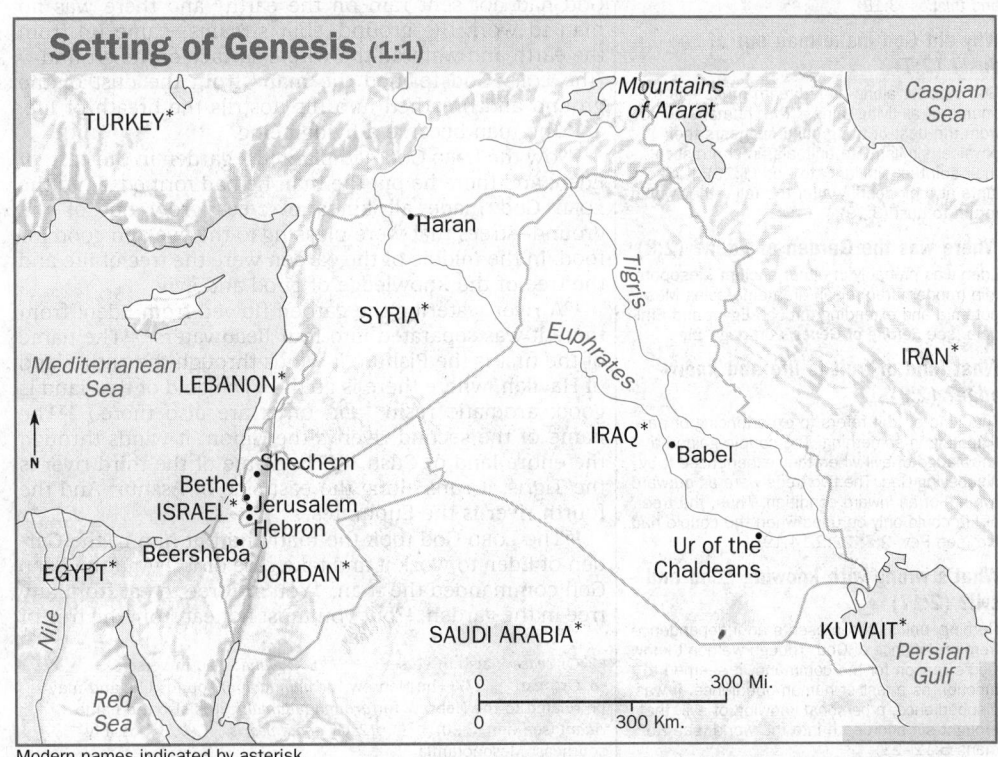

Setting of Genesis (1:1)

TURKEY*
Caspian Sea
Mountains of Ararat
•Haran
SYRIA*
Mediterranean Sea
LEBANON*
Tigris
Euphrates
IRAN*
Shechem
Bethel•
ISRAEL*•Jerusalem
•Hebron
Beersheba•
EGYPT*
JORDAN*
IRAQ*
•Babel
Ur of the Chaldeans•
Nile
SAUDI ARABIA*
KUWAIT*
Persian Gulf
Red Sea

N

0   300 Mi.
0   300 Km.

Modern names indicated by asterisk

male and female he created them.

28God blessed them and said to them, "Be fruitful and increase in number; fill the earth and subdue it. Rule over the fish of the sea and the birds of the air and over every living creature that moves on the ground."

29Then God said, "I give you every seed-bearing plant on the face of the whole earth and every tree that has fruit with seed in it. They will be yours for food. 30And to all the beasts of the earth and all the birds of the air and all the creatures that move on the ground—everything that has the breath of life in it—I give every green plant for food." And it was so.

31God saw all that he had made, and it was very good. And there was evening, and there was morning—the sixth day.

2 Thus the heavens and the earth were completed in all their vast array.

2By the seventh day God had finished the work he had been doing; so on the seventh day he resteda from all his work. 3And God blessed the seventh day and made it holy, because on it he rested from all the work of creating that he had done.

Adam and Eve

4This is the account of the heavens and the earth when they were created.

When the LORD God made the earth and the heavens—5and no shrub of the field had yet appeared on the earthb and no plant of the field had yet sprung up, for the LORD God had not 'sent rain on the earthb and there was no man to work the ground, 6but streamsc came up from the earth and watered the whole surface of the ground—7the LORD God formed the mand from the dust of the ground and breathed into his nostrils the breath of life, and the man became a living being.

8Now the LORD God had planted a garden in the east, in Eden; and there he put the man he had formed. 9And the LORD God made all kinds of trees grow out of the ground—trees that were pleasing to the eye and good for food. In the middle of the garden were the tree of life and the tree of the knowledge of good and evil.

10A river watering the garden flowed from Eden; from there it was separated into four headwaters. 11The name of the first is the Pishon; it winds through the entire land of Havilah, where there is gold. 12(The gold of that land is good; aromatic resine and onyx are also there.) 13The name of the second river is the Gihon; it winds through the entire land of Cush.f 14The name of the third river is the Tigris; it runs along the east side of Asshur. And the fourth river is the Euphrates.

15The LORD God took the man and put him in the Garden of Eden to work it and take care of it. 16And the LORD God commanded the man, "You are free to eat from any tree in the garden; 17but you must not eat from the tree of

---

What does it mean to *subdue* the earth? (1:28)

God entrusted humans to be the custodians of the planet's resources, which suggests using them responsibly. This verse is neither a license to abuse and waste the environment nor a prohibition against its use. God provided animals, minerals, trees, land and water for people to use to improve their lives.

Why did God rest? (2:2)

Not because he was tired. An all-powerful God doesn't need to rest. Perhaps he ceased working in order to mark a division between his work of creation and his later ongoing work in the world. Whatever the reason, it's clear that he modeled a pattern he wanted people to follow—that they would rest one day in seven, setting it apart as holy to the Lord.

Did plants come after humans? (2:5–7)

No. After tracing the creation of the universe (ch. 1), the theme narrows to focus on the humans placed in one particular spot within this universe. Two kinds of plant life are noted here—*shrub of the field* and *plant of the field*. This is not the same vegetation mentioned earlier. Rather these plants precede the *thorns and thistles* (3:18).

Why did God make man out of *dust*? (2:7)

God's power alone—his *breath of life*—is the source of all living things. That humans come from the dust of the ground suggests their physical similarity to animals, in contrast to their spiritual similarity to God (1:26). It also hints at their destiny after the fall—they would return to *dust* (3:19).

Where was the Garden of Eden? (2:8)

Eden was probably in either ancient Mesopotamia (modern Iraq) or an area embracing Mesopotamia and extending through Egypt and Ethiopia (see *Setting of Genesis* on page 3).

What kind of fruit is *life* and *knowledge*? (2:9)

This kind of fruit refers to experiencing or participating in something. The couple gained a knowledge of evil when they experienced it by disobeying God. The two trees were an outward symbol of an inward condition. Thus, the tree of life could only be used when the couple had life (see Rev. 2:7; 22:2,14,19).

What's wrong with knowing good and evil? (2:17)

Nothing, unless it represents an independence from or defiance of God. Though we don't know God's reason for the command, it seemed to function as a test of human obedience. It was disobedience, a *personal* knowing of evil, that brought sin and death into the world (see Romans 5:12–21).

---

a2 Or *ceased*; also in verse 3   b5 Or *land*; also in verse 6
c6 Or *mist*   d7 The Hebrew for *man (adam)* sounds like and may be related to the Hebrew for *ground (adamah)*; it is also the name *Adam* (see Gen. 2:20).   e12 Or *good; pearls*   f13 Possibly southeast Mesopotamia

the knowledge of good and evil, for when you eat of it you will surely die."

18The LORD God said, "It is not good for the man to be alone. I will make a helper suitable for him."

19Now the LORD God had formed out of the ground all the beasts of the field and all the birds of the air. He brought them to the man to see what he would name them; and whatever the man called each living creature, that was its name. **20**So the man gave names to all the livestock, the birds of the air and all the beasts of the field.

But for Adam*a* no suitable helper was found. **21**So the LORD God caused the man to fall into a deep sleep; and while he was sleeping, he took one of the man's ribs*b* and closed up the place with flesh. **22**Then the LORD God made a woman from the rib*c* he had taken out of the man, and he brought her to the man.

23The man said,

"This is now bone of my bones
   and flesh of my flesh;
she shall be called 'woman,*d*'
   for she was taken out of man."

24For this reason a man will leave his father and mother and be united to his wife, and they will become one flesh.

25The man and his wife were both naked, and they felt no shame.

The Fall of Man

3 Now the serpent was more crafty than any of the wild animals the LORD God had made. He said to the woman, "Did God really say, 'You must not eat from any tree in the garden'?"

2The woman said to the serpent, "We may eat fruit from the trees in the garden, **3**but God did say, 'You must not eat fruit from the tree that is in the middle of the garden, and you must not touch it, or you will die.' "

4"You will not surely die," the serpent said to the woman. **5**"For God knows that when you eat of it your eyes will be opened, and you will be like God, knowing good and evil."

a20 Or the man   *b21 Or took part of the man's side*   *c22 Or part*   *d23 The Hebrew for woman sounds like the Hebrew for man.*

What's the reason for marriage? (2:24)

Interpersonal chaos would result from unrestricted, random and casual pairings. The cohesiveness that the family unit offers society would dissolve. To provide a solid basis for the family, God set up this lifetime commitment and relationship between a man and a woman. God intended that the fullest and most satisfying expression of two becoming *one flesh* would be found in the marital covenant.

Why didn't their nakedness embarrass them? (2:25)

Nudity is not in itself a sin or a reason for shame. Only after the first couple fell into sin did they feel shame for their nakedness. This does not mean they lacked discretion prior to the introduction of shame. Sin distorted what God had intended to be beautiful, free of fear or guilt.

Why didn't they die for their sin? (3:2–3)

They did! They became spiritually *dead in . . . transgressions and sins* (Eph. 2:1), before eventually dying physically. The Bible refers to two kinds of death in addition to the physical. *Spiritual death* is the kind that causes guilty persons to hide from the presence of God, as Adam and Eve did. The *second death* refers to total and final separation from God (Rev. 20:14).

Why the unique creation of woman? (2:18–22)

God himself concluded it was not good for the male to be alone. While the animals and other creatures had been created in pairs, the Lord allowed Adam to come to the self-realization that he needed fellowship, friendship and intimacy from a creature corresponding to himself. Thus God made him a *helper.* This does not mean that women are inferior to men or that they are designed merely to be assistants to men. The word *helper* may more accurately mean a *strength* or a *power,* and thus women are comparable to men. Often God himself is designated by the term *helper* or *strength* (see, for example, Psalm 33:20). God, therefore, made woman for the man as his equal and his match as a partner in life. She was taken from *one of the man's ribs,* probably to show an interdependence. She was dependent on the man; men are dependent upon a woman to give birth to them. Some observe that the earliest language of Mesopotamia, Sumerian, has a word for *rib* that also means *life.*

How could fruit give wisdom? (3:6)

The woman, influenced by the serpent, apparently drew this mistaken conclusion.

Was Adam with Eve when she spoke to the serpent? (3:6)

We cannot say for certain. Perhaps Eve approached her husband later. Since Adam had walked and talked with God in the garden, some assume he wouldn't have been tricked as easily as one who was untaught. Paul argues that only the woman was deceived and tricked (1 Tim. 2:13–14). That doesn't flatter Adam, however. He simply disobeyed without any sinister pressure.

How did Adam and Eve realize they were naked? (3:7)

As a result of their loss of innocence, through disobedience. All since Adam and Eve's day have in some manner, and to some degree, carried a sense of shame as a result of the first sin.

Did God literally and visibly walk in the garden? (3:8)

Probably not, since God is spirit. *The sound of the LORD God ... walking in the garden* is a way of describing the infinite God in finite human terms. So real was the presence of God that it was as if they heard God's footsteps.

Is the curse the reason that snakes slither? (3:14)

No, the curse that the serpent would henceforth *crawl on* [his] *belly* was a way of saying that his downfall would be certain. Similar Biblical expressions refer to the abject humility of humans that were likewise conquered (Micah 7:17, for example). It would be wrong to imply from the curse that snakes originally walked upright on feet.

SCRIPTURE LINK (3:15) *He will crush your head, and you will strike his heel*

An early hint of God's plan of salvation through the cross. See Romans 16:20; Rev. 12:9.

What do labor pains have to do with sin? (3:16)

Perhaps nothing; the conception and birth of children would remain a blessing from God (1:28). The emphasis here may be on the sorrow of raising children in a sin-tainted world, rather than on the pain of childbearing itself. However, some believe the consequences of sin ruined creation not only by introducing pain into childbirth but by opening the world to all sorrow, pain and illness.

Your desire will be for your husband (3:16)

Some see this as a warning that women will *turn* (from God) to their husbands, who, in turn, will rule over them. Others see *desire* as a source of conflict between husbands and wives, just as sin *desires* to dominate and control (4:7).

How had the knowledge of good and evil made the man like God? (3:22)

Perhaps irony—a literary device—is employed in the language here. The serpent's promise was at least partly true: Adam and Eve gained an experiential knowledge they had never had

[6] When the woman saw that the fruit of the tree was good for food and pleasing to the eye, and also desirable for gaining wisdom, she took some and ate it. She also gave some to her husband, who was with her, and he ate it. [7] Then the eyes of both of them were opened, and they realized they were naked; so they sewed fig leaves together and made coverings for themselves.

[8] Then the man and his wife heard the sound of the LORD God as he was walking in the garden in the cool of the day, and they hid from the LORD God among the trees of the garden. [9] But the LORD God called to the man, "Where are you?"

[10] He answered, "I heard you in the garden, and I was afraid because I was naked; so I hid."

[11] And he said, "Who told you that you were naked? Have you eaten from the tree that I commanded you not to eat from?"

[12] The man said, "The woman you put here with me—she gave me some fruit from the tree, and I ate it."

[13] Then the LORD God said to the woman, "What is this you have done?"

The woman said, "The serpent deceived me, and I ate."

[14] So the LORD God said to the serpent, "Because you have done this,

> "Cursed are you above all the livestock
>   and all the wild animals!
> You will crawl on your belly
>   and you will eat dust
>   all the days of your life.
> [15] And I will put enmity
>   between you and the woman,
>   and between your offspring[a] and hers;
> he will crush[b] your head,
>   and you will strike his heel."

[16] To the woman he said,

> "I will greatly increase your pains in
>   childbearing;
>   with pain you will give birth to children.
> Your desire will be for your husband,
>   and he will rule over you."

[17] To Adam he said, "Because you listened to your wife and ate from the tree about which I commanded you, 'You must not eat of it,'

> "Cursed is the ground because of you;
>   through painful toil you will eat of it
>   all the days of your life.
> [18] It will produce thorns and thistles for you,
>   and you will eat the plants of the field.
> [19] By the sweat of your brow
>   you will eat your food
> until you return to the ground,
>   since from it you were taken;
> for dust you are
>   and to dust you will return."

[20] Adam[c] named his wife Eve,[d] because she would become the mother of all the living. [21] The LORD God made garments of skin for Adam and his wife and clothed them. [22] And the LORD God said, "The

---

[a] 15 Or *seed*   [b] 15 Or *strike*   [c] 20 Or *The man*   [d] 20 Eve probably means *living*.

man has now become like one of us, knowing good and evil. He must not be allowed to reach out his hand and take also from the tree of life and eat, and live forever." ²³So the LORD God banished him from the Garden of Eden to work the ground from which he had been taken. ²⁴After he drove the man out, he placed on the east side*ᵃ* of the Garden of Eden cherubimᴰ and a flaming sword flashing back and forth to guard the way to the tree of life.

Cain and Abel

4 Adam*ᵇ* lay with his wife Eve, and she became pregnant and gave birth to Cain.*ᶜ* She said, "With the help of the LORD I have brought forth*ᵈ* a man." ²Later she gave birth to his brother Abel.

Now Abel kept flocks, and Cain worked the soil. ³In the course of time Cain brought some of the fruits of the soil as an offering to the LORD. ⁴But Abel brought fat portions from some of the firstbornᴰ of his flock. The LORD looked with favor on Abel and his offering, ⁵but on Cain and his offering he did not look with favor. So Cain was very angry, and his face was downcast.

⁶Then the LORD said to Cain, "Why are you angry? Why is your face downcast? ⁷If you do what is right, will you not be accepted? But if you do not do what is right, sin is crouching at your door; it desires to have you, but you must master it."

⁸Now Cain said to his brother Abel, "Let's go out to the field."*ᵉ* And while they were in the field, Cain attacked his brother Abel and killed him.

⁹Then the LORD said to Cain, "Where is your brother Abel?"

"I don't know," he replied. "Am I my brother's keeper?"

¹⁰The LORD said, "What have you done? Listen! Your brother's blood cries out to me from the ground. ¹¹Now you are under a curse and driven from the ground, which opened its mouth to receive your brother's blood from your hand. ¹²When you work the ground, it will no longer yield its crops for you. You will be a restless wanderer on the earth."

¹³Cain said to the LORD, "My punishment is more than I can bear. ¹⁴Today you are driving me from the land, and I will be hidden from your presence; I will be a restless wanderer on the earth, and whoever finds me will kill me."

¹⁵But the LORD said to him, "Not so*ᶠ*; if anyone kills Cain, he will suffer vengeance seven times over." Then the LORD put a mark on Cain so that no one who found him would kill him. ¹⁶So Cain went out from the LORD's presence and lived in the land of Nod,*ᵍ* east of Eden.

¹⁷Cain lay with his wife, and she became pregnant and gave birth to Enoch. Cain was then building a city, and he named it after his son Enoch. ¹⁸To Enoch was born Irad, and Irad was the father of Mehujael, and Mehujael was the father of Methushael, and Methushael was the father of Lamech.

¹⁹Lamech married two women, one named Adah and the other Zillah. ²⁰Adah gave birth to Jabal; he was the fa-

---

ᵃ24 Or *placed in front*   *ᵇ1* Or *The man*   *ᶜ1 Cain* sounds like the Hebrew for *brought forth* or *acquired.*   *ᵈ1* Or *have acquired*   *ᵉ8* Samaritan Pentateuch, Septuagint, Vulgate and Syriac; Masoretic Text does not have *"Let's go out to the field."*   *ᶠ15* Septuagint, Vulgate and Syriac; Hebrew *Very well*   *ᵍ16 Nod* means *wandering* (see verses 12 and 14).

---

before. But the essence of Satan's deception was that it relied on partial truth. Though their experience expanded their knowledge, Adam and Eve did not achieve divinity or immortality.

One of us (3:22)

See *Why did God say, Let us* [plural] *make man in our image?* (1:26).

Why guard just *the east side*? (3:24)

The Bible doesn't say. Though it seems this was the direction in which people moved away from the garden (see 4:16; 11:2), *east* may have only signified being outside the garden.

What had Cain done wrong? (4:5–7)

Apparently Cain's motives and attitudes were unacceptable to God. The Bible tells us that, because of Abel's faith, his sacrifice was better than Cain's (Heb. 11:4). Abel first offered himself and then brought the best and most expensive portion to God. It was not Cain's offering itself that was wrong; grain offerings and harvest offerings would later be legitimate expressions of worship. But God is pleased with a pure heart, which Cain's was not.

How could Cain master sin? (4:7)

The point of the challenge God put to Cain was that he would have to make a decision about what he would do. (Some say the thrust of these words actually form a question: "Will you master it?") To conquer sinful nature by God's grace requires a decision first that we want to overcome sin.

Of whom was Cain afraid? (4:14)

Some think Cain anticipated that Adam and Eve would quickly produce many relatives who would want to take revenge on him. Others suggest that God perhaps created other humans besides Adam and Eve; Cain could have been afraid of other races. Still others think Cain's fears may have been unfounded.

Why didn't God sentence Cain to death? (4:15)

To protect the sanctity of the family. Because of the small number of people on earth, it would have been virtually impossible to announce capital punishment at this time. The family would have been badly fractured had it been called upon to act as prosecutor, judge, jury, witness and executor all at the same time. Also see article: *Why kill a murderer?* (Deut. 19:13).

What kind of mark did God put on Cain? (4:15)

No one knows, but the meaning of the original Hebrew is that God made a mark *for* Cain, suggesting a sign or a pledge of protection—a complete contrast from being a "marked man" for bounty hunters or the like.

Where did Cain find his wife? (4:17)

Adam had s*ons and daughters* (5:4) so Cain's wife was probably a sister (though some think God may have created other human beings besides Adam and Eve). Marriages between close relatives were at first unavoidable if the whole human race came from a single pair. Only later was marriage between siblings prohibited (Lev. 18:6–18).

Is polygamy okay? (4:19)

See article: *Why did David have so many wives and concubines?* (2 Samuel 5:13).

ther of those who live in tents and raise livestock. [21]His brother's name was Jubal; he was the father of all who play the harp and flute. [22]Zillah also had a son, Tubal-Cain, who forged all kinds of tools out of[a] bronze and iron. Tubal-Cain's sister was Naamah.

[23]Lamech said to his wives,

"Adah and Zillah, listen to me;
  wives of Lamech, hear my words.
I have killed[b] a man for wounding me,
  a young man for injuring me.
  [24]If Cain is avenged[D] seven times,
    then Lamech seventy-seven times."

[25]Adam lay with his wife again, and she gave birth to a son and named him Seth,[c] saying, "God has granted me another child in place of Abel, since Cain killed him." [26]Seth also had a son, and he named him Enosh.

At that time men began to call on[d] the name of the LORD.

From Adam to Noah

5 This is the written account of Adam's line.

When God created man, he made him in the likeness of God. [2]He created them male and female and blessed them. And when they were created, he called them "man.[e]"

[3]When Adam had lived 130 years, he had a son in his own likeness, in his own image; and he named him Seth. [4]After Seth was born, Adam lived 800 years and had other sons and daughters. [5]Altogether, Adam lived 930 years, and then he died.

[6]When Seth had lived 105 years, he became the father[f] of Enosh. [7]And after he became the father of Enosh, Seth lived 807 years and had other sons and daughters. [8]Altogether, Seth lived 912 years, and then he died.

[9]When Enosh had lived 90 years, he became the father of Kenan. [10]And after he became the father of Kenan, Enosh lived 815 years and had other sons and daughters. [11]Altogether, Enosh lived 905 years, and then he died.

[12]When Kenan had lived 70 years, he became the father of Mahalalel. [13]And after he became the father of Mahalalel, Kenan lived 840 years and had other sons and daughters. [14]Altogether, Kenan lived 910 years, and then he died.

[15]When Mahalalel had lived 65 years, he became the father of Jared. [16]And after he became the father of Jared, Mahalalel lived 830 years and had other sons and daughters. [17]Altogether, Mahalalel lived 895 years, and then he died.

[18]When Jared had lived 162 years, he became the father of Enoch. [19]And after he became the father of Enoch, Jared lived 800 years and had other sons and daughters. [20]Altogether, Jared lived 962 years, and then he died.

[21]When Enoch had lived 65 years, he became the father of Methuselah. [22]And after he became the father of Methuselah, Enoch walked with God 300 years and had other sons and daughters. [23]Altogether, Enoch lived 365

Why did people begin to call on God at that time? (4:26)

This was not the first time anyone had ever prayed to God, for certainly Cain and Abel offered prayers along with their sacrifices. Yet this may well have been the first time the name of the Lord—*Yahweh* —was used. See *What did God's name mean to the Israelites?* (Exodus 3:14).

Why call females *man*? (5:2)

The Hebrew word for *man (adam)* is used to designate humanity, or human beings in general.

What good are genealogies? (5:3-32)

Genealogies can demonstrate how God works his plan for history through individuals. Yet this genealogy shows even more: God intended human beings to live forever, but sin destroyed their potential. The decreasing ages at which children were born reveal the deteriorating effect of sin. Also see article: *Why read an ancient list of faceless names?* (1 Chron. 1:1).

What was the secret to such a long life? (5:5)

These men came fresh from the hand of a Creator who had made men and women to be immortal. Nevertheless, death—the result of sin—began its work of making people more and more mortal until we now expect only about 70 years as a normal life span. Some theorize that prior to the flood, the atmosphere was somehow more favorable to prolonging life, perhaps by a cloud cover that more effectively screened radiation from the sun.

---

[a]22 Or *who instructed all who work in*   [b]23 Or *I will kill*
[c]25 *Seth* probably means *granted.*   [d]26 Or *to proclaim*
[e]2 Hebrew *adam*   [f]6 *Father* may mean *ancestor*; also in verses 7-26.

years. **24**Enoch walked with God; then he was no more, because God took him away.

25When Methuselah had lived 187 years, he became the father of Lamech. **26**And after he became the father of Lamech, Methuselah lived 782 years and had other sons and daughters. **27**Altogether, Methuselah lived 969 years, and then he died.

28When Lamech had lived 182 years, he had a son. **29**He named him Noah*a* and said, "He will comfort us in the labor and painful toil of our hands caused by the ground the LORD has cursed." **30**After Noah was born, Lamech lived 595 years and had other sons and daughters. **31**Altogether, Lamech lived 777 years, and then he died.

32After Noah was 500 years old, he became the father of Shem, Ham and Japheth.

The Flood

6 When men began to increase in number on the earth and daughters were born to them, **2**the sons of God saw that the daughters of men were beautiful, and they married any of them they chose. **3**Then the LORD said, "My Spirit will not contend with*b* man forever, for he is mortal*c*; his days will be a hundred and twenty years."

4The Nephilim were on the earth in those days—and also afterward—when the sons of God went to the daughters of men and had children by them. They were the heroes of old, men of renown.

5The LORD saw how great man's wickedness on the earth had become, and that every inclination of the thoughts of his heart was only evil all the time. **6**The LORD was grieved that he had made man on the earth, and his heart was filled with pain. **7**So the LORD said, "I will wipe mankind, whom I have created, from the face of the earth—men and animals, and creatures that move along the ground, and birds of the air—for I am grieved that I have made them." **8**But Noah found favor in the eyes of the LORD.

9This is the account of Noah.

Noah was a righteous*D* man, blameless among the people of his time, and he walked with God. **10**Noah had three sons: Shem, Ham and Japheth.

11Now the earth was corrupt in God's sight and was full of violence. **12**God saw how corrupt the earth had become, for all the people on earth had corrupted their ways. **13**So God said to Noah, "I am going to put an end to all people, for the earth is filled with violence because of them. I am surely going to destroy both them and the earth. **14**So make yourself an ark of cypress*d* wood; make rooms in it and coat it with pitch inside and out. **15**This is how you are to build it: The ark is to be 450 feet long, 75 feet wide and 45 feet high.*e* **16**Make a roof for it and finish*f* the ark to within 18 inches*g* of the top. Put a door in the side of the ark and make lower, middle and upper decks. **17**I am going to bring floodwaters on the earth to destroy all life under the heavens, every creature that has the breath of life in it. Everything on earth will perish.

---

*a*29 Noah sounds like the Hebrew for *comfort.*   *b*3 Or *My spirit will not remain in*   *c*3 Or *corrupt*   *d*14 The meaning of the Hebrew for this word is uncertain.   *e*15 Hebrew *300 cubits long, 50 cubits wide and 30 cubits high* (about 140 meters long, 23 meters wide and 13.5 meters high)   *f*16 Or *Make an opening for light by finishing*   *g*16 Hebrew *a cubit* (about 0.5 meter)

Did Enoch escape death? (5:24)

Yes. The Bible confirms that *Enoch was taken from this life, so that he did not experience death* (Heb. 11:5). Enoch *walked with God,* suggesting an extremely intimate relationship with God that led to an extraordinary departure from this life.

Why did Lamech think Noah would comfort them? (5:29)

It's possible that God inspired Lamech to say what he did in anticipation of the comfort Noah would bring by building an ark and saving the human race. Noah also brought comfort by reinstituting the sacrificial ritual after the flood, having received God's promise never to flood the earth again (8:21).

Who were the sons of God? (6:2)

Some suggest they were supernatural beings such as angels (see NIV text note at Job 1:6). Others say they were godly men descended from Seth who married sinful women descended from Cain. A better interpretation may be that they were human rulers who emerged as heads of city-states in the ancient Middle East and flaunted their power by having large harems. Rulers and judges are often called *gods* or *God* in the Hebrew text (see NIV text notes at Exodus 21:6; 22:8; 1 Samuel 2:25). Also see *What gods does God judge?* (Psalm 82:1).

How does God's Spirit contend with people? (6:3)

Probably by keeping them alive. Though the meaning of the word *contend* is debated, one ancient translation (the Greek Septuagint) puts it: *I will not let my Spirit remain in them* (see NIV text note). If that is the meaning, it suggests that when God would take his Spirit from them, their life on earth would end. This matches the next part of the verse, *for he is mortal.*

Did God set a life span of 120 years? (6:3)

This is debated. Some think so, based on the first part of the verse (see previous note). However, others argue that this can hardly reflect the life span limit of individuals, since many achieved years far exceeding it (ch. 11). Even later Abraham reached 175, Isaac achieved 180 and Jacob 147. The 120 years may refer to the time of reprieve that God gave humanity before sending the flood.

Who were the Nephilim . . . the heroes of old? (6:4)

Nephilim may refer to persons of great physical stature, *giants* (see Num. 13:32–33). But here it probably means princes or aristocrats—men of political stature. *Nephilim* is linked to another term that indicates a heroic person with both power and influence.

How did Noah walk with God? (6:9)

To speak of Noah's "walk" is another way of describing his behavior. He *walked with God* by living righteously and in close communion with the Lord.

Ark (6:14)

The ship Noah built. The English word comes from the Latin *arca,* meaning box. Also see *Why call a chest an ark?* (Exodus 25:14–16).

Why did God establish a covenant with Noah? (6:18)

To promise that he would never again use a flood to wipe out humanity. The covenant God established with Noah (9:1,7) was a renewal of his earlier blessings and instructions that humankind should be *fruitful* and *increase* their numbers (1:28). This is the first reference in the Bible to a covenant.

Clean . . . unclean animal (7:2)

See *Why were some things unclean?* (Lev. 5:2) and article: *Why did God keep some meats off the menu?* (Lev. 11:4–41).

How did Noah know what animals were clean and unclean? (7:2–3)

We don't know for sure. Specific laws regarding what was clean and what wasn't were not given until many years later. See *Why were some things unclean?* (Lev. 5:2). Some suggest that when God gave the law, he may have symbolized religious concepts by using cultural taboos already in existence. If so, Noah could have understood *clean* and *unclean* in cultural terms. Or perhaps God revealed which animals were clean and unclean, but we hear only the summarized version of what God said to Noah.

Why take more clean than unclean animals? (7:2–3)

So Noah and his family could offer sacrifices to God after the flood (8:20). In addition, only clean animals would be used for food. The practice of using clean rather than unclean animals, for both ritual and food purposes, was observed long before Moses' restrictions (Lev. 11–15).

Did God cause the animals to come to Noah? (7:9)

We can't know for sure. Some think Noah went on safaris to gather the animals during the years the ark was under construction. Others believe the animals responded to some sixth sense telling them that disaster was imminent. Still others speculate that a glacial movement of some kind caused a mass migration of animals.

Springs of the great deep (7:11)

Probably refers to tremendous upheaval of the ocean floor or the effects of a great earthquake that caused subterranean water to burst forth in torrents.

How did Noah oversee a floating zoo? (7:14)

Noah had to take on board enough provisions to feed both the eight humans and all the animals on board. Though we cannot say for sure, perhaps some animals went into a period of hibernation. The many questions that arise (How did Noah satisfy the carnivorous animals? Didn't the animals get edgy cooped up for so long?) cannot be answered other than to say that God was in control of the whole affair.

18But I will establish my covenant[D] with you, and you will enter the ark—you and your sons and your wife and your sons' wives with you. **19**You are to bring into the ark two of all living creatures, male and female, to keep them alive with you. **20**Two of every kind of bird, of every kind of animal and of every kind of creature that moves along the ground will come to you to be kept alive. **21**You are to take every kind of food that is to be eaten and store it away as food for you and for them."

22Noah did everything just as God commanded him.

7 The LORD then said to Noah, "Go into the ark, you and your whole family, because I have found you righteous[D] in this generation. **2**Take with you seven[a] of every kind of clean animal, a male and its mate, and two of every kind of unclean[D] animal, a male and its mate, **3**and also seven of every kind of bird, male and female, to keep their various kinds alive throughout the earth. **4**Seven days from now I will send rain on the earth for forty days and forty nights, and I will wipe from the face of the earth every living creature I have made."

5And Noah did all that the LORD commanded him.

6Noah was six hundred years old when the floodwaters came on the earth. **7**And Noah and his sons and his wife and his sons' wives entered the ark to escape the waters of the flood. **8**Pairs of clean and unclean animals, of birds and of all creatures that move along the ground, **9**male and female, came to Noah and entered the ark, as God had commanded Noah. **10**And after the seven days the floodwaters came on the earth.

11In the six hundredth year of Noah's life, on the seventeenth day of the second month—on that day all the springs of the great deep burst forth, and the floodgates of the heavens were opened. **12**And rain fell on the earth forty days and forty nights.

13On that very day Noah and his sons, Shem, Ham and Japheth, together with his wife and the wives of his three sons, entered the ark. **14**They had with them every wild animal according to its kind, all livestock according to their kinds, every creature that moves along the ground according to its kind and every bird according to its kind, everything with wings. **15**Pairs of all creatures that have the breath of life in them came to Noah and entered the ark. **16**The animals going in were male and female of every living thing, as God had commanded Noah. Then the LORD shut him in.

17For forty days the flood kept coming on the earth, and as the waters increased they lifted the ark high above the earth. **18**The waters rose and increased greatly on the earth, and the ark floated on the surface of the water. **19**They rose greatly on the earth, and all the high mountains under the entire heavens were covered. **20**The waters rose and covered the mountains to a depth of more than twenty feet.[b,c] **21**Every living thing that moved on the earth perished—birds, livestock, wild animals, all the creatures that swarm over the earth, and all mankind. **22**Everything on dry land that had the breath of life in its nostrils died. **23**Every living thing on the face of the earth was wiped out; men and animals and the creatures that move along the ground and the birds of the air were

---

[a]2 Or *seven pairs*; also in verse 3   [b]20 Hebrew *fifteen cubits* (about 6.9 meters)   [c]20 Or *rose more than twenty feet, and the mountains were covered*

wiped from the earth. Only Noah was left, and those with him in the ark.

²⁴The waters flooded the earth for a hundred and fifty days.

8 But God remembered Noah and all the wild animals and the livestock that were with him in the ark, and he sent a wind over the earth, and the waters receded. ²Now the springs of the deep and the floodgates of the heavens had been closed, and the rain had stopped falling from the sky. ³The water receded steadily from the earth. At the end of the hundred and fifty days the water had gone down, ⁴and on the seventeenth day of the seventh month the ark came to rest on the mountains of Ararat. ⁵The waters continued to recede until the tenth month, and on the first day of the tenth month the tops of the mountains became visible.

⁶After forty days Noah opened the window he had made in the ark ⁷and sent out a raven, and it kept flying back and forth until the water had dried up from the earth. ⁸Then he sent out a dove to see if the water had receded from the surface of the ground. ⁹But the dove could find no place to set its feet because there was water over all the surface of the earth; so it returned to Noah in the ark. He reached out his hand and took the dove and brought it back to himself in the ark. ¹⁰He waited seven more days and again sent out the dove from the ark. ¹¹When the dove returned to him in the evening, there in its beak was a freshly plucked olive leaf! Then Noah knew that the water had receded from the earth. ¹²He waited seven more days and sent the dove out again, but this time it did not return to him.

¹³By the first day of the first month of Noah's six hundred and first year, the water had dried up from the earth. Noah then removed the covering from the ark and saw that the surface of the ground was dry. ¹⁴By the twenty-seventh day of the second month the earth was completely dry.

¹⁵Then God said to Noah, ¹⁶"Come out of the ark, you and your wife and your sons and their wives. ¹⁷Bring out

God remembered Noah (8:1)

In the Old Testament *to remember* means *to pay attention to*. It emphasizes God's decision to take action according to a previous commitment.

Why did Noah release a raven? (8:6–7)

To discover if land had reappeared. If it did not return, Noah might assume, since ravens feed on carrion, that it had been able to locate corpses that had washed ashore. It did not prove to be a reliable indicator, however, since it was able to fly around waiting for the land to reappear.

Olive leaf (8:11)

From the trees on the lower plains that were sprouting leaves again. The olive branch has become a symbol for peace, perhaps because it signaled the end of God's judgment.

How widespread was the flood? (7:19–20)

The case is strong that this flood covered the whole world: (1) It destroyed all life under the heavens (6:17). (2) The waters rose at least 20 feet above all the high mountains (7:19–20). (3) The flood lasted 371 days, indicating more than just local flooding. (4) The final fiery judgment of the *whole earth* is compared to Noah's flood (2 Peter 3:3–7).

On the other hand, certain questions can be raised in support of a local flood theory: (1) If the flood was indeed global, why did the ark land on Mount Ararat (8:4), floating so few miles from where it started? (2) Why doesn't the original Hebrew use the most common word for *world* even once in the whole account? Why instead does it use a word for *earth* that can also be translated *land* or *country*? (The same word is used later to describe a famine *in all the world,* meaning the world as known from the writer's perspective.)

Some believe the flood was worldwide. Others think it covered a region of the world but is described in universal language—much as we might speak of a world war without precisely meaning that every nation was involved.

Why did God promise not to repeat such judgment? (8:21–22)

It seems likely that his decision was more than just a response to the prayer and sacrifice of Noah. Perhaps God had all of human history in view and wanted to ensure that the normal cycles and processes of nature would continue unabated for as long as the earth would last. People can count on summer and winter, day and night, seedtime and harvest; these will never again cease.

Isn't there anything good about humans? (8:21)

Of course there is. Because God created us we have an undeniable basis for worth and self-esteem. But there is also a pervasive corruption of human nature that constantly pulls against everything our Creator calls us to do.

Why make the animal kingdom fear humans? (9:2)

Perhaps to emphasize the supremacy of human beings over animals. This fear was part of the curse resulting from the fall. But the fact of human supremacy over animals was part of God's created order (1:26,28). Another disruption that took place because of the fall was that animals could now be dangerous to humans.

What was wrong with bloody meat? (9:4)

Life was to be treated as a gift from God. Under no circumstances was it to be regarded in a casual manner. Since the life of the flesh was in the blood (see Lev. 17:11,14; Deut. 12:23), the meat had to be completely drained of its blood before it could be eaten. Also see *Why is blood considered the primary link with life?* (Lev. 17:11).

Does God hold animals accountable for their deeds? (9:5)

Yes, in the sense of being subject to possible punishment. Naturally, animals would not *understand* guilt in the same way humans do. However, just as persons must not treat the blood of animals carelessly by leaving it in the meat they are eating, so animals are to be held accountable for the blood of human beings. This principle was formalized in the Law of Moses in Exodus 21:28–29.

Why does killing require more killing? (9:6)

To instill within people a respect for the image of God in all people. Capital punishment was required because human life is sacred; to destroy human life is to attack the image of God. Such a terrible offense could only be rectified by offering the life of the murderer back to God. Without such a standard, human life would be cheapened and humane causes such as civil rights, gender rights and children's rights would suffer. Also see article: *Why kill a murderer?* (Deut. 19:13). Some believe Jesus later changed the way the criminal code was to be used (see Matt. 5:21–22,38–39). Also see *Why could only the sinless cast the first stone?* (John 8:7).

How can something with a natural explanation be a sign from God? (9:13)

It becomes a sign because of the way God uses it. The rainbow may have been in the sky

every kind of living creature that is with you—the birds, the animals, and all the creatures that move along the ground—so they can multiply on the earth and be fruitful and increase in number upon it."

¹⁸So Noah came out, together with his sons and his wife and his sons' wives. ¹⁹All the animals and all the creatures that move along the ground and all the birds—everything that moves on the earth—came out of the ark, one kind after another.

²⁰Then Noah built an altar to the LORD and, taking some of all the clean animals and clean birds, he sacrificed burnt offerings[D] on it. ²¹The LORD smelled the pleasing aroma and said in his heart: "Never again will I curse the ground because of man, even though[a] every inclination of his heart is evil from childhood. And never again will I destroy all living creatures, as I have done.

> ²²"As long as the earth endures,
>   seedtime and harvest,
>   cold and heat,
>   summer and winter,
>   day and night
>   will never cease."

God's Covenant[D] With Noah

9 Then God blessed Noah and his sons, saying to them, "Be fruitful and increase in number and fill the earth. ²The fear and dread of you will fall upon all the beasts of the earth and all the birds of the air, upon every creature that moves along the ground, and upon all the fish of the sea; they are given into your hands. ³Everything that lives and moves will be food for you. Just as I gave you the green plants, I now give you everything.

⁴"But you must not eat meat that has its lifeblood still in it. ⁵And for your lifeblood I will surely demand an accounting. I will demand an accounting from every animal. And from each man, too, I will demand an accounting for the life of his fellow man.

> ⁶"Whoever sheds the blood of man,
>   by man shall his blood be shed;
> for in the image of God
>   has God made man.

⁷As for you, be fruitful and increase in number; multiply on the earth and increase upon it."

⁸Then God said to Noah and to his sons with him: ⁹"I now establish my covenant with you and with your descendants after you ¹⁰and with every living creature that was with you—the birds, the livestock and all the wild animals, all those that came out of the ark with you—every living creature on earth. ¹¹I establish my covenant with you: Never again will all life be cut off by the waters of a flood; never again will there be a flood to destroy the earth."

¹²And God said, "This is the sign of the covenant I am making between me and you and every living creature with you, a covenant for all generations to come: ¹³I have set my rainbow in the clouds, and it will be the sign of the covenant between me and the earth. ¹⁴Whenever I bring clouds over the earth and the rainbow appears in the clouds, ¹⁵I will remember my covenant between me and you and all living creatures of every kind. Never again

a21 Or man, for

will the waters become a flood to destroy all life. **16**Whenever the rainbow appears in the clouds, I will see it and remember the everlasting covenant^D between God and all living creatures of every kind on the earth."

17So God said to Noah, "This is the sign of the covenant I have established between me and all life on the earth."

The Sons of Noah

18The sons of Noah who came out of the ark were Shem, Ham and Japheth. (Ham was the father of Canaan.) **19**These were the three sons of Noah, and from them came the people who were scattered over the earth.

20Noah, a man of the soil, proceeded^a to plant a vineyard. **21**When he drank some of its wine, he became drunk and lay uncovered inside his tent. **22**Ham, the father of Canaan, saw his father's nakedness and told his two brothers outside. **23**But Shem and Japheth took a garment and laid it across their shoulders; then they walked in backward and covered their father's nakedness. Their faces were turned the other way so that they would not see their father's nakedness.

24When Noah awoke from his wine and found out what his youngest son had done to him, **25**he said,

"Cursed be Canaan!
    The lowest of slaves
    will he be to his brothers."

26He also said,

"Blessed be the LORD, the God of Shem!
    May Canaan be the slave of Shem.^b
27May God extend the territory of Japheth^c;
    may Japheth live in the tents of Shem,
    and may Canaan be his^d slave."

28After the flood Noah lived 350 years. **29**Altogether, Noah lived 950 years, and then he died.

The Table of Nations

10 This is the account of Shem, Ham and Japheth, Noah's sons, who themselves had sons after the flood.

The Japhethites

2The sons^e of Japheth:
    Gomer, Magog, Madai, Javan, Tubal, Meshech and Tiras.
3The sons of Gomer:
    Ashkenaz, Riphath and Togarmah.
4The sons of Javan:
    Elishah, Tarshish, the Kittim and the Rodanim.^f
    5(From these the maritime peoples spread out into their territories by their clans within their nations, each with its own language.)

previously, for the Hebrew grammar is explicit in saying that it was now *to become* a sign. If so, God took what already existed in the heavens to remind people of his promise.

What did Ham do wrong? (9:22–24)
It was no doubt wrong to broadcast his father's nakedness rather than to immediately cover it, perhaps revealing a general disrespect for his father. Some point out that it is Noah (first intoxicated and now hung over), not the Bible, that directly accuses Ham of any wrongdoing. Also see following note.

Why did Noah curse his grandson instead of his son Ham? (9:25)
Some note that children often suffer for their parents' wrongdoing. See *Why punish children for their ancestors' sins?* (Exodus 20:4–5) and article: *Why does God allow innocent children to suffer?* (Lam. 2:11–12). They think Noah may have cursed Ham's son with this in mind. Others suggest that Noah may have recognized tendencies toward sexual perversion in Canaan implied by Ham's behavior. They point out evidence of Canaanite fertility cults (amulets portraying exaggerated genitals and other perversions) for which the Canaanites were later judged.

This is the account of . . . (10:1–32)
See *What good are genealogies?* (5:3–32) and article: *Why read an ancient list of faceless names?* (1 Chron. 1:1).

---

^a20 Or *soil, was the first*   ^b26 Or *be his slave*   ^c27 *Japheth* sounds like the Hebrew for *extend.*   ^d27 Or *their*   ^e2 *Sons* may mean *descendants* or *successors* or *nations*; also in verses 3, 4, 6, 7, 20-23, 29 and 31.   ^f4 Some manuscripts of the Masoretic Text and Samaritan Pentateuch (see also Septuagint and 1 Chron. 1:7); most manuscripts of the Masoretic Text *Dodanim*

The Hamites

6The sons of Ham:

Cush, Mizraim,*a* Put and Canaan.

7The sons of Cush:

Seba, Havilah, Sabtah, Raamah and Sabteca.

The sons of Raamah:

Sheba and Dedan.

8Cush was the father*b* of Nimrod, who grew to be a mighty warrior on the earth. **9**He was a mighty hunter before the LORD; that is why it is said, "Like Nimrod, a mighty hunter before the LORD." **10**The first centers of his kingdom were Babylon, Erech, Akkad and Calneh, in*c* Shinar.*d* **11**From that land he went to Assyria, where he built Nineveh, Rehoboth Ir,*e* Calah **12**and Resen, which is between Nineveh and Calah; that is the great city.

13Mizraim was the father of

the Ludites, Anamites, Lehabites, Naphtuhites, **14**Pathrusites, Casluhites (from whom the Philistines came) and Caphtorites.

15Canaan was the father of

Sidon his firstborn*D,f* and of the Hittites, **16**Jebusites, Amorites, Girgashites, **17**Hivites, Arkites, Sinites, **18**Arvadites, Zemarites and Hamathites.

Later the Canaanite clans scattered **19**and the borders of Canaan reached from Sidon toward Gerar as far as Gaza,

Is this the same Nineveh that Jonah later visited? (10:11)

Yes. Nineveh became the capital city of Assyria in about 700 B.C. and Jonah was reluctantly sent there to call the people to repentance. Though the Ninevites responded to his message (Jonah 3:5), they later reverted to extreme wickedness and were destroyed in 612 B.C. Nineveh's fall is the theme of the book of Nahum.

In what way was the earth divided? (10:25)

Probably by the confusion of languages at the tower of Babel (11:8–9). Since *Peleg* in Hebrew means *to divide,* or *to split* (see NIV text note), he may have received his name in memory of this event.

a6 That is, Egypt; also in verse 13   *b8 Father* may mean *ancestor* or *predecessor* or *founder;* also in verses 13, 15, 24 and 26.   *c10* Or *Erech and Akkad—all of them in*   *d10* That is, Babylonia   *e11* Or *Nineveh with its city squares*   *f15* Or *of the Sidonians, the foremost*

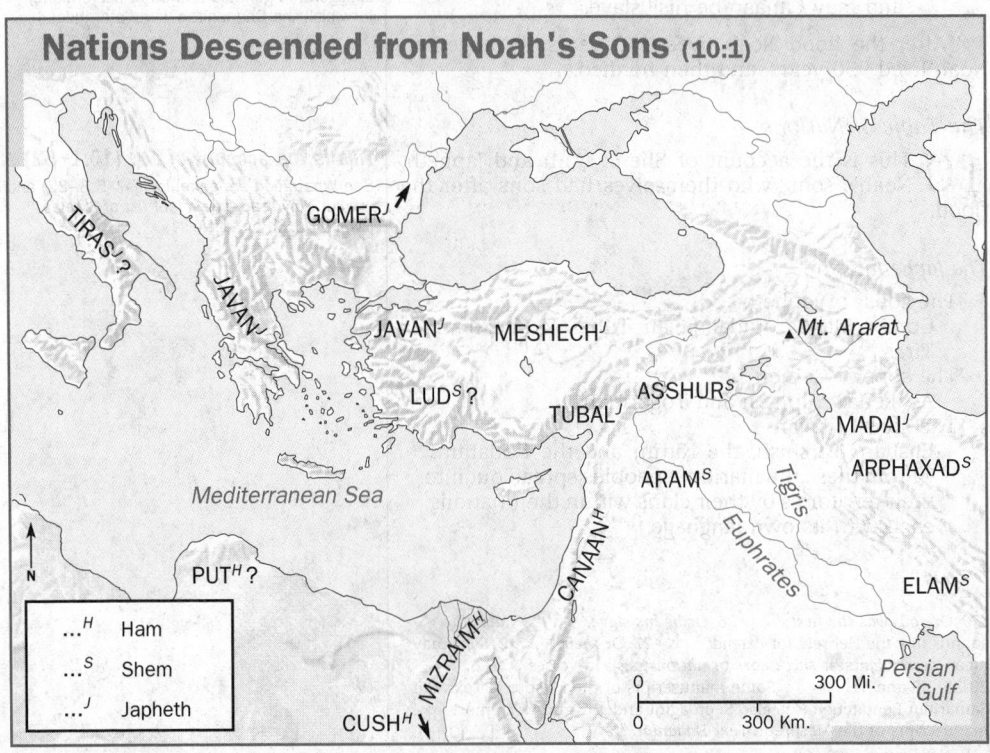

Nations Descended from Noah's Sons (10:1)

TIRAS*J*?

GOMER*J*

JAVAN*J*

JAVAN*J*   MESHECH*J*

▲Mt. Ararat

LUD*S*?

TUBAL*J*   ASSHUR*S*

MADAI*J*

ARPHAXAD*S*

Mediterranean Sea

ARAM*S*

CANAAN*H*

Tigris

Euphrates

N

PUT*H*?

ELAM*S*

Persian Gulf

...*H* Ham
...*S* Shem
...*J* Japheth

MIZRAIM*H*

CUSH*H*↘

0   300 Mi.

0   300 Km.

and then toward Sodom, Gomorrah, Admah and Zeboiim, as far as Lasha.

20These are the sons of Ham by their clans and languages, in their territories and nations.

The Semites

21Sons were also born to Shem, whose older brother was[a] Japheth; Shem was the ancestor of all the sons of Eber.

22The sons of Shem:

Elam, Asshur, Arphaxad, Lud and Aram.

23The sons of Aram:

Uz, Hul, Gether and Meshech.[b]

24Arphaxad was the father of[c] Shelah,

and Shelah the father of Eber.

25Two sons were born to Eber:

One was named Peleg,[d] because in his time the earth was divided; his brother was named Joktan.

26Joktan was the father of

Almodad, Sheleph, Hazarmaveth, Jerah, **27**Hadoram, Uzal, Diklah, **28**Obal, Abimael, Sheba, **29**Ophir, Havilah and Jobab. All these were sons of Joktan.

30The region where they lived stretched from Mesha toward Sephar, in the eastern hill country.

31These are the sons of Shem by their clans and languages, in their territories and nations.

32These are the clans of Noah's sons, according to their lines of descent, within their nations. From these the nations spread out over the earth after the flood.

The Tower of Babel

11 Now the whole world had one language and a common speech. **2**As men moved eastward,[e] they found a plain in Shinar[f] and settled there.

3They said to each other, "Come, let's make bricks and bake them thoroughly." They used brick instead of stone, and tar for mortar. **4**Then they said, "Come, let us build ourselves a city, with a tower that reaches to the heavens, so that we may make a name for ourselves and not be scattered over the face of the whole earth."

5But the LORD came down to see the city and the tower that the men were building. **6**The LORD said, "If as one people speaking the same language they have begun to do this, then nothing they plan to do will be impossible for them. **7**Come, let us go down and confuse their language so they will not understand each other."

8So the LORD scattered them from there over all the earth, and they stopped building the city. **9**That is why it was called Babel[g]—because there the LORD confused the language of the whole world. From there the LORD scattered them over the face of the whole earth.

From Shem to Abram

10This is the account of Shem.

Two years after the flood, when Shem was 100 years

a21 Or Shem, the older brother of   *b23 See Septuagint and 1 Chron. 1:17; Hebrew Mash*   *c24 Hebrew; Septuagint father of Cainan, and Cainan was the father of*   *d25 Peleg means division.*
e2 Or from the east; or in the east   *f2 That is, Babylonia*
g9 That is, Babylon; Babel sounds like the Hebrew for confused.

Who are the modern descendants of Noah's sons? (10:32)

The Semitic peoples are descendants of Shem. Ham's descendants are generally thought to be people from Egypt, Ethiopia, North Africa and Canaan. People with Indo-European roots are usually considered to come from the line of Japheth.

What was the first language? (11:1)

No one really knows for sure. *One language* may mean there was a common language understood by all groups of people at that time, though each group had its own distinct dialect (10:5,20,31).

Why build a tower? (11:4)

Two reasons were given: (1) to make a name for themselves—that is, to accomplish something of lasting significance, and (2) to keep from being scattered over the earth. Perhaps fears left by the flood caused a desire for some form of security. It's more likely, though, that their project reflected their developing paganism as they attempted to placate the gods. One ancient temple-tower (or ziggurat), built for Marduk at Babylon, was supposed to have reached to the heavens.

The Tower of Babel (11:4)

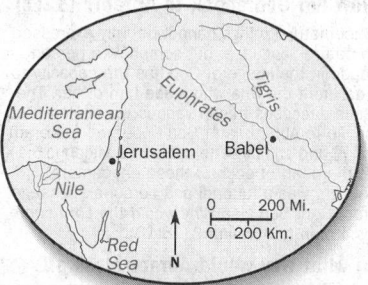

How could building a tower make nothing impossible for humankind? (11:6)

The phrase *nothing . . . will be impossible* refers to their potential for doing evil. It's similar to our figure of speech "anything can happen." When a culture unites, the power that results can be dangerous. History demonstrates the tragic results when people have power but use it the wrong way. God scattered the people to undermine this potential for destructive behavior.

Why does God say, *Come, let us* [plural] *go down?* (11:7)

The battle in the Old Testament is to show that there is only *one* God over all, not *many* gods as was believed by most of the world at that time. For the use of the plural here, see *Why did God say, Let us* [plural] *make man in our image?* (1:26).

Why did God want to divide and scatter people? (11:9)

Large numbers of people concentrated in huge cities seem to bring out the worst in humanity. Crime, social ills and other tragedies seem to accumulate faster when people are crowded together. With this in view, God may have scattered the people for their own good, to protect them from themselves.

old, he became the father[a] of Arphaxad. **11**And after he became the father of Arphaxad, Shem lived 500 years and had other sons and daughters.

12When Arphaxad had lived 35 years, he became the father of Shelah. **13**And after he became the father of Shelah, Arphaxad lived 403 years and had other sons and daughters.[b]

14When Shelah had lived 30 years, he became the father of Eber. **15**And after he became the father of Eber, Shelah lived 403 years and had other sons and daughters.

16When Eber had lived 34 years, he became the father of Peleg. **17**And after he became the father of Peleg, Eber lived 430 years and had other sons and daughters.

18When Peleg had lived 30 years, he became the father of Reu. **19**And after he became the father of Reu, Peleg lived 209 years and had other sons and daughters.

20When Reu had lived 32 years, he became the father of Serug. **21**And after he became the father of Serug, Reu lived 207 years and had other sons and daughters.

22When Serug had lived 30 years, he became the father of Nahor. **23**And after he became the father of Nahor, Serug lived 200 years and had other sons and daughters.

24When Nahor had lived 29 years, he became the father of Terah. **25**And after he became the father of Terah, Nahor lived 119 years and had other sons and daughters.

26After Terah had lived 70 years, he became the father of Abram, Nahor and Haran.

27This is the account of Terah.

Terah became the father of Abram, Nahor and Haran. And Haran became the father of Lot. **28**While his father Terah was still alive, Haran died in Ur of the Chaldeans, in the land of his birth. **29**Abram and Nahor both married. The name of Abram's wife was Sarai, and the name of Nahor's wife was Milcah; she was the daughter of Haran, the father of both Milcah and Iscah. **30**Now Sarai was barren; she had no children.

31Terah took his son Abram, his grandson Lot son of Haran, and his daughter-in-law Sarai, the wife of his son Abram, and together they set out from Ur of the Chaldeans to go to Canaan. But when they came to Haran, they settled there.

32Terah lived 205 years, and he died in Haran.

The Call of Abram

12 The LORD had said to Abram, "Leave your country, your people and your father's household and go to the land I will show you.

2"I will make you into a great nation
and I will bless you;
I will make your name great,
and you will be a blessing.
3I will bless those who bless you,
and whoever curses you I will curse;
and all peoples on earth
will be blessed through you."

Why did Terah set out for Canaan? (11:31)

We don't know why Terah joined Abram in leaving Ur. Abram's ancestors were pagans and did not serve the Lord (Joshua 24:2). But Terah may have been influenced by his son who had heard from God.

How did God speak to Abram? (12:1)

Supernatural things cannot be fully expressed in natural language, but somehow a person made in the image of God has the capacity to hear from the One who made him or her. The Bible describes this in various ways. Here God spoke to Abram; later God appeared to Abram (v. 7) and still later he came in a vision (15:1). At the heart of each of these encounters, though, was a rational and personal message from God. See also *Why would the Lord come as a man to Abraham?* (18:10).

In what way would Abram bless *all peoples on earth*? (12:3)

God would use Abram to express his heart and purpose for all the world. His desire was to redeem humanity from the depths to which they had fallen when Adam sinned. Eventually, through Abram, God would send Jesus to fulfill his plan and offer redemption to the whole world.

Abram's Journeys (12:4)

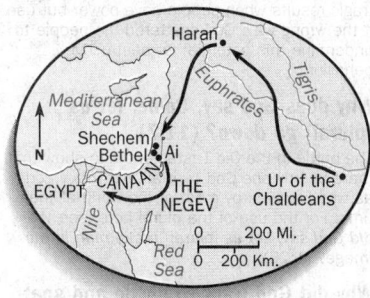

Great tree of Moreh (12:6)

One of several large trees in Canaan that were prominent at sacred places. This was a center for the worship of pagan gods, a spot known to all the locals. Abram built an altar to the real God there—an implicit challenge to the false gods of Canaan.

---

[a] *10 Father* may mean *ancestor*; also in verses 11-25.
[b] *12,13 Hebrew; Septuagint (see also Luke 3:35, 36 and note at Gen. 10:24) 35 years, he became the father of Cainan.* **13***And after he became the father of Cainan, Arphaxad lived 430 years and had other sons and daughters, and then he died. When Cainan had lived 130 years, he became the father of Shelah. And after he became the father of Shelah, Cainan lived 330 years and had other sons and daughters*

⁴So Abram left, as the LORD had told him; and Lot went with him. Abram was seventy-five years old when he set out from Haran. ⁵He took his wife Sarai, his nephew Lot, all the possessions they had accumulated and the people they had acquired in Haran, and they set out for the land of Canaan, and they arrived there.

⁶Abram traveled through the land as far as the site of the great tree of Moreh at Shechem. At that time the Canaanites were in the land. ⁷The LORD appeared to Abram and said, "To your offspring*a* I will give this land." So he built an altar there to the LORD, who had appeared to him.

⁸From there he went on toward the hills east of Bethel and pitched his tent, with Bethel on the west and Ai on the east. There he built an altar to the LORD and called on the name of the LORD. ⁹Then Abram set out and continued toward the Negev.ᴰ

Abram in Egypt

¹⁰Now there was a famine in the land, and Abram went down to Egypt to live there for a while because the famine was severe. ¹¹As he was about to enter Egypt, he said to his wife Sarai, "I know what a beautiful woman you are. ¹²When the Egyptians see you, they will say, 'This is his wife.' Then they will kill me but will let you live. ¹³Say you are my sister, so that I will be treated well for your sake and my life will be spared because of you."

¹⁴When Abram came to Egypt, the Egyptians saw that she was a very beautiful woman. ¹⁵And when Pharaoh's officials saw her, they praised her to Pharaoh, and she was taken into his palace. ¹⁶He treated Abram well for her sake, and Abram acquired sheep and cattle, male and female donkeys, menservants and maidservants, and camels.

¹⁷But the LORD inflicted serious diseases on Pharaoh and his household because of Abram's wife Sarai. ¹⁸So Pharaoh summoned Abram. "What have you done to me?" he said. "Why didn't you tell me she was your wife? ¹⁹Why did you say, 'She is my sister,' so that I took her to be my wife? Now then, here is your wife. Take her and go!" ²⁰Then Pharaoh gave orders about Abram to his men, and they sent him on his way, with his wife and everything he had.

Abram and Lot Separate

13 So Abram went up from Egypt to the Negev, with his wife and everything he had, and Lot went with him. ²Abram had become very wealthy in livestock and in silver and gold.

³From the Negev he went from place to place until he came to Bethel, to the place between Bethel and Ai where his tent had been earlier ⁴and where he had first built an altar. There Abram called on the name of the LORD.

⁵Now Lot, who was moving about with Abram, also had flocks and herds and tents. ⁶But the land could not support them while they stayed together, for their possessions were so great that they were not able to stay together. ⁷And quarreling arose between Abram's herdsmen and the herdsmen of Lot. The Canaanites and Perizzites were also living in the land at that time.

⁸So Abram said to Lot, "Let's not have any quarreling between you and me, or between your herdsmen and mine, for we are brothers. ⁹Is not the whole land before

Why did Abram build altars? (12:7–8)
The normal way to express religious devotion in Canaanite culture was through sacrifices offered on an altar. But because the places and means used to worship false gods were not appropriate for the Lord, Abram built new altars to sacrifice to the true God.

Why did Egypt have food when other countries didn't? (12:10)
The Nile River provided water for irrigating crops. When neighboring lands received no rain, as was often the case, the Nile became the only source of a consistent harvest and made Egypt the breadbasket for the whole region.

What did Pharaoh intend to do with Sarai? (12:15)
Sarai was taken into Pharaoh's harem to become one of his many concubines.

Why would God punish Pharaoh for an unintentional sin? (12:17)
This story illustrates how far God is willing to go to protect his own people when they act foolishly. It also shows that the innocent must suffer sometimes for the sins of others. Here Pharaoh and his house suffered because of Abram's fears and lies. God did this to protect the mother of Israel and to preserve his plan of redemption through Abram.

How did Pharaoh discover the truth about Sarai? (12:18)
Any misfortune in the ancient world was looked upon as an indication of divine displeasure. So when God sent *serious diseases on Pharaoh and his household* (v. 17), Pharaoh and his advisers may have tried to determine when the troubles started. When they traced the troubles to the time of Sarai's arrival, they may have guessed or probed until they arrived at the truth.

Was Abram a nomad? (13:3)
Yes, although there were different kinds of nomads. Some, like Abram, moved about in order to find land on which their cattle, sheep and goats could graze. Abram had to maintain friendly relations with his neighbors so he could graze his livestock on their lands when harvest was completed. Other nomads, such as the Bedouins, were more mobile—and warlike. Using their camels, they would often raid their neighbors.

Why did Abram give Lot first choice? (13:9)
Having returned to the place where he had worshiped God before (12:8), Abram probably recalled God's promise to him with renewed vividness. Also, his humbling experience in Egypt may have helped him see that God intended to take care of him. So Abram demonstrated his confidence in God by giving Lot first choice. God responded to Abram's faith and assured him that all of the land, even what Lot had chosen, would ultimately belong to Abram's descendants.

a 7 Or *seed*

you? Let's part company. If you go to the left, I'll go to the right; if you go to the right, I'll go to the left."

¹⁰Lot looked up and saw that the whole plain of the Jordan was well watered, like the garden of the LORD, like the land of Egypt, toward Zoar. (This was before the LORD destroyed Sodom and Gomorrah.) ¹¹So Lot chose for himself the whole plain of the Jordan and set out toward the east. The two men parted company: ¹²Abram lived in the land of Canaan, while Lot lived among the cities of the plain and pitched his tents near Sodom. ¹³Now the men of Sodom were wicked and were sinning greatly against the LORD.

¹⁴The LORD said to Abram after Lot had parted from him, "Lift up your eyes from where you are and look north and south, east and west. ¹⁵All the land that you see I will give to you and your offspringᵃ forever. ¹⁶I will make your offspring like the dust of the earth, so that if anyone could count the dust, then your offspring could be counted. ¹⁷Go, walk through the length and breadth of the land, for I am giving it to you."

¹⁸So Abram moved his tents and went to live near the great trees of Mamre at Hebron, where he built an altar to the LORD.

Abram Rescues Lot

14 At this time Amraphel king of Shinar,ᵇ Arioch king of Ellasar, Kedorlaomer king of Elam and Tidal king of Goiim ²went to war against Bera king of Sodom, Birsha king of Gomorrah, Shinab king of Admah, Shemeber king of Zeboiim, and the king of Bela (that is, Zoar). ³All these latter kings joined forces in the Valley of Siddim (the Salt Seaᶜ). ⁴For twelve years they had been subject to Kedorlaomer, but in the thirteenth year they rebelled.

⁵In the fourteenth year, Kedorlaomer and the kings allied with him went out and defeated the Rephaites in Ashteroth Karnaim, the Zuzites in Ham, the Emites in Shaveh Kiriathaim ⁶and the Horites in the hill country of Seir, as far as El Paran near the desert. ⁷Then they turned back and went to En Mishpat (that is, Kadesh), and they conquered the whole territory of the Amalekites, as well as the Amorites who were living in Hazazon Tamar.

⁸Then the king of Sodom, the king of Gomorrah, the king of Admah, the king of Zeboiim and the king of Bela (that is, Zoar) marched out and drew up their battle lines in the Valley of Siddim ⁹against Kedorlaomer king of Elam, Tidal king of Goiim, Amraphel king of Shinar and Arioch king of Ellasar—four kings against five. ¹⁰Now the Valley of Siddim was full of tar pits, and when the kings of Sodom and Gomorrah fled, some of the men fell into them and the rest fled to the hills. ¹¹The four kings seized all the goods of Sodom and Gomorrah and all their food; then they went away. ¹²They also carried off Abram's nephew Lot and his possessions, since he was living in Sodom.

¹³One who had escaped came and reported this to Abram the Hebrewᴰ. Now Abram was living near the great trees of Mamre the Amorite, a brotherᵈ of Eshcol and Aner, all of whom were allied with Abram. ¹⁴When Abram heard that his relative had been taken captive, he called out the 318 trained men born in his household and

How did the people of Sodom sin against the LORD? (13:13)

Though we don't know the full extent of Sodom's sin, we know that it was extraordinary. Later there was a great *outcry against Sodom and Gomorrah* (18:20), suggesting perhaps that they oppressed other people with terrible injustice. God spoke of their *grievous* sin (18:20), perhaps referring to their homosexual behavior (19:4–5). Their sexual perversions may have grown out of the practice of pagan fertility cults. See *What did male prostitutes have to do with pagan worship?* (1 Kings 14:24).

Like the dust of the earth (13:16)

This is a figure of speech called hyperbole. It was not meant to be taken literally, but to convey the idea that Abram's descendants would be too many to count. It's possible that this included not just Abram's physical descendants, but also his spiritual heirs (Gal. 3:29). See also 15:5 and article: *Can the Bible exaggerate and still be true?* (2 Chron. 1:9–15).

Great trees (13:18)

See *Great tree of Moreh* (12:6).

Abram . . . built an altar (13:18)

See *Why did Abram build altars?* (12:7–8).

Tar pits (14:10)

Deposits of bitumen, an asphalt-like substance produced naturally in the region. People dug it out for use as a construction material. The kings may have fallen in pits left behind after its removal.

Hebrew (14:13)

See *Where did the term Hebrew come from?* (Exodus 1:15).

Abram Rescues Lot (14:14)

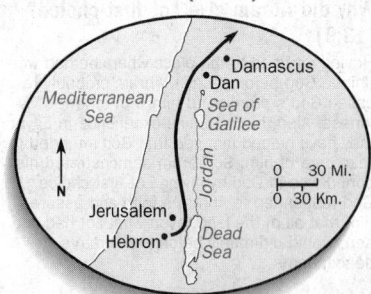

ᵃ15 Or *seed*; also in verse 16   ᵇ1 That is, Babylonia; also in verse 9   ᶜ3 That is, the Dead Sea   ᵈ13 Or *a relative*; or *an ally*

went in pursuit as far as Dan. **15**During the night Abram divided his men to attack them and he routed them, pursuing them as far as Hobah, north of Damascus. **16**He recovered all the goods and brought back his relative Lot and his possessions, together with the women and the other people.

17After Abram returned from defeating Kedorlaomer and the kings allied with him, the king of Sodom came out to meet him in the Valley of Shaveh (that is, the King's Valley).

18Then Melchizedek king of Salem*a* brought out bread and wine. He was priest*D* of God Most High, **19**and he blessed Abram, saying,

> "Blessed be Abram by God Most High,
>   Creator*b* of heaven and earth.
> **20**And blessed be*c* God Most High,
>   who delivered your enemies into your hand."

Then Abram gave him a tenth of everything.

21The king of Sodom said to Abram, "Give me the people and keep the goods for yourself."

22But Abram said to the king of Sodom, "I have raised my hand to the LORD, God Most High, Creator of heaven and earth, and have taken an oath **23**that I will accept nothing belonging to you, not even a thread or the thong of a sandal, so that you will never be able to say, 'I made Abram rich.' **24**I will accept nothing but what my men have eaten and the share that belongs to the men who went with me—to Aner, Eshcol and Mamre. Let them have their share."

God's Covenant With Abram

15 After this, the word of the LORD came to Abram in a vision*D*:

> "Do not be afraid, Abram.
>   I am your shield,*d*
>   your very great reward.*e*"

2But Abram said, "O Sovereign LORD, what can you give me since I remain childless and the one who will inherit*f* my estate is Eliezer of Damascus?" **3**And Abram said, "You have given me no children; so a servant in my household will be my heir."

4Then the word of the LORD came to him: "This man will not be your heir, but a son coming from your own body will be your heir." **5**He took him outside and said, "Look up at the heavens and count the stars—if indeed you can count them." Then he said to him, "So shall your offspring be."

6Abram believed the LORD, and he credited it to him as righteousness*D*.

7He also said to him, "I am the LORD, who brought you out of Ur of the Chaldeans to give you this land to take possession of it."

8But Abram said, "O Sovereign LORD, how can I know that I will gain possession of it?"

9So the LORD said to him, "Bring me a heifer, a goat and a ram, each three years old, along with a dove and a young pigeon."

---

a18 That is, Jerusalem   b19 Or Possessor; also in verse 22
*c20 Or And praise be to   d1 Or sovereign   e1 Or shield; | your
reward will be very great   f2 The meaning of the Hebrew for this
phrase is uncertain.*

Why did the kings of Sodom and Salem meet with Abram? (14:17–18)
Probably to pay him honor and respect. Abram had just defeated their common enemy, and they wanted to express their gratitude to him.

God Most High (14:18)
Melchizedek spoke of *God Most High* but Abram spoke of *the LORD, God Most High, Creator of heaven and earth* (v. 22). Melchizedek probably viewed *God Most High* as the primary God above all others. Melchizedek knew about God and spoke of his *titles*, but Abram knew God personally and used God's *name*. See *By what name did Abraham know God?* (Exodus 6:3).

What kind of priest was Melchizedek? (14:18)
Melchizedek was a Canaanite priest-king, one of the most intriguing persons in the Bible. We know little about him, but the writer of Hebrews uses him as a parable of Christ. He may illustrate that even in a pagan world God can speak to sincere hearts. Also see *The order of Melchizedek* (Heb. 5:6); *How could Melchizedek not have a beginning or end?* (Heb. 7:3) and *If Melchizedek was greater, why did Abraham get the publicity?* (Heb. 7:6–7).

Why did Abram give the king of Salem a tenth of everything? (14:20)
This is the first mention of tithing in the Bible. Abram was full of gratitude to God for his victory and especially for the deliverance of his nephew, Lot. He felt compelled to act out his gratitude by giving a tenth of the spoils to this representative of God Most High.

Why did Abram's allies take spoils when he wouldn't? (14:24)
This refusal to accept any part of the spoils may reflect either royal etiquette or Abram's tentative social status in the country. He was a stranger among them and still needed to develop friendly relations with his neighbors. His wise actions undoubtedly raised their opinion of him.

Why would a *servant* be Abram's heir before his nephew, Lot? (15:2)
Abram was concerned about more than possessions. The issue that concerned him included the preservation of his name down through history. Abram apparently considered Lot to be the namesake of Abram's deceased brother, Haran. Lot could not perpetuate both Abram's and Haran's names. The genealogies could list only one as Lot's father. The customs of the times allowed a servant to be adopted as heir. The servant would care for his adoptive parents in their old age, receive their possessions when they died and continue the family name.

Count the stars (15:5)
This is a figure of speech called hyperbole. It was not meant to be taken literally, but to convey the idea that Abram's descendants would be too many to count. See also 13:16 and article: *Can the Bible exaggerate and still be true?* (2 Chron. 1:9–15).

Why cut animals in half? (15:10)

This was part of the custom of the time when covenants were made between individuals. Other ancient literature tells of killing and dividing animals so that the parties to the covenant could walk between the body parts, signifying that a similar fate should come upon whomever broke the contract (vv. 17–18). It amounted to an oath, made even more serious by the sacrifice of the animals.

Why wait for the Amorites' sin to increase? (15:16)

God's compassion made him slow to act in judgment. He gave the Amorites time so they could repent, not so they could sin all the more. He would not take their land from them and give it to Abram's descendants without first giving them every chance to repent. A holy God will deal with people in a fair and upright manner. See Jonah 3:3–10; 4:11.

Smoking firepot . . . blazing torch (15:17)

This is like God's signature signed to the contract. Fire in the Bible is a consistent symbol of the presence of God. A few other examples include the burning bush (Exodus 3:1–3), the smoke on Mount Sinai (Exodus 19:18), the fire that answered Elijah (1 Kings 18:38), the coal that cleansed Isaiah (Isaiah 6:6) and the fire of Pentecost (Acts 2:1–4).

Why would God promise Abram land belonging to others? (15:18–21)

God answered this question near the end of Moses' life (Deut. 9:1–6). It was not because Israel was more righteous or deserving. God expelled the nations of Canaan because of their wickedness. Later Israel was punished for sin in the same way when Assyria and Babylon took over the land. Also see article: **What right did Israel have to take the land?** (Num. 33:52–53).

Why would a wife urge her husband to have an affair? (16:2)

Because social custom demanded it. The primary purpose of marriage was to have children. If a wife was sterile, it was her responsibility to give one of her maids to her husband

[10]Abram brought all these to him, cut them in two and arranged the halves opposite each other; the birds, however, he did not cut in half. [11]Then birds of prey came down on the carcasses, but Abram drove them away.

[12]As the sun was setting, Abram fell into a deep sleep, and a thick and dreadful darkness came over him. [13]Then the LORD said to him, "Know for certain that your descendants will be strangers in a country not their own, and they will be enslaved and mistreated four hundred years. [14]But I will punish the nation they serve as slaves, and afterward they will come out with great possessions. [15]You, however, will go to your fathers in peace[D] and be buried at a good old age. [16]In the fourth generation your descendants will come back here, for the sin of the Amorites has not yet reached its full measure."

[17]When the sun had set and darkness had fallen, a smoking firepot with a blazing torch appeared and passed between the pieces. [18]On that day the LORD made a covenant[D] with Abram and said, "To your descendants I give this land, from the river[a] of Egypt to the great river, the Euphrates— [19]the land of the Kenites, Kenizzites, Kadmonites, [20]Hittites, Perizzites, Rephaites, [21]Amorites, Canaanites, Girgashites and Jebusites."

Hagar and Ishmael

16 Now Sarai, Abram's wife, had borne him no children. But she had an Egyptian maidservant named Hagar; [2]so she said to Abram, "The LORD has kept me from having children. Go, sleep with my maidservant; perhaps I can build a family through her."

Abram agreed to what Sarai said. [3]So after Abram had been living in Canaan ten years, Sarai his wife took her Egyptian maidservant Hagar and gave her to her husband to be his wife. [4]He slept with Hagar, and she conceived.

When she knew she was pregnant, she began to despise her mistress. [5]Then Sarai said to Abram, "You are responsible for the wrong I am suffering. I put my servant in your arms, and now that she knows she is pregnant, she despises me. May the LORD judge between you and me."

[6]"Your servant is in your hands," Abram said. "Do with

[a]18 Or Wadi

What's so great about Abram's faith? (15:6)

The Bible makes Abram's faith the model for us all. (See, for example, Romans 4; Gal. 3; Heb. 11; James 2.) The surprising thing is that Abram never saw a Bible, had no church, possessed no creed, took no sacrament, heard not even one of the Ten Commandments and knew little about life after death.

Yet Abram's faith shows us what really matters. He heard the voice of God and dared to simply believe he could trust him when he spoke. He risked his life, his security, his reputation, his future and even his son on the word that came from One whom he could not see but in whom he believed. Can there be anything better to demonstrate that it is by faith, and faith alone, that we are saved?

We now have the Bible, the church, the creeds, the sacraments and the Ten Commandments. But God still looks for the basics—God still looks for hearts that will, with reckless abandon, risk all to trust in him.

her whatever you think best." Then Sarai mistreated Hagar; so she fled from her.

7The angel of the LORD found Hagar near a spring in the desert; it was the spring that is beside the road to Shur. **8**And he said, "Hagar, servant of Sarai, where have you come from, and where are you going?"

"I'm running away from my mistress Sarai," she answered.

9Then the angel of the LORD told her, "Go back to your mistress and submit to her." **10**The angel added, "I will so increase your descendants that they will be too numerous to count."

11The angel of the LORD also said to her:

"You are now with child
  and you will have a son.
You shall name him Ishmael,*a*
  for the LORD has heard of your misery.
12He will be a wild donkey of a man;
  his hand will be against everyone
  and everyone's hand against him,
and he will live in hostility
  toward*b* all his brothers."

13She gave this name to the LORD who spoke to her: "You are the God who sees me," for she said, "I have now seen*c* the One who sees me." **14**That is why the well was called Beer Lahai Roi*d*; it is still there, between Kadesh and Bered.

15So Hagar bore Abram a son, and Abram gave the name Ishmael to the son she had borne. **16**Abram was eighty-six years old when Hagar bore him Ishmael.

The Covenant of Circumcision

17 When Abram was ninety-nine years old, the LORD appeared to him and said, "I am God Almighty*e*; walk before me and be blameless. **2**I will confirm my covenant*D* between me and you and will greatly increase your numbers."

3Abram fell facedown, and God said to him, **4**"As for me, this is my covenant with you: You will be the father of many nations. **5**No longer will you be called Abram*f*; your name will be Abraham,*g* for I have made you a father of many nations. **6**I will make you very fruitful; I will make nations of you, and kings will come from you. **7**I will establish my covenant as an everlasting covenant between me and you and your descendants after you for the generations to come, to be your God and the God of your descendants after you. **8**The whole land of Canaan, where you are now an alien*D*, I will give as an everlasting possession to you and your descendants after you; and I will be their God."

9Then God said to Abraham, "As for you, you must keep my covenant, you and your descendants after you for the generations to come. **10**This is my covenant with you and your descendants after you, the covenant you are to keep: Every male among you shall be circumcised*D*. **11**You are to undergo circumcision, and it will be the sign of the covenant between me and you. **12**For the generations to come every male among you who is

so the family name could be continued. Sarai was simply doing her duty according to the culture of that time. In fact, an ancient legal system, the Code of Hammurapi, spelled out the procedures for Sarai's actions.

Why did Hagar despise Sarai? (16:4)
Hagar realized that she was doing for her master what her mistress could not do. So she felt superior to Sarai and began to despise her. Hammurapi's code (see previous note) anticipated such feelings and said that the servant who bore children should be punished if she presumed to be equal to her mistress.

How could Sarai blame Abram? (16:5)
Like many hurting people, Sarai lashed out at someone who was close to her. She might have blamed the system; she might have blamed God for delaying his promise; she might have blamed herself for impatience. Instead, in her distress, she blamed her husband. Wasn't he the head of the family, responsible for everyone in it? Perhaps Sarai appealed to Abram because she knew he could punish Hagar for her insolence.

Did Hagar deserve the treatment she received? (16:6–9)
In one sense, yes. God usually permits the law of the land to prevail, and in this case, God allowed Hagar to suffer for her superior attitude toward Sarai. See *Why did Hagar despise Sarai?* (16:4). Yet God cared compassionately for Hagar and her son. In fact, he blessed her with a promise remarkably like the one he made to Abram (v. 10).

Should people submit to abuse? (16:9)
Every case is different and no general principle can be drawn from one Biblical example. The Bible acknowledges that some will suffer for doing good but says that those who do wrong deserve to be punished (1 Peter 3:17; 4:14–16; Romans 13:3–4). Hagar's actions brought on her own suffering. But when she obeyed God and submitted to Sarai, her change in attitude most likely brought a change in Sarai's actions. Also see *Do we always have to submit?* (1 Peter 2:13–17).

Wild donkey of a man (16:12)
Being wild in the sense of being strong and free was a highly admired trait in that culture. Like a wild donkey in the wilderness, Ishmael would constantly be on the run, hostile to all who would try to come near.

God Almighty (17:1)
El Shaddai, in Hebrew. A special name for God used six times in Genesis, probably meaning *God, the All-powerful One.*

Why did God give Abram a new name? (17:5)
This was the final sealing of the covenant between God and Abram. In ancient Hebrew culture, names carried tremendous significance. Names distinguished a person's status or even a defining circumstance in life. Names were often changed when a person's circumstances changed. In this case, there was not much change in the meaning between *Abram* and *Abraham* (see NIV text notes). But the change did renew and strengthen God's promise as well as deepen the relationship between Abraham and the Lord.

---

a 11 Ishmael means *God hears.*   *b 12* Or *live to the east* / *of*
c 13 Or *seen the back of*   *d 14 Beer Lahai Roi* means *well of the*
Living One who sees me.   *e 1* Hebrew *El-Shaddai*   *f 5 Abram*
means *exalted father.*   *g 5 Abraham* means *father of many.*

The whole land of Canaan . . . I will give you (17:8)

See *Why would God promise Abram land belonging to others?* (15:18–21).

Cut off from his people (17:14)

See *Cut off from my presence* (Lev. 22:3).

Sarai . . . Sarah (17:15)

Like that of Abraham, Sarah's name change probably strengthened the meaning of her name more than it changed her name. Both names seem to convey the idea of *princess*. For more on name changes, see *Why did God give Abram a new name?* (17:5).

Why name a son he laughs? (17:19 and NIV text note)

Some think this was to remind Abraham and Sarah of how they laughed in disbelief when they heard God's promise (v. 17; 18:12). Others suggest that the name was not a rebuke of their unbelief, but a sign of God's joy for the family through whom salvation would come.

eight days old must be circumcised[D], including those born in your household or bought with money from a foreigner—those who are not your offspring. [13]Whether born in your household or bought with your money, they must be circumcised. My covenant in your flesh is to be an everlasting covenant. [14]Any uncircumcised male, who has not been circumcised in the flesh, will be cut off from his people; he has broken my covenant."

[15]God also said to Abraham, "As for Sarai your wife, you are no longer to call her Sarai; her name will be Sarah. [16]I will bless her and will surely give you a son by her. I will bless her so that she will be the mother of nations; kings of peoples will come from her."

[17]Abraham fell facedown; he laughed and said to himself, "Will a son be born to a man a hundred years old? Will Sarah bear a child at the age of ninety?" [18]And Abraham said to God, "If only Ishmael might live under your blessing!"

[19]Then God said, "Yes, but your wife Sarah will bear you a son, and you will call him Isaac.[a] I will establish my covenant with him as an everlasting covenant for his descendants after him. [20]And as for Ishmael, I have heard you: I will surely bless him; I will make him fruitful and will greatly increase his numbers. He will be the father of twelve rulers, and I will make him into a great nation. [21]But my covenant I will establish with Isaac, whom Sarah will bear to you by this time next year." [22]When he had finished speaking with Abraham, God went up from him.

[23]On that very day Abraham took his son Ishmael and all those born in his household or bought with his money, every male in his household, and circumcised them, as God told him. [24]Abraham was ninety-nine years old when he was circumcised, [25]and his son Ishmael was thirteen; [26]Abraham and his son Ishmael were both circumcised on that same day. [27]And every male in Abraham's house-

---

[a]19 *Isaac* means *he laughs.*

Why did God command circumcision? (17:10)

Circumcision was usually practiced in the ancient world as a rite of passage into puberty or marriage, though it does not seem to have been practiced among the Canaanites.

God, however, gave this peculiar custom new meaning when he required it of Abraham. For Abraham, circumcision was a mark of possession, indicating that he belonged to God. It was also a sign of commitment, symbolizing that the Lord alone would be the one he would trust and serve.

Some think it indicated a type of oath: "May I be cut off from my people as my foreskin has been cut off, if I am not faithful to the Lord" (v. 14).

In many ways, God's relationship with Abraham, as symbolized by circumcision, is similar to that of a marriage covenant. The commitment that God intends a husband and a wife to have for each other illustrates the commitment that God wanted from Abraham. Throughout the Old Testament, God characterizes himself as a husband to his people, and adultery is used as a metaphor for their idolatry and unfaithfulness to him (see, for example, Hosea 2:16; 4:15).

hold, including those born in his household or bought from a foreigner, was circumcised[D] with him.

The Three Visitors

18 The LORD appeared to Abraham near the great trees of Mamre while he was sitting at the entrance to his tent in the heat of the day. ²Abraham looked up and saw three men standing nearby. When he saw them, he hurried from the entrance of his tent to meet them and bowed low to the ground.

³He said, "If I have found favor in your eyes, my lord,[a] do not pass your servant by. ⁴Let a little water be brought, and then you may all wash your feet and rest under this tree. ⁵Let me get you something to eat, so you can be refreshed and then go on your way—now that you have come to your servant."

"Very well," they answered, "do as you say."

⁶So Abraham hurried into the tent to Sarah. "Quick," he said, "get three seahs[b] of fine flour and knead it and bake some bread."

⁷Then he ran to the herd and selected a choice, tender calf and gave it to a servant, who hurried to prepare it. ⁸He then brought some curds and milk and the calf that had been prepared, and set these before them. While they ate, he stood near them under a tree.

⁹"Where is your wife Sarah?" they asked him.

"There, in the tent," he said.

¹⁰Then the LORD[c] said, "I will surely return to you about this time next year, and Sarah your wife will have a son."

Now Sarah was listening at the entrance to the tent, which was behind him. ¹¹Abraham and Sarah were already old and well advanced in years, and Sarah was past the age of childbearing. ¹²So Sarah laughed to herself as she thought, "After I am worn out and my master[d] is old, will I now have this pleasure?"

¹³Then the LORD said to Abraham, "Why did Sarah laugh and say, 'Will I really have a child, now that I am old?' ¹⁴Is anything too hard for the LORD? I will return to you at the appointed time next year and Sarah will have a son."

¹⁵Sarah was afraid, so she lied and said, "I did not laugh."

But he said, "Yes, you did laugh."

Abraham Pleads for Sodom

¹⁶When the men got up to leave, they looked down toward Sodom, and Abraham walked along with them to see them on their way. ¹⁷Then the LORD said, "Shall I hide from Abraham what I am about to do? ¹⁸Abraham will surely become a great and powerful nation, and all nations on earth will be blessed through him. ¹⁹For I have chosen him, so that he will direct his children and his household after him to keep the way of the LORD by doing what is right and just, so that the LORD will bring about for Abraham what he has promised him."

²⁰Then the LORD said, "The outcry against Sodom and Gomorrah is so great and their sin so grievous ²¹that I will go down and see if what they have done is as bad as the outcry that has reached me. If not, I will know."

²²The men turned away and went toward Sodom, but

Great trees (18:1)
See *Great tree of Moreh* (12:6).

Why was Abraham so hospitable to strangers? (18:4–5)
Hospitality was one of the most highly regarded virtues of the ancient world. Abraham was undoubtedly a kind and generous man, but he also displayed extraordinary hospitality because of the values and customs of his times.

Why would the Lord come as a man to Abraham? (18:10)
God spoke to his people in many ways—through words (audible or internal), appearances, dreams and visions. He often used prophets as his representatives. Later he would send his Son in the flesh to reveal himself more clearly. God did not limit himself in the ways that he communicated and on rare occasions made physical appearances such as this one (sometimes called a *theophany*). Also see *How did God speak to Abram?* (12:1).

Why did God let Abraham in on his plans? (18:17–19)
Probably because he considered Abraham his friend (Isaiah 41:8). God shared his concerns and plans with Abraham just as friends do. At the same time, it seems that God was also inviting Abraham to intercede on behalf of the righteous people in Sodom and Gomorrah.

Who cried out to God against Sodom and Gomorrah? (18:20)
This appears to be an attempt to describe the ways of God using human expressions and characteristics. So it's possible this simply means that God himself had observed the sinful behavior. But it's also possible that some who were oppressed in the cities cried out for justice, as the Israelites did later in Egypt (Exodus 2:23–25). Also see *How did the people of Sodom sin against the LORD?* (13:13).

Why did God visit the cities in person to check out the facts? (18:21)
This may again be an attempt to describe the ways of God in human terms. An omniscient God does not need to go on fact-finding missions. It's possible this encounter was orchestrated for Abraham's sake, to involve him in the process of interceding for Lot. See *Why did God let Abraham in on his plans?* (18:17–19).

---

*a*3 Or *O Lord*   *b*6 That is, probably about 20 quarts (about 22 liters)   *c*10 Hebrew *Then he*   *d*12 Or *husband*

Is it fair for the righteous to suffer with the wicked? (18:25)

No, it's not fair. But life in a world distorted and ruined by sin is seldom fair. Often the consequences of sinful behavior affect the innocent. Also, in ancient Hebrew culture, people were rewarded or punished as a community, not as individuals. See article: *Why does God allow innocent children to suffer?* (Lam. 2:11–12). In this case, Abraham was pleading for God to overrule standard procedures of judging the whole community. He was asking for God to judge individuals.

Was Abraham bargaining with God? (18:27–32)

In a sense, yes. But in another sense he was interceding earnestly for the city and the few righteous people who might be found in it. Abraham was praying more than he was bargaining.

Why was Lot so hospitable to strangers? (19:2–3)

See *Why was Abraham so hospitable to strangers?* (18:4–5).

Square (19:2)

In the ancient world most towns had no inns or motels as we know them. When a stranger found himself in need of lodging, he would often go to the city square. Ancient laws of hospitality demanded that someone offer lodging.

Why was Sodom filled with homosexuals? (19:4–5)

Canaanite culture was known for many deviant sexual customs, even in its religious worship. See *Shrine prostitute* (Deut. 23:17). It is likely that the addictive nature of such sexual perversion escalated until it reached the proportions described here.

Don't do this wicked thing (19:7)

See *Why does God call homosexual behavior detestable?* (Lev. 18:22).

Why would Lot offer his daughters to be gang raped? (19:8)

Three factors may have contributed to Lot's outrageous proposal: (1) Hospitality was considered to be one of the highest measures of a man. To take a stranger in and let him eat your food was to guarantee his safety—even at personal risk. (2) Wives and daughters were typically viewed as property in his culture. (3) Living as he did in a degenerate society, Lot's values were likely off center. Sin distorts priorities and blurs the line between right and wrong. It was no doubt the combination of these factors that caused Lot to value the safety of his guests more than the well-being of his daughters.

Abraham remained standing before the LORD.*a* **23**Then Abraham approached him and said: "Will you sweep away the righteous*D* with the wicked? **24**What if there are fifty righteous people in the city? Will you really sweep it away and not spare*b* the place for the sake of the fifty righteous people in it? **25**Far be it from you to do such a thing—to kill the righteous with the wicked, treating the righteous and the wicked alike. Far be it from you! Will not the Judge*c* of all the earth do right?"

26The LORD said, "If I find fifty righteous people in the city of Sodom, I will spare the whole place for their sake."

27Then Abraham spoke up again: "Now that I have been so bold as to speak to the Lord, though I am nothing but dust and ashes, **28**what if the number of the righteous is five less than fifty? Will you destroy the whole city because of five people?"

"If I find forty-five there," he said, "I will not destroy it."

29Once again he spoke to him, "What if only forty are found there?"

He said, "For the sake of forty, I will not do it."

30Then he said, "May the Lord not be angry, but let me speak. What if only thirty can be found there?"

He answered, "I will not do it if I find thirty there."

31Abraham said, "Now that I have been so bold as to speak to the Lord, what if only twenty can be found there?"

He said, "For the sake of twenty, I will not destroy it."

32Then he said, "May the Lord not be angry, but let me speak just once more. What if only ten can be found there?"

He answered, "For the sake of ten, I will not destroy it."

33When the LORD had finished speaking with Abraham, he left, and Abraham returned home.

Sodom and Gomorrah Destroyed

19 The two angels arrived at Sodom in the evening, and Lot was sitting in the gateway of the city. When he saw them, he got up to meet them and bowed down with his face to the ground. **2**"My lords," he said, "please turn aside to your servant's house. You can wash your feet and spend the night and then go on your way early in the morning."

"No," they answered, "we will spend the night in the square."

3But he insisted so strongly that they did go with him and entered his house. He prepared a meal for them, baking bread without yeast*D*, and they ate. **4**Before they had gone to bed, all the men from every part of the city of Sodom—both young and old—surrounded the house. **5**They called to Lot, "Where are the men who came to you tonight? Bring them out to us so that we can have sex with them."

6Lot went outside to meet them and shut the door behind him **7**and said, "No, my friends. Don't do this wicked thing. **8**Look, I have two daughters who have never slept with a man. Let me bring them out to you, and you can do what you like with them. But don't do anything to these men, for they have come under the protection of my roof."

9"Get out of our way," they replied. And they said, "This

a22 Masoretic Text; an ancient Hebrew scribal tradition *but the LORD remained standing before Abraham*　　*b24* Or *forgive*; also in verse 26　　*c25* Or *Ruler*

fellow came here as an alien^D, and now he wants to play the judge! We'll treat you worse than them." They kept bringing pressure on Lot and moved forward to break down the door.

¹⁰But the men inside reached out and pulled Lot back into the house and shut the door. ¹¹Then they struck the men who were at the door of the house, young and old, with blindness so that they could not find the door.

¹²The two men said to Lot, "Do you have anyone else here—sons-in-law, sons or daughters, or anyone else in the city who belongs to you? Get them out of here, ¹³because we are going to destroy this place. The outcry to the LORD against its people is so great that he has sent us to destroy it."

¹⁴So Lot went out and spoke to his sons-in-law, who were pledged to marry^a his daughters. He said, "Hurry and get out of this place, because the LORD is about to destroy the city!" But his sons-in-law thought he was joking.

¹⁵With the coming of dawn, the angels urged Lot, saying, "Hurry! Take your wife and your two daughters who are here, or you will be swept away when the city is punished."

¹⁶When he hesitated, the men grasped his hand and the hands of his wife and of his two daughters and led them safely out of the city, for the LORD was merciful to them. ¹⁷As soon as they had brought them out, one of them said, "Flee for your lives! Don't look back, and don't stop anywhere in the plain! Flee to the mountains or you will be swept away!"

¹⁸But Lot said to them, "No, my lords,^b please! ¹⁹Your^c servant has found favor in your^c eyes, and you^c have shown great kindness to me in sparing my life. But I can't flee to the mountains; this disaster will overtake me, and I'll die. ²⁰Look, here is a town near enough to run to, and it is small. Let me flee to it—it is very small, isn't it? Then my life will be spared."

²¹He said to him, "Very well, I will grant this request too; I will not overthrow the town you speak of. ²²But flee there quickly, because I cannot do anything until you reach it." (That is why the town was called Zoar.^d)

²³By the time Lot reached Zoar, the sun had risen over the land. ²⁴Then the LORD rained down burning sulfur on Sodom and Gomorrah—from the LORD out of the heavens. ²⁵Thus he overthrew those cities and the entire plain, including all those living in the cities—and also the vegetation in the land. ²⁶But Lot's wife looked back, and she became a pillar of salt.

²⁷Early the next morning Abraham got up and returned to the place where he had stood before the LORD. ²⁸He looked down toward Sodom and Gomorrah, toward all the land of the plain, and he saw dense smoke rising from the land, like smoke from a furnace.

²⁹So when God destroyed the cities of the plain, he remembered Abraham, and he brought Lot out of the catastrophe that overthrew the cities where Lot had lived.

Lot and His Daughters

³⁰Lot and his two daughters left Zoar and settled in the mountains, for he was afraid to stay in Zoar. He and his two daughters lived in a cave. ³¹One day the older daughter said to the younger, "Our father is old, and there is no

Were Lot's sons-in-law among those struck with blindness? (19:14)

We are not told whether Lot's prospective sons-in-law were smitten by blindness. If they had been, it would seem they might have been more receptive to Lot's warnings. As it was, they dismissed his words as nothing more than a joke.

Burning sulfur (19:24)

Archaeological evidence indicates that Sodom and Gomorrah were buried beneath the shallow waters of the southern part of the Dead Sea (see Map 1 at the back of this Bible). We know that there are deposits of asphalt and sulfur still found in this area. The Lord may have used an earthquake with volcanic-like results to judge these cities.

Why did God turn Lot's wife into a pillar of salt? (19:26)

Lot and his wife never seemed willing to separate themselves from the Canaanite world. Lot wanted to be a part of Sodom even though he knew about its wickedness. When forced to flee, he still preferred to stay in a neighboring town rather than follow God's advice. It was the same kind of reluctance that caused Lot's wife to take one look too many at the life she was leaving behind. As a result, it seems she was buried beneath the falling sulfur and became a pillar of salt.

How could Lot's daughters justify incest with their father? (19:31–32)

Apparently Lot's daughters had themselves been affected by their culture so that their consciences were not bothered by what they proposed. With all that they knew destroyed and little hope for the future, they felt compelled to have children (the primary role for women in that culture) to preserve their father's name and to support themselves in old age.

^a14 Or were married to   ^b18 Or No, Lord; or No, my lord
^c19 The Hebrew is singular.   ^d22 Zoar means small.

man around here to lie with us, as is the custom all over the earth. **32**Let's get our father to drink wine and then lie with him and preserve our family line through our father."

33That night they got their father to drink wine, and the older daughter went in and lay with him. He was not aware of it when she lay down or when she got up.

34The next day the older daughter said to the younger, "Last night I lay with my father. Let's get him to drink wine again tonight, and you go in and lie with him so we can preserve our family line through our father." **35**So they got their father to drink wine that night also, and the younger daughter went and lay with him. Again he was not aware of it when she lay down or when she got up.

36So both of Lot's daughters became pregnant by their father. **37**The older daughter had a son, and she named him Moab*a*; he is the father of the Moabites of today. **38**The younger daughter also had a son, and she named him Ben-Ammi*b*; he is the father of the Ammonites of today.

Abraham and Abimelech

20 Now Abraham moved on from there into the region of the Negev*D* and lived between Kadesh and Shur. For a while he stayed in Gerar, **2**and there Abraham said of his wife Sarah, "She is my sister." Then Abimelech king of Gerar sent for Sarah and took her.

3But God came to Abimelech in a dream one night and said to him, "You are as good as dead because of the woman you have taken; she is a married woman."

4Now Abimelech had not gone near her, so he said, "Lord, will you destroy an innocent nation? **5**Did he not say to me, 'She is my sister,' and didn't she also say, 'He is my brother'? I have done this with a clear conscience and clean hands."

6Then God said to him in the dream, "Yes, I know you did this with a clear conscience, and so I have kept you from sinning against me. That is why I did not let you touch her. **7**Now return the man's wife, for he is a prophet*D*, and he will pray for you and you will live. But if you do not return her, you may be sure that you and all yours will die."

8Early the next morning Abimelech summoned all his officials, and when he told them all that had happened, they were very much afraid. **9**Then Abimelech called Abraham in and said, "What have you done to us? How have I wronged you that you have brought such great guilt upon me and my kingdom? You have done things to me that should not be done." **10**And Abimelech asked Abraham, "What was your reason for doing this?"

11Abraham replied, "I said to myself, 'There is surely no fear of God in this place, and they will kill me because of my wife.' **12**Besides, she really is my sister, the daughter of my father though not of my mother; and she became my wife. **13**And when God had me wander from my father's household, I said to her, 'This is how you can show your love to me: Everywhere we go, say of me, "He is my brother." ' "

14Then Abimelech brought sheep and cattle and male and female slaves and gave them to Abraham, and he re-

SCRIPTURE LINK (20:2)

Sarah, presented as Abraham's sister, had earlier been taken into Pharaoh's harem. See 12:10–15.

Why did Abraham lie again about Sarah? (20:2)

It is a surprise to find this story at this point in Abraham's life—after the renewed covenant was given, after circumcision, after his name change, even after the Lord was a guest at his tent. In reality, though, people often fail at the same point more than once. Weakness can undermine one's ability to trust in God—even after many victories.

Why choose an elderly woman for a wife? (20:2)

There were many reasons for kings to marry in the ancient world other than for beauty and youth. It was a sign of power and wealth to have many wives. Marriage also formed the basis for some treaties, bonding two groups of people. Perhaps Abimelech wanted to extend the courtesy of an agreement between his people and Abraham's by taking Abraham's elderly "sister" as a wife. See article: *Why did David have so many wives and concubines?* (2 Samuel 5:13).

Wasn't Abraham more to blame than Abimelech? (20:7)

Yes. It was Abraham's deception that prompted Abimelech to do what he did. God took Abimelech's innocent motives into account and prevented something worse from happening (v. 6). Nevertheless, he could not be excused from the consequences of his actions now that God had informed him of the actual situation.

---

a37 Moab sounds like the Hebrew for *from father.*   *b38 Ben-Ammi* means *son of my people.*

turned Sarah his wife to him. **15**And Abimelech said, "My land is before you; live wherever you like."

16To Sarah he said, "I am giving your brother a thousand shekels^D^a of silver. This is to cover the offense against you before all who are with you; you are completely vindicated."

17Then Abraham prayed to God, and God healed Abimelech, his wife and his slave girls so they could have children again, **18**for the LORD had closed up every womb in Abimelech's household because of Abraham's wife Sarah.

The Birth of Isaac

21 Now the LORD was gracious to Sarah as he had said, and the LORD did for Sarah what he had promised. **2**Sarah became pregnant and bore a son to Abraham in his old age, at the very time God had promised him. **3**Abraham gave the name Isaac^b to the son Sarah bore him. **4**When his son Isaac was eight days old, Abraham circumcised^D him, as God commanded him. **5**Abraham was a hundred years old when his son Isaac was born to him.

6Sarah said, "God has brought me laughter, and everyone who hears about this will laugh with me." **7**And she added, "Who would have said to Abraham that Sarah would nurse children? Yet I have borne him a son in his old age."

Hagar and Ishmael Sent Away

8The child grew and was weaned, and on the day Isaac was weaned Abraham held a great feast. **9**But Sarah saw that the son whom Hagar the Egyptian had borne to Abraham was mocking, **10**and she said to Abraham, "Get rid of that slave woman and her son, for that slave woman's son will never share in the inheritance with my son Isaac."

11The matter distressed Abraham greatly because it concerned his son. **12**But God said to him, "Do not be so distressed about the boy and your maidservant. Listen to whatever Sarah tells you, because it is through Isaac that your offspring^c will be reckoned. **13**I will make the son of the maidservant into a nation also, because he is your offspring."

14Early the next morning Abraham took some food and a skin of water and gave them to Hagar. He set them on her shoulders and then sent her off with the boy. She went on her way and wandered in the desert of Beersheba.

15When the water in the skin was gone, she put the boy under one of the bushes. **16**Then she went off and sat down nearby, about a bowshot away, for she thought, "I cannot watch the boy die." And as she sat there nearby, she^d began to sob.

17God heard the boy crying, and the angel of God called to Hagar from heaven and said to her, "What is the matter, Hagar? Do not be afraid; God has heard the boy crying as he lies there. **18**Lift the boy up and take him by the hand, for I will make him into a great nation."

19Then God opened her eyes and she saw a well of water. So she went and filled the skin with water and gave the boy a drink.

20God was with the boy as he grew up. He lived in the

How could money pay for the offense against Sarah? (20:16)

Money was simply Abimelech's way of offering his sincere apologies for what was a terrible mistake. He probably hoped that the money would show that he was well-intentioned and did not mean to shame Sarah. He also may have hoped that the gifts would help him gain favor with Abraham and Abraham's God. His wife and concubines had become unable to bear children because he had taken Sarah (v. 18); perhaps he thought a gift would somehow placate God's anger.

How long had Sarah been in Abimelech's house? (20:17–18)

Apparently long enough for Abimelech to notice a disturbing pattern: ever since she arrived, none of Abimelech's wives were able to conceive.

Circumcised . . . as God commanded (21:4)

See article: *Why did God command circumcision?* (17:10).

What was so important about weaning a child? (21:8)

In ancient times, the weaning of a child was a significant rite of passage. In those days, many children died before they reached this age (usually two or three). The weaning indicated that, having survived so far, the child would likely make it to adulthood and become an heir. Since Isaac was the promised son, the event was especially significant for Abraham and Sarah.

Why did God provide for those he banished? (21:13–21)

God intended to create a line of descendants through the child of promise, Isaac. His taking care of Ishmael, whose birth was not divinely sanctioned, showed his mercy and loyalty to Abraham.

Was Abraham an irresponsible father? (21:14)

Abraham here acts only when he is assured by God that both Ishmael's and Hagar's needs will be cared for. Most likely this separation from his son caused him great concern (see v. 11).

Angel of God (21:17)

See *Was this an angel or the Lord?* (Judges 6:11).

---

^a16 That is, about 25 pounds (about 11.5 kilograms)   ^b3 *Isaac* means *he laughs*.   ^c12 Or *seed*   ^d16 Hebrew; Septuagint *the child*

desert and became an archer. [21]While he was living in the Desert of Paran, his mother got a wife for him from Egypt.

The Treaty at Beersheba

[22]At that time Abimelech and Phicol the commander of his forces said to Abraham, "God is with you in everything you do. [23]Now swear to me here before God that you will not deal falsely with me or my children or my descendants. Show to me and the country where you are living as an alien[D] the same kindness I have shown to you."

[24]Abraham said, "I swear it."

[25]Then Abraham complained to Abimelech about a well of water that Abimelech's servants had seized. [26]But Abimelech said, "I don't know who has done this. You did not tell me, and I heard about it only today."

[27]So Abraham brought sheep and cattle and gave them to Abimelech, and the two men made a treaty. [28]Abraham set apart seven ewe lambs from the flock, [29]and Abimelech asked Abraham, "What is the meaning of these seven ewe lambs you have set apart by themselves?"

[30]He replied, "Accept these seven lambs from my hand as a witness that I dug this well."

[31]So that place was called Beersheba,[a] because the two men swore an oath there.

[32]After the treaty had been made at Beersheba, Abimelech and Phicol the commander of his forces returned to the land of the Philistines. [33]Abraham planted a tamarisk tree in Beersheba, and there he called upon the name of the LORD, the Eternal God. [34]And Abraham stayed in the land of the Philistines for a long time.

Abraham Tested

22 Some time later God tested Abraham. He said to him, "Abraham!"

"Here I am," he replied.

[2]Then God said, "Take your son, your only son, Isaac, whom you love, and go to the region of Moriah. Sacrifice[D] him there as a burnt offering[D] on one of the mountains I will tell you about."

[3]Early the next morning Abraham got up and saddled his donkey. He took with him two of his servants and his son Isaac. When he had cut enough wood for the burnt offering, he set out for the place God had told him about. [4]On the third day Abraham looked up and saw the place in the distance. [5]He said to his servants, "Stay here with the donkey while I and the boy go over there. We will worship and then we will come back to you."

[6]Abraham took the wood for the burnt offering and placed it on his son Isaac, and he himself carried the fire and the knife. As the two of them went on together, [7]Isaac spoke up and said to his father Abraham, "Father?"

"Yes, my son?" Abraham replied.

"The fire and wood are here," Isaac said, "but where is the lamb for the burnt offering?"

[8]Abraham answered, "God himself will provide the lamb for the burnt offering, my son." And the two of them went on together.

[9]When they reached the place God had told him about, Abraham built an altar there and arranged the wood on it. He bound his son Isaac and laid him on the altar, on top of the wood. [10]Then he reached out his hand and took the

---

How did ewe lambs guarantee the deal? (21:28–30)

The giving of animals was the ancient equivalent of writing a contract. It was a visible sign that an agreement had been reached. With no police, courts of law or lawyers, people of Abraham's era had to find their own way of guaranteeing agreements.

Called upon the name of the LORD (21:33)

A custom or formality used in sealing a covenant similar to swearing on the Bible in court today. This seems to accompany some physical act. Together, they may have signified to ancient audiences that Abraham was learning to worship God and that God makes and keeps promises.

God tested Abraham (22:1)

See *Does God have to test us to find out what's in our hearts?* (2 Chron. 32:31). Also see articles: *Why did testing come to Job?* (Job 23:10) and *Why does God test us?* (Psalm 81:7).

Did Isaac submit or fight back? (22:9)

No mention is made of Isaac's behavior. This silence may indicate he did not struggle. According to Jewish tradition, Isaac was a willing sacrifice who threw himself on the altar.

---

a31 Beersheba can mean *well of seven* or *well of the oath.*

knife to slay his son. **11**But the angel of the LORD called out to him from heaven, "Abraham! Abraham!"

"Here I am," he replied.

12"Do not lay a hand on the boy," he said. "Do not do anything to him. Now I know that you fear God, because you have not withheld from me your son, your only son."

13Abraham looked up and there in a thicket he saw a ram*a* caught by its horns. He went over and took the ram and sacrificed it as a burnt offering*b* instead of his son. **14**So Abraham called that place The LORD Will Provide. And to this day it is said, "On the mountain of the LORD it will be provided."

15The angel of the LORD called to Abraham from heaven a second time **16**and said, "I swear by myself, declares the LORD, that because you have done this and have not withheld your son, your only son, **17**I will surely bless you and make your descendants as numerous as the stars in the sky and as the sand on the seashore. Your descendants will take possession of the cities of their enemies, **18**and through your offspring*b* all nations on earth will be blessed, because you have obeyed me."

19Then Abraham returned to his servants, and they set off together for Beersheba. And Abraham stayed in Beersheba.

Nahor's Sons

20Some time later Abraham was told, "Milcah is also a mother; she has borne sons to your brother Nahor: **21**Uz the firstborn*D*, Buz his brother, Kemuel (the father of Aram), **22**Kesed, Hazo, Pildash, Jidlaph and Bethuel." **23**Bethuel became the father of Rebekah. Milcah bore these eight sons to Abraham's brother Nahor. **24**His concu-

a13 Many manuscripts of the Masoretic Text, Samaritan Pentateuch, Septuagint and Syriac; most manuscripts of the Masoretic Text *a ram behind ⌊him⌋*   *b18* Or *seed*

Why did Abraham rename this place? (22:14)

Because of the significant act God performed there. The name would be testimony of God's faithfulness to future generations. God had indeed provided. The name is an Old Testament phrase for God, which literally means *the one who will see to it.*

Was God's promise conditional? (22:16–17)

A conditional promise implies one can earn its fulfillment. Some say Abraham did: his sacrifice set in motion God's plan. Others suggest Abraham's faith was tested, but God's promises were not dependent on its authenticity. God's promise was unconditional based on his faithfulness, not Abraham's.

Numerous as the stars . . . and as the sand (22:17)

See article: *Can the Bible exaggerate and still be true?* (2 Chron. 1:9–15).

Would God ever ask us to do wrong? (22:2)

No. But he will push to the limit the boundaries of our commitment to him. The first words of this chapter—*Some time later God tested Abraham*—suggest that God never really intended the sacrifice to take place. The point was the test: Did Abraham really trust God?

We are shocked by this today because we know of the Bible's strong warnings against child sacrifice (Lev. 20:1–5; 2 Kings 23:10; Jer. 32:35). That's what pagan gods demanded, not the holy God of Israel.

Because the Biblical laws against child sacrifice came later, we can't be sure what Abraham understood about it. Still, God had shaped Abraham's sense of values. And this request would not have been consistent with God as he had known him to this point. So perhaps Abraham was somewhat confused or puzzled by the nature of God's command. Abraham's primary concern however was crystal clear: He was being asked to give up the son promised to him.

God's command was harsh (even for the ancients). It raises for us a poignant question: Will we entrust our futures unreservedly to the One who calls us? Or will we doubt God and place our trust in our own understanding?

Our God does not require human sacrifice, but heart sacrifice. God desires in us an obedient heart willing to do what he asks.

bine[D], whose name was Reumah, also had sons: Tebah, Gaham, Tahash and Maacah.

The Death[D] of Sarah

23
Sarah lived to be a hundred and twenty-seven years old. [2]She died at Kiriath Arba (that is, Hebron) in the land of Canaan, and Abraham went to mourn for Sarah and to weep over her.

[3]Then Abraham rose from beside his dead wife and spoke to the Hittites.[a] He said, [4]"I am an alien[D] and a stranger among you. Sell me some property for a burial site here so I can bury my dead."

[5]The Hittites replied to Abraham, [6]"Sir, listen to us. You are a mighty prince among us. Bury your dead in the choicest of our tombs. None of us will refuse you his tomb for burying your dead."

[7]Then Abraham rose and bowed down before the people of the land, the Hittites. [8]He said to them, "If you are willing to let me bury my dead, then listen to me and intercede[D] with Ephron son of Zohar on my behalf [9]so he will sell me the cave of Machpelah, which belongs to him and is at the end of his field. Ask him to sell it to me for the full price as a burial site among you."

[10]Ephron the Hittite was sitting among his people and he replied to Abraham in the hearing of all the Hittites who had come to the gate of his city. [11]"No, my lord," he said. "Listen to me; I give[b] you the field, and I give[b] you the cave that is in it. I give[b] it to you in the presence of my people. Bury your dead."

[12]Again Abraham bowed down before the people of the land [13]and he said to Ephron in their hearing, "Listen to me, if you will. I will pay the price of the field. Accept it from me so I can bury my dead there."

[14]Ephron answered Abraham, [15]"Listen to me, my lord; the land is worth four hundred shekels[D][c] of silver, but what is that between me and you? Bury your dead."

[16]Abraham agreed to Ephron's terms and weighed out for him the price he had named in the hearing of the Hittites: four hundred shekels of silver, according to the weight current among the merchants.

[17]So Ephron's field in Machpelah near Mamre—both the field and the cave in it, and all the trees within the borders of the field—was deeded [18]to Abraham as his property in the presence of all the Hittites who had come to the gate of the city. [19]Afterward Abraham buried his wife Sarah in the cave in the field of Machpelah near Mamre (which is at Hebron) in the land of Canaan. [20]So the field and the cave in it were deeded to Abraham by the Hittites as a burial site.

Isaac and Rebekah

24
Abraham was now old and well advanced in years, and the LORD had blessed him in every way. [2]He said to the chief[d] servant in his household, the one in charge of all that he had, "Put your hand under my thigh. [3]I want you to swear by the LORD, the God of heaven and the God of earth, that you will not get a wife for my son from the daughters of the Canaanites, among whom I am living, [4]but will go to my country and my own relatives and get a wife for my son Isaac."

How did Sarah live so long? (23:1)
See *What was the secret to such a long life?* (5:5).

Was this the usual way to do business at that time? (23:1–18)
Indirection and courtesy were customary in ancient Near East trading practices. Ephron's offer of a gift was not meant to be taken seriously. Ephron knew Abraham would not take a gift, especially since he was a wealthy man. This social pressure was one reason why business deals were made at the gate in front of witnesses. The terms of the agreement were not written down, which was common legal practice. No one could change the terms since a group of witnesses would report what actually was said.

Cave of Machpelah (23:9)
Burial site of Abraham and Sarah and several important descendants including Isaac, Rebekah, Leah and Jacob.

Deeded (23:17)
A deed was a contract made with the whole community. Should either party ever contest it, the community would be called in to testify.

Put your hand under my thigh (24:2)
See *Why put one's hand under someone's thigh?* (47:29).

---

[a]3 Or *the sons of Heth*; also in verses 5, 7, 10, 16, 18 and 20
[b]11 Or *sell*   [c]15 That is, about 10 pounds (about 4.5 kilograms)
[d]2 Or *oldest*

⁵The servant asked him, "What if the woman is unwilling to come back with me to this land? Shall I then take your son back to the country you came from?"

⁶"Make sure that you do not take my son back there," Abraham said. ⁷"The LORD, the God of heaven, who brought me out of my father's household and my native land and who spoke to me and promised me on oath, saying, 'To your offspringᵃ I will give this land'—he will send his angel before you so that you can get a wife for my son from there. ⁸If the woman is unwilling to come back with you, then you will be released from this oath of mine. Only do not take my son back there." ⁹So the servant put his hand under the thigh of his master Abraham and swore an oath to him concerning this matter.

¹⁰Then the servant took ten of his master's camels and left, taking with him all kinds of good things from his master. He set out for Aram Naharaimᵇ and made his way to the town of Nahor. ¹¹He had the camels kneel down near the well outside the town; it was toward evening, the time the women go out to draw water.

¹²Then he prayed, "O LORD, God of my master Abraham, give me success today, and show kindness to my master Abraham. ¹³See, I am standing beside this spring, and the daughters of the townspeople are coming out to draw water. ¹⁴May it be that when I say to a girl, 'Please let down your jar that I may have a drink,' and she says, 'Drink, and I'll water your camels too'—let her be the one you have chosen for your servant Isaac. By this I will know that you have shown kindness to my master."

¹⁵Before he had finished praying, Rebekah came out with her jar on her shoulder. She was the daughter of Bethuel son of Milcah, who was the wife of Abraham's brother Nahor. ¹⁶The girl was very beautiful, a virgin; no man had ever lain with her. She went down to the spring, filled her jar and came up again.

¹⁷The servant hurried to meet her and said, "Please give me a little water from your jar."

ᵃ7 Or *seed*   ᵇ10 That is, Northwest Mesopotamia

Why did Abraham want his son to marry a relative? (24:4)
This refers to marriage within a clan, an acceptable custom of the time. Some think this hints at a later law given to prohibit Israelites from intermarrying with other Canaanite people (Exodus 34:16; Deut. 7:3). This would curtail their pandering after false gods. Others say it can be likened simply to wanting children to marry within their ethnic group.

SCRIPTURE LINK (24:7)
This promise to Abraham is recorded in 12:7.

How was Rebekah related to Isaac? (24:15)
Rebekah would have been Isaac's father's grandniece (see v. 48).

Should we ask for a sign to prove God's will? (24:14)

Abraham's servant did not ask for some extraordinary sign, like fire to fall from heaven. What he asked for was to see some indication of one who would make a valuable wife in that culture—one who was friendly, hospitable and hardworking. The unusual circumstances, however, ultimately proved Rebekah was chosen by God to be Isaac's wife.

Does this Biblical example teach a fail-proof method of knowing God's will? No. God promises us his guidance and his presence, not necessarily external signs. He may choose to grant us events that, upon looking back, we can trace to his leading. But that should not be expected. Much of God's will is learned in the struggle of doubt and faith.

He wants us to live by the principles he's laid down in the Bible. He is concerned about *how we live* as much as *what we do*. That doesn't mean that what we do isn't important, for our actions reflect our allegiance to God. But doing God's will means living one's life in obedience to all that he has revealed to us.

God also gives us his Word and the godly advice of others to discern his will.

How much water would ten camels drink? (24:20)
A lot! The servant had only asked for a little of her water for himself. Her offer was a significant gesture of hospitality.

Nose ring (24:22)
A common article of jewelry for women in the Middle East. The nose may have been pierced.

SCRIPTURE LINK (24:29) Rebekah had a brother named Laban
Rebekah later sent her son Jacob to live with Laban (27:43), and Jacob married his daughters Leah and Rachel (29:14–30).

Why tell the story all over again? (24:34–49)
In Hebrew storytelling, repetition was often used to stress important events. It also may have been used to aid the listeners in memorizing the story. Often the repeated story differed from the first time it was told. Details were likely added for emphasis. Here the story is told to reiterate that God was at work in these events.

18"Drink, my lord," she said, and quickly lowered the jar to her hands and gave him a drink.

19After she had given him a drink, she said, "I'll draw water for your camels too, until they have finished drinking." **20**So she quickly emptied her jar into the trough, ran back to the well to draw more water, and drew enough for all his camels. **21**Without saying a word, the man watched her closely to learn whether or not the LORD had made his journey successful.

22When the camels had finished drinking, the man took out a gold nose ring weighing a beka[a] and two gold bracelets weighing ten shekels[b][b] **23**Then he asked, "Whose daughter are you? Please tell me, is there room in your father's house for us to spend the night?"

24She answered him, "I am the daughter of Bethuel, the son that Milcah bore to Nahor." **25**And she added, "We have plenty of straw and fodder, as well as room for you to spend the night."

26Then the man bowed down and worshiped the LORD, **27**saying, "Praise be to the LORD, the God of my master Abraham, who has not abandoned his kindness and faithfulness to my master. As for me, the LORD has led me on the journey to the house of my master's relatives."

28The girl ran and told her mother's household about these things. **29**Now Rebekah had a brother named Laban, and he hurried out to the man at the spring. **30**As soon as he had seen the nose ring, and the bracelets on his sister's arms, and had heard Rebekah tell what the man said to her, he went out to the man and found him standing by the camels near the spring. **31**"Come, you who are blessed by the LORD," he said. "Why are you standing out here? I have prepared the house and a place for the camels."

32So the man went to the house, and the camels were unloaded. Straw and fodder were brought for the camels, and water for him and his men to wash their feet. **33**Then food was set before him, but he said, "I will not eat until I have told you what I have to say."

"Then tell us," ⌊Laban⌋ said.

34So he said, "I am Abraham's servant. **35**The LORD has blessed my master abundantly, and he has become wealthy. He has given him sheep and cattle, silver and gold, menservants and maidservants, and camels and donkeys. **36**My master's wife Sarah has borne him a son in her[c] old age, and he has given him everything he owns. **37**And my master made me swear an oath, and said, 'You must not get a wife for my son from the daughters of the Canaanites, in whose land I live, **38**but go to my father's family and to my own clan, and get a wife for my son.'

39"Then I asked my master, 'What if the woman will not come back with me?'

40"He replied, 'The LORD, before whom I have walked, will send his angel with you and make your journey a success, so that you can get a wife for my son from my own clan and from my father's family. **41**Then, when you go to my clan, you will be released from my oath even if they refuse to give her to you—you will be released from my oath.'

42"When I came to the spring today, I said, 'O LORD, God of my master Abraham, if you will, please grant success to the journey on which I have come. **43**See, I am

---

[a]22 That is, about 1/5 ounce (about 5.5 grams)   [b]22 That is, about 4 ounces (about 110 grams)   [c]36 Or his

standing beside this spring; if a maiden comes out to draw water and I say to her, "Please let me drink a little water from your jar," **44**and if she says to me, "Drink, and I'll draw water for your camels too," let her be the one the LORD has chosen for my master's son.'

45"Before I finished praying in my heart, Rebekah came out, with her jar on her shoulder. She went down to the spring and drew water, and I said to her, 'Please give me a drink.'

46"She quickly lowered her jar from her shoulder and said, 'Drink, and I'll water your camels too.' So I drank, and she watered the camels also.

47"I asked her, 'Whose daughter are you?'

"She said, 'The daughter of Bethuel son of Nahor, whom Milcah bore to him.'

"Then I put the ring in her nose and the bracelets on her arms, **48**and I bowed down and worshiped the LORD. I praised the LORD, the God of my master Abraham, who had led me on the right road to get the granddaughter of my master's brother for his son. **49**Now if you will show kindness and faithfulness to my master, tell me; and if not, tell me, so I may know which way to turn."

50Laban and Bethuel answered, "This is from the LORD; we can say nothing to you one way or the other. **51**Here is Rebekah; take her and go, and let her become the wife of your master's son, as the LORD has directed."

52When Abraham's servant heard what they said, he bowed down to the ground before the LORD. **53**Then the servant brought out gold and silver jewelry and articles of clothing and gave them to Rebekah; he also gave costly gifts to her brother and to her mother. **54**Then he and the men who were with him ate and drank and spent the night there.

When they got up the next morning, he said, "Send me on my way to my master."

55But her brother and her mother replied, "Let the girl remain with us ten days or so; then you[a] may go."

56But he said to them, "Do not detain me, now that the LORD has granted success to my journey. Send me on my way so I may go to my master."

57Then they said, "Let's call the girl and ask her about it." **58**So they called Rebekah and asked her, "Will you go with this man?"

"I will go," she said.

59So they sent their sister Rebekah on her way, along with her nurse and Abraham's servant and his men. **60**And they blessed Rebekah and said to her,

"Our sister, may you increase
    to thousands upon thousands;
may your offspring possess
    the gates of their enemies."

61Then Rebekah and her maids got ready and mounted their camels and went back with the man. So the servant took Rebekah and left.

62Now Isaac had come from Beer Lahai Roi, for he was living in the Negev[D]. **63**He went out to the field one evening to meditate,[b] and as he looked up, he saw camels approaching. **64**Rebekah also looked up and saw Isaac. She got down from her camel **65**and asked the servant, "Who is that man in the field coming to meet us?"

---

a55 Or *she*   b63 The meaning of the Hebrew for this word is uncertain.

Was this a normal way to find a wife? (24:50–51)
How Rebekah and Isaac met was not typical. The circumstances leading up to their marriage were divinely orchestrated. But the marriage arrangement made between the parents (Abraham represented by the servant) was customary.

Why was Abraham's servant in such a hurry? (24:56)
Some say the servant was afraid to hold back the will of God, which was clearly evident in these events. The outcome could not be delayed. Others say the servant wanted to hurry back to see if Abraham was still alive to witness the union. The servant's early departure, though, was not customary.

What was Rebekah agreeing to? (24:58)
Radical change. She was giving up her life as she knew it for someone she'd never met. She was leaving her ancestral home for a new land and a new life.

What did this blessing do for Rebekah? (24:60)
Some say it confirmed God's leading in the whole matter. The blessing is similar to the one God gave Abraham in 22:17—*Your descendants will take possession of the cities of their enemies*. It showed how carefully and intentionally God had brought the two of them together. Others see the blessing as a customary pronouncement of fertility.

Why did Rebekah cover herself with a veil? (24:65)
Some say the veil was a summer dress with enough material so it could be thrown over the head to conceal her face. Others think it was a head covering used by brides before entering the presence of the bridegroom. Either way, the veiling was an ancient custom, probably symbolizing the bride's modesty and her dependence upon the groom.

With no wedding ceremony, what made this marriage legal? (24:67)

The agreement between the two families. The financial arrangements were specified beforehand. The actual ceremony consisted of the bride's move from her father's house to the bridegroom's residence. The bridal week of celebration followed.

If Isaac's birth was a miracle, were these births also? (25:2)

No. Isaac's birth was a miracle because his mother Sarah had been unable to conceive. God miraculously healed her womb, and Isaac was born. None of these later children shared in Isaac's special status. Isaac was the miracle child through whom God would bless the rest of the nations.

Why did Abraham have concubines? (25:6)

See *Did female servants usually become concubines?* (30:3) and article: *Why did David have so many wives and concubines?* (2 Samuel 5:13).

Why did Abraham send his concubines' sons away? (25:6)

Abraham was physically communicating that Isaac was the sole heir. The torch was being passed on to the new patriarch. Only Isaac would inherit the promise of land, offspring and divine presence (vv. 12–18).

How did Abraham live to be so old? (25:7–8)

See *What was the secret to such a long life?* (5:5).

Gathered to his people (25:8)

A Hebrew expression meaning Abraham joined his ancestors in death (2 Kings 22:20).

Why the hostility? (25:18)

Some think the words *in hostility toward* should be translated *to the east of* (see NIV text note), in which case there was no hostility. Others believe the division between the Ishmaelites (also called Arabs) and their Israelite brothers naturally led to hostility. The conflicts probably arose over land use and border lines.

Are these words a prediction or predestination? (25:23)

Both. This is a prediction of what will be but also an indication of God's divine appointment. The message from God reverses the custom of ancient preference for the firstborn. Traditionally, the younger son should serve the elder, but not so here. God is sovereign over human affairs (Isaiah 46:10), but human actions bring about God's will (Gen. 50:20).

"He is my master," the servant answered. So she took her veil and covered herself.

66Then the servant told Isaac all he had done. **67**Isaac brought her into the tent of his mother Sarah, and he married Rebekah. So she became his wife, and he loved her; and Isaac was comforted after his mother's death.[D]

The Death of Abraham

25 Abraham took[a] another wife, whose name was Keturah. **2**She bore him Zimran, Jokshan, Medan, Midian, Ishbak and Shuah. **3**Jokshan was the father of Sheba and Dedan; the descendants of Dedan were the Asshurites, the Letushites and the Leummites. **4**The sons of Midian were Ephah, Epher, Hanoch, Abida and Eldaah. All these were descendants of Keturah.

5Abraham left everything he owned to Isaac. **6**But while he was still living, he gave gifts to the sons of his concubines[D] and sent them away from his son Isaac to the land of the east.

7Altogether, Abraham lived a hundred and seventy-five years. **8**Then Abraham breathed his last and died at a good old age, an old man and full of years; and he was gathered to his people. **9**His sons Isaac and Ishmael buried him in the cave of Machpelah near Mamre, in the field of Ephron son of Zohar the Hittite, **10**the field Abraham had bought from the Hittites.[b] There Abraham was buried with his wife Sarah. **11**After Abraham's death, God blessed his son Isaac, who then lived near Beer Lahai Roi.

Ishmael's Sons

12This is the account of Abraham's son Ishmael, whom Sarah's maidservant, Hagar the Egyptian, bore to Abraham.

13These are the names of the sons of Ishmael, listed in the order of their birth: Nebaioth the firstborn[D] of Ishmael, Kedar, Adbeel, Mibsam, **14**Mishma, Dumah, Massa, **15**Hadad, Tema, Jetur, Naphish and Kedemah. **16**These were the sons of Ishmael, and these are the names of the twelve tribal rulers according to their settlements and camps. **17**Altogether, Ishmael lived a hundred and thirty-seven years. He breathed his last and died, and he was gathered to his people. **18**His descendants settled in the area from Havilah to Shur, near the border of Egypt, as you go toward Asshur. And they lived in hostility toward[c] all their brothers.

Jacob and Esau

19This is the account of Abraham's son Isaac.

Abraham became the father of Isaac, **20**and Isaac was forty years old when he married Rebekah daughter of Bethuel the Aramean from Paddan Aram[d] and sister of Laban the Aramean.

21Isaac prayed to the LORD on behalf of his wife, because she was barren. The LORD answered his prayer, and his wife Rebekah became pregnant. **22**The babies jostled each other within her, and she said, "Why is this happening to me?" So she went to inquire of the LORD.

23The LORD said to her,

"Two nations are in your womb,

---

a1 Or *had taken*   *b10* Or *the sons of Heth*   *c18* Or *lived to the east of*   *d20* That is, Northwest Mesopotamia

and two peoples from within you will be
   separated;
one people will be stronger than the other,
   and the older will serve the younger."

24When the time came for her to give birth, there were twin boys in her womb. **25**The first to come out was red, and his whole body was like a hairy garment; so they named him Esau.*a* **26**After this, his brother came out, with his hand grasping Esau's heel; so he was named Jacob.*b* Isaac was sixty years old when Rebekah gave birth to them.

27The boys grew up, and Esau became a skillful hunter, a man of the open country, while Jacob was a quiet man, staying among the tents. **28**Isaac, who had a taste for wild game, loved Esau, but Rebekah loved Jacob.

29Once when Jacob was cooking some stew, Esau came in from the open country, famished. **30**He said to Jacob, "Quick, let me have some of that red stew! I'm famished!" (That is why he was also called Edom.*D, c*)

31Jacob replied, "First sell me your birthright.*D*"

32"Look, I am about to die," Esau said. "What good is the birthright to me?"

33But Jacob said, "Swear to me first." So he swore an oath to him, selling his birthright to Jacob.

34Then Jacob gave Esau some bread and some lentil stew. He ate and drank, and then got up and left.

So Esau despised his birthright.

Isaac and Abimelech

26 Now there was a famine in the land—besides the earlier famine of Abraham's time—and Isaac went to Abimelech king of the Philistines in Gerar. **2**The LORD appeared to Isaac and said, "Do not go down to Egypt; live in the land where I tell you to live. **3**Stay in this land for a while, and I will be with you and will bless you. For to you and your descendants I will give all these lands and will confirm the oath I swore to your father Abraham. **4**I will make your descendants as numerous as the stars in the sky and will give them all these lands, and through your offspring*d* all nations on earth will be blessed, **5**because Abraham obeyed me and kept my requirements, my commands, my decrees and my laws." **6**So Isaac stayed in Gerar.

7When the men of that place asked him about his wife, he said, "She is my sister," because he was afraid to say, "She is my wife." He thought, "The men of this place might kill me on account of Rebekah, because she is beautiful."

8When Isaac had been there a long time, Abimelech king of the Philistines looked down from a window and saw Isaac caressing his wife Rebekah. **9**So Abimelech summoned Isaac and said, "She is really your wife! Why did you say, 'She is my sister'?"

Isaac answered him, "Because I thought I might lose my life on account of her."

10Then Abimelech said, "What is this you have done to us? One of the men might well have slept with your wife, and you would have brought guilt upon us."

11So Abimelech gave orders to all the people: "Anyone

Where did Jacob's name come from? (25:26)
The name *Jacob* is a pun on the Hebrew word for *grasp* (see NIV text note).

Is it wrong to give up a birthright? (25:34)
Not so much wrong as foolish. Esau gave up his inheritance rights that favored him as the firstborn son of Isaac. These rights probably involved a greater share of the inheritance and the privileges and responsibilities of family leadership. Esau put immediate gratification before his long-term interests.

As numerous as the stars (26:4)
See *Count the stars* (15:5) and article: *Can the Bible exaggerate and still be true?* (2 Chron. 1:9–15).

SCRIPTURE LINK (26:7) *She is my sister*
Like his father, Isaac was afraid to acknowledge his wife. See 12:11–13.

Why did Isaac make the same mistake as his father? (26:7)
Because of the same problem: lack of faith in God. This is strange in light of God's promise of blessing in vv. 1–4. See *Why did Abraham lie again about Sarah?* (20:2).

---

a25 Esau may mean *hairy*; he was also called Edom, which means *red.*
b26 Jacob means *he grasps the heel* (figuratively, *he deceives*).
c30 Edom means *red.*   *d4* Or *seed*

who molests this man or his wife shall surely be put to death[D]."

[12]Isaac planted crops in that land and the same year reaped a hundredfold, because the LORD blessed him. [13]The man became rich, and his wealth continued to grow until he became very wealthy. [14]He had so many flocks and herds and servants that the Philistines envied him. [15]So all the wells that his father's servants had dug in the time of his father Abraham, the Philistines stopped up, filling them with earth.

[16]Then Abimelech said to Isaac, "Move away from us; you have become too powerful for us."

[17]So Isaac moved away from there and encamped in the Valley of Gerar and settled there. [18]Isaac reopened the wells that had been dug in the time of his father Abraham, which the Philistines had stopped up after Abraham died, and he gave them the same names his father had given them.

[19]Isaac's servants dug in the valley and discovered a well of fresh water there. [20]But the herdsmen of Gerar quarreled with Isaac's herdsmen and said, "The water is ours!" So he named the well Esek,[a] because they disputed with him. [21]Then they dug another well, but they quarreled over that one also; so he named it Sitnah.[b] [22]He moved on from there and dug another well, and no one quarreled over it. He named it Rehoboth,[c] saying, "Now the LORD has given us room and we will flourish in the land."

[23]From there he went up to Beersheba. [24]That night the LORD appeared to him and said, "I am the God of your father Abraham. Do not be afraid, for I am with you; I will bless you and will increase the number of your descendants for the sake of my servant Abraham."

[25]Isaac built an altar there and called on the name of the LORD. There he pitched his tent, and there his servants dug a well.

[26]Meanwhile, Abimelech had come to him from Gerar, with Ahuzzath his personal adviser and Phicol the commander of his forces. [27]Isaac asked them, "Why have you come to me, since you were hostile to me and sent me away?"

[28]They answered, "We saw clearly that the LORD was with you; so we said, 'There ought to be a sworn agreement between us'—between us and you. Let us make a treaty with you [29]that you will do us no harm, just as we did not molest you but always treated you well and sent you away in peace[D]. And now you are blessed by the LORD."

[30]Isaac then made a feast for them, and they ate and drank. [31]Early the next morning the men swore an oath to each other. Then Isaac sent them on their way, and they left him in peace.

[32]That day Isaac's servants came and told him about the well they had dug. They said, "We've found water!" [33]He called it Shibah,[d] and to this day the name of the town has been Beersheba.[e]

[34]When Esau was forty years old, he married Judith daughter of Beeri the Hittite, and also Basemath daughter of Elon the Hittite. [35]They were a source of grief to Isaac and Rebekah.

What frightened Abimelech about Isaac? (26:16)
Isaac's power: his increasing wealth and servants. As his numbers increased, Isaac could conceivably decide to take over the land and even unseat the king. Indirectly, Abimelech also feared the power of God that provided Isaac with his prosperity, but he probably did not distinguish between the two.

Why such fighting over wells? (26:19–20)
In the arid climate of southern Palestine, water was scarce. The little rain that fell was collected in cisterns, which were plastered holding tanks dug in the ground. A spring of fresh water was much more desirable. Ownership of the well may also have meant ownership of the rights to the surrounding pastureland.

Called on the name of the LORD **(26:25)**
See *Called upon the name of the LORD* (21:33).

SCRIPTURE LINK (26:33) *Beersheba*
Isaac's father, Abraham, had also named a place Beersheba (see *Jacob's Journeys* on page 39). See 21:30–31; also see following note.

How could one name have two stories behind it? (26:33; see 21:30–31)
Throughout this chapter, Isaac has been re-tracing Abraham's steps. Isaac's oath with Abimelech at Beersheba, then, is in keeping with Abraham's oath years before. The writer is signaling to the reader that Isaac is indeed the heir of the promises to Abraham, and that Isaac, like Abraham, is learning to trust God through life's trials. The words for *seven* and *oath* sound alike in Hebrew and become the *sheba* of Beersheba (see NIV text note).

How did Esau's wives cause grief for Isaac and Rebekah? (26:35)
Like immigrant parents who want their children to marry within their own ethnic group, Isaac and Rebekah may have wanted the same for Esau. Also, marrying a foreigner potentially threatened one's faith in God. Throughout the Old Testament, intermarriage was prohibited because of the danger of worshiping foreign gods. Isaac and Rebekah may have been upset for both of these reasons. Also see *Why did Abraham want his son to marry a relative?* (24:4).

---

[a]20 *Esek* means *dispute*.   [b]21 *Sitnah* means *opposition*.
[c]22 *Rehoboth* means *room*.   [d]33 *Shibah* can mean *oath* or *seven*.
[e]33 *Beersheba* can mean *well of the oath* or *well of seven*.

Jacob Gets Isaac's Blessing

27 When Isaac was old and his eyes were so weak that he could no longer see, he called for Esau his older son and said to him, "My son."

"Here I am," he answered.

²Isaac said, "I am now an old man and don't know the day of my death^D. ³Now then, get your weapons—your quiver and bow—and go out to the open country to hunt some wild game for me. ⁴Prepare me the kind of tasty food I like and bring it to me to eat, so that I may give you my blessing before I die."

⁵Now Rebekah was listening as Isaac spoke to his son Esau. When Esau left for the open country to hunt game and bring it back, ⁶Rebekah said to her son Jacob, "Look, I overheard your father say to your brother Esau, ⁷'Bring me some game and prepare me some tasty food to eat, so that I may give you my blessing in the presence of the LORD before I die.' ⁸Now, my son, listen carefully and do what I tell you: ⁹Go out to the flock and bring me two choice young goats, so I can prepare some tasty food for your father, just the way he likes it. ¹⁰Then take it to your father to eat, so that he may give you his blessing before he dies."

¹¹Jacob said to Rebekah his mother, "But my brother Esau is a hairy man, and I'm a man with smooth skin. ¹²What if my father touches me? I would appear to be tricking him and would bring down a curse on myself rather than a blessing."

¹³His mother said to him, "My son, let the curse fall on me. Just do what I say; go and get them for me."

¹⁴So he went and got them and brought them to his mother, and she prepared some tasty food, just the way his father liked it. ¹⁵Then Rebekah took the best clothes of Esau her older son, which she had in the house, and put them on her younger son Jacob. ¹⁶She also covered his hands and the smooth part of his neck with the goatskins. ¹⁷Then she handed to her son Jacob the tasty food and the bread she had made.

¹⁸He went to his father and said, "My father."

"Yes, my son," he answered. "Who is it?"

¹⁹Jacob said to his father, "I am Esau your firstborn^D. I have done as you told me. Please sit up and eat some of my game so that you may give me your blessing."

²⁰Isaac asked his son, "How did you find it so quickly, my son?"

"The LORD your God gave me success," he replied.

²¹Then Isaac said to Jacob, "Come near so I can touch you, my son, to know whether you really are my son Esau or not."

²²Jacob went close to his father Isaac, who touched him and said, "The voice is the voice of Jacob, but the hands are the hands of Esau." ²³He did not recognize him, for his hands were hairy like those of his brother Esau; so he blessed him. ²⁴"Are you really my son Esau?" he asked.

"I am," he replied.

²⁵Then he said, "My son, bring me some of your game to eat, so that I may give you my blessing."

Jacob brought it to him and he ate; and he brought some wine and he drank. ²⁶Then his father Isaac said to him, "Come here, my son, and kiss me."

²⁷So he went to him and kissed him. When Isaac caught the smell of his clothes, he blessed him and said,

"Ah, the smell of my son

Blessing before I die (27:4)
Such deathbed blessings had legal force in the ancient Near East.

Why would a mother scheme to steal her son's blessing? (27:10)
Her motives were probably mixed. The loyalties of the parents were divided: Isaac loved Esau, but Rebekah loved Jacob (Gen. 25:28). So she was naturally biased. And besides, Esau was a difficult son to love. He was impulsive, dull and had married two foreign women against his family's wishes. In addition, Rebekah had received the message from God that the elder would serve the younger (Gen. 25:23).

Was the blessing worth risking a curse? (27:12)
Rebekah thought so. In saying that she would take the curse, Rebekah may simply have been stating that she would risk her husband's anger. However Isaac could have pronounced an effective curse of non-prosperity as well.

SCRIPTURE LINK (27:18–30)
Jacob's deceitfulness is reflected in his name. See NIV text note at v. 36.

is like the smell of a field
that the LORD has blessed.
28May God give you of heaven's dew
and of earth's richness—
an abundance of grain and new wine[D].
29May nations serve you
and peoples bow down to you.
Be lord over your brothers,
and may the sons of your mother bow down
to you.
May those who curse you be cursed
and those who bless you be blessed."

30After Isaac finished blessing him and Jacob had scarcely left his father's presence, his brother Esau came in from hunting. **31**He too prepared some tasty food and brought it to his father. Then he said to him, "My father, sit up and eat some of my game, so that you may give me your blessing."

32His father Isaac asked him, "Who are you?"

"I am your son," he answered, "your firstborn[D], Esau."

33Isaac trembled violently and said, "Who was it, then, that hunted game and brought it to me? I ate it just before you came and I blessed him—and indeed he will be blessed!"

34When Esau heard his father's words, he burst out with a loud and bitter cry and said to his father, "Bless me—me too, my father!"

35But he said, "Your brother came deceitfully and took your blessing."

36Esau said, "Isn't he rightly named Jacob[a]? He has deceived me these two times: He took my birthright[D], and now he's taken my blessing!" Then he asked, "Haven't you reserved any blessing for me?"

37Isaac answered Esau, "I have made him lord over you and have made all his relatives his servants, and I have sustained him with grain and new wine. So what can I possibly do for you, my son?"

38Esau said to his father, "Do you have only one blessing, my father? Bless me too, my father!" Then Esau wept aloud.

39His father Isaac answered him,

"Your dwelling will be
away from the earth's richness,
away from the dew of heaven above.
40You will live by the sword
and you will serve your brother.
But when you grow restless,
you will throw his yoke[D]
from off your neck."

Jacob Flees to Laban

41Esau held a grudge against Jacob because of the blessing his father had given him. He said to himself, "The days of mourning for my father are near; then I will kill my brother Jacob."

42When Rebekah was told what her older son Esau had said, she sent for her younger son Jacob and said to him, "Your brother Esau is consoling himself with the thought of killing you. **43**Now then, my son, do what I say: Flee at once to my brother Laban in Haran. **44**Stay with him for a while until your brother's fury subsides. **45**When your

---

Why would God bless a deceitful person? (27:35)
Obviously not because the person was deceitful! For a reason known only to God, he chose to bless Jacob and not Esau. Paul points out that since his choice was made before they were even born, it was not based on their merit (Romans 9:10–13) but on God's sovereign freedom. God's grace and blessing are always undeserved and unexpected. See article: *Does God play favorites?* (Romans 9:8–33).

What was the difference between a birthright and a blessing? (27:36)
Some say there is no difference. Others think the birthright has to do with family inheritance (what the parents have earned), while the blessing has to do with personal success (one's own prosperity).

Why couldn't Isaac bless both sons? (27:38)
Our culture affirms equality and even distribution, which makes Isaac's response difficult to understand. But in that culture only one son could inherit the family blessing. In this case only one son could provide the family line through which the Messiah would come.

SCRIPTURE LINK (27:43) *My brother Laban*
See 24:29.

---

[a]36 *Jacob* means *he grasps the heel* (figuratively, *he deceives*).

brother is no longer angry with you and forgets what you did to him, I'll send word for you to come back from there. Why should I lose both of you in one day?"

⁴⁶Then Rebekah said to Isaac, "I'm disgusted with living because of these Hittite women. If Jacob takes a wife from among the women of this land, from Hittite women like these, my life will not be worth living."

28 So Isaac called for Jacob and blessed[a] him and commanded him: "Do not marry a Canaanite woman. ²Go at once to Paddan Aram,[b] to the house of your mother's father Bethuel. Take a wife for yourself there, from among the daughters of Laban, your mother's brother. ³May God Almighty[c] bless you and make you fruitful and increase your numbers until you become a community of peoples. ⁴May he give you and your descendants the blessing given to Abraham, so that you may take possession of the land where you now live as an alien[D], the land God gave to Abraham." ⁵Then Isaac sent Jacob on his way, and he went to Paddan Aram, to Laban son of Bethuel the Aramean, the brother of Rebekah, who was the mother of Jacob and Esau.

⁶Now Esau learned that Isaac had blessed Jacob and had sent him to Paddan Aram to take a wife from there, and that when he blessed him he commanded him, "Do not marry a Canaanite woman," ⁷and that Jacob had obeyed his father and mother and had gone to Paddan Aram. ⁸Esau then realized how displeasing the Canaanite women were to his father Isaac; ⁹so he went to Ishmael and married Mahalath, the sister of Nebaioth and daughter of Ishmael son of Abraham, in addition to the wives he already had.

Jacob's Dream at Bethel

¹⁰Jacob left Beersheba and set out for Haran. ¹¹When he reached a certain place, he stopped for the night because the sun had set. Taking one of the stones there, he put it under his head and lay down to sleep. ¹²He had a dream in which he saw a stairway[d] resting on the earth, with its top reaching to heaven, and the angels of God were ascending and descending on it. ¹³There above it[e] stood

a 1 Or greeted   b 2 That is, Northwest Mesopotamia; also in verses 5, 6 and 7   c 3 Hebrew El-Shaddai   *d 12 Or* ladder   *e 13 Or There beside him*

Was this a different blessing from the one Jacob stole? (28:4)
Yes. It is intended for Jacob, focusing on his marriage and future family. It also specifically named the promise of land made to Abraham. In delivering this blessing, Isaac was making Jacob heir to the most important family possession—the blessing and friendship of God. Isaac seemed to have accepted the fact that his younger son was the one God would use to fulfill the promise to Abraham.

Why did Esau decide to marry again? (28:9)
Esau was trying to better his own lot by imitating his brother's journey to find a wife among his relatives. As Ishmaelites, these women were grandchildren of Abraham. But they were also excluded from the line of the promise, so Esau was really doing himself no good.

Jacob's Journeys (28:10)

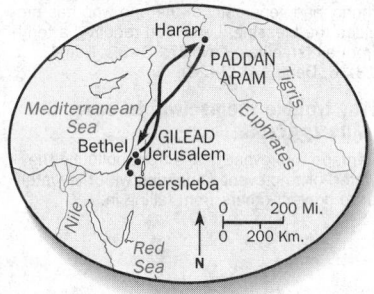

Are dreams messages from God? (28:12-15)

They can be, though they are not always. Here God repeats the promises made to Jacob's father and grandfather. The dream corresponds to the already revealed will of God. Likewise, if God chooses to reveal his will to us in a dream, it will correspond to the teaching of Scripture.

Dreams should never replace sound and well thought-out decisions. Scripture and respected members of the church should be consulted carefully. We shouldn't expect God to tell us in a dream whom to marry or what career track to choose. That isn't God's pattern of revealing his will.

This dream was given to assure Jacob that God was present with him and that God intended to bless him, keeping the promise made to his ancestors. It also marked the beginning of Jacob's lifelong relationship with God.

the LORD, and he said: "I am the LORD, the God of your father Abraham and the God of Isaac. I will give you and your descendants the land on which you are lying. **14**Your descendants will be like the dust of the earth, and you will spread out to the west and to the east, to the north and to the south. All peoples on earth will be blessed through you and your offspring. **15**I am with you and will watch over you wherever you go, and I will bring you back to this land. I will not leave you until I have done what I have promised you."

16When Jacob awoke from his sleep, he thought, "Surely the LORD is in this place, and I was not aware of it." **17**He was afraid and said, "How awesome is this place! This is none other than the house of God; this is the gate of heaven."

18Early the next morning Jacob took the stone he had placed under his head and set it up as a pillar and poured oil on top of it. **19**He called that place Bethel,*a* though the city used to be called Luz.

20Then Jacob made a vow*b*, saying, "If God will be with me and will watch over me on this journey I am taking and will give me food to eat and clothes to wear **21**so that I return safely to my father's house, then the LORD*b* will be my God **22**and*c* this stone that I have set up as a pillar will be God's house, and of all that you give me I will give you a tenth."

Jacob Arrives in Paddan Aram

29 Then Jacob continued on his journey and came to the land of the eastern peoples. **2**There he saw a well in the field, with three flocks of sheep lying near it because the flocks were watered from that well. The stone over the mouth of the well was large. **3**When all the flocks were gathered there, the shepherds would roll the stone away from the well's mouth and water the sheep. Then they would return the stone to its place over the mouth of the well.

4Jacob asked the shepherds, "My brothers, where are you from?"

"We're from Haran," they replied.

5He said to them, "Do you know Laban, Nahor's grandson?"

"Yes, we know him," they answered.

6Then Jacob asked them, "Is he well?"

"Yes, he is," they said, "and here comes his daughter Rachel with the sheep."

7"Look," he said, "the sun is still high; it is not time for the flocks to be gathered. Water the sheep and take them back to pasture."

8"We can't," they replied, "until all the flocks are gathered and the stone has been rolled away from the mouth of the well. Then we will water the sheep."

9While he was still talking with them, Rachel came with her father's sheep, for she was a shepherdess. **10**When Jacob saw Rachel daughter of Laban, his mother's brother, and Laban's sheep, he went over and rolled the stone away from the mouth of the well and watered his uncle's sheep. **11**Then Jacob kissed Rachel and began to weep aloud. **12**He had told Rachel that he was a relative of her

How could Jacob's commitment depend on what God would do for him? (28:20–22)

Some think Jacob was bargaining with God for the very things God had just promised him. Others think this was a general vow given in thankfulness to God, like the ones we find in the Psalms. There the one who prays promises to pay honor and sacrifice to God when the prayer is answered. Even so, Jacob's vow was made in response to a promise of blessing that he did not request!

Why promise a tenth? (28:22)

It seems to be a way of acknowledging the authority and generosity of the one who has provided the blessing. Later God required a tenth from all Israelites (Lev. 27:30–32; Num. 18:26; Deut. 14:22–28).

Why trouble themselves to cover the well? (29:3)

Perhaps to prevent things from polluting the water, or to prevent tampering with the water, or to prevent others from falling in.

---

a 19 Bethel means *house of God.*   *b 20,21* Or *Since God . . . father's house, the* LORD   *c 21,22* Or *house, and the* LORD *will be my God, 22then*

father and a son of Rebekah. So she ran and told her father.

13As soon as Laban heard the news about Jacob, his sister's son, he hurried to meet him. He embraced him and kissed him and brought him to his home, and there Jacob told him all these things. 14Then Laban said to him, "You are my own flesh and blood."

Jacob Marries Leah and Rachel

After Jacob had stayed with him for a whole month, 15Laban said to him, "Just because you are a relative of mine, should you work for me for nothing? Tell me what your wages should be."

16Now Laban had two daughters; the name of the older was Leah, and the name of the younger was Rachel. 17Leah had weak*a* eyes, but Rachel was lovely in form, and beautiful. 18Jacob was in love with Rachel and said, "I'll work for you seven years in return for your younger daughter Rachel."

19Laban said, "It's better that I give her to you than to some other man. Stay here with me." 20So Jacob served seven years to get Rachel, but they seemed like only a few days to him because of his love for her.

21Then Jacob said to Laban, "Give me my wife. My time is completed, and I want to lie with her."

22So Laban brought together all the people of the place and gave a feast. 23But when evening came, he took his daughter Leah and gave her to Jacob, and Jacob lay with her. 24And Laban gave his servant girl Zilpah to his daughter as her maidservant.

25When morning came, there was Leah! So Jacob said to Laban, "What is this you have done to me? I served you for Rachel, didn't I? Why have you deceived me?"

26Laban replied, "It is not our custom here to give the younger daughter in marriage before the older one. 27Finish this daughter's bridal week; then we will give you the younger one also, in return for another seven years of work."

28And Jacob did so. He finished the week with Leah, and then Laban gave him his daughter Rachel to be his wife. 29Laban gave his servant girl Bilhah to his daughter Rachel as her maidservant. 30Jacob lay with Rachel also, and he loved Rachel more than Leah. And he worked for Laban another seven years.

Jacob's Children

31When the LORD saw that Leah was not loved, he opened her womb, but Rachel was barren. 32Leah became pregnant and gave birth to a son. She named him Reuben,*b* for she said, "It is because the LORD has seen my misery. Surely my husband will love me now."

33She conceived again, and when she gave birth to a son she said, "Because the LORD heard that I am not loved, he gave me this one too." So she named him Simeon.*c*

34Again she conceived, and when she gave birth to a son she said, "Now at last my husband will become attached to me, because I have borne him three sons." So he was named Levi.*d*

35She conceived again, and when she gave birth to a

---

a17 Or *delicate*   *b32 Reuben* sounds like the Hebrew for *he has seen my misery;* the name means *see, a son.*   *c33 Simeon* probably means *one who hears.*   *d34 Levi* sounds like and may be derived from the Hebrew for *attached.*

What was wrong with Leah's eyes? (29:17)

Some think she was nearsighted. Others think her eyes lacked sparkle or color. Still others believe the word describing Leah's eyes could be translated *delicate, lovely* or *gentle.* The author might be presenting Leah's best feature before comparing her with her sister: *Leah had nice eyes, but Rachel was a total beauty!*

Was seven years of labor a typical price for a bride? (29:18)

We don't know. Some think this was the way Jacob was compensating her father for the loss of a valuable helper. Rachel had been keeping her father's flocks. Jacob had no money so his labor was used as currency. Others compare it to the stories of suitors who must accomplish great feats to win the women they love.

How could Jacob sleep with Leah and think she was Rachel? (29:23–25)

Some say Jacob would not have been able to see well inside an extremely dark tent. Others suggest that Jacob's senses may have been dulled by the eating and drinking at the wedding feast (v. 22). Perhaps both of these factors were involved, as well as the fact that Leah herself wanted the deception to succeed. Most likely she kept herself veiled through the night.

Bridal week (29:27)

A week of festivities to celebrate a wedding.

Why didn't God open Rachel's womb as well? (29:31)

He did later, only after Leah already had several children. Some say God was caring for Leah, the unloved wife, just as God took care of Hagar, Abraham's concubine who was rejected by Sarah, Abraham's wife. More importantly, both Sarah and Rachel gave birth after a time of infertility; the coming of children was seen as a gift of the Lord who opens and closes the womb.

Why invent names based on circumstances? (29:32–35)

See *Why give a name like this to a child?* (Isaiah 8:3) and *Why choose such odd names for children?* (Hosea 1:4).

son she said, "This time I will praise the LORD." So she named him Judah.[a] Then she stopped having children.

30 When Rachel saw that she was not bearing Jacob any children, she became jealous of her sister. So she said to Jacob, "Give me children, or I'll die!"

[2] Jacob became angry with her and said, "Am I in the place of God, who has kept you from having children?"

[3] Then she said, "Here is Bilhah, my maidservant. Sleep with her so that she can bear children for me and that through her I too can build a family."

[4] So she gave him her servant Bilhah as a wife. Jacob slept with her, [5] and she became pregnant and bore him a son. [6] Then Rachel said, "God has vindicated me; he has listened to my plea and given me a son." Because of this she named him Dan.[b]

[7] Rachel's servant Bilhah conceived again and bore Jacob a second son. [8] Then Rachel said, "I have had a great struggle with my sister, and I have won." So she named him Naphtali.[c]

[9] When Leah saw that she had stopped having children, she took her maidservant Zilpah and gave her to Jacob as a wife. [10] Leah's servant Zilpah bore Jacob a son. [11] Then Leah said, "What good fortune!"[d] So she named him Gad.[e]

[12] Leah's servant Zilpah bore Jacob a second son. [13] Then Leah said, "How happy I am! The women will call me happy." So she named him Asher.[f]

[14] During wheat harvest, Reuben went out into the fields and found some mandrake[D] plants, which he brought to his mother Leah. Rachel said to Leah, "Please give me some of your son's mandrakes."

[15] But she said to her, "Wasn't it enough that you took away my husband? Will you take my son's mandrakes too?"

"Very well," Rachel said, "he can sleep with you tonight in return for your son's mandrakes."

[16] So when Jacob came in from the fields that evening, Leah went out to meet him. "You must sleep with me," she said. "I have hired you with my son's mandrakes." So he slept with her that night.

[17] God listened to Leah, and she became pregnant and bore Jacob a fifth son. [18] Then Leah said, "God has rewarded me for giving my maidservant to my husband." So she named him Issachar.[g]

[19] Leah conceived again and bore Jacob a sixth son. [20] Then Leah said, "God has presented me with a precious gift. This time my husband will treat me with honor, because I have borne him six sons." So she named him Zebulun.[h]

[21] Some time later she gave birth to a daughter and named her Dinah.

[22] Then God remembered Rachel; he listened to her and opened her womb. [23] She became pregnant and gave birth to a son and said, "God has taken away my disgrace." [24] She named him Joseph,[i] and said, "May the LORD add to me another son."

Did female servants usually become concubines? (30:3)

Only when the wife could not bear children. Concubines were slaves in ancient societies and were treated like property. A concubine was more than a servant, but she was not free and did not have the rights of a wife. The taking of concubines was apparently one of many borderline practices God tolerated during Old Testament days. See article: **Why did David have so many wives and concubines?** (2 Samuel 5:13).

Mandrake plants (30:14)

This yellow flowering plant was fragrant and grew wild in the desert areas of Palestine. It was believed to have the power to induce conception, as well as being an aphrodisiac.

God remembered Rachel (30:22)

In the Old Testament *to remember* means *to pay attention to*. It emphasizes God's decision to take action according to a previous commitment.

---

[a]35 *Judah* sounds like and may be derived from the Hebrew for *praise.*
[b]6 *Dan* here means *he has vindicated.*   [c]8 *Naphtali* means *my struggle.*   [d]11 Or *"A troop is coming!"*   [e]11 *Gad* can mean *good fortune* or *a troop.*   [f]13 *Asher* means *happy.*   [g]18 *Issachar* sounds like the Hebrew for *reward.*   [h]20 *Zebulun* probably means *honor.*   [i]24 *Joseph* means *may he add.*

Jacob's Flocks Increase

25After Rachel gave birth to Joseph, Jacob said to Laban, "Send me on my way so I can go back to my own homeland. **26**Give me my wives and children, for whom I have served you, and I will be on my way. You know how much work I've done for you."

27But Laban said to him, "If I have found favor in your eyes, please stay. I have learned by divination[D] that[a] the LORD has blessed me because of you." **28**He added, "Name your wages, and I will pay them."

29Jacob said to him, "You know how I have worked for you and how your livestock has fared under my care. **30**The little you had before I came has increased greatly, and the LORD has blessed you wherever I have been. But now, when may I do something for my own household?"

31"What shall I give you?" he asked.

"Don't give me anything," Jacob replied. "But if you will do this one thing for me, I will go on tending your flocks and watching over them: **32**Let me go through all your flocks today and remove from them every speckled or spotted sheep, every dark-colored lamb and every spotted or speckled goat. They will be my wages. **33**And my honesty will testify for me in the future, whenever you check on the wages you have paid me. Any goat in my possession that is not speckled or spotted, or any lamb that is not dark-colored, will be considered stolen."

34"Agreed," said Laban. "Let it be as you have said." **35**That same day he removed all the male goats that were streaked or spotted, and all the speckled or spotted female goats (all that had white on them) and all the dark-colored lambs, and he placed them in the care of his sons. **36**Then he put a three-day journey between himself and Jacob, while Jacob continued to tend the rest of Laban's flocks.

37Jacob, however, took fresh-cut branches from poplar, almond and plane trees and made white stripes on them by peeling the bark and exposing the white inner wood of the branches. **38**Then he placed the peeled branches in all the watering troughs, so that they would be directly in front of the flocks when they came to drink. When the flocks were in heat and came to drink, **39**they mated in front of the branches. And they bore young that were streaked or speckled or spotted. **40**Jacob set apart the young of the flock by themselves, but made the rest face the streaked and dark-colored animals that belonged to Laban. Thus he made separate flocks for himself and did not put them with Laban's animals. **41**Whenever the stronger females were in heat, Jacob would place the branches in the troughs in front of the animals so they would mate near the branches, **42**but if the animals were weak, he would not place them there. So the weak animals went to Laban and the strong ones to Jacob. **43**In this way the man grew exceedingly prosperous and came to own large flocks, and maidservants and menservants, and camels and donkeys.

Jacob Flees From Laban

31 Jacob heard that Laban's sons were saying, "Jacob has taken everything our father owned and has gained all this wealth from what belonged to our father." **2**And Jacob noticed that Laban's attitude toward him was not what it had been.

[a]27 Or possibly *have become rich and*

Divination (30:27)

The use of either a human intermediary or inanimate objects (such as the examination of animal entrails or looking for pictures in water) to receive messages from the spirit world.

Why did Laban separate himself so far from Jacob? (30:34-36)

Because he was trying to outsmart Jacob. Laban pulled out the spotted goats and dark-colored lambs before Jacob could take them as his wage. Then Laban sent them on a three-day journey so Jacob would never find them and realize he had been cheated.

How do striped sticks produce speckled sheep? (30:37-43)

Jacob was working with a genetic theory of selective breeding (strong produce strong, weak produce weak). He also believed that what the animal saw when mating affected the offspring as well. This latter view was widespread until the twentieth century. But God was the one who made the plan work (see 31:9).

Why did Laban turn against Jacob? (31:2)

Laban had taken advantage of Jacob for 20 years. However, during his final six years, Jacob began to turn the tables on his father-in-law. As a result, Laban's sons felt that Jacob's profiteering threatened their inheritance and Laban came to view his son-in-law as a liability.

3Then the LORD said to Jacob, "Go back to the land of your fathers and to your relatives, and I will be with you."

4So Jacob sent word to Rachel and Leah to come out to the fields where his flocks were. **5**He said to them, "I see that your father's attitude toward me is not what it was before, but the God of my father has been with me. **6**You know that I've worked for your father with all my strength, **7**yet your father has cheated me by changing my wages ten times. However, God has not allowed him to harm me. **8**If he said, 'The speckled ones will be your wages,' then all the flocks gave birth to speckled young; and if he said, 'The streaked ones will be your wages,' then all the flocks bore streaked young. **9**So God has taken away your father's livestock and has given them to me.

10"In breeding season I once had a dream in which I looked up and saw that the male goats mating with the flock were streaked, speckled or spotted. **11**The angel of God said to me in the dream, 'Jacob.' I answered, 'Here I am.' **12**And he said, 'Look up and see that all the male goats mating with the flock are streaked, speckled or spotted, for I have seen all that Laban has been doing to you. **13**I am the God of Bethel, where you anointed[D] a pillar and where you made a vow[D] to me. Now leave this land at once and go back to your native land.' "

14Then Rachel and Leah replied, "Do we still have any share in the inheritance of our father's estate? **15**Does he not regard us as foreigners? Not only has he sold us, but he has used up what was paid for us. **16**Surely all the wealth that God took away from our father belongs to us and our children. So do whatever God has told you."

17Then Jacob put his children and his wives on camels, **18**and he drove all his livestock ahead of him, along with all the goods he had accumulated in Paddan Aram,[a] to go to his father Isaac in the land of Canaan.

19When Laban had gone to shear his sheep, Rachel stole her father's household gods. **20**Moreover, Jacob deceived Laban the Aramean by not telling him he was running away. **21**So he fled with all he had, and crossing the River,[b] he headed for the hill country of Gilead.

Laban Pursues Jacob

22On the third day Laban was told that Jacob had fled. **23**Taking his relatives with him, he pursued Jacob for seven days and caught up with him in the hill country of Gilead. **24**Then God came to Laban the Aramean in a dream at night and said to him, "Be careful not to say anything to Jacob, either good or bad."

25Jacob had pitched his tent in the hill country of Gilead when Laban overtook him, and Laban and his relatives camped there too. **26**Then Laban said to Jacob, "What have you done? You've deceived me, and you've carried off my daughters like captives in war. **27**Why did you run off secretly and deceive me? Why didn't you tell me, so I could send you away with joy and singing to the music of tambourines and harps? **28**You didn't even let me kiss my grandchildren and my daughters good-by. You have done a foolish thing. **29**I have the power to harm you; but last night the God of your father said to me, 'Be careful not to say anything to Jacob, either good or bad.' **30**Now you have gone off because you longed to return to your father's house. But why did you steal my gods?"

31Jacob answered Laban, "I was afraid, because I

How do we know if a dream is from God? (31:11)

God speaks to people in various ways, and many consider dreams to be one of those ways. Because God's Word has come to us fully in the Bible, we know that such dreams will not contradict God's written Word. They will also be edifying to the church, the body of Christ. See article: *Are dreams messages from God?* (28:12–15).

Why did Rachel and Leah feel *sold*? (31:15)

In the culture of their time, contracts for marriages were formal business transactions. The groom usually paid the father of the bride, and the father would frequently give his daughter a gift. Laban treated his daughters no worse than other fathers in those days. Contracting a marriage protected daughters from future neglect or desertion by providing them with legal status. This was especially important in cases such as Leah's, where the husband valued her sister more than her.

Why would Rachel steal her father's pagan gods? (31:19)

Having possession of the household gods may have strengthened Rachel's claim to an inheritance. More likely, though, Rachel wanted her father's idols for the supernatural power she believed they possessed. Later, at Bethel, when Jacob renewed his relationship to God, he commanded his family to rid themselves of all foreign gods—presumably including Rachel's stolen idols (35:2,4).

---

a 18 That is, Northwest Mesopotamia   *b 21* That is, the Euphrates

thought you would take your daughters away from me by force. **32**But if you find anyone who has your gods, he shall not live. In the presence of our relatives, see for yourself whether there is anything of yours here with me; and if so, take it." Now Jacob did not know that Rachel had stolen the gods.

33So Laban went into Jacob's tent and into Leah's tent and into the tent of the two maidservants, but he found nothing. After he came out of Leah's tent, he entered Rachel's tent. **34**Now Rachel had taken the household gods and put them inside her camel's saddle and was sitting on them. Laban searched through everything in the tent but found nothing.

35Rachel said to her father, "Don't be angry, my lord, that I cannot stand up in your presence; I'm having my period." So he searched but could not find the household gods.

36Jacob was angry and took Laban to task. "What is my crime?" he asked Laban. "What sin have I committed that you hunt me down? **37**Now that you have searched through all my goods, what have you found that belongs to your household? Put it here in front of your relatives and mine, and let them judge between the two of us.

38"I have been with you for twenty years now. Your sheep and goats have not miscarried, nor have I eaten rams from your flocks. **39**I did not bring you animals torn by wild beasts; I bore the loss myself. And you demanded payment from me for whatever was stolen by day or night. **40**This was my situation: The heat consumed me in the daytime and the cold at night, and sleep fled from my eyes. **41**It was like this for the twenty years I was in your household. I worked for you fourteen years for your two daughters and six years for your flocks, and you changed my wages ten times. **42**If the God of my father, the God of Abraham and the Fear of Isaac, had not been with me, you would surely have sent me away empty-handed. But God has seen my hardship and the toil of my hands, and last night he rebuked you."

43Laban answered Jacob, "The women are my daughters, the children are my children, and the flocks are my flocks. All you see is mine. Yet what can I do today about these daughters of mine, or about the children they have borne? **44**Come now, let's make a covenant,D you and I, and let it serve as a witness between us."

45So Jacob took a stone and set it up as a pillar. **46**He said to his relatives, "Gather some stones." So they took stones and piled them in a heap, and they ate there by the heap. **47**Laban called it Jegar Sahadutha,*a* and Jacob called it Galeed.*b*

48Laban said, "This heap is a witness between you and me today." That is why it was called Galeed. **49**It was also called Mizpah,*c* because he said, "May the LORD keep watch between you and me when we are away from each other. **50**If you mistreat my daughters or if you take any wives besides my daughters, even though no one is with us, remember that God is a witness between you and me."

51Laban also said to Jacob, "Here is this heap, and here is this pillar I have set up between you and me. **52**This heap is a witness, and this pillar is a witness, that I will not

Why would a menstrual period excuse Rachel from standing up? (31:35)
Laban was probably satisfied that the physical discomfort Rachel was experiencing was reason enough for his daughter to remain seated. Later, Mosaic Law declared any woman ceremonially unclean during her menstrual period —along with anything she sat on (Lev. 15:19–20). It is apparent, however, that Rachel deceived her father to prevent her theft from being discovered.

Why give three different names to one monument? (31:47–49)
Two of the names mean *witness heap*, though expressed in different languages. See the NIV text notes at v. 47. That Laban used the Aramaic language reflects the culture of Paddan Aram where he lived. The third name, *Mizpah*, meaning *watchtower*, was used as a benediction to mean *may God watch between us*. Given the mistrust between Jacob and Laban, *Mizpah* provided a fitting title for a monument that symbolized vows made under God's watchful gaze.

*a*47 The Aramaic *Jegar Sahadutha* means *witness heap.*   *b*47 The Hebrew *Galeed* means *witness heap.*   *c*49 *Mizpah* means *watchtower.*

go past this heap to your side to harm you and that you will not go past this heap and pillar to my side to harm me. ⁵³May the God of Abraham and the God of Nahor, the God of their father, judge between us."

So Jacob took an oath in the name of the Fear of his father Isaac. ⁵⁴He offered a sacrifice^D there in the hill country and invited his relatives to a meal. After they had eaten, they spent the night there.

⁵⁵Early the next morning Laban kissed his grandchildren and his daughters and blessed them. Then he left and returned home.

Jacob Prepares to Meet Esau

32 Jacob also went on his way, and the angels of God met him. ²When Jacob saw them, he said, "This is the camp of God!" So he named that place Mahanaim.^a

³Jacob sent messengers ahead of him to his brother Esau in the land of Seir, the country of Edom^D. ⁴He instructed them: "This is what you are to say to my master Esau: 'Your servant Jacob says, I have been staying with Laban and have remained there till now. ⁵I have cattle and donkeys, sheep and goats, menservants and maidservants. Now I am sending this message to my lord, that I may find favor in your eyes.' "

⁶When the messengers returned to Jacob, they said, "We went to your brother Esau, and now he is coming to meet you, and four hundred men are with him."

⁷In great fear and distress Jacob divided the people who were with him into two groups,^b and the flocks and herds and camels as well. ⁸He thought, "If Esau comes and attacks one group,^c the group^c that is left may escape."

⁹Then Jacob prayed, "O God of my father Abraham, God of my father Isaac, O Lord, who said to me, 'Go back to your country and your relatives, and I will make you prosper,' ¹⁰I am unworthy of all the kindness and faithfulness you have shown your servant. I had only my staff when I crossed this Jordan, but now I have become two groups. ¹¹Save me, I pray, from the hand of my brother Esau, for I am afraid he will come and attack me, and also the mothers with their children. ¹²But you have said, 'I will surely make you prosper and will make your descendants like the sand of the sea, which cannot be counted.' "

¹³He spent the night there, and from what he had with him he selected a gift for his brother Esau: ¹⁴two hundred female goats and twenty male goats, two hundred ewes and twenty rams, ¹⁵thirty female camels with their young, forty cows and ten bulls, and twenty female donkeys and ten male donkeys. ¹⁶He put them in the care of his servants, each herd by itself, and said to his servants, "Go ahead of me, and keep some space between the herds."

¹⁷He instructed the one in the lead: "When my brother Esau meets you and asks, 'To whom do you belong, and where are you going, and who owns all these animals in front of you?' ¹⁸then you are to say, 'They belong to your servant Jacob. They are a gift sent to my lord Esau, and he is coming behind us.' "

¹⁹He also instructed the second, the third and all the others who followed the herds: "You are to say the same thing to Esau when you meet him. ²⁰And be sure to say, 'Your servant Jacob is coming behind us.' " For he

Why did God send angels to Jacob? (32:1-2)

The presence of these angels assured Jacob of God's protection as Esau approached. *Mahanaim* means *two camps*—Jacob's and God's. It is significant that Jacob encountered these angels as he approached the promised land. They were a supernatural indication that God was setting apart the region for his chosen people.

What were Esau's intentions? (32:6)

Twenty years previous to this encounter, Esau had plotted revenge against his brother (27:41). He may have intended here to use his 400 men to slaughter Jacob's clan and take back his inheritance. Apparently, however, Esau had a change of heart, perhaps as a result of Jacob's prayers.

Why give more females than males? (32:14-15)

For breeding practices aimed at increasing the size of the herd, a higher ratio of female to male animals was ideal. Twenty rams could easily impregnate 200 ewes. A reverse ratio would produce a herd 1/10 the size, and would lead to competition and fighting among the rams.

^a2 *Mahanaim* means *two camps*.   ^b7 Or *camps*; also in verse 10   ^c8 Or *camp*

thought, "I will pacify him with these gifts I am sending on ahead; later, when I see him, perhaps he will receive me." **21**So Jacob's gifts went on ahead of him, but he himself spent the night in the camp.

Jacob Wrestles With God

22That night Jacob got up and took his two wives, his two maidservants and his eleven sons and crossed the ford of the Jabbok. **23**After he had sent them across the stream, he sent over all his possessions. **24**So Jacob was left alone, and a man wrestled with him till daybreak. **25**When the man saw that he could not overpower him, he touched the socket of Jacob's hip so that his hip was wrenched as he wrestled with the man. **26**Then the man said, "Let me go, for it is daybreak."

But Jacob replied, "I will not let you go unless you bless me."

27The man asked him, "What is your name?"

"Jacob," he answered.

28Then the man said, "Your name will no longer be Jacob, but Israel,*a* because you have struggled with God and with men and have overcome."

29Jacob said, "Please tell me your name."

But he replied, "Why do you ask my name?" Then he blessed him there.

30So Jacob called the place Peniel,*b* saying, "It is because I saw God face to face, and yet my life was spared."

31The sun rose above him as he passed Peniel,*c* and he was limping because of his hip. **32**Therefore to this day the Israelites do not eat the tendon attached to the socket of the hip, because the socket of Jacob's hip was touched near the tendon.

Jacob Meets Esau

33 Jacob looked up and there was Esau, coming with his four hundred men; so he divided the children among Leah, Rachel and the two maidservants. **2**He put the maidservants and their children in front, Leah and her children next, and Rachel and Joseph in the rear. **3**He himself went on ahead and bowed down to the ground seven times as he approached his brother.

4But Esau ran to meet Jacob and embraced him; he threw his arms around his neck and kissed him. And they wept. **5**Then Esau looked up and saw the women and children. "Who are these with you?" he asked.

Jacob answered, "They are the children God has graciously given your servant."

6Then the maidservants and their children approached and bowed down. **7**Next, Leah and her children came and bowed down. Last of all came Joseph and Rachel, and they too bowed down.

8Esau asked, "What do you mean by all these droves I met?"

"To find favor in your eyes, my lord," he said.

9But Esau said, "I already have plenty, my brother. Keep what you have for yourself."

10"No, please!" said Jacob. "If I have found favor in your eyes, accept this gift from me. For to see your face is like seeing the face of God, now that you have received me favorably. **11**Please accept the present that was brought to

a28 Israel means *he struggles with God.*   *b30 Peniel* means *face of God.*   *c31* Hebrew *Penuel,* a variant of *Peniel*

Who wrestled with Jacob? (32:24,28)
The story seems to indicate that the stranger was a supernatural being. He wrestled with Jacob for several hours without tiring. Then, with simply a touch, he dislocated Jacob's hip. Afterwards, Jacob was grateful his life had been spared because he sensed he had seen the face of God.

Why ask a blessing from someone who had just hurt you? (32:26)
This supernatural being obviously could have done more than cripple Jacob—he could have taken his life. Jacob had been a recipient of his mercy, and now he sought the stranger's blessing and assurance that somehow he would overcome his brother's wrath.

Why did Jacob's name change? (32:28)
The name Israel means *he struggles with God.* Changing a person's name in the ancient Middle East was a rite of passage that marked a significant change in that person's life. Jacob, which means *deceiver,* now had a lifetime reminder of his weakness, God's power and God's blessing.

Why did Jacob believe he had seen God's face? (32:30)
In addition to the unusual occurrences of the nighttime wrestling match, the stranger gave a blessing only God could give. When Jacob asked the man his name, he received a rhetorical question as an answer. After all that had happened, Jacob finally understood that he had been confronted by God himself.

To this day (32:32)
This passage in Genesis likely was written between 1441 and 1400 B.C. Jacob's wrestling match occurred around 1700 B.C. *To this day* reflects the 300 years that had elapsed at the time of the writing. During those years the practice of not eating the hip tendon had become tradition, one which Orthodox Jews still observe.

Why did Jacob arrange his family in this way? (33:2)
Jacob showed preference for Rachel and Joseph by putting them last—in the safest place. If Esau was still angry, he would have destroyed the first groups, giving the latter groups a chance to escape. Jacob placed himself in the greatest danger, however, by leading the procession.

Had God changed Esau's heart? (33:4)
Until this verse, all we know about Esau is that he was plotting to kill his brother for taking his birthright (27:41). Twenty years had passed, and either Esau's heart had softened over time or God had changed it miraculously in response to Jacob's prayers.

you, for God has been gracious to me and I have all I need." And because Jacob insisted, Esau accepted it.

12Then Esau said, "Let us be on our way; I'll accompany you."

13But Jacob said to him, "My lord knows that the children are tender and that I must care for the ewes and cows that are nursing their young. If they are driven hard just one day, all the animals will die. **14**So let my lord go on ahead of his servant, while I move along slowly at the pace of the droves before me and that of the children, until I come to my lord in Seir."

15Esau said, "Then let me leave some of my men with you."

"But why do that?" Jacob asked. "Just let me find favor in the eyes of my lord."

16So that day Esau started on his way back to Seir. **17**Jacob, however, went to Succoth, where he built a place for himself and made shelters for his livestock. That is why the place is called Succoth.*a*

18After Jacob came from Paddan Aram,*b* he arrived safely at the*c* city of Shechem in Canaan and camped within sight of the city. **19**For a hundred pieces of silver,*d* he bought from the sons of Hamor, the father of Shechem, the plot of ground where he pitched his tent. **20**There he set up an altar and called it El Elohe Israel.*e*

Did Jacob lie to Esau? (33:14–17)
Jacob may have intentionally misled his brother, or he may have simply had a change of plans once he settled in Succoth. He knew Esau was prone to violent mood swings and may not have wanted to risk traveling together. Esau did not accuse Jacob of lying when the brothers later met to bury their father (35:29).

Why set up an altar on land bought from the Canaanites? (33:20)
The name of the altar, *El Elohe Israel,* means *God, the God of Israel.* It is significant that this name includes the one given to Jacob by God in his blessing (32:28). He was finally returning to the promised land. Setting up this type of altar indicated that Jacob intended to make this place his permanent home.

Hivites (34:2)
The Hivites, early inhabitants of Syria and Palestine, were descendants of Canaan, one of Ham's sons (10:17; 1 Chron. 1:15). Eventually they settled in the hills of Lebanon (see *Conquest of Canaan* on page 301). They were conscripted as laborers for Solomon's building projects (1 Kings 9:20; 2 Chron. 8:7).

Why couldn't Shechem propose marriage himself? (34:4)
Arranged marriages were the norm in the culture of the ancient Middle East. This was especially true for sons and daughters of different peoples or nations. The political ramifications of such unions were great. Furthermore, in this case, if Shechem had proposed in person, Dinah probably would have refused because he had just raped her. But had the marriage been approved by her father, she would have been required to marry him.

Dinah and the Shechemites

34 Now Dinah, the daughter Leah had borne to Jacob, went out to visit the women of the land. **2**When Shechem son of Hamor the Hivite, the ruler of that area, saw her, he took her and violated her. **3**His heart was drawn to Dinah daughter of Jacob, and he loved the girl and spoke tenderly to her. **4**And Shechem said to his father Hamor, "Get me this girl as my wife."

5When Jacob heard that his daughter Dinah had been defiled, his sons were in the fields with his livestock; so he kept quiet about it until they came home.

6Then Shechem's father Hamor went out to talk with Jacob. **7**Now Jacob's sons had come in from the fields as soon as they heard what had happened. They were filled with grief and fury, because Shechem had done a disgraceful thing in*f* Israel by lying with Jacob's daughter — a thing that should not be done.

8But Hamor said to them, "My son Shechem has his heart set on your daughter. Please give her to him as his wife. **9**Intermarry with us; give us your daughters and take our daughters for yourselves. **10**You can settle among us; the land is open to you. Live in it, trade*g* in it, and acquire property in it."

11Then Shechem said to Dinah's father and brothers, "Let me find favor in your eyes, and I will give you whatever you ask. **12**Make the price for the bride and the gift I am to bring as great as you like, and I'll pay whatever you ask me. Only give me the girl as my wife."

13Because their sister Dinah had been defiled, Jacob's sons replied deceitfully as they spoke to Shechem and his father Hamor. **14**They said to them, "We can't do such a

---

a17 Succoth means *shelters.*   *b18* That is, Northwest Mesopotamia
c18 Or *arrived at Shalem, a*   *d19* Hebrew *hundred kesitahs;* a kesitah was a unit of money of unknown weight and value.
e20 El Elohe Israel can mean *God, the God of Israel* or *mighty is the God of Israel.*   *f7* Or *against*   *g10* Or *move about freely;* also in verse 21

thing; we can't give our sister to a man who is not circumcised[D]. That would be a disgrace to us. **15**We will give our consent to you on one condition only: that you become like us by circumcising all your males. **16**Then we will give you our daughters and take your daughters for ourselves. We'll settle among you and become one people with you. **17**But if you will not agree to be circumcised, we'll take our sister[a] and go."

18Their proposal seemed good to Hamor and his son Shechem. **19**The young man, who was the most honored of all his father's household, lost no time in doing what they said, because he was delighted with Jacob's daughter. **20**So Hamor and his son Shechem went to the gate of their city to speak to their fellow townsmen. **21**"These men are friendly toward us," they said. "Let them live in our land and trade in it; the land has plenty of room for them. We can marry their daughters and they can marry ours. **22**But the men will consent to live with us as one people only on the condition that our males be circumcised, as they themselves are. **23**Won't their livestock, their property and all their other animals become ours? So let us give our consent to them, and they will settle among us."

24All the men who went out of the city gate agreed with Hamor and his son Shechem, and every male in the city was circumcised.

25Three days later, while all of them were still in pain, two of Jacob's sons, Simeon and Levi, Dinah's brothers, took their swords and attacked the unsuspecting city, killing every male. **26**They put Hamor and his son Shechem to the sword and took Dinah from Shechem's house and left. **27**The sons of Jacob came upon the dead bodies and looted the city where[b] their sister had been defiled. **28**They seized their flocks and herds and donkeys and everything else of theirs in the city and out in the fields. **29**They carried off all their wealth and all their women and children, taking as plunder[D] everything in the houses.

30Then Jacob said to Simeon and Levi, "You have brought trouble on me by making me a stench to the Canaanites and Perizzites, the people living in this land. We are few in number, and if they join forces against me and attack me, I and my household will be destroyed."

31But they replied, "Should he have treated our sister like a prostitute?"

Jacob Returns to Bethel

35 Then God said to Jacob, "Go up to Bethel and settle there, and build an altar there to God, who appeared to you when you were fleeing from your brother Esau."

2So Jacob said to his household and to all who were with him, "Get rid of the foreign gods you have with you, and purify[D] yourselves and change your clothes. **3**Then come, let us go up to Bethel, where I will build an altar to God, who answered me in the day of my distress and who has been with me wherever I have gone." **4**So they gave Jacob all the foreign gods they had and the rings in their ears, and Jacob buried them under the oak at Shechem. **5**Then they set out, and the terror of God fell upon the towns all around them so that no one pursued them.

6Jacob and all the people with him came to Luz (that is,

---

a17 Hebrew daughter   *b27 Or because*

Gate of their city (34:20)
The gate of an ancient city was where legal business was handled. Treaties witnessed by the city elders at the gate were as legally binding as written contracts are today.

Did circumcision mean nothing to these pagans? (34:24)
For these Gentiles, circumcision was nothing more than a political gesture, a small price to pay for the wealth they could gain from an alliance with Jacob's clan. On the part of Jacob's sons, the circumcision was part of their plot to avenge the rape of their sister, not an attempt to introduce their neighbors to their God.

Why kill all the men in the city? (34:25)
If Jacob's sons had killed only Shechem, the men of the city would have come after them for revenge. In that civilization, entire communities might be held responsible for one person's wrongdoing, especially if the offense was not condemned by the guilty party's leaders. This was the case with the Hivites. Their leaders, rather than offering amends, took advantage of Israel's tribe.

Had Shechem been holding Dinah against her will? (34:26)
Since Shechem had raped Dinah, she would have been considered unavailable to anyone but him. The proper, though humiliating, response was for Dinah to stay in Shechem's tent until the marriage ceremony was held. Though Shechem tried to win her love, there is no indication that Dinah had any romantic interest in the man who violated her.

What did Jacob's sons do with so many hostages? (34:29)
Along with plundering the town, Jacob's sons likely made the children slaves and the women concubines. Enslaving these people was sure to stir up the anger of neighboring Canaanites and Perizzites. Because of this added risk, Jacob scolded his sons.

Why did Jacob's family have foreign gods? (35:2)
Rachel still had her father's household gods (31:19). The hostages taken from Shechem's city probably brought their idols with them. Prior to the covenant with God at Bethel, Jacob tolerated these foreign gods in his camp. Before then, Jacob's children may have assimilated the religious beliefs of the surrounding cultures.

What did earrings have to do with foreign gods? (35:4)
These earrings probably served as amulets or charms to ward off evil or to bring good fortune. Thought to have magical powers, these earrings were condemned in the Old Testament (Isaiah 3:18–23). Such earrings were used to make the famous golden calf (Exodus 32:2).

Bethel) in the land of Canaan. **7**There he built an altar, and he called the place El Bethel,*a* because it was there that God revealed himself to him when he was fleeing from his brother.

8Now Deborah, Rebekah's nurse, died and was buried under the oak below Bethel. So it was named Allon Bacuth.*b*

9After Jacob returned from Paddan Aram,*c* God appeared to him again and blessed him. **10**God said to him, "Your name is Jacob,*d* but you will no longer be called Jacob; your name will be Israel.*e*" So he named him Israel.

11And God said to him, "I am God Almighty*f*; be fruitful and increase in number. A nation and a community of nations will come from you, and kings will come from your body. **12**The land I gave to Abraham and Isaac I also give to you, and I will give this land to your descendants after you." **13**Then God went up from him at the place where he had talked with him.

14Jacob set up a stone pillar at the place where God had talked with him, and he poured out a drink offering*D* on it; he also poured oil on it. **15**Jacob called the place where God had talked with him Bethel.*g*

The Deaths of Rachel and Isaac

16Then they moved on from Bethel. While they were still some distance from Ephrath, Rachel began to give birth and had great difficulty. **17**And as she was having great difficulty in childbirth, the midwife*D* said to her, "Don't be afraid, for you have another son." **18**As she breathed her last—for she was dying—she named her son Ben-Oni.*h* But his father named him Benjamin.*i*

19So Rachel died and was buried on the way to Ephrath (that is, Bethlehem). **20**Over her tomb Jacob set up a pillar, and to this day that pillar marks Rachel's tomb.

21Israel moved on again and pitched his tent beyond Migdal Eder. **22**While Israel was living in that region, Reuben went in and slept with his father's concubine*D* Bilhah, and Israel heard of it.

Jacob had twelve sons:

23The sons of Leah:

Reuben the firstborn*D* of Jacob,

Simeon, Levi, Judah, Issachar and Zebulun.

24The sons of Rachel:

Joseph and Benjamin.

25The sons of Rachel's maidservant Bilhah:

Dan and Naphtali.

26The sons of Leah's maidservant Zilpah:

Gad and Asher.

These were the sons of Jacob, who were born to him in Paddan Aram.

27Jacob came home to his father Isaac in Mamre, near Kiriath Arba (that is, Hebron), where Abraham and Isaac had stayed. **28**Isaac lived a hundred and eighty years. **29**Then he breathed his last and died and was gathered to

---

Deborah (35:8)
Rebekah's nurse, presumably from her infancy, who accompanied Rebekah when she first met Isaac (24:59).

Why was Jacob's name changed? (35:10)
See *Why did Jacob's name change?* (32:28).

Which community of nations came from Jacob? (35:11)
Literally speaking, Jacob's tribe became only one nation. The *community of nations* could refer to the twelve tribes, but this is doubtful. More likely, this blessing was simply a continuation of the covenant made with Abraham, when God had promised that he would be the father of many nations (17:4–7). This covenant was intended to have a physical and a spiritual fulfillment—Israel was to be a light to the nations, drawing the attention of those communities to the one true God (Isaiah 51:4; 60:3).

Drink offering (35:14)
Usually wine or oil given as a sacrifice of dedication to God to honor him and to express thankfulness. Oil was a valuable commodity and was often used in the religious observances of the Hebrews. Drink offerings generally were given with burnt offerings or fellowship offerings.

Why would Reuben sleep with his father's concubine? (35:22)
The text gives no indication of any animosity between Reuben and his father prior to this occurrence. The encounter was probably an impulsive act of the eldest son—one he did not want his father to know about. Sleeping with the concubine was considered an adulterous and a shameful offense against the father. The seriousness of what he had done is demonstrated later when Jacob, while blessing his sons, said that Reuben would *no longer excel* (49:3–4).

Why would one man have so many wives? (35:23–26)
See article: *Why did David have so many wives and concubines?* (2 Samuel 5:13).

How did Isaac live so long? (35:28)
See *What was the secret to such a long life?* (5:5).

---

a7 El Bethel means *God of Bethel.* *b8 Allon Bacuth* means *oak of weeping.* *c9* That is, Northwest Mesopotamia; also in verse 26 *d10 Jacob* means *he grasps the heel* (figuratively, *he deceives*). *e10 Israel* means *he struggles with God.* *f11* Hebrew *El-Shaddai* *g15 Bethel* means *house of God.* *h18 Ben-Oni* means *son of my trouble.* *i18 Benjamin* means *son of my right hand.*

his people, old and full of years. And his sons Esau and Jacob buried him.

Esau's Descendants

36 This is the account of Esau (that is, Edom^D).

²Esau took his wives from the women of Canaan: Adah daughter of Elon the Hittite, and Oholibamah daughter of Anah and granddaughter of Zibeon the Hivite— ³also Basemath daughter of Ishmael and sister of Nebaioth.

⁴Adah bore Eliphaz to Esau, Basemath bore Reuel, ⁵and Oholibamah bore Jeush, Jalam and Korah. These were the sons of Esau, who were born to him in Canaan.

⁶Esau took his wives and sons and daughters and all the members of his household, as well as his livestock and all his other animals and all the goods he had acquired in Canaan, and moved to a land some distance from his brother Jacob. ⁷Their possessions were too great for them to remain together; the land where they were staying could not support them both because of their livestock. ⁸So Esau (that is, Edom) settled in the hill country of Seir.

⁹This is the account of Esau the father of the Edomites in the hill country of Seir.

¹⁰These are the names of Esau's sons:
Eliphaz, the son of Esau's wife Adah, and Reuel, the son of Esau's wife Basemath.
¹¹The sons of Eliphaz:
Teman, Omar, Zepho, Gatam and Kenaz.
¹²Esau's son Eliphaz also had a concubine^D named Timna, who bore him Amalek. These were grandsons of Esau's wife Adah.
¹³The sons of Reuel:
Nahath, Zerah, Shammah and Mizzah. These were grandsons of Esau's wife Basemath.
¹⁴The sons of Esau's wife Oholibamah daughter of Anah and granddaughter of Zibeon, whom she bore to Esau:
Jeush, Jalam and Korah.

¹⁵These were the chiefs among Esau's descendants:
The sons of Eliphaz the firstborn^D of Esau:
Chiefs Teman, Omar, Zepho, Kenaz, ¹⁶Korah,^a Gatam and Amalek. These were the chiefs descended from Eliphaz in Edom; they were grandsons of Adah.
¹⁷The sons of Esau's son Reuel:
Chiefs Nahath, Zerah, Shammah and Mizzah. These were the chiefs descended from Reuel in Edom; they were grandsons of Esau's wife Basemath.
¹⁸The sons of Esau's wife Oholibamah:
Chiefs Jeush, Jalam and Korah. These were the chiefs descended from Esau's wife Oholibamah daughter of Anah.
¹⁹These were the sons of Esau (that is, Edom), and these were their chiefs.

---

a16 Masoretic Text; Samaritan Pentateuch (see also Gen. 36:11 and 1 Chron. 1:36) does not have *Korah.*

Edom (36:1)

Because of the red stew Esau took from Jacob in exchange for his birthright, the word *Edom,* which means *red,* became associated with Esau. It is uncertain if the name referred to Esau personally, or only to the region southeast of the Dead Sea which became home to Esau's descendants, the Edomites.

Why did Esau marry Canaanite women? (36:2)

Probably because they were nearby and available. Later, however, in an attempt to regain the favor of his parents, he arranged to marry a daughter of Ishmael, Abraham's son (28:8–9). Esau is described as a godless man who did not value the covenants made to his grandfather Abraham and who despised his birthright (Heb. 12:16–17). It's also possible he may have married Canaanite women for political reasons, to make peace with people in the area. See *Why ratify an international treaty with a wedding?* (2 Chron. 18:1).

What is the value of genealogies? (36:2)

See article: *Why read an ancient list of faceless names?* (1 Chron. 1:1).

Why is there so much repetition in these genealogies? (36:2–19)

Even though the names are repeated, each list has its own geographic and historic significance. The first list introduces the family of Esau and describes how it outgrew Jacob's clan. The second list gives the wives and sons again, this time as occupants of the land of Seir. The last list defines the sons as chiefs, establishing Esau's clan as a nation, Edom.

Seir (36:8)

Seir was a mountainous land in the general area of Edom (see *Map 2* at the back of this Bible). Esau's descendants overcame the original inhabitants, the Horites (Deut. 2:12,22). Since one of his wives was a Horite, Esau may have wanted to settle there. Once Esau's descendants controlled the area, it became known as Edom.

20These were the sons of Seir the Horite, who were living in the region:

> Lotan, Shobal, Zibeon, Anah, **21**Dishon, Ezer and Dishan. These sons of Seir in Edom[D] were Horite chiefs.

22The sons of Lotan:

> Hori and Homam.[a] Timna was Lotan's sister.

23The sons of Shobal:

> Alvan, Manahath, Ebal, Shepho and Onam.

24The sons of Zibeon:

> Aiah and Anah. This is the Anah who discovered the hot springs[b] in the desert while he was grazing the donkeys of his father Zibeon.

25The children of Anah:

> Dishon and Oholibamah daughter of Anah.

26The sons of Dishon[c]:

> Hemdan, Eshban, Ithran and Keran.

27The sons of Ezer:

> Bilhan, Zaavan and Akan.

28The sons of Dishan:

> Uz and Aran.

29These were the Horite chiefs:

> Lotan, Shobal, Zibeon, Anah, **30**Dishon, Ezer and Dishan. These were the Horite chiefs, according to their divisions, in the land of Seir.

The Rulers of Edom

31These were the kings who reigned in Edom before any Israelite king reigned[d]:

> **32**Bela son of Beor became king of Edom. His city was named Dinhabah.
>
> **33**When Bela died, Jobab son of Zerah from Bozrah succeeded him as king.
>
> **34**When Jobab died, Husham from the land of the Temanites succeeded him as king.
>
> **35**When Husham died, Hadad son of Bedad, who de-

---

[a]22 Hebrew *Hemam*, a variant of *Homam* (see 1 Chron. 1:39)
[b]24 Vulgate; Syriac *discovered water;* the meaning of the Hebrew for this word is uncertain.   [c]26 Hebrew *Dishan*, a variant of *Dishon*
[d]31 Or *before an Israelite king reigned over them*

What was special about hot springs? (36:24–25)

Anah's discovery of hot springs was important because it increased the value of the land. Water, especially naturally hot water, was a valuable commodity in the ancient Middle East.

Edom (36:31)

See *Why is there so much repetition in these genealogies?* (36:2–19).

What is the spiritual value of secular history? (36:31)

Telling the stories of men like Esau and Ishmael gave Israel an idea of what might have been, had they not been chosen by the Lord. The histories of terrifying, godless people could well have been their own history except for the grace of God.

Secular history, especially that which is recorded in the Bible, also demonstrates God's sovereignty over all nations—whether or not those nations acknowledge God. For example, God used foreign, pagan nations to punish the faithlessness of his own people (Deut. 28:49–57).

Secular history also confirms the truth of the Bible by providing additional evidence for the facts and events it records. Such histories illustrate Biblical truths and principles.

The history of pagan nations also demonstrates that prophecies made about those nations were fulfilled. God wanted to draw the Gentiles to himself through his chosen people. Although in many ways Israel failed in this role, there were always a faithful few who would turn secular history into sacred history.

feated Midian in the country of Moab, succeeded him as king. His city was named Avith.

36When Hadad died, Samlah from Masrekah succeeded him as king.

37When Samlah died, Shaul from Rehoboth on the river*a* succeeded him as king.

38When Shaul died, Baal-Hanan son of Acbor succeeded him as king.

39When Baal-Hanan son of Acbor died, Hadad*b* succeeded him as king. His city was named Pau, and his wife's name was Mehetabel daughter of Matred, the daughter of Me-Zahab.

40These were the chiefs descended from Esau, by name, according to their clans and regions:

Timna, Alvah, Jetheth, **41**Oholibamah, Elah, Pinon, **42**Kenaz, Teman, Mibzar, **43**Magdiel and Iram. These were the chiefs of Edom*D*, according to their settlements in the land they occupied.

This was Esau the father of the Edomites.

Joseph's Dreams

37 Jacob lived in the land where his father had stayed, the land of Canaan.

2This is the account of Jacob.

Joseph, a young man of seventeen, was tending the flocks with his brothers, the sons of Bilhah and the sons of Zilpah, his father's wives, and he brought their father a bad report about them.

3Now Israel loved Joseph more than any of his other sons, because he had been born to him in his old age; and he made a richly ornamented*c* robe for him. **4**When his brothers saw that their father loved him more than any of them, they hated him and could not speak a kind word to him.

5Joseph had a dream, and when he told it to his brothers, they hated him all the more. **6**He said to them, "Listen to this dream I had: **7**We were binding sheaves of grain out in the field when suddenly my sheaf rose and stood upright, while your sheaves gathered around mine and bowed down to it."

8His brothers said to him, "Do you intend to reign over us? Will you actually rule us?" And they hated him all the more because of his dream and what he had said.

9Then he had another dream, and he told it to his brothers. "Listen," he said, "I had another dream, and this time the sun and moon and eleven stars were bowing down to me."

10When he told his father as well as his brothers, his father rebuked him and said, "What is this dream you had? Will your mother and I and your brothers actually come and bow down to the ground before you?" **11**His brothers were jealous of him, but his father kept the matter in mind.

Why does this list of chiefs differ from the list in vv. 15–19? (36:40–43)

Probably because the lists had different purposes. The first (vv. 15–19) lists chiefs according to their genealogy. This one gives different names (for the most part) that show who was in charge of different areas. Only Teman and Kenaz appear in both lists.

Why introduce Joseph's story as the account of Jacob? (37:2)

After the account of Esau and his descendants (ch. 36), we shift to *the account of Jacob*—that is, the account of his descendants. This is primarily the story of Joseph since so much of what happens to the twelve tribes of Israel is based on Joseph's enslavement and eventual rise to power in Egypt.

What bad report did Joseph give? (37:2)

The text does not indicate what Joseph said. Whatever it was, it only fueled his brothers' hatred and his father's favoritism for Joseph. Perhaps the brothers were not doing their job or were scheming against their father. This is the first indication of a strained relationship between Joseph and his brothers.

Richly ornamented robe (37:3)

A long-sleeved, brightly colored robe—a token of Jacob's favoritism of Joseph. While normal work clothes were bland by comparison, this robe symbolized a position of honor and esteem. Wearing this robe probably excused Joseph from jobs that might have caused the garment to lose its luster.

Does God still speak through dreams? (37:5–7,9)

See article: *Does God speak through visions and dreams?* (Daniel 1:17). Also see *Do dreams help us know God's will today?* (Judges 7:15).

---

*a*37 Possibly the Euphrates   *b*39 Many manuscripts of the Masoretic Text, Samaritan Pentateuch and Syriac (see also 1 Chron. 1:50); most manuscripts of the Masoretic Text *Hadar*   *c*3 The meaning of the Hebrew for *richly ornamented* is uncertain; also in verses 23 and 32.

Joseph Sold by His Brothers

12Now his brothers had gone to graze their father's flocks near Shechem, **13**and Israel said to Joseph, "As you know, your brothers are grazing the flocks near Shechem. Come, I am going to send you to them."

"Very well," he replied.

14So he said to him, "Go and see if all is well with your brothers and with the flocks, and bring word back to me." Then he sent him off from the Valley of Hebron.

When Joseph arrived at Shechem, **15**a man found him wandering around in the fields and asked him, "What are you looking for?"

16He replied, "I'm looking for my brothers. Can you tell me where they are grazing their flocks?"

17"They have moved on from here," the man answered. "I heard them say, 'Let's go to Dothan.'"

So Joseph went after his brothers and found them near Dothan. **18**But they saw him in the distance, and before he reached them, they plotted to kill him.

19"Here comes that dreamer!" they said to each other. **20**"Come now, let's kill him and throw him into one of these cisterns^D and say that a ferocious animal devoured him. Then we'll see what comes of his dreams."

21When Reuben heard this, he tried to rescue him from their hands. "Let's not take his life," he said. **22**"Don't shed any blood. Throw him into this cistern here in the desert, but don't lay a hand on him." Reuben said this to rescue him from them and take him back to his father.

23So when Joseph came to his brothers, they stripped him of his robe—the richly ornamented robe he was wearing— **24**and they took him and threw him into the cistern. Now the cistern was empty; there was no water in it.

25As they sat down to eat their meal, they looked up and saw a caravan of Ishmaelites coming from Gilead. Their camels were loaded with spices, balm and myrrh^D, and they were on their way to take them down to Egypt.

26Judah said to his brothers, "What will we gain if we kill our brother and cover up his blood? **27**Come, let's sell him to the Ishmaelites and not lay our hands on him; after all, he is our brother, our own flesh and blood." His brothers agreed.

28So when the Midianite merchants came by, his brothers pulled Joseph up out of the cistern and sold him for twenty shekels^D^a of silver to the Ishmaelites, who took him to Egypt.

29When Reuben returned to the cistern and saw that Joseph was not there, he tore his clothes. **30**He went back to his brothers and said, "The boy isn't there! Where can I turn now?"

31Then they got Joseph's robe, slaughtered a goat and dipped the robe in the blood. **32**They took the ornamented robe back to their father and said, "We found this. Examine it to see whether it is your son's robe."

33He recognized it and said, "It is my son's robe! Some ferocious animal has devoured him. Joseph has surely been torn to pieces."

34Then Jacob tore his clothes, put on sackcloth^D and mourned for his son many days. **35**All his sons and daughters came to comfort him, but he refused to be comforted.

Joseph Sold into Egypt (37:28)

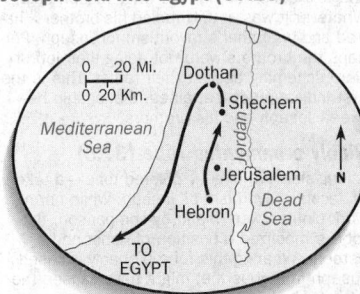

Why did Reuben go along with the cover-up? (37:29–32)
Reuben had already fallen from his father's good graces (for sleeping with one of Jacob's concubines, 35:22). He may have feared being cut off completely from the family and his inheritance if his father found out what happened. Being the oldest son, Reuben would have been held responsible for Joseph's enslavement, even though he did not participate in the sale.

Why did Jacob tear his clothes? (37:34)
See *Where did the custom of ashes and torn clothing come from?* (2 Samuel 13:19).

^a28 That is, about 8 ounces (about 0.2 kilogram)

"No," he said, "in mourning will I go down to the grave[a] to my son." So his father wept for him.

[36]Meanwhile, the Midianites[b] sold Joseph in Egypt to Potiphar, one of Pharaoh's officials, the captain of the guard.

Judah and Tamar

38 At that time, Judah left his brothers and went down to stay with a man of Adullam named Hirah. [2]There Judah met the daughter of a Canaanite man named Shua. He married her and lay with her; [3]she became pregnant and gave birth to a son, who was named Er. [4]She conceived again and gave birth to a son and named him Onan. [5]She gave birth to still another son and named him Shelah. It was at Kezib that she gave birth to him.

[6]Judah got a wife for Er, his firstborn[D], and her name was Tamar. [7]But Er, Judah's firstborn, was wicked in the LORD's sight; so the LORD put him to death[D].

[8]Then Judah said to Onan, "Lie with your brother's wife and fulfill your duty to her as a brother-in-law to produce offspring for your brother." [9]But Onan knew that the offspring would not be his; so whenever he lay with his brother's wife, he spilled his semen on the ground to keep from producing offspring for his brother. [10]What he did was wicked in the LORD's sight; so he put him to death also.

[11]Judah then said to his daughter-in-law Tamar, "Live as a widow in your father's house until my son Shelah grows up." For he thought, "He may die too, just like his brothers." So Tamar went to live in her father's house.

[12]After a long time Judah's wife, the daughter of Shua, died. When Judah had recovered from his grief, he went up to Timnah, to the men who were shearing his sheep, and his friend Hirah the Adullamite went with him.

[13]When Tamar was told, "Your father-in-law is on his way to Timnah to shear his sheep," [14]she took off her widow's clothes, covered herself with a veil to disguise herself, and then sat down at the entrance to Enaim,

[a]35 Hebrew *Sheol*   [b]36 Samaritan Pentateuch, Septuagint, Vulgate and Syriac (see also verse 28); Masoretic Text *Medanites*

Why did Judah leave his family? (38:1)
Perhaps it was hard for Judah to see his father grieving for Joseph, especially with the deception involved. The phrase *left his brothers* may indicate that there was a falling out between Judah and his siblings over Joseph.

Wasn't it wrong to marry a Canaanite woman? (38:2)
Although it later became clear that religious intermarriage would destroy Israel's faithfulness, Jacob apparently did not instruct his sons to avoid marrying Canaanite women. While Jacob's grandfather (24:3) and father (28:1) had prohibited their sons from marrying Canaanites, at this point in their nation's history, marrying someone other than an Israelite did not seem to be wrong in principle. See *Was Joseph wrong to marry the daughter of a pagan priest?* (41:45).

What was Onan's sin? (38:8–10)
Some say this incident illustrates principles relating to the practice of birth control or masturbation, but this is unlikely. Onan's sin was his failure to perpetuate his brother's line of descendants.

Why was Tamar entitled to marry her brother-in-law? (38:14)
Because of a custom intended to perpetuate the line of a deceased brother and provide for the needs of his widow. This was later defined in Mosaic Law so that the brother could back out of the responsibility, but not without some shame (Deut. 25:5–10).

Why did God put some people to death? (38:7–10)

It may seem that God is arbitrary in his punishment. Some men and women have been executed for what seem to be minor offenses; others—perverse criminals—have been allowed to wallow in their wickedness. Why is it that God sometimes appears inconsistent in his discipline?

The Bible reminds us that God takes no pleasure in the death of the wicked. He wants every person to take responsibility for his or her own wrongdoing and to turn from it (Ezek. 33:11). On the other hand, God in his wisdom chooses to make examples of some people, and that may have been the case with the men in these verses. Their punishment reminds us that even relatively minor offenses separate us from God.

Perhaps God allows some of the wicked to live because he wants to give them time to turn from their evil ways, no matter how deeply depraved they may appear to be. He has tolerated the corruption of some for decades or even a lifetime. Some of the most evil people in history have turned from their immoral ways to become great builders of God's kingdom. The apostle Paul is a radiant example of such a person.

Why did Judah not recognize Tamar? (38:15)

It was common for shrine prostitutes to remain veiled during sexual encounters. The practice perpetuated an illusion that the participant was having intercourse with the shrine's goddess. Also see *How did men sacrifice with shrine prostitutes?* (Hosea 4:14).

Was this only a sexual encounter? (38:16)

The Bible does not tell us if Judah's interest in the shrine prostitute was for sexual pleasure alone or if he also hoped to benefit from the superstitions of the fertility cults. (See following note.) We do know that Judah was on his way to shear sheep and would want to gather a lot of wool. It is also clear that idolatry was a temptation to Jacob's family (31:19) and to their descendants for generations to come (Joshua 24:23; Isaiah 46:5–12). See article: *Why would Israelites be tempted by other gods?* (Joshua 23:7) and *Why did people think lifeless idols made by men should be worshiped?* (Psalm 135:15–17).

Shrine prostitutes (38:21)

Shrine prostitutes were used in the fertility cults of the ancient Middle East. These cults believed that harvests and flocks were increased by ritual intercourse with the prostitutes of certain goddesses such as Asherah, Astarte and Anath. Also see *Shrine prostitute* (Deut. 23:17) and *What did male prostitutes have to do with pagan worship?* (1 Kings 14:24).

Did Judah's response reveal a double standard? (38:24)

Absolutely. Promiscuity is never condoned in the Bible. And the absence here of any moral commentary on Judah's sexual activity does not mean that God approved of his actions. When he found out what had happened, Judah took responsibility for his sin and had no further sexual encounters with his daughter-in-law.

Why did Tamar prefer to be a single parent rather than a childless widow? (38:26)

The shame of barrenness was intense in the ancient Middle East. There was less dishonor in being an unwed mother than in being childless and children provided security for the future. Since the sons born belonged to Judah, Tamar was entitled to benefits from his clan, possibly even a partial inheritance. If Tamar were unable to provide for herself in her old age, her sons would be compelled to provide for her.

Which twin was considered the first-born? (38:27–30)

Perez, the first one completely out of the womb, was considered the firstborn (Num. 26:20). It was from the line of Perez that King David was eventually born.

SCRIPTURE LINK (38:27–30)

The struggle of these twins reminds the reader of Jacob grasping at the heel of his brother in birth. See 25:26.

which is on the road to Timnah. For she saw that, though Shelah had now grown up, she had not been given to him as his wife. **15**When Judah saw her, he thought she was a prostitute, for she had covered her face. **16**Not realizing that she was his daughter-in-law, he went over to her by the roadside and said, "Come now, let me sleep with you."

"And what will you give me to sleep with you?" she asked.

17"I'll send you a young goat from my flock," he said.

"Will you give me something as a pledge until you send it?" she asked.

18He said, "What pledge should I give you?"

"Your seal and its cord, and the staff in your hand," she answered. So he gave them to her and slept with her, and she became pregnant by him. **19**After she left, she took off her veil and put on her widow's clothes again.

20Meanwhile Judah sent the young goat by his friend the Adullamite in order to get his pledge back from the woman, but he did not find her. **21**He asked the men who lived there, "Where is the shrine prostitute[D] who was beside the road at Enaim?"

"There hasn't been any shrine prostitute here," they said.

22So he went back to Judah and said, "I didn't find her. Besides, the men who lived there said, 'There hasn't been any shrine prostitute here.'"

23Then Judah said, "Let her keep what she has, or we will become a laughingstock. After all, I did send her this young goat, but you didn't find her."

24About three months later Judah was told, "Your daughter-in-law Tamar is guilty of prostitution, and as a result she is now pregnant."

Judah said, "Bring her out and have her burned to death[D]!"

25As she was being brought out, she sent a message to her father-in-law. "I am pregnant by the man who owns these," she said. And she added, "See if you recognize whose seal and cord and staff these are."

26Judah recognized them and said, "She is more righteous[D] than I, since I wouldn't give her to my son Shelah." And he did not sleep with her again.

27When the time came for her to give birth, there were twin boys in her womb. **28**As she was giving birth, one of them put out his hand; so the midwife[D] took a scarlet thread and tied it on his wrist and said, "This one came out first." **29**But when he drew back his hand, his brother came out, and she said, "So this is how you have broken out!" And he was named Perez.[a] **30**Then his brother, who had the scarlet thread on his wrist, came out and he was given the name Zerah.[b]

Joseph and Potiphar's Wife

39 Now Joseph had been taken down to Egypt. Potiphar, an Egyptian who was one of Pharaoh's officials, the captain of the guard, bought him from the Ishmaelites who had taken him there.

2The LORD was with Joseph and he prospered, and he lived in the house of his Egyptian master. **3**When his master saw that the LORD was with him and that the LORD gave him success in everything he did, **4**Joseph found favor in

---

a29 Perez means *breaking out.*   *b30 Zerah* can mean *scarlet* or *brightness.*

his eyes and became his attendant. Potiphar put him in charge of his household, and he entrusted to his care everything he owned. **5**From the time he put him in charge of his household and of all that he owned, the LORD blessed the household of the Egyptian because of Joseph. The blessing of the LORD was on everything Potiphar had, both in the house and in the field. **6**So he left in Joseph's care everything he had; with Joseph in charge, he did not concern himself with anything except the food he ate.

Now Joseph was well-built and handsome, **7**and after a while his master's wife took notice of Joseph and said, "Come to bed with me!"

8But he refused. "With me in charge," he told her, "my master does not concern himself with anything in the house; everything he owns he has entrusted to my care. **9**No one is greater in this house than I am. My master has withheld nothing from me except you, because you are his wife. How then could I do such a wicked thing and sin against God?" **10**And though she spoke to Joseph day after day, he refused to go to bed with her or even be with her.

11One day he went into the house to attend to his duties, and none of the household servants was inside. **12**She caught him by his cloak and said, "Come to bed with me!" But he left his cloak in her hand and ran out of the house.

13When she saw that he had left his cloak in her hand and had run out of the house, **14**she called her household servants. "Look," she said to them, "this HebrewD has been brought to us to make sport of us! He came in here to sleep with me, but I screamed. **15**When he heard me scream for help, he left his cloak beside me and ran out of the house."

16She kept his cloak beside her until his master came home. **17**Then she told him this story: "That Hebrew slave you brought us came to me to make sport of me. **18**But as soon as I screamed for help, he left his cloak beside me and ran out of the house."

19When his master heard the story his wife told him, saying, "This is how your slave treated me," he burned with anger. **20**Joseph's master took him and put him in prison, the place where the king's prisoners were confined.

But while Joseph was there in the prison, **21**the LORD was with him; he showed him kindness and granted him favor in the eyes of the prison warden. **22**So the warden put Joseph in charge of all those held in the prison, and he was made responsible for all that was done there. **23**The warden paid no attention to anything under Joseph's care, because the LORD was with Joseph and gave him success in whatever he did.

The Cupbearer and the Baker

40 Some time later, the cupbearer and the baker of the king of Egypt offended their master, the king of Egypt. **2**Pharaoh was angry with his two officials, the chief cupbearer and the chief baker, **3**and put them in custody in the house of the captain of the guard, in the same prison where Joseph was confined. **4**The captain of the guard assigned them to Joseph, and he attended them.

After they had been in custody for some time, **5**each of the two men—the cupbearer and the baker of the king of Egypt, who were being held in prison—had a dream the same night, and each dream had a meaning of its own. **6**When Joseph came to them the next morning, he saw that they were dejected. **7**So he asked Pharaoh's officials

How important an official was Potiphar? (39:1)

Potiphar, as captain of the guard—or more literally, *the captain of the executioners*—was a high officer of Pharaoh. In this position, Potiphar supervised the wardens of the prisons in Egypt and was responsible for carrying out Pharaoh's sentences, including executions.

Was it unusual for foreign slaves to be given so much authority? (39:4)

If a foreign slave proved trustworthy over time, he could be given great authority. Daniel was another foreign captive in the Old Testament who was given great responsibility by a foreign oppressor. Ultimately, Joseph succeeded because he cooperated with God's purposes.

Sin against God (39:9)

All sin is ultimately against God because all creation belongs to him. When David sinned, he prayed: *Against you [God], you only, have I sinned and done what is evil in your sight, so that you are proved right when you speak and justified when you judge* (Psalm 51:4). Even before the law was given, God placed a sense of right and wrong in every person's heart.

Hebrew (39:14)

See *Where did the term Hebrew come from?* (Exodus 1:15).

Were the king's prisoners treated better than other prisoners? (39:20)

While most prisons in Egypt were forced-labor camps, the king's prisoners were only under a type of house arrest while they awaited trial. Though they could not leave the compound, they did have considerably more freedom than ordinary prisoners. Stiff sentences were still possible, however, as the execution of the chief baker shows (40:22).

What was done in prison? (39:22)

The pharaohs undertook ambitious building projects that utilized prisoners working under supervision. Some of the pyramids, which were tombs for the pharaohs, took 30 to 40 years to complete. Along with the work projects, some prisoners were given administrative duties, including the daily care and feeding of the prisoners.

Cupbearer (40:2)

Egyptian cupbearers were called *pure of hands*. These servants were trusted confidants of the pharaohs, recognized officials who often wielded great political power. Foreigners were frequently drafted to this position by kings who wanted their wine checked for poison before they would drink. Consequently, some cupbearers died in service.

SCRIPTURE LINK (40:3) *Captain of the guard*

The same title given to Potiphar (39:1). The king's prisoners were placed in the house of the captain of the guard. Perhaps they were placed there because they warranted closer scrutiny. It is unknown whether this captain of the guard was Potiphar.

Like Joseph, Daniel was called upon to interpret dreams and acknowledged God as the source of the interpretation (see Daniel 2:27–28).

Lifted up the heads (40:20)
To lift one's head usually meant to encourage: "Keep your chin up" (see Psalm 3:3, where David says that the Lord lifted up his head). To a prisoner this usually would mean release from prison, as was the case with the cupbearer (vv. 13–21). But the baker's head was lifted off (vv. 19, 22)—a dreadful pun to describe his beheading.

Why would God allow Joseph to be forgotten? (40:23)
Although God may allow people to forget those who have helped them, God never forgets those who belong to him. Perhaps this was a time of spiritual development for Joseph. Although nothing negative is said about Joseph in this account, his heart might not have been ready for the responsibilities God had in store for him.

Was it common to hear from God in dreams? (41:1)
See article: *Does God speak through visions and dreams?* (Daniel 1:17).

who were in custody with him in his master's house, "Why are your faces so sad today?"

8"We both had dreams," they answered, "but there is no one to interpret them."

Then Joseph said to them, "Do not interpretations belong to God? Tell me your dreams."

9So the chief cupbearer told Joseph his dream. He said to him, "In my dream I saw a vine in front of me, **10**and on the vine were three branches. As soon as it budded, it blossomed, and its clusters ripened into grapes. **11**Pharaoh's cup was in my hand, and I took the grapes, squeezed them into Pharaoh's cup and put the cup in his hand."

12"This is what it means," Joseph said to him. "The three branches are three days. **13**Within three days Pharaoh will lift up your head and restore you to your position, and you will put Pharaoh's cup in his hand, just as you used to do when you were his cupbearer. **14**But when all goes well with you, remember me and show me kindness; mention me to Pharaoh and get me out of this prison. **15**For I was forcibly carried off from the land of the Hebrews, and even here I have done nothing to deserve being put in a dungeon."

16When the chief baker saw that Joseph had given a favorable interpretation, he said to Joseph, "I too had a dream: On my head were three baskets of bread.*a* **17**In the top basket were all kinds of baked goods for Pharaoh, but the birds were eating them out of the basket on my head."

18"This is what it means," Joseph said. "The three baskets are three days. **19**Within three days Pharaoh will lift off your head and hang you on a tree.*b* And the birds will eat away your flesh."

20Now the third day was Pharaoh's birthday, and he gave a feast for all his officials. He lifted up the heads of the chief cupbearer and the chief baker in the presence of his officials: **21**He restored the chief cupbearer to his position, so that he once again put the cup into Pharaoh's hand, **22**but he hanged*c* the chief baker, just as Joseph had said to them in his interpretation.

23The chief cupbearer, however, did not remember Joseph; he forgot him.

Pharaoh's Dreams

41 When two full years had passed, Pharaoh had a dream: He was standing by the Nile, **2**when out of the river there came up seven cows, sleek and fat, and they grazed among the reeds. **3**After them, seven other cows, ugly and gaunt, came up out of the Nile and stood beside those on the riverbank. **4**And the cows that were ugly and gaunt ate up the seven sleek, fat cows. Then Pharaoh woke up.

5He fell asleep again and had a second dream: Seven heads of grain, healthy and good, were growing on a single stalk. **6**After them, seven other heads of grain sprouted—thin and scorched by the east wind. **7**The thin heads of grain swallowed up the seven healthy, full heads. Then Pharaoh woke up; it had been a dream.

8In the morning his mind was troubled, so he sent for all the magicians*D* and wise men of Egypt. Pharaoh told

*a16 Or three wicker baskets   b19 Or and impale you on a pole
c22 Or impaled*

them his dreams, but no one could interpret them for him.

9Then the chief cupbearer said to Pharaoh, "Today I am reminded of my shortcomings. **10**Pharaoh was once angry with his servants, and he imprisoned me and the chief baker in the house of the captain of the guard. **11**Each of us had a dream the same night, and each dream had a meaning of its own. **12**Now a young Hebrew^D was there with us, a servant of the captain of the guard. We told him our dreams, and he interpreted them for us, giving each man the interpretation of his dream. **13**And things turned out exactly as he interpreted them to us: I was restored to my position, and the other man was hanged.^a"

14So Pharaoh sent for Joseph, and he was quickly brought from the dungeon. When he had shaved and changed his clothes, he came before Pharaoh.

15Pharaoh said to Joseph, "I had a dream, and no one can interpret it. But I have heard it said of you that when you hear a dream you can interpret it."

16"I cannot do it," Joseph replied to Pharaoh, "but God will give Pharaoh the answer he desires."

17Then Pharaoh said to Joseph, "In my dream I was standing on the bank of the Nile, **18**when out of the river there came up seven cows, fat and sleek, and they grazed among the reeds. **19**After them, seven other cows came up—scrawny and very ugly and lean. I had never seen such ugly cows in all the land of Egypt. **20**The lean, ugly cows ate up the seven fat cows that came up first. **21**But even after they ate them, no one could tell that they had done so; they looked just as ugly as before. Then I woke up.

22"In my dreams I also saw seven heads of grain, full and good, growing on a single stalk. **23**After them, seven other heads sprouted—withered and thin and scorched by the east wind. **24**The thin heads of grain swallowed up the seven good heads. I told this to the magicians^D, but none could explain it to me."

25Then Joseph said to Pharaoh, "The dreams of Pharaoh are one and the same. God has revealed to Pharaoh what he is about to do. **26**The seven good cows are seven years, and the seven good heads of grain are seven years; it is one and the same dream. **27**The seven lean, ugly cows that came up afterward are seven years, and so are the seven worthless heads of grain scorched by the east wind: They are seven years of famine.

28"It is just as I said to Pharaoh: God has shown Pharaoh what he is about to do. **29**Seven years of great abundance are coming throughout the land of Egypt, **30**but seven years of famine will follow them. Then all the abundance in Egypt will be forgotten, and the famine will ravage the land. **31**The abundance in the land will not be remembered, because the famine that follows it will be so severe. **32**The reason the dream was given to Pharaoh in two forms is that the matter has been firmly decided by God, and God will do it soon.

33"And now let Pharaoh look for a discerning and wise man and put him in charge of the land of Egypt. **34**Let Pharaoh appoint commissioners over the land to take a fifth of the harvest of Egypt during the seven years of abundance. **35**They should collect all the food of these good years that are coming and store up the grain under the authority of Pharaoh, to be kept in the cities for food.

Magicians (41:8)

These were people who tried to influence events through their apparently supernatural powers. They kept books of ritual incantations and instructions for the interpretation of dreams. They were often professional advisers to kings, along with wise men (keepers of proverbs and wisdom stories), military advisers, prophets and other specialists.

Why would God speak to a non-believer like Pharaoh? (41:16)

God will work through anyone to accomplish his purposes. Earlier there was Abimelech, the Philistine king to whom God spoke in a dream (Gen. 20:3–7). God influenced mighty leaders like the Babylonian king Nebuchadnezzar (Jer. 25:9), an unnamed Assyrian king (Isaiah 10:5–12) and Cyrus, the founder of the Persian empire (Isaiah 45:1), to accomplish his will.

Seven years of famine (41:27)

An unusual prediction for Egypt, because of the Nile River. See *Why did Egypt have food when other countries didn't?* (12:10).

---

^a 13 Or *impaled*

Did Pharaoh come to believe in the true God? (41:37–39)

Probably not. Ironically, whether or not Pharaoh knew it, he did make a theologically accurate statement. Pharaoh uses the word *Elohim*, a generic name for God that could also be translated *gods*. Here Pharaoh did not necessarily make a confession of faith, but probably only referred to a god or gods generally, according to his understanding. The Babylonians made similar statements about Daniel having *the spirit of the holy gods* (Daniel 4:8).

What position did Joseph hold? (41:41)

Joseph became the administrative head of Pharaoh's kingdom, a position sometimes designated as "vizier." The use of the pharaoh's seal, his signet ring, indicated that Joseph was Pharaoh's primary representative in administrative matters. The extent of the power of this office in Judah is revealed in Isaiah 22:20–24. The position conferred great authority, since Joseph answered only to Pharaoh.

Why did Pharaoh change Joseph's name? (41:45)

To indicate Joseph's complete acceptance into Pharaoh's court and the Egyptian culture. The name change also demonstrated Pharaoh's authority over Joseph and Joseph's allegiance to this new land and life. His associations with the past were to be severed.

Priest of On (41:45)

On was the center of worship for the sun god, Ra (see *Map 1* at the back of this Bible). Because of the crucial role of the sun in agriculture, Ra was considered to be an extremely important deity. Therefore, Ra's priests were a wealthy and powerful group, closely associated politically with many pharaohs' households.

Was Joseph wrong to marry the daughter of a pagan priest? (41:45)

The text makes no judgment about this marriage. In the context of Genesis 41, Joseph's marriage appears positive, underscoring the power and prestige Joseph had gained in Egypt. The marriage was apparently another blessing from God, along with all the other good things happening to him.

Why didn't Joseph send a message to his father? (41:46)

Since his father was an old man when Joseph was born, Joseph might have reasonably assumed his father was now dead. Also, after the rejection by his brothers, the change in his name and the birth of a son named Manasseh (see NIV text note at v. 51), Joseph seemed ready to let go of his painful past, though he undoubtedly still cared for his father.

Why name a child as a reminder that you've forgotten your family? (41:51)

Rather than a reminder of wrongs suffered, perhaps Manasseh would remind Joseph of the ways God had healed him of his family's rejection. The meaning of the boy's name should be read in the context of the chapter: Joseph is now experiencing God's blessing in his life, including a release from the past.

36This food should be held in reserve for the country, to be used during the seven years of famine that will come upon Egypt, so that the country may not be ruined by the famine."

37The plan seemed good to Pharaoh and to all his officials. **38**So Pharaoh asked them, "Can we find anyone like this man, one in whom is the spirit of God*ᵃ*?"

39Then Pharaoh said to Joseph, "Since God has made all this known to you, there is no one so discerning and wise as you. **40**You shall be in charge of my palace, and all my people are to submit to your orders. Only with respect to the throne will I be greater than you."

Joseph in Charge of Egypt

41So Pharaoh said to Joseph, "I hereby put you in charge of the whole land of Egypt." **42**Then Pharaoh took his signet ring*ᵇ* from his finger and put it on Joseph's finger. He dressed him in robes of fine linen and put a gold chain around his neck. **43**He had him ride in a chariot as his second-in-command,*ᵇ* and men shouted before him, "Make way*ᶜ*!" Thus he put him in charge of the whole land of Egypt.

44Then Pharaoh said to Joseph, "I am Pharaoh, but without your word no one will lift hand or foot in all Egypt." **45**Pharaoh gave Joseph the name Zaphenath-Paneah and gave him Asenath daughter of Potiphera, priest*ᴰ* of On,*ᵈ* to be his wife. And Joseph went throughout the land of Egypt.

46Joseph was thirty years old when he entered the service of Pharaoh king of Egypt. And Joseph went out from Pharaoh's presence and traveled throughout Egypt. **47**During the seven years of abundance the land produced plentifully. **48**Joseph collected all the food produced in those seven years of abundance in Egypt and stored it in the cities. In each city he put the food grown in the fields surrounding it. **49**Joseph stored up huge quantities of grain, like the sand of the sea; it was so much that he stopped keeping records because it was beyond measure.

50Before the years of famine came, two sons were born to Joseph by Asenath daughter of Potiphera, priest of On. **51**Joseph named his firstborn*ᴰ* Manasseh*ᵉ* and said, "It is because God has made me forget all my trouble and all my father's household." **52**The second son he named Ephraim*ᶠ* and said, "It is because God has made me fruitful in the land of my suffering."

53The seven years of abundance in Egypt came to an end, **54**and the seven years of famine began, just as Joseph had said. There was famine in all the other lands, but in the whole land of Egypt there was food. **55**When all Egypt began to feel the famine, the people cried to Pharaoh for food. Then Pharaoh told all the Egyptians, "Go to Joseph and do what he tells you."

56When the famine had spread over the whole country, Joseph opened the storehouses and sold grain to the Egyptians, for the famine was severe throughout Egypt. **57**And all the countries came to Egypt to buy grain from Joseph, because the famine was severe in all the world.

ᵃ38 Or of the gods   ᵇ43 Or in the chariot of his second-in-command; or in his second chariot   ᶜ43 Or Bow down   ᵈ45 That is, Heliopolis; also in verse 50   ᵉ51 Manasseh sounds like and may be derived from the Hebrew for forget.   ᶠ52 Ephraim sounds like the Hebrew for twice fruitful.

Joseph's Brothers Go to Egypt

42 When Jacob learned that there was grain in Egypt, he said to his sons, "Why do you just keep looking at each other?" **2**He continued, "I have heard that there is grain in Egypt. Go down there and buy some for us, so that we may live and not die."

3Then ten of Joseph's brothers went down to buy grain from Egypt. **4**But Jacob did not send Benjamin, Joseph's brother, with the others, because he was afraid that harm might come to him. **5**So Israel's sons were among those who went to buy grain, for the famine was in the land of Canaan also.

6Now Joseph was the governor of the land, the one who sold grain to all its people. So when Joseph's brothers arrived, they bowed down to him with their faces to the ground. **7**As soon as Joseph saw his brothers, he recognized them, but he pretended to be a stranger and spoke harshly to them. "Where do you come from?" he asked.

"From the land of Canaan," they replied, "to buy food."

8Although Joseph recognized his brothers, they did not recognize him. **9**Then he remembered his dreams about them and said to them, "You are spies! You have come to see where our land is unprotected."

10"No, my lord," they answered. "Your servants have come to buy food. **11**We are all the sons of one man. Your servants are honest men, not spies."

12"No!" he said to them. "You have come to see where our land is unprotected."

13But they replied, "Your servants were twelve brothers, the sons of one man, who lives in the land of Canaan. The youngest is now with our father, and one is no more."

14Joseph said to them, "It is just as I told you: You are spies! **15**And this is how you will be tested: As surely as Pharaoh lives, you will not leave this place unless your youngest brother comes here. **16**Send one of your number to get your brother; the rest of you will be kept in prison, so that your words may be tested to see if you are telling the truth. If you are not, then as surely as Pharaoh lives, you are spies!" **17**And he put them all in custody for three days.

18On the third day, Joseph said to them, "Do this and you will live, for I fear God: **19**If you are honest men, let one of your brothers stay here in prison, while the rest of you go and take grain back for your starving households. **20**But you must bring your youngest brother to me, so that your words may be verified and that you may not die." This they proceeded to do.

21They said to one another, "Surely we are being punished because of our brother. We saw how distressed he was when he pleaded with us for his life, but we would not listen; that's why this distress has come upon us."

22Reuben replied, "Didn't I tell you not to sin against the boy? But you wouldn't listen! Now we must give an accounting for his blood." **23**They did not realize that Joseph could understand them, since he was using an interpreter.

24He turned away from them and began to weep, but then turned back and spoke to them again. He had Simeon taken from them and bound before their eyes.

25Joseph gave orders to fill their bags with grain, to put each man's silver back in his sack, and to give them provisions for their journey. After this was done for them, **26**they loaded their grain on their donkeys and left.

27At the place where they stopped for the night one of

What became of Manasseh and Ephraim? (41:51–52)
Jacob adopted these two grandsons as his own sons (48:5). As a result, they received inheritances with Jacob's other sons. When their descendants inherited the promised land, they occupied the heartland of Canaan. Manasseh initially possessed the largest, most fertile portion. Eventually, however, Ephraim became the leading tribe among the northern groups (see **Map 4** at the back of this Bible).

In all the world (41:57)
The world known to the Egyptians at this time included areas from modern Turkey to Iran, as well as the rest of the Middle East and Northeastern Africa (modern Libya, Sudan and Ethiopia). See **Map 12** at the back of this Bible.

Why was Jacob so protective of Benjamin? (42:4)
Rachel, the mother of Joseph and Benjamin, had been Jacob's favorite wife. Since Joseph was gone, Benjamin was all he had left from that favored relationship. Perhaps Jacob also feared what had happened once before, with Joseph.

Why wasn't Joseph forthright with his brothers about who he was? (42:7)
The narrative subtly reveals Joseph's loving motive. Joseph's actions helped his brothers deal with their treatment of him. He succeeded as the brothers finally confessed their guilt and Judah offered himself in exchange for Benjamin's safety. This brotherly concern was undoubtedly Joseph's aim.

Your servants (42:10)
Joseph's brothers unknowingly confirmed his prophetic dreams by their own words. Such language was commonly used in addressing powerful leaders. See, for example, Exodus 5:15; Joshua 9:8 and 2 Kings 10:5.

Why did the brothers blame God for an apparent theft? (42:28)

The brothers were acknowledging God's hand in the matter. They likely understood, as did most Biblical characters, that God was sovereign over his world and that nothing took place without his permission. This doesn't mean that God caused the evil circumstance, but that God knew about it and allowed it. The point is emphasized again in 45:7–9 and 50:20.

When do vows go too far? (42:37)

When they cannot be fulfilled. The Bible cautions against making vows, but once made, they should be kept (Eccl. 5:4–5; Deut. 23:21–23). Although his vow seems risky, we can admire Reuben's decisive, strong commitment. He was essentially saying that his namesakes would be destroyed and his family line would come to an end, a grievous penalty in his culture.

SCRIPTURE LINK (43:3)

Judah's leadership among his brothers is evident here and in vv. 8–10. See *How would Judah become a ruler?* (49:10–12). It was through Judah's line that the Messiah came (Matt. 1:2–3).

them opened his sack to get feed for his donkey, and he saw his silver in the mouth of his sack. **28**"My silver has been returned," he said to his brothers. "Here it is in my sack."

Their hearts sank and they turned to each other trembling and said, "What is this that God has done to us?"

29When they came to their father Jacob in the land of Canaan, they told him all that had happened to them. They said, **30**"The man who is lord over the land spoke harshly to us and treated us as though we were spying on the land. **31**But we said to him, 'We are honest men; we are not spies. **32**We were twelve brothers, sons of one father. One is no more, and the youngest is now with our father in Canaan.'

33"Then the man who is lord over the land said to us, 'This is how I will know whether you are honest men: Leave one of your brothers here with me, and take food for your starving households and go. **34**But bring your youngest brother to me so I will know that you are not spies but honest men. Then I will give your brother back to you, and you can trade*a* in the land.' "

35As they were emptying their sacks, there in each man's sack was his pouch of silver! When they and their father saw the money pouches, they were frightened. **36**Their father Jacob said to them, "You have deprived me of my children. Joseph is no more and Simeon is no more, and now you want to take Benjamin. Everything is against me!"

37Then Reuben said to his father, "You may put both of my sons to death*b* if I do not bring him back to you. Entrust him to my care, and I will bring him back."

38But Jacob said, "My son will not go down there with you; his brother is dead and he is the only one left. If harm comes to him on the journey you are taking, you will bring my gray head down to the grave*b* in sorrow."

The Second Journey to Egypt

43 Now the famine was still severe in the land. **2**So when they had eaten all the grain they had brought from Egypt, their father said to them, "Go back and buy us a little more food."

3But Judah said to him, "The man warned us solemnly, 'You will not see my face again unless your brother is with you.' **4**If you will send our brother along with us, we will go down and buy food for you. **5**But if you will not send him, we will not go down, because the man said to us, 'You will not see my face again unless your brother is with you.' "

6Israel asked, "Why did you bring this trouble on me by telling the man you had another brother?"

7They replied, "The man questioned us closely about ourselves and our family. 'Is your father still living?' he asked us. 'Do you have another brother?' We simply answered his questions. How were we to know he would say, 'Bring your brother down here'?"

8Then Judah said to Israel his father, "Send the boy along with me and we will go at once, so that we and you and our children may live and not die. **9**I myself will guarantee his safety; you can hold me personally responsible for him. If I do not bring him back to you and set him here before you, I will bear the blame before you all my life.

a34 Or move about freely   *b38 Hebrew Sheol*

10As it is, if we had not delayed, we could have gone and returned twice."

11Then their father Israel said to them, "If it must be, then do this: Put some of the best products of the land in your bags and take them down to the man as a gift—a little balm and a little honey, some spices and myrrh^D, some pistachio nuts and almonds. **12**Take double the amount of silver with you, for you must return the silver that was put back into the mouths of your sacks. Perhaps it was a mistake. **13**Take your brother also and go back to the man at once. **14**And may God Almighty*a* grant you mercy^D before the man so that he will let your other brother and Benjamin come back with you. As for me, if I am bereaved, I am bereaved."

15So the men took the gifts and double the amount of silver, and Benjamin also. They hurried down to Egypt and presented themselves to Joseph. **16**When Joseph saw Benjamin with them, he said to the steward of his house, "Take these men to my house, slaughter an animal and prepare dinner; they are to eat with me at noon."

17The man did as Joseph told him and took the men to Joseph's house. **18**Now the men were frightened when they were taken to his house. They thought, "We were brought here because of the silver that was put back into our sacks the first time. He wants to attack us and overpower us and seize us as slaves and take our donkeys."

19So they went up to Joseph's steward and spoke to him at the entrance to the house. **20**"Please, sir," they said, "we came down here the first time to buy food. **21**But at the place where we stopped for the night we opened our sacks and each of us found his silver—the exact weight—in the mouth of his sack. So we have brought it back with us. **22**We have also brought additional silver with us to buy food. We don't know who put our silver in our sacks."

23"It's all right," he said. "Don't be afraid. Your God, the God of your father, has given you treasure in your sacks; I received your silver." Then he brought Simeon out to them.

24The steward took the men into Joseph's house, gave them water to wash their feet and provided fodder for their donkeys. **25**They prepared their gifts for Joseph's arrival at noon, because they had heard that they were to eat there.

26When Joseph came home, they presented to him the gifts they had brought into the house, and they bowed down before him to the ground. **27**He asked them how they were, and then he said, "How is your aged father you told me about? Is he still living?"

28They replied, "Your servant our father is still alive and well." And they bowed low to pay him honor.

29As he looked about and saw his brother Benjamin, his own mother's son, he asked, "Is this your youngest brother, the one you told me about?" And he said, "God be gracious to you, my son." **30**Deeply moved at the sight of his brother, Joseph hurried out and looked for a place to weep. He went into his private room and wept there.

31After he had washed his face, he came out and, controlling himself, said, "Serve the food."

32They served him by himself, the brothers by themselves, and the Egyptians who ate with him by themselves, because Egyptians could not eat with Hebrews, for that is detestable to Egyptians. **33**The men had been seat-

a14 Hebrew El-Shaddai

Why bother with gifts from a famine-stricken land? (43:11)

Bearing gifts on a visit, especially to a person of high rank, was normal in this culture (and perhaps indispensable—see 1 Samuel 16:20 and 17:18). Even when the cost was high, such a symbolic gesture was a necessary part of protocol. Besides, these gifts were not staples like bread, grapes or olives but specialty items that Jacob called *the best products of the land.*

Why was an invitation to a ruler's house a cause for fear? (43:18)

Ordinarily an invitation to a person's house was considered a gesture of friendship or normal hospitality in the desert land. But Bedouins were seldom invited to join royalty, so their apprehension is understandable.

How long was Simeon imprisoned? (43:23)

For less than two years, since the famine had only been going on that long (45:6).

Were the ancient Egyptians racially prejudiced? (43:32)

Perhaps, but the reason for separation at the meal was religious. The term *detestable* usually refers to ritual uncleanness. The Egyptians felt Hebrews were unclean because they did not worship the Egyptians' gods. This is similar to the custom of Jews not eating with Gentiles.

Why seat the brothers according to age? (43:33)

We would expect seating by rank at an official dinner. The seat of honor would go to the eldest, with the others following accordingly to their age. Because their host had them seated in exact order from the oldest to the youngest, they were astonished. They could not imagine such an extraordinary coincidence, but neither could they imagine how anyone in the Egyptian court would know their ages.

ed before him in the order of their ages, from the first-born[D] to the youngest; and they looked at each other in astonishment. 34When portions were served to them from Joseph's table, Benjamin's portion was five times as much as anyone else's. So they feasted and drank freely with him.

A Silver Cup in a Sack

Why did Joseph play "mind games" with his brothers? (44:1–5)

To help them deal with the old issue of brother abandonment. This final ploy sets the stage for the moment of truth. The silver cup in his sack would put Benjamin's life in danger. Would the brothers who had sold one brother so ruthlessly abandon another one?

What kind of divination did Joseph do? (44:5,15)

This kind of divination was accomplished by placing oil drops upon water and observing the resulting patterns. Divining God's will through dreams, the budding of plants, sheep fleeces and the casting of lots was not condemned in the Old Testament. People believed God was totally in control and spoke through these means. (The Mosaic Law does not forbid divination, but it condemns consulting the dead through mediums.)

44 Now Joseph gave these instructions to the steward of his house: "Fill the men's sacks with as much food as they can carry, and put each man's silver in the mouth of his sack. 2Then put my cup, the silver one, in the mouth of the youngest one's sack, along with the silver for his grain." And he did as Joseph said.

3As morning dawned, the men were sent on their way with their donkeys. 4They had not gone far from the city when Joseph said to his steward, "Go after those men at once, and when you catch up with them, say to them, 'Why have you repaid good with evil? 5Isn't this the cup my master drinks from and also uses for divination[D]? This is a wicked thing you have done.' "

6When he caught up with them, he repeated these words to them. 7But they said to him, "Why does my lord say such things? Far be it from your servants to do anything like that! 8We even brought back to you from the land of Canaan the silver we found inside the mouths of our sacks. So why would we steal silver or gold from your master's house? 9If any of your servants is found to have it, he will die; and the rest of us will become my lord's slaves."

10"Very well, then," he said, "let it be as you say. Whoever is found to have it will become my slave; the rest of you will be free from blame."

11Each of them quickly lowered his sack to the ground and opened it. 12Then the steward proceeded to search, beginning with the oldest and ending with the youngest. And the cup was found in Benjamin's sack. 13At this, they tore their clothes. Then they all loaded their donkeys and returned to the city.

14Joseph was still in the house when Judah and his brothers came in, and they threw themselves to the ground before him. 15Joseph said to them, "What is this you have done? Don't you know that a man like me can find things out by divination?"

Is favoritism ever a good idea? (43:34)

Joseph showed favoritism by sending extra food to his brother Benjamin. Sending choice food to an honored guest was a common practice in their culture. This was especially true of favoritism shown by, or to, those in powerful positions.

Yet James 2:1–9 admonishes us not to show favoritism. We know that many of Joseph's problems came from the favoritism his father had shown him (ch. 37). However, the Genesis text does not seem to focus on the problem of *showing* favoritism, but upon the problem of how one *responds* when favoritism is shown. Whether or not Joseph and Jacob were out of line to show favoritism, the question in these stories is: How do the brothers respond? In ch. 43, the issue is whether they can stand to have another brother favored. Would they reject him as they had Joseph? Or could they rise above hurt feelings and *rejoice with those who rejoice* (Romans 12:15)?

16"What can we say to my lord?" Judah replied. "What can we say? How can we prove our innocence? God has uncovered your servants' guilt. We are now my lord's slaves—we ourselves and the one who was found to have the cup."

17But Joseph said, "Far be it from me to do such a thing! Only the man who was found to have the cup will become my slave. The rest of you, go back to your father in peace[D]."

18Then Judah went up to him and said: "Please, my lord, let your servant speak a word to my lord. Do not be angry with your servant, though you are equal to Pharaoh himself. **19**My lord asked his servants, 'Do you have a father or a brother?' **20**And we answered, 'We have an aged father, and there is a young son born to him in his old age. His brother is dead, and he is the only one of his mother's sons left, and his father loves him.'

21"Then you said to your servants, 'Bring him down to me so I can see him for myself.' **22**And we said to my lord, 'The boy cannot leave his father; if he leaves him, his father will die.' **23**But you told your servants, 'Unless your youngest brother comes down with you, you will not see my face again.' **24**When we went back to your servant my father, we told him what my lord had said.

25"Then our father said, 'Go back and buy a little more food.' **26**But we said, 'We cannot go down. Only if our youngest brother is with us will we go. We cannot see the man's face unless our youngest brother is with us.'

27"Your servant my father said to us, 'You know that my wife bore me two sons. **28**One of them went away from me, and I said, "He has surely been torn to pieces." And I have not seen him since. **29**If you take this one from me too and harm comes to him, you will bring my gray head down to the grave[a] in misery.'

30"So now, if the boy is not with us when I go back to your servant my father and if my father, whose life is closely bound up with the boy's life, **31**sees that the boy isn't there, he will die. Your servants will bring the gray head of our father down to the grave in sorrow. **32**Your servant guaranteed the boy's safety to my father. I said, 'If I do not bring him back to you, I will bear the blame before you, my father, all my life!'

33"Now then, please let your servant remain here as my lord's slave in place of the boy, and let the boy return with his brothers. **34**How can I go back to my father if the boy is not with me? No! Do not let me see the misery that would come upon my father."

Joseph Makes Himself Known

45 Then Joseph could no longer control himself before all his attendants, and he cried out, "Have everyone leave my presence!" So there was no one with Joseph when he made himself known to his brothers. **2**And he wept so loudly that the Egyptians heard him, and Pharaoh's household heard about it.

3Joseph said to his brothers, "I am Joseph! Is my father still living?" But his brothers were not able to answer him, because they were terrified at his presence.

4Then Joseph said to his brothers, "Come close to me." When they had done so, he said, "I am your brother Joseph, the one you sold into Egypt! **5**And now, do not be distressed and do not be angry with yourselves for selling

---

a29 Hebrew Sheol; *also in verse 31*

What guilt had God uncovered? (44:16)

Judah probably meant they were caught with the goods and therefore must be considered guilty. However, Judah's statement had broader implications, connecting the brothers to the guilt stemming from the mistreatment of Joseph years before. God worked through these events to *uncover* that primary guilt.

My wife bore me two sons (44:27)

Obviously, Jacob had more than two sons. He was the father of 12 sons, from whom the 12 tribes of Israel descended. The two sons Judah refers to here were Joseph and Benjamin, the only sons of Jacob's favorite wife, Rachel.

SCRIPTURE LINK (44:28) *He has surely been torn to pieces*

See 37:33.

What made Joseph more terrifying after his brothers recognized him? (45:3)

First, Joseph burst into tears, which was unexpected from one in his position. Further, they no doubt reasoned their brother might want revenge—and he had the power to implement it. Third, the brothers had probably assumed Joseph was dead, so it was as if a dead man had come back to life. But even if the brothers had known Joseph was in Egypt, they wouldn't have expected him to be in the palace.

me here, because it was to save lives that God sent me ahead of you. ⁶For two years now there has been famine in the land, and for the next five years there will not be plowing and reaping. ⁷But God sent me ahead of you to preserve for you a remnant^D on earth and to save your lives by a great deliverance.^a

⁸"So then, it was not you who sent me here, but God. He made me father to Pharaoh, lord of his entire household and ruler of all Egypt. ⁹Now hurry back to my father and say to him, 'This is what your son Joseph says: God has made me lord of all Egypt. Come down to me; don't delay. ¹⁰You shall live in the region of Goshen and be near me— you, your children and grandchildren, your flocks and herds, and all you have. ¹¹I will provide for you there, because five years of famine are still to come. Otherwise you and your household and all who belong to you will become destitute.'

¹²"You can see for yourselves, and so can my brother Benjamin, that it is really I who am speaking to you. ¹³Tell my father about all the honor accorded me in Egypt and about everything you have seen. And bring my father down here quickly."

¹⁴Then he threw his arms around his brother Benjamin and wept, and Benjamin embraced him, weeping. ¹⁵And he kissed all his brothers and wept over them. Afterward his brothers talked with him.

¹⁶When the news reached Pharaoh's palace that Joseph's brothers had come, Pharaoh and all his officials were pleased. ¹⁷Pharaoh said to Joseph, "Tell your brothers, 'Do this: Load your animals and return to the land of Canaan, ¹⁸and bring your father and your families back to me. I will give you the best of the land of Egypt and you can enjoy the fat of the land.'

¹⁹"You are also directed to tell them, 'Do this: Take some carts from Egypt for your children and your wives, and get your father and come. ²⁰Never mind about your belongings, because the best of all Egypt will be yours.' "

²¹So the sons of Israel did this. Joseph gave them carts, as Pharaoh had commanded, and he also gave them provisions for their journey. ²²To each of them he gave new clothing, but to Benjamin he gave three hundred shekels^{Db} of silver and five sets of clothes. ²³And this is what

Father to Pharaoh (45:8)
The term *father* was commonly used as a title of honor and prestige, perhaps stemming from strong paternal cultural customs.

Why did Joseph want his family to move to Egypt? (45:9)
Because of the famine, Joseph wanted his family members to be where he could provide for them. During the famine, Goshen was probably better grazing land than Canaan because it was in the delta region of the Nile and could produce more vegetation.

Why did Joseph favor Benjamin? (45:22)
See article: *Is favoritism ever a good idea?* (43:34).

^a7 Or *save you as a great band of survivors*   ^b22 That is, about 7 1/2 pounds (about 3.5 kilograms)

Why ignore what Joseph's brothers had done? (45:8)

The brothers had obviously done a great wrong to Joseph years earlier. Joseph does not gloss over the truth of their offense nor their culpability for it. Rather, he focuses his mind, and their minds, on the key message of this saga: God is at work even amid the plans of evil men (50:20; also see this theme in 42:28 and 43:23).

The brothers are responsible for their actions, but they are forgiven. God's original plans did not necessarily include Joseph's rejection, slavery and imprisonment. God allowed these problems to happen and he used them to fulfill his purposes. Yet the brothers did not have to treat Joseph wrongly for God to do what he desired. God's options are infinite. We can now understand Joseph's story in light of Romans 8:28: *In all things God works for the good of those who love him, who have been called according to his purpose.*

he sent to his father: ten donkeys loaded with the best things of Egypt, and ten female donkeys loaded with grain and bread and other provisions for his journey. **24**Then he sent his brothers away, and as they were leaving he said to them, "Don't quarrel on the way!"

25So they went up out of Egypt and came to their father Jacob in the land of Canaan. **26**They told him, "Joseph is still alive! In fact, he is ruler of all Egypt." Jacob was stunned; he did not believe them. **27**But when they told him everything Joseph had said to them, and when he saw the carts Joseph had sent to carry him back, the spirit of their father Jacob revived. **28**And Israel said, "I'm convinced! My son Joseph is still alive. I will go and see him before I die."

Jacob Goes to Egypt

46 So Israel set out with all that was his, and when he reached Beersheba, he offered sacrificesᴰ to the God of his father Isaac.

2And God spoke to Israel in a visionᴰ at night and said, "Jacob! Jacob!"

"Here I am," he replied.

3"I am God, the God of your father," he said. "Do not be afraid to go down to Egypt, for I will make you into a great nation there. **4**I will go down to Egypt with you, and I will surely bring you back again. And Joseph's own hand will close your eyes."

5Then Jacob left Beersheba, and Israel's sons took their father Jacob and their children and their wives in the carts that Pharaoh had sent to transport him. **6**They also took with them their livestock and the possessions they had acquired in Canaan, and Jacob and all his offspring went to Egypt. **7**He took with him to Egypt his sons and grandsons and his daughters and granddaughters—all his offspring.

8These are the names of the sons of Israel (Jacob and his descendants) who went to Egypt:

Reuben the firstbornᴰ of Jacob.
  9The sons of Reuben:
    Hanoch, Pallu, Hezron and Carmi.
  10The sons of Simeon:
    Jemuel, Jamin, Ohad, Jakin, Zohar and Shaul the son of a Canaanite woman.
  11The sons of Levi:
    Gershon, Kohath and Merari.
  12The sons of Judah:
    Er, Onan, Shelah, Perez and Zerah (but Er and Onan had died in the land of Canaan).
    The sons of Perez:
      Hezron and Hamul.
  13The sons of Issachar:
    Tola, Puah,ᵃ Jashubᵇ and Shimron.
  14The sons of Zebulun:
    Sered, Elon and Jahleel.
  15These were the sons Leah bore to Jacob in Paddan Aram,ᶜ besides his daughter Dinah. These sons and daughters of his were thirty-three in all.

16The sons of Gad:

Why did Joseph think his brothers might quarrel? (45:24)

The brothers had a history of quarreling. In fact, all through the narrative, beginning in 37:4, they are pictured as bitter, hateful, quarreling men. But Joseph was hoping this incident might bring harmony among them.

SCRIPTURE LINK (46:2–4) *A vision at night*

God gave Jacob similar promises in a dream the first time he left his homeland many years before. See 28:10–16.

Why list those who had died before the trip? (46:12)

This was a complete list of descendants rather than only a list of those who entered Egypt (compare with Num. 26 and 1 Chron. 1–9). Er and Onan were mentioned because of their connection to David.

ᵃ13 Samaritan Pentateuch and Syriac (see also 1 Chron. 7:1); Masoretic Text *Puvah*   ᵇ13 Samaritan Pentateuch and some Septuagint manuscripts (see also Num. 26:24 and 1 Chron. 7:1); Masoretic Text *Iob*
ᶜ15 That is, Northwest Mesopotamia

Zephon,[a] Haggi, Shuni, Ezbon, Eri, Arodi and Areli.

[17]The sons of Asher:

Imnah, Ishvah, Ishvi and Beriah.

Their sister was Serah.

The sons of Beriah:

Heber and Malkiel.

[18]These were the children born to Jacob by Zilpah, whom Laban had given to his daughter Leah—sixteen in all.

[19]The sons of Jacob's wife Rachel:

Joseph and Benjamin. [20]In Egypt, Manasseh and Ephraim were born to Joseph by Asenath daughter of Potiphera, priest[D] of On.[b]

[21]The sons of Benjamin:

Bela, Beker, Ashbel, Gera, Naaman, Ehi, Rosh, Muppim, Huppim and Ard.

[22]These were the sons of Rachel who were born to Jacob—fourteen in all.

[23]The son of Dan:

Hushim.

[24]The sons of Naphtali:

Jahziel, Guni, Jezer and Shillem.

[25]These were the sons born to Jacob by Bilhah, whom Laban had given to his daughter Rachel—seven in all.

[26]All those who went to Egypt with Jacob—those who were his direct descendants, not counting his sons' wives—numbered sixty-six persons. [27]With the two sons[c] who had been born to Joseph in Egypt, the members of Jacob's family, which went to Egypt, were seventy[d] in all.

[28]Now Jacob sent Judah ahead of him to Joseph to get directions to Goshen. When they arrived in the region of Goshen, [29]Joseph had his chariot made ready and went to Goshen to meet his father Israel. As soon as Joseph appeared before him, he threw his arms around his father[e] and wept for a long time.

[30]Israel said to Joseph, "Now I am ready to die, since I have seen for myself that you are still alive."

[31]Then Joseph said to his brothers and to his father's household, "I will go up and speak to Pharaoh and will say to him, 'My brothers and my father's household, who were living in the land of Canaan, have come to me. [32]The men are shepherds; they tend livestock, and they have brought along their flocks and herds and everything they own.' [33]When Pharaoh calls you in and asks, 'What is your occupation?' [34]you should answer, 'Your servants have tended livestock from our boyhood on, just as our fathers did.' Then you will be allowed to settle in the region of Goshen, for all shepherds are detestable to the Egyptians."

47 Joseph went and told Pharaoh, "My father and brothers, with their flocks and herds and everything they own, have come from the land of Canaan and are now in Goshen." [2]He chose five of his brothers and presented them before Pharaoh.

Was it okay to have several wives and concubines? (46:18)

See article: *Why did David have so many wives and concubines?* (2 Samuel 5:13).

Why such emphasis on the number? (46:26–27)

In this case, 70 corresponds to the number of nations repopulating the earth after the flood. There may be a numerical connection between the repopulation of the earth and the descendants entering the promised land (Deut. 32:8). The entrance of Jacob's family, like the repopulation, was a major moment of re-creation for mankind. It partially fulfilled the promise that God would make Abraham and Jacob into *a great nation.*

Why did Egyptians detest shepherds? (46:34)

Egyptian literature says nothing about their dislike for sheep herders, but it does mention their disdain for cattle and swine herders. The word *detestable* could suggest a religious avoidance; perhaps this occupation made people unclean to participate in religious rites, just as it did later in New Testament times in Israel. See *Why announce the birth of Jesus to shepherds?* (Luke 2:9–12). Another view is that it may reflect the distaste the city dwellers in Egypt had for the harsh conditions endured by the nomads of Canaan—who happened to be sheep herders.

Why didn't Joseph introduce all his brothers to Pharaoh? (47:2)

Egyptians were suspicious of foreigners entering their midst. A large clan like Jacob's could have been troublesome, so presenting only 5 brothers would be less imposing than 11. Emphasizing their pastoral vocation also helped mollify any concerns. Pharaoh would realize that Joseph's shepherd family had no political ambitions and would not disrupt the economy.

a16 Samaritan Pentateuch and Septuagint (see also Num. 26:15); Masoretic Text Ziphion   b20 That is, Heliopolis   c27 Hebrew; Septuagint the nine children   d27 Hebrew (see also Exodus 1:5 and footnote); Septuagint (see also Acts 7:14) seventy-five   e29 Hebrew around him

³Pharaoh asked the brothers, "What is your occupation?"

"Your servants are shepherds," they replied to Pharaoh, "just as our fathers were." ⁴They also said to him, "We have come to live here awhile, because the famine is severe in Canaan and your servants' flocks have no pasture. So now, please let your servants settle in Goshen."

⁵Pharaoh said to Joseph, "Your father and your brothers have come to you, ⁶and the land of Egypt is before you; settle your father and your brothers in the best part of the land. Let them live in Goshen. And if you know of any among them with special ability, put them in charge of my own livestock."

⁷Then Joseph brought his father Jacob in and presented him before Pharaoh. After Jacob blessed*a* Pharaoh, ⁸Pharaoh asked him, "How old are you?"

⁹And Jacob said to Pharaoh, "The years of my pilgrimage are a hundred and thirty. My years have been few and difficult, and they do not equal the years of the pilgrimage of my fathers." ¹⁰Then Jacob blessed*b* Pharaoh and went out from his presence.

¹¹So Joseph settled his father and his brothers in Egypt and gave them property in the best part of the land, the district of Rameses, as Pharaoh directed. ¹²Joseph also provided his father and his brothers and all his father's household with food, according to the number of their children.

Joseph and the Famine

¹³There was no food, however, in the whole region because the famine was severe; both Egypt and Canaan wasted away because of the famine. ¹⁴Joseph collected all the money that was to be found in Egypt and Canaan in payment for the grain they were buying, and he brought it to Pharaoh's palace. ¹⁵When the money of the people of Egypt and Canaan was gone, all Egypt came to Joseph and said, "Give us food. Why should we die before your eyes? Our money is used up."

¹⁶"Then bring your livestock," said Joseph. "I will sell you food in exchange for your livestock, since your money is gone." ¹⁷So they brought their livestock to Joseph, and he gave them food in exchange for their horses, their sheep and goats, their cattle and donkeys. And he brought them through that year with food in exchange for all their livestock.

¹⁸When that year was over, they came to him the following year and said, "We cannot hide from our lord the fact that since our money is gone and our livestock belongs to you, there is nothing left for our lord except our bodies and our land. ¹⁹Why should we perish before your eyes—we and our land as well? Buy us and our land in exchange for food, and we with our land will be in bondage to Pharaoh. Give us seed so that we may live and not die, and that the land may not become desolate."

²⁰So Joseph bought all the land in Egypt for Pharaoh. The Egyptians, one and all, sold their fields, because the famine was too severe for them. The land became Pharaoh's, ²¹and Joseph reduced the people to servitude,*c* from one end of Egypt to the other. ²²However, he did not buy the land of the priests*D*, because they received a reg-

a7 Or greeted   b10 Or said farewell to   c21 Samaritan Pentateuch and Septuagint (see also Vulgate); Masoretic Text and he moved the people into the cities

What happened to the Egyptians living in *the best part of the land?* (47:11)

Pharaoh may have exercised his sovereign right as ruler to relocate the Egyptian inhabitants of Goshen to make room for the Israelites, just as a government today would do to build a highway. Though it's possible some Egyptians stayed to live among the Israelites, the Bible does not say so. In fact, it seems that Goshen became known specifically as Israelite territory (Exodus 8:22–23). See *The Exodus* on page 94.

What kind of "welfare department" did Joseph run? (47:20–21)

The ancient world had no welfare. As long as people could exchange something for food, they gave it—including their lives for slavery, if necessary. (Mosaic Laws did convey the right to buy back land and freedom.) Joseph's measures developed a sort of feudal system of serfs and sharecroppers. With it, Joseph did for the Egyptians what he did for his brothers: he saved their lives.

ular allotment from Pharaoh and had food enough from the allotment Pharaoh gave them. That is why they did not sell their land.

²³Joseph said to the people, "Now that I have bought you and your land today for Pharaoh, here is seed for you so you can plant the ground. ²⁴But when the crop comes in, give a fifth of it to Pharaoh. The other four-fifths you may keep as seed for the fields and as food for yourselves and your households and your children."

²⁵"You have saved our lives," they said. "May we find favor in the eyes of our lord; we will be in bondage to Pharaoh."

²⁶So Joseph established it as a law concerning land in Egypt—still in force today—that a fifth of the produce belongs to Pharaoh. It was only the land of the priests*ᴰ* that did not become Pharaoh's.

²⁷Now the Israelites settled in Egypt in the region of Goshen. They acquired property there and were fruitful and increased greatly in number.

²⁸Jacob lived in Egypt seventeen years, and the years of his life were a hundred and forty-seven. ²⁹When the time drew near for Israel to die, he called for his son Joseph and said to him, "If I have found favor in your eyes, put your hand under my thigh and promise that you will show me kindness and faithfulness. Do not bury me in Egypt, ³⁰but when I rest with my fathers, carry me out of Egypt and bury me where they are buried."

"I will do as you say," he said.

³¹"Swear to me," he said. Then Joseph swore to him, and Israel worshiped as he leaned on the top of his staff.*ᵃ*

Manasseh and Ephraim

48 Some time later Joseph was told, "Your father is ill." So he took his two sons Manasseh and Ephraim along with him. ²When Jacob was told, "Your son Joseph has come to you," Israel rallied his strength and sat up on the bed.

³Jacob said to Joseph, "God Almighty*ᵇ* appeared to me at Luz in the land of Canaan, and there he blessed me ⁴and said to me, 'I am going to make you fruitful and will increase your numbers. I will make you a community of peoples, and I will give this land as an everlasting possession to your descendants after you.'

⁵"Now then, your two sons born to you in Egypt before I came to you here will be reckoned as mine; Ephraim and Manasseh will be mine, just as Reuben and Simeon are mine. ⁶Any children born to you after them will be yours; in the territory they inherit they will be reckoned under the names of their brothers. ⁷As I was returning from Paddan,*ᶜ* to my sorrow Rachel died in the land of Canaan while we were still on the way, a little distance from Ephrath. So I buried her there beside the road to Ephrath" (that is, Bethlehem).

⁸When Israel saw the sons of Joseph, he asked, "Who are these?"

⁹"They are the sons God has given me here," Joseph said to his father.

Then Israel said, "Bring them to me so I may bless them."

¹⁰Now Israel's eyes were failing because of old age, and

Today (47:26)

Assuming Moses wrote this, *today* was more than 400 years later.

Why put one's hand under someone's thigh? (47:29)

This was a covenant ritual, apparently an ancient custom, though no extrabiblical material mentions it. The intimacy that such a practice would require suggests the high level of trust sought in the oath. Twice in the Bible this practice is mentioned; the other time is with Abraham and his chief servant (24:2–9).

How did Israel worship, leaning on the top of his staff? (47:31)

Worship means to bow in submission. Jacob bowed his head after this ceremony, either on his staff or at the head of his bed (see NIV text note). The Hebrew word is *bed;* the ancient Greek translation (the Septuagint) says *staff.* No one can tell if this was a special ritual or simply an old man raising himself to worship.

Why did Jacob claim Joseph's sons for his own? (48:5)

Adoption in the ancient Middle East was common, especially for the purpose of inheritance. Normally the firstborn son received a double portion and then other sons received equal portions of the remainder. In effect, Jacob increased Joseph's inheritance to that of the firstborn. This action would also keep the number of tribes inheriting land in Canaan at 12. (Levi's tribe did not inherit a specific territory.)

---

*ᵃ31 Or Israel bowed down at the head of his bed   *ᵇ3 Hebrew El-Shaddai   *ᶜ7 That is, Northwest Mesopotamia*

he could hardly see. So Joseph brought his sons close to him, and his father kissed them and embraced them.

¹¹Israel said to Joseph, "I never expected to see your face again, and now God has allowed me to see your children too."

¹²Then Joseph removed them from Israel's knees and bowed down with his face to the ground. ¹³And Joseph took both of them, Ephraim on his right toward Israel's left hand and Manasseh on his left toward Israel's right hand, and brought them close to him. ¹⁴But Israel reached out his right hand and put it on Ephraim's head, though he was the younger, and crossing his arms, he put his left hand on Manasseh's head, even though Manasseh was the firstborn ᴰ.

¹⁵Then he blessed Joseph and said,

> "May the God before whom my fathers
>   Abraham and Isaac walked,
> the God who has been my shepherd
>   all my life to this day,
> ¹⁶the Angel who has delivered me from all harm
>   —may he bless these boys.
> May they be called by my name
>   and the names of my fathers Abraham and
>   Isaac,
> and may they increase greatly
>   upon the earth."

¹⁷When Joseph saw his father placing his right hand on Ephraim's head he was displeased; so he took hold of his father's hand to move it from Ephraim's head to Manasseh's head. ¹⁸Joseph said to him, "No, my father, this one is the firstborn; put your right hand on his head." ¹⁹But his father refused and said, "I know, my son, I know. He too will become a people, and he too will become great. Nevertheless, his younger brother will be greater than he, and his descendants will become a group of nations." ²⁰He blessed them that day and said,

> "In your ᵃ name will Israel pronounce this
>   blessing:
> 'May God make you like Ephraim and
>   Manasseh.' "

So he put Ephraim ahead of Manasseh.

²¹Then Israel said to Joseph, "I am about to die, but God will be with you ᵇ and take you ᵇ back to the land of your ᵇ fathers. ²²And to you, as one who is over your brothers, I give the ridge of land ᶜ I took from the Amorites with my sword and my bow."

Jacob Blesses His Sons

49 Then Jacob called for his sons and said: "Gather around so I can tell you what will happen to you in days to come.

> ²"Assemble and listen, sons of Jacob;
>   listen to your father Israel.

> ³"Reuben, you are my firstborn,
>   my might, the first sign of my strength,
>   excelling in honor, excelling in power.

ᵃ20 The Hebrew is singular.   ᵇ21 The Hebrew is plural.
ᶜ22 Or *And to you I give one portion more than to your brothers—the portion*

Angel (48:16)
A reference to God himself. The *angel of the Lᴏʀᴅ* (16:7) frequently refers to God's appearance in visible form. Often passages first label the speaker as the *angel of the Lᴏʀᴅ* and later denote the same speaker as the Lᴏʀᴅ (16:13).

Why did the right hand mean a better blessing? (48:18)
Traditionally the right hand was the hand of strength, privilege, honor and blessing in the Bible, and apparently throughout the ancient Middle East. To sit at the right hand was a sign of being honored (see Psalm 110:1). In the New Testament Jesus described the last judgment, in which the sheep are placed on his right and the goats on his left (Matt. 25:33).

Was Jacob's statement prophecy? (48:19)
To prophesy, in the Bible, usually means to preach. But prophecy can also refer to a predictive message from God, through a human, about the present or future. Jacob conveys God's message about the future, so this is prophecy in the predictive sense. That does not necessarily mean it predetermined the outcome of events. For example, Jonah predicted Nineveh's downfall (Jonah 3:4), but God did not destroy it when its inhabitants repented.

SCRIPTURE LINK (48:19) *His younger brother will be greater than he*
For four generations younger brothers received the family blessing: Isaac instead of Ishmael (17:18–19), Jacob instead of Esau (25:23), Joseph instead of Reuben (49:3–4,26) and now Ephraim instead of Manasseh.

Why did Jacob put the younger ahead of the older? (48:20)
This demonstrated that blessing is not a right, but a gift. God bestows grace at his discretion. Free grace is emphasized because most ancient Middle Eastern religions followed ritual, believing they could place gods under obligation to act on their behalf. That would be manipulation, not worship.

Did people in Bible times expect the dying to see the future? (49:1)
No, but ancient peoples were interested in the dying person's final words, just as we are today. The Bible gives us numerous instances of last words, and their message is typically predictive. The closest parallel to Jacob's speech is Moses' words in Deuteronomy 33.

SCRIPTURE LINK (49:4) *You went up onto your father's bed*
See 35:22.

SCRIPTURE LINK (49:6) *Killed men in their anger*
See 34:25–26.

In what way would Levi and Simeon be scattered? (49:7)
Levi and Simeon were scattered regarding inheritance in the promised land. Levi served priestly functions and was not allotted any region in particular. Instead, his tribe received various villages within the boundaries of other tribes (Joshua 21). Simeon's tribe decreased during the desert wanderings. By the time it arrived in Canaan, it was the smallest tribe and was allotted cities within Judah's boundaries (see *Map 4* at the back of this Bible). Eventually it was assimilated into the tribe of Judah.

Why did Jacob describe his sons as animals? (49:9–27)
Jacob was using word pictures. Comparing people to animals is not uncommon in the Bible. The people were familiar enough with these animals to understand the analogies. The lion denoted strength and leadership; the donkey, submission; the serpent, craftiness; the doe, swiftness with skill; and the wolf, tenacity. These are all good characterizations of these tribes, in light of their unfolding stories.

How would Judah become a ruler? (49:10–12)
Featured throughout the narrative on Joseph, Judah's clan eventually became the dominant tribal group. His actions show his leadership, and Jacob's blessing confirms Judah as leader of the family. We don't know why Judah is chosen over Joseph. Judah was *the strongest of his brothers,* which may refer to the number in his clan or to his quality of leadership. We know God loved Judah (Psalm 78:67–68), but we don't know why he chose him.

⁴Turbulent as the waters, you will no longer excel,
　for you went up onto your father's bed,
　onto my couch and defiled it.

⁵"Simeon and Levi are brothers—
　their swords*ᵃ* are weapons of violence.
⁶Let me not enter their council,
　let me not join their assembly,
for they have killed men in their anger
　and hamstrung oxen as they pleased.
⁷Cursed be their anger, so fierce,
　and their fury, so cruel!
I will scatter them in Jacob
　and disperse them in Israel.

⁸"Judah,*ᵇ* your brothers will praise you;
　your hand will be on the neck of your enemies;
　your father's sons will bow down to you.
⁹You are a lion's cub, O Judah;
　you return from the prey, my son.
Like a lion he crouches and lies down,
　like a lioness—who dares to rouse him?
¹⁰The scepter*ᴰ* will not depart from Judah,
　nor the ruler's staff from between his feet,
until he comes to whom it belongs*ᶜ*
　and the obedience of the nations is his.
¹¹He will tether his donkey to a vine,
　his colt to the choicest branch;
he will wash his garments in wine,
　his robes in the blood of grapes.
¹²His eyes will be darker than wine,
　his teeth whiter than milk.*ᵈ*

¹³"Zebulun will live by the seashore
　and become a haven for ships;
　his border will extend toward Sidon.

¹⁴"Issachar is a rawboned*ᵉ* donkey
　lying down between two saddlebags.*ᶠ*
¹⁵When he sees how good is his resting place
　and how pleasant is his land,
he will bend his shoulder to the burden
　and submit to forced labor.

¹⁶"Dan*ᵍ* will provide justice for his people
　as one of the tribes of Israel.
¹⁷Dan will be a serpent by the roadside,
　a viper along the path,
that bites the horse's heels
　so that its rider tumbles backward.

¹⁸"I look for your deliverance, O LORD.

¹⁹"Gad*ʰ* will be attacked by a band of raiders,
　but he will attack them at their heels.

²⁰"Asher's food will be rich;
　he will provide delicacies fit for a king.

²¹"Naphtali is a doe set free

ᵃ5 The meaning of the Hebrew for this word is uncertain.
ᵇ8 Judah sounds like and may be derived from the Hebrew for praise.
ᶜ10 Or until Shiloh comes; or until he comes to whom tribute belongs
ᵈ12 Or will be dull from wine, / his teeth white from milk   ᵉ14 Or
strong   ᶠ14 Or campfires   ᵍ16 Dan here means he provides
justice.   ʰ19 Gad can mean attack and band of raiders.

that bears beautiful fawns.*a*

22"Joseph is a fruitful vine,
   a fruitful vine near a spring,
   whose branches climb over a wall.*b*
23With bitterness archers attacked him;
   they shot at him with hostility.
24But his bow remained steady,
   his strong arms stayed*c* limber,
because of the hand of the Mighty One of
      Jacob,
   because of the Shepherd, the Rock of Israel,
25because of your father's God, who helps you,
   because of the Almighty,*d* who blesses you
with blessings of the heavens above,
   blessings of the deep that lies below,
   blessings of the breast and womb.
26Your father's blessings are greater
   than the blessings of the ancient mountains,
   than*e* the bounty of the age-old hills.
Let all these rest on the head of Joseph,
   on the brow of the prince among*f* his
      brothers.

27"Benjamin is a ravenous wolf;
   in the morning he devours the prey,
   in the evening he divides the plunder*D*."

28All these are the twelve tribes of Israel, and this is
what their father said to them when he blessed them, giving each the blessing appropriate to him.

The Death of Jacob

29Then he gave them these instructions: "I am about to
be gathered to my people. Bury me with my fathers in the
cave in the field of Ephron the Hittite, **30**the cave in the
field of Machpelah, near Mamre in Canaan, which Abraham bought as a burial place from Ephron the Hittite,
along with the field. **31**There Abraham and his wife Sarah
were buried, there Isaac and his wife Rebekah were buried, and there I buried Leah. **32**The field and the cave in it
were bought from the Hittites.*g*"

33When Jacob had finished giving instructions to his
sons, he drew his feet up into the bed, breathed his last
and was gathered to his people.

50 Joseph threw himself upon his father and wept
over him and kissed him. **2**Then Joseph directed
the physicians in his service to embalm his father Israel.
So the physicians embalmed him, **3**taking a full forty
days, for that was the time required for embalming. And
the Egyptians mourned for him seventy days.

4When the days of mourning had passed, Joseph said to
Pharaoh's court, "If I have found favor in your eyes, speak
to Pharaoh for me. Tell him, **5**'My father made me swear
an oath and said, "I am about to die; bury me in the tomb
I dug for myself in the land of Canaan." Now let me go up
and bury my father; then I will return.' "

6Pharaoh said, "Go up and bury your father, as he made
you swear to do."

7So Joseph went up to bury his father. All Pharaoh's of-

His bow remained steady (49:24)
This blessing likely refers to the military might
of the Ephraimites, descendants of Joseph's
son Ephraim. They were seldom defeated in
battle.

**Why was Jacob buried with only one of
his wives? (49:31)**
Jacob seems to follow the tradition of being
buried with his first wife, Leah, in the family
burial grounds. He was buried with his fathers,
Isaac and Abraham, and their first wives. Rachel, his second wife, died while giving birth to
Benjamin, somewhere in the region of Bethlehem (35:18–20). Apparently she was buried
there instead of at Machpelah because, although she was Jacob's favorite, she was his
second wife and not his first.

**What kind of embalming would take
40 days? (50:2–3)**
The embalming process could take up to 70
days. The number 40 may be symbolic for "a
long time." Embalming was a process the
Egyptians mastered, and no one else has ever
matched the preserving abilities of their process. Some body parts were embalmed separately. After embalming, the body was wrapped
in linen and placed in a wooden case. Mum-
mies unwrapped by archaeologists reveal skin
and hair blackened, but bodies intact.

---

*a21 Or free; / he utters beautiful words   *b22 Or Joseph is a wild
colt, / a wild colt near a spring, / a wild donkey on a terraced hill
*c23,24 Or archers will attack ... will shoot ... will remain ... will stay
*d25 Hebrew Shaddai   *e26 Or of my progenitors, / as great as
*f26 Or the one separated from   *g32 Or the sons of Heth

Why would Egyptians mourn a Hebrew? (50:7)

Joseph was a high official, and showing respect for his father's death was only proper. The extended period of 70 days indicated Joseph's prominence. The Egyptians took death very seriously and provided the best they could for the departed—including food, clothing, pets and other items for use in the world of the dead.

ficials accompanied him—the dignitaries of his court and all the dignitaries of Egypt— **8**besides all the members of Joseph's household and his brothers and those belonging to his father's household. Only their children and their flocks and herds were left in Goshen. **9**Chariots and horsemen*a* also went up with him. It was a very large company.

10When they reached the threshing floor of Atad, near the Jordan, they lamented loudly and bitterly; and there Joseph observed a seven-day period of mourning for his father. **11**When the Canaanites who lived there saw the mourning at the threshing floor of Atad, they said, "The Egyptians are holding a solemn ceremony of mourning." That is why that place near the Jordan is called Abel Mizraim.*b*

12So Jacob's sons did as he had commanded them: **13**They carried him to the land of Canaan and buried him in the cave in the field of Machpelah, near Mamre, which Abraham had bought as a burial place from Ephron the Hittite, along with the field. **14**After burying his father, Joseph returned to Egypt, together with his brothers and all the others who had gone with him to bury his father.

Joseph Reassures His Brothers

Why did the sons of Israel stay in Egypt after the famine? (50:22)

Perhaps the Israelites enjoyed the prosperity and goodness of Egypt. Canaan was more on the frontier, less stable politically and perhaps not as fertile. Since the Israelites lived in Egypt throughout Joseph's lifetime (three generations), they were probably more familiar with Egypt. Also, they may have had some obligation to Pharaoh. Everyone in Pharaoh's land would in some way be indebted to him, even though we see no indication of their slavery until the book of Exodus.

15When Joseph's brothers saw that their father was dead, they said, "What if Joseph holds a grudge against us and pays us back for all the wrongs we did to him?" **16**So they sent word to Joseph, saying, "Your father left these instructions before he died: **17**'This is what you are to say to Joseph: I ask you to forgive your brothers the sins and the wrongs they committed in treating you so badly.' Now please forgive the sins of the servants of the God of your father." When their message came to him, Joseph wept.

18His brothers then came and threw themselves down before him. "We are your slaves," they said.

a9 Or *charioteers*   *b11* Abel Mizraim means *mourning of the Egyptians.*

Does God overrule our intentions? (50:20)

No matter what our intentions, they will not thwart God's working. Accordingly, we can trust him to fulfill his promises. A dominant theme throughout the first five books of the Bible is that God will fulfill his promises to humans. People or circumstances may frustrate God's plan but will never derail it.

For example, Abraham's problems were never too much to overcome. These included nearly losing his wife to Pharaoh, fighting with Lot, being too old to father children and being asked to sacrifice his only son. In each case, God provided. The cycle continues through the patriarchal narratives: The promise is jeopardized by human actions but preserved by God.

The promise to Abraham involved three main elements: descendants, relationship and land. Genesis focuses on God filling his promise of descendants. Exodus and Leviticus focus on preserving the relationship. Numbers and Deuteronomy focus on the promise of land. In Joshua, that promise is fulfilled. At each juncture, God accomplishes his desired result through his own innovative means. The schemes of humans do not destroy God's plans. In fact, he sometimes uses the evil intentions of humans to accomplish his own purposes. The Sovereign Lord will do as he wishes (Prov. 16:4).

19But Joseph said to them, "Don't be afraid. Am I in the place of God? **20**You intended to harm me, but God intended it for good to accomplish what is now being done, the saving of many lives. **21**So then, don't be afraid. I will provide for you and your children." And he reassured them and spoke kindly to them.

The Death of Joseph

22Joseph stayed in Egypt, along with all his father's family. He lived a hundred and ten years **23**and saw the third generation of Ephraim's children. Also the children of Makir son of Manasseh were placed at birth on Joseph's knees.*a*

24Then Joseph said to his brothers, "I am about to die. But God will surely come to your aid and take you up out of this land to the land he promised on oath to Abraham, Isaac and Jacob." **25**And Joseph made the sons of Israel swear an oath and said, "God will surely come to your aid, and then you must carry my bones up from this place."

26So Joseph died at the age of a hundred and ten. And after they embalmed him, he was placed in a coffin in Egypt.

Why place newborns on a grandfather's knees? (50:23)

To "place a child on one's knees" seems to mean the child was accepted as one's own. Here Joseph may be adopting Makir in order to leave an inheritance to him. Since Joseph apparently had no sons beside Manasseh and Ephraim, the adoption of Makir (the firstborn of the firstborn) is understandable. It would be similar in today's society to changing a will so that a grandchild receives as much as a child. The Makir clan is later revealed as having similar status with the rest of the tribal groups (Num. 26:29).

Why did they need help to leave Egypt? (50:24)

The phrase *come to your aid* translates a Hebrew word that often speaks of God coming to people to bring help or judgment. It emphasizes God's decisive action in human history. Joseph predicted God would lead the Hebrews back to Canaan. They did not have to be slaves for God to work in their lives. The Hebrews were apparently not enslaved until several generations after Joseph's death.

SCRIPTURE LINK (50:25) *You must carry my bones up from this place*

Moses later carried out this last request of Joseph. See Exodus 13:19.

---

*a*23 That is, were counted as his

EXODUS

Why read this book?

A spectacular escape and a hair-raising chase scene are only two of the many stories that fill the pages of Exodus. But this book is much more than an epic adventure; it recounts the supernatural rescue of an entire people by their God. Despite God's intervention, the Israelites seem unable to remain loyal to him—even though he produces miracle after miracle for them. But seeing their faltering faith can actually encourage us with a vivid lesson: Even imperfect people can get to know God, who loves them perfectly.

Who wrote this book?

Moses.

Why was it written?

To remind the Israelites how God had rescued them from oppression.

When was it written?

Approximately 1440 B.C.

What was the historical setting for this book?

Jacob had migrated to Egypt with his family to escape a famine in Canaan some four centuries earlier. But the "land of escape" became a "land of bondage" as the Egyptians sought to maintain their dominance over the increasing number of Israelites by forcing them into slave labor. Shortly before his death in the desert, Moses reflected on and penned the swirling events of Israel's escape from Egypt.

What to look for in Exodus:

Exodus spotlights God's direct involvement in human history—how he goes to astonishing lengths to reach those he loves. He helps Moses overcome an incredible inferiority complex, for example, to become a prophet in Israel. Repeatedly, Exodus shows how much God responds to people who, aware of their weaknesses, trust him as their only hope.

When did these things happen?

TIME LINE	2200BC	2100	2000	1900	1800	1700	1600	1500	1400
Moses' birth (c.1526 B.C.)									
The plagues; The Passover (c.1446 B.C.)									
The exodus (c.1446 B.C.)									
Desert wanderings (c.1446-1406 B.C.)									
The Ten Commandments (c.1445 B.C.)									
Book of Exodus written (c.1440 B.C.)									
Moses dies; Joshua becomes leader (c.1406 B.C.)									
Israelites enter Canaan (c.1406 B.C.)									

The Israelites Oppressed

1 These are the names of the sons of Israel who went to Egypt with Jacob, each with his family: [2]Reuben, Simeon, Levi and Judah; [3]Issachar, Zebulun and Benjamin; [4]Dan and Naphtali; Gad and Asher. [5]The descendants of Jacob numbered seventy[a] in all; Joseph was already in Egypt.

[6]Now Joseph and all his brothers and all that generation died, [7]but the Israelites were fruitful and multiplied greatly and became exceedingly numerous, so that the land was filled with them.

[8]Then a new king, who did not know about Joseph, came to power in Egypt. [9]"Look," he said to his people, "the Israelites have become much too numerous for us. [10]Come, we must deal shrewdly with them or they will become even more numerous and, if war breaks out, will join our enemies, fight against us and leave the country."

[11]So they put slave masters over them to oppress them with forced labor, and they built Pithom and Rameses as store cities for Pharaoh. [12]But the more they were oppressed, the more they multiplied and spread; so the Egyptians came to dread the Israelites [13]and worked them ruthlessly. [14]They made their lives bitter with hard labor in brick and mortar and with all kinds of work in the fields; in all their hard labor the Egyptians used them ruthlessly.

[15]The king of Egypt said to the Hebrew[D] midwives[D], whose names were Shiphrah and Puah, [16]"When you help the Hebrew women in childbirth and observe them on the delivery stool, if it is a boy, kill him; but if it is a girl, let her live." [17]The midwives, however, feared God and did not do what the king of Egypt had told them to do; they let the boys live. [18]Then the king of Egypt summoned the midwives and asked them, "Why have you done this? Why have you let the boys live?"

[19]The midwives answered Pharaoh, "Hebrew women are not like Egyptian women; they are vigorous and give birth before the midwives arrive."

[20]So God was kind to the midwives and the people increased and became even more numerous. [21]And because the midwives feared God, he gave them families of their own.

[22]Then Pharaoh gave this order to all his people: "Every boy that is born[b] you must throw into the Nile, but let every girl live."

The Birth of Moses

2 Now a man of the house of Levi married a Levite[D] woman, [2]and she became pregnant and gave birth to a son. When she saw that he was a fine child, she hid him for three months. [3]But when she could hide him no longer, she got a papyrus basket for him and coated it with tar and pitch. Then she placed the child in it and put it among the reeds along the bank of the Nile. [4]His sister stood at a distance to see what would happen to him.

[5]Then Pharaoh's daughter went down to the Nile to bathe, and her attendants were walking along the river bank. She saw the basket among the reeds and sent her slave girl to get it. [6]She opened it and saw the baby. He

How many years had passed since Joseph died? (1:8)

The first seven verses of Exodus cover about 400 years. Joseph's feats had long been erased from the Egyptians' minds.

Did the king have good reason to fear the Israelites? (1:9-10)

No evidence suggests that the Israelites threatened the Egyptians. Even though oppressed, God's people were ethnically distinct, growing in numbers and probably resilient to their enslavement. These factors could have contributed to a widespread Egyptian racism, which Pharaoh used to his advantage.

Where did the term *Hebrew* come from? (1:15)

The term *Hebrew* is used in the Old Testament to describe Semitic people. Noah's son, Shem, the father of the Shemites (later Semites), was an ancestor of Eber (thought to be the origin for the word *Hebrew*). See Gen. 10:21. Applied in a wider sense, the term included other non-Israelites such as the Arameans, Moabites and Ammonites. It may refer to the culture of the people more than to their ethnic identity.

Is lying ever okay? (1:19-20)

Some believe the midwives may not have lied but only told Pharaoh part of the truth. Others, though, believe they did lie but were justified on the grounds that murder is a worse crime than lying. Still others think these women should have told the truth, trusting God to take care of the infants and suffering the consequences for disobeying Pharaoh's edict. Breaking one of God's laws to avoid breaking another one is a complex ethical dilemma. Also see *When is it right to disobey authority?* (Acts 4:19).

Who was Pharaoh's daughter? (2:5)

Many think this woman was Hatshepsut, wife of Thutmose II. Hatshepsut was later named queen and ruled with her brother Thutmose III. He, then, would have been the Pharaoh with the hard heart. Another view is that this woman was the daughter of Rameses II, a Pharaoh who was especially cruel to the Hebrew slaves.

[a]5 Masoretic Text (see also Gen. 46:27); Dead Sea Scrolls and Septuagint (see also Acts 7:14 and note at Gen. 46:27) *seventy-five*
[b]22 Masoretic Text; Samaritan Pentateuch, Septuagint and Targums *born to the Hebrews*

How long did Moses' mother raise him? (2:10)

Moses' mother was paid to take care of him, nursing him for at least his first two years of life. Some think it could possibly have been as long as three or four years.

Did the princess defy Pharaoh's edict? (2:10)

It's unclear why Pharaoh's daughter got away with saving a male Hebrew baby during the time her father had ordered them killed. Some think slave adoption was a common practice for Egyptian nobility. Pharaoh's daughter may have rationalized that she would be raising Moses as an Egyptian, not a Hebrew. Her royal status may also have put her above the law others had to follow.

Was Moses' action justifiable? (2:12)

No. Not even Moses, who became the giver of the law, was justified in murdering one of his captors. The phrase *glancing this way and that* points to Moses' guilty conscience.

Moses Flees to Midian (2:15)

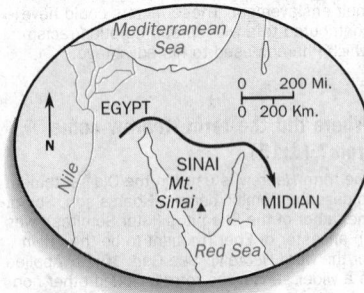

What kind of priest was this? (2:16)

This priest probably served the true God. His tribe, the Midianites, had descended from Abraham through one of his concubines (see Gen. 25:1–2.) Reuel (v. 18) was something of a tribal chief over a nomadic tribe and probably performed dual roles—religious and social. Reuel took Moses in, even giving Moses the hand of one of his daughters in marriage.

Did Moses help the daughters single-handedly? (2:17)

Raised as an Egyptian nobleman, Moses had been trained in sophisticated Egyptian combat. Given his training and the likelihood that he had armed himself before fleeing for his life, a band of shepherds would have been no match for him.

Why the name change? (3:1; see 2:18)

The Bible doesn't explain the use of these two different names. It may not have been unusual at that time to have two or more names. Some think *Jethro* may have been a formal title rather than a name, perhaps meaning *his excellency*.

Why was Horeb called the *mountain of God*? (3:1)

Perhaps because of its immense size. But more likely, Moses, writing years after these events, identified Horeb as it had come to be known. On this mountain God spoke to Moses through the burning bush and also gave him

was crying, and she felt sorry for him. "This is one of the Hebrew^D babies," she said.

7Then his sister asked Pharaoh's daughter, "Shall I go and get one of the Hebrew women to nurse the baby for you?"

8"Yes, go," she answered. And the girl went and got the baby's mother. **9**Pharaoh's daughter said to her, "Take this baby and nurse him for me, and I will pay you." So the woman took the baby and nursed him. **10**When the child grew older, she took him to Pharaoh's daughter and he became her son. She named him Moses,^a saying, "I drew him out of the water."

Moses Flees to Midian

11One day, after Moses had grown up, he went out to where his own people were and watched them at their hard labor. He saw an Egyptian beating a Hebrew, one of his own people. **12**Glancing this way and that and seeing no one, he killed the Egyptian and hid him in the sand. **13**The next day he went out and saw two Hebrews fighting. He asked the one in the wrong, "Why are you hitting your fellow Hebrew?"

14The man said, "Who made you ruler and judge over us? Are you thinking of killing me as you killed the Egyptian?" Then Moses was afraid and thought, "What I did must have become known."

15When Pharaoh heard of this, he tried to kill Moses, but Moses fled from Pharaoh and went to live in Midian, where he sat down by a well. **16**Now a priest^D of Midian had seven daughters, and they came to draw water and fill the troughs to water their father's flock. **17**Some shepherds came along and drove them away, but Moses got up and came to their rescue and watered their flock.

18When the girls returned to Reuel their father, he asked them, "Why have you returned so early today?"

19They answered, "An Egyptian rescued us from the shepherds. He even drew water for us and watered the flock."

20"And where is he?" he asked his daughters. "Why did you leave him? Invite him to have something to eat."

21Moses agreed to stay with the man, who gave his daughter Zipporah to Moses in marriage. **22**Zipporah gave birth to a son, and Moses named him Gershom,^b saying, "I have become an alien^D in a foreign land."

23During that long period, the king of Egypt died. The Israelites groaned in their slavery and cried out, and their cry for help because of their slavery went up to God. **24**God heard their groaning and he remembered his covenant^D with Abraham, with Isaac and with Jacob. **25**So God looked on the Israelites and was concerned about them.

Moses and the Burning Bush

3 Now Moses was tending the flock of Jethro his father-in-law, the priest of Midian, and he led the flock to the far side of the desert and came to Horeb, the mountain of God. **2**There the angel of the LORD appeared to him in flames of fire from within a bush. Moses saw that though the bush was on fire it did not burn up. **3**So Moses thought, "I will go over and see this strange sight—why the bush does not burn up."

^a10 *Moses* sounds like the Hebrew for *draw out*.   ^b22 *Gershom* sounds like the Hebrew for *an alien there*.

4When the LORD saw that he had gone over to look, God called to him from within the bush, "Moses! Moses!"

And Moses said, "Here I am."

5"Do not come any closer," God said. "Take off your sandals, for the place where you are standing is holy ground." **6**Then he said, "I am the God of your father, the God of Abraham, the God of Isaac and the God of Jacob." At this, Moses hid his face, because he was afraid to look at God.

7The LORD said, "I have indeed seen the misery of my people in Egypt. I have heard them crying out because of their slave drivers, and I am concerned about their suffering. **8**So I have come down to rescue them from the hand of the Egyptians and to bring them up out of that land into a good and spacious land, a land flowing with milk and honey—the home of the Canaanites, Hittites, Amorites, Perizzites, Hivites and Jebusites. **9**And now the cry of the Israelites has reached me, and I have seen the way the Egyptians are oppressing them. **10**So now, go. I am sending you to Pharaoh to bring my people the Israelites out of Egypt."

11But Moses said to God, "Who am I, that I should go to Pharaoh and bring the Israelites out of Egypt?"

12And God said, "I will be with you. And this will be the sign to you that it is I who have sent you: When you have brought the people out of Egypt, you*a* will worship God on this mountain."

13Moses said to God, "Suppose I go to the Israelites and say to them, 'The God of your fathers has sent me to you,' and they ask me, 'What is his name?' Then what shall I tell them?"

14God said to Moses, "I AM WHO I AM.*b* This is what you are to say to the Israelites: 'I AM has sent me to you.' "

15God also said to Moses, "Say to the Israelites, 'The LORD,*c* the God of your fathers—the God of Abraham, the God of Isaac and the God of Jacob—has sent me to you.' This is my name forever, the name by which I am to be remembered from generation to generation.

16"Go, assemble the elders of Israel and say to them, 'The LORD, the God of your fathers—the God of Abraham, Isaac and Jacob—appeared to me and said: I have watched over you and have seen what has been done to you in Egypt. **17**And I have promised to bring you up out of your misery in Egypt into the land of the Canaanites, Hittites, Amorites, Perizzites, Hivites and Jebusites—a land flowing with milk and honey.'

18"The elders of Israel will listen to you. Then you and the elders are to go to the king of Egypt and say to him, 'The LORD, the God of the Hebrews, has met with us. Let us take a three-day journey into the desert to offer sacrifices*D* to the LORD our God.' **19**But I know that the king of Egypt will not let you go unless a mighty hand compels him. **20**So I will stretch out my hand and strike the Egyptians with all the wonders that I will perform among them. After that, he will let you go.

21"And I will make the Egyptians favorably disposed toward this people, so that when you leave you will not go empty-handed. **22**Every woman is to ask her neighbor and any woman living in her house for articles of silver and

the Ten Commandments. Mount Horeb was also called Mount Sinai, for the desert region in which it was located.

Why are bare feet considered more holy? (3:5)

Taking off sandals was a cultural and religious symbol of reverence and respect. See *What did bare feet mean to God?* (Joshua 5:15).

Why was Moses afraid to look at God? (3:6)

Staring into the raw power of God struck terror in Moses' soul. He felt unworthy to stand before a holy God and, by looking away, demonstrated his reverence for him.

Why should others have to give up their homes? (3:8)

God originally gave this land to Moses' ancestor, Abraham (Gen. 12:7). Now, after Israel had spent 400 years in Egypt, God promised that they would recover the land they had left behind in Canaan, displacing several tribes in the process. God used Israel to judge these pagan tribes for their idolatry and their sinful ways (Gen. 15:16). Later, God also took the land away from the Israelites when they rejected him (2 Kings 24:2).

How would a trip back to the mountain be a sign? (3:12)

Revisiting the place where his original encounter with the Lord took place would reassure Moses that his vision was indeed legitimate. Returning to the mountain would demonstrate to Moses that he could trust God to keep his promises and bring the Israelites to the promised land.

What did God's name mean to the Israelites? (3:14)

The phrase *I AM WHO I AM*, a wordplay on the name of God, has received much attention. Its precise significance is debated. In most English versions it is translated as *the LORD*; transliterated, it is *Yahweh*. The name *I AM* was the most holy name for God, so revered that later Jewish leaders refused even to speak it. Most likely the name caused the Israelites to think of God's absolute supremacy and their unique relationship to him.

Was God being deceptive? (3:18)

See *Was Moses lying about the three-day trip?* (5:3).

You will plunder the Egyptians (3:21–22)

See *Why would the Egyptians be willing to be looted?* (12:35–36).

---

a 12 The Hebrew is plural.   *b 14* Or *I WILL BE WHAT I WILL BE*
c 15 The Hebrew for LORD sounds like and may be derived from the Hebrew for *I AM* in verse 14.

gold and for clothing, which you will put on your sons and daughters. And so you will plunder[D] the Egyptians."

Signs for Moses

4 Moses answered, "What if they do not believe me or listen to me and say, 'The LORD did not appear to you'?"

2Then the LORD said to him, "What is that in your hand?"

"A staff," he replied.

3The LORD said, "Throw it on the ground."

Moses threw it on the ground and it became a snake, and he ran from it. **4**Then the LORD said to him, "Reach out your hand and take it by the tail." So Moses reached out and took hold of the snake and it turned back into a staff in his hand. **5**"This," said the LORD, "is so that they may believe that the LORD, the God of their fathers—the God of Abraham, the God of Isaac and the God of Jacob—has appeared to you."

6Then the LORD said, "Put your hand inside your cloak." So Moses put his hand into his cloak, and when he took it out, it was leprous,[a] like snow.

7"Now put it back into your cloak," he said. So Moses put his hand back into his cloak, and when he took it out, it was restored, like the rest of his flesh.

8Then the LORD said, "If they do not believe you or pay attention to the first miraculous sign, they may believe the second. **9**But if they do not believe these two signs or listen to you, take some water from the Nile and pour it on the dry ground. The water you take from the river will become blood on the ground."

10Moses said to the LORD, "O Lord, I have never been eloquent, neither in the past nor since you have spoken to your servant. I am slow of speech and tongue."

11The LORD said to him, "Who gave man his mouth? Who makes him deaf or mute? Who gives him sight or makes him blind? Is it not I, the LORD? **12**Now go; I will help you speak and will teach you what to say."

13But Moses said, "O Lord, please send someone else to do it."

14Then the LORD's anger burned against Moses and he said, "What about your brother, Aaron the Levite[D]? I know he can speak well. He is already on his way to meet you, and his heart will be glad when he sees you. **15**You shall speak to him and put words in his mouth; I will help both of you speak and will teach you what to do. **16**He will speak to the people for you, and it will be as if he were your mouth and as if you were God to him. **17**But take this staff in your hand so you can perform miraculous signs with it."

Moses Returns to Egypt

18Then Moses went back to Jethro his father-in-law and said to him, "Let me go back to my own people in Egypt to see if any of them are still alive."

Jethro said, "Go, and I wish you well."

19Now the LORD had said to Moses in Midian, "Go back to Egypt, for all the men who wanted to kill you are dead." **20**So Moses took his wife and sons, put them on a donkey and started back to Egypt. And he took the staff of God in his hand.

Why these particular signs? (4:1–9)

These miracles would validate both God's messenger, Moses, and God's message. There are disagreements over the precise meaning of each of these signs. The first sign, the staff and snake (which some think were Egyptian symbols of power and life), would underscore God's power over Egyptian dominance. The second sign, the leprous hand, would highlight God's power over dread diseases and warn Pharaoh that Moses, an ambassador of God, had the power to inflict sickness. And the last sign, turning water from the Nile (worshiped by Egyptians) into blood would demonstrate God's power over their gods.

Did Moses have a speech impediment? (4:10)

Nothing would suggest Moses had a speech impediment. But his protest was not entirely without foundation. At the very least, he was not a gifted speaker. Whatever his problem, he must have felt strongly about it, since he repeated similar objections later (6:12,30).

Is God responsible for disabilities? (4:11)

The answer is unclear, clouded by the notion that a loving God couldn't permit so much pain, much less cause it. This verse, taken alone, paints a picture of a capricious God, who randomly scars certain people. But three facts help us see a more correct picture: (1) God loves us. (2) All people are scarred, to one degree or another. (3) God works through the weaknesses of wounded, broken people. Our disabilities, however great or insignificant, become a showcase for God's abilities. Because Moses was *slow of speech and tongue* (v. 10), God was better able to speak through him (v. 12). See 2 Cor. 12:9–10.

Why was Moses so reluctant to obey God? (4:13)

His reluctance may have been due to his deep-seated insecurities. But Moses, knowing the ominous task ahead of him, may simply have not wanted any part of it. Raised among the Egyptian governing class, Moses knew about their military prowess. He may have felt that no one could be adequate for the task of releasing the Hebrews from bondage. See also 3:11–13; 4:1,10.

---

[a]6 The Hebrew word was used for various diseases affecting the skin—not necessarily leprosy.

21The LORD said to Moses, "When you return to Egypt, see that you perform before Pharaoh all the wonders I have given you the power to do. But I will harden his heart so that he will not let the people go. **22**Then say to Pharaoh, 'This is what the LORD says: Israel is my firstborn^D son, **23**and I told you, "Let my son go, so he may worship me." But you refused to let him go; so I will kill your firstborn son.' "

24At a lodging place on the way, the LORD met ˌMosesˌ^a and was about to kill him. **25**But Zipporah took a flint knife, cut off her son's foreskin and touched ˌMoses'ˌ feet with it.^b "Surely you are a bridegroom of blood to me," she said. **26**So the LORD let him alone. (At that time she said "bridegroom of blood," referring to circumcision^D.)

27The LORD said to Aaron, "Go into the desert to meet Moses." So he met Moses at the mountain of God and kissed him. **28**Then Moses told Aaron everything the LORD had sent him to say, and also about all the miraculous signs he had commanded him to perform.

29Moses and Aaron brought together all the elders of the Israelites, **30**and Aaron told them everything the LORD had said to Moses. He also performed the signs before the people, **31**and they believed. And when they heard that the LORD was concerned about them and had seen their misery, they bowed down and worshiped.

Bricks Without Straw

5 Afterward Moses and Aaron went to Pharaoh and said, "This is what the LORD, the God of Israel, says: 'Let my people go, so that they may hold a festival to me in the desert.' "

2Pharaoh said, "Who is the LORD, that I should obey him and let Israel go? I do not know the LORD and I will not let Israel go."

3Then they said, "The God of the Hebrews has met with us. Now let us take a three-day journey into the desert to offer sacrifices^D to the LORD our God, or he may strike us with plagues or with the sword."

4But the king of Egypt said, "Moses and Aaron, why are you taking the people away from their labor? Get back to your work!" **5**Then Pharaoh said, "Look, the people of the land are now numerous, and you are stopping them from working."

6That same day Pharaoh gave this order to the slave drivers and foremen in charge of the people: **7**"You are no longer to supply the people with straw for making bricks; let them go and gather their own straw. **8**But require them to make the same number of bricks as before; don't reduce the quota. They are lazy; that is why they are crying out, 'Let us go and sacrifice to our God.' **9**Make the work harder for the men so that they keep working and pay no attention to lies."

10Then the slave drivers and the foremen went out and said to the people, "This is what Pharaoh says: 'I will not give you any more straw. **11**Go and get your own straw wherever you can find it, but your work will not be reduced at all.' " **12**So the people scattered all over Egypt to gather stubble to use for straw. **13**The slave drivers kept pressing them, saying, "Complete the work required of you for each day, just as when you had straw." **14**The Israelite foremen appointed by Pharaoh's slave drivers were

---

^a24 Or ˌMoses' sonˌ; Hebrew him   ^b25 Or and drew near ˌMoses'ˌ feet

---

Why did God make things tougher by hardening Pharaoh's heart? (4:21)

See article: *Who hardened Pharaoh's heart?* (10:1).

Why would God want to kill Moses? (4:24)

This passage is confusing. Some think the word *Moses* should be replaced with *Moses' son.* Others disagree. Either way, the focus is that Moses' disobedience led to dire consequences. Apparently Moses had ignored God's command to circumcise one of his children (Gen. 17:10–14). Some think his wife, Zipporah, a Midianite, was especially opposed to the rite. Circumcision, however, was a symbol of obedience and consecration to God's covenant. Before going to Pharaoh, then, Moses had some unfinished family business to take care of.

Why touch Moses' feet with a bloody foreskin? (4:25)

Many speculate that Zipporah, circumcising her son only to save Moses' life, was repulsed by circumcision. Her actions, in that case, would have been motivated by anger or revulsion. Another view is that her gesture was an act of repentance for Moses' disobedience.

What is a *bridegroom of blood*? (4:25)

No one knows its precise meaning. There is an interesting wordplay between the bloody rite of circumcision and Zipporah's calling Moses a *bridegroom of blood.* Most think it's a term of derision and disgust. See article: *Why did God command circumcision?* (Gen. 17:10).

Did Aaron or Moses perform the signs? (4:30)

It sounds as though *Aaron* did the miracles that God said Moses would do (v. 17). This is not entirely clear. Moses may have done the miracles himself or he may have done them through his representative, Aaron.

Why was Pharaoh unimpressed with the Lord? (5:1–3)

Why should he be impressed? Pharaoh ruled over the Israelites who had been under the thumb of the Egyptians for many years. A man with many gods, Pharaoh obviously did not put much stock in what he would see as the lower-class God of slaves.

Why didn't Moses and Aaron show the signs to Pharaoh on their first visit? (5:3)

Perhaps to give Pharaoh the opportunity to respond voluntarily to their request. Even though God later demonstrated his mighty power and forced Pharaoh's hand, God first let him choose his course of action.

Was Moses lying about the three-day trip? (5:3)

No. Moses was simply countering Pharaoh's refusal of the first request to release the people. Bartering was an important skill. Trying to convince Pharaoh that the Israelites were under God's authority and needed to worship, Moses posed the question differently.

beaten and were asked, "Why didn't you meet your quota of bricks yesterday or today, as before?"

[15]Then the Israelite foremen went and appealed to Pharaoh: "Why have you treated your servants this way? [16]Your servants are given no straw, yet we are told, 'Make bricks!' Your servants are being beaten, but the fault is with your own people."

[17]Pharaoh said, "Lazy, that's what you are—lazy! That is why you keep saying, 'Let us go and sacrifice[D] to the Lord.' [18]Now get to work. You will not be given any straw, yet you must produce your full quota of bricks."

[19]The Israelite foremen realized they were in trouble when they were told, "You are not to reduce the number of bricks required of you for each day." [20]When they left Pharaoh, they found Moses and Aaron waiting to meet them, [21]and they said, "May the Lord look upon you and judge you! You have made us a stench to Pharaoh and his officials and have put a sword in their hand to kill us."

God Promises Deliverance

[22]Moses returned to the Lord and said, "O Lord, why have you brought trouble upon this people? Is this why you sent me? [23]Ever since I went to Pharaoh to speak in your name, he has brought trouble upon this people, and you have not rescued your people at all."

6 Then the Lord said to Moses, "Now you will see what I will do to Pharaoh: Because of my mighty hand he will let them go; because of my mighty hand he will drive them out of his country."

[2]God also said to Moses, "I am the Lord. [3]I appeared to Abraham, to Isaac and to Jacob as God Almighty,[a] but by my name the Lord[b] I did not make myself known to them.[c] [4]I also established my covenant[D] with them to give them the land of Canaan, where they lived as aliens[D]. [5]Moreover, I have heard the groaning of the Israelites, whom the Egyptians are enslaving, and I have remembered my covenant.

[6]"Therefore, say to the Israelites: 'I am the Lord, and I will bring you out from under the yoke[D] of the Egyptians. I will free you from being slaves to them, and I will redeem[D] you with an outstretched arm and with mighty acts of judgment. [7]I will take you as my own people, and I will be your God. Then you will know that I am the Lord your God, who brought you out from under the yoke of the Egyptians. [8]And I will bring you to the land I swore with uplifted hand to give to Abraham, to Isaac and to Jacob. I will give it to you as a possession. I am the Lord.' "

[9]Moses reported this to the Israelites, but they did not listen to him because of their discouragement and cruel bondage.

[10]Then the Lord said to Moses, [11]"Go, tell Pharaoh king of Egypt to let the Israelites go out of his country."

[12]But Moses said to the Lord, "If the Israelites will not listen to me, why would Pharaoh listen to me, since I speak with faltering lips[d]?"

Family Record of Moses and Aaron

[13]Now the Lord spoke to Moses and Aaron about the Israelites and Pharaoh king of Egypt, and he commanded them to bring the Israelites out of Egypt.

By what name did Abraham know God? (6:3)

Before this, God was primarily known as El-Shaddai (see NIV text note), emphasizing God as provider and sustainer. El-Shaddai was not incompatible with Yahweh, but the new name revealed a new understanding of God's character—a closer identification between God and his people. Some think the name Yahweh appears earlier in the Bible because Moses included his fuller understanding of God in his writings, though it would have been more than the views of those he wrote about (see, for example, Gen. 17:1). Others suggest that though they knew the name, they did not know the meaning of God's nature and characteristics. See Why did people begin to call on God at that time? (Gen. 4:26).

What was the significance of a new identity for God? (6:3)

Moses apparently used the various nuances of God's names to communicate specific truths in his writings. The switch to a new name for God may have signaled the start of God's personal relationship with Israel; the divine presence would fulfill the promises made to Abraham, Isaac and Jacob. See previous note.

Redeem you with an outstretched arm (6:6)

An outstretched arm expressed the active role God would play both in Egypt's judgment and the deliverance of the Israelites.

Swore with uplifted hand (6:8)

The uplifted hand was associated with the taking of an oath, just as it is today. This promised that God's word would be good.

---

[a]3 Hebrew El-Shaddai   [b]3 See note at Exodus 3:15.   [c]3 Or Almighty, and by my name the Lord did I not let myself be known to them?   [d]12 Hebrew I am uncircumcised of lips; also in verse 30

14These were the heads of their families[a]:

The sons of Reuben the firstborn[D] son of Israel were Hanoch and Pallu, Hezron and Carmi. These were the clans of Reuben. **15**The sons of Simeon were Jemuel, Jamin, Ohad, Jakin, Zohar and Shaul the son of a Canaanite woman. These were the clans of Simeon. **16**These were the names of the sons of Levi according to their records: Gershon, Kohath and Merari. Levi lived 137 years.

17The sons of Gershon, by clans, were Libni and Shimei.

18The sons of Kohath were Amram, Izhar, Hebron and Uzziel. Kohath lived 133 years.

19The sons of Merari were Mahli and Mushi. These were the clans of Levi according to their records.

20Amram married his father's sister Jochebed, who bore him Aaron and Moses. Amram lived 137 years.

21The sons of Izhar were Korah, Nepheg and Zicri.

22The sons of Uzziel were Mishael, Elzaphan and Sithri.

23Aaron married Elisheba, daughter of Amminadab and sister of Nahshon, and she bore him Nadab and Abihu, Eleazar and Ithamar.

24The sons of Korah were Assir, Elkanah and Abiasaph. These were the Korahite clans.

25Eleazar son of Aaron married one of the daughters of Putiel, and she bore him Phinehas.

These were the heads of the Levite[D] families, clan by clan.

26It was this same Aaron and Moses to whom the LORD said, "Bring the Israelites out of Egypt by their divisions." **27**They were the ones who spoke to Pharaoh king of Egypt about bringing the Israelites out of Egypt. It was the same Moses and Aaron.

Aaron to Speak for Moses

28Now when the LORD spoke to Moses in Egypt, **29**he said to him, "I am the LORD. Tell Pharaoh king of Egypt everything I tell you."

30But Moses said to the LORD, "Since I speak with faltering lips, why would Pharaoh listen to me?"

7 Then the LORD said to Moses, "See, I have made you like God to Pharaoh, and your brother Aaron will be your prophet[D]. **2**You are to say everything I command you, and your brother Aaron is to tell Pharaoh to let the Israelites go out of his country. **3**But I will harden Pharaoh's heart, and though I multiply my miraculous signs and wonders in Egypt, **4**he will not listen to you. Then I will lay my hand on Egypt and with mighty acts of judgment I will bring out my divisions, my people the Israelites. **5**And the Egyptians will know that I am the LORD when I stretch out my hand against Egypt and bring the Israelites out of it."

6Moses and Aaron did just as the LORD commanded them. **7**Moses was eighty years old and Aaron eighty-three when they spoke to Pharaoh.

a 14 The Hebrew for *families* here and in verse 25 refers to units larger than clans.

Why review Moses' pedigree? (6:14–27)

This genealogy interrupts the story about Moses' and Aaron's ongoing dialogue with Pharaoh. Moses probably inserts it to build a case for how it was they happened to be Israel's leaders. Some think that the list points to Moses' and Aaron's priestly heritage as a reason for their being chosen to lead. More likely, the list shows the reverse. God's choosing had nothing to do with natural ability or nobility, so neither Moses nor Aaron could claim special favors. Only by God's grace were they selected to lead.

Was it incest to marry an aunt? (6:20)

Before God gave the law to Moses, marriages with aunts and sisters were allowed. However, in many instances, words like *sons,* for example, refer to descendants, not literal male children. In this case, Amram may have married a distant cousin rather than an aunt.

How was Moses *like God* to Pharaoh? (7:1)

Moses was God's representative to Pharaoh. He came to the Egyptian ruler with divine authority. Pharaoh, revered as a god himself, was slow to recognize Moses' divine authority. But because of the plagues, he eventually grew to fear the power behind Moses.

Why did Moses' political career start so late? (7:7)

The life spans of many Old Testament characters exceeded ours (6:16–20). Moses lived to be 120 (Deut. 34:7). Perhaps Moses, at this critical juncture, was more like a middle-aged man in today's understanding. God took 80 years to prepare Moses to stand before Pharaoh and lead the Israelites. In that sense, this was not the beginning of a career, but the fulfillment of years of preparation.

Aaron's Staff Becomes a Snake

8The LORD said to Moses and Aaron, **9**"When Pharaoh says to you, 'Perform a miracle,' then say to Aaron, 'Take your staff and throw it down before Pharaoh,' and it will become a snake."

10So Moses and Aaron went to Pharaoh and did just as the LORD commanded. Aaron threw his staff down in front of Pharaoh and his officials, and it became a snake. **11**Pharaoh then summoned wise men and sorcerers, and the Egyptian magicians^D also did the same things by their secret arts: **12**Each one threw down his staff and it became a snake. But Aaron's staff swallowed up their staffs. **13**Yet Pharaoh's heart became hard and he would not listen to them, just as the LORD had said.

The Plague of Blood

14Then the LORD said to Moses, "Pharaoh's heart is unyielding; he refuses to let the people go. **15**Go to Pharaoh in the morning as he goes out to the water. Wait on the bank of the Nile to meet him, and take in your hand the staff that was changed into a snake. **16**Then say to him, 'The LORD, the God of the Hebrews, has sent me to say to you: Let my people go, so that they may worship me in the desert. But until now you have not listened. **17**This is what the LORD says: By this you will know that I am the LORD: With the staff that is in my hand I will strike the water of the Nile, and it will be changed into blood. **18**The fish in the Nile will die, and the river will stink; the Egyptians will not be able to drink its water.' "

19The LORD said to Moses, "Tell Aaron, 'Take your staff and stretch out your hand over the waters of Egypt—over the streams and canals, over the ponds and all the reservoirs'—and they will turn to blood. Blood will be everywhere in Egypt, even in the wooden buckets and stone jars."

20Moses and Aaron did just as the LORD had commanded. He raised his staff in the presence of Pharaoh and his officials and struck the water of the Nile, and all the water was changed into blood. **21**The fish in the Nile died, and the river smelled so bad that the Egyptians could not drink its water. Blood was everywhere in Egypt.

22But the Egyptian magicians did the same things by their secret arts, and Pharaoh's heart became hard; he would not listen to Moses and Aaron, just as the LORD had said. **23**Instead, he turned and went into his palace, and did not take even this to heart. **24**And all the Egyptians dug along the Nile to get drinking water, because they could not drink the water of the river.

The Plague of Frogs

8 **25**Seven days passed after the LORD struck the Nile. **1**Then the LORD said to Moses, "Go to Pharaoh and say to him, 'This is what the LORD says: Let my people go, so that they may worship me. **2**If you refuse to let them go, I will plague your whole country with frogs. **3**The Nile will teem with frogs. They will come up into your palace and your bedroom and onto your bed, into the houses of your officials and on your people, and into your ovens and kneading troughs. **4**The frogs will go up on you and your people and all your officials.' "

5Then the LORD said to Moses, "Tell Aaron, 'Stretch out your hand with your staff over the streams and canals and ponds, and make frogs come up on the land of Egypt.' "

What kind of powers did the Egyptian magicians have? (7:11–12,22; 8:7)
The magicians represented Egypt's many gods with their demonic and occultic powers. They may have used hypnosis, sleight-of-hand, rituals, spells, demonic influence or a combination of these. See *Why did the magicians see gnats as the finger of God?* (8:18–19).

Was the water actual blood? (7:20–21)
Some think God literally turned the water to blood. Others, though, believe the river, because of flooding, was polluted with red-colored earth deposits, turning the water the color of blood. The phrase *into blood,* then, would mean *like blood.* Either way, the plague, initiated by God, occurred rapidly.

How did digging along the Nile provide adequate drinking water? (7:24)
With the river contaminated, the only source of water was from makeshift wells dug along the banks of the Nile. This digging may have tapped spring water, or more likely, filtered the contaminated waters of the Nile. This would have also provided the magicians with water to simulate the first plague.

⁶So Aaron stretched out his hand over the waters of Egypt, and the frogs came up and covered the land. ⁷But the magiciansᴰ did the same things by their secret arts; they also made frogs come up on the land of Egypt.

⁸Pharaoh summoned Moses and Aaron and said, "Pray to the LORD to take the frogs away from me and my people, and I will let your people go to offer sacrificesᴰ to the LORD."

⁹Moses said to Pharaoh, "I leave to you the honor of setting the time for me to pray for you and your officials and your people that you and your houses may be rid of the frogs, except for those that remain in the Nile."

¹⁰"Tomorrow," Pharaoh said.

Moses replied, "It will be as you say, so that you may know there is no one like the LORD our God. ¹¹The frogs will leave you and your houses, your officials and your people; they will remain only in the Nile."

¹²After Moses and Aaron left Pharaoh, Moses cried out to the LORD about the frogs he had brought on Pharaoh. ¹³And the LORD did what Moses asked. The frogs died in the houses, in the courtyards and in the fields. ¹⁴They were piled into heaps, and the land reeked of them. ¹⁵But when Pharaoh saw that there was relief, he hardened his heart and would not listen to Moses and Aaron, just as the LORD had said.

The Plague of Gnats

¹⁶Then the LORD said to Moses, "Tell Aaron, 'Stretch out your staff and strike the dust of the ground,' and throughout the land of Egypt the dust will become gnats." ¹⁷They did this, and when Aaron stretched out his hand with the staff and struck the dust of the ground, gnats came upon men and animals. All the dust throughout the land of Egypt became gnats. ¹⁸But when the magicians tried to produce gnats by their secret arts, they could not. And the gnats were on men and animals.

¹⁹The magicians said to Pharaoh, "This is the finger of God." But Pharaoh's heart was hard and he would not listen, just as the LORD had said.

The Plague of Flies

²⁰Then the LORD said to Moses, "Get up early in the morning and confront Pharaoh as he goes to the water and say to him, 'This is what the LORD says: Let my people go, so that they may worship me. ²¹If you do not let my people go, I will send swarms of flies on you and your officials, on your people and into your houses. The houses of the Egyptians will be full of flies, and even the ground where they are.

²²" 'But on that day I will deal differently with the land of Goshen, where my people live; no swarms of flies will be there, so that you will know that I, the LORD, am in this land. ²³I will make a distinctionᵃ between my people and your people. This miraculous sign will occur tomorrow.' "

²⁴And the LORD did this. Dense swarms of flies poured into Pharaoh's palace and into the houses of his officials, and throughout Egypt the land was ruined by the flies.

²⁵Then Pharaoh summoned Moses and Aaron and said, "Go, sacrifice to your God here in the land."

²⁶But Moses said, "That would not be right. The sacrifices we offer the LORD our God would be detestable to the Egyptians. And if we offer sacrifices that are detest-

---

Why would the magicians want to make a plague even worse? (8:7)
In the process of preserving their credibility, these magicians unwittingly made things worse by increasing the number of frogs.

Why did Pharaoh change his mind? (8:15)
A proud and confident leader, he stood to lose on every count if he gave in. These events challenged his position as ruler of Egypt, threatened the local economy by removing his slave-based work force and called into question the authenticity of his Egyptian gods.

Did the dust turn to gnats? (8:17)
No matter how we look at it, this was a powerful miracle. It may be that God created gnats from the dust just as he had made man from the dust (Gen. 2:7). This was, after all, the first plague that forced Pharaoh's magicians to acknowledge God (v. 19; also see following note). More likely, the miracle was that gnats came up out of the dust. *Dust* may refer to the enormous number of gnats, just as when God said Abraham's descendants would be as numerous as *the dust of the earth* (Gen. 13:16).

Why did the magicians see gnats as the finger of God? (8:18–19)
Up until this plague, the magicians had kept pace with Moses' miracles. Their tricks or demonic powers, however, could not simulate hordes of gnats. Consequently, they recognized that a power greater than their own was at work.

Did the Israelites experience these plagues? (8:22–23)
Some think the Israelites were spared from only the plagues where a clear distinction was made, as in this instance (9:4,6,26; 10:23; 11:7). However, Goshen, a region of Egypt where the Israelites lived, may have been spared from all the plagues.

ᵃ23 Septuagint and Vulgate; Hebrew *will put a deliverance*

SCRIPTURE LINK (8:27) *Three-day journey*

See 3:18–19; 5:3–4. Also see *Why didn't Moses accept this offer?* (10:24).

How could Pharaoh just break his word? (8:28–32)

Dictators who rule by the force of power and intimidation seldom relinquish control voluntarily to others. From his youth Pharaoh had become accustomed to getting his own way. To his way of thinking it would have been a sign of weakness to cave in to the wishes of his subjects—especially the Hebrew slaves. Setting himself up as the highest authority, Pharaoh lacked the moral scruples to keep his promise. He had no one to answer to and felt he was within his rights to deceive Moses and manipulate the circumstances.

What did ashes have to do with boils? (9:8–9)

The soot-like ash was taken from a furnace, a symbol of Israel's bondage. As such, it provided a visual aid for Pharaoh. Just as the staff was used to initiate earlier plagues, so this action tied the boils to Moses and the God whom he represented. Some also believe there was a symbolic link between the soot created by the sweat of God's people doing hard labor and the soot that produced boils on Israel's slave masters.

able in their eyes, will they not stone us? **27**We must take a three-day journey into the desert to offer sacrifices[D] to the LORD our God, as he commands us."

28Pharaoh said, "I will let you go to offer sacrifices to the LORD your God in the desert, but you must not go very far. Now pray for me."

29Moses answered, "As soon as I leave you, I will pray to the LORD, and tomorrow the flies will leave Pharaoh and his officials and his people. Only be sure that Pharaoh does not act deceitfully again by not letting the people go to offer sacrifices to the LORD."

30Then Moses left Pharaoh and prayed to the LORD, **31**and the LORD did what Moses asked: The flies left Pharaoh and his officials and his people; not a fly remained. **32**But this time also Pharaoh hardened his heart and would not let the people go.

The Plague on Livestock

9 Then the LORD said to Moses, "Go to Pharaoh and say to him, 'This is what the LORD, the God of the Hebrews, says: "Let my people go, so that they may worship me." **2**If you refuse to let them go and continue to hold them back, **3**the hand of the LORD will bring a terrible plague on your livestock in the field—on your horses and donkeys and camels and on your cattle and sheep and goats. **4**But the LORD will make a distinction between the livestock of Israel and that of Egypt, so that no animal belonging to the Israelites will die.' "

5The LORD set a time and said, "Tomorrow the LORD will do this in the land." **6**And the next day the LORD did it: All the livestock of the Egyptians died, but not one animal belonging to the Israelites died. **7**Pharaoh sent men to investigate and found that not even one of the animals of the Israelites had died. Yet his heart was unyielding and he would not let the people go.

The Plague of Boils

8Then the LORD said to Moses and Aaron, "Take handfuls of soot from a furnace and have Moses toss it into the air in the presence of Pharaoh. **9**It will become fine dust over the whole land of Egypt, and festering boils will break out on men and animals throughout the land."

10So they took soot from a furnace and stood before Pharaoh. Moses tossed it into the air, and festering boils broke out on men and animals. **11**The magicians[D] could not stand before Moses because of the boils that were on them and on all the Egyptians. **12**But the LORD hardened Pharaoh's heart and he would not listen to Moses and Aaron, just as the LORD had said to Moses.

The Plague of Hail

13Then the LORD said to Moses, "Get up early in the morning, confront Pharaoh and say to him, 'This is what the LORD, the God of the Hebrews, says: Let my people go, so that they may worship me, **14**or this time I will send the full force of my plagues against you and against your officials and your people, so you may know that there is no one like me in all the earth. **15**For by now I could have stretched out my hand and struck you and your people with a plague that would have wiped you off the earth. **16**But I have raised you up[a] for this very purpose, that I might show you my power and that my name might be

---

[a]16 Or *have spared you*

proclaimed in all the earth. **17**You still set yourself against my people and will not let them go. **18**Therefore, at this time tomorrow I will send the worst hailstorm that has ever fallen on Egypt, from the day it was founded till now. **19**Give an order now to bring your livestock and everything you have in the field to a place of shelter, because the hail will fall on every man and animal that has not been brought in and is still out in the field, and they will die.' "

20Those officials of Pharaoh who feared the word of the LORD hurried to bring their slaves and their livestock inside. **21**But those who ignored the word of the LORD left their slaves and livestock in the field.

22Then the LORD said to Moses, "Stretch out your hand toward the sky so that hail will fall all over Egypt—on men and animals and on everything growing in the fields of Egypt." **23**When Moses stretched out his staff toward the sky, the LORD sent thunder and hail, and lightning flashed down to the ground. So the LORD rained hail on the land of Egypt; **24**hail fell and lightning flashed back and forth. It was the worst storm in all the land of Egypt since it had become a nation. **25**Throughout Egypt hail struck everything in the fields—both men and animals; it beat down everything growing in the fields and stripped every tree. **26**The only place it did not hail was the land of Goshen, where the Israelites were.

27Then Pharaoh summoned Moses and Aaron. "This time I have sinned," he said to them. "The LORD is in the right, and I and my people are in the wrong. **28**Pray to the LORD, for we have had enough thunder and hail. I will let you go; you don't have to stay any longer."

29Moses replied, "When I have gone out of the city, I will spread out my hands in prayer to the LORD. The thunder will stop and there will be no more hail, so you may know that the earth is the LORD's. **30**But I know that you and your officials still do not fear the LORD God."

31(The flax and barley were destroyed, since the barley had headed and the flax was in bloom. **32**The wheat and spelt, however, were not destroyed, because they ripen later.)

33Then Moses left Pharaoh and went out of the city. He spread out his hands toward the LORD; the thunder and hail stopped, and the rain no longer poured down on the land. **34**When Pharaoh saw that the rain and hail and thunder had stopped, he sinned again: He and his officials hardened their hearts. **35**So Pharaoh's heart was hard and he would not let the Israelites go, just as the LORD had said through Moses.

The Plague of Locusts

10 Then the LORD said to Moses, "Go to Pharaoh, for I have hardened his heart and the hearts of his officials so that I may perform these miraculous signs of mine among them **2**that you may tell your children and grandchildren how I dealt harshly with the Egyptians and how I performed my signs among them, and that you may know that I am the LORD."

3So Moses and Aaron went to Pharaoh and said to him, "This is what the LORD, the God of the Hebrews, says: 'How long will you refuse to humble yourself before me? Let my people go, so that they may worship me. **4**If you refuse to let them go, I will bring locusts^D into your country tomorrow. **5**They will cover the face of the ground so that it cannot be seen. They will devour what little you

Hadn't the livestock been destroyed earlier? (9:19; see v. 6)
The earlier plague destroyed all the livestock *in the field* (v. 3). Some Egyptian officials, believing Moses, saved their livestock by putting them under a shelter (v. 20).

How could Moses travel in and out of the city if it was still hailing? (9:29)
There are several opinions. According to v. 25, the focus of the furious hailstorms was *the fields* of Egypt. Perhaps, then, Moses avoided the disaster areas. Also, the hail may have hit sporadically, something that would have caused even more Egyptians, thinking the hail had ended, to get caught in the storms. Moses likely walked between the cloudbursts, and God granted him safe passage, protecting him in the same way he kept the hail from striking the land of Goshen (v. 26).

Locusts (10:4)
Insects that are similar to grasshoppers, but more aggressive. An army of these insects can devastate entire fields of crops within minutes.

SCRIPTURE LINK (10:6,13–15)
A plague of locusts was also described in Joel 1:2,4,15. Also see *Locusts* (10:4).

How badly had Egypt been damaged by the plagues? (10:7)

It is difficult to accurately assess the extent of the damage. Some of the plagues affected the people directly (boils and biting insects, for instance). But other plagues caused economic setbacks (loss of livestock and crops). Typically even one such catastrophe was enough to cause severe hardship. Pharaoh's own officials believed that the land was *ruined,* suggesting that they expected economic recovery would be long in coming. But perhaps the greatest damage to Egypt was that its religious system was eroded: each plague demonstrated the superiority of the God of Israel and undermined the authority of the false gods of Egypt.

have left after the hail, including every tree that is growing in your fields. **6**They will fill your houses and those of all your officials and all the Egyptians—something neither your fathers nor your forefathers have ever seen from the day they settled in this land till now.' " Then Moses turned and left Pharaoh.

7Pharaoh's officials said to him, "How long will this man be a snare to us? Let the people go, so that they may worship the LORD their God. Do you not yet realize that Egypt is ruined?"

8Then Moses and Aaron were brought back to Pharaoh. "Go, worship the LORD your God," he said. "But just who will be going?"

9Moses answered, "We will go with our young and old, with our sons and daughters, and with our flocks and herds, because we are to celebrate a festival to the LORD."

10Pharaoh said, "The LORD be with you—if I let you go, along with your women and children! Clearly you are bent on evil.*a* **11**No! Have only the men go; and worship the LORD, since that's what you have been asking for." Then Moses and Aaron were driven out of Pharaoh's presence.

12And the LORD said to Moses, "Stretch out your hand over Egypt so that locusts*D* will swarm over the land and devour everything growing in the fields, everything left by the hail."

a10 Or Be careful, trouble is in store for you!

Who hardened Pharaoh's heart? (10:1; see 9:34)

I f Pharaoh was judged as the consequence for his own free will, we'd have no problem; he got what he deserved. But was Pharaoh merely a pawn in God's hands? The Bible seems to suggest that the events—and even his response to them—were not entirely Pharaoh's doing. It describes the hardening of Pharaoh's heart in different ways at different times: (1) in a neutral sense (Exodus 7:13–14; 8:19); (2) as an act of Pharaoh's own choice (Exodus 8:15) and (3) as an act of God's sovereignty (Exodus 9:12).

While several passages describe God as the one hardening Pharaoh's heart, nine other references indicate that Pharaoh hardened his own heart or that circumstances may have helped harden him (7:13,14,22; 8:15,19,32; 9:7,34,35). It was not until the sixth plague that God explicitly hardened Pharaoh's heart (9:12), after several occasions where Pharaoh demonstrated his own stubbornness. Many conclude that the danger of resisting God is that he will eventually give us over to our own choices (see Romans 1:24,26,28). Pharaoh may have resisted God so much that at last he found himself unable to change.

Old Testament writers apparently saw no contradiction in both God's and Pharaoh's simultaneous involvement. To them, Pharaoh's condition could be the result of both his own free will and God's sovereign plan.

Pharaoh was not the hapless victim of God's action, however. God did not drag him against his will kicking and screaming, into disobedience. Pharaoh did, in fact, willfully oppose God.

Ultimately, Pharaoh was responsible for oppressing the Israelites as well as for his own unbelief. At the same time, on another level, God was also at work. Moses, writing years after the events, could say confidently that God was at work even in Pharaoh's hard heart.

Also see article: *Why does God harden some people's hearts?* (11:3).

[13]So Moses stretched out his staff over Egypt, and the LORD made an east wind blow across the land all that day and all that night. By morning the wind had brought the locusts[D]; [14]they invaded all Egypt and settled down in every area of the country in great numbers. Never before had there been such a plague of locusts, nor will there ever be again. [15]They covered all the ground until it was black. They devoured all that was left after the hail—everything growing in the fields and the fruit on the trees. Nothing green remained on tree or plant in all the land of Egypt.

[16]Pharaoh quickly summoned Moses and Aaron and said, "I have sinned against the LORD your God and against you. [17]Now forgive my sin once more and pray to the LORD your God to take this deadly plague away from me."

[18]Moses then left Pharaoh and prayed to the LORD. [19]And the LORD changed the wind to a very strong west wind, which caught up the locusts and carried them into the Red Sea.[a] Not a locust was left anywhere in Egypt. [20]But the LORD hardened Pharaoh's heart, and he would not let the Israelites go.

The Plague of Darkness

[21]Then the LORD said to Moses, "Stretch out your hand toward the sky so that darkness will spread over Egypt—darkness that can be felt." [22]So Moses stretched out his hand toward the sky, and total darkness covered all Egypt for three days. [23]No one could see anyone else or leave his place for three days. Yet all the Israelites had light in the places where they lived.

[24]Then Pharaoh summoned Moses and said, "Go, worship the LORD. Even your women and children may go with you; only leave your flocks and herds behind." [25]But Moses said, "You must allow us to have sacrifices[D] and burnt offerings[D] to present to the LORD our God. [26]Our livestock too must go with us; not a hoof is to be left behind. We have to use some of them in worshiping the LORD our God, and until we get there we will not know what we are to use to worship the LORD."

[27]But the LORD hardened Pharaoh's heart, and he was not willing to let them go. [28]Pharaoh said to Moses, "Get out of my sight! Make sure you do not appear before me again! The day you see my face you will die."

[29]"Just as you say," Moses replied, "I will never appear before you again."

The Plague on the Firstborn

11 Now the LORD had said to Moses, "I will bring one more plague on Pharaoh and on Egypt. After that, he will let you go from here, and when he does, he will drive you out completely. [2]Tell the people that men and women alike are to ask their neighbors for articles of silver and gold." [3](The LORD made the Egyptians favorably disposed toward the people, and Moses himself was highly regarded in Egypt by Pharaoh's officials and by the people.)

[4]So Moses said, "This is what the LORD says: 'About midnight I will go throughout Egypt. [5]Every firstborn[D] son in Egypt will die, from the firstborn son of Pharaoh, who sits on the throne, to the firstborn son of the slave girl, who is at her hand mill, and all the firstborn of the cattle as well. [6]There will be loud wailing throughout

Why didn't Moses accept this offer? (10:24)
Both Moses and Pharaoh clearly understood the implications of Israel's *temporary* worship holiday: Israel was leaving—for good. Pharaoh may have planned to use the animals as leverage to ensure the Israelites' return. Or, he may have wanted to keep their livestock if he had to let them go. After the devastating livestock losses suffered by the Egyptians, the Israelites' animals could have helped Egypt's recovery following the plagues. Whatever their motives, Pharaoh and Moses both knew the stakes.

Why was Pharaoh so obstinate? (10:27–28)
After the plagues had so completely ravaged Egypt, Pharaoh may have thought he needed the Israelites more at this time than ever before. If the slaves were released, Egypt would face a severe economic hardship. Pharaoh was in no position to forfeit such lucrative labor. That, coupled with his wounded pride and loss of power, made Pharaoh more determined than ever to keep his grip on the people.

[a]19 Hebrew *Yam Suph*; that is, Sea of Reeds

Egypt—worse than there has ever been or ever will be again. [7]But among the Israelites not a dog will bark at any man or animal.' Then you will know that the LORD makes a distinction between Egypt and Israel. [8]All these officials of yours will come to me, bowing down before me and saying, 'Go, you and all the people who follow you!' After that I will leave." Then Moses, hot with anger, left Pharaoh.

[9]The LORD had said to Moses, "Pharaoh will refuse to listen to you—so that my wonders may be multiplied in Egypt." [10]Moses and Aaron performed all these wonders before Pharaoh, but the LORD hardened Pharaoh's heart, and he would not let the Israelites go out of his country.

The Passover

12 The LORD said to Moses and Aaron in Egypt, [2]"This month is to be for you the first month, the first month of your year. [3]Tell the whole community of Israel that on the tenth day of this month each man is to take a lamb[a] for his family, one for each household. [4]If any household is too small for a whole lamb, they must share one with their nearest neighbor, having taken into account the number of people there are. You are to determine the amount of lamb needed in accordance with what each person will eat. [5]The animals you choose must be year-old males without defect, and you may take them from the sheep or the goats. [6]Take care of them until the fourteenth day of the month, when all the people of the community of Israel must slaughter them at twilight. [7]Then they are to take some of the blood and put it on the sides and tops of the doorframes of the houses where they eat the lambs. [8]That same night they are to eat the meat roasted over the fire, along with bitter herbs, and

---

[a]3 The Hebrew word can mean *lamb* or *kid*; also in verse 4.

Instead of ten plagues, why not skip right to the last one? (11:9–10)
The number and choice of plagues had both religious and diplomatic significance. The plagues progressively demonstrated God's power over each of Egypt's principal gods (Nile—Hapi; sun/darkness—Ra; cattle—Hathor/Apis; frogs—Hept). Each plague also induced Pharaoh to move closer to Moses' ultimate objective: Israel's freedom. Initially, Pharaoh agreed to let Israel sacrifice *here in the land* (8:25). He then agreed to permit only the men to go (10:11), then to permit all of the people to go but without their livestock and possessions (10:24). Ultimately, Israel was to be "driven out" with not only their own possessions but also the wealth of the Egyptians (11:1–2).

Did the Israelites understand the reasons for the Passover restrictions? (12:1–49)
Perhaps not at this time. The regulations may have been more a test of Israel's complete trust in God. However, each was also necessary because of the situation. Concerns for haste, preparation for travel, group solidarity and recognizing God's grace towards Israel inspired most of the restrictions. Later, the resulting Passover ceremony would answer the children's question, "What does all this mean?" (12:26; 13:3,14; Deut. 4:9).

Why does God harden some people's hearts? (11:3)

God seems to treat people very differently. Though he made many of the Egyptians *favorably disposed* toward Moses and the people of Israel (11:3), *God hardened* Pharaoh's heart (10:27; 11:10).

Why the difference? In one sense, only God knows. As Paul says, "God has mercy on whom he wants to have mercy, and he hardens whom he wants to harden" (Romans 9:18).

From a human point of view, however, we see many factors that help account for the differences. Pharaoh saw the Israelites as free labor—a tool necessary for him to achieve his ambitions. The Egyptian people, on the other hand, were more likely to sympathize with Israel's slavery. See article: *Who hardened Pharaoh's heart?* (10:1).

We know very little about where our deepest feelings come from. How do motivations and desires, prejudices and preferences, begin to form? Are they the result of genetics, environment or chemistry? Or are they consciously chosen?

The Bible teaches that God controls the universe. It also teaches that people can obey or disobey God's commands. How does God's control affect people's free will? If people are perfectly free to choose their own attitudes and biases, it appears to diminish God's absolute power. If, on the other hand, God causes certain individuals to harden their hearts against him, it appears God might be the author of evil.

The connection between God's sovereignty and human freedom remains a mystery.

bread made without yeast^D. ⁹Do not eat the meat raw or cooked in water, but roast it over the fire—head, legs and inner parts. ¹⁰Do not leave any of it till morning; if some is left till morning, you must burn it. ¹¹This is how you are to eat it: with your cloak tucked into your belt, your sandals on your feet and your staff in your hand. Eat it in haste; it is the LORD's Passover.

¹²"On that same night I will pass through Egypt and strike down every firstborn^D—both men and animals—and I will bring judgment on all the gods of Egypt. I am the LORD. ¹³The blood will be a sign for you on the houses where you are; and when I see the blood, I will pass over you. No destructive plague will touch you when I strike Egypt.

¹⁴"This is a day you are to commemorate; for the generations to come you shall celebrate it as a festival to the LORD—a lasting ordinance. ¹⁵For seven days you are to eat bread made without yeast. On the first day remove the yeast from your houses, for whoever eats anything with yeast in it from the first day through the seventh must be cut off from Israel. ¹⁶On the first day hold a sacred assembly^D, and another one on the seventh day. Do no work at all on these days, except to prepare food for everyone to eat—that is all you may do.

¹⁷"Celebrate the Feast of Unleavened Bread, because it was on this very day that I brought your divisions out of Egypt. Celebrate this day as a lasting ordinance for the generations to come. ¹⁸In the first month you are to eat bread made without yeast, from the evening of the fourteenth day until the evening of the twenty-first day. ¹⁹For seven days no yeast is to be found in your houses. And whoever eats anything with yeast in it must be cut off from the community of Israel, whether he is an alien^D or native-born. ²⁰Eat nothing made with yeast. Wherever you live, you must eat unleavened bread."

²¹Then Moses summoned all the elders of Israel and said to them, "Go at once and select the animals for your families and slaughter the Passover lamb. ²²Take a bunch of hyssop^D, dip it into the blood in the basin and put some of the blood on the top and on both sides of the doorframe. Not one of you shall go out the door of his house until morning. ²³When the LORD goes through the land to strike down the Egyptians, he will see the blood on the top and sides of the doorframe and will pass over that doorway, and he will not permit the destroyer to enter your houses and strike you down.

²⁴"Obey these instructions as a lasting ordinance for you and your descendants. ²⁵When you enter the land that the LORD will give you as he promised, observe this ceremony. ²⁶And when your children ask you, 'What does this ceremony mean to you?' ²⁷then tell them, 'It is the Passover sacrifice^D to the LORD, who passed over the houses of the Israelites in Egypt and spared our homes when he struck down the Egyptians.'" Then the people bowed down and worshiped. ²⁸The Israelites did just what the LORD commanded Moses and Aaron.

²⁹At midnight the LORD struck down all the firstborn in Egypt, from the firstborn of Pharaoh, who sat on the throne, to the firstborn of the prisoner, who was in the dungeon, and the firstborn of all the livestock as well. ³⁰Pharaoh and all his officials and all the Egyptians got up during the night, and there was loud wailing in Egypt, for there was not a house without someone dead.

What was wrong with yeast? (12:15)
Baking bread with yeast required saving a portion of soured dough from a previous batch. When added to fresh dough, it would promote fermentation and, over time, cause the dough to rise. The ban on yeast emphasized the need for haste and purity. In the Passover ceremony, yeast came to symbolize sin and contamination (Matt. 16:6; 1 Cor. 5:6–8).

Cut off from Israel (12:15)
This probably meant banishment or shunning. In some cases, however, this phrase refers to execution (Lev. 20:2–3). See *Cut off from my presence* (Lev. 22:3).

The destroyer (12:23)
A spirit sent by God to bring judgment upon the Egyptians, also called *a band of destroying angels* (Psalm 78:49). Some think good angels can bring either blessing or destruction depending on God's instructions. Others suggest this may have been Satan or one of his angels. Either way God *created the destroyer to work havoc* (Isaiah 54:16).

Why did the firstborn have to die? (12:29)
The consequences of opposing God are terrible. This tragedy was necessary to convince Pharaoh to release Israel from slavery. This event becomes an important part of the Bible's theme of redemption, which means to buy back or exchange one life for another. The firstborn among Israel were spared from dying because they offered lambs as their redemption.

The Exodus

[31]During the night Pharaoh summoned Moses and Aaron and said, "Up! Leave my people, you and the Israelites! Go, worship the LORD as you have requested. [32]Take your flocks and herds, as you have said, and go. And also bless me."

[33]The Egyptians urged the people to hurry and leave the country. "For otherwise," they said, "we will all die!" [34]So the people took their dough before the yeast[D] was added, and carried it on their shoulders in kneading troughs wrapped in clothing. [35]The Israelites did as Moses instructed and asked the Egyptians for articles of silver and gold and for clothing. [36]The LORD had made the Egyptians favorably disposed toward the people, and they gave them what they asked for; so they plundered[D] the Egyptians.

[37]The Israelites journeyed from Rameses to Succoth. There were about six hundred thousand men on foot, besides women and children. [38]Many other people went up with them, as well as large droves of livestock, both flocks and herds. [39]With the dough they had brought from Egypt, they baked cakes of unleavened bread. The dough was without yeast because they had been driven out of Egypt and did not have time to prepare food for themselves.

[40]Now the length of time the Israelite people lived in Egypt[a] was 430 years. [41]At the end of the 430 years, to the very day, all the LORD's divisions left Egypt. [42]Because the LORD kept vigil that night to bring them out of Egypt, on this night all the Israelites are to keep vigil to honor the LORD for the generations to come.

Passover Restrictions

[43]The LORD said to Moses and Aaron, "These are the regulations for the Passover:

"No foreigner is to eat of it. [44]Any slave you have bought may eat of it after you have circumcised[D] him, [45]but a temporary resident and a hired worker may not eat of it.

[46]"It must be eaten inside one house; take none of the meat outside the house. Do not break any of the bones. [47]The whole community of Israel must celebrate it.

[48]"An alien[D] living among you who wants to celebrate the LORD's Passover must have all the males in his household circumcised; then he may take part like one born in the land. No uncircumcised[D] male may eat of it. [49]The same law applies to the native-born and to the alien living among you."

[50]All the Israelites did just what the LORD had commanded Moses and Aaron. [51]And on that very day the LORD brought the Israelites out of Egypt by their divisions.

Consecration of the Firstborn

13 The LORD said to Moses, [2]"Consecrate[D] to me every firstborn[D] male. The first offspring of every womb among the Israelites belongs to me, whether man or animal."

[3]Then Moses said to the people, "Commemorate this day, the day you came out of Egypt, out of the land of slavery, because the LORD brought you out of it with a

[a]40 Masoretic Text; Samaritan Pentateuch and Septuagint *Egypt and Canaan*

Why would the Egyptians be willing to be looted? (12:35–36)

Some think the Israelites took advantage of the Egyptians, but most likely the plundering was an Egyptian custom symbolizing the move from slavery to freedom. In some ancient cultures, slave owners bestowed gifts upon slaves being released from bondage. With a long journey before them, the Israelites would also need the aid. In addition, the Egyptians, devastated by the plagues, were probably more than happy to rid themselves of these people and their God.

How many Israelites left Egypt? (12:37)

With a standing army of 603,550 (38:26), the total number of Israelites could have well exceeded two million.

Why did non-Israelites go with them? (12:38)

After the trauma of the plagues, many Egyptians were no doubt eager to leave the disaster area. Some were probably moved to faith by God's mighty acts on behalf of his people. Others, perhaps, were friends of the Israelites.

Why did God wait 430 years to free his people? (12:40)

For most of that time, the Israelites were willing and welcome guests in Egypt. Their enslavement probably began about 125 years before the exodus. Reasons for God's timing can't be known, but God responded when he heard the cry of the Israelites (Exodus 2:23).

How did they consecrate the firstborn males? (13:1–2)

Since God saved Israel's firstborn from the final plague in Egypt, they owed him their lives. To be *consecrated* meant to be *given to God*. Consecrated animals were either killed as sacrifices or (in later years) given to the priests. Instead of the firstborn sons being killed, however, a substitute died in their place. In this way, the lives of the firstborn sons were "redeemed" —that is, bought back. See **Why did the firstborn have to die?** (12:29).

mighty hand. Eat nothing containing yeast[D]. **4**Today, in the month of Abib, you are leaving. **5**When the LORD brings you into the land of the Canaanites, Hittites, Amorites, Hivites and Jebusites—the land he swore to your forefathers to give you, a land flowing with milk and honey—you are to observe this ceremony in this month: **6**For seven days eat bread made without yeast and on the seventh day hold a festival to the LORD. **7**Eat unleavened bread during those seven days; nothing with yeast in it is to be seen among you, nor shall any yeast be seen anywhere within your borders. **8**On that day tell your son, 'I do this because of what the LORD did for me when I came out of Egypt.' **9**This observance will be for you like a sign on your hand and a reminder on your forehead that the law of the LORD is to be on your lips. For the LORD brought you out of Egypt with his mighty hand. **10**You must keep this ordinance at the appointed time year after year.

11"After the LORD brings you into the land of the Canaanites and gives it to you, as he promised on oath to you and your forefathers, **12**you are to give over to the LORD the first offspring of every womb. All the firstborn[D] males of your livestock belong to the LORD. **13**Redeem[D] with a lamb every firstborn donkey, but if you do not redeem it, break its neck. Redeem every firstborn among your sons.

14"In days to come, when your son asks you, 'What does this mean?' say to him, 'With a mighty hand the LORD brought us out of Egypt, out of the land of slavery. **15**When Pharaoh stubbornly refused to let us go, the LORD killed every firstborn in Egypt, both man and animal. This is why I sacrifice[D] to the LORD the first male offspring of every womb and redeem each of my firstborn sons.' **16**And it will be like a sign on your hand and a symbol on your forehead that the LORD brought us out of Egypt with his mighty hand."

Crossing the Sea

17When Pharaoh let the people go, God did not lead them on the road through the Philistine country, though that was shorter. For God said, "If they face war, they might change their minds and return to Egypt." **18**So God led the people around by the desert road toward the Red Sea.[a] The Israelites went up out of Egypt armed for battle.

19Moses took the bones of Joseph with him because Joseph had made the sons of Israel swear an oath. He had said, "God will surely come to your aid, and then you must carry my bones up with you from this place."[b]

20After leaving Succoth they camped at Etham on the edge of the desert. **21**By day the LORD went ahead of them in a pillar of cloud to guide them on their way and by night in a pillar of fire to give them light, so that they could travel by day or night. **22**Neither the pillar of cloud by day nor the pillar of fire by night left its place in front of the people.

14 Then the LORD said to Moses, **2**"Tell the Israelites to turn back and encamp near Pi Hahiroth, between Migdol and the sea. They are to encamp by the sea, directly opposite Baal Zephon. **3**Pharaoh will think, 'The Israelites are wandering around the land in confusion, hemmed in by the desert.' **4**And I will harden Pharaoh's

a18 Hebrew *Yam Suph*; that is, Sea of Reeds   *b19* See Gen. 50:25.

A sign on your hand and a symbol on your forehead (13:9,16)
Centuries later, Jews literally obeyed this command by using *phylacteries*, little boxes containing portions of Scripture and strapped to the forehead or left arm (Matt. 23:5). Here, however, it was the Passover observance that was to be like a sign on the hand or forehead. As a figure of speech—much like we would say, "the word is on the tip of my tongue"—this phrase meant that the Passover would visually symbolize God's mighty power on behalf of his people. See Deut. 6:8.

Why was a death necessary when something belonged to God? (13:13)
God is teaching his people about his holiness. Nothing impure is acceptable in his presence. Anything less than holy, when placed in God's presence, results in death. Fortunately, as a teaching tool, God permitted the life of one creature (the firstborn) to be redeemed by the death of another (an animal). This was the sacrificial system that was ultimately fulfilled in Christ. See *How did they consecrate the firstborn males?* (13:1–2).

Why was Israel *armed for battle* if God led them away from war? (13:17–18)
Though these ex-slaves were mentally unprepared for battle, God wanted them to start seeing themselves as a free nation, belonging to him alone. *Armed for battle* probably meant only that they were equipped with spears, bows and slings and that they marched as a unit in an orderly manner. Few if any swords, shields or protective armor were likely to be found among these former slaves.

Why did God appear as fire and cloud? (13:21–22)
He was assuring his people that he was present, guiding them and providing for them. Yet they did not see God directly, but rather a form of his glory, shrouded by the cloud and fire. Israel's experience was like that of Ezekiel, who saw only *the appearance of the likeness of the glory* of the LORD (Ezek. 1:28).

Why did God lure Pharaoh into pursuing the Israelites? (14:1–4)
God had the Israelites reverse their direction, leading Pharaoh to think they were confused and could be easily captured and returned to slavery. This revealed that Pharaoh's heart had not really changed. He was prepared to pursue the Israelites as long as they were within reach. Perhaps God knew that if they were ever to be rid of the threat of recapture, Pharaoh had to be decisively defeated. Pharaoh continued to resist God and deserved judgment.

Why did God care about gaining glory for himself? (14:4)

See *Why would God be concerned about what the Egyptians think of him?* (Num. 14:13–16).

heart, and he will pursue them. But I will gain glory[D] for myself through Pharaoh and all his army, and the Egyptians will know that I am the LORD." So the Israelites did this.

5When the king of Egypt was told that the people had fled, Pharaoh and his officials changed their minds about them and said, "What have we done? We have let the Israelites go and have lost their services!" **6**So he had his chariot made ready and took his army with him. **7**He took six hundred of the best chariots, along with all the other chariots of Egypt, with officers over all of them. **8**The LORD hardened the heart of Pharaoh king of Egypt, so that he pursued the Israelites, who were marching out boldly. **9**The Egyptians—all Pharaoh's horses and chariots, horsemen[a] and troops—pursued the Israelites and overtook them as they camped by the sea near Pi Hahiroth, opposite Baal Zephon.

10As Pharaoh approached, the Israelites looked up, and there were the Egyptians, marching after them. They were terrified and cried out to the LORD. **11**They said to Moses, "Was it because there were no graves in Egypt that you brought us to the desert to die? What have you done to us by bringing us out of Egypt? **12**Didn't we say to you in Egypt, 'Leave us alone; let us serve the Egyptians'? It would have been better for us to serve the Egyptians than to die in the desert!"

13Moses answered the people, "Do not be afraid. Stand firm and you will see the deliverance the LORD will bring

Did the Israelites really resist leaving slavery? (14:12)

No doubt some feared the risk of running for freedom. While the exact quote in 14:12 isn't mentioned earlier, it is consistent with the fickle attitude that shows up whenever they face difficulties (5:24; 16:3; 17:3; Num. 11:4–5).

---

*a*9 Or *charioteers*; also in verses 17, 18, 23, 26 and 28

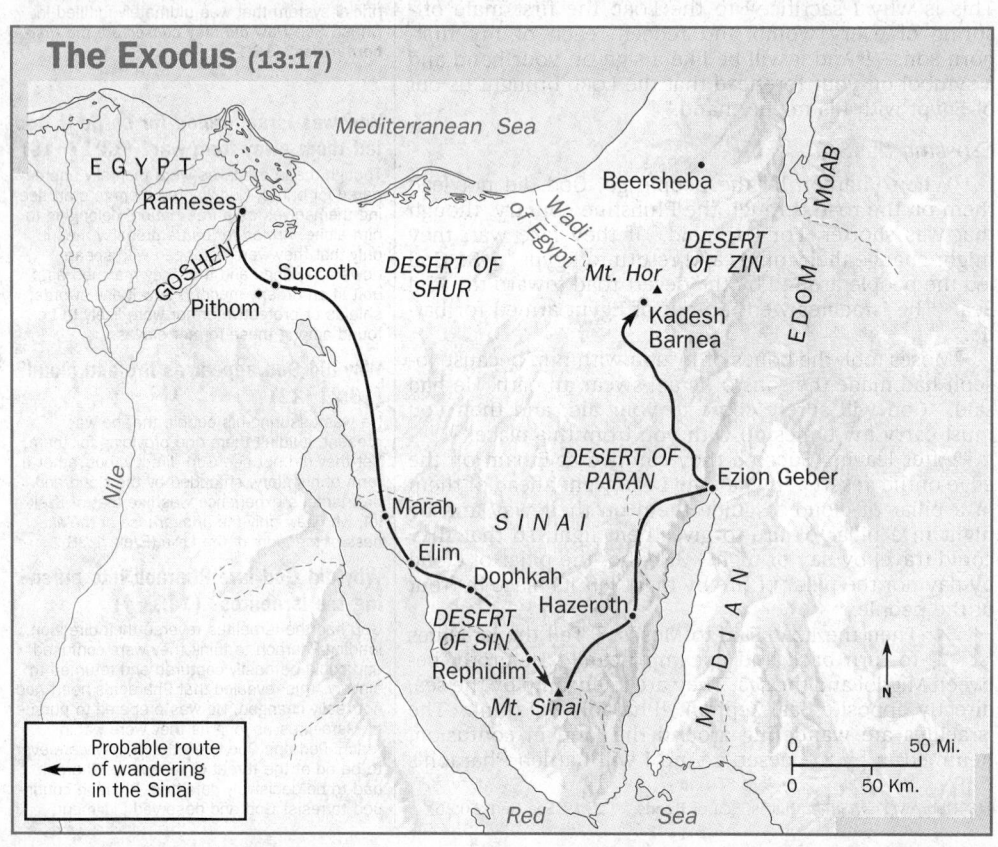

The Exodus (13:17)

Mediterranean Sea

EGYPT

Rameses

GOSHEN

Succoth

Pithom

Nile

DESERT OF SHUR

Wadi of Egypt

Beersheba

Mt. Hor

DESERT OF ZIN

MOAB

EDOM

Kadesh Barnea

Marah

Elim

SINAI

Dophkah

Hazeroth

DESERT OF PARAN

Ezion Geber

MIDIAN

DESERT OF SIN

Rephidim

Mt. Sinai

N

0   50 Mi.

0   50 Km.

Red   Sea

Probable route of wandering in the Sinai

you today. The Egyptians you see today you will never see again. **14**The LORD will fight for you; you need only to be still."

15Then the LORD said to Moses, "Why are you crying out to me? Tell the Israelites to move on. **16**Raise your staff and stretch out your hand over the sea to divide the water so that the Israelites can go through the sea on dry ground. **17**I will harden the hearts of the Egyptians so that they will go in after them. And I will gain glory^D through Pharaoh and all his army, through his chariots and his horsemen. **18**The Egyptians will know that I am the LORD when I gain glory through Pharaoh, his chariots and his horsemen."

19Then the angel of God, who had been traveling in front of Israel's army, withdrew and went behind them. The pillar of cloud also moved from in front and stood behind them, **20**coming between the armies of Egypt and Israel. Throughout the night the cloud brought darkness to the one side and light to the other side; so neither went near the other all night long.

21Then Moses stretched out his hand over the sea, and all that night the LORD drove the sea back with a strong east wind and turned it into dry land. The waters were divided, **22**and the Israelites went through the sea on dry ground, with a wall of water on their right and on their left.

23The Egyptians pursued them, and all Pharaoh's horses and chariots and horsemen followed them into the sea. **24**During the last watch of the night the LORD looked down from the pillar of fire and cloud at the Egyptian army and threw it into confusion. **25**He made the wheels of their chariots come off^a so that they had difficulty driving. And the Egyptians said, "Let's get away from the Israelites! The LORD is fighting for them against Egypt."

26Then the LORD said to Moses, "Stretch out your hand over the sea so that the waters may flow back over the Egyptians and their chariots and horsemen." **27**Moses stretched out his hand over the sea, and at daybreak the sea went back to its place. The Egyptians were fleeing toward^b it, and the LORD swept them into the sea. **28**The water flowed back and covered the chariots and horsemen—the entire army of Pharaoh that had followed the Israelites into the sea. Not one of them survived.

29But the Israelites went through the sea on dry ground, with a wall of water on their right and on their left. **30**That day the LORD saved Israel from the hands of the Egyptians, and Israel saw the Egyptians lying dead on the shore. **31**And when the Israelites saw the great power the LORD displayed against the Egyptians, the people feared the LORD and put their trust in him and in Moses his servant.

The Song of Moses and Miriam

15 Then Moses and the Israelites sang this song to the LORD:

> "I will sing to the LORD,
>   for he is highly exalted.
> The horse and its rider
>   he has hurled into the sea.
> **2**The LORD is my strength and my song;
>   he has become my salvation^D.

What kind of wind could blow a sea dry? (14:21)

Extremely hot sirocco winds from the Arabian desert could displace significant amounts of water and rapidly dry the land. The walling up of the waters on either side, however, was due to God's miraculous hand rather than simply the force of the wind, since Israel would have had to march directly into its gale force (v. 22).

How did anyone know what the Egyptians said? (14:25)

Perhaps some of the Israelites were close enough to the pursuing troops to overhear their shouts. Or perhaps the words were inferred from observing the soldiers' frantic and frustrated actions.

Do Egyptian documents verify this event? (14:28)

None have been found. But it was uncommon for pharaohs to record their defeats. They often would rewrite history, deleting from official records, for instance, the names of traitors and political adversaries. It's not surprising that the Egyptians would not want posterity to know that Pharaoh's army was destroyed chasing runaway slaves.

---

^a25 Or *He jammed the wheels of their chariots* (see Samaritan Pentateuch, Septuagint and Syriac)   ^b27 Or *from*

He is my God, and I will praise him,
   my father's God, and I will exalt him.
³The LORD is a warrior;
   the LORD is his name.
⁴Pharaoh's chariots and his army
   he has hurled into the sea.
The best of Pharaoh's officers
   are drowned in the Red Sea.ᵃ
⁵The deep waters have covered them;
   they sank to the depths like a stone.

⁶"Your right hand, O LORD,
   was majestic in power.
Your right hand, O LORD,
   shattered the enemy.
⁷In the greatness of your majesty
   you threw down those who opposed you.
You unleashed your burning anger;
   it consumed them like stubble.
⁸By the blast of your nostrils
   the waters piled up.
The surging waters stood firm like a wall;
   the deep waters congealed in the heart of the
     sea.

⁹"The enemy boasted,
   'I will pursue, I will overtake them.
I will divide the spoils;
   I will gorge myself on them.
I will draw my sword
   and my hand will destroy them.'
¹⁰But you blew with your breath,
   and the sea covered them.
They sank like lead
   in the mighty waters.

¹¹"Who among the gods is like you, O LORD?
   Who is like you—
   majestic in holiness,
   awesome in gloryᴰ,
   working wonders?
¹²You stretched out your right hand
   and the earth swallowed them.

¹³"In your unfailing love you will lead
   the people you have redeemedᴰ.
In your strength you will guide them
   to your holy dwelling.
¹⁴The nations will hear and tremble;
   anguish will grip the people of Philistia.
¹⁵The chiefs of Edomᴰ will be terrified,
   the leaders of Moab will be seized with
     trembling,
the peopleᵇ of Canaan will melt away;
¹⁶ terror and dread will fall upon them.
By the power of your arm
   they will be as still as a stone—
until your people pass by, O LORD,
   until the people you boughtᶜ pass by.
¹⁷You will bring them in and plant them
   on the mountain of your inheritance—
the place, O LORD, you made for your dwelling,

Your right hand (15:6)

Throughout the Bible, the right hand of God represents his power and authority. Ultimately, God's right hand becomes the seat of authority occupied by the Messiah, Jesus (Matt. 22:44). Also see *The years of the right hand of the Most High* (Psalm 77:10).

Deep waters congealed (15:8)

God made the waters stand firm *like a wall* to allow the Israelites safe passage through the Red Sea.

Why did Moses mention these particular nations? (15:14–16)

The order of the countries mentioned here parallels the order of the nations encountered by the Israelites as they moved toward the promised land after their wandering in the desert.

The chiefs of Edom (15:15)

See *Edom* (Gen. 36:1). Also see Gen. 36:31–43.

ᵃ4 Hebrew *Yam Suph*; that is, Sea of Reeds; also in verse 22
ᵇ15 Or *rulers*   ᶜ16 Or *created*

the sanctuary, O Lord, your hands
    established.
    18The LORD will reign
    for ever and ever."

19When Pharaoh's horses, chariots and horsemen[a]
went into the sea, the LORD brought the waters of the sea
back over them, but the Israelites walked through the sea
on dry ground. **20**Then Miriam the prophetess[b], Aaron's
sister, took a tambourine in her hand, and all the women
followed her, with tambourines and dancing. **21**Miriam
sang to them:

"Sing to the LORD,
    for he is highly exalted.
The horse and its rider
    he has hurled into the sea."

The Waters of Marah and Elim

22Then Moses led Israel from the Red Sea and they
went into the Desert of Shur. For three days they traveled
in the desert without finding water. **23**When they came to
Marah, they could not drink its water because it was bitter. (That is why the place is called Marah.[b]) **24**So the people grumbled against Moses, saying, "What are we to
drink?"

25Then Moses cried out to the LORD, and the LORD
showed him a piece of wood. He threw it into the water,
and the water became sweet.

There the LORD made a decree and a law for them, and
there he tested them. **26**He said, "If you listen carefully to
the voice of the LORD your God and do what is right in his
eyes, if you pay attention to his commands and keep all
his decrees, I will not bring on you any of the diseases I
brought on the Egyptians, for I am the LORD, who heals
you."

27Then they came to Elim, where there were twelve
springs and seventy palm trees, and they camped there
near the water.

Manna and Quail

16 The whole Israelite community set out from Elim
and came to the Desert of Sin, which is between
Elim and Sinai, on the fifteenth day of the second month
after they had come out of Egypt. **2**In the desert the whole
community grumbled against Moses and Aaron. **3**The Israelites said to them, "If only we had died by the LORD's
hand in Egypt! There we sat around pots of meat and ate
all the food we wanted, but you have brought us out into
this desert to starve this entire assembly to death[b]."

4Then the LORD said to Moses, "I will rain down bread
from heaven for you. The people are to go out each day
and gather enough for that day. In this way I will test
them and see whether they will follow my instructions.
5On the sixth day they are to prepare what they bring in,
and that is to be twice as much as they gather on the other
days."

6So Moses and Aaron said to all the Israelites, "In the
evening you will know that it was the LORD who brought
you out of Egypt, **7**and in the morning you will see the
glory[b] of the LORD, because he has heard your grumbling
against him. Who are we, that you should grumble
against us?" **8**Moses also said, "You will know that it was

---

a19 Or *charioteers*   *b23 Marah* means *bitter.*

What was Miriam's role? (15:20)

As a prophetess, Miriam led the people in worship after the victory over the Egyptians. She
also had authority because God spoke through
her (Num. 12:1–6). God used both Miriam and
Aaron as prophets, speaking to them in
dreams and visions. Micah also reports that
Miriam was sent by God to lead Israel
(Micah 6:4).

Was this a miracle or a natural sweet-ener? (15:25)

Some have told accounts of nomadic people
using thornbushes or certain plants to improve
the taste of acrid water. Others say God's power alone improved the water—that the wood
was most likely simply a means to show Moses' obedience. Either way, this event was a
miracle: God intervened in response to Moses'
cry, and Moses obeyed God.

What *decree and law* did God make at Marah? (15:25)

We don't know specifically, but it likely refers
to listening *carefully to the voice of the LORD*
(v. 26). This paves the way for the giving of
the law at Sinai three months later. God was
teaching that *whatever* he commanded, Israel
was to do.

What diseases does God prevent? (15:26)

This may refer to the plagues (chs. 7–11). But
it could also refer to sexually transmitted diseases or other illnesses caused by eating
contaminated food—diseases that would be
prevented if they lived according to God's
standards.

Why did the Israelites distort the facts? (16:3)

The people were fickle. Rather than trusting
God in the face of adversity, they imagined that
he was the source of the problem. In difficult
times it's easy to romanticize the "good ol'
days," even when they weren't so good.

Why does God test them over and over? (16:4)

Perhaps it's more important to ask why the Israelites repeatedly tested God. God had already demonstrated he would care for them
even in difficult situations (the Passover,
crossing the Red Sea, destroying the Egyptian
army, providing fresh water in the desert). It
should have become progressively easier for
the people to trust God—this time for food.
Since they didn't, God needed to continue to
teach them trust through testing.

How serious an offense is grumbling? (16:7)

Grumbling showed Israel's lack of gratitude
and trust, which damages any relationship.

Why does God reward their grumbling by feeding them? (16:8)

Although God was displeased with Israel's ungrateful attitude, his love for them caused him
nonetheless to meet their physical needs.

the LORD when he gives you meat to eat in the evening and all the bread you want in the morning, because he has heard your grumbling against him. Who are we? You are not grumbling against us, but against the LORD."

9Then Moses told Aaron, "Say to the entire Israelite community, 'Come before the LORD, for he has heard your grumbling.' "

10While Aaron was speaking to the whole Israelite community, they looked toward the desert, and there was the gloryᴰ of the LORD appearing in the cloud.

11The LORD said to Moses, **12**"I have heard the grumbling of the Israelites. Tell them, 'At twilight you will eat meat, and in the morning you will be filled with bread. Then you will know that I am the LORD your God.' "

13That evening quailᴰ came and covered the camp, and in the morning there was a layer of dew around the camp. **14**When the dew was gone, thin flakes like frost on the ground appeared on the desert floor. **15**When the Israelites saw it, they said to each other, "What is it?" For they did not know what it was.

Moses said to them, "It is the bread the LORD has given you to eat. **16**This is what the LORD has commanded: 'Each one is to gather as much as he needs. Take an omer*a* for each person you have in your tent.' "

17The Israelites did as they were told; some gathered much, some little. **18**And when they measured it by the omer, he who gathered much did not have too much, and he who gathered little did not have too little. Each one gathered as much as he needed.

19Then Moses said to them, "No one is to keep any of it until morning."

20However, some of them paid no attention to Moses; they kept part of it until morning, but it was full of maggots and began to smell. So Moses was angry with them.

21Each morning everyone gathered as much as he needed, and when the sun grew hot, it melted away. **22**On the sixth day, they gathered twice as much—two omers*b* for each person—and the leaders of the community came and reported this to Moses. **23**He said to them, "This is what the LORD commanded: 'Tomorrow is to be a day of rest, a holy Sabbathᴰ to the LORD. So bake what you want to bake and boil what you want to boil. Save whatever is left and keep it until morning.' "

24So they saved it until morning, as Moses commanded, and it did not stink or get maggots in it. **25**"Eat it today," Moses said, "because today is a Sabbath to the LORD. You will not find any of it on the ground today. **26**Six days you are to gather it, but on the seventh day, the Sabbath, there will not be any."

27Nevertheless, some of the people went out on the seventh day to gather it, but they found none. **28**Then the LORD said to Moses, "How long will you*c* refuse to keep my commands and my instructions? **29**Bear in mind that the LORD has given you the Sabbath; that is why on the sixth day he gives you bread for two days. Everyone is to stay where he is on the seventh day; no one is to go out." **30**So the people rested on the seventh day.

31The people of Israel called the bread mannaᴰ.*d* It was white like coriander seed and tasted like wafers made

Was this the first time the Israelites heard about the Sabbath? (16:23)

This is the first reference to Sabbath observance among the Israelites. While the principle of Sabbath rest is embedded in the creation (Gen. 2:2–3), there is no evidence that God required its observance until the provision of manna and, later, the Ten Commandments.

SCRIPTURE LINK (16:31) *Manna*

This much-needed food was heaven-sent, and in the New Testament, Jesus compares himself to this *bread of life* (John 6:48–51).

What was manna? (16:31)

God's miraculous provision. While some suggest manna still occurs naturally in the Arabian desert (a sweet-tasting liquid produced by insects on tamarisk trees, or a form of edible lichen), no substance today completely matches the manna described here. The fact that it first appeared on a certain day, ended on a particular day (Joshua 5:12), appeared in the appropriate amounts and had unusual spoilage properties (see following note) all point to its supernatural origin.

How could manna not spoil for generations? (16:32)

Leftover manna quickly spoiled and became infested with maggots (v. 20). The spoilage may have been punishment for not trusting God for daily provision. At any rate, he who miraculously provided manna in the first place could certainly preserve a small quantity as a ceremonial remembrance.

---

a16 That is, probably about 2 quarts (about 2 liters); also in verses 18, 32, 33 and 36   *b22* That is, probably about 4 quarts (about 4.5 liters)   *c28* The Hebrew is plural.   *d31 Manna* means *What is it?* (see verse 15).

with honey. **32**Moses said, "This is what the LORD has commanded: 'Take an omer of manna[D] and keep it for the generations to come, so they can see the bread I gave you to eat in the desert when I brought you out of Egypt.' "

33So Moses said to Aaron, "Take a jar and put an omer of manna in it. Then place it before the LORD to be kept for the generations to come."

34As the LORD commanded Moses, Aaron put the manna in front of the Testimony, that it might be kept. **35**The Israelites ate manna forty years, until they came to a land that was settled; they ate manna until they reached the border of Canaan.

36(An omer is one tenth of an ephah.)

Water From the Rock

17 The whole Israelite community set out from the Desert of Sin, traveling from place to place as the LORD commanded. They camped at Rephidim, but there was no water for the people to drink. **2**So they quarreled with Moses and said, "Give us water to drink."

Moses replied, "Why do you quarrel with me? Why do you put the LORD to the test?"

3But the people were thirsty for water there, and they grumbled against Moses. They said, "Why did you bring us up out of Egypt to make us and our children and livestock die of thirst?"

4Then Moses cried out to the LORD, "What am I to do with these people? They are almost ready to stone me."

5The LORD answered Moses, "Walk on ahead of the people. Take with you some of the elders of Israel and take in your hand the staff with which you struck the Nile, and go. **6**I will stand there before you by the rock at Horeb. Strike the rock, and water will come out of it for the people to drink." So Moses did this in the sight of the elders of Israel. **7**And he called the place Massah[a] and Meribah[b] because the Israelites quarreled and because they tested the LORD saying, "Is the LORD among us or not?"

The Amalekites Defeated

8The Amalekites came and attacked the Israelites at Rephidim. **9**Moses said to Joshua, "Choose some of our men and go out to fight the Amalekites. Tomorrow I will stand on top of the hill with the staff of God in my hands."

10So Joshua fought the Amalekites as Moses had ordered, and Moses, Aaron and Hur went to the top of the hill. **11**As long as Moses held up his hands, the Israelites were winning, but whenever he lowered his hands, the Amalekites were winning. **12**When Moses' hands grew tired, they took a stone and put it under him and he sat on it. Aaron and Hur held his hands up—one on one side, one on the other—so that his hands remained steady till sunset. **13**So Joshua overcame the Amalekite army with the sword.

14Then the LORD said to Moses, "Write this on a scroll as something to be remembered and make sure that Joshua hears it, because I will completely blot out the memory of Amalek from under heaven."

15Moses built an altar and called it The LORD is my Banner. **16**He said, "For hands were lifted up to the throne of the LORD. The[c] LORD will be at war against the Amalekites from generation to generation."

a7 Massah means *testing.*   *b7 Meribah* means *quarreling.*
c16 Or *"Because a hand was against the throne of the LORD, the*

The Testimony (16:34)

The stone tablets containing the Ten Commandments and the covenant between God and Israel (34:29). God would later give instructions for building the *ark of the covenant,* also known as the *ark of the Testimony,* to hold the tablets (40:20). The pot of manna and Aaron's staff that had budded (Num. 17:10) were kept together with the tablets in the ark.

What's wrong with wanting water? (17:2)

Israel's sin was not their desire for water, but their attitude toward God. Although God had already demonstrated that he could provide water (15:25), bread (16:15) and meat (16:13), the people were quick to resist Moses' leadership and doubt God's care.

Amalekites (17:8)

Descendants of a grandson of Esau. They were fierce nomads who lived by raiding other tribes, often killing for pleasure.

Why did Moses select Joshua? (17:9)

This is the first time Joshua's name appears. The fact that God later commanded that the curse on Amalek be spoken in Joshua's presence (17:14) indicates that Joshua was already being groomed for leadership. Joshua's preparation involved both anointing and training, military leadership and spiritual leadership.

Who was Hur? (17:10)

The Jewish historian Josephus says that Hur was the husband of Miriam, Moses' sister. He supported Moses during the battle with the Amalekites, and Hur and Aaron were left in charge of Israel when Moses went up to Mount Sinai (24:14). He may also have been the grandfather of Bezalel, the craftsman who supervised the furnishing of the tabernacle (31:2; 35:30).

Why lift Moses' arms and staff? (17:11–12)

Just as God used the staff as a symbol of his power during the plagues in Egypt and over the Red Sea, the staff represented God's power in this battle. In addition, seeing Moses raising the staff on the top of the hill no doubt inspired Israel to fight courageously.

What did Moses write on the scroll? (17:14)

It's not clear if this particular scroll became part of the Bible, but it is clear that Moses was recording the events as they happened. This is one reason he's regarded as the writer of the first five books of the Bible.

If the memory of Amalek was blotted out, why do we still know about Amalekites? (17:14)

Probably because historical records are not the same as *memory* which suggests *renown* or *fame* (as in Hosea 12:5; 14:7). As enemies of God placed under the *ban* (Deut. 25:19; 1 Samuel 15:2–3), the Amalekites were condemned to be destroyed. The sentence *The LORD will be at war against the Amalekites from generation to generation* (v. 16) indicates that God did not intend to execute the sentence immediately. The final remnant of the Amalekites was destroyed during the reign of Hezekiah (1 Chron. 4:41–43).

Jethro Visits Moses

18 Now Jethro, the priest[D] of Midian and father-in-law of Moses, heard of everything God had done for Moses and for his people Israel, and how the LORD had brought Israel out of Egypt.

²After Moses had sent away his wife Zipporah, his father-in-law Jethro received her ³and her two sons. One son was named Gershom,ᵃ for Moses said, "I have become an alien[D] in a foreign land"; ⁴and the other was named Eliezer,ᵇ for he said, "My father's God was my helper; he saved me from the sword of Pharaoh."

⁵Jethro, Moses' father-in-law, together with Moses' sons and wife, came to him in the desert, where he was camped near the mountain of God. ⁶Jethro had sent word to him, "I, your father-in-law Jethro, am coming to you with your wife and her two sons."

⁷So Moses went out to meet his father-in-law and bowed down and kissed him. They greeted each other and then went into the tent. ⁸Moses told his father-in-law about everything the LORD had done to Pharaoh and the Egyptians for Israel's sake and about all the hardships they had met along the way and how the LORD had saved them.

⁹Jethro was delighted to hear about all the good things the LORD had done for Israel in rescuing them from the hand of the Egyptians. ¹⁰He said, "Praise be to the LORD, who rescued you from the hand of the Egyptians and of Pharaoh, and who rescued the people from the hand of the Egyptians. ¹¹Now I know that the LORD is greater than all other gods, for he did this to those who had treated Israel arrogantly." ¹²Then Jethro, Moses' father-in-law, brought a burnt offering[D] and other sacrifices[D] to God, and Aaron came with all the elders of Israel to eat bread with Moses' father-in-law in the presence of God.

¹³The next day Moses took his seat to serve as judge for the people, and they stood around him from morning till evening. ¹⁴When his father-in-law saw all that Moses was doing for the people, he said, "What is this you are doing for the people? Why do you alone sit as judge, while all these people stand around you from morning till evening?"

¹⁵Moses answered him, "Because the people come to me to seek God's will. ¹⁶Whenever they have a dispute, it is brought to me, and I decide between the parties and inform them of God's decrees and laws."

¹⁷Moses' father-in-law replied, "What you are doing is not good. ¹⁸You and these people who come to you will only wear yourselves out. The work is too heavy for you; you cannot handle it alone. ¹⁹Listen now to me and I will give you some advice, and may God be with you. You must be the people's representative before God and bring their disputes to him. ²⁰Teach them the decrees and laws, and show them the way to live and the duties they are to perform. ²¹But select capable men from all the people—men who fear God, trustworthy men who hate dishonest gain—and appoint them as officials over thousands, hundreds, fifties and tens. ²²Have them serve as judges for the people at all times, but have them bring every difficult case to you; the simple cases they can decide themselves. That will make your load lighter, because they will share

---

Why did Moses send his wife and children away? (18:2)

It's unclear, because we don't know at what point he sent them away—before the plagues in Egypt, or during the time in the desert. Perhaps Zipporah returned home after the circumcision of Moses' son (4:24–26), due either to a disagreement or to Moses' fearing for them in Egypt. Num. 12:1 says Miriam and Aaron criticized Moses for taking a Cushite wife—possibly Zipporah. Or perhaps Moses sent them to bring her father, Jethro, to him once they had reached Sinai.

Did Jethro believe in other gods? (18:11)

While Jethro believed in the God of Israel, he may have worshiped him, at least at first, as one of a number of tribal and national gods. This verse shows that he now recognized God as the one and only God. As a priest (2:16), Jethro performed a sacrifice that Moses, Aaron (the eventual high priest) and all the elders participated in (18:12). The fact that God was not displeased by this event indicates that Jethro's faith in God was genuine.

Where did Moses learn the laws of God? (18:15–16)

As leader of Israel, Moses served as judge for civil disputes. With his court training in Egypt, Moses had an extensive background in legal matters. His time in the desert helped him learn God's wisdom. Even though the laws had not yet been written down, God revealed his will in specific cases through Moses. In many ways, the civil laws Moses later wrote down were similar to civil codes of other ancient peoples of the Middle East. Though ancient cultures exchanged some of their customs and values, the human conscience was created by God. Even in pagan societies, God is the source behind a correct interpretation of right and wrong.

ᵃ3 *Gershom* sounds like the Hebrew for *an alien there.*   ᵇ4 *Eliezer* means *my God is helper.*

it with you. ²³If you do this and God so commands, you will be able to stand the strain, and all these people will go home satisfied."

²⁴Moses listened to his father-in-law and did everything he said. ²⁵He chose capable men from all Israel and made them leaders of the people, officials over thousands, hundreds, fifties and tens. ²⁶They served as judges for the people at all times. The difficult cases they brought to Moses, but the simple ones they decided themselves.

²⁷Then Moses sent his father-in-law on his way, and Jethro returned to his own country.

At Mount Sinai

19 In the third month after the Israelites left Egypt—on the very day—they came to the Desert of Sinai. ²After they set out from Rephidim, they entered the Desert of Sinai, and Israel camped there in the desert in front of the mountain.

³Then Moses went up to God, and the LORD called to him from the mountain and said, "This is what you are to say to the house of Jacob and what you are to tell the people of Israel: ⁴'You yourselves have seen what I did to Egypt, and how I carried you on eagles' wings and brought you to myself. ⁵Now if you obey me fully and keep my covenant^D, then out of all nations you will be my treasured possession. Although the whole earth is mine, ⁶you^a will be for me a kingdom of priests^D and a holy nation.' These are the words you are to speak to the Israelites."

⁷So Moses went back and summoned the elders of the people and set before them all the words the LORD had commanded him to speak. ⁸The people all responded together, "We will do everything the LORD has said." So Moses brought their answer back to the LORD.

⁹The LORD said to Moses, "I am going to come to you in a dense cloud, so that the people will hear me speaking with you and will always put their trust in you." Then Moses told the LORD what the people had said.

¹⁰And the LORD said to Moses, "Go to the people and consecrate^D them today and tomorrow. Have them wash their clothes ¹¹and be ready by the third day, because on that day the LORD will come down on Mount Sinai in the sight of all the people. ¹²Put limits for the people around the mountain and tell them, 'Be careful that you do not go up the mountain or touch the foot of it. Whoever touches the mountain shall surely be put to death^D. ¹³He shall surely be stoned or shot with arrows; not a hand is to be laid on him. Whether man or animal, he shall not be permitted to live.' Only when the ram's horn sounds a long blast may they go up to the mountain."

¹⁴After Moses had gone down the mountain to the people, he consecrated them, and they washed their clothes. ¹⁵Then he said to the people, "Prepare yourselves for the third day. Abstain from sexual relations."

¹⁶On the morning of the third day there was thunder and lightning, with a thick cloud over the mountain, and a very loud trumpet blast. Everyone in the camp trembled. ¹⁷Then Moses led the people out of the camp to meet with God, and they stood at the foot of the mountain. ¹⁸Mount Sinai was covered with smoke, because the LORD descended on it in fire. The smoke billowed up from

a5,6 Or *possession, for the whole earth is mine.* 6You

And God so commands (18:23)

Moses' father-in-law wanted to make sure that his advice was confirmed by God.

A kingdom of priests (19:6)

Typically, tribal chiefs were social and religious leaders, serving as mediators between people and God. See, for example, *What kind of priest was this?* (2:16). Here, however, the whole nation was called to mediate God's grace to the world.

SCRIPTURE LINK (19:11) *Mount Sinai*

This place is also known as Mount Horeb, where God earlier spoke to Moses through a burning bush (3:1,12). See *The Exodus* on page 94.

Why did God not want anyone on the mountain? (19:12–13)

The boundaries around the mountain clearly symbolized the vast separation between the holy God and unclean people. Also, the thunder and lightning made the mountain a dangerous place to be.

How is someone *consecrated?* (19:14,22)

Being *consecrated* means being *set apart for God's use.* It involved washing both oneself and one's clothing, symbolizing the need for purity before God. Exodus 29 describes the elaborate ritual for purifying priests to stand before God.

Why no sex for three days? (19:15)

The restriction was designed to allow the Israelites to focus all of their attention and energy on their meeting with God. A similar restriction was placed on soldiers going into battle (1 Samuel 21:4–5; 2 Samuel 11:11). Old Testament law emphasized purity and uncleanness resulting from the discharge of bodily fluids. Also see *Why would God design natural functions to cause uncleanness?* (Lev. 15:16–24).

it like smoke from a furnace, the whole mountain^a trembled violently, **19**and the sound of the trumpet grew louder and louder. Then Moses spoke and the voice of God answered him.^{b}

20The LORD descended to the top of Mount Sinai and called Moses to the top of the mountain. So Moses went up **21**and the LORD said to him, "Go down and warn the people so they do not force their way through to see the LORD and many of them perish. **22**Even the priests^D, who approach the LORD, must consecrate^D themselves, or the LORD will break out against them."

23Moses said to the LORD, "The people cannot come up Mount Sinai, because you yourself warned us, 'Put limits around the mountain and set it apart as holy.'"

24The LORD replied, "Go down and bring Aaron up with you. But the priests and the people must not force their way through to come up to the LORD, or he will break out against them."

25So Moses went down to the people and told them.

The Ten Commandments

20 And God spoke all these words:

2"I am the LORD your God, who brought you out of Egypt, out of the land of slavery.

3"You shall have no other gods before^c me.

4"You shall not make for yourself an idol^D in the form of anything in heaven above or on the earth beneath or in the waters below. **5**You shall not bow down to them or worship them; for I, the LORD your God, am a jealous God, punishing the children for the sin of the fathers to the third and fourth generation of those who hate me, **6**but showing love to a thousand ⌞generations⌟ of those who love me and keep my commandments.

7"You shall not misuse the name of the LORD your God, for the LORD will not hold anyone guiltless who misuses his name.

8"Remember the Sabbath^D day by keeping it holy. **9**Six days you shall labor and do all your work, **10**but the seventh day is a Sabbath to the LORD your God. On it you shall not do any work, neither you, nor your son or daughter, nor your manservant or maidservant, nor your animals, nor the alien^D within your gates. **11**For in six days the LORD made the heavens and the earth, the sea, and all that is in them, but he rested on the seventh day. Therefore the LORD blessed the Sabbath day and made it holy.

12"Honor your father and your mother, so that you may live long in the land the LORD your God is giving you.

13"You shall not murder.

14"You shall not commit adultery.

15"You shall not steal.

16"You shall not give false testimony against your neighbor.

Why were Moses and Aaron permitted to approach the Lord? (19:24)

Because God had called them to the special role of bringing God's message to the people—mediators of the covenant. Still, they must have felt they were risking their lives to dare to approach this awesome God. *The sight was so terrifying that Moses said, "I am trembling with fear"* (Heb. 12:21).

Do all these laws apply to Christians? (20:1–17)

In Jesus, the law is both fulfilled and abolished. See *How is the Law fulfilled?* (Matt. 5:17–18); *Did the good news replace the Law and Prophets?* (Luke 16:16–17) and *Did Jesus abolish the Old Testament Law or fulfill it?* (Eph. 2:15). Thus Christians no longer live under the ceremonial and civil laws that are listed starting in Exodus 21. But the Ten Commandments are different—they reveal God's character, what he values and his expectations for human relationships. The Ten Commandments are timeless truths.

Why punish children for their ancestors' sins? (20:4–5)

Sin has pervasive consequences—children are affected by alcoholic parents, for instance, and many victims of abuse become abusers themselves. The Israelites, with their strong solidarity, knew that good and evil affected whole families, not just individuals. They recognized the ripple effect of sin throughout the generations. Also see article: *Why does God allow innocent children to suffer?* (Lam. 2:11–12).

How can God's name be misused? (20:7)

By swearing oaths in a flippant or disrespectful way. Other ways include profanity and "name-dropping" God's name for personal benefit or to manipulate others. Later, Jews interpreted this command to mean not speaking God's name at all. If while reading Scripture they encountered God's name *Yahweh* (LORD), they substituted the word *Adonai* (Lord).

Should Christians observe the Sabbath? (20:8–11)

See *As Lord of the Sabbath, did Jesus change the rules?* (Luke 6:2–5).

---

^{a}18 Most Hebrew manuscripts; a few Hebrew manuscripts and Septuagint *all the people* ^{b}19 Or *and God answered him with thunder* ^{c}3 Or *besides*

17"You shall not covet your neighbor's house. You shall not covet your neighbor's wife, or his manservant or maidservant, his ox or donkey, or anything that belongs to your neighbor."

18When the people saw the thunder and lightning and heard the trumpet and saw the mountain in smoke, they trembled with fear. They stayed at a distance **19**and said to Moses, "Speak to us yourself and we will listen. But do not have God speak to us or we will die."

20Moses said to the people, "Do not be afraid. God has come to test you, so that the fear of God will be with you to keep you from sinning."

21The people remained at a distance, while Moses approached the thick darkness where God was.

Idols and Altars

22Then the LORD said to Moses, "Tell the Israelites this: 'You have seen for yourselves that I have spoken to you from heaven: **23**Do not make any gods to be alongside me; do not make for yourselves gods of silver or gods of gold.

24" 'Make an altar of earth for me and sacrifice[D] on it your burnt offerings[D] and fellowship offerings[D],[a] your sheep and goats and your cattle. Wherever I cause my name to be honored, I will come to you and bless you. **25**If you make an altar of stones for me, do not build it with dressed stones, for you will defile it if you use a tool on it. **26**And do not go up to my altar on steps, lest your nakedness be exposed on it.'

---

[a]*24* Traditionally *peace offerings*

SCRIPTURE LINK (20:1–17)
A parallel account of the Ten Commandments is found in Deut. 5:6–21.

Wherever I cause my name to be honored (20:24)
God-approved places of worship. God would select only certain sites for Israel to worship (Deut. 12:5; 16:6), unlike the people of Canaan, who would build countless private shrines for Baal, Asherah and other pagan gods. When Israel erected private altars, idol worship usually followed.

Why would tools defile an altar? (20:25)
See *Why were uncut stones needed for the altar?* (Joshua 8:31).

How would *nakedness be exposed* on altar steps? (20:26)
Pagan religions of that day often featured altars with steps. By not allowing such architecture, Israel would be less likely to include paganism in their worship. This phrase may refer to the ritual prostitution that occurred at pagan altars. Also see *Why wear bells and linen underwear?* (28:35) and *Why a lasting ordinance about linen undergarments?* (28:42–43).

Why did God require sacrifices? (20:24)

Many people have wondered how God is honored by an animal being killed. The key to the sacrificial system is not to be found in the animals—or in the gifts of grain, oil or wine—that were used in various Old Testament sacrifices.

Rather, the key concept is this: Holiness requires that sin must not be ignored. Guilt must be dealt with. Someone must pay. Sacrifices were God's way of teaching this spiritual truth to his people.

A second key concept: The innocent can substitute for the guilty. God allows a sin payment on behalf of someone else. In the Old Testament, these payments were animal or food sacrifices. When offered in faith, these pointed to the ultimate sacrifice: Christ's death for the sins of the world (Heb. 10:1–10).

Sacrifices also involved offering something valuable as a token of gratitude to God, just as people today give money to recognize that God is the source of all we have. The people in Old Testament days offered God the best of their flocks and fields to show thanks for his provision.

Finally, the sacrificial system also performed an important community function. Just as the New Testament church celebrated the Lord's Supper (honoring Christ's sacrifice) as part of a *love feast* (Jude 1:12), the Old Testament sacrifices were often performed as part of community meals.

Far from being a wasteful destruction of animals, the food offered as a sacrifice was generally consumed, either by the priests or by the entire worshiping community. Also see articles: *Why was all this blood needed for worship?* (29:11–21) and *Why kill animals to worship God?* (Lev. 1:1).

Why did some Hebrews own *Hebrews*? (21:2)

Though they had all been slaves in Egypt and were now set free, Moses permitted a sort of voluntary slavery to continue. Individuals could sell their services for up to six years to repay debts or make restitution. Hebrew slaves were regarded more as hired hands. The seventh year, their debts were canceled, and they received their freedom.

Why force a servant to choose between freedom and family? (21:4–6)

This would make more sense to us if we could see through the lens of their culture. Their customs required a man to "purchase" a wife by paying a bride-price to her father. If a slave owner purchased a bride for his servant, however, she technically belonged to the one who paid the price. This policy seems harsh, but it was softened by other provisions (see 21:8,11,26–27; Lev. 25).

Why mark a lifelong servant with a pierced ear? (21:6)

Some think this custom carried symbolic meaning: the slave was attached physically to the doorpost of the owner's house to symbolize his emotional attachment there. Pierced ears may also have had a ring or something that identified the one to whom he belonged.

Why would a father sell his daughter as a servant? (21:7–11)

Though this practice clashes with our view of human rights, in those days it provided a daughter protection from the mistreatment common in pagan cultures. A marriage contract ensured that a son-in-law had the means and the will to care for his new wife. Details in the contract guaranteed her food, clothing, conjugal rights and—in case of ill-treatment or neglect—freedom. Such protection was especially important for daughters who were to be concubines since they could be overshadowed by the primary wife.

Why does killing require more killing? (21:12–17)

See *Why does killing require more killing?* (Gen. 9:6). Also see article: *Why kill a murderer?* (Deut. 19:13). Some believe Jesus later changed the way the criminal code was to be used (see Matt. 5:21–22,38–39). Also see *Why could only the sinless cast the first stone?* (John 8:7).

Why execute someone for cursing his parents? (21:17)

A curse was considered more than idle words: it aimed harm and hostility toward a person, even attacking the image of God within that person. As a result, cursing one's parents, along with striking them, was tantamount to murder (vv. 12–15) and was punished accordingly. For more on curses see *Did such blessings and curses work?* (Num. 23:11) and *Do curses have real power?* (Judges 9:57).

The slave is his property (21:20–21)

See article: *Why doesn't the Bible condemn slavery?* (1 Peter 2:18–21).

21 "These are the laws you are to set before them:

Hebrew Servants

2"If you buy a HebrewᴰD servant, he is to serve you for six years. But in the seventh year, he shall go free, without paying anything. **3**If he comes alone, he is to go free alone; but if he has a wife when he comes, she is to go with him. **4**If his master gives him a wife and she bears him sons or daughters, the woman and her children shall belong to her master, and only the man shall go free.

5"But if the servant declares, 'I love my master and my wife and children and do not want to go free,' **6**then his master must take him before the judges.*a* He shall take him to the door or the doorpost and pierce his ear with an awl. Then he will be his servant for life.

7"If a man sells his daughter as a servant, she is not to go free as menservants do. **8**If she does not please the master who has selected her for himself,*b* he must let her be redeemedᴰD. He has no right to sell her to foreigners, because he has broken faith with her. **9**If he selects her for his son, he must grant her the rights of a daughter. **10**If he marries another woman, he must not deprive the first one of her food, clothing and marital rights. **11**If he does not provide her with these three things, she is to go free, without any payment of money.

Personal Injuries

12"Anyone who strikes a man and kills him shall surely be put to deathᴰD. **13**However, if he does not do it intentionally, but God lets it happen, he is to flee to a place I will designate. **14**But if a man schemes and kills another man deliberately, take him away from my altar and put him to death.

15"Anyone who attacks*c* his father or his mother must be put to death.

16"Anyone who kidnaps another and either sells him or still has him when he is caught must be put to death.

17"Anyone who curses his father or mother must be put to death.

18"If men quarrel and one hits the other with a stone or with his fist*d* and he does not die but is confined to bed, **19**the one who struck the blow will not be held responsible if the other gets up and walks around outside with his staff; however, he must pay the injured man for the loss of his time and see that he is completely healed.

20"If a man beats his male or female slave with a rod and the slave dies as a direct result, he must be punished, **21**but he is not to be punished if the slave gets up after a day or two, since the slave is his property.

22"If men who are fighting hit a pregnant woman and she gives birth prematurely*e* but there is no serious injury, the offender must be fined whatever the woman's husband demands and the court allows. **23**But if there is serious injury, you are to take life for life, **24**eye for eye, tooth for tooth, hand for hand, foot for foot, **25**burn for burn, wound for wound, bruise for bruise.

26"If a man hits a manservant or maidservant in the eye and destroys it, he must let the servant go free to compensate for the eye. **27**And if he knocks out the tooth of a

---

*a*6 Or *before God*   *b*8 Or *master so that he does not choose her*
*c*15 Or *kills*   *d*18 Or *with a tool*   *e*22 Or *she has a miscarriage*

manservant or maidservant, he must let the servant go free to compensate for the tooth.

28"If a bull gores a man or a woman to death[D], the bull must be stoned to death, and its meat must not be eaten. But the owner of the bull will not be held responsible. **29**If, however, the bull has had the habit of goring and the owner has been warned but has not kept it penned up and it kills a man or woman, the bull must be stoned and the owner also must be put to death. **30**However, if payment is demanded of him, he may redeem[D] his life by paying whatever is demanded. **31**This law also applies if the bull gores a son or daughter. **32**If the bull gores a male or female slave, the owner must pay thirty shekels[Da] of silver to the master of the slave, and the bull must be stoned.

33"If a man uncovers a pit or digs one and fails to cover it and an ox or a donkey falls into it, **34**the owner of the pit must pay for the loss; he must pay its owner, and the dead animal will be his.

35"If a man's bull injures the bull of another and it dies, they are to sell the live one and divide both the money and the dead animal equally. **36**However, if it was known that the bull had the habit of goring, yet the owner did not keep it penned up, the owner must pay, animal for animal, and the dead animal will be his.

Protection of Property

22 "If a man steals an ox or a sheep and slaughters it or sells it, he must pay back five head of cattle for the ox and four sheep for the sheep.

2"If a thief is caught breaking in and is struck so that he dies, the defender is not guilty of bloodshed; **3**but if it happens[b] after sunrise, he is guilty of bloodshed.

"A thief must certainly make restitution, but if he has nothing, he must be sold to pay for his theft.

4"If the stolen animal is found alive in his possession—whether ox or donkey or sheep—he must pay back double.

5"If a man grazes his livestock in a field or vineyard and lets them stray and they graze in another man's field, he must make restitution from the best of his own field or vineyard.

6"If a fire breaks out and spreads into thornbushes so that it burns shocks of grain or standing grain or the whole field, the one who started the fire must make restitution.

7"If a man gives his neighbor silver or goods for safekeeping and they are stolen from the neighbor's house, the thief, if he is caught, must pay back double. **8**But if the thief is not found, the owner of the house must appear before the judges[c] to determine whether he has laid his hands on the other man's property. **9**In all cases of illegal possession of an ox, a donkey, a sheep, a garment, or any other lost property about which somebody says, 'This is mine,' both parties are to bring their cases before the judges. The one whom the judges declare[d] guilty must pay back double to his neighbor.

10"If a man gives a donkey, an ox, a sheep or any other animal to his neighbor for safekeeping and it dies or is injured or is taken away while no one is looking, **11**the issue between them will be settled by the taking of an oath

Why should a premature birth require a penalty? (21:22–23)
Because harm was done. *Premature birth* could mean either a living baby or a stillborn (see NIV text note)—possibly explaining the range of penalties. Many think the penalties were for injury to the fetus, not the mother. One ancient view was that *no serious injury* meant *no fully-formed fetus.* If so, injury to an undeveloped fetus required a fine, but injury to a fully-formed fetus required retribution in line with the damage done.

Should we demand eye for eye, tooth for tooth? (21:23–25)
This balanced approach to retribution was a tremendous advance over other legal systems of the ancient Middle East. Even today, the principle could prove valid in judicial cases: "bent fender for bent fender"—no more and no less—would put a cap on liability damages, restraining malicious revenge and greed. Of course, Jesus' law of love (Matt. 5:38–39) exceeds these basic Old Testament regulations.

Why couldn't the meat of the bull be eaten? (21:28)
For perhaps two reasons: (1) To eat meat made available only because someone had died would detract from the terrible loss of human life; nothing should be gained by someone's death. (2) A bull that was stoned to death would not have had its blood drained in the proper way and would therefore be ceremonially unclean and unfit to eat.

Why isn't guilt by day also guilt by night? (22:3)
Killing a thief was justified as self-defense only when the thief was armed and dangerous. In the dark a homeowner could not tell if an intruder was armed. In such situations the rule was, protect your family and ask questions later. Killing an unarmed thief was inexcusable in daylight, however. The homeowner could see there was no life-threatening danger from an unarmed intruder.

---

a32 That is, about 12 ounces (about 0.3 kilogram)   b3 Or if he strikes him   c8 Or before God; also in verse 9   d9 Or whom God declares

before the LORD that the neighbor did not lay hands on the other person's property. The owner is to accept this, and no restitution is required. [12]But if the animal was stolen from the neighbor, he must make restitution to the owner. [13]If it was torn to pieces by a wild animal, he shall bring in the remains as evidence and he will not be required to pay for the torn animal.

[14]"If a man borrows an animal from his neighbor and it is injured or dies while the owner is not present, he must make restitution. [15]But if the owner is with the animal, the borrower will not have to pay. If the animal was hired, the money paid for the hire covers the loss.

Social Responsibility

[16]"If a man seduces a virgin who is not pledged to be married and sleeps with her, he must pay the bride-price, and she shall be his wife. [17]If her father absolutely refuses to give her to him, he must still pay the bride-price for virgins.

[18]"Do not allow a sorceress to live.

[19]"Anyone who has sexual relations with an animal must be put to death.[D]

[20]"Whoever sacrifices[D] to any god other than the LORD must be destroyed.[a]

[21]"Do not mistreat an alien[D] or oppress him, for you were aliens in Egypt.

[22]"Do not take advantage of a widow or an orphan. [23]If you do and they cry out to me, I will certainly hear their cry. [24]My anger will be aroused, and I will kill you with the sword; your wives will become widows and your children fatherless.

[25]"If you lend money to one of my people among you who is needy, do not be like a moneylender; charge him no interest.[b] [26]If you take your neighbor's cloak as a pledge, return it to him by sunset, [27]because his cloak is the only covering he has for his body. What else will he sleep in? When he cries out to me, I will hear, for I am compassionate.

[28]"Do not blaspheme[D] God[c] or curse the ruler of your people.

[29]"Do not hold back offerings from your granaries or your vats.[d]

"You must give me the firstborn[D] of your sons. [30]Do the same with your cattle and your sheep. Let them stay with their mothers for seven days, but give them to me on the eighth day.

[31]"You are to be my holy people. So do not eat the meat of an animal torn by wild beasts; throw it to the dogs.

Laws of Justice and Mercy

23 "Do not spread false reports. Do not help a wicked man by being a malicious witness.

[2]"Do not follow the crowd in doing wrong. When you give testimony in a lawsuit, do not pervert justice by siding with the crowd, [3]and do not show favoritism to a poor man in his lawsuit.

[4]"If you come across your enemy's ox or donkey wandering off, be sure to take it back to him. [5]If you see the donkey of someone who hates you fallen down under its

Why pay a bride-price for a seduction? (22:16–17)

Hebrew men contracted their marriages during this era. See **Why would a father sell his daughter as a servant?** (21:7–11). However, a non-virgin was considered "damaged." Her father could no longer get full price for her marriage. The man who seduced her had, in effect, robbed her father. The man would have to pay restitution and keep the woman for his wife. If, however, the father judged the man to be incapable of providing for his daughter, he was entitled to keep the bride-price and his daughter.

Sorceress (22:18)

A woman with evil supernatural power who practiced various occultic activities such as seances, divination and witchcraft. Sorcery was a crime against God because it sought the powers of spirits other than God. Also see Deut. 18:8–14; 1 Samuel 28.

Why didn't God tolerate other lifestyles? (22:18–20)

Idolatry, bestiality and sorcery all were symptoms of a deeper problem: rebellion against God. Bestiality perverted God's natural order for sex and often embraced pagan animal cults or fertility worship—rejecting true worship. Sorcery replaced trust in the Lord with a trust in spirits and incantations. As a direct attack against the Lord's ways, these were punishable by death.

Aliens (22:21)

Foreigners who lived in Israel as an underprivileged class, much as the Israelites had done in Egypt. God called for common decency and justice for aliens in general (23:9) but called for the destruction of foreigners who worshiped idols (v. 20; Deut. 7:1–6).

What's wrong with charging interest? (22:25)

This command focused more on helping the poor than defining business ethics. Making money on our investments is not prohibited (see Matt. 25:17). But we should treat those in need with compassion rather than see them as an opportunity to make a quick profit. Christ urged his followers to make interest-free loans to the poor, even viewing the loans as outright gifts (see Luke 6:34–35).

Give me the firstborn of your sons (22:29)

See **How did they consecrate the firstborn males?** (13:1–2).

---

[a]20 The Hebrew term refers to the irrevocable giving over of things or persons to the LORD, often by totally destroying them.   [b]25 Or *excessive interest*   [c]28 Or *Do not revile the judges*   [d]29 The meaning of the Hebrew for this phrase is uncertain.

load, do not leave it there; be sure you help him with it.

⁶"Do not deny justice to your poor people in their lawsuits. ⁷Have nothing to do with a false charge and do not put an innocent or honest person to death D, for I will not acquit the guilty.

⁸"Do not accept a bribe, for a bribe blinds those who see and twists the words of the righteous D.

⁹"Do not oppress an alien D; you yourselves know how it feels to be aliens, because you were aliens in Egypt.

Sabbath Laws

¹⁰"For six years you are to sow your fields and harvest the crops, ¹¹but during the seventh year let the land lie unplowed and unused. Then the poor among your people may get food from it, and the wild animals may eat what they leave. Do the same with your vineyard and your olive grove.

¹²"Six days do your work, but on the seventh day do not work, so that your ox and your donkey may rest and the slave born in your household, and the alien as well, may be refreshed.

¹³"Be careful to do everything I have said to you. Do not invoke the names of other gods; do not let them be heard on your lips.

The Three Annual Festivals

¹⁴"Three times a year you are to celebrate a festival to me.

¹⁵"Celebrate the Feast of Unleavened Bread; for seven days eat bread made without yeast D, as I commanded you. Do this at the appointed time in the month of Abib, for in that month you came out of Egypt.

"No one is to appear before me empty-handed.

¹⁶"Celebrate the Feast of Harvest with the firstfruits D of the crops you sow in your field.

"Celebrate the Feast of Ingathering at the end of the year, when you gather in your crops from the field.

¹⁷"Three times a year all the men are to appear before the Sovereign LORD.

¹⁸"Do not offer the blood of a sacrifice D to me along with anything containing yeast.

"The fat of my festival offerings must not be kept until morning.

¹⁹"Bring the best of the firstfruits of your soil to the house of the LORD your God.

"Do not cook a young goat in its mother's milk.

God's Angel to Prepare the Way

²⁰"See, I am sending an angel ahead of you to guard you along the way and to bring you to the place I have prepared. ²¹Pay attention to him and listen to what he says. Do not rebel against him; he will not forgive your rebellion, since my Name is in him. ²²If you listen carefully to what he says and do all that I say, I will be an enemy to your enemies and will oppose those who oppose you. ²³My angel will go ahead of you and bring you into the land of the Amorites, Hittites, Perizzites, Canaanites, Hivites and Jebusites, and I will wipe them out. ²⁴Do not bow down before their gods or worship them or follow their practices. You must demolish them and break their sacred stones D to pieces. ²⁵Worship the LORD your God, and his blessing will be on your food and water. I will take away sickness from among you, ²⁶and none will miscarry or be barren in your land. I will give you a full life span.

What did people do for food during the seventh year? (23:10)

See *How could they eat what they weren't permitted to harvest?* (Lev. 25:5–7).

Can't we come to God *empty-handed?* (23:15)

We should come to God expressing our needs. But the focus here is on what God has already done. As an expression of gratitude to God, in an agricultural economy, people could easily worship with something in hand—both the earliest and the final crops of the harvest (v. 16). We can express our worship of God better with offerings than with empty hands.

Who'd want to cook a goat in its mother's milk? (23:19)

Cooking a young goat in its mother's milk was likely linked, not to dietary customs, but to pagan religious practices from the neighboring Canaanites. Details are lacking, but some evidence suggests milk was thought to have magical powers. Pagans would use it in fertility rites, sprinkling it on crops and vineyards to make them more productive. God wanted to distance his people from heathen rituals.

What kind of angel did God send? (23:20–23)

Angel also meant *messenger,* human or divine. Sometimes God spoke through a messenger like Moses or Joshua; sometimes he spoke directly to the people (see Judges 2:1–4). Some think this angel was an Old Testament appearance of Christ. Others think this refers to the mystical cloud and fire which led Israel through the desert (see 13:21). Still others think it may have meant the ark, which bore the name of the Lord.

Is worshiping the Lord a guarantee for health and full life? (23:25–26)

God's promises are often experienced as general principles by those who obey God. God's law, for example, provided for better food distribution and hygiene than what was found in plague-riddled Egypt. Respect for elders and stable families made for a relatively stress-free environment, contributing to childbearing and long life. Still, this was not a blanket guarantee. Sometimes the righteous experience disappointments and tragedies.

Did God really send hornets? (23:28)

Though it's possible this literally meant a plague of hornets, similar to the plagues used earlier by God, it's more likely a figurative expression, perhaps describing either Egyptian troops or some sort of supernatural intervention. See *Did God literally send hornets?* (Joshua 24:12). Whatever the hornets were, they routed Israel's enemies who were pictured as being stung until they panicked and ran.

Wouldn't deserted land be easier to possess than enemy-held territory? (23:29–30)

Israel would have needed a much larger standing army to control the whole land. In unoccupied territory, wild beasts would multiply and run rampant, creating further problems for settlers (see, for example, the problems wild animals caused in 2 Kings 17:25–26). However, gradual inroads into enemy-occupied territory gave time and opportunity to train the next generation of soldiers. See *How could a quick victory cause wild animals to multiply?* (Deut. 7:22).

Nadab and Abihu (24:1,9)

Aaron's two oldest sons, who were later ordained as priests (28:1). They are best known for offering *unauthorized fire before the Lord* and dying as a consequence for their sin (Lev. 10:1–2).

What became of the scroll Moses wrote? (24:4)

See *What did Moses write on the scroll?* (17:14).

Why confirm the covenant in blood? (24:6,8)

Blood could mean different things: on the altar it may have symbolized God's forgiveness (see Lev. 17:11); on the people it may have symbolized death to those who broke the covenant (see Gen. 15). Blood rituals have long solemnized covenants in many cultures, but pagan traditions corrupted the practice after the first animals died as a result of human sin (Gen. 3:21). Blood ultimately points to Christ's death which initiated the new covenant (see Matt. 26:28). See *How could blood atone for sin?* (Lev. 17:11).

The Book of the Covenant (24:7)

Moses wrote what God told him so the people could ratify the actual terms of the agreement. The chapters immediately preceding (20:22—23:33) make up the official *Book*. Perhaps it was viewed as further defining the Ten Commandments (20:1–17). Later, the book of Deuteronomy would provide more comments on the covenant.

Was it possible to see God and live? (24:9–11)

This description of their encounter with the living God was in general, not precise, terms. Since no one could see God's full glory and live, they must have gotten only a partial glimpse. See *How could Moses speak to the Lord face to face?* (33:11).

[27]"I will send my terror ahead of you and throw into confusion every nation you encounter. I will make all your enemies turn their backs and run. [28]I will send the hornet ahead of you to drive the Hivites, Canaanites and Hittites out of your way. [29]But I will not drive them out in a single year, because the land would become desolate and the wild animals too numerous for you. [30]Little by little I will drive them out before you, until you have increased enough to take possession of the land.

[31]"I will establish your borders from the Red Sea[a] to the Sea of the Philistines,[b] and from the desert to the River.[c] I will hand over to you the people who live in the land and you will drive them out before you. [32]Do not make a covenant[D] with them or with their gods. [33]Do not let them live in your land, or they will cause you to sin against me, because the worship of their gods will certainly be a snare to you."

The Covenant Confirmed

24 Then he said to Moses, "Come up to the Lord, you and Aaron, Nadab and Abihu, and seventy of the elders of Israel. You are to worship at a distance, [2]but Moses alone is to approach the Lord; the others must not come near. And the people may not come up with him."

[3]When Moses went and told the people all the Lord's words and laws, they responded with one voice, "Everything the Lord has said we will do." [4]Moses then wrote down everything the Lord had said.

He got up early the next morning and built an altar at the foot of the mountain and set up twelve stone pillars representing the twelve tribes of Israel. [5]Then he sent young Israelite men, and they offered burnt offerings[D] and sacrificed young bulls as fellowship offerings[Dd] to the Lord. [6]Moses took half of the blood and put it in bowls, and the other half he sprinkled on the altar. [7]Then he took the Book of the Covenant and read it to the people. They responded, "We will do everything the Lord has said; we will obey."

[8]Moses then took the blood, sprinkled it on the people and said, "This is the blood of the covenant that the Lord has made with you in accordance with all these words."

[9]Moses and Aaron, Nadab and Abihu, and the seventy elders of Israel went up [10]and saw the God of Israel. Under his feet was something like a pavement made of sapphire,[e] clear as the sky itself. [11]But God did not raise his hand against these leaders of the Israelites; they saw God, and they ate and drank.

[12]The Lord said to Moses, "Come up to me on the mountain and stay here, and I will give you the tablets of stone, with the law and commands I have written for their instruction."

[13]Then Moses set out with Joshua his aide, and Moses went up on the mountain of God. [14]He said to the elders, "Wait here for us until we come back to you. Aaron and Hur are with you, and anyone involved in a dispute can go to them."

[15]When Moses went up on the mountain, the cloud covered it, [16]and the glory[D] of the Lord settled on Mount Sinai. For six days the cloud covered the mountain, and

---

[a]31 Hebrew *Yam Suph*; that is, Sea of Reeds   [b]31 That is, the Mediterranean   [c]31 That is, the Euphrates   [d]5 Traditionally *peace offerings*   [e]10 Or *lapis lazuli*

on the seventh day the LORD called to Moses from within the cloud. **17**To the Israelites the glory^D of the LORD looked like a consuming fire on top of the mountain. **18**Then Moses entered the cloud as he went on up the mountain. And he stayed on the mountain forty days and forty nights.

Offerings for the Tabernacle

25 The LORD said to Moses, **2**"Tell the Israelites to bring me an offering. You are to receive the offering for me from each man whose heart prompts him to give. **3**These are the offerings you are to receive from them: gold, silver and bronze; **4**blue, purple^D and scarlet yarn and fine linen; goat hair; **5**ram skins dyed red and hides of sea cows^{D a}; acacia^D wood; **6**olive oil for the light; spices for the anointing^D oil and for the fragrant incense^D; **7**and onyx stones and other gems to be mounted on the ephod^D and breastpiece^D.

8"Then have them make a sanctuary for me, and I will dwell among them. **9**Make this tabernacle^D and all its furnishings exactly like the pattern I will show you.

The Ark

10"Have them make a chest of acacia wood—two and a half cubits^D long, a cubit and a half wide, and a cubit and a half high.*b* **11**Overlay it with pure gold, both inside and out, and make a gold molding around it. **12**Cast four gold rings for it and fasten them to its four feet, with two rings on one side and two rings on the other. **13**Then make poles of acacia wood and overlay them with gold. **14**Insert the poles into the rings on the sides of the chest to carry it. **15**The poles are to remain in the rings of this ark; they are not to be removed. **16**Then put in the ark the Testimony, which I will give you.

17"Make an atonement^D cover*c* of pure gold—two and a half cubits long and a cubit and a half wide.*d* **18**And make two cherubim^D out of hammered gold at the ends of the cover. **19**Make one cherub on one end and the second cherub on the other; make the cherubim of one piece with the cover, at the two ends. **20**The cherubim are to have their wings spread upward, overshadowing the cover with them. The cherubim are to face each other, looking toward the cover. **21**Place the cover on top of the ark and put in the ark the Testimony, which I will give you. **22**There, above the cover between the two cherubim that are over the ark of the Testimony, I will meet with you and give you all my commands for the Israelites.

The Table

23"Make a table of acacia wood—two cubits long, a cubit wide and a cubit and a half high.*e* **24**Overlay it with pure gold and make a gold molding around it. **25**Also make around it a rim a handbreadth*f* wide and put a gold molding on the rim. **26**Make four gold rings for the table and fasten them to the four corners, where the four legs are. **27**The rings are to be close to the rim to hold the poles

Where did they find a *sea cow* in the desert? (25:5)

This large, aquatic mammal (8 to 15 feet long and up to 1,500 pounds) was related to the manatee and could be found in the Red Sea. Arabs still use leather from its thin but tough underskin to make "name brand" sandals. Bedouins use its coarse upper skin for tent coverings. That such skins are scarce in the desert is significant: nothing but the finest leathers were suitable for God's tabernacle. See *Sea cows* (Num. 4:6).

Why was the tabernacle's design so important? (25:9)

See article: *What was so critical about the pattern?* (25:40).

Acacia wood (25:10)

See *What's so special about acacia wood?* (26:15).

What was the purpose of the ark? (25:10–22)

It served as a portable sanctuary, symbolizing the Lord's presence in the form of a footstool to God's throne or perhaps a miniature temple. It also contained reminders of God's work among them: the stone tablets of the law, a pot of manna and Aaron's staff that budded. It represented God's forgiveness, particularly on the Day of Atonement, when the high priest sprinkled blood on its lid, called the atonement cover (v. 17).

Why call a *chest* an *ark*? (25:14–16)

Both words translate the same Hebrew word for box or coffin (see Gen. 50:26). It is variously referred to as *the ark, ark of the covenant, ark of the LORD, ark of God* and *ark of the Testimony*. The English word *ark*, though meaning simply a box or a box-like boat, has mostly been limited to describe (1) this chest, (2) Noah's boat, (3) the small papyrus boat that held the baby Moses and (4) the cabinet in the synagogue that holds the Torah or Law. Also see *Ark* (Gen. 6:14).

Cherubim (25:18)

The plural of *cherub,* a winged, angelic being who exists primarily to glorify God. Ezekiel describes cherubim (Ezek. 10:12–14), but there are likely several types. Images of cherubim adorned the tabernacle furnishings as symbols of worship to God, not as idols to worship.

---

a5 That is, dugongs   *b10* That is, about 3 3/4 feet (about 1.1 meters) long and 2 1/4 feet (about 0.7 meter) wide and high   *c17* Traditionally *a mercy seat*   *d17* That is, about 3 3/4 feet (about 1.1 meters) long and 2 1/4 feet (about 0.7 meter) wide   *e23* That is, about 3 feet (about 0.9 meter) long and 1 1/2 feet (about 0.5 meter) wide and 2 1/4 feet (about 0.7 meter) high   *f25* That is, about 3 inches (about 8 centimeters)

used in carrying the table. **28**Make the poles of acacia[D] wood, overlay them with gold and carry the table with them. **29**And make its plates and dishes of pure gold, as well as its pitchers and bowls for the pouring out of offerings. **30**Put the bread of the Presence on this table to be before me at all times.

The Lampstand

31"Make a lampstand of pure gold and hammer it out, base and shaft; its flowerlike cups, buds and blossoms shall be of one piece with it. **32**Six branches are to extend from the sides of the lampstand—three on one side and three on the other. **33**Three cups shaped like almond flowers with buds and blossoms are to be on one branch, three on the next branch, and the same for all six branches extending from the lampstand. **34**And on the lampstand there are to be four cups shaped like almond flowers with buds and blossoms. **35**One bud shall be under the first pair of branches extending from the lampstand, a second bud under the second pair, and a third bud under the third pair—six branches in all. **36**The buds and branches shall all be of one piece with the lampstand, hammered out of pure gold.

37"Then make its seven lamps and set them up on it so that they light the space in front of it. **38**Its wick trimmers and trays are to be of pure gold. **39**A talent[a] of pure gold

a39 That is, about 75 pounds (about 34 kilograms)

The bread of the Presence (25:30)

Literally, *the bread of his face.* This was an offering of 12 loaves of bread, symbolizing the 12 tribes of Israel and their devotion to God, kept continually in the Holy Place, in the presence of the Lord. Each week fresh bread was put before the Lord, and the priests were permitted to eat the old bread.

Is this lampstand the same as the Jewish menorah? (25:31–40)

This lampstand may have been a forerunner to the menorah. Its seven lamps (v. 37) and six branches (v. 35) suggest similarities. One difference, however, is that this lampstand was one of a kind, designed to burn only in the holy place of the tabernacle.

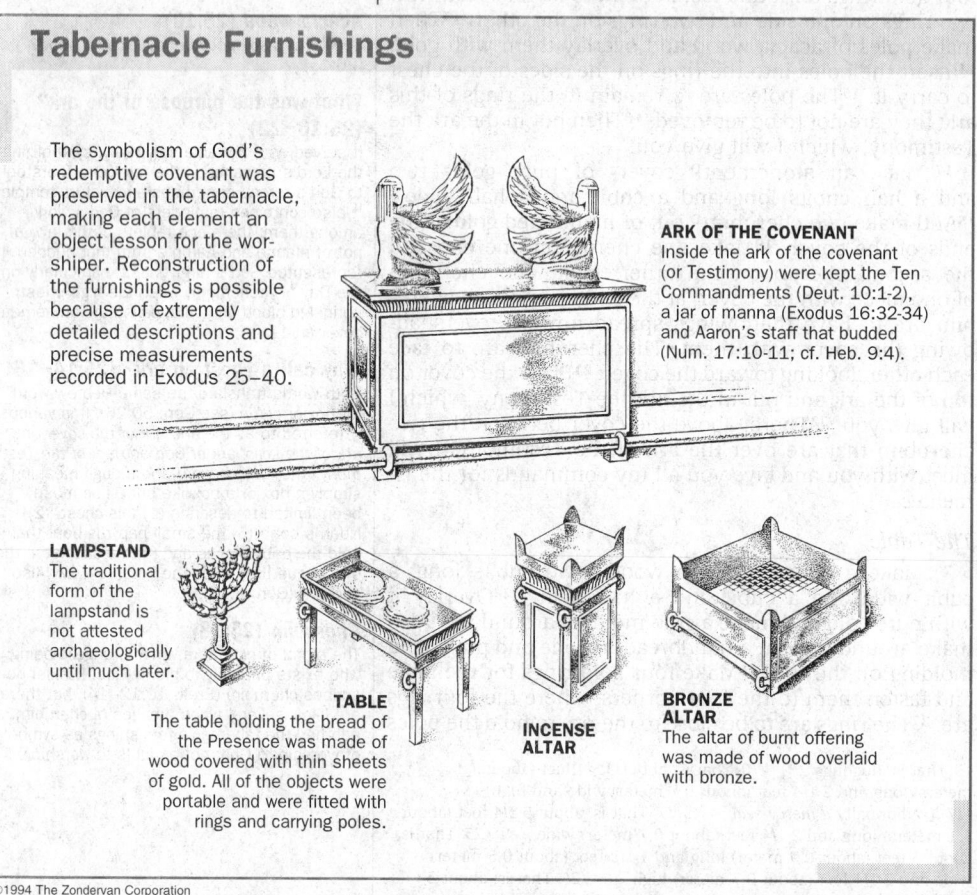

Tabernacle Furnishings

The symbolism of God's redemptive covenant was preserved in the tabernacle, making each element an object lesson for the worshiper. Reconstruction of the furnishings is possible because of extremely detailed descriptions and precise measurements recorded in Exodus 25–40.

ARK OF THE COVENANT
Inside the ark of the covenant (or Testimony) were kept the Ten Commandments (Deut. 10:1-2), a jar of manna (Exodus 16:32-34) and Aaron's staff that budded (Num. 17:10-11; cf. Heb. 9:4).

LAMPSTAND
The traditional form of the lampstand is not attested archaeologically until much later.

TABLE
The table holding the bread of the Presence was made of wood covered with thin sheets of gold. All of the objects were portable and were fitted with rings and carrying poles.

INCENSE ALTAR

BRONZE ALTAR
The altar of burnt offering was made of wood overlaid with bronze.

is to be used for the lampstand and all these accessories. ⁴⁰See that you make them according to the pattern shown you on the mountain.

The Tabernacle

26 "Make the tabernacleᴅ with ten curtains of finely twisted linen and blue, purpleᴅ and scarlet yarn, with cherubimᴅ worked into them by a skilled craftsman. ²All the curtains are to be the same size—twenty-eight cubitsᴅ long and four cubits wide.*ᵃ* ³Join five of the curtains together, and do the same with the other five. ⁴Make loops of blue material along the edge of the end curtain in one set, and do the same with the end curtain in the other set. ⁵Make fifty loops on one curtain and fifty loops on the end curtain of the other set, with the loops opposite each other. ⁶Then make fifty gold clasps and use them to fasten the curtains together so that the tabernacle is a unit.

⁷"Make curtains of goat hair for the tent over the tabernacle—eleven altogether. ⁸All eleven curtains are to be the same size—thirty cubits long and four cubits wide.*ᵇ* ⁹Join five of the curtains together into one set and the other six into another set. Fold the sixth curtain double at the front of the tent. ¹⁰Make fifty loops along the edge of the end curtain in one set and also along the edge of the end curtain in the other set. ¹¹Then make fifty bronze clasps and put them in the loops to fasten the tent together as a unit. ¹²As for the additional length of the tent curtains, the half curtain that is left over is to hang down at the rear of the tabernacle. ¹³The tent curtains will be a cubit*ᶜ* longer on both sides; what is left will hang over the sides of the tabernacle so as to cover it. ¹⁴Make

ᵃ2 That is, about 42 feet (about 12.5 meters) long and 6 feet (about 1.8 meters) wide   ᵇ8 That is, about 45 feet (about 13.5 meters) long and 6 feet (about 1.8 meters) wide   ᶜ13 That is, about 1 1/2 feet (about 0.5 meter)

Is the tabernacle the same thing as the tent of meeting? (26:1)

Not exactly. *Tabernacle* and *tent of meeting* are translations of two different Hebrew terms. There may have been several tents of meeting, temporary structures which were no longer used once the tabernacle was built. Some think that *tent of meeting* was a general descriptive term, encompassing both the temporary tents and the tabernacle.

What was so important about the tabernacle? (26:1)

The tabernacle was the Israelites' place of worship while they were in the desert. It was the holy place where God made his presence known to his people.

Why so much attention to detail? (26:5–11)

See article: *What was so critical about the pattern?* (25:40)

What was so critical about the pattern? (25:40)

We might think a good set of blueprints would have been more helpful. Just what can we learn from these detailed descriptions?

This passage tells us more than *how* the tabernacle was made. It also teaches us *why* it was made: to bring glory to God. From the tabernacle we can learn about God's glory—something far beyond the scope of mere blueprints. The Israelites who first heard these words also saw God's glory in the cloud above the tabernacle. What for us may seem like tedious details probably inspired awe in them.

The Grand Architect who designed the plan of salvation gave Moses its parallel pattern in the tabernacle. The tabernacle held deep symbolic meaning for those who wrote the New Testament, so it should be significant for us as well. See article: *Why such detailed instructions?* (35:4—37:29).

Implied throughout this "blueprint" is a spiritual parallel to Christ and the church. The tabernacle (literally, "dwelling place") points to Christ, who *made his dwelling among us* (John 1:14; see also 2:20–21), tore the curtain of the old covenant in two (Matt. 27:51) and enabled us to enter the Most Holy Place by his sacrifice (Heb. 10:19–22). We can also learn principles about salvation and the church from the pattern of the tabernacle's construction (Eph. 2:21; 1 Peter 2:5).

for the tent a covering of ram skins dyed red, and over that a covering of hides of sea cows.[a]

What's so special about *acacia* wood? (26:15)

The durable acacia wood was readily available in the Sinai Desert and was well-suited for the tabernacle. Because it is harder than oak, wood-eating insects are more likely to avoid it. The trees' branches were protected by "touch-me-not" thorns, perhaps suggesting God's intimidating majesty. The burning bush (3:2) was just one species of acacia. The gum of the acacia tree is used today for both commercial and medicinal purposes.

15"Make upright frames of acacia[D] wood for the tabernacle[D]. **16**Each frame is to be ten cubits[D] long and a cubit and a half wide,[b] **17**with two projections set parallel to each other. Make all the frames of the tabernacle in this way. **18**Make twenty frames for the south side of the tabernacle **19**and make forty silver bases to go under them—two bases for each frame, one under each projection. **20**For the other side, the north side of the tabernacle, make twenty frames **21**and forty silver bases—two under each frame. **22**Make six frames for the far end, that is, the west end of the tabernacle, **23**and make two frames for the corners at the far end. **24**At these two corners they must be double from the bottom all the way to the top, and fitted into a single ring; both shall be like that. **25**So there will be eight frames and sixteen silver bases—two under each frame.

26"Also make crossbars of acacia wood: five for the frames on one side of the tabernacle, **27**five for those on the other side, and five for the frames on the west, at the far end of the tabernacle. **28**The center crossbar is to extend from end to end at the middle of the frames. **29**Overlay the frames with gold and make gold rings to hold the crossbars. Also overlay the crossbars with gold.

30"Set up the tabernacle according to the plan shown you on the mountain.

Where did the Israelites get the materials to make all these things? (26:31–37)

The people donated the materials for the tabernacle from the supplies they brought with them out of Egypt. They gave offerings of *gold, silver and bronze; blue, purple and scarlet yarn and fine linen; goat hair . . .* along with many other objects of value (35:6–9). With 603,550 men (38:26)—meaning about that many families, all living in tents—there would have been more than enough resources to build this tent for the Lord. In fact, the people gave so willingly that the workers had more than they needed; Moses had to tell the people to stop bringing supplies (36:5–7).

Blue, purple and scarlet **(26:31)**
See *Blue, purple and scarlet* (36:8).

SCRIPTURE LINK (27:1–8)
For another account of the altar of burnt offering, see 38:1–7.

31"Make a curtain of blue, purple[D] and scarlet yarn and finely twisted linen, with cherubim[D] worked into it by a skilled craftsman. **32**Hang it with gold hooks on four posts of acacia wood overlaid with gold and standing on four silver bases. **33**Hang the curtain from the clasps and place the ark of the Testimony behind the curtain. The curtain will separate the Holy Place[D] from the Most Holy Place[D]. **34**Put the atonement[D] cover on the ark of the Testimony in the Most Holy Place. **35**Place the table outside the curtain on the north side of the tabernacle and put the lampstand opposite it on the south side.

36"For the entrance to the tent make a curtain of blue, purple and scarlet yarn and finely twisted linen—the work of an embroiderer. **37**Make gold hooks for this curtain and five posts of acacia wood overlaid with gold. And cast five bronze bases for them.

The Altar of Burnt Offering

27 "Build an altar of acacia wood, three cubits[c] high; it is to be square, five cubits long and five cubits wide.[d] **2**Make a horn at each of the four corners, so that the horns and the altar are of one piece, and overlay the altar with bronze. **3**Make all its utensils of bronze—its pots to remove the ashes, and its shovels, sprinkling bowls, meat forks and firepans. **4**Make a grating for it, a bronze network, and make a bronze ring at each of the four corners of the network. **5**Put it under the ledge of the altar so that it is halfway up the altar. **6**Make poles of acacia wood for the altar and overlay them with bronze. **7**The poles are to be inserted into the rings so they will be on two sides of the altar when it is carried.

a14 That is, dugongs   *b16* That is, about 15 feet (about 4.5 meters) long and 2 1/4 feet (about 0.7 meter) wide   *c1* That is, about 4 1/2 feet (about 1.3 meters)   *d1* That is, about 7 1/2 feet (about 2.3 meters) long and wide

⁸Make the altar hollow, out of boards. It is to be made just as you were shown on the mountain.

The Courtyard

⁹"Make a courtyard for the tabernacle^D. The south side shall be a hundred cubits^Dᵃ long and is to have curtains of finely twisted linen, ¹⁰with twenty posts and twenty bronze bases and with silver hooks and bands on the posts. ¹¹The north side shall also be a hundred cubits long and is to have curtains, with twenty posts and twenty bronze bases and with silver hooks and bands on the posts.

¹²"The west end of the courtyard shall be fifty cubitsᵇ wide and have curtains, with ten posts and ten bases. ¹³On the east end, toward the sunrise, the courtyard shall also be fifty cubits wide. ¹⁴Curtains fifteen cubitsᶜ long are to be on one side of the entrance, with three posts and three bases, ¹⁵and curtains fifteen cubits long are to be on the other side, with three posts and three bases.

¹⁶"For the entrance to the courtyard, provide a curtain twenty cubitsᵈ long, of blue, purple and scarlet yarn and finely twisted linen—the work of an embroiderer—with four posts and four bases. ¹⁷All the posts around the courtyard are to have silver bands and hooks, and bronze bases. ¹⁸The courtyard shall be a hundred cubits long and fifty cubits wide,ᵉ with curtains of finely twisted linen five cubitsᶠ high, and with bronze bases. ¹⁹All the other articles used in the service of the tabernacle, whatever their function, including all the tent pegs for it and those for the courtyard, are to be of bronze.

Oil for the Lampstand

²⁰"Command the Israelites to bring you clear oil of pressed olives for the light so that the lamps may be kept burning. ²¹In the Tent of Meeting^D, outside the curtain that is in front of the Testimony, Aaron and his sons are to keep the lamps burning before the LORD from evening till morning. This is to be a lasting ordinance among the Israelites for the generations to come.

The Priestly Garments

28 "Have Aaron your brother brought to you from among the Israelites, along with his sons Nadab and Abihu, Eleazar and Ithamar, so they may serve me as priests^D. ²Make sacred^D garments for your brother Aaron, to give him dignity and honor. ³Tell all the skilled men to whom I have given wisdom in such matters that they are to make garments for Aaron, for his consecration, so he may serve me as priest. ⁴These are the garments they are to make: a breastpiece^D, an ephod^D, a robe, a woven tunic, a turban and a sash. They are to make these sacred garments for your brother Aaron and his sons, so they may serve me as priests. ⁵Have them use gold, and blue, purple and scarlet yarn, and fine linen.

ᵃ9 That is, about 150 feet (about 46 meters); also in verse 11
ᵇ12 That is, about 75 feet (about 23 meters); also in verse 13
ᶜ14 That is, about 22 1/2 feet (about 6.9 meters); also in verse 15
ᵈ16 That is, about 30 feet (about 9 meters)   ᵉ18 That is, about 150 feet (about 46 meters) long and 75 feet (about 23 meters) wide
ᶠ18 That is, about 7 1/2 feet (about 2.3 meters)

SCRIPTURE LINK (27:9–19)
A parallel passage about the courtyard appears in 38:9–20.

Why did God want lamps burning all night? (27:20–21)
These oil lamps were in the Holy Place; their light signified God's presence there. To keep them burning continually symbolized God's perpetual presence.

Why such elaborate garments? (28:1–40)
God intended that the priests' garments would give *dignity and honor* (vv. 2,40). The elaborate designs served to elevate the priests in the eyes of the people. The garments may also have helped the people esteem the worship of God as an awesome and mysterious privilege.

The Ephod

6"Make the ephod^D of gold, and of blue, purple^D and scarlet yarn, and of finely twisted linen—the work of a skilled craftsman. **7**It is to have two shoulder pieces attached to two of its corners, so it can be fastened. **8**Its skillfully woven waistband is to be like it—of one piece with the ephod and made with gold, and with blue, purple and scarlet yarn, and with finely twisted linen.

9"Take two onyx stones and engrave on them the names of the sons of Israel **10**in the order of their birth—six names on one stone and the remaining six on the other. **11**Engrave the names of the sons of Israel on the two stones the way a gem cutter engraves a seal. Then mount the stones in gold filigree settings **12**and fasten them on the shoulder pieces of the ephod as memorial stones for the sons of Israel. Aaron is to bear the names on his shoulders as a memorial before the LORD. **13**Make gold filigree settings **14**and two braided chains of pure gold, like a rope, and attach the chains to the settings.

The Breastpiece

15"Fashion a breastpiece^D for making decisions—the work of a skilled craftsman. Make it like the ephod: of gold, and of blue, purple and scarlet yarn, and of finely twisted linen. **16**It is to be square—a span^a long and a span wide—and folded double. **17**Then mount four rows of precious stones on it. In the first row there shall be a ruby, a topaz and a beryl; **18**in the second row a turquoise, a sapphire^b and an emerald; **19**in the third row a jacinth, an agate and an amethyst; **20**in the fourth row a chrysolite, an onyx and a jasper.^c Mount them in gold filigree settings. **21**There are to be twelve stones, one for each of the names of the sons of Israel, each engraved like a seal with the name of one of the twelve tribes.

22"For the breastpiece make braided chains of pure gold, like a rope. **23**Make two gold rings for it and fasten them to two corners of the breastpiece. **24**Fasten the two gold chains to the rings at the corners of the breastpiece, **25**and the other ends of the chains to the two settings, attaching them to the shoulder pieces of the ephod at the front. **26**Make two gold rings and attach them to the other two corners of the breastpiece on the inside edge next to the ephod. **27**Make two more gold rings and attach them to the bottom of the shoulder pieces on the front of the ephod, close to the seam just above the waistband of the ephod. **28**The rings of the breastpiece are to be tied to the rings of the ephod with blue cord, connecting it to the waistband, so that the breastpiece will not swing out from the ephod.

29"Whenever Aaron enters the Holy Place^D, he will bear the names of the sons of Israel over his heart on the breastpiece of decision as a continuing memorial before the LORD. **30**Also put the Urim^D and the Thummim^D in the breastpiece, so they may be over Aaron's heart whenever he enters the presence of the LORD. Thus Aaron will always bear the means of making decisions for the Israelites over his heart before the LORD.

---

^a16 That is, about 9 inches (about 22 centimeters)   ^b18 Or *lapis lazuli*   ^c20 The precise identification of some of these precious stones is uncertain.

Other Priestly Garments

31"Make the robe of the ephod^D entirely of blue cloth, **32**with an opening for the head in its center. There shall be a woven edge like a collar^a around this opening, so that it will not tear. **33**Make pomegranates of blue, purple^D and scarlet yarn around the hem of the robe, with gold bells between them. **34**The gold bells and the pomegranates are to alternate around the hem of the robe. **35**Aaron must wear it when he ministers. The sound of the bells will be heard when he enters the Holy Place^D before the LORD and when he comes out, so that he will not die.

36"Make a plate of pure gold and engrave on it as on a seal: HOLY TO THE LORD. **37**Fasten a blue cord to it to attach it to the turban; it is to be on the front of the turban. **38**It will be on Aaron's forehead, and he will bear the guilt involved in the sacred^D gifts the Israelites consecrate^D, whatever their gifts may be. It will be on Aaron's forehead continually so that they will be acceptable to the LORD.

39"Weave the tunic of fine linen and make the turban of fine linen. The sash is to be the work of an embroiderer. **40**Make tunics, sashes and headbands for Aaron's sons, to give them dignity and honor. **41**After you put these clothes on your brother Aaron and his sons, anoint^D and ordain them. Consecrate them so they may serve me as priests^D.

42"Make linen undergarments as a covering for the body, reaching from the waist to the thigh. **43**Aaron and his sons must wear them whenever they enter the Tent of Meeting^D or approach the altar to minister in the Holy Place, so that they will not incur guilt and die.

"This is to be a lasting ordinance for Aaron and his descendants.

Consecration of the Priests

29 "This is what you are to do to consecrate them, so they may serve me as priests: Take a young bull and two rams without defect. **2**And from fine wheat flour, without yeast^D, make bread, and cakes mixed with oil, and wafers spread with oil. **3**Put them in a basket and present them in it—along with the bull and the two rams. **4**Then bring Aaron and his sons to the entrance to the Tent of Meeting and wash them with water. **5**Take the garments and dress Aaron with the tunic, the robe of the ephod, the ephod itself and the breastpiece. Fasten the ephod on him by its skillfully woven waistband. **6**Put the turban on his head and attach the sacred diadem to the turban. **7**Take the anointing oil and anoint him by pouring it on his head. **8**Bring his sons and dress them in tunics **9**and put headbands on them. Then tie sashes on Aaron and his sons.^b The priesthood is theirs by a lasting ordinance. In this way you shall ordain Aaron and his sons.

10"Bring the bull to the front of the Tent of Meeting, and Aaron and his sons shall lay their hands on its head. **11**Slaughter it in the LORD's presence at the entrance to the Tent of Meeting. **12**Take some of the bull's blood and put it on the horns of the altar with your finger, and pour out the rest of it at the base of the altar. **13**Then take all the fat around the inner parts, the covering of the liver, and both kidneys with the fat on them, and burn them on the

Why wear bells and linen underwear? (28:35,42–43)

The bells and linen undergarments were part of the high priest's robe that, as a whole, distinguished and protected him. These physical details apparently symbolized the priest's inner, spiritual condition. Without such a covering, he was spiritually "naked," unfit to serve in the presence of a holy God. According to one tradition, the ongoing sound of bells let the people outside know the priest was still ministering within the Holy Place. If this sound stopped, they knew his atonement was inadequate and he had died for his sins. Also see *Why wear linen underwear?* (Lev. 6:10).

Why a *lasting ordinance* about linen undergarments? (28:42–43)

God instituted this *lasting ordinance* to counteract pagan religions of that time, which involved certain rituals of nakedness. To separate them from such practices and encourage holiness in their worship, God instructed the priests to cover their nakedness (see 20:26). Besides ensuring literal modesty, the linen underwear also symbolized a spiritual covering for the flesh or earthly nature (see Col. 3:5–10).

SCRIPTURE LINK (29:1–37)

For more on the consecration of the priests, see Lev. 8:1–36.

Why all the instructions for the various animal parts? (29:13–14)

The sacrifice had symbolic meaning. Some parts of the animal were considered more desirable than others—and were given to God. Other parts, considered undesirable, were identified with sin—and were burned outside the camp.

---

^a32 The meaning of the Hebrew for this word is uncertain.
^b9 Hebrew; Septuagint *on them*

altar. [14]But burn the bull's flesh and its hide and its offal[D] outside the camp. It is a sin offering.

[15]"Take one of the rams, and Aaron and his sons shall lay their hands on its head. [16]Slaughter it and take the blood and sprinkle it against the altar on all sides. [17]Cut the ram into pieces and wash the inner parts and the legs, putting them with the head and the other pieces. [18]Then burn the entire ram on the altar. It is a burnt offering[D] to the LORD, a pleasing aroma, an offering made to the LORD by fire.

[19]"Take the other ram, and Aaron and his sons shall lay their hands on its head. [20]Slaughter it, take some of its blood and put it on the lobes of the right ears of Aaron and his sons, on the thumbs of their right hands, and on the big toes of their right feet. Then sprinkle blood against the altar on all sides. [21]And take some of the blood on the altar and some of the anointing[D] oil and sprinkle it on Aaron and his garments and on his sons and their garments. Then he and his sons and their garments will be consecrated[D].

[22]"Take from this ram the fat, the fat tail, the fat around the inner parts, the covering of the liver, both kidneys with the fat on them, and the right thigh. (This is the ram for the ordination[D].) [23]From the basket of bread made without yeast[D], which is before the LORD, take a loaf, and a cake made with oil, and a wafer. [24]Put all these in the hands of Aaron and his sons and wave them before the LORD as a wave offering[D]. [25]Then take them from their hands and burn them on the altar along with the burnt offering for a pleasing aroma to the LORD, an offering made to the LORD by fire. [26]After you take the breast of the ram for Aaron's ordination, wave it before the LORD as a wave offering, and it will be your share.

[27]"Consecrate those parts of the ordination ram that belong to Aaron and his sons: the breast that was waved and the thigh that was presented. [28]This is always

Why dab blood on Aaron's right ear lobe, thumb and big toe? (29:20)

We know little about this puzzling ceremony (see Lev. 14:14). Perhaps these parts of the anatomy were symbolically cleansed by blood to represent God's desire to direct every part of our lives: *ear lobes* for the things we hear and think, *thumbs* for the things we do and *toes* for the places we go. See *What was special about the priests' right ears, thumbs and big toes?* (Lev. 8:23).

Wave offering (29:22–28)

Part of a fellowship (or peace) offering (see Lev. 7:30–32; 8:25–29). It was lifted up before the Lord and may have been waved—moved back and forth—as a sign that it belonged to the Lord. Then it was eaten by the priest as God's representative, a sign that God would fellowship with the one who offered it. Also see *Why wave an offering?* (Lev. 7:30).

Why was all this blood needed for worship? (29:11–21)

A just and holy God could not ignore sin. There had to be consequences. However, as an act of mercy, God allowed a substitute to take the place of the sinner. The substitute could pay the consequences of sin, so the sinner would not have to die.

This death-for-life substitution was vividly shown in the blood of the sacrificial animal. The blood symbolized life (Lev. 17:11); pour out the blood and you pour out the animal's life. In this way, its life was given in exchange for the death of the sinner. The blood meant death to the animal as payment for sin, but it meant life to the sinner as a sign of forgiveness.

Why did God require such a gruesome payment for sin? He was intent that people should not sidestep the life-and-death seriousness of sin. Anything less than blood and the giving of life would have devalued sin in the eyes of the people (Heb. 9:22). But when a person heard the bleating cries of an innocent lamb, saw its bright red blood spilled on the altar and smelled the smoke of the burnt offering, that person was brought up short by a sobering thought: *I deserved to die for my sin; that sheep died in my place.*

In the New Testament the substitute sacrifice was not ignored. Jesus Christ, the only perfect sacrifice, became the sacrificial Lamb (John 1:29,36), removing the need for ongoing sacrifices of animals (Heb. 7:27; 9:12–14; 10:18).

to be the regular share from the Israelites for Aaron and his sons. It is the contribution the Israelites are to make to the LORD from their fellowship offerings. *a*

²⁹"Aaron's sacred^D garments will belong to his descendants so that they can be anointed^D and ordained in them. ³⁰The son who succeeds him as priest^D and comes to the Tent of Meeting^D to minister in the Holy Place^D is to wear them seven days.

³¹"Take the ram for the ordination^D and cook the meat in a sacred place. ³²At the entrance to the Tent of Meeting, Aaron and his sons are to eat the meat of the ram and the bread that is in the basket. ³³They are to eat these offerings by which atonement^D was made for their ordination and consecration. But no one else may eat them, because they are sacred. ³⁴And if any of the meat of the ordination ram or any bread is left over till morning, burn it up. It must not be eaten, because it is sacred.

³⁵"Do for Aaron and his sons everything I have commanded you, taking seven days to ordain them. ³⁶Sacrifice^D a bull each day as a sin offering^D to make atonement. Purify the altar by making atonement for it, and anoint it to consecrate it. ³⁷For seven days make atonement for the altar and consecrate it. Then the altar will be most holy, and whatever touches it will be holy.

³⁸"This is what you are to offer on the altar regularly each day: two lambs a year old. ³⁹Offer one in the morning and the other at twilight. ⁴⁰With the first lamb offer a tenth of an ephah *b* of fine flour mixed with a quarter of a hin *c* of oil from pressed olives, and a quarter of a hin of wine as a drink offering^D. ⁴¹Sacrifice the other lamb at twilight with the same grain offering^D and its drink offering as in the morning—a pleasing aroma, an offering made to the LORD by fire.

⁴²"For the generations to come this burnt offering^D is to be made regularly at the entrance to the Tent of Meeting before the LORD. There I will meet you and speak to you; ⁴³there also I will meet with the Israelites, and the place will be consecrated by my glory.

⁴⁴"So I will consecrate the Tent of Meeting and the altar and will consecrate Aaron and his sons to serve me as priests. ⁴⁵Then I will dwell among the Israelites and be their God. ⁴⁶They will know that I am the LORD their God, who brought them out of Egypt so that I might dwell among them. I am the LORD their God.

The Altar of Incense

30 "Make an altar of acacia^D wood for burning incense^D. ²It is to be square, a cubit^D long and a cubit wide, and two cubits high *d*—its horns of one piece with it. ³Overlay the top and all the sides and the horns with pure gold, and make a gold molding around it. ⁴Make two gold rings for the altar below the molding—two on opposite sides—to hold the poles used to carry it. ⁵Make the poles of acacia wood and overlay them with gold. ⁶Put the altar in front of the curtain that is before the ark of the Testimony—before the atonement cover that is over the Testimony—where I will meet with you.

⁷"Aaron must burn fragrant incense on the altar every

Why couldn't someone outside Aaron's family be a priest? (29:29–30)
See *Why were Aaron and his sons chosen to be priests?* (Lev. 8:2).

Why take seven days to ordain priests? (29:35)
The seven days of creation, in which God's work was completely finished and perfect, set the precedent for the number seven as a symbol of perfection or completion. For the same reason, some religious feasts lasted for seven days or from Sabbath to Sabbath (Lev. 23:6,34). Taking seven days to ordain a priest (or consecrate an altar, v. 37) indicated a process leading to perfection, making the priest (and the altar) holy—separated from the ordinary to be used for God's purposes.

How did God speak to the Israelites? (29:42–43)
God chose to show himself "by appointment only," as it were, at the Tent of Meeting. God wanted his people to be intentional about meeting with him, *morning and . . . twilight* (29:39). As for how he spoke to them, we cannot say. Perhaps he spoke audibly out of the cloud above the tabernacle; perhaps he spoke only to Moses. See *What kind of angel did God send?* (23:20–23).

---

a28 Traditionally *peace offerings*   *b40* That is, probably about 2 quarts (about 2 liters)   *c40* That is, probably about 1 quart (about 1 liter)   *d2* That is, about 1 1/2 feet (about 0.5 meter) long and wide and about 3 feet (about 0.9 meter) high

morning when he tends the lamps. **8**He must burn incense[D] again when he lights the lamps at twilight so incense will burn regularly before the LORD for the generations to come. **9**Do not offer on this altar any other incense or any burnt offering or grain offering, and do not pour a drink offering[D] on it. **10**Once a year Aaron shall make atonement[D] on its horns. This annual atonement must be made with the blood of the atoning sin offering[D] for the generations to come. It is most holy to the LORD."

Atonement Money

11Then the LORD said to Moses, **12**"When you take a census of the Israelites to count them, each one must pay the LORD a ransom for his life at the time he is counted. Then no plague will come on them when you number them. **13**Each one who crosses over to those already counted is to give a half shekel[D],[a] according to the sanctuary shekel[D], which weighs twenty gerahs. This half shekel is an offering to the LORD. **14**All who cross over, those twenty years old or more, are to give an offering to the LORD. **15**The rich are not to give more than a half shekel and the poor are not to give less when you make the offering to the LORD to atone for your lives. **16**Receive the atonement money from the Israelites and use it for the service of the Tent of Meeting[D]. It will be a memorial for the Israelites before the LORD, making atonement for your lives."

Basin for Washing

17Then the LORD said to Moses, **18**"Make a bronze basin, with its bronze stand, for washing. Place it between the Tent of Meeting and the altar, and put water in it. **19**Aaron and his sons are to wash their hands and feet with water from it. **20**Whenever they enter the Tent of Meeting, they shall wash with water so that they will not die. Also, when they approach the altar to minister by presenting an offering made to the LORD by fire, **21**they shall wash their hands and feet so that they will not die. This is to be a lasting ordinance for Aaron and his descendants for the generations to come."

Anointing Oil

22Then the LORD said to Moses, **23**"Take the following fine spices: 500 shekels[b] of liquid myrrh, half as much (that is, 250 shekels) of fragrant cinnamon, 250 shekels of fragrant cane, **24**500 shekels of cassia—all according to the sanctuary shekel—and a hin[c] of olive oil. **25**Make these into a sacred[D] anointing[D] oil, a fragrant blend, the work of a perfumer. It will be the sacred anointing oil. **26**Then use it to anoint the Tent of Meeting, the ark of the Testimony, **27**the table and all its articles, the lampstand and its accessories, the altar of incense, **28**the altar of burnt offering and all its utensils, and the basin with its stand. **29**You shall consecrate[D] them so they will be most holy, and whatever touches them will be holy.

30"Anoint Aaron and his sons and consecrate them so they may serve me as priests[D]. **31**Say to the Israelites, 'This is to be my sacred anointing oil for the genera-

Why would a census cause a plague? (30:12)

This may have been more of a military conscription than a census (see 2 Samuel 24). God wanted his people to trust him for their security, not their own strength of numbers. When a small *ransom* was paid, however, the census became part of their worship to God and support for the tabernacle service (v. 16; Num. 31:49–54). A plague—decimating their numbers—would have been God's judgment for relying on themselves rather than God. Also see *What was wrong with taking a census?* (2 Samuel 24:3).

How could some Israelites—all ex-slaves—be rich and others poor? (30:15)

Even as slaves, some had been able to accumulate more than others. Now, just a year out of slavery, they owned more livestock, the basic measure of wealth at the time. But the point was that rich and poor alike had the same standing before God. The wealthy were not more important; the poor were not less significant. A half shekel—worth less than a dollar today—was a ransom anyone could afford, a mere token of one's value to God.

Why was God's holiness so threatening? (30:20–21)

Because the people needed a healthy respect for God's holiness in view of their own sinfulness. When carelessness around the holy God brought dire consequences (see 2 Samuel 6:6–8; Lev. 10:1–2), others learned to honor God more. Mere religious ritual, instead of moral and spiritual purity, would not honor God as holy.

---

[a]13 That is, about 1/5 ounce (about 6 grams); also in verse 15
[b]23 That is, about 12 1/2 pounds (about 6 kilograms)   [c]24 That is, probably about 4 quarts (about 4 liters)

tions to come. **32**Do not pour it on men's bodies and do not make any oil with the same formula. It is sacred^D, and you are to consider it sacred. **33**Whoever makes perfume like it and whoever puts it on anyone other than a priest^D must be cut off from his people.' "

Incense

34Then the LORD said to Moses, "Take fragrant spices—gum resin, onycha and galbanum—and pure frankincense, all in equal amounts, **35**and make a fragrant blend of incense^D, the work of a perfumer. It is to be salted and pure and sacred. **36**Grind some of it to powder and place it in front of the Testimony in the Tent of Meeting^D, where I will meet with you. It shall be most holy to you. **37**Do not make any incense with this formula for yourselves; consider it holy to the LORD. **38**Whoever makes any like it to enjoy its fragrance must be cut off from his people."

Bezalel and Oholiab

31 Then the LORD said to Moses, **2**"See, I have chosen Bezalel son of Uri, the son of Hur, of the tribe of Judah, **3**and I have filled him with the Spirit of God, with skill, ability and knowledge in all kinds of crafts— **4**to make artistic designs for work in gold, silver and bronze, **5**to cut and set stones, to work in wood, and to engage in all kinds of craftsmanship. **6**Moreover, I have appointed Oholiab son of Ahisamach, of the tribe of Dan, to help him. Also I have given skill to all the craftsmen to make everything I have commanded you: **7**the Tent of Meeting, the ark of the Testimony with the atonement cover on it, and all the other furnishings of the tent— **8**the table and its articles, the pure gold lampstand and all its accessories, the altar of incense, **9**the altar of burnt offering^D and all its utensils, the basin with its stand— **10**and also the woven garments, both the sacred garments for Aaron the priest and the garments for his sons when they serve as priests, **11**and the anointing oil and fragrant incense for the Holy Place. They are to make them just as I commanded you."

The Sabbath

12Then the LORD said to Moses, **13**"Say to the Israelites, 'You must observe my Sabbaths^D. This will be a sign between me and you for the generations to come, so you may know that I am the LORD, who makes you holy.^a

14" 'Observe the Sabbath, because it is holy to you. Anyone who desecrates^D it must be put to death^D; whoever does any work on that day must be cut off from his people. **15**For six days, work is to be done, but the seventh day is a Sabbath of rest, holy to the LORD. Whoever does any work on the Sabbath day must be put to death. **16**The Israelites are to observe the Sabbath, celebrating it for the generations to come as a lasting covenant^D. **17**It will be a sign between me and the Israelites forever, for in six days the LORD made the heavens and the earth, and on the seventh day he abstained from work and rested.' "

18When the LORD finished speaking to Moses on Mount Sinai, he gave him the two tablets of the Testimony, the tablets of stone inscribed by the finger of God.

---

a13 Or who sanctifies you; or who sets you apart as holy

In what way was Bezalel filled with the Spirit? (31:3)

Bezalel was equipped with extraordinary skill and know-how with arts and crafts (see v. 6 and 36:2). In the Old Testament, God frequently gave a special anointing of his Spirit for the purpose of craftsmanship and building, prophecy (1 Samuel 10:10), and leadership (Judges 6:34). This anointing should not be confused with the indwelling of the Holy Spirit in the New Testament. It may provide a parallel, however, to some passages in Luke and Acts where individuals were filled with the Spirit for specific tasks.

How was the Sabbath a sign? (31:13)

By observing the Sabbath rest, the Israelites showed that they had a unique relationship with the Lord (6:4). The Sabbath each week served as a regular reminder that God had made them a *holy* people.

Do Sabbath restrictions apply to New Testament believers? (31:14–15)

Some are more careful about keeping the Sabbath than others, who consider the principle behind the Sabbath to be more important than the specific details. See *As Lord of the Sabbath, did Jesus change the rules?* (Luke 6:2–5).

Why two tablets instead of one? (31:18)

Many think that one of the tablets was a copy, and that the entire covenant document was contained on one tablet. Following the pattern of ancient covenant agreements, each party retained a copy, one for God and one for Israel. In this instance, both copies were kept in the ark of the covenant (25:21).

How long had Moses been on the mountain? (32:1)

Almost six weeks (24:18).

Why did the Israelites long for gods they could see? (32:1)

The Israelites had lived in Egypt for many years, surrounded by the visible gods of Egypt. Because Moses represented God to the Israelites, they felt far from God when they couldn't see Moses. So while he was on the mountain, they created a substitute they could see—a calf in the style of the Egyptian gods. See article: *Why would Israelites be tempted by other gods?* (Joshua 23:7).

Why did Aaron make a calf for a god? (32:4)

The calf was modeled after Apis, the Egyptian bull-god. For the people of this time, a young bull or calf was a symbol of sexual fertility.

What sort of revelry did they indulge in? (32:6)

Sexual immorality (1 Cor. 10:6–8).

Was God serious in threatening to destroy his chosen people? (32:10)

Yes. God's holiness required punishment for sin. But because of Moses' intercession for the people *the LORD relented* (v. 14). Moses later interceded for the people again, when Korah, Dathan and Abiram instigated a revolt against him (Num. 16:1–50). Moses illustrated the future work of Jesus Christ, the ultimate mediator between God and man (1 Tim. 2:5).

Two tablets (32:15)

See *Why two tablets instead of just one?* (Deut. 9:10).

The Golden Calf

32 When the people saw that Moses was so long in coming down from the mountain, they gathered around Aaron and said, "Come, make us gods*ᵃ* who will go before us. As for this fellow Moses who brought us up out of Egypt, we don't know what has happened to him."

²Aaron answered them, "Take off the gold earrings that your wives, your sons and your daughters are wearing, and bring them to me." ³So all the people took off their earrings and brought them to Aaron. ⁴He took what they handed him and made it into an idolᴰ cast in the shape of a calf, fashioning it with a tool. Then they said, "These are your gods,*ᵇ* O Israel, who brought you up out of Egypt."

⁵When Aaron saw this, he built an altar in front of the calf and announced, "Tomorrow there will be a festival to the LORD." ⁶So the next day the people rose early and sacrificed burnt offeringsᴰ and presented fellowship offeringsᴰ.*ᶜ* Afterward they sat down to eat and drink and got up to indulge in revelry.

⁷Then the LORD said to Moses, "Go down, because your people, whom you brought up out of Egypt, have become corrupt. ⁸They have been quick to turn away from what I commanded them and have made themselves an idol cast in the shape of a calf. They have bowed down to it and sacrificed to it and have said, 'These are your gods, O Israel, who brought you up out of Egypt.'

⁹"I have seen these people," the LORD said to Moses, "and they are a stiff-necked people. ¹⁰Now leave me alone so that my anger may burn against them and that I may destroy them. Then I will make you into a great nation."

¹¹But Moses sought the favor of the LORD his God. "O LORD," he said, "why should your anger burn against your people, whom you brought out of Egypt with great power and a mighty hand? ¹²Why should the Egyptians say, 'It was with evil intent that he brought them out, to kill them in the mountains and to wipe them off the face of the earth'? Turn from your fierce anger; relent and do not bring disaster on your people. ¹³Remember your servants Abraham, Isaac and Israel, to whom you swore by your own self: 'I will make your descendants as numerous as the stars in the sky and I will give your descendants all this land I promised them, and it will be their inheritance forever.' " ¹⁴Then the LORD relented and did not bring on his people the disaster he had threatened.

¹⁵Moses turned and went down the mountain with the two tablets of the Testimony in his hands. They were inscribed on both sides, front and back. ¹⁶The tablets were the work of God; the writing was the writing of God, engraved on the tablets.

¹⁷When Joshua heard the noise of the people shouting, he said to Moses, "There is the sound of war in the camp."

¹⁸Moses replied:

"It is not the sound of victory,
  it is not the sound of defeat;
  it is the sound of singing that I hear."

¹⁹When Moses approached the camp and saw the calf and the dancing, his anger burned and he threw the tablets out of his hands, breaking them to pieces at the foot

---

ᵃ1 Or *a god*; also in verses 23 and 31   *ᵇ4* Or *This is your god*; also in verse 8   *ᶜ6* Traditionally *peace offerings*

of the mountain. **20**And he took the calf they had made and burned it in the fire; then he ground it to powder, scattered it on the water and made the Israelites drink it.

21He said to Aaron, "What did these people do to you, that you led them into such great sin?"

22"Do not be angry, my lord," Aaron answered. "You know how prone these people are to evil. **23**They said to me, 'Make us gods who will go before us. As for this fellow Moses who brought us up out of Egypt, we don't know what has happened to him.' **24**So I told them, 'Whoever has any gold jewelry, take it off.' Then they gave me the gold, and I threw it into the fire, and out came this calf!'

25Moses saw that the people were running wild and that Aaron had let them get out of control and so become a laughingstock to their enemies. **26**So he stood at the entrance to the camp and said, "Whoever is for the LORD, come to me." And all the Levites**D** rallied to him.

27Then he said to them, "This is what the LORD, the God of Israel, says: 'Each man strap a sword to his side. Go back and forth through the camp from one end to the other, each killing his brother and friend and neighbor.' " **28**The Levites did as Moses commanded, and that day about three thousand of the people died. **29**Then Moses said, "You have been set apart to the LORD today, for you were against your own sons and brothers, and he has blessed you this day."

30The next day Moses said to the people, "You have committed a great sin. But now I will go up to the LORD; perhaps I can make atonement**D** for your sin."

31So Moses went back to the LORD and said, "Oh, what a great sin these people have committed! They have made themselves gods of gold. **32**But now, please forgive their

A laughingstock to their enemies (32:25)

For more on Moses' concern about Israel's reputation with the other nations, see *Why did Moses care that Israel be distinct from other nations?* (33:16).

Why did the Levites have to kill brothers, friends and neighbors? (32:27)

Moses ordered the Levites to kill all those who had obviously been sinning, even friends, neighbors and family members if necessary. Possibly the wrongdoers had been observed or they were drunk and easily singled out. Verse 28 says that about 3,000 died that day.

Can our prayers cause God to change his mind? (32:14)

God does not change, but he will adjust his decrees to fit our response. The Bible contains many examples of this—the Hebrews on the outskirts of Canaan (Num. 14:11–23); Hezekiah's repentance on behalf of Israel (2 Chron. 29:3–10,36); the sparing of Nineveh (Jonah 3:1–10).

God's will is dynamic. As with any interpersonal relationship, God's relationship with humanity involves give and take. God accommodates his responses to ours; we adjust our responses to God's. So it can be said that on this level, God sometimes changes his mind in response to our prayers.

At the same time, God's will is determined. There are decrees and promises he has made that do not change. He kept his covenant with the Israelites (Deut. 7:7–8) and keeps his new covenant with us (John 6:37–40,44).

God wants us to follow his will obediently. He has predetermined ways he would like us to respond, but we have the choice to do them or not (Psalm 143:10; Heb. 10:35–39; 1 Thes. 5:16–18; 2 Peter 3:9).

These three aspects of God's will work together. It is not possible for us to understand how, but God is ultimately in control. We might compare the relationship between God, his will and his people to a chess match between a novice player and a master. The novice can make any move he chooses and the master will respond accordingly. But the master will always be in control of the game. The analogy is limited and cannot be pressed further: God's people "win" when the Master's will is done.

How does God blot sinners out of his book? (32:33)

Most believe that the book, when mentioned in the Old Testament, is a list of all those on earth who are part of God's covenant—Hebrews only. When mentioned in the New Testament, the book includes all who are followers of Christ (Phil. 4:3; Rev. 3:5).

Ornaments (33:4–6)

These most likely were items of jewelry—earrings, bracelets, necklaces and anklets—removed as a sign of repentance just as wearing sackcloth was a sign of sorrow. Some speculate these ornaments may have had religious significance as amulets, invoking God's protection.

Was this *"tent of meeting"* the same thing as the tabernacle? (33:7)

Not exactly. The English language does not translate these two Hebrew words specifically. Some believe there were several tents of meeting, all temporary structures which were no longer used once the tabernacle was built. Others believe that "tent of meeting" was a general descriptive term, encompassing both the temporary tents and the tabernacle.

How could Moses speak to the Lord face to face? (33:11)

The phrase *face to face* is a metaphor that, along with the phrase *as a man speaks with his friend,* suggests spiritual communion and intimacy. The image should not be taken literally, especially in view of the fact that God said no one, including Moses, could see his face and live (vv. 19–20). It describes God's straightforward and deep communication with Moses, not his physical presence (Num. 12:6–8).

Why did God say he knew Moses by name? (33:12,17)

This was a way of saying, "You have found favor with me" and "I have chosen you for a special purpose." Jesus used the same phrase to describe all those who have an intimate relationship with him (John 10:1–6).

How did Moses receive God's favor? (33:12)

God's favor or grace cannot be earned. But it can be rejected through disobedience or unfaithfulness. Because Moses remained faithful in serving God, obeying in spite of his own desires and feelings of inadequacy, he found favor with God (vv. 11–14; 4:10–17,29–31; Heb. 11:24–28).

Why did Moses care that Israel be distinct from other nations? (33:16)

Moses saw that God's promise to the Israelites was unique. In fact, it probably would not be understood by the rest of the world. Moses wanted something more tangible—something that would convince aggressive nations to avoid confrontation with the Israelites as they traveled through hostile territory. He wanted evidence of God's power that would cause other nations to fear Israel.

---

sin—but if not, then blot me out of the book you have written."

33The LORD replied to Moses, "Whoever has sinned against me I will blot out of my book. **34**Now go, lead the people to the place I spoke of, and my angel will go before you. However, when the time comes for me to punish, I will punish them for their sin."

35And the LORD struck the people with a plague because of what they did with the calf Aaron had made.

33 Then the LORD said to Moses, "Leave this place, you and the people you brought up out of Egypt, and go up to the land I promised on oath to Abraham, Isaac and Jacob, saying, 'I will give it to your descendants.' **2**I will send an angel before you and drive out the Canaanites, Amorites, Hittites, Perizzites, Hivites and Jebusites. **3**Go up to the land flowing with milk and honey. But I will not go with you, because you are a stiff-necked people and I might destroy you on the way."

4When the people heard these distressing words, they began to mourn and no one put on any ornaments. **5**For the LORD had said to Moses, "Tell the Israelites, 'You are a stiff-necked people. If I were to go with you even for a moment, I might destroy you. Now take off your ornaments and I will decide what to do with you.' " **6**So the Israelites stripped off their ornaments at Mount Horeb.

The Tent of Meeting

7Now Moses used to take a tent and pitch it outside the camp some distance away, calling it the "tent of meetingᴰ." Anyone inquiring of the LORD would go to the tent of meeting outside the camp. **8**And whenever Moses went out to the tent, all the people rose and stood at the entrances to their tents, watching Moses until he entered the tent. **9**As Moses went into the tent, the pillar of cloud would come down and stay at the entrance, while the LORD spoke with Moses. **10**Whenever the people saw the pillar of cloud standing at the entrance to the tent, they all stood and worshiped, each at the entrance to his tent. **11**The LORD would speak to Moses face to face, as a man speaks with his friend. Then Moses would return to the camp, but his young aide Joshua son of Nun did not leave the tent.

Moses and the Glory of the LORD

12Moses said to the LORD, "You have been telling me, 'Lead these people,' but you have not let me know whom you will send with me. You have said, 'I know you by name and you have found favor with me.' **13**If you are pleased with me, teach me your ways so I may know you and continue to find favor with you. Remember that this nation is your people."

14The LORD replied, "My Presence will go with you, and I will give you rest."

15Then Moses said to him, "If your Presence does not go with us, do not send us up from here. **16**How will anyone know that you are pleased with me and with your people unless you go with us? What else will distinguish me and your people from all the other people on the face of the earth?"

17And the LORD said to Moses, "I will do the very thing you have asked, because I am pleased with you and I know you by name."

18Then Moses said, "Now show me your gloryᴰ."

19And the LORD said, "I will cause all my goodness to

pass in front of you, and I will proclaim my name, the LORD, in your presence. I will have mercy[D] on whom I will have mercy, and I will have compassion on whom I will have compassion. **20**But," he said, "you cannot see my face, for no one may see me and live."

21Then the LORD said, "There is a place near me where you may stand on a rock. **22**When my glory[D] passes by, I will put you in a cleft in the rock and cover you with my hand until I have passed by. **23**Then I will remove my hand and you will see my back; but my face must not be seen."

The New Stone Tablets

34 The LORD said to Moses, "Chisel out two stone tablets like the first ones, and I will write on them the words that were on the first tablets, which you broke. **2**Be ready in the morning, and then come up on Mount Sinai. Present yourself to me there on top of the mountain. **3**No one is to come with you or be seen anywhere on the mountain; not even the flocks and herds may graze in front of the mountain."

4So Moses chiseled out two stone tablets like the first ones and went up Mount Sinai early in the morning, as the LORD had commanded him; and he carried the two stone tablets in his hands. **5**Then the LORD came down in the cloud and stood there with him and proclaimed his name, the LORD. **6**And he passed in front of Moses, proclaiming, "The LORD, the LORD, the compassionate and gracious God, slow to anger, abounding in love and faithfulness, **7**maintaining love to thousands, and forgiving wickedness, rebellion and sin. Yet he does not leave the guilty unpunished; he punishes the children and their children for the sin of the fathers to the third and fourth generation."

8Moses bowed to the ground at once and worshiped. **9**"O Lord, if I have found favor in your eyes," he said, "then let the Lord go with us. Although this is a stiff-necked people, forgive our wickedness and our sin, and take us as your inheritance."

10Then the LORD said: "I am making a covenant[D] with you. Before all your people I will do wonders never before done in any nation in all the world. The people you live among will see how awesome is the work that I, the LORD, will do for you. **11**Obey what I command you today. I will drive out before you the Amorites, Canaanites, Hittites, Perizzites, Hivites and Jebusites. **12**Be careful not to make a treaty with those who live in the land where you are going, or they will be a snare among you. **13**Break down their altars, smash their sacred stones[D] and cut down their Asherah poles[D].[a] **14**Do not worship any other god, for the LORD, whose name is Jealous, is a jealous God.

15"Be careful not to make a treaty with those who live in the land; for when they prostitute themselves to their gods and sacrifice[D] to them, they will invite you and you will eat their sacrifices. **16**And when you choose some of their daughters as wives for your sons and those daughters prostitute themselves to their gods, they will lead your sons to do the same.

17"Do not make cast idols[D].

18"Celebrate the Feast of Unleavened Bread. For seven days eat bread made without yeast[D], as I commanded

a13 That is, symbols of the goddess Asherah

Just what did Moses want to see? (33:18—34:7)

Moses wanted to see God's character at its fullness—God's very being. This is more than any man can ever know.

Why indulge Moses so dramatically? (34:6-7)

The Lord made himself known to Moses in dramatic fashion. But this was more than a mere visual revelation. God also presented Moses with an extensive list of his own characteristics (34:6-7). These verses, almost like Theology 101 (a short course on God), are repeated many times throughout the Old Testament. The revelation given to Moses became the foundation of the covenant.

Why would God punish children *for the sin of the fathers*? (34:6-7)

It's hard for us today to appreciate the strong connectedness of families in the traditional Old Testament cultures—for both good and bad. The Bible often mentions the conversion of whole families, indicating that blessings the elders experienced were experienced by the children too. Our modern society is certainly not immune to this. The detrimental effects of child abuse, for example, can be followed from one generation of a family to the next. See article: *Does God punish children for their parents' sins?* (Num. 14:18).

Why would God call himself *Jealous*? (34:14)

God's jealousy springs from love, from a self-less concern for what is best for those he cares for. (Compare Paul's jealousy in 2 Cor. 11:2.) God, therefore, demands our exclusive devotion. The Hebrew word for *jealous* is sometimes translated as *zealous*.

you. Do this at the appointed time in the month of Abib, for in that month you came out of Egypt.

19"The first offspring of every womb belongs to me, including all the firstborn[D] males of your livestock, whether from herd or flock. **20**Redeem[D] the firstborn donkey with a lamb, but if you do not redeem it, break its neck. Redeem all your firstborn sons.

"No one is to appear before me empty-handed.

21"Six days you shall labor, but on the seventh day you shall rest; even during the plowing season and harvest you must rest.

22"Celebrate the Feast of Weeks with the firstfruits[D] of the wheat harvest, and the Feast of Ingathering at the turn of the year.[a] **23**Three times a year all your men are to appear before the Sovereign LORD, the God of Israel. **24**I will drive out nations before you and enlarge your territory, and no one will covet your land when you go up three times each year to appear before the LORD your God.

25"Do not offer the blood of a sacrifice[D] to me along with anything containing yeast[D], and do not let any of the sacrifice from the Passover Feast remain until morning.

26"Bring the best of the firstfruits of your soil to the house of the LORD your God.

"Do not cook a young goat in its mother's milk."

27Then the LORD said to Moses, "Write down these words, for in accordance with these words I have made a covenant[D] with you and with Israel." **28**Moses was there with the LORD forty days and forty nights without eating bread or drinking water. And he wrote on the tablets the words of the covenant—the Ten Commandments.

The Radiant Face of Moses

29When Moses came down from Mount Sinai with the two tablets of the Testimony in his hands, he was not aware that his face was radiant because he had spoken with the LORD. **30**When Aaron and all the Israelites saw Moses, his face was radiant, and they were afraid to come near him. **31**But Moses called to them; so Aaron and all the leaders of the community came back to him, and he spoke to them. **32**Afterward all the Israelites came near him, and he gave them all the commands the LORD had given him on Mount Sinai.

33When Moses finished speaking to them, he put a veil over his face. **34**But whenever he entered the LORD's presence to speak with him, he removed the veil until he came out. And when he came out and told the Israelites what he had been commanded, **35**they saw that his face was radiant. Then Moses would put the veil back over his face until he went in to speak with the LORD.

Sabbath Regulations

35 Moses assembled the whole Israelite community and said to them, "These are the things the LORD has commanded you to do: **2**For six days, work is to be done, but the seventh day shall be your holy day, a Sabbath[D] of rest to the LORD. Whoever does any work on it must be put to death[D]. **3**Do not light a fire in any of your dwellings on the Sabbath day."

Empty-handed (34:20)

See *Can't we come to God empty-handed?* (23:15).

Why didn't his first 40 days make Moses' face radiant? (34:29)

Some think this radiance was the glory Moses prayed for during his second 40 days (33:18). Others believe that Moses' anger when he first descended the mountain (32:19) canceled out any glory that would have appeared on his face. When Moses descended the second time, he was not angry.

SCRIPTURE LINK (34:33) *He put a veil over his face*

This verse was seen by Paul as an illustration of the temporary nature of the old covenant and the permanence of the new. See 2 Cor. 3:7–18.

Why did Moses cover his face after speaking? (34:33)

Moses did not want the people to see the glory fading away (2 Cor. 3:13), so that they would continue to honor him as God's representative and be less likely to turn to idols again.

Why not light a fire on the Sabbath? (35:3)

This may have been a restriction against lighting a *new* fire—which would require considerable work, such as carrying wood and rubbing sticks for the friction to spark a flame. The people could probably keep a fire going that had been started before the Sabbath, so they could cook and have heat.

---

a22 That is, in the fall

Materials for the Tabernacle

4Moses said to the whole Israelite community, "This is what the LORD has commanded: **5**From what you have, take an offering for the LORD. Everyone who is willing is to bring to the LORD an offering of gold, silver and bronze; **6**blue, purple^D and scarlet yarn and fine linen; goat hair; **7**ram skins dyed red and hides of sea cows^Da; acacia^D wood; **8**olive oil for the light; spices for the anointing^D oil and for the fragrant incense^D; **9**and onyx stones and other gems to be mounted on the ephod^D and breastpiece^D.

10"All who are skilled among you are to come and make everything the LORD has commanded: **11**the tabernacle^D with its tent and its covering, clasps, frames, crossbars, posts and bases; **12**the ark with its poles and the atonement^D cover and the curtain that shields it; **13**the table with its poles and all its articles and the bread of the Presence; **14**the lampstand that is for light with its accessories, lamps and oil for the light; **15**the altar of incense with its poles, the anointing oil and the fragrant incense; the curtain for the doorway at the entrance to the tabernacle; **16**the altar of burnt offering with its bronze grating, its poles and all its utensils; the bronze basin with its stand; **17**the curtains of the courtyard with its posts and bases, and the curtain for the entrance to the courtyard; **18**the tent pegs for the tabernacle and for the courtyard, and their ropes; **19**the woven garments worn for ministering in the sanctuary—both the sacred^D garments for Aaron the priest^D and the garments for his sons when they serve as priests."

20Then the whole Israelite community withdrew from Moses' presence, **21**and everyone who was willing and whose heart moved him came and brought an offering to the LORD for the work on the Tent of Meeting^D, for all its service, and for the sacred garments. **22**All who were willing, men and women alike, came and brought gold jewelry of all kinds: brooches, earrings, rings and ornaments. They all presented their gold as a wave offering^D

^a7 That is, dugongs; also in verse 23

SCRIPTURE LINK (35:4–19)
For other verses on offerings for the tabernacle, see 25:1–7 and 39:32–41.

How were the people's hearts moved to give? (35:21)
See *Why did the people give so freely?* (36:4–5).

What was a wave offering? (35:22)
The Lord instituted many kinds of offerings to be given at different times: burnt offerings, fellowship offerings, sin offerings, thank offerings. A wave offering, either meat or grain, got its name because it was probably waved before the Lord as it was presented to him. The offering then usually belonged to the priest and was eaten by him. Also see *Why wave an offering?* (Lev. 7:30).

Why such detailed instructions? (35:4—37:29)

This long passage is almost an exact duplicate of the instructions given earlier about the tabernacle. See article: *What was so critical about the pattern?* (25:40). Repetition was a common literary device in ancient Middle Eastern literature, used to fix the details in the reader's or listener's mind. Some explain the detailed repetition by saying different writers wrote each section, but that is unlikely because other examples of literature from that time contain similar repetitious sections for building projects. The writer of Exodus seems to be following a preexisting format.

How are such details beneficial for us today? Some suggest that parallels can be drawn from passages like this to principles in the New Testament. For example, God is concerned about building the church — his dwelling place among his people today — just as he was concerned about the construction of the tabernacle. Others say that such parts of the Bible were intended for a specific audience and time. They don't feel that applications need to be forced on other situations and that to do so would distort the intended meaning and purpose of Scripture. These people would say that the instructions for the tabernacle should not be applied to any other setting.

to the LORD. **23**Everyone who had blue, purple^D or scarlet yarn or fine linen, or goat hair, ram skins dyed red or hides of sea cows^D brought them. **24**Those presenting an offering of silver or bronze brought it as an offering to the LORD, and everyone who had acacia^D wood for any part of the work brought it. **25**Every skilled woman spun with her hands and brought what she had spun—blue, purple or scarlet yarn or fine linen. **26**And all the women who were willing and had the skill spun the goat hair. **27**The leaders brought onyx stones and other gems to be mounted on the ephod^D and breastpiece^D. **28**They also brought spices and olive oil for the light and for the anointing^D oil and for the fragrant incense^D. **29**All the Israelite men and women who were willing brought to the LORD freewill offerings for all the work the LORD through Moses had commanded them to do.

Bezalel and Oholiab

30Then Moses said to the Israelites, "See, the LORD has chosen Bezalel son of Uri, the son of Hur, of the tribe of Judah, **31**and he has filled him with the Spirit of God, with skill, ability and knowledge in all kinds of crafts— **32**to make artistic designs for work in gold, silver and bronze, **33**to cut and set stones, to work in wood and to engage in all kinds of artistic craftsmanship. **34**And he has given both him and Oholiab son of Ahisamach, of the tribe of Dan, the ability to teach others. **35**He has filled them with skill to do all kinds of work as craftsmen, designers, embroiderers in blue, purple and scarlet yarn and fine linen, and weavers—all of them master craftsmen and designers. **1**So Bezalel, Oholiab and every skilled person to whom the LORD has given skill and ability to know how to carry out all the work of constructing the sanctuary are to do the work just as the Lord has commanded."

2Then Moses summoned Bezalel and Oholiab and every skilled person to whom the LORD had given ability and who was willing to come and do the work. **3**They received from Moses all the offerings the Israelites had brought to carry out the work of constructing the sanctuary. And the people continued to bring freewill offerings morning after morning. **4**So all the skilled craftsmen who were doing all the work on the sanctuary left their work **5**and said to Moses, "The people are bringing more than enough for doing the work the LORD commanded to be done."

6Then Moses gave an order and they sent this word throughout the camp: "No man or woman is to make anything else as an offering for the sanctuary." And so the people were restrained from bringing more, **7**because what they already had was more than enough to do all the work.

The Tabernacle

8All the skilled men among the workmen made the tabernacle^D with ten curtains of finely twisted linen and blue, purple and scarlet yarn, with cherubim worked into them by a skilled craftsman. **9**All the curtains were the same size—twenty-eight cubits^D long and four cubits wide.^a **10**They joined five of the curtains together and did the same with the other five. **11**Then they made loops of blue material along the edge of the end curtain in

---

Why did the people give so freely? (36:4-5)

God may have used recent events to inspire the people to give. They had seen God's power when he punished them for worshiping the golden calf (32:25). They were afraid of Moses, with his radiant face, when he delivered the stone tablets of the law (34:30). Such events may have prompted them to listen all the more closely when Moses outlined plans for building the tabernacle. Whatever means God may have used, it's clear the people caught the vision.

Blue, purple and scarlet (36:8)

Dye obtained from shellfish (*blue*), murex snails' secretions (*purple*) and certain scale insects (*scarlet*).

Cherubim (36:8)

See *Cherubim* (25:18).

SCRIPTURE LINK (36:8-38)

For more on the tabernacle, see 26:1-37.

---

^a9 That is, about 42 feet (about 12.5 meters) long and 6 feet (about 1.8 meters) wide

one set, and the same was done with the end curtain in the other set. **12**They also made fifty loops on one curtain and fifty loops on the end curtain of the other set, with the loops opposite each other. **13**Then they made fifty gold clasps and used them to fasten the two sets of curtains together so that the tabernacleᴰ was a unit.

14They made curtains of goat hair for the tent over the tabernacle—eleven altogether. **15**All eleven curtains were the same size—thirty cubitsᴰ long and four cubits wide.ᵃ **16**They joined five of the curtains into one set and the other six into another set. **17**Then they made fifty loops along the edge of the end curtain in one set and also along the edge of the end curtain in the other set. **18**They made fifty bronze clasps to fasten the tent together as a unit. **19**Then they made for the tent a covering of ram skins dyed red, and over that a covering of hides of sea cows.ᵇ

20They made upright frames of acaciaᴰ wood for the tabernacle. **21**Each frame was ten cubits long and a cubit and a half wide,ᶜ **22**with two projections set parallel to each other. They made all the frames of the tabernacle in this way. **23**They made twenty frames for the south side of the tabernacle **24**and made forty silver bases to go under them—two bases for each frame, one under each projection. **25**For the other side, the north side of the tabernacle, they made twenty frames **26**and forty silver bases—two under each frame. **27**They made six frames for the far end, that is, the west end of the tabernacle, **28**and two frames were made for the corners of the tabernacle at the far end. **29**At these two corners the frames were double from the bottom all the way to the top and fitted into a single ring; both were made alike. **30**So there were eight frames and sixteen silver bases—two under each frame.

31They also made crossbars of acacia wood: five for the frames on one side of the tabernacle, **32**five for those on the other side, and five for the frames on the west, at the far end of the tabernacle. **33**They made the center crossbar so that it extended from end to end at the middle of the frames. **34**They overlaid the frames with gold and made gold rings to hold the crossbars. They also overlaid the crossbars with gold.

35They made the curtain of blue, purpleᴰ and scarlet yarn and finely twisted linen, with cherubimᴰ worked into it by a skilled craftsman. **36**They made four posts of acacia wood for it and overlaid them with gold. They made gold hooks for them and cast their four silver bases. **37**For the entrance to the tent they made a curtain of blue, purple and scarlet yarn and finely twisted linen—the work of an embroiderer; **38**and they made five posts with hooks for them. They overlaid the tops of the posts and their bands with gold and made their five bases of bronze.

The Ark

37 Bezalel made the ark of acacia wood—two and a half cubits long, a cubit and a half wide, and a cubit and a half high.ᵈ **2**He overlaid it with pure gold, both inside and out, and made a gold molding around it.

How did these former slaves get so much gold? (36:13)
Most of the precious metal used in making the furnishings for the tabernacle probably came from the Egyptians. God had caused the Egyptians to become *favorably disposed* toward the Israelites, giving them gifts of silver, gold and clothing as they left the land. Also see *Why would the Egyptians be willing to be looted?* (12:35–36).

Why did they use acacia wood for all these things? (36:20–31)
The durable acacia wood was plentiful in the Sinai Desert and was well-suited for such uses. Because it is harder than oak, it is extremely resistant to insects. The tree's branches were protected by thorns, perhaps suggesting God's intimidating majesty. The burning bush (Exodus 3:2) was one species of acacia.

Why so many details? (36:31–38)
See article: *What was so critical about the pattern?* (25:40)

The ark (37:1)
See *Tabernacle Furnishings* on page 110.

ᵃ15 That is, about 45 feet (about 13.5 meters) long and 6 feet (about 1.8 meters) wide   ᵇ19 That is, dugongs   ᶜ21 That is, about 15 feet (about 4.5 meters) long and 2 1/4 feet (about 0.7 meter) wide   ᵈ1 That is, about 3 3/4 feet (about 1.1 meters) long and 2 1/4 feet (about 0.7 meter) wide and high

[3]He cast four gold rings for it and fastened them to its four feet, with two rings on one side and two rings on the other. [4]Then he made poles of acacia[D] wood and overlaid them with gold. [5]And he inserted the poles into the rings on the sides of the ark to carry it.

[6]He made the atonement[D] cover of pure gold—two and a half cubits[D] long and a cubit and a half wide.[a] [7]Then he made two cherubim[D] out of hammered gold at the ends of the cover. [8]He made one cherub on one end and the second cherub on the other; at the two ends he made them of one piece with the cover. [9]The cherubim had their wings spread upward, overshadowing the cover with them. The cherubim faced each other, looking toward the cover.

The Table

[10]They[b] made the table of acacia wood—two cubits long, a cubit wide, and a cubit and a half high.[c] [11]Then they overlaid it with pure gold and made a gold molding around it. [12]They also made around it a rim a handbreadth[d] wide and put a gold molding on the rim. [13]They cast four gold rings for the table and fastened them to the four corners, where the four legs were. [14]The rings were put close to the rim to hold the poles used in carrying the table. [15]The poles for carrying the table were made of acacia wood and were overlaid with gold. [16]And they made from pure gold the articles for the table—its plates and dishes and bowls and its pitchers for the pouring out of drink offerings.

The Lampstand

[17]They made the lampstand of pure gold and hammered it out, base and shaft; its flowerlike cups, buds and blossoms were of one piece with it. [18]Six branches extended from the sides of the lampstand—three on one side and three on the other. [19]Three cups shaped like almond flowers with buds and blossoms were on one branch, three on the next branch and the same for all six branches extending from the lampstand. [20]And on the lampstand were four cups shaped like almond flowers with buds and blossoms. [21]One bud was under the first pair of branches extending from the lampstand, a second bud under the second pair, and a third bud under the third pair—six branches in all. [22]The buds and the branches were all of one piece with the lampstand, hammered out of pure gold.

[23]They made its seven lamps, as well as its wick trimmers and trays, of pure gold. [24]They made the lampstand and all its accessories from one talent[e] of pure gold.

The Altar of Incense

[25]They made the altar of incense[D] out of acacia wood. It was square, a cubit long and a cubit wide, and two cubits high[f]—its horns of one piece with it. [26]They overlaid the top and all the sides and the horns with pure gold, and made a gold molding around it.

The table (37:10)
See *Tabernacle Furnishings* on page 110.

Is this lampstand the same as the modern menorah? (37:17)
This lampstand may have been a forerunner to the menorah. Its seven lamps (v. 23) and six branches (v. 18) suggest similarities. One difference, however, is that this lampstand was one of a kind, designed to burn only in the holy place of the tabernacle. See *Tabernacle Furnishings* on page 110.

The altar of incense (37:25)
See *Tabernacle Furnishings* on page 110.

---

[a]6 That is, about 3 3/4 feet (about 1.1 meters) long and 2 1/4 feet (about 0.7 meter) wide   [b]10 Or *He*; also in verses 11-29
[c]10 That is, about 3 feet (about 0.9 meter) long, 1 1/2 feet (about 0.5 meter) wide, and 2 1/4 feet (about 0.7 meter) high   [d]12 That is, about 3 inches (about 8 centimeters)   [e]24 That is, about 75 pounds (about 34 kilograms)   [f]25 That is, about 1 1/2 feet (about 0.5 meter) long and wide, and about 3 feet (about 0.9 meter) high

[27]They made two gold rings below the molding—two on opposite sides—to hold the poles used to carry it. [28]They made the poles of acacia[D] wood and overlaid them with gold.

[29]They also made the sacred[D] anointing[D] oil and the pure, fragrant incense[D]—the work of a perfumer.

The Altar of Burnt Offering

38 They[a] built the altar of burnt offering[D] of acacia wood, three cubits[b] high; it was square, five cubits long and five cubits wide.[c] [2]They made a horn at each of the four corners, so that the horns and the altar were of one piece, and they overlaid the altar with bronze. [3]They made all its utensils of bronze—its pots, shovels, sprinkling bowls, meat forks and firepans. [4]They made a grating for the altar, a bronze network, to be under its ledge, halfway up the altar. [5]They cast bronze rings to hold the poles for the four corners of the bronze grating. [6]They made the poles of acacia wood and overlaid them with bronze. [7]They inserted the poles into the rings so they would be on the sides of the altar for carrying it. They made it hollow, out of boards.

Basin for Washing

[8]They made the bronze basin and its bronze stand from the mirrors of the women who served at the entrance to the Tent of Meeting.

The Courtyard

[9]Next they made the courtyard. The south side was a hundred cubits[d] long and had curtains of finely twisted linen, [10]with twenty posts and twenty bronze bases, and with silver hooks and bands on the posts. [11]The north side was also a hundred cubits long and had twenty posts and twenty bronze bases, with silver hooks and bands on the posts.

[12]The west end was fifty cubits[e] wide and had curtains, with ten posts and ten bases, with silver hooks and bands on the posts. [13]The east end, toward the sunrise, was also fifty cubits wide. [14]Curtains fifteen cubits[f] long were on one side of the entrance, with three posts and three bases, [15]and curtains fifteen cubits long were on the other side of the entrance to the courtyard, with three posts and three bases. [16]All the curtains around the courtyard were of finely twisted linen. [17]The bases for the posts were bronze. The hooks and bands on the posts were silver, and their tops were overlaid with silver; so all the posts of the courtyard had silver bands.

[18]The curtain for the entrance to the courtyard was of blue, purple[D] and scarlet yarn and finely twisted linen— the work of an embroiderer. It was twenty cubits[g] long and, like the curtains of the courtyard, five cubits[h] high, [19]with four posts and four bronze bases. Their hooks and bands were silver, and their tops were overlaid with silver. [20]All the tent pegs of the tabernacle[D] and of the surrounding courtyard were bronze.

What were the mirrors of the women? (38:8)

These were not glass mirrors, as we know them, but pieces of highly polished bronze used as we use mirrors today. The women donated these prized objects to help make the basin of bronze.

Who were the women who served at the entrance to the Tent of Meeting? (38:8)

They may have been musicians. Or perhaps they performed domestic responsibilities at the Tent of Meeting. They were not prostitutes as might be found in pagan temples. Prostitution at the Tent of Meeting and tabernacle was clearly forbidden (Deut. 23:17–18).

---

[a]1 Or He; also in verses 2-9   [b]1 That is, about 4 1/2 feet (about 1.3 meters)   [c]1 That is, about 7 1/2 feet (about 2.3 meters) long and wide   [d]9 That is, about 150 feet (about 46 meters)   [e]12 That is, about 75 feet (about 23 meters)   [f]14 That is, about 22 1/2 feet (about 6.9 meters)   [g]18 That is, about 30 feet (about 9 meters)   [h]18 That is, about 7 1/2 feet (about 2.3 meters)

SCRIPTURE LINK (38:22-23)
For more on the work of Bezalel and Oholiab
see 31:1-11.

How did the Levites carry so many heavy objects? (38:24-25,29)
It's estimated there were anywhere from 32,000 to 75,000 adult men in the Levite tribe. The weight of the gold, silver and bronze carried by the Levites was 7.25 tons. If each man carried only two pounds, only 29,000 would have been needed to carry this weight. Furthermore, they most likely relied on other family members to help carry their personal belongings.

What was the value of all this gold, silver and bronze? (38:24-29)
Any calculations are rather inconclusive since ancient Israel did not use a money-based economic system. Furthermore, values are determined by supply-and-demand, so silver could have been nearly as valuable as gold. But at today's market value, for example, the gold would be worth over $40 million.

Why all the fancy clothing? (39:2-7)
The priests' garments were intended to show *dignity and honor*. The elaborate designs served to elevate the priests to a position of stature in the eyes of the people. The garments may also have helped the people esteem the worship of God as an awesome and mysterious privilege.

The Materials Used

21These are the amounts of the materials used for the tabernacle[D], the tabernacle of the Testimony, which were recorded at Moses' command by the Levites[D] under the direction of Ithamar son of Aaron, the priest[D]. **22**(Bezalel son of Uri, the son of Hur, of the tribe of Judah, made everything the LORD commanded Moses; **23**with him was Oholiab son of Ahisamach, of the tribe of Dan—a craftsman and designer, and an embroiderer in blue, purple[D] and scarlet yarn and fine linen.) **24**The total amount of the gold from the wave offering[D] used for all the work on the sanctuary was 29 talents and 730 shekels[D],[a] according to the sanctuary shekel.

25The silver obtained from those of the community who were counted in the census was 100 talents and 1,775 shekels,[b] according to the sanctuary shekel— **26**one beka per person, that is, half a shekel,[c] according to the sanctuary shekel, from everyone who had crossed over to those counted, twenty years old or more, a total of 603,550 men. **27**The 100 talents[d] of silver were used to cast the bases for the sanctuary and for the curtain—100 bases from the 100 talents, one talent for each base. **28**They used the 1,775 shekels[e] to make the hooks for the posts, to overlay the tops of the posts, and to make their bands.

29The bronze from the wave offering was 70 talents and 2,400 shekels.[f] **30**They used it to make the bases for the entrance to the Tent of Meeting[D], the bronze altar with its bronze grating and all its utensils, **31**the bases for the surrounding courtyard and those for its entrance and all the tent pegs for the tabernacle and those for the surrounding courtyard.

The Priestly Garments

39 From the blue, purple and scarlet yarn they made woven garments for ministering in the sanctuary. They also made sacred[D] garments for Aaron, as the LORD commanded Moses.

The Ephod

2They[g] made the ephod[D] of gold, and of blue, purple and scarlet yarn, and of finely twisted linen. **3**They hammered out thin sheets of gold and cut strands to be worked into the blue, purple and scarlet yarn and fine linen—the work of a skilled craftsman. **4**They made shoulder pieces for the ephod, which were attached to two of its corners, so it could be fastened. **5**Its skillfully woven waistband was like it—of one piece with the ephod and made with gold, and with blue, purple and scarlet yarn, and with finely twisted linen, as the LORD commanded Moses.

6They mounted the onyx stones in gold filigree settings and engraved them like a seal with the names of the sons of Israel. **7**Then they fastened them on the shoulder pieces of the ephod as memorial stones for the sons of Israel, as the LORD commanded Moses.

---

a24 The weight of the gold was a little over one ton (about 1 metric ton).   *b25* The weight of the silver was a little over 3 3/4 tons (about 3.4 metric tons).   *c26* That is, about 1/5 ounce (about 5.5 grams)   *d27* That is, about 3 3/4 tons (about 3.4 metric tons)   *e28* That is, about 45 pounds (about 20 kilograms)   *f29* The weight of the bronze was about 2 1/2 tons (about 2.4 metric tons).   *g2* Or *He*; also in verses 7, 8 and 22

The Breastpiece

8They fashioned the breastpiece[D]—the work of a skilled craftsman. They made it like the ephod[D]: of gold, and of blue, purple[D] and scarlet yarn, and of finely twisted linen. **9**It was square—a span[a] long and a span wide—and folded double. **10**Then they mounted four rows of precious stones on it. In the first row there was a ruby, a topaz and a beryl; **11**in the second row a turquoise, a sapphire[b] and an emerald; **12**in the third row a jacinth, an agate and an amethyst; **13**in the fourth row a chrysolite, an onyx and a jasper.[c] They were mounted in gold filigree settings. **14**There were twelve stones, one for each of the names of the sons of Israel, each engraved like a seal with the name of one of the twelve tribes.

15For the breastpiece they made braided chains of pure gold, like a rope. **16**They made two gold filigree settings and two gold rings, and fastened the rings to two of the corners of the breastpiece. **17**They fastened the two gold chains to the rings at the corners of the breastpiece, **18**and the other ends of the chains to the two settings, attaching them to the shoulder pieces of the ephod at the front. **19**They made two gold rings and attached them to the other two corners of the breastpiece on the inside edge next to the ephod. **20**Then they made two more gold rings and attached them to the bottom of the shoulder pieces on the front of the ephod, close to the seam just above the waistband of the ephod. **21**They tied the rings of the breastpiece to the rings of the ephod with blue cord, connecting it to the waistband so that the breastpiece would not swing out from the ephod—as the LORD commanded Moses.

Other Priestly Garments

22They made the robe of the ephod entirely of blue cloth—the work of a weaver— **23**with an opening in the center of the robe like the opening of a collar,[d] and a band around this opening, so that it would not tear. **24**They made pomegranates of blue, purple and scarlet yarn and finely twisted linen around the hem of the robe. **25**And they made bells of pure gold and attached them around the hem between the pomegranates. **26**The bells and pomegranates alternated around the hem of the robe to be worn for ministering, as the LORD commanded Moses.

27For Aaron and his sons, they made tunics of fine linen—the work of a weaver— **28**and the turban of fine linen, the linen headbands and the undergarments of finely twisted linen. **29**The sash was of finely twisted linen and blue, purple and scarlet yarn—the work of an embroiderer—as the LORD commanded Moses.

30They made the plate, the sacred[D] diadem, out of pure gold and engraved on it, like an inscription on a seal: HOLY TO THE LORD. **31**Then they fastened a blue cord to it to attach it to the turban, as the LORD commanded Moses.

Moses Inspects the Tabernacle

32So all the work on the tabernacle[D], the Tent of Meeting[D], was completed. The Israelites did everything just as the LORD commanded Moses. **33**Then they brought the

What was the significance of these gemstones? (39:10–14)

Though it is difficult from the ancient Hebrew to identify with certainty the identity of the stones, it is clear that each was precious, signifying the value God placed upon his people. Each had the name of one of the tribes of Israel engraved upon it: ruby—Reuben, topaz—Simeon, beryl—Levi, turquoise—Judah, sapphire—Issachar, emerald—Zebulun, jacinth—Dan, agate—Naphtali, amethyst—Gad, chrysolite—Asher, onyx—Joseph, jasper—Benjamin.

Pomegranates (39:24)

Not actually fruit, but yarn twisted or knotted as decorative trim to look like pomegranates.

Diadem (39:30)

A crown or headband affixed to the turban, generally used as a sign of royalty. In this case, however, it signified the distinction assigned to the priest as one being *holy to the* LORD.

---

a9 That is, about 9 inches (about 22 centimeters)   *b11* Or *lapis lazuli*   *c13* The precise identification of some of these precious stones is uncertain.   *d23* The meaning of the Hebrew for this word is uncertain.

Sea cows (39:34)

See *Sea cows* (Num. 4:6).

Ark ... table ... lampstand ... altar (39:35–39)

See *Tabernacle Furnishings* on page 110.

What was accomplished by anointing these objects? (40:9)

See *How did anointing oil consecrate the tabernacle?* (Lev. 8:10) and *What did Moses do to anoint and consecrate the tabernacle?* (Num. 7:1).

How long did it take to build the tabernacle? (40:17)

Probably about six months. The first few months after the Israelites had left Egypt were spent traveling to Sinai (19:1), and then waiting there while Moses spent 80 days on the mountain (Deut 9:9,18).

tabernacleᴰ to Moses: the tent and all its furnishings, its clasps, frames, crossbars, posts and bases; **³⁴**the covering of ram skins dyed red, the covering of hides of sea cowsᴰᵃ and the shielding curtain; **³⁵**the ark of the Testimony with its poles and the atonementᴰ cover; **³⁶**the table with all its articles and the bread of the Presence; **³⁷**the pure gold lampstand with its row of lamps and all its accessories, and the oil for the light; **³⁸**the gold altar, the anointingᴰ oil, the fragrant incenseᴰ, and the curtain for the entrance to the tent; **³⁹**the bronze altar with its bronze grating, its poles and all its utensils; the basin with its stand; **⁴⁰**the curtains of the courtyard with its posts and bases, and the curtain for the entrance to the courtyard; the ropes and tent pegs for the courtyard; all the furnishings for the tabernacle, the Tent of Meeting; **⁴¹**and the woven garments worn for ministering in the sanctuary, both the sacredᴰ garments for Aaron the priestᴰ and the garments for his sons when serving as priests.

⁴²The Israelites had done all the work just as the LORD had commanded Moses. **⁴³**Moses inspected the work and saw that they had done it just as the LORD had commanded. So Moses blessed them.

Setting Up the Tabernacle

40 Then the LORD said to Moses: **²**"Set up the tabernacle, the Tent of Meeting, on the first day of the first month. **³**Place the ark of the Testimony in it and shield the ark with the curtain. **⁴**Bring in the table and set out what belongs on it. Then bring in the lampstand and set up its lamps. **⁵**Place the gold altar of incense in front of the ark of the Testimony and put the curtain at the entrance to the tabernacle.

⁶"Place the altar of burnt offeringᴰ in front of the entrance to the tabernacle, the Tent of Meeting; **⁷**place the basin between the Tent of Meeting and the altar and put water in it. **⁸**Set up the courtyard around it and put the curtain at the entrance to the courtyard.

⁹"Take the anointing oil and anoint the tabernacle and everything in it; consecrate it and all its furnishings, and it will be holy. **¹⁰**Then anoint the altar of burnt offering and all its utensils; consecrate the altar, and it will be most holy. **¹¹**Anoint the basin and its stand and consecrate them.

¹²"Bring Aaron and his sons to the entrance to the Tent of Meeting and wash them with water. **¹³**Then dress Aaron in the sacred garments, anoint him and consecrate him so he may serve me as priest. **¹⁴**Bring his sons and dress them in tunics. **¹⁵**Anoint them just as you anointed their father, so they may serve me as priests. Their anointing will be to a priesthood that will continue for all generations to come." **¹⁶**Moses did everything just as the LORD commanded him.

¹⁷So the tabernacle was set up on the first day of the first month in the second year. **¹⁸**When Moses set up the tabernacle, he put the bases in place, erected the frames, inserted the crossbars and set up the posts. **¹⁹**Then he spread the tent over the tabernacle and put the covering over the tent, as the LORD commanded him.

²⁰He took the Testimony and placed it in the ark, attached the poles to the ark and put the atonement cover over it. **²¹**Then he brought the ark into the tabernacle

---

ᵃ34 That is, dugongs

and hung the shielding curtain and shielded the ark of the Testimony, as the LORD commanded him.

²²Moses placed the table in the Tent of Meeting^D on the north side of the tabernacle^D outside the curtain ²³and set out the bread on it before the LORD, as the LORD commanded him.

²⁴He placed the lampstand in the Tent of Meeting opposite the table on the south side of the tabernacle ²⁵and set up the lamps before the LORD, as the LORD commanded him.

²⁶Moses placed the gold altar in the Tent of Meeting in front of the curtain ²⁷and burned fragrant incense^D on it, as the LORD commanded him. ²⁸Then he put up the curtain at the entrance to the tabernacle.

²⁹He set the altar of burnt offering^D near the entrance to the tabernacle, the Tent of Meeting, and offered on it burnt offerings and grain offerings, as the LORD commanded him.

³⁰He placed the basin between the Tent of Meeting and the altar and put water in it for washing, ³¹and Moses and Aaron and his sons used it to wash their hands and feet. ³²They washed whenever they entered the Tent of Meeting or approached the altar, as the LORD commanded Moses.

³³Then Moses set up the courtyard around the tabernacle and altar and put up the curtain at the entrance to the courtyard. And so Moses finished the work.

The Glory of the LORD

³⁴Then the cloud covered the Tent of Meeting, and the glory^D of the LORD filled the tabernacle. ³⁵Moses could not enter the Tent of Meeting because the cloud had settled upon it, and the glory of the LORD filled the tabernacle.

³⁶In all the travels of the Israelites, whenever the cloud lifted from above the tabernacle, they would set out; ³⁷but if the cloud did not lift, they did not set out—until the day it lifted. ³⁸So the cloud of the LORD was over the tabernacle by day, and fire was in the cloud by night, in the sight of all the house of Israel during all their travels.

What was the *ark of the Testimony*? (40:21)

Also called the *ark of the covenant,* this special box contained the covenant between God and Israel. See *The Testimony* (16:34) and *Why call a chest an ark?* (25:14–16).

Was the Tent of Meeting the same thing as the tabernacle? (40:22)

Not exactly. The English language does not translate these two Hebrew words precisely. Some believe there were several tents of meeting, all temporary structures which were no longer used once the tabernacle was built. Others believe that *tent of meeting* was a general descriptive term, encompassing both the temporary tents and the tabernacle.

If Moses couldn't enter the Tent of Meeting, who could? (40:35)

The priests—Aaron and his sons—were the only ones who could enter the tabernacle. Moses was not a priest, so he could not enter.

LEVITICUS

Why read this book?

Most of us find legal documents tedious and frustrating. Still, we know society needs laws or it will disintegrate into anarchy; specialized language with detailed rules and regulations is essential to maintain order. At first glance, Leviticus may seem like an out-of-date legal document full of disgusting customs. But a larger view reveals that it established the rules of maintaining a relationship with God. It provided a sense of order, a means to deal with sin and its consequences. Don't get bogged down in the "legalese" of Leviticus. Instead, read it for the big picture—a better understanding of salvation.

Who wrote this book?

Moses, although it's possible some of his material was shaped and edited by others who came later.

Why and to whom was it written?

God wanted the people of Israel to have instructions for their social and religious life. Leviticus provided them the means to live with each other and with him.

When was it written?

Probably around 1440 B.C.

What was the historical setting for this book?

Moses had led Israel out of Egypt into the desert. There, at the foot of Mount Sinai (see **Map 3** at the back of this Bible), they built the tabernacle to worship God. While they waited for orders to march toward the promised land, God offered these instructions so the Levites could correctly lead worship. (Leviticus means *pertaining to the Levites*.)

What to look for in Leviticus:

While the strict rules detailed in Leviticus may seem senseless to modern readers, they vividly illustrate God's desires. Look for the principles behind the regulations: You'll discover that God wants us to be free from sin and its fatal effects. You'll find he wants to have a personal relationship with us. You'll see that he wants us to be a holy people set apart for him.

The Burnt Offering

1 The LORD called to Moses and spoke to him from the Tent of Meeting[D]. He said, 2"Speak to the Israelites and say to them: 'When any of you brings an offering to the LORD, bring as your offering an animal from either the herd or the flock.

3" 'If the offering is a burnt offering[D] from the herd, he is to offer a male without defect. He must present it at the entrance to the Tent of Meeting so that it[a] will be acceptable to the LORD. 4He is to lay his hand on the head of the burnt offering, and it will be accepted on his behalf to make atonement[D] for him. 5He is to slaughter the young bull before the LORD, and then Aaron's sons the priests[D] shall bring the blood and sprinkle it against the altar on all sides at the entrance to the Tent of Meeting. 6He is to skin the burnt offering and cut it into pieces. 7The sons of Aaron the priest are to put fire on the altar and arrange wood on the fire. 8Then Aaron's sons the priests shall arrange the pieces, including the head and the fat, on the burning wood that is on the altar. 9He is to wash the inner parts and the legs with water, and the priest is to burn all of it on the altar. It is a burnt offering, an offering made by fire, an aroma pleasing to the LORD.

10" 'If the offering is a burnt offering from the flock, from either the sheep or the goats, he is to offer a male without defect. 11He is to slaughter it at the north side of the altar before the LORD, and Aaron's sons the priests shall sprinkle its blood against the altar on all sides. 12He is to cut it into pieces, and the priest shall arrange them, including the head and the fat, on the burning wood that is on the altar. 13He is to wash the inner parts and the legs with water, and the priest is to bring all of it and burn it on the altar. It is a burnt offering, an offering made by fire, an aroma pleasing to the LORD.

14" 'If the offering to the LORD is a burnt offering of birds, he is to offer a dove or a young pigeon. 15The

a3 Or he

Why wash what the priests were just going to burn? (1:9)

Old Testament worshipers washed the entrails and legs of sacrificial animals to cleanse them from excrement. The idea behind this ritual cleansing was that any animal offered on the altar to God should be perfect. Only an unblemished, clean animal could symbolize the purity God demanded.

Why would the *aroma* be important to God? (1:9)

The writer probably drew from a human experience—the pleasant smell of meat cooking—to help us understand God's pleasure with the intent behind an offering. A similar figure of speech was used later in the New Testament describing Christ's sacrifice as a fragrant offering, pleasing to God (Eph. 5:2). The image goes one step further when sacrifices of praise, good deeds and sharing are described as pleasing to God (Heb. 13:15–16).

What was so special about the north side? (1:11)

The north is often associated with God's presence (see NIV text note at Psalm 48:2; see also Ezek. 1:4). The different sides of the altar may have indicated the different types of sacrifices—in this case, it signaled an offering to remove sin. Or it may have merely been a practical matter of space. The east side of the altar was for ashes and the crop of a sacrificial bird (v. 16); the wash basin was on the west side.

Did a bird please God as much as a larger sacrifice? (1:14)

As Jesus taught through the widow's small offering (Luke 21:1–4), God is more concerned with the intent of an offering than with its monetary value. Israelites who couldn't afford a sheep or goat could substitute a bird without penalty. But no one could substitute a half-hearted offering for a sincere one.

Why kill animals to worship God? (1:1)

While animal sacrifice seems repulsive to us who buy our meat in plastic wrap, it was quite normal to the Israelites. Killing animals for religious purposes—to appease or curry favor with angry gods and assure fertility of crops and livestock, for example—was a common practice in the ancient world.

Israel was alone among its neighbors, however, in associating sacrifice with the one true God. Sacrificial worship in Israel also included a strong emphasis on high moral values in contrast to the pagans who used it with cultic prostitution and other perversions.

Animal sacrifices primarily were used as offerings for sin. Every time an animal was sacrificed, it served as a vivid reminder that sin is serious—deadly serious (Gen. 2:17).

When an animal's life was given in exchange for the penalty of sin, however, the guilty person could be cleansed from sin. By placing their hands on the head of the animal to be sacrificed (1:4), worshipers identified themselves with it. They saw clearly that the animal was dying in their place for their sin. Its blood was the cleansing agent that removed sin, since blood represented the life of the animal (17:11). Also see article: *Why was all this blood needed for worship?* (Exodus 29:11–21).

What good was an offering that didn't bleed? (2:1)

The grain offering was presented as a gift, an act of worship rather than restitution for sin. Although the poor could mix grain with an animal sacrifice as a substitute sin offering (Lev. 5:11), the grain offering itself was probably intended simply to remember God's favor and, by remembering, to please him—*an aroma pleasing to the LORD* (v. 2).

Most holy part (2:3)

The unburned portion of the grain offering, set apart (the literal meaning of the word *holy*) for the priests alone. They were to eat it at the sanctuary (6:16–18) rather than bring it home to their families, as allowed with some offerings (Num. 18:8–20).

Why did it matter how the grain was cooked? (2:4–7)

It didn't. The point was that any method was acceptable as long as the grain was mixed with oil and had no yeast (2:11). Oil added value to the sacrifice. Oil and incense symbolized joy, perhaps communicating joyful thanks. See *Oil of joy* (Psalm 45:7). Cooking may also have indicated greater care on the part of the worshiper. (Uncooked grain offerings were used as sin offerings when the person could afford nothing more; see 5:11.)

Why were yeast and honey singled out? (2:11–12)

It's possible honey and yeast were not to be offered because they were used in fermentation. Or *honey* may have been a term for an alcoholic drink, thought to have been used in pagan worship. Yeast was not linked to uncleanness until later Jewish tradition, so it's unlikely that's what was in mind here.

Salt of the covenant (2:13)

Salt was probably used in some ancient cultures to ratify contracts. It was valued as a sign of friendship and as a preservative, a sign that the covenant would last forever. Salt added to offerings reminded the Israelites of God's unchanging love.

How were some offerings for fellowship? (3:1)

Customs of hospitality in the ancient Middle East included elaborate meals. This offering—the only one the worshiper could partake of—symbolized having a meal with the Lord. Traditionally called a peace offering, it was a sign that there was no hostility between the Lord and the one offering the sacrifice. Because it had to be eaten within two days, it was frequently shared with others in need and so also became a means of fellowship between neighbors.

If a female was good enough for one kind of sacrifice, why not for all? (3:1,6)

No one really knows. God specified that males be used for burnt offerings (1:3), but that may have been for practical considerations more than anything else. The future of the herd depended on the number of females more than the number of males. Even a few bulls could keep the herd viable. But with fewer females, the herd's reproductive capabilities would have been greatly diminished.

priest[D] shall bring it to the altar, wring off the head and burn it on the altar; its blood shall be drained out on the side of the altar. **16**He is to remove the crop with its contents[a] and throw it to the east side of the altar, where the ashes are. **17**He shall tear it open by the wings, not severing it completely, and then the priest shall burn it on the wood that is on the fire on the altar. It is a burnt offering[D], an offering made by fire, an aroma pleasing to the LORD.

The Grain Offering

2 " 'When someone brings a grain offering[D] to the LORD, his offering is to be of fine flour. He is to pour oil on it, put incense[D] on it **2**and take it to Aaron's sons the priests. The priest shall take a handful of the fine flour and oil, together with all the incense, and burn this as a memorial portion on the altar, an offering made by fire, an aroma pleasing to the LORD. **3**The rest of the grain offering belongs to Aaron and his sons; it is a most holy part of the offerings made to the LORD by fire.

4" 'If you bring a grain offering baked in an oven, it is to consist of fine flour: cakes made without yeast[D] and mixed with oil, or[b] wafers made without yeast and spread with oil. **5**If your grain offering is prepared on a griddle, it is to be made of fine flour mixed with oil, and without yeast. **6**Crumble it and pour oil on it; it is a grain offering. **7**If your grain offering is cooked in a pan, it is to be made of fine flour and oil. **8**Bring the grain offering made of these things to the LORD; present it to the priest, who shall take it to the altar. **9**He shall take out the memorial portion from the grain offering and burn it on the altar as an offering made by fire, an aroma pleasing to the LORD. **10**The rest of the grain offering belongs to Aaron and his sons; it is a most holy part of the offerings made to the LORD by fire.

11" 'Every grain offering you bring to the LORD must be made without yeast, for you are not to burn any yeast or honey in an offering made to the LORD by fire. **12**You may bring them to the LORD as an offering of the firstfruits[D], but they are not to be offered on the altar as a pleasing aroma. **13**Season all your grain offerings with salt. Do not leave the salt of the covenant[D] of your God out of your grain offerings; add salt to all your offerings.

14" 'If you bring a grain offering of firstfruits to the LORD, offer crushed heads of new grain roasted in the fire. **15**Put oil and incense on it; it is a grain offering. **16**The priest shall burn the memorial portion of the crushed grain and the oil, together with all the incense, as an offering made to the LORD by fire.

The Fellowship Offering

3 " 'If someone's offering is a fellowship offering[D],[c] and he offers an animal from the herd, whether male or female, he is to present before the LORD an animal without defect. **2**He is to lay his hand on the head of his offering and slaughter it at the entrance to the Tent of Meeting[D]. Then Aaron's sons the priests shall sprinkle the blood against the altar on all sides. **3**From the fellowship offering he is to bring a sacrifice made to the LORD by fire: all the fat that covers the inner parts or is

---

a16 Or crop and the feathers; the meaning of the Hebrew for this word is uncertain.   *b4 Or and*   *c1 Traditionally peace offering;* also in verses 3, 6 and 9

connected to them, **4**both kidneys with the fat on them near the loins, and the covering of the liver, which he will remove with the kidneys. **5**Then Aaron's sons are to burn it on the altar on top of the burnt offering^D that is on the burning wood, as an offering made by fire, an aroma pleasing to the LORD.

6" 'If he offers an animal from the flock as a fellowship offering^D to the LORD, he is to offer a male or female without defect. **7**If he offers a lamb, he is to present it before the LORD. **8**He is to lay his hand on the head of his offering and slaughter it in front of the Tent of Meeting^D. Then Aaron's sons shall sprinkle its blood against the altar on all sides. **9**From the fellowship offering he is to bring a sacrifice^D made to the LORD by fire: its fat, the entire fat tail cut off close to the backbone, all the fat that covers the inner parts or is connected to them, **10**both kidneys with the fat on them near the loins, and the covering of the liver, which he will remove with the kidneys. **11**The priest^D shall burn them on the altar as food, an offering made to the LORD by fire.

12" 'If his offering is a goat, he is to present it before the LORD. **13**He is to lay his hand on its head and slaughter it in front of the Tent of Meeting. Then Aaron's sons shall sprinkle its blood against the altar on all sides. **14**From what he offers he is to make this offering to the LORD by fire: all the fat that covers the inner parts or is connected to them, **15**both kidneys with the fat on them near the loins, and the covering of the liver, which he will remove with the kidneys. **16**The priest shall burn them on the altar as food, an offering made by fire, a pleasing aroma. All the fat is the LORD's.

17" 'This is a lasting ordinance for the generations to come, wherever you live: You must not eat any fat or any blood.' "

The Sin Offering

4 The LORD said to Moses, **2**"Say to the Israelites: 'When anyone sins unintentionally and does what is forbidden in any of the LORD's commands—

3" 'If the anointed^D priest sins, bringing guilt on the people, he must bring to the LORD a young bull without defect as a sin offering^D for the sin he has committed. **4**He is to present the bull at the entrance to the Tent of Meeting before the LORD. He is to lay his hand on its head and slaughter it before the LORD. **5**Then the anointed priest shall take some of the bull's blood and carry it into the Tent of Meeting. **6**He is to dip his finger into the blood and sprinkle some of it seven times before the LORD, in front of the curtain of the sanctuary. **7**The priest shall then put some of the blood on the horns of the altar of fragrant incense^D that is before the LORD in the Tent of Meeting. The rest of the bull's blood he shall pour out at the base of the altar of burnt offering at the entrance to the Tent of Meeting. **8**He shall remove all the fat from the bull of the sin offering—the fat that covers the inner parts or is connected to them, **9**both kidneys with the fat on them near the loins, and the covering of the liver, which he will remove with the kidneys— **10**just as the fat is removed from the ox^a sacrificed as a fellowship offering.^b Then the priest shall burn them

Why burn the fat separately? (3:3–5)
The fat was considered a choice portion of the meat and thus the best part of the sacrifice that could be given to God. Because fat smells so good when meat is cooking, it became the *aroma pleasing to the LORD*. Some think burning the fat separately may also have been God's way of limiting cholesterol intake. He later commanded them not to eat fat in certain instances (Lev. 7:23–25).

Why burn food? (3:11,16)
Pagan cultures considered their sacrifices to be food for their gods. The Israelites knew that the Creator did not need their offerings as literal food. But they used the word in a figurative sense. God received their offerings with as much pleasure as one might have when sitting down to an exquisite feast.

Why was all the fat the Lord's? (3:16)
The fatty portions of meat were considered the tastiest. Normally, when they were not sacrificing to the Lord, the Israelites could eat the fatty portions themselves. But by offering all the fat of their sacrifices to the Lord they were offering the best that they had to God.

Lasting ordinance (3:17)
Suggests the ordinance was to be followed as long as God's covenant lasted. Most Christians believe the sacrificial laws were made obsolete by the new covenant. The phrase *lasting ordinance* occurs 17 times in Leviticus.

Why hold someone responsible for an accidental sin? (4:2)
The original word for *unintentionally* meant *wandering away*—as a sheep might wander from the flock. It implied sin that stemmed from the weakness of human character rather than outright rebellion or premeditated evil. We connect guilt with intention, but the ancients connected it with effects.

Anointed priest (4:3)
All priests were anointed with oil to carry out their ministry (Exodus 29:7; Lev. 8:12,30), but only one—the high priest—was referred to as *the anointed priest*.

Why were the people guilty for a priest's sin? (4:3)
From our New Testament perspective, with Christ as our perfect high priest, it's hard to imagine guilt transferring from an individual to the entire community. But in the Old Testament, the priest represented the people before God. As long as he kept himself pure, he could offer sacrifices and provide cleansing for the sins of the nation. If sin made him a flawed representative, however, God saw the people through those flaws—guilty and unclean (also see 10:6).

Why dip fingers in blood? (4:5–7)
God may have wanted the priest to dip his finger in the blood to picture a transfer of guilt: the priest, for himself as well as the people, dipped his finger in blood so he would not have to shed blood. The blood of the sacrifice substituted for the blood of the offender; the sacrifice died so the sinner might live. Putting the blood on the horns of the altar of incense suggests this further since the smoke of the incense went up as an offering to God.

---

^a10 The Hebrew word can include both male and female.
^b10 Traditionally *peace offering*; also in verses 26, 31 and 35

Old Testament Sacrifices

Sacrifice	Old Testament References	Elements	Purpose
BURNT OFFERING	Lev. 1; 6:8-13; 8:18-21; 16:24	Bull, ram or male bird (dove or young pigeon for the poor); wholly consumed; no defect	Voluntary act of worship; atonement for unintentional sin in general; expression of devotion, commitment and complete surrender to God
GRAIN OFFERING	Lev. 2; 6:14-23	Grain, fine flour, olive oil, incense, baked bread (cakes or wafers), salt; no yeast or honey; accompanied burnt offering and fellowship offering (along with drink offering)	Voluntary act of worship; recognition of God's goodness and provisions; devotion to God
FELLOWSHIP OFFERING	Lev. 3; 7:11-34	Any animal without defect from herd or flock; variety of breads	Voluntary act of worship; thanksgiving and fellowship (it included a communal meal)
SIN OFFERING	Lev. 4:1–5:13; 6:24-30; 8:14-17; 16:3-22	1. Young bull: for high priest and congregation 2. Male goat: for leader 3. Female goat or lamb: for common person 4. Dove or pigeon: for the poor 5. Tenth of an ephah of fine flour: for the very poor	Mandatory atonement for specific unintentional sin; confession of sin; forgiveness of sin; cleansing from defilement
GUILT OFFERING	Lev. 5:14–6:7; 7:1-6	Ram or lamb	Mandatory atonement for unintentional sin requiring restitution; cleansing from defilement; make restitution; pay 20% fine

When more than one kind of offering was presented (as in Num. 7:16,17), the procedure was usually as follows: (1) sin offering or guilt offering, (2) burnt offering, (3) fellowship offering and grain offering (along with a drink offering). This sequence furnishes part of the spiritual significance of the sacrificial system. First, sin had to be dealt with (sin offering or guilt offering). Second, the worshiper committed himself completely to God (burnt offering and grain offering). Third, fellowship or communion between the Lord, the priest and the worshiper was established (fellowship offering).

is a guilt offering[D]. [16]He must make restitution for what he has failed to do in regard to the holy things, add a fifth of the value to that and give it all to the priest[D], who will make atonement[D] for him with the ram as a guilt offering, and he will be forgiven.

[17]"If a person sins and does what is forbidden in any of the LORD's commands, even though he does not know it, he is guilty and will be held responsible. [18]He is to bring to the priest as a guilt offering a ram from the flock, one without defect and of the proper value. In this way the priest will make atonement for him for the wrong he has committed unintentionally, and he will be forgiven. [19]It is a guilt offering; he has been guilty of[a] wrongdoing against the LORD."

6 The LORD said to Moses: [2]"If anyone sins and is unfaithful to the LORD by deceiving his neighbor about something entrusted to him or left in his care or stolen, or if he cheats him, [3]or if he finds lost property and lies about it, or if he swears falsely, or if he commits any such sin that people may do— [4]when he thus sins and becomes guilty, he must return what he has stolen or taken by extortion[D], or what was entrusted to him, or the lost property he found, [5]or whatever it was he swore falsely about. He must make restitution in full, add a fifth of the value to it and give it all to the owner on the day he presents his guilt offering. [6]And as a penalty he must bring to the priest, that is, to the LORD, his guilt offering, a ram from the flock, one without defect and of the proper value. [7]In this way the priest will make atonement for him before the LORD, and he will be forgiven for any of these things he did that made him guilty."

The Burnt Offering

[8]The LORD said to Moses: [9]"Give Aaron and his sons this command: 'These are the regulations for the burnt offering[D]: The burnt offering is to remain on the altar hearth throughout the night, till morning, and the fire must be kept burning on the altar. [10]The priest shall then put on his linen clothes, with linen undergarments next to his body, and shall remove the ashes of the burnt offering that the fire has consumed on the altar and place them beside the altar. [11]Then he is to take off these clothes and put on others, and carry the ashes outside the camp to a place that is ceremonially clean. [12]The fire on the altar must be kept burning; it must not go out. Every morning the priest is to add firewood and arrange the burnt offering on the fire and burn the fat of the fellowship offerings[Db] on it. [13]The fire must be kept burning on the altar continuously; it must not go out.

The Grain Offering

[14]" 'These are the regulations for the grain offering[D]: Aaron's sons are to bring it before the LORD, in front of the altar. [15]The priest is to take a handful of fine flour and oil, together with all the incense[D] on the grain offering, and burn the memorial portion on the altar as an aroma pleasing to the LORD. [16]Aaron and his sons shall eat the rest of it, but it is to be eaten without yeast[D] in a holy place; they are to eat it in the courtyard of the Tent of Meeting[D]. [17]It must not be baked with yeast; I have given it as their share of the offerings made to me by fire.

What did the guilt offerings do that other offerings couldn't? (5:15,19)

Guilt offerings absolved the worshiper who had sinned against sacred property, a serious offense. They also distinguished offenses for which restitution could be made (6:2–7). A ram was offered (no substitutes allowed) and complete restitution plus 20 percent was to be paid, satisfying both God and the person wronged. Burnt offerings provided reconciliation; purification or sin offerings provided purification; but only guilt offerings eased guilty consciences with restitution for sin.

Why wear linen underwear? (6:10)

Linen was worn by priests of many nations in the ancient world. Because they were more costly than ordinary clothes, linen garments were considered special. Their white color symbolized purity, explaining why the priests were not allowed to wear their priestly clothes outside the tabernacle. Specialized clothing indicated that the world of the sanctuary and the world outside were to be kept separate.

Why did God want the fire to burn continually? (6:12–13)

The continual fire reminded the Israelites that God was always present with them (Exodus 13:21–22) and that they needed to be constantly mindful of worshiping him. Fire also was a good metaphor for an awesome God (Deut. 4:24; Isaiah 10:17).

Why could only male descendants eat the grain offering? (6:18)

This was simply another way of saying that only the priests could eat the offering. It was not to be used (as some offerings were) as sustenance for the priests' families. Only Aaron's male descendants were designated as priests (Exodus 28:1; 29:9).

How could the priests make things holy merely by their touch? (6:18)

Uncleanness was contagious, but so was cleanness. One could become holy by touching sacred objects (Exodus 30:29). Any other offerings that came into contact with the grain offering also became holy and could only be eaten by Aaron and his sons. While this may sound arbitrary, it communicated the idea of keeping the holy separate from the unholy, the clean from the unclean.

Why did God want the priests to eat some offerings and not others? (6:23)

A priest stood before God on behalf of the people, but he also was God's representative to the people. "Standing in for God," the priest ate from the offerings brought by others. But he couldn't, in the same way, represent God to himself. His own grain offerings had to be burned completely so they would be true sacrifices—completely given over to God. That wouldn't be the case if he got some of the offering back.

Why break clay cooking pots? (6:28)

Because clay was a porous material, it absorbed the juices of the meat, leaving part of the sacrifice in the pot. So the clay pots were broken for the same reasons bronze pots were washed—to get rid of any leftovers. In the same way, any blood that was splattered on a garment had to be washed out (v. 27). By washing or breaking utensils that touched a sacrifice—and were made holy—the sacred and profane were again kept separate.

Most holy (7:1)

See *Most holy part* (2:3).

Like the sin offering[D] and the guilt offering[D], it is most holy. **18**Any male descendant of Aaron may eat it. It is his regular share of the offerings made to the LORD by fire for the generations to come. Whatever touches them will become holy.*a'* "

19The LORD also said to Moses, **20**"This is the offering Aaron and his sons are to bring to the LORD on the day he[b] is anointed[D]: a tenth of an ephah[c] of fine flour as a regular grain offering[D], half of it in the morning and half in the evening. **21**Prepare it with oil on a griddle; bring it well-mixed and present the grain offering broken[d] in pieces as an aroma pleasing to the LORD. **22**The son who is to succeed him as anointed priest shall prepare it. It is the LORD's regular share and is to be burned completely. **23**Every grain offering of a priest shall be burned completely; it must not be eaten."

The Sin Offering

24The LORD said to Moses, **25**"Say to Aaron and his sons: 'These are the regulations for the sin offering: The sin offering is to be slaughtered before the LORD in the place the burnt offering[D] is slaughtered; it is most holy. **26**The priest who offers it shall eat it; it is to be eaten in a holy place, in the courtyard of the Tent of Meeting[D]. **27**Whatever touches any of the flesh will become holy, and if any of the blood is spattered on a garment, you must wash it in a holy place. **28**The clay pot the meat is cooked in must be broken; but if it is cooked in a bronze pot, the pot is to be scoured and rinsed with water. **29**Any male in a priest's family may eat it; it is most holy. **30**But any sin offering whose blood is brought into the Tent of Meeting to make atonement in the Holy Place must not be eaten; it must be burned.

The Guilt Offering

7 " 'These are the regulations for the guilt offering, which is most holy: **2**The guilt offering is to be slaughtered in the place where the burnt offering is slaughtered, and its blood is to be sprinkled against the altar on all sides. **3**All its fat shall be offered: the fat tail and the fat that covers the inner parts, **4**both kidneys with the fat on them near the loins, and the covering of the liver, which is to be removed with the kidneys. **5**The priest shall burn them on the altar as an offering made to the LORD by fire. It is a guilt offering. **6**Any male in a priest's family may eat it, but it must be eaten in a holy place; it is most holy.

7" 'The same law applies to both the sin offering and the guilt offering: They belong to the priest who makes atonement with them. **8**The priest who offers a burnt offering for anyone may keep its hide for himself. **9**Every grain offering baked in an oven or cooked in a pan or on a griddle belongs to the priest who offers it, **10**and every grain offering, whether mixed with oil or dry, belongs equally to all the sons of Aaron.

The Fellowship Offering

11" 'These are the regulations for the fellowship offering[De] a person may present to the LORD:

---

a18 Or *Whoever touches them must be holy*; similarly in verse 27
b20 Or *each*   *c20* That is, probably about 2 quarts (about 2 liters)
d21 The meaning of the Hebrew for this word is uncertain.
e11 Traditionally *peace offering*; also in verses 13-37

¹²" 'If he offers it as an expression of thankfulness, then along with this thank offering^D he is to offer cakes of bread made without yeast^D and mixed with oil, wafers made without yeast and spread with oil, and cakes of fine flour well-kneaded and mixed with oil. ¹³Along with his fellowship offering^D of thanksgiving he is to present an offering with cakes of bread made with yeast. ¹⁴He is to bring one of each kind as an offering, a contribution to the LORD; it belongs to the priest^D who sprinkles the blood of the fellowship offerings. ¹⁵The meat of his fellowship offering of thanksgiving must be eaten on the day it is offered; he must leave none of it till morning.

¹⁶" 'If, however, his offering is the result of a vow^D or is a freewill offering, the sacrifice^D shall be eaten on the day he offers it, but anything left over may be eaten on the next day. ¹⁷Any meat of the sacrifice left over till the third day must be burned up. ¹⁸If any meat of the fellowship offering is eaten on the third day, it will not be accepted. It will not be credited to the one who offered it, for it is impure; the person who eats any of it will be held responsible.

¹⁹" 'Meat that touches anything ceremonially unclean^D must not be eaten; it must be burned up. As for other meat, anyone ceremonially clean may eat it. ²⁰But if anyone who is unclean eats any meat of the fellowship offering belonging to the LORD, that person must be cut off from his people. ²¹If anyone touches something unclean—whether human uncleanness or an unclean animal or any unclean, detestable thing—and then eats any of the meat of the fellowship offering belonging to the LORD, that person must be cut off from his people.' "

Eating Fat and Blood Forbidden

²²The LORD said to Moses, ²³"Say to the Israelites: 'Do not eat any of the fat of cattle, sheep or goats. ²⁴The fat of an animal found dead or torn by wild animals may be used for any other purpose, but you must not eat it. ²⁵Anyone who eats the fat of an animal from which an offering by fire may be^a made to the LORD must be cut off from his people. ²⁶And wherever you live, you must not eat the blood of any bird or animal. ²⁷If anyone eats blood, that person must be cut off from his people.' "

The Priests' Share

²⁸The LORD said to Moses, ²⁹"Say to the Israelites: 'Anyone who brings a fellowship offering to the LORD is to bring part of it as his sacrifice to the LORD. ³⁰With his own hands he is to bring the offering made to the LORD by fire; he is to bring the fat, together with the breast, and wave the breast before the LORD as a wave offering^D. ³¹The priest shall burn the fat on the altar, but the breast belongs to Aaron and his sons. ³²You are to give the right thigh of your fellowship offerings to the priest as a contribution. ³³The son of Aaron who offers the blood and the fat of the fellowship offering shall have the right thigh as his share. ³⁴From the fellowship offerings of the Israelites, I have taken the breast that is waved and the thigh that is presented and have given them to Aaron the priest and his sons as their regular share from the Israelites.' "

³⁵This is the portion of the offerings made to the LORD by fire that were allotted to Aaron and his sons on the day

---

Why could both leavened and unleavened bread be offered for the thank offering? (7:11–14)

Because bread made with yeast was not placed on the altar, it did not violate commands about yeast (2:11; Exodus 23:18). The leavened bread was for the priest to eat. It's debatable why God preferred unleavened bread. Perhaps, without the fermentation of yeast, it was considered more pure. Also see *Why were yeast and honey singled out?* (2:11–12).

Why didn't God want leftovers? (7:15)

Sacrifices had to be eaten before they spoiled. Spoiled meat would have been unclean—and unfit to fulfill its role as a sacrifice. It's not clear why the meat from a fellowship offering had to be eaten the same day, unlike the freewill offering that could be eaten the second day. Perhaps the practice encouraged sharing the food, especially with the poor.

What would make a person unclean? (7:20)

Uncleanness came about through contact with dead or sick people, unclean animals or bodily discharges (see ch. 22 for a list). Anyone who touched any of these things had to go through a purification ritual in order to be declared clean and allowed to participate in worship.

Cut off from his people (7:20)

This phrase refers to direct judgment from God—often death—rather than human punishment. See *Cut off from my presence* (22:3).

What was wrong with eating fat? (7:22–27)

See *Why was all the fat the Lord's?* (3:16).

Why wave an offering? (7:30)

The translation of the word *wave* stems from ancient rabbinic tradition. Though it's possible that portions of sacrifices or small animals (14:12,24) were actually waved back and forth, the word was also used symbolically—as when the Levites were presented as a wave offering (Num. 8:11). The idea probably refers to *lifting* the offering either physically or symbolically as a gift to the Lord. Also see *Wave offering* (Exodus 29:22–28).

---

^a25 Or *fire is*

they were presented to serve the LORD as priests[D]. [36]On the day they were anointed[D], the LORD commanded that the Israelites give this to them as their regular share for the generations to come.

[37]These, then, are the regulations for the burnt offering[D], the grain offering[D], the sin offering[D], the guilt offering[D], the ordination[D] offering and the fellowship offering[D], [38]which the LORD gave Moses on Mount Sinai on the day he commanded the Israelites to bring their offerings to the LORD, in the Desert of Sinai.

The Ordination of Aaron and His Sons

8 The LORD said to Moses, [2]"Bring Aaron and his sons, their garments, the anointing oil, the bull for the sin offering, the two rams and the basket containing bread made without yeast[D], [3]and gather the entire assembly at the entrance to the Tent of Meeting[D]." [4]Moses did as the LORD commanded him, and the assembly gathered at the entrance to the Tent of Meeting.

[5]Moses said to the assembly, "This is what the LORD has commanded to be done." [6]Then Moses brought Aaron and his sons forward and washed them with water. [7]He put the tunic on Aaron, tied the sash around him, clothed him with the robe and put the ephod[D] on him. He also tied the ephod to him by its skillfully woven waistband; so it was fastened on him. [8]He placed the breastpiece[D] on him and put the Urim[D] and Thummim[D] in the breastpiece. [9]Then he placed the turban on Aaron's head and set the gold plate, the sacred[D] diadem, on the front of it, as the LORD commanded Moses.

[10]Then Moses took the anointing oil and anointed the tabernacle[D] and everything in it, and so consecrated[D] them. [11]He sprinkled some of the oil on the altar seven times, anointing the altar and all its utensils and the basin with its stand, to consecrate them. [12]He poured some of the anointing oil on Aaron's head and anointed him to consecrate him. [13]Then he brought Aaron's sons forward, put tunics on them, tied sashes around them and put headbands on them, as the LORD commanded Moses.

[14]He then presented the bull for the sin offering, and Aaron and his sons laid their hands on its head. [15]Moses slaughtered the bull and took some of the blood, and with his finger he put it on all the horns of the altar to purify[D] the altar. He poured out the rest of the blood at the base of the altar. So he consecrated it to make atonement for it. [16]Moses also took all the fat around the inner parts, the covering of the liver, and both kidneys and their fat, and burned it on the altar. [17]But the bull with its hide and its flesh and its offal[D] he burned up outside the camp, as the LORD commanded Moses.

[18]He then presented the ram for the burnt offering, and Aaron and his sons laid their hands on its head. [19]Then Moses slaughtered the ram and sprinkled the blood against the altar on all sides. [20]He cut the ram into pieces and burned the head, the pieces and the fat. [21]He washed the inner parts and the legs with water and burned the whole ram on the altar as a burnt offering, a pleasing aroma, an offering made to the LORD by fire, as the LORD commanded Moses.

[22]He then presented the other ram, the ram for the ordination, and Aaron and his sons laid their hands on its head. [23]Moses slaughtered the ram and took some of its

---

Why were Aaron and his sons chosen to be priests? (8:2)

God instructed Moses to establish an order of priests to serve as mediators, representing God to the people and the people to God. As to why God assigned this awesome responsibility to Aaron and his sons, it is impossible to say. God's sovereign selection of individuals, tribes or even nations often remains a mystery. God decreed that only Levites could take care of the tabernacle and its furnishings (Num. 3:5–9). Only descendants of Aaron (himself a Levite; Num. 26:59) could serve as priests (Num. 3:10). Also see *Why didn't the second in line get what Reuben lost?* (1 Chron. 5:2).

Why all this garb for a priest? (8:7–9)

The priestly garments gave *dignity and honor* (Exodus 28:2), presumably to the priest as God's representative. Even today, clerical garb can communicate the importance and unique nature of the pastoral role. Likewise, Aaron's priestly clothing signified the importance and distinct character of his work as priest.

How did anointing oil consecrate the tabernacle? (8:10)

Anointing was an act of dedication, in this case giving the tabernacle and its furnishings over to God's service and making them holy—set apart for the Lord alone. To the ancients, oil signified joy and well-being (Psalm 104:15). Using oil to consecrate objects or people was also a way to indicate a special honor or role (Judges 9:9). Also see *What did Moses do to anoint and consecrate the tabernacle?* (Num. 7:1).

How could Moses—who wasn't a priest—offer sacrifices? (8:15–19)

Aaron and his sons had not yet been purified or consecrated as priests, so they could not make offerings. At God's command, Moses served as a temporary high priest and set up the ongoing institution of worship and sacrifice. He stepped down once Aaron and his sons were installed.

Ordination (8:22)

The original word literally meant *to fill the hand* and probably referred to offerings placed in their hands. The ritual signified the responsibilities and privileges of the priesthood (v. 27), reminding the Levites that they were set apart for the Lord's service. Ordination of ministers today finds common themes in the roots of this Old Testament practice.

blood and put it on the lobe of Aaron's right ear, on the thumb of his right hand and on the big toe of his right foot. **24**Moses also brought Aaron's sons forward and put some of the blood on the lobes of their right ears, on the thumbs of their right hands and on the big toes of their right feet. Then he sprinkled blood against the altar on all sides. **25**He took the fat, the fat tail, all the fat around the inner parts, the covering of the liver, both kidneys and their fat and the right thigh. **26**Then from the basket of bread made without yeast^D, which was before the LORD, he took a cake of bread, and one made with oil, and a wafer; he put these on the fat portions and on the right thigh. **27**He put all these in the hands of Aaron and his sons and waved them before the LORD as a wave offering^D. **28**Then Moses took them from their hands and burned them on the altar on top of the burnt offering^D as an ordination^D offering, a pleasing aroma, an offering made to the LORD by fire. **29**He also took the breast—Moses' share of the ordination ram—and waved it before the LORD as a wave offering, as the LORD commanded Moses.

30Then Moses took some of the anointing^D oil and some of the blood from the altar and sprinkled them on Aaron and his garments and on his sons and their garments. So he consecrated^D Aaron and his garments and his sons and their garments.

31Moses then said to Aaron and his sons, "Cook the meat at the entrance to the Tent of Meeting^D and eat it there with the bread from the basket of ordination offerings, as I commanded, saying,^a 'Aaron and his sons are to eat it.' **32**Then burn up the rest of the meat and the bread. **33**Do not leave the entrance to the Tent of Meeting for seven days, until the days of your ordination are completed, for your ordination will last seven days. **34**What has been done today was commanded by the LORD to make atonement^D for you. **35**You must stay at the entrance to the Tent of Meeting day and night for seven days and do what the LORD requires, so you will not die; for that is what I have been commanded." **36**So Aaron and his sons did everything the LORD commanded through Moses.

The Priests Begin Their Ministry

9 On the eighth day Moses summoned Aaron and his sons and the elders of Israel. **2**He said to Aaron, "Take a bull calf for your sin offering^D and a ram for your burnt offering, both without defect, and present them before the LORD. **3**Then say to the Israelites: 'Take a male goat for a sin offering, a calf and a lamb—both a year old and without defect—for a burnt offering, **4**and an ox^b and a ram for a fellowship offering^{Dc} to sacrifice^D before the LORD, together with a grain offering^D mixed with oil. For today the LORD will appear to you.'"

5They took the things Moses commanded to the front of the Tent of Meeting, and the entire assembly came near and stood before the LORD. **6**Then Moses said, "This is what the LORD has commanded you to do, so that the glory^D of the LORD may appear to you."

7Moses said to Aaron, "Come to the altar and sacrifice your sin offering and your burnt offering and make

---

^a31 Or *I was commanded*:   ^b4 The Hebrew word can include both male and female; also in verses 18 and 19.   ^c4 Traditionally *peace offering*; also in verses 18 and 22

What was special about the priests' right ears, thumbs and big toes? (8:23)

Many cultures throughout human history have favored the right side over the left, perhaps because most people are right-handed. No one is sure why the right side is often the favored side in Scripture (Gen. 48:17–18; Matt. 25:34,41). As to the significance of these body parts, it's possible that they were symbols for the entire body, just as the horns of the altar apparently stood for the whole altar (v. 15). Putting blood on them symbolized a complete restoration of the priest's relationship with God. Also see *Why dab blood on Aaron's right ear lobe, thumb and big toe?* (Exodus 29:20).

Why was Aaron made a high priest? (8:30)

Aaron had a checkered past. Though he was Moses' brother and aide and had helped confront Pharaoh, Aaron had also made a golden calf idol to appease the people's desires (Exodus 32). Moses accused Aaron, "You led them into such great sin" (Exodus 32:21). The fact of the matter, though, is that there was no one available to be a priest who was not a sinner. And while we cannot say why Aaron was selected, we can see why he needed to be *consecrated*. Like anyone who comes to God, Aaron needed cleansing from sin. Also see *Why were Aaron and his sons chosen to be priests?* (8:2)

What did sacrifices have to do with the Lord's appearing? (9:4)

God was not at the Israelites' beck and call—their sacrifices didn't force him to appear. Rather, the people's sacrifices prepared *them* for his visible appearance, most likely as a cloud or pillar of fire.

atonement[D] for yourself and the people; sacrifice[D] the offering that is for the people and make atonement for them, as the LORD has commanded."

8So Aaron came to the altar and slaughtered the calf as a sin offering[D] for himself. **9**His sons brought the blood to him, and he dipped his finger into the blood and put it on the horns of the altar; the rest of the blood he poured out at the base of the altar. **10**On the altar he burned the fat, the kidneys and the covering of the liver from the sin offering, as the LORD commanded Moses; **11**the flesh and the hide he burned up outside the camp.

12Then he slaughtered the burnt offering[D]. His sons handed him the blood, and he sprinkled it against the altar on all sides. **13**They handed him the burnt offering piece by piece, including the head, and he burned them on the altar. **14**He washed the inner parts and the legs and burned them on top of the burnt offering on the altar.

15Aaron then brought the offering that was for the people. He took the goat for the people's sin offering and slaughtered it and offered it for a sin offering as he did with the first one.

16He brought the burnt offering and offered it in the prescribed way. **17**He also brought the grain offering[D], took a handful of it and burned it on the altar in addition to the morning's burnt offering.

18He slaughtered the ox and the ram as the fellowship offering[D] for the people. His sons handed him the blood, and he sprinkled it against the altar on all sides. **19**But the fat portions of the ox and the ram—the fat tail, the layer of fat, the kidneys and the covering of the liver— **20**these they laid on the breasts, and then Aaron burned the fat on the altar. **21**Aaron waved the breasts and the right thigh before the LORD as a wave offering[D], as Moses commanded.

22Then Aaron lifted his hands toward the people and blessed them. And having sacrificed the sin offering, the burnt offering and the fellowship offering, he stepped down.

23Moses and Aaron then went into the Tent of Meeting[D]. When they came out, they blessed the people; and the glory[D] of the LORD appeared to all the people. **24**Fire came out from the presence of the LORD and consumed the burnt offering and the fat portions on the altar. And when all the people saw it, they shouted for joy and fell facedown.

The Death of Nadab and Abihu

10 Aaron's sons Nadab and Abihu took their censers[D], put fire in them and added incense[D]; and they offered unauthorized fire before the LORD, contrary to his command. **2**So fire came out from the presence of the LORD and consumed them, and they died before the LORD. **3**Moses then said to Aaron, "This is what the LORD spoke of when he said:

" 'Among those who approach me
    I will show myself holy;
in the sight of all the people
    I will be honored.' "

Aaron remained silent.

4Moses summoned Mishael and Elzaphan, sons of Aaron's uncle Uzziel, and said to them, "Come here; carry your cousins outside the camp, away from the front of the

---

What did Moses and Aaron do in the Tent of Meeting? (9:23)

Although the passage doesn't tell us, rabbinic tradition speculates that Moses showed Aaron how to perform the offering or that they both prayed to God. It's a good guess that they prayed since God appeared in glory in the tabernacle (Exodus 40:34–35).

How did the people see the glory of the Lord? (9:23)

Glory suggests an awesome display of power, a tangible representation of God's majestic splendor, perhaps as a cloud. Earlier God's glory had so filled the tabernacle with a cloud that Moses was unable to enter (Exodus 40:34–35). The fire that came out from the Lord's presence was likely another demonstration of God's glory (v. 24).

Unauthorized fire (10:1)

Literally *strange* or *alien* fire, it violated God's command. It may have been taken from a fire other than the altar's, or offered at the wrong time of day, or with the wrong equipment. Though we can't be sure what the deviation was, we know Nadab and Abihu acted presumptuously by making an offering in a manner different from that prescribed by the Lord.

The presence of the LORD (10:2)

This could be translated *from before the face of the LORD*. If the fire that *came out from the presence of the LORD and consumed the burnt offering* was a display of God's glory (9:24), the fire here was a display of God's judgment. God was physically present with his people, inspiring both fear and joy.

sanctuary." **5**So they came and carried them, still in their tunics, outside the camp, as Moses ordered.

6Then Moses said to Aaron and his sons Eleazar and Ithamar, "Do not let your hair become unkempt,*a* and do not tear your clothes, or you will die and the LORD will be angry with the whole community. But your relatives, all the house of Israel, may mourn for those the LORD has destroyed by fire. **7**Do not leave the entrance to the Tent of Meeting*D* or you will die, because the LORD's anointing*D* oil is on you." So they did as Moses said.

8Then the LORD said to Aaron, **9**"You and your sons are not to drink wine or other fermented drink whenever you go into the Tent of Meeting, or you will die. This is a lasting ordinance for the generations to come. **10**You must distinguish between the holy and the common, between the unclean*D* and the clean, **11**and you must teach the Israelites all the decrees the LORD has given them through Moses."

12Moses said to Aaron and his remaining sons, Eleazar and Ithamar, "Take the grain offering*D* left over from the offerings made to the LORD by fire and eat it prepared without yeast*D* beside the altar, for it is most holy. **13**Eat it in a holy place, because it is your share and your sons' share of the offerings made to the LORD by fire; for so I have been commanded. **14**But you and your sons and your daughters may eat the breast that was waved and the thigh that was presented. Eat them in a ceremonially clean place; they have been given to you and your children as your share of the Israelites' fellowship offerings*D.b* **15**The thigh that was presented and the breast that was waved must be brought with the fat portions of the offerings made by fire, to be waved before the LORD as a wave offering*D*. This will be the regular share for you and your children, as the LORD has commanded."

16When Moses inquired about the goat of the sin offering*D* and found that it had been burned up, he was angry with Eleazar and Ithamar, Aaron's remaining sons, and asked, **17**"Why didn't you eat the sin offering in the sanctuary area? It is most holy; it was given to you to take away the guilt of the community by making atonement*D* for them before the LORD. **18**Since its blood was not taken into the Holy Place*D*, you should have eaten the goat in the sanctuary area, as I commanded."

19Aaron replied to Moses, "Today they sacrificed their sin offering and their burnt offering before the LORD, but such things as this have happened to me. Would the LORD have been pleased if I had eaten the sin offering today?" **20**When Moses heard this, he was satisfied.

Clean and Unclean Food

11 The LORD said to Moses and Aaron, **2**"Say to the Israelites: 'Of all the animals that live on land, these are the ones you may eat: **3**You may eat any animal that has a split hoof completely divided and that chews the cud.

4" 'There are some that only chew the cud or only have a split hoof, but you must not eat them. The camel, though it chews the cud, does not have a split hoof; it is ceremonially unclean for you. **5**The coney,*c* though it chews the cud, does not have a split hoof; it is unclean for you. **6**The rabbit, though it chews the cud, does

Why couldn't Aaron and his sons mourn these tragic deaths? (10:6)

The high priest was forbidden from carrying out acts of mourning (21:10–12). The cultural expressions of grief—torn clothing, unkempt grooming, dust and ashes—would have been inappropriate, even defiling, for one dedicated to the Lord. If sacrifices had to be without blemish, so did the priest. A priest in mourning would have been a contradiction in terms, a flaw in the one who represented God.

Why couldn't the priests leave with anointing oil still on them? (10:7)

This figurative language reminded the priests that they were still consecrated to God's service. They belonged to him. In this case, God's anointed priests were to be distanced from the wrongdoing of Nadab and Abihu.

Why abstain from wine while serving before the Lord? (10:9)

Early Jewish commentators suggest that Nadab and Abihu had been drinking before they committed their presumptuous act (v. 1). If so, their drinking could have impaired their judgment, leading to the violation that cost them their lives. That would explain why this command was given here. On the other hand, abstinence was sometimes used as a sign of dedication to the Lord. See *Nazirite* (Judges 13:5) and *What's wrong with grapes and wine?* (Judges 13:14).

What was wrong with burning the offering? (10:16–19)

Aaron's carelessness essentially rendered the sin offering ineffective (6:26). If the priest, standing in as God's representative, did not eat a portion of the offering, it was as though *God* had not accepted it. An unaccepted offering meant the guilt of the people remained. Moses may also have been perturbed because he feared this carelessness might turn out as tragically as Nadab and Abihu's earlier recklessness (vv. 1–2).

What *things* was Aaron referring to? (10:19)

He was probably saying that he and his sons had no appetite because of their grief over the deaths of Nadab and Abihu. Though they had been forbidden to mourn the deaths (v. 6), their hearts were grief-stricken. This was not an act of carelessness or disobedience (as was the case with Nadab and Abihu). Moses could see that they were physically unable to eat the offering.

Ceremonially unclean (11:4)

See *Ceremonially unclean* (5:2).

---

a6 Or Do not uncover your heads   *b14 Traditionally peace offerings*
c5 That is, the hyrax or rock badger

have a split hoof; it is unclean[D] for you. **7**And the pig, though it has a split hoof completely divided, does not chew the cud; it is unclean for you. **8**You must not eat their meat or touch their carcasses; they are unclean for you.

9" 'Of all the creatures living in the water of the seas and the streams, you may eat any that have fins and scales. **10**But all creatures in the seas or streams that do not have fins and scales—whether among all the swarming things or among all the other living creatures in the water—you are to detest. **11**And since you are to detest them, you must not eat their meat and you must detest their carcasses. **12**Anything living in the water that does not have fins and scales is to be detestable to you.

13" 'These are the birds you are to detest and not eat because they are detestable: the eagle, the vulture, the black vulture, **14**the red kite, any kind of black kite, **15**any kind of raven, **16**the horned owl, the screech owl, the gull, any kind of hawk, **17**the little owl, the cormorant, the great owl, **18**the white owl, the desert owl, the osprey, **19**the stork, any kind of heron, the hoopoe and the bat.[a]

20" 'All flying insects that walk on all fours are to be detestable to you. **21**There are, however, some winged creatures that walk on all fours that you may eat: those that have jointed legs for hopping on the ground. **22**Of these you may eat any kind of locust[D], katydid, cricket or

What insects have only four legs? (11:20)

Insects, by definition, have six legs. But it's possible the Israelites didn't count jumping legs as regular legs. We cannot be too concerned about technical definitions when the Bible categorizes animals for religious rather than scientific reasons. Notice that *the bat* is listed as a bird (vv. 13–19; see NIV text note). Also see *What kind of fish swallowed Jonah?* (Jonah 1:17).

---

[a]19 The precise identification of some of the birds, insects and animals in this chapter is uncertain.

Why did God keep some meats off the menu? (11:4–41)

Anyone who touched the meat of certain animals would become unclean—offensive to the holy God (vv. 43–44). How could food separate someone from God? Many believe God forbade these meats for hygienic reasons. While it is true some meats have high potential for transmitting bacteria, not all are clearly harmful. And if health were the primary goal, why not forbid poisonous plants?

Others say these meats were banned because they were used in pagan rituals. But the bull was considered clean even though it was prominent in Canaanite and Egyptian religions.

Still others view the distinction between edible and inedible animals as a "teaching tool." Israel was to remain pure and unadulterated as God's people, not blended with other cultures or polluted by idolatry. To echo this important distinction in the Israelites' daily lives, God outlawed the mixed breeding of animals, mixed plantings, mixed threads (19:19)—and, here, the eating of symbolically "mongrel" creatures.

The forbidden animals are those that in motion or diet don't fit neatly into the "purebred" categories of Genesis 1: birds that fly, fish that swim and land animals that walk (primarily plant-eating). Leviticus 11 bans many meat-eaters, as well as other apparent "mongrels" such as water dwellers without fins or scales. Sheep and goats seem to set the standard for "purebred" land animals. Those that walked or ate in a different manner were forbidden.

Though to us God's restrictions may sound like a real hassle, there is no record that the Israelites felt that way. They got the message: they were God's distinct people and were expected to live like it.

grasshopper. ²³But all other winged creatures that have four legs you are to detest.

²⁴" 'You will make yourselves unclean by these; whoever touches their carcasses will be unclean ᴰ till evening. ²⁵Whoever picks up one of their carcasses must wash his clothes, and he will be unclean till evening.

²⁶" 'Every animal that has a split hoof not completely divided or that does not chew the cud is unclean for you; whoever touches ⌐the carcass of⌐ any of them will be unclean. ²⁷Of all the animals that walk on all fours, those that walk on their paws are unclean for you; whoever touches their carcasses will be unclean till evening. ²⁸Anyone who picks up their carcasses must wash his clothes, and he will be unclean till evening. They are unclean for you.

²⁹" 'Of the animals that move about on the ground, these are unclean for you: the weasel, the rat, any kind of great lizard, ³⁰the gecko, the monitor lizard, the wall lizard, the skink and the chameleon. ³¹Of all those that move along the ground, these are unclean for you. Whoever touches them when they are dead will be unclean till evening. ³²When one of them dies and falls on something, that article, whatever its use, will be unclean, whether it is made of wood, cloth, hide or sackcloth ᴰ. Put it in water; it will be unclean till evening, and then it will be clean. ³³If one of them falls into a clay pot, everything in it will be unclean, and you must break the pot. ³⁴Any food that could be eaten but has water on it from such a pot is unclean, and any liquid that could be drunk from it is unclean. ³⁵Anything that one of their carcasses falls on becomes unclean; an oven or cooking pot must be broken up. They are unclean, and you are to regard them as unclean. ³⁶A spring, however, or a cistern ᴰ for collecting water remains clean, but anyone who touches one of these carcasses is unclean. ³⁷If a carcass falls on any seeds that are to be planted, they remain clean. ³⁸But if water has been put on the seed and a carcass falls on it, it is unclean for you.

³⁹" 'If an animal that you are allowed to eat dies, anyone who touches the carcass will be unclean till evening. ⁴⁰Anyone who eats some of the carcass must wash his clothes, and he will be unclean till evening. Anyone who picks up the carcass must wash his clothes, and he will be unclean till evening.

⁴¹" 'Every creature that moves about on the ground is detestable; it is not to be eaten. ⁴²You are not to eat any creature that moves about on the ground, whether it moves on its belly or walks on all fours or on many feet; it is detestable. ⁴³Do not defile yourselves by any of these creatures. Do not make yourselves unclean by means of them or be made unclean by them. ⁴⁴I am the LORD your God; consecrate ᴰ yourselves and be holy, because I am holy. Do not make yourselves unclean by any creature that moves about on the ground. ⁴⁵I am the LORD who brought you up out of Egypt to be your God; therefore be holy, because I am holy.

⁴⁶" 'These are the regulations concerning animals, birds, every living thing that moves in the water and every creature that moves about on the ground. ⁴⁷You must distinguish between the unclean and the clean, between living creatures that may be eaten and those that may not be eaten.' "

Unclean till evening (11:24)

This time span was probably not a health precaution so much as a corrective measure. Since evening, or sunset, marked the end of one day and the beginning of another, this was probably a ritual period that signified a new beginning. With a clean slate an individual could resume his normal relationship with God.

Why would a carcass cause only some water and seeds to become unclean? (11:36–37)

Some suggest wet seed needed special care because it was likely being soaked to prepare it for cooking. Others think greater care was needed because wet seed is more susceptible to bacteria than dry seed. Still others view these regulations primarily as teaching tools and believe the exceptions were made for practical reasons. If a supply of seed could not be planted, it would mean hardship. If the community water supply was considered polluted, it would mean disaster.

SCRIPTURE LINK (11:43) Do not defile yourselves by any of these creatures

Jesus taught that uncleanness comes not from food, but from within (Mark 7:1–23); Old Testament distinctions between clean and unclean helped Israel learn to distinguish the holy from the profane.

Consecrate yourselves and be holy (11:44–47)

These laws provided the Israelites specific ways to be *holy*—set apart for God. They were to be a distinct people who followed the Lord and demonstrated his character. Performing rituals alone, however, did not bring about holiness. God also desired a proper heart response (Amos 5:21–24).

Why such elaborate ritual? (11:46–47)

See article: *Why did God keep some meats off the menu?* (11:4–41).

Why would a good thing like giving birth require purification? (12:4)

According to the text, *bleeding* made the woman unclean. The birth itself and the baby did not cause the mother's uncleanness. Some suggest this regulation protected women from infection. Others see it as a symbol for a lack of wholeness. Perhaps because *blood* meant life (17:11), *bleeding* implied the opposite, symbolizing death and sin. See *Bodily discharge* (15:2–3).

Why would it take twice as long to purify a woman who gave birth to a girl? (12:5)

We don't really know why God gave this command. Sometimes God's instructions reflected cultural views held during that time. See *Where did Moses learn the laws of God?* (Exodus 18:15–16). Ancient peoples may have believed a woman bled longer after delivering a girl. Or perhaps the passage acknowledges the higher value their culture placed on males. See *Why were men worth more than women?* (27:3–8). Though such a perspective seems unfair today, Biblical teaching raised the status and rights of women far above any other laws or cultures of the time.

Why was atonement needed when no sin had occurred? (12:7)

Uncleanness was uncleanness, whether unintentional or deliberate. It brought defilement into the camp. See *Why hold someone responsible for an accidental sin?* (4:2). This defect in God's people had to be rectified if he was to continue to dwell among them. Any time a person's uncleanness lasted over seven days, a sin offering was required to make atonement. The burnt offering in the case of childbirth also provided the parents an opportunity to show thankfulness for the birth of the child and to renew their own commitment to God. Also see *Why were offerings needed if being sick was not a sin?* (14:10–12).

SCRIPTURE LINK (12:8) *If she cannot afford a lamb . . .*

When Joseph and Mary presented the infant Jesus at the temple, they offered two birds—evidence that they were poor (Luke 2:22–24).

Did the priests serve as doctors? (13:2–3)

Though priests diagnosed skin conditions, they did not attempt to cure them. Instead they guarded the spiritual health of the camp by discerning who was unclean, then determining how long the person should be isolated and what measures needed to be taken for him to return to fellowship.

What kinds of diseases do these medical symptoms indicate? (13:3,13,30,38)

The word for *infectious skin disease* is a general term for skin ailments of various natures, including leprosy (Hansen's disease). Though it's difficult to make medical diagnoses, these verses describe several other possible skin conditions: chronic dermatitis, chronic skin infection, psoriasis, skin cancer or leukoderma. Exodus 4:6 compares the diseased skin to snow, probably referring to its color but perhaps also suggesting flaking.

Purification After Childbirth

12 The LORD said to Moses, [2]"Say to the Israelites: 'A woman who becomes pregnant and gives birth to a son will be ceremonially unclean[D] for seven days, just as she is unclean during her monthly period. [3]On the eighth day the boy is to be circumcised[D]. [4]Then the woman must wait thirty-three days to be purified[D] from her bleeding. She must not touch anything sacred[D] or go to the sanctuary until the days of her purification are over. [5]If she gives birth to a daughter, for two weeks the woman will be unclean, as during her period. Then she must wait sixty-six days to be purified from her bleeding.

[6]"When the days of her purification for a son or daughter are over, she is to bring to the priest[D] at the entrance to the Tent of Meeting[D] a year-old lamb for a burnt offering[D] and a young pigeon or a dove for a sin offering[D]. [7]He shall offer them before the LORD to make atonement[D] for her, and then she will be ceremonially clean from her flow of blood.

"'These are the regulations for the woman who gives birth to a boy or a girl. [8]If she cannot afford a lamb, she is to bring two doves or two young pigeons, one for a burnt offering and the other for a sin offering. In this way the priest will make atonement for her, and she will be clean.'"

Regulations About Infectious Skin Diseases

13 The LORD said to Moses and Aaron, [2]"When anyone has a swelling or a rash or a bright spot on his skin that may become an infectious skin disease,[a] he must be brought to Aaron the priest or to one of his sons[b] who is a priest. [3]The priest is to examine the sore on his skin, and if the hair in the sore has turned white and the sore appears to be more than skin deep,[c] it is an infectious skin disease. When the priest examines him, he shall pronounce him ceremonially unclean. [4]If the spot on his skin is white but does not appear to be more than skin deep and the hair in it has not turned white, the priest is to put the infected person in isolation for seven days. [5]On the seventh day the priest is to examine him, and if he sees that the sore is unchanged and has not spread in the skin, he is to keep him in isolation another seven days. [6]On the seventh day the priest is to examine him again, and if the sore has faded and has not spread in the skin, the priest shall pronounce him clean; it is only a rash. The man must wash his clothes, and he will be clean. [7]But if the rash does spread in his skin after he has shown himself to the priest to be pronounced clean, he must appear before the priest again. [8]The priest is to examine him, and if the rash has spread in the skin, he shall pronounce him unclean; it is an infectious disease.

[9]"When anyone has an infectious skin disease, he must be brought to the priest. [10]The priest is to examine him, and if there is a white swelling in the skin that has turned the hair white and if there is raw flesh in the swelling, [11]it is a chronic skin disease and the priest shall

[a]2 Traditionally *leprosy*; the Hebrew word was used for various diseases affecting the skin—not necessarily leprosy; also elsewhere in this chapter.   [b]2 Or *descendants*   [c]3 Or *be lower than the rest of the skin*; also elsewhere in this chapter

pronounce him unclean[D]. He is not to put him in isolation, because he is already unclean.

[12]"If the disease breaks out all over his skin and, so far as the priest[D] can see, it covers all the skin of the infected person from head to foot, [13]the priest is to examine him, and if the disease has covered his whole body, he shall pronounce that person clean. Since it has all turned white, he is clean. [14]But whenever raw flesh appears on him, he will be unclean. [15]When the priest sees the raw flesh, he shall pronounce him unclean. The raw flesh is unclean; he has an infectious disease. [16]Should the raw flesh change and turn white, he must go to the priest. [17]The priest is to examine him, and if the sores have turned white, the priest shall pronounce the infected person clean; then he will be clean.

[18]"When someone has a boil on his skin and it heals, [19]and in the place where the boil was, a white swelling or reddish-white spot appears, he must present himself to the priest. [20]The priest is to examine it, and if it appears to be more than skin deep and the hair in it has turned white, the priest shall pronounce him unclean. It is an infectious skin disease that has broken out where the boil was. [21]But if, when the priest examines it, there is no white hair in it and it is not more than skin deep and has faded, then the priest is to put him in isolation for seven days. [22]If it is spreading in the skin, the priest shall pronounce him unclean; it is infectious. [23]But if the spot is unchanged and has not spread, it is only a scar from the boil, and the priest shall pronounce him clean.

[24]"When someone has a burn on his skin and a reddish-white or white spot appears in the raw flesh of the burn, [25]the priest is to examine the spot, and if the hair in it has turned white, and it appears to be more than skin deep, it is an infectious disease that has broken out in the burn. The priest shall pronounce him unclean; it is an infectious skin disease. [26]But if the priest examines it and there is no white hair in the spot and if it is not more than skin deep and has faded, then the priest is to put him in isolation for seven days. [27]On the seventh day the priest is to examine him, and if it is spreading in the skin, the priest shall pronounce him unclean; it is an infectious skin disease. [28]If, however, the spot is unchanged and has not spread in the skin but has faded, it is a swelling from the burn, and the priest shall pronounce him clean; it is only a scar from the burn.

[29]"If a man or woman has a sore on the head or on the chin, [30]the priest is to examine the sore, and if it appears to be more than skin deep and the hair in it is yellow and thin, the priest shall pronounce that person unclean; it is an itch, an infectious disease of the head or chin. [31]But if, when the priest examines this kind of sore, it does not seem to be more than skin deep and there is no black hair in it, then the priest is to put the infected person in isolation for seven days. [32]On the seventh day the priest is to examine the sore, and if the itch has not spread and there is no yellow hair in it and it does not appear to be more than skin deep, [33]he must be shaved except for the diseased area, and the priest is to keep him in isolation another seven days. [34]On the seventh day the priest is to examine the itch, and if it has not spread in the skin and appears to be no more than skin deep, the priest shall pronounce him clean. He must wash his clothes, and he will be clean. [35]But if the itch does spread in the skin after he is pronounced clean,

Why were skin conditions considered unclean, but not other illnesses such as fever? (13:3,8)

Just as with bleeding after childbirth (12:4), this command seems to focus on appearance, underscoring the probability that these restrictions were teaching tools that demonstrated God's holiness. See article: *Why did God keep some meats off the menu?* (11:4–41). Any visible sign of a lack of health would cause a person to fall short of God's standard of wholeness and be labeled unclean. Such regulations vividly reminded the Israelites of God's character and perfection.

Isolation (13:4)

The diseased person had to live alone, outside the camp, as long as he remained unclean. See *Why treat someone with a disease in such a callous manner?* (13:46).

Why was someone completely covered by disease declared clean? (13:13)

When a person's skin turned completely white it was perhaps a sign of healed flesh. Raw flesh (inflamed, red or bleeding), on the other hand, was more likely to be infectious and was considered unclean.

Why prevent people from combing their hair? (13:45)

The disheveled appearance of an unclean person warned others to stay away so as not to contaminate themselves. Furthermore, unkempt hair, torn clothes and a covered face were all signs of mourning (see 10:6). Thus, a person afflicted with an infectious disease remained in perpetual mourning. The unkempt appearance would remind people not only of sin but also that repentance was the only appropriate response to sin.

Why treat someone with a disease in such a callous manner? (13:46)

It doesn't seem fair. The ones who lived outside the camp faced great difficulties, since they were completely cut off from society (except for supplies left behind). Yet everyone understood the measure as an unpleasant but necessary way to prevent God's dwelling from being defiled (Num. 5:1–4). On the positive side, these harsh requirements served to protect the unclean person, keeping the holy things at a distance so no one would die for accidentally touching them (10:1–7; 2 Samuel 6:1–11). These rules also protected the rest of the camp, quarantining the disease and preventing its spread. No exceptions were made —even Moses' sister Miriam was exiled (Num. 12:10–15).

What was bad about mildew? (13:49)

The word for mildew here was translated as infectious skin disease earlier (13:2–46). In both cases, a surface area was abnormal and disfigured, perhaps flaking and peeling. Though there may be health benefits to destroying mildewed objects, they were most likely condemned because their appearance displayed a lack of health and wholeness. As such, they could not remain in the camp with the holy God any more than diseased persons could.

Destructive mildew (13:51)

The literal meaning of this phrase is persistent mildew. Certainly any mildew that kept recurring would eventually ruin the material it inhabited.

36the priest[D] is to examine him, and if the itch has spread in the skin, the priest does not need to look for yellow hair; the person is unclean[D]. **37**If, however, in his judgment it is unchanged and black hair has grown in it, the itch is healed. He is clean, and the priest shall pronounce him clean.

38"When a man or woman has white spots on the skin, **39**the priest is to examine them, and if the spots are dull white, it is a harmless rash that has broken out on the skin; that person is clean.

40"When a man has lost his hair and is bald, he is clean. **41**If he has lost his hair from the front of his scalp and has a bald forehead, he is clean. **42**But if he has a reddish-white sore on his bald head or forehead, it is an infectious disease breaking out on his head or forehead. **43**The priest is to examine him, and if the swollen sore on his head or forehead is reddish-white like an infectious skin disease, **44**the man is diseased and is unclean. The priest shall pronounce him unclean because of the sore on his head.

45"The person with such an infectious disease must wear torn clothes, let his hair be unkempt,[a] cover the lower part of his face and cry out, 'Unclean! Unclean!' **46**As long as he has the infection he remains unclean. He must live alone; he must live outside the camp.

Regulations About Mildew

47"If any clothing is contaminated with mildew—any woolen or linen clothing, **48**any woven or knitted material of linen or wool, any leather or anything made of leather— **49**and if the contamination in the clothing, or leather, or woven or knitted material, or any leather article, is greenish or reddish, it is a spreading mildew and must be shown to the priest. **50**The priest is to examine the mildew and isolate the affected article for seven days. **51**On the seventh day he is to examine it, and if the mildew has spread in the clothing, or the woven or knitted material, or the leather, whatever its use, it is a destructive mildew; the article is unclean. **52**He must burn up the clothing, or the woven or knitted material of wool or linen, or any leather article that has the contamination in it, because the mildew is destructive; the article must be burned up.

53"But if, when the priest examines it, the mildew has not spread in the clothing, or the woven or knitted material, or the leather article, **54**he shall order that the contaminated article be washed. Then he is to isolate it for another seven days. **55**After the affected article has been washed, the priest is to examine it, and if the mildew has not changed its appearance, even though it has not spread, it is unclean. Burn it with fire, whether the mildew has affected one side or the other. **56**If, when the priest examines it, the mildew has faded after the article has been washed, he is to tear the contaminated part out of the clothing, or the leather, or the woven or knitted material. **57**But if it reappears in the clothing, or in the woven or knitted material, or in the leather article, it is spreading, and whatever has the mildew must be burned with fire. **58**The clothing, or the woven or knitted material, or any leather article that has been washed and is rid of the mildew, must be washed again, and it will be clean."

59These are the regulations concerning contamination

a45 Or clothes, uncover his head

by mildew in woolen or linen clothing, woven or knitted material, or any leather article, for pronouncing them clean or unclean^D.

Cleansing From Infectious Skin Diseases

14 The LORD said to Moses, **2**"These are the regulations for the diseased person at the time of his ceremonial cleansing, when he is brought to the priest^D: **3**The priest is to go outside the camp and examine him. If the person has been healed of his infectious skin disease,^a **4**the priest shall order that two live clean birds and some cedar wood, scarlet yarn and hyssop^D be brought for the one to be cleansed. **5**Then the priest shall order that one of the birds be killed over fresh water in a clay pot. **6**He is then to take the live bird and dip it, together with the cedar wood, the scarlet yarn and the hyssop, into the blood of the bird that was killed over the fresh water. **7**Seven times he shall sprinkle the one to be cleansed of the infectious disease and pronounce him clean. Then he is to release the live bird in the open fields.

8"The person to be cleansed must wash his clothes, shave off all his hair and bathe with water; then he will be ceremonially clean. After this he may come into the camp, but he must stay outside his tent for seven days. **9**On the seventh day he must shave off all his hair; he must shave his head, his beard, his eyebrows and the rest of his hair. He must wash his clothes and bathe himself with water, and he will be clean.

10"On the eighth day he must bring two male lambs and one ewe lamb a year old, each without defect, along with three-tenths of an ephah^b of fine flour mixed with oil for a grain offering^D, and one log^c of oil. **11**The priest who pronounces him clean shall present both the one to be cleansed and his offerings before the LORD at the entrance to the Tent of Meeting.

12"Then the priest is to take one of the male lambs and offer it as a guilt offering^D, along with the log of oil; he shall wave them before the LORD as a wave offering^D. **13**He is to slaughter the lamb in the holy place where the sin offering^D and the burnt offering^D are slaughtered. Like the sin offering, the guilt offering belongs to the priest; it is most holy. **14**The priest is to take some of the blood of the guilt offering and put it on the lobe of the right ear of the one to be cleansed, on the thumb of his right hand and on the big toe of his right foot. **15**The priest shall then take some of the log of oil, pour it in the palm of his own left hand, **16**dip his right forefinger into the oil in his palm, and with his finger sprinkle some of it before the LORD seven times. **17**The priest is to put some of the oil remaining in his palm on the lobe of the right ear of the one to be cleansed, on the thumb of his right hand and on the big toe of his right foot, on top of the blood of the guilt offering. **18**The rest of the oil in his palm the priest shall put on the head of the one to be cleansed and make atonement^D for him before the LORD.

19"Then the priest is to sacrifice the sin offering and make atonement for the one to be cleansed from his uncleanness^D. After that, the priest shall slaughter

---

What's the meaning of this odd ritual? (14:4–7)
One idea is that the two clean birds represented the person being cleansed. The bird that was killed showed the outcome the person might have suffered—death—but it also atoned for his uncleanness (see 14:49–53). The freed bird symbolized the removal of the guilt and affliction from him (perhaps similar to the scapegoat in 16:20–22). The significance of the other elements of this ceremony (cedar wood, scarlet yarn, hyssop) is not known.

SCRIPTURE LINK (14:4) *Hyssop*
This bushy plant was used to sprinkle blood at the first Passover (Exodus 12:22), and David referred to its cleansing help when he asked for God's forgiveness (Psalm 51:7).

Why make a person live without shelter? (14:8)
This seems to show restoration occurring in stages: at this point, the individual was not yet clean enough to fully participate in community life. Though this sounds harsh, his life had improved considerably over life outside the camp! Such persons living outdoors also served as reminders that God desired restoration and had provided ways for those outside the camp to return to him.

Why were offerings needed if being sick was not a sin? (14:10–12)
Sickness, like sin, disrupted the cleanness of the camp. The issue was not whether one was responsible or not for his condition. The issue was that those who were unclean needed to be cleansed. God had designated offerings as a means to counteract this pollution and make the camp suitable once more for his sustained presence. When God accepted the individual's sacrifice, he enabled him to join in worship and fellowship again. Also see *Why was atonement needed when no sin had occurred?* (12:7).

Wave offering (14:12)
See *Why wave an offering?* (7:30) and *Wave offering* (Exodus 29:22–28).

Were these body parts symbolic? (14:14–18)
See *What was special about the priests' right ears, thumbs and big toes?* (8:23) and *Why dab blood on Aaron's right ear lobe, thumb and big toe?* (Exodus 29:20).

---

^a3 Traditionally *leprosy*; the Hebrew word was used for various diseases affecting the skin—not necessarily leprosy; also elsewhere in this chapter.   ^b10 That is, probably about 6 quarts (about 6.5 liters)   ^c10 That is, probably about 2/3 pint (about 0.3 liter); also in verses 12, 15, 21 and 24

**Guilt offering . . . grain offering . . .
sin offering . . . burnt offering
(14:21–22)**
See *Old Testament Sacrifices* on page 138.

the burnt offering[D] [20]and offer it on the altar, together with the grain offering[D], and make atonement[D] for him, and he will be clean.

[21]"If, however, he is poor and cannot afford these, he must take one male lamb as a guilt offering[D] to be waved to make atonement for him, together with a tenth of an ephah[a] of fine flour mixed with oil for a grain offering, a log of oil, [22]and two doves or two young pigeons, which he can afford, one for a sin offering[D] and the other for a burnt offering.

[23]"On the eighth day he must bring them for his cleansing to the priest[D] at the entrance to the Tent of Meeting[D], before the LORD. [24]The priest is to take the lamb for the guilt offering, together with the log of oil, and wave them before the LORD as a wave offering[D]. [25]He shall slaughter the lamb for the guilt offering and take some of its blood and put it on the lobe of the right ear of the one to be cleansed, on the thumb of his right hand and on the big toe of his right foot. [26]The priest is to pour some of the oil into the palm of his own left hand, [27]and with his right forefinger sprinkle some of the oil from his palm seven times before the LORD. [28]Some of the oil in his palm he is to put on the same places he put the blood of the guilt offering—on the lobe of the right ear of the one to be cleansed, on the thumb of his right hand and on the big toe of his right foot. [29]The rest of the oil in his palm the priest shall put on the head of the one to be cleansed, to make atonement for him before the LORD. [30]Then he shall sacrifice[D] the doves or the young pigeons, which the person can afford, [31]one[b] as a sin offering and the other as a burnt offering, together with the grain offering. In this way the priest will make atonement before the LORD on behalf of the one to be cleansed."

[32]These are the regulations for anyone who has an infectious skin disease and who cannot afford the regular offerings for his cleansing.

Cleansing From Mildew

Why would God give mildew? (14:34)
Sometimes God sent mildew as a form of judgment (see Amos 4:9). In this case, however, it's not clear that judgment was its purpose. This may be nothing more than a statement that God is the source of mildew, just as he is the source of all things.

[33]The LORD said to Moses and Aaron, [34]"When you enter the land of Canaan, which I am giving you as your possession, and I put a spreading mildew in a house in that land, [35]the owner of the house must go and tell the priest, 'I have seen something that looks like mildew in my house.' [36]The priest is to order the house to be emptied before he goes in to examine the mildew, so that nothing in the house will be pronounced unclean[D]. After this the priest is to go in and inspect the house. [37]He is to examine the mildew on the walls, and if it has greenish or reddish depressions that appear to be deeper than the surface of the wall, [38]the priest shall go out the doorway of the house and close it up for seven days. [39]On the seventh day the priest shall return to inspect the house. If the mildew has spread on the walls, [40]he is to order that the contaminated stones be torn out and thrown into an unclean place outside the town. [41]He must have all the inside walls of the house scraped and the material that is scraped off dumped into an unclean place outside the town. [42]Then they are to take other stones to replace these and take new clay and plaster the house.

[43]"If the mildew reappears in the house after the stones

---

[a]21 That is, probably about 2 quarts (about 2 liters)
[b]31 Septuagint and Syriac; Hebrew [31]*such as the person can afford, one*

have been torn out and the house scraped and plastered, **44**the priest[D] is to go and examine it and, if the mildew has spread in the house, it is a destructive mildew; the house is unclean[D]. **45**It must be torn down—its stones, timbers and all the plaster—and taken out of the town to an unclean place.

46"Anyone who goes into the house while it is closed up will be unclean till evening. **47**Anyone who sleeps or eats in the house must wash his clothes.

48"But if the priest comes to examine it and the mildew has not spread after the house has been plastered, he shall pronounce the house clean, because the mildew is gone. **49**To purify[D] the house he is to take two birds and some cedar wood, scarlet yarn and hyssop[D]. **50**He shall kill one of the birds over fresh water in a clay pot. **51**Then he is to take the cedar wood, the hyssop, the scarlet yarn and the live bird, dip them into the blood of the dead bird and the fresh water, and sprinkle the house seven times. **52**He shall purify the house with the bird's blood, the fresh water, the live bird, the cedar wood, the hyssop and the scarlet yarn. **53**Then he is to release the live bird in the open fields outside the town. In this way he will make atonement[D] for the house, and it will be clean."

54These are the regulations for any infectious skin disease, for an itch, **55**for mildew in clothing or in a house, **56**and for a swelling, a rash or a bright spot, **57**to determine when something is clean or unclean.

These are the regulations for infectious skin diseases and mildew.

Discharges Causing Uncleanness

15 The LORD said to Moses and Aaron, **2**"Speak to the Israelites and say to them: 'When any man has a bodily discharge, the discharge is unclean. **3**Whether it continues flowing from his body or is blocked, it will make him unclean. This is how his discharge will bring about uncleanness[D]:

4" 'Any bed the man with a discharge lies on will be unclean, and anything he sits on will be unclean. **5**Anyone who touches his bed must wash his clothes and bathe with water, and he will be unclean till evening. **6**Whoever sits on anything that the man with a discharge sat on must wash his clothes and bathe with water, and he will be unclean till evening.

7" 'Whoever touches the man who has a discharge must wash his clothes and bathe with water, and he will be unclean till evening.

8" 'If the man with the discharge spits on someone who is clean, that person must wash his clothes and bathe with water, and he will be unclean till evening.

9" 'Everything the man sits on when riding will be unclean, **10**and whoever touches any of the things that were under him will be unclean till evening; whoever picks up those things must wash his clothes and bathe with water, and he will be unclean till evening.

11" 'Anyone the man with a discharge touches without rinsing his hands with water must wash his clothes and bathe with water, and he will be unclean till evening.

12" 'A clay pot that the man touches must be broken, and any wooden article is to be rinsed with water.

13" 'When a man is cleansed from his discharge, he is to count off seven days for his ceremonial cleansing; he must wash his clothes and bathe himself with fresh water,

Destructive mildew (14:44)
See *Destructive mildew* (13:51).

Why make atonement for a building? (14:53)
The same standards of holiness that applied to the Israelites in cloth tents were to apply in the future when they built permanent homes in Canaan. And the standards were high. Any appearance of disease and imperfection—even in a building—defiled the Israelites, making them unfit for God's presence. Atonement was needed if they expected God to remain with them.

Bodily discharge (15:2–3)
Bodily can refer to any "fleshly" thing, but it often signifies the reproductive organs. *Discharge* can mean either a runny fluid or a blocked fluid (that is, thickened or coagulated). Discharges from various kinds of infections included diarrhea, urethral discharge (including gonorrhea) and respiratory infections (a runny nose). Notably, such uncleanness is considered more serious than uncleanness from animals or skin diseases.

and he will be clean. ¹⁴On the eighth day he must take two doves or two young pigeons and come before the LORD to the entrance to the Tent of Meeting^D and give them to the priest^D. ¹⁵The priest is to sacrifice them, the one for a sin offering^D and the other for a burnt offering^D. In this way he will make atonement^D before the LORD for the man because of his discharge.

¹⁶" 'When a man has an emission of semen, he must bathe his whole body with water, and he will be unclean^D till evening. ¹⁷Any clothing or leather that has semen on it must be washed with water, and it will be unclean till evening. ¹⁸When a man lies with a woman and there is an emission of semen, both must bathe with water, and they will be unclean till evening.

¹⁹" 'When a woman has her regular flow of blood, the impurity of her monthly period will last seven days, and anyone who touches her will be unclean till evening.

²⁰" 'Anything she lies on during her period will be unclean, and anything she sits on will be unclean. ²¹Whoever touches her bed must wash his clothes and bathe with water, and he will be unclean till evening. ²²Whoever touches anything she sits on must wash his clothes and bathe with water, and he will be unclean till evening. ²³Whether it is the bed or anything she was sitting on, when anyone touches it, he will be unclean till evening.

²⁴" 'If a man lies with her and her monthly flow touches him, he will be unclean for seven days; any bed he lies on will be unclean.

²⁵" 'When a woman has a discharge of blood for many days at a time other than her monthly period or has a discharge that continues beyond her period, she will be unclean as long as she has the discharge, just as in the days of her period. ²⁶Any bed she lies on while her discharge continues will be unclean, as is her bed during her monthly period, and anything she sits on will be unclean, as during her period. ²⁷Whoever touches them will be unclean; he must wash his clothes and bathe with water, and he will be unclean till evening.

²⁸" 'When she is cleansed from her discharge, she must count off seven days, and after that she will be ceremonially clean. ²⁹On the eighth day she must take two doves or two young pigeons and bring them to the priest at the entrance to the Tent of Meeting. ³⁰The priest is to sacrifice one for a sin offering and the other for a burnt offering. In this way he will make atonement for her before the LORD for the uncleanness^D of her discharge.

³¹" 'You must keep the Israelites separate from things that make them unclean, so they will not die in their uncleanness for defiling my dwelling place,^a which is among them.' "

³²These are the regulations for a man with a discharge, for anyone made unclean by an emission of semen, ³³for a woman in her monthly period, for a man or a woman with a discharge, and for a man who lies with a woman who is ceremonially unclean.

Why would God design natural functions to cause uncleanness? (15:16–24)

Sexual intercourse and the menstrual cycle did not cause pollution in a medical sense. Bodily discharges, however, caused symbolic uncleanness—how much depending on the type of discharge. In these two cases, for example, no sacrifices were required for purification. Washing and waiting until evening brought cleanness after intercourse. A menstruating woman became clean when her period ended. However, a woman with an abnormal, long-term discharge needed to offer sacrifices (see vv. 25–30). See also *Why would a good thing like giving birth require purification?* (12:4).

Are sexual relations during a woman's menstrual period wrong? (15:24)

See *Are sexual relations during a woman's menstrual period wrong?* (20:18)

SCRIPTURE LINK (15:25–27) *Unclean as long as she has the discharge*

Uncleanness from a long-term discharge was contagious by touch. But when a woman who had been unclean for 12 years touched Jesus, this touch did not make him unclean. Instead, his touch made her clean—whole in body and spirit (Luke 8:43–48).

How could God, who is spirit, *dwell anywhere?* (15:31)

God is everywhere, but among the Israelites he dwelled in a unique way: he revealed himself to them. At times his presence was overwhelming glory (Exodus 40:34) or judgment (Lev. 10:2). Every day he was present in the pillar of cloud and fire (Exodus 13:21) and the tabernacle (literally, *dwelling place;* see Exodus 25:8–9). Today God's Spirit dwells within each Christian (1 Cor. 6:19). Also see *The presence of the LORD* (10:2).

---

a31 Or my tabernacle

The Day of Atonement^D

16
The LORD spoke to Moses after the death^D of the two sons of Aaron who died when they approached the LORD. **2**The LORD said to Moses: "Tell your brother Aaron not to come whenever he chooses into the Most Holy Place^D behind the curtain in front of the atonement cover on the ark, or else he will die, because I appear in the cloud over the atonement cover.

3"This is how Aaron is to enter the sanctuary area: with a young bull for a sin offering^D and a ram for a burnt offering^D. **4**He is to put on the sacred^D linen tunic, with linen undergarments next to his body; he is to tie the linen sash around him and put on the linen turban. These are sacred garments; so he must bathe himself with water before he puts them on. **5**From the Israelite community he is to take two male goats for a sin offering and a ram for a burnt offering.

6"Aaron is to offer the bull for his own sin offering to make atonement for himself and his household. **7**Then he is to take the two goats and present them before the LORD at the entrance to the Tent of Meeting^D. **8**He is to cast lots for the two goats—one lot for the LORD and the other for the scapegoat.^a **9**Aaron shall bring the goat whose lot falls to the LORD and sacrifice^D it for a sin offering. **10**But the goat chosen by lot as the scapegoat shall be presented alive before the LORD to be used for making atonement by sending it into the desert as a scapegoat.

11"Aaron shall bring the bull for his own sin offering to make atonement for himself and his household, and he is to slaughter the bull for his own sin offering. **12**He is to take a censer^D full of burning coals from the altar before the LORD and two handfuls of finely ground fragrant incense^D and take them behind the curtain. **13**He is to put the incense on the fire before the LORD, and the smoke of the incense will conceal the atonement cover above the Testimony, so that he will not die. **14**He is to take some of the bull's blood and with his finger sprinkle it on the front of the atonement cover; then he shall sprinkle some of it with his finger seven times before the atonement cover.

15"He shall then slaughter the goat for the sin offering for the people and take its blood behind the curtain and do with it as he did with the bull's blood: He shall sprinkle it on the atonement cover and in front of it. **16**In this way he will make atonement for the Most Holy Place because of the uncleanness^D and rebellion of the Israelites, whatever their sins have been. He is to do the same for the Tent of Meeting, which is among them in the midst of their uncleanness. **17**No one is to be in the Tent of Meeting from the time Aaron goes in to make atonement in the Most Holy Place until he comes out, having made atonement for himself, his household and the whole community of Israel.

18"Then he shall come out to the altar that is before the LORD and make atonement for it. He shall take some of the bull's blood and some of the goat's blood and put it on all the horns of the altar. **19**He shall sprinkle some of the blood on it with his finger seven times to cleanse it and to consecrate^D it from the uncleanness of the Israelites.

20"When Aaron has finished making atonement for

---

^a8 That is, the goat of removal; Hebrew *azazel*; also in verses 10 and 26

Why could being close to God cause Aaron to die? (16:2)
God is a holy and righteous God—to be feared as well as loved. His presence in the camp had consequences for everyone, but particularly for the priests. They were delegated with the awesome responsibility of approaching God on behalf of the people. His glory in the Most Holy Place would consume them like fire unless they were properly sanctified. Aaron could approach God safely if he prepared himself, but not whenever he chose.

Atonement cover (16:2)
A flat area on the top of the ark with cherubim on each end, wings outstretched. Though the Hebrew term suggests the idea of lid or cover, it is also seen as a "mercy seat" because God was said to sit enthroned there (Psalm 99:1). In either case, this was where God appeared (Exodus 25:22).

The Testimony (16:13)
Refers to the written revelation of God to Israel: the Ten Commandments, carved on the two stone tablets Moses had brought down from Mount Sinai (Exodus 34:27–29). *The Testimony* (witness) gave evidence of the relationship God had established with them and formed the foundation of their community life.

Why atone for sections of God's house? (16:16)
Because sin is pervasive, even the place of worship itself was tainted, unfit for God's presence until it had been cleansed. Through sacrifices and atonement, God provided a way for the Israelites' relationship with him to be restored.

Why send a goat off into the desert? (16:20–22)
A sacrifice was a substitute, symbolically bearing sin and receiving its consequences. This goat, however, was a living sacrifice—banished from camp as a symbol of guilt removed far from the people and God's presence. The people watched as the goat was led to a distant spot—a striking portrayal of God's promise to remove their sins from them (compare Psalm 103:12).

After all the other sacrifices, why was a Day of Atonement needed? (16:29–30)

Other sacrifices cleansed individuals. Sacrifices on the Day of Atonement cleansed the whole nation of even their unknown transgressions which needed to be removed if God was to continue to dwell among them. This solemn ceremony reminded Israel of how their privileged access to God was threatened by sin. Later Christ's death made the final atonement for believers, making further sacrifices unnecessary (Heb. 9:23–28).

Could a ritual cleanse a nation? (16:30)

The ritual was to encourage the heartfelt repentance of all the people. They were to fast and cease work (implying self-examination and penitence). However, ceremonial repentance did not assure individuals of forgiveness then any more than today's pastoral prayer of confession guarantees that every church member is truly penitent.

Why did God designate a specific, exclusive spot for worship? (17:3–4)

Worship in one location was a precaution to help keep the Israelites from falling into the pagan practices of their neighbors, who worshiped at numerous shrines (Deut. 12:1–5, 29–31). At the tabernacle, their attention would be focused on God's unique revelation and presence among them. He could not be worshiped like a common pagan god!

Guilty of bloodshed (17:4)

Bloodshed commonly refers to ritual slaughter or sacrifice—here it means an improper sacrifice.

Could the Israelites slaughter their own meat? (17:4)

Yes. However, any slaughter of animals had religious implications. They usually ate meat in the context of the fellowship or peace offering (see 7:11–18). Any other time someone killed an animal—even when hunting—he had regulations to follow that reminded him of his relationship with God (17:13–14; Deut. 12:20–25).

Cut off from his people (17:4)

See *Cut off from his people* (7:20) and *Cut off from my presence* (22:3).

Goat idols (17:7)

Some suggest these were related to satyrs, the ancient mythical creatures that were half goat and half human. More probably, they were idols in the shape of a goat, worshiped in Egypt along with bull and calf idols. *Goat idols* are mentioned later along with *calf idols* (2 Chron. 11:15). The term could also refer to demons, as indicated in the text note.

the Most Holy Place[D], the Tent of Meeting[D] and the altar, he shall bring forward the live goat. [21]He is to lay both hands on the head of the live goat and confess over it all the wickedness and rebellion of the Israelites—all their sins—and put them on the goat's head. He shall send the goat away into the desert in the care of a man appointed for the task. [22]The goat will carry on itself all their sins to a solitary place; and the man shall release it in the desert.

[23]"Then Aaron is to go into the Tent of Meeting and take off the linen garments he put on before he entered the Most Holy Place, and he is to leave them there. [24]He shall bathe himself with water in a holy place and put on his regular garments. Then he shall come out and sacrifice[D] the burnt offering[D] for himself and the burnt offering for the people, to make atonement for himself and for the people. [25]He shall also burn the fat of the sin offering[D] on the altar.

[26]"The man who releases the goat as a scapegoat must wash his clothes and bathe himself with water; afterward he may come into the camp. [27]The bull and the goat for the sin offerings, whose blood was brought into the Most Holy Place to make atonement, must be taken outside the camp; their hides, flesh and offal[D] are to be burned up. [28]The man who burns them must wash his clothes and bathe himself with water; afterward he may come into the camp.

[29]"This is to be a lasting ordinance for you: On the tenth day of the seventh month you must deny yourselves[a] and not do any work—whether native-born or an alien[D] living among you— [30]because on this day atonement will be made for you, to cleanse you. Then, before the LORD, you will be clean from all your sins. [31]It is a sabbath[D] of rest, and you must deny yourselves; it is a lasting ordinance. [32]The priest[D] who is anointed[D] and ordained to succeed his father as high priest is to make atonement. He is to put on the sacred linen garments [33]and make atonement for the Most Holy Place, for the Tent of Meeting and the altar, and for the priests and all the people of the community.

[34]"This is to be a lasting ordinance for you: Atonement is to be made once a year for all the sins of the Israelites."

And it was done, as the LORD commanded Moses.

Eating Blood Forbidden

17 The LORD said to Moses, [2]"Speak to Aaron and his sons and to all the Israelites and say to them: 'This is what the LORD has commanded: [3]Any Israelite who sacrifices an ox,[b] a lamb or a goat in the camp or outside of it [4]instead of bringing it to the entrance to the Tent of Meeting to present it as an offering to the LORD in front of the tabernacle[D] of the LORD—that man shall be considered guilty of bloodshed; he has shed blood and must be cut off from his people. [5]This is so the Israelites will bring to the LORD the sacrifices they are now making in the open fields. They must bring them to the priest, that is, to the LORD, at the entrance to the Tent of Meeting and sacrifice them as fellowship offerings.[c] [6]The priest is to sprinkle the blood against the altar of the LORD at the entrance to the Tent of Meeting and burn the fat as an aroma pleasing to the LORD. [7]They must no

---

[a]29 Or *must fast*; also in verse 31   [b]3 The Hebrew word can include both male and female.   [c]5 Traditionally *peace offerings*

longer offer any of their sacrifices^D to the goat idols^Da to whom they prostitute themselves. This is to be a lasting ordinance for them and for the generations to come.'

8"Say to them: 'Any Israelite or any alien^D living among them who offers a burnt offering^D or sacrifice **9**and does not bring it to the entrance to the Tent of Meeting^D to sacrifice it to the LORD—that man must be cut off from his people.

10" 'Any Israelite or any alien living among them who eats any blood—I will set my face against that person who eats blood and will cut him off from his people. **11**For the life of a creature is in the blood, and I have given it to you to make atonement^D for yourselves on the altar; it is the blood that makes atonement for one's life. **12**Therefore I say to the Israelites, "None of you may eat blood, nor may an alien living among you eat blood."

13" 'Any Israelite or any alien living among you who hunts any animal or bird that may be eaten must drain out the blood and cover it with earth, **14**because the life of every creature is its blood. That is why I have said to the Israelites, "You must not eat the blood of any creature, because the life of every creature is its blood; anyone who eats it must be cut off."

15" 'Anyone, whether native-born or alien, who eats anything found dead or torn by wild animals must wash his clothes and bathe with water, and he will be ceremonially unclean^D till evening; then he will be clean. **16**But if he does not wash his clothes and bathe himself, he will be held responsible.' "

Unlawful Sexual Relations

18 The LORD said to Moses, **2**"Speak to the Israelites and say to them: 'I am the LORD your God. **3**You must not do as they do in Egypt, where you used to live, and you must not do as they do in the land of Canaan, where I am bringing you. Do not follow their practices. **4**You must obey my laws and be careful to follow my decrees. I am the LORD your God. **5**Keep my decrees and laws, for the man who obeys them will live by them. I am the LORD.

6" 'No one is to approach any close relative to have sexual relations. I am the LORD.

7" 'Do not dishonor your father by having sexual relations with your mother. She is your mother; do not have relations with her.

8" 'Do not have sexual relations with your father's wife; that would dishonor your father.

9" 'Do not have sexual relations with your sister, either your father's daughter or your mother's daughter, whether she was born in the same home or elsewhere.

10" 'Do not have sexual relations with your son's daughter or your daughter's daughter; that would dishonor you.

11" 'Do not have sexual relations with the daughter of your father's wife, born to your father; she is your sister.

12" 'Do not have sexual relations with your father's sister; she is your father's close relative.

13" 'Do not have sexual relations with your mother's sister, because she is your mother's close relative.

14" 'Do not dishonor your father's brother by approaching his wife to have sexual relations; she is your aunt.

15" 'Do not have sexual relations with your daughter-in-law. She is your son's wife; do not have relations with her.

Why would anyone want to eat blood? (17:10)
Blood was and is a staple food in many cultures around the world. In addition, blood was commonly viewed by ancient pagans as life-giving and even magical. Even today some primitive peoples believe that drinking the blood of a bull, for example, will give them the bull's strength. The Israelites were undoubtedly influenced by such views.

Why is blood considered the primary link with life? (17:11)
Blood is basic to life: cut off the flow of blood to an arm or leg, and the limb dies. You can survive without food for weeks, without water for days and without breath for minutes. But when your heart stops pumping, death comes swiftly. Drain out the blood, and you drain out the life of an animal or person.

How could blood atone for sin? (17:11)
The animal's blood served a sacred purpose. Poured out on the altar, blood was evidence that the animal had paid the price for sin with its very life. It represented a life given in order to spare the life of the sinner. Of course, the substitution of one life for another had to be recognized by God in order to count. Now, God accepts the blood Christ shed on the cross as the means to cleanse us from our sin (Heb. 9:13–14).

Why did God preface these commands with *I am the LORD*? (18:2)
This statement helped the Israelites remember all God had done for them. He had used these same words when he first introduced himself (Exodus 3:13–15), delivered them from Egypt (Exodus 6:2–8) and gave them the Ten Commandments (Exodus 20:2).

SCRIPTURE LINK (18:5) *The man who obeys them* [the laws] *will live by them*
Later Habakkuk says, *The righteous will live by his faith* (Hab. 2:4). These two statements complement one another, for the word translated *faith* also means *faithfulness*. Faithful acts of obedience stem from a heart that responds to God in faith (see also Romans 1:17).

Why list so many negative rules? (18:8–24)
A lot of ink would have been saved if the law had read simply, "Sex is right only when between husband and wife." But the fine points of right and wrong are usually made more clear when a law is stated negatively. Consequently, most laws from ancient times to modern begin similarly to the Ten Commandments: *You shall not . . .*

a7 Or demons

Rival wife (18:18)

Literally, a man is not to marry his wife's sister "in order to distress her." The assumption is that such a marriage would cause distress, just as it had earlier when Jacob married Rachel and Leah (Gen. 29–30). Also see article: *Why did David have so many wives and concubines?* (2 Samuel 5:13).

Are sexual relations during a woman's menstrual period wrong? (18:19)

See *Are sexual relations during a woman's menstrual period wrong?* (20:18).

Sacrificed to Molech (18:21)

This command against sacrificing children to the chief god of the Ammonites was listed along with commands against deviant sexual practices because both were parts of pagan rites of worship. See *Molech* (Jer. 32:35) and *Why would parents sacrifice their children?* (Jer. 19:5).

Why does God call homosexual behavior detestable? (18:22)

Homosexuality—as well as sex with a relative (vv. 6–18), a neighbor's wife (v. 20) or an animal (v. 23)—violates God's boundaries. Since such activities depart from God's created order, they are called *detestable*. Homosexuality was called *wicked* in Sodom (Gen. 19:5–7) and was seen in the New Testament as a sin that separates from God (Romans 1:26–27; 1 Cor. 6:9). For more on the application of these and other laws today, see article: *How are these laws relevant to us today?* (19:18–28).

Vomited out its inhabitants (18:25)

This graphic image personified the land to illustrate God's reaction to the repugnant behavior of the people. The picture shows the sickening nature of sin as well as its consequences—being expelled from the land.

How could the Israelites force others to obey God's commands? (18:26)

They couldn't dictate the consciences of individuals, but they could uphold the law. The assumption here is that the Israelites would be in control of the laws of the land—God's laws. Throughout Israel's history its rulers had the authority to destroy idols and shrines.

Does God expect perfection? (19:2)

The word *holy* does not mean perfect. Rather, it means to be *set aside*—that is, reserved for God's purposes. For more on holiness, see *Consecrate yourselves and be holy* (11:44–47).

16 " 'Do not have sexual relations with your brother's wife; that would dishonor your brother.

17 " 'Do not have sexual relations with both a woman and her daughter. Do not have sexual relations with either her son's daughter or her daughter's daughter; they are her close relatives. That is wickedness.

18 " 'Do not take your wife's sister as a rival wife and have sexual relations with her while your wife is living.

19 " 'Do not approach a woman to have sexual relations during the uncleanness[D] of her monthly period.

20 " 'Do not have sexual relations with your neighbor's wife and defile yourself with her.

21 " 'Do not give any of your children to be sacrificed[a] to Molech[D], for you must not profane[D] the name of your God. I am the LORD.

22 " 'Do not lie with a man as one lies with a woman; that is detestable.

23 " 'Do not have sexual relations with an animal and defile yourself with it. A woman must not present herself to an animal to have sexual relations with it; that is a perversion.

24 " 'Do not defile yourselves in any of these ways, because this is how the nations that I am going to drive out before you became defiled. **25**Even the land was defiled; so I punished it for its sin, and the land vomited out its inhabitants. **26**But you must keep my decrees and my laws. The native-born and the aliens[D] living among you must not do any of these detestable things, **27**for all these things were done by the people who lived in the land before you, and the land became defiled. **28**And if you defile the land, it will vomit you out as it vomited out the nations that were before you.

29 " 'Everyone who does any of these detestable things—such persons must be cut off from their people. **30**Keep my requirements and do not follow any of the detestable customs that were practiced before you came and do not defile yourselves with them. I am the LORD your God.' "

Various Laws

19 The LORD said to Moses, **2**"Speak to the entire assembly of Israel and say to them: 'Be holy because I, the LORD your God, am holy.

3 " 'Each of you must respect his mother and father, and you must observe my Sabbaths[D]. I am the LORD your God.

4 " 'Do not turn to idols[D] or make gods of cast metal for yourselves. I am the LORD your God.

5 " 'When you sacrifice[D] a fellowship offering[D][b] to the LORD, sacrifice it in such a way that it will be accepted on your behalf. **6**It shall be eaten on the day you sacrifice it or on the next day; anything left over until the third day must be burned up. **7**If any of it is eaten on the third day, it is impure and will not be accepted. **8**Whoever eats it will be held responsible because he has desecrated[D] what is holy to the LORD; that person must be cut off from his people.

9 " 'When you reap the harvest of your land, do not reap to the very edges of your field or gather the gleanings of your harvest. **10**Do not go over your vineyard a second

a21 Or to be passed through ⌐the fire⌐   *b5 Traditionally peace offering*

time or pick up the grapes that have fallen. Leave them for the poor and the alien D. I am the LORD your God.

11 " 'Do not steal.

" 'Do not lie.

" 'Do not deceive one another.

12 " 'Do not swear falsely by my name and so profane D the name of your God. I am the LORD.

13 " 'Do not defraud your neighbor or rob him.

" 'Do not hold back the wages of a hired man overnight.

14 " 'Do not curse the deaf or put a stumbling block D in front of the blind, but fear your God. I am the LORD.

15 " 'Do not pervert justice; do not show partiality to the poor or favoritism to the great, but judge your neighbor fairly.

16 " 'Do not go about spreading slander among your people.

" 'Do not do anything that endangers your neighbor's life. I am the LORD.

17 " 'Do not hate your brother in your heart. Rebuke your neighbor frankly so you will not share in his guilt.

18 " 'Do not seek revenge or bear a grudge against one of your people, but love your neighbor as yourself. I am the LORD.

19 " 'Keep my decrees.

" 'Do not mate different kinds of animals.

" 'Do not plant your field with two kinds of seed.

" 'Do not wear clothing woven of two kinds of material.

20 " 'If a man sleeps with a woman who is a slave girl promised to another man but who has not been ransomed or given her freedom, there must be due punishment. Yet they are not to be put to death D, because she had not been freed. **21** The man, however, must bring a

Why did an employee have to be paid daily? (19:13)
It seems that this rule was for the benefit of the poor who lived hand to mouth. Holding back wages for even a day would have created undue hardship for them. See Deut. 24:15.

SCRIPTURE LINK (19:18) *Love your neighbor as yourself*
Jesus cites this as one of the two greatest commandments. See Matt. 22:39.

What was wrong with hybrids? (19:19)
See article: *Why did God keep some meats off the menu?* (11:4–41). Also see *What was wrong with these actions?* (Deut. 22:9–11).

How were slaves treated in Hebrew culture? (19:20–22)
See *Why does God endorse slavery?* (25:44–46).

How are these laws relevant to us today? (19:18–28)

Though some of the laws in Leviticus seem easy to apply today, others do not. It is unsettling to see the mixture of the timeless (*Love your neighbor,* v. 18) with what seems trivial or culture-bound (*Do not cut the hair at the sides of your head,* v. 27). How can we continue to ban homosexual practice (20:13) if we no longer care about blended fabrics of cotton and wool (19:19)?

People attempt to resolve this dilemma in several ways. Some say these laws were superseded when Jesus came. Others still attempt to uphold each one. Still others believe only those regulations mentioned in the New Testament remain binding.

We can gain some insight into the problem by seeing what Jesus said about the law. He told his disciples that not a single letter of the law would disappear *until everything is accomplished* (Matt. 5:17–20). Yet because he followed the true spirit of the law rather than the legalistic views of the religious teachers, Jesus was accused of violating the law (Luke 6:2).

It's best to assume that within each law is an enduring principle that expresses part of God's will for us. Some details, written for Israel's situation, will not fit ours. But the truths behind them are timeless and can still be applied. Jesus upheld the deeper principles of the law when he taught, *You have heard that it was said . . . But I tell you* (Matt. 5).

Old Testament rules that seem to defy explanation often concerned Israel's call to be God's distinct people. In the same way, we should resist pressures to conform to the world (Romans 12:2). We can still apply God's standards to the details of our lives within the context of our culture.

Why was this fruit forbidden? (19:23–25)

The word translated *forbidden* is literally *uncircumcised*. It also suggests the idea of something premature or not yet ready. Fruit trees took time to grow, and produced little or no fruit for the first three years. The first mature harvest—occurring in the fourth year—was to be given to the Lord because it was comparable to offering the *firstfruits* of other, faster-maturing crops (see Deut. 26:1–15). But after the fruit was consecrated to God, the tree's later fruit would be ready for eating.

Why have laws about hairstyles or tattoos? (19:27–28)

To keep the Israelites from imitating the pagan practices of their neighbors. Some people applied tattoos, cut themselves or used disfiguring haircuts as signs of mourning and humiliation to gain favor with their gods. For example, the prophets of Baal cut themselves when they faced Elijah on Mount Carmel (1 Kings 18:25–29). Following the lead of the pagans would not only have honored their gods, it would have dishonored the bodies God had given the Israelites. Also see **Why was shaving considered unholy?** (21:5–6).

Set my face against (20:5)

God's face is used figuratively in the Old Testament to indicate his presence, often in blessing: *The Lord make his face shine upon you* (Num. 6:25). At other times, as here, the image is a frightening one, indicating God's resolve to bring judgment (Ezek. 15:6–8).

Why execute someone merely for saying something bad? (20:9)

This involved more than mere words. It included contempt for one's parents, devaluing them—the very opposite of honoring them, as God had commanded (19:3; Exodus 20:12). Not only did such behavior undermine the family structure, it was an outright challenge to God's authority.

His blood will be on his own head (20:9)

This could be restated, "His guilt is his own." In other words, the individual himself would pay the consequences for his own sin. There could be no substitute or sacrifice.

ram to the entrance to the Tent of Meeting[D] for a guilt offering[D] to the Lord. **22**With the ram of the guilt offering the priest is to make atonement for him before the Lord for the sin he has committed, and his sin will be forgiven.

23 'When you enter the land and plant any kind of fruit tree, regard its fruit as forbidden.[a] For three years you are to consider it forbidden[a]; it must not be eaten. **24**In the fourth year all its fruit will be holy, an offering of praise to the Lord. **25**But in the fifth year you may eat its fruit. In this way your harvest will be increased. I am the Lord your God.

26 'Do not eat any meat with the blood still in it.

" 'Do not practice divination[D] or sorcery[D].

27 'Do not cut the hair at the sides of your head or clip off the edges of your beard.

28 'Do not cut your bodies for the dead or put tattoo marks on yourselves. I am the Lord.

29 'Do not degrade your daughter by making her a prostitute, or the land will turn to prostitution and be filled with wickedness.

30 'Observe my Sabbaths[D] and have reverence[D] for my sanctuary. I am the Lord.

31 'Do not turn to mediums[D] or seek out spiritists, for you will be defiled by them. I am the Lord your God.

32 'Rise in the presence of the aged, show respect for the elderly and revere[D] your God. I am the Lord.

33 'When an alien[D] lives with you in your land, do not mistreat him. **34**The alien living with you must be treated as one of your native-born. Love him as yourself, for you were aliens in Egypt. I am the Lord your God.

35 'Do not use dishonest standards when measuring length, weight or quantity. **36**Use honest scales and honest weights, an honest ephah[b] and an honest hin.[c] I am the Lord your God, who brought you out of Egypt.

37 'Keep all my decrees and all my laws and follow them. I am the Lord.' "

Punishments for Sin

20 The Lord said to Moses, **2**"Say to the Israelites: 'Any Israelite or any alien living in Israel who gives[d] any of his children to Molech[D] must be put to death[D]. The people of the community are to stone him. **3**I will set my face against that man and I will cut him off from his people; for by giving his children to Molech, he has defiled my sanctuary and profaned[D] my holy name. **4**If the people of the community close their eyes when that man gives one of his children to Molech and they fail to put him to death, **5**I will set my face against that man and his family and will cut off from their people both him and all who follow him in prostituting themselves to Molech.

6 'I will set my face against the person who turns to mediums and spiritists to prostitute himself by following them, and I will cut him off from his people.

7 'Consecrate[D] yourselves and be holy, because I am the Lord your God. **8**Keep my decrees and follow them. I am the Lord, who makes you holy.[e]

9 'If anyone curses his father or mother, he must be

---

*a*23 Hebrew *uncircumcised*   *b*36 An ephah was a dry measure.
*c*36 A hin was a liquid measure.   *d*2 Or *sacrifices*; also in verses 3 and 4   *e*8 Or *who sanctifies you*; or *who sets you apart as holy*

put to death[D]. He has cursed his father or his mother, and his blood will be on his own head.

10" 'If a man commits adultery with another man's wife—with the wife of his neighbor—both the adulterer and the adulteress must be put to death.

11" 'If a man sleeps with his father's wife, he has dishonored his father. Both the man and the woman must be put to death; their blood will be on their own heads.

12" 'If a man sleeps with his daughter-in-law, both of them must be put to death. What they have done is a perversion; their blood will be on their own heads.

13" 'If a man lies with a man as one lies with a woman, both of them have done what is detestable. They must be put to death; their blood will be on their own heads.

14" 'If a man marries both a woman and her mother, it is wicked. Both he and they must be burned in the fire, so that no wickedness will be among you.

15" 'If a man has sexual relations with an animal, he must be put to death, and you must kill the animal.

16" 'If a woman approaches an animal to have sexual relations with it, kill both the woman and the animal. They must be put to death; their blood will be on their own heads.

17" 'If a man marries his sister, the daughter of either his father or his mother, and they have sexual relations, it is a disgrace. They must be cut off before the eyes of their people. He has dishonored his sister and will be held responsible.

18" 'If a man lies with a woman during her monthly period and has sexual relations with her, he has exposed the source of her flow, and she has also uncovered it. Both of them must be cut off from their people.

19" 'Do not have sexual relations with the sister of either your mother or your father, for that would dishonor a close relative; both of you would be held responsible.

20" 'If a man sleeps with his aunt, he has dishonored his uncle. They will be held responsible; they will die childless.

21" 'If a man marries his brother's wife, it is an act of impurity; he has dishonored his brother. They will be childless.

22" 'Keep all my decrees and laws and follow them, so that the land where I am bringing you to live may not vomit you out. **23**You must not live according to the customs of the nations I am going to drive out before you. Because they did all these things, I abhorred them. **24**But I said to you, "You will possess their land; I will give it to you as an inheritance, a land flowing with milk and honey." I am the LORD your God, who has set you apart from the nations.

25" 'You must therefore make a distinction between clean and unclean[D] animals and between unclean and clean birds. Do not defile yourselves by any animal or bird or anything that moves along the ground—those which I have set apart as unclean for you. **26**You are to be holy to me[a] because I, the LORD, am holy, and I have set you apart from the nations to be my own.

27" 'A man or woman who is a medium[D] or spiritist among you must be put to death. You are to stone them; their blood will be on their own heads.' "

Why death by burning? (20:14)

No one knows for sure why burning is specifically commanded as the method of execution here. Burning was often associated with sexual offenses (see 21:9; Gen. 38:24). Perhaps it included the idea of purification, because it completely destroyed all remnants of the uncleanness left by the sin.

Didn't Abraham marry his sister? (20:17)

Yes, Sarah was Abraham's half-sister (Gen. 20:11–12). This verse thus outlaws something Israel's patriarch had done long before! There are two ways to deal with this inconsistency: (1) We cannot hold Abraham accountable for laws as yet unrevealed. (2) We do not need to defend Abraham's behavior; not everything he did was right or advisable.

Are sexual relations during a woman's menstrual period wrong? (20:18)

God's reason for this law, as with many others in Leviticus, seems related to religious purposes. Any flow of bodily fluid was considered unclean and would cause ceremonial defilement. See *Bodily discharge* (15:2–3). Because the New Testament believers see the ceremonial requirements of the law fulfilled in Christ, they see the Old Testament law from another perspective. There is not complete agreement on the question, however. See article: *How are these laws relevant to us today?* (19:18–28).

Weren't there times when a man was supposed to marry his brother's wife? (20:21)

Yes, when his brother had died, leaving his wife childless. But this law referred to marrying a brother's wife while the brother was still living. See *Why was a man required to marry his brother's widow?* (Deut. 25:5–9).

---

*a*26 Or *be my holy ones*

Ceremonially unclean (21:1–4)

Family members who prepared a body for burial became unclean. Even entering a place with a corpse in it caused uncleanness (Num. 19:14). Priests were allowed to do this only when close family members had died. High priests could not even go that far (vv. 11–12). Also see *Why couldn't Aaron and his sons mourn these tragic deaths?* (10:6).

Why was shaving considered unholy? (21:5–6)

Shaving wasn't the problem—pagan symbolism was. When mourning for the dead, ancient Canaanites shaved to express deep, hopeless sorrow. It's not known why cutting hair (or, in the extreme, one's body) held such meaning. Some pagan stories told about gods who demonstrated grief by cutting themselves. If the Israelites had mimicked their pagan neighbors, however, they would have denied their God, the Lord of both the living and the dead (Deut. 14:1–2). Also see *Why have laws about hairstyles or tattoos?* (19:27–28).

What does God eat? (21:6,8)

Ancient peoples, believing their gods needed nourishment, had rituals for "feeding" the statues of their gods. Leviticus borrows the conventional terminology of that time to illustrate offerings as God's *food*. The idea is stripped of its mythological overtones, however. God wanted the fellowship and devotion of his people; he didn't need food. The Old Testament ridicules the idea that God has culinary needs (Psalm 50:12–13).

Why couldn't the high priest leave the sanctuary? (21:12)

Usually he could leave—but not to take part in burial customs, even to attend the death of his own parents. This was to prevent the high priest from becoming ceremonially unclean and thus contaminating the sanctuary upon his return. Nothing here suggests that the sanctuary was a type of monastery outside whose walls the high priest could never go.

Why discriminate against the handicapped? (21:17–23)

This rule had nothing to do with individual rights. Serving as a priest was not a *right;* it was a *privilege* reserved for only a few. Those with physical defects were no more discriminated against than were most of the people of Israel: Only men of a certain age, ceremonially clean, without defect, from the tribe of Levi and descended from Aaron were granted the privilege to represent God as priests. At issue was whether the priests would project an image of a holy, perfect God to the people. The uniqueness of the call preserved the image. Nonetheless, Aaron's descendants with defects were not barred from other priestly benefits (v. 22).

Cut off from my presence (22:3)

The penalty for disrespecting the holiness of God. Some say this was excommunication—being cut off from the worship of God. Others say it was ostracism—being banned from the community. Still others say it was the death penalty (v. 9), executed either by the community on God's behalf or by God himself. Some think this phrase included the idea of eternal punishment; the usual formula to describe death, *gathered to his people,* was altered to *cut off from his people.*

Rules for Priests

21 The Lord said to Moses, "Speak to the priests[D], the sons of Aaron, and say to them: 'A priest must not make himself ceremonially unclean[D] for any of his people who die, ²except for a close relative, such as his mother or father, his son or daughter, his brother, ³or an unmarried sister who is dependent on him since she has no husband—for her he may make himself unclean. ⁴He must not make himself unclean for people related to him by marriage,[a] and so defile himself.

⁵" 'Priests must not shave their heads or shave off the edges of their beards or cut their bodies. ⁶They must be holy to their God and must not profane[D] the name of their God. Because they present the offerings made to the Lord by fire, the food of their God, they are to be holy.

⁷" 'They must not marry women defiled by prostitution or divorced from their husbands, because priests are holy to their God. ⁸Regard them as holy, because they offer up the food of your God. Consider them holy, because I the Lord am holy—I who make you holy.[b]

⁹" 'If a priest's daughter defiles herself by becoming a prostitute, she disgraces her father; she must be burned in the fire.

¹⁰" 'The high priest, the one among his brothers who has had the anointing[D] oil poured on his head and who has been ordained to wear the priestly garments, must not let his hair become unkempt[c] or tear his clothes. ¹¹He must not enter a place where there is a dead body. He must not make himself unclean, even for his father or mother, ¹²nor leave the sanctuary of his God or desecrate[D] it, because he has been dedicated by the anointing oil of his God. I am the Lord.

¹³" 'The woman he marries must be a virgin. ¹⁴He must not marry a widow, a divorced woman, or a woman defiled by prostitution, but only a virgin from his own people, ¹⁵so he will not defile his offspring among his people. I am the Lord, who makes him holy.[d]' "

¹⁶The Lord said to Moses, ¹⁷"Say to Aaron: 'For the generations to come none of your descendants who has a defect may come near to offer the food of his God. ¹⁸No man who has any defect may come near: no man who is blind or lame, disfigured or deformed; ¹⁹no man with a crippled foot or hand, ²⁰or who is hunchbacked or dwarfed, or who has any eye defect, or who has festering or running sores or damaged testicles. ²¹No descendant of Aaron the priest who has any defect is to come near to present the offerings made to the Lord by fire. He has a defect; he must not come near to offer the food of his God. ²²He may eat the most holy food of his God, as well as the holy food; ²³yet because of his defect, he must not go near the curtain or approach the altar, and so desecrate my sanctuary. I am the Lord, who makes them holy.[e]' "

²⁴So Moses told this to Aaron and his sons and to all the Israelites.

22 The Lord said to Moses, ²"Tell Aaron and his sons to treat with respect the sacred[D] offerings the Israelites consecrate[D] to me, so they will not profane my holy name. I am the Lord.

³"Say to them: 'For the generations to come, if any of

---

a4 Or *unclean as a leader among his people*   *b8* Or *who sanctify you;* or *who set you apart as holy*   *c10* Or *not uncover his head*   *d15* Or *who sanctifies him;* or *who sets him apart as holy*   *e23* Or *who sanctifies them;* or *who sets them apart as holy*

your descendants is ceremonially unclean[D] and yet comes near the sacred[D] offerings that the Israelites consecrate[D] to the LORD, that person must be cut off from my presence. I am the LORD.

4" 'If a descendant of Aaron has an infectious skin disease[a] or a bodily discharge, he may not eat the sacred offerings until he is cleansed. He will also be unclean if he touches something defiled by a corpse or by anyone who has an emission of semen, **5**or if he touches any crawling thing that makes him unclean, or any person who makes him unclean, whatever the uncleanness may be. **6**The one who touches any such thing will be unclean till evening. He must not eat any of the sacred offerings unless he has bathed himself with water. **7**When the sun goes down, he will be clean, and after that he may eat the sacred offerings, for they are his food. **8**He must not eat anything found dead or torn by wild animals, and so become unclean through it. I am the LORD.

9" 'The priests[D] are to keep my requirements so that they do not become guilty and die for treating them with contempt. I am the LORD, who makes them holy.[b]

10" 'No one outside a priest's family may eat the sacred offering, nor may the guest of a priest or his hired worker eat it. **11**But if a priest buys a slave with money, or if a slave is born in his household, that slave may eat his food. **12**If a priest's daughter marries anyone other than a priest, she may not eat any of the sacred contributions. **13**But if a priest's daughter becomes a widow or is divorced, yet has no children, and she returns to live in her father's house as in her youth, she may eat of her father's food. No unauthorized person, however, may eat any of it.

14" 'If anyone eats a sacred offering by mistake, he must make restitution to the priest for the offering and add a fifth of the value to it. **15**The priests must not desecrate[D] the sacred offerings the Israelites present to the LORD **16**by allowing them to eat the sacred offerings and so bring upon them guilt requiring payment. I am the LORD, who makes them holy.' "

Unacceptable Sacrifices

17The LORD said to Moses, **18**"Speak to Aaron and his sons and to all the Israelites and say to them: 'If any of you—either an Israelite or an alien[D] living in Israel—presents a gift for a burnt offering[D] to the LORD, either to fulfill a vow[D] or as a freewill offering, **19**you must present a male without defect from the cattle, sheep or goats in order that it may be accepted on your behalf. **20**Do not bring anything with a defect, because it will not be accepted on your behalf. **21**When anyone brings from the herd or flock a fellowship offering[Dc] to the LORD to fulfill a special vow or as a freewill offering, it must be without defect or blemish to be acceptable. **22**Do not offer to the LORD the blind, the injured or the maimed, or anything with warts or festering or running sores. Do not place any of these on the altar as an offering made to the LORD by fire. **23**You may, however, present as a freewill offering an ox[d] or a sheep that is deformed or stunted, but it will not

---

Why was skipping a bath a crime when it was okay to own slaves? (22:6,11)

Serving a holy, almighty God should have inspired awe and trembling. A priest coming before God without first being purified was a serious matter. But why could a priest own slaves? At this point in history, it seems that God chose to reform and modify slavery rather than eliminate it. The Old Testament took the lead in world literature, insisting that slaves be treated as human beings for their own sake: a priest's slave was granted privileges (v. 11) that a priest's employees (v. 10) and sometimes children (v. 12) could not enjoy. For more on slavery, see article: *Why doesn't the Bible condemn slavery?* (1 Peter 2:18–21).

Why were there so many religious rules? (22:9)

For at least two reasons: (1) Careful attention to detail meant everything the priests did would better reflect the holy, awesome nature of God. (2) The restrictions they followed established standards of integrity and set Israel's priests apart from the priests of other cultures. Pagan priests, on the other hand, used their religious stature as a means to gain influence and wealth.

What's the difference between a *freewill offering* and a *vow*? (22:23)

The freewill offering, often mentioned along with the vow, was a generic term for many different kinds of contributions which express thanksgiving to God. The freewill offering was entirely voluntary and therefore had fewer stipulations. The vow, on the other hand, made in the form of a sacrifice, stemmed from a prior commitment made by an individual. Its requirements were, therefore, more demanding.

---

[a]4 Traditionally *leprosy*; the Hebrew word was used for various diseases affecting the skin—not necessarily leprosy.   [b]9 Or *who sanctifies them*; or *who sets them apart as holy*; also in verse 16   [c]21 Traditionally *peace offering*   [d]23 The Hebrew word can include both male and female.

What was wrong with an offering not yet eight days old? (22:27)

Some think this rule was for reasons of compassion. But the sacrificial system was designed with judgment, not compassion in mind. Sacrificing a suckling eight-day-old was hardly more compassionate than sacrificing a one- or two-day-old. This law more likely was intended to distinguish life from death. If birth and death came too close, the sacrifice would mean much less. The animal had to live before it could die as a meaningful sacrifice.

Why was it improper to slaughter a cow and its calf on the same day? (22:28)

Some think this rule was for reasons of compassion (see previous note). But slaughtering a cow and its calf on successive days was hardly more compassionate than doing it all at once. It's possible this law was intended to illustrate a distinction between the two sacrifices: the death of a life-giver (cow) was different from that of a life-receiver (calf).

If the Lord made priests holy, why were so many rules needed? (22:32)

Holiness was a joint venture involving God's work and the priests' cooperation. For example, God called on Israel to make the Sabbath holy (Exodus 20:8), something he had already done himself (Exodus 20:11). This didn't mean the priests could attain holiness by their own efforts. But because they had been set apart and called holy, they were enabled to observe God's laws and commandments. Their obedience was a mark of holiness, rather than merit for holiness.

Why have so many festivals? (23:1–44)

For several reasons: (1) Festivals required a pilgrimage—the people were to assemble together. This emphasized the communal nature of their faith and helped keep their religious experience from becoming too private. (2) Festivals focused a great deal on the past acts of God. This tied the faith of one generation to the next, giving hope for the future. (3) Festivals bridged the gap between religious obligation and joyful celebration. Holy days were *commanded,* but they were intended to be happy days.

Sacred assembly (23:2–4)

Behind the word *assembly* is a Hebrew verb meaning *to proclaim, summon, invite.* These were times when the whole community was summoned together for common worship and celebration.

be accepted in fulfillment of a vowᴰ. **24**You must not offer to the Lord an animal whose testicles are bruised, crushed, torn or cut. You must not do this in your own land, **25**and you must not accept such animals from the hand of a foreigner and offer them as the food of your God. They will not be accepted on your behalf, because they are deformed and have defects.' "

26The Lord said to Moses, **27**"When a calf, a lamb or a goat is born, it is to remain with its mother for seven days. From the eighth day on, it will be acceptable as an offering made to the Lord by fire. **28**Do not slaughter a cow or a sheep and its young on the same day.

29"When you sacrificeᴰ a thank offeringᴰ to the Lord, sacrifice it in such a way that it will be accepted on your behalf. **30**It must be eaten that same day; leave none of it till morning. I am the Lord.

31"Keep my commands and follow them. I am the Lord. **32**Do not profaneᴰ my holy name. I must be acknowledged as holy by the Israelites. I am the Lord, who makes*ᵃ* you holy*ᵇ* **33**and who brought you out of Egypt to be your God. I am the Lord."

23

The Lord said to Moses, **2**"Speak to the Israelites and say to them: 'These are my appointed feasts, the appointed feasts of the Lord, which you are to proclaim as sacredᴰ assemblies.

The Sabbath

3" 'There are six days when you may work, but the seventh day is a Sabbathᴰ of rest, a day of sacred assemblyᴰ. You are not to do any work; wherever you live, it is a Sabbath to the Lord.

The Passover and Unleavened Bread

4" 'These are the Lord's appointed feasts, the sacred assemblies you are to proclaim at their appointed times: **5**The Lord's Passover begins at twilight on the fourteenth day of the first month. **6**On the fifteenth day of that month the Lord's Feast of Unleavened Bread begins; for seven days you must eat bread made without yeastᴰ. **7**On the first day hold a sacred assembly and do no regular work. **8**For seven days present an offering made to the Lord by fire. And on the seventh day hold a sacred assembly and do no regular work.' "

Firstfruits

9The Lord said to Moses, **10**"Speak to the Israelites and say to them: 'When you enter the land I am going to give you and you reap its harvest, bring to the priestᴰ a sheaf of the first grain you harvest. **11**He is to wave the sheaf before the Lord so it will be accepted on your behalf; the priest is to wave it on the day after the Sabbath. **12**On the day you wave the sheaf, you must sacrifice as a burnt offeringᴰ to the Lord a lamb a year old without defect, **13**together with its grain offeringᴰ of two-tenths of an ephah*ᶜ* of fine flour mixed with oil—an offering made to the Lord by fire, a pleasing aroma—and its drink offeringᴰ of a quarter of a hin*ᵈ* of wine. **14**You must not eat any bread, or roasted or new grain, until the very day

ᵃ32 Or *made*   *ᵇ32* Or *who sanctifies you; or who sets you apart as holy*   *ᶜ13* That is, probably about 4 quarts (about 4.5 liters); also in verse 17   *ᵈ13* That is, probably about 1 quart (about 1 liter)

you bring this offering to your God. This is to be a lasting ordinance for the generations to come, wherever you live.

Feast of Weeks

¹⁵" 'From the day after the Sabbath ᴰ, the day you brought the sheaf of the wave offering ᴰ, count off seven full weeks. ¹⁶Count off fifty days up to the day after the seventh Sabbath, and then present an offering of new grain to the LORD. ¹⁷From wherever you live, bring two loaves made of two-tenths of an ephah of fine flour, baked with yeast ᴰ, as a wave offering of firstfruits to the LORD. ¹⁸Present with this bread seven male lambs, each a year old and without defect, one young bull and two rams. They will be a burnt offering ᴰ to the LORD, together with their grain offerings ᴰ and drink offerings ᴰ— an offering made by fire, an aroma pleasing to the LORD. ¹⁹Then sacrifice ᴰ one male goat for a sin offering ᴰ and two lambs, each a year old, for a fellowship offering ᴰ,ᵃ ²⁰The priest ᴰ is to wave the two lambs before the LORD as a wave offering, together with the bread of the first-fruits. They are a sacred offering to the LORD for the priest. ²¹On that same day you are to proclaim a sacred assembly ᴰ and do no regular work. This is to be a lasting ordinance for the generations to come, wherever you live.

²²" 'When you reap the harvest of your land, do not reap to the very edges of your field or gather the gleanings of your harvest. Leave them for the poor and the alien ᴰ. I am the LORD your God.' "

Feast of Trumpets

²³The LORD said to Moses, ²⁴"Say to the Israelites: 'On the first day of the seventh month you are to have a day of rest, a sacred assembly commemorated with trumpet blasts. ²⁵Do no regular work, but present an offering made to the LORD by fire.' "

Day of Atonement

²⁶The LORD said to Moses, ²⁷"The tenth day of this seventh month is the Day of Atonement ᴰ. Hold a sacred assembly and deny yourselves,ᵇ and present an offering made to the LORD by fire. ²⁸Do no work on that day, because it is the Day of Atonement, when atonement is made for you before the LORD your God. ²⁹Anyone who does not deny himself on that day must be cut off from his people. ³⁰I will destroy from among his people anyone who does any work on that day. ³¹You shall do no work at all. This is to be a lasting ordinance for the generations to come, wherever you live. ³²It is a sabbath of rest for you, and you must deny yourselves. From the evening of the ninth day of the month until the following evening you are to observe your sabbath."

Feast of Tabernacles

³³The LORD said to Moses, ³⁴"Say to the Israelites: 'On the fifteenth day of the seventh month the LORD's Feast of Tabernacles begins, and it lasts for seven days. ³⁵The first day is a sacred assembly; do no regular work. ³⁶For seven days present offerings made to the LORD by fire, and on the eighth day hold a sacred assembly and present an offering made to the LORD by fire. It is the closing assembly; do no regular work.

ᵃ19 Traditionally *peace offering*   ᵇ27 Or *and fast*; also in verses 29 and 32

Lasting ordinance (23:14)
Comes from a Hebrew verb meaning *to inscribe* or *incise,* and points to the custom of inscribing laws or statutes on stone. Standing alone, then, an *ordinance* meant something permanent. Calling it a *lasting* ordinance served to emphasize not only its permanent status, but also its significance.

What are all these feasts about? (23:15)
See *Old Testament Feasts* on page 168.

SCRIPTURE LINK (23:26–32)
Parallel accounts of the Day of Atonement are found in Lev. 16:2–34 and Num. 29:7–11.

How did the Israelites *deny* themselves? (23:27)
Typically, this has been understood to mean fasting—going without food and beverage. But it may also mean something more, perhaps abstention from things like changing one's clothing, bathing or sex (2 Samuel 12:20).

Old Testament Feasts

Name	Old Testament References	Time	Description	New Testament References
Sabbath	Exodus 20:8-11; 31:12-17; Lev. 23:3; Deut. 5:12-15	7th day	Day of rest; no work	Matt. 12:1-14; Mark 2:23-3:5; Luke 4:16-30; 6:1-10; 13:10-16; 14:1-5; John 5:1-15; 9:1-34; Acts 13:14-48; 17:2; 18:4; Heb. 4:1-11
Sabbath Year	Exodus 23:10-11; Lev. 25:1-7	7th year	Year of rest; fallow fields	
Year of Jubilee	Lev. 25:8-55; 27:17-24; Num. 36:4	50th year	Canceled debts; liberation of slaves and indentured servants; land returned original family owners	
Passover	Exodus 12:1-14; Lev. 23:5; Num. 9:1-14; 28:16; Deut. 16:1-7	1st month (Abib) 14	Slaying and eating a lamb, together with bitter herbs and bread made without yeast, in every household	Matt. 26:1-2,17-29; Mark 14:12-26; Luke 22:7-38; John 2:13-25; 11:55-56; John 13:1-30; 1 Cor. 5:7
Unleavened Bread	Exodus 12:15-20; 13:3-10; 23:15; 34:18; Lev. 23:6-8; Num. 28:17-25; Deut. 16:3-4,8	1st month (Abib) 15-21	Eating bread made without yeast; holding several assemblies; making designated offerings	Matt. 26:17; Mark 14:1,12; Luke 22:1,7; Acts 12:3; 20:6; 1 Cor. 5:6-8
Firstfruits	Lev. 23:9-14	1st month (Abib) 16	Presenting a sheaf of the first of the barley harvest as a wave offering; making a burnt offering and a grain offering	Romans 8:23; 1 Cor. 15:20-23
Weeks (Pentecost)(Harvest)	Exodus 23:16a; 34:22a; Lev. 23:15-21; Num. 28:26-31; Deut. 16:9-12	3rd month (Sivan) 6	A festival of joy; mandatory and voluntary offerings, including the firstfruits of the wheat harvest	Acts 2:1-41; 20:16; 1 Cor. 16:8
Trumpets (Later: Rosh Hashanah-New Year's Day)	Lev. 23:23-25; Num. 29:1-6	7th month (Tishri) 1	An assembly on a day of rest commemorated with trumpet blasts and sacrifices	
Day of Atonement (Yom Kippur)	Lev. 16; 23:26-32; Num. 29:7-11	7th month (Tishri) 10	A day of rest, fasting and sacrifices of atonement for priests and people and atonement for the tabernacle and altar	Acts 27:9; Romans 3:24-26; Heb. 9:1-14,23-26; 10:19-22
Tabernacles (Booths)(Ingathering)	Exodus 23:16b; 34:22b; Lev. 23:33-36,39-43; Num. 29:12-34; Deut. 16:13-15	7th month (Tishri) 15-21	A week of celebration for the harvest; living in booths and offering sacrifices	John 7:2-37
Sacred Assembly	Lev. 23:36; Num. 29:35-38	7th month (Tishri) 22	A day of convocation, rest and offering sacrifices	John 7:37-44
Dedication		9th month	A commemoration of the purification of the temple in the Maccabean era (166-160 B.C.)	John 10:22-39
Purim	Esther 9:18-32	12th month (Adar) 14,15	A day of joy and feasting and giving presents	

37(" 'These are the LORD's appointed feasts, which you are to proclaim as sacred^D assemblies for bringing offerings made to the LORD by fire—the burnt offerings^D and grain offerings^D, sacrifices^D and drink offerings^D required for each day. **38**These offerings are in addition to those for the LORD's Sabbaths^D and^a in addition to your gifts and whatever you have vowed^D and all the freewill offerings you give to the LORD.)

39" 'So beginning with the fifteenth day of the seventh month, after you have gathered the crops of the land, celebrate the festival to the LORD for seven days; the first day is a day of rest, and the eighth day also is a day of rest. **40**On the first day you are to take choice fruit from the trees, and palm fronds, leafy branches and poplars, and rejoice before the LORD your God for seven days. **41**Celebrate this as a festival to the LORD for seven days each year. This is to be a lasting ordinance for the generations to come; celebrate it in the seventh month. **42**Live in booths for seven days: All native-born Israelites are to live in booths **43**so your descendants will know that I had the Israelites live in booths when I brought them out of Egypt. I am the LORD your God.' "

44So Moses announced to the Israelites the appointed feasts of the LORD.

Oil and Bread Set Before the LORD

24 The LORD said to Moses, **2**"Command the Israelites to bring you clear oil of pressed olives for the light so that the lamps may be kept burning continually. **3**Outside the curtain of the Testimony in the Tent of Meeting^D, Aaron is to tend the lamps before the LORD from evening till morning, continually. This is to be a lasting ordinance for the generations to come. **4**The lamps on the pure gold lampstand before the LORD must be tended continually.

5"Take fine flour and bake twelve loaves of bread, using two-tenths of an ephah^b for each loaf. **6**Set them in two rows, six in each row, on the table of pure gold before the LORD. **7**Along each row put some pure incense^D as a memorial portion to represent the bread and to be an offering made to the LORD by fire. **8**This bread is to be set out before the LORD regularly, Sabbath after Sabbath, on behalf of the Israelites, as a lasting covenant^D. **9**It belongs to Aaron and his sons, who are to eat it in a holy place, because it is a most holy part of their regular share of the offerings made to the LORD by fire."

A Blasphemer Stoned

10Now the son of an Israelite mother and an Egyptian father went out among the Israelites, and a fight broke out in the camp between him and an Israelite. **11**The son of the Israelite woman blasphemed^D the Name with a curse; so they brought him to Moses. (His mother's name was Shelomith, the daughter of Dibri the Danite.) **12**They put him in custody until the will of the LORD should be made clear to them.

13Then the LORD said to Moses: **14**"Take the blasphemer outside the camp. All those who heard him are to lay their hands on his head, and the entire assembly is to stone him. **15**Say to the Israelites: 'If anyone curses his God, he will be held responsible; **16**anyone who blasphemes the

Was Aaron on permanent night shift? (24:3)

Not exactly. To *tend the lamps* meant simply that it was Aaron's responsibility (later, that of his descendants) to set up the lamps so they would burn throughout the night. That he was to do this *continually* meant that he was to perform this service regularly. After fulfilling his duties, Aaron could go home to his family.

Were mixed marriages like this common among the Israelites? (24:10)

Probably not. Though marriage with foreigners was forbidden (Deut. 7:3–4), there were a number of foreigners and aliens living among the Israelites (Exodus 12:38; Lev. 18:26). Most intermarriages that we know about involved Israelite men with foreign women (Joseph and his Egyptian wife, Moses and his Midianite wife, Boaz and his Moabite wife, Samson and his Philistine wife, and Solomon with his many foreign wives). This may have been due in part to cultural expectations that a wife would join her husband's people.

Why such a stiff penalty for words spoken in anger? (24:12–16)

Blasphemy involved more than rash words in the heat of a brawl. Blasphemy tarnished God's holy reputation—and God could not allow that to happen. It may seem unfair that the punishment was decided after the crime was committed. But the man broke an established law (Exodus 22:28). Though no penalties had been prescribed, he would have known there would be consequences. Yet, without regard to what those consequences might be, he deliberately went ahead and sinned against God. He was responsible for his actions and would have to face the penalty.

Why did the accusers lay their hands on the head of the condemned? (24:14)

It's difficult to say precisely. Perhaps it suggests that those who heard the blasphemy were polluted by it. Putting their hands on the accused, then, would somehow transfer their contamination back to the source so it could be completely eliminated when he was executed. In the same way the high priest laid his hands on the scapegoat, transferring the sins of the people to the goat before sending it away into the desert (16:21).

What good did it do to "hit back"? (24:20)

It would be wrong to see this as a primitive or barbaric law. This was not restitution gone awry, turned into vengeful retaliation. It's better to see that this law established a foundational principle of justice: the penalty must fit the crime. Too much or too little punishment is a miscarriage of justice. Legal loopholes to avoid prosecution (often available only to the privileged) are wrong. But excessive penalties for minor offenses (often forced upon the poor) are also wrong. Also see *Should we demand eye for eye, tooth for tooth?* (Exodus 21:23–25).

How could they eat what they weren't permitted to harvest? (25:5–7)

These verses seem to contradict each other. How could they *not reap what grows of itself* (v. 5) and then turn around and eat *whatever the land yields during the sabbath year* (v. 6)? The key to resolving this mystery is to see the difference between harvesting and living off the land. Harvesting was for trade and profit; taking just enough to live on was more like subsistence farming—relying on crops that sprouted on their own. During the sabbath year, land owners could take no more than the poor who typically lived off the land.

Jubilee (25:10)

Name (from the Hebrew word for *ram* or *ram's horn*) for the last in a cycle of 50 years, announced by sounding a ram's horn. Jubilee is mentioned only once in the Old Testament outside of Leviticus (Num. 36:4). Some think the Jubilee is seen in the harvest schedule that left Judah so vulnerable during Sennacherib's invasion (701 B.C.). During the 49th and 50th years, the land would have lain fallow for two consecutive years (Isaiah 37:30). Ezekiel called it *the year of freedom* (Ezek. 46:17).

Could land ever change hands? (25:15–16,23)

Yes, but only temporarily. To *buy* or *sell* was never a permanent transaction; we would understand it more as something similar to a lease. This law helped the people remember that God was the real owner of the land. They were simply his tenants, unable to permanently sell something that didn't actually belong to them.

Did the Israelites follow the letter of the law? (25:18)

Apparently not. The prophet Jeremiah rails against Israel for not obeying one of the rules of the Jubilee: freeing Hebrew slaves. That's one of the many reasons he cites why Judah, the southern kingdom of Israel, would be judged by God and carried off into exile (Jer. 34:8–22). The writer of Chronicles hints at the same thing by saying Judah's exile would give the land a chance to recover (2 Chron. 36:21). Most agree that, after returning from exile in Babylon, Judah dropped many of the regulations of Jubilee.

name of the LORD must be put to death^D. The entire assembly must stone him. Whether an alien^D or native-born, when he blasphemes^D the Name, he must be put to death.

17" 'If anyone takes the life of a human being, he must be put to death. **18**Anyone who takes the life of someone's animal must make restitution—life for life. **19**If anyone injures his neighbor, whatever he has done must be done to him: **20**fracture for fracture, eye for eye, tooth for tooth. As he has injured the other, so he is to be injured. **21**Whoever kills an animal must make restitution, but whoever kills a man must be put to death. **22**You are to have the same law for the alien and the native-born. I am the LORD your God.' "

23Then Moses spoke to the Israelites, and they took the blasphemer outside the camp and stoned him. The Israelites did as the LORD commanded Moses.

The Sabbath Year

25 The LORD said to Moses on Mount Sinai, **2**"Speak to the Israelites and say to them: 'When you enter the land I am going to give you, the land itself must observe a sabbath^D to the LORD. **3**For six years sow your fields, and for six years prune your vineyards and gather their crops. **4**But in the seventh year the land is to have a sabbath of rest, a sabbath to the LORD. Do not sow your fields or prune your vineyards. **5**Do not reap what grows of itself or harvest the grapes of your untended vines. The land is to have a year of rest. **6**Whatever the land yields during the sabbath year will be food for you—for yourself, your manservant and maidservant, and the hired worker and temporary resident who live among you, **7**as well as for your livestock and the wild animals in your land. Whatever the land produces may be eaten.

The Year of Jubilee

8" 'Count off seven sabbaths of years—seven times seven years—so that the seven sabbaths of years amount to a period of forty-nine years. **9**Then have the trumpet sounded everywhere on the tenth day of the seventh month; on the Day of Atonement^D sound the trumpet throughout your land. **10**Consecrate^D the fiftieth year and proclaim liberty throughout the land to all its inhabitants. It shall be a jubilee^D for you; each one of you is to return to his family property and each to his own clan. **11**The fiftieth year shall be a jubilee for you; do not sow and do not reap what grows of itself or harvest the untended vines. **12**For it is a jubilee and is to be holy for you; eat only what is taken directly from the fields.

13" 'In this Year of Jubilee everyone is to return to his own property.

14" 'If you sell land to one of your countrymen or buy any from him, do not take advantage of each other. **15**You are to buy from your countryman on the basis of the number of years since the Jubilee. And he is to sell to you on the basis of the number of years left for harvesting crops. **16**When the years are many, you are to increase the price, and when the years are few, you are to decrease the price, because what he is really selling you is the number of crops. **17**Do not take advantage of each other, but fear your God. I am the LORD your God.

18" 'Follow my decrees and be careful to obey my laws, and you will live safely in the land. **19**Then the land will

yield its fruit, and you will eat your fill and live there in safety. **20**You may ask, "What will we eat in the seventh year if we do not plant or harvest our crops?" **21**I will send you such a blessing in the sixth year that the land will yield enough for three years. **22**While you plant during the eighth year, you will eat from the old crop and will continue to eat from it until the harvest of the ninth year comes in.

23" 'The land must not be sold permanently, because the land is mine and you are but aliens^D and my tenants. **24**Throughout the country that you hold as a possession, you must provide for the redemption^D of the land.

25" 'If one of your countrymen becomes poor and sells some of his property, his nearest relative is to come and redeem^D what his countryman has sold. **26**If, however, a man has no one to redeem it for him but he himself prospers and acquires sufficient means to redeem it, **27**he is to determine the value for the years since he sold it and refund the balance to the man to whom he sold it; he can then go back to his own property. **28**But if he does not acquire the means to repay him, what he sold will remain in the possession of the buyer until the Year of Jubilee^D. It will be returned in the Jubilee, and he can then go back to his property.

29" 'If a man sells a house in a walled city, he retains the right of redemption a full year after its sale. During that time he may redeem it. **30**If it is not redeemed before a full year has passed, the house in the walled city shall belong permanently to the buyer and his descendants. It is not to be returned in the Jubilee. **31**But houses in villages without walls around them are to be considered as open country. They can be redeemed, and they are to be returned in the Jubilee.

32" 'The Levites^D always have the right to redeem their houses in the Levitical towns, which they possess. **33**So the property of the Levites is redeemable—that is, a house sold in any town they hold—and is to be returned in the Jubilee, because the houses in the towns of the Levites are their property among the Israelites. **34**But the pastureland belonging to their towns must not be sold; it is their permanent possession.

35" 'If one of your countrymen becomes poor and is unable to support himself among you, help him as you would an alien or a temporary resident, so he can continue to live among you. **36**Do not take interest of any kind^a from him, but fear your God, so that your countryman may continue to live among you. **37**You must not lend him money at interest or sell him food at a profit. **38**I am the LORD your God, who brought you out of Egypt to give you the land of Canaan and to be your God.

39" 'If one of your countrymen becomes poor among you and sells himself to you, do not make him work as a slave. **40**He is to be treated as a hired worker or a temporary resident among you; he is to work for you until the Year of Jubilee. **41**Then he and his children are to be released, and he will go back to his own clan and to the property of his forefathers. **42**Because the Israelites are my servants, whom I brought out of Egypt, they must not be sold as slaves. **43**Do not rule over them ruthlessly, but fear your God.

44" 'Your male and female slaves are to come from the nations around you; from them you may buy slaves.

How were they to "redeem" the land? (25:24)

Land could revert to the original owner in three ways: (1) The seller or members of his family could receive the land without cost in the Year of Jubilee. (2) A relative of the seller could repurchase the land in the seller's behalf. (3) The seller could reclaim his holdings himself, with payment again based on the value of crops until the Year of Jubilee.

Why were the rules of ownership different in a walled city than in the country? (25:29)

One seemed to be a privilege, the other a right. Real estate in the city was always at a premium: space was limited and its value included not just the land but the buildings and walls of fortification. Living there was a privilege. Village property, however, was connected to the surrounding fields, which fell under the guidelines of the Year of Jubilee—owning it was a guaranteed right.

Alien . . . temporary resident (25:35)

An *alien* was a non-Israelite living in Israel. A *temporary resident* could be either a native or a foreigner, typically someone deeply in debt who had to live in the creditor's home to work off his debts. Since aliens and temporary residents did not own property, most of them were poor.

Is it still wrong to charge interest? (25:36–37)

This law reveals God's concern for the poor; it is not a prohibition against business or loan investments. The Hebrew word for *interest* came from a verb meaning *to bite*. Interest took a bite out of the budget and would have inflicted serious damage on the poor who were barely subsisting. Jesus seems to have assumed a legitimate use of interest for loans (see Luke 19:23). Also see *What's wrong with charging interest?* (Exodus 22:25).

---

^a36 Or *take excessive interest*; similarly in verse 37

Why does God endorse slavery? (25:44–46)

God apparently modified a conventional custom rather than doing away with it. His laws greatly improved the institution of slavery over pagan practices. He provided guidelines, set up ethical restrictions and gave slaves their dignity (see, for example, Exodus 21:26–27; Deut. 23:15–16). In many ways, the issue in ancient times would have been viewed like employer-employee issues are viewed today. Still, the Biblical legal system was in the process of development throughout the Old Testament and into the New Testament. As a result, it is often hard for us to understand some of the inequities in the Old Testament. See, for example, *Why force a servant to choose between freedom and family?* (Exodus 21:4–6). Also see article: *Why doesn't the Bible condemn slavery?* (1 Peter 2:18–21).

Year of Jubilee (25:54)

See *Old Testament Feasts* on page 168.

What is a sacred stone? (26:1)

This refers to stone monuments that were used in idol worship. They were often engraved with writing and were intended to be representations of pagan deities. See 2 Kings 3:2.

Dwelling place (26:11)

See *How could God, who is spirit, dwell anywhere?* (15:31).

45You may also buy some of the temporary residents living among you and members of their clans born in your country, and they will become your property. **46**You can will them to your children as inherited property and can make them slaves for life, but you must not rule over your fellow Israelites ruthlessly.

47 'If an alien[D] or a temporary resident among you becomes rich and one of your countrymen becomes poor and sells himself to the alien living among you or to a member of the alien's clan, **48**he retains the right of redemption[D] after he has sold himself. One of his relatives may redeem[D] him: **49**An uncle or a cousin or any blood relative in his clan may redeem him. Or if he prospers, he may redeem himself. **50**He and his buyer are to count the time from the year he sold himself up to the Year of Jubilee[D]. The price for his release is to be based on the rate paid to a hired man for that number of years. **51**If many years remain, he must pay for his redemption a larger share of the price paid for him. **52**If only a few years remain until the Year of Jubilee, he is to compute that and pay for his redemption accordingly. **53**He is to be treated as a man hired from year to year; you must see to it that his owner does not rule over him ruthlessly.

54 'Even if he is not redeemed in any of these ways, he and his children are to be released in the Year of Jubilee, **55**for the Israelites belong to me as servants. They are my servants, whom I brought out of Egypt. I am the LORD your God.

Reward for Obedience

26 " 'Do not make idols[D] or set up an image or a sacred stone[D] for yourselves, and do not place a carved stone in your land to bow down before it. I am the LORD your God.

2 'Observe my Sabbaths[D] and have reverence[D] for my sanctuary. I am the LORD.

3 " 'If you follow my decrees and are careful to obey my commands, **4**I will send you rain in its season, and the ground will yield its crops and the trees of the field their fruit. **5**Your threshing will continue until grape harvest and the grape harvest will continue until planting, and you will eat all the food you want and live in safety in your land.

6 " 'I will grant peace[D] in the land, and you will lie down and no one will make you afraid. I will remove savage beasts from the land, and the sword will not pass through your country. **7**You will pursue your enemies, and they will fall by the sword before you. **8**Five of you will chase a hundred, and a hundred of you will chase ten thousand, and your enemies will fall by the sword before you.

9 " 'I will look on you with favor and make you fruitful and increase your numbers, and I will keep my covenant[D] with you. **10**You will still be eating last year's harvest when you will have to move it out to make room for the new. **11**I will put my dwelling place[a] among you, and I will not abhor you. **12**I will walk among you and be your God, and you will be my people. **13**I am the LORD your God, who brought you out of Egypt so that you would no longer be slaves to the Egyptians; I broke the bars of your yoke[D] and enabled you to walk with heads held high.

a 11 Or my tabernacle

Punishment for Disobedience

14" 'But if you will not listen to me and carry out all these commands, **15**and if you reject my decrees and abhor my laws and fail to carry out all my commands and so violate my covenant^D, **16**then I will do this to you: I will bring upon you sudden terror, wasting diseases and fever that will destroy your sight and drain away your life. You will plant seed in vain, because your enemies will eat it. **17**I will set my face against you so that you will be defeated by your enemies; those who hate you will rule over you, and you will flee even when no one is pursuing you.

18" 'If after all this you will not listen to me, I will punish you for your sins seven times over. **19**I will break down your stubborn pride and make the sky above you like iron and the ground beneath you like bronze. **20**Your strength will be spent in vain, because your soil will not yield its crops, nor will the trees of the land yield their fruit.

21" 'If you remain hostile toward me and refuse to listen to me, I will multiply your afflictions^D seven times over, as your sins deserve. **22**I will send wild animals against you, and they will rob you of your children, destroy your cattle and make you so few in number that your roads will be deserted.

23" 'If in spite of these things you do not accept my correction but continue to be hostile toward me, **24**I myself will be hostile toward you and will afflict^D you for your sins seven times over. **25**And I will bring the sword upon you to avenge^D the breaking of the covenant. When you withdraw into your cities, I will send a plague among you, and you will be given into enemy hands. **26**When I cut off your supply of bread, ten women will be able to

Why such stiff penalties for disobedience? (26:14–33)

This was the other side of God's promise. If obedience would bring blessings, then disobedience would bring consequences. God clearly stipulated these terms of the covenant with his people. Also see *Why such a stiff penalty for words spoken in anger?* (24:12) and article: *How will God judge the world?* (Isaiah 66:15–16).

Why seven times? (26:18,21,24)

In the Bible the number seven is often used to signify completeness or totality. See *What was so special about the number seven?* (2 Chron. 29:21).

Does obedience bring prosperity? (26:3–39)

There is no question that right living has its own rewards. When the people served God, the nation enjoyed better moral and economic climates than when they didn't. Those who live disciplined lives of moderation enjoy the benefits of better health and finances. Insurance companies observe these general principles by basing their premium rates according to the risks of certain lifestyles. However, these are general principles and cannot be forced to apply to specific situations.

The New Testament agrees with the principle, for instance, but differs in its application. It reaffirms that God honors obedience and disdains disobedience. But where the Old Testament insists that a person's character *immediately* determines his circumstance, the New Testament says it will be *eventual*. The Old Testament says the faithful experience the good life *now;* the New Testament says they will *one day* (that is, in heaven).

At the heart of the New Testament is Christ, the only perfect human, whose life ended in the suffering and disgrace of the cross. He was sinless, yet abandoned by God—hardly the picture of prosperity and blessings!

The apostle Paul lists a number of things that cannot separate the believer from Christ (famine, nakedness and so on) in Romans 8:35–39. Interestingly, many items he lists come from the "curse" texts of Leviticus 26 and Deuteronomy 28. In the New Testament, then, to obey does not guarantee an absence of physical problems. The guarantee, however, covers spiritual security despite physical troubles.

Also see articles: *Is success guaranteed to those who obey God?* (Deut. 28:2–6) and *Does seeking God guarantee success?* (2 Chron. 26:5).

How is the anger of God different from ours? (26:28)
God never loses his temper and is always in control. His anger is an appropriate response to faithlessness. Because he is holy and fair, he will not tolerate a lifestyle of disobedience from his people.

How could people *pay for* their sins? (26:41)
To *pay for* sin meant that they would fully accept the guilt of their sin. We might say they would have to *own up* to it. This is accomplished by repentance—*when their uncircumcised hearts are humbled.* It was not the suffering and tragedies sent by the Lord that paid for their sins. Those things merely motivated them to repent. God, looking for a change of heart, then called his judgment to a halt.

Uncircumcised hearts (26:41)
See *What does it mean to circumcise your hearts?* (Jer. 4:4).

What did it mean to dedicate someone to the Lord? (27:2)
This may have referred to the practice of giving oneself, a slave or a child to tabernacle or temple service. Generally, such vows were made when requesting something of God (for example, 1 Samuel 1:11). When the request was granted, the person would then fulfill the vow. That such vows could be converted into payments of money served a practical purpose, providing the sanctuary with necessary operating funds.

bake your bread in one oven, and they will dole out the bread by weight. You will eat, but you will not be satisfied.
27" 'If in spite of this you still do not listen to me but continue to be hostile toward me, **28**then in my anger I will be hostile toward you, and I myself will punish you for your sins seven times over. **29**You will eat the flesh of your sons and the flesh of your daughters. **30**I will destroy your high places^D, cut down your incense^D altars and pile your dead bodies on the lifeless forms of your idols^D, and I will abhor you. **31**I will turn your cities into ruins and lay waste your sanctuaries, and I will take no delight in the pleasing aroma of your offerings. **32**I will lay waste the land, so that your enemies who live there will be appalled. **33**I will scatter you among the nations and will draw out my sword and pursue you. Your land will be laid waste, and your cities will lie in ruins. **34**Then the land will enjoy its sabbath^D years all the time that it lies desolate and you are in the country of your enemies; then the land will rest and enjoy its sabbaths. **35**All the time that it lies desolate, the land will have the rest it did not have during the sabbaths you lived in it.
36" 'As for those of you who are left, I will make their hearts so fearful in the lands of their enemies that the sound of a windblown leaf will put them to flight. They will run as though fleeing from the sword, and they will fall, even though no one is pursuing them. **37**They will stumble over one another as though fleeing from the sword, even though no one is pursuing them. So you will not be able to stand before your enemies. **38**You will perish among the nations; the land of your enemies will devour you. **39**Those of you who are left will waste away in the lands of their enemies because of their sins; also because of their fathers' sins they will waste away.
40" 'But if they will confess their sins and the sins of their fathers—their treachery against me and their hostility toward me, **41**which made me hostile toward them so that I sent them into the land of their enemies—then when their uncircumcised^D hearts are humbled and they pay for their sin, **42**I will remember my covenant^D with Jacob and my covenant with Isaac and my covenant with Abraham, and I will remember the land. **43**For the land will be deserted by them and will enjoy its sabbaths while it lies desolate without them. They will pay for their sins because they rejected my laws and abhorred my decrees. **44**Yet in spite of this, when they are in the land of their enemies, I will not reject them or abhor them so as to destroy them completely, breaking my covenant with them. I am the LORD their God. **45**But for their sake I will remember the covenant with their ancestors whom I brought out of Egypt in the sight of the nations to be their God. I am the LORD.' "
46These are the decrees, the laws and the regulations that the LORD established on Mount Sinai between himself and the Israelites through Moses.

Redeeming What Is the LORD's

27 The LORD said to Moses, **2**"Speak to the Israelites and say to them: 'If anyone makes a special vow^D to dedicate persons to the LORD by giving equivalent values, **3**set the value of a male between the ages of twenty and sixty at fifty shekels^{Da} of silver, according to the

^a3 That is, about 1 1/4 pounds (about 0.6 kilogram); also in verse 16

sanctuary shekel[D][a]; [4]and if it is a female, set her value at thirty shekels[D].[b] [5]If it is a person between the ages of five and twenty, set the value of a male at twenty shekels[c] and of a female at ten shekels.[d] [6]If it is a person between one month and five years, set the value of a male at five shekels[e] of silver and that of a female at three shekels[f] of silver. [7]If it is a person sixty years old or more, set the value of a male at fifteen shekels[g] and of a female at ten shekels. [8]If anyone making the vow is too poor to pay the specified amount, he is to present the person to the priest[D], who will set the value for him according to what the man making the vow can afford.

[9]" 'If what he vowed is an animal that is acceptable as an offering to the LORD, such an animal given to the LORD becomes holy. [10]He must not exchange it or substitute a good one for a bad one, or a bad one for a good one; if he should substitute one animal for another, both it and the substitute become holy. [11]If what he vowed is a ceremonially unclean[D] animal—one that is not acceptable as an offering to the LORD—the animal must be presented to the priest, [12]who will judge its quality as good or bad. Whatever value the priest then sets, that is what it will be. [13]If the owner wishes to redeem[D] the animal, he must add a fifth to its value.

[14]" 'If a man dedicates his house as something holy to the LORD, the priest will judge its quality as good or bad. Whatever value the priest then sets, so it will remain. [15]If the man who dedicates his house redeems it, he must add a fifth to its value, and the house will again become his.

[16]" 'If a man dedicates to the LORD part of his family land, its value is to be set according to the amount of seed required for it—fifty shekels of silver to a homer[h] of barley seed. [17]If he dedicates his field during the Year of Jubilee[D], the value that has been set remains. [18]But if he dedicates his field after the Jubilee, the priest will determine the value according to the number of years that remain until the next Year of Jubilee, and its set value will be reduced. [19]If the man who dedicates the field wishes to redeem it, he must add a fifth to its value, and the field will again become his. [20]If, however, he does not redeem the field, or if he has sold it to someone else, it can never be redeemed. [21]When the field is released in the Jubilee, it will become holy, like a field devoted to the LORD; it will become the property of the priests.[i]

[22]" 'If a man dedicates to the LORD a field he has bought, which is not part of his family land, [23]the priest will determine its value up to the Year of Jubilee, and the man must pay its value on that day as something holy to the LORD. [24]In the Year of Jubilee the field will revert to the person from whom he bought it, the one whose land it was. [25]Every value is to be set according to the sanctuary shekel, twenty gerahs to the shekel.

[26]" 'No one, however, may dedicate the firstborn[D] of an animal, since the firstborn already belongs to the LORD; whether an ox[j] or a sheep, it is the LORD's. [27]If it

[a]3 That is, about 2/5 ounce (about 11.5 grams); also in verse 25   [b]4 That is, about 12 ounces (about 0.3 kilogram)   [c]5 That is, about 8 ounces (about 0.2 kilogram)   [d]5 That is, about 4 ounces (about 110 grams); also in verse 7   [e]6 That is, about 2 ounces (about 55 grams)   [f]6 That is, about 1 1/4 ounces (about 35 grams)   [g]7 That is, about 6 ounces (about 170 grams)   [h]16 That is, probably about 6 bushels (about 220 liters)   [i]21 Or priest   [j]26 The Hebrew word can include both male and female.

Why were men worth more than women? (27:3–8)

These values do not in any way imply that men are more valuable than women. The scale of values was based simply on the amount of work the priests could have expected from the person dedicated to the Lord. Middle-aged workers could be more productive than either the young or elderly; men could handle heavier labor than women. Notice that no distinction was made between free and slave, presumably because both could do the same amount of work.

Why permit someone to take back their vow? (27:13)

Someone could make a vow to the Lord to seek God's favor. After the request was granted, the person could take back whatever had been given by paying the assigned value plus 20 percent. This had two benefits: (1) It provided additional funds for the operations of the sanctuary. (2) It enabled the person asking for God's help to return to business as usual. In other words, the animal, slave, person or land dedicated to the Lord could once again be put to profitable use.

Year of Jubilee (27:24)

See Year of Jubilee (Num. 36:4).

What was the difference between "dedicating" and "devoting" something to the Lord? (27:26–28)

To devote something to the Lord meant either to destroy it completely, or to reserve it exclusively for sanctuary service. This was done as an obligation and the offering would not be redeemed. Since it was most holy to the LORD, it could not be used again for ordinary, everyday purposes. Anything dedicated to the Lord, however, was done so voluntarily and could be redeemed.

Person devoted to destruction (27:29)
A person who was *dedicated* to the Lord was to serve the sanctuary. But one who was *devoted to destruction* was a person who was condemned to die for a serious violation of the law, such as idolatry (Exodus 22:20) or murder (Num. 35:31–34). Such a person had to pay the death penalty and could be neither redeemed nor ransomed.

Tithe (27:30)
Leviticus, regarding the tithe as a type of vow, discusses it here along with other vows. A tithe was typically given in the form of crops or livestock. Animals were sacrificed and could not be redeemed. But the donor could repurchase crop tithes with money plus 20 percent, just as he could other vows or pledges. This might have been done to meet an unexpected shortage.

is one of the unclean D animals, he may buy it back at its set value, adding a fifth of the value to it. If he does not redeem D it, it is to be sold at its set value.

28" 'But nothing that a man owns and devotes a to the LORD—whether man or animal or family land—may be sold or redeemed; everything so devoted is most holy to the LORD.

29" 'No person devoted to destruction b may be ransomed; he must be put to death D.

30" 'A tithe D of everything from the land, whether grain from the soil or fruit from the trees, belongs to the LORD; it is holy to the LORD. 31If a man redeems any of his tithe, he must add a fifth of the value to it. 32The entire tithe of the herd and flock—every tenth animal that passes under the shepherd's rod—will be holy to the LORD. 33He must not pick out the good from the bad or make any substitution. If he does make a substitution, both the animal and its substitute become holy and cannot be redeemed.' "

34These are the commands the LORD gave Moses on Mount Sinai for the Israelites.

---

a28 The Hebrew term refers to the irrevocable giving over of things or persons to the LORD.   b29 The Hebrew term refers to the irrevocable giving over of things or persons to the LORD, often by totally destroying them.

NUMBERS

Why read this book?

A title like Numbers sounds about as exciting as "Dictionary" or "Phone Book." Get ready for a surprise. This book is loaded with powerful stories. It graphically shows what happens when people sin, but it also holds out hope to those who desire God's mercy and want to experience his faithfulness. The book of Numbers reveals a God of devastating wrath, but one who holds his arms wide open for those who repent and turn to him.

Who wrote this book?

Moses.

Why was it written?

Moses wrote about the Israelites' 40 years in the desert to show God's judgment, set against the backdrop of his faithfulness and patience with his beloved Israel.

When was it written?

About 40 years after the exodus from Egypt, just as the Israelites were ready to enter Canaan. Many think Moses penned it about 1400 B.C.

To whom was it written?

The people of God, the children of Israel.

What period of history does it cover?

The book of Numbers covers the 40 years—specifically, 38 years and 9 months—of Israel's wanderings in the desert, from Mount Sinai to the banks of the Jordan River opposite Jericho (1:1; 36:13). For every day the spies spent scouting in Canaan, the people spent one year wandering in judgment for their unfaithfulness (14:33-34).

What to look for in Numbers:

Repeated cycles of sin, judgment and repentance. You'll see human failure, but you'll also see God's response of patience and mercy. This book shows the lengths to which God goes to work with his people.

When did these things happen?

TIME LINE	2200BC	2100	2000	1900	1800	1700	1600	1500	1400
Moses' birth (c.1526 B.C.)								■	
The exodus (c.1446 B.C.)									┠
Desert wanderings (c.1446-1406 B.C.)									■
Exploration of Canaan (c.1443 B.C.)									┠
Book of Numbers written (c.1406 B.C.)									┠
Moses' death; Joshua becomes leader (c.1406 B.C.)									┠
Israelites enter Canaan (c.1406 B.C.)									┨

How did God speak to Moses? (1:1)

On occasion it seems Moses actually heard an audible voice (7:89). Other times he may have experienced a mystical inner sensation or had a mental impression. God communicated with Moses more directly than with the other prophets who received visions or dreams (Num. 12:6–8). In more than 20 ways and over 150 times, Numbers records that God spoke to Moses. Also see *Did God talk to Moses in an audible voice?* (7:89).

Tent of Meeting (1:1)

The Tent of Meeting functioned as a worship place for a people on the move. It was a small tent, 45 feet by 15 feet, situated on a space called the "outer court," about half the size of a football field. Only the priests were allowed in the tent. Also see *Was this "tent of meeting" the same thing as the tabernacle?* (Exodus 33:7).

Why did God order a census? (1:3)

The census served as a draft; Israel's men were no longer slaves, but soldiers. Each of the twelve tribes probably commissioned officers to train the raw recruits.

The Census

1 The LORD spoke to Moses in the Tent of Meeting[D] in the Desert of Sinai on the first day of the second month of the second year after the Israelites came out of Egypt. He said: ²"Take a census of the whole Israelite community by their clans and families, listing every man by name, one by one. ³You and Aaron are to number by their divisions all the men in Israel twenty years old or more who are able to serve in the army. ⁴One man from each tribe, each the head of his family, is to help you. ⁵These are the names of the men who are to assist you:

from Reuben, Elizur son of Shedeur;
⁶from Simeon, Shelumiel son of Zurishaddai;
⁷from Judah, Nahshon son of Amminadab;
⁸from Issachar, Nethanel son of Zuar;
⁹from Zebulun, Eliab son of Helon;
¹⁰from the sons of Joseph:
from Ephraim, Elishama son of Ammihud;
from Manasseh, Gamaliel son of Pedahzur;
¹¹from Benjamin, Abidan son of Gideoni;
¹²from Dan, Ahiezer son of Ammishaddai;
¹³from Asher, Pagiel son of Ocran;
¹⁴from Gad, Eliasaph son of Deuel;
¹⁵from Naphtali, Ahira son of Enan."

¹⁶These were the men appointed from the community, the leaders of their ancestral tribes. They were the heads of the clans of Israel.

¹⁷Moses and Aaron took these men whose names had been given, ¹⁸and they called the whole community together on the first day of the second month. The people indicated their ancestry by their clans and families, and the men twenty years old or more were listed by name, one by one, ¹⁹as the LORD commanded Moses. And so he counted them in the Desert of Sinai:

²⁰From the descendants of Reuben the firstborn[D] son of Israel:
All the men twenty years old or more who were able to serve in the army were listed by name, one by one, according to the records of their clans and families. ²¹The number from the tribe of Reuben was 46,500.

²²From the descendants of Simeon:
All the men twenty years old or more who were able to serve in the army were counted and listed by name, one by one, according to the records of their clans and families. ²³The number from the tribe of Simeon was 59,300.

²⁴From the descendants of Gad:
All the men twenty years old or more who were able to serve in the army were listed by name, according to the records of their clans and families. ²⁵The number from the tribe of Gad was 45,650.

²⁶From the descendants of Judah:
All the men twenty years old or more who were able to serve in the army were listed by name, according to the records of their clans and families. ²⁷The number from the tribe of Judah was 74,600.

²⁸From the descendants of Issachar:
All the men twenty years old or more who were able to serve in the army were listed by name, ac-

cording to the records of their clans and families. **29**The number from the tribe of Issachar was 54,400.

30From the descendants of Zebulun:

All the men twenty years old or more who were able to serve in the army were listed by name, according to the records of their clans and families. **31**The number from the tribe of Zebulun was 57,400.

32From the sons of Joseph:

From the descendants of Ephraim:

All the men twenty years old or more who were able to serve in the army were listed by name, according to the records of their clans and families. **33**The number from the tribe of Ephraim was 40,500.

34From the descendants of Manasseh:

All the men twenty years old or more who were able to serve in the army were listed by name, according to the records of their clans and families. **35**The number from the tribe of Manasseh was 32,200.

36From the descendants of Benjamin:

All the men twenty years old or more who were able to serve in the army were listed by name, according to the records of their clans and families. **37**The number from the tribe of Benjamin was 35,400.

38From the descendants of Dan:

All the men twenty years old or more who were able to serve in the army were listed by name, according to the records of their clans and families. **39**The number from the tribe of Dan was 62,700.

40From the descendants of Asher:

All the men twenty years old or more who were able to serve in the army were listed by name, according to the records of their clans and families. **41**The number from the tribe of Asher was 41,500.

42From the descendants of Naphtali:

All the men twenty years old or more who were able to serve in the army were listed by name, according to the records of their clans and families. **43**The number from the tribe of Naphtali was 53,400.

44These were the men counted by Moses and Aaron and the twelve leaders of Israel, each one representing his family. **45**All the Israelites twenty years old or more who were able to serve in Israel's army were counted according to their families. **46**The total number was 603,550.

47The families of the tribe of Levi, however, were not counted along with the others. **48**The LORD had said to Moses: **49**"You must not count the tribe of Levi or include them in the census of the other Israelites. **50**Instead, appoint the LevitesD to be in charge of the tabernacleD of the Testimony—over all its furnishings and everything belonging to it. They are to carry the tabernacle and all its furnishings; they are to take care of it and encamp around it. **51**Whenever the tabernacle is to move, the Levites are to take it down, and whenever the tabernacle is to be set up, the Levites shall do it. Anyone else who

Why were two sons of Joseph listed in the census? (1:32–34)

Joseph's father Jacob had adopted Ephraim and Manasseh as his own (Gen. 48:5–6). Because the Levites were excluded from the census, the number of tribes was thus kept at 12.

How many Israelites left Egypt? (1:46)

Assuming one woman and two children per male over 20 years old, the Israelite population was nearly 2.5 million.

Why didn't God want the tribe of Levi counted in the census? (1:47–49)

The census was linked to military service, like registering for the draft. God exempted the Levites from military service so they could care for the tabernacle and offer sacrifices. This spiritual support was foundational to Israel's very existence. Before they could achieve victory on the battlefield, they needed a right relationship with God. God's purpose for the Levites was to be the people's direct lifeline to God.

Why kill someone who wanted to come close to God? (1:51-53)

Because God is holy, sin cannot survive in his presence. A sinner will die in the light and power of God's holiness except when God makes special provision. God's ultimate provision was Christ, but here he used the tents of the Levites to form a protective barrier around the tabernacle. The tents were to protect the people, not God, because they prevented the Israelites from accidentally wandering into God's holy presence.

Why is Judah mentioned first? (2:3-4)

Though he was the fourth son of Jacob and Leah, Judah was given the place of honor among his brothers (see Gen. 49:8). It was through the tribe of Judah that the Messiah came (Matt. 1:2-3).

Why should we care about how the Israelites camped and traveled? (2:17)

Details of historical accounts sometimes may seem irrelevant to the hurried reader. But the lessons of history offer more than mere trivia. Here, for example, we can see the value God placed on an ordered society. This was not a haphazard mob traveling across the desert, but an organized nation. We also see that God positioned himself in the middle of his people, with all the tribes camped around the tabernacle. This meant that God had drawn closer to his people, coming down from Mount Sinai to the tent outside the camp (Exodus 33:7-11) and finally to the tabernacle within the camp.

goes near it shall be put to death^D. ⁵²The Israelites are to set up their tents by divisions, each man in his own camp under his own standard. ⁵³The Levites^D, however, are to set up their tents around the tabernacle^D of the Testimony so that wrath will not fall on the Israelite community. The Levites are to be responsible for the care of the tabernacle of the Testimony."

⁵⁴The Israelites did all this just as the LORD commanded Moses.

The Arrangement of the Tribal Camps

2 The LORD said to Moses and Aaron: ²"The Israelites are to camp around the Tent of Meeting^D some distance from it, each man under his standard with the banners of his family."

³On the east, toward the sunrise, the divisions of the camp of Judah are to encamp under their standard. The leader of the people of Judah is Nahshon son of Amminadab. ⁴His division numbers 74,600.

⁵The tribe of Issachar will camp next to them. The leader of the people of Issachar is Nethanel son of Zuar. ⁶His division numbers 54,400.

⁷The tribe of Zebulun will be next. The leader of the people of Zebulun is Eliab son of Helon. ⁸His division numbers 57,400.

⁹All the men assigned to the camp of Judah, according to their divisions, number 186,400. They will set out first.

¹⁰On the south will be the divisions of the camp of Reuben under their standard. The leader of the people of Reuben is Elizur son of Shedeur. ¹¹His division numbers 46,500.

¹²The tribe of Simeon will camp next to them. The leader of the people of Simeon is Shelumiel son of Zurishaddai. ¹³His division numbers 59,300.

¹⁴The tribe of Gad will be next. The leader of the people of Gad is Eliasaph son of Deuel.^a ¹⁵His division numbers 45,650.

¹⁶All the men assigned to the camp of Reuben, according to their divisions, number 151,450. They will set out second.

¹⁷Then the Tent of Meeting and the camp of the Levites will set out in the middle of the camps. They will set out in the same order as they encamp, each in his own place under his standard.

¹⁸On the west will be the divisions of the camp of Ephraim under their standard. The leader of the people of Ephraim is Elishama son of Ammihud. ¹⁹His division numbers 40,500.

²⁰The tribe of Manasseh will be next to them. The leader of the people of Manasseh is Gamaliel son of Pedahzur. ²¹His division numbers 32,200.

²²The tribe of Benjamin will be next. The leader of the people of Benjamin is Abidan son of Gideoni. ²³His division numbers 35,400.

²⁴All the men assigned to the camp of Ephraim, according to their divisions, number 108,100. They will set out third.

^a14 Many manuscripts of the Masoretic Text, Samaritan Pentateuch and Vulgate (see also Num. 1:14); most manuscripts of the Masoretic Text *Reuel*

25On the north will be the divisions of the camp of Dan, under their standard. The leader of the people of Dan is Ahiezer son of Ammishaddai. **26**His division numbers 62,700.

27The tribe of Asher will camp next to them. The leader of the people of Asher is Pagiel son of Ocran. **28**His division numbers 41,500.

29The tribe of Naphtali will be next. The leader of the people of Naphtali is Ahira son of Enan. **30**His division numbers 53,400.

31All the men assigned to the camp of Dan number 157,600. They will set out last, under their standards.

32These are the Israelites, counted according to their families. All those in the camps, by their divisions, number 603,550. **33**The Levites^D, however, were not counted along with the other Israelites, as the LORD commanded Moses.

34So the Israelites did everything the LORD commanded Moses; that is the way they encamped under their standards, and that is the way they set out, each with his clan and family.

The Levites

3 This is the account of the family of Aaron and Moses at the time the LORD talked with Moses on Mount Sinai.

2The names of the sons of Aaron were Nadab the firstborn^D and Abihu, Eleazar and Ithamar. **3**Those were the names of Aaron's sons, the anointed^D priests^D, who were ordained to serve as priests. **4**Nadab and Abihu, however, fell dead before the LORD when they made an offering with unauthorized fire before him in the Desert of Sinai. They had no sons; so only Eleazar and Ithamar served as priests during the lifetime of their father Aaron.

5The LORD said to Moses, **6**"Bring the tribe of Levi and present them to Aaron the priest to assist him. **7**They are to perform duties for him and for the whole community at the Tent of Meeting^D by doing the work of the tabernacle^D. **8**They are to take care of all the furnishings of the Tent of Meeting, fulfilling the obligations of the Israelites by doing the work of the tabernacle. **9**Give the Levites to Aaron and his sons; they are the Israelites who are to be given wholly to him.^a **10**Appoint Aaron and his sons to serve as priests; anyone else who approaches the sanctuary must be put to death^D."

11The LORD also said to Moses, **12**"I have taken the Levites from among the Israelites in place of the first male offspring of every Israelite woman. The Levites are mine, **13**for all the firstborn are mine. When I struck down all the firstborn in Egypt, I set apart for myself every firstborn in Israel, whether man or animal. They are to be mine. I am the LORD."

14The LORD said to Moses in the Desert of Sinai, **15**"Count the Levites by their families and clans. Count every male a month old or more." **16**So Moses counted them, as he was commanded by the word of the LORD.

17These were the names of the sons of Levi:
Gershon, Kohath and Merari.

^a9 Most manuscripts of the Masoretic Text; some manuscripts of the Masoretic Text, Samaritan Pentateuch and Septuagint (see also Num. 8:16) *to me*

How could Israel have an army this size, when only 70 people entered Egypt? (2:32)

With an army this size, the total population is thought to have been about 2.5 million. See *How many Israelites left Egypt?* (1:46). This is a truly remarkable growth from the 70 who had entered Egypt 400 years earlier (Exodus 1:5). No other explanation can be given than that this was the fulfillment of God's promise to his people (Gen. 12:2; 15:5).

Why such specific instructions on where the tribes should travel and camp? (2:34)

God's command for order served the same purpose as numbered seats do in a baseball or football stadium: safety, efficiency and organization. Without it, the Israelites were a disorganized, unruly mob. With it came the discipline and character needed for the nation to be victorious in battle.

SCRIPTURE LINK (3:4)

Nadab and Abihu's unauthorized fire (Lev. 10:1–3) was a reminder that God demands to be treated with respect and honor.

Why do firstborn sons get special honor from God? (3:12–13)

In ancient cultures, the firstborn son occupied a special place of prominence in the family. They believed he symbolized the prime of human vigor and represented the entire offspring. God used a cultural custom during that time to set apart Israel's firstborn, signifying his special claim upon his people.

Why would God command Moses to count the Levites after clearly forbidding him to count them? (3:15; see 1:18,47–49)

This is a different census for a different purpose. The Levites were excluded from the first census because it served as a military draft. The military census only comprised males 20 years old and up, those of a fighting age. This census, however, was for priestly service.

Why not count newborns? (3:15)

Because of high infant mortality in the ancient Middle East, God had Moses count only the babies who were at least a month old and had a better chance of survival.

18These were the names of the Gershonite clans:
Libni and Shimei.
19The Kohathite clans:
Amram, Izhar, Hebron and Uzziel.
20The Merarite clans:
Mahli and Mushi.

These were the Levite^D clans, according to their families.

Why were only males counted? (3:21–22)

There were generally only two reasons for taking a census in ancient Israel. One reason was to determine how many fighting men were available to defend the nation in time of war. This explains why not all the males were counted, but only those old enough to fight (1:45). The other reason was to determine how many were available to serve the Lord in sanctuary service. This census counted all Levite males except those less than a month old, since Levites were exempt from military service. These two reasons for a census satisfied the nation's needs. The census was not intended to devalue women and, in fact, was considered an indicator of the total number of families including women and children (1:45). Also see *Why were men worth more than women?* (Lev. 27:3–8).

21To Gershon belonged the clans of the Libnites and Shimeites; these were the Gershonite clans. **22**The number of all the males a month old or more who were counted was 7,500. **23**The Gershonite clans were to camp on the west, behind the tabernacle^D. **24**The leader of the families of the Gershonites was Eliasaph son of Lael. **25**At the Tent of Meeting^D the Gershonites were responsible for the care of the tabernacle and tent, its coverings, the curtain at the entrance to the Tent of Meeting, **26**the curtains of the courtyard, the curtain at the entrance to the courtyard surrounding the tabernacle and altar, and the ropes—and everything related to their use.

27To Kohath belonged the clans of the Amramites, Izharites, Hebronites and Uzzielites; these were the Kohathite clans. **28**The number of all the males a month old or more was 8,600.^a The Kohathites were responsible for the care of the sanctuary. **29**The Kohathite clans were to camp on the south side of the tabernacle. **30**The leader of the families of the Kohathite clans was Elizaphan son of Uzziel. **31**They were responsible for the care of the ark, the table, the lampstand, the altars, the articles of the sanctuary used in ministering, the curtain, and everything related to their use. **32**The chief leader of the Levites was Eleazar son of Aaron, the priest^D. He was appointed over those who were responsible for the care of the sanctuary.

Ark ... table ... lampstand ... altars (3:31)

See *Tabernacle Furnishings* on page 110.

33To Merari belonged the clans of the Mahlites and the Mushites; these were the Merarite clans. **34**The number of all the males a month old or more who were counted was 6,200. **35**The leader of the families of the Merarite clans was Zuriel son of Abihail; they were to camp on the north side of the tabernacle. **36**The Merarites were appointed to take care of the frames of the tabernacle, its crossbars, posts, bases, all its equipment, and everything related to their use, **37**as well as the posts of the surrounding courtyard with their bases, tent pegs and ropes.

Why penalize anyone who wanted to come close to God? (3:38)

See *Why kill someone who wanted to come close to God?* (1:51–53).

38Moses and Aaron and his sons were to camp to the east of the tabernacle, toward the sunrise, in front of the Tent of Meeting. They were responsible for the care of the sanctuary on behalf of the Israelites. Anyone else who approached the sanctuary was to be put to death^D.

39The total number of Levites counted at the LORD's command by Moses and Aaron according to their clans, including every male a month old or more, was 22,000.

40The LORD said to Moses, "Count all the firstborn^D Israelite males who are a month old or more and make a list of their names. **41**Take the Levites for me in place of all the firstborn of the Israelites, and the livestock of the

---

^a28 Hebrew; some Septuagint manuscripts 8,300

Levites^D in place of all the firstborn^D of the livestock of the Israelites. I am the LORD."

⁴²So Moses counted all the firstborn of the Israelites, as the LORD commanded him. ⁴³The total number of first-born males a month old or more, listed by name, was 22,273.

⁴⁴The LORD also said to Moses, ⁴⁵"Take the Levites in place of all the firstborn of Israel, and the livestock of the Levites in place of their livestock. The Levites are to be mine. I am the LORD. ⁴⁶To redeem^D the 273 first-born Israelites who exceed the number of the Levites, ⁴⁷collect five shekels^{Da} for each one, according to the sanctuary shekel^D, which weighs twenty gerahs. ⁴⁸Give the money for the redemption^D of the additional Israel-ites to Aaron and his sons."

⁴⁹So Moses collected the redemption money from those who exceeded the number redeemed by the Le-vites. ⁵⁰From the firstborn of the Israelites he collect-ed silver weighing 1,365 shekels,^b according to the sanctuary shekel. ⁵¹Moses gave the redemption mon-ey to Aaron and his sons, as he was commanded by the word of the LORD.

The Kohathites

4 The LORD said to Moses and Aaron: ²"Take a census of the Kohathite branch of the Levites by their clans and families. ³Count all the men from thirty to fifty years of age who come to serve in the work in the Tent of Meet-ing.

⁴"This is the work of the Kohathites in the Tent of Meet-ing^D: the care of the most holy things. ⁵When the camp is to move, Aaron and his sons are to go in and take down the shielding curtain and cover the ark of the Testimony with it. ⁶Then they are to cover this with hides of sea cows^{D,c} spread a cloth of solid blue over that and put the poles in place.

⁷"Over the table of the Presence they are to spread a blue cloth and put on it the plates, dishes and bowls, and the jars for drink offerings^D; the bread that is continually there is to remain on it. ⁸Over these they are to spread a scarlet cloth, cover that with hides of sea cows and put its poles in place.

⁹"They are to take a blue cloth and cover the lampstand that is for light, together with its lamps, its wick trimmers and trays, and all its jars for the oil used to supply it. ¹⁰Then they are to wrap it and all its accessories in a cov-ering of hides of sea cows and put it on a carrying frame.

¹¹"Over the gold altar they are to spread a blue cloth and cover that with hides of sea cows and put its poles in place.

¹²"They are to take all the articles used for ministering in the sanctuary, wrap them in a blue cloth, cover that with hides of sea cows and put them on a carrying frame.

¹³"They are to remove the ashes from the bronze altar and spread a purple^D cloth over it. ¹⁴Then they are to place on it all the utensils used for ministering at the altar, including the firepans, meat forks, shovels and sprinkling

---

Why did God substitute the Levites in place of the firstborn from other tribes? (3:45)

Perhaps to keep families and clans together and to avoid the confusion that could have re-sulted from having a mix from different tribes in charge of priestly service and duties. God designated the Levites to handle the priestly duties and be substitutes for the firstborn of each family. See *Why do firstborn sons get special honor from God?* (3:12–13).

Did the ark of the Testimony remain unseen for most people? (4:5)

Yes. The law permitted only the high priest once each year to enter the Most Holy Place, the chamber of the tabernacle housing the ark of the Testimony (Lev. 16:2,34; Heb. 9:7; see also Exodus 30:10). When moving to another campsite, the priests, while disassembling the tabernacle, covered the ark. The closest an or-dinary Israelite could get to the ark was prob-ably the front of the outer court.

Sea cows (4:6)

Sea cows are dugongs, marine animals abounding on the coral banks of the Red Sea and in other tropical waters. A dugong grows to 11 feet long, with a round head, fish-like tail and flippers for forelimbs. Their appearance is similar to seals. Because the Red Sea borders ancient Egypt, it's not surprising that Israel used their hides for various purposes. Also see *Where did they find a sea cow in the desert?* (Exodus 25:5).

---

^a47 That is, about 2 ounces (about 55 grams)   ^b50 That is, about 35 pounds (about 15.5 kilograms)   ^c6 That is, dugongs; also in verses 8, 10, 11, 12, 14 and 25

How big were the holy articles? (4:15; see 4:25,31; 7:6-9)

The ark of the covenant and the altar of incense were roughly the same bulk (and perhaps weight) as a modern living room chair. The 60 wooden pillars, which provided the framework for the outer court, were about 8.5 feet high and were probably the heaviest items. With thousands of men in the three Levite clans (see 4:36,40,44), there was plenty of muscle to move the holy articles. Six wagons also assisted them with transportation. Also see *How did the Levites carry so many heavy objects?* (Exodus 38:24-25).

Why would God kill people because they glanced at holy things? (4:20)

Through strict requirements like these, God impressed upon his people the seriousness of his holiness. These *holy things* symbolized the very presence of God. There was a real danger the Kohathites themselves might grow careless or flippant towards the items while handling them.

bowls. Over it they are to spread a covering of hides of sea cows[D] and put its poles in place.

15"After Aaron and his sons have finished covering the holy furnishings and all the holy articles, and when the camp is ready to move, the Kohathites are to come to do the carrying. But they must not touch the holy things or they will die. The Kohathites are to carry those things that are in the Tent of Meeting.

16"Eleazar son of Aaron, the priest[D], is to have charge of the oil for the light, the fragrant incense[D], the regular grain offering[D] and the anointing[D] oil. He is to be in charge of the entire tabernacle[D] and everything in it, including its holy furnishings and articles."

17The LORD said to Moses and Aaron, **18**"See that the Kohathite tribal clans are not cut off from the Levites[D]. **19**So that they may live and not die when they come near the most holy things, do this for them: Aaron and his sons are to go into the sanctuary and assign to each man his work and what he is to carry. **20**But the Kohathites must not go in to look at the holy things, even for a moment, or they will die."

The Gershonites

21The LORD said to Moses, **22**"Take a census also of the Gershonites by their families and clans. **23**Count all the men from thirty to fifty years of age who come to serve in the work at the Tent of Meeting.

24"This is the service of the Gershonite clans as they work and carry burdens: **25**They are to carry the curtains of the tabernacle, the Tent of Meeting, its covering and the outer covering of hides of sea cows, the curtains for the entrance to the Tent of Meeting, **26**the curtains of the courtyard surrounding the tabernacle and altar, the curtain for the entrance, the ropes and all the equipment used in its service. The Gershonites are to do all that needs to be done with these things. **27**All their service, whether carrying or doing other work, is to be done under the direction of Aaron and his sons. You shall assign to them as their responsibility all they are to carry. **28**This is the service of the Gershonite clans at the Tent of Meeting. Their duties are to be under the direction of Ithamar son of Aaron, the priest.

The Merarites

29"Count the Merarites by their clans and families. **30**Count all the men from thirty to fifty years of age who come to serve in the work at the Tent of Meeting. **31**This is their duty as they perform service at the Tent of Meeting: to carry the frames of the tabernacle, its crossbars, posts and bases, **32**as well as the posts of the surrounding courtyard with their bases, tent pegs, ropes, all their equipment and everything related to their use. Assign to each man the specific things he is to carry. **33**This is the service of the Merarite clans as they work at the Tent of Meeting under the direction of Ithamar son of Aaron, the priest."

The Numbering of the Levite Clans

34Moses, Aaron and the leaders of the community counted the Kohathites by their clans and families. **35**All the men from thirty to fifty years of age who came to serve in the work in the Tent of Meeting, **36**counted by clans, were 2,750. **37**This was the total of all those in the Kohathite clans who served in the Tent of Meeting. Mo-

ses and Aaron counted them according to the LORD's command through Moses.

38The Gershonites were counted by their clans and families. **39**All the men from thirty to fifty years of age who came to serve in the work at the Tent of Meeting^D, **40**counted by their clans and families, were 2,630. **41**This was the total of those in the Gershonite clans who served at the Tent of Meeting. Moses and Aaron counted them according to the LORD's command.

42The Merarites were counted by their clans and families. **43**All the men from thirty to fifty years of age who came to serve in the work at the Tent of Meeting, **44**counted by their clans, were 3,200. **45**This was the total of those in the Merarite clans. Moses and Aaron counted them according to the LORD's command through Moses.

46So Moses, Aaron and the leaders of Israel counted all the Levites^D by their clans and families. **47**All the men from thirty to fifty years of age who came to do the work of serving and carrying the Tent of Meeting **48**numbered 8,580. **49**At the LORD's command through Moses, each was assigned his work and told what to carry.

Thus they were counted, as the LORD commanded Moses.

The Purity of the Camp

5 The LORD said to Moses, **2**"Command the Israelites to send away from the camp anyone who has an infectious skin disease^a or a discharge of any kind, or who is ceremonially unclean^D because of a dead body. **3**Send away male and female alike; send them outside the camp so they will not defile their camp, where I dwell among them." **4**The Israelites did this; they sent them outside the camp. They did just as the LORD had instructed Moses.

Restitution for Wrongs

5The LORD said to Moses, **6**"Say to the Israelites: 'When a man or woman wrongs another in any way^b and so is unfaithful to the LORD, that person is guilty **7**and must confess the sin he has committed. He must make full restitution for his wrong, add one fifth to it and give it all to the person he has wronged. **8**But if that person has no close relative to whom restitution can be made for the wrong, the restitution belongs to the LORD and must be given to the priest^D, along with the ram with which atonement^D is made for him. **9**All the sacred^D contributions the Israelites bring to a priest will belong to him. **10**Each man's sacred gifts are his own, but what he gives to the priest will belong to the priest.' "

The Test for an Unfaithful Wife

11Then the LORD said to Moses, **12**"Speak to the Israelites and say to them: 'If a man's wife goes astray and is unfaithful to him **13**by sleeping with another man, and this is hidden from her husband and her impurity is undetected (since there is no witness against her and she has not been caught in the act), **14**and if feelings of jealousy come over her husband and he suspects his wife and she is impure—or if he is jealous and suspects her even though she is not impure— **15**then he is to take his wife to the priest. He must also take an offering of a tenth of an

Why banish someone for a condition he or she can't avoid? (5:2–3)

This banishment was not meant to suggest the person was responsible for his skin disease or that he was being punished for sin. What was at stake was God's holiness, not which Israelite was responsible for what condition. A serious skin disease, bodily discharge or contact with a dead body defiled the camp where God was present.

Was banishment permanent? (5:2–3)

Not usually. Unclean Israelites probably gathered together outside the camp boundaries, but not too far away. Many of their diseases were not serious. Priests frequently visited their camp and verified those completely healed, clearing them for re-entry into the Israelite camp (see Lev. 14:3).

Did the priests get rich by taking these gifts? (5:10)

These offerings were only received by the priest when there was no one who could be paid for restitution for a wrong (see v. 8). Since priests didn't own land, they couldn't make a living by farming like other Israelites. Though some may have abused the privilege—Eli's sons, for example (1 Samuel 2:12–17)—the priests needed these offerings if they were to devote their total energies to God's service.

Why should an innocent wife go through all this because of a suspicious husband? (5:14–31)

For her own protection. This test actually functioned as a protective measure for a woman falsely accused of having an affair. Without it, the furious husband might harm her—even kill her. The law served as a deterrent against private acts of vengeance and retribution, and ensured justice in a potentially explosive situation.

---

a2 Traditionally *leprosy*; the Hebrew word was used for various diseases affecting the skin—not necessarily leprosy.   *b6* Or *woman commits any wrong common to mankind*

ephah[a] of barley flour on her behalf. He must not pour oil on it or put incense[D] on it, because it is a grain offering[D] for jealousy, a reminder offering to draw attention to guilt.

16" 'The priest[D] shall bring her and have her stand before the LORD. **17**Then he shall take some holy water in a clay jar and put some dust from the tabernacle[D] floor into the water. **18**After the priest has had the woman stand before the LORD, he shall loosen her hair and place in her hands the reminder offering, the grain offering for jealousy, while he himself holds the bitter water that brings a curse. **19**Then the priest shall put the woman under oath and say to her, "If no other man has slept with you and you have not gone astray and become impure while married to your husband, may this bitter water that brings a curse not harm you. **20**But if you have gone astray while married to your husband and you have defiled yourself by sleeping with a man other than your husband"— **21**here the priest is to put the woman under this curse of the oath—"may the LORD cause your people to curse and denounce you when he causes your thigh to waste away and your abdomen to swell.[b] **22**May this water that brings a curse enter your body so that your abdomen swells and your thigh wastes away.[c]"

" 'Then the woman is to say, "Amen. So be it." '

23" 'The priest is to write these curses on a scroll and then wash them off into the bitter water. **24**He shall have the woman drink the bitter water that brings a curse, and this water will enter her and cause bitter suffering. **25**The priest is to take from her hands the grain offering for jealousy, wave it before the LORD and bring it to the altar. **26**The priest is then to take a handful of the grain offering as a memorial offering and burn it on the altar; after that, he is to have the woman drink the water. **27**If she has defiled herself and been unfaithful to her husband, then when she is made to drink the water that brings a curse, it will go into her and cause bitter suffering; her abdomen will swell and her thigh waste away,[d] and she will become accursed among her people. **28**If, however, the woman has not defiled herself and is free from impurity, she will be cleared of guilt and will be able to have children.

29" 'This, then, is the law of jealousy when a woman goes astray and defiles herself while married to her husband, **30**or when feelings of jealousy come over a man because he suspects his wife. The priest is to have her stand before the LORD and is to apply this entire law to her. **31**The husband will be innocent of any wrongdoing, but the woman will bear the consequences of her sin.' "

The Nazirite

6 The LORD said to Moses, **2**"Speak to the Israelites and say to them: 'If a man or woman wants to make a special vow[D], a vow of separation to the LORD as a Nazirite[D], **3**he must abstain from wine and other fermented drink and must not drink vinegar made from wine or from other fermented drink. He must not drink grape juice or eat grapes or raisins. **4**As long as he is a Nazirite,

What did it mean to have a swollen abdomen and a thigh wasted away? (5:22)
This is figurative language for infertility. It indicates a physical malady or reproductive problem that would prevent a woman from bearing children.

How would bitter water accurately prove or disprove adultery? (5:27–28)
God superintended the entire process. Some suggest the process itself may have created enough guilt and shame—if she was guilty, of course—to cause infertility, the ultimate disgrace for a woman during this era. Others see the acrid water as a symbol of the bitterness the woman would face if found guilty.

Were all childless women thought to be accursed for adultery? (5:28)
Not necessarily for adultery, but for some kind of disobedience to the Lord. The Israelites viewed the inability to have children as a divine punishment for personal sin (see Deut. 7:14). God's Word, however, does not make such blanket generalizations. Sarah, for example, bore disgrace for decades, though later she was called *holy* (1 Peter 3:5–6).

Why wasn't there a test for the adulterous man? (5:31)
The test shielded the woman from the husband. See *Why should an innocent wife go through all this because of a suspicious husband?* (5:14–31). In this male-dominated culture, women were especially vulnerable to domestic violence. Men simply didn't need the same protection against false accusations. However, if adultery was discovered, the penalty was the same for both the man and the woman: death (see Lev. 20:10).

What was a Nazirite? (6:2)
The term *Nazirite* means *dedicated one* or *set apart one*. A Nazirite was an individual, male or female, who made an extraordinary vow to God—an extra show of commitment to the Lord. The Mishna, the Jewish digest of oral law, mentions the typical vow as 30 days, though longer periods were not uncommon. Some even took the vow for a lifetime (for example, Samson in Judges 13–14). Those who took a Nazirite vow participated in all aspects of family life except for caring for the burial of a dead relative.

Why stay away from wine, grape juice, grapes and raisins? (6:3–4)
It's unclear. It may be because the fruit of the vine symbolized sensual enjoyment. So abstaining from these pleasures of life, though not evil in themselves, demonstrated a great sacrifice to God. Also see *What's wrong with grapes and wine?* (Judges 13:14).

a15 That is, probably about 2 quarts (about 2 liters)   *b21* Or *causes you to have a miscarrying womb and barrenness*   *c22* Or *body and cause you to be barren and have a miscarrying womb*   *d27* Or *suffering; she will have barrenness and a miscarrying womb*

he must not eat anything that comes from the grapevine, not even the seeds or skins.

5" 'During the entire period of his vow^D of separation no razor may be used on his head. He must be holy until the period of his separation to the LORD is over; he must let the hair of his head grow long. 6Throughout the period of his separation to the LORD he must not go near a dead body. 7Even if his own father or mother or brother or sister dies, he must not make himself ceremonially unclean^D on account of them, because the symbol of his separation to God is on his head. 8Throughout the period of his separation he is consecrated^D to the LORD.

9" 'If someone dies suddenly in his presence, thus defiling the hair he has dedicated, he must shave his head on the day of his cleansing—the seventh day. 10Then on the eighth day he must bring two doves or two young pigeons to the priest^D at the entrance to the Tent of Meeting^D. 11The priest is to offer one as a sin offering and the other as a burnt offering^D to make atonement^D for him because he sinned by being in the presence of the dead body. That same day he is to consecrate his head. 12He must dedicate himself to the LORD for the period of his separation and must bring a year-old male lamb as a guilt offering^D. The previous days do not count, because he became defiled during his separation.

13" 'Now this is the law for the Nazirite^D when the period of his separation is over. He is to be brought to the entrance to the Tent of Meeting. 14There he is to present his offerings to the LORD: a year-old male lamb without defect for a burnt offering, a year-old ewe lamb without defect for a sin offering, a ram without defect for a fellowship offering^D,^a 15together with their grain offerings^D and drink offerings^D, and a basket of bread made without yeast^D—cakes made of fine flour mixed with oil, and wafers spread with oil.

16" 'The priest is to present them before the LORD and make the sin offering and the burnt offering. 17He is to present the basket of unleavened bread and is to sacrifice^D the ram as a fellowship offering to the LORD, together with its grain offering and drink offering.

18" 'Then at the entrance to the Tent of Meeting, the Nazirite must shave off the hair that he dedicated. He is to take the hair and put it in the fire that is under the sacrifice of the fellowship offering.

19" 'After the Nazirite has shaved off the hair of his dedication, the priest is to place in his hands a boiled shoulder of the ram, and a cake and a wafer from the basket, both made without yeast. 20The priest shall then wave them before the LORD as a wave offering^D; they are holy and belong to the priest, together with the breast that was waved and the thigh that was presented. After that, the Nazirite may drink wine.

21" 'This is the law of the Nazirite who vows his offering to the LORD in accordance with his separation, in addition to whatever else he can afford. He must fulfill the vow he has made, according to the law of the Nazirite.' "

The Priestly Blessing

22The LORD said to Moses, 23"Tell Aaron and his sons, 'This is how you are to bless the Israelites. Say to them:

Why would a Nazirite be guilty if someone died in his presence? (6:9–12)

The Nazirites' vow strictly forbade any and all contact with the dead. Their lifestyle depicted, to the Israelite people, the ultimate act of devotion to God. Rules were rules, so even if the contact was accidental, contamination had taken place. The infraction required that the individual be restored to God's standard of holiness.

Why all the different types of offerings? (6:14–15)

See the notes about the offerings in Leviticus 1–7 for a description and explanation of the various types. These offerings were in keeping with the Nazirite vow. They reflected the spirit of absolute commitment to God, central to the vow, and they corresponded to the magnitude of the oath.

^a14 Traditionally *peace offering*; also in verses 17 and 18

" ' "The LORD bless you
  and keep you;
25the LORD make his face shine upon you
  and be gracious to you;
26the LORD turn his face toward you
  and give you peaceD." '

27"So they will put my name on the Israelites, and I will bless them."

Offerings at the Dedication of the Tabernacle

7 When Moses finished setting up the tabernacleD, he anointedD it and consecratedD it and all its furnishings. He also anointed and consecrated the altar and all its utensils. 2Then the leaders of Israel, the heads of families who were the tribal leaders in charge of those who were counted, made offerings. 3They brought as their gifts before the LORD six covered carts and twelve oxen—an ox from each leader and a cart from every two. These they presented before the tabernacle.

4The LORD said to Moses, 5"Accept these from them, that they may be used in the work at the Tent of MeetingD. Give them to the LevitesD as each man's work requires."

6So Moses took the carts and oxen and gave them to the Levites. 7He gave two carts and four oxen to the Gershonites, as their work required, 8and he gave four carts and eight oxen to the Merarites, as their work required. They were all under the direction of Ithamar son of Aaron, the priestD. 9But Moses did not give any to the Kohathites, because they were to carry on their shoulders the holy things, for which they were responsible.

10When the altar was anointed, the leaders brought their offerings for its dedication and presented them before the altar. 11For the LORD had said to Moses, "Each day one leader is to bring his offering for the dedication of the altar."

12The one who brought his offering on the first day was Nahshon son of Amminadab of the tribe of Judah.

13His offering was one silver plate weighing a hundred and thirty shekelsD,a and one silver sprinkling bowl weighing seventy shekels,b both according to the sanctuary shekelD, each filled with fine flour mixed with oil as a grain offeringD; 14one gold dish weighing ten shekels,c filled with incense; 15one young bull, one ram and one male lamb a year old, for a burnt offeringD; 16one male goat for a sin offeringD; 17and two oxen, five rams, five male goats and five male lambs a year old, to be sacrificed as a fellowship offeringD.d This was the offering of Nahshon son of Amminadab.

18On the second day Nethanel son of Zuar, the leader of Issachar, brought his offering.

19The offering he brought was one silver plate weighing a hundred and thirty shekels, and one silver sprinkling bowl weighing seventy shekels, both according to the sanctuary shekel, each filled with fine flour mixed with oil as a grain offering; 20one

In what way did the priests put God's name on the Israelites? (6:27)

The priests simply pronounced to the people the blessings associated with God's name. The name *Yahweh*, translated LORD, was employed by the priests for this blessing. God's name expressed his character. It signified his ongoing relationship with his people and his willingness to act on their behalf.

What did Moses do to *anoint and consecrate* the tabernacle? (7:1)

Moses probably smeared or poured a special olive oil mixture on the altar of the tabernacle (see Exodus 29:36) and possibly over the other holy items. This act marked the tabernacle furnishings as holy articles, designated and separated specifically for God's service.

Why did only a few Levites get carts to carry their loads? (7:9)

It apparently depended on the load—the degree of difficulty in transporting it and its sacred significance. Items like the ark of the covenant and the golden candlestick did not ride on carts; the priests had to carry these precious items on their shoulders. Less sacred and heavier items were more likely to be carried on carts.

Why is the tribe of Judah listed first? (7:12)

The order of these offerings follows that of their marching order (2:3–32). See *Why is Judah mentioned first?* (2:3–4).

Why are all these repetitive offerings listed? (7:12–83)

It would have saved space and time to simply say that each of these leaders brought the same offerings to the Lord. Since the Bible goes to such great lengths to list these identical offerings, we can be sure God had a reason for it. Some suggest that this account was not intended simply to offer us information about what happened. More than that, they say, it helps us feel the magnificence of the ceremony that was taking place. Reading this account conveys something of the ritual pomp and circumstance that accompanied this worship of giving.

---

a13 That is, about 3 1/4 pounds (about 1.5 kilograms); also elsewhere in this chapter   b13 That is, about 1 3/4 pounds (about 0.8 kilogram); also elsewhere in this chapter   c14 That is, about 4 ounces (about 110 grams); also elsewhere in this chapter
d17 Traditionally *peace offering*; also elsewhere in this chapter

gold dish weighing ten shekels[D], filled with incense[D]; **21**one young bull, one ram and one male lamb a year old, for a burnt offering[D]; **22**one male goat for a sin offering[D]; **23**and two oxen, five rams, five male goats and five male lambs a year old, to be sacrificed as a fellowship offering[D]. This was the offering of Nethanel son of Zuar.

24On the third day, Eliab son of Helon, the leader of the people of Zebulun, brought his offering.

25His offering was one silver plate weighing a hundred and thirty shekels, and one silver sprinkling bowl weighing seventy shekels, both according to the sanctuary shekel[D], each filled with fine flour mixed with oil as a grain offering[D]; **26**one gold dish weighing ten shekels, filled with incense; **27**one young bull, one ram and one male lamb a year old, for a burnt offering; **28**one male goat for a sin offering; **29**and two oxen, five rams, five male goats and five male lambs a year old, to be sacrificed as a fellowship offering. This was the offering of Eliab son of Helon.

30On the fourth day Elizur son of Shedeur, the leader of the people of Reuben, brought his offering.

31His offering was one silver plate weighing a hundred and thirty shekels, and one silver sprinkling bowl weighing seventy shekels, both according to the sanctuary shekel, each filled with fine flour mixed with oil as a grain offering; **32**one gold dish weighing ten shekels, filled with incense; **33**one young bull, one ram and one male lamb a year old, for a burnt offering; **34**one male goat for a sin offering; **35**and two oxen, five rams, five male goats and five male lambs a year old, to be sacrificed as a fellowship offering. This was the offering of Elizur son of Shedeur.

36On the fifth day Shelumiel son of Zurishaddai, the leader of the people of Simeon, brought his offering.

37His offering was one silver plate weighing a hundred and thirty shekels, and one silver sprinkling bowl weighing seventy shekels, both according to the sanctuary shekel, each filled with fine flour mixed with oil as a grain offering; **38**one gold dish weighing ten shekels, filled with incense; **39**one young bull, one ram and one male lamb a year old, for a burnt offering; **40**one male goat for a sin offering; **41**and two oxen, five rams, five male goats and five male lambs a year old, to be sacrificed as a fellowship offering. This was the offering of Shelumiel son of Zurishaddai.

42On the sixth day Eliasaph son of Deuel, the leader of the people of Gad, brought his offering.

43His offering was one silver plate weighing a hundred and thirty shekels, and one silver sprinkling bowl weighing seventy shekels, both according to the sanctuary shekel, each filled with fine flour mixed with oil as a grain offering; **44**one gold dish weighing ten shekels, filled with incense; **45**one young bull, one ram and one male lamb a year old, for a burnt offering; **46**one male goat for a sin offering; **47**and two oxen, five rams, five male goats and five male lambs a year old, to be sacrificed as a fel-

Where did the Israelites get all these silver plates, bowls and gold dishes? (7:26–80)

Most of this precious metal probably came from the Egyptians during the exodus. God had caused the Egyptians to become *favorably disposed* toward the Israelites (Exodus 12:36), giving them gifts of silver, gold and clothing as they left the land. Also see *Why would the Egyptians be willing to be looted?* (Exodus 12:35–36).

Grain offering . . . burnt offering . . . sin offering . . . fellowship offering (7:31–80)

See *Old Testament Sacrifices* on page 138.

Why sacrifice all these different kinds of animals? (7:41–80)

Because these were one-time offerings given for the dedication of the tabernacle, it may be that the wide variety of animals (not to mention the gifts of silver and gold utensils, flour and incense) served to represent the whole range of their possessions. In dedicating the tabernacle, the best of everything they had was offered to honor the Lord.

Why are Ephraim and Manasseh listed when they weren't sons of Jacob? (7:48,54)

Jacob had adopted these two sons of Joseph and they received the status of Jacob's own sons. See Gen. 48:5–6.

Did all these animals waiting to be sacrificed turn the tabernacle into a zoo? (7:59–83)

Probably not. The offerings were made over the course of 12 days so the animals were probably not brought to the site until their day had arrived. Since the Israelites raised livestock as a primary occupation, the entire area on which they camped may have looked something like a community of feedlots, dairy farms and sheep farms. For a related note on the dedication of the temple, see *Why so many sacrifices?* (1 Kings 8:5).

lowship offeringᴰ. This was the offering of Eliasaph son of Deuel.

48On the seventh day Elishama son of Ammihud, the leader of the people of Ephraim, brought his offering. **49**His offering was one silver plate weighing a hundred and thirty shekelsᴰ, and one silver sprinkling bowl weighing seventy shekels, both according to the sanctuary shekelᴰ, each filled with fine flour mixed with oil as a grain offeringᴰ; **50**one gold dish weighing ten shekels, filled with incense; **51**one young bull, one ram and one male lamb a year old, for a burnt offeringᴰ; **52**one male goat for a sin offeringᴰ; **53**and two oxen, five rams, five male goats and five male lambs a year old, to be sacrificed as a fellowship offering. This was the offering of Elishama son of Ammihud.

54On the eighth day Gamaliel son of Pedahzur, the leader of the people of Manasseh, brought his offering. **55**His offering was one silver plate weighing a hundred and thirty shekels, and one silver sprinkling bowl weighing seventy shekels, both according to the sanctuary shekel, each filled with fine flour mixed with oil as a grain offering; **56**one gold dish weighing ten shekels, filled with incense; **57**one young bull, one ram and one male lamb a year old, for a burnt offering; **58**one male goat for a sin offering; **59**and two oxen, five rams, five male goats and five male lambs a year old, to be sacrificed as a fellowship offering. This was the offering of Gamaliel son of Pedahzur.

60On the ninth day Abidan son of Gideoni, the leader of the people of Benjamin, brought his offering. **61**His offering was one silver plate weighing a hundred and thirty shekels, and one silver sprinkling bowl weighing seventy shekels, both according to the sanctuary shekel, each filled with fine flour mixed with oil as a grain offering; **62**one gold dish weighing ten shekels, filled with incense; **63**one young bull, one ram and one male lamb a year old, for a burnt offering; **64**one male goat for a sin offering; **65**and two oxen, five rams, five male goats and five male lambs a year old, to be sacrificed as a fellowship offering. This was the offering of Abidan son of Gideoni.

66On the tenth day Ahiezer son of Ammishaddai, the leader of the people of Dan, brought his offering. **67**His offering was one silver plate weighing a hundred and thirty shekels, and one silver sprinkling bowl weighing seventy shekels, both according to the sanctuary shekel, each filled with fine flour mixed with oil as a grain offering; **68**one gold dish weighing ten shekels, filled with incense; **69**one young bull, one ram and one male lamb a year old, for a burnt offering; **70**one male goat for a sin offering; **71**and two oxen, five rams, five male goats and five male lambs a year old, to be sacrificed as a fellowship offering. This was the offering of Ahiezer son of Ammishaddai.

72On the eleventh day Pagiel son of Ocran, the leader of the people of Asher, brought his offering. **73**His offering was one silver plate weighing a hun-

dred and thirty shekels[D], and one silver sprinkling bowl weighing seventy shekels, both according to the sanctuary shekel[D], each filled with fine flour mixed with oil as a grain offering[D]; **74**one gold dish weighing ten shekels, filled with incense; **75**one young bull, one ram and one male lamb a year old, for a burnt offering[D]; **76**one male goat for a sin offering[D]; **77**and two oxen, five rams, five male goats and five male lambs a year old, to be sacrificed as a fellowship offering[D]. This was the offering of Pagiel son of Ocran.

78On the twelfth day Ahira son of Enan, the leader of the people of Naphtali, brought his offering.

79His offering was one silver plate weighing a hundred and thirty shekels, and one silver sprinkling bowl weighing seventy shekels, both according to the sanctuary shekel, each filled with fine flour mixed with oil as a grain offering; **80**one gold dish weighing ten shekels, filled with incense; **81**one young bull, one ram and one male lamb a year old, for a burnt offering; **82**one male goat for a sin offering; **83**and two oxen, five rams, five male goats and five male lambs a year old, to be sacrificed as a fellowship offering. This was the offering of Ahira son of Enan.

84These were the offerings of the Israelite leaders for the dedication of the altar when it was anointed[D]: twelve silver plates, twelve silver sprinkling bowls and twelve gold dishes. **85**Each silver plate weighed a hundred and thirty shekels, and each sprinkling bowl seventy shekels. Altogether, the silver dishes weighed two thousand four hundred shekels,*a* according to the sanctuary shekel. **86**The twelve gold dishes filled with incense weighed ten shekels each, according to the sanctuary shekel. Altogether, the gold dishes weighed a hundred and twenty shekels.*b* **87**The total number of animals for the burnt offering came to twelve young bulls, twelve rams and twelve male lambs a year old, together with their grain offering. Twelve male goats were used for the sin offering. **88**The total number of animals for the sacrifice[D] of the fellowship offering came to twenty-four oxen, sixty rams, sixty male goats and sixty male lambs a year old. These were the offerings for the dedication of the altar after it was anointed.

89When Moses entered the Tent of Meeting[D] to speak with the LORD, he heard the voice speaking to him from between the two cherubim[D] above the atonement[D] cover on the ark of the Testimony. And he spoke with him.

Setting Up the Lamps

8 The LORD said to Moses, **2**"Speak to Aaron and say to him, 'When you set up the seven lamps, they are to light the area in front of the lampstand.' "

3Aaron did so; he set up the lamps so that they faced forward on the lampstand, just as the LORD commanded Moses. **4**This is how the lampstand was made: It was made of hammered gold—from its base to its blossoms. The lampstand was made exactly like the pattern the LORD had shown Moses.

How much was a sanctuary shekel? (7:73)

Before coins were used as money, people often used precious metals, measured by weight, for a currency of exchange. The value of bars or rings of gold or silver was determined according to a commonly accepted standard of measure—the sanctuary shekel, probably weighing 11.5 grams or 2/5 of an ounce.

Ark of the Testimony (7:89)

This ark is variously referred to as *the ark, ark of the covenant, ark of the Lord, ark of God* and *ark of the Testimony*. These names all refer to the cabinet in the tabernacle that holds the stone tablets containing the Ten Commandments, the pot of manna and Aaron's staff that had budded (17:10).

Did God talk to Moses in an audible voice? (7:89)

In this case, yes, but this was an extraordinary occurrence for an extraordinary man. God communicated directly and clearly to the prophets of the Old Testament through visions, dreams, revelations and other kinds of signs, even if he didn't always speak audibly (see 12:6–8). Also see *How did God speak to Moses?* (1:1).

---

a85 That is, about 60 pounds (about 28 kilograms)   *b86* That is, about 3 pounds (about 1.4 kilograms)

What was the value of ritual purification? (8:7)

This process made a person spiritually fit to participate in the worship of God. The Levite priests had to be pure, free from any transgression. This ceremony, which involved washing and prayer, symbolized spiritual cleansing.

In what sense were the Levites *set apart* for God? (8:14)

The Levites, unlike the rest of the Israelites, didn't own and farm the land. Instead, they devoted their lives to the tabernacle and other related responsibilities. Their whole livelihood, then, was given to God for his exclusive use.

Why did God substitute the Levites in place of the firstborn from other tribes? (8:16)

Perhaps to keep families and clans together and to avoid the confusion that could have resulted from having a mix from different tribes in charge of priestly service and duties. God designated the Levites to handle the priestly duties and be substitutes for the firstborn of each family. See *Why do firstborn sons get special honor from God?* (3:12–13).

Why restrict the age that a priest could serve? (8:24–25)

Tabernacle duty was hard work. It included dismantling, hauling and reassembling the tabernacle when the camp moved to another location. It was probably best for the work to be done by this age group, both for the efficiency of the work and for the protection of the priests themselves.

SCRIPTURE LINK (9:1–14)

See Exodus 12 for the account of the first Passover, which was held in Egypt.

The Setting Apart of the Levites

5The LORD said to Moses: **6**"Take the Levites[D] from among the other Israelites and make them ceremonially clean. **7**To purify[D] them, do this: Sprinkle the water of cleansing on them; then have them shave their whole bodies and wash their clothes, and so purify themselves. **8**Have them take a young bull with its grain offering[D] of fine flour mixed with oil; then you are to take a second young bull for a sin offering[D]. **9**Bring the Levites to the front of the Tent of Meeting and assemble the whole Israelite community. **10**You are to bring the Levites before the LORD, and the Israelites are to lay their hands on them. **11**Aaron is to present the Levites before the LORD as a wave offering[D] from the Israelites, so that they may be ready to do the work of the LORD.

12"After the Levites lay their hands on the heads of the bulls, use the one for a sin offering to the LORD and the other for a burnt offering[D], to make atonement[D] for the Levites. **13**Have the Levites stand in front of Aaron and his sons and then present them as a wave offering to the LORD. **14**In this way you are to set the Levites apart from the other Israelites, and the Levites will be mine.

15"After you have purified the Levites and presented them as a wave offering, they are to come to do their work at the Tent of Meeting. **16**They are the Israelites who are to be given wholly to me. I have taken them as my own in place of the firstborn[D], the first male offspring from every Israelite woman. **17**Every firstborn male in Israel, whether man or animal, is mine. When I struck down all the firstborn in Egypt, I set them apart for myself. **18**And I have taken the Levites in place of all the firstborn sons in Israel. **19**Of all the Israelites, I have given the Levites as gifts to Aaron and his sons to do the work at the Tent of Meeting on behalf of the Israelites and to make atonement for them so that no plague will strike the Israelites when they go near the sanctuary."

20Moses, Aaron and the whole Israelite community did with the Levites just as the LORD commanded Moses. **21**The Levites purified themselves and washed their clothes. Then Aaron presented them as a wave offering before the LORD and made atonement for them to purify them. **22**After that, the Levites came to do their work at the Tent of Meeting under the supervision of Aaron and his sons. They did with the Levites just as the LORD commanded Moses.

23The LORD said to Moses, **24**"This applies to the Levites: Men twenty-five years old or more shall come to take part in the work at the Tent of Meeting, **25**but at the age of fifty, they must retire from their regular service and work no longer. **26**They may assist their brothers in performing their duties at the Tent of Meeting, but they themselves must not do the work. This, then, is how you are to assign the responsibilities of the Levites."

The Passover

9 The LORD spoke to Moses in the Desert of Sinai in the first month of the second year after they came out of Egypt. He said, **2**"Have the Israelites celebrate the Passover at the appointed time. **3**Celebrate it at the appointed time, at twilight on the fourteenth day of this month, in accordance with all its rules and regulations."

4So Moses told the Israelites to celebrate the Passover, **5**and they did so in the Desert of Sinai at twilight on the

fourteenth day of the first month. The Israelites did everything just as the LORD commanded Moses.

6But some of them could not celebrate the Passover on
that day because they were ceremonially unclean[D] on
account of a dead body. So they came to Moses and Aaron
that same day **7**and said to Moses, "We have become unclean because of a dead body, but why should we be
kept from presenting the LORD's offering with the other
Israelites at the appointed time?"

8Moses answered them, "Wait until I find out what the
LORD commands concerning you."

9Then the LORD said to Moses, **10**"Tell the Israelites:
'When any of you or your descendants are unclean because of a dead body or are away on a journey, they may
still celebrate the LORD's Passover. **11**They are to celebrate
it on the fourteenth day of the second month at twilight.
They are to eat the lamb, together with unleavened bread
and bitter herbs. **12**They must not leave any of it till morning or break any of its bones. When they celebrate the
Passover, they must follow all the regulations. **13**But if a
man who is ceremonially clean and not on a journey fails
to celebrate the Passover, that person must be cut off
from his people because he did not present the LORD's offering at the appointed time. That man will bear the consequences of his sin.

14" 'An alien[D] living among you who wants to celebrate the LORD's Passover must do so in accordance with
its rules and regulations. You must have the same regulations for the alien and the native-born.' "

The Cloud Above the Tabernacle

15On the day the tabernacle[D], the Tent of the Testimony, was set up, the cloud covered it. From evening till
morning the cloud above the tabernacle looked like fire.
16That is how it continued to be; the cloud covered it, and
at night it looked like fire. **17**Whenever the cloud lifted
from above the Tent, the Israelites set out; wherever the
cloud settled, the Israelites encamped. **18**At the LORD's
command the Israelites set out, and at his command they
encamped. As long as the cloud stayed over the tabernacle, they remained in camp. **19**When the cloud remained over the tabernacle a long time, the Israelites
obeyed the LORD's order and did not set out. **20**Sometimes
the cloud was over the tabernacle only a few days; at
the LORD's command they would encamp, and then at his
command they would set out. **21**Sometimes the cloud
stayed only from evening till morning, and when it lifted
in the morning, they set out. Whether by day or by night,
whenever the cloud lifted, they set out. **22**Whether the
cloud stayed over the tabernacle for two days or a
month or a year, the Israelites would remain in camp and
not set out; but when it lifted, they would set out. **23**At the
LORD's command they encamped, and at the LORD's command they set out. They obeyed the LORD's order, in accordance with his command through Moses.

The Silver Trumpets

10 The LORD said to Moses: **2**"Make two trumpets of
hammered silver, and use them for calling the
community together and for having the camps set out.
3When both are sounded, the whole community is to assemble before you at the entrance to the Tent of Meeting[D]. **4**If only one is sounded, the leaders—the heads of
the clans of Israel—are to assemble before you. **5**When a

Why prohibit breaking any bones of the Passover lamb or keeping it until morning? (9:12)

No reasons are given here or elsewhere for either regulation. The prohibition against breaking a bone parallels the fact that none of
Christ's bones were broken during the crucifixion (John 19:36). Christ is the consummate
Passover lamb, sacrificing himself for the sins
of the people (see John 1:29,36; 1 Cor. 5:7).
The prohibition against saving the leftovers until morning may reflect the holy, inviolable character of the meal. Because the Israelites had
no refrigeration, it may also have been a
precaution against food poisoning.

What does it mean to be *cut off*? (9:13)

The phrase refers to either death precipitated
by God or banishment (excommunication) from
the community. The extreme punishment
stemmed from the significance of the Passover, which recalled the Israelites' deliverance
from Egypt. The exodus was to Old Testament
believers what the cross is to New Testament
Christians—pivotal to the faith. The "crime" of
absenteeism was like denying the faith. See
Cut off from my presence (Lev. 22:3).

Why did God make his presence known in the cloud? (9:15-16)

God's presence in the cloud offered all Israelites an encounter with God. This was a more
general or less direct presence of God than that
in the ark of the Testimony in the tabernacle.

trumpet blast is sounded, the tribes camping on the east are to set out. [6]At the sounding of a second blast, the camps on the south are to set out. The blast will be the signal for setting out. [7]To gather the assembly, blow the trumpets, but not with the same signal.

[8]"The sons of Aaron, the priests[D], are to blow the trumpets. This is to be a lasting ordinance for you and the generations to come. [9]When you go into battle in your own land against an enemy who is oppressing you, sound a blast on the trumpets. Then you will be remembered by the LORD your God and rescued from your enemies. [10]Also at your times of rejoicing—your appointed feasts and New Moon festivals[D]—you are to sound the trumpets over your burnt offerings[D] and fellowship offerings[D],[a] and they will be a memorial for you before your God. I am the LORD your God."

If God "remembers" his people, does that mean he's forgotten them for a time? (10:9)

No, remembering does not always imply forgetfulness. In the Old Testament, it means *to pay attention to,* and emphasizes God's decision to take action according to a previous commitment.

The Israelites Leave Sinai

[11]On the twentieth day of the second month of the second year, the cloud lifted from above the tabernacle[D] of the Testimony. [12]Then the Israelites set out from the Desert of Sinai and traveled from place to place until the cloud came to rest in the Desert of Paran. [13]They set out, this first time, at the LORD's command through Moses.

[14]The divisions of the camp of Judah went first, under their standard. Nahshon son of Amminadab was in command. [15]Nethanel son of Zuar was over the division of the tribe of Issachar, [16]and Eliab son of Helon was over the division of the tribe of Zebulun. [17]Then the tabernacle was taken down, and the Gershonites and Merarites, who carried it, set out.

[18]The divisions of the camp of Reuben went next, under their standard. Elizur son of Shedeur was in command. [19]Shelumiel son of Zurishaddai was over the division of the tribe of Simeon, [20]and Eliasaph son of Deuel was over the division of the tribe of Gad. [21]Then the Kohathites set out, carrying the holy things. The tabernacle was to be set up before they arrived.

How could the tabernacle be set up before the people arrived? (10:21)

The tabernacle was set up before the Kohathites arrived with the holy goods. When moving to another location, the Gershonites and Merarites left before the Kohathites (v. 17). Consequently, they arrived at the new campsite and assembled the tabernacle by the time the Kohathites, who followed the Israelite procession, appeared with the holy objects. All three groups comprised the Levite tribe (see 3:17).

[22]The divisions of the camp of Ephraim went next, under their standard. Elishama son of Ammihud was in command. [23]Gamaliel son of Pedahzur was over the division of the tribe of Manasseh, [24]and Abidan son of Gideoni was over the division of the tribe of Benjamin.

[25]Finally, as the rear guard for all the units, the divisions of the camp of Dan set out, under their standard. Ahiezer son of Ammishaddai was in command. [26]Pagiel son of Ocran was over the division of the tribe of Asher, [27]and Ahira son of Enan was over the division of the tribe of Naphtali. [28]This was the order of march for the Israelite divisions as they set out.

[29]Now Moses said to Hobab son of Reuel the Midianite, Moses' father-in-law, "We are setting out for the place about which the LORD said, 'I will give it to you.' Come with us and we will treat you well, for the LORD has promised good things to Israel."

[30]He answered, "No, I will not go; I am going back to my own land and my own people."

[31]But Moses said, "Please do not leave us. You know where we should camp in the desert, and you can be our eyes. [32]If you come with us, we will share with you whatever good things the LORD gives us."

[33]So they set out from the mountain of the LORD and

[a]10 Traditionally *peace offerings*

traveled for three days. The ark of the covenant[D] of the LORD went before them during those three days to find them a place to rest. [34]The cloud of the LORD was over them by day when they set out from the camp.

[35]Whenever the ark set out, Moses said,

> "Rise up, O LORD!
>   May your enemies be scattered;
>   may your foes flee before you."

[36]Whenever it came to rest, he said,

> "Return, O LORD,
>   to the countless thousands of Israel."

Fire From the LORD

11 Now the people complained about their hardships in the hearing of the LORD, and when he heard them his anger was aroused. Then fire from the LORD burned among them and consumed some of the outskirts of the camp. [2]When the people cried out to Moses, he prayed to the LORD and the fire died down. [3]So that place was called Taberah,[a] because fire from the LORD had burned among them.

Quail From the LORD

[4]The rabble with them began to crave other food, and again the Israelites started wailing and said, "If only we had meat to eat! [5]We remember the fish we ate in Egypt at no cost—also the cucumbers, melons, leeks, onions and garlic. [6]But now we have lost our appetite; we never see anything but this manna[D]!"

[7]The manna was like coriander seed and looked like resin. [8]The people went around gathering it, and then ground it in a handmill or crushed it in a mortar. They cooked it in a pot or made it into cakes. And it tasted like something made with olive oil. [9]When the dew settled on the camp at night, the manna also came down.

[10]Moses heard the people of every family wailing, each at the entrance to his tent. The LORD became exceedingly angry, and Moses was troubled. [11]He asked the LORD, "Why have you brought this trouble on your servant? What have I done to displease you that you put the burden of all these people on me? [12]Did I conceive all these people? Did I give them birth? Why do you tell me to carry them in my arms, as a nurse carries an infant, to the land you promised on oath to their forefathers? [13]Where can I get meat for all these people? They keep wailing to me, 'Give us meat to eat!' [14]I cannot carry all these people by myself; the burden is too heavy for me. [15]If this is how you are going to treat me, put me to death[D] right now—if I have found favor in your eyes—and do not let me face my own ruin."

[16]The LORD said to Moses: "Bring me seventy of Israel's elders who are known to you as leaders and officials among the people. Have them come to the Tent of Meeting[D], that they may stand there with you. [17]I will come down and speak with you there, and I will take of the Spirit that is on you and put the Spirit on them. They will help you carry the burden of the people so that you will not have to carry it alone.

[18]"Tell the people: 'Consecrate[D] yourselves in preparation for tomorrow, when you will eat meat. The LORD

What kind of fire was this? (11:1)
It may have consisted of bolts or flashes of lightning, which then ignited the fires. It probably burned the brush around the camp, as well as some of the Israelites' tents, though the entire camp was not burned. The report of the fire dying down in v. 2 suggests that it had become a raging fire.

The rabble with them (11:4)
See *Why did non-Israelites go with them?* (Exodus 12:38).

Why couldn't the people use some of their flocks and herds for meat? (11:4; see Exodus 12:38)
The livestock were an investment for the Israelites' future. If they consumed their breeding stock, they would have eaten their working capital. That might have solved the present crisis but it would have cast a shadow on their future. It would be difficult, if not impossible, to purchase another herd of cattle or other livestock.

What was *coriander seed* and *resin*? (11:7)
Coriander seeds belonged to a plant closely related to the parsley family. It grew two or three feet high, producing pink or white flowers. Resin, on the other hand, was a waxy substance. No one knows exactly what manna resembled. Israelites compared its appearance and color to familiar objects, such as wafers made with honey (Exodus 16:31). No wonder the Israelites stored a sample in the ark of the covenant for future generations!

---

a 3 Taberah means *burning.*

heard you when you wailed, "If only we had meat to eat! We were better off in Egypt!" Now the LORD will give you meat, and you will eat it. [19]You will not eat it for just one day, or two days, or five, ten or twenty days, [20]but for a whole month—until it comes out of your nostrils and you loathe it—because you have rejected the LORD, who is among you, and have wailed before him, saying, "Why did we ever leave Egypt?" ' "

[21]But Moses said, "Here I am among six hundred thousand men on foot, and you say, 'I will give them meat to eat for a whole month!' [22]Would they have enough if flocks and herds were slaughtered for them? Would they have enough if all the fish in the sea were caught for them?"

[23]The LORD answered Moses, "Is the LORD's arm too short? You will now see whether or not what I say will come true for you."

[24]So Moses went out and told the people what the LORD had said. He brought together seventy of their elders and had them stand around the Tent. [25]Then the LORD came down in the cloud and spoke with him, and he took of the Spirit that was on him and put the Spirit on the seventy elders. When the Spirit rested on them, they prophesied, but they did not do so again.[a]

[26]However, two men, whose names were Eldad and Medad, had remained in the camp. They were listed among the elders, but did not go out to the Tent. Yet the Spirit also rested on them, and they prophesied in the camp. [27]A young man ran and told Moses, "Eldad and Medad are prophesying in the camp."

[28]Joshua son of Nun, who had been Moses' aide since youth, spoke up and said, "Moses, my lord, stop them!"

[29]But Moses replied, "Are you jealous for my sake? I wish that all the LORD's people were prophets[D] and that the LORD would put his Spirit on them!" [30]Then Moses and the elders of Israel returned to the camp.

[31]Now a wind went out from the LORD and drove quail[D] in from the sea. It brought them[b] down all around the camp to about three feet[c] above the ground, as far as a day's walk in any direction. [32]All that day and night and all the next day the people went out and gathered quail. No one gathered less than ten homers.[d] Then they spread them out all around the camp. [33]But while the meat was still between their teeth and before it could be consumed, the anger of the LORD burned against the people, and he struck them with a severe plague. [34]Therefore the place was named Kibroth Hattaavah,[e] because there they buried the people who had craved other food.

[35]From Kibroth Hattaavah the people traveled to Hazeroth and stayed there.

Miriam and Aaron Oppose Moses

12 Miriam and Aaron began to talk against Moses because of his Cushite wife, for he had married a Cushite. [2]"Has the LORD spoken only through Moses?" they asked. "Hasn't he also spoken through us?" And the LORD heard this.

[3](Now Moses was a very humble man, more humble than anyone else on the face of the earth.)

What was the significance of this prophesying? (11:25)

It served as God's endorsement. God's Spirit gave these leaders validity in the eyes of the people. They did not prophesy any new revelations, so they didn't replace Moses as the spokesman for God. It was an authenticating, supernatural rite of passage into leadership of the community.

Why didn't the quail fly away? (11:31)

These quail, small birds of the partridge family, migrated from North Africa through Egypt, Sinai and Canaan. To offset their lack of strength, quail would often coast with the wind. After crossing large bodies of water, the Red Sea in this instance, they landed in a weakened condition and became easy targets for predators.

Why would God grant the people's desire for meat and then punish them for wanting it? (11:33)

God disciplined his whining children for their greed by giving them all they wanted, but allowing it to make them miserable. The answer to their prayers became the source of their punishment. The plague may have been caused by the people eating spoiled meat.

Why did Miriam and Aaron suddenly become opposed to Moses' Cushite wife? (12:1)

Miriam and Aaron became envious of Moses' special position as God's spokesperson (v. 2). They camouflaged the core issue—their jealousy of Moses' prestigious position—by focusing the attention on his Cushite wife.

Why would Moses, the writer of Numbers, brag about his humility? (12:3)

This is probably an editorial addition inserted by a later, unknown writer, but still completely under the guidance of the Holy Spirit. It's also possible that the word for humility could mean afflicted (as in Psalm 10:17, for example) or oppressed (as in Amos 2:7). If Moses wrote it intending this sense of the word, he would have been describing his feelings of persecution rather than his humble character.

---

[a]25 Or prophesied and continued to do so   [b]31 Or They flew
[c]31 Hebrew two cubits (about 1 meter)   [d]32 That is, probably
about 60 bushels (about 2.2 kiloliters)   [e]34 Kibroth Hattaavah
means graves of craving.

4At once the LORD said to Moses, Aaron and Miriam, "Come out to the Tent of Meeting^D, all three of you." So the three of them came out. **5**Then the LORD came down in a pillar of cloud; he stood at the entrance to the Tent and summoned Aaron and Miriam. When both of them stepped forward, **6**he said, "Listen to my words:

> "When a prophet^D of the LORD is among you,
>   I reveal myself to him in visions^D,
>   I speak to him in dreams.
> **7**But this is not true of my servant Moses;
>   he is faithful in all my house.
> **8**With him I speak face to face,
>   clearly and not in riddles;
>   he sees the form of the LORD.
> Why then were you not afraid
>   to speak against my servant Moses?"

9The anger of the LORD burned against them, and he left them.

10When the cloud lifted from above the Tent, there stood Miriam—leprous,^a like snow. Aaron turned toward her and saw that she had leprosy^D; **11**and he said to Moses, "Please, my lord, do not hold against us the sin we have so foolishly committed. **12**Do not let her be like a stillborn infant coming from its mother's womb with its flesh half eaten away."

13So Moses cried out to the LORD, "O God, please heal her!"

14The LORD replied to Moses, "If her father had spit in her face, would she not have been in disgrace for seven days? Confine her outside the camp for seven days; after that she can be brought back." **15**So Miriam was confined outside the camp for seven days, and the people did not move on till she was brought back.

16After that, the people left Hazeroth and encamped in the Desert of Paran.

Exploring Canaan

13 The LORD said to Moses, **2**"Send some men to explore the land of Canaan, which I am giving to the Israelites. From each ancestral tribe send one of its leaders."

3So at the LORD's command Moses sent them out from the Desert of Paran. All of them were leaders of the Israelites. **4**These are their names:

from the tribe of Reuben, Shammua son of Zaccur;
5from the tribe of Simeon, Shaphat son of Hori;
6from the tribe of Judah, Caleb son of Jephunneh;
7from the tribe of Issachar, Igal son of Joseph;
8from the tribe of Ephraim, Hoshea son of Nun;
9from the tribe of Benjamin, Palti son of Raphu;
10from the tribe of Zebulun, Gaddiel son of Sodi;
11from the tribe of Manasseh (a tribe of Joseph), Gaddi son of Susi;
12from the tribe of Dan, Ammiel son of Gemalli;
13from the tribe of Asher, Sethur son of Michael;
14from the tribe of Naphtali, Nahbi son of Vophsi;
15from the tribe of Gad, Geuel son of Maki.

16These are the names of the men Moses sent to explore

How much did Moses see of God? (12:8)

See Exodus 33:20. Also see *How could Moses speak to the Lord face to face?* (Exodus 33:11).

Why was Miriam singled out for God's displeasure when Aaron was just as guilty? (12:10,15)

Miriam may have instigated the whole affair, so she received the brunt of the punishment. Or God may have spared Aaron because of his role as high priest. Miriam's punishment, however, profoundly impacted Aaron. He certainly didn't survive the ordeal emotionally unscathed. Seeing his sister bear the wrath of God for the sins of them both shook him to the core (12:11–12).

Exploring Canaan (13:2)

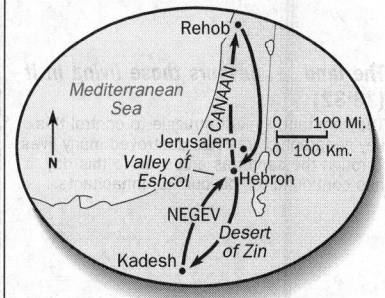

Why did Moses change Hoshea's name? (13:16)

Name changes are often significant in the Bible. See *Why did God give Abram a new name?* (Gen. 17:5).

the land. (Moses gave Hoshea son of Nun the name Joshua.)

¹⁷When Moses sent them to explore Canaan, he said, "Go up through the Negevᴰ and on into the hill country. ¹⁸See what the land is like and whether the people who live there are strong or weak, few or many. ¹⁹What kind of land do they live in? Is it good or bad? What kind of towns do they live in? Are they unwalled or fortified? ²⁰How is the soil? Is it fertile or poor? Are there trees on it or not? Do your best to bring back some of the fruit of the land." (It was the season for the first ripe grapes.)

²¹So they went up and explored the land from the Desert of Zin as far as Rehob, toward Leboᵃ Hamath. ²²They went up through the Negev and came to Hebron, where Ahiman, Sheshai and Talmai, the descendants of Anak, lived. (Hebron had been built seven years before Zoan in Egypt.) ²³When they reached the Valley of Eshcol,ᵇ they cut off a branch bearing a single cluster of grapes. Two of them carried it on a pole between them, along with some pomegranates and figs. ²⁴That place was called the Valley of Eshcol because of the cluster of grapes the Israelites cut off there. ²⁵At the end of forty days they returned from exploring the land.

Report on the Exploration

²⁶They came back to Moses and Aaron and the whole Israelite community at Kadesh in the Desert of Paran. There they reported to them and to the whole assembly and showed them the fruit of the land. ²⁷They gave Moses this account: "We went into the land to which you sent us, and it does flow with milk and honey! Here is its fruit. ²⁸But the people who live there are powerful, and the cities are fortified and very large. We even saw descendants of Anak there. ²⁹The Amalekites live in the Negev; the Hittites, Jebusites and Amorites live in the hill country; and the Canaanites live near the sea and along the Jordan."

³⁰Then Caleb silenced the people before Moses and said, "We should go up and take possession of the land, for we can certainly do it."

What was so alarming about the descendants of Anak? (13:28,33)

The descendants of Anak were exceptionally strong and tall (see Deut. 9:2). The Israelite spies were so afraid that they convinced themselves that the Anakites must have descended from the Nephilim, a race of giants. Hearing the Anakites compared to the Nephilim struck fear in the heart of every Israelite.

³¹But the men who had gone up with him said, "We can't attack those people; they are stronger than we are." ³²And they spread among the Israelites a bad report about the land they had explored. They said, "The land we explored devours those living in it. All the people we saw there are of great size. ³³We saw the Nephilim there (the descendants of Anak come from the Nephilim). We seemed like grasshoppers in our own eyes, and we looked the same to them."

The land . . . devours those living in it (13:32)

The constant, violent struggle to control this key geographic area has destroyed many lives. Through the centuries and even to this day, it has continued to "devour" its inhabitants.

The People Rebel

14 That night all the people of the community raised their voices and wept aloud. ²All the Israelites grumbled against Moses and Aaron, and the whole assembly said to them, "If only we had died in Egypt! Or in this desert! ³Why is the LORD bringing us to this land only to let us fall by the sword? Our wives and children will be taken as plunderᴰ. Wouldn't it be better for us to go back to Egypt?" ⁴And they said to each other, "We should choose a leader and go back to Egypt."

⁵Then Moses and Aaron fell facedown in front of the

ᵃ21 Or *toward the entrance to*   ᵇ23 *Eshcol* means *cluster*; also in verse 24.

whole Israelite assembly gathered there. **6**Joshua son of Nun and Caleb son of Jephunneh, who were among those who had explored the land, tore their clothes **7**and said to the entire Israelite assembly, "The land we passed through and explored is exceedingly good. **8**If the LORD is pleased with us, he will lead us into that land, a land flowing with milk and honey, and will give it to us. **9**Only do not rebel against the LORD. And do not be afraid of the people of the land, because we will swallow them up. Their protection is gone, but the LORD is with us. Do not be afraid of them."

10But the whole assembly talked about stoning them. Then the glory^D of the LORD appeared at the Tent of Meeting^D to all the Israelites. **11**The LORD said to Moses, "How long will these people treat me with contempt? How long will they refuse to believe in me, in spite of all the miraculous signs I have performed among them? **12**I will strike them down with a plague and destroy them, but I will make you into a nation greater and stronger than they."

13Moses said to the LORD, "Then the Egyptians will hear about it! By your power you brought these people up from among them. **14**And they will tell the inhabitants of this land about it. They have already heard that you, O LORD, are with these people and that you, O LORD, have been seen face to face, that your cloud stays over them, and that you go before them in a pillar of cloud by day and a pillar of fire by night. **15**If you put these people to death^D all at one time, the nations who have heard this report about you will say, **16**'The LORD was not able to bring these people into the land he promised them on oath; so he slaughtered them in the desert.'

17"Now may the Lord's strength be displayed, just as you have declared: **18**'The LORD is slow to anger, abounding in love and forgiving sin and rebellion. Yet he does not leave the guilty unpunished; he punishes the children for the sin of the fathers to the third and fourth generation.' **19**In accordance with your great love, forgive the sin of these people, just as you have pardoned them from the time they left Egypt until now."

20The LORD replied, "I have forgiven them, as you asked. **21**Nevertheless, as surely as I live and as surely as the glory of the LORD fills the whole earth, **22**not one of the men who saw my glory and the miraculous signs I performed in Egypt and in the desert but who disobeyed me and tested me ten times— **23**not one of them will ever see the land I promised on oath to their forefathers. No one who has treated me with contempt will ever see it. **24**But because my servant Caleb has a different spirit and follows me wholeheartedly, I will bring him into the land he went to, and his descendants will inherit it. **25**Since the Amalekites and Canaanites are living in the valleys, turn back tomorrow and set out toward the desert along the route to the Red Sea.^a"

26The LORD said to Moses and Aaron: **27**"How long will this wicked community grumble against me? I have heard the complaints of these grumbling Israelites. **28**So tell them, 'As surely as I live, declares the LORD, I will do to you the very things I heard you say: **29**In this desert your bodies will fall—every one of you twenty years old or more who was counted in the census and who has grumbled against me. **30**Not one of you will enter the land I

Tore their clothes (14:6)

For more about mourning customs, see *What did the Israelites do during a 30-day mourning period?* (Deut. 34:8); *Where did the custom of ashes and torn clothing come from?* (2 Samuel 13:19) and *Why shave beards, tear clothes and cut skin?* (Jer. 41:5).

Why would God be concerned about what the Egyptians think of him? (14:13–16)

Even in the Old Testament, God wanted the non-Israelite nations to come to him. In this case, the recent lessons the plagues had taught the Egyptians about God's power were jeopardized. Moses felt that the Egyptians might have dismissed the plagues as coincidence if they learned the Israelites had died in the desert. He wanted God to show how much greater he was than the worthless gods of the Egyptians. Also see *Why did Moses care that Israel be distinct from other nations?* (Exodus 33:16).

If God forgave them, why did the people have to die? (14:20–35)

God's forgiveness does not always remove the consequences of sin. Forgiveness here involved the restoration of God's relationship with the Israelites. Though they were reaffirmed spiritually, however, they still had to pay for their offense. Justice required that they be kept out of the promised land, so they were sentenced to die in the desert. God showed a measure of grace by not eliminating the entire race.

^a25 Hebrew *Yam Suph*; that is, Sea of Reeds

swore with uplifted hand to make your home, except Caleb son of Jephunneh and Joshua son of Nun. ³¹As for your children that you said would be taken as plunder^D, I will bring them in to enjoy the land you have rejected. ³²But you—your bodies will fall in this desert. ³³Your children will be shepherds here for forty years, suffering for your unfaithfulness, until the last of your bodies lies in the desert. ³⁴For forty years—one year for each of the forty days you explored the land—you will suffer for your sins and know what it is like to have me against you.' ³⁵I, the LORD, have spoken, and I will surely do these things to this whole wicked community, which has banded together against me. They will meet their end in this desert; here they will die."

³⁶So the men Moses had sent to explore the land, who returned and made the whole community grumble against him by spreading a bad report about it— ³⁷these men responsible for spreading the bad report about the land were struck down and died of a plague before the LORD. ³⁸Of the men who went to explore the land, only Joshua son of Nun and Caleb son of Jephunneh survived.

³⁹When Moses reported this to all the Israelites, they mourned bitterly. ⁴⁰Early the next morning they went up toward the high hill country. "We have sinned," they said. "We will go up to the place the LORD promised."

⁴¹But Moses said, "Why are you disobeying the LORD's command? This will not succeed! ⁴²Do not go up, because the LORD is not with you. You will be defeated by your enemies, ⁴³for the Amalekites and Canaanites will face you there. Because you have turned away from the LORD, he will not be with you and you will fall by the sword."

⁴⁴Nevertheless, in their presumption they went up toward the high hill country, though neither Moses nor the ark of the LORD's covenant^D moved from the camp.

Why was their late obedience actually disobedience? (14:40–41)

Because they refused to listen to the Lord and to take him seriously. God had rescinded his offer of help, but the people stubbornly pressed ahead with their own plans—though they lacked Moses' support and God's presence. Perhaps they hoped God would change his mind and agree to help them once again. Their old sin of unbelieving despair was replaced by a new sin of presumptuous self-confidence.

Does God punish children for their parents' sins? (14:18)

God punishes people for their own, personal sin. Nowhere in the Bible do righteous believers pay eternally for their parents' sins. In no uncertain terms, God states that a son who acts righteously, even though he has a sinful father, will not die for his father's sin (Ezek. 18:14–20). The law states, *Fathers shall not be put to death for their children, nor children put to death for their fathers; each is to die for his own sin* (Deut. 24:16).

This is not to say, however, that nothing is passed on through the family tree. Sinful patterns of behavior are often passed on to family members. An environment of alcoholism, sexual abuse or violence, for example, can scar children for life. But the children will answer to God for their own lives, not for those of their parents.

There are instances in the Bible where children experience the tragic consequences of their parents' sins. David's affair with Bathsheba, for example, resulted in the death of the son from that union (see 2 Samuel 12:14,18). Today "crack babies" suffer for their mothers' behavior. Until the addictive cycle is broken, generation after generation will be trapped by sin.

The good news of the gospel is that the cycle can be broken. Hezekiah, the son of the wicked King Ahaz, broke the cycle when he turned to God. So did Josiah, the son of the tyrant Amon. When children break the pattern set by sinful parents, they can receive God's blessing. The gospel of Jesus Christ offers power to break sin's grip on families. Also see article: *Why does God allow innocent children to suffer?* (Lam. 2:11–12).

⁴⁵Then the Amalekites and Canaanites who lived in that hill country came down and attacked them and beat them down all the way to Hormah.

Supplementary Offerings

15 The LORD said to Moses, ²"Speak to the Israelites and say to them: 'After you enter the land I am giving you as a home ³and you present to the LORD offerings made by fire, from the herd or the flock, as an aroma pleasing to the LORD—whether burnt offerings^D or sacrifices^D, for special vows^D or freewill offerings or festival offerings— ⁴then the one who brings his offering shall present to the LORD a grain offering^D of a tenth of an ephah^a of fine flour mixed with a quarter of a hin^b of oil. ⁵With each lamb for the burnt offering or the sacrifice, prepare a quarter of a hin of wine as a drink offering.

⁶" 'With a ram prepare a grain offering of two-tenths of an ephah^c of fine flour mixed with a third of a hin^d of oil, ⁷and a third of a hin of wine as a drink offering^D. Offer it as an aroma pleasing to the LORD.

⁸" 'When you prepare a young bull as a burnt offering or sacrifice, for a special vow or a fellowship offering^De to the LORD, ⁹bring with the bull a grain offering of three-tenths of an ephah^f of fine flour mixed with half a hin^g of oil. ¹⁰Also bring half a hin of wine as a drink offering. It will be an offering made by fire, an aroma pleasing to the LORD. ¹¹Each bull or ram, each lamb or young goat, is to be prepared in this manner. ¹²Do this for each one, for as many as you prepare.

¹³" 'Everyone who is native-born must do these things in this way when he brings an offering made by fire as an aroma pleasing to the LORD. ¹⁴For the generations to come, whenever an alien^D or anyone else living among you presents an offering made by fire as an aroma pleasing to the LORD, he must do exactly as you do. ¹⁵The community is to have the same rules for you and for the

---

^a4 That is, probably about 2 quarts (about 2 liters)   ^b4 That is, probably about 1 quart (about 1 liter); also in verse 5   ^c6 That is, probably about 4 quarts (about 4.5 liters)   ^d6 That is, probably about 1 1/4 quarts (about 1.2 liters); also in verse 7   ^e8 Traditionally *peace offering*   ^f9 That is, probably about 6 quarts (about 6.5 liters)   ^g9 That is, probably about 2 quarts (about 2 liters); also in verse 10

How can an aroma be pleasing to God? (15:3)

Most of the offerings are voluntary, sent to God by smoke and fire. The aroma refers to the smoke ascending into the sky. What was pleasing to God was not the odor but the evidence of the obedience of his people. Also see *Why would the aroma be important to God?* (Lev. 1:9).

Drink offering (15:5)

Usually wine or oil given as a sacrifice to honor God and to express thankfulness. Oil was valuable and was often used in Hebrew religious observances. Drink offerings generally were given with burnt offerings or fellowship offerings.

Why offer produce to God? (15:4–5)

In the previous chapter (14:23), God had given some bad news to the people of Israel—no one alive except Caleb and Joshua would see the long-awaited promised land. Yet this chapter begins *After you enter the land I am giving you . . .* , a reassurance that at least the descendants of the existing people would enter the land. Since grain and wine were the produce of Canaan, God, with these instructions for offerings, may be comforting his people: They wouldn't be outlaws forever. His prohibition would be temporary, lasting only one generation.

Another reason may be the deeper significance of sacrifices and offerings. A sacrifice was seen as a substitute for the life of the worshiper. An offering was viewed as a gift to God which spoke of gratitude for his blessings. Together, sacrifices and offerings were means of worshiping God as the giver of life and all its blessings.

alien^D living among you; this is a lasting ordinance for the generations to come. You and the alien shall be the same before the LORD: **16**The same laws and regulations will apply both to you and to the alien living among you.' "

17The LORD said to Moses, **18**"Speak to the Israelites and say to them: 'When you enter the land to which I am taking you **19**and you eat the food of the land, present a portion as an offering to the LORD. **20**Present a cake from the first of your ground meal and present it as an offering from the threshing floor. **21**Throughout the generations to come you are to give this offering to the LORD from the first of your ground meal.

Offerings for Unintentional Sins

22" 'Now if you unintentionally fail to keep any of these commands the LORD gave Moses— **23**any of the LORD's commands to you through him, from the day the LORD gave them and continuing through the generations to come— **24**and if this is done unintentionally without the community being aware of it, then the whole community is to offer a young bull for a burnt offering^D as an aroma pleasing to the LORD, along with its prescribed grain offering^D and drink offering^D, and a male goat for a sin offering^D. **25**The priest^D is to make atonement^D for the whole Israelite community, and they will be forgiven, for it was not intentional and they have brought to the LORD for their wrong an offering made by fire and a sin offering. **26**The whole Israelite community and the aliens living among them will be forgiven, because all the people were involved in the unintentional wrong.

27" 'But if just one person sins unintentionally, he must bring a year-old female goat for a sin offering. **28**The priest is to make atonement before the LORD for the one who erred by sinning unintentionally, and when atonement has been made for him, he will be forgiven. **29**One and the same law applies to everyone who sins unintentionally, whether he is a native-born Israelite or an alien.

30" 'But anyone who sins defiantly, whether native-born or alien, blasphemes the LORD, and that person must be cut off from his people. **31**Because he has despised the LORD's word and broken his commands, that person must surely be cut off; his guilt remains on him.' "

The Sabbath-Breaker Put to Death

32While the Israelites were in the desert, a man was found gathering wood on the Sabbath^D day. **33**Those who found him gathering wood brought him to Moses and Aaron and the whole assembly, **34**and they kept him in custody, because it was not clear what should be done to him. **35**Then the LORD said to Moses, "The man must die. The whole assembly must stone him outside the camp." **36**So the assembly took him outside the camp and stoned him to death, as the LORD commanded Moses.

Tassels on Garments

37The LORD said to Moses, **38**"Speak to the Israelites and say to them: 'Throughout the generations to come you are to make tassels on the corners of your garments, with a blue cord on each tassel. **39**You will have these tassels to look at and so you will remember all the commands of the LORD, that you may obey them and not prostitute yourselves by going after the lusts of your own hearts and

---

Why hold someone responsible for an unintentional sin? (15:22–29)
The original word for *unintentionally* meant *wandering away*—as a sheep might wander from the flock. It implied sin that stemmed from the weakness of human character rather than outright rebellion or premeditated evil. We connect guilt with intention, but the ancients connected it with effects.

Sins defiantly (15:30)
The meaning is picturesque: the word literally means to sin *with a high hand,* as though raising a clenched fist in defiance to God. This was a blatant disregard for God's commands. See Heb. 10:26.

Why the death penalty for this offense? (15:32–36)
God's rules were not ambiguous. In Exodus 31:12–17 and 35:1–3, God clearly spelled out to Israel the penalty for breaking the Sabbath: death. This was an intentional assault on God's law. The stoning would dramatically illustrate to the people that God meant business. Those who sinned *defiantly* would pay with their lives.

How would clothing tassels promote obedience? (15:38–40)
The dangling tassels, which all Jews wore in plain view, constantly reminded them of God's stringent demands, bringing to mind his holiness and commandments. The blue thread most likely represented royalty, a color-coded reminder of their divine pedigree.

eyes. **40**Then you will remember to obey all my commands and will be consecrated[D] to your God. **41**I am the LORD your God, who brought you out of Egypt to be your God. I am the LORD your God.' "

Korah, Dathan and Abiram

16 Korah son of Izhar, the son of Kohath, the son of Levi, and certain Reubenites—Dathan and Abiram, sons of Eliab, and On son of Peleth—became insolent[a] **2**and rose up against Moses. With them were 250 Israelite men, well-known community leaders who had been appointed members of the council. **3**They came as a group to oppose Moses and Aaron and said to them, "You have gone too far! The whole community is holy, every one of them, and the LORD is with them. Why then do you set yourselves above the LORD's assembly?"

4When Moses heard this, he fell facedown. **5**Then he said to Korah and all his followers: "In the morning the LORD will show who belongs to him and who is holy, and he will have that person come near him. The man he chooses he will cause to come near him. **6**You, Korah, and all your followers are to do this: Take censers[D] **7**and tomorrow put fire and incense[D] in them before the LORD. The man the LORD chooses will be the one who is holy. You Levites[D] have gone too far!"

8Moses also said to Korah, "Now listen, you Levites! **9**Isn't it enough for you that the God of Israel has separated you from the rest of the Israelite community and brought you near himself to do the work at the LORD's tabernacle[D] and to stand before the community and minister to them? **10**He has brought you and all your fellow Levites near himself, but now you are trying to get the priesthood too. **11**It is against the LORD that you and all your followers have banded together. Who is Aaron that you should grumble against him?"

12Then Moses summoned Dathan and Abiram, the sons of Eliab. But they said, "We will not come! **13**Isn't it enough that you have brought us up out of a land flowing with milk and honey to kill us in the desert? And now you also want to lord it over us? **14**Moreover, you haven't brought us into a land flowing with milk and honey or given us an inheritance of fields and vineyards. Will you gouge out the eyes of[b] these men? No, we will not come!"

15Then Moses became very angry and said to the LORD, "Do not accept their offering. I have not taken so much as a donkey from them, nor have I wronged any of them."

16Moses said to Korah, "You and all your followers are to appear before the LORD tomorrow—you and they and Aaron. **17**Each man is to take his censer and put incense in it—250 censers in all—and present it before the LORD. You and Aaron are to present your censers also." **18**So each man took his censer, put fire and incense in it, and stood with Moses and Aaron at the entrance to the Tent of Meeting[D]. **19**When Korah had gathered all his followers in opposition to them at the entrance to the Tent of Meeting, the glory of the LORD appeared to the entire assembly. **20**The LORD said to Moses and Aaron, **21**"Separate yourselves from this assembly so I can put an end to them at once."

22But Moses and Aaron fell facedown and cried out, "O

---

a 1 Or *Peleth—took ⌐men⌐*   *b 14* Or *you make slaves of; or you deceive*

What did Korah and the others accuse Moses and Aaron of doing? (16:3)

Korah was jealous of Moses' and Aaron's leadership. Korah and the other revolutionaries—Dathan, Abiram and On—charged that Aaron and Moses had abused their spiritual leadership. Since all of God's people are holy, they reasoned, Moses and Aaron didn't have any special authority to lead Israel (v. 3). Korah came from the priestly tribe of Levi, the family of Kohath, who, among other things, transported the most sacred objects, such as the ark. His family ranked just below the priests (4:1–20). That wasn't good enough, however, for Korah who wanted more prestige for himself.

Why would many be destroyed for the sins of a few? (16:21–22)

Korah's followers included 250 well-known community leaders who had been appointed members of the council. These leaders may have represented the views of a large number of the people. The cancer needed to be cut out before it infected the entire nation of Israel.

God, God of the spirits of all mankind, will you be angry with the entire assembly when only one man sins?"

²³Then the LORD said to Moses, ²⁴"Say to the assembly, 'Move away from the tents of Korah, Dathan and Abiram.' "

²⁵Moses got up and went to Dathan and Abiram, and the elders of Israel followed him. ²⁶He warned the assembly, "Move back from the tents of these wicked men! Do not touch anything belonging to them, or you will be swept away because of all their sins." ²⁷So they moved away from the tents of Korah, Dathan and Abiram. Dathan and Abiram had come out and were standing with their wives, children and little ones at the entrances to their tents.

²⁸Then Moses said, "This is how you will know that the LORD has sent me to do all these things and that it was not my idea: ²⁹If these men die a natural death^D and experience only what usually happens to men, then the LORD has not sent me. ³⁰But if the LORD brings about something totally new, and the earth opens its mouth and swallows them, with everything that belongs to them, and they go down alive into the grave,^a then you will know that these men have treated the LORD with contempt."

³¹As soon as he finished saying all this, the ground under them split apart ³²and the earth opened its mouth and swallowed them, with their households and all Korah's men and all their possessions. ³³They went down alive into the grave, with everything they owned; the earth closed over them, and they perished and were gone from the community. ³⁴At their cries, all the Israelites around them fled, shouting, "The earth is going to swallow us too!"

³⁵And fire came out from the LORD and consumed the 250 men who were offering the incense^D.

³⁶The LORD said to Moses, ³⁷"Tell Eleazar son of Aaron, the priest^D, to take the censers^D out of the smoldering remains and scatter the coals some distance away, for the censers are holy— ³⁸the censers of the men who sinned at the cost of their lives. Hammer the censers into sheets to overlay the altar, for they were presented before the LORD and have become holy. Let them be a sign to the Israelites."

³⁹So Eleazar the priest collected the bronze censers brought by those who had been burned up, and he had them hammered out to overlay the altar, ⁴⁰as the LORD directed him through Moses. This was to remind the Israelites that no one except a descendant of Aaron should come to burn incense before the LORD, or he would become like Korah and his followers.

⁴¹The next day the whole Israelite community grumbled against Moses and Aaron. "You have killed the LORD's people," they said.

⁴²But when the assembly gathered in opposition to Moses and Aaron and turned toward the Tent of Meeting^D, suddenly the cloud covered it and the glory^D of the LORD appeared. ⁴³Then Moses and Aaron went to the front of the Tent of Meeting, ⁴⁴and the LORD said to Moses, ⁴⁵"Get away from this assembly so I can put an end to them at once." And they fell facedown.

⁴⁶Then Moses said to Aaron, "Take your censer and put incense in it, along with fire from the altar, and hurry to the assembly to make atonement^D for them. Wrath

Why would Israel grumble after the events of the preceding day? (16:41)
Their grumbling, despite God's terrible judgment, illustrates how embedded the rebellion had become. Korah's venom had poisoned the community. Their accusation, You (Moses and Aaron) have killed the LORD's people, reveals the community's blindness to God's role in the judgment, vividly demonstrating their deep-rooted sinfulness.

Was God serious in his threat to destroy his chosen people? (16:45)
God was not bullying his people into obedience or playing games. His holiness required punishment for sin. Earlier, when Israel had made a golden calf for an idol, God had also threatened to destroy them (Exodus 32:9–10). But Moses had pled with God on behalf of Israel, and God had granted a reprieve. Here again, Moses interceded for the people and in both cases he illustrated the future work of Jesus Christ, the ultimate mediator between God and man (1 Tim. 2:5).

How did burning incense atone for the sins of the people? (16:46)
Incense was a part of the atonement process spelled out in Leviticus 16:12–13. Because of his holiness, God set up this means of appeasing his wrath whenever Israel sinned. And only Aaron the high priest, or one of his descendants, could offer incense to the Lord.

^a30 Hebrew Sheol; also in verse 33

has come out from the LORD; the plague has started." **47**So Aaron did as Moses said, and ran into the midst of the assembly. The plague had already started among the people, but Aaron offered the incense**D** and made atonement**D** for them. **48**He stood between the living and the dead, and the plague stopped. **49**But 14,700 people died from the plague, in addition to those who had died because of Korah. **50**Then Aaron returned to Moses at the entrance to the Tent of Meeting**D**, for the plague had stopped.

The Budding of Aaron's Staff

17 The LORD said to Moses, **2**"Speak to the Israelites and get twelve staffs from them, one from the leader of each of their ancestral tribes. Write the name of each man on his staff. **3**On the staff of Levi write Aaron's name, for there must be one staff for the head of each ancestral tribe. **4**Place them in the Tent of Meeting in front of the Testimony, where I meet with you. **5**The staff belonging to the man I choose will sprout, and I will rid myself of this constant grumbling against you by the Israelites."

6So Moses spoke to the Israelites, and their leaders gave him twelve staffs, one for the leader of each of their ancestral tribes, and Aaron's staff was among them. **7**Moses placed the staffs before the LORD in the Tent of the Testimony.

8The next day Moses entered the Tent of the Testimony and saw that Aaron's staff, which represented the house of Levi, had not only sprouted but had budded, blossomed and produced almonds. **9**Then Moses brought out all the staffs from the LORD's presence to all the Israelites. They looked at them, and each man took his own staff.

10The LORD said to Moses, "Put back Aaron's staff in front of the Testimony, to be kept as a sign to the rebellious. This will put an end to their grumbling against me, so that they will not die." **11**Moses did just as the LORD commanded him.

12The Israelites said to Moses, "We will die! We are lost, we are all lost! **13**Anyone who even comes near the tabernacle**D** of the LORD will die. Are we all going to die?"

Duties of Priests and Levites

18 The LORD said to Aaron, "You, your sons and your father's family are to bear the responsibility for offenses against the sanctuary, and you and your sons alone are to bear the responsibility for offenses against the priesthood. **2**Bring your fellow Levites**D** from your ancestral tribe to join you and assist you when you and your sons minister before the Tent of the Testimony. **3**They are to be responsible to you and are to perform all the duties of the Tent, but they must not go near the furnishings of the sanctuary or the altar, or both they and you will die. **4**They are to join you and be responsible for the care of the Tent of Meeting—all the work at the Tent—and no one else may come near where you are.

5"You are to be responsible for the care of the sanctuary and the altar, so that wrath will not fall on the Israelites again. **6**I myself have selected your fellow Levites from among the Israelites as a gift to you, dedicated to the LORD to do the work at the Tent of Meeting. **7**But only you and your sons may serve as priests**D** in connection with everything at the altar and inside the curtain. I am giving you the service of the priesthood as a gift. Anyone

Why was a sprouting staff more convincing than fire and plague? (17:5)
Here we see God's loving heart for his people. His previous signs to Israel, precipitated by their rebellion, were meant to crush the uprisings. The budding of Aaron's staff, however, was meant to keep them from sin and its consequences. God (not the people) initiated the test. It pledged God's commitment to his people.

What made the Israelites suddenly afraid? (17:12)
They realized that God, not Moses or Aaron, was the author of the disaster. Numbed, they came to grips with their fatal error. See Num. 16:3,41.

Is this raw fear a healthy attitude toward God? (17:12)
Israel's sin was no small miscue in worship. Theirs was an all-out rebellion against God's holiness. Because of that, they came face to face with the awful wrath of God. When one grasps the utter holiness of God, a reverent fear is the proper response. God is love, but God is also holy. He rightly demands our allegiance and obedience.

Why would the priests die for the Levites' misdeeds? (18:3)
The priests had been ordered to guard the Tent of Meeting and the altar. This kept unauthorized people from crossing the barrier and drawing God's wrath on the entire people. If a priest, through laziness or neglect, allowed a Levite to work in these holy places, the priest and Levite were equally guilty. Both would incur God's judgment.

How was the priesthood a *gift*? (18:7)
The priesthood was God's way of ending the vicious cycle of sin, punishment and death that entrapped Israel. Without the gift of the priesthood to mediate between God's holiness and Israel's failings. God's people would have been destroyed by God's anger. But the priesthood was also a gift for the priests, given the honor and privilege of serving God and having a special relationship with him.

else who comes near the sanctuary must be put to death D."

Offerings for Priests and Levites

8Then the LORD said to Aaron, "I myself have put you in charge of the offerings presented to me; all the holy offerings the Israelites give me I give to you and your sons as your portion and regular share. **9**You are to have the part of the most holy offerings that is kept from the fire. From all the gifts they bring me as most holy offerings, whether grain or sin or guilt offerings D, that part belongs to you and your sons. **10**Eat it as something most holy; every male shall eat it. You must regard it as holy.

11"This also is yours: whatever is set aside from the gifts of all the wave offerings D of the Israelites. I give this to you and your sons and daughters as your regular share. Everyone in your household who is ceremonially clean may eat it.

12"I give you all the finest olive oil and all the finest new wine D and grain they give the LORD as the firstfruits D of their harvest. **13**All the land's firstfruits that they bring to the LORD will be yours. Everyone in your household who is ceremonially clean may eat it.

14"Everything in Israel that is devoted*a* to the LORD is yours. **15**The first offspring of every womb, both man and animal, that is offered to the LORD is yours. But you must redeem D every firstborn D son and every firstborn male of unclean D animals. **16**When they are a month old, you must redeem them at the redemption price set at five shekels D*b* of silver, according to the sanctuary shekel D, which weighs twenty gerahs.

17"But you must not redeem the firstborn of an ox, a sheep or a goat; they are holy. Sprinkle their blood on the altar and burn their fat as an offering made by fire, an aroma pleasing to the LORD. **18**Their meat is to be yours, just as the breast of the wave offering and the right thigh are yours. **19**Whatever is set aside from the holy offerings the Israelites present to the LORD I give to you and your sons and daughters as your regular share. It is an everlasting covenant D of salt before the LORD for both you and your offspring."

20The LORD said to Aaron, "You will have no inheritance in their land, nor will you have any share among them; I am your share and your inheritance among the Israelites.

21"I give to the Levites D all the tithes in Israel as their inheritance in return for the work they do while serving at the Tent of Meeting D. **22**From now on the Israelites must not go near the Tent of Meeting, or they will bear the consequences of their sin and will die. **23**It is the Levites who are to do the work at the Tent of Meeting and bear the responsibility for offenses against it. This is a lasting ordinance for the generations to come. They will receive no inheritance among the Israelites. **24**Instead, I give to the Levites as their inheritance the tithes that the Israelites present as an offering to the LORD. That is why I said concerning them: 'They will have no inheritance among the Israelites.'"

25The LORD said to Moses, **26**"Speak to the Levites and say to them: 'When you receive from the Israelites the tithe I give you as your inheritance, you must present a tenth of that tithe as the LORD's offering. **27**Your offering

Why did God give the people's offerings to the Levites? (18:8)

The Levites were employed by God to perform duties of the clergy. They provided a service necessary for the well-being of Israel. Since God did not give them any portion of the land as an inheritance (18:20), they had limited means of support. Instead God gave them portions from the offerings so they could support their families.

Why could only males eat the most holy offerings? (18:10)

The most holy offerings were the grain, sin and guilt offerings. According to Leviticus 6:16–18,26 and 7:6–7, these offerings could not leave the courtyard of the Tent of Meeting. Since only males were permitted in that area, they alone could eat these most holy offerings.

Everlasting covenant of salt (18:19)

God had instructed the Israelites to salt all of their offerings (Lev. 2:13). He also told them to include salt in their holy incense (Exodus 30:34–38). But its significance is unclear. The phrase *covenant of salt* may refer to the indestructible nature of the pact.

Why weren't Aaron and the Levites permitted to own any land? (18:20,23)

Landowners would need to cultivate or at least supervise the care of the land. Aaron and the other Levites were to devote all of their energy to serving in and around the Tent of Meeting. In addition, their lack of land made them dependent on the people—and on God. If they failed to lead the people in worship, they would lose their means of livelihood. While the Levites did not own a section of tribal land, God did give them towns scattered throughout the territory. See 35:1–8; Joshua 21.

---

a14 The Hebrew term refers to the irrevocable giving over of things or persons to the LORD.   *b16* That is, about 2 ounces (about 55 grams)

will be reckoned to you as grain from the threshing floor or juice from the winepress^D. **28**In this way you also will present an offering to the LORD from all the tithes^D you receive from the Israelites. From these tithes you must give the LORD's portion to Aaron the priest^D. **29**You must present as the LORD's portion the best and holiest part of everything given to you.'

30"Say to the Levites^D: 'When you present the best part, it will be reckoned to you as the product of the threshing floor or the winepress. **31**You and your households may eat the rest of it anywhere, for it is your wages for your work at the Tent of Meeting^D. **32**By presenting the best part of it you will not be guilty in this matter; then you will not defile the holy offerings of the Israelites, and you will not die.' "

The Water of Cleansing

19 The LORD said to Moses and Aaron: **2**"This is a requirement of the law that the LORD has commanded: Tell the Israelites to bring you a red heifer without defect or blemish and that has never been under a yoke^D. **3**Give it to Eleazar the priest; it is to be taken outside the camp and slaughtered in his presence. **4**Then Eleazar the priest is to take some of its blood on his finger and sprinkle it seven times toward the front of the Tent of Meeting. **5**While he watches, the heifer is to be burned—its hide, flesh, blood and offal^D. **6**The priest is to take some cedar wood, hyssop^D and scarlet wool and throw them onto the burning heifer. **7**After that, the priest must wash his clothes and bathe himself with water. He may then come into the camp, but he will be ceremonially unclean^D till evening. **8**The man who burns it must also wash his clothes and bathe with water, and he too will be unclean till evening.

9"A man who is clean shall gather up the ashes of the heifer and put them in a ceremonially clean place outside the camp. They shall be kept by the Israelite community for use in the water of cleansing; it is for purification from sin. **10**The man who gathers up the ashes of the heifer must also wash his clothes, and he too will be unclean till evening. This will be a lasting ordinance both for the Israelites and for the aliens^D living among them.

11"Whoever touches the dead body of anyone will be unclean for seven days. **12**He must purify himself with the water on the third day and on the seventh day; then he will be clean. But if he does not purify himself on the third and seventh days, he will not be clean. **13**Whoever touches the dead body of anyone and fails to purify himself defiles the LORD's tabernacle^D. That person must be cut off from Israel. Because the water of cleansing has not been sprinkled on him, he is unclean; his uncleanness^D remains on him.

14"This is the law that applies when a person dies in a tent: Anyone who enters the tent and anyone who is in it will be unclean for seven days, **15**and every open container without a lid fastened on it will be unclean.

16"Anyone out in the open who touches someone who has been killed with a sword or someone who has died a natural death^D, or anyone who touches a human bone or a grave, will be unclean for seven days.

17"For the unclean person, put some ashes from the burned purification offering into a jar and pour fresh water over them. **18**Then a man who is ceremonially clean is to take some hyssop, dip it in the water and sprinkle the

How did the Levites provide for necessities such as housing and clothing? (18:31)

Not all of the tithes were food offerings. Unclean animals and firstborn children, of course, could not be sacrificed. By paying money, the Israelite families could *redeem* them. Those living too far to transport animals and produce, for example, used cash, bringing the money to the Tent of Meeting. There it was converted into offerings. The Levites may have been free to keep some of these tithes (Deut. 14:22–29).

Why slaughter a red heifer? (19:2–3)

This ritual's purpose was to cleanse someone who had touched a dead body. The red color symbolized blood, which was a Hebrew requisite for cleansing. The sex of the animal—a young female—symbolized the giving of life. The procedure gave life back to the one who had been tainted by death.

Why did touching a dead body make someone unclean? (19:11)

Death and sin were intertwined in the ancient mind. Thousands died during the Korah incident (ch. 16) because of their rebellion against God. The ceremony, then, made provision for any tainting of sin from the bodies. The practice also stemmed the spread of disease. Finally, it allowed time for the surviving family members to grieve.

What made the third and seventh days special? (19:12)

The numbers three and seven appear frequently in Scripture, signifying fullness or completion. See *Why sprinkle blood seven times?* (Lev. 4:5–7).

Why use a dead animal's ashes? (19:17)

The act is not magical but ceremonial—it expresses a deep truth about the need for purification. It could be likened to the Lord's Supper, where Christ took common elements like bread and wine and used them to picture what he would accomplish. Here God used the ashes of a dead animal to communicate his truth. See Heb. 9:13–14.

tent and all the furnishings and the people who were there. He must also sprinkle anyone who has touched a human bone or a grave or someone who has been killed or someone who has died a natural death.D. 19The man who is clean is to sprinkle the uncleanD person on the third and seventh days, and on the seventh day he is to purifyD him. The person being cleansed must wash his clothes and bathe with water, and that evening he will be clean. 20But if a person who is unclean does not purify himself, he must be cut off from the community, because he has defiled the sanctuary of the LORD. The water of cleansing has not been sprinkled on him, and he is unclean. 21This is a lasting ordinance for them.

"The man who sprinkles the water of cleansing must also wash his clothes, and anyone who touches the water of cleansing will be unclean till evening. 22Anything that an unclean person touches becomes unclean, and anyone who touches it becomes unclean till evening."

Water From the Rock

20 In the first month the whole Israelite community arrived at the Desert of Zin, and they stayed at Kadesh. There Miriam died and was buried.

2Now there was no water for the community, and the people gathered in opposition to Moses and Aaron. 3They quarreled with Moses and said, "If only we had died when our brothers fell dead before the LORD! 4Why did you bring the LORD's community into this desert, that we and our livestock should die here? 5Why did you bring us up out of Egypt to this terrible place? It has no grain or figs, grapevines or pomegranates. And there is no water to drink!"

6Moses and Aaron went from the assembly to the entrance to the Tent of MeetingD and fell facedown, and the gloryD of the LORD appeared to them. 7The LORD said to Moses, 8"Take the staff, and you and your brother Aaron gather the assembly together. Speak to that rock before their eyes and it will pour out its water. You will bring water out of the rock for the community so they and their livestock can drink."

9So Moses took the staff from the LORD's presence, just as he commanded him. 10He and Aaron gathered the assembly together in front of the rock and Moses said to them, "Listen, you rebels, must we bring you water out of this rock?" 11Then Moses raised his arm and struck the rock twice with his staff. Water gushed out, and the community and their livestock drank.

12But the LORD said to Moses and Aaron, "Because you did not trust in me enough to honor me as holy in the sight of the Israelites, you will not bring this community into the land I give them."

13These were the waters of Meribah,a where the Israelites quarreled with the LORD and where he showed himself holy among them.

Edom Denies Israel Passage

14Moses sent messengers from Kadesh to the king of Edom, saying:

"This is what your brother Israel says: You know about all the hardships that have come upon us. 15Our forefathers went down into Egypt, and we lived

---

How could Israel complain after the display of God's wrath at Korah's rebellion? (20:3–4)
This band of whiners represents a new generation. Comparing 20:22–29 with 33:38 shows that the time of this rebellion was nearly 40 years after Korah's revolt. Their memory of Korah's wicked end was probably long forgotten.

How did the Lord show himself holy at Meribah? (20:12–13)
By judging Moses and Aaron for their sin, even though they were his chosen leaders. There would be no compromise, no favoritism, no exceptions. He also expressed his holiness (and his grace) by providing ample water for his people—this time in spite of their disobedient leaders.

Why did the Israelites call themselves the brother of Edom? (20:14)
Edom, meaning red, is another name for the land where Esau lived. Esau was the twin brother of Jacob, son of Isaac and grandson of Abraham. The Israelites descended from Jacob; the Edomites descended from Esau. The Israelites inherited the promises God had given to Abraham, but the Edomites did not. The brothers spent much of their lifetime in bitter rivalry, partly because of dispute over that difference. Nearly five hundred years later, their descendants still claimed their relationship to each other—but also the rivalry. See also Gen. 25:23–26,29–34 and 27:36–40.

---

a13 *Meribah* means *quarreling.*

there many years. The Egyptians mistreated us and our fathers, **16**but when we cried out to the LORD, he heard our cry and sent an angel and brought us out of Egypt.

"Now we are here at Kadesh, a town on the edge of your territory. **17**Please let us pass through your country. We will not go through any field or vineyard, or drink water from any well. We will travel along the king's highway and not turn to the right or to the left until we have passed through your territory."

18But Edom[D] answered:

"You may not pass through here; if you try, we will march out and attack you with the sword."

19The Israelites replied:

"We will go along the main road, and if we or our livestock drink any of your water, we will pay for it. We only want to pass through on foot—nothing else."

20Again they answered:

"You may not pass through."

Then Edom came out against them with a large and powerful army. **21**Since Edom refused to let them go through their territory, Israel turned away from them.

The Death of Aaron

22The whole Israelite community set out from Kadesh and came to Mount Hor. **23**At Mount Hor, near the border of Edom, the LORD said to Moses and Aaron, **24**"Aaron will be gathered to his people. He will not enter the land I give the Israelites, because both of you rebelled against my command at the waters of Meribah. **25**Get Aaron and his son Eleazar and take them up Mount Hor. **26**Remove

Why did Edom refuse to allow peaceful traveling? (20:20-21)
Moab, a sister nation to Edom, was already at war with Sihon, king of the Amorites, their warring neighbor to the north. In fact, 21:26 reveals that Sihon had already acquired much of the northern sector of Moab. The Edomites were understandably reluctant to let a potential army pass through their land and possibly turn their country into a battlefield against the Amorites.

Gathered to his people (20:24)
This phrase describes the death of a righteous person who died in old age. It also alludes to the Hebrew view of life after death. The Hebrews anticipated reuniting with family members in a mysterious place called Sheol, the place of the dead. David spoke of this reunion when his baby died (2 Samuel 12:23). A thousand years later, Jesus referred to gathered patriarchs, confirming that ancient believers were indeed still alive. See Matt. 22:32.

Why was Moses punished so harshly? (20:12)

It is not entirely clear why one mistake kept Moses out of the promised land, especially since he had spent forty years putting up with the numerous complaints and rebellions of the ungrateful Israelites. Here are several possible explanations.

First, Moses may have been denied permission to enter the promised land because his personal belief wavered. In v. 12, God indicts him because of his lack of trust—*Because you did not trust in me enough . . .*

Or it may have been because he publicly displayed his distrust, acting as though a mere word were not enough for God to provide water. This may have been what God meant in saying that Moses did not honor God *as holy in the sight of the Israelites.*

Some think Moses did not honor God as holy by taking credit himself for providing the water. He said *Must we bring you water out of this rock?* (v. 10). Others suggest it may have been Moses' disobedience of God's precise instructions that kept him out. God had said, *Gather the assembly and speak to the rock* (v. 8). Moses spoke to the people and hit the rock.

Another suggestion is that Moses' anger may have prevented him from entering the promised land. He called the people *rebels* and struck the rock in a fit of temper (Psalm 106:32-33).

Aaron's garments and put them on his son Eleazar, for Aaron will be gathered to his people; he will die there."

27Moses did as the LORD commanded: They went up Mount Hor in the sight of the whole community. **28**Moses removed Aaron's garments and put them on his son Eleazar. And Aaron died there on top of the mountain. Then Moses and Eleazar came down from the mountain, **29**and when the whole community learned that Aaron had died, the entire house of Israel mourned for him thirty days.

Arad Destroyed

21 When the Canaanite king of Arad, who lived in the Negev^D, heard that Israel was coming along the road to Atharim, he attacked the Israelites and captured some of them. **2**Then Israel made this vow^D to the LORD: "If you will deliver these people into our hands, we will totally destroy^a their cities." **3**The LORD listened to Israel's plea and gave the Canaanites over to them. They completely destroyed them and their towns; so the place was named Hormah.^b

The Bronze Snake

4They traveled from Mount Hor along the route to the Red Sea,^c to go around Edom^D. But the people grew impatient on the way; **5**they spoke against God and against Moses, and said, "Why have you brought us up out of Egypt to die in the desert? There is no bread! There is no water! And we detest this miserable food!"

6Then the LORD sent venomous snakes among them; they bit the people and many Israelites died. **7**The people came to Moses and said, "We sinned when we spoke against the LORD and against you. Pray that the LORD will take the snakes away from us." So Moses prayed for the people.

8The LORD said to Moses, "Make a snake and put it up on a pole; anyone who is bitten can look at it and live." **9**So Moses made a bronze snake and put it up on a pole. Then when anyone was bitten by a snake and looked at the bronze snake, he lived.

The Journey to Moab

10The Israelites moved on and camped at Oboth. **11**Then they set out from Oboth and camped in Iye Abarim, in the desert that faces Moab toward the sunrise. **12**From there they moved on and camped in the Zered Valley. **13**They set out from there and camped alongside the Arnon, which is in the desert extending into Amorite territory. The Arnon is the border of Moab, between Moab and the Amorites. **14**That is why the Book of the Wars of the LORD says:

> ". . . Waheb in Suphah^d and the ravines,
>   the Arnon **15**and^e the slopes of the ravines
>   that lead to the site of Ar
>   and lie along the border of Moab."

16From there they continued on to Beer, the well where

Journey to Moab (21:4)

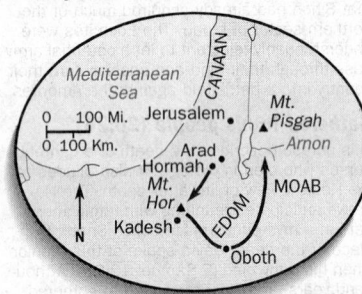

Why was God so strict about complaining? (21:5–6)

The people's complaining was symptomatic of a much deeper problem: distrust of God. Their verbal barrage assaulted God's character. Israel refused to take God at his word.

Why use a symbol of death to bring healing? (21:8)

Perhaps God used a serpent, considered to be a source of death, to drive home a lesson on trust. To judge their sin, God sent venomous snakes to kill the Israelites (v. 6). The people repented, but now they had to trust God's remedy—a brass snake—for healing. Facing death, they found new life. See John 3:14–15.

Book of the Wars of the LORD (21:14)

This book is only mentioned here in the Bible; it is one of seven books mentioned in the Old Testament but not included in the Bible. Most likely it was a collection of war songs. Initially, the songs may have been orally passed from generation to generation but then written down for the sake of preservation.

---

^a2 The Hebrew term refers to the irrevocable giving over of things or persons to the LORD, often by totally destroying them; also in verse 3.   ^b3 *Hormah* means *destruction*.   ^c4 Hebrew *Yam Suph*; that is, Sea of Reeds   ^d14 The meaning of the Hebrew for this phrase is uncertain.   ^e14,15 Or *"I have been given from Suphah and the ravines / of the Arnon* ^15*to*

the LORD said to Moses, "Gather the people together and I will give them water."

¹⁷Then Israel sang this song:

> "Spring up, O well!
>   Sing about it,
> ¹⁸about the well that the princes dug,
>   that the nobles of the people sank—
>   the nobles with scepters^D and staffs."

Then they went from the desert to Mattanah, ¹⁹from Mattanah to Nahaliel, from Nahaliel to Bamoth, ²⁰and from Bamoth to the valley in Moab where the top of Pisgah overlooks the wasteland.

Defeat of Sihon and Og

²¹Israel sent messengers to say to Sihon king of the Amorites:

²²"Let us pass through your country. We will not turn aside into any field or vineyard, or drink water from any well. We will travel along the king's highway until we have passed through your territory."

²³But Sihon would not let Israel pass through his territory. He mustered his entire army and marched out into the desert against Israel. When he reached Jahaz, he fought with Israel. ²⁴Israel, however, put him to the sword and took over his land from the Arnon to the Jabbok, but only as far as the Ammonites, because their border was fortified. ²⁵Israel captured all the cities of the Amorites and occupied them, including Heshbon and all its surrounding settlements. ²⁶Heshbon was the city of Sihon king of the Amorites, who had fought against the former king of Moab and had taken from him all his land as far as the Arnon.

²⁷That is why the poets say:

> "Come to Heshbon and let it be rebuilt;
>   let Sihon's city be restored.
>
> ²⁸"Fire went out from Heshbon,
>   a blaze from the city of Sihon.
> It consumed Ar of Moab,
>   the citizens of Arnon's heights.
> ²⁹Woe to you, O Moab!
>   You are destroyed, O people of Chemosh!
> He has given up his sons as fugitives
>   and his daughters as captives
> to Sihon king of the Amorites.
>
> ³⁰"But we have overthrown them;
>   Heshbon is destroyed all the way to Dibon.
> We have demolished them as far as Nophah,
>   which extends to Medeba."

³¹So Israel settled in the land of the Amorites.
³²After Moses had sent spies to Jazer, the Israelites captured its surrounding settlements and drove out the Amorites who were there. ³³Then they turned and went up along the road toward Bashan, and Og king of Bashan and his whole army marched out to meet them in battle at Edrei.

³⁴The LORD said to Moses, "Do not be afraid of him, for I have handed him over to you, with his whole army and his land. Do to him what you did to Sihon king of the Amorites, who reigned in Heshbon."

³⁵So they struck him down, together with his sons and

SCRIPTURE LINK (21:22)
Israel had requested similar passage from Edom (20:17).

Defeat of Sihon and Og (21:23)

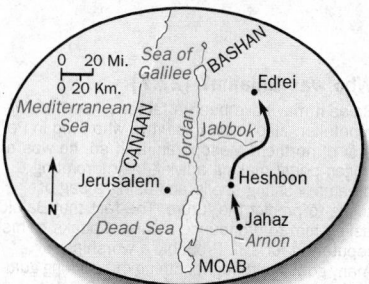

Why sing the enemy's song? (21:27–29)
Victorious Amorites used to taunt their victims by singing this song. The victorious Israelites returned the favor, using this Amorite song to taunt the Amorites. The Israelites then personalized it by adding their own ending (v. 30).

his whole army, leaving them no survivors. And they took possession of his land.

Balak Summons Balaam

22 Then the Israelites traveled to the plains of Moab and camped along the Jordan across from Jericho[D].[a]

[2] Now Balak son of Zippor saw all that Israel had done to the Amorites, [3] and Moab was terrified because there were so many people. Indeed, Moab was filled with dread because of the Israelites.

[4] The Moabites said to the elders of Midian, "This horde is going to lick up everything around us, as an ox licks up the grass of the field."

So Balak son of Zippor, who was king of Moab at that time, [5] sent messengers to summon Balaam son of Beor, who was at Pethor, near the River,[b] in his native land. Balak said:

"A people has come out of Egypt; they cover the face of the land and have settled next to me. [6] Now come and put a curse on these people, because they are too powerful for me. Perhaps then I will be able to defeat them and drive them out of the country. For I know that those you bless are blessed, and those you curse are cursed."

[7] The elders of Moab and Midian left, taking with them the fee for divination[D]. When they came to Balaam, they told him what Balak had said.

[8] "Spend the night here," Balaam said to them, "and I will bring you back the answer the LORD gives me." So the Moabite princes stayed with him.

[9] God came to Balaam and asked, "Who are these men with you?"

[10] Balaam said to God, "Balak son of Zippor, king of Moab, sent me this message: [11] 'A people that has come out of Egypt covers the face of the land. Now come and put a curse on them for me. Perhaps then I will be able to fight them and drive them away.'"

[12] But God said to Balaam, "Do not go with them. You must not put a curse on those people, because they are blessed."

[13] The next morning Balaam got up and said to Balak's princes, "Go back to your own country, for the LORD has refused to let me go with you."

[14] So the Moabite princes returned to Balak and said, "Balaam refused to come with us."

[15] Then Balak sent other princes, more numerous and more distinguished than the first. [16] They came to Balaam and said:

"This is what Balak son of Zippor says: Do not let anything keep you from coming to me, [17] because I will reward you handsomely and do whatever you say. Come and put a curse on these people for me."

[18] But Balaam answered them, "Even if Balak gave me his palace filled with silver and gold, I could not do anything great or small to go beyond the command of the LORD my God. [19] Now stay here tonight as the others did, and I will find out what else the LORD will tell me."

[20] That night God came to Balaam and said, "Since these

Who was Balaam? (22:7)

Balaam may have been a famous Assyrian fortuneteller, also known as Pitru, who lived in Pethor of northern Mesopotamia. If so, he was a pagan priest making a living by interpreting dreams, casting spells and using a bag of tricks to predict the future. The fact that Balak asked him to pronounce a curse speaks of his reputation for evil. Probably a worshiper of many gods, he thought nothing of soliciting guidance from Israel's God (v. 8). See 2 Peter 2:15–16; Jude 11; Rev. 2:14.

Why would a pagan priest call the Lord "his God"? (22:18)

Balaam's greed and treachery proved that his loyalty was to himself—not to Israel or Israel's God (31:15–16). He may have invoked the name of God in a misguided attempt to steal God's power away from Israel for himself. Or he may have thought to add Israel's God to his personal arsenal of deities—one more source of supernatural power.

---

[a] 1 Hebrew *Jordan of Jericho*; possibly an ancient name for the Jordan River   [b] 5 That is, the Euphrates

men have come to summon you, go with them, but do only what I tell you."

Balaam's Donkey

²¹Balaam got up in the morning, saddled his donkey and went with the princes of Moab. ²²But God was very angry when he went, and the angel of the LORD stood in the road to oppose him. Balaam was riding on his donkey, and his two servants were with him. ²³When the donkey saw the angel of the LORD standing in the road with a drawn sword in his hand, she turned off the road into a field. Balaam beat her to get her back on the road.

²⁴Then the angel of the LORD stood in a narrow path between two vineyards, with walls on both sides. ²⁵When the donkey saw the angel of the LORD, she pressed close to the wall, crushing Balaam's foot against it. So he beat her again.

²⁶Then the angel of the LORD moved on ahead and stood in a narrow place where there was no room to turn, either to the right or to the left. ²⁷When the donkey saw the angel of the LORD, she lay down under Balaam, and he was angry and beat her with his staff. ²⁸Then the LORD opened the donkey's mouth, and she said to Balaam, "What have I done to you to make you beat me these three times?"

²⁹Balaam answered the donkey, "You have made a fool of me! If I had a sword in my hand, I would kill you right now."

³⁰The donkey said to Balaam, "Am I not your own donkey, which you have always ridden, to this day? Have I been in the habit of doing this to you?"

"No," he said.

³¹Then the LORD opened Balaam's eyes, and he saw the angel of the LORD standing in the road with his sword drawn. So he bowed low and fell facedown.

³²The angel of the LORD asked him, "Why have you beaten your donkey these three times? I have come here to oppose you because your path is a reckless one before me.ᵃ ³³The donkey saw me and turned away from me these three times. If she had not turned away, I would certainly have killed you by now, but I would have spared her."

³⁴Balaam said to the angel of the LORD, "I have sinned. I did not realize you were standing in the road to oppose me. Now if you are displeased, I will go back."

³⁵The angel of the LORD said to Balaam, "Go with the men, but speak only what I tell you." So Balaam went with the princes of Balak.

³⁶When Balak heard that Balaam was coming, he went out to meet him at the Moabite town on the Arnon border, at the edge of his territory. ³⁷Balak said to Balaam, "Did I not send you an urgent summons? Why didn't you come to me? Am I really not able to reward you?"

³⁸"Well, I have come to you now," Balaam replied. "But can I say just anything? I must speak only what God puts in my mouth."

³⁹Then Balaam went with Balak to Kiriath Huzoth. ⁴⁰Balak sacrificed cattle and sheep, and gave some to Balaam and the princes who were with him. ⁴¹The next morning Balak took Balaam up to Bamoth Baal, and from there he saw part of the people.

ᵃ32 The meaning of the Hebrew for this clause is uncertain.

Why did God tell Balaam to go, then get angry when he went? (22:21–22)

It would appear that God knew something about the attitude of Balaam's heart that we do not. Balaam was clearly told he could not go to curse these people because they had been blessed (v. 12). Yet, when presented with more tempting offers, Balaam asked again to see if God might reconsider (v. 19). Perhaps God allowed Balaam to go so that he could show his displeasure for Balaam's craving. The Bible later says that Balaam *loved the wages of wickedness* (2 Peter 2:15).

Why would God use a donkey? (22:28)

Balaam was in demand. Powerful kings were willing to pay large amounts of money for his services. But not the God of Israel. God was apparently angry with the way Balaam hedged when Moab's princes kept pestering him for his services (v. 22). So God humiliated Balaam by using a beast of burden to get him to obey. Any doubt Balaam might have had about who was working for whom was now clear.

To whom did Balak sacrifice? (22:40)

Some say Balak sacrificed to the gods of Moab. Others think his offering was made to the God of Israel, whose favor he hoped to earn.

What is an oracle? (23:1–24:25)

An announcement or message from God. The word often suggests unwelcome news or judgments.

Balaam's Oracles (23:3)

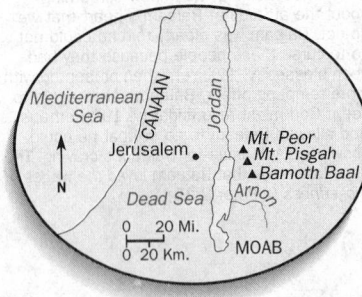

Mediterranean Sea
CANAAN
Jordan
Jerusalem
Mt. Peor
Mt. Pisgah
Bamoth Baal
Dead Sea
Arnon
N
0   20 Mi.
0   20 Km.
MOAB

Did such blessings and curses work? (23:11,25)

In the Old Testament, blessings and curses are always linked to God's control. God cannot be manipulated by human words. In ancient pagan practices, pronouncing a curse invoked the gods to bring calamity on someone. The Bible recognizes that supernatural evil is at work in our world (1 Peter 5:8). But here God used Balaam to do the opposite of Balak's wishes.

If God doesn't change his mind, why does it sometimes appear that way? (23:19)

God chose to create free-thinking human beings. Each of us is unique. To relate to us, God responds dynamically to our choices and actions. As we move through life, God moves with us and in spite of us. Who God is doesn't change, but the way he works to fulfill his grand purposes does. See article: *Why did God change his mind?* (Isaiah 38:1–5).

Balaam's First Oracle

23 Balaam said, "Build me seven altars here, and prepare seven bulls and seven rams for me." **2**Balak did as Balaam said, and the two of them offered a bull and a ram on each altar.

3Then Balaam said to Balak, "Stay here beside your offering while I go aside. Perhaps the LORD will come to meet with me. Whatever he reveals to me I will tell you." Then he went off to a barren height.

4God met with him, and Balaam said, "I have prepared seven altars, and on each altar I have offered a bull and a ram."

5The LORD put a message in Balaam's mouth and said, "Go back to Balak and give him this message."

6So he went back to him and found him standing beside his offering, with all the princes of Moab. **7**Then Balaam uttered his oracle^D:

"Balak brought me from Aram,
    the king of Moab from the eastern
        mountains.
'Come,' he said, 'curse Jacob for me;
    come, denounce Israel.'
8How can I curse
    those whom God has not cursed?
How can I denounce
    those whom the LORD has not denounced?
9From the rocky peaks I see them,
    from the heights I view them.
I see a people who live apart
    and do not consider themselves one of the
        nations.
10Who can count the dust of Jacob
    or number the fourth part of Israel?
Let me die the death^D of the righteous^D,
    and may my end be like theirs!"

11Balak said to Balaam, "What have you done to me? I brought you to curse my enemies, but you have done nothing but bless them!"

12He answered, "Must I not speak what the LORD puts in my mouth?"

Balaam's Second Oracle

13Then Balak said to him, "Come with me to another place where you can see them; you will see only a part but not all of them. And from there, curse them for me." **14**So he took him to the field of Zophim on the top of Pisgah, and there he built seven altars and offered a bull and a ram on each altar.

15Balaam said to Balak, "Stay here beside your offering while I meet with him over there."

16The LORD met with Balaam and put a message in his mouth and said, "Go back to Balak and give him this message."

17So he went to him and found him standing beside his offering, with the princes of Moab. Balak asked him, "What did the LORD say?"

18Then he uttered his oracle:

"Arise, Balak, and listen;
    hear me, son of Zippor.
19God is not a man, that he should lie,
    nor a son of man^D, that he should change
        his mind.

Does he speak and then not act?
 Does he promise and not fulfill?
20I have received a command to bless;
 he has blessed, and I cannot change it.

21"No misfortune is seen in Jacob,
 no misery observed in Israel.*a*
The LORD their God is with them;
 the shout of the King is among them.
22God brought them out of Egypt;
 they have the strength of a wild ox.
23There is no sorcery^D against Jacob,
 no divination^D against Israel.
It will now be said of Jacob
 and of Israel, 'See what God has done!'
24The people rise like a lioness;
 they rouse themselves like a lion
that does not rest till he devours his prey
 and drinks the blood of his victims."

25Then Balak said to Balaam, "Neither curse them at all nor bless them at all!"
26Balaam answered, "Did I not tell you I must do whatever the LORD says?"

Balaam's Third Oracle

27Then Balak said to Balaam, "Come, let me take you to another place. Perhaps it will please God to let you curse them for me from there." **28**And Balak took Balaam to the top of Peor, overlooking the wasteland.
29Balaam said, "Build me seven altars here, and prepare seven bulls and seven rams for me." **30**Balak did as Balaam had said, and offered a bull and a ram on each altar.

24 Now when Balaam saw that it pleased the LORD to bless Israel, he did not resort to sorcery as at other times, but turned his face toward the desert. **2**When Balaam looked out and saw Israel encamped tribe by tribe, the Spirit of God came upon him **3**and he uttered his oracle:

"The oracle of Balaam son of Beor,
 the oracle of one whose eye sees clearly,
4the oracle of one who hears the words of
  God,
who sees a vision^D from the Almighty,*b*
who falls prostrate, and whose eyes are
  opened:

5"How beautiful are your tents, O Jacob,
 your dwelling places, O Israel!

6"Like valleys they spread out,
 like gardens beside a river,
like aloes planted by the LORD,
 like cedars beside the waters.
7Water will flow from their buckets;
 their seed will have abundant water.

"Their king will be greater than Agag;
 their kingdom will be exalted.

8"God brought them out of Egypt;
 they have the strength of a wild ox.
They devour hostile nations

Did God sanction Balaam's use of sorcery? (24:1)
By using Balaam for a good purpose, God was not endorsing Balaam's pagan practices. The Old Testament had strict prohibitions concerning sorcery (Deut. 18:9–13). God issued the blessing, regardless of what Balaam perceived to be its source.

What convinced Balaam that the Lord wanted to bless Israel? (24:1)
The special word translated *God* in v. 4 emphasizes God's power. Most likely Balaam caught a glimpse of the awesome power of God (vv. 2,4). His response, then, was appropriate; Balaam yielded to God's purpose and pronounced God's hope for Israel.

In what sense did the Spirit of God come upon Balaam? (24:2)
The actual process is not clear. God somehow sensitized Balaam's inner "radar" so he could process what God was revealing to him, allowing him to peer into the future.

*a*21 Or *He has not looked on Jacob's offenses / or on the wrongs found in Israel.* *b*4 Hebrew *Shaddai*; also in verse 16

and break their bones in pieces;
  with their arrows they pierce them.
⁹Like a lion they crouch and lie down,
  like a lioness—who dares to rouse them?

"May those who bless you be blessed
  and those who curse you be cursed!"

¹⁰Then Balak's anger burned against Balaam. He struck his hands together and said to him, "I summoned you to curse my enemies, but you have blessed them these three times. ¹¹Now leave at once and go home! I said I would reward you handsomely, but the LORD has kept you from being rewarded."

¹²Balaam answered Balak, "Did I not tell the messengers you sent me, ¹³'Even if Balak gave me his palace filled with silver and gold, I could not do anything of my own accord, good or bad, to go beyond the command of the LORD—and I must say only what the LORD says'? ¹⁴Now I am going back to my people, but come, let me warn you of what this people will do to your people in days to come."

Why does the New Testament paint Balaam in a bad light when he obeyed God? (24:12–14)

There's more to the story. Numbers 31:16 hints at what Balaam did next: he advised Moabite women to seduce the men of Israel (25:1–3). Other Old Testament accounts indicate that Balaam intended all along to curse the people of Israel. See Deut. 23:5–6; Joshua 24:9–10; Neh. 13:1–2. Also see 2 Peter 2:15 and Jude 11.

Balaam's Fourth Oracle

¹⁵Then he uttered his oracle:

"The oracle of Balaam son of Beor,
  the oracle of one whose eye sees clearly,
¹⁶the oracle of one who hears the words of
    God,
  who has knowledge from the Most High,
  who sees a vision^D from the Almighty,
  who falls prostrate, and whose eyes are
    opened:
¹⁷"I see him, but not now;
  I behold him, but not near.
A star will come out of Jacob;
  a scepter^D will rise out of Israel.
He will crush the foreheads of Moab,
  the skulls^a of^b all the sons of Sheth.^c
¹⁸Edom^D will be conquered;
  Seir, his enemy, will be conquered,
  but Israel will grow strong.
¹⁹A ruler will come out of Jacob
  and destroy the survivors of the city."

Who is this oracle talking about? (24:17)

Though this prophecy hints at David—a ruler over Israel who would one day deliver his people from their enemies—that seems to be only part of the interpretation. The Messianic language that describes David also describes the coming Christ who would one day deliver from the enemy everyone who accepts Christ's rule. What is remarkable is that God would use a pagan prophet like Balaam to deliver a true message about the coming Messiah.

Balaam's Final Oracles

²⁰Then Balaam saw Amalek and uttered his oracle:

"Amalek was first among the nations,
  but he will come to ruin at last."

²¹Then he saw the Kenites and uttered his oracle:

"Your dwelling place is secure,
  your nest is set in a rock;
²²yet you Kenites will be destroyed
  when Asshur takes you captive."

²³Then he uttered his oracle:

"Ah, who can live when God does this?^d

---

^a17 Samaritan Pentateuch (see also Jer. 48:45); the meaning of the word in the Masoretic Text is uncertain.   ^b17 Or possibly Moab, / batter   ^c17 Or all the noisy boasters   ^d23 Masoretic Text; with a different word division of the Hebrew A people will gather from the north.

²⁴ Ships will come from the shores of Kittim;
       they will subdue Asshur and Eber,
          but they too will come to ruin."

²⁵Then Balaam got up and returned home and Balak went his own way.

Moab Seduces Israel

25 While Israel was staying in Shittim, the men began to indulge in sexual immorality with Moabite women, ²who invited them to the sacrifices^D to their gods. The people ate and bowed down before these gods. ³So Israel joined in worshiping the Baal^D of Peor. And the LORD's anger burned against them.

⁴The LORD said to Moses, "Take all the leaders of these people, kill them and expose them in broad daylight before the LORD, so that the LORD's fierce anger may turn away from Israel."

⁵So Moses said to Israel's judges, "Each of you must put to death^D those of your men who have joined in worshiping the Baal of Peor."

⁶Then an Israelite man brought to his family a Midianite woman right before the eyes of Moses and the whole assembly of Israel while they were weeping at the entrance to the Tent of Meeting^D. ⁷When Phinehas son of Eleazar, the son of Aaron, the priest^D, saw this, he left the assembly, took a spear in his hand ⁸and followed the Israelite into the tent. He drove the spear through both of them—through the Israelite and into the woman's body. Then the plague against the Israelites was stopped; ⁹but those who died in the plague numbered 24,000.

¹⁰The LORD said to Moses, ¹¹"Phinehas son of Eleazar, the son of Aaron, the priest, has turned my anger away from the Israelites; for he was as zealous as I am for my honor among them, so that in my zeal^D I did not put an end to them. ¹²Therefore tell him I am making my covenant^D of peace^D with him. ¹³He and his descendants will have a covenant of a lasting priesthood, because he was zealous for the honor of his God and made atonement^D for the Israelites."

¹⁴The name of the Israelite who was killed with the Midianite woman was Zimri son of Salu, the leader of a Simeonite family. ¹⁵And the name of the Midianite woman who was put to death was Cozbi daughter of Zur, a tribal chief of a Midianite family.

¹⁶The LORD said to Moses, ¹⁷"Treat the Midianites as enemies and kill them, ¹⁸because they treated you as enemies when they deceived you in the affair of Peor and their sister Cozbi, the daughter of a Midianite leader, the woman who was killed when the plague came as a result of Peor."

The Second Census

26 After the plague the LORD said to Moses and Eleazar son of Aaron, the priest, ²"Take a census of the whole Israelite community by families—all those twenty years old or more who are able to serve in the army of Israel." ³So on the plains of Moab by the Jordan across from Jericho^{D,a} Moses and Eleazar the priest spoke with them and said, ⁴"Take a census of the men

---

^a3 Hebrew *Jordan of Jericho*; possibly an ancient name for the Jordan River; also in verse 63

Why would Israelite men be sleeping with Moabite women? (25:1)

The Midianites and Moabites had formed an alliance against Israel (22:4,7). In an attempt to stop Israel, these two tribes apparently came up with a creative solution: get Israel to abandon their God and consequently lose his protection. To do this, Moabite women invited Israelite men to their fertility festival, which, among other things, involved Baal worship and sex with temple prostitutes. Some of Israel's men obliged. And God breathed fury. See also 31:8,16.

Why would anyone be so cavalier about his sin? (25:6)

This Israelite, named Zimri (v. 14), probably had such little respect for God and his ways that he didn't think anything would happen to him. His public sin, however, resulted in public judgment, warning others who might be similarly tempted. Other leaders who disregarded God's law were also executed (v. 4).

Did the Israelite's sin justify his murder? (25:7–8)

This was not murder but execution. The man's union with the daughter of a Midianite leader symbolized the adultery and idolatry of the people of Israel. These were sins punishable by death. God accepted their execution (at the hand of Phinehas, a priest) as atonement for the sins of the people (v. 13).

Were the Israelites who died in the plague the same ones who worshiped Baal? (25:9)

The Bible does not say. But Baal worship was a national sin. Even those who did not participate were responsible in some sense for the sin, because they could have objected to others doing it. The leaders had particular responsibility, which may explain God's command regarding leaders in v. 4. Just as the sin was corporate, so also was the plague.

Why did Israel need to take another census? (26:2)

God had just announced a military campaign against the Midianites (25:16–18). A census would number the eligible fighting men (26:2). Many changes had occurred since the last census. Adrift for 40 years, the nation had endured two devastating plagues, killing a total of 38,700 people (16:49; 25:9). A whole generation, except for Caleb and Joshua, had died (14:30; 26:65). In addition, the nation was poised to enter the promised land. Tribal population figures were important for the allocation of land.

How can reading a list of names benefit us? (26:4-61)

On the surface, these names seem meaningless. A closer look, however, reveals some nuggets of inspirational treasure. In Genesis 12:1-3, for example, God asked Abraham, a childless, 75-year-old man, to abandon his country and travel a thousand miles to a strange land. God promised him land and descendants. Twenty-five years later, Abraham was still childless and God was still promising (Gen. 17). This census, taken some 500 years later, reveals the character of God: he is faithful; he is a promise-keeper. Also see article: *Why read an ancient list of faceless names?* (1 Chron. 1:1).

SCRIPTURE LINK (26:8-10) *Korah*

For the complete story of Korah's rebellion see 16:1-40.

What good are all these names? (26:12-50)

See article: *Why read an ancient list of faceless names?* (1 Chron. 1:1).

---

twenty years old or more, as the LORD commanded Moses."

These were the Israelites who came out of Egypt:

[5] The descendants of Reuben, the firstborn[D] son of Israel, were:

through Hanoch, the Hanochite clan;
through Pallu, the Palluite clan;
[6] through Hezron, the Hezronite clan;
through Carmi, the Carmite clan.

[7] These were the clans of Reuben; those numbered were 43,730.

[8] The son of Pallu was Eliab, [9] and the sons of Eliab were Nemuel, Dathan and Abiram. The same Dathan and Abiram were the community officials who rebelled against Moses and Aaron and were among Korah's followers when they rebelled against the LORD. [10] The earth opened its mouth and swallowed them along with Korah, whose followers died when the fire devoured the 250 men. And they served as a warning sign. [11] The line of Korah, however, did not die out.

[12] The descendants of Simeon by their clans were:

through Nemuel, the Nemuelite clan;
through Jamin, the Jaminite clan;
through Jakin, the Jakinite clan;
[13] through Zerah, the Zerahite clan;
through Shaul, the Shaulite clan.

[14] These were the clans of Simeon; there were 22,200 men.

[15] The descendants of Gad by their clans were:

through Zephon, the Zephonite clan;
through Haggi, the Haggite clan;
through Shuni, the Shunite clan;
[16] through Ozni, the Oznite clan;
through Eri, the Erite clan;
[17] through Arodi,[a] the Arodite clan;
through Areli, the Arelite clan.

[18] These were the clans of Gad; those numbered were 40,500.

[19] Er and Onan were sons of Judah, but they died in Canaan.

[20] The descendants of Judah by their clans were:

through Shelah, the Shelanite clan;
through Perez, the Perezite clan;
through Zerah, the Zerahite clan.
[21] The descendants of Perez were:

through Hezron, the Hezronite clan;
through Hamul, the Hamulite clan.

[22] These were the clans of Judah; those numbered were 76,500.

[23] The descendants of Issachar by their clans were:

through Tola, the Tolaite clan;
through Puah, the Puite[b] clan;
[24] through Jashub, the Jashubite clan;
through Shimron, the Shimronite clan.

[25] These were the clans of Issachar; those numbered were 64,300.

---

[a]17 Samaritan Pentateuch and Syriac (see also Gen. 46:16); Masoretic Text *Arod*   [b]23 Samaritan Pentateuch, Septuagint, Vulgate and Syriac (see also 1 Chron. 7:1); Masoretic Text *through Puvah, the Punite*

26The descendants of Zebulun by their clans were:

through Sered, the Seredite clan;
through Elon, the Elonite clan;
through Jahleel, the Jahleelite clan.

27These were the clans of Zebulun; those numbered were 60,500.

28The descendants of Joseph by their clans through Manasseh and Ephraim were:

29The descendants of Manasseh:

through Makir, the Makirite clan (Makir was the father of Gilead);
through Gilead, the Gileadite clan.
30These were the descendants of Gilead:
through Iezer, the Iezerite clan;
through Helek, the Helekite clan;
31through Asriel, the Asrielite clan;
through Shechem, the Shechemite clan;
32through Shemida, the Shemidaite clan;
through Hepher, the Hepherite clan.
33(Zelophehad son of Hepher had no sons; he had only daughters, whose names were Mahlah, Noah, Hoglah, Milcah and Tirzah.)

34These were the clans of Manasseh; those numbered were 52,700.

35These were the descendants of Ephraim by their clans:
through Shuthelah, the Shuthelahite clan;
through Beker, the Bekerite clan;
through Tahan, the Tahanite clan.
36These were the descendants of Shuthelah:
through Eran, the Eranite clan.

37These were the clans of Ephraim; those numbered were 32,500.

These were the descendants of Joseph by their clans.

38The descendants of Benjamin by their clans were:
through Bela, the Belaite clan;
through Ashbel, the Ashbelite clan;
through Ahiram, the Ahiramite clan;
39through Shupham,ᵃ the Shuphamite clan;
through Hupham, the Huphamite clan.
40The descendants of Bela through Ard and Naaman were:
through Ard,ᵇ the Ardite clan;
through Naaman, the Naamite clan.

41These were the clans of Benjamin; those numbered were 45,600.

42These were the descendants of Dan by their clans:
through Shuham, the Shuhamite clan.
These were the clans of Dan: **43**All of them were Shuhamite clans; and those numbered were 64,400.

44The descendants of Asher by their clans were:
through Imnah, the Imnite clan;
through Ishvi, the Ishvite clan;
through Beriah, the Beriite clan;
45and through the descendants of Beriah:
through Heber, the Heberite clan;

ᵃ39 A few manuscripts of the Masoretic Text, Samaritan Pentateuch, Vulgate and Syriac (see also Septuagint); most manuscripts of the Masoretic Text *Shephupham*   ᵇ40 Samaritan Pentateuch and Vulgate (see also Septuagint); Masoretic Text does not have *through Ard.*

SCRIPTURE LINK (26:28) *Joseph*
For the story of Joseph's life, see Gen. 37–50.

Why are other daughters not named in this genealogy? (26:33)
As a general rule daughters were not listed here because the purpose of this genealogy was to record the names and numbers of men available to fight in Israel's army (v. 2). Elsewhere other genealogies with different purposes list daughters more frequently (for example, 1 Chron. 2 and 7). But if this explains why other daughters were not mentioned, why would Zelophehad's daughters be listed? Probably simply to set the stage for the account that follows in ch. 27.

How precise is this number? (26:41)
The total for the clans of Benjamin, and for the other clans listed, appears to be a round number (compare v. 7 with v. 34, for example). The total number of men in Israel (see v. 51), although approximate, is consistent with the earlier census figure. See *How does this number compare to the earlier census?* (26:51). That the total did not change dramatically from the time of the first count to the second, demonstrates that the Israelites were remarkably resilient in spite of prolonged hardship. For more on the accuracy of numbers, see *Were there really 500,000 casualties among the Israelites?* (2 Chron. 13:17).

Why is Asher's daughter mentioned? (26:46)

Compared to men, few women are mentioned from this period in Israel's history. Why Serah is listed (she also appears in Genesis 46:17 and 1 Chronicles 7:30) is a mystery. There seems to be no explanation—and no mention of any children or husband she might have had. Some speculate she may have been the only daughter born to Jacob's 12 sons, just as Dinah was the only daughter Jacob had. The odds against that being the case, however, only make the mention of her name all the more remarkable.

How does this number compare to the earlier census? (26:51)

It is almost the same. In spite of all the hardship and loss of life during the 40 years in the desert, the Israelite male population declined by only 1,820—³⁄₁₀ of one percent—from the census taken just after they left Egypt (1:46).

SCRIPTURE LINK (26:61)

Aaron had four sons. Two of them, Nadab and Abihu, died childless while offering *unauthorized fire before the LORD* (Lev. 10:1–2). Because of their disobedience, God destroyed them. Eleazar was one of Aaron's remaining two sons. Eleazar's son Phinehas, then, who had executed Zimri and Cozbi (25:7–8), was Aaron's grandson.

through Malkiel, the Malkielite clan.

46(Asher had a daughter named Serah.)

47These were the clans of Asher; those numbered were 53,400.

48The descendants of Naphtali by their clans were:
    through Jahzeel, the Jahzeelite clan;
    through Guni, the Gunite clan;
49through Jezer, the Jezerite clan;
    through Shillem, the Shillemite clan.
50These were the clans of Naphtali; those numbered were 45,400.

51The total number of the men of Israel was 601,730.

52The LORD said to Moses, **53**"The land is to be allotted to them as an inheritance based on the number of names. **54**To a larger group give a larger inheritance, and to a smaller group a smaller one; each is to receive its inheritance according to the number of those listed. **55**Be sure that the land is distributed by lot. What each group inherits will be according to the names for its ancestral tribe. **56**Each inheritance is to be distributed by lot among the larger and smaller groups."

57These were the LevitesD who were counted by their clans:
    through Gershon, the Gershonite clan;
    through Kohath, the Kohathite clan;
    through Merari, the Merarite clan.
58These also were Levite clans:
    the Libnite clan,
    the Hebronite clan,
    the Mahlite clan,
    the Mushite clan,
    the Korahite clan.
(Kohath was the forefather of Amram; **59**the name of Amram's wife was Jochebed, a descendant of Levi, who was born to the Levites*a* in Egypt. To Amram she bore Aaron, Moses and their sister Miriam. **60**Aaron was the father of Nadab and Abihu, Eleazar and Ithamar. **61**But Nadab and Abihu died when they made an offering before the LORD with unauthorized fire.)

62All the male Levites a month old or more numbered 23,000. They were not counted along with the other Israelites because they received no inheritance among them.

63These are the ones counted by Moses and Eleazar the priestD when they counted the Israelites on the plains of Moab by the Jordan across from JerichoD. **64**Not one of them was among those counted by Moses and Aaron the priest when they counted the Israelites in the Desert of Sinai. **65**For the LORD had told those Israelites they would surely die in the desert, and not one of them was left except Caleb son of Jephunneh and Joshua son of Nun.

Zelophehad's Daughters

27 The daughters of Zelophehad son of Hepher, the son of Gilead, the son of Makir, the son of Manasseh, belonged to the clans of Manasseh son of Joseph. The names of the daughters were Mahlah, Noah, Hoglah, Milcah and Tirzah. They approached **2**the entrance to the

a59 Or Jochebed, a daughter of Levi, who was born to Levi

Tent of Meeting[D] and stood before Moses, Eleazar the priest[D], the leaders and the whole assembly, and said, **3**"Our father died in the desert. He was not among Korah's followers, who banded together against the LORD, but he died for his own sin and left no sons. **4**Why should our father's name disappear from his clan because he had no son? Give us property among our father's relatives."

5So Moses brought their case before the LORD **6**and the LORD said to him, **7**"What Zelophehad's daughters are saying is right. You must certainly give them property as an inheritance among their father's relatives and turn their father's inheritance over to them.

8"Say to the Israelites, 'If a man dies and leaves no son, turn his inheritance over to his daughter. **9**If he has no daughter, give his inheritance to his brothers. **10**If he has no brothers, give his inheritance to his father's brothers. **11**If his father had no brothers, give his inheritance to the nearest relative in his clan, that he may possess it. This is to be a legal requirement for the Israelites, as the LORD commanded Moses.' "

Joshua to Succeed Moses

12Then the LORD said to Moses, "Go up this mountain in the Abarim range and see the land I have given the Israelites. **13**After you have seen it, you too will be gathered to your people, as your brother Aaron was, **14**for when the community rebelled at the waters in the Desert of Zin, both of you disobeyed my command to honor me as holy before their eyes." (These were the waters of Meribah Kadesh, in the Desert of Zin.)

15Moses said to the LORD, **16**"May the LORD, the God of the spirits of all mankind, appoint a man over this community **17**to go out and come in before them, one who will lead them out and bring them in, so the LORD's people will not be like sheep without a shepherd."

18So the LORD said to Moses, "Take Joshua son of Nun, a man in whom is the spirit,[a] and lay your hand on him. **19**Have him stand before Eleazar the priest and the entire assembly and commission him in their presence. **20**Give him some of your authority so the whole Israelite community will obey him. **21**He is to stand before Eleazar the priest, who will obtain decisions for him by inquiring of the Urim[D] before the LORD. At his command he and the entire community of the Israelites will go out, and at his command they will come in."

22Moses did as the LORD commanded him. He took Joshua and had him stand before Eleazar the priest and the whole assembly. **23**Then he laid his hands on him and commissioned him, as the LORD instructed through Moses.

Daily Offerings

28 The LORD said to Moses, **2**"Give this command to the Israelites and say to them: 'See that you present to me at the appointed time the food for my offerings made by fire, as an aroma pleasing to me.' **3**Say to them: 'This is the offering made by fire that you are to present to the LORD: two lambs a year old without defect, as a regular burnt offering[D] each day. **4**Prepare one lamb in the morning and the other at twilight, **5**together with a grain offering[D] of a tenth of an ephah[b] of fine flour

Did God make up the rules as the Israelites went along? (27:5–11)
God gave Moses basic laws of government, worship and civil life, but the laws did not cover every conceivable problem. When a problem arose the law did not directly address, the people brought the case to Moses. If Moses was uncertain, he went to God for direction. The decision then became a precedent for other cases. See also Lev. 24:10–23.

How did the *spirit* make Joshua different? (27:18)
The word translated *spirit* refers to Joshua's inner life, which was sensitized to the things of God. Joshua had godly qualities enabling him to be a spiritual leader. When Moses laid hands on him, Joshua also received the spirit of wisdom (Deut. 34:9), that is, spiritual wisdom to help him lead God's people. Another view is that the word refers to God's Spirit (see NIV text note). When the Holy Spirit dwells within, a person will be dramatically different.

How would an aroma please God? (28:2)
Most of the offerings in ch. 28–29 are voluntary, sent to God by smoke and fire. The aroma refers to the smoke ascending into the sky. See *Why would the aroma be important to God?* (Lev. 1:9).

What does God eat? (28:2)
See *What does God eat?* (Lev. 21:6).

---

a18 Or *Spirit*   *b5* That is, probably about 2 quarts (about 2 liters); also in verses 13, 21 and 29

Burnt offering . . . grain offering (28:6–8)

See *Old Testament Sacrifices* on page 138.

Drink offering (28:7)

Usually wine or oil given as a sacrifice to honor God and to express thankfulness. Oil was valuable and was often used in Hebrew religious observances. Drink offerings generally were given with burnt offerings or fellowship offerings.

How did the Israelites keep track of months? (28:11)

The Hebrews followed a lunar calendar system with an extra month inserted every three years or so to keep pace with the solar year. They had two sequences of months, one sacred and one civil—much as we have a standard calendar along with a fiscal calendar for government and business budgetary purposes.

How did the Israelites remember all these details? (28:14–15)

Several factors may have helped: (1) The priests were entrusted with maintaining the religious ritual and ceremony. They were specialists who were to assist the people in coming to God. (2) The instructions were written down for later reference. (3) Though these instructions sound confusing to our modern ears, the Hebrews would have been quite familiar with these measures as they were part of their everyday life.

mixed with a quarter of a hin[a] of oil from pressed olives. [6]This is the regular burnt offering[D] instituted at Mount Sinai as a pleasing aroma, an offering made to the LORD by fire. [7]The accompanying drink offering[D] is to be a quarter of a hin of fermented drink with each lamb. Pour out the drink offering to the LORD at the sanctuary. [8]Prepare the second lamb at twilight, along with the same kind of grain offering[D] and drink offering that you prepare in the morning. This is an offering made by fire, an aroma pleasing to the LORD.

Sabbath[D] Offerings

[9]" 'On the Sabbath day, make an offering of two lambs a year old without defect, together with its drink offering and a grain offering of two-tenths of an ephah[b] of fine flour mixed with oil. [10]This is the burnt offering for every Sabbath, in addition to the regular burnt offering and its drink offering.

Monthly Offerings

[11]" 'On the first of every month, present to the LORD a burnt offering of two young bulls, one ram and seven male lambs a year old, all without defect. [12]With each bull there is to be a grain offering of three-tenths of an ephah[c] of fine flour mixed with oil; with the ram, a grain offering of two-tenths of an ephah of fine flour mixed with oil; [13]and with each lamb, a grain offering of a tenth of an ephah of fine flour mixed with oil. This is for a burnt offering, a pleasing aroma, an offering made to the LORD by fire. [14]With each bull there is to be a drink offering of half a hin[d] of wine; with the ram, a third of a hin[e]; and with each lamb, a quarter of a hin. This is the monthly burnt offering to be made at each new moon during the year. [15]Besides the regular burnt offering with its drink offering, one male goat is to be presented to the LORD as a sin offering.

The Passover

[16]" 'On the fourteenth day of the first month the LORD's Passover is to be held. [17]On the fifteenth day of this month there is to be a festival; for seven days eat bread made without yeast[D]. [18]On the first day hold a sacred assembly[D] and do no regular work. [19]Present to the LORD an offering made by fire, a burnt offering of two young bulls, one ram and seven male lambs a year old, all without defect. [20]With each bull prepare a grain offering of three-tenths of an ephah of fine flour mixed with oil; with the ram, two-tenths; [21]and with each of the seven lambs, one-tenth. [22]Include one male goat as a sin offering[D] to make atonement[D] for you. [23]Prepare these in addition to the regular morning burnt offering. [24]In this way prepare the food for the offering made by fire every day for seven days as an aroma pleasing to the LORD; it is to be prepared in addition to the regular burnt offering and its drink offering. [25]On the seventh day hold a sacred assembly and do no regular work.

---

[a]5 That is, probably about 1 quart (about 1 liter); also in verses 7 and 14   [b]9 That is, probably about 4 quarts (about 4.5 liters); also in verses 12, 20 and 28   [c]12 That is, probably about 6 quarts (about 6.5 liters); also in verses 20 and 28   [d]14 That is, probably about 2 quarts (about 2 liters)   [e]14 That is, probably about 1 1/4 quarts (about 1.2 liters)

Feast of Weeks

26" 'On the day of firstfruits^D, when you present to the LORD an offering of new grain during the Feast of Weeks, hold a sacred assembly^D and do no regular work. **27**Present a burnt offering^D of two young bulls, one ram and seven male lambs a year old as an aroma pleasing to the LORD. **28**With each bull there is to be a grain offering^D of three-tenths of an ephah of fine flour mixed with oil; with the ram, two-tenths; **29**and with each of the seven lambs, one-tenth. **30**Include one male goat to make atonement^D for you. **31**Prepare these together with their drink offerings^D, in addition to the regular burnt offering and its grain offering. Be sure the animals are without defect.

Feast of Trumpets

29 " 'On the first day of the seventh month hold a sacred assembly and do no regular work. It is a day for you to sound the trumpets. **2**As an aroma pleasing to the LORD, prepare a burnt offering of one young bull, one ram and seven male lambs a year old, all without defect. **3**With the bull prepare a grain offering of three-tenths of an ephah*a* of fine flour mixed with oil; with the ram, two-tenths*b*; **4**and with each of the seven lambs, one-tenth.*c* **5**Include one male goat as a sin offering^D to make atonement for you. **6**These are in addition to the monthly and daily burnt offerings with their grain offerings and drink offerings as specified. They are offerings made to the LORD by fire—a pleasing aroma.

Day of Atonement

7" 'On the tenth day of this seventh month hold a sacred assembly. You must deny yourselves*d* and do no work. **8**Present as an aroma pleasing to the LORD a burnt offering of one young bull, one ram and seven male lambs a year old, all without defect. **9**With the bull prepare a grain offering of three-tenths of an ephah of fine flour mixed with oil; with the ram, two-tenths; **10**and with each of the seven lambs, one-tenth. **11**Include one male goat as a sin offering, in addition to the sin offering for atonement and the regular burnt offering with its grain offering, and their drink offerings.

Feast of Tabernacles

12" 'On the fifteenth day of the seventh month, hold a sacred assembly and do no regular work. Celebrate a festival to the LORD for seven days. **13**Present an offering made by fire as an aroma pleasing to the LORD, a burnt offering of thirteen young bulls, two rams and fourteen male lambs a year old, all without defect. **14**With each of the thirteen bulls prepare a grain offering of three-tenths of an ephah of fine flour mixed with oil; with each of the two rams, two-tenths; **15**and with each of the fourteen lambs, one-tenth. **16**Include one male goat as a sin offering, in addition to the regular burnt offering with its grain offering and drink offering.

17" 'On the second day prepare twelve young bulls, two rams and fourteen male lambs a year old, all without defect. **18**With the bulls, rams and lambs, prepare their grain

What are all these feasts about? (28:26-31)

See *Old Testament Feasts* on page 168.

Why did animals for sacrifices have to be *without defect*? (28:31)

Any animal offered to God on the altar needed to be perfect. Only an unblemished, clean animal could symbolize the purity that a holy God demanded. Anything less would have indicated that the worshiper was not offering his best and most valuable sacrifice to God. Later the Israelites were judged for offering second-rate animals while saving the best for themselves (Mal. 1:13-14).

Sacred assembly (29:1)

Behind the word *assembly* is a Hebrew verb meaning *to proclaim, summon, invite*. These were times when the whole community was summoned together for common worship and celebration.

SCRIPTURE LINK (29:7-11)

The Day of Atonement is also the subject of Lev. 16:2-34 and 23:26-32.

Of what were they to deny themselves? (29:7)

They were to deny themselves food, fasting as a sign of sorrow for their sins. The Day of Atonement was a solemn occasion, considered the most holy day of the year. While other religious rituals were celebrated with feasting, fasting was demanded of those seeking forgiveness of sins.

---

a3 That is, probably about 6 quarts (about 6.5 liters); also in verses 9 and 14   *b3* That is, probably about 4 quarts (about 4.5 liters); also in verses 9 and 14   *c4* That is, probably about 2 quarts (about 2 liters); also in verses 10 and 15   *d7* Or *must fast*

offerings[D] and drink offerings[D] according to the number specified. [19]Include one male goat as a sin offering[D], in addition to the regular burnt offering[D] with its grain offering, and their drink offerings.

[20]" 'On the third day prepare eleven bulls, two rams and fourteen male lambs a year old, all without defect. [21]With the bulls, rams and lambs, prepare their grain offerings and drink offerings according to the number specified. [22]Include one male goat as a sin offering, in addition to the regular burnt offering with its grain offering and drink offering.

[23]" 'On the fourth day prepare ten bulls, two rams and fourteen male lambs a year old, all without defect. [24]With the bulls, rams and lambs, prepare their grain offerings and drink offerings according to the number specified. [25]Include one male goat as a sin offering, in addition to the regular burnt offering with its grain offering and drink offering.

[26]" 'On the fifth day prepare nine bulls, two rams and fourteen male lambs a year old, all without defect. [27]With the bulls, rams and lambs, prepare their grain offerings and drink offerings according to the number specified. [28]Include one male goat as a sin offering, in addition to the regular burnt offering with its grain offering and drink offering.

[29]" 'On the sixth day prepare eight bulls, two rams and fourteen male lambs a year old, all without defect. [30]With the bulls, rams and lambs, prepare their grain offerings and drink offerings according to the number specified. [31]Include one male goat as a sin offering, in addition to the regular burnt offering with its grain offering and drink offering.

[32]" 'On the seventh day prepare seven bulls, two rams and fourteen male lambs a year old, all without defect. [33]With the bulls, rams and lambs, prepare their grain offerings and drink offerings according to the number specified. [34]Include one male goat as a sin offering, in addition to the regular burnt offering with its grain offering and drink offering.

[35]" 'On the eighth day hold an assembly and do no regular work. [36]Present an offering made by fire as an aroma pleasing to the Lord, a burnt offering of one bull, one ram and seven male lambs a year old, all without defect. [37]With the bull, the ram and the lambs, prepare their grain offerings and drink offerings according to the number specified. [38]Include one male goat as a sin offering, in addition to the regular burnt offering with its grain offering and drink offering.

[39]" 'In addition to what you vow[D] and your freewill offerings, prepare these for the Lord at your appointed feasts: your burnt offerings, grain offerings, drink offerings and fellowship offerings.[a]' "

[40]Moses told the Israelites all that the Lord commanded him.

Vows

30 Moses said to the heads of the tribes of Israel: "This is what the Lord commands: [2]When a man makes a vow to the Lord or takes an oath to obligate himself by a pledge, he must not break his word but must do everything he said.

[3]"When a young woman still living in her father's

Why would someone make a vow to God? (30:2)

At this juncture in their journey—preparing to enter long-awaited Canaan—the Israelites wanted to show their devotion to God. They did so with vows and pledges, which were above and beyond what God required of them. A vow was a promise to do something for God; a pledge was a promise to abstain from something or to deny oneself something.

Should we make vows to God today? (30:2)

Little information is given about vows in the New Testament. In fact, Jesus cautioned against reinforcing our promises to God with oaths (Matt. 5:33–37). The New Testament does encourage believers to sacrifice their bodies to God on a daily basis (Romans 12:1; 1 Cor. 6:20). Demonstrating our love for God should not be an occasional habit but a lifestyle of devotion.

Why did some women have to have their vows authorized by men? (30:2,5,8–9,12)

The regulations were given to clear up any confusion at home when fathers and husbands left for war. With the men absent, the women would have to make decisions that would affect the family. These laws retained the right of husbands and fathers to have a say in these matters at a later date. The guidelines freed a woman from possible conflict between obligations to her father or husband and obligations to her God.

---

[a] 39 Traditionally *peace offerings*

house makes a vow[D] to the LORD or obligates herself by a pledge [4]and her father hears about her vow or pledge but says nothing to her, then all her vows and every pledge by which she obligated herself will stand. [5]But if her father forbids her when he hears about it, none of her vows or the pledges by which she obligated herself will stand; the LORD will release her because her father has forbidden her.

[6]"If she marries after she makes a vow or after her lips utter a rash promise by which she obligates herself [7]and her husband hears about it but says nothing to her, then her vows or the pledges by which she obligated herself will stand. [8]But if her husband forbids her when he hears about it, he nullifies the vow that obligates her or the rash promise by which she obligates herself, and the LORD will release her.

[9]"Any vow or obligation taken by a widow or divorced woman will be binding on her.

[10]"If a woman living with her husband makes a vow or obligates herself by a pledge under oath [11]and her husband hears about it but says nothing to her and does not forbid her, then all her vows or the pledges by which she obligated herself will stand. [12]But if her husband nullifies them when he hears about them, then none of the vows or pledges that came from her lips will stand. Her husband has nullified them, and the LORD will release her. [13]Her husband may confirm or nullify any vow she makes or any sworn pledge to deny herself. [14]But if her husband says nothing to her about it from day to day, then he confirms all her vows or the pledges binding on her. He confirms them by saying nothing to her when he hears about them. [15]If, however, he nullifies them some time after he hears about them, then he is responsible for her guilt."

[16]These are the regulations the LORD gave Moses concerning relationships between a man and his wife, and between a father and his young daughter still living in his house.

Vengeance on the Midianites

31 The LORD said to Moses, [2]"Take vengeance on the Midianites for the Israelites. After that, you will be gathered to your people."

[3]So Moses said to the people, "Arm some of your men to go to war against the Midianites and to carry out the LORD's vengeance on them. [4]Send into battle a thousand men from each of the tribes of Israel." [5]So twelve thousand men armed for battle, a thousand from each tribe, were supplied from the clans of Israel. [6]Moses sent them into battle, a thousand from each tribe, along with Phinehas son of Eleazar, the priest[D], who took with him articles from the sanctuary and the trumpets for signaling.

[7]They fought against Midian, as the LORD commanded Moses, and killed every man. [8]Among their victims were Evi, Rekem, Zur, Hur and Reba—the five kings of Midian. They also killed Balaam son of Beor with the sword. [9]The Israelites captured the Midianite women and children and took all the Midianite herds, flocks and goods as plunder[D]. [10]They burned all the towns where the Midianites had settled, as well as all their camps. [11]They took all the plunder and spoils, including the people and animals, [12]and brought the captives, spoils and plunder to Moses and Eleazar the priest and the Israelite assembly at their

What was Balaam still doing among the Midianites? (31:8)

Balaam surfaced with the Midianites in another attempt to sabotage Israel's military power. When God thwarted his effort to curse Israel (24:1–3), Balaam took another approach; he exposed Israel's vulnerability by seducing their men with Midianite women. See v. 16; 25:1–2.

Why could the Israelites keep the plunder from some conquests but not others? (31:9)

Here God instructed them to take the spoils. In the battle against the king of Arad (21:1–3), Israel had vowed that if God were to grant them victory they would raze the Canaanite cities. None of the Israelites profited from the battle in any way but, by demolishing their enemy, they gave all the spoils of war to God.

camp on the plains of Moab, by the Jordan across from Jericho[D].[a] **13**Moses, Eleazar the priest[D] and all the leaders of the community went to meet them outside the camp. **14**Moses was angry with the officers of the army—the commanders of thousands and commanders of hundreds—who returned from the battle.

15"Have you allowed all the women to live?" he asked them. **16**"They were the ones who followed Balaam's advice and were the means of turning the Israelites away from the LORD in what happened at Peor, so that a plague struck the LORD's people. **17**Now kill all the boys. And kill every woman who has slept with a man, **18**but save for yourselves every girl who has never slept with a man.

19"All of you who have killed anyone or touched anyone who was killed must stay outside the camp seven days. On the third and seventh days you must purify[D] yourselves and your captives. **20**Purify every garment as well as everything made of leather, goat hair or wood."

21Then Eleazar the priest said to the soldiers who had gone into battle, "This is the requirement of the law that the LORD gave Moses: **22**Gold, silver, bronze, iron, tin, lead **23**and anything else that can withstand fire must be put through the fire, and then it will be clean. But it must also be purified with the water of cleansing. And whatever cannot withstand fire must be put through that water. **24**On the seventh day wash your clothes and you will be clean. Then you may come into the camp."

Dividing the Spoils

25The LORD said to Moses, **26**"You and Eleazar the priest and the family heads of the community are to count all the people and animals that were captured. **27**Divide the spoils between the soldiers who took part in the battle and the rest of the community. **28**From the soldiers who fought in the battle, set apart as tribute for the LORD one out of every five hundred, whether persons, cattle, donkeys, sheep or goats. **29**Take this tribute from their half share and give it to Eleazar the priest as the LORD's part. **30**From the Israelites' half, select one out of every fifty, whether persons, cattle, donkeys, sheep, goats or other animals. Give them to the Levites[D], who are responsible for the care of the LORD's tabernacle[D]." **31**So Moses and Eleazar the priest did as the LORD commanded Moses.

32The plunder[D] remaining from the spoils that the soldiers took was 675,000 sheep, **33**72,000 cattle, **34**61,000 donkeys **35**and 32,000 women who had never slept with a man.

36The half share of those who fought in the battle was:

> 337,500 sheep, **37**of which the tribute for the LORD was 675;
> **38**36,000 cattle, of which the tribute for the LORD was 72;
> **39**30,500 donkeys, of which the tribute for the LORD was 61;
> **40**16,000 people, of which the tribute for the LORD was 32.

41Moses gave the tribute to Eleazar the priest as the LORD's part, as the LORD commanded Moses.

Why did Balaam make another attempt on God's people? (31:16)

Balaam's motives are not clear. The New Testament suggests that greed drove Balaam's motives (2 Peter 2:14–15). Perhaps he had second thoughts about Balak's lucrative offer (24:11,13).

Why were virgins spared? (31:18)

Midianite women had prompted the war by seducing the men of Israel into idolatry and immorality (ch. 25). In retaliation, Israel spared only the virgins of Midian—those women who could not have participated in the seduction. Most likely the Israelites assimilated these young women into their culture with the kindness prescribed in Deuteronomy 21:10–14.

Why would soldiers obeying God's command become unclean? (31:19; see 31:3)

At war's end, Israelite soldiers had blood on their hands. Though they had killed at God's command, obedience to God didn't annul their responsibility to his other laws. All loss of human life tainted those who came in contact with it, and, the law required cleansing (19:11–13).

What would Eleazar, a priest, do with 32 Midianite virgins? (31:40–41)

Eleazar may have employed these Midianite women to serve at the Tent of Meeting (for example, see Exodus 38:8). In contrast to Midianite worship practices (25:1–3), using these women for sexual exploitation would have been an affront to God.

---

[a]12 Hebrew *Jordan of Jericho*; possibly an ancient name for the Jordan River

⁴²The half belonging to the Israelites, which Moses set apart from that of the fighting men— ⁴³the community's half—was 337,500 sheep, ⁴⁴36,000 cattle, ⁴⁵30,500 donkeys ⁴⁶and 16,000 people. ⁴⁷From the Israelites' half, Moses selected one out of every fifty persons and animals, as the LORD commanded him, and gave them to the LevitesᴰD, who were responsible for the care of the LORD's tabernacleᴰ.

⁴⁸Then the officers who were over the units of the army—the commanders of thousands and commanders of hundreds—went to Moses ⁴⁹and said to him, "Your servants have counted the soldiers under our command, and not one is missing. ⁵⁰So we have brought as an offering to the LORD the gold articles each of us acquired—armlets, bracelets, signet ringsᴰ, earrings and necklaces—to make atonementᴰ for ourselves before the LORD."

⁵¹Moses and Eleazar the priestᴰ accepted from them the gold—all the crafted articles. ⁵²All the gold from the commanders of thousands and commanders of hundreds that Moses and Eleazar presented as a gift to the LORD weighed 16,750 shekelsᴰ.ᵃ ⁵³Each soldier had taken plunderᴰ for himself. ⁵⁴Moses and Eleazar the priest accepted the gold from the commanders of thousands and commanders of hundreds and brought it into the Tent of Meetingᴰ as a memorial for the Israelites before the LORD.

The Transjordan Tribes

32 The Reubenites and Gadites, who had very large herds and flocks, saw that the lands of Jazer and Gilead were suitable for livestock. ²So they came to Moses and Eleazar the priest and to the leaders of the community, and said, ³"Ataroth, Dibon, Jazer, Nimrah, Heshbon, Elealeh, Sebam, Nebo and Beon— ⁴the land the LORD subdued before the people of Israel—are suitable for livestock, and your servants have livestock. ⁵If we have found favor in your eyes," they said, "let this land be given to your servants as our possession. Do not make us cross the Jordan."

⁶Moses said to the Gadites and Reubenites, "Shall your countrymen go to war while you sit here? ⁷Why do you discourage the Israelites from going over into the land the LORD has given them? ⁸This is what your fathers did when I sent them from Kadesh Barnea to look over the land. ⁹After they went up to the Valley of Eshcol and viewed the land, they discouraged the Israelites from entering the land the LORD had given them. ¹⁰The LORD's anger was aroused that day and he swore this oath: ¹¹'Because they have not followed me wholeheartedly, not one of the men twenty years old or more who came up out of Egypt will see the land I promised on oath to Abraham, Isaac and Jacob— ¹²not one except Caleb son of Jephunneh the Kenizzite and Joshua son of Nun, for they followed the LORD wholeheartedly.' ¹³The LORD's anger burned against Israel and he made them wander in the desert forty years, until the whole generation of those who had done evil in his sight was gone.

¹⁴"And here you are, a brood of sinners, standing in the place of your fathers and making the LORD even more angry with Israel. ¹⁵If you turn away from following him, he will again leave all this people in the desert, and you will be the cause of their destruction."

ᵃ52 That is, about 420 pounds (about 190 kilograms)

How could only 12,000 Israelites annihilate a much larger tribe? (31:49)

Some believe the numbers given here were exaggerated intentionally to accent a great victory. Another explanation focuses on God's miraculous power that enabled Israel to rout their enemies (31:3,7). Also see *How can such large numbers be explained?* (1 Chron. 18:4–5); *Were there really 500,000 casualties among the Israelites?* (2 Chron. 13:17) and *Why don't the numbers in the list equal the total figure?* (Neh. 7:66).

Could atonement be bought? (31:50)

In some instances a person facing the death penalty could save his life by paying a ransom, a specified amount of money to compensate for the offense (Exodus 21:28–32). Since God had protected the men who fought against Midian, their offering may have been a way of acknowledging the importance of the life God gave them. In this sense, it may have been a ransom that spared them. See Exodus 30:11–16.

What ignited Moses' anger against these tribes? (32:14)

The two Israelite tribes—the Reubenites and Gadites—asked Moses to give them pastureland outside the boundaries of Canaan, the land that God had promised his people. Moses, who had been denied entrance, could hardly believe his ears. How could anyone permitted to enter paradise choose not to do so? Their request sounded much like the report from the spies in chs. 13–14. At that time the entire nation balked, and the result was 40 years of desert homelessness.

Fortified cities (32:17)

Cities that were well protected. Usually surrounded by walls, such cities were often built on steep hills to provide further protection from hostile forces.

Why did the Gadites and Reubenites want the land east of the Jordan? (32:19–33)

The land the Israelites had already subdued on the east side of the Jordan was extremely fertile and well-suited to the needs of the tribes of Gad and Reuben. They wanted lots of grazing land for their large herds and flocks (vv. 1–4). They were probably weary of traveling and felt this was an opportunity for their families to begin settling down while the rest of the land was being conquered.

What happened to all these cities? (32:34–36)

When the Israelites took them over after defeating the previous inhabitants, they repaired or rebuilt the walls and then occupied the cities. There is archaeological evidence of at least two of the cities, Dibon and Aroer, which were apparently occupied by the Moabites after the Israelites were taken into exile by the Assyrians. Eventually all of these cities fell into disrepair and were abandoned, as was the fate of most smaller ancient cities.

16Then they came up to him and said, "We would like to build pens here for our livestock and cities for our women and children. **17**But we are ready to arm ourselves and go ahead of the Israelites until we have brought them to their place. Meanwhile our women and children will live in fortified cities, for protection from the inhabitants of the land. **18**We will not return to our homes until every Israelite has received his inheritance. **19**We will not receive any inheritance with them on the other side of the Jordan, because our inheritance has come to us on the east side of the Jordan."

20Then Moses said to them, "If you will do this—if you will arm yourselves before the LORD for battle, **21**and if all of you will go armed over the Jordan before the LORD until he has driven his enemies out before him— **22**then when the land is subdued before the LORD, you may return and be free from your obligation to the LORD and to Israel. And this land will be your possession before the LORD.

23"But if you fail to do this, you will be sinning against the LORD; and you may be sure that your sin will find you out. **24**Build cities for your women and children, and pens for your flocks, but do what you have promised."

25The Gadites and Reubenites said to Moses, "We your servants will do as our lord commands. **26**Our children and wives, our flocks and herds will remain here in the cities of Gilead. **27**But your servants, every man armed for battle, will cross over to fight before the LORD, just as our lord says."

28Then Moses gave orders about them to Eleazar the priest[D] and Joshua son of Nun and to the family heads of the Israelite tribes. **29**He said to them, "If the Gadites and Reubenites, every man armed for battle, cross over the Jordan with you before the LORD, then when the land is subdued before you, give them the land of Gilead as their possession. **30**But if they do not cross over with you armed, they must accept their possession with you in Canaan."

31The Gadites and Reubenites answered, "Your servants will do what the LORD has said. **32**We will cross over before the LORD into Canaan armed, but the property we inherit will be on this side of the Jordan."

33Then Moses gave to the Gadites, the Reubenites and the half-tribe of Manasseh son of Joseph the kingdom of Sihon king of the Amorites and the kingdom of Og king of Bashan—the whole land with its cities and the territory around them.

34The Gadites built up Dibon, Ataroth, Aroer, **35**Atroth Shophan, Jazer, Jogbehah, **36**Beth Nimrah and Beth Haran as fortified cities, and built pens for their flocks. **37**And the Reubenites rebuilt Heshbon, Elealeh and Kiriathaim, **38**as well as Nebo and Baal Meon (these names were changed) and Sibmah. They gave names to the cities they rebuilt.

39The descendants of Makir son of Manasseh went to Gilead, captured it and drove out the Amorites who were there. **40**So Moses gave Gilead to the Makirites, the descendants of Manasseh, and they settled there. **41**Jair, a descendant of Manasseh, captured their settlements and called them Havvoth Jair.[a] **42**And Nobah captured Kenath and its surrounding settlements and called it Nobah after himself.

a41 Or them the settlements of Jair

Stages in Israel's Journey

33 Here are the stages in the journey of the Israelites when they came out of Egypt by divisions under the leadership of Moses and Aaron. ²At the LORD's command Moses recorded the stages in their journey. This is their journey by stages:

³The Israelites set out from Rameses on the fifteenth day of the first month, the day after the Passover. They marched out boldly in full view of all the Egyptians, ⁴who were burying all their firstborn^D, whom the LORD had struck down among them; for the LORD had brought judgment on their gods.

⁵The Israelites left Rameses and camped at Succoth.

⁶They left Succoth and camped at Etham, on the edge of the desert.

⁷They left Etham, turned back to Pi Hahiroth, to the east of Baal Zephon, and camped near Migdol.

⁸They left Pi Hahiroth^a and passed through the sea into the desert, and when they had traveled for three days in the Desert of Etham, they camped at Marah.

⁹They left Marah and went to Elim, where there were twelve springs and seventy palm trees, and they camped there.

¹⁰They left Elim and camped by the Red Sea.^b

¹¹They left the Red Sea and camped in the Desert of Sin.

¹²They left the Desert of Sin and camped at Dophkah.

¹³They left Dophkah and camped at Alush.

¹⁴They left Alush and camped at Rephidim, where there was no water for the people to drink.

¹⁵They left Rephidim and camped in the Desert of Sinai.

¹⁶They left the Desert of Sinai and camped at Kibroth Hattaavah.

¹⁷They left Kibroth Hattaavah and camped at Hazeroth.

¹⁸They left Hazeroth and camped at Rithmah.

¹⁹They left Rithmah and camped at Rimmon Perez.

²⁰They left Rimmon Perez and camped at Libnah.

²¹They left Libnah and camped at Rissah.

²²They left Rissah and camped at Kehelathah.

²³They left Kehelathah and camped at Mount Shepher.

²⁴They left Mount Shepher and camped at Haradah.

²⁵They left Haradah and camped at Makheloth.

²⁶They left Makheloth and camped at Tahath.

²⁷They left Tahath and camped at Terah.

²⁸They left Terah and camped at Mithcah.

²⁹They left Mithcah and camped at Hashmonah.

³⁰They left Hashmonah and camped at Moseroth.

³¹They left Moseroth and camped at Bene Jaakan.

³²They left Bene Jaakan and camped at Hor Haggidgad.

By divisions (33:1)

The word translated *divisions* is a military word, sometimes translated *armies* in the NIV and elsewhere. Here it likely communicates that each tribe was an organized body of people, divided into groups for the sake of orderly movement. Also included may be the idea that each division included armed men, ready to defend the tribe.

SCRIPTURE LINK (33:3–4)

See the complete story of the first Passover and the death of all the firstborn of Egypt in Exodus 11–12.

Why did the Israelites move around so much? (33:5–49)

This list of relocations seems more unusual than it is for two reasons: (1) It chronicles the Israelites' movement for the 40 years that they were in the desert. (2) A nomadic lifestyle seems extreme by our standards when in fact it was considered much more the norm from the perspective of the ancient Hebrew: if you wanted your livestock to be watered and fed, you had to go where the water and the pastures were available throughout the seasons of the year. It's possible that Kadesh (vv. 36–37) was the Israelites' central location while they moved around it during their time in the desert.

SCRIPTURE LINK (33:8) *Passed through the sea*

See the story of the Israelites crossing the Red Sea in Exodus 14.

---

^a8 Many manuscripts of the Masoretic Text, Samaritan Pentateuch and Vulgate; most manuscripts of the Masoretic Text *left from before Hahiroth*   ^b10 Hebrew *Yam Suph*; that is, Sea of Reeds; also in verse 11

SCRIPTURE LINK (33:38–39)
For more on the death of Aaron see 20:22–29.

Was Aaron exceptionally old when he died? (33:39)

Although the ancients had lived longer, Aaron was considered advanced in years when he died. Old age was considered a sign of God's blessings upon a person's life. Though Aaron would not be permitted to enter the promised land because of his sin (20:12), God did extend his life to the last year of Israel's wandering in the desert.

Why were all these stopovers recorded in the Bible? (33:49)

This list of place names does not help us understand the geography so much as it helps us to understand the way in which God provided for his people. It was an incredible thing for a nation of 2 to 3 million people to live 40 years in the desert; this was a record of God's leading during that time. Without his help, they never could have survived. The Biblical record helped the Israelites' descendants recall how God had led their ancestors from place to place, providing water and pasture for their herds and flocks as well as manna and quail for them. Today this list reminds us of God's care and leading available to his people.

³³They left Hor Haggidgad and camped at Jotbathah. ³⁴They left Jotbathah and camped at Abronah. ³⁵They left Abronah and camped at Ezion Geber. ³⁶They left Ezion Geber and camped at Kadesh, in the Desert of Zin. ³⁷They left Kadesh and camped at Mount Hor, on the border of Edom.ᴰ ³⁸At the LORD's command Aaron the priestᴰ went up Mount Hor, where he died on the first day of the fifth month of the fortieth year after the Israelites came out of Egypt. ³⁹Aaron was a hundred and twenty-three years old when he died on Mount Hor.

⁴⁰The Canaanite king of Arad, who lived in the Negevᴰ of Canaan, heard that the Israelites were coming.

⁴¹They left Mount Hor and camped at Zalmonah. ⁴²They left Zalmonah and camped at Punon. ⁴³They left Punon and camped at Oboth. ⁴⁴They left Oboth and camped at Iye Abarim, on the border of Moab. ⁴⁵They left Iyimᵃ and camped at Dibon Gad. ⁴⁶They left Dibon Gad and camped at Almon Diblathaim. ⁴⁷They left Almon Diblathaim and camped in the mountains of Abarim, near Nebo. ⁴⁸They left the mountains of Abarim and camped on the plains of Moab by the Jordan across from Jericho.ᴰ ᵇ ⁴⁹There on the plains of Moab they camped along the Jordan from Beth Jeshimoth to Abel Shittim.

⁵⁰On the plains of Moab by the Jordan across from Jericho the LORD said to Moses, ⁵¹"Speak to the Israelites and say to them: 'When you cross the Jordan into Canaan, ⁵²drive out all the inhabitants of the land before you. De-

---

ᵃ45 That is, Iye Abarim   ᵇ48 Hebrew *Jordan of Jericho*; possibly an ancient name for the Jordan River; also in verse 50

What right did Israel have to take the land? (33:52–53)

Israel's conquest of occupied land rankles those who pay rent and taxes, and fight wars to protect their land. The fact that God ordained it makes the Israelites' imperialism only slightly more palatable.

Nearly 500 years prior, though, God had promised the land to Abraham (Gen. 12:1–9). In obedience to God's command, he had pulled up stakes and traveled a thousand miles to Canaan. He and his family occupied the land for four generations.

However, God told Abraham that his descendants would leave the land for 400 years. God promised their return when his patience with the wickedness of the local pagan tribes was ended (Gen. 15:12–21).

The wickedness of Canaan's indigenous tribes did not subside while Abraham's descendants lived in Egypt. They practiced religious rituals particularly offensive to God such as child sacrifice and prostitution (Lev. 18:21; Num. 25:1–5).

In God's timing, Moses pointed Abraham's descendants, the nation of Israel, north to Canaan. Israel's military march, then, recovered the land belonging to Abraham's family. In addition, through his people Israel, God punished the wickedness of the local pagan tribes who inhabited Abraham's land (Deut. 9:4–6).

stroy all their carved images and their cast idols^D, and demolish all their high places^D. **53**Take possession of the land and settle in it, for I have given you the land to possess. **54**Distribute the land by lot, according to your clans. To a larger group give a larger inheritance, and to a smaller group a smaller one. Whatever falls to them by lot will be theirs. Distribute it according to your ancestral tribes.

55" 'But if you do not drive out the inhabitants of the land, those you allow to remain will become barbs in your eyes and thorns in your sides. They will give you trouble in the land where you will live. **56**And then I will do to you what I plan to do to them.' "

Boundaries of Canaan

34 The Lord said to Moses, **2**"Command the Israelites and say to them: 'When you enter Canaan, the land that will be allotted to you as an inheritance will have these boundaries:

3" 'Your southern side will include some of the Desert of Zin along the border of Edom^D. On the east, your southern boundary will start from the end of the Salt Sea,^a **4**cross south of Scorpion^b Pass, continue on to Zin and go south of Kadesh Barnea. Then it will go to Hazar Addar and over to Azmon, **5**where it will turn, join the Wadi of Egypt and end at the Sea.^c

6" 'Your western boundary will be the coast of the Great Sea. This will be your boundary on the west.

7" 'For your northern boundary, run a line from the Great Sea to Mount Hor **8**and from Mount Hor to Lebo^d Hamath. Then the boundary will go to Zedad, **9**continue to Ziphron and end at Hazar Enan. This will be your boundary on the north.

10" 'For your eastern boundary, run a line from Hazar Enan to Shepham. **11**The boundary will go down from Shepham to Riblah on the east side of Ain and continue along the slopes east of the Sea of Kinnereth.^e **12**Then the boundary will go down along the Jordan and end at the Salt Sea.

" 'This will be your land, with its boundaries on every side.' "

13Moses commanded the Israelites: "Assign this land by lot as an inheritance. The Lord has ordered that it be given to the nine and a half tribes, **14**because the families of the tribe of Reuben, the tribe of Gad and the half-tribe of Manasseh have received their inheritance. **15**These two and a half tribes have received their inheritance on the east side of the Jordan of Jericho,^f toward the sunrise."

16The Lord said to Moses, **17**"These are the names of the men who are to assign the land for you as an inheritance: Eleazar the priest^D and Joshua son of Nun. **18**And appoint one leader from each tribe to help assign the land. **19**These are their names:

Caleb son of Jephunneh,
    from the tribe of Judah;
20Shemuel son of Ammihud,
    from the tribe of Simeon;
21Elidad son of Kislon,
    from the tribe of Benjamin;

What are *high places?* (33:52)
Places of worship often associated with pagan religious practices, immorality and human sacrifice. Religious objects were placed on tops of hills to appease pagan gods.

Boundaries of Canaan (34:2)

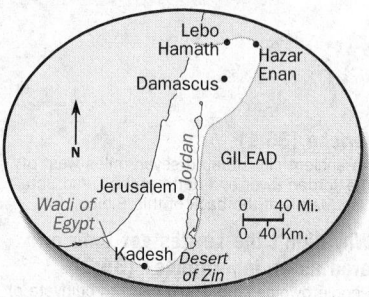

Wadi of Egypt (34:5)
A wadi is an otherwise dry valley through which water runs during the wet seasons of the year. This particular wadi is probably the Wadi el-Arish, located in the northeastern part of the Sinai Peninsula.

How did they assign land by lot? (34:13)
After they had begun the conquest of the land, Joshua cast *lots* to decide what portions of the land would go to which tribes (Joshua 18:10). This may have been done by means of the Urim and the Thummim, stones kept in the ephod worn by the high priest. Whatever the method, it would have been similar to practices we sometimes use to make a selection, such as drawing straws or picking a name out of a hat. They did not, however, view the method as one of chance. They trusted God to guide the outcome of the lots (Prov. 16:33).

---

^a3 That is, the Dead Sea; also in verse 12   ^b4 Hebrew *Akrabbim*
^c5 That is, the Mediterranean; also in verses 6 and 7   ^d8 Or *to the entrance to*   ^e11 That is, Galilee   ^f15 *Jordan of Jericho* was possibly an ancient name for the Jordan River.

²²Bukki son of Jogli,
  the leader from the tribe of Dan;
²³Hanniel son of Ephod,
  the leader from the tribe of Manasseh son of Joseph;
²⁴Kemuel son of Shiphtan,
  the leader from the tribe of Ephraim son of Joseph;
²⁵Elizaphan son of Parnach,
  the leader from the tribe of Zebulun;
²⁶Paltiel son of Azzan,
  the leader from the tribe of Issachar;
²⁷Ahihud son of Shelomi,
  the leader from the tribe of Asher;
²⁸Pedahel son of Ammihud,
  the leader from the tribe of Naphtali."

²⁹These are the men the LORD commanded to assign the inheritance to the Israelites in the land of Canaan.

Towns for the Levites

35 On the plains of Moab by the Jordan across from Jericho,[D,a] the LORD said to Moses, ²"Command the Israelites to give the Levites[D] towns to live in from the inheritance the Israelites will possess. And give them pasturelands around the towns. ³Then they will have towns to live in and pasturelands for their cattle, flocks and all their other livestock.

⁴"The pasturelands around the towns that you give the Levites will extend out fifteen hundred feet[b] from the town wall. ⁵Outside the town, measure three thousand feet[c] on the east side, three thousand on the south side, three thousand on the west and three thousand on the north, with the town in the center. They will have this area as pastureland for the towns.

Cities of Refuge

⁶"Six of the towns you give the Levites will be cities of refuge, to which a person who has killed someone may flee. In addition, give them forty-two other towns. ⁷In all you must give the Levites forty-eight towns, together with their pasturelands. ⁸The towns you give the Levites from the land the Israelites possess are to be given in proportion to the inheritance of each tribe: Take many towns from a tribe that has many, but few from one that has few."

⁹Then the LORD said to Moses: ¹⁰"Speak to the Israelites and say to them: 'When you cross the Jordan into Canaan, ¹¹select some towns to be your cities of refuge, to which a person who has killed someone accidentally may flee. ¹²They will be places of refuge from the avenger, so that a person accused of murder may not die before he stands trial before the assembly. ¹³These six towns you give will be your cities of refuge. ¹⁴Give three on this side of the Jordan and three in Canaan as cities of refuge. ¹⁵These six towns will be a place of refuge for Israelites, aliens[D] and any other people living among them, so that anyone who has killed another accidentally can flee there.

¹⁶" 'If a man strikes someone with an iron object so that he dies, he is a murderer; the murderer shall be put to death[D]. ¹⁷Or if anyone has a stone in his hand that could

Jericho (35:1)
An ancient city situated seven miles west of the Jordan River and north of the Dead Sea. See *Map 4* at the back of this Bible.

Why didn't the Levites get their own area as an inheritance? (35:2)
People owning land would need to cultivate or at least supervise the care of the land. The Levites were to devote all of their energy to serving in and around the Tent of Meeting. In addition, their lack of land made them dependent on the people—and on God. If they failed to lead the people in worship, they would lose their means of livelihood.

Cities of refuge (35:6)
Six cities functioned as jails without walls for those awaiting trial and those found guilty of involuntary manslaughter. They provided a safe place to live and work under the watchful eyes of the Levites. Three cities of refuge were located on either side of the Jordan River, so they would be accessible to any Israelite needing protection from revenge (see *Cities of Refuge* on page 311).

---

a1 Hebrew *Jordan of Jericho*; possibly an ancient name for the Jordan River   *b4* Hebrew *a thousand cubits* (about 450 meters)   *c5* Hebrew *two thousand cubits* (about 900 meters)

kill, and he strikes someone so that he dies, he is a murderer; the murderer shall be put to death[D]. **18**Or if anyone has a wooden object in his hand that could kill, and he hits someone so that he dies, he is a murderer; the murderer shall be put to death. **19**The avenger of blood shall put the murderer to death; when he meets him, he shall put him to death. **20**If anyone with malice aforethought shoves another or throws something at him intentionally so that he dies **21**or if in hostility he hits him with his fist so that he dies, that person shall be put to death; he is a murderer. The avenger of blood shall put the murderer to death when he meets him.

22" 'But if without hostility someone suddenly shoves another or throws something at him unintentionally **23**or, without seeing him, drops a stone on him that could kill him, and he dies, then since he was not his enemy and he did not intend to harm him, **24**the assembly must judge between him and the avenger of blood according to these regulations. **25**The assembly must protect the one accused of murder from the avenger of blood and send him back to the city of refuge to which he fled. He must stay there until the death of the high priest, who was anointed with the holy oil.

26" 'But if the accused ever goes outside the limits of the city of refuge to which he has fled **27**and the avenger of blood finds him outside the city, the avenger of blood may kill the accused without being guilty of murder. **28**The accused must stay in his city of refuge until the death of the high priest; only after the death of the high priest may he return to his own property.

29" 'These are to be legal requirements for you throughout the generations to come, wherever you live.

30" 'Anyone who kills a person is to be put to death as a murderer only on the testimony of witnesses. But no one is to be put to death on the testimony of only one witness.

31" 'Do not accept a ransom for the life of a murderer, who deserves to die. He must surely be put to death.

32" 'Do not accept a ransom for anyone who has fled to a city of refuge and so allow him to go back and live on his own land before the death of the high priest.

33" 'Do not pollute the land where you are. Bloodshed pollutes the land, and atonement[D] cannot be made for the land on which blood has been shed, except by the blood of the one who shed it. **34**Do not defile the land where you live and where I dwell, for I, the LORD, dwell among the Israelites.' "

Inheritance of Zelophehad's Daughters

36 The family heads of the clan of Gilead son of Makir, the son of Manasseh, who were from the clans of the descendants of Joseph, came and spoke before Moses and the leaders, the heads of the Israelite families. **2**They said, "When the LORD commanded my lord to give the land as an inheritance to the Israelites by lot, he ordered you to give the inheritance of our brother Zelophehad to his daughters. **3**Now suppose they marry men from other Israelite tribes; then their inheritance will be taken from our ancestral inheritance and added to that of the tribe they marry into. And so part of the inheritance allotted to us will be taken away. **4**When the Year of Jubilee for the Israelites comes, their inheritance will be added to that of the tribe into which they marry, and their property

Avenger of blood (35:19)

The *avenger of blood*, also called the *kinsman-redeemer*, was the nearest male blood relative to the person who had died. See article: **What was a kinsman-redeemer?** (Ruth 2:20).

How did the judicial process work? (35:24-25)

After killing someone (accidentally or otherwise), an Israelite could flee to a city of refuge safely to await trial. A murder conviction had to be established by more than one witness, and judges were charged with making a thorough investigation of what the witnesses said (Deut. 19:18). If guilty, the person was turned over to the avenger of blood for execution (Deut. 19:11-13). If, however, the assembly found that he had killed accidentally, he was protected in the city of refuge (35:25).

Why banish an innocent man? (35:25)

Innocence here meant innocent of murder but still guilty of manslaughter. Even an accidental killing destroyed a human life made in God's image, polluting the land God had given (v. 33). A person guilty of manslaughter still had to pay.

Year of Jubilee (36:4)

Every 50 years all land reverted to its original owner, and the fields lay fallow. Debts were canceled. Slaves were freed. It was a year of resolution and rest. See notes on Leviticus 25 and Deuteronomy 16.

will be taken from the tribal inheritance of our forefathers."

5Then at the LORD's command Moses gave this order to the Israelites: "What the tribe of the descendants of Joseph is saying is right. 6This is what the LORD commands for Zelophehad's daughters: They may marry anyone they please as long as they marry within the tribal clan of their father. 7No inheritance in Israel is to pass from tribe to tribe, for every Israelite shall keep the tribal land inherited from his forefathers. 8Every daughter who inherits land in any Israelite tribe must marry someone in her father's tribal clan, so that every Israelite will possess the inheritance of his fathers. 9No inheritance may pass from tribe to tribe, for each Israelite tribe is to keep the land it inherits."

10So Zelophehad's daughters did as the LORD commanded Moses. 11Zelophehad's daughters—Mahlah, Tirzah, Hoglah, Milcah and Noah—married their cousins on their father's side. 12They married within the clans of the descendants of Manasseh son of Joseph, and their inheritance remained in their father's clan and tribe.

13These are the commands and regulations the LORD gave through Moses to the Israelites on the plains of Moab by the Jordan across from Jericho.[a]

Why was land valued over love? (36:8)
Land ownership was of extraordinary importance to this five-century-old nation of nomads. Israel was to keep the family's inheritance in the clan and tribe of the family. Not to do so threatened Israel's foundational belief in tribal inheritance. The women appeared to have voiced no objection. They kept the land and their father's name, which had been their original concern. See 27:1–11.

---

a13 Hebrew *Jordan of Jericho*; possibly an ancient name for the Jordan River

DEUTERONOMY

Why read this book?

This book deals with hardship, testing and doubt, but also with promise, hope and trust. It reminds us that faith is not automatic or mechanical. It shows us that faith becomes personal and active when it springs from a living relationship with a loving God. The message of Deuteronomy can be summed up: "Devote yourself wholeheartedly to God." No wonder it's so relevant to the church today.

Who wrote this book?

Moses.

Why was it written?

Deuteronomy records Moses' final words to the Israelites before they entered the promised land. It was his challenge to obey the Lord faithfully and reject all forms of idolatry—a call to the new generation to formally renew the earlier covenant with God that their parents had broken.

When was it written?

Around 1400 B.C.

What was happening in the world at this time?

The Egyptians to the south and the Hittites to the north of Canaan were the powers of the area, although neither nation was particularly menacing. Canaan was a collection of small city-states sharing a common culture under the political control of Egypt. Egypt's power was declining, however, and the political climate was becoming increasingly chaotic.

What to look for in Deuteronomy:

The covenant God made with the Israelites in this book is similar in many respects to the treaties ancient Middle Eastern kings made with their subjects. Such treaties were made when a king imposed certain obligations on his vassals. Vassals were foreign servants, sometimes kings themselves, who were compelled to obey the treaty. Deuteronomy's format suggests that the Israelites were servants to the King of kings.

Arabah (1:1)

A major geographical area of Canaan, a waste-land in the Jordan Valley. *Arabah* means *dry* or *burnt up*. It includes both sides of the Jordan River, extending south from the Sea of Galilee beyond the Dead Sea and angling to the head of the Gulf of Aqaba.

Setting of Deuteronomy (1:1)

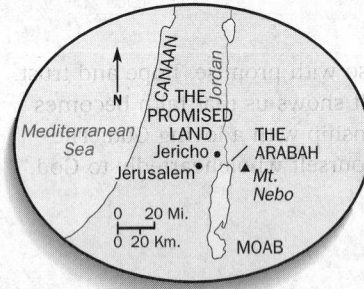

Fortieth year (1:3)

Since they had left Egypt the Israelites had been wandering in the desert for 40 years.

What law did Moses expound? (1:5)

Moses was recalling the law God gave his people at Sinai (Exodus 19–23). But he was also explaining it more fully, in light of their history. More than repeating the law, he was applying it to their situation as they were on the verge of entering the promised land.

SCRIPTURE LINK (1:19–25)

The account of the spies in Canaan and their report to the people is given in Num. 13.

The Command to Leave Horeb

1 These are the words Moses spoke to all Israel in the desert east of the Jordan—that is, in the Arabah—opposite Suph, between Paran and Tophel, Laban, Hazeroth and Dizahab. ²(It takes eleven days to go from Horeb to Kadesh Barnea by the Mount Seir road.)

³In the fortieth year, on the first day of the eleventh month, Moses proclaimed to the Israelites all that the LORD had commanded him concerning them. ⁴This was after he had defeated Sihon king of the Amorites, who reigned in Heshbon, and at Edrei had defeated Og king of Bashan, who reigned in Ashtaroth.

⁵East of the Jordan in the territory of Moab, Moses began to expound this law, saying:

⁶The LORD our God said to us at Horeb, "You have stayed long enough at this mountain. ⁷Break camp and advance into the hill country of the Amorites; go to all the neighboring peoples in the Arabah, in the mountains, in the western foothills, in the Negev[D] and along the coast, to the land of the Canaanites and to Lebanon, as far as the great river, the Euphrates. ⁸See, I have given you this land. Go in and take possession of the land that the LORD swore he would give to your fathers—to Abraham, Isaac and Jacob—and to their descendants after them."

The Appointment of Leaders

⁹At that time I said to you, "You are too heavy a burden for me to carry alone. ¹⁰The LORD your God has increased your numbers so that today you are as many as the stars in the sky. ¹¹May the LORD, the God of your fathers, increase you a thousand times and bless you as he has promised! ¹²But how can I bear your problems and your burdens and your disputes all by myself? ¹³Choose some wise, understanding and respected men from each of your tribes, and I will set them over you."

¹⁴You answered me, "What you propose to do is good."

¹⁵So I took the leading men of your tribes, wise and respected men, and appointed them to have authority over you—as commanders of thousands, of hundreds, of fifties and of tens and as tribal officials. ¹⁶And I charged your judges at that time: Hear the disputes between your brothers and judge fairly, whether the case is between brother Israelites or between one of them and an alien[D]. ¹⁷Do not show partiality in judging; hear both small and great alike. Do not be afraid of any man, for judgment belongs to God. Bring me any case too hard for you, and I will hear it. ¹⁸And at that time I told you everything you were to do.

Spies Sent Out

¹⁹Then, as the LORD our God commanded us, we set out from Horeb and went toward the hill country of the Amorites through all that vast and dreadful desert that you have seen, and so we reached Kadesh Barnea. ²⁰Then I said to you, "You have reached the hill country of the Amorites, which the LORD our God is giving us. ²¹See, the LORD your God has given you the land. Go up and take possession of it as the LORD, the God of your fathers, told you. Do not be afraid; do not be discouraged."

²²Then all of you came to me and said, "Let us send men ahead to spy out the land for us and bring back a report about the route we are to take and the towns we will come to."

ing out from Caphtor*a* destroyed them and settled in their place.)

Defeat of Sihon King of Heshbon

24"Set out now and cross the Arnon Gorge. See, I have given into your hand Sihon the Amorite, king of Heshbon, and his country. Begin to take possession of it and engage him in battle. **25**This very day I will begin to put the terror and fear of you on all the nations under heaven. They will hear reports of you and will tremble and be in anguish because of you."

26From the desert of Kedemoth I sent messengers to Sihon king of Heshbon offering peace*D* and saying, **27**"Let us pass through your country. We will stay on the main road; we will not turn aside to the right or to the left. **28**Sell us food to eat and water to drink for their price in silver. Only let us pass through on foot— **29**as the descendants of Esau, who live in Seir, and the Moabites, who live in Ar, did for us—until we cross the Jordan into the land the LORD our God is giving us." **30**But Sihon king of Heshbon refused to let us pass through. For the LORD your God had made his spirit stubborn and his heart obstinate in order to give him into your hands, as he has now done.

31The LORD said to me, "See, I have begun to deliver Sihon and his country over to you. Now begin to conquer and possess his land."

32When Sihon and all his army came out to meet us in battle at Jahaz, **33**the LORD our God delivered him over to us and we struck him down, together with his sons and his whole army. **34**At that time we took all his towns and completely destroyed*b* them—men, women and children. We left no survivors. **35**But the livestock and the plunder*D* from the towns we had captured we carried off for ourselves. **36**From Aroer on the rim of the Arnon Gorge, and from the town in the gorge, even as far as Gilead, not one town was too strong for us. The LORD our God gave us all of them. **37**But in accordance with the command of the LORD our God, you did not encroach on any

---

a23 That is, Crete   *b34* The Hebrew term refers to the irrevocable giving over of things or persons to the LORD, often by totally destroying them.

How did God terrorize Israel's enemies? (2:25)

The *reports* may refer to the exodus from Egypt, which was understood not only by the Israelites but also by the surrounding nations as the result of divine intervention on Israel's behalf. Even among pagan cultures, military victory was thought to be brought about by divine help. In their view, the god of the defeated nation was not strong enough to save them from the conquering god—in this case, the God of Israel.

Was the king of Heshbon God's unwilling puppet? (2:30)

No. He made his own choices. But there is a point at which a person or a nation becomes so fixed in their rebellion against God that their unwillingness to repent seems to become an inability to repent, almost an addiction. Resist God enough and it becomes a habit hard to break (see Romans 1:24). God allowed the king of Heshbon to become stubborn and obstinate as the consequences of his own decisions to resist God's purposes. Also see article: *Who hardened Pharaoh's heart?* (Exodus 10:1).

Why would God annihilate an entire nation? (2:34; see 3:2)

There are two reasons why God commanded the Israelites to utterly destroy certain nations: (1) the Israelites were God's instruments of judgment on the people's sins, and (2) if these enemies survived, they would turn the hearts of the Israelites away from the Lord and toward their unholy religions (see 20:18).

God told Abram that his descendants would possess the land of the Amorites when the Amorites' sin had *reached its full measure* (Gen. 15:16). It seems implied in this promise that had the Amorites stopped sinning, they could have avoided judgment. Apparently the Amorites' rebellion against God had not yet reached the point where God's judgment on them was irrevocably determined.

But they did not stop sinning. Instead, they fell deeper into sin, and God executed his judgment on the Amorite nation. The conquest, then, was the means by which God both fulfilled his promise of giving land to Israel and punished the Amorites for their sins (see 9:4).

of the land of the Ammonites, neither the land along the course of the Jabbok nor that around the towns in the hills.

Defeat of Og King of Bashan

3 Next we turned and went up along the road toward Bashan, and Og king of Bashan with his whole army marched out to meet us in battle at Edrei. **2**The LORD said to me, "Do not be afraid of him, for I have handed him over to you with his whole army and his land. Do to him what you did to Sihon king of the Amorites, who reigned in Heshbon."

3So the LORD our God also gave into our hands Og king of Bashan and all his army. We struck them down, leaving no survivors. **4**At that time we took all his cities. There was not one of the sixty cities that we did not take from them—the whole region of Argob, Og's kingdom in Bashan. **5**All these cities were fortified with high walls and with gates and bars, and there were also a great many unwalled villages. **6**We completely destroyed[a] them, as we had done with Sihon king of Heshbon, destroying[a] every city—men, women and children. **7**But all the livestock and the plunder[b] from their cities we carried off for ourselves.

8So at that time we took from these two kings of the Amorites the territory east of the Jordan, from the Arnon Gorge as far as Mount Hermon. **9**(Hermon is called Sirion by the Sidonians; the Amorites call it Senir.) **10**We took all the towns on the plateau, and all Gilead, and all Bashan as far as Salecah and Edrei, towns of Og's kingdom in Bashan. **11**(Only Og king of Bashan was left of the remnant[b] of the Rephaites. His bed[b] was made of iron and was more than thirteen feet long and six feet wide.[c] It is still in Rabbah of the Ammonites.)

Division of the Land

12Of the land that we took over at that time, I gave the Reubenites and the Gadites the territory north of Aroer by the Arnon Gorge, including half the hill country of Gilead, together with its towns. **13**The rest of Gilead and also all of Bashan, the kingdom of Og, I gave to the half tribe of Manasseh. (The whole region of Argob in Bashan used to be known as a land of the Rephaites. **14**Jair, a descendant of Manasseh, took the whole region of Argob as far as the border of the Geshurites and the Maacathites; it was named after him, so that to this day Bashan is called Havvoth Jair.[d]) **15**And I gave Gilead to Makir. **16**But to the Reubenites and the Gadites I gave the territory extending from Gilead down to the Arnon Gorge (the middle of the gorge being the border) and out to the Jabbok River, which is the border of the Ammonites. **17**Its western border was the Jordan in the Arabah, from Kinnereth to the Sea of the Arabah (the Salt Sea[e]), below the slopes of Pisgah.

18I commanded you at that time: "The LORD your God has given you this land to take possession of it. But all your able-bodied men, armed for battle, must cross over ahead of your brother Israelites. **19**However, your wives,

Bed was made of iron (3:11)

If this was a literal bed, it was truly a king-sized bed. The NIV text note suggests an alternative view, that it was a *sarcophagus*, a stone coffin for a deceased king. *Iron* could also mean *basalt*. A typical sarcophagus of the period was about ⅖ the size of this one—about 9 feet by 3.5 feet.

Were the women and children left unprotected? (3:18–20)

No. Men under the age of 20 and those over a certain age remained with the camp. Also, in times of war, able-fighting men with new homes, new crops and new fiancées, were exempted from military duty (20:5–8). That also may have been true in this instance.

---

*a*6 The Hebrew term refers to the irrevocable giving over of things or persons to the LORD, often by totally destroying them.   *b*11 Or *sarcophagus*   *c*11 Hebrew *nine cubits long and four cubits wide* (about 4 meters long and 1.8 meters wide)   *d*14 Or *called the settlements of Jair*   *e*17 That is, the Dead Sea

your children and your livestock (I know you have much livestock) may stay in the towns I have given you, **20**until the LORD gives rest to your brothers as he has to you, and they too have taken over the land that the LORD your God is giving them, across the Jordan. After that, each of you may go back to the possession I have given you."

Moses Forbidden to Cross the Jordan

21At that time I commanded Joshua: "You have seen with your own eyes all that the LORD your God has done to these two kings. The LORD will do the same to all the kingdoms over there where you are going. **22**Do not be afraid of them; the LORD your God himself will fight for you."

23At that time I pleaded with the LORD: **24**"O Sovereign LORD, you have begun to show to your servant your greatness and your strong hand. For what god is there in heaven or on earth who can do the deeds and mighty works you do? **25**Let me go over and see the good land beyond the Jordan—that fine hill country and Lebanon."

26But because of you the LORD was angry with me and would not listen to me. "That is enough," the LORD said. "Do not speak to me anymore about this matter. **27**Go up to the top of Pisgah and look west and north and south and east. Look at the land with your own eyes, since you are not going to cross this Jordan. **28**But commission Joshua, and encourage and strengthen him, for he will lead this people across and will cause them to inherit the land that you will see." **29**So we stayed in the valley near Beth Peor.

Obedience Commanded

4 Hear now, O Israel, the decrees and laws I am about to teach you. Follow them so that you may live and may go in and take possession of the land that the LORD, the God of your fathers, is giving you. **2**Do not add to what I command you and do not subtract from it, but keep the commands of the LORD your God that I give you.

3You saw with your own eyes what the LORD did at Baal Peor. The LORD your God destroyed from among you everyone who followed the Baal of Peor, **4**but all of you who held fast to the LORD your God are still alive today.

5See, I have taught you decrees and laws as the LORD my God commanded me, so that you may follow them in the land you are entering to take possession of it. **6**Observe them carefully, for this will show your wisdom and understanding to the nations, who will hear about all these decrees and say, "Surely this great nation is a wise and understanding people." **7**What other nation is so great as to have their gods near them the way the LORD our God is near us whenever we pray to him? **8**And what other nation is so great as to have such righteous[D] decrees and laws as this body of laws I am setting before you today?

9Only be careful, and watch yourselves closely so that you do not forget the things your eyes have seen or let them slip from your heart as long as you live. Teach them to your children and to their children after them. **10**Remember the day you stood before the LORD your God at Horeb, when he said to me, "Assemble the people before me to hear my words so that they may learn to revere[D] me as long as they live in the land and may teach them to their children." **11**You came near and stood at the foot of the mountain while it blazed with fire to the very heav-

How did God fight for Israel? (3:22)

Several things happened: (1) Rahab told the Israelite spies that God had caused Israel's enemies to be paralyzed with fear (Joshua 2:8–11). See *How did God terrorize Israel's enemies?* (2:25). (2) God used the weather to aid Israel in battle—he sent lethal hailstones on the enemy and delayed the sunset until Israel had won the battle (Joshua 10:11–14). (3) God pronounced judgment on the enemy for their sins, allowing their sins finally to destroy them (Joshua 11:20). See *Was the king of Heshbon God's unwilling puppet?* (2:30).

When Moses spoke of other gods was he acknowledging their existence? (3:24)

See *God of gods and Lord of lords* (10:17).

Why did God tell Moses to climb Pisgah? (3:27)

The summit of Pisgah offered a spectacular view of the promised land (see *Balaam's Oracles* on page 214). While God did not permit Moses to enter the land, he allowed him to see it from a distance.

ens, with black clouds and deep darkness. **12**Then the LORD spoke to you out of the fire. You heard the sound of words but saw no form; there was only a voice. **13**He declared to you his covenant[D], the Ten Commandments, which he commanded you to follow and then wrote them on two stone tablets. **14**And the LORD directed me at that time to teach you the decrees and laws you are to follow in the land that you are crossing the Jordan to possess.

Idolatry Forbidden

15You saw no form of any kind the day the LORD spoke to you at Horeb out of the fire. Therefore watch yourselves very carefully, **16**so that you do not become corrupt and make for yourselves an idol[D], an image of any shape, whether formed like a man or a woman, **17**or like any animal on earth or any bird that flies in the air, **18**or like any creature that moves along the ground or any fish in the waters below. **19**And when you look up to the sky and see the sun, the moon and the stars—all the heavenly array— do not be enticed into bowing down to them and worshiping things the LORD your God has apportioned to all the nations under heaven. **20**But as for you, the LORD took you and brought you out of the iron-smelting furnace, out of Egypt, to be the people of his inheritance, as you now are.

21The LORD was angry with me because of you, and he solemnly swore that I would not cross the Jordan and enter the good land the LORD your God is giving you as your inheritance. **22**I will die in this land; I will not cross the Jordan; but you are about to cross over and take possession of that good land. **23**Be careful not to forget the covenant of the LORD your God that he made with you; do not make for yourselves an idol in the form of anything the LORD your God has forbidden. **24**For the LORD your God is a consuming fire, a jealous God.

25After you have had children and grandchildren and have lived in the land a long time—if you then become corrupt and make any kind of idol, doing evil in the eyes of the LORD your God and provoking him to anger, **26**I call heaven and earth as witnesses against you this day that you will quickly perish from the land that you are crossing the Jordan to possess. You will not live there long but will certainly be destroyed. **27**The LORD will scatter you among the peoples, and only a few of you will survive among the nations to which the LORD will drive you. **28**There you will worship man-made gods of wood and stone, which cannot see or hear or eat or smell. **29**But if from there you seek the LORD your God, you will find him if you look for him with all your heart and with all your soul[D]. **30**When you are in distress and all these things have happened to you, then in later days you will return to the LORD your God and obey him. **31**For the LORD your God is a merciful God; he will not abandon or destroy you or forget the covenant with your forefathers, which he confirmed to them by oath.

The LORD Is God

32Ask now about the former days, long before your time, from the day God created man on the earth; ask from one end of the heavens to the other. Has anything so great as this ever happened, or has anything like it ever been heard of? **33**Has any other people heard the voice of God[a] speaking out of fire, as you have, and lived? **34**Has

Why would anyone desire a visible image over an invisible God? (4:15–18; see also 5:8)
People were accustomed to physical representations of gods. Such cultural customs could have become a temptation for the Israelites, since God had revealed himself only in words, not in form (v. 15). Any attempt to portray God's image would have been utterly inadequate and ultimately misleading.

Why was Egypt called an iron-smelting furnace? (4:20)
Iron must be heated to extreme temperatures to rid it of impurities. The Israelites' faith was purified by the heat of their suffering and slavery in Egypt. God delivered them from Egypt, so they might become *the people of his inheritance.*

How is the Lord *a consuming fire*? (4:24)
This pictures the depth of God's feelings when his people are disloyal and turn from him to serve idols. God's righteous jealousy, like fire, *consumes* whatever seeks to undermine his holiness. God initiated his covenant out of love and required Israel to respond in love. Anything that would compete with their allegiance to God would cause him to be *jealous* for their full devotion.

How could God call heaven and earth as witnesses? (4:26)
Summoning witnesses was a standard element of ancient treaties. Typically, the gods of the two parties to the agreement were summoned as witnesses at the time the covenant was made. The gods were thought to have the power necessary to enforce the treaty. In Deuteronomy, God himself is one of the parties to the covenant. Since there is no one above him, he called heaven and earth as reliable, unchanging witnesses—a poetic illustration of God's authority. It is also a reminder that if Israel broke the covenant, they would be threatened with the wrath of heaven and earth—natural disasters, bad harvests and so on (for example, Deut. 28:23–24).

---

a33 Or of a god

any god ever tried to take for himself one nation out of another nation, by testings, by miraculous signs and wonders, by war, by a mighty hand and an outstretched arm, or by great and awesome deeds, like all the things the LORD your God did for you in Egypt before your very eyes?

35You were shown these things so that you might know that the LORD is God; besides him there is no other. **36**From heaven he made you hear his voice to discipline you. On earth he showed you his great fire, and you heard his words from out of the fire. **37**Because he loved your forefathers and chose their descendants after them, he brought you out of Egypt by his Presence and his great strength, **38**to drive out before you nations greater and stronger than you and to bring you into their land to give it to you for your inheritance, as it is today.

39Acknowledge and take to heart this day that the LORD is God in heaven above and on the earth below. There is no other. **40**Keep his decrees and commands, which I am giving you today, so that it may go well with you and your children after you and that you may live long in the land the LORD your God gives you for all time.

Cities of Refuge

41Then Moses set aside three cities east of the Jordan, **42**to which anyone who had killed a person could flee if he had unintentionally killed his neighbor without malice aforethought. He could flee into one of these cities and save his life. **43**The cities were these: Bezer in the desert plateau, for the Reubenites; Ramoth in Gilead, for the Gadites; and Golan in Bashan, for the Manassites.

Introduction to the Law

44This is the law Moses set before the Israelites. **45**These are the stipulations, decrees and laws Moses gave them when they came out of Egypt **46**and were in the valley near Beth Peor east of the Jordan, in the land of Sihon king of the Amorites, who reigned in Heshbon and was defeated by Moses and the Israelites as they came out of Egypt. **47**They took possession of his land and the land of Og king of Bashan, the two Amorite kings east of the Jordan. **48**This land extended from Aroer on the rim of the

SCRIPTURE LINK (4:36) *His great fire*
Read in Exodus 19:16–19 about God speaking from out of the fire to Moses and the Israelites at Mount Sinai. God also spoke to Moses from out of a burning bush in Exodus 3.

Did God give Israel the land *for all time?* **(4:40)**
Yes, but his promise was conditional. Israel eventually lost the land God had given them because they did not keep their side of the bargain outlined in the first part of this verse: to keep the Lord's decrees and commands. The promise was not deficient—the people were.

SCRIPTURE LINK (4:41–43) *Cities of refuge*
For more on the cities of refuge see Num. 35:6–34; Deut. 19:1–14; Joshua 20:1–9. Also see *Cities of refuge* (Num. 35:6).

Did God love Israel more than other nations? (4:33)

Because we cannot comprehend God's ways, what to us seems to be God's special favor is also a unique and challenging assignment. Israel enjoyed great privileges—but those privileges also carried great responsibilities. God made it clear (9:4–5) that there was nothing inherently special or *righteous* about Israel for which they deserved God's favor more than any other nation.

The question may relate more to God's *timing* than to his favor. God gave Israel his special attention at this point in history so that he could use the Israelites as a means to bring his blessings to the whole world (Gen. 12:2–3). God desires everyone everywhere to know him (2 Peter 3:9). So he chose the nation of Israel as a witness to testify to other nations about him.

God loved Israel, but he also loves the whole world. The ultimate expression of God's love—for Israel and the world—was that he sent his Son to die. Also see *Why did God treasure Israel above all other nations?* (26:18).

Arnon Gorge to Mount Siyon[a] (that is, Hermon), [49]and included all the Arabah east of the Jordan, as far as the Sea of the Arabah,[b] below the slopes of Pisgah.

The Ten Commandments

5 Moses summoned all Israel and said:
Hear, O Israel, the decrees and laws I declare in your hearing today. Learn them and be sure to follow them. [2]The LORD our God made a covenant[D] with us at Horeb. [3]It was not with our fathers that the LORD made this covenant, but with us, with all of us who are alive here today. [4]The LORD spoke to you face to face out of the fire on the mountain. [5](At that time I stood between the LORD and you to declare to you the word of the LORD, because you were afraid of the fire and did not go up the mountain.) And he said:

> [6]"I am the LORD your God, who brought you out of Egypt, out of the land of slavery.
> [7]"You shall have no other gods before[c] me.
> [8]"You shall not make for yourself an idol[D] in the form of anything in heaven above or on the earth beneath or in the waters below. [9]You shall not bow down to them or worship them; for I, the LORD your God, am a jealous God, punishing the children for the sin of the fathers to the third and fourth generation of those who hate me, [10]but showing love to a thousand ⌊generations⌋ of those who love me and keep my commandments.
> [11]"You shall not misuse the name of the LORD your God, for the LORD will not hold anyone guiltless who misuses his name.
> [12]"Observe the Sabbath[D] day by keeping it holy, as the LORD your God has commanded you. [13]Six days you shall labor and do all your work, [14]but the seventh day is a Sabbath to the LORD your God. On it you shall not do any work, neither you, nor your son or daughter, nor your manservant or maidservant, nor your ox, your donkey or any of your animals, nor the alien[D] within your gates, so that your manservant and maidservant may rest, as you do. [15]Remember that you were slaves in Egypt and that the LORD your God brought you out of there with a mighty hand and an outstretched arm. Therefore the LORD your God has commanded you to observe the Sabbath day.
> [16]"Honor your father and your mother, as the LORD your God has commanded you, so that you may live long and that it may go well with you in the land the LORD your God is giving you.
> [17]"You shall not murder.
> [18]"You shall not commit adultery.
> [19]"You shall not steal.
> [20]"You shall not give false testimony against your neighbor.
> [21]"You shall not covet your neighbor's wife. You shall not set your desire on your neighbor's house or land, his manservant or maidservant, his ox or

Didn't the Israelites already know the Ten Commandments? (5:1)

Yes, this new generation of Israelites knew the law. But Moses was taking this opportunity (before they entered the promised land) to review the law and to explain it further to the people. This generation had to affirm for themselves the covenant with the Lord. They could not rest on the pledge of their parents.

Face to face (5:4; also 34:10)

This is a Hebrew idiom, not to be taken literally. The people heard God's voice but did not actually see him (4:12). God conceals his glory because to look upon him would destroy us (see Isaiah 6:5). Also see *How could Moses speak to the Lord face to face?* (Exodus 33:11).

Why accuse the people of being afraid to approach God? (5:5)

This was not an accusation. Moses simply recounted their emotions at the time. Their fear was stronger motivation than God's command for them to stay away from the mountain (see Exodus 20:18–19). Fear of God can be either healthy or unhealthy (compare vv. 28–29).

SCRIPTURE LINK (5:6–21)

The Ten Commandments are also recorded in Exodus 20:1–17.

Do these commandments apply to us? (5:6–21)

Yes. The Ten Commandments provide timeless moral principles that form the fabric of the Judeo-Christian ethic. See article: *Should we obey or ignore Old Testament law?* (Gal. 3:1–25).

Why would God punish children for the sin of their parents? (5:9)

Does God hold people accountable for the sins of others? No. This refers more to the *consequences* of sin than *judgment* for sin, though in a sense it is that as well. A generation can be burdened by the sins of their elders. The examples and behavior of some individuals affect the other family members. God, however, only judges a person for his or her own actions (see Ezek. 18:20). See article: *Does God punish children for their parents' sins?* (Num. 14:18).

---

[a]48 Hebrew; Syriac (see also Deut. 3:9) *Sirion*   [b]49 That is, the Dead Sea   [c]7 Or *besides*

donkey, or anything that belongs to your neighbor."

22These are the commandments the LORD proclaimed in a loud voice to your whole assembly there on the mountain from out of the fire, the cloud and the deep darkness; and he added nothing more. Then he wrote them on two stone tablets and gave them to me.

23When you heard the voice out of the darkness, while the mountain was ablaze with fire, all the leading men of your tribes and your elders came to me. **24**And you said, "The LORD our God has shown us his glory^D and his majesty, and we have heard his voice from the fire. Today we have seen that a man can live even if God speaks with him. **25**But now, why should we die? This great fire will consume us, and we will die if we hear the voice of the LORD our God any longer. **26**For what mortal man has ever heard the voice of the living God speaking out of fire, as we have, and survived? **27**Go near and listen to all that the LORD our God says. Then tell us whatever the LORD our God tells you. We will listen and obey."

28The LORD heard you when you spoke to me and the LORD said to me, "I have heard what this people said to you. Everything they said was good. **29**Oh, that their hearts would be inclined to fear me and keep all my commands always, so that it might go well with them and their children forever!

30"Go, tell them to return to their tents. **31**But you stay here with me so that I may give you all the commands, decrees and laws you are to teach them to follow in the land I am giving them to possess."

32So be careful to do what the LORD your God has commanded you; do not turn aside to the right or to the left. **33**Walk in all the way that the LORD your God has commanded you, so that you may live and prosper and prolong your days in the land that you will possess.

Love the LORD Your God

6 These are the commands, decrees and laws the LORD your God directed me to teach you to observe in the land that you are crossing the Jordan to possess, **2**so that you, your children and their children after them may fear the LORD your God as long as you live by keeping all his decrees and commands that I give you, and so that you may enjoy long life. **3**Hear, O Israel, and be careful to obey so that it may go well with you and that you may increase greatly in a land flowing with milk and honey, just as the LORD, the God of your fathers, promised you.

4Hear, O Israel: The LORD our God, the LORD is one.^a **5**Love the LORD your God with all your heart and with all your soul^D and with all your strength. **6**These commandments that I give you today are to be upon your hearts. **7**Impress them on your children. Talk about them when you sit at home and when you walk along the road, when you lie down and when you get up. **8**Tie them as symbols on your hands and bind them on your foreheads. **9**Write them on the doorframes of your houses and on your gates.

10When the LORD your God brings you into the land he swore to your fathers, to Abraham, Isaac and Jacob, to give you—a land with large, flourishing cities you did not

---

a4 Or The LORD our God is one LORD; or The LORD is our God, the LORD is one; or The LORD is our God, the LORD alone

---

What does it mean to misuse God's name? (5:11)
This is usually understood as blasphemy, though it can mean more. The Hebrew phrase translated *misuse* contains two ideas: (1) it is something deceptive—like false testimony, and (2) it is something empty or hollow. Misusing God's name, then, is to devalue his name by using it in a frivolous, deceptive way.

Why does God want us to fear him? (5:29)
See article: *Should we live in terror of God?* (Prov. 1:7).

Flowing with milk and honey (6:3)
This was a metaphor for Canaan used to suggest its prosperous soil and climate. The land had great potential, and prosperity was assured—if Israel continued to obey God.

Did God's love and care for Israel depend on how well they followed the law? (6:3)
God's love for Israel was constant and did not depend on their obedience to the law. He initiated the covenant with them before they ever obeyed, and he still cared for them even when they disobeyed. However, the blessings and curses *were* dependent upon their obedience to the law (see ch. 28). If they turned away from God, they put into motion a negative chain of events and suffered the consequences. If on the other hand they honored God, they enjoyed his abundant provisions.

What does it mean that the LORD is one? (6:4)
In Hebrew these words can be rendered several different ways (see the NIV text note). These words communicate not only the *uniqueness* of God but also his *unity*. They form the clearest possible statement against idolatry and polytheism, the worship of many gods.

What's the difference between heart and soul? (6:5)
See *What's the difference between heart and soul?* (30:6).

Symbols on your hands and . . . foreheads (6:8)
See *A sign on your hand and a symbol on your forehead* (Exodus 13:9,16).

Was it fair to give Israel property others had worked for? (6:10-11)
This was a matter of judgment, not favoritism. God had shown Abraham that he would one day use the Israelites as his instrument of judgment against the sins of the Amorites (Gen. 15:13-16). See article: *What right did Israel have to take the land?* (Num. 33:52-53). Later when the Israelites were judged for sin, they lost their houses and land just as the Amorites had.

SCRIPTURE LINK (6:13) *Oaths in his name*

See *Is it wrong to swear to tell the truth in court?* (Matt. 5:34–37); *If God swore an oath, should we?* (Heb. 6:13) and *Is it wrong to take an oath in court?* (James 5:12).

SCRIPTURE LINK (6:16) *Massah*

See Exodus 17:2.

Why would a God of love command the Israelites to show *no mercy?* (7:2)

God's command to destroy the Canaanites was a warning to the Israelites not to compromise their relationship with him. To make a treaty with the Canaanites would indicate that they at least recognized Canaanite gods. Also, Israel was to destroy the sinful nations as God's judgment against sin. See *Was it fair to give Israel property others had worked for?* (6:10–11).

Why would intermarriage lead Israel to idolatry? (7:3–4)

Why couldn't it just as easily have led to faith for non-Israelites? Because humankind tends to move away from God, not toward him. The Israelites had already experienced this tendency firsthand at Baal Peor (see Num. 25:1–5).

Asherah poles (7:5)

Wooden poles, perhaps carved in the image of the Canaanite goddess Asherah. These poles were placed near the altars in Canaanite worship.

build, [11]houses filled with all kinds of good things you did not provide, wells you did not dig, and vineyards and olive groves you did not plant—then when you eat and are satisfied, [12]be careful that you do not forget the Lord, who brought you out of Egypt, out of the land of slavery.

[13]Fear the Lord your God, serve him only and take your oaths in his name. [14]Do not follow other gods, the gods of the peoples around you; [15]for the Lord your God, who is among you, is a jealous God and his anger will burn against you, and he will destroy you from the face of the land. [16]Do not test the Lord your God as you did at Massah. [17]Be sure to keep the commands of the Lord your God and the stipulations and decrees he has given you. [18]Do what is right and good in the Lord's sight, so that it may go well with you and you may go in and take over the good land that the Lord promised on oath to your forefathers, [19]thrusting out all your enemies before you, as the Lord said.

[20]In the future, when your son asks you, "What is the meaning of the stipulations, decrees and laws the Lord our God has commanded you?" [21]tell him: "We were slaves of Pharaoh in Egypt, but the Lord brought us out of Egypt with a mighty hand. [22]Before our eyes the Lord sent miraculous signs and wonders—great and terrible—upon Egypt and Pharaoh and his whole household. [23]But he brought us out from there to bring us in and give us the land that he promised on oath to our forefathers. [24]The Lord commanded us to obey all these decrees and to fear the Lord our God, so that we might always prosper and be kept alive, as is the case today. [25]And if we are careful to obey all this law before the Lord our God, as he has commanded us, that will be our righteousness[D]."

Driving Out the Nations

7 When the Lord your God brings you into the land you are entering to possess and drives out before you many nations—the Hittites, Girgashites, Amorites, Canaanites, Perizzites, Hivites and Jebusites, seven nations larger and stronger than you— [2]and when the Lord your God has delivered them over to you and you have defeated them, then you must destroy them totally.[a] Make no treaty with them, and show them no mercy[D]. [3]Do not intermarry with them. Do not give your daughters to their sons or take their daughters for your sons, [4]for they will turn your sons away from following me to serve other gods, and the Lord's anger will burn against you and will quickly destroy you. [5]This is what you are to do to them: Break down their altars, smash their sacred stones[D], cut down their Asherah poles[Db] and burn their idols[D] in the fire. [6]For you are a people holy to the Lord your God. The Lord your God has chosen you out of all the peoples on the face of the earth to be his people, his treasured possession.

[7]The Lord did not set his affection on you and choose you because you were more numerous than other peoples, for you were the fewest of all peoples. [8]But it was because the Lord loved you and kept the oath he swore to your forefathers that he brought you out with a mighty hand and redeemed[D] you from the land of slavery, from

---

[a]2 The Hebrew term refers to the irrevocable giving over of things or persons to the Lord, often by totally destroying them; also in verse 26.
[b]5 That is, symbols of the goddess Asherah; here and elsewhere in Deuteronomy

the power of Pharaoh king of Egypt. **9**Know therefore that the LORD your God is God; he is the faithful God, keeping his covenant^D of love to a thousand generations of those who love him and keep his commands. **10**But

> those who hate him he will repay to their face
> by destruction;
> he will not be slow to repay to their face
> those who hate him.

11Therefore, take care to follow the commands, decrees and laws I give you today.

12If you pay attention to these laws and are careful to follow them, then the LORD your God will keep his covenant of love with you, as he swore to your forefathers. **13**He will love you and bless you and increase your numbers. He will bless the fruit of your womb, the crops of your land—your grain, new wine^D and oil—the calves of your herds and the lambs of your flocks in the land that he swore to your forefathers to give you. **14**You will be blessed more than any other people; none of your men or women will be childless, nor any of your livestock without young. **15**The LORD will keep you free from every disease. He will not inflict on you the horrible diseases you knew in Egypt, but he will inflict them on all who hate you. **16**You must destroy all the peoples the LORD your God gives over to you. Do not look on them with pity and do not serve their gods, for that will be a snare to you.

17You may say to yourselves, "These nations are stronger than we are. How can we drive them out?" **18**But do not be afraid of them; remember well what the LORD your God did to Pharaoh and to all Egypt. **19**You saw with your own eyes the great trials, the miraculous signs and wonders, the mighty hand and outstretched arm, with which the LORD your God brought you out. The LORD your God will do the same to all the peoples you now fear. **20**Moreover, the LORD your God will send the hornet among them until even the survivors who hide from you have perished. **21**Do not be terrified by them, for the LORD your God, who is among you, is a great and awesome God. **22**The LORD your God will drive out those nations before you, little by little. You will not be allowed to eliminate them all at once, or the wild animals will multiply around you. **23**But the LORD your God will deliver them over to you, throwing them into great confusion until they are destroyed. **24**He will give their kings into your hand, and you will wipe out their names from under heaven. No one will be able to stand up against you; you will destroy them. **25**The images of their gods are to burn in the fire. Do not covet the silver and gold on them, and do not take it for yourselves, or you will be ensnared by it, for it is detestable to the LORD your God. **26**Do not bring a detestable thing into your house or you, like it, will be set apart for destruction. Utterly abhor and detest it, for it is set apart for destruction.

Do Not Forget the LORD

8 Be careful to follow every command I am giving you today, so that you may live and increase and may enter and possess the land that the LORD promised on oath to your forefathers. **2**Remember how the LORD your God led you all the way in the desert these forty years, to humble you and to test you in order to know what was in your heart, whether or not you would keep his commands. **3**He humbled you, causing you to hunger and then feeding

Why did God tell the people to feel no pity? (7:16)

He wanted them to gain his perspective on the situation. God appointed the Israelites to be his instruments of judgment on the Canaanites, so they were to reflect his zeal and determination. Anything less may have jeopardized their own purity and commitment to God's purposes. Also see *Why would a God of love command the Israelites to show no mercy?* (7:2).

How could the hornet finish off the remaining enemy? (7:20)

The image of being chased by bees may have been meant to remind the people of how the Amorites, *like a swarm of bees*, had chased them off the battlefield (1:44) when the Israelites failed to trust in God. They could reverse the results if they now trusted in the Lord. God would chase away their enemies. Also see *Did God really send hornets?* (Exodus 23:28) and *Did God literally send hornets?* (Joshua 24:12).

How could a quick victory cause wild animals to multiply? (7:22)

This expresses the gradual nature of Israel's military conquest. The *wild animals* may refer to the natural uprising of people in the state of anarchy that sometimes results from a political vacuum. See *Wouldn't deserted land be easier to possess than enemy-held territory?* (Exodus 23:29–30).

Why did God have to test what was in the human heart? (8:2)

God already knows everything, even what is in the hearts of his people (see ch. 32). But he allowed the test so his people could see their true nature. See articles: *Why did testing come to Job?* (Job 23:10) and *Why does God test us?* (Psalm 81:7).

Why describe a dry land like Canaan in such glowing terms? (8:7–8)

Although Canaan is not naturally productive by North American standards, it was better than what the Israelites had known in the desert or in Egypt (which depended on the Nile for agricultural irrigation). Some suggest the land offers less now than it did before several thousand years of use wearied it. See *Flowing with milk and honey* (6:3).

What metals did Israel use? (8:9)

Copper, tin, bronze and iron all could be found in Canaan. At that time iron was considered to be somewhat valuable, and the words *the rocks are iron* figuratively describe the abundance of the land.

What was so great about the Anakites? (9:2)

See *What was so frightening about the Anakites?* (1:28).

How could God hold other nations accountable for what they never knew? (9:4)

God is not only the God of Israel, but also the Lord of all nations. God had revealed himself—his holiness and his judgment—to Noah. Since all people descended from Noah, God's standard of holiness was at one time conveyed to all nations. However, long before God revealed himself again to Israel, the nations had departed from what their ancestors had known.

you with manna^D, which neither you nor your fathers had known, to teach you that man does not live on bread alone but on every word that comes from the mouth of the LORD. **4**Your clothes did not wear out and your feet did not swell during these forty years. **5**Know then in your heart that as a man disciplines his son, so the LORD your God disciplines you.

6Observe the commands of the LORD your God, walking in his ways and revering him. **7**For the LORD your God is bringing you into a good land—a land with streams and pools of water, with springs flowing in the valleys and hills; **8**a land with wheat and barley, vines and fig trees, pomegranates, olive oil and honey; **9**a land where bread will not be scarce and you will lack nothing; a land where the rocks are iron and you can dig copper out of the hills.

10When you have eaten and are satisfied, praise the LORD your God for the good land he has given you. **11**Be careful that you do not forget the LORD your God, failing to observe his commands, his laws and his decrees that I am giving you this day. **12**Otherwise, when you eat and are satisfied, when you build fine houses and settle down, **13**and when your herds and flocks grow large and your silver and gold increase and all you have is multiplied, **14**then your heart will become proud and you will forget the LORD your God, who brought you out of Egypt, out of the land of slavery. **15**He led you through the vast and dreadful desert, that thirsty and waterless land, with its venomous snakes and scorpions. He brought you water out of hard rock. **16**He gave you manna to eat in the desert, something your fathers had never known, to humble and to test you so that in the end it might go well with you. **17**You may say to yourself, "My power and the strength of my hands have produced this wealth for me." **18**But remember the LORD your God, for it is he who gives you the ability to produce wealth, and so confirms his covenant^D, which he swore to your forefathers, as it is today.

19If you ever forget the LORD your God and follow other gods and worship and bow down to them, I testify against you today that you will surely be destroyed. **20**Like the nations the LORD destroyed before you, so you will be destroyed for not obeying the LORD your God.

Not Because of Israel's Righteousness

9 Hear, O Israel. You are now about to cross the Jordan to go in and dispossess nations greater and stronger than you, with large cities that have walls up to the sky. **2**The people are strong and tall—Anakites! You know about them and have heard it said: "Who can stand up against the Anakites?" **3**But be assured today that the LORD your God is the one who goes across ahead of you like a devouring fire. He will destroy them; he will subdue them before you. And you will drive them out and annihilate them quickly, as the LORD has promised you.

4After the LORD your God has driven them out before you, do not say to yourself, "The LORD has brought me here to take possession of this land because of my righteousness^D." No, it is on account of the wickedness of these nations that the LORD is going to drive them out before you. **5**It is not because of your righteousness or your integrity that you are going in to take possession of their land; but on account of the wickedness of these nations, the LORD your God will drive them out before you, to accomplish what he swore to your fathers, to Abraham,

Isaac and Jacob. **6**Understand, then, that it is not because of your righteousness^D that the LORD your God is giving you this good land to possess, for you are a stiff-necked people.

The Golden Calf

7Remember this and never forget how you provoked the LORD your God to anger in the desert. From the day you left Egypt until you arrived here, you have been rebellious against the LORD. **8**At Horeb you aroused the LORD's wrath so that he was angry enough to destroy you. **9**When I went up on the mountain to receive the tablets of stone, the tablets of the covenant^D that the LORD had made with you, I stayed on the mountain forty days and forty nights; I ate no bread and drank no water. **10**The LORD gave me two stone tablets inscribed by the finger of God. On them were all the commandments the LORD proclaimed to you on the mountain out of the fire, on the day of the assembly.

11At the end of the forty days and forty nights, the LORD gave me the two stone tablets, the tablets of the covenant. **12**Then the LORD told me, "Go down from here at once, because your people whom you brought out of Egypt have become corrupt. They have turned away quickly from what I commanded them and have made a cast idol^D for themselves."

13And the LORD said to me, "I have seen this people, and they are a stiff-necked people indeed! **14**Let me alone, so that I may destroy them and blot out their name from under heaven. And I will make you into a nation stronger and more numerous than they."

15So I turned and went down from the mountain while it was ablaze with fire. And the two tablets of the covenant were in my hands.^a **16**When I looked, I saw that you had sinned against the LORD your God; you had made for yourselves an idol cast in the shape of a calf. You had turned aside quickly from the way that the LORD had commanded you. **17**So I took the two tablets and threw them out of my hands, breaking them to pieces before your eyes.

18Then once again I fell prostrate before the LORD for forty days and forty nights; I ate no bread and drank no water, because of all the sin you had committed, doing what was evil in the LORD's sight and so provoking him to anger. **19**I feared the anger and wrath of the LORD, for he was angry enough with you to destroy you. But again the LORD listened to me. **20**And the LORD was angry enough with Aaron to destroy him, but at that time I prayed for Aaron too. **21**Also I took that sinful thing of yours, the calf you had made, and burned it in the fire. Then I crushed it and ground it to powder as fine as dust and threw the dust into a stream that flowed down the mountain.

22You also made the LORD angry at Taberah, at Massah and at Kibroth Hattaavah.

23And when the LORD sent you out from Kadesh Barnea, he said, "Go up and take possession of the land I have given you." But you rebelled against the command of the LORD your God. You did not trust him or obey him. **24**You have been rebellious against the LORD ever since I have known you.

25I lay prostrate before the LORD those forty days and

^a15 Or *And I had the two tablets of the covenant with me, one in each hand*

Stiff-necked people (9:6)

This description of the Israelites illustrates the unworthiness of God's people to receive his favor. The idiom was a farmer's expression for an ox or horse that would not be led or respond to the rope when tugged (see Isaiah 1:3). When God called his people *stiff-necked* (9:13; 10:16; 31:27), he meant they were rebellious and stubborn.

Why two tablets instead of just one? (9:10)

This was common procedure for drawing up a treaty during that time. The two tablets were likely copies of the same words. One copy was for the foreign ruler (in this case God) and one for the servant obliged to submit (Israel). According to ancient custom, a record of the covenant was to be stored in the temple of the god of each party to the agreement. Since God was the God of both parties in this "treaty," both tablets were placed in the ark of the covenant (see 10:8; 31:9).

Why worship a calf? (9:16)

The calf or bull was a symbol of the Canaanite god Baal, the god of fertility and strength, as well as the Egyptian bull-god Apis, with which the Israelites were also familiar. Also see Exodus 32.

Short of a miracle, how could Moses fast for 80 days without food or water? (9:18; see 9:9)

The account in Deuteronomy is a telescoped version of the events in Exodus. These two fasts were actually separated by a period of time (see Exodus 32:34), though certainly the Lord enabled Moses to endure them both.

Does prayer change God's mind? (9:19)

Though God knows before we pray what we will ask and how he will answer, it is spiritually beneficial for us to pray. Moses interceded on behalf of the people, and God, wanting to forgive, heard his prayer. But it seems that God would have destroyed the people, just as he said, had not Moses stood up for them. This is part of the mystery of how God and humankind work together. See article: *Can our prayers cause God to change his mind?* (Exodus 32:14).

SCRIPTURE LINK (9:20) *The LORD was angry enough with Aaron to destroy him*

See Exodus 32:21.

SCRIPTURE LINK (9:22)

For details about what made God angry, see Num. 11:3 (at *Taberah*); Exodus 17:7 (at *Massah*); Num. 11:34 (at *Kibroth Hattaavah*).

forty nights because the LORD had said he would destroy you. **26**I prayed to the LORD and said, "O Sovereign LORD, do not destroy your people, your own inheritance that you redeemed[D] by your great power and brought out of Egypt with a mighty hand. **27**Remember your servants Abraham, Isaac and Jacob. Overlook the stubbornness of this people, their wickedness and their sin. **28**Otherwise, the country from which you brought us will say, 'Because the LORD was not able to take them into the land he had promised them, and because he hated them, he brought them out to put them to death[D] in the desert.' **29**But they are your people, your inheritance that you brought out by your great power and your outstretched arm."

Tablets Like the First Ones

10 At that time the LORD said to me, "Chisel out two stone tablets like the first ones and come up to me on the mountain. Also make a wooden chest.[a] **2**I will write on the tablets the words that were on the first tablets, which you broke. Then you are to put them in the chest."

3So I made the ark out of acacia[D] wood and chiseled out two stone tablets like the first ones, and I went up on the mountain with the two tablets in my hands. **4**The LORD wrote on these tablets what he had written before, the Ten Commandments he had proclaimed to you on the mountain, out of the fire, on the day of the assembly. And the LORD gave them to me. **5**Then I came back down the mountain and put the tablets in the ark I had made, as the LORD commanded me, and they are there now.

6(The Israelites traveled from the wells of the Jaakanites to Moserah. There Aaron died and was buried, and Eleazar his son succeeded him as priest[D]. **7**From there they traveled to Gudgodah and on to Jotbathah, a land with streams of water. **8**At that time the LORD set apart the tribe of Levi to carry the ark of the covenant[D] of the LORD, to stand before the LORD to minister and to pronounce blessings in his name, as they still do today. **9**That is why the Levites[D] have no share or inheritance among their brothers; the LORD is their inheritance, as the LORD your God told them.)

10Now I had stayed on the mountain forty days and nights, as I did the first time, and the LORD listened to me at this time also. It was not his will to destroy you. **11**"Go," the LORD said to me, "and lead the people on their way, so that they may enter and possess the land that I swore to their fathers to give them."

Fear the LORD

12And now, O Israel, what does the LORD your God ask of you but to fear the LORD your God, to walk in all his ways, to love him, to serve the LORD your God with all your heart and with all your soul[D], **13**and to observe the LORD's commands and decrees that I am giving you today for your own good?

14To the LORD your God belong the heavens, even the highest heavens, the earth and everything in it. **15**Yet the LORD set his affection on your forefathers and loved them, and he chose you, their descendants, above all the nations, as it is today. **16**Circumcise[D] your hearts, therefore, and do not be stiff-necked any longer. **17**For the LORD your God is God of gods and Lord of lords, the great God,

---

SCRIPTURE LINK (10:1) *A wooden chest*

The ark of the covenant. See Exodus 25:10–22.

How was God himself the inheritance of the Levites? (10:9)

The Levites lived on what was given to the Lord in temple sacrifice. Though they did not own any property, they did enjoy a special relationship with God, similar to God being Abram's *great reward* (Gen. 15:1).

What does it mean to *circumcise your hearts*? (10:16)

Circumcision symbolized the covenant between God and his people (Gen. 17:9–14). See article: **Why did God command circumcision?** (Gen. 17:10). The people were to learn to love and serve God from their hearts (10:12), a process described figuratively as "circumcision of the heart." Like physical circumcision, this spiritual circumcision required a decision and action from the people. See **How does the Spirit circumcise a heart?** (Romans 2:28–29).

***God of gods and Lord of lords* (10:17)**

This lofty language is typical of Deuteronomy. The phrase essentially means that God is God in the most absolute sense. He transcends our understanding, leaving us in awe of him. This is the basis for a proper attitude toward God. Moses was not acknowledging other gods (which are only false gods), but expressing that there is only one true God.

---

a1 That is, an ark

mighty and awesome, who shows no partiality and accepts no bribes. **18**He defends the cause of the fatherless and the widow, and loves the alienᴰ, giving him food and clothing. **19**And you are to love those who are aliens, for you yourselves were aliens in Egypt. **20**Fear the LORD your God and serve him. Hold fast to him and take your oaths in his name. **21**He is your praise; he is your God, who performed for you those great and awesome wonders you saw with your own eyes. **22**Your forefathers who went down into Egypt were seventy in all, and now the LORD your God has made you as numerous as the stars in the sky.

Love and Obey the LORD

11 Love the LORD your God and keep his requirements, his decrees, his laws and his commands always. **2**Remember today that your children were not the ones who saw and experienced the discipline of the LORD your God: his majesty, his mighty hand, his outstretched arm; **3**the signs he performed and the things he did in the heart of Egypt, both to Pharaoh king of Egypt and to his whole country; **4**what he did to the Egyptian army, to its horses and chariots, how he overwhelmed them with the waters of the Red Seaᵃ as they were pursuing you, and how the LORD brought lasting ruin on them. **5**It was not your children who saw what he did for you in the desert until you arrived at this place, **6**and what he did to Dathan and Abiram, sons of Eliab the Reubenite, when the earth opened its mouth right in the middle of all Israel and swallowed them up with their households, their tents and every living thing that belonged to them. **7**But it was your own eyes that saw all these great things the LORD has done.

8Observe therefore all the commands I am giving you today, so that you may have the strength to go in and take over the land that you are crossing the Jordan to possess, **9**and so that you may live long in the land that the LORD swore to your forefathers to give to them and their descendants, a land flowing with milk and honey. **10**The land you are entering to take over is not like the land of Egypt, from which you have come, where you planted your seed and irrigated it by foot as in a vegetable garden. **11**But the land you are crossing the Jordan to take possession of is a land of mountains and valleys that drinks rain from heaven. **12**It is a land the LORD your God cares for; the eyes of the LORD your God are continually on it from the beginning of the year to its end.

13So if you faithfully obey the commands I am giving you today—to love the LORD your God and to serve him with all your heart and with all your soulᴰ— **14**then I will send rain on your land in its season, both autumn and spring rains, so that you may gather in your grain, new wineᴰ and oil. **15**I will provide grass in the fields for your cattle, and you will eat and be satisfied.

16Be careful, or you will be enticed to turn away and worship other gods and bow down to them. **17**Then the LORD's anger will burn against you, and he will shut the heavens so that it will not rain and the ground will yield no produce, and you will soon perish from the good land the LORD is giving you. **18**Fix these words of mine in your hearts and minds; tie them as symbols on your hands and bind them on your foreheads. **19**Teach them to your chil-

ᵃ4 Hebrew *Yam Suph*; that is, Sea of Reeds

Requirements ... decrees ... laws ... commands (11:1)

God requires specific behavior from his people. While the precise meanings of these words differ slightly from one another, as a whole they represent God's will for those preparing to enter the land of Canaan.

SCRIPTURE LINK (11:6) *Dathan and Abiram ...*

Challenged Moses' authority and joined Korah's rebellion. God judged them by opening the ground beneath them so they were buried alive along with their households and possessions. See Num. 16:1–34.

Flowing with milk and honey (11:9)

See *Flowing with milk and honey* (6:3).

Does God care for the Holy Land more than other places? (11:12)

God was not stating a preference for certain real estate so much as showing a contrast between how Israel had lived in Egypt and how they would live in Canaan. In Canaan they would have to rely by faith on God's provision of rain. In Egypt people took matters into their own hands by irrigating their fields with water from the Nile.

Are blessings such as rain a result of our obedience? (11:17)

See *Is God responsible for disasters?* (Jer. 36:3). Also see article: *Is success guaranteed to those who obey God?* (28:2–6).

Should we wear God's word on our forehead? (11:18)

God commands us first to fix his words in our hearts and minds, signifying a zeal to fulfill God's word. The practice of literally binding God's words on one's forehead and door developed later in Israel's history and was referred to by Jesus when he criticized the religious leaders for their hypocrisy (Matt. 23:5). God has always been interested in the attitude of one's heart, something external symbols cannot guarantee.

dren, talking about them when you sit at home and when you walk along the road, when you lie down and when you get up. **20**Write them on the doorframes of your houses and on your gates, **21**so that your days and the days of your children may be many in the land that the LORD swore to give your forefathers, as many as the days that the heavens are above the earth.

22If you carefully observe all these commands I am giving you to follow—to love the LORD your God, to walk in all his ways and to hold fast to him— **23**then the LORD will drive out all these nations before you, and you will dispossess nations larger and stronger than you. **24**Every place where you set your foot will be yours: Your territory will extend from the desert to Lebanon, and from the Euphrates River to the western sea.*a* **25**No man will be able to stand against you. The LORD your God, as he promised you, will put the terror and fear of you on the whole land, wherever you go.

26See, I am setting before you today a blessing and a curse— **27**the blessing if you obey the commands of the LORD your God that I am giving you today; **28**the curse if you disobey the commands of the LORD your God and turn from the way that I command you today by following other gods, which you have not known. **29**When the LORD your God has brought you into the land you are entering to possess, you are to proclaim on Mount Gerizim the blessings, and on Mount Ebal the curses. **30**As you know, these mountains are across the Jordan, west of the road,*b* toward the setting sun, near the great trees of Moreh, in the territory of those Canaanites living in the Arabah in the vicinity of Gilgal. **31**You are about to cross the Jordan to enter and take possession of the land the LORD your God is giving you. When you have taken it over and are living there, **32**be sure that you obey all the decrees and laws I am setting before you today.

The One Place of Worship

12 These are the decrees and laws you must be careful to follow in the land that the LORD, the God of your fathers, has given you to possess—as long as you live in the land. **2**Destroy completely all the places on the high mountains and on the hills and under every spreading tree where the nations you are dispossessing worship their gods. **3**Break down their altars, smash their sacred stones**D** and burn their Asherah poles**D** in the fire; cut down the idols**D** of their gods and wipe out their names from those places.

4You must not worship the LORD your God in their way. **5**But you are to seek the place the LORD your God will choose from among all your tribes to put his Name there for his dwelling. To that place you must go; **6**there bring your burnt offerings**D** and sacrifices**D**, your tithes**D** and special gifts, what you have vowed**D** to give and your freewill offerings, and the firstborn**D** of your herds and flocks. **7**There, in the presence of the LORD your God, you and your families shall eat and shall rejoice in everything you have put your hand to, because the LORD your God has blessed you.

8You are not to do as we do here today, everyone as he sees fit, **9**since you have not yet reached the resting place and the inheritance the LORD your God is giving you. **10**But you will cross the Jordan and settle in the land the LORD

Why should God's people take land belonging to others? (11:23)

See article: *What right did Israel have to take the land?* (Num. 33:52–53).

SCRIPTURE LINK (11:29) *Proclaim . . . on Mount Ebal the curses*

Read more about these blessings and curses in 27:9–26. See *Map 2* at the back of this Bible.

The Arabah (11:30)

See *Arabah* (1:1).

How can a Name have a place to dwell? (12:5)

God's Name, which he had revealed to Moses (Exodus 3:14–15), was important to Israel because through it they could call on and approach God. By designating a particular place for his Name, God showed the people that he was available to them. However, this dwelling would by no means limit or contain God himself. Also see *Why did God choose a place for his name to dwell?* (26:2).

Why couldn't the Israelites worship anywhere? (12:5)

The Canaanites worshiped their nature-gods wherever they thought they were evident (usually on high hills or under trees). But God was concerned that his people not be drawn away to the practices and false gods of their neighbors. He chose the tabernacle, and later the temple, as the place where he was to be revealed—one place to correspond to one God over Israel. Also see *Why did it matter where they worshiped God?* (2 Kings 18:22).

Was there anarchy in the camp? (12:8)

No. Though everyone did as he saw fit, this indicated that daily offerings could not be offered when Israel was on the move and the tabernacle could not be set up. Once Israel entered Canaan, their wandering days would be over. Then they could settle down and worship God as he had prescribed (vv. 9–13).

SCRIPTURE LINK (12:10) *Rest*

Hebrews 4:1–11 links Israel's rest from fighting and wandering with the future heavenly rest that believers will one day enjoy.

---

a24 That is, the Mediterranean   *b30* Or *Jordan, westward*

your God is giving you as an inheritance, and he will give you rest from all your enemies around you so that you will live in safety. **11**Then to the place the LORD your God will choose as a dwelling for his Name—there you are to bring everything I command you: your burnt offerings^D and sacrifices^D, your tithes^D and special gifts, and all the choice possessions you have vowed^D to the LORD. **12**And there rejoice before the LORD your God, you, your sons and daughters, your menservants and maidservants, and the Levites^D from your towns, who have no allotment or inheritance of their own. **13**Be careful not to sacrifice your burnt offerings anywhere you please. **14**Offer them only at the place the LORD will choose in one of your tribes, and there observe everything I command you.

15Nevertheless, you may slaughter your animals in any of your towns and eat as much of the meat as you want, as if it were gazelle or deer, according to the blessing the LORD your God gives you. Both the ceremonially unclean^D and the clean may eat it. **16**But you must not eat the blood; pour it out on the ground like water. **17**You must not eat in your own towns the tithe of your grain and new wine^D and oil, or the firstborn^D of your herds and flocks, or whatever you have vowed to give, or your freewill offerings or special gifts. **18**Instead, you are to eat them in the presence of the LORD your God at the place the LORD your God will choose—you, your sons and daughters, your menservants and maidservants, and the Levites from your towns—and you are to rejoice before the LORD your God in everything you put your hand to. **19**Be careful not to neglect the Levites as long as you live in your land.

20When the LORD your God has enlarged your territory as he promised you, and you crave meat and say, "I would like some meat," then you may eat as much of it as you want. **21**If the place where the LORD your God chooses to put his Name is too far away from you, you may slaughter animals from the herds and flocks the LORD has given you, as I have commanded you, and in your own towns you may eat as much of them as you want. **22**Eat them as you would gazelle or deer. Both the ceremonially unclean and the clean may eat. **23**But be sure you do not eat the blood, because the blood is the life, and you must not eat the life with the meat. **24**You must not eat the blood; pour it out on the ground like water. **25**Do not eat it, so that it may go well with you and your children after you, because you will be doing what is right in the eyes of the LORD.

26But take your consecrated^D things and whatever you have vowed to give, and go to the place the LORD will choose. **27**Present your burnt offerings on the altar of the LORD your God, both the meat and the blood. The blood of your sacrifices must be poured beside the altar of the LORD your God, but you may eat the meat. **28**Be careful to obey all these regulations I am giving you, so that it may always go well with you and your children after you, because you will be doing what is good and right in the eyes of the LORD your God.

29The LORD your God will cut off before you the nations you are about to invade and dispossess. But when you have driven them out and settled in their land, **30**and after they have been destroyed before you, be careful not to be ensnared by inquiring about their gods, saying, "How do these nations serve their gods? We will do the same." **31**You must not worship the LORD your God in their way,

Ceremonially unclean (12:15)

See *Ceremonially unclean* (Lev. 5:2).

Tithe (12:17)

Ten percent of Israel's crops and animals (Lev. 27:30–32). The tithe was given to the Levites as part of their support, since they had no inheritance as a tribe in Canaan. The Levites, in turn, offered a tithe of the tithe as a sacrifice to God.

Why did the Israelites have to leave their towns to eat the tithe? (12:17)

The Israelites were free to eat ordinary meat any time and in any location, as long as they did not eat the blood. However, the tithe was special. In order to maintain a distinction between ordinary food and the Lord's tithe, a portion of the tithe was to be eaten at the sanctuary, in the presence of the Lord.

Were the Levites on welfare? (12:18–19)

See *How did inheriting priestly duties compare to inheriting land?* (Joshua 13:33).

Consecrated things (12:26)

Sacrifices, offerings or other items designated for the Lord.

SCRIPTURE LINK (12:31) *They even burn their sons and daughters in the fire as sacrifices . . .*

See Jer. 7:31; 19:5; 32:35.

Why did God have to warn his people about sacrificing their own children? (12:31)

Because he knew that they could be influenced by the lower standards of the world around them. God's commands demonstrated his values, including his view of human life. Yet, though God consistently condemned human sacrifice, Israel often adopted the ways of their pagan neighbors in hopes of gaining the favor of false gods. For more on the false hopes that motivated them to such behavior, see *Why would parents sacrifice their children?* (Jer. 19:5).

because in worshiping their gods, they do all kinds of detestable things the LORD hates. They even burn their sons and daughters in the fire as sacrifices^D to their gods.

32See that you do all I command you; do not add to it or take away from it.

Worshiping Other Gods

13 If a prophet^D, or one who foretells by dreams, appears among you and announces to you a miraculous sign or wonder, **2**and if the sign or wonder of which he has spoken takes place, and he says, "Let us follow other gods" (gods you have not known) "and let us worship them," **3**you must not listen to the words of that prophet or dreamer. The LORD your God is testing you to find out whether you love him with all your heart and with all your soul^D. **4**It is the LORD your God you must follow, and him you must revere^D. Keep his commands and obey him; serve him and hold fast to him. **5**That prophet or dreamer must be put to death, because he preached rebellion against the LORD your God, who brought you out of Egypt and redeemed^D you from the land of slavery; he has tried to turn you from the way the LORD your God commanded you to follow. You must purge the evil from among you.

6If your very own brother, or your son or daughter, or the wife you love, or your closest friend secretly entices you, saying, "Let us go and worship other gods" (gods that neither you nor your fathers have known, **7**gods of the peoples around you, whether near or far, from one end of the land to the other), **8**do not yield to him or listen to him. Show him no pity. Do not spare him or shield him. **9**You must certainly put him to death. Your hand must be the first in putting him to death, and then the hands of all the people. **10**Stone him to death, because he tried to turn you away from the LORD your God, who brought you out of Egypt, out of the land of slavery. **11**Then all Is-

---

Is this testing a type of entrapment? (13:3)

No. God never desires his people to fall into sin. But trial comes from many sources: resisting false prophets with their signs and wonders was only one way to prove their allegiance to the Lord. Overcoming false prophets allowed Israel to strengthen their love and obedience to God. Also see *How are temptations different from trials?* (James 1:13).

Why does God have to test us? (13:3)

God does not need to test his people to discover how they will respond. Rather, testing teaches us what we need to know about ourselves. The Israelites needed to learn whether they would remain faithful to God. Testings and trials can strengthen our faith and commitment. Also see *Does God have to test us to find out what's in our hearts?* (2 Chron. 32:31) and the article: *Why did testing come to Job?* (Job 23:10).

Purge the evil (13:5)

See article: *Why kill a murderer?* (19:13).

Does God oppose religious freedom? (13:10)

No. God gives people the chance to choose whether they will follow him or not. But if they decide to go their own way, they must be prepared to suffer the consequences. This was especially true for his people who had entered into a unique covenant relationship with the Lord. If they were to reject God, they would have to break the promise they had made (Exodus 19:7–8).

Did Jesus *take away* from these commandments? (12:32)

No, though it might appear so at first glance. Often in the Gospels it seems that Jesus violated the law (see, for example, Matt. 12:1–8). What, then, was Jesus' view of the law?

Matthew 5:17 holds the key for understanding Jesus' relationship to Old Testament law: *Do not think that I have come to abolish the Law or the Prophets; I have not come to abolish them but to fulfill them.*

Jesus fulfilled the Law and the Prophets by perfectly obeying them, something no other person could ever do. He perfectly loved God with all his heart, soul, mind and strength. His life was a demonstration of loving his neighbor as himself, to the point of dying for his enemies (Romans 5:10).

Jesus uniquely fulfilled the ceremonial requirements of the sacrificial system by becoming both the high priest and the sacrificial Lamb of God. He gave himself as the once-for-all atonement for sin (Heb. 7:27).

The apostle Paul explains how the law, being fulfilled, is no longer in effect: *The law was put in charge to lead us to Christ that we might be justified by faith. Now that faith has come, we are no longer under the supervision of the law* (Gal. 3:24–25).

Also see *How is the law fulfilled?* (Matt. 5:17–18) and *Did Jesus abolish the Old Testament law or fulfill it?* (Eph. 2:15).

rael will hear and be afraid, and no one among you will do such an evil thing again.

¹²If you hear it said about one of the towns the LORD your God is giving you to live in ¹³that wicked men have arisen among you and have led the people of their town astray, saying, "Let us go and worship other gods" (gods you have not known), ¹⁴then you must inquire, probe and investigate it thoroughly. And if it is true and it has been proved that this detestable thing has been done among you, ¹⁵you must certainly put to the sword all who live in that town. Destroy it completely,ᵃ both its people and its livestock. ¹⁶Gather all the plunderᴰ of the town into the middle of the public square and completely burn the town and all its plunder as a whole burnt offering to the LORD your God. It is to remain a ruin forever, never to be rebuilt. ¹⁷None of those condemned thingsᵃ shall be found in your hands, so that the LORD will turn from his fierce anger; he will show you mercyᴰ, have compassion on you, and increase your numbers, as he promised on oath to your forefathers, ¹⁸because you obey the LORD your God, keeping all his commands that I am giving you today and doing what is right in his eyes.

Clean and Unclean Food

14 You are the children of the LORD your God. Do not cut yourselves or shave the front of your heads for the dead, ²for you are a people holy to the LORD your God. Out of all the peoples on the face of the earth, the LORD has chosen you to be his treasured possession.

³Do not eat any detestable thing. ⁴These are the animals you may eat: the ox, the sheep, the goat, ⁵the deer, the gazelle, the roe deer, the wild goat, the ibex, the antelope and the mountain sheep.ᵇ ⁶You may eat any animal that has a split hoof divided in two and that chews the cud. ⁷However, of those that chew the cud or that have a split hoof completely divided you may not eat the camel, the rabbit or the coney.ᶜ Although they chew the cud, they do not have a split hoof; they are ceremonially uncleanᴰ for you. ⁸The pig is also unclean; although it has a split hoof, it does not chew the cud. You are not to eat their meat or touch their carcasses.

⁹Of all the creatures living in the water, you may eat any that has fins and scales. ¹⁰But anything that does not have fins and scales you may not eat; for you it is unclean.

¹¹You may eat any clean bird. ¹²But these you may not eat: the eagle, the vulture, the black vulture, ¹³the red kite, the black kite, any kind of falcon, ¹⁴any kind of raven, ¹⁵the horned owl, the screech owl, the gull, any kind of hawk, ¹⁶the little owl, the great owl, the white owl, ¹⁷the desert owl, the osprey, the cormorant, ¹⁸the stork, any kind of heron, the hoopoe and the bat.

¹⁹All flying insects that swarm are unclean to you; do not eat them. ²⁰But any winged creature that is clean you may eat.

²¹Do not eat anything you find already dead. You may give it to an alienᴰ living in any of your towns, and he

---

Why wipe out the whole town—even animals? (13:15)
See article: *Why kill everything?* (Joshua 6:21).

What's wrong with shaving? (14:1)
See *Why was shaving considered unholy?* (Lev. 21:5–6).

What makes meat kosher? (14:3)
See article: *Why did God keep some meats off the menu?* (Lev. 11:4–41). Also see *Why were some things unclean?* (Lev. 5:2).

Do Jewish laws today still follow these guidelines? (14:3–21)
Food that is ritually correct, prepared according to the dietary laws of Leviticus and Deuteronomy, is called *kosher*, from a Hebrew word meaning *proper*. Although these laws are still observed by Orthodox Jews, they are not kept universally by other Jews.

Could they cook goats in other milk? (14:21)
They probably wouldn't want to. Cooking a goat in milk was more likely related to pagan religious practices than to the culinary arts. See *Who'd want to cook a goat in its mother's milk?* (Exodus 23:19).

ᵃ15,17 The Hebrew term refers to the irrevocable giving over of things or persons to the LORD, often by totally destroying them.   ᵇ5 The precise identification of some of the birds and animals in this chapter is uncertain.   ᶜ7 That is, the hyrax or rock badger

may eat it, or you may sell it to a foreigner. But you are a people holy to the LORD your God.

Do not cook a young goat in its mother's milk.

Tithes

22Be sure to set aside a tenth of all that your fields produce each year. **23**Eat the titheD of your grain, new wineD and oil, and the firstbornD of your herds and flocks in the presence of the LORD your God at the place he will choose as a dwelling for his Name, so that you may learn to revereD the LORD your God always. **24**But if that place is too distant and you have been blessed by the LORD your God and cannot carry your tithe (because the place where the LORD will choose to put his Name is so far away), **25**then exchange your tithe for silver, and take the silver with you and go to the place the LORD your God will choose. **26**Use the silver to buy whatever you like: cattle, sheep, wine or other fermented drink, or anything you wish. Then you and your household shall eat there in the presence of the LORD your God and rejoice. **27**And do not neglect the LevitesD living in your towns, for they have no allotment or inheritance of their own.

28At the end of every three years, bring all the tithes of that year's produce and store it in your towns, **29**so that the Levites (who have no allotment or inheritance of their own) and the aliensD, the fatherless and the widows who live in your towns may come and eat and be satisfied, and so that the LORD your God may bless you in all the work of your hands.

The Year for Canceling Debts

15 At the end of every seven years you must cancel debts. **2**This is how it is to be done: Every creditor shall cancel the loan he has made to his fellow Israelite. He shall not require payment from his fellow Israelite or brother, because the LORD's time for canceling debts has been proclaimed. **3**You may require payment from a foreigner, but you must cancel any debt your brother owes you. **4**However, there should be no poor among you, for in the land the LORD your God is giving you to possess as your inheritance, he will richly bless you, **5**if only you fully obey the LORD your God and are careful to follow all these commands I am giving you today. **6**For the LORD your God will bless you as he has promised, and you will lend to many nations but will borrow from none. You will rule over many nations but none will rule over you.

7If there is a poor man among your brothers in any of the towns of the land that the LORD your God is giving you, do not be hardhearted or tightfisted toward your poor brother. **8**Rather be openhanded and freely lend him whatever he needs. **9**Be careful not to harbor this wicked thought: "The seventh year, the year for canceling debts, is near," so that you do not show ill will toward your needy brother and give him nothing. He may then appeal to the LORD against you, and you will be found guilty of sin. **10**Give generously to him and do so without a grudging heart; then because of this the LORD your God will bless you in all your work and in everything you put your hand to. **11**There will always be poor people in the land. Therefore I command you to be openhanded toward your brothers and toward the poor and needy in your land.

Tithe (14:23)
See *Tithe* (12:17).

Why eat what you give to God? (14:23)
Only the burnt offerings were burned completely so that the entire offering went to the Lord. Other offerings provided food for the priests, Levites, and, on this occasion, to the person offering the sacrifice. Having instructed his people to bring their tithes to him, he invited them to enjoy the tithes in his presence.

Does God approve of drinking alcohol? (14:26)
It's clear from this verse and others that *fermented drink* was an acceptable part of the Israelite diet. But the Bible warns against drunkenness (Gal. 5:21; Eph. 5:18) and urges moderation in using fermented drinks. See **Does Proverbs teach abstinence from alcohol?** (Prov. 20:1).

How can we apply these verses today? (15:1–11; also see Lev. 25:8–38)
The civil and economic laws of ancient Israel were established by God for that time and culture. While we should uphold God's moral and ethical code, other specific instructions no longer apply. What we can learn from these verses is an enduring principle of love and generosity toward the poor. There will always be opportunities for God's people to demonstrate God's love to the needy. Ancient Israel, by periodically canceling debts, provided means for the poor to become productive, responsible members of society. The same goal would be good for us—either as individuals or through government policy.

Seven (15:1)
Seven is an important number in the Bible, and is associated with completion, fulfillment and perfection. See **What was so special about the number seven?** (2 Chron. 29:21).

Does God encourage irresponsibility? (15:1)
There is disagreement about how the term *cancel* should be interpreted. Some believe debts were to be permanently wiped out. However, this could allow debtors to take advantage of the system, and it seems that most people would have been unlikely to grant loans just prior to the seventh year. Others think debts were to be suspended for the seventh year, while the ground lay fallow and there was no income. In this case the debtor would still be responsible for his debt and would resume payments the following year.

Why require payment on a foreigner's loan? (15:3)
Aliens in most lands today do not enjoy the rights and privileges of citizenship, and this verse may reveal the same type of disparity. Or perhaps a foreigner's loan could be collected because he was not required, as the Israelites were, to let his land lie fallow during the sev-

Freeing Servants

12If a fellow Hebrew[D], a man or a woman, sells himself to you and serves you six years, in the seventh year you must let him go free. 13And when you release him, do not send him away empty-handed. 14Supply him liberally from your flock, your threshing floor and your winepress[D]. Give to him as the LORD your God has blessed you. 15Remember that you were slaves in Egypt and the LORD your God redeemed[D] you. That is why I give you this command today.

16But if your servant says to you, "I do not want to leave you," because he loves you and your family and is well off with you, 17then take an awl and push it through his ear lobe into the door, and he will become your servant for life. Do the same for your maidservant.

18Do not consider it a hardship to set your servant free, because his service to you these six years has been worth twice as much as that of a hired hand. And the LORD your God will bless you in everything you do.

The Firstborn Animals

19Set apart for the LORD your God every firstborn[D] male of your herds and flocks. Do not put the firstborn of your oxen to work, and do not shear the firstborn of your sheep. 20Each year you and your family are to eat them in the presence of the LORD your God at the place he will choose. 21If an animal has a defect, is lame or blind, or has any serious flaw, you must not sacrifice[D] it to the LORD your God. 22You are to eat it in your own towns. Both the ceremonially unclean[D] and the clean may eat it, as if it were gazelle or deer. 23But you must not eat the blood; pour it out on the ground like water.

Passover

16 Observe the month of Abib and celebrate the Passover of the LORD your God, because in the month of Abib he brought you out of Egypt by night. 2Sacrifice as the Passover to the LORD your God an animal from your flock or herd at the place the LORD will choose as a dwelling for his Name. 3Do not eat it with bread made with yeast[D], but for seven days eat unleavened bread, the bread of affliction[D], because you left Egypt in haste—so that all the days of your life you may remember the time of your departure from Egypt. 4Let no yeast be found in your possession in all your land for seven days. Do not let any of the meat you sacrifice on the evening of the first day remain until morning.

5You must not sacrifice the Passover in any town the LORD your God gives you 6except in the place he will choose as a dwelling for his Name. There you must sacrifice the Passover in the evening, when the sun goes down, on the anniversary[a] of your departure from Egypt. 7Roast it and eat it at the place the LORD your God will choose. Then in the morning return to your tents. 8For six days eat unleavened bread and on the seventh day hold an assembly to the LORD your God and do no work.

Feast of Weeks

9Count off seven weeks from the time you begin to put the sickle to the standing grain. 10Then celebrate the Feast of Weeks to the LORD your God by giving a freewill offer-

a6 Or down, at the time of day

enth year. He therefore still had the means of earning money to pay his debt. See **Does God encourage irresponsibility?** (15:1).

Is there a cure for poverty? (15:11)

In a perfect world, there would be no poverty. In a perfectly obedient Israel, there would have been no poverty either, but this was never the case. However, the promise of enough for everyone remains strong in prophetic literature (see, for example, Isaiah 55). God's people are to be generous, not to make the poor dependent upon them, but to encourage them to become self-sufficient and independent.

Why disfigure a loyal servant? (15:17)

The ceremony of piercing an ear to the door sounds strange today, but it was a customary practice which held special meaning at that time. The ear was chosen as a symbol of the servant's willingness to listen to and obey the commands of his or her master. The decision to become a servant for life was a voluntary decision made freely by a servant. Also see **Why mark a lifelong servant with a pierced ear?** (Exodus 21:6).

SCRIPTURE LINK (15:17) Push it through his ear lobe

David cites this custom to indicate his willingness to do God's will (Psalm 40:6). The writer of Hebrews, in turn, quotes David to show Christ's willingness as the Servant of the Lord (Heb. 10:5–10).

Month of Abib (16:1)

This month corresponds to March/April on the modern calendar. Later it was changed to the Babylonian name *Nisan*, meaning *beginning*, as found on the contemporary Jewish calendar. It marks the beginning of the religious year with the Feasts of Passover, Unleavened Bread and Firstfruits (Lev. 23:5–6,10).

SCRIPTURE LINK (16:1–8) Passover

Commemorated the historical deliverance of the Jews from Egypt as God's angel passed over the houses of the Israelites and struck dead the firstborn of the Egyptians. See Exodus 12:14–20; Lev. 23:4–8; Num. 28:16–25.

Why is unleavened bread called *the bread of affliction?* (16:3)

Because it reminded the Israelites of their hasty flight from the suffering in Egypt. To escape quickly, they weren't able to allow time for their bread to rise (Exodus 12:34–39).

Why didn't God want leftovers? (16:4)

See *Why didn't God want leftovers?* (Lev. 7:15).

SCRIPTURE LINK (16:9–12) The Feast of Weeks

Also known as the Feast of Harvest, Day of Firstfruits and Pentecost. It was celebrated seven weeks, or 50 days, after the beginning of Passover, and was a time of celebration and joy for the harvest with which the Lord had blessed his people. See Lev. 23:15–23 and Num. 28:26–31.

A harvest thanksgiving festival when people camped out in booths—tents made of branches—to remember how their ancestors had lived in the desert. See Lev. 23:33–43 and Num. 29:12–38.

How could all the men crowd into one place? (16:16)
With hundreds of thousands coming to Jerusalem, it would not have been easy. Several things may have helped, however. Private homes, not just inns, were opened to the travelers. Those who could not find lodging probably camped in the streets or on the outskirts of the city. (Camping in a "tent" made of sticks was a required part of the Feast of Tabernacles.) Furthermore, not every man attended. Men who were sick or elderly, for example, were not expected to make the trip.

Who made the political appointments? (16:18)
Moses had the people choose *wise, understanding and respected men from each of their tribes,* whom he then appointed as judges to help him govern (1:12–18). With Israel scattered throughout the land of Canaan, they were to use similar procedures, probably selecting judges from local elder councils. But we don't know precisely how the selections were made.

Why were executions a community affair? (17:7)
Because idolatry violated God's covenant with his people and posed such danger to the entire community, the whole community was involved in the stoning.

ing in proportion to the blessings the LORD your God has given you. [11]And rejoice before the LORD your God at the place he will choose as a dwelling for his Name—you, your sons and daughters, your menservants and maidservants, the Levites[D] in your towns, and the aliens[D], the fatherless and the widows living among you. [12]Remember that you were slaves in Egypt, and follow carefully these decrees.

Feast of Tabernacles

[13]Celebrate the Feast of Tabernacles for seven days after you have gathered the produce of your threshing floor and your winepress[D]. [14]Be joyful at your Feast—you, your sons and daughters, your menservants and maidservants, and the Levites, the aliens, the fatherless and the widows who live in your towns. [15]For seven days celebrate the Feast to the LORD your God at the place the LORD will choose. For the LORD your God will bless you in all your harvest and in all the work of your hands, and your joy will be complete.

[16]Three times a year all your men must appear before the LORD your God at the place he will choose: at the Feast of Unleavened Bread, the Feast of Weeks and the Feast of Tabernacles. No man should appear before the LORD empty-handed: [17]Each of you must bring a gift in proportion to the way the LORD your God has blessed you.

Judges

[18]Appoint judges and officials for each of your tribes in every town the LORD your God is giving you, and they shall judge the people fairly. [19]Do not pervert justice or show partiality. Do not accept a bribe, for a bribe blinds the eyes of the wise and twists the words of the righteous[D]. [20]Follow justice and justice alone, so that you may live and possess the land the LORD your God is giving you.

Worshiping Other Gods

[21]Do not set up any wooden Asherah pole[Da] beside the altar you build to the LORD your God, [22]and do not erect a sacred stone[D], for these the LORD your God hates.

17 Do not sacrifice[D] to the LORD your God an ox or a sheep that has any defect or flaw in it, for that would be detestable to him.

[2]If a man or woman living among you in one of the towns the LORD gives you is found doing evil in the eyes of the LORD your God in violation of his covenant[D], [3]and contrary to my command has worshiped other gods, bowing down to them or to the sun or the moon or the stars of the sky, [4]and this has been brought to your attention, then you must investigate it thoroughly. If it is true and it has been proved that this detestable thing has been done in Israel, [5]take the man or woman who has done this evil deed to your city gate and stone that person to death[D]. [6]On the testimony of two or three witnesses a man shall be put to death, but no one shall be put to death on the testimony of only one witness. [7]The hands of the witnesses must be the first in putting him to death, and then the hands of all the people. You must purge the evil from among you.

a21 Or Do not plant any tree dedicated to Asherah

Law Courts

8If cases come before your courts that are too difficult for you to judge—whether bloodshed, lawsuits or assaults—take them to the place the LORD your God will choose. **9**Go to the priests[D], who are Levites[D], and to the judge who is in office at that time. Inquire of them and they will give you the verdict. **10**You must act according to the decisions they give you at the place the LORD will choose. Be careful to do everything they direct you to do. **11**Act according to the law they teach you and the decisions they give you. Do not turn aside from what they tell you, to the right or to the left. **12**The man who shows contempt for the judge or for the priest who stands ministering there to the LORD your God must be put to death[D]. You must purge the evil from Israel. **13**All the people will hear and be afraid, and will not be contemptuous again.

The King

14When you enter the land the LORD your God is giving you and have taken possession of it and settled in it, and you say, "Let us set a king over us like all the nations around us," **15**be sure to appoint over you the king the LORD your God chooses. He must be from among your own brothers. Do not place a foreigner over you, one who is not a brother Israelite. **16**The king, moreover, must not acquire great numbers of horses for himself or make the people return to Egypt to get more of them, for the LORD has told you, "You are not to go back that way again." **17**He must not take many wives, or his heart will be led astray. He must not accumulate large amounts of silver and gold.

18When he takes the throne of his kingdom, he is to write for himself on a scroll a copy of this law, taken from that of the priests, who are Levites. **19**It is to be with him, and he is to read it all the days of his life so that he may learn to revere[D] the LORD his God and follow carefully all the words of this law and these decrees **20**and not consider himself better than his brothers and turn from the law to the right or to the left. Then he and his descendants will reign a long time over his kingdom in Israel.

Offerings for Priests and Levites

18 The priests, who are Levites—indeed the whole tribe of Levi—are to have no allotment or inheritance with Israel. They shall live on the offerings made to the LORD by fire, for that is their inheritance. **2**They shall have no inheritance among their brothers; the LORD is their inheritance, as he promised them.

3This is the share due the priests from the people who sacrifice[D] a bull or a sheep: the shoulder, the jowls and the inner parts. **4**You are to give them the firstfruits[D] of your grain, new wine[D] and oil, and the first wool from the shearing of your sheep, **5**for the LORD your God has chosen them and their descendants out of all your tribes to stand and minister in the LORD's name always.

6If a Levite moves from one of your towns anywhere in Israel where he is living, and comes in all earnestness to the place the LORD will choose, **7**he may minister in the name of the LORD his God like all his fellow Levites who serve there in the presence of the LORD. **8**He is to share equally in their benefits, even though he has received money from the sale of family possessions.

Do these instructions work in any form of government? (17:9)
No. This arrangement was designed for a community united by a single, God-ordained law that covered both civil and religious matters. The Israelite system of government apparently called on the priests to handle cases dealing with religious law and the judges to take care of civil cases.

SCRIPTURE LINK (17:14) A king . . . like all the nations
See 1 Samuel 8–9 for the story of how Israel wanted a king despite God's wishes.

Why would God give instructions for something he didn't want done? (17:15)
Because he knew about human weakness. He made allowances to accommodate the desires his people would have for a visible, tangible ruler. He was not recommending a king; he was merely permitting one as a possibility, though he clearly did not want the people to reject him in the process of putting a man on the throne (1 Samuel 8:7).

Why should a king do the work of a scribe? (17:18)
Some think this did not mean that the king wrote out the law himself, but that he received a copy prepared by the priests especially for him. Whether he did the actual writing or simply received his own personal copy of the law, the point was clear: he would depend on the law of God for success as king.

Why couldn't Levites inherit anything? (18:1–2)
See *How did inheriting priestly duties compare to inheriting land?* (Joshua 13:33) and *Why weren't Aaron and the Levites permitted to own any land?* (Num. 18:20).

What would a Levite have to sell? (18:8)
The exact meaning of *sale of family possessions* is unclear. Although Levites were forbidden to sell their pastureland (Lev. 25:33–34), it is possible they could sell or rent their houses if they moved to the central sanctuary. Whatever this phrase means, it's clear the Levites were able to have some sort of personal possessions.

Detestable Practices

9When you enter the land the LORD your God is giving you, do not learn to imitate the detestable ways of the nations there. **10**Let no one be found among you who sacrifices[D] his son or daughter in[a] the fire, who practices divination[D] or sorcery[D], interprets omens, engages in witchcraft[D], **11**or casts spells, or who is a medium[D] or spiritist or who consults the dead. **12**Anyone who does these things is detestable to the LORD, and because of these detestable practices the LORD your God will drive out those nations before you. **13**You must be blameless before the LORD your God.

The Prophet

14The nations you will dispossess listen to those who practice sorcery or divination. But as for you, the LORD your God has not permitted you to do so. **15**The LORD your God will raise up for you a prophet[D] like me from among your own brothers. You must listen to him. **16**For this is what you asked of the LORD your God at Horeb on the day of the assembly when you said, "Let us not hear the voice of the LORD our God nor see this great fire anymore, or we will die."

17The LORD said to me: "What they say is good. **18**I will raise up for them a prophet like you from among their brothers; I will put my words in his mouth, and he will tell them everything I command him. **19**If anyone does not listen to my words that the prophet speaks in my name, I myself will call him to account. **20**But a prophet who presumes to speak in my name anything I have not commanded him to say, or a prophet who speaks in the name of other gods, must be put to death[D]."

21You may say to yourselves, "How can we know when a message has not been spoken by the LORD?" **22**If what a prophet proclaims in the name of the LORD does not take place or come true, that is a message the LORD has not spoken. That prophet has spoken presumptuously. Do not be afraid of him.

Cities of Refuge

19 When the LORD your God has destroyed the nations whose land he is giving you, and when you have driven them out and settled in their towns and houses, **2**then set aside for yourselves three cities centrally located in the land the LORD your God is giving you to possess. **3**Build roads to them and divide into three parts the land the LORD your God is giving you as an inheritance, so that anyone who kills a man may flee there.

4This is the rule concerning the man who kills another and flees there to save his life—one who kills his neighbor unintentionally, without malice aforethought. **5**For instance, a man may go into the forest with his neighbor to cut wood, and as he swings his ax to fell a tree, the head may fly off and hit his neighbor and kill him. That man may flee to one of these cities and save his life. **6**Otherwise, the avenger of blood might pursue him in a rage, overtake him if the distance is too great, and kill him even though he is not deserving of death, since he did it to his neighbor without malice aforethought. **7**This is why I command you to set aside for yourselves three cities. **8**If the LORD your God enlarges your territory, as he

---

How do prophecy and divination differ? (18:14–15)
Divination is a human-initiated attempt to predict the future or discover other things known only to God. Prophecy, on the other hand, was a method chosen by God to communicate with his people.

Who is the *prophet like me*? (18:15)
From the context it seems that this is a reference to all the prophets who would follow Moses in leading God's people. Ultimately it came to refer to the Messiah himself (John 1:21).

How can we know who really speaks for God? (18:21)
The test God gave in Old Testament times to determine whether a prophet was true or false is still valid. Prophecy that proves to be wrong is the sign of a false prophet (v. 22). For example, if a so-called prophet contradicts God's written Word, that person is a false prophet.

SCRIPTURE LINK (19:1–14)
For more on the cities of refuge see Num. 35:6–34; Deut. 4:41–43; Joshua 20:1–9. Also see *Cities of refuge* (Num. 35:6).

Avenger of blood (19:6)
See *What did an avenger of blood do?* (Joshua 20:3).

---

a 10 Or who makes his son or daughter pass through

promised on oath to your forefathers, and gives you the whole land he promised them, **9**because you carefully follow all these laws I command you today—to love the LORD your God and to walk always in his ways—then you are to set aside three more cities. **10**Do this so that innocent blood will not be shed in your land, which the LORD your God is giving you as your inheritance, and so that you will not be guilty of bloodshed.

11But if a man hates his neighbor and lies in wait for him, assaults and kills him, and then flees to one of these cities, **12**the elders of his town shall send for him, bring him back from the city, and hand him over to the avenger of blood to die. **13**Show him no pity. You must purge from Israel the guilt of shedding innocent blood, so that it may go well with you.

14Do not move your neighbor's boundary stone set up by your predecessors in the inheritance you receive in the land the LORD your God is giving you to possess.

Witnesses

15One witness is not enough to convict a man accused of any crime or offense he may have committed. A matter must be established by the testimony of two or three witnesses.

16If a malicious witness takes the stand to accuse a man of a crime, **17**the two men involved in the dispute must stand in the presence of the LORD before the priestsᴰ and the judges who are in office at the time. **18**The judges must make a thorough investigation, and if the witness proves to be a liar, giving false testimony against his brother, **19**then do to him as he intended to do to his brother. You must purge the evil from among you. **20**The rest of the people will hear of this and be afraid, and never again will such an evil thing be done among you. **21**Show no pity:

Boundary stone (19:14)

See *Boundary stone* (27:17).

SCRIPTURE LINK (19:21) *Eye for eye, tooth for tooth*

The law of retaliation was designed to prevent unrestrained vengeance by ensuring that the punishment fit the crime. See *Should we demand eye for eye, tooth for tooth?* (Exodus 21:23–25). Also see Lev. 24:17–22.

Why kill a murderer? (19:13)

There were two primary reasons for capital punishment: (1) The land needed to be cleansed of guilt because innocent blood had been shed. (2) Things would not *go well* for the rest of the community if the guilt was not cleansed. Many see yet another reason for the death penalty—to deter others from murder—though God did not mention this third reason here.

God made it clear that if people tolerated the taking of human life, the whole community would share the guilt and suffer the consequences (21:7–9; Num. 35:33–34). God held life in high esteem and required payment for those who callously snuffed it out (Exodus 21:23–25; Lev. 24:17–22). Murder is particularly offensive to God because it destroys a person who bears the image of God. In this context, capital punishment promotes the sanctity of life and the value of every person created in God's image.

In contrast to the Old Testament policy of *no pity* some say that the New Testament, with its emphasis on grace and individual forgiveness, has preempted the need for capital punishment (see, for example, John 8:3–11). They say that all human life should be respected, even the life of a murderer. Others disagree and insist that in a just society those who refuse to live by the law must pay the consequences, including life for life. Even those who have been forgiven for their sins, they say, must still pay for their crimes (Romans 13:4; Acts 25:11; Matt. 26:52).

Also see *Why didn't God sentence Cain to death?* (Gen. 4:15).

life for life, eye for eye, tooth for tooth, hand for hand, foot for foot.

Going to War

20 When you go to war against your enemies and see horses and chariots and an army greater than yours, do not be afraid of them, because the LORD your God, who brought you up out of Egypt, will be with you. **2**When you are about to go into battle, the priest[D] shall come forward and address the army. **3**He shall say: "Hear, O Israel, today you are going into battle against your enemies. Do not be fainthearted or afraid; do not be terrified or give way to panic before them. **4**For the LORD your God is the one who goes with you to fight for you against your enemies to give you victory."

5The officers shall say to the army: "Has anyone built a new house and not dedicated it? Let him go home, or he may die in battle and someone else may dedicate it. **6**Has anyone planted a vineyard and not begun to enjoy it? Let him go home, or he may die in battle and someone else enjoy it. **7**Has anyone become pledged to a woman and not married her? Let him go home, or he may die in battle and someone else marry her." **8**Then the officers shall add, "Is any man afraid or fainthearted? Let him go home so that his brothers will not become disheartened too." **9**When the officers have finished speaking to the army, they shall appoint commanders over it.

10When you march up to attack a city, make its people an offer of peace[D]. **11**If they accept and open their gates, all the people in it shall be subject to forced labor and shall work for you. **12**If they refuse to make peace and they engage you in battle, lay siege to that city. **13**When the LORD your God delivers it into your hand, put to the sword all the men in it. **14**As for the women, the children, the livestock and everything else in the city, you may take these as plunder[D] for yourselves. And you may use the plunder the LORD your God gives you from your enemies. **15**This is how you are to treat all the cities that are at a distance from you and do not belong to the nations nearby.

16However, in the cities of the nations the LORD your God is giving you as an inheritance, do not leave alive anything that breathes. **17**Completely destroy[a] them— the Hittites, Amorites, Canaanites, Perizzites, Hivites and Jebusites—as the LORD your God has commanded you. **18**Otherwise, they will teach you to follow all the detestable things they do in worshiping their gods, and you will sin against the LORD your God.

19When you lay siege to a city for a long time, fighting against it to capture it, do not destroy its trees by putting an ax to them, because you can eat their fruit. Do not cut them down. Are the trees of the field people, that you should besiege them?[b] **20**However, you may cut down trees that you know are not fruit trees and use them to build siege works[D] until the city at war with you falls.

How can we get God on our side? (20:4)

Believers today cannot claim this verse as a promise for victory in their nations' war efforts. There is a great difference between the wars Israel fought under the direct command of God and the wars nations engage in today, which may or may not be just. Still, individuals can trust God for their personal and spiritual success. The question is not whether God is on our side but whether we have joined his side. See *Don't Christians ever lose?* (Romans 8:37).

Why send all these soldiers home? (20:5–8)

All whose thoughts were occupied with anything other than war were sent home. Israel needed soldiers who could concentrate on the task at hand. Those not at peak performance, or worse, those who might diminish the abilities of others (v. 8) would have been detrimental to the war effort. Better a few determined soldiers than many who could not be trusted.

Why would God's people plunder women and children? (20:14)

It was customary at that time for prisoners of war to become slaves. But Israel was to treat their slaves according to God's standards— not with the brutality that could be found among other nations. See *Why does God endorse slavery?* (Lev. 25:44–46). Women captured by the Israelites were not treated merely as booty; God insisted on certain rights for them and provided for the possibility of their inclusion in the covenant community through marriage (21:10–14).

Do not leave alive anything that breathes (20:16)

See article: *Why kill everything?* (Joshua 6:21).

Aren't human lives more valuable than trees? (20:19)

Of course they are, but that is not the issue here. Israel's enemies were being judged for their sinful ways. Their trees, however, were spared to provide fruit for God's people once they took possession of the land. Other ancient military powers often destroyed indiscriminately, sometimes ruining the productivity of the land for years to come.

Siege works (20:20)

See *Siege works* (Isaiah 29:3). Also see *What happened during a siege?* (2 Kings 17:5).

Why this ritual for an unsolved murder? (21:1–9)

God had declared that *bloodshed pollutes the land* (Num. 35:33–34). So something had to be done to cleanse the land of the guilt of murder. Unplowed land may have symbolized unproductive land. It pictured fields without crops as the consequences of the murder. Running water, then, would have symbolized cleansing. This ritual thus would mean that no plow could uncover any guilt or blood that had soaked into the ground.

---

a 17 The Hebrew term refers to the irrevocable giving over of things or persons to the LORD, often by totally destroying them.   *b 19* Or *down to use in the siege, for the fruit trees are for the benefit of man.*

Atonement for an Unsolved Murder

21 If a man is found slain, lying in a field in the land the LORD your God is giving you to possess, and it is not known who killed him, ²your elders and judges shall go out and measure the distance from the body to the neighboring towns. ³Then the elders of the town nearest the body shall take a heifer that has never been worked and has never worn a yokeᴰ ⁴and lead her down to a valley that has not been plowed or planted and where there is a flowing stream. There in the valley they are to break the heifer's neck. ⁵The priestsᴰ, the sons of Levi, shall step forward, for the LORD your God has chosen them to minister and to pronounce blessings in the name of the LORD and to decide all cases of dispute and assault. ⁶Then all the elders of the town nearest the body shall wash their hands over the heifer whose neck was broken in the valley, ⁷and they shall declare: "Our hands did not shed this blood, nor did our eyes see it done. ⁸Accept this atonementᴰ for your people Israel, whom you have redeemedᴰ, O LORD, and do not hold your people guilty of the blood of an innocent man." And the bloodshed will be atoned for. ⁹So you will purge from yourselves the guilt of shedding innocent blood, since you have done what is right in the eyes of the LORD.

Marrying a Captive Woman

¹⁰When you go to war against your enemies and the LORD your God delivers them into your hands and you take captives, ¹¹if you notice among the captives a beautiful woman and are attracted to her, you may take her as your wife. ¹²Bring her into your home and have her shave her head, trim her nails ¹³and put aside the clothes she was wearing when captured. After she has lived in your house and mourned her father and mother for a full month, then you may go to her and be her husband and she shall be your wife. ¹⁴If you are not pleased with her, let her go wherever she wishes. You must not sell her or treat her as a slave, since you have dishonored her.

The Right of the Firstborn

¹⁵If a man has two wives, and he loves one but not the other, and both bear him sons but the firstbornᴰ is the son of the wife he does not love, ¹⁶when he wills his property to his sons, he must not give the rights of the firstborn to the son of the wife he loves in preference to his actual firstborn, the son of the wife he does not love. ¹⁷He must acknowledge the son of his unloved wife as the firstborn by giving him a double share of all he has. That son is the first sign of his father's strength. The right of the firstborn belongs to him.

A Rebellious Son

¹⁸If a man has a stubborn and rebellious son who does not obey his father and mother and will not listen to them when they discipline him, ¹⁹his father and mother shall take hold of him and bring him to the elders at the gate of his town. ²⁰They shall say to the elders, "This son of ours is stubborn and rebellious. He will not obey us. He is a profligate and a drunkard." ²¹Then all the men of his town shall stone him to deathᴰ. You must purge the evil from among you. All Israel will hear of it and be afraid.

Why could the Israelites marry some foreigners but not others? (21:11)

The warning against intermarrying with other nations was to keep out the influence of foreign religions (7:4). The marriages referred to here would be different in two ways: (1) These women were to be from distant cities, not Canaan. The Canaanites were to be completely destroyed (20:15–16). (2) These marriages could not result from peace treaties between Israel and others (7:2). These women were to be captives of war; their people were to be totally defeated. These foreign wives would have to submit to Israel's ways and Israel's God.

Why shave and manicure a female captive? (21:12)

The newly captured woman was given a month to compose herself before she was married to her Israelite captor. Shaving her head and cutting her nails were elements of a purification ritual (Num. 8:7; Lev. 14:8), indicating her transfer to another life and status. It may have also been part of a mourning ritual for her parents (34:8; Num. 20:29).

Is not being pleased grounds for divorce? (21:14)

Not in the sense that we would think of it today. In Old Testament times, however, this provision would actually have protected the woman from misuse and loss of status on the whim of her husband. It was very generous in comparison with the treatment of women captured by neighboring nations. Also see *Why does God endorse slavery?* (Lev. 25:44–46).

Does God approve of polygamy? (21:15)

See article: *Why did David have so many wives and concubines?* (2 Samuel 5:13).

Right of the firstborn (21:17)

See *What was the difference between a birthright and a blessing?* (Gen. 27:36).

How does fathering a child prove strength? (21:17)

The Israelites considered children to be part of their covenant blessings (Gen. 15:5); they knew that children came from God. The birth of a child, then, signaled a man's reproductive powers as evidence of blessing from God. Also see *Does God cause infertility?* (1 Samuel 1:5).

Why was stoning a son different from sacrificing him? (21:18–21)

The parents who prosecuted their own son before the elders were dealing with a serious threat to the security of the entire community. A son judged to be rebellious was executed by the men of the town for the good of the community. His parents would have had nothing personal to gain from the stoning and would have been filled with grief. By contrast, pagans who sacrificed their children did so to appease their gods in an attempt to gain favor and blessing. See *Why would parents sacrifice their children?* (Jer. 19:5).

Purge the evil (21:21)

See article: *Why kill a murderer?* (19:13).

Various Laws

Anyone who is hung on a tree is under God's curse (21:23)

The man executed for breaking one of God's commands was cursed by God. His corpse hanging on a tree was a public exhibition of judgment. Jesus willingly took this curse on himself by hanging on the cross (Gal. 3:13).

Why does God detest cross-dressing? (22:5)

Some think this passage condemns transvestism since it was associated with homosexuality and certain idolatrous cults. Others think it prohibits the reversal or the blurring of the sex roles of men and women, which would have violated the natural order created by God.

Why not take the mother bird? (22:6–7)

This command may have reflected humanitarian concerns for wildlife, though taking young birds or eggs does not seem terribly humane either. Others suggest this practice helped maintain the food supply. Leaving the hen permitted her to live to lay another batch of eggs.

What was wrong with these actions? (22:9–11)

The mixing of dissimilar things may have been a practice associated with pagan religions, which the Israelites were to avoid. Or it's possible that God intended unblended fabric to symbolize the purity and separation of the Israelites, who were not to blend with their pagan neighbors. Though this requirement seems inappropriate today, the principle it illustrates is seen in the New Testament teaching regarding the undivided loyalty believers should have to God (Matt. 6:24; 2 Cor. 5:15–16; 6:14). See vv. 9–10; Lev. 19:19. Also see article: *Why did God keep some meats off the menu?* (Lev. 11:4–41).

What proof could parents offer that their daughter was a virgin? (22:15)

Most believe the proof of a bride's virginity was a blood-stained sheet or dress resulting from her first sexual intercourse (v. 17). Some think perhaps the word for *virgin* is used here in its more generic sense as a female adolescent. If that is the case, the parents were to present proof of her adolescence—that she was indeed menstruating and was not pregnant.

Is a ruined reputation worse than rape? (22:19,29)

In Israelite culture, a man who raped a virgin was required to pay a penalty (essentially the bride-price her father would have received at her marriage) and to provide marriage protection without possibility of divorce (caring for her and any child born of their union). A man who falsely accused his bride of not being a virgin, however, committed two wrongs: he took her virginity and also defamed her and her family. So he was required to provide the same marriage protection plus pay restitution for damaging her reputation. Also see *Why was marriage part of the punishment for some cases of rape?* (22:29) and *Why would a father sell his daughter as a servant?* (Exodus 21:7–11).

Purge the evil (22:21)

See article: *Why kill a murderer?* (19:13).

22 If a man guilty of a capital offense is put to death[D] and his body is hung on a tree, **23**you must not leave his body on the tree overnight. Be sure to bury him that same day, because anyone who is hung on a tree is under God's curse. You must not desecrate[D] the land the LORD your God is giving you as an inheritance.

22 If you see your brother's ox or sheep straying, do not ignore it but be sure to take it back to him. **2**If the brother does not live near you or if you do not know who he is, take it home with you and keep it until he comes looking for it. Then give it back to him. **3**Do the same if you find your brother's donkey or his cloak or anything he loses. Do not ignore it.

4If you see your brother's donkey or his ox fallen on the road, do not ignore it. Help him get it to its feet.

5A woman must not wear men's clothing, nor a man wear women's clothing, for the LORD your God detests anyone who does this.

6If you come across a bird's nest beside the road, either in a tree or on the ground, and the mother is sitting on the young or on the eggs, do not take the mother with the young. **7**You may take the young, but be sure to let the mother go, so that it may go well with you and you may have a long life.

8When you build a new house, make a parapet around your roof so that you may not bring the guilt of bloodshed on your house if someone falls from the roof.

9Do not plant two kinds of seed in your vineyard; if you do, not only the crops you plant but also the fruit of the vineyard will be defiled.[a]

10Do not plow with an ox and a donkey yoked together. **11**Do not wear clothes of wool and linen woven together.

12Make tassels on the four corners of the cloak you wear.

Marriage Violations

13If a man takes a wife and, after lying with her, dislikes her **14**and slanders her and gives her a bad name, saying, "I married this woman, but when I approached her, I did not find proof of her virginity," **15**then the girl's father and mother shall bring proof that she was a virgin to the town elders at the gate. **16**The girl's father will say to the elders, "I gave my daughter in marriage to this man, but he dislikes her. **17**Now he has slandered her and said, 'I did not find your daughter to be a virgin.' But here is the proof of my daughter's virginity." Then her parents shall display the cloth before the elders of the town, **18**and the elders shall take the man and punish him. **19**They shall fine him a hundred shekels[D] of silver[b] and give them to the girl's father, because this man has given an Israelite virgin a bad name. She shall continue to be his wife; he must not divorce her as long as he lives.

20If, however, the charge is true and no proof of the girl's virginity can be found, **21**she shall be brought to the door of her father's house and there the men of her town shall stone her to death. She has done a disgraceful thing in Israel by being promiscuous while still in her father's house. You must purge the evil from among you.

a 9 Or be forfeited to the sanctuary   *b 19 That is, about 2 1/2 pounds (about 1 kilogram)*

22If a man is found sleeping with another man's wife, both the man who slept with her and the woman must die. You must purge the evil from Israel.

23If a man happens to meet in a town a virgin pledged to be married and he sleeps with her, **24**you shall take both of them to the gate of that town and stone them to deathᴰ—the girl because she was in a town and did not scream for help, and the man because he violated another man's wife. You must purge the evil from among you.

25But if out in the country a man happens to meet a girl pledged to be married and rapes her, only the man who has done this shall die. **26**Do nothing to the girl; she has committed no sin deserving death. This case is like that of someone who attacks and murders his neighbor, **27**for the man found the girl out in the country, and though the betrothed girl screamed, there was no one to rescue her.

28If a man happens to meet a virgin who is not pledged to be married and rapes her and they are discovered, **29**he shall pay the girl's father fifty shekelsᴰ of silver.ᵃ He must marry the girl, for he has violated her. He can never divorce her as long as he lives.

30A man is not to marry his father's wife; he must not dishonor his father's bed.

Exclusion From the Assembly

23 No one who has been emasculated by crushing or cutting may enter the assembly of the LORD.

2No one born of a forbidden marriageᵇ nor any of his descendants may enter the assembly of the LORD, even down to the tenth generation.

3No Ammonite or Moabite or any of his descendants may enter the assembly of the LORD, even down to the tenth generation. **4**For they did not come to meet you with bread and water on your way when you came out of Egypt, and they hired Balaam son of Beor from Pethor in Aram Naharaimᶜ to pronounce a curse on you. **5**However, the LORD your God would not listen to Balaam but turned the curse into a blessing for you, because the LORD your God loves you. **6**Do not seek a treaty of friendship with them as long as you live.

7Do not abhor an Edomite, for he is your brother. Do not abhor an Egyptian, because you lived as an alienᴰ in his country. **8**The third generation of children born to them may enter the assembly of the LORD.

Uncleanness in the Camp

9When you are encamped against your enemies, keep away from everything impure. **10**If one of your men is uncleanᴰ because of a nocturnal emission, he is to go outside the camp and stay there. **11**But as evening approaches he is to wash himself, and at sunset he may return to the camp.

12Designate a place outside the camp where you can go to relieve yourself. **13**As part of your equipment have something to dig with, and when you relieve yourself, dig a hole and cover up your excrement. **14**For the LORD your God moves about in your camp to protect you and to deliver your enemies to you. Your camp must be holy, so that he will not see among you anything indecent and turn away from you.

ᵃ29 That is, about 1 1/4 pounds (about 0.6 kilogram)   ᵇ2 Or *one of illegitimate birth*   ᶜ4 That is, Northwest Mesopotamia

Why the death penalty for adultery? (22:22–25)

The Old Testament is not explicit. Some suggest it had to do with its social effects. Undetected adultery could produce an illegitimate child who then could wrongly receive the family inheritance. In this case, the death penalty is seen as a deterrent to the breakdown of the family. Others say the penalty reflects Israel's belief that adultery was a direct sin against God. The writer of Job equates adultery with murder (Job 24:14–15).

Why was marriage part of the punishment for some cases of rape? (22:29)

The requirement that a man marry the virgin whom he had raped protected the woman, who may have been less desirable for marriage as a result of losing her virginity. It also ensured that the man did not get away with his original intention—sex without the commitment of marriage. Also see *Why pay a bride-price for a seduction?* (Exodus 22:16–17).

Does God discriminate? (23:1)

In some cases, yes—but for good reason. In the idol-worshiping culture in which Israel lived, some would emasculate or mutilate themselves as acts of devotion to their gods. Since God wanted his people to avoid any practice associated with the worship of other gods, he prohibited such things. Later, he would offer special provisions for those accidently emasculated (Isaiah 56:3–6), but for now God wanted his people to honor him and respect his holiness. Also see *Why discriminate against the handicapped?* (Lev. 21:17–23).

Does God reject the children of sinful parents? (23:2)

Some suggest this means God rejected illegitimate children born out of wedlock. Others say a *forbidden marriage* probably was an incestuous affair or a sexual liaison with a cult prostitute in pagan worship. However, excluding descendants for the fault of their ancestors seems extreme, and some see this as a figure of speech (hyperbole) to portray the severity of this sin. The same penalty on the Moabites (v. 3), for example, did not prevent Ruth from becoming a proselyte and an ancestor in the Messiah's family tree (Ruth 1:16; 4:17).

Why hold a grudge? (23:3–6)

God was not encouraging Israel to hold a grudge. It was punishment he demanded! Ammon and Moab had never suffered the consequences for their hostility and lack of hospitality—a grave offense by ancient standards. What appears to be a grudge, then, was in fact an inseparable part of the ancient code of justice.

Nocturnal emission (23:10)

This may have been just a way God taught his people about holiness. See *Why would God design natural functions to cause uncleanness?* (Lev. 15:16–24). Or this may have been part of God's method of community hygiene—just as following instructions dealt with sanitary disposal of sewage (vv. 12–14). Washing oneself outside the camp could cut the risk of contagious disease.

Shrine prostitute (23:17)

Refers to a special class of prostitutes (male and female) that performed sexual acts in the temple of their god as acts of religious devotion. See *What did male prostitutes have to do with pagan worship?* (1 Kings 14:24) and *How did men sacrifice with shrine prostitutes?* (Hosea 4:14).

What's wrong with interest on loans? (23:19)

See *What's wrong with charging interest?* (Exodus 22:25).

SCRIPTURE LINK (23:19) *Do not charge your brother interest*

Further instructions on interest can be found in Lev. 25:35–37; Neh. 5:7,10; Psalm 15:5; Ezek. 18:8,13 and Matt. 25:27.

Why eat the fruit and crops of others? (23:24–25)

It's not clear who was permitted to eat from another's crops. Most think this was a provision made to care for the poor. At the same time, the privilege guarded against abuse: people could eat but not carry produce away in a basket. The Israelites were given other instructions as well on ways to care for the needy among them (24:19–21; Lev. 19:9–10; 23:22).

Was this no-fault divorce? (24:1)

Not really. Some think the word *indecent* means that the woman was ceremonially unclean, having neglected the law's instructions for menstruation (Lev. 15:19–27). Others think it refers to a physical defect, such as being unable to have children. Either way, both were seen as serious problems in the community. This law probably discouraged easy divorce by imposing legal requirements.

What was wrong with remarrying a wife who had married someone else? (24:4)

In some cases remarriage after divorce was not wrong. But a woman who had been divorced from two husbands was not permitted to remarry her first spouse. This may have been intended to discourage husbands from rash actions that led to quick divorces. Or it may have been to protect the woman's reputation—trading husbands suggested immorality or other ulterior motives. A twice-divorced woman was, however, free to marry someone other than her former spouse (v. 2). Also see *Is divorce always wrong?* (Mark 10:1–12).

SCRIPTURE LINK (24:8) *Leprous diseases*

See the detailed instructions given in Lev. 13–14.

SCRIPTURE LINK (24:9) *God punished Miriam with leprosy*

See Num. 12:10.

Is a returned pledge still a pledge? (24:10–13)

Technically, yes. As a special allowance for the poor of the community, such returned items were still considered pledges. The poor were permitted to use what they had pledged during the time they worked to repay their loans.

Miscellaneous Laws

[15]If a slave has taken refuge with you, do not hand him over to his master. [16]Let him live among you wherever he likes and in whatever town he chooses. Do not oppress him.

[17]No Israelite man or woman is to become a shrine prostitute[D]. [18]You must not bring the earnings of a female prostitute or of a male prostitute[a] into the house of the LORD your God to pay any vow[D], because the LORD your God detests them both.

[19]Do not charge your brother interest, whether on money or food or anything else that may earn interest. [20]You may charge a foreigner interest, but not a brother Israelite, so that the LORD your God may bless you in everything you put your hand to in the land you are entering to possess.

[21]If you make a vow to the LORD your God, do not be slow to pay it, for the LORD your God will certainly demand it of you and you will be guilty of sin. [22]But if you refrain from making a vow, you will not be guilty. [23]Whatever your lips utter you must be sure to do, because you made your vow freely to the LORD your God with your own mouth.

[24]If you enter your neighbor's vineyard, you may eat all the grapes you want, but do not put any in your basket. [25]If you enter your neighbor's grainfield, you may pick kernels with your hands, but you must not put a sickle to his standing grain.

24 If a man marries a woman who becomes displeasing to him because he finds something indecent about her, and he writes her a certificate of divorce, gives it to her and sends her from his house, [2]and if after she leaves his house she becomes the wife of another man, [3]and her second husband dislikes her and writes her a certificate of divorce, gives it to her and sends her from his house, or if he dies, [4]then her first husband, who divorced her, is not allowed to marry her again after she has been defiled. That would be detestable in the eyes of the LORD. Do not bring sin upon the land the LORD your God is giving you as an inheritance.

[5]If a man has recently married, he must not be sent to war or have any other duty laid on him. For one year he is to be free to stay at home and bring happiness to the wife he has married.

[6]Do not take a pair of millstones[D]—not even the upper one—as security for a debt, because that would be taking a man's livelihood as security.

[7]If a man is caught kidnapping one of his brother Israelites and treats him as a slave or sells him, the kidnapper must die. You must purge the evil from among you.

[8]In cases of leprous[b] diseases be very careful to do exactly as the priests[D], who are Levites[D], instruct you. You must follow carefully what I have commanded them. [9]Remember what the LORD your God did to Miriam along the way after you came out of Egypt.

[10]When you make a loan of any kind to your neighbor, do not go into his house to get what he is offering as a pledge. [11]Stay outside and let the man to whom you are making the loan bring the pledge out to you. [12]If the man is poor, do not go to sleep with his pledge in your posses-

---

a 18 Hebrew *of a dog*   *b 8* The Hebrew word was used for various diseases affecting the skin—not necessarily leprosy.

sion. [13]Return his cloak to him by sunset so that he may sleep in it. Then he will thank you, and it will be regarded as a righteous[D] act in the sight of the LORD your God.

[14]Do not take advantage of a hired man who is poor and needy, whether he is a brother Israelite or an alien[D] living in one of your towns. [15]Pay him his wages each day before sunset, because he is poor and is counting on it. Otherwise he may cry to the LORD against you, and you will be guilty of sin.

[16]Fathers shall not be put to death[D] for their children, nor children put to death for their fathers; each is to die for his own sin.

[17]Do not deprive the alien or the fatherless of justice, or take the cloak of the widow as a pledge. [18]Remember that you were slaves in Egypt and the LORD your God redeemed[D] you from there. That is why I command you to do this.

[19]When you are harvesting in your field and you overlook a sheaf, do not go back to get it. Leave it for the alien, the fatherless and the widow, so that the LORD your God may bless you in all the work of your hands. [20]When you beat the olives from your trees, do not go over the branches a second time. Leave what remains for the alien, the fatherless and the widow. [21]When you harvest the grapes in your vineyard, do not go over the vines again. Leave what remains for the alien, the fatherless and the widow. [22]Remember that you were slaves in Egypt. That is why I command you to do this.

25 When men have a dispute, they are to take it to court and the judges will decide the case, acquitting the innocent and condemning the guilty. [2]If the guilty man deserves to be beaten, the judge shall make him lie down and have him flogged in his presence with the number of lashes his crime deserves, [3]but he must not give him more than forty lashes. If he is flogged more than that, your brother will be degraded in your eyes.

[4]Do not muzzle an ox while it is treading out the grain.

[5]If brothers are living together and one of them dies without a son, his widow must not marry outside the family. Her husband's brother shall take her and marry her and fulfill the duty of a brother-in-law to her. [6]The first son she bears shall carry on the name of the dead brother so that his name will not be blotted out from Israel.

[7]However, if a man does not want to marry his brother's wife, she shall go to the elders at the town gate and say, "My husband's brother refuses to carry on his brother's name in Israel. He will not fulfill the duty of a brother-in-law to me." [8]Then the elders of his town shall summon him and talk to him. If he persists in saying, "I do not want to marry her," [9]his brother's widow shall go up to him in the presence of the elders, take off one of his sandals, spit in his face and say, "This is what is done to the man who will not build up his brother's family line." [10]That man's line shall be known in Israel as The Family of the Unsandaled.

[11]If two men are fighting and the wife of one of them comes to rescue her husband from his assailant, and she reaches out and seizes him by his private parts, [12]you shall cut off her hand. Show her no pity.

[13]Do not have two differing weights in your bag—one heavy, one light. [14]Do not have two differing measures in your house—one large, one small. [15]You must have accurate and honest weights and measures, so that you may live long in the land the LORD your God is giving you. [16]For

Why have welfare dependent on inefficient harvesting? (24:19–21)

This wasn't exactly a welfare program, though it helped provide for the less fortunate of the community. It might better be called a "make work" program. It offered aliens, widows and orphans an opportunity to work honestly for their food even though they did not own land.

If 41 lashes degraded someone, why wouldn't 40? (25:3)

A limit had to be imposed to prevent excessive punishment. Though the number seems arbitrary, the principle behind it was clear: they were to avoid inhumane punishment that could humiliate the criminal.

Why was a man required to marry his brother's widow? (25:5–9)

A man was required to marry his brother's widow unless she had already borne a son. This preserved the deceased man's name and kept his property within the family. It also served as a social security system, providing the widow a means of support. If a man refused to carry out this duty, the widow could bring him to trial before the town elders (vv. 7–10). If he still refused, then another male relative could assume the responsibility (see Ruth 4:1–12).

Why were the elders at the town gate? (25:7)

Though people lived within the city walls, they worked their fields or cared for their flocks on land surrounding the city. This resulted in a great number of people traveling daily through the town gates. Thus, gates became the place where official business and legal matters were conducted.

How bad was the stigma for a *Family of the Unsandaled*? (25:10)

It was humiliating for the man who refused to marry his brother's widow to be spit upon in public, especially by a woman (v. 9). But the entire community viewed him with complete disdain: How could he allow his brother's name to be blotted out? Such shame would be remembered against this man's family for generations to come.

Why be so harsh about private parts? (25:11–12)

Because injuring a man's sexual organs ran the risk of eliminating his ability to reproduce. Since producing children was a matter of utmost importance in Israelite culture, the penalty for endangering a man's potential offspring was swift and sure. Women were not the only ones punished for such things. A man who maliciously injured another man's genitals would have to suffer his own penalty (Lev. 24:19–20).

What is wrong with *differing weights* and *differing measures*? (25:13–14)

This is not speaking of a legitimate set of weights and measures. Rather this is a warning against having two weights or measures that are supposed to be the same, but where one deviates from the standard. This is a call to honest business practices (v. 15).

Do not forget! (25:19)

See *Why hold a grudge?* (23:3–6).

Firstfruits (26:2)

The first of their crops to ripen. The people were to offer the first of their harvest to God as a testimony of God's faithfulness, their gratitude to him and their confidence in a good harvest to come.

Why did God choose a place for his name to dwell? (26:2)

God does not need a place to dwell, nor can he be confined to any one place. However, he chose to make his presence available to Israel through Moses and, later, the priests. God chose a centralized location as a means of unifying the nation, calling all the people together to worship in one place. This place of worship also served as a witness to neighboring nations that God's presence was in Israel. Also see *Why couldn't the Israelites worship anywhere?* (12:5); and *Why did it matter where they worshiped God?* (2 Kings 18:22).

Aramean (26:5)

An ethnic group located primarily in Syria and northern Palestine. See *David's Victories* on page 407.

Flowing with milk and honey (26:9)

See *Flowing with milk and honey* (6:3).

Why was the third year called *the year of the tithe*? (26:12)

The Israelites tithed their firstfruits every year in Jerusalem (v. 2). One's family, the Levites and the poor would partake of the offerings there (12:5–19; 14:22–27). But every third year they offered the tithe within their own towns rather than in Jerusalem (14:28–29). It was shared with the local Levites and provided food for others who owned no land (aliens, widows and orphans).

Why would anyone offer a tithe to the dead? (26:14)

It's not clear. Some think this was linked to the pagan custom of honoring the dead by offering food to dead relatives or the gods (see Jer. 7:18). Others think this refers to food brought into a house where death had just occurred to be eaten by mourners. Such a house would have been unclean and its food contaminated—unfit for the Lord (see Hosea 9:4).

---

the LORD your God detests anyone who does these things, anyone who deals dishonestly.

¹⁷Remember what the Amalekites did to you along the way when you came out of Egypt. ¹⁸When you were weary and worn out, they met you on your journey and cut off all who were lagging behind; they had no fear of God. ¹⁹When the LORD your God gives you rest from all the enemies around you in the land he is giving you to possess as an inheritance, you shall blot out the memory of Amalek from under heaven. Do not forget!

Firstfruits and Tithes

26 When you have entered the land the LORD your God is giving you as an inheritance and have taken possession of it and settled in it, ²take some of the firstfruits[D] of all that you produce from the soil of the land the LORD your God is giving you and put them in a basket. Then go to the place the LORD your God will choose as a dwelling for his Name ³and say to the priest[D] in office at the time, "I declare today to the LORD your God that I have come to the land the LORD swore to our forefathers to give us." ⁴The priest shall take the basket from your hands and set it down in front of the altar of the LORD your God. ⁵Then you shall declare before the LORD your God: "My father was a wandering Aramean, and he went down into Egypt with a few people and lived there and became a great nation, powerful and numerous. ⁶But the Egyptians mistreated us and made us suffer, putting us to hard labor. ⁷Then we cried out to the LORD, the God of our fathers, and the LORD heard our voice and saw our misery, toil and oppression. ⁸So the LORD brought us out of Egypt with a mighty hand and an outstretched arm, with great terror and with miraculous signs and wonders. ⁹He brought us to this place and gave us this land, a land flowing with milk and honey; ¹⁰and now I bring the firstfruits of the soil that you, O LORD, have given me." Place the basket before the LORD your God and bow down before him. ¹¹And you and the Levites[D] and the aliens[D] among you shall rejoice in all the good things the LORD your God has given to you and your household.

¹²When you have finished setting aside a tenth of all your produce in the third year, the year of the tithe[D], you shall give it to the Levite, the alien, the fatherless and the widow, so that they may eat in your towns and be satisfied. ¹³Then say to the LORD your God: "I have removed from my house the sacred[D] portion and have given it to the Levite, the alien, the fatherless and the widow, according to all you commanded. I have not turned aside from your commands nor have I forgotten any of them. ¹⁴I have not eaten any of the sacred portion while I was in mourning, nor have I removed any of it while I was unclean[D], nor have I offered any of it to the dead. I have obeyed the LORD my God; I have done everything you commanded me. ¹⁵Look down from heaven, your holy dwelling place, and bless your people Israel and the land you have given us as you promised on oath to our forefathers, a land flowing with milk and honey."

Follow the LORD's Commands

¹⁶The LORD your God commands you this day to follow these decrees and laws; carefully observe them with all your heart and with all your soul[D]. ¹⁷You have declared this day that the LORD is your God and that you will walk in his ways, that you will keep his decrees, commands

and laws, and that you will obey him. **18**And the LORD has declared this day that you are his people, his treasured possession as he promised, and that you are to keep all his commands. **19**He has declared that he will set you in praise, fame and honor high above all the nations he has made and that you will be a people holy to the LORD your God, as he promised.

The Altar on Mount Ebal

27 Moses and the elders of Israel commanded the people: "Keep all these commands that I give you today. **2**When you have crossed the Jordan into the land the LORD your God is giving you, set up some large stones and coat them with plaster. **3**Write on them all the words of this law when you have crossed over to enter the land the LORD your God is giving you, a land flowing with milk and honey, just as the LORD, the God of your fathers, promised you. **4**And when you have crossed the Jordan, set up these stones on Mount Ebal, as I command you today, and coat them with plaster. **5**Build there an altar to the LORD your God, an altar of stones. Do not use any iron tool upon them. **6**Build the altar of the LORD your God with fieldstones and offer burnt offerings[D] on it to the LORD your God. **7**Sacrifice[D] fellowship offerings[Da] there, eating them and rejoicing in the presence of the LORD your God. **8**And you shall write very clearly all the words of this law on these stones you have set up."

Curses From Mount Ebal

9Then Moses and the priests[D], who are Levites[D], said to all Israel, "Be silent, O Israel, and listen! You have now become the people of the LORD your God. **10**Obey the LORD your God and follow his commands and decrees that I give you today."

11On the same day Moses commanded the people:

12When you have crossed the Jordan, these tribes shall stand on Mount Gerizim to bless the people: Simeon, Levi, Judah, Issachar, Joseph and Benjamin. **13**And these tribes shall stand on Mount Ebal to pronounce curses: Reuben, Gad, Asher, Zebulun, Dan and Naphtali.

14The Levites shall recite to all the people of Israel in a loud voice:

15"Cursed is the man who carves an image or casts an idol[D]—a thing detestable to the LORD, the work of the craftsman's hands—and sets it up in secret."

Then all the people shall say, "Amen!"

16"Cursed is the man who dishonors his father or his mother."

Then all the people shall say, "Amen!"

17"Cursed is the man who moves his neighbor's boundary stone."

Then all the people shall say, "Amen!"

18"Cursed is the man who leads the blind astray on the road."

Then all the people shall say, "Amen!"

19"Cursed is the man who withholds justice from the alien[D], the fatherless or the widow."

Then all the people shall say, "Amen!"

20"Cursed is the man who sleeps with his father's wife, for he dishonors his father's bed."

Then all the people shall say, "Amen!"

Why did God treasure Israel above all other nations? (26:18)

We cannot always understand the ways God works, but we can say that this was not simply a matter of favoritism. God loves all nations (John 3:16). He singled Israel out for a special blessing because, for reasons known only to him, they were assigned a special responsibility as God's representatives to the world (Gen. 12:2–3). In fact, God intended to bless all nations through Israel's knowledge of the one true God. Also see article: *Did God love Israel more than other nations?* (4:33).

Flowing with milk and honey (27:3)

See *Flowing with milk and honey* (6:3).

All the words of this law (27:3)

Some think this may mean the laws of chs. 12–26. Others suggest it may mean the curses of vv. 15–26, since the laws were written on stones to be erected in the same place where the curses were pronounced (vv. 4,13). It is likely these laws were abbreviated in some form (similar to the Ten Commandments) and would require a long time to read.

What was wrong with using iron tools to build an altar? (27:5)

See *Why were uncut stones needed for the altar?* (Joshua 8:31).

Burnt offerings (27:6)

See *What did the guilt offerings do that other offerings couldn't?* (Lev. 5:15).

Fellowship offerings (27:7)

See *How were some offerings for fellowship?* (Lev. 3:1).

In secret (27:15)

See *Secretly* (27:24).

Boundary stone (27:17)

A marker that established legal property rights. The stone may have had engravings on it stating rights of ownership or even divine curses and blessings. Moving a stone was tantamount to stealing land.

Who would lead the blind astray? (27:18)

The law was intended to protect the less fortunate of the community. People with disabilities, then as now, were particularly vulnerable and easily victimized. The unscrupulous could profit by taking advantage of the blind. The words *on the road* may be figurative as well as literal, suggesting any crime against the blind. In a general sense, this law states it a crime to take advantage of people's disabilities.

---

a 7 Traditionally *peace offerings*

Why were earlier brother-sister marriages permitted? (27:22)

Ancient cultures had their own reasons for such marriages. Foremost among those reasons, perhaps, was to keep property and possessions within the family. God may have allowed the early Hebrews to intermarry to build up their population. Later, after the Israelite nation had become established, he prohibited the practice, perhaps to avoid the adverse effects of prolonged inbreeding. Also see Lev. 18:9; 20:17.

Secretly (27:24)

Many of the curses listed here deal with crimes or sins done in private. But God assured them that any crime hidden from the public eye could not escape his eye—or his punishment.

²¹"Cursed is the man who has sexual relations with any animal."

Then all the people shall say, "Amen!"
²²"Cursed is the man who sleeps with his sister, the daughter of his father or the daughter of his mother."

Then all the people shall say, "Amen!"
²³"Cursed is the man who sleeps with his mother-in-law."

Then all the people shall say, "Amen!"
²⁴"Cursed is the man who kills his neighbor secretly."

Then all the people shall say, "Amen!"
²⁵"Cursed is the man who accepts a bribe to kill an innocent person."

Then all the people shall say, "Amen!"
²⁶"Cursed is the man who does not uphold the words of this law by carrying them out."

Then all the people shall say, "Amen!"

Blessings for Obedience

28 If you fully obey the LORD your God and carefully follow all his commands I give you today, the LORD your God will set you high above all the nations on earth. ²All these blessings will come upon you and accompany you if you obey the LORD your God:

³You will be blessed in the city and blessed in the country.

⁴The fruit of your womb will be blessed, and the crops of your land and the young of your livestock— the calves of your herds and the lambs of your flocks.

⁵Your basket and your kneading trough will be blessed.

Is success guaranteed to those who obey God? (28:2–6)

In a general sense, yes. But the promise was made to the *nation* as a whole, not to *individuals*. Personal fortunes or misfortunes could vary widely apart from the overall prosperity of the nation.

The blessings and curses here are part of the covenant between God and Israel. If Israel obeyed God and kept his laws, God agreed to bless them with success and prosperity. However, if they disobeyed, God would punish them. Such blessings and curses were common in treaties and agreements between nations in ancient times.

The promised prosperity was not primarily for individual comfort. Rather, it was intended to witness to the surrounding nations that Israel served the one true God. God would make Israel powerful, a leader among the others—*the head, not the tail . . . at the top, never at the bottom* (v. 13). In addition, their prosperity was to be shared among the less fortunate of the community so that all might have their needs fulfilled.

We see in these verses a basic principle, not an absolute law. Typically, when we follow God's ways, we will be better off than when we go our own way. Still, suffering may come to those who are righteous—in fact, sometimes it may come because they are righteous.

God has promised to bless those who obey him. When the wicked prosper, two things should be remembered: (1) God's patience and mercy permit many to enjoy things they do not deserve (Matt. 5:45), and (2) justice is not completed in this lifetime.

Also see articles: *Does obedience bring prosperity?* (Lev. 26:3–39) and *Does seeking God guarantee success?* (2 Chron. 26:5).

6You will be blessed when you come in and blessed when you go out.

7The LORD will grant that the enemies who rise up against you will be defeated before you. They will come at you from one direction but flee from you in seven.

8The LORD will send a blessing on your barns and on everything you put your hand to. The LORD your God will bless you in the land he is giving you.

9The LORD will establish you as his holy people, as he promised you on oath, if you keep the commands of the LORD your God and walk in his ways. **10**Then all the peoples on earth will see that you are called by the name of the LORD, and they will fear you. **11**The LORD will grant you abundant prosperity—in the fruit of your womb, the young of your livestock and the crops of your ground—in the land he swore to your forefathers to give you.

12The LORD will open the heavens, the storehouse of his bounty, to send rain on your land in season and to bless all the work of your hands. You will lend to many nations but will borrow from none. **13**The LORD will make you the head, not the tail. If you pay attention to the commands of the LORD your God that I give you this day and carefully follow them, you will always be at the top, never at the bottom. **14**Do not turn aside from any of the commands I give you today, to the right or to the left, following other gods and serving them.

Curses for Disobedience

15However, if you do not obey the LORD your God and do not carefully follow all his commands and decrees I am giving you today, all these curses will come upon you and overtake you:

16You will be cursed in the city and cursed in the country.

17Your basket and your kneading trough will be cursed.

18The fruit of your womb will be cursed, and the crops of your land, and the calves of your herds and the lambs of your flocks.

19You will be cursed when you come in and cursed when you go out.

20The LORD will send on you curses, confusion and rebuke in everything you put your hand to, until you are destroyed and come to sudden ruin because of the evil you have done in forsaking him.*a* **21**The LORD will plague you with diseases until he has destroyed you from the land you are entering to possess. **22**The LORD will strike you with wasting disease, with fever and inflammation, with scorching heat and drought, with blight and mildew, which will plague you until you perish. **23**The sky over your head will be bronze, the ground beneath you iron. **24**The LORD will turn the rain of your country into dust and powder; it will come down from the skies until you are destroyed.

25The LORD will cause you to be defeated before your enemies. You will come at them from one direction but flee from them in seven, and you will become a thing of horror to all the kingdoms on earth. **26**Your carcasses will be food for all the birds of the air and the beasts of the earth, and there will be no one to frighten them away.

Why do these curses mirror the blessings? (28:16–19)

This covenant between God and Israel is similar in style with other legal covenants of ancient times. In such agreements, it was common to balance blessings with curses. This parallel format became the standard for contracts. It is only natural that God would reveal and present his covenant to Israel in the legal language and style of the covenants of that day. See Introduction: *What to look for in Deuteronomy.*

In what sense would the sky be *bronze* and the ground *iron*? (28:23)

This meant a severe drought. The sun would blaze unceasingly, making the cloudless sky appear as bronze. The sun would bake the land and cause it to become extremely dry and hard, like iron. Nothing could grow in such circumstances, and their flocks would starve.

a20 Hebrew me

SCRIPTURE LINK (28:36) *The LORD will drive you*
Fulfilled in 2 Kings 17 and 25.

Can curses be signs and wonders? (28:46)

Yes, curses can be signs of God's power. This kind of miracle, though, would be irrefutable proof to the Israelites that they had failed to obey God. Signs are not always positive.

Iron yoke (28:48)

A yoke was a figurative description of bondage and slavery. An iron yoke (which did not exist) represented an even more terrifying and brutal form of slavery. An iron yoke could not be broken as a wooden one could. Iron pictured permanent slavery (see Jer. 28:13–14).

27The LORD will afflictᴰ you with the boils of Egypt and with tumors, festering sores and the itch, from which you cannot be cured. **28**The LORD will afflict you with madness, blindness and confusion of mind. **29**At midday you will grope about like a blind man in the dark. You will be unsuccessful in everything you do; day after day you will be oppressed and robbed, with no one to rescue you.

30You will be pledged to be married to a woman, but another will take her and ravish her. You will build a house, but you will not live in it. You will plant a vineyard, but you will not even begin to enjoy its fruit. **31**Your ox will be slaughtered before your eyes, but you will eat none of it. Your donkey will be forcibly taken from you and will not be returned. Your sheep will be given to your enemies, and no one will rescue them. **32**Your sons and daughters will be given to another nation, and you will wear out your eyes watching for them day after day, powerless to lift a hand. **33**A people that you do not know will eat what your land and labor produce, and you will have nothing but cruel oppression all your days. **34**The sights you see will drive you mad. **35**The LORD will afflict your knees and legs with painful boils that cannot be cured, spreading from the soles of your feet to the top of your head.

36The LORD will drive you and the king you set over you to a nation unknown to you or your fathers. There you will worship other gods, gods of wood and stone. **37**You will become a thing of horror and an object of scorn and ridicule to all the nations where the LORD will drive you.

38You will sow much seed in the field but you will harvest little, because locustsᴰ will devour it. **39**You will plant vineyards and cultivate them but you will not drink the wine or gather the grapes, because worms will eat them. **40**You will have olive trees throughout your country but you will not use the oil, because the olives will drop off. **41**You will have sons and daughters but you will not keep them, because they will go into captivity. **42**Swarms of locusts will take over all your trees and the crops of your land.

43The alienᴰ who lives among you will rise above you higher and higher, but you will sink lower and lower. **44**He will lend to you, but you will not lend to him. He will be the head, but you will be the tail.

45All these curses will come upon you. They will pursue you and overtake you until you are destroyed, because you did not obey the LORD your God and observe the commands and decrees he gave you. **46**They will be a sign and a wonder to you and your descendants forever. **47**Because you did not serve the LORD your God joyfully and gladly in the time of prosperity, **48**therefore in hunger and thirst, in nakedness and dire poverty, you will serve the enemies the LORD sends against you. He will put an iron yokeᴰ on your neck until he has destroyed you.

49The LORD will bring a nation against you from far away, from the ends of the earth, like an eagle swooping down, a nation whose language you will not understand, **50**a fierce-looking nation without respect for the old or pity for the young. **51**They will devour the young of your livestock and the crops of your land until you are destroyed. They will leave you no grain, new wineᴰ or oil, nor any calves of your herds or lambs of your flocks until you are ruined. **52**They will lay siege to all the cities throughout your land until the high fortified walls in

which you trust fall down. They will besiege all the cities throughout the land the LORD your God is giving you.

⁵³Because of the suffering that your enemy will inflict on you during the siege, you will eat the fruit of the womb, the flesh of the sons and daughters the LORD your God has given you. ⁵⁴Even the most gentle and sensitive man among you will have no compassion on his own brother or the wife he loves or his surviving children, ⁵⁵and he will not give to one of them any of the flesh of his children that he is eating. It will be all he has left because of the suffering your enemy will inflict on you during the siege of all your cities. ⁵⁶The most gentle and sensitive woman among you—so sensitive and gentle that she would not venture to touch the ground with the sole of her foot—will begrudge the husband she loves and her own son or daughter ⁵⁷the afterbirth from her womb and the children she bears. For she intends to eat them secretly during the siege and in the distress that your enemy will inflict on you in your cities.

⁵⁸If you do not carefully follow all the words of this law, which are written in this book, and do not revereᴰ this glorious and awesome name—the LORD your God— ⁵⁹the LORD will send fearful plagues on you and your descendants, harsh and prolonged disasters, and severe and lingering illnesses. ⁶⁰He will bring upon you all the diseases of Egypt that you dreaded, and they will cling to you. ⁶¹The LORD will also bring on you every kind of sickness and disaster not recorded in this Book of the Law, until you are destroyed. ⁶²You who were as numerous as the stars in the sky will be left but few in number, because you did not obey the LORD your God. ⁶³Just as it pleased the LORD to make you prosper and increase in number, so it will please him to ruin and destroy you. You will be uprooted from the land you are entering to possess.

⁶⁴Then the LORD will scatter you among all nations, from one end of the earth to the other. There you will worship other gods—gods of wood and stone, which neither you nor your fathers have known. ⁶⁵Among those nations you will find no repose, no resting place for the sole of your foot. There the LORD will give you an anxious mind, eyes weary with longing, and a despairing heart. ⁶⁶You will live in constant suspense, filled with dread both night and day, never sure of your life. ⁶⁷In the morning you will say, "If only it were evening!" and in the evening, "If only it were morning!"—because of the terror that will fill your hearts and the sights that your eyes will see. ⁶⁸The LORD will send you back in ships to Egypt on a journey I said you should never make again. There you will offer yourselves for sale to your enemies as male and female slaves, but no one will buy you.

Renewal of the Covenant

29 These are the terms of the covenantᴰ the LORD commanded Moses to make with the Israelites in Moab, in addition to the covenant he had made with them at Horeb.

²Moses summoned all the Israelites and said to them:

Your eyes have seen all that the LORD did in Egypt to Pharaoh, to all his officials and to all his land. ³With your own eyes you saw those great trials, those miraculous signs and great wonders. ⁴But to this day the LORD has not given you a mind that understands or eyes that see or ears that hear. ⁵During the forty years that I led you through

SCRIPTURE LINK (28:53) *You will eat . . . sons and daughters*

Cannibalism occurred during a later siege in Israel. See 2 Kings 6:24–29.

Why is God so severe? (28:58–59)

God was concerned that *all the words* of his law be kept. If Israel would not follow his commandments, a God of justice would have to judge them for breaking the covenant. But there is another side to God: just as he is severe, he is also merciful and forgiving. He was willing to restore the covenant blessings if they would repent and turn from their sin (30:1–10).

What were the dreaded diseases of Egypt? (28:60)

They included such things as boils, tumors, diseases of the eyes and bowels, hemorrhoids, skin diseases, venereal diseases, blindness and mental illness (vv. 27–29).

Why does punishment *please* God? (28:63)

Punishment does not please God in the sense of making him feel good. Rather it pleases him that justice is done. If it is right to reward those who do good, it is also right to punish those who do wrong.

How many covenants did God make? (29:1)

Many throughout the Bible. He made covenants with Noah (Gen. 9:11), with Abraham (Gen. 17:7) and with Moses (Exodus 19:5). Now 40 years had passed since the covenant with Moses was made at Mount Sinai (v. 5). Leadership of the people was about to shift to Joshua. Because of that, and because their living conditions had changed during the 40 years, an updated (but not an entirely new) covenant was given.

Can we blame God if we don't understand? (29:4)

God wants us to understand something about him, and he works in ways so that we *might know* (v. 6). But he wants us to repent so he can offer even greater insight to us when we believe by faith. The Israelites had seen many miracles and had been delivered miraculously from Egypt (vv. 2–3). Even so, their hearts remained unrepentant so that they could not understand or appreciate what God had done for them. Though God offered them understanding, he never gave it because of their stubbornness. Now Moses urged them to accept God's covenant and *choose life* (30:19).

the desert, your clothes did not wear out, nor did the sandals on your feet. **6**You ate no bread and drank no wine or other fermented drink. I did this so that you might know that I am the LORD your God.

7When you reached this place, Sihon king of Heshbon and Og king of Bashan came out to fight against us, but we defeated them. **8**We took their land and gave it as an inheritance to the Reubenites, the Gadites and the half-tribe of Manasseh.

9Carefully follow the terms of this covenant[D], so that you may prosper in everything you do. **10**All of you are standing today in the presence of the LORD your God— your leaders and chief men, your elders and officials, and all the other men of Israel, **11**together with your children and your wives, and the aliens[D] living in your camps who chop your wood and carry your water. **12**You are standing here in order to enter into a covenant with the LORD your God, a covenant the LORD is making with you this day and sealing with an oath, **13**to confirm you this day as his people, that he may be your God as he promised you and as he swore to your fathers, Abraham, Isaac and Jacob. **14**I am making this covenant, with its oath, not only with you **15**who are standing here with us today in the presence of the LORD our God but also with those who are not here today.

16You yourselves know how we lived in Egypt and how we passed through the countries on the way here. **17**You saw among them their detestable images and idols[D] of wood and stone, of silver and gold. **18**Make sure there is no man or woman, clan or tribe among you today whose heart turns away from the LORD our God to go and worship the gods of those nations; make sure there is no root among you that produces such bitter poison.

19When such a person hears the words of this oath, he invokes a blessing on himself and therefore thinks, "I will be safe, even though I persist in going my own way." This will bring disaster on the watered land as well as the

What aliens were in the camp? (29:11)

These were people from other nations that joined themselves to Israel and Israel's God. They included Egyptians (Exodus 12:38; Num. 11:4) and Midianites, such as Moses' father-in-law and his relatives (Num. 10:29). These people were eventually assimilated into the nation.

Who were *those who are not here today*? (29:15)

Most likely future generations of Israelites. Both the blessings and the curses of the law would extend to them. God's perpetual concern and love for the nation of Israel was demonstrated when he made this covenant applicable to future generations.

Does God make us anxious? (28:65)

Not directly. But those who disobey his Word can expect to experience mental and emotional stress. Even those who manage to put God completely out of their thoughts can worry about their "indiscretions" coming to light. Sinners have an innate drive to hide their deeds. But cover-ups lead inevitably to anxiety.

Still, God knows that such feelings can be part of the process of bringing people back to him. Just as pain produces a reflex causing us to pull our hand away from a hot stove, so guilt and anxiety can lead to a conviction that causes us to pull away from sinful, destructive behavior. So God has no qualms about allowing sinners to struggle with this kind of anxiety.

God allowed the Israelites to feel anxious when he punished them with exile in foreign lands. But in another sense, they brought despair and worry on themselves by their own sins. God permits anxiety as a consequence for sin and foolish attitudes.

Some people, however, seem to be manipulated by anxieties that God never intended them to have. They worry needlessly about things that will never happen; they imagine things are worse than they really are. God offers relief from this kind of inner turmoil (1 Peter 5:7).

dry.*a* **20**The LORD will never be willing to forgive him; his wrath and zeal*D* will burn against that man. All the curses written in this book will fall upon him, and the LORD will blot out his name from under heaven. **21**The LORD will single him out from all the tribes of Israel for disaster, according to all the curses of the covenant*D* written in this Book of the Law.

22Your children who follow you in later generations and foreigners who come from distant lands will see the calamities that have fallen on the land and the diseases with which the LORD has afflicted*D* it. **23**The whole land will be a burning waste of salt and sulfur—nothing planted, nothing sprouting, no vegetation growing on it. It will be like the destruction of Sodom and Gomorrah, Admah and Zeboiim, which the LORD overthrew in fierce anger. **24**All the nations will ask: "Why has the LORD done this to this land? Why this fierce, burning anger?"

25And the answer will be: "It is because this people abandoned the covenant of the LORD, the God of their fathers, the covenant he made with them when he brought them out of Egypt. **26**They went off and worshiped other gods and bowed down to them, gods they did not know, gods he had not given them. **27**Therefore the LORD's anger burned against this land, so that he brought on it all the curses written in this book. **28**In furious anger and in great wrath the LORD uprooted them from their land and thrust them into another land, as it is now."

29The secret things belong to the LORD our God, but the things revealed belong to us and to our children forever, that we may follow all the words of this law.

Prosperity After Turning to the LORD

30 When all these blessings and curses I have set before you come upon you and you take them to heart wherever the LORD your God disperses you among the nations, **2**and when you and your children return to the LORD your God and obey him with all your heart and with all your soul*D* according to everything I command you today, **3**then the LORD your God will restore your fortunes*b* and have compassion on you and gather you again from all the nations where he scattered you. **4**Even if you have been banished to the most distant land under the heavens, from there the LORD your God will gather you and bring you back. **5**He will bring you to the land that belonged to your fathers, and you will take possession of it. He will make you more prosperous and numerous than your fathers. **6**The LORD your God will circumcise*D* your hearts and the hearts of your descendants, so that you may love him with all your heart and with all your soul, and live. **7**The LORD your God will put all these curses on your enemies who hate and persecute you. **8**You will again obey the LORD and follow all his commands I am giving you today. **9**Then the LORD your God will make you most prosperous in all the work of your hands and in the fruit of your womb, the young of your livestock and the crops of your land. The LORD will again delight in you and make you prosperous, just as he delighted in your fathers, **10**if you obey the LORD your God and keep his commands and decrees that are written in

Is there a limit to God's forgiveness? (29:20)

Though this threat sounds harsh, it should be understood from the perspective of the whole community. Individuals who sinned would affect the community as a whole. Sinners could not expect the blessings of the community to offset their consequences (v. 19). God wanted to protect the people from sin's corruption, so he drew the line at showing mercy to anyone who endangered the whole community.

Admah and Zeboiim (29:23)

Two cities marking the southern border of Canaan (Gen. 10:19). Apparently, they were destroyed for their wickedness at the same time as Sodom and Gomorrah (Gen. 19:23–29). Consequently, they are mentioned as symbols of divine judgment.

SCRIPTURE LINK (29:23) *The destruction of Sodom and Gomorrah*
See *Burning sulfur* (Gen. 19:24).

Secret things . . . things revealed (29:29)

Secret things were probably Israel's unknown future: would they obey and be blessed or disobey and be punished? Only God knows *the secret things*. But Israel possessed *the things revealed*, the law. The Israelites could determine their own future if they faithfully followed God's law.

SCRIPTURE LINK (30:1) *Blessings and curses*
See 27:12—29:29.

What does it mean to *circumcise your hearts?* (30:6)

See *What does it mean to circumcise your hearts?* (10:16) and *How does the Spirit circumcise a heart?* (Romans 2:28–29).

What's the difference between *heart* and *soul?* (30:6)

Heart can mean the human personality or whole being, from which sin needs to be circumcised or cut off. *Heart* can also mean the mind or intellect. *Soul*, by contrast, may mean human desire or will. Though these definitions overlap somewhat, it's only when our heart is circumcised that we can fully love God with our heart (mind) and soul (will).

---

a19 Or way, in order to add drunkenness to thirst."   *b3 Or will bring you back from captivity*

Is the Old Testament law within reach? (30:11)

Moses clearly said so. We find ourselves in a dilemma, though, when we try to explain why no one—except for Christ—has been able to live up to the requirements of the law. We cannot live sinless lives because human nature has been scarred by sin, leaving us spiritually handicapped. God never intended the law to make us righteous, but he uses it to show us our need for Christ (Gal. 3:24). Christ alone gives the new hearts we need to measure up to God's standards.

SCRIPTURE LINK (30:12–14) Who will ascend into heaven

Paul paraphrases these verses in Romans 10:6–8.

How could heaven and earth be witnesses? (30:19)

See How could God call heaven and earth as witnesses? (4:26).

How was Joshua chosen as the new leader? (31:3)

Through Moses, God himself chose Joshua as Moses' successor (vv. 7–8).

How long would it take to publicly read the law? (31:11)

Perhaps only as long as it would take to read a few chapters, although the law may have included much more material and taken considerably longer to read. See All the words of this law (27:3).

---

this Book of the Law and turn to the LORD your God with all your heart and with all your soul.

The Offer of Life or Death

11Now what I am commanding you today is not too difficult for you or beyond your reach. **12**It is not up in heaven, so that you have to ask, "Who will ascend into heaven to get it and proclaim it to us so we may obey it?" **13**Nor is it beyond the sea, so that you have to ask, "Who will cross the sea to get it and proclaim it to us so we may obey it?" **14**No, the word is very near you; it is in your mouth and in your heart so you may obey it.

15See, I set before you today life and prosperity, death and destruction. **16**For I command you today to love the LORD your God, to walk in his ways, and to keep his commands, decrees and laws; then you will live and increase, and the LORD your God will bless you in the land you are entering to possess.

17But if your heart turns away and you are not obedient, and if you are drawn away to bow down to other gods and worship them, **18**I declare to you this day that you will certainly be destroyed. You will not live long in the land you are crossing the Jordan to enter and possess.

19This day I call heaven and earth as witnesses against you that I have set before you life and death, blessings and curses. Now choose life, so that you and your children may live **20**and that you may love the LORD your God, listen to his voice, and hold fast to him. For the LORD is your life, and he will give you many years in the land he swore to give to your fathers, Abraham, Isaac and Jacob.

Joshua to Succeed Moses

31 Then Moses went out and spoke these words to all Israel: **2**"I am now a hundred and twenty years old and I am no longer able to lead you. The LORD has said to me, 'You shall not cross the Jordan.' **3**The LORD your God himself will cross over ahead of you. He will destroy these nations before you, and you will take possession of their land. Joshua also will cross over ahead of you, as the LORD said. **4**And the LORD will do to them what he did to Sihon and Og, the kings of the Amorites, whom he destroyed along with their land. **5**The LORD will deliver them to you, and you must do to them all that I have commanded you. **6**Be strong and courageous. Do not be afraid or terrified because of them, for the LORD your God goes with you; he will never leave you nor forsake you."

7Then Moses summoned Joshua and said to him in the presence of all Israel, "Be strong and courageous, for you must go with this people into the land that the LORD swore to their forefathers to give them, and you must divide it among them as their inheritance. **8**The LORD himself goes before you and will be with you; he will never leave you nor forsake you. Do not be afraid; do not be discouraged."

The Reading of the Law

9So Moses wrote down this law and gave it to the priests, the sons of Levi, who carried the ark of the covenant of the LORD, and to all the elders of Israel. **10**Then Moses commanded them: "At the end of every seven years, in the year for canceling debts, during the Feast of Tabernacles, **11**when all Israel comes to appear before the LORD your God at the place he will choose, you shall read this law before them in their hearing. **12**Assemble the people—men, women and children, and the aliens living in

your towns—so they can listen and learn to fear the LORD your God and follow carefully all the words of this law. ¹³Their children, who do not know this law, must hear it and learn to fear the LORD your God as long as you live in the land you are crossing the Jordan to possess."

Israel's Rebellion Predicted

¹⁴The LORD said to Moses, "Now the day of your deathᴰ is near. Call Joshua and present yourselves at the Tent of Meetingᴰ, where I will commission him." So Moses and Joshua came and presented themselves at the Tent of Meeting.

¹⁵Then the LORD appeared at the Tent in a pillar of cloud, and the cloud stood over the entrance to the Tent. ¹⁶And the LORD said to Moses: "You are going to rest with your fathers, and these people will soon prostitute themselves to the foreign gods of the land they are entering. They will forsake me and break the covenantᴰ I made with them. ¹⁷On that day I will become angry with them and forsake them; I will hide my face from them, and they will be destroyed. Many disasters and difficulties will come upon them, and on that day they will ask, 'Have not these disasters come upon us because our God is not with us?' ¹⁸And I will certainly hide my face on that day because of all their wickedness in turning to other gods.

¹⁹"Now write down for yourselves this song and teach it to the Israelites and have them sing it, so that it may be a witness for me against them. ²⁰When I have brought them into the land flowing with milk and honey, the land I promised on oath to their forefathers, and when they eat their fill and thrive, they will turn to other gods and worship them, rejecting me and breaking my covenant. ²¹And when many disasters and difficulties come upon them, this song will testify against them, because it will

How was Joshua commissioned? (31:14)

The Lord himself spoke to Joshua (v. 23), but he had also commissioned him through Moses. The ceremony is described in Num. 27:18–23.

Why use a song to witness against someone? (31:19–22)

In this ancient culture, songs were used to teach and transmit information. It was easier to learn and remember words that were set to music. This song, found in ch. 32, was to remind the Israelites that God judges disobedience.

***Flowing with milk and honey* (31:20)**

See *Flowing with milk and honey* (6:3).

Why does God allow bad things to happen? (31:16–21)

It's troubling to think that a God who cares would stand idly by and allow something bad to happen if he had the power to intervene. But is the alternative—God forcing people to obey against their will—any better? Finite human minds may never fully understand this dilemma.

It is helpful to remember that God wants a relationship with people. Since the most meaningful relationships are voluntary, God offers us a choice: to reject him or accept him, to go our own way or follow his way. Essential to a meaningful, loving relationship with God is our free will. Love must be voluntary; it can never be forced.

God could have squelched all signs of rebellion in the Israelites. He could have forced them to obey him. But such actions would reduce humanity to little more than automatons—robots that perform as they are programmed. God could have created a world like that, but instead he gave his people options. He wanted them to respond voluntarily to him.

It is not a sign of powerlessness for God to know in advance that something we see as negative will happen and yet not change the course of history—though at times he does intervene in that manner. In this case, God cautioned his people against sin but left obedience up to them.

There is a tension between God's sovereignty and our free will. But that tension makes possible two contrasting truths: God knows and predestines future events, but at the same time makes us responsible for our own choices.

SCRIPTURE LINK (31:23) *Be strong and courageous*

Similar exhortations were given later to Solomon, when he succeeded David as king. See 1 Chron. 22:13; 28:20.

Stiff-necked (31:27)
See *Stiff-necked people* (9:6).

He is the Rock (32:4)
See *How is God like a rock?* (Psalm 18:2).

When did God set up boundaries for all the nations? (32:8)
If the Hebrew is best translated as *sons of Israel*, then God may have set the boundaries of the nations during the exodus, when Israel left Egypt to inherit the promised land. If the Hebrew is best translated as *sons of God*, (see NIV text note) then the boundaries may have been set at an earlier time—before the existence of Israel (see Acts 17:26).

not be forgotten by their descendants. I know what they are disposed to do, even before I bring them into the land I promised them on oath." **22**So Moses wrote down this song that day and taught it to the Israelites.

23The LORD gave this command to Joshua son of Nun: "Be strong and courageous, for you will bring the Israelites into the land I promised them on oath, and I myself will be with you."

24After Moses finished writing in a book the words of this law from beginning to end, **25**he gave this command to the Levites[D] who carried the ark of the covenant[D] of the LORD: **26**"Take this Book of the Law and place it beside the ark of the covenant of the LORD your God. There it will remain as a witness against you. **27**For I know how rebellious and stiff-necked you are. If you have been rebellious against the LORD while I am still alive and with you, how much more will you rebel after I die! **28**Assemble before me all the elders of your tribes and all your officials, so that I can speak these words in their hearing and call heaven and earth to testify against them. **29**For I know that after my death[D] you are sure to become utterly corrupt and to turn from the way I have commanded you. In days to come, disaster will fall upon you because you will do evil in the sight of the LORD and provoke him to anger by what your hands have made."

The Song of Moses

30And Moses recited the words of this song from beginning to end in the hearing of the whole assembly of Israel:

32 Listen, O heavens, and I will speak;
    hear, O earth, the words of my mouth.
2Let my teaching fall like rain
    and my words descend like dew,
  like showers on new grass,
    like abundant rain on tender plants.

3I will proclaim the name of the LORD.
    Oh, praise the greatness of our God!
4He is the Rock, his works are perfect,
    and all his ways are just.
  A faithful God who does no wrong,
    upright and just is he.

5They have acted corruptly toward him;
    to their shame they are no longer his
      children,
    but a warped and crooked generation.[a]
6Is this the way you repay the LORD,
    O foolish and unwise people?
  Is he not your Father, your Creator,[b]
    who made you and formed you?

7Remember the days of old;
    consider the generations long past.
  Ask your father and he will tell you,
    your elders, and they will explain to you.
8When the Most High gave the nations their
      inheritance,
    when he divided all mankind,
  he set up boundaries for the peoples

[a]5 Or *Corrupt are they and not his children, / a generation warped and twisted to their shame*   [b]6 Or *Father, who bought you*

according to the number of the sons of
  Israel.ᵃ
⁹For the LORD's portion is his people,
  Jacob his allotted inheritance.

¹⁰In a desert land he found him,
  in a barren and howling waste.
He shielded him and cared for him;
  he guarded him as the apple of his eye,
¹¹like an eagle that stirs up its nest
  and hovers over its young,
that spreads its wings to catch them
  and carries them on its pinions.
¹²The LORD alone led him;
  no foreign god was with him.

¹³He made him ride on the heights of the land
  and fed him with the fruit of the fields.
He nourished him with honey from the rock,
  and with oil from the flinty crag,
¹⁴with curds and milk from herd and flock
  and with fattened lambs and goats,
with choice rams of Bashan
  and the finest kernels of wheat.
You drank the foaming blood of the grape.

¹⁵Jeshurunᵇ grew fat and kicked;
  filled with food, he became heavy and sleek.
He abandoned the God who made him
  and rejected the Rock his Savior.
¹⁶They made him jealous with their foreign gods
  and angered him with their detestable
    idolsᴰ.
¹⁷They sacrificed to demons, which are not
    God—
  gods they had not known,
  gods that recently appeared,
  gods your fathers did not fear.
¹⁸You deserted the Rock, who fathered you;
  you forgot the God who gave you birth.

¹⁹The LORD saw this and rejected them
  because he was angered by his sons and
    daughters.
²⁰"I will hide my face from them," he said,
  "and see what their end will be;
for they are a perverse generation,
  children who are unfaithful.
²¹They made me jealous by what is no god
  and angered me with their worthless idols.
I will make them envious by those who are not
    a people;
  I will make them angry by a nation that has
    no understanding.
²²For a fire has been kindled by my wrath,
  one that burns to the realm of deathᴰᶜ
    below.
It will devour the earth and its harvests
  and set afire the foundations of the
    mountains.

²³"I will heap calamities upon them

Apple of his eye (32:10)
See *Apple of your eye* (Prov. 7:2).

Honey from the rock (32:13)
Honey from bees that nested among the rocks.
This became a metaphor for God's abundant
provision for Israel, even in the most unlikely of
places.

What did demons have to do with idols? (32:17)
Satan has used many methods to deceive people, including idolatry. Evil spirits can show
themselves through physical objects like idols.
Some think the word *demon* means anything
that replaces God as the object of worship. If
so, idols could be considered demons because
they received devotion belonging to God alone.
Also see 1 Cor. 10:18–22; 1 Tim. 4:1–3.

How could *what is no god* make God jealous? (32:21)
God became jealous and angry because his
people refused him and worshiped lifeless images of stone and wood. The idols did not
evoke such emotion from God; his own people
did. See *Why would God call himself Jealous?*
(Exodus 34:14).

ᵃ8 Masoretic Text; Dead Sea Scrolls (see also Septuagint) *sons of God*
ᵇ15 *Jeshurun* means *the upright one,* that is, Israel.   ᶜ22 Hebrew *to Sheol*

and spend my arrows against them.
24I will send wasting famine against them,
consuming pestilence and deadly plague;
I will send against them the fangs of wild
beasts,
the venom of vipers that glide in the dust.
25In the street the sword will make them
childless;
in their homes terror will reign.
Young men and young women will perish,
infants and gray-haired men.
26I said I would scatter them
and blot out their memory from mankind,
27but I dreaded the taunt of the enemy,
lest the adversary misunderstand
and say, 'Our hand has triumphed;
the LORD has not done all this.' "

28They are a nation without sense,
there is no discernment in them.
29If only they were wise and would understand
this
and discern what their end will be!
30How could one man chase a thousand,
or two put ten thousand to flight,
unless their Rock had sold them,
unless the LORD had given them up?
31For their rock is not like our Rock,
as even our enemies concede.
32Their vine comes from the vine of Sodom
and from the fields of Gomorrah.
Their grapes are filled with poison,
and their clusters with bitterness.
33Their wine is the venom of serpents,
the deadly poison of cobras.

34"Have I not kept this in reserve
and sealed it in my vaults?
35It is mine to avengeD; I will repay.
In due time their foot will slip;
their day of disaster is near
and their doom rushes upon them."

36The LORD will judge his people
and have compassion on his servants
when he sees their strength is gone
and no one is left, slave or free.
37He will say: "Now where are their gods,
the rock they took refuge in,
38the gods who ate the fat of their sacrificesD
and drank the wine of their drink
offeringsD?
Let them rise up to help you!
Let them give you shelter!

39"See now that I myself am He!
There is no god besides me.
I put to deathD and I bring to life,
I have wounded and I will heal,
and no one can deliver out of my hand.
40I lift my hand to heaven and declare:
As surely as I live forever,
41when I sharpen my flashing sword
and my hand grasps it in judgment,
I will take vengeance on my adversaries
and repay those who hate me.

Why would God care what the enemy of Israel thought? (32:27)

See *Why would God be concerned about what the Egyptians think of him?* (Num. 14:13–16).

Unless their Rock had sold them (32:30)

Rock was commonly used as a picture of God (Psalm 18:2). This verse uses two metaphors to show Israel completely overwhelmed by their enemies: (1) They would have no protection without their Rock. (2) They would be powerless when sold (like slaves).

Does God cause death and pain? (32:39)

See article: *Why does God send calamity?* (Lam. 3:38).

Why lift a hand to heaven? (32:40)

This was part of the ritual of giving an oath. After the hand was raised, the oath would be spoken (see Gen. 14:22). In the ancient world a verbal oath functioned similarly to a signed legal document in our day, obligating one to fulfill what was promised.

42I will make my arrows drunk with blood,
    while my sword devours flesh:
the blood of the slain and the captives,
    the heads of the enemy leaders."

43Rejoice, O nations, with his people,*a, b*
    for he will avenge^D the blood of his
        servants;
he will take vengeance on his enemies
    and make atonement^D for his land and
        people.

44Moses came with Joshua*c* son of Nun and spoke all the words of this song in the hearing of the people. **45**When Moses finished reciting all these words to all Israel, **46**he said to them, "Take to heart all the words I have solemnly declared to you this day, so that you may command your children to obey carefully all the words of this law. **47**They are not just idle words for you—they are your life. By them you will live long in the land you are crossing the Jordan to possess."

Moses to Die on Mount Nebo

48On that same day the LORD told Moses, **49**"Go up into the Abarim Range to Mount Nebo in Moab, across from Jericho^D, and view Canaan, the land I am giving the Israelites as their own possession. **50**There on the mountain that you have climbed you will die and be gathered to your people, just as your brother Aaron died on Mount Hor and was gathered to his people. **51**This is because both of you broke faith with me in the presence of the Israelites at the waters of Meribah Kadesh in the Desert of Zin and because you did not uphold my holiness among the Israelites. **52**Therefore, you will see the land only from a distance; you will not enter the land I am giving to the people of Israel."

Moses Blesses the Tribes

33 This is the blessing that Moses the man of God pronounced on the Israelites before his death^D. **2**He said:

  "The LORD came from Sinai
    and dawned over them from Seir;
  he shone forth from Mount Paran.
  He came with*d* myriads of holy ones
    from the south, from his mountain slopes.*e*
3Surely it is you who love the people;
  all the holy ones are in your hand.
  At your feet they all bow down,
    and from you receive instruction,
4the law that Moses gave us,
    the possession of the assembly of Jacob.
5He was king over Jeshurun*f*
  when the leaders of the people assembled,
    along with the tribes of Israel.

  6"Let Reuben live and not die,
    nor*g* his men be few."

a43 Or *Make his people rejoice, O nations*   *b43* Masoretic Text; Dead Sea Scrolls (see also Septuagint) *people, / and let all the angels worship him /*   *c44* Hebrew *Hoshea,* a variant of *Joshua*   *d2* Or *from*   *e2* The meaning of the Hebrew for this phrase is uncertain. *f5 Jeshurun* means *the upright one,* that is, Israel; also in verse 26. *g6* Or *but let*

What does it mean to be *gathered to your people?* (32:50)

This phrase describes the death of a righteous person who died in old age. It also alludes to the Hebrew view of life after death. The Hebrews anticipated reuniting with family members in a mysterious place called Sheol, the place of the dead. David spoke of this reunion when his baby died (2 Samuel 12:23). A thousand years later, Jesus referred to gathered patriarchs, confirming that ancient believers were indeed still alive. See Matt. 22:32.

SCRIPTURE LINK (32:51) *You broke faith with me*

Moses struck the rock instead of speaking to it as God had directed. See Num. 20:1–13.

Why did Moses recite this formal blessing on all the tribes of Israel? (33:1)

In this ancient culture it was customary for a father to pronounce blessings upon his sons before he died (Gen. 27; 49). Moses could be considered a father to the tribes of Israel because of his role as leader.

Holy ones (33:2)

Angels that accompanied God when he gave the law to Moses at Sinai. The New Testament echoes this description of angels at the giving of the law (Gal. 3:19; Heb. 2:2).

SCRIPTURE LINK (33:8) *Massah . . . Meribah*
See Exodus 17:1–7.

Is it okay to ignore one's family for the sake of religious work? (33:9)
No, but that's not what this is talking about. Though it sounds like religious work sabotaged Levite family life, that is not necessarily the case. This poetic language commends the Levites for their commitment to God's law. Protecting the covenant was such a high priority for them that, figuratively speaking, their commitments to their families (which were, in fact, sound) could not compare.

Why bring Ephraim and Manasseh into Joseph's blessing? (33:17)
Ephraim and Manasseh were the sons of Joseph, each the founder of a half-tribe within the tribe of Joseph (Gen. 41:51–52).

[7]And this he said about Judah:

"Hear, O LORD, the cry of Judah;
   bring him to his people.
With his own hands he defends his cause.
   Oh, be his help against his foes!"

[8]About Levi he said:

"Your Thummim[D] and Urim[D] belong
   to the man you favored.
You tested him at Massah;
   you contended with him at the waters of
      Meribah.
[9]He said of his father and mother,
   'I have no regard for them.'
He did not recognize his brothers
   or acknowledge his own children,
but he watched over your word
   and guarded your covenant[D].
[10]He teaches your precepts[D] to Jacob
   and your law to Israel.
He offers incense[D] before you
   and whole burnt offerings[D] on your altar.
[11]Bless all his skills, O LORD,
   and be pleased with the work of his hands.
Smite the loins of those who rise up against
      him;
   strike his foes till they rise no more."

[12]About Benjamin he said:

"Let the beloved of the LORD rest secure in him,
   for he shields him all day long,
and the one the LORD loves rests between his
      shoulders."

[13]About Joseph he said:

"May the LORD bless his land
   with the precious dew from heaven above
   and with the deep waters that lie below;
[14]with the best the sun brings forth
   and the finest the moon can yield;
[15]with the choicest gifts of the ancient mountains
   and the fruitfulness of the everlasting hills;
[16]with the best gifts of the earth and its fullness
   and the favor of him who dwelt in the
      burning bush.
Let all these rest on the head of Joseph,
   on the brow of the prince among[a] his
      brothers.
[17]In majesty he is like a firstborn[D] bull;
   his horns are the horns of a wild ox.
With them he will gore the nations,
   even those at the ends of the earth.
Such are the ten thousands of Ephraim;
   such are the thousands of Manasseh."

[18]About Zebulun he said:

"Rejoice, Zebulun, in your going out,
   and you, Issachar, in your tents.
[19]They will summon peoples to the mountain
   and there offer sacrifices[D] of
      righteousness[D];

[a]16 Or *of the one separated from*

they will feast on the abundance of the seas,
        on the treasures hidden in the sand."

20About Gad he said:

"Blessed is he who enlarges Gad's domain!
        Gad lives there like a lion,
        tearing at arm or head.
21He chose the best land for himself;
        the leader's portion was kept for him.
When the heads of the people assembled,
        he carried out the LORD's righteous[D] will,
        and his judgments concerning Israel."

22About Dan he said:

"Dan is a lion's cub,
        springing out of Bashan."

23About Naphtali he said:

"Naphtali is abounding with the favor of the
        LORD
    and is full of his blessing;
        he will inherit southward to the lake."

24About Asher he said:

"Most blessed of sons is Asher;
        let him be favored by his brothers,
        and let him bathe his feet in oil.
25The bolts of your gates will be iron and bronze,
        and your strength will equal your days.

26"There is no one like the God of Jeshurun,
        who rides on the heavens to help you
        and on the clouds in his majesty.
27The eternal God is your refuge,
        and underneath are the everlasting arms.
He will drive out your enemy before you,
        saying, 'Destroy him!'
28So Israel will live in safety alone;
        Jacob's spring is secure
    in a land of grain and new wine[D],
        where the heavens drop dew.
29Blessed are you, O Israel!
        Who is like you,
        a people saved by the LORD?
He is your shield and helper
        and your glorious sword.
Your enemies will cower before you,
        and you will trample down their high
            places[D].[a]"

The Death of Moses

34 Then Moses climbed Mount Nebo from the plains of Moab to the top of Pisgah, across from Jericho[D]. There the LORD showed him the whole land—from Gilead to Dan, **2**all of Naphtali, the territory of Ephraim and Manasseh, all the land of Judah as far as the western sea,[b] **3**the Negev[D] and the whole region from the Valley of Jericho, the City of Palms, as far as Zoar. **4**Then the LORD said to him, "This is the land I promised on oath to Abraham, Isaac and Jacob when I said, 'I will give it to your descendants.' I have let you see it with your eyes, but you will not cross over into it."

The lake (33:23)
Some think this may mean the Sea of Galilee. Others say it is the Mediterranean. Still others say it could mean the direction west.

What was so great about bathing feet in oil? (33:24)
Since people wore sandals or went barefoot in ancient times, it was a luxury to have one's feet bathed and soothed in oil. This image of oil pictures the prosperity and prominent position of Asher among the other tribes.

Why was Israel so blessed, when they were also so disobedient? (33:29)
Throughout the book of Deuteronomy Moses emphasizes that Israel's special blessing from God did not come about because of the people's righteousness (see 9:1–6). For some reason, known only to God, they were the nation he chose to bring his blessing to the rest of the world. See article: *Did God love Israel more than other nations?* (4:33).

---

a29 Or *will tread upon their bodies*   *b2* That is, the Mediterranean

Why bury Moses in a secret grave? (34:6)

Some think Moses' grave was hidden to prevent the spiritually fickle Israelites from making a shrine out of it. Worship of the dead may have been practiced in some Canaanite religions. See *Why would anyone offer a tithe to the dead?* (26:14).

What did the Israelites do during a 30-day mourning period? (34:8)

Ancient cultures expressed grief in various ways: they would tear their clothes, put ashes or dust on their heads, wear sackcloth, sing funeral songs, screech or wail loudly and sometimes cut or pull out their hair. The Israelites may have done several of these things.

How did Moses' touch transfer wisdom to Joshua? (34:9)

"Laying hands on someone" was a highly significant act in ancient cultures, representing a transfer of authority and the right of leadership. It also symbolized approval from God and the community in commissioning Joshua to lead. Joshua didn't receive wisdom through Moses' touch; he received wisdom from the Lord.

Was Moses the greatest prophet ever? (34:10)

Yes, for two reasons: (1) He had an intimate relationship with God. While God spoke to other prophets through dreams and visions, he spoke to Moses *face to face*. See *How could Moses speak to the Lord face to face?* (Exodus 33:11) and *Face to face* (Deut. 5:4). (2) No other prophet performed miracles that matched the greatness of those in the exodus experience. Moses was surpassed only by Jesus, who most think Moses predicted when he said *a prophet like me* (18:15–18).

⁵And Moses the servant of the Lord died there in Moab, as the Lord had said. ⁶He buried him*ᵃ* in Moab, in the valley opposite Beth Peor, but to this day no one knows where his grave is. ⁷Moses was a hundred and twenty years old when he died, yet his eyes were not weak nor his strength gone. ⁸The Israelites grieved for Moses in the plains of Moab thirty days, until the time of weeping and mourning was over.

⁹Now Joshua son of Nun was filled with the spirit*ᵇ* of wisdom because Moses had laid his hands on him. So the Israelites listened to him and did what the Lord had commanded Moses.

¹⁰Since then, no prophet*ᴰ* has risen in Israel like Moses, whom the Lord knew face to face, ¹¹who did all those miraculous signs and wonders the Lord sent him to do in Egypt—to Pharaoh and to all his officials and to his whole land. ¹²For no one has ever shown the mighty power or performed the awesome deeds that Moses did in the sight of all Israel.

---

*ᵃ*6 Or *He was buried*   *ᵇ*9 Or *Spirit*

JOSHUA

Why read this book?

Have you ever wished for a second chance? Perhaps you squandered a rare opportunity. Maybe you tried something, but your halfhearted attempt failed. Or perhaps you wasted a prime time of life, a precious gift or a valued friendship. The book of Joshua reminds us that God often offers us a second chance. Though the Israelites failed to enter the promised land the first time, and though they wasted 40 years for their failure, God gave them another chance. Having learned their lesson, the results were different the second time around. Their story is inspiring for us all.

Who wrote this book?

Perhaps Joshua and/or the priests Eleazar and Phinehas.

When was it written?

If Joshua wrote it, probably about 1390 B.C.

To whom was it written and why?

To the Israelites, to continue the history of their nation and reassure them that they owed their existence to God.

What to look for in Joshua:

Ancient Biblical history: (1) knowledge about God—about his purpose, his words and how he works in human lives, (2) a deeper appreciation for the grace and mercy of God when we see the requirements the Old Testament law placed on people, (3) encouragement in our own faith when we hear stories about the faith of God's people and their struggles in challenging times, and (4) a spiritual connection to God's people which helps us to identify with them as part of God's family.

When did these things happen?

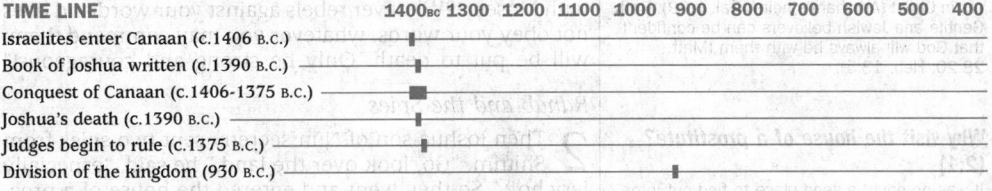

TIME LINE	1400BC	1300	1200	1100	1000	900	800	700	600	500	400
Israelites enter Canaan (c.1406 B.C.)											
Book of Joshua written (c.1390 B.C.)											
Conquest of Canaan (c.1406-1375 B.C.)											
Joshua's death (c.1390 B.C.)											
Judges begin to rule (c.1375 B.C.)											
Division of the kingdom (930 B.C.)											

How did God talk to Joshua? (1:1)

We don't know for sure. He may have spoken audibly or perhaps he impressed his thoughts upon Joshua's conscience. But whatever means he used, the important thing was that he communicated directly to Joshua, affirming him for the task at hand.

Did the territory of Israel ever extend this far? (1:4)

When David became king, the nation enjoyed the necessary strength to subdue the various peoples of Canaan. Even then, the far-flung regions of the kingdom, though controlled, were not annexed or occupied (see 1 Kings 5:1–4). See *Conquest of Canaan* on page 231.

Was it right to take land from others? (1:4)

Why did God endorse such actions—taking land without regard to legal titles, deeds, contracts or payments? If this seems unfair, we should remember that Israel, because of their sin, later lost their land to other nations. In the Old Testament, God took land as punishment for sin, and gave it to others. God took territory away from the Canaanites as a consequence for their immoral living. Note too that non-Hebrews who believed in the Lord were not stripped of their life and possessions, but prospered along with the Israelites. The bottom line is—God controls even what we think is ours. The earth is the Lord's. Also see article: *What right did Israel have to take the land?* (Num. 33:52–53).

Does God promise health and wealth? (1:8)

It would appear so, at least in the Old Testament where God's promises were linked to the land. But God's kingdom is not geographical; it is spiritual and eternal. Some who are called to serve the Lord may have to endure the rigors of poverty and deprivation. Nonetheless, countless Christians testify to a general truth: building one's life on biblical values often leads to material reward.

Do God's promises to Joshua and Israel apply to us? (1:9)

God made two kinds of promises to Joshua and Israel—physical and spiritual. Both look back to God's pledge to give Abraham land, posterity and spiritual blessings (Gen. 12:2–3). The land and posterity were specific, physical promises, made exclusively to Abraham's physical descendants. The promise of spiritual blessing, however, extends to believers in Christ (Abraham's heirs, Gal. 3:29). Both Gentile and Jewish believers can be confident that God will always be with them (Matt. 28:20; Heb. 13:5).

Why visit *the house of a prostitute*? (2:1)

It was no doubt a good place to find out information and blend in with other travelers with no questions asked. Also, a house on the city wall was best for a quick escape, in case they were discovered.

The LORD Commands Joshua

1 After the death[D] of Moses the servant of the LORD, the LORD said to Joshua son of Nun, Moses' aide: **2**"Moses my servant is dead. Now then, you and all these people, get ready to cross the Jordan River into the land I am about to give to them—to the Israelites. **3**I will give you every place where you set your foot, as I promised Moses. **4**Your territory will extend from the desert to Lebanon, and from the great river, the Euphrates—all the Hittite country—to the Great Sea[a] on the west. **5**No one will be able to stand up against you all the days of your life. As I was with Moses, so I will be with you; I will never leave you nor forsake you.

6"Be strong and courageous, because you will lead these people to inherit the land I swore to their forefathers to give them. **7**Be strong and very courageous. Be careful to obey all the law my servant Moses gave you; do not turn from it to the right or to the left, that you may be successful wherever you go. **8**Do not let this Book of the Law depart from your mouth; meditate on it day and night, so that you may be careful to do everything written in it. Then you will be prosperous and successful. **9**Have I not commanded you? Be strong and courageous. Do not be terrified; do not be discouraged, for the LORD your God will be with you wherever you go."

10So Joshua ordered the officers of the people: **11**"Go through the camp and tell the people, 'Get your supplies ready. Three days from now you will cross the Jordan here to go in and take possession of the land the LORD your God is giving you for your own.'"

12But to the Reubenites, the Gadites and the half-tribe of Manasseh, Joshua said, **13**"Remember the command that Moses the servant of the LORD gave you: 'The LORD your God is giving you rest and has granted you this land.' **14**Your wives, your children and your livestock may stay in the land that Moses gave you east of the Jordan, but all your fighting men, fully armed, must cross over ahead of your brothers. You are to help your brothers **15**until the LORD gives them rest, as he has done for you, and until they too have taken possession of the land that the LORD your God is giving them. After that, you may go back and occupy your own land, which Moses the servant of the LORD gave you east of the Jordan toward the sunrise."

16Then they answered Joshua, "Whatever you have commanded us we will do, and wherever you send us we will go. **17**Just as we fully obeyed Moses, so we will obey you. Only may the LORD your God be with you as he was with Moses. **18**Whoever rebels against your word and does not obey your words, whatever you may command them, will be put to death. Only be strong and courageous!"

Rahab and the Spies

2 Then Joshua son of Nun secretly sent two spies from Shittim. "Go, look over the land," he said, "especially Jericho[D]." So they went and entered the house of a prostitute[b] named Rahab[D] and stayed there.

2The king of Jericho was told, "Look! Some of the Israelites have come here tonight to spy out the land." **3**So the king of Jericho sent this message to Rahab: "Bring out the men who came to you and entered your house, because they have come to spy out the whole land."

<hr>

a4 That is, the Mediterranean   b1 Or possibly *an innkeeper*

4But the woman had taken the two men and hidden them. She said, "Yes, the men came to me, but I did not know where they had come from. **5**At dusk, when it was time to close the city gate, the men left. I don't know which way they went. Go after them quickly. You may catch up with them." **6**(But she had taken them up to the roof and hidden them under the stalks of flax she had laid out on the roof.) **7**So the men set out in pursuit of the spies on the road that leads to the fords of the Jordan, and as soon as the pursuers had gone out, the gate was shut.

8Before the spies lay down for the night, she went up on the roof **9**and said to them, "I know that the LORD has given this land to you and that a great fear of you has fallen on us, so that all who live in this country are melting in fear because of you. **10**We have heard how the LORD dried up the water of the Red Sea*a* for you when you came out of Egypt, and what you did to Sihon and Og, the two kings of the Amorites east of the Jordan, whom you completely destroyed.*b* **11**When we heard of it, our hearts melted and everyone's courage failed because of you, for the LORD your God is God in heaven above and on the earth below. **12**Now then, please swear to me by the LORD that you will show kindness to my family, because I have shown kindness to you. Give me a sure sign **13**that you will spare the lives of my father and mother, my brothers and sisters, and all who belong to them, and that you will save us from death*D*."

14"Our lives for your lives!" the men assured her. "If you don't tell what we are doing, we will treat you kindly and faithfully when the LORD gives us the land."

15So she let them down by a rope through the window, for the house she lived in was part of the city wall. **16**Now she had said to them, "Go to the hills so the pursuers will not find you. Hide yourselves there three days until they return, and then go on your way."

17The men said to her, "This oath you made us swear will not be binding on us **18**unless, when we enter the land, you have tied this scarlet cord in the window through which you let us down, and unless you have brought your father and mother, your brothers and all your family into your house. **19**If anyone goes outside your house into the street, his blood will be on his own head; we will not be responsible. As for anyone who is in the house with you, his blood will be on our head if a hand is laid on him. **20**But if you tell what we are doing, we will be released from the oath you made us swear."

21"Agreed," she replied. "Let it be as you say." So she sent them away and they departed. And she tied the scarlet cord in the window.

22When they left, they went into the hills and stayed there three days, until the pursuers had searched all along the road and returned without finding them. **23**Then the two men started back. They went down out of the hills, forded the river and came to Joshua son of Nun and told him everything that had happened to them. **24**They said to Joshua, "The LORD has surely given the whole land into our hands; all the people are melting in fear because of us."

Why were these spies discovered so quickly? (2:2)

Perhaps as a result of their ineptitude. The point of the story is not to show how skilled the Israelites were at military intelligence, but to show how Rahab, a Gentile, became part of the nation of Israel.

Why did God bless Rahab when she told a lie? (2:4–5)

God hates lies (Exodus 20:16; 23:1; Titus 1:13), and did not commend Rahab for hers. God blessed Rahab for acting on her faith by hiding the spies (v. 6) and then sending them away safely (vv. 15–16). She confessed that she believed in Israel's God (vv. 10–13), and she was commended for her faith (Heb. 11:31) and her faithful works (Joshua 6:17,25; James 2:25).

Scarlet cord (2:18)

Some wonder if red cords, like "red light districts" today, advertised the ancient prostitute's business. However, no evidence of this can be found. *Scarlet cord* probably was a decorative roping, colored with a dye made from an insect.

---

a 10 Hebrew *Yam Suph*; that is, Sea of Reeds   *b 10* The Hebrew term refers to the irrevocable giving over of things or persons to the LORD, often by totally destroying them.

The ark of the covenant (3:3)
See Exodus 37:1–9.

Why distance the people from the ark? (3:4)
The ark represented God's holiness and presence. The people had always been kept at a distance from the ark. Only the priests could come closer, serving as intermediaries between the people and the Lord. Some point out that this particular distance—nearly ⅔ of a mile—was about the width of the Jordan's flood plain. Before the people approached the outer banks of the flooded river (v. 15), the water was stopped, and the priests carried the ark to the middle of the Jordan.

How did the people consecrate themselves? (3:5)
With soap, water and sexual abstinence. In Exodus 19:10–15, the people prepared for Moses' return from Sinai by getting clean, which included temporarily avoiding sexual contact. There is no evidence that there was any religious ceremony involved, though these physical actions were undoubtedly performed with a sober attitude. They recognized that God would be doing something extraordinary among them.

What did God have against these groups of people? (3:10)
These various groups living throughout the land of Canaan had worshiped idols and engaged in detestable sins such as religious prostitution and human sacrifice. From God's perspective, the conquest of Canaan occurred because the sin of its inhabitants had reached *full measure* (Gen. 15:16).

How deep was the Jordan at flood stage? (3:15)
Ten to 12 feet in some places.

How did God stop the flow of the Jordan? (3:16)
We don't know, but history records two other similar events. One, in A.D. 1267, resulted from the collapse of high limestone banks, damming the river for 16 hours. In 1927, an earthquake kept parts of the riverbed dry for 21 hours. Some 16 to 19 miles north of Israel's likely crossing were 40-foot banks looming over a narrow stretch of the Jordan. God may have caused their miraculously timed collapse to dam the river and get his people across.

The LORD said to Joshua (4:1)
See *How did God talk to Joshua?* (1:1).

Crossing the Jordan

3 Early in the morning Joshua and all the Israelites set out from Shittim and went to the Jordan, where they camped before crossing over. ²After three days the officers went throughout the camp, ³giving orders to the people: "When you see the ark of the covenant[D] of the LORD your God, and the priests[D], who are Levites[D], carrying it, you are to move out from your positions and follow it. ⁴Then you will know which way to go, since you have never been this way before. But keep a distance of about a thousand yards[a] between you and the ark; do not go near it."

⁵Joshua told the people, "Consecrate[D] yourselves, for tomorrow the LORD will do amazing things among you."

⁶Joshua said to the priests, "Take up the ark of the covenant and pass on ahead of the people." So they took it up and went ahead of them.

⁷And the LORD said to Joshua, "Today I will begin to exalt you in the eyes of all Israel, so they may know that I am with you as I was with Moses. ⁸Tell the priests who carry the ark of the covenant: 'When you reach the edge of the Jordan's waters, go and stand in the river.' "

⁹Joshua said to the Israelites, "Come here and listen to the words of the LORD your God. ¹⁰This is how you will know that the living God is among you and that he will certainly drive out before you the Canaanites, Hittites, Hivites, Perizzites, Girgashites, Amorites and Jebusites. ¹¹See, the ark of the covenant of the Lord of all the earth will go into the Jordan ahead of you. ¹²Now then, choose twelve men from the tribes of Israel, one from each tribe. ¹³And as soon as the priests who carry the ark of the LORD—the Lord of all the earth—set foot in the Jordan, its waters flowing downstream will be cut off and stand up in a heap."

¹⁴So when the people broke camp to cross the Jordan, the priests carrying the ark of the covenant went ahead of them. ¹⁵Now the Jordan is at flood stage all during harvest. Yet as soon as the priests who carried the ark reached the Jordan and their feet touched the water's edge, ¹⁶the water from upstream stopped flowing. It piled up in a heap a great distance away, at a town called Adam in the vicinity of Zarethan, while the water flowing down to the Sea of the Arabah (the Salt Sea[b]) was completely cut off. So the people crossed over opposite Jericho[D]. ¹⁷The priests who carried the ark of the covenant of the LORD stood firm on dry ground in the middle of the Jordan, while all Israel passed by until the whole nation had completed the crossing on dry ground.

4 When the whole nation had finished crossing the Jordan, the LORD said to Joshua, ²"Choose twelve men from among the people, one from each tribe, ³and tell them to take up twelve stones from the middle of the Jordan from right where the priests stood and to carry them over with you and put them down at the place where you stay tonight."

⁴So Joshua called together the twelve men he had appointed from the Israelites, one from each tribe, ⁵and said to them, "Go over before the ark of the LORD your God into the middle of the Jordan. Each of you is to take up a stone on his shoulder, according to the number of the tribes of

---

a4 Hebrew *about two thousand cubits* (about 900 meters)
b16 That is, the Dead Sea

the Israelites, **6**to serve as a sign among you. In the future, when your children ask you, 'What do these stones mean?' **7**tell them that the flow of the Jordan was cut off before the ark of the covenant^D of the LORD. When it crossed the Jordan, the waters of the Jordan were cut off. These stones are to be a memorial to the people of Israel forever."

8So the Israelites did as Joshua commanded them. They took twelve stones from the middle of the Jordan, according to the number of the tribes of the Israelites, as the LORD had told Joshua; and they carried them over with them to their camp, where they put them down. **9**Joshua set up the twelve stones that had been^a in the middle of the Jordan at the spot where the priests^D who carried the ark of the covenant had stood. And they are there to this day.

10Now the priests who carried the ark remained standing in the middle of the Jordan until everything the LORD had commanded Joshua was done by the people, just as Moses had directed Joshua. The people hurried over, **11**and as soon as all of them had crossed, the ark of the LORD and the priests came to the other side while the people watched. **12**The men of Reuben, Gad and the half-tribe of Manasseh crossed over, armed, in front of the Israelites, as Moses had directed them. **13**About forty thousand armed for battle crossed over before the LORD to the plains of Jericho^D for war.

14That day the LORD exalted Joshua in the sight of all Israel; and they revered him all the days of his life, just as they had revered Moses.

15Then the LORD said to Joshua, **16**"Command the priests carrying the ark of the Testimony to come up out of the Jordan."

17So Joshua commanded the priests, "Come up out of the Jordan."

18And the priests came up out of the river carrying the ark of the covenant of the LORD. No sooner had they set their feet on the dry ground than the waters of the Jordan returned to their place and ran at flood stage as before.

19On the tenth day of the first month the people went up from the Jordan and camped at Gilgal on the eastern border of Jericho. **20**And Joshua set up at Gilgal the twelve stones they had taken out of the Jordan. **21**He said to the Israelites, "In the future when your descendants ask their fathers, 'What do these stones mean?' **22**tell them, 'Israel crossed the Jordan on dry ground.' **23**For the LORD your God dried up the Jordan before you until you had crossed over. The LORD your God did to the Jordan just what he had done to the Red Sea^b when he dried it up before us until we had crossed over. **24**He did this so that all the peoples of the earth might know that the hand of the LORD is powerful and so that you might always fear the LORD your God."

Circumcision at Gilgal

5 Now when all the Amorite kings west of the Jordan and all the Canaanite kings along the coast heard how the LORD had dried up the Jordan before the Israelites until we had crossed over, their hearts melted and they no longer had the courage to face the Israelites.

Why was a memorial needed? (4:6–7)

Stone monuments usually outlive the people who erect them. They keep memories alive long after the original players who could tell the stories have left the scene. These stones would remind the people of God's faithfulness at the beginning of their conquests. Together, these twelve stones would also remind them of their national unity.

How old was the memorial when this was written? (4:9)

Some believe eight centuries had lapsed between the crossing of the Jordan and the writing of Joshua. Others think Joshua wrote much of it within a few years. Still others suggest Samuel compiled it.

If the Israelites revered Moses, why did they rebel? (4:14)

Rebellion and reverence often coincide. Most children feel both impulses, as parents will attest. The children of Israel respected Moses for his leadership, but ironically they rebelled for the same reason. Most people who have served God have felt at various times both awe and anger, obedience and stubbornness.

What calendar did the Israelites use? (4:19; see 3:15)

Israel used two calendars, one sacred and one agricultural, much in the same way that a business today will use both a standard and a fiscal calendar. God named Abib (March-April) as the first month—a reminder of deliverance from Egypt and the rebirth of the nation (Exodus 12:2). But the agricultural calendar, which is used in this passage, began with Ethanim (September-October) and dominated the civil affairs of the nation.

---

^a9 Or *Joshua also set up twelve stones*   ^b23 Hebrew *Yam Suph*; that is, Sea of Reeds

Why did Joshua have to circumcise the Israelites? (5:3)

God required each male to be circumcised as a sign of cutting off the old life and beginning anew with God (see Gen. 17:13).

Why had the Israelites ever stopped circumcising? (5:5–7)

Probably because spiritual conditions were at a low ebb. The 40-year desert march was punishment for their unbelief, so the people may have felt some degree of rejection by God. They may have neglected circumcision because they felt the spiritual bond it represented was broken. Also, they may not have felt compelled to identify with the Lord as strongly while isolated in the desert as when facing pagans.

The reproach of Egypt (5:9)

Until they entered the promised land, the Israelites' escape from Egypt was incomplete. If their enterprise failed in the desert, Egypt would ridicule them and the promise God had given them.

Manna (5:12)

The food God miraculously supplied (Exodus 16:14–31) stopped when the people were able to feed themselves. See **What was manna?** (Exodus 16:31) and **What was coriander seed and resin?** (Num. 11:7).

Why did God stop the manna when he did? (5:12)

God gave manna to the Israelites to feed them in the desert as well as to humble them and test them (Deut. 8:16). Its sudden appearance was undeniably supernatural. Its sudden disappearance reminded the new generation of Israelites that manna had been a gift from God—not a natural phenomenon or a product of their own ingenuity. The manna also was stopped because the people had arrived at the promised land, the new source for their sustenance.

Was the commander an angel—or something more? (5:14)

Three things suggest he was more than an angel: (1) Joshua bowed down to worship him, recalling Abraham's response to the Lord (Gen. 17:3; 18:1–2). (2) Joshua was commanded to remove his sandals because he was standing on holy ground (v. 15), just as Moses had been commanded (Exodus 3:5). (3) The commander is called *the Lord*—Yahweh—showing that this was God himself (6:2).

Why wasn't God's commanding officer on Israel's side? (5:14)

God was about to judge the people of Canaan, but that didn't mean that Israel was in the right. God was just, not the people of Israel. Later God would use the Babylonians to judge the people of Judah. See article: **Does God use evil to do good?** (Hab. 1:6,13).

What did bare feet mean to God? (5:15)

Taking off sandals meant putting aside the dirt on them from an impure world. Joshua took off his sandals to acknowledge his own uncleanness.

²At that time the Lord said to Joshua, "Make flint knives and circumcise[D] the Israelites again." ³So Joshua made flint knives and circumcised the Israelites at Gibeath Haaraloth.[a]

⁴Now this is why he did so: All those who came out of Egypt—all the men of military age—died in the desert on the way after leaving Egypt. ⁵All the people that came out had been circumcised, but all the people born in the desert during the journey from Egypt had not. ⁶The Israelites had moved about in the desert forty years until all the men who were of military age when they left Egypt had died, since they had not obeyed the Lord. For the Lord had sworn to them that they would not see the land that he had solemnly promised their fathers to give us, a land flowing with milk and honey. ⁷So he raised up their sons in their place, and these were the ones Joshua circumcised. They were still uncircumcised because they had not been circumcised on the way. ⁸And after the whole nation had been circumcised, they remained where they were in camp until they were healed.

⁹Then the Lord said to Joshua, "Today I have rolled away the reproach[D] of Egypt from you." So the place has been called Gilgal[b] to this day.

¹⁰On the evening of the fourteenth day of the month, while camped at Gilgal on the plains of Jericho[D], the Israelites celebrated the Passover. ¹¹The day after the Passover, that very day, they ate some of the produce of the land: unleavened bread and roasted grain. ¹²The manna[D] stopped the day after[c] they ate this food from the land; there was no longer any manna for the Israelites, but that year they ate of the produce of Canaan.

The Fall of Jericho

¹³Now when Joshua was near Jericho, he looked up and saw a man standing in front of him with a drawn sword in his hand. Joshua went up to him and asked, "Are you for us or for our enemies?"

¹⁴"Neither," he replied, "but as commander of the army of the Lord I have now come." Then Joshua fell facedown to the ground in reverence[D], and asked him, "What message does my Lord[d] have for his servant?"

¹⁵The commander of the Lord's army replied, "Take off your sandals, for the place where you are standing is holy." And Joshua did so.

6 Now Jericho was tightly shut up because of the Israelites. No one went out and no one came in.

²Then the Lord said to Joshua, "See, I have delivered Jericho into your hands, along with its king and its fighting men. ³March around the city once with all the armed men. Do this for six days. ⁴Have seven priests[D] carry trumpets of rams' horns in front of the ark. On the seventh day, march around the city seven times, with the priests blowing the trumpets. ⁵When you hear them sound a long blast on the trumpets, have all the people give a loud shout; then the wall of the city will collapse and the people will go up, every man straight in."

⁶So Joshua son of Nun called the priests and said to them, "Take up the ark of the covenant[D] of the Lord and have seven priests carry trumpets in front of it." ⁷And he ordered the people, "Advance! March around the city, with the armed guard going ahead of the ark of the Lord."

---

a3 Gibeath Haaraloth means *hill of foreskins.*   *b9 Gilgal* sounds like the Hebrew for *roll.*   *c12* Or *the day*   *d14* Or *lord*

8When Joshua had spoken to the people, the seven priests^D carrying the seven trumpets before the LORD went forward, blowing their trumpets, and the ark of the LORD's covenant^D followed them. **9**The armed guard marched ahead of the priests who blew the trumpets, and the rear guard followed the ark. All this time the trumpets were sounding. **10**But Joshua had commanded the people, "Do not give a war cry, do not raise your voices, do not say a word until the day I tell you to shout. Then shout!" **11**So he had the ark of the LORD carried around the city, circling it once. Then the people returned to camp and spent the night there.

12Joshua got up early the next morning and the priests took up the ark of the LORD. **13**The seven priests carrying the seven trumpets went forward, marching before the ark of the LORD and blowing the trumpets. The armed men went ahead of them and the rear guard followed the ark of the LORD, while the trumpets kept sounding. **14**So on the second day they marched around the city once and returned to the camp. They did this for six days.

15On the seventh day, they got up at daybreak and marched around the city seven times in the same manner, except that on that day they circled the city seven times. **16**The seventh time around, when the priests sounded the trumpet blast, Joshua commanded the people, "Shout! For the LORD has given you the city! **17**The city and all that is in it are to be devoted^a to the LORD. Only Rahab^D the prostitute^b and all who are with her in her house shall be spared, because she hid the spies we sent. **18**But keep away from the devoted things, so that you will not bring about your own destruction by taking any of them. Otherwise you will make the camp of Israel liable to destruction and bring trouble on it. **19**All the silver and gold and the articles of bronze and iron are sacred^D to the LORD and must go into his treasury."

20When the trumpets sounded, the people shouted, and at the sound of the trumpet, when the people gave a loud shout, the wall collapsed; so every man charged straight in, and they took the city. **21**They devoted the city to the LORD and destroyed with the sword every living thing in it—men and women, young and old, cattle, sheep and donkeys.

22Joshua said to the two men who had spied out the land, "Go into the prostitute's house and bring her out and all who belong to her, in accordance with your oath to her." **23**So the young men who had done the spying went in and brought out Rahab, her father and mother and brothers and all who belonged to her. They brought out her entire family and put them in a place outside the camp of Israel.

24Then they burned the whole city and everything in it, but they put the silver and gold and the articles of bronze and iron into the treasury of the LORD's house. **25**But Joshua spared Rahab the prostitute, with her family and all who belonged to her, because she hid the men Joshua had sent as spies to Jericho^D—and she lives among the Israelites to this day.

26At that time Joshua pronounced this solemn oath:

a17 The Hebrew term refers to the irrevocable giving over of things or persons to the LORD, often by totally destroying them; also in verses 18 and 21.   *b17* Or possibly *innkeeper*; also in verses 22 and 25

Why did God speak as though victory had already come? (6:2)

Old Testament Hebrew sometimes stated predictions about the future in the present or even the past tense. (Prophecies about Christ's suffering in Isaiah 53 are a good example.) Some say this showed how sure the prediction was—so certain it could be stated as though it had already happened. This was a guarantee: God had resolved absolutely to give Jericho over to the Israelites.

Why did God want them to march around the city? (6:3)

Circling a city was an ancient ritual of siege. In this setting, it raised the fears of Jericho's defenders. For their part, the Israelites learned that God's promises are fulfilled when his conditions are met. By following God's ways, odd or untimely as they might have seemed, the people won the battle.

What kind of trumpets were these? (6:4)

Horns of rams could produce a loud, far-sounding tone and were used to give signals rather than to make music. Shepherds used them to call their flock together. They summoned people to an assembly, announced the start of a feast or led a march into battle.

Why did God want the people to carry the ark around? (6:9)

The ark was not a "magic box" that guaranteed victory. (Later it was even captured by Israel's enemies; see 1 Samuel 4:1–17.) Rather, it was a symbol of the presence of God himself among his people. Inside it were the stone tablets with the Ten Commandments, a jar of manna, and Aaron's staff that budded (Heb. 9:4). The continual presence of the ark was to remind Israel of God's judgment (commandments), his sovereignty (Aaron's staff) and his grace (manna).

What was special about the number seven? (6:13–15)

The final day of the creation week gave the number seven special significance. It symbolized completeness or perfection. In this case the people saw that it meant God's total destruction of Jericho. The first six days of the siege led to its fulfillment on the seventh, God's appointed time.

Was the Sabbath ignored during war? (6:15)

It is unclear whether Jericho fell on the seventh day of the week or the seventh day of the siege. Either way the Sabbath was not observed as usual during that week. It could be that God gave victory on the Sabbath to make Jericho a symbol of ultimate victory. The people took their Sabbath rest by fighting to fulfill God's promise.

Devoted to the LORD (6:17)

Moses "devoted" all the people of Canaan to the Lord (Deut. 20:16–18), not because they were good, but because they were not. Items devoted in this way were destroyed (see NIV text note). Animals, for example, were given to the Lord as sacrifices. The residents of Jericho thus paid the price for the city's long history of corruption and moral rebellion.

What was the purpose of this curse? (6:26)

The curse was to make Jericho a permanent memorial to God's provision and deliverance. It set aside the rubble of a pagan city as testimony to the righteous judgment of God against evil. Some think the city remained a shell for 550 years until Hiel violated the curse and lost two sons (1 Kings 16:34).

What was Joshua doing on his face? (7:6–10)

The ancient Israelites openly expressed their grief in customs that have almost no modern counterparts—tearing clothes, wearing scratchy material called sackcloth, going without sandals or headgear, putting dirt on their heads and rolling in dust or ashes. Joshua was alarmed and grieved to discover that God had abandoned them in their battle against Ai. In anguish he prostrated himself before the ark in the presence of the Lord.

"Cursed before the LORD is the man who undertakes to rebuild this city, Jerichoᴰ:

> "At the cost of his firstbornᴰ son
>   will he lay its foundations;
> at the cost of his youngest
>   will he set up its gates."

²⁷So the LORD was with Joshua, and his fame spread throughout the land.

Achan's Sin

7 But the Israelites acted unfaithfully in regard to the devoted thingsᵃ; Achan son of Carmi, the son of Zimri,ᵇ the son of Zerah, of the tribe of Judah, took some of them. So the LORD's anger burned against Israel.

²Now Joshua sent men from Jericho to Ai, which is near Beth Aven to the east of Bethel, and told them, "Go up and spy out the region." So the men went up and spied out Ai.

³When they returned to Joshua, they said, "Not all the people will have to go up against Ai. Send two or three thousand men to take it and do not weary all the people, for only a few men are there." ⁴So about three thousand men went up; but they were routed by the men of Ai, ⁵who killed about thirty-six of them. They chased the Israelites from the city gate as far as the stone quarriesᶜ and struck them down on the slopes. At this the hearts of the people melted and became like water.

⁶Then Joshua tore his clothes and fell facedown to the ground before the ark of the LORD, remaining there till evening. The elders of Israel did the same, and sprinkled dust on their heads. ⁷And Joshua said, "Ah, Sovereign LORD, why did you ever bring this people across the Jordan to deliver us into the hands of the Amorites to destroy us? If only we had been content to stay on the other side

---

ᵃ1 The Hebrew term refers to the irrevocable giving over of things or persons to the LORD, often by totally destroying them; also in verses 11, 12, 13 and 15.   ᵇ1 See Septuagint and 1 Chron. 2:6; Hebrew *Zabdi*; also in verses 17 and 18.   ᶜ5 Or *as far as Shebarim*

Why kill everything? (6:21)

What was accomplished by annihilating the children, the cattle, the sheep and even the donkeys?

God does not delight in the death of the wicked (Ezek. 18:32; 33:11). He wants them to repent and live. Still, the Bible implies a "point of no return" beyond which judgment is inevitable (see, for example, Jer. 11:11; 14:11–12; 15:1–2).

The Canaanite civilization was so thoroughly degenerate that it was beyond repentance. Chief among their sins was their idol worship, which included sexual perversion and the sacrificial slaughter of infants. Every level of their society was contaminated by evil. Left alone, that evil could have infected the community of God's people. So God dealt with the problem, directly and forcefully.

Still, we are haunted by the killing of infants. Couldn't the babies, at least, have been rescued? We don't know why God included infants with the destruction of the rest of the corrupt Canaanite culture. But because we know *his ways are just* (Deut. 32:4), we must trust God's character in this severe situation. Also, we should remember that the physical death of a baby is not the same as eternal death.

of the Jordan! **8**O Lord, what can I say, now that Israel has been routed by its enemies? **9**The Canaanites and the other people of the country will hear about this and they will surround us and wipe out our name from the earth. What then will you do for your own great name?"

10The LORD said to Joshua, "Stand up! What are you doing down on your face? **11**Israel has sinned; they have violated my covenant^D, which I commanded them to keep. They have taken some of the devoted things; they have stolen, they have lied, they have put them with their own possessions. **12**That is why the Israelites cannot stand against their enemies; they turn their backs and run because they have been made liable to destruction. I will not be with you anymore unless you destroy whatever among you is devoted to destruction.

13"Go, consecrate^D the people. Tell them, 'Consecrate yourselves in preparation for tomorrow; for this is what the LORD, the God of Israel, says: That which is devoted is among you, O Israel. You cannot stand against your enemies until you remove it.

14" 'In the morning, present yourselves tribe by tribe. The tribe that the LORD takes shall come forward clan by clan; the clan that the LORD takes shall come forward family by family; and the family that the LORD takes shall come forward man by man. **15**He who is caught with the devoted things shall be destroyed by fire, along with all that belongs to him. He has violated the covenant of the LORD and has done a disgraceful thing in Israel!' "

16Early the next morning Joshua had Israel come forward by tribes, and Judah was taken. **17**The clans of Judah came forward, and he took the Zerahites. He had the clan of the Zerahites come forward by families, and Zimri was taken. **18**Joshua had his family come forward man by man, and Achan son of Carmi, the son of Zimri, the son of Zerah, of the tribe of Judah, was taken.

19Then Joshua said to Achan, "My son, give glory^D to the LORD,^a the God of Israel, and give him the praise.^b Tell me what you have done; do not hide it from me."

20Achan replied, "It is true! I have sinned against the LORD, the God of Israel. This is what I have done: **21**When I saw in the plunder^D a beautiful robe from Babylonia,^c two hundred shekels^d of silver and a wedge of gold weighing fifty shekels,^e I coveted them and took them. They are hidden in the ground inside my tent, with the silver underneath."

22So Joshua sent messengers, and they ran to the tent, and there it was, hidden in his tent, with the silver underneath. **23**They took the things from the tent, brought them to Joshua and all the Israelites and spread them out before the LORD.

24Then Joshua, together with all Israel, took Achan son of Zerah, the silver, the robe, the gold wedge, his sons and daughters, his cattle, donkeys and sheep, his tent and all that he had, to the Valley of Achor. **25**Joshua said, "Why have you brought this trouble on us? The LORD will bring trouble on you today."

Then all Israel stoned him, and after they had stoned the rest, they burned them. **26**Over Achan they heaped up a large pile of rocks, which remains to this day. Then the

Why blame everybody for one person's sin? (7:11)

Individualism as we know it was not the Israelites' way of thinking. The ancient Israelites would wonder how we could think in any terms other than the community as a whole. Because Achan violated the instructions about Jericho, he broke trust between God and Israel—and the nation as a whole suffered.

Why were the Israelites *liable to destruction*? (7:12)

God threatened their destruction unless they destroyed everything that had been *devoted to destruction*. See NIV text note at 6:17. Also see *What was the difference between "dedicating" and "devoting" something to the Lord?* (Lev. 27:26–28).

Was this justice by lottery? (7:14)

No. In this system, God assumed the role of detective and prosecuting attorney. Achan's confession confirmed the validity of the investigation.

How can confessing sin give glory and praise to God? (7:19)

By confessing sin, the sinner agrees with God that sin is unacceptable. Public confession of that truth glorifies God by acknowledging God to be consistently true and sin to be consistently false.

Why punish Achan's sons and daughters for his sin? (7:24)

They may have helped conceal the plunder. Achan did not fear the curse on Jericho, which is to say that he did not fear God. His attitude would have rubbed off on his family. To cleanse Israel, all that belonged to Achan (including his children) had to be destroyed. Also see *Why punish the children of sinners?* (Jer. 32:18).

---

^a19 A solemn charge to tell the truth   ^b19 Or *and confess to him*
^c21 Hebrew *Shinar*   ^d21 That is, about 5 pounds (about 2.3 kilograms)   ^e21 That is, about 1 1/4 pounds (about 0.6 kilogram)

LORD turned from his fierce anger. Therefore that place has been called the Valley of Achor[a] ever since.

Ai Destroyed

8 Then the LORD said to Joshua, "Do not be afraid; do not be discouraged. Take the whole army with you, and go up and attack Ai. For I have delivered into your hands the king of Ai, his people, his city and his land. [2]You shall do to Ai and its king as you did to Jericho[D] and its king, except that you may carry off their plunder[D] and livestock for yourselves. Set an ambush behind the city."

[3]So Joshua and the whole army moved out to attack Ai. He chose thirty thousand of his best fighting men and sent them out at night [4]with these orders: "Listen carefully. You are to set an ambush behind the city. Don't go very far from it. All of you be on the alert. [5]I and all those with me will advance on the city, and when the men come out against us, as they did before, we will flee from them. [6]They will pursue us until we have lured them away from the city, for they will say, 'They are running away from us as they did before.' So when we flee from them, [7]you are to rise up from ambush and take the city. The LORD your God will give it into your hand. [8]When you have taken the city, set it on fire. Do what the LORD has commanded. See to it; you have my orders."

[9]Then Joshua sent them off, and they went to the place of ambush and lay in wait between Bethel and Ai, to the west of Ai—but Joshua spent that night with the people. [10]Early the next morning Joshua mustered his men, and he and the leaders of Israel marched before them to Ai. [11]The entire force that was with him marched up and approached the city and arrived in front of it. They set up camp north of Ai, with the valley between them and the city. [12]Joshua had taken about five thousand men and set them in ambush between Bethel and Ai, to the west of the city. [13]They had the soldiers take up their positions—all those in the camp to the north of the city and the ambush to the west of it. That night Joshua went into the valley.

[14]When the king of Ai saw this, he and all the men of the city hurried out early in the morning to meet Israel in battle at a certain place overlooking the Arabah. But he did not know that an ambush had been set against him behind the city. [15]Joshua and all Israel let themselves be driven back before them, and they fled toward the desert. [16]All the men of Ai were called to pursue them, and they pursued Joshua and were lured away from the city. [17]Not a man remained in Ai or Bethel who did not go after Israel. They left the city open and went in pursuit of Israel.

[18]Then the LORD said to Joshua, "Hold out toward Ai the javelin that is in your hand, for into your hand I will deliver the city." So Joshua held out his javelin toward Ai. [19]As soon as he did this, the men in the ambush rose quickly from their position and rushed forward. They entered the city and captured it and quickly set it on fire.

[20]The men of Ai looked back and saw the smoke of the city rising against the sky, but they had no chance to escape in any direction, for the Israelites who had been fleeing toward the desert had turned back against their pursuers. [21]For when Joshua and all Israel saw that the ambush had taken the city and that smoke was going up from the city, they turned around and attacked the men of Ai. [22]The men of the ambush also came out of the city

The Battle of Ai (8:1)

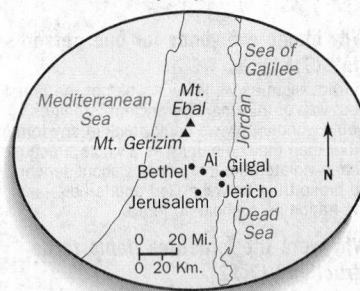

Why could the Israelites plunder Ai, but not Jericho? (8:2)

In ancient times pillaging was a means of resupplying the army with food and equipment. So it was not the battle of Ai that was unusual, but the battle of Jericho. The dedication of Jericho's valuables to the Lord paralleled God's laws about *firstfruits* (see Lev. 2:14): they honored the Lord by giving the first victory to him.

Why rely on military strategy to defeat Ai? (8:3–19)

Why didn't God perform another miracle as he did at Jericho? In reality, both battles had elements of the supernatural and the natural. Israel sent spies into Jericho, clearly a strategic move, as was the use of trumpets, voices and processional marches. At Ai, Joshua's raised javelin was a sign that God would deliver the city into their hands—clearly a supernatural work. God uses a variety of means to achieve his purpose.

---

[a]26 *Achor* means *trouble*.

against them, so that they were caught in the middle, with Israelites on both sides. Israel cut them down, leaving them neither survivors nor fugitives. **23**But they took the king of Ai alive and brought him to Joshua.

24When Israel had finished killing all the men of Ai in the fields and in the desert where they had chased them, and when every one of them had been put to the sword, all the Israelites returned to Ai and killed those who were in it. **25**Twelve thousand men and women fell that day— all the people of Ai. **26**For Joshua did not draw back the hand that held out his javelin until he had destroyed*a* all who lived in Ai. **27**But Israel did carry off for themselves the livestock and plunder*D* of this city, as the LORD had instructed Joshua.

28So Joshua burned Ai and made it a permanent heap of ruins, a desolate place to this day. **29**He hung the king of Ai on a tree and left him there until evening. At sunset, Joshua ordered them to take his body from the tree and throw it down at the entrance of the city gate. And they raised a large pile of rocks over it, which remains to this day.

The Covenant Renewed at Mount Ebal

30Then Joshua built on Mount Ebal an altar to the LORD, the God of Israel, **31**as Moses the servant of the LORD had commanded the Israelites. He built it according to what is written in the Book of the Law of Moses—an altar of un- cut stones, on which no iron tool had been used. On it they offered to the LORD burnt offerings*D* and sacrificed fellowship offerings*D, b* **32**There, in the presence of the Israelites, Joshua copied on stones the law of Moses, which he had written. **33**All Israel, aliens*D* and citizens alike, with their elders, officials and judges, were standing on both sides of the ark of the covenant of the LORD, facing those who carried it—the priests*D*, who were Le- vites*D*. Half of the people stood in front of Mount Gerizim and half of them in front of Mount Ebal, as Moses the ser- vant of the LORD had formerly commanded when he gave instructions to bless the people of Israel.

34Afterward, Joshua read all the words of the law—the blessings and the curses—just as it is written in the Book of the Law. **35**There was not a word of all that Moses had commanded that Joshua did not read to the whole assem- bly of Israel, including the women and children, and the aliens who lived among them.

The Gibeonite Deception

9 Now when all the kings west of the Jordan heard about these things—those in the hill country, in the western foothills, and along the entire coast of the Great Sea*c* as far as Lebanon (the kings of the Hittites, Amo- rites, Canaanites, Perizzites, Hivites and Jebusites)— **2**they came together to make war against Joshua and Israel.

3However, when the people of Gibeon heard what Josh- ua had done to Jericho*D* and Ai, **4**they resorted to a ruse: They went as a delegation whose donkeys were loaded*d* with worn-out sacks and old wineskins*D*, cracked and

Why destroy *everyone*? (8:24–25)
See article: *Why kill everything?* (6:21).

What was done with the dead bodies? (8:24)
To the ancients, leaving bodies unburied was a great dishonor (Eccl. 6:3). Further dishonor re- sulted when birds and beasts ate the dead (Deut. 28:26). What happened to the casual- ties from Ai, after valuables were stripped from the corpses, is unknown. Ancient mass graves have not been found.

Why hang the king in a tree? (8:29)
Since Israel did not execute by hanging, the king was likely killed and his body put on dis- play. See 10:26. The body of a defeated and lifeless king was a trophy for Israel and a warn- ing to surrounding kings. See *Anyone who is hung on a tree is under God's curse* (Deut. 21:23).

Why were uncut stones needed for the altar? (8:31)
The law says *you will defile it* [the altar] *if you use a tool on it* (Exodus 20:25). The defilement may have arisen from the fact that altars to false gods in the surrounding nations often contained elaborate (and erotic) designs. Isra- el's altars would thereby have been distinctive- ly unadorned. The fact that *iron* tools were not to be used to cut the stones (Deut. 27:5–8) suggests that the Israelites (who then pos- sessed no iron) should not depend on any of the surrounding pagan nations to help them worship the true God.

Why make another copy of the com- mandments? (8:32)
Copying the commandments on stone rein- forced the importance of God's laws. Stone would last longer than any other material for writing.

Who were the *aliens who lived among them*? (8:35)
Rahab and her family lived among them, as well as nomads, travelers and vagabonds, who would wander into the Israelite camp for food or shelter. A number of Egyptians and perhaps some non-Hebrew slaves had left Egypt with the Israelites (Exodus 12:38).

---

a26 The Hebrew term refers to the irrevocable giving over of things or persons to the LORD, often by totally destroying them.
b31 Traditionally *peace offerings*   *c1* That is, the Mediterranean
d4 Most Hebrew manuscripts; some Hebrew manuscripts, Vulgate and Syriac (see also Septuagint) *They prepared provisions and loaded their donkeys*

Were the Gibeonites "converts"? (9:9)

Only in the basic sense of acknowledging God's greatness and power. To their credit, the Gibeonites explained Israel's success theologically. They had not, however, become full-fledged members of the covenant. They are portrayed not as brothers, but as shrewd bargainers whose mustard-seed glimpse of God saved their lives. Of such glimpses, however, faith is born.

How should Israel have inquired of the Lord? (9:14)

Perhaps through the Urim and Thummin (see Dictionary), or perhaps through a means similar to what was used to detect Achan's lie (7:14).

Why did the people complain? (9:18)

Israel's strength was still uncertain on the international scene. The people probably doubted their ability to conquer the land if an enemy was allowed to live within their territory. They were upset by the discovery that Joshua and their other leaders had been conned by the Gibeonites. They knew Israel could be devastated if her leaders came to be known as easy marks.

Why honor an oath granted under false pretenses? (9:19)

True, the Israelites had been duped into making the treaty with Gibeon, a violation of Exodus 34:12. But it was made with a people who respected Israel and acknowledged the greatness of God. And breaking an oath was also a violation of the law (Lev. 5:4). See *How could someone take an oath and not know it?* (Lev. 5:4).

Can we admire the resourcefulness of the Gibeonites? (9:25)

Their trickery avoided harm and circumvented bloodshed. The Gibeonites admitted their ruse, submitted to the Israelites and found mercy. Their faith was microscopic, but in Canaan any faith was reason for wonder and admiration.

mended. ⁵The men put worn and patched sandals on their feet and wore old clothes. All the bread of their food supply was dry and moldy. ⁶Then they went to Joshua in the camp at Gilgal and said to him and the men of Israel, "We have come from a distant country; make a treaty with us."

⁷The men of Israel said to the Hivites, "But perhaps you live near us. How then can we make a treaty with you?"

⁸"We are your servants," they said to Joshua.

But Joshua asked, "Who are you and where do you come from?"

⁹They answered: "Your servants have come from a very distant country because of the fame of the LORD your God. For we have heard reports of him: all that he did in Egypt, ¹⁰and all that he did to the two kings of the Amorites east of the Jordan—Sihon king of Heshbon, and Og king of Bashan, who reigned in Ashtaroth. ¹¹And our elders and all those living in our country said to us, 'Take provisions for your journey; go and meet them and say to them, "We are your servants; make a treaty with us." ' ¹²This bread of ours was warm when we packed it at home on the day we left to come to you. But now see how dry and moldy it is. ¹³And these wineskins[D] that we filled were new, but see how cracked they are. And our clothes and sandals are worn out by the very long journey."

¹⁴The men of Israel sampled their provisions but did not inquire of the LORD. ¹⁵Then Joshua made a treaty of peace[D] with them to let them live, and the leaders of the assembly ratified it by oath.

¹⁶Three days after they made the treaty with the Gibeonites, the Israelites heard that they were neighbors, living near them. ¹⁷So the Israelites set out and on the third day came to their cities: Gibeon, Kephirah, Beeroth and Kiriath Jearim. ¹⁸But the Israelites did not attack them, because the leaders of the assembly had sworn an oath to them by the LORD, the God of Israel.

The whole assembly grumbled against the leaders, ¹⁹but all the leaders answered, "We have given them our oath by the LORD, the God of Israel, and we cannot touch them now. ²⁰This is what we will do to them: We will let them live, so that wrath will not fall on us for breaking the oath we swore to them." ²¹They continued, "Let them live, but let them be woodcutters and water carriers for the entire community." So the leaders' promise to them was kept.

²²Then Joshua summoned the Gibeonites and said, "Why did you deceive us by saying, 'We live a long way from you,' while actually you live near us? ²³You are now under a curse: You will never cease to serve as woodcutters and water carriers for the house of my God."

²⁴They answered Joshua, "Your servants were clearly told how the LORD your God had commanded his servant Moses to give you the whole land and to wipe out all its inhabitants from before you. So we feared for our lives because of you, and that is why we did this. ²⁵We are now in your hands. Do to us whatever seems good and right to you."

²⁶So Joshua saved them from the Israelites, and they did not kill them. ²⁷That day he made the Gibeonites woodcutters and water carriers for the community and for the altar of the LORD at the place the LORD would choose. And that is what they are to this day.

The Sun Stands Still

10 Now Adoni-Zedek king of Jerusalem^D heard that Joshua had taken Ai and totally destroyed*a* it, doing to Ai and its king as he had done to Jericho^D and its king, and that the people of Gibeon had made a treaty of peace^D with Israel and were living near them. ²He and his people were very much alarmed at this, because Gibeon was an important city, like one of the royal cities; it was larger than Ai, and all its men were good fighters. ³So Adoni-Zedek king of Jerusalem appealed to Hoham king of Hebron, Piram king of Jarmuth, Japhia king of Lachish and Debir king of Eglon. ⁴"Come up and help me attack Gibeon," he said, "because it has made peace with Joshua and the Israelites."

⁵Then the five kings of the Amorites—the kings of Jerusalem, Hebron, Jarmuth, Lachish and Eglon—joined forces. They moved up with all their troops and took up positions against Gibeon and attacked it.

⁶The Gibeonites then sent word to Joshua in the camp at Gilgal: "Do not abandon your servants. Come up to us quickly and save us! Help us, because all the Amorite kings from the hill country have joined forces against us."

⁷So Joshua marched up from Gilgal with his entire army, including all the best fighting men. ⁸The LORD said to Joshua, "Do not be afraid of them; I have given them into your hand. Not one of them will be able to withstand you."

⁹After an all-night march from Gilgal, Joshua took them by surprise. ¹⁰The LORD threw them into confusion before Israel, who defeated them in a great victory at Gibeon. Israel pursued them along the road going up to Beth Horon and cut them down all the way to Azekah and Makkedah. ¹¹As they fled before Israel on the road down from Beth Horon to Azekah, the LORD hurled large hailstones down on them from the sky, and more of them died from the hailstones than were killed by the swords of the Israelites.

¹²On the day the LORD gave the Amorites over to Israel, Joshua said to the LORD in the presence of Israel:

"O sun, stand still over Gibeon,
    O moon, over the Valley of Aijalon."
¹³So the sun stood still,
    and the moon stopped,
    till the nation avenged^D itself on*b* its
        enemies,

as it is written in the Book of Jashar.

The sun stopped in the middle of the sky and delayed going down about a full day. ¹⁴There has never been a day like it before or since, a day when the LORD listened to a man. Surely the LORD was fighting for Israel!

¹⁵Then Joshua returned with all Israel to the camp at Gilgal.

Five Amorite Kings Killed

¹⁶Now the five kings had fled and hidden in the cave at Makkedah. ¹⁷When Joshua was told that the five kings had been found hiding in the cave at Makkedah, ¹⁸he said, "Roll large rocks up to the mouth of the cave, and post some men there to guard it. ¹⁹But don't stop! Pursue your

a1 The Hebrew term refers to the irrevocable giving over of things or persons to the LORD, often by totally destroying them; also in verses 28, 35, 37, 39 and 40.   *b13* Or *nation triumphed over*

The Battle of Gibeon (10:5)

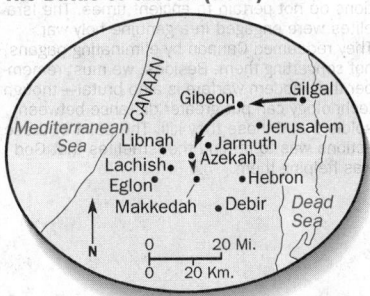

Why did Israel have to defend Gibeon? (10:6–7)

Allies were obliged to help each other. Joshua may have also seen God at work in drawing the armies of five cities together into open battle; it would be less costly to attack them than to besiege five fortified cities individually.

How big were these hailstones? (10:11)

Hail can be the size of softballs and weigh a pound or more. Also, hailstones sometimes stick together as they fall, creating even larger chunks of ice.

Are natural calamities "acts of God"? (10:11)

The Hebrews saw the Creator as the prime cause behind all that happens, including bad as well as good. The events of nature, though initiated by God and often used by him for his purposes, happen in a seemingly random manner, affecting both the righteous and the unrighteous (Matt. 5:45). For a discussion of calamities that strike innocent people, see article: *Are people just pawns in God's chess game?* (Job 1:13–19).

Did Joshua speak to the sun and moon? (10:12)

Joshua spoke to the Lord, not to the things he created. Pagans believed the sun and moon were gods and would pray to them.

How did the sun stop? (10:13–14)

Some believe that God literally made the day last longer. Others say the poem is figurative; that is, so much was accomplished that day that it seemed like an extraordinarily long day.

The Book of Jashar (10:13)

An ancient collection of songs and historical notes on the achievements of national war heroes. See *Book of Jashar* (2 Samuel 1:18).

Why didn't anyone talk against Israel? (10:21)

The ferocity of the Israelites' victories so changed their image that no other people, nation or king dared sound hostile toward that wandering nation.

Wasn't this excessively brutal? (10:24–26)

Yes, by our standards. But modern conventions do not pertain to ancient times. The Israelites were engaged in a genuine holy war. They redeemed Canaan by eliminating pagans, not converting them. Besides, we must remember that modern warfare is also brutal—though technology can put greater distance between soldiers and those they kill. The point of these actions was to remind the Israelites that God was helping them.

What did Joshua do to the king of Jericho? (10:28)

No specific reference is made to the death of Jericho's king. But the king of Ai (who suffered the same fate; see 8:2) was killed and hung on a tree until evening (8:29). It seems that pagan kings were typically killed and hung up for public display and humiliation.

Was this exaggeration? (10:40–43)

It was no exaggeration to say that the Israelites *left no survivors* in certain areas. But to conclude that they had vanquished all their foes and subdued the larger regions is to read too much into this summary. There were still battles to be fought, as the next chapter quickly demonstrates. Also see article: *Can the Bible exaggerate and still be true?* (2 Chron. 1:9–15).

enemies, attack them from the rear and don't let them reach their cities, for the LORD your God has given them into your hand."

²⁰So Joshua and the Israelites destroyed them completely—almost to a man—but the few who were left reached their fortified cities. ²¹The whole army then returned safely to Joshua in the camp at Makkedah, and no one uttered a word against the Israelites.

²²Joshua said, "Open the mouth of the cave and bring those five kings out to me." ²³So they brought the five kings out of the cave—the kings of JerusalemᴰHebron, Jarmuth, Lachish and Eglon. ²⁴When they had brought these kings to Joshua, he summoned all the men of Israel and said to the army commanders who had come with him, "Come here and put your feet on the necks of these kings." So they came forward and placed their feet on their necks.

²⁵Joshua said to them, "Do not be afraid; do not be discouraged. Be strong and courageous. This is what the LORD will do to all the enemies you are going to fight." ²⁶Then Joshua struck and killed the kings and hung them on five trees, and they were left hanging on the trees until evening.

²⁷At sunset Joshua gave the order and they took them down from the trees and threw them into the cave where they had been hiding. At the mouth of the cave they placed large rocks, which are there to this day.

²⁸That day Joshua took Makkedah. He put the city and its king to the sword and totally destroyed everyone in it. He left no survivors. And he did to the king of Makkedah as he had done to the king of Jericho.ᴰ

Southern Cities Conquered

²⁹Then Joshua and all Israel with him moved on from Makkedah to Libnah and attacked it. ³⁰The LORD also gave that city and its king into Israel's hand. The city and everyone in it Joshua put to the sword. He left no survivors there. And he did to its king as he had done to the king of Jericho.

³¹Then Joshua and all Israel with him moved on from Libnah to Lachish; he took up positions against it and attacked it. ³²The LORD handed Lachish over to Israel, and Joshua took it on the second day. The city and everyone in it he put to the sword, just as he had done to Libnah. ³³Meanwhile, Horam king of Gezer had come up to help Lachish, but Joshua defeated him and his army—until no survivors were left.

³⁴Then Joshua and all Israel with him moved on from Lachish to Eglon; they took up positions against it and attacked it. ³⁵They captured it that same day and put it to the sword and totally destroyed everyone in it, just as they had done to Lachish.

³⁶Then Joshua and all Israel with him went up from Eglon to Hebron and attacked it. ³⁷They took the city and put it to the sword, together with its king, its villages and everyone in it. They left no survivors. Just as at Eglon, they totally destroyed it and everyone in it.

³⁸Then Joshua and all Israel with him turned around and attacked Debir. ³⁹They took the city, its king and its villages, and put them to the sword. Everyone in it they totally destroyed. They left no survivors. They did to Debir and its king as they had done to Libnah and its king and to Hebron.

⁴⁰So Joshua subdued the whole region, including the

hill country, the Negev[D], the western foothills and the mountain slopes, together with all their kings. He left no survivors. He totally destroyed all who breathed, just as the LORD, the God of Israel, had commanded. **41**Joshua subdued them from Kadesh Barnea to Gaza and from the whole region of Goshen to Gibeon. **42**All these kings and their lands Joshua conquered in one campaign, because the LORD, the God of Israel, fought for Israel.

43Then Joshua returned with all Israel to the camp at Gilgal.

Northern Kings Defeated

11 When Jabin king of Hazor heard of this, he sent word to Jobab king of Madon, to the kings of Shimron and Acshaph, **2**and to the northern kings who were in the mountains, in the Arabah south of Kinnereth, in the western foothills and in Naphoth Dor[a] on the west; **3**to the Canaanites in the east and west; to the Amorites, Hittites, Perizzites and Jebusites in the hill country; and to the Hivites below Hermon in the region of Mizpah. **4**They came out with all their troops and a large number of horses and chariots—a huge army, as numerous as the sand on the seashore. **5**All these kings joined forces and made camp together at the Waters of Merom, to fight against Israel.

6The LORD said to Joshua, "Do not be afraid of them, because by this time tomorrow I will hand all of them over to Israel, slain. You are to hamstring their horses and burn their chariots."

7So Joshua and his whole army came against them suddenly at the Waters of Merom and attacked them, **8**and the LORD gave them into the hand of Israel. They defeated them and pursued them all the way to Greater Sidon, to Misrephoth Maim, and to the Valley of Mizpah on the east, until no survivors were left. **9**Joshua did to them as the LORD had directed: He hamstrung their horses and burned their chariots.

10At that time Joshua turned back and captured Hazor and put its king to the sword. (Hazor had been the head of all these kingdoms.) **11**Everyone in it they put to the sword. They totally destroyed[b] them, not sparing anything that breathed, and he burned up Hazor itself.

12Joshua took all these royal cities and their kings and put them to the sword. He totally destroyed them, as Moses the servant of the LORD had commanded. **13**Yet Israel did not burn any of the cities built on their mounds—except Hazor, which Joshua burned. **14**The Israelites carried off for themselves all the plunder[D] and livestock of these cities, but all the people they put to the sword until they completely destroyed them, not sparing anyone that breathed. **15**As the LORD commanded his servant Moses, so Moses commanded Joshua, and Joshua did it; he left nothing undone of all that the LORD commanded Moses.

16So Joshua took this entire land: the hill country, all the Negev, the whole region of Goshen, the western foothills, the Arabah and the mountains of Israel with their foothills, **17**from Mount Halak, which rises toward Seir, to Baal Gad in the Valley of Lebanon below Mount Hermon. He captured all their kings and struck them down, putting them to death[D]. **18**Joshua waged war

The Battle of Hazor (11:5)

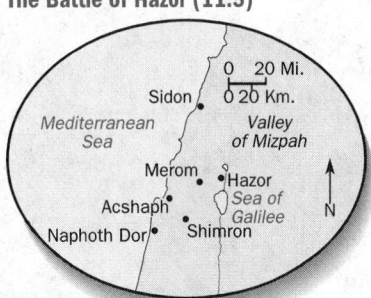

Why hamstring perfectly good horses? (11:6)

God warned his people not to put their trust in chariots and horses—their modern military technologies (Psalm 20:7; 33:17). Rather, Israel was to rely solely on God. God was interested in something far more important than horses—the spiritual condition of the nation of Israel. Healthy horses could be an impediment to their trust in him.

Cities built on their mounds (11:13)

In ancient times many cities were built on the ruins of previous settlements. Over the course of many years, a mound or small hill of accumulated debris would form the foundation for future construction.

---

[a]2 Or *in the heights of Dor*   [b]11 The Hebrew term refers to the irrevocable giving over of things or persons to the LORD, often by totally destroying them; also in verses 12, 20 and 21.

The land had rest from war (11:23)
An expression meaning that the battles for
the conquest of the land had ended. Conflict
had forced the people to live under stressful
situations: normal activities were restricted;
crops were threatened or lost. Just as people
respond to a cease-fire today, the inhabitants
breathed a collective sigh of relief when the
fighting and killing stopped.

against all these kings for a long time. **¹⁹**Except for the Hivites living in Gibeon, not one city made a treaty of
peace[D] with the Israelites, who took them all in battle.
²⁰For it was the LORD himself who hardened their hearts
to wage war against Israel, so that he might destroy them
totally, exterminating them without mercy[D], as the LORD
had commanded Moses.

²¹At that time Joshua went and destroyed the Anakites
from the hill country: from Hebron, Debir and Anab, from
all the hill country of Judah, and from all the hill country
of Israel. Joshua totally destroyed them and their towns.
²²No Anakites were left in Israelite territory; only in Gaza,
Gath and Ashdod did any survive. **²³**So Joshua took the entire land, just as the LORD had directed Moses, and he gave
it as an inheritance to Israel according to their tribal divisions.

Then the land had rest from war.

List of Defeated Kings

12 These are the kings of the land whom the Israelites had defeated and whose territory they took
over east of the Jordan, from the Arnon Gorge to Mount
Hermon, including all the eastern side of the Arabah:

²Sihon king of the Amorites,
who reigned in Heshbon. He ruled from Aroer on the
rim of the Arnon Gorge—from the middle of the
gorge—to the Jabbok River, which is the border of
the Ammonites. This included half of Gilead. **³**He also
ruled over the eastern Arabah from the Sea of Kinnereth[a] to the Sea of the Arabah (the Salt Sea[b]), to

a3 That is, Galilee   *b3* That is, the Dead Sea

Was God responsible for their hard hearts? (11:20)

God works his sovereign will in history, but people are responsible for their
choices. Both truths resound throughout the Bible, but each seems to nullify
the other if pushed to an extreme.

Some argue that God's sovereignty excludes the possibility that Israel's adversaries
had options available to them; they were doomed from the start. According to this view,
history, determined in advance, was immune to change. Both Joshua's obedience and the
opposition of the people in the land were pre-determined by God.

Others say that the responsibility for hard hearts ultimately returns to human choice.
An extreme position might allow God credit for setting things in motion, but makes God a
spectator thereafter. This kind of religion sees God as distant, impersonal and only remotely concerned about how history plays out.

Still others come down somewhere between these two positions. God achieves his
purposes in an open universe with genuine human choices and clear-cut human responsibilities. God's will shall be accomplished—no Christian may doubt it. But evil also occurs, willful rebellion goes on and God grieves because of it.

God shows his power both by helping his people and hardening his enemies (Romans
9:19–26). God finalized the demise of these kings, as part of his sovereign plan, in response to their rebellious choices.

Also see articles: **Who hardened Pharaoh's heart?** (Exodus 10:1) and **Why does God
harden some people's hearts?** (Exodus 11:3).

Beth Jeshimoth, and then southward below the slopes of Pisgah.

⁴And the territory of Og king of Bashan, one of the last of the Rephaites, who reigned in Ashtaroth and Edrei. ⁵He ruled over Mount Hermon, Salecah, all of Bashan to the border of the people of Geshur and Maacah, and half of Gilead to the border of Sihon king of Heshbon.

⁶Moses, the servant of the LORD, and the Israelites conquered them. And Moses the servant of the LORD gave their land to the Reubenites, the Gadites and the half-tribe of Manasseh to be their possession.

⁷These are the kings of the land that Joshua and the Israelites conquered on the west side of the Jordan, from Baal Gad in the Valley of Lebanon to Mount Halak, which rises toward Seir (their lands Joshua gave as an inheritance to the tribes of Israel according to their tribal divisions— ⁸the hill country, the western foothills, the Arabah, the mountain slopes, the desert and the NegevD— the lands of the Hittites, Amorites, Canaanites, Perizzites, Hivites and Jebusites):

⁹the king of JerichoD	one
the king of Ai (near Bethel)	one

SCRIPTURE LINK (12:4) *Og king of Bashan*

Read about the defeat of this king in Deut. 3:1–11.

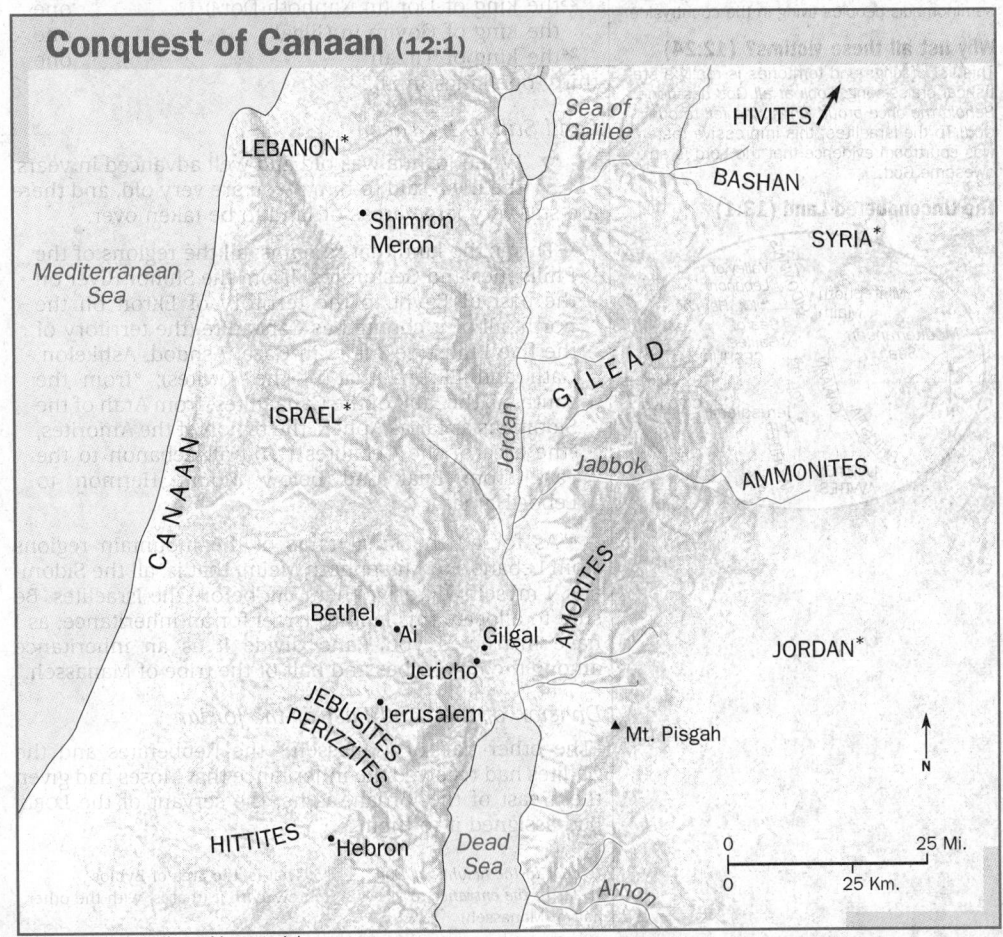

Conquest of Canaan (12:1)

LEBANON*

Sea of Galilee

HIVITES

BASHAN

SYRIA*

Mediterranean Sea

Shimron Meron

GILEAD

ISRAEL*

Jordan

Jabbok

AMMONITES

CANAAN

AMORITES

JORDAN*

Bethel
Ai
Gilgal
Jericho
JEBUSITES
PERIZZITES
Jerusalem

Mt. Pisgah

N

HITTITES   Hebron   Dead Sea

Arnon

0   25 Mi.
0   25 Km.

Modern names indicated by asterisk

¹⁰the king of Jerusalem^D	one
the king of Hebron	one
¹¹the king of Jarmuth	one
the king of Lachish	one
¹²the king of Eglon	one
the king of Gezer	one
¹³the king of Debir	one
the king of Geder	one
¹⁴the king of Hormah	one
the king of Arad	one
¹⁵the king of Libnah	one
the king of Adullam	one
¹⁶the king of Makkedah	one
the king of Bethel	one
¹⁷the king of Tappuah	one
the king of Hepher	one
¹⁸the king of Aphek	one
the king of Lasharon	one
¹⁹the king of Madon	one
the king of Hazor	one
²⁰the king of Shimron Meron	one
the king of Acshaph	one
²¹the king of Taanach	one
the king of Megiddo	one
²²the king of Kedesh	one
the king of Jokneam in Carmel	one
²³the king of Dor (in Naphoth Dor^a)	one
the king of Goyim in Gilgal	one
²⁴the king of Tirzah	one

thirty-one kings in all.

How much power did these kings have? (12:7–24)

These kings were rulers of local city-kingdoms. They were more powerful than city mayors, but less important than pharaohs or empire over-lords. In sparsely settled areas, their influence extended for a radius of several miles. During times of conflict, they came to the aid of the seminomadic peoples living in the countryside.

Why list all these victims? (12:24)

This list of kings and territories is really a statistical praise-song: *Look at all God has done. Behold the once proud kings who fell to our God!* To the Israelites, this impressive roster was courtroom evidence that the Lord is an awesome God.

The Unconquered Land (13:1)

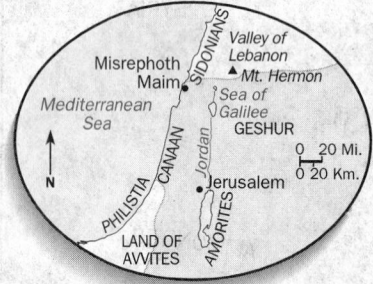

Land Still to Be Taken

13 When Joshua was old and well advanced in years, the LORD said to him, "You are very old, and there are still very large areas of land to be taken over.

²"This is the land that remains: all the regions of the Philistines and Geshurites: ³from the Shihor River on the east of Egypt to the territory of Ekron on the north, all of it counted as Canaanite (the territory of the five Philistine rulers in Gaza, Ashdod, Ashkelon, Gath and Ekron—that of the Avvites); ⁴from the south, all the land of the Canaanites, from Arah of the Sidonians as far as Aphek, the region of the Amorites, ⁵the area of the Gebalites^b; and all Lebanon to the east, from Baal Gad below Mount Hermon to Lebo^c Hamath.

⁶"As for all the inhabitants of the mountain regions from Lebanon to Misrephoth Maim, that is, all the Sidonians, I myself will drive them out before the Israelites. Be sure to allocate this land to Israel for an inheritance, as I have instructed you, ⁷and divide it as an inheritance among the nine tribes and half of the tribe of Manasseh."

Division of the Land East of the Jordan

⁸The other half of Manasseh,^d the Reubenites and the Gadites had received the inheritance that Moses had given them east of the Jordan, as he, the servant of the LORD, had assigned it to them.

---

^a23 Or *in the heights of Dor*   ^b5 That is, the area of Byblos   ^c5 Or *to the entrance to*   ^d8 Hebrew *With it* (that is, with the other half of Manasseh)

⁹It extended from Aroer on the rim of the Arnon Gorge, and from the town in the middle of the gorge, and included the whole plateau of Medeba as far as Dibon, ¹⁰and all the towns of Sihon king of the Amorites, who ruled in Heshbon, out to the border of the Ammonites. ¹¹It also included Gilead, the territory of the people of Geshur and Maacah, all of Mount Hermon and all Bashan as far as Salecah— ¹²that is, the whole kingdom of Og in Bashan, who had reigned in Ashtaroth and Edrei and had survived as one of the last of the Rephaites. Moses had defeated them and taken over their land. ¹³But the Israelites did not drive out the people of Geshur and Maacah, so they continue to live among the Israelites to this day.

¹⁴But to the tribe of Levi he gave no inheritance, since the offerings made by fire to the LORD, the God of Israel, are their inheritance, as he promised them.

¹⁵This is what Moses had given to the tribe of Reuben, clan by clan:

¹⁶The territory from Aroer on the rim of the Arnon Gorge, and from the town in the middle of the gorge, and the whole plateau past Medeba ¹⁷to Heshbon and all its towns on the plateau, including Dibon, Bamoth Baal, Beth Baal Meon, ¹⁸Jahaz, Kedemoth, Mephaath, ¹⁹Kiriathaim, Sibmah, Zereth Shahar on the hill in the valley, ²⁰Beth Peor, the slopes of Pisgah, and Beth Jeshimoth ²¹—all the towns on the plateau and the entire realm of Sihon king of the Amorites, who ruled at Heshbon. Moses had defeated him and the Midianite chiefs, Evi, Rekem, Zur, Hur and Reba— princes allied with Sihon—who lived in that country. ²²In addition to those slain in battle, the Israelites had put to the sword Balaam son of Beor, who practiced divinationᴰ. ²³The boundary of the Reubenites was the bank of the Jordan. These towns and their villages were the inheritance of the Reubenites, clan by clan.

²⁴This is what Moses had given to the tribe of Gad, clan by clan:

²⁵The territory of Jazer, all the towns of Gilead and half the Ammonite country as far as Aroer, near Rabbah; ²⁶and from Heshbon to Ramath Mizpah and Betonim, and from Mahanaim to the territory of Debir; ²⁷and in the valley, Beth Haram, Beth Nimrah, Succoth and Zaphon with the rest of the realm of Sihon king of Heshbon (the east side of the Jordan, the territory up to the end of the Sea of Kinnereth*ᵃ*). ²⁸These towns and their villages were the inheritance of the Gadites, clan by clan.

²⁹This is what Moses had given to the half-tribe of Manasseh, that is, to half the family of the descendants of Manasseh, clan by clan:

³⁰The territory extending from Mahanaim and including all of Bashan, the entire realm of Og king of Bashan—all the settlements of Jair in Bashan, sixty towns, ³¹half of Gilead, and Ashtaroth and Edrei (the royal cities of Og in Bashan). This was for the descendants of Makir son of Manasseh—for half of the sons of Makir, clan by clan.

ᵃ27 That is, Galilee

Dividing the Land (13:8)

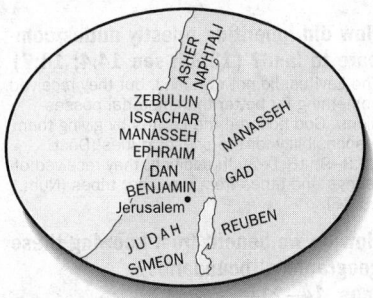

Why were some nations not defeated? (13:13)

The Israelites simply failed to finish the job. They disobeyed God's command to expel all the inhabitants of the land. God promised to drive out their enemies (v. 6), but the promise hinged on their obedience. They also failed later, for the same reason, to drive out some of the inhabitants on the western side of the Jordan (15:63; 16:10).

How did Israel know about Balaam? (13:22)

Even without media or advertising, Balaam's fame had spread. He was well-known as one who earned his living by divination (Num. 22:7). Though he could not bring himself to curse Israel, he advised his clients, the Moabites and the Midianites, to corrupt Israel, enticing them into sexual immorality and idolatry (Num. 25:1–9; 31:16). Perhaps the Israelites heard of Balaam through their intermarriages with the local people. Or perhaps some of the locals, hoping to save their own lives, pointed Balaam out following the battle. Also see *Who was Balaam?* (Num. 22:7).

How did the Reubenites inherit these towns? (13:23)

The division of the land east of the Jordan and the Dead Sea went to the tribes of Reuben, Gad and the half-tribe of Manasseh. Moses had originally assigned this land and these cities (Num. 32:33; Deut. 3:18). Now the Lord commanded Joshua to specify the borders of their inheritance (Joshua 13:7).

How did inheriting priestly duties compare to land? (13:33; see 14:4; 18:7)

The Levites did not own land, but they received something far better than material possessions. God honored the Levites by giving them responsibility for the priestly duties (Deut. 10:8–9; 18:1–2). In addition, they received offerings and tithes from the other tribes (Num. 18:26).

How do we benefit from knowing these geographical boundaries?
(chs. 14–21)

A central theme in Joshua is the fulfillment of God's promise: he would give Israel the land (Deut. 7:18–24; Exodus 23:20–33; Joshua 21:23–45). These geographical details help us appreciate the faithfulness of the Lord. He drove out the inhabitants of the land according to his promise (13:6). Remembering his faithfulness encourages us to trust him more fully.

The land had rest from war (14:15)
See *The land had rest from war* (11:23).

32This is the inheritance Moses had given when he was in the plains of Moab across the Jordan east of Jericho[D]. **33**But to the tribe of Levi, Moses had given no inheritance; the LORD, the God of Israel, is their inheritance, as he promised them.

Division of the Land West of the Jordan

14 Now these are the areas the Israelites received as an inheritance in the land of Canaan, which Eleazar the priest[D], Joshua son of Nun and the heads of the tribal clans of Israel allotted to them. **2**Their inheritances were assigned by lot to the nine-and-a-half tribes, as the LORD had commanded through Moses. **3**Moses had granted the two-and-a-half tribes their inheritance east of the Jordan but had not granted the Levites[D] an inheritance among the rest, **4**for the sons of Joseph had become two tribes—Manasseh and Ephraim. The Levites received no share of the land but only towns to live in, with pasturelands for their flocks and herds. **5**So the Israelites divided the land, just as the LORD had commanded Moses.

Hebron Given to Caleb

6Now the men of Judah approached Joshua at Gilgal, and Caleb son of Jephunneh the Kenizzite said to him, "You know what the LORD said to Moses the man of God at Kadesh Barnea about you and me. **7**I was forty years old when Moses the servant of the LORD sent me from Kadesh Barnea to explore the land. And I brought him back a report according to my convictions, **8**but my brothers who went up with me made the hearts of the people melt with fear. I, however, followed the LORD my God wholeheartedly. **9**So on that day Moses swore to me, 'The land on which your feet have walked will be your inheritance and that of your children forever, because you have followed the LORD my God wholeheartedly.'[a]

10"Now then, just as the LORD promised, he has kept me alive for forty-five years since the time he said this to Moses, while Israel moved about in the desert. So here I am today, eighty-five years old! **11**I am still as strong today as the day Moses sent me out; I'm just as vigorous to go out to battle now as I was then. **12**Now give me this hill country that the LORD promised me that day. You yourself heard then that the Anakites were there and their cities were large and fortified, but, the LORD helping me, I will drive them out just as he said."

13Then Joshua blessed Caleb son of Jephunneh and gave him Hebron as his inheritance. **14**So Hebron has belonged to Caleb son of Jephunneh the Kenizzite ever since, because he followed the LORD, the God of Israel, wholeheartedly. **15**(Hebron used to be called Kiriath Arba after Arba, who was the greatest man among the Anakites.)

Then the land had rest from war.

Allotment for Judah

15 The allotment for the tribe of Judah, clan by clan, extended down to the territory of Edom[D], to the Desert of Zin in the extreme south.

2Their southern boundary started from the bay at the southern end of the Salt Sea,[b] **3**crossed south of Scorpion[c] Pass, continued on to Zin and went over

---

[a]9 Deut. 1:36   [b]2 That is, the Dead Sea; also in verse 5
[c]3 Hebrew *Akrabbim*

to the south of Kadesh Barnea. Then it ran past Hezron up to Addar and curved around to Karka. ⁴It then passed along to Azmon and joined the Wadi of Egypt, ending at the sea. This is their*ᵃ* southern boundary.

⁵The eastern boundary is the Salt Sea as far as the mouth of the Jordan.

The northern boundary started from the bay of the sea at the mouth of the Jordan, ⁶went up to Beth Hoglah and continued north of Beth Arabah to the Stone of Bohan son of Reuben. ⁷The boundary then went up to Debir from the Valley of Achor and turned north to Gilgal, which faces the Pass of Adummim south of the gorge. It continued along to the waters of En Shemesh and came out at En Rogel. ⁸Then it ran up the Valley of Ben Hinnom along the southern slope of the Jebusite city (that is, Jerusalemᴰ). From there it climbed to the top of the hill west of the Hinnom Valley at the northern end of the Valley of Rephaim. ⁹From the hilltop the boundary headed toward the spring of the waters of Nephtoah, came out at the towns of Mount Ephron and went down toward Baalah (that is, Kiriath Jearim). ¹⁰Then it curved westward from Baalah to Mount Seir, ran along the northern slope of Mount Jearim (that is, Kesalon), continued down to Beth Shemesh and crossed to Timnah. ¹¹It went to the northern slope of Ekron, turned toward Shikkeron, passed along to Mount Baalah and reached Jabneel. The boundary ended at the sea.

¹²The western boundary is the coastline of the Great Sea.*ᵇ*

These are the boundaries around the people of Judah by their clans.

¹³In accordance with the LORD's command to him, Joshua gave to Caleb son of Jephunneh a portion in Judah—Kiriath Arba, that is, Hebron. (Arba was the forefather of Anak.) ¹⁴From Hebron Caleb drove out the three Anakites—Sheshai, Ahiman and Talmai—descendants of Anak. ¹⁵From there he marched against the people living in Debir (formerly called Kiriath Sepher). ¹⁶And Caleb said, "I will give my daughter Acsah in marriage to the man who attacks and captures Kiriath Sepher." ¹⁷Othniel son of Kenaz, Caleb's brother, took it; so Caleb gave his daughter Acsah to him in marriage.

¹⁸One day when she came to Othniel, she urged him*ᶜ* to ask her father for a field. When she got off her donkey, Caleb asked her, "What can I do for you?"

¹⁹She replied, "Do me a special favor. Since you have given me land in the Negevᴰ, give me also springs of water." So Caleb gave her the upper and lower springs.

²⁰This is the inheritance of the tribe of Judah, clan by clan:

²¹The southernmost towns of the tribe of Judah in the Negev toward the boundary of Edom were:

Kabzeel, Eder, Jagur, ²²Kinah, Dimonah, Adadah, ²³Kedesh, Hazor, Ithnan, ²⁴Ziph, Telem, Bealoth, ²⁵Hazor Hadattah, Kerioth Hezron (that is, Hazor), ²⁶Amam, Shema, Moladah, ²⁷Hazar Gaddah, Heshmon, Beth Pelet, ²⁸Hazar Shual, Beersheba, Biziothi-

SCRIPTURE LINK (15:15–19)
Similar verses can be found in Judges 1:11–15.

Were Israelite girls treated like property? (15:17)
More or less, yes. Offering one's daughter as a reward for military conquest was customary. It was a practice apparently well-ingrained in the culture, still occurring nearly 400 years later (1 Samuel 17:25; 18:17). Women did have some rights, however. See *What kind of rights did women have?* (17:4).

Why did Acsah have to ask for something as basic as water? (15:19)
Because her father overlooked the fact that the land he offered had no water. Acsah first had her husband, Othniel, ask her father, Caleb, for some land. Although Caleb agreed, the land he offered had no water. He may have noticed his daughter's reaction and asked her what more he could do. It was only then that Acsah requested additional land with water.

---

*ᵃ*4 Hebrew *your*   *ᵇ*12 That is, the Mediterranean; also in verse 47
*ᶜ*18 Hebrew and some Septuagint manuscripts; other Septuagint manuscripts (see also note at Judges 1:14) *Othniel, he urged her*

ah, **29**Baalah, Iim, Ezem, **30**Eltolad, Kesil, Hormah, **31**Ziklag, Madmannah, Sansannah, **32**Lebaoth, Shilhim, Ain and Rimmon—a total of twenty-nine towns and their villages.

33In the western foothills:

Eshtaol, Zorah, Ashnah, **34**Zanoah, En Gannim, Tappuah, Enam, **35**Jarmuth, Adullam, Socoh, Azekah, **36**Shaaraim, Adithaim and Gederah (or Gederothaim)*ᵃ*—fourteen towns and their villages.

37Zenan, Hadashah, Migdal Gad, **38**Dilean, Mizpah, Joktheel, **39**Lachish, Bozkath, Eglon, **40**Cabbon, Lahmas, Kitlish, **41**Gederoth, Beth Dagon, Naamah and Makkedah—sixteen towns and their villages.

42Libnah, Ether, Ashan, **43**Iphtah, Ashnah, Nezib, **44**Keilah, Aczib and Mareshah—nine towns and their villages.

45Ekron, with its surrounding settlements and villages; **46**west of Ekron, all that were in the vicinity of Ashdod, together with their villages; **47**Ashdod, its surrounding settlements and villages; and Gaza, its settlements and villages, as far as the Wadi of Egypt and the coastline of the Great Sea.

48In the hill country:

Shamir, Jattir, Socoh, **49**Dannah, Kiriath Sannah (that is, Debir), **50**Anab, Eshtemoh, Anim, **51**Goshen, Holon and Giloh—eleven towns and their villages.

52Arab, Dumah, Eshan, **53**Janim, Beth Tappuah, Aphekah, **54**Humtah, Kiriath Arba (that is, Hebron) and Zior—nine towns and their villages.

55Maon, Carmel, Ziph, Juttah, **56**Jezreel, Jokdeam, Zanoah, **57**Kain, Gibeah and Timnah—ten towns and their villages.

58Halhul, Beth Zur, Gedor, **59**Maarath, Beth Anoth and Eltekon—six towns and their villages.

60Kiriath Baal (that is, Kiriath Jearim) and Rabbah—two towns and their villages.

61In the desert:

Beth Arabah, Middin, Secacah, **62**Nibshan, the City of Salt and En Gedi—six towns and their villages.

63Judah could not dislodge the Jebusites, who were living in Jerusalem^D; to this day the Jebusites live there with the people of Judah.

Allotment for Ephraim and Manasseh

16 The allotment for Joseph began at the Jordan of Jericho^D,^b east of the waters of Jericho, and went up from there through the desert into the hill country of Bethel. **2**It went on from Bethel (that is, Luz),^c crossed over to the territory of the Arkites in Ataroth, **3**descended westward to the territory of the Japhletites as far as the region of Lower Beth Horon and on to Gezer, ending at the sea.

4So Manasseh and Ephraim, the descendants of Joseph, received their inheritance.

5This was the territory of Ephraim, clan by clan:

The boundary of their inheritance went from Ataroth Addar in the east to Upper Beth Horon **6**and continued to the sea. From Micmethath on the north it

---

Wadi of Egypt (15:47)

A wadi is an otherwise dry valley through which water runs during the wet seasons of the year. This particular wadi is probably the Wadi el-Arish, located in the northeastern part of the Sinai Peninsula (see **Map 2** at the back of this Bible).

Why couldn't Judah drive out the Jebusites? (15:63)

They couldn't because they wouldn't. God had promised to remove the enemy little by little (Exodus 23:29; Deut. 7:22). After six years, however, the conquest of the land was still incomplete (13:1–5). When the Israelites decided to tolerate their enemies rather than expel them, they failed to act on God's promises. They also set a dangerous precedent that eventually resulted in the evil prophesied in Deut. 6:14–15; 7:4 and Exodus 23:32–33.

ᵃ36 Or *Gederah and Gederothaim*   *ᵇ1 Jordan of Jericho* was possibly an ancient name for the Jordan River.   *ᶜ2* Septuagint; Hebrew *Bethel to Luz*

curved eastward to Taanath Shiloh, passing by it to Janoah on the east. **7**Then it went down from Janoah to Ataroth and Naarah, touched Jericho[D] and came out at the Jordan. **8**From Tappuah the border went west to the Kanah Ravine and ended at the sea. This was the inheritance of the tribe of the Ephraimites, clan by clan. **9**It also included all the towns and their villages that were set aside for the Ephraimites within the inheritance of the Manassites.

10They did not dislodge the Canaanites living in Gezer; to this day the Canaanites live among the people of Ephraim but are required to do forced labor.

17 This was the allotment for the tribe of Manasseh as Joseph's firstborn[D], that is, for Makir, Manasseh's firstborn. Makir was the ancestor of the Gileadites, who had received Gilead and Bashan because the Makirites were great soldiers. **2**So this allotment was for the rest of the people of Manasseh—the clans of Abiezer, Helek, Asriel, Shechem, Hepher and Shemida. These are the other male descendants of Manasseh son of Joseph by their clans.

3Now Zelophehad son of Hepher, the son of Gilead, the son of Makir, the son of Manasseh, had no sons but only daughters, whose names were Mahlah, Noah, Hoglah, Milcah and Tirzah. **4**They went to Eleazar the priest[D], Joshua son of Nun, and the leaders and said, "The LORD commanded Moses to give us an inheritance among our brothers." So Joshua gave them an inheritance along with the brothers of their father, according to the LORD's command. **5**Manasseh's share consisted of ten tracts of land besides Gilead and Bashan east of the Jordan, **6**because the daughters of the tribe of Manasseh received an inheritance among the sons. The land of Gilead belonged to the rest of the descendants of Manasseh.

7The territory of Manasseh extended from Asher to Micmethath east of Shechem. The boundary ran southward from there to include the people living at En Tappuah. **8**(Manasseh had the land of Tappuah, but Tappuah itself, on the boundary of Manasseh, belonged to the Ephraimites.) **9**Then the boundary continued south to the Kanah Ravine. There were towns belonging to Ephraim lying among the towns of Manasseh, but the boundary of Manasseh was the northern side of the ravine and ended at the sea. **10**On the south the land belonged to Ephraim, on the north to Manasseh. The territory of Manasseh reached the sea and bordered Asher on the north and Issachar on the east.

11Within Issachar and Asher, Manasseh also had Beth Shan, Ibleam and the people of Dor, Endor, Taanach and Megiddo, together with their surrounding settlements (the third in the list is Naphoth[a]).

12Yet the Manassites were not able to occupy these towns, for the Canaanites were determined to live in that region. **13**However, when the Israelites grew stronger, they subjected the Canaanites to forced labor but did not drive them out completely.

14The people of Joseph said to Joshua, "Why have you given us only one allotment and one portion for an inheritance? We are a numerous people and the LORD has blessed us abundantly."

15"If you are so numerous," Joshua answered, "and if

How did the Israelites get the Canaanites to do forced labor? (16:10)

Israel chose to exploit the Canaanites rather than exterminate them. Though the Lord had commanded total destruction (Deut. 12:2–3; 7:2) and warned of dire consequences for anything short of that (Deut. 12:29; Num. 33:50–56), the Israelites valued the convenience of having slaves more than the importance of obeying God.

What kind of rights did women have? (17:4)

The women of ancient Israel had few rights by today's standards. See *Were Israelite girls treated like property?* (15:17). But the law provided for their care and protection in several important ways: (1) a childless widow was granted the right of a son by her husband's brother (insuring inheritance rights; see Deut. 25:5–6); (2) some kinds of divorce were prohibited totally (for example, Deut. 22:19); (3) women without any brothers could inherit their father's land (Num. 27:3–7); (4) Women were protected from starvation (Deut. 24:19–21). Also see *Why would a father sell his daughter as a servant?* (Exodus 21:7–11).

a11 That is, Naphoth Dor

the hill country of Ephraim is too small for you, go up into the forest and clear land for yourselves there in the land of the Perizzites and Rephaites."

¹⁶The people of Joseph replied, "The hill country is not enough for us, and all the Canaanites who live in the plain have iron chariots, both those in Beth Shan and its settlements and those in the Valley of Jezreel."

¹⁷But Joshua said to the house of Joseph—to Ephraim and Manasseh—"You are numerous and very powerful. You will have not only one allotment ¹⁸but the forested hill country as well. Clear it, and its farthest limits will be yours; though the Canaanites have iron chariots and though they are strong, you can drive them out."

Division of the Rest of the Land

18 The whole assembly of the Israelites gathered at Shiloh and set up the Tent of Meeting ᴰ there. The country was brought under their control, ²but there were still seven Israelite tribes who had not yet received their inheritance.

³So Joshua said to the Israelites: "How long will you wait before you begin to take possession of the land that the LORD, the God of your fathers, has given you? ⁴Appoint three men from each tribe. I will send them out to make a survey of the land and to write a description of it, according to the inheritance of each. Then they will return to me. ⁵You are to divide the land into seven parts. Judah is to remain in its territory on the south and the house of Joseph in its territory on the north. ⁶After you have written descriptions of the seven parts of the land, bring them here to me and I will cast lots for you in the presence of the LORD our God. ⁷The Levites ᴰ, however, do not get a portion among you, because the priestly service of the LORD is their inheritance. And Gad, Reuben and the half-tribe of Manasseh have already received their inheritance on the east side of the Jordan. Moses the servant of the LORD gave it to them."

⁸As the men started on their way to map out the land, Joshua instructed them, "Go and make a survey of the land and write a description of it. Then return to me, and I will cast lots for you here at Shiloh in the presence of the LORD." ⁹So the men left and went through the land. They wrote its description on a scroll, town by town, in seven parts, and returned to Joshua in the camp at Shiloh. ¹⁰Joshua then cast lots for them in Shiloh in the presence of the LORD, and there he distributed the land to the Israelites according to their tribal divisions.

Tent of Meeting (18:1)
A tent that housed the ark of the covenant (Exodus 25:8–22). It was the designated place where God met with his people. It was placed in Shiloh, which was centrally located and probably best situated to help unify the people. See *Tent of Meeting* (Num. 1:1).

What were these seven tribes waiting for? (18:3)
All the land had been subdued by Joshua (11:16–17), meaning the tribes had joined forces and fought together. Not all the land was immediately parceled out, however. Tribal boundaries had yet to be established. Following the general defeat of the Canaanites, individual tribes were expected to eliminate pockets of resistance in their assigned territories. Until they did, the tribes lived together, scattered throughout the land in a loose coalition.

Why cast lots to divide the land? (18:10)
The Israelites could make impartial decisions when they relied on God to direct the outcome of the lots. Most likely, they mixed small marked stones in a jar and drew them out one at a time. Also see Lev. 16:8; 1 Samuel 14:42; Neh. 10:34; Prov. 16:33.

What was so frightening about iron chariots? (17:16)

These were actually iron-plated chariots. Chariots were particularly difficult to fight against on open plains because of their maneuverability and their speed. When fitted with iron, these chariots also became virtually invincible (see Judges 1:19). During the shift from the bronze to the iron age (around 1200 B.C.), the Canaanites jealously guarded the metallurgical secrets they had seized from the Hittites of Asia Minor. Iron became as highly prized as gold and silver!

Iron weapons gave the Philistines a big advantage in their battles against the hill-dwelling Israelites (see 1 Samuel 4:1–2,10).

Allotment for Benjamin

11The lot came up for the tribe of Benjamin, clan by clan. Their allotted territory lay between the tribes of Judah and Joseph:

12On the north side their boundary began at the Jordan, passed the northern slope of Jericho[D] and headed west into the hill country, coming out at the desert of Beth Aven. **13**From there it crossed to the south slope of Luz (that is, Bethel) and went down to Ataroth Addar on the hill south of Lower Beth Horon.

14From the hill facing Beth Horon on the south the boundary turned south along the western side and came out at Kiriath Baal (that is, Kiriath Jearim), a town of the people of Judah. This was the western side.

15The southern side began at the outskirts of Kiriath Jearim on the west, and the boundary came out at the spring of the waters of Nephtoah. **16**The boundary went down to the foot of the hill facing the Valley of Ben Hinnom, north of the Valley of Rephaim. It continued down the Hinnom Valley along the southern slope of the Jebusite city and so to En Rogel. **17**It then curved north, went to En Shemesh, continued to Geliloth, which faces the Pass of Adummim, and ran down to the Stone of Bohan son of Reuben. **18**It continued to the northern slope of Beth Arabah[a] and on down into the Arabah. **19**It then went to the northern slope of Beth Hoglah and came out at the northern bay of the Salt Sea,[b] at the mouth of the Jordan in the south. This was the southern boundary.

20The Jordan formed the boundary on the eastern side.

These were the boundaries that marked out the inheritance of the clans of Benjamin on all sides.

21The tribe of Benjamin, clan by clan, had the following cities:

Jericho, Beth Hoglah, Emek Keziz, **22**Beth Arabah, Zemaraim, Bethel, **23**Avvim, Parah, Ophrah, **24**Kephar Ammoni, Ophni and Geba—twelve towns and their villages.

25Gibeon, Ramah, Beeroth, **26**Mizpah, Kephirah, Mozah, **27**Rekem, Irpeel, Taralah, **28**Zelah, Haeleph, the Jebusite city (that is, Jerusalem[D]), Gibeah and Kiriath—fourteen towns and their villages.

This was the inheritance of Benjamin for its clans.

Allotment for Simeon

19 The second lot came out for the tribe of Simeon, clan by clan. Their inheritance lay within the territory of Judah. **2**It included:

Beersheba (or Sheba),[c] Moladah, **3**Hazar Shual, Balah, Ezem, **4**Eltolad, Bethul, Hormah, **5**Ziklag, Beth Marcaboth, Hazar Susah, **6**Beth Lebaoth and Sharuhen—thirteen towns and their villages;

7Ain, Rimmon, Ether and Ashan—four towns and their villages— **8**and all the villages around these towns as far as Baalath Beer (Ramah in the Negev[D]).

This was the inheritance of the tribe of the Simeonites, clan by clan. **9**The inheritance of the Simeonites was tak-

---

Stone of Bohan son of Reuben (18:17)

Large, naturally occurring stones were often used as boundary markers. We don't know anything about Bohan except that this particular boundary stone was named for him. It was likely located somewhere southeast of Jericho.

How did Judah end up with too much and Simeon with nothing? (19:7–9)

The men of Judah had apparently taken more initiative in conquering sections of land (14:6–12). As a result, Judah (along with four other tribes) acquired territory before the final seven tribes received theirs. Joshua urged the others to overcome their reluctance to fight, and then he cast lots to divide the land (18:3,10). Simeon joined forces with Judah, which apparently had staked claim to more land than it needed (Judges 1:3,17). Their joint venture explains why Simeon settled down within Judah's territory.

---

[a]18 Septuagint; Hebrew *slope facing the Arabah*   [b]19 That is, the Dead Sea   [c]2 Or *Beersheba, Sheba;* 1 Chron. 4:28 does not have *Sheba.*

en from the share of Judah, because Judah's portion was more than they needed. So the Simeonites received their inheritance within the territory of Judah.

Allotment for Zebulun

10The third lot came up for Zebulun, clan by clan:

The boundary of their inheritance went as far as Sarid. **11**Going west it ran to Maralah, touched Dabbesheth, and extended to the ravine near Jokneam. **12**It turned east from Sarid toward the sunrise to the territory of Kisloth Tabor and went on to Daberath and up to Japhia. **13**Then it continued eastward to Gath Hepher and Eth Kazin; it came out at Rimmon and turned toward Neah. **14**There the boundary went around on the north to Hannathon and ended at the Valley of Iphtah El. **15**Included were Kattath, Nahalal, Shimron, Idalah and Bethlehem. There were twelve towns and their villages.

16These towns and their villages were the inheritance of Zebulun, clan by clan.

Allotment for Issachar

17The fourth lot came out for Issachar, clan by clan. **18**Their territory included:

Jezreel, Kesulloth, Shunem, **19**Hapharaim, Shion, Anaharath, **20**Rabbith, Kishion, Ebez, **21**Remeth, En Gannim, En Haddah and Beth Pazzez. **22**The boundary touched Tabor, Shahazumah and Beth Shemesh, and ended at the Jordan. There were sixteen towns and their villages.

23These towns and their villages were the inheritance of the tribe of Issachar, clan by clan.

Allotment for Asher

24The fifth lot came out for the tribe of Asher, clan by clan. **25**Their territory included:

Helkath, Hali, Beten, Acshaph, **26**Allammelech, Amad and Mishal. On the west the boundary touched Carmel and Shihor Libnath. **27**It then turned east toward Beth Dagon, touched Zebulun and the Valley of Iphtah El, and went north to Beth Emek and Neiel, passing Cabul on the left. **28**It went to Abdon,[a] Rehob, Hammon and Kanah, as far as Greater Sidon. **29**The boundary then turned back toward Ramah and went to the fortified city of Tyre, turned toward Hosah and came out at the sea in the region of Aczib, **30**Ummah, Aphek and Rehob. There were twenty-two towns and their villages.

31These towns and their villages were the inheritance of the tribe of Asher, clan by clan.

Allotment for Naphtali

32The sixth lot came out for Naphtali, clan by clan:

33Their boundary went from Heleph and the large tree in Zaanannim, passing Adami Nekeb and Jabneel to Lakkum and ending at the Jordan. **34**The boundary ran west through Aznoth Tabor and came out at Hukkok. It touched Zebulun on the south, Asher on the west and the Jordan[b] on the east. **35**The fortified cities were Ziddim, Zer, Hammath, Rakkath, Kinnereth,

---

[a]28 Some Hebrew manuscripts (see also Joshua 21:30); most Hebrew manuscripts *Ebron*   [b]34 Septuagint; Hebrew *west, and Judah, the Jordan,*

How can towns have villages? (19:15)
Towns typically had villages clustered around them both for convenience and protection. Living outside the town proper made it easier for villagers to work in the fields. But living in smaller, unwalled settlements also made people more vulnerable to enemy attack. So whenever invaders came, the villagers would abandon their homes and gather in the central town where they could be protected by the town walls and mount a concerted effort to defend themselves.

Fortified city (19:29)
A city that was well protected. Usually surrounded by walls, such cities were often built on steep hills to provide further protection from hostile forces.

Why did the Danites go after something other than what they were supposed to? (19:47)
The Danites took it upon themselves to solve their territorial problems. Though God had not instructed them to go elsewhere, he had not specifically prohibited them either. Because they had trouble conquering the small section allotted to them between the territory of Benjamin and the Mediterranean (see *Map 4* at the back of this Bible), they became hemmed in, confined by the Amorites to the hill country (Judges 1:34). The Danites finally found Leshem to the north easier to defeat than the cities in the coastal plain.

36Adamah, Ramah, Hazor, **37**Kedesh, Edrei, En Hazor, **38**Iron, Migdal El, Horem, Beth Anath and Beth She- mesh. There were nineteen towns and their villages. **39**These towns and their villages were the inheritance of the tribe of Naphtali, clan by clan.

Allotment for Dan

40The seventh lot came out for the tribe of Dan, clan by clan. **41**The territory of their inheritance included:

Zorah, Eshtaol, Ir Shemesh, **42**Shaalabbin, Aijalon, Ithlah, **43**Elon, Timnah, Ekron, **44**Eltekeh, Gibbethon, Baalath, **45**Jehud, Bene Berak, Gath Rimmon, **46**Me Jarkon and Rakkon, with the area facing Joppa*ᴰ*.

47(But the Danites had difficulty taking possession of their territory, so they went up and attacked Leshem, took it, put it to the sword and occupied it. They settled in Le- shem and named it Dan after their forefather.) **48**These towns and their villages were the inheritance of the tribe of Dan, clan by clan.

Allotment for Joshua

49When they had finished dividing the land into its al- lotted portions, the Israelites gave Joshua son of Nun an inheritance among them, **50**as the LORD had commanded. They gave him the town he asked for—Timnath Serah*ᵃ* in the hill country of Ephraim. And he built up the town and settled there.

51These are the territories that Eleazar the priest*ᴰ*, Joshua son of Nun and the heads of the tribal clans of Isra- el assigned by lot at Shiloh in the presence of the LORD at the entrance to the Tent of Meeting*ᴰ*. And so they fin- ished dividing the land.

Cities of Refuge

20 Then the LORD said to Joshua: **2**"Tell the Israelites to designate the cities of refuge, as I instructed you through Moses, **3**so that anyone who kills a person acci- dentally and unintentionally may flee there and find pro- tection from the avenger of blood.

4"When he flees to one of these cities, he is to stand in the entrance of the city gate and state his case before the elders of that city. Then they are to admit him into their city and give him a place to live with them. **5**If the avenger of blood pursues him, they must not surrender the one accused, because he killed his neighbor unintentionally and without malice aforethought. **6**He is to stay in that city until he has stood trial before the assembly and until the death*ᴰ* of the high priest who is serving at that time. Then he may go back to his own home in the town from which he fled."

7So they set apart Kedesh in Galilee in the hill country of Naphtali, Shechem in the hill country of Ephraim, and Kiriath Arba (that is, Hebron) in the hill country of Judah. **8**On the east side of the Jordan of Jericho*ᴰᵇ* they desig- nated Bezer in the desert on the plateau in the tribe of Reuben, Ramoth in Gilead in the tribe of Gad, and Golan in Bashan in the tribe of Manasseh. **9**Any of the Israelites or any alien*ᴰ* living among them who killed someone ac- cidentally could flee to these designated cities and not be killed by the avenger of blood prior to standing trial be- fore the assembly.

ᵃ50 Also known as *Timnath Heres* (see Judges 2:9)   *ᵇ8 Jordan of Jericho* was possibly an ancient name for the Jordan River.

Why did Joshua divide and assign land that hadn't yet been conquered? (19:51)

By dividing the land before they actually pos- sessed it, Joshua demonstrated his trust in the Lord's promise. The Lord offered the whole land as an inheritance to Israel (Num. 32:33; Deut. 3:18). Israel, however, was responsible to act in faith and drive out the Canaanites.

Cities of refuge (20:2)

Six cities (three on the east and three on the west side of the Jordan) were established as safe havens for those who had accidentally killed someone (Num. 35:9–34). Anyone ac- cused of murder would be protected in a city of refuge until trial. The victim's avenging rela- tives could not touch him (Num. 35:12). If found innocent, the accused could remain there safely until the death of the high priest. Then he would be permitted to return to his home (Num. 35:28). Also see **How did the judi- cial process work?** (Num. 35:24–25).

Was this the usual method of han- dling accidental deaths? (20:2–3)

Cities of refuge were quite progressive in that day. The system upheld the sanctity for life and imposed limits on retribution, protecting those who killed someone accidentally. Other cul- tures did not show this kind of respect for the accused. This ethic, by contrast, established a principle still valued in civilized lands: "inno- cent until proven guilty." Also see **Why banish an innocent man?** (Num. 35:25).

Cities of Refuge (20:2)

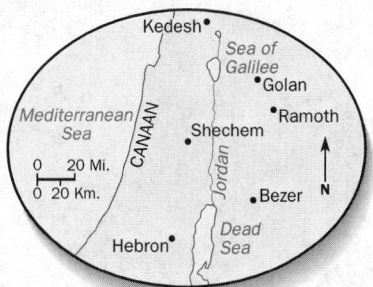

What did an avenger of blood do? (20:3)

When someone was killed, an avenger of blood was obligated to put the killer to death. Typical- ly this was the nearest male relative of the vic- tim. The avenger was not to be a vigilante seeking vengeance, however. His aim instead was retribution, the restoration of life balance in society (Exodus 21:23–25; Lev. 24:17). See **Avenger of blood** (Num. 35:19).

Towns for the Levites

21 Now the family heads of the Levites[D] approached Eleazar the priest[D], Joshua son of Nun, and the heads of the other tribal families of Israel ²at Shiloh in Canaan and said to them, "The LORD commanded through Moses that you give us towns to live in, with pasturelands for our livestock." ³So, as the LORD had commanded, the Israelites gave the Levites the following towns and pasturelands out of their own inheritance:

⁴The first lot came out for the Kohathites, clan by clan. The Levites who were descendants of Aaron the priest were allotted thirteen towns from the tribes of Judah, Simeon and Benjamin. ⁵The rest of Kohath's descendants were allotted ten towns from the clans of the tribes of Ephraim, Dan and half of Manasseh.

⁶The descendants of Gershon were allotted thirteen towns from the clans of the tribes of Issachar, Asher, Naphtali and the half-tribe of Manasseh in Bashan.

⁷The descendants of Merari, clan by clan, received twelve towns from the tribes of Reuben, Gad and Zebulun.

⁸So the Israelites allotted to the Levites these towns and their pasturelands, as the LORD had commanded through Moses.

⁹From the tribes of Judah and Simeon they allotted the following towns by name ¹⁰(these towns were assigned to the descendants of Aaron who were from the Kohathite clans of the Levites, because the first lot fell to them):

¹¹They gave them Kiriath Arba (that is, Hebron), with its surrounding pastureland, in the hill country of Judah. (Arba was the forefather of Anak.) ¹²But the fields and villages around the city they had given to Caleb son of Jephunneh as his possession.

¹³So to the descendants of Aaron the priest they gave Hebron (a city of refuge for one accused of murder), Libnah, ¹⁴Jattir, Eshtemoa, ¹⁵Holon, Debir, ¹⁶Ain, Juttah and Beth Shemesh, together with their pasturelands—nine towns from these two tribes.

¹⁷And from the tribe of Benjamin they gave them Gibeon, Geba, ¹⁸Anathoth and Almon, together with their pasturelands—four towns.

¹⁹All the towns for the priests, the descendants of Aaron, were thirteen, together with their pasturelands.

²⁰The rest of the Kohathite clans of the Levites were allotted towns from the tribe of Ephraim:

²¹In the hill country of Ephraim they were given Shechem (a city of refuge for one accused of murder) and Gezer, ²²Kibzaim and Beth Horon, together with their pasturelands—four towns.

²³Also from the tribe of Dan they received Eltekeh, Gibbethon, ²⁴Aijalon and Gath Rimmon, together with their pasturelands—four towns.

²⁵From half the tribe of Manasseh they received Taanach and Gath Rimmon, together with their pasturelands—two towns.

²⁶All these ten towns and their pasturelands were given to the rest of the Kohathite clans.

²⁷The Levite clans of the Gershonites were given:

from the half-tribe of Manasseh,

Golan in Bashan (a city of refuge for one accused of murder) and Be Eshtarah, together with their pasturelands—two towns;

Were these towns standing vacant? (21:3)

No. Some cities were occupied by Israelites, some by Canaanites (see 18:3). The Canaanites would have been forcibly evicted just as they had been removed from other occupied towns.

Why keep mentioning the towns with their pasturelands? (21:3–42)

See *Why were pasturelands specifically given with towns?* (1 Chron. 6:76)

City of refuge (21:13)

See *Cities of refuge* (20:2). Also see *How did the judicial process work?* (Num. 35:24–25).

28from the tribe of Issachar,
Kishion, Daberath, 29Jarmuth and En Gannim, together with their pasturelands—four towns;
30from the tribe of Asher,
Mishal, Abdon, 31Helkath and Rehob, together with
their pasturelands—four towns;
32from the tribe of Naphtali,
Kedesh in Galilee (a city of refuge for one accused of
murder), Hammoth Dor and Kartan, together with
their pasturelands—three towns.
33All the towns of the Gershonite clans were thirteen, together with their pasturelands.

34The Merarite clans (the rest of the LevitesD) were given:
from the tribe of Zebulun,
Jokneam, Kartah, 35Dimnah and Nahalal, together
with their pasturelands—four towns;
36from the tribe of Reuben,
Bezer, Jahaz, 37Kedemoth and Mephaath, together
with their pasturelands—four towns;
38from the tribe of Gad,
Ramoth in Gilead (a city of refuge for one accused of
murder), Mahanaim, 39Heshbon and Jazer, together
with their pasturelands—four towns in all.
40All the towns allotted to the Merarite clans, who were
the rest of the Levites, were twelve.

41The towns of the Levites in the territory held by the
Israelites were forty-eight in all, together with their pasturelands. 42Each of these towns had pasturelands surrounding it; this was true for all these towns.

43So the LORD gave Israel all the land he had sworn to
give their forefathers, and they took possession of it and
settled there. 44The LORD gave them rest on every side,
just as he had sworn to their forefathers. Not one of their
enemies withstood them; the LORD handed all their enemies over to them. 45Not one of all the LORD's good promises to the house of Israel failed; every one was fulfilled.

Eastern Tribes Return Home

22 Then Joshua summoned the Reubenites, the Gadites and the half-tribe of Manasseh 2and said to
them, "You have done all that Moses the servant of the
LORD commanded, and you have obeyed me in everything
I commanded. 3For a long time now—to this very day—
you have not deserted your brothers but have carried out
the mission the LORD your God gave you. 4Now that the
LORD your God has given your brothers rest as he promised, return to your homes in the land that Moses the servant of the LORD gave you on the other side of the Jordan.
5But be very careful to keep the commandment and the
law that Moses the servant of the LORD gave you: to love
the LORD your God, to walk in all his ways, to obey his
commands, to hold fast to him and to serve him with all
your heart and all your soulD."

6Then Joshua blessed them and sent them away, and
they went to their homes. 7(To the half-tribe of Manasseh
Moses had given land in Bashan, and to the other half of
the tribe Joshua gave land on the west side of the Jordan
with their brothers.) When Joshua sent them home, he
blessed them, 8saying, "Return to your homes with your
great wealth—with large herds of livestock, with silver,
gold, bronze and iron, and a great quantity of clothing—
and divide with your brothers the plunderD from your
enemies."

How could it be said that the LORD handed all their enemies over to them? (21:44)
God offered the land to the Israelites, to take little by little. Israel, however, failed to take all God had provided. The Lord's promise was as good as the deed: he handed their enemies over to them. It's just that they didn't act on his promise.

How long did they fight the campaign? (22:3)
About seven years. The division of the land and assignment of the cities seems to have oc-curred at the same time as Caleb's request (14:10).

Why were the Israelites so quick to go to war over an altar? (22:10–12)

The altar was interpreted to be a threat to the altar of the Lord in Shiloh (vv. 16,29). Ancient Israel couldn't risk divided loyalties. The Israelites felt that if the tribes east of the Jordan departed from the Lord, God would judge all the tribes of Israel (vv. 16–18).

What was the *sin of Peor* and why had the Israelites not yet been cleansed from it? (22:17)

The Israelites had committed sexual immorality with the people of Moab and Midian and had worshiped the Baal of Peor with them (Num. 25:1–3). By admitting they were not yet cleansed, the people acknowledged that the resulting plague had not removed their tendency to sin. Plagues could cause the people to fear the Lord, but plagues could not change sinful hearts into righteous hearts.

Why did they repeat God's names? (22:22)

To show their deep emotion in calling on God as a witness to their innocence. All three names highlighted different aspects of God's attributes including his power as well as his personal convenant with them.

Why did they think the Jordan might one day mark the border of the Lord's territory? (22:25)

The Jordan was a natural border between the eastern tribes (Reuben, Gad and the half-tribe of Manasseh) and the western tribes (13:8). The eastern tribes were afraid future generations of the more numerous western tribes might assume that God had established this border as a limit on his territory.

9So the Reubenites, the Gadites and the half-tribe of Manasseh left the Israelites at Shiloh in Canaan to return to Gilead, their own land, which they had acquired in accordance with the command of the LORD through Moses. **10**When they came to Geliloth near the Jordan in the land of Canaan, the Reubenites, the Gadites and the half-tribe of Manasseh built an imposing altar there by the Jordan. **11**And when the Israelites heard that they had built the altar on the border of Canaan at Geliloth near the Jordan on the Israelite side, **12**the whole assembly of Israel gathered at Shiloh to go to war against them.

13So the Israelites sent Phinehas son of Eleazar, the priest[D], to the land of Gilead—to Reuben, Gad and the half-tribe of Manasseh. **14**With him they sent ten of the chief men, one for each of the tribes of Israel, each the head of a family division among the Israelite clans.

15When they went to Gilead—to Reuben, Gad and the half-tribe of Manasseh—they said to them: **16**"The whole assembly of the LORD says: 'How could you break faith with the God of Israel like this? How could you turn away from the LORD and build yourselves an altar in rebellion against him now? **17**Was not the sin of Peor enough for us? Up to this very day we have not cleansed ourselves from that sin, even though a plague fell on the community of the LORD! **18**And are you now turning away from the LORD?

" 'If you rebel against the LORD today, tomorrow he will be angry with the whole community of Israel. **19**If the land you possess is defiled, come over to the LORD's land, where the LORD's tabernacle[D] stands, and share the land with us. But do not rebel against the LORD or against us by building an altar for yourselves, other than the altar of the LORD our God. **20**When Achan son of Zerah acted unfaithfully regarding the devoted things,[a] did not wrath come upon the whole community of Israel? He was not the only one who died for his sin.' "

21Then Reuben, Gad and the half-tribe of Manasseh replied to the heads of the clans of Israel: **22**"The Mighty One, God, the LORD! The Mighty One, God, the LORD! He knows! And let Israel know! If this has been in rebellion or disobedience to the LORD, do not spare us this day. **23**If we have built our own altar to turn away from the LORD and to offer burnt offerings[D] and grain offerings[D], or to sacrifice[D] fellowship offerings[Db] on it, may the LORD himself call us to account.

24"No! We did it for fear that some day your descendants might say to ours, 'What do you have to do with the LORD, the God of Israel? **25**The LORD has made the Jordan a boundary between us and you—you Reubenites and Gadites! You have no share in the LORD.' So your descendants might cause ours to stop fearing the LORD.

26"That is why we said, 'Let us get ready and build an altar—but not for burnt offerings or sacrifices.' **27**On the contrary, it is to be a witness between us and you and the generations that follow, that we will worship the LORD at his sanctuary with our burnt offerings, sacrifices and fellowship offerings. Then in the future your descendants will not be able to say to ours, 'You have no share in the LORD.'

28"And we said, 'If they ever say this to us, or to our

[a]20 The Hebrew term refers to the irrevocable giving over of things or persons to the LORD, often by totally destroying them.
[b]23 Traditionally *peace offerings*; also in verse 27

descendants, we will answer: Look at the replica of the LORD's altar, which our fathers built, not for burnt offerings[D] and sacrifices[D], but as a witness between us and you.'

²⁹"Far be it from us to rebel against the LORD and turn away from him today by building an altar for burnt offerings, grain offerings and sacrifices, other than the altar of the LORD our God that stands before his tabernacle[D]."

³⁰When Phinehas the priest[D] and the leaders of the community—the heads of the clans of the Israelites—heard what Reuben, Gad and Manasseh had to say, they were pleased. ³¹And Phinehas son of Eleazar, the priest, said to Reuben, Gad and Manasseh, "Today we know that the LORD is with us, because you have not acted unfaithfully toward the LORD in this matter. Now you have rescued the Israelites from the LORD's hand."

³²Then Phinehas son of Eleazar, the priest, and the leaders returned to Canaan from their meeting with the Reubenites and Gadites in Gilead and reported to the Israelites. ³³They were glad to hear the report and praised God. And they talked no more about going to war against them to devastate the country where the Reubenites and the Gadites lived.

³⁴And the Reubenites and the Gadites gave the altar this name: A Witness Between Us that the LORD is God.

Joshua's Farewell to the Leaders

23 After a long time had passed and the LORD had given Israel rest from all their enemies around them, Joshua, by then old and well advanced in years, ²summoned all Israel—their elders, leaders, judges and officials—and said to them: "I am old and well advanced in years. ³You yourselves have seen everything the LORD your God has done to all these nations for your sake; it was the LORD your God who fought for you. ⁴Remember how I have allotted as an inheritance for your tribes all the land of the nations that remain—the nations I conquered—between the Jordan and the Great Sea[a] in the west. ⁵The LORD your God himself will drive them out of your way. He will push them out before you, and you will take possession of their land, as the LORD your God promised you.

⁶"Be very strong; be careful to obey all that is written in the Book of the Law of Moses, without turning aside to the right or to the left. ⁷Do not associate with these nations that remain among you; do not invoke the names of their gods or swear by them. You must not serve them or bow down to them. ⁸But you are to hold fast to the LORD your God, as you have until now.

⁹"The LORD has driven out before you great and powerful nations; to this day no one has been able to withstand you. ¹⁰One of you routs a thousand, because the LORD your God fights for you, just as he promised. ¹¹So be very careful to love the LORD your God.

¹²"But if you turn away and ally yourselves with the survivors of these nations that remain among you and if you intermarry with them and associate with them, ¹³then you may be sure that the LORD your God will no longer drive out these nations before you. Instead, they will become snares and traps for you, whips on your

a4 That is, the Mediterranean

How could Joshua say that some nations remained if he had indeed conquered them? (23:4)
The land as a whole had been conquered, but individual pockets of resistance remained. See *What were these seven tribes waiting for?* (18:3).

Snares and traps (23:13)
Traps usually captured birds and other wild animals by entangling them in nets. Snares sprang shut with flexible branches or ropes which someone pulled. The terms, often used interchangeably, illustrated how Israel was entangled with the idols and affairs of foreign nations, a condition that would lead to destruction.

Thorns in your eyes (23:13)
Before land could be used for crops, it had to be cleared of thistles and thorns. In the process, branches and thorns could easily scratch a person, and eyes would be especially sensitive. Because they didn't clear the Canaanites from the land, the Israelites lost their ability to "see" clearly. Unable to distinguish right from wrong, they stumbled and fell into sin.

backs and thorns in your eyes, until you perish from this good land, which the LORD your God has given you. **14**"Now I am about to go the way of all the earth. You know with all your heart and soul[D] that not one of all the good promises the LORD your God gave you has failed. Every promise has been fulfilled; not one has failed. **15**But just as every good promise of the LORD your God has come true, so the LORD will bring on you all the evil he has threatened, until he has destroyed you from this good land he has given you. **16**If you violate the covenant[D] of the LORD your God, which he commanded you, and go and serve other gods and bow down to them, the LORD's anger will burn against you, and you will quickly perish from the good land he has given you."

The Covenant Renewed at Shechem

24 Then Joshua assembled all the tribes of Israel at Shechem. He summoned the elders, leaders, judges and officials of Israel, and they presented themselves before God.

2Joshua said to all the people, "This is what the LORD, the God of Israel, says: 'Long ago your forefathers, including Terah the father of Abraham and Nahor, lived beyond the River[a] and worshiped other gods. **3**But I took your father Abraham from the land beyond the River and led him throughout Canaan and gave him many descendants. I gave him Isaac, **4**and to Isaac I gave Jacob and Esau. I assigned the hill country of Seir to Esau, but Jacob and his sons went down to Egypt.

5" 'Then I sent Moses and Aaron, and I afflicted[D] the Egyptians by what I did there, and I brought you out. **6**When I brought your fathers out of Egypt, you came to the sea, and the Egyptians pursued them with chariots and horsemen[b] as far as the Red Sea.[c] **7**But they cried to the LORD for help, and he put darkness between you and the Egyptians; he brought the sea over them and covered

---

a2 That is, the Euphrates; also in verses 3, 14 and 15   b6 Or charioteers   c6 Hebrew Yam Suph; that is, Sea of Reeds

---

Why is punishment from God described as evil? (23:15)

God's punishment is just. People bring dire consequences upon themselves when they indulge in wicked behavior. The Lord threatened such consequences—"evil" from the Israelites' perspective—if they failed to keep their part of the covenant (see Lev. 26:14–33; Deut. 28:15–68).

Why would Israelites be tempted by other gods? (23:7)

Although blessed by God as his chosen people, the Israelites seemed to be infatuated with idols and false gods. Several factors probably made such idolatry attractive to them:

(1) Idols were physical objects that could be seen (Lev. 26:1). Israel's God, on the other hand, was unseen. See *Why did the Israelites long for gods they could see?* (Exodus 32:1). (2) Idols could be carried and controlled and confined. Israel's God, however, was an awesome and mysterious God who could not be manipulated by his people. He "moved" when and where he wanted. (3) Foreign gods were thought to have power over crops, a prime concern to the Israelites. The people were superstitious and didn't want to risk their harvest by offending the gods. (4) Some foreign gods were believed to give fertility to the womb. The worship of these gods involved sacred prostitution (1 Kings 14:24) and other sexually immoral practices, which would have appealed to the sensual desires of the Israelites. The Israelites may have concluded that it was better to indulge in these pleasurable activities than to displease the gods of fertility. (5) Idol worship was a cultural norm. The Israelites often found it easier to join in local customs than go against them.

them. You saw with your own eyes what I did to the Egyptians. Then you lived in the desert for a long time.

8" 'I brought you to the land of the Amorites who lived east of the Jordan. They fought against you, but I gave them into your hands. I destroyed them from before you, and you took possession of their land. 9When Balak son of Zippor, the king of Moab, prepared to fight against Israel, he sent for Balaam son of Beor to put a curse on you. 10But I would not listen to Balaam, so he blessed you again and again, and I delivered you out of his hand.

11" 'Then you crossed the Jordan and came to Jericho.D. The citizens of Jericho fought against you, as did also the Amorites, Perizzites, Canaanites, Hittites, Girgashites, Hivites and Jebusites, but I gave them into your hands. 12I sent the hornet ahead of you, which drove them out before you—also the two Amorite kings. You did not do it with your own sword and bow. 13So I gave you a land on which you did not toil and cities you did not build; and you live in them and eat from vineyards and olive groves that you did not plant.'

14"Now fear the LORD and serve him with all faithfulness. Throw away the gods your forefathers worshiped beyond the River and in Egypt, and serve the LORD. 15But if serving the LORD seems undesirable to you, then choose for yourselves this day whom you will serve, whether the gods your forefathers served beyond the River, or the gods of the Amorites, in whose land you are living. But as for me and my household, we will serve the LORD."

16Then the people answered, "Far be it from us to forsake the LORD to serve other gods! 17It was the LORD our God himself who brought us and our fathers up out of Egypt, from that land of slavery, and performed those great signs before our eyes. He protected us on our entire journey and among all the nations through which we traveled. 18And the LORD drove out before us all the nations, including the Amorites, who lived in the land. We too will serve the LORD, because he is our God."

19Joshua said to the people, "You are not able to serve the LORD. He is a holy God; he is a jealous God. He will not forgive your rebellion and your sins. 20If you forsake the LORD and serve foreign gods, he will turn and bring disaster on you and make an end of you, after he has been good to you."

21But the people said to Joshua, "No! We will serve the LORD."

22Then Joshua said, "You are witnesses against yourselves that you have chosen to serve the LORD."

"Yes, we are witnesses," they replied.

23"Now then," said Joshua, "throw away the foreign gods that are among you and yield your hearts to the LORD, the God of Israel."

24And the people said to Joshua, "We will serve the LORD our God and obey him."

25On that day Joshua made a covenantD for the people, and there at Shechem he drew up for them decrees and laws. 26And Joshua recorded these things in the Book of the Law of God. Then he took a large stone and set it up there under the oak near the holy place of the LORD.

27"See!" he said to all the people. "This stone will be a witness against us. It has heard all the words the LORD has said to us. It will be a witness against you if you are untrue to your God."

SCRIPTURE LINK (24:9) *He sent for Balaam . . . to put a curse on you*
See Num. 22.

Did God literally send hornets? (24:12)
Perhaps. Hornets may have made living in the land extremely difficult. But the term could refer to Egyptian troops, since the bee or hornet was one of Pharaoh's symbols. The Egyptians raided Canaan regularly and could have weakened the nation prior to the Israelite invasion. Also see *Did God really send hornets?* (Exodus 23:28) and *How could the hornet finish off the remaining enemy?* (Deut. 7:20).

Why had the Israelites kept the gods of their forefathers? (24:14,23)
As a whole, Israel had clung to the Lord (23:8). But there were many cases of spiritual infidelity in their long history, even as recently as their time in Egypt (see Ezek. 20:7–8; 23:3,8). They were undoubtedly influenced by their idol-worshiping neighbors. Perhaps they wanted something to fall back on in case the Lord didn't come through for them.

Why was Joshua so negative with the people? (24:19)
Joshua rebuked them for their hasty, naive response (vv. 16–18). He wanted the people to be careful about making flippant promises. Joshua wanted them to see their spiritual weakness and inability to please Israel's holy and jealous God. He wanted them to recognize that they needed to depend on him.

Why did the people need new decrees and laws? (24:25)
They didn't. Joshua did not add to the Law (in violation of Deut. 4:2; 12:32) by changing it in any way. Though not precisely spelled out, this covenant apparently reconfirmed the law (Deut. 6:5–6) and reinforced the greatest commandment (see Jesus' comments in Mark 12:28–30).

The Book of the Law of God (24:26)
This probably refers to the Law of Moses.

The holy place of the LORD (24:26)
Perhaps the site of an old altar that stood in Shechem near the oak tree. The same oak appears in Gen. 12:6; 35:4; Deut. 11:30 and Judges 9:6,37. It was located between Mount Ebal and Mount Gerezim near the modern city of Nablus (see **Map 4** at the back of this Bible).

Buried in the Promised Land

28Then Joshua sent the people away, each to his own inheritance.

29After these things, Joshua son of Nun, the servant of the LORD, died at the age of a hundred and ten. **30**And they buried him in the land of his inheritance, at Timnath Serah[a] in the hill country of Ephraim, north of Mount Gaash.

31Israel served the LORD throughout the lifetime of Joshua and of the elders who outlived him and who had experienced everything the LORD had done for Israel.

32And Joseph's bones, which the Israelites had brought up from Egypt, were buried at Shechem in the tract of land that Jacob bought for a hundred pieces of silver[b] from the sons of Hamor, the father of Shechem. This became the inheritance of Joseph's descendants.

33And Eleazar son of Aaron died and was buried at Gibeah, which had been allotted to his son Phinehas in the hill country of Ephraim.

SCRIPTURE LINK (24:32) *Joseph's bones*

For background on why the Israelites had been carrying Joseph's bones around all these years, read Gen. 50:24–26 and Exodus 13:19.

---

[a]30 Also known as *Timnath Heres* (see Judges 2:9) [b]32 Hebrew *hundred kesitahs*; a kesitah was a unit of money of unknown weight and value.

JUDGES

Why read this book?

Judges is filled with sensational stories, as exciting as any of today's headlines. For sheer melodrama—gruesome murders, sexual exploits, superhuman feats of strength, a bizarre mutilation—no tabloid can offer you more. But beneath the sensational stories are eternal lessons you'll never find in a tabloid. The book of Judges shows what can happen when a society slides into moral anarchy. But it also shows God's merciful deliverance when people cry out to him in repentance.

Who wrote this book?

Tradition credits the prophet Samuel, but we don't know for sure who wrote it. The author may have been one of Samuel's associates, perhaps another prophet.

Why was it written?

To recount the stories of Israel's heroes—called judges—and give the nation's history prior to the time it became a kingdom. Six of the 12 judges, one a woman, are described in some detail. More than legal advisers, judges were local leaders who achieved national prominence because of their military victories.

When was it written?

Perhaps as many as 380 years after the events it describes—probably during the days of Israel's first kings, Saul or David (around 1000 B.C.), but before David captured Jerusalem (1:21). The book covers a period of about 350 years.

To whom was it written?

To the people of Israel.

What to look for in Judges:

The repeated cycles of Israel's relationship with God: (1) God's blessing, (2) spiritual complacency, (3) idolatry, (4) suffering at the hands of enemies, (5) repentance and (6) God's deliverance through one of the judges. On the negative side, this book shows the human tendency to sin. On the positive side, it describes God's unrelenting love.

When did these things happen?

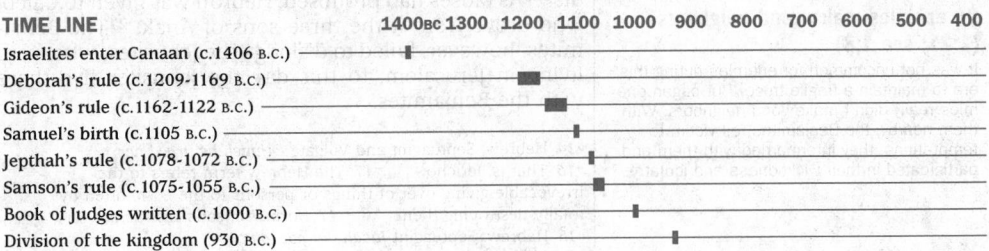

TIME LINE	1400BC	1300	1200	1100	1000	900	800	700	600	500	400
Israelites enter Canaan (c.1406 B.C.)											
Deborah's rule (c.1209-1169 B.C.)											
Gideon's rule (c.1162-1122 B.C.)											
Samuel's birth (c.1105 B.C.)											
Jepthah's rule (c.1078-1072 B.C.)											
Samson's rule (c.1075-1055 B.C.)											
Book of Judges written (c.1000 B.C.)											
Division of the kingdom (930 B.C.)											

Judah's Fight for Land (1:4)

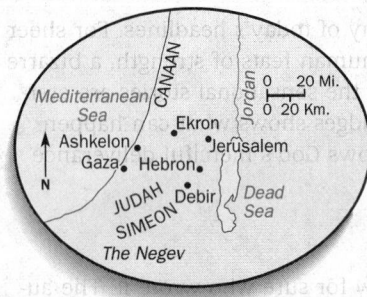

Adoni-Bezek (1:5)
Means *the lord of Bezek*.

Why cut off the king's thumbs and big toes? (1:6)
Judah's soldiers wanted to humiliate and cripple the conquered king. Without thumbs, he would no longer be able to wield a weapon. Without big toes, he would no longer be able to run in battle. This sort of treatment of war prisoners was common among many nations at that time. The defeated king accepted his fate philosophically (1:7). He knew his punishment was no worse than what he had done to those he had conquered.

Why give your daughter as a trophy of war? (1:12–13)
Caleb was essentially hiring someone to lead a victorious attack. His offer stemmed from the customs of the time. Since women were valued for their work, a married daughter meant a worker lost. So a groom would compensate the bride's family for their loss by paying a bride-price and finalizing the marriage contract. By waiving the bride-price for his daughter, he gave any man the chance to gain a wife with heroism rather than wealth. Also see **Were Israelite girls treated like property?** (Joshua 15:17).

Iron chariots (1:19)
See article: **What was so frightening about iron chariots?** (Joshua 17:16).

Do enemies make good neighbors? (1:21; see 1:8)
It was not uncommon for enemies during this era to maintain a fragile truce. But pagan enemies really didn't make good neighbors. With them nearby, the Benjamites fell victim to temptations: they intermarried with them and participated in their wickedness and idolatry.

Israel Fights the Remaining Canaanites

1 After the death[D] of Joshua, the Israelites asked the LORD, "Who will be the first to go up and fight for us against the Canaanites?"

2The LORD answered, "Judah is to go; I have given the land into their hands."

3Then the men of Judah said to the Simeonites their brothers, "Come up with us into the territory allotted to us, to fight against the Canaanites. We in turn will go with you into yours." So the Simeonites went with them.

4When Judah attacked, the LORD gave the Canaanites and Perizzites into their hands and they struck down ten thousand men at Bezek. 5It was there that they found Adoni-Bezek and fought against him, putting to rout the Canaanites and Perizzites. 6Adoni-Bezek fled, but they chased him and caught him, and cut off his thumbs and big toes.

7Then Adoni-Bezek said, "Seventy kings with their thumbs and big toes cut off have picked up scraps under my table. Now God has paid me back for what I did to them." They brought him to Jerusalem[D], and he died there.

8The men of Judah attacked Jerusalem also and took it. They put the city to the sword and set it on fire.

9After that, the men of Judah went down to fight against the Canaanites living in the hill country, the Negev[D] and the western foothills. 10They advanced against the Canaanites living in Hebron (formerly called Kiriath Arba) and defeated Sheshai, Ahiman and Talmai.

11From there they advanced against the people living in Debir (formerly called Kiriath Sepher). 12And Caleb said, "I will give my daughter Acsah in marriage to the man who attacks and captures Kiriath Sepher." 13Othniel son of Kenaz, Caleb's younger brother, took it; so Caleb gave his daughter Acsah to him in marriage.

14One day when she came to Othniel, she urged him[a] to ask her father for a field. When she got off her donkey, Caleb asked her, "What can I do for you?"

15She replied, "Do me a special favor. Since you have given me land in the Negev, give me also springs of water." Then Caleb gave her the upper and lower springs.

16The descendants of Moses' father-in-law, the Kenite, went up from the City of Palms[b] with the men of Judah to live among the people of the Desert of Judah in the Negev near Arad.

17Then the men of Judah went with the Simeonites their brothers and attacked the Canaanites living in Zephath, and they totally destroyed[c] the city. Therefore it was called Hormah.[d] 18The men of Judah also took[e] Gaza, Ashkelon and Ekron—each city with its territory.

19The LORD was with the men of Judah. They took possession of the hill country, but they were unable to drive the people from the plains, because they had iron chariots. 20As Moses had promised, Hebron was given to Caleb, who drove from it the three sons of Anak. 21The Benjamites, however, failed to dislodge the Jebusites, who were living in Jerusalem; to this day the Jebusites live there with the Benjamites.

[a]14 Hebrew; Septuagint and Vulgate *Othniel, he urged her*
[b]16 That is, Jericho   [c]17 The Hebrew term refers to the irrevocable giving over of things or persons to the LORD, often by totally destroying them.   [d]17 *Hormah* means *destruction*.
[e]18 Hebrew; Septuagint *Judah did not take*

22Now the house of Joseph attacked Bethel, and the LORD was with them. **23**When they sent men to spy out Bethel (formerly called Luz), **24**the spies saw a man coming out of the city and they said to him, "Show us how to get into the city and we will see that you are treated well." **25**So he showed them, and they put the city to the sword but spared the man and his whole family. **26**He then went to the land of the Hittites, where he built a city and called it Luz, which is its name to this day.

27But Manasseh did not drive out the people of Beth Shan or Taanach or Dor or Ibleam or Megiddo and their surrounding settlements, for the Canaanites were determined to live in that land. **28**When Israel became strong, they pressed the Canaanites into forced labor but never drove them out completely. **29**Nor did Ephraim drive out the Canaanites living in Gezer, but the Canaanites continued to live there among them. **30**Neither did Zebulun drive out the Canaanites living in Kitron or Nahalol, who remained among them; but they did subject them to forced labor. **31**Nor did Asher drive out those living in Acco or Sidon or Ahlab or Aczib or Helbah or Aphek or Rehob, **32**and because of this the people of Asher lived among the Canaanite inhabitants of the land. **33**Neither did Naphtali drive out those living in Beth Shemesh or Beth Anath; but the Naphtalites too lived among the Canaanite inhabitants of the land, and those living in Beth Shemesh and Beth Anath became forced laborers for them. **34**The Amorites confined the Danites to the hill country, not allowing them to come down into the plain. **35**And the Amorites were determined also to hold out in Mount Heres, Aijalon and Shaalbim, but when the power of the house of Joseph increased, they too were pressed into forced labor. **36**The boundary of the Amorites was from Scorpion[a] Pass to Sela and beyond.

The Angel of the LORD at Bokim

2 The angel of the LORD went up from Gilgal to Bokim and said, "I brought you up out of Egypt and led you into the land that I swore to give to your forefathers. I said, 'I will never break my covenant[D] with you, **2**and you shall not make a covenant with the people of this land, but you shall break down their altars.' Yet you have disobeyed me. Why have you done this? **3**Now therefore I tell you that I will not drive them out before you; they will be ₍thorns₎ in your sides and their gods will be a snare to you."

4When the angel of the LORD had spoken these things to all the Israelites, the people wept aloud, **5**and they called that place Bokim.[b] There they offered sacrifices[D] to the LORD.

Disobedience and Defeat

6After Joshua had dismissed the Israelites, they went to take possession of the land, each to his own inheritance. **7**The people served the LORD throughout the lifetime of Joshua and of the elders who outlived him and who had seen all the great things the LORD had done for Israel.

8Joshua son of Nun, the servant of the LORD, died at the age of a hundred and ten. **9**And they buried him in the land of his inheritance, at Timnath Heres[c] in the hill country of Ephraim, north of Mount Gaash.

Why make slaves of the Canaanites? (1:28)

Probably as a matter of convenience. God had commanded Israel to drive the Canaanites out completely (Joshua 1:4; 3:10; 23:5,12–13). Instead of obeying God, however, the Israelites chose a relative life of ease—acquiring a slave force to do their work for them. The final conquest was not achieved until King David's time. There was a hidden price for enslaving the Canaanites: assimilated into northern Israel, they accelerated Israel's slide into idolatry.

What kind of angel spoke to the nation? (2:1,4)

Some say this was a manifestation of God himself. See *Was this an angel or the Lord?* (6:11). Others think this *angel* may have been a human *messenger,* such as Phinehas the high priest or perhaps a prophet.

How could a whole generation not know the Lord? (2:10)

The Israelites had failed to teach their children. God intended for parents to pass his laws and moral values along to the next generation (Deut. 6:4–9). Gradually influenced by the surrounding paganism, however, the Israelites surrendered to the prevailing cultural and social values, despite the angel's explicit warning.

Why did God decide to stop helping Israel? (2:20–21)

God worked with Israel on the basis of a covenant, or agreement. It specified certain conditions the Israelites had to follow if they wanted to receive God's promised blessings. They could expect life and prosperity or death and destruction, depending on their response to God's commands (Deut. 30:16). God didn't change his mind; he merely fulfilled the covenant.

Why did God test Israel? (2:22)

God's test of Israel was an ongoing examination. It was not a once and done event, like a final exam at the end of a course. Each new test brought a new opportunity to love and serve God. He knew their loyalty would waver over the course of time and from one generation to the next.

Why did God want them to learn warfare? (3:2)

The Lord taught warfare to an inexperienced generation (1) to help them better protect themselves and (2) to test their faith and obedience. Enemies who forced them to fight gave them opportunity to see God's promises at work. In those circumstances, it would have been foolish not to prepare for combat.

¹⁰After that whole generation had been gathered to their fathers, another generation grew up, who knew neither the LORD nor what he had done for Israel. ¹¹Then the Israelites did evil in the eyes of the LORD and served the Baals.ᴰ ¹²They forsook the LORD, the God of their fathers, who had brought them out of Egypt. They followed and worshiped various gods of the peoples around them. They provoked the LORD to anger ¹³because they forsook him and served Baal and the Ashtoreths. ¹⁴In his anger against Israel the LORD handed them over to raiders who plunderedᴰ them. He sold them to their enemies all around, whom they were no longer able to resist. ¹⁵Whenever Israel went out to fight, the hand of the LORD was against them to defeat them, just as he had sworn to them. They were in great distress.

¹⁶Then the LORD raised up judges,ᵃ who saved them out of the hands of these raiders. ¹⁷Yet they would not listen to their judges but prostituted themselves to other gods and worshiped them. Unlike their fathers, they quickly turned from the way in which their fathers had walked, the way of obedience to the LORD's commands. ¹⁸Whenever the LORD raised up a judge for them, he was with the judge and saved them out of the hands of their enemies as long as the judge lived; for the LORD had compassion on them as they groaned under those who oppressed and afflictedᴰ them. ¹⁹But when the judge died, the people returned to ways even more corrupt than those of their fathers, following other gods and serving and worshiping them. They refused to give up their evil practices and stubborn ways.

²⁰Therefore the LORD was very angry with Israel and said, "Because this nation has violated the covenantᴰ that I laid down for their forefathers and has not listened to me, ²¹I will no longer drive out before them any of the nations Joshua left when he died. ²²I will use them to test Israel and see whether they will keep the way of the LORD and walk in it as their forefathers did." ²³The LORD had allowed those nations to remain; he did not drive them out at once by giving them into the hands of Joshua.

3 These are the nations the LORD left to test all those Israelites who had not experienced any of the wars in Canaan ²(he did this only to teach warfare to the descendants of the Israelites who had not had previous battle experience): ³the five rulers of the Philistines, all the Canaanites, the Sidonians, and the Hivites living in the Lebanon mountains from Mount Baal Hermon to Leboᵇ Hamath. ⁴They were left to test the Israelites to see whether they would obey the LORD's commands, which he had given their forefathers through Moses.

⁵The Israelites lived among the Canaanites, Hittites, Amorites, Perizzites, Hivites and Jebusites. ⁶They took their daughters in marriage and gave their own daughters to their sons, and served their gods.

Othniel

⁷The Israelites did evil in the eyes of the LORD; they forgot the LORD their God and served the Baals and the Asherahs. ⁸The anger of the LORD burned against Israel so that he sold them into the hands of Cushan-Rishathaim king of Aram Naharaim,ᶜ to whom the Israelites were subject for eight years. ⁹But when they cried out to the

ᵃ16 Or leaders; similarly in verses 17-19   ᵇ3 Or to the entrance to
ᶜ8 That is, Northwest Mesopotamia

LORD, he raised up for them a deliverer, Othniel son of Kenaz, Caleb's younger brother, who saved them. **10**The Spirit of the LORD came upon him, so that he became Israel's judge*a* and went to war. The LORD gave Cushan-Rishathaim king of Aram into the hands of Othniel, who overpowered him. **11**So the land had peace*b* for forty years, until Othniel son of Kenaz died.

Ehud

12Once again the Israelites did evil in the eyes of the LORD, and because they did this evil the LORD gave Eglon king of Moab power over Israel. **13**Getting the Ammonites and Amalekites to join him, Eglon came and attacked Israel, and they took possession of the City of Palms.*b* **14**The Israelites were subject to Eglon king of Moab for eighteen years.

15Again the Israelites cried out to the LORD, and he gave them a deliverer—Ehud, a left-handed man, the son of Gera the Benjamite. The Israelites sent him with tribute to Eglon king of Moab. **16**Now Ehud had made a double-edged sword about a foot and a half*c* long, which he strapped to his right thigh under his clothing. **17**He presented the tribute to Eglon king of Moab, who was a very fat man. **18**After Ehud had presented the tribute, he sent on their way the men who had carried it. **19**At the idols*d* near Gilgal he himself turned back and said, "I have a secret message for you, O king."

The king said, "Quiet!" And all his attendants left him.

20Ehud then approached him while he was sitting alone in the upper room of his summer palace*e* and said, "I have a message from God for you." As the king rose from his seat, **21**Ehud reached with his left hand, drew the sword from his right thigh and plunged it into the king's belly. **22**Even the handle sank in after the blade, which came out his back. Ehud did not pull the sword out, and the fat closed in over it. **23**Then Ehud went out to the porch*f*; he shut the doors of the upper room behind him and locked them.

24After he had gone, the servants came and found the doors of the upper room locked. They said, "He must be relieving himself in the inner room of the house." **25**They waited to the point of embarrassment, but when he did not open the doors of the room, they took a key and unlocked them. There they saw their lord fallen to the floor, dead.

26While they waited, Ehud got away. He passed by the idols and escaped to Seirah. **27**When he arrived there, he blew a trumpet in the hill country of Ephraim, and the Israelites went down with him from the hills, with him leading them.

28"Follow me," he ordered, "for the LORD has given Moab, your enemy, into your hands." So they followed him down and, taking possession of the fords of the Jordan that led to Moab, they allowed no one to cross over. **29**At that time they struck down about ten thousand Moabites, all vigorous and strong; not a man escaped. **30**That day Moab was made subject to Israel, and the land had peace for eighty years.

---

a10 Or *leader*   *b13* That is, Jericho   *c16* Hebrew *a cubit* (about 0.5 meter)   *d19* Or *the stone quarries;* also in verse 26
e20 The meaning of the Hebrew for this phrase is uncertain.
f23 The meaning of the Hebrew for this word is uncertain.

What were the signs that the Spirit had come upon Othniel? (3:10)

We can't be sure, but Othniel probably displayed unusual leadership abilities. God equipped Othniel with an extraordinary wisdom, courage and strength that would have been evident to all.

How did the Israelites cry out to the Lord? (3:15)

Together and individually, leaders and people turned to God, although we don't know how widespread this spiritual distress call might have been. Their cry to God was twofold: (1) repentance (forsaking pagan deities) and (2) faith (trusting in and worshiping the true God). It seems their cry was primarily a superficial means to escape oppression, because their dedication did not last.

Idols near Gilgal (3:19)

Some think these stones, sculptured or carved, were much larger than typical pagan idols, and were so prominent that they served as landmarks. Others think they were stone quarries or perhaps a local boundary marker (see 3:26). Still another possibility is that they were the stones set up by Joshua to commemorate the miraculous crossing of the Jordan River (Joshua 4:19–24). See *The Battle of Ai* on page 294.

Can assassination be God's will? (3:21)

The Moabites' oppression was broken and Israel's territory freed because of Ehud's courage and cunning. But we don't have to admire his assassination of Eglon or say that God approved it. Other such distasteful scenes in this book reflect the prevailing wickedness of the times. The stories cannot be used to blame God for evil or to sanction it ourselves.

Shamgar

31After Ehud came Shamgar son of Anath, who struck down six hundred Philistines with an oxgoad. He too saved Israel.

Deborah

4 After Ehud died, the Israelites once again did evil in the eyes of the LORD. **2**So the LORD sold them into the hands of Jabin, a king of Canaan, who reigned in Hazor. The commander of his army was Sisera, who lived in Harosheth Haggoyim. **3**Because he had nine hundred iron chariots and had cruelly oppressed the Israelites for twenty years, they cried to the LORD for help.

4Deborah, a prophetess[D], the wife of Lappidoth, was leading[a] Israel at that time. **5**She held court under the Palm of Deborah between Ramah and Bethel in the hill country of Ephraim, and the Israelites came to her to have their disputes decided. **6**She sent for Barak son of Abinoam from Kedesh in Naphtali and said to him, "The LORD, the God of Israel, commands you: 'Go, take with you ten thousand men of Naphtali and Zebulun and lead the way to Mount Tabor. **7**I will lure Sisera, the commander of Jabin's army, with his chariots and his troops to the Kishon River and give him into your hands.' "

8Barak said to her, "If you go with me, I will go; but if you don't go with me, I won't go."

9"Very well," Deborah said, "I will go with you. But because of the way you are going about this,[b] the honor will not be yours, for the LORD will hand Sisera over to a woman." So Deborah went with Barak to Kedesh, **10**where he summoned Zebulun and Naphtali. Ten thousand men followed him, and Deborah also went with him.

11Now Heber the Kenite had left the other Kenites, the descendants of Hobab, Moses' brother-in-law,[c] and pitched his tent by the great tree in Zaanannim near Kedesh.

12When they told Sisera that Barak son of Abinoam had gone up to Mount Tabor, **13**Sisera gathered together his nine hundred iron chariots and all the men with him, from Harosheth Haggoyim to the Kishon River.

14Then Deborah said to Barak, "Go! This is the day the LORD has given Sisera into your hands. Has not the LORD gone ahead of you?" So Barak went down Mount Tabor, followed by ten thousand men. **15**At Barak's advance, the LORD routed Sisera and all his chariots and army by the sword, and Sisera abandoned his chariot and fled on foot. **16**But Barak pursued the chariots and army as far as Harosheth Haggoyim. All the troops of Sisera fell by the sword; not a man was left.

17Sisera, however, fled on foot to the tent of Jael, the wife of Heber the Kenite, because there were friendly relations between Jabin king of Hazor and the clan of Heber the Kenite.

18Jael went out to meet Sisera and said to him, "Come, my lord, come right in. Don't be afraid." So he entered her tent, and she put a covering over him.

19"I'm thirsty," he said. "Please give me some water." She opened a skin of milk, gave him a drink, and covered him up.

20"Stand in the doorway of the tent," he told her. "If

How did the Lord "sell" his people? (4:2)

The Lord *sold them* by allowing them to be defeated by a pagan tribe. Their enemy's domination left them hopeless and in virtual slavery (see 2:14; 3:8; 10:7; 1 Samuel 12:9). Moses used this graphic phrase himself in his prophetic song (Deut. 32:30). Israel had clearly been warned that God would indeed "sell" them to their enemies if they forsook him.

Deborah Defeats King Jabin (4:2)

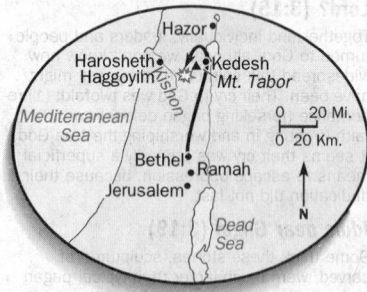

How could a woman be a leader in a patriarchal society? (4:4)

Deborah most likely ascended to prominence because of a power vacuum. With no male leaders stepping forward, Deborah took the initiative. Although it was rare for a woman to do what she did, there was no divine injunction against it (see Miriam, Exodus 15:20, and Huldah, 2 Kings 22:14). In fact, God blessed her for her trust in him, and the people recognized God's hand upon her.

Why did Barak insist that Deborah go along? (4:8)

After twenty years of oppression at the hands of the Canaanites, Barak had reason to be concerned. Deborah, a prophetess, was recognized as one who heard from God. He probably wanted her to come along as insurance that God would go with them and assist them in rebelling against their oppressors.

Why kill an ally? (4:17,21)

Jael knew that her husband Heber, along with the rest of the Kenites, had tried to be friends to both Israel and the Canaanites. But she also knew how wicked Sisera was; perhaps some of her relatives had suffered because of him. She also may have wanted to repay a favor to Deborah or Barak.

---

a4 Traditionally *judging*   *b9* Or *But on the expedition you are undertaking*   *c11* Or *father-in-law*

someone comes by and asks you, 'Is anyone here?' say 'No.' "

²¹But Jael, Heber's wife, picked up a tent peg and a hammer and went quietly to him while he lay fast asleep, exhausted. She drove the peg through his temple into the ground, and he died.

²²Barak came by in pursuit of Sisera, and Jael went out to meet him. "Come," she said, "I will show you the man you're looking for." So he went in with her, and there lay Sisera with the tent peg through his temple—dead.

²³On that day God subdued Jabin, the Canaanite king, before the Israelites. ²⁴And the hand of the Israelites grew stronger and stronger against Jabin, the Canaanite king, until they destroyed him.

The Song of Deborah

5 On that day Deborah and Barak son of Abinoam sang this song:

²"When the princes in Israel take the lead,
    when the people willingly offer themselves—
        praise the LORD!

³"Hear this, you kings! Listen, you rulers!
    I will sing toᵃ the LORD, I will sing;
    I will make music toᵇ the LORD, the God of
        Israel.

⁴"O LORD, when you went out from Seir,
    when you marched from the land of Edomᴰ,
the earth shook, the heavens poured,
    the clouds poured down water.
⁵The mountains quaked before the LORD, the
        One of Sinai,
    before the LORD, the God of Israel.

⁶"In the days of Shamgar son of Anath,
    in the days of Jael, the roads were
        abandoned;
    travelers took to winding paths.
⁷Village lifeᶜ in Israel ceased,
    ceased until I,ᵈ Deborah, arose,
    arose a mother in Israel.
⁸When they chose new gods,
    war came to the city gates,
and not a shield or spear was seen
    among forty thousand in Israel.
⁹My heart is with Israel's princes,
    with the willing volunteers among the
        people.
    Praise the LORD!

¹⁰"You who ride on white donkeys,
    sitting on your saddle blankets,
    and you who walk along the road,
consider ¹¹the voice of the singersᵉ at the
        watering places.
    They recite the righteousᴰ acts of the LORD,
    the righteous acts of his warriorsᶠ in
        Israel.

    "Then the people of the LORD

ᵃ3 Or of   ᵇ3 Or I with song I will praise   ᶜ7 Or Warriors
ᵈ7 Or you   ᵉ11 Or archers; the meaning of the Hebrew for this
word is uncertain.   ᶠ11 Or villagers

Why include a song in a history book? (5:1)

The song of Deborah and Barak was a great celebration of victory intended to inspire praise and adoration for God. It affirmed faith and God's concern for his people. It also taught lessons of national cooperation by commending the tribes that joined in the battle and rebuking those that had not. For people who had suffered 20 years under cruel oppression, the song was a tremendous release. Without books, or any mass media, the song was the best teaching tool available and was often used in Israel's history.

Roads . . . winding paths (5:6)

This offers a clue about difficult and violent times in Israel. Basic communication and travel was disrupted. Commerce was impossible. Those who had to travel would take the back paths to avoid the robbers who commandeered the main roads.

In what way did village life cease? (5:7)

The rampages of the Canaanites threatened farmers who typically lived in small villages near their farmland. Small communities would not have had walls or soldiers to keep out the marauders. Some may have gone into hiding, hoping to farm secluded plots of ground. Others may have sought safety within walled towns. Either way, village life was left in shambles.

What did the Israelites fight with? (5:8)

Part of the Canaanite strategy was to suppress the Israelites by taking all their weapons. Later, Israel's enemies allowed no blacksmiths in the land, preventing them from making spears and swords (1 Samuel 13:19). The song makes it sound like there were no weapons at all in Israel, but that was no doubt a poetic exaggeration, because there were weapons enough to fight the battle at Kishon. However, they probably relied on smaller, concealed weapons, not the larger shields and spears.

went down to the city gates.
¹²'Wake up, wake up, Deborah!
  Wake up, wake up, break out in song!
 Arise, O Barak!
  Take captive your captives, O son of
    Abinoam.'

¹³"Then the men who were left
  came down to the nobles;
 the people of the LORD
  came to me with the mighty.
¹⁴Some came from Ephraim, whose roots were in
    Amalek;
  Benjamin was with the people who followed
    you.
 From Makir captains came down,
  from Zebulun those who bear a
    commander's staff.
¹⁵The princes of Issachar were with Deborah;
  yes, Issachar was with Barak,
  rushing after him into the valley.
 In the districts of Reuben
  there was much searching of heart.
¹⁶Why did you stay among the campfires[a]
  to hear the whistling for the flocks?
 In the districts of Reuben
  there was much searching of heart.
¹⁷Gilead stayed beyond the Jordan.
  And Dan, why did he linger by the ships?
 Asher remained on the coast
  and stayed in his coves.
¹⁸The people of Zebulun risked their very lives;
  so did Naphtali on the heights of the field.

¹⁹"Kings came, they fought;
  the kings of Canaan fought
 at Taanach by the waters of Megiddo,
  but they carried off no silver, no plunder[D].
²⁰From the heavens the stars fought,
  from their courses they fought against Sisera.
²¹The river Kishon swept them away,
  the age-old river, the river Kishon.
  March on, my soul[D]; be strong!
²²Then thundered the horses' hoofs—
  galloping, galloping go his mighty steeds.
²³'Curse Meroz,' said the angel of the LORD.
  'Curse its people bitterly,
 because they did not come to help the LORD,
  to help the LORD against the mighty.'

²⁴"Most blessed of women be Jael,
  the wife of Heber the Kenite,
  most blessed of tent-dwelling women.
²⁵He asked for water, and she gave him milk;
  in a bowl fit for nobles she brought him
    curdled milk.
²⁶Her hand reached for the tent peg,
  her right hand for the workman's hammer.
 She struck Sisera, she crushed his head,
  she shattered and pierced his temple.
²⁷At her feet he sank,
  he fell; there he lay.
 At her feet he sank, he fell;

What did these tribes do? (5:15–17)

Reuben (part of Gilead, the region east of the Jordan), Dan to the south and Asher to the northwest lived some distance from the action. They probably felt relatively secure and preferred to stay home rather than get involved in the battles of others. But that was precisely Deborah's concern. In effect, their disloyalty to fellow Israelites showed that they viewed the tribes of Israel as separate entities rather than as a single nation.

Meroz (5:23)

Perhaps near the Kishon River where the battle was fought. Some think Meroz may have been a Canaanite town that broke an earlier treaty with Manasseh to avoid fighting other Canaanites. The people of Meroz, probably thinking Israel would be defeated, changed their bets to avoid punishment by the Canaanites.

[a] 16 Or saddlebags

where he sank, there he fell—dead.

28"Through the window peered Sisera's mother;
  behind the lattice she cried out,
  'Why is his chariot so long in coming?
  Why is the clatter of his chariots delayed?'
29The wisest of her ladies answer her;
  indeed, she keeps saying to herself,
30'Are they not finding and dividing the spoils:
  a girl or two for each man,
  colorful garments as plunder^D for Sisera,
  colorful garments embroidered,
  highly embroidered garments for my neck—
all this as plunder?'

31"So may all your enemies perish, O LORD!
  But may they who love you be like the sun
  when it rises in its strength."

Then the land had peace^D forty years.

Gideon

6 Again the Israelites did evil in the eyes of the LORD,
and for seven years he gave them into the hands of
the Midianites. ²Because the power of Midian was so oppressive, the Israelites prepared shelters for themselves in
mountain clefts, caves and strongholds^D. ³Whenever the
Israelites planted their crops, the Midianites, Amalekites
and other eastern peoples invaded the country. ⁴They
camped on the land and ruined the crops all the way to
Gaza and did not spare a living thing for Israel, neither
sheep nor cattle nor donkeys. ⁵They came up with their
livestock and their tents like swarms of locusts^D. It was
impossible to count the men and their camels; they invaded the land to ravage it. ⁶Midian so impoverished the Israelites that they cried out to the LORD for help.

⁷When the Israelites cried to the LORD because of Midian, ⁸he sent them a prophet^D, who said, "This is what the
LORD, the God of Israel, says: I brought you up out of
Egypt, out of the land of slavery. ⁹I snatched you from the
power of Egypt and from the hand of all your oppressors.
I drove them from before you and gave you their land. ¹⁰I
said to you, 'I am the LORD your God; do not worship the
gods of the Amorites, in whose land you live.' But you
have not listened to me."

¹¹The angel of the LORD came and sat down under the
oak in Ophrah that belonged to Joash the Abiezrite, where
his son Gideon was threshing wheat in a winepress^D to
keep it from the Midianites. ¹²When the angel of the LORD
appeared to Gideon, he said, "The LORD is with you,
mighty warrior."

¹³"But sir," Gideon replied, "if the LORD is with us, why
has all this happened to us? Where are all his wonders
that our fathers told us about when they said, 'Did not the
LORD bring us up out of Egypt?' But now the LORD has
abandoned us and put us into the hand of Midian."

¹⁴The LORD turned to him and said, "Go in the strength
you have and save Israel out of Midian's hand. Am I not
sending you?"

¹⁵"But Lord,^a" Gideon asked, "how can I save Israel?
My clan is the weakest in Manasseh, and I am the least in
my family."

Why talk about Sisera's mother? (5:28)

This was poetry, not a narrative account. The
singers of this song were unlikely to have any
information about Sisera's mother. But poetically they could express the emotions she was
likely to have felt. This was their way of describing the anguish of their defeated enemies
in contrast to their own exuberant joy.

Why did Midian destroy Israel's crops? (6:4)

This common practice of warfare kept the Israelites in dire straits, constantly scrambling just
to survive. The Midianites wanted Israel to be
too weak to mount a counter-attack. They may
also have used some of the crops for themselves since they lived off the land as semino-
mads.

Was this an angel or the Lord? (6:11,14)

The writer uses both *angel of the LORD* (v. 11)
and *the LORD* (v. 14) interchangeably. The
terms are synonymous in this case. The appearance of God in human or angelic form occurred several times in the Old Testament.
Also, human terms were commonly used to tell
about God's activities and his characteristics.
See *What kind of angel spoke to the nation?*
(2:1).

---

^a15 Or *sir*

16The LORD answered, "I will be with you, and you will strike down all the Midianites together."

17Gideon replied, "If now I have found favor in your eyes, give me a sign that it is really you talking to me. **18**Please do not go away until I come back and bring my offering and set it before you."

And the LORD said, "I will wait until you return."

19Gideon went in, prepared a young goat, and from an ephah*ᵃ* of flour he made bread without yeast*ᴰ*. Putting the meat in a basket and its broth in a pot, he brought them out and offered them to him under the oak.

20The angel of God said to him, "Take the meat and the unleavened bread, place them on this rock, and pour out the broth." And Gideon did so. **21**With the tip of the staff that was in his hand, the angel of the LORD touched the meat and the unleavened bread. Fire flared from the rock, consuming the meat and the bread. And the angel of the LORD disappeared. **22**When Gideon realized that it was the angel of the LORD, he exclaimed, "Ah, Sovereign LORD! I have seen the angel of the LORD face to face!"

23But the LORD said to him, "Peace*ᴰ*! Do not be afraid. You are not going to die."

24So Gideon built an altar to the LORD there and called it The LORD is Peace. To this day it stands in Ophrah of the Abiezrites.

25That same night the LORD said to him, "Take the second bull from your father's herd, the one seven years old.*ᵇ* Tear down your father's altar to Baal*ᴰ* and cut down the Asherah pole*ᴰᶜ* beside it. **26**Then build a proper kind of*ᵈ* altar to the LORD your God on the top of this height. Using the wood of the Asherah pole that you cut down, offer the second*ᵉ* bull as a burnt offering."

27So Gideon took ten of his servants and did as the LORD told him. But because he was afraid of his family and the men of the town, he did it at night rather than in the daytime.

28In the morning when the men of the town got up, there was Baal's altar, demolished, with the Asherah pole beside it cut down and the second bull sacrificed on the newly built altar!

29They asked each other, "Who did this?"

When they carefully investigated, they were told, "Gideon son of Joash did it."

30The men of the town demanded of Joash, "Bring out your son. He must die, because he has broken down Baal's altar and cut down the Asherah pole beside it."

31But Joash replied to the hostile crowd around him, "Are you going to plead Baal's cause? Are you trying to save him? Whoever fights for him shall be put to death*ᴰ* by morning! If Baal really is a god, he can defend himself when someone breaks down his altar." **32**So that day they called Gideon "Jerub-Baal,*ᶠ*" saying, "Let Baal contend with him," because he broke down Baal's altar.

33Now all the Midianites, Amalekites and other eastern peoples joined forces and crossed over the Jordan and camped in the Valley of Jezreel. **34**Then the Spirit of the LORD came upon Gideon, and he blew a trumpet, summoning the Abiezrites to follow him. **35**He sent messen-

Why did God choose someone whose family worshiped Baal? (6:25)

Gideon's family mixed their worship of God with the worship of false gods. Gideon was keenly aware of his own failures and was extremely reluctant to be God's leader. However, because he sensed his own inadequacies, God could use him. God saw his weaknesses, but also saw his potential to be a courageous leader.

Abiezrites (6:34)

Men of Abiezer, Gideon's hometown, were the first to respond to his call to action. They were professed to be the poorest clan in the tribe of Manasseh (vv. 11,15).

ᵃ19 That is, probably about 3/5 bushel (about 22 liters)   *ᵇ25* Or *Take a full-grown, mature bull from your father's herd*   *ᶜ25* That is, a symbol of the goddess Asherah; here and elsewhere in Judges   *ᵈ26* Or *build with layers of stone an*   *ᵉ26* Or *full-grown*; also in verse 28   *ᶠ32* *Jerub-Baal* means *let Baal contend*.

gers throughout Manasseh, calling them to arms, and also into Asher, Zebulun and Naphtali, so that they too went up to meet them.

36Gideon said to God, "If you will save Israel by my hand as you have promised— **37**look, I will place a wool fleece on the threshing floor. If there is dew only on the fleece and all the ground is dry, then I will know that you will save Israel by my hand, as you said." **38**And that is what happened. Gideon rose early the next day; he squeezed the fleece and wrung out the dew—a bowlful of water.

39Then Gideon said to God, "Do not be angry with me. Let me make just one more request. Allow me one more test with the fleece. This time make the fleece dry and the ground covered with dew." **40**That night God did so. Only the fleece was dry; all the ground was covered with dew.

Gideon Defeats the Midianites

7 Early in the morning, Jerub-Baal (that is, Gideon) and all his men camped at the spring of Harod. The camp of Midian was north of them in the valley near the hill of Moreh. **2**The LORD said to Gideon, "You have too many men for me to deliver Midian into their hands. In order that Israel may not boast against me that her own strength has saved her, **3**announce now to the people, 'Anyone who trembles with fear may turn back and leave Mount Gilead.' " So twenty-two thousand men left, while ten thousand remained.

4But the LORD said to Gideon, "There are still too many men. Take them down to the water, and I will sift them for you there. If I say, 'This one shall go with you,' he shall go; but if I say, 'This one shall not go with you,' he shall not go."

5So Gideon took the men down to the water. There the LORD told him, "Separate those who lap the water with their tongues like a dog from those who kneel down to drink." **6**Three hundred men lapped with their hands to

What is "putting out a fleece"? (6:37–40)

Many believers whose faith needs bolstering use the phrase "putting out a fleece" to express their desire to know what God's will is for them. "Putting out a fleece" often describes a specific action that *tests* God's approval or disapproval.

Gideon's Victory (7:1)

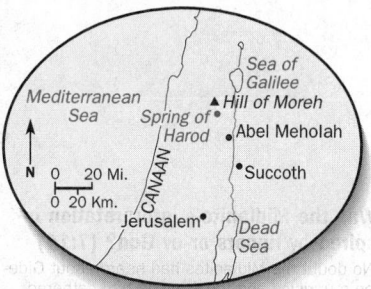

What was significant about the way they drank? (7:5–6)

The drinking test had no special significance or historical precedent. It was simply a way to get the size of the army down to 300. Militarily, the first reduction (described in v. 3) guaranteed good morale; perhaps this second reduction guaranteed alertness. Those who stooped to drink the water were probably less wary than the 300 who kept their heads up while scooping water in their hands.

Can we find God's will by putting out a fleece? (6:37–40)

Without being too hard on Gideon, "putting out a fleece" seems to indicate a lack of faith and courage on his part. God had already assured Gideon of his presence (6:12) and had promised he would use Gideon to deliver Israel (6:14,16). God had also already given Gideon a special sign, at his request, to prove that he was with him (6:17–22). Therefore, the sign of the fleece—not only once, but twice—was Gideon's way of confirming what he already knew.

Similarly, we don't need extraordinary signs to discover God's will. We can be led by the Spirit of God (John 14:26) and find inner peace about life's decisions (Col. 3:15). God also directs us in prayer, by the counsel of godly friends and by the ordering of our circumstances.

Seeking special signs shows a lack of trust in God, because we demand physical evidence as a price for our obedience. By contrast, Christian living is a walk of faith, not sight (Heb. 11:1; 2 Cor. 5:7); Jesus commended those who would believe without seeing (John 20:29). "Putting out a fleece" is never recommended by Jesus nor seen as a means of discovering God's will in the New Testament.

For another view, see *What kind of divination did Joseph do?* (Gen. 44:5,15).

their mouths. All the rest got down on their knees to drink.

7The LORD said to Gideon, "With the three hundred men that lapped I will save you and give the Midianites into your hands. Let all the other men go, each to his own place." **8**So Gideon sent the rest of the Israelites to their tents but kept the three hundred, who took over the provisions and trumpets of the others.

Now the camp of Midian lay below him in the valley. **9**During that night the LORD said to Gideon, "Get up, go down against the camp, because I am going to give it into your hands. **10**If you are afraid to attack, go down to the camp with your servant Purah **11**and listen to what they are saying. Afterward, you will be encouraged to attack the camp." So he and Purah his servant went down to the outposts of the camp. **12**The Midianites, the Amalekites and all the other eastern peoples had settled in the valley, thick as locusts^D. Their camels could no more be counted than the sand on the seashore.

13Gideon arrived just as a man was telling a friend his dream. "I had a dream," he was saying. "A round loaf of barley bread came tumbling into the Midianite camp. It struck the tent with such force that the tent overturned and collapsed."

14His friend responded, "This can be nothing other than the sword of Gideon son of Joash, the Israelite. God has given the Midianites and the whole camp into his hands."

15When Gideon heard the dream and its interpretation, he worshiped God. He returned to the camp of Israel and called out, "Get up! The LORD has given the Midianite camp into your hands." **16**Dividing the three hundred men into three companies, he placed trumpets and empty jars in the hands of all of them, with torches inside.

17"Watch me," he told them. "Follow my lead. When I get to the edge of the camp, do exactly as I do. **18**When I and all who are with me blow our trumpets, then from all around the camp blow yours and shout, 'For the LORD and for Gideon.' "

19Gideon and the hundred men with him reached the edge of the camp at the beginning of the middle watch, just after they had changed the guard. They blew their trumpets and broke the jars that were in their hands. **20**The three companies blew the trumpets and smashed the jars. Grasping the torches in their left hands and holding in their right hands the trumpets they were to blow, they shouted, "A sword for the LORD and for Gideon!" **21**While each man held his position around the camp, all the Midianites ran, crying out as they fled.

22When the three hundred trumpets sounded, the LORD caused the men throughout the camp to turn on each other with their swords. The army fled to Beth Shittah toward Zererah as far as the border of Abel Meholah near Tabbath. **23**Israelites from Naphtali, Asher and all Manasseh were called out, and they pursued the Midianites. **24**Gideon sent messengers throughout the hill country of Ephraim, saying, "Come down against the Midianites and seize the waters of the Jordan ahead of them as far as Beth Barah."

So all the men of Ephraim were called out and they took the waters of the Jordan as far as Beth Barah. **25**They also captured two of the Midianite leaders, Oreb and Zeeb. They killed Oreb at the rock of Oreb, and Zeeb at the winepress^D of Zeeb. They pursued the Midianites and

Was the Midianite's interpretation inspired by rumors or by God? (7:14)

No doubt the Midianites had heard about Gideon's uprising and the army he had gathered, and the dream reinforced what they'd heard. However, God made the interpretation clear to confirm to Gideon that he was with him. Through it, Gideon could see that the surprise attack would cause panic among the Midianites.

How could Gideon understand their language? (7:15)

The Midianites consisted of five families, linked to Abraham through Midian, son of the concubine Keturah. The Midianite language, if not identical with Hebrew, was similar enough for Gideon to understand what the sentries said.

Do dreams help us know God's will today? (7:15)

God's Spirit guides people today through reliable means such as prayer, worship, meditation on Scripture, the counsel of godly friends, and circumstances. Rare incidents do occur where someone is led by a vision or a dream. But if God chooses to reveal his will through a dream, he will also confirm it through other, more reliable means. See article: *Can we find God's will by putting out a fleece?* (6:37–40).

Middle watch (7:19)

Sometime between 10:00 p.m. and 2:00 a.m. The second of three periods during the night when guards were posted to keep watch.

Seize the waters of the Jordan (7:24)

This probably meant that they were to control the places where people could cross the river. In this way they could cut off some of the escape routes of the Midianites and inflict greater losses to their army.

brought the heads of Oreb and Zeeb to Gideon, who was by the Jordan.

Zebah and Zalmunna

8 Now the Ephraimites asked Gideon, "Why have you treated us like this? Why didn't you call us when you went to fight Midian?" And they criticized him sharply.

2But he answered them, "What have I accomplished compared to you? Aren't the gleanings of Ephraim's grapes better than the full grape harvest of Abiezer? **3**God gave Oreb and Zeeb, the Midianite leaders, into your hands. What was I able to do compared to you?" At this, their resentment against him subsided.

4Gideon and his three hundred men, exhausted yet keeping up the pursuit, came to the Jordan and crossed it. **5**He said to the men of Succoth, "Give my troops some bread; they are worn out, and I am still pursuing Zebah and Zalmunna, the kings of Midian."

6But the officials of Succoth said, "Do you already have the hands of Zebah and Zalmunna in your possession? Why should we give bread to your troops?"

7Then Gideon replied, "Just for that, when the LORD has given Zebah and Zalmunna into my hand, I will tear your flesh with desert thorns and briers."

8From there he went up to Peniel*ᵃ* and made the same request of them, but they answered as the men of Succoth had. **9**So he said to the men of Peniel, "When I return in triumph, I will tear down this tower."

10Now Zebah and Zalmunna were in Karkor with a force of about fifteen thousand men, all that were left of the armies of the eastern peoples; a hundred and twenty thousand swordsmen had fallen. **11**Gideon went up by the route of the nomads east of Nobah and Jogbehah and fell upon the unsuspecting army. **12**Zebah and Zalmunna, the two kings of Midian, fled, but he pursued them and captured them, routing their entire army.

13Gideon son of Joash then returned from the battle by the Pass of Heres. **14**He caught a young man of Succoth and questioned him, and the young man wrote down for him the names of the seventy-seven officials of Succoth, the elders of the town. **15**Then Gideon came and said to the men of Succoth, "Here are Zebah and Zalmunna, about whom you taunted me by saying, 'Do you already have the hands of Zebah and Zalmunna in your possession? Why should we give bread to your exhausted men?' " **16**He took the elders of the town and taught the men of Succoth a lesson by punishing them with desert thorns and briers. **17**He also pulled down the tower of Peniel and killed the men of the town.

18Then he asked Zebah and Zalmunna, "What kind of men did you kill at Tabor?"

"Men like you," they answered, "each one with the bearing of a prince."

19Gideon replied, "Those were my brothers, the sons of my own mother. As surely as the LORD lives, if you had spared their lives, I would not kill you." **20**Turning to Jether, his oldest son, he said, "Kill them!" But Jether did not draw his sword, because he was only a boy and was afraid.

21Zebah and Zalmunna said, "Come, do it yourself. 'As is the man, so is his strength.' " So Gideon stepped for-

ᵃ8 Hebrew Penuel, a variant of Peniel; also in verses 9 and 17

Why didn't these towns offer help for a fellow Israelite? (8:6,8)
Gideon's tiny attack force did not appear to offer any prospects for a long-lasting protective army. The people of Succoth and Peniel felt that their security in the long run depended on maintaining good relations with the Midianites (see *Gideon's victory* on page 329). Rather than risk revenge from the Midianites later, they treated Gideon's request coolly and refused to supply him.

What kind of lesson could desert thorns and briers teach? (8:16)
This most likely was capital punishment accomplished by torture. The men of Succoth learned to support Gideon when they saw their elders suffer a painful death, beaten with whips made of thorns and briers.

Was Gideon right to extract such brutal revenge? (8:17)
Yes, at least from Gideon's perspective. As God's leader, he had warned them they would suffer such consequences if they persisted in supporting Israel's enemies (v. 7). The death penalty seemed appropriate because their refusal to help him in battle constituted treason, a capital offense.

ward and killed them, and took the ornaments off their camels' necks.

Gideon's Ephod

22The Israelites said to Gideon, "Rule over us—you, your son and your grandson—because you have saved us out of the hand of Midian."

23But Gideon told them, "I will not rule over you, nor will my son rule over you. The LORD will rule over you." **24**And he said, "I do have one request, that each of you give me an earring from your share of the plunderᴰ." (It was the custom of the Ishmaelites to wear gold earrings.)

25They answered, "We'll be glad to give them." So they spread out a garment, and each man threw a ring from his plunder onto it. **26**The weight of the gold rings he asked for came to seventeen hundred shekelsᴰ,ᵃ not counting the ornaments, the pendants and the purpleᴰ garments worn by the kings of Midian or the chains that were on their camels' necks. **27**Gideon made the gold into an ephodᴰ, which he placed in Ophrah, his town. All Israel prostituted themselves by worshiping it there, and it became a snare to Gideon and his family.

Gideon's Death

28Thus Midian was subdued before the Israelites and did not raise its head again. During Gideon's lifetime, the land enjoyed peaceᴰ forty years.

29Jerub-Baal son of Joash went back home to live. **30**He had seventy sons of his own, for he had many wives. **31**His concubineᴰ, who lived in Shechem, also bore him a son, whom he named Abimelech. **32**Gideon son of Joash died at a good old age and was buried in the tomb of his father Joash in Ophrah of the Abiezrites.

33No sooner had Gideon died than the Israelites again prostituted themselves to the Baals. They set up Baal-Berith as their god and **34**did not remember the LORD their God, who had rescued them from the hands of all their enemies on every side. **35**They also failed to show kindness to the family of Jerub-Baal (that is, Gideon) for all the good things he had done for them.

Abimelech

9 Abimelech son of Jerub-Baal went to his mother's brothers in Shechem and said to them and to all his mother's clan, **2**"Ask all the citizens of Shechem, 'Which is better for you: to have all seventy of Jerub-Baal's sons rule over you, or just one man?' Remember, I am your flesh and blood."

3When the brothers repeated all this to the citizens of Shechem, they were inclined to follow Abimelech, for they said, "He is our brother." **4**They gave him seventy shekelsᵇ of silver from the temple of Baal-Berith, and Abimelech used it to hire reckless adventurers, who became his followers. **5**He went to his father's home in Ophrah and on one stone murdered his seventy brothers, the sons of Jerub-Baal. But Jotham, the youngest son of Jerub-Baal, escaped by hiding. **6**Then all the citizens of Shechem and Beth Millo gathered beside the great tree at the pillar in Shechem to crown Abimelech king.

7When Jotham was told about this, he climbed up on the top of Mount Gerizim and shouted to them, "Listen to

Ephod (8:27)

The original ephod was worn by the high priest (Exodus 39:1–26) and held the Urim and Thummin, used to find God's will (Exodus 28:30; Lev. 8:8). Apparently it later was also a freestanding object. In Gideon's case, it could have been either the garment or the image. The problem was not with the ephod itself, but with what it became in the minds of the people. When they began to worship it, they violated God's command against making and worshiping images.

How could Gideon make such a big mistake? (8:27)

His good intentions notwithstanding (v. 23), Gideon made an ephod that eventually became an idol. Ephods were generally used by priests to discover God's will—a practice Gideon distorted into a form of pagan worship. Perhaps his earlier experiences of seeking specific direction from God later became an obsessive fault for Gideon. He went too far and apparently could not worship the Lord without a visible, material object. Gideon and Israel relied on God to defeat the enemy but then abandoned him when times became good.

Why did Gideon have so many wives? (8:30)

The story of Adam and Eve seems to show that one wife for each husband was God's intention for marriage (Gen. 2:24). But early on, several men married several wives without God's express disapproval, including Abraham, Jacob and David. Though it was not considered a sin to have multiple wives, the practice led to many family problems, breakdowns in relationships and sin. See article: *Why did David have so many wives and concubines?* (2 Samuel 5:13).

Were Abimelech's charges true? (9:2)

Gideon had promised that neither he nor his son would rule over Israel (8:23), so his influence was limited primarily to Ophrah, his hometown. Abimelech apparently played on the fears of his relatives that they could be oppressed by Gideon's many sons, using their fears as a political opportunity to promote himself. Besides selfish ambition, he may also have been motivated by jealousy and hatred. His half-brothers probably looked down on him because he was the son of a slave girl (9:18).

ᵃ26 That is, about 43 pounds (about 19.5 kilograms)   ᵇ4 That is, about 1 3/4 pounds (about 0.8 kilogram)

me, citizens of Shechem, so that God may listen to you. [D]8One day the trees went out to anoint a king for themselves. They said to the olive tree, 'Be our king.'

9"But the olive tree answered, 'Should I give up my oil, by which both gods and men are honored, to hold sway over the trees?'

10"Next, the trees said to the fig tree, 'Come and be our king.'

11"But the fig tree replied, 'Should I give up my fruit, so good and sweet, to hold sway over the trees?'

12"Then the trees said to the vine, 'Come and be our king.'

13"But the vine answered, 'Should I give up my wine, which cheers both gods and men, to hold sway over the trees?'

14"Finally all the trees said to the thornbush, 'Come and be our king.'

15"The thornbush said to the trees, 'If you really want to anoint me king over you, come and take refuge in my shade; but if not, then let fire come out of the thornbush and consume the cedars of Lebanon!'

16"Now if you have acted honorably and in good faith when you made Abimelech king, and if you have been fair to Jerub-Baal and his family, and if you have treated him as he deserves— 17and to think that my father fought for you, risked his life to rescue you from the hand of Midian 18(but today you have revolted against my father's family, murdered his seventy sons on a single stone, and made Abimelech, the son of his slave girl, king over the citizens of Shechem because he is your brother)— 19if then you have acted honorably and in good faith toward Jerub-Baal and his family today, may Abimelech be your joy, and may you be his, too! 20But if you have not, let fire come out from Abimelech and consume you, citizens of Shechem and Beth Millo, and let fire come out from you, citizens of Shechem and Beth Millo, and consume Abimelech!"

21Then Jotham fled, escaping to Beer, and he lived there because he was afraid of his brother Abimelech.

22After Abimelech had governed Israel three years, 23God sent an evil spirit between Abimelech and the citizens of Shechem, who acted treacherously against Abimelech. 24God did this in order that the crime against Jerub-

How could Jotham be heard without getting killed? (9:7)

Being within earshot didn't necessarily mean that he was within bowshot. Jotham climbed the slopes of Mount Gerizim—perhaps shouting down from the top of a cliff or out of a hiding place behind some rocks or in a cave. The rough terrain made it possible to be heard but not easily reached. The walls of the valley also may have served to amplify his voice. Another possibility is that the Shechemites, feasting and drinking, were in no condition to chase Jotham.

How can a holy God send an evil spirit? (9:23)

On the surface, it may seem problematic to read that God used an *evil spirit* to repay Abimelech and the people of Shechem for their wickedness (v. 24). How could a good God use something *evil* to carry out his will?

We may debate whether God *caused* the breakdown of the relationship between Abimelech and the Shechemites or whether he *permitted* them to reap the consequences of their own treacherous ways. The author of Judges, in typical Old Testament fashion, attributes the action to God, in recognition of the truth that God is in control of all history. God, as the ultimate power, can use anything to accomplish his purposes, without regard to its nature (see Gen. 50:20).

Was this *evil spirit* a supernatural being? Some believe that it was, while others maintain that this *spirit* can be interpreted as an attitude of bitterness and distrust that penetrated the relationship and caused the Shechemites to betray Abimelech.

Baal's seventy sons, the shedding of their blood, might be avenged[D] on their brother Abimelech and on the citizens of Shechem, who had helped him murder his brothers. 25In opposition to him these citizens of Shechem set men on the hilltops to ambush and rob everyone who passed by, and this was reported to Abimelech.

26Now Gaal son of Ebed moved with his brothers into Shechem, and its citizens put their confidence in him. 27After they had gone out into the fields and gathered the grapes and trodden them, they held a festival in the temple of their god. While they were eating and drinking, they cursed Abimelech. 28Then Gaal son of Ebed said, "Who is Abimelech, and who is Shechem, that we should be subject to him? Isn't he Jerub-Baal's son, and isn't Zebul his deputy? Serve the men of Hamor, Shechem's father! Why should we serve Abimelech? 29If only this people were under my command! Then I would get rid of him. I would say to Abimelech, 'Call out your whole army!' "[a]

30When Zebul the governor of the city heard what Gaal son of Ebed said, he was very angry. 31Under cover he sent messengers to Abimelech, saying, "Gaal son of Ebed and his brothers have come to Shechem and are stirring up the city against you. 32Now then, during the night you and your men should come and lie in wait in the fields. 33In the morning at sunrise, advance against the city. When Gaal and his men come out against you, do whatever your hand finds to do."

34So Abimelech and all his troops set out by night and took up concealed positions near Shechem in four companies. 35Now Gaal son of Ebed had gone out and was standing at the entrance to the city gate just as Abimelech and his soldiers came out from their hiding place.

36When Gaal saw them, he said to Zebul, "Look, people are coming down from the tops of the mountains!"

Zebul replied, "You mistake the shadows of the mountains for men."

37But Gaal spoke up again: "Look, people are coming down from the center of the land, and a company is coming from the direction of the soothsayers' tree."

38Then Zebul said to him, "Where is your big talk now, you who said, 'Who is Abimelech that we should be subject to him?' Aren't these the men you ridiculed? Go out and fight them!"

39So Gaal led out[b] the citizens of Shechem and fought Abimelech. 40Abimelech chased him, and many fell wounded in the flight—all the way to the entrance to the gate. 41Abimelech stayed in Arumah, and Zebul drove Gaal and his brothers out of Shechem.

42The next day the people of Shechem went out to the fields, and this was reported to Abimelech. 43So he took his men, divided them into three companies and set an ambush in the fields. When he saw the people coming out of the city, he rose to attack them. 44Abimelech and the companies with him rushed forward to a position at the entrance to the city gate. Then two companies rushed upon those in the fields and struck them down. 45All that day Abimelech pressed his attack against the city until he had captured it and killed its people. Then he destroyed the city and scattered salt over it.

46On hearing this, the citizens in the tower of Shechem

Do whatever your hand finds to do (9:33)

Zebul's way of telling Abimelech to take whatever opportunity he could find to regain control of Shechem and turn the tide of rebellion that had risen there. It may have been a common expression at that time (1 Samuel 10:7; Eccl. 9:10).

What kind of tower could hold 1,000 people? (9:46,49)

Some towers were built into the city walls, but larger ones could stand alone as a fortress or citadel. This particular tower or stronghold apparently stood some distance from the city of Shechem. Connected with a pagan temple, it seems to have been more than a mere tower. Shechem had already been destroyed (v. 45), so some think this tower may have been in Beth Millo (v. 6).

a29 Septuagint; Hebrew him." Then he said to Abimelech, "Call out your whole army!"   b39 Or Gaal went out in the sight of

went into the stronghold^D of the temple of El-Berith. **47**When Abimelech heard that they had assembled there, **48**he and all his men went up Mount Zalmon. He took an ax and cut off some branches, which he lifted to his shoulders. He ordered the men with him, "Quick! Do what you have seen me do!" **49**So all the men cut branches and followed Abimelech. They piled them against the stronghold and set it on fire over the people inside. So all the people in the tower of Shechem, about a thousand men and women, also died.

50Next Abimelech went to Thebez and besieged it and captured it. **51**Inside the city, however, was a strong tower, to which all the men and women—all the people of the city—fled. They locked themselves in and climbed up on the tower roof. **52**Abimelech went to the tower and stormed it. But as he approached the entrance to the tower to set it on fire, **53**a woman dropped an upper millstone^D on his head and cracked his skull. **54**Hurriedly he called to his armor-bearer, "Draw your sword and kill me, so that they can't say, 'A woman killed him.'" So his servant ran him through, and he died. **55**When the Israelites saw that Abimelech was dead, they went home.

56Thus God repaid the wickedness that Abimelech had done to his father by murdering his seventy brothers. **57**God also made the men of Shechem pay for all their wickedness. The curse of Jotham son of Jerub-Baal came on them.

Tola

10

After the time of Abimelech a man of Issachar, Tola son of Puah, the son of Dodo, rose to save Israel. He lived in Shamir, in the hill country of Ephraim. **2**He led^a Israel twenty-three years; then he died, and was buried in Shamir.

Jair

3He was followed by Jair of Gilead, who led Israel twenty-two years. **4**He had thirty sons, who rode thirty donkeys. They controlled thirty towns in Gilead, which to this day are called Havvoth Jair.^b **5**When Jair died, he was buried in Kamon.

Jephthah

6Again the Israelites did evil in the eyes of the LORD. They served the Baals and the Ashtoreths, and the gods of Aram, the gods of Sidon, the gods of Moab, the gods of the Ammonites and the gods of the Philistines. And because the Israelites forsook the LORD and no longer served him, **7**he became angry with them. He sold them into the hands of the Philistines and the Ammonites, **8**who that year shattered and crushed them. For eighteen years they oppressed all the Israelites on the east side of the Jordan in Gilead, the land of the Amorites. **9**The Ammonites also crossed the Jordan to fight against Judah, Benjamin and the house of Ephraim; and Israel was in great distress. **10**Then the Israelites cried out to the LORD, "We have sinned against you, forsaking our God and serving the Baals."

11The LORD replied, "When the Egyptians, the Amorites, the Ammonites, the Philistines, **12**the Sidonians, the Ama-

Do curses have real power? (9:57)
In Old Testament history, many curses like Jotham's were fulfilled as the outworking of God's judgment. Moses himself offered the people a choice between blessings and curses (Deut. 27:11–28:68; Joshua 8:33). The power was not in Jotham, but in God. God used him as his spokesman to pronounce judgment. Without God's power, the curses would have been futile.

What was so great about donkeys? (10:4)
Riding on donkeys was a mark of both prestige and power. Horses did not fulfill this role until after King Solomon imported them.

What was the attraction of foreign gods? (10:6)
See article: *Why would Israelites be tempted by other gods?* (Joshua 23:7).

lekites and the Maonites[a] oppressed you and you cried to me for help, did I not save you from their hands? 13But you have forsaken me and served other gods, so I will no longer save you. 14Go and cry out to the gods you have chosen. Let them save you when you are in trouble!"

15But the Israelites said to the LORD, "We have sinned. Do with us whatever you think best, but please rescue us now." 16Then they got rid of the foreign gods among them and served the LORD. And he could bear Israel's misery no longer.

17When the Ammonites were called to arms and camped in Gilead, the Israelites assembled and camped at Mizpah. 18The leaders of the people of Gilead said to each other, "Whoever will launch the attack against the Ammonites will be the head of all those living in Gilead."

11 Jephthah the Gileadite was a mighty warrior. His father was Gilead; his mother was a prostitute. 2Gilead's wife also bore him sons, and when they were grown up, they drove Jephthah away. "You are not going to get any inheritance in our family," they said, "because you are the son of another woman." 3So Jephthah fled from his brothers and settled in the land of Tob, where a group of adventurers gathered around him and followed him.

4Some time later, when the Ammonites made war on Israel, 5the elders of Gilead went to get Jephthah from the land of Tob. 6"Come," they said, "be our commander, so we can fight the Ammonites."

7Jephthah said to them, "Didn't you hate me and drive me from my father's house? Why do you come to me now, when you're in trouble?"

8The elders of Gilead said to him, "Nevertheless, we are turning to you now; come with us to fight the Ammonites, and you will be our head over all who live in Gilead."

9Jephthah answered, "Suppose you take me back to fight the Ammonites and the LORD gives them to me—will I really be your head?"

10The elders of Gilead replied, "The LORD is our witness; we will certainly do as you say." 11So Jephthah went with the elders of Gilead, and the people made him head and commander over them. And he repeated all his words before the LORD in Mizpah.

12Then Jephthah sent messengers to the Ammonite king with the question: "What do you have against us that you have attacked our country?"

13The king of the Ammonites answered Jephthah's messengers, "When Israel came up out of Egypt, they took away my land from the Arnon to the Jabbok, all the way to the Jordan. Now give it back peaceably."

14Jephthah sent back messengers to the Ammonite king, 15saying:

"This is what Jephthah says: Israel did not take the land of Moab or the land of the Ammonites. 16But when they came up out of Egypt, Israel went through the desert to the Red Sea[b] and on to Kadesh. 17Then Israel sent messengers to the king of Edom, saying, 'Give us permission to go through your country,' but the king of Edom would not listen. They sent also to the king of Moab, and he refused. So Israel stayed at Kadesh.

Why did the elders pick an outcast to lead them? (11:4–6)

The elders recruited Jephthah because no leader emerged when the troops assembled at Mizpah (10:17–18). With their very survival at stake, they did not worry about protocol or established policy. The crisis demanded that they do whatever was necessary to protect themselves. Their natural choice was the illegitimate son of Gilead (v. 1), who had proven his charismatic skills as a leader in exile (v. 3).

Why did Jephthah repeat himself? (11:11)

This was Jephthah's formal installation as commander of the Lord's army. He repeated before the troops the vows he had given earlier to the elders. Also, the rank and file confirmed the elders' choice and agreed to the terms of Jephthah's command: if he'd lead them in war, they would follow him in peace as well (vv. 8–10).

---

[a]12 Hebrew; some Septuagint manuscripts *Midianites*   [b]16 Hebrew *Yam Suph*; that is, Sea of Reeds

¹⁸"Next they traveled through the desert, skirted the lands of Edom^D and Moab, passed along the eastern side of the country of Moab, and camped on the other side of the Arnon. They did not enter the territory of Moab, for the Arnon was its border.

¹⁹"Then Israel sent messengers to Sihon king of the Amorites, who ruled in Heshbon, and said to him, 'Let us pass through your country to our own place.' ²⁰Sihon, however, did not trust Israel^a to pass through his territory. He mustered all his men and encamped at Jahaz and fought with Israel.

²¹"Then the LORD, the God of Israel, gave Sihon and all his men into Israel's hands, and they defeated them. Israel took over all the land of the Amorites who lived in that country, ²²capturing all of it from the Arnon to the Jabbok and from the desert to the Jordan.

²³"Now since the LORD, the God of Israel, has driven the Amorites out before his people Israel, what right have you to take it over? ²⁴Will you not take what your god Chemosh gives you? Likewise, whatever the LORD our God has given us, we will possess. ²⁵Are you better than Balak son of Zippor, king of Moab? Did he ever quarrel with Israel or fight with them? ²⁶For three hundred years Israel occupied Heshbon, Aroer, the surrounding settlements and all the towns along the Arnon. Why didn't you retake them during that time? ²⁷I have not wronged you, but you are doing me wrong by waging war against me. Let the LORD, the Judge,^b decide the dispute this day between the Israelites and the Ammonites."

²⁸The king of Ammon, however, paid no attention to the message Jephthah sent him.

²⁹Then the Spirit of the LORD came upon Jephthah. He crossed Gilead and Manasseh, passed through Mizpah of Gilead, and from there he advanced against the Ammonites. ³⁰And Jephthah made a vow^D to the LORD: "If you give the Ammonites into my hands, ³¹whatever comes out of the door of my house to meet me when I return in triumph from the Ammonites will be the LORD's, and I will sacrifice^D it as a burnt offering."

³²Then Jephthah went over to fight the Ammonites, and the LORD gave them into his hands. ³³He devastated twenty towns from Aroer to the vicinity of Minnith, as far as Abel Keramim. Thus Israel subdued Ammon.

³⁴When Jephthah returned to his home in Mizpah, who should come out to meet him but his daughter, dancing to the sound of tambourines! She was an only child. Except for her he had neither son nor daughter. ³⁵When he saw her, he tore his clothes and cried, "Oh! My daughter! You have made me miserable and wretched, because I have made a vow to the LORD that I cannot break."

³⁶"My father," she replied, "you have given your word to the LORD. Do to me just as you promised, now that the LORD has avenged^D you of your enemies, the Ammonites. ³⁷But grant me this one request," she said. "Give me two months to roam the hills and weep with my friends, because I will never marry."

³⁸"You may go," he said. And he let her go for two months. She and the girls went into the hills and wept be-

Was this a legitimate reason for war? (11:23–24)

Jephthah's logic made sense to the cultural mindset of the day. People assumed the god of each nation established its territorial boundaries—stronger gods pushed weaker gods around. Jephthah didn't say he believed in the Ammonite god. But if the Ammonites thought Chemosh was going to give them the land of Israel, Jephthah was determined to defend God's honor. His conviction was that the Lord had given Israel the land they lived in.

If the *Spirit of the Lord* was on Jephthah, how could he make such a stupid vow? (11:29–31)

There is no connection between the Spirit's empowering of Jephthah and his vow. Possessing the Holy Spirit for a special assignment does not guarantee a person will be faultless in other areas of life. Jephthah's vow was an attempt to strike a deal with God instead of trusting him. Also see *How could someone take an oath and not know it?* (Lev. 5:4).

How widespread did this custom become? (11:39–40)

Since there is no other mention of this custom in the Old Testament, the ceremony was likely practiced only in the region where Jephthah's family lived. To call it an *Israelite custom* is perhaps a figure of speech in which overstatement is used for effect.

Why were the men of Ephraim so offended? (12:1)

Not being invited to a fight was an insult to their pride, undermining their role as a leading tribe. Ephraim claimed responsibility for all the northern tribes as well as those east of the Jordan (see *Map 4* at the back of this Bible). They apparently valued themselves highly since they were direct descendants of Joseph. They felt entitled to God's blessings, including part of the glory and spoils of war. Also see 8:1.

Why couldn't the Ephraimites pronounce *Shibboleth*? (12:6)

Shibboleth, meaning *floods*, was chosen as the password, apparently because those living west of the Jordan could not pronounce the *sh* sound. A phonetic limitation of their dialect betrayed them.

cause she would never marry. ³⁹After the two months, she returned to her father and he did to her as he had vowed.ᴰ And she was a virgin.

From this comes the Israelite custom ⁴⁰that each year the young women of Israel go out for four days to commemorate the daughter of Jephthah the Gileadite.

Jephthah and Ephraim

12 The men of Ephraim called out their forces, crossed over to Zaphon and said to Jephthah, "Why did you go to fight the Ammonites without calling us to go with you? We're going to burn down your house over your head."

²Jephthah answered, "I and my people were engaged in a great struggle with the Ammonites, and although I called, you didn't save me out of their hands. ³When I saw that you wouldn't help, I took my life in my hands and crossed over to fight the Ammonites, and the LORD gave me the victory over them. Now why have you come up today to fight me?"

⁴Jephthah then called together the men of Gilead and fought against Ephraim. The Gileadites struck them down because the Ephraimites had said, "You Gileadites are renegades from Ephraim and Manasseh." ⁵The Gileadites captured the fords of the Jordan leading to Ephraim, and whenever a survivor of Ephraim said, "Let me cross over," the men of Gilead asked him, "Are you an Ephraimite?" If he replied, "No," ⁶they said, "All right, say 'Shibboleth.' " If he said, "Sibboleth," because he could not pronounce the word correctly, they seized him and killed him at the fords of the Jordan. Forty-two thousand Ephraimites were killed at that time.

⁷Jephthah ledᵃ Israel six years. Then Jephthah the Gileadite died, and was buried in a town in Gilead.

ᵃ7 Traditionally *judged*; also in verses 8–14

What's behind this bizarre deal with God? (11:31,39)

This story troubles us for several reasons:

(1) Why would a man who was used by God take such risks with his family? Though anointed by God, Jephthah was far from being infallible. He apparently thought God would be impressed by his devotion.

(2) Could God be honored by a sinful act (human sacrifice), if it was to fulfill a vow? No. Fulfilling a vow was a high priority in ancient times (Lev. 5:4; Deut. 23:21–23; Joshua 9:19; Eccl. 5:1–5), and Jephthah apparently didn't want to be humiliated by reversing his promise. But God had outlawed human sacrifice (Lev. 18:21; 20:1–5). God disapproves of sin, even one committed to fulfill a vow.

(3) Why didn't Jephthah take some alternate action? Some think it is not absolutely clear that he kept his vow—that his "sacrifice" meant dedicating his daughter to the Lord for lifelong service and perpetual virginity (vv. 38–39). But since he had vowed to sacrifice a *burnt offering* (v. 31) these explanations seem unlikely.

This whole episode illustrates that even those whom God used as leaders did not always follow his ways. Rather than trust God, Jephthah tried to bargain for God's blessing. What he got instead was grief.

Ibzan, Elon and Abdon

8After him, Ibzan of Bethlehem led Israel. **9**He had thirty sons and thirty daughters. He gave his daughters away in marriage to those outside his clan, and for his sons he brought in thirty young women as wives from outside his clan. Ibzan led Israel seven years. **10**Then Ibzan died, and was buried in Bethlehem.

11After him, Elon the Zebulunite led Israel ten years. **12**Then Elon died, and was buried in Aijalon in the land of Zebulun.

13After him, Abdon son of Hillel, from Pirathon, led Israel. **14**He had forty sons and thirty grandsons, who rode on seventy donkeys. He led Israel eight years. **15**Then Abdon son of Hillel died, and was buried at Pirathon in Ephraim, in the hill country of the Amalekites.

The Birth of Samson

13 Again the Israelites did evil in the eyes of the LORD, so the LORD delivered them into the hands of the Philistines for forty years.

2A certain man of Zorah, named Manoah, from the clan of the Danites, had a wife who was sterile and remained childless. **3**The angel of the LORD appeared to her and said, "You are sterile and childless, but you are going to conceive and have a son. **4**Now see to it that you drink no wine or other fermented drink and that you do not eat anything unclean^D, **5**because you will conceive and give birth to a son. No razor may be used on his head, because the boy is to be a Nazirite^D, set apart to God from birth, and he will begin the deliverance of Israel from the hands of the Philistines."

6Then the woman went to her husband and told him, "A man of God came to me. He looked like an angel of God, very awesome. I didn't ask him where he came from, and he didn't tell me his name. **7**But he said to me, 'You will conceive and give birth to a son. Now then, drink no wine or other fermented drink and do not eat anything unclean, because the boy will be a Nazirite of God from birth until the day of his death^D.' "

8Then Manoah prayed to the LORD: "O Lord, I beg you, let the man of God you sent to us come again to teach us how to bring up the boy who is to be born."

9God heard Manoah, and the angel of God came again to the woman while she was out in the field; but her husband Manoah was not with her. **10**The woman hurried to tell her husband, "He's here! The man who appeared to me the other day!"

11Manoah got up and followed his wife. When he came to the man, he said, "Are you the one who talked to my wife?"

"I am," he said.

12So Manoah asked him, "When your words are fulfilled, what is to be the rule for the boy's life and work?"

13The angel of the LORD answered, "Your wife must do all that I have told her. **14**She must not eat anything that comes from the grapevine, nor drink any wine or other fermented drink nor eat anything unclean. She must do everything I have commanded her."

15Manoah said to the angel of the LORD, "We would like you to stay until we prepare a young goat for you."

16The angel of the LORD replied, "Even though you detain me, I will not eat any of your food. But if you prepare

Who appointed the judges? (12:8,11,13)

The judges were raised up by God in response to the Israelites' cries for help (2:16). Gideon, for example, had a personal encounter with an angelic messenger. Jephthah was selected by the tribal elders and approved by the people. God caused Samson's parents to dedicate him for service to the Lord. The methods may have varied, but in each case God raised the one he wanted to power, and the people recognized the person's leadership.

Were the marriages to outsiders unusual? (12:9)

It was permissible to marry outside a clan or even a tribe as long as the spouse was from another tribe of Israel. But marriage to a foreigner was forbidden by law (Exodus 34:15–17; Deut. 7:1–4). The neighboring nations' worship of pagan gods would dilute Israel's commitment to the Lord.

Donkeys (12:14)

See *What was so great about donkeys?* (10:4).

Nazirite (13:5)

One who demonstrated total consecration to the Lord by observing an ascetic lifestyle: abstaining from grape products, non-kosher foods, haircuts and contact with dead bodies. For Samson (as for Samuel and John the Baptist) this was a lifelong vow. The Bible gives examples of temporary Nazirite vows (Acts 18:18; 21:23–24).

Did Samson's parents do a bad job? (13:8)

Many factors are involved in the way children turn out. It seems that Samson's parents had not instilled their values in their son, though they had asked for God's help in knowing how to raise him. He seemed spoiled, and insistent on getting his own way (Judges 14:2–4). Even with good parents and God's blessings, individuals can choose selfish and destructive ways. See Proverbs 22:6.

What's wrong with grapes and wine? (13:14)

Grapes and wine were delicacies. But to the Nazirite they had spiritual significance: fruit from the vineyard may have symbolized the intoxicating qualities of wine. Perhaps the vineyard was also a reminder of the sins of the Canaanites (who practiced prostitution with their agricultural fertility cults). Though other Israelites could drink wine, a Nazirite could have no hint of impropriety.

How was the angel's name *beyond understanding?* (13:18)

Literally, his name was *wonderful*. This was a way of saying he was something to wonder at, no ordinary messenger. The implication was that he was mysteriously linked to God himself. Later the same phrase names God *Wonderful Counselor* (Isaiah 9:6). Since God is beyond our understanding, any attempt to describe him in human terms will always be inadequate.

How did the Spirit of the Lord begin to stir him? (13:25)

This was an expression that described results more than methods. We can't be sure precisely how Samson encountered the living God. We do know that the Spirit of the Lord equipped Samson to be called as a judge, infusing him with enormous physical strength. Other judges were gifted in other ways—for example, Othniel (see 3:10) and Gideon (see 6:34). See **What were the signs that the Spirit had come upon Othniel?** (3:10).

Did God cause Samson to break a commandment? (14:4)

No. Samson's passions were his own, causing him to desire a wife who, contrary to God's wishes, worshiped idols (Exodus 34:15–17; Deut. 7:1–4). But God remained involved in Samson's life despite his sin. God was committed to using Samson's failures as well as his successes and redeemed the situation to accomplish his purposes (see Romans 8:28). The writer of Judges, writing after the fact, seems to editorialize as he describes God's sovereign involvement.

Does the power of the Spirit give physical strength? (14:6)

It did for Samson. The Spirit gave courage and strength to others as well—for example, David (see 1 Samuel 17:34–37) and Benaiah (see 2 Samuel 23:20). This does not establish some kind of a formula, however. It is better to say that the Lord gives his servants whatever is necessary to accomplish the tasks he has assigned them.

a burnt offering[D], offer it to the LORD." (Manoah did not realize that it was the angel of the LORD.)

17Then Manoah inquired of the angel of the LORD, "What is your name, so that we may honor you when your word comes true?"

18He replied, "Why do you ask my name? It is beyond understanding.[a]" **19**Then Manoah took a young goat, together with the grain offering[D], and sacrificed it on a rock to the LORD. And the LORD did an amazing thing while Manoah and his wife watched: **20**As the flame blazed up from the altar toward heaven, the angel of the LORD ascended in the flame. Seeing this, Manoah and his wife fell with their faces to the ground. **21**When the angel of the LORD did not show himself again to Manoah and his wife, Manoah realized that it was the angel of the LORD.

22"We are doomed to die!" he said to his wife. "We have seen God!"

23But his wife answered, "If the LORD had meant to kill us, he would not have accepted a burnt offering and grain offering from our hands, nor shown us all these things or now told us this."

24The woman gave birth to a boy and named him Samson. He grew and the LORD blessed him, **25**and the Spirit of the LORD began to stir him while he was in Mahaneh Dan, between Zorah and Eshtaol.

Samson's Marriage

14 Samson went down to Timnah and saw there a young Philistine woman. **2**When he returned, he said to his father and mother, "I have seen a Philistine woman in Timnah; now get her for me as my wife."

3His father and mother replied, "Isn't there an acceptable woman among your relatives or among all our people? Must you go to the uncircumcised[D] Philistines to get a wife?"

But Samson said to his father, "Get her for me. She's the right one for me." **4**(His parents did not know that this was from the LORD, who was seeking an occasion to confront the Philistines; for at that time they were ruling over Israel.) **5**Samson went down to Timnah together with his father and mother. As they approached the vineyards of Timnah, suddenly a young lion came roaring toward him. **6**The Spirit of the LORD came upon him in power so that he tore the lion apart with his bare hands as he might have torn a young goat. But he told neither his father nor his mother what he had done. **7**Then he went down and talked with the woman, and he liked her.

8Some time later, when he went back to marry her, he turned aside to look at the lion's carcass. In it was a swarm of bees and some honey, **9**which he scooped out with his hands and ate as he went along. When he rejoined his parents, he gave them some, and they too ate it. But he did not tell them that he had taken the honey from the lion's carcass.

10Now his father went down to see the woman. And Samson made a feast there, as was customary for bridegrooms. **11**When he appeared, he was given thirty companions.

12"Let me tell you a riddle," Samson said to them. "If you can give me the answer within the seven days of the feast, I will give you thirty linen garments and thirty sets

_____
a18 Or *is wonderful*

of clothes. ¹³If you can't tell me the answer, you must give me thirty linen garments and thirty sets of clothes."

"Tell us your riddle," they said. "Let's hear it."

¹⁴He replied,

"Out of the eater, something to eat;
    out of the strong, something sweet."

For three days they could not give the answer.

¹⁵On the fourth*a* day, they said to Samson's wife, "Coax your husband into explaining the riddle for us, or we will burn you and your father's household to death*b*. Did you invite us here to rob us?"

¹⁶Then Samson's wife threw herself on him, sobbing, "You hate me! You don't really love me. You've given my people a riddle, but you haven't told me the answer."

"I haven't even explained it to my father or mother," he replied, "so why should I explain it to you?" ¹⁷She cried the whole seven days of the feast. So on the seventh day he finally told her, because she continued to press him. She in turn explained the riddle to her people.

¹⁸Before sunset on the seventh day the men of the town said to him,

"What is sweeter than honey?
    What is stronger than a lion?"

Samson said to them,

"If you had not plowed with my heifer,
    you would not have solved my riddle."

¹⁹Then the Spirit of the LORD came upon him in power. He went down to Ashkelon, struck down thirty of their men, stripped them of their belongings and gave their clothes to those who had explained the riddle. Burning with anger, he went up to his father's house. ²⁰And Samson's wife was given to the friend who had attended him at his wedding.

Samson's Vengeance on the Philistines

15 Later on, at the time of wheat harvest, Samson took a young goat and went to visit his wife. He said, "I'm going to my wife's room." But her father would not let him go in.

²"I was so sure you thoroughly hated her," he said, "that I gave her to your friend. Isn't her younger sister more attractive? Take her instead."

³Samson said to them, "This time I have a right to get even with the Philistines; I will really harm them." ⁴So he went out and caught three hundred foxes and tied them tail to tail in pairs. He then fastened a torch to every pair of tails, ⁵lit the torches and let the foxes loose in the standing grain of the Philistines. He burned up the shocks and standing grain, together with the vineyards and olive groves.

⁶When the Philistines asked, "Who did this?" they were told, "Samson, the Timnite's son-in-law, because his wife was given to his friend."

So the Philistines went up and burned her and her father to death. ⁷Samson said to them, "Since you've acted like this, I won't stop until I get my revenge on you." ⁸He attacked them viciously and slaughtered many of them. Then he went down and stayed in a cave in the rock of Etam.

Why give someone *sets of clothes*? (14:12–13)

Sets of clothes are mentioned elsewhere in the Bible as gifts of value. See 2 Kings 5:22.

Why would God's Spirit cause Samson to kill people? (14:19)

God undoubtedly gave Samson superhuman strength. But while Samson used it to kill 30 Philistines for his own reasons (to pay off his bet), God had other things in mind. He used Samson's unholy motives to punish the Philistines, a godless nation that held his people hostage.

Samson and the Philistines (15:3)

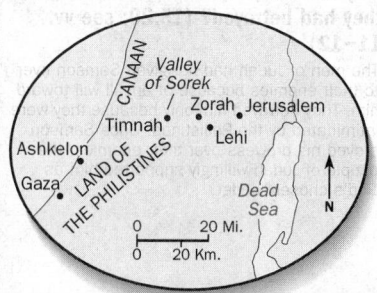

9The Philistines went up and camped in Judah, spreading out near Lehi. **10**The men of Judah asked, "Why have you come to fight us?"

"We have come to take Samson prisoner," they answered, "to do to him as he did to us."

11Then three thousand men from Judah went down to the cave in the rock of Etam and said to Samson, "Don't you realize that the Philistines are rulers over us? What have you done to us?"

He answered, "I merely did to them what they did to me."

12They said to him, "We've come to tie you up and hand you over to the Philistines."

Samson said, "Swear to me that you won't kill me yourselves."

13"Agreed," they answered. "We will only tie you up and hand you over to them. We will not kill you." So they bound him with two new ropes and led him up from the rock. **14**As he approached Lehi, the Philistines came toward him shouting. The Spirit of the LORD came upon him in power. The ropes on his arms became like charred flax, and the bindings dropped from his hands. **15**Finding a fresh jawbone of a donkey, he grabbed it and struck down a thousand men.

16Then Samson said,

> "With a donkey's jawbone
>   I have made donkeys of them.*a*
> With a donkey's jawbone
>   I have killed a thousand men."

17When he finished speaking, he threw away the jawbone; and the place was called Ramath Lehi.*b*

18Because he was very thirsty, he cried out to the LORD, "You have given your servant this great victory. Must I now die of thirst and fall into the hands of the uncircumcisedD?" **19**Then God opened up the hollow place in Lehi, and water came out of it. When Samson drank, his strength returned and he revived. So the spring was called En Hakkore,*c* and it is still there in Lehi.

20Samson led*d* Israel for twenty years in the days of the Philistines.

Samson and Delilah

16 One day Samson went to Gaza, where he saw a prostitute. He went in to spend the night with her. **2**The people of Gaza were told, "Samson is here!" So they surrounded the place and lay in wait for him all night at the city gate. They made no move during the night, saying, "At dawn we'll kill him."

3But Samson lay there only until the middle of the night. Then he got up and took hold of the doors of the city gate, together with the two posts, and tore them loose, bar and all. He lifted them to his shoulders and carried them to the top of the hill that faces Hebron.

4Some time later, he fell in love with a woman in the Valley of Sorek whose name was Delilah. **5**The rulers of the Philistines went to her and said, "See if you can lure him into showing you the secret of his great strength and how we can overpower him so we may tie him up and

---

What did a man like Samson have to fear? (15:12)

In spite of his unusual physical strength, Samson's inner strength was apparently limited by feelings of inadequacy. He wanted to be accepted by those who knew him best. Confronted by 3,000 angry Israelites, he had reason to fear (v. 11).

Did God's miraculous supply of water indicate he approved of Samson's deeds? (15:19)

Yes, although this is difficult for us to accept. Although he was arrogant and violent, Samson was engaged in battle against God's enemies. The En Hakkore springs restored his strength and revived his life—necessary if he was to continue as a protector of God's people against their oppressors.

Why did the people follow someone they had betrayed? (15:20; see vv. 11–12)

The men of Judah had not given Samson over to their enemies because of any ill will toward him. They betrayed him only because they were intimidated by the Philistines. Once Samson proved his prowess over their enemies, the people of Judah willingly supported him as God's chosen leader.

---

a16 Or *made a heap or two*; the Hebrew for *donkey* sounds like the Hebrew for *heap*.   *b17 Ramath Lehi* means *jawbone hill*.
c19 En Hakkore means *caller's spring*.   *d20* Traditionally *judged*

subdue him. Each one of us will give you eleven hundred shekels[D][a] of silver."

6So Delilah said to Samson, "Tell me the secret of your great strength and how you can be tied up and subdued."

7Samson answered her, "If anyone ties me with seven fresh thongs[b] that have not been dried, I'll become as weak as any other man."

8Then the rulers of the Philistines brought her seven fresh thongs that had not been dried, and she tied him with them. **9**With men hidden in the room, she called to him, "Samson, the Philistines are upon you!" But he snapped the thongs as easily as a piece of string snaps when it comes close to a flame. So the secret of his strength was not discovered.

10Then Delilah said to Samson, "You have made a fool of me; you lied to me. Come now, tell me how you can be tied."

11He said, "If anyone ties me securely with new ropes that have never been used, I'll become as weak as any other man."

12So Delilah took new ropes and tied him with them. Then, with men hidden in the room, she called to him, "Samson, the Philistines are upon you!" But he snapped the ropes off his arms as if they were threads.

13Delilah then said to Samson, "Until now, you have been making a fool of me and lying to me. Tell me how you can be tied."

He replied, "If you weave the seven braids of my head into the fabric ⌊on the loom⌋ and tighten it with the pin, I'll become as weak as any other man." So while he was sleeping, Delilah took the seven braids of his head, wove them into the fabric **14**and[c] tightened it with the pin.

Again she called to him, "Samson, the Philistines are upon you!" He awoke from his sleep and pulled up the pin and the loom, with the fabric.

15Then she said to him, "How can you say, 'I love you,' when you won't confide in me? This is the third time you have made a fool of me and haven't told me the secret of your great strength." **16**With such nagging she prodded him day after day until he was tired to death[D].

17So he told her everything. "No razor has ever been used on my head," he said, "because I have been a Nazirite[D] set apart to God since birth. If my head were shaved, my strength would leave me, and I would become as weak as any other man."

18When Delilah saw that he had told her everything, she sent word to the rulers of the Philistines, "Come back once more; he has told me everything." So the rulers of the Philistines returned with the silver in their hands. **19**Having put him to sleep on her lap, she called a man to shave off the seven braids of his hair, and so began to subdue him.[d] And his strength left him.

20Then she called, "Samson, the Philistines are upon you!"

He awoke from his sleep and thought, "I'll go out as before and shake myself free." But he did not know that the LORD had left him.

21Then the Philistines seized him, gouged out his eyes

Why *seven* braids? (16:13)

In ancient Israel the number seven had symbolic significance. Seven was the "perfect" number—indicating completeness or fullness.

Why did Samson give in to Delilah's nagging? (16:17)

Samson was obviously influenced more by his passion than by his will. He was often self-seeking and short-sighted—as when he insisted on a Philistine bride (14:2–4). He was often ruled by his rage (14:19; 15:8). His uncontrolled lust had led to his trysts with Delilah (v. 4). Blinded by his own desires, he could not see God's desires.

After all he'd done, why was a haircut so bad? (16:20)

The Lord had remained with Samson even though he visited prostitutes and sinned in other ways. But the haircut was a renunciation of God's visible presence in his life, a violation of his Nazirite vows.

Did God leave Samson permanently? (16:20)

No. God's love for Samson had not been exhausted, despite Samson's foolishness and sin. Though the symbol of God's power and presence in Samson's life had been cut off, *the hair on his head began to grow again* (v. 22). The new growth suggested that God's plan to deliver Israel from the Philistines had not been abandoned. It also reminded Samson that God continued to care for him.

---

[a]5 That is, about 28 pounds (about 13 kilograms)   [b]7 Or bowstrings; also in verses 8 and 9   [c]13,14 Some Septuagint manuscripts; Hebrew "⌊I can⌋ if you weave the seven braids of my head into the fabric ⌊on the loom⌋." 14So she   [d]19 Hebrew; some Septuagint manuscripts and he began to weaken

and took him down to Gaza. Binding him with bronze shackles, they set him to grinding in the prison. **22**But the hair on his head began to grow again after it had been shaved.

The Death of Samson

23Now the rulers of the Philistines assembled to offer a great sacrifice[D] to Dagon their god and to celebrate, saying, "Our god has delivered Samson, our enemy, into our hands."

24When the people saw him, they praised their god, saying,

> "Our god has delivered our enemy
> into our hands,
> the one who laid waste our land
> and multiplied our slain."

25While they were in high spirits, they shouted, "Bring out Samson to entertain us." So they called Samson out of the prison, and he performed for them.

When they stood him among the pillars, **26**Samson said to the servant who held his hand, "Put me where I can feel the pillars that support the temple, so that I may lean against them." **27**Now the temple was crowded with men and women; all the rulers of the Philistines were there, and on the roof were about three thousand men and women watching Samson perform. **28**Then Samson prayed to the LORD, "O Sovereign LORD, remember me. O God, please strengthen me just once more, and let me with one blow get revenge on the Philistines for my two eyes." **29**Then Samson reached toward the two central pillars on which the temple stood. Bracing himself against them, his right hand on the one and his left hand on the other, **30**Samson said, "Let me die with the Philistines!" Then he pushed with all his might, and down came the temple on the rulers and all the people in it. Thus he killed many more when he died than while he lived.

31Then his brothers and his father's whole family went down to get him. They brought him back and buried him between Zorah and Eshtaol in the tomb of Manoah his father. He had led[a] Israel twenty years.

[a]31 Traditionally *judged*

Who was this god Dagon? (16:23)

Dagon was one of the two most worshiped Philistine gods. His name means *grain* in Hebrew, indicating that he may have been regarded as the giver of crops. The Philistines may have thought that Samson's capture was Dagon's revenge for the burning of the Philistines' fields and vineyards (15:3–5).

How did knocking down two pillars make the whole building collapse? (16:29–30)

Archaeological evidence shows that one type of temple was constructed with two closely-spaced central supporting pillars made of wood. These pillars, standing on marble bases, held most of the weight of the roof. By pushing these pillars off their bases, Samson could have caused the entire roof of the building to come crashing down, killing those beneath and on top (16:27).

Did Samson commit suicide? (16:30)

Samson's death was a casualty of war, not a suicide. His plea *let me die with the Philistines* (v. 30) demonstrates his willingness to see the battle through to the end, even unto death. Samson's prayer was a request to help him in the ongoing fight against his enemies. Like a soldier facing overwhelming odds, Samson accepted his impending death.

In Samson's death the purpose prophesied for his life was realized (see 13:5). God had raised Samson up to punish the sinful Philistines and to begin Israel's deliverance from them. Even on this occasion—in the temple of their god Dagon—the Philistines saw Samson's imprisonment as a sign of Dagon's victory over the God of Israel (vv. 23–24). But while the Philistines were celebrating, God was working through Samson to halt such blasphemy, punish the Philistines and destroy the temple of a false god.

Micah's Idols

17 Now a man named Micah from the hill country of Ephraim ²said to his mother, "The eleven hundred shekels^Da of silver that were taken from you and about which I heard you utter a curse—I have that silver with me; I took it."

Then his mother said, "The LORD bless you, my son!"

³When he returned the eleven hundred shekels of silver to his mother, she said, "I solemnly consecrate^D my silver to the LORD for my son to make a carved image and a cast idol^D. I will give it back to you."

⁴So he returned the silver to his mother, and she took two hundred shekels^b of silver and gave them to a silversmith, who made them into the image and the idol. And they were put in Micah's house.

⁵Now this man Micah had a shrine, and he made an ephod^D and some idols and installed one of his sons as his priest^D. ⁶In those days Israel had no king; everyone did as he saw fit.

⁷A young Levite^D from Bethlehem in Judah, who had been living within the clan of Judah, ⁸left that town in search of some other place to stay. On his way^c he came to Micah's house in the hill country of Ephraim.

⁹Micah asked him, "Where are you from?"

"I'm a Levite from Bethlehem in Judah," he said, "and I'm looking for a place to stay."

¹⁰Then Micah said to him, "Live with me and be my father and priest, and I'll give you ten shekels^d of silver a year, your clothes and your food." ¹¹So the Levite agreed to live with him, and the young man was to him like one of his sons. ¹²Then Micah installed the Levite, and the young man became his priest and lived in his house. ¹³And Micah said, "Now I know that the LORD will be good to me, since this Levite has become my priest."

Danites Settle in Laish

18 In those days Israel had no king.

And in those days the tribe of the Danites was seeking a place of their own where they might settle, because they had not yet come into an inheritance among the tribes of Israel. ²So the Danites sent five warriors from Zorah and Eshtaol to spy out the land and explore it. These men represented all their clans. They told them, "Go, explore the land."

The men entered the hill country of Ephraim and came to the house of Micah, where they spent the night. ³When they were near Micah's house, they recognized the voice of the young Levite; so they turned in there and asked him, "Who brought you here? What are you doing in this place? Why are you here?"

⁴He told them what Micah had done for him, and said, "He has hired me and I am his priest."

⁵Then they said to him, "Please inquire of God to learn whether our journey will be successful."

⁶The priest answered them, "Go in peace. Your journey has the LORD's approval."

⁷So the five men left and came to Laish, where they saw that the people were living in safety, like the Sidonians,

Why would someone worship the Lord by making an idol? (17:1–4)

This was a case of spiritual anarchy: *In those days Israel had no king; everyone did as he saw fit* (v. 6). Happy to have her silver back, Micah's mother dedicated it *to the LORD* to be made into an idol. In reality, they were not worshiping the Lord at all. They were "customizing" their faith by mixing it with pagan practices.

Why did Micah want a personal priest in his own house? (17:5,10,13)

Micah may have sought the services of a personal priest to legitimize his hybrid religion. A priest was necessary to provide mediation in Israel's religion. Micah's error was worsened by recruiting a Levite to serve as a priest, corrupting his sacred role as a servant to the true priestly office.

Danites Move North (18:1)

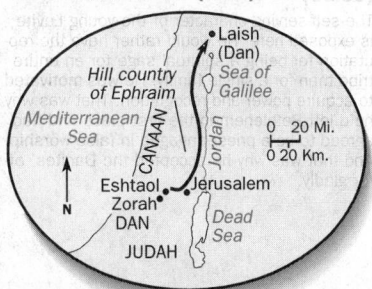

How did the Danites recognize the Levite's voice? (18:3)

It's possible they detected a southern accent since he was some distance from his home. The questions they asked would support such a view. It's also possible that they recognized his religious order by hearing his voice, perhaps as he was chanting a ritual.

---

^a2 That is, about 28 pounds (about 13 kilograms)   ^b4 That is, about 5 pounds (about 2.3 kilograms)   ^c8 Or *To carry on his profession*   ^d10 That is, about 4 ounces (about 110 grams)

unsuspecting and secure. And since their land lacked nothing, they were prosperous.[a] Also, they lived a long way from the Sidonians and had no relationship with anyone else.[b]

8When they returned to Zorah and Eshtaol, their brothers asked them, "How did you find things?"

9They answered, "Come on, let's attack them! We have seen that the land is very good. Aren't you going to do something? Don't hesitate to go there and take it over. **10**When you get there, you will find an unsuspecting people and a spacious land that God has put into your hands, a land that lacks nothing whatever."

11Then six hundred men from the clan of the Danites, armed for battle, set out from Zorah and Eshtaol. **12**On their way they set up camp near Kiriath Jearim in Judah. This is why the place west of Kiriath Jearim is called Mahaneh Dan[c] to this day. **13**From there they went on to the hill country of Ephraim and came to Micah's house.

14Then the five men who had spied out the land of Laish said to their brothers, "Do you know that one of these houses has an ephod[D], other household gods, a carved image and a cast idol[D]? Now you know what to do." **15**So they turned in there and went to the house of the young Levite[D] at Micah's place and greeted him. **16**The six hundred Danites, armed for battle, stood at the entrance to the gate. **17**The five men who had spied out the land went inside and took the carved image, the ephod, the other household gods and the cast idol while the priest and the six hundred armed men stood at the entrance to the gate.

18When these men went into Micah's house and took the carved image, the ephod, the other household gods and the cast idol, the priest said to them, "What are you doing?"

19They answered him, "Be quiet! Don't say a word. Come with us, and be our father and priest. Isn't it better that you serve a tribe and clan in Israel as priest rather than just one man's household?" **20**Then the priest was glad. He took the ephod, the other household gods and the carved image and went along with the people. **21**Putting their little children, their livestock and their possessions in front of them, they turned away and left.

22When they had gone some distance from Micah's house, the men who lived near Micah were called together and overtook the Danites. **23**As they shouted after them, the Danites turned and said to Micah, "What's the matter with you that you called out your men to fight?"

24He replied, "You took the gods I made, and my priest, and went away. What else do I have? How can you ask, 'What's the matter with you?' "

25The Danites answered, "Don't argue with us, or some hot-tempered men will attack you, and you and your family will lose your lives." **26**So the Danites went their way, and Micah, seeing that they were too strong for him, turned around and went back home.

27Then they took what Micah had made, and his priest, and went on to Laish, against a peaceful and unsuspecting people. They attacked them with the sword and burned down their city. **28**There was no one to rescue them because they lived a long way from Sidon and had

Why did the men steal the idols? (18:17)

The Danites thought they could gain supernatural power through the false gods. Later, in their new home, they used Micah's idols for their own religious purposes (v. 31).

Why was the young priest glad? (18:20)

The self-serving character of the young Levite is exposed here. He would rather have the reputation for being a spiritual sage for an entire tribe than for a single family. He was motivated to acquire power and recognition. That was why he'd left Bethlehem in the first place and had agreed to be a priest engaged in false worship. And that was why he accepted the Danites' offer gladly.

Were the Danites right to destroy Laish? (18:27)

What occurred in Laish should never have happened. The Danites had not been overlooked when Joshua originally parceled out Canaan. They had been given the section between the territories of Ephraim and Judah (Joshua 19). Rather than trusting God to help them drive out the Philistines in their allotted territory, the Danites sought an easier way to find themselves a home. They took advantage of an unsuspecting city outside of their territory. Also see *Why did the Danites go after something other than what they were suppose to?* (Joshua 19:47).

---

[a]7 The meaning of the Hebrew for this clause is uncertain.
[b]7 Hebrew; some Septuagint manuscripts *with the Arameans*
[c]12 *Mahaneh Dan* means *Dan's camp.*

no relationship with anyone else. The city was in a valley near Beth Rehob.

The Danites rebuilt the city and settled there. **29**They named it Dan after their forefather Dan, who was born to Israel—though the city used to be called Laish. **30**There the Danites set up for themselves the idols[D], and Jonathan son of Gershom, the son of Moses,[a] and his sons were priests[D] for the tribe of Dan until the time of the captivity of the land. **31**They continued to use the idols Micah had made, all the time the house of God was in Shiloh.

A Levite and His Concubine

19 In those days Israel had no king.

Now a Levite[D] who lived in a remote area in the hill country of Ephraim took a concubine[D] from Bethlehem in Judah. **2**But she was unfaithful to him. She left him and went back to her father's house in Bethlehem, Judah. After she had been there four months, **3**her husband went to her to persuade her to return. He had with him his servant and two donkeys. She took him into her father's house, and when her father saw him, he gladly welcomed him. **4**His father-in-law, the girl's father, prevailed upon him to stay; so he remained with him three days, eating and drinking, and sleeping there.

5On the fourth day they got up early and he prepared to leave, but the girl's father said to his son-in-law, "Refresh yourself with something to eat; then you can go." **6**So the two of them sat down to eat and drink together. Afterward the girl's father said, "Please stay tonight and enjoy yourself." **7**And when the man got up to go, his father-in-law persuaded him, so he stayed there that night. **8**On the morning of the fifth day, when he rose to go, the girl's father said, "Refresh yourself. Wait till afternoon!" So the two of them ate together.

9Then when the man, with his concubine and his servant, got up to leave, his father-in-law, the girl's father, said, "Now look, it's almost evening. Spend the night here; the day is nearly over. Stay and enjoy yourself. Early tomorrow morning you can get up and be on your way home." **10**But, unwilling to stay another night, the man left and went toward Jebus (that is, Jerusalem[D]), with his two saddled donkeys and his concubine.

11When they were near Jebus and the day was almost gone, the servant said to his master, "Come, let's stop at this city of the Jebusites and spend the night."

12His master replied, "No. We won't go into an alien[D] city, whose people are not Israelites. We will go on to Gibeah." **13**He added, "Come, let's try to reach Gibeah or Ramah and spend the night in one of those places." **14**So they went on, and the sun set as they neared Gibeah in Benjamin. **15**There they stopped to spend the night. They went and sat in the city square, but no one took them into his home for the night.

16That evening an old man from the hill country of Ephraim, who was living in Gibeah (the men of the place were Benjamites), came in from his work in the fields. **17**When he looked and saw the traveler in the city square, the old man asked, "Where are you going? Where did you come from?"

18He answered, "We are on our way from Bethlehem in

How could Moses' grandson be involved in idol worship? (18:30–31)

When there is no prophetic voice clarifying the truth and calling the faithful into accountability, the result can be outright heresy. Even Moses' brother slipped into idolatry during Moses' brief absence on Mount Sinai (Exodus 32:1–6). It wasn't that these Israelites intended to reject the Lord; they just didn't think that it mattered if they included other gods in their worship.

Why the forced hospitality? (19:5–10)

In the culture of the ancient Middle East, hospitality was considered an extension of the host himself. Also, because his daughter had disgraced the family name by being unfaithful to her husband and returning to her childhood home, her father was all the more determined to lavish his son-in-law with expressions of apology and regret. Out of respect to his father-in-law and host, the young Levite remained longer than he really wanted to.

---

a 30 An ancient Hebrew scribal tradition, some Septuagint manuscripts and Vulgate; Masoretic Text *Manasseh*

Judah to a remote area in the hill country of Ephraim where I live. I have been to Bethlehem in Judah and now I am going to the house of the LORD. No one has taken me into his house. **19**We have both straw and fodder for our donkeys and bread and wine for ourselves your servants—me, your maidservant, and the young man with us. We don't need anything."

20"You are welcome at my house," the old man said. "Let me supply whatever you need. Only don't spend the night in the square." **21**So he took him into his house and fed his donkeys. After they had washed their feet, they had something to eat and drink.

22While they were enjoying themselves, some of the wicked men of the city surrounded the house. Pounding on the door, they shouted to the old man who owned the house, "Bring out the man who came to your house so we can have sex with him."

23The owner of the house went outside and said to them, "No, my friends, don't be so vile. Since this man is my guest, don't do this disgraceful thing. **24**Look, here is my virgin daughter, and his concubineD. I will bring them out to you now, and you can use them and do to them whatever you wish. But to this man, don't do such a disgraceful thing."

25But the men would not listen to him. So the man took his concubine and sent her outside to them, and they raped her and abused her throughout the night, and at dawn they let her go. **26**At daybreak the woman went back to the house where her master was staying, fell down at the door and lay there until daylight.

27When her master got up in the morning and opened the door of the house and stepped out to continue on his way, there lay his concubine, fallen in the doorway of the house, with her hands on the threshold. **28**He said to her, "Get up; let's go." But there was no answer. Then the man put her on his donkey and set out for home.

29When he reached home, he took a knife and cut up his concubine, limb by limb, into twelve parts and sent them into all the areas of Israel. **30**Everyone who saw it said, "Such a thing has never been seen or done, not since the day the Israelites came up out of Egypt. Think about it! Consider it! Tell us what to do!"

Israelites Fight the Benjamites

20 Then all the Israelites from Dan to Beersheba and from the land of Gilead came out as one man and assembled before the LORD in Mizpah. **2**The leaders of all the people of the tribes of Israel took their places in the assembly of the people of God, four hundred thousand soldiers armed with swords. **3**(The Benjamites heard that the Israelites had gone up to Mizpah.) Then the Israelites said, "Tell us how this awful thing happened."

4So the LeviteD, the husband of the murdered woman, said, "I and my concubine came to Gibeah in Benjamin to spend the night. **5**During the night the men of Gibeah came after me and surrounded the house, intending to kill me. They raped my concubine, and she died. **6**I took my concubine, cut her into pieces and sent one piece to each region of Israel's inheritance, because they committed this lewd and disgraceful act in Israel. **7**Now, all you Israelites, speak up and give your verdict."

8All the people rose as one man, saying, "None of us will go home. No, not one of us will return to his house. **9**But now this is what we'll do to Gibeah: We'll go up

Why sacrifice a daughter to protect a stranger? (19:24)
Influenced by the moral decay in his culture, the old man's priorities were obviously misplaced. As people defined their values for themselves (17:6), society sank as low as human depravity would allow it to go. Though the old man's values said homosexual rape was wrong, he considered the rape of his daughter a necessity to protect his guest. In those days women were often treated as property—objects rather than people. See *Were Israelite girls treated like property?* (Joshua 15:17).

Why was the Levite so outraged, when he was partially to blame? (19:25; 20:6)
In his distorted view, he had given his concubine to the men of Gibeah for sexual entertainment—nothing more. But (he reasoned) they had abused his generosity by raping his concubine to the point of death. He had been thinking only of his own safety when he sent her out to them in the first place. It's possible that now he was at least partially angry with himself, but he vented all his anger at the gang of rapists.

Why did he mutilate her body? (19:29)
Given the fact that she was already dead, the Levite resorted to this grisly act to appeal to the emotions of the surrounding tribes. He hoped to arouse their indignation by graphically illustrating the heinous crime. Their visceral response motivated them to demand justice against the rapists.

against it as the lot directs. [10]We'll take ten men out of every hundred from all the tribes of Israel, and a hundred from a thousand, and a thousand from ten thousand, to get provisions for the army. Then, when the army arrives at Gibeah[a] in Benjamin, it can give them what they deserve for all this vileness done in Israel." [11]So all the men of Israel got together and united as one man against the city.

[12]The tribes of Israel sent men throughout the tribe of Benjamin, saying, "What about this awful crime that was committed among you? [13]Now surrender those wicked men of Gibeah so that we may put them to death[D] and purge the evil from Israel."

But the Benjamites would not listen to their fellow Israelites. [14]From their towns they came together at Gibeah to fight against the Israelites. [15]At once the Benjamites mobilized twenty-six thousand swordsmen from their towns, in addition to seven hundred chosen men from those living in Gibeah. [16]Among all these soldiers there were seven hundred chosen men who were left-handed, each of whom could sling a stone at a hair and not miss.

[17]Israel, apart from Benjamin, mustered four hundred thousand swordsmen, all of them fighting men.

[18]The Israelites went up to Bethel[b] and inquired of God. They said, "Who of us shall go first to fight against the Benjamites?"

The LORD replied, "Judah shall go first."

[19]The next morning the Israelites got up and pitched camp near Gibeah. [20]The men of Israel went out to fight the Benjamites and took up battle positions against them at Gibeah. [21]The Benjamites came out of Gibeah and cut down twenty-two thousand Israelites on the battlefield that day. [22]But the men of Israel encouraged one another and again took up their positions where they had stationed themselves the first day. [23]The Israelites went up and wept before the LORD until evening, and they inquired of the LORD. They said, "Shall we go up again to battle against the Benjamites, our brothers?"

The LORD answered, "Go up against them."

[24]Then the Israelites drew near to Benjamin the second day. [25]This time, when the Benjamites came out from Gibeah to oppose them, they cut down another eighteen thousand Israelites, all of them armed with swords.

[26]Then the Israelites, all the people, went up to Bethel, and there they sat weeping before the LORD. They fasted that day until evening and presented burnt offerings[D] and fellowship offerings[Dc] to the LORD. [27]And the Israelites inquired of the LORD. (In those days the ark of the covenant[D] of God was there, [28]with Phinehas son of Eleazar, the son of Aaron, ministering before it.) They asked, "Shall we go up again to battle with Benjamin our brother, or not?"

The LORD responded, "Go, for tomorrow I will give them into your hands."

[29]Then Israel set an ambush around Gibeah. [30]They went up against the Benjamites on the third day and took up positions against Gibeah as they had done before. [31]The Benjamites came out to meet them and were drawn away from the city. They began to inflict casualties on the Israelites as before, so that about thirty men fell in the

Why did the Benjamites defend the guilty? (20:13-14)

The "law" of the land was that each one did what he felt was right according to his own values (17:6). The Benjamites placed tribal loyalty above bringing the men of Gibeah to justice for their atrocity.

Why, after gaining God's guidance, did the Israelites lose 40,000 people? (20:18-25)

Before they consulted the Lord, the Israelites made several vows (20:8; 21:1,5). This suggests that they were not depending solely on God. So, with mixed motivations, they could not expect the outcome to be without disappointment or disaster.

---

[a]10 One Hebrew manuscript; most Hebrew manuscripts *Geba*, a variant of *Gibeah*   [b]18 Or *to the house of God*; also in verse 26
[c]26 Traditionally *peace offerings*

Although the Bible does not always give such details regarding the ebb and flow of a battle, it is helpful on occasion to see with vivid clarity how things actually occurred. Biblical history seems more real and affects us more when we read details. This is more than words on a page; it's the account of flesh-and-blood people who once lived and breathed and had feelings—just as we do now. Details help us see the emotions behind the history: the sorrow and confusion of the Israelites (vv. 26,28) followed by their scheming (vv. 29,32); and the overconfidence of the Benjamites (vv. 32,34,39), which gave way to terror and panic (vv. 41-42).

Why destroy the whole tribe—even animals—for the sin of a few? (20:48)

The precedent for total annihilation is found in the Lord's words to Moses (Deut. 13:15) and Joshua (Joshua 6:18) concerning the occupation of the land. But limited retribution had been prescribed by the Lord for his own people (Exodus 21:12-36). The Israelites administered justice incorrectly in the case of the Benjamites because of their own defective morality. Also see article: **Why kill everything?** (Joshua 6:21).

open field and on the roads—the one leading to Bethel and the other to Gibeah.

32While the Benjamites were saying, "We are defeating them as before," the Israelites were saying, "Let's retreat and draw them away from the city to the roads."

33All the men of Israel moved from their places and took up positions at Baal Tamar, and the Israelite ambush charged out of its place on the west*a* of Gibeah.*b* **34**Then ten thousand of Israel's finest men made a frontal attack on Gibeah. The fighting was so heavy that the Benjamites did not realize how near disaster was. **35**The LORD defeated Benjamin before Israel, and on that day the Israelites struck down 25,100 Benjamites, all armed with swords. **36**Then the Benjamites saw that they were beaten.

Now the men of Israel had given way before Benjamin, because they relied on the ambush they had set near Gibeah. **37**The men who had been in ambush made a sudden dash into Gibeah, spread out and put the whole city to the sword. **38**The men of Israel had arranged with the ambush that they should send up a great cloud of smoke from the city, **39**and then the men of Israel would turn in the battle.

The Benjamites had begun to inflict casualties on the men of Israel (about thirty), and they said, "We are defeating them as in the first battle." **40**But when the column of smoke began to rise from the city, the Benjamites turned and saw the smoke of the whole city going up into the sky. **41**Then the men of Israel turned on them, and the men of Benjamin were terrified, because they realized that disaster had come upon them. **42**So they fled before the Israelites in the direction of the desert, but they could not escape the battle. And the men of Israel who came out of the towns cut them down there. **43**They surrounded the Benjamites, chased them and easily*c* overran them in the vicinity of Gibeah on the east. **44**Eighteen thousand Benjamites fell, all of them valiant fighters. **45**As they turned and fled toward the desert to the rock of Rimmon, the Israelites cut down five thousand men along the roads. They kept pressing after the Benjamites as far as Gidom and struck down two thousand more.

46On that day twenty-five thousand Benjamite swordsmen fell, all of them valiant fighters. **47**But six hundred men turned and fled into the desert to the rock of Rimmon, where they stayed four months. **48**The men of Israel went back to Benjamin and put all the towns to the sword, including the animals and everything else they found. All the towns they came across they set on fire.

Wives for the Benjamites

21 The men of Israel had taken an oath at Mizpah: "Not one of us will give his daughter in marriage to a Benjamite."

2The people went to Bethel,*d* where they sat before God until evening, raising their voices and weeping bitterly. **3**"O LORD, the God of Israel," they cried, "why has this happened to Israel? Why should one tribe be missing from Israel today?"

4Early the next day the people built an altar and presented burnt offerings*D* and fellowship offerings.*e*

5Then the Israelites asked, "Who from all the tribes of

*a33 Some Septuagint manuscripts and Vulgate; the meaning of the Hebrew for this word is uncertain.   b33 Hebrew Geba, a variant of Gibeah   c43 The meaning of the Hebrew for this word is uncertain. d2 Or to the house of God   e4 Traditionally peace offerings

Israel has failed to assemble before the LORD?" For they had taken a solemn oath that anyone who failed to assemble before the LORD at Mizpah should certainly be put to death^D.

6Now the Israelites grieved for their brothers, the Benjamites. "Today one tribe is cut off from Israel," they said. 7"How can we provide wives for those who are left, since we have taken an oath by the LORD not to give them any of our daughters in marriage?" 8Then they asked, "Which one of the tribes of Israel failed to assemble before the LORD at Mizpah?" They discovered that no one from Jabesh Gilead had come to the camp for the assembly. 9For when they counted the people, they found that none of the people of Jabesh Gilead were there.

10So the assembly sent twelve thousand fighting men with instructions to go to Jabesh Gilead and put to the sword those living there, including the women and children. 11"This is what you are to do," they said. "Kill every male and every woman who is not a virgin." 12They found among the people living in Jabesh Gilead four hundred young women who had never slept with a man, and they took them to the camp at Shiloh in Canaan.

13Then the whole assembly sent an offer of peace^D to the Benjamites at the rock of Rimmon. 14So the Benjamites returned at that time and were given the women of Jabesh Gilead who had been spared. But there were not enough for all of them.

15The people grieved for Benjamin, because the LORD had made a gap in the tribes of Israel. 16And the elders of the assembly said, "With the women of Benjamin destroyed, how shall we provide wives for the men who are left? 17The Benjamite survivors must have heirs," they said, "so that a tribe of Israel will not be wiped out. 18We can't give them our daughters as wives, since we Israelites have taken this oath: 'Cursed be anyone who gives a wife to a Benjamite.' 19But look, there is the annual festival of the LORD in Shiloh, to the north of Bethel, and east of the road that goes from Bethel to Shechem, and to the south of Lebonah."

20So they instructed the Benjamites, saying, "Go and hide in the vineyards 21and watch. When the girls of Shiloh come out to join in the dancing, then rush from the vineyards and each of you seize a wife from the girls of Shiloh and go to the land of Benjamin. 22When their fathers or brothers complain to us, we will say to them, 'Do us a kindness by helping them, because we did not get wives for them during the war, and you are innocent, since you did not give your daughters to them.' "

23So that is what the Benjamites did. While the girls were dancing, each man caught one and carried her off to be his wife. Then they returned to their inheritance and rebuilt the towns and settled in them.

24At that time the Israelites left that place and went home to their tribes and clans, each to his own inheritance.

25In those days Israel had no king; everyone did as he saw fit.

Where was the justice in all this killing? (21:10–11; see 20:47)

The lesson here is that there is no justice when people take morality into their own hands. God never told the Israelites to annihilate the tribe of Benjamin. He never told them to withhold their daughters from marriage to the survivors, or to massacre the men of Jabesh Gilead. This whole account, from beginning to end, shows innocent people suffering because the Israelites put their own interests first (17:6).

Girls of Shiloh . . . dancing (21:19–21)

This dancing was most likely part of the Feast of the Tabernacles, a joyful celebration of God's provisions in the desert. During this time the tabernacle and the ark of the covenant were kept at Shiloh (see *Map 4* of the back of this Bible).

Why kidnap to acquire a wife? (21:21)

This custom was probably borrowed from the pagans. It seemed to be the only way around the thoughtless vow they had made apart from the Lord's guidance (v. 1). They could avoid breaking their vow and still allow the Benjamites to take their daughters in marriage.

RUTH

Why read this book?

If you've ever felt like an outsider struggling to fit in, you'll identify with Ruth, the heroine of this book. In the culture she lived in, Ruth had several strikes against her. At that time, people honored women with children; she had none. Women were dependent on their husbands; she was a widow. Communities were close-knit; she was a foreigner. But this is the story of an outsider who was brought in, saved from poverty and ostracism. So you'll find hope in this book—a picture of God, who wants "outsiders" to come to him for help.

Who wrote this book?

Jewish tradition traces the story to Samuel, but it was likely penned later by an unknown writer.

When was it written?

The events in Ruth probably took place during the period of the judges (1375–1050 B.C.). The date at which the story was written is not known, though it was likely after 1000 B.C.

Why was it written?

To retell an important story and perhaps to encourage the Israelites to include foreigners in their nation (see Isaiah 56:1–8).

To whom was it written?

To the people of Israel.

What to look for in Ruth:

Redemption—the theme permeates this book: Ruth is transformed from poverty to wealth, widow to wife, barren to fertile and foreigner to Israelite. Boaz, a *kinsman-redeemer* who gives Ruth and her mother-in-law, Naomi, a new life, is a key figure.

Naomi and Ruth

1 In the days when the judges ruled,[a] there was a famine in the land, and a man from Bethlehem in Judah, together with his wife and two sons, went to live for a while in the country of Moab. [2]The man's name was Elimelech, his wife's name Naomi, and the names of his two sons were Mahlon and Kilion. They were Ephrathites from Bethlehem, Judah. And they went to Moab and lived there.

[3]Now Elimelech, Naomi's husband, died, and she was left with her two sons. [4]They married Moabite women, one named Orpah and the other Ruth. After they had lived there about ten years, [5]both Mahlon and Kilion also died, and Naomi was left without her two sons and her husband.

[6]When she heard in Moab that the LORD had come to the aid of his people by providing food for them, Naomi and her daughters-in-law prepared to return home from there. [7]With her two daughters-in-law she left the place where she had been living and set out on the road that would take them back to the land of Judah.

[8]Then Naomi said to her two daughters-in-law, "Go back, each of you, to your mother's home. May the LORD show kindness to you, as you have shown to your dead and to me. [9]May the LORD grant that each of you will find rest in the home of another husband."

Then she kissed them and they wept aloud [10]and said to her, "We will go back with you to your people."

[11]But Naomi said, "Return home, my daughters. Why would you come with me? Am I going to have any more sons, who could become your husbands? [12]Return home, my daughters; I am too old to have another husband. Even if I thought there was still hope for me—even if I had a husband tonight and then gave birth to sons— [13]would you wait until they grew up? Would you remain unmarried for them? No, my daughters. It is more bitter for me than for you, because the LORD's hand has gone out against me!"

[14]At this they wept again. Then Orpah kissed her mother-in-law good-by, but Ruth clung to her.

[15]"Look," said Naomi, "your sister-in-law is going back to her people and her gods. Go back with her."

[16]But Ruth replied, "Don't urge me to leave you or to turn back from you. Where you go I will go, and where you stay I will stay. Your people will be my people and your God my God. [17]Where you die I will die, and there I will be buried. May the LORD deal with me, be it ever so severely, if anything but death[b] separates you and me."

[18]When Naomi realized that Ruth was determined to go with her, she stopped urging her.

[19]So the two women went on until they came to Bethlehem. When they arrived in Bethlehem, the whole town was stirred because of them, and the women exclaimed, "Can this be Naomi?"

[20]"Don't call me Naomi,[b]" she told them. "Call me Mara,[c] because the Almighty[d] has made my life very bitter. [21]I went away full, but the LORD has brought me back empty. Why call me Naomi? The LORD has afflicted[D][e] me; the Almighty has brought misfortune upon me."

---

[a]1 Traditionally *judged*   [b]20 *Naomi* means *pleasant*; also in verse 21.   [c]20 *Mara* means *bitter*.   [d]20 Hebrew *Shaddai*; also in verse 21   [e]21 Or *has testified against*

Setting of Ruth (1:1)

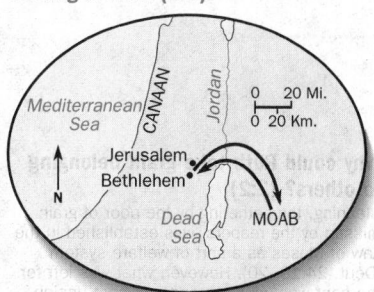

Was it wrong for an Israelite to marry a Moabite? (1:4)

No disapproval by God is implied here. Marriage with the Moabites was not forbidden by God, but no Moabites or their sons to the tenth generation were allowed in the tabernacle (Deut. 23:3). The Moabites, though not Israelites, were considered distant relatives, because they were descendants of Lot, Abraham's nephew (Gen. 19:36–37). As a result, the restrictions against marriage to foreigners did not apply to the Moabites.

Was God to blame for Naomi's bitterness? (1:13,20–21)

It's true that God allowed tragedies to happen to Naomi, but he did not force her to respond with bitterness. She was responsible for that choice, not God.

Why did Naomi tell Ruth to return to her own gods? (1:15)

Why wasn't she more concerned that her daughter-in-law worship the true God? Naomi knew Ruth and Orpah, as foreigners, would socially be at a great disadvantage in Israel. She urged them to go back because she cared about them. In the ancient Middle East, people were seen as an inseparable unit, part and parcel with their land and their gods.

Was Ruth disloyal to her own family and people? (1:16–18)

Obviously, Ruth had to abandon her own people who did not serve the Lord. But she was not being disloyal to them so much as she was being loyal to the Lord. Ruth's decision to leave Moab and go with Naomi was literally a conversion. She vowed to serve Naomi's God. Later Boaz recognized her as a believer (2:12).

Why would Ruth ask God to punish her if she broke her promise? (1:17)

Ruth's words indicate the depth of her loyalty. She recognized that this was a life-and-death decision. Taking a vow of this sort was not uncommon in ancient times. It was an expression of intense feelings.

Why could Ruth take grain belonging to others? (2:2)

Gleaning, the gathering by the poor of grain missed by the reapers, was established in the Law of Moses as a sort of welfare system (Deut. 24:19–20). However, what was left for the poor was usually meager at best (Isaiah 17:5–6). As a favor, Boaz left more for Ruth to pick up (vv. 15–16). See *Why have welfare dependent on inefficient harvesting?* (Deut. 24:19–21).

Was Ruth in danger of being molested? (2:9; also see 2:22)

As a foreigner, as well as a widow with no family who could protect her, Ruth was socially vulnerable. We are not specifically told what might have happened to her, but Boaz's blunt instruction to the men working in the fields suggests that single women were perhaps in danger of harassment—if not worse.

²²So Naomi returned from Moab accompanied by Ruth the Moabitess, her daughter-in-law, arriving in Bethlehem as the barley harvest was beginning.

Ruth Meets Boaz

2 Now Naomi had a relative on her husband's side, from the clan of Elimelech, a man of standing, whose name was Boaz.

²And Ruth the Moabitess said to Naomi, "Let me go to the fields and pick up the leftover grain behind anyone in whose eyes I find favor."

Naomi said to her, "Go ahead, my daughter." ³So she went out and began to glean in the fields behind the harvesters. As it turned out, she found herself working in a field belonging to Boaz, who was from the clan of Elimelech.

⁴Just then Boaz arrived from Bethlehem and greeted the harvesters, "The LORD be with you!"

"The LORD bless you!" they called back.

⁵Boaz asked the foreman of his harvesters, "Whose young woman is that?"

⁶The foreman replied, "She is the Moabitess who came back from Moab with Naomi. ⁷She said, 'Please let me glean and gather among the sheaves behind the harvesters.' She went into the field and has worked steadily from morning till now, except for a short rest in the shelter."

⁸So Boaz said to Ruth, "My daughter, listen to me. Don't go and glean in another field and don't go away from here. Stay here with my servant girls. ⁹Watch the field where the men are harvesting, and follow along after the girls. I have told the men not to touch you. And whenever you are thirsty, go and get a drink from the water jars the men have filled."

¹⁰At this, she bowed down with her face to the ground. She exclaimed, "Why have I found such favor in your eyes that you notice me—a foreigner?"

¹¹Boaz replied, "I've been told all about what you have done for your mother-in-law since the death^D of your husband—how you left your father and mother and your homeland and came to live with a people you did not know before. ¹²May the LORD repay you for what you have done. May you be richly rewarded by the LORD, the God of Israel, under whose wings you have come to take refuge."

¹³"May I continue to find favor in your eyes, my lord," she said. "You have given me comfort and have spoken kindly to your servant—though I do not have the standing of one of your servant girls."

¹⁴At mealtime Boaz said to her, "Come over here. Have some bread and dip it in the wine vinegar."

When she sat down with the harvesters, he offered her some roasted grain. She ate all she wanted and had some left over. ¹⁵As she got up to glean, Boaz gave orders to his men, "Even if she gathers among the sheaves, don't embarrass her. ¹⁶Rather, pull out some stalks for her from the bundles and leave them for her to pick up, and don't rebuke her."

¹⁷So Ruth gleaned in the field until evening. Then she threshed the barley she had gathered, and it amounted to about an ephah.^a ¹⁸She carried it back to town, and her mother-in-law saw how much she had gathered. Ruth

---

^a17 That is, probably about 3/5 bushel (about 22 liters)

also brought out and gave her what she had left over after she had eaten enough.

¹⁹Her mother-in-law asked her, "Where did you glean today? Where did you work? Blessed be the man who took notice of you!"

Then Ruth told her mother-in-law about the one at whose place she had been working. "The name of the man I worked with today is Boaz," she said.

²⁰"The LORD bless him!" Naomi said to her daughter-in-law. "He has not stopped showing his kindness to the living and the dead." She added, "That man is our close relative; he is one of our kinsman-redeemers."

²¹Then Ruth the Moabitess said, "He even said to me, 'Stay with my workers until they finish harvesting all my grain.' "

²²Naomi said to Ruth her daughter-in-law, "It will be good for you, my daughter, to go with his girls, because in someone else's field you might be harmed."

²³So Ruth stayed close to the servant girls of Boaz to glean until the barley and wheat harvests were finished. And she lived with her mother-in-law.

Ruth and Boaz at the Threshing Floor

3 One day Naomi her mother-in-law said to her, "My daughter, should I not try to find a home*a* for you, where you will be well provided for? ²Is not Boaz, with whose servant girls you have been, a kinsman of ours? Tonight he will be winnowing barley on the threshing floor. ³Wash and perfume yourself, and put on your best clothes. Then go down to the threshing floor, but don't let him know you are there until he has finished eating and drinking. ⁴When he lies down, note the place where he is lying. Then go and uncover his feet and lie down. He will tell you what to do."

⁵"I will do whatever you say," Ruth answered. ⁶So she went down to the threshing floor and did everything her mother-in-law told her to do.

⁷When Boaz had finished eating and drinking and was

---

a 1 Hebrew *find rest* (see Ruth 1:9)

Why did Boaz sleep at the threshing floor? (3:7)
There was general disregard for the law during this time. So it's likely that Boaz and others slept at the threshing floor to protect the grain from theft or vandalism.

Was Ruth being immoral? (3:7-8,13-14)
Although this custom may sound questionable to modern ears, Ruth was above reproach. Her actions were simply a ceremonial request for marriage. Anything immoral would have been out of character for her (v. 11).

What was a kinsman-redeemer? (2:20; 3:12; 4:3-6)

A kinsman-redeemer was a close, influential relative to whom members of the extended family could turn for help, usually when the family line or possessions were in danger of being lost. He was supposed to buy back family land sold during a crisis (Lev. 25:25), buy back enslaved relatives (Lev. 25:47-49), provide an heir for a dead brother (Deut. 25:5-10), avenge the killing of a relative (Num. 35:19-21) and care for relatives in difficult circumstances (Jer. 32:6-25).

The idea of the kinsman-redeemer is also used at times to refer to God and his redemption of Israel (Exodus 6:6-8; Job 19:25; Psalms 19:14; 69:18; Isaiah 43:1). In these passages, God is Israel's nearest kinsman, stepping in to bring the nation back into his family when the people could not do it themselves.

The word is also used to prophesy the coming of the Messiah (Isaiah 59:20). Christ is our near kinsman who came to buy us back into God's family. In the New Testament the concept is reflected in the various words for *redeem*, which suggest paying a ransom, making a purchase or saving from loss.

What did it mean to *spread the corner of your garment* over someone? (3:9)

This may have been a play on words in the original language. *Garment* (singular) referred to a custom that had to do with making a marriage proposal. The same word (plural) could mean *wings*—suggesting that, more than marriage, this was a request for protection. Boaz used the term earlier when he said Ruth trusted God by taking refuge under his *wings* (2:12).

How was Ruth being kind to Boaz? (3:10)

Earlier Ruth had shown exceptional kindness toward Naomi (see 2:11). Now she showed an even greater kindness, according to Boaz, by expressing an interest in him when she could have *run after the younger men.* He may also have been impressed that she chose to follow Hebrew law regarding marriage.

Why did Naomi want to sell her land? (4:3)

There are two possible answers: (1) If Naomi's husband had sold the land before they left for Moab (1:1), Naomi still had the right to redeem the property (Lev. 25:23–25). If this was the case, Naomi technically would have been selling her right to repurchase the land—something she could offer only to a close relative. (2) More likely, Naomi still owned the land but was forced to sell because she needed the money it would bring. The law specified that if someone needed to sell property, the kinsman-redeemer could pay to redeem the land. Boaz offered first rights to the property to the one most closely related to Naomi.

If redeeming the land also meant marrying the widow, why didn't Boaz marry Naomi? (4:5)

The reason for marrying the widow was to provide an heir in the name of the deceased. Naomi was presumably beyond childbearing age, so there was no reason for her to remarry. Furthermore, her husband's name already had been passed on to his son, Ruth's deceased husband.

How would his own estate be endangered? (4:6)

This man apparently already had a family of his own who stood to inherit his property. An additional wife and a son by Ruth could possibly have caused a family dispute, undermining the distribution of his estate. There was also the possibility that if a son by Ruth were his only surviving heir, the land he already owned would pass into the family of Elimelech. He must have felt that these factors were too great a risk for him to take. Boaz, by contrast, was willing to endanger his own estate.

in good spirits, he went over to lie down at the far end of the grain pile. Ruth approached quietly, uncovered his feet and lay down. **8**In the middle of the night something startled the man, and he turned and discovered a woman lying at his feet.

9"Who are you?" he asked.

"I am your servant Ruth," she said. "Spread the corner of your garment over me, since you are a kinsman-redeemer."

10"The LORD bless you, my daughter," he replied. "This kindness is greater than that which you showed earlier: You have not run after the younger men, whether rich or poor. **11**And now, my daughter, don't be afraid. I will do for you all you ask. All my fellow townsmen know that you are a woman of noble character. **12**Although it is true that I am near of kin, there is a kinsman-redeemer nearer than I. **13**Stay here for the night, and in the morning if he wants to redeem*D*, good; let him redeem. But if he is not willing, as surely as the LORD lives I will do it. Lie here until morning."

14So she lay at his feet until morning, but got up before anyone could be recognized; and he said, "Don't let it be known that a woman came to the threshing floor."

15He also said, "Bring me the shawl you are wearing and hold it out." When she did so, he poured into it six measures of barley and put it on her. Then he*a* went back to town.

16When Ruth came to her mother-in-law, Naomi asked, "How did it go, my daughter?"

Then she told her everything Boaz had done for her **17**and added, "He gave me these six measures of barley, saying, 'Don't go back to your mother-in-law empty-handed.'"

18Then Naomi said, "Wait, my daughter, until you find out what happens. For the man will not rest until the matter is settled today."

Boaz Marries Ruth

4 Meanwhile Boaz went up to the town gate and sat there. When the kinsman-redeemer he had mentioned came along, Boaz said, "Come over here, my friend, and sit down." So he went over and sat down. **2**Boaz took ten of the elders of the town and said, "Sit here," and they did so. **3**Then he said to the kinsman-redeemer, "Naomi, who has come back from Moab, is selling the piece of land that belonged to our brother Elimelech. **4**I thought I should bring the matter to your attention and suggest that you buy it in the presence of these seated here and in the presence of the elders of my people. If you will redeem it, do so. But if you*b* will not, tell me, so I will know. For no one has the right to do it except you, and I am next in line."

"I will redeem it," he said.

5Then Boaz said, "On the day you buy the land from Naomi and from Ruth the Moabitess, you acquire*c* the dead man's widow, in order to maintain the name of the dead with his property."

6At this, the kinsman-redeemer said, "Then I cannot re-

---

a15 Most Hebrew manuscripts; many Hebrew manuscripts, Vulgate and Syriac *she*   *b4* Many Hebrew manuscripts, Septuagint, Vulgate and Syriac; most Hebrew manuscripts *he*   *c5* Hebrew; Vulgate and Syriac *Naomi, you acquire Ruth the Moabitess,*

deem[D] it because I might endanger my own estate. You redeem it yourself. I cannot do it."

7(Now in earlier times in Israel, for the redemption[D] and transfer of property to become final, one party took off his sandal and gave it to the other. This was the method of legalizing transactions in Israel.)

8So the kinsman-redeemer said to Boaz, "Buy it yourself." And he removed his sandal.

9Then Boaz announced to the elders and all the people, "Today you are witnesses that I have bought from Naomi all the property of Elimelech, Kilion and Mahlon. 10I have also acquired Ruth the Moabitess, Mahlon's widow, as my wife, in order to maintain the name of the dead with his property, so that his name will not disappear from among his family or from the town records. Today you are witnesses!"

11Then the elders and all those at the gate said, "We are witnesses. May the LORD make the woman who is coming into your home like Rachel and Leah, who together built up the house of Israel. May you have standing in Ephrathah and be famous in Bethlehem. 12Through the offspring the LORD gives you by this young woman, may your family be like that of Perez, whom Tamar bore to Judah."

The Genealogy of David

13So Boaz took Ruth and she became his wife. Then he went to her, and the LORD enabled her to conceive, and she gave birth to a son. 14The women said to Naomi: "Praise be to the LORD, who this day has not left you without a kinsman-redeemer. May he become famous throughout Israel! 15He will renew your life and sustain you in your old age. For your daughter-in-law, who loves you and who is better to you than seven sons, has given him birth."

16Then Naomi took the child, laid him in her lap and cared for him. 17The women living there said, "Naomi has a son." And they named him Obed. He was the father of Jesse, the father of David.

18This, then, is the family line of Perez:

Perez was the father of Hezron,
19Hezron the father of Ram,
Ram the father of Amminadab,
20Amminadab the father of Nahshon,
Nahshon the father of Salmon,[a]
21Salmon the father of Boaz,
Boaz the father of Obed,
22Obed the father of Jesse,
and Jesse the father of David.

What kind of blessing is this? (4:12)

First, Perez was Boaz's ancestor, so it would be natural to refer to him in the blessing. Secondly, Tamar's situation was similar to Ruth's. She was a widow facing a childless future (Gen. 38:13–30). Judah did not keep his word by offering his youngest son for Tamar, so she tricked him into having relations with her. Perez, who along with his twin brother was the result of that union, apparently portrayed offspring born into a hopeless situation. Such a blessing would have been a call for good to be redeemed from bad—in this case, the difficulties that Naomi and Ruth had endured.

How was this baby Naomi's kinsman-redeemer? (4:14–15)

Some think the women meant that Boaz was the kinsman-redeemer and the baby was the one who would become famous. Others, however, believe that there was a sense in which the baby joined a line of kinsman-redeemers, with the responsibility passed down through generations. Certainly their hope for Naomi was that this child would renew her life and sustain her in her old age, things a kinsman-redeemer would do.

If Boaz married Ruth to preserve Mahlon's name, why isn't Mahlon in the lineage? (4:21; see 4:10)

In the Bible, genealogies are almost always selective and do not list everyone in the family. We must assume that Mahlon's name was preserved in the town records of the family. The genealogy in 1 Chronicles 2:4–13 is very similar and perhaps was adapted for the end of the book of Ruth.

Why choose a Moabitess to be an ancestor of David? (4:22)

Ruth's faith in the Lord made it possible for her to be an ancestor of David and, eventually, the Messiah. When God chose a Moabitess, he showed that the new covenant would be for all people who believed, not just for the Hebrews.

[a]20 A few Hebrew manuscripts, some Septuagint manuscripts and Vulgate (see also verse 21 and Septuagint of 1 Chron. 2:11); most Hebrew manuscripts Salma

1 SAMUEL

Why read this book?

A great play, according to playwright Arthur Miller, is one in which you discover your own characteristics in the drama's characters. That may also be true of great books. In the two books of Samuel you will find heroic stories and colorful characters. As you experience their tragedies and triumphs, their emotional highs and lows, you'll learn more about yourself—and how God wants to work in your life. A common thread through all these stories is God's undying faithfulness to his people.

Who wrote this book?

The author is anonymous. The prophets Samuel, Nathan, and Gad all kept records (1 Chron. 29:29), which later may have been combined to form 1 and 2 Samuel. Others think official court historians may have chronicled these events (see 2 Samuel 8:16–17; 1 Kings 4:3).

When was it written?

Perhaps around 900 B.C., sometime after the division of the nation into the northern and southern kingdoms in 931 B.C.

Why was it written?

1 Samuel continues the history of God's relationship with his people. It connects the era when the judges ruled Israel to the time of the kings.

What to look for in 1 Samuel:

Each of the book's main characters has flaws and strengths. But some are blessed by God while others receive his judgment. Look for the qualities of the soul that God honors in his people. You also will spot God's amazing grace despite Israel's obstinate ways and wavering commitment.

When did these things happen?

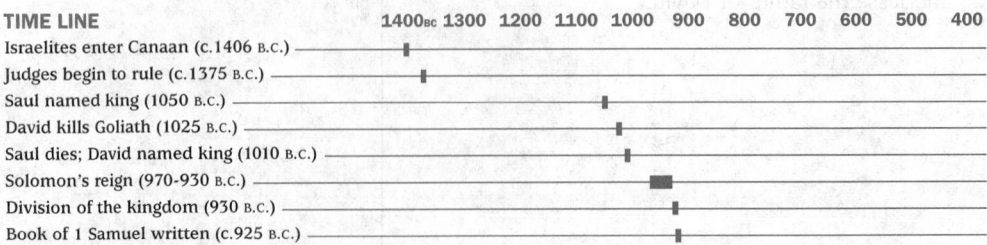

TIME LINE	1400BC	1300	1200	1100	1000	900	800	700	600	500	400
Israelites enter Canaan (c.1406 B.C.)											
Judges begin to rule (c.1375 B.C.)											
Saul named king (1050 B.C.)											
David kills Goliath (1025 B.C.)											
Saul dies; David named king (1010 B.C.)											
Solomon's reign (970-930 B.C.)											
Division of the kingdom (930 B.C.)											
Book of 1 Samuel written (c.925 B.C.)											

The Birth of Samuel

1 There was a certain man from Ramathaim, a Zuphite[a] from the hill country of Ephraim, whose name was Elkanah son of Jeroham, the son of Elihu, the son of Tohu, the son of Zuph, an Ephraimite. **2**He had two wives; one was called Hannah and the other Peninnah. Peninnah had children, but Hannah had none.

3Year after year this man went up from his town to worship and sacrifice[D] to the LORD Almighty at Shiloh, where Hophni and Phinehas, the two sons of Eli, were priests[D] of the LORD. **4**Whenever the day came for Elkanah to sacrifice, he would give portions of the meat to his wife Peninnah and to all her sons and daughters. **5**But to Hannah he gave a double portion because he loved her, and the LORD had closed her womb. **6**And because the LORD had closed her womb, her rival kept provoking her in order to irritate her. **7**This went on year after year. Whenever Hannah went up to the house of the LORD, her rival provoked her till she wept and would not eat. **8**Elkanah her husband would say to her, "Hannah, why are you weeping? Why don't you eat? Why are you downhearted? Don't I mean more to you than ten sons?"

9Once when they had finished eating and drinking in Shiloh, Hannah stood up. Now Eli the priest was sitting on a chair by the doorpost of the LORD's temple.[b] **10**In bitterness of soul[D] Hannah wept much and prayed to the LORD. **11**And she made a vow[D], saying, "O LORD Almighty, if you will only look upon your servant's misery and remember me, and not forget your servant but give her a son, then I will give him to the LORD for all the days of his life, and no razor will ever be used on his head."

12As she kept on praying to the LORD, Eli observed her mouth. **13**Hannah was praying in her heart, and her lips were moving but her voice was not heard. Eli thought she was drunk **14**and said to her, "How long will you keep on getting drunk? Get rid of your wine."

15"Not so, my lord," Hannah replied, "I am a woman who is deeply troubled. I have not been drinking wine or beer; I was pouring out my soul to the LORD. **16**Do not take your servant for a wicked woman; I have been praying here out of my great anguish and grief."

17Eli answered, "Go in peace[D], and may the God of Israel grant you what you have asked of him."

18She said, "May your servant find favor in your eyes." Then she went her way and ate something, and her face was no longer downcast.

19Early the next morning they arose and worshiped before the LORD and then went back to their home at Ramah. Elkanah lay with Hannah his wife, and the LORD remembered her. **20**So in the course of time Hannah conceived and gave birth to a son. She named him Samuel,[c] saying, "Because I asked the LORD for him."

Hannah Dedicates Samuel

21When the man Elkanah went up with all his family to offer the annual sacrifice to the LORD and to fulfill his vow, **22**Hannah did not go. She said to her husband, "After the boy is weaned, I will take him and present him before the LORD, and he will live there always."

23"Do what seems best to you," Elkanah her husband

Why did Elkanah have two wives? (1:2)
Polygamy was a common practice, but monogamy was God's original intent for marriage (Gen. 2:24). See article: *Why did David have so many wives and concubines?* (2 Samuel 5:13).

Did Elkanah worship God only once a year? (1:3)
All male Israelites were commanded to worship at the tabernacle for three feasts annually—Unleavened Bread (or Passover), Weeks (or Pentecost) and Tabernacles (Exodus 34:23; Deut. 16:16). Whether Elkanah's pilgrimage was for one of those feasts isn't clear. Old Testament worship was much more than just visiting the sanctuary. The Israelites' whole lives, including their family and social practices, revolved around worship.

Did God cause Hannah's infertility? (1:5)
Had the Lord literally *closed her womb*? This phrase may have stemmed from a Hebrew view of life that saw God as the primary cause behind everything—even if the outcome was tragic or evil. See article: *How can a holy God send an evil spirit?* (Judges 9:23). Today we might say God *permitted* but did not *cause* Hannah's infertility. Though God may not answer every childless couple as he did Hannah and Elkanah (v. 20), he always has their best interests at heart. Also see *How does fathering a child prove strength?* (Deut. 21:17).

Why would long hair impress God? (1:11)
Uncut hair was one feature of a Nazirite vow. See *Nazirite* (Judges 13:5). In Samuel's case, his mother made the vow for him, setting him aside to perform a special service to God. Ordinarily, Nazirite vows were temporary, but Samuel's was lifelong. Some think that hair, like blood, symbolized life and strength.

Is it better to pray out loud? (1:13)
The Bible does not specify any one correct method or posture for prayer (1 Kings 8:22; Luke 22:41; 1 Tim. 2:8). In ancient Israel, silent, public prayer may have been rare. Most people, seeing someone's lips move, would have expected to hear sound. Eli did and jumped to the conclusion that Hannah was drunk.

---

[a]1 Or *from Ramathaim Zuphim*   [b]9 That is, tabernacle
[c]20 *Samuel* sounds like the Hebrew for *heard of God*.

Hannah Dedicates Samuel (1:24)

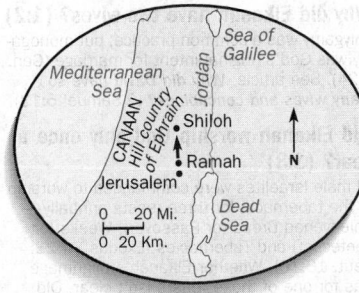

How did Hannah give her toddler *to the Lord*? (1:28)

When Samuel was weaned (perhaps around three years old), Hannah dedicated him to the tabernacle (or worship center) for lifelong service to God (v. 22). See **What did it mean to dedicate someone to the Lord?** (Lev. 27:2). As a young boy, Samuel undoubtedly performed simple tasks such as cleaning and running errands for Eli.

What kind of a *horn* did Hannah have? (2:1)

Hannah's *horn* symbolizes her strength, or dignity (see also NIV text note at Psalm 112:9). In a society where being childless was a disgrace, Hannah was honored and *lifted high* by God's gift of a son.

Was Hannah praying or taunting her enemy? (2:1,3,5)

Praying. In the Old Testament people felt free to express to God their darker sentiments about enemies. Here Hannah was venting her emotions to God, describing her painful journey from social disgrace to honor. Peninnah, the other wife of Hannah's husband, had long needled Hannah. But now, as Samuel's mother, Hannah could freely praise God.

Why would God impoverish people? (2:7)

The focus of this prayer is on God's justice. In a balancing of the scales, Hannah has been lifted up by God; others (deservedly) are brought down by God. When God reverses injustice, the punishment can sometimes come in the form of poverty.

---

told her. "Stay here until you have weaned him; only may the Lord make good his*a* word." So the woman stayed at home and nursed her son until she had weaned him.

²⁴After he was weaned, she took the boy with her, young as he was, along with a three-year-old bull,*b* an ephah*c* of flour and a skin of wine, and brought him to the house of the Lord at Shiloh. ²⁵When they had slaughtered the bull, they brought the boy to Eli, ²⁶and she said to him, "As surely as you live, my lord, I am the woman who stood here beside you praying to the Lord. ²⁷I prayed for this child, and the Lord has granted me what I asked of him. ²⁸So now I give him to the Lord. For his whole life he will be given over to the Lord." And he worshiped the Lord there.

Hannah's Prayer

2 Then Hannah prayed and said:

"My heart rejoices in the Lord;
    in the Lord my horn*d* is lifted high.
My mouth boasts over my enemies,
    for I delight in your deliverance.

²"There is no one holy*e* like the Lord;
    there is no one besides you;
    there is no Rock like our God.

³"Do not keep talking so proudly
    or let your mouth speak such arrogance,
for the Lord is a God who knows,
    and by him deeds are weighed.

⁴"The bows of the warriors are broken,
    but those who stumbled are armed with
        strength.
⁵Those who were full hire themselves out for
        food,
    but those who were hungry hunger no more.
She who was barren has borne seven children,
    but she who has had many sons pines away.

⁶"The Lord brings death*D* and makes alive;
    he brings down to the grave*f* and raises up.
⁷The Lord sends poverty and wealth;
    he humbles and he exalts.
⁸He raises the poor from the dust
    and lifts the needy from the ash heap;
he seats them with princes
    and has them inherit a throne of honor.

"For the foundations of the earth are the
        Lord's;
    upon them he has set the world.
⁹He will guard the feet of his saints*D*,
    but the wicked will be silenced in darkness.

"It is not by strength that one prevails;
¹⁰   those who oppose the Lord will be shattered.
He will thunder against them from heaven;
    the Lord will judge the ends of the earth.

"He will give strength to his king

---

*a*23 Masoretic Text; Dead Sea Scrolls, Septuagint and Syriac *your*
*b*24 Dead Sea Scrolls, Septuagint and Syriac; Masoretic Text *with three bulls*   *c*24 That is, probably about 3/5 bushel (about 22 liters)
*d*1 *Horn* here symbolizes strength; also in verse 10.   *e*2 Or *no Holy One*   *f*6 Hebrew *Sheol*

and exalt the horn of his anointed[D].' "

11Then Elkanah went home to Ramah, but the boy ministered before the LORD under Eli the priest[D].

Eli's Wicked Sons

12Eli's sons were wicked men; they had no regard for the LORD. **13**Now it was the practice of the priests with the people that whenever anyone offered a sacrifice[D] and while the meat was being boiled, the servant of the priest would come with a three-pronged fork in his hand. **14**He would plunge it into the pan or kettle or caldron or pot, and the priest would take for himself whatever the fork brought up. This is how they treated all the Israelites who came to Shiloh. **15**But even before the fat was burned, the servant of the priest would come and say to the man who was sacrificing, "Give the priest some meat to roast; he won't accept boiled meat from you, but only raw."

16If the man said to him, "Let the fat be burned up first, and then take whatever you want," the servant would then answer, "No, hand it over now; if you don't, I'll take it by force."

17This sin of the young men was very great in the LORD's sight, for they[a] were treating the LORD's offering with contempt.

18But Samuel was ministering before the LORD—a boy wearing a linen ephod[D]. **19**Each year his mother made him a little robe and took it to him when she went up with her husband to offer the annual sacrifice. **20**Eli would bless Elkanah and his wife, saying, "May the LORD give you children by this woman to take the place of the one she prayed for and gave to the LORD." Then they would go home. **21**And the LORD was gracious to Hannah; she conceived and gave birth to three sons and two daughters. Meanwhile, the boy Samuel grew up in the presence of the LORD.

22Now Eli, who was very old, heard about everything his sons were doing to all Israel and how they slept with the women who served at the entrance to the Tent of Meeting[D]. **23**So he said to them, "Why do you do such things? I hear from all the people about these wicked deeds of yours. **24**No, my sons; it is not a good report that I hear spreading among the LORD's people. **25**If a man sins against another man, God[b] may mediate for him; but if a man sins against the LORD, who will intercede[D] for him?" His sons, however, did not listen to their father's rebuke, for it was the LORD's will to put them to death[D].

26And the boy Samuel continued to grow in stature and in favor with the LORD and with men.

Prophecy Against the House of Eli

27Now a man of God came to Eli and said to him, "This is what the LORD says: 'Did I not clearly reveal myself to your father's house when they were in Egypt under Pharaoh? **28**I chose your father out of all the tribes of Israel to be my priest, to go up to my altar, to burn incense, and to wear an ephod in my presence. I also gave your father's house all the offerings made with fire by the Israelites. **29**Why do you[c] scorn my sacrifice and offering that I prescribed for my dwelling? Why do you honor your sons more than me by fattening yourselves on the

Who were these women? (2:22)

It is unclear. But these women were neither priestesses nor prostitutes. They served God at the Tent of Meeting in some capacity, perhaps washing utensils or repairing garments. Also see *Who were the women who served at the entrance to the Tent of Meeting?* (Exodus 38:8).

Did God prevent Eli's sons from listening? (2:25)

Did God hinder their possible repentance so he could execute judgment upon them? No. Their punishment was due to their own rebellion. Old Testament writers, though, categorized all events—even disobedience—as falling under God's control. See article: *How can a holy God send an evil spirit?* (Judges 9:23).

---

a17 Or *men*   *b25* Or *the judges*   *c29* The Hebrew is plural

choice parts of every offering made by my people Israel?'

30"Therefore the LORD, the God of Israel, declares: 'I promised that your house and your father's house would minister before me forever.' But now the LORD declares: 'Far be it from me! Those who honor me I will honor, but those who despise me will be disdained. **31**The time is coming when I will cut short your strength and the strength of your father's house, so that there will not be an old man in your family line **32**and you will see distress in my dwelling. Although good will be done to Israel, in your family line there will never be an old man. **33**Every one of you that I do not cut off from my altar will be spared only to blind your eyes with tears and to grieve your heart, and all your descendants will die in the prime of life.

34" 'And what happens to your two sons, Hophni and Phinehas, will be a sign to you—they will both die on the same day. **35**I will raise up for myself a faithful priestᴰ, who will do according to what is in my heart and mind. I will firmly establish his house, and he will minister before my anointedᴰ one always. **36**Then everyone left in your family line will come and bow down before him for a piece of silver and a crust of bread and plead, "Appoint me to some priestly office so I can have food to eat." ' "

The LORD Calls Samuel

3 The boy Samuel ministered before the LORD under Eli. In those days the word of the LORD was rare; there were not many visionsᴰ.

2One night Eli, whose eyes were becoming so weak that he could barely see, was lying down in his usual place. **3**The lamp of God had not yet gone out, and Samuel was lying down in the templeᵃ of the LORD, where the ark of God was. **4**Then the LORD called Samuel.

Samuel answered, "Here I am." **5**And he ran to Eli and said, "Here I am; you called me."

But Eli said, "I did not call; go back and lie down." So he went and lay down.

6Again the LORD called, "Samuel!" And Samuel got up and went to Eli and said, "Here I am; you called me."

"My son," Eli said, "I did not call; go back and lie down."

7Now Samuel did not yet know the LORD: The word of the LORD had not yet been revealed to him.

8The LORD called Samuel a third time, and Samuel got up and went to Eli and said, "Here I am; you called me."

Then Eli realized that the LORD was calling the boy. **9**So Eli told Samuel, "Go and lie down, and if he calls you, say, 'Speak, LORD, for your servant is listening.' " So Samuel went and lay down in his place.

10The LORD came and stood there, calling as at the other times, "Samuel! Samuel!"

Then Samuel said, "Speak, for your servant is listening."

11And the LORD said to Samuel: "See, I am about to do something in Israel that will make the ears of everyone who hears of it tingle. **12**At that time I will carry out against Eli everything I spoke against his family—from beginning to end. **13**For I told him that I would judge his family forever because of the sin he knew about; his sons made themselves contemptible,ᵇ and he failed to restrain them. **14**Therefore, I swore to the house of Eli, 'The guilt

Why should Eli's descendants suffer? (2:31–33)
Biblical writers viewed the devastating effects of sin in a corporate sense. They saw how sin affected many, not just one individual. It was not just the guilty who had to pay a price for sin, but the extended family and community as well (Exodus 20:5–6).

How could Samuel sleep with the ark of God? (3:3)
Wasn't it kept where only the high priest could enter? Though he was near the ark, probably under the same roof, Samuel wasn't in the same room. Both Eli and Samuel slept outside the most holy area of the Tent of Meeting.

In what way did Samuel *not yet know* the LORD? (3:7)
Though he was serving God in the tabernacle, Samuel had experienced no direct personal encounter or revelation from God.

ᵃ3 That is, tabernacle   ᵇ13 Masoretic Text; an ancient Hebrew scribal tradition and Septuagint *sons blasphemed God*

of Eli's house will never be atoned for by sacrifice[D] or offering.' "

15Samuel lay down until morning and then opened the doors of the house of the LORD. He was afraid to tell Eli the vision[D], **16**but Eli called him and said, "Samuel, my son."

Samuel answered, "Here I am."

17"What was it he said to you?" Eli asked. "Do not hide it from me. May God deal with you, be it ever so severely, if you hide from me anything he told you." **18**So Samuel told him everything, hiding nothing from him. Then Eli said, "He is the LORD; let him do what is good in his eyes."

19The LORD was with Samuel as he grew up, and he let none of his words fall to the ground. **20**And all Israel from Dan to Beersheba recognized that Samuel was attested as a prophet[D] of the LORD. **21**The LORD continued to appear at Shiloh, and there he revealed himself to Samuel through his word.

4 And Samuel's word came to all Israel.

The Philistines Capture the Ark

Now the Israelites went out to fight against the Philistines. The Israelites camped at Ebenezer, and the Philistines at Aphek. **2**The Philistines deployed their forces to meet Israel, and as the battle spread, Israel was defeated by the Philistines, who killed about four thousand of them on the battlefield. **3**When the soldiers returned to camp, the elders of Israel asked, "Why did the LORD bring defeat upon us today before the Philistines? Let us bring the ark of the LORD's covenant[D] from Shiloh, so that it[a] may go with us and save us from the hand of our enemies."

4So the people sent men to Shiloh, and they brought back the ark of the covenant of the LORD Almighty, who is enthroned between the cherubim[D]. And Eli's two sons, Hophni and Phinehas, were there with the ark of the covenant of God.

5When the ark of the LORD's covenant came into the camp, all Israel raised such a great shout that the ground shook. **6**Hearing the uproar, the Philistines asked, "What's all this shouting in the Hebrew[D] camp?"

When they learned that the ark of the LORD had come into the camp, **7**the Philistines were afraid. "A god has come into the camp," they said. "We're in trouble! Nothing like this has happened before. **8**Woe to us! Who will deliver us from the hand of these mighty gods? They are the gods who struck the Egyptians with all kinds of plagues in the desert. **9**Be strong, Philistines! Be men, or you will be subject to the Hebrews, as they have been to you. Be men, and fight!"

10So the Philistines fought, and the Israelites were defeated and every man fled to his tent. The slaughter was very great; Israel lost thirty thousand foot soldiers. **11**The ark of God was captured, and Eli's two sons, Hophni and Phinehas, died.

Death of Eli

12That same day a Benjamite ran from the battle line and went to Shiloh, his clothes torn and dust on his head. **13**When he arrived, there was Eli sitting on his chair by the side of the road, watching, because his heart feared for the ark of God. When the man entered the town and told what had happened, the whole town sent up a cry.

Why did Eli threaten Samuel? (3:17)
Presumably, Eli recognized that God was bypassing him (as high priest) to give a rare revelation to Samuel. Yet, Eli was still the high priest, and Samuel was still under his supervision. So he asked Samuel for the uncompromising truth. It was common at that time to take an oath that called for severe repercussions if promises were not kept. See *Why would Ruth ask God to punish her if she broke her promise?* (Ruth 1:17).

He let none of his words fall to the ground (3:19)
The two statements of this verse are most likely parallel and mean essentially the same thing —that God consistently kept all his promises to Samuel (see 3:11–14). God fulfilled all he said he would do. It could also mean that Samuel's words were reliable. People could trust that what he said was the word of God.

How did God speak to Samuel? (3:21)
Probably in much the same way he did the first time, audibly and perhaps visibly (3:10–14).

Travels of the Ark (4:3)

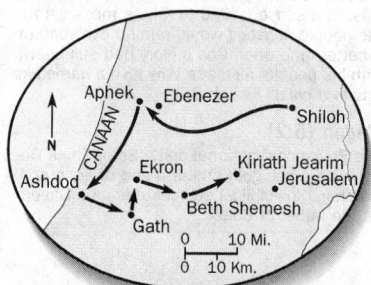

Why did the Israelites lose, when they had the ark? (4:5,7,10)
The Israelites had a lot to learn about God. He was bigger than the box which symbolized his presence. They could not enhance their fortunes by trying to cart him around like a good luck charm. Having the ark didn't mean God was on their side. The more important issue was whether they were on God's side. In this case, God's presence meant judgment rather than blessing.

Why flee to a tent? (4:10)
The expression *to his tent* did not mean to the army tents where the troops were bivouacked. Rather, it meant that they ran from the battlefield and tried to get to their homes (see 1 Kings 12:16). The Philistines routed the Israelites, who scattered every which way in the attempt to escape.

14Eli heard the outcry and asked, "What is the meaning of this uproar?"

The man hurried over to Eli, **15**who was ninety-eight years old and whose eyes were set so that he could not see. **16**He told Eli, "I have just come from the battle line; I fled from it this very day."

Eli asked, "What happened, my son?"

17The man who brought the news replied, "Israel fled before the Philistines, and the army has suffered heavy losses. Also your two sons, Hophni and Phinehas, are dead, and the ark of God has been captured."

18When he mentioned the ark of God, Eli fell backward off his chair by the side of the gate. His neck was broken and he died, for he was an old man and heavy. He had led*a* Israel forty years.

19His daughter-in-law, the wife of Phinehas, was pregnant and near the time of delivery. When she heard the news that the ark of God had been captured and that her father-in-law and her husband were dead, she went into labor and gave birth, but was overcome by her labor pains. **20**As she was dying, the women attending her said, "Don't despair; you have given birth to a son." But she did not respond or pay any attention.

21She named the boy Ichabod,*b* saying, "The glory*D* has departed from Israel"—because of the capture of the ark of God and the deaths of her father-in-law and her husband. **22**She said, "The glory has departed from Israel, for the ark of God has been captured."

The Ark in Ashdod and Ekron

5 After the Philistines had captured the ark of God, they took it from Ebenezer to Ashdod. **2**Then they carried the ark into Dagon's temple and set it beside Dagon. **3**When the people of Ashdod rose early the next day, there was Dagon, fallen on his face on the ground before the ark of the LORD! They took Dagon and put him back in his place. **4**But the following morning when they rose, there was Dagon, fallen on his face on the ground before the ark of the LORD! His head and hands had been broken off and were lying on the threshold; only his body remained. **5**That is why to this day neither the priests*D* of Dagon nor any others who enter Dagon's temple at Ashdod step on the threshold.

6The LORD's hand was heavy upon the people of Ashdod and its vicinity; he brought devastation upon them and afflicted*D* them with tumors.*c* **7**When the men of Ashdod saw what was happening, they said, "The ark of the god of Israel must not stay here with us, because his hand is heavy upon us and upon Dagon our god." **8**So they called together all the rulers of the Philistines and asked them, "What shall we do with the ark of the god of Israel?"

They answered, "Have the ark of the god of Israel moved to Gath." So they moved the ark of the God of Israel.

9But after they had moved it, the LORD's hand was against that city, throwing it into a great panic. He afflicted the people of the city, both young and old, with an outbreak of tumors.*d* **10**So they sent the ark of God to Ekron.

Why such a depressing name? (4:21)
Just as the ark had symbolized God's presence (see Exodus 25:22), this child's unforgettable name would symbolize Israel's traumatic loss of God's presence and glory. Though it seems unfair to burden a child with such a name, he was, in a sense, called to take a message to the people. *Ichabod* would remind everyone of a better time when God's glory had still been with his people. Also see *Why give a name like this to a child?* (Isaiah 8:3).

Dagon (5:2)
The Philistines' national deity. Some think Dagon was a fish god, others a god of grain or weather. Non-biblical sources describe Dagon as the father of Baal.

To this day (5:5)
Obviously some time had lapsed between the time when this occurred (about 1075–1050 B.C.) and when it was written down—probably more than a century.

Why punish the Philistines? (5:6)
The Philistines had wheeled the ark, taken as a trophy of war, into the temple of their pagan god, Dagon. God's holiness could not allow such blasphemy. During the night, God pushed over Dagon (vv. 2–4), breaking off the idol's head and hands. Then, by inflicting the Philistines with tumors, God powerfully demonstrated his absolute supremacy.

---

a18 Traditionally judged   *b21 Ichabod means* no glory.
c6 Hebrew; Septuagint and Vulgate tumors. And rats appeared in their land, and death and destruction were throughout the city   *d9 Or with tumors in the groin (see Septuagint)*

As the ark of God was entering Ekron, the people of Ekron cried out, "They have brought the ark of the god of Israel around to us to kill us and our people." **11**So they called together all the rulers of the Philistines and said, "Send the ark of the god of Israel away; let it go back to its own place, or it*a* will kill us and our people." For death[D] had filled the city with panic; God's hand was very heavy upon it. **12**Those who did not die were afflicted[D] with tumors, and the outcry of the city went up to heaven.

The Ark Returned to Israel

6 When the ark of the LORD had been in Philistine territory seven months, **2**the Philistines called for the priests[D] and the diviners and said, "What shall we do with the ark of the LORD? Tell us how we should send it back to its place."

3They answered, "If you return the ark of the god of Israel, do not send it away empty, but by all means send a guilt offering[D] to him. Then you will be healed, and you will know why his hand has not been lifted from you."

4The Philistines asked, "What guilt offering should we send to him?"

They replied, "Five gold tumors and five gold rats, according to the number of the Philistine rulers, because the same plague has struck both you and your rulers. **5**Make models of the tumors and of the rats that are destroying the country, and pay honor to Israel's god. Perhaps he will lift his hand from you and your gods and your land. **6**Why do you harden your hearts as the Egyptians and Pharaoh did? When he*b* treated them harshly, did they not send the Israelites out so they could go on their way?

7"Now then, get a new cart ready, with two cows that have calved and have never been yoked. Hitch the cows to the cart, but take their calves away and pen them up. **8**Take the ark of the LORD and put it on the cart, and in a chest beside it put the gold objects you are sending back to him as a guilt offering. Send it on its way, **9**but keep watching it. If it goes up to its own territory, toward Beth Shemesh, then the LORD has brought this great disaster on us. But if it does not, then we will know that it was not his hand that struck us and that it happened to us by chance."

10So they did this. They took two such cows and hitched them to the cart and penned up their calves. **11**They placed the ark of the LORD on the cart and along with it the chest containing the gold rats and the models of the tumors. **12**Then the cows went straight up toward Beth Shemesh, keeping on the road and lowing all the way; they did not turn to the right or to the left. The rulers of the Philistines followed them as far as the border of Beth Shemesh.

13Now the people of Beth Shemesh were harvesting their wheat in the valley, and when they looked up and saw the ark, they rejoiced at the sight. **14**The cart came to the field of Joshua of Beth Shemesh, and there it stopped beside a large rock. The people chopped up the wood of the cart and sacrificed the cows as a burnt offering[D] to the LORD. **15**The Levites[D] took down the ark of the LORD, together with the chest containing the gold objects, and placed them on the large rock. On that day the people of Beth Shemesh offered burnt offerings and made sacri-

How were rats *destroying the country?* (6:5)

Some think the destruction had to do with the crops. An ancient philosopher writes about mice destroying an entire harvest in a single night. Others, though, link the devastation to the mysterious disease inflicted on the Philistine people.

How does God show his will? (6:9)

This is a description of how God worked on this occasion, but it does not prescribe a method for discovering God's will. In this case, God revealed himself to the Philistines by working through their superstitions. For God's people, however, he gives Scripture, prayer and the inner witness of the Spirit. Also see article: *Can we find God's will by putting out a fleece?* (Judges 6:37–40).

*a11 Or he   *b6 That is, God

fices[D] to the LORD. [16]The five rulers of the Philistines saw all this and then returned that same day to Ekron.

[17]These are the gold tumors the Philistines sent as a guilt offering[D] to the LORD—one each for Ashdod, Gaza, Ashkelon, Gath and Ekron. [18]And the number of the gold rats was according to the number of Philistine towns belonging to the five rulers—the fortified towns with their country villages. The large rock, on which[a] they set the ark of the LORD, is a witness to this day in the field of Joshua of Beth Shemesh.

[19]But God struck down some of the men of Beth Shemesh, putting seventy[b] of them to death[D] because they had looked into the ark of the LORD. The people mourned because of the heavy blow the LORD had dealt them, [20]and the men of Beth Shemesh asked, "Who can stand in the presence of the LORD, this holy God? To whom will the ark go up from here?"

[21]Then they sent messengers to the people of Kiriath Jearim, saying, "The Philistines have returned the ark of the LORD. Come down and take it up to your place."

7 [1]So the men of Kiriath Jearim came and took up the ark of the LORD. They took it to Abinadab's house on the hill and consecrated[D] Eleazar his son to guard the ark of the LORD.

Samuel Subdues the Philistines at Mizpah

[2]It was a long time, twenty years in all, that the ark remained at Kiriath Jearim, and all the people of Israel mourned and sought after the LORD. [3]And Samuel said to the whole house of Israel, "If you are returning to the LORD with all your hearts, then rid yourselves of the foreign gods and the Ashtoreths[D] and commit yourselves to the LORD and serve him only, and he will deliver you out of the hand of the Philistines." [4]So the Israelites put away their Baals[D] and Ashtoreths, and served the LORD only.

[5]Then Samuel said, "Assemble all Israel at Mizpah and I will intercede[D] with the LORD for you." [6]When they had assembled at Mizpah, they drew water and poured it out before the LORD. On that day they fasted and there they confessed, "We have sinned against the LORD." And Samuel was leader[c] of Israel at Mizpah.

[7]When the Philistines heard that Israel had assembled at Mizpah, the rulers of the Philistines came up to attack them. And when the Israelites heard of it, they were afraid because of the Philistines. [8]They said to Samuel, "Do not stop crying out to the LORD our God for us, that he may rescue us from the hand of the Philistines." [9]Then Samuel took a suckling lamb and offered it up as a whole burnt offering[D] to the LORD. He cried out to the LORD on Israel's behalf, and the LORD answered him.

[10]While Samuel was sacrificing the burnt offering, the Philistines drew near to engage Israel in battle. But that day the LORD thundered with loud thunder against the Philistines and threw them into such a panic that they were routed before the Israelites. [11]The men of Israel rushed out of Mizpah and pursued the Philistines, slaughtering them along the way to a point below Beth Car.

[12]Then Samuel took a stone and set it up between Mizpah and Shen. He named it Ebenezer,[d] saying, "Thus far

Why was God so touchy about the ark? (6:19)
Once again the people had disregarded God's commands, showing no awe or respect for his holiness. Promising death to those who disobeyed, the law prohibited even priests who cared for the ark from glancing at its holy objects (Num. 4:20).

Why send their ark away? (6:20–21)
If the ark was the problem, they reasoned, then they needed to get rid of it. They reacted much the same way the Philistines did (v. 2), not realizing they were the problem, not the ark.

Why pour water before the Lord? (7:6)
This was a symbolic act. Just as they poured out the water, so they poured out their hearts in repentance (see 2 Samuel 23:16; Lam. 2:19). The water also may have symbolized their own resources; they had come to the end of themselves. Their repentance was underscored by going without food and confessing their sins.

How could thunder scare an army? (7:10)
Some think the thunder may have struck out of season (during Israel's dry season). Perhaps lightning killed some of the Philistines, increasing their terror.

What was the meaning of this stone? (7:12)
It marked a spiritual turning point in Israel's history when they turned again to God for help. It may also have served as a sort of boundary marker—indicating the territory of Israel and how far God had helped them chase the Philistines.

---

[a]18 A few Hebrew manuscripts (see also Septuagint); most Hebrew manuscripts *villages as far as Greater Abel, where*   [b]19 A few Hebrew manuscripts; most Hebrew manuscripts and Septuagint *50,070*   [c]6 Traditionally *judge*   [d]12 *Ebenezer* means *stone of help.*

has the LORD helped us." **13**So the Philistines were subdued and did not invade Israelite territory again.

Throughout Samuel's lifetime, the hand of the LORD was against the Philistines. **14**The towns from Ekron to Gath that the Philistines had captured from Israel were restored to her, and Israel delivered the neighboring territory from the power of the Philistines. And there was peace^D between Israel and the Amorites.

15Samuel continued as judge over Israel all the days of his life. **16**From year to year he went on a circuit from Bethel to Gilgal to Mizpah, judging Israel in all those places. **17**But he always went back to Ramah, where his home was, and there he also judged Israel. And he built an altar there to the LORD.

Israel Asks for a King

8 When Samuel grew old, he appointed his sons as judges for Israel. **2**The name of his firstborn^D was Joel and the name of his second was Abijah, and they served at Beersheba. **3**But his sons did not walk in his ways. They turned aside after dishonest gain and accepted bribes and perverted justice.

4So all the elders of Israel gathered together and came to Samuel at Ramah. **5**They said to him, "You are old, and your sons do not walk in your ways; now appoint a king to lead^a us, such as all the other nations have."

6But when they said, "Give us a king to lead us," this displeased Samuel; so he prayed to the LORD. **7**And the LORD told him: "Listen to all that the people are saying to you; it is not you they have rejected, but they have rejected me as their king. **8**As they have done from the day I brought them up out of Egypt until this day, forsaking me and serving other gods, so they are doing to you. **9**Now listen to them; but warn them solemnly and let them know what the king who will reign over them will do."

10Samuel told all the words of the LORD to the people who were asking him for a king. **11**He said, "This is what the king who will reign over you will do: He will take your sons and make them serve with his chariots and horses, and they will run in front of his chariots. **12**Some he will assign to be commanders of thousands and commanders

^a5 Traditionally *judge*; also in verses 6 and 20

Were the actions of Samuel's sons the result of bad parenting? (8:1,3)

The Bible is silent about the reasons for Joel's and Abijah's shady lifestyles. It is interesting to note, though, that their sins were similar to those of the sons of Eli, Samuel's mentor (2:12–17). Also see *Did Samson's parents do a bad job?* (Judges 13:8).

Why was it wrong to want a king? (8:5–9)

The issue wasn't so much which form of government God preferred as it was who would rule their hearts. In rejecting Samuel's sons, irresponsible and sinful though they were, Israel was rejecting God's provision and, once again, his leadership. See *What was the real reason the people wanted a king?* (12:12).

The people had said they wanted a king because they couldn't depend on Samuel's corrupt sons for guidance. Their request was painful to Samuel, though he undoubtedly knew there was a problem with his family. But Samuel also knew what a king symbolized to Israel—an attempt to be like the pagan nations around them and a willingness to reject the Lord as king. As such, he understood the seriousness of their request and attempted to dissuade them (vv. 10–18).

But it was not to be. Though the motive behind Israel's appeal was an offense to God, God let them have their own way.

of fifties, and others to plow his ground and reap his harvest, and still others to make weapons of war and equipment for his chariots. [13]He will take your daughters to be perfumers and cooks and bakers. [14]He will take the best of your fields and vineyards and olive groves and give them to his attendants. [15]He will take a tenth of your grain and of your vintage and give it to his officials and attendants. [16]Your menservants and maidservants and the best of your cattle[a] and donkeys he will take for his own use. [17]He will take a tenth of your flocks, and you yourselves will become his slaves. [18]When that day comes, you will cry out for relief from the king you have chosen, and the LORD will not answer you in that day."

[19]But the people refused to listen to Samuel. "No!" they said. "We want a king over us. [20]Then we will be like all the other nations, with a king to lead us and to go out before us and fight our battles."

[21]When Samuel heard all that the people said, he repeated it before the LORD. [22]The LORD answered, "Listen to them and give them a king."

Then Samuel said to the men of Israel, "Everyone go back to his town."

Samuel Anoints Saul

9 There was a Benjamite, a man of standing, whose name was Kish son of Abiel, the son of Zeror, the son of Becorath, the son of Aphiah of Benjamin. [2]He had a son named Saul, an impressive young man without equal among the Israelites—a head taller than any of the others.

[3]Now the donkeys belonging to Saul's father Kish were lost, and Kish said to his son Saul, "Take one of the servants with you and go and look for the donkeys." [4]So he passed through the hill country of Ephraim and through the area around Shalisha, but they did not find them. They went on into the district of Shaalim, but the donkeys were not there. Then he passed through the territory of Benjamin, but they did not find them.

[5]When they reached the district of Zuph, Saul said to the servant who was with him, "Come, let's go back, or my father will stop thinking about the donkeys and start worrying about us."

[6]But the servant replied, "Look, in this town there is a man of God; he is highly respected, and everything he says comes true. Let's go there now. Perhaps he will tell us what way to take."

[7]Saul said to his servant, "If we go, what can we give the man? The food in our sacks is gone. We have no gift to take to the man of God. What do we have?"

[8]The servant answered him again. "Look," he said, "I have a quarter of a shekel[D][b] of silver. I will give it to the man of God so that he will tell us what way to take." [9](Formerly in Israel, if a man went to inquire of God, he would say, "Come, let us go to the seer[D]," because the prophet[D] of today used to be called a seer.)

[10]"Good," Saul said to his servant. "Come, let's go." So they set out for the town where the man of God was.

[11]As they were going up the hill to the town, they met some girls coming out to draw water, and they asked them, "Is the seer here?"

[12]"He is," they answered. "He's ahead of you. Hurry now; he has just come to our town today, for the people

Why did God give in to Israel? (8:21–22)

God chose to use Israel's request to further his purposes. But this does not mean he gave up on Israel. Even with a king, God would demand their continued allegiance and obedience (12:14).

Samuel Anoints Saul (9:2)

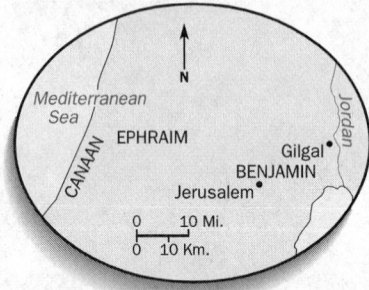

Why was a gift necessary? (9:7)

A customary practice, this gift may have been an "interview fee" (an exchange of goods for services), or simply a gesture of respect to a superior. Such gifts were also brought to the prophets Ahijah and Elisha (1 Kings 14:2–3; 2 Kings 4:42; 5:15).

Why was worship at a *high place* permissible here but wrong elsewhere? (9:12)

Canaanites used high places (such as hilltops) for pagan sacrifices. So when Israel first arrived in Canaan, God commanded them to demolish, along with the Canaanite idols, the high places of sacrifice where the idols were worshiped (Num. 33:52; Deut. 12:2). He also forbade Israel to offer sacrifices anywhere except where he designated (Deut. 12:11–14). In this situation, however, God seems to have tolerated some bending of the rules—perhaps because the designated site of Shiloh had not functioned since the ark had been removed from it (see *Travels of the Ark* on page 363). Later, God visited Solomon in a dream when Solomon worshiped at a high place (1 Kings 3:4–5). Also see *Why couldn't the Israelites worship anywhere?* (Deut. 12:5) and *Why did it matter where they worshiped God?* (2 Kings 18:22).

---

[a]16 Septuagint; Hebrew *young men*   [b]8 That is, about 1/10 ounce (about 3 grams)

have a sacrifice[D] at the high place. [13]As soon as you enter the town, you will find him before he goes up to the high place to eat. The people will not begin eating until he comes, because he must bless the sacrifice; afterward, those who are invited will eat. Go up now; you should find him about this time."

[14]They went up to the town, and as they were entering it, there was Samuel, coming toward them on his way up to the high place.

[15]Now the day before Saul came, the LORD had revealed this to Samuel: [16]"About this time tomorrow I will send you a man from the land of Benjamin. Anoint[D] him leader over my people Israel; he will deliver my people from the hand of the Philistines. I have looked upon my people, for their cry has reached me."

[17]When Samuel caught sight of Saul, the LORD said to him, "This is the man I spoke to you about; he will govern my people."

[18]Saul approached Samuel in the gateway and asked, "Would you please tell me where the seer's[D] house is?"

[19]"I am the seer[D]," Samuel replied. "Go up ahead of me to the high place, for today you are to eat with me, and in the morning I will let you go and will tell you all that is in your heart. [20]As for the donkeys you lost three days ago, do not worry about them; they have been found. And to whom is all the desire of Israel turned, if not to you and all your father's family?"

[21]Saul answered, "But am I not a Benjamite, from the smallest tribe of Israel, and is not my clan the least of all the clans of the tribe of Benjamin? Why do you say such a thing to me?"

[22]Then Samuel brought Saul and his servant into the hall and seated them at the head of those who were invited—about thirty in number. [23]Samuel said to the cook, "Bring the piece of meat I gave you, the one I told you to lay aside."

[24]So the cook took up the leg with what was on it and set it in front of Saul. Samuel said, "Here is what has been kept for you. Eat, because it was set aside for you for this occasion, from the time I said, 'I have invited guests.'" And Saul dined with Samuel that day.

[25]After they came down from the high place to the town, Samuel talked with Saul on the roof of his house. [26]They rose about daybreak and Samuel called to Saul on the roof, "Get ready, and I will send you on your way." When Saul got ready, he and Samuel went outside together. [27]As they were going down to the edge of the town, Samuel said to Saul, "Tell the servant to go on ahead of us"—and the servant did so—"but you stay here awhile, so that I may give you a message from God."

10 Then Samuel took a flask of oil and poured it on Saul's head and kissed him, saying, "Has not the LORD anointed you leader over his inheritance?[a] [2]When you leave me today, you will meet two men near Rachel's tomb, at Zelzah on the border of Benjamin. They will say to you, 'The donkeys you set out to look for have been found. And now your father has stopped thinking about them and is worried about you. He is asking, "What shall I do about my son?"'

---

[a]1 Hebrew; Septuagint and Vulgate *over his people Israel? You will reign over the LORD's people and save them from the power of their enemies round about. And this will be a sign to you that the LORD has anointed you leader over his inheritance:*

What happened to make the Philistines a threat again? (9:16)

In 7:13, the Philistine threat seemed to have been removed completely. While Samuel's leadership kept the Philistines from invading Israel, the Philistines still retained their military dominance. However, from this time forward, the Philistines slowly lost their control, though during Saul's reign they had resurgences of power. King David later defeated them soundly (2 Samuel 8:1).

The desire of Israel turned (9:20)

Some think this refers to all the desirable things the nation had to offer a king (donkeys, possessions, taxes and so forth). Others believe the expression pertains to Israel's desire for a king (8:5). Israel had desired a king, and Samuel prophetically pinpointed Saul to fulfill that function.

3"Then you will go on from there until you reach the great tree of Tabor. Three men going up to God at Bethel will meet you there. One will be carrying three young goats, another three loaves of bread, and another a skin of wine. **4**They will greet you and offer you two loaves of bread, which you will accept from them.

5"After that you will go to Gibeah of God, where there is a Philistine outpost. As you approach the town, you will meet a procession of prophets^D coming down from the high place with lyres^D, tambourines, flutes and harps being played before them, and they will be prophesying. **6**The Spirit of the LORD will come upon you in power, and you will prophesy with them; and you will be changed into a different person. **7**Once these signs are fulfilled, do whatever your hand finds to do, for God is with you.

8"Go down ahead of me to Gilgal. I will surely come down to you to sacrifice^D burnt offerings^D and fellowship offerings^{D, a} but you must wait seven days until I come to you and tell you what you are to do."

Who were these prophets? (10:5)

While most Old Testament prophets received messages directly from God, this group of traveling musicians used musical instruments to accompany their enthusiastic praise of God. Groups like this flourished during the period of the monarchy, contributing to Israel's spiritual development. Israel often inquired of these prophets about future events (1 Kings 22:6).

Saul Made King

9As Saul turned to leave Samuel, God changed Saul's heart, and all these signs were fulfilled that day. **10**When they arrived at Gibeah, a procession of prophets met him; the Spirit of God came upon him in power, and he joined in their prophesying. **11**When all those who had formerly known him saw him prophesying with the prophets, they asked each other, "What is this that has happened to the son of Kish? Is Saul also among the prophets?"

12A man who lived there answered, "And who is their father?" So it became a saying: "Is Saul also among the prophets?" **13**After Saul stopped prophesying, he went to the high place.

14Now Saul's uncle asked him and his servant, "Where have you been?"

"Looking for the donkeys," he said. "But when we saw they were not to be found, we went to Samuel."

15Saul's uncle said, "Tell me what Samuel said to you."

16Saul replied, "He assured us that the donkeys had been found." But he did not tell his uncle what Samuel had said about the kingship.

17Samuel summoned the people of Israel to the LORD at Mizpah **18**and said to them, "This is what the LORD, the God of Israel, says: 'I brought Israel up out of Egypt, and I delivered you from the power of Egypt and all the kingdoms that oppressed you.' **19**But you have now rejected your God, who saves you out of all your calamities and distresses. And you have said, 'No, set a king over us.' So now present yourselves before the LORD by your tribes and clans."

20When Samuel brought all the tribes of Israel near, the tribe of Benjamin was chosen. **21**Then he brought forward the tribe of Benjamin, clan by clan, and Matri's clan was chosen. Finally Saul son of Kish was chosen. But when they looked for him, he was not to be found. **22**So they inquired further of the LORD, "Has the man come here yet?"

And the LORD said, "Yes, he has hidden himself among the baggage."

23They ran and brought him out, and as he stood among the people he was a head taller than any of the

How had Saul changed? (10:9–11)

The Bible doesn't say. In Old Testament times, God's Spirit usually came upon individuals for specific tasks. The change may have been a newly found confidence and power to lead God's people (9:21).

What kind of prophesying did Saul do? (10:10)

Neither here nor in 19:19–24 are we provided with the content of his prophecy. But coming from Saul's mouth, it surprised those who had known Saul previously (v. 11).

How were tribes chosen? (10:20–21)

Probably by casting lots. This was a customary practice, along with the use of the Urim and Thummim, by which God provided specified direction to his people (Exodus 28:30). See also Joshua 18:10; Prov. 16:33.

Why did Saul hide? (10:22)

There is no obvious reason. Saul had also concealed his kingship from his uncle (10:15–16). Most likely, Saul had residual feelings of inferiority and didn't feel capable for the task of leadership (9:21).

How did God reveal Saul's hiding place? (10:22–23)

Probably by casting lots again. Each choice would distinguish between two possibilities at a time, narrowing down the choices over repeated trials, not unlike a guessing game. Numerous options could have been posed by the people before a lot finally pointed to the baggage.

Why was Samuel so eager to crown a king? (10:24)

God commanded Samuel to allow Israel to have a king (8:22). Once that was settled, the Lord had then clarified to Samuel his choice for king (10:1). As God's spokesperson, Samuel was ensuring that God's choice—Saul—would be crowned king.

Regulations of the kingship (10:25)

God's guidelines to monitor the earthly king. At that time, kings tended to be oppressive (see 8:10–17), so there had to be some safeguards to regulate their sovereignty. The regulations would fall in line with Deut. 17:14–20.

^a8 Traditionally *peace offerings*

others. ²⁴Samuel said to all the people, "Do you see the man the LORD has chosen? There is no one like him among all the people."

Then the people shouted, "Long live the king!"

²⁵Samuel explained to the people the regulations of the kingship. He wrote them down on a scroll and deposited it before the LORD. Then Samuel dismissed the people, each to his own home.

²⁶Saul also went to his home in Gibeah, accompanied by valiant men whose hearts God had touched. ²⁷But some troublemakers said, "How can this fellow save us?" They despised him and brought him no gifts. But Saul kept silent.

Saul Rescues the City of Jabesh

11 Nahash the Ammonite went up and besieged Jabesh Gilead. And all the men of Jabesh said to him, "Make a treaty with us, and we will be subject to you."

²But Nahash the Ammonite replied, "I will make a treaty with you only on the condition that I gouge out the right eye of every one of you and so bring disgrace on all Israel."

³The elders of Jabesh said to him, "Give us seven days so we can send messengers throughout Israel; if no one comes to rescue us, we will surrender to you."

⁴When the messengers came to Gibeah of Saul and reported these terms to the people, they all wept aloud. ⁵Just then Saul was returning from the fields, behind his oxen, and he asked, "What is wrong with the people? Why are they weeping?" Then they repeated to him what the men of Jabesh had said.

⁶When Saul heard their words, the Spirit of God came upon him in power, and he burned with anger. ⁷He took a pair of oxen, cut them into pieces, and sent the pieces by messengers throughout Israel, proclaiming, "This is what will be done to the oxen of anyone who does not follow Saul and Samuel." Then the terror of the LORD fell on the people, and they turned out as one man. ⁸When Saul mustered them at Bezek, the men of Israel numbered three hundred thousand and the men of Judah thirty thousand.

⁹They told the messengers who had come, "Say to the men of Jabesh Gilead, 'By the time the sun is hot tomorrow, you will be delivered.'" When the messengers went and reported this to the men of Jabesh, they were elated. ¹⁰They said to the Ammonites, "Tomorrow we will surrender to you, and you can do to us whatever seems good to you."

¹¹The next day Saul separated his men into three divisions; during the last watch of the night they broke into the camp of the Ammonites and slaughtered them until the heat of the day. Those who survived were scattered, so that no two of them were left together.

Saul Confirmed as King

¹²The people then said to Samuel, "Who was it that asked, 'Shall Saul reign over us?' Bring these men to us and we will put them to death.ᴰ"

¹³But Saul said, "No one shall be put to death today, for this day the LORD has rescued Israel."

¹⁴Then Samuel said to the people, "Come, let us go to Gilgal and there reaffirm the kingship." ¹⁵So all the people went to Gilgal and confirmed Saul as king in the presence

Saul Rescues Jabesh (11:1)

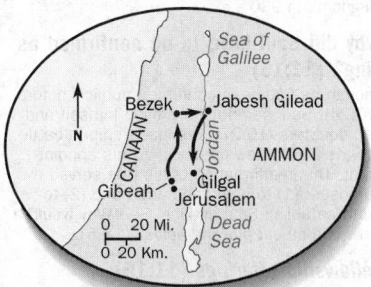

Why demand such brutal conditions for a treaty? (11:2)

Gouging out the right eye would cripple a soldier—since most were right-handed and held their shields in their left hands. With their left eyes concealed, they relied on their right eyes for combat. The Ammonites knew that such a demand also would demoralize the people of Jabesh Gilead. A humiliated people would be even less likely to stand up for themselves.

Why would the Ammonites give the Israelites time to mount a defense? (11:3)

Nahash knew that if he stormed the city, his victory would likely cost the lives of many of his men. By waiting just seven days, he hoped to avoid wasting time, money and men on an extended siege. He probably figured he had a safe bet for at least three reasons: (1) Jabesh Gilead was fairly well isolated from the rest of Israel. (2) Israel apparently had no centralized government (messengers were sent *throughout* Israel). (3) Saul did not yet have an army.

Why would a new king be out plowing fields? (11:5)

In our first glimpse of Saul he has a rather humble assignment, chasing donkeys for his father (9:3). Suddenly, despite his protests, he was catapulted onto the public stage as Israel's first king. After his awkward response at his coronation (10:21–24), he returned home to what was familiar. Gibeah provided him an escape from the glare of the public eye.

How did the Spirit come *upon him in power*? (11:6)

The Holy Spirit suddenly and powerfully overtook Saul so he could perform a specific task given to him by God. Literally, "the Spirit of God *rushed* on Saul." A powerful change was necessary to transform this reluctant king into a dynamic leader.

Are threats an acceptable way to recruit God's army? (11:7)

Drastic action was necessary to galvanize the nation and motivate the people to immediate obedience. The *terror of the LORD* may suggest a fear inspired by God, or it may suggest a fear of God himself. In either case the desired effect was achieved.

Why were the armies of Israel and Judah counted separately when the nation was not yet divided? (11:8)

The fact that Israel and Judah are recognized as distinct entities (see 17:22; 18:16) suggests that 1 Samuel was written after the nation was divided into the northern and southern kingdoms in 930 B.C.

Why did Saul have to be confirmed as king? (11:15)

Though he had been confirmed publicly before (10:24), Saul had not yet proven himself and had doubters (10:27). His leadership in battle, however, gave new credibility to his appointment. This reaffirmation of his rule served two purposes: (1) to unify the nation and (2) to firmly establish Saul as king. See *Why would a new king be out plowing fields?* (11:5).

Fellowship offerings (11:15)

See *Fellowship offerings* (1 Chron. 21:26).

Why was Samuel so negative? (12:1–2)

In the midst of the joyful celebration of Saul's recent victory (11:15), Samuel gave a sober reminder: the people's request for a king—regardless of its apparent success—was evil (v. 17). Neither Samuel (vv. 2–5) nor the Lord himself (vv. 6–11) had ever given them cause to desire a king. In fact, their request was an unspoken rejection of God as their king (v. 12). They needed to repent of their sin and trust in the Lord.

What was the real reason the people wanted a king? (12:12)

Perhaps anticipating Nahash's intentions, the people wanted a strong leader in place before he moved against them. What sparked their original request for a king was that Samuel's sons lacked basic leadership qualities (8:5). However, the nation's history suggests another reason: they repeatedly rejected God's command and grumbled about God's methods. They wanted no more judges, insisting instead on being like other nations and having a king. See article: *Why was it wrong to want a king?* (8:5–9).

of the LORD. There they sacrificed fellowship offerings[D][a] before the LORD, and Saul and all the Israelites held a great celebration.

Samuel's Farewell Speech

12 Samuel said to all Israel, "I have listened to everything you said to me and have set a king over you. ²Now you have a king as your leader. As for me, I am old and gray, and my sons are here with you. I have been your leader from my youth until this day. ³Here I stand. Testify against me in the presence of the LORD and his anointed.[D] Whose ox have I taken? Whose donkey have I taken? Whom have I cheated? Whom have I oppressed? From whose hand have I accepted a bribe to make me shut my eyes? If I have done any of these, I will make it right."

⁴"You have not cheated or oppressed us," they replied. "You have not taken anything from anyone's hand."

⁵Samuel said to them, "The LORD is witness against you, and also his anointed is witness this day, that you have not found anything in my hand."

"He is witness," they said.

⁶Then Samuel said to the people, "It is the LORD who appointed Moses and Aaron and brought your forefathers up out of Egypt. ⁷Now then, stand here, because I am going to confront you with evidence before the LORD as to all the righteous[D] acts performed by the LORD for you and your fathers.

⁸"After Jacob entered Egypt, they cried to the LORD for help, and the LORD sent Moses and Aaron, who brought your forefathers out of Egypt and settled them in this place.

⁹"But they forgot the LORD their God; so he sold them into the hand of Sisera, the commander of the army of Hazor, and into the hands of the Philistines and the king of Moab, who fought against them. ¹⁰They cried out to the LORD and said, 'We have sinned; we have forsaken the LORD and served the Baals[D] and the Ashtoreths.[D] But now deliver us from the hands of our enemies, and we will serve you.' ¹¹Then the LORD sent Jerub-Baal,[b] Barak,[c] Jephthah and Samuel,[d] and he delivered you from the hands of your enemies on every side, so that you lived securely.

¹²"But when you saw that Nahash king of the Ammonites was moving against you, you said to me, 'No, we want a king to rule over us'—even though the LORD your God was your king. ¹³Now here is the king you have chosen, the one you asked for; see, the LORD has set a king over you. ¹⁴If you fear the LORD and serve and obey him and do not rebel against his commands, and if both you and the king who reigns over you follow the LORD your God—good! ¹⁵But if you do not obey the LORD, and if you rebel against his commands, his hand will be against you, as it was against your fathers.

¹⁶"Now then, stand still and see this great thing the LORD is about to do before your eyes! ¹⁷Is it not wheat harvest now? I will call upon the LORD to send thunder and rain. And you will realize what an evil thing you did in the eyes of the LORD when you asked for a king."

¹⁸Then Samuel called upon the LORD, and that same day

---

[a]15 Traditionally *peace offerings*   [b]11 Also called *Gideon*
[c]11 Some Septuagint manuscripts and Syriac; Hebrew *Bedan*
[d]11 Hebrew; some Septuagint manuscripts and Syriac *Samson*

the LORD sent thunder and rain. So all the people stood in awe of the LORD and of Samuel.

¹⁹The people all said to Samuel, "Pray to the LORD your God for your servants so that we will not die, for we have added to all our other sins the evil of asking for a king."

²⁰"Do not be afraid," Samuel replied. "You have done all this evil; yet do not turn away from the LORD, but serve the LORD with all your heart. ²¹Do not turn away after useless idols[D]. They can do you no good, nor can they rescue you, because they are useless. ²²For the sake of his great name the LORD will not reject his people, because the LORD was pleased to make you his own. ²³As for me, far be it from me that I should sin against the LORD by failing to pray for you. And I will teach you the way that is good and right. ²⁴But be sure to fear the LORD and serve him faithfully with all your heart; consider what great things he has done for you. ²⁵Yet if you persist in doing evil, both you and your king will be swept away."

Samuel Rebukes Saul

13 Saul was ⌊thirty⌋[a] years old when he became king, and he reigned over Israel ⌊forty-⌋[b] two years.

²Saul[c] chose three thousand men from Israel; two thousand were with him at Micmash and in the hill country of Bethel, and a thousand were with Jonathan at Gibeah in Benjamin. The rest of the men he sent back to their homes.

³Jonathan attacked the Philistine outpost at Geba, and the Philistines heard about it. Then Saul had the trumpet blown throughout the land and said, "Let the Hebrews hear!" ⁴So all Israel heard the news: "Saul has attacked the Philistine outpost, and now Israel has become a stench to the Philistines." And the people were summoned to join Saul at Gilgal.

⁵The Philistines assembled to fight Israel, with three thousand[d] chariots, six thousand charioteers, and soldiers as numerous as the sand on the seashore. They went up and camped at Micmash, east of Beth Aven. ⁶When the men of Israel saw that their situation was critical and that their army was hard pressed, they hid in caves and thickets, among the rocks, and in pits and cisterns[D]. ⁷Some Hebrews even crossed the Jordan to the land of Gad and Gilead.

Saul remained at Gilgal, and all the troops with him were quaking with fear. ⁸He waited seven days, the time set by Samuel; but Samuel did not come to Gilgal, and Saul's men began to scatter. ⁹So he said, "Bring me the burnt offering[D] and the fellowship offerings.[e]" And Saul offered up the burnt offering. ¹⁰Just as he finished making the offering, Samuel arrived, and Saul went out to greet him.

¹¹"What have you done?" asked Samuel.

Saul replied, "When I saw that the men were scattering, and that you did not come at the set time, and that the Philistines were assembling at Micmash, ¹²I thought, 'Now the Philistines will come down against me at Gilgal,

Is neglecting prayer a sin? (12:23)

Perhaps at times. Neglecting prayer can reveal a sinful attitude of self-sufficiency and independence. It would be wrong to try to straighten out the situation with only human resources. It can be sinful to ignore a problem, choosing instead to "just let things happen." True prayer comes from an attitude of dependence on the Lord, whether celebrating his provision, confessing sin or expressing need.

How many soldiers were stationed in an outpost? (13:3)

Given Jonathan's contingent of 1,000 men (v. 2) and the heralding of his victory, it seems likely that he would have defeated a Philistine garrison of at least comparable size, if not greater. Saul regarded the victory as an outstanding military triumph. The Hebrews fielded men in organized units of 1,000, 100, 50 and 10 (Exodus 18:25). Archaeology suggests that the Philistines may have been organized along similar lines.

Why was Samuel late? (13:11; see 10:8)

He may have been testing Saul's faith and obedience. Saul was instructed to wait until Samuel arrived to tell him how to fight the Philistines. Offering the sacrifice himself demonstrated two flaws: (1) he trusted in the army too much and in God too little and (2) he thought the ritual could substitute for true reliance on God.

---

[a]1 A few late manuscripts of the Septuagint; Hebrew does not have thirty.   [b]1 See the round number in Acts 13:21; Hebrew does not have forty-.   [c]1,2 Or and when he had reigned over Israel two years, ²he   [d]5 Some Septuagint manuscripts and Syriac; Hebrew thirty thousand   [e]9 Traditionally peace offerings

Why was Saul's punishment so severe? (13:14)

Using his authority as king to make a sacrifice was an abuse of his position. He was a king, not a priest. Selfishly, he was more concerned about propping up his base of power than doing what was right. He was more interested in what people thought than in obeying God's command.

and I have not sought the LORD's favor.' So I felt compelled to offer the burnt offering."

13"You acted foolishly," Samuel said. "You have not kept the command the LORD your God gave you; if you had, he would have established your kingdom over Israel for all time. **14**But now your kingdom will not endure; the LORD has sought out a man after his own heart and appointed him leader of his people, because you have not kept the LORD's command."

15Then Samuel left Gilgal*a* and went up to Gibeah in Benjamin, and Saul counted the men who were with him. They numbered about six hundred.

Israel Without Weapons

16Saul and his son Jonathan and the men with them were staying in Gibeah*b* in Benjamin, while the Philistines camped at Micmash. **17**Raiding parties went out from the Philistine camp in three detachments. One turned toward Ophrah in the vicinity of Shual, **18**another toward Beth Horon, and the third toward the borderland overlooking the Valley of Zeboim facing the desert.

19Not a blacksmith could be found in the whole land of Israel, because the Philistines had said, "Otherwise the Hebrews will make swords or spears!" **20**So all Israel went down to the Philistines to have their plowshares, mattocks, axes and sickles*c* sharpened. **21**The price was two thirds of a shekel*d* for sharpening plowshares and mattocks, and a third of a shekel*e* for sharpening forks and axes and for repointing goads.

Without swords or spears, how could the Israelites fight? (13:22)

The Philistines controlled access to the blacksmiths (v. 19) to prevent the Israelites from making weapons. The Israelites probably equipped themselves with axes, sickles, goads and other tools (vv. 20–21). Some may have used bows and arrows or slingshots. Israel needed the supernatural strength of God to help them. Jonathan proved God would help them when he and his armor-bearer, alone and unaided, routed a Philistine garrison at Micmash (14:1–15).

22So on the day of the battle not a soldier with Saul and Jonathan had a sword or spear in his hand; only Saul and his son Jonathan had them.

Jonathan Attacks the Philistines

23Now a detachment of Philistines had gone out to the pass at Micmash. **14** **1**One day Jonathan son of Saul said to the young man bearing his armor, "Come, let's go over to the Philistine outpost on the other side." But he did not tell his father.

2Saul was staying on the outskirts of Gibeah under a pomegranate tree in Migron. With him were about six hundred men, **3**among whom was Ahijah, who was wearing an ephod*D*. He was a son of Ichabod's brother Ahitub son of Phinehas, the son of Eli, the LORD's priest*D* in Shiloh. No one was aware that Jonathan had left.

4On each side of the pass that Jonathan intended to cross to reach the Philistine outpost was a cliff; one was called Bozez, and the other Seneh. **5**One cliff stood to the north toward Micmash, the other to the south toward Geba.

6Jonathan said to his young armor-bearer, "Come, let's go over to the outpost of those uncircumcised*D* fellows. Perhaps the LORD will act in our behalf. Nothing can hinder the LORD from saving, whether by many or by few."

7"Do all that you have in mind," his armor-bearer said. "Go ahead; I am with you heart and soul*D*."

8Jonathan said, "Come, then; we will cross over toward

---

*a*15 Hebrew; Septuagint *Gilgal and went his way; the rest of the people went after Saul to meet the army, and they went out of Gilgal*
*b*16 Two Hebrew manuscripts; most Hebrew manuscripts *Geba,* a variant of *Gibeah*   *c*20 Septuagint; Hebrew *plowshares*
*d*21 Hebrew *pim*; that is, about 1/4 ounce (about 8 grams)
*e*21 That is, about 1/8 ounce (about 4 grams)

the men and let them see us. **9**If they say to us, 'Wait there until we come to you,' we will stay where we are and not go up to them. **10**But if they say, 'Come up to us,' we will climb up, because that will be our sign that the LORD has given them into our hands."

11So both of them showed themselves to the Philistine outpost. "Look!" said the Philistines. "The Hebrews are crawling out of the holes they were hiding in." **12**The men of the outpost shouted to Jonathan and his armor-bearer, "Come up to us and we'll teach you a lesson."

So Jonathan said to his armor-bearer, "Climb up after me; the LORD has given them into the hand of Israel."

13Jonathan climbed up, using his hands and feet, with his armor-bearer right behind him. The Philistines fell before Jonathan, and his armor-bearer followed and killed behind him. **14**In that first attack Jonathan and his armor-bearer killed some twenty men in an area of about half an acre.*a*

Israel Routs the Philistines

15Then panic struck the whole army—those in the camp and field, and those in the outposts and raiding parties—and the ground shook. It was a panic sent by God.*b*

16Saul's lookouts at Gibeah in Benjamin saw the army melting away in all directions. **17**Then Saul said to the men who were with him, "Muster the forces and see who has left us." When they did, it was Jonathan and his armor-bearer who were not there.

18Saul said to Ahijah, "Bring the ark of God." (At that time it was with the Israelites.)*c* **19**While Saul was talking to the priest,*D* the tumult in the Philistine camp increased more and more. So Saul said to the priest, "Withdraw your hand."

20Then Saul and all his men assembled and went to the battle. They found the Philistines in total confusion, striking each other with their swords. **21**Those Hebrews who had previously been with the Philistines and had gone up with them to their camp went over to the Israelites who were with Saul and Jonathan. **22**When all the Israelites who had hidden in the hill country of Ephraim heard that the Philistines were on the run, they joined the battle in hot pursuit. **23**So the LORD rescued Israel that day, and the battle moved on beyond Beth Aven.

Jonathan Eats Honey

24Now the men of Israel were in distress that day, because Saul had bound the people under an oath, saying, "Cursed be any man who eats food before evening comes, before I have avenged*D* myself on my enemies!" So none of the troops tasted food.

25The entire army*d* entered the woods, and there was honey on the ground. **26**When they went into the woods, they saw the honey oozing out, yet no one put his hand to his mouth, because they feared the oath. **27**But Jonathan had not heard that his father had bound the people with the oath, so he reached out the end of the staff that was in his hand and dipped it into the honeycomb. He raised his hand to his mouth, and his eyes brightened.*e*

How could Jonathan be certain this sign was from the Lord? (14:10–12)
Jonathan was neither flippant nor irreverent. He believed God would help his people answer the threat of the superior Philistine military. He trusted God to show him what to do by testing the enemy's courage: if they lacked courage to come to Jonathan, that would signal their defeat, and Jonathan would attack.

Why was the size of the battlefield significant? (14:14)
The relatively small area indicates the battle was probably over quickly.

The ark of God (14:18)
The Philistines had captured the ark in battle (4:11), but now the Israelites again had possession of it. In fact, the Philistines had the ark for only about seven months (6:1).

Why did Saul tell the priest, *Withdraw your hand*? (14:18–19)
Perhaps the priest was consulting the Urim and Thummim—sacred lots used to discern God's will (see Exodus 28:29–30). Hearing sounds of confusion among the Philistines (14:19), Saul would have been saying, in effect, "Forget about casting the lots. I know the will of the Lord now—it's time to attack!"

Why would the Israelites allow traitors to come back? (14:21)
Both traitors (v. 21) and cowards (v. 22) joined in the battle on the side of Israel once Saul's victory was apparent. Perhaps with such a small force under his command, Saul was glad to have additional soldiers join him, and he overlooked their faults. They would have to bear the shame of deserting their own people, but it would have been worse had they remained apart once victory was assured.

Why did Saul make this curse? (14:24)
Because he wanted to take advantage of the situation, Saul impulsively tried to capitalize on his opportunity to rout the enemy. He threatened to kill any soldier who took time out from the battle to eat (see vv. 43–44). It was bad strategy: time gained was strength lost, especially in a long battle.

---

a14 Hebrew *half a yoke*; a "yoke" was the land plowed by a yoke of oxen in one day.   *b15* Or *a terrible panic*   *c18* Hebrew; Septuagint *"Bring the ephod." (At that time he wore the ephod before the Israelites.)*   *d25* Or *Now all the people of the land*   *e27* Or his strength was renewed

Why was eating blood wrong? (14:32–33)

See *Why would anyone want to eat blood?* (Lev. 17:10) and *Why is blood considered the primary link with life?* (Lev. 17:11).

Why did God refuse to answer their inquiries? (14:37)

Perhaps because Jonathan in battle had violated Saul's oath (vv. 27–28). Still, it would be difficult to explain why God would hold the troops to the vow of a foolish man. Another explanation may be that God refused to answer to show his disfavor because the men ate meat with blood still in it (v. 33).

Why did Saul expect God to answer, after he'd just refused? (14:41)

Probably because of the different nature of this request. Saul cast lots to determine the guilty party. He was confident that the Lord would want to reveal what displeased him.

SCRIPTURE LINK (14:44) *May God deal with me . . . if you do not die*

Another strange vow that risked a leader's own child is discussed in the article: *What's behind this bizarre deal with God?* (Judges 11:31,39).

Why was Saul so determined to fulfill a foolish vow? (14:44)

After issuing a command (v. 24), he would have been humiliated as a leader if he went back on his word. To make matters worse, sparing Jonathan would have been an admission that the real offense was his own. Rather than risk that humiliation, he was willing to kill his own son.

28Then one of the soldiers told him, "Your father bound the army under a strict oath, saying, 'Cursed be any man who eats food today!' That is why the men are faint."

29Jonathan said, "My father has made trouble for the country. See how my eyes brightened*a* when I tasted a little of this honey. 30How much better it would have been if the men had eaten today some of the plunder*D* they took from their enemies. Would not the slaughter of the Philistines have been even greater?"

31That day, after the Israelites had struck down the Philistines from Micmash to Aijalon, they were exhausted. 32They pounced on the plunder and, taking sheep, cattle and calves, they butchered them on the ground and ate them, together with the blood. 33Then someone said to Saul, "Look, the men are sinning against the Lord by eating meat that has blood in it."

"You have broken faith," he said. "Roll a large stone over here at once." 34Then he said, "Go out among the men and tell them, 'Each of you bring me your cattle and sheep, and slaughter them here and eat them. Do not sin against the Lord by eating meat with blood still in it.' "

So everyone brought his ox that night and slaughtered it there. 35Then Saul built an altar to the Lord; it was the first time he had done this.

36Saul said, "Let us go down after the Philistines by night and plunder them till dawn, and let us not leave one of them alive."

"Do whatever seems best to you," they replied.

But the priest*D* said, "Let us inquire of God here."

37So Saul asked God, "Shall I go down after the Philistines? Will you give them into Israel's hand?" But God did not answer him that day.

38Saul therefore said, "Come here, all you who are leaders of the army, and let us find out what sin has been committed today. 39As surely as the Lord who rescues Israel lives, even if it lies with my son Jonathan, he must die." But not one of the men said a word.

40Saul then said to all the Israelites, "You stand over there; I and Jonathan my son will stand over here."

"Do what seems best to you," the men replied.

41Then Saul prayed to the Lord, the God of Israel, "Give me the right answer."*b* And Jonathan and Saul were taken by lot, and the men were cleared. 42Saul said, "Cast the lot between me and Jonathan my son." And Jonathan was taken.

43Then Saul said to Jonathan, "Tell me what you have done."

So Jonathan told him, "I merely tasted a little honey with the end of my staff. And now must I die?"

44Saul said, "May God deal with me, be it ever so severely, if you do not die, Jonathan."

45But the men said to Saul, "Should Jonathan die—he who has brought about this great deliverance in Israel? Never! As surely as the Lord lives, not a hair of his head will fall to the ground, for he did this today with God's help." So the men rescued Jonathan, and he was not put to death*D*.

46Then Saul stopped pursuing the Philistines, and they withdrew to their own land.

---

*a*29 Or *my strength was renewed*   *b*41 Hebrew; Septuagint *"Why have you not answered your servant today? If the fault is in me or my son Jonathan, respond with Urim, but if the men of Israel are at fault, respond with Thummim."*

47After Saul had assumed rule over Israel, he fought against their enemies on every side: Moab, the Ammonites, Edom[D], the kings[a] of Zobah, and the Philistines. Wherever he turned, he inflicted punishment on them.[b] **48**He fought valiantly and defeated the Amalekites, delivering Israel from the hands of those who had plundered[D] them.

Saul's Family

49Saul's sons were Jonathan, Ishvi and Malki-Shua. The name of his older daughter was Merab, and that of the younger was Michal. **50**His wife's name was Ahinoam daughter of Ahimaaz. The name of the commander of Saul's army was Abner son of Ner, and Ner was Saul's uncle. **51**Saul's father Kish and Abner's father Ner were sons of Abiel.

52All the days of Saul there was bitter war with the Philistines, and whenever Saul saw a mighty or brave man, he took him into his service.

The LORD Rejects Saul as King

15 Samuel said to Saul, "I am the one the LORD sent to anoint[D] you king over his people Israel; so listen now to the message from the LORD. **2**This is what the LORD Almighty says: 'I will punish the Amalekites for what they did to Israel when they waylaid them as they came up from Egypt. **3**Now go, attack the Amalekites and totally destroy[c] everything that belongs to them. Do not spare them; put to death[D] men and women, children and infants, cattle and sheep, camels and donkeys.' "

4So Saul summoned the men and mustered them at Telaim—two hundred thousand foot soldiers and ten thousand men from Judah. **5**Saul went to the city of Amalek and set an ambush in the ravine. **6**Then he said to the Kenites, "Go away, leave the Amalekites so that I do not destroy you along with them; for you showed kindness to all the Israelites when they came up out of Egypt." So the Kenites moved away from the Amalekites.

7Then Saul attacked the Amalekites all the way from Havilah to Shur, to the east of Egypt. **8**He took Agag king of the Amalekites alive, and all his people he totally destroyed with the sword. **9**But Saul and the army spared Agag and the best of the sheep and cattle, the fat calves[d] and lambs—everything that was good. These they were unwilling to destroy completely, but everything that was despised and weak they totally destroyed.

10Then the word of the LORD came to Samuel: **11**"I am grieved that I have made Saul king, because he has turned away from me and has not carried out my instructions." Samuel was troubled, and he cried out to the LORD all that night.

12Early in the morning Samuel got up and went to meet Saul, but he was told, "Saul has gone to Carmel. There he has set up a monument in his own honor and has turned and gone on down to Gilgal."

13When Samuel reached him, Saul said, "The LORD bless you! I have carried out the LORD's instructions."

Why did God insist on total destruction? (15:2–3)

The Amalekites, like a street gang, lived a lifestyle of intimidation and terrorism. They had preyed upon the weak and helpless (Deut. 25:17–18). God knew Israel could never live peacefully until this threat was eradicated. Also see articles: *Why would God annihilate an entire nation?* (Deut. 2:34) and *Why kill everything?* (Joshua 6:21).

What did Saul plan to do with Agag? (15:8)

Most likely Saul, in his arrogance, simply couldn't resist the temptation to parade his foe before his people and to accumulate even more honor for himself (also see v. 12).

---

a47 Masoretic Text; Dead Sea Scrolls and Septuagint *king*
b47 Hebrew; Septuagint *he was victorious*   *c3* The Hebrew term refers to the irrevocable giving over of things or persons to the LORD, often by totally destroying them; also in verses 8, 9, 15, 18, 20 and 21.
d9 Or *the grown bulls*; the meaning of the Hebrew for this phrase is uncertain.

Why was obedience better than sacrifice? (15:22)
True obedience comes from the heart. Saul claimed to keep the letter of the law, but he ignored its spirit. The sacrifices in which the Lord delights are *a broken spirit, a broken and contrite heart (Psalm 51:17)*. Sacrifices offered in that spirit of humility were the only ones acceptable to God.

Couldn't Saul be forgiven? (15:25–26)
Samuel did not say that Saul couldn't be forgiven, only that his sins had disqualified him from being king. Saul experienced the consequences of his long-term rebellion and arrogance.

Glory of Israel **(15:29)**
Glory means *the Unchanging One*. In this context, the concept of God's unchanging character was particularly appropriate. Samuel stressed how God's decision to replace Saul with another king was irrevocable. Unlike Saul, who had repeatedly demonstrated his unreliability, the Lord, the Unchanging One, was absolutely reliable and could be depended upon to keep his word.

If God is unchanging, why did he make Saul king and then remove him? (15:29)
God did not change—Saul did. God took a humble, self-effacing man and put him on the throne, giving him the chance to prove himself faithful. But Saul failed (13:13), becoming arrogant and rebellious. Had he remained humble, trusting in God for his help and direction, he could have remained king (13:13–14).

How could Samuel—a man of God—kill someone? (15:33)
The Lord often used his people as instruments of righteous judgment (Gen. 9:6; Lev. 24:17–23). There was nothing inconsistent about "a man of God," in response to the clear command of the Lord, putting to death sinners who deserved to die. In this case, Samuel executed Agag (since Saul had refused) to fulfill the Lord's command (15:3).

14But Samuel said, "What then is this bleating of sheep in my ears? What is this lowing of cattle that I hear?"

15Saul answered, "The soldiers brought them from the Amalekites; they spared the best of the sheep and cattle to sacrifice^D to the Lord your God, but we totally destroyed the rest."

16"Stop!" Samuel said to Saul. "Let me tell you what the Lord said to me last night."

"Tell me," Saul replied.

17Samuel said, "Although you were once small in your own eyes, did you not become the head of the tribes of Israel? The Lord anointed^D you king over Israel. **18**And he sent you on a mission, saying, 'Go and completely destroy those wicked people, the Amalekites; make war on them until you have wiped them out.' **19**Why did you not obey the Lord? Why did you pounce on the plunder^D and do evil in the eyes of the Lord?"

20"But I did obey the Lord," Saul said. "I went on the mission the Lord assigned me. I completely destroyed the Amalekites and brought back Agag their king. **21**The soldiers took sheep and cattle from the plunder, the best of what was devoted to God, in order to sacrifice them to the Lord your God at Gilgal."

22But Samuel replied:

"Does the Lord delight in burnt offerings^D and
        sacrifices
    as much as in obeying the voice of the Lord?
To obey is better than sacrifice,
    and to heed is better than the fat of rams.
23For rebellion is like the sin of divination^D,
    and arrogance like the evil of idolatry^D.
Because you have rejected the word of the
        Lord,
    he has rejected you as king."

24Then Saul said to Samuel, "I have sinned. I violated the Lord's command and your instructions. I was afraid of the people and so I gave in to them. **25**Now I beg you, forgive my sin and come back with me, so that I may worship the Lord."

26But Samuel said to him, "I will not go back with you. You have rejected the word of the Lord, and the Lord has rejected you as king over Israel!"

27As Samuel turned to leave, Saul caught hold of the hem of his robe, and it tore. **28**Samuel said to him, "The Lord has torn the kingdom of Israel from you today and has given it to one of your neighbors—to one better than you. **29**He who is the Glory^D of Israel does not lie or change his mind; for he is not a man, that he should change his mind."

30Saul replied, "I have sinned. But please honor me before the elders of my people and before Israel; come back with me, so that I may worship the Lord your God." **31**So Samuel went back with Saul, and Saul worshiped the Lord.

32Then Samuel said, "Bring me Agag king of the Amalekites."

Agag came to him confidently,^a thinking, "Surely the bitterness of death^D is past."

33But Samuel said,

"As your sword has made women childless,

a32 Or him trembling, yet

so will your mother be childless among women."

And Samuel put Agag to death[D] before the LORD at Gilgal.

34Then Samuel left for Ramah, but Saul went up to his home in Gibeah of Saul. **35**Until the day Samuel died, he did not go to see Saul again, though Samuel mourned for him. And the LORD was grieved that he had made Saul king over Israel.

Samuel Anoints David

16 The LORD said to Samuel, "How long will you mourn for Saul, since I have rejected him as king over Israel? Fill your horn with oil and be on your way; I am sending you to Jesse of Bethlehem. I have chosen one of his sons to be king."

2But Samuel said, "How can I go? Saul will hear about it and kill me."

The LORD said, "Take a heifer with you and say, 'I have come to sacrifice[D] to the LORD.' **3**Invite Jesse to the sacrifice, and I will show you what to do. You are to anoint for me the one I indicate."

4Samuel did what the LORD said. When he arrived at Bethlehem, the elders of the town trembled when they met him. They asked, "Do you come in peace[D]?"

5Samuel replied, "Yes, in peace; I have come to sacrifice to the LORD. Consecrate yourselves and come to the sacrifice with me." Then he consecrated Jesse and his sons and invited them to the sacrifice.

6When they arrived, Samuel saw Eliab and thought, "Surely the LORD's anointed stands here before the LORD."

7But the LORD said to Samuel, "Do not consider his appearance or his height, for I have rejected him. The LORD does not look at the things man looks at. Man looks at the outward appearance, but the LORD looks at the heart."

8Then Jesse called Abinadab and had him pass in front of Samuel. But Samuel said, "The LORD has not chosen this one either." **9**Jesse then had Shammah pass by, but Samuel said, "Nor has the LORD chosen this one." **10**Jesse had seven of his sons pass before Samuel, but Samuel said to him, "The LORD has not chosen these." **11**So he asked Jesse, "Are these all the sons you have?"

"There is still the youngest," Jesse answered, "but he is tending the sheep."

Samuel said, "Send for him; we will not sit down[a] until he arrives."

12So he sent and had him brought in. He was ruddy, with a fine appearance and handsome features.

Then the LORD said, "Rise and anoint him; he is the one."

13So Samuel took the horn of oil and anointed him in the presence of his brothers, and from that day on the Spirit of the LORD came upon David in power. Samuel then went to Ramah.

David in Saul's Service

14Now the Spirit of the LORD had departed from Saul, and an evil[b] spirit from the LORD tormented him.

15Saul's attendants said to him, "See, an evil spirit from God is tormenting you. **16**Let our lord command his ser-

---

a11 Some Septuagint manuscripts; Hebrew not gather around
b14 Or injurious; also in verses 15, 16 and 23

Did David and his family know what Samuel was doing? (16:13)

Probably not. Samuel had good reason to keep it a secret—for David's sake as well as for his own (v. 2). David and his family perhaps considered the anointing as a special dedication to God's service.

Does God's Spirit leave people today as he left Saul? (16:14; see 10:10)

The Holy Spirit in the Old Testament is described as coming upon an individual (for example, 10:9–10; 16:13), filling a person for service (Exodus 31:3; 35:31) or being in someone (Num. 27:18; Daniel 4:8). But the presence or absence of the Spirit had nothing to do with salvation. Rather, the presence of the Spirit in the Old Testament indicated only that a person was empowered for service. Since Saul repeatedly acted arrogantly and independently of the Lord, the Spirit left him to his own devices (15:26). Today, the Spirit dwells in everyone who believes in Christ. He dwells permanently, according to some (John 14:17); conditionally, according to others (Heb. 6:4–6).

How can an evil spirit be *from the LORD*? (16:14)

The term *evil spirit* could also mean *a troubling* or *injurious spirit* (see NIV text note), suggesting a sense of depression or gloom. Without a sense of God's presence, Saul may have felt hopeless, a feeling that would have sparked fits of rage (18:10–11). Or his spiritual vacuum may have left him vulnerable to a demonic influence. See article: *How can a holy God send an evil spirit?* (Judges 9:23).

How would the king's servant know the Lord was with David? (16:18)

The servant may not have known specifically about David's spiritual condition, although even then David may have had some reputation for his passionate psalms to God. But more likely the servant used this phrase to convey the common idea that success and skill indicated God's blessing upon a person. *The LORD is with him* was probably the servant's way of saying that David was well-qualified and could do a good job in any of the areas he had just mentioned. Other examples that link success and prosperity to the presence of the Lord include Joseph (Gen. 39:2–3), Joshua (Joshua 1:8–9) and Solomon (2 Chron. 1:1).

David and Goliath (17:1)

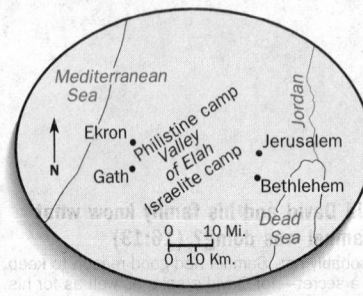

Mediterranean Sea
Ekron
Gath
N
Philistine camp
Valley of Elah
Israelite camp
Jordan
Jerusalem
Bethlehem
Dead Sea
0   10 Mi.
0   10 Km.

Greaves (17:6)

Shin guards used to protect a combatant's legs.

vants here to search for someone who can play the harp. He will play when the evil spirit from God comes upon you, and you will feel better."

17So Saul said to his attendants, "Find someone who plays well and bring him to me."

18One of the servants answered, "I have seen a son of Jesse of Bethlehem who knows how to play the harp. He is a brave man and a warrior. He speaks well and is a fine-looking man. And the LORD is with him."

19Then Saul sent messengers to Jesse and said, "Send me your son David, who is with the sheep." **20**So Jesse took a donkey loaded with bread, a skin of wine and a young goat and sent them with his son David to Saul.

21David came to Saul and entered his service. Saul liked him very much, and David became one of his armor-bearers. **22**Then Saul sent word to Jesse, saying, "Allow David to remain in my service, for I am pleased with him."

23Whenever the spirit from God came upon Saul, David would take his harp and play. Then relief would come to Saul; he would feel better, and the evil spirit would leave him.

David and Goliath

17 Now the Philistines gathered their forces for war and assembled at Socoh in Judah. They pitched camp at Ephes Dammim, between Socoh and Azekah. **2**Saul and the Israelites assembled and camped in the Valley of Elah and drew up their battle line to meet the Philistines. **3**The Philistines occupied one hill and the Israelites another, with the valley between them.

4A champion named Goliath, who was from Gath, came out of the Philistine camp. He was over nine feet*a* tall. **5**He had a bronze helmet on his head and wore a coat of scale armor of bronze weighing five thousand shekels*b*; **6**on his legs he wore bronze greaves, and a bronze javelin was slung on his back. **7**His spear shaft was like a weaver's rod, and its iron point weighed six hundred shekels.*c* His shield bearer went ahead of him.

8Goliath stood and shouted to the ranks of Israel, "Why do you come out and line up for battle? Am I not a Philistine, and are you not the servants of Saul? Choose a man and have him come down to me. **9**If he is able to fight and kill me, we will become your subjects; but if I overcome him and kill him, you will become our subjects and serve us." **10**Then the Philistine said, "This day I defy the ranks of Israel! Give me a man and let us fight each other." **11**On hearing the Philistine's words, Saul and all the Israelites were dismayed and terrified.

12Now David was the son of an Ephrathite named Jesse, who was from Bethlehem in Judah. Jesse had eight sons, and in Saul's time he was old and well advanced in years. **13**Jesse's three oldest sons had followed Saul to the war: The firstborn*D* was Eliab; the second, Abinadab; and the third, Shammah. **14**David was the youngest. The three oldest followed Saul, **15**but David went back and forth from Saul to tend his father's sheep at Bethlehem.

16For forty days the Philistine came forward every morning and evening and took his stand.

17Now Jesse said to his son David, "Take this ephah*d* of

---

*a*4 Hebrew *was six cubits and a span* (about 3 meters)   *b*5 That is, about 125 pounds (about 57 kilograms)   *c*7 That is, about 15 pounds (about 7 kilograms)   *d*17 That is, probably about 3/5 bushel (about 22 liters)

roasted grain and these ten loaves of bread for your brothers and hurry to their camp. [18]Take along these ten cheeses to the commander of their unit.[a] See how your brothers are and bring back some assurance[b] from them. [19]They are with Saul and all the men of Israel in the Valley of Elah, fighting against the Philistines."

[20]Early in the morning David left the flock with a shepherd, loaded up and set out, as Jesse had directed. He reached the camp as the army was going out to its battle positions, shouting the war cry. [21]Israel and the Philistines were drawing up their lines facing each other. [22]David left his things with the keeper of supplies, ran to the battle lines and greeted his brothers. [23]As he was talking with them, Goliath, the Philistine champion from Gath, stepped out from his lines and shouted his usual defiance, and David heard it. [24]When the Israelites saw the man, they all ran from him in great fear.

[25]Now the Israelites had been saying, "Do you see how this man keeps coming out? He comes out to defy Israel. The king will give great wealth to the man who kills him. He will also give him his daughter in marriage and will exempt his father's family from taxes in Israel."

[26]David asked the men standing near him, "What will be done for the man who kills this Philistine and removes this disgrace from Israel? Who is this uncircumcised[D] Philistine that he should defy the armies of the living God?"

[27]They repeated to him what they had been saying and told him, "This is what will be done for the man who kills him."

[28]When Eliab, David's oldest brother, heard him speaking with the men, he burned with anger at him and asked, "Why have you come down here? And with whom did you leave those few sheep in the desert? I know how conceited you are and how wicked your heart is; you came down only to watch the battle."

[29]"Now what have I done?" said David. "Can't I even speak?" [30]He then turned away to someone else and brought up the same matter, and the men answered him as before. [31]What David said was overheard and reported to Saul, and Saul sent for him.

[32]David said to Saul, "Let no one lose heart on account of this Philistine; your servant will go and fight him."

[33]Saul replied, "You are not able to go out against this Philistine and fight him; you are only a boy, and he has been a fighting man from his youth."

[34]But David said to Saul, "Your servant has been keeping his father's sheep. When a lion or a bear came and carried off a sheep from the flock, [35]I went after it, struck it and rescued the sheep from its mouth. When it turned on me, I seized it by its hair, struck it and killed it. [36]Your servant has killed both the lion and the bear; this uncircumcised Philistine will be like one of them, because he has defied the armies of the living God. [37]The LORD who delivered me from the paw of the lion and the paw of the bear will deliver me from the hand of this Philistine."

Saul said to David, "Go, and the LORD be with you."

[38]Then Saul dressed David in his own tunic. He put a coat of armor on him and a bronze helmet on his head. [39]David fastened on his sword over the tunic and tried walking around, because he was not used to them.

"I cannot go in these," he said to Saul, "because I am

Why was David's brother so angry about his questions? (17:28–29)
Eliab was probably jealous of David. The eldest son, Eliab had been bypassed by Samuel when David was anointed (16:6,13). He also was aware of the honor David had received in Saul's court (16:21–23).

How old was David? (17:33)
We can only speculate. Some think David may have been 12 when he first played music for Saul, and 17 or 18 when he fought Goliath.

---

a 18 Hebrew *thousand*   b 18 Or *some token*; or *some pledge of spoils*

not used to them." So he took them off. **40**Then he took his staff in his hand, chose five smooth stones from the stream, put them in the pouch of his shepherd's bag and, with his sling in his hand, approached the Philistine.

41Meanwhile, the Philistine, with his shield bearer in front of him, kept coming closer to David. **42**He looked David over and saw that he was only a boy, ruddy and handsome, and he despised him. **43**He said to David, "Am I a dog, that you come at me with sticks?" And the Philistine cursed David by his gods. **44**"Come here," he said, "and I'll give your flesh to the birds of the air and the beasts of the field!"

45David said to the Philistine, "You come against me with sword and spear and javelin, but I come against you in the name of the LORD Almighty, the God of the armies of Israel, whom you have defied. **46**This day the LORD will hand you over to me, and I'll strike you down and cut off your head. Today I will give the carcasses of the Philistine army to the birds of the air and the beasts of the earth, and the whole world will know that there is a God in Israel. **47**All those gathered here will know that it is not by sword or spear that the LORD saves; for the battle is the LORD's, and he will give all of you into our hands."

48As the Philistine moved closer to attack him, David ran quickly toward the battle line to meet him. **49**Reaching into his bag and taking out a stone, he slung it and struck the Philistine on the forehead. The stone sank into his forehead, and he fell facedown on the ground.

50So David triumphed over the Philistine with a sling and a stone; without a sword in his hand he struck down the Philistine and killed him.

51David ran and stood over him. He took hold of the Philistine's sword and drew it from the scabbard. After he killed him, he cut off his head with the sword.

When the Philistines saw that their hero was dead, they turned and ran. **52**Then the men of Israel and Judah surged forward with a shout and pursued the Philistines to the entrance of Gath*a* and to the gates of Ekron. Their dead were strewn along the Shaaraim road to Gath and Ekron. **53**When the Israelites returned from chasing the Philistines, they plundered*D* their camp. **54**David took the Philistine's head and brought it to Jerusalem*D*, and he put the Philistine's weapons in his own tent.

55As Saul watched David going out to meet the Philistine, he said to Abner, commander of the army, "Abner, whose son is that young man?"

Abner replied, "As surely as you live, O king, I don't know."

56The king said, "Find out whose son this young man is."

57As soon as David returned from killing the Philistine, Abner took him and brought him before Saul, with David still holding the Philistine's head.

58"Whose son are you, young man?" Saul asked him.

David said, "I am the son of your servant Jesse of Bethlehem."

Saul's Jealousy of David

18 After David had finished talking with Saul, Jonathan became one in spirit with David, and he loved him as himself. **2**From that day Saul kept David with him and did not let him return to his father's house. **3**And

What size stone could kill a giant? (17:49)
Archaeologists have found sling stones around fortification systems of the time that are about the size of a baseball—two to three inches in diameter. This may have been the size of those David took from the stream.

Why did David want Goliath's head? (17:54)
It was considered a trophy of war and a reminder of how God can enable his people to overcome overwhelming enemies.

Why didn't Saul recognize David? (17:55,58)
Perhaps a few years had passed since David's service to Saul as a musician and armor-bearer (16:14–23). It could be that Saul did recognize David, but that he needed to be reminded of whose son he was so his family could be rewarded as Saul had promised earlier (v. 25).

---

a52 Some Septuagint manuscripts; Hebrew *a valley*

Jonathan made a covenant[D] with David because he loved him as himself. **4**Jonathan took off the robe he was wearing and gave it to David, along with his tunic, and even his sword, his bow and his belt.

5Whatever Saul sent him to do, David did it so successfully[a] that Saul gave him a high rank in the army. This pleased all the people, and Saul's officers as well.

6When the men were returning home after David had killed the Philistine, the women came out from all the towns of Israel to meet King Saul with singing and dancing, with joyful songs and with tambourines and lutes. **7**As they danced, they sang:

> "Saul has slain his thousands,
>   and David his tens of thousands."

8Saul was very angry; this refrain galled him. "They have credited David with tens of thousands," he thought, "but me with only thousands. What more can he get but the kingdom?" **9**And from that time on Saul kept a jealous eye on David.

10The next day an evil[b] spirit from God came forcefully upon Saul. He was prophesying in his house, while David was playing the harp, as he usually did. Saul had a spear in his hand **11**and he hurled it, saying to himself, "I'll pin David to the wall." But David eluded him twice.

12Saul was afraid of David, because the LORD was with David but had left Saul. **13**So he sent David away from him and gave him command over a thousand men, and David led the troops in their campaigns. **14**In everything he did he had great success,[c] because the LORD was with him. **15**When Saul saw how successful[d] he was, he was afraid of him. **16**But all Israel and Judah loved David, because he led them in their campaigns.

17Saul said to David, "Here is my older daughter Merab. I will give her to you in marriage; only serve me bravely and fight the battles of the LORD." For Saul said to himself, "I will not raise a hand against him. Let the Philistines do that!"

18But David said to Saul, "Who am I, and what is my family or my father's clan in Israel, that I should become the king's son-in-law?" **19**So[e] when the time came for Merab, Saul's daughter, to be given to David, she was given in marriage to Adriel of Meholah.

20Now Saul's daughter Michal was in love with David, and when they told Saul about it, he was pleased. **21**"I will give her to him," he thought, "so that she may be a snare to him and so that the hand of the Philistines may be against him." So Saul said to David, "Now you have a second opportunity to become my son-in-law."

22Then Saul ordered his attendants: "Speak to David privately and say, 'Look, the king is pleased with you, and his attendants all like you; now become his son-in-law.' "

23They repeated these words to David. But David said, "Do you think it is a small matter to become the king's son-in-law? I'm only a poor man and little known."

24When Saul's servants told him what David had said, **25**Saul replied, "Say to David, 'The king wants no other price for the bride than a hundred Philistine foreskins, to take revenge on his enemies.' " Saul's plan was to have David fall by the hands of the Philistines.

26When the attendants told David these things, he was

How much rank was David given? (18:5)

Apparently David was old enough (perhaps 18) to be given command of a portion of the army. His specific rank is not mentioned, but his authority could have been considerable, given the success of his conquests, his friendship with the king's son (vv. 1–4) and his popularity with the people and the servants of the king (v. 6). Before long he would command 1,000 men (v. 13).

What kind of prophesying was Saul doing? (18:10)

Earlier, Saul prophesied after the Spirit of God had come upon him *in power* (10:10). In this case, however, it was an evil spirit that prompted Saul to "prophesy" (or better, *to rave*). His babbling was probably confused and incoherent, revealing that he was tormented by an evil spirit.

How did Saul know the Lord had left him and was with David instead? (18:12)

Samuel had informed Saul earlier that the Lord had rejected him (15:23). Saul must have felt a growing sense of his own diminishing glory. Also, his tormented mind and lack of internal peace must have confirmed his fears that God no longer was with him.

Why did Saul want Philistine foreskins? (18:25–28)

He didn't really want foreskins. He wanted David dead. To receive a bride-price for his daughter's hand in marriage, Saul urged David to go into battle. Saul hoped David would be killed in the attempt to get the Philistine foreskins.

---

[a]5 Or *wisely*   [b]10 Or *injurious*   [c]14 Or *he was very wise*
[d]15 Or *wise*   [e]19 Or *However,*

pleased to become the king's son-in-law. So before the allotted time elapsed, **27**David and his men went out and killed two hundred Philistines. He brought their foreskins and presented the full number to the king so that he might become the king's son-in-law. Then Saul gave him his daughter Michal in marriage.

28When Saul realized that the LORD was with David and that his daughter Michal loved David, **29**Saul became still more afraid of him, and he remained his enemy the rest of his days.

30The Philistine commanders continued to go out to battle, and as often as they did, David met with more success*a* than the rest of Saul's officers, and his name became well known.

Saul Tries to Kill David

19 Saul told his son Jonathan and all the attendants to kill David. But Jonathan was very fond of David **2**and warned him, "My father Saul is looking for a chance to kill you. Be on your guard tomorrow morning; go into hiding and stay there. **3**I will go out and stand with my father in the field where you are. I'll speak to him about you and will tell you what I find out."

4Jonathan spoke well of David to Saul his father and said to him, "Let not the king do wrong to his servant David; he has not wronged you, and what he has done has benefited you greatly. **5**He took his life in his hands when he killed the Philistine. The LORD won a great victory for all Israel, and you saw it and were glad. Why then would you do wrong to an innocent man like David by killing him for no reason?"

6Saul listened to Jonathan and took this oath: "As surely as the LORD lives, David will not be put to death*b*."

7So Jonathan called David and told him the whole conversation. He brought him to Saul, and David was with Saul as before.

8Once more war broke out, and David went out and fought the Philistines. He struck them with such force that they fled before him.

9But an evil*b* spirit from the LORD came upon Saul as he was sitting in his house with his spear in his hand. While David was playing the harp, **10**Saul tried to pin him to the wall with his spear, but David eluded him as Saul drove the spear into the wall. That night David made good his escape.

11Saul sent men to David's house to watch it and to kill him in the morning. But Michal, David's wife, warned him, "If you don't run for your life tonight, tomorrow you'll be killed." **12**So Michal let David down through a window, and he fled and escaped. **13**Then Michal took an idol*D c* and laid it on the bed, covering it with a garment and putting some goats' hair at the head.

14When Saul sent the men to capture David, Michal said, "He is ill."

15Then Saul sent the men back to see David and told them, "Bring him up to me in his bed so that I may kill him." **16**But when the men entered, there was the idol in the bed, and at the head was some goats' hair.

17Saul said to Michal, "Why did you deceive me like this and send my enemy away so that he escaped?"

Evil spirit from the LORD (19:9)
See article: *How can a holy God send an evil spirit?* (Judges 9:23).

Why did David—a man after God's own heart—have an idol in his house? (19:13)
Some argue that Michal, without David's knowledge, kept it in the home. But that is not likely if it was the size suggested here. Such idols played an important role in the culture, indicating who possessed the rights and privileges as leaders of households or clans. Perhaps that is why the early Israelites did not seem concerned that these statues might suggest they were being unfaithful to the Lord. Nevertheless, it remains a mystery why David could have permitted an idol in his own home. Also see *Why would Rachel steal her father's pagan gods?* (Gen. 31:19).

*a*30 Or *David acted more wisely*   *b*9 Or *injurious*   *c*13 Hebrew *teraphim*; also in verse 16

Michal told him, "He said to me, 'Let me get away. Why should I kill you?'"

18When David had fled and made his escape, he went to Samuel at Ramah and told him all that Saul had done to him. Then he and Samuel went to Naioth and stayed there. **19**Word came to Saul: "David is in Naioth at Ramah"; **20**so he sent men to capture him. But when they saw a group of prophets[D] prophesying, with Samuel standing there as their leader, the Spirit of God came upon Saul's men and they also prophesied. **21**Saul was told about it, and he sent more men, and they prophesied too. Saul sent men a third time, and they also prophesied. **22**Finally, he himself left for Ramah and went to the great cistern[D] at Secu. And he asked, "Where are Samuel and David?"

"Over in Naioth at Ramah," they said.

23So Saul went to Naioth at Ramah. But the Spirit of God came even upon him, and he walked along prophesying until he came to Naioth. **24**He stripped off his robes and also prophesied in Samuel's presence. He lay that way all that day and night. This is why people say, "Is Saul also among the prophets?"

David and Jonathan

20 Then David fled from Naioth at Ramah and went to Jonathan and asked, "What have I done? What is my crime? How have I wronged your father, that he is trying to take my life?"

2"Never!" Jonathan replied. "You are not going to die! Look, my father doesn't do anything, great or small, without confiding in me. Why would he hide this from me? It's not so!"

3But David took an oath and said, "Your father knows very well that I have found favor in your eyes, and he has said to himself, 'Jonathan must not know this or he will be grieved.' Yet as surely as the LORD lives and as you live, there is only a step between me and death[D]."

4Jonathan said to David, "Whatever you want me to do, I'll do for you."

5So David said, "Look, tomorrow is the New Moon festival[D], and I am supposed to dine with the king; but let me go and hide in the field until the evening of the day after tomorrow. **6**If your father misses me at all, tell him, 'David earnestly asked my permission to hurry to Bethlehem, his hometown, because an annual sacrifice[D] is being made there for his whole clan.' **7**If he says, 'Very well,' then your servant is safe. But if he loses his temper, you can be sure that he is determined to harm me. **8**As for you, show kindness to your servant, for you have brought him into a covenant[D] with you before the LORD. If I am guilty, then kill me yourself! Why hand me over to your father?"

9"Never!" Jonathan said. "If I had the least inkling that my father was determined to harm you, wouldn't I tell you?"

10David asked, "Who will tell me if your father answers you harshly?"

11"Come," Jonathan said, "let's go out into the field." So they went there together.

12Then Jonathan said to David: "By the LORD, the God of Israel, I will surely sound out my father by this time the day after tomorrow! If he is favorably disposed toward you, will I not send you word and let you know? **13**But if my father is inclined to harm you, may the LORD deal with me, be it ever so severely, if I do not let you know and

What sort of prophesying did Saul's men do when the Spirit of God came upon them? (19:20)

While we are not told what they said, it seems possible they spoke of David's legitimate claim to the throne and/or the evil of Saul's murderous intent. Not only did God thwart the evil purposes of the king and his messengers, but he had them join the company of the prophets whose leader (Samuel) had anointed David as Saul's replacement.

Why would the Spirit of God return to Saul once he had departed? (19:23)

The Holy Spirit originally came on Saul to reveal in him the presence and the power of God (10:10). Later, the Spirit came upon him again, possibly to testify about David's role as God's chosen king. God showed Saul how futile it was to attempt to thwart the Lord's will. No human resistance, not even by the king himself, could withstand the movement of God's hand.

What kind of oath did David make? (20:3)

Jonathan, exhibiting the natural affection of a son for his father, protested that David's accusations must not be true (v. 2). David assured him with an oath, a solemn vow, saying in effect, "I swear, this is true!"

New Moon festival (20:5)

The New Moon was both a religious and a civil festival. It was celebrated at the beginning of each month and is often mentioned in the Old Testament along with the Sabbath (for example, Isaiah 1:13). It was a day of celebration (Hosea 2:11), of rest (Amos 8:5), of increased offerings (Num. 28:11–15; Ezek. 45:17) and of worship (Isaiah 66:23; Ezek. 46:1–7).

send you away safely. May the LORD be with you as he has been with my father. **14**But show me unfailing kindness like that of the LORD as long as I live, so that I may not be killed, **15**and do not ever cut off your kindness from my family—not even when the LORD has cut off every one of David's enemies from the face of the earth."

16So Jonathan made a covenant[D] with the house of David, saying, "May the LORD call David's enemies to account." **17**And Jonathan had David reaffirm his oath out of love for him, because he loved him as he loved himself.

18Then Jonathan said to David: "Tomorrow is the New Moon festival[D]. You will be missed, because your seat will be empty. **19**The day after tomorrow, toward evening, go to the place where you hid when this trouble began, and wait by the stone Ezel. **20**I will shoot three arrows to the side of it, as though I were shooting at a target. **21**Then I will send a boy and say, 'Go, find the arrows.' If I say to him, 'Look, the arrows are on this side of you; bring them here,' then come, because, as surely as the LORD lives, you are safe; there is no danger. **22**But if I say to the boy, 'Look, the arrows are beyond you,' then you must go, because the LORD has sent you away. **23**And about the matter you and I discussed—remember, the LORD is witness between you and me forever."

24So David hid in the field, and when the New Moon festival came, the king sat down to eat. **25**He sat in his customary place by the wall, opposite Jonathan,[a] and Abner sat next to Saul, but David's place was empty. **26**Saul said nothing that day, for he thought, "Something must have happened to David to make him ceremonially unclean[D]—surely he is unclean." **27**But the next day, the second day of the month, David's place was empty again. Then Saul said to his son Jonathan, "Why hasn't the son of Jesse come to the meal, either yesterday or today?"

28Jonathan answered, "David earnestly asked me for permission to go to Bethlehem. **29**He said, 'Let me go, because our family is observing a sacrifice[D] in the town and my brother has ordered me to be there. If I have found favor in your eyes, let me get away to see my brothers.' That is why he has not come to the king's table."

30Saul's anger flared up at Jonathan and he said to him, "You son of a perverse and rebellious woman! Don't I know that you have sided with the son of Jesse to your own shame and to the shame of the mother who bore you? **31**As long as the son of Jesse lives on this earth, neither you nor your kingdom will be established. Now send and bring him to me, for he must die!"

32"Why should he be put to death[D]? What has he done?" Jonathan asked his father. **33**But Saul hurled his spear at him to kill him. Then Jonathan knew that his father intended to kill David.

34Jonathan got up from the table in fierce anger; on that second day of the month he did not eat, because he was grieved at his father's shameful treatment of David.

35In the morning Jonathan went out to the field for his meeting with David. He had a small boy with him, **36**and he said to the boy, "Run and find the arrows I shoot." As the boy ran, he shot an arrow beyond him. **37**When the boy came to the place where Jonathan's arrow had fallen, Jonathan called out after him, "Isn't the arrow beyond you?" **38**Then he shouted, "Hurry! Go quickly! Don't stop!" The boy picked up the arrow and returned to his master.

Was Saul using profanity? (20:30)

We would at least call it coarse language today. What he said was a derogatory term aimed at Jonathan, not at Jonathan's mother.

Why did Jonathan use secret signals? (20:35–40)

Jonathan apparently did not want to take the risk that anyone might see David. Shooting the arrows provided Jonathan with an excuse for being out in the field should anyone have asked about what he was doing. Once the boy returned to the city and it was clear that no one else was around, it was safe for David to briefly come out of hiding.

---

*a*25 Septuagint; Hebrew *wall. Jonathan arose*

39(The boy knew nothing of all this; only Jonathan and David knew.) **40**Then Jonathan gave his weapons to the boy and said, "Go, carry them back to town."

41After the boy had gone, David got up from the south side ⌊of the stone⌋ and bowed down before Jonathan three times, with his face to the ground. Then they kissed each other and wept together—but David wept the most.

42Jonathan said to David, "Go in peace[D], for we have sworn friendship with each other in the name of the LORD, saying, 'The LORD is witness between you and me, and between your descendants and my descendants forever.' " Then David left, and Jonathan went back to the town.

Why did David bow before Jonathan? (20:41)

David approached Jonathan from his hiding place with the attitude of a servant rather than a king. He bowed three times before Jonathan, humbly acknowledging his debt to his friend who had risked so much to warn him of impending danger.

David at Nob

21 David went to Nob, to Ahimelech the priest[D]. Ahimelech trembled when he met him, and asked, "Why are you alone? Why is no one with you?"

2David answered Ahimelech the priest, "The king charged me with a certain matter and said to me, 'No one is to know anything about your mission and your instructions.' As for my men, I have told them to meet me at a certain place. **3**Now then, what do you have on hand? Give me five loaves of bread, or whatever you can find."

4But the priest answered David, "I don't have any ordinary bread on hand; however, there is some consecrated[D] bread here—provided the men have kept themselves from women."

5David replied, "Indeed women have been kept from us, as usual whenever[a] I set out. The men's things[b] are holy even on missions that are not holy. How much more so today!" **6**So the priest gave him the consecrated bread, since there was no bread there except the bread of the Presence that had been removed from before the LORD and replaced by hot bread on the day it was taken away.

7Now one of Saul's servants was there that day, detained before the LORD; he was Doeg the Edomite, Saul's head shepherd.

8David asked Ahimelech, "Don't you have a spear or a sword here? I haven't brought my sword or any other weapon, because the king's business was urgent."

9The priest replied, "The sword of Goliath the Philistine, whom you killed in the Valley of Elah, is here; it is

[a]5 Or *from us in the past few days since*   [b]5 Or *bodies*

Consecrated bread (21:4)

Twelve loaves (representing the twelve tribes of Israel) made of pure wheat flour, this bread of the Presence was placed on a table in the Holy Place of the tabernacle (and later in the temple) each Sabbath. It was a thank offering for the Lord's daily provision. When removed from the Holy Place, the bread could be eaten, but only by the priests (see Exodus 25:30; Lev. 24:5–9).

How could abstaining from women make anyone holy? (21:5)

A man who had sexual contact with a woman was to bathe with water and be considered unclean until evening (Lev. 15:18). The uncleanness relates specifically to ritual purity as defined in the holiness code of Leviticus. It should not be equated with ethical purity, as the term *holy* has come to imply. Military expeditions were considered holy, and they were regularly begun with sacrifices. As such, they required appropriate spiritual preparations.

In what way was Doeg the Edomite detained before the LORD? (21:7)

Doeg's detention at this holy site in Nob must have been for religious reasons. He was likely confined until his period of purification, discipline or the fulfillment of a vow was completed. He would have been disqualified from service until his period of withdrawal from daily activities was completed.

Why did David lie to the priest? (21:2)

I t's not immediately clear why David responded to Ahimelech's question by telling a lie. Two factors may have influenced his decision to deceive: (1) David's life was on the line, and he may have felt justified in resorting to deception to get the help he needed. The Old Testament records other instances of deception to save lives (see, for example, Exodus 1:19 and Joshua 2:5); (2) David may have been trying to protect Ahimelech from any accusation of involvement in David's escape from Saul. Here, David's desire to preserve human life (another's, if not his own) took precedence over the commitment to tell the truth. See *Is lying ever okay?* (Exodus 1:19–20).

It is interesting to note that Jesus later cites the incident of David's request for bread (v. 3) to illustrate the principle that human need takes priority over ceremonial law (Luke 6:3–4).

Why did David go to his enemies for safety? (21:10)

Surely, the last place Saul would look for David would be among the Philistines, especially in the hometown of Goliath (17:4)! If David could just slip in unrecognized among King Achish's troops, there could be no better cover for a man fearing for his life. David's bold willingness to risk living among the Philistines underscores how seriously he viewed Saul's pursuit.

David on the Run (21:10)

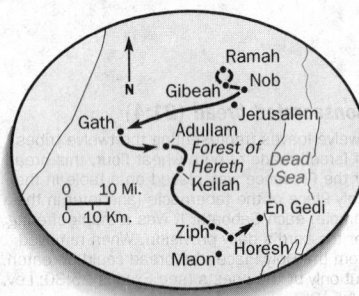

Cave of Adullam (22:1)

The cave was named for the city of Adullam (meaning *retreat, or refuge*), a frontier town between Israel and Philistia, about 12 miles southwest of Bethlehem. The region is one of steep ravines and numerous caves, providing an ideal hiding place combined with exceptional natural defenses. Most likely, one cave served as David's headquarters, but the surrounding area provided abundant shelter for hundreds of men.

What kind of a group was this—men in distress, in debt or discontented? (22:2)

In flight from King Saul, David was officially an outlaw. Others in similar straits were naturally attracted to him. He and his cause became a rallying point for others who felt oppressed. Most were probably men embittered against the system and opposed to the current leadership.

Were David's parents in danger? (22:3)

Possibly. Anyone associated with David would be a natural target, and Bethlehem was much too close to Saul's headquarters in Gibeah. While David's aging parents could find refuge at Adullam for a while, they could never keep pace with the lifestyle of an outlaw. David's Moabite ancestry (Ruth 4:13,22), combined with the Moabite king's animosity toward Saul, made the request for asylum acceptable to Moab.

What kind of stronghold was this? (22:4)

The stronghold probably consisted of a well fortified hilltop, perhaps incorporating one or more of the caves in the region around Adullam. Though Adullam was technically in the territory of Judah, it lay on the very fringe. The *cave of Adullam* and *stronghold* seem to be synonymous (2 Samuel 23:13-14).

wrapped in a cloth behind the ephod[D]. If you want it, take it; there is no sword here but that one."

David said, "There is none like it; give it to me."

David at Gath

[10]That day David fled from Saul and went to Achish king of Gath. [11]But the servants of Achish said to him, "Isn't this David, the king of the land? Isn't he the one they sing about in their dances:

" 'Saul has slain his thousands,
    and David his tens of thousands'?"

[12]David took these words to heart and was very much afraid of Achish king of Gath. [13]So he pretended to be insane in their presence; and while he was in their hands he acted like a madman, making marks on the doors of the gate and letting saliva run down his beard.

[14]Achish said to his servants, "Look at the man! He is insane! Why bring him to me? [15]Am I so short of madmen that you have to bring this fellow here to carry on like this in front of me? Must this man come into my house?"

David at Adullam and Mizpah

22 David left Gath and escaped to the cave of Adullam. When his brothers and his father's household heard about it, they went down to him there. [2]All those who were in distress or in debt or discontented gathered around him, and he became their leader. About four hundred men were with him.

[3]From there David went to Mizpah in Moab and said to the king of Moab, "Would you let my father and mother come and stay with you until I learn what God will do for me?" [4]So he left them with the king of Moab, and they stayed with him as long as David was in the stronghold[D].

[5]But the prophet[D] Gad said to David, "Do not stay in the stronghold. Go into the land of Judah." So David left and went to the forest of Hereth.

Saul Kills the Priests of Nob

[6]Now Saul heard that David and his men had been discovered. And Saul, spear in hand, was seated under the tamarisk tree on the hill at Gibeah, with all his officials standing around him. [7]Saul said to them, "Listen, men of Benjamin! Will the son of Jesse give all of you fields and vineyards? Will he make all of you commanders of thousands and commanders of hundreds? [8]Is that why you have all conspired against me? No one tells me when my son makes a covenant[D] with the son of Jesse. None of you is concerned about me or tells me that my son has incited my servant to lie in wait for me, as he does today."

[9]But Doeg the Edomite, who was standing with Saul's officials, said, "I saw the son of Jesse come to Ahimelech son of Ahitub at Nob. [10]Ahimelech inquired of the LORD for him; he also gave him provisions and the sword of Goliath the Philistine."

[11]Then the king sent for the priest[D] Ahimelech son of Ahitub and his father's whole family, who were the priests at Nob, and they all came to the king. [12]Saul said, "Listen now, son of Ahitub."

"Yes, my lord," he answered.

[13]Saul said to him, "Why have you conspired against me, you and the son of Jesse, giving him bread and a sword and inquiring of God for him, so that he has re-

belled against me and lies in wait for me, as he does today?"

¹⁴Ahimelech answered the king, "Who of all your servants is as loyal as David, the king's son-in-law, captain of
your bodyguard and highly respected in your household?
¹⁵Was that day the first time I inquired of God for him? Of
course not! Let not the king accuse your servant or any of
his father's family, for your servant knows nothing at all
about this whole affair."

¹⁶But the king said, "You will surely die, Ahimelech,
you and your father's whole family."

¹⁷Then the king ordered the guards at his side: "Turn
and kill the priestsᴰ of the LORD, because they too have
sided with David. They knew he was fleeing, yet they did
not tell me."

But the king's officials were not willing to raise a hand
to strike the priests of the LORD.

¹⁸The king then ordered Doeg, "You turn and strike
down the priests." So Doeg the Edomite turned and
struck them down. That day he killed eighty-five men
who wore the linen ephodᴰ. ¹⁹He also put to the sword
Nob, the town of the priests, with its men and women,
its children and infants, and its cattle, donkeys and sheep.

²⁰But Abiathar, a son of Ahimelech son of Ahitub, escaped and fled to join David. ²¹He told David that Saul had
killed the priests of the LORD. ²²Then David said to Abiathar: "That day, when Doeg the Edomite was there, I knew
he would be sure to tell Saul. I am responsible for the
deathᴰ of your father's whole family. ²³Stay with me;
don't be afraid; the man who is seeking your life is seeking mine also. You will be safe with me."

David Saves Keilah

23 When David was told, "Look, the Philistines are
fighting against Keilah and are looting the threshing floors," ²he inquired of the LORD, saying, "Shall I go
and attack these Philistines?"

The LORD answered him, "Go, attack the Philistines and
save Keilah."

³But David's men said to him, "Here in Judah we are
afraid. How much more, then, if we go to Keilah against
the Philistine forces!"

⁴Once again David inquired of the LORD, and the LORD
answered him, "Go down to Keilah, for I am going to give
the Philistines into your hand." ⁵So David and his men
went to Keilah, fought the Philistines and carried off their
livestock. He inflicted heavy losses on the Philistines and
saved the people of Keilah. ⁶(Now Abiathar son of Ahimelech had brought the ephod down with him when he
fled to David at Keilah.)

Saul Pursues David

⁷Saul was told that David had gone to Keilah, and he
said, "God has handed him over to me, for David has imprisoned himself by entering a town with gates and bars."
⁸And Saul called up all his forces for battle, to go down to
Keilah to besiege David and his men.

⁹When David learned that Saul was plotting against
him, he said to Abiathar the priest, "Bring the ephod."
¹⁰David said, "O LORD, God of Israel, your servant has
heard definitely that Saul plans to come to Keilah and destroy the town on account of me. ¹¹Will the citizens of
Keilah surrender me to him? Will Saul come down, as

What responsibilities did David have as captain of the bodyguard? (22:14)

David bore final responsibility for Saul's well-
being and the coordination of the other members of the group. The term translated *bodyguard* derives from a verb that means *to hear*,
or *obey*. The bodyguard consisted of those who
heard and obeyed the personal orders of the
king. They belonged to his inner circle and
were charged with his personal welfare and
comfort.

Why were the officials afraid to obey the king? (22:17)

To kill the priests of the Lord went beyond dealing with David; it constituted a declaration of
war against God himself. Even Saul's officials
—by no means highly sensitive men—understood the danger and the depravity of such action. In their minds, God's anointed priests
were not to be touched.

Ephod (23:6,9)

The ephod, similar to a vest, was a part of the
priestly apparel (Exodus 28:28–29) and served
as the receptacle for the divine objects that
were cast by lot, called Urim and Thummim.
Carefully phrased questions were posed; the
Lord then controlled the lot to provide yes or
no answers.

your servant has heard? O Lord, God of Israel, tell your servant."

And the Lord said, "He will."

12Again David asked, "Will the citizens of Keilah surrender me and my men to Saul?"

And the Lord said, "They will."

13So David and his men, about six hundred in number, left Keilah and kept moving from place to place. When Saul was told that David had escaped from Keilah, he did not go there.

14David stayed in the desert strongholds^D and in the hills of the Desert of Ziph. Day after day Saul searched for him, but God did not give David into his hands.

15While David was at Horesh in the Desert of Ziph, he learned that Saul had come out to take his life. **16**And Saul's son Jonathan went to David at Horesh and helped him find strength in God. **17**"Don't be afraid," he said. "My father Saul will not lay a hand on you. You will be king over Israel, and I will be second to you. Even my father Saul knows this." **18**The two of them made a covenant^D before the Lord. Then Jonathan went home, but David remained at Horesh.

19The Ziphites went up to Saul at Gibeah and said, "Is not David hiding among us in the strongholds at Horesh, on the hill of Hakilah, south of Jeshimon? **20**Now, O king, come down whenever it pleases you to do so, and we will be responsible for handing him over to the king."

21Saul replied, "The Lord bless you for your concern for me. **22**Go and make further preparation. Find out where David usually goes and who has seen him there. They tell me he is very crafty. **23**Find out about all the hiding places he uses and come back to me with definite information.^a Then I will go with you; if he is in the area, I will track him down among all the clans of Judah."

24So they set out and went to Ziph ahead of Saul. Now David and his men were in the Desert of Maon, in the Arabah south of Jeshimon. **25**Saul and his men began the search, and when David was told about it, he went down to the rock and stayed in the Desert of Maon. When Saul heard this, he went into the Desert of Maon in pursuit of David.

26Saul was going along one side of the mountain, and David and his men were on the other side, hurrying to get away from Saul. As Saul and his forces were closing in on David and his men to capture them, **27**a messenger came to Saul, saying, "Come quickly! The Philistines are raiding the land." **28**Then Saul broke off his pursuit of David and went to meet the Philistines. That is why they call this place Sela Hammahlekoth.^b **29**And David went up from there and lived in the strongholds of En Gedi.

David Spares Saul's Life

24 After Saul returned from pursuing the Philistines, he was told, "David is in the Desert of En Gedi." **2**So Saul took three thousand chosen men from all Israel and set out to look for David and his men near the Crags of the Wild Goats.

3He came to the sheep pens along the way; a cave was there, and Saul went in to relieve himself. David and his men were far back in the cave. **4**The men said, "This is the day the Lord spoke of when he said^c to you, 'I will give

---

How did Jonathan help David *find strength in God*? (23:16)

The terminology used here depicts Jonathan as a minister of encouragement to his fearful friend David—one who offers support in the face of a special undertaking. Jonathan's very presence must have lifted David's spirit. Beyond that, there was Jonathan's certainty about God's will for the future; his own resolve to defer to David, and his admission that even Saul, despite his stubborn resistance, knew what God had planned.

Why did they make yet another *covenant before the Lord*? (23:18)

The covenant made here by David and Jonathan goes beyond anything they had yet affirmed (see 18:3; 20:8,14–17). Once Saul was removed from the scene, David as king and Jonathan as second-in-command could rally interest groups from both sides, overcome the deep cleavage developing in the nation and re-unite the people of Israel. Jonathan officially and formally conceded the kingship to David, in a move that hinted at a possible coalition government.

Sheep pens (24:3)

Enclosed with stone walls, permanent sheep pens were shelters for protecting flocks. It is no coincidence that the sheep pens mentioned here were in the same area as a cave. Rough rock walls likely protruded from the mouth of the cave to provide an area for the flock to move about, to prevent escape and to provide protection from predators and inclement weather.

---

^a23 Or *me at Nacon*   ^b28 *Sela Hammahlekoth* means *rock of parting.*   ^c4 Or *"Today the Lord is saying*

your enemy into your hands for you to deal with as you wish.' " Then David crept up unnoticed and cut off a corner of Saul's robe.

⁵Afterward, David was conscience-stricken for having cut off a corner of his robe. ⁶He said to his men, "The LORD forbid that I should do such a thing to my master, the LORD's anointedᴰ, or lift my hand against him; for he is the anointed of the LORD." ⁷With these words David rebuked his men and did not allow them to attack Saul. And Saul left the cave and went his way.

⁸Then David went out of the cave and called out to Saul, "My lord the king!" When Saul looked behind him, David bowed down and prostrated himself with his face to the ground. ⁹He said to Saul, "Why do you listen when men say, 'David is bent on harming you'? ¹⁰This day you have seen with your own eyes how the LORD delivered you into my hands in the cave. Some urged me to kill you, but I spared you; I said, 'I will not lift my hand against my master, because he is the LORD's anointed.' ¹¹See, my father, look at this piece of your robe in my hand! I cut off the corner of your robe but did not kill you. Now understand and recognize that I am not guilty of wrongdoing or rebellion. I have not wronged you, but you are hunting me down to take my life. ¹²May the LORD judge between you and me. And may the LORD avengeᴰ the wrongs you have done to me, but my hand will not touch you. ¹³As the old saying goes, 'From evildoers come evil deeds,' so my hand will not touch you.

¹⁴"Against whom has the king of Israel come out? Whom are you pursuing? A dead dog? A flea? ¹⁵May the LORD be our judge and decide between us. May he consider my cause and uphold it; may he vindicate me by delivering me from your hand."

¹⁶When David finished saying this, Saul asked, "Is that your voice, David my son?" And he wept aloud. ¹⁷"You are more righteousᴰ than I," he said. "You have treated me well, but I have treated you badly. ¹⁸You have just now told me of the good you did to me; the LORD delivered me into your hands, but you did not kill me. ¹⁹When a man finds his enemy, does he let him get away unharmed? May the LORD reward you well for the way you treated me today. ²⁰I know that you will surely be king and that the kingdom of Israel will be established in your hands. ²¹Now swear to me by the LORD that you will not cut off my descendants or wipe out my name from my father's family."

²²So David gave his oath to Saul. Then Saul returned home, but David and his men went up to the strongholdᴰ.

David, Nabal and Abigail

25 Now Samuel died, and all Israel assembled and mourned for him; and they buried him at his home in Ramah.

Then David moved down into the Desert of Maon.ᵃ ²A certain man in Maon, who had property there at Carmel, was very wealthy. He had a thousand goats and three thousand sheep, which he was shearing in Carmel. ³His name was Nabal and his wife's name was Abigail. She was an intelligent and beautiful woman, but her husband, a Calebite, was surly and mean in his dealings.

⁴While David was in the desert, he heard that Nabal was

Why did David feel so guilty about merely cutting off a corner of Saul's robe? (24:5)

In the days of Saul and David, to seize the hem of a garment (Matt. 9:20–21) symbolized loyalty, faith and covenant-making. Cutting off the corner of someone's robe was a symbol of disloyalty and rebellion. David's act was a display of disloyalty toward Saul, something he had continually and carefully guarded against.

What made Saul realize David would become king? (24:20)

David had proved himself the better man, maintaining his composure under provocation and demanding integrity even under pressure. Saul was a beaten warrior who wanted out of the struggle. And he knew that God had chosen David to replace him. See *How did Saul know the Lord had left him and was with David instead?* (18:12).

ᵃ1 Some Septuagint manuscripts; Hebrew *Paran*

Was David's request a form of extortion? (25:7–8)

In a modern society, David's means of supporting his men might be considered "protection money," a form of illegal extortion. But such practices were not uncommon in ancient times, when standing armies and police forces were not available. Wandering bands of marauders—to say nothing of natural predators—posed a tremendous threat to flocks, herds and people. For restraining his own motley band, for warding off Bedouin raids and natural predators, David requested compensation from Nabal. Also see *How frequently were people endangered by bands of raiders?* (27:10).

What hospitality was customary at festive times? (25:8)

Nabal was celebrating the sheep-shearing, the harvest festival of the flock owner. At such festive times, it was the custom to invite and entertain neighbors and friends. A great feast was prepared, and the property owner shared his bounty with all who attended. The poor, the outcast and the needy—in keeping with Israelite tradition—were regularly among those who were helped.

How risky was it for Abigail to make this decision without Nabal's knowledge? (25:19)

There was some risk that she would provoke her husband's anger by defying his decision. But Abigail probably realized it would be a greater risk to do nothing about the potential slaughter of her people. She knew it would do no good to take it to Nabal while he was eating and drinking, celebrating sheep-sheering time (v. 7). Still, after he sobered up, she hid nothing from him and told him what she had done (v. 37). Abigail did the responsible thing in an emergency situation—in spite of her own personal risk.

Why did Abigail say her husband's name was *Fool*? (25:25)

The Hebrew term *nabal* literally means *fool*. Most likely, this was a nickname the man had picked up somewhere—and for good reason! He was the epitome of how an Israelite would define a fool: harsh, ill-mannered, enamored of his possessions, insensitive to his neighbors' needs, disrespectful of others and irreverent toward God. His folly was magnified in his failure to acknowledge David as the prince of Israel.

shearing sheep. **5**So he sent ten young men and said to them, "Go up to Nabal at Carmel and greet him in my name. **6**Say to him: 'Long life to you! Good health to you and your household! And good health to all that is yours!

7 'Now I hear that it is sheep-shearing time. When your shepherds were with us, we did not mistreat them, and the whole time they were at Carmel nothing of theirs was missing. **8**Ask your own servants and they will tell you. Therefore be favorable toward my young men, since we come at a festive time. Please give your servants and your son David whatever you can find for them.' "

9When David's men arrived, they gave Nabal this message in David's name. Then they waited.

10Nabal answered David's servants, "Who is this David? Who is this son of Jesse? Many servants are breaking away from their masters these days. **11**Why should I take my bread and water, and the meat I have slaughtered for my shearers, and give it to men coming from who knows where?"

12David's men turned around and went back. When they arrived, they reported every word. **13**David said to his men, "Put on your swords!" So they put on their swords, and David put on his. About four hundred men went up with David, while two hundred stayed with the supplies.

14One of the servants told Nabal's wife Abigail: "David sent messengers from the desert to give our master his greetings, but he hurled insults at them. **15**Yet these men were very good to us. They did not mistreat us, and the whole time we were out in the fields near them nothing was missing. **16**Night and day they were a wall around us all the time we were herding our sheep near them. **17**Now think it over and see what you can do, because disaster is hanging over our master and his whole household. He is such a wicked man that no one can talk to him."

18Abigail lost no time. She took two hundred loaves of bread, two skins of wine, five dressed sheep, five seahs*a* of roasted grain, a hundred cakes of raisins and two hundred cakes of pressed figs, and loaded them on donkeys. **19**Then she told her servants, "Go on ahead; I'll follow you." But she did not tell her husband Nabal.

20As she came riding her donkey into a mountain ravine, there were David and his men descending toward her, and she met them. **21**David had just said, "It's been useless—all my watching over this fellow's property in the desert so that nothing of his was missing. He has paid me back evil for good. **22**May God deal with David,*b* be it ever so severely, if by morning I leave alive one male of all who belong to him!"

23When Abigail saw David, she quickly got off her donkey and bowed down before David with her face to the ground. **24**She fell at his feet and said: "My lord, let the blame be on me alone. Please let your servant speak to you; hear what your servant has to say. **25**May my lord pay no attention to that wicked man Nabal. He is just like his name—his name is Fool, and folly goes with him. But as for me, your servant, I did not see the men my master sent.

26"Now since the LORD has kept you, my master, from bloodshed and from avenging*D* yourself with your own hands, as surely as the LORD lives and as you live, may your enemies and all who intend to harm my master be

---

a18 That is, probably about a bushel (about 37 liters)   *b22* Some Septuagint manuscripts; Hebrew *with David's enemies*

like Nabal. **27**And let this gift, which your servant has brought to my master, be given to the men who follow you. **28**Please forgive your servant's offense, for the LORD will certainly make a lasting dynasty for my master, because he fights the LORD's battles. Let no wrongdoing be found in you as long as you live. **29**Even though someone is pursuing you to take your life, the life of my master will be bound securely in the bundle of the living by the LORD your God. But the lives of your enemies he will hurl away as from the pocket of a sling. **30**When the LORD has done for my master every good thing he promised concerning him and has appointed him leader over Israel, **31**my master will not have on his conscience the staggering burden of needless bloodshed or of having avenged^D himself. And when the LORD has brought my master success, remember your servant."

32David said to Abigail, "Praise be to the LORD, the God of Israel, who has sent you today to meet me. **33**May you be blessed for your good judgment and for keeping me from bloodshed this day and from avenging myself with my own hands. **34**Otherwise, as surely as the LORD, the God of Israel, lives, who has kept me from harming you, if you had not come quickly to meet me, not one male belonging to Nabal would have been left alive by daybreak."

35Then David accepted from her hand what she had brought him and said, "Go home in peace.^D I have heard your words and granted your request."

36When Abigail went to Nabal, he was in the house holding a banquet like that of a king. He was in high spirits and very drunk. So she told him nothing until daybreak. **37**Then in the morning, when Nabal was sober, his wife told him all these things, and his heart failed him and he became like a stone. **38**About ten days later, the LORD struck Nabal and he died.

39When David heard that Nabal was dead, he said, "Praise be to the LORD, who has upheld my cause against Nabal for treating me with contempt. He has kept his servant from doing wrong and has brought Nabal's wrongdoing down on his own head."

Then David sent word to Abigail, asking her to become his wife. **40**His servants went to Carmel and said to Abigail, "David has sent us to you to take you to become his wife."

41She bowed down with her face to the ground and said, "Here is your maidservant, ready to serve you and wash the feet of my master's servants." **42**Abigail quickly got on a donkey and, attended by her five maids, went with David's messengers and became his wife. **43**David had also married Ahinoam of Jezreel, and they both were his wives. **44**But Saul had given his daughter Michal, David's wife, to Paltiel^a son of Laish, who was from Gallim.

David Again Spares Saul's Life

26 The Ziphites went to Saul at Gibeah and said, "Is not David hiding on the hill of Hakilah, which faces Jeshimon?"

2So Saul went down to the Desert of Ziph, with his three thousand chosen men of Israel, to search there for David. **3**Saul made his camp beside the road on the hill of Hakilah facing Jeshimon, but David stayed in the desert. When he saw that Saul had followed him there, **4**he sent out scouts and learned that Saul had definitely arrived.^b

What does it mean that Nabal *became like a stone*? (25:37)
Nabal apparently suffered a heart attack or a stroke, fell into a coma, lingered for ten days, and then died. How ironic that he who was so morally and socially insensitive became as senseless as a stone.

Both were his wives (25:43)
See article: *Why did David have so many wives and concubines?* (2 Samuel 5:13).

a44 Hebrew Palti, a variant of Paltiel   b4 Or had come to Nacon

Why did David still call Saul *the Lord's anointed*? (26:9)

Saul's royal office carried with it divine sanction by virtue of his anointing. The designation *the Lord's anointed* is used interchangeably in the books of Samuel for *the king* (see 2:10). David, no doubt, used *the Lord's anointed* in this fashion, maintaining his high regard for the office, in spite of the man who held it.

Why did David say the Lord may have incited Saul to kill him? (26:19)

David deals with all the possible causes of Saul's enmity toward him. Could it be David's own fault? *What have I done?* he asks. *And what wrong am I guilty of* (v. 18)? Could other people be the instigators? If so, *may they be cursed before the Lord* (v. 19). Could it somehow be God's doing? If so, then let it be settled with sacrifice (v. 19). The one option he does not identify proves to be the real cause: Saul's sin (v. 21).

Who told David to serve other gods? (26:19)

In David's hypothetical scenario, those responsible for pressuring him to *serve other gods* are the same people who have incited Saul against him. The truth is, however, that no one has incited Saul; Saul himself is to blame. By pursuing David so relentlessly, Saul is pushing him off Israelite soil, away from the sacred worship sites of Almighty God and onto the turf of pagan deities.

⁵Then David set out and went to the place where Saul had camped. He saw where Saul and Abner son of Ner, the commander of the army, had lain down. Saul was lying inside the camp, with the army encamped around him.

⁶David then asked Ahimelech the Hittite and Abishai son of Zeruiah, Joab's brother, "Who will go down into the camp with me to Saul?"

"I'll go with you," said Abishai.

⁷So David and Abishai went to the army by night, and there was Saul, lying asleep inside the camp with his spear stuck in the ground near his head. Abner and the soldiers were lying around him.

⁸Abishai said to David, "Today God has delivered your enemy into your hands. Now let me pin him to the ground with one thrust of my spear; I won't strike him twice."

⁹But David said to Abishai, "Don't destroy him! Who can lay a hand on the Lord's anointed[D] and be guiltless? ¹⁰As surely as the Lord lives," he said, "the Lord himself will strike him; either his time will come and he will die, or he will go into battle and perish. ¹¹But the Lord forbid that I should lay a hand on the Lord's anointed. Now get the spear and water jug that are near his head, and let's go."

¹²So David took the spear and water jug near Saul's head, and they left. No one saw or knew about it, nor did anyone wake up. They were all sleeping, because the Lord had put them into a deep sleep.

¹³Then David crossed over to the other side and stood on top of the hill some distance away; there was a wide space between them. ¹⁴He called out to the army and to Abner son of Ner, "Aren't you going to answer me, Abner?"

Abner replied, "Who are you who calls to the king?"

¹⁵David said, "You're a man, aren't you? And who is like you in Israel? Why didn't you guard your lord the king? Someone came to destroy your lord the king. ¹⁶What you have done is not good. As surely as the Lord lives, you and your men deserve to die, because you did not guard your master, the Lord's anointed. Look around you. Where are the king's spear and water jug that were near his head?"

¹⁷Saul recognized David's voice and said, "Is that your voice, David my son?"

David replied, "Yes it is, my lord the king." ¹⁸And he added, "Why is my lord pursuing his servant? What have I done, and what wrong am I guilty of? ¹⁹Now let my lord the king listen to his servant's words. If the Lord has incited you against me, then may he accept an offering. If, however, men have done it, may they be cursed before the Lord! They have now driven me from my share in the Lord's inheritance and have said, 'Go, serve other gods.' ²⁰Now do not let my blood fall to the ground far from the presence of the Lord. The king of Israel has come out to look for a flea—as one hunts a partridge in the mountains."

²¹Then Saul said, "I have sinned. Come back, David my son. Because you considered my life precious today, I will not try to harm you again. Surely I have acted like a fool and have erred greatly."

²²"Here is the king's spear," David answered. "Let one of your young men come over and get it. ²³The Lord rewards every man for his righteousness[D] and faithfulness. The Lord delivered you into my hands today, but I would

not lay a hand on the LORD's anointed[D]. ²⁴As surely as I valued your life today, so may the LORD value my life and deliver me from all trouble."

²⁵Then Saul said to David, "May you be blessed, my son David; you will do great things and surely triumph."

So David went on his way, and Saul returned home.

David Among the Philistines

27 But David thought to himself, "One of these days I will be destroyed by the hand of Saul. The best thing I can do is to escape to the land of the Philistines. Then Saul will give up searching for me anywhere in Israel, and I will slip out of his hand."

²So David and the six hundred men with him left and went over to Achish son of Maoch king of Gath. ³David and his men settled in Gath with Achish. Each man had his family with him, and David had his two wives: Ahinoam of Jezreel and Abigail of Carmel, the widow of Nabal. ⁴When Saul was told that David had fled to Gath, he no longer searched for him.

⁵Then David said to Achish, "If I have found favor in your eyes, let a place be assigned to me in one of the country towns, that I may live there. Why should your servant live in the royal city with you?"

⁶So on that day Achish gave him Ziklag, and it has belonged to the kings of Judah ever since. ⁷David lived in Philistine territory a year and four months.

⁸Now David and his men went up and raided the Geshurites, the Girzites and the Amalekites. (From ancient times these peoples had lived in the land extending to Shur and Egypt.) ⁹Whenever David attacked an area, he did not leave a man or woman alive, but took sheep and cattle, donkeys and camels, and clothes. Then he returned to Achish.

¹⁰When Achish asked, "Where did you go raiding today?" David would say, "Against the Negev[D] of Judah" or "Against the Negev of Jerahmeel" or "Against the Negev of the Kenites." ¹¹He did not leave a man or woman alive to be brought to Gath, for he thought, "They might inform on us and say, 'This is what David did.' " And such was his practice as long as he lived in Philistine territory. ¹²Achish trusted David and said to himself, "He has become so odious to his people, the Israelites, that he will be my servant forever."

Saul and the Witch of Endor

28 In those days the Philistines gathered their forces to fight against Israel. Achish said to David, "You must understand that you and your men will accompany me in the army."

²David said, "Then you will see for yourself what your servant can do."

Achish replied, "Very well, I will make you my bodyguard for life."

³Now Samuel was dead, and all Israel had mourned for him and buried him in his own town of Ramah. Saul had expelled the mediums[D] and spiritists from the land.

⁴The Philistines assembled and came and set up camp at Shunem, while Saul gathered all the Israelites and set up camp at Gilboa. ⁵When Saul saw the Philistine army, he was afraid; terror filled his heart. ⁶He inquired of the LORD, but the LORD did not answer him by dreams or Urim[D] or prophets[D]. ⁷Saul then said to his attendants,

David Among the Philistines (27:2)

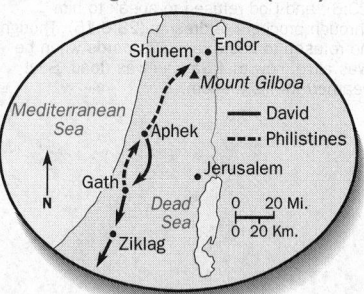

Why did David lie? (27:8–10)

Here David's "lies" were a demonstration of his uncanny ability to outwit the unsuspecting, naïve King Achish. God's hand was surely on this man! While living a protected life in Philistia, he was still able to defeat Israel's enemies (27:8), establish a base for future operations and increase his prosperity. Something important was at stake here—the future of God's people, the survival of the kingdom. Also see article: **Why did David lie to the priest?** (21:2).

How could David follow the Lord and yet be so brutal? (27:9)

David's actions resulted from a combination of theological, cultural and practical concerns. Theologically, the destruction of peoples and cities was considered a religious act, whereby everything was devoted as an offering to God. In this sense, David was continuing the conquest of the land begun under Joshua. Culturally, this was a widely recognized practice, attested to in literature from other ancient societies around Israel. Practically, David was protecting himself against informants who could have passed information to Achish (27:10–11).

How frequently were people endangered by bands of raiders? (27:10)

Marauding bands—such as David's—survived off the plunder accumulated through their raids. New targets were needed regularly. Peoples in and around ancient Israel lived under constant threat of invasion. The construction of walls around cities graphically illustrates how desperately the people sought some form of protection and vigilance. Also see **Was David's request a form of extortion?** (25:7–8).

Why would Achish appoint David to be his bodyguard when he recently thought David was insane? (28:2)

See 21:12–15. In antiquity, insanity was often attributed to spirit possession, which could come and go. People in this condition were usually treated with reverential caution. This, combined with Achish's belief that David had been carrying out successful raids against Philistine enemies, may have contributed to the king's appointment of David to be his bodyguard. Such a position would have put David under constant surveillance.

Why did Saul go to a medium when the Lord would not answer him? (28:6-7)

This was a desperate man's final attempt to coerce contact with God. In keeping with ancient tradition, Saul was seeking divine direction and blessing before engaging his enemies in battle (28:5–6,15). But he no longer had access to the priests and their ephod (22:20; 23:6), and God refused to speak to him through prophets or dreams (28:6,15). Though he refused to heed Samuel's words when he was alive, now that Samuel was dead, Saul yearned for his wisdom.

"Find me a woman who is a medium[D], so I may go and inquire of her."

"There is one in Endor," they said.

8So Saul disguised himself, putting on other clothes, and at night he and two men went to the woman. "Consult a spirit for me," he said, "and bring up for me the one I name."

9But the woman said to him, "Surely you know what Saul has done. He has cut off the mediums and spiritists from the land. Why have you set a trap for my life to bring about my death[D]?"

10Saul swore to her by the LORD, "As surely as the LORD lives, you will not be punished for this."

11Then the woman asked, "Whom shall I bring up for you?"

"Bring up Samuel," he said.

12When the woman saw Samuel, she cried out at the top of her voice and said to Saul, "Why have you deceived me? You are Saul!"

13The king said to her, "Don't be afraid. What do you see?"

The woman said, "I see a spirit[a] coming up out of the ground."

14"What does he look like?" he asked.

"An old man wearing a robe is coming up," she said.

Then Saul knew it was Samuel, and he bowed down and prostrated himself with his face to the ground.

15Samuel said to Saul, "Why have you disturbed me by bringing me up?"

"I am in great distress," Saul said. "The Philistines are fighting against me, and God has turned away from me. He no longer answers me, either by prophets[D] or by dreams. So I have called on you to tell me what to do."

[a]13 Or see spirits; or see gods

Can spirits be called from the dead? (28:12)

Clearly, something supernatural happened in the house of the medium that night. The woman saw a spirit coming up out of the ground. Traditionally a number of perplexing questions have swirled around this passage of Scripture. Was this woman actually able to bring someone up from the dead or was she an expert faker? Did Samuel actually appear or was this old man (v. 14) a demon playing the role of Samuel? Did Samuel appear as a result of the medium's power or did God intervene and raise Samuel himself?

An element of mystery surrounds this story, and it would be presumptuous to claim that we have all the answers. This episode seems to affirm a realm beyond the ordinary physical world—a spiritual realm that can somehow interact with the world in which we live. Though the scientific mind-set of Western culture has numbed our sensitivity to the reality of spiritual forces, the Bible and our experience confirm the reality of the unseen world. In Ephesians 6:10–18, Paul describes the Christian life as a kind of warfare, and he urges his readers to prepare to encounter an opponent not of flesh and blood but of spiritual forces of evil.

We need wisdom to know how to respond to the attacks of the enemy. Occult practices can both intrigue us and frighten us. While acknowledging the reality of the spiritual forces of evil and the deceitful practices of Satan, who masquerades as an angel of light (2 Cor. 11:14), we are urged to resist him and stand firm in the faith (1 Peter 5:9).

¹⁶Samuel said, "Why do you consult me, now that the LORD has turned away from you and become your enemy? ¹⁷The LORD has done what he predicted through me. The LORD has torn the kingdom out of your hands and given it to one of your neighbors—to David. ¹⁸Because you did not obey the LORD or carry out his fierce wrath against the Amalekites, the LORD has done this to you today. ¹⁹The LORD will hand over both Israel and you to the Philistines, and tomorrow you and your sons will be with me. The LORD will also hand over the army of Israel to the Philistines."

²⁰Immediately Saul fell full length on the ground, filled with fear because of Samuel's words. His strength was gone, for he had eaten nothing all that day and night.

²¹When the woman came to Saul and saw that he was greatly shaken, she said, "Look, your maidservant has obeyed you. I took my life in my hands and did what you told me to do. ²²Now please listen to your servant and let me give you some food so you may eat and have the strength to go on your way."

²³He refused and said, "I will not eat."

But his men joined the woman in urging him, and he listened to them. He got up from the ground and sat on the couch.

²⁴The woman had a fattened calf at the house, which she butchered at once. She took some flour, kneaded it and baked bread without yeastᴰ. ²⁵Then she set it before Saul and his men, and they ate. That same night they got up and left.

Achish Sends David Back to Ziklag

29 The Philistines gathered all their forces at Aphek, and Israel camped by the spring in Jezreel. ²As the Philistine rulers marched with their units of hundreds and thousands, David and his men were marching at the rear with Achish. ³The commanders of the Philistines asked, "What about these Hebrews?"

Achish replied, "Is this not David, who was an officer of Saul king of Israel? He has already been with me for over a year, and from the day he left Saul until now, I have found no fault in him."

⁴But the Philistine commanders were angry with him and said, "Send the man back, that he may return to the place you assigned him. He must not go with us into battle, or he will turn against us during the fighting. How better could he regain his master's favor than by taking the heads of our own men? ⁵Isn't this the David they sang about in their dances:

" 'Saul has slain his thousands,
and David his tens of thousands'?"

⁶So Achish called David and said to him, "As surely as the LORD lives, you have been reliable, and I would be pleased to have you serve with me in the army. From the day you came to me until now, I have found no fault in you, but the rulers don't approve of you. ⁷Turn back and go in peaceᴰ; do nothing to displease the Philistine rulers."

⁸"But what have I done?" asked David. "What have you found against your servant from the day I came to you until now? Why can't I go and fight against the enemies of my lord the king?"

⁹Achish answered, "I know that you have been as pleasing in my eyes as an angel of God; nevertheless, the Philis-

Why would evil Saul go to the same place as righteous Samuel when he died? (28:19)

The afterlife was not understood by Old Testament people as a grand and glorious celebration. Rather, it was a shadowy existence in *Sheol*, the subterranean abode of the dead, a place apart from this earth but still accessible to God (Job 26:6; Psalm 139:8; Amos 9:2). The righteous and unrighteous alike were thought to shuffle their way through a dark and gloomy existence (Gen. 37:35; Psalm 9:17; Isaiah 38:10). If this was an evil spirit role-playing as Samuel, we would be less troubled by this conversation. See article: *Can spirits be called from the dead?* (28:12).

Why would a Philistine king swear by Israel's God? (29:6)

By using a familiar oath formula (see 14:39), Achish gave special passion to his appeal to David. But the Philistine king was surely not a believer in Israel's God. His remarks conveyed special praise for David's stellar service and a touch of courtesy, especially since he assumed David was unhappy and upset about not being able to accompany the troops into battle.

What did Achish know about an angel of God? (29:9)

Achish's commendation of David is not an uncommon expression of praise. It need not imply any special insight on Achish's part about angels, or even about God. Achish used this expression to deny any doubt on his part about David's loyalty and to underscore his own desire for David to accompany him into battle.

tine commanders have said, 'He must not go up with us into battle.' [10]Now get up early, along with your master's servants who have come with you, and leave in the morning as soon as it is light."

[11]So David and his men got up early in the morning to go back to the land of the Philistines, and the Philistines went up to Jezreel.

David Destroys the Amalekites

30 David and his men reached Ziklag on the third day. Now the Amalekites had raided the Negev[D] and Ziklag. They had attacked Ziklag and burned it, [2]and had taken captive the women and all who were in it, both young and old. They killed none of them, but carried them off as they went on their way.

[3]When David and his men came to Ziklag, they found it destroyed by fire and their wives and sons and daughters taken captive. [4]So David and his men wept aloud until they had no strength left to weep. [5]David's two wives had been captured—Ahinoam of Jezreel and Abigail, the widow of Nabal of Carmel. [6]David was greatly distressed because the men were talking of stoning him; each one was bitter in spirit because of his sons and daughters. But David found strength in the LORD his God.

[7]Then David said to Abiathar the priest[D], the son of Ahimelech, "Bring me the ephod[D]." Abiathar brought it to him, [8]and David inquired of the LORD, "Shall I pursue this raiding party? Will I overtake them?"

"Pursue them," he answered. "You will certainly overtake them and succeed in the rescue."

[9]David and the six hundred men with him came to the Besor Ravine, where some stayed behind, [10]for two hundred men were too exhausted to cross the ravine. But David and four hundred men continued the pursuit.

[11]They found an Egyptian in a field and brought him to David. They gave him water to drink and food to eat— [12]part of a cake of pressed figs and two cakes of raisins. He ate and was revived, for he had not eaten any food or drunk any water for three days and three nights.

[13]David asked him, "To whom do you belong, and where do you come from?"

He said, "I am an Egyptian, the slave of an Amalekite. My master abandoned me when I became ill three days ago. [14]We raided the Negev of the Kerethites and the territory belonging to Judah and the Negev of Caleb. And we burned Ziklag."

[15]David asked him, "Can you lead me down to this raiding party?"

He answered, "Swear to me before God that you will not kill me or hand me over to my master, and I will take you down to them."

[16]He led David down, and there they were, scattered over the countryside, eating, drinking and reveling because of the great amount of plunder[D] they had taken from the land of the Philistines and from Judah. [17]David fought them from dusk until the evening of the next day, and none of them got away, except four hundred young men who rode off on camels and fled. [18]David recovered everything the Amalekites had taken, including his two wives. [19]Nothing was missing: young or old, boy or girl, plunder or anything else they had taken. David brought everything back. [20]He took all the flocks and herds, and his men drove them ahead of the other livestock, saying, "This is David's plunder."

Why would David's men stone him for something he had no control over? (30:6)

David's men held him ultimately responsible for the tragic raid on Ziklag. His previous assaults on the Amalekites (27:8) must surely have incited their wrath and a desire for vengeance. And to make matters worse, David's decision to take all his troops to Aphek (29:1–2) left his home base at Ziklag unprotected and defenseless against marauding bandits.

How did David find *strength in the LORD*? (30:6)

While his men in bitterness plotted assassination, David in brokenness cried out to the Lord. David's words (Psalm 25:16–17, for example) reflected how he must have felt and how he might have prayed in such a situation. Even in the midst of catastrophe, his communion with God through prayer fortified his faith and stabilized his confidence. See *How did Jonathan help David find strength in God?* (23:16).

How did the Egyptian slave know where to find the Amalekites who had left him behind? (30:15–16)

The trip to Ziklag was surely not the first time this Egyptian slave had accompanied his master on a raid. No doubt he had participated in a number of skirmishes and knew the movements, the campsites and perhaps something of the plans of the Amalekites. Now, left behind to die, he became God's instrument of direction to lead David and his army to the enemy camp (see *David Among the Philistines* on page 395).

How many of David's followers were *evil men and troublemakers*? (30:22)

It's impossible to say, but they may well have been the majority of those returning from battle.

21Then David came to the two hundred men who had been too exhausted to follow him and who were left behind at the Besor Ravine. They came out to meet David and the people with him. As David and his men approached, he greeted them. **22**But all the evil men and troublemakers among David's followers said, "Because they did not go out with us, we will not share with them the plunder[D] we recovered. However, each man may take his wife and children and go."

23David replied, "No, my brothers, you must not do that with what the LORD has given us. He has protected us and handed over to us the forces that came against us. **24**Who will listen to what you say? The share of the man who stayed with the supplies is to be the same as that of him who went down to the battle. All will share alike." **25**David made this a statute and ordinance for Israel from that day to this.

26When David arrived in Ziklag, he sent some of the plunder to the elders of Judah, who were his friends, saying, "Here is a present for you from the plunder of the LORD's enemies."

27He sent it to those who were in Bethel, Ramoth Negev[D] and Jattir; **28**to those in Aroer, Siphmoth, Eshtemoa **29**and Racal; to those in the towns of the Jerahmeelites and the Kenites; **30**to those in Hormah, Bor Ashan, Athach **31**and Hebron; and to those in all the other places where David and his men had roamed.

Saul Takes His Life

31 Now the Philistines fought against Israel; the Israelites fled before them, and many fell slain on Mount Gilboa. **2**The Philistines pressed hard after Saul and his sons, and they killed his sons Jonathan, Abinadab and Malki-Shua. **3**The fighting grew fierce around Saul, and when the archers overtook him, they wounded him critically.

4Saul said to his armor-bearer, "Draw your sword and run me through, or these uncircumcised[D] fellows will come and run me through and abuse me."

But his armor-bearer was terrified and would not do it; so Saul took his own sword and fell on it. **5**When the armor-bearer saw that Saul was dead, he too fell on his sword and died with him. **6**So Saul and his three sons and his armor-bearer and all his men died together that same day.

7When the Israelites along the valley and those across the Jordan saw that the Israelite army had fled and that Saul and his sons had died, they abandoned their towns and fled. And the Philistines came and occupied them.

8The next day, when the Philistines came to strip the dead, they found Saul and his three sons fallen on Mount Gilboa. **9**They cut off his head and stripped off his armor, and they sent messengers throughout the land of the Philistines to proclaim the news in the temple of their idols[D] and among their people. **10**They put his armor in the temple of the Ashtoreths[D] and fastened his body to the wall of Beth Shan.

11When the people of Jabesh Gilead heard of what the Philistines had done to Saul, **12**all their valiant men journeyed through the night to Beth Shan. They took down the bodies of Saul and his sons from the wall of Beth Shan and went to Jabesh, where they burned them. **13**Then they took their bones and buried them under a tamarisk tree at Jabesh, and they fasted seven days.

Why did David share the plunder with the elders of Judah? (30:26)

Probably there were several reasons. (1) His action compensated for losses the elders had suffered at the hands of enemy raiders. (2) It was an expression of gratitude to those who had supported him during his flight from Saul. (3) It was David's alibi against any accusation that he fought with the Philistines against Saul at Gilboa (ch. 31). While that battle raged, David was defeating the Amalekites in the Negev. (4) David was cementing friendly ties with people who would soon crown him king.

What kind of abuse did Saul expect from the Philistines? (31:4)

Various sorts of abuse and torture were not uncommon in the ancient Middle East. Body parts were often cut off or mutilated. Sometimes, captives were skinned alive or had iron hooks, attached to chains, pressed into their flesh so they could be dragged like wild beasts. Such practices were especially reserved for prominent captives (see Judges 16:21–25).

Why did the armor-bearer take his own life? (31:5)

The armor-bearer likely feared a similar fate to Saul's: potential torture and humiliation if captured alive. To retreat—should he actually manage to escape—would have meant shame and reproach from his own people. He had nowhere to turn; his fate seemed sealed. Beyond that, dedication to his king and honor over his death drove him to fall beside Saul and his sons on the field of battle.

Why did the Philistines put Saul's armor in the temple of the Ashtoreths? (31:10)

They placed it there as a kind of sacrifice or offering to their god, in recognition of the help they believed they had received from this deity. Saul's armor—like Goliath's sword in Israel's sanctuary (21:9)—was a trophy celebrating the victory of the god of the Philistines over the Israelites' God.

Why did the men of Jabesh Gilead risk their lives to recover the bodies? (31:12)

These men had never forgotten the great debt they owed Saul and now sought to repay it. Under threat from Nahash the Ammonite, the citizens of Jabesh Gilead had appealed to all Israel for help. The Spirit of God came upon Saul in power, and he rallied hundreds of Israelite warriors, routed the Ammonites, and delivered Jabesh Gilead from a horrible fate (see ch. 11). See *Saul Rescues Jabesh* on page 371.

Why did they burn the bodies before they buried them? (31:12–13)

Several possibilities could account for this. Perhaps they did so to prevent any further decomposition or disfigurement. Or possibly they wanted to ward off any contagion or infection from the rapidly decomposing corpses. But Jews have historically had an aversion to cremation, and when it occurred in the Old Testament, the practice was probably seen as connected to punishment for sin (Lev. 20:14; 21:9). Perhaps the burning affirms the conviction of the men of Jabesh Gilead that Saul and his sons had been rejected by God.

2 SAMUEL

Why read this book?

Sometimes it's hard to look in the mirror. Standing face to face with our own failures, we're shocked to see our flaws and prefer not to look. "After what I've done," some ask, "How could God ever love me?" David, whose story began in 1 Samuel and continues in 2 Samuel, could have asked that question. He knew struggle, sorrow and sin, but he also experienced God's persistent love. David was someone we can all identify with. In this book we see that no matter how great our triumphs, we can't stop at the top; no matter how deep our despair, God's love can always pick us up.

Who wrote this book?

Like 1 Samuel, 2 Samuel was written anonymously. It's possible the author compiled records of Samuel, Nathan and Gad (see 1 Chron. 29:29).

Why was it written?

To trace the history of Israel from the death of Saul to the end of David's reign—approximately 1010 to 970 B.C.

When was it written?

Probably sometime after the death of Solomon and the division of the kingdom—around 930 B.C.

What to look for in 2 Samuel:

Look for God's hand in human events. David rose to power because God selected him. David's heroic exploits were possible because God was with him. And David's disappointments (such as his adultery and the rebellion of his son, Absalom) show God's justice and mercy in response to sin.

When did these things happen?

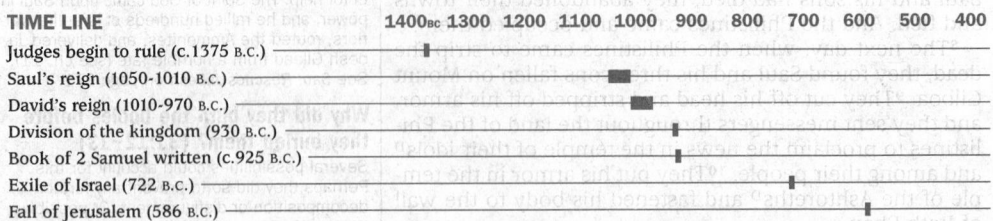

TIME LINE	1400bc	1300	1200	1100	1000	900	800	700	600	500	400
Judges begin to rule (c.1375 B.C.)											
Saul's reign (1050-1010 B.C.)											
David's reign (1010-970 B.C.)											
Division of the kingdom (930 B.C.)											
Book of 2 Samuel written (c.925 B.C.)											
Exile of Israel (722 B.C.)											
Fall of Jerusalem (586 B.C.)											

David Hears of Saul's Death

1 After the death of Saul, David returned from defeating the Amalekites and stayed in Ziklag two days. ²On the third day a man arrived from Saul's camp, with his clothes torn and with dust on his head. When he came to David, he fell to the ground to pay him honor.

³"Where have you come from?" David asked him.

He answered, "I have escaped from the Israelite camp."

⁴"What happened?" David asked. "Tell me."

He said, "The men fled from the battle. Many of them fell and died. And Saul and his son Jonathan are dead."

⁵Then David said to the young man who brought him the report, "How do you know that Saul and his son Jonathan are dead?"

⁶"I happened to be on Mount Gilboa," the young man said, "and there was Saul, leaning on his spear, with the chariots and riders almost upon him. ⁷When he turned around and saw me, he called out to me, and I said, 'What can I do?'

⁸"He asked me, 'Who are you?'

" 'An Amalekite,' I answered.

⁹"Then he said to me, 'Stand over me and kill me! I am in the throes of death, but I'm still alive.'

¹⁰"So I stood over him and killed him, because I knew that after he had fallen he could not survive. And I took the crown that was on his head and the band on his arm and have brought them here to my lord."

¹¹Then David and all the men with him took hold of their clothes and tore them. ¹²They mourned and wept and fasted till evening for Saul and his son Jonathan, and for the army of the LORD and the house of Israel, because they had fallen by the sword.

¹³David said to the young man who brought him the report, "Where are you from?"

"I am the son of an alienᴰ, an Amalekite," he answered.

¹⁴David asked him, "Why were you not afraid to lift your hand to destroy the LORD's anointedᴰ?"

¹⁵Then David called one of his men and said, "Go, strike him down!" So he struck him down, and he died. ¹⁶For David had said to him, "Your blood be on your own head. Your own mouth testified against you when you said, 'I killed the LORD's anointed.' "

David's Lament for Saul and Jonathan

¹⁷David took up this lamentᴰ concerning Saul and his son Jonathan, ¹⁸and ordered that the men of Judah be taught this lament of the bow (it is written in the Book of Jashar):

¹⁹"Your gloryᴰ, O Israel, lies slain on your
    heights.
    How the mighty have fallen!

²⁰"Tell it not in Gath,
    proclaim it not in the streets of Ashkelon,
lest the daughters of the Philistines be glad,
    lest the daughters of the uncircumcisedᴰ
        rejoice.

²¹"O mountains of Gilboa,
    may you have neither dew nor rain,
    nor fields that yield offerings ⌊of grain⌋.
For there the shield of the mighty was defiled,

SCRIPTURE LINK (1:4–12)

See 1 Samuel 31:13; 1 Chron. 10:1–12.

SCRIPTURE LINK (1:10) *So I stood over him and killed him*

The Amalekite was apparently lying. 1 Samuel 31:4 says Saul killed himself. So why did the Amalekite lie? He probably hoped for a reward, thinking David would be glad to hear news of Saul's death.

Why did David execute the Amalekite for doing what Saul asked? (1:10)

David passed judgment on the Amalekite because he claimed to have *killed the LORD's anointed* (v. 16). This is one of several instances when David showed his deep respect for Saul as God's anointed leader (see 1 Samuel 24:1–22).

Why did they mourn their enemy's demise? (1:12)

David and his men mourned the death of Saul and Jonathan because (1) Jonathan was David's close friend; (2) Saul, although corrupt, was nonetheless their king; (3) the death of even a corrupt king meant politically difficult times for Israel and (4) the deaths came from another humiliating defeat at the hands of the Philistines.

Book of Jashar (1:18)

The Israelites apparently kept the *Book of Jashar* to record the exploits of their national heroes. The account of Joshua's defeat of the Amorites on the day the sun stood still (Joshua 10:13), for example, quotes this book. A similar record, called *The Book of the Wars of the LORD*, is mentioned in Numbers 21:14. Although the *Book of Jashar* was familiar to David's contemporaries, it has not survived to modern times.

Why rub shields with oil? (1:21)

Before going into battle the Israelites treated their shields, made of wood or wicker and overlaid with leather, with oil (see Isaiah 21:5). This custom had practical advantages. It protected the shield from weather, made it last longer and caused enemies' swords to glance off. It's likely that, for soldiers of that time, oiling their shields also symbolized preparation and resolve, loosely equivalent to our "roll up your sleeves."

the shield of Saul—no longer rubbed with
    oil.
22From the blood of the slain,
    from the flesh of the mighty,
the bow of Jonathan did not turn back,
    the sword of Saul did not return unsatisfied.

23"Saul and Jonathan—
    in life they were loved and gracious,
    and in deathᴰ they were not parted.
They were swifter than eagles,
    they were stronger than lions.

24"O daughters of Israel,
    weep for Saul,
who clothed you in scarlet and finery,
    who adorned your garments with ornaments
        of gold.

25"How the mighty have fallen in battle!
    Jonathan lies slain on your heights.
26I grieve for you, Jonathan my brother;
    you were very dear to me.
Your love for me was wonderful,
    more wonderful than that of women.

27"How the mighty have fallen!
    The weapons of war have perished!"

David Anointed King Over Judah

2 In the course of time, David inquired of the LORD. "Shall I go up to one of the towns of Judah?" he asked.
The LORD said, "Go up."
David asked, "Where shall I go?"
"To Hebron," the LORD answered.
2So David went up there with his two wives, Ahinoam of Jezreel and Abigail, the widow of Nabal of Carmel. 3David also took the men who were with him, each with his family, and they settled in Hebron and its towns. 4Then the men of Judah came to Hebron and there they anointedᴰ David king over the house of Judah.

When David was told that it was the men of Jabesh Gilead who had buried Saul, 5he sent messengers to the men of Jabesh Gilead to say to them, "The LORD bless you for showing this kindness to Saul your master by burying him. 6May the LORD now show you kindness and faithfulness, and I too will show you the same favor because you have done this. 7Now then, be strong and brave, for Saul your master is dead, and the house of Judah has anointed me king over them."

War Between the Houses of David and Saul

8Meanwhile, Abner son of Ner, the commander of Saul's army, had taken Ish-Bosheth son of Saul and brought him over to Mahanaim. 9He made him king over Gilead, Ashuriᵃ and Jezreel, and also over Ephraim, Benjamin and all Israel.

10Ish-Bosheth son of Saul was forty years old when he became king over Israel, and he reigned two years. The house of Judah, however, followed David. 11The length of time David was king in Hebron over the house of Judah was seven years and six months.

12Abner son of Ner, together with the men of Ish-Bosheth son of Saul, left Mahanaim and went to Gibeon.

What kind of love was better than the love of women? (1:26)

Relationships with the intense loyalty and commitment that shaped the friendship of David and Jonathan were rare between men, but unheard of between men and women. Men typically viewed women as inferiors and considered wives as their possessions. Jonathan loved David *as himself,* sharing his personal possessions—robe, tunic, and even his sword and bow, which were valuable property to a warrior (1 Samuel 18:1–4). Their friendship covenant remained solid even when Jonathan had to defend David from Jonathan's own father (1 Samuel 19:4–5).

Did God speak audibly to David? (2:1)

It's possible David received guidance by using the Urim and Thummim—two stones used by priests to help determine God's will (see Dictionary). It's also possible David consulted one of the prophets—or that he prayed and received an audible answer.

Was David's thanks designed to gain political support? (2:5–7)

David was probably motivated both by political savvy and genuine appreciation to those who had shown respect for God's anointed king. Commanders of the army were some of the strongest power brokers of that culture. So it was politically expedient for David, who hadn't yet consolidated his own power, to thank them for their kindness and continued bravery. But David also respected Saul as the king God had anointed. See *Why did David execute the Amalekite for doing what Saul asked?* (1:10).

ᵃ9 Or *Asher*

¹³Joab son of Zeruiah and David's men went out and met them at the pool of Gibeon. One group sat down on one side of the pool and one group on the other side.

¹⁴Then Abner said to Joab, "Let's have some of the young men get up and fight hand to hand in front of us."

"All right, let them do it," Joab said.

¹⁵So they stood up and were counted off—twelve men for Benjamin and Ish-Bosheth son of Saul, and twelve for David. ¹⁶Then each man grabbed his opponent by the head and thrust his dagger into his opponent's side, and they fell down together. So that place in Gibeon was called Helkath Hazzurim. [a]

¹⁷The battle that day was very fierce, and Abner and the men of Israel were defeated by David's men.

¹⁸The three sons of Zeruiah were there: Joab, Abishai and Asahel. Now Asahel was as fleet-footed as a wild gazelle. ¹⁹He chased Abner, turning neither to the right nor to the left as he pursued him. ²⁰Abner looked behind him and asked, "Is that you, Asahel?"

"It is," he answered.

²¹Then Abner said to him, "Turn aside to the right or to the left; take on one of the young men and strip him of his weapons." But Asahel would not stop chasing him.

²²Again Abner warned Asahel, "Stop chasing me! Why should I strike you down? How could I look your brother Joab in the face?"

²³But Asahel refused to give up the pursuit; so Abner thrust the butt of his spear into Asahel's stomach, and the spear came out through his back. He fell there and died on the spot. And every man stopped when he came to the place where Asahel had fallen and died.

²⁴But Joab and Abishai pursued Abner, and as the sun was setting, they came to the hill of Ammah, near Giah on the way to the wasteland of Gibeon. ²⁵Then the men of Benjamin rallied behind Abner. They formed themselves into a group and took their stand on top of a hill.

²⁶Abner called out to Joab, "Must the sword devour forever? Don't you realize that this will end in bitterness? How long before you order your men to stop pursuing their brothers?"

²⁷Joab answered, "As surely as God lives, if you had not spoken, the men would have continued the pursuit of their brothers until morning. [b]"

²⁸So Joab blew the trumpet, and all the men came to a halt; they no longer pursued Israel, nor did they fight anymore.

²⁹All that night Abner and his men marched through the Arabah. They crossed the Jordan, continued through the whole Bithron [c] and came to Mahanaim.

³⁰Then Joab returned from pursuing Abner and assembled all his men. Besides Asahel, nineteen of David's men were found missing. ³¹But David's men had killed three hundred and sixty Benjamites who were with Abner. ³²They took Asahel and buried him in his father's tomb at Bethlehem. Then Joab and his men marched all night and arrived at Hebron by daybreak.

Why conduct a battle as if it were a sporting event? (2:14–16)

Although this hand-to-hand fight seems like a frivolous skirmish, it's possible Abner and Joab proposed this to prevent all-out civil war. Earlier David's one-on-one battle with Goliath had, in a similar way, provided an alternative to a bigger battle (see Goliath's challenge in 1 Samuel 17:8–10). If this is the case, the contest reflected a value for human life—preventing wholesale slaughter by staging a smaller fight—deadly though it was.

How did the spectators become involved in the battle? (2:17)

Since the smaller battle ended in a tragic stalemate with all 24 men dead, the rest of the men became engaged in the larger battle. Undoubtedly their passions were inflamed by watching their comrades die, triggering an intense desire for revenge.

Why did everyone stop where Asahel died? (2:23)

The men who passed by Asahel's body were stunned by the gruesome manner of his death. No one was killed with the butt of a spear! They were perhaps also disheartened that a man who could run as fast as Asahel would come to such an end. Finally, they may have been stunned to realize that, though they had won the battle (vv. 30–31), even their commander's own brother did not survive. They were all at risk.

---

[a]16 *Helkath Hazzurim* means *field of daggers* or *field of hostilities.*
[b]27 Or *spoken this morning, the men would not have taken up the pursuit of their brothers;* or *spoken, the men would have given up the pursuit of their brothers by morning*   [c]29 Or *morning;* or *ravine;* the meaning of the Hebrew for this word is uncertain.

Why did David have so many wives? (3:2–5)

See article: *Why did David have so many wives and concubines?* (5:13).

Why was Ish-Bosheth angry about whom Abner slept with? (3:7)

A king's wife or concubine was considered his personal property. To sleep with her was viewed not only as an insult, but as a threat to the king's power. Later on, for example, Absalom slept with David's concubines as a sign of his intent to take power away from his father (16:21–22). So when Abner slept with Saul's concubine, Ish-Bosheth considered it treason. As successor to the throne, Ish-Bosheth had exclusive rights to Saul's concubine.

Why was Abner so angry? (3:8–10)

Abner probably felt Ish-Bosheth demonstrated a singular lack of gratitude. Abner, after all, had put Ish-Bosheth in power in the first place (2:8–9). What's more, he had just risked his life and the lives of his men, actually losing 360 of them to keep Ish-Bosheth on the throne. Abner apparently felt that after all he'd done for Ish-Bosheth, he was entitled to a few special privileges.

Why did David want Michal back? (3:14–15)

David may have genuinely loved Michal. We know she had previously been in love with him (1 Samuel 18:20). David also felt he had a prior claim to Michal. He had paid the bride-price, and she was still his wife when Saul in anger gave her to Paltiel. But beyond all that, as Saul's son-in-law once again, David could claim to be a legitimate successor to Saul's throne.

3 The war between the house of Saul and the house of David lasted a long time. David grew stronger and stronger, while the house of Saul grew weaker and weaker.

²Sons were born to David in Hebron:

His firstborn[D] was Amnon the son of Ahinoam of Jezreel;

³his second, Kileab the son of Abigail the widow of Nabal of Carmel;

the third, Absalom the son of Maacah daughter of Talmai king of Geshur;

⁴the fourth, Adonijah the son of Haggith;

the fifth, Shephatiah the son of Abital;

⁵and the sixth, Ithream the son of David's wife Eglah.

These were born to David in Hebron.

Abner Goes Over to David

⁶During the war between the house of Saul and the house of David, Abner had been strengthening his own position in the house of Saul. ⁷Now Saul had had a concubine[D] named Rizpah daughter of Aiah. And Ish-Bosheth said to Abner, "Why did you sleep with my father's concubine?"

⁸Abner was very angry because of what Ish-Bosheth said and he answered, "Am I a dog's head—on Judah's side? This very day I am loyal to the house of your father Saul and to his family and friends. I haven't handed you over to David. Yet now you accuse me of an offense involving this woman! ⁹May God deal with Abner, be it ever so severely, if I do not do for David what the LORD promised him on oath ¹⁰and transfer the kingdom from the house of Saul and establish David's throne over Israel and Judah from Dan to Beersheba." ¹¹Ish-Bosheth did not dare to say another word to Abner, because he was afraid of him.

¹²Then Abner sent messengers on his behalf to say to David, "Whose land is it? Make an agreement with me, and I will help you bring all Israel over to you."

¹³"Good," said David. "I will make an agreement with you. But I demand one thing of you: Do not come into my presence unless you bring Michal daughter of Saul when you come to see me." ¹⁴Then David sent messengers to Ish-Bosheth son of Saul, demanding, "Give me my wife Michal, whom I betrothed to myself for the price of a hundred Philistine foreskins."

¹⁵So Ish-Bosheth gave orders and had her taken away from her husband Paltiel son of Laish. ¹⁶Her husband, however, went with her, weeping behind her all the way to Bahurim. Then Abner said to him, "Go back home!" So he went back.

¹⁷Abner conferred with the elders of Israel and said, "For some time you have wanted to make David your king. ¹⁸Now do it! For the LORD promised David, 'By my servant David I will rescue my people Israel from the hand of the Philistines and from the hand of all their enemies.'"

¹⁹Abner also spoke to the Benjamites in person. Then he went to Hebron to tell David everything that Israel and the whole house of Benjamin wanted to do. ²⁰When Abner, who had twenty men with him, came to David at Hebron, David prepared a feast for him and his men. ²¹Then Abner said to David, "Let me go at once and assemble all Israel for my lord the king, so that they may make a com-

pact with you, and that you may rule over all that your heart desires." So David sent Abner away, and he went in peace[D].

Joab Murders Abner

22Just then David's men and Joab returned from a raid and brought with them a great deal of plunder[D]. But Abner was no longer with David in Hebron, because David had sent him away, and he had gone in peace. **23**When Joab and all the soldiers with him arrived, he was told that Abner son of Ner had come to the king and that the king had sent him away and that he had gone in peace.

24So Joab went to the king and said, "What have you done? Look, Abner came to you. Why did you let him go? Now he is gone! **25**You know Abner son of Ner; he came to deceive you and observe your movements and find out everything you are doing."

26Joab then left David and sent messengers after Abner, and they brought him back from the well of Sirah. But David did not know it. **27**Now when Abner returned to Hebron, Joab took him aside into the gateway, as though to speak with him privately. And there, to avenge[D] the blood of his brother Asahel, Joab stabbed him in the stomach, and he died.

28Later, when David heard about this, he said, "I and my kingdom are forever innocent before the LORD concerning the blood of Abner son of Ner. **29**May his blood fall upon the head of Joab and upon all his father's house! May Joab's house never be without someone who has a running sore or leprosy[Da] or who leans on a crutch or who falls by the sword or who lacks food."

30(Joab and his brother Abishai murdered Abner because he had killed their brother Asahel in the battle at Gibeon.)

31Then David said to Joab and all the people with him, "Tear your clothes and put on sackcloth[D] and walk in mourning in front of Abner." King David himself walked behind the bier. **32**They buried Abner in Hebron, and the king wept aloud at Abner's tomb. All the people wept also.

33The king sang this lament[D] for Abner:

"Should Abner have died as the lawless die?
34   Your hands were not bound,
        your feet were not fettered.
    You fell as one falls before wicked men."

And all the people wept over him again.

35Then they all came and urged David to eat something while it was still day; but David took an oath, saying, "May God deal with me, be it ever so severely, if I taste bread or anything else before the sun sets!"

36All the people took note and were pleased; indeed, everything the king did pleased them. **37**So on that day all the people and all Israel knew that the king had no part in the murder of Abner son of Ner.

38Then the king said to his men, "Do you not realize that a prince and a great man has fallen in Israel this day? **39**And today, though I am the anointed[D] king, I am weak, and these sons of Zeruiah are too strong for me. May the LORD repay the evildoer according to his evil deeds!"

---

a29 The Hebrew word was used for various diseases affecting the skin—not necessarily leprosy.

Why did David curse the commander of his army? (3:29)
David cursed Joab and mourned Abner publicly to show he disapproved of Joab's unjustified revenge. See **What did an avenger of blood do?** (Joshua 20:3). Abner killed Asahel, after repeated warnings, while defending himself in battle. Joab murdered Abner through trickery and deceit. So what Joab did in revenge was not morally equivalent to Abner's deed. What's more, Joab may have been motivated to kill Abner by more than simple revenge. Ambitious man that he was, Joab may have feared Abner's political power.

How much authority did Joab have? (3:39)
With the army behind him, Joab had tremendous power. David may have been recognized as king, but Joab, with his tremendous military and leadership abilities, possessed respect of his own. He took his liberty, for example, in ordering Abner back from the well of Sirah without David's knowledge (3:26). At a time when David had not yet established his own power, Joab was clearly a man to be reckoned with.

Ish-Bosheth Murdered

4 When Ish-Bosheth son of Saul heard that Abner had died in Hebron, he lost courage, and all Israel became alarmed. ²Now Saul's son had two men who were leaders of raiding bands. One was named Baanah and the other Recab; they were sons of Rimmon the Beerothite from the tribe of Benjamin—Beeroth is considered part of Benjamin, ³because the people of Beeroth fled to Gittaim and have lived there as aliensᴰ to this day.

⁴(Jonathan son of Saul had a son who was lame in both feet. He was five years old when the news about Saul and Jonathan came from Jezreel. His nurse picked him up and fled, but as she hurried to leave, he fell and became crippled. His name was Mephibosheth.)

⁵Now Recab and Baanah, the sons of Rimmon the Beerothite, set out for the house of Ish-Bosheth, and they arrived there in the heat of the day while he was taking his noonday rest. ⁶They went into the inner part of the house as if to get some wheat, and they stabbed him in the stomach. Then Recab and his brother Baanah slipped away.

⁷They had gone into the house while he was lying on the bed in his bedroom. After they stabbed and killed him, they cut off his head. Taking it with them, they traveled all night by way of the Arabah. ⁸They brought the head of Ish-Bosheth to David at Hebron and said to the king, "Here is the head of Ish-Bosheth son of Saul, your enemy, who tried to take your life. This day the LORD has avengedᴰ my lord the king against Saul and his offspring."

⁹David answered Recab and his brother Baanah, the sons of Rimmon the Beerothite, "As surely as the LORD lives, who has delivered me out of all trouble, ¹⁰when a man told me, 'Saul is dead,' and thought he was bringing good news, I seized him and put him to deathᴰ in Ziklag. That was the reward I gave him for his news! ¹¹How much more—when wicked men have killed an innocent man in his own house and on his own bed—should I not now demand his blood from your hand and rid the earth of you!"

¹²So David gave an order to his men, and they killed them. They cut off their hands and feet and hung the bodies by the pool in Hebron. But they took the head of Ish-Bosheth and buried it in Abner's tomb at Hebron.

David Becomes King Over Israel

5 All the tribes of Israel came to David at Hebron and said, "We are your own flesh and blood. ²In the past, while Saul was king over us, you were the one who led Israel on their military campaigns. And the LORD said to you, 'You will shepherd my people Israel, and you will become their ruler.' "

³When all the elders of Israel had come to King David at Hebron, the king made a compact with them at Hebron before the LORD, and they anointedᴰ David king over Israel.

⁴David was thirty years old when he became king, and he reigned forty years. ⁵In Hebron he reigned over Judah seven years and six months, and in Jerusalemᴰ he reigned over all Israel and Judah thirty-three years.

David Conquers Jerusalem

⁶The king and his men marched to Jerusalem to attack the Jebusites, who lived there. The Jebusites said to

Why did David execute those who helped him win the throne? (4:12)
David showed his disfavor for the king's murderers and thus gained the respect of those loyal to the king. But political gain was not likely his primary motivation. Time and again, David demonstrated deep regard for God's sovereignty. He knew that God had delivered him in the past and would deliver him now. David didn't need any self-appointed vigilantes taking matters into their own hands.

Why mutilate the bodies before hanging them up for display? (4:12)
This was a common punishment for treason in David's time—and a grisly warning to other would-be assassins. In this case, they cut off the hands of those that murdered Ish-Bosheth. Then they cut off the feet of those that escaped to carry the news to David.

Why were foreigners still in control of Jerusalem? (5:6)
The Jebusites were hard to displace because Jerusalem was a natural fortress—precisely the reason why David wanted to capture it. "The city of Jebus" was located on a hilltop with deep valleys on each side. Others before David had tried to capture the city and had failed. The tribes of Benjamin and Judah, for example, who lived nearby could not dislodge the Jebusites (Judges 1:21).

David, "You will not get in here; even the blind and the lame can ward you off." They thought, "David cannot get in here." ⁷Nevertheless, David captured the fortress of Zion^D, the City of David.

⁸On that day, David said, "Anyone who conquers the Jebusites will have to use the water shaft*a* to reach those 'lame and blind' who are David's enemies.*b*" That is why they say, "The 'blind and lame' will not enter the palace."

⁹David then took up residence in the fortress and called it the City of David. He built up the area around it, from the supporting terraces*c* inward. ¹⁰And he became more and more powerful, because the LORD God Almighty was with him.

¹¹Now Hiram king of Tyre sent messengers to David, along with cedar logs and carpenters and stonemasons, and they built a palace for David. ¹²And David knew that the LORD had established him as king over Israel and had exalted his kingdom for the sake of his people Israel.

¹³After he left Hebron, David took more concubines^D and wives in Jerusalem^D, and more sons and daughters were born to him. ¹⁴These are the names of the children born to him there: Shammua, Shobab, Nathan, Solomon,

Why did David choose to live in Jerusalem? (5:9)

Jerusalem was in David's region. Though located technically in territory belonging to Benjamin (Joshua 18:28), Jerusalem was just five or six miles from David's town of Bethlehem in Judah. Besides being close to his home, Jerusalem offered David a strategic military advantage. And since it was situated in the heart of the promised land, it was accessible to both the northern and southern tribes. By making Jerusalem his capital, David gave himself an edge in uniting the people and putting his own stamp of leadership on the land.

*a*8 Or *use scaling hooks*   *b*8 Or *are hated by David*   *c*9 Or *the Millo*

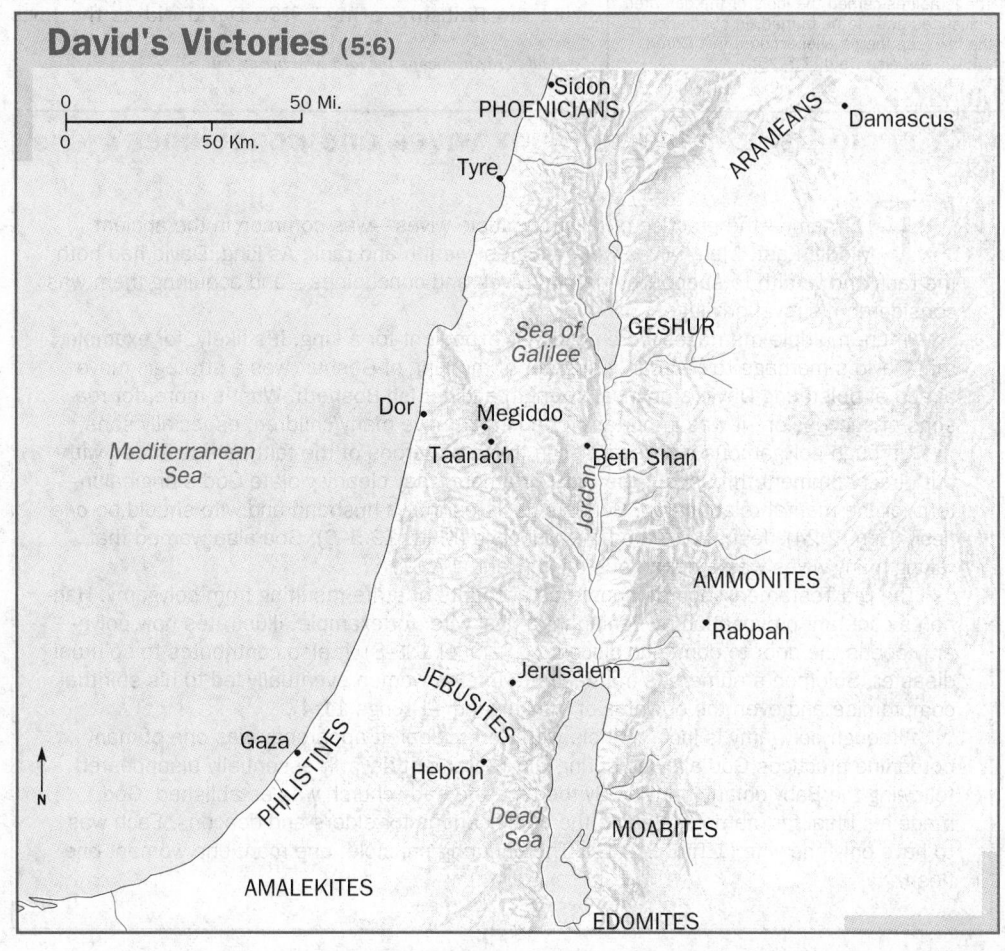

David's Victories (5:6)

0 ——————— 50 Mi.
0 ——————— 50 Km.

Sidon
PHOENICIANS
ARAMEANS   Damascus
Tyre
Sea of Galilee   GESHUR
Dor   Megiddo
Mediterranean Sea   Taanach   Beth Shan
Jordan
AMMONITES
Rabbah
JEBUSITES   Jerusalem
Gaza
PHILISTINES   Hebron
N   Dead Sea   MOABITES
AMALEKITES
EDOMITES

15Ibhar, Elishua, Nepheg, Japhia, 16Elishama, Eliada and Eliphelet.

David Defeats the Philistines

17When the Philistines heard that David had been anointed[D] king over Israel, they went up in full force to search for him, but David heard about it and went down to the stronghold[D]. 18Now the Philistines had come and spread out in the Valley of Rephaim; 19so David inquired of the LORD, "Shall I go and attack the Philistines? Will you hand them over to me?"

The LORD answered him, "Go, for I will surely hand the Philistines over to you."

20So David went to Baal Perazim, and there he defeated them. He said, "As waters break out, the LORD has broken out against my enemies before me." So that place was called Baal Perazim.[a] 21The Philistines abandoned their idols[D] there, and David and his men carried them off.

22Once more the Philistines came up and spread out in the Valley of Rephaim; 23so David inquired of the LORD, and he answered, "Do not go straight up, but circle around behind them and attack them in front of the balsam trees. 24As soon as you hear the sound of marching in the tops of the balsam trees, move quickly, because that will mean the LORD has gone out in front of you to strike the Philistine army." 25So David did as the LORD

a20 *Baal Perazim* means *the lord who breaks out.*

Why did the Philistines carry idols into battle? (5:21)

The Philistines, obviously concerned about David's rise to power, wanted all the help they could get in their battle against his army. They took idols into battle hoping their gods would help them prevail. Bringing a religious symbol into combat was a common practice during this time. The Israelites, for example, brought the ark of the covenant into battle (1 Samuel 4:1–9).

What did David's men do with the idols? (5:21)

The Israelites carried the idols of the defeated Philistines away to be burned, in obedience to the law (see the parallel account in 1 Chron. 14:12; see also Deut. 7:5,25).

Why did David have so many wives and concubines? (5:13)

Polygamy—the practice of taking multiple wives—was common in the ancient Middle East. Many wives were a sign of wealth and rank. As king, David had both the rank and wealth to support numerous wives and concubines—and acquiring them was considered his royal privilege.

Often, multiple marriages were politically expedient for a king. It's likely, for example, that David's marriage to Maacah, daughter of the king of Geshur, was a strategic move aimed at bolstering David's political strength against Ish-Bosheth. What's more, for reasons of succession, it was important for a king to have many children, especially sons.

Although polygamous marriages, even those of heroes of the faith, are recorded without direct comment throughout the Old Testament, they clearly violate God's original intent for the marital relationship. Genesis declares that a husband and wife should be *one flesh* (Gen. 2:24). Jesus reiterated this principle (Matt. 19:5–6). God also warned that taking many wives was a dangerous thing (Deut. 17:17).

The Old Testament records numerous accounts of strife resulting from polygamy. Hannah's constant provocation by Peninnah, a rival wife, for example, illustrates how polygamy opens the door to domestic discord (1 Samuel 1:1–8). It also contributes to spiritual disaster. Solomon's numerous marriages to foreign women eventually led to his spiritual compromise and even the downfall of the kingdom (1 Kings 11:4).

Although polygamy is incompatible with God's ideal, it apparently was one of many borderline practices God allowed during Old Testament days. It essentially disappeared following the Babylonian captivity. By the time the early church was established, God made his ideal for marriage clear in the qualifications for elders and deacons. Each was to have only one wife (1 Tim. 3:2,12). The enduring principle: one man, one woman, one flesh.

commanded him, and he struck down the Philistines all the way from Gibeon*a* to Gezer.

The Ark Brought to Jerusalem

6 David again brought together out of Israel chosen men, thirty thousand in all. ²He and all his men set out from Baalah of Judah*b* to bring up from there the ark of God, which is called by the Name,*c* the name of the LORD Almighty, who is enthroned between the cherubim*D* that are on the ark. ³They set the ark of God on a new cart and brought it from the house of Abinadab, which was on the hill. Uzzah and Ahio, sons of Abinadab, were guiding the new cart ⁴with the ark of God on it,*d* and Ahio was walking in front of it. ⁵David and the whole house of Israel were celebrating with all their might before the LORD, with songs*e* and with harps, lyres*D*, tambourines, sistrums and cymbals.

⁶When they came to the threshing floor of Nacon, Uzzah reached out and took hold of the ark of God, because the oxen stumbled. ⁷The LORD's anger burned against Uzzah because of his irreverent act; therefore God struck him down and he died there beside the ark of God.

⁸Then David was angry because the LORD's wrath had broken out against Uzzah, and to this day that place is called Perez Uzzah.*f*

⁹David was afraid of the LORD that day and said, "How can the ark of the LORD ever come to me?" ¹⁰He was not willing to take the ark of the LORD to be with him in the City of David. Instead, he took it aside to the house of Obed-Edom the Gittite. ¹¹The ark of the LORD remained

a25 Septuagint (see also 1 Chron. 14:16); Hebrew Geba   *b2 That is, Kiriath Jearim; Hebrew Baale Judah, a variant of Baalah of Judah*   *c2 Hebrew; Septuagint and Vulgate do not have the Name.*   *d3,4 Dead Sea Scrolls and some Septuagint manuscripts; Masoretic Text cart ⁴and they brought it with the ark of God from the house of Abinadab, which was on the hill*   *e5 See Dead Sea Scrolls, Septuagint and 1 Chronicles 13:8; Masoretic Text celebrating before the LORD with all kinds of instruments made of pine.*   *f8 Perez Uzzah means outbreak against Uzzah.*

Did David leave the ark with a foreigner—a Gittite? (6:10)

A Gittite was someone from the city of Gath, located in Philistia (see **Map 5** at the back of this Bible). Although it would seem strange for David to leave the ark with a foreigner, it is possible Obed-Edom was one of a number of Gittites who immigrated to Israel to become personal bodyguards for David (15:18). More likely, however, Obed-Edom was a Levite, later appointed as a musician and gatekeeper for the temple (1 Chron. 15:16–26; 16:4–5,38; 26:1–6). A Levite could be called a Gittite if he came from the Levitical city of Gath Rimmon (Joshua 21:20–24).

Why would God kill someone who was trying to help? (6:7)

When David and his 30,000 men moved the ark in a manner contrary to God's instructions, they were all irreverent. In that sense, David set the stage for the subsequent tragedy. But instead of striking 30,000, God struck only the one who came closest and showed the most disregard for his holiness. Uzzah died because he flagrantly violated God's specific instructions about caring for the ark, his good intentions notwithstanding.

Only the Kohathites, a special branch of the tribe of Levi, were allowed to carry the ark—and even they couldn't touch it directly or they would die (Num. 4:15). When Uzzah touched the ark, God acted swiftly and dramatically to protect his holiness before the people.

It's possible that Uzzah, having grown up in the house of Abinidab, where the ark had been kept for many years, had grown too familiar with the sacred object and consequently lacked appropriate reverence for it. Whatever the case, he paid with his life for violating God's standard. Some are careful to note that Uzzah's death sentence tells us nothing about his eternal destination.

in the house of Obed-Edom the Gittite for three months, and the LORD blessed him and his entire household. ¹²Now King David was told, "The LORD has blessed the household of Obed-Edom and everything he has, because of the ark of God." So David went down and brought up the ark of God from the house of Obed-Edom to the City of David with rejoicing. ¹³When those who were carrying the ark of the LORD had taken six steps, he sacrificed a bull and a fattened calf. ¹⁴David, wearing a linen ephodᴰ, danced before the LORD with all his might, ¹⁵while he and the entire house of Israel brought up the ark of the LORD with shouts and the sound of trumpets.

¹⁶As the ark of the LORD was entering the City of David, Michal daughter of Saul watched from a window. And when she saw King David leaping and dancing before the LORD, she despised him in her heart.

¹⁷They brought the ark of the LORD and set it in its place inside the tent that David had pitched for it, and David sacrificed burnt offeringsᴰ and fellowship offeringsᴰᵃ before the LORD. ¹⁸After he had finished sacrificing the burnt offerings and fellowship offerings, he blessed the people in the name of the LORD Almighty. ¹⁹Then he gave a loaf of bread, a cake of dates and a cake of raisins to each person in the whole crowd of Israelites, both men and women. And all the people went to their homes.

²⁰When David returned home to bless his household, Michal daughter of Saul came out to meet him and said, "How the king of Israel has distinguished himself today, disrobing in the sight of the slave girls of his servants as any vulgar fellow would!"

²¹David said to Michal, "It was before the LORD, who chose me rather than your father or anyone from his house when he appointed me ruler over the LORD's people Israel—I will celebrate before the LORD. ²²I will become even more undignified than this, and I will be humiliated in my own eyes. But by these slave girls you spoke of, I will be held in honor."

²³And Michal daughter of Saul had no children to the day of her deathᴰ.

God's Promise to David

7 After the king was settled in his palace and the LORD had given him rest from all his enemies around him, ²he said to Nathan the prophetᴰ, "Here I am, living in a palace of cedar, while the ark of God remains in a tent."

³Nathan replied to the king, "Whatever you have in mind, go ahead and do it, for the LORD is with you."

⁴That night the word of the LORD came to Nathan, saying:

⁵"Go and tell my servant David, 'This is what the LORD says: Are you the one to build me a house to dwell in? ⁶I have not dwelt in a house from the day I brought the Israelites up out of Egypt to this day. I have been moving from place to place with a tent as my dwelling. ⁷Wherever I have moved with all the Israelites, did I ever say to any of their rulers whom I commanded to shepherd my people Israel, "Why have you not built me a house of cedar?" '

⁸"Now then, tell my servant David, 'This is what the LORD Almighty says: I took you from the pasture and

Why did David disrobe for this grand occasion? (6:14)
David took off his linen robe (1 Chron. 15:27) and danced before the ark wearing only an ephod—a short, sleeveless pullover garment. Maybe he wore it simply for practical reasons: reaching only the thighs, the ephod gave him more mobility to dance before the Lord. Since it was a distinctive garment worn by priests who served in the sanctuary (1 Samuel 2:18,28), the ephod was associated with worship. By dressing in a manner like a priest, David perhaps signaled his desire to lead the people of Israel in worship.

Why could David—who wasn't a Levite—sacrifice burnt offerings? (6:17)
Since the priests and Levites were with David (1 Chron. 15:11), it would be unlikely that he would usurp their role, especially since Uzzah's punishment had so recently taught a difficult lesson about ignoring God's law. Undoubtedly, the appropriate priests officiated over David's offerings. David was like any worshiper on whose behalf the priests would perform ritual sacrifices. King Saul, by contrast, incurred God's wrath by disobeying a specific command to wait for Samuel and by offering a sacrifice himself. See 1 Samuel 13:9.

Why was Michal so incensed over David's dancing? (6:20)
Michal accused David of impropriety by disrobing before the slave girls. Though the ephod was short, it wasn't indecent. See *Why did David disrobe for this grand occasion?* (6:14). Michal seemed more upset about behavior she considered unbecoming to a king. A royal daughter herself, she apparently felt it was undignified for a king to dance in front of his subjects with such unbridled enthusiasm. Michal's attitude suggests that she did not understand the depth of David's love for God.

ᵃ17 Traditionally *peace offerings*; also in verse 18

from following the flock to be ruler over my people Israel. **9**I have been with you wherever you have gone, and I have cut off all your enemies from before you. Now I will make your name great, like the names of the greatest men of the earth. **10**And I will provide a place for my people Israel and will plant them so that they can have a home of their own and no longer be disturbed. Wicked people will not oppress them anymore, as they did at the beginning **11**and have done ever since the time I appointed leaders*a* over my people Israel. I will also give you rest from all your enemies.

" 'The LORD declares to you that the LORD himself will establish a house for you: **12**When your days are over and you rest with your fathers, I will raise up your offspring to succeed you, who will come from your own body, and I will establish his kingdom. **13**He is the one who will build a house for my Name, and I will establish the throne of his kingdom forever. **14**I will be his father, and he will be my son. When he does wrong, I will punish him with the rod of men, with floggings inflicted by men. **15**But my love will never be taken away from him, as I took it away from Saul, whom I removed from before you. **16**Your house and your kingdom will endure forever before me*b*; your throne will be established forever.' "

17Nathan reported to David all the words of this entire revelation*D*.

David's Prayer

18Then King David went in and sat before the LORD, and he said:

"Who am I, O Sovereign LORD, and what is my family, that you have brought me this far? **19**And as if this were not enough in your sight, O Sovereign LORD, you have also spoken about the future of the house of your servant. Is this your usual way of dealing with man, O Sovereign LORD?

20"What more can David say to you? For you know your servant, O Sovereign LORD. **21**For the sake of your word and according to your will, you have done

a 11 Traditionally judges   *b 16 Some Hebrew manuscripts and Septuagint; most Hebrew manuscripts you*

Why wouldn't God permit David to build a temple? (7:13)
God had never instructed Israel to build him a temple, and he was not going to ask David to do so now. God used David as a military leader to subdue the enemies of Israel and to establish the kingdom, but not to build God's house. That job would be reserved for David's son, Solomon, a man of peace. Also see *Why would obeying God in war disqualify David from building the temple?* (1 Chron. 22:8).

How has David's house and kingdom endured forever? (7:16)
All the kings who ruled in Jerusalem after David (20 in all) were his descendants. No coup d'etat ever eradicated David's line. Ultimately, however, Christ represents the fulfillment of this promise. Mary was told by an angel that her son, Jesus, would someday occupy David's throne (Luke 1:31–33). It is a beautiful irony that David, who wanted to build a house for God, instead received a promise that God would build *him* a house—the dynasty of kings from which the Messiah would come.

What was God's *usual way of dealing with people?* (7:19)
God dealt in many different ways in the lives of individuals in the Old Testament. However, David recognized that God, by establishing David's family on the throne forever, was bestowing extraordinary blessings on him. David expressed gratitude and astonishment that he, a man of humble origins, should be so privileged.

Does God sometimes play favorites? (7:15)

It may seem unfair that God dealt so harshly with Saul and so mercifully with David. God withheld his love from Saul, but he promised to love David's son always, even when he didn't deserve it. Does God show partiality?

No. The Bible says he shows no partiality (Deut. 10:17; Acts 10:34–35; Romans 2:11). However, God uses certain people, whose hearts are committed to him, to serve him in specific ways. Both David and Saul committed grievous sins, but David's heart continually turned back to God while Saul's continually turned away (1 Kings 15:3). Saul even admitted to David, *You are more righteous than I* (1 Samuel 24:17). Was David, the betrayer of Uriah and seducer of Bathsheba, righteous? In God's eyes, yes—because he repented when he failed and he maintained a humble attitude of faith.

this great thing and made it known to your servant.

22"How great you are, O Sovereign LORD! There is no one like you, and there is no God but you, as we have heard with our own ears. **23**And who is like your people Israel—the one nation on earth that God went out to redeem[D] as a people for himself, and to make a name for himself, and to perform great and awesome wonders by driving out nations and their gods from before your people, whom you redeemed from Egypt?[a] **24**You have established your people Israel as your very own forever, and you, O LORD, have become their God.

25"And now, LORD God, keep forever the promise you have made concerning your servant and his house. Do as you promised, **26**so that your name will be great forever. Then men will say, 'The LORD Almighty is God over Israel!' And the house of your servant David will be established before you.

27"O LORD Almighty, God of Israel, you have revealed this to your servant, saying, 'I will build a house for you.' So your servant has found courage to offer you this prayer. **28**O Sovereign LORD, you are God! Your words are trustworthy, and you have promised these good things to your servant. **29**Now be pleased to bless the house of your servant, that it may continue forever in your sight; for you, O Sovereign LORD, have spoken, and with your blessing the house of your servant will be blessed forever."

David's Victories

8 In the course of time, David defeated the Philistines and subdued them, and he took Metheg Ammah from the control of the Philistines.

2David also defeated the Moabites. He made them lie down on the ground and measured them off with a length of cord. Every two lengths of them were put to death[D], and the third length was allowed to live. So the Moabites became subject to David and brought tribute.

3Moreover, David fought Hadadezer son of Rehob, king of Zobah, when he went to restore his control along the Euphrates River. **4**David captured a thousand of his chariots, seven thousand charioteers[b] and twenty thousand foot soldiers. He hamstrung all but a hundred of the chariot horses.

5When the Arameans of Damascus came to help Hadadezer king of Zobah, David struck down twenty-two thousand of them. **6**He put garrisons in the Aramean kingdom of Damascus, and the Arameans became subject to him and brought tribute. The LORD gave David victory wherever he went.

7David took the gold shields that belonged to the officers of Hadadezer and brought them to Jerusalem[D]. **8**From Tebah[c] and Berothai, towns that belonged to Hadadezer, King David took a great quantity of bronze.

9When Tou[d] king of Hamath heard that David had defeated the entire army of Hadadezer, **10**he sent his son Jo-

Why would David be so brutal? (8:2)

We don't know why David found it necessary—and justifiable—to decimate the Moabite army. On the other hand, compared with many barbaric practices of ancient warfare, it would be just as legitimate to ask why David was so lenient as to let one-third live. It's possible David let some live because the Moabites were his blood relatives through the lineage of Ruth. Also, the Moabites were not among the seven nations God had ordered the Israelites to exterminate when they entered the land of Canaan (Deut. 7:1–2).

Why didn't David save the chariot horses for his own use? (8:4)

The Israelites didn't consider horses that valuable. Partly because of rocky terrain in the area, the Israelite army relied on its infantry instead. So David's main concern was to keep the horses from being of use to the people of Zobah. Furthermore, David obeyed God's decree (Deut. 17:16) that the future king of Israel should not acquire great numbers of horses for himself. Pagan kings might trust in chariots and horses, but the king of Israel was to trust in the Lord (Psalm 20:7).

Garrisons (8:6)

The garrisons David put in Damascus were most likely troops that served as an occupation force. Stationed among the Arameans, such troops would make sure the Arameans complied with David's rule.

a23 See Septuagint and 1 Chron. 17:21; Hebrew *wonders for your land and before your people, whom you redeemed from Egypt, from the nations and their gods.*   *b4* Septuagint (see also Dead Sea Scrolls and 1 Chron. 18:4); Masoretic Text *captured seventeen hundred of his charioteers*   *c8* See some Septuagint manuscripts (see also 1 Chron. 18:8); Hebrew *Betah.*   *d9* Hebrew *Toi*, a variant of *Tou*; also in verse 10

ram*a* to King David to greet him and congratulate him on his victory in battle over Hadadezer, who had been at war with Tou. Joram brought with him articles of silver and gold and bronze.

11King David dedicated these articles to the LORD, as he had done with the silver and gold from all the nations he had subdued: **12**Edom*Db* and Moab, the Ammonites and the Philistines, and Amalek. He also dedicated the plunder*D* taken from Hadadezer son of Rehob, king of Zobah.

13And David became famous after he returned from striking down eighteen thousand Edomites*c* in the Valley of Salt.

14He put garrisons throughout Edom, and all the Edomites became subject to David. The LORD gave David victory wherever he went.

David's Officials

15David reigned over all Israel, doing what was just and right for all his people. **16**Joab son of Zeruiah was over the army; Jehoshaphat son of Ahilud was recorder; **17**Zadok son of Ahitub and Ahimelech son of Abiathar were priests*D*; Seraiah was secretary; **18**Benaiah son of Jehoiada was over the Kerethites and Pelethites; and David's sons were royal advisers.*d*

David and Mephibosheth

9 David asked, "Is there anyone still left of the house of Saul to whom I can show kindness for Jonathan's sake?"

2Now there was a servant of Saul's household named Ziba. They called him to appear before David, and the king said to him, "Are you Ziba?"

"Your servant," he replied.

3The king asked, "Is there no one still left of the house of Saul to whom I can show God's kindness?"

Ziba answered the king, "There is still a son of Jonathan; he is crippled in both feet."

4"Where is he?" the king asked.

Ziba answered, "He is at the house of Makir son of Ammiel in Lo Debar."

5So King David had him brought from Lo Debar, from the house of Makir son of Ammiel.

6When Mephibosheth son of Jonathan, the son of Saul, came to David, he bowed down to pay him honor.

David said, "Mephibosheth!"

"Your servant," he replied.

7"Don't be afraid," David said to him, "for I will surely show you kindness for the sake of your father Jonathan. I will restore to you all the land that belonged to your grandfather Saul, and you will always eat at my table."

8Mephibosheth bowed down and said, "What is your servant, that you should notice a dead dog like me?"

9Then the king summoned Ziba, Saul's servant, and said to him, "I have given your master's grandson everything that belonged to Saul and his family. **10**You and your sons and your servants are to farm the land for him and bring in the crops, so that your master's grandson may be provided for. And Mephibosheth, grandson of your mas-

Why was David permitted to plunder for the Lord? (8:11–12)

Warring nations understood looting and plundering as both risks and profits of war. Unlike others, however, David did not plunder with only himself in mind. He earmarked goods won in this battle for the Lord, as God had instructed Joshua before the battle of Jericho (Joshua 6:18–19). David dedicated himself and his plunder to God, unlike Achan who kept battle spoils for himself (Joshua 7:20–21).

How influential were these positions? (8:16–18)

These were apparently the power elite of David's kingdom. Joab led the army. Jehoshaphat recorded current events as history and perhaps also served as a herald to proclaim the king's decrees. Zadok and Ahimelech were apparently chief priests. As secretary, Seraiah wrote and stored official documents and annals. He may also have had diplomatic functions similar to a modern secretary of state.

Why was Mephibosheth in hiding? (9:4)

Saul's grandson Mephibosheth was probably afraid of David. It was common in the ancient world for kings to seek out their predecessor's surviving family members and put them to death, thus eliminating potential rivals to the throne. Mephibosheth knew David had good reason to hate Saul, who had hunted him down and tried to kill him. It's also possible that Mephibosheth, crippled since the age of five, had simply chosen to live a quiet life of seclusion.

Did Mephibosheth eat with David at every meal? (9:7)

By giving Mephibosheth a permanent place at his table, David made a public gesture of friendship, privilege and acceptance. It was an act of grace, fulfilling his covenant with Jonathan (1 Samuel 20:14–16). Eating at the king's table was a high honor (1 Kings 2:7), although it didn't necessarily mean that the honoree literally sat at the same physical table as the king. When 1 Kings 18:19 says that 850 prophets ate at Jezebel's table, for example, it undoubtedly means they ate at her expense.

What kind of servant was Ziba? (9:9–10)

Ziba most likely held a position equivalent to a middle manager or personal secretary in today's society since he had 20 servants himself. Having previously served in the immediate household of King Saul, Ziba was accustomed to positions of responsibility. He also knew how to play political games for his own advantage—as became apparent later when, in order to get possession of Mephibosheth's lands, he didn't hesitate to make him look bad in David's eyes (16:1–4; 19:26–27).

---

*a*10 A variant of *Hadoram*   *b*12 Some Hebrew manuscripts, Septuagint and Syriac (see also 1 Chron. 18:11); most Hebrew manuscripts *Aram*   *c*13 A few Hebrew manuscripts, Septuagint and Syriac (see also 1 Chron. 18:12); most Hebrew manuscripts *Aram* (that is, Arameans)   *d*18 Or *were priests*

Why shave half a beard and cut off clothes? (10:4–6)

Both were extremely humiliating insults in the ancient world. To Israelite men, beards were symbols of dignity, maturity and manhood. They were also symbols of freedom—men taken as slaves were shaved to indicate their servitude. Since public nakedness was considered shameful, exposing the buttocks was a degrading insult. Both of these acts of humiliation were, in a sense, worse than death.

How were these armies raised and paid? (10:6)

Mercenary armies, relatively common in Old Testament times, were often made up of society's outcasts. When David ran from Saul, for example, he attracted a band of about 400 men—most of whom were discontented, in debt or in distress (1 Samuel 22:1–2). Because of their life circumstances, mercenaries would often do anything for money. When victorious, soldiers could plunder the enemy (1 Samuel 30:23–25). The Ammonites paid one thousand talents of silver to hire chariots and charioteers to fight David's armies for them (1 Chron. 19:6–7).

Why fight a war over shaved beards and cut clothing? (10:6–7)

David took it as a personal affront that his representatives, whom he had sent to Hanun in an act of kindness and good faith, were so deliberately humiliated. He justifiably interpreted Hanun's rebuff as an act of war.

Why aren't Israelite casualties recorded? (10:18)

Scripture does not hesitate to list Israelite casualties in other passages (Joshua 7:4–5; 1 Samuel 4:2), so the omission here should not be seen as a public relations ploy. Apparently, the magnitude of Israel's victory was so great that its losses were scarcely worth mentioning.

Why did they have a season for war? (11:1)

Quarrels with neighboring nations were often left unsettled until after the grain harvest during April and May. Since David did not maintain a large year-round army, it was necessary to summon farmer-soldiers to battle when their crop demands permitted them to go. They would need to return to their fields in time to plant a crop for the fall harvest in September and October.

Didn't David go out to battle any more? (11:1; see 10:7)

Armies have for centuries kept their top generals and leaders safe in the rear ranks or, where short distances were involved, even at home. The Ammonite capital of Rabbah was less than 40 miles from Jerusalem (see *David's Victories* on page 407). David could easily control the battle through reports brought to him from his trusted general Joab. Messengers could be sent out from him to alter strategy if necessary, as recorded in 11:6,14.

ter, will always eat at my table." (Now Ziba had fifteen sons and twenty servants.)

¹¹Then Ziba said to the king, "Your servant will do whatever my lord the king commands his servant to do." So Mephibosheth ate at David's*a* table like one of the king's sons.

¹²Mephibosheth had a young son named Mica, and all the members of Ziba's household were servants of Mephibosheth. ¹³And Mephibosheth lived in Jerusalemᴰ, because he always ate at the king's table, and he was crippled in both feet.

David Defeats the Ammonites

10 In the course of time, the king of the Ammonites died, and his son Hanun succeeded him as king. ²David thought, "I will show kindness to Hanun son of Nahash, just as his father showed kindness to me." So David sent a delegation to express his sympathy to Hanun concerning his father.

When David's men came to the land of the Ammonites, ³the Ammonite nobles said to Hanun their lord, "Do you think David is honoring your father by sending men to you to express sympathy? Hasn't David sent them to you to explore the city and spy it out and overthrow it?" ⁴So Hanun seized David's men, shaved off half of each man's beard, cut off their garments in the middle at the buttocks, and sent them away.

⁵When David was told about this, he sent messengers to meet the men, for they were greatly humiliated. The king said, "Stay at Jerichoᴰ till your beards have grown, and then come back."

⁶When the Ammonites realized that they had become a stench in David's nostrils, they hired twenty thousand Aramean foot soldiers from Beth Rehob and Zobah, as well as the king of Maacah with a thousand men, and also twelve thousand men from Tob.

⁷On hearing this, David sent Joab out with the entire army of fighting men. ⁸The Ammonites came out and drew up in battle formation at the entrance to their city gate, while the Arameans of Zobah and Rehob and the men of Tob and Maacah were by themselves in the open country.

⁹Joab saw that there were battle lines in front of him and behind him; so he selected some of the best troops in Israel and deployed them against the Arameans. ¹⁰He put the rest of the men under the command of Abishai his brother and deployed them against the Ammonites. ¹¹Joab said, "If the Arameans are too strong for me, then you are to come to my rescue; but if the Ammonites are too strong for you, then I will come to rescue you. ¹²Be strong and let us fight bravely for our people and the cities of our God. The LORD will do what is good in his sight."

¹³Then Joab and the troops with him advanced to fight the Arameans, and they fled before him. ¹⁴When the Ammonites saw that the Arameans were fleeing, they fled before Abishai and went inside the city. So Joab returned from fighting the Ammonites and came to Jerusalem.

¹⁵After the Arameans saw that they had been routed by Israel, they regrouped. ¹⁶Hadadezer had Arameans brought from beyond the River*b*; they went to Helam, with Shobach the commander of Hadadezer's army leading them.

a 11 Septuagint; Hebrew my   *b 16 That is, the Euphrates*

17When David was told of this, he gathered all Israel, crossed the Jordan and went to Helam. The Arameans formed their battle lines to meet David and fought against him. **18**But they fled before Israel, and David killed seven hundred of their charioteers and forty thousand of their foot soldiers.*a* He also struck down Shobach the commander of their army, and he died there. **19**When all the kings who were vassals of Hadadezer saw that they had been defeated by Israel, they made peace*D* with the Israelites and became subject to them.

So the Arameans were afraid to help the Ammonites anymore.

David and Bathsheba

11 In the spring, at the time when kings go off to war, David sent Joab out with the king's men and the whole Israelite army. They destroyed the Ammonites and besieged Rabbah. But David remained in Jerusalem*D*.

2One evening David got up from his bed and walked around on the roof of the palace. From the roof he saw a woman bathing. The woman was very beautiful, **3**and David sent someone to find out about her. The man said, "Isn't this Bathsheba, the daughter of Eliam and the wife of Uriah the Hittite?" **4**Then David sent messengers to get her. She came to him, and he slept with her. (She had purified*D* herself from her uncleanness*D*.) Then*b* she went back home. **5**The woman conceived and sent word to David, saying, "I am pregnant."

6So David sent this word to Joab: "Send me Uriah the Hittite." And Joab sent him to David. **7**When Uriah came to him, David asked him how Joab was, how the soldiers were and how the war was going. **8**Then David said to Uriah, "Go down to your house and wash your feet." So Uriah left the palace, and a gift from the king was sent after him. **9**But Uriah slept at the entrance to the palace with all his master's servants and did not go down to his house.

10When David was told, "Uriah did not go home," he asked him, "Haven't you just come from a distance? Why didn't you go home?"

11Uriah said to David, "The ark and Israel and Judah are staying in tents, and my master Joab and my lord's men are camped in the open fields. How could I go to my house to eat and drink and lie with my wife? As surely as you live, I will not do such a thing!"

12Then David said to him, "Stay here one more day, and tomorrow I will send you back." So Uriah remained in Jerusalem that day and the next. **13**At David's invitation, he ate and drank with him, and David made him drunk. But in the evening Uriah went out to sleep on his mat among his master's servants; he did not go home.

14In the morning David wrote a letter to Joab and sent it with Uriah. **15**In it he wrote, "Put Uriah in the front line where the fighting is fiercest. Then withdraw from him so he will be struck down and die."

16So while Joab had the city under siege, he put Uriah at a place where he knew the strongest defenders were. **17**When the men of the city came out and fought against Joab, some of the men in David's army fell; moreover, Uriah the Hittite died.

18Joab sent David a full account of the battle. **19**He in-

---

a18 Some Septuagint manuscripts (see also 1 Chron. 19:18); Hebrew horsemen   b4 Or with her. When she purified herself from her uncleanness,

Why did Bathsheba bathe so openly? (11:2)
This was probably a ritual bath, prescribed by law following menstruation (Lev. 15:19–23). Apparently she thought she would be alone and did not count on observers from the palace roof.

What made David vulnerable to this temptation? (11:2–3)
History shows that many kings have felt themselves above the law since they represent the highest judicial power in the land. Perhaps David felt something of this, but other factors undoubtedly played a part: Perhaps David was in a period of low spiritual vitality since his energies had been engrossed in planning for war. Certainly the temptation developed when he permitted himself to watch Bathsheba bathe.

Was Bathsheba a willing participant? (11:4)
It was common for kings of that day to take whomever they wished for their harem, whether the woman was married or not, though this was against Israelite law. Bathsheba may well have felt obligated to obey the king's summons, which would make this a case of royal rape, not adultery on her part. Some believe she could have protested this act, but the account does not tell what her reaction was.

Why mention Bathsheba's uncleanness? (11:4)
This undoubtedly refers to her menstrual period, showing that she was not pregnant by her husband when David took her.

Why was Uriah—a Hittite—a soldier in the Israelite army? (11:6)
From the time David was a fugitive from King Saul he welcomed society's undesirables into his army (1 Samuel 22:2). Some apparently were foreign mercenary troops (see 15:18). Uriah, known to be one of David's thirty mighty men, seems to have been with David from those early days (23:39). The term *Hittite* in David's time referred to a people who had settled in the area around Hebron before Abraham's arrival (see *Conquest of Canaan* on page 231). But since Uriah's name means "My light is the Lord," it seems likely that his parents were converts to Israel's faith.

Why did Uriah think it such a disgrace to take a break from battle? (11:11)
It was customary in Israel for soldiers to vow to abstain from sexual intercourse while engaged in warfare (1 Samuel 21:5). Rather than expose himself to temptation to break that vow, Uriah chose to stay away from his own home. He could not in good conscience indulge himself and break his vow while his comrades were still facing danger.

Was Joab wrong to obey the king and cause Uriah's death? (11:16)
Joab apparently had no knowledge of any reason why David would want Uriah killed. If he had, he still might have trusted his king to do what was right. In other instances, though, Joab did not hesitate to disobey orders he disapproved of. See *Why didn't Joab follow David's orders?* (18:14). Here Joab probably reasoned that Uriah had done something wrong to incur the king's displeasure.

structed the messenger: "When you have finished giving the king this account of the battle, [20]the king's anger may flare up, and he may ask you, 'Why did you get so close to the city to fight? Didn't you know they would shoot arrows from the wall? [21]Who killed Abimelech son of Jerub-Besheth[a]? Didn't a woman throw an upper millstone[D] on him from the wall, so that he died in Thebez? Why did you get so close to the wall?' If he asks you this, then say to him, 'Also, your servant Uriah the Hittite is dead.'"

[22]The messenger set out, and when he arrived he told David everything Joab had sent him to say. [23]The messenger said to David, "The men overpowered us and came out against us in the open, but we drove them back to the entrance to the city gate. [24]Then the archers shot arrows at your servants from the wall, and some of the king's men died. Moreover, your servant Uriah the Hittite is dead."

[25]David told the messenger, "Say this to Joab: 'Don't let this upset you; the sword devours one as well as another. Press the attack against the city and destroy it.' Say this to encourage Joab."

[26]When Uriah's wife heard that her husband was dead, she mourned for him. [27]After the time of mourning was over, David had her brought to his house, and she became his wife and bore him a son. But the thing David had done displeased the LORD.

Nathan Rebukes David

12 The LORD sent Nathan to David. When he came to him, he said, "There were two men in a certain town, one rich and the other poor. [2]The rich man had a very large number of sheep and cattle, [3]but the poor man had nothing except one little ewe lamb he had bought. He raised it, and it grew up with him and his children. It shared his food, drank from his cup and even slept in his arms. It was like a daughter to him.

[4]"Now a traveler came to the rich man, but the rich man refrained from taking one of his own sheep or cattle to prepare a meal for the traveler who had come to him. Instead, he took the ewe lamb that belonged to the poor man and prepared it for the one who had come to him."

[5]David burned with anger against the man and said to Nathan, "As surely as the LORD lives, the man who did this deserves to die! [6]He must pay for that lamb four times over, because he did such a thing and had no pity."

[7]Then Nathan said to David, "You are the man! This is what the LORD, the God of Israel, says: 'I anointed[D] you king over Israel, and I delivered you from the hand of Saul. [8]I gave your master's house to you, and your master's wives into your arms. I gave you the house of Israel and Judah. And if all this had been too little, I would have given you even more. [9]Why did you despise the word of the LORD by doing what is evil in his eyes? You struck down Uriah the Hittite with the sword and took his wife to be your own. You killed him with the sword of the Ammonites. [10]Now, therefore, the sword will never depart from your house, because you despised me and took the wife of Uriah the Hittite to be your own.'

[11]"This is what the LORD says: 'Out of your own household I am going to bring calamity upon you. Before your very eyes I will take your wives and give them to one who is close to you, and he will lie with your wives in broad

What was Nathan's role in David's court? (12:1)

In ch. 7 he is called Nathan the prophet, and David consulted him about his desire to build a temple for the Lord. As with other prophets in Israel, Nathan was viewed as the ambassador of the Lord, responsible for delivering the word of the Lord wherever he was sent. Although he often encouraged David, here he rebuked the king for his sin.

How many of Saul's wives had David taken to be his own? (12:8)

The only wife of Saul mentioned in Scripture is Ahinoam (1 Samuel 14:50), though a concubine named Rizpah is mentioned in 3:7 and 21:8. There may have been other wives that are not mentioned. The point here is that God had given David all that had been Saul's, yet he still was not satisfied. He stole another man's wife, even committing murder in the process.

Why isn't sin a private matter? (12:9-10)

Our lives affect many others, whether we are conscious of it or not. Nathan told the king that in doing this great sin David had despised the Lord by presuming God would not judge his sin according to his word. David's actions then provided an excuse for the enemies of the Lord, both within and without Israel, to show contempt for God and righteousness. In this way the effects of David's sin reached far beyond David himself.

SCRIPTURE LINK (12:11) He will lie with your wives in broad daylight

See 16:22.

Did God remove David's sin even before he confessed it? (12:13)

No, though it may seem to sound that way, because Nathan declared God's grace the moment David confessed—even before he had made any sin offerings. Notice, however, that forgiveness did not mean David escaped all consequences for his sin.

a21 Also known as Jerub-Baal (that is, Gideon)

daylight. **12**You did it in secret, but I will do this thing in broad daylight before all Israel.' "

13Then David said to Nathan, "I have sinned against the LORD."

Nathan replied, "The LORD has taken away your sin. You are not going to die. **14**But because by doing this you have made the enemies of the LORD show utter contempt,*a* the son born to you will die."

15After Nathan had gone home, the LORD struck the child that Uriah's wife had borne to David, and he became ill. **16**David pleaded with God for the child. He fasted and went into his house and spent the nights lying on the ground. **17**The elders of his household stood beside him to get him up from the ground, but he refused, and he would not eat any food with them.

18On the seventh day the child died. David's servants were afraid to tell him that the child was dead, for they thought, "While the child was still living, we spoke to David but he would not listen to us. How can we tell him the child is dead? He may do something desperate."

19David noticed that his servants were whispering among themselves and he realized the child was dead. "Is the child dead?" he asked.

"Yes," they replied, "he is dead."

20Then David got up from the ground. After he had washed, put on lotions and changed his clothes, he went into the house of the LORD and worshiped. Then he went to his own house, and at his request they served him food, and he ate.

21His servants asked him, "Why are you acting this way? While the child was alive, you fasted and wept, but now that the child is dead, you get up and eat!"

22He answered, "While the child was still alive, I fasted and wept. I thought, 'Who knows? The LORD may be gracious to me and let the child live.' **23**But now that he is dead, why should I fast? Can I bring him back again? I will go to him, but he will not return to me."

24Then David comforted his wife Bathsheba, and he

a 14 Masoretic Text; an ancient Hebrew scribal tradition this you have shown utter contempt for the LORD

If God forgave David, why did his son have to die? (12:14)

We can only speculate about God's mysterious ways. It seems sin often has a price tag in this life, though its eternal consequences have been paid. Some suggest there are two results of sin: (1) It separates a person from God. (2) It produces negative effects in this world. In this view, forgiveness covers the first result of sin but not necessarily the second. And unfortunately for innocent bystanders like David's infant son, the negative effects of sin are not limited to the sinner. See article: *Are the innocent punished for others' sins?* (12:14–15).

Why would the Lord's enemies care about David's sin? (12:14)

People may have raised their eyebrows over David's hasty marriage to the grieving widow. Since a son was born less than nine months later, David's attempt at a cover-up was futile. David's enemies would gloat over news that a godly king had been caught in a sin dishonoring to his God. Though adultery was common among pagans, they could charge that David's religion made him no better than they were. Worse, they could say he was a hypocrite. Also see NIV text note.

What did David mean by saying, *I will go to him?* (12:23)

David may have meant that he would eventually join the child in death. There is good reason, however, for understanding these words in a deeper sense. Though the Old Testament view of life beyond the grave was shadowy and incomplete, still there was hope of a favored condition for the righteous dead (Job 19:25–27) and eternal punishment for the unrighteous (Isaiah 24:21–22). David may have been declaring that he would join his child in a life with God after death.

Are the innocent punished for others' sins? (12:14–15)

The Bible treats both disease and death as universal results of evil. Some infants with AIDS or young victims of drive-by shootings suffer for the sins of others, through no fault of their own. In facing these realities we must remember:

(1) A child's death is not an act of judgment. The child may be spared much agony and pain in this world. Only God, who knows all, can determine whether a death is a tragedy or a blessing.

(2) The loss and pain felt by bereaved parents may be God's instrument to turn their hearts toward him. Sorrow can awaken spiritual insight or cause spiritual growth. This is what seems to have happened to David. His experience refined him and helped him continue more diligently as "a man after God's own heart."

(3) Once we have been forgiven, it is unnecessary self-torture to continue feeling guilty about what our sins have done to others. We should be grateful for forgiveness and seek to minimize the effects of our sin.

Also see article: *Why does God allow innocent children to suffer?* (Lam. 2:11–12).

If God said to name the baby *Jedidiah*, why did they call him *Solomon*? (12:25)

Apparently the baby was given two names, even though only one of them came to be commonly used (just as some today go by their middle name). Jedidiah means *loved by the Lord*. Solomon is a form of the word *shalom*, which means *peace*. Perhaps he was called Jedidiah as a child, but officially adopted the name Solomon upon assuming the throne because God had promised his kingdom would be one of peace (1 Chron. 22:8–9).

went to her and lay with her. She gave birth to a son, and they named him Solomon. The LORD loved him; **25**and because the LORD loved him, he sent word through Nathan the prophet D to name him Jedidiah. *a*

26Meanwhile Joab fought against Rabbah of the Ammonites and captured the royal citadel D. **27**Joab then sent messengers to David, saying, "I have fought against Rabbah and taken its water supply. **28**Now muster the rest of the troops and besiege the city and capture it. Otherwise I will take the city, and it will be named after me."

29So David mustered the entire army and went to Rabbah, and attacked and captured it. **30**He took the crown from the head of their king *b*—its weight was a talent *c* of gold, and it was set with precious stones—and it was placed on David's head. He took a great quantity of plunder D from the city **31**and brought out the people who were there, consigning them to labor with saws and with iron picks and axes, and he made them work at brickmaking. *d* He did this to all the Ammonite towns. Then David and his entire army returned to Jerusalem D.

Amnon and Tamar

13 In the course of time, Amnon son of David fell in love with Tamar, the beautiful sister of Absalom son of David.

2Amnon became frustrated to the point of illness on account of his sister Tamar, for she was a virgin, and it seemed impossible for him to do anything to her.

3Now Amnon had a friend named Jonadab son of Shimeah, David's brother. Jonadab was a very shrewd man. **4**He asked Amnon, "Why do you, the king's son, look so haggard morning after morning? Won't you tell me?"

Amnon said to him, "I'm in love with Tamar, my brother Absalom's sister."

5"Go to bed and pretend to be ill," Jonadab said. "When your father comes to see you, say to him, 'I would like my sister Tamar to come and give me something to eat. Let her prepare the food in my sight so I may watch her and then eat it from her hand.' "

Was it typical to nurse the sick in this way? (13:6)

It's possible, although there is no record of such a custom in Israel. This was a scheme intended to lure Tamar to Amnon's residence under the guise of the king's orders.

6So Amnon lay down and pretended to be ill. When the king came to see him, Amnon said to him, "I would like my sister Tamar to come and make some special bread in my sight, so I may eat from her hand."

7David sent word to Tamar at the palace: "Go to the house of your brother Amnon and prepare some food for him." **8**So Tamar went to the house of her brother Amnon, who was lying down. She took some dough, kneaded it, made the bread in his sight and baked it. **9**Then she took the pan and served him the bread, but he refused to eat.

"Send everyone out of here," Amnon said. So everyone left him. **10**Then Amnon said to Tamar, "Bring the food here into my bedroom so I may eat from your hand." And Tamar took the bread she had prepared and brought it to her brother Amnon in his bedroom. **11**But when she took it to him to eat, he grabbed her and said, "Come to bed with me, my sister."

12"Don't, my brother!" she said to him. "Don't force me. Such a thing should not be done in Israel! Don't do this wicked thing. **13**What about me? Where could I get rid of my disgrace? And what about you? You would be like one

Why would marriage to a man like Amnon have been preferable to rape? (13:13)

Tamar's suggestion seems to be one of desperation, since such a marriage was explicitly prohibited (Lev. 18:11). Perhaps she was buying time, hoping to blunt Amnon's passion for the moment. At any rate, marriage would offer her some degree of social respectability, while rape could only leave her disgraced and personally humiliated.

a25 Jedidiah means loved by the LORD.   *b30 Or of Milcom (that is, Molech)*   *c30 That is, about 75 pounds (about 34 kilograms)*
d31 The meaning of the Hebrew for this clause is uncertain.

of the wicked fools in Israel. Please speak to the king; he will not keep me from being married to you." **14**But he refused to listen to her, and since he was stronger than she, he raped her.

15Then Amnon hated her with intense hatred. In fact, he hated her more than he had loved her. Amnon said to her, "Get up and get out!"

16"No!" she said to him. "Sending me away would be a greater wrong than what you have already done to me."

But he refused to listen to her. **17**He called his personal servant and said, "Get this woman out of here and bolt the door after her." **18**So his servant put her out and bolted the door after her. She was wearing a richly ornamented*a* robe, for this was the kind of garment the virgin daughters of the king wore. **19**Tamar put ashes on her head and tore the ornamented*b* robe she was wearing. She put her hand on her head and went away, weeping aloud as she went.

20Her brother Absalom said to her, "Has that Amnon, your brother, been with you? Be quiet now, my sister; he is your brother. Don't take this thing to heart." And Tamar lived in her brother Absalom's house, a desolate woman.

21When King David heard all this, he was furious. **22**Absalom never said a word to Amnon, either good or bad; he hated Amnon because he had disgraced his sister Tamar.

Absalom Kills Amnon

23Two years later, when Absalom's sheepshearers were at Baal Hazor near the border of Ephraim, he invited all the king's sons to come there. **24**Absalom went to the king and said, "Your servant has had shearers come. Will the king and his officials please join me?"

25"No, my son," the king replied. "All of us should not go; we would only be a burden to you." Although Absalom urged him, he still refused to go, but gave him his blessing.

26Then Absalom said, "If not, please let my brother Amnon come with us."

The king asked him, "Why should he go with you?" **27**But Absalom urged him, so he sent with him Amnon and the rest of the king's sons.

28Absalom ordered his men, "Listen! When Amnon is in high spirits from drinking wine and I say to you, 'Strike Amnon down,' then kill him. Don't be afraid. Have not I given you this order? Be strong and brave." **29**So Absalom's men did to Amnon what Absalom had ordered. Then all the king's sons got up, mounted their mules and fled.

30While they were on their way, the report came to David: "Absalom has struck down all the king's sons; not one of them is left." **31**The king stood up, tore his clothes and lay down on the ground; and all his servants stood by with their clothes torn.

32But Jonadab son of Shimeah, David's brother, said, "My lord should not think that they killed all the princes; only Amnon is dead. This has been Absalom's expressed intention ever since the day Amnon raped his sister Tamar. **33**My lord the king should not be concerned about the report that all the king's sons are dead. Only Amnon is dead."

34Meanwhile, Absalom had fled.

Why did Amnon so quickly hate the one he loved? (13:15)
Such a psychological turnaround clearly proves his so-called "love" was really only lustful passion. Lust sees no objective but its own indulgence.

Why did Tamar want to stay with Amnon? (13:16)
Though Tamar was no longer a virgin, Amnon could spare her some humiliation if he would own up to what he had done to her. By Israelite custom she would be forced to remain unmarried for the rest of her life. She therefore sought to be married to Amnon which, because of his sexual assault, was her right (Deut. 22:28–29).

Where did the custom of ashes and torn clothing come from? (13:19)
These customs date far back in the history of earth's sorrows. Garments represented personalities; to tear them indicated a grievous inner hurt. Ashes spoke of death, since the body returns to dust and ashes at death. Ashes on a person's head meant the individual was grieving as though a death had occurred.

What happened to Tamar? (13:20)
Most likely, she spent her days in virtual widowhood, her chances for an honorable marriage ended. This may seem grossly unfair to us today, but it was in full conformity to social customs of the time. The law required a man who raped a virgin to provide for her as his wife. If her father objected to such a marriage, the rapist still had to pay a bride-price (Exodus 22:16–17). Women, violated and single, usually devoted themselves to social service, often banding together with others like themselves.

If David was furious about what had happened, why didn't he do something? (13:21)
Having recently been exposed in his scandalous behavior with Bathsheba, David may have felt he had no right to rebuke his son. But the ancient Greek translation of the Old Testament (the Septuagint) adds a sentence to this account that suggests another of David's weaknesses: "But he would not hurt Amnon because he was his eldest son and he loved him." This same tendency to fatherly indulgence is seen later in his reaction to Absalom's rebellion.

---

*a*18 The meaning of the Hebrew for this phrase is uncertain.
*b*19 The meaning of the Hebrew for this word is uncertain.

Now the man standing watch looked up and saw many people on the road west of him, coming down the side of the hill. The watchman[D] went and told the king, "I see men in the direction of Horonaim, on the side of the hill."[a]

³⁵Jonadab said to the king, "See, the king's sons are here; it has happened just as your servant said."

³⁶As he finished speaking, the king's sons came in, wailing loudly. The king, too, and all his servants wept very bitterly.

³⁷Absalom fled and went to Talmai son of Ammihud, the king of Geshur. But King David mourned for his son every day.

³⁸After Absalom fled and went to Geshur, he stayed there three years. ³⁹And the spirit of the king[b] longed to go to Absalom, for he was consoled concerning Amnon's death[D].

Absalom Returns to Jerusalem

14 Joab son of Zeruiah knew that the king's heart longed for Absalom. ²So Joab sent someone to Tekoa and had a wise woman brought from there. He said to her, "Pretend you are in mourning. Dress in mourning clothes, and don't use any cosmetic lotions. Act like a woman who has spent many days grieving for the dead. ³Then go to the king and speak these words to him." And Joab put the words in her mouth.

⁴When the woman from Tekoa went[c] to the king, she fell with her face to the ground to pay him honor, and she said, "Help me, O king!"

⁵The king asked her, "What is troubling you?"

She said, "I am indeed a widow; my husband is dead. ⁶I your servant had two sons. They got into a fight with each other in the field, and no one was there to separate them. One struck the other and killed him. ⁷Now the whole clan has risen up against your servant; they say, 'Hand over the one who struck his brother down, so that we may put him to death for the life of his brother whom he killed; then we will get rid of the heir as well.' They would put out the only burning coal I have left, leaving my husband neither name nor descendant on the face of the earth."

⁸The king said to the woman, "Go home, and I will issue an order in your behalf."

⁹But the woman from Tekoa said to him, "My lord the king, let the blame rest on me and on my father's family, and let the king and his throne be without guilt."

¹⁰The king replied, "If anyone says anything to you, bring him to me, and he will not bother you again."

¹¹She said, "Then let the king invoke the LORD his God to prevent the avenger of blood from adding to the destruction, so that my son will not be destroyed."

"As surely as the LORD lives," he said, "not one hair of your son's head will fall to the ground."

¹²Then the woman said, "Let your servant speak a word to my lord the king."

"Speak," he replied.

¹³The woman said, "Why then have you devised a thing like this against the people of God? When the king says this, does he not convict himself, for the king has not

Why didn't David go to Absalom? (13:39)

Two factors may have deterred him from fulfilling his desire to see Absalom: (1) He perhaps realized that justice demanded punishment of some kind for Absalom. David, however, didn't want to punish Absalom and preferred to sidestep the issue. (2) Or perhaps, because Amnon's death put Absalom first in line for the throne, David felt it best to keep Absalom out of public view for awhile until the people would forget his cruelty toward his brother.

Why did Joab go to such great lengths to make his case? (14:2–3)

Since both Nathan the prophet (12:1–4) and Joab, David's general, approached the king in an indirect manner, it may indicate that David's mind could not be changed except by catching him off guard. They helped him gain a truer perspective by using a roundabout approach. Apparently Joab had discussed this matter with the king before, but found him determined to keep Absalom banished. This storytelling technique was common during these times.

Avenger of blood (14:11)

See *Avenger of blood* (Num. 35:19) and *What did an avenger of blood do?* (Joshua 20:3).

---

*a*34 Septuagint; Hebrew does not have this sentence.   *b*39 Dead Sea Scrolls and some Septuagint manuscripts; Masoretic Text *But the spirit of David the king*   *c*4 Many Hebrew manuscripts, Septuagint, Vulgate and Syriac; most Hebrew manuscripts *spoke*

brought back his banished son? **14**Like water spilled on the ground, which cannot be recovered, so we must die. But God does not take away life; instead, he devises ways so that a banished person may not remain estranged from him.

15"And now I have come to say this to my lord the king because the people have made me afraid. Your servant thought, 'I will speak to the king; perhaps he will do what his servant asks. **16**Perhaps the king will agree to deliver his servant from the hand of the man who is trying to cut off both me and my son from the inheritance God gave us.'

17"And now your servant says, 'May the word of my lord the king bring me rest, for my lord the king is like an angel of God in discerning good and evil. May the LORD your God be with you.'"

18Then the king said to the woman, "Do not keep from me the answer to what I am going to ask you."

"Let my lord the king speak," the woman said.

19The king asked, "Isn't the hand of Joab with you in all this?"

The woman answered, "As surely as you live, my lord the king, no one can turn to the right or to the left from anything my lord the king says. Yes, it was your servant Joab who instructed me to do this and who put all these words into the mouth of your servant. **20**Your servant Joab did this to change the present situation. My lord has wisdom like that of an angel of God—he knows everything that happens in the land."

21The king said to Joab, "Very well, I will do it. Go, bring back the young man Absalom."

22Joab fell with his face to the ground to pay him honor, and he blessed the king. Joab said, "Today your servant knows that he has found favor in your eyes, my lord the king, because the king has granted his servant's request."

23Then Joab went to Geshur and brought Absalom back to Jerusalem.[D] **24**But the king said, "He must go to his own house; he must not see my face." So Absalom went to his own house and did not see the face of the king.

25In all Israel there was not a man so highly praised for his handsome appearance as Absalom. From the top of his head to the sole of his foot there was no blemish in him. **26**Whenever he cut the hair of his head—he used to cut his hair from time to time when it became too heavy for him—he would weigh it, and its weight was two hundred shekels[Da] by the royal standard.

27Three sons and a daughter were born to Absalom. The daughter's name was Tamar, and she became a beautiful woman.

28Absalom lived two years in Jerusalem without seeing the king's face. **29**Then Absalom sent for Joab in order to send him to the king, but Joab refused to come to him. So he sent a second time, but he refused to come. **30**Then he said to his servants, "Look, Joab's field is next to mine, and he has barley there. Go and set it on fire." So Absalom's servants set the field on fire.

31Then Joab did go to Absalom's house and he said to him, "Why have your servants set my field on fire?"

32Absalom said to Joab, "Look, I sent word to you and said, 'Come here so I can send you to the king to ask, "Why have I come from Geshur? It would be better for me if I were still there!"' Now then, I want to see the king's

Why was Joab so intent to see Absalom regain the king's favor? (14:22)
There may have been several things that motivated Joab. Perhaps he wanted to do a favor for David who, though thinking he was doing the right thing to have exiled Absalom, had personal feelings for him (v. 1). More likely, Joab was concerned about the political future of the kingdom and with it his own career. As the eldest living son, Absalom would be the heir to David's throne. But as long as Absalom remained out of his father's favor, the potential for battles and political instability increased. Joab may have felt stability in the kingdom could be ensured if Absalom would be returned to Jerusalem and designated crown prince.

Why did David continue to spurn Absalom, refusing to see his face? (14:24)
David apparently wanted to maintain some form of banishment even though he had relented enough to let him return to Jerusalem.

Why did Joab refuse to talk to Absalom? (14:29)
Since David had not reconciled with his son, Joab may have felt that Absalom was *persona non grata*—someone unacceptable to associate with. Or perhaps he felt that he had already done enough for Absalom and did not want to be inconvenienced any further. Or it may be that Joab, before responding, was waiting for an apology or sign of remorse from Absalom for murdering his brother.

---

a26 That is, about 5 pounds (about 2.3 kilograms)

face, and if I am guilty of anything, let him put me to death[D]."

33So Joab went to the king and told him this. Then the king summoned Absalom, and he came in and bowed down with his face to the ground before the king. And the king kissed Absalom.

Absalom's Conspiracy

15 In the course of time, Absalom provided himself with a chariot and horses and with fifty men to run ahead of him. 2He would get up early and stand by the side of the road leading to the city gate. Whenever anyone came with a complaint to be placed before the king for a decision, Absalom would call out to him, "What town are you from?" He would answer, "Your servant is from one of the tribes of Israel." 3Then Absalom would say to him, "Look, your claims are valid and proper, but there is no representative of the king to hear you." 4And Absalom would add, "If only I were appointed judge in the land! Then everyone who has a complaint or case could come to me and I would see that he gets justice."

5Also, whenever anyone approached him to bow down before him, Absalom would reach out his hand, take hold of him and kiss him. 6Absalom behaved in this way toward all the Israelites who came to the king asking for justice, and so he stole the hearts of the men of Israel.

7At the end of four[a] years, Absalom said to the king, "Let me go to Hebron and fulfill a vow[D] I made to the LORD. 8While your servant was living at Geshur in Aram, I made this vow: 'If the LORD takes me back to Jerusalem[D], I will worship the LORD in Hebron.[b]' "

9The king said to him, "Go in peace[D]." So he went to Hebron.

10Then Absalom sent secret messengers throughout the tribes of Israel to say, "As soon as you hear the sound of the trumpets, then say, 'Absalom is king in Hebron.' " 11Two hundred men from Jerusalem had accompanied Absalom. They had been invited as guests and went quite innocently, knowing nothing about the matter. 12While Absalom was offering sacrifices[D], he also sent for Ahithophel the Gilonite, David's counselor, to come from Giloh, his hometown. And so the conspiracy gained strength, and Absalom's following kept on increasing.

David Flees

13A messenger came and told David, "The hearts of the men of Israel are with Absalom."

14Then David said to all his officials who were with him in Jerusalem, "Come! We must flee, or none of us will escape from Absalom. We must leave immediately, or he will move quickly to overtake us and bring ruin upon us and put the city to the sword."

15The king's officials answered him, "Your servants are ready to do whatever our lord the king chooses."

16The king set out, with his entire household following him; but he left ten concubines[D] to take care of the palace. 17So the king set out, with all the people following him, and they halted at a place some distance away. 18All his men marched past him, along with all the Kerethites and Pelethites; and all the six hundred Gittites who had accompanied him from Gath marched before the king.

Why didn't David do something about Absalom's open affront to his authority? (15:2–6)
With a fatherly indulgence, David may have viewed Absalom's activities as appropriate for an heir to the throne. He may not have taken seriously the rebellious faction Absalom gradually was gathering about himself. The account may also indicate some shortcomings in David's court system, which Absalom was able to exploit.

Absalom's Conspiracy (15:6)

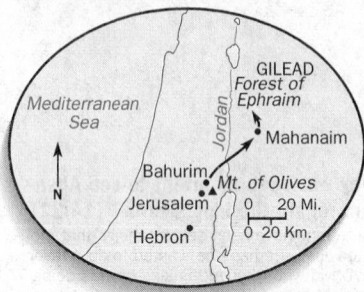

Was it permissible to worship somewhere other than Jerusalem? (15:8)
The feasts and offerings prescribed by the law could be performed only in Jerusalem, but Absalom's sacrifice was to fulfill a vow he allegedly had made while in exile. Since Absalom had been born in Hebron, he may have used that as a reasonable excuse to explain why he wanted to go there.

Why did Absalom pick Hebron? (15:8)
Since it was also the city where David had been made king, Absalom may have felt it was the ideal place for him to begin his coup. Some think Absalom hoped to gain support by capitalizing on resentment that may have existed among the people of Hebron because David had moved his capital to Jerusalem.

---

a7 Some Septuagint manuscripts, Syriac and Josephus; Hebrew *forty*
b8 Some Septuagint manuscripts; Hebrew does not have *in Hebron*.

19The king said to Ittai the Gittite, "Why should you come along with us? Go back and stay with King Absalom. You are a foreigner, an exile[D] from your homeland. **20**You came only yesterday. And today shall I make you wander about with us, when I do not know where I am going? Go back, and take your countrymen. May kindness and faithfulness be with you."

21But Ittai replied to the king, "As surely as the LORD lives, and as my lord the king lives, wherever my lord the king may be, whether it means life or death[D], there will your servant be."

22David said to Ittai, "Go ahead, march on." So Ittai the Gittite marched on with all his men and the families that were with him.

23The whole countryside wept aloud as all the people passed by. The king also crossed the Kidron Valley[D], and all the people moved on toward the desert.

24Zadok was there, too, and all the Levites[D] who were with him were carrying the ark of the covenant[D] of God. They set down the ark of God, and Abiathar offered sacrifices[Da] until all the people had finished leaving the city. **25**Then the king said to Zadok, "Take the ark of God back into the city. If I find favor in the LORD's eyes, he will bring me back and let me see it and his dwelling place again. **26**But if he says, 'I am not pleased with you,' then I am ready; let him do to me whatever seems good to him."

27The king also said to Zadok the priest[D], "Aren't you a seer[D]? Go back to the city in peace[D], with your son Ahimaaz and Jonathan son of Abiathar. You and Abiathar take your two sons with you. **28**I will wait at the fords in the desert until word comes from you to inform me." **29**So Zadok and Abiathar took the ark of God back to Jerusalem[D] and stayed there.

30But David continued up the Mount of Olives, weeping as he went; his head was covered and he was barefoot. All the people with him covered their heads too and were weeping as they went up. **31**Now David had been told, "Ahithophel is among the conspirators with Absalom." So David prayed, "O LORD, turn Ahithophel's counsel into foolishness."

32When David arrived at the summit, where people used to worship God, Hushai the Arkite was there to meet him, his robe torn and dust on his head. **33**David said to him, "If you go with me, you will be a burden to me. **34**But if you return to the city and say to Absalom, 'I will be your servant, O king; I was your father's servant in the past, but now I will be your servant,' then you can help me by frustrating Ahithophel's advice. **35**Won't the priests Zadok and Abiathar be there with you? Tell them anything you hear in the king's palace. **36**Their two sons, Ahimaaz son of Zadok and Jonathan son of Abiathar, are there with them. Send them to me with anything you hear."

37So David's friend Hushai arrived at Jerusalem as Absalom was entering the city.

David and Ziba

16 When David had gone a short distance beyond the summit, there was Ziba, the steward of Mephibosheth, waiting to meet him. He had a string of donkeys saddled and loaded with two hundred loaves of bread, a

Why did David call his son *King* Absalom? (15:19)

It must have appeared to David that Absalom had successfully replaced him as king. He'd been told that the hearts of Israel were with Absalom (v. 13). The city of Hebron had acknowledged Absalom's revolt, and it looked as though 200 citizens of Jerusalem itself had joined him (v. 11). Though David was not giving up his kingdom, he surrendered Jerusalem for the time being. The net result was that Absalom would publicly be acclaimed as king in Judah. David admitted that fact by calling him "king."

Why was covering the head a sign of sorrow? (15:30)

In Israel the uncovered head was a sign of man's honor, pride and freedom before God (see 1 Cor. 11:7). To cover the head, therefore, indicated a loss of freedom—a condition of extreme humiliation. David and his company probably pulled part of their outer garments up over their heads to express their loss and shame. Also see *Head covered in grief* (Esther 6:12).

hundred cakes of raisins, a hundred cakes of figs and a skin of wine.

²The king asked Ziba, "Why have you brought these?"

Ziba answered, "The donkeys are for the king's household to ride on, the bread and fruit are for the men to eat, and the wine is to refresh those who become exhausted in the desert."

³The king then asked, "Where is your master's grandson?"

Ziba said to him, "He is staying in Jerusalem^D, because he thinks, 'Today the house of Israel will give me back my grandfather's kingdom.' "

⁴Then the king said to Ziba, "All that belonged to Mephibosheth is now yours."

"I humbly bow," Ziba said. "May I find favor in your eyes, my lord the king."

Shimei Curses David

⁵As King David approached Bahurim, a man from the same clan as Saul's family came out from there. His name was Shimei son of Gera, and he cursed as he came out. ⁶He pelted David and all the king's officials with stones, though all the troops and the special guard were on David's right and left. ⁷As he cursed, Shimei said, "Get out, get out, you man of blood, you scoundrel! ⁸The LORD has repaid you for all the blood you shed in the household of Saul, in whose place you have reigned. The LORD has handed the kingdom over to your son Absalom. You have come to ruin because you are a man of blood!"

⁹Then Abishai son of Zeruiah said to the king, "Why should this dead dog curse my lord the king? Let me go over and cut off his head."

¹⁰But the king said, "What do you and I have in common, you sons of Zeruiah? If he is cursing because the LORD said to him, 'Curse David,' who can ask, 'Why do you do this?' "

¹¹David then said to Abishai and all his officials, "My son, who is of my own flesh, is trying to take my life. How much more, then, this Benjamite! Leave him alone; let him curse, for the LORD has told him to. ¹²It may be that the LORD will see my distress and repay me with good for the cursing I am receiving today."

¹³So David and his men continued along the road while Shimei was going along the hillside opposite him, cursing as he went and throwing stones at him and showering him with dirt. ¹⁴The king and all the people with him arrived at their destination exhausted. And there he refreshed himself.

The Advice of Hushai and Ahithophel

¹⁵Meanwhile, Absalom and all the men of Israel came to Jerusalem, and Ahithophel was with him. ¹⁶Then Hushai the Arkite, David's friend, went to Absalom and said to him, "Long live the king! Long live the king!"

¹⁷Absalom asked Hushai, "Is this the love you show your friend? Why didn't you go with your friend?"

¹⁸Hushai said to Absalom, "No, the one chosen by the LORD, by these people, and by all the men of Israel—his I will be, and I will remain with him. ¹⁹Furthermore, whom should I serve? Should I not serve the son? Just as I served your father, so I will serve you."

²⁰Absalom said to Ahithophel, "Give us your advice. What should we do?"

²¹Ahithophel answered, "Lie with your father's concu-

Why did David go back on his earlier vows to Mephibosheth? (16:4)

Though David had promised Jonathan's son Mephibosheth royal protection and provision (9:7), he now believed Ziba's story—that Mephibosheth hoped the current political upheaval would help him regain at least part of his grandfather Saul's kingdom. Since David now considered Mephibosheth a traitor, he did not hesitate to assign all of Mephibosheth's property to Ziba. Ziba, however, was acting in his own interests, and this judgment was later revised (19:29).

Why did David think Shimei's curses may have come from God? (16:10-11)

David recognized the armed rebellion in his own family as the consequence for his own actions, part of God's punishment for his sin against Uriah and Bathsheba (see 12:10). He saw affliction as God's means to keep him humble. So he accepted Shimei's curses as coming from the Lord.

binesᴰ whom he left to take care of the palace. Then all Israel will hear that you have made yourself a stench in your father's nostrils, and the hands of everyone with you will be strengthened." **22**So they pitched a tent for Absalom on the roof, and he lay with his father's concubines in the sight of all Israel.

23Now in those days the advice Ahithophel gave was like that of one who inquires of God. That was how both David and Absalom regarded all of Ahithophel's advice.

17 Ahithophel said to Absalom, "I wouldᵃ choose twelve thousand men and set out tonight in pursuit of David. **2**I wouldᵇ attack him while he is weary and weak. I wouldᵇ strike him with terror, and then all the people with him will flee. I wouldᵇ strike down only the king **3**and bring all the people back to you. The deathᴰ of the man you seek will mean the return of all; all the people will be unharmed." **4**This plan seemed good to Absalom and to all the elders of Israel.

5But Absalom said, "Summon also Hushai the Arkite, so we can hear what he has to say." **6**When Hushai came to him, Absalom said, "Ahithophel has given this advice. Should we do what he says? If not, give us your opinion."

7Hushai replied to Absalom, "The advice Ahithophel has given is not good this time. **8**You know your father and his men; they are fighters, and as fierce as a wild bear robbed of her cubs. Besides, your father is an experienced fighter; he will not spend the night with the troops. **9**Even now, he is hidden in a cave or some other place. If he should attack your troops first,ᶜ whoever hears about it will say, 'There has been a slaughter among the troops who follow Absalom.' **10**Then even the bravest soldier, whose heart is like the heart of a lion, will melt with fear, for all Israel knows that your father is a fighter and that those with him are brave.

11"So I advise you: Let all Israel, from Dan to Beersheba—as numerous as the sand on the seashore—be gathered to you, with you yourself leading them into battle. **12**Then we will attack him wherever he may be found, and we will fall on him as dew settles on the ground. Neither he nor any of his men will be left alive. **13**If he withdraws into a city, then all Israel will bring ropes to that city, and we will drag it down to the valley until not even a piece of it can be found."

14Absalom and all the men of Israel said, "The advice of Hushai the Arkite is better than that of Ahithophel." For the LORD had determined to frustrate the good advice of Ahithophel in order to bring disaster on Absalom.

15Hushai told Zadok and Abiathar, the priestsᴰ, "Ahithophel has advised Absalom and the elders of Israel to do such and such, but I have advised them to do so and so. **16**Now send a message immediately and tell David, 'Do not spend the night at the fords in the desert; cross over without fail, or the king and all the people with him will be swallowed up.'"

17Jonathan and Ahimaaz were staying at En Rogel. A servant girl was to go and inform them, and they were to go and tell King David, for they could not risk being seen entering the city. **18**But a young man saw them and told Absalom. So the two of them left quickly and went to the house of a man in Bahurim. He had a well in his courtyard, and they climbed down into it. **19**His wife took a cov-

Why did Absalom sleep with his father's concubines? (16:22)
To demonstrate his power and to try to establish himself as king. Taking over the king's harem indicated to the people that Absalom was taking over the kingship. And it was a bold move, disgracing and challenging his father, David.

SCRIPTURE LINK (17:14)
Absalom's actions were part of God's plans to judge David for his sin. See 12:10–12.

Why bring disaster to someone who was God's instrument of judgment? (17:14; see 12:10–12)
Though Absalom was guilty of wrongdoing, his selfish and sinful agenda was used by God for his divine purposes. Absalom paid for his rebellion and could not be absolved of guilt because he unknowingly had contributed to God's plan.

ᵃ1 Or *Let me*   ᵇ2 Or *will*   ᶜ9 Or *When some of the men fall at the first attack*

ering and spread it out over the opening of the well and scattered grain over it. No one knew anything about it.

20When Absalom's men came to the woman at the house, they asked, "Where are Ahimaaz and Jonathan?"

The woman answered them, "They crossed over the brook."[a] The men searched but found no one, so they returned to Jerusalem[b].

21After the men had gone, the two climbed out of the well and went to inform King David. They said to him, "Set out and cross the river at once; Ahithophel has advised such and such against you." **22**So David and all the people with him set out and crossed the Jordan. By daybreak, no one was left who had not crossed the Jordan.

23When Ahithophel saw that his advice had not been followed, he saddled his donkey and set out for his house in his hometown. He put his house in order and then hanged himself. So he died and was buried in his father's tomb.

24David went to Mahanaim, and Absalom crossed the Jordan with all the men of Israel. **25**Absalom had appointed Amasa over the army in place of Joab. Amasa was the son of a man named Jether,[b] an Israelite[c] who had married Abigail,[d] the daughter of Nahash and sister of Zeruiah the mother of Joab. **26**The Israelites and Absalom camped in the land of Gilead.

27When David came to Mahanaim, Shobi son of Nahash from Rabbah of the Ammonites, and Makir son of Ammiel from Lo Debar, and Barzillai the Gileadite from Rogelim **28**brought bedding and bowls and articles of pottery. They also brought wheat and barley, flour and roasted grain, beans and lentils,[e] **29**honey and curds, sheep, and cheese from cows' milk for David and his people to eat. For they said, "The people have become hungry and tired and thirsty in the desert."

Absalom's Death

18 David mustered the men who were with him and appointed over them commanders of thousands and commanders of hundreds. **2**David sent the troops out—a third under the command of Joab, a third under Joab's brother Abishai son of Zeruiah, and a third under Ittai the Gittite. The king told the troops, "I myself will surely march out with you."

3But the men said, "You must not go out; if we are forced to flee, they won't care about us. Even if half of us die, they won't care; but you are worth ten thousand of us.[f] It would be better now for you to give us support from the city."

4The king answered, "I will do whatever seems best to you."

So the king stood beside the gate while all the men marched out in units of hundreds and of thousands. **5**The king commanded Joab, Abishai and Ittai, "Be gentle with the young man Absalom for my sake." And all the troops heard the king giving orders concerning Absalom to each of the commanders.

Why did Ahithophel hang himself? (17:23)

Perhaps he was bitter because his advice was not followed. More likely he had a hunch that Absalom's revolt would fail. In that case Ahithophel knew he'd be found guilty of treason and decided to avoid execution by killing himself.

Is suicide common in the Bible? (17:23)

Ahithophel is one of five persons mentioned in the Bible who committed suicide: King Saul and his armor-bearer, who both fell on their own swords (1 Samuel 31:4–5); King Zimri, who set his own house on fire (1 Kings 16:18) and Judas, the betrayer of Jesus, who hanged himself (Matt. 27:5). Some say Samson committed suicide; others say his death was equivalent to death in battle (Judges 16:29–30). The Bible does not indicate that suicide is more acceptable than any other murder.

Why was David worth as much as 10,000 soldiers? (18:3)

If David were captured or killed it would mean the end of David's reign and the total loss of his cause. However, if Absalom captured or destroyed even half of David's army, it would not necessarily affect the ultimate outcome of the struggle.

6The army marched into the field to fight Israel, and the battle took place in the forest of Ephraim. **7**There the army of Israel was defeated by David's men, and the casualties that day were great—twenty thousand men. **8**The battle spread out over the whole countryside, and the forest claimed more lives that day than the sword.

9Now Absalom happened to meet David's men. He was riding his mule, and as the mule went under the thick branches of a large oak, Absalom's head got caught in the tree. He was left hanging in midair, while the mule he was riding kept on going.

10When one of the men saw this, he told Joab, "I just saw Absalom hanging in an oak tree."

11Joab said to the man who had told him this, "What! You saw him? Why didn't you strike him to the ground right there? Then I would have had to give you ten shekels^Da of silver and a warrior's belt."

12But the man replied, "Even if a thousand shekels^b were weighed out into my hands, I would not lift my hand against the king's son. In our hearing the king commanded you and Abishai and Ittai, 'Protect the young man Absalom for my sake.^c ' **13**And if I had put my life in jeopardy^d—and nothing is hidden from the king—you would have kept your distance from me."

14Joab said, "I'm not going to wait like this for you." So he took three javelins in his hand and plunged them into Absalom's heart while Absalom was still alive in the oak tree. **15**And ten of Joab's armor-bearers surrounded Absalom, struck him and killed him.

16Then Joab sounded the trumpet, and the troops stopped pursuing Israel, for Joab halted them. **17**They took Absalom, threw him into a big pit in the forest and piled up a large heap of rocks over him. Meanwhile, all the Israelites fled to their homes.

18During his lifetime Absalom had taken a pillar and erected it in the King's Valley as a monument to himself, for he thought, "I have no son to carry on the memory of my name." He named the pillar after himself, and it is called Absalom's Monument to this day.

David Mourns

19Now Ahimaaz son of Zadok said, "Let me run and take the news to the king that the LORD has delivered him from the hand of his enemies."

20"You are not the one to take the news today," Joab told him. "You may take the news another time, but you must not do so today, because the king's son is dead."

21Then Joab said to a Cushite, "Go, tell the king what you have seen." The Cushite bowed down before Joab and ran off.

22Ahimaaz son of Zadok again said to Joab, "Come what may, please let me run behind the Cushite."

But Joab replied, "My son, why do you want to go? You don't have any news that will bring you a reward."

23He said, "Come what may, I want to run."

So Joab said, "Run!" Then Ahimaaz ran by way of the plain^e and outran the Cushite.

How did more men die because of the forest than because of the sword? (18:8)

It is difficult to know just what is meant by this. Besides the dense brush and trees, the soldiers had to contend with rough terrain and large pits (v. 17), perhaps ravines or gullies. Most likely, as individual soldiers became separated from their units during the battle, they tried to escape through the forest and were injured in falls. Others may have been slowed enough that their pursuers finished them off (vv. 9,14).

Why didn't Joab follow David's orders? (18:14)

As David's general, Joab had the interests of the kingdom at heart. David, on the other hand, with a father's love for his son, was more concerned about Absalom. Joab saw Absalom as a dangerous rebel who would continue to threaten the kingdom as long as he lived. David saw Absalom as a reckless young man who had made a foolish mistake. David hoped his son would change as he grew and matured. Joab's single-minded determination to preserve David's throne led him to disobey direct orders.

Didn't Absalom have sons? (18:18)

Absalom had three sons as well as a daughter (14:27), but his sons apparently died as children or even infants.

Why not let Ahimaaz take the news to David? (18:19–20; see 18:27)

Perhaps Joab remembered how David had reacted when an Amalekite brought news of the death of King Saul (1:1–15). Since Ahimaaz was Zadok the priest's son and a close supporter of King David, it may have seemed inappropriate to Joab for Ahimaaz to carry the bad news to the king about Absalom's death. Instead, Joab chose a Cushite, a native of upper Egypt (now known as Ethiopia), to bear the news to the king.

---

^a11 That is, about 4 ounces (about 115 grams)   ^b12 That is, about 25 pounds (about 11 kilograms)   ^c12 A few Hebrew manuscripts, Septuagint, Vulgate and Syriac; most Hebrew manuscripts may be translated *Absalom, whoever you may be.*   ^d13 Or *Otherwise, if I had acted treacherously toward him*   ^e23 That is, the plain of the Jordan

24While David was sitting between the inner and outer gates, the watchman^D went up to the roof of the gateway by the wall. As he looked out, he saw a man running alone. **25**The watchman called out to the king and reported it.

The king said, "If he is alone, he must have good news." And the man came closer and closer.

26Then the watchman saw another man running, and he called down to the gatekeeper, "Look, another man running alone!"

The king said, "He must be bringing good news, too."

27The watchman said, "It seems to me that the first one runs like Ahimaaz son of Zadok."

"He's a good man," the king said. "He comes with good news."

28Then Ahimaaz called out to the king, "All is well!" He bowed down before the king with his face to the ground and said, "Praise be to the Lord your God! He has delivered up the men who lifted their hands against my lord the king."

29The king asked, "Is the young man Absalom safe?"

Ahimaaz answered, "I saw great confusion just as Joab was about to send the king's servant and me, your servant, but I don't know what it was."

30The king said, "Stand aside and wait here." So he stepped aside and stood there.

31Then the Cushite arrived and said, "My lord the king, hear the good news! The Lord has delivered you today from all who rose up against you."

32The king asked the Cushite, "Is the young man Absalom safe?"

The Cushite replied, "May the enemies of my lord the king and all who rise up to harm you be like that young man."

33The king was shaken. He went up to the room over the gateway and wept. As he went, he said: "O my son Absalom! My son, my son Absalom! If only I had died instead of you—O Absalom, my son, my son!"

19 Joab was told, "The king is weeping and mourning for Absalom." **2**And for the whole army the victory that day was turned into mourning, because on that day the troops heard it said, "The king is grieving for his son." **3**The men stole into the city that day as men steal in who are ashamed when they flee from battle. **4**The king covered his face and cried aloud, "O my son Absalom! O Absalom, my son, my son!"

5Then Joab went into the house to the king and said, "Today you have humiliated all your men, who have just saved your life and the lives of your sons and daughters and the lives of your wives and concubines^D. **6**You love those who hate you and hate those who love you. You have made it clear today that the commanders and their men mean nothing to you. I see that you would be pleased if Absalom were alive today and all of us were dead. **7**Now go out and encourage your men. I swear by the Lord that if you don't go out, not a man will be left with you by nightfall. This will be worse for you than all the calamities that have come upon you from your youth till now."

8So the king got up and took his seat in the gateway. When the men were told, "The king is sitting in the gateway," they all came before him.

Why did Ahimaaz evade David's question? (18:29)

Some messengers in ancient times were killed after delivering bad news. Ahimaaz preferred to tell only the good news, perhaps out of a sense of self-preservation. Since Ahimaaz knew the Cushite would tell the king about Absalom's death, he may have simply wanted to be sure David heard about the victory before he heard about his son.

Why was David so anguished for a son he had avoided for years? (18:33)

All along David had a tender heart toward his sons, perhaps too tender. Even though he saw their misbehavior and was angered by their actions, doubtless he also felt a sense of guilt, knowing from Nathan's prophecy that his own sin had exposed his family to great danger. His wish that he had died in Absalom's place expressed both his guilt and his sorrow.

David Returns to Jerusalem

Meanwhile, the Israelites had fled to their homes. [9]Throughout the tribes of Israel, the people were all arguing with each other, saying, "The king delivered us from the hand of our enemies; he is the one who rescued us from the hand of the Philistines. But now he has fled the country because of Absalom; [10]and Absalom, whom we anointed[D] to rule over us, has died in battle. So why do you say nothing about bringing the king back?"

[11]King David sent this message to Zadok and Abiathar, the priests[D]: "Ask the elders of Judah, 'Why should you be the last to bring the king back to his palace, since what is being said throughout Israel has reached the king at his quarters? [12]You are my brothers, my own flesh and blood. So why should you be the last to bring back the king?' [13]And say to Amasa, 'Are you not my own flesh and blood? May God deal with me, be it ever so severely, if from now on you are not the commander of my army in place of Joab.' "

[14]He won over the hearts of all the men of Judah as though they were one man. They sent word to the king, "Return, you and all your men." [15]Then the king returned and went as far as the Jordan.

Now the men of Judah had come to Gilgal to go out and meet the king and bring him across the Jordan. [16]Shimei son of Gera, the Benjamite from Bahurim, hurried down with the men of Judah to meet King David. [17]With him were a thousand Benjamites, along with Ziba, the steward of Saul's household, and his fifteen sons and twenty servants. They rushed to the Jordan, where the king was. [18]They crossed at the ford to take the king's household over and to do whatever he wished.

When Shimei son of Gera crossed the Jordan, he fell prostrate before the king [19]and said to him, "May my lord not hold me guilty. Do not remember how your servant did wrong on the day my lord the king left Jerusalem[D]. May the king put it out of his mind. [20]For I your servant know that I have sinned, but today I have come here as the first of the whole house of Joseph to come down and meet my lord the king."

[21]Then Abishai son of Zeruiah said, "Shouldn't Shimei be put to death[D] for this? He cursed the LORD's anointed."

[22]David replied, "What do you and I have in common, you sons of Zeruiah? This day you have become my adversaries! Should anyone be put to death in Israel today? Do I not know that today I am king over Israel?" [23]So the king said to Shimei, "You shall not die." And the king promised him on oath.

[24]Mephibosheth, Saul's grandson, also went down to meet the king. He had not taken care of his feet or trimmed his mustache or washed his clothes from the day the king left until the day he returned safely. [25]When he came from Jerusalem to meet the king, the king asked him, "Why didn't you go with me, Mephibosheth?"

[26]He said, "My lord the king, since I your servant am lame, I said, 'I will have my donkey saddled and will ride on it, so I can go with the king.' But Ziba my servant betrayed me. [27]And he has slandered your servant to my lord the king. My lord the king is like an angel of God; so do whatever pleases you. [28]All my grandfather's descendants deserved nothing but death from my lord the king, but you gave your servant a place among those who

Why did David demote Joab and recruit the rebel commander? (19:13)
Two factors may lie behind this action: (1) Though David never suggested that he knew Joab killed Absalom, he probably suspected it and was angry at Joab for disobeying his direct order. (2) Appointing Amasa was an attempt to win over those he'd led—the Judeans who had followed Absalom. In this way he hoped to prevent a threatened division between the northern tribes and the southern tribes of Judah and Benjamin.

Why did David have to wait for an invitation? (19:14)
Because the rebellion had begun in Hebron, a chief city of Judah and the place where David himself had been crowned king, it was necessary for David to learn if the Judeans would receive him back as king.

Why did David call a stalwart supporter an adversary? (19:22)
David had already been through this with Abishai once before. See *Why did David think Shimei's curses may have come from God?* (16:10–11). David viewed Abishai as a hothead who could upset the balance of peace and create trouble for David. If Shimei (or, for that matter, any of the Benjamites) were treated harshly, his entire tribe could revolt, leaving David with a fractured kingdom. David called the sons of Zeruiah (that is, Abishai and Joab) adversaries in the sense that their vengeful attitude clashed directly with David's pressing need to repair the rift in his kingdom. Their earlier murder of Abner had caused a political nightmare for David (see 3:30–37). Also see 20:8–10.

Why hadn't Mephibosheth taken care of his personal hygiene? (19:24)
This was a tangible way for him to express his continuing loyalty to David. His physical handicap prevented Mephibosheth from fleeing Jerusalem with David, but his unkempt appearance demonstrated his anguish over the recent events—expressing his support for David.

How did David know whose story was the truth? (19:26–27; see 16:3)
With few clues to go on, the issue had to be decided by the general character of the two men. On the whole, Mephibosheth's loyalty to David seemed real and long-lasting, while Ziba appeared to be an opportunist. It is apparent, however, that David had doubts about both of them. He resolved the problem by dividing the lands between them.

eat at your table. So what right do I have to make any more appeals to the king?"

²⁹The king said to him, "Why say more? I order you and Ziba to divide the fields."

³⁰Mephibosheth said to the king, "Let him take everything, now that my lord the king has arrived home safely."

³¹Barzillai the Gileadite also came down from Rogelim to cross the Jordan with the king and to send him on his way from there. ³²Now Barzillai was a very old man, eighty years of age. He had provided for the king during his stay in Mahanaim, for he was a very wealthy man. ³³The king said to Barzillai, "Cross over with me and stay with me in Jerusalem ᴰ, and I will provide for you."

³⁴But Barzillai answered the king, "How many more years will I live, that I should go up to Jerusalem with the king? ³⁵I am now eighty years old. Can I tell the difference between what is good and what is not? Can your servant taste what he eats and drinks? Can I still hear the voices of men and women singers? Why should your servant be an added burden to my lord the king? ³⁶Your servant will cross over the Jordan with the king for a short distance, but why should the king reward me in this way? ³⁷Let your servant return, that I may die in my own town near the tomb of my father and mother. But here is your servant Kimham. Let him cross over with my lord the king. Do for him whatever pleases you."

³⁸The king said, "Kimham shall cross over with me, and I will do for him whatever pleases you. And anything you desire from me I will do for you."

³⁹So all the people crossed the Jordan, and then the king crossed over. The king kissed Barzillai and gave him his blessing, and Barzillai returned to his home.

⁴⁰When the king crossed over to Gilgal, Kimham crossed with him. All the troops of Judah and half the troops of Israel had taken the king over.

⁴¹Soon all the men of Israel were coming to the king and saying to him, "Why did our brothers, the men of Judah, steal the king away and bring him and his household across the Jordan, together with all his men?"

⁴²All the men of Judah answered the men of Israel, "We did this because the king is closely related to us. Why are you angry about it? Have we eaten any of the king's provisions? Have we taken anything for ourselves?"

⁴³Then the men of Israel answered the men of Judah, "We have ten shares in the king; and besides, we have a greater claim on David than you have. So why do you treat us with contempt? Were we not the first to speak of bringing back our king?"

But the men of Judah responded even more harshly than the men of Israel.

Sheba Rebels Against David

20 Now a troublemaker named Sheba son of Bicri, a Benjamite, happened to be there. He sounded the trumpet and shouted,

"We have no share in David,
  no part in Jesse's son!
Every man to his tent, O Israel!"

²So all the men of Israel deserted David to follow Sheba son of Bicri. But the men of Judah stayed by their king all the way from the Jordan to Jerusalem.

³When David returned to his palace in Jerusalem, he

Why did Barzillai forgo the king's favor? (19:34–37)
Barzillai passed the rewards on to Kimham, one of his sons (see 1 Kings 2:7). Barzillai himself felt too old to enjoy the honors David offered him, but he wanted to retain the advantages for his family. David accepted this substitution out of gratitude to Barzillai for his generous support of David's cause during Absalom's rebellion.

Why did Judah and Israel argue over bringing David back? (19:41–43)
Apparently the men of Israel resented the fact that Judah had led the rebellion against David. Now they felt Judah had no right to treat the king as though he belonged to them alone. Some think the northerners may have based their claim to a greater share of the king on simple math (ten-twelfths of the nation). Another possibility is that their claim was based more on the position than the person: David sat on the throne of Saul, a Benjamite.

Why were David's concubines kept in confinement? (20:3)
They had been publicly dishonored by Absalom's sexual involvement with them (16:21–22). No longer acceptable to David and unsuitable for marriage to anyone else, they were forced to live as widows who could not be married for the rest of their lives. Though this seems unfair, it was consistent with the social practices of the day.

took the ten concubines^D he had left to take care of the palace and put them in a house under guard. He provided for them, but did not lie with them. They were kept in confinement till the day of their death^D, living as widows.

4Then the king said to Amasa, "Summon the men of Judah to come to me within three days, and be here yourself." **5**But when Amasa went to summon Judah, he took longer than the time the king had set for him.

6David said to Abishai, "Now Sheba son of Bicri will do us more harm than Absalom did. Take your master's men and pursue him, or he will find fortified cities and escape from us." **7**So Joab's men and the Kerethites and Pelethites and all the mighty warriors went out under the command of Abishai. They marched out from Jerusalem^D to pursue Sheba son of Bicri.

8While they were at the great rock in Gibeon, Amasa came to meet them. Joab was wearing his military tunic, and strapped over it at his waist was a belt with a dagger in its sheath. As he stepped forward, it dropped out of its sheath.

9Joab said to Amasa, "How are you, my brother?" Then Joab took Amasa by the beard with his right hand to kiss him. **10**Amasa was not on his guard against the dagger in Joab's hand, and Joab plunged it into his belly, and his intestines spilled out on the ground. Without being stabbed again, Amasa died. Then Joab and his brother Abishai pursued Sheba son of Bicri.

11One of Joab's men stood beside Amasa and said, "Whoever favors Joab, and whoever is for David, let him follow Joab!" **12**Amasa lay wallowing in his blood in the middle of the road, and the man saw that all the troops came to a halt there. When he realized that everyone who came up to Amasa stopped, he dragged him from the road into a field and threw a garment over him. **13**After Amasa had been removed from the road, all the men went on with Joab to pursue Sheba son of Bicri.

14Sheba passed through all the tribes of Israel to Abel Beth Maacah^a and through the entire region of the Berites, who gathered together and followed him. **15**All the troops with Joab came and besieged Sheba in Abel Beth Maacah. They built a siege ramp up to the city, and it stood against the outer fortifications. While they were battering the wall to bring it down, **16**a wise woman called from the city, "Listen! Listen! Tell Joab to come here so I can speak to him." **17**He went toward her, and she asked, "Are you Joab?"

"I am," he answered.

She said, "Listen to what your servant has to say."

"I'm listening," he said.

18She continued, "Long ago they used to say, 'Get your answer at Abel,' and that settled it. **19**We are the peaceful and faithful in Israel. You are trying to destroy a city that is a mother in Israel. Why do you want to swallow up the LORD's inheritance?"

20"Far be it from me!" Joab replied, "Far be it from me to swallow up or destroy! **21**That is not the case. A man named Sheba son of Bicri, from the hill country of Ephraim, has lifted up his hand against the king, against David. Hand over this one man, and I'll withdraw from the city."

The woman said to Joab, "His head will be thrown to you from the wall."

Why did Joab kill Amasa? (20:10)

Most likely to regain his position as commander of David's army which had been given to Amasa (19:13). In Joab's defense, some suggest that he may have suspected that Amasa (who had been commander of the rebel army) deliberately failed to carry out David's order and was secretly working against the king (20:5).

Why wasn't Amasa on guard against Joab? (20:10)

Because Joab and Amasa were cousins, Amasa may have seen Joab as a relative instead of a rival. It may also be that Joab's friendly greeting and kiss put Amasa at ease. Typically a man would watch an opponent's right hand—the usual hand for holding a sword. Joab's deception was effective because his right hand was extended in friendship (v. 9) while his left hand delivered the fatal blow.

Wise woman (20:16,22)

Joab earlier had enlisted the help of a wise woman to bear his message to King David (14:2). Here, a wise woman gave her advice to the townspeople of Abel Beth Maacah. Both incidents indicate that such women were highly regarded as counselors in Israel. They may have followed in the example of Deborah, known as a *mother in Israel* who was counselor and guide to Barak (Judges 5).

---

^a14 Or *Abel, even Beth Maacah*; also in verse 15

²²Then the woman went to all the people with her wise advice, and they cut off the head of Sheba son of Bicri and threw it to Joab. So he sounded the trumpet, and his men dispersed from the city, each returning to his home. And Joab went back to the king in Jerusalem ᴅ.

²³Joab was over Israel's entire army; Benaiah son of Jehoiada was over the Kerethites and Pelethites; ²⁴Adoniram ᵃ was in charge of forced labor; Jehoshaphat son of Ahilud was recorder; ²⁵Sheva was secretary; Zadok and Abiathar were priests ᴅ; ²⁶and Ira the Jairite was David's priest.

The Gibeonites Avenged

21 During the reign of David, there was a famine for three successive years; so David sought the face of the Lᴏʀᴅ. The Lᴏʀᴅ said, "It is on account of Saul and his blood-stained house; it is because he put the Gibeonites to death ᴅ."

²The king summoned the Gibeonites and spoke to them. (Now the Gibeonites were not a part of Israel but were survivors of the Amorites; the Israelites had sworn to ⌊spare⌋ them, but Saul in his zeal ᴅ for Israel and Judah had tried to annihilate them.) ³David asked the Gibeonites, "What shall I do for you? How shall I make amends so that you will bless the Lᴏʀᴅ's inheritance?"

⁴The Gibeonites answered him, "We have no right to demand silver or gold from Saul or his family, nor do we have the right to put anyone in Israel to death."

"What do you want me to do for you?" David asked.

⁵They answered the king, "As for the man who destroyed us and plotted against us so that we have been decimated and have no place anywhere in Israel, ⁶let seven of his male descendants be given to us to be killed and

ᵃ24 Some Septuagint manuscripts (see also 1 Kings 4:6 and 5:14); Hebrew *Adoram*

How did God reveal the cause of the famine to them? (21:1)

We don't know for sure. It's possible David called for the high priest who possessed the Urim and Thummin, two stones used to determine the mind of God through a no/yes process (see Dictionary). David may have learned the reason through Nathan, the prophet, who spoke for God by revelation.

Why would God ask for human sacrifices? (21:6,9,14)

God does not require human sacrifice to appease his wrath. But Saul had broken a sacred oath (see Joshua 9). His crimes against the Gibeonites are not mentioned elsewhere in Scripture; our only information comes from v. 2. So God now used a famine to call attention to this injustice—but not until first allowing ample time for Israel to right the wrong.

The Gibeonites felt restitution was required. In a sense, the death of Saul's two sons and five grandsons may be regarded as a judgment of God against Saul for his cruelty, following the principles of the *blood avenger*. See **Avenger of blood** (Num. 35:19) and **What did an avenger of blood do?** (Joshua 20:3). In this case, however, justice was executed by David on behalf of Gibeon, much as human judges are God's agents for law and order today (see Romans 13:4).

We have little difficulty understanding how individuals may enjoy the benefits of the wise choices made by their ancestors. But we balk when it comes to accepting the corollary: personal suffering may be caused by the sins or mistakes of ancestors. However, God makes no mistakes. What appears unfair to us may be the long-range results of evil deliberately chosen by our predecessors. Also see **Why does God allow innocent children to suffer?** (Lam. 2:11–12).

exposed before the LORD at Gibeah of Saul—the LORD's chosen one."

So the king said, "I will give them to you."

7The king spared Mephibosheth son of Jonathan, the son of Saul, because of the oath before the LORD between David and Jonathan son of Saul. **8**But the king took Armoni and Mephibosheth, the two sons of Aiah's daughter Rizpah, whom she had borne to Saul, together with the five sons of Saul's daughter Merab,ᵃ whom she had borne to Adriel son of Barzillai the Meholathite. **9**He handed them over to the Gibeonites, who killed and exposed them on a hill before the LORD. All seven of them fell together; they were put to deathᴰ during the first days of the harvest, just as the barley harvest was beginning.

10Rizpah daughter of Aiah took sackclothᴰ and spread it out for herself on a rock. From the beginning of the harvest till the rain poured down from the heavens on the bodies, she did not let the birds of the air touch them by day or the wild animals by night. **11**When David was told what Aiah's daughter Rizpah, Saul's concubineᴰ, had done, **12**he went and took the bones of Saul and his son Jonathan from the citizens of Jabesh Gilead. (They had taken them secretly from the public square at Beth Shan, where the Philistines had hung them after they struck Saul down on Gilboa.) **13**David brought the bones of Saul and his son Jonathan from there, and the bones of those who had been killed and exposed were gathered up.

14They buried the bones of Saul and his son Jonathan in the tomb of Saul's father Kish, at Zela in Benjamin, and did everything the king commanded. After that, God answered prayer in behalf of the land.

Wars Against the Philistines

15Once again there was a battle between the Philistines and Israel. David went down with his men to fight against the Philistines, and he became exhausted. **16**And Ishbi-Benob, one of the descendants of Rapha, whose bronze spearhead weighed three hundred shekelsᴰᵇ and who was armed with a new ⌊sword⌋, said he would kill David. **17**But Abishai son of Zeruiah came to David's rescue; he struck the Philistine down and killed him. Then David's men swore to him, saying, "Never again will you go out with us to battle, so that the lamp of Israel will not be extinguished."

18In the course of time, there was another battle with the Philistines, at Gob. At that time Sibbecai the Hushathite killed Saph, one of the descendants of Rapha.

19In another battle with the Philistines at Gob, Elhanan son of Jaare-Oregimᶜ the Bethlehemite killed Goliathᵈ the Gittite, who had a spear with a shaft like a weaver's rod.

20In still another battle, which took place at Gath, there was a huge man with six fingers on each hand and six toes on each foot—twenty-four in all. He also was descended from Rapha. **21**When he taunted Israel, Jonathan son of Shimeah, David's brother, killed him.

22These four were descendants of Rapha in Gath, and they fell at the hands of David and his men.

How long did Rizpah keep scavengers away from the bodies? (21:10)

Perhaps for as long as six months! The barley harvest came about mid-April. If the rain refers to the normal early rains of fall, it would not be until October or November. But the rains may well have been an out-of-season shower, marking God's willingness to break the drought and subsequent famine. And Rizpah may have had help in her vigil.

SCRIPTURE LINK (21:15–22)

See 1 Chron. 20:4–8 for a similar account.

How close did David come to being killed? (21:17)

Very close indeed. It was only Abishai's timely intervention that saved David. Abishai was able to slay the giant Philistine warrior. It was such a close call that David's men pleaded with him not to go out to battle any more lest the one they regarded as the very *lamp of Israel* should be extinguished.

ᵃ8 Two Hebrew manuscripts, some Septuagint manuscripts and Syriac (see also 1 Samuel 18:19); most Hebrew and Septuagint manuscripts *Michal*   ᵇ16 That is, about 7 1/2 pounds (about 3.5 kilograms)
ᶜ19 Or *son of Jair the weaver*   ᵈ19 Hebrew and Septuagint;
1 Chron. 20:5 *son of Jair killed Lahmi the brother of Goliath*

Why is a song included in a history book? (22:1-51)

The writer of 2 Samuel gives a full picture of David, Israel's greatest king. He has shown him as a great warrior and a wise leader, as well as an indulgent father and a deliberate sinner. But the record would not be complete without an example of David's skill as a poet and musician. This song (also known as Psalm 18) was composed after David had escaped Saul and assumed the throne, but before his sin with Bathsheba.

The cords of the grave (22:6)

A metaphor for death. Combined with the parallel metaphors in this passage, this may use mythological images that depict a struggle with the Canaanite god of death and god of the sea. David's encounter with pagan forces threatened to ensnare him and pull him down to his death. But God broke the cords and released David from danger. For more on why the Bible would cite pagan mythology see **Why did God break the heads of sea monsters?** (Psalm 74:13-14).

SCRIPTURE LINK (22:1-51)

David's song of praise is also given in Psalm 18:1-50.

David's Song of Praise

22 David sang to the LORD the words of this song when the LORD delivered him from the hand of all his enemies and from the hand of Saul. ²He said:

"The LORD is my rock, my fortress and my
  deliverer;
³ my God is my rock, in whom I take refuge,
  my shield and the horn*a* of my salvation.D
He is my stronghold,D my refuge and my
  savior—
  from violent men you save me.
⁴I call to the LORD, who is worthy of praise,
  and I am saved from my enemies.

⁵"The waves of deathD swirled about me;
  the torrents of destruction overwhelmed me.
⁶The cords of the grave*b* coiled around me;
  the snares of death confronted me.
⁷In my distress I called to the LORD;
  I called out to my God.
From his temple he heard my voice;
  my cry came to his ears.

⁸"The earth trembled and quaked,
  the foundations of the heavens*c* shook;
  they trembled because he was angry.
⁹Smoke rose from his nostrils;
  consuming fire came from his mouth,
  burning coals blazed out of it.
¹⁰He parted the heavens and came down;
  dark clouds were under his feet.
¹¹He mounted the cherubimD and flew;
  he soared*d* on the wings of the wind.
¹²He made darkness his canopy around him—
  the dark*e* rain clouds of the sky.
¹³Out of the brightness of his presence
  bolts of lightning blazed forth.
¹⁴The LORD thundered from heaven;
  the voice of the Most High resounded.
¹⁵He shot arrows and scattered ⌊the enemies⌋,
  bolts of lightning and routed them.
¹⁶The valleys of the sea were exposed
  and the foundations of the earth laid bare
at the rebuke of the LORD,
  at the blast of breath from his nostrils.

¹⁷"He reached down from on high and took hold
  of me;
  he drew me out of deep waters.
¹⁸He rescued me from my powerful enemy,
  from my foes, who were too strong for me.
¹⁹They confronted me in the day of my disaster,
  but the LORD was my support.
²⁰He brought me out into a spacious place;
  he rescued me because he delighted in me.

²¹"The LORD has dealt with me according to my
  righteousness;D

---

a3 Horn here symbolizes strength.   *b6* Hebrew *Sheol*
c8 Hebrew; Vulgate and Syriac (see also Psalm 18:7) *mountains*
d11 Many Hebrew manuscripts (see also Psalm 18:10); most Hebrew manuscripts *appeared*   *e12* Septuagint and Vulgate (see also Psalm 18:11); Hebrew *massed*

according to the cleanness of my hands he
    has rewarded me.
22For I have kept the ways of the LORD;
    I have not done evil by turning from my
        God.
23All his laws are before me;
    I have not turned away from his decrees.
24I have been blameless before him
    and have kept myself from sin.
25The LORD has rewarded me according to my
        righteousness^D,
    according to my cleanness^a in his sight.

26"To the faithful you show yourself faithful,
    to the blameless you show yourself
        blameless,
27to the pure you show yourself pure,
    but to the crooked you show yourself
        shrewd.
28You save the humble,
    but your eyes are on the haughty to bring
        them low.
29You are my lamp, O LORD;
    the LORD turns my darkness into light.
30With your help I can advance against a troop^b;
    with my God I can scale a wall.

31"As for God, his way is perfect;
    the word of the LORD is flawless.
He is a shield
    for all who take refuge in him.
32For who is God besides the LORD?
    And who is the Rock except our God?
33It is God who arms me with strength^c
    and makes my way perfect.
34He makes my feet like the feet of a deer;
    he enables me to stand on the heights.
35He trains my hands for battle;
    my arms can bend a bow of bronze.
36You give me your shield of victory;
    you stoop down to make me great.
37You broaden the path beneath me,
    so that my ankles do not turn.

38"I pursued my enemies and crushed them;
    I did not turn back till they were destroyed.
39I crushed them completely, and they could not
        rise;
    they fell beneath my feet.
40You armed me with strength for battle;
    you made my adversaries bow at my feet.
41You made my enemies turn their backs in
        flight,
    and I destroyed my foes.
42They cried for help, but there was no one to
        save them—
    to the LORD, but he did not answer.
43I beat them as fine as the dust of the earth;
    I pounded and trampled them like mud in
        the streets.

How could David claim to be blameless? (22:24)

David wrote this long before he'd committed the sins of adultery and murder (v. 1). Had he written it later, however, he still might have claimed to be blameless—something quite different from the claim to be sinless. When he sinned, David repented and confessed his sin.

How do sinners see God? (22:27)

Believers see God's capacity for love and forgiveness. Sinners, on the other hand, can expect to see God only as judge and avenger. To them God appears devious, untrustworthy and subject to manipulation. We see God through the grid of our own character. But God remains what he has always been: holy, just, loving, pure and compassionate.

How do bronze bows work? (22:35)

This does not mean that bows were made entirely of bronze. They were made of strong, seasoned wood, then reinforced with bronze or adorned with bronze carvings. Job 20:24 mentions arrows tipped with bronze which would allow for deep penetration.

^{a}25 Hebrew; Septuagint and Vulgate (see also Psalm 18:24) *to the cleanness of my hands* ^{b}30 Or *can run through a barricade*
^{c}33 Dead Sea Scrolls, some Septuagint manuscripts, Vulgate and Syriac (see also Psalm 18:32); Masoretic Text *who is my strong refuge*

44"You have delivered me from the attacks of my
        people;
    you have preserved me as the head of
        nations.
People I did not know are subject to me,
45   and foreigners come cringing to me;
    as soon as they hear me, they obey me.
46They all lose heart;
    they come trembling*a* from their
        strongholds*D*.

47"The LORD lives! Praise be to my Rock!
    Exalted be God, the Rock, my Savior!
48He is the God who avenges*D* me,
    who puts the nations under me,
49   who sets me free from my enemies.
You exalted me above my foes;
    from violent men you rescued me.
50Therefore I will praise you, O LORD, among the
        nations;
    I will sing praises to your name.
51He gives his king great victories;
    he shows unfailing kindness to his
        anointed*D*,
    to David and his descendants forever."

The Last Words of David

23 These are the last words of David:

    "The oracle*D* of David son of Jesse,
        the oracle of the man exalted by the Most
            High,
    the man anointed by the God of Jacob,
        Israel's singer of songs*b*:

2"The Spirit of the LORD spoke through me;
    his word was on my tongue.
3The God of Israel spoke,
    the Rock of Israel said to me:
'When one rules over men in righteousness*D*,
    when he rules in the fear of God,
4he is like the light of morning at sunrise
    on a cloudless morning,
like the brightness after rain
    that brings the grass from the earth.'

5"Is not my house right with God?
    Has he not made with me an everlasting
        covenant*D*,
    arranged and secured in every part?
Will he not bring to fruition my salvation*D*
    and grant me my every desire?
6But evil men are all to be cast aside like
        thorns,
    which are not gathered with the hand.
7Whoever touches thorns
    uses a tool of iron or the shaft of a
        spear;
    they are burned up where they lie."

Were these really the last words that David spoke? (23:1–7)

These are *last words* perhaps only in regard to their vital subject matter—the covenant made with David concerning his dynasty and perpetual throne (ch. 7). Or they may be his *last words* given in a poetic style. Other references to David's *last words* are found in 1 Kings 2:1–9 and 1 Chronicles 23:27.

How many of David's words were inspired by God? (23:2)

Much of what David spoke was tainted with self-interest or mistaken concepts. But David was conscious that God's Spirit was often at work within him, inspiring the words of his psalms. He knew that God had spoken prophetically through him, revealing God's thoughts. We see, however, that even words arising from David's humanity could be recast by the Spirit, corrected to reveal God's truth to us (for example, Psalm 73:2–17).

David's Mighty Men

8These are the names of David's mighty men:

Josheb-Basshebeth,[a] a Tahkemonite,[b] was chief of the Three; he raised his spear against eight hundred men, whom he killed[c] in one encounter.

9Next to him was Eleazar son of Dodai the Ahohite. As one of the three mighty men, he was with David when they taunted the Philistines gathered ⌊at Pas Dammim⌋[d] for battle. Then the men of Israel retreated, **10**but he stood his ground and struck down the Philistines till his hand grew tired and froze to the sword. The LORD brought about a great victory that day. The troops returned to Eleazar, but only to strip the dead.

11Next to him was Shammah son of Agee the Hararite. When the Philistines banded together at a place where there was a field full of lentils, Israel's troops fled from them. **12**But Shammah took his stand in the middle of the field. He defended it and struck the Philistines down, and the LORD brought about a great victory.

13During harvest time, three of the thirty chief men came down to David at the cave of Adullam, while a band of Philistines was encamped in the Valley of Rephaim. **14**At that time David was in the stronghold,[D] and the Philistine garrison was at Bethlehem. **15**David longed for water and said, "Oh, that someone would get me a drink of water from the well near the gate of Bethlehem!" **16**So the three mighty men broke through the Philistine lines, drew water from the well near the gate of Bethlehem and carried it back to David. But he refused to drink it; instead, he poured it out before the LORD. **17**"Far be it from me, O LORD, to do this!" he said. "Is it not the blood of men who went at the risk of their lives?" And David would not drink it.

Such were the exploits of the three mighty men.

18Abishai the brother of Joab son of Zeruiah was chief of the Three.[e] He raised his spear against three hundred men, whom he killed, and so he became as famous as the Three. **19**Was he not held in greater honor than the Three? He became their commander, even though he was not included among them.

20Benaiah son of Jehoiada was a valiant fighter from Kabzeel, who performed great exploits. He struck down two of Moab's best men. He also went down into a pit on a snowy day and killed a lion. **21**And he struck down a huge Egyptian. Although the Egyptian had a spear in his hand, Benaiah went against him with a club. He snatched the spear from the Egyptian's hand and killed him with his own spear. **22**Such were the exploits of Benaiah son of Jehoiada; he too was as famous as the three mighty men. **23**He was held in greater honor than any of the Thirty, but he was not included among the Three. And David put him in charge of his bodyguard.

24Among the Thirty were:

Asahel the brother of Joab,
Elhanan son of Dodo from Bethlehem,

Why do these stories seem out of place? (23:8–39)

The mention in this account of the cave of Adullam and the Valley of Rephaim (v. 13) date these events back to the time when David was a fugitive from Saul or, perhaps, during the early days of his reign while he was still battling the Philistines. The list, like an addendum, gives a more complete picture of David's reign. In a sense, the stories of the mighty men are like a literary flashback.

Why wouldn't David drink the water from the well of Bethlehem? (23:16–17)

By pouring out the water before the Lord, David indicated that in his eyes such life-risking loyalty belonged only to the Lord. He considered the water equivalent to the blood of the men; to use it for trivial refreshment seemed utterly abhorrent to him. Undoubtedly his men understood his sentiments and thought more highly of him for it. Also see *Why would wasting water be better than drinking it?* (1 Chron. 11:18–19).

---

a8 Hebrew; some Septuagint manuscripts suggest *Ish-Bosheth,* that is, *Esh-Baal* (see also 1 Chron. 11:11 *Jashobeam*).   *b8* Probably a variant of *Hacmonite* (see 1 Chron. 11:11)   *c8* Some Septuagint manuscripts (see also 1 Chron. 11:11); Hebrew and other Septuagint manuscripts *Three; it was Adino the Eznite who killed eight hundred men*   *d9* See 1 Chron. 11:13; Hebrew *gathered there.*   *e18* Most Hebrew manuscripts (see also 1 Chron. 11:20); two Hebrew manuscripts and Syriac *Thirty*

²⁵Shammah the Harodite,
    Elika the Harodite,
²⁶Helez the Paltite,
    Ira son of Ikkesh from Tekoa,
²⁷Abiezer from Anathoth,
    Mebunnaiᵃ the Hushathite,
²⁸Zalmon the Ahohite,
    Maharai the Netophathite,
²⁹Heledᵇ son of Baanah the Netophathite,
    Ithai son of Ribai from Gibeah in Benjamin,
³⁰Benaiah the Pirathonite,
    Hiddaiᶜ from the ravines of Gaash,
³¹Abi-Albon the Arbathite,
    Azmaveth the Barhumite,
³²Eliahba the Shaalbonite,
    the sons of Jashen,
    Jonathan ³³son ofᵈ Shammah the Hararite,
    Ahiam son of Shararᵉ the Hararite,
³⁴Eliphelet son of Ahasbai the Maacathite,
    Eliam son of Ahithophel the Gilonite,
³⁵Hezro the Carmelite,
    Paarai the Arbite,
³⁶Igal son of Nathan from Zobah,
    the son of Hagri,ᶠ
³⁷Zelek the Ammonite,
    Naharai the Beerothite, the armor-bearer of Joab
        son of Zeruiah,
³⁸Ira the Ithrite,
    Gareb the Ithrite
³⁹and Uriah the Hittite.
There were thirty-seven in all.

David Counts the Fighting Men

24 Again the anger of the LORD burned against Israel, and he incited David against them, saying, "Go and take a census of Israel and Judah."

²So the king said to Joab and the army commandersᵍ with him, "Go throughout the tribes of Israel from Dan to Beersheba and enroll the fighting men, so that I may know how many there are."

³But Joab replied to the king, "May the LORD your God multiply the troops a hundred times over, and may the eyes of my lord the king see it. But why does my lord the king want to do such a thing?"

⁴The king's word, however, overruled Joab and the army commanders; so they left the presence of the king to enroll the fighting men of Israel.

⁵After crossing the Jordan, they camped near Aroer, south of the town in the gorge, and then went through Gad and on to Jazer. ⁶They went to Gilead and the region of Tahtim Hodshi, and on to Dan Jaan and around toward Sidon. ⁷Then they went toward the fortress of Tyre and all the towns of the Hivites and Canaanites. Finally, they went on to Beersheba in the Negevᴰ of Judah.

⁸After they had gone through the entire land, they came

Why does it say there were 37 men when only 29 names are listed? (23:39; see v. 24)
Some think that the number 37 includes those who were part of *the Thirty* at one time or another. The number of the elite group of warriors may have been maintained at 30 so that whenever a vacancy occurred, a new name was added to the list.

SCRIPTURE LINK (24:1)
The parallel account says *Satan* incited David to take a census of fighting men. See 1 Chron. 21:1.

What was wrong with taking a census? (24:3,10)
David's count of the military shows a shift in focus. Instead of depending solely on God, he began to depend on military power. Joab's uneasiness (v. 3) and David's sense of guilt (v. 10) indicates they knew the danger of depending on human power rather than on the Lord.

ᵃ27 Hebrew; some Septuagint manuscripts (see also 1 Chron. 11:29) *Sibbecai*   ᵇ29 Some Hebrew manuscripts and Vulgate (see also 1 Chron. 11:30); most Hebrew manuscripts *Heleb*   ᶜ30 Hebrew; some Septuagint manuscripts (see also 1 Chron. 11:32) *Hurai*   ᵈ33 Some Septuagint manuscripts (see also 1 Chron. 11:34); Hebrew does not have *son of.*   ᵉ33 Hebrew; some Septuagint manuscripts (see also 1 Chron. 11:35) *Sacar*   ᶠ36 Some Septuagint manuscripts (see also 1 Chron. 11:38); Hebrew *Haggadi*   ᵍ2 Septuagint (see also verse 4 and 1 Chron. 21:2); Hebrew *Joab the army commander*

back to Jerusalem[D] at the end of nine months and twenty days.

⁹Joab reported the number of the fighting men to the king: In Israel there were eight hundred thousand able-bodied men who could handle a sword, and in Judah five hundred thousand.

¹⁰David was conscience-stricken after he had counted the fighting men, and he said to the LORD, "I have sinned greatly in what I have done. Now, O LORD, I beg you, take away the guilt of your servant. I have done a very foolish thing."

¹¹Before David got up the next morning, the word of the LORD had come to Gad the prophet[D], David's seer[D]: ¹²"Go and tell David, 'This is what the LORD says: I am giving you three options. Choose one of them for me to carry out against you.' "

¹³So Gad went to David and said to him, "Shall there come upon you three[a] years of famine in your land? Or three months of fleeing from your enemies while they pursue you? Or three days of plague in your land? Now then, think it over and decide how I should answer the one who sent me."

¹⁴David said to Gad, "I am in deep distress. Let us fall into the hands of the LORD, for his mercy[D] is great; but do not let me fall into the hands of men."

¹⁵So the LORD sent a plague on Israel from that morning until the end of the time designated, and seventy thousand of the people from Dan to Beersheba died. ¹⁶When the angel stretched out his hand to destroy Jerusalem, the LORD was grieved because of the calamity and said to the angel who was afflicting[D] the people, "Enough! Withdraw your hand." The angel of the LORD was then at the threshing floor of Araunah the Jebusite.

¹⁷When David saw the angel who was striking down the people, he said to the LORD, "I am the one who has sinned

Did the punishment fit the crime? (24:15)

It doesn't seem to. But the crime was not merely the census. Some think it was the sinful, rebellious attitude of the people (17:24–26) that brought God's judgment. It may not be entirely accurate, therefore, to say that 70,000 people died for David's sin. See the article: *Why did 70,000 die while the sinner lived?* (1 Chron. 21:14).

---

[a]13 Septuagint (see also 1 Chron. 21:12); Hebrew *seven*

Why would God make someone do wrong? (24:1)

It's not that God *caused* David to do wrong. Like any human, David was capable of doing wrong on his own. Rather, God *permitted* David to pursue his sinful choices and reap the consequences of his actions. "To incite" in this case may have meant that God orchestrated the events that led to David's decision.

To make the question even more confusing, the writer of 1 Chronicles (21:1) says it was not God but Satan that incited David to do wrong. The apparent conflict between the two passages may mean that God sometimes permits Satan to do things that subsequently are viewed as having come from God.

The writer of 2 Samuel reports that God was ultimately behind David's action, probably indicating that God had given David the freedom to choose good or evil. The writer of 1 Chronicles recognizes Satan as the more immediate temptation behind David's decision. Both views are correct.

In the end, God used David's sinful desires to bring judgment for sin upon the nation of Israel. But good also came from these sad events: because of what happened here, the site was acquired where the temple eventually would be built.

Also see *Can Satan incite God's people to do evil?* (1 Chron. 21:1).

and done wrong. These are but sheep. What have they
done? Let your hand fall upon me and my family."

David Builds an Altar

18On that day Gad went to David and said to him, "Go
up and build an altar to the LORD on the threshing floor of
Araunah the Jebusite." 19So David went up, as the LORD
had commanded through Gad. 20When Araunah looked
and saw the king and his men coming toward him, he
went out and bowed down before the king with his face
to the ground.

21Araunah said, "Why has my lord the king come to his
servant?"

"To buy your threshing floor," David answered, "so I can build an altar to the LORD, that the plague on the people may be stopped."

22Araunah said to David, "Let my lord the king take
whatever pleases him and offer it up. Here are oxen for
the burnt offering[D], and here are threshing sledges and
ox yokes[D] for the wood. 23O king, Araunah gives all this
to the king." Araunah also said to him, "May the LORD
your God accept you."

24But the king replied to Araunah, "No, I insist on paying you for it. I will not sacrifice[D] to the LORD my God burnt offerings that cost me nothing."

So David bought the threshing floor and the oxen and
paid fifty shekels[a] of silver for them. 25David built an
altar to the LORD there and sacrificed burnt offerings
and fellowship offerings[D].[b] Then the LORD answered
prayer in behalf of the land, and the plague on Israel was
stopped.

Why did David offer a burnt offering? (24:18,25)

Burnt offerings marked one's total commitment. David, as king, expressed the repentance of the nation and the desire of the people to be completely restored to their God. The fellowship offerings indicated that sin had been judged—that fellowship was now fully established between God and his people.

What's important about this site? (24:18–25)

The threshing floor of Araunah, where David publicly sacrificed for his sin of focusing on military power, became the site God chose as the location for Solomon's temple. This gave the people a new focus for national unity: worshiping the living God.

[a] 24 That is, about 1 1/4 pounds (about 0.6 kilogram)
[b] 25 Traditionally *peace offerings*

1 KINGS

Why read this book?

The story of Solomon—the wisest man ever—is here, along with accounts of other kings of this time. They provide us with both positive examples to follow and mistakes to avoid. It is also here that we learn about the tragic division of Israel into a northern kingdom (Israel) and a southern kingdom (Judah). This division sets the stage for the rest of Biblical history.

Who wrote this book?

Jewish tradition considered the prophet Jeremiah the author. Whoever wrote 1 and 2 Kings probably used preexisting documents such as *the book of the annals of Solomon* (11:41), *the book of the annals of the kings of Israel* (14:19) and *the book of the annals of the kings of Judah* (14:29). Other written sources may have been used as well (see 1 Chron. 29:29; 2 Chron. 9:29; 12:15).

When and why was it written?

Most likely it was written during the Babylonian exile of the Jews, somewhere between 560 and 550 B.C. The book demonstrates the necessity of taking God's commands and promises seriously.

What period of history does this book cover?

This book covers the last days of David, the reign and fall of Solomon and the division of the kingdom between Israel and Judah—approximately the years from 971 to 846 B.C.

Why are there two books of Kings?

Orginally, the two books were one. Primarily because of its length, Kings was divided into two separate books for easier handling.

What to look for in 1 Kings:

Keep an eye open for prophetic warnings—occasionally heeded, but often dismissed. Look for promises of reward for honoring God, contrasted with Israel's neglect of and even contempt for the Lord.

When did these things happen?

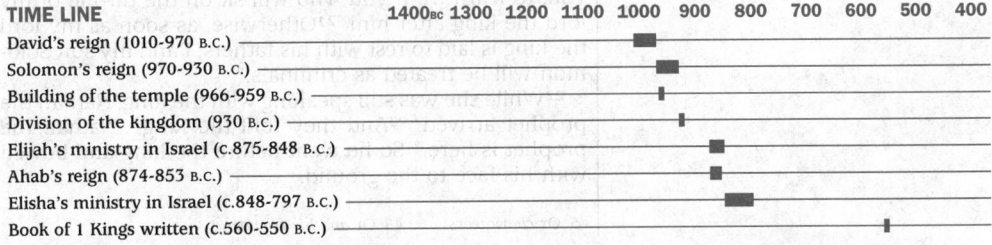

TIME LINE	1400BC	1300	1200	1100	1000	900	800	700	600	500	400
David's reign (1010-970 B.C.)					▬						
Solomon's reign (970-930 B.C.)					▬						
Building of the temple (966-959 B.C.)					▪						
Division of the kingdom (930 B.C.)					▪						
Elijah's ministry in Israel (c.875-848 B.C.)						▪					
Ahab's reign (874-853 B.C.)						▪					
Elisha's ministry in Israel (c.848-797 B.C.)						▬					
Book of 1 Kings written (c.560-550 B.C.)									▪		

Why look for a virgin to warm the king? (1:2)
In his last days, David suffered from the chills, common among the elderly and those who are about to die. David's servants believed that if they could find a virgin to lie naked with him, he would be warmed. They probably considered his wives old and, like him, suffering from poor circulation. They thought a virgin would warm him better. It probably did not help. Though technically considered a concubine, she acted as David's nurse and had no sexual relations with him.

Did an official prophet serve the king? (1:9–10)
The Old Testament describes at least two kinds of prophets: *independent* prophets (like Elijah who opposed Ahab) and *official* prophets who served in the king's court (like Nathan). Could an officially sanctioned prophet speak without compromising his integrity? Nathan's rebuke of David for his adultery shows that it was possible (2 Samuel 12:7–12), and worked to bring the king to repentance. See article: *What influence did prophets have with kings?* (2 Kings 4:13).

How did a latecomer become first lady? (1:11–14)
The Bible does not explain how Bathsheba became first lady in David's court, but it's obvious she wielded a great deal of influence in the kingdom. Perhaps there was some political maneuvering on her part; or perhaps David simply favored her above all his other wives.

Adonijah Sets Himself Up as King

1 When King David was old and well advanced in years, he could not keep warm even when they put covers over him. 2So his servants said to him, "Let us look for a young virgin to attend the king and take care of him. She can lie beside him so that our lord the king may keep warm."

3Then they searched throughout Israel for a beautiful girl and found Abishag, a Shunammite, and brought her to the king. 4The girl was very beautiful; she took care of the king and waited on him, but the king had no intimate relations with her.

5Now Adonijah, whose mother was Haggith, put himself forward and said, "I will be king." So he got chariots and horses*a* ready, with fifty men to run ahead of him. 6(His father had never interfered with him by asking, "Why do you behave as you do?" He was also very handsome and was born next after Absalom.)

7Adonijah conferred with Joab son of Zeruiah and with Abiathar the priest*D*, and they gave him their support. 8But Zadok the priest, Benaiah son of Jehoiada, Nathan the prophet*D*, Shimei and Rei*b* and David's special guard did not join Adonijah.

9Adonijah then sacrificed sheep, cattle and fattened calves at the Stone of Zoheleth near En Rogel. He invited all his brothers, the king's sons, and all the men of Judah who were royal officials, 10but he did not invite Nathan the prophet or Benaiah or the special guard or his brother Solomon.

11Then Nathan asked Bathsheba, Solomon's mother, "Have you not heard that Adonijah, the son of Haggith, has become king without our lord David's knowing it? 12Now then, let me advise you how you can save your own life and the life of your son Solomon. 13Go in to King David and say to him, 'My lord the king, did you not swear to me your servant: "Surely Solomon your son shall be king after me, and he will sit on my throne"? Why then has Adonijah become king?' 14While you are still there talking to the king, I will come in and confirm what you have said."

15So Bathsheba went to see the aged king in his room, where Abishag the Shunammite was attending him. 16Bathsheba bowed low and knelt before the king.

"What is it you want?" the king asked.

17She said to him, "My lord, you yourself swore to me your servant by the LORD your God: 'Solomon your son shall be king after me, and he will sit on my throne.' 18But now Adonijah has become king, and you, my lord the king, do not know about it. 19He has sacrificed great numbers of cattle, fattened calves, and sheep, and has invited all the king's sons, Abiathar the priest and Joab the commander of the army, but he has not invited Solomon your servant. 20My lord the king, the eyes of all Israel are on you, to learn from you who will sit on the throne of my lord the king after him. 21Otherwise, as soon as my lord the king is laid to rest with his fathers, I and my son Solomon will be treated as criminals."

22While she was still speaking with the king, Nathan the prophet arrived. 23And they told the king, "Nathan the prophet is here." So he went before the king and bowed with his face to the ground.

---

a5 Or *charioteers*   *b8* Or *and his friends*

24Nathan said, "Have you, my lord the king, declared that Adonijah shall be king after you, and that he will sit on your throne? 25Today he has gone down and sacrificed great numbers of cattle, fattened calves, and sheep. He has invited all the king's sons, the commanders of the army and Abiathar the priest^D. Right now they are eating and drinking with him and saying, 'Long live King Adonijah!' 26But me your servant, and Zadok the priest, and Benaiah son of Jehoiada, and your servant Solomon he did not invite. 27Is this something my lord the king has done without letting his servants know who should sit on the throne of my lord the king after him?"

David Makes Solomon King

28Then King David said, "Call in Bathsheba." So she came into the king's presence and stood before him.

29The king then took an oath: "As surely as the LORD lives, who has delivered me out of every trouble, 30I will surely carry out today what I swore to you by the LORD, the God of Israel: Solomon your son shall be king after me, and he will sit on my throne in my place."

31Then Bathsheba bowed low with her face to the ground and, kneeling before the king, said, "May my lord King David live forever!"

32King David said, "Call in Zadok the priest, Nathan the prophet^D and Benaiah son of Jehoiada." When they came before the king, 33he said to them: "Take your lord's servants with you and set Solomon my son on my own mule and take him down to Gihon. 34There have Zadok the priest and Nathan the prophet anoint him king over Israel. Blow the trumpet and shout, 'Long live King Solomon!' 35Then you are to go up with him, and he is to come and sit on my throne and reign in my place. I have appointed him ruler over Israel and Judah."

36Benaiah son of Jehoiada answered the king, "Amen! May the LORD, the God of my lord the king, so declare it. 37As the LORD was with my lord the king, so may he be with Solomon to make his throne even greater than the throne of my lord King David!"

38So Zadok the priest, Nathan the prophet, Benaiah son of Jehoiada, the Kerethites and the Pelethites went down and put Solomon on King David's mule and escorted him to Gihon. 39Zadok the priest took the horn of oil from the sacred^D tent and anointed Solomon. Then they sounded the trumpet and all the people shouted, "Long live King Solomon!" 40And all the people went up after him, playing flutes and rejoicing greatly, so that the ground shook with the sound.

41Adonijah and all the guests who were with him heard it as they were finishing their feast. On hearing the sound of the trumpet, Joab asked, "What's the meaning of all the noise in the city?"

42Even as he was speaking, Jonathan son of Abiathar the priest arrived. Adonijah said, "Come in. A worthy man like you must be bringing good news."

43"Not at all!" Jonathan answered. "Our lord King David has made Solomon king. 44The king has sent with him Zadok the priest, Nathan the prophet, Benaiah son of Jehoiada, the Kerethites and the Pelethites, and they have put him on the king's mule, 45and Zadok the priest and Nathan the prophet have anointed him king at Gihon. From there they have gone up cheering, and the city resounds with it. That's the noise you hear. 46Moreover, Solomon has taken his seat on the royal throne. 47Also, the

What did it mean to ride the king's mule? (1:33)
In David's time, the mule was a royal animal reserved for kings. Allowing Solomon to ride the king's mule was a public statement that David wanted his son to inherit the throne.

What did oil signify? (1:39)
Properly applied, the oil signified God's approval of the one being anointed. A unique sacred oil was used to consecrate sanctuaries, priests and kings (Exodus 30:22–33). Typically a prophet or priest performed the ceremony. Also see *Oil of joy* (Psalm 45:7).

How much safety did the horns of the altar provide? (1:50)

Grasping the horns of the altar provided asylum for an accused person while his case was under review. A person could be completely safe there, but only for a time. If a murder was ruled intentional and not accidental, the offender was removed from the altar and executed (Exodus 21:13–14). When Joab refused to let go after being sentenced to die, Benaiah needed special permission to execute him at the altar (2:28–34).

Will God give us prosperity? (2:3)

See articles: *Is success guaranteed to those who obey God?* (Deut. 28:2–6) and *Does seeking God guarantee success?* (2 Chron. 26:5).

Will this promise to David be fulfilled in Christ? (2:4)

See *How has David's house and kingdom endured forever?* (2 Samuel 7:16).

If Joab deserved to die, why leave the job to Solomon? (2:5–6)

Joab had been David's right-hand military man for many years; perhaps the king just couldn't bring himself to execute a once-loyal servant. Or perhaps David may have been reluctant to punish Joab since he was the son of his sister Zeruiah.

Why even the score against Joab? (2:6)

To shed blood *in peacetime as if in battle* (v. 5) was a criminal act. Even though Joab had acted without David's knowledge, the king was still responsible for his commander's actions. David felt that justice should be met in Joab's case, but didn't feel that he should administer it.

royal officials have come to congratulate our lord King David, saying, 'May your God make Solomon's name more famous than yours and his throne greater than yours!' And the king bowed in worship on his bed **48**and said, 'Praise be to the LORD, the God of Israel, who has allowed my eyes to see a successor on my throne today.' "

49At this, all Adonijah's guests rose in alarm and dispersed. **50**But Adonijah, in fear of Solomon, went and took hold of the horns of the altar. **51**Then Solomon was told, "Adonijah is afraid of King Solomon and is clinging to the horns of the altar. He says, 'Let King Solomon swear to me today that he will not put his servant to death^D with the sword.' "

52Solomon replied, "If he shows himself to be a worthy man, not a hair of his head will fall to the ground; but if evil is found in him, he will die." **53**Then King Solomon sent men, and they brought him down from the altar. And Adonijah came and bowed down to King Solomon, and Solomon said, "Go to your home."

David's Charge to Solomon

2 When the time drew near for David to die, he gave a charge to Solomon his son.

2"I am about to go the way of all the earth," he said. "So be strong, show yourself a man, **3**and observe what the LORD your God requires: Walk in his ways, and keep his decrees and commands, his laws and requirements, as written in the Law of Moses, so that you may prosper in all you do and wherever you go, **4**and that the LORD may keep his promise to me: 'If your descendants watch how they live, and if they walk faithfully before me with all their heart and soul^D, you will never fail to have a man on the throne of Israel.'

5"Now you yourself know what Joab son of Zeruiah did to me—what he did to the two commanders of Israel's armies, Abner son of Ner and Amasa son of Jether. He killed them, shedding their blood in peacetime as if in battle, and with that blood stained the belt around his waist and the sandals on his feet. **6**Deal with him according to your wisdom, but do not let his gray head go down to the grave^a in peace^D.

7"But show kindness to the sons of Barzillai of Gilead and let them be among those who eat at your table. They stood by me when I fled from your brother Absalom.

8"And remember, you have with you Shimei son of Gera, the Benjamite from Bahurim, who called down bitter curses on me the day I went to Mahanaim. When he came down to meet me at the Jordan, I swore to him by the LORD: 'I will not put you to death by the sword.' **9**But now, do not consider him innocent. You are a man of wisdom; you will know what to do to him. Bring his gray head down to the grave in blood."

10Then David rested with his fathers and was buried in the City of David. **11**He had reigned forty years over Israel—seven years in Hebron and thirty-three in Jerusalem^D. **12**So Solomon sat on the throne of his father David, and his rule was firmly established.

Solomon's Throne Established

13Now Adonijah, the son of Haggith, went to Bathsheba, Solomon's mother. Bathsheba asked him, "Do you come peacefully?"

a6 Hebrew Sheol; also in verse 9

He answered, "Yes, peacefully." **14**Then he added, "I have something to say to you."

"You may say it," she replied.

15"As you know," he said, "the kingdom was mine. All Israel looked to me as their king. But things changed, and the kingdom has gone to my brother; for it has come to him from the LORD. **16**Now I have one request to make of you. Do not refuse me."

"You may make it," she said.

17So he continued, "Please ask King Solomon—he will not refuse you—to give me Abishag the Shunammite as my wife."

18"Very well," Bathsheba replied, "I will speak to the king for you."

19When Bathsheba went to King Solomon to speak to him for Adonijah, the king stood up to meet her, bowed down to her and sat down on his throne. He had a throne brought for the king's mother, and she sat down at his right hand.

20"I have one small request to make of you," she said. "Do not refuse me."

The king replied, "Make it, my mother; I will not refuse you."

21So she said, "Let Abishag the Shunammite be given in marriage to your brother Adonijah."

22King Solomon answered his mother, "Why do you request Abishag the Shunammite for Adonijah? You might as well request the kingdom for him—after all, he is my older brother—yes, for him and for Abiathar the priestᴰ and Joab son of Zeruiah!"

23Then King Solomon swore by the LORD: "May God deal with me, be it ever so severely, if Adonijah does not pay with his life for this request! **24**And now, as surely as the LORD lives—he who has established me securely on the throne of my father David and has founded a dynasty for me as he promised—Adonijah shall be put to deathᴰ today!" **25**So King Solomon gave orders to Benaiah son of Jehoiada, and he struck down Adonijah and he died.

26To Abiathar the priest the king said, "Go back to your fields in Anathoth. You deserve to die, but I will not put you to death now, because you carried the ark of the Sovereign LORD before my father David and shared all my father's hardships." **27**So Solomon removed Abiathar from the priesthood of the LORD, fulfilling the word the LORD had spoken at Shiloh about the house of Eli.

28When the news reached Joab, who had conspired with Adonijah though not with Absalom, he fled to the tent of the LORD and took hold of the horns of the altar. **29**King Solomon was told that Joab had fled to the tent of the LORD and was beside the altar. Then Solomon ordered Benaiah son of Jehoiada, "Go, strike him down!"

30So Benaiah entered the tent of the LORD and said to Joab, "The king says, 'Come out!'"

But he answered, "No, I will die here."

Benaiah reported to the king, "This is how Joab answered me."

31Then the king commanded Benaiah, "Do as he says. Strike him down and bury him, and so clear me and my father's house of the guilt of the innocent blood that Joab shed. **32**The LORD will repay him for the blood he shed, because without the knowledge of my father David he attacked two men and killed them with the sword. Both of them—Abner son of Ner, commander of Israel's army, and Amasa son of Jether, commander of Judah's army—

Why did Solomon react negatively to his brother's request? (2:22–23)

Though Abishag had no sexual relations with David, she still belonged to his royal harem. Earlier, the rebel Absalom reinforced his claim to power by sleeping with most of David's harem (2 Samuel 16:20–22). Solomon saw Adonijah's request for Abishag in a similar light—as a treasonous claim to the throne.

Was Abishag destined to remain single all her life? (2:22–23)

Since Abishag never had sexual relations with David, she might have been absorbed into Solomon's harem. Some believe she is the Shunammite spoken of in the Song of Songs.

SCRIPTURE LINK (2:27) *The word the Lord had spoken . . . about the house of Eli*

See 1 Samuel 2:27–36.

Why would a king meddle in priestly affairs? (2:27)

God's way of appointing prophets, priests and kings had its own system of checks and balances. David and Solomon appointed prophets and priests, and could remove them. But God's holy men also had authority. Samuel anointed Saul, but deposed him in favor of David.

Why did God wait so long to remove the house of Eli from the priesthood? (2:27)

Perhaps the Lord allowed another generation of Eli's descendants to serve as priests to show how contempt for God can be passed from generation to generation. God had told Eli that his house would be cut off from the priesthood because of his sons' evil behavior. The same disrespect shown by Eli's sons later became evident in Abiathar's contempt for Solomon (1 Samuel 2:30–35).

Why didn't the horns of the altar save Joab? (2:28; see v. 34)

See *How much safety did the horns of the altar provide?* (1:50)

Was Joab's death God's justice? (2:32)

Solomon assured Benaiah that Joab's punishment was sanctioned by God. Since Joab sought asylum at a holy place, Benaiah was hesitant to carry out the death sentence for fear of God's judgment upon himself. Joab had murdered two innocent men for political reasons—a public crime that had stained the integrity of David's administration.

were better men and more upright than he. ³³May the guilt of their blood rest on the head of Joab and his descendants forever. But on David and his descendants, his house and his throne, may there be the LORD's peaceᴰ forever."

³⁴So Benaiah son of Jehoiada went up and struck down Joab and killed him, and he was buried on his own landᵃ in the desert. ³⁵The king put Benaiah son of Jehoiada over the army in Joab's position and replaced Abiathar with Zadok the priestᴰ.

³⁶Then the king sent for Shimei and said to him, "Build yourself a house in Jerusalemᴰ and live there, but do not go anywhere else. ³⁷The day you leave and cross the Kidron Valleyᴰ, you can be sure you will die; your blood will be on your own head."

³⁸Shimei answered the king, "What you say is good. Your servant will do as my lord the king has said." And Shimei stayed in Jerusalem for a long time.

³⁹But three years later, two of Shimei's slaves ran off to Achish son of Maacah, king of Gath, and Shimei was told, "Your slaves are in Gath." ⁴⁰At this, he saddled his donkey and went to Achish at Gath in search of his slaves. So Shimei went away and brought the slaves back from Gath.

⁴¹When Solomon was told that Shimei had gone from Jerusalem to Gath and had returned, ⁴²the king summoned Shimei and said to him, "Did I not make you swear by the LORD and warn you, 'On the day you leave to go anywhere else, you can be sure you will die'? At that time you said to me, 'What you say is good. I will obey.' ⁴³Why then did you not keep your oath to the LORD and obey the command I gave you?"

⁴⁴The king also said to Shimei, "You know in your heart all the wrong you did to my father David. Now the LORD will repay you for your wrongdoing. ⁴⁵But King Solomon will be blessed, and David's throne will remain secure before the LORD forever."

⁴⁶Then the king gave the order to Benaiah son of Jehoiada, and he went out and struck Shimei down and killed him.

The kingdom was now firmly established in Solomon's hands.

Solomon Asks for Wisdom

3 Solomon made an alliance with Pharaoh king of Egypt and married his daughter. He brought her to the City of David until he finished building his palace and the temple of the LORD, and the wall around Jerusalem. ²The people, however, were still sacrificing at the high placesᴰ, because a temple had not yet been built for the Name of the LORD. ³Solomon showed his love for the LORD by walking according to the statutes of his father David, except that he offered sacrificesᴰ and burned incenseᴰ on the high places.

⁴The king went to Gibeon to offer sacrifices, for that was the most important high place, and Solomon offered a thousand burnt offeringsᴰ on that altar. ⁵At Gibeon the LORD appeared to Solomon during the night in a dream, and God said, "Ask for whatever you want me to give you."

⁶Solomon answered, "You have shown great kindness to your servant, my father David, because he was faithful to you and righteousᴰ and upright in heart. You have

ᵃ34 Or *buried in his tomb*

If Shimei deserved to die, why simply confine him to the city? (2:36–37)
Though Shimei had been disloyal to David, even cursing him publicly (2 Samuel 16:5–8), David showed mercy to Shimei. But David may have doubted the wisdom of doing so because when Solomon became king, David warned him to beware of Shimei (2:8–9). Solomon apparently allowed David's mercy to stand, but he wanted to prevent Shimei from stirring up trouble with other Benjamites outside of Jerusalem who may still have held a grudge against David for replacing Saul, their fellow tribesman, as king.

Why did Solomon marry a foreigner? (3:1)
Sometimes a king would marry another king's daughter as a way of guaranteeing the peace. Most of Solomon's 700 marriages were political in nature. However expedient the practice may have been politically, Moses made it clear that the kings of Israel were not to multiply wives for themselves (Deut. 17:17). Solomon's many wives eventually led to his downfall.

What was wrong with worshiping at the high places? (3:3)
The high places were once pagan Canaanite shrines. Even though the Israelites worshiped the Lord at the high places, they often sinned by blending false religions with their worship of the Lord. This was exactly the situation the Law of Moses had addressed when it forbade the use of former pagan shrines to worship the Lord, unless these places were divinely sanctioned (Num. 33:52; Deut. 12:3–8).

What made Gibeon the most important high place? (3:4)
Before the temple was built, Israel's sacred objects were not always together in the same place. The Tent of Meeting and the bronze altar, however, were still at Gibeon, which made it the most significant place of worship (see *The Battle of Gibeon* on page 297).

continued this great kindness to him and have given him a son to sit on his throne this very day.

7"Now, O LORD my God, you have made your servant king in place of my father David. But I am only a little child and do not know how to carry out my duties. **8**Your servant is here among the people you have chosen, a great people, too numerous to count or number. **9**So give your servant a discerning heart to govern your people and to distinguish between right and wrong. For who is able to govern this great people of yours?"

10The Lord was pleased that Solomon had asked for this. **11**So God said to him, "Since you have asked for this and not for long life or wealth for yourself, nor have asked for the death[D] of your enemies but for discernment in administering justice, **12**I will do what you have asked. I will give you a wise and discerning heart, so that there will never have been anyone like you, nor will there ever be. **13**Moreover, I will give you what you have not asked for—both riches and honor—so that in your lifetime you will have no equal among kings. **14**And if you walk in my ways and obey my statutes and commands as David your father did, I will give you a long life." **15**Then Solomon awoke—and he realized it had been a dream.

He returned to Jerusalem[D], stood before the ark of the Lord's covenant[D] and sacrificed burnt offerings[D] and fellowship offerings[D].[a] Then he gave a feast for all his court.

A Wise Ruling

16Now two prostitutes came to the king and stood before him. **17**One of them said, "My lord, this woman and I live in the same house. I had a baby while she was there with me. **18**The third day after my child was born, this woman also had a baby. We were alone; there was no one in the house but the two of us.

19"During the night this woman's son died because she lay on him. **20**So she got up in the middle of the night and took my son from my side while I your servant was asleep. She put him by her breast and put her dead son by my breast. **21**The next morning, I got up to nurse my son—and he was dead! But when I looked at him closely in the morning light, I saw that it wasn't the son I had borne."

22The other woman said, "No! The living one is my son; the dead one is yours."

But the first one insisted, "No! The dead one is yours; the living one is mine." And so they argued before the king.

23The king said, "This one says, 'My son is alive and your son is dead,' while that one says, 'No! Your son is dead and mine is alive.'"

24Then the king said, "Bring me a sword." So they brought a sword for the king. **25**He then gave an order: "Cut the living child in two and give half to one and half to the other."

26The woman whose son was alive was filled with compassion for her son and said to the king, "Please, my lord, give her the living baby! Don't kill him!"

But the other said, "Neither I nor you shall have him. Cut him in two!"

27Then the king gave his ruling: "Give the living baby to the first woman. Do not kill him; she is his mother."

Why did Solomon call himself only a little child? (3:7)
Solomon was only about 20 years old when he began to reign. He had very little administrative experience. The self-imposed label of *little child* points to his honest admission that he had insufficient knowledge, not a lack of confidence.

What did Solomon think when he *realized it had been a dream*? (3:15)
See article: *Does God speak through visions and dreams?* (Daniel 1:17).

*a15 Traditionally *peace offerings*

28When all Israel heard the verdict the king had given, they held the king in awe, because they saw that he had wisdom from God to administer justice.

Solomon's Officials and Governors

4 So King Solomon ruled over all Israel. **2**And these were his chief officials:

Azariah son of Zadok—the priest[D];
3Elihoreph and Ahijah, sons of Shisha—secretaries;
Jehoshaphat son of Ahilud—recorder;
4Benaiah son of Jehoiada—commander in chief;
Zadok and Abiathar—priests;
5Azariah son of Nathan—in charge of the district officers;
Zabud son of Nathan—a priest and personal adviser to the king;
6Ahishar—in charge of the palace;
Adoniram son of Abda—in charge of forced labor.

7Solomon also had twelve district governors over all Israel, who supplied provisions for the king and the royal household. Each one had to provide supplies for one month in the year. **8**These are their names:

Ben-Hur—in the hill country of Ephraim;
9Ben-Deker—in Makaz, Shaalbim, Beth Shemesh and Elon Bethhanan;
10Ben-Hesed—in Arubboth (Socoh and all the land of Hepher were his);
11Ben-Abinadab—in Naphoth Dor[a] (he was married to Taphath daughter of Solomon);
12Baana son of Ahilud—in Taanach and Megiddo, and in all of Beth Shan next to Zarethan below Jezreel, from Beth Shan to Abel Meholah across to Jokmeam;
13Ben-Geber—in Ramoth Gilead (the settlements of Jair son of Manasseh in Gilead were his, as well as the district of Argob in Bashan and its sixty large walled cities with bronze gate bars);
14Ahinadab son of Iddo—in Mahanaim;
15Ahimaaz—in Naphtali (he had married Basemath daughter of Solomon);
16Baana son of Hushai—in Asher and in Aloth;
17Jehoshaphat son of Paruah—in Issachar;
18Shimei son of Ela—in Benjamin;
19Geber son of Uri—in Gilead (the country of Sihon king of the Amorites and the country of Og king of Bashan). He was the only governor over the district.

Solomon's Daily Provisions

20The people of Judah and Israel were as numerous as the sand on the seashore; they ate, they drank and they were happy. **21**And Solomon ruled over all the kingdoms from the River[b] to the land of the Philistines, as far as the border of Egypt. These countries brought tribute and were Solomon's subjects all his life.

22Solomon's daily provisions were thirty cors[c] of fine flour and sixty cors[d] of meal, **23**ten head of stall-fed cattle, twenty of pasture-fed cattle and a hundred sheep and

---

Why was a priest a chief official for the king? (4:2)
See *Why would a king meddle in priestly affairs?* (2:27).

Did Solomon have slaves? (4:6)
Solomon conscripted foreigners as slaves and drafted some Israelites into forced labor as well. Samuel had warned the people of Israel that demanding a king would result in their sons and daughters having to work for the king (1 Samuel 8:11–13).

How did the governors supply provisions for the king? (4:7)
Each of these 12 governors was responsible for supplying the royal court's provisions once a year, gathered as taxes from the landowners in their districts. Samuel had warned the people about the taxes of produce and livestock that would be taken from them. The people later complained to Solomon's son, Rehoboam, revealing their resentment of providing for the king (12:4).

As numerous as the sand on the seashore (4:20)
A figure of speech, poetic hyperbole or exaggeration to express the abundant blessings of God. The people of God are also described as numerous as the dust of the earth (2 Chron. 1:9–15) and the stars in the sky (Gen. 22:17). Also see article: *Can the Bible exaggerate and still be true?* (2 Chron. 1:9–15).

Is *happy* often used to describe the Israelites? (4:20)
No. During the reign of Solomon, Israel experienced unprecedented peace. For a period of time, the absence of war lightened the burden of high taxes. Still, their happiness was not permanent. Eventually they tired of having to pay the bill for their king's projects and comfort (12:4).

Solomon's Kingdom (4:21)

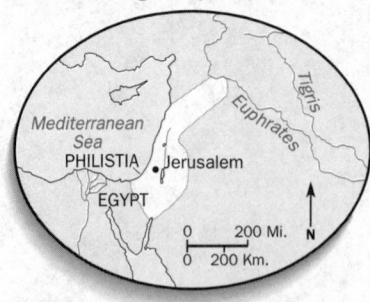

How many people did Solomon feed each day? (4:22–23)
Eventually, Solomon had to feed at least 700 wives, 300 concubines and all their children. Along with these, he also had to provide for the palace servants, court officials and their families.

---

a11 Or *in the heights of Dor*   *b21* That is, the Euphrates; also in verse 24   *c22* That is, probably about 185 bushels (about 6.6 kiloliters)   *d22* That is, probably about 375 bushels (about 13.2 kiloliters)

goats, as well as deer, gazelles, roebucks and choice fowl. [24]For he ruled over all the kingdoms west of the River, from Tiphsah to Gaza, and had peace[D] on all sides. [25]During Solomon's lifetime Judah and Israel, from Dan to Beersheba, lived in safety, each man under his own vine and fig tree.

[26]Solomon had four[a] thousand stalls for chariot horses, and twelve thousand horses.[b]

[27]The district officers, each in his month, supplied provisions for King Solomon and all who came to the king's table. They saw to it that nothing was lacking. [28]They also brought to the proper place their quotas of barley and straw for the chariot horses and the other horses.

Solomon's Wisdom

[29]God gave Solomon wisdom and very great insight, and a breadth of understanding as measureless as the sand on the seashore. [30]Solomon's wisdom was greater than the wisdom of all the men of the East, and greater than all the wisdom of Egypt. [31]He was wiser than any other man, including Ethan the Ezrahite—wiser than Heman, Calcol and Darda, the sons of Mahol. And his fame spread to all the surrounding nations. [32]He spoke three thousand proverbs and his songs numbered a thousand and five. [33]He described plant life, from the cedar of Lebanon to the hyssop[D] that grows out of walls. He also taught about animals and birds, reptiles and fish. [34]Men of all nations came to listen to Solomon's wisdom, sent by all the kings of the world, who had heard of his wisdom.

Preparations for Building the Temple

5 When Hiram king of Tyre heard that Solomon had been anointed[D] king to succeed his father David, he sent his envoys to Solomon, because he had always been on friendly terms with David. [2]Solomon sent back this message to Hiram:

[3]"You know that because of the wars waged against my father David from all sides, he could not build a temple for the Name of the LORD his God until

[a]26 Some Septuagint manuscripts (see also 2 Chron. 9:25); Hebrew forty   [b]26 Or charioteers

---

Each man under his own vine and fig tree (4:25)

Flourishing vines and fig trees signified fertile, prosperous times. To sit under one's own vine and fig tree symbolized peace and security.

What kind of wisdom does God give? (4:29–34)

The Bible describes two types of wisdom: worldly wisdom and wisdom that comes from God. The apostle James says that the wisdom of the world tries to ignore God and the lines he has drawn between right and wrong. People who depend upon this worldly type of wisdom tend to cultivate a type of ambition that is self-destructive.

According to James, the wisdom of God, when used properly, cultivates peaceful relationships. The type of wisdom God gives takes into account the interests of others. It is characterized by sincerity. The wisdom of God helps people become more objective in their decision-making.

This was the type of wisdom that Solomon asked for and received from God. The wisdom described in these verses enabled Solomon to ask probing questions and make knowledgeable decisions. This is the type of wisdom available to anyone who simply asks God for it.

the LORD put his enemies under his feet. **4**But now the LORD my God has given me rest on every side, and there is no adversary or disaster. **5**I intend, therefore, to build a temple for the Name of the LORD my God, as the LORD told my father David, when he said, 'Your son whom I will put on the throne in your place will build the temple for my Name.'

6"So give orders that cedars of Lebanon be cut for me. My men will work with yours, and I will pay you for your men whatever wages you set. You know that we have no one so skilled in felling timber as the Sidonians."

7When Hiram heard Solomon's message, he was greatly pleased and said, "Praise be to the LORD today, for he has given David a wise son to rule over this great nation." **8**So Hiram sent word to Solomon:

"I have received the message you sent me and will do all you want in providing the cedar and pine logs. **9**My men will haul them down from Lebanon to the sea, and I will float them in rafts by sea to the place you specify. There I will separate them and you can take them away. And you are to grant my wish by providing food for my royal household."

10In this way Hiram kept Solomon supplied with all the cedar and pine logs he wanted, **11**and Solomon gave Hiram twenty thousand cors*a* of wheat as food for his household, in addition to twenty thousand baths*b,c* of pressed olive oil. Solomon continued to do this for Hiram year after year. **12**The LORD gave Solomon wisdom, just as he had promised him. There were peaceful relations between Hiram and Solomon, and the two of them made a treaty.

13King Solomon conscripted laborers from all Israel— thirty thousand men. **14**He sent them off to Lebanon in shifts of ten thousand a month, so that they spent one month in Lebanon and two months at home. Adoniram was in charge of the forced labor. **15**Solomon had seventy thousand carriers and eighty thousand stonecutters in the hills, **16**as well as thirty-three hundred*d* foremen who supervised the project and directed the workmen. **17**At the king's command they removed from the quarry large blocks of quality stone to provide a foundation of dressed stone for the temple. **18**The craftsmen of Solomon and Hiram and the men of Gebal*e* cut and prepared the timber and stone for the building of the temple.

Solomon Builds the Temple

6 In the four hundred and eightieth*f* year after the Israelites had come out of Egypt, in the fourth year of Solomon's reign over Israel, in the month of Ziv, the second month, he began to build the temple of the LORD.

2The temple that King Solomon built for the LORD was sixty cubits*D* long, twenty wide and thirty high.*g* **3**The portico at the front of the main hall of the temple extend-

Did Hiram, a non-Jewish king, worship the Lord? (5:7)

It was common for kings that had commercial and political ties to recognize each other's gods. Of course, faithful Jews were to never acknowledge pagan deities, though Solomon eventually fell into this trap. It is possible that Hiram genuinely praised the Lord, just as the Queen of Sheba did. During the dedication of the temple, Solomon prayed that foreigners would personally come to know the God of Israel (8:43).

Why be allies with pagans? (5:12)

Win-win treaties with pagan tribes were not an option under the law. Israel was to subdue its pagan neighbors. There was, however, an exception to the rule for nations at a distance from Israel, but Tyre and Sidon should have been excluded from covenant consideration since they were within the original boundaries of the promised land (Deut. 20:12–15; see *Map 5* at the back of this Bible). Perhaps Hiram's acknowledgement of the Lord persuaded Solomon that the pagan king could be an acceptable partner.

Were Solomon's conscripted laborers slaves? (5:13)

Solomon made no slaves of Israelites (9:22), but he did draft them into forced labor. This fulfilled Samuel's warnings about the burdens a king would impose (1 Samuel 8:16). The 30,000 male Israelites, however, are distinguished from the true slaves (v. 15). The 70,000 carriers and 80,000 stonecutters, though residents of the land, were not Israelites (2 Chron. 2:17–18).

Four hundred and eightieth year (6:1)

Probably around 966 B.C. If the date is taken literally, the exodus occurred around 1446 B.C. Some believe the 480 years mentioned here is a general figure to describe 12 generations, which would allow for a later date for the exodus, around 1290 B.C.

Where did Solomon get the plans for the temple? (6:2–9)

Key characteristics of Solomon's temple reflect the desert tabernacle, one that Moses built *exactly like the pattern* God showed him (Exodus 25:9). Solomon's temple was nearly twice as large and had an additional portico. Canaanite and Phoenician temples from that era were markedly similar. Hiram's architects may have contributed to the design of the temple as well as to its construction.

*a*11 That is, probably about 125,000 bushels (about 4,400 kiloliters)   *b*11 Septuagint (see also 2 Chron. 2:10); Hebrew *twenty cors*   *c*11 That is, about 115,000 gallons (about 440 kiloliters)   *d*16 Hebrew; some Septuagint manuscripts (see also 2 Chron. 2:2, 18) *thirty-six hundred*   *e*18 That is, Byblos   *f*1 Hebrew; Septuagint *four hundred and fortieth*   *g*2 That is, about 90 feet (about 27 meters) long and 30 feet (about 9 meters) wide and 45 feet (about 13.5 meters) high

ed the width of the temple, that is twenty cubits[D],[a] and projected ten cubits[b] from the front of the temple. **4**He made narrow clerestory windows in the temple. **5**Against the walls of the main hall and inner sanctuary he built a structure around the building, in which there were side rooms. **6**The lowest floor was five cubits[c] wide, the middle floor six cubits[d] and the third floor seven.[e] He made offset ledges around the outside of the temple so that nothing would be inserted into the temple walls.

7In building the temple, only blocks dressed at the quarry were used, and no hammer, chisel or any other iron tool was heard at the temple site while it was being built.

8The entrance to the lowest[f] floor was on the south side of the temple; a stairway led up to the middle level and from there to the third. **9**So he built the temple and completed it, roofing it with beams and cedar planks. **10**And he built the side rooms all along the temple. The height of each was five cubits, and they were attached to the temple by beams of cedar.

11The word of the LORD came to Solomon: **12**"As for this temple you are building, if you follow my decrees, carry out my regulations and keep all my commands and obey them, I will fulfill through you the promise I gave to David your father. **13**And I will live among the Israelites and will not abandon my people Israel."

14So Solomon built the temple and completed it. **15**He lined its interior walls with cedar boards, paneling them from the floor of the temple to the ceiling, and covered the floor of the temple with planks of pine. **16**He partitioned off twenty cubits[a] at the rear of the temple with cedar boards from floor to ceiling to form within the temple an inner sanctuary, the Most Holy Place[D]. **17**The main hall in front of this room was forty cubits[g] long. **18**The inside of the temple was cedar, carved with gourds and open flowers. Everything was cedar; no stone was to be seen.

19He prepared the inner sanctuary within the temple to set the ark of the covenant[D] of the LORD there. **20**The inner sanctuary was twenty cubits long, twenty wide and twenty high.[h] He overlaid the inside with pure gold, and he also overlaid the altar of cedar. **21**Solomon covered the inside of the temple with pure gold, and he extended gold chains across the front of the inner sanctuary, which was overlaid with gold. **22**So he overlaid the whole interior with gold. He also overlaid with gold the altar that belonged to the inner sanctuary.

23In the inner sanctuary he made a pair of cherubim[D] of olive wood, each ten cubits[b] high. **24**One wing of the first cherub was five cubits long, and the other wing five cubits—ten cubits from wing tip to wing tip. **25**The second cherub also measured ten cubits, for the two cherubim were identical in size and shape. **26**The height of each cherub was ten cubits. **27**He placed the cherubim inside the innermost room of the temple, with their wings spread out. The wing of one cherub

Clerestory (6:4)

The upper portion of the inner walls that rose above the adjacent siderooms to the temple. Its windows brought light into the temple proper.

Why weren't tools used at the temple site? (6:7)

At the time of Moses, the use of iron on rock was closely associated with pagan practices. Shaped stones were forbidden in the building of an altar (Exodus 20:25). Perhaps uncut stones were considered a symbol for purity. For the temple, tools were only forbidden at the construction site, not at the quarry. Using pre-fitted stones made the construction go much faster. Also see *Why were uncut stones needed for the altar?* (Joshua 8:31).

---

[a]3,16 That is, about 30 feet (about 9 meters)   [b]3,23 That is, about 15 feet (about 4.5 meters)   [c]6 That is, about 7 1/2 feet (about 2.3 meters); also in verses 10 and 24   [d]6 That is, about 9 feet (about 2.7 meters)   [e]6 That is, about 10 1/2 feet (about 3.1 meters)   [f]8 Septuagint; Hebrew *middle*   [g]17 That is, about 60 feet (about 18 meters)   [h]20 That is, about 30 feet (about 9 meters) long, wide and high

SCRIPTURE LINK (6:29–35) *He carved cherubim*
The second commandment prohibited images to be worshiped (Exodus 20:4–5). In contrast, Solomon's use of decorative art work in the temple is recorded without condemnation. Art that promotes the worship of God gives God pleasure.

Why did Solomon spend more time building his own house than God's house? (7:1; see 6:38)
The contrast between the times taken to build the temple and the king's palace may be a subtle criticism of Solomon's priorities. As Solomon's power grew, he began to distance himself from the Lord.

Why did Pharaoh's daughter, Solomon's wife, need a separate palace? (7:8)
Chronicles, in its single reference to the king's wives, states that Solomon wouldn't allow Pharaoh's daughter to live in the holy places where the ark of the Lord had been (2 Chron. 8:11). Ironically, though Solomon separated her from Israel's God, he eventually joined his foreign wives in worshiping their gods.

touched one wall, while the wing of the other touched the other wall, and their wings touched each other in the middle of the room. **28**He overlaid the cherubim[D] with gold.

29On the walls all around the temple, in both the inner and outer rooms, he carved cherubim, palm trees and open flowers. **30**He also covered the floors of both the inner and outer rooms of the temple with gold.

31For the entrance of the inner sanctuary he made doors of olive wood with five-sided jambs. **32**And on the two olive wood doors he carved cherubim, palm trees and open flowers, and overlaid the cherubim and palm trees with beaten gold. **33**In the same way he made four-sided jambs of olive wood for the entrance to the main hall. **34**He also made two pine doors, each having two leaves that turned in sockets. **35**He carved cherubim, palm trees and open flowers on them and overlaid them with gold hammered evenly over the carvings.

36And he built the inner courtyard of three courses of dressed stone and one course of trimmed cedar beams.

37The foundation of the temple of the LORD was laid in the fourth year, in the month of Ziv. **38**In the eleventh year in the month of Bul, the eighth month, the temple was finished in all its details according to its specifications. He had spent seven years building it.

Solomon Builds His Palace

7 It took Solomon thirteen years, however, to complete the construction of his palace. **2**He built the Palace of the Forest of Lebanon a hundred cubits[D] long, fifty wide and thirty high,[a] with four rows of cedar columns supporting trimmed cedar beams. **3**It was roofed with cedar above the beams that rested on the columns—forty-five beams, fifteen to a row. **4**Its windows were placed high in sets of three, facing each other. **5**All the doorways had rectangular frames; they were in the front part in sets of three, facing each other.[b]

6He made a colonnade fifty cubits long and thirty wide.[c] In front of it was a portico, and in front of that were pillars and an overhanging roof.

7He built the throne hall, the Hall of Justice, where he was to judge, and he covered it with cedar from floor to ceiling.[d] **8**And the palace in which he was to live, set farther back, was similar in design. Solomon also made a palace like this hall for Pharaoh's daughter, whom he had married.

9All these structures, from the outside to the great courtyard and from foundation to eaves, were made of blocks of high-grade stone cut to size and trimmed with a saw on their inner and outer faces. **10**The foundations were laid with large stones of good quality, some measuring ten cubits[e] and some eight.[f] **11**Above were high-grade stones, cut to size, and cedar beams. **12**The great courtyard was surrounded by a wall of three courses of dressed stone and one course of trimmed cedar beams, as was the inner courtyard of the temple of the LORD with its portico.

---

[a]2 That is, about 150 feet (about 46 meters) long, 75 feet (about 23 meters) wide and 45 feet (about 13.5 meters) high   [b]5 The meaning of the Hebrew for this verse is uncertain.   [c]6 That is, about 75 feet (about 23 meters) long and 45 feet (about 13.5 meters) wide   [d]7 Vulgate and Syriac; Hebrew *floor*   [e]10 That is, about 15 feet (about 4.5 meters)   [f]10 That is, about 12 feet (about 3.6 meters)

The Temple's Furnishings

13King Solomon sent to Tyre and brought Huram,[a] **14**whose mother was a widow from the tribe of Naphtali and whose father was a man of Tyre and a craftsman in bronze. Huram was highly skilled and experienced in all kinds of bronze work. He came to King Solomon and did all the work assigned to him.

15He cast two bronze pillars, each eighteen cubits[D] high and twelve cubits around,[b] by line. **16**He also made two capitals of cast bronze to set on the tops of the pillars; each capital was five cubits[c] high. **17**A network of interwoven chains festooned the capitals on top of the pillars, seven for each capital. **18**He made pomegranates in two rows[d] encircling each network to decorate the capitals on top of the pillars.[e] He did the same for each capital. **19**The capitals on top of the pillars in the portico were in the shape of lilies, four cubits[f] high. **20**On the capitals of both pillars, above the bowl-shaped part next to the network, were the two hundred pomegranates in rows all around. **21**He erected the pillars at the portico of the temple. The pillar to the south he named Jakin[g] and the one to the north Boaz.[h] **22**The capitals on top were in the shape of lilies. And so the work on the pillars was completed.

a13 Hebrew *Hiram,* a variant of *Huram;* also in verses 40 and 45
b15 That is, about 27 feet (about 8.1 meters) high and 18 feet (about 5.4 meters) around   *c16* That is, about 7 1/2 feet (about 2.3 meters); also in verse 23   *d18* Two Hebrew manuscripts and Septuagint; most Hebrew manuscripts *made the pillars, and there were two rows*   *e18* Many Hebrew manuscripts and Syriac; most Hebrew manuscripts *pomegranates*   *f19* That is, about 6 feet (about 1.8 meters); also in verse 38   *g21* Jakin probably means *he establishes.*   *h21* Boaz probably means *in him is strength.*

Could children of mixed marriages fit into Israel? (7:14)

Moses forbade anyone born of a foreign marriage to *enter the assembly of the LORD* (Deut. 23:1–6). But exceptions dot the history of God's people. Ruth, the Moabite, was an ancestor of David and appears in Jesus' genealogy (Matt. 1:5). Rehoboam, Solomon's successor, had an Ammonite mother (14:21,31). God was more concerned about a person's heart than his or her parentage. Also see *Does God reject the children of sinful parents?* (Deut. 23:2).

Why give names to pillars? (7:21)

See *Why give names to pillars?* (2 Chron. 3:17).

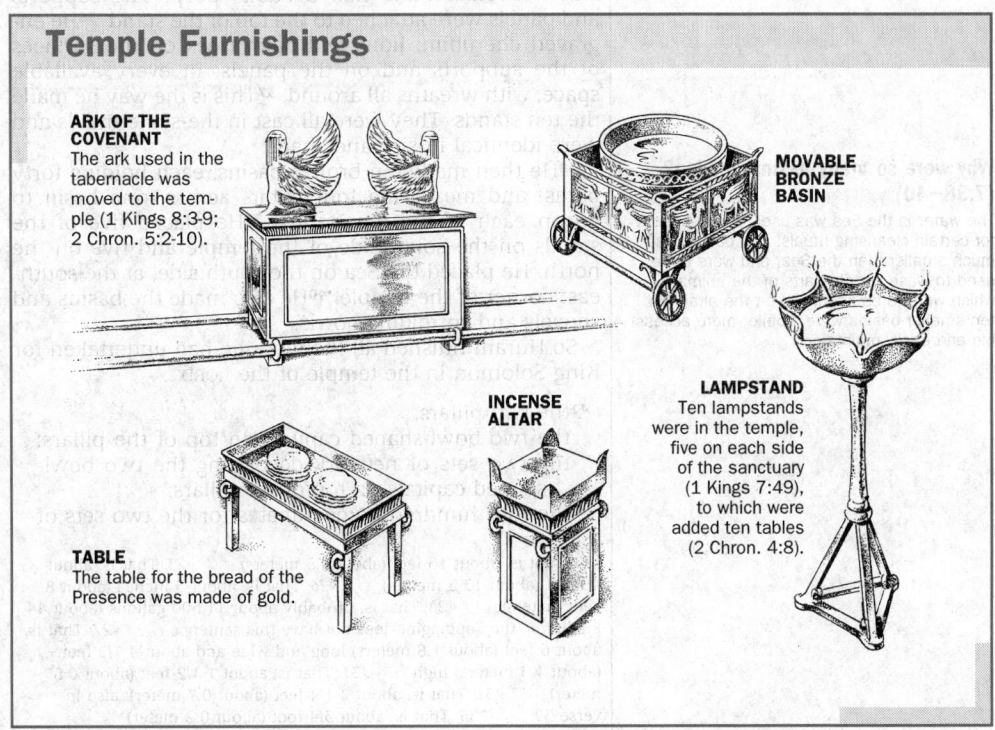

Temple Furnishings

ARK OF THE COVENANT
The ark used in the tabernacle was moved to the temple (1 Kings 8:3-9; 2 Chron. 5:2-10).

MOVABLE BRONZE BASIN

INCENSE ALTAR

LAMPSTAND
Ten lampstands were in the temple, five on each side of the sanctuary (1 Kings 7:49), to which were added ten tables (2 Chron. 4:8).

TABLE
The table for the bread of the Presence was made of gold.

The Sea (7:23)

Huge basin or reservoir used by priests to cleanse their hand and feet. Its capacity was approximately 10,000 gallons.

Why have bulls in the temple? (7:25)

Since the bull is associated with Canaan's fertility god Baal, it seems like a dangerous symbol to have in the Lord's temple. But these bulls were symbols of God's power—and nothing more. They were not objects of worship and were therefore acceptable forms of religious art for Israel.

Why were so many basins needed? (7:38–40)

The water in the Sea was used by the priests for certain cleansing rituals. The basins were much smaller than the Sea, and were to be used to wash certain parts of the animals which were to be sacrificed on the altar. The ten smaller basins were mobile, more accessible and easily maintained.

23He made the Sea of cast metal, circular in shape, measuring ten cubits[D][a] from rim to rim and five cubits high. It took a line of thirty cubits[b] to measure around it. **24**Below the rim, gourds encircled it—ten to a cubit. The gourds were cast in two rows in one piece with the Sea.

25The Sea stood on twelve bulls, three facing north, three facing west, three facing south and three facing east. The Sea rested on top of them, and their hindquarters were toward the center. **26**It was a handbreadth[c] in thickness, and its rim was like the rim of a cup, like a lily blossom. It held two thousand baths.[d]

27He also made ten movable stands of bronze; each was four cubits long, four wide and three high.[e] **28**This is how the stands were made: They had side panels attached to uprights. **29**On the panels between the uprights were lions, bulls and cherubim[D]—and on the uprights as well. Above and below the lions and bulls were wreaths of hammered work. **30**Each stand had four bronze wheels with bronze axles, and each had a basin resting on four supports, cast with wreaths on each side. **31**On the inside of the stand there was an opening that had a circular frame one cubit[f] deep. This opening was round, and with its basework it measured a cubit and a half.[g] Around its opening there was engraving. The panels of the stands were square, not round. **32**The four wheels were under the panels, and the axles of the wheels were attached to the stand. The diameter of each wheel was a cubit and a half. **33**The wheels were made like chariot wheels; the axles, rims, spokes and hubs were all of cast metal.

34Each stand had four handles, one on each corner, projecting from the stand. **35**At the top of the stand there was a circular band half a cubit[h] deep. The supports and panels were attached to the top of the stand. **36**He engraved cherubim, lions and palm trees on the surfaces of the supports and on the panels, in every available space, with wreaths all around. **37**This is the way he made the ten stands. They were all cast in the same molds and were identical in size and shape.

38He then made ten bronze basins, each holding forty baths[i] and measuring four cubits across, one basin to go on each of the ten stands. **39**He placed five of the stands on the south side of the temple and five on the north. He placed the Sea on the south side, at the southeast corner of the temple. **40**He also made the basins and shovels and sprinkling bowls.

So Huram finished all the work he had undertaken for King Solomon in the temple of the LORD:

41the two pillars;
   the two bowl-shaped capitals on top of the pillars;
   the two sets of network decorating the two bowl-shaped capitals on top of the pillars;
42the four hundred pomegranates for the two sets of

---

[a]23 That is, about 15 feet (about 4.5 meters)   [b]23 That is, about 45 feet (about 13.5 meters)   [c]26 That is, about 3 inches (about 8 centimeters)   [d]26 That is, probably about 11,500 gallons (about 44 kiloliters); the Septuagint does not have this sentence.   [e]27 That is, about 6 feet (about 1.8 meters) long and wide and about 4 1/2 feet (about 1.3 meters) high   [f]31 That is, about 1 1/2 feet (about 0.5 meter)   [g]31 That is, about 2 1/4 feet (about 0.7 meter); also in verse 32   [h]35 That is, about 3/4 foot (about 0.2 meter)   [i]38 That is, about 230 gallons (about 880 liters)

network (two rows of pomegranates for each network, decorating the bowl-shaped capitals on top of the pillars);
43the ten stands with their ten basins;
44the Sea and the twelve bulls under it;
45the pots, shovels and sprinkling bowls.

All these objects that Huram made for King Solomon for the temple of the LORD were of burnished bronze. **46**The king had them cast in clay molds in the plain of the Jordan between Succoth and Zarethan. **47**Solomon left all these things unweighed, because there were so many; the weight of the bronze was not determined.
48Solomon also made all the furnishings that were in the LORD's temple:

the golden altar;
the golden table on which was the bread of the Presence;
49the lampstands of pure gold (five on the right and five on the left, in front of the inner sanctuary);
the gold floral work and lamps and tongs;
50the pure gold basins, wick trimmers, sprinkling bowls, dishes and censersᴰ;
and the gold sockets for the doors of the innermost room, the Most Holy Placeᴰ, and also for the doors of the main hall of the temple.

51When all the work King Solomon had done for the temple of the LORD was finished, he brought in the things his father David had dedicated—the silver and gold and the furnishings—and he placed them in the treasuries of the LORD's temple.

The Ark Brought to the Temple

8 Then King Solomon summoned into his presence at Jerusalemᴰ the elders of Israel, all the heads of the tribes and the chiefs of the Israelite families, to bring up the ark of the LORD's covenantᴰ from Zionᴰ, the City of David. **2**All the men of Israel came together to King Solomon at the time of the festival in the month of Ethanim, the seventh month.
3When all the elders of Israel had arrived, the priestsᴰ took up the ark, **4**and they brought up the ark of the LORD and the Tent of Meetingᴰ and all the sacredᴰ furnishings in it. The priests and Levites carried them up, **5**and King Solomon and the entire assembly of Israel that had gathered about him were before the ark, sacrificing so many sheep and cattle that they could not be recorded or counted.
6The priests then brought the ark of the LORD's covenant to its place in the inner sanctuary of the temple, the Most Holy Place, and put it beneath the wings of the cherubimᴰ. **7**The cherubim spread their wings over the place of the ark and overshadowed the ark and its carrying poles. **8**These poles were so long that their ends could be seen from the Holy Placeᴰ in front of the inner sanctuary, but not from outside the Holy Place; and they are still there today. **9**There was nothing in the ark except the two stone tablets that Moses had placed in it at Horeb, where the LORD made a covenant with the Israelites after they came out of Egypt.
10When the priests withdrew from the Holy Place, the cloud filled the temple of the LORD. **11**And the priests

What objects had David dedicated to the temple? (7:51)

David's gifts to the temple appear to have been raw materials—supplies for building and decorating (1 Chron. 29:1–5). The gold, silver and bronze David contributed came from defeated nations. According to 1 Chronicles 18:8, Solomon used the bronze to make the Sea, the pillars and various vessels.

Where had the ark been before being placed in the temple? (8:1–6)

From Shiloh, its first *home* in Canaan, the ark went to the Philistines for seven months, and then briefly to Beth Shemesh. From there it was transferred to Abinadab in Kiriath Jearim where it stayed for 20 years. After it was moved to the house of Obed-Edom the Gittite for a brief period, David took it to a tent in Jerusalem, where it stayed until it was brought to Solomon's temple.

Why did they offer so many sacrifices? (8:5)

The number of sacrifices at the dedication of the temple reflects Israel's gratitude for a central and permanent place of worship. The statement that these sacrifices were so numerous that they couldn't be recorded or counted is likely a poetic exaggeration.

Cherubim (8:6)

These larger cherubim were not the same as the cherubim on the cover of the ark itself.

Who raided the ark? (8:9)

The Bible doesn't reveal what happened to the jar of manna and Aaron's staff that were once in the ark (Exodus 16:32–34). These items may have been taken by the Philistines during the seven months they held the ark, though if they were, it's not clear how the theft could have occurred without consequences for touching the ark. See article: **Why would God kill someone who was trying to help?** (2 Samuel 6:7). Or perhaps at some point God instructed the priests to remove the manna and staff. Both possibilities are speculative.

When the priests could minister, did that mean God's glory had departed? (8:10–13)

No. On special occasions, though, the manifestation of God's glory was so intense that it paralyzed human activity. Moses, for example, was held at bay when God's glory descended upon the tabernacle in the desert (Exodus 40:35).

could not perform their service because of the cloud, for the glory[D] of the LORD filled his temple.

[12]Then Solomon said, "The LORD has said that he would dwell in a dark cloud; [13]I have indeed built a magnificent temple for you, a place for you to dwell forever."

[14]While the whole assembly of Israel was standing there, the king turned around and blessed them. [15]Then he said:

"Praise be to the LORD, the God of Israel, who with his own hand has fulfilled what he promised with his own mouth to my father David. For he said, [16]'Since the day I brought my people Israel out of Egypt, I have not chosen a city in any tribe of Israel to have a temple built for my Name to be there, but I have chosen David to rule my people Israel.'

[17]"My father David had it in his heart to build a temple for the Name of the LORD, the God of Israel. [18]But the LORD said to my father David, 'Because it was in your heart to build a temple for my Name, you did well to have this in your heart. [19]Nevertheless, you are not the one to build the temple, but your son, who is your own flesh and blood—he is the one who will build the temple for my Name.'

[20]"The LORD has kept the promise he made: I have succeeded David my father and now I sit on the throne of Israel, just as the LORD promised, and I have built the temple for the Name of the LORD, the God of Israel. [21]I have provided a place there for the ark, in which is the covenant[D] of the LORD that he made with our fathers when he brought them out of Egypt."

Solomon's Prayer of Dedication

[22]Then Solomon stood before the altar of the LORD in front of the whole assembly of Israel, spread out his hands toward heaven [23]and said:

"O LORD, God of Israel, there is no God like you in heaven above or on earth below—you who keep your covenant of love with your servants who continue wholeheartedly in your way. [24]You have kept your promise to your servant David my father; with your mouth you have promised and with your hand you have fulfilled it—as it is today. [25]"Now LORD, God of Israel, keep for your servant David my father the promises you made to him when you said, 'You shall never fail to have a man to sit before me on the throne of Israel, if only your sons are careful in all they do to walk before me as you have done.' [26]And now, O God of Israel, let your word that you promised your servant David my father come true.

[27]"But will God really dwell on earth? The heavens, even the highest heaven, cannot contain you. How much less this temple I have built! [28]Yet give attention to your servant's prayer and his plea for mercy[D], O LORD my God. Hear the cry and the prayer that your servant is praying in your presence this day. [29]May your eyes be open toward this temple night and day, this place of which you said, 'My Name shall be there,' so that you will hear the prayer your servant prays toward this place. [30]Hear the supplication of your servant and of your people Israel

Was there a difference between a temple for God and a temple for his Name? (8:27,29)

Yes. A temple for God suggests that God dwells only in the temple. But Solomon made it clear that God could not be contained within a building. The king, therefore, dedicated the temple to God's name, which represented his character and nature. God would still be present in a special way, but not confined to the temple proper. Also see *Why did God choose a place for his name to dwell?* (Deut. 26:2).

when they pray toward this place. Hear from heaven, your dwelling place, and when you hear, forgive. ³¹"When a man wrongs his neighbor and is required to take an oath and he comes and swears the oath before your altar in this temple, ³²then hear from heaven and act. Judge between your servants, condemning the guilty and bringing down on his own head what he has done. Declare the innocent not guilty, and so establish his innocence.

³³"When your people Israel have been defeated by an enemy because they have sinned against you, and when they turn back to you and confess your name, praying and making supplication to you in this temple, ³⁴then hear from heaven and forgive the sin of your people Israel and bring them back to the land you gave to their fathers.

³⁵"When the heavens are shut up and there is no rain because your people have sinned against you, and when they pray toward this place and confess your name and turn from their sin because you have afflictedᴰ them, ³⁶then hear from heaven and forgive the sin of your servants, your people Israel. Teach them the right way to live, and send rain on the land you gave your people for an inheritance.

³⁷"When famine or plague comes to the land, or blight or mildew, locustsᴰ or grasshoppers, or when an enemy besieges them in any of their cities, whatever disaster or disease may come, ³⁸and when a prayer or plea is made by any of your people Israel— each one aware of the afflictionsᴰ of his own heart, and spreading out his hands toward this temple— ³⁹then hear from heaven, your dwelling place. Forgive and act; deal with each man according to all he does, since you know his heart (for you alone know the hearts of all men), ⁴⁰so that they will fear you all the time they live in the land you gave our fathers.

⁴¹"As for the foreigner who does not belong to

How did God reveal who was guilty and who was innocent? (8:31–32)

The Law of Moses provided several methods: judicial inquiry (Deut. 13:12–14); physical symptoms that were supernaturally induced (Num. 5:11–31); a direct word from God (Num. 15:35) and the casting of lots (1 Samuel 14:40–42).

Are disasters God's judgments? (8:37–38)

See article: *Why does God send calamity?* (Lam. 3:38).

Does it matter where we pray? (8:29–30)

The Lord can hear our prayers no matter where we are. Jonah discovered that the Lord heard his prayer even from the belly of a fish. Even *in the depths,* the Lord is with us (Psalm 139:8).

Talking with God in certain places or positions can have a positive effect on our prayers. Locations that we consider holy, like a church or place of personal devotions, can enhance our feeling of reverence for God. Kneeling when we pray or bowing our heads can affect our sense of humility. Holding our hands open to heaven can increase our sense of submission to God.

Solomon's dedication of the temple as a place of prayer reminds us that *holy places* enrich our worship. There are many such holy places described in the Bible, for example: Jacob's pillar, which he called *the house of God* (Gen. 28:10–22); the site of the burning bush where Moses removed his sandals (Exodus 3:5); Daniel's place of prayer in pagan Babylon, where he always faced Jerusalem (Daniel 6:10) and the garden of Gethsemane, where Jesus wrestled with the prospect of suffering and death (Matt. 26:36).

God does not want people of prayer to rely too much on sacred places. Even the temple was not immune from destruction when the hearts of the Israelites wandered too far from God.

Was Solomon unusually generous in his prayer for foreigners? (8:43)

God intended to reach the world through his chosen people. Israel was to be a light to the nations, drawing all men to the true and living God. God told Abraham that all the peoples of the earth would be blessed through him (Gen. 12:3). Moses said other nations would admire Israel's divinely given laws (Deut. 4:6). Solomon's prayer, that Gentiles would be drawn to the temple in order to worship the God of Israel, is the fulfillment of God's promise.

your people Israel but has come from a distant land because of your name— **42**for men will hear of your great name and your mighty hand and your outstretched arm—when he comes and prays toward this temple, **43**then hear from heaven, your dwelling place, and do whatever the foreigner asks of you, so that all the peoples of the earth may know your name and fear you, as do your own people Israel, and may know that this house I have built bears your Name.

44"When your people go to war against their enemies, wherever you send them, and when they pray to the LORD toward the city you have chosen and the temple I have built for your Name, **45**then hear from heaven their prayer and their plea, and uphold their cause.

46"When they sin against you—for there is no one who does not sin—and you become angry with them and give them over to the enemy, who takes them captive to his own land, far away or near; **47**and if they have a change of heart in the land where they are held captive, and repent[D] and plead with you in the land of their conquerors and say, 'We have sinned, we have done wrong, we have acted wickedly'; **48**and if they turn back to you with all their heart and soul[D] in the land of their enemies who took them captive, and pray to you toward the land you gave their fathers, toward the city you have chosen and the temple I have built for your Name; **49**then from heaven, your dwelling place, hear their prayer and their plea, and uphold their cause. **50**And forgive your people, who have sinned against you; forgive all the offenses they have committed against you, and cause their conquerors to show them mercy[D]; **51**for they are your people and your inheritance, whom you brought out of Egypt, out of that iron-smelting furnace.

52"May your eyes be open to your servant's plea and to the plea of your people Israel, and may you listen to them whenever they cry out to you. **53**For you singled them out from all the nations of the world to be your own inheritance, just as you declared through your servant Moses when you, O Sovereign LORD, brought our fathers out of Egypt."

54When Solomon had finished all these prayers and supplications to the LORD, he rose from before the altar of the LORD, where he had been kneeling with his hands spread out toward heaven. **55**He stood and blessed the whole assembly of Israel in a loud voice, saying:

56"Praise be to the LORD, who has given rest to his people Israel just as he promised. Not one word has failed of all the good promises he gave through his servant Moses. **57**May the LORD our God be with us as he was with our fathers; may he never leave us nor forsake us. **58**May he turn our hearts to him, to walk in all his ways and to keep the commands, decrees and regulations he gave our fathers. **59**And may these words of mine, which I have prayed before the LORD, be near to the LORD our God day and night, that he may uphold the cause of his servant and the cause of his people Israel according to each day's need, **60**so that all the peoples of the earth may know that the LORD is God and that there is no other. **61**But your

Is God responsible to *turn our hearts to him?* (8:58)

People need God's help to make the right decisions. In fact, though God gives individuals a free will, none could exercise that free will unless God extended his grace. The fall left humankind trapped by sin, which distorts our thinking and decision-making process. That's why God takes the first step to turn our hearts to himself. But we must respond. Sadly, many ignore God's overtures to them. See article: *If God chooses us, do we have any choice?* (Eph. 1:4–5).

hearts must be fully committed to the LORD our God, to live by his decrees and obey his commands, as at this time."

The Dedication of the Temple

62Then the king and all Israel with him offered sacrifices[D] before the LORD. **63**Solomon offered a sacrifice of fellowship offerings[Da] to the LORD: twenty-two thousand cattle and a hundred and twenty thousand sheep and goats. So the king and all the Israelites dedicated the temple of the LORD.

64On that same day the king consecrated[D] the middle part of the courtyard in front of the temple of the LORD, and there he offered burnt offerings[D], grain offerings[D] and the fat of the fellowship offerings, because the bronze altar before the LORD was too small to hold the burnt offerings, the grain offerings and the fat of the fellowship offerings.

65So Solomon observed the festival at that time, and all Israel with him—a vast assembly, people from Lebo[b] Hamath to the Wadi of Egypt. They celebrated it before the LORD our God for seven days and seven days more, fourteen days in all. **66**On the following day he sent the people away. They blessed the king and then went home, joyful and glad in heart for all the good things the LORD had done for his servant David and his people Israel.

The LORD Appears to Solomon

9 When Solomon had finished building the temple of the LORD and the royal palace, and had achieved all he had desired to do, **2**the LORD appeared to him a second time, as he had appeared to him at Gibeon. **3**The LORD said to him:

"I have heard the prayer and plea you have made before me; I have consecrated this temple, which you have built, by putting my Name there forever. My eyes and my heart will always be there.

4"As for you, if you walk before me in integrity of heart and uprightness, as David your father did, and do all I command and observe my decrees and laws, **5**I will establish your royal throne over Israel forever, as I promised David your father when I said, 'You shall never fail to have a man on the throne of Israel.'

6"But if you[c] or your sons turn away from me and do not observe the commands and decrees I have given you[c] and go off to serve other gods and worship them, **7**then I will cut off Israel from the land I have given them and will reject this temple I have consecrated for my Name. Israel will then become a byword[D] and an object of ridicule among all peoples. **8**And though this temple is now imposing, all who pass by will be appalled and will scoff and say, 'Why has the LORD done such a thing to this land and to this temple?' **9**People will answer, 'Because they have forsaken the LORD their God, who brought their fathers out of Egypt, and have embraced other gods, worshiping and serving them—that is why the LORD brought all this disaster on them.' "

Why so many sacrifices? (8:63)
See *Why did they offer so many sacrifices?* (8:5).

Burnt offerings . . . grain offerings . . . fellowship offerings (8:64)
See *Old Testament Sacrifices* on page 138.

---

*a*63 Traditionally *peace offerings*; also in verse 64   *b*65 Or *from the entrance to*   *c*6 The Hebrew is plural.

Why didn't Hiram appreciate the cities Solomon gave him? (9:12–14)

Apparently, Solomon had become quite indebted to Hiram during his 20-year building project. Solomon gave these cities to Hiram for collateral, but it seems Solomon's neighbor did not consider the towns valuable enough to back up Israel's debt. Hiram returned the towns to Solomon, who eventually rebuilt them (2 Chron. 8:2).

Was it right for Solomon to enslave these people? (9:20–21)

Moses had made it clear to the people of Israel that they were to completely destroy the Amorites, Hittites, Perizzites, Hivites and Jebusites (Deut. 20:16–18; see *Conquest of Canaan* on page 231). These people practiced shrine prostitution and child sacrifice—if they were spared, these practices would seep into Israel's religious customs. Enslaving some of these people was an unacceptable compromise. As Moses warned, the people of Israel were soon participating in the pagan rituals of their captives.

Ophir (9:28)

A country known for its fine gold, as well as silver, ivory and peacocks. Its location is uncertain. Sites in South Arabia, East Africa and North India have been suggested.

Where was Sheba? (10:1)

The most probable location was the home of the ancient Sabaeans, which is present-day Yemen (see *Map 12* at the back of this Bible).

Why did the queen want to test Solomon? (10:1)

The queen of Sheba knew there was some connection between Solomon's success and the God of Israel. Perhaps she wanted to see what this powerful God was all about. When she saw for herself all that God had accomplished through Solomon, she praised the Lord and acknowledged his eternal love for Israel (v. 9). The genuineness of her query was supported by Jesus (Matt. 12:42).

What piqued the queen's curiosity about the Lord? (10:1)

The queen heard of Solomon's *relation to the name of the Lord*. Solomon made it clear that his success was due to the blessing of the Lord.

Why such a large caravan? (10:2)

The spices, gold and precious stones brought by the queen also suggest that she wanted a trade agreement.

Solomon's Other Activities

10At the end of twenty years, during which Solomon built these two buildings—the temple of the LORD and the royal palace— **11**King Solomon gave twenty towns in Galilee to Hiram king of Tyre, because Hiram had supplied him with all the cedar and pine and gold he wanted. **12**But when Hiram went from Tyre to see the towns that Solomon had given him, he was not pleased with them. **13**"What kind of towns are these you have given me, my brother?" he asked. And he called them the Land of Cabul,*a* a name they have to this day. **14**Now Hiram had sent to the king 120 talents*b* of gold.

15Here is the account of the forced labor King Solomon conscripted to build the LORD's temple, his own palace, the supporting terraces,*c* the wall of Jerusalem,*D* and Hazor, Megiddo and Gezer. **16**(Pharaoh king of Egypt had attacked and captured Gezer. He had set it on fire. He killed its Canaanite inhabitants and then gave it as a wedding gift to his daughter, Solomon's wife. **17**And Solomon rebuilt Gezer.) He built up Lower Beth Horon, **18**Baalath, and Tadmor*d* in the desert, within his land, **19**as well as all his store cities and the towns for his chariots and for his horses*e*—whatever he desired to build in Jerusalem, in Lebanon and throughout all the territory he ruled.

20All the people left from the Amorites, Hittites, Perizzites, Hivites and Jebusites (these peoples were not Israelites), **21**that is, their descendants remaining in the land, whom the Israelites could not exterminate*f*—these Solomon conscripted for his slave labor force, as it is to this day. **22**But Solomon did not make slaves of any of the Israelites; they were his fighting men, his government officials, his officers, his captains, and the commanders of his chariots and charioteers. **23**They were also the chief officials in charge of Solomon's projects—550 officials supervising the men who did the work.

24After Pharaoh's daughter had come up from the City of David to the palace Solomon had built for her, he constructed the supporting terraces.

25Three times a year Solomon sacrificed burnt offerings*D* and fellowship offerings*D g* on the altar he had built for the LORD, burning incense*D* before the LORD along with them, and so fulfilled the temple obligations.

26King Solomon also built ships at Ezion Geber, which is near Elath in Edom,*D* on the shore of the Red Sea.*h* **27**And Hiram sent his men—sailors who knew the sea—to serve in the fleet with Solomon's men. **28**They sailed to Ophir and brought back 420 talents*i* of gold, which they delivered to King Solomon.

The Queen of Sheba Visits Solomon

10 When the queen of Sheba heard about the fame of Solomon and his relation to the name of the LORD, she came to test him with hard questions. **2**Arriving at Jerusalem with a very great caravan—with camels carrying spices, large quantities of gold, and precious stones—

---

a13 Cabul sounds like the Hebrew for *good-for-nothing.*   *b14* That is, about 4 1/2 tons (about 4 metric tons)   *c15* Or *the Millo*; also in verse 24   *d18* The Hebrew may also be read *Tamar.*   *e19* Or *charioteers*   *f21* The Hebrew term refers to the irrevocable giving over of things or persons to the LORD, often by totally destroying them.   *g25* Traditionally *peace offerings*   *h26* Hebrew *Yam Suph*; that is, Sea of Reeds   *i28* That is, about 16 tons (about 14.5 metric tons)

she came to Solomon and talked with him about all that she had on her mind. ³Solomon answered all her questions; nothing was too hard for the king to explain to her. ⁴When the queen of Sheba saw all the wisdom of Solomon and the palace he had built, ⁵the food on his table, the seating of his officials, the attending servants in their robes, his cupbearers, and the burnt offerings^D he made at^a the temple of the LORD, she was overwhelmed.

⁶She said to the king, "The report I heard in my own country about your achievements and your wisdom is true. ⁷But I did not believe these things until I came and saw with my own eyes. Indeed, not even half was told me; in wisdom and wealth you have far exceeded the report I heard. ⁸How happy your men must be! How happy your officials, who continually stand before you and hear your wisdom! ⁹Praise be to the LORD your God, who has delighted in you and placed you on the throne of Israel. Because of the LORD's eternal love for Israel, he has made you king, to maintain justice and righteousness^D."

¹⁰And she gave the king 120 talents^b of gold, large quantities of spices, and precious stones. Never again were so many spices brought in as those the queen of Sheba gave to King Solomon.

¹¹(Hiram's ships brought gold from Ophir; and from there they brought great cargoes of almugwood^c and precious stones. ¹²The king used the almugwood to make supports for the temple of the LORD and for the royal palace, and to make harps and lyres^D for the musicians. So much almugwood has never been imported or seen since that day.)

¹³King Solomon gave the queen of Sheba all she desired and asked for, besides what he had given her out of his royal bounty. Then she left and returned with her retinue to her own country.

Solomon's Splendor

¹⁴The weight of the gold that Solomon received yearly was 666 talents,^d ¹⁵not including the revenues from merchants and traders and from all the Arabian kings and the governors of the land.

¹⁶King Solomon made two hundred large shields of hammered gold; six hundred bekas^e of gold went into each shield. ¹⁷He also made three hundred small shields of hammered gold, with three minas^f of gold in each shield. The king put them in the Palace of the Forest of Lebanon.

¹⁸Then the king made a great throne inlaid with ivory and overlaid with fine gold. ¹⁹The throne had six steps, and its back had a rounded top. On both sides of the seat were armrests, with a lion standing beside each of them. ²⁰Twelve lions stood on the six steps, one at either end of each step. Nothing like it had ever been made for any other kingdom. ²¹All King Solomon's goblets were gold, and all the household articles in the Palace of the Forest of Lebanon were pure gold. Nothing was made of silver, because silver was considered of little value in Solomon's days. ²²The king had a fleet of trading ships^g at sea along

Almugwood (10:12)

See *What made algumwood so outstanding?* (2 Chron. 9:11).

What were the golden shields used for? (10:16–17)

The large shields covered the whole body and were used by the infantry. The smaller shields were used by the archers. These shields were probably carried only on ceremonial occasions and may have doubled as a sort of royal treasury—a form of storing Solomon's wealth.

---

^a5 Or *the ascent by which he went up to*   ^b10 That is, about 4 1/2 tons (about 4 metric tons)   ^c11 Probably a variant of *algumwood*; also in verse 12   ^d14 That is, about 25 tons (about 23 metric tons)   ^e16 That is, about 7 1/2 pounds (about 3.5 kilograms)   ^f17 That is, about 3 3/4 pounds (about 1.7 kilograms)   ^g22 Hebrew *of ships of Tarshish*

The whole world (10:24)

The entire known world. During Solomon's reign, Israel became a superpower that had trading relationships with countries all over the known earth. This fulfilled God's promise to Solomon that he would have no equal among kings (3:13).

SCRIPTURE LINK (10:26) Twelve thousand horses

See Deut. 17:16 for God's instructions about Israel's restrictions on horses.

What was Solomon's real problem? (11:1–4)

Moses had said that no king of Israel was to multiply wives for himself (Deut. 17:17). And Solomon's downfall was helped by the fact that he had too many of the wrong kind of wives. Though Solomon's multiple marriages were primarily political in nature, he became quite attached to these women—and eventually to their gods. Many years later, Nehemiah rebuked the men of Israel for taking foreign wives as Solomon did: *Was it not because of marriages like these that Solomon king of Israel sinned?* (Neh. 13:26).

Why did Solomon's wisdom and insight fail him in the end? (11:4–8)

The possession of wisdom does not guarantee that it will be used. By the end of his life, Solomon had broken most of the proverbs he had written. If wisdom is the application of knowledge, then obedience is the application of wisdom. Solomon's wisdom did not fail him; he failed to follow it.

Did Solomon believe in false gods or merely accommodate his wives' beliefs? (11:5–8)

Solomon's construction of shrines to foreign gods was no mere political gesture. Solomon participated in the worship of his wives' gods, which might have included shrine prostitution and child sacrifice. As his intimacy with his wives grew, so did his compulsion to honor their gods.

with the ships of Hiram. Once every three years it returned, carrying gold, silver and ivory, and apes and baboons.

²³King Solomon was greater in riches and wisdom than all the other kings of the earth. ²⁴The whole world sought audience with Solomon to hear the wisdom God had put in his heart. ²⁵Year after year, everyone who came brought a gift—articles of silver and gold, robes, weapons and spices, and horses and mules.

²⁶Solomon accumulated chariots and horses; he had fourteen hundred chariots and twelve thousand horses,[a] which he kept in the chariot cities and also with him in Jerusalem[D]. ²⁷The king made silver as common in Jerusalem as stones, and cedar as plentiful as sycamore-fig trees in the foothills. ²⁸Solomon's horses were imported from Egypt[b] and from Kue[c]—the royal merchants purchased them from Kue. ²⁹They imported a chariot from Egypt for six hundred shekels[d] of silver, and a horse for a hundred and fifty.[e] They also exported them to all the kings of the Hittites and of the Arameans.

Solomon's Wives

11 King Solomon, however, loved many foreign women besides Pharaoh's daughter—Moabites, Ammonites, Edomites, Sidonians and Hittites. ²They were from nations about which the LORD had told the Israelites, "You must not intermarry with them, because they will surely turn your hearts after their gods." Nevertheless, Solomon held fast to them in love. ³He had seven hundred wives of royal birth and three hundred concubines[D], and his wives led him astray. ⁴As Solomon grew old, his wives turned his heart after other gods, and his heart was not fully devoted to the LORD his God, as the heart of David his father had been. ⁵He followed Ashtoreth[D] the goddess of the Sidonians, and Molech[Df] the detestable god of the Ammonites. ⁶So Solomon did evil in the eyes of the LORD; he did not follow the LORD completely, as David his father had done.

⁷On a hill east of Jerusalem, Solomon built a high place for Chemosh the detestable god of Moab, and for Molech the detestable god of the Ammonites. ⁸He did the same for all his foreign wives, who burned incense[D] and offered sacrifices[D] to their gods.

⁹The LORD became angry with Solomon because his heart had turned away from the LORD, the God of Israel, who had appeared to him twice. ¹⁰Although he had forbidden Solomon to follow other gods, Solomon did not keep the LORD's command. ¹¹So the LORD said to Solomon, "Since this is your attitude and you have not kept my covenant[D] and my decrees, which I commanded you, I will most certainly tear the kingdom away from you and give it to one of your subordinates. ¹²Nevertheless, for the sake of David your father, I will not do it during your lifetime. I will tear it out of the hand of your son. ¹³Yet I will not tear the whole kingdom from him, but will give him one tribe for the sake of David my servant and for the sake of Jerusalem, which I have chosen."

---

a26 Or *charioteers*   *b28* Or possibly *Muzur*, a region in Cilicia; also in verse 29   *c28* Probably *Cilicia*   *d29* That is, about 15 pounds (about 7 kilograms)   *e29* That is, about 3 3/4 pounds (about 1.7 kilograms)   *f5* Hebrew *Milcom*; also in verse 33

Solomon's Adversaries

14Then the LORD raised up against Solomon an adversary, Hadad the Edomite, from the royal line of Edom[D]. **15**Earlier when David was fighting with Edom, Joab the commander of the army, who had gone up to bury the dead, had struck down all the men in Edom. **16**Joab and all the Israelites stayed there for six months, until they had destroyed all the men in Edom. **17**But Hadad, still only a boy, fled to Egypt with some Edomite officials who had served his father. **18**They set out from Midian and went to Paran. Then taking men from Paran with them, they went to Egypt, to Pharaoh king of Egypt, who gave Hadad a house and land and provided him with food.

19Pharaoh was so pleased with Hadad that he gave him a sister of his own wife, Queen Tahpenes, in marriage. **20**The sister of Tahpenes bore him a son named Genubath, whom Tahpenes brought up in the royal palace. There Genubath lived with Pharaoh's own children.

21While he was in Egypt, Hadad heard that David rested with his fathers and that Joab the commander of the army was also dead. Then Hadad said to Pharaoh, "Let me go, that I may return to my own country."

22"What have you lacked here that you want to go back to your own country?" Pharaoh asked.

"Nothing," Hadad replied, "but do let me go!"

23And God raised up against Solomon another adversary, Rezon son of Eliada, who had fled from his master, Hadadezer king of Zobah. **24**He gathered men around him and became the leader of a band of rebels when David destroyed the forces[a] of Zobah; the rebels went to Damascus, where they settled and took control. **25**Rezon was Israel's adversary as long as Solomon lived, adding to the trouble caused by Hadad. So Rezon ruled in Aram and was hostile toward Israel.

[a]24 Hebrew *destroyed them*

Why would Pharaoh have been so pleased with Hadad, a boy? (11:17–19)

Probably because Hadad, the young and inexperienced king of Edom, pledged to serve Pharaoh and support the interests of Egypt. Hadad and some Edomite officials had fled to Egypt for safety because David's troops had devastated Edom. Once there, they undoubtedly sought Pharaoh's backing so they could regain control over Edom. Pharaoh, for his part, could use the loyalty of the Edomites to expand Egyptian influence to foreign territory. The understanding that they worked out was sealed with a marriage between the two sides. See *Why ratify an international treaty with a wedding?* (2 Chron. 18:1).

Did Solomon get away with idolatry? (11:10–12)

Even though the kingdom of Israel did not split during Solomon's lifetime, the king was severely disciplined by the Lord for worshiping other gods. After years of peace, the Lord gave Solomon several powerful enemies to contend with. Some think the book of Ecclesiastes describes Solomon's descent into despair as he lost his devotion to God. Without a growing and dynamic relationship with the Lord, his life became meaningless and empty. Solomon's wealth and knowledge exceeded that of his contemporaries, but God took away his ability to enjoy them.

Even forgiven sin has its consequences. Those whom God loves he disciplines, as a good parent corrects his or her children. The goal of God's loving discipline is always restoration—never condemnation. After all Solomon suffered as a result of his sin, he acknowledged that only by knowing and obeying God can anyone have a meaningful life (Eccl. 12:13). God did not allow the ten tribes of Israel to secede during Solomon's lifetime because this would have placed a historical stigma upon David. When Solomon died, however, the kingdom was torn to pieces because the wisest man in the world had lost his full devotion to God.

Where was the twelfth piece? (11:30-32)

The ten tribes of Israel and the one tribe of Judah only add up to eleven. Some believe the twelfth tribe was Simeon's, which disappeared into Judah's territory and virtually ceased to exist. Some believe the tribe of Levi was excluded, because they had no separate allotment of land. The twelfth tribe could also have been Benjamin's, since they had divided loyalties between Israel and Judah, and could not be counted on by either side (see *Map 4* at the back of this Bible).

Lamp before me (11:36)

The lamp was symbolic of God's living presence. God had promised David that he would always have a living representative upon the throne in Jerusalem. This was considered a Messianic promise, and was ultimately fulfilled by Jesus Christ. Several passages use this metaphor in connection with David and his house (15:4; 2 Kings 8:19; 2 Samuel 21:17).

The annals of Solomon (11:41)

Probably a more comprehensive and detailed account than the typical annals of the kings of Judah and Israel. The author of Kings no doubt used these sources, though they are no longer available to us. They were probably lost during the destruction of Jerusalem or during the chaos of the exile.

Jeroboam Rebels Against Solomon

26Also, Jeroboam son of Nebat rebelled against the king. He was one of Solomon's officials, an Ephraimite from Zeredah, and his mother was a widow named Zeruah.

27Here is the account of how he rebelled against the king: Solomon had built the supporting terraces[a] and had filled in the gap in the wall of the city of David his father. **28**Now Jeroboam was a man of standing, and when Solomon saw how well the young man did his work, he put him in charge of the whole labor force of the house of Joseph.

29About that time Jeroboam was going out of Jerusalem[D], and Ahijah the prophet[D] of Shiloh met him on the way, wearing a new cloak. The two of them were alone out in the country, **30**and Ahijah took hold of the new cloak he was wearing and tore it into twelve pieces. **31**Then he said to Jeroboam, "Take ten pieces for yourself, for this is what the LORD, the God of Israel, says: 'See, I am going to tear the kingdom out of Solomon's hand and give you ten tribes. **32**But for the sake of my servant David and the city of Jerusalem, which I have chosen out of all the tribes of Israel, he will have one tribe. **33**I will do this because they have[b] forsaken me and worshiped Ashtoreth[D] the goddess of the Sidonians, Chemosh the god of the Moabites, and Molech[D] the god of the Ammonites, and have not walked in my ways, nor done what is right in my eyes, nor kept my statutes and laws as David, Solomon's father, did.

34" 'But I will not take the whole kingdom out of Solomon's hand; I have made him ruler all the days of his life for the sake of David my servant, whom I chose and who observed my commands and statutes. **35**I will take the kingdom from his son's hands and give you ten tribes. **36**I will give one tribe to his son so that David my servant may always have a lamp before me in Jerusalem, the city where I chose to put my Name. **37**However, as for you, I will take you, and you will rule over all that your heart desires; you will be king over Israel. **38**If you do whatever I command you and walk in my ways and do what is right in my eyes by keeping my statutes and commands, as David my servant did, I will be with you. I will build you a dynasty as enduring as the one I built for David and will give Israel to you. **39**I will humble David's descendants because of this, but not forever.' "

40Solomon tried to kill Jeroboam, but Jeroboam fled to Egypt, to Shishak the king, and stayed there until Solomon's death[D].

Solomon's Death

41As for the other events of Solomon's reign—all he did and the wisdom he displayed—are they not written in the book of the annals of Solomon? **42**Solomon reigned in Jerusalem over all Israel forty years. **43**Then he rested with his fathers and was buried in the city of David his father. And Rehoboam his son succeeded him as king.

---

*a*27 Or *the Millo*   *b*33 Hebrew; Septuagint, Vulgate and Syriac
because he has

Israel Rebels Against Rehoboam

12 Rehoboam went to Shechem, for all the Israelites had gone there to make him king. **2**When Jeroboam son of Nebat heard this (he was still in Egypt, where he had fled from King Solomon), he returned from[a] Egypt. **3**So they sent for Jeroboam, and he and the whole assembly of Israel went to Rehoboam and said to him: **4**"Your father put a heavy yoke[D] on us, but now lighten the harsh labor and the heavy yoke he put on us, and we will serve you."

5Rehoboam answered, "Go away for three days and then come back to me." So the people went away.

6Then King Rehoboam consulted the elders who had served his father Solomon during his lifetime. "How would you advise me to answer these people?" he asked. **7**They replied, "If today you will be a servant to these people and serve them and give them a favorable answer, they will always be your servants."

8But Rehoboam rejected the advice the elders gave him and consulted the young men who had grown up with him and were serving him. **9**He asked them, "What is your advice? How should we answer these people who say to me, 'Lighten the yoke your father put on us'?"

10The young men who had grown up with him replied, "Tell these people who have said to you, 'Your father put a heavy yoke on us, but make our yoke lighter'—tell them, 'My little finger is thicker than my father's waist. **11**My father laid on you a heavy yoke; I will make it even heavier. My father scourged you with whips; I will scourge you with scorpions.' "

12Three days later Jeroboam and all the people returned to Rehoboam, as the king had said, "Come back to me in three days." **13**The king answered the people harshly. Rejecting the advice given him by the elders, **14**he followed the advice of the young men and said, "My father made your yoke heavy; I will make it even heavier. My father scourged you with whips; I will scourge you with scorpions." **15**So the king did not listen to the people, for this turn of events was from the LORD, to fulfill the word the LORD had spoken to Jeroboam son of Nebat through Ahijah the Shilonite.

16When all Israel saw that the king refused to listen to them, they answered the king:

> "What share do we have in David,
>   what part in Jesse's son?
> To your tents, O Israel!
>   Look after your own house, O David!"

So the Israelites went home. **17**But as for the Israelites who were living in the towns of Judah, Rehoboam still ruled over them.

18King Rehoboam sent out Adoniram,[b] who was in charge of forced labor, but all Israel stoned him to death[D]. King Rehoboam, however, managed to get into his chariot and escape to Jerusalem[D]. **19**So Israel has been in rebellion against the house of David to this day.

20When all the Israelites heard that Jeroboam had returned, they sent and called him to the assembly and made him king over all Israel. Only the tribe of Judah remained loyal to the house of David.

a2 Or *he remained in*   *b18* Some Septuagint manuscripts and Syriac (see also 1 Kings 4:6 and 5:14); Hebrew *Adoram*

What was the heavy yoke Solomon had imposed on the people? (12:4)

Ancient kings often built their monuments and military garrisons with the labor of captured enemies. But Solomon's peaceful reign denied him this labor pool. Instead, he enslaved foreigners (9:15), and drafted citizens to work one month out of every three (5:13–15). He also divided the kingdom into twelve districts, each responsible for providing one month of supplies for the king and his extravagant royal household (4:7,22–23,27–28).

Did God cause Rehoboam to reject the people's request? (12:15)

Yes and no. On the one hand, Rehoboam made his decision and had to live with the consequences. On the other hand, God worked in and through the circumstances that led to Rehoboam's decision. In this sense *this turn of events was from the* LORD. Also see article: **Did God cause Rehoboam's foolish choice?** (2 Chron. 10:15).

Why didn't Rehoboam enforce his authority? (12:16)

He tried (vv. 18, 21). But with ten of the twelve tribes of Israel in rebellion against him, Rehoboam no longer had the resources he had begun with. His authority existed only because the people had entrusted him with it. By leaving the kingdom, they took power away from the king.

The Divided Kingdom (12:16)

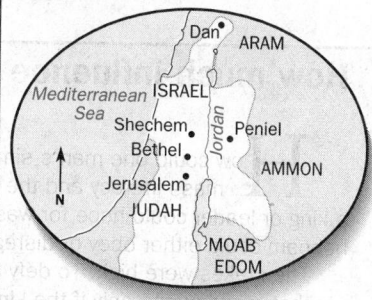

Forced labor (12:18)

Before the mid–1800s, slavery was a common institution. All kings turned prisoners of war and conquered populations into permanent slaves. It is not surprising that David, Solomon and other leaders of Israel depended on human slaves for building their empires and infrastructure. In Israel, Solomon imposed a program of national service within a certain time frame—similar to the modern military draft—to do forced labor.

21When Rehoboam arrived in Jerusalem[D], he mustered the whole house of Judah and the tribe of Benjamin—a hundred and eighty thousand fighting men—to make war against the house of Israel and to regain the kingdom for Rehoboam son of Solomon.

22But this word of God came to Shemaiah the man of God: 23"Say to Rehoboam son of Solomon king of Judah, to the whole house of Judah and Benjamin, and to the rest of the people, 24'This is what the LORD says: Do not go up to fight against your brothers, the Israelites. Go home, every one of you, for this is my doing.'" So they obeyed the word of the LORD and went home again, as the LORD had ordered.

Golden Calves at Bethel and Dan

25Then Jeroboam fortified Shechem in the hill country of Ephraim and lived there. From there he went out and built up Peniel.[a]

26Jeroboam thought to himself, "The kingdom will now likely revert to the house of David. 27If these people go up to offer sacrifices[D] at the temple of the LORD in Jerusalem, they will again give their allegiance to their lord, Rehoboam king of Judah. They will kill me and return to King Rehoboam."

Here are your gods, O Israel (12:28–33)
Jeroboam's blatant sin was to institute false gods so his people would not depend on Jerusalem for their religious needs.

28After seeking advice, the king made two golden calves. He said to the people, "It is too much for you to go up to Jerusalem. Here are your gods, O Israel, who brought you up out of Egypt." 29One he set up in Bethel, and the other in Dan. 30And this thing became a sin; the people went even as far as Dan to worship the one there.

31Jeroboam built shrines on high places[D] and appointed priests[D] from all sorts of people, even though they were not Levites[D]. 32He instituted a festival on the fifteenth day of the eighth month, like the festival held in Judah, and offered sacrifices on the altar. This he did in Bethel, sacrificing to the calves he had made. And at Bethel he also installed priests at the high places he had made. 33On the fifteenth day of the eighth month, a month of his own choosing, he offered sacrifices on the

a25 Hebrew Penuel, a variant of Peniel

How much influence did prophets have? (12:24)

How could one man's simple speech halt an entire army ready for battle? Before mass literacy and the written revelation of Scripture, the only word from God a king or leader could hope for was counsel from a prophet. When Shemaiah spoke, Rehoboam could either obey or disregard him.

The stakes were high. To defy a true prophet was to fight with God himself. Ignoring a prophet made sense only if the king believed the prophet to be insincere, uninformed or mistaken. How could a king know if a prophet was reliable or phony? Only by trial and error—watching to see if a prophet's words came true or not.

Today we compare the words of a "prophet" (preacher, counselor or others) with the Scriptures. We also look for sincerity, empathy, conviction, compassion, integrity and other virtues. So, in many ways, our methods of evaluating spiritual pronouncements are similar to those of the ancients. The chief difference is that we also have access to God's written Word.

altar he had built at Bethel. So he instituted the festival for the Israelites and went up to the altar to make offerings.

The Man of God From Judah

13 By the word of the LORD a man of God came from Judah to Bethel, as Jeroboam was standing by the altar to make an offering. **2**He cried out against the altar by the word of the LORD: "O altar, altar! This is what the LORD says: 'A son named Josiah will be born to the house of David. On you he will sacrifice**D** the priests**D** of the high places**D** who now make offerings here, and human bones will be burned on you.' " **3**That same day the man of God gave a sign: "This is the sign the LORD has declared: The altar will be split apart and the ashes on it will be poured out."

4When King Jeroboam heard what the man of God cried out against the altar at Bethel, he stretched out his hand from the altar and said, "Seize him!" But the hand he stretched out toward the man shriveled up, so that he could not pull it back. **5**Also, the altar was split apart and its ashes poured out according to the sign given by the man of God by the word of the LORD.

6Then the king said to the man of God, "Intercede with the LORD your God and pray for me that my hand may be restored." So the man of God interceded**D** with the LORD, and the king's hand was restored and became as it was before.

7The king said to the man of God, "Come home with me and have something to eat, and I will give you a gift."

8But the man of God answered the king, "Even if you were to give me half your possessions, I would not go with you, nor would I eat bread or drink water here. **9**For I was commanded by the word of the LORD: 'You must not eat bread or drink water or return by the way you came.' " **10**So he took another road and did not return by the way he had come to Bethel.

11Now there was a certain old prophet**D** living in Bethel, whose sons came and told him all that the man of God had done there that day. They also told their father what he had said to the king. **12**Their father asked them, "Which way did he go?" And his sons showed him which road the man of God from Judah had taken. **13**So he said to his sons, "Saddle the donkey for me." And when they had saddled the donkey for him, he mounted it **14**and rode after the man of God. He found him sitting under an oak tree and asked, "Are you the man of God who came from Judah?"

"I am," he replied.

15So the prophet said to him, "Come home with me and eat."

16The man of God said, "I cannot turn back and go with you, nor can I eat bread or drink water with you in this place. **17**I have been told by the word of the LORD: 'You must not eat bread or drink water there or return by the way you came.' "

18The old prophet answered, "I too am a prophet, as you are. And an angel said to me by the word of the LORD: 'Bring him back with you to your house so that he may eat bread and drink water.' " (But he was lying to him.) **19**So the man of God returned with him and ate and drank in his house.

20While they were sitting at the table, the word of the LORD came to the old prophet who had brought him back. **21**He cried out to the man of God who had come

Who was the anonymous prophet? (13:1–10)

The term *man of God* is a common title for a prophet (see 12:22). Though his name is unknown, his ministry was significant. He appeared to be anti-social (v. 8), but only because he was determined to obey God and not be flattered or rewarded—and thus bought off —by Jeroboam, for whom the prophet had an unsettling message from God.

Why would the old prophet lie? (13:18)

He may have been testing the man from Judah to see if his message was, in fact, from the Lord. Though the man from Judah failed to prove his message by his own obedience to it, the old prophet could announce a second, more dramatic, test of truth: the man's judgment. If he survived and returned home, his word at Bethel would be meaningless, since God would have taken no steps to punish his disobedience. But his death would prove God cared about the integrity of his message and would warn Jeroboam that disobedience carried an awful price.

Why would God kill the man of God for trusting a lying prophet? (13:18)

It seems unfair that a prophet would trick someone and cause judgment to come upon him. But this incident is a somber reminder: we are always responsible to carefully evaluate messages supposedly from God, especially when they contradict what God has previously revealed.

Were lions common in Israel? (13:24)

Yes, lions roamed throughout Canaan. Samson killed one bare-handed, aided by supernatural strength from the Holy Spirit (Judges 14:6). David killed one with primitive weapons —a sign of courage (1 Samuel 17:34).

Why didn't the lion kill the donkey or eat the man? (13:24–25)

If its natural instincts had been at work, the lion would have done more. But because God had directed this lion to be an instrument of his judgment, what happened was quite unnatural. The miracle of a lion standing passively over a kill, with a donkey standing near and humans passing by, should have sent a message to Jeroboam about the authenticity of God's message.

Why did the old prophet mourn the death he intentionally caused? (13:29–30)

The old prophet's response holds the key to this story. If the old prophet were a trickster, he would not have grieved. But he was seeking truth. If the man's prophecy against Jeroboam were true, God would have to punish the man's disobedience, just as the prophecy promised punishment for Jeroboam's disobedience. By this death, the old prophet realized how true the man's words were, how powerful God was and the seriousness of Jeroboam's stubbornness.

With judgment promised against false priests, why would anyone want to be one? (13:33)

Jeroboam's priests were politically and perhaps financially motivated. Accepting such an office would require skepticism, if not complete disbelief, that God would speak through a prophet. These priests were, therefore, unafraid of the prophet's prediction of doom (v. 2).

How could Ahijah say David did only what was right? (14:8)

There was no question that David sinned. It was a matter of public knowledge. But to show a clear distinction between a godly king and an evil ruler, Ahijah described David as good and Jeroboam as bad.

from Judah, "This is what the LORD says: 'You have defied the word of the LORD and have not kept the command the LORD your God gave you. ²²You came back and ate bread and drank water in the place where he told you not to eat or drink. Therefore your body will not be buried in the tomb of your fathers.'"

²³When the man of God had finished eating and drinking, the prophet^D who had brought him back saddled his donkey for him. ²⁴As he went on his way, a lion met him on the road and killed him, and his body was thrown down on the road, with both the donkey and the lion standing beside it. ²⁵Some people who passed by saw the body thrown down there, with the lion standing beside the body, and they went and reported it in the city where the old prophet lived.

²⁶When the prophet who had brought him back from his journey heard of it, he said, "It is the man of God who defied the word of the LORD. The LORD has given him over to the lion, which has mauled him and killed him, as the word of the LORD had warned him."

²⁷The prophet said to his sons, "Saddle the donkey for me," and they did so. ²⁸Then he went out and found the body thrown down on the road, with the donkey and the lion standing beside it. The lion had neither eaten the body nor mauled the donkey. ²⁹So the prophet picked up the body of the man of God, laid it on the donkey, and brought it back to his own city to mourn for him and bury him. ³⁰Then he laid the body in his own tomb, and they mourned over him and said, "Oh, my brother!"

³¹After burying him, he said to his sons, "When I die, bury me in the grave where the man of God is buried; lay my bones beside his bones. ³²For the message he declared by the word of the LORD against the altar in Bethel and against all the shrines on the high places^D in the towns of Samaria will certainly come true."

³³Even after this, Jeroboam did not change his evil ways, but once more appointed priests^D for the high places from all sorts of people. Anyone who wanted to become a priest he consecrated for the high places. ³⁴This was the sin of the house of Jeroboam that led to its downfall and to its destruction from the face of the earth.

Ahijah's Prophecy Against Jeroboam

14 At that time Abijah son of Jeroboam became ill, ²and Jeroboam said to his wife, "Go, disguise yourself, so you won't be recognized as the wife of Jeroboam. Then go to Shiloh. Ahijah the prophet is there—the one who told me I would be king over this people. ³Take ten loaves of bread with you, some cakes and a jar of honey, and go to him. He will tell you what will happen to the boy." ⁴So Jeroboam's wife did what he said and went to Ahijah's house in Shiloh.

Now Ahijah could not see; his sight was gone because of his age. ⁵But the LORD had told Ahijah, "Jeroboam's wife is coming to ask you about her son, for he is ill, and you are to give her such and such an answer. When she arrives, she will pretend to be someone else."

⁶So when Ahijah heard the sound of her footsteps at the door, he said, "Come in, wife of Jeroboam. Why this pretense? I have been sent to you with bad news. ⁷Go, tell Jeroboam that this is what the LORD, the God of Israel, says: 'I raised you up from among the people and made you a leader over my people Israel. ⁸I tore the kingdom away from the house of David and gave it to you, but you

have not been like my servant David, who kept my commands and followed me with all his heart, doing only what was right in my eyes. **9**You have done more evil than all who lived before you. You have made for yourself other gods, idols[D] made of metal; you have provoked me to anger and thrust me behind your back.

10" 'Because of this, I am going to bring disaster on the house of Jeroboam. I will cut off from Jeroboam every last male in Israel—slave or free. I will burn up the house of Jeroboam as one burns dung, until it is all gone. **11**Dogs will eat those belonging to Jeroboam who die in the city, and the birds of the air will feed on those who die in the country. The LORD has spoken!'

12"As for you, go back home. When you set foot in your city, the boy will die. **13**All Israel will mourn for him and bury him. He is the only one belonging to Jeroboam who will be buried, because he is the only one in the house of Jeroboam in whom the LORD, the God of Israel, has found anything good.

14"The LORD will raise up for himself a king over Israel who will cut off the family of Jeroboam. This is the day! What? Yes, even now.[a] **15**And the LORD will strike Israel, so that it will be like a reed swaying in the water. He will uproot Israel from this good land that he gave to their forefathers and scatter them beyond the River,[b] because they provoked the LORD to anger by making Asherah poles.[c] **16**And he will give Israel up because of the sins Jeroboam has committed and has caused Israel to commit."

17Then Jeroboam's wife got up and left and went to Tirzah. As soon as she stepped over the threshold of the house, the boy died. **18**They buried him, and all Israel mourned for him, as the LORD had said through his servant the prophet[D] Ahijah.

19The other events of Jeroboam's reign, his wars and how he ruled, are written in the book of the annals of the kings of Israel. **20**He reigned for twenty-two years and then rested with his fathers. And Nadab his son succeeded him as king.

Rehoboam King of Judah

21Rehoboam son of Solomon was king in Judah. He was forty-one years old when he became king, and he reigned seventeen years in Jerusalem[D], the city the LORD had chosen out of all the tribes of Israel in which to put his Name. His mother's name was Naamah; she was an Ammonite.

22Judah did evil in the eyes of the LORD. By the sins they committed they stirred up his jealous anger more than their fathers had done. **23**They also set up for themselves high places[D], sacred stones[D] and Asherah poles on every high hill and under every spreading tree. **24**There were even male shrine prostitutes[D] in the land; the people engaged in all the detestable practices of the nations the LORD had driven out before the Israelites.

25In the fifth year of King Rehoboam, Shishak king of Egypt attacked Jerusalem. **26**He carried off the treasures of the temple of the LORD and the treasures of the royal palace. He took everything, including all the gold shields Solomon had made. **27**So King Rehoboam made bronze shields to replace them and assigned these to the com-

---

a 14 The meaning of the Hebrew for this sentence is uncertain.   *b 15* That is, the Euphrates   *c 15* That is, symbols of the goddess Asherah; here and elsewhere in 1 Kings

What happened to the immediate judgment—*even now?* (14:14)

Why did Jeroboam die in a ripe old age and his son succeed him, apparently contradicting Ahijah's warning? Ahijah pronounced God's judgment as effective without delay, but not all judgment falls with suddenness. For Jeroboam, the immediate future included the death of a son. The long-range future included the sure prospect that all his efforts would lead to disaster and shame. It was a sentence of lifetime frustration and failure, and it must have been like a dark cloud over Jeroboam's head, every day of his life.

Book of the annals (14:19)

A record of the nation's history available to the writers of Kings, but apparently lost today.

High places; sacred stones (14:23)

The top of a rise, hill or mountain gave ancient worshipers a sense of distance from the mundane things of life. It also moved them closer to the sky, where they believed the gods resided. This led to the custom of placing religious objects on hills to appease the gods. But this was a pagan practice forbidden to the Israelites (Exodus 23:24; Lev. 26:1; Deut. 16:21–22).

What did male prostitutes have to do with pagan worship? (14:24)

The pagans viewed prostitution as more than simply sinful pleasure. They believed that prostitutes, taking on the role of gods of nature, could force the gods to do certain things. Prostitution became their way of "praying" for a good harvest. Intercourse symbolized the fertile reproduction of their crops; semen symbolized rain sent by the gods. Some think male prostitutes were used for "religious intercourse" with women worshipers. Others think male prostitutes, representing male gods, committed homosexual acts. Also see *How did men sacrifice with shrine prostitutes?* (Hosea 4:14).

manders of the guard on duty at the entrance to the royal palace. [28]Whenever the king went to the LORD's temple, the guards bore the shields, and afterward they returned them to the guardroom.

[29]As for the other events of Rehoboam's reign, and all he did, are they not written in the book of the annals of the kings of Judah? [30]There was continual warfare between Rehoboam and Jeroboam. [31]And Rehoboam rested with his fathers and was buried with them in the City of David. His mother's name was Naamah; she was an Ammonite. And Abijah[a] his son succeeded him as king.

Abijah King of Judah

15 In the eighteenth year of the reign of Jeroboam son of Nebat, Abijah[b] became king of Judah, [2]and he reigned in Jerusalem[D] three years. His mother's name was Maacah daughter of Abishalom.[c]

[3]He committed all the sins his father had done before him; his heart was not fully devoted to the LORD his God, as the heart of David his forefather had been. [4]Nevertheless, for David's sake the LORD his God gave him a lamp in Jerusalem by raising up a son to succeed him and by making Jerusalem strong. [5]For David had done what was right in the eyes of the LORD and had not failed to keep any of the LORD's commands all the days of his life—except in the case of Uriah the Hittite.

[6]There was war between Rehoboam[d] and Jeroboam throughout ⌊Abijah's⌋ lifetime. [7]As for the other events of Abijah's reign, and all he did, are they not written in the book of the annals of the kings of Judah? There was war between Abijah and Jeroboam. [8]And Abijah rested with his fathers and was buried in the City of David. And Asa his son succeeded him as king.

Asa King of Judah

[9]In the twentieth year of Jeroboam king of Israel, Asa became king of Judah, [10]and he reigned in Jerusalem forty-one years. His grandmother's name was Maacah daughter of Abishalom.

[11]Asa did what was right in the eyes of the LORD, as his father David had done. [12]He expelled the male shrine prostitutes[D] from the land and got rid of all the idols[D] his fathers had made. [13]He even deposed his grandmother Maacah from her position as queen mother, because she had made a repulsive Asherah pole[D]. Asa cut the pole down and burned it in the Kidron Valley[D]. [14]Although he did not remove the high places[D], Asa's heart was fully committed to the LORD all his life. [15]He brought into the temple of the LORD the silver and gold and the articles that he and his father had dedicated.

[16]There was war between Asa and Baasha king of Israel throughout their reigns. [17]Baasha king of Israel went up against Judah and fortified Ramah to prevent anyone from leaving or entering the territory of Asa king of Judah. [18]Asa then took all the silver and gold that was left in the treasuries of the LORD's temple and of his own palace. He entrusted it to his officials and sent them to Ben-Ha-

---

Lamp (15:4)

See *Lamp before me* (11:36).

SCRIPTURE LINK (15:5) *Uriah the Hittite*

See 2 Samuel 11.

If Asa was so good, why did he send temple treasure to a pagan king? (15:18–19)

Baasha was in control of Ramah, only four miles north of Jerusalem. Baasha threatened to control the trade routes and isolate Judah's capital. Asa turned the tide by forging an alliance with the pagan ruler Ben-Hadad of Aram (Syria). The prophet Hanani marked Asa's alliance as sin (2 Chron. 16:7–9). Asa's last years are described as painful, stubborn and repressive (2 Chron. 16:10–12).

---

[a]31 Some Hebrew manuscripts and Septuagint (see also 2 Chron. 12:16); most Hebrew manuscripts *Abijam*   [b]1 Some Hebrew manuscripts and Septuagint (see also 2 Chron. 12:16); most Hebrew manuscripts *Abijam*; also in verses 7 and 8   [c]2 A variant of *Absalom*; also in verse 10   [d]6 Most Hebrew manuscripts; some Hebrew manuscripts and Syriac *Abijam* (that is, Abijah)

dad son of Tabrimmon, the son of Hezion, the king of Aram, who was ruling in Damascus. **19**"Let there be a treaty between me and you," he said, "as there was between my father and your father. See, I am sending you a gift of silver and gold. Now break your treaty with Baasha king of Israel so he will withdraw from me."

20Ben-Hadad agreed with King Asa and sent the commanders of his forces against the towns of Israel. He conquered Ijon, Dan, Abel Beth Maacah and all Kinnereth in addition to Naphtali. **21**When Baasha heard this, he stopped building Ramah and withdrew to Tirzah. **22**Then King Asa issued an order to all Judah—no one was exempt—and they carried away from Ramah the stones and timber Baasha had been using there. With them King Asa built up Geba in Benjamin, and also Mizpah.

23As for all the other events of Asa's reign, all his achievements, all he did and the cities he built, are they not written in the book of the annals of the kings of Judah? In his old age, however, his feet became diseased. **24**Then Asa rested with his fathers and was buried with them in the city of his father David. And Jehoshaphat his son succeeded him as king.

Nadab King of Israel

25Nadab son of Jeroboam became king of Israel in the second year of Asa king of Judah, and he reigned over Israel two years. **26**He did evil in the eyes of the LORD, walking in the ways of his father and in his sin, which he had caused Israel to commit.

27Baasha son of Ahijah of the house of Issachar plotted against him, and he struck him down at Gibbethon, a Philistine town, while Nadab and all Israel were besieging it. **28**Baasha killed Nadab in the third year of Asa king of Judah and succeeded him as king.

29As soon as he began to reign, he killed Jeroboam's whole family. He did not leave Jeroboam anyone that breathed, but destroyed them all, according to the word of the LORD given through his servant Ahijah the Shilonite— **30**because of the sins Jeroboam had committed and had caused Israel to commit, and because he provoked the LORD, the God of Israel, to anger.

31As for the other events of Nadab's reign, and all he did, are they not written in the book of the annals of the kings of Israel? **32**There was war between Asa and Baasha king of Israel throughout their reigns.

Baasha King of Israel

33In the third year of Asa king of Judah, Baasha son of Ahijah became king of all Israel in Tirzah, and he reigned twenty-four years. **34**He did evil in the eyes of the LORD, walking in the ways of Jeroboam and in his sin, which he had caused Israel to commit.

16 Then the word of the LORD came to Jehu son of Hanani against Baasha: **2**"I lifted you up from the dust and made you leader of my people Israel, but you walked in the ways of Jeroboam and caused my people Israel to sin and to provoke me to anger by their sins. **3**So I am about to consume Baasha and his house, and I will make your house like that of Jeroboam son of Nebat. **4**Dogs will eat those belonging to Baasha who die in the city, and the birds of the air will feed on those who die in the country."

5As for the other events of Baasha's reign, what he did and his achievements, are they not written in the book of

---

Is Ahijah of Issachar the same as the prophet Ahijah who lived in Shiloh? (15:27,29; see 14:2,10–16)

Probably not. Ahijah, which means *my brother is Yahweh,* is a name that apparently belonged to three Bible figures: the priest under Saul (1 Samuel 14:3), the famous prophet of Shiloh (11:29) and the father of Baasha, king of Israel (v. 33). The writer was careful to make the distinction: the prophet was the one from Shiloh (in Ephraim, not Issachar).

Why would God use an evil person? (15:34)

God is not limited to using only good people for his purposes. God can redirect evil intended for selfish ends so that it accomplishes unexpected good. Baasha thus became God's instrument to punish Jeroboam's family (v. 29; see 14:10–16). Also see **Is God guilty of lying?** (22:20–22) and article: **Does God use evil to do good?** (Hab. 1:6,13).

Why did God punish Baasha? (16:7)

Baasha's violence accomplished God's purpose (see previous note), but that one act did not make him a servant of God. God held him accountable for his evil intentions, not for inadvertently fulfilling God's will. Baasha had wiped out Jeroboam's clan to increase his power base, not to honor God.

Was Zimri an agent of God's anger? (16:11-12)

See *Why would God use an evil person?* (15:34).

the annals of the kings of Israel? **6**Baasha rested with his fathers and was buried in Tirzah. And Elah his son succeeded him as king.

7Moreover, the word of the LORD came through the prophet[D] Jehu son of Hanani to Baasha and his house, because of all the evil he had done in the eyes of the LORD, provoking him to anger by the things he did, and becoming like the house of Jeroboam—and also because he destroyed it.

Elah King of Israel

8In the twenty-sixth year of Asa king of Judah, Elah son of Baasha became king of Israel, and he reigned in Tirzah two years.

9Zimri, one of his officials, who had command of half his chariots, plotted against him. Elah was in Tirzah at the time, getting drunk in the home of Arza, the man in charge of the palace at Tirzah. **10**Zimri came in, struck him down and killed him in the twenty-seventh year of Asa king of Judah. Then he succeeded him as king.

11As soon as he began to reign and was seated on the throne, he killed off Baasha's whole family. He did not spare a single male, whether relative or friend. **12**So Zimri destroyed the whole family of Baasha, in accordance with the word of the LORD spoken against Baasha through the prophet Jehu— **13**because of all the sins Baasha and his son Elah had committed and had caused Israel to commit, so that they provoked the LORD, the God of Israel, to anger by their worthless idols[D].

14As for the other events of Elah's reign, and all he did, are they not written in the book of the annals of the kings of Israel?

Zimri King of Israel

15In the twenty-seventh year of Asa king of Judah, Zimri reigned in Tirzah seven days. The army was encamped near Gibbethon, a Philistine town. **16**When the Israelites in the camp heard that Zimri had plotted against the king and murdered him, they proclaimed Omri, the commander of the army, king over Israel that very day there in the camp. **17**Then Omri and all the Israelites with him withdrew from Gibbethon and laid siege to Tirzah. **18**When Zimri saw that the city was taken, he went into the citadel[D] of the royal palace and set the palace on fire around him. So he died, **19**because of the sins he had committed, doing evil in the eyes of the LORD and walking in the ways of Jeroboam and in the sin he had committed and had caused Israel to commit.

20As for the other events of Zimri's reign, and the rebellion he carried out, are they not written in the book of the annals of the kings of Israel?

Omri King of Israel

21Then the people of Israel were split into two factions; half supported Tibni son of Ginath for king, and the other half supported Omri. **22**But Omri's followers proved stronger than those of Tibni son of Ginath. So Tibni died and Omri became king.

23In the thirty-first year of Asa king of Judah, Omri became king of Israel, and he reigned twelve years, six of them in Tirzah. **24**He bought the hill of Samaria from Shemer for two talents[a] of silver and built a city on the hill,

---

[a]*24* That is, about 150 pounds (about 70 kilograms)

calling it Samaria, after Shemer, the name of the former owner of the hill.

²⁵But Omri did evil in the eyes of the LORD and sinned more than all those before him. ²⁶He walked in all the ways of Jeroboam son of Nebat and in his sin, which he had caused Israel to commit, so that they provoked the LORD, the God of Israel, to anger by their worthless idols.ᴰ

²⁷As for the other events of Omri's reign, what he did and the things he achieved, are they not written in the book of the annals of the kings of Israel? ²⁸Omri rested with his fathers and was buried in Samaria. And Ahab his son succeeded him as king.

Ahab Becomes King of Israel

²⁹In the thirty-eighth year of Asa king of Judah, Ahab son of Omri became king of Israel, and he reigned in Samaria over Israel twenty-two years. ³⁰Ahab son of Omri did evil in the eyes of the LORD than any of those before him. ³¹He not only considered it trivial to commit the sins of Jeroboam son of Nebat, but he also married Jezebel daughter of Ethbaal king of the Sidonians, and began to serve Baalᴰ and worship him. ³²He set up an altar for Baal in the temple of Baal that he built in Samaria. ³³Ahab also made an Asherah poleᴰ and did more to provoke the LORD, the God of Israel, to anger than did all the kings of Israel before him.

³⁴In Ahab's time, Hiel of Bethel rebuilt Jericho.ᴰ He laid its foundations at the cost of his firstbornᴰ son Abiram, and he set up its gates at the cost of his youngest son Segub, in accordance with the word of the LORD spoken by Joshua son of Nun.

Elijah Fed by Ravens

17 Now Elijah the Tishbite, from Tishbeᵃ in Gilead, said to Ahab, "As the LORD, the God of Israel, lives, whom I serve, there will be neither dew nor rain in the next few years except at my word."

²Then the word of the LORD came to Elijah: ³"Leave here, turn eastward and hide in the Kerith Ravine, east of the Jordan. ⁴You will drink from the brook, and I have ordered the ravens to feed you there."

⁵So he did what the LORD had told him. He went to the Kerith Ravine, east of the Jordan, and stayed there. ⁶The ravens brought him bread and meat in the morning and bread and meat in the evening, and he drank from the brook.

The Widow at Zarephath

⁷Some time later the brook dried up because there had been no rain in the land. ⁸Then the word of the LORD came to him: ⁹"Go at once to Zarephath of Sidon and stay there. I have commanded a widow in that place to supply you with food." ¹⁰So he went to Zarephath. When he came to the town gate, a widow was there gathering sticks. He called to her and asked, "Would you bring me a little water in a jar so I may have a drink?" ¹¹As she was going to get it, he called, "And bring me, please, a piece of bread."

¹²"As surely as the LORD your God lives," she replied, "I don't have any bread—only a handful of flour in a jar and a little oil in a jug. I am gathering a few sticks to take

---

ᵃ1 Or *Tishbite, of the settlers*

Sins of Jeroboam (16:31)

This became a catch-all phrase used by the prophets and Biblical writers to refer to the sins of Israel. See *Here are your gods, O Israel* (12:28–33).

What was so bad about marrying Jezebel? (16:31)

Quite apart from her strong-willed and arrogant personality, Jezebel brought grief to God-fearing Israelites through her efforts to promote Baal worship. Jezebel was the daughter of king-priest Ethbaal of Tyre. Like Solomon's foreign wives, Jezebel was given a temple in which to practice her paganism. Soon Baal worship enjoyed royal sanction throughout Israel.

Baal (16:32)

Best known of the Canaanite gods. In the pagan family of gods, El was the father (a mild-mannered fellow whose only role was to settle sibling squabbles) and Asherah was the mother. Baal (meaning *master* or *lord*) was one of their seventy offspring, the fertility god responsible for germinating crops, increasing flocks and adding children to the community. Baal worship, accordingly, included religious prostitution, male and female. See *What did male prostitutes have to do with pagan worship?* (14:24). Also see *Consult the Baals* (2 Chron. 17:3).

What killed Hiel's sons? (16:34)

Perhaps a construction accident. Perhaps they were killed to pacify gods in the ancient Middle East. Sometimes infants were bottled and entombed within city walls, which is what probably happened here, though the immediate cause of death is unknown.

SCRIPTURE LINK (16:34)

Joshua had warned that rebuilding the walls of Jericho would cost lives. See Joshua 6:26.

Why did Elijah need to hide? (17:3)

Primarily because God told him to. Prophets were to obey the Lord first and ask questions later. In this case, hiding was a means of showing the Israelites the cost of selling out to Baal. While the nation was starving and thirsty, God's prophet had enough food and water. Could a lesson be clearer? God was not the cause of the people's hardship; they were the cause when they broke their covenant with God.

Elijah and Ahab (17:3)

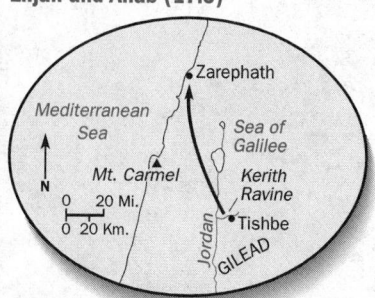

Why did God send Elijah to a foreign woman? (17:9)

The blessings of life and prosperity that came to this Gentile widow formed a stark contrast to the starvation faced by Israel. The widow showed enough faith to feed Elijah and refer to his God as *the* LORD (v. 12). Though she wrongly thought later that her sins caused her son's illness, she still recognized God as the judge over all (v. 18). Finally, her testimony (v. 24) is exactly what God wanted to hear from the Israelite nation.

What sin was the widow referring to? (17:18)

We don't know. Because of her son's illness, she assumed she must have done something wrong.

Why blame Elijah for the son's illness and death? (17:18,20)

The woman, knowing the prophet represented God, may have figured that having the prophet live in her house was ample protection. Elijah was like health and life insurance to her. When her son stopped breathing, she lashed out at God's representative. Or she may have felt that because Elijah was in her house he had called God's attention to her sin and now God was punishing her.

Why didn't she trust Elijah before? (17:24)

Though the widow had enjoyed a miraculous supply of oil and flour, it took the return of her son for her to believe. Some who are confronted with a miracle do not take it to heart. Skeptics may even rationalize the supernatural away, increasing their doubts rather than their faith.

Who were the prophets killed by Jezebel? (18:4,13)

These prophets represented true worship in Israel. Jezebel's actions are not explained, so we can only infer that the prophets posed a threat to her power—or to her conscience. Perhaps Jezebel was a bit unnerved to see the weaker Ahab vacillating again toward his old religious roots and away from her Baal worship.

home and make a meal for myself and my son, that we may eat it—and die."

[13]Elijah said to her, "Don't be afraid. Go home and do as you have said. But first make a small cake of bread for me from what you have and bring it to me, and then make something for yourself and your son. [14]For this is what the LORD, the God of Israel, says: 'The jar of flour will not be used up and the jug of oil will not run dry until the day the LORD gives rain on the land.'"

[15]She went away and did as Elijah had told her. So there was food every day for Elijah and for the woman and her family. [16]For the jar of flour was not used up and the jug of oil did not run dry, in keeping with the word of the LORD spoken by Elijah.

[17]Some time later the son of the woman who owned the house became ill. He grew worse and worse, and finally stopped breathing. [18]She said to Elijah, "What do you have against me, man of God? Did you come to remind me of my sin and kill my son?"

[19]"Give me your son," Elijah replied. He took him from her arms, carried him to the upper room where he was staying, and laid him on his bed. [20]Then he cried out to the LORD, "O LORD my God, have you brought tragedy also upon this widow I am staying with, by causing her son to die?" [21]Then he stretched himself out on the boy three times and cried to the LORD, "O LORD my God, let this boy's life return to him!"

[22]The LORD heard Elijah's cry, and the boy's life returned to him, and he lived. [23]Elijah picked up the child and carried him down from the room into the house. He gave him to his mother and said, "Look, your son is alive!"

[24]Then the woman said to Elijah, "Now I know that you are a man of God and that the word of the LORD from your mouth is the truth."

Elijah and Obadiah

18 After a long time, in the third year, the word of the LORD came to Elijah: "Go and present yourself to Ahab, and I will send rain on the land." [2]So Elijah went to present himself to Ahab.

Now the famine was severe in Samaria, [3]and Ahab had summoned Obadiah, who was in charge of his palace. (Obadiah was a devout believer in the LORD. [4]While Jezebel was killing off the LORD's prophets[D], Obadiah had taken a hundred prophets and hidden them in two caves, fifty in each, and had supplied them with food and water.) [5]Ahab had said to Obadiah, "Go through the land to all the springs and valleys. Maybe we can find some grass to keep the horses and mules alive so we will not have to kill any of our animals." [6]So they divided the land they were to cover, Ahab going in one direction and Obadiah in another.

[7]As Obadiah was walking along, Elijah met him. Obadiah recognized him, bowed down to the ground, and said, "Is it really you, my lord Elijah?"

[8]"Yes," he replied. "Go tell your master, 'Elijah is here.'"

[9]"What have I done wrong," asked Obadiah, "that you are handing your servant over to Ahab to be put to death[D]? [10]As surely as the LORD your God lives, there is not a nation or kingdom where my master has not sent someone to look for you. And whenever a nation or kingdom claimed you were not there, he made them swear they could not find you. [11]But now you tell me to go to my

master and say, 'Elijah is here.' 12I don't know where the Spirit of the LORD may carry you when I leave you. If I go and tell Ahab and he doesn't find you, he will kill me. Yet I your servant have worshiped the LORD since my youth. 13Haven't you heard, my lord, what I did while Jezebel was killing the prophetsD of the LORD? I hid a hundred of the LORD's prophets in two caves, fifty in each, and supplied them with food and water. 14And now you tell me to go to my master and say, 'Elijah is here.' He will kill me!"

15Elijah said, "As the LORD Almighty lives, whom I serve, I will surely present myself to Ahab today."

Elijah on Mount Carmel

16So Obadiah went to meet Ahab and told him, and Ahab went to meet Elijah. 17When he saw Elijah, he said to him, "Is that you, you troubler of Israel?"

18"I have not made trouble for Israel," Elijah replied. "But you and your father's family have. You have abandoned the LORD's commands and have followed the BaalsD. 19Now summon the people from all over Israel to meet me on Mount Carmel. And bring the four hundred and fifty prophets of Baal and the four hundred prophets of Asherah, who eat at Jezebel's table."

20So Ahab sent word throughout all Israel and assembled the prophets on Mount Carmel. 21Elijah went before the people and said, "How long will you waver between two opinions? If the LORD is God, follow him; but if Baal is God, follow him."

But the people said nothing. 22Then Elijah said to them, "I am the only one of the LORD's prophets left, but Baal has four hundred and fifty prophets. 23Get two bulls for us. Let them choose one for themselves, and let them cut it into pieces and put it on the wood but not set fire to it. I will prepare the other bull and put it on the wood but not set fire to it. 24Then you call on the name of your god, and I will call on the name of the LORD. The god who answers by fire—he is God."

Then all the people said, "What you say is good."

25Elijah said to the prophets of Baal, "Choose one of the bulls and prepare it first, since there are so many of you. Call on the name of your god, but do not light the fire." 26So they took the bull given them and prepared it.

Then they called on the name of Baal from morning till noon. "O Baal, answer us!" they shouted. But there was no response; no one answered. And they danced around the altar they had made.

27At noon Elijah began to taunt them. "Shout louder!" he said. "Surely he is a god! Perhaps he is deep in thought, or busy, or traveling. Maybe he is sleeping and must be awakened." 28So they shouted louder and slashed themselves with swords and spears, as was their custom, until their blood flowed. 29Midday passed, and they continued their frantic prophesying until the time for the evening sacrificeD. But there was no response, no one answered, no one paid attention.

30Then Elijah said to all the people, "Come here to me." They came to him, and he repaired the altar of the LORD, which was in ruins. 31Elijah took twelve stones, one for each of the tribes descended from Jacob, to whom the word of the LORD had come, saying, "Your name shall be Israel." 32With the stones he built an altar in the name of the LORD, and he dug a trench around it large enough to

Why didn't Ahab arrest Elijah? (18:17)
First, because Ahab was an opportunist. More important than ridding the country of Elijah was solving the problem of drought. Ahab would listen to anybody who might have an answer. Second, because God had other plans for Elijah. The tyrannical moods of Ahab were held at bay so that Elijah (whose very name is also his message: The Lord is my God) could call the Israelites back to God.

Why did the prophets of Baal cut themselves? (18:28)
With the king's patience growing thin, the prophets of Baal accelerated the frenzy of their prayers by cutting themselves—a common practice among ancient pagan prophets, but forbidden in Levitical law. They hoped such self-sacrifice would convince the gods they were fervent and deserving of an answer.

Why did Elijah use so much water during a drought? (18:33–34)

Probably to make a point: by drenching the sacrifice, Elijah was stacking the deck against God igniting the sacrifice. There could be no doubt that only a miracle could burn the water-soaked sacrifice. Baal, said to be the god of fire, storm, vegetation, fertility and life, should have been able to send rain. By pouring out the precious water—a resource Baal had failed to provide for 3 ½ years—Elijah only added to Baal's humiliation. The water was probably drawn from an underground fountain, a natural reservoir protected by rock from the sun.

Why did Ahab allow Elijah to kill the queen's prophets? (18:40–42)

The prophets of Baal had failed, humiliating themselves, their god and their queen. Ahab, most likely sensing the mood of the people, realized the 450 prophets were a political liability. Under such circumstances, Elijah could take his holy vengeance without interference.

What happened to the 400 prophets of Asherah? (18:40; see v. 19)

It's hard to say. The writer gives only limited information. Possibly, the label prophets of Baal could have been used in a generic sense to include the prophets of Asherah as well. If so, they would have been executed as well. It seems unlikely, since Elijah now had the upper hand, that he would have allowed them to escape.

How could Elijah outrun a chariot? (18:46)

Could Ahab take his chariot full-tilt down a mountain for 20 miles? Was the roadway to Jezreel crowded with other vehicles and pedestrians? Was Ahab dazed over the events that just transpired? Would Ahab have purposely kept his chariot behind the running prophet, in holy awe? However it happened, Elijah's run to Jezreel was empowered by God, and symbolized the superiority of the Lord above all other contenders.

Broom tree (19:4)

A low, bushy desert plant whose embers burn far longer than the wood of other species. The white broom is used as a symbol of scorn in Job 30:4 (digging its roots for livelihood), and of long-lasting fire in Psalm 120:4.

hold two seahs^a of seed. **33**He arranged the wood, cut the bull into pieces and laid it on the wood. Then he said to them, "Fill four large jars with water and pour it on the offering and on the wood."

34"Do it again," he said, and they did it again.

"Do it a third time," he ordered, and they did it the third time. **35**The water ran down around the altar and even filled the trench.

36At the time of sacrifice^D, the prophet^D Elijah stepped forward and prayed: "O LORD, God of Abraham, Isaac and Israel, let it be known today that you are God in Israel and that I am your servant and have done all these things at your command. **37**Answer me, O LORD, answer me, so these people will know that you, O LORD, are God, and that you are turning their hearts back again."

38Then the fire of the LORD fell and burned up the sacrifice, the wood, the stones and the soil, and also licked up the water in the trench.

39When all the people saw this, they fell prostrate and cried, "The LORD—he is God! The LORD—he is God!"

40Then Elijah commanded them, "Seize the prophets of Baal^D. Don't let anyone get away!" They seized them, and Elijah had them brought down to the Kishon Valley and slaughtered there.

41And Elijah said to Ahab, "Go, eat and drink, for there is the sound of a heavy rain." **42**So Ahab went off to eat and drink, but Elijah climbed to the top of Carmel, bent down to the ground and put his face between his knees.

43"Go and look toward the sea," he told his servant. And he went up and looked.

"There is nothing there," he said.

Seven times Elijah said, "Go back."

44The seventh time the servant reported, "A cloud as small as a man's hand is rising from the sea."

So Elijah said, "Go and tell Ahab, 'Hitch up your chariot and go down before the rain stops you.' "

45Meanwhile, the sky grew black with clouds, the wind rose, a heavy rain came on and Ahab rode off to Jezreel. **46**The power of the LORD came upon Elijah and, tucking his cloak into his belt, he ran ahead of Ahab all the way to Jezreel.

Elijah Flees to Horeb

19 Now Ahab told Jezebel everything Elijah had done and how he had killed all the prophets with the sword. **2**So Jezebel sent a messenger to Elijah to say, "May the gods deal with me, be it ever so severely, if by this time tomorrow I do not make your life like that of one of them."

3Elijah was afraid^b and ran for his life. When he came to Beersheba in Judah, he left his servant there, **4**while he himself went a day's journey into the desert. He came to a broom tree, sat down under it and prayed that he might die. "I have had enough, LORD," he said. "Take my life; I am no better than my ancestors." **5**Then he lay down under the tree and fell asleep.

All at once an angel touched him and said, "Get up and eat." **6**He looked around, and there by his head was a cake of bread baked over hot coals, and a jar of water. He ate and drank and then lay down again.

7The angel of the LORD came back a second time and

---

^{a}32 That is, probably about 13 quarts (about 15 liters) ^{b}3 Or Elijah saw

touched him and said, "Get up and eat, for the journey is too much for you." **8**So he got up and ate and drank. Strengthened by that food, he traveled forty days and forty nights until he reached Horeb, the mountain of God. **9**There he went into a cave and spent the night.

The LORD Appears to Elijah

And the word of the LORD came to him: "What are you doing here, Elijah?"

10He replied, "I have been very zealous for the LORD God Almighty. The Israelites have rejected your covenantᴅ, broken down your altars, and put your prophetsᴅ to death with the sword. I am the only one left, and now they are trying to kill me too."

11The LORD said, "Go out and stand on the mountain in the presence of the LORD, for the LORD is about to pass by."

Then a great and powerful wind tore the mountains apart and shattered the rocks before the LORD, but the LORD was not in the wind. After the wind there was an earthquake, but the LORD was not in the earthquake. **12**After the earthquake came a fire, but the LORD was not in the fire. And after the fire came a gentle whisper. **13**When Elijah heard it, he pulled his cloak over his face and went out and stood at the mouth of the cave.

Then a voice said to him, "What are you doing here, Elijah?"

14He replied, "I have been very zealous for the LORD God Almighty. The Israelites have rejected your covenant, broken down your altars, and put your prophets to death with the sword. I am the only one left, and now they are trying to kill me too."

15The LORD said to him, "Go back the way you came, and go to the Desert of Damascus. When you get there, anointᴅ Hazael king over Aram. **16**Also, anoint Jehu son of Nimshi king over Israel, and anoint Elisha son of Shaphat from Abel Meholah to succeed you as prophet. **17**Jehu will put to death any who escape the sword of Hazael, and Elisha will put to death any who escape the sword of Jehu. **18**Yet I reserve seven thousand in Israel— all whose knees have not bowed down to Baalᴅ and all whose mouths have not kissed him."

How could an Israelite prophet anoint a king in Aram? (19:15)

At this stage in Israel's history, it was uncommon for prophets to have much influence outside the nation. But news of Elijah's triumph at Carmel over the prophets of Baal undoubtedly spread quickly and created an international reputation.

Why was Elijah afraid, after his great victory? (19:3)

Even individuals of great courage and conviction have moments when they feel discouraged. After the euphoric victory on Mount Carmel, it seems that Elijah's emotions fell. He was not indestructible. He had human weaknesses. *Elijah was a man just like us* (James 5:17).

We might think that in the rush of victory, Elijah would have felt invincible. Instead, it seems, he felt exhausted. We might think Elijah would have welcomed Jezebel's challenge as an opportunity to attack his enemy at its source. Instead, he retreated.

It may be that Elijah was facing a personal crisis of faith, identity and vision. Now that he had won his lifelong battle against the prophets of Baal, why was his life still in danger? Didn't he deserve a little rest? Hadn't he earned the right to retire in peace? Sometimes the thought of another battle, after just finishing one, is overwhelming.

We can only speculate about what actually fueled Elijah's fears. But we can readily see that he was human.

How could Elisha plow with twelve yoke of oxen? (19:19)

He was actually driving only the last pair of oxen. It seems that others were driving the first 11 pairs since farming was often done as a community activity. Apparently the land or the oxen or both belonged to Elisha's family. If so, he would have been in charge of the work and could be said accurately to be *plowing with twelve yoke of oxen.*

Why did Elijah throw his cloak around Elisha? (19:19)

A cloak of animal hair, although occasionally worn by kings, was generally recognized as prophet's clothing. By laying his cloak over Elisha, Elijah gave him a new identity and set him apart for a prophetic mission—like pastoral candidates set apart for ministry by an ordination ceremony. With prophetic power upon him, Elisha was thereafter a different person. Later he inherited Elijah's cloak as a sign that he was to carry on Elijah's prophetic work (see 2 Kings 2:13–14).

Was Ben-Hadad trying to pick a fight? (20:4–6)

Although his first demands were met with ceremonial acceptance by Ahab, Ben-Hadad showed that his intentions were to take everything he could. Ahab's payoff, the common practice when strong armies intimidated weak cities, would not be enough. When Ahab realized he could never satisfy Beh-Hadad, he decided to resist.

The Call of Elisha

19So Elijah went from there and found Elisha son of Shaphat. He was plowing with twelve yokeᴰ of oxen, and he himself was driving the twelfth pair. Elijah went up to him and threw his cloak around him. **20**Elisha then left his oxen and ran after Elijah. "Let me kiss my father and mother good-by," he said, "and then I will come with you."

"Go back," Elijah replied. "What have I done to you?"

21So Elisha left him and went back. He took his yoke of oxen and slaughtered them. He burned the plowing equipment to cook the meat and gave it to the people, and they ate. Then he set out to follow Elijah and became his attendant.

Ben-Hadad Attacks Samaria

20 Now Ben-Hadad king of Aram mustered his entire army. Accompanied by thirty-two kings with their horses and chariots, he went up and besieged Samaria and attacked it. **2**He sent messengers into the city to Ahab king of Israel, saying, "This is what Ben-Hadad says: **3**'Your silver and gold are mine, and the best of your wives and children are mine.' "

4The king of Israel answered, "Just as you say, my lord the king. I and all I have are yours."

5The messengers came again and said, "This is what Ben-Hadad says: 'I sent to demand your silver and gold, your wives and your children. **6**But about this time tomorrow I am going to send my officials to search your palace and the houses of your officials. They will seize everything you value and carry it away.' "

7The king of Israel summoned all the elders of the land and said to them, "See how this man is looking for trouble! When he sent for my wives and my children, my silver and my gold, I did not refuse him."

8The elders and the people all answered, "Don't listen to him or agree to his demands."

9So he replied to Ben-Hadad's messengers, "Tell my lord the king, 'Your servant will do all you demanded the first time, but this demand I cannot meet.' " They left and took the answer back to Ben-Hadad.

10Then Ben-Hadad sent another message to Ahab: "May the gods deal with me, be it ever so severely, if enough dust remains in Samaria to give each of my men a handful."

11The king of Israel answered, "Tell him: 'One who puts on his armor should not boast like one who takes it off.' "

12Ben-Hadad heard this message while he and the kings were drinking in their tents,ᵃ and he ordered his men: "Prepare to attack." So they prepared to attack the city.

Ahab Defeats Ben-Hadad

13Meanwhile a prophetᴰ came to Ahab king of Israel and announced, "This is what the LORD says: 'Do you see this vast army? I will give it into your hand today, and then you will know that I am the LORD.' "

14"But who will do this?" asked Ahab.

The prophet replied, "This is what the LORD says: 'The young officers of the provincial commanders will do it.' "

"And who will start the battle?" he asked.

The prophet answered, "You will."

ᵃ12 Or *in Succoth;* also in verse 16

¹⁵So Ahab summoned the young officers of the provincial commanders, 232 men. Then he assembled the rest of the Israelites, 7,000 in all. ¹⁶They set out at noon while Ben-Hadad and the 32 kings allied with him were in their tents getting drunk. ¹⁷The young officers of the provincial commanders went out first.

Now Ben-Hadad had dispatched scouts, who reported, "Men are advancing from Samaria."

¹⁸He said, "If they have come out for peace^D, take them alive; if they have come out for war, take them alive."

¹⁹The young officers of the provincial commanders marched out of the city with the army behind them ²⁰and each one struck down his opponent. At that, the Arameans fled, with the Israelites in pursuit. But Ben-Hadad king of Aram escaped on horseback with some of his horsemen. ²¹The king of Israel advanced and overpowered the horses and chariots and inflicted heavy losses on the Arameans.

²²Afterward, the prophet^D came to the king of Israel and said, "Strengthen your position and see what must be done, because next spring the king of Aram will attack you again."

²³Meanwhile, the officials of the king of Aram advised him, "Their gods are gods of the hills. That is why they were too strong for us. But if we fight them on the plains, surely we will be stronger than they. ²⁴Do this: Remove all the kings from their commands and replace them with other officers. ²⁵You must also raise an army like the one you lost—horse for horse and chariot for chariot—so we can fight Israel on the plains. Then surely we will be stronger than they." He agreed with them and acted accordingly.

²⁶The next spring Ben-Hadad mustered the Arameans and went up to Aphek to fight against Israel. ²⁷When the Israelites were also mustered and given provisions, they marched out to meet them. The Israelites camped opposite them like two small flocks of goats, while the Arameans covered the countryside.

²⁸The man of God came up and told the king of Israel, "This is what the LORD says: 'Because the Arameans think the LORD is a god of the hills and not a god of the valleys, I will deliver this vast army into your hands, and you will know that I am the LORD.' "

²⁹For seven days they camped opposite each other, and on the seventh day the battle was joined. The Israelites inflicted a hundred thousand casualties on the Aramean foot soldiers in one day. ³⁰The rest of them escaped to the city of Aphek, where the wall collapsed on twenty-seven thousand of them. And Ben-Hadad fled to the city and hid in an inner room.

³¹His officials said to him, "Look, we have heard that the kings of the house of Israel are merciful. Let us go to the king of Israel with sackcloth^D around our waists and ropes around our heads. Perhaps he will spare your life."

³²Wearing sackcloth around their waists and ropes around their heads, they went to the king of Israel and said, "Your servant Ben-Hadad says: 'Please let me live.' "

The king answered, "Is he still alive? He is my brother."

³³The men took this as a good sign and were quick to pick up his word. "Yes, your brother Ben-Hadad!" they said.

"Go and get him," the king said. When Ben-Hadad came out, Ahab had him come up into his chariot.

Why did Ben-Hadad want to take prisoners? (20:18)

He probably intended to humiliate, perhaps torture and certainly execute the army of Israel. But such a strategy put his own soldiers at greater risk. Trying to overpower the Israelites without killing them would make the Arameans much more vulnerable in battle.

Why did they fear a god of the hills? (20:23)

The Israelites fought better in the hills, away from the level plains where the Aramean chariots had more effect. Ben-Hadad was looking for excuses for his battle losses. So the Aramites rationalized that the Israelites had a hill-god who had protected them. They thought they would outsmart the hill-god by moving the battle to the plains.

How had Ahab gained a reputation for being merciful? (20:31)

Perhaps Israel's kings were considered merciful by comparison to the ruthless tyrants of Aram. Perhaps the Arameans recalled peace talks in the past with Israel. Some say Ahab was known as an indecisive leader, possibly leading the Arameans to think he would not be forceful in his dealings with them.

Why did Ahab set Ben-Hadad free? (20:34)

Perhaps his greed at the prospect of a trade agreement caused Ahab not to carry out the death sentence. But that mistake would cost Ahab his life (22:35).

Sons of the prophets (20:35)

See *Company of the prophets* (2 Kings 2:3).

Why such a violent end for a nonviolent man? (20:36)

The prophets lived in a different dimension of justice. Many of their pronouncements bore symbolic weight, and frequently that weight intended to tell the people that God would not allow compromise. The fate of the man who refused to obey the prophet was a clear message to Ahab and others: to reject God's word was to sacrifice life itself.

Why couldn't Naboth make a deal? (21:3)

Naboth rightly regarded his inherited land as a trust. The land itself was the Lord's; Naboth and his family were stewards. To sell would, in strict interpretation, violate the land laws of Leviticus 25. So Naboth's refusal was a twofold sting to Ahab: (1) he accused the king of trying to break the covenant law; (2) he didn't want to associate with the royal house.

34"I will return the cities my father took from your father," Ben-Hadad offered. "You may set up your own market areas in Damascus, as my father did in Samaria."

ˌAhab said,ˌ "On the basis of a treaty I will set you free." So he made a treaty with him, and let him go.

A Prophet Condemns Ahab

35By the word of the LORD one of the sons of the prophetsᴰ said to his companion, "Strike me with your weapon," but the man refused.

36So the prophet said, "Because you have not obeyed the LORD, as soon as you leave me a lion will kill you." And after the man went away, a lion found him and killed him.

37The prophet found another man and said, "Strike me, please." So the man struck him and wounded him. **38**Then the prophet went and stood by the road waiting for the king. He disguised himself with his headband down over his eyes. **39**As the king passed by, the prophet called out to him, "Your servant went into the thick of the battle, and someone came to me with a captive and said, 'Guard this man. If he is missing, it will be your life for his life, or you must pay a talent*ᵃ* of silver.' **40**While your servant was busy here and there, the man disappeared."

"That is your sentence," the king of Israel said. "You have pronounced it yourself."

41Then the prophet quickly removed the headband from his eyes, and the king of Israel recognized him as one of the prophets. **42**He said to the king, "This is what the LORD says: 'You have set free a man I had determined should die.*ᵇ* Therefore it is your life for his life, your people for his people.' " **43**Sullen and angry, the king of Israel went to his palace in Samaria.

Naboth's Vineyard

21 Some time later there was an incident involving a vineyard belonging to Naboth the Jezreelite. The vineyard was in Jezreel, close to the palace of Ahab king of Samaria. **2**Ahab said to Naboth, "Let me have your vineyard to use for a vegetable garden, since it is close to my palace. In exchange I will give you a better vineyard or, if you prefer, I will pay you whatever it is worth."

3But Naboth replied, "The LORD forbid that I should give you the inheritance of my fathers."

4So Ahab went home, sullen and angry because Naboth the Jezreelite had said, "I will not give you the inheritance of my fathers." He lay on his bed sulking and refused to eat.

5His wife Jezebel came in and asked him, "Why are you so sullen? Why won't you eat?"

6He answered her, "Because I said to Naboth the Jezreelite, 'Sell me your vineyard; or if you prefer, I will give you another vineyard in its place.' But he said, 'I will not give you my vineyard.' "

7Jezebel his wife said, "Is this how you act as king over Israel? Get up and eat! Cheer up. I'll get you the vineyard of Naboth the Jezreelite."

8So she wrote letters in Ahab's name, placed his seal on

ᵃ39 That is, about 75 pounds (about 34 kilograms)   *ᵇ42* The Hebrew term refers to the irrevocable giving over of things or persons to the LORD, often by totally destroying them.

them, and sent them to the elders and nobles who lived in Naboth's city with him. **9**In those letters she wrote:

"Proclaim a day of fasting and seat Naboth in a prominent place among the people. **10**But seat two scoundrels opposite him and have them testify that he has cursed both God and the king. Then take him out and stone him to death⁰."

11So the elders and nobles who lived in Naboth's city did as Jezebel directed in the letters she had written to them. **12**They proclaimed a fast and seated Naboth in a prominent place among the people. **13**Then two scoundrels came and sat opposite him and brought charges against Naboth before the people, saying, "Naboth has cursed both God and the king." So they took him outside the city and stoned him to death. **14**Then they sent word to Jezebel: "Naboth has been stoned and is dead."

15As soon as Jezebel heard that Naboth had been stoned to death, she said to Ahab, "Get up and take possession of the vineyard of Naboth the Jezreelite that he refused to sell you. He is no longer alive, but dead." **16**When Ahab heard that Naboth was dead, he got up and went down to take possession of Naboth's vineyard.

17Then the word of the LORD came to Elijah the Tishbite: **18**"Go down to meet Ahab king of Israel, who rules in Samaria. He is now in Naboth's vineyard, where he has gone to take possession of it. **19**Say to him, 'This is what the LORD says: Have you not murdered a man and seized his property?' Then say to him, 'This is what the LORD says: In the place where dogs licked up Naboth's blood, dogs will lick up your blood—yes, yours!' "

20Ahab said to Elijah, "So you have found me, my enemy!"

"I have found you," he answered, "because you have sold yourself to do evil in the eyes of the LORD. **21**'I am going to bring disaster on you. I will consume your descendants and cut off from Ahab every last male in Israel—slave or free. **22**I will make your house like that of Jeroboam son of Nebat and that of Baasha son of Ahijah, because you have provoked me to anger and have caused Israel to sin.'

23"And also concerning Jezebel the LORD says: 'Dogs will devour Jezebel by the wall ofᵃ Jezreel.'

24"Dogs will eat those belonging to Ahab who die in the city, and the birds of the air will feed on those who die in the country."

25(There was never a man like Ahab, who sold himself to do evil in the eyes of the LORD, urged on by Jezebel his wife. **26**He behaved in the vilest manner by going after idols⁰, like the Amorites the LORD drove out before Israel.)

27When Ahab heard these words, he tore his clothes, put on sackcloth⁰ and fasted. He lay in sackcloth and went around meekly.

28Then the word of the LORD came to Elijah the Tishbite: **29**"Have you noticed how Ahab has humbled himself before me? Because he has humbled himself, I will not bring this disaster in his day, but I will bring it on his house in the days of his son."

Why proclaim a day of fasting? (21:9)

People often fasted to avert disaster or to regain God's favor. This fast, however, was a religious pretense to disguise Jezebel's murder plot. The fast gave Jezebel's plot an aura of respectability, except to those who knew her scheme.

What about Naboth's heirs? (21:16)

Naboth's sons were also murdered in this heinous scheme, eliminating any heirs to the land (2 Kings 9:26). Furthermore, traitors forfeited their property to the king.

Was Ahab's repentance sincere? (21:27)

God declared that Ahab's repentance was sincere (v. 29). Later, however, Ahab resisted God's prophet Micaiah, once again demonstrating his lack of backbone (ch. 22). He drifted with the tides; his mind and will never found a settled home.

ᵃ23 Most Hebrew manuscripts; a few Hebrew manuscripts, Vulgate and Syriac (see also 2 Kings 9:26) *the plot of ground at*

Micaiah Prophesies Against Ahab

22 For three years there was no war between Aram and Israel. 2But in the third year Jehoshaphat king of Judah went down to see the king of Israel. 3The king of Israel had said to his officials, "Don't you know that Ramoth Gilead belongs to us and yet we are doing nothing to retake it from the king of Aram?"

4So he asked Jehoshaphat, "Will you go with me to fight against Ramoth Gilead?"

Jehoshaphat replied to the king of Israel, "I am as you are, my people as your people, my horses as your horses." 5But Jehoshaphat also said to the king of Israel, "First seek the counsel of the LORD."

6So the king of Israel brought together the prophetsᴰ— about four hundred men—and asked them, "Shall I go to war against Ramoth Gilead, or shall I refrain?"

"Go," they answered, "for the Lord will give it into the king's hand."

7But Jehoshaphat asked, "Is there not a prophet of the LORD here whom we can inquire of?"

8The king of Israel answered Jehoshaphat, "There is still one man through whom we can inquire of the LORD, but I hate him because he never prophesies anything good about me, but always bad. He is Micaiah son of Imlah."

"The king should not say that," Jehoshaphat replied.

9So the king of Israel called one of his officials and said, "Bring Micaiah son of Imlah at once."

10Dressed in their royal robes, the king of Israel and Jehoshaphat king of Judah were sitting on their thrones at the threshing floor by the entrance of the gate of Samaria, with all the prophets prophesying before them. 11Now Zedekiah son of Kenaanah had made iron horns and he declared, "This is what the LORD says: 'With these you will gore the Arameans until they are destroyed.' "

12All the other prophets were prophesying the same thing. "Attack Ramoth Gilead and be victorious," they said, "for the LORD will give it into the king's hand."

13The messenger who had gone to summon Micaiah said to him, "Look, as one man the other prophets are predicting success for the king. Let your word agree with theirs, and speak favorably."

14But Micaiah said, "As surely as the LORD lives, I can tell him only what the LORD tells me."

15When he arrived, the king asked him, "Micaiah, shall we go to war against Ramoth Gilead, or shall I refrain?"

"Attack and be victorious," he answered, "for the LORD will give it into the king's hand."

16The king said to him, "How many times must I make you swear to tell me nothing but the truth in the name of the LORD?"

17Then Micaiah answered, "I saw all Israel scattered on the hills like sheep without a shepherd, and the LORD said, 'These people have no master. Let each one go home in peaceᴰ.' "

18The king of Israel said to Jehoshaphat, "Didn't I tell you that he never prophesies anything good about me, but only bad?"

19Micaiah continued, "Therefore hear the word of the LORD: I saw the LORD sitting on his throne with all the host of heaven standing around him on his right and on his left. 20And the LORD said, 'Who will entice Ahab into attacking Ramoth Gilead and going to his deathᴰ there?'

"One suggested this, and another that. 21Finally, a spirit

How did Jehoshaphat recognize these were false prophets? (22:6–7)

Perhaps he had a healthy suspicion for any "prophet" who enjoyed favor with Ahab. Perhaps Jehoshaphat's network of contacts in the north kept him abreast of genuine prophets and phonies. Perhaps spiritual discernment showed him that not everyone who speaks of the Lord is the Lord's.

Why did Micaiah deliberately give a false prophecy? (22:15)

Micaiah seemed at first to be lying. But no one believed his words, including Ahab, who had the greatest interest in them. From this we can conclude that Micaiah was mocking Ahab by mimicking the pseudo-prophets. The sarcasm in his voice must have conveyed his real message, since even Ahab demanded a more direct answer.

Does God have a council? (22:19–20)

See *Was this a parable or a literal event in heaven?* (2 Chron. 18:18–21).

Is God guilty of lying? (22:20–22)

No. God allowed 400 prophets to prophesy falsehoods. He used them much as he sometimes used heathen nations to punish Israel (see Hab. 1:2–11). Remember that Micaiah denounced the false prophets. God didn't trick Ahab; he offered him a choice—believe a lie or believe the truth. See article: *How can a holy God send an evil spirit?* (Judges 9:23). Also see *Why would God use a lie to accomplish his purpose?* (2 Chron. 18:22).

came forward, stood before the LORD and said, 'I will entice him.'

22" 'By what means?' the LORD asked.

" 'I will go out and be a lying spirit in the mouths of all his prophets[D],' he said.

" 'You will succeed in enticing him,' said the LORD. 'Go and do it.'

23"So now the LORD has put a lying spirit in the mouths of all these prophets of yours. The LORD has decreed disaster for you."

24Then Zedekiah son of Kenaanah went up and slapped Micaiah in the face. "Which way did the spirit from[a] the LORD go when he went from me to speak to you?" he asked.

25Micaiah replied, "You will find out on the day you go to hide in an inner room."

26The king of Israel then ordered, "Take Micaiah and send him back to Amon the ruler of the city and to Joash the king's son **27**and say, 'This is what the king says: Put this fellow in prison and give him nothing but bread and water until I return safely.' "

28Micaiah declared, "If you ever return safely, the LORD has not spoken through me." Then he added, "Mark my words, all you people!"

Ahab Killed at Ramoth Gilead

29So the king of Israel and Jehoshaphat king of Judah went up to Ramoth Gilead. **30**The king of Israel said to Jehoshaphat, "I will enter the battle in disguise, but you wear your royal robes." So the king of Israel disguised himself and went into battle.

31Now the king of Aram had ordered his thirty-two chariot commanders, "Do not fight with anyone, small or great, except the king of Israel." **32**When the chariot commanders saw Jehoshaphat, they thought, "Surely this is the king of Israel." So they turned to attack him, but when Jehoshaphat cried out, **33**the chariot commanders saw that he was not the king of Israel and stopped pursuing him.

34But someone drew his bow at random and hit the king of Israel between the sections of his armor. The king told his chariot driver, "Wheel around and get me out of the fighting. I've been wounded." **35**All day long the battle raged, and the king was propped up in his chariot facing the Arameans. The blood from his wound ran onto the floor of the chariot, and that evening he died. **36**As the sun was setting, a cry spread through the army: "Every man to his town; everyone to his land!"

37So the king died and was brought to Samaria, and they buried him there. **38**They washed the chariot at a pool in Samaria (where the prostitutes bathed),[b] and the dogs licked up his blood, as the word of the LORD had declared.

39As for the other events of Ahab's reign, including all he did, the palace he built and inlaid with ivory, and the cities he fortified, are they not written in the book of the annals of the kings of Israel? **40**Ahab rested with his fathers. And Ahaziah his son succeeded him as king.

Jehoshaphat King of Judah

41Jehoshaphat son of Asa became king of Judah in the fourth year of Ahab king of Israel. **42**Jehoshaphat was thir-

Why didn't Ahab get any medical attention? (22:35)
Perhaps he did in ways that enabled him to be propped up in the chariot and inspire his soldiers during the daylong battle. Likely Ahab recognized his wound as fatal, and if we read the story generously, we can see a failed king who finally submitted to God's will. If Ahab understood his wound as being from God, he seems not to have resisted in his last hours.

a 24 Or *Spirit of*   *b 38* Or *Samaria and cleaned the weapons*

ty-five years old when he became king, and he reigned in Jerusalem[D] twenty-five years. His mother's name was Azubah daughter of Shilhi. **43**In everything he walked in the ways of his father Asa and did not stray from them; he did what was right in the eyes of the LORD. The high places[D], however, were not removed, and the people continued to offer sacrifices[D] and burn incense[D] there. **44**Jehoshaphat was also at peace[D] with the king of Israel.

45As for the other events of Jehoshaphat's reign, the things he achieved and his military exploits, are they not written in the book of the annals of the kings of Judah? **46**He rid the land of the rest of the male shrine prostitutes[D] who remained there even after the reign of his father Asa. **47**There was then no king in Edom[D]; a deputy ruled.

48Now Jehoshaphat built a fleet of trading ships[a] to go to Ophir for gold, but they never set sail—they were wrecked at Ezion Geber. **49**At that time Ahaziah son of Ahab said to Jehoshaphat, "Let my men sail with your men," but Jehoshaphat refused.

50Then Jehoshaphat rested with his fathers and was buried with them in the city of David his father. And Jehoram his son succeeded him.

Ahaziah King of Israel

51Ahaziah son of Ahab became king of Israel in Samaria in the seventeenth year of Jehoshaphat king of Judah, and he reigned over Israel two years. **52**He did evil in the eyes of the LORD, because he walked in the ways of his father and mother and in the ways of Jeroboam son of Nebat, who caused Israel to sin. **53**He served and worshiped Baal[D] and provoked the LORD, the God of Israel, to anger, just as his father had done.

Male shrine prostitutes (22:46)
See *What did male prostitutes have to do with pagan worship?* (14:24).

2 KINGS

Why read this book?

We can learn a lot about human nature from this historical book. We'll meet fascinating characters like Elisha and Elijah. We'll also see lesser known but intriguing examples of God's power and providence (see, for example, 4:1–7; 4:42–44; 7:3–11).

Who wrote this book?

We can't be sure. According to ancient Jewish tradition, Jeremiah did. Whoever wrote 1 and 2 Kings probably used preexisting documents such as *the book of the annals of Solomon* (11:41), *the book of the annals of the kings of Israel* (14:19) and *the book of the annals of the kings of Judah* (14:29). Other written sources may have been used as well (see 1 Chron. 29:29; 2 Chron. 9:29; 12:15).

To whom and why was it written?

Originally it was written to preserve the history of Israel and Judah for the Jews living in exile in Babylon. The author wanted his readers to learn the lessons of history, reminding them of the consequences of unfaithfulness to God.

When did these events occur and when was this book written?

2 Kings covers events between 853 B.C. and 562 B.C. Originally, the book was part of 1 Kings and was probably written after the fall of Jerusalem in 586 B.C., but before 550 B.C.

Why is Kings split into two books?

This was done in the third century B.C. by those who translated the Old Testament into Greek (a version called the Septuagint). One scroll had been sufficient for the Hebrew (without vowels). But the Greek (with vowels) required nearly twice the space.

What to look for in 2 Kings:

The tragic consequences of idolatry: Israel's defeat and captivity in Assyria, and Judah's defeat and captivity in Babylon. Look for summary statements (17:7–23; 24:8–20) which sadly detail the terrible losses God's people endured because of their sin.

When did these things happen?

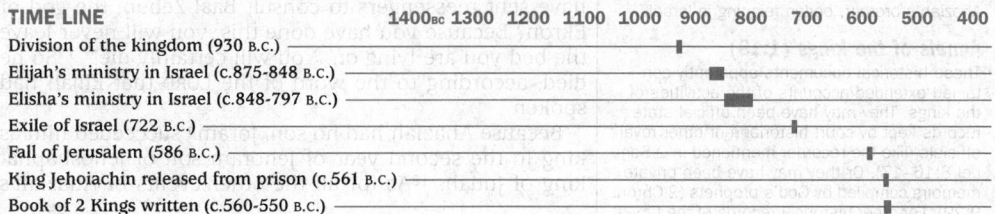

TIME LINE	1400BC	1300	1200	1100	1000	900	800	700	600	500	400
Division of the kingdom (930 B.C.)											
Elijah's ministry in Israel (c.875-848 B.C.)											
Elisha's ministry in Israel (c.848-797 B.C.)											
Exile of Israel (722 B.C.)											
Fall of Jerusalem (586 B.C.)											
King Jehoiachin released from prison (c.561 B.C.)											
Book of 2 Kings written (c.560-550 B.C.)											

Was the king involved in Satan worship? (1:2)

No, but he did worship idols, which could be considered a form of Satanism. Baal-Zebub, a popular pagan deity, was actually *Baal-Zebul* (meaning *lord or master, the prince*). But the Lord's people ridiculed him as *Baal-Zebub* (meaning *lord of the flies*). Since this term implied both false worship and moral filth, a variation of it was used for Satan in New Testament times. See Matt. 12:24.

Why did prophets wear eccentric clothes? (1:8)

Elijah's coarse garments demonstrated the unvarnished toughness of his godly character. His way of dressing was an ethical statement—a stark contrast to the self-indulgent luxury enjoyed by the evil kings of his time. Elijah also may have intended that his uncomfortable clothes show his sorrow over the people's unfaithfulness. Ancient prophets were often recognized by their rough, animal-skin garments, as was John the Baptist in later times (Matt. 3:4; Heb. 11:37).

Why did God destroy 102 men? (1:10,12)

God's action seems harsh, since the captains and their men were simply following orders. Yet they knew Elijah was a man of God (1:9,11). They most likely knew of Elijah's conflicts with King Ahab and Queen Jezebel and God's previous judgment on Mount Carmel (1 Kings 18:16–46). The soldiers had a choice: obey the orders of an evil king (encouraging the idolatrous rebellion against God) or do the right thing. There are times we *must obey God rather than men* (Acts 5:29).

Why would Elijah fear the captain? (1:15)

Elijah's life was in danger. Apparently, the king intended to arrest, imprison or even kill him. Earlier, Elijah had run for his life because of the death threats of Jezebel (1 Kings 19:1–3), the present king's mother.

Who was really king? (1:17)

At this point, both Israel and Judah had rulers with similar names. Jehoram reigned in Judah, apparently as co-regent during the latter part of his father Jehoshaphat's reign (see 3:1). Meanwhile, Joram (a variation of the name *Jehoram*), Ahaziah's brother, began reigning in Israel.

Annals of the kings (1:18)

These historical documents apparently contained extended accounts of the activities of the kings. They may have been official state records kept by court historians or other royal officials (like the recorder mentioned in 2 Samuel 8:16–17). Or they may have been private memoirs compiled by God's prophets (2 Chron. 9:29). For other historical records of the times, see 1 Kings 11:41; 14:29.

The LORD's Judgment on Ahaziah

1 After Ahab's death[D], Moab rebelled against Israel. ²Now Ahaziah had fallen through the lattice of his upper room in Samaria and injured himself. So he sent messengers, saying to them, "Go and consult Baal-Zebub, the god of Ekron, to see if I will recover from this injury."

³But the angel of the LORD said to Elijah the Tishbite, "Go up and meet the messengers of the king of Samaria and ask them, 'Is it because there is no God in Israel that you are going off to consult Baal-Zebub, the god of Ekron?' ⁴Therefore this is what the LORD says: 'You will not leave the bed you are lying on. You will certainly die!' " So Elijah went.

⁵When the messengers returned to the king, he asked them, "Why have you come back?"

⁶"A man came to meet us," they replied. "And he said to us, 'Go back to the king who sent you and tell him, "This is what the LORD says: Is it because there is no God in Israel that you are sending men to consult Baal-Zebub, the god of Ekron? Therefore you will not leave the bed you are lying on. You will certainly die!" ' "

⁷The king asked them, "What kind of man was it who came to meet you and told you this?"

⁸They replied, "He was a man with a garment of hair and with a leather belt around his waist."

The king said, "That was Elijah the Tishbite."

⁹Then he sent to Elijah a captain with his company of fifty men. The captain went up to Elijah, who was sitting on the top of a hill, and said to him, "Man of God, the king says, 'Come down!' "

¹⁰Elijah answered the captain, "If I am a man of God, may fire come down from heaven and consume you and your fifty men!" Then fire fell from heaven and consumed the captain and his men.

¹¹At this the king sent to Elijah another captain with his fifty men. The captain said to him, "Man of God, this is what the king says, 'Come down at once!' "

¹²"If I am a man of God," Elijah replied, "may fire come down from heaven and consume you and your fifty men!" Then the fire of God fell from heaven and consumed him and his fifty men.

¹³So the king sent a third captain with his fifty men. This third captain went up and fell on his knees before Elijah. "Man of God," he begged, "please have respect for my life and the lives of these fifty men, your servants! ¹⁴See, fire has fallen from heaven and consumed the first two captains and all their men. But now have respect for my life!"

¹⁵The angel of the LORD said to Elijah, "Go down with him; do not be afraid of him." So Elijah got up and went down with him to the king.

¹⁶He told the king, "This is what the LORD says: Is it because there is no God in Israel for you to consult that you have sent messengers to consult Baal-Zebub, the god of Ekron? Because you have done this, you will never leave the bed you are lying on. You will certainly die!" ¹⁷So he died, according to the word of the LORD that Elijah had spoken.

Because Ahaziah had no son, Joram[a] succeeded him as king in the second year of Jehoram son of Jehoshaphat king of Judah. ¹⁸As for all the other events of Ahaziah's

a17 Hebrew Jehoram, a variant of Joram

reign, and what he did, are they not written in the book of the annals of the kings of Israel?

Elijah Taken Up to Heaven

2 When the LORD was about to take Elijah up to heaven in a whirlwind, Elijah and Elisha were on their way from Gilgal. ²Elijah said to Elisha, "Stay here; the LORD has sent me to Bethel."

But Elisha said, "As surely as the LORD lives and as you live, I will not leave you." So they went down to Bethel.

³The company of the prophets[D] at Bethel came out to Elisha and asked, "Do you know that the LORD is going to take your master from you today?"

"Yes, I know," Elisha replied, "but do not speak of it."

⁴Then Elijah said to him, "Stay here, Elisha; the LORD has sent me to Jericho[D]."

And he replied, "As surely as the LORD lives and as you live, I will not leave you." So they went to Jericho.

⁵The company of the prophets at Jericho went up to Elisha and asked him, "Do you know that the LORD is going to take your master from you today?"

"Yes, I know," he replied, "but do not speak of it."

⁶Then Elijah said to him, "Stay here; the LORD has sent me to the Jordan."

And he replied, "As surely as the LORD lives and as you live, I will not leave you." So the two of them walked on.

⁷Fifty men of the company of the prophets went and stood at a distance, facing the place where Elijah and Elisha had stopped at the Jordan. ⁸Elijah took his cloak, rolled it up and struck the water with it. The water divided to the right and to the left, and the two of them crossed over on dry ground.

⁹When they had crossed, Elijah said to Elisha, "Tell me, what can I do for you before I am taken from you?"

"Let me inherit a double portion of your spirit," Elisha replied.

¹⁰"You have asked a difficult thing," Elijah said, "yet if you see me when I am taken from you, it will be yours—otherwise not."

¹¹As they were walking along and talking together, suddenly a chariot of fire and horses of fire appeared and separated the two of them, and Elijah went up to heaven in a whirlwind. ¹²Elisha saw this and cried out, "My father! My father! The chariots and horsemen of Israel!" And Elisha saw him no more. Then he took hold of his own clothes and tore them apart.

¹³He picked up the cloak that had fallen from Elijah and went back and stood on the bank of the Jordan. ¹⁴Then he took the cloak that had fallen from him and struck the water with it. "Where now is the LORD, the God of Elijah?" he asked. When he struck the water, it divided to the right and to the left, and he crossed over.

¹⁵The company of the prophets from Jericho, who were watching, said, "The spirit of Elijah is resting on Elisha." And they went to meet him and bowed to the ground before him. ¹⁶"Look," they said, "we your servants have fifty able men. Let them go and look for your master. Perhaps the Spirit of the LORD has picked him up and set him down on some mountain or in some valley."

"No," Elisha replied, "do not send them."

¹⁷But they persisted until he was too ashamed to refuse. So he said, "Send them." And they sent fifty men, who searched for three days but did not find him. ¹⁸When they

SCRIPTURE LINK (2:1) Elisha
Elijah's aide. See 1 Kings 19:19–21.

Why did Elisha insist on staying with Elijah? (2:2,4,6)
Elisha, Elijah's personal attendant and companion, was heir-apparent to Elijah's role as a leading prophet. Evidently, Elisha realized (either through a personal premonition or a direct revelation from God) that his mentor's time on earth was nearing an end, so he wanted to stay at Elijah's side during these final moments.

Why didn't Elijah want Elisha to go with him? (2:2,4,6)
Elijah may have been testing Elisha's faithfulness and love. Or perhaps he simply wished to spend his last days in solitude. Elisha, however, was determined to see exactly what would happen to Elijah and receive any last-minute instructions. This incident shows the interaction between two godly but strong-willed personalities.

Company of the prophets (2:3,5)
Beginning with the time of Samuel, prophets gathered in groups sometimes known as "schools of prophets" or "sons of prophets." Experienced prophets were mentors for younger ones and they lived and worked together in the Lord's service. These companies of prophets were used by God on occasion (9:1–10). Although we do not know how many such companies existed, there were sizable groups in places like Bethel, Gilgal and Jericho (2:3,5; 4:38; see Map 6 at the back of this Bible). The total number of prophets exceeded 100 (see 4:38–43; 1 Samuel 19:20–21; 1 Kings 18:4).

Why did Elisha tell them not to speak? (2:3,5)
The younger prophets were too brazen and eager about something so sober and sacred. What they said was true, but their exuberance needed to be tempered by wisdom, patience and perhaps humility. Furthermore, Elisha did not need them to inform him about such matters.

What did Elisha want? (2:9)
Elisha was requesting either twice the spiritual power that Elijah had or twice the power of any of the remaining prophets—just as the eldest son would inherit a double portion of his father's property (Deut. 21:17). In any case, Elisha wanted divine strength to fulfill his new role as spiritual leader of the nation (2:15).

What is a chariot of fire? (2:11)
See What were these horses and chariots? (6:17).

Why the dramatic exit? (2:11)
It was a sign of divine favor and power. Instead of dying, Elijah ascended bodily into the heavenly realms, much like Enoch and Jesus (Gen. 5:24; Acts 1:9). Whirlwinds and fire were associated with the power and presence of God (Job 38:1; 40:6; Isaiah 29:6). Years later, on the day of Pentecost, wind and fire accompanied the coming of the Holy Spirit (Acts 2:1–4).

Why form a search party? (2:16)

The company of prophets may have thought God put Elijah down alive nearby. Or perhaps they believed Elijah was dead, and they wanted to locate his body. Elisha let them look, perhaps thinking it would help them accept their loss when they saw that Elijah was really gone.

Why put salt in the spring? (2:21)

While God could have healed the water in a different way, the clean new bowl and the salt were appropriate symbols of purification and holiness (Lev. 2:13; Matt. 5:13).

Sacred stone of Baal (3:2)

Joram's father, Ahab, had aroused God's anger by his unabashed idolatry. He built an altar and temple that included a stone—an engraved image dedicated to Baal (1 Kings 16:32–33). Whatever Joram did with this stone, it was not completely destroyed until Jehu's men later charred the stone with fire and demolished it (see 10:26–27).

The sins of Jeroboam (3:3)

See *Sins of Jeroboam* (1 Kings 16:31).

Moab Revolts (3:5)

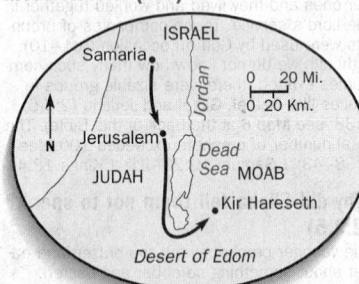

returned to Elisha, who was staying in Jericho[D], he said to them, "Didn't I tell you not to go?"

Healing of the Water

19The men of the city said to Elisha, "Look, our lord, this town is well situated, as you can see, but the water is bad and the land is unproductive."

20"Bring me a new bowl," he said, "and put salt in it." So they brought it to him.

21Then he went out to the spring and threw the salt into it, saying, "This is what the LORD says: 'I have healed this water. Never again will it cause death[D] or make the land unproductive.'" **22**And the water has remained wholesome to this day, according to the word Elisha had spoken.

Elisha Is Jeered

23From there Elisha went up to Bethel. As he was walking along the road, some youths came out of the town and jeered at him. "Go on up, you baldhead!" they said. "Go on up, you baldhead!" **24**He turned around, looked at them and called down a curse on them in the name of the LORD. Then two bears came out of the woods and mauled forty-two of the youths. **25**And he went on to Mount Carmel and from there returned to Samaria.

Moab Revolts

3 Joram[a] son of Ahab became king of Israel in Samaria in the eighteenth year of Jehoshaphat king of Judah, and he reigned twelve years. **2**He did evil in the eyes of the LORD, but not as his father and mother had done. He got rid of the sacred stone[D] of Baal[D] that his father had made. **3**Nevertheless he clung to the sins of Jeroboam son of Nebat, which he had caused Israel to commit; he did not turn away from them.

4Now Mesha king of Moab raised sheep, and he had to supply the king of Israel with a hundred thousand lambs and with the wool of a hundred thousand rams. **5**But after Ahab died, the king of Moab rebelled against the king of Israel. **6**So at that time King Joram set out from Samaria

---

a1 Hebrew *Jehoram,* a variant of *Joram;* also in verse 6

Was this personal revenge on harmless youths? (2:23–24)

Probably not, for the following reasons:

(1) Very likely these were young men (the word translated *youths* often refers to people in their late teens), not little children. To Elisha, the group of at least 42 youths must have appeared a formidable mob.

(2) Their mockery represented the irreverence of a generation growing up with increasing contempt for God and his laws (Lev. 19:32).

(3) Their insults targeted not just Elisha's baldness but the God whom he represented. In taunting Elisha and rejecting his prophetic authority, the youths were taunting God and rejecting his authority. *Go on up* may have been a way of saying "Get lost!" or perhaps, "If you are really a prophet like Elijah, go on up to heaven as he did."

(4) Elisha did not take personal revenge but called on the Lord, who seems to have used the bears to warn a corrupt generation that blasphemy against God would be met with swift consequences.

and mobilized all Israel. **7**He also sent this message to Je-hoshaphat king of Judah: "The king of Moab has rebelled against me. Will you go with me to fight against Moab?"

"I will go with you," he replied. "I am as you are, my people as your people, my horses as your horses."

8"By what route shall we attack?" he asked.

"Through the Desert of Edom[D]," he answered.

9So the king of Israel set out with the king of Judah and the king of Edom. After a roundabout march of seven days, the army had no more water for themselves or for the animals with them.

10"What!" exclaimed the king of Israel. "Has the LORD called us three kings together only to hand us over to Moab?"

11But Jehoshaphat asked, "Is there no prophet[D] of the LORD here, that we may inquire of the LORD through him?"

An officer of the king of Israel answered, "Elisha son of Shaphat is here. He used to pour water on the hands of Elijah.[a]"

12Jehoshaphat said, "The word of the LORD is with him." So the king of Israel and Jehoshaphat and the king of Edom went down to him.

13Elisha said to the king of Israel, "What do we have to do with each other? Go to the prophets of your father and the prophets of your mother."

"No," the king of Israel answered, "because it was the LORD who called us three kings together to hand us over to Moab."

14Elisha said, "As surely as the LORD Almighty lives, whom I serve, if I did not have respect for the presence of Jehoshaphat king of Judah, I would not look at you or even notice you. **15**But now bring me a harpist."

While the harpist was playing, the hand of the LORD came upon Elisha **16**and he said, "This is what the LORD says: Make this valley full of ditches. **17**For this is what the LORD says: You will see neither wind nor rain, yet this valley will be filled with water, and you, your cattle and your other animals will drink. **18**This is an easy thing in the eyes of the LORD; he will also hand Moab over to you. **19**You will overthrow every fortified city and every major town. You will cut down every good tree, stop up all the springs, and ruin every good field with stones."

20The next morning, about the time for offering the sacrifice[D], there it was—water flowing from the direction of Edom! And the land was filled with water.

21Now all the Moabites had heard that the kings had come to fight against them; so every man, young and old, who could bear arms was called up and stationed on the border. **22**When they got up early in the morning, the sun was shining on the water. To the Moabites across the way, the water looked red—like blood. **23**"That's blood!" they said. "Those kings must have fought and slaughtered each other. Now to the plunder[D], Moab!"

24But when the Moabites came to the camp of Israel, the Israelites rose up and fought them until they fled. And the Israelites invaded the land and slaughtered the Moabites. **25**They destroyed the towns, and each man threw a stone on every good field until it was covered. They stopped up all the springs and cut down every good tree. Only Kir Hareseth was left with its stones in place, but men armed with slings surrounded it and attacked it as well.

a11 That is, he was Elijah's personal servant.

Why did Joram blame the Lord for his troubles? (3:10)

It is human nature to shift the blame from oneself. Joram, like many (Prov. 19:3), blamed God for problems of his own making. There is no evidence that God had sanctioned this expedition, as Joram claimed. The kings did not pray or consult a prophet for advice until they were in desperate straits (v. 11). Initially motivated by political self-interest, the three kings now saw that they needed God's help.

Does music enhance our spiritual lives? (3:15)

In this case, the music of the harp evidently calmed Elisha, who was so angry he could hardly look at King Joram (v. 14). Settled in his spirit, he could focus his heart and hear from God. Prophecy and music went together on other occasions (1 Samuel 10:5; 1 Chron. 25:1–3). Music is also a way of expressing worship and praise (2 Chron. 5:12–14; Psalm 147:7; Eph. 5:19).

How might God have caused this flow of water? (3:20)

As Elisha noted, it was *an easy thing* (v. 18) for the Lord to supply drinking water. Since this water flowed from the direction of Edom, it appears that the Lord caused heavy rains to fall in the mountains of Edom, some distance south of Moab. Because no rain actually fell in Moab, the Moabites did not expect to find pools of water and mistook the reflected red of the morning sun for blood (v. 22).

Why such destruction? (3:25)

The soldiers were following conventional tactics of ancient warfare. The intent was to cripple the agricultural capability of their enemies, so that it would take years to recover from the devastation. But the drastic measures described here were more than just standard operating procedure. They were necessary measures taken to combat the dangerous threat of Moab's idolatry and wickedness.

SCRIPTURE LINK (3:27)

See *Why sacrifice the heir to the throne?*
(16:3) and *Why would parents sacrifice their
children?* (Jer. 19:5).

What did human sacrifice have to do with the Israelites' withdrawal? (3:27)

By sacrificing his son, the Moabite king made a final and desperate appeal to his god, Chemosh. The Moabites got the results they wanted, not because Chemosh answered their prayers, but because they were so stirred by the sacrifice of the crown prince that they fought with greater intensity and fury. The Israelites, having accomplished their main objectives, had no reason to prolong the battle and withdrew.

Why this elaborate way to raise funds? (4:2–7)

This method compelled the woman to put her faith into action by obeying the prophet's instructions. As she poured the oil into jar after jar, she saw God turn small blessings into bountiful provisions. The story became an object lesson of God's care for his people and undoubtedly encouraged the Jews when they were slaves in Babylon.

Miracle at Shunem (4:8)

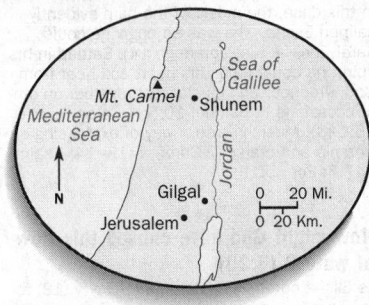

Why didn't Elisha talk directly to this woman? (4:13)

We don't know why, but it was not uncommon for Elisha to employ a servant as an intermediary. He probably wasn't trying to preserve some sort of prophetic honor or authority since later he used a messenger to communicate even with the highly-respected Naaman (5:9–10). He spoke directly with her later (v. 16).

26When the king of Moab saw that the battle had gone against him, he took with him seven hundred swordsmen to break through to the king of Edom^D, but they failed. **27**Then he took his firstborn^D son, who was to succeed him as king, and offered him as a sacrifice^D on the city wall. The fury against Israel was great; they withdrew and returned to their own land.

The Widow's Oil

4 The wife of a man from the company of the prophets^D cried out to Elisha, "Your servant my husband is dead, and you know that he revered the LORD. But now his creditor is coming to take my two boys as his slaves."

2Elisha replied to her, "How can I help you? Tell me, what do you have in your house?"

"Your servant has nothing there at all," she said, "except a little oil."

3Elisha said, "Go around and ask all your neighbors for empty jars. Don't ask for just a few. **4**Then go inside and shut the door behind you and your sons. Pour oil into all the jars, and as each is filled, put it to one side."

5She left him and afterward shut the door behind her and her sons. They brought the jars to her and she kept pouring. **6**When all the jars were full, she said to her son, "Bring me another one."

But he replied, "There is not a jar left." Then the oil stopped flowing.

7She went and told the man of God, and he said, "Go, sell the oil and pay your debts. You and your sons can live on what is left."

The Shunammite's Son Restored to Life

8One day Elisha went to Shunem. And a well-to-do woman was there, who urged him to stay for a meal. So whenever he came by, he stopped there to eat. **9**She said to her husband, "I know that this man who often comes our way is a holy man of God. **10**Let's make a small room on the roof and put in it a bed and a table, a chair and a lamp for him. Then he can stay there whenever he comes to us."

11One day when Elisha came, he went up to his room and lay down there. **12**He said to his servant Gehazi, "Call the Shunammite." So he called her, and she stood before him. **13**Elisha said to him, "Tell her, 'You have gone to all this trouble for us. Now what can be done for you? Can we speak on your behalf to the king or the commander of the army?' "

She replied, "I have a home among my own people."

14"What can be done for her?" Elisha asked.

Gehazi said, "Well, she has no son and her husband is old."

15Then Elisha said, "Call her." So he called her, and she stood in the doorway. **16**"About this time next year," Elisha said, "you will hold a son in your arms."

"No, my lord," she objected. "Don't mislead your servant, O man of God!"

17But the woman became pregnant, and the next year about that same time she gave birth to a son, just as Elisha had told her.

18The child grew, and one day he went out to his father, who was with the reapers. **19**"My head! My head!" he said to his father.

His father told a servant, "Carry him to his mother." **20**After the servant had lifted him up and carried him to

his mother, the boy sat on her lap until noon, and then he died. ²¹She went up and laid him on the bed of the man of God, then shut the door and went out.

²²She called her husband and said, "Please send me one of the servants and a donkey so I can go to the man of God quickly and return."

²³"Why go to him today?" he asked. "It's not the New Moon or the Sabbath ᴰ."

"It's all right," she said.

²⁴She saddled the donkey and said to her servant, "Lead on; don't slow down for me unless I tell you." ²⁵So she set out and came to the man of God at Mount Carmel.

When he saw her in the distance, the man of God said to his servant Gehazi, "Look! There's the Shunammite! ²⁶Run to meet her and ask her, 'Are you all right? Is your husband all right? Is your child all right?' "

"Everything is all right," she said.

²⁷When she reached the man of God at the mountain, she took hold of his feet. Gehazi came over to push her away, but the man of God said, "Leave her alone! She is in bitter distress, but the LORD has hidden it from me and has not told me why."

²⁸"Did I ask you for a son, my lord?" she said. "Didn't I tell you, 'Don't raise my hopes'?"

²⁹Elisha said to Gehazi, "Tuck your cloak into your belt, take my staff in your hand and run. If you meet anyone, do not greet him, and if anyone greets you, do not answer. Lay my staff on the boy's face."

³⁰But the child's mother said, "As surely as the LORD lives and as you live, I will not leave you." So he got up and followed her.

³¹Gehazi went on ahead and laid the staff on the boy's face, but there was no sound or response. So Gehazi went back to meet Elisha and told him, "The boy has not awakened."

³²When Elisha reached the house, there was the boy lying dead on his couch. ³³He went in, shut the door on the two of them and prayed to the LORD. ³⁴Then he got on the bed and lay upon the boy, mouth to mouth, eyes to eyes, hands to hands. As he stretched himself out upon him, the boy's body grew warm. ³⁵Elisha turned away and walked back and forth in the room and then got on the

Did prophets keep visiting hours? (4:23)
While Elisha may have been available at other times, the New Moon and the Sabbath day provided regular monthly and weekly occasions for God's people to assemble and hear the word of God from the prophet.

What influence did prophets have with kings? (4:13)

God used inspired men who fearlessly proclaimed his word and provided spiritual guidance, not only for the nation but for the nation's rulers as well.

Good kings like David, Solomon and Hezekiah welcomed the prophets' support and maintained close ties with the prophets who counseled and instructed them (2 Samuel 7:1–17; 1 Kings 1:22–27; 2 Kings 19:20). David even accepted rebukes and correction from prophets, humbly repenting before Nathan and Gad (2 Samuel 12:1–14; 24:10–25). Other prophets offered valuable counsel in times of war (1 Kings 12:21–24; 2 Kings 6:8–10).

Bold individuals like Elijah and Elisha might have been harassed or despised by wicked kings, but they could not be ignored; they dared to confront the kings with news from God that inevitably proved true. God's prophets reminded kings that they were accountable to the higher law of the King of kings. See article: *How much influence did prophets have?* (1 Kings 12:24).

bed and stretched out upon him once more. The boy sneezed seven times and opened his eyes.

[36]Elisha summoned Gehazi and said, "Call the Shunammite." And he did. When she came, he said, "Take your son." [37]She came in, fell at his feet and bowed to the ground. Then she took her son and went out.

Death in the Pot

[38]Elisha returned to Gilgal and there was a famine in that region. While the company of the prophets[D] was meeting with him, he said to his servant, "Put on the large pot and cook some stew for these men."

[39]One of them went out into the fields to gather herbs and found a wild vine. He gathered some of its gourds and filled the fold of his cloak. When he returned, he cut them up into the pot of stew, though no one knew what they were. [40]The stew was poured out for the men, but as they began to eat it, they cried out, "O man of God, there is death[D] in the pot!" And they could not eat it.

[41]Elisha said, "Get some flour." He put it into the pot and said, "Serve it to the people to eat." And there was nothing harmful in the pot.

Feeding of a Hundred

[42]A man came from Baal Shalishah, bringing the man of God twenty loaves of barley bread baked from the first ripe grain, along with some heads of new grain. "Give it to the people to eat," Elisha said.

[43]"How can I set this before a hundred men?" his servant asked.

But Elisha answered, "Give it to the people to eat. For this is what the LORD says: 'They will eat and have some left over.'" [44]Then he set it before them, and they ate and had some left over, according to the word of the LORD.

Naaman Healed of Leprosy

5 Now Naaman was commander of the army of the king of Aram. He was a great man in the sight of his master and highly regarded, because through him the LORD had given victory to Aram. He was a valiant soldier, but he had leprosy[D].[a]

[2]Now bands from Aram had gone out and had taken captive a young girl from Israel, and she served Naaman's wife. [3]She said to her mistress, "If only my master would see the prophet who is in Samaria! He would cure him of his leprosy."

[4]Naaman went to his master and told him what the girl from Israel had said. [5]"By all means, go," the king of Aram replied. "I will send a letter to the king of Israel." So Naaman left, taking with him ten talents[b] of silver, six thousand shekels[Dc] of gold and ten sets of clothing. [6]The letter that he took to the king of Israel read: "With this letter I am sending my servant Naaman to you so that you may cure him of his leprosy."

[7]As soon as the king of Israel read the letter, he tore his robes and said, "Am I God? Can I kill and bring back to life? Why does this fellow send someone to me to be cured of his leprosy? See how he is trying to pick a quarrel with me!"

Company of the prophets (4:38)
See Company of the prophets (2:3).

What was wrong with the stew? (4:40)
It was either too bitter to eat or poisonous. In either case, Elisha's divine powers were displayed when he made the food safe by using ordinary flour to turn it into something good to eat. Similarly he used salt to purify water (2:19–22) and oil to solve a widow's credit problems (4:7). In Elisha we see vivid displays of God's ability to salvage and transform.

Did the Lord give victory to the enemy? (5:1)
Yes, but probably not at Israel's expense. This victory probably refers to Naaman's skirmishes with the Assyrians who threatened to overtake Aram (Syria) during this period. Naaman did not realize it, but it was the help of God, not just his military skill, that contributed to his nation's success.

Why would leprosy strike someone God had favored? (5:1)
When God uses people for good, he doesn't necessarily insulate them from life's other experiences, even harsh ones. Paul had a thorn in the flesh (2 Cor. 12:7–9) and Timothy was often sick (1 Tim. 5:23), yet the Lord enabled them to serve effectively. Though leprosy sometimes represented divine punishment (5:27; 2 Chron. 26:16–23), Naaman's suffering led to a dramatic encounter with the power of God (5:15,17). We cannot know all the reasons for suffering, but we can trust that the outcome will ultimately reflect God's glory and purpose. Also see article: Does God allow pain in order to display his power? (John 9:3).

---

[a]1 The Hebrew word was used for various diseases affecting the skin—not necessarily leprosy; also in verses 3, 6, 7, 11 and 27.
[b]5 That is, about 750 pounds (about 340 kilograms)   [c]5 That is, about 150 pounds (about 70 kilograms)

8When Elisha the man of God heard that the king of Israel had torn his robes, he sent him this message: "Why have you torn your robes? Have the man come to me and he will know that there is a prophet^D in Israel." **9**So Naaman went with his horses and chariots and stopped at the door of Elisha's house. **10**Elisha sent a messenger to say to him, "Go, wash yourself seven times in the Jordan, and your flesh will be restored and you will be cleansed."

11But Naaman went away angry and said, "I thought that he would surely come out to me and stand and call on the name of the LORD his God, wave his hand over the spot and cure me of my leprosy^D. **12**Are not Abana and Pharpar, the rivers of Damascus, better than any of the waters of Israel? Couldn't I wash in them and be cleansed?" So he turned and went off in a rage.

13Naaman's servants went to him and said, "My father, if the prophet had told you to do some great thing, would you not have done it? How much more, then, when he tells you, 'Wash and be cleansed'!" **14**So he went down and dipped himself in the Jordan seven times, as the man of God had told him, and his flesh was restored and became clean like that of a young boy.

15Then Naaman and all his attendants went back to the man of God. He stood before him and said, "Now I know that there is no God in all the world except in Israel. Please accept now a gift from your servant."

16The prophet answered, "As surely as the LORD lives, whom I serve, I will not accept a thing." And even though Naaman urged him, he refused.

17"If you will not," said Naaman, "please let me, your servant, be given as much earth as a pair of mules can carry, for your servant will never again make burnt offerings^D and sacrifices^D to any other god but the LORD. **18**But may the LORD forgive your servant for this one thing: When my master enters the temple of Rimmon to bow down and he is leaning on my arm and I bow there also—when I bow down in the temple of Rimmon, may the LORD forgive your servant for this."

19"Go in peace^D," Elisha said.

After Naaman had traveled some distance, **20**Gehazi, the servant of Elisha the man of God, said to himself, "My master was too easy on Naaman, this Aramean, by not accepting from him what he brought. As surely as the LORD lives, I will run after him and get something from him."

21So Gehazi hurried after Naaman. When Naaman saw him running toward him, he got down from the chariot to meet him. "Is everything all right?" he asked.

22"Everything is all right," Gehazi answered. "My master sent me to say, 'Two young men from the company of the prophets have just come to me from the hill country of Ephraim. Please give them a talent^a of silver and two sets of clothing.'"

23"By all means, take two talents," said Naaman. He urged Gehazi to accept them, and then tied up the two talents of silver in two bags, with two sets of clothing. He gave them to two of his servants, and they carried them ahead of Gehazi. **24**When Gehazi came to the hill, he took the things from the servants and put them away in the house. He sent the men away and they left. **25**Then he went in and stood before his master Elisha.

"Where have you been, Gehazi?" Elisha asked.

"Your servant didn't go anywhere," Gehazi answered.

What did Naaman have against the Jordan? (5:10-12)

Compared to his own nation's rivers, Naaman found the Jordan muddy and unappealing. God was apparently testing Naaman to see if he would obey even if it cost him his pride. The Lord must have known that this military officer needed faith more than physical healing.

Why did Naaman want dirt from the holy land? (5:17)

Evidently he now considered the land of Israel "holy ground," and intended to spread the soil over a plot of ground in his homeland. That spot would then serve as a special place to worship the Lord. In those days, many believed individual gods ruled only over certain geographic areas. This request may have been Naaman's first halting step toward worshiping the true God on foreign soil.

Did Elisha accept Naaman's excuse? (5:18-19)

Naaman realized his new faith would be tested when he returned home. He intended to worship the Lord God only, but would be required to accompany his king to the temple of Rimmon. Elisha neither denied nor affirmed Naaman's wish. *Go in peace* could mean simply that Naaman was not to worry: the God who had healed him would also give him wisdom to deal with this problem.

---

^a22 That is, about 75 pounds (about 34 kilograms)

How did Elisha's spirit go with Gehazi? (5:26)

Though he had not left his house, Elisha's prophetic insight gave him knowledge of everything Gehazi had done.

Why such anxiety over an axhead? (6:5)

The worker was especially upset because he was responsible for someone else's property. Whether the axhead was finely crafted, borrowed from a poor man or unique in some other way, we don't know. It is clear, though, that the problem was not too small to receive Elisha's attention.

Why throw a stick into the river? (6:6)

It marked the location of the axhead and served to demonstrate that just as wood can float naturally, even iron could float when God's miraculous power intervened.

What were these horses and chariots? (6:17)

Most likely they were angels, spirit beings who serve God in the heavenly realms where spiritual battles occur (see Eph. 6:12; Heb. 1:14). In this case, the angelic host appeared as horses and chariots to assure Elisha's servant that God's forces were more powerful than the troops and chariots of Aram. *Fire* probably means they glowed, reflecting God's heavenly glory. A similar angelic band comprised Elijah's special escort to heaven. See 2:11–12.

26But Elisha said to him, "Was not my spirit with you when the man got down from his chariot to meet you? Is this the time to take money, or to accept clothes, olive groves, vineyards, flocks, herds, or menservants and maidservants? **27**Naaman's leprosy[D] will cling to you and to your descendants forever." Then Gehazi went from Elisha's presence and he was leprous, as white as snow.

An Axhead Floats

6 The company of the prophets[D] said to Elisha, "Look, the place where we meet with you is too small for us. **2**Let us go to the Jordan, where each of us can get a pole; and let us build a place there for us to live."

And he said, "Go."

3Then one of them said, "Won't you please come with your servants?"

"I will," Elisha replied. **4**And he went with them.

They went to the Jordan and began to cut down trees. **5**As one of them was cutting down a tree, the iron axhead fell into the water. "Oh, my lord," he cried out, "it was borrowed!"

6The man of God asked, "Where did it fall?" When he showed him the place, Elisha cut a stick and threw it there, and made the iron float. **7**"Lift it out," he said. Then the man reached out his hand and took it.

Elisha Traps Blinded Arameans

8Now the king of Aram was at war with Israel. After conferring with his officers, he said, "I will set up my camp in such and such a place."

9The man of God sent word to the king of Israel: "Beware of passing that place, because the Arameans are going down there." **10**So the king of Israel checked on the place indicated by the man of God. Time and again Elisha warned the king, so that he was on his guard in such places.

11This enraged the king of Aram. He summoned his officers and demanded of them, "Will you not tell me which of us is on the side of the king of Israel?"

12"None of us, my lord the king," said one of his officers, "but Elisha, the prophet who is in Israel, tells the king of Israel the very words you speak in your bedroom."

13"Go, find out where he is," the king ordered, "so I can send men and capture him." The report came back: "He is in Dothan." **14**Then he sent horses and chariots and a strong force there. They went by night and surrounded the city.

15When the servant of the man of God got up and went out early the next morning, an army with horses and chariots had surrounded the city. "Oh, my lord, what shall we do?" the servant asked.

16"Don't be afraid," the prophet answered. "Those who are with us are more than those who are with them."

17And Elisha prayed, "O LORD, open his eyes so he may see." Then the LORD opened the servant's eyes, and he looked and saw the hills full of horses and chariots of fire all around Elisha.

18As the enemy came down toward him, Elisha prayed to the LORD, "Strike these people with blindness." So he struck them with blindness, as Elisha had asked.

19Elisha told them, "This is not the road and this is not the city. Follow me, and I will lead you to the man you are looking for." And he led them to Samaria.

20After they entered the city, Elisha said, "LORD, open

the eyes of these men so they can see." Then the LORD opened their eyes and they looked, and there they were, inside Samaria.

21When the king of Israel saw them, he asked Elisha, "Shall I kill them, my father? Shall I kill them?"

22"Do not kill them," he answered. "Would you kill men you have captured with your own sword or bow? Set food and water before them so that they may eat and drink and then go back to their master." **23**So he prepared a great feast for them, and after they had finished eating and drinking, he sent them away, and they returned to their master. So the bands from Aram stopped raiding Israel's territory.

Famine in Besieged Samaria

24Some time later, Ben-Hadad king of Aram mobilized his entire army and marched up and laid siege to Samaria. **25**There was a great famine in the city; the siege lasted so long that a donkey's head sold for eighty shekels^D*a* of silver, and a quarter of a cab*b* of seed pods*c* for five shekels.*d*

26As the king of Israel was passing by on the wall, a woman cried to him, "Help me, my lord the king!"

27The king replied, "If the LORD does not help you, where can I get help for you? From the threshing floor? From the winepress^D?" **28**Then he asked her, "What's the matter?"

She answered, "This woman said to me, 'Give up your son so we may eat him today, and tomorrow we'll eat my son.' **29**So we cooked my son and ate him. The next day I said to her, 'Give up your son so we may eat him,' but she had hidden him."

30When the king heard the woman's words, he tore his robes. As he went along the wall, the people looked, and there, underneath, he had sackcloth^D on his body. **31**He said, "May God deal with me, be it ever so severely, if the head of Elisha son of Shaphat remains on his shoulders today!"

32Now Elisha was sitting in his house, and the elders were sitting with him. The king sent a messenger ahead, but before he arrived, Elisha said to the elders, "Don't you see how this murderer is sending someone to cut off my head? Look, when the messenger comes, shut the door and hold it shut against him. Is not the sound of his master's footsteps behind him?"

33While he was still talking to them, the messenger came down to him. And ⌊the king⌋ said, "This disaster is from the LORD. Why should I wait for the LORD any longer?"

7 Elisha said, "Hear the word of the LORD. This is what the LORD says: About this time tomorrow, a seah*e* of flour will sell for a shekel*f* and two seahs*g* of barley for a shekel at the gate of Samaria."

2The officer on whose arm the king was leaning said to the man of God, "Look, even if the LORD should open the floodgates of the heavens, could this happen?"

---

a25 That is, about 2 pounds (about 1 kilogram)   *b25* That is, probably about 1/2 pint (about 0.3 liter)   *c25* Or *of dove's dung*   *d25* That is, about 2 ounces (about 55 grams)   *e1* That is, probably about 7 quarts (about 7.3 liters); also in verses 16 and 18   *f1* That is, about 2/5 ounce (about 11 grams); also in verses 16 and 18   *g1* That is, probably about 13 quarts (about 15 liters); also in verses 16 and 18

Why did the king call Elisha *my father?* (6:21)

Father was a term of honor and respect. The king recognized the prophet's spiritual authority (see 13:14). In the same way, Elisha had also called his mentor Elijah *my father* (2:12), and the servants of Naaman referred to their master in a similar way (5:13).

Why did the king wear sackcloth under his robes? (6:30)

Coarse sackcloth was usually worn next to the skin as an indication of sorrow or repentance. Either the king was too proud to repent openly, or perhaps he wanted to preserve some sense of royal dignity as he led his people during a bitter famine.

What did the king have against Elisha? (6:32–33)

There are several possibilities. He may have resented Elisha for his earlier advice which allowed the army of Aram to escape (6:21–23) —the same army now besieging Samaria. Or perhaps the king was perturbed that Elisha had had not performed a miracle, providing food and deliverance. At the very least, the king wanted a scapegoat for his troubles.

How had the king been waiting for the Lord? (6:33)

He was not known to be a man of prayer. He had simply been waiting for the Lord to intervene and resolve the crisis. But now the king had run out of patience.

Why did the king need someone to lean on? (7:2)

Perhaps he was physically weak and needed someone to prop him up. More likely, this is an expression that implies the officer was the king's personal attendant, adviser and "right hand man." Similarly, the king of Aram leaned on Naaman's arm (5:18).

"You will see it with your own eyes," answered Elisha, "but you will not eat any of it!"

The Siege Lifted

3Now there were four men with leprosy[Da] at the entrance of the city gate. They said to each other, "Why stay here until we die? **4**If we say, 'We'll go into the city'—the famine is there, and we will die. And if we stay here, we will die. So let's go over to the camp of the Arameans and surrender. If they spare us, we live; if they kill us, then we die."

5At dusk they got up and went to the camp of the Arameans. When they reached the edge of the camp, not a man was there, **6**for the Lord had caused the Arameans to hear the sound of chariots and horses and a great army, so that they said to one another, "Look, the king of Israel has hired the Hittite and Egyptian kings to attack us!" **7**So they got up and fled in the dusk and abandoned their tents and their horses and donkeys. They left the camp as it was and ran for their lives.

8The men who had leprosy reached the edge of the camp and entered one of the tents. They ate and drank, and carried away silver, gold and clothes, and went off and hid them. They returned and entered another tent and took some things from it and hid them also.

9Then they said to each other, "We're not doing right. This is a day of good news and we are keeping it to ourselves. If we wait until daylight, punishment will overtake us. Let's go at once and report this to the royal palace."

10So they went and called out to the city gatekeepers and told them, "We went into the Aramean camp and not a man was there—not a sound of anyone—only tethered horses and donkeys, and the tents left just as they were." **11**The gatekeepers shouted the news, and it was reported within the palace.

12The king got up in the night and said to his officers, "I will tell you what the Arameans have done to us. They know we are starving; so they have left the camp to hide in the countryside, thinking, 'They will surely come out, and then we will take them alive and get into the city.' "

13One of his officers answered, "Have some men take five of the horses that are left in the city. Their plight will be like that of all the Israelites left here—yes, they will only be like all these Israelites who are doomed. So let us send them to find out what happened."

14So they selected two chariots with their horses, and the king sent them after the Aramean army. He commanded the drivers, "Go and find out what has happened." **15**They followed them as far as the Jordan, and they found the whole road strewn with the clothing and equipment the Arameans had thrown away in their headlong flight. So the messengers returned and reported to the king. **16**Then the people went out and plundered[D] the camp of the Arameans. So a seah of flour sold for a shekel[D], and two seahs of barley sold for a shekel, as the LORD had said.

17Now the king had put the officer on whose arm he leaned in charge of the gate, and the people trampled him in the gateway, and he died, just as the man of God had foretold when the king came down to his house. **18**It happened as the man of God had said to the king: "About this

---

Why were these men with leprosy camped outside the city gate? (7:3)
According to the Law of Moses, people with leprosy were supposed to live outside the city, keeping the disease away from the general population (Lev. 13:46; Num. 5:2–3). Living near the gate, these men would normally have received food from relatives and friends. However, if the famine caused desperation for ordinary inhabitants, the lepers' situation was hopeless.

Why didn't the Arameans use their horses for the quickest escape? (7:7)
The horses left behind were probably chariot horses (6:15). Chariots might be useful in battle, but they were no good for hasty escapes. In the dim light and confusion, there was no time to harness horses and prepare chariots. Panic set in, and the men simply ran.

---

a3 The Hebrew word is used for various diseases affecting the skin—not necessarily leprosy; also in verse 8.

time tomorrow, a seah of flour will sell for a shekel[D] and two seahs of barley for a shekel at the gate of Samaria."

19The officer had said to the man of God, "Look, even if the LORD should open the floodgates of the heavens, could this happen?" The man of God had replied, "You will see it with your own eyes, but you will not eat any of it!" **20**And that is exactly what happened to him, for the people trampled him in the gateway, and he died.

The Shunammite's Land Restored

8 Now Elisha had said to the woman whose son he had restored to life, "Go away with your family and stay for a while wherever you can, because the LORD has decreed a famine in the land that will last seven years." **2**The woman proceeded to do as the man of God said. She and her family went away and stayed in the land of the Philistines seven years.

3At the end of the seven years she came back from the land of the Philistines and went to the king to beg for her house and land. **4**The king was talking to Gehazi, the servant of the man of God, and had said, "Tell me about all the great things Elisha has done." **5**Just as Gehazi was telling the king how Elisha had restored the dead to life, the woman whose son Elisha had brought back to life came to beg the king for her house and land.

Gehazi said, "This is the woman, my lord the king, and this is her son whom Elisha restored to life." **6**The king asked the woman about it, and she told him.

Then he assigned an official to her case and said to him, "Give back everything that belonged to her, including all the income from her land from the day she left the country until now."

Hazael Murders Ben-Hadad

7Elisha went to Damascus, and Ben-Hadad king of Aram was ill. When the king was told, "The man of God has come all the way up here," **8**he said to Hazael, "Take a gift with you and go to meet the man of God. Consult the LORD through him; ask him, 'Will I recover from this illness?'"

9Hazael went to meet Elisha, taking with him as a gift forty camel-loads of all the finest wares of Damascus. He went in and stood before him, and said, "Your son Ben-Hadad king of Aram has sent me to ask, 'Will I recover from this illness?'"

10Elisha answered, "Go and say to him, 'You will certainly recover'; but[a] the LORD has revealed to me that he will in fact die." **11**He stared at him with a fixed gaze until Hazael felt ashamed. Then the man of God began to weep.

12"Why is my lord weeping?" asked Hazael.

"Because I know the harm you will do to the Israelites," he answered. "You will set fire to their fortified places, kill their young men with the sword, dash their little children to the ground, and rip open their pregnant women."

13Hazael said, "How could your servant, a mere dog, accomplish such a feat?"

"The LORD has shown me that you will become king of Aram," answered Elisha.

14Then Hazael left Elisha and returned to his master. When Ben-Hadad asked, "What did Elisha say to you?" Hazael replied, "He told me that you would certainly re-

---

SCRIPTURE LINK (8:1) *Woman whose son he had restored to life*
See 4:8–37.

Who took the woman's land while she was away? (8:3)
Some think the culprit was an unnamed neighbor. Others believe the king himself may have seized the property. In either case, the king had the power to restore the land to its rightful owner.

Why should the woman get income for work she didn't do? (8:6)
Since the woman's land had been taken unlawfully, it was proper for her to receive what the land had produced in her absence—as though it had been leased out. Since it was a time of famine, however, her land probably had not produced much.

Hazael (8:8)
Hazael was a personal assistant to the king of Aram. Ambitious and treacherous, Hazael succeeded Ben-Hadad and eventually fulfilled Elisha's tearful prediction by inflicting painful defeats upon both Israel and Judah (8:11–15; 10:32–33; 13:3–7). See also Amos 1:3–4.

Why was the king of Aram called Elisha's son? (8:9)
See *Why did the king call Elisha my father?* (6:21).

Did Elisha tell Hazael to lie? (8:10)
Elisha truthfully stated that the king would not die of his present illness. Presumably, the king would have recovered had the illness been allowed to run its course. Assassination, not illness, caused the king's death.

---

*a*10 The Hebrew may also be read *Go and say, 'You will certainly not recover,' for.*

cover." **15**But the next day he took a thick cloth, soaked it in water and spread it over the king's face, so that he died. Then Hazael succeeded him as king.

Jehoram King of Judah

16In the fifth year of Joram son of Ahab king of Israel, when Jehoshaphat was king of Judah, Jehoram son of Jehoshaphat began his reign as king of Judah. **17**He was thirty-two years old when he became king, and he reigned in Jerusalem^D eight years. **18**He walked in the ways of the kings of Israel, as the house of Ahab had done, for he married a daughter of Ahab. He did evil in the eyes of the LORD. **19**Nevertheless, for the sake of his servant David, the LORD was not willing to destroy Judah. He had promised to maintain a lamp for David and his descendants forever.

20In the time of Jehoram, Edom^D rebelled against Judah and set up its own king. **21**So Jehoram^a went to Zair with all his chariots. The Edomites surrounded him and his chariot commanders, but he rose up and broke through by night; his army, however, fled back home. **22**To this day Edom has been in rebellion against Judah. Libnah revolted at the same time.

23As for the other events of Jehoram's reign, and all he did, are they not written in the book of the annals of the kings of Judah? **24**Jehoram rested with his fathers and was buried with them in the City of David. And Ahaziah his son succeeded him as king.

Ahaziah King of Judah

25In the twelfth year of Joram son of Ahab king of Israel, Ahaziah son of Jehoram king of Judah began to reign. **26**Ahaziah was twenty-two years old when he became king, and he reigned in Jerusalem one year. His mother's name was Athaliah, a granddaughter of Omri king of Israel. **27**He walked in the ways of the house of Ahab and did evil in the eyes of the LORD, as the house of Ahab had done, for he was related by marriage to Ahab's family.

28Ahaziah went with Joram son of Ahab to war against Hazael king of Aram at Ramoth Gilead. The Arameans wounded Joram; **29**so King Joram returned to Jezreel to recover from the wounds the Arameans had inflicted on him at Ramoth^b in his battle with Hazael king of Aram.

Then Ahaziah son of Jehoram king of Judah went down to Jezreel to see Joram son of Ahab, because he had been wounded.

Jehu Anointed King of Israel

9 The prophet^D Elisha summoned a man from the company of the prophets and said to him, "Tuck your cloak into your belt, take this flask of oil with you and go to Ramoth Gilead. **2**When you get there, look for Jehu son of Jehoshaphat, the son of Nimshi. Go to him, get him away from his companions and take him into an inner room. **3**Then take the flask and pour the oil on his head and declare, 'This is what the LORD says: I anoint^D you king over Israel.' Then open the door and run; don't delay!"

4So the young man, the prophet, went to Ramoth Gilead. **5**When he arrived, he found the army officers sitting together. "I have a message for you, commander," he said.

Who was really king? (8:16)
See *Who was really king?* (1:17).

The ways of the kings of Israel (8:18)
The kings of Israel had all turned from the Lord and followed after idols. Jehoram followed their ways instead of following his father, Jehoshaphat, a good king of Judah. He led the people of Judah into idolatry—a deed for which God struck him with a fatal illness (2 Chron. 21:5–19).

Annals of the kings (8:23)
See *Annals of the kings* (1:18).

---

^a21 Hebrew *Joram*, a variant of *Jehoram*; also in verses 23 and 24
^b29 Hebrew *Ramah*, a variant of *Ramoth*

"For which of us?" asked Jehu.

"For you, commander," he replied.

⁶Jehu got up and went into the house. Then the proph-et[D] poured the oil on Jehu's head and declared, "This is what the LORD, the God of Israel, says: 'I anoint[D] you king over the LORD's people Israel. ⁷You are to destroy the house of Ahab your master, and I will avenge[D] the blood of my servants the prophets and the blood of all the LORD's servants shed by Jezebel. ⁸The whole house of Ahab will perish. I will cut off from Ahab every last male in Israel—slave or free. ⁹I will make the house of Ahab like the house of Jeroboam son of Nebat and like the house of Baasha son of Ahijah. ¹⁰As for Jezebel, dogs will devour her on the plot of ground at Jezreel, and no one will bury her.' " Then he opened the door and ran.

¹¹When Jehu went out to his fellow officers, one of them asked him, "Is everything all right? Why did this madman come to you?"

"You know the man and the sort of things he says," Jehu replied.

¹²"That's not true!" they said. "Tell us."

Jehu said, "Here is what he told me: 'This is what the LORD says: I anoint you king over Israel.' "

¹³They hurried and took their cloaks and spread them under him on the bare steps. Then they blew the trumpet and shouted, "Jehu is king!"

Jehu Kills Joram and Ahaziah

¹⁴So Jehu son of Jehoshaphat, the son of Nimshi, con-spired against Joram. (Now Joram and all Israel had been defending Ramoth Gilead against Hazael king of Aram, ¹⁵but King Joram[a] had returned to Jezreel to recover from the wounds the Arameans had inflicted on him in the battle with Hazael king of Aram.) Jehu said, "If this is the way you feel, don't let anyone slip out of the city to go and tell the news in Jezreel." ¹⁶Then he got into his chariot and rode to Jezreel, because Joram was resting there and Ahaziah king of Judah had gone down to see him.

¹⁷When the lookout standing on the tower in Jezreel saw Jehu's troops approaching, he called out, "I see some troops coming."

"Get a horseman," Joram ordered. "Send him to meet them and ask, 'Do you come in peace[D]?' "

¹⁸The horseman rode off to meet Jehu and said, "This is what the king says: 'Do you come in peace?' "

"What do you have to do with peace?" Jehu replied. "Fall in behind me."

The lookout reported, "The messenger has reached them, but he isn't coming back."

¹⁹So the king sent out a second horseman. When he came to them he said, "This is what the king says: 'Do you come in peace?' "

Jehu replied, "What do you have to do with peace? Fall in behind me."

²⁰The lookout reported, "He has reached them, but he isn't coming back either. The driving is like that of Jehu son of Nimshi—he drives like a madman."

²¹"Hitch up my chariot," Joram ordered. And when it was hitched up, Joram king of Israel and Ahaziah king of Judah rode out, each in his own chariot, to meet Jehu. They met him at the plot of ground that had belonged to

---

King Jehu's Mission (9:6)

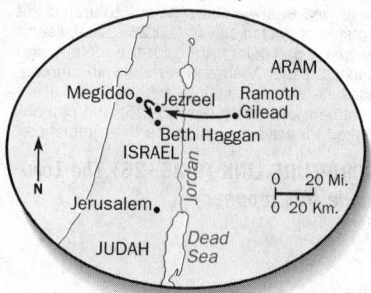

SCRIPTURE LINK (9:7) Blood . . . shed by Jezebel

See 1 Kings 18:4.

Why did they call the prophet a madman? (9:11)

The prophet's behavior seemed odd and bi-zarre. He arrived unexpectedly, conducted his business secretly and then ran away abruptly. Prophets, who dressed peculiarly and lived apart from much of society, were sometimes considered "on the fringe" (see, for example, 1:8; 1 Samuel 19:20–24).

When did Jehu become concerned about witchcraft and idolatry? (9:22)

Jehu was a man of mixed loyalties. Later he destroyed Baal worship, but still tolerated the worship of golden calves (10:28–31). Evidently he had a particular hatred for the idolatry and witchcraft that Ahab and Jezebel had promoted. Jehu had personally witnessed their ill treatment of Naboth (vv. 25–26) and probably looked for ways to undermine their influence.

SCRIPTURE LINK (9:25–26) The LORD made this prophecy

See 1 Kings 21:19.

Why did Jezebel call Jehu *Zimri*? (9:31)

Several years earlier a trusted royal official named Zimri had plotted against Elah, the king of Israel. Zimri killed Elah and became king in his place (1 Kings 16:8–20). Jezebel recognized what Jehu was up to.

Naboth the Jezreelite. ²²When Joram saw Jehu he asked, "Have you come in peaceᴰ, Jehu?"

"How can there be peace," Jehu replied, "as long as all the idolatryᴰ and witchcraftᴰ of your mother Jezebel abound?"

²³Joram turned about and fled, calling out to Ahaziah, "Treachery, Ahaziah!"

²⁴Then Jehu drew his bow and shot Joram between the shoulders. The arrow pierced his heart and he slumped down in his chariot. ²⁵Jehu said to Bidkar, his chariot officer, "Pick him up and throw him on the field that belonged to Naboth the Jezreelite. Remember how you and I were riding together in chariots behind Ahab his father when the LORD made this prophecyᴰ about him: ²⁶'Yesterday I saw the blood of Naboth and the blood of his sons, declares the LORD, and I will surely make you pay for it on this plot of ground, declares the LORD.'ᵃ Now then, pick him up and throw him on that plot, in accordance with the word of the LORD."

²⁷When Ahaziah king of Judah saw what had happened, he fled up the road to Beth Haggan.ᵇ Jehu chased him, shouting, "Kill him too!" They wounded him in his chariot on the way up to Gur near Ibleam, but he escaped to Megiddo and died there. ²⁸His servants took him by chariot to Jerusalemᴰ and buried him with his fathers in his tomb in the City of David. ²⁹(In the eleventh year of Joram son of Ahab, Ahaziah had become king of Judah.)

Jezebel Killed

³⁰Then Jehu went to Jezreel. When Jezebel heard about it, she painted her eyes, arranged her hair and looked out of a window. ³¹As Jehu entered the gate, she asked, "Have you come in peace, Zimri, you murderer of your master?"ᶜ

³²He looked up at the window and called out, "Who is on my side? Who?" Two or three eunuchsᴰ looked down at him. ³³"Throw her down!" Jehu said. So they threw her down, and some of her blood spattered the wall and the horses as they trampled her underfoot.

³⁴Jehu went in and ate and drank. "Take care of that cursed woman," he said, "and bury her, for she was a king's daughter." ³⁵But when they went out to bury her, they found nothing except her skull, her feet and her hands. ³⁶They went back and told Jehu, who said, "This is the word of the LORD that he spoke through his servant Elijah the Tishbite: On the plot of ground at Jezreel dogs will devour Jezebel's flesh.ᵈ ³⁷Jezebel's body will be like refuse on the ground in the plot at Jezreel, so that no one will be able to say, 'This is Jezebel.'"

Ahab's Family Killed

10 Now there were in Samaria seventy sons of the house of Ahab. So Jehu wrote letters and sent them to Samaria: to the officials of Jezreel,ᵉ to the elders and to the guardians of Ahab's children. He said, ²"As soon as this letter reaches you, since your master's sons are with you and you have chariots and horses, a fortified city and weapons, ³choose the best and most worthy of

---

ᵃ26 See 1 Kings 21:19.   ᵇ27 Or *fled by way of the garden house*
ᶜ31 Or *"Did Zimri have peace, who murdered his master?"*   ᵈ36 See 1 Kings 21:23.   ᵉ1 Hebrew; some Septuagint manuscripts and Vulgate *of the city*

your master's sons and set him on his father's throne. Then fight for your master's house."

4But they were terrified and said, "If two kings could not resist him, how can we?"

5So the palace administrator, the city governor, the elders and the guardians sent this message to Jehu: "We are your servants and we will do anything you say. We will not appoint anyone as king; you do whatever you think best."

6Then Jehu wrote them a second letter, saying, "If you are on my side and will obey me, take the heads of your master's sons and come to me in Jezreel by this time tomorrow."

Now the royal princes, seventy of them, were with the leading men of the city, who were rearing them. **7**When the letter arrived, these men took the princes and slaughtered all seventy of them. They put their heads in baskets and sent them to Jehu in Jezreel. **8**When the messenger arrived, he told Jehu, "They have brought the heads of the princes."

Then Jehu ordered, "Put them in two piles at the entrance of the city gate until morning."

9The next morning Jehu went out. He stood before all the people and said, "You are innocent. It was I who conspired against my master and killed him, but who killed all these? **10**Know then, that not a word the LORD has spoken against the house of Ahab will fail. The LORD has done what he promised through his servant Elijah." **11**So Jehu killed everyone in Jezreel who remained of the house of Ahab, as well as all his chief men, his close friends and his priests^D, leaving him no survivor.

12Jehu then set out and went toward Samaria. At Beth Eked of the Shepherds, **13**he met some relatives of Ahaziah king of Judah and asked, "Who are you?"

They said, "We are relatives of Ahaziah, and we have come down to greet the families of the king and of the queen mother."

14"Take them alive!" he ordered. So they took them alive and slaughtered them by the well of Beth Eked—forty-two men. He left no survivor.

15After he left there, he came upon Jehonadab son of Recab, who was on his way to meet him. Jehu greeted him and said, "Are you in accord with me, as I am with you?"

"I am," Jehonadab answered.

"If so," said Jehu, "give me your hand." So he did, and Jehu helped him up into the chariot. **16**Jehu said, "Come with me and see my zeal^D for the LORD." Then he had him ride along in his chariot.

17When Jehu came to Samaria, he killed all who were left there of Ahab's family; he destroyed them, according to the word of the LORD spoken to Elijah.

Ministers of Baal Killed

18Then Jehu brought all the people together and said to them, "Ahab served Baal^D a little; Jehu will serve him much. **19**Now summon all the prophets^D of Baal, all his ministers and all his priests. See that no one is missing, because I am going to hold a great sacrifice^D for Baal. Anyone who fails to come will no longer live." But Jehu was acting deceptively in order to destroy the ministers of Baal.

20Jehu said, "Call an assembly in honor of Baal." So they proclaimed it. **21**Then he sent word throughout Isra-

Why such barbaric behavior? (10:8)
Jehu wanted to waste no time in establishing himself as king, nor did he want to leave any doubt about his power and will to rule. It was not unusual for kings to display the heads of defeated rivals in this manner, though Jehu appears to have been particularly ruthless.

Why did Jehu kill so many people? (10:11,17)
These princes (sons or advisers of Ahab) could each have made a persuasive claim to the throne. Jehu wanted to take no chances.

Why did Jehu want to impress Jehonadab with how good he was? (10:16)
Jehonadab (also known as Jonadab) was a respected leader of the Recabite clan, which was known for a strict, conservative lifestyle. They lived in tents instead of houses, refused to plant crops or vineyards and avoided drinking wine (Jer. 35:6–10). Jehonadab's public approval would lend credence to Jehu's revolution. Jehonadab, for his part, was apparently glad to endorse anyone as king who would overturn the idolatry of Ahab's household. Jehu's zeal for the Lord was mixed with political ambition.

Is it okay to lie to get rid of evil? (10:19)
Jehu's ultimate goal was right: to remove Baal worship from the land. Even killing the Baal worshipers was justified, since idolatry was punishable by death under the Law of Moses (Deut. 17:2–6). However, Jehu's deceitful tactics (pretending to worship Baal, then killing the prophets who came at his invitation) were unethical and cannot be justified.

el, and all the ministers of Baal[D] came; not one stayed away. They crowded into the temple of Baal until it was full from one end to the other. [22]And Jehu said to the keeper of the wardrobe, "Bring robes for all the ministers of Baal." So he brought out robes for them.

[23]Then Jehu and Jehonadab son of Recab went into the temple of Baal. Jehu said to the ministers of Baal, "Look around and see that no servants of the LORD are here with you—only ministers of Baal." [24]So they went in to make sacrifices[D] and burnt offerings[D]. Now Jehu had posted eighty men outside with this warning: "If one of you lets any of the men I am placing in your hands escape, it will be your life for his life."

[25]As soon as Jehu had finished making the burnt offering, he ordered the guards and officers: "Go in and kill them; let no one escape." So they cut them down with the sword. The guards and officers threw the bodies out and then entered the inner shrine of the temple of Baal. [26]They brought the sacred stone[D] out of the temple of Baal and burned it. [27]They demolished the sacred stone of Baal and tore down the temple of Baal, and people have used it for a latrine to this day.

[28]So Jehu destroyed Baal worship in Israel. [29]However, he did not turn away from the sins of Jeroboam son of Nebat, which he had caused Israel to commit—the worship of the golden calves at Bethel and Dan.

[30]The LORD said to Jehu, "Because you have done well in accomplishing what is right in my eyes and have done to the house of Ahab all I had in mind to do, your descendants will sit on the throne of Israel to the fourth generation." [31]Yet Jehu was not careful to keep the law of the LORD, the God of Israel, with all his heart. He did not turn away from the sins of Jeroboam, which he had caused Israel to commit.

[32]In those days the LORD began to reduce the size of Israel. Hazael overpowered the Israelites throughout their territory [33]east of the Jordan in all the land of Gilead (the region of Gad, Reuben and Manasseh), from Aroer by the Arnon Gorge through Gilead to Bashan.

[34]As for the other events of Jehu's reign, all he did, and all his achievements, are they not written in the book of the annals of the kings of Israel?

[35]Jehu rested with his fathers and was buried in Samaria. And Jehoahaz his son succeeded him as king. [36]The time that Jehu reigned over Israel in Samaria was twenty-eight years.

Athaliah and Joash

11 When Athaliah the mother of Ahaziah saw that her son was dead, she proceeded to destroy the whole royal family. [2]But Jehosheba, the daughter of King Jehoram[a] and sister of Ahaziah, took Joash son of Ahaziah and stole him away from among the royal princes, who were about to be murdered. She put him and his nurse in a bedroom to hide him from Athaliah; so he was not killed. [3]He remained hidden with his nurse at the temple of the LORD for six years while Athaliah ruled the land.

[4]In the seventh year Jehoiada sent for the commanders of units of a hundred, the Carites and the guards and had them brought to him at the temple of the LORD. He made a covenant[D] with them and put them under oath at the

---

Sacred stone (10:26)
See *Sacred stone of Baal* (3:2).

Why did Jehu get rid of Baal but not the golden calves? (10:29)
For political purposes, Jehu's religious reforms were incomplete. Though he hated Baal worship, he saw the political advantage of keeping the golden calves as a rallying-point for the people. Like Jeroboam who set up the golden calves (1 Kings 12:26–33), Jehu wanted the northern tribes to distinguish themselves from the people of Judah, who worshiped the Lord in Jerusalem. Sadly, the kind of mixed loyalty found in Jehu was common during this time period (17:41).

Annals of the kings (10:34)
See *Annals of the kings* (1:18).

Why would a grandmother murder her own grandchildren? (11:1–2)
In those days a king's harem existed primarily to provide insurance that the dynasty would be preserved. It hardly fostered family relationships. As a result, Athaliah had no emotional attachment to her son's children. To the contrary, she would have seen them as potential threats to her own future. Her actions, though appalling to us, would have been understood completely by others steeped in paganism and with little regard for human life.

Jehoiada (11:4)
The high priest, a strong and able leader (2 Chron. 23:1). He influenced Joash for good as long as he lived (12:2) and helped retain the throne of Judah for David's line.

Carites (11:4)
Some say these foreigners were from the region of southwest Asia Minor called Caria. Soldiers from there served as mercenaries in other parts of the ancient world. Others say these were descendants of the Kerethites—Philistine mercenaries who faithfully served through several coup attempts as bodyguards to David and Solomon. If these were their descendants, they would have overthrown Athaliah because of their long-standing loyalty to the house of David.

---

a2 Hebrew Joram, *a variant of* Jehoram

temple of the LORD. Then he showed them the king's son. [5]He commanded them, saying, "This is what you are to do: You who are in the three companies that are going on duty on the Sabbath[D]—a third of you guarding the royal palace, [6]a third at the Sur Gate, and a third at the gate behind the guard, who take turns guarding the temple— [7]and you who are in the other two companies that normally go off Sabbath duty are all to guard the temple for the king. [8]Station yourselves around the king, each man with his weapon in his hand. Anyone who approaches your ranks[a] must be put to death[D]. Stay close to the king wherever he goes."

[9]The commanders of units of a hundred did just as Jehoiada the priest[D] ordered. Each one took his men— those who were going on duty on the Sabbath and those who were going off duty—and came to Jehoiada the priest. [10]Then he gave the commanders the spears and shields that had belonged to King David and that were in the temple of the LORD. [11]The guards, each with his weapon in his hand, stationed themselves around the king— near the altar and the temple, from the south side to the north side of the temple.

[12]Jehoiada brought out the king's son and put the crown on him; he presented him with a copy of the covenant[D] and proclaimed him king. They anointed[D] him, and the people clapped their hands and shouted, "Long live the king!"

[13]When Athaliah heard the noise made by the guards and the people, she went to the people at the temple of the LORD. [14]She looked and there was the king, standing by the pillar, as the custom was. The officers and the trumpeters were beside the king, and all the people of the land were rejoicing and blowing trumpets. Then Athaliah tore her robes and called out, "Treason! Treason!"

[15]Jehoiada the priest ordered the commanders of units of a hundred, who were in charge of the troops: "Bring her out between the ranks[b] and put to the sword anyone who follows her." For the priest had said, "She must not be put to death in the temple of the LORD." [16]So they seized her as she reached the place where the horses enter the palace grounds, and there she was put to death.

[17]Jehoiada then made a covenant between the LORD and the king and people that they would be the LORD's people. He also made a covenant between the king and the people. [18]All the people of the land went to the temple of Baal[D] and tore it down. They smashed the altars and idols[D] to pieces and killed Mattan the priest of Baal in front of the altars.

Then Jehoiada the priest posted guards at the temple of the LORD. [19]He took with him the commanders of hundreds, the Carites, the guards and all the people of the land, and together they brought the king down from the temple of the LORD and went into the palace, entering by way of the gate of the guards. The king then took his place on the royal throne, [20]and all the people of the land rejoiced. And the city was quiet, because Athaliah had been slain with the sword at the palace.

[21]Joash[c] was seven years old when he began to reign.

Why did the military support a priest's coup? (11:9)

It's possible in a patriarchal culture that soldiers would prefer to have a man on the throne. (Athaliah was the only woman to rule in Judah.) Perhaps it was even more important that Athaliah was not from Judah, but from the northern kingdom of Israel, the daughter of King Ahab and probably Queen Jezebel. As a foreigner she would have had limited support from within Judah.

What covenant did the young king receive? (11:12)

Israel's rulers were to have and to study a copy of the Law (Deut. 17:18–20). At the very least this would have been the regulations for the king (Deut. 17). More likely, Joash received the entire book of Deuteronomy—and possibly the entire collection of the Law, Genesis through Deuteronomy.

Why did kings stand by a certain temple pillar? (11:14)

This was a traditional place where pronouncements and decrees could be uttered, perhaps the bronze pillar near the entrance to the temple grounds (1 Kings 7:15). The roots of this custom have been lost in Israel's history.

---

[a]8 Or *approaches the precincts*   [b]15 Or *out from the precincts*
[c]21 Hebrew *Jehoash*, a variant of *Joash*

Joash Repairs the Temple

12 In the seventh year of Jehu, Joash[a] became king, and he reigned in Jerusalem[D] forty years. His mother's name was Zibiah; she was from Beersheba. [2]Joash did what was right in the eyes of the LORD all the years Jehoiada the priest[D] instructed him. [3]The high places[D], however, were not removed; the people continued to offer sacrifices[D] and burn incense[D] there.

[4]Joash said to the priests, "Collect all the money that is brought as sacred[D] offerings to the temple of the LORD—the money collected in the census, the money received from personal vows[D] and the money brought voluntarily to the temple. [5]Let every priest receive the money from one of the treasurers, and let it be used to repair whatever damage is found in the temple."

[6]But by the twenty-third year of King Joash the priests still had not repaired the temple. [7]Therefore King Joash summoned Jehoiada the priest and the other priests and asked them, "Why aren't you repairing the damage done to the temple? Take no more money from your treasurers, but hand it over for repairing the temple." [8]The priests agreed that they would not collect any more money from the people and that they would not repair the temple themselves.

[9]Jehoiada the priest took a chest and bored a hole in its lid. He placed it beside the altar, on the right side as one enters the entrance of the LORD. The priests who guarded the entrance put into the chest all the money that was brought to the temple of the LORD. [10]Whenever they saw that there was a large amount of money in the chest, the royal secretary and the high priest came, counted the money that had been brought into the temple of the LORD and put it into bags. [11]When the amount had been determined, they gave the money to the men appointed to supervise the work on the temple. With it they paid those who worked on the temple of the LORD—the carpenters and builders, [12]the masons and stonecutters. They purchased timber and dressed stone for the repair of the temple of the LORD, and met all the other expenses of restoring the temple.

[13]The money brought into the temple was not spent for making silver basins, wick trimmers, sprinkling bowls, trumpets or any other articles of gold or silver for the temple of the LORD; [14]it was paid to the workmen, who used it to repair the temple. [15]They did not require an accounting from those to whom they gave the money to pay the workers, because they acted with complete honesty. [16]The money from the guilt offerings[D] and sin offerings[D] was not brought into the temple of the LORD; it belonged to the priests.

[17]About this time Hazael king of Aram went up and attacked Gath and captured it. Then he turned to attack Jerusalem. [18]But Joash king of Judah took all the sacred objects dedicated by his fathers—Jehoshaphat, Jehoram and Ahaziah, the kings of Judah—and the gifts he himself had dedicated and all the gold found in the treasuries of the temple of the LORD and of the royal palace, and he sent them to Hazael king of Aram, who then withdrew from Jerusalem.

[19]As for the other events of the reign of Joash, and all he did, are they not written in the book of the annals of

---

Why were the high places allowed to remain? (12:3)

Though the people were thrilled by Athaliah's death and responded by tearing down her beloved temple of Baal (11:18), the high places were quite another matter. Many had been shrines to Canaanite gods before Israel had arrived in the land. They remained popular with local people, farmers who considered them essential to successful farming on Canaan's land. Kings could bring reform by destroying religious symbols (Asherim, pillars and altars), but the people often continued to practice their localized idolatry at the high places.

Why hadn't the priests repaired the temple? (12:6–8)

It's possible the priests considered offerings for *the service of the Tent of Meeting* (Exodus 30:16) to be part of their income. If so, young Joash's earlier command (vv. 4–5) would have seemed unreasonable to them—he was meddling with their terms of employment. They could easily have ignored it. Now that Joash was 30—the age of full manhood—he would have been much harder to ignore. So the priests would have complied with his order. See *Why did the Levites take so long to collect the money?* (2 Chron. 24:5).

Why did Joash plunder the newly refurbished temple? (12:18)

Hazael was a serious threat to the continued safety of Joash, Jerusalem and the temple. Several neighboring peoples, including Israel, had already been overwhelmed. To make matters worse, this foreign assault was God's judgment upon Judah for backsliding and murdering Zechariah, son of the priest, Jehoida (2 Chron. 24:17–24). Under judgment and unwilling to repent, Joash had no hope of God's help. All he could do was pay Hazael to leave him alone.

Annals of the kings (12:19)

See *Annals of the kings* (1:18).

---

a1 Hebrew *Jehoash*, a variant of *Joash*; also in verses 2, 4, 6, 7 and 18

the kings of Judah? **20**His officials conspired against him and assassinated him at Beth Millo, on the road down to Silla. **21**The officials who murdered him were Jozabad son of Shimeath and Jehozabad son of Shomer. He died and was buried with his fathers in the City of David. And Amaziah his son succeeded him as king.

Jehoahaz King of Israel

13 In the twenty-third year of Joash son of Ahaziah king of Judah, Jehoahaz son of Jehu became king of Israel in Samaria, and he reigned seventeen years. **2**He did evil in the eyes of the LORD by following the sins of Jeroboam son of Nebat, which he had caused Israel to commit, and he did not turn away from them. **3**So the LORD's anger burned against Israel, and for a long time he kept them under the power of Hazael king of Aram and Ben-Hadad his son.

4Then Jehoahaz sought the LORD's favor, and the LORD listened to him, for he saw how severely the king of Aram was oppressing Israel. **5**The LORD provided a deliverer for Israel, and they escaped from the power of Aram. So the Israelites lived in their own homes as they had before. **6**But they did not turn away from the sins of the house of Jeroboam, which he had caused Israel to commit; they continued in them. Also, the Asherah pole[D]a remained standing in Samaria.

7Nothing had been left of the army of Jehoahaz except fifty horsemen, ten chariots and ten thousand foot soldiers, for the king of Aram had destroyed the rest and made them like the dust at threshing time.

8As for the other events of the reign of Jehoahaz, all he did and his achievements, are they not written in the book of the annals of the kings of Israel? **9**Jehoahaz rested with his fathers and was buried in Samaria. And Jehoash[b] his son succeeded him as king.

Jehoash King of Israel

10In the thirty-seventh year of Joash king of Judah, Jehoash son of Jehoahaz became king of Israel in Samaria, and he reigned sixteen years. **11**He did evil in the eyes of the LORD and did not turn away from any of the sins of Jeroboam son of Nebat, which he had caused Israel to commit; he continued in them.

12As for the other events of the reign of Jehoash, all he did and his achievements, including his war against Amaziah king of Judah, are they not written in the book of the annals of the kings of Israel? **13**Jehoash rested with his fathers, and Jeroboam succeeded him on the throne. Jehoash was buried in Samaria with the kings of Israel.

14Now Elisha was suffering from the illness from which he died. Jehoash king of Israel went down to see him and wept over him. "My father! My father!" he cried. "The chariots and horsemen of Israel!"

15Elisha said, "Get a bow and some arrows," and he did so. **16**"Take the bow in your hands," he said to the king of Israel. When he had taken it, Elisha put his hands on the king's hands.

17"Open the east window," he said, and he opened it. "Shoot!" Elisha said, and he shot. "The LORD's arrow of

---

a6 That is, a symbol of the goddess Asherah; here and elsewhere in 2 Kings   b9 Hebrew *Joash,* a variant of *Jehoash*; also in verses 12-14 and 25

The sins of Jeroboam (13:2)

See *Sins of Jeroboam* (1 Kings 16:31).

Was Jehoahaz evil or good? (13:2,4)

Jehoahaz called on the Lord when he was in trouble, but he never turned away from his other gods. This was why he was considered *evil.* Jehoahaz was like many of his subjects: they looked to God for help but never recognized the need to worship only him. Here we read that Jehoahaz called for help, but we never read that he repented. God answered and helped him in spite of his sin—evidence of God's grace more than of a man's repentance. Also see article: *How did God judge the kings?* (2 Chron. 25:2).

Why would an evil king honor a godly prophet? (13:14)

Even an evil king could recognize and respect God's power. Elisha had stood for God and against Israel's enemies for approximately 50 years. Jehoash had heard the stories of what Elisha had done. Now, knowing that Elisha was near death, the king regretted the grave loss to the nation.

Why call Elisha Israel's *chariots and horsemen?* (13:14)

This may have been a saying that originated with Elisha as he watched the chariots of the Lord escort Elijah to heaven (2:12). One ancient interpretation of this expression was that Elijah, through his prayers, was more help to Israel than all its chariots and horsemen. In this case Jehoahaz mourned for Elisha, recognizing that the prophet meant more to the nation than he and all his armies did. Also see *What were these horses and chariots?* (6:17).

Did the king know why he was to hit the ground? (13:18–19)

He should have. Ancient people often saw the flight of arrows as omens of the future. Shooting an arrow out the window was a sign Jehoash would understand, especially when Elisha explained it meant victory over his enemies (v. 17). Striking the ground with the arrows should have been an obvious connection to the LORD's *arrow of victory* over the Arameans. Jehoash's half-hearted response demonstrated a lack of faith in Elisha's promise of victory.

Why would God's power remain in Elisha's bones? (13:21)

Elisha's life was marked by the miraculous, but this was not a miracle accomplished by power still in Elisha's remains. If anything, it was a sign that Elisha's God lived—even though the prophet had been reduced to a pile of bones.

To this day (13:23)

The phrase implies that Samaria still stood when this book was written. That had to be before 722 B.C., when Assyria destroyed the northern kingdom. But it would seem that the author of Kings wrote after 562 B.C., quoting from an earlier source. He retained the original comment even though Samaria had been gone for over 160 years.

Why did Amaziah challenge Jehoash to a fight? (14:8)

Amaziah had hired mercenaries from Israel while preparing for an attack on Edom. But then he dismissed them before the battle, taking away their chance to loot Edom. Angry, they retaliated by plundering the undefended towns of Judah on their way home, killing 3,000 people (2 Chron. 25:5–13). Amaziah probably challenged Jehoash in order to regain some of his losses to the marauding Israelite soldiers and possibly to defend his honor.

victory, the arrow of victory over Aram!" Elisha declared. "You will completely destroy the Arameans at Aphek."

18Then he said, "Take the arrows," and the king took them. Elisha told him, "Strike the ground." He struck it three times and stopped. **19**The man of God was angry with him and said, "You should have struck the ground five or six times; then you would have defeated Aram and completely destroyed it. But now you will defeat it only three times."

20Elisha died and was buried.

Now Moabite raiders used to enter the country every spring. **21**Once while some Israelites were burying a man, suddenly they saw a band of raiders; so they threw the man's body into Elisha's tomb. When the body touched Elisha's bones, the man came to life and stood up on his feet.

22Hazael king of Aram oppressed Israel throughout the reign of Jehoahaz. **23**But the LORD was gracious to them and had compassion and showed concern for them because of his covenant[D] with Abraham, Isaac and Jacob. To this day he has been unwilling to destroy them or banish them from his presence.

24Hazael king of Aram died, and Ben-Hadad his son succeeded him as king. **25**Then Jehoash son of Jehoahaz recaptured from Ben-Hadad son of Hazael the towns he had taken in battle from his father Jehoahaz. Three times Jehoash defeated him, and so he recovered the Israelite towns.

Amaziah King of Judah

14 In the second year of Jehoash[a] son of Jehoahaz king of Israel, Amaziah son of Joash king of Judah began to reign. **2**He was twenty-five years old when he became king, and he reigned in Jerusalem[D] twenty-nine years. His mother's name was Jehoaddin; she was from Jerusalem. **3**He did what was right in the eyes of the LORD, but not as his father David had done. In everything he followed the example of his father Joash. **4**The high places[D], however, were not removed; the people continued to offer sacrifices[D] and burn incense[D] there.

5After the kingdom was firmly in his grasp, he executed the officials who had murdered his father the king. **6**Yet he did not put the sons of the assassins to death[D], in accordance with what is written in the Book of the Law of Moses where the LORD commanded: "Fathers shall not be put to death for their children, nor children put to death for their fathers; each is to die for his own sins."[b]

7He was the one who defeated ten thousand Edomites in the Valley of Salt and captured Sela in battle, calling it Joktheel, the name it has to this day.

8Then Amaziah sent messengers to Jehoash son of Jehoahaz, the son of Jehu, king of Israel, with the challenge: "Come, meet me face to face."

9But Jehoash king of Israel replied to Amaziah king of Judah: "A thistle in Lebanon sent a message to a cedar in Lebanon, 'Give your daughter to my son in marriage.' Then a wild beast in Lebanon came along and trampled the thistle underfoot. **10**You have indeed defeated Edom[D] and now you are arrogant. Glory in your victory, but stay at home! Why ask for trouble and cause your own downfall and that of Judah also?"

---

*a*1 Hebrew *Joash*, a variant of *Jehoash*; also in verses 13, 23 and 27
*b*6 Deut. 24:16

¹¹Amaziah, however, would not listen, so Jehoash king of Israel attacked. He and Amaziah king of Judah faced each other at Beth Shemesh in Judah. ¹²Judah was routed by Israel, and every man fled to his home. ¹³Jehoash king of Israel captured Amaziah king of Judah, the son of Joash, the son of Ahaziah, at Beth Shemesh. Then Jehoash went to Jerusalem^D and broke down the wall of Jerusalem from the Ephraim Gate to the Corner Gate—a section about six hundred feet long.^a ¹⁴He took all the gold and silver and all the articles found in the temple of the LORD and in the treasuries of the royal palace. He also took hostages and returned to Samaria.

¹⁵As for the other events of the reign of Jehoash, what he did and his achievements, including his war against Amaziah king of Judah, are they not written in the book of the annals of the kings of Israel? ¹⁶Jehoash rested with his fathers and was buried in Samaria with the kings of Israel. And Jeroboam his son succeeded him as king.

¹⁷Amaziah son of Joash king of Judah lived for fifteen years after the death^D of Jehoash son of Jehoahaz king of Israel. ¹⁸As for the other events of Amaziah's reign, are they not written in the book of the annals of the kings of Judah?

¹⁹They conspired against him in Jerusalem, and he fled to Lachish, but they sent men after him to Lachish and killed him there. ²⁰He was brought back by horse and was buried in Jerusalem with his fathers, in the City of David.

²¹Then all the people of Judah took Azariah,^b who was sixteen years old, and made him king in place of his father Amaziah. ²²He was the one who rebuilt Elath and restored it to Judah after Amaziah rested with his fathers.

Jeroboam II King of Israel

²³In the fifteenth year of Amaziah son of Joash king of Judah, Jeroboam son of Jehoash king of Israel became king in Samaria, and he reigned forty-one years. ²⁴He did evil in the eyes of the LORD and did not turn away from any of the sins of Jeroboam son of Nebat, which he had caused Israel to commit. ²⁵He was the one who restored the boundaries of Israel from Lebo^c Hamath to the Sea of the Arabah,^d in accordance with the word of the LORD, the God of Israel, spoken through his servant Jonah son of Amittai, the prophet^D from Gath Hepher.

²⁶The LORD had seen how bitterly everyone in Israel, whether slave or free, was suffering; there was no one to help them. ²⁷And since the LORD had not said he would blot out the name of Israel from under heaven, he saved them by the hand of Jeroboam son of Jehoash.

²⁸As for the other events of Jeroboam's reign, all he did, and his military achievements, including how he recovered for Israel both Damascus and Hamath, which had belonged to Yaudi,^e are they not written in the book of the annals of the kings of Israel? ²⁹Jeroboam rested with his fathers, the kings of Israel. And Zechariah his son succeeded him as king.

Why repeat these verses, almost word for word? (14:15–16; see 13:12–13)
English readers often find repetitions in the Old Testament to be pointless. Ancient Hebrews, however, used them as literary devices, indicators of something more. These verses appear as a standardized summary of the king's career—first to introduce Jehoash's account, and then to conclude it.

The sins of Jeroboam (14:24)
See *Sins of Jeroboam* (1 Kings 16:31).

Is this the same Jonah who was swallowed by the fish? (14:25)
Yes. This verse gives us some clues about the time of Jonah's ministry—prior to or during the reign of Jeroboam II (793–753 B.C.).

Yaudi (14:28)
This probably refers to Judah, although Judah is usually spelled differently in Hebrew. This form resembles the Assyrian spelling, although no one can say why it is used here. Hamath and Damascus were part of that territory when the Judean kings David and Solomon had ruled a united Israel.

---

^a13 Hebrew *four hundred cubits* (about 180 meters)   ^b21 Also called *Uzziah*   ^c25 Or *from the entrance to*   ^d25 That is, the Dead Sea   ^e28 Or *Judah*

Azariah King of Judah

15 In the twenty-seventh year of Jeroboam king of Israel, Azariah son of Amaziah king of Judah began to reign. ²He was sixteen years old when he became king, and he reigned in Jerusalem[D] fifty-two years. His mother's name was Jecoliah; she was from Jerusalem. ³He did what was right in the eyes of the LORD, just as his father Amaziah had done. ⁴The high places[D], however, were not removed; the people continued to offer sacrifices[D] and burn incense[D] there.

⁵The LORD afflicted[D] the king with leprosy[Da] until the day he died, and he lived in a separate house.[b] Jotham the king's son had charge of the palace and governed the people of the land.

⁶As for the other events of Azariah's reign, and all he did, are they not written in the book of the annals of the kings of Judah? ⁷Azariah rested with his fathers and was buried near them in the City of David. And Jotham his son succeeded him as king.

Zechariah King of Israel

⁸In the thirty-eighth year of Azariah king of Judah, Zechariah son of Jeroboam became king of Israel in Samaria, and he reigned six months. ⁹He did evil in the eyes of the LORD, as his fathers had done. He did not turn away from the sins of Jeroboam son of Nebat, which he had caused Israel to commit.

¹⁰Shallum son of Jabesh conspired against Zechariah. He attacked him in front of the people,[c] assassinated him and succeeded him as king. ¹¹The other events of Zechariah's reign are written in the book of the annals of the kings of Israel. ¹²So the word of the LORD spoken to Jehu was fulfilled: "Your descendants will sit on the throne of Israel to the fourth generation."[d]

Shallum King of Israel

¹³Shallum son of Jabesh became king in the thirty-ninth year of Uzziah king of Judah, and he reigned in Samaria one month. ¹⁴Then Menahem son of Gadi went from Tirzah up to Samaria. He attacked Shallum son of Jabesh in Samaria, assassinated him and succeeded him as king.

¹⁵The other events of Shallum's reign, and the conspiracy he led, are written in the book of the annals of the kings of Israel.

¹⁶At that time Menahem, starting out from Tirzah, attacked Tiphsah and everyone in the city and its vicinity, because they refused to open their gates. He sacked Tiphsah and ripped open all the pregnant women.

Menahem King of Israel

¹⁷In the thirty-ninth year of Azariah king of Judah, Menahem son of Gadi became king of Israel, and he reigned in Samaria ten years. ¹⁸He did evil in the eyes of the LORD. During his entire reign he did not turn away from the sins of Jeroboam son of Nebat, which he had caused Israel to commit.

¹⁹Then Pul[e] king of Assyria invaded the land, and Men-

Why allow assassins to become kings? (15:10,14)

Military coups are nothing new. In the ancient world those who seized a throne by force were often relatives of the king. Sometimes they were military men. In either case, they had a strong power base to complete the takeover of power, something the assassination alone could not have done. People didn't have much choice about accepting the rule of a murdering dictator if he had gained enough support. The adage, "Might makes right," seemed especially true.

Why not unlock the city gates? (15:16)

For reasons we don't know, the city was not prepared to accept Menahem as Israel's new king. It's possible the people had been displeased with him earlier when he was stationed in their region as a commander of Zechariah's army (v. 14). Suspicious of his intentions, they refused to open their city to him. Menahem ruthlessly crushed their opposition, determined to make them an example to others who might be reluctant to acknowledge him as king.

Why rip open pregnant women? (15:16)

Most people today would consider this a senseless brutality. But in the twisted logic of ancient warfare, it made a great deal of sense: babies could grow up to be younger, stronger warriors.

---

a5 The Hebrew word was used for various diseases affecting the skin—not necessarily leprosy.   *b5* Or *in a house where he was relieved of responsibility*   *c10* Hebrew; some Septuagint manuscripts *in Ibleam*   *d12* 2 Kings 10:30   *e19* Also called *Tiglath-Pileser*

ahem gave him a thousand talents[a] of silver to gain his support and strengthen his own hold on the kingdom. [20]Menahem exacted this money from Israel. Every wealthy man had to contribute fifty shekels[Db] of silver to be given to the king of Assyria. So the king of Assyria withdrew and stayed in the land no longer.

[21]As for the other events of Menahem's reign, and all he did, are they not written in the book of the annals of the kings of Israel? [22]Menahem rested with his fathers. And Pekahiah his son succeeded him as king.

Pekahiah King of Israel

[23]In the fiftieth year of Azariah king of Judah, Pekahiah son of Menahem became king of Israel in Samaria, and he reigned two years. [24]Pekahiah did evil in the eyes of the LORD. He did not turn away from the sins of Jeroboam son of Nebat, which he had caused Israel to commit. [25]One of his chief officers, Pekah son of Remaliah, conspired against him. Taking fifty men of Gilead with him, he assassinated Pekahiah, along with Argob and Arieh, in the citadel[D] of the royal palace at Samaria. So Pekah killed Pekahiah and succeeded him as king.

[26]The other events of Pekahiah's reign, and all he did, are written in the book of the annals of the kings of Israel.

Pekah King of Israel

[27]In the fifty-second year of Azariah king of Judah, Pekah son of Remaliah became king of Israel in Samaria, and he reigned twenty years. [28]He did evil in the eyes of the LORD. He did not turn away from the sins of Jeroboam son of Nebat, which he had caused Israel to commit.

[29]In the time of Pekah king of Israel, Tiglath-Pileser king of Assyria came and took Ijon, Abel Beth Maacah, Janoah, Kedesh and Hazor. He took Gilead and Galilee, including all the land of Naphtali, and deported the people to Assyria. [30]Then Hoshea son of Elah conspired against Pekah son of Remaliah. He attacked and assassinated him, and then succeeded him as king in the twentieth year of Jotham son of Uzziah.

[31]As for the other events of Pekah's reign, and all he did, are they not written in the book of the annals of the kings of Israel?

Jotham King of Judah

[32]In the second year of Pekah son of Remaliah king of Israel, Jotham son of Uzziah king of Judah began to reign. [33]He was twenty-five years old when he became king, and he reigned in Jerusalem[D] sixteen years. His mother's name was Jerusha daughter of Zadok. [34]He did what was right in the eyes of the LORD, just as his father Uzziah had done. [35]The high places[D], however, were not removed; the people continued to offer sacrifices[D] and burn incense[D] there. Jotham rebuilt the Upper Gate of the temple of the LORD.

[36]As for the other events of Jotham's reign, and what he did, are they not written in the book of the annals of the kings of Judah? [37](In those days the LORD began to send Rezin king of Aram and Pekah son of Remaliah against Judah.) [38]Jotham rested with his fathers and was buried with them in the City of David, the city of his father. And Ahaz his son succeeded him as king.

When were the first hostages taken from Israel? (15:29)

This deportation was carried out by Tiglath-Pileser III and took place around 733 B.C. More refugees than hostages, the captives were forced to relocate to a foreign land, shaking their sense of ethnic and national identity.

Why does the writer abruptly switch, using Uzziah for Azariah? (15:30)

It's uncertain why the two names are used. It could be that Uzziah was a throne name (assumed when he took the throne) and Azariah was the name he used all his life. The author gathered his information on Azariah from two books, the *Annals of the kings of Judah* and the *Annals of the kings of Israel*. It's possible he simply used the form of the name that appeared in each of these two annals.

---

[a]19 That is, about 37 tons (about 34 metric tons)   [b]20 That is, about 1 1/4 pounds (about 0.6 kilogram)

Why sacrifice the heir to the throne? (16:3)

From ancient times those who have tried to manipulate the spirit world have considered human sacrifice the most dreadful and most powerful of all sacrifices. If a god would give assistance for payment of a goat or bull, it was reasoned, a human life would buy a much stronger favor. In a time of national and personal crisis, Ahaz tried to buy the help of the nature gods of Canaan with the life of his son. Also see *What did human sacrifice have to do with the Israelites' withdrawal?* (3:27) and *Why would parents sacrifice their children?* (Jer. 19:5).

To this day (16:6)

See *To this day* (13:23).

Were new altars the latest fad? (16:10)

Visiting Damascus, probably to pay tribute to Tiglath-Pileser III, Ahaz noticed an altar to Asshur, worshiped by the Assyrians. The altar appealed to him, perhaps for no reason other than that he was an enthusiastic idolater. According to ancient theology, the Assyrian god had proven his power by conquering the gods of other lands. On the other hand, Ahaz may have copied this altar as an expression of his submission to Assyria.

How did Ahaz plan to use the bronze altar to guide him? (16:15)

Sacrifices for divination included careful inspections of the organs of sacrificial animals —especially livers—placed upon an altar. Unusual shapes, colors or markings were thought to reveal messages from the gods about the future. By blending elements of Canaanite, Assyrian and Israelite religions, Ahaz hoped to attain the best possible guidance. However, his worship was worthless in God's eyes.

Sabbath canopy (16:18)

Sometimes called the *covered way*, the Sabbath canopy is mentioned only here in the Bible. It may have been a special place for the king to attend Sabbath services, a special entry for the priests or a covered place for teaching.

Why would the king of Assyria restrict Ahaz's worship? (16:18)

Unafraid of Israel's God (whom he did not consider a threat), the Assyrian king probably removed Ahaz's special entry into the temple for political reasons rather than spiritual. It was a symbolic act demonstrating that Ahaz had no royal privileges except those permitted by Tiglath-Pileser III. It may have had some military significance as well: Temples, usually built with heavy walls on the highest point in a city could offer the last line of defense for a city under attack; perhaps the royal entrance was the king's escape route.

Annals of the kings (16:19)

See *Annals of the kings* (1:18).

Ahaz King of Judah

16 In the seventeenth year of Pekah son of Remaliah, Ahaz son of Jotham king of Judah began to reign. ²Ahaz was twenty years old when he became king, and he reigned in Jerusalem^D sixteen years. Unlike David his father, he did not do what was right in the eyes of the LORD his God. ³He walked in the ways of the kings of Israel and even sacrificed his son in^a the fire, following the detestable ways of the nations the LORD had driven out before the Israelites. ⁴He offered sacrifices^D and burned incense^D at the high places^D, on the hilltops and under every spreading tree.

⁵Then Rezin king of Aram and Pekah son of Remaliah king of Israel marched up to fight against Jerusalem and besieged Ahaz, but they could not overpower him. ⁶At that time, Rezin king of Aram recovered Elath for Aram by driving out the men of Judah. Edomites then moved into Elath and have lived there to this day.

⁷Ahaz sent messengers to say to Tiglath-Pileser king of Assyria, "I am your servant and vassal. Come up and save me out of the hand of the king of Aram and of the king of Israel, who are attacking me." ⁸And Ahaz took the silver and gold found in the temple of the LORD and in the treasuries of the royal palace and sent it as a gift to the king of Assyria. ⁹The king of Assyria complied by attacking Damascus and capturing it. He deported its inhabitants to Kir and put Rezin to death^D.

¹⁰Then King Ahaz went to Damascus to meet Tiglath-Pileser king of Assyria. He saw an altar in Damascus and sent to Uriah the priest^D a sketch of the altar, with detailed plans for its construction. ¹¹So Uriah the priest built an altar in accordance with all the plans that King Ahaz had sent from Damascus and finished it before King Ahaz returned. ¹²When the king came back from Damascus and saw the altar, he approached it and presented offerings^b on it. ¹³He offered up his burnt offering^D and grain offering^D, poured out his drink offering^D, and sprinkled the blood of his fellowship offerings^Dc on the altar. ¹⁴The bronze altar that stood before the LORD he brought from the front of the temple—from between the new altar and the temple of the LORD—and put it on the north side of the new altar.

¹⁵King Ahaz then gave these orders to Uriah the priest: "On the large new altar, offer the morning burnt offering and the evening grain offering, the king's burnt offering and his grain offering, and the burnt offering of all the people of the land, and their grain offering and their drink offering. Sprinkle on the altar all the blood of the burnt offerings and sacrifices. But I will use the bronze altar for seeking guidance." ¹⁶And Uriah the priest did just as King Ahaz had ordered.

¹⁷King Ahaz took away the side panels and removed the basins from the movable stands. He removed the Sea from the bronze bulls that supported it and set it on a stone base. ¹⁸He took away the Sabbath^D canopy^d that had been built at the temple and removed the royal entryway outside the temple of the LORD, in deference to the king of Assyria.

¹⁹As for the other events of the reign of Ahaz, and what

---

^a3 Or *even made his son pass through*   ^b12 Or *and went up*
^c13 Traditionally *peace offerings*   ^d18 Or *the dais of his throne* (see Septuagint)

he did, are they not written in the book of the annals of the kings of Judah? **20**Ahaz rested with his fathers and was buried with them in the City of David. And Hezekiah his son succeeded him as king.

Hoshea Last King of Israel

17 In the twelfth year of Ahaz king of Judah, Hoshea son of Elah became king of Israel in Samaria, and he reigned nine years. **2**He did evil in the eyes of the LORD, but not like the kings of Israel who preceded him.

3Shalmaneser king of Assyria came up to attack Hoshea, who had been Shalmaneser's vassal and had paid him tribute. **4**But the king of Assyria discovered that Hoshea was a traitor, for he had sent envoys to So*a* king of Egypt, and he no longer paid tribute to the king of Assyria, as he had done year by year. Therefore Shalmaneser seized him and put him in prison. **5**The king of Assyria invaded the entire land, marched against Samaria and laid siege to it for three years. **6**In the ninth year of Hoshea, the king of Assyria captured Samaria and deported the Israelites to Assyria. He settled them in Halah, in Gozan on the Habor River and in the towns of the Medes.

Israel Exiled Because of Sin

7All this took place because the Israelites had sinned against the LORD their God, who had brought them up out of Egypt from under the power of Pharaoh king of Egypt. They worshiped other gods **8**and followed the practices of the nations the LORD had driven out before them, as well as the practices that the kings of Israel had introduced. **9**The Israelites secretly did things against the LORD their God that were not right. From watchtower[D] to fortified city they built themselves high places[D] in all their towns. **10**They set up sacred stones[D] and Asherah poles[D] on every high hill and under every spreading tree. **11**At every high place they burned incense[D], as the nations whom the LORD had driven out before them had done. They did

*a*4 Or *to Sais, to the*; *So* is possibly an abbreviation for *Osorkon*.

What happened during a siege? (17:5)

A siege cut off all traffic into a city. Supplies were kept out in an attempt to starve the population within the fortified walls until they would surrender. A three-year siege was unusual, but not unheard of. Tyre, built on an island and supplied by boat, survived a Babylonian siege of 13 years. Jerusalem fell after a siege of 18 months. Any siege, successful or not, meant terrible suffering (see, for example, 18:27).

Exile of Israel (17:7)

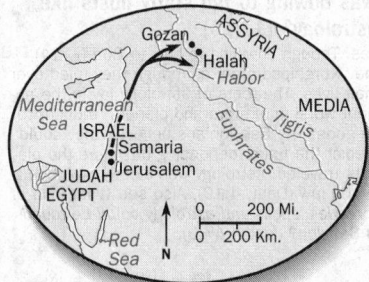

How did the Israelites sin secretly? (17:9)

This probably was a reference to the pointless deception pursued through their idolatry. They continued to worship God as if he didn't know they were also worshiping idols. The Bible describes people who think they can sin in secret (Psalms 73:11; 94:7; Isaiah 5:18–21). They almost seem to be challenging God to discover their sin, but their sinful lives are as futile as the idea that God can't see them.

Why didn't Uriah resist the king's idolatry? (16:15–16)

Apparently Uriah was a weak religious leader with little backbone for controversy. While he supported Isaiah (Isaiah 8:1–4), Uriah found it difficult to stand against the orders of the idolatrous King Ahaz. Perhaps he rationalized that if he wanted to maintain his influence for the Lord and retain his position as priest he would have to suspend his convictions from time to time. If that's what he thought, his influence for God would have been severely damaged.

Uriah may also have been a product of his time. Rather than opposing the popular culture of idolatry, he may have tried to relate to it. Idolatry was an integral part of life in the northern kingdom, and its influence had already become deeply entrenched in Judah where Uriah served. Though people worshiped the Lord at the temple, they worshiped false gods as well—a fact borne out by archaeological discoveries of household idols in the homes of ancient Judah. Perhaps Uriah hoped his tolerance for the people's worship of idols would prevent them from abandoning the Lord altogether.

Whatever his reasons, Uriah's compromise seems to be another symptom of the severe sickness that was at the heart of Judah's spiritual life.

What was the difference between a prophet and a seer? (17:13)

It seems there wasn't much difference. In earlier times, prophets were called seers (1 Samuel 9:9). It may be that as Israel developed from a tribal confederation to a kingdom and as people turned from God, the prophetic ministry and its name changed. Or perhaps the language just changed.

Stiff-necked (17:14)

A stiff-necked people couldn't humble themselves enough to admit they were wrong and change their ways (Prov. 29:1; Jer. 17:23). See *Stiff-necked people* (Deut. 9:6).

Was bowing to the starry hosts like astrology? (17:16)

Yes. Though unwilling to bow to God (v. 14), they worshiped stars as though they ruled over their lives. The roots of astrology lay in the ancient worship of stars and planets, thought to be gods. The Babylonians believed they could predict the future depending on where the planets traveled. Astrology was clearly prohibited by the law (Deut. 4:19). Also see *What kind of sorceries, spells and astrology could be found in Babylon?* (Isaiah 47:9).

Why force some people out, only to bring others in? (17:24)

As the Assyrian empire grew, the expanding lands and various peoples became more difficult to control. So, to strengthen their hold over them, Assyria used a form of "ethnic cleansing," deporting whole populations to alien territory in an attempt to wipe out their ethnic and national identities. Such state-sponsored terrorism helped diminish the possibility of rebellion.

Why did God expect foreigners to worship him? (17:25)

It might seem God expected too much from these new arrivals. Why should pagans be more spiritually mature than those who knew the law? Some suggest the writer of Kings was merely repeating the people's view that marauding lions were divine punishment (v. 26). Others say God can use any means—including fear of judgment—to draw people to the truth. The other side of judgment, however, is grace. Since these foreigners had moved to the land God reserved for his people, he extended the blessings of the land to them—if they were willing to worship him.

What did the priest teach about worship? (17:28)

A priest from the northern kingdom would not have taught anything that pleased God. The people had been judged by God and deported from their land because of their adulterated religion (vv. 22–23). Most likely, the priest taught the religion of Jeroboam (see 1 Kings 12:26–33). As a result, the newcomers thought of themselves as Jews while they continued to worship other gods (v. 33). The long-standing division between Jews and Samaritans began here. See *Why the tension between Jews and Samaritans?* (John 4:9).

wicked things that provoked the LORD to anger. 12They worshiped idols^D, though the LORD had said, "You shall not do this."^a 13The LORD warned Israel and Judah through all his prophets^D and seers^D: "Turn from your evil ways. Observe my commands and decrees, in accordance with the entire Law that I commanded your fathers to obey and that I delivered to you through my servants the prophets."

14But they would not listen and were as stiff-necked as their fathers, who did not trust in the LORD their God. 15They rejected his decrees and the covenant^D he had made with their fathers and the warnings he had given them. They followed worthless idols and themselves became worthless. They imitated the nations around them although the LORD had ordered them, "Do not do as they do," and they did the things the LORD had forbidden them to do.

16They forsook all the commands of the LORD their God and made for themselves two idols cast in the shape of calves, and an Asherah pole^D. They bowed down to all the starry hosts^D, and they worshiped Baal^D. 17They sacrificed their sons and daughters in^b the fire. They practiced divination^D and sorcery^D and sold themselves to do evil in the eyes of the LORD, provoking him to anger.

18So the LORD was very angry with Israel and removed them from his presence. Only the tribe of Judah was left, 19and even Judah did not keep the commands of the LORD their God. They followed the practices Israel had introduced. 20Therefore the LORD rejected all the people of Israel; he afflicted^D them and gave them into the hands of plunderers, until he thrust them from his presence.

21When he tore Israel away from the house of David, they made Jeroboam son of Nebat their king. Jeroboam enticed Israel away from following the LORD and caused them to commit a great sin. 22The Israelites persisted in all the sins of Jeroboam and did not turn away from them 23until the LORD removed them from his presence, as he had warned through all his servants the prophets. So the people of Israel were taken from their homeland into exile^D in Assyria, and they are still there.

Samaria Resettled

24The king of Assyria brought people from Babylon, Cuthah, Avva, Hamath and Sepharvaim and settled them in the towns of Samaria to replace the Israelites. They took over Samaria and lived in its towns. 25When they first lived there, they did not worship the LORD; so he sent lions among them and they killed some of the people. 26It was reported to the king of Assyria: "The people you deported and resettled in the towns of Samaria do not know what the god of that country requires. He has sent lions among them, which are killing them off, because the people do not know what he requires."

27Then the king of Assyria gave this order: "Have one of the priests^D you took captive from Samaria go back to live there and teach the people what the god of the land requires." 28So one of the priests who had been exiled from Samaria came to live in Bethel and taught them how to worship the LORD.

29Nevertheless, each national group made its own gods in the several towns where they settled, and set them up

^a12 Exodus 20:4, 5   ^b17 Or *They made their sons and daughters pass through*

in the shrines the people of Samaria had made at the high places[D]. [30]The men from Babylon made Succoth Benoth, the men from Cuthah made Nergal, and the men from Hamath made Ashima; [31]the Avvites made Nibhaz and Tartak, and the Sepharvites burned their children in the fire as sacrifices[D] to Adrammelech and Anammelech, the gods of Sepharvaim. [32]They worshiped the LORD, but they also appointed all sorts of their own people to officiate for them as priests[D] in the shrines at the high places. [33]They worshiped the LORD, but they also served their own gods in accordance with the customs of the nations from which they had been brought.

[34]To this day they persist in their former practices. They neither worship the LORD nor adhere to the decrees and ordinances, the laws and commands that the LORD gave the descendants of Jacob, whom he named Israel. [35]When the LORD made a covenant[D] with the Israelites, he commanded them: "Do not worship any other gods or bow down to them, serve them or sacrifice to them. [36]But the LORD, who brought you up out of Egypt with mighty power and outstretched arm, is the one you must worship. To him you shall bow down and to him offer sacrifices. [37]You must always be careful to keep the decrees and ordinances, the laws and commands he wrote for you. Do not worship other gods. [38]Do not forget the covenant I have made with you, and do not worship other gods. [39]Rather, worship the LORD your God; it is he who will deliver you from the hand of all your enemies."

[40]They would not listen, however, but persisted in their former practices. [41]Even while these people were worshiping the LORD, they were serving their idols[D]. To this day their children and grandchildren continue to do as their fathers did.

Hezekiah King of Judah

18 In the third year of Hoshea son of Elah king of Israel, Hezekiah son of Ahaz king of Judah began to reign. [2]He was twenty-five years old when he became king, and he reigned in Jerusalem[D] twenty-nine years. His mother's name was Abijah[a] daughter of Zechariah. [3]He did what was right in the eyes of the LORD, just as his father David had done. [4]He removed the high places, smashed the sacred stones[D] and cut down the Asherah poles[D]. He broke into pieces the bronze snake Moses had made, for up to that time the Israelites had been burning incense[D] to it. (It was called[b] Nehushtan.[c])

[5]Hezekiah trusted in the LORD, the God of Israel. There was no one like him among all the kings of Judah, either before him or after him. [6]He held fast to the LORD and did not cease to follow him; he kept the commands the LORD had given Moses. [7]And the LORD was with him; he was successful in whatever he undertook. He rebelled against the king of Assyria and did not serve him. [8]From watchtower[D] to fortified city, he defeated the Philistines, as far as Gaza and its territory.

[9]In King Hezekiah's fourth year, which was the seventh year of Hoshea son of Elah king of Israel, Shalmaneser king of Assyria marched against Samaria and laid siege to it. [10]At the end of three years the Assyrians took it. So Samaria was captured in Hezekiah's sixth year, which was

Why did they think they could worship idols and also the Lord? (17:41)

From our vantage point of history, it's hard to understand how difficult it was for the people to abandon their idols. The prevailing mindset of the ancient world was polytheism—a belief in many gods—making it difficult for God's people to grasp the concept of one God alone, though they knew it from the law (Deut. 6:4). Also see article: *Why would Israelites be tempted by other gods?* (Joshua 23:7).

How could something good be used for evil? (18:4)

Sin often can be seen as a distortion or a perversion of something good: Eating is good, but gluttony is sin; God created sex, but adultery is sin; it's good to talk, but gossip destroys. In this case, *Nehushtan* illustrates the tendency humans have to worship things God gives rather than to worship him alone. Over time, the people probably had begun to think of the bronze snake as something that could help them as it had in the past. Gradually, it acquired the status of an idol with supernatural powers.

---

*a*2 Hebrew *Abi,* a variant of *Abijah*   *b*4 Or *He called it*
*c*4 *Nehushtan* sounds like the Hebrew for *bronze* and *snake* and *unclean thing.*

the ninth year of Hoshea king of Israel. **11**The king of Assyria deported Israel to Assyria and settled them in Halah, in Gozan on the Habor River and in towns of the Medes. **12**This happened because they had not obeyed the LORD their God, but had violated his covenant**D**—all that Moses the servant of the LORD commanded. They neither listened to the commands nor carried them out.

13In the fourteenth year of King Hezekiah's reign, Sennacherib king of Assyria attacked all the fortified cities of Judah and captured them. **14**So Hezekiah king of Judah sent this message to the king of Assyria at Lachish: "I have done wrong. Withdraw from me, and I will pay whatever you demand of me." The king of Assyria exacted from Hezekiah king of Judah three hundred talents*a* of silver and thirty talents*b* of gold. **15**So Hezekiah gave him all the silver that was found in the temple of the LORD and in the treasuries of the royal palace.

16At this time Hezekiah king of Judah stripped off the gold with which he had covered the doors and doorposts of the temple of the LORD, and gave it to the king of Assyria.

Sennacherib Threatens Jerusalem

17The king of Assyria sent his supreme commander, his chief officer and his field commander with a large army, from Lachish to King Hezekiah at Jerusalem**D**. They came up to Jerusalem and stopped at the aqueduct of the Upper Pool, on the road to the Washerman's Field. **18**They called for the king; and Eliakim son of Hilkiah the palace administrator, Shebna the secretary, and Joah son of Asaph the recorder went out to them.

19The field commander said to them, "Tell Hezekiah:

" 'This is what the great king, the king of Assyria, says: On what are you basing this confidence of yours? **20**You say you have strategy and military strength—but you speak only empty words. On whom are you depending, that you rebel against me? **21**Look now, you are depending on Egypt, that splintered reed of a staff, which pierces a man's hand and wounds him if he leans on it! Such is Pharaoh king of Egypt to all who depend on him. **22**And if you say to me, "We are depending on the LORD our God"—isn't he the one whose high places**D** and altars Hezekiah removed, saying to Judah and Jerusalem, "You must worship before this altar in Jerusalem"?

23" 'Come now, make a bargain with my master, the king of Assyria: I will give you two thousand horses—if you can put riders on them! **24**How can you repulse one officer of the least of my master's officials, even though you are depending on Egypt for chariots and horsemen*c*? **25**Furthermore, have I come to attack and destroy this place without word from the LORD? The LORD himself told me to march against this country and destroy it.' "

26Then Eliakim son of Hilkiah, and Shebna and Joah said to the field commander, "Please speak to your servants in Aramaic**D**, since we understand it. Don't speak to us in Hebrew**D** in the hearing of the people on the wall."

27But the commander replied, "Was it only to your master and you that my master sent me to say these things,

Was Hezekiah right when he said he was wrong? (18:14)

Yes and no. It was right to trust in the Lord instead of the king of Assyria (v. 7). But from Sennacherib's perspective, Hezekiah was wrong to rebel against him. Now, threatened by Assyria, Hezekiah stated that he had been wrong—a last ditch effort to appease Sennacherib and avoid war. In the final analysis, however, Hezekiah escaped Assyria's wrath by relying on God (19:32–36), not by paying tribute.

Why did it matter where they worshiped God? (18:22)

People had worshiped God in high places—but they had worshiped idols there as well. Many earlier reforms had not gone far enough and had permitted idolatry to persist. Hezekiah tore down the high places others had overlooked, hoping to return the people to worshiping God alone. God's people could still pray anywhere, but they could sacrifice only in Jerusalem. Also see *Why were the high places allowed to remain?* (12:3) and *How was this high place different from others that displeased God?* (1 Chron. 16:39).

Why would the king of Assyria claim to have marching orders from the Lord? (18:25)

This was Sennacherib's claim, not God's. To intimidate the people, the Assyrian commander first claimed to be ordained by God and then bragged that God couldn't stop him. Neither statement was prophetic but merely part of a propaganda campaign. He knew enough about the Israelites to know what kind of information might demoralize them. Still, God used Assyria's evil intentions to accomplish his own purposes, though Assyria would not have known this (v. 12). Also see *Why did God "ordain" Assyria to devastate other nations?* (19:25).

Why did Assyria continue to threaten Jerusalem after Hezekiah had paid tribute? (18:25)

It's possible the Assyrians wanted to punish their disobedient subjects, even though Hezekiah tried to appease Sennacherib by paying everything he could (vv. 14–16). Ultimately, though, this may have been a case of "too little, too late."

Was Hebrew well-known? (18:26–28)

Aramaic, the language of international affairs during this time, was known by most people in government service. Some think the field commander may have used a translator to deliver his message in the lesser known Hebrew in order to frighten the common people. However, language skills were highly developed and it would not have been unthinkable for a field commander of a leading world power to know Hebrew.

a14 That is, about 11 tons (about 10 metric tons)   *b14* That is, about 1 ton (about 1 metric ton)   *c24* Or *charioteers*

and not to the men sitting on the wall—who, like you, will have to eat their own filth and drink their own urine?"

28Then the commander stood and called out in Hebrew[D]: "Hear the word of the great king, the king of Assyria! **29**This is what the king says: Do not let Hezekiah deceive you. He cannot deliver you from my hand. **30**Do not let Hezekiah persuade you to trust in the LORD when he says, 'The LORD will surely deliver us; this city will not be given into the hand of the king of Assyria.'

31"Do not listen to Hezekiah. This is what the king of Assyria says: Make peace[D] with me and come out to me. Then every one of you will eat from his own vine and fig tree and drink water from his own cistern[D], **32**until I come and take you to a land like your own, a land of grain and new wine[D], a land of bread and vineyards, a land of olive trees and honey. Choose life and not death[D]!

"Do not listen to Hezekiah, for he is misleading you when he says, 'The LORD will deliver us.' **33**Has the god of any nation ever delivered his land from the hand of the king of Assyria? **34**Where are the gods of Hamath and Arpad? Where are the gods of Sepharvaim, Hena and Ivvah? Have they rescued Samaria from my hand? **35**Who of all the gods of these countries has been able to save his land from me? How then can the LORD deliver Jerusalem[D] from my hand?"

36But the people remained silent and said nothing in reply, because the king had commanded, "Do not answer him."

37Then Eliakim son of Hilkiah the palace administrator, Shebna the secretary and Joah son of Asaph the recorder went to Hezekiah, with their clothes torn, and told him what the field commander had said.

Jerusalem's Deliverance Foretold

19 When King Hezekiah heard this, he tore his clothes and put on sackcloth[D] and went into the temple of the LORD. **2**He sent Eliakim the palace administrator, Shebna the secretary and the leading priests[D], all wearing sackcloth, to the prophet Isaiah son of Amoz. **3**They told him, "This is what Hezekiah says: This day is a day of distress and rebuke and disgrace, as when children come to the point of birth and there is no strength to deliver them. **4**It may be that the LORD your God will hear all the words of the field commander, whom his master, the king of Assyria, has sent to ridicule the living God, and that he will rebuke him for the words the LORD your God has heard. Therefore pray for the remnant[D] that still survives."

5When King Hezekiah's officials came to Isaiah, **6**Isaiah said to them, "Tell your master, 'This is what the LORD says: Do not be afraid of what you have heard—those words with which the underlings of the king of Assyria have blasphemed[D] me. **7**Listen! I am going to put such a spirit in him that when he hears a certain report, he will return to his own country, and there I will have him cut down with the sword.' "

8When the field commander heard that the king of Assyria had left Lachish, he withdrew and found the king fighting against Libnah.

9Now Sennacherib received a report that Tirhakah, the Cushite[a] king ⌊of Egypt⌋, was marching out to fight against him. So he again sent messengers to Hezekiah

---

What drove the Assyrians to insult the Lord? (18:30,35)
The Assyrians believed the supernatural world included gods who ruled over limited territories. They thought that weaker gods could be conquered by more powerful gods. The Assyrians also believed they could increase their power base by adding the gods of their victims to their collection of gods. To the Assyrians, the Lord was just another one of many gods on their list to be defeated.

Why did they go to the king in torn clothes? (18:37)
Garments represented personalities; torn garments indicated a grievous inner hurt. In this case, Eliakim and Shebna were likely grieved by the Assyrian commander's disregard for God.

---

a 9 That is, from the upper Nile region

with this word: **10**"Say to Hezekiah king of Judah: Do not let the god you depend on deceive you when he says, 'Jerusalem^D will not be handed over to the king of Assyria.' **11**Surely you have heard what the kings of Assyria have done to all the countries, destroying them completely. And will you be delivered? **12**Did the gods of the nations that were destroyed by my forefathers deliver them: the gods of Gozan, Haran, Rezeph and the people of Eden who were in Tel Assar? **13**Where is the king of Hamath, the king of Arpad, the king of the city of Sepharvaim, or of Hena or Ivvah?"

Hezekiah's Prayer

14Hezekiah received the letter from the messengers and read it. Then he went up to the temple of the LORD and spread it out before the LORD. **15**And Hezekiah prayed to the LORD: "O LORD, God of Israel, enthroned between the cherubim^D, you alone are God over all the kingdoms of the earth. You have made heaven and earth. **16**Give ear, O LORD, and hear; open your eyes, O LORD, and see; listen to the words Sennacherib has sent to insult the living God.

17"It is true, O LORD, that the Assyrian kings have laid waste these nations and their lands. **18**They have thrown their gods into the fire and destroyed them, for they were not gods but only wood and stone, fashioned by men's hands. **19**Now, O LORD our God, deliver us from his hand, so that all kingdoms on earth may know that you alone, O LORD, are God."

Isaiah Prophesies Sennacherib's Fall

20Then Isaiah son of Amoz sent a message to Hezekiah: "This is what the LORD, the God of Israel, says: I have heard your prayer concerning Sennacherib king of Assyria. **21**This is the word that the LORD has spoken against him:

" 'The Virgin Daughter of Zion^D
      despises you and mocks you.
  The Daughter of Jerusalem
      tosses her head as you flee.
22Who is it you have insulted and blasphemed^D?
      Against whom have you raised your voice
  and lifted your eyes in pride?
      Against the Holy One of Israel!
23By your messengers
      you have heaped insults on the Lord.
  And you have said,
      "With my many chariots
  I have ascended the heights of the mountains,
      the utmost heights of Lebanon.
  I have cut down its tallest cedars,
      the choicest of its pines.
  I have reached its remotest parts,
      the finest of its forests.
24I have dug wells in foreign lands
      and drunk the water there.
  With the soles of my feet
      I have dried up all the streams of Egypt."

25" 'Have you not heard?
      Long ago I ordained it.
  In days of old I planned it;
      now I have brought it to pass,
  that you have turned fortified cities
      into piles of stone.

Why did God "ordain" Assyria to devastate other nations? (19:25)
Because God is sovereign, he can use whatever means he wishes to accomplish his purposes. Sometimes he used natural events to judge nations—withholding rain, for example. Other times he used human agents—allowing one nation to punish another. All nations, having descended from Noah, could be held to account and judged by God. See *How could God hold other nations accountable for what they never knew?* (Deut. 9:4). Also see article: *Does God use evil to do good?* (Hab. 1:6,13).

²⁶Their people, drained of power,
 are dismayed and put to shame.
They are like plants in the field,
 like tender green shoots,
like grass sprouting on the roof,
 scorched before it grows up.

²⁷" 'But I know where you stay
 and when you come and go
 and how you rage against me.
²⁸Because you rage against me
 and your insolence has reached my ears,
I will put my hook in your nose
 and my bit in your mouth,
and I will make you return
 by the way you came.'

²⁹"This will be the sign for you, O Hezekiah:

"This year you will eat what grows by itself,
 and the second year what springs from that.
But in the third year sow and reap,
 plant vineyards and eat their fruit.
³⁰Once more a remnant^D of the house of Judah
 will take root below and bear fruit above.
³¹For out of Jerusalem^D will come a remnant,
 and out of Mount Zion^D a band of survivors.

The zeal^D of the LORD Almighty will accomplish this.

³²"Therefore this is what the LORD says concerning the king of Assyria:

"He will not enter this city
 or shoot an arrow here.
He will not come before it with shield
 or build a siege ramp against it.
³³By the way that he came he will return;
 he will not enter this city,
       declares the LORD.
³⁴I will defend this city and save it,
 for my sake and for the sake of David my
   servant."

³⁵That night the angel of the LORD went out and put to death^D a hundred and eighty-five thousand men in the Assyrian camp. When the people got up the next morning—there were all the dead bodies! ³⁶So Sennacherib king of Assyria broke camp and withdrew. He returned to Nineveh and stayed there.

³⁷One day, while he was worshiping in the temple of his god Nisroch, his sons Adrammelech and Sharezer cut him down with the sword, and they escaped to the land of Ararat. And Esarhaddon his son succeeded him as king.

Hezekiah's Illness

20 In those days Hezekiah became ill and was at the point of death. The prophet Isaiah son of Amoz went to him and said, "This is what the LORD says: Put your house in order, because you are going to die; you will not recover."

²Hezekiah turned his face to the wall and prayed to the LORD, ³"Remember, O LORD, how I have walked before you faithfully and with wholehearted devotion and have done what is good in your eyes." And Hezekiah wept bitterly.

⁴Before Isaiah had left the middle court, the word of the

Did Hezekiah's prayer change God's mind? (20:1–6)

It would appear so, although God would have anticipated the final outcome. Without ignoring what actually preceded a impending death, Isaiah's instructions addressed the problems too saying that God had dealt directly to prayer. Whatever God's reasons were, Hezekiah's prayers do not have been logical unless God had not anything. God gives power to his people through prayer. (See also 1 Kings 21 and 1 above his prayer, Isaiah 38:1–8).

Why did Hezekiah need a sign? (20:8–11)

In this case, Hezekiah was a double-minded God came confused about which message he would embrace. Hezekiah asked for a sign that would accompany/verify that he would live.

Did the earth suddenly reverse its rotation? (20:11)

We know from the effect, not the mechanism that may have involved the earth's rotation. But in any case other possible explanations exist. Without a precise mechanism that could have acted as a lens to bend the rays of the sun. No in that way could we speak are this was a provisional display—God's answer to his request was a visible taking of that God's timing here.

When did Hezekiah show foolishness, everything he had? (20:12)

Self-centre and pride may be a not sign this do (v. 3). Looking at his character's relentless displayed seven years to form the day (chaps 17:2 — 18:4) of his overthrow. To Hezekiah's (ch. 19) was prophecy he needed to so tough in about structure, instead as even to restrain God have wanted to suspect his posture [...]'s that second, and from a human believe.

How could Hezekiah tell prophecy?

A correct respect precedes hectoring, this

What kind of plague did God send? (19:35)

Josephus, an ancient historian, writes that this incident was accompanied by an infestation of mice and rats. As a result, some wonder if this may have been a form of the bubonic plague. With limited information, we can't say for sure. Whatever means God gave the angel to kill 185,000 in a single night, it was swift and effective.

Why wasn't Hezekiah—a godly king—prepared to face death? (20:2–3)

Israelites considered a long life to be a sign of God's favor. Death in mid-life was therefore thought to show God's judgment. Hezekiah seemed to hint at this view when he prayed, reminding God of how he had faithfully served him all his life. Perhaps it wasn't the idea of death that Hezekiah struggled with, but the thought of being judged after a life of devotion to God's service.

Did Hezekiah's prayer change God's mind? (20:5–6)

It would appear so, although God would have known beforehand the final outcome of this incident. After announcing Hezekiah's impending death, Isaiah returned to reverse his proclamation saying that God had heard Hezekiah's prayer. Whatever God's reasons were for acting on Hezekiah's request, it seems Hezekiah would not have been healed unless first he had prayed. God gives power to his people through prayer. See article: *Why did God change his mind?* (Isaiah 38:1–5).

Why did Hezekiah need a sign? (20:8–11)

In this case, a sign was a demonstration of God's grace. Confused about which message he should embrace, Hezekiah asked for a sign and God showed conclusively that he would live.

Did the earth actually reverse its rotation? (20:11)

We know only the effect, not the cause of this sign. God could have reversed the earth's rotation, but there are other possible explanations as well. Some have suggested some sort of atmospheric anomaly. Water or gases, perhaps, could have acted as a lens to bend the light of the sun. No matter what cause we speculate, this was a supernatural display—God's miracle. The result was a shadow falling where it shouldn't have been.

Why did Hezekiah show foreigners everything he had? (20:13)

Both politics and pride may have motivated this display. Babylon's Merodach-Baladan had troubled Assyria for years before being deposed (721–710 b.c.). His overtures to Hezekiah (v. 12) were probably made in an attempt to win Judah's support against Assyria. Hezekiah would have wanted to impress this potential ally. In that context and from a human perspective, it would have made sense to display Jerusalem's wealth.

How could Hezekiah call this prophecy good? (20:16–19)

A cynic might presume Hezekiah thought the prophecy good because it enabled him to escape the outcome of his foolish act. But it's possible that he declared it good to express his humble submission to God's will. The prophecy could be called good because it was God's word, not because Hezekiah was pleased with it. His relief at temporary prospects for peace and security would have stemmed more out of gratitude for the delay in consequences than the knowledge that his heirs would have to face such horrors.

What sort of water works did Hezekiah construct? (20:20)

Hezekiah's water tunnel was a remarkable feat of ancient engineering. It brought water from a hidden spring outside Jerusalem to a pool in the city where people could have a continuous source of water. To do this, his workers had to tunnel almost ⅖ of a mile through solid rock. According to an inscription found in the tunnel, workers started from both ends and, after digging to within ten feet of one another, chiseled their way toward the sound of their hammers. The tunnel is about 6 ½ feet high and provided ample water for Jerusalem.

LORD came to him: 5"Go back and tell Hezekiah, the leader of my people, 'This is what the LORD, the God of your father David, says: I have heard your prayer and seen your tears; I will heal you. On the third day from now you will go up to the temple of the LORD. 6I will add fifteen years to your life. And I will deliver you and this city from the hand of the king of Assyria. I will defend this city for my sake and for the sake of my servant David.' "

7Then Isaiah said, "Prepare a poultice of figs." They did so and applied it to the boil, and he recovered.

8Hezekiah had asked Isaiah, "What will be the sign that the LORD will heal me and that I will go up to the temple of the LORD on the third day from now?"

9Isaiah answered, "This is the LORD's sign to you that the LORD will do what he has promised: Shall the shadow go forward ten steps, or shall it go back ten steps?"

10"It is a simple matter for the shadow to go forward ten steps," said Hezekiah. "Rather, have it go back ten steps."

11Then the prophetD Isaiah called upon the LORD, and the LORD made the shadow go back the ten steps it had gone down on the stairway of Ahaz.

Envoys From Babylon

12At that time Merodach-Baladan son of Baladan king of Babylon sent Hezekiah letters and a gift, because he had heard of Hezekiah's illness. 13Hezekiah received the messengers and showed them all that was in his storehouses—the silver, the gold, the spices and the fine oil—his armory and everything found among his treasures. There was nothing in his palace or in all his kingdom that Hezekiah did not show them.

14Then Isaiah the prophet went to King Hezekiah and asked, "What did those men say, and where did they come from?"

"From a distant land," Hezekiah replied. "They came from Babylon."

15The prophet asked, "What did they see in your palace?"

"They saw everything in my palace," Hezekiah said. "There is nothing among my treasures that I did not show them."

16Then Isaiah said to Hezekiah, "Hear the word of the LORD: 17The time will surely come when everything in your palace, and all that your fathers have stored up until this day, will be carried off to Babylon. Nothing will be left, says the LORD. 18And some of your descendants, your own flesh and blood, that will be born to you, will be taken away, and they will become eunuchsD in the palace of the king of Babylon."

19"The word of the LORD you have spoken is good," Hezekiah replied. For he thought, "Will there not be peaceD and security in my lifetime?"

20As for the other events of Hezekiah's reign, all his achievements and how he made the pool and the tunnel by which he brought water into the city, are they not written in the book of the annals of the kings of Judah? 21Hezekiah rested with his fathers. And Manasseh his son succeeded him as king.

Manasseh King of Judah

21 Manasseh was twelve years old when he became king, and he reigned in JerusalemD fifty-five years. His mother's name was Hephzibah. 2He did evil in the eyes of the LORD, following the detestable practices of

the nations the LORD had driven out before the Israelites. ³He rebuilt the high places^D his father Hezekiah had destroyed; he also erected altars to Baal^D and made an Asherah pole^D, as Ahab king of Israel had done. He bowed down to all the starry hosts^D and worshiped them. ⁴He built altars in the temple of the LORD, of which the LORD had said, "In Jerusalem^D I will put my Name." ⁵In both courts of the temple of the LORD, he built altars to all the starry hosts. ⁶He sacrificed his own son in^a the fire, practiced sorcery^D and divination^D, and consulted mediums^D and spiritists. He did much evil in the eyes of the LORD, provoking him to anger.

⁷He took the carved Asherah pole he had made and put it in the temple, of which the LORD had said to David and to his son Solomon, "In this temple and in Jerusalem, which I have chosen out of all the tribes of Israel, I will put my Name forever. ⁸I will not again make the feet of the Israelites wander from the land I gave their forefathers, if only they will be careful to do everything I commanded them and will keep the whole Law that my servant Moses gave them." ⁹But the people did not listen. Manasseh led them astray, so that they did more evil than the nations the LORD had destroyed before the Israelites.

¹⁰The LORD said through his servants the prophets^D: ¹¹"Manasseh king of Judah has committed these detestable sins. He has done more evil than the Amorites who preceded him and has led Judah into sin with his idols^D. ¹²Therefore this is what the LORD, the God of Israel, says: I am going to bring such disaster on Jerusalem and Judah that the ears of everyone who hears of it will tingle. ¹³I will stretch out over Jerusalem the measuring line used against Samaria and the plumb line used against the house of Ahab. I will wipe out Jerusalem as one wipes a dish, wiping it and turning it upside down. ¹⁴I will forsake the remnant^D of my inheritance and hand them over to their enemies. They will be looted and plundered^D by all their foes, ¹⁵because they have done evil in my eyes and have provoked me to anger from the day their forefathers came out of Egypt until this day."

¹⁶Moreover, Manasseh also shed so much innocent blood that he filled Jerusalem from end to end—besides the sin that he had caused Judah to commit, so that they did evil in the eyes of the LORD.

¹⁷As for the other events of Manasseh's reign, and all he did, including the sin he committed, are they not written in the book of the annals of the kings of Judah? ¹⁸Manasseh rested with his fathers and was buried in his palace garden, the garden of Uzza. And Amon his son succeeded him as king.

Amon King of Judah

¹⁹Amon was twenty-two years old when he became king, and he reigned in Jerusalem two years. His mother's name was Meshullemeth daughter of Haruz; she was from Jotbah. ²⁰He did evil in the eyes of the LORD, as his father Manasseh had done. ²¹He walked in all the ways of his father; he worshiped the idols his father had worshiped, and bowed down to them. ²²He forsook the LORD, the God of his fathers, and did not walk in the way of the LORD.

²³Amon's officials conspired against him and assassinated the king in his palace. ²⁴Then the people of the land

---

Annals of the kings (20:20)

See *Annals of the kings* (1:18).

Starry hosts (21:3)

See *Was bowing to the starry hosts like astrology?* (17:16).

How were the Israelites more evil than the nations before them? (21:9)

The problem wasn't that the Israelites did things the nations before them hadn't done. It was that they should have known better. Their evil deeds were all the more appalling because they rejected God's covenant to fall on their faces in front of sticks and stones. Israel abandoned God, taking up the worship of Canaan's gods in spite of a full knowledge of the truth.

SCRIPTURE LINK (21:13) *Measuring line used against Samaria and the plumb line used against the house of Ahab*

This was a way of saying that Judah would be punished in the same way that the northern kingdom had been. See 17:1–6.

Who were Manasseh's innocent victims? (21:16)

Like Ahaz before him, Manasseh sacrificed sons, probably to the god Molech. His example may have led others to sacrifice their own children. They too would have been his victims. Ancient Jewish tradition also blames him for the death of Isaiah. Some think Isaiah's death is meant when the book of Hebrews talks about those sawed in two for their faith (Heb. 11:37).

Annals of the kings (21:17)

See *Annals of the kings* (1:18).

---

^a6 Or *He made his own son pass through*

killed all who had plotted against King Amon, and they made Josiah his son king in his place. **25**As for the other events of Amon's reign, and what he did, are they not written in the book of the annals of the kings of Judah? **26**He was buried in his grave in the garden of Uzza. And Josiah his son succeeded him as king.

The Book of the Law Found

22 Josiah was eight years old when he became king, and he reigned in Jerusalem[D] thirty-one years. His mother's name was Jedidah daughter of Adaiah; she was from Bozkath. **2**He did what was right in the eyes of the LORD and walked in all the ways of his father David, not turning aside to the right or to the left.

3In the eighteenth year of his reign, King Josiah sent the secretary, Shaphan son of Azaliah, the son of Meshullam, to the temple of the LORD. He said: **4**"Go up to Hilkiah the high priest[D] and have him get ready the money that has been brought into the temple of the LORD, which the door-keepers have collected from the people. **5**Have them entrust it to the men appointed to supervise the work on the temple. And have these men pay the workers who repair the temple of the LORD— **6**the carpenters, the builders and the masons. Also have them purchase timber and dressed stone to repair the temple. **7**But they need not account for the money entrusted to them, because they are acting faithfully."

8Hilkiah the high priest said to Shaphan the secretary, "I have found the Book of the Law in the temple of the LORD." He gave it to Shaphan, who read it. **9**Then Shaphan the secretary went to the king and reported to him: "Your officials have paid out the money that was in the temple of the LORD and have entrusted it to the workers and supervisors at the temple." **10**Then Shaphan the secretary informed the king, "Hilkiah the priest has given me a book." And Shaphan read from it in the presence of the king.

11When the king heard the words of the Book of the Law, he tore his robes. **12**He gave these orders to Hilkiah the priest, Ahikam son of Shaphan, Acbor son of Micaiah, Shaphan the secretary and Asaiah the king's attendant: **13**"Go and inquire of the LORD for me and for the people and for all Judah about what is written in this book that has been found. Great is the LORD's anger that burns against us because our fathers have not obeyed the words of this book; they have not acted in accordance with all that is written there concerning us."

14Hilkiah the priest, Ahikam, Acbor, Shaphan and Asaiah went to speak to the prophetess[D] Huldah, who was the wife of Shallum son of Tikvah, the son of Harhas, keeper of the wardrobe. She lived in Jerusalem, in the Second District.

15She said to them, "This is what the LORD, the God of Israel, says: Tell the man who sent you to me, **16**'This is what the LORD says: I am going to bring disaster on this place and its people, according to everything written in the book the king of Judah has read. **17**Because they have forsaken me and burned incense[D] to other gods and provoked me to anger by all the idols[D] their hands have made,[a] my anger will burn against this place and will not be quenched.' **18**Tell the king of Judah, who sent you to inquire of the LORD, 'This is what the LORD, the God of Is-

---

How was Josiah able to overcome negative influences and do *what was right*? (22:2)

For most of the world, our Western concept of functional, individual families makes little sense. Children are the responsibility of the extended family, not merely the nuclear family. As with royal sons throughout the ancient world, Josiah was probably raised by people who were not his biological family. Anonymous people in the royal court probably deserve the credit for introducing Josiah to the God of Israel. They nurtured the character that made him a worthy heir to David's throne.

How could the priests have lost the Book of the Law? (22:8)

Reverence for God's Word goes hand in hand with reverence for God. The reign of Manasseh, lasting 55 years, erased knowledge of God's law from the minds of all but the oldest priests. Since God seemed unnecessary to the people, his law became irrelevant. Manasseh's fanatical dedication to idolatry exerted a powerful and negative influence on the people. With so many false gods, they had no interest in God's book.

How common were prophetesses in Judah? (22:14)

Prophetesses were rare in the Old Testament. Miriam (Exodus 15:20), Deborah (Judges 4:4) and Isaiah's wife (Isaiah 8:3) are the only other ones mentioned. In a patriarchal culture, it seems remarkable that even four women were used by God to speak for him. See article: *Why silence the women?* (1 Tim. 2:11). Also see *Why can't a woman teach a man?* (1 Tim. 2:12).

---

a17 Or by everything they have done

rael, says concerning the words you heard: [19]Because your heart was responsive and you humbled yourself before the LORD when you heard what I have spoken against this place and its people, that they would become accursed and laid waste, and because you tore your robes and wept in my presence, I have heard you, declares the LORD. [20]Therefore I will gather you to your fathers, and you will be buried in peace[D]. Your eyes will not see all the disaster I am going to bring on this place.' "

So they took her answer back to the king.

Josiah Renews the Covenant

23 Then the king called together all the elders of Judah and Jerusalem[D]. [2]He went up to the temple of the LORD with the men of Judah, the people of Jerusalem, the priests and the prophets—all the people from the least to the greatest. He read in their hearing all the words of the Book of the Covenant[D], which had been found in the temple of the LORD. [3]The king stood by the pillar and renewed the covenant in the presence of the LORD—to follow the LORD and keep his commands, regulations and decrees with all his heart and all his soul[D], thus confirming the words of the covenant written in this book. Then all the people pledged themselves to the covenant.

[4]The king ordered Hilkiah the high priest, the priests next in rank and the doorkeepers to remove from the temple of the LORD all the articles made for Baal[D] and Asherah and all the starry hosts[D]. He burned them outside Jerusalem in the fields of the Kidron Valley[D] and took the ashes to Bethel. [5]He did away with the pagan priests appointed by the kings of Judah to burn incense[D] on the high places[D] of the towns of Judah and on those around Jerusalem—those who burned incense to Baal, to the sun and moon, to the constellations and to all the starry hosts. [6]He took the Asherah pole[D] from the temple of the LORD to the Kidron Valley outside Jerusalem and burned it there. He ground it to powder and scattered the dust over the graves of the common people. [7]He also tore down the quarters of the male shrine prostitutes[D], which were in the temple of the LORD and where women did weaving for Asherah.

[8]Josiah brought all the priests from the towns of Judah and desecrated[D] the high places, from Geba to Beersheba, where the priests had burned incense. He broke down the shrines[a] at the gates—at the entrance to the Gate of Joshua, the city governor, which is on the left of the city gate. [9]Although the priests of the high places did not serve at the altar of the LORD in Jerusalem, they ate unleavened bread with their fellow priests.

[10]He desecrated Topheth[D], which was in the Valley of Ben Hinnom, so no one could use it to sacrifice[D] his son or daughter in[b] the fire to Molech[D]. [11]He removed from the entrance to the temple of the LORD the horses that the kings of Judah had dedicated to the sun. They were in the court near the room of an official named Nathan-Melech. Josiah then burned the chariots dedicated to the sun.

[12]He pulled down the altars the kings of Judah had erected on the roof near the upper room of Ahaz, and the altars Manasseh had built in the two courts of the temple

---

The pillar (23:3)
See *Why did kings stand by a certain temple pillar?* (11:14).

Why have male shrine prostitutes? (23:7)
See *What did male prostitutes have to do with pagan worship?* (1 Kings 14:24).

What did the women weave for Asherah? (23:7)
It's not clear. Some have suggested the women wove garments for images of Asherah. In some religions today it is part of the ritual to "clothe and feed" the idol. Others suggest they may have made some kind of a cloth screen to enclose the images of Asherah.

---

a 8 Or high places   *b 10 Or to make his son or daughter pass through*

Hill of Corruption (23:13)

Called the Mount of Olives in the New Testament (see **Setting of the Gospels** on page 1332), it was *the Mount of Ointment* in ancient Israel. The writer of Kings, however, used a play on words—a pun—to turn the name around. How could he call a place to worship foreign gods a place of oil—a place of anointing and blessing? No, this was a place of corruption.

SCRIPTURE LINK (23:13) *High places . . . Solomon king of Israel had built for Ashtoreth*

See 1 Kings 11:5.

Why have a cemetery connected with a high place? (23:17)

Usually cemeteries and high places had little in common. But the shrine at Bethel was not merely another high place. It was a temple built by Jeroboam I to rival the true temple in Jerusalem. Perhaps it was used in religious ceremonies for the dead, requiring a burial ground to be located nearby. More likely, the cemetery contained the bones of priests from Jeroboam's renegade temple.

SCRIPTURE LINK (23:17) *The man of God who came from Judah*

A prophet who predicted these events. See 1 Kings 13:1–2.

Why burn human bones on an altar? (23:20)

If the cemetery was for the false priests from Jeroboam's shrine, Josiah's action was doubly effective. First, he fulfilled the prophecy (see previous note). Second, contact with the dead desecrated the altar and its location, so that it would never be usable as a sanctuary again.

What good did Josiah's revival do? (23:24–26)

Josiah's attempted reform may have been the most extensive and thorough of any of Judah's reforms, but unfortunately, it had no lasting effect. Manasseh's lengthy reign, marked by his persistent determination to suppress Israel's true faith left no one at the grass roots to support the movement. When Josiah died everyone went back to business—and religion—as usual. God postponed judgment on Judah, however, as an act of grace during the rule of the godly king.

Why did Josiah butt into someone else's fight? (23:29)

Josiah hoped to preserve Judah, possibly by playing the spoiler's role in the clash between two superpowers. Egypt wanted to help Assyria, probably because a strong Assyria could serve as a buffer between Egypt and the rising threat of the region, Babylon. While this made good political sense for Egypt, Josiah knew it would be disastrous for Judah. What hope did his tiny kingdom have, wedged between Egypt and Assyria? For Judah, support for a distant power like Babylon must have seemed the only choice.

of the LORD. He removed them from there, smashed them to pieces and threw the rubble into the Kidron Valley^D. ¹³The king also desecrated^D the high places^D that were east of Jerusalem^D on the south of the Hill of Corruption—the ones Solomon king of Israel had built for Ashtoreth^D the vile goddess of the Sidonians, for Chemosh the vile god of Moab, and for Molech^{Da} the detestable god of the people of Ammon. ¹⁴Josiah smashed the sacred stones^D and cut down the Asherah poles^D and covered the sites with human bones.

¹⁵Even the altar at Bethel, the high place made by Jeroboam son of Nebat, who had caused Israel to sin—even that altar and high place he demolished. He burned the high place and ground it to powder, and burned the Asherah pole also. ¹⁶Then Josiah looked around, and when he saw the tombs that were there on the hillside, he had the bones removed from them and burned on the altar to defile it, in accordance with the word of the LORD proclaimed by the man of God who foretold these things.

¹⁷The king asked, "What is that tombstone I see?"

The men of the city said, "It marks the tomb of the man of God who came from Judah and pronounced against the altar of Bethel the very things you have done to it."

¹⁸"Leave it alone," he said. "Don't let anyone disturb his bones." So they spared his bones and those of the prophet^D who had come from Samaria.

¹⁹Just as he had done at Bethel, Josiah removed and defiled all the shrines at the high places that the kings of Israel had built in the towns of Samaria that had provoked the LORD to anger. ²⁰Josiah slaughtered all the priests^D of those high places on the altars and burned human bones on them. Then he went back to Jerusalem.

²¹The king gave this order to all the people: "Celebrate the Passover to the LORD your God, as it is written in this Book of the Covenant^D." ²²Not since the days of the judges who led Israel, nor throughout the days of the kings of Israel and the kings of Judah, had any such Passover been observed. ²³But in the eighteenth year of King Josiah, this Passover was celebrated to the LORD in Jerusalem.

²⁴Furthermore, Josiah got rid of the mediums^D and spiritists, the household gods, the idols^D and all the other detestable things seen in Judah and Jerusalem. This he did to fulfill the requirements of the law written in the book that Hilkiah the priest had discovered in the temple of the LORD. ²⁵Neither before nor after Josiah was there a king like him who turned to the LORD as he did—with all his heart and with all his soul^D and with all his strength, in accordance with all the Law of Moses.

²⁶Nevertheless, the LORD did not turn away from the heat of his fierce anger, which burned against Judah because of all that Manasseh had done to provoke him to anger. ²⁷So the LORD said, "I will remove Judah also from my presence as I removed Israel, and I will reject Jerusalem, the city I chose, and this temple, about which I said, 'There shall my Name be.'^b"

²⁸As for the other events of Josiah's reign, and all he did, are they not written in the book of the annals of the kings of Judah?

²⁹While Josiah was king, Pharaoh Neco king of Egypt went up to the Euphrates River to help the king of Assyria. King Josiah marched out to meet him in battle, but Neco

^a13 Hebrew *Milcom*   ^b27 1 Kings 8:29

faced him and killed him at Megiddo. **30**Josiah's servants brought his body in a chariot from Megiddo to Jerusalem[D] and buried him in his own tomb. And the people of the land took Jehoahaz son of Josiah and anointed[D] him and made him king in place of his father.

Jehoahaz King of Judah

31Jehoahaz was twenty-three years old when he became king, and he reigned in Jerusalem three months. His mother's name was Hamutal daughter of Jeremiah; she was from Libnah. **32**He did evil in the eyes of the LORD, just as his fathers had done. **33**Pharaoh Neco put him in chains at Riblah in the land of Hamath[a] so that he might not reign in Jerusalem, and he imposed on Judah a levy of a hundred talents[b] of silver and a talent[c] of gold. **34**Pharaoh Neco made Eliakim son of Josiah king in place of his father Josiah and changed Eliakim's name to Jehoiakim. But he took Jehoahaz and carried him off to Egypt, and there he died. **35**Jehoiakim paid Pharaoh Neco the silver and gold he demanded. In order to do so, he taxed the land and exacted the silver and gold from the people of the land according to their assessments.

Jehoiakim King of Judah

36Jehoiakim was twenty-five years old when he became king, and he reigned in Jerusalem eleven years. His mother's name was Zebidah daughter of Pedaiah; she was from Rumah. **37**And he did evil in the eyes of the LORD, just as his fathers had done.

24 During Jehoiakim's reign, Nebuchadnezzar king of Babylon invaded the land, and Jehoiakim became his vassal for three years. But then he changed his mind and rebelled against Nebuchadnezzar. **2**The LORD sent Babylonian,[d] Aramean, Moabite and Ammonite raiders against him. He sent them to destroy Judah, in accordance with the word of the LORD proclaimed by his servants the prophets[D]. **3**Surely these things happened to Judah according to the LORD's command, in order to remove them from his presence because of the sins of Manasseh and all he had done, **4**including the shedding of innocent blood. For he had filled Jerusalem with innocent blood, and the LORD was not willing to forgive.

5As for the other events of Jehoiakim's reign, and all he did, are they not written in the book of the annals of the kings of Judah? **6**Jehoiakim rested with his fathers. And Jehoiachin his son succeeded him as king.

7The king of Egypt did not march out from his own country again, because the king of Babylon had taken all his territory, from the Wadi of Egypt to the Euphrates River.

Jehoiachin King of Judah

8Jehoiachin was eighteen years old when he became king, and he reigned in Jerusalem three months. His mother's name was Nehushta daughter of Elnathan; she was from Jerusalem. **9**He did evil in the eyes of the LORD, just as his father had done.

10At that time the officers of Nebuchadnezzar king of Babylon advanced on Jerusalem and laid siege to it,

---

Why did Pharaoh Neco chain Jehoahaz in Riblah? (23:33)

Probably to demonstrate his authority over Judah. By summoning Judah's new king to his field headquarters and replacing him on the throne with his brother, Neco proved that Egypt, not Judah, was in control. Jehoahaz was sent to Egypt, probably as a hostage, where he eventually died.

Why did Neco install the king's brother as the new king? (23:34)

It was fairly common for a conqueror from this period to replace a king with another member of the same family. Elevating someone new to the throne increased the likelihood that the king would remain loyal to the conqueror. At the same time, the possibility that the people would rebel was diminished by keeping the original royal family in place.

Why change Eliakim's name? (23:34)

Every Hebrew name has a meaning, but it doesn't always have significance. Eliakim may mean *God establishes* while Jehoiakim means *The LORD has established*. Neither was particularly appropriate for a king under the control of foreign powers. It's possible *Jehoiakim* was Eliakim's official throne name. But it seems more likely that Neco II wanted to show he had the power to make a new king with a new identity.

Was Jehoiakim serving Egypt and Babylon at the same time? (24:1)

No. In the international conflict between Babylon and Egypt, Babylon was the victor. Judah was part of the spoils. Jehoiakim had been a vassal king under Neco of Egypt and now he would be a vassal king under Nebuchadnezzar of Babylon. 2 Kings shows us the transfer of control over Judah in this verse.

Annals of the kings (24:5)

See *Annals of the kings* (1:18).

---

a33 Hebrew; Septuagint (see also 2 Chron. 36:3) *Neco at Riblah in Hamath removed him*   *b33* That is, about 3 3/4 tons (about 3.4 metric tons)   *c33* That is, about 75 pounds (about 34 kilograms)
d2 Or *Chaldean*

11and Nebuchadnezzar himself came up to the city while his officers were besieging it. 12Jehoiachin king of Judah, his mother, his attendants, his nobles and his officials all surrendered to him.

In the eighth year of the reign of the king of Babylon, he took Jehoiachin prisoner. 13As the LORD had declared, Nebuchadnezzar removed all the treasures from the temple of the LORD and from the royal palace, and took away all the gold articles that Solomon king of Israel had made for the temple of the LORD. 14He carried into exileᴰ all Jerusalemᴰ: all the officers and fighting men, and all the craftsmen and artisans—a total of ten thousand. Only the poorest people of the land were left.

15Nebuchadnezzar took Jehoiachin captive to Babylon. He also took from Jerusalem to Babylon the king's mother, his wives, his officials and the leading men of the land. 16The king of Babylon also deported to Babylon the entire force of seven thousand fighting men, strong and fit for war, and a thousand craftsmen and artisans. 17He made Mattaniah, Jehoiachin's uncle, king in his place and changed his name to Zedekiah.

Zedekiah King of Judah

18Zedekiah was twenty-one years old when he became king, and he reigned in Jerusalem eleven years. His mother's name was Hamutal daughter of Jeremiah; she was from Libnah. 19He did evil in the eyes of the LORD, just as Jehoiakim had done. 20It was because of the LORD's anger that all this happened to Jerusalem and Judah, and in the end he thrust them from his presence.

The Fall of Jerusalem

Now Zedekiah rebelled against the king of Babylon.

25 So in the ninth year of Zedekiah's reign, on the tenth day of the tenth month, Nebuchadnezzar king of Babylon marched against Jerusalem with his whole army. He encamped outside the city and built siege worksᴰ all around it. 2The city was kept under siege until the eleventh year of King Zedekiah. 3By the ninth day of

---

Why leave the poor behind? (24:14)

The Babylonian conquests could have flooded Babylon with slaves. They became selective because too many slaves could have been counterproductive, causing a drain on their economy. Slaves with skills or trades were more desirable since they could contribute to Babylon's economy. Untrained and uneducated, the poorest would not have made the best slaves for Babylon.

What did this name change accomplish? (24:17)

See *Why change Eliakim's name?* (23:34).

Exile of Judah (25:1)

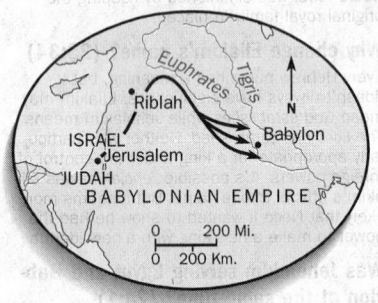

Why was the Lord unwilling to forgive? (24:4)

The prophets make it clear that God was always willing to forgive. But he was not willing to forgive those who refused to repent (Jer. 8:4–5). Even the reforms of Josiah were not permanent; they embodied a form of religion but didn't change people's hearts (Jer. 3:10). See *What good did Josiah's revival do?* (23:24–26).

God had promised his people either blessings or curses, depending on whether they obeyed or disobeyed (Deut. 28). According to the terms of his covenant with his people, God was within his rights to destroy the nation.

But God did not judge his people hastily. He was patient, continually giving them opportunities to mend their ways and turn to him with their whole hearts. But though he disciplined them in every way possible, the people would not respond (Jer. 2:30).

God's final decision to destroy Jerusalem, the temple and the nation was an act of judgment that swept the land clean. After a cleansing judgment, God could start anew with a righteous remnant of his people (Isaiah 11:11–12).

Even in the end, God held out the opportunity for individuals to repent (Ezek. 18:30–32). But the people rejected God's forgiveness by rejecting him.

the ⌊fourth⌋ᵃ month the famine in the city had become so severe that there was no food for the people to eat. ⁴Then the city wall was broken through, and the whole army fled at night through the gate between the two walls near the king's garden, though the Babyloniansᵇ were surrounding the city. They fled toward the Arabah,ᶜ ⁵but the Babylonianᵈ army pursued the king and overtook him in the plains of JerichoᴰÞ. All his soldiers were separated from him and scattered, ⁶and he was captured. He was taken to the king of Babylon at Riblah, where sentence was pronounced on him. ⁷They killed the sons of Zedekiah before his eyes. Then they put out his eyes, bound him with bronze shackles and took him to Babylon.

⁸On the seventh day of the fifth month, in the nineteenth year of Nebuchadnezzar king of Babylon, Nebuzaradan commander of the imperial guard, an official of the king of Babylon, came to JerusalemᴰÞ. ⁹He set fire to the temple of the LORD, the royal palace and all the houses of Jerusalem. Every important building he burned down. ¹⁰The whole Babylonian army, under the commander of the imperial guard, broke down the walls around Jerusalem. ¹¹Nebuzaradan the commander of the guard carried into exileᴰ the people who remained in the city, along with the rest of the populace and those who had gone over to the king of Babylon. ¹²But the commander left behind some of the poorest people of the land to work the vineyards and fields.

¹³The Babylonians broke up the bronze pillars, the movable stands and the bronze Sea that were at the temple of the LORD and they carried the bronze to Babylon. ¹⁴They also took away the pots, shovels, wick trimmers, dishes and all the bronze articles used in the temple service. ¹⁵The commander of the imperial guard took away the censersᴰ and sprinkling bowls—all that were made of pure gold or silver.

¹⁶The bronze from the two pillars, the Sea and the movable stands, which Solomon had made for the temple of the LORD, was more than could be weighed. ¹⁷Each pillar was twenty-seven feetᵉ high. The bronze capital on top of one pillar was four and a half feetᶠ high and was decorated with a network and pomegranates of bronze all around. The other pillar, with its network, was similar.

¹⁸The commander of the guard took as prisoners Seraiah the chief priestᴰ, Zephaniah the priest next in rank and the three doorkeepers. ¹⁹Of those still in the city, he took the officer in charge of the fighting men and five royal advisers. He also took the secretary who was chief officer in charge of conscripting the people of the land and sixty of his men who were found in the city. ²⁰Nebuzaradan the commander took them all and brought them to the king of Babylon at Riblah. ²¹There at Riblah, in the land of Hamath, the king had them executed.

So Judah went into captivity, away from her land.

²²Nebuchadnezzar king of Babylon appointed Gedaliah son of Ahikam, the son of Shaphan, to be over the people he had left behind in Judah. ²³When all the army officers and their men heard that the king of Babylon had appointed Gedaliah as governor, they came to Gedaliah at Mizpah—Ishmael son of Nethaniah, Johanan son of Kare-

Why did they spare Zedekiah's life? (25:7)

This was a world where empires rose to power on the strengths of policies that today would be called terrorism. A captive king, chained, blinded and bereaved, made a powerful object lesson. Zedekiah was used to demonstrate what happened to subjects who rebelled against Nebuchadnezzar.

Why didn't the Babylonians finish the job the first time? (25:8–9)

Nebuchadnezzar's first concern was to capture and punish a rebel king. As with extortionists and terrorists today, fear proved an effective weapon against would-be opponents. Jerusalem and the temple could wait. The king who had rebelled, however, had to be dealt with. His escape or any sign of mercy toward him might have been interpreted as weakness and might have triggered further rebellion.

ᵃ3 See Jer. 52:6.   ᵇ4 Or *Chaldeans*; also in verses 13, 25 and 26
ᶜ4 Or *the Jordan Valley*   ᵈ5 Or *Chaldean*; also in verses 10 and 24
ᵉ17 Hebrew *eighteen cubits* (about 8.1 meters)   ᶠ17 Hebrew *three cubits* (about 1.3 meters)

ah, Seraiah son of Tanhumeth the Netophathite, Jaazaniah the son of the Maacathite, and their men. **24**Gedaliah took an oath to reassure them and their men. "Do not be afraid of the Babylonian officials," he said. "Settle down in the land and serve the king of Babylon, and it will go well with you."

25In the seventh month, however, Ishmael son of Nethaniah, the son of Elishama, who was of royal blood, came with ten men and assassinated Gedaliah and also the men of Judah and the Babylonians who were with him at Mizpah. **26**At this, all the people from the least to the greatest, together with the army officers, fled to Egypt for fear of the Babylonians.

Jehoiachin Released

27In the thirty-seventh year of the exile^D of Jehoiachin king of Judah, in the year Evil-Merodach^a became king of Babylon, he released Jehoiachin from prison on the twenty-seventh day of the twelfth month. **28**He spoke kindly to him and gave him a seat of honor higher than those of the other kings who were with him in Babylon. **29**So Jehoiachin put aside his prison clothes and for the rest of his life ate regularly at the king's table. **30**Day by day the king gave Jehoiachin a regular allowance as long as he lived.

What did Ishmael achieve by assassinating Gedaliah? (25:25)

Perhaps Ishmael thought he could become ruler over what was left of the land. Related to the royal family and formerly one of the king's officers (Jer. 41:1), Ishmael had some grounds for his ambitions. With the backing of Baalis, king of the Ammonites, who probably hoped to create further trouble for Judah (Jer. 40:14), Ishmael was encouraged to ruthlessly pursue his political goals.

Why release a king after 37 years in prison? (25:27–30)

Crowned when he was only 18, Jehoiachin was taken to Babylon only three months later. Released at age 55, Jehoiachin would have posed no threat to his captors. The simultaneous release of several other captive kings suggests a general amnesty to celebrate Evil-Merodach's coronation.

---

a27 Also called *Amel-Marduk*

Kings of Israel and Judah

This chart depicts the reigns of the kings of Israel and Judah from Jeroboam of Israel and Rehoboam of Judah until the fall of Jerusalem. As best can be determined, the dates reflect the official reign of each king and not any years of his co-regency with another king. The center column is divided into increments of twenty years; the outside columns give the passages in 1 and 2 Kings and 2 Chronicles where the reign of each king is described. By using this chart, you can see at a glance both the length of each reign and the kings in Israel and Judah who were contemporaries. The final column depicts when the major prophets lived and ministered.

PASSAGES	KINGS OF ISRAEL	DATE B.C.	KINGS OF JUDAH	PASSAGES		PROPHETS
1 Kings				1 Kings	2 Chron.	
12:25–14:20	JEROBOAM 1	930	REHOBOAM	12:1-24; 14:21-31	10:1–12:16	
			ABIJAH	15:1-8	13:1–14:1	
15:25-31	NADAB	910	ASA	15:9-24	14:2–16:14	
15:32–16:7	BAASHA					
		890				
16:8-14	ELAH					
16:15-22	ZIMRI, TIBNI/OMRI					
16:23-28	OMRI					
16:29–22:40	AHAB					Elijah
		870	JEHOSHAPHAT	22:41-50	17:1–21:3	
2 Kings						
1:1-18	AHAZIAH					
3:1–8:15	JORAM	850				Elisha

Kings of Israel and Judah (continued)

PASSAGES 2 Kings	KINGS OF ISRAEL	DATE B.C.	KINGS OF JUDAH	2 Kings	2 Chron.	PROPHETS
		850				Elisha (cont.)
			JEHORAM	8:16-24	21:4-20	
9:30–10:36	JEHU		AHAZIAH	8:25-29	22:1-9	
			ATHALIAH	11:1-21	22:10–23:21	
			JOASH	12:1-21	24:1-27	
		830				
13:1-9	JEHOAHAZ					
		810				
13:10-25	JEHOASH					
			AMAZIAH	14:1-22	25:1-28	
		790				
14:23-29	JEROBOAM II					Jonah
		770				
			AZARIAH (UZZIAH)	15:1-7	26:1-23	
						Amos
15:8-15	ZECHARIAH, SHALLUM					Hosea
15:16-22	MENAHEM	750				

PASSAGES	KINGS OF ISRAEL	DATE B.C.	KINGS OF JUDAH	PASSAGES		PROPHETS
2 Kings		750		2 Kings	2 Chron.	
15:23-26	PEKAHIAH					
15:27-31	PEKAH		JOTHAM	15:32-38	27:1-8	
17:1-6	HOSHEA	730	AHAZ	16:1-20	28:1-27	
	FALL OF SAMARIA	722				
			HEZEKIAH	18:1–20:21	29:1–32:33	
		710				
		690				
			MANASSEH	21:1-18	33:1-20	
		670				
		650				

Prophets (right column, vertical bars): Isaiah, Micah, Hosea (cont.), Nahum

Kings of Israel and Judah (continued)

PASSAGES	KINGS OF ISRAEL	DATE B.C.	KINGS OF JUDAH	PASSAGES		PROPHETS
				2 Kings	2 Chron.	Nahum (cont.)
		650				
			AMON	21:19-26	33:21-25	Zephaniah
			JOSIAH	22:1–23:30	34:1–35:27	
		630				Jeremiah
		610				Habakkuk
			JEHOAHAZ	23:31-33	36:1-4	
			JEHOIAKIM	23:36–24:7	36:5-8	Daniel
			JEHOIACHIN	24:8-17	36:9-10	
			ZEDEKIAH	24:18–25:21	36:11-21	Ezekiel
		590				
		586	FALL OF JERUSALEM	25:8-17	36:15-19	
		570				
		550				

1 CHRONICLES

Why read this book?

When you find your old school yearbook, whose face do you look for first? Chances are, it's your own—or at least those of your closest friends. There is a universal human need to belong. The Israelites were no different. The books of Chronicles showed the Israelites how they fit into God's plan. These books still show us the principles of how to belong to God.

Who wrote this book?

Traditionally, it's been thought that Ezra wrote Chronicles. But an unknown priest or Levite may have been the author.

When and why was it written?

Chronicles was written around 450 to 400 B.C.—more than six centuries after the first events it records, about 100–150 years after the last events in 2 Chronicles 36. The two books (originally one) re-examine the history of Israel. The writer's apparent goal was for the Israelites to recognize their godly roots and to rediscover their heritage.

What period of history does it cover?

1 Chronicles looks at genealogical records from the beginning of recorded history until after the Babylonian exile. The remaining chapters focus on the reign of King David.

Why repeat material from 2 Samuel and 2 Kings?

Chronicles is not just a rehash of other Old Testament texts. Samuel and Kings were written to a people in exile, who wondered how and why they got there. Chronicles was written to a people returned from exile, who wondered if they still fit into God's plan.

What to look for in 1 Chronicles:

This genealogy (chs. 1–9) connected the Israelites just returned from exile with their ancestors and with the promises their ancestors had received from God. Also, watch for David's role in leading Israel to worship God, and look for ways to enhance your own worship.

When did these things happen?

TIME LINE	1400 BC	1300	1200	1100	1000	900	800	700	600	500	400
Saul's reign (1050-1010 B.C.)											
David's reign (1010-970 B.C.)											
Solomon's reign (970-930 B.C.)											
Building of the temple (966-959 B.C.)											
Division of the kingdom (930 B.C.)											
Exile of Israel (722 B.C.)											
Fall of Jerusalem (586 B.C.)											
Book of 1 Chronicles written (c.450-400 B.C.)											

Historical Records From Adam to Abraham

To Noah's Sons

1 Adam, Seth, Enosh, **2**Kenan, Mahalalel, Jared, **3**Enoch, Methuselah, Lamech, Noah.

4The sons of Noah:*a*
Shem, Ham and Japheth.

The Japhethites

5The sons*b* of Japheth:
Gomer, Magog, Madai, Javan, Tubal, Meshech and Tiras.
6The sons of Gomer:
Ashkenaz, Riphath*c* and Togarmah.
7The sons of Javan:
Elishah, Tarshish, the Kittim and the Rodanim.

The Hamites

8The sons of Ham:
Cush, Mizraim,*d* Put and Canaan.
9The sons of Cush:
Seba, Havilah, Sabta, Raamah and Sabteca.
The sons of Raamah:
Sheba and Dedan.
10Cush was the father*e* of Nimrod, who grew to be a mighty warrior on earth.

a4 Septuagint; Hebrew does not have *The sons of Noah*:   *b5 Sons*
may mean *descendants* or *successors* or *nations*; also in verses 6-10, 17
and 20.   *c6* Many Hebrew manuscripts and Vulgate (see also
Septuagint and Gen. 10:3); most Hebrew manuscripts *Diphath*
d8. That is, Egypt; also in verse 11   *e10 Father* may mean *ancestor*
or *predecessor* or *founder*; also in verses 11, 13, 18 and 20.

Why are only sons listed? (1:5)

In Israelite culture, the sons received the inheritance. Through the sons the father's name was carried on. These genealogies were given to help the Israelites stay connected with their history. The names of the males represented entire families that people could relate to, even though mothers' and daughters' names weren't often mentioned.

Why is Nimrod described when hardly anyone else is? (1:10)

Genealogies occasionally provided glimpses into the character, circumstances, accomplishments or misdeeds of the people listed. Such details remind us that this is not a meaningless list; these were people as real as we are. Nimrod had apparently become well known for his military prowess. But Nimrod is not the only one with an expanded record in this genealogy. See, for example, Peleg who was named for the *division of the earth* (v. 19), Er who was so wicked that he was put to death by the Lord (2:3) and Jabez *who was more honorable than his brothers* (4:9–10).

Why read an ancient list of faceless names? (1:1)

If we can learn from history, then we can learn from Biblical genealogies as well. How? By putting ourselves in the place of the original readers. If we can discover what *they* gained, we'll gain something too.

How did genealogies encourage and inspire the Israelites? In several ways: (1) Genealogies established their heritage—including their rights of inheritance and property, claims to the throne, priesthood and clan leadership. (2) Genealogies helped them organize—determining how they pitched their tents, chose their spies, parceled out the promised land and so on. (3) Genealogies kept them in touch with what God had done for their ancestors.

The writer of Chronicles used this list of names to show how God had chosen Israel for a prominent role in history. He wanted to encourage those who had just returned from exile and were struggling to rebuild their ruined nation. These names showed that God accomplished his purposes through their ancestors—before David, Moses or even Abraham. In fact, God's plan began with Adam.

This genealogy helped the surviving Jews see that God could use them too, that God's purposes were still in effect. The nation had been chosen and brought back to the promised land for a reason! Identify with those first readers, and you'll see a lesson that applies to us today: God still has a purpose, and he still has a people—Abraham's true descendants by faith (Gal. 3:29)—to fulfill his plan. *He chose us in him before the creation of the world* (Eph. 1:4).

11Mizraim was the father of
the Ludites, Anamites, Lehabites, Naphtuhites,
12Pathrusites, Casluhites (from whom the Philistines came) and Caphtorites.
13Canaan was the father of
Sidon his firstborn^D,^a and of the Hittites, **14**Jebusites, Amorites, Girgashites, **15**Hivites, Arkites, Sinites, **16**Arvadites, Zemarites and Hamathites.

The Semites

17The sons of Shem:
Elam, Asshur, Arphaxad, Lud and Aram.
The sons of Aram^b:
Uz, Hul, Gether and Meshech.
18Arphaxad was the father of Shelah,
and Shelah the father of Eber.
19Two sons were born to Eber:
One was named Peleg,^c because in his time the earth was divided; his brother was named Joktan.
20Joktan was the father of
Almodad, Sheleph, Hazarmaveth, Jerah, **21**Hadoram, Uzal, Diklah, **22**Obal,^d Abimael, Sheba, **23**Ophir, Havilah and Jobab. All these were sons of Joktan.

24Shem, Arphaxad,^e Shelah,
25Eber, Peleg, Reu,
26Serug, Nahor, Terah
27and Abram (that is, Abraham).

The Family of Abraham

28The sons of Abraham:
Isaac and Ishmael.

Descendants of Hagar

29These were their descendants:
Nebaioth the firstborn of Ishmael, Kedar, Adbeel, Mibsam, **30**Mishma, Dumah, Massa, Hadad, Tema, **31**Jetur, Naphish and Kedemah. These were the sons of Ishmael.

Descendants of Keturah

32The sons born to Keturah, Abraham's concubine^D:
Zimran, Jokshan, Medan, Midian, Ishbak and Shuah.
The sons of Jokshan:
Sheba and Dedan.
33The sons of Midian:
Ephah, Epher, Hanoch, Abida and Eldaah.
All these were descendants of Keturah.

Descendants of Sarah

34Abraham was the father of Isaac.
The sons of Isaac:
Esau and Israel.

In what way was the earth divided in Peleg's time? (1:19)
Some speculate that this may refer to what is called continental drift—the dividing of the continents. Others think this was a division of people—either populations that migrated in opposite directions (as happened at the Tower of Babel, Gen. 11:1–9) or populations that divided in hostility against each other. Since *Peleg* also can mean *canal* or *channel,* some think the divided earth refers to a well-watered area such as Babylonia, perhaps where the waters of the Euphrates River were divided into an irrigation canal.

Why include concubines in a genealogy? (1:32)
Family-based cultures like the Israelites listed concubines, and including them was necessary to include the whole family. It also guaranteed a concubine's social and legal rights, though it listed her in a branch of the family with less status.

^a13 Or *of the Sidonians, the foremost*   ^b17 One Hebrew manuscript and some Septuagint manuscripts (see also Gen. 10:23); most Hebrew manuscripts do not have this line.   ^c19 *Peleg* means *division.*
^d22 Some Hebrew manuscripts and Syriac (see also Gen. 10:28); most Hebrew manuscripts *Ebal*   ^e24 Hebrew; some Septuagint manuscripts *Arphaxad, Cainan* (see also note at Gen. 11:10)

Esau's Sons

35The sons of Esau:
Eliphaz, Reuel, Jeush, Jalam and Korah.
36The sons of Eliphaz:
Teman, Omar, Zepho,[a] Gatam and Kenaz;
by Timna: Amalek.[b]
37The sons of Reuel:
Nahath, Zerah, Shammah and Mizzah.

The People of Seir in Edom

38The sons of Seir:
Lotan, Shobal, Zibeon, Anah, Dishon, Ezer and Di-
shan.
39The sons of Lotan:
Hori and Homam. Timna was Lotan's sister.
40The sons of Shobal:
Alvan,[c] Manahath, Ebal, Shepho and Onam.
The sons of Zibeon:
Aiah and Anah.
41The son of Anah:
Dishon.
The sons of Dishon:
Hemdan,[d] Eshban, Ithran and Keran.
42The sons of Ezer:
Bilhan, Zaavan and Akan.[e]
The sons of Dishan[f]:
Uz and Aran.

The Rulers of Edom

43These were the kings who reigned in Edom[D] before
any Israelite king reigned[g]:
Bela son of Beor, whose city was named Dinha-
bah.
44When Bela died, Jobab son of Zerah from Bozrah
succeeded him as king.
45When Jobab died, Husham from the land of the Te-
manites succeeded him as king.
46When Husham died, Hadad son of Bedad, who defeated Midian in the country of Moab, succeeded
him as king. His city was named Avith.
47When Hadad died, Samlah from Masrekah succeeded him as king.
48When Samlah died, Shaul from Rehoboth on the river[h] succeeded him as king.
49When Shaul died, Baal-Hanan son of Acbor succeeded him as king.
50When Baal-Hanan died, Hadad succeeded him as
king. His city was named Pau,[i] and his wife's
name was Mehetabel daughter of Matred, the
daughter of Me-Zahab. **51**Hadad also died.

**Why list nations other than Israel?
(1:43–54)**
The writer followed the pattern found in Genesis, where God's chosen people were listed after others. Including Edom's kings (who came
from the line of Esau, Jacob's brother) may
have revealed another perspective on God's
election: they were *not chosen*. Also, current
events may have caused the original readers of
Chronicles to have special interest in Edom.

---

[a]36 Many Hebrew manuscripts, some Septuagint manuscripts and
Syriac (see also Gen. 36:11); most Hebrew manuscripts *Zephi*
[b]36 Some Septuagint manuscripts (see also Gen. 36:12); Hebrew
Gatam, Kenaz, Timna and Amalek   [c]40 Many Hebrew manuscripts
and some Septuagint manuscripts (see also Gen. 36:23); most Hebrew
manuscripts *Alian*   [d]41 Many Hebrew manuscripts and some
Septuagint manuscripts (see also Gen. 36:26); most Hebrew
manuscripts *Hamran*   [e]42 Many Hebrew and Septuagint
manuscripts (see also Gen. 36:27); most Hebrew manuscripts *Zaavan,
Jaakan*   [f]42 Hebrew *Dishon*, a variant of *Dishan*   [g]43 Or *before
an Israelite king reigned over them*   [h]48 Possibly the Euphrates
[i]50 Many Hebrew manuscripts, some Septuagint manuscripts, Vulgate
and Syriac (see also Gen. 36:39); most Hebrew manuscripts *Pai*

The chiefs of Edom[D] were:
Timna, Alvah, Jetheth, [52]Oholibamah, Elah, Pinon, [53]Kenaz, Teman, Mibzar, [54]Magdiel and Iram. These were the chiefs of Edom.

Israel's Sons

2 These were the sons of Israel:
Reuben, Simeon, Levi, Judah, Issachar, Zebulun, [2]Dan, Joseph, Benjamin, Naphtali, Gad and Asher.

Judah

To Hezron's Sons

[3]The sons of Judah:
Er, Onan and Shelah. These three were born to him by a Canaanite woman, the daughter of Shua. Er, Judah's firstborn[D], was wicked in the LORD's sight; so the LORD put him to death[D]. [4]Tamar, Judah's daughter-in-law, bore him Perez and Zerah. Judah had five sons in all.

[5]The sons of Perez:
Hezron and Hamul.
[6]The sons of Zerah:
Zimri, Ethan, Heman, Calcol and Darda[a]—five in all.
[7]The son of Carmi:
Achar,[b] who brought trouble on Israel by violating the ban on taking devoted things.[c]
[8]The son of Ethan:
Azariah.
[9]The sons born to Hezron were:
Jerahmeel, Ram and Caleb.[d]

From Ram Son of Hezron

[10]Ram was the father of
Amminadab, and Amminadab the father of Nahshon, the leader of the people of Judah. [11]Nahshon was the father of Salmon,[e] Salmon the father of Boaz, [12]Boaz the father of Obed and Obed the father of Jesse.
[13]Jesse was the father of
Eliab his firstborn; the second son was Abinadab, the third Shimea, [14]the fourth Nethanel, the fifth Raddai, [15]the sixth Ozem and the seventh David. [16]Their sisters were Zeruiah and Abigail. Zeruiah's three sons were Abishai, Joab and Asahel. [17]Abigail was the mother of Amasa, whose father was Jether the Ishmaelite.

Caleb Son of Hezron

[18]Caleb son of Hezron had children by his wife Azubah (and by Jerioth). These were her sons: Jesher, Shobab and Ardon. [19]When Azubah died, Caleb married Ephrath, who bore him Hur. [20]Hur was the father of Uri, and Uri the father of Bezalel.
[21]Later, Hezron lay with the daughter of Makir the fa-

---

a6 Many Hebrew manuscripts, some Septuagint manuscripts and Syriac (see also 1 Kings 4:31); most Hebrew manuscripts *Dara*
b7 *Achar* means *trouble*; *Achar* is called *Achan* in Joshua.   *c7* The Hebrew term refers to the irrevocable giving over of things or persons to the LORD, often by totally destroying them.   *d9* Hebrew *Kelubai,* a variant of *Caleb*   *e11* Septuagint (see also Ruth 4:21); Hebrew *Salma*

How was a chief different from a king? (1:51)

Apparently there could be more than one chief at a time. This suggests that the chiefs were most likely key leaders under the king, in charge of certain regions or districts. It's also possible that they were leaders of tribes or clans.

Why list the offspring Judah had by his son's wife? (2:4)

See *Why was Tamar entitled to marry her brother-in-law?* (Gen. 38:14).

Why are David's sisters mentioned? (2:16)

Probably because their children played such central roles in the formation and development of the nation of Israel. Zeruiah's sons, David's nephews, supported him in battle as he rose to the throne. Joab served as the general of his army. Abigail's son, Amasa, became the general for David's son, Absalom, when he led the rebellion against his father. Later, Amasa was appointed commander over David's army —until he was treacherously murdered by Joab, his cousin and the man whom he replaced (2 Samuel 20:9–10).

Was it unusual to marry at 60 years old? (2:21)

Probably no more so than today. Hezron had been married before and had already fathered children (v. 9). Isaac was 40 years old when he married Rebekah (Gen. 25:20). Generally, fathers in ancient Hebrew culture made arrangements as to whom their sons and daughters would marry. Often the couples, especially the brides, were quite young, a custom that eventually prompted Jewish rabbis to set a minimum age of 12 for the wife and 13 for the husband.

ther of Gilead (he had married her when he was sixty years old), and she bore him Segub. **22**Segub was the father of Jair, who controlled twenty-three towns in Gilead. **23**(But Geshur and Aram captured Havvoth Jair,*a* as well as Kenath with its surrounding settlements—sixty towns.) All these were descendants of Makir the father of Gilead.

24After Hezron died in Caleb Ephrathah, Abijah the wife of Hezron bore him Ashhur the father*b* of Tekoa.

Jerahmeel Son of Hezron

25The sons of Jerahmeel the firstborn**D** of Hezron:
Ram his firstborn, Bunah, Oren, Ozem and*c* Ahijah. **26**Jerahmeel had another wife, whose name was Atarah; she was the mother of Onam.
27The sons of Ram the firstborn of Jerahmeel:
Maaz, Jamin and Eker.
28The sons of Onam:
Shammai and Jada.
The sons of Shammai:
Nadab and Abishur.
29Abishur's wife was named Abihail, who bore him Ahban and Molid.
30The sons of Nadab:
Seled and Appaim. Seled died without children.
31The son of Appaim:
Ishi, who was the father of Sheshan.
Sheshan was the father of Ahlai.
32The sons of Jada, Shammai's brother:
Jether and Jonathan. Jether died without children.
33The sons of Jonathan:
Peleth and Zaza.
These were the descendants of Jerahmeel.
34Sheshan had no sons—only daughters.
He had an Egyptian servant named Jarha. **35**Sheshan gave his daughter in marriage to his servant Jarha, and she bore him Attai.
36Attai was the father of Nathan,
Nathan the father of Zabad,
37Zabad the father of Ephlal,
Ephlal the father of Obed,
38Obed the father of Jehu,
Jehu the father of Azariah,
39Azariah the father of Helez,
Helez the father of Eleasah,
40Eleasah the father of Sismai,
Sismai the father of Shallum,
41Shallum the father of Jekamiah,
and Jekamiah the father of Elishama.

The Clans of Caleb

42The sons of Caleb the brother of Jerahmeel:
Mesha his firstborn, who was the father of Ziph, and his son Mareshah,*d* who was the father of Hebron.
43The sons of Hebron:
Korah, Tappuah, Rekem and Shema. **44**Shema was the father of Raham, and Raham the father of Jor-

Why mention that someone died without children? (2:32)

For two reasons: (1) to explain why none of Jether's sons were listed in the next section of the genealogy; (2) because having no children was seen as a great misfortune in Hebrew culture. Anyone reading this genealogy would be reminded that Jether was an unfortunate man.

Why have your daughter marry your slave? (2:34–35)

This was a way to keep your property and possessions within the family. Because Sheshan had no sons, he could bequeath the family land to his daughters (Num. 27:1–8). After marriage, however, control over the property would transfer to their husbands. Sheshan's other option was to designate his servant as his adopted heir—just as Abraham considered doing before he had a son of his own (Gen. 15:2–3). Sheshan apparently exercised both options, adopting his Egyptian servant, Jarha, and then giving his daughter in marriage to him.

---

a23 Or captured the settlements of Jair   *b24 Father may mean civic leader or military leader; also in verses 42, 45, 49-52 and possibly elsewhere.*   *c25 Or Oren and Ozem, by*   *d42 The meaning of the Hebrew for this phrase is uncertain.*

keam. Rekem was the father of Shammai. **45**The son of Shammai was Maon, and Maon was the father of Beth Zur.

46Caleb's concubine*D* Ephah was the mother of Haran, Moza and Gazez. Haran was the father of Gazez.

47The sons of Jahdai:

Regem, Jotham, Geshan, Pelet, Ephah and Shaaph.

48Caleb's concubine Maacah was the mother of Sheber and Tirhanah. **49**She also gave birth to Shaaph the father of Madmannah and to Sheva the father of Macbenah and Gibea. Caleb's daughter was Acsah. **50**These were the descendants of Caleb.

The sons of Hur the firstborn*D* of Ephrathah:

Shobal the father of Kiriath Jearim, **51**Salma the father of Bethlehem, and Hareph the father of Beth Gader.

52The descendants of Shobal the father of Kiriath Jearim were:

Haroeh, half the Manahathites, **53**and the clans of Kiriath Jearim: the Ithrites, Puthites, Shumathites and Mishraites. From these descended the Zorathites and Eshtaolites.

54The descendants of Salma:

Bethlehem, the Netophathites, Atroth Beth Joab, half the Manahathites, the Zorites, **55**and the clans of scribes*a* who lived at Jabez: the Tirathites, Shimeathites and Sucathites. These are the Kenites who came from Hammath, the father of the house of Recab.*b*

The Sons of David

3 These were the sons of David born to him in Hebron:

The firstborn was Amnon the son of Ahinoam of Jezreel;

the second, Daniel the son of Abigail of Carmel;

2the third, Absalom the son of Maacah daughter of Talmai king of Geshur;

the fourth, Adonijah the son of Haggith;

3the fifth, Shephatiah the son of Abital;

and the sixth, Ithream, by his wife Eglah.

4These six were born to David in Hebron, where he reigned seven years and six months.

David reigned in Jerusalem*D* thirty-three years, **5**and these were the children born to him there:

Shammua,*c* Shobab, Nathan and Solomon. These four were by Bathsheba*d* daughter of Ammiel. **6**There were also Ibhar, Elishua,*e* Eliphelet, **7**Nogah, Nepheg, Japhia, **8**Elishama, Eliada and Eliphelet—nine in all. **9**All these were the sons of David, besides his sons by his concubines. And Tamar was their sister.

The Kings of Judah

10Solomon's son was Rehoboam,

Abijah his son,

Asa his son,

Why are the sons of concubines included in this list? (2:46)

Family-based cultures such as the Israelites considered concubines and their children to be members of the family. Although a concubine had fewer privileges than a primary wife, being on the genealogical list guaranteed her and her children certain rights: proper care, including food and clothing, and freedom, in case of ill-treatment or neglect.

Is this Daniel the same person as in the book of Daniel? (3:1)

No. This was David's second son (called Kileab in 2 Samuel 3:2). He lived about 400 years before the prophet Daniel.

---

a55 Or *of the Sopherites*   *b55* Or *father of Beth Recab*
c5 Hebrew *Shimea,* a variant of *Shammua*   *d5* One Hebrew manuscript and Vulgate (see also Septuagint and 2 Samuel 11:3); most Hebrew manuscripts *Bathshua*   *e6* Two Hebrew manuscripts (see also 2 Samuel 5:15 and 1 Chron. 14:5); most Hebrew manuscripts *Elishama*

Why was Zedekiah listed as a successor of Jehoiakim and not a son? (3:16)

Because Zedekiah was Jehoiakim's uncle, not his son. During the closing days of Judah's history, the transition from one king to the next was sometimes made under less than ideal circumstances. In this case the king of Babylon conquered Jerusalem, took Jehoiachin captive to Babylon and set Zedekiah up as the puppet ruler. With the exile into Babylonia, the reign of Zedekiah—the last king of Judah—came to an end.

Why are the totals listed for some descendants and not for others? (3:22)

This may have been a stylistic technique—bringing closure to one part of the list before going on to the next. But why it is used on some occasions and not others is unclear. In v. 22, the total given is one more than the names listed, meaning perhaps that one name has been omitted from the list. Another explanation is that Shemaiah's sons are not listed and that this list of five are sons of Shecaniah. If so, there then would be six names given as sons of Shecaniah.

Jehoshaphat his son,
[11]Jehoram[a] his son,
Ahaziah his son,
Joash his son,
[12]Amaziah his son,
Azariah his son,
Jotham his son,
[13]Ahaz his son,
Hezekiah his son,
Manasseh his son,
[14]Amon his son,
Josiah his son.
[15]The sons of Josiah:
Johanan the firstborn[D],
Jehoiakim the second son,
Zedekiah the third,
Shallum the fourth.
[16]The successors of Jehoiakim:
Jehoiachin[b] his son,
and Zedekiah.

The Royal Line After the Exile

[17]The descendants of Jehoiachin the captive:
Shealtiel his son, [18]Malkiram, Pedaiah, Shenazzar, Jekamiah, Hoshama and Nedabiah.
[19]The sons of Pedaiah:
Zerubbabel and Shimei.
The sons of Zerubbabel:
Meshullam and Hananiah.
Shelomith was their sister.
[20]There were also five others:
Hashubah, Ohel, Berekiah, Hasadiah and Jushab-Hesed.
[21]The descendants of Hananiah:
Pelatiah and Jeshaiah, and the sons of Rephaiah, of Arnan, of Obadiah and of Shecaniah.
[22]The descendants of Shecaniah:
Shemaiah and his sons:
Hattush, Igal, Bariah, Neariah and Shaphat—six in all.
[23]The sons of Neariah:
Elioenai, Hizkiah and Azrikam—three in all.
[24]The sons of Elioenai:
Hodaviah, Eliashib, Pelaiah, Akkub, Johanan, Delaiah and Anani—seven in all.

Other Clans of Judah

4 The descendants of Judah:
Perez, Hezron, Carmi, Hur and Shobal.
[2]Reaiah son of Shobal was the father of Jahath, and Jahath the father of Ahumai and Lahad. These were the clans of the Zorathites.
[3]These were the sons[c] of Etam:
Jezreel, Ishma and Idbash. Their sister was named Hazzelelponi. [4]Penuel was the father of Gedor, and Ezer the father of Hushah.
These were the descendants of Hur, the firstborn of Ephrathah and father[d] of Bethlehem.

[a]11 Hebrew *Joram*, a variant of *Jehoram*   [b]16 Hebrew *Jeconiah*, a variant of *Jehoiachin*; also in verse 17   [c]3 Some Septuagint manuscripts (see also Vulgate); Hebrew *father*   [d]4 *Father* may mean *civic leader* or *military leader*; also in verses 12, 14, 17, 18 and possibly elsewhere.

⁵Ashhur the father of Tekoa had two wives, Helah and Naarah. ⁶Naarah bore him Ahuzzam, Hepher, Temeni and Haahashtari. These were the descendants of Naarah.
⁷The sons of Helah:
Zereth, Zohar, Ethnan, ⁸and Koz, who was the father of Anub and Hazzobebah and of the clans of Aharhel son of Harum.

⁹Jabez was more honorable than his brothers. His mother had named him Jabez,ᵃ saying, "I gave birth to him in pain." ¹⁰Jabez cried out to the God of Israel, "Oh, that you would bless me and enlarge my territory! Let your hand be with me, and keep me from harm so that I will be free from pain." And God granted his request.

¹¹Kelub, Shuhah's brother, was the father of Mehir, who was the father of Eshton. ¹²Eshton was the father of Beth Rapha, Paseah and Tehinnah the father of Ir Nahash.ᵇ These were the men of Recah.

¹³The sons of Kenaz:
Othniel and Seraiah.
The sons of Othniel:
Hathath and Meonothai.ᶜ ¹⁴Meonothai was the father of Ophrah.
Seraiah was the father of Joab,
the father of Ge Harashim.ᵈ It was called this because its people were craftsmen.
¹⁵The sons of Caleb son of Jephunneh:
Iru, Elah and Naam.
The son of Elah:
Kenaz.
¹⁶The sons of Jehallelel:
Ziph, Ziphah, Tiria and Asarel.
¹⁷The sons of Ezrah:
Jether, Mered, Epher and Jalon. One of Mered's wives gave birth to Miriam, Shammai and Ishbah the father of Eshtemoa. ¹⁸(His Judean wife gave birth to Jered the father of Gedor, Heber the father of Soco, and Jekuthiel the father of Zanoah.) These were the children of Pharaoh's daughter Bithiah, whom Mered had married.
¹⁹The sons of Hodiah's wife, the sister of Naham:
the father of Keilah the Garmite, and Eshtemoa the Maacathite.
²⁰The sons of Shimon:
Amnon, Rinnah, Ben-Hanan and Tilon.
The descendants of Ishi:
Zoheth and Ben-Zoheth.
²¹The sons of Shelah son of Judah:
Er the father of Lecah, Laadah the father of Mareshah and the clans of the linen workers at Beth Ashbea, ²²Jokim, the men of Cozeba, and Joash and Saraph, who ruled in Moab and Jashubi Lehem. (These records are from ancient times.) ²³They were the potters who lived at Netaim and Gederah; they stayed there and worked for the king.

Why give Jabez extra attention? (4:9-10)
It was not uncommon to insert historical comments in genealogies. But why comment on Jabez? To the Hebrew's way of thinking, Jabez was a "born loser." His name literally meant *pain*. But in spite of this dysfunctional beginning, he was honored because of his relationship with God. This was a valuable lesson for a people struggling with their own identity. See article: *Why read an ancient list of faceless names?* (1:1).

SCRIPTURE LINK (4:13) *Othniel*
See Judges 3:9,11.

How could an Israelite slave marry Pharaoh's daughter? (4:17-18)
Apparently this happened long before Moses' time, when Israel was still in favor with Egypt. It also indicated that Mered was a man of some distinction.

ᵃ9 *Jabez* sounds like the Hebrew for *pain*.   ᵇ12 Or *of the city of Nahash*   ᶜ13 Some Septuagint manuscripts and Vulgate; Hebrew does not have *and Meonothai*.   ᵈ14 *Ge Harashim* means *valley of craftsmen*.

Simeon

²⁴The descendants of Simeon:

Nemuel, Jamin, Jarib, Zerah and Shaul;

²⁵Shallum was Shaul's son, Mibsam his son and Mishma his son.

²⁶The descendants of Mishma:

Hammuel his son, Zaccur his son and Shimei his son.

²⁷Shimei had sixteen sons and six daughters, but his brothers did not have many children; so their entire clan did not become as numerous as the people of Judah. ²⁸They lived in Beersheba, Moladah, Hazar Shual, ²⁹Bilhah, Ezem, Tolad, ³⁰Bethuel, Hormah, Ziklag, ³¹Beth Marcaboth, Hazar Susim, Beth Biri and Shaaraim. These were their towns until the reign of David. ³²Their surrounding villages were Etam, Ain, Rimmon, Token and Ashan—five towns— ³³and all the villages around these towns as far as Baalath.ᵃ These were their settlements. And they kept a genealogical record.

³⁴Meshobab, Jamlech, Joshah son of Amaziah, ³⁵Joel, Jehu son of Joshibiah, the son of Seraiah, the son of Asiel, ³⁶also Elioenai, Jaakobah, Jeshohaiah, Asaiah, Adiel, Jesimiel, Benaiah, ³⁷and Ziza son of Shiphi, the son of Allon, the son of Jedaiah, the son of Shimri, the son of Shemaiah.

³⁸The men listed above by name were leaders of their clans. Their families increased greatly, ³⁹and they went to the outskirts of Gedor to the east of the valley in search of pasture for their flocks. ⁴⁰They found rich, good pasture, and the land was spacious, peaceful and quiet. Some Hamites had lived there formerly.

⁴¹The men whose names were listed came in the days of Hezekiah king of Judah. They attacked the Hamites in their dwellings and also the Meunites who were there and completely destroyedᵇ them, as is evident to this day. Then they settled in their place, because there was pasture for their flocks. ⁴²And five hundred of these Simeonites, led by Pelatiah, Neariah, Rephaiah and Uzziel, the sons of Ishi, invaded the hill country of Seir. ⁴³They killed the remaining Amalekites who had escaped, and they have lived there to this day.

Reuben

5 The sons of Reuben the firstbornᴰ of Israel (he was the firstborn, but when he defiled his father's marriage bed, his rights as firstborn were given to the sons of Joseph son of Israel; so he could not be listed in the genealogical record in accordance with his birthrightᴰ, ²and though Judah was the strongest of his brothers and a ruler came from him, the rights of the firstborn belonged to Joseph)— ³the sons of Reuben the firstborn of Israel:

Hanoch, Pallu, Hezron and Carmi.

⁴The descendants of Joel:

Shemaiah his son, Gog his son,
Shimei his son, ⁵Micah his son,
Reaiah his son, Baal his son,
⁶and Beerah his son, whom Tiglath-Pileserᶜ king

As a firstborn son, what rights would Reuben have had? (5:1)

The firstborn son was typically assigned two things: clan leadership and covenant blessing. He succeeded his father as head of the family or tribe and received twice as much of his father's property as any of his brothers. His younger siblings were under his authority and he cared for his mother and unmarried sisters, as if he were their father. Some say Reuben's actions also may have lost the priesthood for his descendants, but that is highly speculative.

Why didn't the second in line get what Reuben lost? (5:2)

The second and third sons, Simeon and Levi, were not permitted to lead the Israelites because their vengeance had endangered the clan's safety (Gen. 34:25,30). Judah, Jacob's fourth son, became the clan's leader. Joseph's sons received the covenant blessings, perhaps because Joseph was the firstborn of Jacob's favorite wife, Rachel. The priesthood later went to the tribe of Levi, maybe because Levi's wrath represented God's response to sin or perhaps simply because Moses and Aaron, chosen for a special purpose, were Levites.

ᵃ33 Some Septuagint manuscripts (see also Joshua 19:8); Hebrew *Baal*   ᵇ41 The Hebrew term refers to the irrevocable giving over of things or persons to the LORD, often by totally destroying them.   ᶜ6 Hebrew *Tilgath-Pilneser*, a variant of *Tiglath-Pileser*; also in verse 26

of Assyria took into exile^D. Beerah was a leader of the Reubenites.

⁷Their relatives by clans, listed according to their genealogical records:

Jeiel the chief, Zechariah, ⁸and Bela son of Azaz, the son of Shema, the son of Joel. They settled in the area from Aroer to Nebo and Baal Meon. ⁹To the east they occupied the land up to the edge of the desert that extends to the Euphrates River, because their livestock had increased in Gilead.

¹⁰During Saul's reign they waged war against the Hagrites, who were defeated at their hands; they occupied the dwellings of the Hagrites throughout the entire region east of Gilead.

Gad

¹¹The Gadites lived next to them in Bashan, as far as Salecah:

¹²Joel was the chief, Shapham the second, then Janai and Shaphat, in Bashan.

¹³Their relatives, by families, were:

Michael, Meshullam, Sheba, Jorai, Jacan, Zia and Eber—seven in all.

¹⁴These were the sons of Abihail son of Huri, the son of Jaroah, the son of Gilead, the son of Michael, the son of Jeshishai, the son of Jahdo, the son of Buz.

¹⁵Ahi son of Abdiel, the son of Guni, was head of their family.

¹⁶The Gadites lived in Gilead, in Bashan and its outlying villages, and on all the pasturelands of Sharon as far as they extended.

¹⁷All these were entered in the genealogical records during the reigns of Jotham king of Judah and Jeroboam king of Israel.

¹⁸The Reubenites, the Gadites and the half-tribe of Manasseh had 44,760 men ready for military service—able-bodied men who could handle shield and sword, who could use a bow, and who were trained for battle. ¹⁹They waged war against the Hagrites, Jetur, Naphish and Nodab. ²⁰They were helped in fighting them, and God handed the Hagrites and all their allies over to them, because they cried out to him during the battle. He answered their prayers, because they trusted in him. ²¹They seized the livestock of the Hagrites—fifty thousand camels, two hundred fifty thousand sheep and two thousand donkeys. They also took one hundred thousand people captive, ²²and many others fell slain, because the battle was God's. And they occupied the land until the exile.

The Half-Tribe of Manasseh

²³The people of the half-tribe of Manasseh were numerous; they settled in the land from Bashan to Baal Hermon, that is, to Senir (Mount Hermon).

²⁴These were the heads of their families: Epher, Ishi, Eliel, Azriel, Jeremiah, Hodaviah and Jahdiel. They were brave warriors, famous men, and heads of their families. ²⁵But they were unfaithful to the God of their fathers and prostituted themselves to the gods of the peoples of the land, whom God had destroyed before them. ²⁶So the God of Israel stirred up the spirit of Pul king of Assyria (that is, Tiglath-Pileser king of Assyria), who took the Reubenites, the Gadites and the half-tribe of Manasseh into exile. He

Why would these tribes want 100,000 captives? (5:21)

Probably to use as slaves, just as Egypt had earlier used Israel. It was common practice in the ancient Middle East to decimate enemy populations by forcing them into slavery. Although the writer does not mention slavery here, most slaves in Israel were POWs. Compared with slaves elsewhere during that era, those in Israel were relatively well-treated because they were protected by Mosaic Law.

Did God inspire the king of Assyria to go to war? (5:26)

Yes, but Tiglath-Pileser probably had no idea God was using him as an instrument to punish the Israelites. The king likely thought his military power and strategy along with his own gods had given him victory. However, God was working behind the scenes, formulating the concept and finalizing the conclusion of Assyria's battles. This is a theme throughout Chronicles: God blesses those who trust him and punishes those who follow other gods. See article: *Why does a merciful God punish anyone?* (Nahum 2:13).

took them to Halah, Habor, Hara and the river of Gozan, where they are to this day.

Levi

6 The sons of Levi:
Gershon, Kohath and Merari.
²The sons of Kohath:
Amram, Izhar, Hebron and Uzziel.
³The children of Amram:
Aaron, Moses and Miriam.
The sons of Aaron:
Nadab, Abihu, Eleazar and Ithamar.
⁴Eleazar was the father of Phinehas,
Phinehas the father of Abishua,
⁵Abishua the father of Bukki,
Bukki the father of Uzzi,
⁶Uzzi the father of Zerahiah,
Zerahiah the father of Meraioth,
⁷Meraioth the father of Amariah,
Amariah the father of Ahitub,
⁸Ahitub the father of Zadok,
Zadok the father of Ahimaaz,
⁹Ahimaaz the father of Azariah,
Azariah the father of Johanan,
¹⁰Johanan the father of Azariah (it was he who served as priest^D in the temple Solomon built in Jerusalem^D),
¹¹Azariah the father of Amariah,
Amariah the father of Ahitub,
¹²Ahitub the father of Zadok,
Zadok the father of Shallum,
¹³Shallum the father of Hilkiah,
Hilkiah the father of Azariah,
¹⁴Azariah the father of Seraiah,
and Seraiah the father of Jehozadak.
¹⁵Jehozadak was deported when the LORD sent Judah and Jerusalem into exile by the hand of Nebuchadnezzar.

¹⁶The sons of Levi:
Gershon,^a Kohath and Merari.
¹⁷These are the names of the sons of Gershon:
Libni and Shimei.
¹⁸The sons of Kohath:
Amram, Izhar, Hebron and Uzziel.
¹⁹The sons of Merari:
Mahli and Mushi.
These are the clans of the Levites^D listed according to their fathers:
²⁰Of Gershon:
Libni his son, Jehath his son,
Zimmah his son, ²¹Joah his son,
Iddo his son, Zerah his son
and Jeatherai his son.
²²The descendants of Kohath:
Amminadab his son, Korah his son,
Assir his son, ²³Elkanah his son,
Ebiasaph his son, Assir his son,
²⁴Tahath his son, Uriel his son,
Uzziah his son and Shaul his son.
²⁵The descendants of Elkanah:

SCRIPTURE LINK (6:3)
The birth of Moses is told in Exodus 2.

---

a 16 Hebrew *Gershom,* a variant of *Gershon;* also in verses 17, 20, 43, 62 and 71

Amasai, Ahimoth,
26Elkanah his son,[a] Zophai his son,
Nahath his son, **27**Eliab his son,
Jeroham his son, Elkanah his son
and Samuel his son.[b]
28The sons of Samuel:
Joel[c] the firstborn[D]
and Abijah the second son.
29The descendants of Merari:
Mahli, Libni his son,
Shimei his son, Uzzah his son,
30Shimea his son, Haggiah his son
and Asaiah his son.

The Temple Musicians

31These are the men David put in charge of the music in the house of the LORD after the ark came to rest there. **32**They ministered with music before the tabernacle[D], the Tent of Meeting[D], until Solomon built the temple of the LORD in Jerusalem[D]. They performed their duties according to the regulations laid down for them.

33Here are the men who served, together with their sons:

From the Kohathites:
Heman, the musician,
the son of Joel, the son of Samuel,
34the son of Elkanah, the son of Jeroham,
the son of Eliel, the son of Toah,
35the son of Zuph, the son of Elkanah,
the son of Mahath, the son of Amasai,
36the son of Elkanah, the son of Joel,
the son of Azariah, the son of Zephaniah,
37the son of Tahath, the son of Assir,
the son of Ebiasaph, the son of Korah,
38the son of Izhar, the son of Kohath,
the son of Levi, the son of Israel;
39and Heman's associate Asaph, who served at his right hand:
Asaph son of Berekiah, the son of Shimea,
40the son of Michael, the son of Baaseiah,[d]
the son of Malkijah, **41**the son of Ethni,
the son of Zerah, the son of Adaiah,
42the son of Ethan, the son of Zimmah,
the son of Shimei, **43**the son of Jahath,
the son of Gershon, the son of Levi;
44and from their associates, the Merarites, at his left hand:
Ethan son of Kishi, the son of Abdi,
the son of Malluch, **45**the son of Hashabiah,
the son of Amaziah, the son of Hilkiah,
46the son of Amzi, the son of Bani,
the son of Shemer, **47**the son of Mahli,
the son of Mushi, the son of Merari,
the son of Levi.

48Their fellow Levites[D] were assigned to all the other

Why make a specific list of the musicians? (6:31)

This genealogy proved their pure origins from the tribe of Levi and legitimized their role as worship leaders. Remarkably, nothing is mentioned about musical talent being required, though we may assume they had musical abilities. They were first of all Levites—like the priests and temple caretakers who served in other capacities. Each of the three clans of Levi provided musicians for the temple.

Asaph (6:39)

Sometimes called "the other psalmist," since several psalms are attributed to him (Psalms 50, 73–83). Asaph sounded cymbals when the ark was finally brought from the house of Obed-Edom (15:16–19) and was assigned the permanent office of sounding cymbals at worship in Jerusalem. Asaph performed and taught music. He also composed poetry and like other Levitical musicians, was considered to hold a prophetic role (25:1; 2 Chron. 29:30).

---

a26 Some Hebrew manuscripts, Septuagint and Syriac; most Hebrew manuscripts *Ahimoth 26and Elkanah. The sons of Elkanah:*
b27 Some Septuagint manuscripts (see also 1 Samuel 1:19,20 and 1 Chron. 6:33,34); Hebrew does not have *and Samuel his son.*
c28 Some Septuagint manuscripts and Syriac (see also 1 Samuel 8:2 and 1 Chron. 6:33); Hebrew does not have *Joel.*   *d40* Most Hebrew manuscripts; some Hebrew manuscripts, one Septuagint manuscript and Syriac *Maaseiah*

duties of the tabernacle[D], the house of God. **49**But Aaron and his descendants were the ones who presented offerings on the altar of burnt offering[D] and on the altar of incense[D] in connection with all that was done in the Most Holy Place[D], making atonement[D] for Israel, in accordance with all that Moses the servant of God had commanded.

50These were the descendants of Aaron:
Eleazar his son, Phinehas his son,
Abishua his son, **51**Bukki his son,
Uzzi his son, Zerahiah his son,
52Meraioth his son, Amariah his son,
Ahitub his son, **53**Zadok his son
and Ahimaaz his son.

Why list the towns of the Levites? (6:54)

The Levites were a reminder that God had given the promised land to Israel. Since the Levites inherited no specific territory like the other tribes but were scattered in towns throughout the land, the Israelites could pay their tithes to the Levites—living symbols of God in the land. Giving a portion of what they earned from the land was a way the people could acknowledge that the land belonged to God.

SCRIPTURE LINK (6:57) *City of refuge*
See Deut. 19:1–10.

54These were the locations of their settlements allotted as their territory (they were assigned to the descendants of Aaron who were from the Kohathite clan, because the first lot was for them):

55They were given Hebron in Judah with its surrounding pasturelands. **56**But the fields and villages around the city were given to Caleb son of Jephunneh.

57So the descendants of Aaron were given Hebron (a city of refuge), and Libnah,[a] Jattir, Eshtemoa, **58**Hilen, Debir, **59**Ashan, Juttah[b] and Beth Shemesh, together with their pasturelands. **60**And from the tribe of Benjamin they were given Gibeon,[c] Geba, Alemeth and Anathoth, together with their pasturelands.

These towns, which were distributed among the Kohathite clans, were thirteen in all.

61The rest of Kohath's descendants were allotted ten towns from the clans of half the tribe of Manasseh.

62The descendants of Gershon, clan by clan, were allotted thirteen towns from the tribes of Issachar, Asher and Naphtali, and from the part of the tribe of Manasseh that is in Bashan.

63The descendants of Merari, clan by clan, were allotted twelve towns from the tribes of Reuben, Gad and Zebulun.

64So the Israelites gave the Levites[D] these towns and their pasturelands. **65**From the tribes of Judah, Simeon and Benjamin they allotted the previously named towns.

66Some of the Kohathite clans were given as their territory towns from the tribe of Ephraim.

67In the hill country of Ephraim they were given Shechem (a city of refuge), and Gezer,[d] **68**Jokmeam, Beth Horon, **69**Aijalon and Gath Rimmon, together with their pasturelands.

70And from half the tribe of Manasseh the Israelites gave Aner and Bileam, together with their pasturelands, to the rest of the Kohathite clans.

71The Gershonites received the following:
From the clan of the half-tribe of Manasseh
they received Golan in Bashan and also Ashtaroth, together with their pasturelands;
72from the tribe of Issachar

---

[a]57 See Joshua 21:13; Hebrew *given the cities of refuge: Hebron, Libnah.*   [b]59 Syriac (see also Septuagint and Joshua 21:16); Hebrew does not have *Juttah.*   [c]60 See Joshua 21:17; Hebrew does not have *Gibeon.*   [d]67 See Joshua 21:21; Hebrew *given the cities of refuge: Shechem, Gezer.*

they received Kedesh, Daberath, [73]Ramoth and Anem, together with their pasturelands;

[74]from the tribe of Asher
    they received Mashal, Abdon, [75]Hukok and Rehob, together with their pasturelands;

[76]and from the tribe of Naphtali
    they received Kedesh in Galilee, Hammon and Kiriathaim, together with their pasturelands.

[77]The Merarites (the rest of the Levites[D]) received the following:
    From the tribe of Zebulun
    they received Jokneam, Kartah,[a] Rimmono and Tabor, together with their pasturelands;

[78]from the tribe of Reuben across the Jordan east of Jericho[D]
    they received Bezer in the desert, Jahzah, [79]Kedemoth and Mephaath, together with their pasturelands;

[80]and from the tribe of Gad
    they received Ramoth in Gilead, Mahanaim, [81]Heshbon and Jazer, together with their pasturelands.

Issachar

7 The sons of Issachar:
    Tola, Puah, Jashub and Shimron—four in all.
[2]The sons of Tola:
    Uzzi, Rephaiah, Jeriel, Jahmai, Ibsam and Samuel—heads of their families. During the reign of David, the descendants of Tola listed as fighting men in their genealogy[D] numbered 22,600.
[3]The son of Uzzi:
    Izrahiah.
    The sons of Izrahiah:
    Michael, Obadiah, Joel and Isshiah. All five of them were chiefs. [4]According to their family genealogy, they had 36,000 men ready for battle, for they had many wives and children.
[5]The relatives who were fighting men belonging to all the clans of Issachar, as listed in their genealogy, were 87,000 in all.

Benjamin

[6]Three sons of Benjamin:
    Bela, Beker and Jediael.
[7]The sons of Bela:
    Ezbon, Uzzi, Uzziel, Jerimoth and Iri, heads of families—five in all. Their genealogical record listed 22,034 fighting men.
[8]The sons of Beker:
    Zemirah, Joash, Eliezer, Elioenai, Omri, Jeremoth, Abijah, Anathoth and Alemeth. All these were the sons of Beker. [9]Their genealogical record listed the heads of families and 20,200 fighting men.
[10]The son of Jediael:
    Bilhan.
    The sons of Bilhan:
    Jeush, Benjamin, Ehud, Kenaanah, Zethan, Tarshish and Ahishahar. [11]All these sons of Jediael

Why were pasturelands specifically given with towns? (6:76)

Though people lived in towns and villages, their society remained primarily agricultural. Each morning they would leave their towns and villages to work in their fields or to herd their livestock. The land necessary to practice these occupations was considered part of the territory for each town. See *How can towns have villages?* (Joshua 19:15).

Why list the fighting men? (7:2)

See *What was wrong with taking a census?* (21:1).

---

a 77 See Septuagint and Joshua 21:34; Hebrew does not have *Jokneam, Kartah.*

were heads of families. There were 17,200 fighting men ready to go out to war. [12]The Shuppites and Huppites were the descendants of Ir, and the Hushites the descendants of Aher.

Naphtali

[13]The sons of Naphtali:

Jahziel, Guni, Jezer and Shillem[a]—the descendants of Bilhah.

Manasseh

[14]The descendants of Manasseh:

Asriel was his descendant through his Aramean concubine[D]. She gave birth to Makir the father of Gilead. [15]Makir took a wife from among the Huppites and Shuppites. His sister's name was Maacah.

Another descendant was named Zelophehad, who had only daughters.

[16]Makir's wife Maacah gave birth to a son and named him Peresh. His brother was named Sheresh, and his sons were Ulam and Rakem.

[17]The son of Ulam:

Bedan.

These were the sons of Gilead son of Makir, the son of Manasseh. [18]His sister Hammoleketh gave birth to Ishhod, Abiezer and Mahlah. [19]The sons of Shemida were:

Ahian, Shechem, Likhi and Aniam.

Ephraim

[20]The descendants of Ephraim:

Shuthelah, Bered his son,
Tahath his son, Eleadah his son,
Tahath his son, [21]Zabad his son
and Shuthelah his son.

Ezer and Elead were killed by the native-born men of Gath, when they went down to seize their livestock. [22]Their father Ephraim mourned for them many days, and his relatives came to comfort him. [23]Then he lay with his wife again, and she became pregnant and gave birth to a son. He named him Beriah,[b] because there had been misfortune in his family. [24]His daughter was Sheerah, who built Lower and Upper Beth Horon as well as Uzzen Sheerah. [25]Rephah was his son, Resheph his son,[c]
Telah his son, Tahan his son,
[26]Ladan his son, Ammihud his son,
Elishama his son, [27]Nun his son
and Joshua his son.

[28]Their lands and settlements included Bethel and its surrounding villages, Naaran to the east, Gezer and its villages to the west, and Shechem and its villages all the way to Ayyah and its villages. [29]Along the borders of Manasseh were Beth Shan, Taanach, Megiddo and Dor, together with their villages. The descendants of Joseph son of Israel lived in these towns.

Was it normal for a woman to take charge of a construction project in those days? (7:24)

No. Sheerah, whose name meant *kinswoman*, must have been an outstanding woman to have been mentioned at all, let alone by name, in this patriarchal society. Her supervision of a construction project, however, may not be entirely unique (see Prov. 31:10–31). Still, little is known of Sheerah.

[a]13 Some Hebrew and Septuagint manuscripts (see also Gen. 46:24 and Num. 26:49); most Hebrew manuscripts *Shallum*   [b]23 *Beriah* sounds like the Hebrew for *misfortune.*   [c]25 Some Septuagint manuscripts; Hebrew does not have *his son.*

Asher

30The sons of Asher:

Imnah, Ishvah, Ishvi and Beriah. Their sister was Serah.

31The sons of Beriah:

Heber and Malkiel, who was the father of Birzaith.

32Heber was the father of Japhlet, Shomer and Hotham and of their sister Shua.

33The sons of Japhlet:

Pasach, Bimhal and Ashvath.

These were Japhlet's sons.

34The sons of Shomer:

Ahi, Rohgah,*a* Hubbah and Aram.

35The sons of his brother Helem:

Zophah, Imna, Shelesh and Amal.

36The sons of Zophah:

Suah, Harnepher, Shual, Beri, Imrah, **37**Bezer, Hod, Shamma, Shilshah, Ithran*b* and Beera.

38The sons of Jether:

Jephunneh, Pispah and Ara.

39The sons of Ulla:

Arah, Hanniel and Rizia.

40All these were descendants of Asher—heads of families, choice men, brave warriors and outstanding leaders. The number of men ready for battle, as listed in their genealogy*D*, was 26,000.

The Genealogy of Saul the Benjamite

8 Benjamin was the father of Bela his firstborn*D*, Ashbel the second son, Aharah the third, **2**Nohah the fourth and Rapha the fifth.

3The sons of Bela were:

Addar, Gera, Abihud,*c* **4**Abishua, Naaman, Ahoah, **5**Gera, Shephuphan and Huram.

6These were the descendants of Ehud, who were heads of families of those living in Geba and were deported to Manahath:

7Naaman, Ahijah, and Gera, who deported them and who was the father of Uzza and Ahihud.

8Sons were born to Shaharaim in Moab after he had divorced his wives Hushim and Baara. **9**By his wife Hodesh he had Jobab, Zibia, Mesha, Malcam, **10**Jeuz, Sakia and Mirmah. These were his sons, heads of families. **11**By Hushim he had Abitub and Elpaal.

12The sons of Elpaal:

Eber, Misham, Shemed (who built Ono and Lod with its surrounding villages), **13**and Beriah and Shema, who were heads of families of those living in Aijalon and who drove out the inhabitants of Gath.

14Ahio, Shashak, Jeremoth, **15**Zebadiah, Arad, Eder, **16**Michael, Ishpah and Joha were the sons of Beriah.

17Zebadiah, Meshullam, Hizki, Heber, **18**Ishmerai, Izliah and Jobab were the sons of Elpaal.

19Jakim, Zicri, Zabdi, **20**Elienai, Zillethai, Eliel, **21**Adaiah, Beraiah and Shimrath were the sons of Shimei.

22Ishpan, Eber, Eliel, **23**Abdon, Zicri, Hanan, **24**Hanani-

Why list divorced wives? (8:8)
There is no way to know why these divorced wives are included in this list. If Shaharaim divorced them because they failed to bear children, he was breaking Mosaic Law which allowed divorce only when a husband found "uncleanness" in his wife (Deut. 24:1). They may have been listed to maintain their legal rights. See *Why include concubines in a genealogy?* (1:32).

---

*a*34 Or *of his brother Shomer: Rohgah*   *b*37 Possibly a variant of *Jether*   *c*3 Or *Gera the father of Ehud*

ah, Elam, Anthothijah, **25**Iphdeiah and Penuel
were the sons of Shashak.

26Shamsherai, Shehariah, Athaliah, **27**Jaareshiah, Elijah and Zicri were the sons of Jeroham.

28All these were heads of families, chiefs as listed in
their genealogy^D, and they lived in Jerusalem^D.

29Jeiel^a the father^b of Gibeon lived in Gibeon.
His wife's name was Maacah, **30**and his firstborn^D
son was Abdon, followed by Zur, Kish, Baal,
Ner,^c Nadab, **31**Gedor, Ahio, Zeker **32**and Mikloth,
who was the father of Shimeah. They too lived
near their relatives in Jerusalem.

33Ner was the father of Kish, Kish the father of Saul,
and Saul the father of Jonathan, Malki-Shua, Abinadab and Esh-Baal.^d

34The son of Jonathan:
Merib-Baal,^e who was the father of Micah.

35The sons of Micah:
Pithon, Melech, Tarea and Ahaz.

36Ahaz was the father of Jehoaddah, Jehoaddah was
the father of Alemeth, Azmaveth and Zimri, and
Zimri was the father of Moza. **37**Moza was the father of Binea; Raphah was his son, Eleasah his son
and Azel his son.

38Azel had six sons, and these were their names:
Azrikam, Bokeru, Ishmael, Sheariah, Obadiah and
Hanan. All these were the sons of Azel.

39The sons of his brother Eshek:
Ulam his firstborn, Jeush the second son and
Eliphelet the third. **40**The sons of Ulam were brave
warriors who could handle the bow. They had
many sons and grandsons—150 in all.
All these were the descendants of Benjamin.

The book of the kings of Israel (9:1)
This may be a reference to the books of 1 and
2 Kings. The writer of Chronicles certainly used
these books as a resource, among many other
sources which have since disappeared including prophetic books such as the records of
Samuel, Nathan and Gad (29:29) and official
court records such as Jehu's in the book of the
kings of Israel (2 Chron. 20:34).

9 All Israel was listed in the genealogies recorded in
the book of the kings of Israel.

The People in Jerusalem

The people of Judah were taken captive to Babylon because of their unfaithfulness. **2**Now the first to resettle on
their own property in their own towns were some Israelites, priests^D, Levites^D and temple servants.

3Those from Judah, from Benjamin, and from Ephraim
and Manasseh who lived in Jerusalem were:

4Uthai son of Ammihud, the son of Omri, the son of
Imri, the son of Bani, a descendant of Perez son of
Judah.

5Of the Shilonites:
Asaiah the firstborn and his sons.

6Of the Zerahites:
Jeuel.
The people from Judah numbered 690.

7Of the Benjamites:
Sallu son of Meshullam, the son of Hodaviah, the
son of Hassenuah;
8Ibneiah son of Jeroham; Elah son of Uzzi, the son
of Micri; and Meshullam son of Shephatiah, the
son of Reuel, the son of Ibnijah.

^a29 Some Septuagint manuscripts (see also 1 Chron. 9:35); Hebrew
does not have *Jeiel*.　　^b29 *Father* may mean *civic leader* or *military
leader.*　　^c30 Some Septuagint manuscripts (see also 1 Chron. 9:36);
Hebrew does not have *Ner.*　　^d33 Also known as *Ish-Bosheth*
^e34 Also known as *Mephibosheth*

9The people from Benjamin, as listed in their genealogy[D], numbered 956. All these men were heads of their families.

10Of the priests[D]:

Jedaiah; Jehoiarib; Jakin;

11Azariah son of Hilkiah, the son of Meshullam, the son of Zadok, the son of Meraioth, the son of Ahitub, the official in charge of the house of God;

12Adaiah son of Jeroham, the son of Pashhur, the son of Malkijah; and Maasai son of Adiel, the son of Jahzerah, the son of Meshullam, the son of Meshillemith, the son of Immer.

13The priests, who were heads of families, numbered 1,760. They were able men, responsible for ministering in the house of God.

14Of the Levites[D]:

Shemaiah son of Hasshub, the son of Azrikam, the son of Hashabiah, a Merarite; **15**Bakbakkar, Heresh, Galal and Mattaniah son of Mica, the son of Zicri, the son of Asaph; **16**Obadiah son of Shemaiah, the son of Galal, the son of Jeduthun; and Berekiah son of Asa, the son of Elkanah, who lived in the villages of the Netophathites.

17The gatekeepers:

Shallum, Akkub, Talmon, Ahiman and their brothers, Shallum their chief **18**being stationed at the King's Gate on the east, up to the present time. These were the gatekeepers belonging to the camp of the Levites. **19**Shallum son of Kore, the son of Ebiasaph, the son of Korah, and his fellow gatekeepers from his family (the Korahites) were responsible for guarding the thresholds of the Tent[a] just as their fathers had been responsible for guarding the entrance to the dwelling of the LORD. **20**In earlier times Phinehas son of Eleazar was in charge of the gatekeepers, and the LORD was with him. **21**Zechariah son of Meshelemiah was the gatekeeper at the entrance to the Tent of Meeting.

22Altogether, those chosen to be gatekeepers at the thresholds numbered 212. They were registered by genealogy in their villages. The gatekeepers had been assigned to their positions of trust by David and Samuel the seer[D]. **23**They and their descendants were in charge of guarding the gates of the house of the LORD—the house called the Tent. **24**The gatekeepers were on the four sides: east, west, north and south. **25**Their brothers in their villages had to come from time to time and share their duties for seven-day periods. **26**But the four principal gatekeepers, who were Levites, were entrusted with the responsibility for the rooms and treasuries in the house of God. **27**They would spend the night stationed around the house of God, because they had to guard it; and they had charge of the key for opening it each morning.

28Some of them were in charge of the articles used in the temple service; they counted them when they were brought in and when they were taken out. **29**Others were assigned to take care of the furnishings and all the other articles of the sanctuary, as well as the flour and wine, and the oil, incense[D] and spices. **30**But some of the priests took care of mixing the spices. **31**A Levite named Mattithiah, the firstborn[D] son of Shallum the Ko-

Why were all the men who were taken from Benjamin the *heads of their families*? (9:9)

The phrase *all these men* does not refer only to the Benjamites. It refers to those taken from all the tribes listed here (vv. 3–9), including some remnants of the northern kingdom—represented by Manasseh and Ephraim. As to why the Babylonians would selectively take heads of families captive: By deporting clan leaders (or in some cases, killing them), a conquering army could greatly reduce the chance that a defeated nation would mount any rebellion against its new masters. Without leaders, a nation typically would be more submissive.

Is this Obadiah the prophet who wrote the book of Obadiah? (9:16)

No. *Obadiah* was a common name in the Old Testament. At least ten other Bible characters had the same name.

Is this Zechariah the prophet who wrote the book of Zechariah? (9:21)

No. *Zechariah* was an extremely common name in the Old Testament. At least 30 other Bible characters had the same name.

---

a19 That is, the temple; also in verses 21 and 23

rahite, was entrusted with the responsibility for baking the offering bread. [32]Some of their Kohathite brothers were in charge of preparing for every Sabbath[D] the bread set out on the table.

[33]Those who were musicians, heads of Levite[D] families, stayed in the rooms of the temple and were exempt from other duties because they were responsible for the work day and night.

[34]All these were heads of Levite families, chiefs as listed in their genealogy[D], and they lived in Jerusalem[D].

The Genealogy of Saul

[35]Jeiel the father[a] of Gibeon lived in Gibeon.
His wife's name was Maacah, [36]and his firstborn[D] son was Abdon, followed by Zur, Kish, Baal, Ner, Nadab, [37]Gedor, Ahio, Zechariah and Mikloth. [38]Mikloth was the father of Shimeam. They too lived near their relatives in Jerusalem.

[39]Ner was the father of Kish, Kish the father of Saul, and Saul the father of Jonathan, Malki-Shua, Abinadab and Esh-Baal.[b]

[40]The son of Jonathan:
Merib-Baal,[c] who was the father of Micah.

[41]The sons of Micah:
Pithon, Melech, Tahrea and Ahaz.[d]

[42]Ahaz was the father of Jadah, Jadah[e] was the father of Alemeth, Azmaveth and Zimri, and Zimri was the father of Moza. [43]Moza was the father of Binea; Rephaiah was his son, Eleasah his son and Azel his son.

[44]Azel had six sons, and these were their names:
Azrikam, Bokeru, Ishmael, Sheariah, Obadiah and Hanan. These were the sons of Azel.

Saul Takes His Life

10 Now the Philistines fought against Israel; the Israelites fled before them, and many fell slain on Mount Gilboa. [2]The Philistines pressed hard after Saul and his sons, and they killed his sons Jonathan, Abinadab and Malki-Shua. [3]The fighting grew fierce around Saul, and when the archers overtook him, they wounded him.

[4]Saul said to his armor-bearer, "Draw your sword and run me through, or these uncircumcised[D] fellows will come and abuse me."

But his armor-bearer was terrified and would not do it; so Saul took his own sword and fell on it. [5]When the armor-bearer saw that Saul was dead, he too fell on his sword and died. [6]So Saul and his three sons died, and all his house died together.

[7]When all the Israelites in the valley saw that the army had fled and that Saul and his sons had died, they abandoned their towns and fled. And the Philistines came and occupied them.

[8]The next day, when the Philistines came to strip the dead, they found Saul and his sons fallen on Mount Gilboa. [9]They stripped him and took his head and his armor, and sent messengers throughout the land of the Philis-

Why repeat Saul's genealogy? (9:35–44)

Though this repetition of 8:29–40 seems unnecessary by our standards, the writer uses Saul's genealogy this second time simply as a transition. He wants to tell the story of Saul's death before moving on to tell the story of David, his primary concern.

---

[a]35 Father may mean civic leader or military leader.   [b]39 Also known as Ish-Bosheth   [c]40 Also known as Mephibosheth   [d]41 Vulgate and Syriac (see also Septuagint and 1 Chron. 8:35); Hebrew does not have and Ahaz.   [e]42 Some Hebrew manuscripts and Septuagint (see also 1 Chron. 8:36); most Hebrew manuscripts Jarah, Jarah

tines to proclaim the news among their idols^D and their people. ¹⁰They put his armor in the temple of their gods and hung up his head in the temple of Dagon.

¹¹When all the inhabitants of Jabesh Gilead heard of everything the Philistines had done to Saul, ¹²all their valiant men went and took the bodies of Saul and his sons and brought them to Jabesh. Then they buried their bones under the great tree in Jabesh, and they fasted seven days.

¹³Saul died because he was unfaithful to the LORD; he did not keep the word of the LORD and even consulted a medium^D for guidance, ¹⁴and did not inquire of the LORD. So the LORD put him to death^D and turned the kingdom over to David son of Jesse.

David Becomes King Over Israel

11 All Israel came together to David at Hebron and said, "We are your own flesh and blood. ²In the past, even while Saul was king, you were the one who led Israel on their military campaigns. And the LORD your God said to you, 'You will shepherd my people Israel, and you will become their ruler.' "

³When all the elders of Israel had come to King David at Hebron, he made a compact with them at Hebron before the LORD, and they anointed^D David king over Israel, as the LORD had promised through Samuel.

David Conquers Jerusalem

⁴David and all the Israelites marched to Jerusalem^D (that is, Jebus). The Jebusites who lived there ⁵said to David, "You will not get in here." Nevertheless, David captured the fortress of Zion^D, the City of David.

⁶David had said, "Whoever leads the attack on the Jebusites will become commander-in-chief." Joab son of Zeruiah went up first, and so he received the command.

⁷David then took up residence in the fortress, and so it was called the City of David. ⁸He built up the city around it, from the supporting terraces^a to the surrounding wall, while Joab restored the rest of the city. ⁹And David became more and more powerful, because the LORD Almighty was with him.

David's Mighty Men

¹⁰These were the chiefs of David's mighty men—they, together with all Israel, gave his kingship strong support to extend it over the whole land, as the LORD had promised— ¹¹this is the list of David's mighty men:

Jashobeam,^b a Hacmonite, was chief of the officers^c; he raised his spear against three hundred men, whom he killed in one encounter.

¹²Next to him was Eleazar son of Dodai the Ahohite, one of the three mighty men. ¹³He was with David at Pas Dammim when the Philistines gathered there for battle. At a place where there was a field full of barley, the troops fled from the Philistines. ¹⁴But they took their stand in the middle of the field. They defended it and struck the Philistines down, and the LORD brought about a great victory.

¹⁵Three of the thirty chiefs came down to David to the rock at the cave of Adullam, while a band of Philistines was encamped in the Valley of Rephaim. ¹⁶At that time David was in the stronghold^D, and the Philistine garrison was at Bethlehem. ¹⁷David longed for water and said, "Oh,

How could one man kill 300 men? (11:11)

We can't know for sure whether these numbers are literal or figurative (see 12:14). It's possible Jashobeam, as chief of the officers, received credit for something they all did together—just as a coach today receives credit when his team wins a victory. On the other hand, it's also possible this describes a miraculous victory given by God. Either way, the victorious results show that Jashobeam's actions were inspired by faith.

Why would wasting water be better than drinking it? (11:18–19)

Pouring out the water was like pouring out a drink offering of wine in the sanctuary (see Num. 28:7). Recognizing he was not worthy of the kind of sacrifice the Three had made, David offered the water up to God. His men would not think because the water was poured out that their perilous journey had been in vain. Rather, they would realize it had been devoted to an even greater cause than their leader's thirst—they had risked their lives for the Lord himself. Also see *Why wouldn't David drink the water from the well of Bethlehem?* (2 Samuel 23:16–17).

Why list David's recruits? (11:26–12:40)

The writer wanted his readers to see how David inspired loyalty in *all Israel,* even among Saul's kinsmen. By listing the variety of men who joined David he showed David's appeal. This list from the past was also the writer's way of pointing to the future. Israel could anticipate a golden era again if they would only have faith and follow God as David had.

that someone would get me a drink of water from the well near the gate of Bethlehem!" [18]So the Three broke through the Philistine lines, drew water from the well near the gate of Bethlehem and carried it back to David. But he refused to drink it; instead, he poured it out before the LORD. [19]"God forbid that I should do this!" he said. "Should I drink the blood of these men who went at the risk of their lives?" Because they risked their lives to bring it back, David would not drink it.

Such were the exploits of the three mighty men.

[20]Abishai the brother of Joab was chief of the Three. He raised his spear against three hundred men, whom he killed, and so he became as famous as the Three. [21]He was doubly honored above the Three and became their commander, even though he was not included among them.

[22]Benaiah son of Jehoiada was a valiant fighter from Kabzeel, who performed great exploits. He struck down two of Moab's best men. He also went down into a pit on a snowy day and killed a lion. [23]And he struck down an Egyptian who was seven and a half feet[a] tall. Although the Egyptian had a spear like a weaver's rod in his hand, Benaiah went against him with a club. He snatched the spear from the Egyptian's hand and killed him with his own spear. [24]Such were the exploits of Benaiah son of Jehoiada; he too was as famous as the three mighty men. [25]He was held in greater honor than any of the Thirty, but he was not included among the Three. And David put him in charge of his bodyguard.

[26]The mighty men were:
Asahel the brother of Joab,
Elhanan son of Dodo from Bethlehem,
[27]Shammoth the Harorite,
Helez the Pelonite,
[28]Ira son of Ikkesh from Tekoa,
Abiezer from Anathoth,
[29]Sibbecai the Hushathite,
Ilai the Ahohite,
[30]Maharai the Netophathite,
Heled son of Baanah the Netophathite,
[31]Ithai son of Ribai from Gibeah in Benjamin,
Benaiah the Pirathonite,
[32]Hurai from the ravines of Gaash,
Abiel the Arbathite,
[33]Azmaveth the Baharumite,
Eliahba the Shaalbonite,
[34]the sons of Hashem the Gizonite,
Jonathan son of Shagee the Hararite,
[35]Ahiam son of Sacar the Hararite,
Eliphal son of Ur,
[36]Hepher the Mekerathite,
Ahijah the Pelonite,
[37]Hezro the Carmelite,
Naarai son of Ezbai,
[38]Joel the brother of Nathan,
Mibhar son of Hagri,
[39]Zelek the Ammonite,
Naharai the Berothite, the armor-bearer of Joab son of Zeruiah,
[40]Ira the Ithrite,
Gareb the Ithrite,

---

[a]23 Hebrew *five cubits* (about 2.3 meters)

41Uriah the Hittite,
Zabad son of Ahlai,
42Adina son of Shiza the Reubenite, who was chief
of the Reubenites, and the thirty with him,
43Hanan son of Maacah,
Joshaphat the Mithnite,
44Uzzia the Ashterathite,
Shama and Jeiel the sons of Hotham the Aroerite,
45Jediael son of Shimri,
his brother Joha the Tizite,
46Eliel the Mahavite,
Jeribai and Joshaviah the sons of Elnaam,
Ithmah the Moabite,
47Eliel, Obed and Jaasiel the Mezobaite.

Warriors Join David

12 These were the men who came to David at Ziklag, while he was banished from the presence of Saul son of Kish (they were among the warriors who helped him in battle; **2**they were armed with bows and were able to shoot arrows or to sling stones right-handed or left-handed; they were kinsmen of Saul from the tribe of Benjamin):

3Ahiezer their chief and Joash the sons of Shemaah the Gibeathite; Jeziel and Pelet the sons of Azmaveth; Beracah, Jehu the Anathothite, **4**and Ishmaiah the Gibeonite, a mighty man among the Thirty, who was a leader of the Thirty; Jeremiah, Jahaziel, Johanan, Jozabad the Gederathite, **5**Eluzai, Jerimoth, Bealiah, Shemariah and Shephatiah the Haruphite; **6**Elkanah, Isshiah, Azarel, Joezer and Jashobeam the Korahites; **7**and Joelah and Zebadiah the sons of Jeroham from Gedor.

8Some Gadites defected to David at his strongholdᴰ in the desert. They were brave warriors, ready for battle and able to handle the shield and spear. Their faces were the faces of lions, and they were as swift as gazelles in the mountains.
9Ezer was the chief,
Obadiah the second in command, Eliab the third,
10Mishmannah the fourth, Jeremiah the fifth,
11Attai the sixth, Eliel the seventh,
12Johanan the eighth, Elzabad the ninth,
13Jeremiah the tenth and Macbannai the eleventh.
14These Gadites were army commanders; the least was a match for a hundred, and the greatest for a thousand. **15**It was they who crossed the Jordan in the first month when it was overflowing all its banks, and they put to flight everyone living in the valleys, to the east and to the west.

16Other Benjamites and some men from Judah also came to David in his stronghold. **17**David went out to meet them and said to them, "If you have come to me in peaceᴰ, to help me, I am ready to have you unite with me. But if you have come to betray me to my enemies when my hands are free from violence, may the God of our fathers see it and judge you."
18Then the Spirit came upon Amasai, chief of the Thirty, and he said:

"We are yours, O David!
We are with you, O son of Jesse!
Success, success to you,

SCRIPTURE LINK (11:41) *Uriah the Hittite*

The first husband of David's wife Bathsheba. See 2 Samuel 11:6.

How unique were ambidextrous warriors in those days? (12:2)

They were unique enough to receive special mention. The writer considered these skilled warriors as another sign of the blessings God gave to David. Their ambidextrous skills proved that they were well trained, but their left-handedness may also have had some hereditary basis. The Benjamites were known for their left-handed fighters. Ehud, the Benjamite judge was left-handed (Judges 3:15), as were 700 warriors who could *sling a stone at a hair and not miss* (Judges 20:16).

Why would Saul's own kinsmen defect to David? (12:2)

The writer's theme of *all Israel* (v. 38) becomes most obvious when he tells how even Saul's kinsmen joined David's army. Many of Saul's own tribe could see that the hand of God was on David and joined with *all Israel* in following him.

Why was God's Spirit needed to announce loyalty to David? (12:18)

In the Old Testament, *Spirit* most often refers to the spirit of prophecy. This psalm, credited to Amasai, expressed the popular mood of the people throughout the country. David did not automatically trust the Benjamites, Saul's kinsmen. This prophecy, however, enabled David and the Benjamites to gain more confidence in one another.

and success to those who help you,
for your God will help you."

So David received them and made them leaders of his raiding bands.

[19]Some of the men of Manasseh defected to David when he went with the Philistines to fight against Saul. (He and his men did not help the Philistines because, after consultation, their rulers sent him away. They said, "It will cost us our heads if he deserts to his master Saul.") [20]When David went to Ziklag, these were the men of Manasseh who defected to him: Adnah, Jozabad, Jediael, Michael, Jozabad, Elihu and Zillethai, leaders of units of a thousand in Manasseh. [21]They helped David against raiding bands, for all of them were brave warriors, and they were commanders in his army. [22]Day after day men came to help David, until he had a great army, like the army of God.[a]

Others Join David at Hebron

[23]These are the numbers of the men armed for battle who came to David at Hebron to turn Saul's kingdom over to him, as the LORD had said:

[24]men of Judah, carrying shield and spear—6,800 armed for battle;

[25]men of Simeon, warriors ready for battle—7,100;

[26]men of Levi—4,600, [27]including Jehoiada, leader of the family of Aaron, with 3,700 men, [28]and Zadok, a brave young warrior, with 22 officers from his family;

[29]men of Benjamin, Saul's kinsmen—3,000, most of whom had remained loyal to Saul's house until then;

[30]men of Ephraim, brave warriors, famous in their own clans—20,800;

[31]men of half the tribe of Manasseh, designated by name to come and make David king—18,000;

[32]men of Issachar, who understood the times and knew what Israel should do—200 chiefs, with all their relatives under their command;

[33]men of Zebulun, experienced soldiers prepared for battle with every type of weapon, to help David with undivided loyalty—50,000;

[34]men of Naphtali—1,000 officers, together with 37,000 men carrying shields and spears;

[35]men of Dan, ready for battle—28,600;

[36]men of Asher, experienced soldiers prepared for battle—40,000;

[37]and from east of the Jordan, men of Reuben, Gad and the half-tribe of Manasseh, armed with every type of weapon—120,000.

[38]All these were fighting men who volunteered to serve in the ranks. They came to Hebron fully determined to make David king over all Israel. All the rest of the Israelites were also of one mind to make David king. [39]The men spent three days there with David, eating and drinking, for their families had supplied provisions for them. [40]Also, their neighbors from as far away as Issachar, Zebulun and Naphtali came bringing food on donkeys, camels, mules and oxen. There were plentiful supplies of flour, fig cakes, raisin cakes, wine, oil, cattle and sheep, for there was joy in Israel.

The army of God (12:22)
An army or host of angels, usually unseen (Joshua 5:13–15; 2 Kings 6:8–17). Jesus said he could call 12 legions of angels to defend him, a legion being 3,000 to 6,000 Roman soldiers. (Matt. 26:53).

How was David's army like *the army of God*? (12:22)
Though they were not as numerous as the army of God, they represented many more of their kinsmen back home who had pledged their full support to David. Besides suggesting a large number, the expression also speaks of the high quality of these soldiers. Some say David and his men pictured the Messiah as commander of God's army.

Designated by name (12:31)
This could mean *expressly named* or *nominated*. The phrase probably did not mean a military draft since those nominated most likely had volunteered and were honored to be chosen by name.

Why list Manasseh twice? (12:31,37)
The tribe of Manasseh was split into two halves—half was east of the Jordan River where they had settled with the tribes of Reuben and Gad (see Num. 32) and half was west of the Jordan in northern Israel (see *Map 4* at the back of this Bible).

How were the men of Issachar able to understand the times? (12:32)
This is perhaps a description of a kind of God-inspired common sense. Others may have looked to them as men trained by the Spirit to see events from God's perspective. Some suggest they may have practiced divination, such as astrology (see Esther 1:13). But since such things were condemned in Israel, it's more likely this merely recognizes their political savvy in joining David early in his reign.

---

[a]22 Or *a great and mighty army*

Bringing Back the Ark

13 David conferred with each of his officers, the commanders of thousands and commanders of hundreds. ²He then said to the whole assembly of Israel, "If it seems good to you and if it is the will of the LORD our God, let us send word far and wide to the rest of our brothers throughout the territories of Israel, and also to the priests[D] and Levites[D] who are with them in their towns and pasturelands, to come and join us. ³Let us bring the ark of our God back to us, for we did not inquire of[a] it[b] during the reign of Saul." ⁴The whole assembly agreed to do this, because it seemed right to all the people.

⁵So David assembled all the Israelites, from the Shihor River in Egypt to Lebo[c] Hamath, to bring the ark of God from Kiriath Jearim. ⁶David and all the Israelites with him went to Baalah of Judah (Kiriath Jearim) to bring up from there the ark of God the LORD, who is enthroned between the cherubim[D]—the ark that is called by the Name.

⁷They moved the ark of God from Abinadab's house on a new cart, with Uzzah and Ahio guiding it. ⁸David and all the Israelites were celebrating with all their might before God, with songs and with harps, lyres[D], tambourines, cymbals and trumpets.

⁹When they came to the threshing floor of Kidon, Uzzah reached out his hand to steady the ark, because the oxen stumbled. ¹⁰The LORD's anger burned against Uzzah, and he struck him down because he had put his hand on the ark. So he died there before God.

¹¹Then David was angry because the LORD's wrath had broken out against Uzzah, and to this day that place is called Perez Uzzah.[d]

¹²David was afraid of God that day and asked, "How can I ever bring the ark of God to me?" ¹³He did not take the ark to be with him in the City of David. Instead, he took

---

[a]3 Or *we neglected*   [b]3 Or *him*   [c]5 Or *to the entrance to*
[d]11 *Perez Uzzah* means *outbreak against Uzzah.*

How did they plan to inquire of the ark? (13:3)
It's not known for sure, but it's possible the high priest stood before the ark in the presence of the Lord to use the Urim and Thummim. These were stones held in a fold or pocket beneath the priest's breastplate. They apparently gave "yes" or "no" answers in a way similar to secular methods such as drawing straws or flipping coins, though the results were governed by God, not chance.

Why punish someone who was only trying to help? (13:9–10)
Uzzah's good intentions could not make up for his carelessness. The ark, representing the very throne of God, required special care and handling (Exodus 25:10–22). But taking their cue from the pagan Philistines, the Israelites put the ark on a cart (see 1 Samuel 6:10–11), which showed no awe for God's presence or commands. Uzzah violated God's instructions (Num. 4:15), but others who merely looked at it deserved to die as well (Num. 4:20). The question could well be, "Why didn't God punish more people than he did?"

How was the ark put on the cart in the first place without being touched? (13:10)
We don't know for sure. It's possible that poles were used to pick up the ark and place it into the cart.

With whom was David angry? (13:11)
David became angry with God for striking down Uzzah. But he may have been angry with himself as well, thinking that he had indirectly caused Uzzah's death. Perhaps he was also angry with Uzzah for being so careless.

Obed-Edom (13:13)
See *Did David leave the ark with a foreigner—a Gittite?* (2 Samuel 6:10).

What power did the ark have? (13:10,14)

The ark, in and of itself, was simply an ornate box with no supernatural power. However, as a representation of God's presence among his people, it reflected God's holiness and caused his people to be filled with awe. Still, it was *God* they were to respect, not the *symbol* of his presence.

The ark illustrated several things about God:

(1) No one could approach him on a whim; proper preparation was necessary. The high priest, for example, could come before God's presence in the Most Holy Place only once a year, and then only after careful ritual cleansing.

(2) God's power could save. On occasion, God instructed the people to take the ark (God's chariot; 28:18) into battle (Joshua 3:3; 6:12–13; Num. 10:35). When the Israelites used the ark as a "good luck charm" and brought it into battle on their own (1 Samuel 4:3–11), they were defeated.

(3) God's power was both fearful and desirable. His power came as judgment when some died for looking into the ark (1 Samuel 6:19) or when Uzzah disregarded God's holiness and touched it. But when the ark was left at the home of Obed-Edom, God's power blessed his whole household. Those who had reverence for the ark as a symbol of the holy God enjoyed blessings; those who viewed it as good luck flirted with disaster.

it aside to the house of Obed-Edom the Gittite. **¹⁴**The ark of God remained with the family of Obed-Edom in his house for three months, and the LORD blessed his household and everything he had.

David's House and Family

14 Now Hiram king of Tyre sent messengers to David, along with cedar logs, stonemasons and carpenters to build a palace for him. **²**And David knew that the LORD had established him as king over Israel and that his kingdom had been highly exalted for the sake of his people Israel.

³In Jerusalem*ᴰ* David took more wives and became the father of more sons and daughters. **⁴**These are the names of the children born to him there: Shammua, Shobab, Nathan, Solomon, **⁵**Ibhar, Elishua, Elpelet, **⁶**Nogah, Nepheg, Japhia, **⁷**Elishama, Beeliada*ᵃ* and Eliphelet.

David Defeats the Philistines

⁸When the Philistines heard that David had been anointed*ᴰ* king over all Israel, they went up in full force to search for him, but David heard about it and went out to meet them. **⁹**Now the Philistines had come and raided the Valley of Rephaim; **¹⁰**so David inquired of God: "Shall I go and attack the Philistines? Will you hand them over to me?"

The LORD answered him, "Go, I will hand them over to you."

¹¹So David and his men went up to Baal Perazim, and there he defeated them. He said, "As waters break out, God has broken out against my enemies by my hand." So that place was called Baal Perazim.*ᵇ* **¹²**The Philistines had abandoned their gods there, and David gave orders to burn them in the fire.

¹³Once more the Philistines raided the valley; **¹⁴**so David inquired of God again, and God answered him, "Do not go straight up, but circle around them and attack them in front of the balsam trees. **¹⁵**As soon as you hear the sound of marching in the tops of the balsam trees, move out to battle, because that will mean God has gone out in front of you to strike the Philistine army." **¹⁶**So David did as God commanded him, and they struck down the Philistine army, all the way from Gibeon to Gezer.

¹⁷So David's fame spread throughout every land, and the LORD made all the nations fear him.

The Ark Brought to Jerusalem

15 After David had constructed buildings for himself in the City of David, he prepared a place for the ark of God and pitched a tent for it. **²**Then David said, "No one but the Levites*ᴰ* may carry the ark of God, because the LORD chose them to carry the ark of the LORD and to minister before him forever."

³David assembled all Israel in Jerusalem to bring up the ark of the LORD to the place he had prepared for it. **⁴**He called together the descendants of Aaron and the Levites:

⁵From the descendants of Kohath,
Uriel the leader and 120 relatives;
⁶from the descendants of Merari,
Asaiah the leader and 220 relatives;

Why did Hiram, king of Tyre, endorse David? (14:1-2)

He must have felt it was in his best interest to be David's friend. The tribute he sent was an offer of friendship so that their nations could have a treaty between them. David saw God at work behind Hiram's actions, further evidence that God was blessing David.

Why would David want so many wives? (14:3)

Although God's ideal was one husband for one wife, God's blessing was also measured in David's time by having a large number of sons and daughters, something virtually ensured by having many wives. Also see article: *Why did David have so many wives and concubines?* (2 Samuel 5:13).

How did David inquire of God? (14:10,14)

Throughout Israel's history the people had inquired of the Lord in several ways: through the pillar of cloud, the Urim and Thummim and prophecy. Most likely David went to the high priest and inquired of God using the Urim and Thummim. See *How did they plan to inquire of the ark?* (13:3).

How did God give David a detailed battle plan? (14:10,14)

Assuming David used the Urim and Thummim, he would have asked questions of God, which would be answered by the high priest after he had consulted the stones, although we can't say how. See *How did they plan to inquire of the ark?* (13:3).

How did David discover the proper way to move the ark? (15:2)

After David's anger at God subsided, David apparently had the priests and Levites look into the sacred scrolls containing the Mosaic Laws. There they would have rediscovered the Lord's regulations about the ark, its treatment and movement. See v. 13.

ᵃ 7 A variant of *Eliada*   *ᵇ 11 Baal Perazim* means *the lord who breaks out.*

⁷from the descendants of Gershon,ᵃ
  Joel the leader and 130 relatives;
⁸from the descendants of Elizaphan,
  Shemaiah the leader and 200 relatives;
⁹from the descendants of Hebron,
  Eliel the leader and 80 relatives;
¹⁰from the descendants of Uzziel,
  Amminadab the leader and 112 relatives.

¹¹Then David summoned Zadok and Abiathar the priests D, and Uriel, Asaiah, Joel, Shemaiah, Eliel and Amminadab the Levites D. ¹²He said to them, "You are the heads of the Levitical families; you and your fellow Levites are to consecrate yourselves and bring up the ark of the LORD, the God of Israel, to the place I have prepared for it. ¹³It was because you, the Levites, did not bring it up the first time that the LORD our God broke out in anger against us. We did not inquire of him about how to do it in the prescribed way." ¹⁴So the priests and Levites consecrated themselves in order to bring up the ark of the LORD, the God of Israel. ¹⁵And the Levites carried the ark of God with the poles on their shoulders, as Moses had commanded in accordance with the word of the LORD.

¹⁶David told the leaders of the Levites to appoint their brothers as singers to sing joyful songs, accompanied by musical instruments: lyres D, harps and cymbals.

¹⁷So the Levites appointed Heman son of Joel; from his brothers, Asaph son of Berekiah; and from their brothers the Merarites, Ethan son of Kushaiah; ¹⁸and with them their brothers next in rank: Zechariah,ᵇ Jaaziel, Shemiramoth, Jehiel, Unni, Eliab, Benaiah, Maaseiah, Mattithiah, Eliphelehu, Mikneiah, Obed-Edom and Jeiel,ᶜ the gatekeepers.

¹⁹The musicians Heman, Asaph and Ethan were to sound the bronze cymbals; ²⁰Zechariah, Aziel, Shemiramoth, Jehiel, Unni, Eliab, Maaseiah and Benaiah were to play the lyres according to alamoth,ᵈ ²¹and Mattithiah, Eliphelehu, Mikneiah, Obed-Edom, Jeiel and Azaziah were to play the harps, directing according to sheminith.ᵈ ²²Kenaniah the head Levite was in charge of the singing; that was his responsibility because he was skillful at it.

²³Berekiah and Elkanah were to be doorkeepers for the ark. ²⁴Shebaniah, Joshaphat, Nethanel, Amasai, Zechariah, Benaiah and Eliezer the priests were to blow trumpets before the ark of God. Obed-Edom and Jehiah were also to be doorkeepers for the ark.

²⁵So David and the elders of Israel and the commanders of units of a thousand went to bring up the ark of the covenant D of the LORD from the house of Obed-Edom, with rejoicing. ²⁶Because God had helped the Levites who were carrying the ark of the covenant of the LORD, seven bulls and seven rams were sacrificed. ²⁷Now David was clothed in a robe of fine linen, as were all the Levites who were carrying the ark, and as were the singers, and Kenaniah, who was in charge of the singing of the choirs. David also wore a linen ephod D. ²⁸So all Israel brought up the ark of the covenant of the LORD with

Why did David wear an ephod? (15:27)
Ephods were typically worn by priests. David may have been wearing one to show his devotion to God. David considered it an honor to worship the Lord. Some think that the king clothed in a priestly ephod was a picture of the coming Christ who would be both priest and king.

ᵃ7 Hebrew Gershom, a variant of Gershon   ᵇ18 Three Hebrew manuscripts and most Septuagint manuscripts (see also verse 20 and 1 Chron. 16:5); most Hebrew manuscripts Zechariah son and or Zechariah, Ben and   ᶜ18 Hebrew; Septuagint (see also verse 21) Jeiel and Azaziah   ᵈ20,21 Probably a musical term

Why did Michal despise David for dancing? (15:29)

David's wife spoke sarcastically of the king's *disrobing* (2 Samuel 6:20–23). But nothing suggests David was clothed indecently. Michal was probably upset that he had violated kingly dignity by removing his royal robes and lowering himself to the level of a priest. In her view, he had made a fool of himself before the slave girls. She was more concerned about David's maintaining his reputation than about the arrival of the ark of the Lord.

Why did David act like a priest? (16:2)

Other kings were punished when they offered sacrifices, something only the priests were supposed to do. Saul lost his kingdom (1 Samuel 13:9–14) and Uzziah was afflicted with leprosy (2 Chron. 26:16–21). Some think David was permitted to offer sacrifices in this unique instance because he was a man after God's own heart. It is much more likely, however, that though David *offered* sacrifices, he did it *through* the priests who actually killed the animals and burned them on the altar.

shouts, with the sounding of rams' horns and trumpets, and of cymbals, and the playing of lyres[D] and harps.

[29]As the ark of the covenant[D] of the LORD was entering the City of David, Michal daughter of Saul watched from a window. And when she saw King David dancing and celebrating, she despised him in her heart.

16 They brought the ark of God and set it inside the tent that David had pitched for it, and they presented burnt offerings[D] and fellowship offerings[Da] before God. [2]After David had finished sacrificing the burnt offerings and fellowship offerings, he blessed the people in the name of the LORD. [3]Then he gave a loaf of bread, a cake of dates and a cake of raisins to each Israelite man and woman.

[4]He appointed some of the Levites[D] to minister before the ark of the LORD, to make petition, to give thanks, and to praise the LORD, the God of Israel: [5]Asaph was the chief, Zechariah second, then Jeiel, Shemiramoth, Jehiel, Mattithiah, Eliab, Benaiah, Obed-Edom and Jeiel. They were to play the lyres and harps, Asaph was to sound the cymbals, [6]and Benaiah and Jahaziel the priests[D] were to blow the trumpets regularly before the ark of the covenant of God.

David's Psalm of Thanks

[7]That day David first committed to Asaph and his associates this psalm of thanks to the LORD:

[8]Give thanks to the LORD, call on his name;
    make known among the nations what he has
        done.
[9]Sing to him, sing praise to him;
    tell of all his wonderful acts.
[10]Glory in his holy name;
    let the hearts of those who seek the LORD
        rejoice.
[11]Look to the LORD and his strength;
    seek his face always.
[12]Remember the wonders he has done,
    his miracles, and the judgments he
        pronounced,
[13]O descendants of Israel his servant,
    O sons of Jacob, his chosen ones.

[14]He is the LORD our God;
    his judgments are in all the earth.
[15]He remembers[b] his covenant forever,
    the word he commanded, for a thousand
        generations,
[16]the covenant he made with Abraham,
    the oath he swore to Isaac.
[17]He confirmed it to Jacob as a decree,
    to Israel as an everlasting covenant:
[18]"To you I will give the land of Canaan
    as the portion you will inherit."

[19]When they were but few in number,
    few indeed, and strangers in it,
[20]they[c] wandered from nation to nation,
    from one kingdom to another.

---

a1 Traditionally *peace offerings*; also in verse 2   *b15* Some Septuagint manuscripts (see also Psalm 105:8); Hebrew *Remember*   *c18-20* One Hebrew manuscript, Septuagint and Vulgate (see also Psalm 105:12); most Hebrew manuscripts *inherit, / 19though you are but few in number, / few indeed, and strangers in it." / 20They*

²¹He allowed no man to oppress them;
    for their sake he rebuked kings:
²²"Do not touch my anointed^D ones;
    do my prophets^D no harm."

²³Sing to the LORD, all the earth;
    proclaim his salvation^D day after day.
²⁴Declare his glory^D among the nations,
    his marvelous deeds among all peoples.
²⁵For great is the LORD and most worthy of
    praise;
    he is to be feared above all gods.
²⁶For all the gods of the nations are idols^D,
    but the LORD made the heavens.
²⁷Splendor and majesty are before him;
    strength and joy in his dwelling place.
²⁸Ascribe to the LORD, O families of nations,
    ascribe to the LORD glory and strength,
²⁹   ascribe to the LORD the glory due his name.
Bring an offering and come before him;
    worship the LORD in the splendor of his^a
    holiness.
³⁰Tremble before him, all the earth!
    The world is firmly established; it cannot be
    moved.
³¹Let the heavens rejoice, let the earth be glad;
    let them say among the nations, "The LORD
    reigns!"
³²Let the sea resound, and all that is in it;
    let the fields be jubilant, and everything in
    them!
³³Then the trees of the forest will sing,
    they will sing for joy before the LORD,
    for he comes to judge the earth.

³⁴Give thanks to the LORD, for he is good;
    his love endures forever.
³⁵Cry out, "Save us, O God our Savior;
    gather us and deliver us from the nations,
    that we may give thanks to your holy name,
    that we may glory in your praise."
³⁶Praise be to the LORD, the God of Israel,
    from everlasting to everlasting.

Then all the people said "Amen" and "Praise the LORD."

³⁷David left Asaph and his associates before the ark of the covenant^D of the LORD to minister there regularly, according to each day's requirements. ³⁸He also left Obed-Edom and his sixty-eight associates to minister with them. Obed-Edom son of Jeduthun, and also Hosah, were gatekeepers.

³⁹David left Zadok the priest^D and his fellow priests before the tabernacle^D of the LORD at the high place in Gibeon ⁴⁰to present burnt offerings^D to the LORD on the altar of burnt offering regularly, morning and evening, in accordance with everything written in the Law of the LORD, which he had given Israel. ⁴¹With them were Heman and Jeduthun and the rest of those chosen and designated by name to give thanks to the LORD, "for his love endures forever." ⁴²Heman and Jeduthun were responsible for the sounding of the trumpets and cymbals and for the playing of the other instruments for sacred^D song. The sons of Jeduthun were stationed at the gate.

^a29 Or LORD with the splendor of

Why was the tabernacle still at Gibeon after the ark was moved to Jerusalem? (16:39)

Gibeon (a hill or hill city) had been important throughout Israel's history, probably because it was considered a high place of worship (see Map 4 at the back of this Bible). It was at Gibeon that Solomon later sacrificed and received a message from God through a dream. Gibeon continued as a worship center until Solomon completed the temple in Jerusalem. Some suggest David brought the ark to Jerusalem instead of Gibeon because it helped him solidify his political support.

How was this high place different from others that displeased God? (16:39)

God had commanded that all high places be destroyed (Deut. 12:2–4). But those dedicated to the Lord were considered good—the difference between true worship and heathen worship. Later, when the temple was built, even high places dedicated to the Lord were denounced for several reasons: (1) Worship at one temple fostered a national spirit of unity. (2) One location helped prevent borrowed pagan practices from creeping into worship. (3) The magnificent temple ensured God's glory and majesty would not be devalued.

How did David bless his family? (16:43)

God assigned priests to bless the nation. The head of the family, though, could function like a priest to the family, praying God's blessings upon each member. Blessings could be prophetic predictions as when Jacob had blessed his sons (Gen. 49:1–28). Or they could be an expression of good wishes and a prayer. Blessing also could be the giving of gifts and favors, just as David blessed the people and gave each of them a loaf of bread, a cake of dates and a cake of raisins. (vv. 2–3).

Did Nathan advise David without first seeking God's will? (17:2)

Probably. It was evident to Nathan that God was with David in all he did. He saw no sin in David's intent to build a great temple for the Lord. God had other plans, however, and so inspired the vision by which Nathan halted David's plans to build the temple (v. 4).

Why did God decide to change his dwelling from a tent to a temple? (17:5–6,12)

Some think that the tabernacle, which was transported through the desert, was replaced with a permanent, unmovable temple after Israel became firmly established in the promised land. Others suggest a more symbolic view—that the tabernacle paralleled the nomadic tent-dwelling descendants of Abraham. The temple, established firmly on a foundation, pointed forward to the coming Messiah—the rock of salvation. With hindsight it can be seen that the Old Testament hinted at New Testament events yet to come.

Haven't the Jews been disturbed many times throughout Israel's tragic history? (17:9)

Yes, they have. But this promise is not just about the physical nation of Israel. The writer of Chronicles had the kingdom of God in mind more than the kingdom of David. Even though David's heirs later lost their kingdom, God has always had his kingdom. God's kingdom will never be thwarted. His people will not be disturbed when this promise is fulfilled through the Son of David, the Messiah.

43Then all the people left, each for his own home, and David returned home to bless his family.

God's Promise to David

17 After David was settled in his palace, he said to Nathan the prophet[D], "Here I am, living in a palace of cedar, while the ark of the covenant[D] of the LORD is under a tent."

2Nathan replied to David, "Whatever you have in mind, do it, for God is with you."

3That night the word of God came to Nathan, saying:

4"Go and tell my servant David, 'This is what the LORD says: You are not the one to build me a house to dwell in. **5**I have not dwelt in a house from the day I brought Israel up out of Egypt to this day. I have moved from one tent site to another, from one dwelling place to another. **6**Wherever I have moved with all the Israelites, did I ever say to any of their leaders[a] whom I commanded to shepherd my people, "Why have you not built me a house of cedar?" '

7"Now then, tell my servant David, 'This is what the LORD Almighty says: I took you from the pasture and from following the flock, to be ruler over my people Israel. **8**I have been with you wherever you have gone, and I have cut off all your enemies from before you. Now I will make your name like the names of the greatest men of the earth. **9**And I will provide a place for my people Israel and will plant them so that they can have a home of their own and no longer be disturbed. Wicked people will not oppress them anymore, as they did at the beginning **10**and have done ever since the time I appointed leaders over my people Israel. I will also subdue all your enemies.

" 'I declare to you that the LORD will build a house for you: **11**When your days are over and you go to be with your fathers, I will raise up your offspring to succeed you, one of your own sons, and I will establish his kingdom. **12**He is the one who will build a house for me, and I will establish his throne forever. **13**I will be his father, and he will be my son. I will never take my love away from him, as I took it away from your predecessor. **14**I will set him over my house and my kingdom forever; his throne will be established forever.' "

15Nathan reported to David all the words of this entire revelation[D].

David's Prayer

16Then King David went in and sat before the LORD, and he said:

"Who am I, O LORD God, and what is my family, that you have brought me this far? **17**And as if this were not enough in your sight, O God, you have spoken about the future of the house of your servant. You have looked on me as though I were the most exalted of men, O LORD God.

18"What more can David say to you for honoring your servant? For you know your servant, **19**O LORD. For the sake of your servant and according to your

---

a6 Traditionally *judges*; also in verse 10

will, you have done this great thing and made known all these great promises.

²⁰"There is no one like you, O LORD, and there is no God but you, as we have heard with our own ears. ²¹And who is like your people Israel—the one nation on earth whose God went out to redeem[D] a people for himself, and to make a name for yourself, and to perform great and awesome wonders by driving out nations from before your people, whom you redeemed from Egypt? ²²You made your people Israel your very own forever, and you, O LORD, have become their God.

²³"And now, LORD, let the promise you have made concerning your servant and his house be established forever. Do as you promised, ²⁴so that it will be established and that your name will be great forever. Then men will say, 'The LORD Almighty, the God over Israel, is Israel's God!' And the house of your servant David will be established before you.

²⁵"You, my God, have revealed to your servant that you will build a house for him. So your servant has found courage to pray to you. ²⁶O LORD, you are God! You have promised these good things to your servant. ²⁷Now you have been pleased to bless the house of your servant, that it may continue forever in your sight; for you, O LORD, have blessed it, and it will be blessed forever."

David's Victories

18 In the course of time, David defeated the Philistines and subdued them, and he took Gath and its surrounding villages from the control of the Philistines.

²David also defeated the Moabites, and they became subject to him and brought tribute.

³Moreover, David fought Hadadezer king of Zobah, as far as Hamath, when he went to establish his control along the Euphrates River. ⁴David captured a thousand of his chariots, seven thousand charioteers and twenty thousand foot soldiers. He hamstrung all but a hundred of the chariot horses.

⁵When the Arameans of Damascus came to help Hadadezer king of Zobah, David struck down twenty-two thousand of them. ⁶He put garrisons in the Aramean kingdom of Damascus, and the Arameans became subject to him and brought tribute. The LORD gave David victory everywhere he went.

⁷David took the gold shields carried by the officers of Hadadezer and brought them to Jerusalem[D]. ⁸From Tebah[a] and Cun, towns that belonged to Hadadezer, David took a great quantity of bronze, which Solomon used to make the bronze Sea, the pillars and various bronze articles.

⁹When Tou king of Hamath heard that David had defeated the entire army of Hadadezer king of Zobah, ¹⁰he sent his son Hadoram to King David to greet him and congratulate him on his victory in battle over Hadadezer, who had been at war with Tou. Hadoram brought all kinds of articles of gold and silver and bronze.

¹¹King David dedicated these articles to the LORD, as he had done with the silver and gold he had taken from all these nations: Edom[D] and Moab, the Ammonites and the Philistines, and Amalek.

How can such large numbers be explained? (18:4–5)
The scribes who copied the Bible in past centuries sometimes misread the numerals. Numbers in the thousands were indicated by dots above the digit letter. In a worn manuscript the number of dots could be difficult to read. Such copying errors, however, do not undermine the authority of the Bible; differences in numbers do not challenge the Bible's critical essence. Also see *Were there really 500,000 casualties among the Israelites?* (2 Chron. 13:17) and *Why don't the numbers in the list equal the total figure?* (Neh. 7:66).

Why hamstring valuable horses rather than using them? (18:4)
David knew God had prohibited the kings of Israel from acquiring great numbers of horses (Deut. 17:16). Perhaps he recalled the time that Joshua obeyed God by hamstringing horses the Israelites had captured (Joshua 11:6,9).

ᵃ8 Hebrew *Tibhath,* a variant of *Tebah*

Abishai (18:12)

Brother of Joab, David's top general. Abishai became commander of *the Three* of David's mighty men (11:20–21).

Valley of Salt (18:12)

Named for the high salt content in the soil and rocks of the area, it was south and southwest of the Dead Sea, toward the land of Edom. The salt marsh there may have slowed the fleeing Edomites.

Why did David put an official in charge of foreigners? (18:17)

It wasn't that he needed an official in charge of foreigners. David simply needed someone in charge of his royal bodyguard which was made up of Kerethites and Pelethites, foreign soldiers who formerly had helped him against Saul.

What kindness had Nahash done for David? (19:1–2)

We are not told the exact nature of the kindness, but Nahash had probably aided David during his troubles with King Saul. The Hebrew word used here for kindness reflects deep devotion to a solemn mutual obligation.

Why humiliate suspected spies? (19:3–5)

Instead of accepting David's delegation at face value—as an expression of sympathy—Hanun became paranoid, speculating about David's motives. His judgment may have been clouded since, by deliberately humiliating David's men, he brought about the very thing he feared. Dishonoring them was like a challenge to war. The psychological impact of humiliating the messengers was certainly stronger than imprisoning them—perhaps even stronger than killing them.

Why fight a war over shaved beards and cut clothing? (19:6–9)

See *Why fight a war over shaved beards and cut clothing?* (2 Samuel 10:6–7).

Were the Arameans living in more than one country? (19:6,16)

Yes. The Arameans lived in Syria, north of the Ammonites, beyond Damascus into Naharaim, northwest Mesopotamia, and beyond the Euphrates River (see *Map 5* at the back of this Bible). A different king ruled each of the Aramean states which were named for the walled city within each state: Naharaim, Maacah, Zobah, Beth Rehob and Tob (see 2 Samuel 10:6).

12Abishai son of Zeruiah struck down eighteen thousand Edomites in the Valley of Salt. **13**He put garrisons in Edom[D], and all the Edomites became subject to David. The LORD gave David victory everywhere he went.

David's Officials

14David reigned over all Israel, doing what was just and right for all his people. **15**Joab son of Zeruiah was over the army; Jehoshaphat son of Ahilud was recorder; **16**Zadok son of Ahitub and Ahimelech[a] son of Abiathar were priests[D]; Shavsha was secretary; **17**Benaiah son of Jehoiada was over the Kerethites and Pelethites; and David's sons were chief officials at the king's side.

The Battle Against the Ammonites

19 In the course of time, Nahash king of the Ammonites died, and his son succeeded him as king. **2**David thought, "I will show kindness to Hanun son of Nahash, because his father showed kindness to me." So David sent a delegation to express his sympathy to Hanun concerning his father.

When David's men came to Hanun in the land of the Ammonites to express sympathy to him, **3**the Ammonite nobles said to Hanun, "Do you think David is honoring your father by sending men to you to express sympathy? Haven't his men come to you to explore and spy out the country and overthrow it?" **4**So Hanun seized David's men, shaved them, cut off their garments in the middle at the buttocks, and sent them away.

5When someone came and told David about the men, he sent messengers to meet them, for they were greatly humiliated. The king said, "Stay at Jericho[D] till your beards have grown, and then come back."

6When the Ammonites realized that they had become a stench in David's nostrils, Hanun and the Ammonites sent a thousand talents[b] of silver to hire chariots and charioteers from Aram Naharaim,[c] Aram Maacah and Zobah. **7**They hired thirty-two thousand chariots and charioteers, as well as the king of Maacah with his troops, who came and camped near Medeba, while the Ammonites were mustered from their towns and moved out for battle.

8On hearing this, David sent Joab out with the entire army of fighting men. **9**The Ammonites came out and drew up in battle formation at the entrance to their city, while the kings who had come were by themselves in the open country.

10Joab saw that there were battle lines in front of him and behind him; so he selected some of the best troops in Israel and deployed them against the Arameans. **11**He put the rest of the men under the command of Abishai his brother, and they were deployed against the Ammonites. **12**Joab said, "If the Arameans are too strong for me, then you are to rescue me; but if the Ammonites are too strong for you, then I will rescue you. **13**Be strong and let us fight bravely for our people and the cities of our God. The LORD will do what is good in his sight."

14Then Joab and the troops with him advanced to fight the Arameans, and they fled before him. **15**When the Ammonites saw that the Arameans were fleeing, they too fled

---

[a]16 Some Hebrew manuscripts, Vulgate and Syriac (see also 2 Samuel 8:17); most Hebrew manuscripts *Abimelech*   [b]6 That is, about 37 tons (about 34 metric tons)   [c]6 That is, Northwest Mesopotamia

before his brother Abishai and went inside the city. So Joab went back to Jerusalem.ᴰ

16After the Arameans saw that they had been routed by Israel, they sent messengers and had Arameans brought from beyond the River,ᵃ with Shophach the commander of Hadadezer's army leading them.

17When David was told of this, he gathered all Israel and crossed the Jordan; he advanced against them and formed his battle lines opposite them. David formed his lines to meet the Arameans in battle, and they fought against him. **18**But they fled before Israel, and David killed seven thousand of their charioteers and forty thousand of their foot soldiers. He also killed Shophach the commander of their army.

19When the vassals of Hadadezer saw that they had been defeated by Israel, they made peaceᴰ with David and became subject to him.

So the Arameans were not willing to help the Ammonites anymore.

The Capture of Rabbah

20 In the spring, at the time when kings go off to war, Joab led out the armed forces. He laid waste the land of the Ammonites and went to Rabbah and besieged it, but David remained in Jerusalem. Joab attacked Rabbah and left it in ruins. **2**David took the crown from the head of their kingᵇ—its weight was found to be a talentᶜ of gold, and it was set with precious stones—and it was placed on David's head. He took a great quantity of plunderᴰ from the city **3**and brought out the people who were there, consigning them to labor with saws and with iron picks and axes. David did this to all the Ammonite towns. Then David and his entire army returned to Jerusalem.

War With the Philistines

4In the course of time, war broke out with the Philistines, at Gezer. At that time Sibbecai the Hushathite killed Sippai, one of the descendants of the Rephaites, and the Philistines were subjugated.

5In another battle with the Philistines, Elhanan son of Jair killed Lahmi the brother of Goliath the Gittite, who had a spear with a shaft like a weaver's rod.

6In still another battle, which took place at Gath, there was a huge man with six fingers on each hand and six toes on each foot—twenty-four in all. He also was descended from Rapha. **7**When he taunted Israel, Jonathan son of Shimea, David's brother, killed him.

8These were descendants of Rapha in Gath, and they fell at the hands of David and his men.

David Numbers the Fighting Men

21 Satan rose up against Israel and incited David to take a census of Israel. **2**So David said to Joab and the commanders of the troops, "Go and count the Israelites from Beersheba to Dan. Then report back to me so that I may know how many there are."

3But Joab replied, "May the LORD multiply his troops a hundred times over. My lord the king, are they not all my lord's subjects? Why does my lord want to do this? Why should he bring guilt on Israel?"

4The king's word, however, overruled Joab; so Joab left

ᵃ16 That is, the Euphrates   ᵇ2 Or *of Milcom,* that is, Molech
ᶜ2 That is, about 75 pounds (about 34 kilograms)

Why was spring a time for war? (20:1)
This apparently became a custom mostly as a matter of tactical convenience. The onset of the rainy season in October had probably delayed the battle to capture Rabbah, the Ammonite capital. During the winter the king and his generals likely plotted battle plans. Then, when the farmers gathered their harvests at the beginning of the dry season in May, Joab could advance to Rabbah, living off the land along the way.

Why did David join his troops after the worst of the fighting was over? (20:1–2)
The author gives no reason for David's delay. He chooses not to tell about the Bathsheba affair which occurred at this time (see 2 Samuel 11)—one possible explanation for David's lack of involvement in the fighting. David did arrive in time to get credit for the victory, following the advice of Joab (see 2 Samuel 12:26–28). See *Didn't David go out to battle anymore?* (2 Samuel 11:1).

Why wear a 75-pound crown? (20:2)
Taking the crown (possibly a ceremonial crown) from the defeated Ammonite king and putting it on David symbolized David's complete victory and Rabbah's total surrender and humiliation. Some think the word for *king* was a name—Milcom the god of the Ammonites, perhaps also known as Molech (see NIV text note). If so, this heavy crown could originally have sat on the head of an idol. Either way, David probably wore it only briefly, with assistance, to celebrate his victory.

Why were there so many battles? (20:4–8)
The Philistines continued their taunts during the early years of David's reign. In each case, defeating one of the giants, a descendant of Rapha, made the incident worth recording.

SCRIPTURE LINK (21:1)
The parallel account says *God* incited David to take a census of fighting men. See 2 Samuel 24:1.

Can Satan incite God's people to do evil? (21:1)
Yes. Since the Garden of Eden Satan has tempted humankind to do evil. But people choose their own responses to Satan's temptation. Satan preys upon the evil desires of individuals. If they give in to his urging, they can become ensnared in sin, which leads to death (James 1:13–15). Though David was committed to the Lord, he was also influenced by his own human weakness. In this case, his pride responded to Satan's suggestion. God's people, susceptible to their own human shortcomings, must guard against Satan's seductive logic. Also see article: *Why would God make someone do wrong?* (2 Samuel 24:1).

What was wrong with taking a census? (21:1,6–7)

God instructed Moses how to take a census in a way that would avoid a plague: each man was to pay a census tax to support the tabernacle service (Exodus 30:11–12; Num. 31:48–50). God ordered a census before preparing an army to conquer the promised land (Num. 1:2). Therefore, there was a right way and a wrong way, a right reason and a wrong reason for taking a census. David's sin was not in taking a census per se but his wrong *motive* for taking it. After extensive military victories, he seemed inclined to trust in a strong army rather than in an all-powerful God.

Why didn't David listen to his general's advice? (21:3–4)

David's persistence toward sin in the face of Joab's advice seems out of character. He had listened to others before: Abigail (1 Samuel 25:4–35), the prophet Gad (1 Samuel 22:5), Joab (2 Samuel 19:1–8) and Nathan (2 Samuel 12:1–12). In a time of prosperity and strength, arrogance and self-reliance can make us deaf to God's warnings.

Seer (21:9)

A person who prophesies future events; a prophet. See *What was the difference between a prophet and a seer?* (2 Kings 17:13).

and went throughout Israel and then came back to Jerusalem[D]. [5]Joab reported the number of the fighting men to David: In all Israel there were one million one hundred thousand men who could handle a sword, including four hundred and seventy thousand in Judah.

[6]But Joab did not include Levi and Benjamin in the numbering, because the king's command was repulsive to him. [7]This command was also evil in the sight of God; so he punished Israel.

[8]Then David said to God, "I have sinned greatly by doing this. Now, I beg you, take away the guilt of your servant. I have done a very foolish thing."

[9]The LORD said to Gad, David's seer[D], [10]"Go and tell David, 'This is what the LORD says: I am giving you three options. Choose one of them for me to carry out against you.' "

[11]So Gad went to David and said to him, "This is what the LORD says: 'Take your choice: [12]three years of famine, three months of being swept away[a] before your enemies, with their swords overtaking you, or three days of the sword of the LORD—days of plague in the land, with the angel of the LORD ravaging every part of Israel.' Now then, decide how I should answer the one who sent me."

[13]David said to Gad, "I am in deep distress. Let me fall into the hands of the LORD, for his mercy[D] is very great; but do not let me fall into the hands of men."

[14]So the LORD sent a plague on Israel, and seventy thousand men of Israel fell dead. [15]And God sent an angel to destroy Jerusalem. But as the angel was doing so, the LORD saw it and was grieved because of the calamity and said to the angel who was destroying the people, "Enough! Withdraw your hand." The angel of the LORD

---

[a]12 Hebrew; Septuagint and Vulgate (see also 2 Samuel 24:13) *of fleeing*

Why did 70,000 die while the sinner lived? (21:14)

It doesn't seem fair. Even David was distressed by the consequences his sin had on innocent people (21:17). We may make our own choices, but we cannot control the extent of the consequences of sin.

Because of our Western individualism we struggle to understand the Eastern tradition in which the head of a family, tribe or nation represented the people under them. The members were treated as a whole, sharing in the blessings or punishments resulting from the actions of their leaders. When Achan sinned, God said *Israel has sinned* (Joshua 7:11). Joshua had to identify the tribe, clan and family to which the sinner belonged.

In this case, it may have been Israel's sin as a nation that led to David's sin. The Lord was angry with Israel *before* David was incited to take a census (2 Samuel 24:1). For this reason, some see this as a plague upon a nation of people who had themselves sinned. See *Did the punishment fit the crime?* (2 Samuel 24:15).

David's sin deserved personal punishment, but David's death might have been worse for the nation than the plague. Political turmoil in Israel could have brought invading armies that would have killed even more people. David suffered remorse and grief. Along with the leaders who may have supported his call for a census, David mourned and repented. God graciously forgave him and intervened to spare Jerusalem. Later, the temple was built on the site where David offered his sacrifice and saw the plague halted.

was then standing at the threshing floor of Araunah[a] the Jebusite. **16**David looked up and saw the angel of the LORD standing between heaven and earth, with a drawn sword in his hand extended over Jerusalem[D]. Then David and the elders, clothed in sackcloth[D], fell facedown.

17David said to God, "Was it not I who ordered the fighting men to be counted? I am the one who has sinned and done wrong. These are but sheep. What have they done? O LORD my God, let your hand fall upon me and my family, but do not let this plague remain on your people."

18Then the angel of the LORD ordered Gad to tell David to go up and build an altar to the LORD on the threshing floor of Araunah the Jebusite. **19**So David went up in obedience to the word that Gad had spoken in the name of the LORD.

20While Araunah was threshing wheat, he turned and saw the angel; his four sons who were with him hid themselves. **21**Then David approached, and when Araunah looked and saw him, he left the threshing floor and bowed down before David with his face to the ground.

22David said to him, "Let me have the site of your threshing floor so I can build an altar to the LORD, that the plague on the people may be stopped. Sell it to me at the full price."

23Araunah said to David, "Take it! Let my lord the king do whatever pleases him. Look, I will give the oxen for the burnt offerings[D], the threshing sledges for the wood, and the wheat for the grain offering[D]. I will give all this."

24But King David replied to Araunah, "No, I insist on paying the full price. I will not take for the LORD what is yours, or sacrifice[D] a burnt offering that costs me nothing."

25So David paid Araunah six hundred shekels[D][b] of gold for the site. **26**David built an altar to the LORD there and sacrificed burnt offerings and fellowship offerings[D].[c] He called on the LORD, and the LORD answered him with fire from heaven on the altar of burnt offering. **27**Then the LORD spoke to the angel, and he put his sword back into its sheath. **28**At that time, when David saw that the LORD had answered him on the threshing floor of Araunah the Jebusite, he offered sacrifices there. **29**The tabernacle of the LORD, which Moses had made in the desert, and the altar of burnt offering were at that time on the high place at Gibeon. **30**But David could not go before it to inquire of God, because he was afraid of the sword of the angel of the LORD.

22 Then David said, "The house of the LORD God is to be here, and also the altar of burnt offering for Israel."

Preparations for the Temple

2So David gave orders to assemble the aliens[D] living in Israel, and from among them he appointed stonecutters to prepare dressed stone for building the house of God. **3**He provided a large amount of iron to make nails for the doors of the gateways and for the fittings, and more bronze than could be weighed. **4**He also provided more cedar logs than could be counted, for the Sidonians and Tyrians had brought large numbers of them to David.

---

[a]15 Hebrew *Ornan*, a variant of *Araunah*; also in verses 18–28
[b]25 That is, about 15 pounds (about 7 kilograms)
[c]26 Traditionally *peace offerings*

Why would God be grieved by something he himself initiated? (21:15)

Just as a parent finds it painful but necessary to discipline a beloved child, God is troubled when we suffer the consequences of going against his will. He looks on us with compassion and love; he does not delight in destruction but works to save and heal. Because he is holy, sin must be punished but because of his mercy, the repentant can be spared.

Why would God use land owned by someone who wasn't an Israelite? (21:15)

Who owned the land was not as significant as its location. The word *site* (v. 22) suggests it was already considered a holy place. Tradition connects it with Mount Moriah where Abraham offered Isaac (Gen. 22:2). God chose this site for the temple, graciously allowing a pagan farmer to have a part in God's plan (see 2 Chron. 3:1).

Burnt offerings (21:26)

To make payment for sins, a person voluntarily brought a perfect animal to the priest, then laid his hand on the head of the animal to symbolize that the animal was a substitute for the sinner. The priest then killed it, sprinkled its blood and burned it, symbolizing the person's total devotion to God. See Lev. 1.

Fellowship offerings (21:26)

To express gratitude to God, a person sacrificed a perfect animal. Part was burned but part could be eaten by the person, symbolizing peace and fellowship with God. See Lev. 3.

Why build the temple where God's judgment stopped? (22:1)

The site was significant not just as the place where judgment stopped, but also as the place where mercy began. What more appropriate place for the temple than where God's judgment and mercy met? The holy, righteous God of Israel would have compassion on his people in this place. Also see *Why would God use land owned by someone who wasn't an Israelite?* (21:15).

How young was Solomon? (22:5)

Solomon was probably not more than 18 years old. Some suggest he may have been only 14.

Why would obeying God in war disqualify David from building the temple? (22:8)

Obedience was not the issue. The issue was God's purpose and timing: building the temple belonged to a time of peace. God gives each person abilities for specific situations or tasks. David, for example, was gifted as a fighter and a leader, and these abilities made possible the peace that enabled Solomon to reign with his gifts of wisdom and administration.

Sacred articles **(22:19)**

Utensils used in the tabernacle, including a gold-covered incense altar, a table for the showbread, gold dishes, spoons, bowls, lampstands, copper pots, shovels, basins, meat forks and firepans.

SCRIPTURE LINK (23:1)

Read about Solomon's rise to the throne in 1 Kings 1:11–40.

Why was it okay to count the Levites, when a census was wrong? (23:3; see 21:6–7)

Because the motives were completely different. The general census was prompted by proud self-reliance and a shift away from trusting in God. See **What was wrong with taking a census?** (21:1,6–7). By contrast, counting the Levites, the tribe set apart for God's service, enabled leaders to organize the work of the temple.

Why count Levites of different ages? (23:3,27)

The first count included Levites 30 years old or more; the second included those 20 and older. The difference may have been due to the transition from the tabernacle to the temple. In the tabernacle Levites served from age 30 to 50 (Num. 4:3). Apparently, more Levites were needed for the work of the larger temple so David lowered the age to 20. Also, the type of work would be lighter (see vv. 4–5) since they did not have to carry the tabernacle from place to place.

[5]David said, "My son Solomon is young and inexperienced, and the house to be built for the LORD should be of great magnificence and fame and splendor in the sight of all the nations. Therefore I will make preparations for it." So David made extensive preparations before his death[D].

[6]Then he called for his son Solomon and charged him to build a house for the LORD, the God of Israel. [7]David said to Solomon: "My son, I had it in my heart to build a house for the Name of the LORD my God. [8]But this word of the LORD came to me: 'You have shed much blood and have fought many wars. You are not to build a house for my Name, because you have shed much blood on the earth in my sight. [9]But you will have a son who will be a man of peace[D] and rest, and I will give him rest from all his enemies on every side. His name will be Solomon,[a] and I will grant Israel peace and quiet during his reign. [10]He is the one who will build a house for my Name. He will be my son, and I will be his father. And I will establish the throne of his kingdom over Israel forever.'

[11]"Now, my son, the LORD be with you, and may you have success and build the house of the LORD your God, as he said you would. [12]May the LORD give you discretion and understanding when he puts you in command over Israel, so that you may keep the law of the LORD your God. [13]Then you will have success if you are careful to observe the decrees and laws that the LORD gave Moses for Israel. Be strong and courageous. Do not be afraid or discouraged.

[14]"I have taken great pains to provide for the temple of the LORD a hundred thousand talents[b] of gold, a million talents[c] of silver, quantities of bronze and iron too great to be weighed, and wood and stone. And you may add to them. [15]You have many workmen: stonecutters, masons and carpenters, as well as men skilled in every kind of work [16]in gold and silver, bronze and iron—craftsmen beyond number. Now begin the work, and the LORD be with you."

[17]Then David ordered all the leaders of Israel to help his son Solomon. [18]He said to them, "Is not the LORD your God with you? And has he not granted you rest on every side? For he has handed the inhabitants of the land over to me, and the land is subject to the LORD and to his people. [19]Now devote your heart and soul[D] to seeking the LORD your God. Begin to build the sanctuary of the LORD God, so that you may bring the ark of the covenant[D] of the LORD and the sacred[D] articles belonging to God into the temple that will be built for the Name of the LORD."

The Levites

23 When David was old and full of years, he made his son Solomon king over Israel.

[2]He also gathered together all the leaders of Israel, as well as the priests[D] and Levites[D]. [3]The Levites thirty years old or more were counted, and the total number of men was thirty-eight thousand. [4]David said, "Of these, twenty-four thousand are to supervise the work of the temple of the LORD and six thousand are to be officials and judges. [5]Four thousand are to be gatekeepers and four thousand are to praise the LORD with the musical instruments I have provided for that purpose."

[a]9 *Solomon* sounds like and may be derived from the Hebrew for *peace.*   [b]14 That is, about 3,750 tons (about 3,450 metric tons)   [c]14 That is, about 37,500 tons (about 34,500 metric tons)

⁶David divided the Levites[D] into groups corresponding to the sons of Levi: Gershon, Kohath and Merari.

Gershonites

⁷Belonging to the Gershonites:
Ladan and Shimei.
⁸The sons of Ladan:
Jehiel the first, Zetham and Joel—three in all.
⁹The sons of Shimei:
Shelomoth, Haziel and Haran—three in all.
These were the heads of the families of Ladan.
¹⁰And the sons of Shimei:
Jahath, Ziza,[a] Jeush and Beriah.
These were the sons of Shimei—four in all.
¹¹Jahath was the first and Ziza the second, but Jeush and Beriah did not have many sons; so they were counted as one family with one assignment.

Kohathites

¹²The sons of Kohath:
Amram, Izhar, Hebron and Uzziel—four in all.
¹³The sons of Amram:
Aaron and Moses.
Aaron was set apart, he and his descendants forever, to consecrate[D] the most holy things, to offer sacrifices[D] before the LORD, to minister before him and to pronounce blessings in his name forever. ¹⁴The sons of Moses the man of God were counted as part of the tribe of Levi.
¹⁵The sons of Moses:
Gershom and Eliezer.
¹⁶The descendants of Gershom:
Shubael was the first.
¹⁷The descendants of Eliezer:
Rehabiah was the first.
Eliezer had no other sons, but the sons of Rehabiah were very numerous.
¹⁸The sons of Izhar:
Shelomith was the first.
¹⁹The sons of Hebron:
Jeriah the first, Amariah the second, Jahaziel the third and Jekameam the fourth.
²⁰The sons of Uzziel:
Micah the first and Isshiah the second.

Merarites

²¹The sons of Merari:
Mahli and Mushi.
The sons of Mahli:
Eleazar and Kish.
²²Eleazar died without having sons: he had only daughters. Their cousins, the sons of Kish, married them.
²³The sons of Mushi:
Mahli, Eder and Jerimoth—three in all.

²⁴These were the descendants of Levi by their families—the heads of families as they were registered under their names and counted individually, that is, the workers twenty years old or more who served in the temple of the LORD. ²⁵For David had said, "Since the LORD, the God of

---

a 10 One Hebrew manuscript, Septuagint and Vulgate (see also verse 11); most Hebrew manuscripts *Zina*

Why do we need to know the names of all these Levites? (23:7–23)

The days of the Levites being in charge of moving the tabernacle were over. Soon they would be ministering in the new temple. David was forming divisions to perform different tasks. By listing all the names, he let every family know of their importance and made sure everyone knew their tasks. From this list we can be reminded that we are all important to God, too, and that serving him is our task as well.

SCRIPTURE LINK (23:13)

Read how Aaron was set apart as a priest in Exodus 29–30.

What kind of job description did a Levite have? (23:26,28-32)

Levites assisted the priests as janitors for the sanctuary. They maintained the equipment in the sanctuary, moved the furnishings and baked the showbread. They were storekeepers of the supplies for the offerings. They were also musicians, administrators and assistants to the priests in ceremonies and sacrifices. Also see 9:28-32 and Num. 18:1-4.

Israel, has granted rest to his people and has come to dwell in Jerusalem[D] forever, [26]the Levites[D] no longer need to carry the tabernacle[D] or any of the articles used in its service." [27]According to the last instructions of David, the Levites were counted from those twenty years old or more.

[28]The duty of the Levites was to help Aaron's descendants in the service of the temple of the LORD: to be in charge of the courtyards, the side rooms, the purification of all sacred[D] things and the performance of other duties at the house of God. [29]They were in charge of the bread set out on the table, the flour for the grain offerings[D], the unleavened wafers, the baking and the mixing, and all measurements of quantity and size. [30]They were also to stand every morning to thank and praise the LORD. They were to do the same in the evening [31]and whenever burnt offerings[D] were presented to the LORD on Sabbaths[D] and at New Moon festivals[D] and at appointed feasts. They were to serve before the LORD regularly in the proper number and in the way prescribed for them.

[32]And so the Levites carried out their responsibilities for the Tent of Meeting[D], for the Holy Place[D] and, under their brothers the descendants of Aaron, for the service of the temple of the LORD.

The Divisions of Priests

24 These were the divisions of the sons of Aaron:
The sons of Aaron were Nadab, Abihu, Eleazar and Ithamar. [2]But Nadab and Abihu died before their father did, and they had no sons; so Eleazar and Ithamar served as the priests[D]. [3]With the help of Zadok a descendant of Eleazar and Ahimelech a descendant of Ithamar, David separated them into divisions for their appointed order of ministering. [4]A larger number of leaders were found among Eleazar's descendants than among Ithamar's, and they were divided accordingly: sixteen heads of families from Eleazar's descendants and eight heads of families from Ithamar's descendants. [5]They divided them impartially by drawing lots, for there were officials of the sanctuary and officials of God among the descendants of both Eleazar and Ithamar.

[6]The scribe Shemaiah son of Nethanel, a Levite, recorded their names in the presence of the king and of the officials: Zadok the priest, Ahimelech son of Abiathar and the heads of families of the priests and of the Levites—one family being taken from Eleazar and then one from Ithamar.

Why rely on chance to select the priests who would serve before God? (24:5)

In the Old Testament lots were cast to discover God's will (see Lev. 16:6-8; Joshua 18:8). Since God instructed Moses to use this method, God would control the outcome. The lots provided equal opportunities for service to the descendants of Eleazer and Ithamar. For more on casting lots, see *Why use a lottery to pick an apostle?* (Acts 1:26) and *How can God work through such an arbitrary process?* (Prov. 18:18).

How were officials of the sanctuary different from officials of God? (24:5)

The distinction between these is not clear. Some think the officials of the sanctuary offered sacrifices and conducted religious ceremonies while the officials of God represented the people before God. Another view is that the sanctuary officials were Levites who took care of facilities and utensils while the officials of God were priests who actually made the sacrifices. See *What kind of job description did a Levite have?* (23:26,28-32).

[7]The first lot fell to Jehoiarib,
the second to Jedaiah,
[8]the third to Harim,
the fourth to Seorim,
[9]the fifth to Malkijah,
the sixth to Mijamin,
[10]the seventh to Hakkoz,
the eighth to Abijah,
[11]the ninth to Jeshua,
the tenth to Shecaniah,
[12]the eleventh to Eliashib,
the twelfth to Jakim,
[13]the thirteenth to Huppah,
the fourteenth to Jeshebeab,
[14]the fifteenth to Bilgah,
the sixteenth to Immer,

15the seventeenth to Hezir,
  the eighteenth to Happizzez,
16the nineteenth to Pethahiah,
  the twentieth to Jehezkel,
17the twenty-first to Jakin,
  the twenty-second to Gamul,
18the twenty-third to Delaiah
  and the twenty-fourth to Maaziah.

19This was their appointed order of ministering when they entered the temple of the LORD, according to the regulations prescribed for them by their forefather Aaron, as the LORD, the God of Israel, had commanded him.

The Rest of the Levites

20As for the rest of the descendants of Levi:
  from the sons of Amram: Shubael;
    from the sons of Shubael: Jehdeiah.
  21As for Rehabiah, from his sons:
    Isshiah was the first.
22From the Izharites: Shelomoth;
  from the sons of Shelomoth: Jahath.
23The sons of Hebron: Jeriah the first,ª Amariah the second, Jahaziel the third and Jekameam the fourth.
24The son of Uzziel: Micah;
  from the sons of Micah: Shamir.
  25The brother of Micah: Isshiah;
    from the sons of Isshiah: Zechariah.
26The sons of Merari: Mahli and Mushi.
  The son of Jaaziah: Beno.
27The sons of Merari:
  from Jaaziah: Beno, Shoham, Zaccur and Ibri.
28From Mahli: Eleazar, who had no sons.
29From Kish: the son of Kish:
  Jerahmeel.
30And the sons of Mushi: Mahli, Eder and Jerimoth.

These were the Levites^D, according to their families.
31They also cast lots, just as their brothers the descendants of Aaron did, in the presence of King David and of Zadok, Ahimelech, and the heads of families of the priests^D and of the Levites. The families of the oldest brother were treated the same as those of the youngest.

The Singers

25 David, together with the commanders of the army, set apart some of the sons of Asaph, Heman and Jeduthun for the ministry of prophesying, accompanied by harps, lyres^D and cymbals. Here is the list of the men who performed this service:

2From the sons of Asaph:
  Zaccur, Joseph, Nethaniah and Asarelah. The sons of Asaph were under the supervision of Asaph, who prophesied under the king's supervision.
3As for Jeduthun, from his sons:
  Gedaliah, Zeri, Jeshaiah, Shimei,^b Hashabiah and Mattithiah, six in all, under the supervision of their father Jeduthun, who prophesied, using the harp in thanking and praising the LORD.

ª23 Two Hebrew manuscripts and some Septuagint manuscripts (see also 1 Chron. 23:19); most Hebrew manuscripts *The sons of Jeriah:*
^b3 One Hebrew manuscript and some Septuagint manuscripts (see also verse 17); most Hebrew manuscripts do not have *Shimei.*

SCRIPTURE LINK (24:19)
See the regulations God gave Aaron in Lev. 16; 21–22.

Was it unusual to treat the youngest and oldest the same? (24:31)
Yes, according to the customs of inheritance. See *As a firstborn son, what rights would Reuben have had?* (5:1). In serving God, every Levite shared equally.

What did a *seer* do for David? (25:5)

David looked to a *seer* (prophet) who revealed the will of God for certain situations and served as a check-and-balance on David's actions as king (2 Samuel 7:2–17; 12:1–25). In addition, prophetic ministry could at times include aspects of musical worship to the Lord: Heman's ministry of prophesying was *accompanied by harps, lyres and cymbals* (v. 1). Perhaps for this reason, some think that there could be a distinction between a prophetic ministry (hearing and delivering a message from God) and a prophetic office (a position to fulfill a function or service).

4As for Heman, from his sons:
Bukkiah, Mattaniah, Uzziel, Shubael and Jerimoth; Hananiah, Hanani, Eliathah, Giddalti and Romamti-Ezer; Joshbekashah, Mallothi, Hothir and Mahazioth. **5**All these were sons of Heman the king's seer[D]. They were given him through the promises of God to exalt him.[a] God gave Heman fourteen sons and three daughters.

6All these men were under the supervision of their fathers for the music of the temple of the LORD, with cymbals, lyres[D] and harps, for the ministry at the house of God. Asaph, Jeduthun and Heman were under the supervision of the king. **7**Along with their relatives—all of them trained and skilled in music for the LORD—they numbered 288. **8**Young and old alike, teacher as well as student, cast lots for their duties.

9The first lot, which was for Asaph, fell to Joseph,
his sons and relatives,[b]   12[c]
the second to Gedaliah,
he and his relatives and sons,   12
10the third to Zaccur,
his sons and relatives,   12
11the fourth to Izri,[d]
his sons and relatives,   12
12the fifth to Nethaniah,
his sons and relatives,   12
13the sixth to Bukkiah,
his sons and relatives,   12

a5 Hebrew *exalt the horn*   *b9* See Septuagint; Hebrew does not have *his sons and relatives*.   *c9* See the total in verse 7; Hebrew does not have *twelve*.   *d11* A variant of *Zeri*

What was *the ministry of prophesying?* (25:1,6–7)

Prophecy, among other things, was a declaration of God's message to the people, which sometimes included a message about future events. Prophets, uniquely empowered by the Spirit of God, spoke from their firsthand experience and knowledge of him.

The Bible describes in detail the call and work of some prophets like Moses or Samuel. But the ministry of prophesying was also given to other anonymous individuals who worshiped and spoke in groups. See *Company of the prophets* (2 Kings 2:3). On occasion, unlikely people were given the ability to prophesy. When Saul sent soldiers to capture David, the Spirit of God came upon them when they saw a group of prophets with Samuel, causing Saul's men to prophesy (1 Samuel 19:20).

What did prophesying sound like? Sometimes it was a ringing declaration of God's word for that moment. Other times prophecy pronounced spiritual truth with authority, warned of impending judgment or reassured people of God's deliverance. Often delivered in poetic or figurative language, Old Testament prophecy repeatedly focused on God's character and power. Sometimes prophets like Isaiah or Ezekiel seemed rather eccentric as they acted out an object lesson to underscore their message from God (see, for example, Isaiah 20:2; Ezek. 4:14–15).

Read aloud one of the psalms of the prophet Asaph (Psalms 75–83) and you may be able to picture the singers and instrumentalists in their ministry of prophesying.

14the seventh to Jesarelah,[a]
   his sons and relatives,   12
15the eighth to Jeshaiah,
   his sons and relatives,   12
16the ninth to Mattaniah,
   his sons and relatives,   12
17the tenth to Shimei,
   his sons and relatives,   12
18the eleventh to Azarel,[b]
   his sons and relatives,   12
19the twelfth to Hashabiah,
   his sons and relatives,   12
20the thirteenth to Shubael,
   his sons and relatives,   12
21the fourteenth to Mattithiah,
   his sons and relatives,   12
22the fifteenth to Jerimoth,
   his sons and relatives,   12
23the sixteenth to Hananiah,
   his sons and relatives,   12
24the seventeenth to Joshbekashah,
   his sons and relatives,   12
25the eighteenth to Hanani,
   his sons and relatives,   12
26the nineteenth to Mallothi,
   his sons and relatives,   12
27the twentieth to Eliathah,
   his sons and relatives,   12
28the twenty-first to Hothir,
   his sons and relatives,   12
29the twenty-second to Giddalti,
   his sons and relatives,   12
30the twenty-third to Mahazioth,
   his sons and relatives,   12
31the twenty-fourth to Romamti-Ezer,
   his sons and relatives,   12

The Gatekeepers

26 The divisions of the gatekeepers:

From the Korahites: Meshelemiah son of Kore, one of the sons of Asaph.
2Meshelemiah had sons:
   Zechariah the firstborn[D],
   Jediael the second,
   Zebadiah the third,
   Jathniel the fourth,
   3Elam the fifth,
   Jehohanan the sixth
   and Eliehoenai the seventh.
4Obed-Edom also had sons:
   Shemaiah the firstborn,
   Jehozabad the second,
   Joah the third,
   Sacar the fourth,
   Nethanel the fifth,
   5Ammiel the sixth,
   Issachar the seventh
   and Peullethai the eighth.
   (For God had blessed Obed-Edom.)

6His son Shemaiah also had sons, who were leaders

What kinds of duties did these lots represent? (25:9–31)

These lots determined the times at which each group of musicians would have their turn to minister. There were 288 (representing 24 groups of 12) who led the sacred singing and playing of instruments in the temple service (vv. 6–7), apparently at two-week intervals. Since there were 4,000 Levites designated to offer musical praises to the Lord (23:5), we can assume that those listed here were the leaders or the most skilled of the musicians, leaving 3,712 who assisted them.

What did gatekeepers do? (26:1)

Among their duties was guarding the temple entrances. But they apparently did much more, including the gathering of people's monetary offerings and perhaps even physically taking care of the temple.

---

[a] *14 A variant of *Asarelah*   [b] *18 A variant of *Uzziel*

in their father's family because they were very capable men. [7]The sons of Shemaiah: Othni, Raphael, Obed and Elzabad; his relatives Elihu and Semakiah were also able men. [8]All these were descendants of Obed-Edom; they and their sons and their relatives were capable men with the strength to do the work—descendants of Obed-Edom, 62 in all.

[9]Meshelemiah had sons and relatives, who were able men—18 in all.

How could a father *appoint* a firstborn son? (26:10)

The rights of a firstborn son might be shifted if his conduct had made him undeserving. See *As a firstborn son, what rights would Reuben have had?* (5:1). His rights, however, could not be taken away just to be given to the son of a more favored wife.

[10]Hosah the Merarite had sons: Shimri the first (although he was not the firstborn[D], his father had appointed him the first), [11]Hilkiah the second, Tabaliah the third and Zechariah the fourth. The sons and relatives of Hosah were 13 in all.

[12]These divisions of the gatekeepers, through their chief men, had duties for ministering in the temple of the LORD, just as their relatives had. [13]Lots were cast for each gate, according to their families, young and old alike.

[14]The lot for the East Gate fell to Shelemiah.[a] Then lots were cast for his son Zechariah, a wise counselor, and the lot for the North Gate fell to him. [15]The lot for the South Gate fell to Obed-Edom, and the lot for the storehouse fell to his sons. [16]The lots for the West Gate and the Shalleketh Gate on the upper road fell to Shuppim and Hosah.

Guard was alongside of guard: [17]There were six Levites[D] a day on the east, four a day on the north, four a day on the south and two at a time at the storehouse. [18]As for the court to the west, there were four at the road and two at the court itself.

[19]These were the divisions of the gatekeepers who were descendants of Korah and Merari.

The Treasurers and Other Officials

[20]Their fellow Levites were[b] in charge of the treasuries of the house of God and the treasuries for the dedicated things.

[21]The descendants of Ladan, who were Gershonites through Ladan and who were heads of families belonging to Ladan the Gershonite, were Jehieli, [22]the sons of Jehieli, Zetham and his brother Joel. They were in charge of the treasuries of the temple of the LORD.

[23]From the Amramites, the Izharites, the Hebronites and the Uzzielites:

[24]Shubael, a descendant of Gershom son of Moses, was the officer in charge of the treasuries. [25]His relatives through Eliezer: Rehabiah his son, Jeshaiah his son, Joram his son, Zicri his son and Shelomith his son. [26]Shelomith and his relatives were in charge of all the treasuries for the things dedicated by King David, by the heads of families who were the commanders of thousands and commanders of hundreds, and by the other army commanders. [27]Some of the plunder[D] taken in battle they dedicated for the repair of the temple of the LORD. [28]And everything dedicated by Samuel the seer[D] and by Saul son of Kish, Abner son of Ner and Joab son of Zeruiah, and all the other dedicated things were in the care of Shelomith and his relatives.

[a]14 A variant of *Meshelemiah*　　[b]20 Septuagint; Hebrew *As for the Levites, Ahijah was*

²⁹From the Izharites: Kenaniah and his sons were assigned duties away from the temple, as officials and judges over Israel. ³⁰From the Hebronites: Hashabiah and his relatives—seventeen hundred able men—were responsible in Israel west of the Jordan for all the work of the LORD and for the king's service. ³¹As for the Hebronites, Jeriah was their chief according to the genealogical records of their families. In the fortieth year of David's reign a search was made in the records, and capable men among the Hebronites were found at Jazer in Gilead. ³²Jeriah had twenty-seven hundred relatives, who were able men and heads of families, and King David put them in charge of the Reubenites, the Gadites and the half-tribe of Manasseh for every matter pertaining to God and for the affairs of the king.

Army Divisions

27 This is the list of the Israelites—heads of families, commanders of thousands and commanders of hundreds, and their officers, who served the king in all that concerned the army divisions that were on duty month by month throughout the year. Each division consisted of 24,000 men.

²In charge of the first division, for the first month, was Jashobeam son of Zabdiel. There were 24,000 men in his division. ³He was a descendant of Perez and chief of all the army officers for the first month.

⁴In charge of the division for the second month was Dodai the Ahohite; Mikloth was the leader of his division. There were 24,000 men in his division.

⁵The third army commander, for the third month, was Benaiah son of Jehoiada the priest^D. He was chief and there were 24,000 men in his division. ⁶This was the Benaiah who was a mighty man among the Thirty and was over the Thirty. His son Ammizabad was in charge of his division.

⁷The fourth, for the fourth month, was Asahel the brother of Joab; his son Zebadiah was his successor. There were 24,000 men in his division.

⁸The fifth, for the fifth month, was the commander Shamhuth the Izrahite. There were 24,000 men in his division.

⁹The sixth, for the sixth month, was Ira the son of Ikkesh the Tekoite. There were 24,000 men in his division.

¹⁰The seventh, for the seventh month, was Helez the Pelonite, an Ephraimite. There were 24,000 men in his division.

¹¹The eighth, for the eighth month, was Sibbecai the Hushathite, a Zerahite. There were 24,000 men in his division.

¹²The ninth, for the ninth month, was Abiezer the Anathothite, a Benjamite. There were 24,000 men in his division.

¹³The tenth, for the tenth month, was Maharai the Netophathite, a Zerahite. There were 24,000 men in his division.

¹⁴The eleventh, for the eleventh month, was Benaiah the Pirathonite, an Ephraimite. There were 24,000 men in his division.

¹⁵The twelfth, for the twelfth month, was Heldai the Ne-

Why did these tribes need someone besides David in charge of them? (26:32)

The tribes of Reuben, Gad and the half-tribe of Manasseh had settled east of the Jordan River and were apparently beyond the jurisdiction of the Levites who administered the tribes west of the river. By this time (the 40th year of his reign was his last) David had become more feeble, perhaps prompting him to delegate more of the administrative tasks. Or perhaps he wanted to prepare for an orderly transition when his son would become king.

The Thirty (27:6)

Refers to David's mighty men, known for their strength, courage and loyalty. See their description in 11:10–47 and 2 Samuel 23:8–39.

tophathite, from the family of Othniel. There were 24,000 men in his division.

Officers of the Tribes

16The officers over the tribes of Israel:

over the Reubenites: Eliezer son of Zicri;
over the Simeonites: Shephatiah son of Maacah;
17over Levi: Hashabiah son of Kemuel;
over Aaron: Zadok;
18over Judah: Elihu, a brother of David;
over Issachar: Omri son of Michael;
19over Zebulun: Ishmaiah son of Obadiah;
over Naphtali: Jerimoth son of Azriel;
20over the Ephraimites: Hoshea son of Azaziah;
over half the tribe of Manasseh: Joel son of Pedaiah;
21over the half-tribe of Manasseh in Gilead: Iddo son of Zechariah;
over Benjamin: Jaasiel son of Abner;
22over Dan: Azarel son of Jeroham.
These were the officers over the tribes of Israel.

23David did not take the number of the men twenty years old or less, because the LORD had promised to make Israel as numerous as the stars in the sky. 24Joab son of Zeruiah began to count the men but did not finish. Wrath came on Israel on account of this numbering, and the number was not entered in the book[a] of the annals of King David.

The King's Overseers

25Azmaveth son of Adiel was in charge of the royal storehouses.

Jonathan son of Uzziah was in charge of the storehouses in the outlying districts, in the towns, the villages and the watchtowers[b].

26Ezri son of Kelub was in charge of the field workers who farmed the land.

27Shimei the Ramathite was in charge of the vineyards.

Zabdi the Shiphmite was in charge of the produce of the vineyards for the wine vats.

28Baal-Hanan the Gederite was in charge of the olive and sycamore-fig trees in the western foothills.

Joash was in charge of the supplies of olive oil.

29Shitrai the Sharonite was in charge of the herds grazing in Sharon.

Shaphat son of Adlai was in charge of the herds in the valleys.

30Obil the Ishmaelite was in charge of the camels.

Jehdeiah the Meronothite was in charge of the donkeys.

31Jaziz the Hagrite was in charge of the flocks.

All these were the officials in charge of King David's property.

32Jonathan, David's uncle, was a counselor, a man of insight and a scribe. Jehiel son of Hacmoni took care of the king's sons.

33Ahithophel was the king's counselor.

Hushai the Arkite was the king's friend. 34Ahithophel was succeeded by Jehoiada son of Benaiah and by Abiathar.

Joab was the commander of the royal army.

a24 Septuagint; Hebrew number

Wrath came on Israel on account of this numbering (27:24)
See *What was wrong with taking a census?* (21:1).

Why list *friend* as an official position? (27:33)
The title may have been given to a special personal adviser. In this case, it may have been an honor given to Hushai for his part in frustrating Absalom's plot against David (2 Samuel 15:31–37).

David's Plans for the Temple

28 David summoned all the officials of Israel to assemble at Jerusalem[D]: the officers over the tribes, the commanders of the divisions in the service of the king, the commanders of thousands and commanders of hundreds, and the officials in charge of all the property and livestock belonging to the king and his sons, together with the palace officials, the mighty men and all the brave warriors.

²King David rose to his feet and said: "Listen to me, my brothers and my people. I had it in my heart to build a house as a place of rest for the ark of the covenant[D] of the LORD, for the footstool[D] of our God, and I made plans to build it. ³But God said to me, 'You are not to build a house for my Name, because you are a warrior and have shed blood.'

⁴"Yet the LORD, the God of Israel, chose me from my whole family to be king over Israel forever. He chose Judah as leader, and from the house of Judah he chose my family, and from my father's sons he was pleased to make me king over all Israel. ⁵Of all my sons—and the LORD has given me many—he has chosen my son Solomon to sit on the throne of the kingdom of the LORD over Israel. ⁶He said to me: 'Solomon your son is the one who will build my house and my courts, for I have chosen him to be my son, and I will be his father. ⁷I will establish his kingdom forever if he is unswerving in carrying out my commands and laws, as is being done at this time.'

⁸"So now I charge you in the sight of all Israel and of the assembly of the LORD, and in the hearing of our God: Be careful to follow all the commands of the LORD your God, that you may possess this good land and pass it on as an inheritance to your descendants forever.

⁹"And you, my son Solomon, acknowledge the God of your father, and serve him with wholehearted devotion and with a willing mind, for the LORD searches every heart and understands every motive behind the thoughts. If you seek him, he will be found by you; but if you forsake him, he will reject you forever. ¹⁰Consider now, for the LORD has chosen you to build a temple as a sanctuary. Be strong and do the work."

¹¹Then David gave his son Solomon the plans for the portico of the temple, its buildings, its storerooms, its upper parts, its inner rooms and the place of atonement[D]. ¹²He gave him the plans of all that the Spirit had put in his mind for the courts of the temple of the LORD and all the surrounding rooms, for the treasuries of the temple of God and for the treasuries for the dedicated things. ¹³He gave him instructions for the divisions of the priests[D] and Levites[D], and for all the work of serving in the temple of the LORD, as well as for all the articles to be used in its service. ¹⁴He designated the weight of gold for all the gold articles to be used in various kinds of service, and the weight of silver for all the silver articles to be used in various kinds of service: ¹⁵the weight of gold for the gold lampstands and their lamps, with the weight for each lampstand and its lamps; and the weight of silver for each silver lampstand and its lamps, according to the use of each lampstand; ¹⁶the weight of gold for each table for consecrated[D] bread; the weight of silver for the silver tables; ¹⁷the weight of pure gold for the forks, sprinkling bowls and pitchers; the weight of gold for each gold dish; the weight of silver for each silver dish; ¹⁸and the weight

How did the Spirit give David the plans for the temple? (28:12,19)

God gave Moses a vision of the tabernacle—including descriptions as detailed as a blueprint. For years David dreamed of building the temple. He credited the Spirit with giving him this vision, down to the details of the plan, revealed in 2 Chronicles 3–4.

Was this chariot something new? (28:18)

No. The golden cherubim on the cover of the ark of the covenant (Exodus 25:17–22) were considered God's chariot. It was a figurative way to describe their wings spread over the ark —where God's holy presence was. The Bible speaks of God *enthroned between the cherubim* (Psalm 99:1) and says that *he mounted* (a word drawn from the word for *chariot*) *the cherubim and flew* (Psalm 18:10).

of the refined gold for the altar of incense[D]. He also gave him the plan for the chariot, that is, the cherubim[D] of gold that spread their wings and shelter the ark of the covenant[D] of the LORD.

19"All this," David said, "I have in writing from the hand of the LORD upon me, and he gave me understanding in all the details of the plan."

20David also said to Solomon his son, "Be strong and courageous, and do the work. Do not be afraid or discouraged, for the LORD God, my God, is with you. He will not fail you or forsake you until all the work for the service of the temple of the LORD is finished. **21**The divisions of the priests[D] and Levites[D] are ready for all the work on the temple of God, and every willing man skilled in any craft will help you in all the work. The officials and all the people will obey your every command."

How was the hand of the Lord upon David? (28:19)

This at least means that God inspired David to write these things, much as he did other Biblical writers. David seems to be implying a similarity between the way he received the plan from the Lord and the way Moses received the Law from God.

Gifts for Building the Temple

29 Then King David said to the whole assembly: "My son Solomon, the one whom God has chosen, is young and inexperienced. The task is great, because this palatial structure is not for man but for the LORD God. **2**With all my resources I have provided for the temple of my God—gold for the gold work, silver for the silver, bronze for the bronze, iron for the iron and wood for the wood, as well as onyx for the settings, turquoise,[a] stones of various colors, and all kinds of fine stone and marble—all of these in large quantities. **3**Besides, in my devotion to the temple of my God I now give my personal treasures of gold and silver for the temple of my God, over and above everything I have provided for this holy temple: **4**three thousand talents[b] of gold (gold of Ophir) and seven thousand talents[c] of refined silver, for the overlaying of the walls of the buildings, **5**for the gold work and the silver work, and for all the work to be done by the craftsmen. Now, who is willing to consecrate[D] himself today to the LORD?"

How much was all this gold, silver, bronze and iron worth? (29:3–7)

Any calculations are rather inconclusive since ancient Israel did not use a money-based economic system. But calculating simply by the weight and today's approximate market value, the total of the gold alone (v. 7) would be worth over $7 billion.

6Then the leaders of families, the officers of the tribes of Israel, the commanders of thousands and commanders of hundreds, and the officials in charge of the king's work gave willingly. **7**They gave toward the work on the temple of God five thousand talents[d] and ten thousand darics[e] of gold, ten thousand talents[f] of silver, eighteen thousand talents[g] of bronze and a hundred thousand talents[h] of iron. **8**Any who had precious stones gave them to the treasury of the temple of the LORD in the custody of Jehiel the Gershonite. **9**The people rejoiced at the willing response of their leaders, for they had given freely and wholeheartedly to the LORD. David the king also rejoiced greatly.

David's Prayer

10David praised the LORD in the presence of the whole assembly, saying,

"Praise be to you, O LORD,
    God of our father Israel,

---

*a*2 The meaning of the Hebrew for this word is uncertain.
*b*4 That is, about 110 tons (about 100 metric tons)   *c*4 That is, about 260 tons (about 240 metric tons)   *d*7 That is, about 190 tons (about 170 metric tons)   *e*7 That is, about 185 pounds (about 84 kilograms)   *f*7 That is, about 375 tons (about 345 metric tons)   *g*7 That is, about 675 tons (about 610 metric tons)   *h*7 That is, about 3,750 tons (about 3,450 metric tons)

from everlasting to everlasting.
¹¹Yours, O LORD, is the greatness and the power
   and the glory^D and the majesty and the
      splendor,
   for everything in heaven and earth is yours.
   Yours, O LORD, is the kingdom;
      you are exalted as head over all.
¹²Wealth and honor come from you;
      you are the ruler of all things.
   In your hands are strength and power
      to exalt and give strength to all.
¹³Now, our God, we give you thanks,
      and praise your glorious name.

¹⁴"But who am I, and who are my people, that we should be able to give as generously as this? Everything comes from you, and we have given you only what comes from your hand. ¹⁵We are aliens^D and strangers in your sight, as were all our forefathers. Our days on earth are like a shadow, without hope. ¹⁶O LORD our God, as for all this abundance that we have provided for building you a temple for your Holy Name, it comes from your hand, and all of it belongs to you. ¹⁷I know, my God, that you test the heart and are pleased with integrity. All these things have I given willingly and with honest intent. And now I have seen with joy how willingly your people who are here have given to you. ¹⁸O LORD, God of our fathers Abraham, Isaac and Israel, keep this desire in the hearts of your people forever, and keep their hearts loyal to you. ¹⁹And give my son Solomon the wholehearted devotion to keep your commands, requirements and decrees and to do everything to build the palatial structure for which I have provided."

²⁰Then David said to the whole assembly, "Praise the LORD your God." So they all praised the LORD, the God of their fathers; they bowed low and fell prostrate before the LORD and the king.

Solomon Acknowledged as King

²¹The next day they made sacrifices^D to the LORD and presented burnt offerings^D to him: a thousand bulls, a thousand rams and a thousand male lambs, together with their drink offerings^D, and other sacrifices in abundance for all Israel. ²²They ate and drank with great joy in the presence of the LORD that day.

Then they acknowledged Solomon son of David as king a second time, anointing^D him before the LORD to be ruler and Zadok to be priest^D. ²³So Solomon sat on the throne of the LORD as king in place of his father David. He prospered and all Israel obeyed him. ²⁴All the officers and mighty men, as well as all of King David's sons, pledged their submission to King Solomon.

²⁵The LORD highly exalted Solomon in the sight of all Israel and bestowed on him royal splendor such as no king over Israel ever had before.

The Death of David

²⁶David son of Jesse was king over all Israel. ²⁷He ruled over Israel forty years—seven in Hebron and thirty-three in Jerusalem^D. ²⁸He died at a good old age, having enjoyed long life, wealth and honor. His son Solomon succeeded him as king.

²⁹As for the events of King David's reign, from begin-

How does God test the heart? (29:17)
The Lord searches every heart, David said, *and understands every motive behind the thoughts* (28:9). David knew appearances might impress people, but God sees beneath the surface. God knows our hidden faults and our honorable motives (Psalms 19:12; 90:8). Just as God searched the motives of David, Solomon and the people then, he searches our thoughts and motives, testing them against his standard of integrity and purity. See article: **Why did testing come to Job?** (Job 23:10).

Why did they acknowledge Solomon as king a second time? (29:22)
The first time was a hurried, emergency coronation (1 Kings 1). Some believe there was a period of co-regency when Solomon and David ruled together due to Solomon's youth.

What are the records of Samuel, Nathan and Gad? (29:29)
As prophets and seers, these men served as national historians. The records may refer to material which found its way into the books of 1 and 2 Samuel.

Do any of these records still exist? (29:29)

No, except for what was taken from them and recorded in Scripture. Apparently the person writing 1 and 2 Chronicles drew from many sources, including several other existing Bible books.

ning to end, they are written in the records of Samuel the seer[D], the records of Nathan the prophet[D] and the records of Gad the seer, [30]together with the details of his reign and power, and the circumstances that surrounded him and Israel and the kingdoms of all the other lands.

2 CHRONICLES

Why read this book?

At first glance, 2 Chronicles seems to be a rather dry record of historical facts. But 2 Chronicles is to history what the space shuttle is to a hang glider. The "extras" you'll find featured in its pages offer a higher vantage point. By looking at God's dealings with his people, a nation caught in sin and decline, 2 Chronicles helps us understand a bit of the scope of human events: even when life unravels, God still has a purpose for his people.

Who wrote this book?

Probably Ezra, a priest and scribe who also wrote the book that bears his name. Some suggest, however, that an unknown priest or Levite may have been the author.

When was it written?

The late 400s B.C., though this book covers the period from Solomon's reign (about 970 B.C.) to the fall of Jerusalem (586 B.C.).

What was happening at the time?

After the Babylonians destroyed Jerusalem, the Jews were taken as captives to Babylon where they lived for 70 years. Then, after the Persians conquered Babylon, several groups of Jews were allowed to return to their homeland.

To whom was it written and why?

To those who resettled in Judah and were essentially rebuilding their society. Studying the early, prosperous days of their nation reinforced their faith in the promises God had given them as a people. God also wanted them to learn from their mistakes so they would not be destined to repeat the past.

What to look for in 2 Chronicles:

You'll find history with a moral: a nation that honors God will see success. Focusing mainly on Judah, the southern kingdom, the writer tells us about the temple, the priesthood, God's covenant and the kings to reinforce his central theme. By the end of the book you'll have read about the downfall of the nation—the result of rulers and people straying from God.

When did these things happen?

TIME LINE	1400 BC	1300	1200	1100	1000	900	800	700	600	500	400
Solomon's reign (970-930 B.C.)											
Building of the temple (966-959 B.C.)											
Division of the kingdom (930 B.C.)											
Exile of Israel (722 B.C.)											
Fall of Jerusalem (586 B.C.)											
First return of exiles to Jerusalem (538 B.C.)											
Book of 2 Chronicles written (c.450-400 B.C.)											

Why did Solomon worship at a high place? (1:3)

Typically such hilltop locations, with their symbolic stones and other objects of pagan worship, were forbidden to the Israelites (Num. 33:52). But because the Tent of Meeting (or tabernacle) was at Gibeon (see *Map 4* at the back of this Bible), it was a legitimate place for Solomon to seek God's favor. Still, some think the Israelites compromised their standards in the first place by pitching the tabernacle at a high place—one example of the Israelites adopting Canaanite religious customs.

Why did David remove the ark of God from the Tent of Meeting? (1:4)

He didn't. It had been removed years before during an ill-conceived plan to use it as a sort of good luck charm during battles against the Philistines (1 Samuel 4:1–11). It ended up at Kiriath Jearim in the house of Abinadab (1 Samuel 7:1) where David later retrieved it.

Why did David set up a new worship center in Jerusalem? (1:4)

In 6:6, we hear David's own explanation for his decision: God had chosen Jerusalem. This was the place where Abraham had obeyed God in faith and offered his son as a sacrifice centuries earlier (Gen. 22). In addition to its religious significance, David may have wanted Jerusalem for his capital because it was a good military site, easily defended by his army. He probably wanted to bring together the political and religious centers of Israel.

Solomon Asks for Wisdom

1 Solomon son of David established himself firmly over his kingdom, for the LORD his God was with him and made him exceedingly great.

²Then Solomon spoke to all Israel—to the commanders of thousands and commanders of hundreds, to the judges and to all the leaders in Israel, the heads of families— ³and Solomon and the whole assembly went to the high place at Gibeon, for God's Tent of Meeting^D was there, which Moses the LORD's servant had made in the desert. ⁴Now David had brought up the ark of God from Kiriath Jearim to the place he had prepared for it, because he had pitched a tent for it in Jerusalem^D. ⁵But the bronze altar that Bezalel son of Uri, the son of Hur, had made was in Gibeon in front of the tabernacle^D of the LORD; so Solomon and the assembly inquired of him there. ⁶Solomon went up to the bronze altar before the LORD in the Tent of Meeting and offered a thousand burnt offerings on it.

⁷That night God appeared to Solomon and said to him, "Ask for whatever you want me to give you."

⁸Solomon answered God, "You have shown great kindness to David my father and have made me king in his place. ⁹Now, LORD God, let your promise to my father David be confirmed, for you have made me king over a people who are as numerous as the dust of the earth. ¹⁰Give me wisdom and knowledge, that I may lead this people, for who is able to govern this great people of yours?"

¹¹God said to Solomon, "Since this is your heart's desire and you have not asked for wealth, riches or honor, nor for the death^D of your enemies, and since you have not asked for a long life but for wisdom and knowledge to govern my people over whom I have made you king, ¹²therefore wisdom and knowledge will be given you. And I will also give you wealth, riches and honor, such as no

Can the Bible exaggerate and still be true? (1:9–15)

In a word, yes. When Solomon said the people were *as numerous as the dust of the earth,* he didn't have an exact figure in mind. Solomon was using a figure of speech called hyperbole—an exaggeration not meant to be interpreted literally. He simply meant that there were a lot of people!

The writers of the Bible's 66 books used all the richness and variety of human language to communicate God's message. To understand the Bible accurately, its various literary devices and figures of speech must be seen for what they are. Interpret them at face value and the intended meaning may be missed completely.

The writer of Chronicles reports that Solomon *made silver and gold as common . . . as stones, and cedar* (a rare and costly wood) *as plentiful as sycamore-fig trees* (a commonplace tree). His point was not to be exact, but to indicate great wealth—numbers that would boggle the mind.

There are many passages—especially in 1 and 2 Chronicles—where the Bible offers precise information. But when God promises Abraham as many children as there are stars or grains of sand (Gen. 15:5), or when Mark says that *all the people of Jerusalem* went out to see John the Baptist (Mark 1:5), or even when Paul claims to be *the worst* of sinners (1 Tim. 1:15), the context and language indicate a meaning beneath the surface. In such cases, the Bible simply uses the richness of human language to express what's true.

king who was before you ever had and none after you will have."

¹³Then Solomon went to Jerusalem^D from the high place at Gibeon, from before the Tent of Meeting^D. And he reigned over Israel.

¹⁴Solomon accumulated chariots and horses; he had fourteen hundred chariots and twelve thousand horses,^a which he kept in the chariot cities and also with him in Jerusalem. ¹⁵The king made silver and gold as common in Jerusalem as stones, and cedar as plentiful as syca-more-fig trees in the foothills. ¹⁶Solomon's horses were imported from Egypt^b and from Kue^c—the royal merchants purchased them from Kue. ¹⁷They imported a chariot from Egypt for six hundred shekels^d of silver, and a horse for a hundred and fifty.^e They also exported them to all the kings of the Hittites and of the Arameans.

Preparations for Building the Temple

2 Solomon gave orders to build a temple for the Name of the Lord and a royal palace for himself. ²He conscripted seventy thousand men as carriers and eighty thousand as stonecutters in the hills and thirty-six hundred as foremen over them.

³Solomon sent this message to Hiram^f king of Tyre:

"Send me cedar logs as you did for my father David when you sent him cedar to build a palace to live in. ⁴Now I am about to build a temple for the Name of the Lord my God and to dedicate it to him for burning fragrant incense^D before him, for setting out the consecrated^D bread regularly, and for making burnt offerings^D every morning and evening and on Sabbaths^D and New Moons and at the appointed feasts of the Lord our God. This is a lasting ordinance for Israel.

⁵"The temple I am going to build will be great, because our God is greater than all other gods. ⁶But who is able to build a temple for him, since the heavens, even the highest heavens, cannot contain him? Who then am I to build a temple for him, except as a place to burn sacrifices^D before him?

⁷"Send me, therefore, a man skilled to work in gold and silver, bronze and iron, and in purple^D, crimson and blue yarn, and experienced in the art of engraving, to work in Judah and Jerusalem with my skilled craftsmen, whom my father David provided.

⁸"Send me also cedar, pine and algum^g logs from Lebanon, for I know that your men are skilled in cutting timber there. My men will work with yours ⁹to provide me with plenty of lumber, because the temple I build must be large and magnificent. ¹⁰I will give your servants, the woodsmen who cut the timber, twenty thousand cors^h of ground wheat, twenty thousand cors of barley, twenty thousand baths^i of wine and twenty thousand baths of olive oil."

¹¹Hiram king of Tyre replied by letter to Solomon:

---

a14 Or *charioteers*   *b16* Or possibly *Muzur,* a region in Cilicia; also in verse 17   *c16* Probably Cilicia   *d17* That is, about 15 pounds (about 7 kilograms)   *e17* That is, about 3 3/4 pounds (about 1.7 kilograms)   *f3* Hebrew *Huram,* a variant of *Hiram;* also in verses 11 and 12   *g8* Probably a variant of *almug;* possibly juniper   *h10* That is, probably about 125,000 bushels (about 4,400 kiloliters)   *i10* That is, probably about 115,000 gallons (about 440 kiloliters)

Did 1,000 sacrifices help Solomon hear from God? (1:5–6)

No, Solomon did not "earn" a hearing with God by offering so many sacrifices. But the large number was a dramatic sign to the public that Solomon meant business and realized he needed God's guidance in his reign.

Wisdom . . . will be given you (1:12)

See article: *What kind of wisdom does God give?* (1 Kings 4:29–34).

Why build a temple for the *Name* of the Lord? (2:1)

In Hebrew thinking, a person's name was an extension of himself. To speak of God's name, therefore, was to speak of God himself. His *Name* was considered holy, just as God is holy. Also included in the idea of a person's name was one's reputation. Solomon wanted to build a magnificent temple to gain respect for God from the surrounding nations, strengthening God's reputation. See Deut. 12:5. Also see *Was there a difference between a temple for God and a temple for his Name?* (1 Kings 8:27).

Did the king of Tyre believe in God? (2:12)

Not necessarily. It was a common diplomatic courtesy at that time for rulers of one nation to speak well of the gods of another nation (see, for example, 1 Kings 10:9).

Did Solomon treat the aliens fairly? (2:17)

There is nothing to say that he didn't, at least by the standards of the ancient world (where forced labor was considered a fact of life). These aliens were descendants of those who had lost their land to the Israelites many years before (8:8). Many Canaanites had been killed by the conquering Israelites, so the survivors' descendants may have felt lucky to be alive. Since Solomon fed the visiting laborers from Tyre (v. 10), it's reasonable to assume that he did at least as much for his own slaves.

Why build the temple on Mount Moriah? (3:1)

Historically, it had been the site of two significant encounters with God. To stop a deadly plague, David had been instructed to build an altar and offer a sacrifice at Araunah's threshing floor (2 Samuel 24:18), overlooking Jerusalem from Mount Moriah. It was also the site where Abraham had nearly sacrificed Isaac (Gen. 22). Also see *Why build the temple where God's judgment stopped?* (1 Chron. 22:1).

Cubit of the old standard (3:3)

This was 20–21 inches long, a handbreadth larger than the "common cubit." The old cubit, or "long cubit" (Ezek. 40:5; 43:13), seems to have been used for sacred purposes.

Gold of Parvaim (3:6)

Parvaim may be the name of a place in Yemen and southeast Arabia (see *Map 12* at the back of this Bible). The context indicates its gold was more precious than ordinary gold, perhaps because it had fewer impurities or perhaps because it was imported from a distant, exotic location.

"Because the LORD loves his people, he has made you their king."

¹²And Hiram added:

"Praise be to the LORD, the God of Israel, who made heaven and earth! He has given King David a wise son, endowed with intelligence and discernment, who will build a temple for the LORD and a palace for himself.

¹³"I am sending you Huram-Abi, a man of great skill, ¹⁴whose mother was from Dan and whose father was from Tyre. He is trained to work in gold and silver, bronze and iron, stone and wood, and with purple^D and blue and crimson yarn and fine linen. He is experienced in all kinds of engraving and can execute any design given to him. He will work with your craftsmen and with those of my lord, David your father.

¹⁵"Now let my lord send his servants the wheat and barley and the olive oil and wine he promised, ¹⁶and we will cut all the logs from Lebanon that you need and will float them in rafts by sea down to Joppa^D. You can then take them up to Jerusalem^D."

¹⁷Solomon took a census of all the aliens^D who were in Israel, after the census his father David had taken; and they were found to be 153,600. ¹⁸He assigned 70,000 of them to be carriers and 80,000 to be stonecutters in the hills, with 3,600 foremen over them to keep the people working.

Solomon Builds the Temple

3 Then Solomon began to build the temple of the LORD in Jerusalem on Mount Moriah, where the LORD had appeared to his father David. It was on the threshing floor of Araunah^a the Jebusite, the place provided by David. ²He began building on the second day of the second month in the fourth year of his reign.

³The foundation Solomon laid for building the temple of God was sixty cubits^D long and twenty cubits wide^b (using the cubit of the old standard). ⁴The portico at the front of the temple was twenty cubits^c long across the width of the building and twenty cubits^d high.

He overlaid the inside with pure gold. ⁵He paneled the main hall with pine and covered it with fine gold and decorated it with palm tree and chain designs. ⁶He adorned the temple with precious stones. And the gold he used was gold of Parvaim. ⁷He overlaid the ceiling beams, doorframes, walls and doors of the temple with gold, and he carved cherubim^D on the walls.

⁸He built the Most Holy Place^D, its length corresponding to the width of the temple—twenty cubits long and twenty cubits wide. He overlaid the inside with six hundred talents^e of fine gold. ⁹The gold nails weighed fifty shekels.^f He also overlaid the upper parts with gold.

¹⁰In the Most Holy Place he made a pair of sculptured cherubim and overlaid them with gold. ¹¹The total wingspan of the cherubim was twenty cubits. One

---

a1 Hebrew *Ornan,* a variant of *Araunah*   *b3* That is, about 90 feet (about 27 meters) long and 30 feet (about 9 meters) wide   *c4* That is, about 30 feet (about 9 meters); also in verses 8, 11 and 13   *d4* Some Septuagint and Syriac manuscripts; Hebrew *and a hundred and twenty*   *e8* That is, about 23 tons (about 21 metric tons)   *f9* That is, about 1 1/4 pounds (about 0.6 kilogram)

wing of the first cherub^D was five cubits^{Da} long and touched the temple wall, while its other wing, also five cubits long, touched the wing of the other cherub. ¹²Similarly one wing of the second cherub was five cubits long and touched the other temple wall, and its other wing, also five cubits long, touched the wing of the first cherub. ¹³The wings of these cherubim extended twenty cubits. They stood on their feet, facing the main hall.^b

¹⁴He made the curtain of blue, purple^D and crimson yarn and fine linen, with cherubim worked into it.

¹⁵In the front of the temple he made two pillars, which ⌊together⌋ were thirty-five cubits^c long, each with a capital on top measuring five cubits. ¹⁶He made interwoven chains^d and put them on top of the pillars. He also made a hundred pomegranates and attached them to the chains. ¹⁷He erected the pillars in the front of the temple, one to the south and one to the north. The one to the south he named Jakin^e and the one to the north Boaz.^f

The Temple's Furnishings

4 He made a bronze altar twenty cubits long, twenty cubits wide and ten cubits high.^g ²He made the Sea of cast metal, circular in shape, measuring ten cubits from rim to rim and five cubits^h high. It took a line of thirty cubitsⁱ to measure around it. ³Below the

Why give names to pillars? (3:17)
These pillars in front of the temple were more like monuments or national markers. They didn't hold up anything in the temple structure, but were apparently free-standing. They had symbolic meaning, as their names indicate (see NIV text notes). Jakin and Boaz were monuments to God's promise to keep the temple standing.

The Sea of cast metal (4:2)
A large bronze basin for the priests' ceremonial washing. It was like a small inland "sea." See NIV text notes for its dimensions.

---

^a11 That is, about 7 1/2 feet (about 2.3 meters); also in verse 15
^b13 Or *facing inward*   ^c15 That is, about 52 feet (about 16 meters)
^d16 Or possibly *made chains in the inner sanctuary*; the meaning of the Hebrew for this phrase is uncertain.   ^e17 *Jakin* probably means *he establishes*.   ^f17 *Boaz* probably means *in him is strength*.
^g1 That is, about 30 feet (about 9 meters) long and wide, and about 15 feet (about 4.5 meters) high   ^h2 That is, about 7 1/2 feet (about 2.3 meters)   ⁱ2 That is, about 45 feet (about 13.5 meters)

What is the significance of the temple? (3:3–17)

It is important for us to understand what the temple meant to the ancient Israelites. First, the temple provided a focus for Israel's worship. For years the tabernacle had been in one place, the ark in another. To make matters worse, some Israelites were worshiping at the pagan high places. The temple centralized the nation's worship and redirected it back to the Lord.

The temple also represented the only way God provided for his people to have a relationship with him. Sacrifices for sin were offered there by priests who served as mediators before God on behalf of the people.

Even though the temple no longer exists, the principles behind it do. Studying the temple can teach us certain parallel New Testament concepts: (1) Though we have different traditions, our worship must be centralized, focused on Jesus. (2) Just as Solomon spared no expense to build the temple, today we should hold nothing back in our commitment to God. God deserves the best—then and now. (3) The temple was God's means of meeting with his people, just as he now meets with us through the death and resurrection of Jesus. (4) Finally, the temple is used in the New Testament to illustrate Jesus himself —where we meet God (John 2:19; 14:6–10). "Temple" is also used to describe the church—the people of God (1 Cor. 3:17; 6:19–20; see Matt. 18:20). Also see *In what sanctuary does Jesus serve?* (Heb. 8:2).

rim, figures of bulls encircled it—ten to a cubit[D].[a] The bulls were cast in two rows in one piece with the Sea.

4The Sea stood on twelve bulls, three facing north, three facing west, three facing south and three facing east. The Sea rested on top of them, and their hindquarters were toward the center. **5**It was a handbreadth[b] in thickness, and its rim was like the rim of a cup, like a lily blossom. It held three thousand baths.[c]

6He then made ten basins for washing and placed five on the south side and five on the north. In them the things to be used for the burnt offerings[D] were rinsed, but the Sea was to be used by the priests[D] for washing.

7He made ten gold lampstands according to the specifications for them and placed them in the temple, five on the south side and five on the north.

8He made ten tables and placed them in the temple, five on the south side and five on the north. He also made a hundred gold sprinkling bowls.

9He made the courtyard of the priests, and the large court and the doors for the court, and overlaid the doors with bronze. **10**He placed the Sea on the south side, at the southeast corner.

11He also made the pots and shovels and sprinkling bowls.

So Huram finished the work he had undertaken for King Solomon in the temple of God:

12the two pillars;
    the two bowl-shaped capitals on top of the pillars;
    the two sets of network decorating the two bowl-shaped capitals on top of the pillars;
13the four hundred pomegranates for the two sets of network (two rows of pomegranates for each network, decorating the bowl-shaped capitals on top of the pillars);
14the stands with their basins;
15the Sea and the twelve bulls under it;
16the pots, shovels, meat forks and all related articles.

All the objects that Huram-Abi made for King Solomon for the temple of the LORD were of polished bronze. **17**The king had them cast in clay molds in the plain of the Jordan between Succoth and Zarethan.[d] **18**All these things that Solomon made amounted to so much that the weight of the bronze was not determined.

19Solomon also made all the furnishings that were in God's temple:

    the golden altar;
    the tables on which was the bread of the Presence;
20the lampstands of pure gold with their lamps, to burn in front of the inner sanctuary as prescribed;
21the gold floral work and lamps and tongs (they were solid gold);
22the pure gold wick trimmers, sprinkling bowls, dishes and censers[D]; and the gold doors of the temple: the inner doors to the Most Holy Place[D] and the doors of the main hall.

How were all these items used in temple worship? (4:6–16)

Temple worship could be viewed as an "industry" of sorts. There was a lot of physical labor involved in offering the animal sacrifices—and in cleaning up afterward. The *basins* were filled from the reservoir and used for cleaning. The *lampstands* held the golden oil-burning lamps that gave light within the temple. The *tables* displayed the consecrated bread each Sabbath (Lev. 24:5–8). The priests collected blood from the sacrifices and sprinkled the altar, using *sprinkling bowls* (Exodus 24:6). The *pots* and *meat forks* were probably used in cooking the meat of the animals sacrificed. The *shovels*, no doubt, were used to clean up the ashes.

[a]3 That is, about 1 1/2 feet (about 0.5 meter)   [b]5 That is, about 3 inches (about 8 centimeters)   [c]5 That is, about 17,500 gallons (about 66 kiloliters)   [d]17 Hebrew *Zeredatha*, a variant of *Zarethan*

5 When all the work Solomon had done for the temple of the LORD was finished, he brought in the things his father David had dedicated—the silver and gold and all the furnishings—and he placed them in the treasuries of God's temple.

The Ark Brought to the Temple

²Then Solomon summoned to Jerusalem^D the elders of Israel, all the heads of the tribes and the chiefs of the Israelite families, to bring up the ark of the LORD's covenant^D from Zion^D, the City of David. ³And all the men of Israel came together to the king at the time of the festival in the seventh month.

⁴When all the elders of Israel had arrived, the Levites^D took up the ark, ⁵and they brought up the ark and the Tent of Meeting^D and all the sacred^D furnishings in it. The priests^D, who were Levites, carried them up; ⁶and King Solomon and the entire assembly of Israel that had gathered about him were before the ark, sacrificing so many sheep and cattle that they could not be recorded or counted.

⁷The priests then brought the ark of the LORD's covenant to its place in the inner sanctuary of the temple, the Most Holy Place^D, and put it beneath the wings of the cherubim^D. ⁸The cherubim spread their wings over the place of the ark and covered the ark and its carrying poles. ⁹These poles were so long that their ends, extending from the ark, could be seen from in front of the inner sanctuary, but not from outside the Holy Place^D; and they are still there today. ¹⁰There was nothing in the ark except the two tablets that Moses had placed in it at Horeb, where the LORD made a covenant with the Israelites after they came out of Egypt.

¹¹The priests then withdrew from the Holy Place. All the priests who were there had consecrated themselves, regardless of their divisions. ¹²All the Levites who were musicians—Asaph, Heman, Jeduthun and their sons and relatives—stood on the east side of the altar, dressed in fine linen and playing cymbals, harps and lyres^D. They were accompanied by 120 priests sounding trumpets. ¹³The trumpeters and singers joined in unison, as with one voice, to give praise and thanks to the LORD. Accompanied by trumpets, cymbals and other instruments, they raised their voices in praise to the LORD and sang:

> "He is good;
>   his love endures forever."

Then the temple of the LORD was filled with a cloud, ¹⁴and the priests could not perform their service because of the cloud, for the glory^D of the LORD filled the temple of God.

6 Then Solomon said, "The LORD has said that he would dwell in a dark cloud; ²I have built a magnificent temple for you, a place for you to dwell forever."

³While the whole assembly of Israel was standing there, the king turned around and blessed them. ⁴Then he said:

"Praise be to the LORD, the God of Israel, who with his hands has fulfilled what he promised with his mouth to my father David. For he said, ⁵'Since the day I brought my people out of Egypt, I have not chosen a city in any tribe of Israel to have a temple built for my Name to be there, nor have I chosen anyone

SCRIPTURE LINK (5:10) *Nothing in the ark except . . .*

At one time the ark also held a golden jar of manna (Exodus 16:32–34) and Aaron's staff which had miraculously budded (Num. 17:10–11). See Heb. 9:4.

Who raided the ark? (5:10)

Some speculate that God at some point may have instructed the priests to remove the manna and staff, leaving only his law for their attention. Others wonder if, to teach Israel a lesson, God allowed the Philistines to raid the ark (see 1 Samuel 4:11) without striking them for their disrespect. Still others object to both these guesses and say we simply don't know.

Why did God's glory appear as a cloud? (5:13–14)

God sometimes appeared to his people as a dazzling, white cloud—merely an image of his glory since he was too holy to be seen face to face (Exodus 33:20). He had appeared in the cloud that led the Israelites through the desert (Exodus 14:19–20) and had covered the tabernacle at its dedication (Exodus 24:15–18). It appeared in the temple as a sign that God was present there.

Wasn't limiting worship to one location a step backward? (6:5–6)

No. The Israelites had never been permitted to worship God indiscriminately—at any place and in any way they chose. There was a danger that the fertility cult practiced at many high places could infiltrate Israel's worship. They needed the limits of a centralized location to help them resist pagan influences. Until Jerusalem, the tabernacle filled this role at Gibeon (see *Map 4* at the back of this Bible).

to be the leader over my people Israel. **6**But now I have chosen Jerusalem^D for my Name to be there, and I have chosen David to rule my people Israel.'

7"My father David had it in his heart to build a temple for the Name of the LORD, the God of Israel. **8**But the LORD said to my father David, 'Because it was in your heart to build a temple for my Name, you did well to have this in your heart. **9**Nevertheless, you are not the one to build the temple, but your son, who is your own flesh and blood—he is the one who will build the temple for my Name.'

10"The LORD has kept the promise he made. I have succeeded David my father and now I sit on the throne of Israel, just as the LORD promised, and I have built the temple for the Name of the LORD, the God of Israel. **11**There I have placed the ark, in which is the covenant^D of the LORD that he made with the people of Israel."

Solomon's Prayer of Dedication

12Then Solomon stood before the altar of the LORD in front of the whole assembly of Israel and spread out his hands. **13**Now he had made a bronze platform, five cubits^{Da} long, five cubits wide and three cubits^b high, and had placed it in the center of the outer court. He stood on the platform and then knelt down before the whole assembly of Israel and spread out his hands toward heaven. **14**He said:

"O LORD, God of Israel, there is no God like you in heaven or on earth—you who keep your covenant of love with your servants who continue wholeheartedly in your way. **15**You have kept your promise to your servant David my father; with your mouth you have promised and with your hand you have fulfilled it—as it is today.

16"Now LORD, God of Israel, keep for your servant David my father the promises you made to him when you said, 'You shall never fail to have a man to sit before me on the throne of Israel, if only your sons are careful in all they do to walk before me according to my law, as you have done.' **17**And now, O LORD, God of Israel, let your word that you promised your servant David come true.

18"But will God really dwell on earth with men? The heavens, even the highest heavens, cannot contain you. How much less this temple I have built! **19**Yet give attention to your servant's prayer and his plea for mercy^D, O LORD my God. Hear the cry and the prayer that your servant is praying in your presence. **20**May your eyes be open toward this temple day and night, this place of which you said you would put your Name there. May you hear the prayer your servant prays toward this place. **21**Hear the supplications of your servant and of your people Israel when they pray toward this place. Hear from heaven, your dwelling place; and when you hear, forgive.

22"When a man wrongs his neighbor and is required to take an oath and he comes and swears the oath before your altar in this temple, **23**then hear from heaven and act. Judge between your servants,

---

Did Solomon show us the proper posture for prayer? (6:13)

Kneeling is a universal sign of submission. When the king knelt down, he was admitting publicly that he was God's servant. Reaching out his hands—a gesture not unlike that a beggar might make—indicated he was asking for something from God. But his example does not indicate a formula for prayer. Scripture shows many postures for prayer—bowing the head (Gen. 24:26), looking up (Mark 6:41) and lying prostrate (Joshua 7:6) are some others. What matters more than the position of the body is the attitude of the heart.

Why pray toward a specific site? (6:21)

There was no magic involved in praying in a certain direction. But it reminded the person who was praying of the *destination* of the prayers. The people were not praying to some vague fertility god on any one of numerous hilltops. They were praying to the true God who met his people in the temple at Jerusalem.

---

^a13 That is, about 7 1/2 feet (about 2.3 meters)   ^b13 That is, about 4 1/2 feet (about 1.3 meters)

repaying the guilty by bringing down on his own head what he has done. Declare the innocent not guilty and so establish his innocence.

²⁴"When your people Israel have been defeated by an enemy because they have sinned against you and when they turn back and confess your name, praying and making supplication before you in this temple, ²⁵then hear from heaven and forgive the sin of your people Israel and bring them back to the land you gave to them and their fathers.

²⁶"When the heavens are shut up and there is no rain because your people have sinned against you, and when they pray toward this place and confess your name and turn from their sin because you have afflicted[D] them, ²⁷then hear from heaven and forgive the sin of your servants, your people Israel. Teach them the right way to live, and send rain on the land you gave your people for an inheritance.

²⁸"When famine or plague comes to the land, or blight or mildew, locusts[D] or grasshoppers, or when enemies besiege them in any of their cities, whatever disaster or disease may come, ²⁹and when a prayer or plea is made by any of your people Israel—each one aware of his afflictions[D] and pains, and spreading out his hands toward this temple— ³⁰then hear from heaven, your dwelling place. Forgive, and deal with each man according to all he does, since you know his heart (for you alone know the hearts of men), ³¹so that they will fear you and walk in your ways all the time they live in the land you gave our fathers.

³²"As for the foreigner who does not belong to your people Israel but has come from a distant land because of your great name and your mighty hand and your outstretched arm—when he comes and prays toward this temple, ³³then hear from heaven, your dwelling place, and do whatever the foreigner asks of you, so that all the peoples of the earth may know your name and fear you, as do your own people Israel, and may know that this house I have built bears your Name.

³⁴"When your people go to war against their enemies, wherever you send them, and when they pray to you toward this city you have chosen and the temple I have built for your Name, ³⁵then hear from heaven their prayer and their plea, and uphold their cause.

³⁶"When they sin against you—for there is no one who does not sin—and you become angry with them and give them over to the enemy, who takes them captive to a land far away or near; ³⁷and if they have a change of heart in the land where they are held captive, and repent[D] and plead with you in the land of their captivity and say, 'We have sinned, we have done wrong and acted wickedly'; ³⁸and if they turn back to you with all their heart and soul[D] in the land of their captivity where they were taken, and pray toward the land you gave their fathers, toward the city you have chosen and toward the temple I have built for your Name; ³⁹then from heaven, your dwelling place, hear their prayer and their pleas, and uphold their cause. And forgive your people, who have sinned against you.

Did the Israelites become missionaries to other nations? (6:33)

Yes and no. Solomon's prayer presents a picture echoed by several prophets—that the whole world would be attracted to worship of the true God at Jerusalem (Isaiah 56:6–8). This did happen, not through the nation per se, but through Jesus, crucified in Jerusalem. Through him, the whole world is invited into a relationship with God.

Why call the temple God's *resting place*? (6:41)

The Tent of Meeting had been moved a number of times over the years, first through the desert and then to various locations within Canaan. Finally God chose a permanent place where he could "settle down" among his people. This same theme of God's resting place in Jerusalem is echoed again in Psalm 132:13-18.

How long would it take to offer 142,000 sacrifices? (7:5)

Probably the entire length of the festival, which lasted two weeks. The entire courtyard was used to perform these sacrifices, since the single bronze altar was too small (1 Kings 8:64).

40"Now, my God, may your eyes be open and your ears attentive to the prayers offered in this place.

41"Now arise, O LORD God, and come to your
　　resting place,
　　you and the ark of your might.
May your priests[D], O LORD God, be clothed
　　with salvation[D],
　　may your saints[D] rejoice in your
　　goodness.
42O LORD God, do not reject your anointed[D]
　　one.
　　Remember the great love promised to
　　David your servant."

The Dedication of the Temple

7 When Solomon finished praying, fire came down from heaven and consumed the burnt offering[D] and the sacrifices[D], and the glory[D] of the LORD filled the temple. **2**The priests could not enter the temple of the LORD because the glory of the LORD filled it. **3**When all the Israelites saw the fire coming down and the glory of the LORD above the temple, they knelt on the pavement with their faces to the ground, and they worshiped and gave thanks to the LORD, saying,

　　"He is good;
　　　his love endures forever."

4Then the king and all the people offered sacrifices before the LORD. **5**And King Solomon offered a sacrifice of twenty-two thousand head of cattle and a hundred and twenty thousand sheep and goats. So the king and all the people dedicated the temple of God. **6**The priests took their positions, as did the Levites[D] with the LORD's musical instruments, which King David had made for praising the LORD and which were used when he gave thanks, saying, "His love endures forever." Opposite the Levites, the priests blew their trumpets, and all the Israelites were standing.

7Solomon consecrated[D] the middle part of the courtyard in front of the temple of the LORD, and there he offered burnt offerings and the fat of the fellowship offerings[D],[a] because the bronze altar he had made could not hold the burnt offerings, the grain offerings and the fat portions.

8So Solomon observed the festival at that time for seven days, and all Israel with him—a vast assembly, people from Lebo[b] Hamath to the Wadi of Egypt. **9**On the eighth day they held an assembly, for they had celebrated the dedication of the altar for seven days and the festival for seven days more. **10**On the twenty-third day of the seventh month he sent the people to their homes, joyful and glad in heart for the good things the LORD had done for David and Solomon and for his people Israel.

The LORD Appears to Solomon

11When Solomon had finished the temple of the LORD and the royal palace, and had succeeded in carrying out all he had in mind to do in the temple of the LORD and in his own palace, **12**the LORD appeared to him at night and said:

---

a 7 Traditionally *peace offerings*　　*b 8* Or *from the entrance to*

"I have heard your prayer and have chosen this place for myself as a temple for sacrifices^D.

¹³"When I shut up the heavens so that there is no rain, or command locusts^D to devour the land or send a plague among my people, ¹⁴if my people, who are called by my name, will humble themselves and pray and seek my face and turn from their wicked ways, then will I hear from heaven and will forgive their sin and will heal their land. ¹⁵Now my eyes will be open and my ears attentive to the prayers offered in this place. ¹⁶I have chosen and consecrated^D this temple so that my Name may be there forever. My eyes and my heart will always be there.

¹⁷"As for you, if you walk before me as David your father did, and do all I command, and observe my decrees and laws, ¹⁸I will establish your royal throne, as I covenanted^D with David your father when I said, 'You shall never fail to have a man to rule over Israel.'

¹⁹"But if you[a] turn away and forsake the decrees and commands I have given you[a] and go off to serve other gods and worship them, ²⁰then I will uproot Israel from my land, which I have given them, and will reject this temple I have consecrated for my Name. I will make it a byword^D and an object of ridicule among all peoples. ²¹And though this temple is now so imposing, all who pass by will be appalled and say, 'Why has the LORD done such a thing to this land and to this temple?' ²²People will answer, 'Because they have forsaken the LORD, the God of their fathers, who brought them out of Egypt, and have embraced other gods, worshiping and serving them—that is why he brought all this disaster on them.' "

[a] 19 The Hebrew is plural.

SCRIPTURE LINK (7:11–22)

Much of this same prayer by Solomon is recorded in 1 Kings 9:1–9.

What did this promise to Solomon mean? (7:18)

This promise could have meant several things to Solomon. First, it would have been an encouragement for him to know that God would answer his prayer so directly. His father, David, had enjoyed a close relationship with the Lord. Now Solomon had some indication that God desired the same kind of relationship with him. But more than that, God reiterated a promise made in the past and brought it into the present. Solomon would not have to rely on God's previous work. He could expect God's continued involvement. By the same token, this promise also served as a warning to Solomon: there were conditions attached requiring his faithful obedience.

Do Israel's promises apply to us today? (7:14)

Yes, in that the basic principles behind God's promises to Israel can be applied to our own situations. But we need to be careful how far we take them; general principles cannot always be forced to fit specific cases.

For example, God told Solomon he would send drought or plagues when the people turned away from him. What is the broad application still in effect? Sin produces trouble. However, one cannot say that every drought or plague is the result of sin.

The general rule is that we can make a broad application from a passage of Scripture when it is reinforced in other ways from other parts of the Bible. The idea that sin produces trouble is a principle supported by other Biblical statements: *A man reaps what he sows* (Gal. 6:7), for instance.

Sometimes principles will apply to individuals: one will suffer in life because of straying from God. They can also apply to nations: when people drift into wickedness, serious problems will destroy the fabric of their society.

God has built certain "laws" into creation. The Bible uses various means to teach them to us—examples from history, proverbs, prophetic warnings, direct teachings and so on. God wants us to know from Israel's example that things will go better for us (as individuals or nations) when we follow God's ways.

Solomon's Other Activities

8 At the end of twenty years, during which Solomon built the temple of the LORD and his own palace, ²Solomon rebuilt the villages that Hiram[a] had given him, and settled Israelites in them. ³Solomon then went to Hamath Zobah and captured it. ⁴He also built up Tadmor in the desert and all the store cities he had built in Hamath. ⁵He rebuilt Upper Beth Horon and Lower Beth Horon as fortified cities, with walls and with gates and bars, ⁶as well as Baalath and all his store cities, and all the cities for his chariots and for his horses[b]—whatever he desired to build in Jerusalem[D], in Lebanon and throughout all the territory he ruled.

⁷All the people left from the Hittites, Amorites, Perizzites, Hivites and Jebusites (these peoples were not Israelites), ⁸that is, their descendants remaining in the land, whom the Israelites had not destroyed—these Solomon conscripted for his slave labor force, as it is to this day. ⁹But Solomon did not make slaves of the Israelites for his work; they were his fighting men, commanders of his captains, and commanders of his chariots and charioteers. ¹⁰They were also King Solomon's chief officials—two hundred and fifty officials supervising the men.

¹¹Solomon brought Pharaoh's daughter up from the City of David to the palace he had built for her, for he said, "My wife must not live in the palace of David king of Israel, because the places the ark of the LORD has entered are holy."

¹²On the altar of the LORD that he had built in front of the portico, Solomon sacrificed burnt offerings[D] to the LORD, ¹³according to the daily requirement for offerings commanded by Moses for Sabbaths[D], New Moons and the three annual feasts—the Feast of Unleavened Bread, the Feast of Weeks and the Feast of Tabernacles. ¹⁴In keeping with the ordinance of his father David, he appointed the divisions of the priests[D] for their duties, and the Levites[D] to lead the praise and to assist the priests according to each day's requirement. He also appointed the gatekeepers by divisions for the various gates, because this was what David the man of God had ordered. ¹⁵They did not deviate from the king's commands to the priests or to the Levites in any matter, including that of the treasuries.

¹⁶All Solomon's work was carried out, from the day the foundation of the temple of the LORD was laid until its completion. So the temple of the LORD was finished.

¹⁷Then Solomon went to Ezion Geber and Elath on the coast of Edom[D]. ¹⁸And Hiram sent him ships commanded by his own officers, men who knew the sea. These, with Solomon's men, sailed to Ophir and brought back four hundred and fifty talents[c] of gold, which they delivered to King Solomon.

The Queen of Sheba Visits Solomon

9 When the queen of Sheba heard of Solomon's fame, she came to Jerusalem to test him with hard questions. Arriving with a very great caravan—with camels carrying spices, large quantities of gold, and precious stones—she came to Solomon and talked with him about all she had on her mind. ²Solomon answered all her ques-

Slave labor (8:8)
See *Did Solomon treat the aliens fairly?* (2:17).

Why couldn't the king's wife live in David's palace? (8:11)
Solomon's wife was a foreigner who did not serve the God of Israel. As a result, Solomon may have been sensitive about having an idol worshiper in a place where the holy ark of God had been housed. Or he may have been fending off criticism from worshipers who would be offended by a pagan queen in that holy site. It's possible he was afraid it would be dangerous for her to be too close to the ark.

What did Solomon give in exchange for all this gold? (8:18)
Some think the Israelites mined and refined various metals of their own, such as copper, for export. But Solomon also acted as a middleman. He gave Hiram of Tyre access to eastern timber buyers and took a cut of the profits.

Sheba (9:1)
Probably a region in southern Arabia, though some have suggested Ethiopia (see *Map 12* at the back of this Bible). In any case, the queen probably traveled some 1,000 miles to see Solomon, who may have been threatening some of her trading contracts with Tyre and other nations.

Why did this queen want to test Solomon? (9:1)
Her *hard questions* were riddles. Asking riddles was an Arabic custom—sort of a friendly competition of wits. Also see *Why did the queen want to test Solomon?* (1 Kings 10:1).

---

[a]2 Hebrew *Huram*, a variant of *Hiram*; also in verse 18   [b]6 Or *charioteers*   [c]18 That is, about 17 tons (about 16 metric tons)

tions; nothing was too hard for him to explain to her. ³When the queen of Sheba saw the wisdom of Solomon, as well as the palace he had built, ⁴the food on his table, the seating of his officials, the attending servants in their robes, the cupbearers in their robes and the burnt offerings ᴰ he made at ᵃ the temple of the Lᴏʀᴅ, she was overwhelmed.

⁵She said to the king, "The report I heard in my own country about your achievements and your wisdom is true. ⁶But I did not believe what they said until I came and saw with my own eyes. Indeed, not even half the greatness of your wisdom was told me; you have far exceeded the report I heard. ⁷How happy your men must be! How happy your officials, who continually stand before you and hear your wisdom! ⁸Praise be to the Lᴏʀᴅ your God, who has delighted in you and placed you on his throne as king to rule for the Lᴏʀᴅ your God. Because of the love of your God for Israel and his desire to uphold them forever, he has made you king over them, to maintain justice and righteousness ᴰ."

⁹Then she gave the king 120 talents ᵇ of gold, large quantities of spices, and precious stones. There had never been such spices as those the queen of Sheba gave to King Solomon.

¹⁰(The men of Hiram and the men of Solomon brought gold from Ophir; they also brought algumwood ᶜ and precious stones. ¹¹The king used the algumwood to make steps for the temple of the Lᴏʀᴅ and for the royal palace, and to make harps and lyres ᴰ for the musicians. Nothing like them had ever been seen in Judah.)

¹²King Solomon gave the queen of Sheba all she desired and asked for; he gave her more than she had brought to him. Then she left and returned with her retinue to her own country.

Solomon's Splendor

¹³The weight of the gold that Solomon received yearly was 666 talents, ᵈ ¹⁴not including the revenues brought in by merchants and traders. Also all the kings of Arabia and the governors of the land brought gold and silver to Solomon.

¹⁵King Solomon made two hundred large shields of hammered gold; six hundred bekas ᵉ of hammered gold went into each shield. ¹⁶He also made three hundred small shields of hammered gold, with three hundred bekas ᶠ of gold in each shield. The king put them in the Palace of the Forest of Lebanon.

¹⁷Then the king made a great throne inlaid with ivory and overlaid with pure gold. ¹⁸The throne had six steps, and a footstool ᴰ of gold was attached to it. On both sides of the seat were armrests, with a lion standing beside each of them. ¹⁹Twelve lions stood on the six steps, one at either end of each step. Nothing like it had ever been made for any other kingdom. ²⁰All King Solomon's goblets were gold, and all the household articles in the Palace of the Forest of Lebanon were pure gold. Nothing was made of silver, because silver was considered of little value in Solomon's day. ²¹The king had a fleet of trading

What motivated the queen of Sheba to give gifts to Solomon? (9:9)

She was obviously impressed by his wisdom and wealth. This may also have been the beginning of a trade agreement that profited them both.

What made algumwood so outstanding? (9:11)

The name is a variation on *almugwood* (1 Kings 10:11)—both forms are Hebrew since English does not have any equivalent. Although algumwood cannot be identified with certainty, the context suggests that it was a type of wood prized for making musical instruments. Since it was from Ophir, some think it was red sandalwood which provided decoration for Solomon's building projects.

Where did Solomon's revenue come from? (9:13–14)

From taxes, tribute and trade. A later rebellion against Solomon's son suggests that Solomon not only had drafted construction laborers but that he also had put a *heavy yoke* of taxes on the people (10:4). The gold totaled here appears to have come from taxes alone; additional funds were raised by tribute (fees paid by nations to their conquerors) and trade (including profits on goods, sales taxes and tolls on traveling caravans).

---

a4 Or *the ascent by which he went up to*   *b9* That is, about 4 1/2 tons (about 4 metric tons)   *c10* Probably a variant of *almugwood*   *d13* That is, about 25 tons (about 23 metric tons)   *e15* That is, about 7 1/2 pounds (about 3.5 kilograms)   *f16* That is, about 3 3/4 pounds (about 1.7 kilograms)

ships[a] manned by Hiram's[b] men. Once every three years it returned, carrying gold, silver and ivory, and apes and baboons. **22**King Solomon was greater in riches and wisdom than all the other kings of the earth. **23**All the kings of the earth sought audience with Solomon to hear the wisdom God had put in his heart. **24**Year after year, everyone who came brought a gift—articles of silver and gold, and robes, weapons and spices, and horses and mules.

25Solomon had four thousand stalls for horses and chariots, and twelve thousand horses,[c] which he kept in the chariot cities and also with him in Jerusalem[D]. **26**He ruled over all the kings from the River[d] to the land of the Philistines, as far as the border of Egypt. **27**The king made silver as common in Jerusalem as stones, and cedar as plentiful as sycamore-fig trees in the foothills. **28**Solomon's horses were imported from Egypt[e] and from all other countries.

Solomon's Death

29As for the other events of Solomon's reign, from beginning to end, are they not written in the records of Nathan the prophet[D], in the prophecy[D] of Ahijah the Shilonite and in the visions[D] of Iddo the seer[D] concerning Jeroboam son of Nebat? **30**Solomon reigned in Jerusalem over all Israel forty years. **31**Then he rested with his fathers and was buried in the city of David his father. And Rehoboam his son succeeded him as king.

Israel Rebels Against Rehoboam

10 Rehoboam went to Shechem, for all the Israelites had gone there to make him king. **2**When Jeroboam son of Nebat heard this (he was in Egypt, where he had fled from King Solomon), he returned from Egypt. **3**So they sent for Jeroboam, and he and all Israel went to Rehoboam and said to him: **4**"Your father put a heavy yoke[D] on us, but now lighten the harsh labor and the heavy yoke he put on us, and we will serve you."

5Rehoboam answered, "Come back to me in three days." So the people went away.

6Then King Rehoboam consulted the elders who had served his father Solomon during his lifetime. "How would you advise me to answer these people?" he asked.

7They replied, "If you will be kind to these people and please them and give them a favorable answer, they will always be your servants."

8But Rehoboam rejected the advice the elders gave him and consulted the young men who had grown up with him and were serving him. **9**He asked them, "What is your advice? How should we answer these people who say to me, 'Lighten the yoke your father put on us'?"

10The young men who had grown up with him replied, "Tell the people who have said to you, 'Your father put a heavy yoke on us, but make our yoke lighter'—tell them, 'My little finger is thicker than my father's waist. **11**My father laid on you a heavy yoke; I will make it even heavier. My father scourged you with whips; I will scourge you with scorpions.'"

12Three days later Jeroboam and all the people returned to Rehoboam, as the king had said, "Come back to me in

What happened to these written records? (9:29)
We don't know. It is possible much of their content has been included in the books of Kings and Chronicles, but otherwise these books are lost to us.

SCRIPTURE LINK (9:29) The other events of Solomon's reign
The writer of Chronicles ignores Solomon's personal and spiritual failures. See 1 Kings 11:1–10.

Why omit Solomon's failures? (9:29)
The writer of Chronicles seems more interested in national implications than personal problems. (He leaves out David's sins as well.) Solomon's initial public devotion to the Lord brought about the nation's great success. Solomon's personal failings, though impacting the nation negatively, did not change the fact that he had once been effective in leading the nation through prosperous times.

Why was Rehoboam so unsympathetic? (10:8–11)
The older counselors, who may have known David and his humble beginnings, advised leniency toward the common people. But Rehoboam, raised in the prosperity of his father's reign, would have been extremely unaware of the plight of the commoner. In addition, political adversaries had plagued Solomon's final years (1 Kings 11:14–40). Rehoboam, worried that adversaries would try to take advantage of him during his transition to power, responded harshly to all criticism.

Who were the young men who had grown up with Rehoboam? (10:10)
These may have been other sons of Solomon, born and raised in the luxury of the royal court. Or they may have been sons of court aristocrats. It was customary in some countries that heirs to the throne would be trained alongside children of nobles. Whoever they were, they were out of touch with the feelings of the common people.

a21 Hebrew of ships that could go to Tarshish   b21 Hebrew Huram, a variant of *Hiram   c25 Or charioteers   d26 That is, the* Euphrates   *e28 Or possibly Muzur, a region in Cilicia*

three days." ¹³The king answered them harshly. Rejecting the advice of the elders, ¹⁴he followed the advice of the young men and said, "My father made your yoke ᴰ heavy; I will make it even heavier. My father scourged you with whips; I will scourge you with scorpions." ¹⁵So the king did not listen to the people, for this turn of events was from God, to fulfill the word the LORD had spoken to Jeroboam son of Nebat through Ahijah the Shilonite.

¹⁶When all Israel saw that the king refused to listen to them, they answered the king:

"What share do we have in David,
    what part in Jesse's son?
To your tents, O Israel!
    Look after your own house, O David!"

So all the Israelites went home. ¹⁷But as for the Israelites who were living in the towns of Judah, Rehoboam still ruled over them.

¹⁸King Rehoboam sent out Adoniram,ᵃ who was in charge of forced labor, but the Israelites stoned him to death ᴰ. King Rehoboam, however, managed to get into his chariot and escape to Jerusalem ᴰ. ¹⁹So Israel has been in rebellion against the house of David to this day.

11 When Rehoboam arrived in Jerusalem, he mustered the house of Judah and Benjamin—a hundred and eighty thousand fighting men—to make war against Israel and to regain the kingdom for Rehoboam. ²But this word of the LORD came to Shemaiah the man of God: ³"Say to Rehoboam son of Solomon king of Judah and to all the Israelites in Judah and Benjamin, ⁴'This is what the LORD says: Do not go up to fight against your brothers. Go home, every one of you, for this is my doing.'" So they obeyed the words of the LORD and turned back from marching against Jeroboam.

Rehoboam Fortifies Judah

⁵Rehoboam lived in Jerusalem and built up towns for defense in Judah: ⁶Bethlehem, Etam, Tekoa, ⁷Beth Zur,

---

ᵃ18 Hebrew *Hadoram*, a variant of *Adoniram*

Was this a taxpayers' revolt, or something more? (10:14–16)

On a popular level, yes, it was a taxpayers' revolt. The rulers had become tyrants, and the people stood up for their own rights. But the writer also notes that *this turn of events was from God.* The writer of 1 Kings is more direct, stating that God tore the ten tribes away from Solomon's son because of Solomon's idolatry (1 Kings 11:29–39).

SCRIPTURE LINK (10:15) *The word the LORD had spoken . . . through Ahijah the Shilonite*

See 1 Kings 11:29–39.

Why would an entire army sacrifice their national pride to listen to a lone prophet? (11:4)

See article: *How much influence did prophets have?* (1 Kings 12:24).

Did God cause Rehoboam's foolish choice? (10:15)

I f *this turn of events was from God,* does that mean he caused Rehoboam to make a foolish choice?

The same kind of question applies to other situations, most notably the hardening of Pharaoh's heart prior to the exodus from Egypt (Exodus 4:21).

There's no easy answer. We can only acknowledge two truths that seem contradictory. On the one hand, human beings are given the choice to follow God or not (see Joshua 24:15). If we choose wrongly, we might face disaster. On the other hand, God ultimately controls all of human history. He is always working out the purposes of his own will.

So Pharaoh, Rehoboam and others are all responsible for their own bad choices. And yet God uses all human choices to do what *he* wants. Rehoboam's bad decision brought about the rebellion, but God used Rehoboam's choice to punish Solomon's court for its idolatry.

Also see article: *Why does God harden some people's hearts?* (Exodus 11:3).

Were the priests right to abandon Israel? (11:13–14)

Who abandoned whom? While God may have put Jeroboam's revolt into motion, Jeroboam abandoned the worship of God and set up a counterfeit religion. The priests felt their only recourse was to return to Jerusalem, where true worship was still practiced and they could remain faithful to God.

Did religion—more than politics—drive the wedge between Israel and Judah? (11:16)

It turned out that way. Jeroboam feared that if the people remained loyal to Jerusalem as a center of worship, then his political power might be weakened (1 Kings 12:26–27). So he set up alternate worship centers. This forced the issue among the northerners who wished to remain faithful to the God of Israel and sent many of them packing for the south. The influx of loyal worshipers was responsible for a period of piety and prosperity in Judah (v. 17).

Why didn't God condemn polygamy? (11:21)

See article: *Why did David have so many wives and concubines?* (2 Samuel 5:13).

Soco, Adullam, [8]Gath, Mareshah, Ziph, [9]Adoraim, Lachish, Azekah, [10]Zorah, Aijalon and Hebron. These were fortified cities in Judah and Benjamin. [11]He strengthened their defenses and put commanders in them, with supplies of food, olive oil and wine. [12]He put shields and spears in all the cities, and made them very strong. So Judah and Benjamin were his.

[13]The priests[D] and Levites[D] from all their districts throughout Israel sided with him. [14]The Levites even abandoned their pasturelands and property, and came to Judah and Jerusalem[D] because Jeroboam and his sons had rejected them as priests of the LORD. [15]And he appointed his own priests for the high places and for the goat and calf idols[D] he had made. [16]Those from every tribe of Israel who set their hearts on seeking the LORD, the God of Israel, followed the Levites to Jerusalem to offer sacrifices[D] to the LORD, the God of their fathers. [17]They strengthened the kingdom of Judah and supported Rehoboam son of Solomon three years, walking in the ways of David and Solomon during this time.

Rehoboam's Family

[18]Rehoboam married Mahalath, who was the daughter of David's son Jerimoth and of Abihail, the daughter of Jesse's son Eliab. [19]She bore him sons: Jeush, Shemariah and Zaham. [20]Then he married Maacah daughter of Absalom, who bore him Abijah, Attai, Ziza and Shelomith. [21]Rehoboam loved Maacah daughter of Absalom more than any of his other wives and concubines[D]. In all, he had eighteen wives and sixty concubines, twenty-eight sons and sixty daughters.

[22]Rehoboam appointed Abijah son of Maacah to be the chief prince among his brothers, in order to make him king. [23]He acted wisely, dispersing some of his sons throughout the districts of Judah and Benjamin, and to all the fortified cities. He gave them abundant provisions and took many wives for them.

Shishak Attacks Jerusalem

12 After Rehoboam's position as king was established and he had become strong, he and all Israel[a] with him abandoned the law of the LORD. [2]Because they had been unfaithful to the LORD, Shishak king of Egypt attacked Jerusalem in the fifth year of King Rehoboam. [3]With twelve hundred chariots and sixty thousand horsemen and the innumerable troops of Libyans, Sukkites and Cushites[b] that came with him from Egypt, [4]he captured the fortified cities of Judah and came as far as Jerusalem.

[5]Then the prophet[D] Shemaiah came to Rehoboam and to the leaders of Judah who had assembled in Jerusalem for fear of Shishak, and he said to them, "This is what the LORD says, 'You have abandoned me; therefore, I now abandon you to Shishak.'"

[6]The leaders of Israel and the king humbled themselves and said, "The LORD is just."

[7]When the LORD saw that they humbled themselves, this word of the LORD came to Shemaiah: "Since they have humbled themselves, I will not destroy them but will soon give them deliverance. My wrath will not be poured out on Jerusalem through Shishak. [8]They will, however, be-

---

[a]1 That is, Judah, as frequently in 2 Chronicles   [b]3 That is, people from the upper Nile region

come subject to him, so that they may learn the difference between serving me and serving the kings of other lands."

⁹When Shishak king of Egypt attacked Jerusalem^D, he carried off the treasures of the temple of the LORD and the treasures of the royal palace. He took everything, including the gold shields Solomon had made. ¹⁰So King Rehoboam made bronze shields to replace them and assigned these to the commanders of the guard on duty at the entrance to the royal palace. ¹¹Whenever the king went to the LORD's temple, the guards went with him, bearing the shields, and afterward they returned them to the guardroom.

¹²Because Rehoboam humbled himself, the LORD's anger turned from him, and he was not totally destroyed. Indeed, there was some good in Judah.

¹³King Rehoboam established himself firmly in Jerusalem and continued as king. He was forty-one years old when he became king, and he reigned seventeen years in Jerusalem, the city the LORD had chosen out of all the tribes of Israel in which to put his Name. His mother's name was Naamah; she was an Ammonite. ¹⁴He did evil because he had not set his heart on seeking the LORD.

¹⁵As for the events of Rehoboam's reign, from beginning to end, are they not written in the records of Shemaiah the prophet^D and of Iddo the seer^D that deal with genealogies^D? There was continual warfare between Rehoboam and Jeroboam. ¹⁶Rehoboam rested with his fathers and was buried in the City of David. And Abijah his son succeeded him as king.

Abijah King of Judah

13 In the eighteenth year of the reign of Jeroboam, Abijah became king of Judah, ²and he reigned in Jerusalem three years. His mother's name was Maacah,^a a daughter^b of Uriel of Gibeah.

There was war between Abijah and Jeroboam. ³Abijah went into battle with a force of four hundred thousand able fighting men, and Jeroboam drew up a battle line against him with eight hundred thousand able troops.

⁴Abijah stood on Mount Zemaraim, in the hill country of Ephraim, and said, "Jeroboam and all Israel, listen to me! ⁵Don't you know that the LORD, the God of Israel, has given the kingship of Israel to David and his descendants forever by a covenant^D of salt? ⁶Yet Jeroboam son of Nebat, an official of Solomon son of David, rebelled against his master. ⁷Some worthless scoundrels gathered around him and opposed Rehoboam son of Solomon when he was young and indecisive and not strong enough to resist them.

⁸"And now you plan to resist the kingdom of the LORD, which is in the hands of David's descendants. You are indeed a vast army and have with you the golden calves that Jeroboam made to be your gods. ⁹But didn't you drive out the priests^D of the LORD, the sons of Aaron, and the Levites^D, and make priests of your own as the peoples of other lands do? Whoever comes to consecrate^D himself with a young bull and seven rams may become a priest of what are not gods.

¹⁰"As for us, the LORD is our God, and we have not forsaken him. The priests who serve the LORD are sons of

How could bronze take the place of gold? (12:10)

It couldn't really. Other articles of value taken from the temple probably were replaced by cheaper substitutes as well. Such humiliation and loss of grandeur apparently caused a change of heart that brought about *some good* (v. 12). Perhaps the people discovered that true worship required a humble heart more than gold.

What kind of evil did Rehoboam do?(12:14)

Rehoboam's reign saw the spread of Canaanite idolatry in Judah (1 Kings 14:22–24). His pride (revealed by his initial response to Jeroboam in 10:14) may also have led to the sin of self-sufficiency—so that he failed to turn to God for help.

The records of Shemaiah (12:15)

See *What happened to these written records?* (9:29).

Covenant of salt (13:5)

Salt, a valuable preservative, was included with many sacrifices (Lev. 2:13; Ezek. 43:24). Part of the sacrificial meat was given to the priests as a covenant of salt. See *Everlasting covenant of salt* (Num. 18:19). The phrase may have suggested that the promise, like other things salted, would be preserved. God's promise to David was everlasting (2 Samuel 7:8–16).

Why *become a priest of what are not gods?* (13:9)

Then, as now, unscrupulous people aimed to profit by engaging in counterfeit ministries. Since their religion was contrived to begin with, the priests felt no qualms about using their position for their personal benefit. Abijah's point was that because Israel had rejected God and accepted a false religion, the Lord was not on their side.

---

^a2 Most Septuagint manuscripts and Syriac (see also 2 Chron. 11:20 and 1 Kings 15:2); Hebrew *Micaiah*   ^b2 Or *granddaughter*

Aaron, and the Levites[D] assist them. [11]Every morning and evening they present burnt offerings[D] and fragrant incense[D] to the LORD. They set out the bread on the ceremonially clean table and light the lamps on the gold lampstand every evening. We are observing the requirements of the LORD our God. But you have forsaken him. [12]God is with us; he is our leader. His priests[D] with their trumpets will sound the battle cry against you. Men of Israel, do not fight against the LORD, the God of your fathers, for you will not succeed."

[13]Now Jeroboam had sent troops around to the rear, so that while he was in front of Judah the ambush was behind them. [14]Judah turned and saw that they were being attacked at both front and rear. Then they cried out to the LORD. The priests blew their trumpets [15]and the men of Judah raised the battle cry. At the sound of their battle cry, God routed Jeroboam and all Israel before Abijah and Judah. [16]The Israelites fled before Judah, and God delivered them into their hands. [17]Abijah and his men inflicted heavy losses on them, so that there were five hundred thousand casualties among Israel's able men. [18]The men of Israel were subdued on that occasion, and the men of Judah were victorious because they relied on the LORD, the God of their fathers.

[19]Abijah pursued Jeroboam and took from him the towns of Bethel, Jeshanah and Ephron, with their surrounding villages. [20]Jeroboam did not regain power during the time of Abijah. And the LORD struck him down and he died.

[21]But Abijah grew in strength. He married fourteen wives and had twenty-two sons and sixteen daughters. [22]The other events of Abijah's reign, what he did and what he said, are written in the annotations of the prophet[D] Iddo.

14 And Abijah rested with his fathers and was buried in the City of David. Asa his son succeeded him as king, and in his days the country was at peace[D] for ten years.

Asa King of Judah

[2]Asa did what was good and right in the eyes of the LORD his God. [3]He removed the foreign altars and the high places[D], smashed the sacred stones[D] and cut down the Asherah poles[D].[a] [4]He commanded Judah to seek the LORD, the God of their fathers, and to obey his laws and commands. [5]He removed the high places and incense altars in every town in Judah, and the kingdom was at peace under him. [6]He built up the fortified cities of Judah, since the land was at peace. No one was at war with him during those years, for the LORD gave him rest.

[7]"Let us build up these towns," he said to Judah, "and put walls around them, with towers, gates and bars. The land is still ours, because we have sought the LORD our God; we sought him and he has given us rest on every side." So they built and prospered.

[8]Asa had an army of three hundred thousand men from Judah, equipped with large shields and with spears, and two hundred and eighty thousand from Benjamin, armed with small shields and with bows. All these were brave fighting men.

[9]Zerah the Cushite marched out against them with a

Were there really 500,000 casualties among the Israelites? (13:17)

This seems an extraordinary figure. (Total U.S. deaths in World War II amounted to 405,000.) Some say the word *thousand* could be translated as *chiefs* or even *specially trained warriors*. If so, the number slain would have been only 500. Others point out that numbers were susceptible to scribal errors; Hebrew writers were not as precise with numbers as we tend to be. In their culture, the word *thousand* could simply convey the idea of *a lot*. Also see *How can such large numbers be explained?* (1 Chron. 18:4–5) and *Why don't the numbers in the list equal the total figure?* (Neh. 7:66).

The annotations of the prophet Iddo (13:22)

See *What happened to these written records?* (9:29).

How could a small nation support such a large army? (14:8)

The figures for Asa's army total 580,000—more than the 537,000 sent to the 1991 Gulf War by the U.S. For more about the large numbers, see *Were there really 500,000 casualties among the Israelites?* (13:17).

---

[a]3 That is, symbols of the goddess Asherah; here and elsewhere in 2 Chronicles

vast army[a] and three hundred chariots, and came as far as Mareshah. ¹⁰Asa went out to meet him, and they took up battle positions in the Valley of Zephathah near Mareshah.

¹¹Then Asa called to the LORD his God and said, "LORD, there is no one like you to help the powerless against the mighty. Help us, O LORD our God, for we rely on you, and in your name we have come against this vast army. O LORD, you are our God; do not let man prevail against you."

¹²The LORD struck down the Cushites before Asa and Judah. The Cushites fled, ¹³and Asa and his army pursued them as far as Gerar. Such a great number of Cushites fell that they could not recover; they were crushed before the LORD and his forces. The men of Judah carried off a large amount of plunder[D]. ¹⁴They destroyed all the villages around Gerar, for the terror of the LORD had fallen upon them. They plundered all these villages, since there was much booty there. ¹⁵They also attacked the camps of the herdsmen and carried off droves of sheep and goats and camels. Then they returned to Jerusalem[D].

Asa's Reform

15 The Spirit of God came upon Azariah son of Oded. ²He went out to meet Asa and said to him, "Listen to me, Asa and all Judah and Benjamin. The LORD is with you when you are with him. If you seek him, he will be found by you, but if you forsake him, he will forsake you. ³For a long time Israel was without the true God, without a priest[D] to teach and without the law. ⁴But in their distress they turned to the LORD, the God of Israel, and sought him, and he was found by them. ⁵In those days it was not safe to travel about, for all the inhabitants of the lands were in great turmoil. ⁶One nation was being crushed by another and one city by another, because God was troubling them with every kind of distress. ⁷But as for you, be strong and do not give up, for your work will be rewarded."

⁸When Asa heard these words and the prophecy[D] of Azariah son of[b] Oded the prophet[D], he took courage. He removed the detestable idols[D] from the whole land of Judah and Benjamin and from the towns he had captured in the hills of Ephraim. He repaired the altar of the LORD that was in front of the portico of the LORD's temple.

⁹Then he assembled all Judah and Benjamin and the people from Ephraim, Manasseh and Simeon who had settled among them, for large numbers had come over to him from Israel when they saw that the LORD his God was with him.

¹⁰They assembled at Jerusalem in the third month of the fifteenth year of Asa's reign. ¹¹At that time they sacrificed to the LORD seven hundred head of cattle and seven thousand sheep and goats from the plunder they had brought back. ¹²They entered into a covenant[D] to seek the LORD, the God of their fathers, with all their heart and soul[D]. ¹³All who would not seek the LORD, the God of Israel, were to be put to death[D], whether small or great, man or woman. ¹⁴They took an oath to the LORD with loud acclamation, with shouting and with trumpets and horns. ¹⁵All Judah rejoiced about the oath because they had

Asa Defeats the Cushites (14:10)

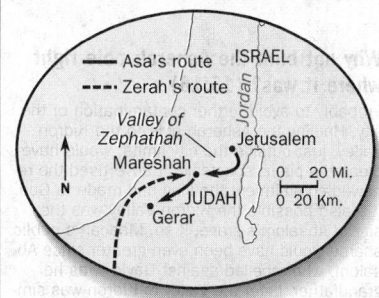

The terror of the LORD (14:14–15)

Indicates a sort of psychological paralysis—an inability to fight—on the part of Judah's foes (17:10; 20:29). Since Judah's army was fighting with the Lord's power, their enemies realized they could not withstand it.

How did the Spirit of God come upon Azariah? (15:1)

See *How did the Spirit of the LORD come upon Jahaziel?* (20:14).

What time in Israel's history was Azariah talking about? (15:3–6)

Probably the period of the judges. See, for instance, Judges 13:1; 21:25.

Why was a new covenant necessary? (15:12)

The nation had plunged into idolatry and had neglected the worship of the Lord. Asa saw that a heartfelt revival was needed. The covenant Israel had made with God at Sinai had already been renewed several times as the nation recommitted itself to the Lord (Deut. 29:1; Joshua 8:30–35; 24:1–27; 1 Samuel 11:14).

How did Asa depose his grandmother? (15:16)

It is unclear what power belonged to queen mothers in Judah, but it was considerable. Later, Queen Athaliah was able to usurp the throne after her son Ahaziah's death (2 Kings 11:1–4). Asa's bold move to remove his grandmother from her position was both symbolic and political. He stripped her of whatever powers or influence she had, perhaps consigning her to house arrest.

---

a9 Hebrew *with an army of a thousand thousands* or *with an army of thousands upon thousands*   b8 Vulgate and Syriac (see also Septuagint and verse 1); Hebrew does not have *Azariah son of*.

Why not burn the Asherah pole right where it was? (15:16)

Probably to avoid further contamination of the city. Hauling the Asherah pole to the Kidron Valley, just outside the city limits, would have created a public spectacle. It advertised the renewed commitment the king had made to God. It's also possible the Kidron Valley was the site of Absalom's grave. If so, Maacah's public shame would have been even greater since Absalom, who rebelled against David, was her grandfather. Later the Valley of Kidron was similarly used in other reforms (29:16; 30:14 2 Kings 23:4–6).

How much did it cost to rent an army? (16:2–4)

See *How much did soldiers get paid?* (25:6).

Hanani the seer (16:7)

Presumably, this is the same Hanani whose son, Jehu, ministered to Asa's son, Jehoshaphat (19:2). Nothing else is known about him.

Do these verses classify Asa as a good or bad king? (16:7–12)

The writer of Chronicles sees the kings—some good, some bad—as spiritual role models for his readers. Asa's treaty with the king of Aram and his refusal to ask God for healing are interpreted negatively. For most of his life, Asa was good, but near the end of his life, he turned from God and was punished for his sins. The generalized summary of his life (15:17), however, did not take into account his later failures, leaving the general feeling that he was considered as one of the good kings of Judah.

sworn it wholeheartedly. They sought God eagerly, and he was found by them. So the LORD gave them rest on every side.

¹⁶King Asa also deposed his grandmother Maacah from her position as queen mother, because she had made a repulsive Asherah pole⁰. Asa cut the pole down, broke it up and burned it in the Kidron Valley⁰. ¹⁷Although he did not remove the high places⁰ from Israel, Asa's heart was fully committed ⌊to the LORD⌋ all his life. ¹⁸He brought into the temple of God the silver and gold and the articles that he and his father had dedicated.

¹⁹There was no more war until the thirty-fifth year of Asa's reign.

Asa's Last Years

16 In the thirty-sixth year of Asa's reign Baasha king of Israel went up against Judah and fortified Ramah to prevent anyone from leaving or entering the territory of Asa king of Judah.

²Asa then took the silver and gold out of the treasuries of the LORD's temple and of his own palace and sent it to Ben-Hadad king of Aram, who was ruling in Damascus. ³"Let there be a treaty between me and you," he said, "as there was between my father and your father. See, I am sending you silver and gold. Now break your treaty with Baasha king of Israel so he will withdraw from me."

⁴Ben-Hadad agreed with King Asa and sent the commanders of his forces against the towns of Israel. They conquered Ijon, Dan, Abel Maim⁰ and all the store cities of Naphtali. ⁵When Baasha heard this, he stopped building Ramah and abandoned his work. ⁶Then King Asa brought all the men of Judah, and they carried away from

a4 Also known as *Abel Beth Maacah*

Why did Israel and Judah fight each other? (16:1)

Conflict had been the hallmark of the Israel–Judah relationship from the time the empire ruled over by Solomon was divided in 930 B.C. The two nations were plagued by chronic hostility, fighting over the border territory to the north of Jerusalem. Why couldn't two kingdoms that had been one get along? Why did they fight each other?

Although the writer of Chronicles could have pointed to the political or sociological tensions common to neighboring countries, he chose to focus on the religious issues that had been set in motion by Israel's first king, Jeroboam. The author of Kings records how Jeroboam set up two golden calves in the northern kingdom (Israel), allowing pagan practices to infiltrate the religious ceremonies of the Israelites (1 Kings 12:25–30). The source of much of the conflict between Israel and Judah stems, according to the writer of Chronicles, from the different religious practices of the two nations. Note the Chronicler's description of the migration to Judah of those who wanted to be faithful to the Lord (11:13–17), as well as his characterization of the open hostilities between Israel and Judah (13:8–20).

Even when Judah allied itself with Israel (18:1), the results were disastrous—because, as the Chronicler indicates, Judah's alliance with Israel was with *those who hate the LORD* (19:2). Again, the differences in faithfulness to the Lord are accented.

In the end, the Chronicler doesn't seem surprised that these two neighboring nations feuded. His focus was on religious issues, and so he offers little explanation of the political circumstances behind the wars between Israel and Judah.

Ramah the stones and timber Baasha had been using. With them he built up Geba and Mizpah.

⁷At that time Hanani the seer^D came to Asa king of Judah and said to him: "Because you relied on the king of Aram and not on the LORD your God, the army of the king of Aram has escaped from your hand. ⁸Were not the Cushites^a and Libyans a mighty army with great numbers of chariots and horsemen^b? Yet when you relied on the LORD, he delivered them into your hand. ⁹For the eyes of the LORD range throughout the earth to strengthen those whose hearts are fully committed to him. You have done a foolish thing, and from now on you will be at war."

¹⁰Asa was angry with the seer because of this; he was so enraged that he put him in prison. At the same time Asa brutally oppressed some of the people.

¹¹The events of Asa's reign, from beginning to end, are written in the book of the kings of Judah and Israel. ¹²In the thirty-ninth year of his reign Asa was afflicted^D with a disease in his feet. Though his disease was severe, even in his illness he did not seek help from the LORD, but only from the physicians. ¹³Then in the forty-first year of his reign Asa died and rested with his fathers. ¹⁴They buried him in the tomb that he had cut out for himself in the City of David. They laid him on a bier covered with spices and various blended perfumes, and they made a huge fire in his honor.

Jehoshaphat King of Judah

17 Jehoshaphat his son succeeded him as king and strengthened himself against Israel. ²He stationed troops in all the fortified cities of Judah and put garrisons in Judah and in the towns of Ephraim that his father Asa had captured.

³The LORD was with Jehoshaphat because in his early years he walked in the ways his father David had followed. He did not consult the Baals^D ⁴but sought the God of his father and followed his commands rather than the practices of Israel. ⁵The LORD established the kingdom under his control; and all Judah brought gifts to Jehoshaphat, so that he had great wealth and honor. ⁶His heart was devoted to the ways of the LORD; furthermore, he removed the high places^D and the Asherah poles^D from Judah.

⁷In the third year of his reign he sent his officials Ben-Hail, Obadiah, Zechariah, Nethanel and Micaiah to teach in the towns of Judah. ⁸With them were certain Levites^D—Shemaiah, Nethaniah, Zebadiah, Asahel, Shemiramoth, Jehonathan, Adonijah, Tobijah and Tob-Adonijah—and the priests^D Elishama and Jehoram. ⁹They taught throughout Judah, taking with them the Book of the Law of the LORD; they went around to all the towns of Judah and taught the people.

¹⁰The fear of the LORD fell on all the kingdoms of the lands surrounding Judah, so that they did not make war with Jehoshaphat. ¹¹Some Philistines brought Jehoshaphat gifts and silver as tribute, and the Arabs brought him flocks: seven thousand seven hundred rams and seven thousand seven hundred goats.

¹²Jehoshaphat became more and more powerful; he built forts and store cities in Judah ¹³and had large supplies in the towns of Judah. He also kept experienced fighting men in Jerusalem^D. ¹⁴Their enrollment by families was as follows:

^a8 That is, people from the upper Nile region   ^b8 Or charioteers

What sort of foot disease was this? (16:12)

There are three reasonable possibilities: gout, dropsy or senile gangrene. However, there are not enough symptoms given for anyone to determine the disease with certainty.

What was wrong with going to physicians? (16:12)

This is not an indictment against the medical profession. It is an indictment against Asa for not seeking the Lord. Disease was a means God used as a spiritual wake-up call. God wanted to get Asa's attention and bring him back to trusting him. God was displeased that Asa was now relying solely on natural solutions instead of seeking the Lord (v. 7).

Did Asa turn away from God? (16:12)

Why, if Asa's heart was fully committed ⌊to the LORD⌋ all his life (15:17), did he seem to reject God at the end? Asa began as a good king whose life was mostly characterized by his trust in God. Sadly, the last events of Asa's life were less impressive. He rejected God's word given through Hanani and became an oppressive ruler (v. 10). He refused to seek God's help in times of national (v. 7) and personal crises. Perhaps Asa, like many others who have enjoyed God's blessings, allowed his faith to be gradually eroded by complacency. Though he could be called fully committed for his lifetime average, at the end he may have taken God for granted. See following note.

Why have a bonfire at a funeral? (16:14)

Apparently it was customary to honor the dead with a memorial fire (see 21:19; Jer. 34:5). Perhaps the fire included spices, incense and perfume, and the body may have been buried upon a bed of the aromatic ashes. Some think that Asa was cremated, though that is unlikely (Lev. 20:14; 21:9). But cremations were done in some cases. See *Why did they burn the bodies before they buried them?* (1 Samuel 31:12–13) and *Why cremate the dead?* (Amos 6:10).

Consult the Baals (17:3)

Seeking guidance for the future was a common practice of idol worship. *Baal* means *lord* or *master* and can refer to several gods. Baal to the Canaanites was normally Hadad, the god of storms. The prophets of Baal who competed with Elijah (1 Kings 18) served another Baal, probably Melqart, the god of the underworld. Ahab, the king of Israel during Jehoshaphat's reign in Judah, also worshiped Melqart, perhaps prompting the writer to note that Jehoshaphat did not. Also see *Baal* (1 Kings 16:32).

What could average citizens give a king? (17:5)

The gifts they brought were tribute, more a symbol of allegiance than a substantial gift. They would have been equivalent to taxes (see 1 Samuel 8:14–17).

How did people learn about God before these teachers came? (17:7)

Typically, people traveled to the prophets, as Saul went to Samuel (1 Samuel 9:6–10) and the Shunammite woman went to Elisha (2 Kings 4:22–23). Sometimes they went to priests (1 Samuel 1:3). Priests were in charge of sacrifice and worship but also taught moral, legal and social traditions.

Store cities (17:12)
Fortresses along the frontier of the nation used for defense. Provisions and weapons were stored in them to provide an emergency supply in case of attack.

Why ratify an international treaty with a wedding? (18:1)
This was a widespread custom in ancient times. The wedding sealed the treaty with a relationship. The idea was that a king would be less likely to break treaties if doing so would endanger his family members who now lived with his former enemies. Psalm 45 was written with just such a treaty and royal wedding in mind.

Ahab Killed (18:3)

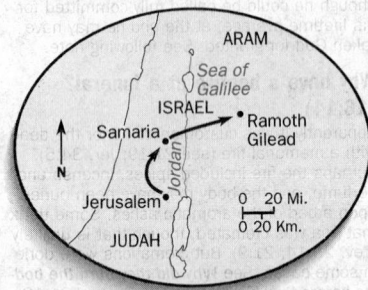

Why did Jehoshaphat find these prophets unsatisfactory? (18:5–6)
Somehow Jehoshaphat suspected these 400 prophets were "yes men." Perhaps their unified voice made him suspicious. Or perhaps Jehoshaphat, as a Judean king from the south, was uncertain about the northern prophets. It may be that he questioned their word because they didn't use the name of God, the LORD.

What is this *prophesying*? (18:9)
We don't know if these prophets were speaking all at once or taking turns, speaking in a trance-like chant or in some other way. We do know they were attempting to predict future events. Sometimes prophecy was accompanied by exuberant behavior such as making music, dancing or falling faint on the ground (for example, 1 Samuel 10:5; 19:24). But it is not known if anything like that occurred here.

Was Micaiah lying or being sarcastic? (18:14)
Micaiah was apparently role-playing, pretending to be another of the king's "yes men," perhaps to ridicule the king. It's possible that he spoke in a falsetto voice. Even if not, it's clear that something about his voice or mannerism let King Ahab know immediately that he was being mocked (v. 15).

From Judah, commanders of units of 1,000:
Adnah the commander, with 300,000 fighting men;
15next, Jehohanan the commander, with 280,000;
16next, Amasiah son of Zicri, who volunteered himself for the service of the LORD, with 200,000.
17From Benjamin:
Eliada, a valiant soldier, with 200,000 men armed with bows and shields;
18next, Jehozabad, with 180,000 men armed for battle.
19These were the men who served the king, besides those he stationed in the fortified cities throughout Judah.

Micaiah Prophesies Against Ahab

18 Now Jehoshaphat had great wealth and honor, and he allied himself with Ahab by marriage. **2**Some years later he went down to visit Ahab in Samaria. Ahab slaughtered many sheep and cattle for him and the people with him and urged him to attack Ramoth Gilead. **3**Ahab king of Israel asked Jehoshaphat king of Judah, "Will you go with me against Ramoth Gilead?"

Jehoshaphat replied, "I am as you are, and my people as your people; we will join you in the war." **4**But Jehoshaphat also said to the king of Israel, "First seek the counsel of the LORD."

5So the king of Israel brought together the prophetsᴰ— four hundred men—and asked them, "Shall we go to war against Ramoth Gilead, or shall I refrain?"

"Go," they answered, "for God will give it into the king's hand."

6But Jehoshaphat asked, "Is there not a prophet of the LORD here whom we can inquire of?"

7The king of Israel answered Jehoshaphat, "There is still one man through whom we can inquire of the LORD, but I hate him because he never prophesies anything good about me, but always bad. He is Micaiah son of Imlah."

"The king should not say that," Jehoshaphat replied.

8So the king of Israel called one of his officials and said, "Bring Micaiah son of Imlah at once."

9Dressed in their royal robes, the king of Israel and Jehoshaphat king of Judah were sitting on their thrones at the threshing floor by the entrance to the gate of Samaria, with all the prophets prophesying before them. **10**Now Zedekiah son of Kenaanah had made iron horns, and he declared, "This is what the LORD says: 'With these you will gore the Arameans until they are destroyed.'"

11All the other prophets were prophesying the same thing. "Attack Ramoth Gilead and be victorious," they said, "for the LORD will give it into the king's hand."

12The messenger who had gone to summon Micaiah said to him, "Look, as one man the other prophets are predicting success for the king. Let your word agree with theirs, and speak favorably."

13But Micaiah said, "As surely as the LORD lives, I can tell him only what my God says."

14When he arrived, the king asked him, "Micaiah, shall we go to war against Ramoth Gilead, or shall I refrain?"

"Attack and be victorious," he answered, "for they will be given into your hand."

15The king said to him, "How many times must I make you swear to tell me nothing but the truth in the name of the LORD?"

16Then Micaiah answered, "I saw all Israel scattered on the hills like sheep without a shepherd, and the LORD said, 'These people have no master. Let each one go home in peace^D.' "

17The king of Israel said to Jehoshaphat, "Didn't I tell you that he never prophesies anything good about me, but only bad?"

18Micaiah continued, "Therefore hear the word of the LORD: I saw the LORD sitting on his throne with all the host of heaven standing on his right and on his left. **19**And the LORD said, 'Who will entice Ahab king of Israel into attacking Ramoth Gilead and going to his death^D there?'

"One suggested this, and another that. **20**Finally, a spirit came forward, stood before the LORD and said, 'I will entice him.'

" 'By what means?' the LORD asked.

21" 'I will go and be a lying spirit in the mouths of all his prophets^D,' he said.

" 'You will succeed in enticing him,' said the LORD. 'Go and do it.'

22"So now the LORD has put a lying spirit in the mouths of these prophets of yours. The LORD has decreed disaster for you."

23Then Zedekiah son of Kenaanah went up and slapped Micaiah in the face. "Which way did the spirit from^a the LORD go when he went from me to speak to you?" he asked.

24Micaiah replied, "You will find out on the day you go to hide in an inner room."

25The king of Israel then ordered, "Take Micaiah and send him back to Amon the ruler of the city and to Joash the king's son, **26**and say, 'This is what the king says: Put this fellow in prison and give him nothing but bread and water until I return safely.' "

27Micaiah declared, "If you ever return safely, the LORD has not spoken through me." Then he added, "Mark my words, all you people!"

Ahab Killed at Ramoth Gilead

28So the king of Israel and Jehoshaphat king of Judah went up to Ramoth Gilead. **29**The king of Israel said to Jehoshaphat, "I will enter the battle in disguise, but you wear your royal robes." So the king of Israel disguised himself and went into battle.

30Now the king of Aram had ordered his chariot commanders, "Do not fight with anyone, small or great, except the king of Israel." **31**When the chariot commanders saw Jehoshaphat, they thought, "This is the king of Israel." So they turned to attack him, but Jehoshaphat cried out, and the LORD helped him. God drew them away from him, **32**for when the chariot commanders saw that he was not the king of Israel, they stopped pursuing him.

33But someone drew his bow at random and hit the king of Israel between the sections of his armor. The king told the chariot driver, "Wheel around and get me out of the fighting. I've been wounded." **34**All day long the battle raged, and the king of Israel propped himself up in his chariot facing the Arameans until evening. Then at sunset he died.

^a23 Or *Spirit of*

Was this a parable or a literal event in heaven? (18:18–21)

Perhaps a little of both. Communicating through images familiar to their culture, God had Micaiah describe a heavenly conference parallel to the one King Ahab was conducting. The two kings sat regally on their thrones with the false prophets before them (v. 9). The king of heaven was pictured similarly, in a way consistent with the view of Middle Eastern culture: gods conferring together with one as the chairperson.

Why would God use a lie to accomplish his purposes? (18:22)

Ahab, though unwilling to follow the Lord, tried to get God to endorse his plan through the prophets. He deceived himself and got exactly what he wanted—confirmation of his war strategy. If he had been open to the true word from the Lord, however, he would have recognized that the false prophets were simply echoing his personal desires. In the final analysis, God did not deceive Ahab. He gave Ahab the choice between believing a lie and believing the truth. But Ahab already had his mind made up and chose what he wanted to believe. See *Is God guilty of lying?* (1 Kings 22:20–22) and article: *How can a holy God send an evil spirit?* (Judges 9:23).

What happened to Micaiah? (18:25–26)

We're not told whether the king's wishes were carried out, since the king never returned safely. His orders would have amounted to a life sentence for Micaiah. But it's possible that once Micaiah's words were vindicated, others would have made sure that he was released from prison. The writer's main focus was that Micaiah was a true prophet. Details concerning Micaiah's fate had nothing to do with the more important point he wanted to make.

After going to so much trouble to find a true prophet, why did Jehoshaphat ignore his warning? (18:28)

Several possibilities exist. Perhaps he felt the social pressure to go along with the crowd—everyone but Micaiah had heartily endorsed Ahab's plan. Or perhaps he felt some social obligation to comply with the host who had just entertained him so lavishly. Or it may be that out of sheer stubbornness he decided to do what he knew to be wrong. He was later rebuked for his disobedience (19:2).

Why did the king of Israel disguise himself? (18:29)

It appears Ahab was acting on a hunch that he would be singled out as a target by the Arameans, which actually happened (v. 30). If this was why he disguised himself, then he deliberately set Jehoshaphat up to take the brunt of the attack. Ahab was known for his self-serving and deceptive character.

Why did the soldiers spare Jehoshaphat? (18:32)

Because their quarrel wasn't with him. They knew that if they could get Ahab, the battle would be over. In fact, their king had told them to fight no one except Ahab (v. 30). Jehoshaphat was merely an auxiliary king leading supporting troops. Nonetheless, it was God working in all these circumstances who made it possible for Jehoshaphat to escape (v. 31).

How could the soldiers tell that the king of Judah was not the king of Israel? (18:32)

It's possible the two kings wore different styles of royal clothing—perhaps with their own national symbols that would not have been recognized from a distance. It's doubtful the Arameans would have recognized a king most of them had never seen by facial features or physical stature. When the king of Aram instructed his soldiers to fight only the king of Israel (v. 30), he may have given them some sort of intelligence gathered by spies that would help them recognize him.

SCRIPTURE LINK (19:2) *Jehu . . . the son of Hanani*

Hanani had earlier confronted another king (Asa) when he turned from God (16:7). There is no evidence that prophetic callings were regularly transferred from a father to his son, even though the priesthood was.

What did revival have to do with appointing judges? (19:4-5)

Revival would have brought a renewed sense of right and wrong, setting the stage for honest and effective judges to work for justice. God wanted his people to be righteous and just. But without a strong spiritual foundation, a society's judicial system would fall short.

What distinguished the king's concerns from the Lord's? (19:11)

It was the difference between secular and religious cases. There seem to have been separate judges for these two categories of cases (see Deut. 17:9-12). Still, it's unknown where the lines were drawn in cases that could fall in either category.

Meunites (20:1)

Probably an ethnic group east of the Jordan River which came from the vicinity of Mount Seir—another name for Edom (v. 10).

How near was this threatening army? (20:2)

They were at En Gedi, half way up the west coast of the Dead Sea or about 25 aerial miles from Jerusalem as the crow flies (see *Map 4* at the back of this Bible). It would have been a bit further on the road.

Was it unusual for kings to pray publicly? (20:5-12)

We don't really know. At special times, the kings led prayers—David, for example, praised God before *the whole assembly* (1 Chron. 29:10-19), Solomon dedicated the temple (6:12-42) and Josiah led the people in a renewal of the covenant with God (34:29-31). The king was known as God's anointed one, representing God's leadership. Perhaps that's why the king often stood in a prominent place in the temple (23:13). Despite this role, the king's actions were ceremonial and not routine.

19 When Jehoshaphat king of Judah returned safely to his palace in Jerusalem[D], [2]Jehu the seer[D], the son of Hanani, went out to meet him and said to the king, "Should you help the wicked and love[a] those who hate the LORD? Because of this, the wrath of the LORD is upon you. [3]There is, however, some good in you, for you have rid the land of the Asherah poles[D] and have set your heart on seeking God."

Jehoshaphat Appoints Judges

[4]Jehoshaphat lived in Jerusalem, and he went out again among the people from Beersheba to the hill country of Ephraim and turned them back to the LORD, the God of their fathers. [5]He appointed judges in the land, in each of the fortified cities of Judah. [6]He told them, "Consider carefully what you do, because you are not judging for man but for the LORD, who is with you whenever you give a verdict. [7]Now let the fear of the LORD be upon you. Judge carefully, for with the LORD our God there is no injustice or partiality or bribery."

[8]In Jerusalem also, Jehoshaphat appointed some of the Levites[D], priests[D] and heads of Israelite families to administer the law of the LORD and to settle disputes. And they lived in Jerusalem. [9]He gave them these orders: "You must serve faithfully and wholeheartedly in the fear of the LORD. [10]In every case that comes before you from your fellow countrymen who live in the cities—whether bloodshed or other concerns of the law, commands, decrees or ordinances—you are to warn them not to sin against the LORD; otherwise his wrath will come on you and your brothers. Do this, and you will not sin.

[11]"Amariah the chief priest will be over you in any matter concerning the LORD, and Zebadiah son of Ishmael, the leader of the tribe of Judah, will be over you in any matter concerning the king, and the Levites will serve as officials before you. Act with courage, and may the LORD be with those who do well."

Jehoshaphat Defeats Moab and Ammon

20 After this, the Moabites and Ammonites with some of the Meunites[b] came to make war on Jehoshaphat.

[2]Some men came and told Jehoshaphat, "A vast army is coming against you from Edom[D,c] from the other side of the Sea.[d] It is already in Hazazon Tamar" (that is, En Gedi). [3]Alarmed, Jehoshaphat resolved to inquire of the LORD, and he proclaimed a fast for all Judah. [4]The people of Judah came together to seek help from the LORD; indeed, they came from every town in Judah to seek him.

[5]Then Jehoshaphat stood up in the assembly of Judah and Jerusalem at the temple of the LORD in the front of the new courtyard [6]and said:

"O LORD, God of our fathers, are you not the God who is in heaven? You rule over all the kingdoms of the nations. Power and might are in your hand, and no one can withstand you. [7]O our God, did you not drive out the inhabitants of this land before your people Israel and give it forever to the descendants of Abraham your friend? [8]They have lived in it and have

---

[a]2 Or *and make alliances with*   [b]1 Some Septuagint manuscripts; Hebrew *Ammonites*   [c]2 One Hebrew manuscript; most Hebrew manuscripts, Septuagint and Vulgate *Aram*   [d]2 That is, the Dead Sea

built in it a sanctuary for your Name, saying, ⁹'If calamity comes upon us, whether the sword of judgment, or plague or famine, we will stand in your
presence before this temple that bears your Name
and will cry out to you in our distress, and you will
hear us and save us.'

¹⁰"But now here are men from Ammon, Moab and
Mount Seir, whose territory you would not allow Israel to invade when they came from Egypt; so they
turned away from them and did not destroy them.
¹¹See how they are repaying us by coming to drive us
out of the possession you gave us as an inheritance.
¹²O our God, will you not judge them? For we have
no power to face this vast army that is attacking us.
We do not know what to do, but our eyes are upon
you."

¹³All the men of Judah, with their wives and children
and little ones, stood there before the LORD.

¹⁴Then the Spirit of the LORD came upon Jahaziel son of
Zechariah, the son of Benaiah, the son of Jeiel, the son of
Mattaniah, a Levite⁰ and descendant of Asaph, as he
stood in the assembly.

¹⁵He said: "Listen, King Jehoshaphat and all who live in
Judah and Jerusalem⁰! This is what the LORD says to you:
'Do not be afraid or discouraged because of this vast
army. For the battle is not yours, but God's. ¹⁶Tomorrow
march down against them. They will be climbing up by
the Pass of Ziz, and you will find them at the end of the
gorge in the Desert of Jeruel. ¹⁷You will not have to fight
this battle. Take up your positions; stand firm and see the
deliverance the LORD will give you, O Judah and Jerusalem. Do not be afraid; do not be discouraged. Go out to
face them tomorrow, and the LORD will be with you.'"

¹⁸Jehoshaphat bowed with his face to the ground, and
all the people of Judah and Jerusalem fell down in worship before the LORD. ¹⁹Then some Levites from the Kohathites and Korahites stood up and praised the LORD, the
God of Israel, with very loud voice.

²⁰Early in the morning they left for the Desert of Tekoa.
As they set out, Jehoshaphat stood and said, "Listen to me,
Judah and people of Jerusalem! Have faith in the LORD
your God and you will be upheld; have faith in his prophets⁰ and you will be successful." ²¹After consulting the
people, Jehoshaphat appointed men to sing to the LORD
and to praise him for the splendor of hisᵃ holiness as
they went out at the head of the army, saying:

"Give thanks to the LORD,
    for his love endures forever."

²²As they began to sing and praise, the LORD set am-
bushes against the men of Ammon and Moab and Mount
Seir who were invading Judah, and they were defeated.
²³The men of Ammon and Moab rose up against the men
from Mount Seir to destroy and annihilate them. After
they finished slaughtering the men from Seir, they helped
to destroy one another.

²⁴When the men of Judah came to the place that overlooks the desert and looked toward the vast army, they
saw only dead bodies lying on the ground; no one had
escaped. ²⁵So Jehoshaphat and his men went to carry off
their plunder⁰, and they found among them a great

ᵃ21 Or *him with the splendor of*

How did the Spirit of the Lord come upon Jahaziel? (20:14)

Although we can't be sure how God's Spirit
came upon Jahaziel, it was clear to the people
who heard him that he was speaking God's
message with authority. As a descendant of
Asaph (see **Asaph**; 1 Chron. 6:39), Jahaziel
was one of the Levites assigned to make music for the temple worship and had probably
not been a prophet before this time. Also see
**What were the signs that the Spirit had come
upon Othniel?** (Judges 3:10).

Why have a choir lead soldiers into battle? (20:21)

Soldiers typically would shout war cries or
chant and sing in rhythm to the marching. Jehoshaphat had the Israelites do the same, but
their shouts were to summon the help of the
Lord instead of their own courage. He wanted
them to see that they weren't the warriors; God
was fighting for them! Joshua (Joshua 6:20),
Gideon (Judges 7:20) and Abijah
(13:14–15) commanded similar processions
or war shouts that glorified God.

Why would allies ambush each other? (20:22–23)

They didn't. They were ambushed by God. The
ambush, some kind of sudden surprise, frightened Judah's enemies and sent them into panicked confusion. Their fear and confusion
caused them to fight each other. Some think
God used angels or some other supernatural
means to ambush them.

amount of equipment and clothing*ᵃ* and also articles of value—more than they could take away. There was so much plunderᴰ that it took three days to collect it. **²⁶**On the fourth day they assembled in the Valley of Beracah, where they praised the Lᴏʀᴅ. This is why it is called the Valley of Beracah*ᵇ* to this day.

²⁷Then, led by Jehoshaphat, all the men of Judah and Jerusalemᴰ returned joyfully to Jerusalem, for the Lᴏʀᴅ had given them cause to rejoice over their enemies. **²⁸**They entered Jerusalem and went to the temple of the Lᴏʀᴅ with harps and lutes and trumpets.

²⁹The fear of God came upon all the kingdoms of the countries when they heard how the Lᴏʀᴅ had fought against the enemies of Israel. **³⁰**And the kingdom of Jehoshaphat was at peaceᴰ, for his God had given him rest on every side.

The End of Jehoshaphat's Reign

³¹So Jehoshaphat reigned over Judah. He was thirty-five years old when he became king of Judah, and he reigned in Jerusalem twenty-five years. His mother's name was Azubah daughter of Shilhi. **³²**He walked in the ways of his father Asa and did not stray from them; he did what was right in the eyes of the Lᴏʀᴅ. **³³**The high placesᴰ, however, were not removed, and the people still had not set their hearts on the God of their fathers.

³⁴The other events of Jehoshaphat's reign, from beginning to end, are written in the annals of Jehu son of Hanani, which are recorded in the book of the kings of Israel.

³⁵Later, Jehoshaphat king of Judah made an alliance with Ahaziah king of Israel, who was guilty of wickedness. **³⁶**He agreed with him to construct a fleet of trading ships.*ᶜ* After these were built at Ezion Geber, **³⁷**Eliezer son of Dodavahu of Mareshah prophesied against Jehoshaphat, saying, "Because you have made an alliance with Ahaziah, the Lᴏʀᴅ will destroy what you have made." The ships were wrecked and were not able to set sail to trade.*ᵈ*

21 Then Jehoshaphat rested with his fathers and was buried with them in the City of David. And Jehoram his son succeeded him as king. **²**Jehoram's brothers, the sons of Jehoshaphat, were Azariah, Jehiel, Zechariah, Azariahu, Michael and Shephatiah. All these were sons of Jehoshaphat king of Israel.*ᵉ* **³**Their father had given them many gifts of silver and gold and articles of value, as well as fortified cities in Judah, but he had given the kingdom to Jehoram because he was his firstbornᴰ son.

Jehoram King of Judah

⁴When Jehoram established himself firmly over his father's kingdom, he put all his brothers to the sword along with some of the princes of Israel. **⁵**Jehoram was thirty-two years old when he became king, and he reigned in Jerusalem eight years. **⁶**He walked in the ways of the kings of Israel, as the house of Ahab had done, for he married a daughter of Ahab. He did evil in the eyes of the Lᴏʀᴅ. **⁷**Nevertheless, because of the covenantᴰ the Lᴏʀᴅ had made with David, the Lᴏʀᴅ was not willing to destroy

Why would the son of a godly king murder his brothers? (21:4)
Jehoram killed his brothers because they were potential political rivals. Although this violent path to power was more often the pattern in the northern kingdom, it was not unheard of in Judah. Solomon, for example, had his brother Adonijah killed to remove him as a political opponent (1 Kings 2:23–25).

Did Jehoram's marriage cause his evil ways? (21:6)
Many factors shape a person's life, the choice of a mate being one of the most persuasive. The writer of Chronicles saw Jehoram's wife (who would have brought her idolatrous practices with her) as a primary influence upon his life, causing him to turn away from God (v. 11). Ironically, Jehoram's marriage may have been arranged by his godly father, Jehoshaphat (see 18:1).

ᵃ25 Some Hebrew manuscripts and Vulgate; most Hebrew manuscripts *corpses*   *ᵇ26 Beracah* means *praise.*   *ᶜ36* Hebrew *of ships that could go to Tarshish*   *ᵈ37* Hebrew *sail for Tarshish*   *ᵉ2* That is, Judah, as frequently in 2 Chronicles

the house of David. He had promised to maintain a lamp for him and his descendants forever.

8In the time of Jehoram, Edom[D] rebelled against Judah and set up its own king. **9**So Jehoram went there with his officers and all his chariots. The Edomites surrounded him and his chariot commanders, but he rose up and broke through by night. **10**To this day Edom has been in rebellion against Judah.

Libnah revolted at the same time, because Jehoram had forsaken the LORD, the God of his fathers. **11**He had also built high places[D] on the hills of Judah and had caused the people of Jerusalem[D] to prostitute themselves and had led Judah astray.

12Jehoram received a letter from Elijah the prophet[D], which said:

"This is what the LORD, the God of your father David, says: 'You have not walked in the ways of your father Jehoshaphat or of Asa king of Judah. **13**But you have walked in the ways of the kings of Israel, and you have led Judah and the people of Jerusalem to prostitute themselves, just as the house of Ahab did. You have also murdered your own brothers, members of your father's house, men who were better than you. **14**So now the LORD is about to strike your people, your sons, your wives and everything that is yours, with a heavy blow. **15**You yourself will be very ill with a lingering disease of the bowels, until the disease causes your bowels to come out.' "

16The LORD aroused against Jehoram the hostility of the Philistines and of the Arabs who lived near the Cushites. **17**They attacked Judah, invaded it and carried off all the goods found in the king's palace, together with his sons and wives. Not a son was left to him except Ahaziah,[a] the youngest.

18After all this, the LORD afflicted[D] Jehoram with an incurable disease of the bowels. **19**In the course of time, at the end of the second year, his bowels came out because of the disease, and he died in great pain. His people made no fire in his honor, as they had for his fathers.

20Jehoram was thirty-two years old when he became king, and he reigned in Jerusalem eight years. He passed away, to no one's regret, and was buried in the City of David, but not in the tombs of the kings.

Ahaziah King of Judah

22 The people of Jerusalem made Ahaziah, Jehoram's youngest son, king in his place, since the raiders, who came with the Arabs into the camp, had killed all the older sons. So Ahaziah son of Jehoram king of Judah began to reign.

2Ahaziah was twenty-two[b] years old when he became king, and he reigned in Jerusalem one year. His mother's name was Athaliah, a granddaughter of Omri.

3He too walked in the ways of the house of Ahab, for his mother encouraged him in doing wrong. **4**He did evil in the eyes of the LORD, as the house of Ahab had done, for after his father's death[D] they became his advisers, to his undoing. **5**He also followed their counsel when he went with Joram[c] son of Ahab king of Israel to war against

---

Libnah (21:10)

The exact location of Libnah, on the border between Judah and Philistia (2 Kings 8:22), is unknown (see **Map 3** at the back of this Bible).

Why didn't Elijah meet with Jehoram face to face? (21:12)

We don't know. It was not unusual for prophets to relay their messages through a servant or aide. Since Elijah was a prophet in the northern kingdom, distance or difficulties in border crossing may have been contributing factors. Perhaps his age or limited mobility were others. This letter was likely written shortly before Elijah was taken up from the earth.

What disease afflicted Jehoram? (21:15)

Although there is no way to tell with certainty, Jehoram's symptoms may describe a cancer of the rectum or possibly a condition called a rectal prolapse in which the rectum turns inside out. Over the course of time, the blood flow is cut off and the rectum becomes gangrenous.

Who advised Ahaziah—the house of Ahab? (22:4)

The royal counselors from the northern court had a great deal of influence over the southern king. Ahaziah's mother, Ahab's daughter, was a member of the northern dynasty (21:6).

---

*a*17 Hebrew *Jehoahaz,* a variant of *Ahaziah*   *b*2 Some Septuagint manuscripts and Syriac (see also 2 Kings 8:26); Hebrew *forty-two*
*c*5 Hebrew *Jehoram,* a variant of *Joram*; also in verses 6 and 7

Hazael king of Aram at Ramoth Gilead. The Arameans wounded Joram; **6**so he returned to Jezreel to recover from the wounds they had inflicted on him at Ramoth*ᵃ* in his battle with Hazael king of Aram.

Then Ahaziah*ᵇ* son of Jehoram king of Judah went down to Jezreel to see Joram son of Ahab because he had been wounded.

7Through Ahaziah's visit to Joram, God brought about Ahaziah's downfall. When Ahaziah arrived, he went out with Joram to meet Jehu son of Nimshi, whom the LORD had anointed*ᴰ* to destroy the house of Ahab. **8**While Jehu was executing judgment on the house of Ahab, he found the princes of Judah and the sons of Ahaziah's relatives, who had been attending Ahaziah, and he killed them. **9**He then went in search of Ahaziah, and his men captured him while he was hiding in Samaria. He was brought to Jehu and put to death*ᴰ*. They buried him, for they said, "He was a son of Jehoshaphat, who sought the LORD with all his heart." So there was no one in the house of Ahaziah powerful enough to retain the kingdom.

Athaliah and Joash

10When Athaliah the mother of Ahaziah saw that her son was dead, she proceeded to destroy the whole royal family of the house of Judah. **11**But Jehosheba,*ᶜ* the daughter of King Jehoram, took Joash son of Ahaziah and stole him away from among the royal princes who were about to be murdered and put him and his nurse in a bedroom. Because Jehosheba,*ᶜ* the daughter of King Jehoram and wife of the priest*ᴰ* Jehoiada, was Ahaziah's sister, she hid the child from Athaliah so she could not kill him. **12**He remained hidden with them at the temple of God for six years while Athaliah ruled the land.

23 In the seventh year Jehoiada showed his strength. He made a covenant*ᴰ* with the commanders of units of a hundred: Azariah son of Jeroham, Ishmael son of Jehohanan, Azariah son of Obed, Maaseiah son of Adaiah, and Elishaphat son of Zicri. **2**They went throughout Judah and gathered the Levites*ᴰ* and the heads of Israelite families from all the towns. When they came to Jerusalem*ᴰ*, **3**the whole assembly made a covenant with the king at the temple of God.

Jehoiada said to them, "The king's son shall reign, as the LORD promised concerning the descendants of David. **4**Now this is what you are to do: A third of you priests and Levites who are going on duty on the Sabbath are to keep watch at the doors, **5**a third of you at the royal palace and a third at the Foundation Gate, and all the other men are to be in the courtyards of the temple of the LORD. **6**No one is to enter the temple of the LORD except the priests and Levites on duty; they may enter because they are consecrated*ᴰ*, but all the other men are to guard what the LORD has assigned to them.*ᵈ* **7**The Levites are to station themselves around the king, each man with his weapons in his hand. Anyone who enters the temple must be put to death. Stay close to the king wherever he goes."

8The Levites and all the men of Judah did just as Je-

Why would Ahaziah's mother destroy the royal family? (22:10)

Athaliah was making a bid for political survival. If one of her grandsons became king, she would be eased off the stage of national politics. Though married into Judah's royal family, Athaliah had no legal claim to the throne. But by removing all legitimate heirs to the throne, she hoped to take full advantage of being the daughter of a northern king. Also see **Why would a grandmother murder her own grandchildren?** (2 Kings 11:1–2).

How could a public place like the temple be safe from Athaliah? (22:12)

This part of the temple—the priests' private quarters—wasn't that public. For her part, Athaliah and her attendants cared nothing about going to the temple to worship the Lord.

Foundation Gate (23:5)

It's not known which temple gate this was or how it got its name. It is also called the Sur Gate (2 Kings 11:6), but neither name appears any other place in the Bible. Some speculate that it may have led from the palace to the temple area.

Divisions (23:8)

The priests and Levites were organized into 24 divisions, each division taking turns at serving in the temple (1 Chron. 24:1–4). When they weren't on duty, they lived in various towns assigned to the Levites. To gain extra manpower for the coup, Jehoiada recruited those coming on temple duty to join those that had just finished. Also see **Why did the military support a priest's coup?** (2 Kings 11:9).

---

*ᵃ*6 Hebrew *Ramah,* a variant of *Ramoth*   *ᵇ*6 Some Hebrew manuscripts, Septuagint, Vulgate and Syriac (see also 2 Kings 8:29); most Hebrew manuscripts *Azariah*   *ᶜ*11 Hebrew *Jehoshabeath,* a variant of *Jehosheba*   *ᵈ*6 Or *to observe the LORD's command ⌊not to enter⌋*

hoiada the priest[D] ordered. Each one took his men—those who were going on duty on the Sabbath[D] and those who were going off duty—for Jehoiada the priest had not released any of the divisions. **9**Then he gave the commanders of units of a hundred the spears and the large and small shields that had belonged to King David and that were in the temple of God. **10**He stationed all the men, each with his weapon in his hand, around the king—near the altar and the temple, from the south side to the north side of the temple.

11Jehoiada and his sons brought out the king's son and put the crown on him; they presented him with a copy of the covenant[D] and proclaimed him king. They anointed[D] him and shouted, "Long live the king!"

12When Athaliah heard the noise of the people running and cheering the king, she went to them at the temple of the LORD. **13**She looked, and there was the king, standing by his pillar at the entrance. The officers and the trumpeters were beside the king, and all the people of the land were rejoicing and blowing trumpets, and singers with musical instruments were leading the praises. Then Athaliah tore her robes and shouted, "Treason! Treason!"

14Jehoiada the priest sent out the commanders of units of a hundred, who were in charge of the troops, and said to them: "Bring her out between the ranks[a] and put to the sword anyone who follows her." For the priest had said, "Do not put her to death[D] at the temple of the LORD." **15**So they seized her as she reached the entrance of the Horse Gate on the palace grounds, and there they put her to death.

16Jehoiada then made a covenant that he and the people and the king[b] would be the LORD's people. **17**All the people went to the temple of Baal[D] and tore it down. They smashed the altars and idols[D] and killed Mattan the priest of Baal in front of the altars.

18Then Jehoiada placed the oversight of the temple of the LORD in the hands of the priests, who were Levites[D], to whom David had made assignments in the temple, to present the burnt offerings[D] of the LORD as written in the Law of Moses, with rejoicing and singing, as David had ordered. **19**He also stationed doorkeepers at the gates of the LORD's temple so that no one who was in any way unclean[D] might enter.

20He took with him the commanders of hundreds, the nobles, the rulers of the people and all the people of the land and brought the king down from the temple of the LORD. They went into the palace through the Upper Gate and seated the king on the royal throne, **21**and all the people of the land rejoiced. And the city was quiet, because Athaliah had been slain with the sword.

Joash Repairs the Temple

24 Joash was seven years old when he became king, and he reigned in Jerusalem[D] forty years. His mother's name was Zibiah; she was from Beersheba. **2**Joash did what was right in the eyes of the LORD all the years of Jehoiada the priest. **3**Jehoiada chose two wives for him, and he had sons and daughters.

4Some time later Joash decided to restore the temple of the LORD. **5**He called together the priests and Levites and said to them, "Go to the towns of Judah and collect

---

a 14 Or *out from the precincts*   *b 16* Or *covenant between ⌊the LORD⌋ and the people and the king that they* (see 2 Kings 11:17)

Why would weapons be stored in a place of worship? (23:9)

Pagan temples in ancient times were, to some extent, considered religious museums as they contained relics to commemorate times the gods had supposedly helped the people. The temple in Jerusalem, dedicated to the one true God, displayed weapons as trophies of God's grace. They were signs of praise and thanksgiving for past victories. Various items taken as plunder in battle also were dedicated to the Lord as an honor to him (1 Chron. 18:7–11; 26:26–27).

Horse Gate (23:15)

This was a royal gate in the palace complex. (There was a different horse gate in the city wall.) It probably got its name because it was close to the royal stables and would be the usual entrance used by the king's horses.

Was this a spiritual or a political covenant? (23:16)

Both. The writer sees these as two sides to the same coin. The Israelites were both a covenant people and a political nation. When they declared their allegiance to the young king God had preserved for them, they also destroyed the Baal worship favored by Athaliah (v. 17).

How could the priests see who was unclean? (23:19)

In general, they couldn't. Uncleanness was seldom visible by external means. Perhaps they were to permit only consecrated priests and Levites to enter the temple (v. 6). More likely, the doorkeepers were to stop everyone entering the temple with a reminder that they had to be ceremonially clean. They may have even asked those coming in to declare their cleanness.

Upper Gate (23:20)

This temple gate was called *Upper* because it was higher than the outer court of the royal complex. Located on the south side of the temple, one had to go down some steps to enter the palace quarters. Actually, this gate hadn't yet been built when these events took place. It was built later during the reign of Jotham (27:3). But the writer used a site familiar to his readers to show how Joash went directly from the temple to the palace throne.

Why did Jehoiada choose two wives for Joash? (24:3)

Athaliah had killed off the royal family, almost extinguishing the dynasty. Jehoiada chose two wives to ensure progeny and to rebuild the royal family. See article: **Why did David have so many wives and concubines?** (2 Samuel 5:13).

Why did the Levites take so long to collect the money? (24:5)

We don't know why the Levites delayed collecting money for temple renovations. Although he did not issue his order when he first came to the throne, Joash had been king 23 years before he called the priests and Levites to account for holding up the project (2 Kings 12:6). Some think it's possible they had their own personal priorities in mind for the funds.

the money due annually from all Israel, to repair the temple of your God. Do it now." But the Levites[D] did not act
at once.

Could objects defiled by Baal worship be reconsecrated to the Lord? (24:7)

The sacred items later removed from the temple by Ahaz for his evil purposes were reconsecrated during Hezekiah's reign (29:19).

6Therefore the king summoned Jehoiada the chief priest[D] and said to him, "Why haven't you required the Levites to bring in from Judah and Jerusalem the tax imposed by Moses the servant of the LORD and by the assembly of Israel for the Tent of the Testimony?"

7Now the sons of that wicked woman Athaliah had broken into the temple of God and had used even its sacred[D] objects for the Baals[D].

8At the king's command, a chest was made and placed outside, at the gate of the temple of the LORD. **9**A proclamation was then issued in Judah and Jerusalem that they should bring to the LORD the tax that Moses the servant of God had required of Israel in the desert. **10**All the officials and all the people brought their contributions gladly, dropping them into the chest until it was full. **11**Whenever the chest was brought in by the Levites to the king's officials and they saw that there was a large amount of money, the royal secretary and the officer of the chief priest would come and empty the chest and carry it back to its place. They did this regularly and collected a great amount of money. **12**The king and Jehoiada gave it to the men who carried out the work required for the temple of the LORD. They hired masons and carpenters to restore the LORD's temple, and also workers in iron and bronze to repair the temple.

13The men in charge of the work were diligent, and the repairs progressed under them. They rebuilt the temple of God according to its original design and reinforced it. **14**When they had finished, they brought the rest of the money to the king and Jehoiada, and with it were made articles for the LORD's temple: articles for the service and for the burnt offerings[D], and also dishes and other objects of gold and silver. As long as Jehoiada lived, burnt offerings were presented continually in the temple of the LORD.

15Now Jehoiada was old and full of years, and he died at the age of a hundred and thirty. **16**He was buried with the kings in the City of David, because of the good he had done in Israel for God and his temple.

Why would a priest be buried with the kings? (24:16)

Because of the good he had done meant he had enormous impact on the nation. Jehoiada was the human agent God used to restore the line of David to the throne. He also had instructed the young king and had carried considerable clout in royal affairs (24:2). It was because he played a role so much larger than that of priest that Jehoiada was buried with the kings.

How could Joash so quickly and so completely abandon his upbringing? (24:18)

As hard as it is to understand Joash's lack of commitment to the Lord, his is a pattern familiar in Chronicles. The writer used Joash, along with several other kings, as examples to warn his readers that spiritual commitment could not be taken for granted. He wanted them to avoid the mistakes made by Joash.

How did the Spirit of God come upon Zechariah? (24:20)

See *How did the Spirit of the Lord come upon Jahaziel?* (20:14).

The Wickedness of Joash

17After the death[D] of Jehoiada, the officials of Judah came and paid homage to the king, and he listened to them. **18**They abandoned the temple of the LORD, the God of their fathers, and worshiped Asherah poles[D] and idols[D]. Because of their guilt, God's anger came upon Judah and Jerusalem. **19**Although the LORD sent prophets[D] to the people to bring them back to him, and though they testified against them, they would not listen.

20Then the Spirit of God came upon Zechariah son of Jehoiada the priest. He stood before the people and said, "This is what God says: 'Why do you disobey the LORD's commands? You will not prosper. Because you have forsaken the LORD, he has forsaken you.'"

21But they plotted against him, and by order of the king they stoned him to death in the courtyard of the LORD's temple. **22**King Joash did not remember the kindness Zechariah's father Jehoiada had shown him but killed his son, who said as he lay dying, "May the LORD see this and call you to account."

²³At the turn of the year,ᵃ the army of Aram marched against Joash; it invaded Judah and JerusalemᴰD and killed all the leaders of the people. They sent all the plunderᴰ to their king in Damascus. ²⁴Although the Aramean army had come with only a few men, the LORD delivered into their hands a much larger army. Because Judah had forsaken the LORD, the God of their fathers, judgment was executed on Joash. ²⁵When the Arameans withdrew, they left Joash severely wounded. His officials conspired against him for murdering the son of Jehoiada the priestᴰ, and they killed him in his bed. So he died and was buried in the City of David, but not in the tombs of the kings.

²⁶Those who conspired against him were Zabad,ᵇ son of Shimeath an Ammonite woman, and Jehozabad, son of Shimrithᶜ a Moabite woman. ²⁷The account of his sons, the many propheciesᴰ about him, and the record of the restoration of the temple of God are written in the annotations on the book of the kings. And Amaziah his son succeeded him as king.

Amaziah King of Judah

25 Amaziah was twenty-five years old when he became king, and he reigned in Jerusalem twenty-nine years. His mother's name was Jehoaddinᵈ; she was from Jerusalem. ²He did what was right in the eyes of the LORD, but not wholeheartedly. ³After the kingdom was firmly in his control, he executed the officials who had murdered his father the king. ⁴Yet he did not put their sons to deathᴰ, but acted in accordance with what is written in the Law, in the Book of Moses, where the LORD commanded: "Fathers shall not be put to death for their children, nor children put to death for their fathers; each is to die for his own sins."ᵉ

⁵Amaziah called the people of Judah together and as-

ᵃ23 Probably in the spring   ᵇ26 A variant of *Jozabad*   ᶜ26 A variant of *Shomer*   ᵈ1 Hebrew *Jehoaddan*, a variant of *Jehoaddin*   ᵉ4 Deut. 24:16

Why wasn't Joash buried with the kings? (24:25)

The writer saw the burial places of the kings as a significant footnote to their lives—a report card on their reign. Just as Jehoiada had been honored in his burial (v. 16), Joash was dishonored. A similar lack of respect was shown for King Jehoram who likewise was not buried in the tombs of the kings (21:20).

How did God judge the kings? (25:2)

What was *right in the eyes of the LORD*? Did God judge Amaziah for his personal piety or for his policies in the political arena? Although we can't know God's mind, the Chronicler seems to indicate that God doesn't separate the two but sees public actions as external indicators of personal faith.

By and large, the accounts of the kings' reigns recorded in Chronicles reveal that kings judged as doing what was *right in the eyes of the LORD* demonstrated their faith by supporting temple worship, encouraging the priests and Levites and opposing idol worship. Many of these faithful kings enjoyed the blessings of prosperity, fame and military victory.

On the other hand, kings judged to have done what was *evil in the eyes of the LORD* neglected the temple and supported idol worship (see 33:1–9). Many of these unfaithful kings suffered the consequences, experiencing sickness and military defeat.

Although not every good king always met with success (32:24-26) and not every evil king always met with failure (33:13), the Chronicler does draw special attention to the good moments when kings turned to God and God responded with an outpouring of blessings.

signed them according to their families to commanders of thousands and commanders of hundreds for all Judah and Benjamin. He then mustered those twenty years old or more and found that there were three hundred thousand men ready for military service, able to handle the spear and shield. **6**He also hired a hundred thousand fighting men from Israel for a hundred talents[a] of silver.

7But a man of God came to him and said, "O king, these troops from Israel must not march with you, for the LORD is not with Israel—not with any of the people of Ephraim. **8**Even if you go and fight courageously in battle, God will overthrow you before the enemy, for God has the power to help or to overthrow."

9Amaziah asked the man of God, "But what about the hundred talents I paid for these Israelite troops?"

The man of God replied, "The LORD can give you much more than that."

10So Amaziah dismissed the troops who had come to him from Ephraim and sent them home. They were furious with Judah and left for home in a great rage.

11Amaziah then marshaled his strength and led his army to the Valley of Salt, where he killed ten thousand men of Seir. **12**The army of Judah also captured ten thousand men alive, took them to the top of a cliff and threw them down so that all were dashed to pieces.

13Meanwhile the troops that Amaziah had sent back and had not allowed to take part in the war raided Judean towns from Samaria to Beth Horon. They killed three thousand people and carried off great quantities of plunderᴰ.

14When Amaziah returned from slaughtering the Edomites, he brought back the gods of the people of Seir. He set them up as his own gods, bowed down to them and burned sacrificesᴰ to them. **15**The anger of the LORD burned against Amaziah, and he sent a prophetᴰ to him, who said, "Why do you consult this people's gods, which could not save their own people from your hand?"

16While he was still speaking, the king said to him, "Have we appointed you an adviser to the king? Stop! Why be struck down?"

So the prophet stopped but said, "I know that God has determined to destroy you, because you have done this and have not listened to my counsel."

17After Amaziah king of Judah consulted his advisers, he sent this challenge to Jehoash[b] son of Jehoahaz, the son of Jehu, king of Israel: "Come, meet me face to face."

18But Jehoash king of Israel replied to Amaziah king of Judah: "A thistle in Lebanon sent a message to a cedar in Lebanon, 'Give your daughter to my son in marriage.' Then a wild beast in Lebanon came along and trampled the thistle underfoot. **19**You say to yourself that you have defeated Edomᴰ, and now you are arrogant and proud. But stay at home! Why ask for trouble and cause your own downfall and that of Judah also?"

20Amaziah, however, would not listen, for God so worked that he might hand them over to ⌊Jehoash⌋, because they sought the gods of Edom. **21**So Jehoash king of Israel attacked. He and Amaziah king of Judah faced each other at Beth Shemesh in Judah. **22**Judah was routed by Israel, and every man fled to his home. **23**Jehoash king

---

How much did soldiers get paid? (25:6)

The going rate, which probably fluctuated due to supply and demand, was approximately one talent per thousand men which is about three shekels of silver (a bit more than an ounce) each. Soldiers for hire would also receive food and supplies plus the loot they won in battle.

Why were the mercenaries so angry? (25:10)

Though they received their pay, they were denied the chance to win any loot in battle. They became upset because they expected much more. In retaliation, they plundered the countryside of Judah, the nation that had hired them in the first place (v. 13).

Why kill prisoners of war? (25:12)

Because Judah nursed an ongoing grudge with Edom—and had since the time of Jacob and Esau, their ancestors. Their antagonism was fueled by Judah's conviction that Edomites were the enemies of God. Since the Edomites lived in high, rocky places (Obad. v. 3), a cliff was a quick, convenient means for Judah to dispose of their enemies—even if such actions seem inhumane by today's standards.

Wasn't Samaria part of the northern kingdom? (25:13)

Yes. Since no town by this name was known in Judah, this may either be a copyist's error or it may be that the mercenaries assembled in Samaria and launched their raids on the Judean towns from there.

Why did Amaziah worship defeated gods? (25:14)

It was common for victorious nations in ancient times to cart off the idols of their defeated foes. They assumed their victory was due in part to the gods of their enemies switching sides in battle. So they would add them to all the other gods they worshiped to give thanks for helping them win. Similarly, Ahaz worshiped "victorious" foreign gods in an attempt to increase his military strength (28:23). God played off this line of thinking to warn his people: if they were unfaithful to him, he himself would bring foreigners to attack them (Deut. 28:49–52).

Why did Jehoash answer Amaziah with an allegory? (25:18–19)

Parables were sometimes used to make a point indirectly or to add subtle shades of meaning. Jehoash answered Amaziah with a story, not only to communicate his answer to the challenge but to send his insults and sentiments as well: *you're no better than a common noxious weed.*

Did Jehoash leave Amaziah on the throne in Jerusalem? (25:23)

Apparently, although he left him in a weakened and vulnerable condition, breaking down part of the city wall and taking hostages away (v. 24). Since Amaziah refused to listen when told to stay home (v. 19), he was forced against his will to be subject to King Jehoash.

---

*a*6 That is, about 3 3/4 tons (about 3.4 metric tons); also in verse 9
*b*17 Hebrew *Joash,* a variant of *Jehoash*; also in verses 18, 21, 23 and 25

of Israel captured Amaziah king of Judah, the son of Joash, the son of Ahaziah,[a] at Beth Shemesh. Then Jehoash brought him to Jerusalem[D] and broke down the wall of Jerusalem from the Ephraim Gate to the Corner Gate—a section about six hundred feet[b] long. ²⁴He took all the gold and silver and all the articles found in the temple of God that had been in the care of Obed-Edom, together with the palace treasures and the hostages, and returned to Samaria.

²⁵Amaziah son of Joash king of Judah lived for fifteen years after the death[D] of Jehoash son of Jehoahaz king of Israel. ²⁶As for the other events of Amaziah's reign, from beginning to end, are they not written in the book of the kings of Judah and Israel? ²⁷From the time that Amaziah turned away from following the LORD, they conspired against him in Jerusalem and he fled to Lachish, but they sent men after him to Lachish and killed him there. ²⁸He was brought back by horse and was buried with his fathers in the City of Judah.

Uzziah King of Judah

26 Then all the people of Judah took Uzziah,[c] who was sixteen years old, and made him king in place of his father Amaziah. ²He was the one who rebuilt Elath and restored it to Judah after Amaziah rested with his fathers.

³Uzziah was sixteen years old when he became king, and he reigned in Jerusalem fifty-two years. His mother's name was Jecoliah; she was from Jerusalem. ⁴He did what was right in the eyes of the LORD, just as his father Amaziah had done. ⁵He sought God during the days of Zechariah, who instructed him in the fear[d] of God. As long as he sought the LORD, God gave him success.

⁶He went to war against the Philistines and broke down the walls of Gath, Jabneh and Ashdod. He then rebuilt towns near Ashdod and elsewhere among the Philistines. ⁷God helped him against the Philistines and against the Arabs who lived in Gur Baal and against the Meunites. ⁸The Ammonites brought tribute to Uzziah, and his fame

---

a23 Hebrew *Jehoahaz,* a variant of *Ahaziah*   *b23* Hebrew *four hundred cubits* (about 180 meters)   *c1* Also called *Azariah*   *d5* Many Hebrew manuscripts, Septuagint and Syriac; other Hebrew manuscripts *vision*

Zechariah (26:5)

Served as spiritual mentor to King Uzziah, just as Jehoiada had served Joash earlier (24:2). The Bible mentions 30 different men by this name. The book of Zechariah was written by a prophet who lived 200 years after this Zechariah.

What is *the fear of God?* (26:5)

Proverbs calls it the beginning of knowledge (Prov. 1:7). Zechariah gave Uzziah insight into the nature and character of God, helping him to see God as the one true God, not just one of many deities that ruled over various territories, as was commonly believed at that time. *The fear of God* taught Uzziah awe and respect for God, the Sovereign Lord, Creator and Sustainer of all life. Also see article: *Should we live in terror of God?* (Prov. 1:7).

Does seeking God guarantee success? (26:5)

Yes and no. Faithfulness in seeking God does not guarantee that he will grant us success if we define success in terms of acquiring wealth, prestige and power. That is not to say, however, that God couldn't bless us with those gifts, as we see in King Uzziah's case. What God does guarantee is that when we seek him, we will enjoy the *success* of finding the source of love and peace and the reason for hope.

Whether or not God blesses us with those commonly recognized signs of success that our society cherishes, the writer of Chronicles makes it clear that we must focus not on seeking success but on seeking God.

Also see articles: *Does obedience bring prosperity?* (Lev. 26:3-39) and *Is success guaranteed to those who obey God?* (Deut. 28:2-6). See also *Does God promise health and wealth?* (Joshua 1:8).

Why build towers in the desert? (26:10)

Towers in remote regions served several important purposes. Armies used them for defense, lookout posts and signaling. Farmers used towers to store crops (as silos do today), water (as above ground cisterns) or farm tools. Some towers were used as shelter for travelers or farm workers. Uzziah's success as a military leader and administrator required an infrastructure that included roads, water systems and towers.

Why would a king want to do a priest's job? (26:18)

Probably, in this case, Uzziah's royal ego inflated his estimation of his own importance. *Pride led to his downfall,* the writer says (v. 16). Apparently he began to think that as king he could do whatever he wanted, even those sacred duties reserved only for priests who were consecrated and authorized by God (see Num. 16:39–40).

Why did God use a disease as a punishment? (26:19)

The writer doesn't explain why God pronounced this judgment against Uzziah. But it's easy to see that the punishment fit the crime. Proud Uzziah was humbled immediately, taken from high-life to low-life, from honor to disgrace, from notoriety to quarantine. Uzziah's remaining days reminded everyone that God, not man, was in charge. Also see *Does God make us sick when he is angry with us?* (Psalm 38:3).

How was Uzziah's burial different from other kings? (26:23)

Even in death and burial, the quarantined king remained apart. Normally a king's body would be laid in the royal sepulchers as a final honor. Uzziah was a great king in his prime, but in death as in his last days, he was tainted with the disease that no one wanted—a sign of God's anger.

What was wrong with going into the temple? (27:2)

Nothing, unless it was done at the wrong time and for the wrong purposes. Furthermore, certain areas of the temple were restricted to priests alone. Uzziah's mistake was to do what only priests were commissioned to do, and Jotham is commended here for not repeating it.

What were these *corrupt practices*? (27:2)

Probably the worst thing the people did was to persist in the pagan worship common in the region. Jotham did not remove the high places where such worship occurred (2 Kings 15:35). Pagan worship led to other dreadful activities —violence against children and sexual misconduct.

spread as far as the border of Egypt, because he had become very powerful.

⁹Uzziah built towers in Jerusalem[D] at the Corner Gate, at the Valley Gate and at the angle of the wall, and he fortified them. ¹⁰He also built towers in the desert and dug many cisterns[D], because he had much livestock in the foothills and in the plain. He had people working his fields and vineyards in the hills and in the fertile lands, for he loved the soil.

¹¹Uzziah had a well-trained army, ready to go out by divisions according to their numbers as mustered by Jeiel the secretary and Maaseiah the officer under the direction of Hananiah, one of the royal officials. ¹²The total number of family leaders over the fighting men was 2,600. ¹³Under their command was an army of 307,500 men trained for war, a powerful force to support the king against his enemies. ¹⁴Uzziah provided shields, spears, helmets, coats of armor, bows and slingstones for the entire army. ¹⁵In Jerusalem he made machines designed by skillful men for use on the towers and on the corner defenses to shoot arrows and hurl large stones. His fame spread far and wide, for he was greatly helped until he became powerful.

¹⁶But after Uzziah became powerful, his pride led to his downfall. He was unfaithful to the Lord his God, and entered the temple of the Lord to burn incense[D] on the altar of incense. ¹⁷Azariah the priest with eighty other courageous priests of the Lord followed him in. ¹⁸They confronted him and said, "It is not right for you, Uzziah, to burn incense to the Lord. That is for the priests, the descendants of Aaron, who have been consecrated[D] to burn incense. Leave the sanctuary, for you have been unfaithful; and you will not be honored by the Lord God."

¹⁹Uzziah, who had a censer[D] in his hand ready to burn incense, became angry. While he was raging at the priests in their presence before the incense altar in the Lord's temple, leprosy[D][a] broke out on his forehead. ²⁰When Azariah the chief priest and all the other priests looked at him, they saw that he had leprosy on his forehead, so they hurried him out. Indeed, he himself was eager to leave, because the Lord had afflicted[D] him. ²¹King Uzziah had leprosy until the day he died. He lived in a separate house[b]—leprous, and excluded from the temple of the Lord. Jotham his son had charge of the palace and governed the people of the land.

²²The other events of Uzziah's reign, from beginning to end, are recorded by the prophet[D] Isaiah son of Amoz. ²³Uzziah rested with his fathers and was buried near them in a field for burial that belonged to the kings, for people said, "He had leprosy." And Jotham his son succeeded him as king.

Jotham King of Judah

27 Jotham was twenty-five years old when he became king, and he reigned in Jerusalem sixteen years. His mother's name was Jerusha daughter of Zadok. ²He did what was right in the eyes of the Lord, just as his father Uzziah had done, but unlike him he did not enter the temple of the Lord. The people, however, continued their corrupt practices. ³Jotham rebuilt the Upper Gate of

[a]19 The Hebrew word was used for various diseases affecting the skin—not necessarily leprosy; also in verses 20, 21 and 23.
[b]21 Or *in a house where he was relieved of responsibilities*

the temple of the LORD and did extensive work on the wall at the hill of Ophel. **4**He built towns in the Judean hills and forts and towers in the wooded areas.

5Jotham made war on the king of the Ammonites and conquered them. That year the Ammonites paid him a hundred talents*a* of silver, ten thousand cors*b* of wheat and ten thousand cors of barley. The Ammonites brought him the same amount also in the second and third years.

6Jotham grew powerful because he walked steadfastly before the LORD his God.

7The other events in Jotham's reign, including all his wars and the other things he did, are written in the book of the kings of Israel and Judah. **8**He was twenty-five years old when he became king, and he reigned in Jerusalem*D* sixteen years. **9**Jotham rested with his fathers and was buried in the City of David. And Ahaz his son succeeded him as king.

Ahaz King of Judah

28 Ahaz was twenty years old when he became king, and he reigned in Jerusalem sixteen years. Unlike David his father, he did not do what was right in the eyes of the LORD. **2**He walked in the ways of the kings of Israel and also made cast idols*D* for worshiping the Baals*D*. **3**He burned sacrifices*D* in the Valley of Ben Hinnom and sacrificed his sons in the fire, following the detestable ways of the nations the LORD had driven out before the Israelites. **4**He offered sacrifices and burned incense at the high places*D*, on the hilltops and under every spreading tree.

5Therefore the LORD his God handed him over to the king of Aram. The Arameans defeated him and took many of his people as prisoners and brought them to Damascus.

He was also given into the hands of the king of Israel, who inflicted heavy casualties on him. **6**In one day Pekah son of Remaliah killed a hundred and twenty thousand soldiers in Judah—because Judah had forsaken the LORD, the God of their fathers. **7**Zicri, an Ephraimite warrior, killed Maaseiah the king's son, Azrikam the officer in charge of the palace, and Elkanah, second to the king. **8**The Israelites took captive from their kinsmen two hundred thousand wives, sons and daughters. They also took a great deal of plunder*D*, which they carried back to Samaria.

9But a prophet*D* of the LORD named Oded was there, and he went out to meet the army when it returned to Samaria. He said to them, "Because the LORD, the God of your fathers, was angry with Judah, he gave them into your hand. But you have slaughtered them in a rage that reaches to heaven. **10**And now you intend to make the men and women of Judah and Jerusalem your slaves. But aren't you also guilty of sins against the LORD your God? **11**Now listen to me! Send back your fellow countrymen you have taken as prisoners, for the LORD's fierce anger rests on you."

12Then some of the leaders in Ephraim—Azariah son of Jehohanan, Berekiah son of Meshillemoth, Jehizkiah son of Shallum, and Amasa son of Hadlai—confronted those who were arriving from the war. **13**"You must not bring those prisoners here," they said, "or we will be guilty before the LORD. Do you intend to add to our sin and guilt?

*a*5 That is, about 3 3/4 tons (about 3.4 metric tons)   *b*5 That is, probably about 62,000 bushels (about 2,200 kiloliters)

Do those who faithfully serve God always grow powerful? (27:6)

Nobody grows powerful in life without God, though many people think they do because they have gained money and prestige. Those who serve God may or may not become wealthy. What makes them powerful is not their money or fame but their relationship with the Lord.

Valley of Ben Hinnom (28:3)

West and south of Jerusalem, it was the old border between Judah and Benjamin (Joshua 15:8). During the period covered in the Chronicles, it became a place of idol worship and child sacrifice.

Why would anyone want to sacrifice their children? (28:3)

See *Why would parents sacrifice their children?* (Jer. 19:5).

Arameans (28:5)

Descendants of Shem (Semites), who lived north of Canaan in the vicinity of Damascus (see *David's Victories* on page 407). Saul clashed with them, David defeated them and Solomon lost to them before they were defeated by the Assyrians in 732 B.C. But their language lived on: Jesus spoke Aramaic.

Is defeat a sign of God's displeasure? (28:5)

It was in this case but it's not always a certain sign. A sovereign God does not insure that good always wins and evil always loses—except in the long run. While the battle is the Lord's, smaller skirmishes may be lost for a number of reasons: human error, wrong timing, less than ideal circumstances, talented opposition and so on. Losses need not mean defeat, however. Instead they can be an opportunity to take stock, reconsider strategy and determine if God's plan is being followed.

Oded (28:9)

A prophet who protested Israel's violent treatment of Judah in wartime, helping to convince the soldiers to return their prisoners. Another prophet named Oded appears in 15:9, but there is no apparent connection between the two.

Can anyone go too far in doing God's will? (28:9–10)

No. God's will is perfect. But we can step outside of God's will even while righteously thinking we're still in it. Apparently that's what happened here. God had permitted Israel to wage war against Judah. But Israel stepped outside of God's will when they used cruel and unjust means to accomplish it. It was a case of the end not justifying the means.

City of Palms (28:15)

Jericho lay 820 feet below the level of the Mediterranean Sea, near powerful springs that gave it a subtropical climate. Balsam, sycamore and palms all flourished there, lending the city its nickname.

Edomites (28:17)

Descendants of Esau (Gen 36:1,8). The Edomites were a group of federated tribes that lived south of the Dead Sea amid reddish sandstone of the Rift Valley, perhaps leading to their name which meant *red* (see **Map 5** at the back of this Bible). They worshiped gods of fertility and developed an economy based on agriculture and trade routes.

Did anyone protest the king's actions? (28:24–25)

No doubt some did, but no protest is recorded here. Probably the doors of the inner temple, the Holy Place, were shut, not the temple complex as a whole. Thus, some may have continued to worship the true God in the outer courts. See following question.

Why wasn't Ahaz buried in the kings' tombs? (28:27)

Here the protest against Ahaz took tangible form. His actions were offensive enough to a sufficient group of powerful people (especially his heirs to power) that they separated his remains and his memory from the honor typically given to national leaders.

Who taught Hezekiah to serve the Lord? (29:3)

The writer gives only hints. Any king who served God did so in light of the example of David, who preceded Hezekiah by 300 years. Faithful priests, prophets and other persons close to Hezekiah must have kept the vision of David alive. It's certain Hezekiah did not learn faithfulness from his own father. Others close to the child must have nurtured him in the truth. Also see **What made Hezekiah's faith so strong?** (32:7–8).

For our guilt is already great, and his fierce anger rests on Israel." **14**So the soldiers gave up the prisoners and plunder[D] in the presence of the officials and all the assembly. **15**The men designated by name took the prisoners, and from the plunder they clothed all who were naked. They provided them with clothes and sandals, food and drink, and healing balm. All those who were weak they put on donkeys. So they took them back to their fellow countrymen at Jericho[D], the City of Palms, and returned to Samaria.

16At that time King Ahaz sent to the king[a] of Assyria for help. **17**The Edomites had again come and attacked Judah and carried away prisoners, **18**while the Philistines had raided towns in the foothills and in the Negev[D] of Judah. They captured and occupied Beth Shemesh, Aijalon and Gederoth, as well as Soco, Timnah and Gimzo, with their surrounding villages. **19**The LORD had humbled Judah because of Ahaz king of Israel,[b] for he had promoted wickedness in Judah and had been most unfaithful to the LORD. **20**Tiglath-Pileser[c] king of Assyria came to him, but he gave him trouble instead of help. **21**Ahaz took some of the things from the temple of the LORD and from the royal palace and from the princes and presented them to the king of Assyria, but that did not help him.

22In his time of trouble King Ahaz became even more unfaithful to the LORD. **23**He offered sacrifices[D] to the gods of Damascus, who had defeated him; for he thought, "Since the gods of the kings of Aram have helped them, I will sacrifice to them so they will help me." But they were his downfall and the downfall of all Israel.

24Ahaz gathered together the furnishings from the temple of God and took them away.[d] He shut the doors of the LORD's temple and set up altars at every street corner in Jerusalem[D]. **25**In every town in Judah he built high places[D] to burn sacrifices to other gods and provoked the LORD, the God of his fathers, to anger.

26The other events of his reign and all his ways, from beginning to end, are written in the book of the kings of Judah and Israel. **27**Ahaz rested with his fathers and was buried in the city of Jerusalem, but he was not placed in the tombs of the kings of Israel. And Hezekiah his son succeeded him as king.

Hezekiah Purifies the Temple

29 Hezekiah was twenty-five years old when he became king, and he reigned in Jerusalem twenty-nine years. His mother's name was Abijah daughter of Zechariah. **2**He did what was right in the eyes of the LORD, just as his father David had done.

3In the first month of the first year of his reign, he opened the doors of the temple of the LORD and repaired them. **4**He brought in the priests[D] and the Levites[D], assembled them in the square on the east side **5**and said: "Listen to me, Levites! Consecrate yourselves now and consecrate the temple of the LORD, the God of your fathers. Remove all defilement from the sanctuary. **6**Our fathers were unfaithful; they did evil in the eyes of the LORD our God and forsook him. They turned their faces away from the LORD's dwelling place and turned their

<hr/>

a16 One Hebrew manuscript, Septuagint and Vulgate (see also 2 Kings 16:7); most Hebrew manuscripts *kings*   *b19* That is, Judah, as frequently in 2 Chronicles   *c20* Hebrew *Tilgath-Pilneser,* a variant of *Tiglath-Pileser*   *d24* Or *and cut them up*

backs on him. **7**They also shut the doors of the portico and put out the lamps. They did not burn incense^D or present any burnt offerings^D at the sanctuary to the God of Israel. **8**Therefore, the anger of the LORD has fallen on Judah and Jerusalem^D; he has made them an object of dread and horror and scorn, as you can see with your own eyes. **9**This is why our fathers have fallen by the sword and why our sons and daughters and our wives are in captivity. **10**Now I intend to make a covenant^D with the LORD, the God of Israel, so that his fierce anger will turn away from us. **11**My sons, do not be negligent now, for the LORD has chosen you to stand before him and serve him, to minister before him and to burn incense."

12Then these Levites^D set to work:

from the Kohathites,
    Mahath son of Amasai and Joel son of Azariah;
from the Merarites,
    Kish son of Abdi and Azariah son of Jehallelel;
from the Gershonites,
    Joah son of Zimmah and Eden son of Joah;
13from the descendants of Elizaphan,
    Shimri and Jeiel;
from the descendants of Asaph,
    Zechariah and Mattaniah;
14from the descendants of Heman,
    Jehiel and Shimei;
from the descendants of Jeduthun,
    Shemaiah and Uzziel.

15When they had assembled their brothers and consecrated^D themselves, they went in to purify^D the temple of the LORD, as the king had ordered, following the word of the LORD. **16**The priests^D went into the sanctuary of the LORD to purify it. They brought out to the courtyard of the LORD's temple everything unclean^D that they found in the temple of the LORD. The Levites took it and carried it out to the Kidron Valley^D. **17**They began the consecration on the first day of the first month, and by the eighth day of the month they reached the portico of the LORD. For eight more days they consecrated the temple of the LORD itself, finishing on the sixteenth day of the first month.

18Then they went in to King Hezekiah and reported: "We have purified the entire temple of the LORD, the altar of burnt offering with all its utensils, and the table for setting out the consecrated bread, with all its articles. **19**We have prepared and consecrated all the articles that King Ahaz removed in his unfaithfulness while he was king. They are now in front of the LORD's altar."

20Early the next morning King Hezekiah gathered the city officials together and went up to the temple of the LORD. **21**They brought seven bulls, seven rams, seven male lambs and seven male goats as a sin offering^D for the kingdom, for the sanctuary and for Judah. The king commanded the priests, the descendants of Aaron, to offer these on the altar of the LORD. **22**So they slaughtered the bulls, and the priests took the blood and sprinkled it on the altar; next they slaughtered the rams and sprinkled their blood on the altar; then they slaughtered the lambs and sprinkled their blood on the altar. **23**The goats for the sin offering were brought before the king and the assembly, and they laid their hands on them. **24**The priests then slaughtered the goats and presented their blood on the altar for a sin offering to atone for all Isra-

What was needed to consecrate themselves and the temple? (29:15–17)
The Bible doesn't say specifically. No provisions had been made to cleanse the temple of the Lord from pagan influence. Idolatry in the temple courts was never supposed to happen. Earlier instructions to cleanse the land required the destruction of all pagan sites and equipment (Deut. 12:2–3).

Kidron Valley (29:16)
Just east of Jerusalem, between the city and the Mount of Olives (see **Map 8** at the back of this Bible). Pagan relics were destroyed there under Asa, Hezekiah and Josiah.

What was so special about the number seven? (29:21)
Even among pagans, the number seven had been especially recognized throughout the region for centuries, perhaps because of the religious rituals attached to the phases of the moon. Among the Hebrews, however, from the time of creation, *seven* signified something that was complete or perfect.

el, because the king had ordered the burnt offering[D] and the sin offering[D] for all Israel.

25He stationed the Levites[D] in the temple of the LORD with cymbals, harps and lyres[D] in the way prescribed by David and Gad the king's seer[D] and Nathan the prophet[D]; this was commanded by the LORD through his prophets. 26So the Levites stood ready with David's instruments, and the priests[D] with their trumpets.

27Hezekiah gave the order to sacrifice[D] the burnt offering on the altar. As the offering began, singing to the LORD began also, accompanied by trumpets and the instruments of David king of Israel. 28The whole assembly bowed in worship, while the singers sang and the trumpeters played. All this continued until the sacrifice of the burnt offering was completed.

29When the offerings were finished, the king and everyone present with him knelt down and worshiped. 30King Hezekiah and his officials ordered the Levites to praise the LORD with the words of David and of Asaph the seer. So they sang praises with gladness and bowed their heads and worshiped.

31Then Hezekiah said, "You have now dedicated yourselves to the LORD. Come and bring sacrifices and thank offerings[D] to the temple of the LORD." So the assembly brought sacrifices and thank offerings, and all whose hearts were willing brought burnt offerings.

32The number of burnt offerings the assembly brought was seventy bulls, a hundred rams and two hundred male lambs—all of them for burnt offerings to the LORD. 33The animals consecrated[D] as sacrifices amounted to six hundred bulls and three thousand sheep and goats. 34The priests, however, were too few to skin all the burnt offerings; so their kinsmen the Levites helped them until the task was finished and until other priests had been consecrated, for the Levites had been more conscientious in consecrating themselves than the priests had been. 35There were burnt offerings in abundance, together with the fat of the fellowship offerings[Da] and the drink offerings[D] that accompanied the burnt offerings.

So the service of the temple of the LORD was reestablished. 36Hezekiah and all the people rejoiced at what God had brought about for his people, because it was done so quickly.

Hezekiah Celebrates the Passover

30 Hezekiah sent word to all Israel and Judah and also wrote letters to Ephraim and Manasseh, inviting them to come to the temple of the LORD in Jerusalem[D] and celebrate the Passover to the LORD, the God of Israel. 2The king and his officials and the whole assembly in Jerusalem decided to celebrate the Passover in the second month. 3They had not been able to celebrate it at the regular time because not enough priests had consecrated themselves and the people had not assembled in Jerusalem. 4The plan seemed right both to the king and to the whole assembly. 5They decided to send a proclamation throughout Israel, from Beersheba to Dan, calling the people to come to Jerusalem and celebrate the Passover to the LORD, the God of Israel. It had not been celebrated in large numbers according to what was written.

6At the king's command, couriers went throughout Isra-

How could worship be legislated? (29:30)

Because independent thinking is highly valued today, it's hard for us to see how a king's command could force people to worship God sincerely. A couple of factors may be involved: (1) Ancient cultures often focused on the community more than the individual. People accepted the collective wisdom of their community and yielded to their leaders' thinking much more readily than we do. (2) Simply obeying the king's orders did not make for sincere worship. The Levites were genuinely glad to worship God —command or no command—and did so from their hearts.

Why weren't the priests more conscientious? (29:34)

The writer does not tell the whole story. Perhaps the priests, closer to influential circles, had been corrupted by the worldly ways of Ahaz, Hezekiah's father. Perhaps religious ritual for the priests had become more ritual and less genuine.

Regular time (30:3)

The Passover was usually celebrated on the 14th day of the first month, Abib (mid-March to mid-April).

Was Hezekiah's invitation purely religious—or did it have political overtones? (30:6)

Nothing in Israel was purely religious or purely political. The separation of church and state is a modern concept that would have baffled Hezekiah. To recover worship of the true God would also be to recover national unity and strength, in Hezekiah's mind. Citizens of the northern kingdom, under the thumb of Assyria, undoubtedly understood the message clearly.

---

a35 Traditionally *peace offerings*

el and Judah with letters from the king and from his officials, which read:

"People of Israel, return to the LORD, the God of Abraham, Isaac and Israel, that he may return to you who are left, who have escaped from the hand of the kings of Assyria. **7**Do not be like your fathers and brothers, who were unfaithful to the LORD, the God of their fathers, so that he made them an object of horror, as you see. **8**Do not be stiff-necked, as your fathers were; submit to the LORD. Come to the sanctuary, which he has consecrated^D forever. Serve the LORD your God, so that his fierce anger will turn away from you. **9**If you return to the LORD, then your brothers and your children will be shown compassion by their captors and will come back to this land, for the LORD your God is gracious and compassionate. He will not turn his face from you if you return to him."

10The couriers went from town to town in Ephraim and Manasseh, as far as Zebulun, but the people scorned and ridiculed them. **11**Nevertheless, some men of Asher, Manasseh and Zebulun humbled themselves and went to Jerusalem^D. **12**Also in Judah the hand of God was on the people to give them unity of mind to carry out what the king and his officials had ordered, following the word of the LORD.

13A very large crowd of people assembled in Jerusalem to celebrate the Feast of Unleavened Bread in the second month. **14**They removed the altars in Jerusalem and cleared away the incense^D altars and threw them into the Kidron Valley.

15They slaughtered the Passover lamb on the fourteenth day of the second month. The priests^D and the Levites^D were ashamed and consecrated themselves and brought burnt offerings^D to the temple of the LORD. **16**Then they took up their regular positions as prescribed in the Law of Moses the man of God. The priests sprinkled the blood handed to them by the Levites. **17**Since many in the crowd had not consecrated themselves, the Levites had to kill the Passover lambs for all those who were not ceremonially clean and could not consecrate ⌊their lambs⌋ to the LORD. **18**Although most of the many people who came from Ephraim, Manasseh, Issachar and Zebulun had not purified^D themselves, yet they ate the Passover, contrary to what was written. But Hezekiah prayed for them, saying, "May the LORD, who is good, pardon everyone **19**who sets his heart on seeking God—the LORD, the God of his fathers—even if he is not clean according to the rules of the sanctuary." **20**And the LORD heard Hezekiah and healed the people.

21The Israelites who were present in Jerusalem celebrated the Feast of Unleavened Bread for seven days with great rejoicing, while the Levites and priests sang to the LORD every day, accompanied by the LORD's instruments of praise.^a

22Hezekiah spoke encouragingly to all the Levites, who showed good understanding of the service of the LORD. For the seven days they ate their assigned portion and offered fellowship offerings^{Db} and praised the LORD, the God of their fathers.

23The whole assembly then agreed to celebrate the fes-

Why were the couriers harassed? (30:10)

Probably for two reasons: (1) The people of the northern kingdom had a long history of going against God and (2) they were afraid of the possible political consequences. Those who worshiped other gods opposed Hezekiah's couriers meddling in their affairs. Nervous officials, however, were probably more concerned about potential repercussions from their Assyrian masters. They hoped that humiliating the couriers would appease the Assyrians.

Feast of Unleavened Bread (30:13)

Another name for Passover, usually celebrated on the 14th day of the first month to commemorate Israel's deliverance from Egypt. It was the first of three annual feasts which required all men to come to the sanctuary.

What altars were removed? (30:14)

Ahaz had erected an altar in the temple, perhaps to Rimmon, the Aramean god of storm and war, known in other lands as Baal (2 Kings 5:18). Or, the altar may have been in honor of the Assyrian king, Ahaz's master (2 Kings 16:10). Ahaz probably used altars as he worshiped *the gods of Damascus* (28:23) and sacrificed his sons to the Ammonite god, Molech (28:3).

Kidron Valley (30:14)

See *Kidron Valley* (29:16).

Healed (30:20)

Not physical, but spiritual healing. Solomon's prayer described this healing (7:14). David had asked for it (Psalm 41:4). It is the renewing of a relationship between God and his people, restoring hope and love. With the weight of sin and guilt removed, the people could freely rejoice (v. 21).

What were the Lord's instruments? (30:21)

There were three types: stringed (lyre and harp), wind (flute and horn) and percussion (tambourine and cymbal). Horns had a common military usage; cymbals signaled important events and tambourines were widely used to keep the beat in public singing.

---

^a21 Or *priests praised the LORD every day with resounding instruments belonging to the LORD*   ^b22 Traditionally *peace offerings*

What causes prayers to reach God? (30:27)

The phrase, *God heard them, for their prayer reached heaven,* shows how limited human language is when it comes to explaining the supernatural. God hears and knows everything. But when he *ignores* some prayers for certain reasons, human language might say that God does not *hear* those prayers. These prayers were effective because those who prayed had submitted to God and were dependent upon him. Their earnest requests were squared with God's will and purpose. Selfish or doubting prayers are exercises in futility. Also see article: *When does God refuse to hear our prayers?* (Jer. 11:11).

Was the portion due priests like a tax? (31:4)

In a sense, yes. Certain amounts were to be given at certain times. But there was a difference: their giving was to be an act of worship, springing from grateful hearts—unlike taxes, often given out of obligation. As a sign of revival and renewed obedience, Hezekiah wanted the old system of giving to be reinstated. The people's generous response was quite unlike the typical response to paying taxes (vv. 5–8). Also see *Why did God give the people's offerings to the Levites?* (Num. 18:8).

Tithe (31:5)

One-tenth of one's income. Giving a *tithe* was an ancient system widespread in the region for supporting religious professionals, though some cultures required less than a tenth. The Israelites devoted a *tithe* to support the Levites, freeing them to serve the Lord (Num. 18:21; Lev. 27:30).

tival seven more days; so for another seven days they celebrated joyfully. **24**Hezekiah king of Judah provided a thousand bulls and seven thousand sheep and goats for the assembly, and the officials provided them with a thousand bulls and ten thousand sheep and goats. A great number of priests^D consecrated^D themselves. **25**The entire assembly of Judah rejoiced, along with the priests and Levites^D and all who had assembled from Israel, including the aliens^D who had come from Israel and those who lived in Judah. **26**There was great joy in Jerusalem^D, for since the days of Solomon son of David king of Israel there had been nothing like this in Jerusalem. **27**The priests and the Levites stood to bless the people, and God heard them, for their prayer reached heaven, his holy dwelling place.

31 When all this had ended, the Israelites who were there went out to the towns of Judah, smashed the sacred stones^D and cut down the Asherah poles^D. They destroyed the high places^D and the altars throughout Judah and Benjamin and in Ephraim and Manasseh. After they had destroyed all of them, the Israelites returned to their own towns and to their own property.

Contributions for Worship

2Hezekiah assigned the priests and Levites to divisions—each of them according to their duties as priests or Levites—to offer burnt offerings and fellowship offerings^{D,a} to minister, to give thanks and to sing praises at the gates of the LORD's dwelling. **3**The king contributed from his own possessions for the morning and evening burnt offerings and for the burnt offerings on the Sabbaths^D, New Moons and appointed feasts as written in the Law of the LORD. **4**He ordered the people living in Jerusalem to give the portion due the priests and Levites so they could devote themselves to the Law of the LORD. **5**As soon as the order went out, the Israelites generously gave the firstfruits^D of their grain, new wine^D, oil and honey and all that the fields produced. They brought a great amount, a tithe^D of everything. **6**The men of Israel and Judah who lived in the towns of Judah also brought a tithe of their herds and flocks and a tithe of the holy things dedicated to the LORD their God, and they piled them in heaps. **7**They began doing this in the third month and finished in the seventh month. **8**When Hezekiah and his officials came and saw the heaps, they praised the LORD and blessed his people Israel.

9Hezekiah asked the priests and Levites about the heaps; **10**and Azariah the chief priest, from the family of Zadok, answered, "Since the people began to bring their contributions to the temple of the LORD, we have had enough to eat and plenty to spare, because the LORD has blessed his people, and this great amount is left over."

11Hezekiah gave orders to prepare storerooms in the temple of the LORD, and this was done. **12**Then they faithfully brought in the contributions, tithes and dedicated gifts. Conaniah, a Levite, was in charge of these things, and his brother Shimei was next in rank. **13**Jehiel, Azaziah, Nahath, Asahel, Jerimoth, Jozabad, Eliel, Ismakiah, Mahath and Benaiah were supervisors under Conaniah and Shimei his brother, by appointment of King Hezekiah and Azariah the official in charge of the temple of God. **14**Kore son of Imnah the Levite, keeper of the East

---

a2 Traditionally peace offerings

Gate, was in charge of the freewill offerings given to God, distributing the contributions made to the LORD and also the consecrated[D] gifts. [15]Eden, Miniamin, Jeshua, Shemaiah, Amariah and Shecaniah assisted him faithfully in the towns of the priests[D], distributing to their fellow priests according to their divisions, old and young alike.

[16]In addition, they distributed to the males three years old or more whose names were in the genealogical records—all who would enter the temple of the LORD to perform the daily duties of their various tasks, according to their responsibilities and their divisions. [17]And they distributed to the priests enrolled by their families in the genealogical records and likewise to the Levites[D] twenty years old or more, according to their responsibilities and their divisions. [18]They included all the little ones, the wives, and the sons and daughters of the whole community listed in these genealogical records. For they were faithful in consecrating themselves.

[19]As for the priests, the descendants of Aaron, who lived on the farm lands around their towns or in any other towns, men were designated by name to distribute portions to every male among them and to all who were recorded in the genealogies[D] of the Levites.

[20]This is what Hezekiah did throughout Judah, doing what was good and right and faithful before the LORD his God. [21]In everything that he undertook in the service of God's temple and in obedience to the law and the commands, he sought his God and worked wholeheartedly. And so he prospered.

Sennacherib Threatens Jerusalem

32 After all that Hezekiah had so faithfully done, Sennacherib king of Assyria came and invaded Judah. He laid siege to the fortified cities, thinking to conquer them for himself. [2]When Hezekiah saw that Sennacherib had come and that he intended to make war on Jerusalem[D], [3]he consulted with his officials and military staff about blocking off the water from the springs outside the city, and they helped him. [4]A large force of men assembled, and they blocked all the springs and the stream that flowed through the land. "Why should the kings[a] of Assyria come and find plenty of water?" they said. [5]Then he worked hard repairing all the broken sections of the wall and building towers on it. He built another wall outside that one and reinforced the supporting terraces[b] of the City of David. He also made large numbers of weapons and shields.

[6]He appointed military officers over the people and assembled them before him in the square at the city gate and encouraged them with these words: [7]"Be strong and courageous. Do not be afraid or discouraged because of the king of Assyria and the vast army with him, for there is a greater power with us than with him. [8]With him is only the arm of flesh, but with us is the LORD our God to help us and to fight our battles." And the people gained confidence from what Hezekiah the king of Judah said.

[9]Later, when Sennacherib king of Assyria and all his forces were laying siege to Lachish, he sent his officers to Jerusalem with this message for Hezekiah king of Judah and for all the people of Judah who were there:

[10]"This is what Sennacherib king of Assyria says:

Why were children as young as three paid tithes though they were not yet priests? (31:16)
Levites coming to serve the temple brought their sons with them. Room, board and childcare evidently came from their sons' allotments.

Will those who are faithful be rewarded with prosperity? (31:21)
See article: *Does seeking God guarantee success?* (26:5).

Sennacherib (32:1)
King of Assyria (705–681 B.C.). To stabilize his empire, he launched an ambitious western campaign demanding first tribute and then surrender from Hezekiah. God intervened (v. 21) and Sennacherib returned to Nineveh where he was assassinated by two sons in 681 B.C.

Supporting terraces (32:5)
A landfill structure built up like a mound to help defend the city, sometimes called the Millo (see NIV text note). It was there when David took Jerusalem, was rebuilt by Solomon, strengthened by Hezekiah and finally leveled by Nebuchadnezzar.

What made Hezekiah's faith so strong? (32:7–8)
Hezekiah did not receive spiritual training from his father, the wicked King Ahaz (28:22–25). Hezekiah, influenced more by others, served the Lord instead of his father's idols. His godly upbringing became clear in the first priority of his reign—to undo the evil his father had done (29:3). His mother, Abijah, may have been one of those responsible for his spiritual roots. She was the daughter of Zechariah (29:1)—perhaps the godly adviser to his great-grandfather Uzziah (26:5) or the Levite later recruited to help restore the temple (29:13).

---

*a*4 Hebrew; Septuagint and Syriac *king*   *b*5 Or *the Millo*

Had Hezekiah actually removed altars to the Lord? (32:12)

Yes. But the altars he removed were unauthorized, so Sennacherib's charges were not really accurate. Many Israelites had used pagan high places to worship false gods as well as to worship the Lord (2 Kings 17:32–33). Hezekiah urged them to return to the temple as the sole place of worship (30:8). Sennacherib may also have intended to paint Hezekiah as a hypocrite since he had taken silver and gold from the temple to pay tribute (2 Kings 18:15–16). Also see article: *What is the significance of the temple?* (3:3–17).

What drove the Assyrians to insult the Lord? (32:16–19)

The Assyrians believed the supernatural world included gods who ruled over limited territories. They thought that weaker gods would be conquered by more powerful gods. The Assyrians also believed that they could increase their power base by adding the gods of their victims to their collection of gods. To the Assyrians, the Lord was just another one of many gods on their list to be defeated.

What kind of angel annihilates people? (32:21)

An angel who is instructed by God to impart justice. Only rarely did God intervene with such lethal force in human affairs. After David's ill-advised census, an angel brought a plague that killed 70,000 (2 Samuel 24:15–17). Here God's angel rescued Jerusalem from the Assyrians, killing 185,000 (2 Kings 19:35). John's visions of the future (Rev. 15:1) suggest that similar judgments carried out by angels are still to come.

SCRIPTURE LINK (32:24) *Miraculous sign*

The shadow of the sun went backwards. See Isaiah 38:7–8.

Why did Hezekiah and his people become proud? (32:25–26)

Some think this pride stemmed from the growing power and success enjoyed by Hezekiah and his people. Such success could have occurred before his illness and the Assyrian invasion (see 2 Kings 20:6, which suggests a different sequence of events). If it came later, God's miraculous rescue probably raised Hezekiah's reputation (v. 23) and perhaps tempted him to think of himself as "God's special gift" to humanity.

On what are you basing your confidence, that you remain in Jerusalem[D] under siege? [11]When Hezekiah says, 'The LORD our God will save us from the hand of the king of Assyria,' he is misleading you, to let you die of hunger and thirst. [12]Did not Hezekiah himself remove this god's high places[D] and altars, saying to Judah and Jerusalem, 'You must worship before one altar and burn sacrifices[D] on it'?

[13]"Do you not know what I and my fathers have done to all the peoples of the other lands? Were the gods of those nations ever able to deliver their land from my hand? [14]Who of all the gods of these nations that my fathers destroyed has been able to save his people from me? How then can your god deliver you from my hand? [15]Now do not let Hezekiah deceive you and mislead you like this. Do not believe him, for no god of any nation or kingdom has been able to deliver his people from my hand or the hand of my fathers. How much less will your god deliver you from my hand!"

[16]Sennacherib's officers spoke further against the LORD God and against his servant Hezekiah. [17]The king also wrote letters insulting the LORD, the God of Israel, and saying this against him: "Just as the gods of the peoples of the other lands did not rescue their people from my hand, so the god of Hezekiah will not rescue his people from my hand." [18]Then they called out in Hebrew[D] to the people of Jerusalem who were on the wall, to terrify them and make them afraid in order to capture the city. [19]They spoke about the God of Jerusalem as they did about the gods of the other peoples of the world—the work of men's hands.

[20]King Hezekiah and the prophet[D] Isaiah son of Amoz cried out in prayer to heaven about this. [21]And the LORD sent an angel, who annihilated all the fighting men and the leaders and officers in the camp of the Assyrian king. So he withdrew to his own land in disgrace. And when he went into the temple of his god, some of his sons cut him down with the sword.

[22]So the LORD saved Hezekiah and the people of Jerusalem from the hand of Sennacherib king of Assyria and from the hand of all others. He took care of them[a] on every side. [23]Many brought offerings to Jerusalem for the LORD and valuable gifts for Hezekiah king of Judah. From then on he was highly regarded by all the nations.

Hezekiah's Pride, Success and Death

[24]In those days Hezekiah became ill and was at the point of death[D]. He prayed to the LORD, who answered him and gave him a miraculous sign. [25]But Hezekiah's heart was proud and he did not respond to the kindness shown him; therefore the LORD's wrath was on him and on Judah and Jerusalem. [26]Then Hezekiah repented of the pride of his heart, as did the people of Jerusalem; therefore the LORD's wrath did not come upon them during the days of Hezekiah.

[27]Hezekiah had very great riches and honor, and he made treasuries for his silver and gold and for his precious stones, spices, shields and all kinds of valuables. [28]He also made buildings to store the harvest of grain, new wine[D] and oil; and he made stalls for various kinds

a22 Hebrew; Septuagint and Vulgate *He gave them rest*

of cattle, and pens for the flocks. ²⁹He built villages and acquired great numbers of flocks and herds, for God had given him very great riches.

³⁰It was Hezekiah who blocked the upper outlet of the Gihon spring and channeled the water down to the west side of the City of David. He succeeded in everything he undertook. ³¹But when envoys were sent by the rulers of Babylon to ask him about the miraculous sign that had occurred in the land, God left him to test him and to know everything that was in his heart.

³²The other events of Hezekiah's reign and his acts of devotion are written in the vision^D of the prophet^D Isaiah son of Amoz in the book of the kings of Judah and Israel. ³³Hezekiah rested with his fathers and was buried on the hill where the tombs of David's descendants are. All Judah and the people of Jerusalem^D honored him when he died. And Manasseh his son succeeded him as king.

Manasseh King of Judah

33 Manasseh was twelve years old when he became king, and he reigned in Jerusalem fifty-five years. ²He did evil in the eyes of the LORD, following the detestable practices of the nations the LORD had driven out before the Israelites. ³He rebuilt the high places^D his father Hezekiah had demolished; he also erected altars to the Baals^D and made Asherah poles^D. He bowed down to all the starry hosts^D and worshiped them. ⁴He built altars in the temple of the LORD, of which the LORD had said, "My Name will remain in Jerusalem forever." ⁵In both courts of the temple of the LORD, he built altars to all the starry hosts. ⁶He sacrificed his sons in^a the fire in the Valley of Ben Hinnom, practiced sorcery^D, divination^D and witchcraft^D, and consulted mediums^D and spiritists. He did much evil in the eyes of the LORD, provoking him to anger.

⁷He took the carved image he had made and put it in God's temple, of which God had said to David and to his son Solomon, "In this temple and in Jerusalem, which I have chosen out of all the tribes of Israel, I will put my Name forever. ⁸I will not again make the feet of the Israelites leave the land I assigned to your forefathers, if only they will be careful to do everything I commanded them concerning all the laws, decrees and ordinances given through Moses." ⁹But Manasseh led Judah and the people of Jerusalem astray, so that they did more evil than the nations the LORD had destroyed before the Israelites.

¹⁰The LORD spoke to Manasseh and his people, but they paid no attention. ¹¹So the LORD brought against them the army commanders of the king of Assyria, who took Manasseh prisoner, put a hook in his nose, bound him with bronze shackles and took him to Babylon. ¹²In his distress he sought the favor of the LORD his God and humbled himself greatly before the God of his fathers. ¹³And when he prayed to him, the LORD was moved by his entreaty and listened to his plea; so he brought him back to Jerusalem and to his kingdom. Then Manasseh knew that the LORD is God.

¹⁴Afterward he rebuilt the outer wall of the City of David, west of the Gihon spring in the valley, as far as the entrance of the Fish Gate and encircling the hill of Ophel;

a6 Or He made his sons pass through

In what way did God leave Hezekiah? (32:31)

God often tested the righteous in the Old Testament to reveal their true loyalties. In this case, God left Hezekiah by not guiding him and by allowing him to make his own choices. When the Babylonians came looking for an ally to help them fight against Assyria, God did not stop Hezekiah from making a foolish decision. Nor did he protect him from the consequences of his decision. The Babylonian envoys carried back news of Israel's wealth. Later, Babylonian soldiers would take Israel's wealth as well as Israelite prisoners (2 Kings 20:14–18).

Does God have to test us to find out what's in our hearts? (32:31)

No, he doesn't. But tests of faith are not to enlighten God; they're to teach us. Tests help uncover our real motives, clarify our deep loyalties, eliminate deceit and nurture genuine faith. Also see article: *Why did testing come to Job?* (Job 23:10).

Why did God permit an evil king to rule so long? (33:1–2)

A long tenure is normally a sign of God's blessing. Still, Manasseh was punished for his sins, not rewarded. It was only after he had repented that he was later restored to the throne (vv. 12–13). If he had not turned to God, Manasseh would have remained a prisoner in Babylon and his reign as king would not have been so long.

Who taught Manasseh to serve pagan gods? (33:3–6)

Manasseh was probably influenced by several things: (1) the customs of his pagan neighbors; (2) a respect for powerful, idol-worshiping nations (such as Assyria); (3) the political advantages of showing loyalty to those successful nations (by worshiping their gods); (4) the pattern of his own nation's history—many of his own ancestors had earlier been involved with idolatry.

How did God speak to Manasseh and the people? (33:10)

God spoke through prophets, or seers (v. 18) and through the Law of Moses (v. 8). As far we know, Manasseh never personally heard God's voice or saw a vision.

How was Manasseh released from captivity and restored as king? (33:13)

We can only guess how God worked through the events. The Assyrians may have released Manasseh if he agreed to pay tribute and serve under Assyria's heavy thumb. Or they may have only intended Manasseh's captivity to be something like a "re-education camp" to teach him who was boss. When sufficiently "re-educated" he could then return to rule, but with greater respect for his overlords. As he learned to submit politically, Manasseh learned spiritual humility as well. Because he repented, God forgave him and returned him to the throne.

Why was it wrong to worship the Lord at the high places? (33:17)

Primarily because such worship confused the distinction between true and false worship. The high places were built by ancient Canaanites for pagan worship and ritual. Using the same places for true worship would only confuse the distinction between God and Baal.

Do we still have Manasseh's prayer? (33:18-19)

The only suggested possibility is found in the Apocrypha (meaning *things that are hidden* and referring to a collection of non-Biblical books) —a short book called The Prayer of Manasseh. Because it reads like a psalm and speaks of repentance and God's glory, some think it contains the words referred to here. Others remain doubtful about its authenticity.

Annals of the kings of Israel (33:18)

A history—a record book (see 2 Kings 1:18) —much like the annals of the kings of Judah (see 2 Kings 15:36). These records were accessible to the writer of 1 and 2 Kings, but are lost today.

Records of the seers (33:19)

One of several of the prophets' annals, this one perhaps was associated with an otherwise unknown prophet named Hozai (see NIV text note).

How could Josiah recognize the graves of idol worshipers? (34:4)

These were likely the new graves of wicked priests killed in the recent purge. It's also possible these may have been the older graves of false priests, perhaps those of priests known to have cooperated with Manasseh or Amon. Most likely, only those who served idols would have been permitted to be buried near the worship site. See *Why have a cemetery connected with a high place?* (2 Kings 23:17).

Did Josiah order priests to be killed? (34:5)

Yes (2 Kings 23:20), but this may also refer to bones taken from older graves (v. 4). Others— Jehu (2 Kings 10) and Jehoiada (2 Kings 11:18) —led similar purgings as part of their reforms. They were following the letter of the law (Deut. 13; 17:2-7).

Why did Josiah try to reform places outside of Judah? (34:6-7)

The time was ripe for Josiah to try to extend his influence into the northern kingdom of Israel. The international political scene had given him an opening: The Assyrian empire was crumbling and Nineveh was under siege. Mountain tribes were raiding Assyrian territory at will. Babylon had already won independence. If Israel and Judah could be reunited, this seemed a favorable time.

he also made it much higher. He stationed military commanders in all the fortified cities in Judah.

¹⁵He got rid of the foreign gods and removed the image from the temple of the LORD, as well as all the altars he had built on the temple hill and in Jerusalem^D; and he threw them out of the city. ¹⁶Then he restored the altar of the LORD and sacrificed fellowship offerings^Da and thank offerings^D on it, and told Judah to serve the LORD, the God of Israel. ¹⁷The people, however, continued to sacrifice^D at the high places^D, but only to the LORD their God.

¹⁸The other events of Manasseh's reign, including his prayer to his God and the words the seers^D spoke to him in the name of the LORD, the God of Israel, are written in the annals of the kings of Israel.^b ¹⁹His prayer and how God was moved by his entreaty, as well as all his sins and unfaithfulness, and the sites where he built high places and set up Asherah poles^D and idols^D before he humbled himself—all are written in the records of the seers.^c ²⁰Manasseh rested with his fathers and was buried in his palace. And Amon his son succeeded him as king.

Amon King of Judah

²¹Amon was twenty-two years old when he became king, and he reigned in Jerusalem two years. ²²He did evil in the eyes of the LORD, as his father Manasseh had done. Amon worshiped and offered sacrifices to all the idols Manasseh had made. ²³But unlike his father Manasseh, he did not humble himself before the LORD; Amon increased his guilt.

²⁴Amon's officials conspired against him and assassinated him in his palace. ²⁵Then the people of the land killed all who had plotted against King Amon, and they made Josiah his son king in his place.

Josiah's Reforms

34 Josiah was eight years old when he became king, and he reigned in Jerusalem thirty-one years. ²He did what was right in the eyes of the LORD and walked in the ways of his father David, not turning aside to the right or to the left.

³In the eighth year of his reign, while he was still young, he began to seek the God of his father David. In his twelfth year he began to purge Judah and Jerusalem of high places, Asherah poles, carved idols and cast images. ⁴Under his direction the altars of the Baals^D were torn down; he cut to pieces the incense^D altars that were above them, and smashed the Asherah poles, the idols and the images. These he broke to pieces and scattered over the graves of those who had sacrificed to them. ⁵He burned the bones of the priests^D on their altars, and so he purged Judah and Jerusalem. ⁶In the towns of Manasseh, Ephraim and Simeon, as far as Naphtali, and in the ruins around them, ⁷he tore down the altars and the Asherah poles and crushed the idols to powder and cut to pieces all the incense altars throughout Israel. Then he went back to Jerusalem.

⁸In the eighteenth year of Josiah's reign, to purify^D the land and the temple, he sent Shaphan son of Azaliah and

---

^a 16 Traditionally *peace offerings*   ^b 18 That is, Judah, as frequently in 2 Chronicles   ^c 19 One Hebrew manuscript and Septuagint; most Hebrew manuscripts *of Hozai*

Maaseiah the ruler of the city, with Joah son of Joahaz, the recorder, to repair the temple of the LORD his God.

9They went to Hilkiah the high priest^D and gave him the money that had been brought into the temple of God, which the Levites^D who were the doorkeepers had collected from the people of Manasseh, Ephraim and the entire remnant^D of Israel and from all the people of Judah and Benjamin and the inhabitants of Jerusalem^D. **10**Then they entrusted it to the men appointed to supervise the work on the LORD's temple. These men paid the workers who repaired and restored the temple. **11**They also gave money to the carpenters and builders to purchase dressed stone, and timber for joists and beams for the buildings that the kings of Judah had allowed to fall into ruin.

12The men did the work faithfully. Over them to direct them were Jahath and Obadiah, Levites descended from Merari, and Zechariah and Meshullam, descended from Kohath. The Levites—all who were skilled in playing musical instruments— **13**had charge of the laborers and supervised all the workers from job to job. Some of the Levites were secretaries, scribes and doorkeepers.

The Book of the Law Found

14While they were bringing out the money that had been taken into the temple of the LORD, Hilkiah the priest found the Book of the Law of the LORD that had been given through Moses. **15**Hilkiah said to Shaphan the secretary, "I have found the Book of the Law in the temple of the LORD." He gave it to Shaphan.

16Then Shaphan took the book to the king and reported to him: "Your officials are doing everything that has been committed to them. **17**They have paid out the money that was in the temple of the LORD and have entrusted it to the supervisors and workers." **18**Then Shaphan the secretary informed the king, "Hilkiah the priest has given me a book." And Shaphan read from it in the presence of the king.

19When the king heard the words of the Law, he tore his robes. **20**He gave these orders to Hilkiah, Ahikam son of Shaphan, Abdon son of Micah,*a* Shaphan the secretary and Asaiah the king's attendant: **21**"Go and inquire of the LORD for me and for the remnant in Israel and Judah about what is written in this book that has been found. Great is the LORD's anger that is poured out on us because our fathers have not kept the word of the LORD; they have not acted in accordance with all that is written in this book."

22Hilkiah and those the king had sent with him*b* went to speak to the prophetess^D Huldah, who was the wife of Shallum son of Tokhath,*c* the son of Hasrah,*d* keeper of the wardrobe. She lived in Jerusalem, in the Second District.

23She said to them, "This is what the LORD, the God of Israel, says: Tell the man who sent you to me, **24**'This is what the LORD says: I am going to bring disaster on this place and its people—all the curses written in the book that has been read in the presence of the king of Judah. **25**Because they have forsaken me and burned incense^D to other gods and provoked me to anger by all that their

---

Why use musicians to oversee a construction project? (34:12–13)
The Levites appear to have supervised and managed the workers, but they may also have provided music to work by.

Why did Josiah rip his robes? (34:19)
This was a cultural expression of grief and mourning. See *Where did the custom of ashes and torn clothing come from?* (2 Samuel 13:19).

Why was Huldah known as a prophetess? (34:22)
Nothing is known about her except the information here. She is the only prophetess mentioned in Kings or Chronicles. As respected as she was, she was obviously effective and influential. Her prophecy of a peaceful death for Josiah (v. 28) may seem to have failed when he died in battle (35:22–24), but some think the prophecy required Josiah's obedience. It was canceled when Josiah failed to listen to God (35:22).

---

a20 Also called *Acbor son of Micaiah*   *b22* One Hebrew manuscript, Vulgate and Syriac; most Hebrew manuscripts do not have *had sent with him.*   *c22* Also called *Tikvah*   *d22* Also called *Harhas*

What good was a temporary reprieve? (34:27–28)

Any reprieve from God's judgment, even of the inevitable, is better than immediate misery. The writer of Chronicles frequently stresses God's immediate punishment for wrongdoing, so a reprieve was a sign of mercy and hope. Through faithful obedience, a reprieve may have even been extended. In Judah's case, further disobedience brought punishment about 25 years after Josiah died.

What was the king's pillar? (34:31)

Possibly one of the bronze pillars Solomon placed at the entrance to the temple (1 Kings 7:15). This appears to be the place where the king commonly issued important public statements.

How could worship be legislated? (34:33)

See *How could worship be legislated?* (29:30).

Why was the ark out of the temple in the first place? (35:3)

It probably had been removed or hidden for safe-keeping during the pagan reigns of Manasseh or Amon. On the other hand, Josiah may have planned a re-installation so that his reforms would parallel Solomon's dedication celebration.

hands have made,ᵃ my anger will be poured out on this place and will not be quenched.' ²⁶Tell the king of Judah, who sent you to inquire of the LORD, 'This is what the LORD, the God of Israel, says concerning the words you heard: ²⁷Because your heart was responsive and you humbled yourself before God when you heard what he spoke against this place and its people, and because you humbled yourself before me and tore your robes and wept in my presence, I have heard you, declares the LORD. ²⁸Now I will gather you to your fathers, and you will be buried in peaceᴰ. Your eyes will not see all the disaster I am going to bring on this place and on those who live here.'"

So they took her answer back to the king.

²⁹Then the king called together all the elders of Judah and Jerusalemᴰ. ³⁰He went up to the temple of the LORD with the men of Judah, the people of Jerusalem, the priestsᴰ and the Levitesᴰ—all the people from the least to the greatest. He read in their hearing all the words of the Book of the Covenantᴰ, which had been found in the temple of the LORD. ³¹The king stood by his pillar and renewed the covenant in the presence of the LORD—to follow the LORD and keep his commands, regulations and decrees with all his heart and all his soulᴰ, and to obey the words of the covenant written in this book.

³²Then he had everyone in Jerusalem and Benjamin pledge themselves to it; the people of Jerusalem did this in accordance with the covenant of God, the God of their fathers.

³³Josiah removed all the detestable idolsᴰ from all the territory belonging to the Israelites, and he had all who were present in Israel serve the LORD their God. As long as he lived, they did not fail to follow the LORD, the God of their fathers.

Josiah Celebrates the Passover

35 Josiah celebrated the Passover to the LORD in Jerusalem, and the Passover lamb was slaughtered on the fourteenth day of the first month. ²He appointed the priests to their duties and encouraged them in the service of the LORD's temple. ³He said to the Levites, who instructed all Israel and who had been consecratedᴰ to the LORD: "Put the sacredᴰ ark in the temple that Solomon son of David king of Israel built. It is not to be carried about on your shoulders. Now serve the LORD your God and his people Israel. ⁴Prepare yourselves by families in your divisions, according to the directions written by David king of Israel and by his son Solomon.

⁵"Stand in the holy place with a group of Levites for each subdivision of the families of your fellow countrymen, the lay people. ⁶Slaughter the Passover lambs, consecrate yourselves and prepare ⌊the lambs⌋ for your fellow countrymen, doing what the LORD commanded through Moses."

⁷Josiah provided for all the lay people who were there a total of thirty thousand sheep and goats for the Passover offerings, and also three thousand cattle—all from the king's own possessions.

⁸His officials also contributed voluntarily to the people and the priests and Levites. Hilkiah, Zechariah and Jehiel, the administrators of God's temple, gave the priests twenty-six hundred Passover offerings and three

ᵃ25 Or *by everything they have done*

hundred cattle. **9**Also Conaniah along with Shemaiah and Nethanel, his brothers, and Hashabiah, Jeiel and Jozabad, the leaders of the Levites[D], provided five thousand Passover offerings and five hundred head of cattle for the Levites.

10The service was arranged and the priests[D] stood in their places with the Levites in their divisions as the king had ordered. **11**The Passover lambs were slaughtered, and the priests sprinkled the blood handed to them, while the Levites skinned the animals. **12**They set aside the burnt offerings[D] to give them to the subdivisions of the families of the people to offer to the LORD, as is written in the Book of Moses. They did the same with the cattle. **13**They roasted the Passover animals over the fire as prescribed, and boiled the holy offerings in pots, caldrons and pans and served them quickly to all the people. **14**After this, they made preparations for themselves and for the priests, because the priests, the descendants of Aaron, were sacrificing the burnt offerings and the fat portions until nightfall. So the Levites made preparations for themselves and for the Aaronic priests.

15The musicians, the descendants of Asaph, were in the places prescribed by David, Asaph, Heman and Jeduthun the king's seer[D]. The gatekeepers at each gate did not need to leave their posts, because their fellow Levites made the preparations for them.

16So at that time the entire service of the LORD was carried out for the celebration of the Passover and the offering of burnt offerings on the altar of the LORD, as King Josiah had ordered. **17**The Israelites who were present celebrated the Passover at that time and observed the Feast of Unleavened Bread for seven days. **18**The Passover had not been observed like this in Israel since the days of the prophet[D] Samuel; and none of the kings of Israel had ever celebrated such a Passover as did Josiah, with the priests, the Levites and all Judah and Israel who were there with the people of Jerusalem[D]. **19**This Passover was celebrated in the eighteenth year of Josiah's reign.

The Death of Josiah

20After all this, when Josiah had set the temple in order, Neco king of Egypt went up to fight at Carchemish on the Euphrates, and Josiah marched out to meet him in battle. **21**But Neco sent messengers to him, saying, "What quarrel is there between you and me, O king of Judah? It is not you I am attacking at this time, but the house with which I am at war. God has told me to hurry; so stop opposing God, who is with me, or he will destroy you."

22Josiah, however, would not turn away from him, but disguised himself to engage him in battle. He would not listen to what Neco had said at God's command but went to fight him on the plain of Megiddo.

23Archers shot King Josiah, and he told his officers, "Take me away; I am badly wounded." **24**So they took him out of his chariot, put him in the other chariot he had and brought him to Jerusalem, where he died. He was buried in the tombs of his fathers, and all Judah and Jerusalem mourned for him.

25Jeremiah composed laments[D] for Josiah, and to this day all the men and women singers commemorate Josiah in the laments. These became a tradition in Israel and are written in the Laments.

26The other events of Josiah's reign and his acts of devotion, according to what is written in the Law of the

How did the king of Egypt know what God wanted him to do? (35:21-22)
We don't know. The sovereign God in his grace can break through and communicate with whomever he wishes. Some suggest Neco was speaking about God in a generic sense without claiming special revelation from the Lord in particular. On the other hand, Josiah was faulted for failing to recognize this as the Lord's instruction.

This day (35:25)
The Chronicles were written during the latter half of the fifth century B.C., more than 150 years after Josiah's death. See Introduction: *When was it written?*

LORD— **27**all the events, from beginning to end, are written in the book of the kings of Israel and Judah.

36

1And the people of the land took Jehoahaz son of Josiah and made him king in JerusalemᴰD in place of his father.

Jehoahaz King of Judah

2Jehoahaz*ᵃ* was twenty-three years old when he became king, and he reigned in Jerusalem three months. **3**The king of Egypt dethroned him in Jerusalem and imposed on Judah a levy of a hundred talents*ᵇ* of silver and a talent*ᶜ* of gold. **4**The king of Egypt made Eliakim, a brother of Jehoahaz, king over Judah and Jerusalem and changed Eliakim's name to Jehoiakim. But Neco took Eliakim's brother Jehoahaz and carried him off to Egypt.

Jehoiakim King of Judah

5Jehoiakim was twenty-five years old when he became king, and he reigned in Jerusalem eleven years. He did evil in the eyes of the LORD his God. **6**Nebuchadnezzar king of Babylon attacked him and bound him with bronze shackles to take him to Babylon. **7**Nebuchadnezzar also took to Babylon articles from the temple of the LORD and put them in his temple*ᵈ* there.

8The other events of Jehoiakim's reign, the detestable things he did and all that was found against him, are written in the book of the kings of Israel and Judah. And Jehoiachin his son succeeded him as king.

Jehoiachin King of Judah

9Jehoiachin was eighteen*ᵉ* years old when he became king, and he reigned in Jerusalem three months and ten days. He did evil in the eyes of the LORD. **10**In the spring, King Nebuchadnezzar sent for him and brought him to Babylon, together with articles of value from the temple of the LORD, and he made Jehoiachin's uncle,*ᶠ* Zedekiah, king over Judah and Jerusalem.

Zedekiah King of Judah

11Zedekiah was twenty-one years old when he became king, and he reigned in Jerusalem eleven years. **12**He did evil in the eyes of the LORD his God and did not humble himself before Jeremiah the prophetᴰ, who spoke the word of the LORD. **13**He also rebelled against King Nebuchadnezzar, who had made him take an oath in God's name. He became stiff-necked and hardened his heart and would not turn to the LORD, the God of Israel. **14**Furthermore, all the leaders of the priestsᴰ and the people became more and more unfaithful, following all the detestable practices of the nations and defiling the temple of the LORD, which he had consecratedᴰ in Jerusalem.

The Fall of Jerusalem

15The LORD, the God of their fathers, sent word to them through his messengers again and again, because he had pity on his people and on his dwelling place. **16**But they mocked God's messengers, despised his words and

---

Why did the king of Egypt change Eliakim's name? (36:4)

Name changes like this signaled a monarch's authority over a puppet-ruler. Three of the last four kings of Judah were known by at least two names. Both Jehoiakim and Zedekiah were names given to them by the rulers who installed them.

Why didn't the Egyptians defend the king they'd installed in Jerusalem? (36:4,6)

Because things had changed. Neco had been defeated at the Battle of Carchemish in 605 B.C. (see *Map 7* at the back of this Bible). That prompted Jehoiakim to transfer his allegiance to Nebuchadnezzar, king of Babylon. Judah lived in peace for three years, but then Jehoiakim rebelled against Babylon. When Nebuchadnezzar's army came to put down the rebellion, Egypt was either too smart or too weak to become involved. The Babylonians removed Jehoiakim from the throne and perhaps took him as a prisoner to Babylon.

Stiff-necked (36:13)
See *Stiff-necked* (2 Kings 17:14).

ᵃ2 Hebrew *Joahaz*, a variant of *Jehoahaz*; also in verse 4   *ᵇ3* That is, about 3 3/4 tons (about 3.4 metric tons)   *ᶜ3* That is, about 75 pounds (about 34 kilograms)   *ᵈ7* Or *palace*   *ᵉ9* One Hebrew manuscript, some Septuagint manuscripts and Syriac (see also 2 Kings 24:8); most Hebrew manuscripts *eight*   *ᶠ10* Hebrew *brother*, that is, relative (see 2 Kings 24:17)

scoffed at his prophets[D] until the wrath of the LORD was aroused against his people and there was no remedy. [17]He brought up against them the king of the Babylonians,[a] who killed their young men with the sword in the sanctuary, and spared neither young man nor young woman, old man or aged. God handed all of them over to Nebuchadnezzar. [18]He carried to Babylon all the articles from the temple of God, both large and small, and the treasures of the LORD's temple and the treasures of the king and his officials. [19]They set fire to God's temple and broke down the wall of Jerusalem[D]; they burned all the palaces and destroyed everything of value there.

[20]He carried into exile[D] to Babylon the remnant[D], who escaped from the sword, and they became servants to him and his sons until the kingdom of Persia came to power. [21]The land enjoyed its sabbath[D] rests; all the time of its desolation it rested, until the seventy years were completed in fulfillment of the word of the LORD spoken by Jeremiah.

[22]In the first year of Cyrus[D] king of Persia, in order to fulfill the word of the LORD spoken by Jeremiah, the LORD moved the heart of Cyrus king of Persia to make a proclamation throughout his realm and to put it in writing:

[23]"This is what Cyrus king of Persia says:

" 'The LORD, the God of heaven, has given me all the kingdoms of the earth and he has appointed me to build a temple for him at Jerusalem in Judah. Anyone of his people among you—may the LORD his God be with him, and let him go up.' "

Sabbath rests (36:21)

The people were supposed to honor God by allowing their land to lie fallow every seventh year. This period of not growing crops was considered a *sabbath of rest* (Lev. 25:4). But because they failed to do this through the centuries, God judged them and took all the *sabbath rests* at one time. The land would lie dormant during the Babylonian captivity (Lev. 26:34–35,43).

SCRIPTURE LINK (36:21) *Word . . . spoken by Jeremiah*

See his prophecy about the length of their captivity in Jer. 29:10.

Why would a pagan king want to build a temple for the Lord? (36:23)

See article: *Why build a temple for a God you don't worship?* (Ezra 1:1–2).

EZRA

Why read this book?

Have you ever dreamed of being a hero? Most of us are ordinary people hoping some-how to make our lives count. This book offers encouragement for ordinary people look-ing for their niche in God's world. It focuses on the team effort rather than the heroics of a few. Ezra, a humble, low-profile leader, was simply a part of the community at large. The main characters here are the people—everyone from priests to servants—who work together.

Who wrote this book?

Some think Ezra wrote it along with the book of Nehemiah. Others believe it was com-piled anonymously by someone who may have drawn from material written previously. In that case this book could have been part of several other books, including 1 and 2 Chronicles and Nehemiah.

What historical events surrounded it?

Good news! After years of living in exile because of the Babylonians, the Israelites saw Cyrus the Persian (539 B.C.) conquer Babylon. He allowed the Jewish exiles to return to Jerusalem to rebuild the temple.

When was it written?

Ezra and Nehemiah were linked together as a single book in the original Hebrew Bible. The events in Nehemiah were completed sometime after 440 B.C.

What to look for in Ezra:

Ezra reveals God as the power behind earthly events, moving even pagan kings accord-ing to his purposes (1:1; 6:22; 7:6,27). Ezra also contrasts purity with compromise. The lure of secular values is seen in the way the local religions seduced the returned exiles. The drastic measures required to purge the exiles of impurity remind us of God's holi-ness: *O LORD, God of Israel, you are righteous!* (9:15).

When did these things happen?

TIME LINE	1400BC	1300	1200	1100	1000	900	800	700	600	500	400
Fall of Jerusalem (586 B.C.)											
Persia's conquest of Babylon (539 B.C.)											
First return of exiles to Jerusalem (538 B.C.)											
Ministries of Haggai and Zechariah (c.520-480 B.C.)											
Completion of temple (516 B.C.)											
Second return to Jerusalem under Ezra (458 B.C.)											
Third return to Jerusalem under Nehemiah (445 B.C.)											
Book of Ezra written (c.440 B.C.)											

Cyrus Helps the Exiles to Return

1 In the first year of Cyrus[D] king of Persia, in order to fulfill the word of the LORD spoken by Jeremiah, the LORD moved the heart of Cyrus king of Persia to make a proclamation throughout his realm and to put it in writing:

2"This is what Cyrus king of Persia says:

" 'The LORD, the God of heaven, has given me all the kingdoms of the earth and he has appointed me to build a temple for him at Jerusalem[D] in Judah. **3**Anyone of his people among you—may his God be with him, and let him go up to Jerusalem in Judah and build the temple of the LORD, the God of Israel, the God who is in Jerusalem. **4**And the people of any place where survivors may now be living are to provide him with silver and gold, with goods and livestock, and with freewill offerings for the temple of God in Jerusalem.' "

5Then the family heads of Judah and Benjamin, and the priests[D] and Levites[D]—everyone whose heart God had moved—prepared to go up and build the house of the LORD in Jerusalem. **6**All their neighbors assisted them with articles of silver and gold, with goods and livestock, and with valuable gifts, in addition to all the freewill offerings. **7**Moreover, King Cyrus brought out the articles belonging to the temple of the LORD, which Nebuchadnezzar had carried away from Jerusalem and had placed in the temple of his god.[a] **8**Cyrus king of Persia had them brought by Mithredath the treasurer, who counted them out to Sheshbazzar the prince of Judah.

9This was the inventory:

gold dishes	30
silver dishes	1,000

[a]7 Or *gods*

What prophecy did Cyrus fulfill? (1:1)

Certainly he fulfilled the prophecy about Babylon's fall and the end of the exile (Jer. 25:12; 29:10). But the phrase *moved the heart* suggests even more specific prophecies. Jeremiah used the same word (translated *stirred up*) to speak of the Medes conquering Babylon, bringing vengeance for their destruction of God's temple (Jer. 51:11). Isaiah prophesied the Lord would *stir up* a conqueror (Isaiah 41:2,25) and specifically named *Cyrus* as the one who would rebuild the temple (Isaiah 44:28; 45:1,13).

Return from Exile (1:3)

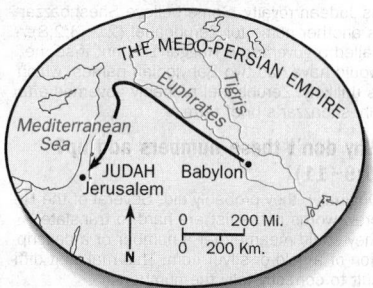

Why did neighbors help with the moving expenses? (1:4–6)

Most of these generous neighbors were probably Jews who had chosen to remain in Babylon, but wanted to contribute to the rebuilding of the temple. Others in Persia may have contributed as well, perhaps to imitate their ruler, who supported the restoration of many temples throughout his empire.

Why build a temple for a God you don't worship? (1:1–2)

U nlike the Assyrian and Babylonian rulers who took the Israelites captive and destroyed the temple, King Cyrus of Persia allowed the Israelites to return home and even encouraged them to rebuild their temple.

Cyrus's motive for honoring the God of Israel in this way was undoubtedly both political and religious. Not only would Cyrus's policy of tolerance earn him the favor of the Israelites and all other people subject to him, it could very well endear him to many different gods worshiped by these subjects.

Although a worshiper of the Babylonian god Marduk, Cyrus may have hoped to carry the favor of as many gods as possible. One inscription attributed to Cyrus reads, "May all the gods whom I have resettled in their sacred cities ask daily Bel and Nebo for a long life for me and may they recommend me to Marduk, my Lord . . . "

As recorded in Ezra, the Persian rulers Darius and Artaxerxes later exhibited a similar tolerance in an attempt to please all the gods they could. Darius asked the priests in Jerusalem to pray for him and his sons (6:10). Artaxerxes asked Ezra to be sure God was worshiped properly because he wanted to avoid God's wrath (7:23).

Ironically, God used such religious pluralism to get his people back to Jerusalem so they would worship him alone.

Why didn't all Jews want to return? (1:5)

The majority of living Jews had never seen their native land. More than 60 years had passed since Nebuchadnezzar had wrenched their parents and grandparents from their homes, planting them in Babylonia. For two or three generations they had settled into the Babylonian way of life. Most felt no urge to leave familiar surroundings, travel a thousand miles, and rebuild from scratch in a war-ravaged land.

Sheshbazzar the prince of Judah (1:8)

Probably the first Persian-appointed governor of Judah. Sheshbazzar is not listed elsewhere as Judean royalty. Some believe Sheshbazzar is another name for Zerubbabel (2:2; 3:2,8), called a *governor* in Haggai 1:1, but if so, he would have had two Babylonian names, which is unlikely. Zerubbabel probably governed *after* Sheshbazzar's brief term.

Why don't these numbers add up? (1:9–11)

Originally, they probably did. Several of the Hebrew words in the list are hard to translate: they could mean either a number or a description of a gold or silver item. This makes it difficult to correctly tally the numbers.

How did Jews born in Babylon go to their own towns? (2:1)

They returned to the towns of their ancestors. Land was considered the permanent possession of a family. Jews remaining in Judah would recognize such family rights.

Nehemiah . . . Mordecai (2:2)

These are probably not the same men we see later in the books of Nehemiah and Esther. The book of Nehemiah begins its account 90 years after v. 2. If these two Mordecais are the same, Esther's guardian would have first journeyed to Jerusalem and later returned to Persia—not too likely since Esther's story begins over 50 years after v. 2.

Why list all these names? (2:2-61)

These names represented people—thousands of them—going back to where they belonged. The detailed list of the names and towns of the returning families shows that God didn't limit his focus to a few leaders. Every individual was important.

silver pans[a]	29
[10]gold bowls	30
matching silver bowls	410
other articles	1,000

[11]In all, there were 5,400 articles of gold and of silver. Sheshbazzar brought all these along when the exiles[D] came up from Babylon to Jerusalem[D].

The List of the Exiles Who Returned

2 Now these are the people of the province who came up from the captivity of the exiles, whom Nebuchadnezzar king of Babylon had taken captive to Babylon (they returned to Jerusalem and Judah, each to his own town, [2]in company with Zerubbabel, Jeshua, Nehemiah, Seraiah, Reelaiah, Mordecai, Bilshan, Mispar, Bigvai, Rehum and Baanah):

The list of the men of the people of Israel:

[3]the descendants of Parosh	2,172
[4]of Shephatiah	372
[5]of Arah	775
[6]of Pahath-Moab (through the line of Jeshua and Joab)	2,812
[7]of Elam	1,254
[8]of Zattu	945
[9]of Zaccai	760
[10]of Bani	642
[11]of Bebai	623
[12]of Azgad	1,222
[13]of Adonikam	666
[14]of Bigvai	2,056
[15]of Adin	454
[16]of Ater (through Hezekiah)	98
[17]of Bezai	323
[18]of Jorah	112
[19]of Hashum	223
[20]of Gibbar	95
[21]the men of Bethlehem	123
[22]of Netophah	56
[23]of Anathoth	128
[24]of Azmaveth	42
[25]of Kiriath Jearim,[b] Kephirah and Beeroth	743
[26]of Ramah and Geba	621
[27]of Micmash	122
[28]of Bethel and Ai	223
[29]of Nebo	52
[30]of Magbish	156
[31]of the other Elam	1,254
[32]of Harim	320
[33]of Lod, Hadid and Ono	725
[34]of Jericho[D]	345
[35]of Senaah	3,630
[36]The priests[D]:	
the descendants of Jedaiah (through the family of Jeshua)	973
[37]of Immer	1,052
[38]of Pashhur	1,247
[39]of Harim	1,017

[a]9 The meaning of the Hebrew for this word is uncertain.
[b]25 See Septuagint (see also Neh. 7:29); Hebrew *Kiriath Arim*.

40The Levites[D]:

the descendants of Jeshua and Kadmiel
    (through the line of Hodaviah)   74

41The singers:

the descendants of Asaph   128

42The gatekeepers of the temple:

the descendants of
    Shallum, Ater, Talmon,
    Akkub, Hatita and Shobai   139

43The temple servants:

the descendants of
    Ziha, Hasupha, Tabbaoth,
44Keros, Siaha, Padon,
45Lebanah, Hagabah, Akkub,
46Hagab, Shalmai, Hanan,
47Giddel, Gahar, Reaiah,
48Rezin, Nekoda, Gazzam,
49Uzza, Paseah, Besai,
50Asnah, Meunim, Nephussim,
51Bakbuk, Hakupha, Harhur,
52Bazluth, Mehida, Harsha,
53Barkos, Sisera, Temah,
54Neziah and Hatipha

55The descendants of the servants of Solomon:

the descendants of
    Sotai, Hassophereth, Peruda,
56Jaala, Darkon, Giddel,
57Shephatiah, Hattil,
    Pokereth-Hazzebaim and Ami

58The temple servants and the descendants of
    the servants of Solomon   392

59The following came up from the towns of Tel Me-
lah, Tel Harsha, Kerub, Addon and Immer, but they
could not show that their families were descended
from Israel:

60The descendants of
    Delaiah, Tobiah and Nekoda   652

61And from among the priests[D]:

The descendants of
    Hobaiah, Hakkoz and Barzillai (a man who had
    married a daughter of Barzillai the Gileadite
    and was called by that name).
62These searched for their family records, but they
could not find them and so were excluded from the
priesthood as unclean[D]. **63**The governor ordered
them not to eat any of the most sacred[D] food until
there was a priest ministering with the Urim and
Thummim[D].

64The whole company numbered 42,360, **65**besides their 7,337 menservants and maidservants; and
they also had 200 men and women singers. **66**They
had 736 horses, 245 mules, **67**435 camels and 6,720
donkeys.

68When they arrived at the house of the LORD in Jerusalem[D], some of the heads of the families gave freewill offerings toward the rebuilding of the house of God on its

Descendants of the servants of Solomon (2:55,58)
These people were probably descendants of slaves who served Solomon, perhaps drawn from the native Canaanites (1 Kings 9:20–21,27). It's unclear why they were named for their master rather than the head of their family.

Why was ancestry so important? (2:59)
Such records were essential in matters of property inheritance, but they were also important spiritually. Jews who could demonstrate their family purity after two or three generations in a foreign land showed that they had not mingled with pagans and (by implication) pagan gods.

Why couldn't those without family records serve as priests? (2:62)
The strict requirements for the priesthood symbolized the purity and holiness needed to come into God's presence. Any priest who attempted to minister while "unclean" risked death (Lev. 8–10). Without family records, it was impossible to prove that anyone was of priestly lineage. One of the families mentioned—that of Hakkoz—was later included among the priests (8:33; Neh. 3:4,21), presumably after finding the proper records.

Urim and Thummim (2:63)
Divinely approved devices with which a priest could discern God's will (Exodus 28:30). They were possibly sacred lots or stones cast like dice to determine an answer from God (Lev. 8:8). Some speculate that *Urim* means *light* and suggest that a sparkle or glow from one or both of the stones would signal the answer. Others think *Urim* means *curses*—giving a "no" answer—and *Thummim* means *perfections* giving a "yes."

If 42,360 returned, how many stayed in Babylon? (2:64)
Biblical tallies of Judeans exiled to Babylon (2 Kings 24:14–16; Jer. 52:28–30) total about 15,000. However, the numbers may represent only men of a certain standing, or perhaps heads of families. Most agree that the 42,360 who returned to Jerusalem were a minority. Many more chose to stay in Babylon.

site. **69**According to their ability they gave to the treasury for this work 61,000 drachmas*a* of gold, 5,000 minas*b* of silver and 100 priestly garments.

70The priests**D**, the Levites**D**, the singers, the gatekeepers and the temple servants settled in their own towns, along with some of the other people, and the rest of the Israelites settled in their towns.

Rebuilding the Altar

3 When the seventh month came and the Israelites had settled in their towns, the people assembled as one man in Jerusalem**D**. **2**Then Jeshua son of Jozadak and his fellow priests and Zerubbabel son of Shealtiel and his associates began to build the altar of the God of Israel to sacrifice**D** burnt offerings**D** on it, in accordance with what is written in the Law of Moses the man of God. **3**Despite their fear of the peoples around them, they built the altar on its foundation and sacrificed burnt offerings on it to the LORD, both the morning and evening sacrifices. **4**Then in accordance with what is written, they celebrated the Feast of Tabernacles with the required number of burnt offerings prescribed for each day. **5**After that, they presented the regular burnt offerings, the New Moon sacrifices and the sacrifices for all the appointed sacred**D** feasts of the LORD, as well as those brought as freewill offerings to the LORD. **6**On the first day of the seventh month they began to offer burnt offerings to the LORD, though the foundation of the LORD's temple had not yet been laid.

Rebuilding the Temple

7Then they gave money to the masons and carpenters, and gave food and drink and oil to the people of Sidon and Tyre, so that they would bring cedar logs by sea from Lebanon to Joppa**D**, as authorized by Cyrus**D** king of Persia.

8In the second month of the second year after their arrival at the house of God in Jerusalem, Zerubbabel son of Shealtiel, Jeshua son of Jozadak and the rest of their brothers (the priests and the Levites and all who had returned from the captivity to Jerusalem) began the work, appointing Levites twenty years of age and older to supervise the building of the house of the LORD. **9**Jeshua and his sons and brothers and Kadmiel and his sons (descendants of Hodaviah*c*) and the sons of Henadad and their sons and brothers—all Levites—joined together in supervising those working on the house of God.

10When the builders laid the foundation of the temple of the LORD, the priests in their vestments and with trumpets, and the Levites (the sons of Asaph) with cymbals, took their places to praise the LORD, as prescribed by David king of Israel. **11**With praise and thanksgiving they sang to the LORD:

"He is good;
his love to Israel endures forever."

And all the people gave a great shout of praise to the LORD, because the foundation of the house of the LORD was laid. **12**But many of the older priests and Levites and family heads, who had seen the former temple, wept aloud when

Since they had the king's endorsement, why were the builders afraid? (3:3)
By building an altar and sacrificing on it, the returning exiles signaled that they had come to stay. The surrounding peoples had likely claimed the land for themselves (Ezek. 25) and would fight to prevent the new arrivals from reclaiming it. Although the Jews had the king's backing, he was a thousand miles away.

Why did the older Israelites weep? (3:12)
They apparently realized the rebuilt temple would not match the splendor of the temple they had once known. Even though it was twice as high as Solomon's temple, it was inferior in all other respects.

*a*69 That is, about 1,100 pounds (about 500 kilograms)   *b*69 That is, about 3 tons (about 2.9 metric tons)   *c*9 Hebrew *Yehudah*, probably a variant of *Hodaviah*

they saw the foundation of this temple being laid, while many others shouted for joy. ¹³No one could distinguish the sound of the shouts of joy from the sound of weeping, because the people made so much noise. And the sound was heard far away.

Opposition to the Rebuilding

4 When the enemies of Judah and Benjamin heard that the exilesᴰ were building a temple for the LORD, the God of Israel, ²they came to Zerubbabel and to the heads of the families and said, "Let us help you build because, like you, we seek your God and have been sacrificing to him since the time of Esarhaddon king of Assyria, who brought us here."

³But Zerubbabel, Jeshua and the rest of the heads of the families of Israel answered, "You have no part with us in building a temple to our God. We alone will build it for the LORD, the God of Israel, as King Cyrusᴰ, the king of Persia, commanded us."

⁴Then the peoples around them set out to discourage the people of Judah and make them afraid to go on building.ᵃ ⁵They hired counselors to work against them and frustrate their plans during the entire reign of Cyrus king of Persia and down to the reign of Darius king of Persia.

Later Opposition Under Xerxes and Artaxerxes

⁶At the beginning of the reign of Xerxes,ᵇ they lodged an accusation against the people of Judah and Jerusalemᴰ.

⁷And in the days of Artaxerxes king of Persia, Bishlam, Mithredath, Tabeel and the rest of his associates wrote a letter to Artaxerxes. The letter was written in Aramaicᴰ script and in the Aramaic language.ᶜ,ᵈ

⁸Rehum the commanding officer and Shimshai the secretary wrote a letter against Jerusalem to Artaxerxes the king as follows:

⁹Rehum the commanding officer and Shimshai the secretary, together with the rest of their associates— the judges and officials over the men from Tripolis, Persia,ᵉ Erech and Babylon, the Elamites of Susa, ¹⁰and the other people whom the great and honorable Ashurbanipalᶠ deported and settled in the city of Samaria and elsewhere in Trans-Euphrates.

¹¹(This is a copy of the letter they sent him.)

To King Artaxerxes,

From your servants, the men of Trans-Euphrates:

¹²The king should know that the Jewsᴰ who came up to us from you have gone to Jerusalem and are rebuilding that rebellious and wicked city. They are restoring the walls and repairing the foundations.

¹³Furthermore, the king should know that if this city is built and its walls are restored, no more taxes, tribute or duty will be paid, and the royal revenues will suffer. ¹⁴Now since we are under obligation to the palace and it is not proper for us to see the king

Why would their enemies want to help build the temple? (4:1–2)

These *enemies* were probably Gentiles, descendants of captives brought into the territory by the Assyrians. They had intermarried with the local peoples (possibly even Jews) and mingled religions (2 Kings 17:24–41). Their offer to help was probably politically motivated. Either they wanted to gain influence among the newcomers or sabotage their plans.

Why wouldn't the Jews accept their help? (4:3)

They had both political and religious reasons for refusing. They alone were authorized by Cyrus to rebuild—and it was good policy to follow the king's commands precisely. In addition, they realized that accepting help would represent spiritual compromise, since these neighboring peoples had tainted their worship of God by mixing it with idol worship.

Who were these *counselors*, and what did they do? (4:5)

They were probably advisers to the Persian king. These particular officials seem to have been corrupt, accepting bribes and speaking against the cause of the returning exiles whenever they could.

What were these accusations all about? (4:6–23)

The accusations mentioned in v. 6 came perhaps ten years after the events in vv. 1–5, and the protest in v. 7 came about 60 years later. The writer is not as concerned with chronology as he is with explaining the work stoppage. After telling us how Judeans rejected their neighbors' help (4:3), the writer takes a detour to show that such action was justified because of the neighbors' recurring sabotage of their plans.

Trans-Euphrates (4:10)

This was the largest of the 20 Persian provinces. The name translated literally means *beyond the river*. The province encompassed the massive area west of the Euphrates River all the way to the Mediterranean Sea, including the entire area that had once been Israel and Judah (see *Map 7* at the back of this Bible).

ᵃ4 Or *and troubled them as they built*   ᵇ6 Hebrew *Ahasuerus,* a variant of Xerxes' Persian name   ᶜ7 Or *written in Aramaic and translated*   ᵈ7 The text of Ezra 4:8—6:18 is in Aramaic.   ᵉ9 Or *officials, magistrates and governors over the men from*   ᶠ10 Aramaic *Osnappar,* a variant of *Ashurbanipal*

dishonored, we are sending this message to inform the king, **15**so that a search may be made in the archives of your predecessors. In these records you will find that this city is a rebellious city, troublesome to kings and provinces, a place of rebellion from ancient times. That is why this city was destroyed. **16**We inform the king that if this city is built and its walls are restored, you will be left with nothing in Trans-Euphrates.

17The king sent this reply:

To Rehum the commanding officer, Shimshai the secretary and the rest of their associates living in Samaria and elsewhere in Trans-Euphrates:

Greetings.

18The letter you sent us has been read and translated in my presence. **19**I issued an order and a search was made, and it was found that this city has a long history of revolt against kings and has been a place of rebellion and sedition. **20**Jerusalem[D] has had powerful kings ruling over the whole of Trans-Euphrates, and taxes, tribute and duty were paid to them. **21**Now issue an order to these men to stop work, so that this city will not be rebuilt until I so order. **22**Be careful not to neglect this matter. Why let this threat grow, to the detriment of the royal interests?

23As soon as the copy of the letter of King Artaxerxes was read to Rehum and Shimshai the secretary and their associates, they went immediately to the Jews[D] in Jerusalem and compelled them by force to stop.

24Thus the work on the house of God in Jerusalem came to a standstill until the second year of the reign of Darius king of Persia.

Tattenai's Letter to Darius

5 Now Haggai the prophet[D] and Zechariah the prophet, a descendant of Iddo, prophesied to the Jews in Judah and Jerusalem in the name of the God of Israel, who was over them. **2**Then Zerubbabel son of Shealtiel and Jeshua son of Jozadak set to work to rebuild the house of God in Jerusalem. And the prophets of God were with them, helping them.

3At that time Tattenai, governor of Trans-Euphrates, and Shethar-Bozenai and their associates went to them and asked, "Who authorized you to rebuild this temple and restore this structure?" **4**They also asked, "What are the names of the men constructing this building?"*a* **5**But the eye of their God was watching over the elders of the Jews, and they were not stopped until a report could go to Darius and his written reply be received.

6This is a copy of the letter that Tattenai, governor of Trans-Euphrates, and Shethar-Bozenai and their associates, the officials of Trans-Euphrates, sent to King Darius. **7**The report they sent him read as follows:

To King Darius:

Cordial greetings.

Why did Artaxerxes order the work stopped? (4:21–22)
Persian policy favored the kind of rebuilding going on in Jerusalem, both of the temple and of the city. But the Jews were framed by their enemies who claimed the Jews planned to rebel. With major revolts in Egypt and Athens at the time, the king took the accusation seriously. However, he did not completely override the prior edict, simply ordering the work stopped temporarily—*until I so order.* Later he let it resume (6:14; Neh. 2:1–10).

How long did the work remain at a standstill? (4:24)
The construction was halted for some 16 years, from early in Cyrus's reign (536 B.C.) to the second year of Darius (520 B.C.).

The eye of their God was watching (5:5)
This poetic expression shows God's watchfulness over his people, much as *the hand of the* Lord (7:6) illustrates his personal care. Interestingly, Persian inspectors in that day were popularly known as "the king's eyes." Thus the use of the word *eye* shows that God's knowledge and power were superior to the king's.

---

a4 See Septuagint; Aramaic *4We told them the names of the men constructing this building.*

8The king should know that we went to the district of Judah, to the temple of the great God. The people are building it with large stones and placing the timbers in the walls. The work is being carried on with diligence and is making rapid progress under their direction.

9We questioned the elders and asked them, "Who authorized you to rebuild this temple and restore this structure?" **10**We also asked them their names, so that we could write down the names of their leaders for your information.

11This is the answer they gave us:

"We are the servants of the God of heaven and earth, and we are rebuilding the temple that was built many years ago, one that a great king of Israel built and finished. **12**But because our fathers angered the God of heaven, he handed them over to Nebuchadnezzar the Chaldean, king of Babylon, who destroyed this temple and deported the people to Babylon.

13"However, in the first year of Cyrus[D] king of Babylon, King Cyrus issued a decree to rebuild this house of God. **14**He even removed from the temple[a] of Babylon the gold and silver articles of the house of God, which Nebuchadnezzar had taken from the temple in Jerusalem[D] and brought to the temple[a] in Babylon.

"Then King Cyrus gave them to a man named Sheshbazzar, whom he had appointed governor, **15**and he told him, 'Take these articles and go and deposit them in the temple in Jerusalem. And rebuild the house of God on its site.' **16**So this Sheshbazzar came and laid the foundations of the house of God in Jerusalem. From that day to the present it has been under construction but is not yet finished."

17Now if it pleases the king, let a search be made in the royal archives of Babylon to see if King Cyrus did in fact issue a decree to rebuild this house of God in Jerusalem. Then let the king send us his decision in this matter.

The Decree of Darius

6 King Darius then issued an order, and they searched in the archives stored in the treasury at Babylon. **2**A scroll was found in the citadel[D] of Ecbatana in the province of Media, and this was written on it:

Memorandum:

3In the first year of King Cyrus, the king issued a decree concerning the temple of God in Jerusalem:

Let the temple be rebuilt as a place to present sacrifices[D], and let its foundations be laid. It is to be ninety feet[b] high and ninety feet wide, **4**with three courses of large stones and one of timbers. The costs are to be paid by the royal treasury. **5**Also, the gold and silver articles of the house of God, which Nebuchadnezzar took from the temple in Jerusalem and brought to Babylon, are to be returned to their places in the temple in Jerusalem; they are to be deposited in the house of God.

Why is Cyrus called the *king of Babylon*? (5:13)

The Judean elders probably used this title to contrast Cyrus with the former king of Babylon, Nebuchadnezzar (v. 12). The term was not incorrect: Cyrus, as ruler of the Persian empire, could be called the king of any number of nations that were subject to him. In one ancient text he refers to himself not only as the "king of Babylon" but as "king of the world," listing other lands over which he ruled.

The citadel of Ecbatana (6:2)

Ecbatana was a large fortified city in Media, where precious metals and documents could be stored separately from Babylon's treasuries (see *Map 7* at the back of this Bible). Because the city was the summer residence of the Persian kings, many royal documents originated there as well.

Why would Darius finance this project from the royal treasury? (6:4)

Darius was simply continuing the policy of Cyrus, which he quotes in v. 4. The money in the royal treasury ultimately came out of the pockets of the people of Trans-Euphrates through taxes (6:8). The returning exiles' neighbors in Babylon had donated to the temple fund voluntarily (1:6). Their new neighbors would be contributing whether they wanted to or not.

*a*14 Or *palace*   *b*3 Aramaic *sixty cubits* (about 27 meters)

6Now then, Tattenai, governor of Trans-Euphrates, and Shethar-Bozenai and you, their fellow officials of that province, stay away from there. **7**Do not interfere with the work on this temple of God. Let the governor of the Jews[D] and the Jewish elders rebuild this house of God on its site.

8Moreover, I hereby decree what you are to do for these elders of the Jews in the construction of this house of God:

The expenses of these men are to be fully paid out of the royal treasury, from the revenues of Trans-Euphrates, so that the work will not stop. **9**Whatever is needed—young bulls, rams, male lambs for burnt offerings[D] to the God of heaven, and wheat, salt, wine and oil, as requested by the priests[D] in Jerusalem[D]—must be given them daily without fail, **10**so that they may offer sacrifices[D] pleasing to the God of heaven and pray for the well-being of the king and his sons.

11Furthermore, I decree that if anyone changes this edict[D], a beam is to be pulled from his house and he is to be lifted up and impaled on it. And for this crime his house is to be made a pile of rubble. **12**May God, who has caused his Name to dwell there, overthrow any king or people who lifts a hand to change this decree or to destroy this temple in Jerusalem.

I Darius have decreed it. Let it be carried out with diligence.

Completion and Dedication of the Temple

13Then, because of the decree King Darius had sent, Tattenai, governor of Trans-Euphrates, and Shethar-Bozenai and their associates carried it out with diligence. **14**So the elders of the Jews continued to build and prosper under the preaching of Haggai the prophet[D] and Zechariah, a descendant of Iddo. They finished building the temple according to the command of the God of Israel and the decrees of Cyrus[D], Darius and Artaxerxes, kings of Persia. **15**The temple was completed on the third day of the month Adar, in the sixth year of the reign of King Darius.

16Then the people of Israel—the priests, the Levites and the rest of the exiles[D]—celebrated the dedication of the house of God with joy. **17**For the dedication of this house of God they offered a hundred bulls, two hundred rams, four hundred male lambs and, as a sin offering[D] for all Israel, twelve male goats, one for each of the tribes of Israel. **18**And they installed the priests in their divisions and the Levites in their groups for the service of God at Jerusalem, according to what is written in the Book of Moses.

The Passover

19On the fourteenth day of the first month, the exiles celebrated the Passover. **20**The priests and Levites had purified[D] themselves and were all ceremonially clean. The Levites slaughtered the Passover lamb for all the exiles, for their brothers the priests and for themselves. **21**So the Israelites who had returned from the exile ate it, together with all who had separated themselves from the unclean[D] practices of their Gentile[D] neighbors in order to seek the LORD, the God of Israel. **22**For seven days they celebrated with joy the Feast of Unleavened Bread, because the LORD had filled them with joy by changing the attitude of the king of Assyria, so that he

---

Why would Darius want Jews praying to their God for him? (6:10)

Like Cyrus, Darius believed broadly in many deities, and was glad to have anyone pray to any god on his behalf. See article: *Why build a temple for a God you don't worship?* (1:1–2). He may also have felt that God owed him some favors for his assistance in building the temple.

Why such a strange penalty? (6:11)

It was standard procedure for a royal decree to include a penalty clause. If the offense were major, the penalty often included both death and the destruction of the person's property (see Daniel 2:5). But this punishment was gruesome even by Persian standards, showing that Darius took this matter seriously. He wanted to avoid civil war within his empire.

Who *separated themselves* from their neighbors' *unclean practices*? (6:21)

Any or all of the following: Judeans who had remained in the land, Israelites from the former northern kingdom or foreign converts who now worshiped God alone. Most think this refers to the converts because it occurred during Passover, a feast in which circumcised foreigners could traditionally be included (Exodus 12:44,48).

King of Assyria (6:22)

Though writing about the Persian Cyrus or Darius (or both), the writer uses *king of Assyria* as a generic term for "foreign conqueror." It had been nearly two centuries since the Assyrians marched through Israel, but they had not been forgotten (see Neh. 9:32). And since the Persians now ruled the former Assyrian domains, a Persian emperor could rightfully be called the king of Assyria. See *Why is Cyrus called the king of Babylon?* (5:13).

assisted them in the work on the house of God, the God of Israel.

Ezra Comes to Jerusalem

7 After these things, during the reign of Artaxerxes king of Persia, Ezra son of Seraiah, the son of Azariah, the son of Hilkiah, ²the son of Shallum, the son of Zadok, the son of Ahitub, ³the son of Amariah, the son of Azariah, the son of Meraioth, ⁴the son of Zerahiah, the son of Uzzi, the son of Bukki, ⁵the son of Abishua, the son of Phinehas, the son of Eleazar, the son of Aaron the chief priest^D— ⁶this Ezra came up from Babylon. He was a teacher well versed in the Law of Moses, which the LORD, the God of Israel, had given. The king had granted him everything he asked, for the hand of the LORD his God was on him. ⁷Some of the Israelites, including priests, Levites, singers, gatekeepers and temple servants, also came up to Jerusalem^D in the seventh year of King Artaxerxes.

⁸Ezra arrived in Jerusalem in the fifth month of the seventh year of the king. ⁹He had begun his journey from Babylon on the first day of the first month, and he arrived in Jerusalem on the first day of the fifth month, for the gracious hand of his God was on him. ¹⁰For Ezra had devoted himself to the study and observance of the Law of the LORD, and to teaching its decrees and laws in Israel.

King Artaxerxes' Letter to Ezra

¹¹This is a copy of the letter King Artaxerxes had given to Ezra the priest and teacher, a man learned in matters concerning the commands and decrees of the LORD for Israel:

¹²^aArtaxerxes, king of kings,

To Ezra the priest, a teacher of the Law of the God of heaven:

Greetings.

¹³Now I decree that any of the Israelites in my kingdom, including priests and Levites, who wish to go to Jerusalem with you, may go. ¹⁴You are sent by the king and his seven advisers to inquire about Judah and Jerusalem with regard to the Law of your God, which is in your hand. ¹⁵Moreover, you are to take with you the silver and gold that the king and his advisers have freely given to the God of Israel, whose dwelling is in Jerusalem, ¹⁶together with all the silver and gold you may obtain from the province of Babylon, as well as the freewill offerings of the people and priests for the temple of their God in Jerusalem. ¹⁷With this money be sure to buy bulls, rams and male lambs, together with their grain offerings^D and drink offerings^D, and sacrifice^D them on the altar of the temple of your God in Jerusalem. ¹⁸You and your brother Jews^D may then do whatever seems best with the rest of the silver and gold, in accordance with the will of your God. ¹⁹Deliver to the God of Jerusalem all the articles entrusted to you for worship in the temple of your God. ²⁰And anything else needed for the temple of your God that you may have occasion to supply, you may provide from the royal treasury.

²¹Now I, King Artaxerxes, order all the treasurers

Why did Artaxerxes suddenly help the Jewish cause? (7:12–15)

Artaxerxes' earlier halt to the building program was a departure from the norm. Persian leaders typically encouraged such projects. The work stoppage had been prompted by rumors of a rebellion in Judah. See *Why did Artaxerxes order the work stopped?* (4:21–22). The writer does not explain why Artaxerxes resumed his favorable stance toward the Jews, except to say that *the hand of the LORD* was on Ezra (7:6).

Did Artaxerxes give Ezra a blank check? (7:16)

No. *All the silver and gold you may obtain* meant that Ezra had permission to solicit gifts from the king and his advisers (v. 15) as well as from the people and priests in Jerusalem (v. 16).

---

^a12 The text of Ezra 7:12-26 is in Aramaic.

Was Artaxerxes trying to win God's protection? (7:23)

Probably so. Persian kings often sought the favor of foreign gods—and the goodwill of their worshipers—by such policies. See article: *Why build a temple for a God you don't worship?* (1:1–2). It wasn't unusual for a Middle Eastern ruler to fear the wrath of a deity who was being worshiped improperly. Ironically, Artaxerxes seemed to have more fear of displeasing God than many Jews did.

Why give Jewish religious leaders a "tax exemption"? (7:24)

This was not uncommon in Persia. One inscription from the time of Darius chides a local governor for taxing the priests of Apollo. Subsidizing priests and temple workers was part of the Persian policy of reestablishing native religions in an attempt to keep the empire stable.

Did Artaxerxes want the whole region to live by the law of God? (7:25–26)

No. He modified the phrase *all the people of Trans-Euphrates* by adding *all who know the laws of your God:* that is, the Jews. It made political sense to teach and enforce local community laws. Such action would promote stability throughout Artaxerxes' empire. Religiously, Artaxerxes may also have hoped to gain God's favor by assuring that the Jews obeyed God's laws.

Why does the narrative suddenly shift to first person? (7:28)

Many think a writer compiled this account using a number of sources. Having told us about Ezra, the writer now quotes from Ezra's own memoirs, offering an inside perspective.

of Trans-Euphrates to provide with diligence whatever Ezra the priest[D], a teacher of the Law of the God of heaven, may ask of you— [22]up to a hundred talents[a] of silver, a hundred cors[b] of wheat, a hundred baths[c] of wine, a hundred baths[c] of olive oil, and salt without limit. [23]Whatever the God of heaven has prescribed, let it be done with diligence for the temple of the God of heaven. Why should there be wrath against the realm of the king and of his sons? [24]You are also to know that you have no authority to impose taxes, tribute or duty on any of the priests, Levites[D], singers, gatekeepers, temple servants or other workers at this house of God.

[25]And you, Ezra, in accordance with the wisdom of your God, which you possess, appoint magistrates and judges to administer justice to all the people of Trans-Euphrates—all who know the laws of your God. And you are to teach any who do not know them. [26]Whoever does not obey the law of your God and the law of the king must surely be punished by death[D], banishment, confiscation of property, or imprisonment.

[27]Praise be to the LORD, the God of our fathers, who has put it into the king's heart to bring honor to the house of the LORD in Jerusalem[D] in this way [28]and who has extended his good favor to me before the king and his advisers and all the king's powerful officials. Because the hand of the LORD my God was on me, I took courage and gathered leading men from Israel to go up with me.

List of the Family Heads Returning With Ezra

8 These are the family heads and those registered with them who came up with me from Babylon during the reign of King Artaxerxes:

[2]of the descendants of Phinehas, Gershom;
   of the descendants of Ithamar, Daniel;
   of the descendants of David, Hattush [3]of the descendants of Shecaniah;

   of the descendants of Parosh, Zechariah, and with him were registered 150 men;
[4]of the descendants of Pahath-Moab, Eliehoenai son of Zerahiah, and with him 200 men;
[5]of the descendants of Zattu,[d] Shecaniah son of Jahaziel, and with him 300 men;
[6]of the descendants of Adin, Ebed son of Jonathan, and with him 50 men;
[7]of the descendants of Elam, Jeshaiah son of Athaliah, and with him 70 men;
[8]of the descendants of Shephatiah, Zebadiah son of Michael, and with him 80 men;
[9]of the descendants of Joab, Obadiah son of Jehiel, and with him 218 men;
[10]of the descendants of Bani,[e] Shelomith son of Josiphiah, and with him 160 men;
[11]of the descendants of Bebai, Zechariah son of Bebai, and with him 28 men;

---

[a]22 That is, about 3 3/4 tons (about 3.4 metric tons)   [b]22 That is, probably about 600 bushels (about 22 kiloliters)   [c]22 That is, probably about 600 gallons (about 2.2 kiloliters)   [d]5 Some Septuagint manuscripts (also 1 Esdras 8:32); Hebrew does not have *Zattu*.   [e]10 Some Septuagint manuscripts (also 1 Esdras 8:36); Hebrew does not have *Bani*.

¹²of the descendants of Azgad, Johanan son of Hakkatan, and with him 110 men;

¹³of the descendants of Adonikam, the last ones, whose names were Eliphelet, Jeuel and Shemaiah, and with them 60 men;

¹⁴of the descendants of Bigvai, Uthai and Zaccur, and with them 70 men.

The Return to Jerusalem

¹⁵I assembled them at the canal that flows toward Ahava, and we camped there three days. When I checked among the people and the priests[D], I found no Levites[D] there. ¹⁶So I summoned Eliezer, Ariel, Shemaiah, Elnathan, Jarib, Elnathan, Nathan, Zechariah and Meshullam, who were leaders, and Joiarib and Elnathan, who were men of learning, ¹⁷and I sent them to Iddo, the leader in Casiphia. I told them what to say to Iddo and his kinsmen, the temple servants in Casiphia, so that they might bring attendants to us for the house of our God. ¹⁸Because the gracious hand of our God was on us, they brought us Sherebiah, a capable man, from the descendants of Mahli son of Levi, the son of Israel, and Sherebiah's sons and brothers, 18 men; ¹⁹and Hashabiah, together with Jeshaiah from the descendants of Merari, and his brothers and nephews, 20 men. ²⁰They also brought 220 of the temple servants—a body that David and the officials had established to assist the Levites. All were registered by name.

²¹There, by the Ahava Canal, I proclaimed a fast, so that we might humble ourselves before our God and ask him for a safe journey for us and our children, with all our possessions. ²²I was ashamed to ask the king for soldiers and horsemen to protect us from enemies on the road, because we had told the king, "The gracious hand of our God is on everyone who looks to him, but his great anger is against all who forsake him." ²³So we fasted and petitioned our God about this, and he answered our prayer.

²⁴Then I set apart twelve of the leading priests, together with Sherebiah, Hashabiah and ten of their brothers, ²⁵and I weighed out to them the offering of silver and gold and the articles that the king, his advisers, his officials and all Israel present there had donated for the house of our God. ²⁶I weighed out to them 650 talents[a] of silver, silver articles weighing 100 talents,[b] 100 talents[b] of gold, ²⁷20 bowls of gold valued at 1,000 darics,[c] and two fine articles of polished bronze, as precious as gold.

²⁸I said to them, "You as well as these articles are consecrated[D] to the LORD. The silver and gold are a freewill offering to the LORD, the God of your fathers. ²⁹Guard them carefully until you weigh them out in the chambers of the house of the LORD in Jerusalem[D] before the leading priests and the Levites and the family heads of Israel." ³⁰Then the priests and Levites received the silver and gold and sacred[D] articles that had been weighed out to be taken to the house of our God in Jerusalem.

³¹On the twelfth day of the first month we set out from the Ahava Canal to go to Jerusalem. The hand of our God was on us, and he protected us from enemies and bandits along the way. ³²So we arrived in Jerusalem, where we rested three days.

Why was Ezra worried about the lack of Levites? (8:15)

The Levites' role was to do menial labor around the temple. Ezra knew very few had returned to Jerusalem earlier (2:40–42). He must have felt the need for more Levites to serve at the upcoming temple celebration.

---

[a]26 That is, about 25 tons (about 22 metric tons)   [b]26 That is, about 3 3/4 tons (about 3.4 metric tons)   [c]27 That is, about 19 pounds (about 8.5 kilograms)

Royal satraps (8:36)
Pronounced *SAY-traps.* A *satrap* was a Persian administrative district similar to a province (Trans-Euphrates was one of 20). It also referred to the official who ruled over such a district.

What were the *detestable practices* of the surrounding peoples? (9:1)
They involved worshiping pagan gods, probably fertilility rites that may have included sacrifices or ritual prostitution. These rites were detestable, whatever form they took, because they involved unfaithfulness to God. Because such compromises were so tempting, intermarriage with the Canaanite nations mentioned had been forbidden (Deut. 7:1–4).

Why did Ezra confess guilt as though he himself had sinned? (9:6)
Like a modern pastor, Ezra led a public prayer of confession. He did not personally commit the sins mentioned from the pulpit, but Ezra saw himself vitally linked to the community—even in its sin. Ezra showed care and responsibility for his people rather than setting himself above them.

33On the fourth day, in the house of our God, we weighed out the silver and gold and the sacredᴰ articles into the hands of Meremoth son of Uriah, the priestᴰ. Eleazar son of Phinehas was with him, and so were the Levitesᴰ Jozabad son of Jeshua and Noadiah son of Binnui. **34**Everything was accounted for by number and weight, and the entire weight was recorded at that time.

35Then the exilesᴰ who had returned from captivity sacrificed burnt offeringsᴰ to the God of Israel: twelve bulls for all Israel, ninety-six rams, seventy-seven male lambs and, as a sin offeringᴰ, twelve male goats. All this was a burnt offering to the LORD. **36**They also delivered the king's orders to the royal satrapsᴰ and to the governors of Trans-Euphrates, who then gave assistance to the people and to the house of God.

Ezra's Prayer About Intermarriage

9 After these things had been done, the leaders came to me and said, "The people of Israel, including the priests and the Levites, have not kept themselves separate from the neighboring peoples with their detestable practices, like those of the Canaanites, Hittites, Perizzites, Jebusites, Ammonites, Moabites, Egyptians and Amorites. **2**They have taken some of their daughters as wives for themselves and their sons, and have mingled the holy race with the peoples around them. And the leaders and officials have led the way in this unfaithfulness."

3When I heard this, I tore my tunic and cloak, pulled hair from my head and beard and sat down appalled. **4**Then everyone who trembled at the words of the God of Israel gathered around me because of this unfaithfulness of the exiles. And I sat there appalled until the evening sacrificeᴰ.

5Then, at the evening sacrifice, I rose from my self-abasement, with my tunic and cloak torn, and fell on my knees with my hands spread out to the LORD my God **6**and prayed:

"O my God, I am too ashamed and disgraced to lift up my face to you, my God, because our sins are higher than our heads and our guilt has reached to the heavens. **7**From the days of our forefathers until now, our guilt has been great. Because of our sins, we and our kings and our priests have been subjected to the sword and captivity, to pillage and humiliation at the hand of foreign kings, as it is today.

8"But now, for a brief moment, the LORD our God has been gracious in leaving us a remnantᴰ and giving us a firm place in his sanctuary, and so our God gives light to our eyes and a little relief in our bondage. **9**Though we are slaves, our God has not deserted us in our bondage. He has shown us kindness in the sight of the kings of Persia: He has granted us new life to rebuild the house of our God and repair its ruins, and he has given us a wall of protection in Judah and Jerusalemᴰ.

10"But now, O our God, what can we say after this? For we have disregarded the commands **11**you gave through your servants the prophetsᴰ when you said: 'The land you are entering to possess is a land polluted by the corruption of its peoples. By their detestable practices they have filled it with their impurity from one end to the other. **12**Therefore, do not give your daughters in marriage to their sons or take their

daughters for your sons. Do not seek a treaty of friendship with them at any time, that you may be strong and eat the good things of the land and leave it to your children as an everlasting inheritance.'

¹³"What has happened to us is a result of our evil deeds and our great guilt, and yet, our God, you have punished us less than our sins have deserved and have given us a remnantᴰ like this. ¹⁴Shall we again break your commands and intermarry with the peoples who commit such detestable practices? Would you not be angry enough with us to destroy us, leaving us no remnant or survivor? ¹⁵O Lᴏʀᴅ, God of Israel, you are righteousᴰ! We are left this day as a remnant. Here we are before you in our guilt, though because of it not one of us can stand in your presence."

The People's Confession of Sin

10 While Ezra was praying and confessing, weeping and throwing himself down before the house of God, a large crowd of Israelites—men, women and children—gathered around him. They too wept bitterly. ²Then Shecaniah son of Jehiel, one of the descendants of Elam, said to Ezra, "We have been unfaithful to our God by marrying foreign women from the peoples around us. But in spite of this, there is still hope for Israel. ³Now let us make a covenantᴰ before our God to send away all these women and their children, in accordance with the counsel of my lord and of those who fear the commands of our God. Let it be done according to the Law. ⁴Rise up; this matter is in your hands. We will support you, so take courage and do it."

⁵So Ezra rose up and put the leading priestsᴰ and Levitesᴰ and all Israel under oath to do what had been suggested. And they took the oath. ⁶Then Ezra withdrew from before the house of God and went to the room of Jehohanan son of Eliashib. While he was there, he ate no food and drank no water, because he continued to mourn over the unfaithfulness of the exilesᴰ.

Why did Ezra act this way? (10:1)
We don't know if Ezra was intentionally drawing attention to himself as an object lesson, or if his distress was just so great that he was in agony before the Lord. Whatever his intentions, Ezra's actions resulted in others joining him in repentance (vv. 1–4).

Wasn't abandonment a rather harsh solution? (10:3)

The relationships Shecaniah referred to were not true marriages, nor were the women innocent victims of the men's wrongdoing. The word translated *marry* in 10:2 is not the usual word for marriage, but means *give a home to*. Some think the words *foreign women* implies *harlots*. Even legitimate marriage to members of the Canaanite races was illegal under Mosaic Law specifically because of the danger of religious compromise. See *What were the detestable practices of the surrounding peoples?* (9:1). Clearly, the Jewish men involved did not take God's laws seriously, and the women were willing to accept a tenuous and less-than-legal status in these men's homes. Severing the relationships meant ending something that had been wrong from the beginning.

Although sending these women and their children away seems drastic, the people themselves chose this solution as the best option available to them (10:1–5,12–14). They were determined to separate themselves from their sin. Ezra endorsed their plan. The writer does not tell us what happened to the women and children. It is clear, however, that each case was considered carefully. Any cases in which the foreign women had actually turned from idol worship to the worship of God could have been taken into account.

7A proclamation was then issued throughout Judah and Jerusalem[D] for all the exiles[D] to assemble in Jerusalem. 8Anyone who failed to appear within three days would forfeit all his property, in accordance with the decision of the officials and elders, and would himself be expelled from the assembly of the exiles.

9Within the three days, all the men of Judah and Benjamin had gathered in Jerusalem. And on the twentieth day of the ninth month, all the people were sitting in the square before the house of God, greatly distressed by the occasion and because of the rain. 10Then Ezra the priest[D] stood up and said to them, "You have been unfaithful; you have married foreign women, adding to Israel's guilt. 11Now make confession to the LORD, the God of your fathers, and do his will. Separate yourselves from the peoples around you and from your foreign wives."

12The whole assembly responded with a loud voice: "You are right! We must do as you say. 13But there are many people here and it is the rainy season; so we cannot stand outside. Besides, this matter cannot be taken care of in a day or two, because we have sinned greatly in this thing. 14Let our officials act for the whole assembly. Then let everyone in our towns who has married a foreign woman come at a set time, along with the elders and judges of each town, until the fierce anger of our God in this matter is turned away from us." 15Only Jonathan son of Asahel and Jahzeiah son of Tikvah, supported by Meshullam and Shabbethai the Levite[D], opposed this.

16So the exiles did as was proposed. Ezra the priest selected men who were family heads, one from each family division, and all of them designated by name. On the first day of the tenth month they sat down to investigate the cases, 17and by the first day of the first month they finished dealing with all the men who had married foreign women.

Those Guilty of Intermarriage

18Among the descendants of the priests, the following had married foreign women:

From the descendants of Jeshua son of Jozadak, and his brothers: Maaseiah, Eliezer, Jarib and Gedaliah. 19(They all gave their hands in pledge to put away their wives, and for their guilt they each presented a ram from the flock as a guilt offering.)

20From the descendants of Immer:
Hanani and Zebadiah.

21From the descendants of Harim:
Maaseiah, Elijah, Shemaiah, Jehiel and Uzziah.

22From the descendants of Pashhur:
Elioenai, Maaseiah, Ishmael, Nethanel, Jozabad and Elasah.

23Among the Levites:

Jozabad, Shimei, Kelaiah (that is, Kelita), Pethahiah, Judah and Eliezer.

24From the singers:
Eliashib.
From the gatekeepers:
Shallum, Telem and Uri.

25And among the other Israelites:

From the descendants of Parosh:

Fierce anger of our God (10:14)
The writer does not mention any specific displays of God's anger: deaths, wars, or pestilences. But the people felt sure that such wrath was an imminent danger. They were trying to avoid God's anger by willingly changing their idolatrous ways before God acted to punish them as he had in previous generations (for example, Hosea 9:10–17; Amos 4:6–11).

Why did some disagree with the majority opinion? (10:15)
We don't know whether these men disagreed with the verdict itself (sending the foreign wives away) or only with the proposed method of carrying it out (case-by-case, over a period of months). None of these four critics appears conclusively on the list of men with foreign wives. And there is no record that they were rebuked for their objections. It's likely the four were hard-liners, wanting the intermarriage problem dealt with then and there, not with a process.

Why did it take so long to settle the issue? (10:17)
The council took three months to determine the guilt in the 110 cases listed. Their careful investigation showed that they did not take the breakups of these households lightly. Their verdict may have been innocence in some cases (perhaps because a woman had been converted to worship the God of the Jews).

Ramiah, Izziah, Malkijah, Mijamin, Eleazar, Malkijah and Benaiah.

26From the descendants of Elam:

Mattaniah, Zechariah, Jehiel, Abdi, Jeremoth and
Elijah.

27From the descendants of Zattu:

Elioenai, Eliashib, Mattaniah, Jeremoth, Zabad and
Aziza.

28From the descendants of Bebai:

Jehohanan, Hananiah, Zabbai and Athlai.

29From the descendants of Bani:

Meshullam, Malluch, Adaiah, Jashub, Sheal and
Jeremoth.

30From the descendants of Pahath-Moab:

Adna, Kelal, Benaiah, Maaseiah, Mattaniah, Bezalel, Binnui and Manasseh.

31From the descendants of Harim:

Eliezer, Ishijah, Malkijah, Shemaiah, Shimeon,
32Benjamin, Malluch and Shemariah.

33From the descendants of Hashum:

Mattenai, Mattattah, Zabad, Eliphelet, Jeremai, Manasseh and Shimei.

34From the descendants of Bani:

Maadai, Amram, Uel, 35Benaiah, Bedeiah, Keluhi,
36Vaniah, Meremoth, Eliashib, 37Mattaniah, Mattenai and Jaasu.

38From the descendants of Binnui:a

Shimei, 39Shelemiah, Nathan, Adaiah, 40Macnade-
bai, Shashai, Sharai, 41Azarel, Shelemiah, Shemariah, 42Shallum, Amariah and Joseph.

43From the descendants of Nebo:

Jeiel, Mattithiah, Zabad, Zebina, Jaddai, Joel and
Benaiah.

44All these had married foreign women, and some of
them had children by these wives.b

Was this list intended to embarrass the offenders? (10:18–43)

Not necessarily. Their deeds were already known in the community, leading to their indictment by Ezra (v. 10) and their confession (vv. 12–13). More likely this list contained the official findings of the tribunal commissioned to make careful judgments regarding each family's case (v. 16). Like court documents today, this list may have served as a record of legal proceedings and decisions. It also may have served to clear the names of the innocent: they could point to the list to show that their names were not included.

---

a37,38 See Septuagint (also 1 Esdras 9:34); Hebrew Jaasu 38and Bani
and Binnui,   b44 Or and they sent them away with their children

NEHEMIAH

Why read this book?

If you've ever faced an overwhelming task or felt inadequate to meet a challenge, you'll be able to identify with Nehemiah. He struggled with issues still with us today: motivation, fatigue, criticism. But this book also offers inspiration and vision. Without neglecting the practical, Nehemiah shows how to tackle God's difficult assignments and survive both opposition and apathy.

Who wrote this book?

Probably the writer of Ezra (which was originally combined with Nehemiah) who many think also wrote 1 and 2 Chronicles. He likely drew from Nehemiah's memoirs and from census records.

What were the historical circumstances surrounding it?

The Babylonians conquered Israel in 586 B.C. Persia, in turn, conquered Babylon (539 B.C.) and later allowed the Jews to return to Jerusalem. By 445 B.C., however, the challenges of rebuilding their homeland had demoralized them. Under Ezra, they had rebuilt the temple, but the walls of the city remained in rubble.

Why was it written?

To remind God's people of their spiritual heritage and to keep them from becoming careless toward the Lord.

When was it written?

The incidents occurred between 444 and 432 B.C. The book was probably compiled about 430 B.C., though no one knows for sure.

What to look for in Nehemiah:

A shining example of one man's methods of accomplishing his goals. Watch for the ways he balanced his spirituality with down-to-earth action. One example: *we prayed to our God and posted a guard* (4:9).

When did these things happen?

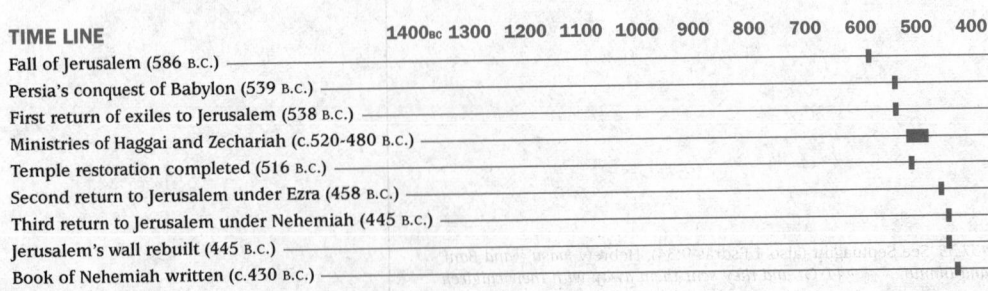

TIME LINE	1400BC	1300	1200	1100	1000	900	800	700	600	500	400
Fall of Jerusalem (586 B.C.)											
Persia's conquest of Babylon (539 B.C.)											
First return of exiles to Jerusalem (538 B.C.)											
Ministries of Haggai and Zechariah (c.520-480 B.C.)											
Temple restoration completed (516 B.C.)											
Second return to Jerusalem under Ezra (458 B.C.)											
Third return to Jerusalem under Nehemiah (445 B.C.)											
Jerusalem's wall rebuilt (445 B.C.)											
Book of Nehemiah written (c.430 B.C.)											

Nehemiah's Prayer

1 The words of Nehemiah son of Hacaliah:

In the month of Kislev in the twentieth year, while I was in the citadelᴰ of Susa, **2**Hanani, one of my brothers, came from Judah with some other men, and I questioned them about the Jewish remnantᴰ that survived the exileᴰ, and also about Jerusalemᴰ.

3They said to me, "Those who survived the exile and are back in the province are in great trouble and disgrace. The wall of Jerusalem is broken down, and its gates have been burned with fire."

4When I heard these things, I sat down and wept. For some days I mourned and fasted and prayed before the God of heaven. **5**Then I said:

"O Lᴏʀᴅ, God of heaven, the great and awesome God, who keeps his covenantᴰ of love with those who love him and obey his commands, **6**let your ear be attentive and your eyes open to hear the prayer your servant is praying before you day and night for your servants, the people of Israel. I confess the sins we Israelites, including myself and my father's house, have committed against you. **7**We have acted very wickedly toward you. We have not obeyed the commands, decrees and laws you gave your servant Moses.

8"Remember the instruction you gave your servant Moses, saying, 'If you are unfaithful, I will scatter you among the nations, **9**but if you return to me and obey my commands, then even if your exiled people are at the farthest horizon, I will gather them from there and bring them to the place I have chosen as a dwelling for my Name.'

10"They are your servants and your people, whom you redeemedᴰ by your great strength and your mighty hand. **11**O Lord, let your ear be attentive to the prayer of this your servant and to the prayer of your servants who delight in revering your name. Give your servant success today by granting him favor in the presence of this man."

I was cupbearer to the king.

Artaxerxes Sends Nehemiah to Jerusalem

2 In the month of Nisan in the twentieth year of King Artaxerxes, when wine was brought for him, I took the wine and gave it to the king. I had not been sad in his presence before; **2**so the king asked me, "Why does your face look so sad when you are not ill? This can be nothing but sadness of heart."

I was very much afraid, **3**but I said to the king, "May the king live forever! Why should my face not look sad when the city where my fathers are buried lies in ruins, and its gates have been destroyed by fire?"

4The king said to me, "What is it you want?"

Then I prayed to the God of heaven, **5**and I answered the king, "If it pleases the king and if your servant has found favor in his sight, let him send me to the city in Judah where my fathers are buried so that I can rebuild it."

6Then the king, with the queen sitting beside him, asked me, "How long will your journey take, and when

The month of Kislev (1:1)
From mid-November to mid-December. The Jewish calendar had 12 months, with the year beginning in mid-March (the month of Nisan).

Twentieth year (1:1)
Of the reign of Artaxerxes I, that is, 445 ʙ.ᴄ.

The citadel of Susa (1:1)
Susa was the winter capital of the Persian empire, located about 150 miles north of the Persian Gulf on today's border between Iran and Iraq (see **Map 7** at the back of this Bible). Susa was southeast of Baghdad and nearly 1000 miles from Jerusalem. It was also the site of the story of Esther.

Why grieve for a place you've never seen? (1:4)
Nehemiah's passion for Jerusalem was rooted in his commitment to the God of Israel. Nehemiah feared that his people, lacking the protection of walls and without commitment to God's laws, could be assimilated into the surrounding nations. He was concerned that they might lose their God-given identity, purpose and hope.

What sins did Nehemiah confess? (1:6)
Nehemiah was most concerned about the basic sinfulness of the human heart. He grieved because sin had infected the whole nation, including himself, with apathy toward God's *commands, decrees and laws* (v. 7). The pattern of disobedience that had stained him had its origin in the sins committed by his forefathers. He confessed to sin because he was part of that history. His personal revival prepared the way for national revival.

What did a *cupbearer* do? (1:11)
The cupbearer to the king was a position somewhat parallel to the U.S. Secret Service, which protects the President. Assassination plots were a constant concern to the king. It was Nehemiah's job to taste-test the food and drink served to the king, a position that required the greatest trust. Quite possibly, Nehemiah doubled as a confidant and adviser to the king. Thanks in part to Nehemiah's good work, Artaxerxes I reigned 40 years and died of natural causes—a rarity in the dynasty to which he belonged.

The month of Nisan (2:1)
Since the month of Nisan extended from mid-March to mid-April, Nehemiah had prayed earnestly about this matter for about four months. See **The month of Kislev** (1:1). It was likely he mourned and fasted at various times throughout those months.

Why was Nehemiah afraid? (2:2)
Perhaps Nehemiah feared that the display of his personal feelings would jeopardize his position. Kings were not to be bothered with the concerns of their subjects. But more likely, he was afraid because he planned to make two bold requests: (1) He would ask permission to be released from his duties as cupbearer to become governor of Jerusalem. (2) He would also ask for the king's help to restore a city which, in the king's view, would have had a reputation for being troublesome.

What had happened to the city wall of Jerusalem? (2:5–8)

In 586 B.C. Jerusalem had fallen to the Babylonians. Besieged, attacked and burned, Jerusalem was left in ruins. Ezra the priest had apparently rallied a small group of Jews to begin rebuilding the wall (458 B.C.), but they were stopped by the opposition of the Samaritans (Ezra 4:12–23).

Trans-Euphrates (2:7)

See *Trans-Euphrates* (Ezra 4:10).

Why were Sanballat and Tobiah opposed to rebuilding Jerusalem? (2:10,19)

Sanballat was probably the governor of Samaria, the region immediately to the north of Jerusalem. Tobiah, probably the governor of Ammon, the region just to the east of Jerusalem across the Jordan River, was most likely Sanballat's friend and business partner. Although under the thumb of the Persians, these men had become rich and powerful, exercising control over Jerusalem and its inhabitants. Most likely they didn't appreciate someone else moving in on their territory.

Why had Nehemiah kept his mission secret? (2:12)

Two factors may explain Nehemiah's secrecy: (1) Jerusalem, without its protecting walls, was populated with many non-Jews and was a hotbed of political intrigue. Spies would be willing to sell secrets to enemies of the Jews. (2) Any attempt to rally the demoralized Jews to rebuild the walls without a clear plan would breed skepticism among those he needed to inspire.

Why did Nehemiah have only one horse in his group? (2:12)

More horses would have jeopardized the secrecy of their mission. Still, a horse (or mule, another possible translation) put Nehemiah in a better position to scout out the situation. The few men that were with him were trusted aides who probably had a better knowledge of the terrain than he did.

Were the Jews encouraged to build because of danger or because of disgrace? (2:17)

Both would have been powerful motivations. Without city walls, the inhabitants were vulnerable to enemies and thieves who could come and go freely. But it was the disgrace that Nehemiah particularly noted. All of their national pride was centered in "the city of David." Others would think their situation meant they had a weak God (false) or that their God was displeased with them (true)—a humiliating judgment.

What was involved in rebuilding the wall? (3:1–32)

Apparently the northern and western portions of the wall needed only to be renovated. The eastern wall, however, may have required completely new construction since it was located further up the mountainside from its earlier position. The wall, about eight feet thick at its base, was crudely constructed from uncut stone and rubble—explaining why it was mocked. It may have been 20 to 30 feet high and nearly two miles long, enclosing about 90 acres.

will you get back?" It pleased the king to send me; so I set a time.

7I also said to him, "If it pleases the king, may I have letters to the governors of Trans-Euphrates, so that they will provide me safe-conduct until I arrive in Judah? **8**And may I have a letter to Asaph, keeper of the king's forest, so he will give me timber to make beams for the gates of the citadelᴰ by the temple and for the city wall and for the residence I will occupy?" And because the gracious hand of my God was upon me, the king granted my requests. **9**So I went to the governors of Trans-Euphrates and gave them the king's letters. The king had also sent army officers and cavalry with me.

10When Sanballat the Horonite and Tobiah the Ammonite official heard about this, they were very much disturbed that someone had come to promote the welfare of the Israelites.

Nehemiah Inspects Jerusalem's Walls

11I went to Jerusalemᴰ, and after staying there three days **12**I set out during the night with a few men. I had not told anyone what my God had put in my heart to do for Jerusalem. There were no mounts with me except the one I was riding on. **13**By night I went out through the Valley Gate toward the Jackalᵃ Well and the Dung Gate, examining the walls of Jerusalem, which had been broken down, and its gates, which had been destroyed by fire. **14**Then I moved on toward the Fountain Gate and the King's Pool, but there was not enough room for my mount to get through; **15**so I went up the valley by night, examining the wall. Finally, I turned back and reentered through the Valley Gate. **16**The officials did not know where I had gone or what I was doing, because as yet I had said nothing to the Jewsᴰ or the priestsᴰ or nobles or officials or any others who would be doing the work.

17Then I said to them, "You see the trouble we are in: Jerusalem lies in ruins, and its gates have been burned with fire. Come, let us rebuild the wall of Jerusalem, and we will no longer be in disgrace." **18**I also told them about the gracious hand of my God upon me and what the king had said to me.

They replied, "Let us start rebuilding." So they began this good work.

19But when Sanballat the Horonite, Tobiah the Ammonite official and Geshem the Arab heard about it, they mocked and ridiculed us. "What is this you are doing?" they asked. "Are you rebelling against the king?"

20I answered them by saying, "The God of heaven will give us success. We his servants will start rebuilding, but as for you, you have no share in Jerusalem or any claim or historic right to it."

Builders of the Wall

3 Eliashib the high priest and his fellow priests went to work and rebuilt the Sheep Gate. They dedicated it and set its doors in place, building as far as the Tower of the Hundred, which they dedicated, and as far as the Tower of Hananel. **2**The men of Jerichoᴰ built the adjoining section, and Zaccur son of Imri built next to them.

ᵃ13 Or *Serpent* or *Fig*

³The Fish Gate was rebuilt by the sons of Hassenaah. They laid its beams and put its doors and bolts and bars in place. ⁴Meremoth son of Uriah, the son of Hakkoz, repaired the next section. Next to him Meshullam son of Berekiah, the son of Meshezabel, made repairs, and next to him Zadok son of Baana also made repairs. ⁵The next section was repaired by the men of Tekoa, but their nobles would not put their shoulders to the work under their supervisors.ᵃ

⁶The Jeshanahᵇ Gate was repaired by Joiada son of Paseah and Meshullam son of Besodeiah. They laid its beams and put its doors and bolts and bars in place. ⁷Next to them, repairs were made by men from Gibeon and Mizpah—Melatiah of Gibeon and Jadon of Meronoth—places under the authority of the governor of Trans-Euphrates. ⁸Uzziel son of Harhaiah, one of the goldsmiths, repaired the next section; and Hananiah, one of the perfume-makers, made repairs next to that. They restoredᶜ Jerusalemᴰ as far as the Broad Wall. ⁹Rephaiah son of Hur, ruler of a half-district of Jerusalem, repaired the next section. ¹⁰Adjoining this, Jedaiah son of Harumaph made repairs opposite his house, and Hattush son of Hashabneiah made repairs next to him. ¹¹Malkijah son of Harim and Hasshub son of Pahath-Moab repaired another section and the Tower of the Ovens. ¹²Shallum son of Hallohesh, ruler of a half-district of Jerusalem, repaired the next section with the help of his daughters.

¹³The Valley Gate was repaired by Hanun and the residents of Zanoah. They rebuilt it and put its doors and bolts and bars in place. They also repaired five hundred yardsᵈ of the wall as far as the Dung Gate.

¹⁴The Dung Gate was repaired by Malkijah son of Recab, ruler of the district of Beth Hakkerem. He rebuilt it and put its doors and bolts and bars in place.

ᵃ5 Or *their Lord* or *the governor*   ᵇ6 Or *Old*   ᶜ8 Or *They left out part of*   ᵈ13 Hebrew *a thousand cubits* (about 450 meters)

Rebuilding the Wall (3:1)

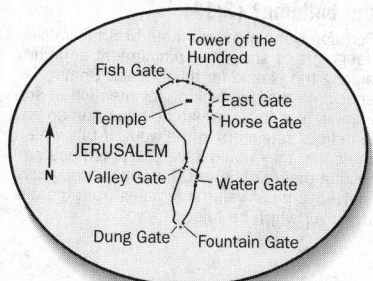

Why did the nobles of Tekoa refuse to work? (3:5)

Since they were not listed among those who immigrated with Nehemiah, they were probably long-time residents, who were perhaps jealous of the newcomers. Another possibility is that these nobles may have felt threatened by Geshem the Arab (see 2:19) since Tekoa was a southern outpost of Judea and therefore closer to Arabia (see *Map 6* at the back of this Bible). Perhaps they refused to work so they would not aggravate Geshem and his countrymen.

What kind of perfume did Hananiah make? (3:8)

Perfume makers of that day used ingredients such as aloes, balm, calamus, cassia and cinnamon. They also traded for sap, bark, flowers and roots from as far away as India. These various scents were made into perfume, incense and ointment for personal hygiene, funerals and religious purposes.

What can we learn from this project? (3:1–32)

On the surface, the details of a long-ago construction project may seem irrelevant. But this account is more than a collection of minor facts. By studying this passage carefully, we can learn principles which apply to modern-day projects: beginning a new church, building a new facility, launching a missions outreach and so forth.

Recurring ideas, pivotal phrases, summary statements and spiritual characteristics all offer themes for us to learn. For example, the repeated phrase *next to them* shows the level of coordination that is needed for a job this big. Also we might learn from Nehemiah's example how a leader can motivate people; he apparently did this by enlisting most workers to build near their own homes. Finally, from Nehemiah's careful record of personal names, we see a leader who noticed individuals; he knew their names and noted their achievements.

On the spiritual level we know that now, as then, physical situations can affect spiritual well-being. Limited resources or direct opposition can challenge the plans of believers now just as surely as opponents challenged the Jews back then. The details of the Jews' encounter offer examples for us, showing us how to meet and overcome such obstacles (see Romans 15:4).

Why did Shallum's daughters help with the building? (3:12)

Perhaps Nehemiah took note of Shallum's daughters to show the commitment and unity among the people for this project. Some speculate that the lack of any mention of sons implies that Shallum had no sons and so enlisted his daughters in the work. If this were the case, they would have been his heirs protecting their birthright. Others think *daughter* may have meant all the females from the district over which he ruled.

15The Fountain Gate was repaired by Shallun son of Col-Hozeh, ruler of the district of Mizpah. He rebuilt it, roofing it over and putting its doors and bolts and bars in place. He also repaired the wall of the Pool of Siloam,[a] by the King's Garden, as far as the steps going down from the City of David. 16Beyond him, Nehemiah son of Azbuk, ruler of a half-district of Beth Zur, made repairs up to a point opposite the tombs[b] of David, as far as the artificial pool and the House of the Heroes.

17Next to him, the repairs were made by the Levites[D] under Rehum son of Bani. Beside him, Hashabiah, ruler of half the district of Keilah, carried out repairs for his district. 18Next to him, the repairs were made by their countrymen under Binnui[c] son of Henadad, ruler of the other half-district of Keilah. 19Next to him, Ezer son of Jeshua, ruler of Mizpah, repaired another section, from a point facing the ascent to the armory as far as the angle. 20Next to him, Baruch son of Zabbai zealously repaired another section, from the angle to the entrance of the house of Eliashib the high priest[D]. 21Next to him, Meremoth son of Uriah, the son of Hakkoz, repaired another section, from the entrance of Eliashib's house to the end of it.

22The repairs next to him were made by the priests from the surrounding region. 23Beyond them, Benjamin and Hasshub made repairs in front of their house; and next to them, Azariah son of Maaseiah, the son of Ananiah, made repairs beside his house. 24Next to him, Binnui son of Henadad repaired another section, from Azariah's house to the angle and the corner, 25and Palal son of Uzai worked opposite the angle and the tower projecting from the upper palace near the court of the guard. Next to him, Pedaiah son of Parosh 26and the temple servants living on the hill of Ophel made repairs up to a point opposite the Water Gate toward the east and the projecting tower. 27Next to them, the men of Tekoa repaired another section, from the great projecting tower to the wall of Ophel.

28Above the Horse Gate, the priests made repairs, each in front of his own house. 29Next to them, Zadok son of Immer made repairs opposite his house. Next to him, Shemaiah son of Shecaniah, the guard at the East Gate, made repairs. 30Next to him, Hananiah son of Shelemiah, and Hanun, the sixth son of Zalaph, repaired another section. Next to them, Meshullam son of Berekiah made repairs opposite his living quarters. 31Next to him, Malkijah, one of the goldsmiths, made repairs as far as the house of the temple servants and the merchants, opposite the Inspection Gate, and as far as the room above the corner; 32and between the room above the corner and the Sheep Gate the goldsmiths and merchants made repairs.

Opposition to the Rebuilding

Why was Sanballat so upset that the Jews were rebuilding their wall? (4:1–2)

See *Why were Sanballat and Tobiah opposed to rebuilding Jerusalem?* (2:10).

4 When Sanballat heard that we were rebuilding the wall, he became angry and was greatly incensed. He ridiculed the Jews[D], 2and in the presence of his associates and the army of Samaria, he said, "What are those feeble Jews doing? Will they restore their wall? Will they offer sacrifices[D]? Will they finish in a day? Can they bring the stones back to life from those heaps of rubble—burned as they are?"

[a]15 Hebrew *Shelah,* a variant of *Shiloah,* that is, Siloam
[b]16 Hebrew; Septuagint, some Vulgate manuscripts and Syriac *tomb*
[c]18 Two Hebrew manuscripts and Syriac (see also Septuagint and verse 24); most Hebrew manuscripts *Bavvai*

³Tobiah the Ammonite, who was at his side, said, "What they are building—if even a fox climbed up on it, he would break down their wall of stones!"

⁴Hear us, O our God, for we are despised. Turn their insults back on their own heads. Give them over as plunder^D in a land of captivity. ⁵Do not cover up their guilt or blot out their sins from your sight, for they have thrown insults in the face of^a the builders.

⁶So we rebuilt the wall till all of it reached half its height, for the people worked with all their heart.

⁷But when Sanballat, Tobiah, the Arabs, the Ammonites and the men of Ashdod heard that the repairs to Jerusalem's walls had gone ahead and that the gaps were being closed, they were very angry. ⁸They all plotted together to come and fight against Jerusalem and stir up trouble against it. ⁹But we prayed to our God and posted a guard day and night to meet this threat.

¹⁰Meanwhile, the people in Judah said, "The strength of the laborers is giving out, and there is so much rubble that we cannot rebuild the wall."

¹¹Also our enemies said, "Before they know it or see us, we will be right there among them and will kill them and put an end to the work."

¹²Then the Jews^D who lived near them came and told us ten times over, "Wherever you turn, they will attack us."

¹³Therefore I stationed some of the people behind the lowest points of the wall at the exposed places, posting them by families, with their swords, spears and bows. ¹⁴After I looked things over, I stood up and said to the nobles, the officials and the rest of the people, "Don't be afraid of them. Remember the Lord, who is great and awesome, and fight for your brothers, your sons and your daughters, your wives and your homes."

¹⁵When our enemies heard that we were aware of their plot and that God had frustrated it, we all returned to the wall, each to his own work.

¹⁶From that day on, half of my men did the work, while the other half were equipped with spears, shields, bows and armor. The officers posted themselves behind all the people of Judah ¹⁷who were building the wall. Those who carried materials did their work with one hand and held a weapon in the other, ¹⁸and each of the builders wore his sword at his side as he worked. But the man who sounded the trumpet stayed with me.

¹⁹Then I said to the nobles, the officials and the rest of the people, "The work is extensive and spread out, and we are widely separated from each other along the wall. ²⁰Wherever you hear the sound of the trumpet, join us there. Our God will fight for us!"

²¹So we continued the work with half the men holding spears, from the first light of dawn till the stars came out. ²²At that time I also said to the people, "Have every man and his helper stay inside Jerusalem at night, so they can serve us as guards by night and workmen by day." ²³Neither I nor my brothers nor my men nor the guards with me took off our clothes; each had his weapon, even when he went for water.^b

Why did Nehemiah pray such vindictive prayers? (4:4–5)

Nehemiah had a keen sense that Sanballat and his supporters were not just his personal enemies—they were enemies of God, bent on discouraging God's people and frustrating the work God had assigned. Such attacks had worked some 15 or 20 years earlier (Ezra 4:12–23), and Nehemiah was determined not to let that happen again. Note that he did not retaliate personally against his enemies; he simply prayed for God's intervention and judgment.

What kind of a plot were Sanballat and Tobiah hatching? (4:7–8)

The actual details of their plot were unclear. The Jews suspected a direct surprise attack on some especially weak part of the wall, perhaps by night, as indicated by their defensive plan (v. 13). Other Jews living near Judah's borders repeatedly told Nehemiah how threatened they felt. An attack on a border area could have had a devastating effect on the building efforts in Jerusalem.

Why were the builders losing their strength? (4:10)

Manually building a wall from large stones was work that would tax the strongest laborer. Many were not accustomed to such work, especially considering their long hours (v. 21). Furthermore, their morale suffered under the persistent mockery and threats (v. 5). Physical exhaustion, work sites strewn with rubble, a job far from completion and debilitating verbal abuse all contributed to their lost strength.

How vulnerable were the workers? (4:16–23)

Their precautions effectively diminished the threat of surprise attack. Interestingly, the dual assignments of guard duty and working on the construction did more than provide protection. It also gave some variety to the workers, resting them and improving their morale. Militarily, of course, the alliance of leaders mentioned in v. 7 could completely surround and overwhelm the Jews. But the plotters knew Nehemiah had the support of the powerful Persian government, which they feared. Of course, the greatest protection the Jews had was their faith in God.

How long did the men go without changing clothes? (4:23)

Nehemiah and his men worked and slept in their clothes, ready at any moment for a surprise attack. Since it took 52 days to complete the walls (6:15), it's possible they went without clean clothes and baths for nearly two months.

How did internal bickering surface amid danger from outside attack? (5:1–5)

To some degree, taking defensive measures diminished the sense of immediate danger. Once that external threat was slightly relieved, other frustrations just beneath the surface began to appear. The threat of famine became nearly as frightening as that of enemy attack. Animosity between the "haves" and the "have-nots" became more acute, despite their cooperation on the wall.

Why were some Jews selling their sons and daughters into slavery? (5:5)

Sometimes ancient peoples, having little property to mortgage, would be forced to use family members as collateral for loans. If the loan wasn't repaid, the creditor gained the pledged person as a slave for a period of time equivalent to the balance of the loan. This slavery wasn't necessarily cruel, and such servants were not necessarily separated from their homes. But they were obligated to serve their new masters.

Usury (5:7)

Although commercial loans could be charged interest, the Law of Moses prohibited charging interest on loans to the poor (Exodus 22:25–27; Lev. 25:35–37; Deut. 23:19–20; 24:10–13). God expected his people to help the poor by giving them loans without charge.

Did Nehemiah put the banks out of business? (5:10–11)

There were no banks then as we know them now. There were, however, wealthy people who made money at the expense of the poor. Nehemiah insisted on two major changes: (1) Creditors should no longer hold or use collateral until the debt was repaid. (2) They should stop charging the *hundredth part*, usually thought to be one percent per month or 12 percent annually.

Where did Nehemiah get his money? (5:14–18)

Nehemiah was probably quite wealthy when he came from Persia. In addition, money in the treasury could perhaps have been used without exacting more tax. Also, there may have been other sources of revenue, such as subsidies from the Persian capital.

Nehemiah Helps the Poor

5 Now the men and their wives raised a great outcry against their Jewish brothers. [2]Some were saying, "We and our sons and daughters are numerous; in order for us to eat and stay alive, we must get grain."

[3]Others were saying, "We are mortgaging our fields, our vineyards and our homes to get grain during the famine."

[4]Still others were saying, "We have had to borrow money to pay the king's tax on our fields and vineyards. [5]Although we are of the same flesh and blood as our countrymen and though our sons are as good as theirs, yet we have to subject our sons and daughters to slavery. Some of our daughters have already been enslaved, but we are powerless, because our fields and our vineyards belong to others."

[6]When I heard their outcry and these charges, I was very angry. [7]I pondered them in my mind and then accused the nobles and officials. I told them, "You are exacting usury[D] from your own countrymen!" So I called together a large meeting to deal with them [8]and said: "As far as possible, we have bought back our Jewish brothers who were sold to the Gentiles[D]. Now you are selling your brothers, only for them to be sold back to us!" They kept quiet, because they could find nothing to say.

[9]So I continued, "What you are doing is not right. Shouldn't you walk in the fear of our God to avoid the reproach[D] of our Gentile enemies? [10]I and my brothers and my men are also lending the people money and grain. But let the exacting of usury stop! [11]Give back to them immediately their fields, vineyards, olive groves and houses, and also the usury you are charging them—the hundredth part of the money, grain, new wine[D] and oil."

[12]"We will give it back," they said. "And we will not demand anything more from them. We will do as you say."

Then I summoned the priests[D] and made the nobles and officials take an oath to do what they had promised. [13]I also shook out the folds of my robe and said, "In this way may God shake out of his house and possessions every man who does not keep this promise. So may such a man be shaken out and emptied!"

At this the whole assembly said, "Amen," and praised the LORD. And the people did as they had promised.

[14]Moreover, from the twentieth year of King Artaxerxes, when I was appointed to be their governor in the land of Judah, until his thirty-second year—twelve years—neither I nor my brothers ate the food allotted to the governor. [15]But the earlier governors—those preceding me—placed a heavy burden on the people and took forty shekels[Da] of silver from them in addition to food and wine. Their assistants also lorded it over the people. But out of reverence[D] for God I did not act like that. [16]Instead, I devoted myself to the work on this wall. All my men were assembled there for the work; we[b] did not acquire any land.

[17]Furthermore, a hundred and fifty Jews[D] and officials ate at my table, as well as those who came to us from the surrounding nations. [18]Each day one ox, six choice sheep and some poultry were prepared for me, and every ten

---

[a]15 That is, about 1 pound (about 0.5 kilogram)   [b]16 Most Hebrew manuscripts; some Hebrew manuscripts, Septuagint, Vulgate and Syriac *I*

days an abundant supply of wine of all kinds. In spite of all this, I never demanded the food allotted to the governor, because the demands were heavy on these people.

¹⁹Remember me with favor, O my God, for all I have done for these people.

Further Opposition to the Rebuilding

6 When word came to Sanballat, Tobiah, Geshem the Arab and the rest of our enemies that I had rebuilt the wall and not a gap was left in it—though up to that time I had not set the doors in the gates— ²Sanballat and Geshem sent me this message: "Come, let us meet together in one of the villages^a on the plain of Ono."

But they were scheming to harm me; ³so I sent messengers to them with this reply: "I am carrying on a great project and cannot go down. Why should the work stop while I leave it and go down to you?" ⁴Four times they sent me the same message, and each time I gave them the same answer.

⁵Then, the fifth time, Sanballat sent his aide to me with the same message, and in his hand was an unsealed letter ⁶in which was written:

"It is reported among the nations—and Geshem^b says it is true—that you and the Jews^D are plotting to revolt, and therefore you are building the wall. Moreover, according to these reports you are about to become their king ⁷and have even appointed prophets^D to make this proclamation about you in Jerusalem^D: 'There is a king in Judah!' Now this report will get back to the king; so come, let us confer together."

⁸I sent him this reply: "Nothing like what you are saying is happening; you are just making it up out of your head."

⁹They were all trying to frighten us, thinking, "Their hands will get too weak for the work, and it will not be completed."

⌊But I prayed,⌋ "Now strengthen my hands."

¹⁰One day I went to the house of Shemaiah son of Delaiah, the son of Mehetabel, who was shut in at his home. He said, "Let us meet in the house of God, inside the temple, and let us close the temple doors, because men are coming to kill you—by night they are coming to kill you."

¹¹But I said, "Should a man like me run away? Or should one like me go into the temple to save his life? I will not go!" ¹²I realized that God had not sent him, but that he had prophesied against me because Tobiah and Sanballat had hired him. ¹³He had been hired to intimidate me so that I would commit a sin by doing this, and then they would give me a bad name to discredit me.

¹⁴Remember Tobiah and Sanballat, O my God, because of what they have done; remember also the prophetess Noadiah and the rest of the prophets who have been trying to intimidate me.

The Completion of the Wall

¹⁵So the wall was completed on the twenty-fifth of Elul, in fifty-two days. ¹⁶When all our enemies heard about this, all the surrounding nations were afraid and lost their self-confidence, because they realized that this work had been done with the help of our God.

Unsealed letter (6:5)

Official correspondence of the day was written on papyrus or leather parchment, tied and sealed with clay. This *unsealed letter* was clearly meant not only to menace Nehemiah but, as an open or public letter, to fuel rumors about Nehemiah's intentions.

Why was Shemaiah *shut in at his home*? (6:10)

This was apparently part of a complicated plot by Shemaiah, Tobiah and Sanballat to trap Nehemiah (v. 13). Shemaiah pretended to be hiding from danger in his house. We don't know to what extent he played this role, but it's possible he bolted the door and glanced secretly out the windows before warning Nehemiah they were both in danger and should flee to the temple.

Why would it be a sin to be intimidated? (6:13)

It could be that Shemaiah, who may have been a priest, tried to frighten Nehemiah and lure him into the temple where only priests were permitted to go. But the altar was known as a place of refuge for those threatened with execution (Exodus 21:14; 1 Kings 1:50–51; 2:28; 2 Kings 11:15). Most likely, Nehemiah's sin would have been to live in fear of threats rather than by trusting God. Had he yielded to Shemaiah's pressures, he would have lost the respect and support of the people who looked to him for leadership.

Who were these prophets? (6:14)

We know nothing at all of Noadiah the prophetess or who *the rest of the prophets* were. However, we can conclude that both political and religious pressures were brought to bear upon Nehemiah. While Nehemiah proclaimed God's intention was for the people to finish the walls, other religious leaders were saying just the opposite.

Why were surrounding nations afraid? (6:15–16)

The erection of the wall in such a short time was perceived as nothing short of a miracle. Neighboring nations recognized this unmistakable act of God as a sign that the Jews, far from being rejected, had God's special favor. Potential enemies realized they would have to deal with more than Judah's wall. They would have to deal with Judah's God. They may also have feared some sort of retaliation since they had been so antagonistic toward Judah. Their loss of confidence may have been an answer to Nehemiah's prayer in 4:4–5.

^a2 Or in Kephirim   ^b6 Hebrew *Gashmu*, a variant of *Geshem*

Why was Tobiah so opposed to the Jews? (6:17–18)

While Tobiah was well-connected to the Jews, his power and wealth were rooted in his leadership over the Ammonites. He also thrived because of his relationship with Sanballat and the Samaritans. He used his Jewish connections only to strengthen his position. He didn't mind the Jews living in the area, but neither did he want them becoming independently powerful. That would diminish his own strength.

What would be gained by registering all the people? (7:5)

God accomplished several things by bringing the people together: Leadership was shifted from city rulers to the traditional heads of family clans; key leaders were named to populate Jerusalem and restore its credibility as a capital city; impurity in the priesthood was cleaned out; a new national identity was established and funds were raised for the work. Ultimately, this census helped promote a great revival (chs. 8–10).

How does Nehemiah's list compare to the one found in Ezra? (7:6–73)

Of 153 numbers, 29 differ. Most of the discrepancies appear in the count of the laymen. Perhaps errors occurred in the process of copying subsequent manuscripts. Or the lists may have been made under slightly different circumstances: Ezra perhaps listed those who announced their intentions to return to Judah while Nehemiah may have listed those who actually arrived.

Mordecai (7:7)

It may be remotely possible that this Mordecai was Esther's cousin (Esther 2:5–7), but most think that this is a different man. See *Nehemiah . . . Mordecai* (Ezra 2:2).

17Also, in those days the nobles of Judah were sending many letters to Tobiah, and replies from Tobiah kept coming to them. **18**For many in Judah were under oath to him, since he was son-in-law to Shecaniah son of Arah, and his son Jehohanan had married the daughter of Meshullam son of Berekiah. **19**Moreover, they kept reporting to me his good deeds and then telling him what I said. And Tobiah sent letters to intimidate me.

7 After the wall had been rebuilt and I had set the doors in place, the gatekeepers and the singers and the Levites^D were appointed. **2**I put in charge of Jerusalem^D my brother Hanani, along with^a Hananiah the commander of the citadel^D, because he was a man of integrity and feared God more than most men do. **3**I said to them, "The gates of Jerusalem are not to be opened until the sun is hot. While the gatekeepers are still on duty, have them shut the doors and bar them. Also appoint residents of Jerusalem as guards, some at their posts and some near their own houses."

The List of the Exiles Who Returned

4Now the city was large and spacious, but there were few people in it, and the houses had not yet been rebuilt. **5**So my God put it into my heart to assemble the nobles, the officials and the common people for registration by families. I found the genealogical record of those who had been the first to return. This is what I found written there:

6These are the people of the province who came up from the captivity of the exiles^D whom Nebuchadnezzar king of Babylon had taken captive (they returned to Jerusalem and Judah, each to his own town, **7**in company with Zerubbabel, Jeshua, Nehemiah, Azariah, Raamiah, Nahamani, Mordecai, Bilshan, Mispereth, Bigvai, Nehum and Baanah):

The list of the men of Israel:

8the descendants of Parosh	2,172
9of Shephatiah	372
10of Arah	652
11of Pahath-Moab (through the line of Jeshua and Joab)	2,818
12of Elam	1,254
13of Zattu	845
14of Zaccai	760
15of Binnui	648
16of Bebai	628
17of Azgad	2,322
18of Adonikam	667
19of Bigvai	2,067
20of Adin	655
21of Ater (through Hezekiah)	98
22of Hashum	328
23of Bezai	324
24of Hariph	112
25of Gibeon	95
26the men of Bethlehem and Netophah	188
27of Anathoth	128
28of Beth Azmaveth	42
29of Kiriath Jearim, Kephirah and Beeroth	743
30of Ramah and Geba	621
31of Micmash	122

^a2 Or *Hanani, that is,*

³²of Bethel and Ai 123
³³of the other Nebo 52
³⁴of the other Elam 1,254
³⁵of Harim 320
³⁶of Jericho^D 345
³⁷of Lod, Hadid and Ono 721
³⁸of Senaah 3,930

³⁹The priests^D:

the descendants of Jedaiah (through the
family of Jeshua) 973
⁴⁰of Immer 1,052
⁴¹of Pashhur 1,247
⁴²of Harim 1,017

⁴³The Levites^D:

the descendants of Jeshua (through Kadmiel
through the line of Hodaviah) 74

⁴⁴The singers:

the descendants of Asaph 148

⁴⁵The gatekeepers:

the descendants of
Shallum, Ater, Talmon, Akkub, Hatita and
Shobai 138

⁴⁶The temple servants:

the descendants of
Ziha, Hasupha, Tabbaoth,
⁴⁷Keros, Sia, Padon,
⁴⁸Lebana, Hagaba, Shalmai,
⁴⁹Hanan, Giddel, Gahar,
⁵⁰Reaiah, Rezin, Nekoda,
⁵¹Gazzam, Uzza, Paseah,
⁵²Besai, Meunim, Nephussim,
⁵³Bakbuk, Hakupha, Harhur,
⁵⁴Bazluth, Mehida, Harsha,
⁵⁵Barkos, Sisera, Temah,
⁵⁶Neziah and Hatipha

⁵⁷The descendants of the servants of Solomon:

the descendants of
Sotai, Sophereth, Perida,
⁵⁸Jaala, Darkon, Giddel,
⁵⁹Shephatiah, Hattil,
Pokereth-Hazzebaim and Amon

⁶⁰The temple servants and the descendants of
the servants of Solomon 392

⁶¹The following came up from the towns of Tel Me-
lah, Tel Harsha, Kerub, Addon and Immer, but they
could not show that their families were descended
from Israel:

⁶²the descendants of
Delaiah, Tobiah and Nekoda 642

⁶³And from among the priests:

the descendants of
Hobaiah, Hakkoz and Barzillai (a man who had
married a daughter of Barzillai the Gileadite
and was called by that name).

⁶⁴These searched for their family records, but they

Why were these people identified as descendants of servants of Solomon? (7:57)

These people weren't likely descended simply
from Solomon's court servants. More likely this
refers to Canaanite people Solomon had
forced into slavery and who had eventually become part of the Israelite nation.

Why were these priests disqualified? (7:64)

See *Why couldn't those without family records
serve as priests?* (Ezra 2:62).

How would the Urim and Thummim allow them to eat the sacred food? (7:65)

The *Urim and Thummim,* used to discern the will of God, could determine which priests were acceptable to God. However, the Urim and Thummim had been lost for many years. Ancient Jewish writings indicate that the Jews believed the Urim and Thummim would be found and restored to use only after the Messiah had come.

Why don't the numbers in the list equal the total figure? (7:66)

Neither Nehemiah's total (31,089) nor Ezra's (29,818) match their stated total (42,360). The number of women may account for the difference, but that would mean three times as many men returned as women. Others suggest the difference represents the number of children under 12 or Jews from tribes other than Judah and Benjamin. Still others think errors in copying the text created the problem. Since both Ezra and Nehemiah use the same grand total, that number is presumed to be accurate. Also see *How can such large numbers be explained?* (1 Chron. 18:4–5); *How could only 12,000 Israelites annihilate a much larger tribe?* (Num. 31:49) and *Were there really 500,000 casualties among the Israelites?* (2 Chron. 13:17).

Did Ezra read the entire Law of Moses? (8:2–3)

The Law, the first five books of the Bible, was far too much for Ezra to read aloud in six hours or so. He read perhaps from Deuteronomy, Moses' own summary of the Law, or perhaps he read selected passages which he felt the people most needed to hear. Since this reading continued for seven or eight days (8:18), it may be that he did systematically read through the entire Law.

Why have such a marathon reading of the Book of the Law? (8:3)

The people apparently wanted this prolonged reading of the Scriptures. Only four or five days had passed since they had finished the walls, and they all shared a keen sense of being part of a miracle (6:16). Ezra had taught them the Law (Ezra 7:10), but finishing the walls seemed to galvanize a new interest among them to discover what God expected of them.

Why were so many Levites required to teach the people? (8:7)

There are at least three possibilities: (1) Ezra read from the original Hebrew, and the Levites translated into Aramaic, the language more familiar to Jews who had just returned from Babylon. (2) Ezra read a verse and paused to allow the Levites to explain it. (3) The Levites arranged themselves in a circle around Ezra to repeat in unison the phrases he read as a sort of public address system.

could not find them and so were excluded from the priesthood as unclean.^D ⁶⁵The governor, therefore, ordered them not to eat any of the most sacred^D food until there should be a priest^D ministering with the Urim^D and Thummim.^D

⁶⁶The whole company numbered 42,360, ⁶⁷besides their 7,337 menservants and maidservants; and they also had 245 men and women singers. ⁶⁸There were 736 horses, 245 mules,*a* ⁶⁹435 camels and 6,720 donkeys.

⁷⁰Some of the heads of the families contributed to the work. The governor gave to the treasury 1,000 drachmas*b* of gold, 50 bowls and 530 garments for priests. ⁷¹Some of the heads of the families gave to the treasury for the work 20,000 drachmas*c* of gold and 2,200 minas*d* of silver. ⁷²The total given by the rest of the people was 20,000 drachmas of gold, 2,000 minas*e* of silver and 67 garments for priests. ⁷³The priests, the Levites, the gatekeepers, the singers and the temple servants, along with certain of the people and the rest of the Israelites, settled in their own towns.

Ezra Reads the Law

When the seventh month came and the Israelites had settled in their towns, ¹all the people assembled as one man in the square before the Water Gate. They told Ezra the scribe to bring out the Book of the Law of Moses, which the LORD had commanded for Israel.

²So on the first day of the seventh month Ezra the priest brought the Law before the assembly, which was made up of men and women and all who were able to understand. ³He read it aloud from daybreak till noon as he faced the square before the Water Gate in the presence of the men, women and others who could understand. And all the people listened attentively to the Book of the Law.

⁴Ezra the scribe stood on a high wooden platform built for the occasion. Beside him on his right stood Mattithiah, Shema, Anaiah, Uriah, Hilkiah and Maaseiah; and on his left were Pedaiah, Mishael, Malkijah, Hashum, Hashbaddanah, Zechariah and Meshullam.

⁵Ezra opened the book. All the people could see him because he was standing above them; and as he opened it, the people all stood up. ⁶Ezra praised the LORD, the great God; and all the people lifted their hands and responded, "Amen! Amen!" Then they bowed down and worshiped the LORD with their faces to the ground.

⁷The Levites—Jeshua, Bani, Sherebiah, Jamin, Akkub, Shabbethai, Hodiah, Maaseiah, Kelita, Azariah, Jozabad, Hanan and Pelaiah—instructed the people in the Law while the people were standing there. ⁸They read from the Book of the Law of God, making it clear*f* and giving the meaning so that the people could understand what was being read.

⁹Then Nehemiah the governor, Ezra the priest and

---

*a68 Some Hebrew manuscripts (see also Ezra 2:66); most Hebrew manuscripts do not have this verse.   *b70 That is, about 19 pounds (about 8.5 kilograms)   *c71 That is, about 375 pounds (about 170 kilograms); also in verse 72   *d71 That is, about 1 1/3 tons (about 1.2 metric tons)   *e72 That is, about 1 1/4 tons (about 1.1 metric tons)   *f8 Or God, translating it*

scribe, and the Levites[D] who were instructing the people said to them all, "This day is sacred[D] to the LORD your God. Do not mourn or weep." For all the people had been weeping as they listened to the words of the Law.

[10]Nehemiah said, "Go and enjoy choice food and sweet drinks, and send some to those who have nothing prepared. This day is sacred to our Lord. Do not grieve, for the joy of the LORD is your strength."

[11]The Levites calmed all the people, saying, "Be still, for this is a sacred day. Do not grieve."

[12]Then all the people went away to eat and drink, to send portions of food and to celebrate with great joy, because they now understood the words that had been made known to them.

[13]On the second day of the month, the heads of all the families, along with the priests[D] and the Levites, gathered around Ezra the scribe to give attention to the words of the Law. [14]They found written in the Law, which the LORD had commanded through Moses, that the Israelites were to live in booths during the feast of the seventh month [15]and that they should proclaim this word and spread it throughout their towns and in Jerusalem[D]: "Go out into the hill country and bring back branches from olive and wild olive trees, and from myrtles, palms and shade trees, to make booths"—as it is written.[a]

[16]So the people went out and brought back branches and built themselves booths on their own roofs, in their courtyards, in the courts of the house of God and in the square by the Water Gate and the one by the Gate of Ephraim. [17]The whole company that had returned from exile[D] built booths and lived in them. From the days of Joshua son of Nun until that day, the Israelites had not celebrated it like this. And their joy was very great.

[18]Day after day, from the first day to the last, Ezra read from the Book of the Law of God. They celebrated the feast for seven days, and on the eighth day, in accordance with the regulation, there was an assembly.

The Israelites Confess Their Sins

9 On the twenty-fourth day of the same month, the Israelites gathered together, fasting and wearing sackcloth[D] and having dust on their heads. [2]Those of Israelite descent had separated themselves from all foreigners. They stood in their places and confessed their sins and the wickedness of their fathers. [3]They stood where they were and read from the Book of the Law of the LORD their God for a quarter of the day, and spent another quarter in confession and in worshiping the LORD their God. [4]Standing on the stairs were the Levites—Jeshua, Bani, Kadmiel, Shebaniah, Bunni, Sherebiah, Bani and Kenani—who called with loud voices to the LORD their God. [5]And the Levites—Jeshua, Kadmiel, Bani, Hashabneiah, Sherebiah, Hodiah, Shebaniah and Pethahiah—said: "Stand up and praise the LORD your God, who is from everlasting to everlasting.[b]"

"Blessed be your glorious name, and may it be exalted above all blessing and praise. [6]You alone are the LORD. You made the heavens, even the highest heavens, and all their starry host[D], the earth and all that is on it, the seas and all that is in them. You give life

Why were the people weeping? (8:9-11)

They were probably grief stricken to realize how they had failed God. They had not lived up to his holy expectations. But in a beautiful example of God's grace, their leaders exhorted them to stop weeping, not because they weren't sinful, but because *the joy of the LORD is your strength.* They could delight in the joy of the Lord because he is *a forgiving God, gracious and compassionate* (9:17).

Why had the Feast of Booths been so neglected through the years? (8:17)

Perhaps because it had lost its significance during their years in exile. The feast was to remind those in the promised land what it had been like to live in the desert. In captivity, however, the Jews couldn't celebrate the joy of living in their own land. Now they had come home and could once again celebrate. The ancient rabbis said, "He who has not seen Jerusalem during the Feast of Tabernacles [Booths] does not know what rejoicing means."

What was the purpose of this group prayer? (9:5-38)

After nearly a month of spiritual preparation, the Jews were ready to make a *binding agreement* before God (v. 38). This prayer was a summary of all the hours of Scriptural teaching they had received. It unflinchingly recounted their historic tendency to sin and God's tendency for mercy. This perspective was essential so they would not waver in their resolutions to serve God.

---

[a]15 See Lev. 23:37-40.   [b]5 Or *God for ever and ever*

Why does God swear with an *uplifted hand*? (9:15)

In his prayer, the speaker described God's actions or characteristics in distinctly human terms. The Lord used this expression about himself (Exodus 6:8) to show that his promise about the land was a formal vow, like a person raising his or her right hand to declare the solemn truth.

Stiff-necked (9:16)

Stubborn people unwilling to submit to God's will were often compared to stubborn oxen or other animals which refused to be led by their masters. Their "stiff necks" would not bend the way they were directed. It was also an expression which brought to mind rebellious children resisting the pull of a parent's hand. Also see Exodus 32:9; Deut. 10:16.

to everything, and the multitudes of heaven worship you.

7"You are the LORD God, who chose Abram and brought him out of Ur of the Chaldeans and named him Abraham. **8**You found his heart faithful to you, and you made a covenant[D] with him to give to his descendants the land of the Canaanites, Hittites, Amorites, Perizzites, Jebusites and Girgashites. You have kept your promise because you are righteous[D].

9"You saw the suffering of our forefathers in Egypt; you heard their cry at the Red Sea.[a] **10**You sent miraculous signs and wonders against Pharaoh, against all his officials and all the people of his land, for you knew how arrogantly the Egyptians treated them. You made a name for yourself, which remains to this day. **11**You divided the sea before them, so that they passed through it on dry ground, but you hurled their pursuers into the depths, like a stone into mighty waters. **12**By day you led them with a pillar of cloud, and by night with a pillar of fire to give them light on the way they were to take.

13"You came down on Mount Sinai; you spoke to them from heaven. You gave them regulations and laws that are just and right, and decrees and commands that are good. **14**You made known to them your holy Sabbath[D] and gave them commands, decrees and laws through your servant Moses. **15**In their hunger you gave them bread from heaven and in their thirst you brought them water from the rock; you told them to go in and take possession of the land you had sworn with uplifted hand to give them.

16"But they, our forefathers, became arrogant and stiff-necked, and did not obey your commands. **17**They refused to listen and failed to remember the miracles you performed among them. They became stiff-necked and in their rebellion appointed a leader in order to return to their slavery. But you are a forgiving God, gracious and compassionate, slow to anger and abounding in love. Therefore you did not desert them, **18**even when they cast for themselves an image of a calf and said, 'This is your god, who brought you up out of Egypt,' or when they committed awful blasphemies[D].

19"Because of your great compassion you did not abandon them in the desert. By day the pillar of cloud did not cease to guide them on their path, nor the pillar of fire by night to shine on the way they were to take. **20**You gave your good Spirit to instruct them. You did not withhold your manna[D] from their mouths, and you gave them water for their thirst. **21**For forty years you sustained them in the desert; they lacked nothing, their clothes did not wear out nor did their feet become swollen.

22"You gave them kingdoms and nations, allotting to them even the remotest frontiers. They took over the country of Sihon[b] king of Heshbon and the country of Og king of Bashan. **23**You made their sons as numerous as the stars in the sky, and you brought them into the land that you told their fathers to enter and possess. **24**Their sons went in and took posses-

---

a9 Hebrew *Yam Suph*; that is, Sea of Reeds   *b22* One Hebrew manuscript and Septuagint; most Hebrew manuscripts *Sihon, that is, the country of the*

sion of the land. You subdued before them the Canaanites, who lived in the land; you handed the Canaanites over to them, along with their kings and the peoples of the land, to deal with them as they pleased. 25They captured fortified cities and fertile land; they took possession of houses filled with all kinds of good things, wells already dug, vineyards, olive groves and fruit trees in abundance. They ate to the full and were well-nourished; they reveled in your great goodness.

26"But they were disobedient and rebelled against you; they put your law behind their backs. They killed your prophetsᴰ, who had admonished them in order to turn them back to you; they committed awful blasphemiesᴰ. 27So you handed them over to their enemies, who oppressed them. But when they were oppressed they cried out to you. From heaven you heard them, and in your great compassion you gave them deliverers, who rescued them from the hand of their enemies.

28"But as soon as they were at rest, they again did what was evil in your sight. Then you abandoned them to the hand of their enemies so that they ruled over them. And when they cried out to you again, you heard from heaven, and in your compassion you delivered them time after time.

29"You warned them to return to your law, but they became arrogant and disobeyed your commands. They sinned against your ordinances, by which a man will live if he obeys them. Stubbornly they turned their backs on you, became stiff-necked and refused to listen. 30For many years you were patient with them. By your Spirit you admonished them through your prophets. Yet they paid no attention, so you handed them over to the neighboring peoples. 31But in your great mercyᴰ you did not put an end to them or abandon them, for you are a gracious and merciful God.

32"Now therefore, O our God, the great, mighty and awesome God, who keeps his covenantᴰ of love, do not let all this hardship seem trifling in your eyes—the hardship that has come upon us, upon our kings and leaders, upon our priestsᴰ and prophets, upon our fathers and all your people, from the days of the kings of Assyria until today. 33In all that has happened to us, you have been just; you have acted faithfully, while we did wrong. 34Our kings, our leaders, our priests and our fathers did not follow your law; they did not pay attention to your commands or the warnings you gave them. 35Even while they were in their kingdom, enjoying your great goodness to them in the spacious and fertile land you gave them, they did not serve you or turn from their evil ways.

36"But see, we are slaves today, slaves in the land you gave our forefathers so they could eat its fruit and the other good things it produces. 37Because of our sins, its abundant harvest goes to the kings you have placed over us. They rule over our bodies and our cattle as they please. We are in great distress.

The Agreement of the People

38"In view of all this, we are making a binding agreement, putting it in writing, and our leaders, our Levitesᴰ and our priests are affixing their seals to it."

Put your law behind their backs (9:26)
We would say, "They turned their backs on your law." This phrase describes an act of defiant disobedience. See 1 Kings 14:9; Ezek. 23:35.

What were they binding themselves to? (9:38)
The *binding agreement* to which these leaders comitted themselves is given in 10:28–39. It was a solemn pledge to strictly obey God's law, keep the Sabbath, bring offerings necessary to maintain the temple and not to intermarry with their pagan neighbors. Sadly, they eventually broke each of these vows.

10 Those who sealed it were:

Nehemiah the governor, the son of Hacaliah.

Zedekiah, [2]Seraiah, Azariah, Jeremiah,
[3]Pashhur, Amariah, Malkijah,
[4]Hattush, Shebaniah, Malluch,
[5]Harim, Meremoth, Obadiah,
[6]Daniel, Ginnethon, Baruch,
[7]Meshullam, Abijah, Mijamin,
[8]Maaziah, Bilgai and Shemaiah.
These were the priests[D].

[9]The Levites[D]:

Jeshua son of Azaniah, Binnui of the sons of Henadad, Kadmiel,
[10]and their associates: Shebaniah,
  Hodiah, Kelita, Pelaiah, Hanan,
[11]Mica, Rehob, Hashabiah,
[12]Zaccur, Sherebiah, Shebaniah,
[13]Hodiah, Bani and Beninu.

[14]The leaders of the people:

Parosh, Pahath-Moab, Elam, Zattu, Bani,
[15]Bunni, Azgad, Bebai,
[16]Adonijah, Bigvai, Adin,
[17]Ater, Hezekiah, Azzur,
[18]Hodiah, Hashum, Bezai,
[19]Hariph, Anathoth, Nebai,
[20]Magpiash, Meshullam, Hezir,
[21]Meshezabel, Zadok, Jaddua,
[22]Pelatiah, Hanan, Anaiah,
[23]Hoshea, Hananiah, Hasshub,
[24]Hallohesh, Pilha, Shobek,
[25]Rehum, Hashabnah, Maaseiah,
[26]Ahiah, Hanan, Anan,
[27]Malluch, Harim and Baanah.

[28]"The rest of the people—priests, Levites, gatekeepers, singers, temple servants and all who separated themselves from the neighboring peoples for the sake of the Law of God, together with their wives and all their sons and daughters who are able to understand— [29]all these now join their brothers the nobles, and bind themselves with a curse and an oath to follow the Law of God given through Moses the servant of God and to obey carefully all the commands, regulations and decrees of the LORD our Lord.

[30]"We promise not to give our daughters in marriage to the peoples around us or take their daughters for our sons.

[31]"When the neighboring peoples bring merchandise or grain to sell on the Sabbath[D], we will not buy from them on the Sabbath or on any holy day. Every seventh year we will forgo working the land and will cancel all debts.

[32]"We assume the responsibility for carrying out the commands to give a third of a shekel[Da] each year for the service of the house of our God: [33]for the bread set out on the table; for the regular grain offerings[D] and burnt offerings[D]; for the offerings on the Sabbaths, New Moon festivals and appointed

Why would the people bind themselves with a curse and an oath? (10:29)
The oath signified a formal promise, a solemn agreement. With the curse they invited God's judgment on themselves if they did not keep their word.

SCRIPTURE LINK (10:30–31)
The promises made here were rooted in God's commands given earlier. See Exodus 20:8–11; Lev. 25:4; Deut. 5:12–15.

New Moon festivals (10:33)
See *New Moon festival* (1 Samuel 20:5).

---

a32 That is, about 1/8 ounce (about 4 grams)

feasts; for the holy offerings; for sin offerings[D] to make atonement[D] for Israel; and for all the duties of the house of our God.

34"We—the priests[D], the Levites[D] and the people—have cast lots to determine when each of our families is to bring to the house of our God at set times each year a contribution of wood to burn on the altar of the LORD our God, as it is written in the Law.

35"We also assume responsibility for bringing to the house of the LORD each year the firstfruits[D] of our crops and of every fruit tree.

36"As it is also written in the Law, we will bring the firstborn[D] of our sons and of our cattle, of our herds and of our flocks to the house of our God, to the priests ministering there.

37"Moreover, we will bring to the storerooms of the house of our God, to the priests, the first of our ground meal, of our ⌐grain⌐ offerings, of the fruit of all our trees and of our new wine[D] and oil. And we will bring a tithe[D] of our crops to the Levites, for it is the Levites who collect the tithes in all the towns where we work. **38**A priest descended from Aaron is to accompany the Levites when they receive the tithes, and the Levites are to bring a tenth of the tithes up to the house of our God, to the storerooms of the treasury. **39**The people of Israel, including the Levites, are to bring their contributions of grain, new wine and oil to the storerooms where the articles for the sanctuary are kept and where the ministering priests, the gatekeepers and the singers stay.

"We will not neglect the house of our God."

The New Residents of Jerusalem

11 Now the leaders of the people settled in Jerusalem[D], and the rest of the people cast lots to bring one out of every ten to live in Jerusalem, the holy city, while the remaining nine were to stay in their own towns. **2**The people commended all the men who volunteered to live in Jerusalem.

3These are the provincial leaders who settled in Jerusalem (now some Israelites, priests, Levites, temple servants and descendants of Solomon's servants lived in the towns of Judah, each on his own property in the various towns, **4**while other people from both Judah and Benjamin lived in Jerusalem):

From the descendants of Judah:

Athaiah son of Uzziah, the son of Zechariah, the son of Amariah, the son of Shephatiah, the son of Mahalalel, a descendant of Perez; **5**and Maaseiah son of Baruch, the son of Col-Hozeh, the son of Hazaiah, the son of Adaiah, the son of Joiarib, the son of Zechariah, a descendant of Shelah. **6**The descendants of Perez who lived in Jerusalem totaled 468 able men.

7From the descendants of Benjamin:

Sallu son of Meshullam, the son of Joed, the son of Pedaiah, the son of Kolaiah, the son of Maaseiah, the son of Ithiel, the son of Jeshaiah, **8**and his followers, Gabbai and Sallai—928 men. **9**Joel son of Zicri was their chief officer, and Judah son of Hassenuah was over the Second District of the city.

Cast lots (10:34)
See *How can God work through such an arbitrary process?* (Prov. 18:18).

Why did they bring firstborn sons to the priests? (10:36)
God wanted his people to make him their top priority. They needed to remember that everything, including themselves, belonged to God. To symbolize this fact, the law required that firstborns be brought to God (Exodus 22:29–30; 34:19). People brought the firstborn animals to the priests to be sacrificed. Parents offered these sacrifices in place of their firstborn sons and then took their sons home to raise. This law reminded them of how God had spared Israel's firstborn sons during the Passover in Egypt (Exodus 13:14–16).

Why did they have to draft "volunteers" to live in Jerusalem? (11:1–2)
Seldom do people enjoy moving into insecure situations. So the leaders took extra measures to ensure that Jerusalem would be re-populated. If the city was to regain its influence and the ability to defend itself, it had to thrive. It's estimated this recruitment effort left Jerusalem with a population of 5,000 to 8,000. A total of 3,044 men are mentioned in vv. 4–18. The ancient Jewish historian Josephus said Nehemiah "prepared houses for them at his own expense," though this can't be verified.

Does this list tell us anything we need to know? (11:3–19)
These names may not seem significant to us, but it's helpful to remember that most were chosen by lot. This meant they were selected, not by blind luck, but by divine appointment. God brought a very particular blend of people into his *holy city,* a mix of both personalities and roles—just as he does in churches and organizations today. The lessons from this list come more by example and implication than specific principle. See article: *What can we learn from this building project?* (3:1–32).

¹⁰From the priests[D]:

Jedaiah; the son of Joiarib; Jakin; ¹¹Seraiah son of Hilkiah, the son of Meshullam, the son of Zadok, the son of Meraioth, the son of Ahitub, supervisor in the house of God, ¹²and their associates, who carried on work for the temple—822 men; Adaiah son of Jeroham, the son of Pelaliah, the son of Amzi, the son of Zechariah, the son of Pashhur, the son of Malkijah, ¹³and his associates, who were heads of families— 242 men; Amashsai son of Azarel, the son of Ahzai, the son of Meshillemoth, the son of Immer, ¹⁴and his[a] associates, who were able men—128. Their chief officer was Zabdiel son of Haggedolim.

¹⁵From the Levites[D]:

Shemaiah son of Hasshub, the son of Azrikam, the son of Hashabiah, the son of Bunni; ¹⁶Shabbethai and Jozabad, two of the heads of the Levites, who had charge of the outside work of the house of God; ¹⁷Mattaniah son of Mica, the son of Zabdi, the son of Asaph, the director who led in thanksgiving and prayer; Bakbukiah, second among his associates; and Abda son of Shammua, the son of Galal, the son of Jeduthun. ¹⁸The Levites in the holy city totaled 284.

¹⁹The gatekeepers:

Akkub, Talmon and their associates, who kept watch at the gates—172 men.

²⁰The rest of the Israelites, with the priests and Levites, were in all the towns of Judah, each on his ancestral property.

²¹The temple servants lived on the hill of Ophel, and Ziha and Gishpa were in charge of them.

²²The chief officer of the Levites in Jerusalem was Uzzi son of Bani, the son of Hashabiah, the son of Mattaniah, the son of Mica. Uzzi was one of Asaph's descendants, who were the singers responsible for the service of the house of God. ²³The singers were under the king's orders, which regulated their daily activity.

²⁴Pethahiah son of Meshezabel, one of the descendants of Zerah son of Judah, was the king's agent in all affairs relating to the people.

²⁵As for the villages with their fields, some of the people of Judah lived in Kiriath Arba and its surrounding settlements, in Dibon and its settlements, in Jekabzeel and its villages, ²⁶in Jeshua, in Moladah, in Beth Pelet, ²⁷in Hazar Shual, in Beersheba and its settlements, ²⁸in Ziklag, in Meconah and its settlements, ²⁹in En Rimmon, in Zorah, in Jarmuth, ³⁰Zanoah, Adullam and their villages, in Lachish and its fields, and in Azekah and its settlements. So they were living all the way from Beersheba to the Valley of Hinnom.

³¹The descendants of the Benjamites from Geba lived in Micmash, Aija, Bethel and its settlements, ³²in Anathoth, Nob and Ananiah, ³³in Hazor, Ramah and Gittaim, ³⁴in Hadid, Zeboim and Neballat, ³⁵in Lod and Ono, and in the Valley of the Craftsmen.

³⁶Some of the divisions of the Levites of Judah settled in Benjamin.

Why did the king of Persia regulate the temple singers? (11:23)
Unlike kings of other empires who sought to scatter and/or assimilate conquered peoples, the king of Persia had a political interest in preserving the religious life of those under his rule. This would help him maintain peace throughout his kingdom. *The king's orders* in this case directed the Jews to follow their religious practices. This phrase may also imply that the king funded the support of these singers. See article: *Why build a temple for a God you don't worship?* (Ezra 1:1–2).

ᵃ14 Most Septuagint manuscripts; Hebrew *their*

Priests and Levites

12 These were the priests[D] and Levites[D] who returned with Zerubbabel son of Shealtiel and with
Jeshua:

Seraiah, Jeremiah, Ezra,
[2]Amariah, Malluch, Hattush,
[3]Shecaniah, Rehum, Meremoth,
[4]Iddo, Ginnethon,[a] Abijah,
[5]Mijamin,[b] Moadiah, Bilgah,
[6]Shemaiah, Joiarib, Jedaiah,
[7]Sallu, Amok, Hilkiah and Jedaiah.

These were the leaders of the priests and their associates in the days of Jeshua.

[8]The Levites were Jeshua, Binnui, Kadmiel, Sherebiah, Judah, and also Mattaniah, who, together with his associates, was in charge of the songs of thanksgiving. [9]Bak-
bukiah and Unni, their associates, stood opposite them in
the services.

[10]Jeshua was the father of Joiakim, Joiakim the father of
Eliashib, Eliashib the father of Joiada, [11]Joiada the father
of Jonathan, and Jonathan the father of Jaddua.

[12]In the days of Joiakim, these were the heads of the
priestly families:

of Seraiah's family, Meraiah;
of Jeremiah's, Hananiah;
[13]of Ezra's, Meshullam;
of Amariah's, Jehohanan;
[14]of Malluch's, Jonathan;
of Shecaniah's,[c] Joseph;
[15]of Harim's, Adna;
of Meremoth's,[d] Helkai;
[16]of Iddo's, Zechariah;
of Ginnethon's, Meshullam;
[17]of Abijah's, Zicri;
of Miniamin's and of Moadiah's, Piltai;
[18]of Bilgah's, Shammua;
of Shemaiah's, Jehonathan;
[19]of Joiarib's, Mattenai;
of Jedaiah's, Uzzi;
[20]of Sallu's, Kallai;
of Amok's, Eber;
[21]of Hilkiah's, Hashabiah;
of Jedaiah's, Nethanel.

[22]The family heads of the Levites in the days of Eliashib, Joiada, Johanan and Jaddua, as well as those of the
priests, were recorded in the reign of Darius the Persian. [23]The family heads among the descendants of Levi
up to the time of Johanan son of Eliashib were recorded
in the book of the annals. [24]And the leaders of the Levites were Hashabiah, Sherebiah, Jeshua son of Kadmiel, and their associates, who stood opposite them to give
praise and thanksgiving, one section responding to the
other, as prescribed by David the man of God.

[25]Mattaniah, Bakbukiah, Obadiah, Meshullam, Talmon
and Akkub were gatekeepers who guarded the storerooms at the gates. [26]They served in the days of Joiakim

Why was it important to list all these names? (12:1)

Nehemiah was not just leading a rebuilding expedition; he was attempting to lead the people
in following the Lord. The priests and Levites
were Israel's direct link to God, and Nehemiah
wanted to be sure the people remembered
they had priests and Levites to minister for
them.

Darius the Persian (12:22)

This was either Darius III Codomannus
(336–331 B.C.) or Darius II Nothus (423–
404 B.C.).

---

[a]4 Many Hebrew manuscripts and Vulgate (see also Neh. 12:16); most
Hebrew manuscripts *Ginnethoi*   [b]5 A variant of *Miniamin*
[c]14 Very many Hebrew manuscripts, some Septuagint manuscripts and
Syriac (see also Neh. 12:3); most Hebrew manuscripts *Shebaniah's*
[d]15 Some Septuagint manuscripts (see also Neh. 12:3); Hebrew
Meraioth's

son of Jeshua, the son of Jozadak, and in the days of Nehemiah the governor and of Ezra the priest[D] and scribe.

What can we learn from the details of this dedication ceremony? (12:27–43)

When we work with God on any great endeavor, we're not done until we celebrate and dedicate that work. Celebration involves the entire congregation and takes full advantage of music and ceremony to heighten the sense of joy and worship. Dedication reminds us of our dependence on God and invites him to guard the work accomplished by his help. Such a time often marks a fresh beginning for God's people —with a renewed sense of purpose, identity, worth and the security of his care.

Why did the singers settle together in villages? (12:29)

The singers all worked at the temple in Jerusalem, so it was natural that they would want to live near their work. Furthermore, since the singers were from the tribe of Levi, it was also expected that they would live in the same community—just as the people of other tribes often did.

How did the priests and Levites purify themselves? (12:30)

While it's not exactly clear what they did, purification rites typically included fasting, sexual abstinence and the washing of garments. Such outward acts alone would not be sufficient to purify anyone. But they were expected to be accompanied by inward acts of self-examination, repentance and recommitment to God.

Dedication of the Wall of Jerusalem

27At the dedication of the wall of Jerusalem[D], the Levites[D] were sought out from where they lived and were brought to Jerusalem to celebrate joyfully the dedication with songs of thanksgiving and with the music of cymbals, harps and lyres[D]. **28**The singers also were brought together from the region around Jerusalem— from the villages of the Netophathites, **29**from Beth Gilgal, and from the area of Geba and Azmaveth, for the singers had built villages for themselves around Jerusalem. **30**When the priests and Levites had purified themselves ceremonially, they purified the people, the gates and the wall.

31I had the leaders of Judah go up on top[a] of the wall. I also assigned two large choirs to give thanks. One was to proceed on top[b] of the wall to the right, toward the Dung Gate. **32**Hoshaiah and half the leaders of Judah followed them, **33**along with Azariah, Ezra, Meshullam, **34**Judah, Benjamin, Shemaiah, Jeremiah, **35**as well as some priests with trumpets, and also Zechariah son of Jonathan, the son of Shemaiah, the son of Mattaniah, the son of Micaiah, the son of Zaccur, the son of Asaph, **36**and his associates—Shemaiah, Azarel, Milalai, Gilalai, Maai, Nethanel, Judah and Hanani—with musical instruments prescribed by, David the man of God. Ezra the scribe led the procession. **37**At the Fountain Gate they continued directly up the steps of the City of David on the ascent to the wall and passed above the house of David to the Water Gate on the east.

38The second choir proceeded in the opposite direction. I followed them on top[c] of the wall, together with half the people—past the Tower of the Ovens to the Broad Wall, **39**over the Gate of Ephraim, the Jeshanah[d] Gate, the Fish Gate, the Tower of Hananel and the Tower of the Hundred, as far as the Sheep Gate. At the Gate of the Guard they stopped.

40The two choirs that gave thanks then took their places in the house of God; so did I, together with half the officials, **41**as well as the priests—Eliakim, Maaseiah, Miniamin, Micaiah, Elioenai, Zechariah and Hananiah with their trumpets— **42**and also Maaseiah, Shemaiah, Eleazar, Uzzi, Jehohanan, Malkijah, Elam and Ezer. The choirs sang under the direction of Jezrahiah. **43**And on that day they offered great sacrifices[D], rejoicing because God had given them great joy. The women and children also rejoiced. The sound of rejoicing in Jerusalem could be heard far away.

44At that time men were appointed to be in charge of the storerooms for the contributions, firstfruits[D] and tithes[D]. From the fields around the towns they were to bring into the storerooms the portions required by the Law for the priests and the Levites, for Judah was pleased with the ministering priests and Levites. **45**They performed the service of their God and the service of purification, as did also the singers and gatekeepers, according to the commands of David and his son Solomon. **46**For long ago, in the days of David and Asaph, there had been directors for the singers and for the songs

a 31 Or go alongside   b 31 Or proceed alongside   c 38 Or them alongside   d 39 Or Old

of praise and thanksgiving to God. **47**So in the days of Zerubbabel and of Nehemiah, all Israel contributed the daily portions for the singers and gatekeepers. They also set aside the portion for the other Levites^D, and the Levites set aside the portion for the descendants of Aaron.

Nehemiah's Final Reforms

13 On that day the Book of Moses was read aloud in the hearing of the people and there it was found written that no Ammonite or Moabite should ever be admitted into the assembly of God, **2**because they had not met the Israelites with food and water but had hired Balaam to call a curse down on them. (Our God, however, turned the curse into a blessing.) **3**When the people heard this law, they excluded from Israel all who were of foreign descent.

4Before this, Eliashib the priest^D had been put in charge of the storerooms of the house of our God. He was closely associated with Tobiah, **5**and he had provided him with a large room formerly used to store the grain offerings^D and incense^D and temple articles, and also the tithes^D of grain, new wine^D and oil prescribed for the Levites, singers and gatekeepers, as well as the contributions for the priests.

6But while all this was going on, I was not in Jerusalem^D, for in the thirty-second year of Artaxerxes king of Babylon I had returned to the king. Some time later I asked his permission **7**and came back to Jerusalem. Here I learned about the evil thing Eliashib had done in providing Tobiah a room in the courts of the house of God. **8**I was greatly displeased and threw all Tobiah's household goods out of the room. **9**I gave orders to purify^D the rooms, and then I put back into them the equipment of the house of God, with the grain offerings and the incense.

The Book of Moses (13:1)

The book of Deuteronomy (see Joshua 23:3–6).

Why offer a room in the temple for Tobiah the Ammonite? (13:4–5)

Tobiah remained well-connected in Jerusalem despite Nehemiah's strong feelings against him (6:17–19). When Nehemiah returned to Persia, Tobiah apparently used his influence over various nobles who owed him favors. He wheedled his way, not just back into Jerusalem, but into a large apartment in the very temple of God! Eliashib, the high priest (see v. 28), was obviously part of this conspiracy and may also have been related to Tobiah by marriage.

Why exclude outsiders? (13:1-3)

The Bible is filled with stern warnings about outsiders. This was not bigotry, but caution. God recognized that human weakness would draw his people toward the sinful behavior of others more than they would draw others to righteousness. Old Testament history bears this out: God's people frequently fell into compromise with the world around them.

God's plan, by contrast, was to choose a people for himself and set them apart in order to reach outsiders. He wanted his people to demonstrate to others the benefits of righteousness and fellowship with God. He wanted their example to attract neighboring nations to the Lord. The great acts of God have been for all the nations, not just Israel —his covenant with Abraham (Gen. 12:2–3), the building of the temple (2 Chron. 6:32–33) and the promise of the Messiah (Isaiah 11:10–11).

Of course, God's love for the world is spelled out in even more detail in the New Testament (John 3:16), including the command to believers to *go and make disciples of all nations* (Matt. 28:19). God promises that heaven will be filled with the redeemed *from every tribe and language and people and nation* (Rev. 5:9–10).

God still expects us to be wary of compromise in our relationships with unsaved people (2 Cor. 6:14–18). But while he wants us to maintain spiritual integrity and holiness, he also wants us to be in contact with "outsiders," so we can draw them to the Savior of the world.

What happened to the earlier vows to care for the temple? (13:10)

Although the people had promised passionately to support and maintain the temple (10:32–33), in time they gradually forgot their good intentions. Apparently the leaders during Nehemiah's absence lacked either the will or the ability to constantly challenge the Jews to faithful stewardship. After a while, the people and the Levites had become more interested in establishing comfortable lifestyles for themselves than in providing for God's house.

Why did Nehemiah ask God to remember him? (13:14,22)

The original word for *remember* implies not only that God should recall what Nehemiah had done, but that he should intervene on his behalf. Nehemiah was not demanding repayment for his good works, but he did make a humble plea for God's mercy in light of his faithful and self-sacrificing service. Just like Christians today, Nehemiah longed to one day hear God say, *Well done, good and faithful servant! . . . Come and share your master's happiness!* (Matt. 25:21).

Why would a good leader treat people this way? (13:25–28)

It is easy to misinterpret Nehemiah's actions as some sort of back-alley brawl. The word *rebuked* implies not only strong words but a strong argument against the behavior of these men. When they dedicated the walls, the people themselves had invited curses to come upon them if they became disobedient (10:29). This beating was probably not life-threatening so much as attention-getting.

How did foreign women cause Solomon to sin? (13:26)

In disobedience to God, Solomon had initially used marriages with foreign princesses as a way of strengthening political alliances. But in time he married literally hundreds of foreign wives who enticed him to build altars and idols so they could worship as they had in their own lands. Eventually he even joined his wives in worshiping those foreign gods. For a summary of the sordid result, see *What was Solomon's real problem?* (1 Kings 11:1–4).

10I also learned that the portions assigned to the Levites had not been given to them, and that all the Levites and singers responsible for the service had gone back to their own fields. **11**So I rebuked the officials and asked them, "Why is the house of God neglected?" Then I called them together and stationed them at their posts.

12All Judah brought the tithes of grain, new wine and oil into the storerooms. **13**I put Shelemiah the priest, Zadok the scribe, and a Levite named Pedaiah in charge of the storerooms and made Hanan son of Zaccur, the son of Mattaniah, their assistant, because these men were considered trustworthy. They were made responsible for distributing the supplies to their brothers.

14Remember me for this, O my God, and do not blot out what I have so faithfully done for the house of my God and its services.

15In those days I saw men in Judah treading winepresses^D on the Sabbath^D and bringing in grain and loading it on donkeys, together with wine, grapes, figs and all other kinds of loads. And they were bringing all this into Jerusalem on the Sabbath. Therefore I warned them against selling food on that day. **16**Men from Tyre who lived in Jerusalem were bringing in fish and all kinds of merchandise and selling them in Jerusalem on the Sabbath to the people of Judah. **17**I rebuked the nobles of Judah and said to them, "What is this wicked thing you are doing—desecrating^D the Sabbath day? **18**Didn't your forefathers do the same things, so that our God brought all this calamity upon us and upon this city? Now you are stirring up more wrath against Israel by desecrating^D the Sabbath^D."

19When evening shadows fell on the gates of Jerusalem^D before the Sabbath, I ordered the doors to be shut and not opened until the Sabbath was over. I stationed some of my own men at the gates so that no load could be brought in on the Sabbath day. **20**Once or twice the merchants and sellers of all kinds of goods spent the night outside Jerusalem. **21**But I warned them and said, "Why do you spend the night by the wall? If you do this again, I will lay hands on you." From that time on they no longer came on the Sabbath. **22**Then I commanded the Levites^D to purify^D themselves and go and guard the gates in order to keep the Sabbath day holy.

Remember me for this also, O my God, and show mercy^D to me according to your great love.

23Moreover, in those days I saw men of Judah who had married women from Ashdod, Ammon and Moab. **24**Half of their children spoke the language of Ashdod or the language of one of the other peoples, and did not know how to speak the language of Judah. **25**I rebuked them and called curses down on them. I beat some of the men and pulled out their hair. I made them take an oath in God's name and said: "You are not to give your daughters in marriage to their sons, nor are you to take their daughters in marriage for your sons or for yourselves. **26**Was it not because of marriages like these that Solomon king of Israel sinned? Among the many nations there was no king like him. He was loved by his God, and God made him king over all Israel, but even he was led into sin by foreign women. **27**Must we hear now that you too are doing all this terrible wickedness and are being unfaithful to our God by marrying foreign women?"

²⁸One of the sons of Joiada son of Eliashib the high priest^D was son-in-law to Sanballat the Horonite. And I drove him away from me.

²⁹Remember them, O my God, because they defiled the priestly office and the covenant^D of the priesthood and of the Levites.

³⁰So I purified the priests and the Levites of everything foreign, and assigned them duties, each to his own task. ³¹I also made provision for contributions of wood at designated times, and for the firstfruits^D.

Remember me with favor, O my God.

Why did Nehemiah drive the high priest's grandson away? (13:28)

It was a sin for any Jew to marry an outsider. But it was even more serious an offense for a high priest, since marriage restrictions for high priests were quite stringent (Lev. 21:14). Since a high priest's son could eventually become high priest, this man's sin removed him from consideration for the position. To make matters worse, he had married the daughter of Sanballat, Nehemiah's enemy. This marriage could have given Sanballat direct access to the highest office in Judaism. This man had demonstrated, by unlawfully marrying a foreigner, that he was unfit for spiritual leadership.

ESTHER

Why read this book?

Have you ever wondered if God is really involved in the circumstances of your life? If so, you may wonder why life is such a struggle. The book of Esther, like much of the Bible, tells the story of God's involvement with his people. Unlike the rest of the Bible, however, this book shows God's work indirectly. In fact, God's name is not mentioned once, though his influence permeates the narrative. The book demonstrates how God works in the lives of his people, both then and now.

Who wrote this book?

The author is unknown, but it is clear, from the tone and details throughout, that the author is a devout Jew. Possibly Mordecai, Ezra or Nehemiah wrote it.

Why was it written?

As a history, to record the events leading to the establishment of the Jewish observance of Purim (9:24–32), and as a way to assure the Jews of God's protection.

When and where was it written?

In Persia, sometime between 460 and 350 B.C. Esther became queen in 479 B.C.

What to look for in Esther:

A revealing of God's character, his faithfulness and how he provides for those who trust him, even through events most of us would see as tragic. Notice the indirect allusions to God's involvement in the life of his people (4:14,16).

When did these things happen?

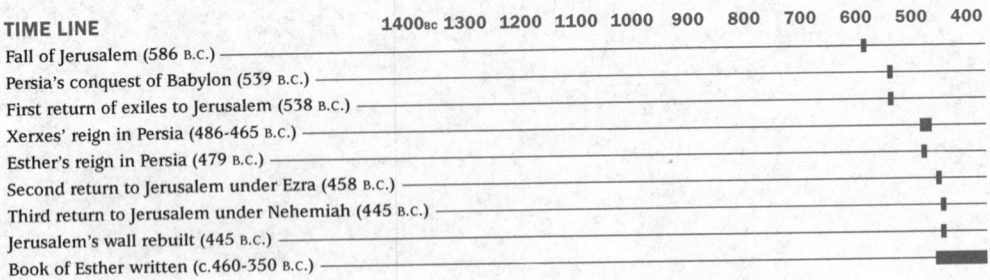

TIME LINE	1400bc 1300 1200 1100 1000 900 800 700 600 500 400
Fall of Jerusalem (586 B.C.)	
Persia's conquest of Babylon (539 B.C.)	
First return of exiles to Jerusalem (538 B.C.)	
Xerxes' reign in Persia (486-465 B.C.)	
Esther's reign in Persia (479 B.C.)	
Second return to Jerusalem under Ezra (458 B.C.)	
Third return to Jerusalem under Nehemiah (445 B.C.)	
Jerusalem's wall rebuilt (445 B.C.)	
Book of Esther written (c.460-350 B.C.)	

Queen Vashti Deposed

1 This is what happened during the time of Xerxes,[a] the Xerxes who ruled over 127 provinces stretching from India to Cush[b]: ²At that time King Xerxes reigned from his royal throne in the citadel[D] of Susa, ³and in the third year of his reign he gave a banquet for all his nobles and officials. The military leaders of Persia and Media, the princes, and the nobles of the provinces were present.

⁴For a full 180 days he displayed the vast wealth of his kingdom and the splendor and glory[D] of his majesty. ⁵When these days were over, the king gave a banquet, lasting seven days, in the enclosed garden of the king's palace, for all the people from the least to the greatest, who were in the citadel of Susa. ⁶The garden had hangings of white and blue linen, fastened with cords of white linen and purple[D] material to silver rings on marble pillars. There were couches of gold and silver on a mosaic pavement of porphyry, marble, mother-of-pearl and other costly stones. ⁷Wine was served in goblets of gold, each one different from the other, and the royal wine was abundant, in keeping with the king's liberality. ⁸By the king's command each guest was allowed to drink in his own way, for the king instructed all the wine stewards to serve each man what he wished.

⁹Queen Vashti also gave a banquet for the women in the royal palace of King Xerxes.

¹⁰On the seventh day, when King Xerxes was in high spirits from wine, he commanded the seven eunuchs[D] who served him—Mehuman, Biztha, Harbona, Bigtha, Abagtha, Zethar and Carcas— ¹¹to bring before him Queen Vashti, wearing her royal crown, in order to display her beauty to the people and nobles, for she was lovely to look at. ¹²But when the attendants delivered the king's command, Queen Vashti refused to come. Then the king became furious and burned with anger.

¹³Since it was customary for the king to consult experts in matters of law and justice, he spoke with the wise men who understood the times ¹⁴and were closest to the king—Carshena, Shethar, Admatha, Tarshish, Meres, Marsena and Memucan, the seven nobles of Persia and Media who had special access to the king and were highest in the kingdom.

¹⁵"According to law, what must be done to Queen Vashti?" he asked. "She has not obeyed the command of King Xerxes that the eunuchs have taken to her."

¹⁶Then Memucan replied in the presence of the king and the nobles, "Queen Vashti has done wrong, not only against the king but also against all the nobles and the peoples of all the provinces of King Xerxes. ¹⁷For the queen's conduct will become known to all the women, and so they will despise their husbands and say, 'King Xerxes commanded Queen Vashti to be brought before him, but she would not come.' ¹⁸This very day the Persian and Median women of the nobility who have heard about the queen's conduct will respond to all the king's nobles in the same way. There will be no end of disrespect and discord.

¹⁹"Therefore, if it pleases the king, let him issue a royal decree and let it be written in the laws of Persia and Media, which cannot be repealed, that Vashti is never again

---

[a]1 Hebrew *Ahasuerus*, a variant of Xerxes' Persian name; here and throughout Esther   [b]1 That is, the upper Nile region

Xerxes (1:1)

Xerxes is Greek for "Ahasuerus," which in turn is Hebrew for his Persian name, Khshayar-shan. Xerxes ruled the Persian empire from 485 to 465 B.C. This vast realm (1:1) was the dominant military and economic power of its time. Xerxes was the son and successor of Darius I, whose reign (521–486 B.C.) saw the restoration of the Jerusalem temple in 516 B.C. (Ezra 5–6).

Setting of Esther (1:1)

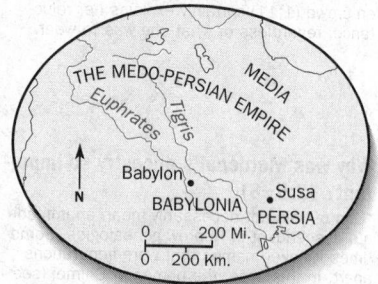

Where is Susa? (1:2)

The mounds of ruins that were once the city of Susa are located about 150 miles north of the Persian Gulf in southwestern Iran—an area known today as Khuzistan.

What kind of "display" would go on for six months? (1:4–5)

Xerxes spent the early days of his reign suppressing revolts in Egypt and Babylon. This display of his acquired wealth (see Daniel 11:2) was probably part of a victory celebration. Its length would have given Xerxes opportunity to reward his military commanders for service and to plan future campaigns. This display of wealth would also have served to impress friend and foe alike. The seven-day banquet was probably the culmination of the celebration.

What did it mean to *drink in his own way*? (1:8)

According to Persian law, guests at the king's table could drink only when he drank. Xerxes set aside that law, giving permission for his guests to drink as much as they liked. This indicates both the extravagance and the revelry of Xerxes' banquet.

Why was there a separate banquet for women? (1:9)

It doesn't appear that such segregation was the norm in Persia. Perhaps the atmosphere at the king's banquet, which involved serious drinking (see previous note), was deemed too vulgar for the presence of noblewomen. In any case, this verse makes it clear that Vashti was not at Xerxes' banquet, setting the stage for his summons (1:11) and her subsequent refusal (1:12).

Had the king's top aides been castrated? (1:10–12)

It is not clear. The Hebrew word translated here as "eunuch" can mean either an officer or a castrated male or both. Since these men had access to the king's harem, they may have

been castrated to protect the king's interests, but the title may also reflect their close relationship to the king.

Why did Queen Vashti refuse the king's summons? (1:12)

Considering the importance of the occasion and her position, she may have had a political motive. Or she may have anticipated an unpleasant situation. According to Jewish historians, Vashti was to appear wearing *only* her crown. The prospect of being ogled by a drunken crowd (1:11) certainly explains her reluctance, regardless of what she was to wear.

Why was Mordecai's ancestry so important? (2:5–6)

"Son of" did not necessarily mean an immediate descendant in Hebrew genealogies. Sometimes it linked names that were generations apart. In this case, the names of Shimei (see 2 Samuel 16:5–14) and Kish (see 1 Samuel 9:1) established Mordecai's kinship with the tribe and family of King Saul. This was significant to the conflict between Mordecai and Haman, who was a descendant of Agag—an ancient enemy of Saul and Israel. See *Agagite* (3:1).

Why did Esther have two names? (2:7)

Hadassah (meaning *myrtle*) was her Hebrew name; Esther was her Persian name. Some think her Persian name may have been related to the Persian *stara* (meaning *star*) or to *Ishtar,* the Babylonian goddess of love and fertility. Many Hebrew exiles had two such names, including Daniel (Daniel 1:7). In concealing her *nationality and family background* (2:10), Esther would also have kept her Hebrew name secret. It makes sense that the author would use her Persian name since this was how she would have been known, even among the Jews.

Did the girls selected for the harem have any choice in the matter? (2:8)

Probably not. This decree demonstrated the prevailing attitudes toward women in ancient Persia. By abducting young virgins from all over the empire, Xerxes issued a painful reminder to all his subjects about the "proper" behavior of women—and the supremacy of his own will.

Why did Mordecai forbid Esther to mention her nationality? (2:10)

Mordecai was aware that Esther's ethnic background could put her at a disadvantage, even in danger, because of potential anti-Jewish sentiment in the palace. The existence of this hostility throughout the empire is demonstrated by the large numbers of enemies slain by the Jews in ch. 9.

What was a Jewish girl doing in a harem? (2:12–16)

It appears that she had no choice in the matter. In keeping with the royal edict, she was simply *taken to the king's palace* (2:8) along with the other virgins to await Xerxes' call for sexual favors. She made such an impression on the king, however, that she became more than a member of the harem and was named queen.

to enter the presence of King Xerxes. Also let the king give her royal position to someone else who is better than she. ²⁰Then when the king's edict[D] is proclaimed throughout all his vast realm, all the women will respect their husbands, from the least to the greatest."

²¹The king and his nobles were pleased with this advice, so the king did as Memucan proposed. ²²He sent dispatches to all parts of the kingdom, to each province in its own script and to each people in its own language, proclaiming in each people's tongue that every man should be ruler over his own household.

Esther Made Queen

2 Later when the anger of King Xerxes had subsided, he remembered Vashti and what she had done and what he had decreed about her. ²Then the king's personal attendants proposed, "Let a search be made for beautiful young virgins for the king. ³Let the king appoint commissioners in every province of his realm to bring all these beautiful girls into the harem at the citadel[D] of Susa. Let them be placed under the care of Hegai, the king's eunuch[D], who is in charge of the women; and let beauty treatments be given to them. ⁴Then let the girl who pleases the king be queen instead of Vashti." This advice appealed to the king, and he followed it.

⁵Now there was in the citadel of Susa a Jew of the tribe of Benjamin, named Mordecai son of Jair, the son of Shimei, the son of Kish, ⁶who had been carried into exile[D] from Jerusalem[D] by Nebuchadnezzar king of Babylon, among those taken captive with Jehoiachin[a] king of Judah. ⁷Mordecai had a cousin named Hadassah, whom he had brought up because she had neither father nor mother. This girl, who was also known as Esther, was lovely in form and features, and Mordecai had taken her as his own daughter when her father and mother died.

⁸When the king's order and edict had been proclaimed, many girls were brought to the citadel of Susa and put under the care of Hegai. Esther also was taken to the king's palace and entrusted to Hegai, who had charge of the harem. ⁹The girl pleased him and won his favor. Immediately he provided her with her beauty treatments and special food. He assigned to her seven maids selected from the king's palace and moved her and her maids into the best place in the harem.

¹⁰Esther had not revealed her nationality and family background, because Mordecai had forbidden her to do so. ¹¹Every day he walked back and forth near the courtyard of the harem to find out how Esther was and what was happening to her.

¹²Before a girl's turn came to go in to King Xerxes, she had to complete twelve months of beauty treatments prescribed for the women, six months with oil of myrrh[D] and six with perfumes and cosmetics. ¹³And this is how she would go to the king: Anything she wanted was given her to take with her from the harem to the king's palace. ¹⁴In the evening she would go there and in the morning return to another part of the harem to the care of Shaashgaz, the king's eunuch who was in charge of the concubines[D]. She would not return to the king unless he was pleased with her and summoned her by name.

¹⁵When the turn came for Esther (the girl Mordecai had adopted, the daughter of his uncle Abihail) to go to the

---

[a]6 Hebrew *Jeconiah,* a variant of *Jehoiachin*

king, she asked for nothing other than what Hegai, the king's eunuch[D] who was in charge of the harem, suggested. And Esther won the favor of everyone who saw her. [16]She was taken to King Xerxes in the royal residence in the tenth month, the month of Tebeth, in the seventh year of his reign.

[17]Now the king was attracted to Esther more than to any of the other women, and she won his favor and approval more than any of the other virgins. So he set a royal crown on her head and made her queen instead of Vashti. [18]And the king gave a great banquet, Esther's banquet, for all his nobles and officials. He proclaimed a holiday throughout the provinces and distributed gifts with royal liberality.

Mordecai Uncovers a Conspiracy

[19]When the virgins were assembled a second time, Mordecai was sitting at the king's gate. [20]But Esther had kept secret her family background and nationality just as Mordecai had told her to do, for she continued to follow Mordecai's instructions as she had done when he was bringing her up.

[21]During the time Mordecai was sitting at the king's gate, Bigthana[a] and Teresh, two of the king's officers who guarded the doorway, became angry and conspired to assassinate King Xerxes. [22]But Mordecai found out about the plot and told Queen Esther, who in turn reported it to the king, giving credit to Mordecai. [23]And when the report was investigated and found to be true, the two officials were hanged on a gallows.[b] All this was recorded in the book of the annals in the presence of the king.

Haman's Plot to Destroy the Jews

3 After these events, King Xerxes honored Haman son of Hammedatha, the Agagite, elevating him and giving him a seat of honor higher than that of all the other nobles. [2]All the royal officials at the king's gate knelt down and paid honor to Haman, for the king had commanded this concerning him. But Mordecai would not kneel down or pay him honor.

[3]Then the royal officials at the king's gate asked Mordecai, "Why do you disobey the king's command?" [4]Day after day they spoke to him but he refused to comply. Therefore they told Haman about it to see whether Mordecai's behavior would be tolerated, for he had told them he was a Jew[D].

[5]When Haman saw that Mordecai would not kneel down or pay him honor, he was enraged. [6]Yet having learned who Mordecai's people were, he scorned the idea of killing only Mordecai. Instead Haman looked for a way to destroy all Mordecai's people, the Jews, throughout the whole kingdom of Xerxes.

[7]In the twelfth year of King Xerxes, in the first month, the month of Nisan, they cast the *pur* (that is, the lot) in the presence of Haman to select a day and month. And the lot fell on[c] the twelfth month, the month of Adar.

[8]Then Haman said to King Xerxes, "There is a certain

Why wasn't Esther's background investigated before she became queen? (2:17)

The king was apparently so impressed with her beauty that he did not inquire further about her background. Also Esther had won the favor of the king's eunuch (v. 9) and of everyone else in the royal court (v. 15), so probably no one questioned her appointment as queen.

Why did Mordecai sit at the king's gate? (2:19)

The gate of an ancient city was its center of commercial and legal activity. It is likely that Mordecai had gained a position in the king's service that kept him at the gate. This is supported by Mordecai's association with court officials (see 3:2–4) and his knowledge of events transpiring within the palace (see 2:19–23; 4:6–8). Ancient records indicate a minor official of Xerxes' administration with a similar name (Mardukaya).

Agagite (3:1)

Haman was a descendant of Agag, an ancient Amalekite king. The Amalekites had tried to annihilate the Israelites as they journeyed from Egypt to the promised land (Exodus 17:8–16). The Lord had commanded Israel to retaliate by annihilating the Amalekites after Israel had gained control of the land (Deut. 25:17–19), but King Saul failed to obey that command when he spared Agag (1 Samuel 15:9) and apparently, some of his offspring (see 1 Chron. 4:42–43).

Why did Mordecai disobey the king's command? (3:2–5)

He refused to honor Haman because he recognized him as an enemy of his people. This also explains Haman's desire to destroy not only Mordecai but all the Jews (3:6).

Why did Mordecai reveal his nationality when he had told Esther to conceal hers? (3:4)

Mordecai's command to his adopted daughter was for her own protection—see *Why did Mordecai forbid Esther to mention her nationality?* (2:10); however, his refusal to obey a direct command of the king required an explanation (3:3). Since Mordecai's only reason for refusing to honor Haman was the ancient enmity of Jews and Amalekites, Mordecai *told them he was a Jew*. See *Agagite* (3:1).

Month of Adar (3:7)

Adar is the Persian name given to the twelfth and last month of the Hebrew calendar. It falls in the February/March period of the modern Western calendar. Ancient Middle Eastern rulers would plan their calendars a year in advance at the beginning of the new year. Dice (pur) were cast to determine dates for important events. See *Purim . . . pur* (9:26).

---

a21 Hebrew Bigthan, a variant of *Bigthana*   *b23* Or *were hung* (or *impaled*) *on poles*; similarly elsewhere in Esther   *c7* Septuagint; Hebrew does not have *And the lot fell on.*

How much was 10,000 talents of silver? (3:9)

The talent was equivalent to 75 pounds (91.1 troy pounds). If a troy ounce of silver costs about $5.00, then 10,000 talents would be worth nearly $55,000,000 in today's market. Either Haman had recognized the prosperity of the Jews and was offering their great wealth to Xerxes as an "incentive," or Haman himself was extremely wealthy.

Signet ring (3:10)

Signet rings were used by people in authority in the ancient world as official seals. They were engraved with the wearer's personal insignia, which would be used to make an impression upon soft wax or clay in order to authorize important documents (3:12). By giving Haman his signet ring, Xerxes gave him authority to do whatever he wished in the king's name.

Why was the city of Susa bewildered? (3:15)

This edict decreed the wholesale slaughter of an entire ethnic group for no apparent reason. The average citizen was most likely unaware of the ancient animosity between the Jews and Amalekites, which lay behind the decree. Furthermore, the Jews were industrious and supportive citizens, seeking the peace and prosperity of Persia. The decree probably made no sense to the larger segment of the population that had no apparent reason to hate the Jews.

Why did Mordecai tear his clothes? (4:1-2)

The tearing of one's clothes and wearing of sackcloth and ashes were universal signs of intense grief in the Middle East. Sackcloth was made of goat or camel hair and was probably worn because it was coarse and black.

Why did Esther need the edict explained? (4:8)

Perhaps she didn't understand the implications of the legal terminology. It's also possible that, as a woman in that culture, Esther had never been taught to read.

How often would a queen typically see the king? (4:11)

A queen was often little more than the king's favored concubine, with little or no real administrative power. It seems reasonable to assume that, as Xerxes' favorite, Esther was with him frequently. However, given the number of his concubines, it is possible that she was not often called. Her protest here might also indicate that she was no longer in his highest favor.

people dispersed and scattered among the peoples in all the provinces of your kingdom whose customs are different from those of all other people and who do not obey the king's laws; it is not in the king's best interest to tolerate them. ⁹If it pleases the king, let a decree be issued to destroy them, and I will put ten thousand talents*a* of silver into the royal treasury for the men who carry out this business."

¹⁰So the king took his signet ring*D* from his finger and gave it to Haman son of Hammedatha, the Agagite, the enemy of the Jews*D*. ¹¹"Keep the money," the king said to Haman, "and do with the people as you please."

¹²Then on the thirteenth day of the first month the royal secretaries were summoned. They wrote out in the script of each province and in the language of each people all Haman's orders to the king's satraps*D*, the governors of the various provinces and the nobles of the various peoples. These were written in the name of King Xerxes himself and sealed with his own ring. ¹³Dispatches were sent by couriers to all the king's provinces with the order to destroy, kill and annihilate all the Jews—young and old, women and little children—on a single day, the thirteenth day of the twelfth month, the month of Adar, and to plunder*D* their goods. ¹⁴A copy of the text of the edict*D* was to be issued as law in every province and made known to the people of every nationality so they would be ready for that day.

¹⁵Spurred on by the king's command, the couriers went out, and the edict was issued in the citadel of Susa. The king and Haman sat down to drink, but the city of Susa was bewildered.

Mordecai Persuades Esther to Help

4 When Mordecai learned of all that had been done, he tore his clothes, put on sackcloth*D* and ashes, and went out into the city, wailing loudly and bitterly. ²But he went only as far as the king's gate, because no one clothed in sackcloth was allowed to enter it. ³In every province to which the edict*D* and order of the king came, there was great mourning among the Jews*D*, with fasting, weeping and wailing. Many lay in sackcloth and ashes.

⁴When Esther's maids and eunuchs*D* came and told her about Mordecai, she was in great distress. She sent clothes for him to put on instead of his sackcloth, but he would not accept them. ⁵Then Esther summoned Hathach, one of the king's eunuchs assigned to attend her, and ordered him to find out what was troubling Mordecai and why.

⁶So Hathach went out to Mordecai in the open square of the city in front of the king's gate. ⁷Mordecai told him everything that had happened to him, including the exact amount of money Haman had promised to pay into the royal treasury for the destruction of the Jews. ⁸He also gave him a copy of the text of the edict for their annihilation, which had been published in Susa, to show to Esther and explain it to her, and he told him to urge her to go into the king's presence to beg for mercy*D* and plead with him for her people.

⁹Hathach went back and reported to Esther what Mordecai had said. ¹⁰Then she instructed him to say to Mordecai, ¹¹"All the king's officials and the people of the royal

---

a9 That is, about 375 tons (about 345 metric tons)

provinces know that for any man or woman who approaches the king in the inner court without being summoned the king has but one law: that he be put to death[D]. The only exception to this is for the king to extend the gold scepter[D] to him and spare his life. But thirty days have passed since I was called to go to the king."

[12]When Esther's words were reported to Mordecai, [13]he sent back this answer: "Do not think that because you are in the king's house you alone of all the Jews will escape. [14]For if you remain silent at this time, relief and deliverance for the Jews will arise from another place, but you and your father's family will perish. And who knows but that you have come to royal position for such a time as this?"

[15]Then Esther sent this reply to Mordecai: [16]"Go, gather together all the Jews who are in Susa, and fast for me. Do not eat or drink for three days, night or day. I and my maids will fast as you do. When this is done, I will go to the king, even though it is against the law. And if I perish, I perish."

[17]So Mordecai went away and carried out all of Esther's instructions.

Esther's Request to the King

5 On the third day Esther put on her royal robes and stood in the inner court of the palace, in front of the king's hall. The king was sitting on his royal throne in the

Couldn't the *queen* escape such an edict? (4:14)

A royal edict in ancient Persia was irrevocable and no respecter of status. It's possible that some of Esther's attendants may have suspected she was a Jew. Given the king's treatment of Vashti, it's unlikely Esther would have been spared.

From what "other place" would deliverance for the Jews come? (4:14)

The phrase *from another place* appears to be a veiled reference to the Lord. Mordecai was expressing his faith that the Lord would not permit the annihilation of his people—regardless of Esther's decision. See article: **Is the book of Esther "Godless"?** (4:16).

Why was Mordecai so sure Esther would die if she kept silent? (4:14)

Mordecai's warning alluded to God's hand in the situation. If the Lord was not working for his people's salvation (as Mordecai implied by referring to Esther's royal position), then surely he was working for their destruction. If so, Esther would certainly not escape that destruction.

Is the book of Esther "Godless"? (4:16)

Why isn't God mentioned at all in this book? This question has been a source of controversy for centuries. Some have even questioned the book's place in the Bible because of it. However, at several points in the narrative, the author alludes to God's hand in the events. For example, Mordecai's contention that deliverance would come *from another place* (4:14) is probably the author's way of saying the Lord would intervene for his people. Esther's request that they all fast (4:16) was no doubt a reference to prayer to the Lord on her behalf. The Jews' refusal to plunder their enemies (9:10,16) indicated that they fought for the Lord, not themselves.

In addition, the writer shows God's involvement through an incredible string of "coincidences": (1) Esther selected from among many to become queen, (2) Mordecai "accidently" discovering a plot against the king, (3) Esther defying the law to gain uninvited entrance to see the king and (4) Mordecai given Haman's position of power by which he could turn an unalterable law upside down and deliver the Jews. The reader is left saying, "Nobody could be so lucky. Something else must have been going on." The story points to God as the one behind the scenes, orchestrating the events.

Esther, too, is in the mold of other Old Testament heroes who were clearly guided by the Lord. She, like Joseph, was imprisoned but found favor with her captors and rose to a position of power to save the Jews (Gen. 39–50). In addition, Mordecai, like both Joseph and Daniel, came to a position of power second only to the king (Gen. 41:41–44; Daniel 6:2).

Still, the question remains: Did the writer deliberately edit God out of the story? We can only speculate. Perhaps the author was employing the literary device of understatement to emphasize that nothing short of God's direct intervention in these circumstances could possibly explain the way things worked out. More importantly, since the book was written in Persia, the author may have been aware of certain laws against non-Persian religions or may not have wanted to risk having the book destroyed by the government.

Was the king literally promising half his kingdom to Esther? (5:3)

Probably not. Xerxes' oath to Esther appears to have been a stock phrase used by ancient monarchs to express favor. It's a promise to grant "anything you ask." Xerxes knew Esther would not dare approach him unless she had a very important reason. Esther had succeeded in arousing both his admiration and his curiosity.

Why did Esther wait for the second banquet to make her request? (5:8)

It may have been a strategic decision by Esther, who was hoping to please the king sufficiently to grant this major request. Or, Esther may have simply (and understandably) lost her courage the first time. Or, perhaps Esther was led by God to postpone her request, thus setting up the timing of Xerxes' discovery of Mordecai's valor (6:1-2).

Why build such a high gallows? (5:14)

Perhaps the gallows were on top of a wall or house, making it a total of 75 feet, since a free-standing, 75-foot gallows would be difficult to construct in one night. The Hebrew word literally means *tree*, so this implement of death might have actually been a stake upon which Mordecai was to be impaled (see NIV text note on 2:23) in keeping with Persian custom. Its height indicates Haman's intense hatred for Mordecai and his desire to make Mordecai's death a warning to all. Hebrew law also identified this form of death as an indication of God's curse, making the death of Haman and his sons (7:10; 9:13) all the more significant.

Why had Mordecai gone unrewarded for saving the king's life? (6:2-3)

No one knows for sure. Those who helped a king in extraordinary ways were considered benefactors who deserved almost a legal right to a reward, though it was often granted after a period of time. Some, like Haman, undoubtedly would have made claim on their reward. Others, like Mordecai, were not so self-promoting.

hall, facing the entrance. ²When he saw Queen Esther standing in the court, he was pleased with her and held out to her the gold scepter that was in his hand. So Esther approached and touched the tip of the scepter.

³Then the king asked, "What is it, Queen Esther? What is your request? Even up to half the kingdom, it will be given you."

⁴"If it pleases the king," replied Esther, "let the king, together with Haman, come today to a banquet I have prepared for him."

⁵"Bring Haman at once," the king said, "so that we may do what Esther asks."

So the king and Haman went to the banquet Esther had prepared. ⁶As they were drinking wine, the king again asked Esther, "Now what is your petition? It will be given you. And what is your request? Even up to half the kingdom, it will be granted."

⁷Esther replied, "My petition and my request is this: ⁸If the king regards me with favor and if it pleases the king to grant my petition and fulfill my request, let the king and Haman come tomorrow to the banquet I will prepare for them. Then I will answer the king's question."

Haman's Rage Against Mordecai

⁹Haman went out that day happy and in high spirits. But when he saw Mordecai at the king's gate and observed that he neither rose nor showed fear in his presence, he was filled with rage against Mordecai. ¹⁰Nevertheless, Haman restrained himself and went home.

Calling together his friends and Zeresh, his wife, ¹¹Haman boasted to them about his vast wealth, his many sons, and all the ways the king had honored him and how he had elevated him above the other nobles and officials. ¹²"And that's not all," Haman added. "I'm the only person Queen Esther invited to accompany the king to the banquet she gave. And she has invited me along with the king tomorrow. ¹³But all this gives me no satisfaction as long as I see that Jewᴰ Mordecai sitting at the king's gate."

¹⁴His wife Zeresh and all his friends said to him, "Have a gallows built, seventy-five feetᵃ high, and ask the king in the morning to have Mordecai hanged on it. Then go with the king to the dinner and be happy." This suggestion delighted Haman, and he had the gallows built.

Mordecai Honored

6 That night the king could not sleep; so he ordered the book of the chronicles, the record of his reign, to be brought in and read to him. ²It was found recorded there that Mordecai had exposed Bigthana and Teresh, two of the king's officers who guarded the doorway, who had conspired to assassinate King Xerxes.

³"What honor and recognition has Mordecai received for this?" the king asked.

"Nothing has been done for him," his attendants answered.

⁴The king said, "Who is in the court?" Now Haman had just entered the outer court of the palace to speak to the king about hanging Mordecai on the gallows he had erected for him.

ᵃ14 Hebrew *fifty cubits* (about 23 meters)

[5]His attendants answered, "Haman is standing in the court."

"Bring him in," the king ordered.

[6]When Haman entered, the king asked him, "What should be done for the man the king delights to honor?"

Now Haman thought to himself, "Who is there that the king would rather honor than me?" [7]So he answered the king, "For the man the king delights to honor, [8]have them bring a royal robe the king has worn and a horse the king has ridden, one with a royal crest placed on its head. [9]Then let the robe and horse be entrusted to one of the king's most noble princes. Let them robe the man the king delights to honor, and lead him on the horse through the city streets, proclaiming before him, 'This is what is done for the man the king delights to honor!'"

[10]"Go at once," the king commanded Haman. "Get the robe and the horse and do just as you have suggested for Mordecai the Jew, who sits at the king's gate. Do not neglect anything you have recommended."

[11]So Haman got the robe and the horse. He robed Mordecai, and led him on horseback through the city streets, proclaiming before him, "This is what is done for the man the king delights to honor!"

[12]Afterward Mordecai returned to the king's gate. But Haman rushed home, with his head covered in grief, [13]and told Zeresh his wife and all his friends everything that had happened to him.

His advisers and his wife Zeresh said to him, "Since Mordecai, before whom your downfall has started, is of Jewish origin, you cannot stand against him—you will surely come to ruin!" [14]While they were still talking with him, the king's eunuchs[D] arrived and hurried Haman away to the banquet Esther had prepared.

Haman Hanged

7 So the king and Haman went to dine with Queen Esther, [2]and as they were drinking wine on that second day, the king again asked, "Queen Esther, what is your petition? It will be given you. What is your request? Even up to half the kingdom, it will be granted."

[3]Then Queen Esther answered, "If I have found favor with you, O king, and if it pleases your majesty, grant me my life—this is my petition. And spare my people—this is my request. [4]For I and my people have been sold for destruction and slaughter and annihilation. If we had merely been sold as male and female slaves, I would have kept quiet, because no such distress would justify[D] disturbing the king.[a]"

[5]King Xerxes asked Queen Esther, "Who is he? Where is the man who has dared to do such a thing?"

[6]Esther said, "The adversary and enemy is this vile Haman."

Then Haman was terrified before the king and queen. [7]The king got up in a rage, left his wine and went out into the palace garden. But Haman, realizing that the king had already decided his fate, stayed behind to beg Queen Esther for his life.

[8]Just as the king returned from the palace garden to the banquet hall, Haman was falling on the couch where Esther was reclining.

[a]4 Or quiet, but the compensation our adversary offers cannot be compared with the loss the king would suffer

---

What was so special about wearing a hand-me-down from the king? (6:8)

The kings' garment had great significance in the ancient world. It was an outward, physical representation of his power and glory. To wear something belonging to another signified sharing a part of that person's stature and honor (see, for example, 2 Kings 2:13–14). Haman made this suggestion because he could flatter the king and at the same time (he assumed) maneuver to gain greater recognition and authority for himself.

Head covered in grief (6:12)

Covering one's head was a typical expression of sorrow in ancient times (2 Samuel 15:30; Jer. 14:3). It may have been to hide one's tears or perhaps to show a desire to mourn in private. Haman grieved for two reasons: (1) He could not dare now to kill the favored Mordecai. (2) He had been publicly humiliated before his enemy.

Why did Haman's advisers think Mordecai's Jewish origin ensured Haman's ruin? (6:13)

What had seemed like ideal circumstances for Haman's revenge (5:14) had now been miraculously altered. The significance of this disastrous turn of events (vv. 10–11) was not lost on Haman's advisers. They probably knew the ancient history of Israel and Amalek. See *Agagite* (3:1). They knew how the Jews had been protected during the exile. It seems they also recognized that the Lord's judgment was at hand for Haman.

Would Esther really have kept quiet at being sold into slavery? (7:4)

Slavery in ancient culture did not carry the same dread connotations it bears today, so she would not have risked death at the threat of slavery. Further, Esther might have been hinting that it was in Xerxes' own best interest to prevent the Jews, who were productive workers in his realm, from being annihilated. See NIV text note.

Why did they cover Haman's face? (7:8–9)

It was customary among the Greeks and Romans to cover the face of a person sentenced to death. The attendants who were present covered Haman's face as soon as the word left the king's mouth—presumably the execution order.

The king exclaimed, "Will he even molest the queen while she is with me in the house?"

As soon as the word left the king's mouth, they covered Haman's face. 9Then Harbona, one of the eunuchsᴰ attending the king, said, "A gallows seventy-five feetᵃ high stands by Haman's house. He had it made for Mordecai, who spoke up to help the king."

The king said, "Hang him on it!" 10So they hanged Haman on the gallows he had prepared for Mordecai. Then the king's fury subsided.

The King's Edict in Behalf of the Jews

8 That same day King Xerxes gave Queen Esther the estate of Haman, the enemy of the Jewsᴰ. And Mordecai came into the presence of the king, for Esther had told how he was related to her. 2The king took off his signet ringᴰ, which he had reclaimed from Haman, and presented it to Mordecai. And Esther appointed him over Haman's estate.

3Esther again pleaded with the king, falling at his feet and weeping. She begged him to put an end to the evil plan of Haman the Agagite, which he had devised against the Jews. 4Then the king extended the gold scepter to Esther and she arose and stood before him.

5"If it pleases the king," she said, "and if he regards me with favor and thinks it the right thing to do, and if he is pleased with me, let an order be written overruling the dispatches that Haman son of Hammedatha, the Agagite, devised and wrote to destroy the Jews in all the king's provinces. 6For how can I bear to see disaster fall on my people? How can I bear to see the destruction of my family?"

7King Xerxes replied to Queen Esther and to Mordecai the Jewᴰ, "Because Haman attacked the Jews, I have given his estate to Esther, and they have hanged him on the gallows. 8Now write another decree in the king's name in behalf of the Jews as seems best to you, and seal it with the king's signet ringᴰ—for no document written in the king's name and sealed with his ring can be revoked."

9At once the royal secretaries were summoned—on the twenty-third day of the third month, the month of Sivan. They wrote out all Mordecai's orders to the Jews, and to the satrapsᴰ, governors and nobles of the 127 provinces stretching from India to Cush.ᵇ These orders were written in the script of each province and the language of each people and also to the Jews in their own script and language. 10Mordecai wrote in the name of King Xerxes, sealed the dispatches with the king's signet ring, and sent them by mounted couriers, who rode fast horses especially bred for the king.

11The king's edictᴰ granted the Jews in every city the right to assemble and protect themselves; to destroy, kill and annihilate any armed force of any nationality or province that might attack them and their women and children; and to plunderᴰ the property of their enemies. 12The day appointed for the Jews to do this in all the provinces of King Xerxes was the thirteenth day of the twelfth month, the month of Adar. 13A copy of the text of the edict was to be issued as law in every province and made known to the people of every nationality so that the

Why did Esther still have to plead with Xerxes? (8:3)

Esther was making her general request from 7:3 more explicit, drawing Xerxes' attention back to the larger issue at hand. The decree Haman had written and sealed with the king's signet ring was still in effect even though Haman was dead. The immediate threat to Mordecai had been averted, but the Jews were still facing annihilation. By extending his scepter, Xerxes indicated his favorable response to her plea (v. 4).

Why couldn't the king change his own decrees? (8:8)

A royal decree—one *written in the king's name and sealed with his ring*—was irrevocable, even by the king. This had been a fact of Persian law for generations (see Daniel 6:12). The most that could be done to counter such a decree was to write another that would supersede it, which is precisely what Xerxes allowed Esther and Mordecai to do (8:8–14).

ᵃ9 Hebrew *fifty cubits* (about 23 meters)   ᵇ9 That is, the upper Nile region

Jews would be ready on that day to avenge themselves on their enemies.

¹⁴The couriers, riding the royal horses, raced out, spurred on by the king's command. And the edict was also issued in the citadel D of Susa.

¹⁵Mordecai left the king's presence wearing royal garments of blue and white, a large crown of gold and a purpleD robe of fine linen. And the city of Susa held a joyous celebration. ¹⁶For the Jews it was a time of happiness and joy, gladness and honor. ¹⁷In every province and in every city, wherever the edict of the king went, there was joy and gladness among the Jews, with feasting and celebrating. And many people of other nationalities became Jews because fear of the Jews had seized them.

Triumph of the Jews

9 On the thirteenth day of the twelfth month, the month of Adar, the edict commanded by the king was to be carried out. On this day the enemies of the Jews had hoped to overpower them, but now the tables were turned and the Jews got the upper hand over those who hated them. ²The Jews assembled in their cities in all the provinces of King Xerxes to attack those seeking their destruction. No one could stand against them, because the people of all the other nationalities were afraid of them. ³And all the nobles of the provinces, the satraps, the governors and the king's administrators helped the Jews, because fear of Mordecai had seized them. ⁴Mordecai was prominent in the palace; his reputation spread throughout the provinces, and he became more and more powerful.

⁵The Jews struck down all their enemies with the sword, killing and destroying them, and they did what they pleased to those who hated them. ⁶In the citadel of Susa, the JewsD killed and destroyed five hundred men. ⁷They also killed Parshandatha, Dalphon, Aspatha, ⁸Poratha, Adalia, Aridatha, ⁹Parmashta, Arisai, Aridai and Vaizatha, ¹⁰the ten sons of Haman son of Hammedatha, the enemy of the Jews. But they did not lay their hands on the plunderD.

¹¹The number of those slain in the citadelD of Susa was reported to the king that same day. ¹²The king said to Queen Esther, "The Jews have killed and destroyed five hundred men and the ten sons of Haman in the citadel of Susa. What have they done in the rest of the king's provinces? Now what is your petition? It will be given you. What is your request? It will also be granted."

¹³"If it pleases the king," Esther answered, "give the Jews in Susa permission to carry out this day's edict tomorrow also, and let Haman's ten sons be hanged on gallows."

¹⁴So the king commanded that this be done. An edict was issued in Susa, and they hanged the ten sons of Haman. ¹⁵The Jews in Susa came together on the fourteenth day of the month of Adar, and they put to deathD in Susa three hundred men, but they did not lay their hands on the plunder.

¹⁶Meanwhile, the remainder of the Jews who were in the king's provinces also assembled to protect themselves and get relief from their enemies. They killed seventy-five thousand of them but did not lay their hands on the plunder. ¹⁷This happened on the thirteenth day of the month of Adar, and on the fourteenth they rested and made it a day of feasting and joy.

How could a non-Jew become a Jew? (8:17)

To become a Jew meant to accept and obey the entirety of Jewish ceremonial, civil and moral law (Num. 15:14–16). Some of these laws would have been irrelevant in exile due to the lack of a temple or an autonomous government. Many would still apply, however, including circumcision (Exodus 12:48), observance of holy days (Lev. 16:29) and dietary laws (Lev. 17:12). The *fear of the Jews* mentioned here was not fear of Jewish aggression, since the edict only permitted the Jews to protect themselves (8:11). It was more likely an awed recognition that the Jews had been granted divine favor and protection.

Fear of Mordecai (9:3–4)

Mordecai's sudden advancement was recognized as supernatural. To oppose such a person was to oppose the gods and ensure one's doom. The rulers of the provinces were filled with awe by a power they could not identify but could clearly perceive—the sovereign power of God.

Did the Jews initiate this attack on their enemies? (9:5–10)

The edict allowed Jews to *protect themselves* against those who *might attack them and their women and children* (8:11). These may have been preemptive strikes, but this was not random violence, nor were they slaying women and children or looting (9:6,12,15).

Why did the Jews need to kill 75,000 people? (9:6,15–16)

That the Jews would kill so many aggressors indicates that the threat of hostility against them had been increasing since the edict against them had been issued (3:15). It's possible that this number is an exaggeration used to emphasize the Jews' victory. Given the vast extent of the empire, however, 75,000 is not an inconceivable number, especially considering that 800 were killed in Susa alone. The failure to mention Jewish casualties is almost certainly intended to communicate the Jews' overwhelming success rather than an absence of losses.

Why didn't the Jews take any plunder? (9:10,15)

This was a holy war—a war commanded by the Lord in judgment on great evil. It is distinguished from normal warfare by the ban on taking plunder, which demonstrates that the aggression is not for financial gain but only to carry out God's sentence.

Why hang Haman's sons, already dead, on the gallows? (9:13)

First, it made an example of them as a deterrent to any who would think to attack the Jews again. Second, given that hanging on a tree was a sign of the Lord's vengeance upon a person (Deut. 21:23; Gal. 3:13), it would have especially communicated to the Jews of Susa that the Lord's ancient curse against the Amalekites had been fulfilled by Saul's descendants (1 Samuel 15:17–19).

Purim Celebrated

18The Jews in Susa, however, had assembled on the thirteenth and fourteenth, and then on the fifteenth they rested and made it a day of feasting and joy.

19That is why rural Jews—those living in villages—observe the fourteenth of the month of Adar as a day of joy and feasting, a day for giving presents to each other.

20Mordecai recorded these events, and he sent letters to all the Jews throughout the provinces of King Xerxes, near and far, **21**to have them celebrate annually the fourteenth and fifteenth days of the month of Adar **22**as the time when the Jews got relief from their enemies, and as the month when their sorrow was turned into joy and their mourning into a day of celebration. He wrote them to observe the days as days of feasting and joy and giving presents of food to one another and gifts to the poor.

23So the Jews agreed to continue the celebration they had begun, doing what Mordecai had written to them. **24**For Haman son of Hammedatha, the Agagite, the enemy of all the Jews, had plotted against the Jews to destroy them and had cast the *pur* (that is, the lot) for their ruin and destruction. **25**But when the plot came to the king's attention,[a] he issued written orders that the evil scheme Haman had devised against the Jews should come back onto his own head, and that he and his sons should be hanged on the gallows. **26**(Therefore these days were called Purim, from the word *pur*.) Because of everything written in this letter and because of what they had seen and what had happened to them, **27**the Jews took it upon themselves to establish the custom that they and their descendants and all who join them should without fail observe these two days every year, in the way prescribed and at the time appointed. **28**These days should be remembered and observed in every generation by every family, and in every province and in every city. And these days of Purim should never cease to be celebrated by the Jews[b], nor should the memory of them die out among their descendants.

29So Queen Esther, daughter of Abihail, along with Mordecai the Jew, wrote with full authority to confirm this second letter concerning Purim. **30**And Mordecai sent letters to all the Jews in the 127 provinces of the kingdom of Xerxes—words of goodwill and assurance— **31**to establish these days of Purim at their designated times, as Mordecai the Jew and Queen Esther had decreed for them, and as they had established for themselves and their descendants in regard to their times of fasting and lamentation. **32**Esther's decree confirmed these regulations about Purim, and it was written down in the records.

The Greatness of Mordecai

10 King Xerxes imposed tribute throughout the empire, to its distant shores. **2**And all his acts of power and might, together with a full account of the greatness of Mordecai to which the king had raised him, are they not written in the book of the annals of the kings of Media and Persia? **3**Mordecai the Jew was second in rank to King Xerxes, preeminent among the Jews, and held in high esteem by his many fellow Jews, because he worked for the good of his people and spoke up for the welfare of all the Jews.

Purim . . . pur (9:26)

Purim is a combination of the Persian word for "lot" (*pur*) with the Hebrew plural ending (*-im*). The day was chosen by lot (see 3:7) originally as the day an attack was to be launched against the Jews. Instead, in a dramatic turn of events, it became a Jewish holiday which is observed to this day. An explanation of the name was necessary because the word would not have been recognized by non-Persian Jews.

Annals of the kings of Media and Persia (10:2)

Historical records not yet recovered by archaeologists. There is ancient evidence, however, of a man who had a name similar to Mordecai during the early part of Xerxes' reign. See *Why did Mordecai sit at the king's gate?* (2:19).

How much power would Mordecai have as second in rank to the king? (10:3)

Plenty. Mordecai could not only act frequently on his own, he also enjoyed the confidence and trust of the king who had relied on him more than any of his nobles and advisers. Mordecai would have had virtually unlimited opportunity to shape the policies and administration of the empire. His high position guaranteed the welfare of the Jews while they lived in a foreign land—similar to the accounts of Joseph (Gen. 41:43) and Daniel (Daniel 6:2–3).

---

a25 Or when Esther came before the king

JOB

Why read this book?

To explore the most difficult questions of life—questions most people ask at some time or another: Why is there evil in the world? Why is there pain, suffering and heartache? Why do the righteous suffer? If you've puzzled over such questions—or perhaps been disappointed by simplistic answers—you'll appreciate the honest way the book of Job looks at God's mysterious ways.

Who wrote this book?

Probably an unknown Israelite, though no one knows for sure. Some speculate about many names as possible authors: Job (though he was not an Israelite), Elihu, Moses, Solomon, Isaiah, Hezekiah, or Baruch (Jeremiah's friend).

When was it written?

This too is uncertain. The cultural and historical settings seem to reflect the times of Genesis 12–50, the second millennium B.C. Some think the story of Job was passed down orally from generation to generation and only later put into writing.

Why was it written?

To address the question of suffering. The writer tells Job's story in a way that allows readers to identify with his spiritual and philosophical struggles. Like a counselor to those who suffer, the writer of Job vividly illustrates the inadequacy of human logic to explain the reality and nature of evil in the world.

What to look for in Job:

Consider carefully the various voices found throughout the book. Job's friends, for example, make profound statements—but they also make some classic errors in judgment. Also watch for the wide range of literary techniques used in this book: dialogue, poetry, proverbs, riddles, laments, curses and word pictures. Some parts read like court proceedings, as if Job were on trial. As you read keep in mind the context of the book as a whole. The voice of the narrator (chs. 1–2,42) helps us see things that Job and his friends did not.

Location of Uz (1:1)

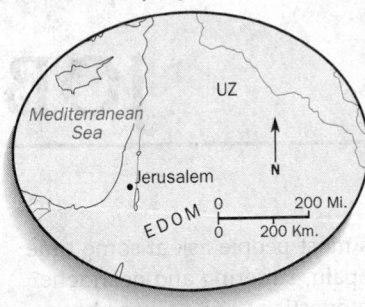

Uz (1:1)

A region east of Canaan.

The East (1:3)

A reference to the region east of Canaan, often referred to as the Near East.

Can we ask God to forgive someone else? (1:5)

Not exactly, but we can pray for others. In the ancient times of the patriarchs, the father acted as priest for his family. Here Job served as a priest by offering sacrifices on behalf of his children. The Bible contains numerous instances where people interceded for others: for example, Moses prayed for the sins of the Israelites (Num. 14:19) as did Nehemiah (Neh. 1:4–11). Also see *What sin leads to death?* (1 John 5:16–17).

What do we know about heavenly councils? (1:6)

Not much, though there are other examples in the Bible (1 Kings 22:19; Psalm 89:5; Jer. 23:18,22, for instance). Some think this may be figurative language using images from ancient culture to describe spiritual realities in terms that humans can understand: God is King and all spiritual beings answer to him. Also see *Why did Satan mingle with God's angels?* (2:1).

Why did God point out Job to Satan? (1:8)

The text does not reveal why God initiated the dialogue. Perhaps God was giving Job a greater opportunity to honor him with his allegiance. If so, the testing of God's servant was also a greater opportunity for God to prove his faithfulness. Satan's assault was ultimately on God, directed through Job.

Was God giving Satan permission to hurt Job? (1:12)

Yes. God allowed Satan to destroy Job's wealth, family and health. But God set limits on what Satan could destroy and demonstrated his sovereign control.

Prologue

1 In the land of Uz there lived a man whose name was Job. This man was blameless and upright; he feared God and shunned evil. ²He had seven sons and three daughters, ³and he owned seven thousand sheep, three thousand camels, five hundred yoke^D of oxen and five hundred donkeys, and had a large number of servants. He was the greatest man among all the people of the East.

⁴His sons used to take turns holding feasts in their homes, and they would invite their three sisters to eat and drink with them. ⁵When a period of feasting had run its course, Job would send and have them purified^D. Early in the morning he would sacrifice^D a burnt offering^D for each of them, thinking, "Perhaps my children have sinned and cursed God in their hearts." This was Job's regular custom.

Job's First Test

⁶One day the angels^a came to present themselves before the LORD, and Satan^b also came with them. ⁷The LORD said to Satan, "Where have you come from?"

Satan answered the LORD, "From roaming through the earth and going back and forth in it."

⁸Then the LORD said to Satan, "Have you considered my servant Job? There is no one on earth like him; he is blameless and upright, a man who fears God and shuns evil."

⁹"Does Job fear God for nothing?" Satan replied. ¹⁰"Have you not put a hedge around him and his household and everything he has? You have blessed the work of his hands, so that his flocks and herds are spread throughout the land. ¹¹But stretch out your hand and strike everything he has, and he will surely curse you to your face."

¹²The LORD said to Satan, "Very well, then, everything he has is in your hands, but on the man himself do not lay a finger."

Then Satan went out from the presence of the LORD.

¹³One day when Job's sons and daughters were feasting and drinking wine at the oldest brother's house, ¹⁴a messenger came to Job and said, "The oxen were plowing and the donkeys were grazing nearby, ¹⁵and the Sabeans attacked and carried them off. They put the servants to the sword, and I am the only one who has escaped to tell you!"

¹⁶While he was still speaking, another messenger came and said, "The fire of God fell from the sky and burned up the sheep and the servants, and I am the only one who has escaped to tell you!"

¹⁷While he was still speaking, another messenger came and said, "The Chaldeans formed three raiding parties and swept down on your camels and carried them off. They put the servants to the sword, and I am the only one who has escaped to tell you!"

¹⁸While he was still speaking, yet another messenger came and said, "Your sons and daughters were feasting and drinking wine at the oldest brother's house, ¹⁹when suddenly a mighty wind swept in from the desert and struck the four corners of the house. It collapsed on them and they are dead, and I am the only one who has escaped to tell you!"

---

^a 6 Hebrew *the sons of God*   ^b 6 *Satan* means *accuser.*

20At this, Job got up and tore his robe and shaved his head. Then he fell to the ground in worship **21**and said:

"Naked I came from my mother's womb,
    and naked I will depart. *a*
The LORD gave and the LORD has taken away;
    may the name of the LORD be praised."

22In all this, Job did not sin by charging God with wrongdoing.

Job's Second Test

2 On another day the angels *b* came to present themselves before the LORD, and Satan also came with them to present himself before him. **2**And the LORD said to Satan, "Where have you come from?"

Satan answered the LORD, "From roaming through the earth and going back and forth in it."

3Then the LORD said to Satan, "Have you considered my servant Job? There is no one on earth like him; he is blameless and upright, a man who fears God and shuns evil. And he still maintains his integrity, though you incited me against him to ruin him without any reason."

4"Skin for skin!" Satan replied. "A man will give all he has for his own life. **5**But stretch out your hand and strike his flesh and bones, and he will surely curse you to your face."

6The LORD said to Satan, "Very well, then, he is in your hands; but you must spare his life."

a21 Or *will return there*   *b1* Hebrew *the sons of God*

Why did Job tear his clothes and shave his head? (1:20)

These were symbols of grief and mourning in Job's culture. His actions demonstrated not only his overwhelming grief but also his total resignation to God's sovereign will. Also see *Why shave beards, tear clothes and cut skin?* (Jer. 41:5).

Why did Satan mingle with God's angels? (2:1)

Angels literally means *sons of God* (see NIV text note). Though hard to imagine, Satan himself was a *son of God* created originally to serve the Lord. As a spirit being, he could come with the others to talk to God. On the other hand, some note that Satan's purpose in coming was to accuse (see NIV text note at 1:6). They suggest that the phrase *with them* means that Satan came as an intruder. Also see *What do we know about heavenly councils?* (1:6).

How did Satan incite God? (2:3)

This is typical Old Testament language explaining supernatural things in human terms. However, this does not imply that God can be urged to do anything against his will. It was God, in fact, who pointed Job out to Satan (1:8; 2:3)—not the other way around. As it was, God used Satan's evil intentions against Job to provide an opportunity for both God and Job to prove their faithfulness to each other. See article: *Is God responsible for what Satan does?* (19:8–12).

Are people just pawns in God's chess game? (1:13–19)

I t often seems that people are caught in events beyond their control, manipulated by God or Satan. They may feel forced into situations they would not choose if they were given a chance. While this seems unfair, there is another way—a higher way—to interpret the circumstances of life. We can see them as God-given opportunities to cooperate with his plans and, by serving him, to fulfill something far more significant than our own little schemes ever could. We're more than pawns in a chess game. We can honor Almighty God by the way we live and die.

Still, many unanswered questions remain. Only God knows why dozens of bystanders had to die in this unfolding drama between Satan and God. We struggle with the fact that some who are righteous have short, tragic lives while others who are wicked enjoy wealth and long life. One thing we can affirm, however: what seems unfair in this life will be made right in eternity. Our questions will be resolved.

God has permitted Satan certain freedoms. He is called the *prince of this world* (John 14:30) and the *ruler of the kingdom of the air* (Eph. 2:2). Satan can sometimes use the forces of nature, sickness, plagues and wicked people. Though Jesus dealt a fatal blow to Satan through his death and resurrection, the struggle between God and Satan continues until the end (Romans 16:20).

There are two sides to the suffering of the righteous: the earthly and the heavenly. The apostle Paul understood the tension of living in a corrupt world as one controlled by the Spirit. He placed his trust in God and things eternal—God's justice, mercy and love—not in the temporary things of this world—success, wealth and fame. Paul recognized that *our struggle is not against flesh and blood* (Eph. 6:12) and took courage in knowing that *our citizenship is in heaven* (Phil. 3:20).

What kind of sores did Job have? (2:7-8)

We don't know Job's actual ailment, but some of his symptoms may be described throughout the book, suggesting a combination of physical problems: disfigurement (v. 12), parasites (7:5), skin infections (7:5), hallucinations (7:14), emaciation (19:20), sharp pains (30:17) and fever (30:30). Job's sores may have been boils—painful bacterial infections of the skin.

Does God send trouble as well as good? (2:10)

In a sense, yes. Because Job trusted in God, he concluded that trouble from God was better than comfort and ease without God. He was confident that God had his best interest at heart, even though he could not understand how.

Where did Job's friends come from? (2:11)

Only the homeland of Eliphaz can be located with certainty. Teman was an Edomite city south of the Dead Sea (see *Map 2* at the back of this Bible), considered a center of wisdom at that time (Jer. 49:7). Bildad may have descended from the eastern tribe of Shuah, Abraham's youngest son (Gen. 25:2). Some think that Zophar the Naamathite (a word which occurs nowhere else in the Bible) came from Arabia.

Were Job's friends unusually good friends? (2:11-13)

Job lived in a much slower-paced culture than our modern society. Hospitality was considered one of the highest virtues. Job's friends may have been exceptionally good ones, but to sit in silent mourning for a week was also much more typical of their culture than ours.

Cursed the day of his birth (3:1)

The phrase is a figure of speech, full of power and poignancy, expressing deeply felt emotions. Though Job never curses God, in his despair he seems to challenge God's sovereign wisdom in permitting his birth (see 10:18; Jer. 20:14).

Why does the narrative switch to poetry? (3:3)

The unknown author probably felt that Job's deep emotions could best be expressed in lyrical poetry. Biblical poetry (such as the Psalms) typically conveys the spiritual dimensions of human feelings and the quest for a relationship with God far better than narrative techniques, which communicate facts and information.

Those who curse days (3:8)

This is probably a general reference to the professional sorcerers believed to have the power to make a day unlucky—like Balaam (Num. 24:1). It would be similar to those today who read people's palms or horoscopes.

[7]So Satan went out from the presence of the LORD and afflicted[D] Job with painful sores from the soles of his feet to the top of his head. [8]Then Job took a piece of broken pottery and scraped himself with it as he sat among the ashes.

[9]His wife said to him, "Are you still holding on to your integrity? Curse God and die!"

[10]He replied, "You are talking like a foolish[a] woman. Shall we accept good from God, and not trouble?"

In all this, Job did not sin in what he said.

Job's Three Friends

[11]When Job's three friends, Eliphaz the Temanite, Bildad the Shuhite and Zophar the Naamathite, heard about all the troubles that had come upon him, they set out from their homes and met together by agreement to go and sympathize with him and comfort him. [12]When they saw him from a distance, they could hardly recognize him; they began to weep aloud, and they tore their robes and sprinkled dust on their heads. [13]Then they sat on the ground with him for seven days and seven nights. No one said a word to him, because they saw how great his suffering was.

Job Speaks

3 After this, Job opened his mouth and cursed the day of his birth. [2]He said:

[3]"May the day of my birth perish,
    and the night it was said, 'A boy is born!'
[4]That day—may it turn to darkness;
    may God above not care about it;
    may no light shine upon it.
[5]May darkness and deep shadow[b] claim it once
        more;
    may a cloud settle over it;
    may blackness overwhelm its light.
[6]That night—may thick darkness seize it;
    may it not be included among the days of
        the year
    nor be entered in any of the months.
[7]May that night be barren;
    may no shout of joy be heard in it.
[8]May those who curse days[c] curse that day,
    those who are ready to rouse Leviathan[D].
[9]May its morning stars become dark;
    may it wait for daylight in vain
    and not see the first rays of dawn,
[10]for it did not shut the doors of the womb on
        me
    to hide trouble from my eyes.

[11]"Why did I not perish at birth,
    and die as I came from the womb?
[12]Why were there knees to receive me
    and breasts that I might be nursed?
[13]For now I would be lying down in peace[D];
    I would be asleep and at rest
[14]with kings and counselors of the earth,
    who built for themselves places now lying in
        ruins,
[15]with rulers who had gold,

---

[a]10 The Hebrew word rendered *foolish* denotes moral deficiency.
[b]5 Or *and the shadow of death*   [c]8 Or *the sea*

who filled their houses with silver.
¹⁶Or why was I not hidden in the ground like a
　　stillborn child,
　like an infant who never saw the light of
　　day?
¹⁷There the wicked cease from turmoil,
　and there the weary are at rest.
¹⁸Captives also enjoy their ease;
　they no longer hear the slave driver's shout.
¹⁹The small and the great are there,
　and the slave is freed from his master.

²⁰"Why is light given to those in misery,
　and life to the bitter of soul^D,
²¹to those who long for death^D that does not
　　come,
　who search for it more than for hidden
　　treasure,
²²who are filled with gladness
　and rejoice when they reach the grave?
²³Why is life given to a man
　whose way is hidden,
　whom God has hedged in?
²⁴For sighing comes to me instead of food;
　my groans pour out like water.
²⁵What I feared has come upon me;
　what I dreaded has happened to me.
²⁶I have no peace^D, no quietness;
　I have no rest, but only turmoil."

Eliphaz

4 Then Eliphaz the Temanite replied:

²"If someone ventures a word with you, will you
　　be impatient?
　But who can keep from speaking?
³Think how you have instructed many,
　how you have strengthened feeble hands.
⁴Your words have supported those who
　　stumbled;
　you have strengthened faltering knees.
⁵But now trouble comes to you, and you are
　　discouraged;
　it strikes you, and you are dismayed.
⁶Should not your piety be your confidence
　and your blameless ways your hope?

⁷"Consider now: Who, being innocent, has ever
　　perished?
　Where were the upright ever destroyed?
⁸As I have observed, those who plow evil
　and those who sow trouble reap it.
⁹At the breath of God they are destroyed;
　at the blast of his anger they perish.
¹⁰The lions may roar and growl,
　yet the teeth of the great lions are broken.
¹¹The lion perishes for lack of prey,
　and the cubs of the lioness are scattered.

¹²"A word was secretly brought to me,
　my ears caught a whisper of it.
¹³Amid disquieting dreams in the night,
　when deep sleep falls on men,
¹⁴fear and trembling seized me
　and made all my bones shake.

Leviathan (3:8)

This may be a reference to a popular mythological dragon thought to cause eclipses by twisting itself around the sun. Or it could refer to a creature said by ancient mythical sources to have been defeated by God at creation. Later *leviathan* means the crocodile (41:1). For more on why the Bible would cite ancient mythology, see *Why did God break the heads of sea monsters?* (Psalm 74:13–14).

Is no life better than a troubled life? (3:10–16)

In his misery, Job might have thought so. But the Bible's message throughout is that life—all life—is a gift from God. Even in terrible suffering, God's glory can be revealed.

How had God *hedged in* Job? (3:23)

Satan accused God of putting a barrier around Job to protect him (1:10). Job saw things differently—that God's hedge meant there could be no escape from whatever God sent, including suffering as well as protection (1:21).

How had Job helped others? (4:3–4)

Job's godly lifestyle had been an example to many. He was a respected and influential leader, he helped those in need, and he saw that justice was done (29:7–17). Also see 31:13–22.

Don't the innocent ever die? (4:7–8)

See *Who would believe that bad things don't happen to good people?* (5:27).

Did Eliphaz see a ghost? (4:12–16)

It is unclear whether this language is meant to be understood figuratively or literally. There is nothing that can verify Eliphaz's experience as a genuine revelation.

Did Eliphaz mean no one could be perfect? (4:17–19)

Yes. But at the same time, ironically, Eliphaz acknowledged that Job was, as far as was humanly possible, *blameless* (v. 6).

Holy ones (5:1)

A reference to the angels, God's servants, similar to those in the heavenly council who stand in God's presence (1:6).

A fool ... the simple (5:2)

One who ignores God (Psalm 14:1) in contrast to the wise person who fears God and is able to judge between good and evil (Prov. 1:7). These terms refer to moral, not intellectual measurements. See NIV text note at 2:10.

¹⁵A spirit glided past my face,
  and the hair on my body stood on end.
¹⁶It stopped,
  but I could not tell what it was.
A form stood before my eyes,
  and I heard a hushed voice:
¹⁷'Can a mortal be more righteous[D] than God?
  Can a man be more pure than his Maker?
¹⁸If God places no trust in his servants,
  if he charges his angels with error,
¹⁹how much more those who live in houses of
    clay,
  whose foundations are in the dust,
  who are crushed more readily than a
    moth!
²⁰Between dawn and dusk they are broken to
    pieces;
  unnoticed, they perish forever.
²¹Are not the cords of their tent pulled up,
  so that they die without wisdom?'[a]

5 "Call if you will, but who will answer you?
     To which of the holy ones will you turn?
²Resentment kills a fool,
  and envy slays the simple.
³I myself have seen a fool taking root,
  but suddenly his house was cursed.
⁴His children are far from safety,
  crushed in court without a defender.

[a]21 Some interpreters end the quotation after verse 17.

What can we learn from Job's friends? (4:1)

Job's friends came to console him by sharing in his grief. But they soon began to accuse him, rigidly applying general principles to Job's specific situation. By distorting the truth in this way, Job's friends only added to his suffering.

So what are we to make of the large sections of this book that come from the lips of Job's friends (15 chapters compared to 20 for Job)? How much of what they say is true? How can we tell when they distort or misapply the truth to arrive at a wrong conclusion?

The key to understanding these passages in Job is *context*. Taken apart from the whole, the words of Eliphaz and the others can be misleading. For example, when Eliphaz suggests that the innocent and the upright are never destroyed (v. 7), we should remember that the Bible as a whole teaches that the righteous may at times suffer undeserved calamities, persecutions or even death. On the other hand, when Eliphaz says that God *performs wonders that cannot be fathomed, miracles that cannot be counted* (5:9), we can see the thought to be consistent with the rest of the Bible. Even Job echoes the same words (9:10).

Beyond comparing what Job's friends say with the rest of the Bible, we can learn from their faulty logic. If sin causes suffering, they reasoned, then all suffering must be caused by sin. Not so. Jesus contradicted such simplistic explanations when he showed his disciples that some suffering comes not because of sin, but to bring glory to God (John 9:1–3).

We can also learn from the example of Job's friends that we should not pass judgment on those who suffer. Rather than attempt to offer short-sighted explanations, Job's friends would have helped Job more to simply share his grief and admit that they did not know all the "whys" of life.

⁵The hungry consume his harvest,
   taking it even from among thorns,
   and the thirsty pant after his wealth.
⁶For hardship does not spring from the soil,
   nor does trouble sprout from the ground.
⁷Yet man is born to trouble
   as surely as sparks fly upward.

⁸"But if it were I, I would appeal to God;
   I would lay my cause before him.
⁹He performs wonders that cannot be
      fathomed,
   miracles that cannot be counted.
¹⁰He bestows rain on the earth;
   he sends water upon the countryside.
¹¹The lowly he sets on high,
   and those who mourn are lifted to safety.
¹²He thwarts the plans of the crafty,
   so that their hands achieve no success.
¹³He catches the wise in their craftiness,
   and the schemes of the wily are swept
      away.
¹⁴Darkness comes upon them in the daytime;
   at noon they grope as in the night.
¹⁵He saves the needy from the sword in their
      mouth;
   he saves them from the clutches of the
      powerful.
¹⁶So the poor have hope,
   and injustice shuts its mouth.

¹⁷"Blessed is the man whom God corrects;
   so do not despise the discipline of the
      Almighty.ᵃ
¹⁸For he wounds, but he also binds up;
   he injures, but his hands also heal.
¹⁹From six calamities he will rescue you;
   in seven no harm will befall you.
²⁰In famine he will ransom you from deathᴰ,
   and in battle from the stroke of the sword.
²¹You will be protected from the lash of the
      tongue,
   and need not fear when destruction comes.
²²You will laugh at destruction and famine,
   and need not fear the beasts of the earth.
²³For you will have a covenantᴰ with the stones
      of the field,
   and the wild animals will be at peaceᴰ with
      you.
²⁴You will know that your tent is secure;
   you will take stock of your property and find
      nothing missing.
²⁵You will know that your children will be
      many,
   and your descendants like the grass of the
      earth.
²⁶You will come to the grave in full vigor,
   like sheaves gathered in season.

²⁷"We have examined this, and it is true.
   So hear it and apply it to yourself."

Is trouble going to come no matter what we do? (5:7)

In essence, yes. Trouble is certain. In a world fallen due to sin, no one can escape the trouble inherent in this life. Some may seem to have more trouble than others, but all face something sooner or later. Eliphaz makes a direct connection between moral evil and physical evil—that trouble comes from doing wrong. This is only one explanation of suffering, however, and it wasn't the right one for Job's circumstances.

Why did Eliphaz advise Job to appeal his case to God? (5:8)

There is more a tone of judgment than concern in Eliphaz's advice. Ironically, Job wanted to have God hear his case too (13:3). Some think Eliphaz was suggesting that God would remove Job's troubles or show him where he had gone wrong.

Does God always lift the lowly and thwart the crafty? (5:11–12)

See *Who would believe that bad things don't happen to good people?* (5:27).

The sword in their mouth (5:15)

Although the precise meaning of this phrase is unclear, Eliphaz's intent seems to be that God saves those who are oppressed and needy. *The sword*, then, may mean the threat of violence.

Why did Eliphaz think God was disciplining Job? (5:17–18)

This was the only explanation that would fit the conventional views of the day. If Job was suffering, Eliphaz reasoned, it was clear Job had sinned and was receiving God's judgment.

From six . . . in seven (5:19)

This kind of language is common in the Old Testament—a number mentioned within the framework of a second number which represented a limit or extreme. For the Hebrews, the number *seven* symbolized perfection or completion. The idea is that because God is able to rescue from many troubles (six), he is able to deliver from them all.

Who would believe that bad things don't happen to good people? (5:27)

Most everyone at that time. Eliphaz articulated the conventional wisdom of the day. His rather simplistic view (4:7–8) must have added to Job's already intense pain. Job and his friends did not know what we know from chs. 1–2: bad things do happen to good people. In fact, it is Job's experience, recounted through the inspiration of the Spirit, that helps us see things differently.

ᵃ17 Hebrew *Shaddai*; here and throughout Job

Were Job's troubles due to God's arrows—God's terrors? (6:4)

In a sense, yes. Since God allowed the troubles, he can be seen as the one ultimately responsible. What Job had difficulty seeing (as we do too) is that troubles are not just a result of sin, and that God can use our troubles to accomplish an even greater good. See *How did Satan incite God?* (2:3).

What was Job's point about a braying donkey and a bellowing ox? (6:5)

This is a word picture. As donkeys and oxen make noise when they have no food, Job felt he had a right to complain (that is, to make noise) about his suffering. If someone could give him an explanation for his troubles, Job said, he would stop his bellowing. As it was, he was starved for words to encourage and sustain him, rather than the *tasteless* accusations Eliphaz offered (v. 6).

What did Job want? (6:8–13)

Job wanted to die. Since God seemed inaccessible, Job felt death was the only escape from his suffering and pain. But even more than an escape, Job wanted to remain faithful to God by not denying him while he was in his weakened condition.

Why were Job's friends undependable? (6:15–17)

With their limited knowledge and experience, they were unqualified to judge Job's situation (vv. 21,26). They were more interested in defending their assumptions about sin and suffering than they were in caring for their friend and what he was feeling. Job needed *the devotion of his friends* (v. 14). What he got was criticism and condemnation.

Caravans of Tema . . . merchants of Sheba (6:19)

This is another word picture (see v. 5). Tema was an oasis in northern Arabia; Sheba was probably in southern Arabia (see *Map 1* at the back of this Bible). Caravans crossed the deserts with the hopes of finding an oasis so they could finish the journey. Just as those caravans would be *distressed* and *disappointed* (v. 20) if they didn't find water in the place they expected, Job was distressed not to find devotion from those he assumed would stand by him—his friends.

What did Job hope to learn? (6:24)

There was perhaps a touch of sarcasm in this challenge Job issued to his friends. In his mind they were as cruel as those who would collect debts by making servants out of orphans or even friends (v. 27). Job wanted more than their pat answers to the question of suffering.

Job

6 Then Job replied:

2 "If only my anguish could be weighed
    and all my misery be placed on the scales!
3 It would surely outweigh the sand of the seas—
    no wonder my words have been impetuous.
4 The arrows of the Almighty are in me,
    my spirit drinks in their poison;
    God's terrors are marshaled against me.
5 Does a wild donkey bray when it has grass,
    or an ox bellow when it has fodder?
6 Is tasteless food eaten without salt,
    or is there flavor in the white of an egg*a*?
7 I refuse to touch it;
    such food makes me ill.

8 "Oh, that I might have my request,
    that God would grant what I hope for,
9 that God would be willing to crush me,
    to let loose his hand and cut me off!
10 Then I would still have this consolation—
    my joy in unrelenting pain—
    that I had not denied the words of the Holy One.

11 "What strength do I have, that I should still hope?
    What prospects, that I should be patient?
12 Do I have the strength of stone?
    Is my flesh bronze?
13 Do I have any power to help myself,
    now that success has been driven from me?

14 "A despairing man should have the devotion of his friends,
    even though he forsakes the fear of the Almighty.
15 But my brothers are as undependable as intermittent streams,
    as the streams that overflow
16 when darkened by thawing ice
    and swollen with melting snow,
17 but that cease to flow in the dry season,
    and in the heat vanish from their channels.
18 Caravans turn aside from their routes;
    they go up into the wasteland and perish.
19 The caravans of Tema look for water,
    the traveling merchants of Sheba look in hope.
20 They are distressed, because they had been confident;
    they arrive there, only to be disappointed.
21 Now you too have proved to be of no help;
    you see something dreadful and are afraid.
22 Have I ever said, 'Give something on my behalf,
    pay a ransom for me from your wealth,
23 deliver me from the hand of the enemy,
    ransom me from the clutches of the ruthless'?

24 "Teach me, and I will be quiet;
    show me where I have been wrong.

---

a 6 The meaning of the Hebrew for this phrase is uncertain.

25How painful are honest words!
But what do your arguments prove?
26Do you mean to correct what I say,
and treat the words of a despairing man as
wind?
27You would even cast lots for the fatherless
and barter away your friend.

28"But now be so kind as to look at me.
Would I lie to your face?
29Relent, do not be unjust;
reconsider, for my integrity is at stake.[a]
30Is there any wickedness on my lips?
Can my mouth not discern malice?

7 "Does not man have hard service on earth?
Are not his days like those of a hired man?
2Like a slave longing for the evening shadows,
or a hired man waiting eagerly for his wages,
3so I have been allotted months of futility,
and nights of misery have been assigned to
me.
4When I lie down I think, 'How long before I get
up?'
The night drags on, and I toss till dawn.
5My body is clothed with worms and scabs,
my skin is broken and festering.

6"My days are swifter than a weaver's shuttle,
and they come to an end without hope.
7Remember, O God, that my life is but a breath;
my eyes will never see happiness again.
8The eye that now sees me will see me no
longer;
you will look for me, but I will be no more.
9As a cloud vanishes and is gone,
so he who goes down to the grave[b] does not
return.
10He will never come to his house again;
his place will know him no more.

11"Therefore I will not keep silent;
I will speak out in the anguish of my spirit,
I will complain in the bitterness of my
soul.D
12Am I the sea, or the monster of the deep,
that you put me under guard?
13When I think my bed will comfort me
and my couch will ease my complaint,
14even then you frighten me with dreams
and terrify me with visions,D
15so that I prefer strangling and death,D
rather than this body of mine.
16I despise my life; I would not live forever.
Let me alone; my days have no meaning.

17"What is man that you make so much of him,
that you give him so much attention,
18that you examine him every morning
and test him every moment?
19Will you never look away from me,
or let me alone even for an instant?
20If I have sinned, what have I done to you,
O watcher of men?

How is life like slavery? (7:1–2)
This is another word picture. Job wants his suffering to end, describing his desire like that of
a slave or servant who longs for the end of the
workday or, better still, for payday. A troubled
life is like slavery because there seems to be
no escape and the end is nowhere in sight.

What kind of disease did Job have? (7:5)
See *What kind of sores did Job have?* (2:7–8).

Weaver's shuttle (7:6)
An instrument used with a loom to weave the
cross (woof) threads of a piece of fabric between the (warp) threads held lengthwise in
the loom. The speed with which a weaver
throws the shuttle from one side to the other is
a striking illustration of the passing of life.

Had Job given up hope? (7:8–10)
Job looked to death as his hope for relief from
pain and suffering. In his despair he saw no
other basis for hope in this life.

Does God send nightmares? (7:14)
The Bible speaks of God's use of dreams to
communicate messages. See article: *Does God
speak through visions and dreams?* (Daniel
1:17). However, nightmares are another matter. Perhaps this is meant to be understood figuratively—one of several ways Job expresses
his view that God is responsible for his suffering.

Can those who trust in God get so depressed? (7:15–16)
Yes, even those with great faith have their moments of despair. Moses wanted to die (Num.
11:15) as did Elijah (1 Kings 19:4), and Jeremiah wished he'd never been born (Jer.
20:14). Job wanted release from his suffering.

Does God continually test us? (7:18)
No, at least not in the unmerciful sense that
Job implies here. We should remember that
these are the words of a deeply despondent
man, one who saw death as preferable to life
(3:17–22). Those whom God delivers from the
depths of despair see things differently. Some
see Job's words (vv. 17–18) as a parody on the
theme of Psalm 8:4: *What is man that you are
mindful of him, the son of man that you care
for him?* As to the purpose of being tested, see
article: *Why did testing come to Job?* (23:10).

a29 Or *my righteousness still stands*   b9 Hebrew *Sheol*

Why couldn't Job receive any assurance of forgiveness? (7:21)

Job had no external, physical evidence that his life was approved by God. According to the views of the day, he was continually being judged. So it seemed that not only was he guilty of sin, but that his sacrifices and prayers had amounted to nothing. Also see article: *Why did testing come to Job?* (23:10).

Why ask questions with obvious answers? (8:3)

Used correctly, a rhetorical question can be an effective communication tool. Bildad, however, uses these questions to viciously undercut what little remaining hope Job might have had that he could receive any encouragement from his "friends." Far from empathizing with Job, Bildad attacks him for daring to express his complaints to God.

Did God restore Job to his rightful place? (8:6–7)

See *Why did God reward Job with material prosperity?* (42:12–13).

What do the godless trust in that is fragile? (8:13–14)

The word for *godless* here means something like *hypocrite*. One who hopes in false pretensions or superficial appearances depends on that which is unreliable and temporary—like a spider's web.

Why do some blameless suffer and some evildoers succeed? (8:20)

See *Who would believe that bad things don't happen to good people?* (5:27).

Why have you made me your target?
Have I become a burden to you?[a]
²¹Why do you not pardon my offenses
and forgive my sins?
For I will soon lie down in the dust;
you will search for me, but I will be no
more."

Bildad

8 Then Bildad the Shuhite replied:

²"How long will you say such things?
Your words are a blustering wind.
³Does God pervert justice?
Does the Almighty pervert what is right?
⁴When your children sinned against him,
he gave them over to the penalty of their sin.
⁵But if you will look to God
and plead with the Almighty,
⁶if you are pure and upright,
even now he will rouse himself on your
behalf
and restore you to your rightful place.
⁷Your beginnings will seem humble,
so prosperous will your future be.

⁸"Ask the former generations
and find out what their fathers learned,
⁹for we were born only yesterday and know
nothing,
and our days on earth are but a shadow.
¹⁰Will they not instruct you and tell you?
Will they not bring forth words from their
understanding?
¹¹Can papyrus grow tall where there is no
marsh?
Can reeds thrive without water?
¹²While still growing and uncut,
they wither more quickly than grass.
¹³Such is the destiny of all who forget God;
so perishes the hope of the godless.
¹⁴What he trusts in is fragile[b];
what he relies on is a spider's web.
¹⁵He leans on his web, but it gives way;
he clings to it, but it does not hold.
¹⁶He is like a well-watered plant in the sunshine,
spreading its shoots over the garden;
¹⁷it entwines its roots around a pile of rocks
and looks for a place among the stones.
¹⁸But when it is torn from its spot,
that place disowns it and says, 'I never saw
you.'
¹⁹Surely its life withers away,
and[c] from the soil other plants grow.

²⁰"Surely God does not reject a blameless man
or strengthen the hands of evildoers.
²¹He will yet fill your mouth with laughter
and your lips with shouts of joy.

---

[a]20 A few manuscripts of the Masoretic Text, an ancient Hebrew scribal tradition and Septuagint; most manuscripts of the Masoretic Text *I have become a burden to myself.*   [b]14 The meaning of the Hebrew for this word is uncertain.   [c]19 Or *Surely all the joy it has / is that*

²²Your enemies will be clothed in shame,
  and the tents of the wicked will be no more."

Job

9 Then Job replied:

²"Indeed, I know that this is true.
  But how can a mortal be righteous^D before
      God?
³Though one wished to dispute with him,
  he could not answer him one time out of a
      thousand.
⁴His wisdom is profound, his power is vast.
  Who has resisted him and come out
      unscathed?
⁵He moves mountains without their knowing it
  and overturns them in his anger.
⁶He shakes the earth from its place
  and makes its pillars tremble.
⁷He speaks to the sun and it does not shine;
  he seals off the light of the stars.
⁸He alone stretches out the heavens
  and treads on the waves of the sea.
⁹He is the Maker of the Bear and Orion,
  the Pleiades and the constellations of the
      south.
¹⁰He performs wonders that cannot be fathomed,
  miracles that cannot be counted.
¹¹When he passes me, I cannot see him;
  when he goes by, I cannot perceive him.
¹²If he snatches away, who can stop him?
  Who can say to him, 'What are you doing?'
¹³God does not restrain his anger;
  even the cohorts of Rahab^D cowered at his
      feet.

¹⁴"How then can I dispute with him?
  How can I find words to argue with him?
¹⁵Though I were innocent, I could not answer
      him;
  I could only plead with my Judge for
      mercy.^D
¹⁶Even if I summoned him and he responded,
  I do not believe he would give me a hearing.
¹⁷He would crush me with a storm
  and multiply my wounds for no reason.
¹⁸He would not let me regain my breath
  but would overwhelm me with misery.
¹⁹If it is a matter of strength, he is mighty!
  And if it is a matter of justice, who will
      summon him^a?
²⁰Even if I were innocent, my mouth would
      condemn me;
  if I were blameless, it would pronounce me
      guilty.

²¹"Although I am blameless,
  I have no concern for myself;
  I despise my own life.
²²It is all the same; that is why I say,
  'He destroys both the blameless and the
      wicked.'
²³When a scourge brings sudden death,^D

^a19 See Septuagint; Hebrew *me*.

Did Job concede Bildad's argument? (9:2)

Job was probably referring to the general idea that God is just and holy in all he does. In other words, he conceded the overall facts of Bildad's argument, but still raised the larger question about how a person can be righteous in God's sight. See article: *Are we responsible for inborn sin?* (25:4).

SCRIPTURE LINK (9:2,10)

Job echoes the earlier words of Eliphaz (see 4:17; 5:9), perhaps to counter Bildad's simplistic explanations: "What you say is true, but what Eliphaz said is also true. No one can be righteous before a holy God."

What would Job have known about the constellations? (9:9)

His words probably reflect the common knowledge of ancient people and the prevailing view of astronomy at that time. Just as mountains, seas and other physical landmarks were named, the ancients mapped out the skies and gave names to the various combinations of stars.

Does God hide from us? (9:11)

Sometimes it may seem so. The Psalms express this frustration. See *Does God have a physical body?* (Psalm 13:1). Job says that while he can sense God's presence all around him and while he can see the evidence of God's work (vv. 5–10), the sovereign God of the universe is somehow elusive. Job was not speaking of a God who hides so much as he was expressing poetically the awesome grandeur of God.

Rahab (9:13)

A mythological sea monster (the name itself means *storm*). See *Rahab* (Psalm 89:10).

Boats of papyrus (9:26)
Boats made of the tall, grass-like plants that grew in marshes. The papyrus stalks were woven together and waterproofed. The basket boat that carried Moses as a baby was a smaller version (Exodus 2:3).

Was Job guilty until proven innocent? (9:29–31)
Job's unrelieved suffering was proof to Job's friends that he had sinned and refused to repent. But Job was honest enough to insist he knew of nothing he had done for which he should repent. Since he was apparently being judged and he knew of no way to purge himself before God, Job may have resigned himself to suffering. Why seek vindication when God seemed determined to hold him guilty?

Why did Job long for a mediator between him and God? (9:33–35)
Confident of his clear conscience but seemingly unable to gain a hearing with God, Job longed for an arbitrator to decide his case with God. It was a whimsical request; Job knew there was no one who could make an appeal to God on his behalf. Yet his desire for an advocate is a powerful example of our need for a Savior.

Was Job's request for an explanation unreasonable? (10:2)
No. Job was not being rebellious or arrogant. He simply wanted to understand the reasons for his suffering. But the larger issue, which is not mentioned until later, is that the sovereign God can decide to withhold information from us. Though we understand the reasons behind Job's suffering (from chs. 1–2), we don't know why God thought it best to leave Job in the dark.

he mocks the despair of the innocent.
²⁴When a land falls into the hands of the wicked,
   he blindfolds its judges.
   If it is not he, then who is it?

²⁵"My days are swifter than a runner;
   they fly away without a glimpse of joy.
²⁶They skim past like boats of papyrus,
   like eagles swooping down on their prey.
²⁷If I say, 'I will forget my complaint,
   I will change my expression, and smile,'
²⁸I still dread all my sufferings,
   for I know you will not hold me innocent.
²⁹Since I am already found guilty,
   why should I struggle in vain?
³⁰Even if I washed myself with soap*ᵃ*
   and my hands with washing soda,
³¹you would plunge me into a slime pit
   so that even my clothes would detest me.

³²"He is not a man like me that I might answer him,
   that we might confront each other in court.
³³If only there were someone to arbitrate between us,
   to lay his hand upon us both,
³⁴someone to remove God's rod from me,
   so that his terror would frighten me no more.
³⁵Then I would speak up without fear of him,
   but as it now stands with me, I cannot.

10 "I loathe my very life;
   therefore I will give free rein to my complaint
   and speak out in the bitterness of my soul*ᵇ*.
²I will say to God: Do not condemn me,
   but tell me what charges you have against me.

ᵃ30 Or snow

Is God guilty of neglect? (9:22–24)

No. But to those who have hit bottom and feel abandoned, God might appear neglectful. See **Does God help us out of all troubles?** (Psalm 34:17).

In his despair Job paints a horrifying—and incorrect—picture of God, saying that he afflicts *for no reason* (v. 17), overwhelms people with misery (v. 18), destroys both the righteous and the unrighteous indiscriminately (v. 22), laughs at the pain of the innocent (v. 23) and allows injustice (v. 24). Job's fear of this tyrannical deity could force him to confess to sins he had not committed (v. 20)!

But these are the words of a despondent, discouraged Job. On the whole, Job had a higher view of God than this. The major difference between Job's view of God and that of his friends was his belief that afflictions in this life come to both the righteous and the unrighteous—that suffering could not always be explained in terms of what one deserved.

Severe and sudden calamity is no more a sign of disfavor with God than sustained prosperity indicates God's approval and blessing. But in the next life God promises to balance the scales and make right all that has been perverted by sin here on earth. God is not guilty of neglect, but he allows some suffering to accomplish his greater purposes, often beyond human comprehension.

³Does it please you to oppress me,
    to spurn the work of your hands,
    while you smile on the schemes of the
        wicked?
⁴Do you have eyes of flesh?
    Do you see as a mortal sees?
⁵Are your days like those of a mortal
    or your years like those of a man,
⁶that you must search out my faults
    and probe after my sin—
⁷though you know that I am not guilty
    and that no one can rescue me from your
        hand?

⁸"Your hands shaped me and made me.
    Will you now turn and destroy me?
⁹Remember that you molded me like clay.
    Will you now turn me to dust again?
¹⁰Did you not pour me out like milk
    and curdle me like cheese,
¹¹clothe me with skin and flesh
    and knit me together with bones and sinews?
¹²You gave me life and showed me kindness,
    and in your providence watched over my
        spirit.

¹³"But this is what you concealed in your heart,
    and I know that this was in your mind:
¹⁴If I sinned, you would be watching me
    and would not let my offense go unpunished.
¹⁵If I am guilty—woe to me!
    Even if I am innocent, I cannot lift my head,
    for I am full of shame
    and drowned in^a my affliction.^b
¹⁶If I hold my head high, you stalk me like a lion
    and again display your awesome power
        against me.
¹⁷You bring new witnesses against me
    and increase your anger toward me;
    your forces come against me wave upon
        wave.

¹⁸"Why then did you bring me out of the womb?
    I wish I had died before any eye saw me.
¹⁹If only I had never come into being,
    or had been carried straight from the womb
        to the grave!
²⁰Are not my few days almost over?
    Turn away from me so I can have a
        moment's joy
²¹before I go to the place of no return,
    to the land of gloom and deep shadow,^b
²²to the land of deepest night,
    of deep shadow and disorder,
    where even the light is like darkness."

Zophar

11 Then Zophar the Naamathite replied:

²"Are all these words to go unanswered?
    Is this talker to be vindicated?
³Will your idle talk reduce men to silence?

_a15 Or_ and aware of   _b21 Or_ and the shadow of death; _also in_
verse 22

Does God watch to catch us sinning? (10:13–14)
God's eye is on us continually, but not in the sense of trying to get us. Rather, God's love and concern cause him to watch us continually (Psalm 34:15, for example). Job's words, however, express his darkest thoughts and fears. More than likely, Job did not have access to any of God's written Word that could have encouraged him with God's watchful mercy. All Job had, for the moment, was his experience of suffering.

Is it better to have lived with trouble than never to have lived at all? (10:18–19)
See _Is no life better than a troubled life?_ (3:10–16).

What did Job believe about the afterlife? (10:21–22)
See _What did Job believe about the afterlife?_ (19:25–27).

How is light like darkness in the next life? (10:22)
In ancient times little was known about what happened after death. Lack of knowledge was frequently characterized as darkness; knowledge was enlightenment. The mysteries of the hereafter seemed like deep darkness to people in Job's time. The land of the dead was considered as absolute night without a hint of light.

Did Zophar think Job might vindicate himself? (11:2)
Zophar wasn't worried that Job might be proven innocent of the charge of sin leveled against him. He simply didn't want Job's latest words to go unchallenged. He couldn't imagine that Job was being honest with himself. Zophar regarded Job's protests of innocence as pure mockery.

Does God forget our sins? (11:6)

Nothing escapes God. He sees all sins and in-justices in the world. Zophar, however, seems to imply sarcastically that Job's punishment would be much worse if God had not forgotten some of his sin. In reality, though God does not forget as we understand forgetfulness, he does choose to not remember our sins and to mercifully wipe the slate clean (Isaiah 43:25).

Why did Zophar accuse Job of claiming to understand God? (11:7)

Zophar continues to misinterpret what Job has said. Job did not claim to be able to fathom the depths of God's mind. He knew that humanity could never comprehend the purposes of God. Job only sought an answer to why he was suf-fering.

Did Zophar think Job's troubles would be solved? (11:16)

Zophar erroneously and arrogantly suggested that if Job repented, all his problems would be solved. He assumed he knew the reasons for Job's suffering, and his limited knowledge caused him to be simplistic in his solution.

Was Job being sarcastic? (12:2-3)

Yes. He was fed up with Zophar's attacks about his sins (11:6,14) and lack of wisdom (11:7,12). After being called a *witless man,* Job rose up to defend himself, using both sarcasm and logic. He was as intelligent as Zophar, and obviously Zophar did not have a corner on wis-dom. *You are the people* means the only peo-ple who count.

How had Job become a laughingstock? (12:4)

Job suffered ridicule because of his horren-dous personal losses. The assumption was that he suffered because of sin. In those days the basic theology was that God blessed the righteous and cursed the wicked. Job never wa-vered, however. He maintained his innocence throughout.

How could Job claim to be *righteous and blameless?* (12:4)

He was not claiming absolute perfection on a par with God's holiness. But the general tenor of his life pleased God; his claim on righteous-ness was validated by God (1:1,8). Even after calamity struck he worshiped God (1:20). He did not sin by cursing God for what had hap-pened to him (1:22; 2:10).

Will no one rebuke you when you mock?
⁴You say to God, 'My beliefs are flawless
 and I am pure in your sight.'
⁵Oh, how I wish that God would speak,
 that he would open his lips against you
⁶and disclose to you the secrets of wisdom,
 for true wisdom has two sides.
 Know this: God has even forgotten some of
  your sin.

⁷"Can you fathom the mysteries^D of God?
 Can you probe the limits of the Almighty?
⁸They are higher than the heavens—what can
  you do?
 They are deeper than the depths of the
  grave^a—what can you know?
⁹Their measure is longer than the earth
 and wider than the sea.

¹⁰"If he comes along and confines you in prison
 and convenes a court, who can oppose him?
¹¹Surely he recognizes deceitful men;
 and when he sees evil, does he not take
  note?
¹²But a witless man can no more become wise
 than a wild donkey's colt can be born a
  man.^b

¹³"Yet if you devote your heart to him
 and stretch out your hands to him,
¹⁴if you put away the sin that is in your hand
 and allow no evil to dwell in your tent,
¹⁵then you will lift up your face without shame;
 you will stand firm and without fear.
¹⁶You will surely forget your trouble,
 recalling it only as waters gone by.
¹⁷Life will be brighter than noonday,
 and darkness will become like morning.
¹⁸You will be secure, because there is hope;
 you will look about you and take your rest in
  safety.
¹⁹You will lie down, with no one to make you
  afraid,
 and many will court your favor.
²⁰But the eyes of the wicked will fail,
 and escape will elude them;
 their hope will become a dying gasp."

Job

12 Then Job replied:

²"Doubtless you are the people,
 and wisdom will die with you!
³But I have a mind as well as you;
 I am not inferior to you.
 Who does not know all these things?

⁴"I have become a laughingstock to my friends,
 though I called upon God and he answered—
 a mere laughingstock, though righteous^D
  and blameless!
⁵Men at ease have contempt for misfortune
 as the fate of those whose feet are slipping.
⁶The tents of marauders are undisturbed,

^a8 Hebrew *than Sheol*   ^b12 Or *wild donkey can be born tame*

and those who provoke God are secure—
those who carry their god in their hands.[a]

7"But ask the animals, and they will teach you,
or the birds of the air, and they will tell you;
8or speak to the earth, and it will teach you,
or let the fish of the sea inform you.
9Which of all these does not know
that the hand of the LORD has done this?
10In his hand is the life of every creature
and the breath of all mankind.
11Does not the ear test words
as the tongue tastes food?
12Is not wisdom found among the aged?
Does not long life bring understanding?

13"To God belong wisdom and power;
counsel and understanding are his.
14What he tears down cannot be rebuilt;
the man he imprisons cannot be released.
15If he holds back the waters, there is drought;
if he lets them loose, they devastate the land.
16To him belong strength and victory;
both deceived and deceiver are his.
17He leads counselors away stripped
and makes fools of judges.
18He takes off the shackles put on by kings
and ties a loincloth[b] around their waist.
19He leads priests[D] away stripped
and overthrows men long established.
20He silences the lips of trusted advisers
and takes away the discernment of elders.
21He pours contempt on nobles
and disarms the mighty.
22He reveals the deep things of darkness
and brings deep shadows into the light.
23He makes nations great, and destroys them;
he enlarges nations, and disperses them.
24He deprives the leaders of the earth of their
reason;
he sends them wandering through a trackless
waste.
25They grope in darkness with no light;
he makes them stagger like drunkards.

13 "My eyes have seen all this,
my ears have heard and understood it.
2What you know, I also know;
I am not inferior to you.
3But I desire to speak to the Almighty
and to argue my case with God.
4You, however, smear me with lies;
you are worthless physicians, all of you!
5If only you would be altogether silent!
For you, that would be wisdom.
6Hear now my argument;
listen to the plea of my lips.
7Will you speak wickedly on God's behalf?
Will you speak deceitfully for him?
8Will you show him partiality?
Will you argue the case for God?
9Would it turn out well if he examined you?

Who carry their god in their hands (12:6)
The meaning of this phrase is unclear. It may
mean the marauders worship only their own
power—in which case the *god in their hands*
would be their swords.

Why the rhetorical questions? (12:11–12)
Rhetorical questions are the normal fare of
skillful debaters. They contain irony and sometimes sarcasm. See *Why ask questions with
obvious answers?* (8:3).

Why is God unpredictable? (12:15–16,22–23)
Because he is God, and we are frail human beings with limited understanding. As Job groped
for some resolution of his dilemma, he could
find no integrating principle. Even so, people of
faith hold to the belief that God knows what he
is doing as he works out the details of his
plans.

Is it presumptuous to want an audi-ence with God? (13:3)
Not at all. That is the essence of prayer. Prayer
is our avenue to communicate with God, and it
should include our appeals as well as our worship. Because we desire answers to our *why*
questions, we confess our ignorance and ask
God for his enlightenment. Of course, it is presumptuous if our purpose is self-justification,
to prove that we are right and God is wrong.

a6 Or secure / in what God's hand brings them   b18 Or shackles of
kings / and ties a belt

Could you deceive him as you might deceive
    men?
[10]He would surely rebuke you
    if you secretly showed partiality.
[11]Would not his splendor terrify you?
    Would not the dread of him fall on you?
[12]Your maxims are proverbs of ashes;
    your defenses are defenses of clay.

[13]"Keep silent and let me speak;
    then let come to me what may.
[14]Why do I put myself in jeopardy
    and take my life in my hands?
[15]Though he slay me, yet will I hope in him;[a]
    I will surely[a] defend my ways to his face.
[16]Indeed, this will turn out for my deliverance,
    for no godless man would dare come before
      him!
[17]Listen carefully to my words;
    let your ears take in what I say.
[18]Now that I have prepared my case,
    I know I will be vindicated.
[19]Can anyone bring charges against me?
    If so, I will be silent and die.

[20]"Only grant me these two things, O God,
    and then I will not hide from you:
[21]Withdraw your hand far from me,
    and stop frightening me with your terrors.
[22]Then summon me and I will answer,
    or let me speak, and you reply.
[23]How many wrongs and sins have I committed?
    Show me my offense and my sin.
[24]Why do you hide your face
    and consider me your enemy?
[25]Will you torment a windblown leaf?
    Will you chase after dry chaff[D]?
[26]For you write down bitter things against me
    and make me inherit the sins of my youth.
[27]You fasten my feet in shackles;
    you keep close watch on all my paths
    by putting marks on the soles of my feet.

[28]"So man wastes away like something rotten,
    like a garment eaten by moths.

14

"Man born of woman
    is of few days and full of trouble.
[2]He springs up like a flower and withers away;
    like a fleeting shadow, he does not endure.
[3]Do you fix your eye on such a one?
    Will you bring him[b] before you for
      judgment?
[4]Who can bring what is pure from the impure?
    No one!
[5]Man's days are determined;
    you have decreed the number of his months
    and have set limits he cannot exceed.
[6]So look away from him and let him alone,
    till he has put in his time like a hired man.

[7]"At least there is hope for a tree:
    If it is cut down, it will sprout again,

In what way was Job laying his life on the line? (13:14)

Job realized that any confrontation with the Almighty carried considerable risk. Suppose he pled his case and lost? Would God punish him further? Job had such an exalted view of God that he knew he was moving on dangerous ground.

Did Job believe God would kill him? (13:15)

Probably not. Job was a realist who professed his hope in God no matter what the outcome. Death comes to all, but death is no reason to abandon hope in God. Job trusted God because he recognized God's control over every detail of his life.

Would God grant Job's requests? (13:20-22)

Job's argument adopts a courtroom stance. He appeals to God as his judge and makes two reasonable requests: the removal of God's heavy hand from him, and the end of God's frightening terrors. Obviously, he hoped for a quick end to his suffering, but he received no such assurance from God. In that sense, his requests were not granted immediately. In due course, however, they were.

Does God torment people? (13:25)

No. However, sinners under the Holy Spirit's conviction often believe God is hounding them. In the end, when they confess their sins and see their offenses against God, often they are frightened of the consequences. In this case, Job did not think his youthful sins (v. 26) merited such treatment.

Why did Job think God focused on his sins? (13:26)

Job saw himself under God's indictment. Because he had suffered so much, he thought that God must have had a huge charge against him. It is easy when under judgment to think the judge has forgotten all the good things and picked out only the bad things. Job thought God was unfair to make such a fuss over his youthful recklessness.

Marks on the soles of my feet (13:27)

Some think ancient slave owners branded their names on the feet of their slaves. Others believe this has the more generic meaning of examine my footprints.

What does God decree for each person? (14:5)

The Bible presents God as sovereign, controlling the destiny of all humanity. When it comes to moral choices, some say even these are determined. However, the prophets, Jesus and the apostles all appealed for people to make their own choice by repenting of sin and exercising faith. Of course, God creates the boundaries within which these choices are made.

[a]15 Or He will surely slay me; I have no hope — / yet I will
[b]3 Septuagint, Vulgate and Syriac; Hebrew me

and its new shoots will not fail.
8Its roots may grow old in the ground
   and its stump die in the soil,
9yet at the scent of water it will bud
   and put forth shoots like a plant.
10But man dies and is laid low;
   he breathes his last and is no more.
11As water disappears from the sea
   or a riverbed becomes parched and dry,
12so man lies down and does not rise;
   till the heavens are no more, men will not
      awake
   or be roused from their sleep.

13"If only you would hide me in the grave*a*
   and conceal me till your anger has passed!
   If only you would set me a time
   and then remember me!
14If a man dies, will he live again?
   All the days of my hard service
   I will wait for my renewal*b* to come.
15You will call and I will answer you;
   you will long for the creature your hands
      have made.
16Surely then you will count my steps
   but not keep track of my sin.
17My offenses will be sealed up in a bag;
   you will cover over my sin.

18"But as a mountain erodes and crumbles
   and as a rock is moved from its place,
19as water wears away stones
   and torrents wash away the soil,
   so you destroy man's hope.
20You overpower him once for all, and he is
      gone;
   you change his countenance and send him
      away.
21If his sons are honored, he does not know it;
   if they are brought low, he does not see it.
22He feels but the pain of his own body
   and mourns only for himself."

Eliphaz

15 Then Eliphaz the Temanite replied:

2"Would a wise man answer with empty notions
   or fill his belly with the hot east wind?
3Would he argue with useless words,
   with speeches that have no value?
4But you even undermine piety
   and hinder devotion to God.
5Your sin prompts your mouth;
   you adopt the tongue of the crafty.
6Your own mouth condemns you, not mine;
   your own lips testify against you.

7"Are you the first man ever born?
   Were you brought forth before the hills?
8Do you listen in on God's council?
   Do you limit wisdom to yourself?
9What do you know that we do not know?

Renewal (14:14)
Release or relief. In his depression Job could
not be consoled, so he would go on asking for
relief from his suffering.

How did Eliphaz think Job was hinder-ing devotion to God? (15:4)
He thought Job was keeping people from their
piety because he persistently refused to acknowledge his sins. To Eliphaz's mind, Job was
a terrible example. The truly pious would confess their sins and seek God's mercy, not ask
for a hearing before God Almighty. If Job would
accept the charges of his critics, Eliphaz reasoned, devotion to God would increase.

*a*13 Hebrew *Sheol*   *b*14 Or *release*

What insights do you have that we do not
            have?

[10]The gray-haired and the aged are on our side,
            men even older than your father.

[11]Are God's consolations not enough for you,
            words spoken gently to you?

[12]Why has your heart carried you away,
            and why do your eyes flash,

[13]so that you vent your rage against God
            and pour out such words from your mouth?

[14]"What is man, that he could be pure,
            or one born of woman, that he could be
            righteous[D]?

[15]If God places no trust in his holy ones,
            if even the heavens are not pure in his eyes,

[16]how much less man, who is vile and corrupt,
            who drinks up evil like water!

Who was given the land? (15:19)

The fathers of the wise men, the patriarchs beginning with Abraham.

What kind of torment do the wicked suffer? (15:20)

Eliphaz is speaking of psychological torment—
guilt for sin, insecurity, lack of peace and fear
of death and judgment (vv. 23–26; John 16:8;
Isaiah 57:21). He paints a dark picture of their
inner life. Ultimately, the wicked are judged by
God at the end of the age (Rev. 20:11–15).

Were Job's troubles like those that come to the wicked? (15:24–33)

Eliphaz's intent was to shake Job up. He
paints a terrifying picture of judgment on the
wicked. It was supposed to motivate Job to
confess his sins. His friends had already tried
and convicted him, and now they pronounced
judgment. Their theology was filled with half-
truths: the wicked would be punished, true
enough. But that didn't mean that Job was being punished or that he was wicked. In actual
fact, Job was *blameless* and *upright* (1:1).

[17]"Listen to me and I will explain to you;
            let me tell you what I have seen,

[18]what wise men have declared,
            hiding nothing received from their fathers

[19](to whom alone the land was given
            when no alien[D] passed among them):

[20]All his days the wicked man suffers torment,
            the ruthless through all the years stored up
                for him.

[21]Terrifying sounds fill his ears;
            when all seems well, marauders attack him.

[22]He despairs of escaping the darkness;
            he is marked for the sword.

[23]He wanders about—food for vultures[a];
            he knows the day of darkness is at hand.

[24]Distress and anguish fill him with terror;
            they overwhelm him, like a king poised to
                attack,

[a]23 Or *about, looking for food*

Is it wrong to be angry with God? (15:13)

No. The problem comes when legitimate feelings of anger are not handled correctly and lead to inappropriate bitterness and rebellion that sometimes accompany anger. The Bible realistically portrays the frustration and anger of God's people
when things go wrong or when they cannot understand why certain things happen. This
was the reason for Job's anger. Not only did he feel he was being treated unjustly by God,
but he could get no explanation from him.

Jonah's anger over Nineveh's repentance and the death of the shade-giving vine was
inappropriate (Jonah 4). Twice the Lord rebuked him, "Have you any right to be angry?"
(vv. 4,9). The prophet Jeremiah grew angry with God because of his persecution and the
lack of response to his preaching. But he went too far when he accused God of lying (Jer.
15:18). Immediately, God told him to repent and stop uttering foolish words (15:19).

Ultimately, that is where Job ended up. Though his suffering caused many questions
and anguish, he went too far when he insisted that he had a right to an explanation. In
the end, God spoke to Job and set him straight: God had the right to question Job, not
the other way around (38:1–3). Job realized he had been arrogant and that his anger was
unjustified. When confronted by the awesomeness of God, Job repented (42:6).

²⁵because he shakes his fist at God
    and vaunts himself against the Almighty,
²⁶defiantly charging against him
    with a thick, strong shield.

²⁷"Though his face is covered with fat
    and his waist bulges with flesh,
²⁸he will inhabit ruined towns
    and houses where no one lives,
    houses crumbling to rubble.
²⁹He will no longer be rich and his wealth will
        not endure,
    nor will his possessions spread over the land.
³⁰He will not escape the darkness;
    a flame will wither his shoots,
    and the breath of God's mouth will carry him
        away.
³¹Let him not deceive himself by trusting what is
        worthless,
    for he will get nothing in return.
³²Before his time he will be paid in full,
    and his branches will not flourish.
³³He will be like a vine stripped of its unripe
        grapes,
    like an olive tree shedding its blossoms.
³⁴For the company of the godless will be barren,
    and fire will consume the tents of those who
        love bribes.
³⁵They conceive trouble and give birth to evil;
    their womb fashions deceit."

Job

16 Then Job replied:

²"I have heard many things like these;
    miserable comforters are you all!
³Will your long-winded speeches never end?
    What ails you that you keep on arguing?
⁴I also could speak like you,
    if you were in my place;
    I could make fine speeches against you
        and shake my head at you.
⁵But my mouth would encourage you;
    comfort from my lips would bring you relief.

⁶"Yet if I speak, my pain is not relieved;
    and if I refrain, it does not go away.
⁷Surely, O God, you have worn me out;
    you have devastated my entire household.
⁸You have bound me—and it has become a
        witness;
    my gauntness rises up and testifies against
        me.
⁹God assails me and tears me in his anger
    and gnashes his teeth at me;
    my opponent fastens on me his piercing
        eyes.
¹⁰Men open their mouths to jeer at me;
    they strike my cheek in scorn
    and unite together against me.
¹¹God has turned me over to evil men
    and thrown me into the clutches of the
        wicked.
¹²All was well with me, but he shattered me;
    he seized me by the neck and crushed me.

What's the purpose of endless pain? (16:6)

The purposes of pain are hidden in God's wisdom. The great heroes of the Bible all seem to have suffered. Sometimes pain brought people like Jacob, when he wrestled with God, to yield their pride (Gen. 32:22–30). Jeremiah's unending pain and incurable wound drove him back to God's call (Jer. 15:18). Pain showed the apostle Paul that his sufficiency was in Christ (2 Cor. 12:9–10). Perhaps pain's greatest lesson is obedience (Heb. 5:8).

Was God angry? (16:9)

Job thought so. Often we feel this way when God seems to be treating us unfairly. God was not angry at Job; God was testing him (1:8). Such subtle distinctions are hard to sort out while facing severe suffering, however. In the process of refining our faith, God often chooses to keep his purposes hidden.

Who are the evil men? (16:10–11)

Job's persecutors are not named, but since Job knew God was in control of his destiny, he believed God had turned him over to them. From the human standpoint, Job's persecutors seemed to be God's instruments.

Pierces my kidneys . . . spills my gall (16:13)

A poetic description of the intensity of Job's pain. It was like having his internal organs cut apart.

He has made me his target;

13 his archers surround me.
Without pity, he pierces my kidneys
    and spills my gall on the ground.

14Again and again he bursts upon me;
    he rushes at me like a warrior.

15"I have sewed sackclothD over my skin
    and buried my brow in the dust.

16My face is red with weeping,
    deep shadows ring my eyes;

17yet my hands have been free of violence
    and my prayer is pure.

Who pled Job's case before God? (16:19)

Job may be talking about himself since he appealed to God on his own behalf. Through his prayer he is bringing his case before God. However, another view is that Job longed for—and expressed confidence that he would have—a heavenly mediator to stand between him and God.

18"O earth, do not cover my blood;
    may my cry never be laid to rest!

19Even now my witness is in heaven;
    my advocate is on high.

20My intercessor is my frienda
    as my eyes pour out tears to God;

21on behalf of a man he pleads with God
    as a man pleads for his friend.

22"Only a few years will pass
    before I go on the journey of no return.

17 1My spirit is broken,
    my days are cut short,
    the grave awaits me.

2Surely mockers surround me;
    my eyes must dwell on their hostility.

Why did Job want a pledge from God? (17:3)

Job wanted God to be his guarantee of security. Certainly none of Job's friends would guarantee his innocence. Job wanted assurance that ultimately he would be vindicated. As he saw his life ebbing away, he became desperate for some word of affirmation from God.

3"Give me, O God, the pledge you demand.
    Who else will put up security for me?

4You have closed their minds to understanding;
    therefore you will not let them triumph.

5If a man denounces his friends for reward,
    the eyes of his children will fail.

Byword (17:6)

An object of notoriety, a nickname or term of verbal abuse. Apparently Job's reputation, because of his severe suffering, preceded him. He was the object of scorn and ridicule.

6"God has made me a bywordD to everyone,
    a man in whose face people spit.

a20 Or *My friends treat me with scorn*

What makes prayer pure? (16:17)

Pure motives. Job said his prayers were sincere: he was honestly seeking answers from God without ulterior motives. He was not lying to God; his heart was clean (6:28).

One of the temptations of prayer is self-gratification. We are inclined to ask repeatedly for things we *want*, not just things we *need*. The line between selfish and unselfish prayer is often fuzzy. Scrutinizing our motives can help sort through self-deceit.

Confession is a prerequisite to sincere prayers. Jesus taught us not to pray if we are carrying a grudge. The psalmist wrote that if there is sin in our hearts, God will not hear us (Psalm 66:18). Cleaning up unfinished business with family or fellow workers clears the deck so we can pray with purer motives.

We'll never be able to fully evaluate every prayer we pray. Motives are like mercury; getting a grip on them is next to impossible. But God's people are not left alone. Asking the Holy Spirit to search our motives puts us on the right track (Psalm 139:23–24). The Holy Spirit promises to work on our behalf while we seek God in prayer (Romans 8:26–27).

⁷My eyes have grown dim with grief;
    my whole frame is but a shadow.
⁸Upright men are appalled at this;
    the innocent are aroused against the
        ungodly.
⁹Nevertheless, the righteous^D will hold to their
        ways,
    and those with clean hands will grow
        stronger.

¹⁰"But come on, all of you, try again!
    I will not find a wise man among you.
¹¹My days have passed, my plans are shattered,
    and so are the desires of my heart.
¹²These men turn night into day;
    in the face of darkness they say, 'Light is
        near.'
¹³If the only home I hope for is the grave,^a
    if I spread out my bed in darkness,
¹⁴if I say to corruption, 'You are my father,'
    and to the worm, 'My mother' or 'My sister,'
¹⁵where then is my hope?
    Who can see any hope for me?
¹⁶Will it go down to the gates of death^{Da}?
    Will we descend together into the dust?"

Bildad

18 Then Bildad the Shuhite replied:

²"When will you end these speeches?
    Be sensible, and then we can talk.
³Why are we regarded as cattle
    and considered stupid in your sight?
⁴You who tear yourself to pieces in your anger,
    is the earth to be abandoned for your sake?
    Or must the rocks be moved from their
        place?

⁵"The lamp of the wicked is snuffed out;
    the flame of his fire stops burning.
⁶The light in his tent becomes dark;
    the lamp beside him goes out.
⁷The vigor of his step is weakened;
    his own schemes throw him down.
⁸His feet thrust him into a net
    and he wanders into its mesh.
⁹A trap seizes him by the heel;
    a snare holds him fast.
¹⁰A noose is hidden for him on the ground;
    a trap lies in his path.
¹¹Terrors startle him on every side
    and dog his every step.
¹²Calamity is hungry for him;
    disaster is ready for him when he falls.
¹³It eats away parts of his skin;
    death's firstborn devours his limbs.
¹⁴He is torn from the security of his tent
    and marched off to the king of terrors.
¹⁵Fire resides^b in his tent;
    burning sulfur is scattered over his dwelling.
¹⁶His roots dry up below
    and his branches wither above.
¹⁷The memory of him perishes from the earth;

What appalled people so much? (17:7–8)

Job's apparent innocence yet horrifying suffering. The suffering of righteous people can cause others to wonder what might befall them. They can become indignant; such suffering violates their theology—good people are blessed, wicked people are punished. Their bewilderment was partly due to the physical horror of Job's suffering and partly due to their confusion of how they thought life was supposed to work.

How had Job's friends brought light? (17:12)

Job may be using sarcasm here: it was just like his friends to speak of cheer in the middle of tragedy. Or Job may be speaking of the futility of his friends who were trying admirably to cheer him up.

What hope is there for the discouraged or depressed? (17:15)

That we are not alone. God is present with us even in the depths of our despair (Psalm 139). We also need to be reminded that many stretches of depression or discouragement are not forever but only for a season. Our ultimate hope, though, lies in Christ, who promises one day to wipe away every tear (Rev. 21:4).

Why were Job's friends so intent on getting him to come to his senses? (18:2)

Rather than empathizing with him, they saw Job as their opponent in a gigantic theological debate. Determined to win, they pounded away at his faults. The issue at stake was their pride.

How was Job tearing himself to pieces? (18:4)

Bildad is using sarcasm, throwing Job's words back in his face. Job had accused God of tearing him to pieces (16:9), but Bildad was trying to set the record straight—claiming that Job was tearing himself to pieces by refusing to admit to the many charges placed against him.

Death's firstborn (18:13)

A poetic description of a dreaded disease.

^a13,16 Hebrew *Sheol* — ^b15 Or *Nothing he had remains*

Men of the west . . . men of the east (18:20)

A poetic way to describe men everywhere. Bildad was trying to prove that Job had become a universal horror.

Was Bildad saying Job was an unbeliever? (18:21)

What Bildad said was true generally of the wicked, but whether he meant Job specifically is not clear. He probably meant to warn Job, saying in essence, "You'd better examine your relationship with God."

Ten times (19:3)

Another way to say *often*. The expression was commonly used as a synonym for *often* or *many*, or sometimes as a round number (Gen. 31:7; Eccl. 7:19).

Why are some people pleased when others have trouble? (19:5)

Because of a perverse form of spiritual pride, which believes those suffering are getting what they deserve. To Job's friends, that God blessed the righteous and punished the ungodly was only good theology. They didn't have another category for what was happening to Job.

Why is God sometimes silent when we cry for help? (19:7)

The short answer might be that God's silence can deepen our faith. The long answer is that we don't know. God's silence has puzzled his people from the earliest times until now. God, even in his matchless love for his people, sometimes allows us to drift, seemingly alone.

Crown from my head (19:9)

A possible metaphor for honor. Job had fallen from a position of respect in his community to a homeless vagrant. His honor had been replaced by dishonor. Some have also suggested that *crown* may represent Job's hair, which he had shaved off (1:20). That would symbolize great humiliation.

he has no name in the land.
18He is driven from light into darkness
and is banished from the world.
19He has no offspring or descendants among his people,
no survivor where once he lived.
20Men of the west are appalled at his fate;
men of the east are seized with horror.
21Surely such is the dwelling of an evil man;
such is the place of one who knows not God."

Job

19

Then Job replied:

2"How long will you torment me
and crush me with words?
3Ten times now you have reproached[D] me;
shamelessly you attack me.
4If it is true that I have gone astray,
my error remains my concern alone.
5If indeed you would exalt yourselves above me
and use my humiliation against me,
6then know that God has wronged me
and drawn his net around me.

7"Though I cry, 'I've been wronged!' I get no response;
though I call for help, there is no justice.
8He has blocked my way so I cannot pass;
he has shrouded my paths in darkness.
9He has stripped me of my honor
and removed the crown from my head.
10He tears me down on every side till I am gone;
he uproots my hope like a tree.
11His anger burns against me;
he counts me among his enemies.
12His troops advance in force;
they build a siege ramp against me
and encamp around my tent.

Is God responsible for what Satan does? (19:8–12)

God permitted Satan to attack Job, so in that sense he was responsible (1:12; 2:6). But God is not morally responsible for Satan's wickedness. Since God is holy, we know he does not devise evil (James 1:13–15). He cannot be made a scapegoat for Satan's destructive activities.

Satan is the great liar who chose to defy God and was banished from God's presence with the fallen angels. The New Testament calls him the *prince of this world* (John 12:31). Christ's entrance onto the human stage was the long-promised part of God's plan to recover Satan's "playground," the world. Satan's final judgment awaits the return of Christ and the consummation of the age when Satan is cast into the abyss (Rev. 20:10).

Tracing evil back to God has been the subject of much debate throughout the centuries. Theologically, we can only say that God is holy and reigns supreme, yet Satan has certain limits of power within the parameters of God's permission. Evil in no way can be traced back to God; he cannot be even remotely connected to evil.

13"He has alienated my brothers from me;
  my acquaintances are completely estranged
    from me.
14My kinsmen have gone away;
  my friends have forgotten me.
15My guests and my maidservants count me a
    stranger;
  they look upon me as an alien.D
16I summon my servant, but he does not answer,
  though I beg him with my own mouth.
17My breath is offensive to my wife;
  I am loathsome to my own brothers.
18Even the little boys scorn me;
  when I appear, they ridicule me.
19All my intimate friends detest me;
  those I love have turned against me.
20I am nothing but skin and bones;
  I have escaped with only the skin of my
    teeth.*a*

21"Have pity on me, my friends, have pity,
  for the hand of God has struck me.
22Why do you pursue me as God does?
  Will you never get enough of my flesh?

23"Oh, that my words were recorded,
  that they were written on a scroll,
24that they were inscribed with an iron tool on*b*
    lead,
  or engraved in rock forever!
25I know that my Redeemer*Dc* lives,
  and that in the end he will stand upon the
    earth.*d*
26And after my skin has been destroyed,
  yet*e* in*f* my flesh I will see God;
27I myself will see him
  with my own eyes—I, and not another.
  How my heart yearns within me!

28"If you say, 'How we will hound him,
  since the root of the trouble lies in him,*g*'
29you should fear the sword yourselves;
  for wrath will bring punishment by the
    sword,
  and then you will know that there is
    judgment.*h*"

Zophar

20

Then Zophar the Naamathite replied:

2"My troubled thoughts prompt me to answer
  because I am greatly disturbed.
3I hear a rebuke that dishonors me,
  and my understanding inspires me to reply.

4"Surely you know how it has been from of
    old,
  ever since man*i* was placed on the earth,

Why would God alienate his friend? (19:11)

These are words of feeling, not fact. Job felt like an enemy of God, but God had not deserted him. We have the good fortune of knowing the beginning of the story—that God delights in Job (1:8; 2:3) and that Job's actual enemy is the Accuser, Satan.

Why would family and friends abandon one who suffers? (19:13–20)

Some can't handle the intense environment—they don't want to be around pain and suffering. It's too uncomfortable. Others have little sympathy and hear everything as whining. Still others leave perhaps because they think the sufferer deserves what has happened.

Iron tool on lead (19:24)

The precise meaning is uncertain. Apparently Job wanted his words engraved on a monument of some sort so that his case could be judged later by others whom he deemed more honest than his friends. Specifically how iron tools were used to inscribe on lead or rock is not clear.

Who did Job consider to be his *Redeemer*? (19:25)

Some say this person was human; others say divine. We cannot be certain. Whomever it was, Job saw himself on trial and was sure someone would come to his defense. This role of Job's *Redeemer* is similar to that of Christ's in the New Testament (1 John 2:1). However, Job was probably speaking of God himself.

What turned Job's despair into hope? (19:25)

We aren't told. After looking at the past and finding no comfort there, Job decided to look to the future. His friends were poor comforters, so his only recourse was to trust God for future vindication. Nothing had changed outwardly, but by some powerful inner dynamic he surmounted his despair. This is a demonstration of faith: being certain of something that, on the surface doesn't make sense (Heb. 11:1).

What did Job believe about the afterlife? (19:25–27)

He probably had a general hope of life beyond the grave. It's uncertain, though, whether he thought in terms of a physical resurrection as taught later in the New Testament (1 Cor. 15). Job merely expressed a strong confidence that somehow, somewhere, he would meet God face to face. Also see *Does Proverbs teach about life after death?* (Prov. 2:18) and *How did the Old Testament view resurrection?* (Daniel 12:2).

Did Job wish his friends would get what he got? (19:29)

No. He was deeply hurt by their charges, so in a spirit of accountability he stated the general principle that wrongdoers are judged. This is a warning: in due course they would be punished for falsely accusing him.

---

*a*20 Or *only my gums*   *b*24 Or *and*   *c*25 Or *defender*
*d*25 Or *upon my grave*   *e*26 Or *And after I awake, / though this*
⌊*body*⌋ *has been destroyed, / then*   *f*26 Or / *apart from*
*g*28 Many Hebrew manuscripts, Septuagint and Vulgate; most Hebrew
manuscripts *me*   *h*29 Or *I that you may come to know the Almighty*
*i*4 Or *Adam*

Who thinks the joy of the wicked is *but a moment?* (20:5–9)

Zophar, for one, and other Biblical writers like James (James 1:11). The joy of the wicked, though, certainly doesn't seem brief to godly people who are suffering. Scripture, however, always points us to a larger time frame: 70 years is a drop in the bucket compared to an ocean of eternity.

Who makes the wicked pay restitution? (20:10,18–19)

Zophar seems to appeal to a larger divine principle of judgment by God who sees that the wicked will restore what rightfully belongs to their victims. Of course, this doesn't always work out in real life. Many rich, wicked people go to their grave shaking their fist at God and terrorizing the poor. God, though, does have the last word.

Rivers flowing with honey and cream (20:17)

A figurative expression to picture the good life (Psalm 36:8). It represented the wicked's overwhelming abundance of good things to eat and drink. Canaan was said to be a land flowing with milk and honey (Exodus 13:5).

When does God settle his accounts with the wicked? (20:23–29)

Zophar probably saw God settling his accounts with Job in the terrible things he had suffered. In some instances (not Job's), God judges the wicked in this life. They reap what they sow. However, ultimate judgment, according to the New Testament, comes after death when one's eternal destiny is settled (Matt. 25:46). Then the scales of justice will be finally balanced.

⁵that the mirth of the wicked is brief,
  the joy of the godless lasts but a moment.
⁶Though his pride reaches to the heavens
  and his head touches the clouds,
⁷he will perish forever, like his own dung;
  those who have seen him will say, 'Where is he?'
⁸Like a dream he flies away, no more to be found,
  banished like a visionᴰ of the night.
⁹The eye that saw him will not see him again;
  his place will look on him no more.
¹⁰His children must make amends to the poor;
  his own hands must give back his wealth.
¹¹The youthful vigor that fills his bones
  will lie with him in the dust.

¹²"Though evil is sweet in his mouth
  and he hides it under his tongue,
¹³though he cannot bear to let it go
  and keeps it in his mouth,
¹⁴yet his food will turn sour in his stomach;
  it will become the venom of serpents within him.
¹⁵He will spit out the riches he swallowed;
  God will make his stomach vomit them up.
¹⁶He will suck the poison of serpents;
  the fangs of an adder will kill him.
¹⁷He will not enjoy the streams,
  the rivers flowing with honey and cream.
¹⁸What he toiled for he must give back uneaten;
  he will not enjoy the profit from his trading.
¹⁹For he has oppressed the poor and left them destitute;
  he has seized houses he did not build.

²⁰"Surely he will have no respite from his craving;
  he cannot save himself by his treasure.
²¹Nothing is left for him to devour;
  his prosperity will not endure.
²²In the midst of his plenty, distress will overtake him;
  the full force of misery will come upon him.
²³When he has filled his belly,
  God will vent his burning anger against him
  and rain down his blows upon him.
²⁴Though he flees from an iron weapon,
  a bronze-tipped arrow pierces him.
²⁵He pulls it out of his back,
  the gleaming point out of his liver.
  Terrors will come over him;
²⁶ total darkness lies in wait for his treasures.
  A fire unfanned will consume him
  and devour what is left in his tent.
²⁷The heavens will expose his guilt;
  the earth will rise up against him.
²⁸A flood will carry off his house,
  rushing watersᵃ on the day of God's wrath.
²⁹Such is the fate God allots the wicked,
  the heritage appointed for them by God."

ᵃ28 Or *The possessions in his house will be carried off, / washed away*

Job

21

Then Job replied:

2"Listen carefully to my words;
    let this be the consolation you give me.
3Bear with me while I speak,
    and after I have spoken, mock on.

4"Is my complaint directed to man?
    Why should I not be impatient?
5Look at me and be astonished;
    clap your hand over your mouth.
6When I think about this, I am terrified;
    trembling seizes my body.
7Why do the wicked live on,
    growing old and increasing in power?
8They see their children established around
        them,
    their offspring before their eyes.
9Their homes are safe and free from fear;
    the rod of God is not upon them.
10Their bulls never fail to breed;
    their cows calve and do not miscarry.
11They send forth their children as a flock;
    their little ones dance about.
12They sing to the music of tambourine and
        harp;
    they make merry to the sound of the flute.
13They spend their years in prosperity
    and go down to the grave*a* in peace.*b*
14Yet they say to God, 'Leave us alone!
    We have no desire to know your ways.
15Who is the Almighty, that we should serve
        him?
    What would we gain by praying to him?'
16But their prosperity is not in their own hands,
    so I stand aloof from the counsel of the
        wicked.

17"Yet how often is the lamp of the wicked
        snuffed out?
    How often does calamity come upon them,
    the fate God allots in his anger?
18How often are they like straw before the wind,
    like chaff*D* swept away by a gale?
19It is said, 'God stores up a man's punishment
        for his sons.'
    Let him repay the man himself, so that he
        will know it!
20Let his own eyes see his destruction;
    let him drink of the wrath of the Almighty.*c*
21For what does he care about the family he
        leaves behind
    when his allotted months come to an end?

22"Can anyone teach knowledge to God,
    since he judges even the highest?
23One man dies in full vigor,
    completely secure and at ease,
24his body*d* well nourished,
    his bones rich with marrow.

Why are wicked people so successful? (21:13)

Usually they are smart and pragmatic in devious ways. They may know how to take advantage of people and make shrewd decisions. Many view life not in moral terms but in what they can get out of it for themselves. If they have no scruples, anything standing in the way of prosperity can be removed with a vengeance. Winners take all.

Who controls the prosperity of the wicked? (21:16)

God does. This verse points to God's ultimate control over the destiny of the wicked.

How is death the great equalizer? (21:23–26)

Everyone will eventually die—both the wicked and the righteous. But although our physical fate may be the same, there's no parity after death in the spiritual realm. Faith in Jesus Christ makes the difference between eternal death and eternal life (Matt. 25:46).

*a13 Hebrew Sheol   b13 Or in an instant   c17-20 Verses 17 and 18 may be taken as exclamations and 19 and 20 as declarations.
d24 The meaning of the Hebrew for this word is uncertain.*

²⁵Another man dies in bitterness of soul^D,
    never having enjoyed anything good.
²⁶Side by side they lie in the dust,
    and worms cover them both.

²⁷"I know full well what you are thinking,
    the schemes by which you would wrong me.
²⁸You say, 'Where now is the great man's house,
    the tents where wicked men lived?'
²⁹Have you never questioned those who travel?
    Have you paid no regard to their accounts—
³⁰that the evil man is spared from the day of
      calamity,
    that he is delivered from^a the day of wrath?
³¹Who denounces his conduct to his face?
    Who repays him for what he has done?
³²He is carried to the grave,
    and watch is kept over his tomb.
³³The soil in the valley is sweet to him;
    all men follow after him,
    and a countless throng goes^b before him.

³⁴"So how can you console me with your
      nonsense?
    Nothing is left of your answers but
      falsehood!"

Eliphaz

22

Then Eliphaz the Temanite replied:

²"Can a man be of benefit to God?
    Can even a wise man benefit him?
³What pleasure would it give the Almighty if
      you were righteous^D?
    What would he gain if your ways were
      blameless?

⁴"Is it for your piety that he rebukes you
    and brings charges against you?
⁵Is not your wickedness great?
    Are not your sins endless?
⁶You demanded security from your brothers for
      no reason;
    you stripped men of their clothing, leaving
      them naked.
⁷You gave no water to the weary
    and you withheld food from the hungry,
⁸though you were a powerful man, owning
      land—
    an honored man, living on it.
⁹And you sent widows away empty-handed
    and broke the strength of the fatherless.
¹⁰That is why snares are all around you,
    why sudden peril terrifies you,
¹¹why it is so dark you cannot see,
    and why a flood of water covers you.

¹²"Is not God in the heights of heaven?
    And see how lofty are the highest stars!
¹³Yet you say, 'What does God know?
    Does he judge through such darkness?
¹⁴Thick clouds veil him, so he does not see us
    as he goes about in the vaulted heavens.'

Why accuse Job of such crimes? (22:6-9)

Eliphaz was on a witch hunt. He was trying to drag out of Job's closet skeletons that weren't even there (1:8). He was still snooping for the reason for Job's suffering.

When did Job say this? (22:13-14)

We don't know. He may never have said these exact words. Perhaps Eliphaz paraphrased or summarized what he thought was the thrust of Job's previous answers. These words, attributed to Job, convinced Eliphaz that Job was stubborn, proud and unrepentant.

---

^a30 Or *man is reserved for the day of calamity, / that he is brought forth to*   ^b33 Or *I as a countless throng went*

15Will you keep to the old path
    that evil men have trod?
16They were carried off before their time,
    their foundations washed away by a flood.
17They said to God, 'Leave us alone!
    What can the Almighty do to us?'
18Yet it was he who filled their houses with good
      things,
    so I stand aloof from the counsel of the
      wicked.

19"The righteousᴰ see their ruin and rejoice;
    the innocent mock them, saying,
20'Surely our foes are destroyed,
    and fire devours their wealth.'

21"Submit to God and be at peaceᴰ with him;
    in this way prosperity will come to you.
22Accept instruction from his mouth
    and lay up his words in your heart.
23If you return to the Almighty, you will be
      restored:
    If you remove wickedness far from your tent
24and assign your nuggets to the dust,
    your gold of Ophir to the rocks in the
      ravines,
25then the Almighty will be your gold,
    the choicest silver for you.
26Surely then you will find delight in the
      Almighty
    and will lift up your face to God.
27You will pray to him, and he will hear you,
    and you will fulfill your vowsᴰ.
28What you decide on will be done,
    and light will shine on your ways.
29When men are brought low and you say, 'Lift
      them up!'
    then he will save the downcast.
30He will deliver even one who is not innocent,
    who will be delivered through the cleanness
      of your hands."

Job

23

Then Job replied:

2"Even today my complaint is bitter;
    his handᵃ is heavy in spite ofᵇ my
      groaning.
3If only I knew where to find him;
    if only I could go to his dwelling!
4I would state my case before him
    and fill my mouth with arguments.
5I would find out what he would answer me,
    and consider what he would say.
6Would he oppose me with great power?
    No, he would not press charges against me.
7There an upright man could present his case
      before him,
    and I would be delivered forever from my
      judge.

8"But if I go to the east, he is not there;

ᵃ2 Septuagint and Syriac; Hebrew *l the hand on me*   ᵇ2 Or *heavy on me in*

SCRIPTURE LINK (22:17-18)

Here Eliphaz is quoting Job, using Job's own words (21:14-16), probably to put a certain spin on his theology. Job and Eliphaz seemed to agree about the prosperity of the wicked. Their difference had to do with the application of that theology. Eliphaz believed Job was guilty of some sin and should repent. Job refused to acknowledge any wrongdoing.

Can we become prosperous by following God? (22:21-25)

Yes, we can become *spiritually* prosperous, but not necessarily *materially* wealthy. In the Old Testament, the prevailing principle was that God prospered the righteous. Moses warned about the blessings or curses that would follow either obedience or disobedience to God (Deut. 4:1-4). In the New Testament teachings of Christ and the apostles, however, spiritual prosperity is promised for faith and obedience (John 4:13; 1 Peter 1:3-5)—along with promises of hardships (Matt. 5:10-11; 2 Tim. 3:12; 1 Peter 4:12).

Did Eliphaz offer good advice? (22:21)

Yes. His advice was solid, though misdirected. It fit the general theme of obedience to God as being the best way to live. But suffering, not prosperity, is often the outcome of obedience. As far as Job was concerned, he had followed God and prospered, but now he was destitute. Eliphaz was wrong to assume Job was to blame.

Is God heavy-handed? (23:2)

Though Job felt God was heavy-handed, God is always fair. Job did not know about the discussions between God and Satan (1:8-11), so he assumed his affliction came directly from God. In reality, it was the work of Satan. But Job's statement poetically captures the truth that God sometimes permits suffering to befall us (1:12). To Job's credit, though feeling that God's *hand is heavy*, Job did not *curse God and die* (2:9).

Was Job claiming innocence? (23:7)

Job never claimed to be sinless, only *upright*. The author of Job agrees: *This man was blameless and upright; he feared God and shunned evil* (1:1). Job knew no hidden, heinous sin had led to his present calamity. Job believed if he could just present his case before God, he would be judged innocent of all charges.

Does God hide? (23:8-9)

God is present at all times and in all places (Psalm 139:7-12). But like Job, we all experience moments when God seems far away. In suffering, we may not recognize God's work, his ways or even his presence, though he is always with us. Also see *Does God hide from us?* (9:11).

if I go to the west, I do not find him.
⁹When he is at work in the north, I do not see
  him;
  when he turns to the south, I catch no
    glimpse of him.
¹⁰But he knows the way that I take;
  when he has tested me, I will come forth as
    gold.
¹¹My feet have closely followed his steps;
  I have kept to his way without turning aside.
¹²I have not departed from the commands of his
    lips;
  I have treasured the words of his mouth
    more than my daily bread.

¹³"But he stands alone, and who can oppose
    him?
  He does whatever he pleases.
¹⁴He carries out his decree against me,
  and many such plans he still has in store.
¹⁵That is why I am terrified before him;
  when I think of all this, I fear him.
¹⁶God has made my heart faint;
  the Almighty has terrified me.
¹⁷Yet I am not silenced by the darkness,
  by the thick darkness that covers my face.

Was Job's attitude right? (23:13–17)

Job was right that God can do whatever he
wants, and nobody can stop him. When the all-
powerful God allows suffering in our lives, it's
understandable that we would be *terrified before him*. But Job, in his great pain, was losing
sight of the fact that God is also the source of
our blessings (1:21; 2:10).

Is it right to fear God's plans for us?
(23:14–15)

Job was in utter agony; he had no idea when all
this suffering would end. It was natural for him
to feel anxious about the future. But we need
to balance Job's statement with the broader
teaching in the Bible that God always has our
best interest at heart (Jer. 29:11). Job himself
discovered this when God restored and doubled everything Job had lost (42:12). We never
need to fear God's ultimate plans for us.

Why doesn't God put an end to injus-
tice? (24:1–12)

God does deal with the wicked, as Job himself
admits later in the chapter (vv. 18–24). In
these verses, Job simply cries in anguish
about the cruelty and unfairness he sees in the
world around him. Today, we may watch the
evening news and feel the same way. Ultimately, though, the wicked will be judged; God's
eyes are on their ways (v. 23) and they will be
brought low (v. 24).

24 "Why does the Almighty not set times for
        judgment?
  Why must those who know him look in vain
    for such days?
²Men move boundary stones;
  they pasture flocks they have stolen.
³They drive away the orphan's donkey
  and take the widow's ox in pledge.
⁴They thrust the needy from the path

Why did testing come to Job? (23:10)

Why believers undergo prolonged and difficult suffering has no one, simple
explanation. But the Bible offers several reasons.

First, testing strengthens our character. James says, *the testing of your faith develops
perseverance* (James 1:2–3). Painful situations produce character the same way regular
exercise builds muscle tone.

Peter adds that testing proves our faith is genuine (1 Peter 1:7). When the heat is on,
who we actually are, and what we truly believe are revealed. He also suggests that this
tested faith gives honor to God. Remaining faithful despite prolonged agony testifies to
others how much we value God.

Job notes that testing can get rid of unrefined qualities in our lives (23:10). Much the
way a blast furnace brings out impurities in metals, testing removes sinful attitudes in us,
and we *come forth as gold*.

The writer of Hebrews (12:6–8) says that testing proves we are God's children. Every
parent disciplines a child, in love, to help the child develop. When God brings testing, it
reminds us that we are his children.

Why did testing come to Job? Job never realized that God allowed it because he was
proud of him: *Have you considered my servant Job? There is no one on earth like him*
(1:8). There may be no reason behind our testing other than that God is proud of us. He
may want to demonstrate to others that our devotion to him is real and unshakable.

and force all the poor of the land into hiding.
⁵Like wild donkeys in the desert,
the poor go about their labor of foraging
food;
the wasteland provides food for their
children.
⁶They gather fodder in the fields
and glean in the vineyards of the wicked.
⁷Lacking clothes, they spend the night naked;
they have nothing to cover themselves in the
cold.
⁸They are drenched by mountain rains
and hug the rocks for lack of shelter.
⁹The fatherless child is snatched from the
breast;
the infant of the poor is seized for a debt.
¹⁰Lacking clothes, they go about naked;
they carry the sheaves, but still go hungry.
¹¹They crush olives among the terraces*a*;
they tread the winepresses*D*, yet suffer
thirst.
¹²The groans of the dying rise from the city,
and the souls*D* of the wounded cry out for
help.
But God charges no one with wrongdoing.

¹³"There are those who rebel against the light,
who do not know its ways
or stay in its paths.
¹⁴When daylight is gone, the murderer rises up
and kills the poor and needy;
in the night he steals forth like a thief.
¹⁵The eye of the adulterer watches for dusk;
he thinks, 'No eye will see me,'
and he keeps his face concealed.
¹⁶In the dark, men break into houses,
but by day they shut themselves in;
they want nothing to do with the light.
¹⁷For all of them, deep darkness is their
morning*b*;
they make friends with the terrors of
darkness.*c*

¹⁸"Yet they are foam on the surface of the water;
their portion of the land is cursed,
so that no one goes to the vineyards.
¹⁹As heat and drought snatch away the melted
snow,
so the grave*d* snatches away those who have
sinned.
²⁰The womb forgets them,
the worm feasts on them;
evil men are no longer remembered
but are broken like a tree.
²¹They prey on the barren and childless woman,
and to the widow show no kindness.
²²But God drags away the mighty by his power;
though they become established, they have
no assurance of life.
²³He may let them rest in a feeling of security,

What is fodder? (24:6)

Generally a coarse feed for animals. It could be almost any kind of grain or hay. Here it likely refers to what was left in the fields after the owners had harvested their crops.

Foam on the surface of the water (24:18)

A metaphor for the temporary nature of the wicked: Like foam whipped by the waves, sinners will soon be gone. Some wonder why Job would say this and thereby lend force to his friends' argument that sin reaps a swift penalty. Others suggest that Job's point of view, more complex than his friends', allowed for exceptions to the general rule that the righteous are rewarded and the wicked punished. Some think this may have been an expression of Job's desire to see the wicked judged—like *foam on the surface of the water.*

a 11 Or olives between the millstones; the meaning of the Hebrew for this word is uncertain.   b 17 Or them, their morning is like the shadow of death   c 17 Or of the shadow of death   d 19 Hebrew Sheol

Did Job finally agree with his friends' viewpoint? (24:24)

Job's friends had argued that suffering is God's punishment for wickedness (22:15–16). Therefore, they reasoned, since Job was suffering, he must have committed some evil. Here, Job agrees with his friends only that at some point evil people are *cut off like heads of grain.* Job refuses to grant that his suffering is proof of his own guilt. There must be another reason, though for the moment, he doesn't know what it is.

Shuhite (25:1)

Little is known about the Shuhite tribe. Abraham and his concubine Keturah had a son named Shuah (Gen. 25:2; 1 Chron. 1:32). Shuah and his brothers went to *the land of the east* (Gen. 25:6). Bildad was likely from this area, which carried the original settler's name.

What are God's *forces*? (25:3)

The term refers to *armed troops.* It could mean angels or other heavenly armies (Matt. 26:53), or it could mean the military forces of nations, which are ultimately under God's control. The point is that God possesses the resources to carry out his orders and defeat his enemies. See Isaiah 45:6.

Are people only *maggots* or *worms*? (25:6)

In comparison to the power and holy majesty of God, humans seem little more than lowly insects. But it's important not to confuse our lowly human faculties with our value to God. Our value to God is beyond description. He was willing to give even his Son for us (John 3:16).

Do the dead suffer? (26:5)

Yes, although it's uncertain whether Job, with his Old Testament perspective, had any idea of how much (see Matt. 13:42; Mark 9:47–48). When Job says *The dead are in deep anguish,* he probably means that even the spirits of the dead must tremble before God's majesty. Thus, Job was challenging Bildad and saying that he didn't go far enough in describing God's awesome power (25:2–6). Not only the heavens and earth, but even the shadowy world of the dead, bow to his dominion. See article: *Where are the dead?* (1 Thes. 4:14).

but his eyes are on their ways.
²⁴For a little while they are exalted, and then
    they are gone;
they are brought low and gathered up like all
    others;
they are cut off like heads of grain.

²⁵"If this is not so, who can prove me false
    and reduce my words to nothing?"

Bildad

25

Then Bildad the Shuhite replied:

²"Dominion and awe belong to God;
    he establishes order in the heights of heaven.
³Can his forces be numbered?
    Upon whom does his light not rise?
⁴How then can a man be righteous[D] before
    God?
    How can one born of woman be pure?
⁵If even the moon is not bright
    and the stars are not pure in his eyes,
⁶how much less man, who is but a maggot—
    a son of man[D], who is only a worm!"

Job

26

Then Job replied:

²"How you have helped the powerless!
    How you have saved the arm that is feeble!
³What advice you have offered to one without
    wisdom!
    And what great insight you have displayed!
⁴Who has helped you utter these words?
    And whose spirit spoke from your mouth?

⁵"The dead are in deep anguish,
    those beneath the waters and all that live in
    them.
⁶Death[a] is naked before God;
    Destruction[b] lies uncovered.

[a]6 Hebrew *Sheol*   [b]6 Hebrew *Abaddon*

Are we responsible for inborn sin? (25:4)

How then can a man be righteous before God? is the most important question in life. The answer is obvious: no one can claim a personal righteousness equal to God's purity. Paul recognizes that *all have sinned and fall short of the glory of God* (Romans 3:23).

The problem is, we are born in a sinful condition. David described what some call original sin: *Surely I was sinful at birth, sinful from the time my mother conceived me* (Psalm 51:5).

Isn't that unfair? How can we be held accountable for something we inherit? The question instead should be: What do we do with the sinful nature we inherit? Do we indulge it? Or do we trust in the way God has provided to overcome it? Through faith in the saving work of Jesus Christ on the cross, we can be given a brand new nature and righteous standing before God.

7He spreads out the northern ⌞skies⌟ over empty
space;
he suspends the earth over nothing.
8He wraps up the waters in his clouds,
yet the clouds do not burst under their
weight.
9He covers the face of the full moon,
spreading his clouds over it.
10He marks out the horizon on the face of the
waters
for a boundary between light and darkness.
11The pillars of the heavens quake,
aghast at his rebuke.
12By his power he churned up the sea;
by his wisdom he cut Rahab^D to pieces.
13By his breath the skies became fair;
his hand pierced the gliding serpent.
14And these are but the outer fringe of his works;
how faint the whisper we hear of him!
Who then can understand the thunder of his
power?"

27 And Job continued his discourse:

2"As surely as God lives, who has denied me
justice,
the Almighty, who has made me taste
bitterness of soul^D,
3as long as I have life within me,
the breath of God in my nostrils,
4my lips will not speak wickedness,
and my tongue will utter no deceit.
5I will never admit you are in the right;
till I die, I will not deny my integrity.
6I will maintain my righteousness^D and never
let go of it;
my conscience will not reproach^D me as
long as I live.

7"May my enemies be like the wicked,
my adversaries like the unjust!
8For what hope has the godless when he is cut
off,
when God takes away his life?
9Does God listen to his cry
when distress comes upon him?
10Will he find delight in the Almighty?
Will he call upon God at all times?

11"I will teach you about the power of God;
the ways of the Almighty I will not conceal.
12You have all seen this yourselves.
Why then this meaningless talk?

13"Here is the fate God allots to the wicked,
the heritage a ruthless man receives from the
Almighty:
14However many his children, their fate is the
sword;
his offspring will never have enough to eat.
15The plague will bury those who survive him,
and their widows will not weep for them.
16Though he heaps up silver like dust
and clothes like piles of clay,
17what he lays up the righteous^D will wear,
and the innocent will divide his silver.

Death . . . Destruction (26:6)

In Hebrew the word *Death* (*Sheol*) refers to the
grave or death itself. See **Depths** (Psalm
139:8). *Destruction* (*Abaddon*) means the
place where souls perish or come to ruin. Job
is simply saying that even in the lowest and
darkest regions of creation, God still sees everything.

Why does Job talk about nature? (26:7–14)

To emphasize God's enormous power. The unending vastness of the sky, the clouds that
carry immeasurable volumes of water, the dazzling brilliance of the horizon and the fury of
the raging sea, are but a *whisper* of God's overwhelming strength. Also see Romans 1:20.

Gliding serpent (26:13)

Ancient Middle Eastern stories told of the sea
monster *Rahab* (v. 12) and the *gliding serpent*
Leviathan. In the Bible, these monsters poetically symbolize the forces of nature that wreak
havoc on the earth (Isaiah 27:1). The verse declares that God is more powerful than the wild-
est force nature can unleash. See also **Rahab**
(Psalm 89:10).

Why would a just God deny justice? (27:1–2)

God does not ultimately deny justice, though
he sometimes delays it. Job desperately wanted God to establish his innocence in the sight
of his friends (which God later did) and restore
his losses (which God later did). But Job had to
wait for God's timing. While he waited, feeling
despair, Job could not see how God could be
just. But Job did not completely abandon faith
in God. Later in the chapter he affirms that
God will judge the wicked.

The breath of God in my nostrils (27:3)

This refers to life itself. Job is saying, "as long
as I live." The creation account tells us God
breathed into Adam *the breath of life* (Gen.
2:7). If God withdrew his breath from creation
it would perish at once (34:14–15).

Is it okay to pray against your enemies? (27:7)

Not for their harm. Not everything a Bible character says or does is to be imitated. Jesus
taught clearly how we should treat our enemies: love them and pray for them (Matt.
5:44). See article: *Is it right to pray for revenge?* (Psalm 58:6–8). Also see **Should we
pray for God's judgment to fall on sinners?**
(Psalm 140:10).

Will the righteous get the riches of the wicked? (27:13–17)

Job is describing a general principle, a way that
God's justice operates in life. A wicked person often engages in conduct that brings about his
own death or destruction. The righteous, who
do not engage in such conduct, may not experience early death or destruction. Naturally, general rules don't apply in every case.

East wind (27:21)

The *sirocco*, a blistering wind off the desert. It was the *mighty wind* that collapsed the house where Job's children were feasting (1:19).

Why a lecture on mining ore? (28:1–23)

Job is making a comparison. He's saying, in effect: "Though it is extremely difficult to mine iron or copper, humans have managed it. But it is much harder to mine *wisdom* and *understanding* (v. 12). Only God can do that (v. 23)." Job is pointing out how hard it is to become wise, and that wisdom can be found only with God. (Interestingly, archaeologists know that mining operations were conducted in regions throughout the Middle East as far back as 4500 B.C.)

¹⁸The house he builds is like a moth's cocoon,
  like a hut made by a watchman^D.
¹⁹He lies down wealthy, but will do so no more;
  when he opens his eyes, all is gone.
²⁰Terrors overtake him like a flood;
  a tempest snatches him away in the night.
²¹The east wind carries him off, and he is gone;
  it sweeps him out of his place.
²²It hurls itself against him without mercy^D
  as he flees headlong from its power.
²³It claps its hands in derision
  and hisses him out of his place.

28 "There is a mine for silver
  and a place where gold is refined.
²Iron is taken from the earth,
  and copper is smelted from ore.
³Man puts an end to the darkness;
  he searches the farthest recesses
  for ore in the blackest darkness.
⁴Far from where people dwell he cuts a shaft,
  in places forgotten by the foot of man;
  far from men he dangles and sways.
⁵The earth, from which food comes,
  is transformed below as by fire;
⁶sapphires^a come from its rocks,
  and its dust contains nuggets of gold.
⁷No bird of prey knows that hidden path,
  no falcon's eye has seen it.
⁸Proud beasts do not set foot on it,
  and no lion prowls there.
⁹Man's hand assaults the flinty rock
  and lays bare the roots of the mountains.
¹⁰He tunnels through the rock;
  his eyes see all its treasures.
¹¹He searches^b the sources of the rivers
  and brings hidden things to light.

¹²"But where can wisdom be found?
  Where does understanding dwell?
¹³Man does not comprehend its worth;
  it cannot be found in the land of the living.
¹⁴The deep says, 'It is not in me';
  the sea says, 'It is not with me.'
¹⁵It cannot be bought with the finest gold,
  nor can its price be weighed in silver.
¹⁶It cannot be bought with the gold of Ophir,
  with precious onyx or sapphires.
¹⁷Neither gold nor crystal can compare with it,
  nor can it be had for jewels of gold.
¹⁸Coral and jasper are not worthy of mention;
  the price of wisdom is beyond rubies.
¹⁹The topaz of Cush cannot compare with it;
  it cannot be bought with pure gold.

²⁰"Where then does wisdom come from?
  Where does understanding dwell?
²¹It is hidden from the eyes of every living thing,
  concealed even from the birds of the air.
²²Destruction^c and Death^D say,
  'Only a rumor of it has reached our ears.'
²³God understands the way to it

_a6 Or *lapis lazuli*; also in verse 16   _b11 Septuagint, Aquila and Vulgate; Hebrew *He dams up*   _c22 Hebrew *Abaddon*

and he alone knows where it dwells,
²⁴for he views the ends of the earth
and sees everything under the heavens.
²⁵When he established the force of the wind
and measured out the waters,
²⁶when he made a decree for the rain
and a path for the thunderstorm,
²⁷then he looked at wisdom and appraised it;
he confirmed it and tested it.
²⁸And he said to man,
'The fear of the Lord^D—that is wisdom,
and to shun evil is understanding.' "

29

Job continued his discourse:

²"How I long for the months gone by,
for the days when God watched over me,
³when his lamp shone upon my head
and by his light I walked through darkness!
⁴Oh, for the days when I was in my prime,
when God's intimate friendship blessed my
house,
⁵when the Almighty was still with me
and my children were around me,
⁶when my path was drenched with cream
and the rock poured out for me streams of
olive oil.

⁷"When I went to the gate of the city
and took my seat in the public square,
⁸the young men saw me and stepped aside
and the old men rose to their feet;
⁹the chief men refrained from speaking
and covered their mouths with their hands;
¹⁰the voices of the nobles were hushed,
and their tongues stuck to the roof of their
mouths.
¹¹Whoever heard me spoke well of me,
and those who saw me commended me,
¹²because I rescued the poor who cried for help,
and the fatherless who had none to assist
him.
¹³The man who was dying blessed me;
I made the widow's heart sing.
¹⁴I put on righteousness^D as my clothing;
justice was my robe and my turban.
¹⁵I was eyes to the blind
and feet to the lame.
¹⁶I was a father to the needy;
I took up the case of the stranger.
¹⁷I broke the fangs of the wicked
and snatched the victims from their teeth.

¹⁸"I thought, 'I will die in my own house,
my days as numerous as the grains of sand.
¹⁹My roots will reach to the water,
and the dew will lie all night on my
branches.
²⁰My glory^D will remain fresh in me,
the bow ever new in my hand.'

²¹"Men listened to me expectantly,
waiting in silence for my counsel.
²²After I had spoken, they spoke no more;
my words fell gently on their ears.
²³They waited for me as for showers

Why is it wise to be afraid of God? (28:28)

The fear of the Lord does not mean only cowering in terror before a powerful deity. It means living in reverence and respect before a holy God. Until you recognize that God is terrifyingly powerful and gloriously holy, you will never have a strong enough incentive to halt sinful choices and behavior—in other words, live wisely. See article: **Should we live in terror of God?** (Prov. 1:7).

Does God ever stop watching over us? (29:2)

Job thought so. He longed for the days when God watched over me. But God always watches over those who trust him, even when they are not aware of his care. One temptation during extended suffering is to think, as Job did, that God has turned his back on us. We can resist that temptation only by choosing to trust the Word of God in spite of appearances.

Who would want cream on their path? (29:6)

In Job's day, cream was a scarce luxury. This phrase is a poetic way of saying that God had once blessed Job so abundantly that even life's sweetest luxuries were as common as the dirt he walked on.

Seat in the public square (29:7)

In ancient Middle Eastern cities, this was the place of official government business. It compares to courthouses and city hall chambers today.

Why was silence a sign of respect? (29:9–10)

Some ancient cultures required people to literally hold their hand over their mouth to show respect and honor to the ruler. It was the custom in Job's day to remain quiet until the leading official had spoken. We follow much the same protocol today when a presiding judge enters a court room or the President of the United States appears to make a public statement. Silence recognizes the importance of the authority figure.

Why does Job seem to brag about his good deeds? (29:12–17)

Job is not boasting, but rather explaining why he used to be honored (vv. 7–11). He had used his power and influence to help people in need. While other officials may have used their position to pad their wallets or their power base, Job used his office to serve.

My glory will remain fresh in me (29:20)

The word glory here refers to the honor given to an individual. Job had been considered the greatest man among all the peoples of the East (1:3), and he had thought he would enjoy that honor for a long time.

and drank in my words as the spring rain.
24When I smiled at them, they scarcely believed
    it;
    the light of my face was precious to them.*a*
25I chose the way for them and sat as their chief;
    I dwelt as a king among his troops;
    I was like one who comforts mourners.

Whom is Job attacking? (30:1–8)
The outcasts of society. Now, even they taunt
and humiliate poor Job, adding further insult to
his unbearable injuries.

30
"But now they mock me,
    men younger than I,
whose fathers I would have disdained
    to put with my sheep dogs.
2Of what use was the strength of their hands to
    me,
    since their vigor had gone from them?
3Haggard from want and hunger,
    they roamed*b* the parched land
    in desolate wastelands at night.
4In the brush they gathered salt herbs,
    and their food*c* was the root of the broom
        tree.
5They were banished from their fellow men,
    shouted at as if they were thieves.
6They were forced to live in the dry stream
        beds,
    among the rocks and in holes in the ground.
7They brayed among the bushes
    and huddled in the undergrowth.
8A base and nameless brood,
    they were driven out of the land.

Base and nameless brood (30:8)
The ancestry of Job's new tormentors. Perhaps
the worst insult of Job's day was to put down a
person's family or ancestry. Job is saying that
his new tormentors were so low, they lacked
even the dignity of a family name. It's also possible that Job is simply referring to an unnamed mob or tribe of people.

How had God *unstrung* Job's *bow*?
(30:11)
The bow and arrow, a premier weapon and
hunting tool in Job's time, was a symbol of
strength. A bow without the bowstring was useless. So this phrase means that God allowed
Job to become weak and humiliated. All the former trappings of Job's might, reputation and
honor have been stripped from him.

9"And now their sons mock me in song;
    I have become a byword*D* among them.
10They detest me and keep their distance;
    they do not hesitate to spit in my face.
11Now that God has unstrung my bow and
        afflicted*D* me,
    they throw off restraint in my presence.
12On my right the tribe*d* attacks;
    they lay snares for my feet,
    they build their siege ramps against me.
13They break up my road;
    they succeed in destroying me—
    without anyone's helping them.*e*
14They advance as through a gaping breach;
    amid the ruins they come rolling in.
15Terrors overwhelm me;
    my dignity is driven away as by the wind,
    my safety vanishes like a cloud.

16"And now my life ebbs away;
    days of suffering grip me.
17Night pierces my bones;
    my gnawing pains never rest.
18In his great power ⌊God⌋ becomes like clothing
        to me*f*;
    he binds me like the neck of my garment.
19He throws me into the mud,
    and I am reduced to dust and ashes.

---

a24 The meaning of the Hebrew for this clause is uncertain.
b3 Or *gnawed*   *c4* Or *fuel*   *d12* The meaning of the Hebrew for
this word is uncertain.   *e13* Or *me. / 'No one can help him,' ⌊they
say⌋.*   *f18* Hebrew; Septuagint ⌊*God*⌋ *grasps my clothing*

²⁰"I cry out to you, O God, but you do not
    answer;
  I stand up, but you merely look at me.
²¹You turn on me ruthlessly;
  with the might of your hand you attack me.
²²You snatch me up and drive me before the
    wind;
  you toss me about in the storm.
²³I know you will bring me down to death^D,
  to the place appointed for all the living.

²⁴"Surely no one lays a hand on a broken man
  when he cries for help in his distress.
²⁵Have I not wept for those in trouble?
  Has not my soul^D grieved for the poor?
²⁶Yet when I hoped for good, evil came;
  when I looked for light, then came darkness.
²⁷The churning inside me never stops;
  days of suffering confront me.
²⁸I go about blackened, but not by the sun;
  I stand up in the assembly and cry for
    help.
²⁹I have become a brother of jackals,
  a companion of owls.
³⁰My skin grows black and peels;
  my body burns with fever.
³¹My harp is tuned to mourning,
  and my flute to the sound of wailing.

31 "I made a covenant^D with my eyes
    not to look lustfully at a girl.
²For what is man's lot from God above,
  his heritage from the Almighty on high?
³Is it not ruin for the wicked,
  disaster for those who do wrong?
⁴Does he not see my ways
  and count my every step?

Does God refuse to answer a helpless person's cry? (30:20)
Job is not the only one who has felt that God does not answer prayer (Psalm 22:2). But God *does not ignore the cry of the afflicted* (Psalm 9:12). He does hear it and will answer. As Job discovered later, God's answer was "wait." God's timing is different from ours, and often when we think he is saying "no," he is saying only "not yet."

Blackened (30:28)
Job may have had some kind of a wasting disease, accompanied by fever (v. 30), that changed his normal complexion to an unnatural pigment. Or perhaps the scabs from his sores (2:7–8) may have changed his coloring.

Covenant with my eyes (31:1)
Job had sworn a solemn promise not to use his eyes to feed lust in his life. He wisely recognized that resisting temptation involves an act of our will.

Is it okay to swear an oath against ourselves? (ch. 31)

Through this entire chapter, Job calls down great harm upon himself—broken arms, farm calamities, even death—if he has sinned. Should we follow his example?

The answer can be found if we understand something of Job's society. They did not have lie-detector tests or contracts written in triplicate. The only way they could prove their innocence was to swear an oath. Thus, oath-taking was permitted, and even God was said to swear oaths (Deut. 7:8).

But the Old Testament strictly warns against abusing oaths. Since some people said, "I swear by God," when they weren't telling the truth, God warned not to *swear falsely by my name* (Lev. 19:12). Other passages warn people to fulfill any vows they make (Eccl. 5:4–6).

In the New Testament, Jesus raises the stakes: we should live lives of such integrity that we shouldn't have to use oaths to prove our truthfulness. Instead, we should be able to simply say *yes* or *no* and leave it at that (Matt. 5:33–37; James 5:12). Following these passages, some Christians refuse to take oaths in court; other Christians permit such oaths as long as they are said truthfully.

Today, there is no reason we need to call down harm upon ourselves in order to prove we are telling the truth.

If . . . then . . . (31:5–8)

Job invoked the most serious oath a person in his time could swear. If he had lied, cheated someone or stolen, Job said, God should judge him without mercy and allow terrible consequences to befall him. Other "if . . . then . . ." statements follow and were Job's last, desperate attempt to prove his innocence.

5"If I have walked in falsehood
    or my foot has hurried after deceit—
6let God weigh me in honest scales
    and he will know that I am blameless—
7if my steps have turned from the path,
    if my heart has been led by my eyes,
    or if my hands have been defiled,
8then may others eat what I have sown,
    and may my crops be uprooted.

9"If my heart has been enticed by a woman,
    or if I have lurked at my neighbor's door,
10then may my wife grind another man's grain,
    and may other men sleep with her.
11For that would have been shameful,
    a sin to be judged.
12It is a fire that burns to Destruction*a*;
    it would have uprooted my harvest.

13"If I have denied justice to my menservants and
        maidservants
    when they had a grievance against me,
14what will I do when God confronts me?
    What will I answer when called to account?
15Did not he who made me in the womb make
        them?
    Did not the same one form us both within
        our mothers?

16"If I have denied the desires of the poor
    or let the eyes of the widow grow weary,
17if I have kept my bread to myself,
    not sharing it with the fatherless—
18but from my youth I reared him as would a
        father,
    and from my birth I guided the widow—
19if I have seen anyone perishing for lack of
        clothing,
    or a needy man without a garment,
20and his heart did not bless me
    for warming him with the fleece from my
        sheep,
21if I have raised my hand against the fatherless,
    knowing that I had influence in court,
22then let my arm fall from the shoulder,
    let it be broken off at the joint.
23For I dreaded destruction from God,
    and for fear of his splendor I could not do
        such things.

24"If I have put my trust in gold
    or said to pure gold, 'You are my security,'
25if I have rejoiced over my great wealth,
    the fortune my hands had gained,
26if I have regarded the sun in its radiance
    or the moon moving in splendor,
27so that my heart was secretly enticed
    and my hand offered them a kiss of homage,
28then these also would be sins to be judged,
    for I would have been unfaithful to God on
        high.

29"If I have rejoiced at my enemy's misfortune

Is fear of punishment a good motivation? (31:23)

While love for God is a powerful enticement to live a godly life, so is the sobering truth that God is a holy and just God who does not leave sin unpunished. *Do not be deceived: God cannot be mocked. A man reaps what he sows* (Gal. 6:7). It is better to do good out of fear than not to do it at all, though ideally one's motives will be more positive.

Why link money and the moon? (31:24–28)

Putting our trust in either one is idolatry. If we base our security on either our wealth or our horoscope, we are *unfaithful to God on high*. God alone deserves our faith and trust, and he will not share his glory with either gold or the galaxies.

Kiss of homage (31:27)

In Job's culture, people kissed idols to show their worship and submission. In the prophet Elijah's day there were only 7,000 people *whose mouths had not kissed* Baal (1 Kings 19:18).

a12 Hebrew *Abaddon*

or gloated over the trouble that came to
    him—
³⁰I have not allowed my mouth to sin
    by invoking a curse against his life—
³¹if the men of my household have never said,
    'Who has not had his fill of Job's meat?'—
³²but no stranger had to spend the night in the
    street,
    for my door was always open to the
        traveler—
³³if I have concealed my sin as men do,^a
    by hiding my guilt in my heart
³⁴because I so feared the crowd
    and so dreaded the contempt of the clans
    that I kept silent and would not go outside

³⁵("Oh, that I had someone to hear me!
    I sign now my defense—let the Almighty
        answer me;
    let my accuser put his indictment in writing.
³⁶Surely I would wear it on my shoulder,
    I would put it on like a crown.
³⁷I would give him an account of my every step;
    like a prince I would approach him.)—

³⁸"if my land cries out against me
    and all its furrows are wet with tears,
³⁹if I have devoured its yield without payment
    or broken the spirit of its tenants,
⁴⁰then let briers come up instead of wheat
    and weeds instead of barley."

The words of Job are ended.

Elihu

32 So these three men stopped answering Job, be-
cause he was righteous^D in his own eyes. ²But Elihu son of Barakel the Buzite, of the family of Ram, became very angry with Job for justifying^D himself rather
than God. ³He was also angry with the three friends, because they had found no way to refute Job, and yet had
condemned him.^b ⁴Now Elihu had waited before speaking to Job because they were older than he. ⁵But when he
saw that the three men had nothing more to say, his anger was aroused.

⁶So Elihu son of Barakel the Buzite said:

"I am young in years,
    and you are old;
that is why I was fearful,
    not daring to tell you what I know.
⁷I thought, 'Age should speak;
    advanced years should teach wisdom.'
⁸But it is the spirit^c in a man,
    the breath of the Almighty, that gives him
        understanding.
⁹It is not only the old^d who are wise,
    not only the aged who understand what is
        right.
¹⁰"Therefore I say: Listen to me;
    I too will tell you what I know.

Sign . . . my defense (31:35)
Job may have actually put his signature to a
document that detailed the arguments for his
innocence. But more probably he is speaking
symbolically.

Accuser (31:35)
The context suggests Job is referring to God.
God had not actually accused Job of anything.
In fact, only Satan, the *accuser* (see NIV text
note at 1:6), had accused Job. He had charged
that Job followed God only because it benefited him—therefore, Job was really self-serving.
But in his pain, Job assumed that God was
against him. "Why else," he probably asked
himself, "would God have allowed these calamities?"

How do you pay farmland for its yield?
(31:39)
Payment does not go to the land itself, but to
those who have worked to produce its harvest.
Job claimed that he had never sinned by under-
paying laborers for their hard work.

Elihu (32:2)
The last of Job's challengers to appear. He is
the only one with a Hebrew name; it means *He
is my God.* He was called a *Buzite*—a descendant of Abraham's nephew (Gen. 22:20–21).
The name Elihu also belonged to Samuel's
great-grandfather (1 Samuel 1:1), though there
is no evidence to connect the two.

What made Elihu angry? (32:2–5)
Elihu was furious for two reasons. First, Job
had claimed to be innocent and that God had
no reason to be punishing him in this way. That
claim called God's character into question.
Second, Job's friends had mishandled the debate and lost the argument: *not one of you has
proved Job wrong; none of you has answered
his arguments* (v. 12).

---

^a33 Or *as Adam did*   ^b3 Masoretic Text; an ancient Hebrew scribal
tradition *Job, and so had condemned God*   ^c8 Or *Spirit*; also in
verse 18   ^d9 Or *many;* or *great*

Did Job win the debate? (32:12)

To Elihu, Job's three friends failed miserably in refuting Job's arguments that he was innocent. But Elihu wouldn't concede that Job was innocent, only that Job's friends had failed in their strategy and tactics.

What did Elihu say different from the others? (32:14)

Elihu believed Job's suffering was an act of discipline intended to point him back to righteousness: *God does all these things to a man—twice, even three times—to turn back his soul from the pit, that the light of life may shine on him* (33:29–30). It's a good insight, but it doesn't apply to Job. Job was suffering not for his sin, but for his righteousness.

Wineskins (32:19)

Wine, as it ferments, gives off gases that can burst a container. In a similar way, Elihu said that his anger and agitation had been bottled up and building inside him. His zeal to defend God's character was a pressure that had to be relieved by allowing him to speak.

Why did Elihu spend so much time defending his right to speak? (33:2–7)

Elihu was the youngest of Job's four friends, and it was considered disrespectful for a man under 30 to express his opinion in the presence of his elders. Even though the three older friends already had asserted their seniority (15:10), Elihu felt compelled to speak because he believed that Job and the others were misrepresenting God.

Was Elihu right? Was Job justifying himself? (33:8–9)

Though Elihu does not quote Job word for word, he does accurately summarize Job's statement in 13:23–27. However, though Job believed he was innocent, he was not claiming to be sinless. There were times, in fact, when Job admitted he was a sinner (7:21; 13:26). Job only wanted his day in court so that he could prove that his suffering was unjust. In the end, God stood behind Job.

Is it wrong to complain to God? (33:13)

See article: *Is it okay to argue with God?* (Hab. 2:1).

What good is it if no one recognizes when God speaks? (33:13–14)

Elihu states that people may not realize when God is speaking to them, but also recognizes that God can *turn man from wrongdoing* (v. 17) even when his voice is not recognized. It is sometimes hard to hear God's voice in the busyness of life, but God always hears our concerns, even when he sometimes appears silent or hidden.

Does God still speak in dreams and visions? (33:15)

See article: *Does God speak through visions and dreams?* (Daniel 1:17).

11I waited while you spoke,
   I listened to your reasoning;
   while you were searching for words,
12 I gave you my full attention.
But not one of you has proved Job wrong;
   none of you has answered his arguments.
13Do not say, 'We have found wisdom;
   let God refute him, not man.'
14But Job has not marshaled his words against me,
   and I will not answer him with your arguments.

15"They are dismayed and have no more to say;
   words have failed them.
16Must I wait, now that they are silent,
   now that they stand there with no reply?
17I too will have my say;
   I too will tell what I know.
18For I am full of words,
   and the spirit within me compels me;
19inside I am like bottled-up wine,
   like new wineskinsᴰ ready to burst.
20I must speak and find relief;
   I must open my lips and reply.
21I will show partiality to no one,
   nor will I flatter any man;
22for if I were skilled in flattery,
   my Maker would soon take me away.

33 "But now, Job, listen to my words;
   pay attention to everything I say.
2I am about to open my mouth;
   my words are on the tip of my tongue.
3My words come from an upright heart;
   my lips sincerely speak what I know.
4The Spirit of God has made me;
   the breath of the Almighty gives me life.
5Answer me then, if you can;
   prepare yourself and confront me.
6I am just like you before God;
   I too have been taken from clay.
7No fear of me should alarm you,
   nor should my hand be heavy upon you.

8"But you have said in my hearing—
   I heard the very words—
9'I am pure and without sin;
   I am clean and free from guilt.
10Yet God has found fault with me;
   he considers me his enemy.
11He fastens my feet in shackles;
   he keeps close watch on all my paths.'

12"But I tell you, in this you are not right,
   for God is greater than man.
13Why do you complain to him
   that he answers none of man's wordsᵃ?
14For God does speak—now one way, now another—
   though man may not perceive it.
15In a dream, in a visionᴰ of the night,
   when deep sleep falls on men
   as they slumber in their beds,

ᵃ13 Or *that he does not answer for any of his actions*

16he may speak in their ears
and terrify them with warnings,
17to turn man from wrongdoing
and keep him from pride,
18to preserve his soul[D] from the pit,[a]
his life from perishing by the sword.[b]
19Or a man may be chastened on a bed of pain
with constant distress in his bones,
20so that his very being finds food repulsive
and his soul loathes the choicest meal.
21His flesh wastes away to nothing,
and his bones, once hidden, now stick out.
22His soul draws near to the pit,[c]
and his life to the messengers of death[D,d]

23"Yet if there is an angel on his side
as a mediator, one out of a thousand,
to tell a man what is right for him,
24to be gracious to him and say,
'Spare him from going down to the pit[e];
I have found a ransom for him'—
25then his flesh is renewed like a child's;
it is restored as in the days of his youth.
26He prays to God and finds favor with him,
he sees God's face and shouts for joy;
he is restored by God to his righteous[D] state.
27Then he comes to men and says,
'I sinned, and perverted what was right,
but I did not get what I deserved.
28He redeemed[D] my soul from going down to
the pit,[f]
and I will live to enjoy the light.'

29"God does all these things to a man—
twice, even three times—
30to turn back his soul from the pit,[g]
that the light of life may shine on him.

31"Pay attention, Job, and listen to me;
be silent, and I will speak.
32If you have anything to say, answer me;
speak up, for I want you to be cleared.
33But if not, then listen to me;
be silent, and I will teach you wisdom."

34
Then Elihu said:

2"Hear my words, you wise men;
listen to me, you men of learning.
3For the ear tests words
as the tongue tastes food.
4Let us discern for ourselves what is right;
let us learn together what is good.

5"Job says, 'I am innocent,
but God denies me justice.
6Although I am right,
I am considered a liar;
although I am guiltless,
his arrow inflicts an incurable wound.'
7What man is like Job,

How does God warn us against doing wrong? (33:16–17)

Jesus taught that one role of the Holy Spirit was to convict those who contemplate doing wrong (John 16:8). The apostle Paul says that God has placed a knowledge of himself in every human being (Romans 1:19–20). Because people are created in the image of God, each person knows the difference between right and wrong, even if they have never read a word in the Bible.

How does pain speak to us? (33:19)

Pain in our lives has a way of focusing our attention upon God and leading us to examine ourselves. As in Job's case, suffering is not always punitive or corrective. Sometimes it is used to instruct. It is wrong to call all suffering the judgment of God; the Lord's final rebuke of Job's friends is proof of that.

Do angels defend us before God? (33:23–24)

It is ironic that the exact opposite of Elihu's claim occurred in the prologue. There, a fallen angel approaches God and accuses his blameless servant. Job would have gladly accepted an angelic mediator to present his case before God (9:33). However, the New Testament tells us there is *one mediator between God and men, the man Christ Jesus* (1 Tim. 2:5).

Doesn't Elihu merely echo the wrong ideas of the other three? (33:27)

Like the others, Elihu believed that Job was suffering for some wrong that he committed. However, Elihu, unlike the others, makes concessions for God's mercy. If Job would only take responsibility for whatever brought these difficulties upon him, then he would find grace. Contrary to Eliphaz, Elihu believed that a supernatural mediator could speak on Job's behalf.

Why would Elihu want Job's name cleared? (33:32)

The other three friends seemed interested only in quieting Job and defending God's right to punish the wicked. Elihu was concerned about justice, as well, not only to clear Job but to clear up the negative view of God presented so far. Elihu believed that God was gracious and would redeem Job if he would repent.

Drinks scorn like water (34:7)

Scorn is open and unqualified contempt for a person or thing. Elihu accused Job of indulging in his scorn for God like a parched man in the desert takes in water.

---

a 18 Or *preserve him from the grave*   *b 18* Or *from crossing the River*   *c 22* Or *He draws near to the grave*   *d 22* Or *to the dead*   *e 24* Or *grave*   *f 28* Or *redeemed me from going down to the grave*   *g 30* Or *turn him back from the grave*

Why accuse Job of associating with evildoers? (34:8)

Although Elihu is more merciful than the others in his rebuke of Job, he maintains many of the same assumptions. Since Job, in his bitterness, claims that it is useless to attempt to please God, Elihu assumes Job's attitude reflects an association with evil men. Because in ch. 24 Job rails against the activities of evil men, it is unlikely he would have associated with such people. Rather, he made sure to *stand aloof from the counsel of the wicked* (21:15–18).

Unthinkable (34:12)

Some philosophers who debate the problem of evil insist that God must be either unloving or impotent. For Elihu, it was impossible for God to be either. In his view, the blame had to rest on Job in some way.

who drinks scorn like water?
⁸He keeps company with evildoers;
   he associates with wicked men.
⁹For he says, 'It profits a man nothing
   when he tries to please God.'

¹⁰"So listen to me, you men of understanding.
   Far be it from God to do evil,
   from the Almighty to do wrong.
¹¹He repays a man for what he has done;
   he brings upon him what his conduct deserves.
¹²It is unthinkable that God would do wrong,
   that the Almighty would pervert justice.
¹³Who appointed him over the earth?
   Who put him in charge of the whole world?
¹⁴If it were his intention
   and he withdrew his spirit[a] and breath,
¹⁵all mankind would perish together
   and man would return to the dust.

¹⁶"If you have understanding, hear this;
   listen to what I say.
¹⁷Can he who hates justice govern?
   Will you condemn the just and mighty One?
¹⁸Is he not the One who says to kings, 'You are worthless,'
   and to nobles, 'You are wicked,'
¹⁹who shows no partiality to princes
   and does not favor the rich over the poor,
   for they are all the work of his hands?
²⁰They die in an instant, in the middle of the night;
   the people are shaken and they pass away;
   the mighty are removed without human hand.
²¹"His eyes are on the ways of men;
   he sees their every step.
²²There is no dark place, no deep shadow,

---

a 14 Or Spirit

Is life fair? Is God fair? (34:19)

Is life fair? In a world where there are drive-by shootings, child abuse and other indescribable forms of evil, it is difficult to speak of life being fair. It seems that too often good people go unrewarded, and evil people go unpunished.

Is God fair? Absolutely. The justice of God is a theme that threads itself throughout the Old and New Testaments. At times, God punished evil people moments after they carried out their schemes. Good people were rewarded with prosperity and health. But these occurrences seem to be rare. How can we maintain that God is just in a world so full of injustice?

Justice delayed is still justice. Even in our court systems, where crimes are punished years after they are committed and medals of honor are awarded decades after a war, justice is done. God promises that no evil will go unpunished; no good act will go unrewarded. As Solomon said, *God will bring every deed into judgment, including every hidden thing, whether it is good or evil* (Eccl. 12:14). If there is anything we can count on, it's God's justice. Waiting for it to come, however, can at times seem unbearable.

where evildoers can hide.
²³God has no need to examine men further,
    that they should come before him for
      judgment.
²⁴Without inquiry he shatters the mighty
    and sets up others in their place.
²⁵Because he takes note of their deeds,
    he overthrows them in the night and they
      are crushed.
²⁶He punishes them for their wickedness
    where everyone can see them,
²⁷because they turned from following him
    and had no regard for any of his ways.
²⁸They caused the cry of the poor to come
      before him,
    so that he heard the cry of the needy.
²⁹But if he remains silent, who can condemn
      him?
    If he hides his face, who can see him?
    Yet he is over man and nation alike,
³⁰ to keep a godless man from ruling,
    from laying snares for the people.

³¹"Suppose a man says to God,
    'I am guilty but will offend no more.
³²Teach me what I cannot see;
    if I have done wrong, I will not do so again.'
³³Should God then reward you on your terms,
    when you refuse to repentᴰ?
    You must decide, not I;
    so tell me what you know.

³⁴"Men of understanding declare,
    wise men who hear me say to me,
³⁵'Job speaks without knowledge;
    his words lack insight.'
³⁶Oh, that Job might be tested to the utmost
    for answering like a wicked man!
³⁷To his sin he adds rebellion;
    scornfully he claps his hands among us
    and multiplies his words against God."

35 Then Elihu said:

²"Do you think this is just?
    You say, 'I will be cleared by God.ᵃ'
³Yet you ask him, 'What profit is it to me,ᵇ
    and what do I gain by not sinning?'

⁴"I would like to reply to you
    and to your friends with you.
⁵Look up at the heavens and see;
    gaze at the clouds so high above you.
⁶If you sin, how does that affect him?
    If your sins are many, what does that do to
      him?
⁷If you are righteousᴰ, what do you give to
      him,
    or what does he receive from your hand?
⁸Your wickedness affects only a man like
      yourself,
    and your righteousnessᴰ only the sons of
      men.

Why is God silent and distant at times? (34:29)

The silence of God is a difficult thing for a suffering person to endure. Why would God remain hidden when his comforting presence is needed the most? Perhaps because the answer to a person's suffering is so complex that God does not ask that person to try to understand it; instead, God silently sustains that person through the pain. Or perhaps the answer is so simple that God leads the person to discover the answer for himself or herself by remaining silent.

Where do godless rulers come from if God indeed is in control? (34:29–30)

Elihu claims that God would keep the godless from ruling. We know, however, that God allows some evil people to attain positions of authority. Jesus told Pontius Pilate, *You would have no power over me if it were not given to you from above* (John 19:11). Perhaps God allows the godless to rule to test the loyalty of those who claim to follow him. But even if the wicked rule, God remains in control.

Was Job rebelling against God? (34:37)

No. Elihu, in his ignorance, was looking for a simplistic explanation for Job's suffering. Job was actually rebelling against injustice in his life, not against God himself. By demanding his day in court, Job was complaining that God allowed the injustices against him to go unanswered. Other Biblical figures, such as Jeremiah and Habakkuk, similarly expressed their disappointment in God without denying him.

Does sin affect God? (35:6)

In the Bible, God's relationship with people is often described as a marriage. When a man or a woman sins against God, God is deeply grieved. Here, however, Elihu emphasizes God's transcendence. He says that man's actions will not change God himself.

ᵃ2 Or *My righteousness is more than God's*   ᵇ3 Or *you*

What kind of prayer is Elihu suggesting? (35:12–13)

Elihu is claiming that the prayers of the wicked and arrogant are not heard by God. (Elihu believes that God does not respond to Job because Job refuses to admit his guilt.) The Bible teaches that God will not respond to the prayers of his people if they harbor sin in their lives (Isaiah 1:11–15). See article: *When does God refuse to hear our prayers?* (Jer. 11:11).

Does God withdraw when we question his ways? (35:12–13)

God withdraws from questions that are asked in an arrogant and insulting manner. Job never sinned against God with his words. He complained bitterly, but he never blamed God for his situation. As can be seen in God's eventual reply to Job, God did not withdraw from Job because of his questioning. The same was true of the prophets Jeremiah and Habakkuk when they complained to God.

Why did Elihu act so smart? (36:3–4)

Perhaps he felt insecure as the youngest member of the group and tried to compensate through his boasting, implying that his insights were supernaturally inspired and that what he spoke was without error. Or possibly he was speaking ironically—mimicking what he thought was Job's arrogant, self-righteous attitude (33:8–9).

What are a victim's rights? (36:6)

Those who are afflicted have a right to justice and restitution. They have the right to prove that they did not deserve what was done to them. God created human beings with a free will. One consequence of disobedience is that innocent people suffer. Even though the wait for justice might seem unbearable, God one day will restore those who have suffered without cause.

How are the righteous enthroned? (36:7)

This may have been Elihu's poetic way of saying that God would one day reward the righteous for their faithfulness. In the book of Revelation, the apostle John says that in the age to come, those who trust in Christ will reign with him (Rev. 20:6).

Didn't Elihu make the same mistaken assumptions as the others? (36:9–11)

Yes. He assumes that the righteous always prosper and the wicked always are punished. Ultimately, this is true: on the day of judgment, God will reward the righteous and punish the wicked. In the meantime, however, this balance is not always achieved. None of the four friends ever addressed the suffering of the innocent.

Male prostitutes (36:14)

See *What did male prostitutes have to do with pagan worship?* (1 Kings 14:24).

9"Men cry out under a load of oppression;
   they plead for relief from the arm of the
   powerful.
10But no one says, 'Where is God my Maker,
   who gives songs in the night,
11who teaches more to us than to*a* the beasts of
      the earth
   and makes us wiser than*b* the birds of the
      air?'
12He does not answer when men cry out
   because of the arrogance of the wicked.
13Indeed, God does not listen to their empty plea;
   the Almighty pays no attention to it.
14How much less, then, will he listen
   when you say that you do not see him,
   that your case is before him
   and you must wait for him,
15and further, that his anger never punishes
   and he does not take the least notice of
      wickedness.*c*
16So Job opens his mouth with empty talk;
   without knowledge he multiplies words."

36 Elihu continued:

2"Bear with me a little longer and I will show
      you
   that there is more to be said in God's behalf.
3I get my knowledge from afar;
   I will ascribe justice to my Maker.
4Be assured that my words are not false;
   one perfect in knowledge is with you.

5"God is mighty, but does not despise men;
   he is mighty, and firm in his purpose.
6He does not keep the wicked alive
   but gives the afflictedᴰ their rights.
7He does not take his eyes off the righteousᴰ;
   he enthrones them with kings
   and exalts them forever.
8But if men are bound in chains,
   held fast by cords of afflictionᴰ,
9he tells them what they have done—
   that they have sinned arrogantly.
10He makes them listen to correction
   and commands them to repentᴰ of their
      evil.
11If they obey and serve him,
   they will spend the rest of their days in
      prosperity
   and their years in contentment.
12But if they do not listen,
   they will perish by the sword*d*
   and die without knowledge.

13"The godless in heart harbor resentment;
   even when he fetters them, they do not cry
      for help.
14They die in their youth,
   among male prostitutes of the shrines.

a11 Or *teaches us by*   *b11* Or *us wise by*   *c15* Symmachus,
Theodotion and Vulgate; the meaning of the Hebrew for this word is
uncertain.   *d12* Or *will cross the River*

15But those who suffer he delivers in their
        suffering;
    he speaks to them in their affliction D.

16"He is wooing you from the jaws of distress
        to a spacious place free from restriction,
        to the comfort of your table laden with
            choice food.
17But now you are laden with the judgment due
        the wicked;
    judgment and justice have taken hold of you.
18Be careful that no one entices you by riches;
    do not let a large bribe turn you aside.
19Would your wealth
        or even all your mighty efforts
    sustain you so you would not be in distress?
20Do not long for the night,
    to drag people away from their homes. a
21Beware of turning to evil,
    which you seem to prefer to affliction.

22"God is exalted in his power.
    Who is a teacher like him?
23Who has prescribed his ways for him,
    or said to him, 'You have done wrong'?
24Remember to extol D his work,
    which men have praised in song.
25All mankind has seen it;
    men gaze on it from afar.
26How great is God—beyond our understanding!
    The number of his years is past finding out.

27"He draws up the drops of water,
    which distill as rain to the streams b;
28the clouds pour down their moisture
    and abundant showers fall on mankind.
29Who can understand how he spreads out the
        clouds,
    how he thunders from his pavilion?
30See how he scatters his lightning about him,
    bathing the depths of the sea.
31This is the way he governs c the nations
    and provides food in abundance.
32He fills his hands with lightning
    and commands it to strike its mark.

a20 The meaning of the Hebrew for verses 18-20 is uncertain.
b27 Or distill from the mist as rain   c31 Or nourishes

Had Job been trusting in his wealth? (36:19)

Job did not put any kind of ultimate security in his wealth. Job said, "If I have put my trust in gold or said to pure gold, 'You are my security' . . . then these also would be sins to be judged" (31:24,28). Since God himself described Job as blameless, we can assume Job was accurate in his self-evaluation. He showed great concern for the poor, and helped them out whenever he could (31:16–20).

Why would Job have dragged people from their homes? (36:20–21)

He probably didn't. This may have been simply another accusation by a so-called friend groping for some explanation to Job's suffering. To the contrary, Job was generous with his money, having mercy on those who were indebted to him. (See NIV text note on v. 20.)

Does God aim his bolts of lightning? (36:32)

See article: Why does God send calamity? (Lam. 3:38).

Why seek a God who is beyond understanding? (36:26)

There are many things about God that we will never comprehend. What does it mean for God to be self-existent—to have no beginning and no end? Such a mystery is beyond understanding. But the fact that we can never comprehend God for all that he is does not mean we cannot have a meaningful relationship with him.

God has revealed himself to us through his Son Jesus Christ. Jesus said, Anyone who has seen me has seen the Father (John 14:9). By pursuing and cultivating a relationship with Jesus Christ, we come to know God through a being of flesh and blood. As Moses said to the people of Israel, The secret things belong to the LORD our God, but the things revealed belong to us and our children forever (Deut. 29:29).

33His thunder announces the coming storm;
  even the cattle make known its approach.[a]

37 "At this my heart pounds
  and leaps from its place.
2Listen! Listen to the roar of his voice,
  to the rumbling that comes from his mouth.
3He unleashes his lightning beneath the whole
      heaven
  and sends it to the ends of the earth.
4After that comes the sound of his roar;
  he thunders with his majestic voice.
  When his voice resounds,
  he holds nothing back.
5God's voice thunders in marvelous ways;
  he does great things beyond our
      understanding.
6He says to the snow, 'Fall on the earth,'
  and to the rain shower, 'Be a mighty
      downpour.'
7So that all men he has made may know his
      work,
  he stops every man from his labor.[b]
8The animals take cover;
  they remain in their dens.
9The tempest comes out from its chamber,
  the cold from the driving winds.
10The breath of God produces ice,
  and the broad waters become frozen.
11He loads the clouds with moisture;
  he scatters his lightning through them.
12At his direction they swirl around
  over the face of the whole earth
  to do whatever he commands them.
13He brings the clouds to punish men,
  or to water his earth[c] and show his love.

14"Listen to this, Job;
  stop and consider God's wonders.
15Do you know how God controls the clouds
  and makes his lightning flash?
16Do you know how the clouds hang poised,
  those wonders of him who is perfect in
      knowledge?
17You who swelter in your clothes
  when the land lies hushed under the south
      wind,
18can you join him in spreading out the skies,
  hard as a mirror of cast bronze?

19"Tell us what we should say to him;
  we cannot draw up our case because of our
      darkness.
20Should he be told that I want to speak?
  Would any man ask to be swallowed up?
21Now no one can look at the sun,
  bright as it is in the skies
  after the wind has swept them clean.
22Out of the north he comes in golden splendor;
  God comes in awesome majesty.

Why must humans stop working to see God's work? (37:7)

It seems that in every age, people become so focused on their own plans that they lose sight of God. Elihu knew that God's storms (vv. 1–6) can easily halt men's plans, forcing them to remain inside for shelter. Busy schedules and hectic activities allow people little time to give to God or to see what he is doing. When bad weather forces the cancellation of our plans, perhaps God wants to slow us down a bit so we will notice him.

How can God use the same thing for both punishment and reward? (37:13)

God can use his creation for any purpose. At times, God is neutral in his treatment of humans. Jesus said that God sends the rain on the righteous and the unrighteous (Matt. 5:45). At other times, God uses nature to discipline. The same rain that waters the crops can also flood them. However, it is unwise to assume that all natural disasters are God's judgment. God may be testing a person's faith, as he did with Job.

Have the explanations of science diminished God's wonders? (37:14–16)

Scientific discoveries can be used to explain God away or to point to his purposeful design in the universe. Elihu questions Job about his knowledge of the weather in order to expose his ignorance. Today, we have scientific explanations for many of Elihu's questions. But what we have discovered can only make us marvel the more at God and his creation. Both the answered and the unanswered mysteries of the universe point to the presence of a purposeful and intelligent Designer.

Why compare God to the sun? (37:21)

God's glory is often described in the Bible as brilliant and unapproachable, just like the powerful rays of the sun. God is sometimes described as a consuming fire (Deut. 4:24; Heb. 12:29). In a natural, physical sense, the sun serves as a good metaphor for God because of its power and glory. Some cultures have worshiped the sun instead of its Creator.

---

a 33 Or *announces his coming—* / *the One zealous against evil*
b 7 Or / *he fills all men with fear by his power*   *c 13* Or *to favor them*

²³The Almighty is beyond our reach and exalted
  in power;
  in his justice and great righteousness^D, he
    does not oppress.
²⁴Therefore, men revere^D him,
  for does he not have regard for all the wise
    in heart?^a"

The LORD Speaks

38 Then the LORD answered Job out of the storm. He
said:

²"Who is this that darkens my counsel
  with words without knowledge?
³Brace yourself like a man;
  I will question you,
  and you shall answer me.

⁴"Where were you when I laid the earth's
    foundation?
  Tell me, if you understand.
⁵Who marked off its dimensions? Surely you
    know!
  Who stretched a measuring line^D across it?
⁶On what were its footings set,
  or who laid its cornerstone—
⁷while the morning stars sang together
  and all the angels^b shouted for joy?

⁸"Who shut up the sea behind doors
  when it burst forth from the womb,
⁹when I made the clouds its garment
  and wrapped it in thick darkness,
¹⁰when I fixed limits for it
  and set its doors and bars in place,
¹¹when I said, 'This far you may come and no
    farther;
  here is where your proud waves halt'?

¹²"Have you ever given orders to the morning,
  or shown the dawn its place,

^a24 Or *for he does not have regard for any who think they are wise.*
^b7 Hebrew *the sons of God*

Does God stay *beyond our reach?* (37:23)

See article: *Why seek a God who is beyond understanding?* (36:26).

Who is *wise in heart?* (37:24)

Throughout this book, wisdom is humbly accepting whatever God sends, prosperity or calamity. Godly wisdom is not intellectual ability but a conviction in one's heart that God knows and cares for us. According to Elihu however, the wise in heart are those who believe that God never oppresses the righteous or allows them to be troubled. After reading Satan's request of God at the beginning of Job, we know that this is false. What Elihu wants is for Job to let go of his claims to innocence and become *wise in heart* by worshiping God who is just. Also see article: *How can we develop wise hearts?* (Prov. 23:15).

How did God speak to Job out of a storm? (38:1)

In the Old Testament, we have accounts of God appearing to humans in a visible or audible manner. To some God appeared in angelic or human form. To Moses God appeared in a burning bush. Here God speaks to Job out of a storm. Because in the last chapter of Job we read that God spoke to three of the four friends, we can assume that God spoke to Job in an audible voice that could be heard by everyone present.

How had Job darkened God's counsel? (38:2)

In the bitterness of his pain and discomfort, Job had expressed rage over the injustice he was experiencing. He claimed that God was angry with him, and had become his enemy. From the events in the prologue, the reader knows that these assumptions were false. Job's biggest problem was his ignorance. He could not comprehend the complexity of God or the world he had created.

Does God answer Job's charges? (chs. 38–41)

In all that God says in his speeches, he makes no reference to Job's troubles, or even to the reason why he was suffering. The book of Job illustrates a basic human question of why there is evil in the world. Some have argued that the presence of evil proves that God cannot be all-powerful and all-loving at the same time. If God is all-loving, they say, then it's clear he does not have the power to suppress evil. On the other hand, they say, if God is all-powerful but yet allows evil to run rampant, he cannot be all-loving.

In the divine speeches, God demonstrates that he is all-powerful *and* all-loving, and leaves the paradox unresolved. He never really answers Job's charges. But neither does God reverse his opinion that Job is blameless. In the end, God stands by Job and rebukes his friends, leaving their sentence in the hands of the man they have been accusing. Job, in his righteousness, forgives those who accused him unjustly and prays for them. God gave Job a degree of vindication, but only after he no longer demanded it.

Gates of death (38:17)

In ancient literature of the Mesopotamian area, all who entered the netherworld after death passed through a series of seven gates. In the Bible, the gates of death are a poetic description of the passageway through which people pass when they die. The metaphor is also used in Psalm 9:13; 107:18 and Isaiah 38:10.

Abode of light . . . darkness (38:19)

In this passage, light and darkness are personified as living in places unknown to humans.

Was God being sarcastic? (38:21)

Even though God makes statements of irony throughout his speeches in Job, he is working not to embarrass or humiliate Job, but to instruct him. If embarrassment were his intention, God could have taken up Job's arguments and refuted them one by one, as the friends had done.

Pleiades . . . Orion (38:31)

See *What would Job have known about the constellations?* (9:9).

13that it might take the earth by the edges
and shake the wicked out of it?
14The earth takes shape like clay under a seal;
its features stand out like those of a garment.
15The wicked are denied their light,
and their upraised arm is broken.

16"Have you journeyed to the springs of the sea
or walked in the recesses of the deep?
17Have the gates of deathᴰ been shown to you?
Have you seen the gates of the shadow of
deathᵃ?
18Have you comprehended the vast expanses of
the earth?
Tell me, if you know all this.

19"What is the way to the abode of light?
And where does darkness reside?
20Can you take them to their places?
Do you know the paths to their dwellings?
21Surely you know, for you were already born!
You have lived so many years!

22"Have you entered the storehouses of the snow
or seen the storehouses of the hail,
23which I reserve for times of trouble,
for days of war and battle?
24What is the way to the place where the
lightning is dispersed,
or the place where the east winds are
scattered over the earth?
25Who cuts a channel for the torrents of rain,
and a path for the thunderstorm,
26to water a land where no man lives,
a desert with no one in it,
27to satisfy a desolate wasteland
and make it sprout with grass?
28Does the rain have a father?
Who fathers the drops of dew?
29From whose womb comes the ice?
Who gives birth to the frost from the
heavens
30when the waters become hard as stone,
when the surface of the deep is frozen?

31"Can you bind the beautifulᵇ Pleiades?
Can you loose the cords of Orion?
32Can you bring forth the constellations in their
seasonsᶜ
or lead out the Bearᵈ with its cubs?
33Do you know the laws of the heavens?
Can you set up ⌞God'sᵉ⌟ dominion over the
earth?

34"Can you raise your voice to the clouds
and cover yourself with a flood of water?
35Do you send the lightning bolts on their way?
Do they report to you, 'Here we are'?
36Who endowed the heartᶠ with wisdom
or gave understanding to the mindᶠ?
37Who has the wisdom to count the clouds?

ᵃ17 Or *gates of deep shadows*   ᵇ31 Or *the twinkling;* or *the chains of the*   ᶜ32 Or *the morning star in its season*   ᵈ32 Or *out Leo*
ᵉ33 Or *his;* or *their*   ᶠ36 The meaning of the Hebrew for this word is uncertain.

Who can tip over the water jars of the
heavens
³⁸when the dust becomes hard
and the clods of earth stick together?

³⁹"Do you hunt the prey for the lioness
and satisfy the hunger of the lions
⁴⁰when they crouch in their dens
or lie in wait in a thicket?
⁴¹Who provides food for the raven
when its young cry out to God
and wander about for lack of food?

39

"Do you know when the mountain goats give
birth?
Do you watch when the doe bears her fawn?
²Do you count the months till they bear?
Do you know the time they give birth?
³They crouch down and bring forth their young;
their labor pains are ended.
⁴Their young thrive and grow strong in the
wilds;
they leave and do not return.

⁵"Who let the wild donkey go free?
Who untied his ropes?
⁶I gave him the wasteland as his home,
the salt flats as his habitat.
⁷He laughs at the commotion in the town;
he does not hear a driver's shout.
⁸He ranges the hills for his pasture
and searches for any green thing.

⁹"Will the wild ox consent to serve you?
Will he stay by your manger at night?
¹⁰Can you hold him to the furrow with a
harness?
Will he till the valleys behind you?
¹¹Will you rely on him for his great strength?
Will you leave your heavy work to him?
¹²Can you trust him to bring in your grain
and gather it to your threshing floor?

¹³"The wings of the ostrich flap joyfully,
but they cannot compare with the pinions
and feathers of the stork.
¹⁴She lays her eggs on the ground
and lets them warm in the sand,
¹⁵unmindful that a foot may crush them,
that some wild animal may trample them.
¹⁶She treats her young harshly, as if they were
not hers;
she cares not that her labor was in vain,
¹⁷for God did not endow her with wisdom
or give her a share of good sense.
¹⁸Yet when she spreads her feathers to run,
she laughs at horse and rider.

¹⁹"Do you give the horse his strength
or clothe his neck with a flowing mane?
²⁰Do you make him leap like a locust^D,
striking terror with his proud snorting?
²¹He paws fiercely, rejoicing in his strength,
and charges into the fray.
²²He laughs at fear, afraid of nothing;
he does not shy away from the sword.
²³The quiver rattles against his side,

What does the animal kingdom tell us about God? (39:1–30)

The animal kingdom shows us the pleasure that God derives from variety. It testifies to God's loving sovereignty and power over all of creation. God did not simply get things running and then leave his creation to fend for itself. He is as intimately involved in the survival of these creatures as he is in the lives of humans.

Why didn't God give the ostrich common sense? (39:17)

The ostrich has an extremely small brain, though it has sufficient sense for survival. Its legs are strong enough to run at incredible speeds to defend against predators. Why would God create a bird that can't fly? The lesson for Job is that there are many unexplainable things, but that they exist solely for the pleasure of God.

along with the flashing spear and lance.
²⁴In frenzied excitement he eats up the ground;
  he cannot stand still when the trumpet
    sounds.
²⁵At the blast of the trumpet he snorts, 'Aha!'
  He catches the scent of battle from afar,
    the shout of commanders and the battle cry.

²⁶"Does the hawk take flight by your wisdom
  and spread his wings toward the south?
²⁷Does the eagle soar at your command
  and build his nest on high?
²⁸He dwells on a cliff and stays there at night;
  a rocky crag is his stronghold.^D
²⁹From there he seeks out his food;
  his eyes detect it from afar.
³⁰His young ones feast on blood,
  and where the slain are, there is he."

40

The LORD said to Job:

²"Will the one who contends with the Almighty
    correct him?
  Let him who accuses God answer him!"

³Then Job answered the LORD:

⁴"I am unworthy—how can I reply to you?
  I put my hand over my mouth.
⁵I spoke once, but I have no answer—
  twice, but I will say no more."

⁶Then the LORD spoke to Job out of the storm:

⁷"Brace yourself like a man;
  I will question you,
    and you shall answer me.

⁸"Would you discredit my justice?
  Would you condemn me to justify^D
    yourself?
⁹Do you have an arm like God's,
  and can your voice thunder like his?
¹⁰Then adorn yourself with glory^D and splendor,
  and clothe yourself in honor and majesty.
¹¹Unleash the fury of your wrath,
  look at every proud man and bring him low,
¹²look at every proud man and humble him,
  crush the wicked where they stand.
¹³Bury them all in the dust together;
  shroud their faces in the grave.
¹⁴Then I myself will admit to you
  that your own right hand can save you.

¹⁵"Look at the behemoth,^a
  which I made along with you
    and which feeds on grass like an ox.
¹⁶What strength he has in his loins,
  what power in the muscles of his belly!
¹⁷His tail^b sways like a cedar;
  the sinews of his thighs are close-knit.
¹⁸His bones are tubes of bronze,
  his limbs like rods of iron.
¹⁹He ranks first among the works of God,

Did God want Job to be silent about his doubts? (40:2)

A healthy skepticism is good for determining what is true. In Job's case, however, his doubts were becoming destructive as he began to question God's integrity and love for him. Because these doubts were leading Job to believe things that were not true, God wanted to silence them. It is not wrong to doubt if you are genuinely seeking the truth. Truth is unchangeable and will withstand any challenge.

Was Job admitting he was wrong? (40:4)

Not exactly. The word *unworthy* can mean *small* or *insignificant*. It was an ancient custom to cover one's mouth to show respect and submission before a powerful ruler. Perhaps Job was saying that he had been presumptuous to dare to complain to God.

Why did God continue to rebuke Job? (40:7)

It may be that God continued to rebuke Job because he had not yet repented (42:6). Or perhaps God wanted to address the moral issues raised earlier between Job and his friends. It may be that God wanted to convince Job that he could trust the Lord to be his friend. When God was finished, Job repented and his doubts disappeared—even though some of his questions remained unanswered.

Was God bragging to Job? (40:8–14)

Throughout his complaint, Job had insisted that if he could only have an audience with God, he could prove his innocence. Job had wanted to do what God apparently was not doing—vindicating the innocent. In response the Lord challenges Job to take on the characteristics of deity if he can. These verses show that Job was helpless against the forces of evil in the world; God was not.

Had Job condemned God? (40:8)

Yes, on at least two counts. First he felt that God had wronged him by allowing him to suffer without cause (19:6). But Job also felt that God had refused him the chance to be vindicated. Job wanted to have his day in court and accused God of denying him that privilege.

---

^a15 Possibly the hippopotamus or the elephant   ^b17 Possibly trunk

yet his Maker can approach him with his
    sword.
²⁰The hills bring him their produce,
    and all the wild animals play nearby.
²¹Under the lotus plants he lies,
    hidden among the reeds in the marsh.
²²The lotuses conceal him in their shadow;
    the poplars by the stream surround him.
²³When the river rages, he is not alarmed;
    he is secure, though the Jordan should surge
        against his mouth.
²⁴Can anyone capture him by the eyes,ᵃ
    or trap him and pierce his nose?

41 "Can you pull in the leviathanᴰᵇ with a
    fishhook
    or tie down his tongue with a rope?
²Can you put a cord through his nose
    or pierce his jaw with a hook?
³Will he keep begging you for mercyᴰ?
    Will he speak to you with gentle words?
⁴Will he make an agreement with you
    for you to take him as your slave for life?
⁵Can you make a pet of him like a bird
    or put him on a leash for your girls?
⁶Will traders barter for him?
    Will they divide him up among the
        merchants?
⁷Can you fill his hide with harpoons
    or his head with fishing spears?
⁸If you lay a hand on him,
    you will remember the struggle and never do
        it again!
⁹Any hope of subduing him is false;
    the mere sight of him is overpowering.
¹⁰No one is fierce enough to rouse him.
    Who then is able to stand against me?
¹¹Who has a claim against me that I must pay?
    Everything under heaven belongs to me.

¹²"I will not fail to speak of his limbs,
    his strength and his graceful form.
¹³Who can strip off his outer coat?
    Who would approach him with a bridle?
¹⁴Who dares open the doors of his mouth,
    ringed about with his fearsome teeth?
¹⁵His back hasᶜ rows of shields
    tightly sealed together;
¹⁶each is so close to the next
    that no air can pass between.
¹⁷They are joined fast to one another;
    they cling together and cannot be parted.
¹⁸His snorting throws out flashes of light;
    his eyes are like the rays of dawn.
¹⁹Firebrands stream from his mouth;
    sparks of fire shoot out.
²⁰Smoke pours from his nostrils
    as from a boiling pot over a fire of reeds.
²¹His breath sets coals ablaze,
    and flames dart from his mouth.
²²Strength resides in his neck;
    dismay goes before him.

How does the leviathan prove no one can stand up to God? (41:10)

In the literature of the era, the leviathan was used to symbolize evil political powers. The non-mythological leviathan was the crocodile. In this speech, the Lord describes his sovereignty over the moral order, using the leviathan to represent something that Job was powerless over. Man could never form an alliance with this creature, either by treaty or by force. If one could not stand up to this creature, how could one stand up to its Creator?

Had Job claimed God owed him something? (41:11)

Job had insisted that God owed him an explanation. He wanted to know the charges against him (7:20), and he wanted God to put them in writing (31:35). Job claimed he could do what God was failing to do—prove his innocence. Job insisted that God owed him this. It is clear from God's speech that God is never obligated to explain himself.

Was this fire-breathing dragon real? (41:18–21)

No. This describes the leviathan or crocodile symbolically to represent evil political empires (as, for example, in Psalm 74:14). It was also used to picture an evil power that raises itself up against God in the end times (Isaiah 27:1). In Job, the leviathan appears in God's discourse about his sovereignty. What Job could not tame, God could hold at bay.

ᵃ24 Or by a water hole   ᵇ1 Possibly the crocodile   ᶜ15 Or His
pride is his

Lower millstone (41:24)

This is one of a set of two cylindrical stones used for grinding grain. With this method, which is among the oldest and most common ways of grinding grain, the kernels are spread over the lower millstone while the upper millstone is rolled along the edge of the lower millstone until the grain is crushed into flour.

Threshing sledge (41:30)

The threshing sledge was a large, weighted implement that was driven over wheat to dislodge the grain from the straw. This was usually done on high ground so that the wind would carry the light chaff away.

Why did God answer questions with questions? (42:4)

Questions can help students discover truths for themselves. In Job's case, God used a series of pointed questions to guide Job to the truth and to free him from his bitterness.

Was Job actually able to see God? (42:5)

Now my eyes have seen you could mean that Job had a vision of God, or simply that his spiritual eyes had been opened to the truth about God. We do know that God spoke to Job out of a whirlwind, which presumably could be seen and heard. See *How could Moses speak to the Lord face to face?* (Exodus 33:11).

23The folds of his flesh are tightly joined;
   they are firm and immovable.
24His chest is hard as rock,
   hard as a lower millstoneD.
25When he rises up, the mighty are terrified;
   they retreat before his thrashing.
26The sword that reaches him has no effect,
   nor does the spear or the dart or the javelin.
27Iron he treats like straw
   and bronze like rotten wood.
28Arrows do not make him flee;
   slingstones are like chaffD to him.
29A club seems to him but a piece of straw;
   he laughs at the rattling of the lance.
30His undersides are jagged potsherds,
   leaving a trail in the mud like a threshing
     sledge.
31He makes the depths churn like a boiling
     caldron
   and stirs up the sea like a pot of ointment.
32Behind him he leaves a glistening wake;
   one would think the deep had white hair.
33Nothing on earth is his equal—
   a creature without fear.
34He looks down on all that are haughty;
   he is king over all that are proud."

Job

42 Then Job replied to the LORD:

2"I know that you can do all things;
   no plan of yours can be thwarted.
3⌊You asked,⌋ 'Who is this that obscures my
     counsel without knowledge?'
   Surely I spoke of things I did not understand,
   things too wonderful for me to know.

4⌊"You said,⌋ 'Listen now, and I will speak;
   I will question you,
   and you shall answer me.'

How had Job changed? (42:2)

Earlier, Job was convinced that God was angry with him and that he had become God's enemy. He cursed the day of his birth because of the suffering he was experiencing. He was angry at God's silence and demanded that his arguments be heard. He wanted to do what God had failed to do—provide his vindication.

But after God had finished speaking, Job acknowledged he had been talking over his head—beyond his understanding (v. 3). Even though Job never received a reason for his suffering, it was sufficient for him to know that a reason existed. If he had to do it over, Job probably would have tried to trust God a little more and complain a whole lot less.

Part of Job's problem had been with what he did not know. Now that he had encountered the sovereign God, Job regretted the presumptuous statements he had made about God. Job had come to realize that God was sovereign over the moral order of the world, and that nothing could happen apart from his permission.

Perhaps the most comforting revelation of all for Job was that God was still his friend. Though he seemed silent or even absent, God was no mere spectator of Job's suffering. He was with him through the experience.

⁵My ears had heard of you
   but now my eyes have seen you.
⁶Therefore I despise myself
   and repent^D in dust and ashes."

Epilogue

⁷After the LORD had said these things to Job, he said to Eliphaz the Temanite, "I am angry with you and your two friends, because you have not spoken of me what is right, as my servant Job has. ⁸So now take seven bulls and seven rams and go to my servant Job and sacrifice^D a burnt offering^D for yourselves. My servant Job will pray for you, and I will accept his prayer and not deal with you according to your folly. You have not spoken of me what is right, as my servant Job has." ⁹So Eliphaz the Temanite, Bildad the Shuhite and Zophar the Naamathite did what the LORD told them; and the LORD accepted Job's prayer.

¹⁰After Job had prayed for his friends, the LORD made him prosperous again and gave him twice as much as he had before. ¹¹All his brothers and sisters and everyone who had known him before came and ate with him in his house. They comforted and consoled him over all the trouble the LORD had brought upon him, and each one gave him a piece of silver^a and a gold ring.

¹²The LORD blessed the latter part of Job's life more than the first. He had fourteen thousand sheep, six thousand camels, a thousand yoke^D of oxen and a thousand donkeys. ¹³And he also had seven sons and three daughters. ¹⁴The first daughter he named Jemimah, the second Keziah and the third Keren-Happuch. ¹⁵Nowhere in all the land were there found women as beautiful as Job's daughters, and their father granted them an inheritance along with their brothers.

¹⁶After this, Job lived a hundred and forty years; he saw his children and their children to the fourth generation. ¹⁷And so he died, old and full of years.

Despise myself (42:6)

The verb for *despise myself* can be translated *I reject what I said*. Job had made many rash statements about God's apparent sloth in vindicating him, and now he was taking them back.

Dust and ashes (42:6)

In the ancient Middle East, a grieving person would don burlap and pour dust and ashes over his or her head as a sign of distress. Here Job does the same to signify his sorrow.

You and your two friends (42:7)

God was referring to Eliphaz, Bildad and Zophar. Although Elihu echoed many of the same sentiments as these three, he was quite distinct from them.

Why did God appoint Job as mediator for his three friends? (42:8)

To some extent, putting Job in this position gave him a taste of the vindication he had longed for. These three had falsely accused him of sin and had added to his grief. By praying for his enemies, Job's healing would become complete (v. 10; Matt. 5:44).

How had Job's friends misrepresented God? (42:8)

The basic assumption of the three friends was that the righteous always prosper and the wicked are always punished. They implied that no one ever suffers innocently.

Did the Lord or Satan bring trouble to Job? (42:11)

See article: *Is God responsible for what Satan does?* (19:8–12).

Why does God restore double his cattle but only the identical number of children? (42:12–13)

Property can be replaced, but there is no substitute for children. Perhaps Job would one day again see the children he had lost to death.

Why did God reward Job with material prosperity? (42:12–13)

We can only speculate about why God not only restored Job's wealth, but doubled it. Perhaps it was meant to be a sign to all that just because the innocent suffer, it does not mean that God has abandoned them. Job handled his wealth well (31:24), and so it probably never interfered with his relationship with God.

Why tell about Job's daughters, but not his sons? (42:14–15)

In the epic literature of Job's era, it was common to speak of the hero's beautiful daughters as a sign of divine blessing. Daughters in this culture were generally denied an inheritance. Making an exception for them shows how precious they were to Job.

---

^a11 Hebrew *him a kesitah*; a kesitah was a unit of money of unknown weight and value.

PSALMS

Why read this book?

This book can help you give voice to your feelings. Expressing emotions can be frustrating—especially if you're also trying to maintain spiritual balance. Is it okay to be "sometimes up and sometimes down"? Can you shout for joy when God gets you out of a jam? And what can you say when you feel abandoned by God? Whatever you feel—joy or sorrow, peace or anguish—you'll find your feelings expressed somewhere in Psalms. You'll find comfort and strength when you identify with the Old Testament saints who wrote these prayers and songs.

Who wrote this book?

David—Israel's most celebrated king—is connected to 73 of the psalms, either as writer or recipient. Asaph, the Sons of Korah, Solomon, Moses and others wrote psalms as well.

Why was it written?

Some authors originally may have intended their psalms for solitary singing or meditation. Others meant their psalms for group singing—some even for soldiers to sing while marching to battle. As their value for spiritual encouragement became apparent, the psalms were collected as helps for worship, prayer and instruction about God.

What to look for in Psalms:

The psalms are poetry, not doctrinal essays. Their writers usually were more interested in how something felt than what it meant. Think of the psalms as entries in a diary—they reflect people's most intimate dealings with God. Watch for figures of speech, exaggerations and repetitions. Poetic language calls for you to read with your heart as well as your mind.

BOOK I
Psalms 1-41

Psalm 1

¹Blessed is the man
  who does not walk in the counsel of the
    wicked
or stand in the way of sinners
  or sit in the seat of mockers.
²But his delight is in the law of the LORD,
  and on his law he meditates day and night.
³He is like a tree planted by streams of water,
  which yields its fruit in season
and whose leaf does not wither.
  Whatever he does prospers.

⁴Not so the wicked!
  They are like chaffᴰ
  that the wind blows away.
⁵Therefore the wicked will not stand in the
    judgment,
  nor sinners in the assembly of the
    righteousᴰ.

⁶For the LORD watches over the way of the
    righteous,
  but the way of the wicked will perish.

Psalm 2

¹Why do the nations conspireᵃ
  and the peoples plot in vain?
²The kings of the earth take their stand
  and the rulers gather together
against the LORD

ᵃ1 Hebrew; Septuagint rage

Blessed (1:1)
See *Blessed* (32:1).

Counsel . . . way . . . seat (1:1)
Counsel means advice. *Way* means behavior. *Seat* means position or mental attitude.

Why should we meditate? (1:2)
When we meditate by wrapping our hearts and minds around God's revelation of himself in his Word (law), we'll find spiritual stability, depth of character and divine blessing. Also see article: *Isn't meditation used by some other religions?* (77:12).

Does following God bring success? (1:3–4)
This psalm offers a *principle,* not a *guarantee* of success. The ancient Hebrews did not limit their definition of success to purely financial terms. They valued other factors as well: a positive reputation and community respect, for example. For the righteous, success is measured not in the accumulation of wealth but in the experience of God's blessing on their words and deeds. Also see article: *Are proverbs iron-clad promises?* (Prov. 3:1–4).

Chaff (1:4)
After wheat was harvested, the chaff (stems, leaves, husks and dust) was blown away from the grain in a process called winnowing. The worthless *chaff* symbolized the wicked, who would be separated from the righteous at judgment. See **Winnowing fork** (Luke 3:17).

Anointed One (2:2)
Messiah comes from the Hebrew word for *Anointed.* When the Israelites read this, they thought of their king. But the early followers of Jesus recognized these words as a foreshadowing of the Son of God. See NIV text note at Matt. 1:17.

How should we understand Biblical poetry? (1:1)

With its highly symbolic language and frequent use of metaphors, Biblical poetry can sometimes be difficult to understand. Learning a few basics, however, can help. One important characteristic of ancient Hebrew poetry is *parallelism—* verses or lines expressing the same thought in parallel structure. For example, in Psalm 1 we read that the blessed man doesn't *walk in the counsel of the wicked* or *stand in the way of sinners* or *sit in the seat of mockers.* The idea of associating with godless people is expressed with different verbs, but in the same grammatical structure.

The impact of some other poetic devices is lost with the translation from ancient Hebrew into modern English. *Acrostics,* for example, are discussed in **Why is there a Hebrew character and word at the start of each section?** (119:1–176).

The poetry of the psalms focuses largely on human feelings. Poetry reveals a range of emotions experienced by sincere but sinful people who struggle to follow God and understand his place in their lives. For this reason, the psalms can be quite varied: some are uplifting, others depressing—but all are real. Why? Because the writers of the psalms bared their souls to God as well as to their readers.

Though we can learn a great deal from Biblical poetry, its primary purpose is not so much to *teach* us as to *reach* us.

Who planned the revolt *against the Lord and his Anointed One*? (2:2)

David, God's anointed king, was a warrior who had to contend with many challenges to his power. This revolt could have been organized by nearby Philistines, Phoenicians, Syrians, Moabites, Ammonites, other assorted desert tribes or an alliance of these groups. At various times, David fought against all of these.

Holy hill (2:6)

See *Where was God's holy mountain?* (43:3).

Why did the Lord call the king his Son? (2:7)

In the sense that God is our Creator, all of us are his children. But the king had a unique relationship to God based on the position God had assigned him. God gave the king the authority to rule, like a father to a son (2 Samuel 7:14).

Why would the king want to *dash the nations to pieces*? (2:8–9)

God's harsh action was a direct response to the gathering of the nations against his chosen people and their king. Some say the harshness of this battle rhetoric foreshadows Christ's judgment of the world and his final victory over evil described in the book of Revelation.

Why should other kings kiss the Son? (2:12)

Unlike a handshake, which often is a greeting between equals, a kiss in ancient times was a sign of giving honor and homage to someone with greater power or authority. Such honor was especially due God's chosen king (see 110:1–2).

Is God easily angered? (2:12)

It's a matter of perspective. Humanly speaking, God's retribution may seem like a sudden surprise. On the other hand, it is not unusual for God to withhold his wrath for a long time, waiting for people to repent. Based on God's holy standard, perhaps we should be more surprised that his wrath against stubborn sinners is not more sudden and severe.

SCRIPTURE LINK (3:1) *How many are my foes*

David's son, Absalom, led a rebellion against David, forcing the king to flee from Jerusalem. See 2 Samuel 15–18 for the background to this psalm.

Holy hill (3:4)

See *Where was God's holy mountain?* (43:3).

Why did David pray his enemies would have their teeth broken? (3:7)

David's prayer was probably framed by his feelings that his enemies were biting and chewing on him and his kingdom. Such inflammatory language shows that David was a passionate person. But we must also remember that David was God's anointed king and God took attacks on David very seriously. See articles: *Is it right to pray for revenge?* (58:6–8) and *Who would smash babies for revenge?* (137:8–9).

and against his Anointed[D] One.[a]

³"Let us break their chains," they say,
   "and throw off their fetters."

⁴The One enthroned in heaven laughs;
   the Lord scoffs at them.
⁵Then he rebukes them in his anger
   and terrifies them in his wrath, saying,
⁶"I have installed my King[b]
   on Zion[D], my holy hill."

⁷I will proclaim the decree of the Lord:

He said to me, "You are my Son[c];
   today I have become your Father.[d]
⁸Ask of me,
   and I will make the nations your
      inheritance,
   the ends of the earth your possession.
⁹You will rule them with an iron scepter[De];
   you will dash them to pieces like pottery."

¹⁰Therefore, you kings, be wise;
   be warned, you rulers of the earth.
¹¹Serve the Lord with fear
   and rejoice with trembling.
¹²Kiss the Son, lest he be angry
   and you be destroyed in your way,
for his wrath can flare up in a moment.
   Blessed are all who take refuge in him.

Psalm 3

A psalm of David. When he fled from his son Absalom.

¹O Lord, how many are my foes!
   How many rise up against me!
²Many are saying of me,
   "God will not deliver him."   *Selah*[Df]

³But you are a shield around me, O Lord;
   you bestow glory[D] on me and lift[g] up my
      head.
⁴To the Lord I cry aloud,
   and he answers me from his holy hill.
                                             Selah

⁵I lie down and sleep;
   I wake again, because the Lord sustains
      me.
⁶I will not fear the tens of thousands
   drawn up against me on every side.

⁷Arise, O Lord!
   Deliver me, O my God!
Strike all my enemies on the jaw;
   break the teeth of the wicked.

⁸From the Lord comes deliverance.
   May your blessing be on your people. *Selah*

---

a2 Or *anointed one*   *b6* Or *king*   *c7* Or *son*; also in verse 12
d7 Or *have begotten you*   *e9* Or *will break them with a rod of iron*
f2 A word of uncertain meaning, occurring frequently in the Psalms; possibly a musical term   *g3* Or *Lord, / my Glorious One, who lifts*

Psalm 4

For the director of music. With stringed instruments.
A psalm of David.

1Answer me when I call to you,
    O my righteous[D] God.
Give me relief from my distress;
    be merciful to me and hear my prayer.

2How long, O men, will you turn my glory[D]
    into shame[a]?
How long will you love delusions and seek
    false gods[b]?   Selah[D]
3Know that the LORD has set apart the godly for
    himself;
the LORD will hear when I call to him.

4In your anger do not sin;
    when you are on your beds,
    search your hearts and be silent.   Selah
5Offer right sacrifices[D]
    and trust in the LORD.

6Many are asking, "Who can show us any
    good?"
Let the light of your face shine upon us,
    O LORD.
7You have filled my heart with greater joy
    than when their grain and new wine[D]
    abound.
8I will lie down and sleep in peace[D],
    for you alone, O LORD,
    make me dwell in safety.

a2 Or *you dishonor my Glorious One*   *b2* Or *seek lies*

Why, in the middle of a prayer, did David talk to *men*? (4:2–5)

There is disagreement about why these words to *men* appear in a prayer to God. Some think David was quoting a proverb or passage familiar to his hearers. Others think this was a congregational psalm in which the priest first addressed God and then turned to address the congregation. Still others say this psalm may have been formed by combining parts of more than one psalm.

Set apart (4:3)

From a Hebrew word meaning *separate,* which seldom appears in the Old Testament. Godly people are uniquely chosen among the entire human race and have a distinctive relationship with God.

Right sacrifices (4:5)

Sacrifices that (1) met the requirements laid down by God and (2) arose from correct motives of reverence for God (see 51:17; 2 Cor. 9:6–7).

What are the different kinds of psalms? (3:1)

There are many ways to categorize the psalms. Some focus on content (trouble or trust, praise or prayer, joy or repentance). Others emphasize the use of the psalms (public ceremonies, private prayers and so on). Still others analyze style and technique (such as parallelism and acrostics). Here are some general categories:

(1) *Hymns of praise.* Many psalms were used in temple worship and some even include directions for the song leader. Many are still used as the basis for modern hymns and praise choruses.

(2) *Complaints.* Life is tough and many of the psalms reflect that fact. People turn to the psalms in times of distress because the psalms dare to be honest and meet them right where they are.

(3) *Royal* or *Messianic.* Many psalms revolved around the king and were intended to be used for public occasions in the life of the nation of Israel. Early Christian teachers, however, recognized that these psalms contained prophetic allusions to Christ, the King of kings.

(4) *Occasional.* "Songs of ascent" (120–134) were so named because they were sung by Israelite pilgrims as they *went up* to Jerusalem for the annual feasts. Other special occasions often had their own psalms as well.

(5) *Wisdom.* A few psalms illustrate the difference between human folly and godly wisdom, between sinful and righteous behavior.

Other categories could also be listed: *historical, repentance, curse* and *nature.*

Psalm 5

For the director of music. For flutes. A psalm of David.

¹Give ear to my words, O LORD,
    consider my sighing.
²Listen to my cry for help,
    my King and my God,
    for to you I pray.
³In the morning, O LORD, you hear my voice;
    in the morning I lay my requests before you
    and wait in expectation.

⁴You are not a God who takes pleasure in evil;
    with you the wicked cannot dwell.
⁵The arrogant cannot stand in your presence;
    you hate all who do wrong.
⁶You destroy those who tell lies;
    bloodthirsty and deceitful men
    the LORD abhors.

⁷But I, by your great mercyᴰ,
    will come into your house;
in reverenceᴰ will I bow down
    toward your holy temple.
⁸Lead me, O LORD, in your righteousnessᴰ
    because of my enemies—
    make straight your way before me.

⁹Not a word from their mouth can be trusted;
    their heart is filled with destruction.
Their throat is an open grave;
    with their tongue they speak deceit.
¹⁰Declare them guilty, O God!
    Let their intrigues be their downfall.
Banish them for their many sins,
    for they have rebelled against you.

¹¹But let all who take refuge in you be glad;

Were David's enemies really that evil? (5:9)

The psalms express people's feelings, but they do not necessarily offer objective analysis. David felt so passionately about his enemies that though they undoubtedly were cruel, he may have overstated his case a bit.

Is the God of love also a God of hate? (5:5)

Yes. He hates sin and, at least in one sense, those who revel in their evil and rebellion. In the Old Testament, God's hatred of evil led him to favor one brother over another (Jacob over Esau), destroy cities (Sodom and Gomorrah) and flood the entire earth. See *How can God hate?* (Mal. 1:2–3).

Nevertheless, God distinguishes the fine line between hating the sinner and hating the sinner's sinful characteristics. It is not a contradiction that God loves the sinner at the same time that he hates sin. *God demonstrates his own love for us in this: While we were still sinners, Christ died for us* (Romans 5:8).

In the Bible, God's *love* and *hate* often represent more than mere emotion. The words illustrate the condition of a person's relationship with God—someone is either on God's side or not. See *Is hatred sometimes a good thing?* (139:21–22).

Whether we suffer the consequences of God's hatred or the benefits of his love, then, depends on our response. Those who persist in doing evil by setting themselves against God are destined to encounter God's wrath—as did those whom David mentions here, the *wicked . . . arrogant . . . bloodthirsty . . .* and *deceitful.* Those who seek God in humility, bowing down before him, can enjoy God's mercy (v. 7). God is loving and forgiving, but at the same time he is opposed to those who are opposed to him.

let them ever sing for joy.
Spread your protection over them,
    that those who love your name may rejoice
      in you.
¹²For surely, O LORD, you bless the righteous^D;
    you surround them with your favor as with a
      shield.

Psalm 6

For the director of music. With stringed instruments.
According to sheminith.^a A psalm of David.

¹O LORD, do not rebuke me in your anger
    or discipline me in your wrath.
²Be merciful to me, LORD, for I am faint;
    O LORD, heal me, for my bones are in agony.
³My soul^D is in anguish.
    How long, O LORD, how long?

⁴Turn, O LORD, and deliver me;
    save me because of your unfailing love.
⁵No one remembers you when he is dead.
    Who praises you from the grave^b?

⁶I am worn out from groaning;
    all night long I flood my bed with weeping
    and drench my couch with tears.
⁷My eyes grow weak with sorrow;
    they fail because of all my foes.

⁸Away from me, all you who do evil,
    for the LORD has heard my weeping.
⁹The LORD has heard my cry for mercy^D;
    the LORD accepts my prayer.
¹⁰All my enemies will be ashamed and dismayed;
    they will turn back in sudden disgrace.

Psalm 7

A shiggaion^c of David, which he sang to the LORD
concerning Cush, a Benjamite.

¹O LORD my God, I take refuge in you;
    save and deliver me from all who pursue me,
²or they will tear me like a lion
    and rip me to pieces with no one to rescue
      me.

³O LORD my God, if I have done this
    and there is guilt on my hands—
⁴if I have done evil to him who is at peace^D
    with me
    or without cause have robbed my foe—
⁵then let my enemy pursue and overtake me;
    let him trample my life to the ground
    and make me sleep in the dust.   *Selah*^D

⁶Arise, O LORD, in your anger;
    rise up against the rage of my enemies.
    Awake, my God; decree justice.
⁷Let the assembled peoples gather around you.
    Rule over them from on high;
⁸ let the LORD judge the peoples.

How does God discipline people? (6:1)
God is like a good father who spanks his disobedient child. Neither one enjoys disciplining his children. Sometimes God uses physical suffering to discipline his people. (David wanted healing because his bones were *in agony*, v. 2.) Other times God causes emotional distress to make his point (David's soul was *in anguish*, v. 3). But God also teaches us by his Word, through the counsel of other believers or through specific circumstances. Also see *Is affliction a good thing?* (119:67–75).

Was David physically sick? (6:2–7)
David's severe sorrow caused faintness, agony, anguish, groaning and weeping. He was speaking with poetic flair, probably exaggerating his emotional state. Producing enough tears to drench a couch is a figure of speech (v. 6).

Didn't David believe in life after death? (6:5)
David believed in life after death (Psalm 23), but he seemed somewhat uncertain about specifics. Such hesitation was not unusual for Old Testament saints. See *Why would evil Saul go to the same place as righteous Samuel when he died?* (1 Samuel 28:19). The emphasis in the psalms primarily is on reward and punishment in this life, not the next.

Does God hear our prayers better when we are emotional? (6:8)
God hears our prayers regardless of their emotional intensity. David was an emotional person, so his prayers reflected that passion. He was honest with God and opened his heart to God. It's that type of *intimacy*—not necessarily emotional outbursts—that God desires in our prayers.

Who was Cush and what had he done to David? (7:title)
We don't know who Cush was, since he isn't explained here and no such individual is mentioned elsewhere in the Bible. Usually, Cush refers to Ethiopia or northern Sudan and could refer to people from those regions (see **Map 12** at the back of this Bible).

Why did David want to stir God up? (7:6)
David wanted action—some kind of a response from God. From his perspective his enemies had gone unchallenged; nothing was being done about the injustice around him. It may have seemed to David that God wasn't doing anything, so he tried to stir up God's wrath against sinners.

---

^aTitle: Probably a musical term   ^b5 Hebrew *Sheol*   ^cTitle: Probably a literary or musical term

Judge me, O LORD, according to my
     righteousness[D],
  according to my integrity, O Most High.
[9]O righteous[D] God,
  who searches minds and hearts,
  bring to an end the violence of the wicked
  and make the righteous secure.

[10]My shield[a] is God Most High,
  who saves the upright in heart.
[11]God is a righteous judge,
  a God who expresses his wrath every day.
[12]If he does not relent,
  he[b] will sharpen his sword;
  he will bend and string his bow.
[13]He has prepared his deadly weapons;
  he makes ready his flaming arrows.

[14]He who is pregnant with evil
  and conceives trouble gives birth to
     disillusionment.
[15]He who digs a hole and scoops it out
  falls into the pit he has made.
[16]The trouble he causes recoils on himself;
  his violence comes down on his own head.

[17]I will give thanks to the LORD because of his
     righteousness
  and will sing praise to the name of the LORD
     Most High.

Psalm 8

For the director of music. According to *gittith*.[c]
A psalm of David.

[1]O LORD, our Lord,
  how majestic is your name in all the earth!

You have set your glory[D]
  above the heavens.
[2]From the lips of children and infants
  you have ordained praise[d]
because of your enemies,
  to silence the foe and the avenger.

[3]When I consider your heavens,
  the work of your fingers,
  the moon and the stars,
  which you have set in place,
[4]what is man that you are mindful of him,
  the son of man[D] that you care for him?
[5]You made him a little lower than the heavenly
     beings[e]
  and crowned him with glory and honor.

[6]You made him ruler over the works of your
     hands;
  you put everything under his feet:
[7]all flocks and herds,
  and the beasts of the field,
[8]the birds of the air,

Why is righteousness so often expressed as wrath? (7:11)

Because righteousness requires judgment for sin. A holy, righteous God must judge wickedness and rebellion fairly. Even God's mercy satisfies the requirements of justice. Old Testament mercy was given when judgment came upon sacrifices; New Testament mercy came when Christ paid the price for our sins. God's righteousness, then, is revealed both as wrath and as love.

How does God punish sinners? (7:13,16)

When people sin, they can expect two basic reactions. One is supernatural: God invades human endeavors—the picture is of war—with his sword, bow, weapons and arrows. The other consequence of sin is natural: Wickedness tends to boomerang; sinners shouldn't be surprised when they get caught in their own schemes. Also see *Pit they have dug . . . net they have hidden* (9:15).

How do babies praise God? (8:2)

Even a newborn's first cry can be an eloquent expression of praise to the God who made us. If mountains, hills and trees can "sing" the praises of God (Isaiah 55:12), then why not infants?

What *heavenly beings* are humans slightly below? (8:5)

Some see them as angels. Others see them more generally as supernatural beings in spiritual realms, perhaps the various ranks of angelic beings. This verse is not a lesson on angels; it illustrates the contrast between God's majesty and our relative insignificance.

In what sense do humans rule over creation? (8:6)

God told Adam to *fill the earth and subdue it* and to *rule over . . . every living creature* (Gen. 1:28). Later God told Noah that *fear and dread* of humans would fall upon all living creatures (Gen. 9:2). The power God has given humans over nature involves both privileges and responsibilities. Some use their abilities and knowledge to exploit the earth's resources. Others, however, remain good stewards of all that God has entrusted to their care.

---

a 10 Or *sovereign*   *b 12* Or *If a man does not repent, / God*
c Title: Probably a musical term   *d 2* Or *strength*   *e 5* Or *than God*

and the fish of the sea,
all that swim the paths of the seas.

9O LORD, our Lord,
how majestic is your name in all the earth!

Psalm 9ᵃ

For the director of music. To ⌊the tune of⌋ "The
Death^D of the Son." A psalm of David.

1I will praise you, O LORD, with all my heart;
I will tell of all your wonders.
2I will be glad and rejoice in you;
I will sing praise to your name, O Most High.

3My enemies turn back;
they stumble and perish before you.
4For you have upheld my right and my cause;
you have sat on your throne, judging
righteously^D.
5You have rebuked the nations and destroyed
the wicked;
you have blotted out their name for ever and
ever.
6Endless ruin has overtaken the enemy,
you have uprooted their cities;
even the memory of them has perished.

7The LORD reigns forever;
he has established his throne for judgment.
8He will judge the world in righteousness^D;
he will govern the peoples with justice.
9The LORD is a refuge for the oppressed,
a stronghold^D in times of trouble.
10Those who know your name will trust in you,
for you, LORD, have never forsaken those
who seek you.

11Sing praises to the LORD, enthroned in Zion^D;
proclaim among the nations what he has
done.
12For he who avenges^D blood remembers;
he does not ignore the cry of the afflicted^D.

13O LORD, see how my enemies persecute me!
Have mercy^D and lift me up from the gates
of death,
14that I may declare your praises
in the gates of the Daughter of Zion
and there rejoice in your salvation^D.
15The nations have fallen into the pit they have
dug;
their feet are caught in the net they have
hidden.
16The LORD is known by his justice;
the wicked are ensnared by the work of their
hands.   *Higgaion.*ᵇ Selah^D
17The wicked return to the grave,ᶜ
all the nations that forget God.
18But the needy will not always be forgotten,
nor the hope of the afflicted ever perish.

Are the wicked completely erased from history? (9:5–6)

This is figurative language, and refers to "redemptive history," not actual history. The Bible
speaks of blotting the names of the wicked out
of the book of life (69:28). Also see *Book of
life* (Rev. 3:5).

Gates of death (9:13)

A poetic term for the edge of the grave or being
near death.

Pit they have dug . . . net they have hidden (9:15)

Ancient hunters trapped animals by camouflag-
ing holes in the ground or hanging nets from
trees. David used the term to describe how the
efforts of his enemies had backfired on them.

ᵃPsalms 9 and 10 may have been originally a single acrostic poem, the
stanzas of which begin with the successive letters of the Hebrew
alphabet. In the Septuagint they constitute one psalm.   ᵇ16 Or
Meditation; possibly a musical notation   ᶜ17 Hebrew *Sheol*

19Arise, O Lord, let not man triumph;
　　let the nations be judged in your presence.
20Strike them with terror, O Lord;
　　let the nations know they are but men.

*Selah*D

Psalm 10ᵃ

1Why, O Lord, do you stand far off?
　　Why do you hide yourself in times of
　　　　trouble?

2In his arrogance the wicked man hunts down
　　　　the weak,
　　who are caught in the schemes he devises.
3He boasts of the cravings of his heart;
　　he blesses the greedy and reviles the Lord.
4In his pride the wicked does not seek him;
　　in all his thoughts there is no room for God.
5His ways are always prosperous;
　　he is haughty and your laws are far from
　　　　him;
　　he sneers at all his enemies.
6He says to himself, "Nothing will shake me;
　　I'll always be happy and never have trouble."
7His mouth is full of curses and lies and threats;
　　trouble and evil are under his tongue.
8He lies in wait near the villages;
　　from ambush he murders the innocent,
　　watching in secret for his victims.

ᵃPsalms 9 and 10 may have been originally a single acrostic poem, the stanzas of which begin with the successive letters of the Hebrew alphabet. In the Septuagint they constitute one psalm.

Why did the writer feel abandoned by God? (10:1)

There is no way of knowing the specific circumstances that led to the feelings expressed in this psalm. However, when we go through dark times, we can be encouraged by knowing that this experience is not uncommon. Even those who trust in God can encounter times of spiritual despair.

Curses (10:7)

Negative pronouncements, oaths or swearing. People of the ancient world believed words had power for affirming people or hurting them. They took oaths as seriously as people today take legal contracts.

Does God sometimes hide from us? (10:1)

It would seem so. Our prayers may go unanswered year after year. We may wrestle continually with a problem and never find spiritual insight to explain it. Or we may endure ongoing suffering with no relief in sight.

Many factors can contribute to such a dilemma. Though we may discover some reasons for this problem, there may be other factors that are impossible to determine in this life. See article: *When does God refuse to hear our prayers?* (Jer. 11:11).

David's poetry often expresses a feeling of abandonment by God. He was not alone with such feelings: Job, Moses, Jeremiah, Elijah and other Biblical people of faith echoed David's emotions. Even Jesus felt this way when he quoted David's haunting cry, *My God, my God, why have you forsaken me?* (22:1). If those with such great faith rode emotional waves like these, we can at least know we're in good company when we experience similar frustrations.

Ironically, David paints an entirely different picture in other psalms. He describes God as always being with him, for example, when he asks, *Where can I go from your Spirit? Where can I flee from your presence?* (139:7).

At times, we may sense God's presence covering us like a warm blanket of love and protection. At other times, we may feel nothing but an eerie and depressing silence. Psalms such as this one show us that such feelings of abandonment are not unusual. But as David reminds us elsewhere, we can be certain God is always with us no matter how we feel.

9He lies in wait like a lion in cover;
  he lies in wait to catch the helpless;
  he catches the helpless and drags them off in
    his net.
10His victims are crushed, they collapse;
  they fall under his strength.
11He says to himself, "God has forgotten;
  he covers his face and never sees."

12Arise, LORD! Lift up your hand, O God.
  Do not forget the helpless.
13Why does the wicked man revile God?
  Why does he say to himself,
  "He won't call me to account"?
14But you, O God, do see trouble and grief;
  you consider it to take it in hand.
The victim commits himself to you;
  you are the helper of the fatherless.
15Break the arm of the wicked and evil man;
  call him to account for his wickedness
  that would not be found out.

16The LORD is King for ever and ever;
  the nations will perish from his land.
17You hear, O LORD, the desire of the afflicted[D];
  you encourage them, and you listen to their
    cry,
18defending the fatherless and the oppressed,
  in order that man, who is of the earth, may
    terrify no more.

Psalm 11

For the director of music. Of David.

1In the LORD I take refuge.
  How then can you say to me:
  "Flee like a bird to your mountain.
2For look, the wicked bend their bows;
  they set their arrows against the strings
to shoot from the shadows
  at the upright in heart.
3When the foundations are being destroyed,
  what can the righteous[D] do[a]?"

4The LORD is in his holy temple;
  the LORD is on his heavenly throne.
He observes the sons of men;
  his eyes examine them.
5The LORD examines the righteous,
  but the wicked[b] and those who love
    violence
his soul[D] hates.
6On the wicked he will rain
  fiery coals and burning sulfur;
  a scorching wind will be their lot.

7For the LORD is righteous,
  he loves justice;
  upright men will see his face.

What did Israelite society do for the fatherless and the oppressed? (10:18)

God's people have always been told to care for the poor, the orphaned and the oppressed. They were to reflect God's own deep concern for the afflicted of society (Deut. 15:7–11; Prov. 14:31; 19:17). But they did not always live up to God's commands. The prophets of Israel frequently called their society to task for neglecting God's clear commands about caring for the underprivileged (Amos 5:11–12, for example).

Who advised David to flee? (11:1)

We can't tell who gave this advice to David or why. There were times David did *flee like a bird* —from Saul (1 Samuel 21:10), and later from his son Absalom (2 Samuel 15:14). In this case, however, it seems David was rejecting advice to flee because he was determined to trust in God no matter how discouraging his advisers thought things were.

Foundations (11:3)

The moral foundations of a society based on God's law. Some feared these foundations were threatened by increasing rebellion and the growing aggressiveness of the wicked.

How can a God of love hate the wicked? (11:5)

See article: *Is the God of love also a God of hate?* (5:5).

Fiery coals . . . burning sulfur . . . scorching wind (11:6)

This could refer to (1) God's destruction of Sodom and Gomorrah (Gen. 19:24), (2) God's coming judgment upon the whole world or (3) a desert dweller's worst nightmare of punishment.

*a*3 Or *what is the Righteous One doing*   *b*5 Or *The LORD, the
Righteous One, examines the wicked, /*

Why were there no godly people left? (12:1)

There were still godly people, but David is exaggerating for emphasis (a figure of speech known as *hyperbole*). See **Was David physically sick?** (6:2–7). David *felt* like there was no one left who was faithful and would stand with him.

Didn't they have a right to freedom of speech? (12:3–4)

Yes, but their speech revealed the proud attitudes that motivated them. By announcing their freedom to *say* what they wanted, these people showed their desire to *do* what they wanted. Their loose lips revealed their rebellious hearts.

Who was maligning whom? (12:5)

The rich and powerful were verbally attacking the oppressed and weak. Perhaps they wanted to justify their own lack of compassion and failure to help the poor. It may be that they unfairly blamed the poor for their own problems, perhaps accusing them of laziness.

What vile things were people honoring? (12:8)

Apparently the wealthy arrogantly paraded their riches while neglecting the poor. God was displeased with their pompous self-centeredness and their desire to use their wealth to court people's favor.

Does God have a physical body? (13:1)

No, at least not in the human sense. When David writes of God hiding his *face*, he is writing figuratively to describe his feelings that God had apparently neglected him. Biblical poetry frequently illustrates God's personality or spiritual characteristics by referring to God's hands, arms, eyes and ears.

Light to my eyes (13:3)

Light is associated with life and darkness with death. David was seeking God's help for a military victory, but he knew that divine encouragement and assurance were most important.

Psalm 12

For the director of music. According to *sheminith.* [a]
A psalm of David.

¹Help, LORD, for the godly are no more;
   the faithful have vanished from among men.
²Everyone lies to his neighbor;
   their flattering lips speak with deception.

³May the LORD cut off all flattering lips
   and every boastful tongue
⁴that says, "We will triumph with our tongues;
   we own our lips[b]—who is our master?"

⁵"Because of the oppression of the weak
   and the groaning of the needy,
I will now arise," says the LORD.
   "I will protect them from those who malign them."
⁶And the words of the LORD are flawless,
   like silver refined in a furnace of clay,
   purified[D] seven times.

⁷O LORD, you will keep us safe
   and protect us from such people forever.
⁸The wicked freely strut about
   when what is vile is honored among men.

Psalm 13

For the director of music. A psalm of David.

¹How long, O LORD? Will you forget me forever?
   How long will you hide your face from me?
²How long must I wrestle with my thoughts
   and every day have sorrow in my heart?
   How long will my enemy triumph over me?

³Look on me and answer, O LORD my God.
   Give light to my eyes, or I will sleep in death[D];

[a]Title: Probably a musical term   [b]4 Or / our lips are our plowshares

Why was David so up and down? (13:1–5)

Within five verses David moves from spiritual despair to hope, from gut-wrenching, internal wrestlings to complete trust and from deep sorrow to rejoicing. What causes the dramatic turnabout?

One explanation may be that David's psalms are simply snapshots of his feelings. As he gradually worked through the issues, he returned to his confidence in God. But it may have happened more slowly than it would appear from reading the compressed account in these few verses.

Another explanation may be that David knew how to express feelings and faith simultaneously. Perhaps David revealed his emotions on one level while on another level he told what he actually believed.

David's mood changes reflect the feelings of normal people struggling with their faith. Perhaps that's why so many people can identify with Psalms with all its ups and downs.

4my enemy will say, "I have overcome him,"
   and my foes will rejoice when I fall.

5But I trust in your unfailing love;
   my heart rejoices in your salvation[D].
6I will sing to the LORD,
   for he has been good to me.

Psalm 14

For the director of music. Of David.

1The fool[a] says in his heart,
   "There is no God."
They are corrupt, their deeds are vile;
   there is no one who does good.

2The LORD looks down from heaven
   on the sons of men
to see if there are any who understand,
   any who seek God.
3All have turned aside,
   they have together become corrupt;
there is no one who does good,
   not even one.

4Will evildoers never learn—
   those who devour my people as men eat
      bread
and who do not call on the LORD?
5There they are, overwhelmed with dread,
   for God is present in the company of the
      righteous[D].
6You evildoers frustrate the plans of the poor,
   but the LORD is their refuge.

7Oh, that salvation for Israel would come out
      of Zion[D]!
   When the LORD restores the fortunes of his
      people,
   let Jacob rejoice and Israel be glad!

Psalm 15

A psalm of David.

1LORD, who may dwell in your sanctuary?
   Who may live on your holy hill?

2He whose walk is blameless
   and who does what is righteous,
who speaks the truth from his heart
3   and has no slander on his tongue,
who does his neighbor no wrong
   and casts no slur on his fellowman,
4who despises a vile man
   but honors those who fear the LORD,
who keeps his oath
   even when it hurts,
5who lends his money without usury[D]
   and does not accept a bribe against the
      innocent.

---

a 1 The Hebrew words rendered *fool* in Psalms denote one who is
morally deficient.

Wasn't there *even one* who did good? (14:3)

Though David was using exaggeration to describe his immediate situation, the Bible does teach clearly that everyone is a sinner (Romans 3:23). See *Why were there no godly people left?* (12:1).

How is the *dread* of the Lord different from the fear of the Lord? (14:5)

Though occasionally used in place of the word *fear,* the word *dread* conveys a greater sense of foreboding. The righteous have a fear or healthy respect for God. The wicked, however, have a dread when they consider God's judgment and wrath.

Sanctuary (15:1)

Literally, *tent,* meaning the tabernacle. Jerusalem's temple wasn't built until after David's death. (Compare the definition of a different Hebrew word for *sanctuary* in 20:2.)

Holy hill (15:1)

See *Where was God's holy mountain?* (43:3).

Usury (15:5)

Ancient Israelites were commanded to lend without charging exorbitant interest (Lev. 25:36–37; Deut. 23:19). Applying this to modern finance is difficult, though some suggest Christians should charge other believers no more than the rate of inflation. See *What's wrong with charging interest?* (Exodus 22:25).

He who does these things
will never be shaken.

Psalm 16

A *miktam*[a] of David.

[1]Keep me safe, O God,
for in you I take refuge.

[2]I said to the LORD, "You are my Lord;
apart from you I have no good thing."
[3]As for the saints[b] who are in the land,
they are the glorious ones in whom is all my
delight.[b]
[4]The sorrows of those will increase
who run after other gods.
I will not pour out their libations of blood
or take up their names on my lips.

[5]LORD, you have assigned me my portion and
my cup;
you have made my lot secure.
[6]The boundary lines have fallen for me in
pleasant places;
surely I have a delightful inheritance.

[7]I will praise the LORD, who counsels me;
even at night my heart instructs me.
[8]I have set the LORD always before me.
Because he is at my right hand,
I will not be shaken.

[9]Therefore my heart is glad and my tongue
rejoices;
my body also will rest secure,
[10]because you will not abandon me to the
grave,[c]
nor will you let your Holy One[d] see decay.
[11]You have made[e] known to me the path of life;
you will fill me with joy in your presence,
with eternal pleasures at your right hand.

Psalm 17

A prayer of David.

[1]Hear, O LORD, my righteous[b] plea;
listen to my cry.
Give ear to my prayer—
it does not rise from deceitful lips.
[2]May my vindication come from you;
may your eyes see what is right.

[3]Though you probe my heart and examine me
at night,
though you test me, you will find nothing;
I have resolved that my mouth will not sin.
[4]As for the deeds of men—
by the word of your lips
I have kept myself
from the ways of the violent.

Saints (16:3)

Means *holy*—often applied to God himself.
When referring to people, the word does not
mean sinless perfection. Rather it means
those who are God's people, set apart through
dedication and service to God.

Pour out . . . libations of blood (16:4)

David was declaring his allegiance to the Lord:
He would never make sacrifices to other gods.

My portion and my cup (16:5)

Guests at ancient banquets received their portion (of food) and their cup (of drink). Comparing God to the host of a banquet, David expressed satisfaction with his lot in life.

How did David's heart instruct him even at night? (16:7)

Perhaps David meant that long after he had
meditated upon the Word of God, his inner being continued to digest and apply it. Even his
subconscious mind was uplifted by God's
Word. Or he may have been recalling the times
when, as a shepherd alone at night under the
stars, he marveled at God's handiwork. David's nightly meditations may have inspired
several psalms (see 8:3, for example).

SCRIPTURE LINK (16:8–11) *Nor will you let your Holy One see decay*

The apostles saw David's words as a prophetic
allusion to the resurrection of Christ. See Acts
2:25–28; 13:35.

What did David mean by saying God would not abandon him to the grave? (16:10)

The most direct answer is that David was
thanking God for his protection—for sparing
him from death. But David also spoke of *eternal pleasures* (v. 11)—he anticipated being
with God forever after death.

How could David claim to be without sin? (17:3–5)

David was speaking poetically. He considered
himself innocent of wrongdoing—at least when
he compared himself to the violence and wickedness of those around him (v. 4). On other occasions, however, when he saw himself in light
of God's holiness, he confessed his sin before
God (51:3–4). See *How could David claim to
be blameless?* (26:1).

---

[a]Title: Probably a literary or musical term   [b]3 Or *As for the pagan
priests who are in the land / and the nobles in whom all delight, I said:*
[c]10 Hebrew *Sheol*   [d]10 Or *your faithful one*   [e]11 Or *You will
make*

⁵My steps have held to your paths;
　　my feet have not slipped.

⁶I call on you, O God, for you will answer me;
　　give ear to me and hear my prayer.
⁷Show the wonder of your great love,
　　you who save by your right hand
　　those who take refuge in you from their foes.
⁸Keep me as the apple of your eye;
　　hide me in the shadow of your wings
⁹from the wicked who assail me,
　　from my mortal enemies who surround me.

¹⁰They close up their callous hearts,
　　and their mouths speak with arrogance.
¹¹They have tracked me down, they now
　　　surround me,
　　with eyes alert, to throw me to the ground.
¹²They are like a lion hungry for prey,
　　like a great lion crouching in cover.

¹³Rise up, O LORD, confront them, bring them
　　　down;
　　rescue me from the wicked by your sword.
¹⁴O LORD, by your hand save me from such men,
　　from men of this world whose reward is in
　　　this life.

You still the hunger of those you cherish;
　　their sons have plenty,
　　and they store up wealth for their children.
¹⁵And I—in righteousnessᴅ I will see your face;
　　when I awake, I will be satisfied with seeing
　　　your likeness.

Psalm 18

For the director of music. Of David the servant of the
LORD. He sang to the LORD the words of this song when
　the LORD delivered him from the hand of all his
　enemies and from the hand of Saul. He said:

¹I love you, O LORD, my strength.

²The LORD is my rock, my fortress and my
　　　deliverer;
　　my God is my rock, in whom I take refuge.
　　He is my shield and the hornᵃ of my
　　　salvationᴅ, my strongholdᴅ.
³I call to the LORD, who is worthy of praise,
　　and I am saved from my enemies.

⁴The cords of deathᴅ entangled me;
　　the torrents of destruction overwhelmed me.
⁵The cords of the graveᵇ coiled around me;
　　the snares of death confronted me.
⁶In my distress I called to the LORD;
　　I cried to my God for help.
From his temple he heard my voice;
　　my cry came before him, into his ears.

⁷The earth trembled and quaked,
　　and the foundations of the mountains shook;
　　they trembled because he was angry.
⁸Smoke rose from his nostrils;
　　consuming fire came from his mouth,

Apple of your eye (17:8)

Suggests the pupil of the eye—used as a
metaphor to describe something that is protected and guarded carefully. See *Apple of your
eye* (Prov. 7:2).

Shadow of your wings (17:8)

This is poetic language that borrows the characteristics of a protective bird to describe the
way David wants God to take care of him. It is
symbolic of the love and protection of God that
surrounded David.

When did David hope to see the Lord? (17:15)

David was not writing a detailed analysis of life
after death, so we can't really draw much from
these few words. But we do know that David
saw a glimmer of eternity; he expected to
awaken from death's dark sleep so that he
could see God.

How is God like a rock? (18:2)

God is firm, solid, impregnable and immovable
—just the kind of stability needed by an emotional man like David. He writes of a rock large
enough that he could hide on top of it from his
enemies below. A few soldiers could defend a
high rock bluff against a much larger army. Perhaps David was recalling the rocks and caves
that kept him safe from Saul (1 Samuel
23:25).

Where was the temple in David's day? (18:6)

The Jerusalem temple was not built until after
David's death. There are several possible interpretations: (1) The tabernacle may have been
called a temple. (2) This psalm may have been
written by another, later author. (3) A later editor changed *tabernacle* to *temple*. (4) The word
is a more general reference to creation as
God's temple (see 29:9). (5) David saw God's
dwelling place in the heavens as a *temple* (see
11:4).

Why did God appear in such frighten-
ing ways? (18:7–15)

Because God, by his very nature, so far transcends mere human experience, those who encounter his glory, majesty and power are overwhelmed. Furthermore, the limitations of
human language—even with poetic figures of
speech—do not do justice to such an awesome, holy God.

ᵃ2 *Horn* here symbolizes strength.　　ᵇ5 Hebrew *Sheol*

burning coals blazed out of it.
⁹He parted the heavens and came down;
    dark clouds were under his feet.
¹⁰He mounted the cherubim ᴰ and flew;
    he soared on the wings of the wind.
¹¹He made darkness his covering, his canopy
        around him—
    the dark rain clouds of the sky.
¹²Out of the brightness of his presence clouds
        advanced,
    with hailstones and bolts of lightning.
¹³The Lᴏʀᴅ thundered from heaven;
    the voice of the Most High resounded. ᵃ
¹⁴He shot his arrows and scattered ⌊the enemies⌋,
    great bolts of lightning and routed them.
¹⁵The valleys of the sea were exposed
    and the foundations of the earth laid bare
  at your rebuke, O Lᴏʀᴅ,
    at the blast of breath from your nostrils.

¹⁶He reached down from on high and took hold
        of me;
    he drew me out of deep waters.
¹⁷He rescued me from my powerful enemy,
    from my foes, who were too strong for me.
¹⁸They confronted me in the day of my disaster,
    but the Lᴏʀᴅ was my support.
¹⁹He brought me out into a spacious place;
    he rescued me because he delighted in me.

²⁰The Lᴏʀᴅ has dealt with me according to my
        righteousness ᴰ;
    according to the cleanness of my hands he
        has rewarded me.
²¹For I have kept the ways of the Lᴏʀᴅ;
    I have not done evil by turning from my
        God.
²²All his laws are before me;
    I have not turned away from his decrees.
²³I have been blameless before him
    and have kept myself from sin.
²⁴The Lᴏʀᴅ has rewarded me according to my
        righteousness,
    according to the cleanness of my hands in
        his sight.

²⁵To the faithful you show yourself faithful,
    to the blameless you show yourself
        blameless,
²⁶to the pure you show yourself pure,
    but to the crooked you show yourself
        shrewd.
²⁷You save the humble
    but bring low those whose eyes are haughty.
²⁸You, O Lᴏʀᴅ, keep my lamp burning;
    my God turns my darkness into light.
²⁹With your help I can advance against a troop ᵇ;
    with my God I can scale a wall.

³⁰As for God, his way is perfect;
    the word of the Lᴏʀᴅ is flawless.
  He is a shield

Valleys of the sea ... foundations of the earth (18:15)

A possible reference to the canyon-scarred Judean desert or, perhaps, God's parting of the Red Sea. The intent of this image is to convey God's awesome power.

Spacious place (18:19)

A figure of speech meaning a place of comfort and ease. We still use the contrasting figure of speech to speak of trouble when we say that someone is in a "tight spot" or "backed into a corner."

How could David claim to be blameless? (18:23)

See *How could David claim to be without sin?* (17:3–5).

Why is God sometimes shrewd? (18:25–26)

Nobody can outsmart God. He is always in control, even when he deals with con artists and schemers. Though God's righteous character means he is not deceptive or crooked, he can still deal with people in ways that relate to the way they deal with him.

ᵃ13 Some Hebrew manuscripts and Septuagint (see also 2 Samuel 22:14); most Hebrew manuscripts *resounded, / amid hailstones and bolts of lightning*   ᵇ29 Or *can run through a barricade*

for all who take refuge in him.
³¹For who is God besides the LORD?
    And who is the Rock except our God?
³²It is God who arms me with strength
    and makes my way perfect.
³³He makes my feet like the feet of a deer;
    he enables me to stand on the heights.
³⁴He trains my hands for battle;
    my arms can bend a bow of bronze.
³⁵You give me your shield of victory,
    and your right hand sustains me;
    you stoop down to make me great.
³⁶You broaden the path beneath me,
    so that my ankles do not turn.

³⁷I pursued my enemies and overtook them;
    I did not turn back till they were destroyed.
³⁸I crushed them so that they could not rise;
    they fell beneath my feet.
³⁹You armed me with strength for battle;
    you made my adversaries bow at my feet.
⁴⁰You made my enemies turn their backs in
        flight,
    and I destroyed my foes.
⁴¹They cried for help, but there was no one to
        save them—
    to the LORD, but he did not answer.
⁴²I beat them as fine as dust borne on the wind;
    I poured them out like mud in the streets.

⁴³You have delivered me from the attacks of the
        people;
    you have made me the head of nations;
    people I did not know are subject to me.
⁴⁴As soon as they hear me, they obey me;
    foreigners cringe before me.
⁴⁵They all lose heart;
    they come trembling from their
        strongholdsᴰ.

⁴⁶The LORD lives! Praise be to my Rock!
    Exalted be God my Savior!
⁴⁷He is the God who avengesᴰ me,
    who subdues nations under me,
⁴⁸   who saves me from my enemies.
You exalted me above my foes;
    from violent men you rescued me.
⁴⁹Therefore I will praise you among the nations,
        O LORD;
    I will sing praises to your name.
⁵⁰He gives his king great victories;
    he shows unfailing kindness to his
        anointedᴰ,
    to David and his descendants forever.

Psalm 19

For the director of music. A psalm of David.

¹The heavens declare the gloryᴰ of God;
    the skies proclaim the work of his hands.
²Day after day they pour forth speech;
    night after night they display knowledge.
³There is no speech or language

How is God a rock? (18:31)
The picture is of a huge rock, so hard and strong that no one can damage it. It has been in its spot since the beginning of the earth and will always remain there. This is the kind of God we have: strong, enduring, trustworthy. He will always be there when we need him.

Is David being boastful here? (18:44–45)
Not really. Though he acknowledged the victories he had gained and the people who had submitted to him, he gave credit to the Lord for all his success: *You have delivered me . . . you have made me the head of nations . . . Praise be to my Rock!* (vv. 43,46). An honest appraisal of accomplishments is not bragging, especially when God is honored as the source of those achievements.

How does the law revive someone? (19:7)

The word *reviving* means *restoring* (as it is used in 23:3). But it can also mean *convert* or *turn back* (as it is used in 51:13). So this is a picture of renewal and transformation. The law teaches God's principles so we can be shaped continually by them to live according to his pattern. When we allow God's word to have its effect on us, we will be invigorated by his strength and refreshed with his wisdom.

How is the fear of the Lord like the law? (19:7–9)

They are linked together. The fear, or respect, of the Lord is the beginning of wisdom (Job 28:28; Prov. 1:7; Eccl. 12:13). Studying God's law, with its specific requirements for human behavior and its harsh punishments for disobedience, leads us to a greater respect for God and increases our desire to serve him.

Does God hold us accountable for sins we aren't aware of? (19:12)

God makes his will known to us, though he knows our understanding and obedience will be imperfect. That's why prayers like this one are so important. They open hidden aspects of our lives to God's examination and grace so we will no longer be ignorant. (Compare 139:23–24.)

What was David's standard for innocence? (19:13)

In this verse, David defined innocence as freedom from committing willful sins. In contrast with sins that are unintentional, these sins are those committed in overt rebellion against God. David felt that if he avoided such sins he could approach God with a clear conscience.

How is God like a rock? (19:14)

See *How is God like a rock?* (18:2).

How does God's *name* offer protection? (20:1)

God's name is not a magical charm, but it represents his authority and all that he is. His name is synonymous with his power and protects us, much as the name of the president or the governor can authorize privileges for citizens.

Sanctuary (20:2)

Means *holy place,* suggesting (1) the tent in Jerusalem that housed the ark, the symbol of God's presence, or (2) Zion, the holy mountain where the temple was later built.

Does knowing God guarantee success? (20:4)

See articles: *Does seeking God guarantee success?* (2 Chron. 26:5) and *Is success guaranteed to those who obey God?* (Deut. 28:2–6).

His anointed (20:6)

The king of Israel. See *Anointed One* (2:2).

Why refer to God's right hand? (20:6)

This was a figurative way to speak of God's great strength (see Exodus 15:6). Also see *The years of the right hand of the Most High* (77:10).

where their voice is not heard.[a]
⁴Their voice[b] goes out into all the earth,
    their words to the ends of the world.

In the heavens he has pitched a tent for the
        sun,
⁵ which is like a bridegroom coming forth
        from his pavilion,
    like a champion rejoicing to run his course.
⁶It rises at one end of the heavens
    and makes its circuit to the other;
    nothing is hidden from its heat.

⁷The law of the LORD is perfect,
    reviving the soul[D].
The statutes of the LORD are trustworthy,
    making wise the simple.
⁸The precepts[D] of the LORD are right,
    giving joy to the heart.
The commands of the LORD are radiant,
    giving light to the eyes.
⁹The fear of the LORD is pure,
    enduring forever.
The ordinances of the LORD are sure
    and altogether righteous[D].
¹⁰They are more precious than gold,
    than much pure gold;
they are sweeter than honey,
    than honey from the comb.
¹¹By them is your servant warned;
    in keeping them there is great reward.

¹²Who can discern his errors?
    Forgive my hidden faults.
¹³Keep your servant also from willful sins;
    may they not rule over me.
Then will I be blameless,
    innocent of great transgression.

¹⁴May the words of my mouth and the
        meditation of my heart
    be pleasing in your sight,
    O LORD, my Rock and my Redeemer[D].

Psalm 20

For the director of music. A psalm of David.

¹May the LORD answer you when you are in
        distress;
    may the name of the God of Jacob protect
        you.
²May he send you help from the sanctuary
    and grant you support from Zion[D].
³May he remember all your sacrifices[D]
    and accept your burnt offerings[D].   *Selah*[D]
⁴May he give you the desire of your heart
    and make all your plans succeed.
⁵We will shout for joy when you are victorious
    and will lift up our banners in the name of
        our God.
    May the LORD grant all your requests.

⁶Now I know that the LORD saves his anointed[D];

---

[a]3 Or *They have no speech, there are no words; / no sound is heard
    from them*   [b]4 Septuagint, Jerome and Syriac; Hebrew *line*

he answers him from his holy heaven
  with the saving power of his right hand.
⁷Some trust in chariots and some in horses,
  but we trust in the name of the LORD our
    God.
⁸They are brought to their knees and fall,
  but we rise up and stand firm.

⁹O LORD, save the king!
  Answer*a* us when we call!

Psalm 21

For the director of music. A psalm of David.

¹O LORD, the king rejoices in your strength.
  How great is his joy in the victories you give!
²You have granted him the desire of his heart
  and have not withheld the request of his lips.
                                                    *Selah*D

³You welcomed him with rich blessings
  and placed a crown of pure gold on his head.
⁴He asked you for life, and you gave it to him—
  length of days, for ever and ever.
⁵Through the victories you gave, his gloryD is
    great;
  you have bestowed on him splendor and
    majesty.
⁶Surely you have granted him eternal blessings
  and made him glad with the joy of your
    presence.
⁷For the king trusts in the LORD;
  through the unfailing love of the Most High
  he will not be shaken.

⁸Your hand will lay hold on all your enemies;
  your right hand will seize your foes.
⁹At the time of your appearing
  you will make them like a fiery furnace.
  In his wrath the LORD will swallow them up,
  and his fire will consume them.
¹⁰You will destroy their descendants from the
    earth,
  their posterity from mankind.
¹¹Though they plot evil against you
  and devise wicked schemes, they cannot
    succeed;
¹²for you will make them turn their backs
  when you aim at them with drawn bow.

¹³Be exalted, O LORD, in your strength;
  we will sing and praise your might.

Psalm 22

For the director of music. To ⌊the tune of⌋ "The Doe of
    the Morning." A psalm of David.

¹My God, my God, why have you forsaken me?
  Why are you so far from saving me,
    so far from the words of my groaning?
²O my God, I cry out by day, but you do not
    answer,
  by night, and am not silent.

a9 Or save! / O King, answer

What does it mean to trust God's name? (20:7)
Trusting God's *name* means placing one's confidence in who he is. See **How does God's name offer protection?** (20:1).

Were they praying for the king's salvation? (20:9)
Yes, in the physical sense. This psalm is a prayer for the king as he goes out to battle. Its original intent—a prayer of blessing sung by the ancient Israelites on behalf of their king—shows a principle that can be paralleled today: we can pray for our leaders. When Israel had a godly, successful king whose prayers were answered, the whole nation benefited (see 2 Chron. 20:1–30). Now our King, Jesus Christ, offers requests on our behalf (Romans 8:34).

What were these *victories*? (21:1)
We don't know precisely what historical events led to this psalm. David won control of the kingdom and overcame the hostilities of the Philistines and other enemies (1 Chron. 11,14, 18–20). If this psalm was not written for one of those victories, it would have been written for one like them.

Life . . . for ever and ever (21:4)
This may have been a figure of speech—similar to "long live the king"—rather than a direct statement about eternity. Still, David had a concept of life after death. See **Didn't David believe in life after death?** (6:5).

Fiery furnace (21:9)
A typical picture of God's judgment and destruction of the wicked. Here it describes the defeat of David's enemies.

SCRIPTURE LINK (22:1) *My God, my God, why have you forsaken me*
Christ quoted these words as he hung from the cross (see Matt. 27:46). David's experience in this psalm spoke in a prophetic way about the crucifixion. See vv. 6–8,12–18.

Had God forsaken David? (22:1–2)
No, but it appeared that way to David. However, David still affirmed his convictions that God was in control (v. 3) and soon regained his assurance that God would personally answer him (v. 24). Psalms such as this one frequently alternate between the writer's emotional despair and his faith in the solid truth about God. Also see articles: **Does God sometimes hide from us?** (10:1) and **Why was David so up and down?** (13:1–5).

Did David have poor self-esteem? (22:6–7)

Sometimes. David was generally confident and led a highly successful life: He enjoyed great military victories and became king over all Israel. Still, he also faced difficulties, temptations and sorrows. Great honors did not insulate him from trouble; if anything, his critics and enemies increased with his success. See article: *Why was David so up and down?* (13:1–5).

What kind of trust could an infant have in God? (22:9–10)

David's parents committed him to God from birth and apparently taught him well. As a youngster he likely heard Israel's history and the stories of faith. So he speaks here of his consistent relationship with God; he had never served any other god. Also see *How do babies praise God?* (8:2).

Bulls of Bashan (22:12)

In David's time the lush grasslands of Bashan, known today as the Golan Heights, were ideal for livestock. Bashan's well-fed bulls were famous for their size and, apparently, for their mean disposition. David uses the *bulls* along with *lions* (v. 13) and *dogs* (v. 16) to portray his enemies.

How did David have his hands and feet pierced? (22:16)

We don't really know. Some think David is continuing his metaphor of the *dogs*: his enemies, like attacking dogs, "bit" his hands and feet as he tried to hold them off. God used David's poetic allusions to foreshadow Christ being nailed to the cross.

Great assembly (22:25)

The congregation gathered to worship God. Some suggest this anticipates a future gathering of all those around the world who serve the Lord.

What kind of vows had David made? (22:25)

These were probably vows to publicly worship God with offerings to honor him for his deliverance (see v. 22). David was not trying to buy God's help; his vows were sincere. He genuinely wanted to praise God and tell people of God's greatness.

What did David know about the nations submitting to the Lord? (22:27)

We can't really say, though it's apparent that David foresaw a time when the whole world would recognize the sovereignty of the Lord. Sometimes the psalms speak of military conquest over other nations (135:10, for example). But they also speak of a coming time when nations will voluntarily bow in worship before God (86:9).

³Yet you are enthroned as the Holy One;
     you are the praise of Israel.ᵃ
⁴In you our fathers put their trust;
     they trusted and you delivered them.
⁵They cried to you and were saved;
     in you they trusted and were not
         disappointed.

⁶But I am a worm and not a man,
     scorned by men and despised by the people.
⁷All who see me mock me;
     they hurl insults, shaking their heads:
⁸"He trusts in the LORD;
     let the LORD rescue him.
Let him deliver him,
     since he delights in him."

⁹Yet you brought me out of the womb;
     you made me trust in you
     even at my mother's breast.
¹⁰From birth I was cast upon you;
     from my mother's womb you have been my
         God.
¹¹Do not be far from me,
     for trouble is near
     and there is no one to help.

¹²Many bulls surround me;
     strong bulls of Bashan encircle me.
¹³Roaring lions tearing their prey
     open their mouths wide against me.
¹⁴I am poured out like water,
     and all my bones are out of joint.
My heart has turned to wax;
     it has melted away within me.
¹⁵My strength is dried up like a potsherd,
     and my tongue sticks to the roof of my
         mouth;
     you lay meᵇ in the dust of death.ᴰ
¹⁶Dogs have surrounded me;
     a band of evil men has encircled me,
     they have piercedᶜ my hands and my feet.
¹⁷I can count all my bones;
     people stare and gloat over me.
¹⁸They divide my garments among them
     and cast lots for my clothing.

¹⁹But you, O LORD, be not far off;
     O my Strength, come quickly to help me.
²⁰Deliver my life from the sword,
     my precious life from the power of the dogs.
²¹Rescue me from the mouth of the lions;
     saveᵈ me from the horns of the wild oxen.

²²I will declare your name to my brothers;
     in the congregation I will praise you.
²³You who fear the LORD, praise him!
     All you descendants of Jacob, honor him!
     Revereᴰ him, all you descendants of Israel!
²⁴For he has not despised or disdained
     the suffering of the afflictedᴰ one;

ᵃ3 Or *Yet you are holy, / enthroned on the praises of Israel*   ᵇ15 Or */ I am laid*   ᶜ16 Some Hebrew manuscripts, Septuagint and Syriac; most Hebrew manuscripts */ like the lion,*   ᵈ21 Or */ you have heard*

he has not hidden his face from him
  but has listened to his cry for help.

25From you comes the theme of my praise in the
      great assembly;
  before those who fear you[a] will I fulfill my
      vows[D].
26The poor will eat and be satisfied;
  they who seek the LORD will praise him—
  may your hearts live forever!
27All the ends of the earth
  will remember and turn to the LORD,
and all the families of the nations
  will bow down before him,
28for dominion belongs to the LORD
  and he rules over the nations.

29All the rich of the earth will feast and worship;
  all who go down to the dust will kneel
      before him—
  those who cannot keep themselves alive.
30Posterity will serve him;
  future generations will be told about the
      Lord.
31They will proclaim his righteousness[D]
  to a people yet unborn—
  for he has done it.

Psalm 23

A psalm of David.

1The LORD is my shepherd, I shall not be in
      want.
2 He makes me lie down in green pastures,
he leads me beside quiet waters,
3 he restores my soul[D].
He guides me in paths of righteousness
  for his name's sake.
4Even though I walk
  through the valley of the shadow of
      death[D,b]
I will fear no evil,
  for you are with me;
your rod and your staff,
  they comfort me.

5You prepare a table before me
  in the presence of my enemies.
You anoint[D] my head with oil;
  my cup overflows.
6Surely goodness and love will follow me
  all the days of my life,
and I will dwell in the house of the LORD
  forever.

Psalm 24

Of David. A psalm.

1The earth is the LORD's, and everything in it,
  the world, and all who live in it;
2for he founded it upon the seas
  and established it upon the waters.

Go down to the dust (22:29)
A picture of death (see Gen. 3:19).

How did future worshipers encourage David? (22:30–31)
God allowed David to glimpse future generations praising God for the things done for David. It was encouraging for him to see that his
current troubles would provide opportunities
for God to work. David was also able to look at
the big picture, seeing future praise for God's
faithfulness to all of Israel.

He has done it (22:31)
This may be the phrase David saw echoing
through coming years—God being praised for
each thing he accomplished. Or this may be an
example of the Hebrew "prophetic perfect
tense," in which a future event is translated
as past tense to stress the certainty of the
coming events. See *Why did God speak as
though victory had already come?* (Joshua 6:2).

Does God intend that we have no "wants"? (23:1)
This word does not mean we will never want
anything, but that we will not be *in* want. That
is, we can trust God for the essentials of life.

How does God restore our souls? (23:3)
David paints a picture of sheep being nourished with food and water. In the same way,
God nourishes us spiritually and emotionally.
His loving care puts our minds at ease so we
can rest peacefully. To be restored means to
be refreshed and strengthened.

How does God guide us? (23:3)
God does not reveal every detail of his plan for
our lives. Nevertheless, there is an inner assurance that comes when we do his will. Developing a close, dependent relationship with the
Lord will help us follow his way. And if we do
the things we know God wants us to do, we'll
discover more details about his will for us.

How could God's rod and staff bring comfort? (23:4)
The shepherd used his staff to guide the
sheep, directing them and setting boundaries
for them. He also used his rod as a weapon
against predators. By guiding them into safe
places and by fighting enemies, the shepherd's rod and staff were a comfort for the
sheep.

Why eat a meal when your enemies are nearby? (23:5)
This picture may be understood as: (1) A description of God's protection and power, as David could feast in safety and security even
though he was surrounded by enemies, or (2) a
victory feast where David celebrated the defeat
of his enemies—prisoners without weapons
and no longer dangerous.

Anoint (23:5)
In Biblical times a good host would wash the
guest's feet and anoint his head prior to the
meal. See *Anointed One* (2:2).

---

[a]25 Hebrew *him*   [b]4 Or *through the darkest valley*

The hill of the LORD (24:3)

Mount Zion, on which the temple was built. The *holy place* can refer to any area of the temple courts, but most specifically to the first room inside the temple. Also see *Where was God's holy mountain?* (43:3).

How can a heart be made pure? (24:3–4)

This is a descriptive way to speak about pure motives. We must sincerely desire God's mercy and forgiveness; otherwise we cannot approach him. In fact, the only way to have a *pure heart* is through the grace of God, granted in response to our faith and obedience.

What gates and doors did the Lord enter? (24:7)

In ancient times when a king returned victorious from battle, the gates of the city would be opened and the citizens would receive him with adoration and praise. David uses this metaphor to describe the Lord entering the gates of Jerusalem—to the cheers and praises of his people—so he can live among them.

How can a soul be lifted up to God? (25:1)

David speaks of his inner being, his emotional and spiritual condition as well as his attitude. Other times David admits that his soul is *in anguish* (6:3), *downcast* (42:5) or *full of trouble* (88:3). But David makes a conscious decision about the focus of his soul—he decides to look to God, not to circumstances. He will trust in the Lord rather than fear his enemies (v. 2).

Why remind God of his promises? (25:6)

Remember is a strong covenant word. Asking God to remember does not imply that he has forgotten. It is asking God to act *now* on the basis of his promises.

How does it help to be humble? (25:9)

God will not give what we are too proud to receive. Pride is like a barrier that blocks out the very things God desires to do in our lives. *God opposes the proud but gives grace to the humble* (James 4:6).

What *covenant* must we keep? (25:10)

More than likely this refers to the laws of Moses, containing God's covenant with his people. Following God's *loving and faithful* ways, David says, is the best way to live. We have been given the new covenant since these words were written, but the principle remains the same: we can express our love for God by submitting to his ways and obeying him (see John 14:15). Also see *Did Jesus abolish the Old Testament law or fulfill it?* (Eph. 2:15).

Why appeal for mercy on the basis of God's name? (25:11)

The Lord's character and reputation are expressed in his name. On the basis of his character, we can count on him to forgive. To preserve his reputation he will act on behalf of his people. Also see *How does God's name offer protection?* (20:1).

³Who may ascend the hill of the LORD?
  Who may stand in his holy place?
⁴He who has clean hands and a pure heart,
  who does not lift up his soul[D] to an idol[D]
  or swear by what is false.[a]
⁵He will receive blessing from the LORD
  and vindication from God his Savior.
⁶Such is the generation of those who seek him,
  who seek your face, O God of Jacob.[b]

                                        Selah[D]

⁷Lift up your heads, O you gates;
  be lifted up, you ancient doors,
  that the King of glory[D] may come in.
⁸Who is this King of glory?
  The LORD strong and mighty,
  the LORD mighty in battle.
⁹Lift up your heads, O you gates;
  lift them up, you ancient doors,
  that the King of glory may come in.
¹⁰Who is he, this King of glory?
  The LORD Almighty—
  he is the King of glory.   *Selah*

Psalm 25[c]

Of David.

¹To you, O LORD, I lift up my soul;
² in you I trust, O my God.
  Do not let me be put to shame,
  nor let my enemies triumph over me.
³No one whose hope is in you
  will ever be put to shame,
  but they will be put to shame
  who are treacherous without excuse.

⁴Show me your ways, O LORD,
  teach me your paths;
⁵guide me in your truth and teach me,
  for you are God my Savior,
  and my hope is in you all day long.
⁶Remember, O LORD, your great mercy[D] and
    love,
  for they are from of old.
⁷Remember not the sins of my youth
  and my rebellious ways;
  according to your love remember me,
  for you are good, O LORD.

⁸Good and upright is the LORD;
  therefore he instructs sinners in his ways.
⁹He guides the humble in what is right
  and teaches them his way.
¹⁰All the ways of the LORD are loving and faithful
  for those who keep the demands of his
    covenant[D].
¹¹For the sake of your name, O LORD,
  forgive my iniquity, though it is great.

---

[a]4 Or *swear falsely*   [b]6 Two Hebrew manuscripts and Syriac (see also Septuagint); most Hebrew manuscripts *face, Jacob*   [c]This psalm is an acrostic poem, the verses of which begin with the successive letters of the Hebrew alphabet.

¹²Who, then, is the man that fears the LORD?
　He will instruct him in the way chosen for
　　him.
¹³He will spend his days in prosperity,
　and his descendants will inherit the land.
¹⁴The LORD confides in those who fear him;
　he makes his covenant[D] known to them.
¹⁵My eyes are ever on the LORD,
　for only he will release my feet from the
　　snare.

¹⁶Turn to me and be gracious to me,
　for I am lonely and afflicted[D].
¹⁷The troubles of my heart have multiplied;
　free me from my anguish.
¹⁸Look upon my affliction[D] and my distress
　and take away all my sins.
¹⁹See how my enemies have increased
　and how fiercely they hate me!
²⁰Guard my life and rescue me;
　let me not be put to shame,
　for I take refuge in you.
²¹May integrity and uprightness protect
　　me,
　because my hope is in you.

²²Redeem[D] Israel, O God,
　from all their troubles!

Psalm 26

Of David.

¹Vindicate me, O LORD,
　for I have led a blameless life;
I have trusted in the LORD
　without wavering.
²Test me, O LORD, and try me,
　examine my heart and my mind;
³for your love is ever before me,
　and I walk continually in your truth.
⁴I do not sit with deceitful men,
　nor do I consort with hypocrites;
⁵I abhor the assembly of evildoers
　and refuse to sit with the wicked.
⁶I wash my hands in innocence,
　and go about your altar, O LORD,
⁷proclaiming aloud your praise
　and telling of all your wonderful
　　deeds.
⁸I love the house where you live, O LORD,
　the place where your glory[D] dwells.

⁹Do not take away my soul[D] along with
　　sinners,
　my life with bloodthirsty men,
¹⁰in whose hands are wicked schemes,
　whose right hands are full of bribes.
¹¹But I lead a blameless life;
　redeem me and be merciful to me.

¹²My feet stand on level ground;
　in the great assembly I will praise the
　　LORD.

How much of our lives does God plan for us? (25:12)

David is not saying that God makes decisions for us leaving us with no choice. Rather David is talking about how God lays out before us the best way to go. It's up to us to decide whether we follow his ways or not.

Does godliness lead to prosperity? (25:13)

See articles: *Does seeking God guarantee success?* (2 Chron. 26:5) and *Is success guaranteed to those who obey God?* (Deut. 28:2–6).

Why would Almighty God *confide* in people? (25:14)

This metaphor pictures an intimate communion with God—as though mere humans could sit in on God's heavenly council (89:7). God's love for people causes him to long for fellowship with them.

What does it mean to *fear* the Lord? (25:14)

To *fear* the Lord does not exactly mean to be afraid of him. It means to revere him for who he is and to live in a manner that honors him. See article: *Should we live in terror of God?* (Prov. 1:7).

How could David claim to be blameless? (26:1)

Though he was not perfect, David was a man of integrity. *A blameless life* is not a claim that he never sinned. It is rather David's claim to be genuine—sincere in his attempts to honor and serve God. Also see *How could David claim to be without sin?* (17:3–5).

Could David avoid dealing with *deceitful men* and *hypocrites*? (26:4–5)

David does not mean that he never had contact with them but that he did not follow their examples or adopt their ways of thinking. David would have faced the same sort of people and temptations that can be found today in places of power and influence. Deceit and hypocrisy can be found everywhere.

How does God's glory dwell on earth? (26:8)

In David's day the ark of the covenant and the tabernacle were physical signs of God's presence—they were tangible structures that helped people visualize God's glory. Yet people knew God could not be confined to a box or a temple (8:1; 24:1; 1 Kings 8:27). Today God's presence dwells in a special way within his people (1 Cor. 3:16; Eph. 2:22).

Level ground (26:12)

A place of confidence and security, where one does not trip and fall over temptations or evil. It may also refer literally to the level courtyards where the godly gathered to worship the Lord.

Great assembly (26:12)

See *Great assembly* (22:25).

Stronghold (27:1)

A military image—a tower, fortress or fortified hilltop from which an enemy could be resisted. David uses it as a metaphor for refuge and security: God saves and protects us from evil.

Were David's enemies cannibals? (27:2)

No. *Devour my flesh* is probably a metaphor to say that his enemies wanted to kill him. Enemies were often pictured as carnivorous animals (see 22:13,16, for example).

What was David confident about? (27:3)

David was probably convinced he would be physically safe in battle. He had a strong sense of God's plans for his life—how could he be killed before his time? His confidence in God's protection probably was enhanced by the string of victories God gave him. It may be that David was also thinking of his eternal safety.

Straight path (27:11)

A path without twists and turns, rocks or holes. God wants to keep those who follow him safe from stumbling and injury in a spiritual sense. Also see *Level ground* (26:12).

Where is the *land of the living*? (27:13)

David was not referring to a location here, but he was expressing confidence that he would live to see God's blessings in this life.

What does it mean to *wait for the LORD*? (27:14)

Waiting for the Lord suggests trust in God's goodness and timing. God sees things differently than we do, so answers to prayer may not always come in the way we want or as quickly as we want. David waited on God—he depended on him alone for his needs and looked expectantly to him. David also discovered the value of patience; he trusted God to send the answer when—and only when—the time was right.

Psalm 27

Of David.

¹The LORD is my light and my salvation^D—
   whom shall I fear?
The LORD is the stronghold^D of my life—
   of whom shall I be afraid?
²When evil men advance against me
   to devour my flesh,ᵃ
when my enemies and my foes attack
      me,
   they will stumble and fall.
³Though an army besiege me,
   my heart will not fear;
though war break out against me,
   even then will I be confident.

⁴One thing I ask of the LORD,
   this is what I seek:
that I may dwell in the house of the LORD
   all the days of my life,
to gaze upon the beauty of the LORD
   and to seek him in his temple.
⁵For in the day of trouble
   he will keep me safe in his dwelling;
he will hide me in the shelter of his
      tabernacle^D
   and set me high upon a rock.
⁶Then my head will be exalted
   above the enemies who surround me;
at his tabernacle will I sacrifice with shouts
      of joy;
   I will sing and make music to the LORD.

⁷Hear my voice when I call, O LORD;
   be merciful to me and answer me.
⁸My heart says of you, "Seek his^b face!"
   Your face, LORD, I will seek.
⁹Do not hide your face from me,
   do not turn your servant away in anger;
   you have been my helper.
Do not reject me or forsake me,
   O God my Savior.
¹⁰Though my father and mother forsake
      me,
   the LORD will receive me.
¹¹Teach me your way, O LORD;
   lead me in a straight path
   because of my oppressors.
¹²Do not turn me over to the desire of my
      foes,
   for false witnesses rise up against me,
   breathing out violence.

¹³I am still confident of this:
   I will see the goodness of the LORD
   in the land of the living.
¹⁴Wait for the LORD;
   be strong and take heart
   and wait for the LORD.

ᵃ2 Or *to slander me*   ᵇ8 Or *To you, O my heart, he has said, "Seek my*

Psalm 28

Of David.

¹To you I call, O L ORD my Rock;
  do not turn a deaf ear to me.
For if you remain silent,
  I will be like those who have gone down to
    the pit.
²Hear my cry for mercy[D]
  as I call to you for help,
as I lift up my hands
  toward your Most Holy Place[D].

³Do not drag me away with the wicked,
  with those who do evil,
who speak cordially with their neighbors
  but harbor malice in their hearts.
⁴Repay them for their deeds
  and for their evil work;
repay them for what their hands have done
  and bring back upon them what they
    deserve.
⁵Since they show no regard for the works of the
    L ORD
  and what his hands have done,
he will tear them down
  and never build them up again.

⁶Praise be to the L ORD,
  for he has heard my cry for mercy.
⁷The L ORD is my strength and my shield;
  my heart trusts in him, and I am helped.
My heart leaps for joy
  and I will give thanks to him in song.

⁸The L ORD is the strength of his people,
  a fortress of salvation[D] for his anointed[D]
    one.
⁹Save your people and bless your inheritance;
  be their shepherd and carry them forever.

Psalm 29

A psalm of David.

¹Ascribe to the L ORD, O mighty ones,
  ascribe to the L ORD glory[D] and strength.
²Ascribe to the L ORD the glory due his name;
  worship the L ORD in the splendor of his[a]
    holiness.

³The voice of the L ORD is over the waters;
  the God of glory thunders,
  the L ORD thunders over the mighty waters.
⁴The voice of the L ORD is powerful;
  the voice of the L ORD is majestic.
⁵The voice of the L ORD breaks the cedars;
  the L ORD breaks in pieces the cedars of
    Lebanon.
⁶He makes Lebanon skip like a calf,
  Sirion[b] like a young wild ox.
⁷The voice of the L ORD strikes
  with flashes of lightning.

Rock (28:1)
See *How is God like a rock?* (18:2).

Pit (28:1)
Pits were dug to bury the dead (graves were dug into the sides of the hole). In this way, *pit* became a figure of speech for death—the meaning David intends here. See *What kind of pit was David in?* (40:2).

Is it right to pray for revenge? (28:4)
See article: *Is it right to pray for revenge?* (58:6–8).

Anointed one (28:8)
See *Anointed One* (2:2).

Mighty ones (29:1)
Literally, *sons of God* (Gen. 6:2). Also translated as *heavenly beings* (89:6) and *angels* (Job 1:6). This most likely refers to those beings who inhabit the spiritual realms.

What does it mean to worship *in the splendor of his holiness?* (29:2)
It's not entirely clear. Many think this means to worship *in holy attire*. It may also be related to the idea of a holy assembly—*arrayed in holy majesty* (110:3). However this is understood, the primary thrust is that we are to praise God properly, as he deserves.

Skip like a calf (29:6)
A figure of speech for an earthquake, a display of God's power in nature. Language that depicts an earthquake could also be used to describe political or social upheaval. See *Was this an actual earthquake?* (46:2–3).

Why is God's glory so terrifying? (29:7–9)
The pagan nations saw the powerful forces of nature as indicators that the gods were angry. By contrast, David saw lightning and thunder as expressions of the power of the true God. Also see *Why did God appear in such frightening ways?* (18:7–15).

---

a2 Or L ORD *with the splendor of*   *b6 That is, Mount Hermon*

8The voice of the LORD shakes the desert;
 the LORD shakes the Desert of Kadesh.
9The voice of the LORD twists the oaks*a*
 and strips the forests bare.
And in his temple all cry, "Glory*D*!"

10The LORD sits*b* enthroned over the flood;
 the LORD is enthroned as King forever.
11The LORD gives strength to his people;
 the LORD blesses his people with peace*D*.

How is God enthroned over the flood? (29:10)

David paints a mental picture of God as a king ruling over his creation. God's rule over the flood may refer to (1) his word of creation over the formless waters (v. 3; Gen. 1:2), or (2) his control—ruling and judging—during the flood of Noah's time (Gen. 6:17). It's also possible this may refer to flash floods caused by sudden cloudbursts (see v. 7)—a fairly common occurrence in a land with many dry creek beds.

From what depths did God lift David? (30:1)

From the depths of death. David praises God for keeping him alive, perhaps saving him from a grave illness or mortal danger. See v. 3.

Grave . . . pit (30:3)
See *Pit* (28:1).

Saints (30:4)
See *Saints* (16:3).

Psalm 30

A psalm. A song. For the dedication of the temple.c
Of David.

1I will exalt you, O LORD,
 for you lifted me out of the depths
 and did not let my enemies gloat over me.
2O LORD my God, I called to you for help
 and you healed me.
3O LORD, you brought me up from the grave*d*;
 you spared me from going down into the pit.

4Sing to the LORD, you saints*D* of his;
 praise his holy name.
5For his anger lasts only a moment,
 but his favor lasts a lifetime;
weeping may remain for a night,
 but rejoicing comes in the morning.

6When I felt secure, I said,
 "I will never be shaken."
7O LORD, when you favored me,
 you made my mountain*e* stand firm;
but when you hid your face,
 I was dismayed.

8To you, O LORD, I called;
 to the Lord I cried for mercy*D*:
9"What gain is there in my destruction,*f*
 in my going down into the pit?
Will the dust praise you?
 Will it proclaim your faithfulness?
10Hear, O LORD, and be merciful to me;
 O LORD, be my help."

11You turned my wailing into dancing;
 you removed my sackcloth*D* and clothed me
  with joy,
12that my heart may sing to you and not be
  silent.
 O LORD my God, I will give you thanks
  forever.

Why wasn't David more confident about life after death? (30:9)

In the face of death's unknown mysteries, people in ancient times could find little comfort. See *Why would evil Saul go to the same place as righteous Samuel when he died?* (1 Samuel 28:19). They just did not know much about the afterlife. What they could see were the rewards of a long, prosperous life. Nonetheless, there were glimmers of revelation about eternity in God's presence, and we know David believed in life after death (17:15).

Psalm 31

For the director of music. A psalm of David.

1In you, O LORD, I have taken refuge;
 let me never be put to shame;
 deliver me in your righteousness*D*.
2Turn your ear to me,

Rock (31:2)
See *How is God like a rock?* (18:2).

a9 Or LORD makes the deer give birth   *b10 Or sat*   *cTitle: Or palace*   *d3 Hebrew Sheol*   *e7 Or hill country*   *f9 Or there if I am silenced*

come quickly to my rescue;
be my rock of refuge,
    a strong fortress to save me.
³Since you are my rock and my fortress,
    for the sake of your name lead and guide
        me.
⁴Free me from the trap that is set for me,
    for you are my refuge.
⁵Into your hands I commit my spirit;
    redeem^D me, O LORD, the God of truth.

⁶I hate those who cling to worthless idols^D;
    I trust in the LORD.
⁷I will be glad and rejoice in your love,
    for you saw my affliction^D
    and knew the anguish of my soul^D.
⁸You have not handed me over to the enemy
    but have set my feet in a spacious place.

⁹Be merciful to me, O LORD, for I am in distress;
    my eyes grow weak with sorrow,
    my soul and my body with grief.
¹⁰My life is consumed by anguish
    and my years by groaning;
my strength fails because of my affliction,^{a}
    and my bones grow weak.
¹¹Because of all my enemies,
    I am the utter contempt of my neighbors;
I am a dread to my friends—
    those who see me on the street flee from
        me.
¹²I am forgotten by them as though I were dead;
    I have become like broken pottery.
¹³For I hear the slander of many;
    there is terror on every side;
they conspire against me
    and plot to take my life.

¹⁴But I trust in you, O LORD;
    I say, "You are my God."
¹⁵My times are in your hands;
    deliver me from my enemies
    and from those who pursue me.
¹⁶Let your face shine on your servant;
    save me in your unfailing love.
¹⁷Let me not be put to shame, O LORD,
    for I have cried out to you;
but let the wicked be put to shame
    and lie silent in the grave.^{b}
¹⁸Let their lying lips be silenced,
    for with pride and contempt
    they speak arrogantly against the righteous^D.

¹⁹How great is your goodness,
    which you have stored up for those who fear
        you,
which you bestow in the sight of men
    on those who take refuge in you.
²⁰In the shelter of your presence you hide them
    from the intrigues of men;
in your dwelling you keep them safe
    from accusing tongues.

Why appeal to the name of the Lord? (31:3)
See *How does God's name offer protection?* (20:1).

Was it right for David to hate his enemies? (31:6)
Just as the Lord hates sin and wickedness (5:5), David hated idolatry and rebellion against God. His passion was in line with what he knew to be God's will. Rightly or wrongly, hatred of sin typically was transferred to the sinner. We cannot hold David accountable for a standard of love that was unknown until Christ came. Also see article: *Is the God of love also a God of hate?* (5:5).

Spacious place (31:8)
See *Spacious place* (18:19).

What made David so loathsome to his neighbors? (31:11)
This may refer to times when David's enemies forced him to flee for his life, hiding in caves and living in primitive conditions—a loathsome situation. More likely this means that David was slandered and despised because of false charges made by his adversaries (v. 13; 27:12).

How was David like broken pottery? (31:12)
Broken pieces of pottery were practically worthless and were used in menial ways as scrapers, scoops or sometimes to write on as "scratch paper." David uses the image of *broken pottery* to describe his impression that people had lost all respect for him.

What *times* did David place in the Lord's hands? (31:15)
The times of his life—his day by day circumstances and events. This is another way of saying that he was committing his spirit into the hands of the Lord (v. 5)—that he was trusting his life to God.

^{a}10 Or *guilt* ^{b}17 Hebrew *Sheol*

Cut off from your sight (31:22)

Probably a figure of speech referring to a life-threatening situation, perhaps one of those occasions when David felt like he had been abandoned by God.

Blessed (32:1)

Full of joy, happy. To be blessed, however, is much more than a feeling, because it is the result of having a right relationship with God.

What's good about covering up sin? (32:1)

We cannot sweep sins under the rug and think everything is fine because they're hidden. When God "covers" sins, he does away with them completely; he doesn't conceal sins, he eradicates them. The image of covering sin was linked to the blood of the sacrifice that *covered* one's sin. When God saw the blood, he no longer saw the sin—and since God sees everything, what he does not see does not exist.

Why would silence waste David's bones away? (32:3)

Because his silence was something like denial—a refusal to admit what he had done wrong. As long as David could not face up to his own sinfulness, he suffered internal guilt and anguish.

Is there a time when the Lord *can't* be found? (32:6)

God is always present, but he may *seem* more approachable at some times than at others. Those who sincerely seek the Lord will find him (Jer. 29:13–14)—but those who seek him only when they are desperate for his help may discover that he has become "unavailable." See article: *Does God sometimes hide from us?* (10:1).

How is the Lord a *hiding place*? (32:7)

Like other word pictures in the psalms (such as refuge, rock and fortress), David speaks of the Lord as his *hiding place*—a place of security. Though David was probably thinking mostly of safety from physical threats, God also provides safety from spiritual trouble. He delivers us from the penalty of sin.

Does God sometimes control us like a horse or mule? (32:9)

No. This graphic image looks at human response, not God's methods. It acknowledges that people can be stubborn as mules but does not imply that God forces them to go against their will. He offers instruction and counsel (v. 8), not spiritual coercion (*bit and bridle*). God wants our willing trust and obedience. At the same time, however, God is still sovereign. See *Does God sometimes frustrate people's plans?* (33:10).

²¹Praise be to the LORD,
  for he showed his wonderful love to me
  when I was in a besieged city.
²²In my alarm I said,
  "I am cut off from your sight!"
Yet you heard my cry for mercy^D
  when I called to you for help.

²³Love the LORD, all his saints^D!
  The LORD preserves the faithful,
  but the proud he pays back in full.
²⁴Be strong and take heart,
  all you who hope in the LORD.

Psalm 32

Of David. A *maskil.*[a]

¹Blessed is he
  whose transgressions are forgiven,
  whose sins are covered.
²Blessed is the man
  whose sin the LORD does not count against
    him
  and in whose spirit is no deceit.

³When I kept silent,
  my bones wasted away
  through my groaning all day long.
⁴For day and night
  your hand was heavy upon me;
my strength was sapped
  as in the heat of summer.   *Selah*^D
⁵Then I acknowledged my sin to you
  and did not cover up my iniquity.
I said, "I will confess
  my transgressions to the LORD"—
and you forgave
  the guilt of my sin.   *Selah*

⁶Therefore let everyone who is godly pray to
    you
  while you may be found;
surely when the mighty waters rise,
  they will not reach him.
⁷You are my hiding place;
  you will protect me from trouble
  and surround me with songs of deliverance.
     Selah

⁸I will instruct you and teach you in the way
    you should go;
  I will counsel you and watch over you.
⁹Do not be like the horse or the mule,
  which have no understanding
but must be controlled by bit and bridle
  or they will not come to you.
¹⁰Many are the woes of the wicked,
  but the LORD's unfailing love
  surrounds the man who trusts in him.

---

[a]Title: Probably a literary or musical term

¹¹Rejoice in the LORD and be glad, you
    righteous^D;
  sing, all you who are upright in heart!

Psalm 33

¹Sing joyfully to the LORD, you righteous;
  it is fitting for the upright to praise him.
²Praise the LORD with the harp;
  make music to him on the ten-stringed
    lyre^D.
³Sing to him a new song;
  play skillfully, and shout for joy.

⁴For the word of the LORD is right and true;
  he is faithful in all he does.
⁵The LORD loves righteousness^D and justice;
  the earth is full of his unfailing love.

⁶By the word of the LORD were the heavens
    made,
  their starry host^D by the breath of his
    mouth.
⁷He gathers the waters of the sea into jars[a];
  he puts the deep into storehouses.
⁸Let all the earth fear the LORD;
  let all the people of the world revere^D him.
⁹For he spoke, and it came to be;
  he commanded, and it stood firm.
¹⁰The LORD foils the plans of the nations;
  he thwarts the purposes of the peoples.
¹¹But the plans of the LORD stand firm forever,
  the purposes of his heart through all
    generations.

¹²Blessed is the nation whose God is the LORD,
  the people he chose for his inheritance.
¹³From heaven the LORD looks down
  and sees all mankind;
¹⁴from his dwelling place he watches
  all who live on earth—
¹⁵he who forms the hearts of all,
  who considers everything they do.
¹⁶No king is saved by the size of his army;
  no warrior escapes by his great strength.
¹⁷A horse is a vain hope for deliverance;
  despite all its great strength it cannot save.
¹⁸But the eyes of the LORD are on those who fear
    him,
  on those whose hope is in his unfailing
    love,
¹⁹to deliver them from death^D
  and keep them alive in famine.

²⁰We wait in hope for the LORD;
  he is our help and our shield.
²¹In him our hearts rejoice,
  for we trust in his holy name.
²²May your unfailing love rest upon us,
    O LORD,
  even as we put our hope in you.

Ten-stringed lyre (33:2)
A harp-like instrument distinguished by its
number of strings. *Lyres* typically had a sound
board over which the vibrating strings could
resonate.

Are new songs better than old? (33:3)
A *new* song probably indicates the freshness of
one's experience with God more than the age
of one's music. A new song that doesn't honor
God is worthless as a song of worship; on the
other hand, an old song that describes God's
personal and current involvement has tremendous worship value.

**In what sense is the earth filled with
God's unfailing love? (33:5)**
In the sense that there is no shortage of God's
love. He has mercy and grace enough for all
the world. Even the undeserving experience his
love. The sorrow, disappointment and judgment we see on earth can also be understood
as an expression of God's love because such
things can prepare hearts to receive God's
mercy.

**Does God sometimes frustrate peo-
ple's plans? (33:10)**
Absolutely—but not in a capricious or arbitrary
manner. God is sovereign; he can overrule the
plans of individuals and accomplish a far greater good through his own purposes. See Prov.
16:9.

**Does this promise of blessing apply to
any nation that follows the Lord?
(33:12)**
The *principle* described here is true for individuals, families, communities and even entire
nations: those who serve God will benefit from
their close relationship with him. This *specific*
promise, however, applied to Israel, the nation
chosen as God's inheritance.

**Does God constantly watch us?
(33:14–15)**
Yes, God is always present (*omnipresent*) and
knows everything (*omniscient*); he perceives
our thoughts and hidden motives. But he
doesn't watch us to try to catch us doing
something wrong. Though he judges wrongdoing when he sees it, his reason for keeping an
eye on us is because he loves us and wants to
help us (2 Chron. 16:9).

**Do godly people never starve?
(33:18–19)**
There are times when even the godly starve.
Tragedies often strike in a random manner;
those who deserve less trouble sometimes receive more. In these verses, God's character is
painted in broad strokes, describing the general pattern of his work, but they do not provide a
mechanical formula for every situation. Also
see article: **Are proverbs iron-clad promises?**
(Prov. 3:1–4).

ᵃ7 Or *sea as into a heap*

Psalm 34[a]

Of David. When he pretended to be insane before
Abimelech, who drove him away, and he left.

¹I will extol[D] the LORD at all times;
  his praise will always be on my lips.
²My soul[D] will boast in the LORD;
  let the afflicted[D] hear and rejoice.
³Glorify the LORD with me;
  let us exalt his name together.

⁴I sought the LORD, and he answered me;
  he delivered me from all my fears.
⁵Those who look to him are radiant;
  their faces are never covered with shame.
⁶This poor man called, and the LORD heard him;
  he saved him out of all his troubles.
⁷The angel of the LORD encamps around those
    who fear him,
  and he delivers them.

⁸Taste and see that the LORD is good;
  blessed is the man who takes refuge in him.
⁹Fear the LORD, you his saints[D],
  for those who fear him lack nothing.
¹⁰The lions may grow weak and hungry,
  but those who seek the LORD lack no good
    thing.

¹¹Come, my children, listen to me;
  I will teach you the fear of the LORD.
¹²Whoever of you loves life
  and desires to see many good days,
¹³keep your tongue from evil
  and your lips from speaking lies.
¹⁴Turn from evil and do good;
  seek peace[D] and pursue it.

¹⁵The eyes of the LORD are on the righteous[D]
  and his ears are attentive to their cry;
¹⁶the face of the LORD is against those who do
    evil,
  to cut off the memory of them from the
    earth.

¹⁷The righteous cry out, and the LORD hears
    them;
  he delivers them from all their troubles.
¹⁸The LORD is close to the brokenhearted
  and saves those who are crushed in spirit.

¹⁹A righteous man may have many troubles,
  but the LORD delivers him from them all;
²⁰he protects all his bones,
  not one of them will be broken.

²¹Evil will slay the wicked;
  the foes of the righteous will be
    condemned.
²²The LORD redeems[D] his servants;
  no one will be condemned who takes refuge
    in him.

The angel of the LORD (34:7)

Sometimes indistinguishable from the Lord
himself (Exodus 3:2–4, for example). Other
times this means the *messenger* of the Lord,
speaking or acting in his name (Num. 22:22).
Some think this verse may anticipate Jesus'
continual presence with us (see Matt. 28:20).

If someone is in need, does that mean they don't fear God? (34:9–10)

A person's need does not indicate that he or
she didn't seek God enough. In fact, God consistently shows deep compassion for the poor
and afflicted of society (Prov. 14:31; 19:17).
David's statement is intended as a general
principle of God's care and provision, not an
absolute guarantee for every situation.

What does it mean for God's face to be *against* someone? (34:16)

A person's disposition and emotions usually
can be read from the expression on his or her
face. Thus, God's *face* is used as a poetic way
of describing God's favor or his judgment toward someone. A sign of God's blessing is that
his face "shines" (4:6); a sign of God's displeasure and judgment is that his face is hidden (30:7) or *against* someone. Also see **Does
God have a physical body?** (13:1).

Does God help us out of *all* our troubles? (34:17)

Not exactly—as life's sorrows and heartaches
easily demonstrate. But the Lord does not promise so much to remove our difficulties as to
see us *through* them. God can use even trouble
to accomplish his purposes; Jesus was made
perfect through suffering (Heb. 2:10). With
God's help, troubles can mature us. The bottom line is that God changes something—if
it's not our troubles, then he changes us.

---

[a]This psalm is an acrostic poem, the verses of which begin with the
successive letters of the Hebrew alphabet.

Psalm 35

Of David.

¹Contend, O Lord, with those who contend with
    me;
    fight against those who fight against me.
²Take up shield and buckler;
    arise and come to my aid.
³Brandish spear and javelin*a*
    against those who pursue me.
Say to my soul*D*,
    "I am your salvation*D*."

⁴May those who seek my life
    be disgraced and put to shame;
may those who plot my ruin
    be turned back in dismay.
⁵May they be like chaff*D* before the wind,
    with the angel of the Lord driving them
        away;
⁶may their path be dark and slippery,
    with the angel of the Lord pursuing them.
⁷Since they hid their net for me without cause
    and without cause dug a pit for me,
⁸may ruin overtake them by surprise—
    may the net they hid entangle them,
    may they fall into the pit, to their ruin.
⁹Then my soul will rejoice in the Lord
    and delight in his salvation.
¹⁰My whole being will exclaim,
    "Who is like you, O Lord?
You rescue the poor from those too strong for
        them,
    the poor and needy from those who rob
        them."

¹¹Ruthless witnesses come forward;
    they question me on things I know nothing
        about.
¹²They repay me evil for good
    and leave my soul forlorn.
¹³Yet when they were ill, I put on sackcloth*D*
    and humbled myself with fasting.
When my prayers returned to me unanswered,
¹⁴   I went about mourning
    as though for my friend or brother.
I bowed my head in grief
    as though weeping for my mother.
¹⁵But when I stumbled, they gathered in glee;
    attackers gathered against me when I was
        unaware.
    They slandered me without ceasing.
¹⁶Like the ungodly they maliciously mocked*b*;
    they gnashed their teeth at me.
¹⁷O Lord, how long will you look on?
    Rescue my life from their ravages,
    my precious life from these lions.
¹⁸I will give you thanks in the great assembly;
    among throngs of people I will praise you.

¹⁹Let not those gloat over me
    who are my enemies without cause;

Buckler (35:2)

Often translated *shield,* this was a specific type
of shield—one that was quite large and used
to cover the whole body, often carried by a
shield bearer. The first *shield* mentioned in this
verse was a smaller version, round or oblong
and more mobile. This was David's figurative
way of saying that God is our complete defense—he protects us in every way.

Chaff (35:5)
See *Chaff* (1:4).

The angel of the Lord (35:5)
See *The angel of the Lord* (34:7).

How were nets and pits used in war-
fare? (35:7)

Pits, nets and other types of traps were set to
capture—and sometimes injure—enemies.
David used these images to picture his opponents' schemes; he prayed that they would be
caught by their own evil plots (v. 8).

Why were David's kindnesses repaid
with evil? (35:11–16)

We can't be sure who these adversaries were
or why they turned against David. It may be
that, like most leaders, he faced unfair criticisms from disgruntled followers. David, for his
part, often repaid evil with good. For example,
when King Saul tried to murder him, David
would not retaliate, even though others believed he had the right to do so (1 Samuel
24:10). See *Why did David pray his enemies
would have their teeth broken?* (3:7). Also see
articles: *Is it right to pray for revenge?* (58:6–8)
and *Who would smash babies for revenge?*
(137:8–9).

Great assembly (35:18)
See *Great assembly* (22:25).

---

*a*3 Or *and block the way*   *b*16 Septuagint; Hebrew may mean
ungodly circle of mockers.

let not those who hate me without reason
   maliciously wink the eye.
20They do not speak peaceably,
   but devise false accusations
   against those who live quietly in the land.
21They gape at me and say, "Aha! Aha!
   With our own eyes we have seen it."

22O LORD, you have seen this; be not silent.
   Do not be far from me, O Lord.
23Awake, and rise to my defense!
   Contend for me, my God and Lord.
24Vindicate me in your righteousnessᴰ, O LORD
     my God;
   do not let them gloat over me.
25Do not let them think, "Aha, just what we
     wanted!"
   or say, "We have swallowed him up."

26May all who gloat over my distress
   be put to shame and confusion;
   may all who exalt themselves over me
   be clothed with shame and disgrace.
27May those who delight in my vindication
   shout for joy and gladness;
   may they always say, "The LORD be exalted,
   who delights in the well-being of his
     servant."
28My tongue will speak of your righteousness
   and of your praises all day long.

Psalm 36

For the director of music. Of David the servant of the
                  LORD.

Oracle (36:1)
An announcement from God. The word often
suggests unwelcome news or judgment.

1An oracleᴰ is within my heart
   concerning the sinfulness of the wicked:ᵃ
There is no fear of God
   before his eyes.
2For in his own eyes he flatters himself
   too much to detect or hate his sin.
3The words of his mouth are wicked and
     deceitful;
   he has ceased to be wise and to do good.
4Even on his bed he plots evil;
   he commits himself to a sinful course
   and does not reject what is wrong.

5Your love, O LORD, reaches to the heavens,
   your faithfulness to the skies.
6Your righteousness is like the mighty
     mountains,
   your justice like the great deep.
O LORD, you preserve both man and beast.
7 How priceless is your unfailing love!
Both high and low among men
   findᵇ refuge in the shadow of your wings.
8They feast on the abundance of your house;
   you give them drink from your river of
     delights.
9For with you is the fountain of life;
   in your light we see light.

Shadow of your wings (36:7)
See **Shadow of your wings** (17:8).

ᵃ1 Or heart: / Sin proceeds from the wicked.   ᵇ7 Or love, O God! /
Men find; or love! / Both heavenly beings and men / find

¹⁰Continue your love to those who know you,
your righteousness^D to the upright in heart.
¹¹May the foot of the proud not come against
me,
nor the hand of the wicked drive me away.
¹²See how the evildoers lie fallen—
thrown down, not able to rise!

Psalm 37ᵃ

Of David.

¹Do not fret because of evil men
or be envious of those who do wrong;
²for like the grass they will soon wither,
like green plants they will soon die away.

³Trust in the LORD and do good;
dwell in the land and enjoy safe pasture.
⁴Delight yourself in the LORD
and he will give you the desires of your
heart.

⁵Commit your way to the LORD;
trust in him and he will do this:
⁶He will make your righteousness shine like
the dawn,
the justice of your cause like the noonday
sun.

⁷Be still before the LORD and wait patiently for
him;
do not fret when men succeed in their ways,
when they carry out their wicked schemes.

⁸Refrain from anger and turn from wrath;
do not fret—it leads only to evil.
⁹For evil men will be cut off,

ᵃThis psalm is an acrostic poem, the stanzas of which begin with the
successive letters of the Hebrew alphabet.

Does God give us anything we desire? (37:4)

No. But he will give us our desires when they
first are shaped by a delight in the Lord. To receive this promise, we must first meet the conditions attached to it: By loving God above all
else, our desires will become what he desires
for us. Then our greatest longing will be to conform our lives to his will.

Cut off (37:9)

A common figure of speech to describe (1) the
breaking off of a relationship, as in excom-
municating or alienating someone from the
community; or (2) a sentence of divine judgment which eliminated someone by execution.

If we trust in God, are we guaranteed safety? (37:3–25)

This is a general promise, not a specific one. *Safe pasture* sounds like physical
safety, but other passages in the Bible suggest a broader interpretation. We
can conclude that spiritual safety is always guaranteed even if physical safety sometimes
is not.

The Bible speaks not only of those who were saved from physical threats, but also of
those who were not. The book of Hebrews recounts the stories of nameless martyrs
(11:35–38), and Jesus told his followers that some would be killed (John 16:2). Even
Jesus experienced physical suffering and death.

Throughout history, many righteous people have tragically lost their lives. God did not
always rescue them. Members of the early church were tortured and died cruel deaths.
Such maltreatment has continued even into the present. Some point out that more died
as Christian martyrs in the twentieth century than in any previous century.

The writer of this psalm had seen the wicked thrive and the righteous suffer. But in
spite of that, he still could speak of safety for the righteous because he chose to focus
on God and his goodness. Though the reasons behind life's tragedies often remain a
mystery, the psalmist, by faith, could assert that God would not abandon his people.

What was the significance of inheriting land? (37:9)

Land in the Old Testament symbolized more than just a piece of property. It often represented the blessing and presence of God. God's promise is that one day the tables will be turned: those who are well off may not be in the future; those who suffer will one day be comforted. Ultimately the righteous will be rewarded and the wicked will be brought to ruin. Jesus made the same point in saying that the meek will inherit the earth (Matt. 5:5).

Gnash their teeth (37:12)

See *What does it mean to gnash teeth?* (112:10).

Perish . . . vanish like smoke (37:20)

See *Cut off* (37:9).

Dwell in the land (37:27)

See *What was the significance of inheriting land?* (37:9).

but those who hope in the LORD will inherit the land.

¹⁰A little while, and the wicked will be no more;
though you look for them, they will not be found.
¹¹But the meek will inherit the land
and enjoy great peace.ᴰ

¹²The wicked plot against the righteousᴰ
and gnash their teeth at them;
¹³but the Lord laughs at the wicked,
for he knows their day is coming.

¹⁴The wicked draw the sword
and bend the bow
to bring down the poor and needy,
to slay those whose ways are upright.
¹⁵But their swords will pierce their own hearts,
and their bows will be broken.

¹⁶Better the little that the righteous have
than the wealth of many wicked;
¹⁷for the power of the wicked will be broken,
but the LORD upholds the righteous.

¹⁸The days of the blameless are known to the LORD,
and their inheritance will endure forever.
¹⁹In times of disaster they will not wither;
in days of famine they will enjoy plenty.

²⁰But the wicked will perish:
The LORD's enemies will be like the beauty of the fields,
they will vanish—vanish like smoke.

²¹The wicked borrow and do not repay,
but the righteous give generously;
²²those the LORD blesses will inherit the land,
but those he curses will be cut off.

²³If the LORD delights in a man's way,
he makes his steps firm;
²⁴though he stumble, he will not fall,
for the LORD upholds him with his hand.

²⁵I was young and now I am old,
yet I have never seen the righteous forsaken
or their children begging bread.
²⁶They are always generous and lend freely;
their children will be blessed.

²⁷Turn from evil and do good;
then you will dwell in the land forever.
²⁸For the LORD loves the just
and will not forsake his faithful ones.

They will be protected forever,
but the offspring of the wicked will be cut off;
²⁹the righteous will inherit the land
and dwell in it forever.

³⁰The mouth of the righteous man utters wisdom,
and his tongue speaks what is just.
³¹The law of his God is in his heart;
his feet do not slip.

32The wicked lie in wait for the righteous[D],
 seeking their very lives;
33but the LORD will not leave them in their power
 or let them be condemned when brought to
  trial.

34Wait for the LORD
 and keep his way.
He will exalt you to inherit the land;
 when the wicked are cut off, you will see it.

35I have seen a wicked and ruthless man
 flourishing like a green tree in its native soil,
36but he soon passed away and was no more;
 though I looked for him, he could not be
  found.

37Consider the blameless, observe the upright;
 there is a future[a] for the man of peace[D].
38But all sinners will be destroyed;
 the future[b] of the wicked will be cut off.

39The salvation[D] of the righteous comes from
  the LORD;
 he is their stronghold[D] in time of trouble.
40The LORD helps them and delivers them;
 he delivers them from the wicked and saves
  them,
 because they take refuge in him.

Psalm 38

A psalm of David. A petition.

1O LORD, do not rebuke me in your anger
 or discipline me in your wrath.
2For your arrows have pierced me,
 and your hand has come down upon me.
3Because of your wrath there is no health in my
  body;
 my bones have no soundness because of my
  sin.
4My guilt has overwhelmed me
 like a burden too heavy to bear.

5My wounds fester and are loathsome
 because of my sinful folly.
6I am bowed down and brought very low;
 all day long I go about mourning.
7My back is filled with searing pain;
 there is no health in my body.
8I am feeble and utterly crushed;
 I groan in anguish of heart.

9All my longings lie open before you, O Lord;
 my sighing is not hidden from you.
10My heart pounds, my strength fails me;
 even the light has gone from my eyes.
11My friends and companions avoid me because
  of my wounds;
 my neighbors stay far away.
12Those who seek my life set their traps,
 those who would harm me talk of my ruin;
 all day long they plot deception.

Does God make us sick when he is angry with us? (38:3)

Some Bible passages suggest that sickness can come as a result of sin (for example, 2 Samuel 24:13). But sickness can also strike those who are righteous in God's sight (for example, John 9:1–3 and the book of Job). Some illness may have caused David to look within his heart and see his sin. Or he may have used poetic language to describe his spiritual condition as a sickness. Also see *Why did God use a disease as a punishment?* (2 Chron. 26:19).

What is the purpose of guilt? (38:4)

Guilt can bring us to repentance. David felt troubled by his sin. Guilt led him to confess it (v. 18) and then ask God for help (vv. 21–22).

The light . . . gone from my eyes (38:10)

See *Light to my eyes* (13:3).

---

a 37 Or there will be posterity   *b 38 Or posterity*

13I am like a deaf man, who cannot hear,
    like a mute, who cannot open his mouth;
14I have become like a man who does not hear,
    whose mouth can offer no reply.
15I wait for you, O LORD;
    you will answer, O Lord my God.
16For I said, "Do not let them gloat
    or exalt themselves over me when my foot
        slips."

17For I am about to fall,
    and my pain is ever with me.
18I confess my iniquity;
    I am troubled by my sin.
19Many are those who are my vigorous enemies;
    those who hate me without reason are
        numerous.
20Those who repay my good with evil
    slander me when I pursue what is good.

21O LORD, do not forsake me;
    be not far from me, O my God.
22Come quickly to help me,
    O Lord my Savior.

Psalm 39

For the director of music. For Jeduthun. A psalm
of David.

1I said, "I will watch my ways
    and keep my tongue from sin;
I will put a muzzle on my mouth
    as long as the wicked are in my presence."
2But when I was silent and still,
    not even saying anything good,
    my anguish increased.
3My heart grew hot within me,
    and as I meditated, the fire burned;
    then I spoke with my tongue:

4"Show me, O LORD, my life's end
    and the number of my days;
    let me know how fleeting is my life.
5You have made my days a mere handbreadth;
    the span of my years is as nothing before
        you.
    Each man's life is but a breath.   SelahD
6Man is a mere phantom as he goes to and fro:
    He bustles about, but only in vain;
    he heaps up wealth, not knowing who will
        get it.

7"But now, Lord, what do I look for?
    My hope is in you.
8Save me from all my transgressions;
    do not make me the scorn of fools.
9I was silent; I would not open my mouth,
    for you are the one who has done this.
10Remove your scourge from me;
    I am overcome by the blow of your hand.
11You rebuke and discipline men for their sin;
    you consume their wealth like a moth—
    each man is but a breath.   Selah

Why were the wicked with David? (39:1)

It's not unusual for those in public positions of authority to have many lurking around who look for an opportunity to bring them down. Whether it was enemies or unfaithful friends who intended to betray him, David felt the pressure of evil and a great need to maintain his spiritual purity.

Did God physically hurt David? (39:10)

Just because David blamed God for his suffering doesn't mean that God mistreated him. Those in agony—often lash out at those closest to them. This apparently was the case with David. At the same time, though, David admitted his sin and his need for God (v. 8). David may have thought God's dealings with him were heavy-handed, but he still clung to God as his hope of salvation.

¹²"Hear my prayer, O LORD,
　　listen to my cry for help;
　　be not deaf to my weeping.
For I dwell with you as an alienᴰ,
　　a stranger, as all my fathers were.
¹³Look away from me, that I may rejoice
　　　again
　　before I depart and am no more."

Psalm 40

For the director of music. Of David. A psalm.

¹I waited patiently for the LORD;
　　he turned to me and heard my cry.
²He lifted me out of the slimy pit,
　　out of the mud and mire;
he set my feet on a rock
　　and gave me a firm place to stand.
³He put a new song in my mouth,
　　a hymn of praise to our God.
Many will see and fear
　　and put their trust in the LORD.

⁴Blessed is the man
　　who makes the LORD his trust,
who does not look to the proud,
　　to those who turn aside to false gods.ᵃ
⁵Many, O LORD my God,
　　are the wonders you have done.
The things you planned for us
　　no one can recount to you;
were I to speak and tell of them,
　　they would be too many to declare.

⁶Sacrificeᴰ and offering you did not desire,
　　but my ears you have pierced ᵇ,ᶜ;
burnt offeringsᴰ and sin offeringsᴰ
　　you did not require.
⁷Then I said, "Here I am, I have come—
　　it is written about me in the scroll.ᵈ
⁸I desire to do your will, O my God;
　　your law is within my heart."

⁹I proclaim righteousnessᴰ in the great
　　　assembly;
I do not seal my lips,
　　as you know, O LORD.
¹⁰I do not hide your righteousness in my
　　　heart;
I speak of your faithfulness and salvationᴰ.
I do not conceal your love and your truth
　　from the great assembly.

¹¹Do not withhold your mercyᴰ from me,
　　O LORD;
may your love and your truth always protect
　　me.
¹²For troubles without number surround me;
　　my sins have overtaken me, and I cannot
　　see.

Why did David want God to look away from him? (39:13)

He didn't. This was his way of asking for mercy, of repenting of his sin. David was asking God to direct his angry, penetrating gaze elsewhere. Though he wanted God to stop focusing on his sin, David also begged God to pay attention to him (v. 12).

What kind of pit was David in? (40:2)

David's graphic description of this pit probably reminded his readers of pits dug for water. Or *pit* could mean a dungeon (Exodus 12:29), a trap (9:15) or be used as a metaphor for death itself (28:1). Some graves were dug in the sides of a deep hole. No matter which image comes to mind, the symbolism is clear: God rescued him out of a desperate, hopeless situation.

Why didn't God want David's offerings? (40:6)

It's not that God didn't want David's offerings, it's that he wanted sincere worship and obedience even more. Going through the motions of religious ritual does not please God. The desire to do his will must come from the heart (v. 8).

Why did God pierce David's ears? (40:6)

Hebrew servants who pledged to serve a master for life were marked by having an ear held against a doorpost and pierced with an awl (Exodus 21:5-6). Thus some think David's "pierced ears" suggested a wholehearted commitment to serve God. Others, however, believe *pierced* means *opened* (see NIV text note), indicating ears ready to hear (and obey) God's word (Jer. 6:10).

SCRIPTURE LINK (40:6-8) *It is written about me in the scroll*

The writer of Hebrews saw in David's words another meaning: a prediction of the coming Messiah. See Heb. 10:5-7.

What was written about David? (40:7)

David was not referring to a prophecy about himself. Instead, he was remembering the copy of the law he received when he was crowned king. He recognized that being king was a position of great responsibility God had given him. So he declared that the law he received was binding upon him (see Deut. 17:18-20).

ᵃ4 Or *to falsehood*　　ᵇ6 Hebrew; Septuagint *but a body you have prepared for me* (see also Symmachus and Theodotion)　　ᶜ6 Or *opened*　　ᵈ7 Or *come / with the scroll written for me*

They are more than the hairs of my head,
  and my heart fails within me.

¹³Be pleased, O LORD, to save me;
  O LORD, come quickly to help me.
¹⁴May all who seek to take my life
  be put to shame and confusion;
may all who desire my ruin
  be turned back in disgrace.
¹⁵May those who say to me, "Aha! Aha!"
  be appalled at their own shame.
¹⁶But may all who seek you
  rejoice and be glad in you;
may those who love your salvation^D always
    say,
  "The LORD be exalted!"

¹⁷Yet I am poor and needy;
  may the Lord think of me.
You are my help and my deliverer;
  O my God, do not delay.

Why would David call himself *poor and needy*? (40:17)

As king, David was not financially poor. He may have felt overwhelmed by the obligations of caring for an entire nation. Or he may have been acknowledging his spiritual need, using an expression of humility. *Poor and needy* in the Old Testament sometimes refers to *the righteous*. If David used the phrase this way, it would have been his way of showing his dependence on God.

Did David need healing because he'd sinned? (41:4)

Yes, but probably not for a physical ailment. Literally this means *heal my soul.*

Lifted up his heel against me (41:9)

An expression similar to "walked out on me" or "kicked me when I was down." It suggests some sort of betrayal, most likely involving slander. Jesus used these same words (John 13:18) to describe his betrayal.

Amen and Amen (41:13)

Each of the five "books" (or sub-collections) of the Psalms ends with an expression of praise. Here it was a congregational response: *Amen and Amen,* confirming their agreement with the words that preceded it.

Psalm 41

For the director of music. A psalm of David.

¹Blessed is he who has regard for the weak;
  the LORD delivers him in times of trouble.
²The LORD will protect him and preserve his
    life;
  he will bless him in the land
  and not surrender him to the desire of his
    foes.
³The LORD will sustain him on his sickbed
  and restore him from his bed of illness.

⁴I said, "O LORD, have mercy^D on me;
  heal me, for I have sinned against you."
⁵My enemies say of me in malice,
  "When will he die and his name perish?"
⁶Whenever one comes to see me,
  he speaks falsely, while his heart gathers
    slander;
  then he goes out and spreads it abroad.

⁷All my enemies whisper together against me;
  they imagine the worst for me, saying,
⁸"A vile disease has beset him;
  he will never get up from the place where he
    lies."
⁹Even my close friend, whom I trusted,
  he who shared my bread,
  has lifted up his heel against me.

¹⁰But you, O LORD, have mercy on me;
  raise me up, that I may repay them.
¹¹I know that you are pleased with me,
  for my enemy does not triumph over me.
¹²In my integrity you uphold me
  and set me in your presence forever.

¹³Praise be to the LORD, the God of Israel,
  from everlasting to everlasting.
    Amen and Amen.

BOOK II
Psalms 42-72

Psalm 42[a]

For the director of music. A *maskil*[b] of the Sons of Korah.

[1] As the deer pants for streams of water,
  so my soul[D] pants for you, O God.
[2] My soul thirsts for God, for the living God.
  When can I go and meet with God?
[3] My tears have been my food
  day and night,
while men say to me all day long,
  "Where is your God?"
[4] These things I remember
  as I pour out my soul:
how I used to go with the multitude,
  leading the procession to the house of God,
with shouts of joy and thanksgiving
  among the festive throng.

[5] Why are you downcast, O my soul?
  Why so disturbed within me?
Put your hope in God,
  for I will yet praise him,
  my Savior and [6] my God.

My[c] soul is downcast within me;
  therefore I will remember you
from the land of the Jordan,
  the heights of Hermon—from Mount Mizar.
[7] Deep calls to deep
  in the roar of your waterfalls;
all your waves and breakers
  have swept over me.

[8] By day the LORD directs his love,
  at night his song is with me—
  a prayer to the God of my life.

[9] I say to God my Rock,
  "Why have you forgotten me?
Why must I go about mourning,
  oppressed by the enemy?"
[10] My bones suffer mortal agony
  as my foes taunt me,
saying to me all day long,
  "Where is your God?"

[11] Why are you downcast, O my soul?
  Why so disturbed within me?
Put your hope in God,
  for I will yet praise him,
  my Savior and my God.

Psalm 43[a]

[1] Vindicate me, O God,
  and plead my cause against an ungodly
    nation;

---

[a]In many Hebrew manuscripts Psalms 42 and 43 constitute one psalm.
[b]Title: Probably a literary or musical term   [c]5,6 A few Hebrew manuscripts, Septuagint and Syriac; most Hebrew manuscripts *praise him for his saving help. / [6]O my God, my*

Who were the *Sons of Korah*? (42:title)
See *Sons of Korah* (84:title).

Why are the Psalms divided into books? (42:1)
Ancient scribes collected and organized the psalms into categories—five books in all. The first two books seem to be primarily earlier psalms, written before the Babylonian exile. Others are grouped together because of language similarities, such as *the LORD reigns* or *Praise the LORD*. Others are linked by their titles (*of David*, for example). Still, some seem to have been grouped in an arbitrary manner, perhaps simply as a matter of convenience.

What was the psalmist's problem? (42:3-4)
Most likely he was exiled far from Jerusalem, causing him to mourn the fact that he no longer could lead in worshiping God in the temple. Worse, in a foreign land and surrounded by foreign gods, he felt cut off from the presence of the Lord.

The heights of Hermon . . . Mount Mizar (42:6)
The Jordan River flows from its source, Mount Hermon, north of Israel (see *Map 4* at the back of this Bible). At about 9,100 feet, it is the highest mountain in Syria. Mount Mizar is more difficult to identify. Meaning literally *little mountain*, it was probably a peak near Mount Hermon. Referring to these foreign mountains underscores the writer's exile from Israel.

Deep calls to deep (42:7)
Perhaps this phrase alludes to God's boundless supply: the *deep* above from which water was said to fall into the rivers and seas and the *deep* below. Or it could describe the waters of the upper Jordan spilling down the mountain. In either case it is a picture of water that is potentially destructive (69:1–2). The writer sees God's flood covering him and sweeping him away.

God my rock (42:9)
See *How is God like a rock?* (18:2).

rescue me from deceitful and wicked men.
²You are God my stronghold[D].
  Why have you rejected me?
Why must I go about mourning,
  oppressed by the enemy?
³Send forth your light and your truth,
  let them guide me;
let them bring me to your holy mountain,
  to the place where you dwell.
⁴Then will I go to the altar of God,
  to God, my joy and my delight.
I will praise you with the harp,
  O God, my God.

⁵Why are you downcast, O my soul[D]?
  Why so disturbed within me?
Put your hope in God,
  for I will yet praise him,
  my Savior and my God.

Where was God's holy mountain? (43:3)

The psalmists often refer to Mount Zion as a *holy hill* or *holy mountain* (see 2:6; 3:4; 15:1; 48:2). Mount Zion was the site of the Jerusalem temple, God's dwelling. It was thought that this was the same mountain where God tested Abraham and provided a sacrifice (Gen. 22:13–14).

Psalm 44

For the director of music. Of the Sons of Korah. A *maskil.*[a]

¹We have heard with our ears, O God;
  our fathers have told us
what you did in their days,
  in days long ago.
²With your hand you drove out the nations
  and planted our fathers;
you crushed the peoples
  and made our fathers flourish.
³It was not by their sword that they won the land,
  nor did their arm bring them victory;
it was your right hand, your arm,
  and the light of your face, for you loved them.

SCRIPTURE LINK (44:2) *Drove out the nations*

The Israelite conquest of Canaan is recounted in the book of Joshua.

Your right hand . . . arm . . . face (44:3)

See *Does God have a physical body?* (13:1).

⁴You are my King and my God,
  who decrees[b] victories for Jacob.
⁵Through you we push back our enemies;
  through your name we trample our foes.
⁶I do not trust in my bow,
  my sword does not bring me victory;
⁷but you give us victory over our enemies,
  you put our adversaries to shame.
⁸In God we make our boast all day long,
  and we will praise your name forever.
                                    Selah[D]

⁹But now you have rejected and humbled us;
  you no longer go out with our armies.
¹⁰You made us retreat before the enemy,
  and our adversaries have plundered[D] us.
¹¹You gave us up to be devoured like sheep
  and have scattered us among the nations.
¹²You sold your people for a pittance,
  gaining nothing from their sale.
¹³You have made us a reproach[D] to our
  neighbors,

What made the blessing go sour? (44:9,17)

In the mind of the writer, there doesn't seem to be any reason. From what he could tell, the nation had been faithful to God and consequently deserved God's blessings. So the troubles that had hit his nation confused him. The reality of the situation didn't fit his theology. Still, national disgrace motivated him to pray even when he couldn't understand (vv. 23–26), trusting the God who had helped them in the past.

---

[a]Title: Probably a literary or musical term and Syriac; Hebrew *King, O God;* / command   [b]4 Septuagint, Aquila

the scorn and derision of those around us.
14You have made us a byword[D] among the
    nations;
    the peoples shake their heads at us.
15My disgrace is before me all day long,
    and my face is covered with shame
16at the taunts of those who reproach[D] and
    revile me,
    because of the enemy, who is bent on
    revenge.

17All this happened to us,
    though we had not forgotten you
    or been false to your covenant[D].
18Our hearts had not turned back;
    our feet had not strayed from your path.
19But you crushed us and made us a haunt for
    jackals
    and covered us over with deep darkness.

20If we had forgotten the name of our God
    or spread out our hands to a foreign god,
21would not God have discovered it,
    since he knows the secrets of the heart?
22Yet for your sake we face death[D] all day long;
    we are considered as sheep to be
    slaughtered.

23Awake, O Lord! Why do you sleep?
    Rouse yourself! Do not reject us forever.
24Why do you hide your face
    and forget our misery and oppression?

25We are brought down to the dust;
    our bodies cling to the ground.
26Rise up and help us;
    redeem[D] us because of your unfailing love.

Psalm 45

For the director of music. To ⌊the tune of⌋ "Lilies." Of
  the Sons of Korah. A *maskil.* [a] A wedding song.

1My heart is stirred by a noble theme
    as I recite my verses for the king;
    my tongue is the pen of a skillful writer.

2You are the most excellent of men
    and your lips have been anointed[D] with
    grace[D],
    since God has blessed you forever.
3Gird your sword upon your side, O mighty one;
    clothe yourself with splendor and majesty.
4In your majesty ride forth victoriously
    in behalf of truth, humility and
    righteousness[D];
    let your right hand display awesome deeds.
5Let your sharp arrows pierce the hearts of the
    king's enemies;
    let the nations fall beneath your feet.
6Your throne, O God, will last for ever and ever;
    a scepter[D] of justice will be the scepter of
    your kingdom.
7You love righteousness and hate wickedness;

[a]Title: Probably a literary or musical term

**SCRIPTURE LINK (44:22) We face
death all day long**
Paul quotes this to describe his confidence in
God despite present circumstances. See Romans 8:36.

**Why does God sometimes hide him-
self? (44:24)**
See article: *Does God sometimes hide from
us?* (10:1).

**Why have a poem in the Bible to honor
an earthly ruler? (45:1–17)**
Because it contains additional layers of meaning. It was composed originally to celebrate the
marriage of a king. In Israel, the king symbolized the nation: to celebrate the king was to
celebrate God's people. Later, this psalm took
on a larger meaning, referring not just to the
king—ritually anointed for his office—but to
the Anointed One, the Messiah.

Why call the king God? (45:6–7)
The king was not literally considered to be a
god, but he may have been seen as God's representative, ruling in God's place. David's intimate relationship with God probably set a high
standard of expectation for his ruling descendants. God had declared that David's son
would be his own son when he came to the
throne (2 Samuel 7:14).

**SCRIPTURE LINK (45:6–7) Your
throne, O God, will last for ever and
ever**
Quoted in Heb. 1:8–9 to refer to Christ.

Oil of joy (45:7)

This may speak of the anointing of the king for his duties of office. It may also refer to the fragrant oil people often applied as an expression of joy during a festive occasion. Oil typically was used in grooming; lack of oil was a sign of mourning (2 Samuel 14:2; Isaiah 61:3).

Honored women (45:9)

These women were those in the bridal party and those who were honored guests for the king's wedding.

Gold of Ophir (45:9)

This was thought to be the finest gold (see Isaiah 13:12). The location of Ophir is unknown. Saudi Arabia, East Africa and India have been suggested.

Was this an actual earthquake? (46:2–3)

Perhaps. But Biblical writers often used poetic language, portraying political or social chaos as a shaking of the earth and seas. The image of a trembling earth and sky was also used to describe the final tumult of the *day of the LORD* (Joel 3:14–16).

The city of God (46:4)

Jerusalem, also called Zion. The city was fortified by God's presence.

Is dawn the best time to get God's help? (46:5)

Not necessarily. Attacks generally were launched against cities at dawn, allowing the entire day for the battle to be decided. God's help arrived on time, *at break of day,* just as the battle would have been starting. God's help comes when we need it most.

What international turmoil does this describe? (46:6)

It's impossible to say. There are no clues to identify the specific historical crisis that prompted the writing of this psalm. In general, though, it covers several kinds of conflicts: with nature (vv. 1–3), enemies (vv. 4–7) and the world (vv. 8–11).

Why does God bring *desolations*? (46:8)

To frustrate the instruments of evil and injustice: wars, bows and spears would be broken (v. 9). God would be victorious when human wickedness was defeated. The writer sees sin and evil conquered by the judgment of God: fighting and killing will come to an end when God finally exerts his power. Also see **Why use destruction as an image for God?** (50:3).

therefore God, your God, has set you above
  your companions
by anointing[D] you with the oil of joy.
[8]All your robes are fragrant with myrrh[D] and
  aloes and cassia;
from palaces adorned with ivory
  the music of the strings makes you glad.
[9]Daughters of kings are among your honored
  women;
at your right hand is the royal bride in gold
  of Ophir.

[10]Listen, O daughter, consider and give ear:
  Forget your people and your father's house.
[11]The king is enthralled by your beauty;
  honor him, for he is your lord.
[12]The Daughter of Tyre will come with a gift,[a]
  men of wealth will seek your favor.

[13]All glorious is the princess within ⌊her
  chamber⌋;
  her gown is interwoven with gold.
[14]In embroidered garments she is led to the king;
  her virgin companions follow her
  and are brought to you.
[15]They are led in with joy and gladness;
  they enter the palace of the king.

[16]Your sons will take the place of your fathers;
  you will make them princes throughout the
  land.
[17]I will perpetuate your memory through all
  generations;
therefore the nations will praise you for ever
  and ever.

Psalm 46

For the director of music. Of the Sons of Korah.
According to *alamoth.*[b] A song.

[1]God is our refuge and strength,
  an ever-present help in trouble.
[2]Therefore we will not fear, though the earth
  give way
  and the mountains fall into the heart of the
  sea,
[3]though its waters roar and foam
  and the mountains quake with their surging.
                                              Selah[D]

[4]There is a river whose streams make glad the
  city of God,
  the holy place where the Most High dwells.
[5]God is within her, she will not fall;
  God will help her at break of day.
[6]Nations are in uproar, kingdoms fall;
  he lifts his voice, the earth melts.

[7]The LORD Almighty is with us;
  the God of Jacob is our fortress.   *Selah*

[8]Come and see the works of the LORD,
  the desolations he has brought on the earth.

---

[a]12 Or *A Tyrian robe is among the gifts*   [b]Title: Probably a musical
term

⁹He makes wars cease to the ends of the earth;
　he breaks the bow and shatters the spear,
　he burns the shields*a* with fire.
¹⁰"Be still, and know that I am God;
　I will be exalted among the nations,
　I will be exalted in the earth."
¹¹The Lord Almighty is with us;
　the God of Jacob is our fortress.   *Selah*D

Psalm 47

*For the director of music. Of the Sons of Korah.
A psalm.*

¹Clap your hands, all you nations;
　shout to God with cries of joy.
²How awesome is the Lord Most High,
　the great King over all the earth!
³He subdued nations under us,
　peoples under our feet.
⁴He chose our inheritance for us,
　the pride of Jacob, whom he loved.   *Selah*

⁵God has ascended amid shouts of joy,
　the Lord amid the sounding of trumpets.
⁶Sing praises to God, sing praises;
　sing praises to our King, sing praises.

⁷For God is the King of all the earth;
　sing to him a psalm*b* of praise.
⁸God reigns over the nations;
　God is seated on his holy throne.
⁹The nobles of the nations assemble
　as the people of the God of Abraham,
for the kings*c* of the earth belong to God;
　he is greatly exalted.

Psalm 48

A song. A psalm of the Sons of Korah.

¹Great is the Lord, and most worthy of praise,
　in the city of our God, his holy mountain.
²It is beautiful in its loftiness,
　the joy of the whole earth.
Like the utmost heights of Zaphon*d* is Mount
　Zion D,
　the*e* city of the Great King.
³God is in her citadels D;
　he has shown himself to be her fortress.

⁴When the kings joined forces,
　when they advanced together,
⁵they saw ⌊her⌋ and were astounded;
　they fled in terror.
⁶Trembling seized them there,
　pain like that of a woman in labor.
⁷You destroyed them like ships of Tarshish
　shattered by an east wind.

**How could foreigners be called *people
of the God of Abraham*? (47:9)**
In one sense God, as Creator of all, is the God
of all people. On another level, however, the
psalmist recognized a coming time when all
ethnic groups—*the nations*—would be included in God's covenant with his people.

City of our God (48:1)
See *The city of God* (46:4).

Holy mountain (48:1)
See *Where was God's holy mountain?* (43:3).

Ships of Tarshish (48:7)
This phrase most likely identifies a type of
ship, not the home port. They were large, sea-
worthy ships capable of long voyages. As such,
they symbolized the wealth and power of God's
enemies. *Tarshish* is also thought to be a specific location, possibly in Spain. Some suggest
Tarshish may also refer to the type of cargo
such ships carried, perhaps copper ore.

---

*a*9 Or *chariots*   *b*7 Or *a maskil* (probably a literary or musical
term)   *c*9 Or *shields*   *d*2 *Zaphon* can refer to a sacred mountain
or the direction north.   *e*2 Or *earth, / Mount Zion, on the northern
side / of the*

How *secure* is Jerusalem? (48:8)

Very secure—provided its inhabitants trust in God. God's promise came with a stipulation: As long as their trust was in God, they would be safe. But if they were to rely on anything less or refuse to serve the Lord, their security would evaporate (see Jer. 7:3–15). The wars and turmoil that have stained Jerusalem's history do not disprove God's promise of security; they prove the people's unfaithfulness.

How has God's name and praise reached the ends of the earth? (48:10)

This poetic language describes God's influence and power demonstrated throughout the world, probably through creation. Many have not yet heard the gospel, but they have seen God's handiwork (Romans 1:19–20). Some suggest that the religious tendencies in all cultures throughout the history of humankind, though at times distorted, have shown that God's reality has indeed touched *the ends of the earth.*

Why wasn't the psalmist afraid of powerful and wicked people? (49:5–9)

Because he knew their power was limited. He realized the wicked and their schemes could not last forever. Because he knew God is sovereign and in control, he was confident God would ultimately set things right.

⁸As we have heard,
　　so have we seen
in the city of the Lord Almighty,
　　in the city of our God:
　　God makes her secure forever.　　　*Selah*ᴰ

⁹Within your temple, O God,
　　we meditate on your unfailing love.
¹⁰Like your name, O God,
　　your praise reaches to the ends of the earth;
　　your right hand is filled with righteousnessᴰ.
¹¹Mount Zionᴰ rejoices,
　　the villages of Judah are glad
　　because of your judgments.

¹²Walk about Zion, go around her,
　　count her towers,
¹³consider well her ramparts,
　　view her citadelsᴰ,
　　that you may tell of them to the next
　　　generation.
¹⁴For this God is our God for ever and ever;
　　he will be our guide even to the end.

Psalm 49

For the director of music. Of the Sons of Korah.
A psalm.

¹Hear this, all you peoples;
　　listen, all who live in this world,
²both low and high,
　　rich and poor alike:
³My mouth will speak words of wisdom;
　　the utterance from my heart will give
　　　understanding.
⁴I will turn my ear to a proverb;
　　with the harp I will expound my riddle:

⁵Why should I fear when evil days come,
　　when wicked deceivers surround me—
⁶those who trust in their wealth
　　and boast of their great riches?
⁷No man can redeemᴰ the life of another
　　or give to God a ransom for him—
⁸the ransom for a life is costly,
　　no payment is ever enough—
⁹that he should live on forever
　　and not see decay.

¹⁰For all can see that wise men die;
　　the foolish and the senseless alike perish
　　and leave their wealth to others.
¹¹Their tombs will remain their housesᵃ forever,
　　their dwellings for endless generations,
　　though they hadᵇ named lands after
　　　themselves.

¹²But man, despite his riches, does not endure;
　　he isᶜ like the beasts that perish.

¹³This is the fate of those who trust in
　　themselves,

ᵃ11 Septuagint and Syriac; Hebrew *In their thoughts their houses will remain*　　　ᵇ11 Or *I for they have*　　　ᶜ12 Hebrew; Septuagint and Syriac read verse 12 the same as verse 20.

and of their followers, who approve their
    sayings.   *Selah*[D]

[14]Like sheep they are destined for the grave,[a]
  and death[D] will feed on them.
The upright will rule over them in the morning;
  their forms will decay in the grave,[a]
  far from their princely mansions.
[15]But God will redeem[D] my life[b] from the
    grave;
  he will surely take me to himself.   *Selah*

[16]Do not be overawed when a man grows rich,
  when the splendor of his house increases;
[17]for he will take nothing with him when he
    dies,
  his splendor will not descend with him.
[18]Though while he lived he counted himself
    blessed—
  and men praise you when you prosper—
[19]he will join the generation of his fathers,
  who will never see the light ⌊of life⌋.

[20]A man who has riches without understanding
  is like the beasts that perish.

Psalm 50

A psalm of Asaph.

[1]The Mighty One, God, the LORD,
  speaks and summons the earth
  from the rising of the sun to the place where
    it sets.
[2]From Zion[D], perfect in beauty,
  God shines forth.
[3]Our God comes and will not be silent;
  a fire devours before him,
  and around him a tempest rages.
[4]He summons the heavens above,
  and the earth, that he may judge his people:
[5]"Gather to me my consecrated[D] ones,
  who made a covenant[D] with me by
    sacrifice[D]."
[6]And the heavens proclaim his righteousness[D],
  for God himself is judge.   *Selah*

[7]"Hear, O my people, and I will speak,
  O Israel, and I will testify against you:
  I am God, your God.
[8]I do not rebuke you for your sacrifices
  or your burnt offerings[D], which are ever
    before me.
[9]I have no need of a bull from your stall
  or of goats from your pens,
[10]for every animal of the forest is mine,
  and the cattle on a thousand hills.
[11]I know every bird in the mountains,
  and the creatures of the field are mine.
[12]If I were hungry I would not tell you,
  for the world is mine, and all that is in it.
[13]Do I eat the flesh of bulls
  or drink the blood of goats?
[14]Sacrifice thank offerings to God,

Before Christ, how did people go to God when they died? (49:15)

The Old Testament does not say much about life beyond the grave. Still, certain Old Testament passages see God's eternal nature as an assurance of our immortality. Accordingly, some say this verse speaks of eternal life. Others, however, say it refers to rescue from present trouble—being taken to God could then mean a return to Jerusalem from exile. Also see *You will take me into glory* (73:24).

Light (49:19)

Often used to symbolize God's presence. Darkness, then, can mean banishment from God— the destiny of the wicked.

Why repeat God's name? (50:1)

Repeating words or similar phrases was a common practice in Hebrew poetry called "parallelism." See article: *How should we understand Biblical poetry?* (1:1). It helps the reader to grasp the emotions behind the words. *The Mighty One, God, the LORD* emphasizes God's glory and power, helping us feel a bit of his majesty.

Why use destruction as an image for God? (50:3)

Though images of destruction may be frightening—or even offensive to some—they describe God accurately. True, he is a God of love and mercy; but he is also a God of justice and judgment. Those who suffer because of evil will rejoice when God's judgment finally destroys it. But those who reject God's offer of grace will eventually have to face his wrath. Also see *Why does God bring desolations?* (46:8).

Why did it take a sacrifice to confirm a covenant? (50:5)

Sacrifices demonstrated people's determination to fulfill their vows to God. Paying a price indicated they were in earnest, committed to their promises. They didn't just mouth empty words; they did what it took to turn words into actions. The Old Testament stresses that sinful people could be put into right relationship with God when the blood of an animal was poured out in their behalf. See *How could blood atone for sin?* (Lev. 17:11).

---

[a]14 Hebrew *Sheol*; also in verse 15   [b]15 Or *soul*

Were the wicked trying to force blessings from God? (50:16)

Yes. Many viewed God something like a merchant with whom they could do business. They thought God's covenant promises could be used as bargaining tools to get what they wanted. They reasoned that if they offered sacrifices (which they thought God needed), God would be forced to bless them. But they had forgotten that he was the sovereign Lord of the universe who needed nothing (v. 12). He would not be manipulated.

How did sacrifices *prepare* the way of salvation? (50:23)

Sacrifices brought people to a place where spiritual commitment could be made. Sacrifices, in and of themselves, were physical activities. But something more needed to occur beneath the surface for salvation to take place. Effective sacrifices included a spiritual dimension: sincere, repentant hearts.

SCRIPTURE LINK (51:title)

The story of David's sin with Bathsheba is told in 2 Samuel 11–12.

Why wasn't David put to death for his sin? (51:1)

David was guilty of murder and adultery, both punishable by death according to the law (Exodus 21:23–25; Lev. 20:10). But God's mercy frequently superseded his judgment, even in the Old Testament. Those who sincerely repented of their sin and renewed their trust in God, looking to him for forgiveness, often found the letter of the law set aside. See, for example, Exodus 32:11–14; 2 Chron. 33:10–13; Jer. 18:7–8. Also see *Save me from bloodguilt* (51:14).

Blot out (51:1)

Wipe away, as removing writing from a book (see also Exodus 32:32; Num. 5:23). Ink in ancient times was typically a mixture of water with soot or powdered charcoal. Though it made black writing, it could be easily wiped away with a damp cloth.

fulfill your vows[D] to the Most High,
15and call upon me in the day of trouble;
    I will deliver you, and you will honor me."

16But to the wicked, God says:

"What right have you to recite my laws
    or take my covenant[D] on your lips?
17You hate my instruction
    and cast my words behind you.
18When you see a thief, you join with him;
    you throw in your lot with adulterers.
19You use your mouth for evil
    and harness your tongue to deceit.
20You speak continually against your brother
    and slander your own mother's son.
21These things you have done and I kept silent;
    you thought I was altogether[a] like you.
But I will rebuke you
    and accuse you to your face.

22"Consider this, you who forget God,
    or I will tear you to pieces, with none to rescue:
23He who sacrifices[D] thank offerings[D] honors me,
    and he prepares the way
    so that I may show him[b] the salvation[D] of God."

Psalm 51

For the director of music. A psalm of David. When the prophet[D] Nathan came to him after David had committed adultery with Bathsheba.

1Have mercy[D] on me, O God,
    according to your unfailing love;
according to your great compassion
    blot out my transgressions.
2Wash away all my iniquity
    and cleanse me from my sin.

3For I know my transgressions,

a21 Or thought the 'I AM' was   b23 Or and to him who considers his way / I will show

Does God demand or despise sacrifices? (50:8–15; 40:6)

Almost from the beginning of time, God required sacrifices as an expression of repentance and faith. God did not need sacrifices. Rather, God desired them as a means by which people could worship him. Sacrifices demonstrated obedient, contrite and thankful hearts.

Sacrifices could lose their effectiveness, however, if they were performed merely as empty, religious rituals. God despised such superficial practices. He wanted his people to sacrifice with a sincere heart. He desired an attitude of humility and trust from those who came to him. Anything less would have reduced the covenant between God and his people to mere bargaining. God doesn't want to make a deal with us; he wants to have a relationship with us. See *Why didn't God want David's offerings?* (40:6) and, for a New Testament perspective, *Why are some prayers wrong?* (Matt. 6:7).

and my sin is always before me.
⁴Against you, you only, have I sinned
  and done what is evil in your sight,
 so that you are proved right when you speak
  and justifiedᴰ when you judge.
⁵Surely I was sinful at birth,
  sinful from the time my mother conceived
  me.
⁶Surely you desire truth in the inner parts*a*;
  you teach*b* me wisdom in the inmost place.

⁷Cleanse me with hyssopᴰ, and I will be clean;
  wash me, and I will be whiter than snow.
⁸Let me hear joy and gladness;
  let the bones you have crushed rejoice.
⁹Hide your face from my sins
  and blot out all my iniquity.

¹⁰Create in me a pure heart, O God,
  and renew a steadfast spirit within me.
¹¹Do not cast me from your presence
  or take your Holy Spirit from me.
¹²Restore to me the joy of your salvationᴰ
  and grant me a willing spirit, to sustain me.

¹³Then I will teach transgressors your ways,
  and sinners will turn back to you.
¹⁴Save me from bloodguiltᴰ, O God,
  the God who saves me,
  and my tongue will sing of your
  righteousnessᴰ.
¹⁵O Lord, open my lips,
  and my mouth will declare your praise.
¹⁶You do not delight in sacrificeᴰ, or I would
  bring it;
  you do not take pleasure in burnt offeringsᴰ.
¹⁷The sacrifices of God are*c* a broken spirit;
  a broken and contrite heart,
  O God, you will not despise.

¹⁸In your good pleasure make Zionᴰ prosper;
  build up the walls of Jerusalemᴰ.
¹⁹Then there will be righteousᴰ sacrifices,
  whole burnt offerings to delight you;
  then bulls will be offered on your altar.

Psalm 52

For the director of music. A *maskil*ᵈ of David. When
Doeg the Edomite had gone to Saul and told him:
"David has gone to the house of Ahimelech."

¹Why do you boast of evil, you mighty man?
  Why do you boast all day long,
  you who are a disgrace in the eyes of God?
²Your tongue plots destruction;
  it is like a sharpened razor,
  you who practice deceit.
³You love evil rather than good,
  falsehood rather than speaking the truth.
                                                    *Selah*ᴰ

---

*a*6 The meaning of the Hebrew for this phrase is uncertain.   *b*6 Or
you desired . . . ; / you taught   *c*17 Or *My sacrifice, O God, is*
*d*Title: Probably a literary or musical term

How could David say he had sinned *only* against God? (51:4)

David could not deny that he had sinned against Uriah and Bathsheba (see 2 Samuel 11). But in a figurative sense, victimizing others is a sin against God who created all people in his own image. This was probably poetic exaggeration—a way David could express his intense sorrow for violating God's laws. It underscored what sin—any sin—really is: an offense, first and foremost, against God.

Hyssop (51:7)

A plant that was used for a ritual cleansing ceremony. It was dipped in sacrificial blood which was then brushed or sprinkled on the object or person being cleansed (see Exodus 12:22; Lev. 14:6–7). Here it symbolizes spiritual cleansing from sin.

Save me from bloodguilt (51:14)

Bloodguilt probably meant that the death penalty should have been imposed for David's sins. Most likely this was David's plea for mercy so that he would be spared from vengeance and death.

Why wouldn't sacrifices satisfy the Lord as they once had? (51:16)

See article: *Does God demand or despise sacrifices?* (50:8–15). See also *Why didn't God want David's offerings?* (40:6).

Why pray for Jerusalem's well-being while confessing sin? (51:18)

Some suggest that the welfare of the nation hinged on the welfare of the king. If he was in trouble, the whole country would suffer.

Why promise sacrifices if God cared nothing about them? (51:19)

Though David claimed that God did not delight in sacrifices (v. 16), what God had actually rejected was the empty ritual of insincere sacrifices. Those who offered sacrifices along with genuine repentance would be accepted by the Lord. Now it is Christ's sacrifice that establishes our relationship with God—when we come with a sincere heart in true repentance (Heb. 10:19–22).

SCRIPTURE LINK (52:title)

See 1 Samuel 22:9–19.

4You love every harmful word,
  O you deceitful tongue!

5Surely God will bring you down to everlasting
      ruin:
  He will snatch you up and tear you from
      your tent;
  he will uproot you from the land of the
      living.   *Selah*ᴰ
6The righteousᴰ will see and fear;
  they will laugh at him, saying,
7"Here now is the man
  who did not make God his strongholdᴰ
but trusted in his great wealth
  and grew strong by destroying others!"

8But I am like an olive tree
  flourishing in the house of God;
I trust in God's unfailing love
  for ever and ever.
9I will praise you forever for what you have
      done;
  in your name I will hope, for your name is
      good.
  I will praise you in the presence of your
      saintsᴰ.

Psalm 53

For the director of music. According to *mahalath*.ᵃ A
                    *maskil*ᵇ of David.

1The fool says in his heart,
  "There is no God."
They are corrupt, and their ways are vile;
  there is no one who does good.

2God looks down from heaven
  on the sons of men
to see if there are any who understand,
  any who seek God.
3Everyone has turned away,
  they have together become corrupt;
there is no one who does good,
  not even one.

4Will the evildoers never learn—
  those who devour my people as men eat
      bread
  and who do not call on God?
5There they were, overwhelmed with dread,
  where there was nothing to dread.
God scattered the bones of those who attacked
      you;
  you put them to shame, for God despised
      them.

6Oh, that salvationᴰ for Israel would come out
      of Zionᴰ!
  When God restores the fortunes of his
      people,
  let Jacob rejoice and Israel be glad!

How was David like an olive tree? (52:8)

Ancient Hebrews honored the olive tree as "king of trees" and considered it a symbol of beauty, virility, prosperity and divine blessing. By comparing himself to this splendid tree, David was acknowledging God as the source of his strength and fruitfulness. David, more than a king, was a warrior, singer, poet and a man of God.

SCRIPTURE LINK (53:1–6) *The fool says in his heart*

The same thoughts can be found in 14:1–7.

Why are some verses repeated in Scripture? (53:1–6)

This psalm seems to be a repetition and revision of Psalm 14. One difference—*God* is used in place of Lᴏʀᴅ—leads some to believe this psalm was written a few centuries later, possibly during the reign of Hezekiah. By that time many regarded Yahweh (Lᴏʀᴅ) as more than just the God of Israel. Others, however, wonder if David may have made slight revisions so the psalm could be used for another occasion or with different music. Whatever the reason, the result is that the truth is emphasized. See *Why repeat these verses, almost word for word?* (2 Kings 14:15–16) and *Why is this information repeated?* (Jer. 52:1–24).

Everyone? (53:3)

Yes, everyone. Even those who try to do right and obey God's commands fail sooner or later. Sin has been part of human nature since Adam and Eve. We all turn away from God, since by nature we are corrupt. That's why we need a Savior.

How and when did God restore Israel's fortunes? (53:6)

This is a generic prayer that would fit numerous situations in Israel's history. Some suggest it refers to the time that Israel was restored when the Arameans, hearing the sound of chariots and horses even though there were none, abandoned a siege of Samaria (2 Kings 7:6–7).

ᵃTitle: Probably a musical term   ᵇTitle: Probably a literary or musical term

Psalm 54

For the director of music. With stringed instruments. A *maskil*[a] of David. When the Ziphites had gone to Saul and said, "Is not David hiding among us?"

¹Save me, O God, by your name;
   vindicate me by your might.
²Hear my prayer, O God;
   listen to the words of my mouth.

³Strangers are attacking me;
   ruthless men seek my life—
   men without regard for God.   *Selah*[D]

⁴Surely God is my help;
   the Lord is the one who sustains me.

⁵Let evil recoil on those who slander me;
   in your faithfulness destroy them.

⁶I will sacrifice[D] a freewill offering to you;
   I will praise your name, O LORD,
   for it is good.
⁷For he has delivered me from all my troubles,
   and my eyes have looked in triumph on my
     foes.

Psalm 55

For the director of music. With stringed instruments. A *maskil*[a] of David.

¹Listen to my prayer, O God,
   do not ignore my plea;
² hear me and answer me.
My thoughts trouble me and I am distraught
³ at the voice of the enemy,
   at the stares of the wicked;
for they bring down suffering upon me
   and revile me in their anger.

[a]Title: Probably a literary or musical term

SCRIPTURE LINK (54:title)
See 1 Samuel 23:19–25.

How does faithfulness lead to destruction? (54:5)

God, to be faithful, must maintain truth and carry out justice. If he tolerated sin and allowed the wicked to go unpunished, he would not be faithful. Faithfulness, then, when used to dispense justice, brings about the destruction of the wicked.

Why does David move so quickly from petition to praise? (54:6–7)

Offering praise to God is always right, regardless of the circumstances. Here David calls for help and, in the same breath, declares God as his helper. David was a poet and musician: poetry expressed his feelings, not necessarily his logic; his music could be melancholy (vv. 1–5) or joyful (vv. 6–7). Perhaps he shifted the melodies to indicate these changes.

Why was David so afraid? (55:2–5,11–14)

The specific reason isn't stated, but strife and violence were not unusual during David's time. On this occasion, his fears were not merely due to enemies (v. 3) but to a friend who had turned against him (v. 13). Some have speculated that this psalm alludes to David's adviser, Ahithophel, who joined Absalom's rebellion against David (2 Samuel 15:12).

How does God rescue people? (54:7)

Many psalms, like this one, plead for God's deliverance from a specific problem or threat. Yet these psalms describe God's help in general ways. They state with assurance that God's people can count on him to rescue them. It seems clear that God preserved lessons from specific incidents to teach us larger spiritual truths that can be applied more broadly in many kinds of situations. This psalm, then, promises much more than rescue from the Ziphites (see the title). Even without Ziphites around to harass us, God still rescues his people.

Sometimes God protects us from physical dangers—from human threats (like those David often faced), and from misfortunes such as sickness and accidents. Other times his protection prevents spiritual troubles from overtaking us. Jesus taught his disciples to pray, *Deliver us from the evil one* (Matt. 6:13).

Because God is infinite, he can deliver us in infinite ways, whether the danger is physical or spiritual. God's most important rescue, however, is through the work of Christ on the cross—setting people free from sin and death.

SCRIPTURE LINK (55:4–8) *I would flee far away*
Similar to what David actually experienced in 2 Samuel 15–17.

4My heart is in anguish within me;
  the terrors of death[D] assail me.
5Fear and trembling have beset me;
  horror has overwhelmed me.
6I said, "Oh, that I had the wings of a dove!
  I would fly away and be at rest—
7I would flee far away
  and stay in the desert;   Selah[D]
8I would hurry to my place of shelter,
  far from the tempest and storm."

9Confuse the wicked, O Lord, confound their
    speech,
  for I see violence and strife in the city.
10Day and night they prowl about on its walls;
  malice and abuse are within it.
11Destructive forces are at work in the city;
  threats and lies never leave its streets.

12If an enemy were insulting me,
  I could endure it;
if a foe were raising himself against me,
  I could hide from him.
13But it is you, a man like myself,
  my companion, my close friend,
14with whom I once enjoyed sweet fellowship
  as we walked with the throng at the house of
    God.

Why would David want his enemies buried alive? (55:15)

It's not unusual to wish that someone would be "removed from the scene." But it's probably not accurate to say that David wanted to bury his enemies alive. Death by surprise and going alive to the grave (*Sheol*, see 139:8; Job 26:6), were probably ways of asking for God's judgment to overtake one's enemies. David felt that they deserved an early death.

15Let death take my enemies by surprise;
  let them go down alive to the grave,[a]
  for evil finds lodging among them.

16But I call to God,
  and the LORD saves me.
17Evening, morning and noon
  I cry out in distress,
  and he hears my voice.
18He ransoms me unharmed
  from the battle waged against me,
  even though many oppose me.
19God, who is enthroned forever,
  will hear them and afflict[D] them—   Selah
men who never change their ways
  and have no fear of God.

20My companion attacks his friends;
  he violates his covenant[D].
21His speech is smooth as butter,
  yet war is in his heart;
his words are more soothing than oil,
  yet they are drawn swords.

22Cast your cares on the LORD
  and he will sustain you;
  he will never let the righteous[D] fall.
23But you, O God, will bring down the wicked
  into the pit of corruption;
  bloodthirsty and deceitful men
    will not live out half their days.

But as for me, I trust in you.

Pit of corruption (55:23)

Pits, sinkholes and cisterns were common features of the ancient landscape. David uses the image of a pit as a metaphor for death and the grave (see previous note).

a 15 Hebrew *Sheol*

Psalm 56

For the director of music. To ˌthe tune ofˌ "A Dove on Distant Oaks." Of David. A *miktam.ᵃ* When the Philistines had seized him in Gath.

¹Be merciful to me, O God, for men hotly
    pursue me;
  all day long they press their attack.
²My slanderers pursue me all day long;
  many are attacking me in their pride.

³When I am afraid,
  I will trust in you.
⁴In God, whose word I praise,
  in God I trust; I will not be afraid.
  What can mortal man do to me?

⁵All day long they twist my words;
  they are always plotting to harm me.
⁶They conspire, they lurk,
  they watch my steps,
  eager to take my life.
⁷On no account let them escape;
  in your anger, O God, bring down the
    nations.
⁸Record my lamentᴰ;
  list my tears on your scrollᵇ—
  are they not in your record?

⁹Then my enemies will turn back
  when I call for help.
  By this I will know that God is for me.
¹⁰In God, whose word I praise,
  in the LORD, whose word I praise—
¹¹in God I trust; I will not be afraid.
  What can man do to me?

¹²I am under vowsᴰ to you, O God;
  I will present my thank offeringsᴰ to you.
¹³For you have delivered meᶜ from deathᴰ
  and my feet from stumbling,
  that I may walk before God
  in the light of life.ᵈ

Psalm 57

For the director of music. ˌTo the tune ofˌ "Do Not Destroy." Of David. A *miktam.ᵃ* When he had fled from Saul into the cave.

¹Have mercyᴰ on me, O God, have mercy on
    me,
  for in you my soulᴰ takes refuge.
  I will take refuge in the shadow of your wings
  until the disaster has passed.

²I cry out to God Most High,
  to God, who fulfills ˌhis purposeˌ for me.
³He sends from heaven and saves me,
  rebuking those who hotly pursue me; *Selah*ᴰ
  God sends his love and his faithfulness.

⁴I am in the midst of lions;

SCRIPTURE LINK (56:title)
See 1 Samuel 21:10–15.

What kind of records does God keep? (56:8)
God keeps an account of all the thoughts and deeds of humanity (see Rev. 20:12). God also keeps a record of those who are saved by faith, whose names are in the book of life (69:28; Rev. 3:5; 21:27).

SCRIPTURE LINK (57:title)
See 1 Samuel 22:1.

Shadow of your wings (57:1)
An image of God's protection and care. As a shadow provides relief from the merciless sun, as a bird covers her young in the nest, so God provides a place of refuge. Jesus expressed his concern for the people of Jerusalem in a similar manner: *as a hen gathers her chicks under her wings* (Matt. 23:37).

ᵃTitle: Probably a literary or musical term   ᵇ8 Or *I put my tears in your wineskin*   ᶜ13 Or *my soul*   ᵈ13 Or *the land of the living*

I lie among ravenous beasts—
  men whose teeth are spears and arrows,
  whose tongues are sharp swords.

⁵Be exalted, O God, above the heavens;
  let your glory^D be over all the earth.

⁶They spread a net for my feet—
  I was bowed down in distress.
They dug a pit in my path—
  but they have fallen into it themselves.
                              Selah^D

⁷My heart is steadfast, O God,
  my heart is steadfast;
  I will sing and make music.
⁸Awake, my soul^D!
  Awake, harp and lyre^D!
  I will awaken the dawn.

⁹I will praise you, O Lord, among the nations;
  I will sing of you among the peoples.
¹⁰For great is your love, reaching to the heavens;
  your faithfulness reaches to the skies.

¹¹Be exalted, O God, above the heavens;
  let your glory be over all the earth.

Psalm 58

For the director of music. ⌞To the tune of⌟ "Do Not
    Destroy." Of David. A *miktam.*^a

¹Do you rulers indeed speak justly?
  Do you judge uprightly among men?
²No, in your heart you devise injustice,
  and your hands mete out violence on the
    earth.
³Even from birth the wicked go astray;
  from the womb they are wayward and speak
    lies.
⁴Their venom is like the venom of a snake,
  like that of a cobra that has stopped its ears,
⁵that will not heed the tune of the charmer,
  however skillful the enchanter may be.

⁶Break the teeth in their mouths, O God;
  tear out, O Lᴏʀᴅ, the fangs of the lions!
⁷Let them vanish like water that flows away;
  when they draw the bow, let their arrows be
    blunted.
⁸Like a slug melting away as it moves along,
  like a stillborn child, may they not see the
    sun.

⁹Before your pots can feel ⌞the heat of⌟ the
    thorns—
  whether they be green or dry—the wicked
    will be swept away.^b
¹⁰The righteous^D will be glad when they are
    avenged^D,
  when they bathe their feet in the blood of
    the wicked.
¹¹Then men will say,

What were the unjust rulers doing? (58:1-2)

Most likely, they were distorting justice. Perhaps these were judges or other leaders who had accepted bribes or misused their powers. Whatever they had done, David expressed frustration over his inability to weed out these bureaucrats who were creating havoc. Even though he was king, David couldn't always control the actions of those under him.

Why heat pots with thorns? (58:9)

As a quick-burning fuel, thorns were popular in the ancient world and are still popular among Bedouin Arabs. The immediate heat produced by burning thorns pictured God's even quicker judgment.

Why be glad about a bloodbath? (58:10)

In the ancient world victorious armies seldom hesitated to wreak grisly retribution upon their enemies. But even when they did not, accounts of victory often were exaggerated outrageously. It may be that the psalmist used the same terminology to illustrate how great the joy of the righteous would be when God's justice finally arrived.

^aTitle: Probably a literary or musical term   ^b9 The meaning of the
Hebrew for this verse is uncertain.

"Surely the righteous[D] still are rewarded;
   surely there is a God who judges the earth."

Psalm 59

For the director of music. ⌊To the tune of⌋ "Do Not
Destroy." Of David. A *miktam*.[a] When Saul had sent
men to watch David's house in order to kill him.

1Deliver me from my enemies, O God;
   protect me from those who rise up against
   me.
2Deliver me from evildoers
   and save me from bloodthirsty men.

3See how they lie in wait for me!
   Fierce men conspire against me
   for no offense or sin of mine, O LORD.
4I have done no wrong, yet they are ready to
   attack me.
   Arise to help me; look on my plight!
5O LORD God Almighty, the God of Israel,
   rouse yourself to punish all the nations;
   show no mercy[D] to wicked traitors.   *Selah*[D]

6They return at evening,
   snarling like dogs,
   and prowl about the city.
7See what they spew from their mouths—
   they spew out swords from their lips,
   and they say, "Who can hear us?"

[a]Title: Probably a literary or musical term

SCRIPTURE LINK (59:title)
See 1 Samuel 19:11.

What was David afraid of? (59:2)
He was afraid of losing his life. The title of this
psalm links it to David's narrow escape from
Saul's men—one of several occasions when
Saul tried to have David killed. See 1 Samuel
19:11–13.

Is it right to pray for revenge? (58:6–8)

Several psalms call upon God to take revenge on the enemy. Yet Jesus taught
that we should love our enemies (Matt. 5:44). And the apostle Paul wrote, *Do
not take revenge, my friends, but leave room for God's wrath . . .* (Romans 12:19). How,
then, do we interpret psalms that call a curse on the enemy?

Several points help put this question into perspective:

(1) Cursing the wicked was, for Old Testament saints, more a plea for God's justice
than a cry for personal revenge. Their reasoning: sinners tarnish God's honor when they
cause the innocent to suffer. The writers of the psalms could not tolerate the idea of God
standing by, permitting these wrongs to go unpunished. They begged for his justice and
his wrath to be carried out.

(2) Though David asked God to show no mercy to the wicked (59:5, for example), he
himself showed mercy several times when he could have taken revenge on the guilty: to
Saul (1 Samuel 24:8–13; 26:8–11), to Shimei (2 Samuel 16:5–13) and to Absalom
(2 Samuel 18:5). In those cases, David left the judgment of sinners in the hands of God,
the Judge of the earth (94:2).

(3) The writers of the psalms, though they had the benefit of Old Testament law, had
not experienced the new dimensions that were given through Christ. It's hardly fair to expect Old Testament people to act "Christian" before Christ even came.

No, we should not pray for revenge. Like the psalmists, we must trust God to right the
wrongs of this world. And with Christ's help, we can love and pray for those who mistreat
us.

Was it right for David to gloat? (59:10)

Some think that *gloat* is too strong a word—that David simply meant to *look* or *gaze* triumphantly upon his enemies. Still, it's clear from the context that he meant to look down on his defeated enemies. Others suggest that God's scornful laughter (v. 8; also see 2:4–5; 37:13) and David's gloating are symbolic ways of describing the foolishness and eventual defeat of the wicked.

SCRIPTURE LINK (60:title)

See 2 Samuel 8:13.

How and why had God rejected Israel? (60:1)

The language of this psalm, along with its title, suggests that David was mourning a military setback which he interpreted as God's rejection. David may have felt abandoned by God, but that does not mean he actually was. God rejected Saul as king because Saul had rejected his word (1 Samuel 15:23). But David's defeats were temporary, perhaps because he constantly sought God's favor in prayers such as these.

Why would God raise a banner? (60:4)

Flags and banners were carried into battle to rally the troops and raise their morale. This word picture describes the confidence God could give his people—like a banner *unfurled against the bow*, the bow representing a formidable enemy.

8But you, O Lord, laugh at them;
you scoff at all those nations.

9O my Strength, I watch for you;
you, O God, are my fortress, **10**my loving God.

God will go before me
and will let me gloat over those who slander me.
11But do not kill them, O Lord our shield,[a]
or my people will forget.
In your might make them wander about,
and bring them down.
12For the sins of their mouths,
for the words of their lips,
let them be caught in their pride.
For the curses and lies they utter,
13   consume them in wrath,
consume them till they are no more.
Then it will be known to the ends of the earth
that God rules over Jacob.   *Selah*[D]

14They return at evening,
snarling like dogs,
and prowl about the city.
15They wander about for food
and howl if not satisfied.
16But I will sing of your strength,
in the morning I will sing of your love;
for you are my fortress,
my refuge in times of trouble.

17O my Strength, I sing praise to you;
you, O God, are my fortress, my loving God.

Psalm 60

For the director of music. To ⌊the tune of⌋ "The Lily of the Covenant." A *miktam*[b] of David. For teaching. When he fought Aram Naharaim[c] and Aram Zobah,[d] and when Joab returned and struck down twelve thousand Edomites in the Valley of Salt.

1You have rejected us, O God, and burst forth upon us;
you have been angry—now restore us!
2You have shaken the land and torn it open;
mend its fractures, for it is quaking.
3You have shown your people desperate times;
you have given us wine that makes us stagger.

4But for those who fear you, you have raised a banner
to be unfurled against the bow.   *Selah*

5Save us and help us with your right hand,
that those you love may be delivered.
6God has spoken from his sanctuary:
"In triumph I will parcel out Shechem
and measure off the Valley of Succoth.
7Gilead is mine, and Manasseh is mine;
Ephraim is my helmet,

---

[a]11 Or *sovereign*   [b]Title: Probably a literary or musical term
[c]Title: That is, Arameans of Northwest Mesopotamia   [d]Title: That is, Arameans of central Syria

Judah my scepter[D].

[8]Moab is my washbasin,
  upon Edom[D] I toss my sandal;
  over Philistia I shout in triumph."

[9]Who will bring me to the fortified city?
  Who will lead me to Edom?
[10]Is it not you, O God, you who have rejected us
  and no longer go out with our armies?
[11]Give us aid against the enemy,
  for the help of man is worthless.
[12]With God we will gain the victory,
  and he will trample down our enemies.

Psalm 61

For the director of music. With stringed instruments.
  Of David.

[1]Hear my cry, O God;
  listen to my prayer.

[2]From the ends of the earth I call to you,
  I call as my heart grows faint;
  lead me to the rock that is higher than I.
[3]For you have been my refuge,
  a strong tower against the foe.

[4]I long to dwell in your tent forever
  and take refuge in the shelter of your wings.
                                    Selah[D]
[5]For you have heard my vows[D], O God;
  you have given me the heritage of those who
    fear your name.

[6]Increase the days of the king's life,
  his years for many generations.
[7]May he be enthroned in God's presence
    forever;
  appoint your love and faithfulness to protect
    him.

[8]Then will I ever sing praise to your name
  and fulfill my vows day after day.

Psalm 62

For the director of music. For Jeduthun. A psalm
  of David.

[1]My soul[D] finds rest in God alone;
  my salvation[D] comes from him.
[2]He alone is my rock and my salvation;
  he is my fortress, I will never be shaken.

[3]How long will you assault a man?
  Would all of you throw him down—
  this leaning wall, this tottering fence?
[4]They fully intend to topple him
  from his lofty place;
  they take delight in lies.
With their mouths they bless,
  but in their hearts they curse.   Selah

[5]Find rest, O my soul, in God alone;
  my hope comes from him.
[6]He alone is my rock and my salvation;
  he is my fortress, I will not be shaken.

Did God disdain certain countries? (60:8)

Moab, Edom and Philistia were perpetual enemies on Israel's eastern, southern and western borders (see *David's Victories* on page 407). David's point, however, was not that God despised certain people. Rather it was that God is sovereign over all. In the same way David described Gilead, Manasseh, Ephraim and Judah—all tribes of Israel—as possessions belonging to the Lord. David was saying that God could give them victory because he ruled over all nations and rulers.

Why did David say he was calling from the ends of the earth? (61:2)

He was not referring to a literal place but to his own emotional condition. We might say he was "out in the middle of nowhere" or "at the end of his rope." Many believe David wrote this psalm at Mahanaim, where he had fled during Absalom's rebellion (2 Samuel 17:27), yearning to return to Jerusalem.

Rock . . . higher than I (61:2)

A rock—a cliff or stone bluff—provided a safe place for warriors. They could launch their raids from a rock and retreat back to its safe caves and steep heights. David used this image to describe his need for God's protection and help, at the same time admitting his own weakness and insecurity.

Shelter of your wings (61:4)

See *Shadow of your wings* (57:1).

Rock (62:2)

See *How is God like a rock?* (18:2).

Why did David refer to himself as a leaning wall and a tottering fence? (62:3-6)

Many think David was describing the way his enemies regarded him—either as a young, inexperienced and unstable king or as a tottering, old ruler about to collapse and fall from power. They fully intended to topple him (v. 4). David, however, saw himself standing firm and unshaken on God, his rock (v. 6).

Who was threatening David's position? (62:3-4)

We can't be sure. During his early days, he was challenged for the throne by Ish-Bosheth, Saul's son (2 Samuel 2:8—3:1). When he was much older, his son, Absalom, led an insurrection against him (2 Samuel 15–18).

What kind of lies had David heard? (62:4)

David probably had to put up with two kinds of lies: (1) false information from outside sources —rumors and exaggerations about his enemies and (2) smooth reassurances from so-called supporters who said the right things but inwardly despised his authority.

7My salvation[D] and my honor depend on
        God[a];
    he is my mighty rock, my refuge.
8Trust in him at all times, O people;
    pour out your hearts to him,
    for God is our refuge.   *Selah*[D]

9Lowborn men are but a breath,
    the highborn are but a lie;
if weighed on a balance, they are nothing;
    together they are only a breath.
10Do not trust in extortion[D]
    or take pride in stolen goods;
though your riches increase,
    do not set your heart on them.

11One thing God has spoken,
    two things have I heard:
that you, O God, are strong,
12   and that you, O Lord, are loving.
    Surely you will reward each person
        according to what he has done.

Psalm 63

A psalm of David. When he was in the Desert
        of Judah.

1O God, you are my God,
    earnestly I seek you;
my soul[D] thirsts for you,
    my body longs for you,
in a dry and weary land
    where there is no water.

2I have seen you in the sanctuary
    and beheld your power and your glory[D].
3Because your love is better than life,
    my lips will glorify you.
4I will praise you as long as I live,
    and in your name I will lift up my hands.
5My soul will be satisfied as with the richest
        of foods;
    with singing lips my mouth will praise you.

6On my bed I remember you;
    I think of you through the watches of the
        night.
7Because you are my help,
    I sing in the shadow of your wings.
8My soul clings to you;
    your right hand upholds me.

9They who seek my life will be destroyed;
    they will go down to the depths of the
        earth.
10They will be given over to the sword
    and become food for jackals.

11But the king will rejoice in God;
    all who swear by God's name will praise
        him,
    while the mouths of liars will be silenced.

SCRIPTURE LINK (63:title)
This psalm may have been written when David
fled from Jerusalem during Absalom's rebellion
(2 Samuel 15:23–28).

How is physical thirst like spiritual thirst? (63:1)
David used physical thirst as a metaphor for
spiritual longing. Both are caused by a keenly
felt need. Both, if not quenched, can lead to
death—one physical, the other spiritual. David's spiritual thirst was satisfied by God's
presence in the sanctuary (v. 2), by praising
God (v. 3) and by reflecting on God (vv. 6–7).

Why lift up hands to worship God? (63:4)
From ancient times, upraised hands have revealed both praise and petition. The Hebrews
used their hands to express both their dependence on God and their respect for him.
Lifting their hands symbolized an expectant attitude and trust in God—that he would fill their
empty hands with his blessings. One of the Hebrew words for *praise*, derived from the word
for *hand*, could mean *holding out hands in worship*.

Shadow of your wings (63:7)
See *Shadow of your wings* (57:1).

---

[a]7 Or *I God Most High is my salvation and my honor*

Psalm 64

For the director of music. A psalm of David.

1Hear me, O God, as I voice my complaint;
    protect my life from the threat of the enemy.
2Hide me from the conspiracy of the wicked,
    from that noisy crowd of evildoers.

3They sharpen their tongues like swords
    and aim their words like deadly arrows.
4They shoot from ambush at the innocent man;
    they shoot at him suddenly, without fear.

5They encourage each other in evil plans,
    they talk about hiding their snares;
    they say, "Who will see them*ᵃ*?"
6They plot injustice and say,
    "We have devised a perfect plan!"
    Surely the mind and heart of man are
        cunning.

7But God will shoot them with arrows;
    suddenly they will be struck down.
8He will turn their own tongues against them
    and bring them to ruin;
    all who see them will shake their heads in
        scorn.

9All mankind will fear;
    they will proclaim the works of God
    and ponder what he has done.
10Let the righteousᴰ rejoice in the LORD
    and take refuge in him;
    let all the upright in heart praise him!

Psalm 65

For the director of music. A psalm of David. A song.

1Praise awaitsᵇ you, O God, in Zionᴰ;
    to you our vowsᴰ will be fulfilled.
2O you who hear prayer,
    to you all men will come.
3When we were overwhelmed by sins,
    you forgaveᶜ our transgressions.
4Blessed are those you choose
    and bring near to live in your courts!
    We are filled with the good things of your
        house,
    of your holy temple.

5You answer us with awesome deeds of
        righteousnessᴰ,
    O God our Savior,
    the hope of all the ends of the earth
    and of the farthest seas,
6who formed the mountains by your power,
    having armed yourself with strength,
7who stilled the roaring of the seas,
    the roaring of their waves,
    and the turmoil of the nations.
8Those living far away fear your wonders;

How harmful can words be? (64:3–6)
Extremely harmful—words can kill as surely as bullets. Words can do emotional damage that will impact an entire life. The more prominent one is, as David was, the more criticism there will be. David struggled with detractors throughout his career, so it's difficult to link this psalm to any specific time. Perhaps the most harmful words came from his own son, Absalom (2 Samuel 15:1–6). Eventually those words forced David to flee for his life (2 Samuel 15:13–14; see *David on the Run* on page 388).

Who could live in God's house? (65:4)
Only Levites, those commissioned to care for the temple or serve as priests. But this seems to be speaking in a broader sense, describing the blessings of those who were privileged to come into God's presence.

Why would David talk about the temple when there was no temple during his lifetime? (65:4)
Most scholars feel that David did not write this psalm, despite the credit given to him in the title. Some think the phrase *of David* may have meant *in the manner or style of David*. Others observe that some titles were added years later, after the exile in Babylon, and such additions occasionally may have been inaccurate. Also see *Where was the temple in David's day?* (18:6).

Did non-Jews fear God in the sense of worshiping him? (65:8)
Some may have feared God as the Egyptians did. They recognized his power, but did not submit voluntarily to him (Exodus 8:19). Others may have acknowledged the Lord, but viewed him as just one more god to worship. See article: *Why build a temple for a God you don't worship?* (Ezra 1:1–2). Still others may have worshiped God exclusively, despite cultural pressures to do otherwise (Naaman, for example, 2 Kings 5:17). Also see *If God doesn't show favoritism, why were the Jews the chosen people?* (Romans 2:10–11) and *What happens to good people who never had a chance to hear?* (Romans 2:14–16).

ᵃ5 Or us   ᵇ1 Or befits; the meaning of the Hebrew for this word is uncertain.   *ᶜ3 Or made atonement for*

How can meadows and valleys shout for joy? (65:13)
See *Why describe inanimate objects as rejoicing?* (96:11–13).

where morning dawns and evening fades
　　you call forth songs of joy.
⁹You care for the land and water it;
　　you enrich it abundantly.
The streams of God are filled with water
　　to provide the people with grain,
　　for so you have ordained it. *ᵃ*
¹⁰You drench its furrows
　　and level its ridges;
you soften it with showers
　　and bless its crops.
¹¹You crown the year with your bounty,
　　and your carts overflow with abundance.
¹²The grasslands of the desert overflow;
　　the hills are clothed with gladness.
¹³The meadows are covered with flocks
　　and the valleys are mantled with grain;
　　they shout for joy and sing.

Psalm 66

For the director of music. A song. A psalm.

¹Shout with joy to God, all the earth!
² 　Sing the glory ᴰ of his name;
　　make his praise glorious!
³Say to God, "How awesome are your deeds!
　　So great is your power
　　that your enemies cringe before you.
⁴All the earth bows down to you;
　　they sing praise to you,
　　they sing praise to your name." 　　*Selah* ᴰ

⁵Come and see what God has done,
　　how awesome his works in man's behalf!
⁶He turned the sea into dry land,
　　they passed through the waters on foot—
　　come, let us rejoice in him.
⁷He rules forever by his power,
　　his eyes watch the nations—
　　let not the rebellious rise up against him.
　　　　　　　　　　　　　　　　Selah

SCRIPTURE LINK (66:6) *They passed through the waters on foot*
See Exodus 14:22.

⁸Praise our God, O peoples,
　　let the sound of his praise be heard;
⁹he has preserved our lives
　　and kept our feet from slipping.
¹⁰For you, O God, tested us;
　　you refined us like silver.
¹¹You brought us into prison
　　and laid burdens on our backs.
¹²You let men ride over our heads;
　　we went through fire and water,
　　but you brought us to a place of abundance.

What's good about being tested? (66:10)
Human character and behavior can be refined by difficulties and hardships. As impurities can be drawn out of silver in the fire, flaws in our character can be revealed by testing. God can use the tests we face to continue his spiritual work within. Hardships can also discipline us so that we'll be stronger and better equipped to accomplish God's purposes (Heb. 12:11).

¹³I will come to your temple with burnt offerings ᴰ
　　and fulfill my vows ᴰ to you—
¹⁴vows my lips promised and my mouth spoke
　　when I was in trouble.
¹⁵I will sacrifice ᴰ fat animals to you
　　and an offering of rams;
　　I will offer bulls and goats. 　　*Selah*

What had the psalmist endured? (66:11–12)
It is not known for sure. Some think this was praise offered to God for breaking the Assyrian siege on Jerusalem (2 Kings 19:35–36). Others simply say it describes a king of Judah who was saved from military defeat.

ᵃ9 Or for that is how you prepare the land

¹⁶Come and listen, all you who fear God;
let me tell you what he has done for me.
¹⁷I cried out to him with my mouth;
his praise was on my tongue.
¹⁸If I had cherished sin in my heart,
the Lord would not have listened;
¹⁹but God has surely listened
and heard my voice in prayer.
²⁰Praise be to God,
who has not rejected my prayer
or withheld his love from me!

Psalm 67

For the director of music. With stringed instruments.
A psalm. A song.

¹May God be gracious to us and bless us
and make his face shine upon us,   *Selah*ᴰ
²that your ways may be known on earth,
your salvationᴰ among all nations.

³May the peoples praise you, O God;
may all the peoples praise you.
⁴May the nations be glad and sing for joy,
for you rule the peoples justly
and guide the nations of the earth.   *Selah*
⁵May the peoples praise you, O God;
may all the peoples praise you.

⁶Then the land will yield its harvest,
and God, our God, will bless us.
⁷God will bless us,
and all the ends of the earth will fear him.

Psalm 68

For the director of music. Of David. A psalm. A song.

¹May God arise, may his enemies be scattered;
may his foes flee before him.
²As smoke is blown away by the wind,
may you blow them away;
as wax melts before the fire,
may the wicked perish before God.
³But may the righteousᴰ be glad
and rejoice before God;
may they be happy and joyful.

⁴Sing to God, sing praise to his name,
extolᴰ him who rides on the cloudsᵃ—
his name is the LORD—
and rejoice before him.
⁵A father to the fatherless, a defender of
widows,
is God in his holy dwelling.
⁶God sets the lonely in families,ᵇ
he leads forth the prisoners with singing;
but the rebellious live in a sun-scorched
land.

⁷When you went out before your people, O God,
when you marched through the wasteland,   *Selah*

Does God sometimes ignore the prayers of sinners? (66:18)

See article: *When does God refuse to hear our prayers?* (Jer. 11:11).

How does God's *face shine upon us?* (67:1)

This expression is a picture of God's tender mercies being shown to his people. See 4:6. Also see *What does it mean for God's face to be against someone?* (34:16).

Why would foreign nations worship Israel's God? (67:2)

The writer demonstrates his confidence that foreigners would serve the Lord once they recognized his ways. He displays no petty nationalistic pride. He wants all the people to be blessed by God and enabled to sing for joy to the Lord.

Do poor crops indicate that people have not praised God? (67:5–6)

Poor crops can come for many reasons. We know that the sun shines and the rain falls on both the righteous and the unrighteous (Matt. 5:45). But the writer of this psalm is speaking in general terms—that those who serve the Lord will be more productive and enjoy more blessings.

Him who rides on the clouds (68:4)

Ancient literature frequently speaks of a god with storm clouds for a chariot. The Hebrews seem to have discarded pagan mythology but kept the poetic imagery. To portray the living God in strength and action, the writer pictures him riding the clouds.

ᵃ4 Or *I prepare the way for him who rides through the deserts*
ᵇ6 Or *the desolate in a homeland*

Sinai (68:8)
The mountain where God gave the law to Moses, accompanied by an awesome display of power, perhaps a volcanic eruption (Exodus 19:16–19).

Who or what is God's dove? (68:13)
Perhaps this means the nation of Israel (74:19). Some suggest an allusion here to the Song of Deborah which was sung following a decisive Israelite victory over the Canaanites. Deborah chided the tribe of Reuben for failing to fight, for staying *among the campfires* (Judges 5:16). Here the silver and gold which line the wings of the dove may refer to the wealth of spoils Israel acquired in the battle—even for all those who stayed *among the campfires*. Another view suggests that this may refer to a practice of releasing doves to signal news of a victorious battle.

What did the mountains envy? (68:16)
In poetic language, the writer describes the surrounding mountains being envious of Mount Zion, a rather insignificant hill that God chose for his throne. Also see **Why describe inanimate objects as rejoicing?** (96:11–13).

Does God take hostages? (68:18)
This is a symbolic way of describing a victorious, triumphant God. Just as conquering kings of that era returned to their courts with the spoils of war, God is pictured returning to the courts of heaven following his victories against the enemies of his people. In a more literal sense, Israel enjoyed most of the spoils of the conquest of Canaan. Still, some of the spoils were *devoted . . . to the* LORD (Joshua 6:18–19).

SCRIPTURE LINK (68:18) When you ascended on high
Paul uses this passage to describe Christ's majestic rule and authority over sin. See Eph. 4:8–13.

Why go to Bashan? (68:22)
Bashan was a high, rocky desert area east of the Jordan where the Canaanites would have fled from God's army (see **Conquest of Canaan** on page 231). This expands on the figurative picture of God's victories, in this case the "mopping up" of the scattered resistance—God chasing down Israel's foes and bringing them back to punish them.

Why dip one's feet in the blood of an enemy? (68:23)
Shocking words—but such barbaric actions make a poetic point, not a literal one: God is the overwhelming conqueror. Some suggest that this pictured the end of a war—the stamping of feet to shake off the blood from the battle. Also see **Why be glad about a bloodbath?** (58:10).

Why have a parade to worship God? (68:24–25)
The language here continues to describe God as a triumphant warrior. The victory procession, however, developed into a tangible expression of worship for the Hebrews, who sang psalms as they went in a procession to the temple gates. Some think this may have been connected to the procession that brought the ark to Jerusalem (2 Samuel 6:16).

⁸the earth shook,
 the heavens poured down rain,
before God, the One of Sinai,
 before God, the God of Israel.
⁹You gave abundant showers, O God;
 you refreshed your weary inheritance.
¹⁰Your people settled in it,
 and from your bounty, O God, you provided
  for the poor.

¹¹The Lord announced the word,
 and great was the company of those who
  proclaimed it:
¹²"Kings and armies flee in haste;
 in the camps men divide the plunderᴰ.
¹³Even while you sleep among the campfires,ᵃ
 the wings of ⌐my⌐ dove are sheathed with
  silver,
 its feathers with shining gold."
¹⁴When the Almightyᵇ scattered the kings in the
  land,
 it was like snow fallen on Zalmon.

¹⁵The mountains of Bashan are majestic
  mountains;
 rugged are the mountains of Bashan.
¹⁶Why gaze in envy, O rugged mountains,
 at the mountain where God chooses to reign,
 where the LORD himself will dwell forever?
¹⁷The chariots of God are tens of thousands
 and thousands of thousands;
 the Lord ⌐has come⌐ from Sinai into his
  sanctuary.
¹⁸When you ascended on high,
 you led captives in your train;
 you received gifts from men,
even fromᶜ the rebellious—
 that you,ᵈ O LORD God, might dwell there.

¹⁹Praise be to the Lord, to God our Savior,
 who daily bears our burdens.   *Selah*ᴰ
²⁰Our God is a God who saves;
 from the Sovereign LORD comes escape from
  deathᴰ.

²¹Surely God will crush the heads of his enemies,
 the hairy crowns of those who go on in their
  sins.
²²The Lord says, "I will bring them from Bashan;
 I will bring them from the depths of the sea,
²³that you may plunge your feet in the blood of
  your foes,
 while the tongues of your dogs have their
  share."

²⁴Your procession has come into view, O God,
 the procession of my God and King into the
  sanctuary.
²⁵In front are the singers, after them the
  musicians;
 with them are the maidens playing
  tambourines.
²⁶Praise God in the great congregation;

ᵃ13 Or *saddlebags*   ᵇ14 Hebrew *Shaddai*   ᶜ18 Or *gifts for men,*
/ *even*   ᵈ18 Or *they*

praise the LORD in the assembly of Israel.
²⁷There is the little tribe of Benjamin, leading
   them,
   there the great throng of Judah's princes,
   and there the princes of Zebulun and of
      Naphtali.

²⁸Summon your power, O God^a;
   show us your strength, O God, as you have
      done before.
²⁹Because of your temple at Jerusalem^D
   kings will bring you gifts.
³⁰Rebuke the beast among the reeds,
   the herd of bulls among the calves of the
      nations.
   Humbled, may it bring bars of silver.
   Scatter the nations who delight in war.
³¹Envoys will come from Egypt;
   Cush^b will submit herself to God.

³²Sing to God, O kingdoms of the earth,
   sing praise to the Lord,   *Selah*^D
³³to him who rides the ancient skies above,
   who thunders with mighty voice.
³⁴Proclaim the power of God,
   whose majesty is over Israel,
   whose power is in the skies.
³⁵You are awesome, O God, in your sanctuary;
   the God of Israel gives power and strength to
      his people.

   Praise be to God!

Psalm 69

For the director of music. To ⌊the tune of⌋ "Lilies."
   Of David.

¹Save me, O God,
   for the waters have come up to my neck.
²I sink in the miry depths,
   where there is no foothold.
I have come into the deep waters;
   the floods engulf me.
³I am worn out calling for help;
   my throat is parched.
My eyes fail,
   looking for my God.
⁴Those who hate me without reason
   outnumber the hairs of my head;
many are my enemies without cause,
   those who seek to destroy me.
I am forced to restore
   what I did not steal.

⁵You know my folly, O God;
   my guilt is not hidden from you.

⁶May those who hope in you
   not be disgraced because of me,
   O Lord, the LORD Almighty;
may those who seek you
   not be put to shame because of me,

Beast among the reeds (68:30)
The beast (a crocodile or, perhaps, a hip-
popotamus) probably symbolizes Egypt (v. 31)
or Egypt's leader. The bulls and calves refer to
people of other nations who did not believe in
Israel's God. Curiously, they are not to be
slaughtered but merely rebuked.

**How could David have been so de-
pressed? (69:1–3)**
We don't know what specific problem discouraged David and prompted him to write this
psalm. What we learn from this psalm is that
even God's people will encounter seasons of
doubt. Such feelings are part of the human experience and do not cancel out the reality of
our relationship with God. David could be de-
pressed because he was human. But he could
pray about his depression because he belonged to God.

**What had David done to disgrace
God's people? (69:5–6)**
King David might possibly have composed
these verses after his adulterous affair with
Bathsheba (2 Samuel 11–12). But it is not entirely clear that this psalm was written by David, since some of the psalm titles are of questionable authenticity. See *Why would David
talk about the temple when there was no temple during his lifetime?* (65:4).

^a28 Many Hebrew manuscripts, Septuagint and Syriac; most Hebrew
manuscripts *Your God has summoned power for you*   ^b31 That is,
the upper Nile region

O God of Israel.
7For I endure scorn for your sake,
   and shame covers my face.
8I am a stranger to my brothers,
   an alien[D] to my own mother's sons;
9for zeal[D] for your house consumes me,
   and the insults of those who insult you fall
      on me.
10When I weep and fast,
   I must endure scorn;
11when I put on sackcloth[D],
   people make sport of me.
12Those who sit at the gate mock me,
   and I am the song of the drunkards.

13But I pray to you, O LORD,
   in the time of your favor;
 in your great love, O God,
   answer me with your sure salvation[D].
14Rescue me from the mire,
   do not let me sink;
 deliver me from those who hate me,
   from the deep waters.
15Do not let the floodwaters engulf me
   or the depths swallow me up
   or the pit close its mouth over me.
16Answer me, O LORD, out of the goodness of
      your love;
   in your great mercy[D] turn to me.
17Do not hide your face from your servant;
   answer me quickly, for I am in trouble.
18Come near and rescue me;
   redeem[D] me because of my foes.

19You know how I am scorned, disgraced and
      shamed;
   all my enemies are before you.
20Scorn has broken my heart
   and has left me helpless;
 I looked for sympathy, but there was none,
   for comforters, but I found none.
21They put gall in my food
   and gave me vinegar for my thirst.

22May the table set before them become a snare;
   may it become retribution[D] and[a] a trap.
23May their eyes be darkened so they cannot see,
   and their backs be bent forever.
24Pour out your wrath on them;
   let your fierce anger overtake them.
25May their place be deserted;
   let there be no one to dwell in their tents.
26For they persecute those you wound
   and talk about the pain of those you hurt.
27Charge them with crime upon crime;
   do not let them share in your salvation.
28May they be blotted out of the book of life
   and not be listed with the righteous[D].

29I am in pain and distress;
   may your salvation, O God, protect me.

30I will praise God's name in song
   and glorify him with thanksgiving.

Zeal for your house (69:9)

Describes the writer's enthusiasm and devotion for God. He was willing to do whatever it took to please God, even if it meant that others would ridicule him.

SCRIPTURE LINK (69:9) *Zeal for your house*

This descriptive phrase was linked to Christ in John 2:17.

SCRIPTURE LINK (69:9) *The insults of those who insult you fall on me*

The apostle Paul described Christ with these words in Romans 15:3.

Why would people make fun of the king? (69:10–12)

When a leader blunders, few sympathize. *The song of the drunkards* may be roughly equivalent to political jokes or satire today.

Is it right to pray for revenge? (69:22–28)

See article: *Is it right to pray for revenge?* (58:6–8).

Book of life (69:28)

See *What kind of records does God keep?* (56:8).

---

[a]22 Or *snare / and their fellowship become*

³¹This will please the Lord more than an ox,
 more than a bull with its horns and hoofs.
³²The poor will see and be glad—
 you who seek God, may your hearts live!
³³The Lord hears the needy
 and does not despise his captive people.

³⁴Let heaven and earth praise him,
 the seas and all that move in them,
³⁵for God will save Zion^D
 and rebuild the cities of Judah.
 Then people will settle there and possess it;
³⁶ the children of his servants will inherit it,
 and those who love his name will dwell
 there.

Psalm 70

For the director of music. Of David. A petition.

¹Hasten, O God, to save me;
 O Lord, come quickly to help me.
²May those who seek my life
 be put to shame and confusion;
 may all who desire my ruin
 be turned back in disgrace.
³May those who say to me, "Aha! Aha!"
 turn back because of their shame.
⁴But may all who seek you
 rejoice and be glad in you;
 may those who love your salvation^D always
 say,
 "Let God be exalted!"

⁵Yet I am poor and needy;
 come quickly to me, O God.
 You are my help and my deliverer;
 O Lord, do not delay.

Psalm 71

¹In you, O Lord, I have taken refuge;
 let me never be put to shame.
²Rescue me and deliver me in your
 righteousness^D;
 turn your ear to me and save me.
³Be my rock of refuge,
 to which I can always go;
 give the command to save me,
 for you are my rock and my fortress.
⁴Deliver me, O my God, from the hand of the
 wicked,
 from the grasp of evil and cruel men.

⁵For you have been my hope, O Sovereign Lord,
 my confidence since my youth.
⁶From birth I have relied on you;
 you brought me forth from my mother's
 womb.
 I will ever praise you.
⁷I have become like a portent to many,
 but you are my strong refuge.
⁸My mouth is filled with your praise,
 declaring your splendor all day long.

Why did the cities of Judah need to be rebuilt? (69:35)

This may refer to the situation in Judah after the Babylonian exile, four centuries after David's reign. All of Judah had been decimated by Nebuchadnezzar's armies (2 Kings 25). Some think the writer of this psalm, rather than David, could have been the prophet Jeremiah, who wrote his *Lamentations* in response to Jerusalem's fall. These words seem to predict a time when the Jews would return to Judah to reclaim their inheritance and resettle the land.

Is it okay to ask God to hurry? (70:1,5)

God wants us to be patient and accept his timing, but he understands and is pleased when we call to him for help. Our need for God to help us—and help us right now—demonstrates our vulnerability and God's strength.

What does this psalm say to us if our lives are not in jeopardy? (70:2)

Even though David spoke of literal human enemies, it is valid for us to apply this to other situations, including spiritual struggles. All of life is a battle and our ultimate enemy is Satan himself (Eph. 6:10–20). As long as we live in this evil world, our lives are in jeopardy, even though we may face no physical threat.

Aha! Aha! (70:3)

David quoted the mocking laughter of his enemies who ridiculed him, primarily for his godliness.

In what way was David poor and needy? (70:5)

Though as king of Israel, David was wealthy and famous, he saw through these surface realities and knew that he was spiritually poor and desperately needed the help of the Lord.

Rock of refuge (71:3)

An image of safety and protection. We usually think of a *rock* as something relatively small. The Hebrews, however, could see the term as a huge rock face or cliff—a way to keep enemies at bay. The geography of Israel includes high, rock-faced natural strongholds. No wonder the writer of this psalm sees God, who protects his people, as a *rock of refuge.* Also see *How is God like a rock?* (18:2).

Why do we need deliverance? (71:4)

The writer of this psalm needed help because he was physically threatened by flesh-and-blood enemies. He knew God alone could save him, so he called to him for help. We, too, need deliverance, perhaps occasionally from flesh-and-blood enemies, but always from wickedness and evil. Also see *What does this psalm say to us if our lives are not in jeopardy?* (70:2).

Portent (71:7)

We would more likely say *example* or *witness.* The psalmist saw his troubles as a warning to others, but he was determined to trust in God despite his difficulties.

⁹Do not cast me away when I am old;
    do not forsake me when my strength is
        gone.
¹⁰For my enemies speak against me;
    those who wait to kill me conspire together.
¹¹They say, "God has forsaken him;
    pursue him and seize him,
    for no one will rescue him."
¹²Be not far from me, O God;
    come quickly, O my God, to help me.
¹³May my accusers perish in shame;
    may those who want to harm me
    be covered with scorn and disgrace.

¹⁴But as for me, I will always have hope;
    I will praise you more and more.
¹⁵My mouth will tell of your righteousnessᴰ,
    of your salvationᴰ all day long,
    though I know not its measure.
¹⁶I will come and proclaim your mighty acts,
    O Sovereign LORD;
    I will proclaim your righteousness, yours
        alone.
¹⁷Since my youth, O God, you have taught me,
    and to this day I declare your marvelous
        deeds.
¹⁸Even when I am old and gray,
    do not forsake me, O God,
    till I declare your power to the next generation,
    your might to all who are to come.

¹⁹Your righteousness reaches to the skies,
    O God,
    you who have done great things.
    Who, O God, is like you?
²⁰Though you have made me see troubles, many
        and bitter,
    you will restore my life again;
    from the depths of the earth
    you will again bring me up.

What did the psalmist know about salvation? (71:15)

He knew much about salvation—primarily physical, but also spiritual. There is no question that he was thinking here first of physical salvation. He recalled many times in his own past when God had rescued him from physical danger. Furthermore, he knew history well: God had rescued his people from great physical dangers. The Old Testament writers also knew about God's salvation from sin and guilt (Psalm 51), although that is not the primary focus of this psalm.

Why ask God to remain faithful? (71:9–18)

On one level, it is totally unnecessary to call on God to remain faithful. He is faithful to all of his promises. There is no chance that God will forsake his people.

However, our circumstances do not always seem to conform to this truth. We see evil in the world and trouble in our own lives and we wonder, *Is God truly with us?*

The writer of this psalm had had confidence in God from his youth (vv. 5–6), but now that he had grown old he was worried because his enemies had sensed his weakness and had closed in on him. Their assessment was that God had forsaken him in his old age.

From this perspective—pouring out his honest emotions—the psalmist called on God to protect him. He asked God to remember his promise not to forsake him. He also asked the Lord to punish those who were persecuting him. But not only did he appeal to God's promise; he also made one of his own: If God would rescue him, then he would tell the next generation about God's power (v. 18).

The writer was confident the Lord would save him. He repeatedly expressed this firm conviction (vv. 14–17, 19–21) and concluded his prayer with a song of praise (vv. 22–24).

²¹You will increase my honor
    and comfort me once again.

²²I will praise you with the harp
    for your faithfulness, O my God;
  I will sing praise to you with the lyre^D,
    O Holy One of Israel.
²³My lips will shout for joy
    when I sing praise to you—
  I, whom you have redeemed^D.
²⁴My tongue will tell of your righteous^D acts
    all day long,
  for those who wanted to harm me
    have been put to shame and confusion.

Psalm 72

Of Solomon.

¹Endow the king with your justice, O God,
    the royal son with your righteousness^D.
²He will^a judge your people in righteousness,
    your afflicted^D ones with justice.
³The mountains will bring prosperity to the
        people,
    the hills the fruit of righteousness.
⁴He will defend the afflicted among the people
    and save the children of the needy;
  he will crush the oppressor.

⁵He will endure^b as long as the sun,
    as long as the moon, through all generations.
⁶He will be like rain falling on a mown field,
    like showers watering the earth.
⁷In his days the righteous will flourish;
    prosperity will abound till the moon is no
        more.

---

^a2 Or *May he*; similarly in verses 3-11 and 17   ^b5 Septuagint;
Hebrew *You will be feared*

Of Solomon (72:title)

It is not known for sure what *of* means in the
psalm titles. Was this poem about Solomon?
Or was he the author? It would appear here
that Solomon was both the author and the subject of this prayer of dedication. (Compare the
use of *of* in 18:title; Hab. 3:1.)

**Why would Solomon brag about him-
self? (72:5)**

This language is poetic, so we can expect
some exaggeration—a figure of speech known
as *hyperbole*. But Solomon has high hopes
rooted in God's promise to David—a promise
of a dynasty that would last forever (1 Samuel
7). The strong language of this psalm, echoing
what God had said, pointed beyond Israel's human kings to the divine king, the Messiah, also
known as a son of David (Romans 1:3).

Does God send troubles? (71:20)

We have trouble in the world and in our lives because of humanity's sinful nature. The book of Job, however, shows that troubles do not necessarily
come in direct proportion to our sin. Troubles may come when someone else sins against
us—not always because we have committed a particular sin.

In this psalm the writer looks back on his life and admits that God has allowed him to
experience some bitter troubles. Though God is not the cause or origin of evil in the
world, he is more than a passive observer. God sometimes *permits* trouble in people's
lives. Other times he seems to deliberately bring people to a place where they will experience difficulties.

God may have many reasons for allowing the godly to experience suffering, such as
(1) to lead someone away from sin and closer to him (Heb. 12:4–13), (2) to build up a
person's character (James 1:2–8) or (3) to provide a means to glorify God (John 9:1–5).

Then again, there is the lesson of Job: explanations cannot always be found. At times
we may not understand why God allows us to experience troubles, but even without answers it is good to say with the psalmist, *You will restore my life again . . . you will again
bring me up.*

Desert tribes (72:9)

Most likely peoples who lived near Israel—perhaps nomadic Bedouin tribes that were not part of any particular nation. These tribes would often harass settled nations like Israel that lived in areas with better resources.

Kings of Tarshish . . . Sheba and Seba (72:10)

Nations far from Israel. Tarshish may be Iberia, modern Spain, known also for its massive ocean-going ships. Sheba is far to the south (often identified with modern Yemen). Sheba's queen once visited Solomon, the probable writer of this psalm (1 Kings 10:1–3). Seba is variously located near Sheba or in north Africa (see **Map 12** at the back of this Bible).

Prayers of David son of Jesse (72:20)

Over several centuries, before the sequence of the psalms was finalized, the book of Psalms underwent many editorial changes. Most think this verse did indeed conclude the Davidic collection at one time. But then, as other psalms were added, it was dislodged from its place. This verse does not mean David wrote all the psalms up to this point (see, for instance, 42–50). Furthermore, some later psalms (138–145) are credited to David.

Asaph (73:title)

Asaph was the worship music leader, a Levite appointed by King David (1 Chron. 16:4–6). He apparently composed songs as well; 12 psalms are ascribed to him (50; 73–83). Some think the Asaph of David's time wrote all 12. Others think perhaps a later Asaph who lived during the time of the Babylonian exile wrote some of them. Still others say that *Asaph* in a psalm title is a "guild name"—so that the credit goes to a group of musicians. Asaph's descendants (either biological or professional—we cannot be sure) were still involved with holy music after the Jews returned from exile (Ezra 3:10).

⁸He will rule from sea to sea
and from the River*ᵃ* to the ends of the earth.*ᵇ*
⁹The desert tribes will bow before him
and his enemies will lick the dust.
¹⁰The kings of Tarshish and of distant shores
will bring tribute to him;
the kings of Sheba and Seba
will present him gifts.
¹¹All kings will bow down to him
and all nations will serve him.

¹²For he will deliver the needy who cry out,
the afflicted*ᴅ* who have no one to help.
¹³He will take pity on the weak and the needy
and save the needy from death*ᴅ*.
¹⁴He will rescue them from oppression and violence,
for precious is their blood in his sight.

¹⁵Long may he live!
May gold from Sheba be given him.
May people ever pray for him
and bless him all day long.
¹⁶Let grain abound throughout the land;
on the tops of the hills may it sway.
Let its fruit flourish like Lebanon;
let it thrive like the grass of the field.
¹⁷May his name endure forever;
may it continue as long as the sun.

All nations will be blessed through him,
and they will call him blessed.

¹⁸Praise be to the Lᴏʀᴅ God, the God of Israel,
who alone does marvelous deeds.
¹⁹Praise be to his glorious name forever;
may the whole earth be filled with his glory*ᴅ*.
Amen and Amen.

²⁰This concludes the prayers of David son of Jesse.

BOOK III
Psalms 73–89

Psalm 73

A psalm of Asaph.

¹Surely God is good to Israel,
to those who are pure in heart.

²But as for me, my feet had almost slipped;
I had nearly lost my foothold.
³For I envied the arrogant
when I saw the prosperity of the wicked.

⁴They have no struggles;
their bodies are healthy and strong.*ᶜ*

ᵃ8 That is, the Euphrates   *ᵇ8* Or *the end of the land*   *ᶜ4* With a different word division of the Hebrew; Masoretic Text *struggles at their death; / their bodies are healthy*

⁵They are free from the burdens common to
　　man;
　　they are not plagued by human ills.
⁶Therefore pride is their necklace;
　　they clothe themselves with violence.
⁷From their callous hearts comes iniquity*ᵃ;
　　the evil conceits of their minds know no
　　limits.
⁸They scoff, and speak with malice;
　　in their arrogance they threaten oppression.
⁹Their mouths lay claim to heaven,
　　and their tongues take possession of the
　　earth.
¹⁰Therefore their people turn to them
　　and drink up waters in abundance.ᵇ
¹¹They say, "How can God know?
　　Does the Most High have knowledge?"

¹²This is what the wicked are like—
　　always carefree, they increase in wealth.

¹³Surely in vain have I kept my heart pure;
　　in vain have I washed my hands in
　　innocence.
¹⁴All day long I have been plagued;
　　I have been punished every morning.

¹⁵If I had said, "I will speak thus,"
　　I would have betrayed your children.
¹⁶When I tried to understand all this,
　　it was oppressive to me
¹⁷till I entered the sanctuary of God;
　　then I understood their final destiny.

¹⁸Surely you place them on slippery ground;
　　you cast them down to ruin.
¹⁹How suddenly are they destroyed,

ᵃ7 Syriac (see also Septuagint); Hebrew *Their eyes bulge with fat*
ᵇ10 The meaning of the Hebrew for this verse is uncertain.

Their people (73:10)
The context of this verse describes the riches
and arrogance of the wicked. The psalmist
seems to be saying that the wicked have a following of people who crowd around them to
drink from their wealth and prosperity—pictured by the phrase, *waters in abundance*.

Why be good? (73:13)
Because there's more to life than meets the
eye. A righteous life does not guarantee
health, wealth and earthly pleasures. Nor do
such things give a life meaning and purpose.
The reason for being good is not found in this
world. The meaning of life and the source of
true happiness are found only in God.

What does worship teach us? (73:17)
Worship allows us to meet with God. When we
have an encounter with God, our perspective
changes. When the psalmist came into God's
presence, he suddenly saw things from an
eternal perspective. He discovered that bringing his grievances to God while submitting to
him in worship can clarify life's issues and
point to spiritual realities.

Why does life seem unfair? (73:3–5)

Because we see only one part of the picture. It appears to us that success often
has nothing to do with godliness: Those who ignore or even hate God may
have more wealth and power than those who love him. Many Christians suffer while non-
Christians seem relatively unaffected by life's difficulties.

The writer of this psalm struggled with such feelings. He saw arrogant, violent individuals who lived in ease and prosperity (vv. 3–12). What he saw even caused him to question the validity of his own faith (v. 2). He felt cheated. Why try to live right? It never
seemed to pay off in tangible ways (v. 13).

But when he finally sat down to write, he wrote about how his attitude had changed.
What had happened?

He had begun to look at life from a spiritual point of view rather than from a worldly
one (v. 17). Life will always seem unfair when we measure it by earthly standards of
health, wealth and power. But when we encounter God in a personal, intimate way—as
the psalmist did in the sanctuary—we can gain a heavenly perspective. We'll begin to see
the other part of the picture—that the rewards of this life are temporary and, as a matter
of fact, can even hinder us from discovering what is really important.

How was the writer senseless and ignorant? (73:22)

He had complained about the apparent success of the arrogant and rich (vv. 4–12). Jealousy had consumed him as he saw them prosper. Once he saw things from God's perspective, though, he realized how far off the mark he had been. He described his earlier inability to understand by comparing himself to a *brute beast*—a dumb animal with no spiritual sensitivity or insight.

You will take me into glory (73:24)

The Hebrew word for *glory* may refer simply to the climax of God's blessing—often meaning earthly authority and fame. Nonetheless, the context here supports the view that the writer meant *eternal* glory, that is, heaven (vv. 25–26). Also see *Before Christ, how did people go to God when they died?* (49:15).

Asaph (74:title)

See *Asaph* (73:title).

SCRIPTURE LINK (74:3–8) *All this destruction the enemy has brought*

The Babylonians conquered Jerusalem (586 B.C.) and ransacked the temple. To the writer, these were signs that God had abandoned his people because of their sins. See 2 Kings 25.

Where had all the prophets gone? (74:9)

It seemed that God had stopped speaking. Prophet after prophet had warned the people to turn away from false gods and turn back to the Lord—or they would be destroyed. Once judgment came, though, God was silent. Technically, we know there were still prophets— Ezekiel, Jeremiah and Daniel, for instance. But this psalm may have been composed from the perspective of one still on the scene, surveying the ruins. Any remaining prophets would have been taken away to foreign lands.

completely swept away by terrors!
20As a dream when one awakes,
    so when you arise, O Lord,
    you will despise them as fantasies.

21When my heart was grieved
    and my spirit embittered,
22I was senseless and ignorant;
    I was a brute beast before you.

23Yet I am always with you;
    you hold me by my right hand.
24You guide me with your counsel,
    and afterward you will take me into glory.D
25Whom have I in heaven but you?
    And earth has nothing I desire besides you.
26My flesh and my heart may fail,
    but God is the strength of my heart
    and my portion forever.

27Those who are far from you will perish;
    you destroy all who are unfaithful to you.
28But as for me, it is good to be near God.
    I have made the Sovereign LORD my refuge;
    I will tell of all your deeds.

Psalm 74

A maskila of Asaph.

1Why have you rejected us forever, O God?
    Why does your anger smolder against the
      sheep of your pasture?
2Remember the people you purchased of old,
    the tribe of your inheritance, whom you
      redeemedD—
    Mount ZionD, where you dwelt.
3Turn your steps toward these everlasting ruins,
    all this destruction the enemy has brought
      on the sanctuary.

4Your foes roared in the place where you met
      with us;
    they set up their standards as signs.
5They behaved like men wielding axes
    to cut through a thicket of trees.
6They smashed all the carved paneling
    with their axes and hatchets.
7They burned your sanctuary to the ground;
    they defiled the dwelling place of your Name.
8They said in their hearts, "We will crush them
      completely!"
    They burned every place where God was
      worshiped in the land.
9We are given no miraculous signs;
    no prophetsD are left,
    and none of us knows how long this will be.

10How long will the enemy mock you, O God?
    Will the foe revile your name forever?
11Why do you hold back your hand, your right
      hand?
    Take it from the folds of your garment and
      destroy them!

aTitle: Probably a literary or musical term

¹²But you, O God, are my king from of old;
    you bring salvation^D upon the earth.
¹³It was you who split open the sea by your
        power;
    you broke the heads of the monster in the
        waters.
¹⁴It was you who crushed the heads of
        Leviathan^D
    and gave him as food to the creatures of the
        desert.
¹⁵It was you who opened up springs and
        streams;
    you dried up the ever flowing rivers.
¹⁶The day is yours, and yours also the night;
    you established the sun and moon.
¹⁷It was you who set all the boundaries of the
        earth;
    you made both summer and winter.

¹⁸Remember how the enemy has mocked you,
        O LORD,
    how foolish people have reviled your name.
¹⁹Do not hand over the life of your dove to wild
        beasts;
    do not forget the lives of your afflicted^D
        people forever.
²⁰Have regard for your covenant^D,
    because haunts of violence fill the dark
        places of the land.
²¹Do not let the oppressed retreat in disgrace;
    may the poor and needy praise your name.

²²Rise up, O God, and defend your cause;
    remember how fools mock you all day long.
²³Do not ignore the clamor of your adversaries,
    the uproar of your enemies, which rises
        continually.

Psalm 75

For the director of music. ⌊To the tune of⌋ "Do Not
    Destroy." A psalm of Asaph. A song.

¹We give thanks to you, O God,
    we give thanks, for your Name is near;
    men tell of your wonderful deeds.

²You say, "I choose the appointed time;
    it is I who judge uprightly.
³When the earth and all its people quake,
    it is I who hold its pillars firm.   Selah^D
⁴To the arrogant I say, 'Boast no more,'
    and to the wicked, 'Do not lift up your
        horns.
⁵Do not lift up your horns against heaven;
    do not speak with outstretched neck.' "

⁶No one from the east or the west
    or from the desert can exalt a man.
⁷But it is God who judges:
    He brings one down, he exalts another.
⁸In the hand of the LORD is a cup
    full of foaming wine mixed with spices;
he pours it out, and all the wicked of the earth
    drink it down to its very dregs^D.

SCRIPTURE LINK (74:13) *Split open the sea*
God divided the waters of the Red Sea. See Exodus 14:21.

Why did God break the heads of sea monsters? (74:13–14)
This poetic language borrows images from the ancient mythology of Israel's neighbors. They believed that their gods (Marduk in Mesopotamia, Baal in Canaan) defeated the sea and created the universe by splitting it into the heavens and the earth. The psalmist did not believe these stories. He merely used familiar traditions to make a strong statement: the God of Israel is Creator—not mythical gods.

What did the writer want from God? (74:20–23)
Upset to see haughty pagans demolishing Jerusalem and the temple, he wanted the enemies put out so God's reputation would be protected. Though he knew that unrepented sin leads inevitably to judgment, he couldn't understand why God allowed his own name to be tarnished. Perhaps he hoped God's promise of a returning remnant would be the means to turn the tide—and he prayed that it would quickly happen.

Haunts of violence (74:20)
The land of Israel is peppered with caves. When law and order had broken down because there was no strong government, robbers and other criminals would use these caves as hideouts, launching their acts of violence from them.

The appointed time (75:2)
A time when God will judge evil. The writer of this psalm had seen the arrogant boasting of the wicked (vv. 4–5) and writes to exalt the ultimate judge of all—the Lord God (v. 7).

Horns (75:4)
See *Horn* (112:9).

Outstretched neck (75:5)
This is an image of the arrogance of the wicked. The writer describes them as a bull that proudly stretches out its neck and lifts its horns in a menacing way.

Foaming wine mixed with spices (75:8)
This describes a very strong drink. This image is found in several psalms and prophets (for example, 60:3; Isaiah 51:17); it is often called the cup of God's wrath. It may taste good initially, but those who drink it are soon intoxicated.

Why would anyone sing a song like this? (75:10)

The writer of this psalm wanted to see the wicked removed from power. This was his cry for justice, a call for God to judge the wicked and reward the righteous. Though the psalmist may sound vindictive, there's no need to apologize for a song of justice. See article: *Is it right to pray for revenge?* (58:6–8).

Salem (76:2)

Salem is the short name for the city of Jerusalem. The verse refers to God's sanctuary in Jerusalem where God had made his presence known to his people.

Why did the writer praise God? (76:3–4)

He was celebrating a great military victory over Israel's enemies. It was obvious to him that the Lord won the battle on Israel's behalf. We do not know which of Israel's many victories inspired this psalm. It probably was written generically so it could be used after any victory.

How does God's wrath bring him praise? (76:10)

He is praised because he is a just and holy God who will not tolerate the ungodly who oppress his people. God's wrath is directed toward unrepentant sinners—in this case, the enemies of his people. God's victory is accomplished by his wrath, which, in turn, saves his people. His people, then, praise him for their rescue.

Asaph (77:title)

See *Asaph* (73:title).

Why read this psalm if we're not in distress? (77:2)

Because life is full of ups and downs. Eventually, distress of some sort comes to everyone—whether personal, family, community or global. This psalm can help us anticipate times of trouble as well as articulate our current anxieties and fears. If we can't identify with the writer at least we can learn from him.

⁹As for me, I will declare this forever;
　I will sing praise to the God of Jacob.
¹⁰I will cut off the horns of all the wicked,
　but the horns of the righteousᴰ will be lifted up.

Psalm 76

For the director of music. With stringed instruments.
A psalm of Asaph. A song.

¹In Judah God is known;
　his name is great in Israel.
²His tent is in Salem,
　his dwelling place in Zionᴰ.
³There he broke the flashing arrows,
　the shields and the swords, the weapons of war.　　*Selah*ᴰ
⁴You are resplendent with light,
　more majestic than mountains rich with game.
⁵Valiant men lie plunderedᴰ,
　they sleep their last sleep;
not one of the warriors
　can lift his hands.
⁶At your rebuke, O God of Jacob,
　both horse and chariot lie still.
⁷You alone are to be feared.
　Who can stand before you when you are angry?
⁸From heaven you pronounced judgment,
　and the land feared and was quiet—
⁹when you, O God, rose up to judge,
　to save all the afflictedᴰ of the land.　　*Selah*
¹⁰Surely your wrath against men brings you praise,
　and the survivors of your wrath are restrained.ᵃ

¹¹Make vowsᴰ to the Lᴏʀᴅ your God and fulfill them;
　let all the neighboring lands
　bring gifts to the One to be feared.
¹²He breaks the spirit of rulers;
　he is feared by the kings of the earth.

Psalm 77

For the director of music. For Jeduthun. Of Asaph.
A psalm.

¹I cried out to God for help;
　I cried out to God to hear me.
²When I was in distress, I sought the Lord;
　at night I stretched out untiring hands
　and my soulᴰ refused to be comforted.

³I remembered you, O God, and I groaned;
　I mused, and my spirit grew faint.　　*Selah*
⁴You kept my eyes from closing;
　I was too troubled to speak.
⁵I thought about the former days,
　the years of long ago;

ᵃ10 Or *Surely the wrath of men brings you praise, / and with the remainder of wrath you arm yourself*

⁶I remembered my songs in the night.
My heart mused and my spirit inquired:

⁷"Will the Lord reject forever?
Will he never show his favor again?
⁸Has his unfailing love vanished forever?
Has his promise failed for all time?
⁹Has God forgotten to be merciful?
Has he in anger withheld his compassion?"
*Selah*D

¹⁰Then I thought, "To this I will appeal:
the years of the right hand of the Most
High."
¹¹I will remember the deeds of the LORD;
yes, I will remember your miracles of long
ago.
¹²I will meditate on all your works
and consider all your mighty deeds.

¹³Your ways, O God, are holy.
What god is so great as our God?
¹⁴You are the God who performs miracles;
you display your power among the peoples.
¹⁵With your mighty arm you redeemedD your
people,
the descendants of Jacob and Joseph.   *Selah*

¹⁶The waters saw you, O God,
the waters saw you and writhed;
the very depths were convulsed.
¹⁷The clouds poured down water,
the skies resounded with thunder;
your arrows flashed back and forth.
¹⁸Your thunder was heard in the whirlwind,
your lightning lit up the world;
the earth trembled and quaked.
¹⁹Your path led through the sea,
your way through the mighty waters,
though your footprints were not seen.
²⁰You led your people like a flock
by the hand of Moses and Aaron.

The years of the right hand of the Most High (77:10)

This was a picture of God's power to save his people (Exodus 15:6). The *right hand* was typically considered the hand of strength, authority and honor. Apparently the writer of this psalm, while reciting his troubles, suddenly remembered how God had saved and protected his people in the past. The past years, then, could serve as evidence that God protects his people. So the psalmist determined to view his present difficulties by appealing to the testimony of the past. If God helped before, why not now?

SCRIPTURE LINK (77:19) *Your path led through the sea*

God took his people through the Red Sea. See Exodus 14:21–22.

Isn't meditation used by some other religions? (77:12)

Many other religions practice meditation. Is it risky to do what they do? Not necessarily. Meditation is merely a tool—neither good nor bad. The tool becomes bad only when it's used in the wrong way.

Simply put, meditation is focused, repetitive thinking. When people meditate, they concentrate on a single subject, blocking out distractions. So how can focused thinking be bad or good? In the same way worship can be good (if it's directed to God) or bad (if to idols). Meditation can center on the things of God or the things of evil.

It's good to meditate if we do it as the psalmist did. He determined that he would meditate on the works of God—he would focus on God's miracles and displays of power.

Meditation accomplished something wonderful for him. Though at first he was absorbed by his problems and anxieties, he was able to turn his attitude around. He went from complaining to praise simply by focusing on God's past mighty works. He gained faith and insight to deal with his troubles because of a proper use of meditation. See article: *How does a person meditate on God's Word?* (119:15).

What is a parable? (78:2)

A *parable* in this context means history with important practical applications. In other words, the psalms, though they frequently describe the great events of the past, do so to honor God and to show us how to live in the present. Matthew refers to this verse to describe Jesus' teaching in parables (Matt. 13:35).

Did the law teach trust in God? (78:5–7)

The law came with certain consequences: blessings for obedience and curses for disobedience (Deut. 28). As generation after generation saw that God was true to his word, that he brought good things to those who obeyed and troubles to those who did not, they could see he was a God they could rely on.

How had Ephraim lacked courage? (78:9–10)

Ephraim lacked courage in battle. Though the psalm is not specific about which battle or why they lacked courage, we can guess from later allusions (vv. 56–64) that this may have referred to the battles that took place during the final days of the judges, which resulted in the loss of the ark to the Philistines (1 Samuel 4:10–11).

Region of Zoan (78:12)

Zoan was a city in Egypt (Num. 13:22), where God did miracles that led to Israel's release from bondage (v. 13). The exact location and identification of the city is disputed, though the Septuagint, the ancient Greek translation of the Old Testament, translated it *Tanis,* a city on the Nile delta (see *Map 1* at the back of this Bible).

SCRIPTURE LINK (78:13–16) *He divided the sea and led them through*

God brought his people out of Egypt and miraculously provided for their needs in the desert. See Exodus 13:21; 14:21–22; Num. 20:11.

SCRIPTURE LINK (78:17) *Rebelling in the desert*

Israel rebelled repeatedly after God brought them out of Egypt. See Exodus 15:24; 17:2; Num. 11:4; 21:5.

What does it mean to *put God to the test?* (78:18)

It implies a lack of trust in God's goodness or his power. The people of Israel tested God during their desert wanderings by challenging him to meet their demands. They seemed to be threatening that if he did not satisfy their ultimatum, they would not believe in his ability or willingness to help them.

SCRIPTURE LINK (78:21) *Fire broke out*

See Num. 11:1.

Psalm 78

A *maskil*[a] of Asaph.

¹O my people, hear my teaching;
  listen to the words of my mouth.
²I will open my mouth in parables[D],
  I will utter hidden things, things from of
    old—
³what we have heard and known,
  what our fathers have told us.
⁴We will not hide them from their children;
  we will tell the next generation
the praiseworthy deeds of the LORD,
  his power, and the wonders he has done.
⁵He decreed statutes for Jacob
  and established the law in Israel,
which he commanded our forefathers
  to teach their children,
⁶so the next generation would know them,
  even the children yet to be born,
  and they in turn would tell their children.
⁷Then they would put their trust in God
  and would not forget his deeds
  but would keep his commands.
⁸They would not be like their forefathers—
  a stubborn and rebellious generation,
whose hearts were not loyal to God,
  whose spirits were not faithful to him.

⁹The men of Ephraim, though armed with bows,
  turned back on the day of battle;
¹⁰they did not keep God's covenant[D]
  and refused to live by his law.
¹¹They forgot what he had done,
  the wonders he had shown them.
¹²He did miracles in the sight of their fathers
  in the land of Egypt, in the region of Zoan.
¹³He divided the sea and led them through;
  he made the water stand firm like a wall.
¹⁴He guided them with the cloud by day
  and with light from the fire all night.
¹⁵He split the rocks in the desert
  and gave them water as abundant as the
    seas;
¹⁶he brought streams out of a rocky crag
  and made water flow down like rivers.

¹⁷But they continued to sin against him,
  rebelling in the desert against the Most High.
¹⁸They willfully put God to the test
  by demanding the food they craved.
¹⁹They spoke against God, saying,
  "Can God spread a table in the desert?
²⁰When he struck the rock, water gushed out,
  and streams flowed abundantly.
But can he also give us food?
  Can he supply meat for his people?"
²¹When the LORD heard them, he was very angry;
  his fire broke out against Jacob,
  and his wrath rose against Israel,
²²for they did not believe in God
  or trust in his deliverance.

---

[a]Title: Probably a literary or musical term

23Yet he gave a command to the skies above
    and opened the doors of the heavens;
24he rained down manna[D] for the people to
        eat,
    he gave them the grain of heaven.
25Men ate the bread of angels;
    he sent them all the food they could eat.
26He let loose the east wind from the heavens
    and led forth the south wind by his power.
27He rained meat down on them like dust,
    flying birds like sand on the seashore.
28He made them come down inside their camp,
    all around their tents.
29They ate till they had more than enough,
    for he had given them what they craved.
30But before they turned from the food they
        craved,
    even while it was still in their mouths,
31God's anger rose against them;
    he put to death[D] the sturdiest among
        them,
    cutting down the young men of Israel.

32In spite of all this, they kept on sinning;
    in spite of his wonders, they did not
        believe.
33So he ended their days in futility
    and their years in terror.
34Whenever God slew them, they would seek
        him;
    they eagerly turned to him again.
35They remembered that God was their Rock,
    that God Most High was their Redeemer[D].
36But then they would flatter him with their
        mouths,
    lying to him with their tongues;
37their hearts were not loyal to him,
    they were not faithful to his covenant[D].
38Yet he was merciful;
    he forgave their iniquities
    and did not destroy them.
Time after time he restrained his anger
    and did not stir up his full wrath.
39He remembered that they were but flesh,
    a passing breeze that does not return.

40How often they rebelled against him in the
        desert
    and grieved him in the wasteland!
41Again and again they put God to the test;
    they vexed the Holy One of Israel.
42They did not remember his power—
    the day he redeemed[D] them from the
        oppressor,
43the day he displayed his miraculous signs in
        Egypt,
    his wonders in the region of Zoan.
44He turned their rivers to blood;
    they could not drink from their streams.
45He sent swarms of flies that devoured them,
    and frogs that devastated them.
46He gave their crops to the grasshopper,
    their produce to the locust[D].
47He destroyed their vines with hail
    and their sycamore-figs with sleet.

SCRIPTURE LINK (78:24) Manna
See Exodus 16:4.

SCRIPTURE LINK (78:27) Meat
See Num. 11:31.

SCRIPTURE LINK (78:31) Put to death
See Num. 11:33.

With God's power all around them, why couldn't the people believe? (78:32)
It's hard to sympathize with people who witnessed God's miracles and possessed God's law—and still did not believe. But in their defense, they never doubted God's existence. The problem was that they often worshiped other gods as well. They simply wanted to hedge their bets: in case God didn't come through for them, perhaps one of the other gods would. Also see *What was the attraction of foreign gods?* (Judges 10:6) and article: *Why would Israelites be tempted by other gods?* (Joshua 23:7).

What causes people to turn to God? (78:34)
God's judgment, unfortunately, is often the only thing that can get the attention of sinners. When we come to the end of ourselves and recognize our weakness and guilt, we finally see that there is nowhere to turn but to God. A lot of trouble could be avoided if people would learn to seek God diligently during the good times instead of waiting for the bad. The Israelites' superficial faith allowed them to abandon God when things were going well.

Does God kill? (78:34)
Yes. The Bible leaves no doubt that God, who gives life, also pronounces judgment that takes life. Some wonder how God who said, *You shall not murder* (Exodus 20:13), can himself take life. This is not a dilemma for at least two reasons: (1) When God's judgment takes life it is not murder; it is justice. (2) The commandment against murder is for humans, not God. We have no right to take the life of another arbitrarily; a righteous God, on the other hand, must administer justice.

What does God expect of flesh? (78:39)
God expects *flesh* to worship him. But because human beings are flesh, he recognizes their limitations and restrains his anger. He is merciful and forgiving (v. 38) because he knows we are unable to live up to his fullest expectations. He sees us as mortal creatures whose lifespans are already cut short. God is patient, but eventually his justice will come.

Tents of Ham (78:51)

Another name for Egypt (see also 105:23,27; 106:22). The table of nations, specifically Gen. 10:6, tells us that one of Ham's sons was named *Mizraim,* which in Hebrew means *Egypt.*

Why did God give Israel land belonging to others? (78:55)

See *Was it right to take land from others?* (Joshua 1:4). Also see article: *What right did Israel have to take the land?* (Num. 33:52–53).

Why was Israel compared to a faulty bow? (78:57)

The word *faulty* indicates a slack bow, one that lacks the power to shoot an arrow and hit the target. Just as a slack bow was considered an unreliable weapon for a warrior, so Israel was unreliable in its relationship with God. Though God brought them safely into the promised land (v. 55), he could not depend upon them to be faithful (v. 56).

SCRIPTURE LINK (78:60–61) *Abandoned the tabernacle of Shiloh*

See Joshua 18:1; 1 Samuel 4:3,11. See *Travels of the Ark* on page 363.

---

⁴⁸He gave over their cattle to the hail,
  their livestock to bolts of lightning.
⁴⁹He unleashed against them his hot
        anger,
    his wrath, indignation and hostility—
    a band of destroying angels.
⁵⁰He prepared a path for his anger;
    he did not spare them from death ᴰ
    but gave them over to the plague.
⁵¹He struck down all the firstborn ᴰ of Egypt,
    the firstfruits ᴰ of manhood in the tents of
        Ham.
⁵²But he brought his people out like a flock;
    he led them like sheep through the desert.
⁵³He guided them safely, so they were unafraid;
    but the sea engulfed their enemies.
⁵⁴Thus he brought them to the border of his holy
        land,
    to the hill country his right hand had taken.
⁵⁵He drove out nations before them
    and allotted their lands to them as an
        inheritance;
    he settled the tribes of Israel in their
        homes.

⁵⁶But they put God to the test
    and rebelled against the Most High;
    they did not keep his statutes.
⁵⁷Like their fathers they were disloyal and
        faithless,
    as unreliable as a faulty bow.
⁵⁸They angered him with their high places ᴰ;
    they aroused his jealousy with their idols ᴰ.
⁵⁹When God heard them, he was very angry;
    he rejected Israel completely.
⁶⁰He abandoned the tabernacle ᴰ of Shiloh,
    the tent he had set up among men.
⁶¹He sent ⌊the ark of⌋ his might into captivity,
    his splendor into the hands of the enemy.
⁶²He gave his people over to the sword;
    he was very angry with his inheritance.
⁶³Fire consumed their young men,
    and their maidens had no wedding songs;
⁶⁴their priests ᴰ were put to the sword,
    and their widows could not weep.

⁶⁵Then the Lord awoke as from sleep,
    as a man wakes from the stupor of wine.
⁶⁶He beat back his enemies;
    he put them to everlasting shame.
⁶⁷Then he rejected the tents of Joseph,
    he did not choose the tribe of Ephraim;
⁶⁸but he chose the tribe of Judah,
    Mount Zion ᴰ, which he loved.
⁶⁹He built his sanctuary like the heights,
    like the earth that he established forever.
⁷⁰He chose David his servant
    and took him from the sheep pens;
⁷¹from tending the sheep he brought him
    to be the shepherd of his people Jacob,
    of Israel his inheritance.
⁷²And David shepherded them with integrity of
        heart;
    with skillful hands he led them.

Psalm 79

A psalm of Asaph.

¹O God, the nations have invaded your
    inheritance;
  they have defiled your holy temple,
  they have reduced Jerusalem^D to rubble.
²They have given the dead bodies of your
    servants
    as food to the birds of the air,
    the flesh of your saints^D to the beasts of the
      earth.
³They have poured out blood like water
    all around Jerusalem,
  and there is no one to bury the dead.
⁴We are objects of reproach^D to our neighbors,
  of scorn and derision to those around us.

⁵How long, O LORD? Will you be angry forever?
  How long will your jealousy burn like fire?
⁶Pour out your wrath on the nations
    that do not acknowledge you,
  on the kingdoms
    that do not call on your name;
⁷for they have devoured Jacob
  and destroyed his homeland.
⁸Do not hold against us the sins of the fathers;
  may your mercy^D come quickly to meet us,
  for we are in desperate need.

⁹Help us, O God our Savior,
  for the glory^D of your name;
  deliver us and forgive our sins
  for your name's sake.
¹⁰Why should the nations say,

Asaph (79:title)

See *Asaph* (73:title).

SCRIPTURE LINK (79:1–4) *Defiled your holy temple . . . reduced Jerusalem to rubble*

The Babylonians conquered Jerusalem in 586 B.C. and ransacked the temple. See 2 Kings 25.

Do we serve an angry God? (79:5)

Yes, we do. While it is true that God is love and is the source of all love, we cannot escape the fact that God is also holy. Love does not distort his righteousness. He hates sin and directs his wrath against those who defiantly rebel against him. It is a distortion to speak of God only as love without mentioning his wrath. God's judgment is real, as Israel discovered.

Did God make children suffer for their fathers' sins? (79:8)

This psalm was sung by the survivors of the destruction of Jerusalem, the remnant. They pleaded with God to change his attitude toward his people. Repentance began as they distanced themselves from the sins of the previous generations. In fact, the repentance of the remnant children led to the restoration. Nonetheless, it is true that children suffer the effects of their parents' sins.

Why does God choose some and reject others? (78:67–68)

It's unlikely that we will find a completely satisfactory answer to this question. To be sure, there are several factors we can identify: The transfer of favor from Ephraim to Judah may reveal God's punishing hand as well his grace. After all, the sanctuary at Shiloh in the hill country of Ephraim was full of corruption and incompetence. The sons of the high priest did not treat God's ark with respect but as a mere magic charm. There is little question that the destruction of Shiloh was an act of God's anger (vv. 56–64).

It was Israel's unfaithfulness and misuse of God's blessings that led to the capture of the ark of the Lord by the Philistines (vv. 60–61; 1 Samuel 4:11). It was the presumption and disobedience of the people themselves that removed the symbol of God's presence and blessing from Shiloh. And it was David, trusting in God, who defeated the Philistines and eventually brought the ark to Jerusalem (2 Samuel 5:17–25; 6:17).

Still, the broader question of God's choice remains. The apostle Paul discussed it by examining God's relationship with Jacob and Esau. His conclusion was that humans are limited in what they can understand about an incomprehensible God (Romans 9:13–15): *I will have mercy on whom I have mercy and I will have compassion on whom I have compassion.*

See article: *Does God play favorites?* (Romans 9:8–33). Also see *How can God hate?* (Mal. 1:2–3).

"Where is their God?"
Before our eyes, make known among the
        nations
    that you avenge^D the outpoured blood of
        your servants.
¹¹May the groans of the prisoners come before
        you;
    by the strength of your arm
    preserve those condemned to die.

¹²Pay back into the laps of our neighbors seven
        times
    the reproach^D they have hurled at you,
        O Lord.
¹³Then we your people, the sheep of your
        pasture,
    will praise you forever;
from generation to generation
    we will recount your praise.

Psalm 80

For the director of music. To ⌐the tune of⌐ "The Lilies
        of the Covenant." Of Asaph. A psalm.

¹Hear us, O Shepherd of Israel,
    you who lead Joseph like a flock;
you who sit enthroned between the
        cherubim^D, shine forth
²   before Ephraim, Benjamin and Manasseh.
Awaken your might;
    come and save us.

³Restore us, O God;
    make your face shine upon us,
    that we may be saved.

⁴O LORD God Almighty,
    how long will your anger smolder
    against the prayers of your people?
⁵You have fed them with the bread of tears;
    you have made them drink tears by the
        bowlful.
⁶You have made us a source of contention to
        our neighbors,
    and our enemies mock us.

⁷Restore us, O God Almighty;
    make your face shine upon us,
    that we may be saved.

⁸You brought a vine out of Egypt;
    you drove out the nations and planted it.
⁹You cleared the ground for it,
    and it took root and filled the land.
¹⁰The mountains were covered with its shade,
    the mighty cedars with its branches.
¹¹It sent out its boughs to the Sea,^a
    its shoots as far as the River.^b

¹²Why have you broken down its walls
    so that all who pass by pick its grapes?
¹³Boars from the forest ravage it
    and the creatures of the field feed on it.
¹⁴Return to us, O God Almighty!

Was the writer a prisoner? (79:11)

The writer of this psalm was likely one of the
exiles, carried away from his home to live in a
foreign land. In this sense, he would have been
a prisoner. Also see *Asaph* (73:title).

What prayers make God angry? (80:4)

God's anger was directed more at the past
sins of the Israelites than at their current
prayers. The psalmist seems to be saying,
"Enough is enough. Haven't we paid enough
for our sins?" The writer wants God to restore
Israel to the way it was before the enemy invasions.

Why sing about the troubles God sends? (80:6)

See article: *If God is in control, why do things
go wrong?* (93:1–5).

SCRIPTURE LINK (80:8) *A vine out of Egypt*

This image of Israel suggests God planted the
nation and tends it like a vinedresser or gardener would care for a vine. He expects the nation to *bear fruit*. See Gen. 49:22; Isaiah
5:1–7; Matt. 20:1–16.

^a11 Probably the Mediterranean   ^b11 That is, the Euphrates

Look down from heaven and see!
Watch over this vine,
15 the root your right hand has planted,
the son[a] you have raised up for yourself.

16Your vine is cut down, it is burned with fire;
at your rebuke your people perish.
17Let your hand rest on the man at your right
hand,
the son of man[b] you have raised up for
yourself.
18Then we will not turn away from you;
revive us, and we will call on your name.

19Restore us, O LORD God Almighty;
make your face shine upon us,
that we may be saved.

Psalm 81

For the director of music. According to *gittith.*[b]
Of Asaph.

1Sing for joy to God our strength;
shout aloud to the God of Jacob!
2Begin the music, strike the tambourine,
play the melodious harp and lyre[b].

3Sound the ram's horn at the New Moon,
and when the moon is full, on the day of our
Feast;
4this is a decree for Israel,
an ordinance of the God of Jacob.
5He established it as a statute for Joseph
when he went out against Egypt,
where we heard a language we did not
understand.[c]

6He says, "I removed the burden from their
shoulders;
their hands were set free from the basket.
7In your distress you called and I rescued you,

---

[a]15 Or *branch*   [b]Title: Probably a musical term   [c]5 Or *I and we
heard a voice we had not known*

Son of man (80:17)

Some say this simply refers to the nation of Israel, which is like a son to God (v. 15). Others suggest it points to a king, specifically to the coming Messiah (Matt. 12:40).

Which comes first—revival or calling on God? (80:18)

You would think that God begins to move when people pray first. But this verse suggests the reverse: the people will call on God *after* revival happens. True revival is always initiated by God's Spirit, not by human effort.

New Moon (81:3)

See *New Moon festival* (1 Samuel 20:5).

What was this heavy basket? (81:6)

It symbolized the weight the Israelites carried as slaves during their captivity in Egypt (Exodus 1:11–14). Though none are mentioned in the Exodus account, the baskets were probably used to carry supplies like bricks and mortar, or grain from the fields, during their forced labor.

SCRIPTURE LINK (81:7) *The waters of Meribah*

The Israelites, after being miraculously delivered from Egypt, complained about their lack of water in Exodus 17:1–7. God told Moses to strike a rock with his staff. When he did, water came out of it. Moses named the place *Meribah,* which literally means strife or quarreling.

Why does God test us? (81:7)

God was testing the Israelites' faith, whether they trusted in his ability to provide for them. They had seen his incredible power in the plagues, the crossing of the Red Sea, the manna and quail and in so many other ways. Yet they were still grumbling and complaining. In this way they failed their test.

Life is a *laboratory* of faith. God tests us to confirm the strength of our faith and the sincerity of our commitment to him. Another example of this was when God tested Abraham (Gen. 22:1). Would he trust God even if it required the sacrifice of his beloved son?

It's important to distinguish between testing and temptation. We know God *tempts* no one (James 1:13). Rather, Satan is the tempter (Matt. 4:3; 1 Cor. 7:5). Yet God can use Satan's temptations to *test* us; God redeems what Satan intended for evil and uses it to accomplish something good.

Why would God's people ignore him? (81:11)

Because of hardened and stubborn hearts. God had given the Israelites ample evidence of his grace and power, yet they repeatedly chose not to submit to him. Each of us has a penchant to live by our own rules rather than God's.

Honey from the rock (81:16)

A phrase reminiscent of a song Moses sang where he described honey coming from the rocks (Deut. 32:13). Sometimes bees built their hives in the rocky cliffs. Their rich and valuable honey is contrasted with the naturally barren cliffs.

Asaph (82:title)

See *Asaph* (73:title).

Great assembly (82:1)

Possibly a figurative gathering of all earthly rulers who are before God's throne to give an account of the way they used or abused their authority. It could also refer to a collection of deities other nations worshiped.

What *gods* does God judge? (82:1)

Probably human rulers who live and die like everyone else. Often leaders elevate themselves (or are elevated by their subjects) to lofty positions of power. In this way they can be thought of as *gods* who compete with the one true God for loyalty. God rightly judges the actions of all earthly rulers. Other interpretations say the *gods* are spiritual beings that promote earthly evils or that they were the pagan deities of Israel's heathen neighbors.

Who's partial? (82:2-4)

The human rulers, the *gods* (see previous note). They promote injustice, showing themselves to be evil. Instead of protecting the innocent, they're covering for the guilty. God has a special place in his heart for the defenseless. He expects their rights to be protected by the earthly powers.

SCRIPTURE LINK (82:6) *Sons of the Most High*

All humans (rulers included) are created by God. Through creation we are all *sons of God*. But in another sense, we need to become *sons of God* through Jesus Christ (Gal. 3:26). Jesus quotes this verse in John 10:34-35 where the religious leaders accuse him of blasphemy for claiming to be one with the Father. Jesus shows that all leaders on earth are divinely appointed by God.

Rise up (82:8)

A call for immediate action on God's part.

Why would God give us the silent treatment? (83:1)

To teach us to trust him. Often God's silence, though, is a matter of timing. It might seem to us that God doesn't hear or answer our prayers. But God acts according to his timetable, not ours.

Why were these nations enemies of God? (83:2,6-8)

They were neighboring countries with whom Israel had border disputes, who sought to plunder and destroy God's people. On another lev-

I answered you out of a thundercloud;
  I tested you at the waters of Meribah.   *Selah*[D]

[8]"Hear, O my people, and I will warn you—
  if you would but listen to me, O Israel!
[9]You shall have no foreign god among you;
  you shall not bow down to an alien[D] god.
[10]I am the LORD your God,
  who brought you up out of Egypt.
  Open wide your mouth and I will fill it.

[11]"But my people would not listen to me;
  Israel would not submit to me.
[12]So I gave them over to their stubborn hearts
  to follow their own devices.

[13]"If my people would but listen to me,
  if Israel would follow my ways,
[14]how quickly would I subdue their enemies
  and turn my hand against their foes!
[15]Those who hate the LORD would cringe before
    him,
  and their punishment would last forever.
[16]But you would be fed with the finest of wheat;
  with honey from the rock I would satisfy
    you."

Psalm 82

A psalm of Asaph.

[1]God presides in the great assembly;
  he gives judgment among the "gods":

[2]"How long will you[a] defend the unjust
  and show partiality to the wicked?   *Selah*
[3]Defend the cause of the weak and fatherless;
  maintain the rights of the poor and
    oppressed.
[4]Rescue the weak and needy;
  deliver them from the hand of the wicked.

[5]"They know nothing, they understand nothing.
  They walk about in darkness;
  all the foundations of the earth are shaken.

[6]"I said, 'You are "gods";
  you are all sons of the Most High.'
[7]But you will die like mere men;
  you will fall like every other ruler."

[8]Rise up, O God, judge the earth,
  for all the nations are your inheritance.

Psalm 83

A song. A psalm of Asaph.

[1]O God, do not keep silent;
  be not quiet, O God, be not still.
[2]See how your enemies are astir,
  how your foes rear their heads.
[3]With cunning they conspire against your
    people;
  they plot against those you cherish.

a2 The Hebrew is plural.

4"Come," they say, "let us destroy them as a
    nation,
that the name of Israel be remembered no
    more."

5With one mind they plot together;
    they form an alliance against you—
6the tents of EdomD and the Ishmaelites,
    of Moab and the Hagrites,
7Gebal,a Ammon and Amalek,
    Philistia, with the people of Tyre.
8Even Assyria has joined them
    to lend strength to the descendants of Lot.
                                SelahD

9Do to them as you did to Midian,
    as you did to Sisera and Jabin at the river
    Kishon,
10who perished at Endor
    and became like refuse on the ground.
11Make their nobles like Oreb and Zeeb,
    all their princes like Zebah and Zalmunna,
12who said, "Let us take possession
    of the pasturelands of God."

13Make them like tumbleweed, O my God,
    like chaffD before the wind.
14As fire consumes the forest
    or a flame sets the mountains ablaze,
15so pursue them with your tempest
    and terrify them with your storm.
16Cover their faces with shame
    so that men will seek your name, O LORD.

17May they ever be ashamed and dismayed;
    may they perish in disgrace.
18Let them know that you, whose name is the
    LORD—
that you alone are the Most High over all the
    earth.

Psalm 84

For the director of music. According to gittith.b Of the
    Sons of Korah. A psalm.

1How lovely is your dwelling place,
    O LORD Almighty!
2My soulD yearns, even faints,
    for the courts of the LORD;
my heart and my flesh cry out
    for the living God.

3Even the sparrow has found a home,
    and the swallow a nest for herself,
    where she may have her young—
a place near your altar,
    O LORD Almighty, my King and my God.
4Blessed are those who dwell in your house;
    they are ever praising you.   Selah

5Blessed are those whose strength is in you,
    who have set their hearts on pilgrimage.
6As they pass through the Valley of Baca,
    they make it a place of springs;

a7 That is, Byblos   bTitle: Probably a musical term

el, they were instruments of Satan in a
spiritual war to thwart God's plan of redemption through the nation of Israel.

Descendants of Lot (83:8)
Moab and Ammon were both descendants of
Lot (Gen. 19:36–38). They were the sons of
Lot's daughters and were fathered by Lot
himself!

SCRIPTURE LINK (83:9) As you did to
Midian . . . Sisera and Jabin
The past defeats of Israel's enemies recorded
in the book of Judges. Midian refers to Gideon's victory in Judges 7. Sisera and Jabin refer
to Barak's victory over the Canaanites in
Judges 4.

SCRIPTURE LINK (83:11) Like Oreb
and Zeeb . . . Zebah and Zalmunna
Oreb and Zeeb were two Midianite leaders who
were captured and killed by the men of Ephraim after Gideon's victory. See Judges 7:25. Zebah and Zalmunna were other Midianites killed
by Gideon in Judges 8:21.

Was he right to ask God to destroy his
enemies? (83:13–16)
It's best to think of this as the psalmist's personal journal in which he's venting his anger
about these enemy nations. Ultimately, he's
leaving the action up to God and not taking
matters into his own hands or resorting to violence (Romans 12:19). See article: *Is it right to
pray for revenge?* (58:6–8).

Sons of Korah (84:title)
A choir of Levites that King David appointed to
serve in the temple worship. These were
descendants of Korah, who was the grandson
of Levi, the head of one of the twelve tribes of
Israel. The Levites were the tribe responsible
for temple worship. Korah got into a dispute
with Moses and was eventually swallowed alive
by the ground (Num. 16:1–33).

Where does God live? (84:1)
See *Where does God live?* (Micah 1:3).

Why was this psalmist so homesick for
the temple? (84:2)
The writer was probably someone who normally
served in the temple but was prevented from
doing so for some reason. Perhaps this psalm
was written when Sennacherib, the king of Assyria, was threatening the temple in Jerusalem. Or it might refer to being in captivity in another country.

Valley of Baca (84:6)
The meaning is uncertain. It may refer to a valley of balsam trees that grow in dry areas. Or it
might be an imaginary valley full of dryness and
sorrow.

Who is their shield? (84:9)

The *anointed one,* the king in Jerusalem. The word *shield* could also be translated *sovereign* (see NIV text note). The king's duty was to protect the people within his charge. Perhaps the king was in some sort of danger when this psalm was first written.

How is God like a shield? (84:11)

Ancient shields protected the body during warfare. Likewise, God protects his people from the fiery darts of the evil one, from fear and from the danger of the unknown.

Whose walk is blameless? (84:11)

The walk of those who seek God's will. This doesn't imply perfection, but undivided loyalty. No one is completely blameless before the Lord since we've all sinned (53:1–3). But when God grants forgiveness, we become blameless in his sight. See *How could David claim to be blameless?* (26:1).

Sons of Korah (85:title)

See *Sons of Korah* (84:title).

How had God's people displeased him? (85:4)

By spurning God's love. Israel had a long history of pandering after every god but their own. They repeatedly kicked and screamed against the God who created them and called them his own. When they rebelled, God punished them by sending invading armies, famine and pestilence. This time the nation may have been experiencing a famine (v. 12).

Whose responsibility is revival—God's or ours? (85:6)

See *Which comes first—revival or calling on God?* (80:18).

Fear him (85:9)

See article: *Should we live in terror of God?* (Prov. 1:7).

What kind of kiss is this? (85:10–11)

This poetic imagery suggests a close association between love and faithfulness and between righteousness and peace. Righteousness refers to moral perfection. Peace can be seen as a wholesome state of well-being or as the complete absence of hostility. The image suggests a state of joy and harmony.

Does a good harvest require obedience as much as it requires rain? (85:12)

Here it does. The drought seems to be linked to prior disobedience, so returning to a state of obedience to expect God's blessings is only reasonable. Verses 8–9 imply that God's blessings come to those who fear (honor, respect, obey) him. However, God also sends rain on the righteous *and* the unrighteous (Matt. 5:45). We can't assume all droughts result from human disobedience.

the autumn rains also cover it with
pools. [a]
[7]They go from strength to strength,
till each appears before God in Zion[D].

[8]Hear my prayer, O Lord God Almighty;
listen to me, O God of Jacob.   *Selah*[D]
[9]Look upon our shield,[b] O God;
look with favor on your anointed[D] one.

[10]Better is one day in your courts
than a thousand elsewhere;
I would rather be a doorkeeper in the house of
my God
than dwell in the tents of the wicked.
[11]For the Lord God is a sun and shield;
the Lord bestows favor and honor;
no good thing does he withhold
from those whose walk is blameless.

[12]O Lord Almighty,
blessed is the man who trusts in you.

Psalm 85

For the director of music. Of the Sons of Korah.
A psalm.

[1]You showed favor to your land, O Lord;
you restored the fortunes of Jacob.
[2]You forgave the iniquity of your people
and covered all their sins.   *Selah*
[3]You set aside all your wrath
and turned from your fierce anger.

[4]Restore us again, O God our Savior,
and put away your displeasure toward
us.
[5]Will you be angry with us forever?
Will you prolong your anger through all
generations?
[6]Will you not revive us again,
that your people may rejoice in you?
[7]Show us your unfailing love, O Lord,
and grant us your salvation[D].

[8]I will listen to what God the Lord will say;
he promises peace[D] to his people, his
saints[D]—
but let them not return to folly.
[9]Surely his salvation is near those who fear
him,
that his glory[D] may dwell in our land.

[10]Love and faithfulness meet together;
righteousness[D] and peace kiss each other.
[11]Faithfulness springs forth from the earth,
and righteousness looks down from
heaven.
[12]The Lord will indeed give what is good,
and our land will yield its harvest.
[13]Righteousness goes before him
and prepares the way for his steps.

[a]6 Or *blessings*   [b]9 Or *sovereign*

Psalm 86

A prayer of David.

[1]Hear, O LORD, and answer me,
for I am poor and needy.
[2]Guard my life, for I am devoted to you.
You are my God; save your servant
who trusts in you.
[3]Have mercy[D] on me, O Lord,
for I call to you all day long.
[4]Bring joy to your servant,
for to you, O Lord,
I lift up my soul[D].

[5]You are forgiving and good, O Lord,
abounding in love to all who call to you.
[6]Hear my prayer, O LORD;
listen to my cry for mercy.
[7]In the day of my trouble I will call to you,
for you will answer me.

[8]Among the gods there is none like you, O Lord;
no deeds can compare with yours.
[9]All the nations you have made
will come and worship before you, O Lord;
they will bring glory[D] to your name.
[10]For you are great and do marvelous deeds;
you alone are God.

[11]Teach me your way, O LORD,
and I will walk in your truth;
give me an undivided heart,
that I may fear your name.
[12]I will praise you, O Lord my God, with all my
heart;
I will glorify your name forever.
[13]For great is your love toward me;
you have delivered me from the depths of
the grave.[a]

[14]The arrogant are attacking me, O God;

[a]13 Hebrew *Sheol*

In what way was David poor and needy? (86:1)

In the spiritual sense. This kind of poverty is a recognition of complete dependence on God, that we have no resources to save ourselves (34:6; 35:10). It doesn't refer to a lack of money or possessions.

How can a soul be lifted up to God? (86:4)

See *How can a soul be lifted up to God?* (25:1).

Did David think there were other gods? (86:8)

The neighboring Canaanite tribes were filled with pagan gods, but David knew his God to be the one, true God (115:3–7; 135:13–17). He knew that all other gods were mere idols, made by human hands.

When will all nations come to worship God? (86:9)

This is a theme common throughout the book of Psalms, as well as the rest of the Bible (Phil. 2:9–11; Rev. 15:4). This has happened in the past 2,000 years as Christianity has spread throughout the world. And while it's true that people around the world now worship Jesus Christ, this prophecy will reach its ultimate fulfillment after his second coming.

Depths of the grave (86:13)

This image refers to complete distress—even to the point of death itself. Elsewhere in the Old Testament, this idea is called the pit, or Sheol. It is described as darkness, destruction and corruption. David's expression here could refer to something that *has happened* or something that *will happen* in the future. If it refers to the future, it probably refers to physical death and resurrection.

Who wanted David dead? (86:14)

The expressions *arrogant* and *band of ruthless men* may symbolize the various types of adversaries David had faced in his life. It may not point to one specific event, though throughout his life many people wanted him dead (including Goliath, Saul, descendants of Saul, the Ammonites and even his own son, Absalom).

How do I know if my heart is divided? (86:11)

Throughout the psalms, the word *heart* refers to the center of the human soul or spirit. From this center flow all a person's emotions, thoughts and attitudes. An *undivided heart* means that these expressions reveal a heart that is pure and unselfish, not corrupted in any way.

The prophet Jeremiah wrote in a similar vein, telling us that God wants us to return to him with all our heart (Jer. 24:7). He called this concept *singleness of heart and action* (Jer. 32:39). Ezekiel also spoke of God giving *an undivided heart and . . . a new spirit* (Ezek. 11:19).

Only God can give someone an undivided heart; it's not something we get on our own. Still, we must accept God's offer; we must want an undivided heart. The surest way to know whether one's heart is undivided may be to echo David's prayer: *Search me, O God and know my heart; test me and know my anxious thoughts* (139:23). Only God can tell whether or not our hearts are pure.

What sign was David looking for? (86:17)

Visible proof of God's goodness. He wanted his enemies to see that God was involved. David had already affirmed God's goodness, forgiveness and love (vv. 5,13), his great deeds (v. 10) and his divine attributes (v. 15). Now he wanted his enemies to see some evidence of this, too. Perhaps he wanted to clear his own name or put his enemies to shame (35:4).

Sons of Korah (87:title)

See *Sons of Korah* (84:title).

Holy mountain (87:1)

Mount Zion, the place where God himself has established a city (Isaiah 28:16). The Hebrew word for mountain is plural, which may point to all the hills around Jerusalem or the absolute majesty surrounding God's holy mountain.

Did these nations actually turn to God? (87:4)

The nations listed here are symbolic of all Gentile nations. Rahab is a poetic name for Egypt. Egypt and Babylon were two of Israel's fiercest enemies. Some see this as a prophecy that someday all nations will acknowledge the one, true God. Others say it refers to individuals within all these countries who turn to God.

Born in Zion (87:4–6)

God will treat these people as though they were native citizens of his holy city. Even though they are converts, they will enjoy all the privileges and benefits of citizenship.

Why would they say, *All my fountains are in you?* (87:7)

Fountains (or springs) can be taken as a metaphor for the source of all that gives life and blessing. This may be related to another metaphor of a river running through Zion that makes people glad (36:8; 46:4).

Who can sing this psalm? (87:7)

Anyone who has found new life in Jesus Christ should be able to echo the joyful sentiment expressed in this song. For through Christ, we can live as citizens in the city of God and enjoy all its blessings.

Sons of Korah (88:title)

See *Sons of Korah* (84:title).

What trouble is the psalmist in? (88:3)

This person was suffering from physical as well as emotional pain. This is one of the saddest psalms in the whole book. Whoever wrote it appears to have been close to death and had been that way for some time (v. 15). He had also lost his closest friends (vv. 8,18).

Why say God forgets the dead? (88:5)

This is a psalm of emotion; this is how the psalmist *feels*. The writer was in a dark tunnel and couldn't see much hope. This psalm is in the Bible to show us that God can handle our words of despair as well as our words of praise. He doesn't expect us to wear rose-colored glasses and go through life pretending it isn't difficult or painful.

a band of ruthless men seeks my life—
men without regard for you.
15But you, O Lord, are a compassionate and
gracious God,
slow to anger, abounding in love and
faithfulness.
16Turn to me and have mercy[D] on me;
grant your strength to your servant
and save the son of your maidservant.[a]
17Give me a sign of your goodness,
that my enemies may see it and be put to
shame,
for you, O LORD, have helped me and
comforted me.

Psalm 87

Of the Sons of Korah. A psalm. A song.

1He has set his foundation on the holy
mountain;
2   the LORD loves the gates of Zion[D]
more than all the dwellings of Jacob.
3Glorious things are said of you,
O city of God: *Selah*[D]
4"I will record Rahab[Db] and Babylon
among those who acknowledge me—
Philistia too, and Tyre, along with Cush[c]—
and will say, 'This[d] one was born in
Zion.' "
5Indeed, of Zion it will be said,
"This one and that one were born in her,
and the Most High himself will establish
her."
6The LORD will write in the register of the
peoples:
"This one was born in Zion."   *Selah*
7As they make music they will sing,
"All my fountains are in you."

Psalm 88

*A song. A psalm of the Sons of Korah. For the director
of music. According to* mahalath leannoth.[e] *A* maskil[f]
of Heman the Ezrahite.

1O LORD, the God who saves me,
day and night I cry out before you.
2May my prayer come before you;
turn your ear to my cry.

3For my soul[D] is full of trouble
and my life draws near the grave.[g]
4I am counted among those who go down to the
pit;
I am like a man without strength.
5I am set apart with the dead,
like the slain who lie in the grave,

---

a16 Or save your faithful son   *b4 A poetic name for Egypt*
c4 That is, the upper Nile region   *d4 Or "O Rahab and Babylon, /
Philistia, Tyre and Cush, / I will record concerning those who
acknowledge me: / 'This*   *e Title: Possibly a tune, "The Suffering of
Affliction"*   *f Title: Probably a literary or musical term*
g3 Hebrew Sheol

whom you remember no more,
  who are cut off from your care.

⁶You have put me in the lowest pit,
  in the darkest depths.
⁷Your wrath lies heavily upon me;
  you have overwhelmed me with all your
    waves.   *Selah*ᴰ
⁸You have taken from me my closest friends
  and have made me repulsive to them.
I am confined and cannot escape;
⁹ my eyes are dim with grief.

I call to you, O LORD, every day;
  I spread out my hands to you.
¹⁰Do you show your wonders to the dead?
  Do those who are dead rise up and praise
    you?   *Selah*
¹¹Is your love declared in the grave,
  your faithfulness in Destructionᵃ?
¹²Are your wonders known in the place of
    darkness,
  or your righteousᴰ deeds in the land of
    oblivion?

¹³But I cry to you for help, O LORD;
  in the morning my prayer comes before you.
¹⁴Why, O LORD, do you reject me
  and hide your face from me?

¹⁵From my youth I have been afflictedᴰ and
    close to deathᴰ;
  I have suffered your terrors and am in
    despair.
¹⁶Your wrath has swept over me;
  your terrors have destroyed me.
¹⁷All day long they surround me like a flood;
  they have completely engulfed me.
¹⁸You have taken my companions and loved
    ones from me;
  the darkness is my closest friend.

Psalm 89

A *maskil*ᵇ of Ethan the Ezrahite.

¹I will sing of the LORD's great love forever;
  with my mouth I will make your faithfulness
    known through all generations.
²I will declare that your love stands firm forever,
  that you established your faithfulness in
    heaven itself.

³You said, "I have made a covenantᴰ with my
    chosen one,
  I have sworn to David my servant,
⁴'I will establish your line forever
  and make your throne firm through all
    generations.' "   *Selah*
⁵The heavens praise your wonders, O LORD,
  your faithfulness too, in the assembly of the
    holy ones.
⁶For who in the skies above can compare with
    the LORD?

Why would God put someone in the pit? (88:6)
The psalmist has no other explanation for his awful circumstances, so he blames God. His words resemble those of Jesus, who also felt forsaken by men and by God (Matt. 27:46).

Is it okay to be so negative? (88:10-12)
Genuine faith forces us to wrestle with God in prayer, especially during difficult times. This is precisely what the psalmist is doing. God wants us to bring our toughest questions to him.

What does the Old Testament teach about the resurrection? (88:10)
See *Gathered to his people* (Num. 20:24) and *How did the Old Testament view resurrection?* (Daniel 12:2).

What can we do if we feel like God has rejected us? (88:14)
Tell him how we're feeling. The psalmist may feel like he's been rejected by God, but at least he's still crying to the Lord for help (v. 13). Even in the midst of terrible circumstances, he recognizes that there's nowhere else to turn.

Ethan (89:title)
The name *Ethan* appears in two other places (1 Chron. 6:42; 15:17–19). Whether either can be connected to this *Ethan* is not certain. Ethan was probably associated with the choir worship. Some connect him to Jeduthun, the person to whom Psalm 39 is dedicated.

SCRIPTURE LINK (89:3) *I have made a covenant*
God entered into a special covenant relationship with his chosen servant, David, promising to establish his throne (kingdom) forever (2 Samuel 7:8–16). Jesus was the ultimate fulfillment of God's promise to David.

Assembly of the holy ones (89:5)
See *Great assembly* (82:1).

ᵃ11 Hebrew *Abaddon*   ᵇTitle: Probably a literary or musical term

Who is like the LORD among the heavenly
    beings?
⁷In the council of the holy ones God is greatly
    feared;
  he is more awesome than all who surround
    him.
⁸O LORD God Almighty, who is like you?
  You are mighty, O LORD, and your
    faithfulness surrounds you.

⁹You rule over the surging sea;
  when its waves mount up, you still them.
¹⁰You crushed Rahab^D like one of the slain;
  with your strong arm you scattered your
    enemies.
¹¹The heavens are yours, and yours also the
    earth;
  you founded the world and all that is in it.
¹²You created the north and the south;
  Tabor and Hermon sing for joy at your
    name.
¹³Your arm is endued with power;
  your hand is strong, your right hand exalted.

¹⁴Righteousness^D and justice are the foundation
    of your throne;
  love and faithfulness go before you.
¹⁵Blessed are those who have learned to acclaim
    you,
  who walk in the light of your presence,
    O LORD.
¹⁶They rejoice in your name all day long;
  they exult in your righteousness.
¹⁷For you are their glory^D and strength,
  and by your favor you exalt our horn.^a
¹⁸Indeed, our shield^b belongs to the LORD,
  our king to the Holy One of Israel.

¹⁹Once you spoke in a vision^D,
  to your faithful people you said:
  "I have bestowed strength on a warrior;
    I have exalted a young man from among the
      people.
²⁰I have found David my servant;
  with my sacred^D oil I have anointed^D him.
²¹My hand will sustain him;
  surely my arm will strengthen him.
²²No enemy will subject him to tribute;
  no wicked man will oppress him.
²³I will crush his foes before him
  and strike down his adversaries.
²⁴My faithful love will be with him,
  and through my name his horn^c will be
    exalted.
²⁵I will set his hand over the sea,
  his right hand over the rivers.
²⁶He will call out to me, 'You are my Father,
  my God, the Rock my Savior.'
²⁷I will also appoint him my firstborn^D,
  the most exalted of the kings of the earth.
²⁸I will maintain my love to him forever,
  and my covenant^D with him will never fail.

Rahab (89:10)

A name used to symbolize the sea or a mythical sea monster that neighboring countries believed in. The name is used in multiple ways to
symbolize outward hostility toward God's people. This mythical sea monster (which the Israelites didn't believe in) was associated with
Baal worship. The crushing of Rahab may refer
to God's control over the sea, or to Israel's escape from Egypt via the sea. See also 87:4;
Job 9:13; Isaiah 30:7.

Firstborn (89:27)

David, Israel's greatest king. David wasn't
really a firstborn child, but God bestowed on
him all the privileges associated with being the
firstborn. God's promises to David were fully
realized in the coming of Jesus to earth. Jesus
is the true *firstborn*.

Who would fulfill this prediction? (89:27)

See *How can a dead king rule?* (Ezek.
37:24–25).

---

^a 17 *Horn* here symbolizes strong one.   ^b 18 Or *sovereign*
^c 24 *Horn* here symbolizes strength.

29I will establish his line forever,
  his throne as long as the heavens endure.

30"If his sons forsake my law
  and do not follow my statutes,
31if they violate my decrees
  and fail to keep my commands,
32I will punish their sin with the rod,
  their iniquity with flogging;
33but I will not take my love from him,
  nor will I ever betray my faithfulness.
34I will not violate my covenant[D]
  or alter what my lips have uttered.
35Once for all, I have sworn by my holiness—
  and I will not lie to David—
36that his line will continue forever
  and his throne endure before me like the
    sun;
37it will be established forever like the moon,
  the faithful witness in the sky."   *Selah*[D]

38But you have rejected, you have spurned,
  you have been very angry with your
    anointed[D] one.
39You have renounced the covenant with your
    servant
  and have defiled his crown in the dust.
40You have broken through all his walls
  and reduced his strongholds[D] to ruins.
41All who pass by have plundered[D] him;
  he has become the scorn of his neighbors.
42You have exalted the right hand of his foes;
  you have made all his enemies rejoice.
43You have turned back the edge of his sword
  and have not supported him in battle.
44You have put an end to his splendor
  and cast his throne to the ground.
45You have cut short the days of his youth;
  you have covered him with a mantle of
    shame.   *Selah*

46How long, O LORD? Will you hide yourself
    forever?
  How long will your wrath burn like fire?
47Remember how fleeting is my life.
  For what futility you have created all men!
48What man can live and not see death[D],
  or save himself from the power of the
    grave[a]?   *Selah*
49O Lord, where is your former great love,
  which in your faithfulness you swore to
    David?
50Remember, Lord, how your servant has[b] been
    mocked,
  how I bear in my heart the taunts of all the
    nations,
51the taunts with which your enemies have
    mocked, O LORD,
  with which they have mocked every step of
    your anointed one.

52Praise be to the LORD forever!
  Amen and Amen.

a48 Hebrew Sheol   *b50 Or your servants have*

Why the sudden shift in tone? (89:38)
In vv. 1–37, the psalmist seemed so positive,
while vv. 38–51 focus on the negative. All the
evidence seemed to suggest to the writer that
God had forgotten about his earlier promises.
The psalmist felt that the nation had been
judged too harshly. This expression of up-and-
down emotions is a characteristic of poetry.

**Why does the psalmist think God went
back on his word? (89:39)**
This psalm was probably written after the
downfall of David's dynasty. Therefore, it appeared humanly impossible that God would fulfill the covenant to establish an everlasting
kingdom through David. The writer was thinking
of an earthly kingdom, not a spiritual one. God
didn't go back on his word; he just didn't go
about it in the way the people expected.

SCRIPTURE LINK (89:40) *You have
broken through all his walls*
This may refer to the attacks on Jerusalem by
King Nebuchadnezzar in 597 B.C. (2 Kings
24:8–17) or to the fall of Jerusalem (2 Kings
25:1–10).

Is this verse out of place? (89:52)
Not really. Note that this verse concludes Book
III of the Psalms (73–89), so it's really a formula of praise or doxology to the whole section, not just this particular psalm. Similar
positive verses end Books I and II (41:13;
72:19). These doxologies were likely added by
those who compiled the psalms into their
present arrangement.

BOOK IV

Psalms 90–106

Psalm 90

A prayer of Moses the man of God.

¹Lord, you have been our dwelling place
  throughout all generations.
²Before the mountains were born
  or you brought forth the earth and the
    world,
  from everlasting to everlasting you are God.

³You turn men back to dust,
  saying, "Return to dust, O sons of men."
⁴For a thousand years in your sight
  are like a day that has just gone by,
  or like a watch in the night.
⁵You sweep men away in the sleep of death[D];
  they are like the new grass of the morning—
⁶though in the morning it springs up new,
  by evening it is dry and withered.

⁷We are consumed by your anger
  and terrified by your indignation.
⁸You have set our iniquities before you,
  our secret sins in the light of your presence.
⁹All our days pass away under your wrath;
  we finish our years with a moan.
¹⁰The length of our days is seventy years—
  or eighty, if we have the strength;
yet their span[a] is but trouble and sorrow,
  for they quickly pass, and we fly away.

¹¹Who knows the power of your anger?
  For your wrath is as great as the fear that is
    due you.
¹²Teach us to number our days aright,
  that we may gain a heart of wisdom.

¹³Relent, O LORD! How long will it be?
  Have compassion on your servants.
¹⁴Satisfy us in the morning with your unfailing
    love,
  that we may sing for joy and be glad all our
    days.
¹⁵Make us glad for as many days as you have
    afflicted[D] us,
  for as many years as we have seen trouble.
¹⁶May your deeds be shown to your servants,
  your splendor to their children.

¹⁷May the favor[b] of the Lord our God rest upon
    us;
  establish the work of our hands for us—
  yes, establish the work of our hands.

Psalm 91

¹He who dwells in the shelter of the Most High
  will rest in the shadow of the Almighty.[c]

Moses (90:title)
That Moses actually crafted this psalm seems strange; he lived so much earlier than the other psalm writers. Perhaps it was passed down from generation to generation and finally recorded here. The songs of Moses in Exodus 15 and Deuteronomy 32 show Moses to be poetic. Some doubt this was written by Moses, saying it was written "in the spirit" of Moses or as a tribute to him.

Why compare people to dry grass? (90:5-6)
Both have a short life. Compared to the scope of eternity, a person's days on earth are brief. Compared to the greatness of God, people are nothing more than grass. These verses put life into perspective.

Secret sins (90:8)
The sins we try to keep hidden from others—and possibly even ourselves. But God knows everything, so nothing is hidden to him.

Can we sing about our troubles in worship? (90:9-10)
Certainly. But there are also times when our singing should be full of joy. Time on earth does pass quickly and there are a lot of things to moan about. But even with all the negatives, God gives us a reason to sing with joy and gladness. We sing not because of sadness and the seeming futility of life, but because of God's unfailing love for us.

Do God's love and God's anger work together? (90:11-14)
Because God is perfectly righteous, he will always be angry about sin. Yet, when he forgives our sin, it is removed as far as the east is from the west (103:12). We can only experience God's great love when our sins have been forgiven. Our sins can only be forgiven through God's own sacrifice to appease his anger, Jesus Christ.

How does God establish the work of our hands? (90:17)
By teaching us this wisdom: our lives are brief in the scope of eternity. What we do, though it often appears insignificant, is made significant by God. He takes our efforts and gives us success and hope, infusing even the mundane with eternal value.

---

*a*10 Or *yet the best of them*   *b*17 Or *beauty*   *c*1 Hebrew *Shaddai*

²I will say*ᵃ* of the LORD, "He is my refuge and
    my fortress,
  my God, in whom I trust."

³Surely he will save you from the fowler's snare
    and from the deadly pestilence.
⁴He will cover you with his feathers,
    and under his wings you will find refuge;
  his faithfulness will be your shield and
    rampart.
⁵You will not fear the terror of night,
    nor the arrow that flies by day,
⁶nor the pestilence that stalks in the darkness,
    nor the plague that destroys at midday.
⁷A thousand may fall at your side,
    ten thousand at your right hand,
  but it will not come near you.
⁸You will only observe with your eyes
    and see the punishment of the wicked.

⁹If you make the Most High your dwelling—
    even the LORD, who is my refuge—
¹⁰then no harm will befall you,
    no disaster will come near your tent.
¹¹For he will command his angels concerning
    you
  to guard you in all your ways;
¹²they will lift you up in their hands,
    so that you will not strike your foot against a
    stone.
¹³You will tread upon the lion and the cobra;
    you will trample the great lion and the
    serpent.

¹⁴"Because he loves me," says the LORD, "I will
    rescue him;
  I will protect him, for he acknowledges my
    name.
¹⁵He will call upon me, and I will answer him;
    I will be with him in trouble,
    I will deliver him and honor him.
¹⁶With long life will I satisfy him
    and show him my salvation*ᴰ*."

Psalm 92

A psalm. A song. For the Sabbath*ᴰ* day.

¹It is good to praise the LORD
    and make music to your name, O Most High,
²to proclaim your love in the morning
    and your faithfulness at night,
³to the music of the ten-stringed lyre*ᴰ*
    and the melody of the harp.

⁴For you make me glad by your deeds, O LORD;
    I sing for joy at the works of your hands.
⁵How great are your works, O LORD,
    how profound your thoughts!
⁶The senseless man does not know,
    fools do not understand,
⁷that though the wicked spring up like grass

ᵃ2 Or He says

Fowler (91:3)
The enemy of a fowl. The *fowler's snare* refers
to any type of danger from an enemy, such
as plots our enemies might devise to cause
us harm.

Why compare God to a bird? (91:4)
Mother birds are known for the protection they
give their young, especially beneath their own
wings. Jesus used a similar metaphor when he
longed to gather the city of Jerusalem under
his wings (Luke 13:34). The softness of a
bird's protection is balanced by the hard, solid
protection of a shield in the second half of the
verse. God provides both for his people.

How can we become immune to harm? (91:10)
If you read these verses in isolation, you could
conclude that God's people will be protected
from any type of harm. But this isn't the case.
This isn't referring simply to physical safety but
to God's general providence in our lives. Whatever happens to us, God is ultimately in control
and cares for us.

Does everyone have a guardian angel? (91:11)
Some would argue that every believer is protected by a guardian angel. Others would say
that God's angels protect people in a general
sense but aren't assigned to specific people.

Why walk on snakes or trample lions? (91:13)
These images are used to symbolize all types
of mortal threats. The lion could represent
strength and the cobra could represent cunning or evil. They might even represent evil
people (58:3–6).

What about those who have short lives? (91:16)
Obviously, not all those who trust in God are
guaranteed a long life on earth. Illness, accidents and violence can cut anyone's life short.
But ultimately God will provide everlasting life
(salvation) to those who belong to him.

How can we know God's thoughts? (92:4–5)
The psalmist isn't claiming to know God's
thoughts. Rather, he's marveling at how profound or deep they must be. What God has
done (his deeds) and what he's created (the
works of his hands) are evidence of that.
Though God gives us a glimpse of his thoughts
in his Word, no person can completely understand the mind of God or comprehend his acts
of love (Isaiah 40:13–14; 55:8; Romans
11:33–34).

and all evildoers flourish,
they will be forever destroyed.

8But you, O LORD, are exalted forever.

9For surely your enemies, O LORD,
surely your enemies will perish;
all evildoers will be scattered.
10You have exalted my horn[a] like that of a wild
ox;
fine oils have been poured upon me.
11My eyes have seen the defeat of my
adversaries;
my ears have heard the rout of my wicked
foes.

12The righteous[b] will flourish like a palm tree,
they will grow like a cedar of Lebanon;
13planted in the house of the LORD,
they will flourish in the courts of our God.
14They will still bear fruit in old age,
they will stay fresh and green,
15proclaiming, "The LORD is upright;
he is my Rock, and there is no wickedness in
him."

What kind of fruit can we bear in old age? (92:14–15)
Like a tree that continues to bear fruit, elderly people are useful to God. Shortly before his death at age 120, Moses' *eyes were not weak nor his strength gone* (Deut. 34:7). It doesn't mean that the person stays forever youthful but that he or she stays useful to God.

Psalm 93

1The LORD reigns, he is robed in majesty;
the LORD is robed in majesty
and is armed with strength.
The world is firmly established;
it cannot be moved.
2Your throne was established long ago;
you are from all eternity.

3The seas have lifted up, O LORD,
the seas have lifted up their voice;
the seas have lifted up their pounding waves.
4Mightier than the thunder of the great waters,
mightier than the breakers of the sea—
the LORD on high is mighty.

a 10 Horn here symbolizes strength.

If God is in control, why do things go wrong? (93:1–5)

This psalm affirms that God is majestic and mighty. He created the world and continues to hold it together. His control keeps the world and its laws in place. God is also eternal (v. 2). Our limited perspective might cause us to question God's control; only he has the big picture.

This psalm also acknowledges that God is mightier than his creation, more powerful than the greatest ocean waves (vv. 3–4). This is a visual reminder of God's power. Finally, we see that God's statutes (that is, his laws and his covenant relationship with his people) are also firmly established. Though we mess up and break our end of the bargain, God won't renege on his.

Although God will always be in control, many things in creation seem out of control because God doesn't force his "subjects" to worship him—and many choose not to. In spite of the problems this creates, it in no way negates his kingship.

5Your statutes stand firm;
  holiness adorns your house
    for endless days, O LORD.

Psalm 94

1O LORD, the God who avenges[D],
  O God who avenges, shine forth.
2Rise up, O Judge of the earth;
  pay back to the proud what they deserve.
3How long will the wicked, O LORD,
  how long will the wicked be jubilant?

4They pour out arrogant words;
  all the evildoers are full of boasting.
5They crush your people, O LORD;
  they oppress your inheritance.
6They slay the widow and the alien[D];
  they murder the fatherless.
7They say, "The LORD does not see;
  the God of Jacob pays no heed."

8Take heed, you senseless ones among the
      people;
  you fools, when will you become wise?
9Does he who implanted the ear not hear?
  Does he who formed the eye not see?
10Does he who disciplines nations not punish?
  Does he who teaches man lack knowledge?
11The LORD knows the thoughts of man;
  he knows that they are futile.

12Blessed is the man you discipline, O LORD,
  the man you teach from your law;
13you grant him relief from days of trouble,
  till a pit is dug for the wicked.
14For the LORD will not reject his people;
  he will never forsake his inheritance.
15Judgment will again be founded on
      righteousness[D],
  and all the upright in heart will follow it.

16Who will rise up for me against the wicked?
  Who will take a stand for me against
      evildoers?
17Unless the LORD had given me help,
  I would soon have dwelt in the silence of
      death[D].
18When I said, "My foot is slipping,"
  your love, O LORD, supported me.
19When anxiety was great within me,
  your consolation brought joy to my soul[D].

20Can a corrupt throne be allied with you—
  one that brings on misery by its decrees?
21They band together against the righteous[D]
  and condemn the innocent to death.
22But the LORD has become my fortress,
  and my God the rock in whom I take
      refuge.
23He will repay them for their sins
  and destroy them for their wickedness;
    the LORD our God will destroy them.

How firm are God's statutes? (93:5)

The word *statutes* can also mean *testimonies* or *affirmations*, and is closely related in meaning to God's commands, decrees and covenants. Statutes are more than a set of rules, though the concept includes God's laws. As God's guidelines for human conduct, they are reliable and trustworthy.

Why does God want to avenge? (94:1–3)

God is the rightful judge over all creation. As judge, God sets right the wrongs that have been committed. Our human concept of vengeance is usually associated with getting even or getting back at someone. The motivation is often selfish. But God's motives are pure and whatever punishment he inflicts against wickedness or injustice is always warranted.

Why overlook wickedness for so long? (94:3–7)

Because God is patient. Some might think God is blind to evil (v. 7) or has made some type of agreement with those who do evil to let them get away with it (v. 20). But these ideas are far from the truth. The psalmist was tired of the evil he saw in the world and he wanted God to do something about it right away. But *the LORD is compassionate and gracious, slow to anger, abounding in love* (103:8).

Why is God's discipline a blessing? (94:12–13)

Discipline involves much more than punishment or correction; it also involves teaching. Without it we have no basis for proper conduct. God punishes and teaches us for our own benefit, not to ruin our fun.

What kind of stand should we take against evil? (94:16)

These questions are rhetorical and have but one answer. The only real stand we can take against wickedness is to bring our appeal before the Lord and plead with him to take action. Only the Lord can provide the help, support and consolation we need (vv. 17,19). This isn't to say we should ignore or simply tolerate evil in the world. But we do need to recognize that repaying evildoers is God's role, not ours (v. 23).

How should we view bad government? (94:20–23)

Our first recourse is to do as the psalmist did—bring our case to God himself. It's up to God, not us, to bring judgment upon corrupt governments. Governments, like people, are prone to corruption. Yet, God has established human government and we should submit to it (Romans 13:1–7) unless it directly violates Christian principles (Acts 4:19). In a democracy, we also can vote and hold elected officials accountable, using the system to make changes.

How can we tell when we hear God's voice? (95:7)

We have to begin by wanting to hear his voice. The most likely way we'll hear God speak is through his written Word (78:1–2). But he can communicate with us in other ways too—circumstances, the counsel of trusted Christians or by his Holy Spirit prompting our spirit. Often God's message is hard to hear. If you question whether you're hearing God's voice or your own thoughts, check the message against Scripture. God never contradicts himself.

SCRIPTURE LINK (95:8–9) Meribah . . . Massah

Meribah means quarreling or strife and Massah means testing. Both refer to where Moses drew water from the rock to satisfy the thirst of the grumbling Israelites. These places symbolize a generation of unbelieving Israelites. Also see article: Why does God test us? (81:7).

Does God hold grudges? (95:10)

Not in the way that people do. God's dealings with us are based in righteousness and justice. But his holiness cannot tolerate sin. Even though God was angry with his people for 40 years, he continued to protect them and provide for them in the desert (Num. 14:1–35).

What can we learn about worship from this psalm? (95:11)

Verses 1–5 describe a joyful celebration complete with thanksgiving, music and song. This is the image most people have of worship. Verses 6–7a describe a more reflective aspect of worship—kneeling and bowing down before God, probably in silence. Out of this we hear God's voice which leads us to another aspect of worship—our response (vv. 7b–11).

What kind of rest did God withhold? (95:11)

In Joshua 1:13,15, the promised land is called a place of rest. All the people who didn't believe the promised land could be conquered were not allowed to enter it. They all died in the desert over the next 40 years.

What's wrong with old songs? (96:1–3)

Nothing. The point here is to offer fresh outpourings of praise to God. Since God's mercies are new every morning (Lam. 3:23), we always have something new to sing about. We especially need to avoid growing stale and predictable in our worship. The new song here may refer to this psalm itself. Also see Are new songs better than old? (33:3).

Ascribe (96:7–8)

To offer a concrete expression of praise to God. It involves telling him that we recognize his greatness, majesty and strength. This can be done through singing, praying and praising in worship, or through the giving of our money, time and talents to him. Note that the word ascribe appears three times in vv. 7–8, which matches the three-fold sing to the LORD in vv. 1–2.

Can we worship without giving an offering? (96:8)

The word offering sometimes conjures up images of obligations that smack of taxes and paying bills. But the word can also be translated gift, something we lovingly offer out of grati-

Psalm 95

[1]Come, let us sing for joy to the LORD;
  let us shout aloud to the Rock of our
    salvation[D].
[2]Let us come before him with thanksgiving
  and extol[D] him with music and song.

[3]For the LORD is the great God,
  the great King above all gods.
[4]In his hand are the depths of the earth,
  and the mountain peaks belong to him.
[5]The sea is his, for he made it,
  and his hands formed the dry land.

[6]Come, let us bow down in worship,
  let us kneel before the LORD our Maker;
[7]for he is our God
  and we are the people of his pasture,
  the flock under his care.

  Today, if you hear his voice,
[8] do not harden your hearts as you did at
      Meribah,[a]
  as you did that day at Massah[b] in the desert,
[9]where your fathers tested and tried me,
  though they had seen what I did.
[10]For forty years I was angry with that
    generation;
  I said, "They are a people whose hearts go
    astray,
  and they have not known my ways."
[11]So I declared on oath in my anger,
  "They shall never enter my rest."

Psalm 96

[1]Sing to the LORD a new song;
  sing to the LORD, all the earth.
[2]Sing to the LORD, praise his name;
  proclaim his salvation day after day.
[3]Declare his glory[D] among the nations,
  his marvelous deeds among all peoples.

[4]For great is the LORD and most worthy of
    praise;
  he is to be feared above all gods.
[5]For all the gods of the nations are idols[D],
  but the LORD made the heavens.
[6]Splendor and majesty are before him;
  strength and glory are in his sanctuary.

[7]Ascribe to the LORD, O families of nations,
  ascribe to the LORD glory and strength.
[8]Ascribe to the LORD the glory due his name;
  bring an offering and come into his courts.
[9]Worship the LORD in the splendor of his[c]
    holiness;
  tremble before him, all the earth.

[10]Say among the nations, "The LORD reigns."
  The world is firmly established, it cannot be
    moved;
  he will judge the peoples with equity.

---

[a]8 Meribah means quarreling.   [b]8 Massah means testing.
[c]9 Or LORD with the splendor of

[11]Let the heavens rejoice, let the earth be glad;
   let the sea resound, and all that is in it;
[12] let the fields be jubilant, and everything in
         them.
   Then all the trees of the forest will sing for joy;
[13] they will sing before the LORD, for he comes,
      he comes to judge the earth.
   He will judge the world in righteousness[D]
      and the peoples in his truth.

Psalm 97

[1]The LORD reigns, let the earth be glad;
   let the distant shores rejoice.

[2]Clouds and thick darkness surround him;
   righteousness and justice are the
      foundation of his throne.
[3]Fire goes before him
   and consumes his foes on every side.
[4]His lightning lights up the world;
   the earth sees and trembles.
[5]The mountains melt like wax before the LORD,
   before the Lord of all the earth.
[6]The heavens proclaim his righteousness,
   and all the peoples see his glory[D].

[7]All who worship images are put to shame,
   those who boast in idols[D]—
   worship him, all you gods!

[8]Zion[D] hears and rejoices
   and the villages of Judah are glad
   because of your judgments, O LORD.
[9]For you, O LORD, are the Most High over all the
      earth;
   you are exalted far above all gods.

[10]Let those who love the LORD hate evil,
   for he guards the lives of his faithful ones
   and delivers them from the hand of the
      wicked.
[11]Light is shed upon the righteous[D]
   and joy on the upright in heart.
[12]Rejoice in the LORD, you who are righteous,
   and praise his holy name.

Psalm 98

A psalm.

[1]Sing to the LORD a new song,
   for he has done marvelous things;
   his right hand and his holy arm
   have worked salvation[D] for him.
[2]The LORD has made his salvation known
   and revealed his righteousness to the
      nations.
[3]He has remembered his love
   and his faithfulness to the house of Israel;
   all the ends of the earth have seen
      the salvation of our God.

[4]Shout for joy to the LORD, all the earth,
   burst into jubilant song with music;
[5]make music to the LORD with the harp,

tude to Christ, who has given us everything already. Giving gifts to God, then, is a necessary and natural part of true worship.

Why describe inanimate objects as rejoicing? (96:11–13)
This is called personification, a literary technique common in the Bible (especially in Psalms and Isaiah). *Rejoice* means to give joy or to feel great joy or delight. Obviously, inanimate objects don't "feel" joy the way people do, but they certainly give joy to their Creator. Creation stands as a testimony to the awesome power and majesty of God (98:7–8; 148:3–13; Isaiah 35:1).

What do these graphic pictures say about God? (97:2–5)
This is poetic language, meant to emphasize God's majesty rather than to describe the technical details of his appearance or his activities. It is meant to create a feeling *about* God, rather than draw a blueprint *of* him.

Who are God's foes? (97:3)
The wicked—all those who oppose him and resist his purposes. Yet God loves his enemies (Romans 5:8–10) and wants them to repent (2 Peter 3:9). The Hebrews often viewed things from a nationalistic perspective and counted Israel's enemies as God's enemies.

In what ways do people worship images? (97:7)
In ancient times idol worshipers prayed to images and offered sacrifices to them. Idols may not be so obvious today but they still compete for our allegiance—just as the ancient idols did. When materialism, status, emotional well-being, pleasures and other things drive a wedge between a person and God, those things become a means of contemporary idol worship.

How much protection does God give? (97:10)
God *guards* and *delivers*, but he probably views the protection he offers differently than we do. While we'd like a guarantee of a safe life, free of risk and danger, God is more interested in our eternal safety. Sometimes he allows tragedies or pain in our lives because he is accomplishing something far greater and more permanent than our finite minds can understand (Romans 8:28).

Right hand (98:1)
The right hand symbolized strength, power, love, honor and authority. See *The years of the right hand of the Most High* (77:10).

In what sense has all the earth seen God's salvation? (98:2–3)
In one sense salvation has been shown to the nations through God's works for Israel. But in another sense, this psalm can be read as prophecy—looking forward to the end times when God will judge and all will see his salvation.

Why describe inanimate objects as rejoicing? (98:8–9)

See *Why describe inanimate objects as rejoicing?* (96:11–13).

Why celebrate the coming judgment? (98:9)

Although the judgment of God is described as *a cruel day, with wrath and fierce anger* (Isaiah 13:9), it will accomplish great good. Sin will be judged and justice will be established. Ever since sin was introduced in the Garden of Eden, it has brought terrible consequences to the world. The day it is finally eliminated will be a day for great rejoicing.

SCRIPTURE LINK (99:1) *Enthroned between the cherubim*

God dwelt between the two cherubim on the cover of the ark. See Exodus 25:22.

What's so awesome about a name? (99:3)

A name in Hebrew was often used to signify the collected attributes, characteristics or the essence of the person (or object) named. This is especially true with the names of God, both for the Father and the Son. To know the name of God is to know God himself—and to be in awe of his holiness and power.

How can we worship at God's footstool? (99:5)

Sometimes God's *footstool* was linked specifically to the temple (1 Chron. 28:2). But in a broader sense, the earth can be called God's footstool, using the same figure of speech that symbolizes heaven as God's throne (Isaiah 66:1). To worship at God's footstool does not mean going to a certain location. Rather, it suggests an attitude of submission and humility before the majesty of God.

In what ways was Moses a priest? (99:6)

Moses had a unique calling that included many of the duties of a priest—sprinkling the blood of the covenant (Exodus 24:6–8), consecrating Aaron and his sons (Lev. 8) and serving in the sanctuary (Exodus 40:22–27). Also, Moses interceded with God on behalf of the people, just as a priest would (Exodus 32:30–32).

Should *we* go to God's holy mountain to worship? (99:9)

Because of Christ, we don't have to. God no longer requires his people to worship him from just one location, the temple. Instead God looks for worshipers whose hearts are oriented toward him, whether or not they are physically in Jerusalem (John 4:21,23).

How are God's people like sheep? (100:3)

Sheep are very dependent animals. They need a shepherd to protect them and guide them to good pasture and water. Like sheep, people need someone to lead them. When people follow the Lord, they find spiritual safety and nourishment. When they follow their own sinful desires, they risk eternal death caused by spiritual hunger and thirst or spiritual predators.

with the harp and the sound of singing,
⁶with trumpets and the blast of the ram's
horn—
shout for joy before the LORD, the King.

⁷Let the sea resound, and everything in it,
the world, and all who live in it.
⁸Let the rivers clap their hands,
let the mountains sing together for joy;
⁹let them sing before the LORD,
for he comes to judge the earth.
He will judge the world in righteousness[D]
and the peoples with equity.

Psalm 99

¹The LORD reigns,
let the nations tremble;
he sits enthroned between the cherubim[D],
let the earth shake.
²Great is the LORD in Zion[D];
he is exalted over all the nations.
³Let them praise your great and awesome
name—
he is holy.

⁴The King is mighty, he loves justice—
you have established equity;
in Jacob you have done
what is just and right.
⁵Exalt the LORD our God
and worship at his footstool[D];
he is holy.

⁶Moses and Aaron were among his priests[D],
Samuel was among those who called on his
name;
they called on the LORD
and he answered them.
⁷He spoke to them from the pillar of cloud;
they kept his statutes and the decrees he
gave them.

⁸O LORD our God,
you answered them;
you were to Israel[a] a forgiving God,
though you punished their misdeeds.[b]
⁹Exalt the LORD our God
and worship at his holy mountain,
for the LORD our God is holy.

Psalm 100

A psalm. For giving thanks.

¹Shout for joy to the LORD, all the earth.
²   Worship the LORD with gladness;
come before him with joyful songs.
³Know that the LORD is God.
It is he who made us, and we are his[c];
we are his people, the sheep of his pasture.

---

[a]8 Hebrew *them*   [b]8 Or *I an avenger of the wrongs done to them*
[c]3 Or *and not we ourselves*

⁴Enter his gates with thanksgiving
    and his courts with praise;
    give thanks to him and praise his name.
⁵For the LORD is good and his love endures
        forever;
    his faithfulness continues through all
        generations.

Psalm 101

Of David. A psalm.

¹I will sing of your love and justice;
    to you, O LORD, I will sing praise.
²I will be careful to lead a blameless life—
    when will you come to me?

I will walk in my house
    with blameless heart.
³I will set before my eyes
    no vile thing.

The deeds of faithless men I hate;
    they will not cling to me.
⁴Men of perverse heart shall be far from me;
    I will have nothing to do with evil.

⁵Whoever slanders his neighbor in secret,
    him will I put to silence;
whoever has haughty eyes and a proud
        heart,
    him will I not endure.

⁶My eyes will be on the faithful in the land,
    that they may dwell with me;
he whose walk is blameless
    will minister to me.

⁷No one who practices deceit
    will dwell in my house;
no one who speaks falsely
    will stand in my presence.

⁸Every morning I will put to silence
    all the wicked in the land;
I will cut off every evildoer
    from the city of the LORD.

Where are God's gates and courts? (100:4)

These words borrow from practices familiar to ancient culture. Gates were often used as places to conduct legal business; the open enclosures of courtyards were used for large assemblies of people. The temple gates and courts symbolized the idea of meeting with God. See *Should we go to God's holy mountain to worship?* (99:9).

Who can be blameless? (101:2)

Only the one who loves God and is forgiven. David loved God so much that he wanted to please God more than anything else. But it is impossible to do the will of God perfectly and consistently without divine empowerment. Perhaps that is why he immediately follows his vow to be blameless with an urgent plea: *When will you come to me?*

Vile thing (101:3)

This is the Hebrew word *Belial,* meaning *without profit*—that is, something that is worthless or wicked. Personified, it became linked with Satan (2 Cor. 6:15). The statement here can also be stated in the affirmative: "I will focus on God."

Should we isolate ourselves from the world? (101:4)

No, but neither should we immerse ourselves in it. The New Testament helps clarify this principle: Jesus expects us to be in the world, but *not of the world* (John 17:15–16). By this he meant God's people could penetrate and influence the world with their transformed hearts and values. At the same time, however, he cautioned Christians against being so intimate with the world that they would sacrifice their spiritual dynamic, the very power capable of transforming the world.

Cut off (101:8)

For the Hebrews, this was a form of excommunication from the community. It can refer, in one way or another, to a break in relationship: banishment, loss of privileges or even death. See *Cut off from my presence* (Lev. 22:3).

How can we be joyful when we're really sad? (100:2)

Unlike much of contemporary society, the Bible does not confuse joy with happiness. Happiness is an emotional state typically dependent upon external circumstances; the Biblical concept of joy involves a deeper reality. Joy includes a condition of genuine well-being, marked by confidence, hope and trust that extends far beyond our own finite perceptions.

Happiness is often temporary; joy is more of a process, often developed most profoundly during periods of chaos and suffering. The deep, sustaining joy of the Lord comes from an assurance that he is with us and will deliver us—from present difficulties as well as from this scarred and stained world. Such joy is able to express its hope, even in the middle of legitimate sadness.

Weeping may remain for a night, but rejoicing comes in the morning (30:5).

Psalm 102

A prayer of an afflicted man. When he is faint and pours out his lament before the LORD.

¹Hear my prayer, O LORD;
  let my cry for help come to you.
²Do not hide your face from me
  when I am in distress.
 Turn your ear to me;
  when I call, answer me quickly.

³For my days vanish like smoke;
  my bones burn like glowing embers.
⁴My heart is blighted and withered like grass;
  I forget to eat my food.
⁵Because of my loud groaning
  I am reduced to skin and bones.
⁶I am like a desert owl,
  like an owl among the ruins.
⁷I lie awake; I have become
  like a bird alone on a roof.
⁸All day long my enemies taunt me;
  those who rail against me use my name as a
    curse.
⁹For I eat ashes as my food
  and mingle my drink with tears
¹⁰because of your great wrath,
  for you have taken me up and thrown me
    aside.
¹¹My days are like the evening shadow;
  I wither away like grass.

¹²But you, O LORD, sit enthroned forever;
  your renown endures through all
    generations.
¹³You will arise and have compassion on Zion[D],
  for it is time to show favor to her;
  the appointed time has come.
¹⁴For her stones are dear to your servants;

What was this man's problem? (102:3–5)

These powerful, poetic images could describe a number of things. Most likely, the psalmist was expressing his emotional suffering and turmoil, not just his physical symptoms. He felt completely separated from God, left alone to deal with his sin and to confront his enemies.

How was the psalmist like a desert owl or a bird alone on a roof? (102:6–7)

Both of these images present a graphic picture of loneliness. The writer felt abandoned by God, desolate and forsaken. Though he scanned the horizon for help, all he could see were ruins and barrenness. Alone and hopeless, he was like a solitary bird.

Why would God discard someone? (102:9–10)

Because of his wrath and judgment—or even because of his mercy. He may bring those he loves through hard times to motivate them to seek him. When people become desperate enough and at the end of themselves, they may repent and humbly turn to God. Feeling discarded and worthless can be a strong motivation to seek genuine significance.

What made it time to show favor to Zion? (102:13–14)

We don't know enough details to tell why the writer was so confident that the time had come for Zion to be restored. But we can say God generally restores relationships when suffering and solitude cause people to repent and sincerely depend upon him.

What prevents God from hearing our prayers? (102:1–2)

God's hearing is never impaired (94:9). But the language of Biblical poetry sometimes pictures God as though he were deaf (Deut. 1:45). This was simply a figurative way to say that God does not always respond to requests as people might hope. Sometimes answers come only after long delays; other times answers may come in an unrecognized form or in a manner the petitioner would not have wanted.

Effective prayer requires that the one praying have the right attitudes: reverence, humility, proper motivation, purity. Ineffectual prayer—that which God seems to ignore—often results from the lack of such qualities. Here are a few examples:

Irreverence: God may ignore those who are irreverent (50:21). *Pride:* God wants to help those who are humble in spirit, not those who are proud (James 4:6). *Self-seeking:* When people pray for selfish reasons, God may refuse their requests (James 4:3). *Sin:* Disobeying God can separate someone from God and cause prayers to go "unanswered" (Isaiah 59:1–2). *Unbelief:* Spiritual instability can undermine prayers (James 1:6–7). *Broken relationships:* A husband's prayers may be neutralized if he has treated his wife disrespectfully (1 Peter 3:7).

Also see article: **When does God refuse to hear our prayers?** (Jer. 11:11).

her very dust moves them to pity.
¹⁵The nations will fear the name of the LORD,
    all the kings of the earth will revere[D] your
        glory[D].
¹⁶For the LORD will rebuild Zion[D]
    and appear in his glory.
¹⁷He will respond to the prayer of the destitute;
    he will not despise their plea.

¹⁸Let this be written for a future generation,
    that a people not yet created may praise the
        LORD:
¹⁹"The LORD looked down from his sanctuary on
        high,
    from heaven he viewed the earth,
²⁰to hear the groans of the prisoners
    and release those condemned to death[D]."
²¹So the name of the LORD will be declared in
        Zion
    and his praise in Jerusalem[D]
²²when the peoples and the kingdoms
    assemble to worship the LORD.

²³In the course of my life[a] he broke my
        strength;
    he cut short my days.
²⁴So I said:
    "Do not take me away, O my God, in the
        midst of my days;
    your years go on through all generations.
²⁵In the beginning you laid the foundations of
        the earth,
    and the heavens are the work of your hands.
²⁶They will perish, but you remain;
    they will all wear out like a garment.
Like clothing you will change them
    and they will be discarded.
²⁷But you remain the same,
    and your years will never end.
²⁸The children of your servants will live in your
        presence;
    their descendants will be established before
        you."

Psalm 103

Of David.

¹Praise the LORD, O my soul[D];
    all my inmost being, praise his holy name.
²Praise the LORD, O my soul,
    and forget not all his benefits—
³who forgives all your sins
    and heals all your diseases,
⁴who redeems[D] your life from the pit
    and crowns you with love and compassion,
⁵who satisfies your desires with good things
    so that your youth is renewed like the
        eagle's.

⁶The LORD works righteousness[D]
    and justice for all the oppressed.

⁷He made known his ways to Moses,

a23 Or By his power

What prompted the writing of this psalm? (102:16-18)

Many believe this psalm was penned by one of the exiles living in Babylon. The nation of Israel had been defeated by the Babylonians, who had demolished Jerusalem and the temple and left the nation a wasteland. The exile, alone and friendless and without a country, probably wrote to express his sorrow and, more importantly, his hope that the Lord would one day restore himself and his country.

When will kingdoms *assemble to worship the Lord* in Jerusalem? (102:21-22)

Some believe that Jesus, after his second coming, will establish a kingdom on earth with Jerusalem as its capital city. His earthly reign will last 1,000 years and will include all the nations of the earth. Others view this more figuratively and think it may possibly refer to the new Jerusalem (Rev. 21:2).

Does this predict the end of the world? (102:25-26)

Maybe. The Bible makes it clear that the world is not here to stay. But more than the temporary nature of the earth, these verses emphasize the the unchanging nature of God.

Does God guarantee healing from any disease? (103:3)

There are several different opinions. Some say that God promises healing unequivocally, with the cure often dependent only upon the strength of our faith. Others believe that in some cases physical healing may not always be God's first priority. Sometimes physical sickness and suffering may, in fact, accomplish God's greater good—a spiritual healing, perhaps. The apostle Paul, for one, speaks of an affliction that God chose not to heal (2 Cor. 12:7-9).

What desires does God satisfy? (103:5)

Desires that are rooted in what pleases him. We cannot expect God to answer prayers for sinful or selfish desires (James 4:3). See *Does God give us anything we desire?* (37:4).

What do our sins deserve? (103:10)

Sin deserves death (Romans 6:23), sometimes defined as eternal separation from God. Unconfessed and unforgiven sin will bring judgment and prevent us from standing before a holy God (Matt. 25:41; Rev. 21:8).

Does God want us to be afraid of him? (103:11)

Fear of, or respect for, God is a good thing. Without it, people are presumptuous before God. Those who do not fear God will fail to respect his awesome power and righteousness, and they will not recognize the infinite distance between their sins and his holiness. See article: *Should we live in terror of God?* (Prov. 1:7).

As far as the east is from the west (103:12)

A metaphor used to picture an infinite distance. When the Lord removes sin, it no longer exists anywhere.

Why call human beings dust? (103:14)

God formed humanity from the dust of the earth (Gen. 2:7), showing the insignificance and brevity of physical life. Yet he values humans so much that he stamped his own image on us (Gen. 1:27) and sent his Son to die for us (John 3:16).

Why does God reward children and grandchildren for something they didn't do? (103:17–18)

Just as the destructive effects of sin seep into succeeding generations (Jer. 32:18), righteousness influences generations to come in positive ways. Godly people not only provide a healthy, stable environment for their families, they also model a vital relationship with God and train their children in righteousness.

Who's really in charge? (103:19)

God is. At the same time, however, God gives us the free will to make our own decisions—for good or bad. God created everything good (Gen. 1:31) but risked it all to give humankind the capacity to choose between right and wrong. Because God entrusted humans with a choice, sin was able to get a foothold (Gen. 3:17–19). But because of Jesus, creation one day *will be liberated from its bondage to decay* (Romans 8:21).

What is the psalmist saying about God? (104:2–9)

As with the poetic language of so many of the psalms, these verses use metaphors and personification to paint a sweeping vision of the sovereignty, rule and power of a holy Creator.

Is this literally the way the earth was formed? (104:6–9)

Most likely it is a figurative description of creation. However, some speculate a more literal view, that when God first made the earth, it was covered with water (v. 9)—either as one global ocean or perhaps shrouded by a blanket of mist and fog. Either way, dry ground had not yet appeared. Then God raised the dry land up out of the waters and formed continents. The waters flowed down from the land and formed separate oceans.

his deeds to the people of Israel:
8The Lord is compassionate and gracious,
   slow to anger, abounding in love.
9He will not always accuse,
   nor will he harbor his anger forever;
10he does not treat us as our sins deserve
   or repay us according to our iniquities.
11For as high as the heavens are above the earth,
   so great is his love for those who fear him;
12as far as the east is from the west,
   so far has he removed our transgressions
      from us.
13As a father has compassion on his children,
   so the Lord has compassion on those who
      fear him;
14for he knows how we are formed,
   he remembers that we are dust.
15As for man, his days are like grass,
   he flourishes like a flower of the field;
16the wind blows over it and it is gone,
   and its place remembers it no more.
17But from everlasting to everlasting
   the Lord's love is with those who fear him,
   and his righteousness^D with their children's
      children—
18with those who keep his covenant^D
   and remember to obey his precepts.^D

19The Lord has established his throne in heaven,
   and his kingdom rules over all.

20Praise the Lord, you his angels,
   you mighty ones who do his bidding,
   who obey his word.
21Praise the Lord, all his heavenly hosts,
   you his servants who do his will.
22Praise the Lord, all his works
   everywhere in his dominion.

Praise the Lord, O my soul.^D

Psalm 104

1Praise the Lord, O my soul.

O Lord my God, you are very great;
   you are clothed with splendor and majesty.
2He wraps himself in light as with a garment;
   he stretches out the heavens like a tent
3 and lays the beams of his upper chambers
      on their waters.
He makes the clouds his chariot
   and rides on the wings of the wind.
4He makes winds his messengers,^a
   flames of fire his servants.

5He set the earth on its foundations;
   it can never be moved.
6You covered it with the deep as with a
      garment;
   the waters stood above the mountains.
7But at your rebuke the waters fled,
   at the sound of your thunder they took to
      flight;

---

a4 Or angels

[8]they flowed over the mountains,
    they went down into the valleys,
    to the place you assigned for them.
[9]You set a boundary they cannot cross;
    never again will they cover the earth.

[10]He makes springs pour water into the ravines;
    it flows between the mountains.
[11]They give water to all the beasts of the field;
    the wild donkeys quench their thirst.
[12]The birds of the air nest by the waters;
    they sing among the branches.
[13]He waters the mountains from his upper chambers;
    the earth is satisfied by the fruit of his work.
[14]He makes grass grow for the cattle,
    and plants for man to cultivate—
    bringing forth food from the earth:
[15]wine that gladdens the heart of man,
    oil to make his face shine,
    and bread that sustains his heart.
[16]The trees of the LORD are well watered,
    the cedars of Lebanon that he planted.
[17]There the birds make their nests;
    the stork has its home in the pine trees.
[18]The high mountains belong to the wild goats;
    the crags are a refuge for the coneys.[a]

[19]The moon marks off the seasons,
    and the sun knows when to go down.
[20]You bring darkness, it becomes night,
    and all the beasts of the forest prowl.
[21]The lions roar for their prey
    and seek their food from God.
[22]The sun rises, and they steal away;
    they return and lie down in their dens.
[23]Then man goes out to his work,
    to his labor until evening.

[24]How many are your works, O LORD!
    In wisdom you made them all;
    the earth is full of your creatures.
[25]There is the sea, vast and spacious,
    teeming with creatures beyond number—
    living things both large and small.
[26]There the ships go to and fro,
    and the leviathan[D], which you formed to frolic there.

[27]These all look to you
    to give them their food at the proper time.
[28]When you give it to them,
    they gather it up;
when you open your hand,
    they are satisfied with good things.
[29]When you hide your face,
    they are terrified;
when you take away their breath,
    they die and return to the dust.
[30]When you send your Spirit,
    they are created,
    and you renew the face of the earth.

[31]May the glory[D] of the LORD endure forever;

[a]18 That is, the hyrax or rock badger

What and where are God's chambers? (104:13)

Continuing with his poetic metaphors, the psalmist describes the clouds as the foundation of God's *upper chambers* (v. 3). This figurative language does not refer to one specific location, but is intended rather to emphasize God's majesty and power.

How much gladness of heart can wine give? (104:14–15)

The verses in this psalm are centered on God's provision—for people, animals and all of life. Wine is included as one of God's provisions that makes life good. Why, then, are so many today faced with horrible addictions to wine and many other substances? How can something God intended for good ruin lives and relationships? Because even God's good things require us to use them responsibly. God-given gifts can be twisted and perverted by Satan, who tempts us to excess. Too much of a good thing leads to misery instead of gladness. Also see *Does Proverbs teach abstinence from alcohol?* (Prov. 20:1).

Cedars of Lebanon (104:16)

Trees that grew abundantly in Lebanon. Tall and stately, they were often used in the construction of palaces and temples. Because they were often used to build objects of human pride and wealth, they sometimes pictured God's coming judgment (Isaiah 2:12–18).

Does God's creation still need him? (104:16–30)

Although God created natural and immutable laws to govern and control the universe, he is still the divine center that holds it all together (Col. 1:16–17). He is also the center of life; whether we acknowledge it or not, each of us depends upon God for our next breath (Job 12:10; Acts 17:25).

Leviathan (104:26)

A great aquatic animal, possibly a crocodile, a serpent, a sea monster or a whale. *Leviathan* is used only in the poetic passages of the Bible, leading some to think that it was a borrowed metaphor from ancient creation myths. For more about this, see *Leviathan . . . serpent . . . monster* (Isaiah 27:1).

How does God's Spirit create living things? (104:30)

He is the source of all life. He is the cause behind the effect, the basis for every created being (Gen. 1:2).

SCRIPTURE LINK (104:32) Who touches the mountains and they smoke

Mount Sinai was covered with smoke when God gave the law to Moses there. See Exodus 19:18.

Why was history important? (105:1)

God reminded the people of his miracles interwoven throughout their history—how he had delivered them from their enemies and cared for them in times of need. He had rescued them from Egyptian bondage and given the entire nation a new birth. Using history was a means to call Israel back to its roots, warning the people of judgment and exhorting them to repent.

SCRIPTURE LINK (105:8–10) His covenant

The promise that the people of Israel would possess the land of Canaan (v. 11). This promise was made to Abraham (Gen. 22:15–18), Isaac (Gen. 26:3) and Jacob (Gen. 35:11–12).

My anointed ones (105:15)

Generally means specially set apart and consecrated for God's use alone. In this case it refers to the prophets. Messiah and Christ both mean the Anointed One (see NIV text note at Matt. 1:17).

SCRIPTURE LINK (105:17)

Joseph's story can be found in Gen. 37, 39–48.

---

may the LORD rejoice in his works—
³²he who looks at the earth, and it trembles,
  who touches the mountains, and they smoke.

³³I will sing to the LORD all my life;
  I will sing praise to my God as long as I live.
³⁴May my meditation be pleasing to him,
  as I rejoice in the LORD.
³⁵But may sinners vanish from the earth
  and the wicked be no more.

Praise the LORD, O my soul.ᴰ

Praise the LORD.ᵃ

Psalm 105

¹Give thanks to the LORD, call on his name;
  make known among the nations what he has
    done.
²Sing to him, sing praise to him;
  tell of all his wonderful acts.
³Gloryᴰ in his holy name;
  let the hearts of those who seek the LORD
    rejoice.
⁴Look to the LORD and his strength;
  seek his face always.

⁵Remember the wonders he has done,
  his miracles, and the judgments he
    pronounced,
⁶O descendants of Abraham his servant,
  O sons of Jacob, his chosen ones.
⁷He is the LORD our God;
  his judgments are in all the earth.

⁸He remembers his covenantᴰ forever,
  the word he commanded, for a thousand
    generations,
⁹the covenant he made with Abraham,
  the oath he swore to Isaac.
¹⁰He confirmed it to Jacob as a decree,
  to Israel as an everlasting covenant:
¹¹"To you I will give the land of Canaan
  as the portion you will inherit."

¹²When they were but few in number,
  few indeed, and strangers in it,
¹³they wandered from nation to nation,
  from one kingdom to another.
¹⁴He allowed no one to oppress them;
  for their sake he rebuked kings:
¹⁵"Do not touch my anointedᴰ ones;
  do my prophetsᴰ no harm."

¹⁶He called down famine on the land
  and destroyed all their supplies of food;
¹⁷and he sent a man before them—
  Joseph, sold as a slave.
¹⁸They bruised his feet with shackles,
  his neck was put in irons,
¹⁹till what he foretold came to pass,
  till the word of the LORD proved him true.
²⁰The king sent and released him,

ᵃ35 Hebrew Hallelu Yah; in the Septuagint this line stands at the beginning of Psalm 105.

the ruler of peoples set him free.
[21]He made him master of his household,
     ruler over all he possessed,
[22]to instruct his princes as he pleased
     and teach his elders wisdom.

[23]Then Israel entered Egypt;
     Jacob lived as an alien[D] in the land of Ham.
[24]The LORD made his people very fruitful;
     he made them too numerous for their foes,
[25]whose hearts he turned to hate his people,
     to conspire against his servants.
[26]He sent Moses his servant,
     and Aaron, whom he had chosen.
[27]They performed his miraculous signs among
          them,
     his wonders in the land of Ham.
[28]He sent darkness and made the land dark—
     for had they not rebelled against his words?
[29]He turned their waters into blood,
     causing their fish to die.
[30]Their land teemed with frogs,
     which went up into the bedrooms of their
          rulers.
[31]He spoke, and there came swarms of flies,
     and gnats throughout their country.
[32]He turned their rain into hail,
     with lightning throughout their land;
[33]he struck down their vines and fig trees
     and shattered the trees of their country.
[34]He spoke, and the locusts[D] came,
     grasshoppers without number;
[35]they ate up every green thing in their land,
     ate up the produce of their soil.
[36]Then he struck down all the firstborn[D] in their
          land,
     the firstfruits[D] of all their manhood.

[37]He brought out Israel, laden with silver and
          gold,
     and from among their tribes no one faltered.
[38]Egypt was glad when they left,
     because dread of Israel had fallen on them.
[39]He spread out a cloud as a covering,
     and a fire to give light at night.
[40]They asked, and he brought them quail[D]
     and satisfied them with the bread of heaven.
[41]He opened the rock, and water gushed out;
     like a river it flowed in the desert.

[42]For he remembered his holy promise
     given to his servant Abraham.
[43]He brought out his people with rejoicing,
     his chosen ones with shouts of joy;
[44]he gave them the lands of the nations,
     and they fell heir to what others had toiled
          for—
[45]that they might keep his precepts[D]
     and observe his laws.

     Praise the LORD.[a]

a45 Hebrew *Hallelu Yah*

SCRIPTURE LINK (105:24–45)
The stories of Israel's deliverance from Egypt,
travels in the desert and entrance into the land
of Canaan are told in Exodus and Numbers.

**Why did God give Israel the lands of
other people? (105:44)**
It was not because Israel was more righteous
or deserving. God expelled the nations of Canaan because of their wickedness. Later Israel
was punished for sin in the same way when Assyria and Babylon took over the land. Also see
article: *What right did Israel have to take the
land?* (Num. 33:52–53).

Psalm 106

¹Praise the LORD.*ᵃ*

Give thanks to the LORD, for he is good;
  his love endures forever.
²Who can proclaim the mighty acts of the LORD
  or fully declare his praise?
³Blessed are they who maintain justice,
  who constantly do what is right.
⁴Remember me, O LORD, when you show favor
    to your people,
  come to my aid when you save them,
⁵that I may enjoy the prosperity of your chosen
    ones,
  that I may share in the joy of your nation
  and join your inheritance in giving praise.

⁶We have sinned, even as our fathers did;
  we have done wrong and acted wickedly.
⁷When our fathers were in Egypt,
  they gave no thought to your miracles;
they did not remember your many kindnesses,
  and they rebelled by the sea, the Red Sea.*ᵇ*
⁸Yet he saved them for his name's sake,
  to make his mighty power known.
⁹He rebuked the Red Sea, and it dried up;
  he led them through the depths as through a
    desert.
¹⁰He saved them from the hand of the foe;
  from the hand of the enemy he redeemedᴰ
    them.
¹¹The waters covered their adversaries;
  not one of them survived.
¹²Then they believed his promises
  and sang his praise.

¹³But they soon forgot what he had done
  and did not wait for his counsel.
¹⁴In the desert they gave in to their craving;
  in the wasteland they put God to the test.
¹⁵So he gave them what they asked for,
  but sent a wasting disease upon them.

¹⁶In the camp they grew envious of Moses
  and of Aaron, who was consecratedᴰ to the
    LORD.
¹⁷The earth opened up and swallowed Dathan;
  it buried the company of Abiram.
¹⁸Fire blazed among their followers;
  a flame consumed the wicked.

¹⁹At Horeb they made a calf
  and worshiped an idolᴰ cast from metal.
²⁰They exchanged their Gloryᴰ
  for an image of a bull, which eats grass.
²¹They forgot the God who saved them,
  who had done great things in Egypt,
²²miracles in the land of Ham
  and awesome deeds by the Red Sea.
²³So he said he would destroy them—
  had not Moses, his chosen one,

What kind of prosperity do God's chosen ones enjoy? (106:3–5)

God promises to prosper those who follow his laws and obey his commands. His laws lead to health, righteousness, selfless living, inner joy, and God's protection and provision. Prosperity, by God's definition, is not physical wealth and success squandered on selfish interests. See article: *Does obedience bring prosperity?* (Lev. 26:3–39).

Why recount past failures? (106:7–43)

The old maxim, "Those who forget history are bound to repeat it," was just as true then as it is now. God recounts their failures to remind the Israelites that they are a people who are naturally inclined to sin. God continued dealing with his people even though they continued the cycle of sinning, repenting, trusting, growing complacent and then sinning again.

SCRIPTURE LINK (106:7) *They rebelled by the sea*

See Exodus 14:10–13.

SCRIPTURE LINK (106:14) *They gave in to their craving*

For three examples, see Exodus 15:22–24; 17:2; 32:1–6.

SCRIPTURE LINK (106:19) *At Horeb they made a calf*

See Exodus 32.

Glory (106:20)

Used as a synonym for God. Also see *Glory of Israel* (1 Samuel 15:29); *How did the people see the glory of the Lord?* (Lev. 9:23) and *Glory of the Lord* (Ezek. 43:4–5).

How could Moses change God's mind? (106:23)

The Bible is filled with incidents where God's mind was changed by the prayers and often the repentance of godly people. It is no threat to God's sovereignty that *the prayer of a righteous man is powerful and effective* (James 5:16). Also see article: *Can our prayers cause God to change his mind?* (Exodus 32:14).

---

*ᵃ*1 Hebrew *Hallelu Yah*; also in verse 48   *ᵇ*7 Hebrew *Yam Suph*; that is, Sea of Reeds; also in verses 9 and 22

stood in the breach before him
to keep his wrath from destroying them.

²⁴Then they despised the pleasant land;
they did not believe his promise.
²⁵They grumbled in their tents
and did not obey the LORD.
²⁶So he swore to them with uplifted hand
that he would make them fall in the desert,
²⁷make their descendants fall among the nations
and scatter them throughout the lands.

²⁸They yoked themselves to the Baalᴰ of Peor
and ate sacrificesᴰ offered to lifeless gods;
²⁹they provoked the LORD to anger by their
wicked deeds,
and a plague broke out among them.
³⁰But Phinehas stood up and intervened,
and the plague was checked.
³¹This was credited to him as righteousnessᴰ
for endless generations to come.

³²By the waters of Meribah they angered the
LORD,
and trouble came to Moses because of them;
³³for they rebelled against the Spirit of God,
and rash words came from Moses' lips.ᵃ

³⁴They did not destroy the peoples
as the LORD had commanded them,
³⁵but they mingled with the nations
and adopted their customs.
³⁶They worshiped their idolsᴰ,
which became a snare to them.
³⁷They sacrificed their sons
and their daughters to demons.
³⁸They shed innocent blood,
the blood of their sons and daughters,
whom they sacrificed to the idols of Canaan,
and the land was desecratedᴰ by their
blood.
³⁹They defiled themselves by what they did;
by their deeds they prostituted themselves.

ᵃ33 Or against his spirit, / and rash words came from his lips

SCRIPTURE LINK (106:24) *Then they despised the pleasant land*
See Num. 14:26–35.

SCRIPTURE LINK (106:28) *They yoked themselves to the Baal of Peor*
See Num. 25:1–9.

Baal of Peor (106:28)
A Moabite deity worshiped on Mount Peor with immoral rites, including prostitution.

How did Phinehas intervene to halt the punishment? (106:30)
Phinehas, a priest and the grandson of Aaron, obeyed the Lord's command to put to death those who were worshiping Baal through immoral sexual rites. He ran a spear through an Israelite man and a Moabite woman engaged in sexual intercourse. For his action, the Lord halted a plague he had sent on Israel. See Num. 25:7–11.

SCRIPTURE LINK (106:32) *They angered the LORD*
See Num. 20:2–13.

SCRIPTURE LINK (106:34) *They did not destroy the peoples*
For the command that Israel failed to perform, see Exodus 23:32–33.

They sacrificed their sons and their daughters to demons (106:37)
See *Why would parents sacrifice their children?* (Jer. 19:5).

Can righteousness be credited to our account? (106:31)

Yes, when it is the outgrowth of faith. By daring to act on God's Word, Phinehas showed that he had faith in God's Word. But if his righteous acts had been offered in an attempt to earn salvation, they would have been the outgrowth of a lack of faith. Those who depend on their own good efforts will not have righteousness credited to their accounts.

The apostle Paul says that it is faith—not good works—that is credited as righteousness (Romans 4:5). He uses Abraham as an example: Abraham did not earn credit with God by doing righteous works. Instead, Abraham simply trusted God. *Abraham believed God* (Romans 4:3); it was his faith that was credited to his account as righteousness.

We can also have righteousness credited to our accounts—when we trust God and believe in Jesus Christ.

What nations did they need to be gathered from? (106:47)

Many believe this psalm was written after Judah was conquered by Babylon. To reduce the threat of rebellion, Babylon made it a practice to "disperse" the conquered people. The Israelites were taken into captivity in Babylon, primarily in its eastern provinces.

What circumstances prompted this psalm to be written? (107:1-7)

This was probably written when the Israelites were allowed to return to their homeland from their Babylonian captivity. Once exiles, living in foreign lands and suffering distress and often imprisonment, they were now free to celebrate God's help to them.

In what way did Israel rebel? (107:11)

Rebelling against God and despising his counsel go hand in hand. Israel forgot that God's laws were for their own protection. They began to chafe under his instructions until they became contemptuous about the law and hated God for the boundaries he imposed on their behavior. They rejected God's wisdom (as in Prov. 1:30) and rejected God himself by turning to other gods that seemed to offer to make them feel good (Deut. 31:20).

---

⁴⁰Therefore the LORD was angry with his people
    and abhorred his inheritance.
⁴¹He handed them over to the nations,
    and their foes ruled over them.
⁴²Their enemies oppressed them
    and subjected them to their power.
⁴³Many times he delivered them,
    but they were bent on rebellion
    and they wasted away in their sin.
⁴⁴But he took note of their distress
    when he heard their cry;
⁴⁵for their sake he remembered his covenant[D]
    and out of his great love he relented.
⁴⁶He caused them to be pitied
    by all who held them captive.

⁴⁷Save us, O LORD our God,
    and gather us from the nations,
that we may give thanks to your holy name
    and glory in your praise.

⁴⁸Praise be to the LORD, the God of Israel,
    from everlasting to everlasting.
Let all the people say, "Amen!"

Praise the LORD.

BOOK V

Psalms 107-150

Psalm 107

¹Give thanks to the LORD, for he is good;
    his love endures forever.
²Let the redeemed[D] of the LORD say this—
    those he redeemed from the hand of the
      foe,
³those he gathered from the lands,
    from east and west, from north and south.[a]

⁴Some wandered in desert wastelands,
    finding no way to a city where they could
      settle.
⁵They were hungry and thirsty,
    and their lives ebbed away.
⁶Then they cried out to the LORD in their
      trouble,
    and he delivered them from their distress.
⁷He led them by a straight way
    to a city where they could settle.
⁸Let them give thanks to the LORD for his
      unfailing love
    and his wonderful deeds for men,
⁹for he satisfies the thirsty
    and fills the hungry with good things.

¹⁰Some sat in darkness and the deepest gloom,
    prisoners suffering in iron chains,
¹¹for they had rebelled against the words of God
    and despised the counsel of the Most High.
¹²So he subjected them to bitter labor;
    they stumbled, and there was no one to help.
¹³Then they cried to the LORD in their trouble,

---

[a]3 Hebrew *north and the sea*

and he saved them from their distress.
¹⁴He brought them out of darkness and the
    deepest gloom
and broke away their chains.
¹⁵Let them give thanks to the LORD for his
    unfailing love
and his wonderful deeds for men,
¹⁶for he breaks down gates of bronze
    and cuts through bars of iron.

¹⁷Some became fools through their rebellious
    ways
and suffered affliction^D because of their
    iniquities.
¹⁸They loathed all food
    and drew near the gates of death^D.
¹⁹Then they cried to the LORD in their trouble,
    and he saved them from their distress.
²⁰He sent forth his word and healed them;
    he rescued them from the grave.
²¹Let them give thanks to the LORD for his
    unfailing love
and his wonderful deeds for men.
²²Let them sacrifice^D thank offerings^D
    and tell of his works with songs of joy.

²³Others went out on the sea in ships;
    they were merchants on the mighty
        waters.
²⁴They saw the works of the LORD,
    his wonderful deeds in the deep.
²⁵For he spoke and stirred up a tempest
    that lifted high the waves.
²⁶They mounted up to the heavens and went
    down to the depths;
in their peril their courage melted away.
²⁷They reeled and staggered like drunken men;
    they were at their wits' end.
²⁸Then they cried out to the LORD in their
    trouble,
and he brought them out of their distress.
²⁹He stilled the storm to a whisper;
    the waves of the sea were hushed.
³⁰They were glad when it grew calm,
    and he guided them to their desired haven.
³¹Let them give thanks to the LORD for his
    unfailing love
and his wonderful deeds for men.
³²Let them exalt him in the assembly of the
    people
and praise him in the council of the elders.

³³He turned rivers into a desert,
    flowing springs into thirsty ground,
³⁴and fruitful land into a salt waste,
    because of the wickedness of those who
        lived there.
³⁵He turned the desert into pools of water
    and the parched ground into flowing
        springs;
³⁶there he brought the hungry to live,
    and they founded a city where they could
        settle.
³⁷They sowed fields and planted vineyards
    that yielded a fruitful harvest;

Gates of bronze ... bars of iron (107:16)

This may be a metaphor borrowed from the prophet Isaiah who described, in a general sense, how God would free Israel from Babylon (Isaiah 45:2). The phrase, however, could be taken literally since Babylon was a city of great wealth and may have had gates covered with bronze. Also many Israelites were imprisoned, probably behind bars of iron.

Why would God ruin the environment to punish people for their sins? (107:33-34)

Sin unleashes all sorts of destruction as part of its consequences—on land as well as people. After sin entered the world through Adam, for example, the ground was cursed (Gen. 3:17). Later, God warned Israel that if their sins defiled the land, it would vomit them out (Lev. 18:28).

How does this psalm teach us about the love of the Lord? (107:33-43)

It shows a familiar pattern in the relationship between God and his people: His people repent; God forgives and blesses; his people become spiritually comfortable and apathetic and eventually sin against God; God sends judgment; his people repent. This psalm describes this cycle, demonstrating God's great patience. He judges his people to bring them back to himself.

38he blessed them, and their numbers greatly
increased,
and he did not let their herds diminish.

39Then their numbers decreased, and they were
humbled
by oppression, calamity and sorrow;
40he who pours contempt on nobles
made them wander in a trackless waste.
41But he lifted the needy out of their affliction[D]
and increased their families like flocks.
42The upright see and rejoice,
but all the wicked shut their mouths.

43Whoever is wise, let him heed these things
and consider the great love of the LORD.

Psalm 108

A song. A psalm of David.

1My heart is steadfast, O God;
I will sing and make music with all my
soul[D].
2Awake, harp and lyre[D]!
I will awaken the dawn.
3I will praise you, O LORD, among the nations;
I will sing of you among the peoples.
4For great is your love, higher than the heavens;
your faithfulness reaches to the skies.
5Be exalted, O God, above the heavens,
and let your glory[D] be over all the earth.

6Save us and help us with your right hand,
that those you love may be delivered.
7God has spoken from his sanctuary:
"In triumph I will parcel out Shechem
and measure off the Valley of Succoth.
8Gilead is mine, Manasseh is mine;
Ephraim is my helmet,
Judah my scepter[D].
9Moab is my washbasin,
upon Edom[D] I toss my sandal;
over Philistia I shout in triumph."

10Who will bring me to the fortified city?
Who will lead me to Edom?
11Is it not you, O God, you who have rejected us
and no longer go out with our armies?
12Give us aid against the enemy,
for the help of man is worthless.
13With God we will gain the victory,
and he will trample down our enemies.

Psalm 109

For the director of music. Of David. A psalm.

1O God, whom I praise,
do not remain silent,
2for wicked and deceitful men
have opened their mouths against me;
they have spoken against me with lying
tongues.
3With words of hatred they surround me;
they attack me without cause.

Right hand (108:6)
See *The years of the right hand of the Most
High* (77:10) and *Withdrawn his right hand*
(Lam. 2:3).

Where was God's sanctuary? (108:7)
It's not so much God's location that's important as it is his character. The point is that God
speaks from a perspective different than ours.
God's *sanctuary* serves to remind us of his holiness.

Besides Israel, were all these nations also chosen by God? (108:7–9)
God created and owns everything. He often
demonstrated his sovereignty over other countries by using them to do his will, even when
they were not aware of it. However, God did not
select these other nations in the same way
that he had chosen Israel. He wanted a special
relationship with Israel as an example to the
world (Gen. 12:3). He chose them by his grace,
not because they were the most qualified nation (Deut. 7:6–7).

Why did David ask who would bring him to the fortified city? (108:10)
David was looking to God for safety from his
enemies. The rhetorical question *Who will bring
me to the fortified city?* is David's way of expressing his confidence in God. Only God can
protect and keep his people, even though it
sometimes seems that he has abandoned
them. David is saying that without the power
and protection of God no man-made city (or
any other invention) can provide safety and victory (v. 12).

Why did David think God had rejected his people? (108:11)
David may have experienced some military set-
back that caused him to believe they were being punished by God.

What prompted David to write this psalm? (109:1–3)
It is impossible to say for sure. It seems to
have been written to denounce the actions of
one particular enemy, not enemies in general.
Perhaps it was someone who betrayed David
while he was king—perhaps Ahithophel
(2 Samuel 15:31), Shimei (2 Samuel 16:5–8)
or Sheba (2 Samuel 20:1). In any case, David
felt deeply betrayed; he released his pain before God, asking God for justice.

4In return for my friendship they accuse me,
  but I am a man of prayer.
5They repay me evil for good,
  and hatred for my friendship.

6Appoint[a] an evil man[b] to oppose him;
  let an accuser[c] stand at his right hand.
7When he is tried, let him be found guilty,
  and may his prayers condemn him.
8May his days be few;
  may another take his place of leadership.
9May his children be fatherless
  and his wife a widow.
10May his children be wandering beggars;
  may they be driven[d] from their ruined
    homes.
11May a creditor seize all he has;
  may strangers plunder[D] the fruits of his
    labor.
12May no one extend kindness to him
  or take pity on his fatherless children.
13May his descendants be cut off,
  their names blotted out from the next
    generation.
14May the iniquity of his fathers be remembered
    before the LORD;
  may the sin of his mother never be blotted
    out.
15May their sins always remain before the LORD,
  that he may cut off the memory of them
    from the earth.

16For he never thought of doing a kindness,
  but hounded to death[D] the poor
  and the needy and the brokenhearted.
17He loved to pronounce a curse—
  may it[e] come on him;
  he found no pleasure in blessing—
  may it be[f] far from him.
18He wore cursing as his garment;
  it entered into his body like water,
  into his bones like oil.
19May it be like a cloak wrapped about him,
  like a belt tied forever around him.
20May this be the LORD's payment to my
    accusers,
  to those who speak evil of me.

21But you, O Sovereign LORD,
  deal well with me for your name's sake;
  out of the goodness of your love, deliver me.
22For I am poor and needy,
  and my heart is wounded within me.
23I fade away like an evening shadow;
  I am shaken off like a locust[D].
24My knees give way from fasting;
  my body is thin and gaunt.
25I am an object of scorn to my accusers;
  when they see me, they shake their heads.

26Help me, O LORD my God;

Is it right to pray for revenge? (109:6–20)

See article: *Is it right to pray for revenge?* (58:6–8).

In what way could David's situation be good for God's name? (109:21)

David believed that what happened to him reflected on the reputation of God's name. If things went well for him, then God would receive the credit. If, on the other hand, David experienced bad times, he believed God's reputation would suffer because he had declared his trust in God. In this way, then, David asked for God's righteousness and blessings in his life.

---

*a*6 Or ⌊*They say:*⌋ "*Appoint* (with quotation marks at the end of verse 19)   *b*6 Or *the Evil One*   *c*6 Or *let Satan*   *d*10 Septuagint; Hebrew *sought*   *e*17 Or *curse, / and it has*   *f*17 Or *blessing, / and it is*

What did it mean for God to stand *at the right hand of the needy?* (109:31)

Just as God's right hand is a place of honor representing his power and authority, God becomes the *right hand* to those in need. In other words, he stands ready to serve those in need who will trust in him.

What did this psalm mean to David? (110:1)

King David wrote this to be sung at the crowning of future kings of Israel. He probably did not fully understand that one of those kings would be Jesus, the Messiah from God.

SCRIPTURE LINK (110:1) *The L*ORD *says to my Lord*

Jesus quoted this scripture to explain that the Christ (the Messiah) was greater than King David himself, even though Christ came later in history. See Matt. 22:44.

Whom was David talking about? (110:1)

LORD with all capitals is the Hebrew name for God, *Yahweh.* Lord with only the *L* capitalized is a title for the king. Though David was the reigning king, he could refer to a future ruler of Israel as *my Lord.* David acknowledged the coming Messiah as his king.

Scepter (110:2)

A staff or pole which the king held as a symbol of his royal authority. This promise means that God would expand the king's rule far beyond Jerusalem.

Why did the Lord swear? (110:4)

To guarantee his promise. When the Lord swore an oath that would never change, he made an unbreakable promise: the Messiah would be permanently appointed as king and priest. He would reign forever!

SCRIPTURE LINK (110:4) *Melchizedek*

Centuries before David, Melchizedek had been a king and priest of Salem (later called Jerusalem). Abraham brought offerings to this amazing man (Gen. 14:18–20). The New Testament quotes this passage to show that Jesus would be a priest forever. See Heb. 5:6; 7:21.

What kind of a priest was Melchizedek? (110:4)

Melchizedek's name means *king of righteousness.* Since he was the king of Salem (which means *peace*), he was also the *king of peace.* In addition to governing and judging the people, he was a priest who stood before God to make sacrifices on behalf of the people.

Extol (111:1)

Another way of saying *praise.* Every verse of this psalm finds a different way to say *Praise the L*ORD, or *Hallelujah.* (See NIV text note.)

Council of the upright (111:1)

Probably not any formal group. *Council* suggests something more intimate while *assembly* conveys the idea of something more public. In poetic terms, this simply says that everyone will praise God—from the smallest gathering of righteous people to an assembly of the entire nation of Israel.

save me in accordance with your love.
²⁷Let them know that it is your hand,
    that you, O LORD, have done it.
²⁸They may curse, but you will bless;
    when they attack they will be put to shame,
    but your servant will rejoice.
²⁹My accusers will be clothed with disgrace
    and wrapped in shame as in a cloak.

³⁰With my mouth I will greatly extol[D] the LORD;
    in the great throng I will praise him.
³¹For he stands at the right hand of the needy
        one,
    to save his life from those who condemn
        him.

Psalm 110

Of David. A psalm.

¹The LORD says to my Lord:
    "Sit at my right hand
until I make your enemies
    a footstool[D] for your feet."

²The LORD will extend your mighty scepter[D]
        from Zion[D];
    you will rule in the midst of your enemies.
³Your troops will be willing
    on your day of battle.
Arrayed in holy majesty,
    from the womb of the dawn
    you will receive the dew of your youth.[a]

⁴The LORD has sworn
    and will not change his mind:
"You are a priest[D] forever,
    in the order of Melchizedek."

⁵The Lord is at your right hand;
    he will crush kings on the day of his wrath.
⁶He will judge the nations, heaping up the dead
    and crushing the rulers of the whole earth.
⁷He will drink from a brook beside the way[b];
    therefore he will lift up his head.

Psalm 111[c]

¹Praise the LORD.[d]

I will extol the LORD with all my heart
    in the council of the upright and in the
        assembly.

²Great are the works of the LORD;
    they are pondered by all who delight in
        them.
³Glorious and majestic are his deeds,
    and his righteousness[D] endures forever.
⁴He has caused his wonders to be remembered;
    the LORD is gracious and compassionate.
⁵He provides food for those who fear him;

---

[a]3 Or *I your young men will come to you like the dew*   [b]7 Or *I The One who grants succession will set him in authority*   [c]This psalm is an acrostic poem, the lines of which begin with the successive letters of the Hebrew alphabet.   [d]1 Hebrew *Hallelu Yah*

he remembers his covenant^D forever.
6He has shown his people the power of his
    works,
    giving them the lands of other nations.
7The works of his hands are faithful and just;
    all his precepts^D are trustworthy.
8They are steadfast for ever and ever,
    done in faithfulness and uprightness.
9He provided redemption^D for his people;
    he ordained his covenant forever—
    holy and awesome is his name.

10The fear of the LORD is the beginning of
    wisdom;
    all who follow his precepts have good
      understanding.
    To him belongs eternal praise.

Psalm 112ᵃ

1Praise the LORD.ᵇ

Blessed is the man who fears the LORD,
    who finds great delight in his commands.

2His children will be mighty in the land;
    the generation of the upright will be blessed.
3Wealth and riches are in his house,
    and his righteousness^D endures forever.
4Even in darkness light dawns for the upright,
    for the gracious and compassionate and
      righteous^D man.ᶜ
5Good will come to him who is generous and
    lends freely,
    who conducts his affairs with justice.
6Surely he will never be shaken;

ᵃThis psalm is an acrostic poem, the lines of which begin with the
successive letters of the Hebrew alphabet.   ᵇ1 Hebrew *Hallelu Yah*
ᶜ4 Or *I for ⌐the LORD⌐ is gracious and compassionate and righteous*

What covenant is this? (111:5–9)

The psalmist is saying, "God keeps his word."
The primary covenant that would come to
mind, however, would be God's covenant with
Abram (Gen. 17:4–8). There God promised to
bless and multiply Abram's descendants and
give them the land.

What is the fear of the Lord? (111:10)

See article: ***Should we live in terror of God?***
(Prov. 1:7).

How does light dawn for the upright? (112:4)

In Hebrew poetry *darkness* often refers to calamity, *light* to well-being. God brings good to
the upright person even during tragedy. Sometimes light dawns through positive new circumstances. At other times God's comfort becomes like bright rays in the middle of
adversity. The upright person is someone who
focuses on God, seeks to live for him, praises
him and delights in his commands (v. 1).

How does trust make a heart steadfast? (112:6–7)

When we are convinced everything is under
control, our hearts become calm. We become
solid instead of shaky, confident instead of
anxious. Though the problems may still exist
for the moment, and even though circumstances have not changed immediately, trust
provides a settled assurance that God is working things out.

Can we take these statements as promises? (112:2–8)

Great children, wealth, good will, never shaken, no fears, steady and secure—
this man appears to have everything. But these pleasant things are not the
focus of this psalm. The subject of this psalm is found in its first words: *Praise the LORD.*

This is a song about God and the good he does. It's not a list of promises to claim,
but a list of reasons to praise God for his greatness and generosity.

This man *fears the LORD* and *finds great delight in his commands.* In other words, he is
more interested in God for his own sake than in what he can get from God. The benefits
are great but should not be our focus. They should remind us to praise God. This psalm
encourages us to look at the good things in our lives and count them as gifts from God.
We can read or sing this list and then add our own items.

Faithfulness to God doesn't always make life easy. Righteous people can experience
both good and bad. They go through times of *darkness* (v. 4) and hear *bad news* (v. 7).
Those who live for God, however, will find that the *light dawns* in the darkness. They can
look forward to triumph in the end. Whether times are good or bad, they can praise the
Lord.

Also see article: ***Are proverbs iron-clad promises?*** (Prov. 3:1–4).

Horn (112:9)

A symbol of power and strength, often used to portray military power or the authority of a king. Also see NIV text note.

What does it mean to gnash teeth? (112:10)

Gnashing teeth is the same as grinding teeth together. In ancient cultures a person could express malice toward someone by gnashing his teeth at that person. Envy was another sentiment sometimes expressed by gnashing teeth.

Does God sit on a throne? (113:5)

If not literally, then at least figuratively. This poetic language conveys an image of a king ruling over the people. The writer of this psalm wanted to portray God as the King of kings, ruling over all the world.

How does God raise the poor and lift the needy? (113:7-9)

God, in his greatness, shows his concern for the poor and needy. He steps down from his throne (see previous question) to help hurting people. These words come from Hannah (1 Samuel 2:8) who prayed desperately for a child. When God gave her a son, she felt like God had raised her from the dust by removing the reproach of barrenness from her.

Why the distinction between Israel and Jacob? (114:1)

Hebrew poetry often contains parallel thoughts expressing the same thing two different ways. See article: *How should we understand Biblical poetry?* (1:1). Israel and Jacob were two names for the same person, used here as names for the nation which he fathered.

In what sense was Judah God's sanctuary, Israel his dominion? (114:2)

As God's sanctuary, God lived among them, first in the tabernacle and later in the temple. They were also God's dominion, his kingdom on earth. Because of God's presence, they were given a lofty position—they were the people among whom God chose to dwell. This is remarkable, since when the Hebrew people left Egypt (v. 2), they were destitute of earthly status.

Do these verses describe a specific event? (114:3-6)

Not literally. The psalmist is using personification to show that all of creation gets excited over God's great acts. These verses describe nature's response as God led his people out of Egypt and established his dominion over them.

a righteous^D man will be remembered forever.

7He will have no fear of bad news;
  his heart is steadfast, trusting in the LORD.
8His heart is secure, he will have no fear;
  in the end he will look in triumph on his foes.
9He has scattered abroad his gifts to the poor,
  his righteousness^D endures forever;
  his horn*a* will be lifted high in honor.

10The wicked man will see and be vexed,
  he will gnash his teeth and waste away;
  the longings of the wicked will come to nothing.

Psalm 113

1Praise the LORD.*b*

Praise, O servants of the LORD,
  praise the name of the LORD.
2Let the name of the LORD be praised,
  both now and forevermore.
3From the rising of the sun to the place where it sets,
  the name of the LORD is to be praised.

4The LORD is exalted over all the nations,
  his glory^D above the heavens.
5Who is like the LORD our God,
  the One who sits enthroned on high,
6who stoops down to look
  on the heavens and the earth?

7He raises the poor from the dust
  and lifts the needy from the ash heap;
8he seats them with princes,
  with the princes of their people.
9He settles the barren woman in her home
  as a happy mother of children.

Praise the LORD.

Psalm 114

1When Israel came out of Egypt,
  the house of Jacob from a people of foreign tongue,
2Judah became God's sanctuary,
  Israel his dominion.

3The sea looked and fled,
  the Jordan turned back;
4the mountains skipped like rams,
  the hills like lambs.

5Why was it, O sea, that you fled,
  O Jordan, that you turned back,
6you mountains, that you skipped like rams,
  you hills, like lambs?

7Tremble, O earth, at the presence of the Lord,
  at the presence of the God of Jacob,

a9 Horn here symbolizes dignity.   b1 Hebrew Hallelu Yah; also in verse 9

8who turned the rock into a pool,
  the hard rock into springs of water.

Psalm 115

1Not to us, O LORD, not to us
  but to your name be the gloryD,
  because of your love and faithfulness.

2Why do the nations say,
  "Where is their God?"
3Our God is in heaven;
  he does whatever pleases him.
4But their idolsD are silver and gold,
  made by the hands of men.
5They have mouths, but cannot speak,
  eyes, but they cannot see;
6they have ears, but cannot hear,
  noses, but they cannot smell;
7they have hands, but cannot feel,
  feet, but they cannot walk;
  nor can they utter a sound with their throats.
8Those who make them will be like them,
  and so will all who trust in them.

9O house of Israel, trust in the LORD—
  he is their help and shield.
10O house of Aaron, trust in the LORD—
  he is their help and shield.
11You who fear him, trust in the LORD—
  he is their help and shield.

12The LORD remembers us and will bless us:
  He will bless the house of Israel,
  he will bless the house of Aaron,
13he will bless those who fear the LORD—
  small and great alike.

14May the LORD make you increase,
  both you and your children.
15May you be blessed by the LORD,
  the Maker of heaven and earth.

16The highest heavens belong to the LORD,
  but the earth he has given to man.
17It is not the dead who praise the LORD,
  those who go down to silence;
18it is we who extolD the LORD,
  both now and forevermore.

Praise the LORD.a

Psalm 116

1I love the LORD, for he heard my voice;
  he heard my cry for mercyD.
2Because he turned his ear to me,
  I will call on him as long as I live.

3The cords of deathD entangled me,
  the anguish of the graveb came upon me;
  I was overcome by trouble and sorrow.
4Then I called on the name of the LORD:
  "O LORD, save me!"

5The LORD is gracious and righteousD;

Why did other nations have doubts about Israel's God? (115:2)
Israel had many difficult experiences—40 years in the desert, famines, floods and judgments from God. During those tough times, the neighboring nations taunted Israel, suggesting that God had abandoned them.

Why did people worship man-made idols? (115:4–7)
People who made idols and worshiped them felt they were in control and more closely connected to their gods. They really believed (or at least tried to convince themselves) that a real god—a spirit—moved into what they made. When they worshiped these idols, they believed they could get supernatural powers to work for their benefit.

How would idol worshipers become like idols? (115:8)
The psalmist taunts idol makers and worshipers (reversing their earlier roles). See *Why did other nations have doubts about Israel's God?* (115:2). He says they will end up just like their idols—blind, powerless, lifeless and helpless. The prophet Isaiah develops the same theme with great detail describing how craftsmen fashion their idols (44:9–20).

House of Aaron (115:10,12)
Refers to the priests descended from Aaron, the first high priest of the nation of Israel.

In what sense did God give the earth to humans? (115:16)
God has loaned us the earth to care for as our home. God still owns the earth, but he has entrusted it for a time to us.

Cords of death (116:3)
The writer pictures himself as being tied up like a prisoner, trapped by death itself.

---

a18 Hebrew *Hallelu Yah*   b3 Hebrew *Sheol*

our God is full of compassion.
6The LORD protects the simplehearted;
when I was in great need, he saved me.

7Be at rest once more, O my soul[D],
for the LORD has been good to you.

8For you, O LORD, have delivered my soul
from death[D],
my eyes from tears,
my feet from stumbling,
9that I may walk before the LORD
in the land of the living.
10I believed; therefore[a] I said,
"I am greatly afflicted[D]."
11And in my dismay I said,
"All men are liars."

12How can I repay the LORD
for all his goodness to me?
13I will lift up the cup of salvation[D]
and call on the name of the LORD.
14I will fulfill my vows[D] to the LORD
in the presence of all his people.

15Precious in the sight of the LORD
is the death of his saints.
16O LORD, truly I am your servant;
I am your servant, the son of your
maidservant[b];
you have freed me from my chains.

17I will sacrifice[D] a thank offering[D] to you
and call on the name of the LORD.
18I will fulfill my vows to the LORD
in the presence of all his people,
19in the courts of the house of the LORD—
in your midst, O Jerusalem[D].

Praise the LORD.[c]

Psalm 117

1Praise the LORD, all you nations;
extol[D] him, all you peoples.
2For great is his love toward us,
and the faithfulness of the LORD endures
forever.

Praise the LORD.[c]

Psalm 118

1Give thanks to the LORD, for he is good;
his love endures forever.

2Let Israel say:
"His love endures forever."
3Let the house of Aaron say:
"His love endures forever."
4Let those who fear the LORD say:
"His love endures forever."

5In my anguish I cried to the LORD,
and he answered by setting me free.

Why would the psalmist say he is afflicted because he believed? (116:10)
The psalmist didn't have to sugarcoat reality. Because he had such strong faith, he felt free to declare the truth of his situation. Acknowledging his afflictions did not in any way diminish his faith in God. He still recognized God's power and control over his life.

The cup of salvation (116:13)
During Hebrew religious ceremonies, a cup of wine was lifted to God as an expression of thanksgiving. The writer celebrates God's goodness in saving him and publicly acknowledges his gratitude.

What kind of vows had the psalmist made? (116:14–18)
We aren't told what his specific vows were, but he seems to suggest that he had promised to publicly praise God for saving him (vv. 18–19).

Why would our death be precious to the Lord? (116:15)
This doesn't necessarily mean death is something pleasant or desirable. Precious can mean expensive or costly. God doesn't take the death of a righteous person lightly. He feels our pain and grieves with us. Some suggest another interpretation: that God is eager for his loved ones to come to him and rejoices when we arrive.

Who was the Lord's maidservant? (116:16)
This does not refer to an actual person. Rather the writer is painting a poetic picture. The first two lines in this verse suggest that he is not merely a servant, but a servant from birth—one born to the master's servant. See NIV text note.

Thank offerings (116:17)
Thank offerings were brought to the temple to express gratitude to God for deliverance from trouble, healing of sickness, answers to prayer or some other blessing. See Lev. 7:12–15.

Why repeat phrases over and over? (118:1–4)
Repetitions may seem awkward to read, but they were very effective when sung. Many psalms were written for worship, for thousands of people gathered together from all of Israel. The leader would sing, Let Israel say, and the people then respond, His love endures forever. The leader would continue, Let the house of Aaron say, and just the priests would sing, His love endures forever. The repetitions involved everyone in worship.

a 10 Or *believed even when*   *b 16* Or *servant, your faithful son*
c 19,2 Hebrew *Hallelu Yah*

⁶The LORD is with me; I will not be afraid.
  What can man do to me?
⁷The LORD is with me; he is my helper.
  I will look in triumph on my enemies.

⁸It is better to take refuge in the LORD
  than to trust in man.
⁹It is better to take refuge in the LORD
  than to trust in princes.

¹⁰All the nations surrounded me,
  but in the name of the LORD I cut them off.
¹¹They surrounded me on every side,
  but in the name of the LORD I cut them off.
¹²They swarmed around me like bees,
  but they died out as quickly as burning
    thorns;
  in the name of the LORD I cut them off.

¹³I was pushed back and about to fall,
  but the LORD helped me.
¹⁴The LORD is my strength and my song;
  he has become my salvationD.

¹⁵Shouts of joy and victory
  resound in the tents of the righteousD:
  "The LORD's right hand has done mighty things!
¹⁶ The LORD's right hand is lifted high;
  the LORD's right hand has done mighty
    things!"

¹⁷I will not die but live,
  and will proclaim what the LORD has done.
¹⁸The LORD has chastened me severely,
  but he has not given me over to deathD.

¹⁹Open for me the gates of righteousnessD;
  I will enter and give thanks to the LORD.
²⁰This is the gate of the LORD
  through which the righteous may enter.
²¹I will give you thanks, for you answered me;
  you have become my salvation.

²²The stone the builders rejected
  has become the capstoneD;
²³the LORD has done this,
  and it is marvelous in our eyes.
²⁴This is the day the LORD has made;
  let us rejoice and be glad in it.

²⁵O LORD, save us;
  O LORD, grant us success.
²⁶Blessed is he who comes in the name of the
    LORD.
  From the house of the LORD we bless you.a
²⁷The LORD is God,
  and he has made his light shine upon us.
  With boughs in hand, join in the festal
    procession
  upb to the horns of the altar.

²⁸You are my God, and I will give you thanks;
  you are my God, and I will exalt you.

²⁹Give thanks to the LORD, for he is good;
  his love endures forever.

a26 The Hebrew is plural.   b27 Or Bind the festal sacrifice with
ropes / and take it

Just what *can* man do to me? (118:6)
History records many persecutions against those loyal to the Lord, so this is not a guarantee of divine protection against any abuse. The psalmist's rhetorical question shows his confidence that no matter what any humans do to him, his life will remain within God's control. God has promised to be with us always, even when things appear bleak.

How did the psalmist *cut them off?* (118:10–13)
The writer reflects back on a situation where everything seemed hopeless for the nation of Israel. But then the enemy was grandly defeated. Apparently the psalmist was the military leader of the victorious conflict.

Why would God chasten the one he rescued? (118:18)
First God chastened him, *then* he rescued him. In a literary technique similar to a flashback, the writer reflects on the time before the victory, when Israel was surrounded and everything seemed hopeless. He saw that time as a chastening experience in his life, one which God used to teach him important lessons about life, danger and trust in God.

SCRIPTURE LINK (118:22) *The stone the builders rejected*
Jesus used these words to describe himself. Although he was rejected by many people, he is the *capstone,* the key part of the structure. See Mark 12:10.

What stone did the builders reject? (118:22)
We understand this to mean Christ, rejected by many. But the writer probably used this metaphor to speak of himself. Foreign armies showed their disrespect by attacking him. His victory, however, put him over them all. Another view is that the nation of Israel itself had been despised and was now honored.

Capstone (118:22)
The capstone was probably the most important stone in a building. It could have been a large stone over a doorway like a lintel; a keystone, holding up an arch; or a cornerstone, at the base of perpendicular walls. See Mark 12:10; 1 Peter 2:6–7.

SCRIPTURE LINK (118:26) *Blessed is he who comes in the name of the Lord*
These words were used to greet travelers coming to Jerusalem for the Feast of Unleavened Bread (Passover). The crowd shouted these words with additional vigor when Jesus triumphantly entered Jerusalem before Passover. See Luke 19:38.

What was the festal procession? (118:27)
It was like a parade, lending a festive atmosphere to the Hebrew religious festivals. People would join together and march through the streets, ending up at the temple where the celebrations would begin.

Psalm 119[a]

א Aleph

Why is this psalm so much longer than the average? (119:1–176)

This poet apparently was overflowing with zeal for the Word of God. The result of his intense passion is the longest chapter in the Bible. He looks at God's Word in a highly structured manner and from every conceivable angle. Because of its length, it may have been intended for reading rather than for singing.

Why is there a Hebrew character and word at the start of each section? (119:1–176)

This poem is expressed in a creative literary form known as the acrostic poem, fun and easy to remember. It is structured alphabetically, with a stanza for each of the 22 letters of the Hebrew alphabet (Aleph is like our A, Beth is like B and so on). The psalmist may have wanted to show that God's Word is so great that it takes every letter of the alphabet to talk about it. Or perhaps it was his way of covering his subject, as we would say, "from A to Z."

How do we hide God's Word in our hearts? (119:11)

By studying God's Word, memorizing his promises and meditating on and understanding their meaning. When we know God's Word well, it becomes part of us—shaping our values and our behavior.

How does God's Word keep us from sin? (119:11)

Sin, in this case, isn't deliberate evil, but failure to do what God requires. Knowing God's Word is a way to know his will, and we will more likely please God by doing what is right when we understand what he wants.

1Blessed are they whose ways are blameless,
who walk according to the law of the LORD.
2Blessed are they who keep his statutes
and seek him with all their heart.
3They do nothing wrong;
they walk in his ways.
4You have laid down precepts[D]
that are to be fully obeyed.
5Oh, that my ways were steadfast
in obeying your decrees!
6Then I would not be put to shame
when I consider all your commands.
7I will praise you with an upright heart
as I learn your righteous[D] laws.
8I will obey your decrees;
do not utterly forsake me.

ב Beth

9How can a young man keep his way pure?
By living according to your word.
10I seek you with all my heart;
do not let me stray from your commands.
11I have hidden your word in my heart
that I might not sin against you.
12Praise be to you, O LORD;
teach me your decrees.
13With my lips I recount
all the laws that come from your mouth.
14I rejoice in following your statutes
as one rejoices in great riches.
15I meditate on your precepts
and consider your ways.
16I delight in your decrees;
I will not neglect your word.

[a]This psalm is an acrostic poem; the verses of each stanza begin with the same letter of the Hebrew alphabet.

How do these terms for God's Word differ? (119:1–176)

These words are only slightly different in their meaning and are often translated interchangeably.

Law meaning *teaching* or *instruction* is used most frequently. It can mean a specific order from God, the Old Testament portion of the Bible called the Law, or the whole Bible in general.

Statutes are a record of God's stated will and give guidance and instruction. The word sometimes refers to the Ten Commandments.

Precepts are regulations of a covenant established by the Lord.

Decrees are a synonym for *law,* but with an emphasis on civil and ritual ordinances. These laws distinguished the Hebrews from other people.

Commands refer to words from God with a special focus on God's authority.

Word is a more general term that summarizes all the others. It refers to all God's truth, no matter how it's presented.

Promise is derived from the verb *say.* If God said it, it will come true.

ג   Gimel

17Do good to your servant, and I will live;
    I will obey your word.
18Open my eyes that I may see
    wonderful things in your law.
19I am a stranger on earth;
    do not hide your commands from me.
20My soul[D] is consumed with longing
    for your laws at all times.
21You rebuke the arrogant, who are cursed
    and who stray from your commands.
22Remove from me scorn and contempt,
    for I keep your statutes.
23Though rulers sit together and slander
        me,
    your servant will meditate on your
        decrees.
24Your statutes are my delight;
    they are my counselors.

ד   Daleth

25I am laid low in the dust;
    preserve my life according to your word.
26I recounted my ways and you answered
        me;
    teach me your decrees.
27Let me understand the teaching of your
        precepts[D];
    then I will meditate on your wonders.
28My soul is weary with sorrow;
    strengthen me according to your word.
29Keep me from deceitful ways;
    be gracious to me through your law.
30I have chosen the way of truth;
    I have set my heart on your laws.
31I hold fast to your statutes, O LORD;
    do not let me be put to shame.
32I run in the path of your commands,
    for you have set my heart free.

What makes the law wonderful? (119:18)

Just as God's miracles and creation inspire amazement and wonder, so does his law. Those who look carefully into God's law will discover its order and design for living and, as a result, will be filled with awe. Not only does God's law guide us to live in a way that pleases God, it also offers us what we need to know to get the most out of life—for now and for eternity.

Why are God's people strangers on earth? (119:19)

Stranger means *alien*—one belonging to another place. Those who belong to God will not feel completely at home in this world. Their loyalties and longings will be focused on the kingdom of God: they are citizens of heaven (Phil. 3:20).

How can a heart be free if it's restricted by commands? (119:32)

Literally, *set my heart free* means *enlarged my heart.* We might express the same idea by saying, "My heart could burst for joy." This joyful, carefree heart comes from the security of knowing what our boundaries are. When we stay within the limits of God's plan, we can be confident that we're in the best place possible.

How does a person meditate on God's Word? (119:15)

Meditation is a combination of reviewing, repeating, reflecting, thinking, analyzing, feeling and even enjoying. It is a physical, intellectual and emotional activity.

In some ways, meditation doesn't easily fit into Western culture. We value action and busyness more than stopping and considering. The author of this psalm was from another time and culture, one with a tradition that valued meditation. As a result, meditation came more naturally for him and others with his Middle Eastern background. We have to overcome some cultural obstacles to learn to meditate.

There are many ways to meditate on God's Word. Some possibilities include: (1) Take time to read a verse or passage over and over. (2) Begin to memorize all or part of it. (3) Listen—quiet your heart to allow the Holy Spirit to speak to you through God's Word. (4) Consider how it fits with the rest of the Bible and life in general. (5) Become emotionally involved—allow yourself to feel what God feels, his desires expressed through his words. (6) Move from meditation to application—connect your thoughts to action. Consider how the truth and power of the Word of God should affect your behavior.

ה   He

33Teach me, O Lord, to follow your decrees;
  then I will keep them to the end.
34Give me understanding, and I will keep your
  law
  and obey it with all my heart.
35Direct me in the path of your commands,
  for there I find delight.
36Turn my heart toward your statutes
  and not toward selfish gain.
37Turn my eyes away from worthless things;
  preserve my life according to your word. [a]
38Fulfill your promise to your servant,
  so that you may be feared.
39Take away the disgrace I dread,
  for your laws are good.
40How I long for your precepts[D]!
  Preserve my life in your righteousness[D].

ו   Waw

41May your unfailing love come to me, O Lord,
  your salvation[D] according to your promise;
42then I will answer the one who taunts me,
  for I trust in your word.
43Do not snatch the word of truth from my
  mouth,
  for I have put my hope in your laws.
44I will always obey your law,
  for ever and ever.
45I will walk about in freedom,
  for I have sought out your precepts.
46I will speak of your statutes before kings
  and will not be put to shame,
47for I delight in your commands
  because I love them.
48I lift up my hands to[b] your commands, which
  I love,
  and I meditate on your decrees.

ז   Zayin

49Remember your word to your servant,
  for you have given me hope.
50My comfort in my suffering is this:
  Your promise preserves my life.
51The arrogant mock me without restraint,
  but I do not turn from your law.
52I remember your ancient laws, O Lord,
  and I find comfort in them.
53Indignation grips me because of the wicked,
  who have forsaken your law.
54Your decrees are the theme of my song
  wherever I lodge.
55In the night I remember your name, O Lord,
  and I will keep your law.
56This has been my practice:
  I obey your precepts.

ח   Heth

57You are my portion, O Lord;
  I have promised to obey your words.

Why would God snatch the truth from our mouths? (119:43)

The psalmist is not implying that God would want to snatch truth away from him. Rather this is an expression of the psalmist's gratitude for the privilege of speaking God's truth. He feels honored to speak the truth of God to others, especially those who taunt him (v. 42). He prays that he will always have the privilege of speaking God's Word to other people.

How can ancient laws be relevant today? (119:52)

God's ancient laws are relevant because they provide unchanging, absolute truth in an age of relativity. God's truth remains solid and dependable when nothing else can be trusted. Some today claim there are no absolutes. But ethics and morality cannot exist in a vacuum; society cannot be built upon standards that shift with popular opinion. That's why we need the firm foundation of God's ancient laws.

Portion (119:57)

Refers to what one possesses. Others may have money and land, but the writer is delighted that he has the Lord. Having a close personal relationship with God is more valuable than anything else.

a37 Two manuscripts of the Masoretic Text and Dead Sea Scrolls; most
manuscripts of the Masoretic Text *life in your way*   *b48* Or *for*

⁵⁸I have sought your face with all my heart;
  be gracious to me according to your promise.
⁵⁹I have considered my ways
  and have turned my steps to your statutes.
⁶⁰I will hasten and not delay
  to obey your commands.
⁶¹Though the wicked bind me with ropes,
  I will not forget your law.
⁶²At midnight I rise to give you thanks
  for your righteousᴰ laws.
⁶³I am a friend to all who fear you,
  to all who follow your preceptsᴰ.
⁶⁴The earth is filled with your love, O LORD;
  teach me your decrees.

ט Teth

⁶⁵Do good to your servant
  according to your word, O LORD.
⁶⁶Teach me knowledge and good judgment,
  for I believe in your commands.
⁶⁷Before I was afflictedᴰ I went astray,
  but now I obey your word.
⁶⁸You are good, and what you do is good;
  teach me your decrees.
⁶⁹Though the arrogant have smeared me with
    lies,
  I keep your precepts with all my heart.
⁷⁰Their hearts are callous and unfeeling,
  but I delight in your law.
⁷¹It was good for me to be afflicted
  so that I might learn your decrees.
⁷²The law from your mouth is more precious to
    me
  than thousands of pieces of silver and gold.

י Yodh

⁷³Your hands made me and formed me;
  give me understanding to learn your
    commands.
⁷⁴May those who fear you rejoice when they see
    me,
  for I have put my hope in your word.
⁷⁵I know, O LORD, that your laws are righteous,
  and in faithfulness you have afflicted me.
⁷⁶May your unfailing love be my comfort,
  according to your promise to your servant.
⁷⁷Let your compassion come to me that I may
    live,
  for your law is my delight.
⁷⁸May the arrogant be put to shame for wronging
    me without cause;
  but I will meditate on your precepts.
⁷⁹May those who fear you turn to me,
  those who understand your statutes.
⁸⁰May my heart be blameless toward your
    decrees,
  that I may not be put to shame.

כ Kaph

⁸¹My soulᴰ faints with longing for your
    salvationᴰ,
  but I have put my hope in your word.
⁸²My eyes fail, looking for your promise;

Is affliction a good thing?
(119:67-75)
Often it is, or at least, it can be. Among several
positive benefits, affliction can teach us to appreciate God's presence, his truth and his
faithfulness. Affliction can also motivate us to
study and obey God's Word. Many insist that
difficulties bring them closer to God than do
pleasures and prosperity. We don't necessarily
desire affliction, but with the right attitude, we
can make the most of it when it comes.

Wineskin in the smoke (119:83)

Wineskins, used as bottles, were often hung from rafters. Smoke from the continual cooking fires would cover the skins with soot and eventually leave them dry and shriveled. The psalmist says that even if life leaves him unused, smudged and shriveled, he won't forget God's decrees.

Why was the psalmist persecuted? (119:86)

Because he was so committed to obeying God's Word, the writer ran into opposition from those who opposed it. They probably persecuted him with taunting words and actions, although we don't know the specifics.

What's the limit of perfection? (119:96)

In the Bible *perfect* often conveys the idea of something that is *completed* or *finished*. That's probably the meaning here. This is a poetic way of saying that there is no limit to what the commands of God can teach us. Since God is infinite, there can be no end to the things we can learn from him.

Why do we need teachers if we have God's commands? (119:99)

We can always benefit from the right kinds of teachers. In fact, because teaching is needed, God gives some individuals a special ability in teaching (Eph. 4:11). The point here is simply that God's truth is greater than human teachers.

Lamp to my feet (119:105)

The ancient lamp was small and flat with a wick and oil. It gave just enough light to see a short distance ahead. Similarly, God's Word gives light enough for each step in making moral decisions.

I say, "When will you comfort me?"
83Though I am like a wineskinD in the smoke,
  I do not forget your decrees.
84How long must your servant wait?
  When will you punish my persecutors?
85The arrogant dig pitfalls for me,
  contrary to your law.
86All your commands are trustworthy;
  help me, for men persecute me without
    cause.
87They almost wiped me from the earth,
  but I have not forsaken your preceptsD.
88Preserve my life according to your love,
  and I will obey the statutes of your mouth.

ל   Lamedh

89Your word, O LORD, is eternal;
  it stands firm in the heavens.
90Your faithfulness continues through all
    generations;
  you established the earth, and it endures.
91Your laws endure to this day,
  for all things serve you.
92If your law had not been my delight,
  I would have perished in my afflictionD.
93I will never forget your precepts,
  for by them you have preserved my life.
94Save me, for I am yours;
  I have sought out your precepts.
95The wicked are waiting to destroy me,
  but I will ponder your statutes.
96To all perfection I see a limit;
  but your commands are boundless.

מ   Mem

97Oh, how I love your law!
  I meditate on it all day long.
98Your commands make me wiser than my
    enemies,
  for they are ever with me.
99I have more insight than all my teachers,
  for I meditate on your statutes.
100I have more understanding than the elders,
  for I obey your precepts.
101I have kept my feet from every evil path
  so that I might obey your word.
102I have not departed from your laws,
  for you yourself have taught me.
103How sweet are your words to my taste,
  sweeter than honey to my mouth!
104I gain understanding from your precepts;
  therefore I hate every wrong path.

נ   Nun

105Your word is a lamp to my feet
  and a light for my path.
106I have taken an oath and confirmed it,
  that I will follow your righteousD laws.
107I have suffered much;
  preserve my life, O LORD, according to your
    word.
108Accept, O LORD, the willing praise of my mouth,
  and teach me your laws.

[109]Though I constantly take my life in my hands,
    I will not forget your law.
[110]The wicked have set a snare for me,
    but I have not strayed from your precepts[D].
[111]Your statutes are my heritage forever;
    they are the joy of my heart.
[112]My heart is set on keeping your decrees
    to the very end.

ס   Samekh

[113]I hate double-minded men,
    but I love your law.
[114]You are my refuge and my shield;
    I have put my hope in your word.
[115]Away from me, you evildoers,
    that I may keep the commands of my God!
[116]Sustain me according to your promise, and I will
    live;
    do not let my hopes be dashed.
[117]Uphold me, and I will be delivered;
    I will always have regard for your decrees.
[118]You reject all who stray from your decrees,
    for their deceitfulness is in vain.
[119]All the wicked of the earth you discard like
    dross[D];
    therefore I love your statutes.
[120]My flesh trembles in fear of you;
    I stand in awe of your laws.

ע   Ayin

[121]I have done what is righteous[D] and just;
    do not leave me to my oppressors.
[122]Ensure your servant's well-being;
    let not the arrogant oppress me.
[123]My eyes fail, looking for your salvation[D],
    looking for your righteous promise.
[124]Deal with your servant according to your love
    and teach me your decrees.
[125]I am your servant; give me discernment
    that I may understand your statutes.
[126]It is time for you to act, O Lord;
    your law is being broken.
[127]Because I love your commands
    more than gold, more than pure gold,
[128]and because I consider all your precepts right,
    I hate every wrong path.

פ   Pe

[129]Your statutes are wonderful;
    therefore I obey them.
[130]The unfolding of your words gives light;
    it gives understanding to the simple.
[131]I open my mouth and pant,
    longing for your commands.
[132]Turn to me and have mercy[D] on me,
    as you always do to those who love your
    name.
[133]Direct my footsteps according to your word;
    let no sin rule over me.
[134]Redeem[D] me from the oppression of men,
    that I may obey your precepts.
[135]Make your face shine upon your servant
    and teach me your decrees.

Double-minded (119:113)
Double-minded people are those who hold two different opinions at the same time. They think they're playing it safe by not making a commitment or decision. See James 1:6–8.

Dross (119:119)
The worthless by-product left over after refining precious metals like gold or silver ore. *Dross* is thrown out.

How can God's words be *unfolded*? (119:130)
By being *opened*, that is, by being interpreted and explained. This word picture also may suggest simply that God's words are presented so they can be heard and taken to heart.

136Streams of tears flow from my eyes,
    for your law is not obeyed.

צ Tsadhe

137RighteousD are you, O LORD,
    and your laws are right.
138The statutes you have laid down are righteous;
    they are fully trustworthy.
139My zealD wears me out,
    for my enemies ignore your words.
140Your promises have been thoroughly tested,
    and your servant loves them.
141Though I am lowly and despised,
    I do not forget your preceptsD.
142Your righteousnessD is everlasting
    and your law is true.
143Trouble and distress have come upon me,
    but your commands are my delight.
144Your statutes are forever right;
    give me understanding that I may live.

ק Qoph

145I call with all my heart; answer me, O LORD,
    and I will obey your decrees.
146I call out to you; save me
    and I will keep your statutes.
147I rise before dawn and cry for help;
    I have put my hope in your word.
148My eyes stay open through the watches of the
        night,
    that I may meditate on your promises.
149Hear my voice in accordance with your love;
    preserve my life, O LORD, according to your
        laws.
150Those who devise wicked schemes are near,
    but they are far from your law.
151Yet you are near, O LORD,
    and all your commands are true.
152Long ago I learned from your statutes
    that you established them to last forever.

ר Resh

153Look upon my suffering and deliver me,
    for I have not forgotten your law.
154Defend my cause and redeemD me;
    preserve my life according to your promise.
155SalvationD is far from the wicked,
    for they do not seek out your decrees.
156Your compassion is great, O LORD;
    preserve my life according to your laws.
157Many are the foes who persecute me,
    but I have not turned from your statutes.
158I look on the faithless with loathing,
    for they do not obey your word.
159See how I love your precepts;
    preserve my life, O LORD, according to your
        love.
160All your words are true;
    all your righteous laws are eternal.

שׂ Sin and Shin

161Rulers persecute me without cause,
    but my heart trembles at your word.

How is prayer connected with God's Word? (119:145–146)

Obeying God's commands isn't always easy. That may be why the writer called out to God for help. He knew that if God answered his prayer, he would be able to obey God's statutes. God's Word becomes more effective in our lives when it is coupled with prayer.

Watches of the night (119:148)

Night watchmen in ancient times usually did not have to work a full shift. The Hebrews divided the hours from sunset to sunrise into three watches consisting of about four hours each. The practice was that guards were relieved after their four hours, since no one was expected to remain alert all night. The writer of this psalm, however, was so thrilled to mediate on God's promises that he couldn't sleep! His enthusiasm for God's Word kept him alert all night.

162I rejoice in your promise
    like one who finds great spoil.
163I hate and abhor falsehood
    but I love your law.
164Seven times a day I praise you
    for your righteousD laws.
165Great peaceD have they who love your law,
    and nothing can make them stumble.
166I wait for your salvationD, O LORD,
    and I follow your commands.
167I obey your statutes,
    for I love them greatly.
168I obey your preceptsD and your statutes,
    for all my ways are known to you.

ת   Taw

169May my cry come before you, O LORD;
    give me understanding according to your
    word.
170May my supplication come before you;
    deliver me according to your promise.
171May my lips overflow with praise,
    for you teach me your decrees.
172May my tongue sing of your word,
    for all your commands are righteous.
173May your hand be ready to help me,
    for I have chosen your precepts.
174I long for your salvation, O LORD,
    and your law is my delight.
175Let me live that I may praise you,
    and may your laws sustain me.
176I have strayed like a lost sheep.
    Seek your servant,
    for I have not forgotten your commands.

Psalm 120

A song of ascents.

1I call on the LORD in my distress,
    and he answers me.
2Save me, O LORD, from lying lips
    and from deceitful tongues.

3What will he do to you,
    and what more besides, O deceitful tongue?
4He will punish you with a warrior's sharp
    arrows,
    with burning coals of the broom tree.

5Woe to me that I dwell in Meshech,
    that I live among the tents of Kedar!
6Too long have I lived
    among those who hate peace.
7I am a man of peace;
    but when I speak, they are for war.

Psalm 121

A song of ascents.

1I lift up my eyes to the hills—
    where does my help come from?
2My help comes from the LORD,
    the Maker of heaven and earth.

Great spoil (119:162)

The writer compares his experience with God's Word to be like that of a soldier who wins a battle and is able to take home the spoils of war. The Bible offers great riches to its readers.

Why did the psalmist praise God seven times each day? (119:164)

Seven is often used in the Bible to represent fullness or completeness (see, for example, 12:6). The writer is expressing the importance of praising God continually, not just *seven times*.

What is the psalmist praying for? (119:169)

Reading and knowing God's Word is one thing. Fully understanding it is something more. The writer of this psalm yearned to have a deep *understanding* of God's Word. He wasn't satisfied merely to hear God's truth; he wanted to better understand God himself.

How can we stray if we remember God's commands? (119:176)

This verse shows the writer to be a humble and honest man. He admits that his behavior does not always match his heart's desire. He is like a sheep that wanders away from the shepherd that it loves, even though, in his heart, he has not forgotten nor forsaken the Lord and his Word. We too may stray from God for a time, but his Word will remain with us.

Song of ascents (120:title)

Ascents means *steps* and could refer to any one of the following: (1) music that went up in pitch; (2) the place of the singing—on steps leading up to the temple; (3) the steps of the Jews returning from captivity or (4) the steps of a pilgrim singing these psalms.

Meshech . . . Kedar (120:5)

Meshech was in Asia Minor (modern Turkey); Kedar was south of Damascus. Since the writer couldn't possibly live in two distant places simultaneously, this is probably his figurative way of saying that he feels surrounded by hostile strangers.

Why look to the hills? (121:1)

As worshipers approached Jerusalem, they could see the hills around the city. In ancient times, some of those hills were used as *high places* for altars to pagan deities. As they looked to those hills and asked where their help came from, they were reminded that their real help didn't come from idols. It came instead from the Lord, the true God, the Creator.

How could the moon be harmful? (121:4–6)

This is poetic language to describe God's protection, which includes every extreme—light to dark, sun to moon and everything in between. It may be the writer knew stories of individuals harmed during the night and expressed the conviction that God can protect even in the most dangerous times. He is always alert, never sleeping (v. 4).

SCRIPTURE LINK (122:3–4) *According to the statute given to Israel*

Though Jerusalem was not named in the statute itself, it was clear that God called for his people to worship from a single, central location (Deut. 12:13–14). Jerusalem was later selected when David brought the ark there (2 Samuel 6:12). Solomon eventually built the temple there as well (1 Kings 6:1).

Thrones for judgment (122:5)

During his reign, David had developed a system of judgment with representatives of the king determining civil and criminal matters. The king, however, was ultimately responsible for justice in the kingdom. The term *throne* did not have to mean a literal chair made especially for a ruler. The term could be used as a metaphor to picture any position of authority, including that of a priest, a judge or a military leader.

Are we like slaves begging the master for mercy? (123:2–4)

In one sense, we are like slaves before the master in our relationship to God. God has power over all things and we are ultimately dependent on God for everything. So it is fitting that we relate to God in humility and submission. However, we shouldn't assume the negative and abusive aspects of slavery in this analogy. God is a loving and kind master, one who is a joy to serve.

³He will not let your foot slip—
 he who watches over you will not
 slumber;
⁴indeed, he who watches over Israel
 will neither slumber nor sleep.

⁵The LORD watches over you—
 the LORD is your shade at your right
 hand;
⁶the sun will not harm you by day,
 nor the moon by night.

⁷The LORD will keep you from all harm—
 he will watch over your life;
⁸the LORD will watch over your coming and
 going
 both now and forevermore.

Psalm 122

A song of ascents. Of David.

¹I rejoiced with those who said to me,
 "Let us go to the house of the LORD."
²Our feet are standing
 in your gates, O Jerusalem.ᴰ

³Jerusalem is built like a city
 that is closely compacted together.
⁴That is where the tribes go up,
 the tribes of the LORD,
to praise the name of the LORD
 according to the statute given to Israel.
⁵There the thrones for judgment stand,
 the thrones of the house of David.

⁶Pray for the peaceᴰ of Jerusalem:
 "May those who love you be secure.
⁷May there be peace within your walls
 and security within your citadels.ᴰ"
⁸For the sake of my brothers and friends,
 I will say, "Peace be within you."
⁹For the sake of the house of the LORD our
 God,
 I will seek your prosperity.

Psalm 123

A song of ascents.

¹I lift up my eyes to you,
 to you whose throne is in heaven.
²As the eyes of slaves look to the hand of their
 master,
 as the eyes of a maid look to the hand of her
 mistress,
so our eyes look to the LORD our God,
 till he shows us his mercy.ᴰ

³Have mercy on us, O LORD, have mercy on
 us,
 for we have endured much contempt.
⁴We have endured much ridicule from the
 proud,
 much contempt from the arrogant.

Psalm 124

A song of ascents. Of David.

¹If the LORD had not been on our side—
    let Israel say—
²if the LORD had not been on our side
    when men attacked us,
³when their anger flared against us,
    they would have swallowed us alive;
⁴the flood would have engulfed us,
    the torrent would have swept over us,
⁵the raging waters
    would have swept us away.

⁶Praise be to the LORD,
    who has not let us be torn by their teeth.
⁷We have escaped like a bird
    out of the fowler's snare;
the snare has been broken,
    and we have escaped.
⁸Our help is in the name of the LORD,
    the Maker of heaven and earth.

Psalm 125

A song of ascents.

¹Those who trust in the LORD are like Mount
        Zion^D,
    which cannot be shaken but endures forever.
²As the mountains surround Jerusalem^D,
    so the LORD surrounds his people
    both now and forevermore.

³The scepter^D of the wicked will not remain
    over the land allotted to the righteous^D,
for then the righteous might use
    their hands to do evil.

⁴Do good, O LORD, to those who are good,
    to those who are upright in heart.
⁵But those who turn to crooked ways
    the LORD will banish with the evildoers.

    Peace^D be upon Israel.

Psalm 126

A song of ascents.

¹When the LORD brought back the captives to^a
        Zion,
    we were like men who dreamed.^b
²Our mouths were filled with laughter,
    our tongues with songs of joy.
Then it was said among the nations,
    "The LORD has done great things for them."
³The LORD has done great things for us,
    and we are filled with joy.

⁴Restore our fortunes,^c O LORD,
    like streams in the Negev^D.
⁵Those who sow in tears

Song of ascents (124:title)
See *Song of ascents* (120:title).

Fowler's snare (124:7)
See *Fowler* (91:3).

Scepter (125:3)
See *Scepter* (110:2).

How might a wicked government tempt the righteous to do evil? (125:3)

Israel endured many wicked governments, both those of Hebrew rulers and foreign conquerors. Those wicked governments encouraged the people to worship false gods, break the commandments of God and otherwise do evil. The pressures and temptations were at times so great that even the righteous would give in to the prevailing mindset. Ungodly leaders may also have used the threat of punishment for those who sought to follow God's ways.

What events were behind this psalm? (126:1)

This probably refers to the return of the Jews from Babylon to Jerusalem in 538 B.C. Thousands had been uprooted and taken to Babylon. Living in a foreign land, away from their homeland, they had dreamed of one day being able to return to Zion (that is, Jerusalem). When after 70 years or so the dream finally came true, they could hardly believe it had happened.

Negev (126:4)

The Negev is the area to the far south of Palestine (see **Map 2** at the back of this Bible). It is usually desert-like. But at times there are seasons of rain that leave standing pools of water and rivers of flowing water—a metaphor for God's blessings.

Why would anyone weep while planting seed? (126:5–6)

During times of drought, sowing seed was accompanied by anxiety. Were they just wasting the seed? Or would rains come and bring a harvest? This psalm reminded the people that bleak days, such as those in captivity, had turned to joy. It also encouraged those still living with tears and fears to anticipate God's future joy.

---

^a1 Or LORD *restored the fortunes of*   ^b1 Or *men restored to health*
^c4 Or *Bring back our captives*

Of Solomon (127:title)
Solomon is credited with this psalm and Psalm 72. See *Of Solomon* (72:title).

If everything depends on God, what's the use of trying? (127:1–2)
The point is not that we shouldn't do our best, but that our efforts mean nothing apart from God. People can achieve worldly riches, fame and a sense of security, only to find it is all in vain, unless God has been directing them (v. 2). See Deut. 8:17–18.

Does insomnia indicate a spiritual problem? (127:2)
Not necessarily. This psalm speaks about dealing with our anxieties in view of God's continual care. Generally, those who trust in God will rest more easily than those who don't. This psalm does not discuss other factors, however, that can contribute to an inability to sleep.

How was a large family a sign of God's blessing? (127:3–5)
In the ancient Middle Eastern culture, having many children ensured parents that they would be cared for in their old age. Also, the ability to support a large family was seen as evidence that God had provided the resources to do so. Sons were considered a particular blessing (v. 3) because they carried on the family name.

Song of ascents (128:title)
See *Song of ascents* (120:title).

What's good about fearing the Lord? (128:1)
See article: *Should we live in terror of God?* (Prov. 1:7).

Why define God's blessings in material terms? (128:2)
God wants us to enjoy the fruit of our labor as a gift from him. But these promises of prosperity to those who work hard depend on a person's reverence (*fear of the LORD*) and obedience (*walking in his ways*). Usually those who honor and obey God and work hard will enjoy material gain. There are, of course, exceptions to this general principle of life. See article: *Are proverbs iron-clad promises?* (Prov. 3:1–4).

Who had oppressed Israel for so long? (129:1–2)
We can't be sure since it's difficult to know for certain when this psalm was written. Perhaps the psalmist is recounting Israel's long history of oppression, from the days of slavery in Egypt to the exile in Babylon. This is a lament, expressing to God the struggles, suffering and disappointments of the community.

will reap with songs of joy.
⁶He who goes out weeping,
    carrying seed to sow,
will return with songs of joy,
    carrying sheaves with him.

Psalm 127

A song of ascents. Of Solomon.

¹Unless the LORD builds the house,
    its builders labor in vain.
Unless the LORD watches over the city,
    the watchmen^D stand guard in vain.
²In vain you rise early
    and stay up late,
toiling for food to eat—
    for he grants sleep to^a those he loves.

³Sons are a heritage from the LORD,
    children a reward from him.
⁴Like arrows in the hands of a warrior
    are sons born in one's youth.
⁵Blessed is the man
    whose quiver is full of them.
They will not be put to shame
    when they contend with their enemies in the
      gate.

Psalm 128

A song of ascents.

¹Blessed are all who fear the LORD,
    who walk in his ways.
²You will eat the fruit of your labor;
    blessings and prosperity will be yours.
³Your wife will be like a fruitful vine
    within your house;
your sons will be like olive shoots
    around your table.
⁴Thus is the man blessed
    who fears the LORD.

⁵May the LORD bless you from Zion^D
    all the days of your life;
may you see the prosperity of Jerusalem^D,
⁶   and may you live to see your children's
      children.

Peace^D be upon Israel.

Psalm 129

A song of ascents.

¹They have greatly oppressed me from my
      youth—
    let Israel say—
²they have greatly oppressed me from my
      youth,
    but they have not gained the victory over
      me.
³Plowmen have plowed my back

---

^a2 Or *eat— / for while they sleep he provides for*

and made their furrows long.
⁴But the LORD is righteousᴰ;
    he has cut me free from the cords of the
      wicked.

⁵May all who hate Zionᴰ
    be turned back in shame.
⁶May they be like grass on the roof,
    which withers before it can grow;
⁷with it the reaper cannot fill his hands,
    nor the one who gathers fill his arms.
⁸May those who pass by not say,
    "The blessing of the LORD be upon you;
    we bless you in the name of the LORD."

Psalm 130

A song of ascents.

¹Out of the depths I cry to you, O LORD;
²   O Lord, hear my voice.
Let your ears be attentive
    to my cry for mercyᴰ.

³If you, O LORD, kept a record of sins,
    O Lord, who could stand?
⁴But with you there is forgiveness;
    therefore you are feared.

⁵I wait for the LORD, my soulᴰ waits,
    and in his word I put my hope.
⁶My soul waits for the Lord
    more than watchmenᴰ wait for the morning,
    more than watchmen wait for the morning.

⁷O Israel, put your hope in the LORD,
    for with the LORD is unfailing love
    and with him is full redemptionᴰ.
⁸He himself will redeemᴰ Israel
    from all their sins.

Psalm 131

A song of ascents. Of David.

¹My heart is not proud, O LORD,
    my eyes are not haughty;
I do not concern myself with great matters
    or things too wonderful for me.
²But I have stilled and quieted my soul;
    like a weaned child with its mother,
    like a weaned child is my soul within me.

³O Israel, put your hope in the LORD
    both now and forevermore.

Psalm 132

A song of ascents.

¹O LORD, remember David
    and all the hardships he endured.

²He swore an oath to the LORD
    and made a vowᴰ to the Mighty One of
      Jacob:

Why worry about the wicked? (129:4–8)

Even though the writer of this psalm acknowledges that the Lord had cut Israel *free from the cords of the wicked*, his following words still sound spiteful and retaliatory. Such language was frequently used to call for judgment of evil. The psalmist makes his case to God just as a plaintiff in court would argue for justice before a judge. Also see article: *Who would smash babies for revenge?* (137:8–9).

The depths (130:1)

See *From what depths did God lift David?* (30:1).

Doesn't God keep records? (130:3–4)

Yes, he does. Yet, even in the Old Testament, God wanted to obliterate records of sin. God's mercy provided a means for his people to start over again with a clean record: they could present sin offerings along with their sincere repentance. Also see *What kind of records does God keep?* (56:8).

Why did the psalmist yearn so intensely? (130:5–6)

God's offer of forgiveness apparently awakened a deep desire within the psalmist to know God more intimately. He poured out his heart to God because he was certain of his love and care—more certain than night watchmen were that night would end and dawn would come.

Why repeat these words? (130:6)

See *Why repeat phrases over and over?* (118:1–4) and article: *How should we understand Biblical poetry?* (1:1).

What did redemption mean in the Old Testament? (130:7–8)

In Israel's early history, God redeemed his people from Egyptian slavery; later he redeemed them from Babylonian captivity. In both cases *redemption* was applied to the entire nation, not to individuals. But there were hints of individual responsibility for sin (Ezek. 18:14–20, for example). The understanding of redemption continued to develop throughout Old Testament history, culminating in Jesus Christ.

Why did David seem so proud of his humility? (131:1–2)

When David said his heart was *not proud*, it was his way of saying he was submitted to God and dependent upon him.

How was David like a *weaned child with its mother*? (131:2)

Some suggest this means a *satisfied infant* rather than a *weaned child*; as a nursing baby is comforted at its mother's breast, so David was content to depend upon God. Others, however, say that the word *weaned* pictures a child that no longer cries and fusses for its milk; David had matured and better learned to trust God for his needs.

Song of ascents (132:title)

See *Song of ascents* (120:title).

Ephrathah . . . Jaar (132:6)

Ephrathah was another name for Bethlehem (Micah 5:2); Jaar was also known as Kiriath Jearim (1 Samuel 7:1). This psalm recounts how the exciting news had spread through the land that the ark of the covenant (here referred to as *it*) was finally being brought to rest in Jerusalem. See 2 Samuel 6:12–19.

Footstool (132:7)

See *How can we worship at God's footstool?* (99:5).

How could David's descendants reign forever? (132:12)

When David wanted to erect a house (a temple) for the Lord, God promised to preserve his house (descendants) forever. It was God's way of saying that the Messiah would come from the family of David. See *How has David's house and kingdom endured forever?* (2 Samuel 7:16).

What occasion prompted the writing of this psalm? (133:1)

Some think this may have been written by David to commemorate the time all Israel joined together at Hebron to make him king (2 Samuel 5:1–10). Others think it may simply refer to the time that the people came together to celebrate the feasts at Jerusalem.

Does *unity* mean total agreement? (133:1)

No. Biblical unity does not depend on conformity but on harmony. In spite of differences in style and opinion, believers can come together in submission to the Lord and worship him. Also see *Would like-minded Christians have no disagreements?* (Phil. 2:2–5).

What was *good and pleasant* about oil poured on the head? (133:2)

Though it might seem messy to us, oil symbolized luxury, abundance and joy in ancient cultures. It was used for cosmetic and grooming purposes; no oil was a sign of mourning. This picture describes the joy of harmony among God's people. Also see *How did anointing oil consecrate the tabernacle?* (Lev. 8:10).

What was significant about the dew of Hermon? (133:3)

Mount Hermon, the highest mountain in Israel, was known for its heavy dew (see *Map 5* at the back of this Bible). Its dew was considered a blessing from God (see Gen. 27:28) because it helped the land to be fruitful.

3"I will not enter my house
   or go to my bed—
4I will allow no sleep to my eyes,
   no slumber to my eyelids,
5till I find a place for the LORD,
   a dwelling for the Mighty One of Jacob."

6We heard it in Ephrathah,
   we came upon it in the fields of Jaar[a; b]
7"Let us go to his dwelling place;
   let us worship at his footstool[D]—
8arise, O LORD, and come to your resting
      place,
   you and the ark of your might.
9May your priests[D] be clothed with
      righteousness[D];
   may your saints[D] sing for joy."

10For the sake of David your servant,
   do not reject your anointed[D] one.

11The LORD swore an oath to David,
   a sure oath that he will not revoke:
"One of your own descendants
   I will place on your throne—
12if your sons keep my covenant[D]
   and the statutes I teach them,
then their sons will sit
   on your throne for ever and ever."

13For the LORD has chosen Zion[D],
   he has desired it for his dwelling:
14"This is my resting place for ever and ever;
   here I will sit enthroned, for I have desired
      it—
15I will bless her with abundant provisions;
   her poor will I satisfy with food.
16I will clothe her priests with salvation,
   and her saints will ever sing for joy.

17"Here I will make a horn[c] grow for David
   and set up a lamp for my anointed one.
18I will clothe his enemies with shame,
   but the crown on his head will be
      resplendent."

Psalm 133

A song of ascents. Of David.

1How good and pleasant it is
   when brothers live together in unity!
2It is like precious oil poured on the head,
   running down on the beard,
running down on Aaron's beard,
   down upon the collar of his robes.
3It is as if the dew of Hermon
   were falling on Mount Zion.
For there the LORD bestows his blessing,
   even life forevermore.

---

[a]6 That is, Kiriath Jearim   [b]6 Or *heard of it in Ephrathah, / we found it in the fields of Jaar.* (And no quotes around verses 7-9)   [c]17 *Horn* here symbolizes strong one, that is, king.

Psalm 134

A song of ascents.

[1]Praise the LORD, all you servants of the LORD
    who minister by night in the house of the
    LORD.
[2]Lift up your hands in the sanctuary
    and praise the LORD.

[3]May the LORD, the Maker of heaven and earth,
    bless you from Zion[D].

Psalm 135

[1]Praise the LORD.[a]

Praise the name of the LORD;
    praise him, you servants of the LORD,
[2]you who minister in the house of the LORD,
    in the courts of the house of our God.

[3]Praise the LORD, for the LORD is good;
    sing praise to his name, for that is pleasant.
[4]For the LORD has chosen Jacob to be his own,
    Israel to be his treasured possession.

[5]I know that the LORD is great,
    that our Lord is greater than all gods.
[6]The LORD does whatever pleases him,
    in the heavens and on the earth,
    in the seas and all their depths.
[7]He makes clouds rise from the ends of the
        earth;
    he sends lightning with the rain
    and brings out the wind from his
        storehouses.

[8]He struck down the firstborn[D] of Egypt,
    the firstborn of men and animals.
[9]He sent his signs and wonders into your midst,
        O Egypt,
    against Pharaoh and all his servants.
[10]He struck down many nations
    and killed mighty kings—
[11]Sihon king of the Amorites,
    Og king of Bashan
    and all the kings of Canaan—
[12]and he gave their land as an inheritance,
    an inheritance to his people Israel.

[13]Your name, O LORD, endures forever,
    your renown, O LORD, through all
        generations.
[14]For the LORD will vindicate his people
    and have compassion on his servants.

[15]The idols[D] of the nations are silver and gold,
    made by the hands of men.
[16]They have mouths, but cannot speak,
    eyes, but they cannot see;
[17]they have ears, but cannot hear,
    nor is there breath in their mouths.
[18]Those who make them will be like them,
    and so will all who trust in them.

[a]1 Hebrew *Hallelu Yah*; also in verses 3 and 21

Did some priests work at night? (134:1)

Some priestly singers served God in the temple *day and night* (1 Chron. 9:33). Other Levites were assigned morning and evening duties and were to assist whenever burnt offerings were presented on Sabbaths, New Moon festivals and feasts. They were instructed to keep the fire burning continually on the altar (Lev. 6:13) and the golden lampstands (Lev. 24:2–4).

Why lift hands to praise the Lord? (134:2)

See *Why lift up hands to worship God?* (63:4).

SCRIPTURE LINK (135:8–9) *He sent his signs and wonders into your midst, O Egypt*

Read about the plagues God sent upon Egypt and his deliverance of Israel in Exodus 7–14.

SCRIPTURE LINK (135:10–12) *He struck down many nations*

The story of the conquest of Canaan is told in the book of Joshua. Read about Israel's defeat of Sihon and Og in Num. 21:21–35.

Why did people think lifeless idols made by men should be worshiped? (135:15–17)

Though the concept sounds foolish to us, they were only doing what so many still strive to do: manipulate or control the circumstances of their lives. Whether someone trusts in superstitions or hard work, anything that comes between that person and God becomes an idol. Also see article: *Why would Israelites be tempted by other gods?* (Joshua 23:7). Also see *What was the attraction of foreign gods?* (Judges 10:6).

19O house of Israel, praise the LORD;
　O house of Aaron, praise the LORD;
20O house of Levi, praise the LORD;
　you who fear him, praise the LORD.
21Praise be to the LORD from Zion[D],
　to him who dwells in Jerusalem[D].

　Praise the LORD.

Psalm 136

1Give thanks to the LORD, for he is good.
　　　　　His love endures forever.
2Give thanks to the God of gods.
　　　　　His love endures forever.
3Give thanks to the Lord of lords:
　　　　　His love endures forever.

4to him who alone does great wonders,
　　　　　His love endures forever.
5who by his understanding made the heavens,
　　　　　His love endures forever.
6who spread out the earth upon the waters,
　　　　　His love endures forever.
7who made the great lights—
　　　　　His love endures forever.
8the sun to govern the day,
　　　　　His love endures forever.
9the moon and stars to govern the night;
　　　　　His love endures forever.

10to him who struck down the firstborn[D] of
　　　Egypt
　　　　　His love endures forever.
11and brought Israel out from among them
　　　　　His love endures forever.
12with a mighty hand and outstretched arm;
　　　　　His love endures forever.
13to him who divided the Red Sea[a] asunder
　　　　　His love endures forever.
14and brought Israel through the midst of it,
　　　　　His love endures forever.
15but swept Pharaoh and his army into the
　　　Red Sea;
　　　　　His love endures forever.

16to him who led his people through the desert,
　　　　　His love endures forever.
17who struck down great kings,
　　　　　His love endures forever.
18and killed mighty kings—
　　　　　His love endures forever.
19Sihon king of the Amorites
　　　　　His love endures forever.
20and Og king of Bashan—
　　　　　His love endures forever.
21and gave their land as an inheritance,
　　　　　His love endures forever.
22an inheritance to his servant Israel;
　　　　　His love endures forever.

23to the One who remembered us in our low
　　　estate
　　　　　His love endures forever.

Why say the same thing over and over? (136:1–26)

See *Why repeat phrases over and over?* (118:1–4).

SCRIPTURE LINK (136:10–27)

These incidents from Israel's history are drawn from Exodus 7–14 and Num. 21:21–35.

---

a 13 Hebrew *Yam Suph*; that is, Sea of Reeds; also in verse 15

²⁴and freed us from our enemies,
> *His love endures forever.*
²⁵and who gives food to every creature.
> *His love endures forever.*

²⁶Give thanks to the God of heaven.
> *His love endures forever.*

Psalm 137

¹By the rivers of Babylon we sat and wept
  when we remembered Zion^D.
²There on the poplars
  we hung our harps,
³for there our captors asked us for songs,
  our tormentors demanded songs of joy;
  they said, "Sing us one of the songs of
    Zion!"

⁴How can we sing the songs of the LORD
  while in a foreign land?
⁵If I forget you, O Jerusalem^D,
  may my right hand forget ⌊its skill⌋.
⁶May my tongue cling to the roof of my mouth
  if I do not remember you,
  if I do not consider Jerusalem
    my highest joy.

⁷Remember, O LORD, what the Edomites did
  on the day Jerusalem fell.
"Tear it down," they cried,
  "tear it down to its foundations!"

⁸O Daughter of Babylon, doomed to destruction,
  happy is he who repays you
  for what you have done to us—

What occasion prompted the writing of this psalm? (137:1–4)

This psalm expresses the pain felt by the Israelites during their exile in Babylon (sometime after 586 B.C.). To their way of thinking, to be taken away from Jerusalem meant they had been separated from God, who was thought to dwell there in a special sense—*How can we sing the songs of the LORD while in a foreign land?* (v. 4). In reality, most Israelites had been separated from God even before Jerusalem fell. God's judgment, however, executed by the Babylonians, made them aware of their separation from God.

Why sing a song about why they couldn't sing? (137:4)

In actuality, their question expressed the Israelites' recommitment to the Lord. Though the Babylonians wanted to be entertained by Israelite songs, God's people refused to allow their God to be mocked with *songs of joy* (v. 3). They knew this was a time for repentance, a time for songs of lament.

Why was it important to remember Jerusalem? (137:5–6)

To the Israelites, Jerusalem was the place where God met his people. A free Jerusalem represented their identity as an independent nation. These words were more than a fond recollection of their city; they expressed their longing for a lost golden age.

What did the Edomites do? (137:7)

Even though they were distant relatives to the Israelites, they actively cheered Judah's demise. They captured Israelite refugees and turned them over to their enemies. See *Why was God so angry with Edom?* (Obad. vv. 10–11).

Who would smash babies for revenge? (137:8–9)

Those who would want to see enemy infants dashed against the rocks would typically be those who have seen their own infants suffer the atrocities of war. We don't have to defend the feelings of the psalmist to understand them. One side commits war crimes and genocide in exchange for the other side's holocausts and massacres. Atrocities and escalating revenge should be expected where forgiveness cannot be found. In a world fueled by hate and untouched by the peace of Christ, we should not be surprised when wars kill and maim the innocent, displace families and slowly starve refugees to death.

What is difficult for Christians to understand, however, is how such sentiments could be contained in the Bible. Such graphic violence seems out of place in a book we look to for hope and comfort. Such suffering seems inexplicable when we think of God's forgiveness and love. But we cannot simply dismiss these words because they seem too offensive.

Those who wrote what are often called imprecatory or curse psalms were concerned about something far more significant than revenge. They were concerned first for God's holiness—and recognized that he was offended by the atrocities committed against his people. They were also concerned about justice. They knew that right will triumph only when evil has been overthrown and punished.

Also see article: *Is it right to pray for revenge?* (58:6–8). Also see *Why does God permit the innocent to suffer?* (Isaiah 13:16).

Daughter of Babylon (137:8)

This term could have a literal meaning—referring to the Babylonian people—or a figurative meaning, implying those who exhibited the same characteristics as the Babylonians. Those, then, who were cruel and vindictive, like the Babylonians, were *daughters of Babylon*.

How has God exalted his name and Word? (138:2)

The *name* of the Lord refers to the manifestation of his character and nature—*your love and your faithfulness*. God's *name* is exalted because of who God is. God's *word* refers to his promises, which are like an extension of himself. When these promises are fulfilled, God is exalted by all who witness them (vv. 3–4).

How did *the kings of the earth* hear God's Word? (138:4)

Some think this may express the *hope* that one day all the rulers of the earth will praise God. Others think this may express the *certainty* that the rulers will worship the Lord (Phil. 2:9–11). In either case, the reality of God will be revealed to the world.

Right hand (138:7)

The right hand symbolized strength, power, love, honor and authority. See *The years of the right hand of the Most High* (77:10).

Was there a chance God might abandon his people? (138:8)

See article: *Why ask God to remain faithful?* (71:9–18).

How does God search us? (139:1)

God examines our hearts and minds to discover everything about us: our true personalities, our secret fantasies, our hidden motives. God knows the *reality* of our inner life—which sometimes has nothing to do with how we feel. See Heb. 4:12–13.

Why did God hem David in? (139:5)

Though today we use this to express a feeling of confinement or restricted freedom, David meant just the opposite. When God hemmed David in, David was grateful for God's close contact. Wherever he turned, he found God. As a result, David was both comforted and awestruck by God's care and protection (v. 6).

Why did David want to run from God? (139:7)

David did not really want to escape God's presence. It's possible that these are rhetorical questions, asked merely to make the point that God is omnipresent—he can be found everywhere. Or perhaps David's reaction can be compared to others who, in the presence of the Almighty, became painfully aware of their sin and unworthiness (Isaiah 6:5; Luke 5:8).

Depths (139:8)

Or *Sheol* (see NIV text note), poetically pictured in several ways: as a vast grave (Ezek. 32:18–32), a stronghold (9:13; 107:18; Matt. 16:18), a wasteland (Job 10:22) and a beast of prey (Isaiah 5:14). *Sheol*, traditionally translated as *hell*, generally means just the place of the dead, without implying either reward or punishment. David is saying that God's sovereignty extends even to the grave and beyond.

9he who seizes your infants
  and dashes them against the rocks.

Psalm 138

Of David.

1I will praise you, O Lord, with all my heart;
  before the "gods" I will sing your praise.
2I will bow down toward your holy temple
  and will praise your name
  for your love and your faithfulness,
for you have exalted above all things
  your name and your word.
3When I called, you answered me;
  you made me bold and stouthearted.

4May all the kings of the earth praise you,
  O Lord,
  when they hear the words of your mouth.
5May they sing of the ways of the Lord,
  for the glory[D] of the Lord is great.

6Though the Lord is on high, he looks upon the
  lowly,
  but the proud he knows from afar.
7Though I walk in the midst of trouble,
  you preserve my life;
you stretch out your hand against the anger of
  my foes,
  with your right hand you save me.
8The Lord will fulfill ⌐his purpose⌐ for me;
  your love, O Lord, endures forever—
  do not abandon the works of your hands.

Psalm 139

For the director of music. Of David. A psalm.

1O Lord, you have searched me
  and you know me.
2You know when I sit and when I rise;
  you perceive my thoughts from afar.
3You discern my going out and my lying down;
  you are familiar with all my ways.
4Before a word is on my tongue
  you know it completely, O Lord.

5You hem me in—behind and before;
  you have laid your hand upon me.
6Such knowledge is too wonderful for me,
  too lofty for me to attain.

7Where can I go from your Spirit?
  Where can I flee from your presence?
8If I go up to the heavens, you are there;
  if I make my bed in the depths,[a] you are
  there.
9If I rise on the wings of the dawn,
  if I settle on the far side of the sea,
10even there your hand will guide me,
  your right hand will hold me fast.
11If I say, "Surely the darkness will hide me
  and the light become night around me,"

a8 Hebrew Sheol

¹²even the darkness will not be dark to you;
　　the night will shine like the day,
　　for darkness is as light to you.

¹³For you created my inmost being;
　　you knit me together in my mother's womb.
¹⁴I praise you because I am fearfully and
　　　wonderfully made;
　　your works are wonderful,
　　I know that full well.
¹⁵My frame was not hidden from you
　　when I was made in the secret place.
　　When I was woven together in the depths of
　　　the earth,
¹⁶　your eyes saw my unformed body.
　　All the days ordained for me
　　were written in your book
　　before one of them came to be.

¹⁷How precious to*a* me are your thoughts,
　　　O God!
　　How vast is the sum of them!
¹⁸Were I to count them,
　　they would outnumber the grains of sand.
　　When I awake,
　　I am still with you.

¹⁹If only you would slay the wicked, O God!
　　Away from me, you bloodthirsty men!
²⁰They speak of you with evil intent;
　　your adversaries misuse your name.
²¹Do I not hate those who hate you, O LORD,
　　and abhor those who rise up against you?
²²I have nothing but hatred for them;
　　I count them my enemies.

²³Search me, O God, and know my heart;
　　test me and know my anxious thoughts.
²⁴See if there is any offensive way in me,
　　and lead me in the way everlasting.

a 17 Or concerning

My inmost being (139:13)
Literally, *kidneys*. The Hebrews used *kidneys* for the center of a person's emotions and conscience.

Depths of the earth (139:15)
This phrase is a metaphor for the womb, echoing the earlier thoughts of v. 13. This is a different Hebrew word for *depths* than is used in v. 8.

Do we have any choice in how our lives turn out? (139:16)
This is a poetic way of speaking about God's intentions and best wishes for people. David is not saying that the script for our lives has been written in indelible ink. David simply acknowledges God's plans for his life—including the number of days God would give.

Why the abrupt change of tone from praise to vengeance? (139:19–22)
David is saying in essence, "I hate evil just as you do, Lord." Though angry, his words are couched in humility (vv. 23–24). David knew that God alone is fit to judge sin. This kind of curse language is discussed in the article: *Is it right to pray for revenge?* (58:6–8).

Why doesn't God *slay the wicked*? (139:19)
The Bible constantly challenges us to see things from God's perspective. The issue of judgment is no different. Though David longed for God to correct injustice, there is a confidence expressed throughout the psalms that God, whether in this life or the next, will judge evil. Sometimes it is because of his mercy that God allows sin to continue for a time (2 Peter 3:8–9).

Is hatred sometimes a good thing? (139:21–22)
Understood the proper way, some hatred could be considered good. Hatred of evil, for example, is seen here as zeal for God's honor. The words *hate* and *love* sometimes are used differently in the Bible than we normally use

Does God create each unborn child? (139:13–16)

We may bring more questions to these verses than they were meant to answer, though one general theme permeates every line: God is somehow involved in every detail of our lives, including our formation. Poetic language is used to express the unfathomable, that God sovereignly crafts us according to his will.

This general theme of God's role in our development can at least set the stage for understanding how to approach some of the difficult issues concerning the unborn. Issues such as: Are birth defects God's will? What about miscarriages? Are some methods of birth control acceptable or are they all just attempts to control what belongs to the Creator of life?

Certainly, prenatal and neonatal technologies have extended the range of ethical concerns for our day (such as abortion on demand, artificial insemination and in vitro fertilization). Psalm 139 provides a good foundation on which to build a Biblical framework for addressing these tough issues. But more than anything else, these verses assure us that God is deeply and personally concerned for each human life—even before birth.

them. David used these words as he passionately announced his loyalty to God. His *love* meant he wanted to be on God's side; his *hate* meant he wanted nothing to do with those opposed to the Lord. See **How can God hate?** (Mal. 1:2–3) and article: **Does Jesus really want us to hate our families?** (Luke 14:26).

Why sing a psalm about fears? (140:1–11)

Because even admitting our fears can bring honor and glory to God. Part of the beauty of the psalms is their breadth of emotion—from joy to sorrow, from confidence to fear. The psalmist's fears led him to worship God. Dangers provided a reason to tell about God's great power and his loving care. Expressing his fears gave the writer a chance to also express his confidence in the Lord (vv. 12–13).

Should we pray for God's judgment to fall on sinners? (140:10)

We might feel like praying that sinners would be judged—and it is okay to tell God our honest emotions. But we can also trust God to judge fairly and eventually set right all injustices. Believers know that bitterness or an unforgiving heart can damage their own spirits (Matt. 6:14–15; Heb. 12:14–15). As a result, they will want to be free of such emotions and even try to bless their enemies (Matt. 5:44). The use of this kind of imprecatory or curse language in the psalms is discussed in the article: **Is it right to pray for revenge?** (58:6–8).

Psalm 140

For the director of music. A psalm of David.

¹Rescue me, O LORD, from evil men;
   protect me from men of violence,
²who devise evil plans in their hearts
   and stir up war every day.
³They make their tongues as sharp as a
      serpent's;
   the poison of vipers is on their lips.   *Selah*D

⁴Keep me, O LORD, from the hands of the
      wicked;
   protect me from men of violence
   who plan to trip my feet.
⁵Proud men have hidden a snare for me;
   they have spread out the cords of their net
   and have set traps for me along my path.
                                             Selah

⁶O LORD, I say to you, "You are my God."
   Hear, O LORD, my cry for mercyD.
⁷O Sovereign LORD, my strong deliverer,
   who shields my head in the day of battle—
⁸do not grant the wicked their desires, O LORD;
   do not let their plans succeed,
   or they will become proud.   *Selah*

⁹Let the heads of those who surround me
   be covered with the trouble their lips have
      caused.
¹⁰Let burning coals fall upon them;
   may they be thrown into the fire,
   into miry pits, never to rise.
¹¹Let slanderers not be established in the land;
   may disaster hunt down men of violence.

¹²I know that the LORD secures justice for the
      poor
   and upholds the cause of the needy.
¹³Surely the righteousD will praise your name
   and the upright will live before you.

Why is there still injustice? (140:12)

This passage probably refers more to God's ultimate judgment than to present circumstances.

Sin doesn't always incur immediate punishment, but it always has eternal consequences. That is why the psalmists could say confidently that God would avenge evildoers. Some will face the consequences for their actions in this life, but all will face them in the next life.

When the Bible speaks of justice, it means that God will be the judge and everyone who refuses to repent will get what he or she deserves. It may seem to us that the wicked go unpunished and their schemes unchallenged. It may seem that no one pleads the case of the poor. Yet God has a plan to balance the scales.

Throughout their history of oppression, the Israelites found comfort in knowing that God had a plan to bring about justice. Such hope can also be a source of encouragement to us when we face hardships at the hands of evil people and powers.

Psalm 141

A psalm of David.

1O LORD, I call to you; come quickly to me.
  Hear my voice when I call to you.
2May my prayer be set before you like
    incense[D];
  may the lifting up of my hands be like the
    evening sacrifice[D].

3Set a guard over my mouth, O LORD;
  keep watch over the door of my lips.
4Let not my heart be drawn to what is evil,
  to take part in wicked deeds
with men who are evildoers;
  let me not eat of their delicacies.

5Let a righteous[D] man[a] strike me—it is a
    kindness;
  let him rebuke me—it is oil on my head.
  My head will not refuse it.

Yet my prayer is ever against the deeds of
    evildoers;
6 their rulers will be thrown down from the
    cliffs,
  and the wicked will learn that my words
    were well spoken.
7⌊They will say,⌋ "As one plows and breaks up
    the earth,
  so our bones have been scattered at the
    mouth of the grave.[b]"

8But my eyes are fixed on you, O Sovereign
    LORD;
  in you I take refuge—do not give me over to
    death[D].
9Keep me from the snares they have laid for
    me,
  from the traps set by evildoers.
10Let the wicked fall into their own nets,
  while I pass by in safety.

Psalm 142

A maskil[c] of David. When he was in the cave.
A prayer.

1I cry aloud to the LORD;
  I lift up my voice to the LORD for mercy[D].
2I pour out my complaint before him;
  before him I tell my trouble.

3When my spirit grows faint within me,
  it is you who know my way.
In the path where I walk
  men have hidden a snare for me.
4Look to my right and see;
  no one is concerned for me.
I have no refuge;
  no one cares for my life.

5I cry to you, O LORD;
  I say, "You are my refuge,

How is incense like prayer? (141:2)

Incense apparently had symbolized prayers since the time Aaron first burned it on the altar of incense (Exodus 30:1–8). David's hope was that his prayers would rise up to God, just as the smoke of the incense rises upward. He also hoped that his prayers would be pleasing to God, like the pleasing fragrance of the incense. Also see Rev. 5:8.

What was David afraid he might say? (141:3)

David was probably concerned because he knew his own tendency to sin (51:5). Though we can't say the specific words David might have feared he would say, we can guess he wanted to avoid words that would reveal evil within his heart (v. 4). David wanted wholesome words because he wanted pure motives.

Why is it good to be struck by a righteous man? (141:5)

This is a figure of speech—to be "struck" is to be disciplined. We are wise to welcome correction that comes from a righteous person (Prov. 9:8).

Thrown down from the cliffs (141:6)

See *Why kill prisoners of war?* (2 Chron. 25:12).

SCRIPTURE LINK (142:title)

This psalm may have been written when David fled from Saul and hid in a cave. See 1 Samuel 22:1.

Does God want to hear our complaints? (142:2)

See article: *Is it okay to argue with God?* (Hab. 2:1).

---

[a]5 Or *Let the Righteous One*   [b]7 Hebrew *Sheol*   [c]Title: Probably a literary or musical term

How does reading about desperate need encourage us? (142:6)

Desperate need frames a message of faith and hope. The depth of David's need vividly displayed David's trust in God. If we could not read about his need, we could never fully appreciate the degree of confidence that David had in God. The psalms encourage us to entrust our fears and cares to him.

SCRIPTURE LINK (143:title)

See 2 Samuel 11:1—12:25.

Was David pleading for mercy because he was in danger of judgment? (143:1–2)

Perhaps. But the one who acknowledges sin is the one who receives mercy. David often expressed his sin and sought God's *faithfulness and righteousness* (51:2–3). Some think David did not intend to repent for a specific sin here but for all his sins.

Why *spread out my hands* to God? (143:6)

His gesture is clarified by the second half of the verse: *my soul thirsts for you* . . . Extending one's hands was a gesture that illustrated one's need for God. Also see *Why lift up hands to worship God?* (63:4).

Rock (144:1)

See *How is God like a rock?* (18:2).

Why would God run a boot camp for soldiers? (144:1)

The harsh realities of life in David's time included enemies who would have been happy to conquer and loot Israel. David gives God credit for helping the nation thrive in spite of such threats. That's why he refers to him as *my loving God . . . my fortress . . . my deliverer* (v. 2). But part of a strong defense is a strong offense, so God trained David for war and prepared him for battle. In addition, every victory for Israel confirmed the Lord's superiority over the pagan gods of Israel's neighbors. David was not merely engaged in war; he was fighting for God's righteous cause, inflicting judgment upon sinful nations.

my portion in the land of the living."
⁶Listen to my cry,
    for I am in desperate need;
rescue me from those who pursue me,
    for they are too strong for me.
⁷Set me free from my prison,
    that I may praise your name.

Then the righteousᴰ will gather about me
    because of your goodness to me.

Psalm 143

A psalm of David.

¹O LORD, hear my prayer,
    listen to my cry for mercyᴰ;
in your faithfulness and righteousnessᴰ
    come to my relief.
²Do not bring your servant into judgment,
    for no one living is righteous before you.

³The enemy pursues me,
    he crushes me to the ground;
he makes me dwell in darkness
    like those long dead.
⁴So my spirit grows faint within me;
    my heart within me is dismayed.

⁵I remember the days of long ago;
    I meditate on all your works
    and consider what your hands have done.
⁶I spread out my hands to you;
    my soulᴰ thirsts for you like a parched land.
                                        *Selah*ᴰ

⁷Answer me quickly, O LORD;
    my spirit fails.
Do not hide your face from me
    or I will be like those who go down to the
        pit.
⁸Let the morning bring me word of your
        unfailing love,
    for I have put my trust in you.
Show me the way I should go,
    for to you I lift up my soul.
⁹Rescue me from my enemies, O LORD,
    for I hide myself in you.
¹⁰Teach me to do your will,
    for you are my God;
may your good Spirit
    lead me on level ground.

¹¹For your name's sake, O LORD, preserve my
        life;
    in your righteousness, bring me out of
        trouble.
¹²In your unfailing love, silence my enemies;
    destroy all my foes,
    for I am your servant.

Psalm 144

Of David.

¹Praise be to the LORD my Rock,
    who trains my hands for war,

my fingers for battle.
2He is my loving God and my fortress,
my stronghold[D] and my deliverer,
my shield, in whom I take refuge,
who subdues peoples[a] under me.

3O Lord, what is man that you care for him,
the son of man[D] that you think of him?
4Man is like a breath;
his days are like a fleeting shadow.

5Part your heavens, O Lord, and come down;
touch the mountains, so that they smoke.
6Send forth lightning and scatter ˪the enemies˩;
shoot your arrows and rout them.
7Reach down your hand from on high;
deliver me and rescue me
from the mighty waters,
from the hands of foreigners
8whose mouths are full of lies,
whose right hands are deceitful.

9I will sing a new song to you, O God;
on the ten-stringed lyre[D] I will make music
to you,
10to the One who gives victory to kings,
who delivers his servant David from the
deadly sword.

11Deliver me and rescue me
from the hands of foreigners
whose mouths are full of lies,
whose right hands are deceitful.

12Then our sons in their youth
will be like well-nurtured plants,
and our daughters will be like pillars
carved to adorn a palace.
13Our barns will be filled
with every kind of provision.
Our sheep will increase by thousands,
by tens of thousands in our fields;
14 our oxen will draw heavy loads.[b]
There will be no breaching of walls,
no going into captivity,
no cry of distress in our streets.

15Blessed are the people of whom this is true;
blessed are the people whose God is the
Lord.

Psalm 145[c]

A psalm of praise. Of David.

1I will exalt you, my God the King;
I will praise your name for ever and ever.
2Every day I will praise you
and extol[D] your name for ever and ever.

3Great is the Lord and most worthy of praise;
his greatness no one can fathom.

Ten-stringed lyre (144:9)
A musical instrument made of wood, probably
of Syrian origin. It may have looked something
like the guitar and been played in a manner
similar to the harp.

---

*a*2 Many manuscripts of the Masoretic Text, Dead Sea Scrolls, Aquila,
Jerome and Syriac; most manuscripts of the Masoretic Text *subdues my
people*   *b*14 Or *our chieftains will be firmly established*   *c*This
psalm is an acrostic poem, the verses of which (including verse 13b)
begin with the successive letters of the Hebrew alphabet.

⁴One generation will commend your works to
  another;
  they will tell of your mighty acts.
⁵They will speak of the glorious splendor of
  your majesty,
  and I will meditate on your wonderful
  works.ᵃ
⁶They will tell of the power of your awesome
  works,
  and I will proclaim your great deeds.
⁷They will celebrate your abundant goodness
  and joyfully sing of your righteousnessᴰ.

⁸The LORD is gracious and compassionate,
  slow to anger and rich in love.
⁹The LORD is good to all;
  he has compassion on all he has made.
¹⁰All you have made will praise you, O LORD;
  your saintsᴰ will extolᴰ you.
¹¹They will tell of the gloryᴰ of your kingdom
  and speak of your might,
¹²so that all men may know of your mighty acts
  and the glorious splendor of your kingdom.
¹³Your kingdom is an everlasting kingdom,
  and your dominion endures through all
  generations.

The LORD is faithful to all his promises
  and loving toward all he has made.ᵇ
¹⁴The LORD upholds all those who fall
  and lifts up all who are bowed down.
¹⁵The eyes of all look to you,
  and you give them their food at the proper
  time.
¹⁶You open your hand
  and satisfy the desires of every living thing.

¹⁷The LORD is righteousᴰ in all his ways
  and loving toward all he has made.
¹⁸The LORD is near to all who call on him,
  to all who call on him in truth.
¹⁹He fulfills the desires of those who fear him;
  he hears their cry and saves them.
²⁰The LORD watches over all who love him,
  but all the wicked he will destroy.

²¹My mouth will speak in praise of the LORD.
  Let every creature praise his holy name
  for ever and ever.

Psalm 146

¹Praise the LORD.ᶜ

Praise the LORD, O my soulᴰ.
² I will praise the LORD all my life;
  I will sing praise to my God as long as I live.

³Do not put your trust in princes,
  in mortal men, who cannot save.

How can a loving, compassionate God ever be angry? (145:8–9)
See *Why couldn't God's love overcome his wrath?* (Jer. 30:22–24) and *Did God punish out of anger?* (Ezek. 5:13).

When will everyone praise God? (145:10)
Although we can't say when this will be exactly, we know that at the end of time all creation will praise God. Even those opposed to God will have to bow before Jesus (Phil. 2:10–11).

Everlasting kingdom (145:13)
David recognized the eternal nature of God's reign, but was limited in his understanding of it. Most likely his point was simply that God was the King over all human kings (v. 1) and his kingdom would endure long after all earthly kingdoms had crumbled.

How can we reconcile reality with these bold statements of God's care? (145:14–16)
It seems that the Lord does not uphold all those who fall. It seems that many are bowed down who are never lifted at all. And countless numbers of people starve and even die without their desires being satisfied. But we can see these words as poetry—figurative expressions of God's care which is often shown in spiritual and eternal ways, if not in physical ways. See article: *Why is there still injustice?* (140:12).

Is no one to be trusted? (146:3–4)
Not when it means abandoning trust in God. If you have to choose between God and human leaders, trust God every time. Human nature has been permanently damaged by sin, making it dangerous to put our faith in individuals.

ᵃ5 Dead Sea Scrolls and Syriac (see also Septuagint); Masoretic Text *On the glorious splendor of your majesty / and on your wonderful works I will meditate*   ᵇ13 One manuscript of the Masoretic Text, Dead Sea Scrolls and Syriac (see also Septuagint); most manuscripts of the Masoretic Text do not have the last two lines of verse 13.
ᶜ1 Hebrew *Hallelu Yah*; also in verse 10

⁴When their spirit departs, they return to the
        ground;
    on that very day their plans come to nothing.

⁵Blessed is he whose help is the God of Jacob,
    whose hope is in the LORD his God,
⁶the Maker of heaven and earth,
    the sea, and everything in them—
    the LORD, who remains faithful forever.
⁷He upholds the cause of the oppressed
    and gives food to the hungry.
The LORD sets prisoners free,
⁸   the LORD gives sight to the blind,
    the LORD lifts up those who are bowed down,
    the LORD loves the righteousᴰ.
⁹The LORD watches over the alienᴰ
    and sustains the fatherless and the widow,
    but he frustrates the ways of the wicked.

¹⁰The LORD reigns forever,
    your God, O Zionᴰ, for all generations.

    Praise the LORD.

Psalm 147

¹Praise the LORD.ᵃ

How good it is to sing praises to our God,
    how pleasant and fitting to praise him!

²The LORD builds up Jerusalemᴰ;
    he gathers the exilesᴰ of Israel.
³He heals the brokenhearted
    and binds up their wounds.
⁴He determines the number of the stars
    and calls them each by name.
⁵Great is our Lord and mighty in power;
    his understanding has no limit.
⁶The LORD sustains the humble
    but casts the wicked to the ground.

⁷Sing to the LORD with thanksgiving;
    make music to our God on the harp.
⁸He covers the sky with clouds;
    he supplies the earth with rain
    and makes grass grow on the hills.
⁹He provides food for the cattle
    and for the young ravens when they call.

¹⁰His pleasure is not in the strength of the horse,
    nor his delight in the legs of a man;
¹¹the LORD delights in those who fear him,
    who put their hope in his unfailing love.

¹²Extolᴰ the LORD, O Jerusalem;
    praise your God, O Zion,
¹³for he strengthens the bars of your gates
    and blesses your people within you.
¹⁴He grants peaceᴰ to your borders
    and satisfies you with the finest of wheat.

¹⁵He sends his command to the earth;
    his word runs swiftly.
¹⁶He spreads the snow like wool
    and scatters the frost like ashes.

ᵃ1 Hebrew *Hallelu Yah*; also in verse 20

Why are tyranny and starvation still problems? (146:7–9)
See *How can we reconcile reality with these bold statements of God's care?* (145:14–16).

How did God *build up* Jerusalem? (147:2)
The date of this psalm is uncertain, but it was probably written after the Babylonian exile. If so, then this verse may express thanks to God for bringing his people back to Jerusalem and enabling them to reconstruct the walls around the city (see Neh. 2:11–20).

Does God want us to be afraid of him? (147:11)
See article: *Should we live in terror of God?* (Prov. 1:7).

If God gives peace to Jerusalem, why have there been so many battles there? (147:14)
Depending on when it was written, this psalm could be either a confident expectation of peace or a thanksgiving for the peace that the Israelites enjoyed after the exile. In either case God was praised as the giver of peace. The opposite is also true: the Israelites viewed the lack of peace as a sign of God's displeasure with his people (2 Kings 17:7–20). Their turning away from him resulted in the battles over Jerusalem.

Why did God play favorites? (147:20)
See *If God doesn't show favoritism, why were the Jews the chosen people?* (Romans 2:10–11) and article: *Does God play favorites?* (Romans 9:8–33).

How can things praise God? (148:1–10)
This is poetic language. The heavens (sun, moon, stars) are personified to paint a picture of God's control over all creation. Though only humans can consciously and verbally express their praise to God (v. 14), the rest of creation gives its praise to God by being what he has made it to be—*for he commanded and they were created* (v. 5). Also see **Why describe inanimate objects as rejoicing?** (96:11–13).

Assembly of the saints (149:1)
Since this psalm was probably written after the time of the Babylonian captivity, *assembly* would refer to the faithful remnant who returned from Babylon. The *saints* were those who honored God by living according to his will.

How does dancing honor God? (149:3)
Dancing and making music was just one legitimate Biblical expression of worship (see Exodus 15:19–20; 2 Samuel 6:14–15, for example). Voices, hands, body position and movement all can express feelings of joy, thankfulness and praise to God.

Why sing in bed? (149:5)
This may be a figurative way of describing an ability to sleep peacefully at night without fear and with a clear conscience (4:8; 127:2). Some think this may be a picture of reclining (as was the custom) to eat a festal meal—especially if the theme of the festival was God's ultimate victory.

Can we praise God while inflicting vengeance? (149:6–9)
The vengeance discussed here was focused on the appropriate target—evil. The psalmists understood that evil had to be eradicated if righteousness were to fully prevail. So there was no contradiction seen between praising God and wanting to avenge his enemies. Read about curse language in the article: *Is it right to pray for revenge?* (58:6–8).

17He hurls down his hail like pebbles.
Who can withstand his icy blast?
18He sends his word and melts them;
he stirs up his breezes, and the waters flow.

19He has revealed his word to Jacob,
his laws and decrees to Israel.
20He has done this for no other nation;
they do not know his laws.

Praise the LORD.

Psalm 148

1Praise the LORD.*a*

Praise the LORD from the heavens,
praise him in the heights above.
2Praise him, all his angels,
praise him, all his heavenly hosts.
3Praise him, sun and moon,
praise him, all you shining stars.
4Praise him, you highest heavens
and you waters above the skies.
5Let them praise the name of the LORD,
for he commanded and they were created.
6He set them in place for ever and ever;
he gave a decree that will never pass away.

7Praise the LORD from the earth,
you great sea creatures and all ocean depths,
8lightning and hail, snow and clouds,
stormy winds that do his bidding,
9you mountains and all hills,
fruit trees and all cedars,
10wild animals and all cattle,
small creatures and flying birds,
11kings of the earth and all nations,
you princes and all rulers on earth,
12young men and maidens,
old men and children.

13Let them praise the name of the LORD,
for his name alone is exalted;
his splendor is above the earth and the heavens.
14He has raised up for his people a horn,*b*
the praise of all his saintsᴰ,
of Israel, the people close to his heart.

Praise the LORD.

Psalm 149

1Praise the LORD.*c*

Sing to the LORD a new song,
his praise in the assembly of the saints.

2Let Israel rejoice in their Maker;
let the people of Zionᴰ be glad in their King.
3Let them praise his name with dancing
and make music to him with tambourine and harp.

a1 Hebrew *Hallelu Yah*; also in verse 14   *b14* Horn here symbolizes strong one, that is, king.   *c1* Hebrew *Hallelu Yah*; also in verse 9

4For the LORD takes delight in his people;
  he crowns the humble with salvation^D.
5Let the saints^D rejoice in this honor
  and sing for joy on their beds.

6May the praise of God be in their mouths
  and a double-edged sword in their hands,
7to inflict vengeance on the nations
  and punishment on the peoples,
8to bind their kings with fetters,
  their nobles with shackles of iron,
9to carry out the sentence written against them.
  This is the glory^D of all his saints.

  Praise the LORD.

Psalm 150

1Praise the LORD. ^a

  Praise God in his sanctuary;
    praise him in his mighty heavens.
2Praise him for his acts of power;
    praise him for his surpassing greatness.
3Praise him with the sounding of the trumpet,
    praise him with the harp and lyre^D,
4praise him with tambourine and dancing,
    praise him with the strings and flute,
5praise him with the clash of cymbals,
    praise him with resounding cymbals.

6Let everything that has breath praise the LORD.

  Praise the LORD.

Where should we praise God? (150:1)
The *sanctuary* refers to the temple in Jerusalem, the basic center of worship. The *mighty heavens* refers to the sky. In essence, the message is: Let praises to God be given everywhere!

Why should we praise God? (150:2)
(1) For his *acts of power*, referring primarily to his acts of deliverance (20:6), though perhaps also to his power in creation (65:6). (2) For his *surpassing greatness*, meaning we can focus our adoration on who God is.

Lyre (150:3)
See *Ten-stringed lyre* (144:9).

How should we praise God? (150:3–5)
With everything we have. God is worthy of the best we can do in our worship.

Dancing (150:4)
See *How does dancing honor God?* (149:3).

Who should praise God? (150:6)
The poetic expression *everything that has breath* beautifully summarizes the variety of praises that God's creation can give to Him. Also see *How can things praise God?* (148:1–10).

PROVERBS

Why read this book?

Giving advice is big business. From daytime talk shows to advice columns and self-help books, our culture is glutted with knowledge—but often starved for wisdom. One reason is the complexity of life; we need practical counsel that is also spiritual. Proverbs offers this spiritual depth to issues ranging from managing money to the dangers of adultery to learning how to identify true friends. Here you can find wisdom that works and insights that won't wear out.

Who wrote this book?

Solomon, the wisest king to rule Israel, wrote much of it. Agur, son of Jakeh, and Lemuel (probably a non-Israelite king) are also contributors.

To whom was it written?

The people of Israel, particularly young people just starting out on life's journey.

When was it written?

Solomon reigned during the tenth century B.C., but many of the proverbs were not compiled and edited until several centuries later—around 700 B.C.

Why was it written?

To show how godly wisdom merges with real life (1:2–6).

What is a proverb?

A proverb, sometimes called a "maxim," is a truth condensed into a few words and stated in a memorable fashion which has application to a variety of situations in life.

What to look for in Proverbs:

Watch for contrasting issues such as foolishness and wisdom, laziness and diligence, adultery and faithfulness, and true and false friendships. Also look for principles of building strong marriages, parenting and relationships on the job. Pay close attention to the differing outcomes of those who follow God's wisdom and those who don't.

Prologue: Purpose and Theme

1 The proverbs of Solomon son of David, king of Israel:

²for attaining wisdom and discipline;
    for understanding words of insight;
³for acquiring a disciplined and prudent life,
    doing what is right and just and fair;
⁴for giving prudence to the simple,
    knowledge and discretion to the young—
⁵let the wise listen and add to their learning,
    and let the discerning get guidance—
⁶for understanding proverbs and parablesᴰ,
    the sayings and riddles of the wise.

⁷The fear of the LORD is the beginning of
    knowledge,
    but foolsᵃ despise wisdom and discipline.

Exhortations to Embrace Wisdom

Warning Against Enticement

⁸Listen, my son, to your father's instruction
    and do not forsake your mother's teaching.
⁹They will be a garland to graceᴰ your head
    and a chain to adorn your neck.

¹⁰My son, if sinners entice you,
    do not give in to them.
¹¹If they say, "Come along with us;
    let's lie in wait for someone's blood,
    let's waylay some harmless soulᴰ;
¹²let's swallow them alive, like the grave,ᵇ
    and whole, like those who go down to the
        pit;
¹³we will get all sorts of valuable things
    and fill our houses with plunderᴰ;
¹⁴throw in your lot with us,
    and we will share a common purse"—

ᵃ7 The Hebrew words rendered *fool* in Proverbs, and often elsewhere
in the Old Testament, denote one who is morally deficient.
ᵇ12 Hebrew *Sheol*

What is wisdom? (1:2)

The basic idea behind *wisdom* is *skill*. The term is used in the Old Testament to describe the abilities of garment makers, craftsmen, goldsmiths, sailors—even professional mourners at funerals. The book of Proverbs uses the word to speak of the skill of living life in a way that honors God. A wise person has the ability to adapt his or her life to God's pattern. What distinguishes Biblical wisdom from the so-called wisdom of the other ancient nations is its foundation in the fear of God (v. 7). Since God is the source of wisdom, reverence for God is the controlling principle for applying these wise observations about the way life works.

My son (1:8)

In ancient times, writings of instruction or wisdom frequently used *my son* to refer to a person open to instruction and eager for knowledge. Here Solomon is addressing all individuals hungry for wisdom in spiritual and practical matters.

Should we live in terror of God? (1:7)

The phrase *the fear of the LORD is the beginning of . . . wisdom* is the cornerstone of Proverbs. *Fear* is actually another word for reverence or worship, suggesting that wisdom begins when we properly acknowledge who God is and offer him the worship he deserves. It reminds us that life's true significance is discovered when we approach God with an attitude of humility and awe, not dread and fright.

The remainder of Proverbs explains how we can *fear* God in our daily lives. Whether the topic is wealth, work, or marriage, we are called to give God the honor due him by obeying his will in each of these areas. A wise person will humbly seek God's perspective on a matter before acting, but the fool will throw caution to the wind and act on his own impulses. What's the result of ignoring God and doing it our way? *There is a way that seems right to a man, but in the end it leads to death* (14:12).

But the person who *fears* God, who daily worships and honors him, has nothing to fear in either life or death. Also see 9:10; Job 28:28; Psalm 111:10.

15my son, do not go along with them,
  do not set foot on their paths;
16for their feet rush into sin,
  they are swift to shed blood.
17How useless to spread a net
  in full view of all the birds!
18These men lie in wait for their own blood;
  they waylay only themselves!
19Such is the end of all who go after ill-gotten
  gain;
  it takes away the lives of those who get it.

Warning Against Rejecting Wisdom

20Wisdom calls aloud in the street,
  she raises her voice in the public squares;
21at the head of the noisy streets*a* she cries out,
  in the gateways of the city she makes her
  speech:

22"How long will you simple ones*b* love your
  simple ways?
  How long will mockers delight in mockery
  and fools hate knowledge?
23If you had responded to my rebuke,
  I would have poured out my heart to you
  and made my thoughts known to you.
24But since you rejected me when I called
  and no one gave heed when I stretched out
  my hand,
25since you ignored all my advice
  and would not accept my rebuke,
26I in turn will laugh at your disaster;
  I will mock when calamity overtakes you—
27when calamity overtakes you like a storm,
  when disaster sweeps over you like a
  whirlwind,
  when distress and trouble overwhelm you.

28"Then they will call to me but I will not
  answer;
  they will look for me but will not find me.
29Since they hated knowledge
  and did not choose to fear the LORD,
30since they would not accept my advice
  and spurned my rebuke,
31they will eat the fruit of their ways
  and be filled with the fruit of their schemes.
32For the waywardness of the simple will kill
  them,
  and the complacency of fools will destroy
  them;
33but whoever listens to me will live in safety
  and be at ease, without fear of harm."

Moral Benefits of Wisdom

2 My son, if you accept my words
  and store up my commands within you,
2turning your ear to wisdom
  and applying your heart to understanding,
3and if you call out for insight
  and cry aloud for understanding,

Why is wisdom pictured as a woman? (1:20)

Proverbs presents wisdom not just as an idea but as a person. Some think a woman is chosen to represent wisdom because in the Hebrew language the word for wisdom is feminine. Others believe that since the aim of this book is to train young people, a woman—like a nurturing mother—would make a lasting impression on tender minds. Still others point to a pagan goddess of education and training, suggesting that the writer may have borrowed similar terms to contrast true wisdom with pagan wisdom.

Are these terms—*simple, mockers* and *fools*—identical? (1:22)

They are closely related. "Parallelism" is a literary device used frequently by Old Testament writers. The writer chooses words that are similar or parallel in meaning to emphasize a certain truth. The root meaning of *simple* is *to be wide open*—that is, to be naive, accepting anything. A *mocker* is someone who cynically scoffs at morality. The *fool* is a person insensitive to moral truth, who reaps the sad consequences of short-sighted living.

What is the difference between *wisdom, understanding* and *insight*? (2:1-4)

Though closely related, each casts a slightly different hue. *Wisdom* seems to be a more general term meaning knowledge that leads to the knowledge of God. *Understanding* conveys discernment, and *insight* refers to a basic grasp of moral and ethical principles as they apply to life. Also see *What is wisdom?* (1:2).

a21 Hebrew; Septuagint / on the tops of the walls   b22 The Hebrew word rendered simple in Proverbs generally denotes one without moral direction and inclined to evil.

⁴and if you look for it as for silver
    and search for it as for hidden treasure,
⁵then you will understand the fear of the LORD
    and find the knowledge of God.
⁶For the LORD gives wisdom,
    and from his mouth come knowledge and
        understanding.
⁷He holds victory in store for the upright,
    he is a shield to those whose walk is
        blameless,
⁸for he guards the course of the just
    and protects the way of his faithful ones.

⁹Then you will understand what is right and just
    and fair—every good path.
¹⁰For wisdom will enter your heart,
    and knowledge will be pleasant to your
        soul.ᴰ
¹¹Discretion will protect you,
    and understanding will guard you.

¹²Wisdom will save you from the ways of wicked
    men,
    from men whose words are perverse,
¹³who leave the straight paths
    to walk in dark ways,
¹⁴who delight in doing wrong
    and rejoice in the perverseness of evil,
¹⁵whose paths are crooked
    and who are devious in their ways.

¹⁶It will save you also from the adulteress,
    from the wayward wife with her seductive
        words,
¹⁷who has left the partner of her youth
    and ignored the covenantᴰ she made before
        God.ᵃ
¹⁸For her house leads down to deathᴰ
    and her paths to the spirits of the dead.
¹⁹None who go to her return
    or attain the paths of life.

²⁰Thus you will walk in the ways of good men
    and keep to the paths of the righteous.ᴰ
²¹For the upright will live in the land,
    and the blameless will remain in it;
²²but the wicked will be cut off from the land,
    and the unfaithful will be torn from it.

Further Benefits of Wisdom

3 My son, do not forget my teaching,
    but keep my commands in your heart,
²for they will prolong your life many years
    and bring you prosperity.

³Let love and faithfulness never leave you;
    bind them around your neck,
    write them on the tablet of your heart.
⁴Then you will win favor and a good name
    in the sight of God and man.

⁵Trust in the LORD with all your heart
    and lean not on your own understanding;

ᵃ17 Or *covenant of her God*

What are the immediate consequences of adultery? (2:16–19)
See article: *What's wrong with adultery?* (5:3–10).

Does Proverbs teach about life after death? (2:18)
Not explicitly. But it assumes that both punishment and reward follow this life. The destiny of a person caught up in a lifestyle of sexual infidelity, for example, is *Sheol* or the underworld of the dead. But for those who live rightly according to God's commandments, *along that path is immortality* (12:28).

What land are the wicked cut off from? (2:22)
According to the Law of Moses, adulterers were to be put to death (Lev. 20:10) or prematurely cut off from the land of the living. The phrase can also refer to forfeiting the opportunity to live a life filled with the blessings the righteous enjoy. The inevitable outcome of adultery is broken promises, shattered trust and ruined relationships.

Does trusting God mean ignoring our own common sense? (3:5–6)
God's wisdom is not at war with common sense. But often common sense alone isn't enough to give the needed direction for a particular decision. That's why filling our minds with the perfect Word of God is so important (Psalm 18:30). By grounding our common sense in God's Word, we rely on him, not ourselves.

⁶in all your ways acknowledge him,
and he will make your paths straight.^a

⁷Do not be wise in your own eyes;
fear the LORD and shun evil.
⁸This will bring health to your body
and nourishment to your bones.

⁹Honor the LORD with your wealth,
with the firstfruits^D of all your crops;
¹⁰then your barns will be filled to overflowing,
and your vats will brim over with new
wine.^D

¹¹My son, do not despise the LORD's discipline
and do not resent his rebuke,
¹²because the LORD disciplines those he loves,
as a father^b the son he delights in.

¹³Blessed is the man who finds wisdom,
the man who gains understanding,
¹⁴for she is more profitable than silver
and yields better returns than gold.
¹⁵She is more precious than rubies;
nothing you desire can compare with her.
¹⁶Long life is in her right hand;
in her left hand are riches and honor.
¹⁷Her ways are pleasant ways,
and all her paths are peace.^D
¹⁸She is a tree of life to those who embrace her;
those who lay hold of her will be blessed.

¹⁹By wisdom the LORD laid the earth's
foundations,
by understanding he set the heavens in
place;
²⁰by his knowledge the deeps were divided,
and the clouds let drop the dew.

²¹My son, preserve sound judgment and
discernment,
do not let them out of your sight;
²²they will be life for you,

^a6 Or *will direct your paths*   ^b12 Hebrew; Septuagint / *and he punishes*

Should we give God a portion of every paycheck? (3:9–10)

Yes, although the amount to give is debated. Giving the *firstfruits* of harvest was part of the law (Exodus 23:19). Many believe the Old Testament principle to give God one-tenth of our income is reaffirmed in the New Testament. Others believe the percentage we give God, because of the New Testament principle of grace, isn't important. Either way a portion of everything we earn should be set aside for God's work.

Is there a difference between *discipline* and *punishment*? (3:11–12)

The reason for discipline is to teach. Punishment is intended to inflict consequences for past misbehavior. Through discipline God wants to instruct his people about himself. Its purpose is to enhance our character and strengthen our faith (Psalm 119:17).

Are proverbs iron-clad promises? (3:1–4)

Proverbs are principles of right living and general descriptions of life's realities, rather than sure-fire promises or guarantees. For example, Prov. 3:1 appears to promise a long life and prosperity to those who *do not forget my teaching, but keep my commands in your heart.* Yet some godly people live in poverty and die at a young age. Does this mean God doesn't keep his word?

This proverb isn't offering immunity from illness, accidents or financial troubles. Rather, proverbs such as this point to a general principle, which if applied consistently to our lives, will save us from unnecessary pain and suffering. While we aren't guaranteed we'll never contract cancer or go broke, we can avoid the foolish choices that can prematurely cut our life short or cause financial ruin.

While Proverbs observes the way life works time after time, exceptions to the general rules are evident in the books of Ecclesiastes and Job.

an ornament to grace^D your neck.
²³Then you will go on your way in safety,
  and your foot will not stumble;
²⁴when you lie down, you will not be afraid;
  when you lie down, your sleep will be sweet.
²⁵Have no fear of sudden disaster
  or of the ruin that overtakes the wicked,
²⁶for the LORD will be your confidence
  and will keep your foot from being snared.

²⁷Do not withhold good from those who deserve
    it,
  when it is in your power to act.
²⁸Do not say to your neighbor,
  "Come back later; I'll give it tomorrow"—
  when you now have it with you.

²⁹Do not plot harm against your neighbor,
  who lives trustfully near you.
³⁰Do not accuse a man for no reason—
  when he has done you no harm.

³¹Do not envy a violent man
  or choose any of his ways,
³²for the LORD detests a perverse man
  but takes the upright into his confidence.

³³The LORD's curse is on the house of the wicked,
  but he blesses the home of the righteous^D.
³⁴He mocks proud mockers
  but gives grace to the humble.
³⁵The wise inherit honor,
  but fools he holds up to shame.

Wisdom Is Supreme

4 Listen, my sons, to a father's instruction;
  pay attention and gain understanding.
²I give you sound learning,
  so do not forsake my teaching.
³When I was a boy in my father's house,
  still tender, and an only child of my mother,
⁴he taught me and said,
  "Lay hold of my words with all your heart;
  keep my commands and you will live.
⁵Get wisdom, get understanding;
  do not forget my words or swerve from
    them.
⁶Do not forsake wisdom, and she will protect
    you;
  love her, and she will watch over you.
⁷Wisdom is supreme; therefore get wisdom.
  Though it cost all you have,^a get
    understanding.
⁸Esteem her, and she will exalt you;
  embrace her, and she will honor you.
⁹She will set a garland of grace on your head
  and present you with a crown of splendor."

¹⁰Listen, my son, accept what I say,
  and the years of your life will be many.
¹¹I guide you in the way of wisdom
  and lead you along straight paths.
¹²When you walk, your steps will not be
    hampered;

Does God actually curse certain house-holds? (3:33)
This *curse* is a consequence of sin, an announcement of punishment. Humanity was placed under the curse of suffering and death when Adam and Eve sinned (Gen. 4:11). Moses warned of specific curses for disobeying God's law (Deut. 11:26). The writer is warning the wicked that because of their disobedience, judgment rests on their lives. Though they may prosper for a season, ultimately their gains will be erased.

Is this a reference to Solomon's father? (4:3–4)
Yes. King David was a primary source of Solomon's instruction (1:1).

^a7 Or *Whatever else you get*

when you run, you will not stumble.
¹³Hold on to instruction, do not let it go;
    guard it well, for it is your life.
¹⁴Do not set foot on the path of the wicked
    or walk in the way of evil men.
¹⁵Avoid it, do not travel on it;
    turn from it and go on your way.
¹⁶For they cannot sleep till they do evil;
    they are robbed of slumber till they make
        someone fall.
¹⁷They eat the bread of wickedness
    and drink the wine of violence.

¹⁸The path of the righteousᴰ is like the first
        gleam of dawn,
    shining ever brighter till the full light of day.
¹⁹But the way of the wicked is like deep
        darkness;
    they do not know what makes them stumble.

²⁰My son, pay attention to what I say;
    listen closely to my words.
²¹Do not let them out of your sight,
    keep them within your heart;
²²for they are life to those who find them
    and health to a man's whole body.
²³Above all else, guard your heart,
    for it is the wellspring of life.
²⁴Put away perversity from your mouth;
    keep corrupt talk far from your lips.
²⁵Let your eyes look straight ahead,
    fix your gaze directly before you.
²⁶Make levelᵃ paths for your feet
    and take only ways that are firm.
²⁷Do not swerve to the right or the left;
    keep your foot from evil.

Warning Against Adultery

5 My son, pay attention to my wisdom,
        listen well to my words of insight,
²that you may maintain discretion
    and your lips may preserve knowledge.
³For the lips of an adulteress drip honey,
    and her speech is smoother than oil;
⁴but in the end she is bitter as gall,
    sharp as a double-edged sword.
⁵Her feet go down to deathᴰ;
    her steps lead straight to the grave.ᵇ
⁶She gives no thought to the way of life;
    her paths are crooked, but she knows it not.

⁷Now then, my sons, listen to me;
    do not turn aside from what I say.
⁸Keep to a path far from her,
    do not go near the door of her house,
⁹lest you give your best strength to others
    and your years to one who is cruel,
¹⁰lest strangers feast on your wealth
    and your toil enrich another man's house.
¹¹At the end of your life you will groan,
    when your flesh and body are spent.
¹²You will say, "How I hated discipline!
    How my heart spurned correction!

Wellspring of life (4:23)
A metaphor for the heart, believed at that time to be the source of intelligence and the place where life-changing decisions were made. Just as a source of water could go bad, one's thinking could become corrupted if it was not guarded.

Make level paths (4:26)
We *make level paths* by avoiding things that might trip us up. The proverb suggests that we consider options carefully and make choices consistent with God's will. See NIV text note. Also see **Level ground** (Psalm 26:12).

ᵃ26 Or *Consider the*   ᵇ5 Hebrew *Sheol*

¹³I would not obey my teachers
   or listen to my instructors.
¹⁴I have come to the brink of utter ruin
   in the midst of the whole assembly."

¹⁵Drink water from your own cistern^D,
   running water from your own well.
¹⁶Should your springs overflow in the streets,
   your streams of water in the public
      squares?
¹⁷Let them be yours alone,
   never to be shared with strangers.
¹⁸May your fountain be blessed,
   and may you rejoice in the wife of your
      youth.
¹⁹A loving doe, a graceful deer—
   may her breasts satisfy you always,
   may you ever be captivated by her love.
²⁰Why be captivated, my son, by an adulteress?
   Why embrace the bosom of another man's
      wife?
²¹For a man's ways are in full view of the
      LORD,
   and he examines all his paths.
²²The evil deeds of a wicked man ensnare him;
   the cords of his sin hold him fast.
²³He will die for lack of discipline,
   led astray by his own great folly.

Warnings Against Folly

6 My son, if you have put up security for your
      neighbor,
   if you have struck hands in pledge for
      another,
²if you have been trapped by what you said,
   ensnared by the words of your mouth,
³then do this, my son, to free yourself,
   since you have fallen into your neighbor's
      hands:
   Go and humble yourself;
      press your plea with your neighbor!
⁴Allow no sleep to your eyes,
   no slumber to your eyelids.

Is sex intended for more than procreation? (5:18–19)

Sex has at least three God-given benefits: to provide pleasure, intimacy and children. Pleasure and intimacy are mentioned in these verses. Within marriage, the physical delights of sex are fully realized: enjoyment, closeness and a secure, satisfying relationship.

Why didn't Solomon follow his own advice? (5:18–19)

Perhaps Solomon learned some of his lessons the hard way. With 700 wives and 300 concubines, he knew firsthand the complications of entangled relationships. This may be an example of Solomon's wisdom surpassing his practices.

Ensnare . . . hold him fast (5:22–23)

The snare pictures captivity or subjection. Adultery can be habit-forming and its addictive grip becomes increasingly harder to break. It enslaves the sinner and brings premature destruction. Breaking free is nearly impossible without God's help.

Is co-signing a loan sinful? (6:1–5)

Proverbs simply warns the young person who might be gullible or impulsive. Putting up money for someone who is a bad risk will jeopardize the future. The practice itself isn't wrong, but wisdom is needed to minimize bad debt. Poor judgment may result in a lifetime of repayment.

What's wrong with adultery? (5:3–10)

First, it violates God's holy standard (Exodus 20:14). Second, its consequences are devastating. Proverbs takes this approach, stressing the practical reasons why adultery should be avoided at all costs.

The writer acknowledges the powerful and tantalizing appeal of adultery. It pretends to offer pleasure and sexual release with few risks. The secrecy, intrigue and forbidden nature of the act only seem to add to its relentless pull.

Yet appearances are deceiving. What begins as sweet desire quickly turns bitter. Adultery destroys reputations, character and marriages; the permanent costs immeasurably outweigh the momentary rewards.

It ruins relationships, crushes the wronged spouse and cuts a deep gash in the marriage. Even adultery done and kept in secret is fully exposed to a God who judges righteously.

⁵Free yourself, like a gazelle from the hand of
the hunter,
like a bird from the snare of the fowler.

⁶Go to the ant, you sluggard;
consider its ways and be wise!
⁷It has no commander,
no overseerᴰ or ruler,
⁸yet it stores its provisions in summer
and gathers its food at harvest.

⁹How long will you lie there, you sluggard?
When will you get up from your sleep?
¹⁰A little sleep, a little slumber,
a little folding of the hands to rest—
¹¹and poverty will come on you like a bandit
and scarcity like an armed man.ᵃ

Is there no forgiveness for a divisive person? (6:12–15)

Not if he doesn't repent. The description is of the unrepentant *scoundrel* (v. 12), meaning someone without worth. Such a person deliberately divides people from one another, using subtle, manipulative gestures and words. God hates division and strife and those who deliberately cause it in friendships, families or churches can expect God's judgment.

Are these the sins God hates most? (6:16–19)

Many believe the formula *six things the LORD hates, seven that are detestable to him* is a poetic way of suggesting a specific but not exhaustive catalog of sins. These represent sins God finds particularly offensive. See also 30:15–31.

¹²A scoundrel and villain,
who goes about with a corrupt mouth,
13   who winks with his eye,
signals with his feet
and motions with his fingers,
14   who plots evil with deceit in his heart—
he always stirs up dissension.
¹⁵Therefore disaster will overtake him in an
instant;
he will suddenly be destroyed—without
remedy.

¹⁶There are six things the LORD hates,
seven that are detestable to him:
17   haughty eyes,
a lying tongue,
hands that shed innocent blood,
18   a heart that devises wicked schemes,
feet that are quick to rush into evil,

ᵃ11 Or *like a vagrant / and scarcity like a beggar*

Is hard work the secret to success? (6:6–11)

There is no formula or shortcut to success. But self-discipline is certainly a character trait of all successful people. Here the ant is offered as an example of unsupervised, uncoerced self-discipline. Without any outside pressure, this tiny creature both stores and gathers provisions to see it through future days when food will be scarce.

The writer suggests there is wisdom in hard work motivated by a spirit of foresight and diligence. By avoiding procrastination and doing what we ought to when we ought to, we'll discover a great deal of freedom from a fear of the future. We'll worry much less about scarcity and needs.

The *sluggard*, however, is lazy, short-sighted and destined for poverty and want. Such a person avoids taking responsibility for the future, shuns hard work and even lacks motivation to get out of bed. Rather than demonstrating initiative and effort, the sluggard finds it a chore to lift food from the plate to the mouth (19:24). The principle of success is summarized in 14:23: *All hard work brings a profit, but mere talk leads only to poverty.*

Though these verses focus on the human side of success, other verses in Proverbs underscore the importance of a commitment to the Lord. Following God is the primary quality of one who is successful in God's eyes (see 16:3, for example).

¹⁹a false witness who pours out lies
and a man who stirs up dissension among
brothers.

Warning Against Adultery

²⁰My son, keep your father's commands
and do not forsake your mother's teaching.
²¹Bind them upon your heart forever;
fasten them around your neck.
²²When you walk, they will guide you;
when you sleep, they will watch over you;
when you awake, they will speak to you.
²³For these commands are a lamp,
this teaching is a light,
and the corrections of discipline
are the way to life,
²⁴keeping you from the immoral woman,
from the smooth tongue of the wayward wife.
²⁵Do not lust in your heart after her beauty
or let her captivate you with her eyes,
²⁶for the prostitute reduces you to a loaf of
bread,
and the adulteress preys upon your very life.
²⁷Can a man scoop fire into his lap
without his clothes being burned?
²⁸Can a man walk on hot coals
without his feet being scorched?
²⁹So is he who sleeps with another man's wife;
no one who touches her will go unpunished.

³⁰Men do not despise a thief if he steals
to satisfy his hunger when he is starving.
³¹Yet if he is caught, he must pay sevenfold,
though it costs him all the wealth of his
house.
³²But a man who commits adultery lacks
judgment;
whoever does so destroys himself.
³³Blows and disgrace are his lot,
and his shame will never be wiped away;
³⁴for jealousy arouses a husband's fury,
and he will show no mercyᴰ when he takes
revenge.
³⁵He will not accept any compensation;
he will refuse the bribe, however great it is.

Warning Against the Adulteress

7 My son, keep my words
and store up my commands within you.
²Keep my commands and you will live;
guard my teachings as the apple of your eye.
³Bind them on your fingers;
write them on the tablet of your heart.
⁴Say to wisdom, "You are my sister,"
and call understanding your kinsman;
⁵they will keep you from the adulteress,
from the wayward wife with her seductive
words.

⁶At the window of my house
I looked out through the lattice.
⁷I saw among the simple,
I noticed among the young men,
a youth who lacked judgment.

Apple of your eye (7:2)
Apple is a metaphor for the center or pupil of
the eye. The highly sensitive pupil is guarded
fiercely by our eyelids and quick reflex systems. Damage to the pupil could result in
blindness. We're to be as concerned about the
teachings of Proverbs as the body is about the
pupil. Without wisdom, we live in darkness,
spiritually blind.

Are women the initiators of adultery?
(7:4–5)
No. Either sex can seduce the other and both
bear responsibility for the sin. The characters
in this scenario happen to be a simpleton and
a prostitute. The man is guilty of pandering after forbidden fruit and the woman is guilty of
seducing him.

Fellowship offerings (7:14–23)

Ceremonial law required that meat used in such a sacrifice had to be eaten the same day. None could be left until morning (Lev. 7:15). The seductive woman lures this foolish man by suggesting she has a sumptuous dinner that has to be eaten before daybreak. She perversely turns an act of worship into an occasion for sexual sin.

⁸He was going down the street near her corner,
    walking along in the direction of her house
⁹at twilight, as the day was fading,
    as the dark of night set in.

¹⁰Then out came a woman to meet him,
    dressed like a prostitute and with crafty
      intent.
¹¹(She is loud and defiant,
    her feet never stay at home;
¹²now in the street, now in the squares,
    at every corner she lurks.)
¹³She took hold of him and kissed him
    and with a brazen face she said:

¹⁴"I have fellowship offerings[D][a] at home;
    today I fulfilled my vows[D].
¹⁵So I came out to meet you;
    I looked for you and have found you!
¹⁶I have covered my bed
    with colored linens from Egypt.
¹⁷I have perfumed my bed
    with myrrh[D], aloes and cinnamon.
¹⁸Come, let's drink deep of love till morning;
    let's enjoy ourselves with love!
¹⁹My husband is not at home;
    he has gone on a long journey.
²⁰He took his purse filled with money
    and will not be home till full moon."

²¹With persuasive words she led him astray;
    she seduced him with her smooth talk.
²²All at once he followed her
    like an ox going to the slaughter,
    like a deer[b] stepping into a noose[c]
²³   till an arrow pierces his liver,
    like a bird darting into a snare,
    little knowing it will cost him his life.

²⁴Now then, my sons, listen to me;
    pay attention to what I say.
²⁵Do not let your heart turn to her ways
    or stray into her paths.
²⁶Many are the victims she has brought down;
    her slain are a mighty throng.
²⁷Her house is a highway to the grave,[d]
    leading down to the chambers of death[D].

Wisdom's Call

8   Does not wisdom call out?
    Does not understanding raise her voice?
²On the heights along the way,
    where the paths meet, she takes her stand;
³beside the gates leading into the city,
    at the entrances, she cries aloud:
⁴"To you, O men, I call out;
    I raise my voice to all mankind.
⁵You who are simple, gain prudence;
    you who are foolish, gain understanding.
⁶Listen, for I have worthy things to say;
    I open my lips to speak what is right.
⁷My mouth speaks what is true,

---

a14 Traditionally *peace offerings*   *b22* Syriac (see also Septuagint); Hebrew *fool*   *c22* The meaning of the Hebrew for this line is uncertain.   *d27* Hebrew *Sheol*

for my lips detest wickedness.
8All the words of my mouth are just;
 none of them is crooked or perverse.
9To the discerning all of them are right;
 they are faultless to those who have
 knowledge.
10Choose my instruction instead of silver,
 knowledge rather than choice gold,
11for wisdom is more precious than rubies,
 and nothing you desire can compare with
 her.

12"I, wisdom, dwell together with prudence;
 I possess knowledge and discretion.
13To fear the LORD is to hate evil;
 I hate pride and arrogance,
 evil behavior and perverse speech.
14Counsel and sound judgment are mine;
 I have understanding and power.
15By me kings reign
 and rulers make laws that are just;
16by me princes govern,
 and all nobles who rule on earth.*a*
17I love those who love me,
 and those who seek me find me.
18With me are riches and honor,
 enduring wealth and prosperity.
19My fruit is better than fine gold;
 what I yield surpasses choice silver.
20I walk in the way of righteousness*b*,
 along the paths of justice,
21bestowing wealth on those who love me
 and making their treasuries full.

22"The LORD brought me forth as the first of his
 works,*b, c*
 before his deeds of old;
23I was appointed*d* from eternity,
 from the beginning, before the world began.
24When there were no oceans, I was given birth,
 when there were no springs abounding with
 water;
25before the mountains were settled in place,
 before the hills, I was given birth,
26before he made the earth or its fields
 or any of the dust of the world.
27I was there when he set the heavens in place,
 when he marked out the horizon on the face
 of the deep,
28when he established the clouds above
 and fixed securely the fountains of the deep,
29when he gave the sea its boundary
 so the waters would not overstep his
 command,
 and when he marked out the foundations of
 the earth.
30 Then I was the craftsman at his side.
 I was filled with delight day after day,
 rejoicing always in his presence,

Why is wisdom better than wealth? (8:10–11)

While money can buy some of life's pleasures, it cannot purchase character, a good reputation or a meaningful relationship with God. Wealth is volatile and fleeting, but wisdom is eternal and not only brings meaning and joy to our lives but gains us the priceless favor of the Lord (8:35).

Who is speaking here? (8:12)

The speaker is wisdom personified. See *Why is wisdom pictured as a woman?* (1:20).

What role did wisdom play in creation? (8:22–31)

It was the organizing force behind all of creation. The beauty and order of the world is obviously the work of a superior designer. Like a skilled architect who carefully crafts plans for a magnificent structure, God's wisdom ordered the scheme of creation before it appeared.

a16 Many Hebrew manuscripts and Septuagint; most Hebrew manuscripts *and nobles—all righteous rulers*   *b22* Or *way;* or *dominion*   *c22* Or *The LORD possessed me at the beginning of his work;* or *The LORD brought me forth at the beginning of his work*   *d23* Or *fashioned*

³¹rejoicing in his whole world
    and delighting in mankind.

³²"Now then, my sons, listen to me;
    blessed are those who keep my ways.
³³Listen to my instruction and be wise;
    do not ignore it.
³⁴Blessed is the man who listens to me,
    watching daily at my doors,
    waiting at my doorway.
³⁵For whoever finds me finds life
    and receives favor from the LORD.
³⁶But whoever fails to find me harms himself;
    all who hate me love death ᴰ."

Invitations of Wisdom and of Folly

9 Wisdom has built her house;
    she has hewn out its seven pillars.
²She has prepared her meat and mixed her
    wine;
    she has also set her table.
³She has sent out her maids, and she calls
    from the highest point of the city.
⁴"Let all who are simple come in here!"
    she says to those who lack judgment.
⁵"Come, eat my food
    and drink the wine I have mixed.
⁶Leave your simple ways and you will live;
    walk in the way of understanding.

⁷"Whoever corrects a mocker invites insult;
    whoever rebukes a wicked man incurs
    abuse.
⁸Do not rebuke a mocker or he will hate you;
    rebuke a wise man and he will love you.
⁹Instruct a wise man and he will be wiser still;
    teach a righteous ᴰ man and he will add to
    his learning.

¹⁰"The fear of the LORD is the beginning of
    wisdom,
    and knowledge of the Holy One is
    understanding.
¹¹For through me your days will be many,
    and years will be added to your life.
¹²If you are wise, your wisdom will reward
    you;
    if you are a mocker, you alone will suffer."

¹³The woman Folly is loud;
    she is undisciplined and without knowledge.
¹⁴She sits at the door of her house,
    on a seat at the highest point of the city,
¹⁵calling out to those who pass by,
    who go straight on their way.
¹⁶"Let all who are simple come in here!"
    she says to those who lack judgment.
¹⁷"Stolen water is sweet;
    food eaten in secret is delicious!"
¹⁸But little do they know that the dead are
    there,
    that her guests are in the depths of the
    grave.ᵃ

ᵃ18 Hebrew *Sheol*

What's the significance of *seven pillars*? (9:1)

Some think this alludes to the seven-pillared shrines of an ancient pagan religion. The writer, then, would be contrasting true wisdom with the so-called wisdom of a false religion. Others believe the pillars symbolize the seven days of creation or perhaps the sun, moon and the five planets then known to exist. Or since seven is considered a perfect number, some believe this verse may refer to the perfect world that wisdom can build. It is also possible, however, that the number has no significance here. It may have been a common architectural practice to use seven pillars when building a beautiful home or building.

Should we give up on *mockers*? (9:7–9)

Yes, if they deliberately and arrogantly reject the truth. To do otherwise wastes time and only invites insults and abuse. Such people are better off left alone. Of course, if the mocker is more receptive, we should instruct him or her in God's wisdom.

Stolen water ... food eaten in secret (9:17)

The intrigue and danger of being found out can add to sexual temptation. Doing something considered out of bounds offers a thrill or heightened sense of excitement. The euphoria, however, is short-lived and soon gives way to shame, self-loathing and regret.

Proverbs of Solomon

10 The proverbs of Solomon:

A wise son brings joy to his father,
  but a foolish son grief to his mother.

²Ill-gotten treasures are of no value,
  but righteousness^D delivers from death^D.

³The LORD does not let the righteous^D go
    hungry
  but he thwarts the craving of the wicked.

⁴Lazy hands make a man poor,
  but diligent hands bring wealth.

⁵He who gathers crops in summer is a wise son,
  but he who sleeps during harvest is a
    disgraceful son.

⁶Blessings crown the head of the righteous,
  but violence overwhelms the mouth of the
    wicked. ª

⁷The memory of the righteous will be a
    blessing,
  but the name of the wicked will rot.

⁸The wise in heart accept commands,
  but a chattering fool comes to ruin.

⁹The man of integrity walks securely,
  but he who takes crooked paths will be
    found out.

¹⁰He who winks maliciously causes grief,
  and a chattering fool comes to ruin.

¹¹The mouth of the righteous is a fountain of
    life,
  but violence overwhelms the mouth of the
    wicked.

¹²Hatred stirs up dissension,
  but love covers over all wrongs.

¹³Wisdom is found on the lips of the discerning,
  but a rod is for the back of him who lacks
    judgment.

¹⁴Wise men store up knowledge,
  but the mouth of a fool invites ruin.

¹⁵The wealth of the rich is their fortified city,
  but poverty is the ruin of the poor.

¹⁶The wages of the righteous bring them life,
  but the income of the wicked brings them
    punishment.

¹⁷He who heeds discipline shows the way to life,
  but whoever ignores correction leads others
    astray.

¹⁸He who conceals his hatred has lying lips,
  and whoever spreads slander is a fool.

¹⁹When words are many, sin is not absent,
  but he who holds his tongue is wise.

How are these *proverbs of Solomon* different from those in the first nine chapters? (10:1)
The first nine chapters are extended lessons on the value of wisdom. The book then shifts gears and begins to apply that wisdom to everyday life. Switching from the philosophical to the practical, chs. 10–22 offer straightforward advice, warnings and principles to live by.

Does this verse promise that the righteous will never starve? (10:3)
No. Godly people throughout history have suffered severe deprivation and death because of war, famine or oppression. The proverb states a general principle that God's people will be blessed. See article: *Are proverbs iron-clad promises?* (3:1–4).

Overwhelms the mouth (10:6)
Probably refers to the way evil betrays itself. We might say their guilt was "written all over their faces." Just as the blessings of the righteous are plain to see, so are the violent deeds of the wicked.

Do we earn our salvation? (10:16)
This verse is not referring to salvation and eternal life. Elsewhere the Bible clearly teaches that our salvation is a gift from God, unearned and undeserved. Rather, this verse points to the blessings we can expect in this life from godly conduct and actions.

ª6 Or *but the mouth of the wicked conceals violence*; also in verse 11

²⁰The tongue of the righteousᴰ is choice silver,
  but the heart of the wicked is of little value.

²¹The lips of the righteous nourish many,
  but fools die for lack of judgment.

²²The blessing of the LORD brings wealth,
  and he adds no trouble to it.

²³A fool finds pleasure in evil conduct,
  but a man of understanding delights in
    wisdom.

²⁴What the wicked dreads will overtake him;
  what the righteous desire will be granted.

²⁵When the storm has swept by, the wicked are
    gone,
  but the righteous stand firm forever.

²⁶As vinegar to the teeth and smoke to the eyes,
  so is a sluggard to those who send him.

²⁷The fear of the LORD adds length to life,
  but the years of the wicked are cut short.

²⁸The prospect of the righteous is joy,
  but the hopes of the wicked come to
    nothing.

²⁹The way of the LORD is a refuge for the
    righteous,
  but it is the ruin of those who do evil.

³⁰The righteous will never be uprooted,
  but the wicked will not remain in the land.

³¹The mouth of the righteous brings forth
    wisdom,
  but a perverse tongue will be cut out.

³²The lips of the righteous know what is fitting,
  but the mouth of the wicked only what is
    perverse.

Why do some righteous people die young? (10:27)

Like other proverbs this is not a guaranteed promise so much as a general observation about how life usually works. See article: *Are proverbs iron-clad promises?* (3:1–4). This proverb does not offer to the righteous an immunity from ever meeting an untimely death. Nor does it guarantee that the wicked will always die young. Rather, this outlines general principles of life: If we live a righteous life, we can avoid many foolish actions that prematurely may cut our lives short. By contrast, if we follow God's ways, as a rule we will lead happier, healthier and longer lives.

Can my mouth ruin my life? (10:18–21)

Yes! Our mouths have the potential to make our lives miserable and affect our destiny. A *chattering fool*, says Proverbs, *comes to ruin* (v. 10).

The more we talk, the more likely we are going to stray into areas of gossip and slander (10:19). Slander is the spreading of false and damaging information about another person as if it were true. Only a fool does that, because sooner or later truth wins out and the slanderer will be discredited and punished (v. 18). Gossip, which is the sharing of rumors or information of an intimate, personal or sensational nature, ultimately destroys friendships and creates friction (16:28).

The wise person, however, speaks frugally. The tongue rightly used can *nourish* or *feed* others. A compliment or word of encouragement can brighten someone's outlook or motivate a person to pursue a dream. Sharing the Word of God is another life-giving use. Our tongue doesn't affect only *our* destiny; it can also change the destiny of those we bless or curse.

That's why Proverbs advocates an economy of speech. It's a wise person who bridles his urge to blurt out everything on his mind. Even fools are thought to be wise when they keep their mouth shut (17:28).

11

The Lᴏʀᴅ abhors dishonest scales,
     but accurate weights are his delight.

2When pride comes, then comes disgrace,
     but with humility comes wisdom.

3The integrity of the upright guides them,
     but the unfaithful are destroyed by their
         duplicity.

4Wealth is worthless in the day of wrath,
     but righteousnessᴅ delivers from deathᴅ.

5The righteousness of the blameless makes a
         straight way for them,
     but the wicked are brought down by their
         own wickedness.

6The righteousness of the upright delivers
         them,
     but the unfaithful are trapped by evil desires.

7When a wicked man dies, his hope perishes;
     all he expected from his power comes to
         nothing.

8The righteousᴅ man is rescued from trouble,
     and it comes on the wicked instead.

9With his mouth the godless destroys his
         neighbor,
     but through knowledge the righteous
         escape.

10When the righteous prosper, the city rejoices;
     when the wicked perish, there are shouts of
         joy.

11Through the blessing of the upright a city is
         exalted,
     but by the mouth of the wicked it is
         destroyed.

12A man who lacks judgment derides his
         neighbor,
     but a man of understanding holds his tongue.

13A gossip betrays a confidence,
     but a trustworthy man keeps a secret.

14For lack of guidance a nation falls,
     but many advisers make victory sure.

15He who puts up security for another will surely
         suffer,
     but whoever refuses to strike hands in pledge
         is safe.

16A kindhearted woman gains respect,
     but ruthless men gain only wealth.

17A kind man benefits himself,
     but a cruel man brings trouble on himself.

18The wicked man earns deceptive wages,
     but he who sows righteousness reaps a
         sure reward.

19The truly righteous man attains life,
     but he who pursues evil goes to his death.

20The Lᴏʀᴅ detests men of perverse heart

Day of wrath (11:4)

The day of judgment, when the consequences for actions finally are realized. Money won't help pay off spiritual debts on that day.

Does God actually bless entire cities? (11:10–11)

As just, honest and compassionate people gain influence in a community, the morality of public life is raised, as well as the quality of life for the citizens. Blessings are the results of good influences, just as curses are consequences for wrong actions. See *Does God actually curse certain households?* (3:33).

but he delights in those whose ways are
    blameless.

²¹Be sure of this: The wicked will not go
    unpunished,
but those who are righteousᴰ will go free.

Why such a strong figure of speech? (11:22)

The writer uses hyperbole, or overstatement, to emphasize how wrong it is to put beauty together with indiscretion. The Old Testament ceremonial law considered a pig to be an *unclean* animal. The absurdity of linking outward beauty with inward indiscretion is obvious.

²²Like a gold ring in a pig's snout
    is a beautiful woman who shows no
    discretion.

²³The desire of the righteous ends only in
    good,
but the hope of the wicked only in wrath.

²⁴One man gives freely, yet gains even more;
    another withholds unduly, but comes to
    poverty.

²⁵A generous man will prosper;
    he who refreshes others will himself be
    refreshed.

²⁶People curse the man who hoards grain,
    but blessing crowns him who is willing to
    sell.

²⁷He who seeks good finds goodwill,
    but evil comes to him who searches for it.

²⁸Whoever trusts in his riches will fall,
    but the righteous will thrive like a green
    leaf.

²⁹He who brings trouble on his family will
    inherit only wind,
    and the fool will be servant to the wise.

He who wins souls (11:30)

Refers to the person who persuades others with godly wisdom, convincing them of the value of righteous and wise living. This verse does not refer to winning souls to Christ, which is a New Testament concept.

³⁰The fruit of the righteous is a tree of life,
    and he who wins soulsᴰ is wise.

³¹If the righteous receive their due on earth,
    how much more the ungodly and the sinner!

How can I achieve financial security? (11:25–28)

One of the great deceptions of wealth is its false sense of security. If the stock market crashes, millionaires can become paupers in one day. Also, there will come a time when we will have to account for our lives before God; on that day our money will be utterly useless (v. 4). A person whose hope is in riches is headed for a fall (v. 28). Only trust in God offers true security.

Yet the book of Proverbs offers principles that apply to our finances. First, we should recognize that whatever we have is not ours and is the result of God's blessing.

That means we should hold our money with an open hand and give generously. God expects us to honor him with our wealth, returning to him a portion of our *firstfruits* by giving to his work on a planned, consistent and priority basis (3:9).

Second, we should work hard, earning our money honestly and spending it frugally. God hates dishonest business practices while he delights in those who conduct their financial affairs with integrity and honesty (v. 1). Third, we should save in the good times for the times of need—retirement, unemployment, college or any time when our income might be reduced. He who gathers money little by little makes it grow (13:11).

12 Whoever loves discipline loves knowledge,
    but he who hates correction is stupid.

²A good man obtains favor from the LORD,
    but the LORD condemns a crafty man.

³A man cannot be established through
        wickedness,
    but the righteous⁰ cannot be uprooted.

⁴A wife of noble character is her husband's
        crown,
    but a disgraceful wife is like decay in his
        bones.

⁵The plans of the righteous are just,
    but the advice of the wicked is deceitful.

⁶The words of the wicked lie in wait for blood,
    but the speech of the upright rescues them.

⁷Wicked men are overthrown and are no more,
    but the house of the righteous stands firm.

⁸A man is praised according to his wisdom,
    but men with warped minds are despised.

⁹Better to be a nobody and yet have a servant
    than pretend to be somebody and have no
        food.

¹⁰A righteous man cares for the needs of his
        animal,
    but the kindest acts of the wicked are cruel.

¹¹He who works his land will have abundant
        food,
    but he who chases fantasies lacks judgment.

¹²The wicked desire the plunder⁰ of evil men,
    but the root of the righteous flourishes.

¹³An evil man is trapped by his sinful talk,
    but a righteous man escapes trouble.

¹⁴From the fruit of his lips a man is filled with
        good things
    as surely as the work of his hands rewards
        him.

¹⁵The way of a fool seems right to him,
    but a wise man listens to advice.

¹⁶A fool shows his annoyance at once,
    but a prudent man overlooks an insult.

¹⁷A truthful witness gives honest testimony,
    but a false witness tells lies.

¹⁸Reckless words pierce like a sword,
    but the tongue of the wise brings healing.

¹⁹Truthful lips endure forever,
    but a lying tongue lasts only a moment.

²⁰There is deceit in the hearts of those who plot
        evil,
    but joy for those who promote peace⁰.

²¹No harm befalls the righteous,
    but the wicked have their fill of trouble.

²²The LORD detests lying lips,
    but he delights in men who are truthful.

How can I welcome correction when it hurts? (12:1)

Swallowing our pride and choking down the hard truth about ourselves is never easy. But the wise person will sift through the chaff for the grain of truth. Being able to accept criticism is a sure sign of a growing, emotionally healthy person.

What are the characteristics of a woman with noble character? (12:4)

See *Is the wife of noble character a realistic model for today's woman?* (31:10–31).

Should I think of myself as a *nobody?* (12:9)

The advice is to accept ourselves as we are, giving up the charade of trying to pretend we're something we're not. Living within our means is better than spending what we don't have and ending up financially strapped.

How is caring for animals a righteous act? (12:10)

The point is that godly wisdom affects all of life —even how we treat the rest of creation. How we treat animals may be a reflection on how we treat our family and friends.

How do I know if I'm *chasing fantasies?* (12:11)

See *How do I know if I'm chasing fantasies?* (28:19).

How can I make a wise decision? (12:15)

Wise decisions flow from a reservoir of spiritual wisdom: they are made by wise people— those who honor and fear God (1:7; 2:6). Nevertheless, Proverbs outlines certain principles that characterize the choices made by wise people: Wise decisions are made with the advice and instruction of others (9:9; 11:14). They stem from a life of discipline and obedience (10:8; 29:11). Some of the basic qualities that help shape wise decisions include peace, humility and a conciliatory attitude (10:19; 11:2; 16:14). Also see *Why make a decision if God always has the final say?* (16:1–9).

Is it best to just always keep quiet? (12:23)

See article: *Can my mouth ruin my life?* (10:18–21).

Am I obligated to obey my father when I am an adult? (13:1)

The statement—*A wise son heeds his father's instruction*—praises the virtue of being teachable, but it doesn't imply obligatory obedience throughout life. In this scenario, the son is a member of his father's household, so listening to his instruction only makes good sense.

Is instant gratification good for us? (13:12)

That's not what this verse is saying. This is a general observation on life: a legitimate longing that is delayed indefinitely grows wearisome. People naturally tire of persistently unmet expectations. Proverbs that offer general observations should not be accepted as absolute principles to be applied in every situation. Instant gratification, when satisfying an inappropriate desire or feeding an impatient attitude, is detrimental to a person's character.

23A prudent man keeps his knowledge to himself,
but the heart of fools blurts out folly.

24Diligent hands will rule,
but laziness ends in slave labor.

25An anxious heart weighs a man down,
but a kind word cheers him up.

26A righteous[D] man is cautious in friendship,[a]
but the way of the wicked leads them astray.

27The lazy man does not roast[b] his game,
but the diligent man prizes his possessions.

28In the way of righteousness[D] there is life;
along that path is immortality.

13 A wise son heeds his father's instruction,
but a mocker does not listen to rebuke.

2From the fruit of his lips a man enjoys good things,
but the unfaithful have a craving for violence.

3He who guards his lips guards his life,
but he who speaks rashly will come to ruin.

4The sluggard craves and gets nothing,
but the desires of the diligent are fully satisfied.

5The righteous hate what is false,
but the wicked bring shame and disgrace.

6Righteousness guards the man of integrity,
but wickedness overthrows the sinner.

7One man pretends to be rich, yet has nothing;
another pretends to be poor, yet has great wealth.

8A man's riches may ransom his life,
but a poor man hears no threat.

9The light of the righteous shines brightly,
but the lamp of the wicked is snuffed out.

10Pride only breeds quarrels,
but wisdom is found in those who take advice.

11Dishonest money dwindles away,
but he who gathers money little by little makes it grow.

12Hope deferred makes the heart sick,
but a longing fulfilled is a tree of life.

13He who scorns instruction will pay for it,
but he who respects a command is rewarded.

14The teaching of the wise is a fountain of life,
turning a man from the snares of death[D].

15Good understanding wins favor,
but the way of the unfaithful is hard.[c]

a26 Or *man is a guide to his neighbor*   *b27* The meaning of the Hebrew for this word is uncertain.   *c15* Or *unfaithful does not endure*

¹⁶Every prudent man acts out of knowledge,
    but a fool exposes his folly.

¹⁷A wicked messenger falls into trouble,
    but a trustworthy envoy brings healing.

¹⁸He who ignores discipline comes to poverty
      and shame,
    but whoever heeds correction is honored.

¹⁹A longing fulfilled is sweet to the soul[D],
    but fools detest turning from evil.

²⁰He who walks with the wise grows wise,
    but a companion of fools suffers harm.

²¹Misfortune pursues the sinner,
    but prosperity is the reward of the
      righteous[D].

²²A good man leaves an inheritance for his
      children's children,
    but a sinner's wealth is stored up for the
      righteous.

²³A poor man's field may produce abundant
      food,
    but injustice sweeps it away.

²⁴He who spares the rod hates his son,
    but he who loves him is careful to discipline
      him.

²⁵The righteous eat to their hearts' content,
    but the stomach of the wicked goes hungry.

14 The wise woman builds her house,
    but with her own hands the foolish one tears
      hers down.

²He whose walk is upright fears the Lord,
    but he whose ways are devious despises him.

³A fool's talk brings a rod to his back,
    but the lips of the wise protect them.

⁴Where there are no oxen, the manger is empty,
    but from the strength of an ox comes an
      abundant harvest.

⁵A truthful witness does not deceive,
    but a false witness pours out lies.

⁶The mocker seeks wisdom and finds none,
    but knowledge comes easily to the
      discerning.

⁷Stay away from a foolish man,
    for you will not find knowledge on his lips.

⁸The wisdom of the prudent is to give thought
      to their ways,
    but the folly of fools is deception.

⁹Fools mock at making amends for sin,
    but goodwill is found among the upright.

¹⁰Each heart knows its own bitterness,
    and no one else can share its joy.

¹¹The house of the wicked will be destroyed,
    but the tent of the upright will flourish.

How is seeking forgiveness beneficial? (14:9)

When a wrong is committed, a barrier of guilt is erected. Unconfessed sin disrupts not only our relationships with others but with God as well. Forgiveness reignites a spirit of goodwill and harmony between individuals and reconnects our communication with God.

Can we ever trust our own judgment? (14:12)

No, not unless our judgment has been shaped by a relationship with God. The *way* in this verse suggests a road apart from the wisdom of God. Our own sense of what is right or wrong, apart from God, is not always reliable. Life may seem to make perfect sense to someone who doesn't *fear the Lord* (1:7). That's why we've been given a guide that is perfectly reliable: God's Word. From it we acquire wisdom to walk down the right path.

¹²There is a way that seems right to a man,
  but in the end it leads to death[D].

¹³Even in laughter the heart may ache,
  and joy may end in grief.

¹⁴The faithless will be fully repaid for their ways,
  and the good man rewarded for his.

¹⁵A simple man believes anything,
  but a prudent man gives thought to his steps.

¹⁶A wise man fears the LORD and shuns evil,
  but a fool is hotheaded and reckless.

¹⁷A quick-tempered man does foolish things,
  and a crafty man is hated.

¹⁸The simple inherit folly,
  but the prudent are crowned with
    knowledge.

¹⁹Evil men will bow down in the presence of the
    good,
  and the wicked at the gates of the
    righteous[D].

²⁰The poor are shunned even by their neighbors,
  but the rich have many friends.

²¹He who despises his neighbor sins,
  but blessed is he who is kind to the needy.

²²Do not those who plot evil go astray?
  But those who plan what is good find[a] love
    and faithfulness.

²³All hard work brings a profit,
  but mere talk leads only to poverty.

²⁴The wealth of the wise is their crown,
  but the folly of fools yields folly.

²⁵A truthful witness saves lives,
  but a false witness is deceitful.

²⁶He who fears the LORD has a secure fortress,
  and for his children it will be a refuge.

²⁷The fear of the LORD is a fountain of life,
  turning a man from the snares of death.

²⁸A large population is a king's glory[D],
  but without subjects a prince is ruined.

²⁹A patient man has great understanding,
  but a quick-tempered man displays folly.

³⁰A heart at peace[D] gives life to the body,
  but envy rots the bones.

³¹He who oppresses the poor shows contempt
    for their Maker,
  but whoever is kind to the needy honors
    God.

³²When calamity comes, the wicked are brought
    down,
  but even in death the righteous have a
    refuge.

³³Wisdom reposes in the heart of the discerning

*a*22 Or *show*

and even among fools she lets herself be known.*a*

34Righteousness*D* exalts a nation,
but sin is a disgrace to any people.

35A king delights in a wise servant,
but a shameful servant incurs his wrath.

15 A gentle answer turns away wrath,
but a harsh word stirs up anger.

2The tongue of the wise commends knowledge,
but the mouth of the fool gushes folly.

3The eyes of the LORD are everywhere,
keeping watch on the wicked and the good.

4The tongue that brings healing is a tree of life,
but a deceitful tongue crushes the spirit.

5A fool spurns his father's discipline,
but whoever heeds correction shows
prudence.

6The house of the righteous*D* contains great
treasure,
but the income of the wicked brings them
trouble.

7The lips of the wise spread knowledge;
not so the hearts of fools.

8The LORD detests the sacrifice*D* of the wicked,
but the prayer of the upright pleases him.

9The LORD detests the way of the wicked
but he loves those who pursue
righteousness.

a33 Hebrew; Septuagint and Syriac / but in the heart of fools she is not known

Can a *nation* be considered righteous? (14:34)

The word *exalts* refers to the moral benefits godly people bring to a country. When the wicked are in power, injustice flourishes unbridled. But righteous leaders can set a tone of justice and concern for the poor, values that are near to the heart of God. This builds up the well-being of the entire community.

Great treasure (15:6)

This could refer to physical wealth, but if so it is only a general statement of principle, not an absolute guarantee. See article: *Are proverbs iron-clad promises?* (3:1–4). But *treasure* can refer to many things—one can be wealthy in values, personal character, relationships and so on. By contrast, the wicked, though they may have physical riches, will also have troubles along with them—if not now, later.

How can the wicked ever find God if their worship is rejected? (15:8)

They can find God when they abandon their insincerity to genuinely seek God. As long as their *sacrifice* is a sham, a ruse to try to attain God's favor, God will reject their false worship. Money, church attendance and other religious acts do not automatically offer the humility of spirit that acknowledges sin and a need for repentance. Those who sincerely seek God will find him.

Should I bottle up my feelings? (14:29)

Not necessarily. Emotions are neither good nor bad. They're simply a part of our makeup. But depending on how emotions are used, they can either help or harm us in life. Proverbs makes the case for handling our emotions properly—they should not be denied or buried, but they should be governed by reason and an *even temper* (17:27).

For example, it's certainly not sinful to feel upset when insulted. But to spew out anger in retaliation, says Proverbs, is foolish (12:16). Proverbs repeatedly condemns hotheaded individuals (vv. 16–17). Throttling high-running emotions and resisting the temptation to say something rash are vital to preserving our personal well-being (13:3).

The ability to give a gentle answer in the face of an angry confrontation is a sign of deep character.

The opposite of reckless anger is patience. Patience recognizes that a violent temper makes matters worse, inflicting further damage to relationships and even causing internal distress. A heart at peace gives life to the body (v. 30).

Feelings are healthy. Telling others how we feel is appropriate. How we do that, however, should be consistent with the wisdom described in Proverbs.

10Stern discipline awaits him who leaves the
path;
he who hates correction will die.

11Death[D] and Destruction[a] lie open before the
LORD—
how much more the hearts of men!

12A mocker resents correction;
he will not consult the wise.

13A happy heart makes the face cheerful,
but heartache crushes the spirit.

14The discerning heart seeks knowledge,
but the mouth of a fool feeds on folly.

15All the days of the oppressed are wretched,
but the cheerful heart has a continual feast.

16Better a little with the fear of the LORD
than great wealth with turmoil.

17Better a meal of vegetables where there is love
than a fattened calf with hatred.

18A hot-tempered man stirs up dissension,
but a patient man calms a quarrel.

19The way of the sluggard is blocked with thorns,
but the path of the upright is a highway.

20A wise son brings joy to his father,
but a foolish man despises his mother.

21Folly delights a man who lacks judgment,
but a man of understanding keeps a straight
course.

**Must I always check with others be-
fore making plans? (15:22)**

No, but this is a general rule of thumb. There is
safety in numbers. Groups tend to make better
decisions than individuals. The more important
the decision, the more important it is that we
seek the advice of others. Also see following
note.

22Plans fail for lack of counsel,
but with many advisers they succeed.

23A man finds joy in giving an apt reply—
and how good is a timely word!

24The path of life leads upward for the wise
to keep him from going down to the grave.[b]

25The LORD tears down the proud man's house
but he keeps the widow's boundaries intact.

26The LORD detests the thoughts of the wicked,
but those of the pure are pleasing to him.

27A greedy man brings trouble to his family,
but he who hates bribes will live.

28The heart of the righteous[D] weighs its
answers,
but the mouth of the wicked gushes evil.

29The LORD is far from the wicked
but he hears the prayer of the righteous.

30A cheerful look brings joy to the heart,
and good news gives health to the bones.

31He who listens to a life-giving rebuke
will be at home among the wise.

32He who ignores discipline despises himself,
but whoever heeds correction gains
understanding.

a 11 Hebrew *Sheol and Abaddon*   *b 24* Hebrew *Sheol*

[33]The fear of the LORD teaches a man wisdom,[a]
and humility comes before honor.

16

To man belong the plans of the heart,
but from the LORD comes the reply of the
tongue.

[2]All a man's ways seem innocent to him,
but motives are weighed by the LORD.

[3]Commit to the LORD whatever you do,
and your plans will succeed.

[4]The LORD works out everything for his own
ends—
even the wicked for a day of disaster.

[5]The LORD detests all the proud of heart.
Be sure of this: They will not go unpunished.

[6]Through love and faithfulness sin is atoned for;
through the fear of the LORD a man avoids
evil.

[7]When a man's ways are pleasing to the LORD,
he makes even his enemies live at peace[D]
with him.

[8]Better a little with righteousness[D]
than much gain with injustice.

[9]In his heart a man plans his course,
but the LORD determines his steps.

[10]The lips of a king speak as an oracle[D],
and his mouth should not betray justice.

[11]Honest scales and balances are from the LORD;
all the weights in the bag are of his making.

[12]Kings detest wrongdoing,
for a throne is established through
righteousness.

[13]Kings take pleasure in honest lips;
they value a man who speaks the truth.

[14]A king's wrath is a messenger of death[D],
but a wise man will appease it.

[15]When a king's face brightens, it means life;
his favor is like a rain cloud in spring.

[16]How much better to get wisdom than gold,
to choose understanding rather than silver!

[17]The highway of the upright avoids evil;
he who guards his way guards his life.

[18]Pride goes before destruction,
a haughty spirit before a fall.

[19]Better to be lowly in spirit and among the
oppressed
than to share plunder[D] with the proud.

[20]Whoever gives heed to instruction prospers,
and blessed is he who trusts in the LORD.

[21]The wise in heart are called discerning,
and pleasant words promote instruction.[b]

Why make a decision if God always has the final say? (16:1–9)

God's overriding veto sounds strange in a book about how to make wise choices. But it is consistent with the rest of the Bible. We are urged to act wisely, for our life's outcome depends on these decisions. Yet, despite what we decide to do, God has the final word. For the wise, this is a comforting thought: God is in control. For the foolish, however, it's a sign of frustration, because God will overrule their plans.

How can love and faithfulness atone for sin? (16:6)

Good deeds or pure motives can never remove guilt. Only the shedding of blood can accomplish that (Heb. 9:22). The writer is describing the *results* of repentance, not the *means* to be reconciled to God. To *fear the Lord* (1:7) motivates the believer to turn from evil.

[a]33 Or *Wisdom teaches the fear of the LORD*   [b]21 Or *words make a man persuasive*

²²Understanding is a fountain of life to those
  who have it,
  but folly brings punishment to fools.

²³A wise man's heart guides his mouth,
  and his lips promote instruction.^a

²⁴Pleasant words are a honeycomb,
  sweet to the soul^D and healing to the bones.

²⁵There is a way that seems right to a man,
  but in the end it leads to death.^D

²⁶The laborer's appetite works for him;
  his hunger drives him on.

²⁷A scoundrel plots evil,
  and his speech is like a scorching fire.

²⁸A perverse man stirs up dissension,
  and a gossip separates close friends.

²⁹A violent man entices his neighbor
  and leads him down a path that is not good.

³⁰He who winks with his eye is plotting
    perversity;
  he who purses his lips is bent on evil.

³¹Gray hair is a crown of splendor;
  it is attained by a righteous^D life.

³²Better a patient man than a warrior,
  a man who controls his temper than one
    who takes a city.

³³The lot is cast into the lap,
  but its every decision is from the LORD.

17 Better a dry crust with peace^D and quiet
  than a house full of feasting,^b with strife.

²A wise servant will rule over a disgraceful son,
  and will share the inheritance as one of the
    brothers.

³The crucible for silver and the furnace for gold,
  but the LORD tests the heart.

⁴A wicked man listens to evil lips;
  a liar pays attention to a malicious tongue.

⁵He who mocks the poor shows contempt for
    their Maker;
  whoever gloats over disaster will not go
    unpunished.

⁶Children's children are a crown to the aged,
  and parents are the pride of their children.

⁷Arrogant^c lips are unsuited to a fool—
  how much worse lying lips to a ruler!

⁸A bribe is a charm to the one who gives it;
  wherever he turns, he succeeds.

⁹He who covers over an offense promotes love,
  but whoever repeats the matter separates
    close friends.

Is old age a reward? (16:31)
Rather than seeing the aging process as something to be delayed, Solomon treats it as a status symbol. The general principle is that longevity is one mark of a godly life. Evil men and women reach old age too, but their paths may have been marred by the consequences of their lifestyle.

How does God test the heart? (17:3)
Both gold and silver are refined by high heat. The impurities float to the top and are skimmed off, improving the purity and quality of the metal. In the same way, suffering allows the moral impurities in our character to surface. The heat of hard times is designed to improve us, drawing us closer to the heart of God.

Is bribery encouraged? (17:8)
This proverb is merely describing reality: how the one who bribes feels about what he does. Bribery is sometimes effective, but this verse is not extolling its benefits. The Bible clearly condemns bribery as a perversion of justice (v. 23).

---

^a23 Or mouth / and makes his lips persuasive   ^b1 Hebrew sacrifices
^c7 Or Eloquent

¹⁰A rebuke impresses a man of discernment
    more than a hundred lashes a fool.

¹¹An evil man is bent only on rebellion;
    a merciless official will be sent against him.

¹²Better to meet a bear robbed of her cubs
    than a fool in his folly.

¹³If a man pays back evil for good,
    evil will never leave his house.

¹⁴Starting a quarrel is like breaching a dam;
    so drop the matter before a dispute breaks
        out.

¹⁵Acquitting the guilty and condemning the
        innocent—
    the LORD detests them both.

¹⁶Of what use is money in the hand of a fool,
    since he has no desire to get wisdom?

¹⁷A friend loves at all times,
    and a brother is born for adversity.

¹⁸A man lacking in judgment strikes hands in
        pledge
    and puts up security for his neighbor.

¹⁹He who loves a quarrel loves sin;
    he who builds a high gate invites destruction.

²⁰A man of perverse heart does not prosper;
    he whose tongue is deceitful falls into
        trouble.

²¹To have a fool for a son brings grief;
    there is no joy for the father of a fool.

²²A cheerful heart is good medicine,
    but a crushed spirit dries up the bones.

²³A wicked man accepts a bribe in secret
    to pervert the course of justice.

Why is building a *high gate* so dangerous? (17:19)

The word *gate* literally means *opening*. It could refer to the mouth of an impulsive and boisterous person whose loud mouth consistently gets him in trouble. Or it could refer to the construction of a gaudy and pretentious home whose sole purpose is to impress others. The arrogant display of wealth invites negative reactions as well.

How can I know who my friends are? (17:17)

One way is a test of loyalty. A genuine friend loves us through the best and worst of times. In fact, a friend's true colors are revealed when we go through unusually difficult or painful circumstances.

According to Proverbs it's preferable to have one or two close, intimate companions than a host of superficial acquaintances. The person who maintains only surface relationships with a wide number of people may eventually face ruin for lack of good advice when it is really needed (18:24).

True friends also wound us. They're willing to tell us the hard truth, even when it hurts. We can trust their honest feedback, but an enemy only *multiplies kisses* (27:6). Beware of someone who does not have the courage to confront you when you need it.

Some people make poor friends—those who would *entice* us to join them in crime, for example (1:10–19). Drunkards and gluttons are also on the list of people to avoid (23:20–21). Less dangerous, but nonetheless unreliable, are those drawn to us because of our material possessions or wealth. When financial hardship strikes, they disappear (19:4,7). Gossips should also be shunned. Their habit of sharing inappropriate and private matters inevitably separates close friends (16:28).

24A discerning man keeps wisdom in view,
  but a fool's eyes wander to the ends of the
    earth.

25A foolish son brings grief to his father
  and bitterness to the one who bore him.

26It is not good to punish an innocent man,
  or to flog officials for their integrity.

27A man of knowledge uses words with restraint,
  and a man of understanding is
    even-tempered.

28Even a fool is thought wise if he keeps silent,
  and discerning if he holds his tongue.

18 An unfriendly man pursues selfish ends;
  he defies all sound judgment.

2A fool finds no pleasure in understanding
  but delights in airing his own opinions.

3When wickedness comes, so does contempt,
  and with shame comes disgrace.

4The words of a man's mouth are deep waters,
  but the fountain of wisdom is a bubbling
    brook.

5It is not good to be partial to the wicked
  or to deprive the innocent of justice.

6A fool's lips bring him strife,
  and his mouth invites a beating.

7A fool's mouth is his undoing,
  and his lips are a snare to his soulD.

8The words of a gossip are like choice morsels;
  they go down to a man's inmost parts.

9One who is slack in his work
  is brother to one who destroys.

10The name of the LORD is a strong tower;
  the righteousD run to it and are safe.

11The wealth of the rich is their fortified city;
  they imagine it an unscalable wall.

12Before his downfall a man's heart is proud,
  but humility comes before honor.

13He who answers before listening—
  that is his folly and his shame.

14A man's spirit sustains him in sickness,
  but a crushed spirit who can bear?

15The heart of the discerning acquires
    knowledge;
  the ears of the wise seek it out.

16A gift opens the way for the giver
  and ushers him into the presence of the
    great.

17The first to present his case seems right,
  till another comes forward and questions
    him.

18Casting the lot settles disputes
  and keeps strong opponents apart.

Why call gossip *choice morsels*? (18:8)
See *Why call gossip choice morsels?* (26:22).

Are shoddy work habits a moral problem? (18:9)
Yes. Failing to do things the right way can lead to the ruin of a business, the destruction of a good reputation and the loss of means to provide for one's family. Being slothful is also a form of deception. By drawing a paycheck we don't deserve, we rob our employer.

How can God work through such an arbitrary process? (18:18)
Casting lots was a means used to settle disputed questions. In the absence of clear moral justification for deciding one way or another, this ancient equivalent of "flipping a coin" resolved the matter quickly and decisively. Though the means might appear arbitrary, participants fully believed God was involved: *The lot is cast into the lap, but its every decision is from the LORD* (16:33). God could certainly have directed the results of any such process. Also see *Why use a lottery to pick an apostle?* (Acts 1:26).

19An offended brother is more unyielding than a
        fortified city,
    and disputes are like the barred gates of a
        citadelᴰ.

20From the fruit of his mouth a man's stomach is
        filled;
    with the harvest from his lips he is satisfied.

21The tongue has the power of life and deathᴰ,
    and those who love it will eat its fruit.

22He who finds a wife finds what is good
    and receives favor from the LORD.

23A poor man pleads for mercyᴰ,
    but a rich man answers harshly.

24A man of many companions may come to ruin,
    but there is a friend who sticks closer than a
        brother.

19 Better a poor man whose walk is blameless
        than a fool whose lips are perverse.

2It is not good to have zealᴰ without
        knowledge,
    nor to be hasty and miss the way.

3A man's own folly ruins his life,
    yet his heart rages against the LORD.

4Wealth brings many friends,
    but a poor man's friend deserts him.

5A false witness will not go unpunished,
    and he who pours out lies will not go free.

6Many curry favor with a ruler,
    and everyone is the friend of a man who
        gives gifts.

7A poor man is shunned by all his relatives—
    how much more do his friends avoid him!
Though he pursues them with pleading,
    they are nowhere to be found.ᵃ

8He who gets wisdom loves his own soulᴰ;
    he who cherishes understanding prospers.

9A false witness will not go unpunished,
    and he who pours out lies will perish.

10It is not fitting for a fool to live in luxury—
    how much worse for a slave to rule over
        princes!

11A man's wisdom gives him patience;
    it is to his gloryᴰ to overlook an offense.

12A king's rage is like the roar of a lion,
    but his favor is like dew on the grass.

13A foolish son is his father's ruin,
    and a quarrelsome wife is like a constant
        dripping.

14Houses and wealth are inherited from parents,
    but a prudent wife is from the LORD.

15Laziness brings on deep sleep,
    and the shiftless man goes hungry.

Is being single a sign of God's disfavor? (18:22)

The expression is simply an upbeat comment about finding a wife, not a jab at those who are single. Marriage is not a reward for something done but a generous gift from God. In the New Testament, the apostle Paul argues that being single may be the better choice (1 Cor. 7:8).

Why do we blame God for our mistakes? (19:3)

It's human nature. Instead of accepting responsibility for our mistakes, we tend to blame others. In doing so, we attempt to avoid the consequences of our foolish behavior.

Why can't a person enjoy their money if they've earned it? (19:10)

Apparently this *fool* didn't earn his money; he fell into it along the way. A fool with money is an absurdity. He lacks the character and wisdom to earn it honestly or use it wisely. Most likely it will be squandered.

ᵃ7 The meaning of the Hebrew for this sentence is uncertain.

Why does God so closely identify with the poor? (19:17)

One reason is God's passion for justice; so often the poor are victims of injustice and oppression. Another reason is his love for those he created. Since the poor do not have access to the luxuries of the world, many consider them unlovable. But they still bear the image of God. Who would look out for the poor if not God? The poor also often exhibit the values God is looking for: a spirit of brokenness, trust and complete dependence upon him.

16He who obeys instructions guards his life,
but he who is contemptuous of his ways will die.

17He who is kind to the poor lends to the LORD,
and he will reward him for what he has done.

18Discipline your son, for in that there is hope;
do not be a willing party to his deathᴰ.

19A hot-tempered man must pay the penalty;
if you rescue him, you will have to do it again.

20Listen to advice and accept instruction,
and in the end you will be wise.

21Many are the plans in a man's heart,
but it is the LORD's purpose that prevails.

22What a man desires is unfailing loveᵃ;
better to be poor than a liar.

23The fear of the LORD leads to life:
Then one rests content, untouched by trouble.

24The sluggard buries his hand in the dish;
he will not even bring it back to his mouth!

25Flog a mocker, and the simple will learn prudence;
rebuke a discerning man, and he will gain knowledge.

26He who robs his father and drives out his mother
is a son who brings shame and disgrace.

ᵃ22 Or A man's greed is his shame

How should children be disciplined? (19:18)

Proverbs begins with the assumption that children are born in need of correction. They enter the world with a bent toward doing the wrong things. Fathers and mothers are expected to lovingly but firmly train children in the ways of wisdom, responsibility and righteousness. The direction children receive at home sets the course for their entire lives—*Train a child in the way he should go and when he is old he will not turn from it* (22:6). This isn't a blanket promise that godly parents won't have wayward children, but it does underscore the general principle that good parenting can have a life-long impact.

Parents who fail in their duty to discipline their children bear a heavy responsibility. The writer sees them as a *willing party* to their child's death (19:18). In ancient Israel the penalty for several crimes was capital punishment, so failing to properly control a child could indirectly lead to his death. Parents who ignore their children or fail to give them the discipline they need consign them to a bleak and dismal future.

There is disagreement today over disciplinary methods. Proverbs appears to favor the stronger forms of discipline—*He who spares the rod hates his son, but he who loves him is careful to discipline him* (13:24). Taken to an extreme, of course, such punishment could become abuse, which the Bible never encourages. The other side of the coin, of course, is that children who never learn that their actions carry consequences will eventually come to even more grief.

²⁷Stop listening to instruction, my son,
　　and you will stray from the words of
　　knowledge.

²⁸A corrupt witness mocks at justice,
　　and the mouth of the wicked gulps down
　　evil.

²⁹Penalties are prepared for mockers,
　　and beatings for the backs of fools.

20 Wine is a mocker and beer a brawler;
　　whoever is led astray by them is not wise.

²A king's wrath is like the roar of a lion;
　　he who angers him forfeits his life.

³It is to a man's honor to avoid strife,
　　but every fool is quick to quarrel.

⁴A sluggard does not plow in season;
　　so at harvest time he looks but finds nothing.

⁵The purposes of a man's heart are deep waters,
　　but a man of understanding draws them out.

⁶Many a man claims to have unfailing love,
　　but a faithful man who can find?

⁷The righteousᴰ man leads a blameless life;
　　blessed are his children after him.

⁸When a king sits on his throne to judge,
　　he winnows out all evil with his eyes.

⁹Who can say, "I have kept my heart pure;
　　I am clean and without sin"?

¹⁰Differing weights and differing measures—
　　the Lᴏʀᴅ detests them both.

¹¹Even a child is known by his actions,
　　by whether his conduct is pure and right.

¹²Ears that hear and eyes that see—
　　the Lᴏʀᴅ has made them both.

¹³Do not love sleep or you will grow poor;
　　stay awake and you will have food to spare.

¹⁴"It's no good, it's no good!" says the buyer;
　　then off he goes and boasts about his
　　purchase.

¹⁵Gold there is, and rubies in abundance,
　　but lips that speak knowledge are a rare
　　jewel.

¹⁶Take the garment of one who puts up security
　　for a stranger;
　　hold it in pledge if he does it for a wayward
　　woman.

¹⁷Food gained by fraud tastes sweet to a man,
　　but he ends up with a mouth full of gravel.

¹⁸Make plans by seeking advice;
　　if you wage war, obtain guidance.

¹⁹A gossip betrays a confidence;
　　so avoid a man who talks too much.

²⁰If a man curses his father or mother,
　　his lamp will be snuffed out in pitch
　　darkness.

Does Proverbs teach abstinence from alcohol? (20:1)

No. But it strongly warns of the dangerous consequences of alcohol abuse. The key phrase is *whoever is led astray by them is not wise.* Rulers are advised against drinking alcohol; it can affect their decisions (31:4–7). While not commanded of everyone, abstinence guarantees avoidance of the pitfalls of alcohol abuse.

Does *blameless* mean we must measure up to a list of rules? (20:7)

Blameless does not imply perfection but integrity. Someone with integrity believes in God and strives constantly to align his life with God's.

Why take a garment for security? (20:16)

See *Why take a garment for security?* (27:13).

21An inheritance quickly gained at the beginning
will not be blessed at the end.

22Do not say, "I'll pay you back for this wrong!"
Wait for the LORD, and he will deliver you.

23The LORD detests differing weights,
and dishonest scales do not please him.

24A man's steps are directed by the LORD.
How then can anyone understand his own
way?

25It is a trap for a man to dedicate something
rashly
and only later to consider his vows[D].

26A wise king winnows out the wicked;
he drives the threshing wheel over them.

27The lamp of the LORD searches the spirit of a
man[a];
it searches out his inmost being.

28Love and faithfulness keep a king safe;
through love his throne is made secure.

29The glory[D] of young men is their strength,
gray hair the splendor of the old.

30Blows and wounds cleanse away evil,
and beatings purge the inmost being.

21 The king's heart is in the hand of the LORD;
he directs it like a watercourse wherever he
pleases.

2All a man's ways seem right to him,
but the LORD weighs the heart.

3To do what is right and just
is more acceptable to the LORD than
sacrifice[D].

4Haughty eyes and a proud heart,
the lamp of the wicked, are sin!

5The plans of the diligent lead to profit
as surely as haste leads to poverty.

6A fortune made by a lying tongue
is a fleeting vapor and a deadly snare.[b]

7The violence of the wicked will drag them
away,
for they refuse to do what is right.

8The way of the guilty is devious,
but the conduct of the innocent is upright.

9Better to live on a corner of the roof
than share a house with a quarrelsome wife.

10The wicked man craves evil;
his neighbor gets no mercy[D] from him.

11When a mocker is punished, the simple gain
wisdom;
when a wise man is instructed, he gets
knowledge.

Lamp of the LORD (20:27)
The picture is of a lamp searching out the darkest corners of a room. Some think this refers to the all-knowing and probing Spirit of God. Others believe it refers to the inner world of an individual—perhaps the spiritual nature by which it is possible to know God, or the conscience by which we can search our motives.

Lamp of the wicked (21:4)
A small, palm-size bowl with oil and a wick to provide light. Here it is used as sort of a reversed metaphor: light typically pictures inspiration or godly guidance. The wicked, by contrast, look to their own pride for guidance.

Don't diligent people work quickly? (21:5)
The issue here is not how long it takes a person to do a job, but how long he or she takes to prepare and plan for it. Skilled workers can work quickly (see 22:29, where the word *skilled* means *quick, prompt*—compare Isaiah 16:5 where the same Hebrew word is translated *speeds*). This proverb, though, warns against hurrying into agreements or projects without adequate preparation. A wise person makes careful plans before building, investing, hiring, lending or jumping into other ventures.

Why pick on wives? (21:9)
Proverbs, directing its wisdom to the young man, frequently warns about quarrelsome wives (see also 19:13; 21:19; 25:24; 27:15). A young man needs to exercise great care in his choice of a marriage partner, fully aware of the problems a quarrelsome wife can generate in a marriage. What is not said is that the reverse also is true for a young woman. She should beware of choosing a husband who will be abusive, lazy, financially irresponsible or plagued by other destructive habits.

---

*a*27 Or *The spirit of man is the LORD's lamp*   *b*6 Some Hebrew manuscripts, Septuagint and Vulgate; most Hebrew manuscripts *vapor for those who seek death*

¹²The RighteousᴰOneᵃ takes note of the house
   of the wicked
and brings the wicked to ruin.

¹³If a man shuts his ears to the cry of the poor,
   he too will cry out and not be answered.

¹⁴A gift given in secret soothes anger,
   and a bribe concealed in the cloak pacifies
      great wrath.

¹⁵When justice is done, it brings joy to the
   righteous
but terror to evildoers.

¹⁶A man who strays from the path of
   understanding
comes to rest in the company of the dead.

¹⁷He who loves pleasure will become poor;
   whoever loves wine and oil will never be
      rich.

¹⁸The wicked become a ransom for the
   righteous,
and the unfaithful for the upright.

¹⁹Better to live in a desert
   than with a quarrelsome and ill-tempered
      wife.

²⁰In the house of the wise are stores of choice
   food and oil,
but a foolish man devours all he has.

²¹He who pursues righteousnessᴰ and love
   finds life, prosperityᵇ and honor.

²²A wise man attacks the city of the mighty
   and pulls down the strongholdᴰ in which
      they trust.

²³He who guards his mouth and his tongue
   keeps himself from calamity.

²⁴The proud and arrogant man—"Mocker" is his
   name;
he behaves with overweening pride.

²⁵The sluggard's craving will be the deathᴰ of
   him,
because his hands refuse to work.

²⁶All day long he craves for more,
   but the righteous give without sparing.

²⁷The sacrificeᴰ of the wicked is detestable—
   how much more so when brought with evil
      intent!

²⁸A false witness will perish,
   and whoever listens to him will be destroyed
      forever.ᶜ

²⁹A wicked man puts up a bold front,
   but an upright man gives thought to his
      ways.

³⁰There is no wisdom, no insight, no plan
   that can succeed against the LORD.

Why aren't more wicked people "ruined"? (21:12)

God brings wicked people to ruin according to his timetable, not ours. Sometimes we misinterpret God's graciousness and slowness to anger as an unwillingness or an inability to deal with evil people. However, God tells us not to fret over people who do evil. Instead, we're to wait patiently until he deals with them (Psalm 37:1,7).

Does this proverb condone bribes? (21:14)

The Old Testament clearly condemns giving and receiving bribes (17:23; Exodus 23:8; Deut. 16:19; Isaiah 5:23). This proverb merely makes an observation; it does not offer advice to follow. Also, there is a fine line separating a *gift* (a neutral term in the original language) from a *bribe:* though a gift may pacify someone's anger, when does a gift become a bribe? See *Why give gifts to the rich?* (22:16).

What's wrong with enjoying the finer things in life? (21:17)

Nothing—as long as they're kept in perspective. God's blessing may include the finer things in life (10:22). But this proverb warns against an obsession with pleasure and luxuries. People who must always have the most expensive, state-of-the-art possessions will deplete their financial resources.

Why would a wise man attack a strong city? (21:22)

This is an analogy meaning simply that wise tactics bring success. Cities in Bible times were often built on hills and surrounded by thick, high walls of cut stone. With ample food and water, a city could withstand a long siege. Babylon had food enough for 20 years and a constant water supply from the Euphrates River (see *Map 7* at the back of this Bible). Yet the Persians conquered Babylon by diverting the water supply and sneaking in via a "dry" river bed. The point is that employing wisdom can be more effective than using strength alone.

ᵃ12 Or *The righteous man*   ᵇ21 Or *righteousness*   ᶜ28 Or / *but
the words of an obedient man will live on*

How can I acquire a good name? (22:1)

In a sense, this is what Proverbs is all about. A good name develops from the pursuit and practice of wisdom. Wise people earn a good reputation as they learn to handle finances carefully, avoid sexual impurity, control their emotions and speech and work hard. Those who ignore wisdom and wind up in debt, sexual immorality, laziness and drunkenness will find their names on bad credit reports, pink slips and even police blotters!

Why does God make some rich and others poor? (22:2)

This is a mystery. But the rich should take caution and the poor should take comfort in the implications of this proverb: rich and poor are equal before God as his creatures. Their economic status does not make them better or worse in God's sight. What's most important is knowing God (Jer. 9:23–24). Thus, we should not be overly impressed when people are wealthy (Psalm 49:16–20). Nor should we devalue the poor (James 2:1–13).

What is the explanation for God-fearing people who are poor or unhealthy? (22:4)

Like other proverbs, this one makes a general observation about life which is usually true. Occasionally, though, God allows God-fearing people to suffer so that he might display his mighty works through them (John 9:1–3). God may also use poverty or poor health to test our loyalties (Deut. 8:2), to keep us dependent upon his grace (2 Cor. 12:7–10) or to develop character in us (James 1:2–4).

Will good training guarantee that children will not rebel? (22:6)

Some suggest that *way* in this proverb refers to a child's personality or bent. More likely it means (as it does throughout Proverbs) a moral path—the way of wisdom. Again, this proverb makes a general observation about the way life usually works: children whose parents start them out down the right pathway of life will not abandon it. There are occasional exceptions, but these do not cancel out the general principle or give an excuse not to follow it.

Is it wrong to borrow money? (22:7)

Proverbs does not categorically prohibit borrowing, but it does remind us that debt is a form of bondage. The ancient Israelites sometimes sold themselves into slavery to pay off debts (Exodus 21:2–7). Today, if we can't pay on time or pay at all, the lender can garnish our wages or personal possessions. In a society where credit cards and loan opportunities abound, extreme caution about borrowing money is needed.

Why give gifts to the rich? (22:16)

Giving gifts to the rich was apparently a form of bribery. This practice results in poverty because the "investment" yields no return. You're wasting your money trying to manipulate wealthy people! According to the first line of the proverb, it's about as effective as stealing from the poor!

³¹The horse is made ready for the day of battle,
but victory rests with the LORD.

22 A good name is more desirable than great riches;
to be esteemed is better than silver or gold.

²Rich and poor have this in common:
The LORD is the Maker of them all.

³A prudent man sees danger and takes refuge,
but the simple keep going and suffer for it.

⁴Humility and the fear of the LORD
bring wealth and honor and life.

⁵In the paths of the wicked lie thorns and snares,
but he who guards his soulᴰ stays far from them.

⁶Trainᵃ a child in the way he should go,
and when he is old he will not turn from it.

⁷The rich rule over the poor,
and the borrower is servant to the lender.

⁸He who sows wickedness reaps trouble,
and the rod of his fury will be destroyed.

⁹A generous man will himself be blessed,
for he shares his food with the poor.

¹⁰Drive out the mocker, and out goes strife;
quarrels and insults are ended.

¹¹He who loves a pure heart and whose speech is gracious
will have the king for his friend.

¹²The eyes of the LORD keep watch over knowledge,
but he frustrates the words of the unfaithful.

¹³The sluggard says, "There is a lion outside!"
or, "I will be murdered in the streets!"

¹⁴The mouth of an adulteress is a deep pit;
he who is under the LORD's wrath will fall into it.

¹⁵Folly is bound up in the heart of a child,
but the rod of discipline will drive it far from him.

¹⁶He who oppresses the poor to increase his wealth
and he who gives gifts to the rich—both come to poverty.

Sayings of the Wise

¹⁷Pay attention and listen to the sayings of the wise;
apply your heart to what I teach,
¹⁸for it is pleasing when you keep them in your heart
and have all of them ready on your lips.
¹⁹So that your trust may be in the LORD,
I teach you today, even you.

ᵃ6 Or *Start*

²⁰Have I not written thirty^a sayings for you,
  sayings of counsel and knowledge,
²¹teaching you true and reliable words,
  so that you can give sound answers
    to him who sent you?

²²Do not exploit the poor because they are poor
  and do not crush the needy in court,
²³for the LORD will take up their case
  and will plunder^D those who plunder
    them.

²⁴Do not make friends with a hot-tempered man,
  do not associate with one easily angered,
²⁵or you may learn his ways
  and get yourself ensnared.

²⁶Do not be a man who strikes hands in pledge
  or puts up security for debts;
²⁷if you lack the means to pay,
  your very bed will be snatched from under
    you.

²⁸Do not move an ancient boundary stone
  set up by your forefathers.

²⁹Do you see a man skilled in his work?
  He will serve before kings;
  he will not serve before obscure men.

23 When you sit to dine with a ruler,
  note well what^b is before you,
²and put a knife to your throat
  if you are given to gluttony.
³Do not crave his delicacies,
  for that food is deceptive.

⁴Do not wear yourself out to get rich;
  have the wisdom to show restraint.
⁵Cast but a glance at riches, and they are gone,
  for they will surely sprout wings
  and fly off to the sky like an eagle.

⁶Do not eat the food of a stingy man,
  do not crave his delicacies;
⁷for he is the kind of man
  who is always thinking about the cost.^c
"Eat and drink," he says to you,
  but his heart is not with you.
⁸You will vomit up the little you have eaten
  and will have wasted your compliments.

⁹Do not speak to a fool,
  for he will scorn the wisdom of your words.

¹⁰Do not move an ancient boundary stone
  or encroach on the fields of the fatherless,
¹¹for their Defender is strong;
  he will take up their case against you.

¹²Apply your heart to instruction
  and your ears to words of knowledge.

¹³Do not withhold discipline from a child;
  if you punish him with the rod, he will not
    die.

What are the *sayings of the wise?* (22:17)

The sayings of the wise (22:17–24:22) show striking similarities to an Egyptian text slightly older than Proverbs, known as *The Wisdom of Amenemope*. Several of the sayings (on oppression, the tongue, getting rich and others) are almost identical. Why would God include secular wisdom in the Bible? There are several possible explanations: (1) All truth is God's truth, no matter where it is found. (2) These proverbs were first sifted through the grid of Israel's faith before being included in the Bible. (3) God could have chosen to reveal his truth to an Egyptian sage, perhaps even one who believed in the true God.

Thirty sayings (22:20)

This section from *The Wisdom of Amenemope* (see previous note) is divided into about 30 units or sayings. The reference to *thirty sayings* also occurs in the Egyptian text.

Striking hands in a pledge (22:26)

Similar to our practice of shaking hands to make an agreement. In a culture that did not rely on written contracts for personal agreements, striking hands in a pledge bound a person to a course of action, in this case the payment of a debt.

Is it wrong to put up security for a debt? (22:26)

While this proverb does not make an absolute prohibition, it issues a strong warning against casual co-signing. See **Is co-signing a loan sinful?** (6:1–5).

How were property lines established? (22:28)

The land was considered a gift from God to his people (Deut. 19:14). The tribes of Israel were allotted land according to boundaries God established through Moses (Num. 34:1—35:8). The specific portions were assigned by lot (Num. 33:54) and then subdivided by tribal leaders. People used large stones or stone pillars to mark these boundaries.

Who are *rulers* today? (23:1–3)

This is anyone in a higher position, especially one inclined to use or manipulate others. The point is, don't overindulge yourself on the privileges or delicacies such individuals offer. You'll make an unfavorable impression and you may play into their plans to manipulate you.

Why not eat the food of a stingy man? (23:6)

It's unwise to ask for or even to accept a favor from a stingy person. Whether you eat his food, borrow something from him or enlist his time and efforts on a project, his manners and attitude may make the experience miserable.

^a20 Or *not formerly written*; or *not written excellent*   ^b1 Or *who*
^c7 Or *for as he thinks within himself, / so he is*; or *for as he puts on a
feast, / so he is*

Who has truth for sale? (23:23)

This proverb uses the imagery of commerce—buying and selling—to emphasize the priority of acquiring truth and its companions. Like a person who would spend a great deal of effort bartering for an item, a wise person will work hard to get truth, wisdom, discipline and understanding. These are items to savor, not to resell.

Deep pit ... narrow well (23:27)

In ancient times, people would bore holes into the ground—even into solid limestone rock—to catch rainwater. Such pits or other wells could be used to trap animals or to keep people prisoners (see Gen. 37:22; Jer. 18:20,22). Marital infidelity is often glamorized, but in reality, it's a prison from which you can't escape.

Can unfaithful men blame prostitutes for their sins? (23:28)

Absolutely not! The cunning of prostitutes provides a reason for fleeing rather than an excuse for failing. Men should avoid places and situations where sexual temptation will be most intense (5:8). No matter how devious the trap, God holds both men and women accountable for their sexual conduct.

Was alcoholism a problem in this culture? (23:29–35)

Alcoholism is not only a modern phenomenon; it troubled people in the ancient Middle East as well. The symptoms described here can be seen still today: those under the influence of alcohol pick fights, ruin their health and lose control of their lives—they endure *woe ... sorrow ... strife ... complaints ... needless bruises ... bloodshot eyes.* Also see 31:4–7.

¹⁴Punish him with the rod
and save his soulᴰ from deathᴰ.ᵃ

¹⁵My son, if your heart is wise,
then my heart will be glad;
¹⁶my inmost being will rejoice
when your lips speak what is right.

¹⁷Do not let your heart envy sinners,
but always be zealous for the fear of the
Lᴏʀᴅ.
¹⁸There is surely a future hope for you,
and your hope will not be cut off.

¹⁹Listen, my son, and be wise,
and keep your heart on the right path.
²⁰Do not join those who drink too much wine
or gorge themselves on meat,
²¹for drunkards and gluttonsᴰ become poor,
and drowsiness clothes them in rags.

²²Listen to your father, who gave you life,
and do not despise your mother when she is
old.
²³Buy the truth and do not sell it;
get wisdom, discipline and understanding.
²⁴The father of a righteousᴰ man has great joy;
he who has a wise son delights in him.
²⁵May your father and mother be glad;
may she who gave you birth rejoice!

²⁶My son, give me your heart
and let your eyes keep to my ways,
²⁷for a prostitute is a deep pit
and a wayward wife is a narrow well.
²⁸Like a bandit she lies in wait,
and multiplies the unfaithful among men.

²⁹Who has woe? Who has sorrow?
Who has strife? Who has complaints?
Who has needless bruises? Who has
bloodshot eyes?
³⁰Those who linger over wine,
who go to sample bowls of mixed wine.

ᵃ14 Hebrew *Sheol*

How can we develop wise hearts? (23:15)

Developing a heart that is skilled in following God's ways requires exceptional commitment. Because of sin, we enter this world with spiritual "heart disease" (see Jer. 17:9). Our heart, the inner control center that thinks, feels and makes choices, is clogged with all kinds of evil thoughts, sexual perversions, deceit, pride and foolishness (compare Mark 7:21–23).

Bringing healing to our hearts begins with a passionate *fear of the Lᴏʀᴅ* (v. 17). It requires distancing ourselves from people who will lead us into a life overdosed on pleasure (vv. 21–22). We must weed out evil thoughts, desires and motives (4:23), and fill our minds with true, pure, admirable thoughts (Phil. 4:8). We must listen carefully to the right sources of input (vv. 19,22). Believers who are aware of God's wrath against sin and the brevity of life will give their days to the pursuit of a heart of wisdom (Psalm 90:12).

Also see *Why make a decision if God always has the final say?* (16:1).

³¹Do not gaze at wine when it is red,
   when it sparkles in the cup,
   when it goes down smoothly!
³²In the end it bites like a snake
   and poisons like a viper.
³³Your eyes will see strange sights
   and your mind imagine confusing things.
³⁴You will be like one sleeping on the high seas,
   lying on top of the rigging.
³⁵"They hit me," you will say, "but I'm not hurt!
   They beat me, but I don't feel it!
When will I wake up
   so I can find another drink?"

24 Do not envy wicked men,
      do not desire their company;
²for their hearts plot violence,
   and their lips talk about making trouble.

³By wisdom a house is built,
   and through understanding it is established;
⁴through knowledge its rooms are filled
   with rare and beautiful treasures.

⁵A wise man has great power,
   and a man of knowledge increases strength;
⁶for waging war you need guidance,
   and for victory many advisers.

⁷Wisdom is too high for a fool;
   in the assembly at the gate he has nothing to
      say.

⁸He who plots evil
   will be known as a schemer.
⁹The schemes of folly are sin,
   and men detest a mocker.

¹⁰If you falter in times of trouble,
   how small is your strength!

¹¹Rescue those being led away to deathᴰ;
   hold back those staggering toward slaughter.
¹²If you say, "But we knew nothing about this,"
   does not he who weighs the heart perceive
      it?
Does not he who guards your life know it?
   Will he not repay each person according to
      what he has done?

¹³Eat honey, my son, for it is good;
   honey from the comb is sweet to your taste.
¹⁴Know also that wisdom is sweet to your soulᴰ;
   if you find it, there is a future hope for you,
   and your hope will not be cut off.

¹⁵Do not lie in wait like an outlaw against a
      righteousᴰ man's house,
   do not raid his dwelling place;
¹⁶for though a righteous man falls seven times,
      he rises again,
   but the wicked are brought down by
      calamity.

¹⁷Do not gloat when your enemy falls;
   when he stumbles, do not let your heart
      rejoice,
¹⁸or the LORD will see and disapprove
   and turn his wrath away from him.

Assembly at the gate (24:7)

To make a city gate difficult for enemy armies to penetrate, gates were built with a series of two or even three doorways with massive wooden doors. In times of peace, these gates were open. Between the doorways were benches upon which the elders would sit and conduct business and discuss community issues. The point is: A fool has nothing meaningful to contribute when the wise leaders gather for such a meeting.

When trouble hits don't we all falter at times? (24:10)

Certainly! Even heroes of the faith like Abraham (Gen. 12:10–20), David (2 Samuel 11:2–4; 1 Chron. 21:14–17), the Gospel writer John Mark (Acts 15:37–38) and Peter (Matt. 26:69–75) failed when tough times hit. This proverb simply recognizes that difficulties and hardships reveal our character. Anyone can appear strong when times are good.

How can we rescue those being led away to death? (24:11)

This advice may have referred to helping those unjustly condemned to die. Today there are many people on the road to death whom we can rescue in a variety of ways: through education, protesting, sharing our material resources, opening our homes and so on. Our efforts should not be limited to those headed for physical death through drugs, alcohol, disease, abortion, hunger or violence. We may also help those destined for spiritual death. Ultimately, people need to hear the life-changing message of the gospel.

Why, of all possible foods, is honey endorsed by God? (24:13)

This is an analogy encouraging the reader to get wisdom (v. 14). Like honey, wisdom is desirable because of its life-giving properties and its sweetness. Just as honey satisfies a person's taste, wisdom satisfies a person's life, providing hope that a foolish person does not have.

19Do not fret because of evil men
  or be envious of the wicked,
20for the evil man has no future hope,
  and the lamp of the wicked will be snuffed
    out.

21Fear the LORD and the king, my son,
  and do not join with the rebellious,
22for those two will send sudden destruction
    upon them,
  and who knows what calamities they can
    bring?

Further Sayings of the Wise

23These also are sayings of the wise:

To show partiality in judging is not good:
24Whoever says to the guilty, "You are
    innocent"—
  peoples will curse him and nations denounce
    him.
25But it will go well with those who convict the
    guilty,
  and rich blessing will come upon them.

26An honest answer
  is like a kiss on the lips.

27Finish your outdoor work
  and get your fields ready;
  after that, build your house.

28Do not testify against your neighbor without
    cause,
  or use your lips to deceive.
29Do not say, "I'll do to him as he has done to
    me;
  I'll pay that man back for what he did."

30I went past the field of the sluggard,
  past the vineyard of the man who lacks
    judgment;
31thorns had come up everywhere,
  the ground was covered with weeds,

How does an honest answer resemble a kiss on the lips? (24:26)

Like a kiss, an honest answer demonstrates affection and love, the marks of genuine friendship.

Why plow your field before building a house? (24:27)

The principle is to get your financial and vocational life in order before you undertake a project like building a house. Many believe that building a house is a figure of speech for marriage. Thus, make sure you're able to provide for a family before you begin one.

When are rest and sleep okay? (24:30–34)

Some people tend to be lazy, but others are bent towards workaholism. Either extreme can distort labor all out of proportion; both greed and the desire to escape work are wrong.

Yet rest has been part of God's design for work from the beginning. After God worked on creation for six days, he stopped work on the seventh. God designed the world with a cycle of work and rest. He intended that the Sabbath would provide rest and refreshment for the workers (Exodus 23:12).

Jesus, who had a great sense of urgency for ministry, took time off (Mark 6:30–32). In fact, busyness can distract us from cultivating an intimate relationship with Christ (see Luke 10:38–42).

Leisure must not dominate us, but it must be part of our lives. Rest, used appropriately, works *for* workers, not against them. A proper balance between labor and rest can make us more efficient than when we constantly work without any rest.

and the stone wall was in ruins.
32I applied my heart to what I observed
and learned a lesson from what I saw:
33A little sleep, a little slumber,
a little folding of the hands to rest—
34and poverty will come on you like a bandit
and scarcity like an armed man.*a*

More Proverbs of Solomon

25 These are more proverbs of Solomon, copied by the men of Hezekiah king of Judah:

2It is the glory*D* of God to conceal a matter;
to search out a matter is the glory of kings.

3As the heavens are high and the earth is deep,
so the hearts of kings are unsearchable.

4Remove the dross*D* from the silver,
and out comes material for*b* the silversmith;
5remove the wicked from the king's presence,
and his throne will be established through
righteousness*D*.

6Do not exalt yourself in the king's presence,
and do not claim a place among great men;
7it is better for him to say to you, "Come up
here,"
than for him to humiliate you before a
nobleman.

What you have seen with your eyes
8   do not bring*c* hastily to court,
for what will you do in the end
if your neighbor puts you to shame?

9If you argue your case with a neighbor,
do not betray another man's confidence,
10or he who hears it may shame you
and you will never lose your bad reputation.

11A word aptly spoken
is like apples of gold in settings of silver.

12Like an earring of gold or an ornament of fine
gold
is a wise man's rebuke to a listening ear.

13Like the coolness of snow at harvest time
is a trustworthy messenger to those who
send him;
he refreshes the spirit of his masters.

14Like clouds and wind without rain
is a man who boasts of gifts he does not
give.

15Through patience a ruler can be persuaded,
and a gentle tongue can break a bone.

16If you find honey, eat just enough—
too much of it, and you will vomit.

17Seldom set foot in your neighbor's house—
too much of you, and he will hate you.

18Like a club or a sword or a sharp arrow

Men of Hezekiah (25:1)
Scribes or scholars who served in King Hezekiah's royal court, approximately 250 years after Solomon's reign. The study of wisdom was a royal pursuit. Kings would often sponsor wisdom conferences and have their own scribes and scholars sift through bits and pieces of wisdom. Under the Holy Spirit's direction, these scholars re-worked some of Solomon's material for further usage by God's people.

What's so glorious about God concealing matters? (25:2)
A king must search out matters to be a good leader. The mysteries of God, though, cannot be fully known. God has not told us everything about himself. He has preserved an element of mystery surrounding his personality and his purposes, leaving us in awe of him. It's because we cannot know everything about God that he is even more glorious.

SCRIPTURE LINK (25:7)
While dining at the house of a prominent religious leader, Jesus used the teaching of this proverb to rebuke guests who sought places of honor at the host's table. See Luke 14:7–11.

Apples of gold in settings of silver (25:11)
This suggests some kind of decorative piece or centerpiece on a table. Or, this may refer to a carving done in gold over silver. Either way, the emphasis is on an exquisite beauty, value and artistry which our speech should resemble.

Was snow at harvest desired? (25:13)
A source of coolness on a hot harvest day would be refreshing and welcome—just like news from a trustworthy messenger. Since snow at harvest time would be highly unusual, the metaphor may refer to several things—snow brought down from mountains and stored in an ice hole, cool air blowing down from snow-capped mountains or a mountain snow shower, or some other imagined refreshment.

Can you get too much of a good thing? (25:16)
Too much of any good thing will bring negative side-effects. Moderation is essential to the enjoyment of life's good pleasures.

Should we avoid visiting neighbors? (25:17)
Visiting friends and neighbors can be a delightful experience. But we can hinder relationships when we visit too frequently or for too long a time. Even our best friends need some space and privacy to care for their own affairs and spend time with their own families.

---

a 34 Or *like a vagrant / and scarcity like a beggar*   *b* 4 Or *comes a vessel from*   *c* 7,8 Or *nobleman / on whom you had set your eyes. / 8Do not go*

What's wrong with encouraging somebody who's down? (25:20)

People who are discouraged may benefit more if we weep with them (Romans 12:15) than if we spout jovial or light-hearted admonitions like "Don't worry; be happy." This proverb discourages superficial cheer.

Is it right to do good deeds in order to hurt someone? (25:21–22)

In this case, the good deeds will not produce harm. The *burning coals* symbolize the sharp pain of regret and shame a person experiences after seeing the error of his or her ways. The point is that good deeds and not revenge will prick an enemy's conscience.

SCRIPTURE LINK (25:21–22)

Jesus stressed the principle of this proverb and the apostle Paul quoted it directly. Both emphasized the need to love one's enemy and to overcome evil with good. See Matt. 5:44; Romans 12:20.

How is a man lacking self-control like a city with broken-down walls? (25:28)

A city with broken-down walls is defenseless against attacks by the enemy. Likewise, a person with no self-control has no defenses against the attacks of temptation. Those who can't control their lust, for example, are vulnerable to sexual temptation. People who can't control spending are vulnerable to indebtedness. People who can't control eating habits are vulnerable to weight gain and health problems.

An undeserved curse (26:2)

In ancient times many believed that words of blessing or cursing had mystical powers to accomplish their intentions. This proverb dismantles this superstition, picturing the curse as a fluttering bird that doesn't want to land.

Does this proverb mean fools should be beaten? (26:3)

Not exactly. This proverb simply observes that fools are like horses and donkeys which cannot be controlled by reason. Only physical force (whips, halters, rods) can produce any effect. Likewise, only physical punishment can subdue or control some fools.

Can one proverb contradict another? (26:4, compare with 26:5)

Some ancient Jewish scholars had doubts about the authenticity of Proverbs because of supposed contradictions. The fact that these two proverbs lie side by side helps to resolve the problem—this clash was intended! The point is that you have to adapt your approach depending on the kind of fool you're dealing with. Some fools should be answered (v. 5), others should be ignored (v. 4).

How are a fool's proverbs like a lame man's legs? (26:7)

A fool is verbally disabled and wisdom-impaired. Just as a lame man can get nowhere on his legs, a fool can do nothing with a proverb. He can't put truth into practice in his personal life, let alone teach it to someone else.

is the man who gives false testimony against
his neighbor.

¹⁹Like a bad tooth or a lame foot
is reliance on the unfaithful in times of
trouble.

²⁰Like one who takes away a garment on a cold day,
or like vinegar poured on soda,
is one who sings songs to a heavy heart.

²¹If your enemy is hungry, give him food to eat;
if he is thirsty, give him water to drink.
²²In doing this, you will heap burning coals on
his head,
and the LORD will reward you.

²³As a north wind brings rain,
so a sly tongue brings angry looks.

²⁴Better to live on a corner of the roof
than share a house with a quarrelsome wife.

²⁵Like cold water to a weary soulᴰ
is good news from a distant land.

²⁶Like a muddied spring or a polluted well
is a righteousᴰ man who gives way to the
wicked.

²⁷It is not good to eat too much honey,
nor is it honorable to seek one's own honor.

²⁸Like a city whose walls are broken down
is a man who lacks self-control.

26 Like snow in summer or rain in harvest,
honor is not fitting for a fool.

²Like a fluttering sparrow or a darting swallow,
an undeserved curse does not come to rest.

³A whip for the horse, a halter for the donkey,
and a rod for the backs of fools!

⁴Do not answer a fool according to his folly,
or you will be like him yourself.

⁵Answer a fool according to his folly,
or he will be wise in his own eyes.

⁶Like cutting off one's feet or drinking violence
is the sending of a message by the hand of a
fool.

⁷Like a lame man's legs that hang limp
is a proverb in the mouth of a fool.

⁸Like tying a stone in a sling
is the giving of honor to a fool.

⁹Like a thornbush in a drunkard's hand
is a proverb in the mouth of a fool.

¹⁰Like an archer who wounds at random
is he who hires a fool or any passer-by.

¹¹As a dog returns to its vomit,
so a fool repeats his folly.

¹²Do you see a man wise in his own eyes?
There is more hope for a fool than for him.

[13]The sluggard says, "There is a lion in the road,
a fierce lion roaming the streets!"

[14]As a door turns on its hinges,
so a sluggard turns on his bed.

[15]The sluggard buries his hand in the dish;
he is too lazy to bring it back to his mouth.

[16]The sluggard is wiser in his own eyes
than seven men who answer discreetly.

[17]Like one who seizes a dog by the ears
is a passer-by who meddles in a quarrel not
his own.

[18]Like a madman shooting
firebrands or deadly arrows
[19]is a man who deceives his neighbor
and says, "I was only joking!"

[20]Without wood a fire goes out;
without gossip a quarrel dies down.

[21]As charcoal to embers and as wood to fire,
so is a quarrelsome man for kindling strife.

[22]The words of a gossip are like choice morsels;
they go down to a man's inmost parts.

[23]Like a coating of glaze[a] over earthenware
are fervent lips with an evil heart.

[24]A malicious man disguises himself with his lips,
but in his heart he harbors deceit.
[25]Though his speech is charming, do not believe
him,
for seven abominations[b] fill his heart.
[26]His malice may be concealed by deception,
but his wickedness will be exposed in the
assembly.

[27]If a man digs a pit, he will fall into it;
if a man rolls a stone, it will roll back on
him.

[28]A lying tongue hates those it hurts,
and a flattering mouth works ruin.

27 Do not boast about tomorrow,
for you do not know what a day may bring
forth.

[2]Let another praise you, and not your own
mouth;
someone else, and not your own lips.

[3]Stone is heavy and sand a burden,
but provocation by a fool is heavier than
both.

[4]Anger is cruel and fury overwhelming,
but who can stand before jealousy?

[5]Better is open rebuke
than hidden love.

[6]Wounds from a friend can be trusted,
but an enemy multiplies kisses.

[a]23 With a different word division of the Hebrew; Masoretic Text *of silver dross*

How does honoring a fool resemble tying a stone in a sling? (26:8)

Both actions are absurd! Tying a stone in a slingshot defeats its purpose. Likewise, honoring a fool accomplishes nothing. The fool is still a fool. Some suggest that the stone might even slip out and harm the thrower. Similarly, honoring a fool may come back to harm you, perhaps causing you embarrassment, a bad reputation or the consequences of having placed a fool in a position of authority.

Why call gossip *choice morsels*? (26:22)

Choice delicacies are relished and eagerly devoured. Unfortunately so is gossip. Like *choice morsels*, gossip is something that stimulates the desire for more. People who gossip can't stop saying: "You'll never believe what I just found out."

Seven abominations (26:25)

The number *seven* often represents many, several or countless (see also v. 16). Here it may refer specifically to the seven abominations enumerated in 6:16–19.

What's the point of warning against digging a pit or rolling a stone? (26:27)

It's a warning that our intentions may boomerang. Intending to harm someone else may cause us harm instead. We may fall into our own trap or be the victim of our own plans. This proverb is sandwiched between warnings about wrongful speech, so it might relate to the harmful effect our wrongful speech against someone else can have on us.

SCRIPTURE LINK (27:1)

The apostle James warned about the same problem: arrogant presumption about the future with no regard for God. What we need is to humbly acknowledge the shortness and uncertainty of life. See James 4:13–16.

Why is it better to let someone else praise you? (27:2)

If you deserve praise, someone else will notice and will praise you! If you brag about yourself, you are acting in pride and will probably turn others off. Besides, the praise of others carries more weight; they will be more objective about your accomplishments and your character qualities.

How can we trust injuries caused by a friend? (27:6)

These are rebukes or criticism intended to correct (see 25:12). Even though they are painful, they are of more use than the flattery or insincerity of an enemy. Somebody else who criticizes may be trying to harm, whereas friends do it to build up. See article: *How can I know who my friends are?* (17:17).

Why go to a friend for help rather than a family member? (27:10)
This proverb speaks about the value of maintaining friendships. It does not suggest abandoning families as means of help. Develop a network of friendships and you'll have a base of support.

Why take a garment for security? (27:13)
This is equivalent to giving someone a secured loan—demanding security because he or she is a risk. In ancient times, before mass production, garments held considerable value because of the time, effort and materials invested in making them. Thus, they served well as collateral—just as vehicles or houses serve for collateral in today's economy.

In what ways do people sharpen each other? (27:17)
This expression has to do with personality. People sharpen each other through exchanging information, discussing issues and critiquing each other's ideas. Different people can bring different perspectives and strengths to a discussion. Like a knife blade rubbed on steel, this process in a friendship may sometimes cause the sparks to fly! Yet the result is good! A true friend sharpens the personality of his or her friend.

How are we tested by the praise of others? (27:21)
We are tested by the manner in which we respond to praise. Does it trigger arrogance and pride? Or does praise cause humility? Praise, more than criticisms, can be a severe test that reveals our character.

7He who is full loathes honey,
but to the hungry even what is bitter tastes sweet.

8Like a bird that strays from its nest
is a man who strays from his home.

9Perfume and incenseᴰ bring joy to the heart,
and the pleasantness of one's friend springs from his earnest counsel.

10Do not forsake your friend and the friend of your father,
and do not go to your brother's house when disaster strikes you—
better a neighbor nearby than a brother far away.

11Be wise, my son, and bring joy to my heart;
then I can answer anyone who treats me with contempt.

12The prudent see danger and take refuge,
but the simple keep going and suffer for it.

13Take the garment of one who puts up security for a stranger;
hold it in pledge if he does it for a wayward woman.

14If a man loudly blesses his neighbor early in the morning,
it will be taken as a curse.

15A quarrelsome wife is like
a constant dripping on a rainy day;
16restraining her is like restraining the wind
or grasping oil with the hand.

17As iron sharpens iron,
so one man sharpens another.

18He who tends a fig tree will eat its fruit,
and he who looks after his master will be honored.

19As water reflects a face,
so a man's heart reflects the man.

20Deathᴰ and Destructionᵃ are never satisfied,
and neither are the eyes of man.

21The crucible for silver and the furnace for gold,
but man is tested by the praise he receives.

22Though you grind a fool in a mortar,
grinding him like grain with a pestle,
you will not remove his folly from him.

23Be sure you know the condition of your flocks,
give careful attention to your herds;
24for riches do not endure forever,
and a crown is not secure for all generations.
25When the hay is removed and new growth appears
and the grass from the hills is gathered in,
26the lambs will provide you with clothing,
and the goats with the price of a field.
27You will have plenty of goats' milk

ᵃ20 Hebrew *Sheol and Abaddon*

to feed you and your family
and to nourish your servant girls.

28 The wicked man flees though no one pursues,
but the righteous[D] are as bold as a lion.

2When a country is rebellious, it has many
rulers,
but a man of understanding and knowledge
maintains order.

3A ruler[a] who oppresses the poor
is like a driving rain that leaves no crops.

4Those who forsake the law praise the wicked,
but those who keep the law resist them.

5Evil men do not understand justice,
but those who seek the LORD understand it
fully.

6Better a poor man whose walk is blameless
than a rich man whose ways are perverse.

7He who keeps the law is a discerning son,
but a companion of gluttons[D] disgraces his
father.

8He who increases his wealth by exorbitant
interest
amasses it for another, who will be kind to
the poor.

9If anyone turns a deaf ear to the law,
even his prayers are detestable.

10He who leads the upright along an evil path
will fall into his own trap,
but the blameless will receive a good
inheritance.

11A rich man may be wise in his own eyes,
but a poor man who has discernment sees
through him.

12When the righteous triumph, there is great
elation;
but when the wicked rise to power, men go
into hiding.

13He who conceals his sins does not prosper,
but whoever confesses and renounces them
finds mercy[D].

14Blessed is the man who always fears the LORD,
but he who hardens his heart falls into
trouble.

15Like a roaring lion or a charging bear
is a wicked man ruling over a helpless
people.

16A tyrannical ruler lacks judgment,
but he who hates ill-gotten gain will enjoy a
long life.

17A man tormented by the guilt of murder
will be a fugitive till death[D];
let no one support him.

18He whose walk is blameless is kept safe,

a3 Or *A poor man*

How do *many rulers* show that a country is rebellious? (28:2)

During times of rebellion, a lack of political stability generates a frequent change of rulers. Various factions or individuals grasp for power. For example, the rebellious northern kingdom of Israel had nine different ruling families in just over two centuries. Each one came into power through an assassination and none of them obeyed God (see Hosea 7:7). For more than three centuries, by contrast, Judah had only one ruling family.

What's the best way to confess sins? (28:13)

God's people should honestly and openly tell him when they sin. Though he knows when they sin, he wants them to admit it so he can help. David's prayers in Psalm 32 and Psalm 51 provide a model for confessing to God. These psalms (as well as 1 John 1:6–9) indicate the value of acknowledging our sin: the sooner we confess, the sooner we can experience God's forgiveness.

What does it mean to harden one's heart? (28:14)

This means stubbornly resisting God's ways and commands. The term *harden* was first used to describe the stubborn resistance of oxen to the yoke around their necks. Thus, it pictures the resistance of a person's heart—mind, will and emotions—to God's control. The same word is used to picture the rebellious, those with "hardened" or "stiff" necks (29:1).

How do I know if I'm *chasing fantasies*? (28:19)

This proverb warns against abandoning diligence and hard work to chase pipe dreams. Fantasies or "get-rich-quick" schemes try to shortcut the process of diligent work. But even daring, venturous ideas require work. Beware of anything that promises a great return for a little investment of time or energy.

Stiff-necked (29:1)

Describes a stubborn person who resists correction or challenges to his character. The opposite would be a submissive attitude pictured by a bending neck. The same term is applied in 28:14 to a rebellious person who is described as having a "stiff" or "hard" heart.

A net for his feet (29:5)

A net of woven cords was designed to catch birds or sometimes, when spread over an open pit, animals. This proverb uses the concept of a net in a figurative way to describe being caught off guard by flattering words.

but he whose ways are perverse will
    suddenly fall.

¹⁹He who works his land will have abundant
    food,
  but the one who chases fantasies will have
    his fill of poverty.

²⁰A faithful man will be richly blessed,
  but one eager to get rich will not go
    unpunished.

²¹To show partiality is not good—
  yet a man will do wrong for a piece of bread.

²²A stingy man is eager to get rich
  and is unaware that poverty awaits him.

²³He who rebukes a man will in the end gain
    more favor
  than he who has a flattering tongue.

²⁴He who robs his father or mother
  and says, "It's not wrong"—
  he is partner to him who destroys.

²⁵A greedy man stirs up dissension,
  but he who trusts in the LORD will prosper.

²⁶He who trusts in himself is a fool,
  but he who walks in wisdom is kept safe.

²⁷He who gives to the poor will lack nothing,
  but he who closes his eyes to them receives
    many curses.

²⁸When the wicked rise to power, people go into
    hiding;
  but when the wicked perish, the righteous[D]
    thrive.

29 A man who remains stiff-necked after many
    rebukes
  will suddenly be destroyed—without remedy.

²When the righteous thrive, the people rejoice;
  when the wicked rule, the people groan.

³A man who loves wisdom brings joy to his
    father,
  but a companion of prostitutes squanders his
    wealth.

⁴By justice a king gives a country stability,
  but one who is greedy for bribes tears it
    down.

⁵Whoever flatters his neighbor
  is spreading a net for his feet.

⁶An evil man is snared by his own sin,
  but a righteous one can sing and be glad.

⁷The righteous care about justice for the poor,
  but the wicked have no such concern.

⁸Mockers stir up a city,
  but wise men turn away anger.

⁹If a wise man goes to court with a fool,
  the fool rages and scoffs, and there is no
    peace[D].

¹⁰Bloodthirsty men hate a man of integrity
    and seek to kill the upright.

¹¹A fool gives full vent to his anger,
    but a wise man keeps himself under control.

¹²If a ruler listens to lies,
    all his officials become wicked.

¹³The poor man and the oppressor have this in
        common:
    The LORD gives sight to the eyes of both.

¹⁴If a king judges the poor with fairness,
    his throne will always be secure.

¹⁵The rod of correction imparts wisdom,
    but a child left to himself disgraces his
        mother.

¹⁶When the wicked thrive, so does sin,
    but the righteousᴰ will see their downfall.

¹⁷Discipline your son, and he will give you
        peaceᴰ;
    he will bring delight to your soulᴰ.

¹⁸Where there is no revelationᴰ, the people cast
        off restraint;
    but blessed is he who keeps the law.

¹⁹A servant cannot be corrected by mere words;
    though he understands, he will not respond.

²⁰Do you see a man who speaks in haste?
    There is more hope for a fool than for him.

²¹If a man pampers his servant from youth,
    he will bring griefᵃ in the end.

²²An angry man stirs up dissension,
    and a hot-tempered one commits many sins.

²³A man's pride brings him low,
    but a man of lowly spirit gains honor.

²⁴The accomplice of a thief is his own enemy;
    he is put under oath and dare not testify.

²⁵Fear of man will prove to be a snare,
    but whoever trusts in the LORD is kept safe.

²⁶Many seek an audience with a ruler,
    but it is from the LORD that man gets justice.

²⁷The righteous detest the dishonest;
    the wicked detest the upright.

Sayings of Agur

30 The sayings of Agur son of Jakeh—an oracleᴰᵇ:

This man declared to Ithiel,
    to Ithiel and to Ucal:ᶜ

²"I am the most ignorant of men;
    I do not have a man's understanding.
³I have not learned wisdom,
    nor have I knowledge of the Holy One.

ᵃ21 The meaning of the Hebrew for this word is uncertain.   ᵇ1 Or
Jakeh of Massa   ᶜ1 Masoretic Text; with a different word division
of the Hebrew *declared, "I am weary, O God; / I am weary, O God, and
faint.*

Do the poor and the oppressor have the same standing before God? (29:13)
See *Why does God make some rich and others poor?* (22:2).

Rod (29:15)
A stick which could be used for farming, fighting, shepherding or correcting. Used as a paddle in correcting, it came to symbolize physical discipline in general. Also see article: *How should children be disciplined?* (19:18).

What does it mean for people to *cast off restraint*? (29:18)
It means that they run wild and break loose from submission to authority. This results in spiritual and political chaos. Such chaos is prevented when revelation from God gives direction and guidance in God's way.

How do we get others to respond to constructive criticism? (29:19)
Not everyone is mature enough to handle criticism. In ancient times, most slaves needed to be corrected at one time or another, not pampered (v. 21). Similarly there may be times when we have to do more than issue verbal correction. We may have to withhold privileges or establish penalties to hold immature people accountable. Real consequences lend force to words.

Why listen to Agur—an ignorant man who didn't know God? (30:2-3)
Agur uses exaggeration for the sake of effect. His confession of ignorance is actually an expression of humility. He draws a contrast between his lowliness and God's greatness and majesty (v. 4). All this is preparation for the affirmation that humans have no ability or right to add anything to God's Word (vv. 5–6). We can't know God from our own ideas—only from God's revelation about himself.

SCRIPTURE LINK (30:4)
While talking with Nicodemus, a leading Bible scholar of the day, Jesus applied this statement to himself—an astounding claim of his deity. See John 3:13.

Three things . . . four (30:15)
This pattern signifies that the list, while specific, is not exhaustive. In other words, it could be extended. Some believe that pattern also stresses the final item as the end result or product of the previous items.

⁴Who has gone up to heaven and come down?
  Who has gathered up the wind in the hollow
    of his hands?
Who has wrapped up the waters in his cloak?
  Who has established all the ends of the
    earth?
What is his name, and the name of his son?
  Tell me if you know!

⁵"Every word of God is flawless;
  he is a shield to those who take refuge in
    him.
⁶Do not add to his words,
  or he will rebuke you and prove you a liar.

⁷"Two things I ask of you, O LORD;
  do not refuse me before I die:
⁸Keep falsehood and lies far from me;
  give me neither poverty nor riches,
  but give me only my daily bread.
⁹Otherwise, I may have too much and disown
    you
  and say, 'Who is the LORD?'
Or I may become poor and steal,
  and so dishonor the name of my God.

¹⁰"Do not slander a servant to his master,
  or he will curse you, and you will pay for it.

¹¹"There are those who curse their fathers
  and do not bless their mothers;
¹²those who are pure in their own eyes
  and yet are not cleansed of their filth;
¹³those whose eyes are ever so haughty,
  whose glances are so disdainful;
¹⁴those whose teeth are swords
  and whose jaws are set with knives
to devour the poor from the earth,
  the needy from among mankind.

¹⁵"The leech has two daughters.
  'Give! Give!' they cry.

"There are three things that are never satisfied,
  four that never say, 'Enough!':
¹⁶the grave,^a the barren womb,
  land, which is never satisfied with water,
  and fire, which never says, 'Enough!'

¹⁷"The eye that mocks a father,
  that scorns obedience to a mother,
will be pecked out by the ravens of the valley,
  will be eaten by the vultures.

¹⁸"There are three things that are too amazing
    for me,
  four that I do not understand:
¹⁹the way of an eagle in the sky,
  the way of a snake on a rock,
  the way of a ship on the high seas,
  and the way of a man with a maiden.

²⁰"This is the way of an adulteress:
  She eats and wipes her mouth
  and says, 'I've done nothing wrong.'

^a16 Hebrew *Sheol*

21"Under three things the earth trembles,
      under four it cannot bear up:
22a servant who becomes king,
      a fool who is full of food,
23an unloved woman who is married,
      and a maidservant who displaces her
            mistress.

24"Four things on earth are small,
      yet they are extremely wise:
25Ants are creatures of little strength,
      yet they store up their food in the summer;
26coneys*a* are creatures of little power,
      yet they make their home in the crags;
27locusts*b* have no king,
      yet they advance together in ranks;
28a lizard can be caught with the hand,
      yet it is found in kings' palaces.

29"There are three things that are stately in their
            stride,
      four that move with stately bearing:
30a lion, mighty among beasts,
      who retreats before nothing;
31a strutting rooster, a he-goat,
      and a king with his army around him.*b*

32"If you have played the fool and exalted
            yourself,
      or if you have planned evil,
      clap your hand over your mouth!
33For as churning the milk produces butter,
      and as twisting the nose produces blood,
      so stirring up anger produces strife."

Sayings of King Lemuel

31 The sayings of King Lemuel—an oracle*c* his
      mother taught him:

2"O my son, O son of my womb,
      O son of my vows*d*,
3do not spend your strength on women,
      your vigor on those who ruin kings.

4"It is not for kings, O Lemuel—
      not for kings to drink wine,
      not for rulers to crave beer,
5lest they drink and forget what the law
            decrees,
      and deprive all the oppressed of their
            rights.
6Give beer to those who are perishing,
      wine to those who are in anguish;
7let them drink and forget their poverty
      and remember their misery no more.

8"Speak up for those who cannot speak for
            themselves,
      for the rights of all who are destitute.
9Speak up and judge fairly;
      defend the rights of the poor and needy."

What is so frightening about these four things? (30:21–23)

The potential for harm. In each example someone is elevated to prominent status without being prepared for it. These cases describe people who likely had been oppressed, but were now put in power where they could take out their frustration on others. The maidservant who displeases her mistress brings to mind Hagar, who "displaced" her mistress Sarah by having Abraham's child (Gen. 16:1–6).

What's the lesson of these four creatures? (30:24–28)

Nature has many object lessons for us. Ants teach us the wisdom of preparing today for the future. Coneys, akin to our woodchucks or marmots, teach us the wisdom of knowing where to find protection. Locusts teach us the wisdom of pooling our resources for results. Lizards teach us the wisdom of seizing opportunities either through determination, boldness or cunning.

What can we learn from four things stately in their stride? (30:29–31)

As these images suggest, it is a grand, majestic sight to watch a leader move confidently forward to meet a challenge! A king's real leadership is not seen while he is seated on his throne, but when he leads his army to face the enemy. These examples teach us that boldness and courage are virtues to be desired.

King Lemuel (31:1)

No one knows who King Lemuel was. He was not a king in Israel or Judah unless his name, which means *belonging to God*, is a nickname. Lemuel shares wisdom that came from his mother, stressing the role a mother can have in building character into her children.

What does it mean to *spend strength on women?* (31:3)

This warning, given to a future king by his mother, concerns adultery—or at least the heavy investment of time, energy and money needed to court women. Kings in the ancient Middle East were especially susceptible to this weakness. They had wealth, prestige and the permission of their culture to marry many wives. They could even justify taking foreign princesses as wives to seal treaties.

a26 That is, the hyrax or rock badger   *b31* Or *king secure against revolt*   *c1* Or *of Lemuel king of Massa, which*   *d2* Or / *the answer to my prayers*

Is the wife of noble character a realistic model for today's woman? (31:10–31)

With poetic flair this passage shows that a godly woman can find fulfillment in her home, in the community, and in a career. This passage does not limit a woman's role to any one of these areas. Nor does it create unrealistic expectations for women, calling them to do everything in all these areas. Some women will focus more on one of these aspects than on the others. Rather than presenting an impossible dream, this epilogue to Proverbs lays out some of the possible opportunities for women who are married and have children. The *wife of noble character* puts wisdom into the fabric of her life.

Distaff . . . spindle (31:19)

These items were used in the process of twisting wool or flax fibers into thread. The distaff, a rod or stick, held the wool or flax. This was spun by turning the spindle, a small flywheel positioned at the lower end of the stick.

Why is her husband at the city gate? (31:23)

He's at the city gate to conduct business, like a leader of the city. See *Assembly at the gate* (24:7). Because his wife does her work well, he can be free to do his.

Epilogue: The Wife of Noble Character

10^aA wife of noble character who can find?
 She is worth far more than rubies.
11Her husband has full confidence in her
 and lacks nothing of value.
12She brings him good, not harm,
 all the days of her life.
13She selects wool and flax
 and works with eager hands.
14She is like the merchant ships,
 bringing her food from afar.
15She gets up while it is still dark;
 she provides food for her family
 and portions for her servant girls.
16She considers a field and buys it;
 out of her earnings she plants a vineyard.
17She sets about her work vigorously;
 her arms are strong for her tasks.
18She sees that her trading is profitable,
 and her lamp does not go out at night.
19In her hand she holds the distaff
 and grasps the spindle with her fingers.
20She opens her arms to the poor
 and extends her hands to the needy.
21When it snows, she has no fear for her household;
 for all of them are clothed in scarlet.
22She makes coverings for her bed;
 she is clothed in fine linen and purple.^D
23Her husband is respected at the city gate,
 where he takes his seat among the elders of the land.
24She makes linen garments and sells them,
 and supplies the merchants with sashes.
25She is clothed with strength and dignity;
 she can laugh at the days to come.
26She speaks with wisdom,
 and faithful instruction is on her tongue.
27She watches over the affairs of her household
 and does not eat the bread of idleness.
28Her children arise and call her blessed;
 her husband also, and he praises her:
29"Many women do noble things,
 but you surpass them all."
30Charm is deceptive, and beauty is fleeting;
 but a woman who fears the LORD is to be praised.
31Give her the reward she has earned,
 and let her works bring her praise at the city gate.

^a10 Verses 10-31 are an acrostic, each verse beginning with a successive letter of the Hebrew alphabet.

ECCLESIASTES

Why read this book?

If the deep and perplexing issues of life intrigue you, take a look at Ecclesiastes—but be prepared for a few surprises. On the surface, Ecclesiastes seems to challenge essential biblical truths. It dares to face hard questions. It shows the unglamorized life of a sinful world. It offers a glimpse at the secular mind. It looks at suffering and struggles to find meaning in it all. But most importantly, in the end Ecclesiastes points us to a solution.

Who wrote this book?

Solomon, according to tradition, though many now doubt this view. Some believe the writer was an unnamed *Teacher* or *assembly leader* who merely played the role of a king (1:1). Others say a wise man collected the views of the Teacher as a means to instruct his son (12:11–12).

When was it written?

It is impossible to say. Those who think Solomon wrote it, place it in the tenth century B.C. Others think it was compiled some time later.

Why was it written?

Ecclesiastes offers a philosophy of life—and shows how God fits into it. Part of the wisdom literature of the Old Testament, Ecclesiastes was used by the Hebrews as a book of instruction. It showed them how to find spiritual significance in a life that would otherwise be meaningless (12:8,13).

What to look for in Ecclesiastes:

Expect surprises. Ecclesiastes has lots of them: honest confessions of doubts, struggles with faith and disillusionment. A prologue (1:1–11) and an epilogue (12:9–14) frame its contents to reveal a proper, God-fearing attitude toward life. Watch out for isolated statements. They must be understood within the context of the whole book and, ultimately, that of the whole Bible.

Everything Is Meaningless

The Teacher, son of David, king in Jerusalem (1:1)

See Introduction: *Who wrote this book?*

1 The words of the Teacher,[a] son of David, king in Jerusalem[b]:

2"Meaningless! Meaningless!"
    says the Teacher.
"Utterly meaningless!
    Everything is meaningless."

3What does man gain from all his labor
    at which he toils under the sun?
4Generations come and generations go,
    but the earth remains forever.
5The sun rises and the sun sets,
    and hurries back to where it rises.

Does nothing satisfy? (1:6–8)

The Teacher looks at nature and observes cycles that are never completed: the wind keeps blowing in circles; water goes from streams to the sea and then back again. People are the same way, he concludes. They are never satisfied in this life and are always looking for more —more excitement, more money, more recognition, more love. Unless we rise above this fallen world, life will prove frustrating and unsatisfying.

6The wind blows to the south
    and turns to the north;
round and round it goes,
    ever returning on its course.
7All streams flow into the sea,
    yet the sea is never full.
To the place the streams come from,
    there they return again.
8All things are wearisome,
    more than one can say.
The eye never has enough of seeing,
    nor the ear its fill of hearing.

Why does the writer say nothing is new? (1:9–10)

While there may be new circumstances and new lifestyles, people are just like those in the days of the Teacher. There has been no new development in the areas of human nature and sin. Still, the Teacher's dour perspective needs amending—the Bible tells of God *doing a new thing* (Isaiah 43:19); in Christ *the new has come* (2 Cor. 5:17).

9What has been will be again,
    what has been done will be done
        again;
    there is nothing new under the sun.
10Is there anything of which one can say,
    "Look! This is something new"?
It was here already, long ago;
    it was here before our time.
11There is no remembrance of men of old,
    and even those who are yet to come
will not be remembered
    by those who follow.

a1 Or leader of the assembly; also in verses 2 and 12

Is life meaningless? (1:2)

I t can be, if we look for meaning in the wrong places. The Teacher tells of his
    search in various pursuits—wisdom, work, pleasure, prestige—and how he came
up empty every time. *Meaningless* can literally mean *vapor* or *breath*. It stresses the nothingness of life apart from God. The Teacher echoes this refrain throughout his book, beginning and ending on this note (1:2; 12:8).

Many think the Teacher, though wise, was a skeptic who based his view of life on what he observed around him. When he speaks of life *under the sun* (1:3) he means life apart from God, describing a fallen world under the curse of sin.

The Teacher is correct, then, but only up to a point: apart from God, life is meaningless. However, this is not the final word of the book of Ecclesiastes. According to its conclusion, there is meaning in life right now in the present (12:9–14). Some say this upbeat summary came from a wise man who used the Teacher's pessimistic views as a starting place for his son's instruction.

Wisdom Is Meaningless

[12]I, the Teacher, was king over Israel in Jerusalem[D]. [13]I devoted myself to study and to explore by wisdom all that is done under heaven. What a heavy burden God has laid on men! [14]I have seen all the things that are done under the sun; all of them are meaningless, a chasing after the wind.

> [15]What is twisted cannot be straightened;
> what is lacking cannot be counted.

[16]I thought to myself, "Look, I have grown and increased in wisdom more than anyone who has ruled over Jerusalem before me; I have experienced much of wisdom and knowledge." [17]Then I applied myself to the understanding of wisdom, and also of madness and folly, but I learned that this, too, is a chasing after the wind.

> [18]For with much wisdom comes much sorrow;
> the more knowledge, the more grief.

Pleasures Are Meaningless

2 I thought in my heart, "Come now, I will test you with pleasure to find out what is good." But that also proved to be meaningless. [2]"Laughter," I said, "is foolish. And what does pleasure accomplish?" [3]I tried cheering myself with wine, and embracing folly—my mind still guiding me with wisdom. I wanted to see what was worthwhile for men to do under heaven during the few days of their lives.

[4]I undertook great projects: I built houses for myself and planted vineyards. [5]I made gardens and parks and planted all kinds of fruit trees in them. [6]I made reservoirs to water groves of flourishing trees. [7]I bought male and female slaves and had other slaves who were born in my house. I also owned more herds and flocks than anyone in Jerusalem before me. [8]I amassed silver and gold for myself, and the treasure of kings and provinces. I acquired men and women singers, and a harem[a] as well—the delights of the heart of man. [9]I became greater by far than anyone in Jerusalem before me. In all this my wisdom stayed with me.

> [10]I denied myself nothing my eyes desired;
> I refused my heart no pleasure.
> My heart took delight in all my work,
> and this was the reward for all my labor.
> [11]Yet when I surveyed all that my hands had done
> and what I had toiled to achieve,
> everything was meaningless, a chasing after the wind;
> nothing was gained under the sun.

Wisdom and Folly Are Meaningless

> [12]Then I turned my thoughts to consider wisdom,
> and also madness and folly.
> What more can the king's successor do
> than what has already been done?
> [13]I saw that wisdom is better than folly,
> just as light is better than darkness.
> [14]The wise man has eyes in his head,
> while the fool walks in the darkness;

[a]8 The meaning of the Hebrew for this phrase is uncertain.

Has God put a burden on us? (1:13–14)

Yes—according to the Teacher or according to the perspective of the one apart from God. In fact, the Hebrew literally says that God has given men and women an *evil burden*. The Teacher will proceed to support his contention by citing death, the inability to know the future and political oppression as factors that contribute to the hardship of life. But keep in mind the different conclusion (12:8–14).

What is twisted cannot be straightened (1:15)

A proverb cited by the Teacher to support his point, a technique he uses occasionally throughout the book. The thrust of this proverb is that there is something fundamentally wrong with life on earth. This fatalistic view says that God has burdened humanity with unsolvable problems (v. 13).

Why does wisdom cause sorrow? (1:18)

In a sense, "ignorance is bliss"; the fool can live life without a clear vision of the end. But the wise person knows death will come. There are human limitations that even wisdom cannot overcome (2:12–16). Wisdom has value, but it still cannot change the fate that awaits everyone.

What's wrong with pleasure? (2:1–2)

Pleasure does not give meaning to life. It is short-lived and superficial. At best, it serves as an anesthetic to the harsh realities of life.

What's worth doing? (2:3–11)

The Teacher explored many different things in an attempt to find meaning in life. He tried sensual pleasures and wealth but concluded that, while they might grant temporary enjoyment, the results do not last. As we read these words we must constantly keep in mind that the Teacher is speaking of things apart from God —things *under the sun*. As a whole the Bible teaches that meaning for life can be found in Jesus Christ.

Is insanity an option? (2:12)

The Teacher intended to explore everything *under the sun* (v. 11). He determined to consider all options, to leave no stone unturned in his search for meaning. If he could not find life's purpose in the highest forms of wisdom, he would consider the other extremes—folly and even insanity. His conclusion: life's meaning is found in neither wisdom nor insanity.

Are the wise no better than fools? (2:13–16)

The Teacher acknowledged that wisdom had its advantages over folly. But he was looking for more: life's ultimate meaning. To his way of thinking, wisdom could not provide meaning for life because death brought it to an end. The Teacher believed death made everything in life insignificant. His understanding was limited, though. He could not foresee that Jesus would triumph over death so we might live forever.

but I came to realize
 that the same fate overtakes them both.

¹⁵Then I thought in my heart,

 "The fate of the fool will overtake me also.
  What then do I gain by being wise?"
 I said in my heart,
  "This too is meaningless."
¹⁶For the wise man, like the fool, will not be long
  remembered;
 in days to come both will be forgotten.
Like the fool, the wise man too must die!

Toil Is Meaningless

¹⁷So I hated life, because the work that is done under the sun was grievous to me. All of it is meaningless, a chasing after the wind. ¹⁸I hated all the things I had toiled for under the sun, because I must leave them to the one who comes after me. ¹⁹And who knows whether he will be a wise man or a fool? Yet he will have control over all the work into which I have poured my effort and skill under the sun. This too is meaningless. ²⁰So my heart began to despair over all my toilsome labor under the sun. ²¹For a man may do his work with wisdom, knowledge and skill, and then he must leave all he owns to someone who has not worked for it. This too is meaningless and a great misfortune. ²²What does a man get for all the toil and anxious striving with which he labors under the sun? ²³All his days his work is pain and grief; even at night his mind does not rest. This too is meaningless.

²⁴A man can do nothing better than to eat and drink and find satisfaction in his work. This too, I see, is from the hand of God, ²⁵for without him, who can eat or find enjoyment? ²⁶To the man who pleases him, God gives wisdom, knowledge and happiness, but to the sinner he gives the task of gathering and storing up wealth to hand it over to the one who pleases God. This too is meaningless, a chasing after the wind.

A Time for Everything

3 There is a time for everything,
  and a season for every activity under heaven:

 ² a time to be born and a time to die,
  a time to plant and a time to uproot,
 ³ a time to kill and a time to heal,
  a time to tear down and a time to build,
 ⁴ a time to weep and a time to laugh,
  a time to mourn and a time to dance,
 ⁵ a time to scatter stones and a time to gather
   them,
  a time to embrace and a time to refrain,
 ⁶ a time to search and a time to give up,
  a time to keep and a time to throw away,
 ⁷ a time to tear and a time to mend,
  a time to be silent and a time to speak,
 ⁸ a time to love and a time to hate,
  a time for war and a time for peace.ᴰ

⁹What does the worker gain from his toil? ¹⁰I have seen the burden God has laid on men. ¹¹He has made everything beautiful in its time. He has also set eternity in the hearts of men; yet they cannot fathom what God has done from beginning to end. ¹²I know that there is nothing bet-

What gives contentment? (2:24–25)

Concluding that life was meaningless, the Teacher advised going after as much pleasure as possible. "Live life to the full," he seems to say. "Work hard and play hard. Do whatever God enables you to do." His general pessimism, however, suggests the Teacher was unable to follow his own advice. Deep-thinking people often find that simple pleasures fail to satisfy. A better answer comes in the conclusion of the book: contentment comes through a life of faith and obedience.

What's the sinner's assignment? (2:26)

The sinner who strives to accumulate wealth is destined to futility: someone else eventually will get it—if not sooner, then certainly when death comes. This theme is common in Old Testament wisdom literature (for example, Prov. 11:4,7; 13:9,21–22). Some suggest the Teacher is not describing penalties for sin but God's seemingly arbitrary ways. They say the Teacher felt God was unfair, favoring some and not others—another meaningless thing about life.

Does this describe a balanced life? (3:1)

Though the Teacher seems to outline a formula for a balanced life, it's much more likely he is telling what life *is*—not what it *should* be. These verses describe life, but they don't offer advice for life. The fact that life contains such a wide range of experiences leads the Teacher pessimistically to a rhetorical question: *What does the worker gain from his toil?* (v. 9)—in other words, "Why fight it?"

When is it time to kill? (3:3)

The Teacher is not saying there is a time when killing is desirable. He is simply saying that killing happens. It is true, however, that under certain conditions killing was considered appropriate—as punishment for some crimes under the Law of Moses, for instance, or during times of war or defending oneself from deadly force.

What kind of burden has God put on us? (3:10)

See *Has God put a burden on us?* (1:13–14).

How does God implant eternity? (3:11)

Human beings have an awareness of something beyond them, something bigger than they are. Fully understanding this can lead to a dissatisfaction with life. Though God placed eternity in the Teacher's heart, it led to his frustration rather than to contentment—*yet they cannot fathom what God has done.*

ter for men than to be happy and do good while they live. [13]That everyone may eat and drink, and find satisfaction in all his toil—this is the gift of God. [14]I know that everything God does will endure forever; nothing can be added to it and nothing taken from it. God does it so that men will revere[D] him.

[15]Whatever is has already been,
    and what will be has been before;
and God will call the past to account.[a]

[16]And I saw something else under the sun:

In the place of judgment—wickedness was
    there,
in the place of justice—wickedness was
    there.

[17]I thought in my heart,

"God will bring to judgment
    both the righteous[D] and the wicked,
for there will be a time for every activity,
    a time for every deed."

[18]I also thought, "As for men, God tests them so that they may see that they are like the animals. [19]Man's fate is like that of the animals; the same fate awaits them both: As one dies, so dies the other. All have the same breath[b]; man has no advantage over the animal. Everything is meaningless. [20]All go to the same place; all come from dust, and to dust all return. [21]Who knows if the spirit of man rises upward and if the spirit of the animal[c] goes down into the earth?"

[22]So I saw that there is nothing better for a man than to enjoy his work, because that is his lot. For who can bring him to see what will happen after him?

Oppression, Toil, Friendlessness

4 Again I looked and saw all the oppression that was taking place under the sun:

I saw the tears of the oppressed—
    and they have no comforter;
power was on the side of their oppressors—
    and they have no comforter.
[2]And I declared that the dead,
    who had already died,
are happier than the living,
    who are still alive.
[3]But better than both
    is he who has not yet been,
who has not seen the evil
    that is done under the sun.

[4]And I saw that all labor and all achievement spring from man's envy of his neighbor. This too is meaningless, a chasing after the wind.

[5]The fool folds his hands
    and ruins himself.
[6]Better one handful with tranquillity
    than two handfuls with toil
    and chasing after the wind.

[a]*15 Or God calls back the past*   [b]*19 Or spirit*   [c]*21 Or Who knows the spirit of man, which rises upward, or the spirit of the animal, which*

What gives contentment? (3:13)
See *What gives contentment?* (2:24–25).

How does God compel us to honor him? (3:14)
An attitude of reverence for God flows out of an awareness that our security is found not in the fleeting pleasures of this world but in the God who made and controls all things. While God might seem to force us to revere him, he leaves the response up to us. His part is to demonstrate to us that it is in him that joy and satisfaction ultimately can be found.

How will God judge? (3:17)
The Teacher seems to draw upon his upbringing and early training to say that God will bring justice to a crooked world. Yet, he sees oppression and injustice in the world: inept or corrupt courts (v. 16), for instance, or authorities who abuse their power (4:1–3). He sees death—the great equalizer—bringing down everyone, including the wicked (vv. 18–22). Though he seems to imply here that death alone does not bring justice, the conclusion of the book underscores the certainty of final judgment (12:14).

Do people die like animals? (3:18)
The Teacher did not have a clear understanding of the afterlife (see also 9:10). To him, death ended it all, taking all meaning out of life. To the mind of the Teacher, human beings have no advantage over animals in death. Once again, however, the Teacher's perspective is limited to the physical realms. He does not see the spiritual or eternal. The Bible as a whole teaches that humans will live eternally.

Why would a Biblical writer offer no hope in death? (3:20–22)
See article: *What can we believe in this book?* (9:4–6).

Is it better not to be born? (4:1–3)
Unable to find an answer to explain oppression and injustice, the Teacher despairingly concludes that death—or no existence at all—is better than life in a rotten world. His viewpoint, however, is riveted to an earthly perspective; *under the sun* (v. 1), he cannot rise above it. He looks for "quality of life" apart from God. The Bible, on the other hand, teaches that those who trust in God can see good come out of suffering (1 Peter 4:19).

Is the economy fueled by envy? (4:4–6)
Often it is, in the natural order of things. The Teacher turns his jaundiced view to the economy and sees only envy. He believes that people work primarily to get ahead of their neighbors. But his comment is more about human character than the economy. Beneath the virtue of hard work he sees self-serving human nature. He underscores the futility of it all by quoting two contrasting proverbs—the first advising against laziness (v. 5), the second advising against empty activity (v. 6).

Why mention the value of companionship? (4:9–12)

Though the Teacher was a pessimist and seems down on life, he was also practical. So while talking about a corrupt world full of troubles, he goes on to suggest one way of coping: people are better off when they have friends to help them with the challenges of life. In fact, the more difficult life is, the more valuable friends become.

Why would a ruler be honored by one generation, despised by the next? (4:13–16)

The Teacher doesn't say. Indeed, he seems puzzled himself by the course of events. Perhaps he is bothered by the unfairness of life— so much that happens seems arbitrary. It may be that he describes this situation to illustrate that the value of wisdom is only temporary.

Sacrifice of fools (5:1)

A sacrifice offered without faith, performed only because of cultural or traditional demands. The Teacher warned that it is dangerous to unthinkingly offer sacrifices. He advises people to be more cautious in approaching God.

Is it better to have no intentions than unachieved good intentions? (5:4–6)

Good intentions are one thing; vows are something more. A vow was a promise or commitment, a religious tribute to God. Worshipers often vowed to do something unusual if God answered their prayer request. Vows were not required but, once made, it was imperative that a vow be fulfilled. Careless vows made without counting the cost still had to be performed. Thus, the Teacher felt it was better not to make a vow than to make one and not fulfill it. (See Prov. 20:25.)

7Again I saw something meaningless under the sun:

8There was a man all alone;
  he had neither son nor brother.
There was no end to his toil,
  yet his eyes were not content with his
    wealth.
"For whom am I toiling," he asked,
  "and why am I depriving myself of
    enjoyment?"
This too is meaningless—
  a miserable business!

9Two are better than one,
  because they have a good return for their
    work:
10If one falls down,
  his friend can help him up.
But pity the man who falls
  and has no one to help him up!
11Also, if two lie down together, they will keep
    warm.
  But how can one keep warm alone?
12Though one may be overpowered,
  two can defend themselves.
A cord of three strands is not quickly broken.

Advancement Is Meaningless

13Better a poor but wise youth than an old but foolish king who no longer knows how to take warning. **14**The youth may have come from prison to the kingship, or he may have been born in poverty within his kingdom. **15**I saw that all who lived and walked under the sun followed the youth, the king's successor. **16**There was no end to all the people who were before them. But those who came later were not pleased with the successor. This too is meaningless, a chasing after the wind.

Stand in Awe of God

5 Guard your steps when you go to the house of God. Go near to listen rather than to offer the sacrifice[D] of fools, who do not know that they do wrong.

2Do not be quick with your mouth,
  do not be hasty in your heart
    to utter anything before God.
God is in heaven
  and you are on earth,
    so let your words be few.
3As a dream comes when there are many cares,
  so the speech of a fool when there are many
    words.

4When you make a vow[D] to God, do not delay in fulfilling it. He has no pleasure in fools; fulfill your vow. **5**It is better not to vow than to make a vow and not fulfill it. **6**Do not let your mouth lead you into sin. And do not protest to the ⌊temple⌋ messenger, "My vow was a mistake." Why should God be angry at what you say and destroy the work of your hands? **7**Much dreaming and many words are meaningless. Therefore stand in awe of God.

Riches Are Meaningless

8If you see the poor oppressed in a district, and justice and rights denied, do not be surprised at such things; for one official is eyed by a higher one, and over them both

are others higher still. **9**The increase from the land is taken by all; the king himself profits from the fields.

10Whoever loves money never has money
enough;
whoever loves wealth is never satisfied with
his income.
This too is meaningless.

11As goods increase,
so do those who consume them.
And what benefit are they to the owner
except to feast his eyes on them?

12The sleep of a laborer is sweet,
whether he eats little or much,
but the abundance of a rich man
permits him no sleep.

13I have seen a grievous evil under the sun:

wealth hoarded to the harm of its owner,
14   or wealth lost through some misfortune,
so that when he has a son
there is nothing left for him.
15Naked a man comes from his mother's womb,
and as he comes, so he departs.
He takes nothing from his labor
that he can carry in his hand.

16This too is a grievous evil:

As a man comes, so he departs,
and what does he gain,
since he toils for the wind?
17All his days he eats in darkness,
with great frustration, affliction**D** and anger.

18Then I realized that it is good and proper for a man to eat and drink, and to find satisfaction in his toilsome labor under the sun during the few days of life God has given him—for this is his lot. **19**Moreover, when God gives any man wealth and possessions, and enables him to enjoy them, to accept his lot and be happy in his work—this is a gift of God. **20**He seldom reflects on the days of his life, because God keeps him occupied with gladness of heart.

6 I have seen another evil under the sun, and it weighs heavily on men: **2**God gives a man wealth, possessions and honor, so that he lacks nothing his heart desires, but God does not enable him to enjoy them, and a stranger enjoys them instead. This is meaningless, a grievous evil.

3A man may have a hundred children and live many years; yet no matter how long he lives, if he cannot enjoy his prosperity and does not receive proper burial, I say that a stillborn child is better off than he. **4**It comes without meaning, it departs in darkness, and in darkness its name is shrouded. **5**Though it never saw the sun or knew anything, it has more rest than does that man— **6**even if he lives a thousand years twice over but fails to enjoy his prosperity. Do not all go to the same place?

7All man's efforts are for his mouth,
yet his appetite is never satisfied.
8What advantage has a wise man
over a fool?
What does a poor man gain

Does nothing satisfy? (5:10)
See *Does nothing satisfy?* (1:6–8).

What's wrong with buying things? (5:11)
The Teacher realized that spending money could never satisfy a person or give meaning to life. No matter how much money a person has, it can never be enough (v. 10). As a matter of fact, the more wealth someone acquires, the faster the money gets spent (v. 11). A large estate and many possessions require more employees to care for it all. The larger the income, the greater the expense. The Teacher says this is a never-ending cycle.

Grievous evil (5:13)
A terrible injustice, more than unfair. *Grievous* may suggest the idea of *sickening*—the Teacher was sick about what he saw.

What gives contentment? (5:18)
See *What gives contentment?* (2:24–25).

Why accuse God of preventing people from reflecting on life? (5:19–20)
God seems to be responsible for advocating an unexamined life, but what we leave unexamined makes all the difference. The thought here is not that life will be so quiet that no reflection takes place but that life will be so *occupied with gladness* that the meaninglessness of life will nearly be forgotten. While the frustrations of life can be preoccupying, the life of faith and joy can be even more preoccupying.

Why was a proper burial important? (6:3)
In the ancient world, a proper burial brought closure to one's life. It signified that one had died peacefully and in prosperity. The alternative to proper burial—rotting in the open countryside after dying in battle or in poverty— meant that one's life was not prosperous or successful.

Does nothing satisfy? (6:7)
See *Does nothing satisfy?* (1:6–8).

What's the difference between a roving appetite and *what the eye sees*? (6:9)

What the eye sees is at hand—perhaps within grasp. But a roving appetite is not satisfied with what is at hand. It impatiently looks for something new, something better or something that is not certain. The Teacher's proverb is similar to the more familiar, "A bird in the hand is worth two in the bush." See Prov. 17:24.

What cheapens words? (6:10–11)

The Teacher sees mindless repetition of words as meaningless. Fools may think they sound important because they use lots of words. The book of Proverbs, however, values words used sparingly (for example, 10:8,19; 17:27–28). The Teacher, however, may be even more forceful. Everything has already been said, he says, so it is pointless to argue with *one who is stronger*—perhaps referring to God. In this view, more words mean nothing.

Why didn't the writer know what was good for life? (6:12)

The Teacher did not know what was good for life because his perspective remained earth-bound—*under the sun* (v. 13). In this world apart from God there is no meaning. With such a limited perspective, it's no wonder he struggled trying to find moral absolutes.

Why the change to poetry? (7:1–29)

Some think the Teacher has stopped analyzing the dilemma of life and is now giving practical advice. They see his list of proverbs as perhaps something of an answer to his question: *Who knows what is good for a man in life?* (6:12). Others point out, however, that his dark tone continues: death is better than life (vv. 1-2), the futility of righteousness (vv. 15–16), the impossibility of being wise (v. 23) and so on. Either way, it is helpful to remember that proverbs are not intended to be absolute, unalterable principles but generalized observations on life. See article: *Are proverbs iron-clad promises?* (Prov. 3:1–4).

What's good about being sad? (7:3)

Life is a serious matter, says the Teacher. Sadness reflects realities that touch on something far deeper than good times. We live in a fallen world that has no hope to offer. Those who search only for good feelings will be out of touch with what really matters in life (5:20). It's true that lasting happiness does not come through anything this world has to offer, but through eternal realities found in Christ.

Why is it unwise to recall "the good old days"? (7:10)

A person who thinks it was better in the past than in the present is self-deceived. After all, *there is nothing new under the sun* (1:9). It is only our forgetfulness that makes us think things have gotten worse. In a world of sin, things have always been bad. Wishing for what never was is not helpful in dealing with issues of right and wrong.

by knowing how to conduct himself before others?
⁹Better what the eye sees
than the roving of the appetite.
This too is meaningless,
a chasing after the wind.

¹⁰Whatever exists has already been named,
and what man is has been known;
no man can contend
with one who is stronger than he.
¹¹The more the words,
the less the meaning,
and how does that profit anyone?

¹²For who knows what is good for a man in life, during the few and meaningless days he passes through like a shadow? Who can tell him what will happen under the sun after he is gone?

Wisdom

7   A good name is better than fine perfume,
and the day of death ᴰ better than the day of birth.
²It is better to go to a house of mourning
than to go to a house of feasting,
for death is the destiny of every man;
the living should take this to heart.
³Sorrow is better than laughter,
because a sad face is good for the heart.
⁴The heart of the wise is in the house of mourning,
but the heart of fools is in the house of pleasure.
⁵It is better to heed a wise man's rebuke
than to listen to the song of fools.
⁶Like the crackling of thorns under the pot,
so is the laughter of fools.
This too is meaningless.

⁷Extortion ᴰ turns a wise man into a fool,
and a bribe corrupts the heart.

⁸The end of a matter is better than its beginning,
and patience is better than pride.
⁹Do not be quickly provoked in your spirit,
for anger resides in the lap of fools.

¹⁰Do not say, "Why were the old days better than these?"
For it is not wise to ask such questions.

¹¹Wisdom, like an inheritance, is a good thing
and benefits those who see the sun.
¹²Wisdom is a shelter
as money is a shelter,
but the advantage of knowledge is this:
that wisdom preserves the life of its possessor.

¹³Consider what God has done:

Who can straighten
what he has made crooked?
¹⁴When times are good, be happy;
but when times are bad, consider:

God has made the one
    as well as the other.
Therefore, a man cannot discover
    anything about his future.

15In this meaningless life of mine I have seen both of these:

  a righteous^D man perishing in his
       righteousness,
  and a wicked man living long in his
       wickedness.

16Do not be overrighteous,
    neither be overwise—
  why destroy yourself?
17Do not be overwicked,
    and do not be a fool—
  why die before your time?
18It is good to grasp the one
    and not let go of the other.
  The man who fears God will avoid all
    ⌊extremes⌋.ᵃ

19Wisdom makes one wise man more powerful
    than ten rulers in a city.

20There is not a righteous man on earth
    who does what is right and never sins.

21Do not pay attention to every word people say,
    or you may hear your servant cursing you—
22for you know in your heart
    that many times you yourself have cursed
       others.

23All this I tested by wisdom and I said,

  "I am determined to be wise"—
    but this was beyond me.
24Whatever wisdom may be,
    it is far off and most profound—
  who can discover it?
25So I turned my mind to understand,
    to investigate and to search out wisdom and
       the scheme of things
  and to understand the stupidity of wickedness
    and the madness of folly.

26I find more bitter than death^D
    the woman who is a snare,
  whose heart is a trap
    and whose hands are chains.
  The man who pleases God will escape her,
    but the sinner she will ensnare.

27"Look," says the Teacher,ᵇ "this is what I have discovered:

  "Adding one thing to another to discover the
    scheme of things—
28 while I was still searching
    but not finding—
  I found one ⌊upright⌋ man among a thousand,
    but not one ⌊upright⌋ woman among them
       all.
29This only have I found:
    God made mankind upright,

ᵃ18 Or *will follow them both*   ᵇ27 Or *leader of the assembly*

Is God to blame for bad times? (7:13–14)

In one sense, yes. God himself took credit for creating darkness as well as light, and for causing disaster as well as prosperity (Isaiah 45:7). God is sovereign over all that he has created. The Teacher echoes what Job said: *Shall we accept good from God, and not trouble?* (Job 2:10). The conclusion of Ecclesiastes, however, reminds us that God one day will judge everything, both good and evil (12:14). Also see article: **Why does God send calamity?** (Lam. 3:38).

How can we be too righteous? (7:16)

We can't be too righteous—if our righteousness comes from God. But those who use their own human effort to work hard at doing good, those who try to earn salvation, those who base their righteousness on legalism, will end up frustrated. In that sense, some people (the Pharisees of the New Testament, for example) are so righteous that they miss God. The Teacher, however, may have simply been disillusioned about the inequities of life, saying, in essence, "Being good doesn't offer any guarantees, so don't bother trying to be perfect."

How is it possible to ignore unfair criticism? (7:21)

The Teacher is not talking about ignoring criticism. He only advises us not to go out of the way to get it. Don't eavesdrop; don't listen in on every conversation. If you do, sooner or later you'll be disappointed by what you hear said about you.

How did the writer know about deceitful women? (7:26)

Some think that the Teacher was Solomon (see Introduction: **Who wrote this book?**) and feel that he is here reflecting on his own sad history with women who snared him into false worship (1 Kings 11:1–6). Others say the Teacher (not Solomon) was simply commenting on women in general, by saying that men are trapped by women. Still others think this is a warning against adultery (Prov. 6:20–7:27).

If God made humans upright, why are we so flawed? (7:29)

The Teacher himself answers this question: *men have gone in search of many schemes.* He understood that people, distorted by temptation and sin, tampered with God's design. Though God created men and women in his image, sinful humanity willfully disobeyed him and plunged the world into curse and despair.

but men have gone in search of many
schemes."

8 Who is like the wise man?
Who knows the explanation of things?
Wisdom brightens a man's face
and changes its hard appearance.

Obey the King

²Obey the king's command, I say, because you took an oath before God. ³Do not be in a hurry to leave the king's presence. Do not stand up for a bad cause, for he will do whatever he pleases. ⁴Since a king's word is supreme, who can say to him, "What are you doing?"

⁵Whoever obeys his command will come to no
harm,
and the wise heart will know the proper time
and procedure.
⁶For there is a proper time and procedure for
every matter,
though a man's misery weighs heavily upon
him.

⁷Since no man knows the future,
who can tell him what is to come?
⁸No man has power over the wind to contain
it *a*;
so no one has power over the day of his
death*b*.
As no one is discharged in time of war,
so wickedness will not release those who
practice it.

⁹All this I saw, as I applied my mind to everything done under the sun. There is a time when a man lords it over others to his own*b* hurt. ¹⁰Then too, I saw the wicked buried—those who used to come and go from the holy place and receive praise*c* in the city where they did this. This too is meaningless.
¹¹When the sentence for a crime is not quickly carried out, the hearts of the people are filled with schemes to do wrong. ¹²Although a wicked man commits a hundred crimes and still lives a long time, I know that it will go better with God-fearing men, who are reverent before God. ¹³Yet because the wicked do not fear God, it will not go well with them, and their days will not lengthen like a shadow.
¹⁴There is something else meaningless that occurs on earth: righteous*b* men who get what the wicked deserve, and wicked men who get what the righteous deserve. This too, I say, is meaningless. ¹⁵So I commend the enjoyment of life, because nothing is better for a man under the sun than to eat and drink and be glad. Then joy will accompany him in his work all the days of the life God has given him under the sun.
¹⁶When I applied my mind to know wisdom and to observe man's labor on earth—his eyes not seeing sleep day or night— ¹⁷then I saw all that God has done. No one can comprehend what goes on under the sun. Despite all his efforts to search it out, man cannot discover its meaning.

a8 Or *over his spirit to retain it*　*b9* Or *to their*　*c10* Some Hebrew manuscripts and Septuagint (Aquila); most Hebrew manuscripts *and are forgotten*

Are some rulers beyond accountability? (8:2–6)
It would appear so, at least for a time. While in power, they pretty much do what they want. The Teacher is not claiming that rulers are infallible. He simply implies that those in a position of authority are there because God intended them to be. That's why people pledged before God their loyalty to the king (v. 2). See Psalm 75:6–7; Daniel 2:21; 4:25; Romans 13:1–7.

Buried (8:10)
See *Why was a proper burial important?* (6:3).

Does *meaningless* include injustice? (8:14)
Yes. According to the Teacher, rampant injustice in the world contributes to his verdict that everything is meaningless. If the wise and the godly are not rewarded, what meaning is there in a wise and godly lifestyle (9:11–17)? In such cases, again, purpose and meaning have to be found after this life is over and the final accounts are settled (12:14).

What gives contentment? (8:15)
See *What gives contentment?* (2:24–25).

Is life meaningless without purpose? (8:16–17)
Yes. For life to have purpose, we must grasp something larger than life and deeper than humankind. The Teacher says that the secrets of life's meaning belong to God. The Teacher casts doubt on the traditional view that wise teachers could know the ways of the world, understand its meaning and know how to act. He is not so confident and says no one can discover life's meaning, not even the acknowledged teacher of wisdom.

Even if a wise man claims he knows, he cannot really comprehend it.

A Common Destiny for All

9 So I reflected on all this and concluded that the righteous[D] and the wise and what they do are in God's hands, but no man knows whether love or hate awaits him. ²All share a common destiny—the righteous and the wicked, the good and the bad,[a] the clean and the unclean[D], those who offer sacrifices[D] and those who do not.

> As it is with the good man,
>> so with the sinner;
> as it is with those who take oaths,
>> so with those who are afraid to take them.

³This is the evil in everything that happens under the sun: The same destiny overtakes all. The hearts of men, moreover, are full of evil and there is madness in their hearts while they live, and afterward they join the dead. ⁴Anyone who is among the living has hope[b]—even a live dog is better off than a dead lion!

> ⁵For the living know that they will die,
>> but the dead know nothing;
> they have no further reward,
>> and even the memory of them is forgotten.
> ⁶Their love, their hate
>> and their jealousy have long since vanished;

---

[a]2 Septuagint (Aquila), Vulgate and Syriac; Hebrew does not have *and the bad.*   [b]4 Or *What then is to be chosen? With all who live, there is hope*

What is our *common destiny*? (9:1–3)
Death, according to the Teacher. And, from his limited perspective, nothing certain lies beyond the grave (vv. 5–6). Since both good and bad meet the same fate, in his view, he concludes God is unfair: *this is the evil in everything that happens under the sun* (v. 3). Also see ***Do people die like animals?*** (3:18).

What can we believe in this book? (9:4–6)

It's one thing to see the Teacher's pessimism for life *under the sun*—on this side of eternity. But it's something quite different to face his pessimism about life and justice after death. What are we to think of statements like these? How do they fit with the rest of the Bible?

People disagree about how to understand this book. Some say the Teacher is essentially faithful to the truth but dares to grapple with hard questions and doubts. They see his skeptical words, then, as honest questions raised during a lifetime of learning and maturing.

Another view is that this book is full of error and can be discounted because it was written by Solomon after he had fallen away from God (1 Kings 11:1–6). Those who hold this opinion see the concluding verses (12:9–14) as Solomon's final repentance and trust in God.

Still others divide the teaching of this book similarly, but with different players. They see the Teacher who, though wise, is a skeptic. They see a second, unnamed wise man who uses the Teacher's bitter words to instruct his son. This second man, they say, wrote 1:1 and 12:9–14 to put the book into context.

Whatever view is taken, two things should be kept in mind: (1) This book should be taken as a whole; isolated verses can contradict the truth of the Bible. (2) Any philosophy taken from this book should be evaluated by the teaching of the whole Bible.

For a related question, see article: ***What can we learn from Job's friends?*** (Job 4:1).

never again will they have a part
in anything that happens under the sun.

7Go, eat your food with gladness, and drink your wine with a joyful heart, for it is now that God favors what you do. **8**Always be clothed in white, and always anoint[D] your head with oil. **9**Enjoy life with your wife, whom you love, all the days of this meaningless life that God has given you under the sun— all your meaningless days. For this is your lot in life and in your toilsome labor under the sun. **10**Whatever your hand finds to do, do it with all your might, for in the grave,[a] where you are going, there is neither working nor planning nor knowledge nor wisdom.

11I have seen something else under the sun:

The race is not to the swift
    or the battle to the strong,
nor does food come to the wise
    or wealth to the brilliant
    or favor to the learned;
but time and chance happen to them all.

12Moreover, no man knows when his hour will come:

As fish are caught in a cruel net,
    or birds are taken in a snare,
so men are trapped by evil times
    that fall unexpectedly upon them.

Wisdom Better Than Folly

13I also saw under the sun this example of wisdom that greatly impressed me: **14**There was once a small city with only a few people in it. And a powerful king came against it, surrounded it and built huge siegeworks against it. **15**Now there lived in that city a man poor but wise, and he saved the city by his wisdom. But nobody remembered that poor man. **16**So I said, "Wisdom is better than strength." But the poor man's wisdom is despised, and his words are no longer heeded.

17The quiet words of the wise are more to be
        heeded
    than the shouts of a ruler of fools.
18Wisdom is better than weapons of war,
    but one sinner destroys much good.

10 As dead flies give perfume a bad smell,
    so a little folly outweighs wisdom and honor.
2The heart of the wise inclines to the right,
    but the heart of the fool to the left.
3Even as he walks along the road,
    the fool lacks sense
    and shows everyone how stupid he is.
4If a ruler's anger rises against you,
    do not leave your post;
    calmness can lay great errors to rest.

5There is an evil I have seen under the sun,
    the sort of error that arises from a ruler:
6Fools are put in many high positions,
    while the rich occupy the low ones.
7I have seen slaves on horseback,
    while princes go on foot like slaves.

a 10 Hebrew *Sheol*

Clothed in white . . . anoint your head with oil (9:8)

Symbolized festive times of joy and celebration. White clothes, which reflected rather than absorbed the sun, and oil, which protected against dry skin, both helped people battle the dry, hot climate of Palestine. The context suggests that this is the Teacher's way of urging people to enjoy life to the full since he felt that there was nothing after death.

What do we do in the next life? (9:10)

According to the Teacher, we do nothing— there is no afterlife. In his opinion, if we are going to have any joy, we will have to find it in the present life. We have to turn to the rest of the Bible, primarily the New Testament, to learn about the resurrection life. (See, for example, 1 Cor. 15.)

What role does luck play in our lives? (9:11–12)

So often it seems that we have no control over the events of our lives, that blind chance determines who succeeds. But this viewpoint looks only at things *under the sun*—from an earthbound perspective. The Teacher sees the arbitrary events of life as a sign that God is unconcerned and is unfair in his dealings with humanity. The Bible as a whole, however, teaches the opposite. God is concerned about everyone and deals with people fairly. What we don't see is that accounts are not all settled in this lifetime.

If wisdom is so great, why is it despised? (9:13–16)

The Teacher simply is saying that credit is not always given where credit is due. Human nature doesn't always appreciate wise counsel, even if its value is proven beyond all doubt— as in this example where wisdom spared a city under attack. Human nature often forgets good advice once the problem has been solved.

Right . . . left (10:2)

This has nothing to do with our modern use of these terms to label political liberals or conservatives. This basically says that wisdom and folly go in two opposite directions. In the ancient world, *right* symbolized power, honor, authority and strength (Gen. 48:18; Isaiah 41:10); *left* represented the opposite—weakness or even evil. Also see *The years of the right hand of the Most High* (Psalm 77:10).

Why are fools in high positions? (10:6)

Not everyone in a place of authority deserves to be there. Circumstances and injustice sometimes bring honor to fools, raising them to power. When fools are given positions of authority, the whole society suffers. Nevertheless, God uses all governments to accomplish his purposes (Daniel 2:21; Romans 13:1–7), even corrupt ones. See article: *Does God use evil to do good?* (Hab. 1:6,13). This continues the Teacher's observations that life doesn't always turn out to be fair in our eyes. Some get more than they deserve, others far less. Also see Prov. 19:10; 28:28.

8Whoever digs a pit may fall into it;
    whoever breaks through a wall may be bitten
        by a snake.
9Whoever quarries stones may be injured by
        them;
    whoever splits logs may be endangered by
        them.

10If the ax is dull
    and its edge unsharpened,
more strength is needed
    but skill will bring success.

11If a snake bites before it is charmed,
    there is no profit for the charmer.

12Words from a wise man's mouth are
        gracious,
    but a fool is consumed by his own lips.
13At the beginning his words are folly;
    at the end they are wicked madness—
14   and the fool multiplies words.

No one knows what is coming—
    who can tell him what will happen after
        him?

15A fool's work wearies him;
    he does not know the way to town.

16Woe to you, O land whose king was a
        servant[a]
and whose princes feast in the morning.
17Blessed are you, O land whose king is of noble
        birth
and whose princes eat at a proper time—
    for strength and not for drunkenness.

18If a man is lazy, the rafters sag;
    if his hands are idle, the house leaks.

19A feast is made for laughter,
    and wine makes life merry,
    but money is the answer for everything.

20Do not revile the king even in your thoughts,
    or curse the rich in your bedroom,
because a bird of the air may carry your
        words,
    and a bird on the wing may report what you
        say.

Bread Upon the Waters

11 Cast your bread upon the waters,
    for after many days you will find it again.
2Give portions to seven, yes to eight,
    for you do not know what disaster may
        come upon the land.

3If clouds are full of water,
    they pour rain upon the earth.
Whether a tree falls to the south or to the
        north,
    in the place where it falls, there will it lie.
4Whoever watches the wind will not plant;
    whoever looks at the clouds will not reap.

a 16 Or king is a child

Can we live without risks? (10:8–11)
No. To be diligent and industrious, the Teacher says, we have to risk loss, perhaps even injury. No matter how carefully you work, disaster could strike at any time. Some say the Teacher is simply observing life—"accidents will happen"—and urging caution to avoid trouble if possible. Others say mishaps, in the Teacher's mind, are another example of life's unfairness and God's lack of concern.

What makes a noble ruler? (10:16–17)
According to the Teacher, a noble ruler should be: (1) a descendant of rulers (not from *servant* classes); (2) disciplined, avoiding excess. Though this seems elitist to us, general principles can be made: rulers should have a healthy upbringing, have adequate resources, be well-trained and be prepared and equipped for the responsibilities of leadership.

Feast in the morning . . . eat at a proper time (10:16–17)
An image of bad rulers compared to good ones. The first priority for bad rulers is to fulfill their own appetites and desires. Good rulers, on the other hand, are disciplined. They enjoy good things, but in moderation, so they can concentrate on governing well.

Why would the writer declare money is the answer for everything? (10:19)
There may be a note of sarcasm in the Teacher's voice. Throughout this book he has taught that there is no answer for anything. On the other hand, though, lots of money would help anyone searching for pleasure in an attempt to escape life's harsh realities. See *What gives contentment?* (2:24–25).

What's wrong with criticizing those in power? (10:20)
The Teacher lived in a world where the king's word, on the human level, was final. A ruthless ruler could have his subjects executed simply for expressing an opinion that opposed the king's. Things may not always be like that, but the principle remains: be careful what you think; sooner or later others will hear what you say.

Why throw bread away? (11:1)
This may be an expression describing business ventures—like investing and taking risks, perhaps in ocean-going trade. Such a view would fit the teaching in this section (vv. 1–6): though the world is uncertain and humans cannot control what happens, it is still better to take action than to be paralyzed with fear and do nothing.

How does giving prepare us for disaster? (11:2)
The world is uncertain and humans are unable to control what happens around them. Life is one risk after another. Because of this, the Teacher warns his readers not to "put all their eggs in one basket." If one venture fails, the others still have a chance to succeed.

What can we really understand about God? (11:5)

Some think the Teacher meant to demonstrate the futility of typical approaches to wisdom—to show that God cannot be apprehended by human reason. Others see his words as a sign of his resistance to God—that he refused to let God's revelation shape his understanding. Either way, though our knowledge is incomplete, because of Jesus we understand more about God than the writer of Ecclesiastes did (Heb. 1:1–4).

Why remember dark days? (11:8)

To keep perspective. If the only goal people have in life is to be happy, they will not find meaning and purpose. But hard times—coupled with a serious view of life—can help people find God as well as purpose in life. Also see **What's good about being sad?** (7:3).

Follow the ways of your heart: Is this advice or a warning? (11:9)

Perhaps both. With his pessimistic view of life's hazards, the Teacher seems to say it doesn't really matter what one does. He advises young people to enjoy life as much as possible. But he footnotes his advice with a warning: don't be surprised at how short and meaningless it all seems when the harsh realities of old age, death and judgment overtake you.

Can we banish anxiety from our hearts? (11:10)

Not really, although our choice of lifestyle and attitude can have a tremendous influence on our own peace of mind. The Teacher tells us to relax and enjoy life: Don't worry about anything, he says. It's all meaningless anyway. The Bible as a whole, however, teaches that inner peace can only be found by trusting in the Lord (Isaiah 26:3; 1 Peter 5:7).

Is it meaningless to remember God when you're young? (12:1,6–8)

The Teacher seems to have grown cynical in his old age. Still, he says that if we don't remember God in our youth, we probably won't remember him when our life draws to a close. So others see the Teacher in a more positive light as he advises us to give our best years to God. It's when we don't that one day everything becomes meaningless.

Keepers of the house . . . grinders . . . doors . . . almond tree . . . grasshopper (12:3–5)

Metaphors to illustrate old age. Some say *keepers of the house* are arms; *strong men*, legs or bent back; *grinders*, teeth; *windows*, eyes; *doors*, ears; *almond tree* (in blossom), white hair; and *grasshopper* (in cold weather), slow movement. The picture is of a person slowly dying.

What did the writer mean by eternal home? (12:5)

He simply meant the grave, not anything like we would think of regarding eternity in the presence of God. With the *mourners* in the streets, this is a picture of the old man's funeral procession.

⁵As you do not know the path of the wind,
    or how the body is formed[a] in a mother's womb,
so you cannot understand the work of God,
    the Maker of all things.

⁶Sow your seed in the morning,
    and at evening let not your hands be idle,
for you do not know which will succeed,
    whether this or that,
    or whether both will do equally well.

Remember Your Creator While Young

⁷Light is sweet,
    and it pleases the eyes to see the sun.
⁸However many years a man may live,
    let him enjoy them all.
But let him remember the days of darkness,
    for they will be many.
    Everything to come is meaningless.

⁹Be happy, young man, while you are young,
    and let your heart give you joy in the days of your youth.
Follow the ways of your heart
    and whatever your eyes see,
but know that for all these things
    God will bring you to judgment.
¹⁰So then, banish anxiety from your heart
    and cast off the troubles of your body,
    for youth and vigor are meaningless.

12 Remember your Creator
    in the days of your youth,
before the days of trouble come
    and the years approach when you will say,
    "I find no pleasure in them"—
²before the sun and the light
    and the moon and the stars grow dark,
    and the clouds return after the rain;
³when the keepers of the house tremble,
    and the strong men stoop,
when the grinders cease because they are few,
    and those looking through the windows grow dim;
⁴when the doors to the street are closed
    and the sound of grinding fades;
when men rise up at the sound of birds,
    but all their songs grow faint;
⁵when men are afraid of heights
    and of dangers in the streets;
when the almond tree blossoms
    and the grasshopper drags himself along
    and desire no longer is stirred.
Then man goes to his eternal home
    and mourners go about the streets.

⁶Remember him—before the silver cord is severed,
    or the golden bowl is broken;

ᵃ5 Or *know how life* (or *the spirit*) / *enters the body being formed*

before the pitcher is shattered at the spring,
   or the wheel broken at the well,
⁷and the dust returns to the ground it came
      from,
   and the spirit returns to God who gave it.

⁸"Meaningless! Meaningless!" says the Teacher.ᵃ
   "Everything is meaningless!"

The Conclusion of the Matter

⁹Not only was the Teacher wise, but also he imparted knowledge to the people. He pondered and searched out and set in order many proverbs. ¹⁰The Teacher searched to find just the right words, and what he wrote was upright and true.

¹¹The words of the wise are like goads, their collected sayings like firmly embedded nails—given by one Shepherd. ¹²Be warned, my son, of anything in addition to them.

Of making many books there is no end, and much study wearies the body.

¹³Now all has been heard;
   here is the conclusion of the matter:
Fear God and keep his commandments,
   for this is the whole ⌊duty⌋ of man.
¹⁴For God will bring every deed into
      judgment,
   including every hidden thing,
   whether it is good or evil.

ᵃ8 Or *the leader of the assembly*; also in verses 9 and 10

Silver cord . . . golden bowl . . . pitcher . . . wheel (12:6)

Another metaphor for death, comparing it to the destruction of valuable but perishable items. In this way he illustrates that life has value but is also fragile. In the end, what is useful for life is destroyed.

How does our spirit return to God? (12:7)

The Old Testament understanding of life recognized that God provided the breath (or spirit) of life (Gen. 2:7). It stands to reason, then, from an Old Testament perspective, that death is the same process in reverse. When life goes, it is because God takes back the breath (see Psalm 104:29). This verse does not refer to the heavenly afterlife we would typically envision.

Meaningless (12:8)

See article: *Is life meaningless?* (1:2).

Why would a Shepherd (instead of a carpenter) be hammering nails? (12:11–12)

We have a mixed metaphor here. Some think *Shepherd* refers to God, the source of all wisdom. It can be understood, however, as the collected wisdom of all the wise teachers of Israel. Others think it refers to the Scriptures—writings that cannot be compared to the countless books composed by humans (v. 12). As for the firmly implanted nails, some take them to symbolize the stability of the wisdom teaching. Others suggest the nails (like the *goads*) can mean the painful lessons of life taught by the teachers.

Why fear God? (12:13–14)

Some say that this conclusion only makes sense if the speaker has been transformed or is someone completely new. See article: *What can we believe in this book?* (9:4–6). Others say that this is simply the final conclusion of the Teacher's hard, unblinking look at life. They say that though this book asks the difficult questions and is often cynical, it also shows sparks of faith. Indeed, this is not the first time we are urged to fear God (see 8:12–13). Now, however, faith is clearly favored over doubt.

Some think this conclusion was written by a wise man or editor other than the Teacher. They suggest he uses the writings of the Teacher primarily to demonstrate how futile they were. His intent, then, is to teach his son (or disciple: *my son* was a conventional way for a teacher to speak to his student, v. 12) the better way—to fear God (vv. 13–14).

Either way, the doctrine of the Old Testament is summarized in a few short phrases. The reader is urged (1) to have a right relationship with God (*fear God*); (2) to maintain that relationship by following the law (*keep his commandments*) and (3) to anticipate a final and future judgment (*God will bring every deed into judgment*).

SONG OF SONGS

Why read this book?

A lot of people have wondered why a poem of love and sexual intimacy is included in the Bible. Some suggest, therefore, that we read it only symbolically, as a picture of God's unconditional love. Others take it at face value and find a treasure of marital delights in it. Perhaps there is value in both approaches. At any rate, Song of Songs is a beautiful picture of the physical side of love and its sensual words applaud sexuality as part of God's wonderful creation.

Who wrote this book?

Tradition has long named Solomon as the author, based on the phrase *Solomon's Song of Songs* (1:1). However, this could have several possible meanings. See ***Did Solomon write this Song?*** (1:1). Some think an unknown writer composed it and set it to music. Others say it could have been a collection of poems by a number of different writers, including Solomon.

To whom was it written?

It was written to God's people, to celebrate his gift of love and sexuality and to reflect on the intimacies of God's love.

When was it written?

It may have been written during or just after King Solomon's reign around the tenth century B.C. Some think it may have been compiled at a later date.

What to look for in Song of Songs:

Poetic language that conveys feelings more than facts. Watch for word pictures and turns of phrases that capture the moods of love. And remember that poetry was entertainment in ancient times—just as videos and compact discs are today.

1

Solomon's Song of Songs.

Beloved[a]

²Let him kiss me with the kisses of his mouth—
  for your love is more delightful than wine.
³Pleasing is the fragrance of your perfumes;
  your name is like perfume poured out.
  No wonder the maidens love you!
⁴Take me away with you—let us hurry!
  Let the king bring me into his chambers.

Friends

We rejoice and delight in you[b];
  we will praise your love more than wine.

Beloved

How right they are to adore you!

⁵Dark am I, yet lovely,
  O daughters of Jerusalem[D],
  dark like the tents of Kedar,
  like the tent curtains of Solomon.[c]
⁶Do not stare at me because I am dark,
  because I am darkened by the sun.
  My mother's sons were angry with me
  and made me take care of the vineyards;
  my own vineyard I have neglected.
⁷Tell me, you whom I love, where you graze
      your flock

[a]Primarily on the basis of the gender of the Hebrew pronouns used,
male and female speakers are indicated in the margins by the captions
Lover and *Beloved* respectively. The words of others are marked
Friends. In some instances the divisions and their captions are
debatable.   [b]4 The Hebrew is masculine singular.   [c]5 Or *Salma*

Did Solomon write this Song? (1:1)

King Solomon's relationship to this poem has been debated for centuries. Some say he wrote it (see 1 Kings 4:32). Others say it was written about him. Still others say it might have been neither by him nor about him. The poem may have been "his" simply in the sense that it was a literary work dedicated to him as a wedding present.

Why is a poem about romance and sex in the Bible? (1:2)

We might just as well ask why not. After all, God created sex. Romance was his idea. The distortion that sin has given this subject should not make us forget that sexual intimacy is his gift to us—to be enjoyed when used as he intended.

Who are these maidens? (1:3)

The word *love* used here does not necessarily imply that they were lovers; *maidens* could also be translated *virgins* (see Isaiah 7:14). Perhaps the young woman was expressing her lover's appeal and her joy that she was the one who caught him.

Why did she pursue him so aggressively? (1:4)

See *Why did she pursue him so aggressively?* (3:2).

Tents of Kedar (1:5)

An area in the Arabian Desert where Bedouin tents were commonly made of black goat skins.

Does this describe a love affair? (1:4)

The references to the king, the daughters of Jerusalem, the queens, concubines and virgins seem to suggest that this is the story of a maiden's love affair with King Solomon. Some think Solomon wrote this song in his youth, before he acquired his extensive harem.

Others say it reflects the love between a young Israelite shepherd and his bride, a maiden from the hill country of northern Israel. They think the two lovers may simply have been fantasizing—using images of royalty to enhance their affection for each other. To the chaste and beautiful bride, her beloved was the royal monarch in all his majesty, surrounded by his troops and riding in his upholstered carriage. This was her man, her "Solomon," her "king." The young shepherd responded by describing his beloved as a *prince's daughter* (7:1), unique among the many queens who would praise her (6:9). This is the exaggerated language of love, with lavish images from the privacy and passion of the bedroom.

Still others, uncomfortable about the poem's graphic sexual imagery, have wanted to dismiss both possibilities and call it an allegory of God's love for Israel. They insist that the early rabbis would never have accepted the book as anything but allegory because of the prominence and dignity it gives to the woman.

Regardless of one's interpretation, the poem is a timeless expression of the joy and intimacy of love, the gift of our Creator.

Why was dark skin considered unattractive? (1:6)

The young woman was pretty—*Dark am I, yet lovely* (v. 5)—but she felt self-conscious about her position in society. The girls with darker skin were those who had to work out in the sun, in the fields or vineyards. More privileged girls could be recognized by their lighter complexions.

Why were her brothers angry? (1:6)

We aren't told the cause. We're told only that they punished her by making her take care of the family vineyards. Long days in the vineyard, probably planted on a hillside to catch the sun's rays, caused her to tan darker. Caring for the vineyard, she neglected her personal appearance, described poetically as her own vineyard. See *Who tended the bride's fruit?* (8:12).

What was wrong with wearing a veil? (1:7)

Some suggest that prostitutes wearing veils wandered from flock to flock, looking for shepherds willing to buy their services (see Gen. 38:15). A young woman, committed to the love of one man would not want to be mistaken for a loose, wandering woman so she asked her shepherd lover where she could readily find him while he watched his sheep.

Is her lover her husband? (1:13)

The term *lover* appears 30 times in this poem, but the terms *husband* or *wife* don't appear even once. Other cultures may use the word *lover* outside the context of marriage, but the Biblical perspective is that one's lover is one's spouse. When the Bible uses *love* to describe adultery, it clearly labels it as sin. That is not the case here. In intimate conversation (and this is a very intimate poem) spouses go beyond terms like *husband* and *wife* to words like *sweetheart, darling* and *beloved.*

Myrrh (1:13)

In this sensual metaphor, one of the most graphic in the poem, the woman compares her lover to a sweet-smelling ointment used by royalty at that time to scent their wedding robes (Psalm 45:8). It was also used as an enticing perfume. In her view her lover took the place of perfume.

What's the plot to this story? (2:1)

Since poets do not necessarily follow a sequence of events, the Song while disjointed at times by poetic license, may still reflect a single, unified plot. Some, however, see gaps and uneven transitions in this poetry as evidence that it is really a random collection of several love poems with no discernible plot. Also see the following note.

and where you rest your sheep at midday.
Why should I be like a veiled woman
     beside the flocks of your friends?

Friends

   8If you do not know, most beautiful of women,
        follow the tracks of the sheep
   and graze your young goats
        by the tents of the shepherds.

Lover

   9I liken you, my darling, to a mare
        harnessed to one of the chariots of Pharaoh.
   10Your cheeks are beautiful with earrings,
        your neck with strings of jewels.
   11We will make you earrings of gold,
        studded with silver.

Beloved

   12While the king was at his table,
        my perfume spread its fragrance.
   13My lover is to me a sachet of myrrhᴰ
        resting between my breasts.
   14My lover is to me a cluster of henna blossoms
        from the vineyards of En Gedi.

Lover

   15How beautiful you are, my darling!
        Oh, how beautiful!
        Your eyes are doves.

Beloved

   16How handsome you are, my lover!
        Oh, how charming!
        And our bed is verdant.

Lover

   17The beams of our house are cedars;
        our rafters are firs.

*Beloved*ᵃ

2   I am a roseᵇ of Sharon,
        a lily of the valleys.

Lover

   2Like a lily among thorns
        is my darling among the maidens.

Beloved

   3Like an apple tree among the trees of the forest
        is my lover among the young men.
   I delight to sit in his shade,
        and his fruit is sweet to my taste.
   4He has taken me to the banquet hall,
        and his banner over me is love.
   5Strengthen me with raisins,
        refresh me with apples,
        for I am faint with love.
   6His left arm is under my head,
        and his right arm embraces me.

ᵃ1 Or *Lover*   ᵇ1 Possibly a member of the crocus family

[7]Daughters of Jerusalem[D], I charge you
   by the gazelles and by the does of the field:
Do not arouse or awaken love
   until it so desires.

[8]Listen! My lover!
Look! Here he comes,
   leaping across the mountains,
   bounding over the hills.
[9]My lover is like a gazelle or a young stag.
Look! There he stands behind our wall,
gazing through the windows,
   peering through the lattice.
[10]My lover spoke and said to me,
   "Arise, my darling,
   my beautiful one, and come with me.
[11]See! The winter is past;
   the rains are over and gone.
[12]Flowers appear on the earth;
   the season of singing has come,
the cooing of doves
   is heard in our land.
[13]The fig tree forms its early fruit;
   the blossoming vines spread their fragrance.
Arise, come, my darling;
   my beautiful one, come with me."

Lover

[14]My dove in the clefts of the rock,
   in the hiding places on the mountainside,
show me your face,
   let me hear your voice;
for your voice is sweet,
   and your face is lovely.
[15]Catch for us the foxes,
   the little foxes
that ruin the vineyards,
   our vineyards that are in bloom.

Beloved

[16]My lover is mine and I am his;
   he browses among the lilies.
[17]Until the day breaks
   and the shadows flee,
turn, my lover,
   and be like a gazelle
or like a young stag
   on the rugged hills.[a]

3   All night long on my bed
   I looked for the one my heart loves;
   I looked for him but did not find him.
[2]I will get up now and go about the city,
   through its streets and squares;
I will search for the one my heart loves.
   So I looked for him but did not find him.
[3]The watchmen[D] found me
   as they made their rounds in the city.
   "Have you seen the one my heart loves?"
[4]Scarcely had I passed them
   when I found the one my heart loves.
I held him and would not let him go

[a]17 Or the hills of Bether

Daughters of Jerusalem (2:7; see 3:5,10; 5:8; 8:4)

The poet creates a literary device to highlight the admirable qualities of the two lovers. The bride speaks to others, possibly those in King Solomon's harem or the privileged ladies of the court. She instructs them in the way of true love, telling them that sexual intimacy cannot be forced. Love and lust are not the same. Many think the repetition of these words throughout the Song provides evidence of the poem's fundamental unity.

What do foxes have to do with romance? (2:15)

The lover tells about small foxes that attack and destroy the vines when they are in bloom. Little foxes apparently liked to dig around the blossom-covered vines. The lover's warning was that little things (such as perfectionism or jealousy, for example) could creep into a beautiful marriage relationship, gnawing at it until the love vine lies in ruins. The lover wanted those little things caught before serious damage was done.

Browses among the lilies (2:16)

The lilies in the garden were the charms of the young woman herself (v. 2). The lover is compared to a gazelle (v. 17) who, in a leisurely way, is free to enjoy her delicacies (also see 6:3).

Why did she pursue him so aggressively? (3:2,4)

In a culture where marriage contracts were typically arranged by parents, romantic feelings seldom entered into the negotiations. Those emotions usually came later, after the marriage was consummated. Prior to that neither the young woman nor the man pursued the other. These verses may then describe the desires of two people already married and deeply in love. Or they could recall a dream in which the woman longs for her marriage to be consummated. If so, then poetry reveals her private desires where culture would insist she be more reserved. Also see *Could these verses describe a dream?* (5:2–8).

Why go to the place where she was conceived? (3:4)

This may have been connected with their upcoming marriage ceremony. Bringing her future husband to her mother's home would have demonstrated the purity of their love. In 8:5 they return to the home of the bride's mother, perhaps an indication that the wedding festivities had ended and their married life together had begun: there the bride pays tribute to love in a faithful marriage (8:6–7,9).

till I had brought him to my mother's house,
　　to the room of the one who conceived me.
[5]Daughters of Jerusalem[D], I charge you
　　by the gazelles and by the does of the field:
Do not arouse or awaken love
　　until it so desires.

[6]Who is this coming up from the desert
　　like a column of smoke,
perfumed with myrrh[D] and incense[D]
　　made from all the spices of the merchant?
[7]Look! It is Solomon's carriage,
　　escorted by sixty warriors,
　　the noblest of Israel,
[8]all of them wearing the sword,
　　all experienced in battle,
each with his sword at his side,
　　prepared for the terrors of the night.
[9]King Solomon made for himself the carriage;
　　he made it of wood from Lebanon.
[10]Its posts he made of silver,
　　its base of gold.
Its seat was upholstered with purple[D],
　　its interior lovingly inlaid
　　by[a] the daughters of Jerusalem.
[11]Come out, you daughters of Zion[D],
　　and look at King Solomon wearing the
　　　　crown,
　　the crown with which his mother crowned
　　　　him
on the day of his wedding,
　　the day his heart rejoiced.

Lover

4　How beautiful you are, my darling!
　　Oh, how beautiful!
　　Your eyes behind your veil are doves.
Your hair is like a flock of goats
　　descending from Mount Gilead.
[2]Your teeth are like a flock of sheep just shorn,
　　coming up from the washing.
Each has its twin;
　　not one of them is alone.
[3]Your lips are like a scarlet ribbon;
　　your mouth is lovely.
Your temples behind your veil
　　are like the halves of a pomegranate.
[4]Your neck is like the tower of David,
　　built with elegance[b];
on it hang a thousand shields,
　　all of them shields of warriors.
[5]Your two breasts are like two fawns,
　　like twin fawns of a gazelle
　　that browse among the lilies.
[6]Until the day breaks
　　and the shadows flee,
I will go to the mountain of myrrh
　　and to the hill of incense.
[7]All beautiful you are, my darling;
　　there is no flaw in you.

[8]Come with me from Lebanon, my bride,

Was Solomon the lover? (3:11)

Many have thought so. But others think Solomon was probably too busy with his royal duties to engage in a pastoral romance with a country peasant. The *King Solomon* here may have been a commoner—"king for a day" at his wedding feast. The bridegroom even wore a *crown*, a wedding wreath his mother placed on his head at some point during the celebration. Traditional Syrian marriage customs even today include week-long wedding festivities where the groom and his bride are entertained as "king and queen" for the occasion.

This is a *compliment*? (4:1–4)

What woman wants to be compared to sheep, goats and pomegranates? These images do not typically appeal to our modern imaginations because we are so far removed from the simple country beauty from which they are drawn. But to people of an earlier time and more rural culture, these images would easily be seen as attractive. For example, a flock of goats streaming down a hillside at sunset looks curiously like a woman's long, flowing hair.

Mountain of myrrh . . . hill of incense (4:6)

See *Myrrh* (1:13).

Amana . . . Hermon (4:8)

Summits in a range of mountains north of Israel. (Senir is another name for Mount Hermon.) The poet colors his work, just as modern songwriters might include a certain city in a song. The bride seems to have lived with her family among the vineyards of northern Israel.

---

[a]10 Or *its inlaid interior a gift of love / from*　　　[b]4 The meaning of the Hebrew for this word is uncertain.

come with me from Lebanon.
Descend from the crest of Amana,
    from the top of Senir, the summit of
        Hermon,
from the lions' dens
    and the mountain haunts of the leopards.
⁹You have stolen my heart, my sister, my bride;
    you have stolen my heart
with one glance of your eyes,
    with one jewel of your necklace.
¹⁰How delightful is your love, my sister, my
        bride!
    How much more pleasing is your love than
        wine,
    and the fragrance of your perfume than any
        spice!
¹¹Your lips drop sweetness as the honeycomb,
        my bride;
    milk and honey are under your tongue.
    The fragrance of your garments is like that of
        Lebanon.
¹²You are a garden locked up, my sister, my
        bride;
    you are a spring enclosed, a sealed fountain.
¹³Your plants are an orchard of pomegranates
    with choice fruits,
    with henna and nard,
¹⁴   nard and saffron,
    calamusᴰ and cinnamon,
    with every kind of incenseᴰ tree,
    with myrrhᴰ and aloes
    and all the finest spices.
¹⁵You areᵃ a garden fountain,
    a well of flowing water
    streaming down from Lebanon.

Beloved

¹⁶Awake, north wind,
    and come, south wind!
Blow on my garden,
    that its fragrance may spread abroad.
Let my lover come into his garden
    and taste its choice fruits.

Lover

5 I have come into my garden, my sister, my bride;
    I have gathered my myrrh with my spice.
I have eaten my honeycomb and my honey;
    I have drunk my wine and my milk.

Friends

Eat, O friends, and drink;
    drink your fill, O lovers.

Beloved

²I slept but my heart was awake.
    Listen! My lover is knocking:
"Open to me, my sister, my darling,
    my dove, my flawless one.
My head is drenched with dew,
    my hair with the dampness of the night."

ᵃ15 Or *I am* (spoken by the *Beloved*)

Why call a lover a sister? (4:9)

Such terms of endearment were not limited to their specific technical definitions and were commonly used in ancient Middle Eastern literature.

How is the bride like a locked garden? (4:12)

The lover was apparently describing his bride on their wedding night. She was a virgin whose garden was about to be unlocked for the first time. Until then she had remained a *spring enclosed . . . a sealed fountain*. The consummation of the marriage is beautifully described in 4:16–5:1.

Why do friends cheer them on? (5:1)

Wedding feasts were gala social events that often lasted for seven days. During that time the guests took part celebrating the consummated marriage.

Could these verses describe a dream? (5:2–8)

Yes. The opening words of these verses, *I slept but my heart was awake* are a poetic way to describe a dream. These verses show that the pleasures of marriage do not guarantee there will be no disappointments.

Why did her passion cool? (5:3)

Even love stories have conflict. When the honeymoon is over, the thrill of romance can fade if it isn't nurtured. These verses (5:2–7) describe an incident—some say a dream—that occurred early in their marriage. For some reason the bride and groom were separated. When he returned, she was so drowsy with sleep she did not respond quickly enough for him. By the time she responded, he had come and gone. Now it was her turn to seek her beloved.

Was this a gang rape? (5:7)

Probably not. If this literally described a brutal attack on his wife, the lover would then have taken a completely different role in this poem—not as a loving husband, but as a vengeful man robbed of his prize. It is more plausible that these verses describe incidents from a dream. By the time the watchmen appeared in the dream, it had become a nightmare.

Why emphasize physical appearance? (5:10–16)

Throughout the poem the spotlight on physical beauty has caused many to interpret it allegorically. But it does not glorify the flesh at the expense of the spiritual. The human body and sex were designed by God. The Bible teaches here that the body is a thing of beauty, a masterpiece of creation.

³I have taken off my robe—
  must I put it on again?
I have washed my feet—
  must I soil them again?
⁴My lover thrust his hand through the
      latch-opening;
  my heart began to pound for him.
⁵I arose to open for my lover,
  and my hands dripped with myrrhᴰ,
my fingers with flowing myrrh,
  on the handles of the lock.
⁶I opened for my lover,
  but my lover had left; he was gone.
  My heart sank at his departure.ᵃ
I looked for him but did not find him.
  I called him but he did not answer.
⁷The watchmenᴰ found me
  as they made their rounds in the city.
They beat me, they bruised me;
  they took away my cloak,
  those watchmen of the walls!
⁸O daughters of Jerusalemᴰ, I charge
      you—
  if you find my lover,
what will you tell him?
  Tell him I am faint with love.

Friends

⁹How is your beloved better than others,
  most beautiful of women?
How is your beloved better than others,
  that you charge us so?

Beloved

¹⁰My lover is radiant and ruddy,
  outstanding among ten thousand.
¹¹His head is purest gold;
  his hair is wavy
  and black as a raven.
¹²His eyes are like doves
  by the water streams,
washed in milk,
  mounted like jewels.
¹³His cheeks are like beds of spice
  yielding perfume.
His lips are like lilies
  dripping with myrrh.
¹⁴His arms are rods of gold
  set with chrysolite.
His body is like polished ivory
  decorated with sapphires.ᵇ
¹⁵His legs are pillars of marble
  set on bases of pure gold.
His appearance is like Lebanon,
  choice as its cedars.
¹⁶His mouth is sweetness itself;
  he is altogether lovely.
This is my lover, this my friend,
  O daughters of Jerusalem.

ᵃ6 Or *heart had gone out to him when he spoke*   ᵇ14 Or *lapis lazuli*

Friends

6

Where has your lover gone,
    most beautiful of women?
Which way did your lover turn,
    that we may look for him with you?

Beloved

²My lover has gone down to his garden,
    to the beds of spices,
to browse in the gardens
    and to gather lilies.
³I am my lover's and my lover is mine;
    he browses among the lilies.

Lover

⁴You are beautiful, my darling, as Tirzah,
    lovely as Jerusalem^D,
    majestic as troops with banners.
⁵Turn your eyes from me;
    they overwhelm me.
Your hair is like a flock of goats
    descending from Gilead.
⁶Your teeth are like a flock of sheep
    coming up from the washing.
Each has its twin,
    not one of them is alone.
⁷Your temples behind your veil
    are like the halves of a pomegranate.
⁸Sixty queens there may be,
    and eighty concubines^D,
    and virgins beyond number;
⁹but my dove, my perfect one, is unique,
    the only daughter of her mother,
    the favorite of the one who bore her.
The maidens saw her and called her blessed;
    the queens and concubines praised her.

Friends

¹⁰Who is this that appears like the dawn,
    fair as the moon, bright as the sun,
    majestic as the stars in procession?

Lover

¹¹I went down to the grove of nut trees
    to look at the new growth in the valley,
to see if the vines had budded
    or the pomegranates were in bloom.
¹²Before I realized it,
    my desire set me among the royal chariots of
        my people.ᵃ

Friends

¹³Come back, come back, O Shulammite;
    come back, come back, that we may gaze on
        you!

Lover

Why would you gaze on the Shulammite
    as on the dance of Mahanaim?

ᵃ12 Or *among the chariots of Amminadab*; or *among the chariots of the people of the prince*

Browse in the gardens . . . gather lilies (6:2)
See *Browses among the lilies* (2:16).

Did she have more than 140 competitors? (6:8)
Some believe Solomon wrote this poem when he was still young, before he had 700 foreign wives and 300 concubines (1 Kings 11:3). Others, who think this poem is about a common shepherd and his bride, believe the comparison to 60 queens and 80 concubines is similar to lovers who might say their love is "one in a million." The young shepherd boasted that his bride was more desirable than the occupants of a royal household.

Why take a chariot ride? (6:12)
People disagree about who is speaking in these verses. If it is the bride, it may be she was carried off in chariots, which could account for v. 13. However, this might describe her fantasy: wandering into the vineyards to see the new growth, she may have imagined herself riding off in a royal chariot with her "prince charming." If it is the lover who is speaking about his desires, the chariots may picture his racing heartbeat.

Shulammite (6:13)
Some say this is the name of the young bride. Others say it only tells that she came from Shunem, a village near Jezreel. Still others maintain the name Shulammite is a feminine form of Solomon, meaning a woman belonging to Solomon.

Dance of Mahanaim (6:13)
Wedding festivals were filled with music and dancing. It would not be unusual for the guests to watch the bride, the center of attention, as she danced in celebration. Some think this dance was part of the bride's fantasy, but that her husband now joined in the fantasy. If so, then the bride danced for him and he described her graceful figure (7:1–9). Others interpret the original use of the word *Mahanaim* to suggest a dance of angels (see Gen. 32:1–2).

Setting of Song of Songs (6:13)

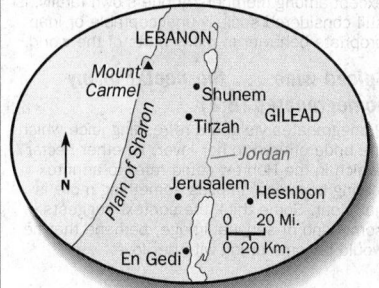

Was the bride a daughter of a prince? (7:1)

Some think she was a maiden engaged to marry a king (see Psalm 45:13–15). Others see the Song of Songs as a poem filled with romantic fantasy where the groom called his bride a princess even though she was merely a rustic girl. Because of her beautiful qualities, her shepherd-husband considered her far more attractive than all the queens in Solomon's harem. See article: *Does this describe a love affair?* (1:4).

What's so appealing about a nose like a tower? (7:2–9)

It would be surprising if these descriptions of beauty appealed to the modern reader, considering the gaps of time and distance between our culture and theirs. If we could be more familiar with the physical environment of this book, we might better appreciate its imagery. Was there an elegance or flowing lines about the tower of Lebanon? Were newborn gazelle fawns especially soft and warm? Did the pools of Heshbon reflect a dark, mysterious beauty?

Does this describe sexual intercourse? (7:8–9)

Yes, though in imaginative, poetic language rather than technical terms. When the Bible uses poetry as its medium of truth, it can be understood in ways far deeper than what lies on the surface.

Mandrakes (7:13)

Mandrake plants (with forked roots that resembled the lower part of a human body) have been used for centuries as love potions and aphrodisiacs (see Gen. 30:14–16). This verse refers to their aroma which was also stimulating.

Couldn't a woman kiss her husband in public? (8:1)

Obviously not in that culture. Kissing in public, except among members of one's own family, is still considered socially unacceptable or inappropriate behavior in many parts of the world.

Spiced wine . . . the nectar of my pomegranates (8:2)

Pomegranates yielded a refreshing juice which the bride offered to her lover. Whether *nectar* (which in the Hebrew could refer to an intoxicating beverage) implies something more is not clear. Some think the context suggests some kind of sensual image, perhaps that he would become drunk with her love.

7 How beautiful your sandaled feet,
  O prince's daughter!
Your graceful legs are like jewels,
  the work of a craftsman's hands.
²Your navel is a rounded goblet
  that never lacks blended wine.
Your waist is a mound of wheat
  encircled by lilies.
³Your breasts are like two fawns,
  twins of a gazelle.
⁴Your neck is like an ivory tower.
Your eyes are the pools of Heshbon
  by the gate of Bath Rabbim.
Your nose is like the tower of Lebanon
  looking toward Damascus.
⁵Your head crowns you like Mount Carmel.
  Your hair is like royal tapestry;
  the king is held captive by its tresses.
⁶How beautiful you are and how pleasing,
  O love, with your delights!
⁷Your stature is like that of the palm,
  and your breasts like clusters of fruit.
⁸I said, "I will climb the palm tree;
  I will take hold of its fruit."
May your breasts be like the clusters of the vine,
  the fragrance of your breath like apples,
⁹ and your mouth like the best wine.

Beloved

May the wine go straight to my lover,
  flowing gently over lips and teeth.ᵃ
¹⁰I belong to my lover,
  and his desire is for me.
¹¹Come, my lover, let us go to the countryside,
  let us spend the night in the villages.ᵇ
¹²Let us go early to the vineyards
  to see if the vines have budded,
if their blossoms have opened,
  and if the pomegranates are in bloom—
  there I will give you my love.
¹³The mandrakesᴰ send out their fragrance,
  and at our door is every delicacy,
both new and old,
  that I have stored up for you, my lover.

8 If only you were to me like a brother,
  who was nursed at my mother's breasts!
Then, if I found you outside,
  I would kiss you,
  and no one would despise me.
²I would lead you
  and bring you to my mother's house—
  she who has taught me.
I would give you spiced wine to drink,
  the nectar of my pomegranates.
³His left arm is under my head
  and his right arm embraces me.
⁴Daughters of Jerusalemᴰ, I charge you:
  Do not arouse or awaken love
  until it so desires.

ᵃ9 Septuagint, Aquila, Vulgate and Syriac; Hebrew *lips of sleepers*
ᵇ11 Or *henna bushes*

Friends

⁵Who is this coming up from the desert
   leaning on her lover?

Beloved

Under the apple tree I roused you;
   there your mother conceived you,
   there she who was in labor gave you birth.
⁶Place me like a seal over your heart,
   like a seal on your arm;
for love is as strong as death^D,
   its jealousy^a unyielding as the grave.^b
It burns like blazing fire,
   like a mighty flame.^c
⁷Many waters cannot quench love;
   rivers cannot wash it away.
If one were to give
   all the wealth of his house for love,
   it^d would be utterly scorned.

Friends

⁸We have a young sister,
   and her breasts are not yet grown.
What shall we do for our sister
   for the day she is spoken for?
⁹If she is a wall,
   we will build towers of silver on her.
If she is a door,
   we will enclose her with panels of cedar.

Beloved

¹⁰I am a wall,
   and my breasts are like towers.
Thus I have become in his eyes
   like one bringing contentment.
¹¹Solomon had a vineyard in Baal Hamon;
   he let out his vineyard to tenants.
Each was to bring for its fruit
   a thousand shekels^{De} of silver.
¹²But my own vineyard is mine to give;
   the thousand shekels are for you,
      O Solomon,
   and two hundred^f are for those who tend
      its fruit.

Lover

¹³You who dwell in the gardens
   with friends in attendance,
   let me hear your voice!

Beloved

¹⁴Come away, my lover,
   and be like a gazelle
   or like a young stag
   on the spice-laden mountains.

Why go to the place where she was conceived? (8:5)

This may be a poetic way of referring to the home of the bride's mother. See *Why go to the place where she was conceived?* (3:4).

How could she seal her husband's heart? (8:6)

The bride wanted to put her mark of ownership on her husband. In Biblical times an engraved stone or metal seal was used to identify the owner of something. It gave the owner free access to his or her possessions—and it kept others out. Not only would her husband be identified as her property, he would be reserved for her alone. She belonged to him and he to her.

Why compare a sister to a wall? (8:9)

Some speculate the sister was the couple's daughter. Others see her as the bride's sister. Still others think this recalls an earlier time when the bride was cared for by her brothers before she was married. The *wall* suggests purity—shutting out sexual temptation. The *door* on the other hand, suggests openness and vulnerability, someone needing protection. The bride affirms she has been faithful—a strong *wall*—open only to her beloved (v. 10).

Who tended the bride's fruit? (8:12)

There are many opinions. One plausible explanation is that the bride compared her figurative vineyard (her body and her love) to Solomon's real vineyard. He rented his vineyard to tenants who paid him with its fruit, keeping 20 percent for themselves. But her vineyard was priceless by comparison and she was not for sale. Instead she would give herself freely to her husband.

---

^a6 Or *ardor*   ^b6 Hebrew *Sheol*   ^c6 Or / *like the very flame of the* Lord   ^d7 Or *he*   ^e11 That is, about 25 pounds (about 11.5 kilograms); also in verse 12   ^f12 That is, about 5 pounds (about 2.3 kilograms)

ISAIAH

Why read this book?

Have you known Christians who lived double lives? Who only seemed to be playing with God? Isaiah knew people who lived a double life—the nation of Israel—and he shared God's hatred for their compromise. He challenged them to shape up and love God with all their hearts and minds. Isaiah hoped that his readers might clearly see their hypocrisy and change their ways.

Who wrote this book?

Isaiah, the son of Amoz. Some claim that he could not have written later material in the book, describing events that occurred after the prophet's death. But others think such a view discounts the supernatural element of God's revelation. Prophecy, given by the inspiration of God, can predict future events.

To whom was it written and why?

Isaiah lived in Judah, the southern kingdom of the divided nation of Israel. He was a prophet to four kings of Judah from about 740 B.C. to 681 B.C., but he preached repentance and salvation to the whole nation.

What was happening during this time?

Israel had faded from its former prominence and was now a second-rate nation. Though Judah was threatened by Assyria and Egypt, it was spared from their destruction, largely through Isaiah's influence. The northern kingdom, however, was demolished by Assyrian forces.

What to look for in Isaiah:

Paradox. Isaiah was a piercing poet, who understood the two-sided nature of God's character: mercy and judgment, grace and discipline, justice and forgiveness, exile and salvation. The tension of these great paradoxes fills the pages of Isaiah's writings, awaiting a resolution only the reader can bring—faith or unbelief.

When did these things happen?

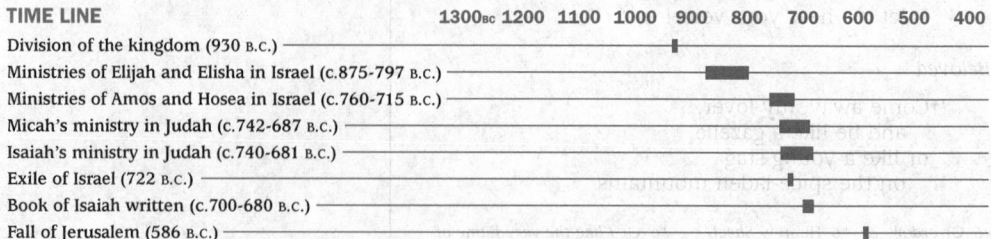

TIME LINE	1300BC	1200	1100	1000	900	800	700	600	500	400
Division of the kingdom (930 B.C.)										
Ministries of Elijah and Elisha in Israel (c.875-797 B.C.)										
Ministries of Amos and Hosea in Israel (c.760-715 B.C.)										
Micah's ministry in Judah (c.742-687 B.C.)										
Isaiah's ministry in Judah (c.740-681 B.C.)										
Exile of Israel (722 B.C.)										
Book of Isaiah written (c.700-680 B.C.)										
Fall of Jerusalem (586 B.C.)										

1 The vision[D] concerning Judah and Jerusalem[D] that Isaiah son of Amoz saw during the reigns of Uzziah, Jotham, Ahaz and Hezekiah, kings of Judah.

A Rebellious Nation

2Hear, O heavens! Listen, O earth!
  For the LORD has spoken:
"I reared children and brought them up,
  but they have rebelled against me.
3The ox knows his master,
  the donkey his owner's manger,
but Israel does not know,
  my people do not understand."

4Ah, sinful nation,
  a people loaded with guilt,
a brood of evildoers,
  children given to corruption!
They have forsaken the LORD;
  they have spurned the Holy One of Israel
  and turned their backs on him.

5Why should you be beaten anymore?
  Why do you persist in rebellion?
Your whole head is injured,
  your whole heart afflicted[D].
6From the sole of your foot to the top of your
      head
  there is no soundness—
only wounds and welts
  and open sores,
not cleansed or bandaged
  or soothed with oil.

7Your country is desolate,
  your cities burned with fire;
your fields are being stripped by foreigners

Vision (1:1)

A supernatural revelation, message, or insight communicated through images seen only within a person's mind or spirit. The pictures seen in a vision may illustrate spiritual truths or future events.

How should we understand prophetic visions? (1:1)

It's clear that the book of Isaiah cannot be read like a typical novel. Transitions are lacking, time frames jump dramatically and threads of plot or direction are often severed without warning. Confusion often results. The book of Isaiah is primarily a collection of visions. Although the words must be regarded as authentic history, prophecy and poetry, they must first and foremost be understood as visions.

The problem with understanding visions is not with the text, but in our limited understanding of how God communicated with prophets: *When a prophet of the Lord is among you, I reveal myself to him in visions, I speak to him in dreams* (Num. 12:6). Prophets then relayed those visions to the people.

The purpose of a vision was not straight-line communication. It was to create an impression of God upon a person. Prophetic words, then, primarily carry the power of the message, not necessarily a smooth flow of logic. That is why poetry, with its graphic images and exaggeration, was often the preferred literary form of the prophets. The story line was abandoned in favor of more tumultuous language.

This was certainly true with Isaiah. He was especially concerned with revealing the paradoxical character of God, between his mercy and his discipline, for example. To communicate such tensions, Isaiah chose to describe what he saw, possibly hoping to impress people with God's holiness by contrasting it with Judah's sin.

Daughter of Zion (1:8)

A reference to Jerusalem. Cities were commonly personified as women and *daughters* of the country to which they belonged.

SCRIPTURE LINK (1:9) *Sodom and Gomorrah*

See Gen. 18–19.

Why was God tired of sacrifices? (1:11–14)

Because the Israelites' hearts were hard, set against obeying God. Though they outwardly did what he had commanded (Exodus 23:15, Deut. 16:16), they resisted God inwardly. God wanted their inner motives to be pure (Psalm 51:17, Hosea 6:6) even more than he wanted their sacrifices. Clearly, Israel had not humbled itself before God.

right before you,
laid waste as when overthrown by strangers.
⁸The Daughter of Zion^D is left
like a shelter in a vineyard,
like a hut in a field of melons,
like a city under siege.
⁹Unless the LORD Almighty
had left us some survivors,
we would have become like Sodom,
we would have been like Gomorrah.

¹⁰Hear the word of the LORD,
you rulers of Sodom;
listen to the law of our God,
you people of Gomorrah!
¹¹"The multitude of your sacrifices^D—
what are they to me?" says the LORD.
"I have more than enough of burnt offerings^D,
of rams and the fat of fattened animals;
I have no pleasure
in the blood of bulls and lambs and goats.
¹²When you come to appear before me,
who has asked this of you,
this trampling of my courts?
¹³Stop bringing meaningless offerings!
Your incense^D is detestable to me.
New Moons, Sabbaths^D and convocations—
I cannot bear your evil assemblies.
¹⁴Your New Moon festivals^D and your appointed feasts
my soul^D hates.
They have become a burden to me;
I am weary of bearing them.
¹⁵When you spread out your hands in prayer,
I will hide my eyes from you;
even if you offer many prayers,
I will not listen.
Your hands are full of blood;
¹⁶ wash and make yourselves clean.
Take your evil deeds
out of my sight!
Stop doing wrong,
¹⁷ learn to do right!
Seek justice,
encourage the oppressed.^a
Defend the cause of the fatherless,
plead the case of the widow.
¹⁸"Come now, let us reason together,"
says the LORD.
"Though your sins are like scarlet,
they shall be as white as snow;
though they are red as crimson,
they shall be like wool.
¹⁹If you are willing and obedient,
you will eat the best from the land;
²⁰but if you resist and rebel,
you will be devoured by the sword."
For the mouth of the LORD has spoken.

²¹See how the faithful city
has become a harlot!
She once was full of justice;

a 17 Or / rebuke the oppressor

righteousness[D] used to dwell in her—
  but now murderers!
22Your silver has become dross[D],
  your choice wine is diluted with water.
23Your rulers are rebels,
  companions of thieves;
they all love bribes
  and chase after gifts.
They do not defend the cause of the fatherless;
  the widow's case does not come before
    them.
24Therefore the Lord, the LORD Almighty,
  the Mighty One of Israel, declares:
"Ah, I will get relief from my foes
  and avenge[D] myself on my enemies.
25I will turn my hand against you;
  I will thoroughly purge away your dross
  and remove all your impurities.
26I will restore your judges as in days of old,
  your counselors as at the beginning.
Afterward you will be called
  the City of Righteousness,
  the Faithful City."

27Zion[D] will be redeemed[D] with justice,
  her penitent ones with righteousness.
28But rebels and sinners will both be broken,
  and those who forsake the LORD will perish.

29"You will be ashamed because of the sacred[D]
    oaks
  in which you have delighted;
you will be disgraced because of the gardens
  that you have chosen.
30You will be like an oak with fading leaves,
  like a garden without water.
31The mighty man will become tinder
  and his work a spark;
both will burn together,
  with no one to quench the fire."

The Mountain of the LORD

2 This is what Isaiah son of Amoz saw concerning Judah and Jerusalem[D]:

2In the last days

the mountain of the LORD's temple will be
    established
  as chief among the mountains;
it will be raised above the hills,
  and all nations will stream to it.

3Many peoples will come and say,

"Come, let us go up to the mountain of the
    LORD,
  to the house of the God of Jacob.
He will teach us his ways,
  so that we may walk in his paths."
The law will go out from Zion,
  the word of the LORD from Jerusalem.
4He will judge between the nations
  and will settle disputes for many peoples.
They will beat their swords into plowshares
  and their spears into pruning hooks.

Does God have enemies? (1:24)
Yes. The enemies of God are all those who oppose him, who sin against him and who insist on going their own way instead of his. In this instance, Israel is his enemy.

Sacred oaks . . . gardens (1:29)
In the ancient Middle East, gardens shaded by oak trees were often used as places for religious gatherings. There, under the trees, various kinds of idol worship took place, including some religious rituals that actually involved indiscriminate sexual intercourse.

Last days (2:2)
Some believe the *last days* refer to a future time of God's judgment (*the Day of the* LORD) followed by Christ's direct rule from Jerusalem. Others believe the *last days* began at the time of Christ and his rule in human hearts and will continue until Christ's second coming.

Nation will not take up sword against nation,
    nor will they train for war anymore.

⁵Come, O house of Jacob,
    let us walk in the light of the LORD.

The Day of the LORD

⁶You have abandoned your people,
    the house of Jacob.
They are full of superstitions from the East;
    they practice divination^D like the Philistines
    and clasp hands with pagans.
⁷Their land is full of silver and gold;
    there is no end to their treasures.
Their land is full of horses;
    there is no end to their chariots.
⁸Their land is full of idols^D;
    they bow down to the work of their hands,
    to what their fingers have made.
⁹So man will be brought low
    and mankind humbled—
    do not forgive them.^a

¹⁰Go into the rocks,
    hide in the ground
from dread of the LORD
    and the splendor of his majesty!
¹¹The eyes of the arrogant man will be humbled
    and the pride of men brought low;
    the LORD alone will be exalted in that day.

¹²The LORD Almighty has a day in store
    for all the proud and lofty,
    for all that is exalted
    (and they will be humbled),
¹³for all the cedars of Lebanon, tall and lofty,
    and all the oaks of Bashan,
¹⁴for all the towering mountains
    and all the high hills,
¹⁵for every lofty tower
    and every fortified wall,
¹⁶for every trading ship^b
    and every stately vessel.
¹⁷The arrogance of man will be brought low
    and the pride of men humbled;
    the LORD alone will be exalted in that day,
¹⁸ and the idols will totally disappear.

¹⁹Men will flee to caves in the rocks
    and to holes in the ground
from dread of the LORD
    and the splendor of his majesty,
    when he rises to shake the earth.
²⁰In that day men will throw away
    to the rodents and bats
their idols of silver and idols of gold,
    which they made to worship.
²¹They will flee to caverns in the rocks
    and to the overhanging crags
from dread of the LORD
    and the splendor of his majesty,
    when he rises to shake the earth.

²²Stop trusting in man,

Why the dramatic change of tone? (2:6)

For impact. Isaiah wanted Israel to know that God's rule would not come before God purged sin. These sudden shifts in language or scenes occur throughout this book.

Superstitions ... divination ... clasp hands with pagans (2:6)

The nations of the Middle East traded not only their goods and services but also their religious traditions and idolatry. The customs from foreign religions had polluted Israel's worship of the Lord.

How did materialism impact Israel? (2:7–8)

It caused the people to become less dependent on the Lord. They grew more confident in their own resources. This led to arrogance (v. 17) and self-sufficiency (v. 22). Their tendency toward idolatry, then, is not surprising (v. 8), since idolatry is little more than worshiping the works of one's own hands.

Why did Isaiah ask God to not forgive? (2:9–10)

Genuine forgiveness must be preceded by admitting sin and desiring to change. Isaiah could see no signs of repentance from the rampant sin throughout the land. So he asked God not to forgive the nation, so that it would be humbled.

---

^a9 Or *not raise them up*   ^b16 Hebrew *every ship of Tarshish*

who has but a breath in his nostrils.
Of what account is he?

Judgment on Jerusalem and Judah

3 See now, the Lord,
the LORD Almighty,
is about to take from Jerusalem[D] and Judah
both supply and support:
all supplies of food and all supplies of water,
2 the hero and warrior,
the judge and prophet[D],
the soothsayer and elder,
3the captain of fifty and man of rank,
the counselor, skilled craftsman and clever
enchanter.

4I will make boys their officials;
mere children will govern them.
5People will oppress each other—
man against man, neighbor against neighbor.
The young will rise up against the old,
the base against the honorable.

6A man will seize one of his brothers
at his father's home, and say,
"You have a cloak, you be our leader;
take charge of this heap of ruins!"
7But in that day he will cry out,
"I have no remedy.
I have no food or clothing in my house;
do not make me the leader of the people."

8Jerusalem staggers,
Judah is falling;
their words and deeds are against the LORD,
defying his glorious presence.
9The look on their faces testifies against them;
they parade their sin like Sodom;
they do not hide it.
Woe to them!
They have brought disaster upon themselves.

10Tell the righteous[D] it will be well with them,
for they will enjoy the fruit of their deeds.
11Woe to the wicked! Disaster is upon them!
They will be paid back for what their hands
have done.

12Youths oppress my people,
women rule over them.
O my people, your guides lead you astray;
they turn you from the path.

13The LORD takes his place in court;
he rises to judge the people.
14The LORD enters into judgment
against the elders and leaders of his people:
"It is you who have ruined my vineyard;
the plunder[D] from the poor is in your
houses.
15What do you mean by crushing my people
and grinding the faces of the poor?"
declares the Lord, the LORD Almighty.

16The LORD says,
"The women of Zion[D] are haughty,
walking along with outstretched necks,

What was Isaiah predicting? (3:1)
Some think Isaiah was referring to the series of Assyrian invasions culminating in the sacking of the northern kingdom of Israel in 722 B.C. Others point to the Babylonian's attack on Jerusalem and subsequent exile of the southern kingdom of Judah in 586 B.C.

What was meant by child rulers? (3:4,12)
The thought of children or women ruling over them was unthinkable; it was an indication that their Jewish society would be in chaos and upheaval. In a culture where men dominated the power structures, anything less would be a sign of a devastated, ruined country. Isaiah's prediction may have also pointed to the future carnage of war: if most of the men would be killed in battle, only children and women would be left to rule.

Why would a cloak make someone a leader? (3:6)
This graphic image underscored the devastation Isaiah predicted for Israel. He claimed that the nation would become so impoverished that anyone left with even a stitch of clothing would be considered privileged and thus a candidate for leadership.

Of what, exactly, were the women guilty? (3:16–23)
Some think the term women personifies a class of people—Jerusalem's self-indulgent rich—who cared little for anything but their own comfort. Others believe Isaiah spoke to a literal upper class of women. Either way, Isaiah's descriptions—outstretched necks, flirting eyes—were symptoms of their self-centered lives and inward moral decay.

How would they be punished? (3:24–26)

The stench, rope, baldness and branding described the treatment given to a people defeated in war and forced into foreign captivity. Reports of the squalor and hardships of modern war refugees offer some analogies.

Was being single a disgrace? (4:1)

Most likely these seven women were widows, their husbands having been killed in the war. In ancient times widows were treated poorly and were exposed to oppression. However, because these widows claimed to have their own financial resources, their disgrace probably stemmed from being childless. In Hebrew culture there was no greater humiliation than to be a woman with no children of her own. These women apparently wanted children to remove their disgrace.

SCRIPTURE LINK (4:2) *Branch of the* Lord

See Jer. 23:5; Zech. 6:12. Also see *Why call Jesse's descendant a branch?* (11:1).

Why call them *holy?* (4:2–3)

The word *holy* means to be reserved by God for his own use. By judging Jerusalem, God purified his people, setting them apart for his glory. He separated his precious ones from the perpetrators of evil in Jerusalem.

Why focus on the filthiness of women? (4:4)

Perhaps Isaiah wanted the women to see they could no longer hide their own personal responsibilities behind their husbands or rulers. The *bloodstains from Jerusalem* could refer to meaningless sacrifices (1:15), murders (1:21) or even child sacrifices (57:5)—things the women participated in. Or Isaiah may have singled the women out because they were the only ones *left in Zion, who remain in Jerusalem* (v. 3). Most of the males would have been killed in battle or captured by the enemy.

What sort of canopy is this? (4:5)

Some see this *canopy*, or covering, as representing God's continual presence in the day of Jerusalem's salvation, still in the future. Others seem to think of it as a promise of God's general protection during the times that followed Israel's troubles.

Why the sudden shift to a love song? (5:1)

Isaiah was moving from the hope of a future time (4:2–6) to the painful reality of the moment. In this poetic shift, the emotions of God —especially his feelings of pain and longing— are dramatically highlighted. Also see *Why the dramatic change of tone?* (2:6).

flirting with their eyes,
tripping along with mincing steps,
with ornaments jingling on their ankles.
[17]Therefore the Lord will bring sores on the
heads of the women of Zion[D];
the Lord will make their scalps bald."

[18]In that day the Lord will snatch away their finery: the bangles and headbands and crescent necklaces, [19]the earrings and bracelets and veils, [20]the headdresses and ankle chains and sashes, the perfume bottles and charms, [21]the signet rings[D] and nose rings, [22]the fine robes and the capes and cloaks, the purses [23]and mirrors, and the linen garments and tiaras and shawls.

[24]Instead of fragrance there will be a stench;
instead of a sash, a rope;
instead of well-dressed hair, baldness;
instead of fine clothing, sackcloth[D];
instead of beauty, branding.
[25]Your men will fall by the sword,
your warriors in battle.
[26]The gates of Zion will lament and mourn;
destitute, she will sit on the ground.

4 In that day seven women
will take hold of one man
and say, "We will eat our own food
and provide our own clothes;
only let us be called by your name.
Take away our disgrace!"

The Branch of the Lord

[2]In that day the Branch of the Lord will be beautiful and glorious, and the fruit of the land will be the pride and glory[D] of the survivors in Israel. [3]Those who are left in Zion, who remain in Jerusalem, will be called holy, all who are recorded among the living in Jerusalem. [4]The Lord will wash away the filth of the women of Zion; he will cleanse the bloodstains from Jerusalem by a spirit[a] of judgment and a spirit[a] of fire. [5]Then the Lord will create over all of Mount Zion and over those who assemble there a cloud of smoke by day and a glow of flaming fire by night; over all the glory will be a canopy. [6]It will be a shelter and shade from the heat of the day, and a refuge and hiding place from the storm and rain.

The Song of the Vineyard

5 I will sing for the one I love
a song about his vineyard:
My loved one had a vineyard
on a fertile hillside.
[2]He dug it up and cleared it of stones
and planted it with the choicest vines.
He built a watchtower[D] in it
and cut out a winepress[D] as well.
Then he looked for a crop of good grapes,
but it yielded only bad fruit.

[3]"Now you dwellers in Jerusalem and men of
Judah,
judge between me and my vineyard.
[4]What more could have been done for my
vineyard

[a]4 Or *the Spirit*

than I have done for it?
When I looked for good grapes,
   why did it yield only bad?
⁵Now I will tell you
   what I am going to do to my vineyard:
I will take away its hedge,
   and it will be destroyed;
I will break down its wall,
   and it will be trampled.
⁶I will make it a wasteland,
   neither pruned nor cultivated,
   and briers and thorns will grow there.
I will command the clouds
   not to rain on it."

⁷The vineyard of the LORD Almighty
   is the house of Israel,
and the men of Judah
   are the garden of his delight.
And he looked for justice, but saw bloodshed;
   for righteousnessᴰ, but heard cries of
      distress.

Woes and Judgments

⁸Woe to you who add house to house
   and join field to field
till no space is left
   and you live alone in the land.

⁹The LORD Almighty has declared in my hearing:

"Surely the great houses will become desolate,
   the fine mansions left without occupants.
¹⁰A ten-acreᵃ vineyard will produce only a
      bathᵇ of wine,
   a homerᶜ of seed only an ephahᵈ of grain."

¹¹Woe to those who rise early in the morning
   to run after their drinks,
who stay up late at night
   till they are inflamed with wine.
¹²They have harps and lyresᴰ at their banquets,
   tambourines and flutes and wine,
but they have no regard for the deeds of the
      LORD,
   no respect for the work of his hands.
¹³Therefore my people will go into exileᴰ
   for lack of understanding;
their men of rank will die of hunger
   and their masses will be parched with thirst.
¹⁴Therefore the graveᵉ enlarges its appetite
   and opens its mouth without limit;
into it will descend their nobles and masses
   with all their brawlers and revelers.
¹⁵So man will be brought low
   and mankind humbled,
   the eyes of the arrogant humbled.
¹⁶But the LORD Almighty will be exalted by his
      justice,
   and the holy God will show himself holy by
      his righteousness.

ᵃ10 Hebrew ten-yoke, that is, the land plowed by 10 yoke of oxen in
one day   ᵇ10 That is, probably about 6 gallons (about 22 liters)
ᶜ10 That is, probably about 6 bushels (about 220 liters)   ᵈ10 That
is, probably about 3/5 bushel (about 22 liters)   ᵉ14 Hebrew Sheol

When does productivity become wrong? (5:8)

When the desire to accumulate wealth possesses people and causes them to walk over others. Many in Judah had become self-indulgent, caring only for themselves in a mad pursuit for pleasure. Justice, love and respect for others had been sacrificed on the altar of pleasure, self and greed.

Exile (5:13)

They would be banished from their own country, taken captive to a foreign land. God used exile in the Old Testament to punish his people, purging them of their sinful and rebellious ways.

How would Jerusalem's judgment exalt God? (5:15–16)

Because Jerusalem's punishment was deserved. It was right, and therefore honoring to God, that this sinful people be punished. God's judgment revealed his holiness as well as his power to act according to his character. Judging sin is consistent with who God is.

¹⁷Then sheep will graze as in their own pasture;
  lambs will feed^a among the ruins of the
    rich.

Why condemn those wanting to see God's work? (5:18–19)

They were condemned because they were not sincere; their words dripped with deceit, scorn and sarcasm. They had grown so arrogant they even mocked God's power and holiness. Because they had prospered in their sin, they did not believe God was capable of judging them.

¹⁸Woe to those who draw sin along with cords of
    deceit,
  and wickedness as with cart ropes,
¹⁹to those who say, "Let God hurry,
  let him hasten his work
  so we may see it.
Let it approach,
  let the plan of the Holy One of Israel come,
  so we may know it."

²⁰Woe to those who call evil good
    and good evil,
  who put darkness for light
    and light for darkness,
  who put bitter for sweet
    and sweet for bitter.

²¹Woe to those who are wise in their own eyes
    and clever in their own sight.

²²Woe to those who are heroes at drinking wine
    and champions at mixing drinks,
²³who acquit the guilty for a bribe,
    but deny justice to the innocent.
²⁴Therefore, as tongues of fire lick up straw
    and as dry grass sinks down in the flames,
  so their roots will decay
    and their flowers blow away like dust;
  for they have rejected the law of the LORD
      Almighty
    and spurned the word of the Holy One of
      Israel.
²⁵Therefore the LORD's anger burns against his
      people;
  his hand is raised and he strikes them down.
The mountains shake,
    and the dead bodies are like refuse in the
      streets.

Yet for all this, his anger is not turned away,
  his hand is still upraised.

What role does a banner play? (5:26)

The word *banner* literally meant *conspicuous* or *easily seen*. Standards and symbols lifted on poles, hilltops or other highly visible places were used to rally troops and armies. For God to raise a banner for distant nations was a figurative way of saying that he was calling them to battle against Israel. God frequently employed other nations to discipline his people, often through war.

²⁶He lifts up a banner for the distant nations,
  he whistles for those at the ends of the earth.
Here they come,
  swiftly and speedily!
²⁷Not one of them grows tired or stumbles,
  not one slumbers or sleeps;
not a belt is loosened at the waist,
  not a sandal thong is broken.
²⁸Their arrows are sharp,
  all their bows are strung;
their horses' hoofs seem like flint,
  their chariot wheels like a whirlwind.
²⁹Their roar is like that of the lion,
  they roar like young lions;
they growl as they seize their prey
  and carry it off with no one to rescue.
³⁰In that day they will roar over it
  like the roaring of the sea.
And if one looks at the land,

^a17 Septuagint; Hebrew / *strangers will eat*

he will see darkness and distress;
even the light will be darkened by the
clouds.

Isaiah's Commission

6 In the year that King Uzziah died, I saw the Lord seated on a throne, high and exalted, and the train of his robe filled the temple. ²Above him were seraphs, each with six wings: With two wings they covered their faces, with two they covered their feet, and with two they were flying. ³And they were calling to one another:

"Holy, holy, holy is the LORD Almighty;
the whole earth is full of his glory^D."

⁴At the sound of their voices the doorposts and thresholds shook and the temple was filled with smoke.

⁵"Woe to me!" I cried. "I am ruined! For I am a man of unclean^D lips, and I live among a people of unclean lips, and my eyes have seen the King, the LORD Almighty."

⁶Then one of the seraphs flew to me with a live coal in his hand, which he had taken with tongs from the altar. ⁷With it he touched my mouth and said, "See, this has touched your lips; your guilt is taken away and your sin atoned for."

⁸Then I heard the voice of the Lord saying, "Whom shall I send? And who will go for us?"

And I said, "Here am I. Send me!"

⁹He said, "Go and tell this people:

" 'Be ever hearing, but never understanding;
be ever seeing, but never perceiving.'

¹⁰Make the heart of this people calloused;
make their ears dull
and close their eyes.^a
Otherwise they might see with their eyes,
hear with their ears,
understand with their hearts,
and turn and be healed."

¹¹Then I said, "For how long, O Lord?"

And he answered:

"Until the cities lie ruined
and without inhabitant,
until the houses are left deserted
and the fields ruined and ravaged,
¹²until the LORD has sent everyone far away
and the land is utterly forsaken.
¹³And though a tenth remains in the land,
it will again be laid waste.
But as the terebinth and oak
leave stumps when they are cut down,
so the holy seed will be the stump in the
land."

The Sign of Immanuel

7 When Ahaz son of Jotham, the son of Uzziah, was king of Judah, King Rezin of Aram and Pekah son of Remaliah king of Israel marched up to fight against Jerusalem^D, but they could not overpower it. ²Now the house of David was told, "Aram has allied it-

---

^a 9,10 Hebrew; Septuagint 'You will be ever hearing, but never understanding; / you will be ever seeing, but never perceiving.' / ¹⁰This people's heart has become calloused; / they hardly hear with their ears, / and they have closed their eyes

---

Why isn't Isaiah's "call" at the beginning of the book? (6:1–8)
The first five chapters of the book are used to clearly establish Judah's sinful condition. In much the same way that a writer establishes context, Isaiah may have delayed this chapter for the sake of impact. Seeing the condition of *a people of unclean lips* (v. 5) helps us to better understand the anguish Isaiah felt about standing before an awesome and holy God.

Did this actually happen to Isaiah? (6:1)
If taken literally, the phrases *I saw the Lord* (v. 1) and *he touched my mouth* (v. 7) seem to indicate an actual event. But it may have been a vision where Isaiah saw things in another realm. Either way, its effect on Isaiah was both dramatic and genuine.

Seraphs (6:2)
Some think these creatures were winged serpents with certain human features. They could be compared to the cherubim (see Dictionary) in the inner sanctuary of the Jerusalem temple (1 Kings 6:23–28).

Unclean lips (6:5)
Sinful. The mouth expresses the sinful intentions of the human heart. See James 3:5 and Matt. 12:34.

How can a hot coal take away guilt? (6:6–7)
The hot coal symbolized both God's wrath and his process of purification. In order for sin to be forgiven, God's wrath, which both destroys and purifies, must be released against the sin. The hot coal that cauterized Isaiah's lips caused him to experience the full heat of God's wrath and thus to experience his forgiveness.

Did God not want his people to repent? (6:9–13)
Some ancient translators saw these commands as statements (see NIV text note). The Bible record is clear on two things, however: (1) God had long wanted his people's affections; (2) Israel consistently spurned him. It seems that at this juncture, God was at long last responding in judgment. Israel had crossed the line; no matter how much they repented, they would still face the wrath of God.

Holy seed . . . stump (6:13)
In this symbolic language lies the heart of Isaiah's message: through God's punishment, a small group of people (a remnant) would return, purified and holy. With this obedient remnant, God would work his plan of redemption. Also see **Stump of Jesse (11:1).**

What war was this? (7:1)
This was called the Syro-Ephraimite war and was fought during King Ahaz's reign in Judah in 734–733 B.C. Many nations in the region, including Israel (the northern kingdom), were controlled by Assyria. In order to throw off Assyria's yoke, Israel and Aram formed an alliance. They then attempted to force Judah (the southern kingdom also lived in the shadow of the Assyrian threat) to join their conspiracy. Their coercion resulted in war.

self with[a] Ephraim"; so the hearts of Ahaz and his people were shaken, as the trees of the forest are shaken by the wind.

[3]Then the LORD said to Isaiah, "Go out, you and your son Shear-Jashub,[b] to meet Ahaz at the end of the aqueduct of the Upper Pool, on the road to the Washerman's Field. [4]Say to him, 'Be careful, keep calm and don't be afraid. Do not lose heart because of these two smoldering stubs of firewood—because of the fierce anger of Rezin and Aram and of the son of Remaliah. [5]Aram, Ephraim and Remaliah's son have plotted your ruin, saying, [6]"Let us invade Judah; let us tear it apart and divide it among ourselves, and make the son of Tabeel king over it." [7]Yet this is what the Sovereign LORD says:

> " 'It will not take place,
>   it will not happen,
> [8]for the head of Aram is Damascus,
>   and the head of Damascus is only Rezin.
> Within sixty-five years
>   Ephraim will be too shattered to be a people.
> [9]The head of Ephraim is Samaria,
>   and the head of Samaria is only Remaliah's
>   son.
> If you do not stand firm in your faith,
>   you will not stand at all.' "

[10]Again the LORD spoke to Ahaz, [11]"Ask the LORD your God for a sign, whether in the deepest depths or in the highest heights."

[12]But Ahaz said, "I will not ask; I will not put the LORD to the test."

[13]Then Isaiah said, "Hear now, you house of David! Is it not enough to try the patience of men? Will you try the patience of my God also? [14]Therefore the Lord himself will give you[c] a sign: The virgin will be with child and will give birth to a son, and[d] will call him Immanuel.[e] [15]He will eat curds and honey when he knows enough to reject the wrong and choose the right. [16]But before the boy knows enough to reject the wrong and choose the right, the land of the two kings you dread will be laid waste. [17]The LORD will bring on you and on your people and on the house of your father a time unlike any since Ephraim broke away from Judah—he will bring the king of Assyria."

[18]In that day the LORD will whistle for flies from the distant streams of Egypt and for bees from the land of Assyria. [19]They will all come and settle in the steep ravines and in the crevices in the rocks, on all the thornbushes and at all the water holes. [20]In that day the Lord will use a razor hired from beyond the River[f]—the king of Assyria—to shave your head and the hair of your legs, and to take off your beards also. [21]In that day, a man will keep alive a young cow and two goats. [22]And because of the abundance of the milk they give, he will have curds to eat. All who remain in the land will eat curds and honey. [23]In that day, in every place where there were a thousand vines worth a thousand silver shekels[D],[g] there will be only briers and thorns. [24]Men will go there with bow and ar-

Why did God want Isaiah's son to go with Isaiah? (7:3)

The name of Isaiah's son was a message from God to Ahaz (see NIV text note). Some think God wanted to assure Ahaz that the armies of Israel and Aram would be defeated and reduced to a *remnant* (2 Kings 15:29). Others think God wanted to warn Ahaz that if he allied with Israel and Aram, only a *remnant* of Judah would survive the bloodletting. Still others believe Shear-Jashub's name offered hope concerning a future beyond the present disaster.

Why did God offer a sign for Ahaz? (7:11)

It was a last-ditch offer from God to give Ahaz a way out, saving the nation from needless tragedy—as though the Lord were saying, "What will it take to prove this to you?" The offer of a sign revealed God's grace and ongoing concern for Judah's destiny.

Is this a prediction of the Messiah? (7:14–16)

Like many prophecies, this passage seems to have a double meaning. First, a child, perhaps another son of Isaiah, would be born to a virgin (which could simply refer to a young woman) during the time of Ahaz. By the time he was grown, Judah's two enemies (Israel and Aram) would be destroyed. The second meaning was later applied to the birth of Christ (Matt. 1:23). The name *Immanuel, God with us,* became a title for the Messiah.

Why shave the hair of the Israelites? (7:20)

This was a metaphor that pictured the great shame Israel would experience at the hands of the Assyrians. Shaving, which here also included the genital areas, totally disgraced a soldier in the ancient world. Isaiah's prophecy meant that the Assyrians would leave Ahaz with nothing—not even the hairs on his body.

---

[a]2 Or *has set up camp in*   [b]3 *Shear-Jashub* means *a remnant will return.*   [c]14 The Hebrew is plural.   [d]14 Masoretic Text; Dead Sea Scrolls *and he* or *and they*   [e]14 *Immanuel* means *God with us.* [f]20 That is, the Euphrates   [g]23 That is, about 25 pounds (about 11.5 kilograms)

row, for the land will be covered with briers and thorns. ²⁵As for all the hills once cultivated by the hoe, you will no longer go there for fear of the briers and thorns; they will become places where cattle are turned loose and where sheep run.

Assyria, the LORD's Instrument

8 The LORD said to me, "Take a large scroll and write on it with an ordinary pen: Maher-Shalal-Hash-Baz.ᵃ ²And I will call in Uriah the priestᴰ and Zechariah son of Jeberekiah as reliable witnesses for me."

³Then I went to the prophetessᴰ, and she conceived and gave birth to a son. And the LORD said to me, "Name him Maher-Shalal-Hash-Baz. ⁴Before the boy knows how to say 'My father' or 'My mother,' the wealth of Damascus and the plunderᴰ of Samaria will be carried off by the king of Assyria."

⁵The LORD spoke to me again:

⁶"Because this people has rejected
  the gently flowing waters of Shiloah
and rejoices over Rezin
  and the son of Remaliah,
⁷therefore the Lord is about to bring against
    them
  the mighty floodwaters of the Riverᵇ—
  the king of Assyria with all his pomp.
It will overflow all its channels,
  run over all its banks
⁸and sweep on into Judah, swirling over it,
  passing through it and reaching up to the
    neck.
Its outspread wings will cover the breadth of
    your land,
  O Immanuelᶜ!"

⁹Raise the war cry,ᵈ you nations, and be
    shattered!
Listen, all you distant lands.
Prepare for battle, and be shattered!
Prepare for battle, and be shattered!
¹⁰Devise your strategy, but it will be thwarted;
  propose your plan, but it will not stand,
  for God is with us.ᵉ

Fear God

¹¹The LORD spoke to me with his strong hand upon me, warning me not to follow the way of this people. He said:

¹²"Do not call conspiracy
  everything that these people call
    conspiracyᶠ;
do not fear what they fear,
  and do not dread it.
¹³The LORD Almighty is the one you are to regard
    as holy,
  he is the one you are to fear,
  he is the one you are to dread,
¹⁴and he will be a sanctuary;
  but for both houses of Israel he will be
  a stone that causes men to stumble

Why give a name like this to a child? (8:3)

To the Israelites names were often connected with special characteristics or events and sometimes were even prophetic. In this case, God intended the child's name to signal the coming Assyrian conquest of Israel (see NIV text note, v. 1). Although we may think the name unusual, it marked a turning point in Israel's history, giving the child special significance. Actually this name suggested warrior-like qualities of strength and daring, far more desirable than some other Biblical names. See, for example, *Wouldn't a name that means not loved harm a child's self-esteem?* (Hosea 1:6).

Shiloah (8:6)

This slow stream flowed from the spring of Gihon along the southeast wall of Jerusalem. It was sharply contrasted to the *mighty floodwaters of the River* (v. 7), referring to the Euphrates, which flowed through the Assyrian capital. The *Shiloah* represented the peace of the Lord; the *floodwaters* represented the surging armies of Assyria.

The River (8:7)

The Euphrates (see *Map 7* at the back of this Bible). The river symbolizes the coming Assyrian destruction. See previous note.

Why does God seem to side with Israel's enemies? (8:7–8)

He had given Israel and Judah their chance, but they refused to put their trust in him. To punish his people, God permitted Assyria to ravage Israel.

Why the dramatic shift from utter defeat to victory? (8:9–10)

This dramatic shift plays on the phrase, *God with us,* or *Immanuel* (see NIV text note at 7:14). Isaiah delivered his message of coming judgment, but he could not help moving quickly, without transition, to a future time when the remnant of God's people (see NIV text note at 7:3) would return and God would be with Israel in victory.

ᵃ1 *Maher-Shalal-Hash-Baz* means *quick to the plunder, swift to the spoil*; also in verse 3.   ᵇ7 That is, the Euphrates   ᶜ8 *Immanuel* means *God with us.*   ᵈ9 Or *Do your worst*   ᵉ10 Hebrew *Immanuel*
ᶠ12 Or *Do not call for a treaty / every time these people call for a treaty*

and a rock that makes them fall.
And for the people of Jerusalem^D he will be
    a trap and a snare.
¹⁵Many of them will stumble;
    they will fall and be broken,
    they will be snared and captured."

¹⁶Bind up the testimony
    and seal up the law among my disciples^D.
¹⁷I will wait for the LORD,
    who is hiding his face from the house of
      Jacob.
    I will put my trust in him.

¹⁸Here am I, and the children the LORD has given me.
We are signs and symbols in Israel from the LORD Almighty, who dwells on Mount Zion^D.

¹⁹When men tell you to consult mediums^D and spiritists, who whisper and mutter, should not a people inquire of their God? Why consult the dead on behalf of the living? ²⁰To the law and to the testimony! If they do not speak according to this word, they have no light of dawn. ²¹Distressed and hungry, they will roam through the land; when they are famished, they will become enraged and, looking upward, will curse their king and their God. ²²Then they will look toward the earth and see only distress and darkness and fearful gloom, and they will be thrust into utter darkness.

To Us a Child Is Born

9 Nevertheless, there will be no more gloom for those who were in distress. In the past he humbled the land of Zebulun and the land of Naphtali, but in the future he will honor Galilee of the Gentiles, by the way of the sea, along the Jordan—

²The people walking in darkness
    have seen a great light;
on those living in the land of the shadow of
      death^{Da}
    a light has dawned.
³You have enlarged the nation
    and increased their joy;
they rejoice before you
    as people rejoice at the harvest,
as men rejoice
    when dividing the plunder^D.
⁴For as in the day of Midian's defeat,
    you have shattered
the yoke^D that burdens them,
    the bar across their shoulders,
    the rod of their oppressor.
⁵Every warrior's boot used in battle
    and every garment rolled in blood
will be destined for burning,
    will be fuel for the fire.
⁶For to us a child is born,
    to us a son is given,
    and the government will be on his shoulders.
And he will be called
    Wonderful Counselor,^b Mighty God,
    Everlasting Father, Prince of Peace^D.
⁷Of the increase of his government and peace

Seal up the law (8:16)

Some think this refers to the *large scroll* of v. 1 on which the judgment of Israel was written. If so, this would have been God's way of preserving the pronouncement of judgment that Ahaz refused to hear. Later, when it was fulfilled, it could prove that God was behind both the prophecy and the judgment.

How were Isaiah and his children signs and symbols? (8:18)

Isaiah and his sons and daughters were living testimonies to God's workings with his people. The meaning of their names would constantly put God's plan before the people of Israel. (See NIV text notes, 7:3,14; 8:1.) Isaiah later became a sign to the nation with his object lesson sermons. (See, for example, 20:2–3.)

Mediums and spiritists (8:19)

People through whom the spirit of a dead person was believed to communicate with the living. This practice was widespread among Israel's neighbors and was a constant temptation for Israel, especially when they were under the judgment of God.

Galilee of the Gentiles (9:1)

The name of one of the three provinces of the northern kingdom created by Tiglath-Pileser, the Assyrian general, when he plundered Israel in 733 B.C.

A great light (9:2)

Some see this phrase as a metaphor of God's saving action, believing it referred to future kings of Judah—like Hezekiah and Josiah—who would lead Israel back to God. Many, though, believe Isaiah was looking ahead to the future Messiah we now know to be Jesus Christ, who would arrive on the scene to break the bondage of sin. See 49:6; Luke 2:32; John 1:5 and 8:12.

How would God break the yoke of his people? (9:4)

Some think this prophecy referred to Israel's future liberation from foreigners who oppressed them. Others, though, believe the word yoke was a symbol for the heart's bondage to sin. It is in this sense that the Messiah, Jesus Christ, broke the yoke for all people with his death on the cross.

What child is this? (9:6)

Unlike the prophecy of 7:14–16 which had an immediate application as well as the later one, this prophecy spoke specifically of a coming Messiah. The names given to this child—Mighty God, Everlasting Father, Prince of Peace—allow no possibility for it to mean any other person.

^a2 Or *land of darkness*   ^b6 Or *Wonderful, Counselor*

as men gather abandoned eggs,
   so I gathered all the countries;
not one flapped a wing,
   or opened its mouth to chirp.' "

¹⁵Does the ax raise itself above him who swings
      it,
   or the saw boast against him who uses it?
As if a rod were to wield him who lifts it up,
   or a club brandish him who is not wood!
¹⁶Therefore, the Lord, the Lᴏʀᴅ Almighty,
   will send a wasting disease upon his sturdy
      warriors;
under his pomp a fire will be kindled
   like a blazing flame.
¹⁷The Light of Israel will become a fire,
   their Holy One a flame;
in a single day it will burn and consume
   his thorns and his briers.
¹⁸The splendor of his forests and fertile fields
   it will completely destroy,
   as when a sick man wastes away.
¹⁹And the remaining trees of his forests will be
      so few
   that a child could write them down.

The Remnant of Israel

²⁰In that day the remnantᴰ of Israel,
   the survivors of the house of Jacob,
will no longer rely on him
   who struck them down
but will truly rely on the Lᴏʀᴅ,
   the Holy One of Israel.
²¹A remnant will return,ᵃ a remnant of
      Jacob
   will return to the Mighty God.
²²Though your people, O Israel, be like the sand
      by the sea,
   only a remnant will return.
Destruction has been decreed,
   overwhelming and righteousᴰ.
²³The Lord, the Lᴏʀᴅ Almighty, will carry out
   the destruction decreed upon the whole land.

²⁴Therefore, this is what the Lord, the Lᴏʀᴅ Almighty,
says:

   "O my people who live in Zionᴰ,
      do not be afraid of the Assyrians,
   who beat you with a rod
      and lift up a club against you, as Egypt did.
²⁵Very soon my anger against you will end
   and my wrath will be directed to their
      destruction."

²⁶The Lᴏʀᴅ Almighty will lash them with a whip,
   as when he struck down Midian at the rock
      of Oreb;
and he will raise his staff over the waters,
   as he did in Egypt.
²⁷In that day their burden will be lifted from
      your shoulders,
   their yokeᴰ from your neck;

Who would be the remnant? (10:20)

Some believe the remnant was either the survivors of the fall of the northern kingdom or those who survived Nebuchadnezzar's invasion and sack of Jerusalem in 586 ʙ.ᴄ. Others, though, point to a future time when a remnant of Jewish people will return to a deep trust in God.

Why not fear the Assyrians? (10:24)

What Judah should fear is not the Assyrians—or any other enemy—but the Holy One of Israel (8:13). Here Isaiah was prophesying that a believing remnant would be saved. Even in the midst of judgment God offered comfort to his people. He called them to faith, not fear.

ᵃ21 Hebrew *shear-jashub*; also in verse 22

Why list these places? (10:28–34)

As we read these names, the details of this invasion begin to build the tension. These names trace the advancing Assyrian forces as they approached Jerusalem, from north to south (see *Assyria Threatens Jerusalem* on page 986). Then, just when the end was in sight, God decisively stepped in to halt the invaders at a foothill of Mount Zion.

the yoke^D will be broken
   because you have grown so fat.^a

28They enter Aiath;
   they pass through Migron;
   they store supplies at Micmash.
29They go over the pass, and say,
   "We will camp overnight at Geba."
Ramah trembles;
   Gibeah of Saul flees.
30Cry out, O Daughter of Gallim!
   Listen, O Laishah!
   Poor Anathoth!
31Madmenah is in flight;
   the people of Gebim take cover.
32This day they will halt at Nob;
   they will shake their fist
   at the mount of the Daughter of Zion^D,
   at the hill of Jerusalem^D.

33See, the Lord, the LORD Almighty,
   will lop off the boughs with great power.
The lofty trees will be felled,
   the tall ones will be brought low.
34He will cut down the forest thickets with an ax;
   Lebanon will fall before the Mighty One.

The Branch From Jesse

Stump of Jesse (11:1)

A picture of a family tree chopped down. God had promised David, Jesse's son, that his descendants would rule forever (2 Samuel 7:12–16). But when those descendants failed to meet the conditions of the promise, the tree was cut down.

Why call Jesse's descendant a branch? (11:1)

Isaiah played on the picture of a family tree. From the *stump of Jesse* a new branch would sprout, a future Messiah whom we now know as Jesus Christ (Matt. 16:16; Romans 1:2–4). Since the Messiah would be a branch of Jesse's family tree, the word *branch* became a Messianic title. The *Branch of the LORD* (4:2) also suggests the spiritual fruit produced by the Messiah.

When will justice finally occur? (11:4–5)

Isaiah anticipated a time when Christ would completely right all wrongs. While on earth, Christ began to establish justice by what he said and taught. His written Word continues to bring justice today wherever it is obeyed. Though justice on earth has begun, the scales won't be completely balanced until Christ returns the second time.

How can wolves live with lambs? (11:6–9)

Some believe this scene pictures a future time of universal peace—the *Millennium*—an earthly kingdom to be set up by Christ when he returns (see Rev. 20:1–6). Others think wolves may describe sinners who turn from their predatory ways to live in harmony with God's people, the lambs (Ezek. 34:25). This could refer to spiritual changes that bring individuals into God's kingdom now.

11 A shoot will come up from the stump of Jesse;
   from his roots a Branch will bear fruit.
2The Spirit of the LORD will rest on him—
   the Spirit of wisdom and of understanding,
   the Spirit of counsel and of power,
   the Spirit of knowledge and of the fear of the
      LORD—
3and he will delight in the fear of the LORD.

He will not judge by what he sees with his
      eyes,
   or decide by what he hears with his ears;
4but with righteousness^D he will judge the
      needy,
   with justice he will give decisions for the
      poor of the earth.
He will strike the earth with the rod of his
      mouth;
   with the breath of his lips he will slay the
      wicked.
5Righteousness will be his belt
   and faithfulness the sash around his waist.

6The wolf will live with the lamb,
   the leopard will lie down with the goat,
the calf and the lion and the yearling^b
      together;
   and a little child will lead them.
7The cow will feed with the bear,
   their young will lie down together,
   and the lion will eat straw like the ox.
8The infant will play near the hole of the cobra,
   and the young child put his hand into the
      viper's nest.
9They will neither harm nor destroy

a27 Hebrew; Septuagint broken / from your shoulders   *b6 Hebrew;
Septuagint lion will feed*

on all my holy mountain,
for the earth will be full of the knowledge of
the LORD
as the waters cover the sea.

¹⁰In that day the Root of Jesse will stand as a banner for the peoples; the nations will rally to him, and his place of rest will be glorious. ¹¹In that day the Lord will reach out his hand a second time to reclaim the remnant[D] that is left of his people from Assyria, from Lower Egypt, from Upper Egypt,[a] from Cush,[b] from Elam, from Babylonia,[c] from Hamath and from the islands of the sea.

¹²He will raise a banner for the nations
and gather the exiles[D] of Israel;
he will assemble the scattered people of Judah
from the four quarters of the earth.
¹³Ephraim's jealousy will vanish,
and Judah's enemies[d] will be cut off;
Ephraim will not be jealous of Judah,
nor Judah hostile toward Ephraim.
¹⁴They will swoop down on the slopes of
Philistia to the west;
together they will plunder[D] the people to
the east.
They will lay hands on Edom[D] and Moab,
and the Ammonites will be subject to them.
¹⁵The LORD will dry up
the gulf of the Egyptian sea;
with a scorching wind he will sweep his hand
over the Euphrates River.[e]
He will break it up into seven streams
so that men can cross over in sandals.
¹⁶There will be a highway for the remnant of
his people
that is left from Assyria,
as there was for Israel
when they came up from Egypt.

Songs of Praise

12 In that day you will say:

"I will praise you, O LORD.
Although you were angry with me,
your anger has turned away
and you have comforted me.
²Surely God is my salvation[D];
I will trust and not be afraid.
The LORD, the LORD, is my strength and my
song;
he has become my salvation."
³With joy you will draw water
from the wells of salvation.

⁴In that day you will say:

"Give thanks to the LORD, call on his name;
make known among the nations what he has
done,
and proclaim that his name is exalted.
⁵Sing to the LORD, for he has done glorious
things;
let this be known to all the world.

a11 Hebrew *from Pathros*   *b11* That is, the upper Nile region
c11 Hebrew *Shinar*   *d13* Or *hostility*   *e15* Hebrew *the River*

That day (11:10)

See *The day of the LORD* (13:6).

Is the second time yet to come? (11:11)

God first reclaimed Israel when he rescued them from Egypt. Some believe the second time is still in the future, when ethnic Jews will gather after Christ returns. Others, though, think the second time was when God's people, after being defeated and exiled to Babylon, were sent home by Cyrus, a Persian king, in 538 B.C.

What caused the feud between Ephraim and Judah? (11:13)

Following the rebellion that split Israel in two, Ephraim in the north remained rivals of Judah in the south (see *Map 4* at the back of this Bible). In Isaiah's day, animosity led to war when Ahaz, king of Judah, refused to join an alliance with Ephraim and Syria against their common enemy, Assyria. Some think the prophecy of an end to the feud was fulfilled when the Jews returned from captivity. Others, though, look ahead to a future Jewish reconciliation when Christ returns.

Why tell people what they will say? (12:1–6)

Isaiah was offering the people a broader perspective than the sufferings they were enduring. He wanted to encourage them with hope from God. A similar song of salvation came out of the first exodus (Exodus 15). In a sense, Isaiah compared Israel's new exodus from the nations with the old exodus from Egypt.

Was Isaiah a prophet or a poet? (12:1–6)

Both. Almost all prophecy is couched in poetry. This hymn, though, was probably not used in worship. It functioned solely as a prophetic tool to tell of future salvation.

That day (12:1)

See *The day of the LORD* (13:6).

Why are God's emotions so volatile? (12:1)

God is not distant and uninvolved; he cares intensely about his relationship with us. If he were indifferent about our sin, for example, his apathy would show he didn't care about us as his people. To increase the impact of his writing, Isaiah intentionally pictured God's emotions from opposite ends of the spectrum.

⁶Shout aloud and sing for joy, people of Zion^D,
    for great is the Holy One of Israel among
        you."

A Prophecy Against Babylon

13 An oracle^D concerning Babylon that Isaiah son of
    Amoz saw:

²Raise a banner on a bare hilltop,
    shout to them;
beckon to them
    to enter the gates of the nobles.
³I have commanded my holy ones;
    I have summoned my warriors to carry out
        my wrath—
    those who rejoice in my triumph.

⁴Listen, a noise on the mountains,
    like that of a great multitude!
Listen, an uproar among the kingdoms,
    like nations massing together!
The LORD Almighty is mustering
    an army for war.
⁵They come from faraway lands,
    from the ends of the heavens—
the LORD and the weapons of his wrath—
    to destroy the whole country.

⁶Wail, for the day of the LORD^D is near;
    it will come like destruction from the
        Almighty.^a
⁷Because of this, all hands will go limp,
    every man's heart will melt.
⁸Terror will seize them,
    pain and anguish will grip them;
    they will writhe like a woman in labor.
They will look aghast at each other,
    their faces aflame.

⁹See, the day of the LORD is coming
    —a cruel day, with wrath and fierce anger—
to make the land desolate
    and destroy the sinners within it.
¹⁰The stars of heaven and their constellations
    will not show their light.
The rising sun will be darkened
    and the moon will not give its light.
¹¹I will punish the world for its evil,
    the wicked for their sins.
I will put an end to the arrogance of the
        haughty
    and will humble the pride of the ruthless.
¹²I will make man scarcer than pure gold,
    more rare than the gold of Ophir.
¹³Therefore I will make the heavens tremble;
    and the earth will shake from its place
at the wrath of the LORD Almighty,
    in the day of his burning anger.

¹⁴Like a hunted gazelle,
    like sheep without a shepherd,
each will return to his own people,
    each will flee to his native land.
¹⁵Whoever is captured will be thrust through;

Oracle (13:1)

A message from God; in some cases, the word suggests unwelcome news or judgment.

Why was Babylon's future important to Isaiah? (13:1)

Babylon's future directly affected Jerusalem's future. Though God had earlier defeated Israel's enemies, he was now handing his people over to them. Isaiah's readers, seeing Babylon as a symbol of pagan religion and culture, needed assurance that Jerusalem and the Lord would triumph, not Babylon and its god, Marduk.

Who are God's warriors? (13:3)

The victorious armies of the earth used by God to judge evil nations—including unrepentant Israel. These victorious armies are called *holy ones* not because of their righteous behavior, but because God had sanctified them to carry out judgment. The armies may or may not have been aware of their special role.

The day of the Lord (13:6)

Any specific time when God, the divine Warrior, is victorious (Ezek. 30:2–4; Amos 5:18). This is different from the phrase *in that day*, which refers to the day of Israel's blessings (11:10; 12:1). Here *the day of the Lord* is equated with impending judgment against Babylon.

Why hold the world accountable for sin? (13:9–11)

Why punish those who never heard God's Word? Even though God did not put his law into writing for the whole world, he did plant moral principles in their hearts (Romans 2:14–15). See article: *What happens to good people who never had a chance to hear?* (Romans 2:14–16). Also see *Will judgment be easier for some than others?* (Matt. 11:22).

Why darken the sun, moon and stars? (13:10)

To judge the world. These graphic images illustrate doomsday language in the extreme—a picture of absolute devastation. Many see these words fulfilled figuratively during Isaiah's time. For them, the cosmic darkness, associated with *the day of the Lord*, is a literary symbol of God's dark judgment—the coming captivity. Others, though, see this as a literal darkness that will be fulfilled in a future tribulation. See also Jer. 4:23; Joel 2:10,31; Rev. 6:12–13.

Who would flee? (13:14)

The Assyrians. As their empire broke apart, their imperial army, which consisted of mercenaries hired from conquered nations, also would dissolve.

---

^a6 Hebrew *Shaddai*

all who are caught will fall by the sword.
16Their infants will be dashed to pieces before
their eyes;
their houses will be looted and their wives
ravished.

17See, I will stir up against them the Medes,
who do not care for silver
and have no delight in gold.
18Their bows will strike down the young men;
they will have no mercyᴰ on infants
nor will they look with compassion on
children.
19Babylon, the jewel of kingdoms,
the gloryᴰ of the Babylonians'ᵃ pride,
will be overthrown by God
like Sodom and Gomorrah.
20She will never be inhabited
or lived in through all generations;
no Arab will pitch his tent there,
no shepherd will rest his flocks there.
21But desert creatures will lie there,
jackals will fill her houses;
there the owls will dwell,
and there the wild goats will leap about.
22Hyenas will howl in her strongholdsᴰ,
jackals in her luxurious palaces.
Her time is at hand,
and her days will not be prolonged.

14 The LORD will have compassion on Jacob;
once again he will choose Israel
and will settle them in their own land.
Aliens will join them
and unite with the house of Jacob.
2Nations will take them
and bring them to their own place.
And the house of Israel will possess the nations
as menservants and maidservants in the
LORD's land.
They will make captives of their captors
and rule over their oppressors.

ᵃ19 Or *Chaldeans'*

Why does God permit the innocent to suffer? (13:16)

There are no simple answers, but several things can be considered in this case: (1) Isaiah may have been using extreme imagery to demonstrate how terrible the day of the Lord would be. (2) Isaiah may have been speaking literally. In his day people did not see children and women as individuals, but as a part of their culture. (3) This was strictly a matter of justice—an eye for an eye, a tooth for a tooth. What the Babylonians had done to others would now be done to them. Also see article: *Who would smash babies for revenge?* (Psalm 137:8–9).

Has Babylon remained uninhabitable? (13:19–20)

The Medes destroyed Babylon in 539 B.C. and it remained insignificant until it was completely abandoned sometime after A.D. 100. Not much of Babylon has ever even been found. It is thought to be buried under silt from the Tigris River.

How were Israelites to treat their neighbors? (14:1–2)

God used the Israelites as his instrument to dispense either judgment or grace on their neighbors. God instructed Israel to first make an offer of peace to those whom they marched against (Deut. 20:10–18). If peace was accepted, the Israelites then laid down their arms. If not, they stormed the city and killed the inhabitants. In this way, Israel became an agent of divine wrath and was called to punish those who resisted God's plan and worshiped idols.

On the other hand, the Israelites were to treat their repentant neighbors as partners of God's promises. In the exodus from Egypt, the Israelites welcomed those nations that joined them in their faith (Exodus 12:38). In the second exodus from Babylon, they gratefully acknowledged the help of those nations that played a role in helping them return to their homeland (41:1–29; 44:28–45:1). Also see 55:5; 60:1–7; 66:19–20.

Why describe the destruction of these nations? (14:3–27)

After unleashing his anger against his own people, God expressed his anger against the nations who had relished their role in punishing Israel. At one time, the nations feared Israel's God because he had given military victories to Israel. Now they would recognize his sovereign power through the words of his prophets. Also see *Why was Babylon's future important to Isaiah?* (13:1).

Does this describe the fall of Satan? (14:12–15)

Some think this should be linked to Satan's fall (Luke 10:18). Others see the morning star —meaning the planet Venus—as a metaphor that describes the king of Babylon (v. 4). The planet aspired to climb to the highest point in the sky, just as the Assyrian king Sennacherib —who conquered Babylon and called himself the "king of Babylon"—desired to rule the entire world. Venus's light was extinguished by the increasing brightness of the rising sun just as Sennacherib's plans were frustrated and dimmed. Also see *Is this a picture of Satan?* (Ezek. 28:13).

³On the day the Lord gives you relief from suffering and turmoil and cruel bondage, ⁴you will take up this taunt against the king of Babylon:

How the oppressor has come to an end!
  How his fury[a] has ended!
⁵The Lord has broken the rod of the wicked,
  the scepter[D] of the rulers,
⁶which in anger struck down peoples
  with unceasing blows,
and in fury subdued nations
  with relentless aggression.
⁷All the lands are at rest and at peace[D];
  they break into singing.
⁸Even the pine trees and the cedars of Lebanon
  exult over you and say,
"Now that you have been laid low,
  no woodsman comes to cut us down."

⁹The grave[b] below is all astir
  to meet you at your coming;
it rouses the spirits of the departed to greet
      you—
  all those who were leaders in the world;
it makes them rise from their thrones—
  all those who were kings over the nations.
¹⁰They will all respond,
  they will say to you,
"You also have become weak, as we are;
  you have become like us."
¹¹All your pomp has been brought down to the
      grave,
  along with the noise of your harps;
maggots are spread out beneath you
  and worms cover you.

¹²How you have fallen from heaven,
  O morning star, son of the dawn!
You have been cast down to the earth,
  you who once laid low the nations!
¹³You said in your heart,
  "I will ascend to heaven;
I will raise my throne
  above the stars of God;
I will sit enthroned on the mount of assembly,
  on the utmost heights of the sacred[D]
      mountain.[c]
¹⁴I will ascend above the tops of the clouds;
  I will make myself like the Most High."
¹⁵But you are brought down to the grave,
  to the depths of the pit.

¹⁶Those who see you stare at you,
  they ponder your fate:
"Is this the man who shook the earth
  and made kingdoms tremble,
¹⁷the man who made the world a desert,
  who overthrew its cities
and would not let his captives go home?"

¹⁸All the kings of the nations lie in state,
  each in his own tomb.

---

a4 Dead Sea Scrolls, Septuagint and Syriac; the meaning of the word in the Masoretic Text is uncertain.   *b9* Hebrew *Sheol*; also in verses 11 and 15   *c13* Or *the north*; Hebrew *Zaphon*

¹⁹But you are cast out of your tomb
  like a rejected branch;
you are covered with the slain,
  with those pierced by the sword,
  those who descend to the stones of the pit.
Like a corpse trampled underfoot,
²⁰ you will not join them in burial,
for you have destroyed your land
  and killed your people.

The offspring of the wicked
  will never be mentioned again.
²¹Prepare a place to slaughter his sons
  for the sins of their forefathers;
they are not to rise to inherit the land
  and cover the earth with their cities.

²²"I will rise up against them,"
  declares the LORD Almighty.
"I will cut off from Babylon her name and
    survivors,
  her offspring and descendants,"
                    declares the LORD.
²³"I will turn her into a place for owls
  and into swampland;
I will sweep her with the broom of
    destruction,"
  declares the LORD Almighty.

A Prophecy Against Assyria

²⁴The LORD Almighty has sworn,

"Surely, as I have planned, so it will be,
  and as I have purposed, so it will stand.
²⁵I will crush the Assyrian in my land;
  on my mountains I will trample him down.
His yoke[D] will be taken from my people,
  and his burden removed from their
    shoulders."

²⁶This is the plan determined for the whole
    world;
  this is the hand stretched out over all
    nations.
²⁷For the LORD Almighty has purposed, and who
    can thwart him?
His hand is stretched out, and who can turn
    it back?

A Prophecy Against the Philistines

²⁸This oracle[D] came in the year King Ahaz died:

²⁹Do not rejoice, all you Philistines,
  that the rod that struck you is broken;
from the root of that snake will spring up a
    viper,
  its fruit will be a darting, venomous serpent.
³⁰The poorest of the poor will find pasture,
  and the needy will lie down in safety.
But your root I will destroy by famine;
  it will slay your survivors.

³¹Wail, O gate! Howl, O city!
  Melt away, all you Philistines!
A cloud of smoke comes from the north,
  and there is not a straggler in its ranks.

Why should children pay for the sins of their father? (14:21)
See the articles: *Does God punish children for their parents' sins?* (Num. 14:18) and *Why does God allow innocent children to suffer?* (Lam. 2:11–12).

Oracle (14:28)
See *Oracle* (13:1).

Why did the Philistines want to rejoice? (14:29)
They rejoiced because the rod that struck them —King Sargon II of Assyria (10:5)—had died. The Philistines celebrated the temporary weakness in the Assyrian dominance. The viper probably refers to Sargon II's son Sennacherib, who would quickly end the Philistines' rejoicing. Also see *Sargon* (20:1).

³²What answer shall be given
   to the envoys of that nation?
"The Lord has established Zion^D,
   and in her his afflicted^D people will find
      refuge."

A Prophecy Against Moab

15 An oracle^D concerning Moab:

Ar in Moab is ruined,
   destroyed in a night!
Kir in Moab is ruined,
   destroyed in a night!
²Dibon goes up to its temple,
   to its high places^D to weep;
Moab wails over Nebo and Medeba.
Every head is shaved
   and every beard cut off.
³In the streets they wear sackcloth^D;
   on the roofs and in the public squares
they all wail,
   prostrate with weeping.
⁴Heshbon and Elealeh cry out,
   their voices are heard all the way to Jahaz.
Therefore the armed men of Moab cry out,
   and their hearts are faint.

⁵My heart cries out over Moab;
   her fugitives flee as far as Zoar,
   as far as Eglath Shelishiyah.
They go up the way to Luhith,
   weeping as they go;
on the road to Horonaim
   they lament^D their destruction.
⁶The waters of Nimrim are dried up
   and the grass is withered;
the vegetation is gone
   and nothing green is left.
⁷So the wealth they have acquired and stored up

Why detail Moab's destruction? (15:1–4)

See *Why describe the destruction of these nations?* (14:3–27).

Why did Isaiah feel so bad about Moab's plight? (15:5)

Several reasons may have softened Isaiah's heart to Moab's pain. Israel and Moab shared the same ancestral father, Terah (Gen. 11:27; 19:37; Deut. 2:9), and King David's great-grandmother, Ruth, had come from Moab (1 Samuel 22:3–4). Furthermore, unlike Edom, the Bible never mentions Moab rejoicing over Israel's misfortunes.

What do ancient oracles have to do with us today? (15:1–9)

Isaiah's oracles teach several important truths, still relevant centuries later. First, God rules over all nations; he's not a local deity or a territorial god. Despite appearances at times to the contrary, God has his hand in the intricate details of our lives as well as the broad strokes of human history. God's message of hope is for people of all nations and ethnic backgrounds.

Second, God rules by his prophetic Word, which is sharp and powerful (Heb. 4:12–13). Through obedience to God's Word, we can promote God's will in our lives and bring justice to our neighborhoods.

Third, God has the last word. The pretenses and rebellion of modern society will burst like a soap bubble. Those who ignore God's Word will be judged at the end of the age. All evil will have its day in court.

Finally, those who have trusted Christ, living in obedience to his Word, are not under judgment. If we personally and intimately know the One who gives prophetic words, and if we live by his mercy, we can rest securely in his unconditional love. Also see article: *What do ancient visions mean to us today?* (Zech. 1:8).

they carry away over the Ravine of the
  Poplars.
8Their outcry echoes along the border of Moab;
  their wailing reaches as far as Eglaim,
  their lamentation as far as Beer Elim.
9Dimon's*a* waters are full of blood,
  but I will bring still more upon Dimon*a*—
a lion upon the fugitives of Moab
  and upon those who remain in the land.

16 Send lambs as tribute
  to the ruler of the land,
from Sela, across the desert,
  to the mount of the Daughter of Zion^D.
2Like fluttering birds
  pushed from the nest,
so are the women of Moab
  at the fords of the Arnon.

3"Give us counsel,
  render a decision.
Make your shadow like night—
  at high noon.
Hide the fugitives,
  do not betray the refugees.
4Let the Moabite fugitives stay with you;
  be their shelter from the destroyer."

The oppressor will come to an end,
  and destruction will cease;
  the aggressor will vanish from the land.
5In love a throne will be established;
  in faithfulness a man will sit on it—
one from the house*b* of David—
one who in judging seeks justice
  and speeds the cause of righteousness^D.

6We have heard of Moab's pride—
  her overweening pride and conceit,
her pride and her insolence—
  but her boasts are empty.
7Therefore the Moabites wail,
  they wail together for Moab.
Lament and grieve
  for the men*c* of Kir Hareseth.
8The fields of Heshbon wither,
  the vines of Sibmah also.
The rulers of the nations
  have trampled down the choicest vines,
which once reached Jazer
  and spread toward the desert.
Their shoots spread out
  and went as far as the sea.
9So I weep, as Jazer weeps,
  for the vines of Sibmah.
O Heshbon, O Elealeh,
  I drench you with tears!
The shouts of joy over your ripened fruit
  and over your harvests have been stilled.
10Joy and gladness are taken away from the
  orchards;

Why aid Moabites under God's judgment? (16:3–5)

Moab's fugitives wanted to escape judgment by submitting to the Lord's rule (v. 1). Called to be a light to the nations, in this case Israel fulfilled its role as an agent of God's mercy. Like Israel, Moab—in contrast to Babylon, Assyria and Philistia—had a remnant (14:30), a small group of faithful believers.

How could Moabites belong to Israel's Messiah? (16:5)

Moab, having come to Zion and suffered injustices at the hands of a tyrannical oppressor, would find justice through Israel's Messiah. This passage promises that the Messiah will bring salvation to all the earth—including the fugitives from Moab. In fact, the hope of the world lies in Israel's God (9:2–7; 11:1–9).

What did Moab have to boast about? (16:6)

This insignificant nation was only a whimper compared to the roaring of other nations such as Assyria. Moab's pride was based on its own feelings of self-importance, not reality. Inflated opinions of oneself, particularly when set alongside shriveled resources and abilities, demonstrate how ridiculous human boasting is.

How was Moab trampled down? (16:8)

The Assyrian king, Sargon II, put down a rebellion along its western border states (716 B.C.) and probably squelched Moab in the process.

a9 Masoretic Text; Dead Sea Scrolls, some Septuagint manuscripts and Vulgate *Dibon*   *b5* Hebrew *tent*   *c7* Or *"raisin cakes,"* a wordplay

no one sings or shouts in the vineyards;
no one treads out wine at the presses,
    for I have put an end to the shouting.
¹¹My heart laments^D for Moab like a harp,
    my inmost being for Kir Hareseth.
¹²When Moab appears at her high place,
    she only wears herself out;
when she goes to her shrine to pray,
    it is to no avail.

¹³This is the word the LORD has already spoken concerning Moab. ¹⁴But now the LORD says: "Within three years, as a servant bound by contract would count them, Moab's splendor and all her many people will be despised, and her survivors will be very few and feeble."

An Oracle Against Damascus

17 An oracle^D concerning Damascus:

"See, Damascus will no longer be a city
    but will become a heap of ruins.
²The cities of Aroer will be deserted
    and left to flocks, which will lie down,
    with no one to make them afraid.
³The fortified city will disappear from Ephraim,
    and royal power from Damascus;
the remnant^D of Aram will be
    like the glory^D of the Israelites,"
            declares the LORD Almighty.

⁴"In that day the glory of Jacob will fade;
    the fat of his body will waste away.
⁵It will be as when a reaper gathers the standing
        grain
    and harvests the grain with his arm—
as when a man gleans heads of grain
    in the Valley of Rephaim.
⁶Yet some gleanings will remain,
    as when an olive tree is beaten,
leaving two or three olives on the topmost
        branches,
    four or five on the fruitful boughs,"
            declares the LORD, the God of Israel.

⁷In that day men will look to their Maker
    and turn their eyes to the Holy One of Israel.
⁸They will not look to the altars,
    the work of their hands,
and they will have no regard for the Asherah
        poles^{Da}
    and the incense^D altars their fingers have
        made.

⁹In that day their strong cities, which they left because of the Israelites, will be like places abandoned to thickets and undergrowth. And all will be desolation.

¹⁰You have forgotten God your Savior;
    you have not remembered the Rock, your
        fortress.
Therefore, though you set out the finest plants
    and plant imported vines,
¹¹though on the day you set them out, you make
        them grow,

Oracle (17:1)
See *Oracle* (13:1).

How was Damascus reduced to ruins? (17:1)
In 732 B.C., the Assyrian king, Tiglath-Pileser III, responding to pleas from Judah's king Ahaz for military support, razed Damascus (7:16; 2 Kings 16:9).

Aroer (17:2)
A Moabite city east of the Dead Sea on the Arnon River which flows into the Dead Sea (see **Map 4** at the back of this Bible).

Why was Ephraim included in the oracle against Damascus? (17:3)
Ephraim—a tribe representative of the northern kingdom of Israel—had joined in a military alliance with Damascus (7:1). As a result, the prophecy was given against both kingdoms.

How would Aram's remnant *be like the glory of the Israelites*? (17:3–6)
Isaiah is being sarcastic—and goes on to describe what he really means—exactly the opposite (vv. 4–6). *Glory* was used to describe any power or splendor that gives social weight, respect and esteem. The remnant of Aram (Syria), those surviving Assyria's destruction of Damascus and their nation, would have no glory whatsoever.

Whom did this revival describe? (17:7–8)
Since Damascus, the capital of Aram (Syria), was allied with Ephraim (the northern kingdom), the oracle was against both of them (see **Map 4** at the back of this Bible). This revival, then, primarily referred to Israelites returning to their God. A remnant of Aram may also have found salvation along with Israel—like Moab's fugitives (16:3–4). No information exists, however, about whether or not a small group from Damascus might have looked to Israel for salvation.

Hadn't Damascus always been pagan? (17:10)
Yes, but this oracle was directed at Damascus *and* Ephraim. This indictment was directed against the northern kingdom (17:4). The Israelites had *forgotten God* their Savior.

---

^a8 That is, symbols of the goddess Asherah

and on the morning when you plant them,
    you bring them to bud,
yet the harvest will be as nothing
    in the day of disease and incurable pain.

¹²Oh, the raging of many nations—
    they rage like the raging sea!
Oh, the uproar of the peoples—
    they roar like the roaring of great waters!
¹³Although the peoples roar like the roar of
        surging waters,
    when he rebukes them they flee far away,
driven before the wind like chaffᴰ on the hills,
    like tumbleweed before a gale.
¹⁴In the evening, sudden terror!
    Before the morning, they are gone!
This is the portion of those who loot us,
    the lot of those who plunderᴰ us.

A Prophecy Against Cush

18 Woe to the land of whirring wingsᵃ
        along the rivers of Cush,ᵇ
    ²which sends envoys by sea
        in papyrus boats over the water.

Go, swift messengers,
to a people tall and smooth-skinned,
    to a people feared far and wide,
an aggressive nation of strange speech,
    whose land is divided by rivers.

³All you people of the world,
    you who live on the earth,
when a banner is raised on the mountains,
    you will see it,
and when a trumpet sounds,
    you will hear it.
⁴This is what the LORD says to me:
    "I will remain quiet and will look on from
        my dwelling place,
like shimmering heat in the sunshine,
    like a cloud of dew in the heat of harvest."
⁵For, before the harvest, when the blossom is
        gone
    and the flower becomes a ripening grape,
he will cut off the shoots with pruning knives,
    and cut down and take away the spreading
        branches.
⁶They will all be left to the mountain birds of
        prey
    and to the wild animals;
the birds will feed on them all summer,
    the wild animals all winter.

⁷At that time gifts will be brought to the LORD Almighty

from a people tall and smooth-skinned,
    from a people feared far and wide,
an aggressive nation of strange speech,
    whose land is divided by rivers—

the gifts will be brought to Mount Zionᴰ, the place of the
Name of the LORD Almighty.

The land of whirring wings (18:1)
This may refer either to insects (locusts) or
ships. Some ancient translations of this passage interpreted *whirring wings* as a figure of
speech for boats with canvas sails flapping in
the wind.

**Who were these tall and smooth-
skinned people? (18:2)**
The Hebrew is uncertain here, making the identification of these people difficult. Some think
it might refer to the peoples along the Nile River. Or the reference could be to the Assyrians
or Medes. Or the phrase might possibly be a
figure of speech to mean human kingdoms in
general.

**Why would foreigners give gifts to the
Lord? (18:7)**
Grateful to the Lord for defeating the Assyrians, these people would give gifts that
amounted to tribute (2 Chron. 32:22–23). Giving tribute included the idea of submission,
just as a defeated nation submits to the conquering nation. These peoples would give because they would submit to the Lord.

ᵃ1 Or *of locusts*   ᵇ1 That is, the upper Nile region

A Prophecy About Egypt

Oracle (19:1)
See *Oracle* (13:1).

19 An oracle[D] concerning Egypt:

See, the LORD rides on a swift cloud
    and is coming to Egypt.
The idols[D] of Egypt tremble before him,
    and the hearts of the Egyptians melt within
        them.

²"I will stir up Egyptian against Egyptian—
    brother will fight against brother,
    neighbor against neighbor,
    city against city,
    kingdom against kingdom.
³The Egyptians will lose heart,
    and I will bring their plans to nothing;
they will consult the idols and the spirits of
        the dead,
    the mediums[D] and the spiritists.
⁴I will hand the Egyptians over
    to the power of a cruel master,
and a fierce king will rule over them,"
    declares the Lord, the LORD Almighty.

⁵The waters of the river will dry up,
    and the riverbed will be parched and dry.
⁶The canals will stink;
    the streams of Egypt will dwindle and dry
        up.
The reeds and rushes will wither,
⁷   also the plants along the Nile,
    at the mouth of the river.
Every sown field along the Nile
    will become parched, will blow away and be
        no more.
⁸The fishermen will groan and lament[D],
    all who cast hooks into the Nile;
those who throw nets on the water
    will pine away.
⁹Those who work with combed flax will despair,
    the weavers of fine linen will lose hope.
¹⁰The workers in cloth will be dejected,
    and all the wage earners will be sick at heart.

¹¹The officials of Zoan are nothing but fools;
    the wise counselors of Pharaoh give
        senseless advice.
How can you say to Pharaoh,
    "I am one of the wise men,
    a disciple[D] of the ancient kings"?

¹²Where are your wise men now?
    Let them show you and make known
what the LORD Almighty
    has planned against Egypt.
¹³The officials of Zoan have become fools,
    the leaders of Memphis[a] are deceived;
the cornerstones of her peoples
    have led Egypt astray.
¹⁴The LORD has poured into them
    a spirit of dizziness;
they make Egypt stagger in all that she does,
    as a drunkard staggers around in his vomit.

What happened to the Egyptians? (19:5–10)
In addition to being invaded by Sargon II, the Egyptians had most likely experienced a drought. The so-called gods of Egypt had failed. The Nile had dried up and caused economic collapse throughout the country.

Why use the term *women* as a put-down? (19:16)
In Isaiah's world, women were defenseless. With no means of protecting themselves, women often suffered the brunt of horrific abuse from conquering armies. Facing such calamities, women became consumed with terror. To compare the Egyptians to women was an insult to the men, who, like defenseless women, would be defenseless and afraid before the wrath of the Lord.

Why would Egyptians speak Hebrew? (19:18)
To show their submission. By abandoning their own language and speaking like God's people, they surrendered their own ways to follow God's ways. Their speech revealed a radical transformation—former enemies would become allies. Some see this as something yet to come in the future. Others believe it was fulfilled when God miraculously spared Jerusalem under King Hezekiah (see ch. 37). Still others apply it to Christ's kingdom today, as all have opportunity to worship God (2:2–4; Romans 10:12–13).

a 13 Hebrew *Noph*

15There is nothing Egypt can do—
    head or tail, palm branch or reed.

16In that day the Egyptians will be like women. They will shudder with fear at the uplifted hand that the LORD Almighty raises against them. **17**And the land of Judah will bring terror to the Egyptians; everyone to whom Judah is mentioned will be terrified, because of what the LORD Almighty is planning against them.

18In that day five cities in Egypt will speak the language of Canaan and swear allegiance to the LORD Almighty. One of them will be called the City of Destruction.ᵃ

19In that day there will be an altar to the LORD in the heart of Egypt, and a monument to the LORD at its border. **20**It will be a sign and witness to the LORD Almighty in the land of Egypt. When they cry out to the LORD because of their oppressors, he will send them a savior and defender, and he will rescue them. **21**So the LORD will make himself known to the Egyptians, and in that day they will acknowledge the LORD. They will worship with sacrificesᴰ and grain offeringsᴰ; they will make vowsᴰ to the LORD and keep them. **22**The LORD will strike Egypt with a plague; he will strike them and heal them. They will turn to the LORD, and he will respond to their pleas and heal them.

23In that day there will be a highway from Egypt to Assyria. The Assyrians will go to Egypt and the Egyptians to Assyria. The Egyptians and Assyrians will worship together. **24**In that day Israel will be the third, along with Egypt and Assyria, a blessing on the earth. **25**The LORD Almighty will bless them, saying, "Blessed be Egypt my people, Assyria my handiwork, and Israel my inheritance."

A Prophecy Against Egypt and Cush

20 In the year that the supreme commander, sent by Sargon king of Assyria, came to Ashdod and attacked and captured it— **2**at that time the LORD spoke through Isaiah son of Amoz. He said to him, "Take off the sacklothᴰ from your body and the sandals from your feet." And he did so, going around stripped and barefoot.

3Then the LORD said, "Just as my servant Isaiah has gone stripped and barefoot for three years, as a sign and portent against Egypt and Cush,ᵇ **4**so the king of Assyria will lead away stripped and barefoot the Egyptian captives and Cushite exilesᴰ, young and old, with buttocks bared—to Egypt's shame. **5**Those who trusted in Cush and boasted in Egypt will be afraid and put to shame. **6**In that day the people who live on this coast will say, 'See what has happened to those we relied on, those we fled to for help and deliverance from the king of Assyria! How then can we escape?' "

A Prophecy Against Babylon

21 An oracleᴰ concerning the Desert by the Sea:

    Like whirlwinds sweeping through the
        southland,
    an invader comes from the desert,
        from a land of terror.

    2A dire visionᴰ has been shown to me:

ᵃ18 Most manuscripts of the Masoretic Text; some manuscripts of the Masoretic Text, Dead Sea Scrolls and Vulgate *City of the Sun* (that is, Heliopolis)   ᵇ3 That is, the upper Nile region; also in verse 5

The City of Destruction (19:18)

Most likely this refers to the Egyptian city called Heliopolis (see **Map 3** at the back of this Bible), which literally meant the *city of the sun*. The Hebrew word for *sun* is almost identical to the word for *destruction*. Some think Isaiah and other Jewish writers used the similar sounds as a play on words to insult the city.

Did Isaiah expect revival among the pagans? (19:19–25)

Yes. God promised as much when he called Abraham to be a light to the nations, promising blessings through his provision (Gen. 12:2–3). Today nations are being converted to the God of Israel through the ministry of the church (Matt. 28:18–20; Romans 15:8–12).

Why strike worshipers only to heal them again? (19:22)

Some confusion may arise because these verses are not arranged in strict chronological order. This verse explains the circumstances that caused Egypt to turn to the Lord (v. 21). Egypt was disciplined *before* their salvation, not *after*, as the order of the verses seems to suggest. Divine discipline often serves to draw one closer to the Lord (30:26; Hosea 6:1).

Sargon (20:1)

From 721 to 705 B.C., Sargon II ruled Assyria. Ashdod, a leading Philistine city, had rebelled against Assyria but succumbed to Sargon II in 711 B.C. An inscription mentioning Sargon by name has been unearthed at Ashdod. Also see *Why did the Philistines want to rejoice?* (14:29).

Why did God have Isaiah take off his clothes? (20:2)

Drastic measures were needed to make an important point—that Judah could not rely on Egypt and Cush nor join in their rebellion against Assyria. Using the object lesson of a captive stripped naked, Isaiah vividly warned Hezekiah about what could happen. The phrase *three years* (v. 3) actually meant *involving three years*, at least 14 months.

Did Isaiah go completely nude? (20:2)

Isaiah was role-playing the part of captives, often stripped of their clothes and belongings as they were herded into exile. Though probably not completely nude, he was undoubtedly shamed. *Stripped* means uncovered buttocks, a sign of humiliation (2 Samuel 10:4). At the very least, Isaiah took off his sackcloth, the distinctive garb of prophets (Zech. 13:4). Also see *Why did prophets wear eccentric clothes?* (2 Kings 1:8).

Why prohibit a military alliance with Egypt and Cush? (20:5–6)

For two reasons: (1) Isaiah foresaw that an insurrection against Assyria would end in failure. That, in fact, proved to be the case. (2) Isaiah wanted Hezekiah to choose between trusting foreign allies or trusting God. He could not do both at the same time.

Desert by the Sea (21:1)

This mysterious description could be a reference to Babylon, a desert empire just north of the Persian Gulf (see **Map 7** at the back of this Bible).

What caused Isaiah to tremble? (21:3–4)

These words might symbolize the horrors Babylon would suffer when foreign armies would invade it. More likely they describe Isaiah's reaction to his vision of seeing the Babylonians die. He showed great compassion for the enemy, though God had said Babylon would utterly destroy Jerusalem. Like other prophets, Isaiah waited anxiously for the *twilight*—the fall of Babylon. But he was unprepared for the gruesome images of Babylon's dying human beings.

SCRIPTURE LINK (21:5) They set the tables

Read about a feast in the royal courts of Babylon the night before it fell (Daniel 5:1–4).

Oil the shields (21:5)

Most shields in Old Testament times were made of wood or wicker frames covered with hides. Some were reinforced with metal in the center and around the edges. Left unoiled, the leather covering became brittle and easier to pierce in combat.

The traitor betrays, the looter takes loot.
Elam, attack! Media, lay siege!
  I will bring to an end all the groaning she
    caused.

³At this my body is racked with pain,
  pangs seize me, like those of a woman in
    labor;
I am staggered by what I hear,
  I am bewildered by what I see.
⁴My heart falters,
  fear makes me tremble;
the twilight I longed for
  has become a horror to me.

⁵They set the tables,
  they spread the rugs,
  they eat, they drink!
Get up, you officers,
  oil the shields!

⁶This is what the Lord says to me:

"Go, post a lookout
  and have him report what he sees.
⁷When he sees chariots
  with teams of horses,
riders on donkeys
  or riders on camels,
let him be alert,
  fully alert."

⁸And the lookout*ᵃ* shouted,

"Day after day, my lord, I stand on the
    watchtower*ᴰ*;
every night I stay at my post.
⁹Look, here comes a man in a chariot
  with a team of horses.
And he gives back the answer:
  'Babylon has fallen, has fallen!

ᵃ8 Dead Sea Scrolls and Syriac; Masoretic Text *A lion*

What can we learn from ancient prophecies? (21:1)

Prophecy teaches us lessons, much as history does. When we see the parallels between our times and the Israelites', we can benefit from the things they learned.

For instance, prophecy offers a glimpse of how seriously God takes sin. A holy God cannot leave sin unpunished indefinitely. Sinners must either be forgiven or face a day of judgment.

Prophecy also reveals the danger of specific sins. Israel, for example, desiring to be self-sufficient, often was reluctant to trust in God. If their crops didn't grow or their wives didn't conceive, they would turn to fertility gods for solutions. If neighboring armies strapped on body armor, the Israelites would make treaties with pagan allies instead of trusting in God (Lev. 26:7–8; Isaiah 31:1).

Prophecies sometimes show us examples of God's patience and mercy. He often used prophecy to call Israel back to him—his last attempt to avoid punishing them for their failure to follow him.

All the images of its gods
  lie shattered on the ground!' "

¹⁰O my people, crushed on the threshing floor,
  I tell you what I have heard
from the LORD Almighty,
  from the God of Israel.

A Prophecy Against Edom

¹¹An oracleᴅ concerning Dumahᵃ:

Someone calls to me from Seir,
  "Watchmanᴅ, what is left of the night?
Watchman, what is left of the night?"
¹²The watchman replies,
  "Morning is coming, but also the night.
If you would ask, then ask;
  and come back yet again."

A Prophecy Against Arabia

¹³An oracle concerning Arabia:

You caravans of Dedanites,
  who camp in the thickets of Arabia,
¹⁴ bring water for the thirsty;
you who live in Tema,
  bring food for the fugitives.
¹⁵They flee from the sword,
  from the drawn sword,
from the bent bow
  and from the heat of battle.

¹⁶This is what the Lord says to me: "Within one year, as a servant bound by contract would count it, all the pomp of Kedar will come to an end. ¹⁷The survivors of the bowmen, the warriors of Kedar, will be few." The LORD, the God of Israel, has spoken.

A Prophecy About Jerusalem

22 An oracle concerning the Valley of Vision:

What troubles you now,
  that you have all gone up on the roofs,
²O town full of commotion,
  O city of tumult and revelry?
Your slain were not killed by the sword,
  nor did they die in battle.
³All your leaders have fled together;
  they have been captured without using the
    bow.
All you who were caught were taken prisoner
    together,
  having fled while the enemy was still far
    away.
⁴Therefore I said, "Turn away from me;
  let me weep bitterly.
Do not try to console me
  over the destruction of my people."

⁵The Lord, the LORD Almighty, has a day
  of tumult and trampling and terror
    in the Valley of Vision,
a day of battering down walls
  and of crying out to the mountains.

ᵃ11 Dumah means silence or stillness, a wordplay on Edom.

Dumah . . . Seir (21:11)

Seir is Edom, Esau's homeland southeast of the Dead Sea (Gen. 32:3). *Dumah* could be a play on words, referring to Edom. In Hebrew it looks similar to Edom and means *silence*, a good description of what may have been an unclear prophecy even in Isaiah's day. Dumah could also be an oasis in northern Arabia. Either way, the prophecy was a warning to the desert people southeast of Jerusalem.

Why were the people of Kedar so pompous? (21:16)

Kedar, in northwestern Arabia not far from Judah, was known as a land of Arabian princes, prosperous caravan merchants and wealthy herdsmen (Ezek. 27:21). But Kedar's glory days were about to end. Assyria and Babylon each led campaigns into northern Arabia with Nebuchadnezzar's army finally defeating Kedar (Jer. 49:28–29).

Valley of Vision (22:1)

A surprising way to introduce a prophecy about Jerusalem, often referred to as a *mountain* (10:32). A mountain provides a commanding view, but little can be seen from a valley. This could be sarcasm—Isaiah saying the people have no vision. They celebrate a temporary victory and fail to see the coming destruction. The phrase could also mean a specific valley in which Isaiah had this vision.

Why did the people go to the roof? (22:1)

It was not uncommon for flat roofs to be used as multi-purpose family rooms—sometimes for work, sometimes for relaxing in the cool evening breezes. In this case, however, the people simply wanted a good look at the distant hills. They may have watched in alarm as foreign soldiers surrounded the city, or they may have been celebrating the invaders' retreat, perhaps after the unsuccessful Assyrian attack in 701 B.C. (2 Chron. 32).

How did they die? (22:2–3)

In 588 B.C. Babylon surrounded Jerusalem in a blockade that lasted about two years. The city ran out of food causing many to starve or die of disease. The night Babylon finally broke through the wall, Jerusalem's rulers tried to escape, but the king was chased down and captured 16 miles away in Jericho (v. 3; 2 Kings 25:3–5).

Palace of the Forest (22:8–11)
Solomon's palace, built of cedars shipped from the forests of Lebanon (1 Kings 7:2). Part of this palace served as an armory (39:2). Isaiah lists the palace with its weapons, their ingeniously engineered water supply (v. 9) and their reinforced walls (v. 10) as evidence that they were trusting in themselves rather than in God.

SCRIPTURE LINK (22:13) *Let us eat and drink ... for tomorrow we die*
Jesus (Luke 12:18–20) and Paul (1 Cor. 15:32) refer to this cavalier attitude that some people have toward death.

Shebna (22:15)
A royal official in Hezekiah's day, perhaps both prime minister and palace administrator, second in power to the king. He was eventually demoted and replaced by Eliakim (2 Kings 18:18). Isaiah saw in Shebna an example of proud, self-confident Judah.

⁶Elam takes up the quiver,
   with her charioteers and horses;
   Kir uncovers the shield.
⁷Your choicest valleys are full of chariots,
   and horsemen are posted at the city gates;
⁸   the defenses of Judah are stripped away.

And you looked in that day
   to the weapons in the Palace of the Forest;
⁹you saw that the City of David
   had many breaches in its defenses;
you stored up water
   in the Lower Pool.
¹⁰You counted the buildings in Jerusalem^D
   and tore down houses to strengthen the wall.
¹¹You built a reservoir between the two walls
   for the water of the Old Pool,
but you did not look to the One who made it,
   or have regard for the One who planned it
      long ago.

¹²The Lord, the LORD Almighty,
   called you on that day
to weep and to wail,
   to tear out your hair and put on sackcloth^D.
¹³But see, there is joy and revelry,
   slaughtering of cattle and killing of sheep,
   eating of meat and drinking of wine!
"Let us eat and drink," you say,
   "for tomorrow we die!"

¹⁴The LORD Almighty has revealed this in my hearing: "Till your dying day this sin will not be atoned for," says the Lord, the LORD Almighty.

¹⁵This is what the Lord, the LORD Almighty, says:

"Go, say to this steward,
   to Shebna, who is in charge of the palace:
¹⁶What are you doing here and who gave you
      permission
   to cut out a grave for yourself here,
hewing your grave on the height
   and chiseling your resting place in the rock?

How could God be so unforgiving? (22:14)

Because the nation of Judah was so unrepentant. If God had forgiven this unrepentant people, it would have been the same as if he had approved of their sin. As it was, God had shown incredible patience toward them, even though they had repeatedly broken their covenant with him.

Through the prophets God tried again and again to restore the relationship the people had severed. But the people rejected his prophets and his message. Even the annihilation of the northern kingdom of Israel (722 B.C.) failed to convince the masses of the southern kingdom to repent.

God may have appeared unforgiving. In reality, Isaiah was only declaring what the people had already decided: they would not repent; they would not change their sinful way of life; and they would not seek God.

The result? They would remain unforgiven and pay the price for their own sinful choices.

17"Beware, the LORD is about to take firm hold of
    you
    and hurl you away, O you mighty man.
18He will roll you up tightly like a ball
    and throw you into a large country.
There you will die
    and there your splendid chariots will
        remain—
    you disgrace to your master's house!
19I will depose you from your office,
    and you will be ousted from your position.

20"In that day I will summon my servant, Eliakim son of
Hilkiah. **21**I will clothe him with your robe and fasten your
sash around him and hand your authority over to him. He
will be a father to those who live in JerusalemD and to the
house of Judah. **22**I will place on his shoulder the key to the
house of David; what he opens no one can shut, and
what he shuts no one can open. **23**I will drive him like a
peg into a firm place; he will be a seat*a* of honor for the
house of his father. **24**All the gloryD of his family will
hang on him: its offspring and offshoots—all its lesser
vessels, from the bowls to all the jars.

25"In that day," declares the LORD Almighty, "the peg
driven into the firm place will give way; it will be sheared
off and will fall, and the load hanging on it will be cut
down." The LORD has spoken.

A Prophecy About Tyre

23 An oracleD concerning Tyre:

Wail, O ships of Tarshish!
    For Tyre is destroyed
    and left without house or harbor.
From the land of Cyprus*b*
    word has come to them.

2Be silent, you people of the island
    and you merchants of Sidon,
    whom the seafarers have enriched.
3On the great waters
    came the grain of the Shihor;
the harvest of the Nile*c* was the revenue of
        Tyre,
    and she became the marketplace of the
        nations.

4Be ashamed, O Sidon, and you, O fortress of
        the sea,
    for the sea has spoken:
"I have neither been in labor nor given birth;
    I have neither reared sons nor brought up
        daughters."
5When word comes to Egypt,
    they will be in anguish at the report from
        Tyre.

6Cross over to Tarshish;
    wail, you people of the island.
7Is this your city of revelry,
    the old, old city,

**SCRIPTURE LINK (22:22) *What he
opens no one can shut***

Jesus used similar words to illustrate authority
given by God. See Matt. 16:19; Rev. 3:7.

How was Tyre destroyed? (23:1–5)

Tyre's island fortress half a mile offshore
made it seem unconquerable. If the mainland
portion of the city fell, as it did to Babylon in
572 B.C., the people would retreat to the island
until the invaders left—13 years later in Babylon's case. But centuries later, Alexander the
Great defeated mainland Tyre. Then, using the
timber and stones from its ruins, he built a
road across the water to the island city. The
fortress finally fell in 332 B.C. Alexander crucified 2,000 and sold 30,000 into slavery. Also
see *What's left in place of Tyre today?* (Ezek.
26:14).

**Why would the sea say these things to
Sidon? (23:4)**

This is symbolic language, expressing the fact
that the economy of the entire Mediterranean
coastal world depended heavily on Tyre, a hub
of commerce. This was especially true of Sidon, Tyre's sister Phoenician city 20 miles
north (see *Map 5* at the back of this Bible).
With Tyre suddenly gone, Sidon was as alone
as a childless woman—a terrible stigma in Isaiah's day.

---

*a*23 Or *throne*   *b*1 Hebrew *Kittim*   *c*2,3 Masoretic Text; one
Dead Sea Scroll *Sidon, / who cross over the sea; / your envoys* *3are on
the great waters. / The grain of the Shihor, / the harvest of the Nile,*

whose feet have taken her
    to settle in far-off lands?
[8]Who planned this against Tyre,
    the bestower of crowns,
whose merchants are princes,
    whose traders are renowned in the earth?
[9]The LORD Almighty planned it,
    to bring low the pride of all glory[D]
    and to humble all who are renowned on the
      earth.

[10]Till[a] your land as along the Nile,
    O Daughter of Tarshish,
    for you no longer have a harbor.
[11]The LORD has stretched out his hand over the
      sea
    and made its kingdoms tremble.
He has given an order concerning Phoenicia[b]
    that her fortresses be destroyed.
[12]He said, "No more of your reveling,
    O Virgin Daughter of Sidon, now crushed!

"Up, cross over to Cyprus[c];
    even there you will find no rest."
[13]Look at the land of the Babylonians,[d]
    this people that is now of no account!
The Assyrians have made it
    a place for desert creatures;
they raised up their siege towers,
    they stripped its fortresses bare
    and turned it into a ruin.

[14]Wail, you ships of Tarshish;
    your fortress is destroyed!

[15]At that time Tyre will be forgotten for seventy years, the span of a king's life. But at the end of these seventy years, it will happen to Tyre as in the song of the prostitute:

[16]"Take up a harp, walk through the city,
    O prostitute forgotten;
play the harp well, sing many a song,
    so that you will be remembered."

[17]At the end of seventy years, the LORD will deal with Tyre. She will return to her hire as a prostitute and will ply her trade with all the kingdoms on the face of the earth. [18]Yet her profit and her earnings will be set apart for the LORD; they will not be stored up or hoarded. Her profits will go to those who live before the LORD, for abundant food and fine clothes.

The LORD's Devastation of the Earth

24 See, the LORD is going to lay waste the earth
    and devastate it;
he will ruin its face
    and scatter its inhabitants—
[2]it will be the same
    for priest[D] as for people,
    for master as for servant,
    for mistress as for maid,
    for seller as for buyer,

Why call Sidon a *Virgin Daughter*? (23:12)

Simply to show the contrast between what Sidon was and what she would become. Sidon, with all Phoenicia, would no longer be like a happy-go-lucky young girl, enjoying the pampered life. She would be captured, beaten and raped.

What could Cyprus offer? (23:12)

The king of Sidon hoped to escape Sennacherib and the Assyrians by finding safety among allies on the island of Cyprus. But any such rest would be short-lived. Sidon's defeat to the Assyrians was as inevitable as the defeats handed to the not-yet-powerful Babylon (710 and 689 B.C.). See v. 13.

Why would a forgotten prostitute sing in public? (23:15–16)

Perhaps to drum up business. An older prostitute, feeling less attractive, would use entertainment or whatever other means possible to get the attention she needed to make a living.

How was Tyre like a prostitute? (23:17)

In two ways: (1) figuratively, by compromising ethical standards for the sake of making a profit and building a thriving business with merchants from many nations; (2) literally, by using temple prostitutes to worship Baal. Tyre returned to its prostitution when Ptolemy II, an Egyptian ruler sympathetic to Jews, began rebuilding Tyre (274 B.C.).

---

[a]10 Dead Sea Scrolls and some Septuagint manuscripts; Masoretic Text *Go through*   [b]11 Hebrew *Canaan*   [c]12 Hebrew *Kittim*
[d]13 Or *Chaldeans*

for borrower as for lender,
    for debtor as for creditor.
³The earth will be completely laid waste
    and totally plunderedᴰ.
          The Lᴏʀᴅ has spoken this word.

⁴The earth dries up and withers,
    the world languishes and withers,
    the exalted of the earth languish.
⁵The earth is defiled by its people;
    they have disobeyed the laws,
  violated the statutes
    and broken the everlasting covenantᴰ.
⁶Therefore a curse consumes the earth;
    its people must bear their guilt.
  Therefore earth's inhabitants are burned up,
    and very few are left.
⁷The new wineᴰ dries up and the vine withers;
    all the merrymakers groan.
⁸The gaiety of the tambourines is stilled,
    the noise of the revelers has stopped,
    the joyful harp is silent.
⁹No longer do they drink wine with a song;
    the beer is bitter to its drinkers.
¹⁰The ruined city lies desolate;
    the entrance to every house is barred.
¹¹In the streets they cry out for wine;
    all joy turns to gloom,
    all gaiety is banished from the earth.
¹²The city is left in ruins,
    its gate is battered to pieces.
¹³So will it be on the earth
    and among the nations,
  as when an olive tree is beaten,
    or as when gleanings are left after the grape
       harvest.

¹⁴They raise their voices, they shout for joy;
    from the west they acclaim the Lᴏʀᴅ's
       majesty.
¹⁵Therefore in the east give gloryᴰ to the Lᴏʀᴅ;
    exalt the name of the Lᴏʀᴅ, the God of Israel,
    in the islands of the sea.

What city was ruined? (24:10–12)

Some think this meant Jerusalem, which fell in 586 ʙ.ᴄ.—over a century after Isaiah's time. Some say that *ruined city* could literally mean *city of chaos*, perhaps suggesting the chaos when God began creation. The God who created out of chaos, they say, will undo it all and begin again. Others think that *city* refers to all the cities of the world—implying an end to human civilization.

Who would praise God with destruction all around? (24:14–16)

Perhaps the righteous who escape, as few in number as the *olives* and *grapes* missed during a harvest (v. 13). No one else would have reason to be happy about judgment. God's wrath will terrorize the wicked and excite those who have been anticipating and praying for God to act. Still, their praise will not be about destruction, but about what comes next—the fulfillment of God's kingdom.

How and when would God destroy the whole earth? (24:1–6)

To this point, Isaiah's warnings were about God's judgment upon specific cities. But here he broadens the word of doom to encompass the entire world: destruction comes to all who sin.

The picture he paints is of devastation so complete it will rival the flood. *Ruin its face* (v. 1) suggests a disaster that will change the contours of the planet, much like the flood did. Earthquakes, droughts and crashing meteorites each have the potential to do that. This much is clear: it is God, not soldiers, laying waste to the planet. It is God judging human beings for their sins (v. 5).

We don't know when this destruction will happen. But Isaiah seems to say that after God turns his creation into chaos, he will make a new creation (26:1). This could be in the last days of human history, when God defeats evil once and for all. So many have interpreted the message this way that chs. 24–27 are known as the Apocalypse of Isaiah.

Why did Isaiah feel betrayed? (24:16)

He was appalled at the immense human tragedy in his vision. After *Woe to me*, Isaiah uses a
poetic device—five words that sound quite
similar in Hebrew. The technique seems to underscore his complaint that everywhere he
looked he saw treachery. Though appropriate
to rejoice about the coming victory of good over
evil, Isaiah found himself engulfed in the misery of those defeated.

Is this a description of the end of the world? (24:18–20)

Perhaps not literally the end of the planet, but
perhaps the end of human society. Isaiah borrows a description from the early days of history to describe the last days: *floodgates of the
heavens* pictures the flood—God's judgment
(Gen. 7:11). Then, in poetry that pushes the
language to its limit, Isaiah says that those
who trust only in this world will find themselves
with nothing.

Powers in the heavens (24:21–22)

This may mean Satan and the fallen angels.
Later Jewish end-time writings pick up the idea
of warfare among supernatural beings. The
idea also is found in the New Testament (Eph.
6:12; Rev. 12:7–9; 20:2–3). The phrase might
refer, however, to the stars. Many believed the
stars had power over individuals and nations.

Will God literally reign in Jerusalem? (24:23)

Some believe the Messiah will come to earth,
rebuild the Jerusalem temple and reign over
the world. But others think this may describe
the new Jerusalem after the destruction of
earth (Rev. 21:1–2). Either way, the message
remains the same: God will reign.

Why praise God for destruction and devastation? (25:2)

See *Who would praise God with destruction all
around?* (24:14–16).

Who are the people at the feast? (25:6–7)

The people of God who join in an unrestrained
celebration. The picture is of an inaugural banquet for a king, with the Lord as King. It also
could suggest a wedding celebration, with Isaiah hinting about the marriage supper of the
Lamb (Luke 14:15; Rev. 19:7–9).

---

¹⁶From the ends of the earth we hear singing:
  "Glory^D to the Righteous^D One."

But I said, "I waste away, I waste away!
  Woe to me!
The treacherous betray!
  With treachery the treacherous betray!"
¹⁷Terror and pit and snare await you,
  O people of the earth.
¹⁸Whoever flees at the sound of terror
  will fall into a pit;
whoever climbs out of the pit
  will be caught in a snare.

The floodgates of the heavens are opened,
  the foundations of the earth shake.
¹⁹The earth is broken up,
  the earth is split asunder,
  the earth is thoroughly shaken.
²⁰The earth reels like a drunkard,
  it sways like a hut in the wind;
so heavy upon it is the guilt of its rebellion
  that it falls—never to rise again.

²¹In that day the Lord will punish
  the powers in the heavens above
  and the kings on the earth below.
²²They will be herded together
  like prisoners bound in a dungeon;
they will be shut up in prison
  and be punished^a after many days.
²³The moon will be abashed, the sun ashamed;
  for the Lord Almighty will reign
on Mount Zion^D and in Jerusalem^D,
  and before its elders, gloriously.

Praise to the Lord

25 O Lord, you are my God;
  I will exalt you and praise your name,
for in perfect faithfulness
  you have done marvelous things,
  things planned long ago.
²You have made the city a heap of rubble,
  the fortified town a ruin,
the foreigners' stronghold^D a city no more;
  it will never be rebuilt.
³Therefore strong peoples will honor you;
  cities of ruthless nations will revere^D you.
⁴You have been a refuge for the poor,
  a refuge for the needy in his distress,
a shelter from the storm
  and a shade from the heat.
For the breath of the ruthless
  is like a storm driving against a wall
⁵ and like the heat of the desert.
You silence the uproar of foreigners;
  as heat is reduced by the shadow of a cloud,
so the song of the ruthless is stilled.

⁶On this mountain the Lord Almighty will
    prepare
  a feast of rich food for all peoples,
  a banquet of aged wine—

---

^a22 Or *released*

the best of meats and the finest of wines.
7On this mountain he will destroy
    the shroud that enfolds all peoples,
  the sheet that covers all nations;
8   he will swallow up death[D] forever.
The Sovereign LORD will wipe away the tears
    from all faces;
he will remove the disgrace of his people
    from all the earth.
               The LORD has spoken.

9In that day they will say,

"Surely this is our God;
  we trusted in him, and he saved us.
This is the LORD, we trusted in him;
  let us rejoice and be glad in his salvation[D]."

10The hand of the LORD will rest on this
      mountain;
but Moab will be trampled under him
  as straw is trampled down in the manure.
11They will spread out their hands in it,
  as a swimmer spreads out his hands to swim.
God will bring down their pride
  despite the cleverness[a] of their hands.
12He will bring down your high fortified walls
  and lay them low;
he will bring them down to the ground,
  to the very dust.

A Song of Praise

26 In that day this song will be sung in the land of
Judah:

We have a strong city;
  God makes salvation
  its walls and ramparts.
2Open the gates
  that the righteous[D] nation may enter,
  the nation that keeps faith.
3You will keep in perfect peace[D]
  him whose mind is steadfast,
  because he trusts in you.
4Trust in the LORD forever,
  for the LORD, the LORD, is the Rock eternal.
5He humbles those who dwell on high,
  he lays the lofty city low;
he levels it to the ground
  and casts it down to the dust.
6Feet trample it down—
  the feet of the oppressed,
  the footsteps of the poor.

7The path of the righteous is level;
  O upright One, you make the way of the
      righteous smooth.
8Yes, LORD, walking in the way of your laws,[b]
  we wait for you;
your name and renown
  are the desire of our hearts.
9My soul[D] yearns for you in the night;
  in the morning my spirit longs for you.

---

a 11 The meaning of the Hebrew for this word is uncertain.   *b 8* Or
judgments

What covers the nations? (25:7)

Death, portrayed through the image of a
shroud that wraps a corpse. The Hebrew combines rhyming words with similar meanings and
poetic parallelism (in which the second thought
repeats the first). All this emphasizes that
death will be destroyed (v. 8).

SCRIPTURE LINK (25:8) *He will swal-low up death forever*

Paul quoted this (1 Cor. 15:54) to show that
God's ultimate victory will end death and the
mourning it causes. John linked this with the
new Jerusalem (Rev. 21:2–4).

How many righteous people must there be for a nation to be called *righteous*? (26:2)

It's impossible to say exactly. After Abraham's
pleading, ten righteous people would have
been enough to save Sodom and Gomorrah
from judgment (Gen. 18:32). But Isaiah's point
is not that a few godly people provide access
to the new Jerusalem. His point is that *faith* is
the entrance pass. Only those who have it may
come in.

SCRIPTURE LINK (26:4) *The LORD . . . is the Rock eternal*

The Old Testament often describes God as a
rock—a source of water, shade and protection. See 32:2; Exodus 17:6; Psalm 18:2.

Does *judgment* teach righteousness better than *grace*? (26:9–10)

In a way, yes. When everything seems fine,
people may neglect God, because they don't
feel a need for him. Judgment, on the other
hand, usually gets a person's attention. In this
way, judgment can be a form of grace, when it
starts us moving toward God.

When your judgments come upon the earth,
  the people of the world learn
    righteousness[D].
[10]Though grace[D] is shown to the wicked,
  they do not learn righteousness;
even in a land of uprightness they go on doing
    evil
  and regard not the majesty of the LORD.
[11]O LORD, your hand is lifted high,
  but they do not see it.
Let them see your zeal[D] for your people and
    be put to shame;
  let the fire reserved for your enemies
    consume them.

[12]LORD, you establish peace[D] for us;
  all that we have accomplished you have
    done for us.
[13]O LORD, our God, other lords besides you have
    ruled over us,
  but your name alone do we honor.
[14]They are now dead, they live no more;
  those departed spirits do not rise.
You punished them and brought them to
    ruin;
  you wiped out all memory of them.
[15]You have enlarged the nation, O LORD;
  you have enlarged the nation.
You have gained glory[D] for yourself;
  you have extended all the borders of the
    land.

[16]LORD, they came to you in their distress;
  when you disciplined them,
  they could barely whisper a prayer.[a]
[17]As a woman with child and about to give
    birth
  writhes and cries out in her pain,
  so were we in your presence, O LORD.
[18]We were with child, we writhed in pain,
  but we gave birth to wind.
We have not brought salvation[D] to the earth;
  we have not given birth to people of the
    world.

[19]But your dead will live;
  their bodies will rise.
You who dwell in the dust,
  wake up and shout for joy.
Your dew is like the dew of the morning;
  the earth will give birth to her dead.

[20]Go, my people, enter your rooms
  and shut the doors behind you;
hide yourselves for a little while
  until his wrath has passed by.
[21]See, the LORD is coming out of his dwelling
    to punish the people of the earth for their
    sins.
The earth will disclose the blood shed upon
    her;
  she will conceal her slain no longer.

What other lords had Israel served? (26:13)

Isaiah was not talking here about other gods. He was talking about foreign rulers, dead and forgotten, unlike the Lord who remained very much alive. These invaders came from nations such as Egypt, Assyria and Babylon. Each took a turn ruling the land, but the hearts of righteous Hebrews remained loyal to God.

Gave birth to wind (26:18)

Instead of turning to God, the Jews relied on their own resources and cunning to save themselves from the invaders. Their efforts were as unproductive as a woman straining to give birth, but delivering nothing but wind.

To what resurrection does Isaiah refer? (26:19)

Perhaps this is the resurrection of the righteous dead in the last days (Daniel 12:2; 1 Cor. 15:51–52). But in the context of the surrounding verses, in which Isaiah complains about the distress Judah is suffering, it seems that he is speaking about the resurrection—the restoration—of the nation.

SCRIPTURE LINK (26:19) Dead will live ... bodies will rise

This imagery parallels that of Ezek. 37:1–11. There, dry bones coming to life represented Israel.

---

[a]16 The meaning of the Hebrew for this clause is uncertain.

Deliverance of Israel

27 In that day,

the LORD will punish with his sword,
his fierce, great and powerful sword,
Leviathan[D] the gliding serpent,
Leviathan the coiling serpent;
he will slay the monster of the sea.

[2]In that day—

"Sing about a fruitful vineyard:
[3] I, the LORD, watch over it;
I water it continually.
I guard it day and night
so that no one may harm it.
[4] I am not angry.
If only there were briers and thorns
confronting me!
I would march against them in battle;
I would set them all on fire.
[5]Or else let them come to me for refuge;
let them make peace[D] with me,
yes, let them make peace with me."

[6]In days to come Jacob will take root,
Israel will bud and blossom
and fill all the world with fruit.

[7]Has ⌊the LORD⌋ struck her
as he struck down those who struck her?
Has she been killed
as those were killed who killed her?
[8]By warfare[a] and exile[D] you contend with
her—
with his fierce blast he drives her out,
as on a day the east wind blows.
[9]By this, then, will Jacob's guilt be atoned for,
and this will be the full fruitage of the
removal of his sin:
When he makes all the altar stones
to be like chalk stones crushed to pieces,
no Asherah poles[Db] or incense[D] altars
will be left standing.
[10]The fortified city stands desolate,
an abandoned settlement, forsaken like the
desert;
there the calves graze,
there they lie down;
they strip its branches bare.
[11]When its twigs are dry, they are broken off
and women come and make fires with them.
For this is a people without understanding;
so their Maker has no compassion on them,
and their Creator shows them no favor.

[12]In that day the LORD will thresh from the flowing Euphrates[c] to the Wadi of Egypt, and you, O Israelites, will be gathered up one by one. [13]And in that day a great trumpet will sound. Those who were perishing in Assyria and those who were exiled in Egypt will come and worship the LORD on the holy mountain in Jerusalem[D].

---

[a]8 See Septuagint; the meaning of the Hebrew for this word is uncertain.   [b]9 That is, symbols of the goddess Asherah
[c]12 Hebrew *River*

Leviathan . . . serpent . . . monster (27:1)
Creation myths from several ancient Middle Eastern nations tell of a god defeating a sea monster before the creation could be completed. Here, similar words seem to portray an image of an end-time battle in which God defeats evil before he completes a new creation. Also see *Rahab* (30:7).

SCRIPTURE LINK (27:2) A fruitful vineyard
Used elsewhere to describe Israel. See 5:1–7; Luke 20:9–19.

Why would God prefer briers and thorns in his vineyard? (27:2–5)
This could mean that God would rather battle wicked nations than unfaithful Israel, the one he had chosen. On the other hand, this might be God's expression of how much he cares for his newly planted vineyard—enough to protect it from thorns that no longer exist.

How has Israel blossomed? (27:6)
Perhaps the *blossom* is a symbol of life in the new Jerusalem, with the Messiah as King (4:2). *Israel* would then mean all those who are faithful to God, Jew and Gentile alike (Gal. 3:28; 6:16). Some, however, suggest that this refers to the restoration and worldwide influence of the Jewish nation, either after the exile in Babylon or sometime in the future.

How could banishing refugees atone for sin? (27:8–9)
Atonement contains the idea of reconciling a broken relationship. A sacrifice atoned for sin because it meant someone had repented and desired to return to God. Though Judah had refused to repent, its defeat and exile to a foreign land, coming about a century after Isaiah's death, would turn the hearts of the nation back to God once again. God's judgment became a means of bringing God's grace. See *Does judgment teach righteousness better than grace?* (26:9–10).

Why didn't God show compassion for those who couldn't understand? (27:10–11)
It's not that the people *couldn't* understand—they *wouldn't*. They were seeking direction from idols instead of the one, true God. Their lack of discernment was self-inflicted and deserved judgment rather than compassion.

Why *thresh* from the Euphrates River to Egypt? (27:12)
This was a promise of a coming harvest: though they would be scattered from Egypt to Babylon, God's people would again be gathered back to the promised land. Because *threshing* was often used as an image of punishment, some suggest this also contains the idea of judgment upon the nations that carried Israel away. Others see an allusion to a coming golden age: *from the Euphrates to Egypt* represented the boundaries of Israel at its peak (1 Kings 4:21).

Wreath (28:1)

This pictured Samaria, capital of the northern kingdom of Israel, destroyed by Assyria in 722 B.C. Like a crown or *wreath* some wore at ancient parties, Samaria sat proudly on a hill at the northern end of a fertile valley.

Ephraim (28:1)

A prominent tribe of Israel. For Isaiah and Hosea it became another name for the northern kingdom (7:2; Hosea 5:3).

What battle was fought at the gate? (28:6)

Isaiah probably meant no specific battle. Many battles were fought, at least in part, *at the gate*, usually the most vulnerable part of the wall. Isaiah may have been looking beyond the fall of Samaria and Jerusalem to a new beginning when God would give strength to the surviving remnant, enabling them to do what Israel and Judah had failed to do: resist evil.

Who was teaching whom? (28:9–10)

Isaiah was quoting what the drunken priests and prophets had said to mock and criticize him. They argued they were old enough to know the difference between right and wrong. They mocked Isaiah's teachings as being too basic and too simplistic. They thought they knew it all.

How would God use foreigners to speak to his people? (28:11)

If they couldn't understand plain Hebrew, God would teach in another language. They would not understand the speech of their cruel Assyrian conquerors as they were beaten and dragged into captivity, but they would quickly learn the lesson God had wanted them to learn all along—that he was serious about their sins and their need for repentance.

Did God replace spiritual rest with legalism? (28:12–13)

No. The Israelites had replaced their dependence on God with self-sufficiency. God had brought them into the promised land, but they had rejected his promises. Instead of rest and freedom, then, they were forced to submit to Assyria. They had, in effect, exchanged God's ways for the oppressive rule of a foreign invader.

Woe to Ephraim

28 Woe to that wreath, the pride of Ephraim's
        drunkards,
    to the fading flower, his glorious beauty,
set on the head of a fertile valley—
    to that city, the pride of those laid low by
        wine!
²See, the Lord has one who is powerful and
        strong.
Like a hailstorm and a destructive wind,
like a driving rain and a flooding downpour,
    he will throw it forcefully to the ground.
³That wreath, the pride of Ephraim's drunkards,
    will be trampled underfoot.
⁴That fading flower, his glorious beauty,
    set on the head of a fertile valley,
will be like a fig ripe before harvest—
    as soon as someone sees it and takes it in his
        hand,
    he swallows it.

⁵In that day the Lord Almighty
    will be a glorious crown,
a beautiful wreath
    for the remnantᴰ of his people.
⁶He will be a spirit of justice
    to him who sits in judgment,
a source of strength
    to those who turn back the battle at the gate.

⁷And these also stagger from wine
    and reel from beer:
Priests and prophetsᴰ stagger from beer
    and are befuddled with wine;
they reel from beer,
    they stagger when seeing visionsᴰ,
    they stumble when rendering decisions.
⁸All the tables are covered with vomit
    and there is not a spot without filth.

⁹"Who is it he is trying to teach?
    To whom is he explaining his message?
To children weaned from their milk,
    to those just taken from the breast?
¹⁰For it is:
    Do and do, do and do,
    rule on rule, rule on ruleᵃ;
    a little here, a little there."

¹¹Very well then, with foreign lips and strange
        tongues
    God will speak to this people,
¹²to whom he said,
    "This is the resting place, let the weary rest";
and, "This is the place of repose"—
    but they would not listen.
¹³So then, the word of the Lord to them will
        become:
    Do and do, do and do,
    rule on rule, rule on rule;
    a little here, a little there—

ᵃ10 Hebrew / *sav lasav sav lasav / kav lakav kav lakav* (possibly meaningless sounds; perhaps a mimicking of the prophet's words); also in verse 13

so that they will go and fall backward,
    be injured and snared and captured.

14Therefore hear the word of the LORD, you
    scoffers
who rule this people in JerusalemᴰD.
15You boast, "We have entered into a covenantᴰ
    with deathᴰ,
with the grave*a* we have made an
    agreement.
When an overwhelming scourge sweeps by,
    it cannot touch us,
for we have made a lie our refuge
    and falsehood*b* our hiding place."

16So this is what the Sovereign LORD says:

"See, I lay a stone in Zionᴰ,
    a tested stone,
a precious cornerstone for a sure foundation;
    the one who trusts will never be dismayed.
17I will make justice the measuring lineᴰ
    and righteousnessᴰ the plumb line;
hail will sweep away your refuge, the lie,
    and water will overflow your hiding place.
18Your covenant with death will be annulled;
    your agreement with the grave will not
    stand.
When the overwhelming scourge sweeps by,
    you will be beaten down by it.
19As often as it comes it will carry you away;
    morning after morning, by day and by night,
    it will sweep through."

The understanding of this message
    will bring sheer terror.
20The bed is too short to stretch out on,
    the blanket too narrow to wrap around you.
21The LORD will rise up as he did at Mount
    Perazim,
he will rouse himself as in the Valley of
    Gibeon—
to do his work, his strange work,
    and perform his task, his alienᴰ task.
22Now stop your mocking,
    or your chains will become heavier;
the Lord, the LORD Almighty, has told me
    of the destruction decreed against the whole
    land.

23Listen and hear my voice;
    pay attention and hear what I say.
24When a farmer plows for planting, does he
    plow continually?
Does he keep on breaking up and harrowing
    the soil?
25When he has leveled the surface,
    does he not sow caraway and scatter
    cummin?
Does he not plant wheat in its place,*c*
    barley in its plot,*c*
    and spelt in its field?

Why did they make a covenant with death? (28:14–15)

This may have been Isaiah's poetic way of describing a venture that was doomed to failure. The word *covenant* could mean a treaty—an agreement between Judah and Egypt (see 20:5; 30:2; 31:1), perhaps guaranteed by the Egyptian goddess of death, Osiris. Some think this related to some idolatrous perversion—necromancy or attempts to gain immortality (see 65:4). Whatever the explanation, Isaiah's message was to trust God, not pagan beliefs.

What kind of cornerstone did God lay? (28:16)

The temple was built over a large rock used as a threshing floor (1 Chron. 21:28–22:1). The rock may have been called a *tested stone* because threshing—a symbol of judgment and God's testing—took place on it. *Tested stone* could also mean a standard—a rock to which other cut stones were tested for accurate sizing. This image of the cornerstone was later applied to Christ (see 1 Peter 2:6–7).

What did a short bed and narrow blanket have to do with Judah? (28:20)

Using a proverb of the day, Isaiah said that Judah would find no rest or comfort in their treaty (v. 18).

SCRIPTURE LINK (28:21)

At Perazim, God gave David victory over the Philistines (see 2 Samuel 5:20). At Gibeon, God sent hail and then stopped the sun in the sky to help Joshua defeat the Amorites (see Joshua 10:9–13).

Why all these references to agriculture? (28:24–29)

Threshing was a well-known symbol of judgment. Perhaps the point is that God will not *thresh*, or punish, Israel forever. Or it could mean that just as God has provided a strategy and instructions for the farmer to produce a good harvest (v. 29), he also has a strategy and instructions for the nation to produce righteousness.

---

*a*15 Hebrew *Sheol*; also in verse 18   *b*15 Or *false gods*
*c*25 The meaning of the Hebrew for this word is uncertain.

Ariel (29:1)
A nickname for Jerusalem. In Hebrew it sounds like the word for *altar hearth* and originally may have meant that. Since people came to Jerusalem to worship at the temple altar, the word became synonymous for the city. *Ariel* also sounds similar to *lion of God* and that meaning may be suggested as well. Other Scriptures describe Israel as a lion (Gen. 49:9).

Siege works (29:3)
Military equipment used to capture a walled city. Assyrian art shows wheeled battering rams and huge, wheeled towers packed with archers. Soldiers pushed these towers against the wall and used them as protected ladders.

Are natural disasters signs of God's judgment? (29:6)
See *Is God responsible for disasters?* (Jer. 36:3) and article: *Why does God send calamity?* (Lam. 3:38).

Why did God prevent the religious leaders from understanding? (29:9–10)
For so long and in such callous ways they had rejected him, that this might have been God's way of saying, "Okay, have it your way." Or it could be an exaggerated way of saying that the people were so blind it was as though God himself had put them to sleep. For more on their blindness see 6:9–10.

²⁶His God instructs him
  and teaches him the right way.

²⁷Caraway is not threshed with a sledge,
  nor is a cartwheel rolled over cummin;
caraway is beaten out with a rod,
  and cummin with a stick.
²⁸Grain must be ground to make bread;
  so one does not go on threshing it forever.
Though he drives the wheels of his threshing
    cart over it,
  his horses do not grind it.
²⁹All this also comes from the LORD Almighty,
  wonderful in counsel and magnificent in
    wisdom.

Woe to David's City

29 Woe to you, Ariel, Ariel,
  the city where David settled!
Add year to year
  and let your cycle of festivals go on.
²Yet I will besiege Ariel;
  she will mourn and lament,ᴰ
  she will be to me like an altar hearth.ᵃ
³I will encamp against you all around;
  I will encircle you with towers
  and set up my siege worksᴰ against you.
⁴Brought low, you will speak from the ground;
  your speech will mumble out of the dust.
Your voice will come ghostlike from the earth;
  out of the dust your speech will whisper.

⁵But your many enemies will become like fine
    dust,
  the ruthless hordes like blown chaff.ᴰ
Suddenly, in an instant,
⁶ the LORD Almighty will come
  with thunder and earthquake and great noise,
  with windstorm and tempest and flames of a
    devouring fire.
⁷Then the hordes of all the nations that fight
    against Ariel,
  that attack her and her fortress and besiege
    her,
will be as it is with a dream,
  with a visionᴰ in the night—
⁸as when a hungry man dreams that he is
    eating,
  but he awakens, and his hunger remains;
as when a thirsty man dreams that he is
    drinking,
  but he awakens faint, with his thirst
    unquenched.
So will it be with the hordes of all the nations
  that fight against Mount Zion.ᴰ

⁹Be stunned and amazed,
  blind yourselves and be sightless;
be drunk, but not from wine,
  stagger, but not from beer.
¹⁰The LORD has brought over you a deep sleep:
  He has sealed your eyes (the prophets);
  he has covered your heads (the seers).

ᵃ2 The Hebrew for *altar hearth* sounds like the Hebrew for *Ariel*.

11For you this whole vision[D] is nothing but words sealed in a scroll. And if you give the scroll to someone who can read, and say to him, "Read this, please," he will answer, "I can't; it is sealed." **12**Or if you give the scroll to someone who cannot read, and say, "Read this, please," he will answer, "I don't know how to read."

13The Lord says:

"These people come near to me with their
        mouth
    and honor me with their lips,
        but their hearts are far from me.
Their worship of me
    is made up only of rules taught by men.[a]
14Therefore once more I will astound these
        people
    with wonder upon wonder;
the wisdom of the wise will perish,
    the intelligence of the intelligent will vanish."

15Woe to those who go to great depths
        to hide their plans from the LORD,
who do their work in darkness and think,
    "Who sees us? Who will know?"
16You turn things upside down,
    as if the potter were thought to be like the
        clay!
Shall what is formed say to him who formed it,
    "He did not make me"?
Can the pot say of the potter,
    "He knows nothing"?

17In a very short time, will not Lebanon be
        turned into a fertile field
    and the fertile field seem like a forest?
18In that day the deaf will hear the words of the
        scroll,
    and out of gloom and darkness
        the eyes of the blind will see.
19Once more the humble will rejoice in the LORD;
    the needy will rejoice in the Holy One of
        Israel.
20The ruthless will vanish,
    the mockers will disappear,
    and all who have an eye for evil will be cut
        down—
21those who with a word make a man out to be
        guilty,
    who ensnare the defender in court
    and with false testimony deprive the
        innocent of justice.

22Therefore this is what the LORD, who redeemed[D] Abraham, says to the house of Jacob:

"No longer will Jacob be ashamed;
    no longer will their faces grow pale.
23When they see among them their children,
    the work of my hands,
they will keep my name holy;
    they will acknowledge the holiness of the
        Holy One of Jacob,
    and will stand in awe of the God of Israel.

---

a 13 Hebrew; Septuagint *They worship me in vain, / their teachings are
but rules taught by men*

SCRIPTURE LINK (29:13) *Honor me with their lips, but their hearts are far from me*

Jesus used this verse to describe the hypocrisy in his day. See Matt. 15:8–9; Mark 7:6–7.

What *rules* had they substituted for genuine worship? (29:13)

The rules outlined by Moses in Leviticus: rules about what to sacrifice and when, how to honor the Sabbath, what not to eat and so on. Though these rules were given by God and had a purpose, the people missed the point entirely. They were only going through the motions—and that wasn't enough. David had been concerned about empty religious ritual long before Isaiah (Psalm 40:6–8; 51:16–17).

Who was planning what? (29:15–16)

To offset the threat of enemies, kings often relied on intricate international schemes that obligated them to allies. Hezekiah dialogued with Egypt to counteract the Assyrian menace to Jerusalem (2 Kings 18:21). See *What was wrong with asking for Egyptian support?* (30:1–2).

SCRIPTURE LINK (29:16) *Potter . . . like the clay*

Jeremiah and Paul used this same idea to talk about God's sovereignty. See Jer. 18; Romans 9:20.

24Those who are wayward in spirit will gain
            understanding;
        those who complain will accept instruction."

Woe to the Obstinate Nation

30 "Woe to the obstinate children,"
        declares the LORD,
    "to those who carry out plans that are not
            mine,
        forming an alliance, but not by my Spirit,
        heaping sin upon sin;
2who go down to Egypt
        without consulting me;
    who look for help to Pharaoh's protection,
        to Egypt's shade for refuge.
3But Pharaoh's protection will be to your shame,
        Egypt's shade will bring you disgrace.
4Though they have officials in Zoan
        and their envoys have arrived in Hanes,
5everyone will be put to shame
        because of a people useless to them,
    who bring neither help nor advantage,
        but only shame and disgrace."

6An oracleᴰ concerning the animals of the Negevᴰ:

    Through a land of hardship and distress,
        of lions and lionesses,
        of adders and darting snakes,
    the envoys carry their riches on donkeys'
            backs,
        their treasures on the humps of camels,
    to that unprofitable nation,
7   to Egypt, whose help is utterly useless.
    Therefore I call her
        Rahabᴰ the Do-Nothing.

8Go now, write it on a tablet for them,
        inscribe it on a scroll,
    that for the days to come
        it may be an everlasting witness.
9These are rebellious people, deceitful children,
        children unwilling to listen to the LORD's
            instruction.
10They say to the seersᴰ,
        "See no more visionsᴰ!"
    and to the prophetsᴰ,
        "Give us no more visions of what is right!
    Tell us pleasant things,
        prophesy illusions.
11Leave this way,
        get off this path,
    and stop confronting us
        with the Holy One of Israel!"

12Therefore, this is what the Holy One of Israel says:

    "Because you have rejected this message,
        relied on oppression
        and depended on deceit,
13this sin will become for you
        like a high wall, cracked and bulging,
        that collapses suddenly, in an instant.
14It will break in pieces like pottery,
        shattered so mercilessly

What was wrong with asking for Egyptian support? (30:1–2)

The problem was that the Jewish leaders hadn't consulted God. God alone was to be their source of security, but the people wanted a backup plan—just in case something went wrong or God didn't come through. So to hedge their bets with God, they made a treaty with Egypt (2 Kings 18:21).

Rahab (30:7)

Mythical sea monster that ruled over the chaos that existed at the time of creation; also a nickname for Egypt (Psalm 87:4). God proved his power over this supposed monster at creation (Job 26:12; Psalm 89:10). Also see *Leviathan . . . serpent . . . monster* (27:1).

that among its pieces not a fragment will be
    found
  for taking coals from a hearth
  or scooping water out of a cistern^D."

¹⁵This is what the Sovereign LORD, the Holy One of Israel, says:

"In repentance^D and rest is your salvation^D,
  in quietness and trust is your strength,
  but you would have none of it.
¹⁶You said, 'No, we will flee on horses.'
  Therefore you will flee!
You said, 'We will ride off on swift horses.'
  Therefore your pursuers will be swift!
¹⁷A thousand will flee
  at the threat of one;
at the threat of five
  you will all flee away,
till you are left
  like a flagstaff on a mountaintop,
  like a banner on a hill."

¹⁸Yet the LORD longs to be gracious to you;
  he rises to show you compassion.
For the LORD is a God of justice.
  Blessed are all who wait for him!

¹⁹O people of Zion^D, who live in Jerusalem^D, you will weep no more. How gracious he will be when you cry for help! As soon as he hears, he will answer you. ²⁰Although the Lord gives you the bread of adversity and the water of affliction^D, your teachers will be hidden no more; with your own eyes you will see them. ²¹Whether you turn to the right or to the left, your ears will hear a voice behind you, saying, "This is the way; walk in it." ²²Then you will defile your idols^D overlaid with silver and your images covered with gold; you will throw them away like a menstrual cloth and say to them, "Away with you!"

²³He will also send you rain for the seed you sow in the ground, and the food that comes from the land will be rich and plentiful. In that day your cattle will graze in broad meadows. ²⁴The oxen and donkeys that work the soil will eat fodder and mash, spread out with fork and shovel. ²⁵In the day of great slaughter, when the towers fall, streams of water will flow on every high mountain and every lofty hill. ²⁶The moon will shine like the sun, and the sunlight will be seven times brighter, like the light of seven full days, when the LORD binds up the bruises of his people and heals the wounds he inflicted.

²⁷See, the Name of the LORD comes from afar,
  with burning anger and dense clouds of
    smoke;
his lips are full of wrath,
  and his tongue is a consuming fire.
²⁸His breath is like a rushing torrent,
  rising up to the neck.
He shakes the nations in the sieve of
    destruction;
  he places in the jaws of the peoples
  a bit that leads them astray.
²⁹And you will sing
  as on the night you celebrate a holy festival;
your hearts will rejoice
  as when people go up with flutes

What does it mean to *wait* for the Lord? (30:18)

It means to trust him when a situation looks hopeless—even when it seems he is gone (40:27–31). For Judah, having failed to repent when it had opportunity to do so, mercy would have to wait for justice to be completed. But after justice there would again be God's mercy and blessing (40:2).

How will the sun be *seven times brighter*? (30:26)

Perhaps in the sense that the entire universe will take part in God's new reign and that everything good for God's people will be magnified. (Seven was considered a picture of completeness or perfection.) This symbolism of a brighter sun stands in contrast to when the sun and moon were ashamed while God executed judgment on the world (24:23).

Why would God lead people astray? (30:28)

This is likely a reference to pulling the reigns back on Assyria and halting her destructive stampede. God would use Assyria to punish Israel, but after the punishment it would be time for that powerful empire to face the consequences of her own sin. Babylon defeated the last Assyrian army in 609 B.C.

to the mountain of the LORD,
    to the Rock of Israel.
30The LORD will cause men to hear his majestic
        voice
    and will make them see his arm coming
        down
with raging anger and consuming fire,
    with cloudburst, thunderstorm and hail.
31The voice of the LORD will shatter Assyria;
    with his scepter[D] he will strike them down.
32Every stroke the LORD lays on them
    with his punishing rod
will be to the music of tambourines and harps,
    as he fights them in battle with the blows of
        his arm.
33Topheth[D] has long been prepared;
    it has been made ready for the king.
Its fire pit has been made deep and wide,
    with an abundance of fire and wood;
the breath of the LORD,
    like a stream of burning sulfur,
    sets it ablaze.

Woe to Those Who Rely on Egypt

31 Woe to those who go down to Egypt for help,
        who rely on horses,
who trust in the multitude of their chariots
    and in the great strength of their horsemen,
but do not look to the Holy One of Israel,
    or seek help from the LORD.
2Yet he too is wise and can bring disaster;
    he does not take back his words.
He will rise up against the house of the wicked,
    against those who help evildoers.
3But the Egyptians are men and not God;
    their horses are flesh and not spirit.
When the LORD stretches out his hand,
    he who helps will stumble,
    he who is helped will fall;
    both will perish together.

4This is what the LORD says to me:

"As a lion growls,
    a great lion over his prey—
and though a whole band of shepherds
    is called together against him,
he is not frightened by their shouts
    or disturbed by their clamor—
so the LORD Almighty will come down
    to do battle on Mount Zion[D] and on its
        heights.
5Like birds hovering overhead,
    the LORD Almighty will shield Jerusalem[D];
he will shield it and deliver it,
    he will 'pass over' it and will rescue it."

6Return to him you have so greatly revolted against, O
Israelites. **7**For in that day every one of you will reject the
idols[D] of silver and gold your sinful hands have made.

8"Assyria will fall by a sword that is not of man;
    a sword, not of mortals, will devour them.
They will flee before the sword

Topheth (30:33)

A garbage dump outside Jerusalem, used to
burn trash. During times of unfaithfulness it
was used as a place for human sacrifices
(2 Kings 23:10; Jer. 7:31–32). Because of
such atrocities, the Hebrews associated
Topheth with shameful abominations.

What was wrong with recruiting Egyptian support? (31:1)

See *What was wrong with asking for Egyptian
support?* (30:1–2).

Why did God not want Israel to have a strong national defense? (31:1)

God wanted the people to trust him and seek
his help. If their defenses were weak, then
there would be no doubt that their help came
from God alone.

Why did God judge the Assyrians? (31:8–9)

Isaiah returns to this common theme, that the
Assyrians would be judged (10:12; 14:25;
30:31–33). Even though he used the Assyrians to accomplish his own purposes, God detested their pride, later described by Isaiah
(37:21–29). They also went too far in their
vicious treatment of their victims (Nahum
3:1–5).

How did God judge the Assyrians? (31:8–9)

The *sword that is not of man* suggests supernatural judgment: the angel of the Lord put to
death 185,000 Assyrian soldiers (37:36). The
Assyrian *stronghold* probably refers to Nineveh,
which was destroyed by the Medes and Babylonians around 612 B.C.

and their young men will be put to forced
labor.
⁹Their stronghold⁰ will fall because of terror;
at sight of the battle standard their
commanders will panic,"
declares the LORD,
whose fire is in Zion⁰,
whose furnace is in Jerusalem⁰.

The Kingdom of Righteousness

32 See, a king will reign in righteousness⁰
and rulers will rule with justice.
²Each man will be like a shelter from the wind
and a refuge from the storm,
like streams of water in the desert
and the shadow of a great rock in a thirsty
land.
³Then the eyes of those who see will no longer
be closed,
and the ears of those who hear will listen.
⁴The mind of the rash will know and
understand,
and the stammering tongue will be fluent
and clear.
⁵No longer will the fool be called noble
nor the scoundrel be highly respected.
⁶For the fool speaks folly,
his mind is busy with evil:
He practices ungodliness
and spreads error concerning the LORD;
the hungry he leaves empty
and from the thirsty he withholds water.
⁷The scoundrel's methods are wicked,
he makes up evil schemes
to destroy the poor with lies,
even when the plea of the needy is just.
⁸But the noble man makes noble plans,
and by noble deeds he stands.

The Women of Jerusalem

⁹You women who are so complacent,
rise up and listen to me;
you daughters who feel secure,
hear what I have to say!
¹⁰In little more than a year
you who feel secure will tremble;
the grape harvest will fail,
and the harvest of fruit will not come.
¹¹Tremble, you complacent women;
shudder, you daughters who feel secure!
Strip off your clothes,
put sackcloth⁰ around your waists.
¹²Beat your breasts for the pleasant fields,
for the fruitful vines
¹³and for the land of my people,
a land overgrown with thorns and briers—
yes, mourn for all houses of merriment
and for this city of revelry.
¹⁴The fortress will be abandoned,
the noisy city deserted;
citadel⁰ and watchtower⁰ will become a
wasteland forever,
the delight of donkeys, a pasture for flocks,

What sort of *furnace* was in Jerusalem? (31:9)
This may refer to the fire that burned continual-
ly upon the altar in the temple in Jerusalem.
Some also see in the word *furnace* a symbol of
God's wrath against his enemies. Others think
it may mean his intense glory.

What king would *reign in righteousness?* (32:1)
Whether or not Isaiah's original readers understood it, this pertained to the coming Messiah,
not an ordinary king. A perfect government
could only be established under the rule of the
Messiah (9:7). His righteousness would even
be reflected by those who served him, his rulers or governmental officials.

How would men become shelters and refuges? (32:2)
The words *each man* most likely refer to the
rulers of this righteous government. These rulers would reflect the protective and sheltering
character of the Lord, their king (see 25:4).
Some would see this as an allusion to believers in Christ who have become a *royal priesthood* (1 Peter 2:9). They may also be the leaders in the church, those who *govern diligently*
(Romans 12:8).

Whose eyes will be opened? (32:3)
To all who earnestly seek to follow him, Christ
gives eyes to see and ears to hear spiritual
truth. If we receive him, we'll be receptive to
God's truth. Isaiah had warned that the people's eyes and ears would be shut to God's
truth (6:9–10). Their hearts would be hardened
to his message. Here, however, Isaiah promises that the Messiah will heal such spiritual
blindness and deafness.

Why would fools be considered noble? (32:5–6)
Because the people didn't know any better.
When people are spiritually blind and deaf,
they often allow ungodly people (*fool* means
someone who prefers sin over righteousness
—someone who is wicked) to assume noble
positions of leadership. Nations often get the
leaders they deserve (see 3:4–7).

Why did the women feel so complacent and secure? (32:9–10)
Because they were so caught up in their easy
lives of luxury. They ignored deeper, spiritual
needs—both their own and their nation's. Isaiah called attention to their complacency as
just one example of society's twisted values
during his day.

What was to happen in little more than a year? (32:10)
We can't say with certainty. Some think this
was perhaps a prophecy of an invasion by the
Assyrian king Sennacherib in 701 B.C. Whatever the coming trouble, it's clear that the things
that once gave pleasure and feelings of security would soon be gone.

¹⁵till the Spirit is poured upon us from on high,
  and the desert becomes a fertile field,
  and the fertile field seems like a forest.
¹⁶Justice will dwell in the desert
  and righteousness^D live in the fertile field.
¹⁷The fruit of righteousness will be peace;
  the effect of righteousness will be quietness
  and confidence forever.
¹⁸My people will live in peaceful dwelling places,
  in secure homes,
  in undisturbed places of rest.
¹⁹Though hail flattens the forest
  and the city is leveled completely,
²⁰how blessed you will be,
  sowing your seed by every stream,
  and letting your cattle and donkeys range
  free.

Distress and Help

33 Woe to you, O destroyer,
  you who have not been destroyed!
Woe to you, O traitor,
  you who have not been betrayed!
When you stop destroying,
  you will be destroyed;
when you stop betraying,
  you will be betrayed.

²O LORD, be gracious to us;
  we long for you.
Be our strength every morning,
  our salvation^D in time of distress.
³At the thunder of your voice, the peoples flee;
  when you rise up, the nations scatter.
⁴Your plunder^D, O nations, is harvested as by
  young locusts^D;
  like a swarm of locusts men pounce on it.

⁵The LORD is exalted, for he dwells on high;
  he will fill Zion^D with justice and
  righteousness.
⁶He will be the sure foundation for your times,
  a rich store of salvation and wisdom and
  knowledge;
  the fear of the LORD is the key to this
  treasure.^a

⁷Look, their brave men cry aloud in the streets;
  the envoys of peace weep bitterly.
⁸The highways are deserted,
  no travelers are on the roads.
The treaty is broken,
  its witnesses^b are despised,
  no one is respected.
⁹The land mourns^c and wastes away,
  Lebanon is ashamed and withers;
Sharon is like the Arabah,
  and Bashan and Carmel drop their leaves.

¹⁰"Now will I arise," says the LORD.
  "Now will I be exalted;
  now will I be lifted up.
¹¹You conceive chaff^D,

Destroyer (33:1)
Probably the nation of Assyria. Up to this time, the Assyrians had always been victorious. This was about to change.

Fear of the Lord (33:6)
See article: *Should we live in terror of God?* (Prov. 1:7).

Why did brave men cry? (33:7–9)
Brave men crying—along with the images that follow—were graphic, poetic expressions to describe the utter despair that engulfed the land: The brave men of Judah would cry over the destruction brought about by the Assyrians. The destruction came because of a broken *treaty*, probably the agreement between Hezekiah, king of Judah and Sennacherib, king of Assyria (2 Kings 18:14). The hopelessness of the people was heightened because the Assyrians totally ignored their overtures toward peace.

Chaff . . . straw . . . fire (33:11)
Chaff and straw were the unusable portions of crops—what was left after the grain had been harvested and threshed. This is a picture of futility: their own efforts would accomplish nothing and, in fact, would end up being fuel for the fire. After the harvest, the straw stubble left in the field was torched, sending towering clouds of smoke and flame into the air.

---

^a6 Or *is a treasure from him*   ^b8 Dead Sea Scrolls; Masoretic Text / *the cities*   ^c9 Or *dries up*

you give birth to straw;
   your breath is a fire that consumes you.
¹²The peoples will be burned as if to lime;
   like cut thornbushes they will be set ablaze."

¹³You who are far away, hear what I have done;
   you who are near, acknowledge my power!
¹⁴The sinners in Zion^D are terrified;
   trembling grips the godless:
"Who of us can dwell with the consuming
      fire?
   Who of us can dwell with everlasting
      burning?"
¹⁵He who walks righteously^D
   and speaks what is right,
who rejects gain from extortion^D
   and keeps his hand from accepting bribes,
who stops his ears against plots of murder
   and shuts his eyes against contemplating
      evil—
¹⁶this is the man who will dwell on the heights,
   whose refuge will be the mountain fortress.
His bread will be supplied,
   and water will not fail him.

¹⁷Your eyes will see the king in his beauty
   and view a land that stretches afar.
¹⁸In your thoughts you will ponder the former
      terror:
"Where is that chief officer?
   Where is the one who took the revenue?
   Where is the officer in charge of the
      towers?"
¹⁹You will see those arrogant people no more,
   those people of an obscure speech,
   with their strange, incomprehensible tongue.

²⁰Look upon Zion, the city of our festivals;
   your eyes will see Jerusalem^D,

To lime (33:12)
See *To lime* (Amos 2:1).

Does *the consuming fire* refer to hell? (33:14)
No, it refers to God. God's presence, especially when judgment is involved, is often associated with fire (29:6; 30:27,30; Exodus 24:17; Heb. 12:29).

How would the innocent in Jerusalem escape its judgment? (33:15–16)
Those who live righteously *dwell on the heights*, a symbol of the security found only in God. While *sinners in Zion are terrified* (v. 14), the righteous enjoy refuge. This may have meant primarily a spiritual sort of security, since the atrocities of war inevitably cause innocents to suffer.

Does this describe the end of the foreign domination over Israel? (33:17–19)
Isaiah again seems to be describing the future Messianic age when God's people would be safe at last. The *king* refers to the Messiah, or possibly to God himself. Even though the ultimate fulfillment of this prophecy was many years away, it must have provided great comfort to those facing the immediate threat posed by Assyria. The clear message was that no matter what happens, God is in control.

What is this vision of? (33:20–24)

Isaiah painted a wonderful picture of a new Jerusalem with a peace-filled future, speaking of both spiritual and material blessings to come. In contrast to the impending judgment and destruction (vv. 7–9), God's holy city would be safe and secure in the coming Messianic age. It would be restored again as a peaceful place for religious feasts.

Knowing their city would one day be like *a tent that will not be moved* (v. 20) must have comforted people who were threatened with being uprooted. Though Jerusalem wasn't protected by *broad rivers and streams* (v. 21), it would then be as safe as if it were. Wide rivers, shallow and slow, made cities unreachable by deeper sailing war ships. Their waters also helped protect from land attack from one or more sides. God would be more than protector; he would also govern the city as a *judge, lawgiver* and *king* (v. 22).

Verse 23 seems to be parenthetical. Isaiah contrasts the future security and the present danger. What was to come did not change the reality of the people's sin. Their rebellion against God had left them vulnerable to the enemy. But verse 24 shifts again to the future where sin and sickness would be removed.

For New Testament prophecies about the new Jerusalem, see Heb. 12:22; Rev. 3:12; 21:1–5.

a peaceful abode, a tent that will not be
moved;
its stakes will never be pulled up,
nor any of its ropes broken.
21There the Lord will be our Mighty One.
It will be like a place of broad rivers and
streams.
No galley with oars will ride them,
no mighty ship will sail them.
22For the Lord is our judge,
the Lord is our lawgiver,
the Lord is our king;
it is he who will save us.

23Your rigging hangs loose:
The mast is not held secure,
the sail is not spread.
Then an abundance of spoils will be divided
and even the lame will carry off plunder[D].
24No one living in Zion[D] will say, "I am ill";
and the sins of those who dwell there will be
forgiven.

Judgment Against the Nations

34 Come near, you nations, and listen;
    pay attention, you peoples!
Let the earth hear, and all that is in it,
the world, and all that comes out of it!
2The Lord is angry with all nations;
his wrath is upon all their armies.
He will totally destroy[a] them,
he will give them over to slaughter.
3Their slain will be thrown out,
their dead bodies will send up a stench;
the mountains will be soaked with their
blood.
4All the stars of the heavens will be dissolved
and the sky rolled up like a scroll;
all the starry host[D] will fall
like withered leaves from the vine,
like shriveled figs from the fig tree.

5My sword has drunk its fill in the heavens;
see, it descends in judgment on Edom[D],
the people I have totally destroyed.
6The sword of the Lord is bathed in blood,
it is covered with fat—
the blood of lambs and goats,
fat from the kidneys of rams.
For the Lord has a sacrifice[D] in Bozrah
and a great slaughter in Edom.
7And the wild oxen will fall with them,
the bull calves and the great bulls.
Their land will be drenched with blood,
and the dust will be soaked with fat.

8For the Lord has a day of vengeance,
a year of retribution[D], to uphold Zion's
cause.
9Edom's streams will be turned into pitch,
her dust into burning sulfur;
her land will become blazing pitch!

Why was God angry with *all* nations? (34:1–3)
God's anger targets all nations that refuse to honor him, but especially those that show hostility to the people that belong to him. The *armies* of these nations bear the brunt of God's wrath, probably because a nation's military so often reflects its self-sufficiency and deep-seated arrogance.

What does this poetic language describe? (34:4)
It pictures the extent of God's judgment—affecting heaven as well as earth. Though it can be taken literally, for God can do things in ways we cannot comprehend, it is also possible that such language, typical for divine judgment, is to be understood symbolically. This future judgment, also known as *the day of the Lord* is further described in Matt. 24:29; 2 Peter 3:10; Rev. 6:12–14.

Edom (34:5)
Although this was a specific nation (see *Edom*, Gen. 36:1, and *Edomites*, 2 Chron. 28:17), here it symbolizes all the enemies of God and his people.

Why was the sword of the Lord covered in fat? (34:6–7)
This sword represents God's judgment against enemy nations—even those living in luxury and ease. Fat symbolized excess—having more than was needed. It was a metaphor for enjoying comfortable circumstances. Fat was also considered the choice part of the meat and in some cases was completely burned as an offering of one's best to God. Therefore, God's judgment would extend to all people of enemy nations, even the "best"—those who were well-off and well-protected. No enemy would be spared.

---

a2 The Hebrew term refers to the irrevocable giving over of things or persons to the Lord, often by totally destroying them; also in verse 5.

¹⁰It will not be quenched night and day;
  its smoke will rise forever.
From generation to generation it will lie
    desolate;
  no one will ever pass through it again.
¹¹The desert owl*a* and screech owl*a* will
    possess it;
  the great owl*a* and the raven will nest there.
God will stretch out over Edom*D*
  the measuring line*D* of chaos
  and the plumb line of desolation.
¹²Her nobles will have nothing there to be called
    a kingdom,
  all her princes will vanish away.
¹³Thorns will overrun her citadels*D*,
  nettles and brambles her strongholds*D*.
She will become a haunt for jackals,
  a home for owls.
¹⁴Desert creatures will meet with hyenas,
  and wild goats will bleat to each other;
there the night creatures will also repose
  and find for themselves places of rest.
¹⁵The owl will nest there and lay eggs,
  she will hatch them, and care for her young
    under the shadow of her wings;
there also the falcons will gather,
  each with its mate.

¹⁶Look in the scroll of the LORD and read:

None of these will be missing,
  not one will lack her mate.
For it is his mouth that has given the order,
  and his Spirit will gather them together.
¹⁷He allots their portions;
  his hand distributes them by measure.
They will possess it forever
  and dwell there from generation to
    generation.

Joy of the Redeemed

35 The desert and the parched land will be glad;
  the wilderness will rejoice and blossom.
Like the crocus, ²it will burst into bloom;
  it will rejoice greatly and shout for joy.
The glory*D* of Lebanon will be given to it,
  the splendor of Carmel and Sharon;
they will see the glory of the LORD,
  the splendor of our God.

³Strengthen the feeble hands,
  steady the knees that give way;
⁴say to those with fearful hearts,
  "Be strong, do not fear;
your God will come,
  he will come with vengeance;
with divine retribution*D*
  he will come to save you."

⁵Then will the eyes of the blind be opened
  and the ears of the deaf unstopped.
⁶Then will the lame leap like a deer,
  and the mute tongue shout for joy.

a11 The precise identification of these birds is uncertain.

What scroll were the people supposed to study? (34:16)

Some suggest that this scroll was the book of life (Psalm 139:16; Mal. 3:16) or possibly other parts of Isaiah. It's more likely that it refers to a scroll containing this prophecy against Edom. Since it was written down, when it happens it will demonstrate God's part in the final judgment.

What did blossoms in the desert mean? (35:1–2)

The land once devastated by the enemy would again become vibrant and beautiful, much as a desert bursts into life with plants and flowers following a rare rainfall. Isaiah may have had some of the areas of Judah in mind when he wrote this, such as the desert regions to the east. It is also possible that the metaphor pictured the time of the Jews returning from exile. The ultimate fulfillment will be when Christ comes again.

When will God come? (35:4)

Isaiah doesn't pinpoint an exact time, but whenever God comes, he's involved in both vengeance (judgment) and salvation. Again, the ultimate fulfillment of these words will be realized only when the Messianic kingdom is established. God not only saves his people from physical enemies, he delivers them from their greatest enemy—sin.

Did this foretell Jesus? (35:5–10)

Yes, this is another reference to the kingdom of the Messiah, ushered in by Jesus Christ. Just as the land will be changed (v. 1), the people themselves will undergo a glorious transformation.

What kind of highway is this? (35:8)

Most roads common to Isaiah's day were mere trails that left travelers vulnerable to dangers along the way. But Isaiah describes a highway that is completely safe and available only to God's redeemed people. It leads to Jerusalem, God's holy city and symbolizes the return of his people to the place where he reigns.

From where would those who were ransomed return? (35:10)

Although Isaiah doesn't say, he might be referring to the return to Jerusalem of those who were in captivity. Words like *everlasting joy* suggest that some future redemptive work of God is also in mind—where people return to him from their sin. Zion represents all the blessings God has in store for his redeemed people. Since we live on this side of the cross, we can see that this redemption is fully possible only through Jesus Christ.

SCRIPTURE LINK (chs. 36–39)

This portion of Isaiah is nearly identical to material found in 2 Kings 18:13—20:19. Many say Isaiah adapted this material from 2 Kings, while others point out both writers could have borrowed from a third, unknown source.

Why did Isaiah switch his writing style? (36:1)

Up to this point, the writing style has mostly been poetry. Suddenly it's prose—a straight narration of history. The events narrated in chs. 36–39, however, parallel the prophecies just given. In many ways, these chapters provide a transition between prophecies about an Assyrian threat and a more potent Babylonian threat which begins in ch. 40 but is hinted at in chs. 38–39.

Assyria Threatens Jerusalem (36:1)

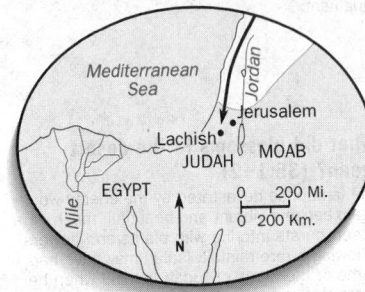

How did Hezekiah rebel against Assyria? (36:4–5)

Perhaps Hezekiah resisted the Assyrian invasion and did not surrender completely and quickly. Or he may have contemplated recruiting Egyptian assistance (v. 6). The Assyrians, under King Sennacherib, had conquered every major city in Judah, except Jerusalem. Finally, Hezekiah paid Sennacherib a sizable tribute, hoping to appease the Assyrians (2 Kings 18:14–16). The Assyrians, however, were not bought off so easily.

Was Hezekiah depending on Egypt as charged? (36:6)

See *Was the report of Egyptian aid true?* (37:9).

Water will gush forth in the wilderness
   and streams in the desert.
7The burning sand will become a pool,
   the thirsty ground bubbling springs.
In the haunts where jackals once lay,
   grass and reeds and papyrus will grow.

8And a highway will be there;
   it will be called the Way of Holiness.
The unclean[D] will not journey on it;
   it will be for those who walk in that Way;
   wicked fools will not go about on it.[a]
9No lion will be there,
   nor will any ferocious beast get up on it;
   they will not be found there.
But only the redeemed[D] will walk there,
10   and the ransomed of the LORD will return.
They will enter Zion[D] with singing;
   everlasting joy will crown their heads.
Gladness and joy will overtake them,
   and sorrow and sighing will flee away.

Sennacherib Threatens Jerusalem

36 In the fourteenth year of King Hezekiah's reign, Sennacherib king of Assyria attacked all the fortified cities of Judah and captured them. 2Then the king of Assyria sent his field commander with a large army from Lachish to King Hezekiah at Jerusalem[D]. When the commander stopped at the aqueduct of the Upper Pool, on the road to the Washerman's Field, 3Eliakim son of Hilkiah the palace administrator, Shebna the secretary, and Joah son of Asaph the recorder went out to him.

4The field commander said to them, "Tell Hezekiah,

" 'This is what the great king, the king of Assyria, says: On what are you basing this confidence of yours? 5You say you have strategy and military strength—but you speak only empty words. On whom are you depending, that you rebel against me? 6Look now, you are depending on Egypt, that splintered reed of a staff, which pierces a man's hand and wounds him if he leans on it! Such is Pharaoh king of Egypt to all who depend on him. 7And if you say to me, "We are depending on the LORD our God"—isn't he the one whose high places[D] and altars Hezekiah removed, saying to Judah and Jerusalem, "You must worship before this altar"?

8" 'Come now, make a bargain with my master, the king of Assyria: I will give you two thousand horses—if you can put riders on them! 9How then can you repulse one officer of the least of my master's officials, even though you are depending on Egypt for chariots and horsemen? 10Furthermore, have I come to attack and destroy this land without the LORD? The LORD himself told me to march against this country and destroy it.' "

11Then Eliakim, Shebna and Joah said to the field commander, "Please speak to your servants in Aramaic[D], since we understand it. Don't speak to us in Hebrew[D] in the hearing of the people on the wall."

12But the commander replied, "Was it only to your master and you that my master sent me to say these things,

---

a8 Or / the simple will not stray from it

and not to the men sitting on the wall—who, like you, will have to eat their own filth and drink their own urine?"

¹³Then the commander stood and called out in Hebrew^D, "Hear the words of the great king, the king of Assyria! ¹⁴This is what the king says: Do not let Hezekiah deceive you. He cannot deliver you! ¹⁵Do not let Hezekiah persuade you to trust in the LORD when he says, 'The LORD will surely deliver us; this city will not be given into the hand of the king of Assyria.'

¹⁶"Do not listen to Hezekiah. This is what the king of Assyria says: Make peace^D with me and come out to me. Then every one of you will eat from his own vine and fig tree and drink water from his own cistern^D, ¹⁷until I come and take you to a land like your own—a land of grain and new wine^D, a land of bread and vineyards.

¹⁸"Do not let Hezekiah mislead you when he says, 'The LORD will deliver us.' Has the god of any nation ever delivered his land from the hand of the king of Assyria? ¹⁹Where are the gods of Hamath and Arpad? Where are the gods of Sepharvaim? Have they rescued Samaria from my hand? ²⁰Who of all the gods of these countries has been able to save his land from me? How then can the LORD deliver Jerusalem^D from my hand?"

²¹But the people remained silent and said nothing in reply, because the king had commanded, "Do not answer him."

²²Then Eliakim son of Hilkiah the palace administrator, Shebna the secretary, and Joah son of Asaph the recorder went to Hezekiah, with their clothes torn, and told him what the field commander had said.

Jerusalem's Deliverance Foretold

37 When King Hezekiah heard this, he tore his clothes and put on sackcloth^D and went into the temple of the LORD. ²He sent Eliakim the palace administrator, Shebna the secretary, and the leading priests^D, all wearing sackcloth, to the prophet Isaiah son of Amoz. ³They told him, "This is what Hezekiah says: This day is a day of distress and rebuke and disgrace, as when children come to the point of birth and there is no strength to deliver them. ⁴It may be that the LORD your God will hear the words of the field commander, whom his master, the king of Assyria, has sent to ridicule the living God, and that he will rebuke him for the words the LORD your God has heard. Therefore pray for the remnant^D that still survives."

⁵When King Hezekiah's officials came to Isaiah, ⁶Isaiah said to them, "Tell your master, 'This is what the LORD says: Do not be afraid of what you have heard—those words with which the underlings of the king of Assyria have blasphemed^D me. ⁷Listen! I am going to put a spirit in him so that when he hears a certain report, he will return to his own country, and there I will have him cut down with the sword.' "

⁸When the field commander heard that the king of Assyria had left Lachish, he withdrew and found the king fighting against Libnah.

⁹Now Sennacherib received a report that Tirhakah, the Cushite^a king ₗof Egypt₎, was marching out to fight against him. When he heard it, he sent messengers to Hezekiah with this word: ¹⁰"Say to Hezekiah king of Judah: Do not let the god you depend on deceive you when

---

^a9 That is, from the upper Nile region

Why did Hezekiah restrict worship of God? (36:7)

The Assyrian commander was referring to the time when Hezekiah removed all the *high places and altars* where the people of Judah worshiped God (2 Kings 18:4). What the commander didn't say was that these high places and altars were also often used by people to worship false gods. The commander was trying to make the people of Judah doubt Hezekiah's commitment to God.

Why did Sennacherib claim to follow the Lord's directions? (36:10)

Such a claim would have struck terror into the hearts of the people of Judah—to think that this enemy was actually following the Lord's command! It's true that the Lord did use Assyria to punish the people of Israel and Judah, but the Assyrian commander didn't realize Assyria itself was about to feel the heat of God's judgment.

Was this war propaganda effective? (36:16–17)

This is military propaganda at its finest. Fortunately, Hezekiah's people didn't take the bait (v. 21).

Tore his clothes (37:1)

See *Where did the custom of ashes and torn clothing come from?* (2 Samuel 13:19); *Why did Mordecai tear his clothes?* (Esther 4:1–2) and *Why shave beards, tear clothes and cut skin?* (Jer. 41:5).

As a prophet, what role did Isaiah play in government? (37:2)

Isaiah had no official role in the government. Technically, he was merely a private citizen. Nevertheless, King Hezekiah recognized Isaiah as a prophet—one who spoke for God. Hezekiah sought Isaiah's help because he hoped to receive direction from the Lord.

What *spirit* would God put in Sennacherib? (37:7)

What God put in Sennacherib was not the Holy Spirit or even an evil spirit. This *spirit* was most likely a general compulsion. God apparently intended to use Sennacherib's own anxieties or other feelings to cause him to return to his own land.

Was the report of Egyptian aid true? (37:9)

Sennacherib heard a rumor that Egypt was coming to the aid of Judah. Whether this rumor was true or not isn't known. Either way, the rumor made the Assyrians even more desperate to capture Jerusalem.

Why didn't Hezekiah go to Isaiah again? (37:14)
Isaiah may have been unavailable, or perhaps there wasn't enough time. What is significant is that Hezekiah was able to approach God directly. Since he had a relationship with God himself, he didn't need a prophet to act on his behalf when he faced troubles.

Did God base his decision on Hezekiah's prayer? (37:21)
God clearly wanted Hezekiah to know his prayer would be answered. We also know that God had already promised to deliver his people. Some say God may change his methods in response to prayer, but that he never alters his purpose. Others note that God makes both absolute decrees (unchanged regardless of what humans do with them) and conditional decrees (which invite—even depend upon—human interaction). Either way, God does not change. His character and purpose are settled. Also see article: *When does God refuse to hear our prayers?* (Jer. 11:11).

he says, 'Jerusalem[D] will not be handed over to the king of Assyria.' [11]Surely you have heard what the kings of Assyria have done to all the countries, destroying them completely. And will you be delivered? [12]Did the gods of the nations that were destroyed by my forefathers deliver them—the gods of Gozan, Haran, Rezeph and the people of Eden who were in Tel Assar? [13]Where is the king of Hamath, the king of Arpad, the king of the city of Sepharvaim, or of Hena or Ivvah?"

Hezekiah's Prayer

[14]Hezekiah received the letter from the messengers and read it. Then he went up to the temple of the LORD and spread it out before the LORD. [15]And Hezekiah prayed to the LORD: [16]"O LORD Almighty, God of Israel, enthroned between the cherubim[D], you alone are God over all the kingdoms of the earth. You have made heaven and earth. [17]Give ear, O LORD, and hear; open your eyes, O LORD, and see; listen to all the words Sennacherib has sent to insult the living God.

[18]"It is true, O LORD, that the Assyrian kings have laid waste all these peoples and their lands. [19]They have thrown their gods into the fire and destroyed them, for they were not gods but only wood and stone, fashioned by human hands. [20]Now, O LORD our God, deliver us from his hand, so that all kingdoms on earth may know that you alone, O LORD, are God.[a]"

Sennacherib's Fall

[21]Then Isaiah son of Amoz sent a message to Hezekiah: "This is what the LORD, the God of Israel, says: Because you have prayed to me concerning Sennacherib king of Assyria, [22]this is the word the LORD has spoken against him:

"The Virgin Daughter of Zion[D]
    despises and mocks you.
The Daughter of Jerusalem
    tosses her head as you flee.
[23]Who is it you have insulted and blasphemed[D]?
    Against whom have you raised your voice
and lifted your eyes in pride?
    Against the Holy One of Israel!
[24]By your messengers
    you have heaped insults on the Lord.
And you have said,
    'With my many chariots
I have ascended the heights of the mountains,
    the utmost heights of Lebanon.
I have cut down its tallest cedars,
    the choicest of its pines.
I have reached its remotest heights,
    the finest of its forests.
[25]I have dug wells in foreign lands[b]
    and drunk the water there.
With the soles of my feet
    I have dried up all the streams of Egypt.'

[26]"Have you not heard?
    Long ago I ordained it.
In days of old I planned it;

---

a20 Dead Sea Scrolls (see also 2 Kings 19:19); Masoretic Text *alone are the* LORD   *b25* Dead Sea Scrolls (see also 2 Kings 19:24); Masoretic Text does not have *in foreign lands.*

now I have brought it to pass,
that you have turned fortified cities
into piles of stone.
27Their people, drained of power,
are dismayed and put to shame.
They are like plants in the field,
like tender green shoots,
like grass sprouting on the roof,
scorched[a] before it grows up.

28"But I know where you stay
and when you come and go
and how you rage against me.
29Because you rage against me
and because your insolence has reached my
ears,
I will put my hook in your nose
and my bit in your mouth,
and I will make you return
by the way you came.

30"This will be the sign for you, O Hezekiah:

"This year you will eat what grows by itself,
and the second year what springs from
that.
But in the third year sow and reap,
plant vineyards and eat their fruit.
31Once more a remnant[D] of the house of
Judah
will take root below and bear fruit above.
32For out of Jerusalem[D] will come a remnant,
and out of Mount Zion[D] a band of survivors.
The zeal[D] of the LORD Almighty
will accomplish this.

33"Therefore this is what the LORD says concerning the
king of Assyria:

"He will not enter this city
or shoot an arrow here.
He will not come before it with shield
or build a siege ramp against it.
34By the way that he came he will return;
he will not enter this city,"
declares the LORD.
35"I will defend this city and save it,
for my sake and for the sake of David my
servant!"

36Then the angel of the LORD went out and put to
death[D] a hundred and eighty-five thousand men in the
Assyrian camp. When the people got up the next morning—there were all the dead bodies! 37So Sennacherib
king of Assyria broke camp and withdrew. He returned to
Nineveh and stayed there.
38One day, while he was worshiping in the temple
of his god Nisroch, his sons Adrammelech and Sharezer
cut him down with the sword, and they escaped to the
land of Ararat. And Esarhaddon his son succeeded him as
king.

---

a27 Some manuscripts of the Masoretic Text, Dead Sea Scrolls and
some Septuagint manuscripts (see also 2 Kings 19:26); most
manuscripts of the Masoretic Text roof / and terraced fields

My hook . . . my bit (37:29)

Refers to the cruel treatment that the Assyrians often used on their captives. Sometimes
they placed rings through their captives' noses
so one soldier could lead many captives by running a rope through all the rings. Now, God was
about to give Sennacherib a taste of his own
medicine. The king of Assyria would be completely under God's control.

How did the angel put so many to death? (37:36)

We are not told the exact details, but some
suggest it was a plague, possibly the bubonic
plague. Whatever it was, it was obvious that
this was a direct punishment from the Lord.
Also see *What kind of plague did God send?*
(2 Kings 19:35).

How much later was Sennacherib as-
sassinated? (37:38)

About 20 years elapsed between the Assyrians' retreat from Jerusalem and Sennacherib's downfall.

Wasn't the Assyrian threat resolved in the last chapter? (38:6)

Yes, it was. That's why many believe that the events in chs. 38–39 actually took place before those described in chs. 36–37. One reason why the chapters might have been arranged in this order is that the focus of the book now shifts from Assyria to Babylon. The words *in those days* (v. 1) might simply refer to the lifetime of Hezekiah, not the next event in chronological order.

How did the sun's shadow go back? (38:7–8)

We can only guess what might have happened. Some point out that untold physical consequences would have occurred if the sun went backward because of an actual reversal of the earth's rotation. They suggest the shadow moved perhaps as the result of some type of refraction or reflection of sunlight. Yet, nothing is outside God's power and there are many instances in the Bible where God contradicts the natural laws he established.

Why was this sign even necessary? (38:7–8)

Hezekiah asked for a sign (v. 22; 2 Kings 20:8), perhaps because he felt his faith needed to be strengthened. After all, he had heard two opposite predictions (vv. 1,5). God obliged the king's request as a pledge that he would perform what he promised.

Hezekiah's Illness

38 In those days Hezekiah became ill and was at the point of death[D]. The prophet[D] Isaiah son of Amoz went to him and said, "This is what the LORD says: Put your house in order, because you are going to die; you will not recover."

²Hezekiah turned his face to the wall and prayed to the LORD, ³"Remember, O LORD, how I have walked before you faithfully and with wholehearted devotion and have done what is good in your eyes." And Hezekiah wept bitterly.

⁴Then the word of the LORD came to Isaiah: ⁵"Go and tell Hezekiah, 'This is what the LORD, the God of your father David, says: I have heard your prayer and seen your tears; I will add fifteen years to your life. ⁶And I will deliver you and this city from the hand of the king of Assyria. I will defend this city.

⁷"'This is the LORD's sign to you that the LORD will do what he has promised: ⁸I will make the shadow cast by the sun go back the ten steps it has gone down on the stairway of Ahaz.'" So the sunlight went back the ten steps it had gone down.

⁹A writing of Hezekiah king of Judah after his illness and recovery:

¹⁰I said, "In the prime of my life
    must I go through the gates of death[a]
    and be robbed of the rest of my years?"
¹¹I said, "I will not again see the LORD,
    the LORD, in the land of the living;
  no longer will I look on mankind,

a10 Hebrew Sheol

Why did God change his mind? (38:1–5)

Some say God cannot change his mind without contradicting his unchanging nature. They say that maybe God intended all along to heal Hezekiah. Withholding that news from Hezekiah, then, served to stimulate the intensity of his prayer. In this view, Hezekiah didn't change God's mind. But prayer helped him discover God's purpose so he could align his life and actions to it.

Others, however, have another view. They agree that God doesn't change his mind the way people do. But they suggest a sovereign God can predetermine to change his course of action in response to our prayers. His ultimate purposes are unchangeable, they say, but he builds options into his purposes from the start. They see flexibility in the outcome to accommodate the various responses of people. In this view, God is something like a traveler who plans a destination but allows freedom to change the route or make spontaneous side trips along the way. God's methods, they say, aren't necessarily set in concrete: people's actions can make a difference in the way God works.

The Bible recounts other examples of times that God seemed to change his mind: After saying he would destroy Nineveh, he didn't because they repented (Jonah 3:10–4:2). Earlier he had intended to destroy the Israelites but did not when Moses interceded for them (Exodus 32:9–14). On the other hand, God did not seem to respond to David's repentance (2 Samuel 12:13–23). And he told Jeremiah and Ezekiel that he would not even listen to requests of leniency for Judah (Jer. 7:16; 15:1; Ezek. 14:12–14). Also see article: *Can our prayers cause God to change his mind?* (Exodus 32:14).

or be with those who now dwell in this
    world.*a*

¹²Like a shepherd's tent my house
    has been pulled down and taken from me.
Like a weaver I have rolled up my life,
    and he has cut me off from the loom;
    day and night you made an end of me.
¹³I waited patiently till dawn,
    but like a lion he broke all my bones;
    day and night you made an end of me.
¹⁴I cried like a swift or thrush,
    I moaned like a mourning dove.
My eyes grew weak as I looked to the heavens.
    I am troubled; O Lord, come to my aid!"

¹⁵But what can I say?
    He has spoken to me, and he himself has
        done this.
I will walk humbly all my years
    because of this anguish of my soulᴰ.
¹⁶Lord, by such things men live;
    and my spirit finds life in them too.
You restored me to health
    and let me live.
¹⁷Surely it was for my benefit
    that I suffered such anguish.
In your love you kept me
    from the pit of destruction;
you have put all my sins
    behind your back.
¹⁸For the grave*b* cannot praise you,
    deathᴰ cannot sing your praise;
those who go down to the pit
    cannot hope for your faithfulness.
¹⁹The living, the living—they praise you,
    as I am doing today;
fathers tell their children
    about your faithfulness.

²⁰The Lord will save me,
    and we will sing with stringed instruments
all the days of our lives
    in the temple of the Lord.

²¹Isaiah had said, "Prepare a poultice of figs and apply it to the boil, and he will recover." ²²Hezekiah had asked, "What will be the sign that I will go up to the temple of the Lord?"

Envoys From Babylon

39 At that time Merodach-Baladan son of Baladan king of Babylon sent Hezekiah letters and a gift, because he had heard of his illness and recovery. ²Hezekiah received the envoys gladly and showed them what was in his storehouses—the silver, the gold, the spices, the fine oil, his entire armory and everything found among his treasures. There was nothing in his palace or in all his kingdom that Hezekiah did not show them.

³Then Isaiah the prophetᴰ went to King Hezekiah and asked, "What did those men say, and where did they come from?"

*a*11 A few Hebrew manuscripts; most Hebrew manuscripts *in the place of cessation*   *b*18 Hebrew *Sheol*

Is it okay to fear death? (38:10–14)

Hezekiah's words may reflect despair more than fear. Some think he worried that a short life (he was possibly in his late 30s) indicated he had failed to live a good life. (In Old Testament times, long life was considered a blessing.) His concern also may have been heightened if he did not yet have an heir to the throne. It's not unusual to be anxious about something we don't fully understand. Still, we have resources to face death that Hezekiah didn't (Heb. 2:14–15).

What did Hezekiah think would happen after death? (38:18)

Hezekiah's words echo the psalmists' sentiments (Psalms 6:5; 115:17). It was common then for people, even godly ones, to think their sins would keep them apart from God after death. They were therefore understandably nervous about what would happen when they died. The New Testament, however, assures us that through Christ our sins can be totally forgiven, allowing us to live with God forever.

Why do these verses seem out of order? (38:21–22)

Perhaps they serve as a footnote—clarifying what prompted Hezekiah's writing (vv. 9–20). These verses tie up the loose ends to the story. Writers today sometimes use this technique, called a flashback, to depart from the natural sequence and tell about an earlier event.

Why was Hezekiah so eager to show his wealth to a potential enemy? (39:1–2)

Perhaps Hezekiah was demonstrating that he had something to offer as a potential ally against the Assyrians. If so, he may have been wooing the Babylonians, hoping their protection might prevent further trouble with Assyria. Or, he may have been putting too much stock in his wealth and not enough in God's power. Either way he was trusting in human resources rather than the Lord—a foolish move on his part.

"From a distant land," Hezekiah replied. "They came to me from Babylon."

[4]The prophet[D] asked, "What did they see in your palace?"

"They saw everything in my palace," Hezekiah said. "There is nothing among my treasures that I did not show them."

[5]Then Isaiah said to Hezekiah, "Hear the word of the LORD Almighty: [6]The time will surely come when everything in your palace, and all that your fathers have stored up until this day, will be carried off to Babylon. Nothing will be left, says the LORD. [7]And some of your descendants, your own flesh and blood who will be born to you, will be taken away, and they will become eunuchs[D] in the palace of the king of Babylon."

[8]"The word of the LORD you have spoken is good," Hezekiah replied. For he thought, "There will be peace[D] and security in my lifetime."

Why would Hezekiah think God's judgment was good? (39:5–8)

Maybe Hezekiah pronounced this judgment *good* because he felt he deserved much worse. God could have brought all this about during Hezekiah's own lifetime. Another possibility is that *good* simply meant that he felt the judgment was appropriate. Just because he agreed with the judgment doesn't mean Hezekiah didn't care about the future of his descendants. Yes, he would enjoy peace and security in his lifetime, but he would have to live with the knowledge that hard times were in store for his descendants. It's unlikely Hezekiah was thinking only of himself.

Is there any connection between this chapter and what came before? (40:1)

Yes. Both touch on the coming Babylonian captivity. The historical account of ch. 39 foreshadows it while the poetry of ch. 40 offers hopeful words to contrast with the despair it would bring.

What service had Jerusalem completed? (40:2)

A bonded servant typically worked seven years to pay off a debt. Once the service was completed, the servant was set free. Israel had a debt to pay to the Lord and would work it off by being taken as captives to Babylon. Although these words sound like the exile was over and past, Isaiah penned them before the exile. He used the past tense in a hopeful sense, looking forward to when the captivity would be over. In a broader sense, this *service* could refer to all the time up until the coming of the Messiah.

Double for all her sins (40:2)

Israel had paid the consequences for its sins. This expression indicated that the people had been punished more than enough.

How were these promises fulfilled? (40:3–5,9)

Those who heard Isaiah's prophecy associated it with the return of the exiles from Babylon to Jerusalem. We can see another fulfillment, however, because of the New Testament. Isaiah's words anticipated John the Baptist and the good news announcing the coming Messiah.

Whose voice was this? (40:3,6)

We know from the New Testament that this prophecy looked ahead to the voice of John the Baptist (Matt. 3:3). John, a cousin of Jesus, helped prepare the way for Jesus' ministry by preaching about the need for repentance. As people became aware of their sin, the stage was set for Christ's saving work.

Comfort for God's People

40 Comfort, comfort my people,
        says your God.
[2]Speak tenderly to Jerusalem[D],
        and proclaim to her
that her hard service has been completed,
        that her sin has been paid for,
that she has received from the LORD's hand
        double for all her sins.

[3]A voice of one calling:
"In the desert prepare
        the way for the LORD[a];
make straight in the wilderness
        a highway for our God.[b]
[4]Every valley shall be raised up,
        every mountain and hill made low;
the rough ground shall become level,
        the rugged places a plain.
[5]And the glory[D] of the LORD will be revealed,
        and all mankind together will see it.
                        For the mouth of the
                        LORD has spoken."

[6]A voice says, "Cry out."
        And I said, "What shall I cry?"

"All men are like grass,
        and all their glory is like the flowers of the
                field.
[7]The grass withers and the flowers fall,
        because the breath of the LORD blows on them.
        Surely the people are grass.
[8]The grass withers and the flowers fall,
        but the word of our God stands forever."

[9]You who bring good tidings to Zion[D],
        go up on a high mountain.
You who bring good tidings to Jerusalem,[c]
        lift up your voice with a shout,
lift it up, do not be afraid;
        say to the towns of Judah,

---

[a]3 Or *A voice of one calling in the desert: / "Prepare the way for the LORD*   [b]3 Hebrew; Septuagint *make straight the paths of our God*   [c]9 Or *O Zion, bringer of good tidings, / go up on a high mountain. / O Jerusalem, bringer of good tidings*

"Here is your God!"

¹⁰See, the Sovereign LORD comes with power,
   and his arm rules for him.
See, his reward is with him,
   and his recompense accompanies him.
¹¹He tends his flock like a shepherd:
   He gathers the lambs in his arms
and carries them close to his heart;
   he gently leads those that have young.

¹²Who has measured the waters in the hollow of
      his hand,
   or with the breadth of his hand marked off
      the heavens?
Who has held the dust of the earth in a basket,
   or weighed the mountains on the scales
   and the hills in a balance?
¹³Who has understood the mind*ᵃ* of the LORD,
   or instructed him as his counselor?
¹⁴Whom did the LORD consult to enlighten him,
   and who taught him the right way?
Who was it that taught him knowledge
   or showed him the path of understanding?

¹⁵Surely the nations are like a drop in a bucket;
   they are regarded as dust on the scales;
he weighs the islands as though they were
      fine dust.
¹⁶Lebanon is not sufficient for altar fires,
   nor its animals enough for burnt offeringsᴰ.
¹⁷Before him all the nations are as nothing;
   they are regarded by him as worthless
   and less than nothing.

¹⁸To whom, then, will you compare God?
   What image will you compare him to?
¹⁹As for an idolᴰ, a craftsman casts it,
   and a goldsmith overlays it with gold
   and fashions silver chains for it.
²⁰A man too poor to present such an offering
   selects wood that will not rot.
He looks for a skilled craftsman
   to set up an idol that will not topple.

²¹Do you not know?
   Have you not heard?
Has it not been told you from the beginning?
   Have you not understood since the earth was
      founded?
²²He sits enthroned above the circle of the earth,
   and its people are like grasshoppers.
He stretches out the heavens like a canopy,
   and spreads them out like a tent to live in.
²³He brings princes to naught
   and reduces the rulers of this world to
      nothing.
²⁴No sooner are they planted,
   no sooner are they sown,
   no sooner do they take root in the ground,
than he blows on them and they wither,
   and a whirlwind sweeps them away like
      chaffᴰ.

²⁵"To whom will you compare me?

ᵃ13 Or *Spirit*; or *spirit*

How is God a powerful ruler and, at the same time, a gentle shepherd? (40:10–11)

There's no contradiction here, for the Lord's strong arm is used both to rule and to protect his people. The Lord cherishes those who follow him; he also displays his power and his resolve to effectively lead. Jesus demonstrated both strength and gentleness—a good shepherd needs both (John 10:11).

Why does God consider all nations to be worthless? (40:17)

Saying that nations are *worthless* and *less than nothing* doesn't mean that God cares nothing about nations. This is a literary device known as hyperbole—acknowledged exaggeration to emphasize a point. In comparison to the Lord's greatness, the nations are nothing more than a drop in the bucket or a heap of dust.

Circle of the earth (40:22)

The horizon. This is the only time this phrase appears in the Bible.

Does God manipulate political events? (40:23)

Yes, God can manipulate political events and sometimes does so in a dramatic fashion. But humans are not mere puppets on a string. They still have the responsibility to respond to what God does and says. Also see *Is God responsible for bad government?* (Daniel 5:18) and article: *Does God support bad government?* (Romans 13:1–7).

Or who is my equal?" says the Holy One.
²⁶Lift your eyes and look to the heavens:
　Who created all these?
He who brings out the starry host[D] one by
　　one,
　and calls them each by name.
Because of his great power and mighty
　　strength,
　not one of them is missing.

²⁷Why do you say, O Jacob,
　and complain, O Israel,
"My way is hidden from the LORD;
　my cause is disregarded by my God"?
²⁸Do you not know?
　Have you not heard?
The LORD is the everlasting God,
　the Creator of the ends of the earth.
He will not grow tired or weary,
　and his understanding no one can fathom.
²⁹He gives strength to the weary
　and increases the power of the weak.
³⁰Even youths grow tired and weary,
　and young men stumble and fall;
³¹but those who hope in the LORD
　will renew their strength.
They will soar on wings like eagles;
　they will run and not grow weary,
　they will walk and not be faint.

The Helper of Israel

41 "Be silent before me, you islands!
　　Let the nations renew their strength!
Let them come forward and speak;
　let us meet together at the place of judgment.

²"Who has stirred up one from the east,
　calling him in righteousness[D] to his
　　service[a]?
He hands nations over to him
　and subdues kings before him.
He turns them to dust with his sword,
　to windblown chaff[D] with his bow.
³He pursues them and moves on unscathed,
　by a path his feet have not traveled before.
⁴Who has done this and carried it through,
　calling forth the generations from the
　　beginning?
I, the LORD—with the first of them
　and with the last—I am he."

⁵The islands have seen it and fear;
　the ends of the earth tremble.
They approach and come forward;
⁶　each helps the other
　and says to his brother, "Be strong!"
⁷The craftsman encourages the goldsmith,
　and he who smooths with the hammer
　spurs on him who strikes the anvil.
He says of the welding, "It is good."
　He nails down the idol[D] so it will not topple.

⁸"But you, O Israel, my servant,

What does it mean to *hope in the Lord?* (40:31)

The word *hope* implies both trust and patience. Trust involves confidence in God's power to deliver and faith that he will keep his promises. Hoping in the Lord also implies the patience to wait for God's promises since God works according to his own timing.

One from the east (41:2)

Cyrus the Great, ruler of Persia, from the area of modern-day Iran. This would be not only east of Israel, but somewhat east of Babylon, where the Jews languished in exile before Cyrus came to power (see *Setting of Esther* on page 666). His Persians conquered the Babylonians in 539 B.C. and he later allowed the Jews to return to their homeland.

Why talk about those who make idols? (41:7)

In a world where people worshiped many different deities, God regularly asked his people to compare the one true God with the false gods (see 1 Kings 18:16–45, for example). Here we see the whole world trembling in response to God's mighty actions (v. 5). But instead of turning to the true God, the idolmakers try to console each other—and even try to anchor their idols so that they will not be shaken by God's shock waves.

*a*2 Or *I whom victory meets at every step*

Jacob, whom I have chosen,
you descendants of Abraham my friend,
⁹I took you from the ends of the earth,
from its farthest corners I called you.
I said, 'You are my servant';
I have chosen you and have not rejected you.
¹⁰So do not fear, for I am with you;
do not be dismayed, for I am your God.
I will strengthen you and help you;
I will uphold you with my righteousᴰ right
hand.

¹¹"All who rage against you
will surely be ashamed and disgraced;
those who oppose you
will be as nothing and perish.
¹²Though you search for your enemies,
you will not find them.
Those who wage war against you
will be as nothing at all.
¹³For I am the LORD, your God,
who takes hold of your right hand
and says to you, Do not fear;
I will help you.
¹⁴Do not be afraid, O worm Jacob,
O little Israel,
for I myself will help you," declares the LORD,
your Redeemerᴰ, the Holy One of Israel.
¹⁵"See, I will make you into a threshing sledge,
new and sharp, with many teeth.
You will thresh the mountains and crush them,
and reduce the hills to chaffᴰ.
¹⁶You will winnow them, the wind will pick
them up,
and a gale will blow them away.
But you will rejoice in the LORD
and glory in the Holy One of Israel.

¹⁷"The poor and needy search for water,
but there is none;
their tongues are parched with thirst.
But I the LORD will answer them;
I, the God of Israel, will not forsake them.
¹⁸I will make rivers flow on barren heights,
and springs within the valleys.
I will turn the desert into pools of water,
and the parched ground into springs.
¹⁹I will put in the desert
the cedar and the acaciaᴰ, the myrtle and
the olive.
I will set pines in the wasteland,
the fir and the cypress together,
²⁰so that people may see and know,
may consider and understand,
that the hand of the LORD has done this,
that the Holy One of Israel has created it.

²¹"Present your case," says the LORD.
"Set forth your arguments," says Jacob's
King.
²²"Bring in ᴸ your idolsᴰ ᴶ to tell us
what is going to happen.
Tell us what the former things were,
so that we may consider them
and know their final outcome.

Why does God call his people a *worm*? (41:14)

It's obvious from the context that God was not
scolding his people. They already must have
been considering themselves as insignificant
as worms. He was comforting them and offering new hope. They may have been little and insignificant compared to the great nations battling for power, but God would still use Israel in
mighty ways.

Threshing sledge (41:15)

After grain was harvested, it was usually dried
and taken to a threshing floor to be crushed in
order to separate the stalks and husks from
the edible kernels. This was often done with
large sleds, or sledges, drawn by animals. Not
only would the weight of the sledges crush the
grain, but some sledges were fitted with sharp
teeth to rip the grain apart. This is an image of
great power. Little Israel would become a huge
sledge, threshing the *mountains,* the surrounding nations.

When did God *turn the desert into pools of water?* (41:18)

We must look at these prophecies in three
ways: spiritual, historical and future-kingdom.
Spiritually, God turns a dry heart into a *spring
of water welling up to eternal life* (John 4:14).
Historically, we might find *some* fulfillment in
Israel's return to its land after the Babylonian
captivity (or in the twentieth century). But God
regularly uses this image to describe his future
kingdom, in which the earth itself will be transformed (see 35:6–7).

Or declare to us the things to come,
23   tell us what the future holds,
        so we may know that you are gods.
Do something, whether good or bad,
        so that we will be dismayed and filled with
            fear.
24But you are less than nothing
        and your works are utterly worthless;
        he who chooses you is detestable.

25"I have stirred up one from the north, and he
        comes—
    one from the rising sun who calls on my
        name.
He treads on rulers as if they were mortar,
        as if he were a potter treading the clay.
26Who told of this from the beginning, so we
        could know,
    or beforehand, so we could say, 'He was
        right'?
No one told of this,
        no one foretold it,
        no one heard any words from you.
27I was the first to tell ZionD, 'Look, here they
        are!'
    I gave to JerusalemD a messenger of good
        tidings.
28I look but there is no one—
        no one among them to give counsel,
        no one to give answer when I ask them.
29See, they are all false!
        Their deeds amount to nothing;
        their images are but wind and confusion.

The Servant of the LORD

42 "Here is my servant, whom I uphold,
        my chosen one in whom I delight;
    I will put my Spirit on him
        and he will bring justice to the nations.
2He will not shout or cry out,

One from the north (41:25)

This is Cyrus again, described also as *one
from the rising sun.* Before his takeover of
Babylon, he had already defeated the northern Medes and the northwestern Lydians, so
the threat of this eastern ruler came from
the north. Cyrus appears as a redeemer of
Israel, calling on God's name. Historical sources
show Cyrus as one who honored the gods of
any nation he was conquering at the time. See
One from the east (41:2).

Why did potters tread in clay? (41:25)

To remove air bubbles. Potters found clay in
the ground, added water and some fine sand
to get the right consistency, then removed the
water. But it then had to be stomped to
squash any air pockets that would weaken the
final product. Builders used a similar process
in making mortar for construction with stones
or bricks (see Nahum 3:14).

Who was the servant? (42:1)

At first glance, it seems that this servant might have been Cyrus. God had already talked of using this *one from the east* (41:2) for his purposes and Cyrus
would do great things to redeem God's people, to set them free and to restore their
homeland. Yet throughout Scripture we often find prophecies with multiple fulfillment and
Cyrus, obviously not Israel's Messiah, merely stands as a prototype of the *Anointed* ruler
to come.

Many Jewish scholars see the servant as Israel itself, suffering for the sins of humanity. To some extent, this fits. For example, the servant is identified by name as *Jacob* or
Israel (44:1; 45:4, for example). But ch. 49 adds a new angle. The servant's purpose is
to *bring Jacob back to him* [God] (v. 5) and to be *a light for the Gentiles* (v. 6).

Of course, Christians have always understood the servant to be Jesus Christ. In fact,
at Jesus' baptism the divine voice alluded to Isaiah, saying: *This is my Son, whom I love;
with him I am well pleased* (Matt. 3:17). (Allowing for translation from Hebrew to Greek,
this phrase is the same as *in whom I delight.*) The Servant Song is quoted several times
in the New Testament in reference to Jesus.

or raise his voice in the streets.
³A bruised reed he will not break,
    and a smoldering wick he will not snuff out.
In faithfulness he will bring forth justice;
⁴   he will not falter or be discouraged
till he establishes justice on earth.
    In his law the islands will put their hope."

⁵This is what God the LORD says—
he who created the heavens and stretched
        them out,
    who spread out the earth and all that comes
        out of it,
who gives breath to its people,
    and life to those who walk on it:
⁶"I, the LORD, have called you in
        righteousness^D;
    I will take hold of your hand.
I will keep you and will make you
    to be a covenant^D for the people
    and a light for the Gentiles^D,
⁷to open eyes that are blind,
    to free captives from prison
    and to release from the dungeon those who
        sit in darkness.

⁸"I am the LORD; that is my name!
    I will not give my glory^D to another
    or my praise to idols^D.
⁹See, the former things have taken place,
    and new things I declare;
before they spring into being
    I announce them to you."

Song of Praise to the LORD

¹⁰Sing to the LORD a new song,
    his praise from the ends of the earth,
you who go down to the sea, and all that is in
        it,
    you islands, and all who live in them.
¹¹Let the desert and its towns raise their voices;
    let the settlements where Kedar lives rejoice.
Let the people of Sela sing for joy;
    let them shout from the mountaintops.
¹²Let them give glory to the LORD
    and proclaim his praise in the islands.
¹³The LORD will march out like a mighty man,
    like a warrior he will stir up his zeal^D;
with a shout he will raise the battle cry
    and will triumph over his enemies.

¹⁴"For a long time I have kept silent,
    I have been quiet and held myself back.
But now, like a woman in childbirth,
    I cry out, I gasp and pant.
¹⁵I will lay waste the mountains and hills
    and dry up all their vegetation;
I will turn rivers into islands
    and dry up the pools.
¹⁶I will lead the blind by ways they have not
        known,
    along unfamiliar paths I will guide them;
I will turn the darkness into light before them
    and make the rough places smooth.
These are the things I will do;

**In what way would the servant be *a
light for the Gentiles*? (42:6)**
He would welcome Gentiles as well as Jews
into the family of God, through his sacrificial
atonement. Jesus Christ, who died for the sins
of all humanity, fulfilled God's purpose of
reaching out to the whole world through his
chosen people and through his promised Messiah (see 60:1–14).

Kedar ... Sela (42:11)
Kedar was a nomadic tribe that settled in
northern Arabia. Sela was the Edomite capital,
probably set on a towering plateau south of the
Dead Sea. Isaiah gives us a topography lesson
—islands and desert (*Kedar*) and mountains
(*Sela*) will all welcome the victorious Lord.

**Why was God silent for so long?
(42:14)**
God stood by as his people went into captivity.
Perhaps God felt the tension of a parent who
must punish a beloved child. After the period
of silence—God's inaction—God would again
express himself mightily, *crying out* in judgment against Babylon and causing a miraculous restoration of his people.

I will not forsake them.
¹⁷But those who trust in idols^D,
    who say to images, 'You are our gods,'
    will be turned back in utter shame.

Israel Blind and Deaf

¹⁸"Hear, you deaf;
    look, you blind, and see!
¹⁹Who is blind but my servant,
    and deaf like the messenger I send?
Who is blind like the one committed to me,
    blind like the servant of the LORD?
²⁰You have seen many things, but have paid no
        attention;
    your ears are open, but you hear nothing."
²¹It pleased the LORD
    for the sake of his righteousness^D
    to make his law great and glorious.
²²But this is a people plundered^D and looted,
    all of them trapped in pits
    or hidden away in prisons.
They have become plunder,
    with no one to rescue them;
they have been made loot,
    with no one to say, "Send them back."

²³Which of you will listen to this
    or pay close attention in time to come?
²⁴Who handed Jacob over to become loot,
    and Israel to the plunderers?
Was it not the LORD,
    against whom we have sinned?
For they would not follow his ways;
    they did not obey his law.
²⁵So he poured out on them his burning anger,
    the violence of war.
It enveloped them in flames, yet they did not
        understand;
    it consumed them, but they did not take it to
        heart.

Israel's Only Savior

43 But now, this is what the LORD says—
    he who created you, O Jacob,
    he who formed you, O Israel:
"Fear not, for I have redeemed^D you;
    I have summoned you by name; you are
        mine.
²When you pass through the waters,
    I will be with you;
and when you pass through the rivers,
    they will not sweep over you.
When you walk through the fire,
    you will not be burned;
    the flames will not set you ablaze.
³For I am the LORD, your God,
    the Holy One of Israel, your Savior;
I give Egypt for your ransom,
    Cush^a and Seba in your stead.
⁴Since you are precious and honored in my
        sight,
    and because I love you,

What made the Lord's servant blind? (42:18–20)

The servant in this context appears to be Israel and the blindness seems to be a willful resistance to the truth. They see, but they don't pay attention. Elsewhere, the Lord comments on a similar blindness and deafness of his people (see 6:9–10). God expresses some frustration in these verses, but also his determination to *turn the darkness into light* (v. 16).

How was Israel plundered and looted? (42:22)

The Assyrians overran the northern kingdom of Israel in 722 B.C., deporting its people. The Babylonians raided the southern kingdom of Judah in a series of invasions, 606–586 B.C., looting and taking prisoners each time. Thus, the nation was not only looted, but the people themselves were *made loot*, being taken by force from their homeland.

What good is punishment that doesn't hurt? (43:2)

If God brought these disasters upon his people as punishment (42:24–25), does it make sense for him to protect them from those same disasters? Yes! The whole point is that they must learn to rely on him. He will protect his people *if they let him*. If they don't, disaster awaits.

Why make Egypt, Cush and Seba pay for Israel's sin? (43:3)

This text implies that God allowed Persia to conquer these surrounding nations in exchange (*ransom*) for Persia's allowing the Jews to return home. Was this fair? As several of the prophets pointed out, every nation had its own sins to pay for (see Zeph. 2, for instance).

---

^a3 That is, the upper Nile region

I will give men in exchange for you,
and people in exchange for your life.
⁵Do not be afraid, for I am with you;
I will bring your children from the east
and gather you from the west.
⁶I will say to the north, 'Give them up!'
and to the south, 'Do not hold them back.'
Bring my sons from afar
and my daughters from the ends of the
earth—
⁷everyone who is called by my name,
whom I created for my glory,ᴰ
whom I formed and made."

⁸Lead out those who have eyes but are blind,
who have ears but are deaf.
⁹All the nations gather together
and the peoples assemble.
Which of them foretold this
and proclaimed to us the former things?
Let them bring in their witnesses to prove they
were right,
so that others may hear and say, "It is true."
¹⁰"You are my witnesses," declares the LORD,
"and my servant whom I have chosen,
so that you may know and believe me
and understand that I am he.
Before me no god was formed,
nor will there be one after me.
¹¹I, even I, am the LORD,
and apart from me there is no savior.
¹²I have revealed and saved and proclaimed—
I, and not some foreign god among you.
You are my witnesses," declares the LORD, "that
I am God.
¹³   Yes, and from ancient days I am he.
No one can deliver out of my hand.
When I act, who can reverse it?"

God's Mercy and Israel's Unfaithfulness

¹⁴This is what the LORD says—
your Redeemer,ᴰ the Holy One of Israel:
"For your sake I will send to Babylon
and bring down as fugitives all the
Babylonians,ᵃ
in the ships in which they took pride.
¹⁵I am the LORD, your Holy One,
Israel's Creator, your King."

¹⁶This is what the LORD says—
he who made a way through the sea,
a path through the mighty waters,
¹⁷who drew out the chariots and horses,
the army and reinforcements together,
and they lay there, never to rise again,
extinguished, snuffed out like a wick:
¹⁸"Forget the former things;
do not dwell on the past.
¹⁹See, I am doing a new thing!
Now it springs up; do you not perceive it?
I am making a way in the desert
and streams in the wasteland.

ᵃ14 Or *Chaldeans*

From the east ... from the west ... the north ... the south (43:5–6)
Isaiah looks forward to a future gathering, when the Root of Jesse (the Messiah) draws together the scattered remnant of Israel (11:11). Some say this happened when Jesus came; others point to Pentecost (Acts 2:8–11). It will certainly happen in the coming kingdom.

Who would be God's witnesses? (43:10)
Israel is the witness, the servant who will testify of God's power. God is setting up a court battle between himself and idols. Did any of the idols predict the recent events? Could any of them save the Israelites? Of course not; they can produce no witnesses to support their case.

When would the Babylonians flee in ships? (43:14)
When the Persians took over in 539 B.C. The Babylonians had boasted of their great navy and sea trading. Now they would become "boat people."

SCRIPTURE LINK (43:16–17) *He who made a way through the sea*
See Exodus 14–15. The crossing of the Red Sea had been the definitive miracle that God had worked for his people. This release from Babylon was another major miracle.

SCRIPTURE LINK (43:23)

Compare with 29:13. Were the Israelites busy doing religious things or weren't they? This apparent contradiction has two possible solutions. In 43:23–24, God could be agreeing that they made offerings and prayers, adding that these were not *for him*. A second possibility is that these two texts were written for very different times. In the 700s B.C., when ch. 29 was written, there was a lot of empty religion in Israel. In the 500s, the time for which ch. 43 was written, the Jews—separated from their temple—had let their religion lapse.

Calamus (43:24)

The stalk of a marsh herb was crushed to produce this fragrant oil, which was used in incense offerings.

Why would God forget their sins when they had not repented? (43:25)

This verse does not promise forgiveness without repentance. God speaks of his basic character here (*I am he who . . .*); he maintains a willingness to forgive and forget, should the people repent. He calls his people to acknowledge their wrongdoing, accept his forgiveness and enter a renewed relationship.

First father (43:27)

Possibly Adam or Abraham (51:2), but Jacob might make even more sense. Remember that Israel was named after Jacob and Jacob had practiced more than his share of deceit.

Spokesmen (43:27)

This may refer to Moses and Aaron and their occasional sins (Exodus 32; Num. 20), or to the more recent generations of false priests and prophets.

Jeshurun (44:2)

Another name for Israel, meaning *one who is upright*, or perhaps *one who is pleasing*. It is used only three other times, all in Deuteronomy. This may be an intentional allusion to a time when Jeshurun became proud, abandoned God, suffered and was then restored (Deut. 32:15–43).

Why did they write God's name on their hands? (44:5)

The Israelites had a custom of putting reminders of God's law on their hands and foreheads (Exodus 13:9,16). But this may allude to a pagan practice of branding a slave with his owner's name. See an interesting parallel in 49:16, where God writes their names on his hands.

²⁰The wild animals honor me,
  the jackals and the owls,
because I provide water in the desert
  and streams in the wasteland,
to give drink to my people, my chosen,
²¹ the people I formed for myself
  that they may proclaim my praise.

²²"Yet you have not called upon me, O Jacob,
  you have not wearied yourselves for me,
    O Israel.
²³You have not brought me sheep for burnt
    offerings,ᴰ
  nor honored me with your sacrifices.
I have not burdened you with grain offerings
  nor wearied you with demands for incense.
²⁴You have not bought any fragrant calamusᴰ
    for me,
  or lavished on me the fat of your sacrifices.
But you have burdened me with your sins
  and wearied me with your offenses.

²⁵"I, even I, am he who blots out
  your transgressions, for my own sake,
  and remembers your sins no more.
²⁶Review the past for me,
  let us argue the matter together;
  state the case for your innocence.
²⁷Your first father sinned;
  your spokesmen rebelled against me.
²⁸So I will disgrace the dignitaries of your
    temple,
  and I will consign Jacob to destructionª
  and Israel to scorn.

Israel the Chosen

44 "But now listen, O Jacob, my servant,
  Israel, whom I have chosen.
²This is what the LORD says—
  he who made you, who formed you in the
    womb,
  and who will help you:
Do not be afraid, O Jacob, my servant,
  Jeshurun, whom I have chosen.
³For I will pour water on the thirsty land,
  and streams on the dry ground;
I will pour out my Spirit on your offspring,
  and my blessing on your descendants.
⁴They will spring up like grass in a meadow,
  like poplar trees by flowing streams.
⁵One will say, 'I belong to the LORD';
  another will call himself by the name of
    Jacob;
still another will write on his hand, 'The
    LORD's,'
  and will take the name Israel.

The LORD, Not Idols

⁶"This is what the LORD says—
  Israel's King and Redeemer,ᴰ the LORD
    Almighty:

ª28 The Hebrew term refers to the irrevocable giving over of things or persons to the LORD, often by totally destroying them.

I am the first and I am the last;
   apart from me there is no God.
[7]Who then is like me? Let him proclaim it.
   Let him declare and lay out before me
what has happened since I established my
      ancient people,
   and what is yet to come—
   yes, let him foretell what will come.
[8]Do not tremble, do not be afraid.
   Did I not proclaim this and foretell it long
      ago?
You are my witnesses. Is there any God besides
      me?
   No, there is no other Rock; I know not one."

[9]All who make idols[D] are nothing,
   and the things they treasure are worthless.
Those who would speak up for them are blind;
   they are ignorant, to their own shame.
[10]Who shapes a god and casts an idol,
   which can profit him nothing?
[11]He and his kind will be put to shame;
   craftsmen are nothing but men.
Let them all come together and take their
      stand;
   they will be brought down to terror and
      infamy.

[12]The blacksmith takes a tool
   and works with it in the coals;
he shapes an idol with hammers,
   he forges it with the might of his arm.
He gets hungry and loses his strength;
   he drinks no water and grows faint.
[13]The carpenter measures with a line
   and makes an outline with a marker;
he roughs it out with chisels
   and marks it with compasses.
He shapes it in the form of man,
   of man in all his glory[D],
   that it may dwell in a shrine.
[14]He cut down cedars,
   or perhaps took a cypress or oak.
He let it grow among the trees of the forest,
   or planted a pine, and the rain made it grow.
[15]It is man's fuel for burning;
   some of it he takes and warms himself,
   he kindles a fire and bakes bread.
But he also fashions a god and worships it;
   he makes an idol and bows down to it.
[16]Half of the wood he burns in the fire;
   over it he prepares his meal,
   he roasts his meat and eats his fill.
He also warms himself and says,
   "Ah! I am warm; I see the fire."
[17]From the rest he makes a god, his idol;
   he bows down to it and worships.
He prays to it and says,
   "Save me; you are my god."
[18]They know nothing, they understand nothing;
   their eyes are plastered over so they cannot
      see,
   and their minds closed so they cannot
      understand.
[19]No one stops to think,

Why was Isaiah sarcastic? (44:16–17)

To modern minds, it might seem improper to mock other religions, but this was common practice in the ancient world. God regularly showed his people that idol-worship made no sense, since those gods had no real power. Often he used humor to do this (see 1 Kings 18:27; Psalm 115:4–8).

no one has the knowledge or understanding
  to say,
"Half of it I used for fuel;
  I even baked bread over its coals,
  I roasted meat and I ate.
Shall I make a detestable thing from what is
  left?
Shall I bow down to a block of wood?"
20He feeds on ashes, a deluded heart misleads
  him;
he cannot save himself, or say,
  "Is not this thing in my right hand a lie?"

21"Remember these things, O Jacob,
  for you are my servant, O Israel.
I have made you, you are my servant;
  O Israel, I will not forget you.
22I have swept away your offenses like a cloud,
  your sins like the morning mist.
Return to me,
  for I have redeemed[D] you."

23Sing for joy, O heavens, for the LORD has done
  this;
shout aloud, O earth beneath.
Burst into song, you mountains,
  you forests and all your trees,
for the LORD has redeemed Jacob,
  he displays his glory[D] in Israel.

Jerusalem to Be Inhabited

24"This is what the LORD says—
  your Redeemer[D], who formed you in the
  womb:

I am the LORD,
  who has made all things,
who alone stretched out the heavens,
  who spread out the earth by myself,

25who foils the signs of false prophets[D]
  and makes fools of diviners,
who overthrows the learning of the wise
  and turns it into nonsense,
26who carries out the words of his servants
  and fulfills the predictions of his messengers,

who says of Jerusalem[D], 'It shall be inhabited,'
  of the towns of Judah, 'They shall be built,'
  and of their ruins, 'I will restore them,'
27who says to the watery deep, 'Be dry,
  and I will dry up your streams,'
28who says of Cyrus[D], 'He is my shepherd
  and will accomplish all that I please;
he will say of Jerusalem, "Let it be rebuilt,"
  and of the temple, "Let its foundations be
  laid." '

45 "This is what the LORD says to his anointed[D],
  to Cyrus, whose right hand I take hold of
to subdue nations before him
  and to strip kings of their armor,
to open doors before him
  so that gates will not be shut:
2I will go before you

How can mountains sing? (44:23)
See *Why describe inanimate objects as rejoicing?* (Psalm 96:11–13).

Cyrus (44:28)
Cyrus II (the Great) ruled Persia from 558 to 530 B.C. Whereas previous empires had dominated the Middle East with military might, Cyrus combined might with diplomacy by allowing various captive nations to return home and by setting up a decentralized government. God used this leader's rise to power to save his people (Ezra 1:2–4) and spark the rebuilding of the temple. See *One from the east* (41:2).

How was Cyrus *anointed*? (45:1)
Cyrus's anointing is figurative, to be sure, but God was empowering him for the task of returning the Jews to their homeland. The word Messiah means *anointed*—because God would specially prepare that special One to redeem his people—but Cyrus was not the Messiah. He was just a leader prepared by God for a unique task.

and will level the mountains[a];
I will break down gates of bronze
   and cut through bars of iron.
³I will give you the treasures of darkness,
   riches stored in secret places,
so that you may know that I am the LORD,
   the God of Israel, who summons you by
      name.
⁴For the sake of Jacob my servant,
   of Israel my chosen,
I summon you by name
   and bestow on you a title of honor,
   though you do not acknowledge me.
⁵I am the LORD, and there is no other;
   apart from me there is no God.
I will strengthen you,
   though you have not acknowledged me,
⁶so that from the rising of the sun
   to the place of its setting
men may know there is none besides me.
   I am the LORD, and there is no other.
⁷I form the light and create darkness,
   I bring prosperity and create disaster;
   I, the LORD, do all these things.

⁸"You heavens above, rain down
      righteousness[D];
   let the clouds shower it down.
Let the earth open wide,
   let salvation[D] spring up,
let righteousness grow with it;
   I, the LORD, have created it.

⁹"Woe to him who quarrels with his Maker,
   to him who is but a potsherd among the
      potsherds on the ground.
Does the clay say to the potter,
   'What are you making?'
Does your work say,
   'He has no hands'?
¹⁰Woe to him who says to his father,
   'What have you begotten?'
or to his mother,
   'What have you brought to birth?'

¹¹"This is what the LORD says—
   the Holy One of Israel, and its Maker:
Concerning things to come,
   do you question me about my children,
   or give me orders about the work of my
      hands?
¹²It is I who made the earth
   and created mankind upon it.
My own hands stretched out the heavens;
   I marshaled their starry hosts[D].
¹³I will raise up Cyrus[Db] in my righteousness:
   I will make all his ways straight.
He will rebuild my city
   and set my exiles[D] free,
but not for a price or reward,
   says the LORD Almighty."

¹⁴This is what the LORD says:

Treasures of darkness, riches stored in secret places (45:3)

As Cyrus conquered nations, building his empire, he took possession of great wealth. Ancient writers commented on the legendary wealth of Lydia, which Cyrus conquered in 546 B.C. God was both equipping and rewarding Cyrus for the great deed of freeing Israel. (This may, however, be an allusion to the treasures that the Babylonians stole from the Jerusalem temple, which Cyrus found and then returned to the Jews; Ezra 5:14–15.)

Why would a loving God create disaster? (45:7)

The best answer might rest in the image of God as a loving parent, who offers care but insists on obedience. The specific disaster in the minds of the readers was the captivity of the Jews, which was clearly intended as a lesson for Israel, one that would draw them into greater obedience. Also see article: **Why does God send calamity?** (Lam. 3:38).

What should we do with our doubts and complaints? (45:9)

The word for *quarrel* here conveys the idea of picking a fight. There is a rich Biblical tradition of faithful people expressing their honest disagreements with God. Abraham, Moses, David, Job, Jeremiah and others all did this. But their complaints actually served to bring them closer to God, while the quarrels mentioned here are points of division. We can tell God how we feel without picking a fight and turning away from him.

Potsherd (45:9)

A broken piece of pottery. See **How was David like broken pottery?** (Psalms 31:12).

---

a2 Dead Sea Scrolls and Septuagint; the meaning of the word in the Masoretic Text is uncertain.   *b13* Hebrew *him*

Why would God *hide himself?* (45:15)

The surrounding verses speak of other nations, idol-worshipers, coming to Israel's God. From their perspective, Israel's God is different because he is not made of wood or stone. He is invisible—or *hidden* from their eyes. God responds by saying he is *not* hiding—he reveals himself to his people (vv. 18–19). Also see article: *Does God sometimes hide from us?* (Psalm 10:1).

Why would God swear by himself? (45:23)

First, to emphasize the total truth of what he says here. Second, to portray the utter uniqueness of God. In those days, as today, people would swear to God (or say: "By God") to indicate their truthfulness. Who could God swear by? Himself, of course, since *there is no other* (v. 22). See Heb. 6:13.

SCRIPTURE LINK (45:23)

See Romans 14:11; Phil. 2:10–11. The Bible foretells a time when everyone will bow before God as judge. In Romans, Paul quotes this text to show how we should avoid judging each other. In Philippians, he poetically places Jesus in this picture as the recipient of honor.

"The products of Egypt and the merchandise of
    Cush,[a]
    and those tall Sabeans—
they will come over to you
    and will be yours;
they will trudge behind you,
    coming over to you in chains.
They will bow down before you
    and plead with you, saying,
'Surely God is with you, and there is no other;
    there is no other god.' "

[15]Truly you are a God who hides himself,
    O God and Savior of Israel.
[16]All the makers of idols[D] will be put to shame
        and disgraced;
    they will go off into disgrace together.
[17]But Israel will be saved by the LORD
    with an everlasting salvation[D];
you will never be put to shame or disgraced,
    to ages everlasting.

[18]For this is what the LORD says—
    he who created the heavens,
    he is God;
he who fashioned and made the earth,
    he founded it;
he did not create it to be empty,
    but formed it to be inhabited—
he says:
"I am the LORD,
    and there is no other.
[19]I have not spoken in secret,
    from somewhere in a land of darkness;
I have not said to Jacob's descendants,
    'Seek me in vain.'
I, the LORD, speak the truth;
    I declare what is right.

[20]"Gather together and come;
    assemble, you fugitives from the nations.
Ignorant are those who carry about idols of
        wood,
    who pray to gods that cannot save.
[21]Declare what is to be, present it—
    let them take counsel together.
Who foretold this long ago,
    who declared it from the distant past?
Was it not I, the LORD?
And there is no God apart from me,
a righteous[D] God and a Savior;
    there is none but me.

[22]"Turn to me and be saved,
    all you ends of the earth;
for I am God, and there is no other.
[23]By myself I have sworn,
    my mouth has uttered in all integrity
    a word that will not be revoked:
Before me every knee will bow;
    by me every tongue will swear.
[24]They will say of me, 'In the LORD alone
    are righteousness[D] and strength.' "
    All who have raged against him

[a]14 That is, the upper Nile region

will come to him and be put to shame.
²⁵But in the LORD all the descendants of Israel
will be found righteous^D and will exult.

Gods of Babylon

46 Bel bows down, Nebo stoops low;
their idols^D are borne by beasts of burden.^a
The images that are carried about are
burdensome,
a burden for the weary.
²They stoop and bow down together;
unable to rescue the burden,
they themselves go off into captivity.

³"Listen to me, O house of Jacob,
all you who remain of the house of Israel,
you whom I have upheld since you were
conceived,
and have carried since your birth.
⁴Even to your old age and gray hairs
I am he, I am he who will sustain you.
I have made you and I will carry you;
I will sustain you and I will rescue you.

⁵"To whom will you compare me or count me
equal?
To whom will you liken me that we may be
compared?
⁶Some pour out gold from their bags
and weigh out silver on the scales;
they hire a goldsmith to make it into a god,
and they bow down and worship it.
⁷They lift it to their shoulders and carry it;
they set it up in its place, and there it
stands.
From that spot it cannot move.
Though one cries out to it, it does not answer;
it cannot save him from his troubles.

⁸"Remember this, fix it in mind,
take it to heart, you rebels.
⁹Remember the former things, those of long
ago;
I am God, and there is no other;
I am God, and there is none like me.
¹⁰I make known the end from the beginning,
from ancient times, what is still to come.
I say: My purpose will stand,
and I will do all that I please.
¹¹From the east I summon a bird of prey;
from a far-off land, a man to fulfill my
purpose.
What I have said, that will I bring about;
what I have planned, that will I do.
¹²Listen to me, you stubborn-hearted,
you who are far from righteousness^D.
¹³I am bringing my righteousness near,
it is not far away;
and my salvation^D will not be delayed.
I will grant salvation to Zion,
my splendor to Israel.

Bel ... Nebo (46:1)

Gods of Babylon. Bel means *lord* and referred to Marduk, the chief god of Babylon. Nebo (sometimes called Nabu) was Marduk's son, honored in the name of Babylonian kings such as Nebuchadnezzar. Here the prophet may be seeing a procession of refugees, fleeing the conquering Persians, with their idols unable to save them.

Bird of prey (46:11)

Cyrus the Great, who swooped in to conquer Babylon. Historian Xenophon says Cyrus had an eagle depicted on his royal banner.

^a1 Or *are but beasts and cattle*

The Fall of Babylon

Why link wicked Babylon with a *Virgin Daughter*? (47:1)
This chapter is a mocking poem, taunting the Babylonians with news of their fall from power and privilege. The *Virgin Daughter* is untouched, a pampered princess in the royal palace. Our Biblical glimpses of Babylon fit this picture (see Daniel 5)—the Babylonian leaders seemed proud of their position and unconcerned. But those days of ease are over, the prophet says.

47 "Go down, sit in the dust,
  Virgin Daughter of Babylon;
sit on the ground without a throne,
  Daughter of the Babylonians.ᵃ
No more will you be called
  tender or delicate.
²Take millstonesᴰ and grind flour;
  take off your veil.
Lift up your skirts, bare your legs,
  and wade through the streams.
³Your nakedness will be exposed
  and your shame uncovered.
I will take vengeance;
  I will spare no one."

⁴Our Redeemerᴰ—the LORD Almighty is his
    name—
  is the Holy One of Israel.

⁵"Sit in silence, go into darkness,
  Daughter of the Babylonians;
no more will you be called
  queen of kingdoms.

How did God *desecrate* his inheritance? (47:6)
The word means to take a holy thing and do something unholy with it. His inheritance is Israel, his people—he wants them to live in a holy relationship with him. In his anger, God handed them over to the Babylonians, to teach them a lesson.

⁶I was angry with my people
  and desecratedᴰ my inheritance;
I gave them into your hand,
  and you showed them no mercyᴰ.
Even on the aged
  you laid a very heavy yokeᴰ.
⁷You said, 'I will continue forever—
  the eternal queen!'
But you did not consider these things
  or reflect on what might happen.

⁸"Now then, listen, you wanton creature,
  lounging in your security
and saying to yourself,
  'I am, and there is none besides me.
I will never be a widow
  or suffer the loss of children.'
⁹Both of these will overtake you
  in a moment, on a single day:
  loss of children and widowhood.
They will come upon you in full measure,
  in spite of your many sorceriesᴰ
  and all your potent spells.

SCRIPTURE LINK (47:8,10)
God made a similar boast earlier (45:5–6), but *he* could back it up. Babylon was only concerned for itself and proudly set itself up above all others.

¹⁰You have trusted in your wickedness
  and have said, 'No one sees me.'
Your wisdom and knowledge mislead you
  when you say to yourself,
  'I am, and there is none besides me.'
¹¹Disaster will come upon you,
  and you will not know how to conjure it
    away.
A calamity will fall upon you
  that you cannot ward off with a ransom;
a catastrophe you cannot foresee
  will suddenly come upon you.

What kind of sorceries, spells and astrology could be found in Babylon? (47:9,12–13)
Many ancient writers refer to Babylon as a source of the magic arts. With various charms and ritual incantations, sorcerers sought to manipulate the spirit world for their own benefit. Astrologers charted the stars and advised kings. Daniel, with his own source of spiritual knowledge, was added to the ranks of Babylonian astrologers (Daniel 1:17,20; 2:2). The magi who visited Jesus may have been heirs of this tradition. Also see *What were the frightening signs in the sky?* (Jer. 10:1–2).

¹²"Keep on, then, with your magic spells
  and with your many sorceries,
  which you have labored at since childhood.

ᵃ1 Or *Chaldeans*; also in verse 5

Perhaps you will succeed,
    perhaps you will cause terror.
¹³All the counsel you have received has only
        worn you out!
    Let your astrologers come forward,
    those stargazers who make predictions month
        by month,
    let them save you from what is coming upon
        you.
¹⁴Surely they are like stubble;
    the fire will burn them up.
They cannot even save themselves
    from the power of the flame.
Here are no coals to warm anyone;
    here is no fire to sit by.
¹⁵That is all they can do for you—
    these you have labored with
    and trafficked with since childhood.
Each of them goes on in his error;
    there is not one that can save you.

Stubborn Israel

48 "Listen to this, O house of Jacob,
    you who are called by the name of Israel
    and come from the line of Judah,
you who take oaths in the name of the LORD
    and invoke the God of Israel—
    but not in truth or righteousnessᴰ—
²you who call yourselves citizens of the holy
        city
    and rely on the God of Israel—
    the LORD Almighty is his name:
³I foretold the former things long ago,
    my mouth announced them and I made
        them known;
    then suddenly I acted, and they came to
        pass.
⁴For I knew how stubborn you were;
    the sinews of your neck were iron,
    your forehead was bronze.
⁵Therefore I told you these things long ago;
    before they happened I announced them to
        you
so that you could not say,
    'My idolsᴰ did them;
    my wooden image and metal god ordained
        them.'
⁶You have heard these things; look at them all.
    Will you not admit them?

"From now on I will tell you of new things,
    of hidden things unknown to you.
⁷They are created now, and not long ago;
    you have not heard of them before today.
So you cannot say,
    'Yes, I knew of them.'
⁸You have neither heard nor understood;
    from of old your ear has not been open.
Well do I know how treacherous you are;
    you were called a rebel from birth.
⁹For my own name's sake I delay my wrath;
    for the sake of my praise I hold it back from
        you,
    so as not to cut you off.

What kind of oaths did God's people take? (48:1)

People took oaths to affirm loyalty to someone (Neh. 6:18), to testify in court (Exodus 22:11) or to promise something to God or another person (Joshua 2:17–20). This text seems to refer to religious or interpersonal oaths that were not kept, or that were wrongly taken (such as an oath of vengeance).

What *new things . . . hidden things* were coming? (48:6)

The "new exodus"—that is, the release from Babylon and the return to Judah. God wanted his people to pay attention and not to assume they had heard this before. It is also possible that these *new things* are the prophecies about the Servant-Messiah.

How does affliction refine God's people? (48:10)

Metal such as silver was refined with fire. Impurities were burned off. In the same way, the seven-decade captivity in Babylon was intended to burn away the sins, such as idolatry and corruption, that had tainted Israel. *Though not as silver* may indicate God's frustration that his people had not forsaken their sins yet and thus were not yet like pure silver.

SCRIPTURE LINK (48:12)

See Rev. 1:17. God is at the beginning of the creation and at its end. In Revelation, Jesus uses the same phrase to describe himself.

Whom did God choose as his ally? (48:14)

Cyrus, king of Persia. See article: **Who was the servant?** (42:1). The Hebrew word for *ally* is a strong one, meaning *loved one* or *good friend*.

Why did God tell his people to escape from the Babylonians? (48:20)

After Cyrus conquered Babylon, he allowed the Jews to return to Judah. Escape was not necessary, which is why they could *flee . . . with shouts of joy*.

SCRIPTURE LINK (48:21)

See Exodus 17:1–7. When the Israelites wandered through the Sinai desert, God miraculously provided water from a rock. This text may allude to the Arabian desert that separated Babylon from Judah.

10See, I have refined you, though not as silver;
I have tested you in the furnace of affliction.[D]
11For my own sake, for my own sake, I do this.
How can I let myself be defamed?
I will not yield my glory[D] to another.

Israel Freed

12"Listen to me, O Jacob,
Israel, whom I have called:
I am he;
I am the first and I am the last.
13My own hand laid the foundations of the earth,
and my right hand spread out the heavens;
when I summon them,
they all stand up together.

14"Come together, all of you, and listen:
Which of ⌊the idols⌋ has foretold these things?
The LORD's chosen ally
will carry out his purpose against Babylon;
his arm will be against the Babylonians.[a]
15I, even I, have spoken;
yes, I have called him.
I will bring him,
and he will succeed in his mission.

16"Come near me and listen to this:

"From the first announcement I have not spoken in secret;
at the time it happens, I am there."

And now the Sovereign LORD has sent me,
with his Spirit.

17This is what the LORD says—
your Redeemer,[D] the Holy One of Israel:
"I am the LORD your God,
who teaches you what is best for you,
who directs you in the way you should go.
18If only you had paid attention to my commands,
your peace[D] would have been like a river,
your righteousness[D] like the waves of the sea.
19Your descendants would have been like the sand,
your children like its numberless grains;
their name would never be cut off
nor destroyed from before me."

20Leave Babylon,
flee from the Babylonians!
Announce this with shouts of joy
and proclaim it.
Send it out to the ends of the earth;
say, "The LORD has redeemed[D] his servant Jacob."
21They did not thirst when he led them through the deserts;
he made water flow for them from the rock;
he split the rock
and water gushed out.

a14 Or *Chaldeans*; also in verse 20

²²"There is no peace D," says the LORD, "for the
   wicked."

The Servant of the LORD

49 Listen to me, you islands;
        hear this, you distant nations:
   Before I was born the LORD called me;
        from my birth he has made mention of my
        name.
²He made my mouth like a sharpened sword,
   in the shadow of his hand he hid me;
he made me into a polished arrow
   and concealed me in his quiver.
³He said to me, "You are my servant,
   Israel, in whom I will display my splendor."
⁴But I said, "I have labored to no purpose;
   I have spent my strength in vain and for
      nothing.
Yet what is due me is in the LORD's hand,
   and my reward is with my God."

⁵And now the LORD says—
   he who formed me in the womb to be his
      servant
to bring Jacob back to him
   and gather Israel to himself,
for I am honored in the eyes of the LORD
   and my God has been my strength—
⁶he says:
"It is too small a thing for you to be my
      servant
   to restore the tribes of Jacob
   and bring back those of Israel I have kept.
I will also make you a light for the Gentiles D,
   that you may bring my salvation D to the
      ends of the earth."

⁷This is what the LORD says—
   the Redeemer D and Holy One of Israel—
to him who was despised and abhorred by the
      nation,
   to the servant of rulers:
"Kings will see you and rise up,
   princes will see and bow down,
because of the LORD, who is faithful,
   the Holy One of Israel, who has chosen
      you."

Restoration of Israel

⁸This is what the LORD says:

"In the time of my favor I will answer you,
   and in the day of salvation I will help you;
I will keep you and will make you
   to be a covenant D for the people,
to restore the land
   and to reassign its desolate inheritances,
⁹to say to the captives, 'Come out,'
   and to those in darkness, 'Be free!'

"They will feed beside the roads
   and find pasture on every barren hill.
¹⁰They will neither hunger nor thirst,
   nor will the desert heat or the sun beat upon
      them.

Who is speaking? (49:1–5)

The speaker seems at first to be Israel, telling
what the Lord said (v. 3). But then the speaker
seems to be commissioned with the task of restoring Israel to God (v. 5). This could be seen
in several ways: (1) as an idealized image of Israel; (2) as a righteous remnant of Israelites
(possibly including Isaiah) who have stayed
true to God or (3) as the future Servant-
Messiah, who identifies with Israel. The Messianic tone is strong in this text and in the following chapters.

The time of my favor (49:8)

The time when God decides to redeem his people. The phrase may have been used for the
Year of Jubilee (Lev. 25:10), every fiftieth year
when slaves were freed and land returned to
its original owners. In the New Testament, Paul
quoted 49:8, adding, *Now is the time of God's
favor* (2 Cor. 6:2). God was doing a whole new
work of redemption through Jesus.

North . . . west . . . Aswan (49:12)
God would draw his people back to their land, not only from Babylon in the east, but also from other places where they had scattered. Assyria had forcibly scattered the northern Israelites in 722 B.C., but many others had emigrated when times got tough. There were already Jewish settlements in many areas of the Mediterranean world, even Aswan, in southern Egypt.

Why did God engrave them on his hands? (49:16)
To remember them. Tattooing was common in the ancient Middle East for religious and personal reasons. A person might tattoo the name of a loved one on his body, or a religious name or text. Also, some slaves were marked with the names of their masters. See *Why did they write God's name on their hands?* (44:5). God used this symbol to express his constant concern for Jerusalem.

Your walls (49:16)
The walls of Jerusalem, which were broken down during the captivity (Neh. 1:3). God envisioned an established, secure Jerusalem.

What did God promise that the Gentiles would do for the Israelites? (49:22)
The Gentiles would assist in the regathering of the Jews to their land. This was fulfilled, in a way, as the Jews were aided by Cyrus, a Gentile. Some would see later fulfillment in the twentieth-century establishment of Israel.

He who has compassion on them will guide them
and lead them beside springs of water.
¹¹I will turn all my mountains into roads,
and my highways will be raised up.
¹²See, they will come from afar—
some from the north, some from the west,
some from the region of Aswan.ᵃ"

¹³Shout for joy, O heavens;
rejoice, O earth;
burst into song, O mountains!
For the LORD comforts his people
and will have compassion on his afflictedᴰ
ones.

¹⁴But Zionᴰ said, "The LORD has forsaken me,
the Lord has forgotten me."

¹⁵"Can a mother forget the baby at her breast
and have no compassion on the child she
has borne?
Though she may forget,
I will not forget you!
¹⁶See, I have engraved you on the palms of my
hands;
your walls are ever before me.
¹⁷Your sons hasten back,
and those who laid you waste depart from
you.
¹⁸Lift up your eyes and look around;
all your sons gather and come to you.
As surely as I live," declares the LORD,
"you will wear them all as ornaments;
you will put them on, like a bride.

¹⁹"Though you were ruined and made desolate
and your land laid waste,
now you will be too small for your people,
and those who devoured you will be far
away.
²⁰The children born during your bereavement
will yet say in your hearing,
'This place is too small for us;
give us more space to live in.'
²¹Then you will say in your heart,
'Who bore me these?
I was bereaved and barren;
I was exiledᴰ and rejected.
Who brought these up?
I was left all alone,
but these—where have they come from?' "

²²This is what the Sovereign LORD says:

"See, I will beckon to the Gentilesᴰ,
I will lift up my banner to the peoples;
they will bring your sons in their arms
and carry your daughters on their shoulders.
²³Kings will be your foster fathers,
and their queens your nursing mothers.
They will bow down before you with their
faces to the ground;
they will lick the dust at your feet.

ᵃ12 Dead Sea Scrolls; Masoretic Text *Sinim*

Then you will know that I am the LORD;
   those who hope in me will not be
      disappointed."

²⁴Can plunderᴰ be taken from warriors,
   or captives rescued from the fierceᵃ?

²⁵But this is what the LORD says:

"Yes, captives will be taken from warriors,
   and plunder retrieved from the fierce;
I will contend with those who contend with
      you,
   and your children I will save.
²⁶I will make your oppressors eat their own
      flesh;
   they will be drunk on their own blood, as
      with wine.
Then all mankind will know
   that I, the LORD, am your Savior,
   your Redeemerᴰ, the Mighty One of Jacob."

Israel's Sin and the Servant's Obedience

50 This is what the LORD says:

"Where is your mother's certificate of divorce
      with which I sent her away?
Or to which of my creditors
   did I sell you?
Because of your sins you were sold;
   because of your transgressions your mother
      was sent away.
²When I came, why was there no one?
   When I called, why was there no one to
      answer?
Was my arm too short to ransom you?
   Do I lack the strength to rescue you?
By a mere rebuke I dry up the sea,
   I turn rivers into a desert;
their fish rot for lack of water
   and die of thirst.
³I clothe the sky with darkness
   and make sackclothᴰ its covering."

⁴The Sovereign LORD has given me an instructed
      tongue,
   to know the word that sustains the weary.
He wakens me morning by morning,
   wakens my ear to listen like one being
      taught.
⁵The Sovereign LORD has opened my ears,
   and I have not been rebellious;
   I have not drawn back.
⁶I offered my back to those who beat me,
   my cheeks to those who pulled out my
      beard;
I did not hide my face
   from mocking and spitting.
⁷Because the Sovereign LORD helps me,
   I will not be disgraced.
Therefore have I set my face like flint,
   and I know I will not be put to shame.
⁸He who vindicates me is near.

Certificate of divorce (50:1)
Jewish law allowed a man to divorce his wife by writing out a certificate. There was some debate about acceptable grounds for divorce; the view that prevailed allowed *for any and every reason* (Matt. 19:3,7). The divorce, though, was irrevocable. Here, God explains that there is no certificate and thus his separation from his people can be rescinded.

How was Isaiah physically and verbally abused? (50:4–6)
Although Jeremiah was abused (Jer. 36–38) and other prophets insulted, we don't have any record of Isaiah being mistreated. This text must refer to the servant, who would be faithful to God despite the abuse that might result. Verse 6 describes treatment Jesus endured before his crucifixion (see Matt. 26:67,68; 27:30,31).

Flint (50:7)
A hard rock abundant in the Middle East. Its hardness made it useful in tools such as hammers, chisels and knives. It also became a symbol for stubborn endurance, as it is used here.

ᵃ24 Dead Sea Scrolls, Vulgate and Syriac (see also Septuagint and verse 25); Masoretic Text *righteous*

Who then will bring charges against me?
Let us face each other!
Who is my accuser?
Let him confront me!
⁹It is the Sovereign LORD who helps me.
Who is he that will condemn me?
They will all wear out like a garment;
the moths will eat them up.

¹⁰Who among you fears the LORD
and obeys the word of his servant?
Let him who walks in the dark,
who has no light,
trust in the name of the LORD
and rely on his God.
¹¹But now, all you who light fires
and provide yourselves with flaming torches,
go, walk in the light of your fires
and of the torches you have set ablaze.
This is what you shall receive from my hand:
You will lie down in torment.

Why torment those with torches and reward those who walk in darkness? (50:10–11)

The Jews in Babylonian captivity must have felt that they were in the dark. God asked for their trust—he would lead them. But many were tempted to abandon God, to try to find their own way, to *light fires*. (Ironically, this phrase could read *play with fire*.) This would only lead to disaster.

Everlasting Salvation for Zion

51 "Listen to me, you who pursue righteousnessᴰ
and who seek the LORD:
Look to the rock from which you were cut
and to the quarry from which you were hewn;
²look to Abraham, your father,
and to Sarah, who gave you birth.
When I called him he was but one,
and I blessed him and made him many.
³The LORD will surely comfort Zionᴰ
and will look with compassion on all her ruins;
he will make her deserts like Eden,
her wastelands like the garden of the LORD.
Joy and gladness will be found in her,
thanksgiving and the sound of singing.

⁴"Listen to me, my people;
hear me, my nation:
The law will go out from me;
my justice will become a light to the nations.
⁵My righteousness draws near speedily,
my salvationᴰ is on the way,
and my arm will bring justice to the nations.
The islands will look to me
and wait in hope for my arm.
⁶Lift up your eyes to the heavens,
look at the earth beneath;
the heavens will vanish like smoke,
the earth will wear out like a garment
and its inhabitants die like flies.
But my salvation will last forever,
my righteousness will never fail.

⁷"Hear me, you who know what is right,
you people who have my law in your hearts:
Do not fear the reproachᴰ of men
or be terrified by their insults.
⁸For the moth will eat them up like a garment;
the worm will devour them like wool.
But my righteousness will last forever,
my salvation through all generations."

⁹Awake, awake! Clothe yourself with strength,
    O arm of the LORD;
awake, as in days gone by,
    as in generations of old.
Was it not you who cut Rahab[D] to pieces,
    who pierced that monster through?
¹⁰Was it not you who dried up the sea,
    the waters of the great deep,
who made a road in the depths of the sea
    so that the redeemed[D] might cross over?
¹¹The ransomed of the LORD will return.
    They will enter Zion[D] with singing;
    everlasting joy will crown their heads.
Gladness and joy will overtake them,
    and sorrow and sighing will flee away.

¹²"I, even I, am he who comforts you.
    Who are you that you fear mortal men,
    the sons of men, who are but grass,
¹³that you forget the LORD your Maker,
    who stretched out the heavens
    and laid the foundations of the earth,
that you live in constant terror every day
    because of the wrath of the oppressor,
    who is bent on destruction?
For where is the wrath of the oppressor?
¹⁴   The cowering prisoners will soon be set free;
    they will not die in their dungeon,
    nor will they lack bread.
¹⁵For I am the LORD your God,
    who churns up the sea so that its waves
        roar—
    the LORD Almighty is his name.
¹⁶I have put my words in your mouth
    and covered you with the shadow of my
        hand—
I who set the heavens in place,
    who laid the foundations of the earth,
    and who say to Zion, 'You are my
        people.' "

The Cup of the LORD's Wrath

¹⁷Awake, awake!
    Rise up, O Jerusalem[D],
you who have drunk from the hand of the
        LORD
    the cup of his wrath,
you who have drained to its dregs[D]
    the goblet that makes men stagger.
¹⁸Of all the sons she bore
    there was none to guide her;
of all the sons she reared
    there was none to take her by the hand.
¹⁹These double calamities have come upon
        you—
    who can comfort you?—
ruin and destruction, famine and sword—
    who can[a] console you?
²⁰Your sons have fainted;
    they lie at the head of every street,
    like antelope caught in a net.

---

a19 Dead Sea Scrolls, Septuagint, Vulgate and Syriac; Masoretic Text /
how can I

Rahab . . . that monster (51:9)
A sea monster in ancient mythology, Rahab also became a name for Egypt (30:7). In this description of God's power, it could mean either or both. According to the Babylonian creation myth, the god Marduk cut a monster in two, dividing heaven and earth. Here the prophet may be implying that it was really the God of the Jews who did that.

SCRIPTURE LINK (51:10)
See Exodus 14:29. The prophet begs the Lord to act again as he did when he parted the Red Sea.

They are filled with the wrath of the LORD
    and the rebuke of your God.

21Therefore hear this, you afflicted[D] one,
    made drunk, but not with wine.
22This is what your Sovereign LORD says,
    your God, who defends his people:
"See, I have taken out of your hand
    the cup that made you stagger;
from that cup, the goblet of my wrath,
    you will never drink again.
23I will put it into the hands of your tormentors,
    who said to you,
    'Fall prostrate that we may walk over you.'
And you made your back like the ground,
    like a street to be walked over."

Uncircumcised (52:1)
See article: *Why did God command circumcision?* (Gen. 17:10).

52 Awake, awake, O Zion[D],
    clothe yourself with strength.
Put on your garments of splendor,
    O Jerusalem[D], the holy city.
The uncircumcised[D] and defiled
    will not enter you again.
2Shake off your dust;
    rise up, sit enthroned, O Jerusalem.
Free yourself from the chains on your neck,
    O captive Daughter of Zion.

3For this is what the LORD says:

"You were sold for nothing,
    and without money you will be redeemed[D]."

4For this is what the Sovereign LORD says:

"At first my people went down to Egypt to live;
    lately, Assyria has oppressed them.

5"And now what do I have here?" declares the LORD.

"For my people have been taken away for
        nothing,
    and those who rule them mock,[a]"
                            declares the LORD.
"And all day long
    my name is constantly blasphemed[D].
6Therefore my people will know my name;
    therefore in that day they will know
that it is I who foretold it.
    Yes, it is I."

What's so beautiful about feet? (52:7)
It is beautiful to see the running of a bringer of good news, because we anticipate the good news. This poetic device focuses on one aspect of a beautiful situation.

7How beautiful on the mountains
    are the feet of those who bring good news,
who proclaim peace[D],
    who bring good tidings,
    who proclaim salvation[D],
who say to Zion,
    "Your God reigns!"
8Listen! Your watchmen[D] lift up their voices;
    together they shout for joy.
When the LORD returns to Zion,
    they will see it with their own eyes.
9Burst into songs of joy together,
    you ruins of Jerusalem,
for the LORD has comforted his people,
    he has redeemed Jerusalem.

Why did God bare his arm? (52:10)
Throughout the Bible, God's arm is associated with his great power. So when he *lay*[s] *bare his holy arm,* he is in fact "rolling up his sleeves" to do something powerful—namely, to redeem his people.

*a*5 Dead Sea Scrolls and Vulgate; Masoretic Text *wail*

10The LORD will lay bare his holy arm
   in the sight of all the nations,
and all the ends of the earth will see
   the salvation[D] of our God.

11Depart, depart, go out from there!
   Touch no unclean[D] thing!
Come out from it and be pure,
   you who carry the vessels of the LORD.
12But you will not leave in haste
   or go in flight;
for the LORD will go before you,
   the God of Israel will be your rear guard.

The Suffering and Glory of the Servant

13See, my servant will act wisely[a];
   he will be raised and lifted up and highly
   exalted.
14Just as there were many who were appalled at
   him[b]—
   his appearance was so disfigured beyond that
   of any man
   and his form marred beyond human
   likeness—
15so will he sprinkle many nations,[c]
   and kings will shut their mouths because of
   him.
For what they were not told, they will see,
   and what they have not heard, they will
   understand.

53 Who has believed our message
   and to whom has the arm of the LORD been
   revealed?
2He grew up before him like a tender shoot,
   and like a root out of dry ground.
He had no beauty or majesty to attract us to
   him,
   nothing in his appearance that we should
   desire him.
3He was despised and rejected by men,
   a man of sorrows, and familiar with
   suffering.
Like one from whom men hide their faces
   he was despised, and we esteemed him not.

4Surely he took up our infirmities
   and carried our sorrows,
yet we considered him stricken by God,
   smitten by him, and afflicted[D].
5But he was pierced for our transgressions,
   he was crushed for our iniquities;
the punishment that brought us peace[D] was
   upon him,
   and by his wounds we are healed.
6We all, like sheep, have gone astray,
   each of us has turned to his own way;
and the LORD has laid on him
   the iniquity of us all.

7He was oppressed and afflicted,
   yet he did not open his mouth;
he was led like a lamb to the slaughter,

Vessels of the Lord (52:11)

Lampstands, lamps, wick trimmers, trays, basins, jars—items used in the temple rituals (Num. 4:9). These were regarded as holy and put in the charge of priests and Levites, who were specially consecrated (Lev. 21).

Servant (52:13)

See article: *Who was the servant?* (42:1).

How did God's servant become so disfigured? (52:14)

It would make sense that the violence described in 50:6 caused this. If the servant is Israel, this disfigurement could be understood as the displacement, scattering and captivity of the nation. It would be amazing that Israel, after being ravaged by the Assyrians and Babylonians, would still exist—especially back in their homeland. Christians, of course, see that this also refers to the crucifixion of Jesus.

What does it mean to *sprinkle* nations? (52:15)

In Old Testament rituals, people and items were sometimes ceremonially cleansed by sprinkling with blood or oil (Lev. 4:6; 8:11). Thus this sprinkling would somehow make the nations—that is, Gentiles—righteous. This was always part of Israel's mission (Gen. 12:3) and it was perfectly fulfilled in Jesus Christ (Luke 2:30–32; Eph. 2:13).

SCRIPTURE LINK (53:1)

See John 12:38; Romans 10:16. John and Paul both quote this verse as they show that many Jews did not believe the Good News about Christ.

Who is Isaiah describing? (53:2)

This could be the nation (or faithful remnant) of Israel, but it becomes clearer that Isaiah is describing an individual, the Messiah, who would bear the sins of the world. The surprise is that the individual is so vulnerable—*a tender shoot . . . a root out of dry ground*. It is amazing that God could work through tiny Israel and even more so through a lowly carpenter.

SCRIPTURE LINK (53:4–5)

See Matt. 8:17; 1 Peter 2:24. Matthew saw Jesus healing people and thought of this text. Peter extended the image—when Christ died, he *bore our sins in his body* on the cross.

How can a substitute suffer the punishment for our sins? (53:5)

By killing innocent animals, the Israelites made a covering for their sins before the coming of the perfect sacrifice. In retrospect, the writer of Hebrews declares it *impossible for the blood of bulls and goats to take away sins.* These were merely symbols of Christ, who was *sacrificed once to take away the sins of many people* (Heb. 9:28; 10:4).

How are we healed by wounds given to someone else? (53:5)

A modern analogy might be a heart transplant: one person lives because another dies. That physical analogy pictures the spiritual healing God makes available to us. The Bible shows humanity with a heart condition—our hearts are evil, incapable of the wholeness and holiness God intended. The Servant, pure of heart, suffers and dies so that we can live.

---

a 13 Or will prosper   b 14 Hebrew you   c 15 Hebrew; Septuagint
so will many nations marvel at him

How are we like sheep? (53:6-7)

We go astray. The Bible depicts sheep as helpless and rather ignorant. They do not keep themselves safe, but wander into dangerous situations.

SCRIPTURE LINK (53:7)

See John 1:29. John the Baptist hailed Jesus as the *Lamb of God, who takes away the sin of the world*, alluding to the Passover sacrifice (Exodus 12) and to this text. At the beginning of his public ministry, Jesus was already heading toward his sacrificial death.

SCRIPTURE LINK (53:7-8)

See Acts 8:32-35. This text from Isaiah was being read by the Ethiopian official when Philip approached him. Like some modern readers, the official wasn't sure who the passage was describing. Philip explained that it was about Jesus.

SCRIPTURE LINK (53:9)

See 1 Peter 2:22. Peter was writing to suffering Christians. But he wanted to make sure they were suffering righteously and not just being punished for wrongs they had done. He used this verse from Isaiah as an image of righteous suffering and silent endurance.

Guilt offering (53:10)

In the Israelite sacrificial system, a guilt offering was made for unintentional (or even unknown) violations. The person brought an untainted ram to the priest for sacrifice, made restitution as necessary and paid a fine (Lev. 5:14-19).

How would God reward his suffering servant? (53:12)

If Israel is the servant, the reward is a return to their own land and the new freedom and wealth that would result. But Christians see a hint of resurrection in this verse. Though the Servant-Messiah dies in disgrace, great honor awaits him (Phil. 2:6-11). This is the language of a conquering king sharing the spoils of victory.

and as a sheep before her shearers is silent,
   so he did not open his mouth.
[8]By oppression[a] and judgment he was taken
      away.
   And who can speak of his descendants?
For he was cut off from the land of the living;
   for the transgression of my people he was
      stricken.[b]
[9]He was assigned a grave with the wicked,
   and with the rich in his deathD,
though he had done no violence,
   nor was any deceit in his mouth.

[10]Yet it was the LORD's will to crush him and
      cause him to suffer,
   and though the LORD makes[c] his life a guilt
      offeringD,
he will see his offspring and prolong his days,
   and the will of the LORD will prosper in his
      hand.
[11]After the suffering of his soulD,
   he will see the light ⌊of life⌋[d] and be
      satisfied[e];
by his knowledge[f] my righteousD servant will
      justifyD many,
   and he will bear their iniquities.
[12]Therefore I will give him a portion among the
      great,[g]
   and he will divide the spoils with the
      strong,[h]
because he poured out his life unto death,
   and was numbered with the transgressors.

---

[a]8 Or *From arrest*   [b]8 Or *away. / Yet who of his generation
considered / that he was cut off from the land of the living / for the
transgression of my people, / to whom the blow was due?*
[c]10 Hebrew *though you make*   [d]11 Dead Sea Scrolls (see also
Septuagint); Masoretic Text does not have *the light ⌊of life⌋*   [e]11 Or
(with Masoretic Text) [11]*He will see the result of the suffering of his soul
/ and be satisfied*   [f]11 Or *by knowledge of him*   [g]12 Or *many*
[h]12 Or *numerous*

Why did God cause his servant to suffer? (53:10)

Isaiah emphasizes the *purpose of God*. Something great is happening here, the prophet says. Cyrus will make it happen, the servant will make it happen, but it will happen because God wills it (55:11). Though this part of Isaiah is clearly written to the Jews in Babylonian captivity, *the nations are part of this drama, too. All of humanity* is in captivity, in one sense or another.

It is God's purpose to set us free. The whole Bible is this phenomenal love story—God creates people, people turn away, God woos people back. Israel is the microcosm of humanity. God plays the love scene again and again through Moses, David, Elijah, Hosea and Isaiah. But too often his love goes unrequited.

The sin of rejecting divine love requires sacrifice and God decided to make the sacrifice himself. He would send his innocent Servant to bear the weight of the world's sin. This would clear the way for a new relationship between God and the people he loves so much. It might seem gruesome on the face of it—unjust and bloodthirsty. But it is God's purpose. The suffering of God's Servant is the key to his plan: *that God was reconciling the world to himself in Christ, not counting men's sins against them* (2 Cor. 5:19).

For he bore the sin of many,
and made intercession for the transgressors.

The Future Glory of Zion

54 "Sing, O barren woman,
you who never bore a child;
burst into song, shout for joy,
you who were never in labor;
because more are the children of the desolate
woman
than of her who has a husband,"
says the LORD.

2 "Enlarge the place of your tent,
stretch your tent curtains wide,
do not hold back;
lengthen your cords,
strengthen your stakes.
3 For you will spread out to the right and to the
left;
your descendants will dispossess nations
and settle in their desolate cities.

4 "Do not be afraid; you will not suffer shame.
Do not fear disgrace; you will not be
humiliated.
You will forget the shame of your youth
and remember no more the reproach D of
your widowhood.
5 For your Maker is your husband—
the LORD Almighty is his name—
the Holy One of Israel is your Redeemer D;
he is called the God of all the earth.
6 The LORD will call you back
as if you were a wife deserted and distressed
in spirit—
a wife who married young,
only to be rejected," says your God.
7 "For a brief moment I abandoned you,
but with deep compassion I will bring you
back.
8 In a surge of anger
I hid my face from you for a moment,
but with everlasting kindness

Who is the barren woman? (54:1–6)

The woman is a metaphor for Jerusalem and Jerusalem represents the people of God. Isaiah describes the city as a childless, husbandless woman who has suffered a great deal (see v. 11). God's people had nothing—like a widow (v. 4) or a deserted wife (v. 6). In ancient times, it was a disgrace to be childless. Widows without family were left destitute and were often held in contempt. Some say society insinuated that widows were being punished for sin.

What kind of tents can be expanded? (54:2)

A typical nomad's tent had nine poles in three rows and was divided into two rooms by a curtain—one for men, one for women. Such a tent could be enlarged by adding another row of poles to make another room. However, this more likely meant, as much as possible, to straighten the poles and stretch the fabric tight. Though people lived in houses during Isaiah's day, they saw this as a metaphor for a coming time of growth and blessing.

Shame of your youth . . . reproach of your widowhood (54:4)

Jerusalem was like a woman disgraced for sin committed when she was young. God's people were like a destitute widow with no resources. Yet God promised to reverse their shame and humiliation. See *Who is the barren woman?* (54:1–6).

Who called Israel's God *the God of all the earth*? (54:5)

Only the people of God, having heard the message of his prophets, would know that the Lord was truly the God of all the earth. Other people did not have much respect for the God of Israel because he could not be seen as their own idols could (see Psalm 115:2–13).

What is God promising? (54:1–17)

Two things, primarily: (1) a period when great trouble will come to God's people and (2) a later time when the problems will end and God will again bless his people. The images in this chapter vividly show the contrasts. Nearly deserted, Jerusalem will again be full of people. It will go from poverty to wealth, humiliation to respect, weakness to power, captivity to freedom.

These predictions were fulfilled when Jerusalem fell to the Babylonians in the sixth century B.C. and when many descendants of the captives later returned to Jerusalem under Ezra and Nehemiah.

These promises can also be understood in terms of a general principle for the people of God. Jerusalem can be a metaphor for those who serve God. When God's people drift from their commitment to him, they will face his judgment. When they return to him, they will again experience God's blessings.

What are the limits of God's patience? (54:7)

His patience is limitless. God commanded the Israelites to be holy and gave them the law and prophets to help them. When they persisted in their sins, he had to punish them because he is holy. Still, he could not leave it at that. He forgave them and received them back with great compassion. He still does that for anyone who sins today.

Does God allow things to happen that he doesn't like? (54:15)

Yes, he does. God is all-powerful and can control everything that happens in his world. However, he gives humans freedom to decide some things for themselves. When they sin, for example, they have only themselves to blame for the consequences. Of course, God could prevent evil—including the enemy attacks he mentions here. But having given humankind certain authority, God often allows them to play out their own drama.

How can we buy without money? (55:1)

If a merchant were to set the price of wine, milk and bread at zero, then the poor who have no money could buy it. The merchant's work would be unprofitable, but his generosity would help the poor. This is a picture in material terms of what the Lord has done spiritually for his people.

Why was another covenant necessary? (55:3)

God made (and sometimes renewed) covenants with his people through Noah, Abraham, Moses, Joshua, David and others. Some were conditional and could be canceled if God's people failed to live up to them (Deut. 6:1-19). Others were unconditional (2 Sam. 7:1-16). Jesus Christ fulfilled God's promise to David that his descendant would rule forever. Israel had broken the covenant given through Moses but a new covenant was given—Jesus Christ, described by Isaiah as the *everlasting covenant*— to allow them to once again become God's people (see Jer. 31:31; 1 Cor. 11:25).

I will have compassion on you,"
  says the LORD your Redeemer[D].

9"To me this is like the days of Noah,
    when I swore that the waters of Noah would
      never again cover the earth.
So now I have sworn not to be angry with you,
      never to rebuke you again.
10Though the mountains be shaken
    and the hills be removed,
yet my unfailing love for you will not be
      shaken
    nor my covenant[D] of peace[D] be removed,"
  says the LORD, who has compassion on you.

11"O afflicted[D] city, lashed by storms and not
      comforted,
    I will build you with stones of turquoise,[a]
      your foundations with sapphires.[b]
12I will make your battlements of rubies,
    your gates of sparkling jewels,
    and all your walls of precious stones.
13All your sons will be taught by the LORD,
    and great will be your children's peace.
14In righteousness[D] you will be established:
  Tyranny will be far from you;
    you will have nothing to fear.
  Terror will be far removed;
    it will not come near you.
15If anyone does attack you, it will not be my
      doing;
    whoever attacks you will surrender to you.

16"See, it is I who created the blacksmith
    who fans the coals into flame
    and forges a weapon fit for its work.
And it is I who have created the destroyer to
      work havoc;
17   no weapon forged against you will prevail,
    and you will refute every tongue that accuses
      you.
This is the heritage of the servants of the LORD,
    and this is their vindication from me,"
                                        declares the LORD.

Invitation to the Thirsty

55 "Come, all you who are thirsty,
    come to the waters;
and you who have no money,
    come, buy and eat!
  Come, buy wine and milk
    without money and without cost.
2Why spend money on what is not bread,
    and your labor on what does not satisfy?
  Listen, listen to me, and eat what is good,
    and your soul[D] will delight in the richest of
      fare.
3Give ear and come to me;
    hear me, that your soul may live.
  I will make an everlasting covenant with you,
    my faithful love promised to David.
4See, I have made him a witness to the peoples,

---

a 11 The meaning of the Hebrew for this word is uncertain.
b 11 Or *lapis lazuli*

a leader and commander of the peoples.
⁵Surely you will summon nations you know not,
　　and nations that do not know you will
　　　　hasten to you,
　because of the LORD your God,
　　the Holy One of Israel,
　　for he has endowed you with splendor."

⁶Seek the LORD while he may be found;
　　call on him while he is near.
⁷Let the wicked forsake his way
　　and the evil man his thoughts.
Let him turn to the LORD, and he will have
　　mercyᴰ on him,
　and to our God, for he will freely pardon.

⁸"For my thoughts are not your thoughts,
　　neither are your ways my ways,"
　　　　　　　　　　　　declares the LORD.
⁹"As the heavens are higher than the earth,
　　so are my ways higher than your ways
　　and my thoughts than your thoughts.
¹⁰As the rain and the snow
　　come down from heaven,
　and do not return to it
　　without watering the earth
　and making it bud and flourish,
　　so that it yields seed for the sower and bread
　　　for the eater,
¹¹so is my word that goes out from my mouth:
　　It will not return to me empty,
　but will accomplish what I desire
　　and achieve the purpose for which I sent it.
¹²You will go out in joy
　　and be led forth in peaceᴰ;
　the mountains and hills
　　will burst into song before you,
　and all the trees of the field
　　will clap their hands.
¹³Instead of the thornbush will grow the pine
　　tree,
　and instead of briers the myrtle will grow.
This will be for the LORD's renown,
　　for an everlasting sign,
　　which will not be destroyed."

Salvation for Others

56 This is what the LORD says:

　"Maintain justice
　　and do what is right,
　for my salvationᴰ is close at hand
　　and my righteousnessᴰ will soon be
　　　revealed.
²Blessed is the man who does this,
　　the man who holds it fast,
　who keeps the Sabbathᴰ without desecratingᴰ
　　it,
　and keeps his hand from doing any evil."

³Let no foreigner who has bound himself to the
　　LORD say,
　　"The LORD will surely exclude me from his
　　　people."

How did God give his people *splendor*? (55:5)

Typically nations that were conquered and taken into captivity lost their national identity forever. They would be assimilated into other peoples and simply disappear as a distinct people. God gave splendor to Israel by (1) preserving its national and religious identity while in exile and (2) returning them to Jerusalem after humiliation at the hands of the Babylonians. God's people would again be able to hold their heads high.

My word (55:11)

During Isaiah's lifetime, God's people primarily heard the word of God through his prophets—an oral word. After the exile, they came to think more and more of the *written* word of the Lord, the Scriptures. Thus, they became known as the people of "the Book."

In what sense does God's word not fail —even when people reject it? (55:11)

Like a sovereign king in an ancient culture, the Lord can achieve his purposes by issuing decrees and giving orders. His plans are mysterious to human beings, too high for us to understand (v. 9). It stands to reason, then, that God does not need human beings to accomplish his purpose. His word alone is enough.

How will nature praise God? (55:13)

This may be figurative language to describe the breadth of the new order that God will create. Chapter 54 speaks of God's people being restored. Chapter 55 is broader in scope, encompassing all of creation. The fallen world, trapped under the curse of human sin, will be set free—no more thorns or briers (Gen. 3:17–18; Romans 8:19–22). Even now, nature testifies to the glory of God (Psalm 19:1), but nothing like what will take place in the new world.

Why give observance of the Sabbath such importance? (56:2)

In Hebrew law, moral requirements (such as not committing murder) are found alongside ritual requirements (such as keeping the Sabbath). Isaiah here refers to both. He expected the people to uphold the moral code (to *maintain justice and do what is right*; v. 1) as well as the rituals (*the Sabbath*). Some say this suggests the entire law will be kept in the coming age.

How would having heirs encourage spiritual commitment? (56:3)

The Hebrew people thought of having children as a sign of God's blessing. No children, then, indicated no blessing from God. See *Who is the barren woman?* (54:1–6). This may have been at least part of the reason why eunuchs, who were unable to father children, were not allowed to enter the temple. Their unblessed condition would pollute the temple. But the Lord here promises blessings to even eunuchs. They too will be allowed to come into his presence (vv. 4–5). Also see *Does God discriminate?* (Deut. 23:1).

And let not any eunuch[D] complain,
"I am only a dry tree."

[4]For this is what the LORD says:

"To the eunuchs who keep my Sabbaths,
  who choose what pleases me
  and hold fast to my covenant[D]—
[5]to them I will give within my temple and its
  walls
  a memorial and a name
  better than sons and daughters;
I will give them an everlasting name
  that will not be cut off.
[6]And foreigners who bind themselves to the
  LORD
  to serve him,
to love the name of the LORD,
  and to worship him,
all who keep the Sabbath without
  desecrating[D] it
  and who hold fast to my covenant—
[7]these I will bring to my holy mountain
  and give them joy in my house of prayer.
Their burnt offerings[D] and sacrifices[D]
  will be accepted on my altar;
for my house will be called
  a house of prayer for all nations."
[8]The Sovereign LORD declares—
  he who gathers the exiles[D] of Israel:
"I will gather still others to them
  besides those already gathered."

God's Accusation Against the Wicked

[9]Come, all you beasts of the field,
  come and devour, all you beasts of the
  forest!
[10]Israel's watchmen[D] are blind,
  they all lack knowledge;
they are all mute dogs,
  they cannot bark;
they lie around and dream,
  they love to sleep.
[11]They are dogs with mighty appetites;
  they never have enough.
They are shepherds who lack understanding;
  they all turn to their own way,
  each seeks his own gain.
[12]"Come," each one cries, "let me get wine!
  Let us drink our fill of beer!
And tomorrow will be like today,
  or even far better."

57 The righteous[D] perish,
  and no one ponders it in his heart;
devout men are taken away,
  and no one understands
that the righteous are taken away
  to be spared from evil.
[2]Those who walk uprightly
  enter into peace[D];
  they find rest as they lie in death[D].

[3]"But you—come here, you sons of a sorceress,
  you offspring of adulterers and prostitutes!

My holy mountain (56:7)
Refers to Jerusalem, specifically Mount Zion, where the temple was located. This promised access to the Lord to those who had formerly been excluded.

Israel's watchmen (56:10)
Israel's civil and religious leaders. Like watchmen whose job it is to protect a city from invaders, Israel's leaders were entrusted in the guarding against spiritual attack. But they were spiritually blind or asleep and failed to warn the people or lead them in following the Lord.

Is death a means of escape? (57:1–2)
When the righteous suffer persecution and eventually are martyred for their faith, Isaiah says that they will find relief in death. This is not the same as saying that all suffering is bad or that suicide is an option for believers who want to escape physical pain. It is simply saying that those who are obedient to God, no matter what the cost, will one day be rewarded for their faithfulness. Also see *Is no life better than a troubled life?* (Job 3:10–16).

⁴Whom are you mocking?
  At whom do you sneer
  and stick out your tongue?
Are you not a brood of rebels,
  the offspring of liars?
⁵You burn with lust among the oaks
  and under every spreading tree;
you sacrifice[D] your children in the ravines
  and under the overhanging crags.
⁶⌊The idols⌋ among the smooth stones of the
    ravines are your portion;
  they, they are your lot.
Yes, to them you have poured out drink
    offerings[D]
  and offered grain offerings[D].
In the light of these things, should I relent?
⁷You have made your bed on a high and lofty
    hill;
  there you went up to offer your sacrifices.
⁸Behind your doors and your doorposts
  you have put your pagan symbols.
Forsaking me, you uncovered your bed,
  you climbed into it and opened it wide;
you made a pact with those whose beds you
    love,
  and you looked on their nakedness.
⁹You went to Molech[D][a] with olive oil
  and increased your perfumes.
You sent your ambassadors[b] far away;
  you descended to the grave[c] itself!
¹⁰You were wearied by all your ways,
  but you would not say, 'It is hopeless.'
You found renewal of your strength,
  and so you did not faint.

¹¹"Whom have you so dreaded and feared
  that you have been false to me,
and have neither remembered me
  nor pondered this in your hearts?
Is it not because I have long been silent
  that you do not fear me?
¹²I will expose your righteousness[D] and your
    works,
  and they will not benefit you.
¹³When you cry out for help,
  let your collection ⌊of idols⌋ save you!
The wind will carry all of them off,
  a mere breath will blow them away.
But the man who makes me his refuge
  will inherit the land
  and possess my holy mountain."

Comfort for the Contrite

¹⁴And it will be said:

"Build up, build up, prepare the road!
  Remove the obstacles out of the way of my
    people."
¹⁵For this is what the high and lofty One says—
  he who lives forever, whose name is holy:
"I live in a high and holy place,
  but also with him who is contrite and lowly
    in spirit,

a9 Or to the king   b9 Or idols   c9 Hebrew Sheol

What was going on among the oaks? (57:5)

Idolatry. See *Sacred oaks . . . gardens* (1:29).

What sort of pagan symbols did they use? (57:8)

In the law, the people of God were commanded to place God's commands on their doors to remind them of the Lord continually (Deut. 6:9). Here the prophet says that, instead of God's commands, they had placed the symbols of idolatry on their doors. Since the idolatry included sexual orgies, it is possible the symbols were themselves sexual in nature.

Molech (57:9)

Molech was the primary god of the Ammonites and was worshiped by some Canaanites. Worship of Molech included human sacrifice. See *Molech* (Jer. 32:35).

Where does God live? (57:15)

The Bible often describes heaven as God's home (Matt. 6:9, for example). It also speaks of God living among or within his people (John 1:14, for example). Here Isaiah combines both ideas in a beautiful way: God lives in heaven, but he also lives with humble people to give them hope and confidence. Also see *Where does God live?* (Micah 1:3).

Why didn't punishment do any good? (57:17)

One way God punishes his people is to withdraw his presence from them. Often those who are abandoned by God suddenly recognize their need for him and repent. Other times, however, people are so stubborn and determined to go their own way that they refuse to admit their need. Punishment sometimes galvanizes the resistance of those who want to rebel.

What does fasting do? (58:3)

The law called for fasting on the Day of Atonement as a sign of humility and sincere repentance. Fasting meant focusing their hearts on God and expressing their deep sorrow for their sins. Over time, however, some Hebrews began to see fasting as a ritual that could earn God's favor: "If we fast," they thought, "God will bless us." Isaiah knew rituals were pointless unless they were motivated by sincere faith and obedience to God's moral law. The "fasting" God wants most is not ritual, but action: feed the hungry, clothe the naked and so on (vv. 6–7).

How did the Israelites exploit people? (58:3)

In many ways, perhaps. They may have overworked their servants, been inhospitable to strangers, ignored the needs of the poor or used bribes to get their own way in the community. They had no regard for God or the law and consequently abused the system horribly.

Can social works replace spiritual disciplines? (58:6–7)

No. Works—no matter how good—cannot replace spirituality. But religious rituals cannot replace them either and that is what Isaiah was speaking against. Some Israelites became lax about the moral side of the law. They thought they could deliberately disobey it and still be forgiven simply by going through the motions of ritual sacrifices. Prophets like Isaiah taught that God despises empty rituals done by insincere people. God wants righteous living that stems from wholehearted commitment.

to revive the spirit of the lowly
    and to revive the heart of the contrite.
¹⁶I will not accuse forever,
    nor will I always be angry,
for then the spirit of man would grow faint
        before me—
    the breath of man that I have created.
¹⁷I was enraged by his sinful greed;
    I punished him, and hid my face in anger,
    yet he kept on in his willful ways.
¹⁸I have seen his ways, but I will heal him;
    I will guide him and restore comfort to him,
¹⁹   creating praise on the lips of the mourners in
        Israel.
  Peace[D], peace, to those far and near,"
    says the LORD. "And I will heal them."
²⁰But the wicked are like the tossing sea,
    which cannot rest,
    whose waves cast up mire and mud.
²¹"There is no peace," says my God, "for the
        wicked."

True Fasting

58 "Shout it aloud, do not hold back.
    Raise your voice like a trumpet.
  Declare to my people their rebellion
    and to the house of Jacob their sins.
²For day after day they seek me out;
    they seem eager to know my ways,
  as if they were a nation that does what is right
    and has not forsaken the commands of its
        God.
  They ask me for just decisions
    and seem eager for God to come near them.
³'Why have we fasted,' they say,
    'and you have not seen it?
  Why have we humbled ourselves,
    and you have not noticed?'

  "Yet on the day of your fasting, you do as you
        please
    and exploit all your workers.
⁴Your fasting ends in quarreling and strife,
    and in striking each other with wicked fists.
  You cannot fast as you do today
    and expect your voice to be heard on high.
⁵Is this the kind of fast I have chosen,
    only a day for a man to humble himself?
  Is it only for bowing one's head like a reed
    and for lying on sackcloth[D] and ashes?
  Is that what you call a fast,
    a day acceptable to the LORD?

⁶"Is not this the kind of fasting I have chosen:
    to loose the chains of injustice
    and untie the cords of the yoke[D],
  to set the oppressed free
    and break every yoke?
⁷Is it not to share your food with the hungry
    and to provide the poor wanderer with
        shelter—
  when you see the naked, to clothe him,
    and not to turn away from your own flesh
        and blood?

⁸Then your light will break forth like the dawn,
 and your healing will quickly appear;
then your righteousness^Da will go before you,
 and the glory^D of the LORD will be your rear
  guard.
⁹Then you will call, and the LORD will answer;
 you will cry for help, and he will say: Here
  am I.

"If you do away with the yoke^D of oppression,
 with the pointing finger and malicious talk,
¹⁰and if you spend yourselves in behalf of the
  hungry
 and satisfy the needs of the oppressed,
then your light will rise in the darkness,
 and your night will become like the
  noonday.
¹¹The LORD will guide you always;
 he will satisfy your needs in a sun-scorched
  land
 and will strengthen your frame.
You will be like a well-watered garden,
 like a spring whose waters never fail.
¹²Your people will rebuild the ancient ruins
 and will raise up the age-old foundations;
you will be called Repairer of Broken Walls,
 Restorer of Streets with Dwellings.

¹³"If you keep your feet from breaking the
  Sabbath^D
 and from doing as you please on my holy
  day,
if you call the Sabbath a delight
 and the LORD's holy day honorable,
and if you honor it by not going your own way
 and not doing as you please or speaking idle
  words,
¹⁴then you will find your joy in the LORD,
 and I will cause you to ride on the heights of
  the land
 and to feast on the inheritance of your father
  Jacob."
       The mouth of the LORD has spoken.

Sin, Confession and Redemption

59 Surely the arm of the LORD is not too short to
     save,
 nor his ear too dull to hear.
²But your iniquities have separated
 you from your God;
your sins have hidden his face from you,
 so that he will not hear.
³For your hands are stained with blood,
 your fingers with guilt.
Your lips have spoken lies,
 and your tongue mutters wicked things.
⁴No one calls for justice;
 no one pleads his case with integrity.
They rely on empty arguments and speak lies;
 they conceive trouble and give birth to evil.
⁵They hatch the eggs of vipers
 and spin a spider's web.

Your light will break forth . . . your light will rise in the darkness (58:8,10)
For the Israelites in Isaiah's day, darkness halted most activities and brought all sorts of threats and dangers. In figurative language, then, darkness became a symbol for evil; light, on the other hand, represented goodness. Here light first represents God's salvation—to protect and heal (v. 8); then it represents the people's genuine acts of righteousness.

What ancient ruins would be rebuilt? (58:12)
The ruins of Jerusalem. Isaiah foretold its destruction and its restoration. It would be rebuilt by the people, a sure sign that God would be with them once more. The faithful workers who would rebuild the city are called the *Repairer*[s] and *Restorer*[s] of the city. The rebuilding of Jerusalem would be evidence that God had restored the people of Israel.

How would they *ride on the heights of the land*? (58:14)
This was a figure of speech that describes how God lifts us, spiritually and emotionally, above our troubles and hardships. It may be taken from the image of an eagle carrying its young from the nest up into the sky—to *ride on the heights of the land* (Deut. 32:10–13).

What were the people guilty of? (59:3)
Among other things listed here, the people were guilty of violence, lying, injustice, hostility, rebellion, treachery, oppressing the weak and turning away from God (vv. 3–21).

ᵃ8 Or *your righteous One*

Whoever eats their eggs will die,
    and when one is broken, an adder is
        hatched.
⁶Their cobwebs are useless for clothing;
    they cannot cover themselves with what they
        make.
Their deeds are evil deeds,
    and acts of violence are in their hands.
⁷Their feet rush into sin;
    they are swift to shed innocent blood.
Their thoughts are evil thoughts;
    ruin and destruction mark their ways.
⁸The way of peaceᴰ they do not know;
    there is no justice in their paths.
They have turned them into crooked roads;
    no one who walks in them will know
        peace.

⁹So justice is far from us,
    and righteousnessᴰ does not reach us.
We look for light, but all is darkness;
    for brightness, but we walk in deep shadows.
¹⁰Like the blind we grope along the wall,
    feeling our way like men without eyes.
At midday we stumble as if it were twilight;
    among the strong, we are like the dead.
¹¹We all growl like bears;
    we moan mournfully like doves.
We look for justice, but find none;
    for deliverance, but it is far away.

¹²For our offenses are many in your sight,
    and our sins testify against us.
Our offenses are ever with us,
    and we acknowledge our iniquities:
¹³rebellion and treachery against the LORD,
    turning our backs on our God,
    fomenting oppression and revolt,

Why did Isaiah talk as though he were as guilty as everyone else? (59:12)
Because he identified with the entire nation. In Western culture, we tend to think of wrongdoing in terms of the individual: this person did it, not that one. In ancient Israel, the tendency was to think of wrongdoing in terms of the entire community: we all did it; no one is totally innocent.

Why won't God listen to sinners? (59:2)

God does listen to sinners when they genuinely repent of their sins and ask God for forgiveness, for example, God listens and answers. So Isaiah's statement needs to be understood within its context.

Isaiah was telling the people of his day that even though God could help them, he chose not to. God would not listen to their prayers and religious rituals. They wanted God to help them when they were in trouble, but they didn't want to serve him with all their hearts. They didn't want to abandon their wicked ways or their foreign idols. If they wouldn't listen to him, why should he listen to them?

The Bible teaches that God answers prayers. Jesus tells us that we can speak to God as a child speaks to his father (Matt. 6:6). God cares for his people and responds to their prayers simply because he loves them. The irony is that when he refuses to answer requests, it's for the same reason—because of his love.

A father shows love when he allows his child to learn from mistakes. If he always protects his child, how will that child ever learn and mature? God responds in love when he does not come to the rescue of people who continue to live their lives in disobedience to his commands.

Also see article: *When does God refuse to hear our prayers?* (Jer. 11:11).

uttering lies our hearts have conceived.
14So justice is driven back,
    and righteousness^D stands at a distance;
truth has stumbled in the streets,
    honesty cannot enter.
15Truth is nowhere to be found,
    and whoever shuns evil becomes a prey.

The LORD looked and was displeased
    that there was no justice.
16He saw that there was no one,
    he was appalled that there was no one to
        intervene;
so his own arm worked salvation^D for him,
    and his own righteousness sustained him.
17He put on righteousness as his breastplate,
    and the helmet of salvation on his head;
he put on the garments of vengeance
    and wrapped himself in zeal^D as in a cloak.
18According to what they have done,
    so will he repay
wrath to his enemies
    and retribution^D to his foes;
he will repay the islands their due.
19From the west, men will fear the name of the
        LORD,
    and from the rising of the sun, they will
        revere^D his glory^D.
For he will come like a pent-up flood
    that the breath of the LORD drives along.^a

20"The Redeemer^D will come to Zion^D,
    to those in Jacob who repent^D of their sins,"
        declares the LORD.

21"As for me, this is my covenant^D with them," says
the LORD. "My Spirit, who is on you, and my words that I
have put in your mouth will not depart from your mouth,
or from the mouths of your children, or from the mouths
of their descendants from this time on and forever," says
the LORD.

The Glory of Zion

60
"Arise, shine, for your light has come,
    and the glory of the LORD rises upon you.
2See, darkness covers the earth
    and thick darkness is over the peoples,
but the LORD rises upon you
    and his glory appears over you.
3Nations will come to your light,
    and kings to the brightness of your dawn.

4"Lift up your eyes and look about you:
    All assemble and come to you;
your sons come from afar,
    and your daughters are carried on the arm.
5Then you will look and be radiant,
    your heart will throb and swell with joy;
the wealth on the seas will be brought to you,
    to you the riches of the nations will come.
6Herds of camels will cover your land,
    young camels of Midian and Ephah.
And all from Sheba will come,

Who did God expect to intervene? (59:16)
Though this could refer to all the people of God, it likely means that God expected their leaders to intervene. But the king, his aides, the priests and even many of the prophets of Israel failed to defend those who were being oppressed by the injustice committed throughout the land.

SCRIPTURE LINK (59:17) *Righteousness as his breastplate*
God is described as a warrior who wears a breastplate of righteousness and a helmet of salvation. Later, Paul uses these same terms to instruct Christians about their spiritual armor. See Eph. 6:14,17.

How do the warnings of this chapter fit with the reassurances of chs. 54–56? (59:18)
In the Old Testament we see a recurring pattern in the life of the Hebrew people: They sin; God judges them; they repent; God forgives them. Then the cycle begins all over again. God's nature includes both judgment and forgiveness, both warnings and reassurances. The Israelites sometimes needed judgment, sometimes forgiveness. Both were equally important in God's formation of the spiritual life of their nation.

How could God promise that their descendants would never reject his Spirit or his word? (59:21)
He didn't. He simply promised that he would never withdraw his Spirit from his people. This was God's side of the covenant. But the other side of the deal, on the part of the people, included their own commitment to the relationship. As long as they remained faithful to the Lord, he would remain with them. His promise was to those *who repent of their sins* (v. 20). Many also see this as a prophecy of the new covenant. God gave his Spirit permanently to the church of Christ at Pentecost (Acts 2:1–4).

How will Israel give light to the nations? (60:3)
Isaiah paints a picture of the sun shining brightly on the temple high atop Mount Zion while the surrounding valleys remained in darkness (see v. 7). This represented the way God would come in glory to his people. Those in spiritual darkness will look to the light shining through God's people—light characterized by lives of integrity, compassion and peace. Jesus said, *You are the light of the world* (Matt. 5:14). Also see *Your light will break forth . . . your light will rise in the darkness* (58:8).

Why will Israel's sons be so far away? (60:4)
Isaiah was probably thinking of how Jerusalem would fall to the Babylonians and the people would be taken into exile. But he was actually looking through that tragic period of Israel's history to see what would come later. Isaiah saw the immense joy their sons and daughters would have when they returned to Jerusalem out of exile.

a19 Or When the enemy comes in like a flood, / the Spirit of the LORD will put him to flight

Wealth . . . riches . . . camels . . . gold (60:5–7)

God's blessings upon his people—demonstrating the miraculous way in which God would restore them to Jerusalem. When they returned, the Israelites received many valuable gifts (Ezra 1:6–7; 7:15–22). Their wealth also symbolized the great spiritual blessings God would give them. He would save them and restore them to a right relationship with himself.

Midian . . . Ephah . . . Sheba . . . Kedar . . . Nebaioth (60:6–7)

Peoples who lived in Arabia (modern Jordan, Saudi Arabia and Yemen), all known for their wealth (see *Map 12* at the back of this Bible). The descendants of Ephah, a son of Midian, were traders who became wealthy by transporting goods. The people of Kedar and Nebaioth, a son of Ishmael, were famous for their sheep.

When will Israel rule the world? (60:12)

Some think this is a description of the coming millennial age when Christ will rule from Jerusalem. Others see this in a more figurative sense—that Jesus, the Son of David, representing the people of Israel, rules over all those who acknowledge him as Lord. Those who do not *will perish.*

The milk of nations . . . nursed at royal breasts (60:16)

A metaphor to describe the salvation God gives his people. Though its images seem foreign to us, its basic meaning is clear enough: God's salvation will be extravagant and abundant. Breasts represented nurture and care, a perpetual source for everything a child would need. Royalty represented the best anywhere, second to none.

Is this a prophecy about Israel or eternity? (60:19)

It could be both. This figure of speech could indicate the salvation of Israel upon earth—God's light would protect the nation from darkness, foreign threats and internal injustice. Whether or not this prophecy applies to physical Israel, it certainly applies to God's people in eternity. John used it to write of the heavenly city (Rev. 21:23).

bearing gold and incense[D]
and proclaiming the praise of the LORD.
[7]All Kedar's flocks will be gathered to you,
the rams of Nebaioth will serve you;
they will be accepted as offerings on my altar,
and I will adorn my glorious temple.

[8]"Who are these that fly along like clouds,
like doves to their nests?
[9]Surely the islands look to me;
in the lead are the ships of Tarshish,[a]
bringing your sons from afar,
with their silver and gold,
to the honor of the LORD your God,
the Holy One of Israel,
for he has endowed you with splendor.

[10]"Foreigners will rebuild your walls,
and their kings will serve you.
Though in anger I struck you,
in favor I will show you compassion.
[11]Your gates will always stand open,
they will never be shut, day or night,
so that men may bring you the wealth of the
nations—
their kings led in triumphal procession.
[12]For the nation or kingdom that will not serve
you will perish;
it will be utterly ruined.

[13]"The glory[D] of Lebanon will come to you,
the pine, the fir and the cypress together,
to adorn the place of my sanctuary;
and I will glorify the place of my feet.
[14]The sons of your oppressors will come bowing
before you;
all who despise you will bow down at your
feet
and will call you the City of the LORD,
Zion[D] of the Holy One of Israel.

[15]"Although you have been forsaken and hated,
with no one traveling through,
I will make you the everlasting pride
and the joy of all generations.
[16]You will drink the milk of nations
and be nursed at royal breasts.
Then you will know that I, the LORD, am your
Savior,
your Redeemer[D], the Mighty One of Jacob.
[17]Instead of bronze I will bring you gold,
and silver in place of iron.
Instead of wood I will bring you bronze,
and iron in place of stones.
I will make peace[D] your governor
and righteousness[D] your ruler.
[18]No longer will violence be heard in your land,
nor ruin or destruction within your borders,
but you will call your walls Salvation[D]
and your gates Praise.
[19]The sun will no more be your light by day,
nor will the brightness of the moon shine on
you,

[a]9 Or *the trading ships*

for the LORD will be your everlasting light,
    and your God will be your glory[D].
20Your sun will never set again,
    and your moon will wane no more;
the LORD will be your everlasting light,
    and your days of sorrow will end.
21Then will all your people be righteous[D]
    and they will possess the land forever.
They are the shoot I have planted,
    the work of my hands,
    for the display of my splendor.
22The least of you will become a thousand,
    the smallest a mighty nation.
I am the LORD;
    in its time I will do this swiftly."

The Year of the LORD's Favor

61 The Spirit of the Sovereign LORD is on me,
    because the LORD has anointed[D] me
to preach good news to the poor.
He has sent me to bind up the brokenhearted,
    to proclaim freedom for the captives
    and release from darkness for the
        prisoners,[a]
2to proclaim the year of the LORD's favor
    and the day of vengeance of our God,
to comfort all who mourn,
3 and provide for those who grieve in Zion[D]—
to bestow on them a crown of beauty
    instead of ashes,
the oil of gladness
    instead of mourning,
and a garment of praise
    instead of a spirit of despair.
They will be called oaks of righteousness[D],
    a planting of the LORD
    for the display of his splendor.

4They will rebuild the ancient ruins
    and restore the places long devastated;
they will renew the ruined cities
    that have been devastated for generations.
5Aliens will shepherd your flocks;
    foreigners will work your fields and
        vineyards.
6And you will be called priests[D] of the LORD,
    you will be named ministers of our God.
You will feed on the wealth of nations,
    and in their riches you will boast.

7Instead of their shame
    my people will receive a double portion,
and instead of disgrace
    they will rejoice in their inheritance;
and so they will inherit a double portion in
        their land,
    and everlasting joy will be theirs.

8"For I, the LORD, love justice;
    I hate robbery and iniquity.
In my faithfulness I will reward them
    and make an everlasting covenant[D] with
        them.

a 1 Hebrew; Septuagint *the blind*

SCRIPTURE LINK (61:1–2)
When Jesus preached his first sermon in his hometown synagogue, he read these verses and said that they were fulfilled that day. See Luke 4:16–19.

Why wear ashes? (61:3)
In the Bible, the ashes left behind after a fire had burned out were, understandably, a sign of destruction. When people experienced troubles, they sometimes sat on an ash pile (58:5) or put ashes on their heads (2 Samuel 13:19) as a sign of mourning. But God promises his people that their mourning will end; in place of ashes, they will be well-groomed with oil, a symbol of joy and celebration. Also see *What was good and pleasant about oil poured on the head?* (Psalm 133:2).

Was it a benefit to have alien and foreign workers? (61:5)
Yes. It was a sign of prosperity to have many servants. Life was very hard for most people in the ancient world and the promise of having others to do your work for you was a wonderful picture of God's salvation. These most likely were domestic servants from other nations, not slaves captured in war.

How did bridegrooms dress like priests? (61:10)

A bridegroom in Isaiah's day wore a turban or crown of some sort (Song 3:11). Priests also wore turbans (Exodus 28:4).

Why the new names? (62:4)

In ancient times, names were used to do much more than identify a person. Names revealed something about people—their characteristics, for example, or the circumstances surrounding their lives. Changing names was a vivid way to express a change in circumstances. See NIV text notes for the meanings. Also see *Why give a name like this to a child?* (8:3).

How can land *be married*? (62:4)

In a figurative sense. Since marriage was considered a blessing, this was a picture of God's blessings upon the people of God who lived in the land. This promise was especially significant to people who had been described as childless widows (54:1,4–5).

Why use incest to picture God's blessings? (62:5)

Metaphors have limitations and this one was probably not meant to be stretched too far. The word *sons* may have meant *Builder* (see NIV text note). The word *marry* may mean *take possession of*. This was simply a picture of the people of the Lord returning to Jerusalem and loving and caring for that city as their own.

Can we tire God out with our prayers? (62:7)

No. But the Bible sometimes pictures God as having physical human characteristics. This verse simply urges God's people to pray until their prayers are answered. Though prayers do not literally wear God out, he does respond to persistence (Luke 18:1–8).

⁹Their descendants will be known among the
nations
  and their offspring among the peoples.
All who see them will acknowledge
  that they are a people the LORD has blessed."

¹⁰I delight greatly in the LORD;
  my soul[D] rejoices in my God.
For he has clothed me with garments of
  salvation[D]
  and arrayed me in a robe of righteousness[D],
as a bridegroom adorns his head like a priest[D],
  and as a bride adorns herself with her jewels.
¹¹For as the soil makes the sprout come up
  and a garden causes seeds to grow,
so the Sovereign LORD will make
  righteousness and praise
  spring up before all nations.

Zion's New Name

62 For Zion's[D] sake I will not keep silent,
  for Jerusalem's sake I will not remain quiet,
till her righteousness shines out like the
  dawn,
  her salvation like a blazing torch.
²The nations will see your righteousness,
  and all kings your glory[D];
you will be called by a new name
  that the mouth of the LORD will bestow.
³You will be a crown of splendor in the LORD's
  hand,
  a royal diadem in the hand of your God.
⁴No longer will they call you Deserted,
  or name your land Desolate.
But you will be called Hephzibah,*ᵃ*
  and your land Beulah*ᵇ*;
for the LORD will take delight in you,
  and your land will be married.
⁵As a young man marries a maiden,
  so will your sons*ᶜ* marry you;
as a bridegroom rejoices over his bride,
  so will your God rejoice over you.

⁶I have posted watchmen[D] on your walls,
  O Jerusalem;
they will never be silent day or night.
You who call on the LORD,
  give yourselves no rest,
⁷and give him no rest till he establishes
  Jerusalem
  and makes her the praise of the earth.

⁸The LORD has sworn by his right hand
  and by his mighty arm:
"Never again will I give your grain
  as food for your enemies,
and never again will foreigners drink the new
  wine[D]
  for which you have toiled;
⁹but those who harvest it will eat it
  and praise the LORD,

ᵃ4 Hephzibah means *my delight is in her.*   *ᵇ4 Beulah* means
married.   *ᶜ5 Or Builder*

and those who gather the grapes will drink it
    in the courts of my sanctuary."

10Pass through, pass through the gates!
    Prepare the way for the people.
Build up, build up the highway!
    Remove the stones.
Raise a banner for the nations.

11The LORD has made proclamation
    to the ends of the earth:
"Say to the Daughter of ZionD,
    'See, your Savior comes!
See, his reward is with him,
    and his recompense accompanies him.' "
12They will be called the Holy People,
    the RedeemedD of the LORD;
and you will be called Sought After,
    the City No Longer Deserted.

God's Day of Vengeance and Redemption

63 Who is this coming from EdomD,
    from Bozrah, with his garments stained
      crimson?
Who is this, robed in splendor,
    striding forward in the greatness of his
      strength?

"It is I, speaking in righteousnessD,
    mighty to save."

2Why are your garments red,
    like those of one treading the winepressD?

3"I have trodden the winepress alone;
    from the nations no one was with me.
I trampled them in my anger
    and trod them down in my wrath;
their blood spattered my garments,
    and I stained all my clothing.
4For the day of vengeance was in my heart,
    and the year of my redemptionD has come.
5I looked, but there was no one to help,
    I was appalled that no one gave support;
so my own arm worked salvationD for me,
    and my own wrath sustained me.
6I trampled the nations in my anger;
    in my wrath I made them drunk
    and poured their blood on the ground."

Praise and Prayer

7I will tell of the kindnesses of the LORD,
    the deeds for which he is to be praised,
    according to all the LORD has done for us—
yes, the many good things he has done
    for the house of Israel,
    according to his compassion and many
      kindnesses.
8He said, "Surely they are my people,
    sons who will not be false to me";
    and so he became their Savior.
9In all their distress he too was distressed,
    and the angel of his presence saved them.
In his love and mercyD he redeemed them;
    he lifted them up and carried them
    all the days of old.

Why build a road for the people? (62:10)
Rebuilding the fallen city of Jerusalem pictures
salvation. The road repairs illustrate the Israelites' return to Jerusalem, the way that leads to
salvation. God would make his salvation available to all of his people.

Holy People (62:12)
Here we have four more names for God's people (see vv. 2–4 for others). These names, like
the earlier ones, make it quite clear that the
status of the people has changed. Their salvation will clearly define them as God's people.

Edom . . . Bozrah (63:1)
Bozrah, which means fortress, was the capital
city of Edom, to the south and east of Israel.

Who is talking to whom? (63:1–6)
Isaiah, as a prophet, plays the role of a watchman guarding the city of Jerusalem. He asks,
in effect, "Who goes there?" and discovers it
is the Lord, speaking in righteousness, mighty
to save.

Winepress (63:2)
A large vat or trough where several people
could work together stomping on grapes to
squeeze out the juice so it could be drained off
and collected. The process left their feet and
clothing stained by the red grape juice.

SCRIPTURE LINK (63:5)
This verse is similar to 59:16 and the meaning
of the two verses is the same: God rescues his
people himself because there is no one else to
do it.

How can God be grieved? (63:10)

The Bible often speaks of God's passion and deep emotions. He loves people; he hates sin. He shows compassion and mercy; he grows angry. God's emotions demonstrate his personal nature. God is not an omnipotent machine looking dispassionately on the world. He longs to be involved in our lives and is grieved when people reject him. This personal side of God's Spirit is revealed more clearly in this passage than anywhere else in the Old Testament. Also see *What grieves the Holy Spirit?* (Eph. 4:30).

Why did God care about public relations? (63:12,14)

When people want to *gain . . . renown* or *make . . . a glorious name* for themselves, they are usually driven by less than pure motives including pride, self-centeredness and lust for power. But God's motives are entirely pure. He wants people to know the truth—that he alone is God, that other so-called gods are false. Only when people know the truth about God and honor him as God will they find their deepest needs met.

Why would God cause people to stray from his ways? (63:17)

Some say this simply means that God *allowed* his people to stray—he gave them the opportunity. God is not the author of sin; he does not cause people to sin. Though the Hebrews did not always distinguish it so carefully, there is a vast difference between what God allows to happen, which can include sin, and what God causes to happen. For further discussion on this, see article: *How can a holy God send an evil spirit?* (Judges 9:23).

What happens when God comes down? (64:1–3)

Who can say? With God, there is no limit as to what can happen. Isaiah wanted God to demonstrate his great power and reveal his glory to all nations, not just to his own people. He wanted God both to judge the evil nations and to bless his people Israel. When God comes in power to do *awesome things that we did not expect* (v. 3), the wicked and the righteous both tremble before him.

---

¹⁰Yet they rebelled
   and grieved his Holy Spirit.
So he turned and became their enemy
   and he himself fought against them.

¹¹Then his people recalled[a] the days of old,
   the days of Moses and his people—
where is he who brought them through the
     sea,
   with the shepherd of his flock?
Where is he who set
   his Holy Spirit among them,
¹²who sent his glorious arm of power
   to be at Moses' right hand,
who divided the waters before them,
   to gain for himself everlasting renown,
¹³who led them through the depths?
Like a horse in open country,
   they did not stumble;
¹⁴like cattle that go down to the plain,
   they were given rest by the Spirit of the
     LORD.
This is how you guided your people
   to make for yourself a glorious name.

¹⁵Look down from heaven and see
   from your lofty throne, holy and glorious.
Where are your zeal[D] and your might?
   Your tenderness and compassion are
     withheld from us.
¹⁶But you are our Father,
   though Abraham does not know us
   or Israel acknowledge us;
you, O LORD, are our Father,
   our Redeemer[D] from of old is your name.
¹⁷Why, O LORD, do you make us wander from
     your ways
   and harden our hearts so we do not revere[D]
     you?
Return for the sake of your servants,
   the tribes that are your inheritance.
¹⁸For a little while your people possessed your
     holy place,
   but now our enemies have trampled down
     your sanctuary.
¹⁹We are yours from of old;
   but you have not ruled over them,
   they have not been called by your name.[b]

64 Oh, that you would rend the heavens and
     come down,
   that the mountains would tremble before
     you!
²As when fire sets twigs ablaze
   and causes water to boil,
come down to make your name known to your
     enemies
   and cause the nations to quake before you!
³For when you did awesome things that we did
     not expect,
   you came down, and the mountains trembled
     before you.

---

a11 Or But may he recall   *b19 Or We are like those you have never ruled, / like those never called by your name*

4Since ancient times no one has heard,
no ear has perceived,
no eye has seen any God besides you,
who acts on behalf of those who wait for
him.
5You come to the help of those who gladly do
right,
who remember your ways.
But when we continued to sin against them,
you were angry.
How then can we be saved?
6All of us have become like one who is
uncleanD,
and all our righteousD acts are like filthy
rags;
we all shrivel up like a leaf,
and like the wind our sins sweep us away.
7No one calls on your name
or strives to lay hold of you;
for you have hidden your face from us
and made us waste away because of our sins.

8Yet, O LORD, you are our Father.
We are the clay, you are the potter;
we are all the work of your hand.
9Do not be angry beyond measure, O LORD;
do not remember our sins forever.
Oh, look upon us, we pray,
for we are all your people.
10Your sacredD cities have become a desert;
even ZionD is a desert, JerusalemD a
desolation.
11Our holy and glorious temple, where our
fathers praised you,
has been burned with fire,
and all that we treasured lies in ruins.
12After all this, O LORD, will you hold yourself
back?
Will you keep silent and punish us beyond
measure?

Judgment and Salvation

65 "I revealed myself to those who did not ask for
me;
I was found by those who did not seek me.
To a nation that did not call on my name,
I said, 'Here am I, here am I.'
2All day long I have held out my hands
to an obstinate people,
who walk in ways not good,
pursuing their own imaginations—
3a people who continually provoke me
to my very face,
offering sacrificesD in gardens
and burning incenseD on altars of brick;
4who sit among the graves
and spend their nights keeping secret vigil;
who eat the flesh of pigs,
and whose pots hold broth of unclean
meat;
5who say, 'Keep away; don't come near me,
for I am too sacred for you!'
Such people are smoke in my nostrils,
a fire that keeps burning all day.

How can we *wait for him*? (64:4)

To wait for God means to trust him, to be faithful to him and to commit oneself to him (see, for example, Psalm 37:3–7). Waiting for God means, in particular, to keep on trusting even when things are going badly—when you have not yet been delivered from your troubles. God does not always intervene immediately when we call on him for help.

How could something so righteous be so dirty? (64:6)

Isaiah says that the best and most righteous things we do are distorted and overwhelmed by our sinful nature. Good deeds alone cannot counteract wickedness any more than dry leaves can resist the wind. The Bible presents two contrasting views of humanity: though human beings are made in the image of God, they are also vile sinners.

Father (64:8)

A picture of God with several wonderful implications: God gives us life, loves us, protects us and provides for us. The word *Father* depicts the special relationship we can have with God (1 John 3:1). It also offers us a better understanding of his relationship with Jesus, the Son of God (Matt. 3:16–17).

If the potter shapes the clay, how is the clay responsible? (64:8)

It is hard to blame the clay for the shape it is in. And if this were the only picture we had of the relationship between God and people, it would be difficult to see how people can be held accountable for their condition. But metaphors have limitations and cannot illustrate every side of a particular truth. The Bible uses many analogies to help us understand God: God *the potter* shows his sovereign control over creation; God *our Father* (also in this verse) suggests a relationship where children can choose to be obedient or rebellious.

Did this predict the destruction of Jerusalem and the temple? (64:10–11)

Yes. Isaiah's vivid language has prompted some to think parts of this book were written and added later, after the fact. They doubt prophecy can be so specific. Others believe this book was the work of a single prophet. They see no problem with either Isaiah's precise words or use of the past tense to describe the future. The Hebrew "prophetic perfect tense," translated as past tense, stresses the certainty of the coming events. For more on this use of language see *What service had Jerusalem completed?* (40:2) and *Why did God speak as though victory had already come?* (Joshua 6:2).

Why did God come to those who didn't care? (65:1)

God came to them not because of, but in spite of, the fact that they did not care. Left to ourselves, none of us would care about God. But he initiates a relationship; he comes despite our inability to see our own need. In fact, the human heart cannot respond to God until after God has somehow touched it. Some speak of God's "prevenient grace"—grace that comes before we can move toward God (1 John 4:19).

How did they provoke the Lord? (65:3–4)

Other than worshiping idols, it's not entirely clear what the people were doing. Some suggest they may have been practicing some sort of nature cults in the gardens or perhaps even necromancy in the graveyards. Furthermore, God had commanded that their altar be of uncut stone, not brick (Exodus 20:25) and that they eat clean meat, not unclean (Lev. 11). Also see *Why were uncut stones needed for the altar?* (Joshua 8:31).

Why would people think they were too holy for God? (65:5)

Because of their idolatry. Some Israelites had tried in the past to serve both the Lord and the false gods. But these people no longer attempted to play that game. They had dedicated themselves to worshiping idols and wanted nothing at all to do with the one true God. Apparently they thought that if they associated with the Lord as well, the effectiveness of their idolatry and incantations would be canceled.

What did it mean to pay *back into their laps?* (65:6–7)

This pictures someone seated with a cloth or shawl in his or her lap, into which grain was poured (Ruth 3:15). It symbolized the judgment God would pour upon those who had committed these terrible idolatries.

Sharon . . . Valley of Achor (65:10)

Sharon was a swamp beside the Mediterranean south of Mount Carmel (see *Map 2* at the back of this Bible). Achor, which means *trouble*, was a desert area near the Dead Sea. Both were unsuitable for grazing land. But God's salvation would transform the land as dramatically as turning these two places into good pasture.

6 "See, it stands written before me:
  I will not keep silent but will pay back in
    full;
  I will pay it back into their laps—
7 both your sins and the sins of your fathers,"
  says the LORD.
  "Because they burned sacrifices[D] on the
    mountains
  and defied me on the hills,
  I will measure into their laps
  the full payment for their former deeds."

8 This is what the LORD says:

  "As when juice is still found in a cluster of
    grapes
  and men say, 'Don't destroy it,
    there is yet some good in it,'
  so will I do in behalf of my servants;
  I will not destroy them all.
9 I will bring forth descendants from Jacob,
  and from Judah those who will possess my
    mountains;
  my chosen people will inherit them,
  and there will my servants live.
10 Sharon will become a pasture for flocks,
  and the Valley of Achor a resting place for
    herds,
  for my people who seek me.

11 "But as for you who forsake the LORD
  and forget my holy mountain,
  who spread a table for Fortune
  and fill bowls of mixed wine for Destiny,
12 I will destine you for the sword,
  and you will all bend down for the slaughter;
  for I called but you did not answer,
  I spoke but you did not listen.
  You did evil in my sight
  and chose what displeases me."

13 Therefore this is what the Sovereign LORD says:

  "My servants will eat,
    but you will go hungry;
  my servants will drink,
    but you will go thirsty;
  my servants will rejoice,
    but you will be put to shame.
14 My servants will sing
  out of the joy of their hearts,
  but you will cry out
    from anguish of heart
  and wail in brokenness of spirit.
15 You will leave your name
  to my chosen ones as a curse;
  the Sovereign LORD will put you to death[D],
  but to his servants he will give another
    name.
16 Whoever invokes a blessing in the land
  will do so by the God of truth;
  he who takes an oath in the land
  will swear by the God of truth.
  For the past troubles will be forgotten
  and hidden from my eyes.

New Heavens and a New Earth

17"Behold, I will create
    new heavens and a new earth.
The former things will not be remembered,
    nor will they come to mind.
18But be glad and rejoice forever
    in what I will create,
for I will create Jerusalem^D to be a delight
    and its people a joy.
19I will rejoice over Jerusalem
    and take delight in my people;
the sound of weeping and of crying
    will be heard in it no more.

20"Never again will there be in it
    an infant who lives but a few days,
    or an old man who does not live out his
        years;
he who dies at a hundred
    will be thought a mere youth;
he who fails to reach^a a hundred
    will be considered accursed.
21They will build houses and dwell in them;
    they will plant vineyards and eat their
        fruit.
22No longer will they build houses and others
    live in them,
    or plant and others eat.
For as the days of a tree,
    so will be the days of my people;
my chosen ones will long enjoy
    the works of their hands.
23They will not toil in vain
    or bear children doomed to misfortune;
for they will be a people blessed by the
    LORD,
    they and their descendants with them.
24Before they call I will answer;
    while they are still speaking I will hear.
25The wolf and the lamb will feed together,
    and the lion will eat straw like the ox,
    but dust will be the serpent's food.
They will neither harm nor destroy
    on all my holy mountain,"
                       says the LORD.

Judgment and Hope

66 This is what the LORD says:

"Heaven is my throne,
    and the earth is my footstool.^D
Where is the house you will build for me?
    Where will my resting place be?
2Has not my hand made all these things,
    and so they came into being?"
                     declares the LORD.

"This is the one I esteem:
    he who is humble and contrite in spirit,
    and trembles at my word.
3But whoever sacrifices^D a bull
    is like one who kills a man,

a20 Or l the sinner who reaches

New heavens and a new earth (65:17)

It's possible Isaiah was thinking of the end of this present heaven and earth, with God beginning all over again. But it's much more likely that he was using the word *create* to mean *transform*. If so, he was saying that when God brings salvation to his people everything will be completely transformed.

Why consider 100-year-olds as mere youths? (65:20)

Some see this as the new order in the kingdom or millennial age. Others see this in more general terms, as a figure of speech. Either way, when God transforms his world, there will be no untimely deaths. No one will die in infancy and 100-year-olds will be considered young. These images portray one central truth: the new world is going to be better than the old.

Why answer before someone calls? (65:24)

This illustrates the changes that are coming. In this present, fallen world, it sometimes seems that God's answers don't come or, at best, are delayed. The psalmist prayed, *Why, O LORD, do you stand far off? Why do you hide yourself in times of trouble?* (Psalm 10:1). But when God makes his world anew, things will be different. Then God will answer even before his people finish praying to him.

SCRIPTURE LINK (65:25) *The wolf and the lamb*

When God saves his people, the world will be transformed, including the world of nature. Creation itself will be redeemed. See this similar theme in 11:6–9.

Why did Isaiah criticize sacrifices? (66:3)

One of the themes of the prophets of Israel was that God detests human efforts to please him by keeping ritual laws without respecting his moral laws. Sacrifices meant nothing to God if they were offered by merciless, unjust people. Morality is more important than ritual. People without morals are not genuinely religious when they perform rituals; they are merely being superstitious.

and whoever offers a lamb,
  like one who breaks a dog's neck;
whoever makes a grain offering[D]
  is like one who presents pig's blood,
and whoever burns memorial incense[D],
  like one who worships an idol[D].
They have chosen their own ways,
  and their souls[D] delight in their
    abominations[D];
4So I also will choose harsh treatment for
    them
  and will bring upon them what they dread.
For when I called, no one answered,
  when I spoke, no one listened.
They did evil in my sight
  and chose what displeases me."

5Hear the word of the LORD,
  you who tremble at his word:
"Your brothers who hate you,
  and exclude you because of my name, have
    said,
'Let the LORD be glorified,
  that we may see your joy!'
Yet they will be put to shame.
6Hear that uproar from the city,
  hear that noise from the temple!
It is the sound of the LORD
  repaying his enemies all they deserve.

7"Before she goes into labor,
  she gives birth;
before the pains come upon her,
  she delivers a son.
8Who has ever heard of such a thing?
  Who has ever seen such things?
Can a country be born in a day
  or a nation be brought forth in a moment?
Yet no sooner is Zion[D] in labor
  than she gives birth to her children.
9Do I bring to the moment of birth
  and not give delivery?" says the LORD.
"Do I close up the womb
  when I bring to delivery?" says your God.
10"Rejoice with Jerusalem[D] and be glad for
    her,
  all you who love her;
rejoice greatly with her,
  all you who mourn over her.
11For you will nurse and be satisfied
  at her comforting breasts;
you will drink deeply
  and delight in her overflowing abundance."

12For this is what the LORD says:

"I will extend peace[D] to her like a river,
  and the wealth of nations like a flooding
    stream;
you will nurse and be carried on her arm
  and dandled on her knees.
13As a mother comforts her child,
  so will I comfort you;
and you will be comforted over Jerusalem."

Has Zion given birth to a nation? (66:8)

Yes. The city of Jerusalem *gives birth* to Israel with the Lord as the midwife (v. 9). Isaiah uses many images and metaphors. Earlier he compares the Lord to a woman giving birth to the nation of Israel (42:14). Here, Isaiah promises a quick and effortless delivery, contrary to what one would expect. When Cyrus of Persia allowed the Jews to return and rebuild Jerusalem (538 B.C.), it was a miraculous rebirth of the nation. Also see *How did God give his people splendor?* (55:5).

¹⁴When you see this, your heart will rejoice
    and you will flourish like grass;
  the hand of the LORD will be made known to
        his servants,
    but his fury will be shown to his foes.
¹⁵See, the LORD is coming with fire,
    and his chariots are like a whirlwind;
  he will bring down his anger with fury,
    and his rebuke with flames of fire.
¹⁶For with fire and with his sword
    the LORD will execute judgment upon all
        men,
    and many will be those slain by the
        LORD.

¹⁷"Those who consecrate[D] and purify[D] themselves to go into the gardens, following the one in the midst of[a] those who eat the flesh of pigs and rats and other abominable things—they will meet their end together," declares the LORD.

¹⁸"And I, because of their actions and their imaginations, am about to come[b] and gather all nations and tongues, and they will come and see my glory[D].

¹⁹"I will set a sign among them, and I will send some of those who survive to the nations—to Tarshish, to the Libyans[c] and Lydians (famous as archers), to Tubal and Greece, and to the distant islands that have not heard of my fame or seen my glory. They will proclaim my glory among the nations. ²⁰And they will bring all your brothers, from all the nations, to my holy mountain in Jerusalem[D] as an offering to the LORD—on horses, in chariots and wagons, and on mules and camels," says the LORD. "They will bring them, as the Israelites bring their grain offerings[D], to the temple of the LORD in ceremonially clean vessels. ²¹And I will select some of them also to be priests[D] and Levites[D]," says the LORD.

ª17 Or *gardens behind one of your temples, and*   ᵇ18 The meaning of the Hebrew for this clause is uncertain.   ᶜ19 Some Septuagint manuscripts *Put* (Libyans); Hebrew *Pul*

SCRIPTURE LINK (66:17) *Abominable things*

Similar to those things listed in 65:3–4, detestable things associated with idol worship, superstition and immorality.

Tarshish . . . Libyans . . . Lydians . . . Tubal . . . Greece (66:19)

Tarshish was probably in Spain. Libya was part of North Africa west of Egypt. Lydia and Tubal were in what today is Turkey, near the Black Sea (see *Map 12* at the back of this Bible). These, together with the islands, represent all the earth, the point being that God will send the news of his glory to all the world.

Priests and Levites (66:21)

Some say these are the Jews, brought by Gentiles to be dedicated to the Lord (v. 20). Others say these are the Gentiles who made the offering—perhaps a picture of the largely Gentile church leading Jewish people to faith in Christ. In ancient Israel only male Levites descended from Aaron could be priests. But God held out the promise that one day all could become priests (61:6; Exodus 19:5–6). Today, all who trust in Christ can come as priests directly to the Lord (1 Peter 2:9).

How will God judge the world? (66:15–16)

For Isaiah and other Old Testament prophets, God was clearly a God of both judgment and salvation. They knew nothing of a salvation that did not involve judgment. In fact, they saw God's judgment as a sign that he cared enough to save.

The Bible describes judgment for sin in various ways: It is a place of fire and worms (Mark 9:48) and a place of darkness (Matt. 8:12). It is a sentence pronounced by the righteous judge (Matt. 25:31–33). It is harvesting what you have sown (Gal. 6:7). It is separation from God (Matt. 7:23). Here, Isaiah pictures judgment as a mighty warrior; God is riding a whirlwind for a chariot, destroying his enemies with fire and a sword. The message is clear: God does not ignore sinners; he punishes them.

Perhaps Isaiah is speaking here of the final judgment of God, at the end of the world when sinners will be separated from God in hell. Or perhaps he is speaking of the judgment that continues to cycle throughout history—nations falling from power, defeated for their injustices. In either case God's judgment is shown to be devastating.

Their worm will not die, nor will their fire be quenched (66:24)

A metaphor of judgment upon those who attack Jerusalem: following a major battle, it was difficult to bury all the bodies. Usually fallen corpses would decay (pictured by worms) or be heaped into piles and burned. This image of perpetual decay and burning probably was meant to convey the idea of casualties too great to number. But the image also expresses a broader meaning, one of eternal punishment in hell. Jesus quoted this verse with that meaning when he spoke of hell (Mark 9:47–48).

[22]"As the new heavens and the new earth that I make will endure before me," declares the LORD, "so will your name and descendants endure. [23]From one New Moon to another and from one Sabbath[D] to another, all mankind will come and bow down before me," says the LORD. [24]"And they will go out and look upon the dead bodies of those who rebelled against me; their worm will not die, nor will their fire be quenched, and they will be loathsome to all mankind."

JEREMIAH

Why read this book?

If you've ever wondered what God wanted or if you've felt you might have missed his purpose for you, you're in good company. Jeremiah was a young man who struggled to know God's plan for his life. Even after he'd made his choice, additional pressures made him wonder if he'd done the right thing. But what Jeremiah discovered can give us insight and perspective when we feel stressed out about serving God in difficult times.

Who wrote this book?

Jeremiah, a priest and prophet. Jeremiah's aide, Baruch, actually wrote down the prophecies as they were dictated by Jeremiah.

When was it written?

Over the course of Jeremiah's ministry (626 to 585 B.C.). The last verses were added after 561 B.C., about 25 years after the destruction of Jerusalem.

What were the key events of Jeremiah's life and times?

Born in a village about an hour's walk from Jerusalem, Jeremiah, while still young, was called by God to be a prophet. Jeremiah saw his nation disintegrating morally from within and being destroyed militarily from without. He saw the siege and sack of Jerusalem (586 B.C.), and he saw many of his people taken captive to foreign lands. All this time, his warnings and pleas that Israel should turn back to God fell on deaf ears. After Jerusalem fell, Jeremiah was forced to flee to Egypt, where it is assumed he died.

What to look for in Jeremiah:

Jeremiah's grim speeches, in both poetry and prose, continually warned Judah about God's approaching judgment. Yet, intermingled with all the dark messages, there are words of hope about Judah's future redemption. Watch for Jeremiah's encouragement—prophecies that are still being fulfilled today, whenever sinful hearts are transformed by God.

When did these things happen?

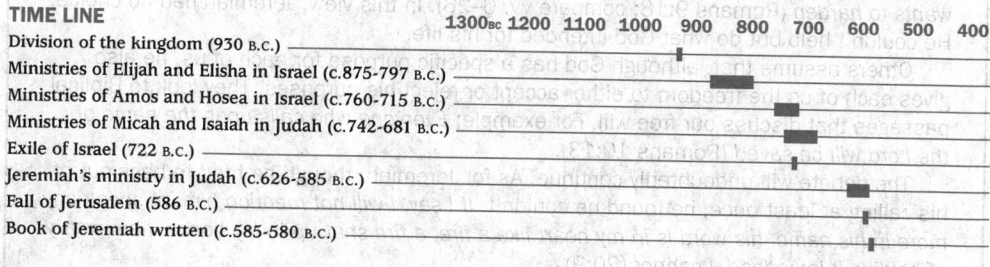

TIME LINE — 1300 BC 1200 1100 1000 900 800 700 600 500 400

Division of the kingdom (930 B.C.)

Ministries of Elijah and Elisha in Israel (c.875-797 B.C.)

Ministries of Amos and Hosea in Israel (c.760-715 B.C.)

Ministries of Micah and Isaiah in Judah (c.742-681 B.C.)

Exile of Israel (722 B.C.)

Jeremiah's ministry in Judah (c.626-585 B.C.)

Fall of Jerusalem (586 B.C.)

Book of Jeremiah written (c.585-580 B.C.)

When did Jeremiah preach? (1:1–3)

Jeremiah actually preached during the reigns of five kings (only the most important are noted here), who reigned from 627 to 587 B.C. After the fall of Jerusalem, Jeremiah also preached for a few years when exiled in Egypt.

How old was Jeremiah when he sensed God's call? (1:6)

Jeremiah described himself as a child, but childhood was a broader term then than it is now. It probably referred to anyone who was not yet fully mature. Jeremiah may have been between his early teens and early twenties.

What exactly did God want Jeremiah to do? (1:10)

Four of the six words used to describe Jeremiah's call were pessimistic. The bulk of Jeremiah's preaching was to be the announcement of Judah's destruction: *uproot . . . tear down . . . destroy . . . overthrow.* But Jeremiah was also called to proclaim hope—a redemption that was to follow: *build . . . plant.* Jeremiah himself did not destroy or build, but God did. Jeremiah's ministry was to announce the things God would be doing in Judah.

Why use a pun? (1:11–12; see NIV text note)

A play on words was a popular technique used by several prophets. It not only got people's attention, it helped them remember the message.

What northern kingdoms would attack Judah? (1:14–15)

In particular, Babylon and her allies. Although Babylon was actually located east of Judah, the normal military route from there to Judah was not on a straight east-west line. Instead, the Babylonians would travel around the expansive Arabian Desert that lay between them and Judah. The attackers from the east would consequently enter Judah from the north (see **Map 7** at the back of this Bible).

1 The words of Jeremiah son of Hilkiah, one of the priests[D] at Anathoth in the territory of Benjamin. ²The word of the LORD came to him in the thirteenth year of the reign of Josiah son of Amon king of Judah, ³and through the reign of Jehoiakim son of Josiah king of Judah, down to the fifth month of the eleventh year of Zedekiah son of Josiah king of Judah, when the people of Jerusalem[D] went into exile[D].

The Call of Jeremiah

⁴The word of the LORD came to me, saying,

⁵"Before I formed you in the womb I knew[a]
      you,
   before you were born I set you apart;
   I appointed you as a prophet[D] to the
      nations."

⁶"Ah, Sovereign LORD," I said, "I do not know how to speak; I am only a child."

⁷But the LORD said to me, "Do not say, 'I am only a child.' You must go to everyone I send you to and say whatever I command you. ⁸Do not be afraid of them, for I am with you and will rescue you," declares the LORD.

⁹Then the LORD reached out his hand and touched my mouth and said to me, "Now, I have put my words in your mouth. ¹⁰See, today I appoint you over nations and kingdoms to uproot and tear down, to destroy and overthrow, to build and to plant."

¹¹The word of the LORD came to me: "What do you see, Jeremiah?"

"I see the branch of an almond tree," I replied.

¹²The LORD said to me, "You have seen correctly, for I am watching[b] to see that my word is fulfilled."

¹³The word of the LORD came to me again: "What do you see?"

"I see a boiling pot, tilting away from the north," I answered.

¹⁴The LORD said to me, "From the north disaster will be

[a]5 Or *chose*   [b]12 The Hebrew for *watching* sounds like the Hebrew for *almond tree.*

How can God appoint someone not yet born? (1:5)

G od "appoints" people before they are born in the sense that he has a plan and purpose for each person.

Some believe this divine plan cannot be resisted. They look to Paul's argument for support: *God has mercy on whom he wants to have mercy, and he hardens whom he wants to harden* (Romans 9:18; compare vv. 6–26). In this view, Jeremiah had no choice. He couldn't help but do what God intended for his life.

Others assume that, although God has a specific purpose for each of us, he also gives each of us the freedom to either accept or reject his purposes. They look to Biblical passages that discuss our free will. For example: *Everyone who calls upon the name of the Lord will be saved* (Romans 10:13).

The debate will undoubtedly continue. As for Jeremiah, though he tried to back out of his calling at least once, he found he couldn't: *If I say, I will not mention him, or speak any more in his name, his word is in my heart like a fire, a fire shut up in my bones. I am weary of holding it in; indeed, I cannot* (20:9).

poured out on all who live in the land. **15**I am about to summon all the peoples of the northern kingdoms," declares the LORD.

> "Their kings will come and set up their thrones
>   in the entrance of the gates of Jerusalem[D];
> they will come against all her surrounding
>   walls
>   and against all the towns of Judah.
> **16**I will pronounce my judgments on my people
>   because of their wickedness in forsaking me,
> in burning incense[D] to other gods
>   and in worshiping what their hands have
>   made.

17"Get yourself ready! Stand up and say to them whatever I command you. Do not be terrified by them, or I will terrify you before them. **18**Today I have made you a fortified city, an iron pillar and a bronze wall to stand against the whole land—against the kings of Judah, its officials, its priests[D] and the people of the land. **19**They will fight against you but will not overcome you, for I am with you and will rescue you," declares the LORD.

Israel Forsakes God

2 The word of the LORD came to me: **2**"Go and proclaim in the hearing of Jerusalem:

> " 'I remember the devotion of your youth,
>   how as a bride you loved me
> and followed me through the desert,
>   through a land not sown.
> **3**Israel was holy to the LORD,
>   the firstfruits[D] of his harvest;
> all who devoured her were held guilty,
>   and disaster overtook them,' "
>
> declares the LORD.

> **4**Hear the word of the LORD, O house of Jacob,
>   all you clans of the house of Israel.

5This is what the LORD says:

> "What fault did your fathers find in me,
>   that they strayed so far from me?
> They followed worthless idols[D]
>   and became worthless themselves.
> **6**They did not ask, 'Where is the LORD,
>   who brought us up out of Egypt
> and led us through the barren wilderness,
>   through a land of deserts and rifts,
> a land of drought and darkness,[a]
>   a land where no one travels and no one
>   lives?'
> **7**I brought you into a fertile land
>   to eat its fruit and rich produce.
> But you came and defiled my land
>   and made my inheritance detestable.
> **8**The priests did not ask,
>   'Where is the LORD?'
> Those who deal with the law did not know me;
>   the leaders rebelled against me.
> The prophets[D] prophesied by Baal[D],
>   following worthless idols.

a6 Or and the shadow of death

Why accuse innocent grandchildren? (2:9)

This probably expresses the idea that Judah's sins would have long-lasting consequences, affecting generations to come. This was, in fact, exactly what happened: Judah was exiled for several generations. See *Why 70 years?* (25:11–12). It could mean that just as God would contend with the present generation of sinners, so he would also contend with future generations of sinners. See *Why punish the children of sinners?* (32:18).

Why would anyone choose a cistern over a fresh spring? (2:13)

This was Jeremiah's point precisely. In parched Palestine, cool spring water was extremely rare and highly valued. Most people had to use cisterns, hewed out of rock, to store water. No one would deliberately choose a cistern if a clean spring were available. Yet Judah, in deserting God, had abandoned a gushing spring for a leaking cistern!

Who are the *lions* that *have roared?* (2:15)

The lion typically was seen as a symbol of power and ferocity. These roaring lions probably referred to Assyria, the dominant nation of the time. Assyria invaded the northern nation of Israel, destroying it in 722 B.C. Its ominous, threatening roars could still be heard in nearby Judah when Jeremiah prophesied a century later.

Why did these men shave the heads of Israel? (2:16)

Memphis and Tahpanhes, cities of ancient Egypt, symbolized the whole nation of Egypt— just as Washington, D.C., could be understood in certain contexts to mean the United States. Since shaving the head was a sign of mourning or shame, this passage probably described Josiah's humiliating defeat at the hands of the Egyptians in 609 B.C. Also see *Why shave beards, tear clothes and cut skin?* (41:5).

What had they done *in the valley?* (2:23)

This was likely Jeremiah's way of recalling the people's participation in various pagan rituals. Child sacrifice and other detestable practices were carried out in the Valley of Ben Hinnom, just outside Jerusalem. On the other hand, the phrase could simply set the scene for the following metaphor of the she-camel.

⁹"Therefore I bring charges against you again,"
                    declares the LORD.
"And I will bring charges against your
    children's children.
¹⁰Cross over to the coasts of Kittim*ᵃ* and look,
    send to Kedar*ᵇ* and observe closely;
    see if there has ever been anything like this:
¹¹Has a nation ever changed its gods?
    (Yet they are not gods at all.)
But my people have exchanged their*ᶜ* Glory*ᴰ*
    for worthless idols*ᴰ*.
¹²Be appalled at this, O heavens,
    and shudder with great horror,"
                    declares the LORD.
¹³"My people have committed two sins:
They have forsaken me,
    the spring of living water,
and have dug their own cisterns*ᴰ*,
    broken cisterns that cannot hold water.
¹⁴Is Israel a servant, a slave by birth?
    Why then has he become plunder*ᴰ*?
¹⁵Lions have roared;
    they have growled at him.
They have laid waste his land;
    his towns are burned and deserted.
¹⁶Also, the men of Memphis*ᵈ* and Tahpanhes
    have shaved the crown of your head.*ᵉ*
¹⁷Have you not brought this on yourselves
    by forsaking the LORD your God
    when he led you in the way?
¹⁸Now why go to Egypt
    to drink water from the Shihor*ᶠ*?
And why go to Assyria
    to drink water from the River*ᵍ*?
¹⁹Your wickedness will punish you;
    your backsliding*ᴰ* will rebuke you.
Consider then and realize
    how evil and bitter it is for you
when you forsake the LORD your God
    and have no awe of me,"
                    declares the Lord, the LORD Almighty.

²⁰"Long ago you broke off your yoke*ᴰ*
    and tore off your bonds;
    you said, 'I will not serve you!'
Indeed, on every high hill
    and under every spreading tree
    you lay down as a prostitute.
²¹I had planted you like a choice vine
    of sound and reliable stock.
How then did you turn against me
    into a corrupt, wild vine?
²²Although you wash yourself with soda
    and use an abundance of soap,
    the stain of your guilt is still before me,"
                    declares the Sovereign LORD.
²³"How can you say, 'I am not defiled;
    I have not run after the Baals'?
See how you behaved in the valley;

ᵃ10 That is, Cyprus and western coastlands   *ᵇ10* The home of Bedouin tribes in the Syro-Arabian desert   *ᶜ11* Masoretic Text; an ancient Hebrew scribal tradition *my*   *ᵈ16* Hebrew *Noph*   *ᵉ16* Or *have cracked your skull*   *ᶠ18* That is, a branch of the Nile   *ᵍ18* That is, the Euphrates

consider what you have done.
You are a swift she-camel
running here and there,
²⁴a wild donkey accustomed to the desert,
sniffing the wind in her craving—
in her heat who can restrain her?
Any males that pursue her need not tire
themselves;
at mating time they will find her.
²⁵Do not run until your feet are bare
and your throat is dry.
But you said, 'It's no use!
I love foreign gods,
and I must go after them.'

²⁶"As a thief is disgraced when he is caught,
so the house of Israel is disgraced—
they, their kings and their officials,
their priests^D and their prophets^D.
²⁷They say to wood, 'You are my father,'
and to stone, 'You gave me birth.'
They have turned their backs to me
and not their faces;
yet when they are in trouble, they say,
'Come and save us!'
²⁸Where then are the gods you made for
yourselves?
Let them come if they can save you
when you are in trouble!
For you have as many gods
as you have towns, O Judah.

²⁹"Why do you bring charges against me?
You have all rebelled against me,"
declares the LORD.
³⁰"In vain I punished your people;
they did not respond to correction.
Your sword has devoured your prophets
like a ravening lion.

³¹"You of this generation, consider the word of the
LORD:

"Have I been a desert to Israel
or a land of great darkness?
Why do my people say, 'We are free to roam;
we will come to you no more'?
³²Does a maiden forget her jewelry,
a bride her wedding ornaments?
Yet my people have forgotten me,
days without number.
³³How skilled you are at pursuing love!
Even the worst of women can learn from
your ways.
³⁴On your clothes men find
the lifeblood of the innocent poor,
though you did not catch them breaking in.
Yet in spite of all this
³⁵   you say, 'I am innocent;
he is not angry with me.'
But I will pass judgment on you
because you say, 'I have not sinned.'
³⁶Why do you go about so much,
changing your ways?
You will be disappointed by Egypt
as you were by Assyria.

Why did the people bring charges against God? (2:29)

They probably blamed him for not protecting them from defeat in their recent battle against Egypt. They may also have accused God for neglecting Judah and permitting the nation to be made subject to Assyria.

What had Judah done to the poor? (2:34)

Innocent lives were being lost—probably as the result of social injustice, or perhaps due to the practice of child sacrifice. There was no defense for such atrocities.

How had Judah been disappointed? (2:36)

On more than one occasion, Judah had looked to other nations, including Assyria, for political and military support, only to be betrayed. God wanted his people to trust him, not the military powers of foreign nations.

37You will also leave that place
with your hands on your head,
for the LORD has rejected those you trust;
you will not be helped by them.

3   "If a man divorces his wife
and she leaves him and marries another
man,
should he return to her again?
Would not the land be completely defiled?
But you have lived as a prostitute with many
lovers—
would you now return to me?"
declares the LORD.
2"Look up to the barren heights and see.
Is there any place where you have not been
ravished?
By the roadside you sat waiting for lovers,
sat like a nomad*a* in the desert.
You have defiled the land
with your prostitution and wickedness.
3Therefore the showers have been withheld,
and no spring rains have fallen.
Yet you have the brazen look of a prostitute;
you refuse to blush with shame.
4Have you not just called to me:
'My Father, my friend from my youth,
5will you always be angry?
Will your wrath continue forever?'
This is how you talk,
but you do all the evil you can."

Did God want the people to return to him? (3:1)

Absolutely. Though he wanted the people of Judah to renew their commitment to him, God used strong language to show how badly they had sinned. No one else in God's position, dealing with such extreme unfaithfulness in a spouse, would ever accept the feeble apologies and excuses Judah seemed inclined to make. Apart from his own grace and mercy, God had no reason to receive them back.

Does God use drought to punish? (3:3)

In this and other Old Testament passages, it appears so. But the New Testament suggests that weather is not necessarily linked to disobedience (see Matt. 5:45). Perhaps it's best to see drought, to name just one example, as an opportunity to examine our lives. If drought calls our attention to spiritual dryness, we can look afresh to God for the living water of his Spirit. Also see *Does God cause natural calamities because of people's sin?* (5:25).

Unfaithful Israel

6During the reign of King Josiah, the LORD said to me, "Have you seen what faithless Israel has done? She has gone up on every high hill and under every spreading tree and has committed adultery there. **7**I thought that after she had done all this she would return to me but she did not, and her unfaithful sister Judah saw it. **8**I gave faithless Israel her certificate of divorce and sent her away because of all her adulteries. Yet I saw that her unfaithful sister Judah had no fear; she also went out and committed adultery. **9**Because Israel's immorality mattered so little to her, she defiled the land and committed adultery with stone and wood. **10**In spite of all this, her unfaithful sister Judah did not return to me with all her heart, but only in pretense," declares the LORD.

11The LORD said to me, "Faithless Israel is more righteousᴰ than unfaithful Judah. **12**Go, proclaim this message toward the north:

" 'Return, faithless Israel,' declares the LORD,
'I will frown on you no longer,
for I am merciful,' declares the LORD,
'I will not be angry forever.
13Only acknowledge your guilt—
you have rebelled against the LORD your God,
you have scattered your favors to foreign gods
under every spreading tree,
and have not obeyed me,' "
declares the LORD.

14"Return, faithless people," declares the LORD, "for I

How was Israel more righteous than Judah? (3:11)

When the northern kingdom of Israel abandoned the Lord about a century before Jeremiah's time, it ignored the warnings of the prophets. The southern kingdom of Judah, however, ignored not only the prophets but also the example of what had happened to Israel. They could see how the northern kingdom had been destroyed, its people taken captive to Assyria. Yet even with that vivid illustration, they persisted in their sin, which made them less righteous than faithless Israel.

When did the *faithless people* return and have godly leaders? (3:14–16)

This promise hinged on the repentance of the people. Since they never fully repented, they never got the godly leaders. The promise can be understood more completely when it is seen as a metaphor for the coming kingdom of God. In this sense, the return to Zion speaks of a spiritual journey climaxed by the second coming of Christ. *Shepherds after my own heart* probably speaks of a Messianic government, but may suggest ministers under the new covenant.

a2 Or an Arab

am your husband. I will choose you—one from a town and two from a clan—and bring you to Zion.ᴰ ¹⁵Then I will give you shepherds after my own heart, who will lead you with knowledge and understanding. ¹⁶In those days, when your numbers have increased greatly in the land," declares the Lᴏʀᴅ, "men will no longer say, 'The ark of the covenantᴰ of the Lᴏʀᴅ.' It will never enter their minds or be remembered; it will not be missed, nor will another one be made. ¹⁷At that time they will call Jerusalemᴰ The Throne of the Lᴏʀᴅ, and all nations will gather in Jerusalem to honor the name of the Lᴏʀᴅ. No longer will they follow the stubbornness of their evil hearts. ¹⁸In those days the house of Judah will join the house of Israel, and together they will come from a northern land to the land I gave your forefathers as an inheritance.

¹⁹"I myself said,

" 'How gladly would I treat you like sons
    and give you a desirable land,
    the most beautiful inheritance of any nation.'
I thought you would call me 'Father'
    and not turn away from following me.
²⁰But like a woman unfaithful to her husband,
    so you have been unfaithful to me, O house
        of Israel,"
                                        declares the Lᴏʀᴅ.

²¹A cry is heard on the barren heights,
    the weeping and pleading of the people of
        Israel,
because they have perverted their ways
    and have forgotten the Lᴏʀᴅ their God.

²²"Return, faithless people;
    I will cure you of backsliding.ᴰ"

"Yes, we will come to you,
    for you are the Lᴏʀᴅ our God.
²³Surely the ⌐idolatrous⌐ commotion on the hills
        and mountains is a deception;
surely in the Lᴏʀᴅ our God
    is the salvationᴰ of Israel.
²⁴From our youth shameful gods have consumed
        the fruits of our fathers' labor—
their flocks and herds,
    their sons and daughters.
²⁵Let us lie down in our shame,
    and let our disgrace cover us.
We have sinned against the Lᴏʀᴅ our God,
        both we and our fathers;
from our youth till this day
    we have not obeyed the Lᴏʀᴅ our God."

4   "If you will return, O Israel,
        return to me,"
                                        declares the Lᴏʀᴅ.
"If you put your detestable idolsᴰ out of my
            sight
    and no longer go astray,
²and if in a truthful, just and righteousᴰ way
    you swear, 'As surely as the Lᴏʀᴅ lives,'
then the nations will be blessed by him
    and in him they will glory.ᴰ"

³This is what the Lᴏʀᴅ says to the men of Judah and to Jerusalem:

Why would people say, *The ark of the covenant of the Lᴏʀᴅ?* (3:16)

It was a physical, tangible way to identify God's presence in Israel. The ark carried the Ten Commandments, God's covenant with his people. Even more, the atonement cover of the ark symbolized God's very throne where he met with Moses (Exodus 25:17–22). But in the last days, no ark of the covenant would be needed to demonstrate God's presence. God would be enthroned directly in the lives of his people (v. 17; see Rev. 21:3).

Who agreed to come to the Lord? (3:22)

Some responded in a positive way to Jeremiah's preaching, at least early in his ministry. His message was not entirely rejected, although he was often distraught by the limited response he got (see 15:10; 20:7–8).

How did pagan gods "consume" animals and people? (3:24)

This likely is a reference to the sacrifices, animal and human, that were made to them. Sacrifices were considered "food" for the gods, even though it was the fire that consumed them. See *What does God eat?* (Lev. 21:6).

What does it mean to *circumcise your hearts*? (4:4)

This was a figurative way to call the people to cut sinful impurities from their lives, just as in physical circumcision the foreskin was removed. Jeremiah was advising the people of Judah to remove the sinful practices that hinder spiritual growth. The apostle Paul also used the metaphor of a circumcised heart (see Romans 2:28–29; Col. 2:11).

Why did disaster come after they had repented? (4:6; see 3:24–25)

The sayings and stories of this book are not arranged chronologically. We don't know when or to what degree repentance took place. Before the fall of Jerusalem, some people may have responded to Jeremiah's message, but the sin and hard-heartedness of the rest of the people no doubt remained. So Jeremiah continued to warn about coming judgment.

Why did Jeremiah accuse God of deception? (4:10)

Because God had allowed false prophets to announce that there was nothing to be concerned about, Jeremiah, passionately concerned about his people, was upset that God would in this way permit Judah to become deceived. Later Jeremiah gained a better perspective—that because God had not sent the false prophets and because they spoke their own delusions, they, too, would be punished (see 14:13–16; 23:21,26). See also *Why did Jeremiah accuse God of deception?* (20:7).

What was special about this wind? (4:11–12)

Even today, a hot, dry southeasterly wind can blow across Palestine for three days to two weeks. Fine dust fills the air, making life extremely trying for both humans and vegetation. A normal wind can blow away chaff, *to winnow or cleanse,* helping the harvesting process. But this hot wind destroyed the crops. For Jeremiah, this natural phenomenon was a metaphor for the fierceness of God's judgment.

Why did a warning come from Dan? (4:15–18)

Dan was traditionally considered the northern limits of the promised land (Deut. 34:1). The hills of Ephraim lay about ten miles north of Jerusalem. In short, the enemy was traveling through the northern outposts of the land, rushing south to attack Jerusalem (see *Map 4* at the back of this Bible). The voice from the north traveled like a shock wave just ahead of the invading army.

"Break up your unplowed ground
    and do not sow among thorns.
⁴Circumcise[D] yourselves to the LORD,
    circumcise your hearts,
    you men of Judah and people of Jerusalem[D],
or my wrath will break out and burn like fire
    because of the evil you have done—
    burn with no one to quench it.

Disaster From the North

⁵"Announce in Judah and proclaim in
        Jerusalem and say:
    'Sound the trumpet throughout the land!'
    Cry aloud and say:
    'Gather together!
    Let us flee to the fortified cities!'
⁶Raise the signal to go to Zion[D]!
    Flee for safety without delay!
For I am bringing disaster from the north,
    even terrible destruction."

⁷A lion has come out of his lair;
    a destroyer of nations has set out.
He has left his place
    to lay waste your land.
Your towns will lie in ruins
    without inhabitant.
⁸So put on sackcloth[D],
    lament[D] and wail,
for the fierce anger of the LORD
    has not turned away from us.

⁹"In that day," declares the LORD,
    "the king and the officials will lose heart,
the priests[D] will be horrified,
    and the prophets[D] will be appalled."

¹⁰Then I said, "Ah, Sovereign LORD, how completely you have deceived this people and Jerusalem by saying, 'You will have peace[D],' when the sword is at our throats."

¹¹At that time this people and Jerusalem will be told, "A scorching wind from the barren heights in the desert blows toward my people, but not to winnow or cleanse; ¹²a wind too strong for that comes from me.[a] Now I pronounce my judgments against them."

¹³Look! He advances like the clouds,
    his chariots come like a whirlwind,
his horses are swifter than eagles.
    Woe to us! We are ruined!
¹⁴O Jerusalem, wash the evil from your heart
        and be saved.
    How long will you harbor wicked thoughts?
¹⁵A voice is announcing from Dan,
    proclaiming disaster from the hills of
        Ephraim.
¹⁶"Tell this to the nations,
    proclaim it to Jerusalem:
    'A besieging army is coming from a distant
        land,
    raising a war cry against the cities of Judah.
¹⁷They surround her like men guarding a field,

ᵃ12 Or *comes at my command*

because she has rebelled against me,' "
declares the LORD.

18"Your own conduct and actions
have brought this upon you.
This is your punishment.
How bitter it is!
How it pierces to the heart!"

19Oh, my anguish, my anguish!
I writhe in pain.
Oh, the agony of my heart!
My heart pounds within me,
I cannot keep silent.
For I have heard the sound of the trumpet;
I have heard the battle cry.
20Disaster follows disaster;
the whole land lies in ruins.
In an instant my tents are destroyed,
my shelter in a moment.
21How long must I see the battle standard
and hear the sound of the trumpet?

22"My people are fools;
they do not know me.
They are senseless children;
they have no understanding.
They are skilled in doing evil;
they know not how to do good."

23I looked at the earth,
and it was formless and empty;
and at the heavens,
and their light was gone.
24I looked at the mountains,
and they were quaking;
all the hills were swaying.
25I looked, and there were no people;
every bird in the sky had flown away.
26I looked, and the fruitful land was a desert;
all its towns lay in ruins
before the LORD, before his fierce anger.

27This is what the LORD says:

"The whole land will be ruined,
though I will not destroy it completely.
28Therefore the earth will mourn
and the heavens above grow dark,
because I have spoken and will not relent,
I have decided and will not turn back."

29At the sound of horsemen and archers
every town takes to flight.
Some go into the thickets;
some climb up among the rocks.
All the towns are deserted;
no one lives in them.

30What are you doing, O devastated one?
Why dress yourself in scarlet
and put on jewels of gold?
Why shade your eyes with paint?
You adorn yourself in vain.
Your lovers despise you;
they seek your life.

31I hear a cry as of a woman in labor,
a groan as of one bearing her first child—

Why did Jeremiah have to endure such anguish? (4:19-26)

Because he dearly loved the people of Judah. Jeremiah didn't speak the harsh, prophetic word of God's judgment because he was an angry man. He identified with his people; it troubled him deeply to have to speak as he did, knowing what was to befall Judah.

Why was God so final? (4:28)

Apparently, by the time this oracle was spoken, the time for repentance had run out. Some speculate that this section, or at least large portions of it, were spoken just before the fall of Jerusalem. In terms of just Jeremiah's ministry—not to mention the other prophets— Judah had had at least 40 years of warning.

How did Judah dress up? (4:30)

Jeremiah compared Judah with a prostitute who hoped to attract a lover with alluring clothes, make-up, jewels and perfume. The Israelites were trying to appease a nation (most likely Babylon) that, though they did not know it at the time, would eventually destroy them. This same metaphor is used and developed extensively in Ezekiel 23.

the cry of the Daughter of Zion^D gasping for
>breath,
stretching out her hands and saying,
"Alas! I am fainting;
>my life is given over to murderers."

Not One Is Upright

5 "Go up and down the streets of Jerusalem^D,
>look around and consider,
>search through her squares.
If you can find but one person
>who deals honestly and seeks the truth,
>I will forgive this city.
²Although they say, 'As surely as the LORD lives,'
>still they are swearing falsely."

³O LORD, do not your eyes look for truth?
>You struck them, but they felt no pain;
>you crushed them, but they refused
>>correction.
They made their faces harder than stone
>and refused to repent^D.
⁴I thought, "These are only the poor;
>they are foolish,
for they do not know the way of the LORD,
>the requirements of their God.
⁵So I will go to the leaders
>and speak to them;
surely they know the way of the LORD,
>the requirements of their God."
But with one accord they too had broken off
>>the yoke^D
>and torn off the bonds.
⁶Therefore a lion from the forest will attack
>>them,
>a wolf from the desert will ravage them,
a leopard will lie in wait near their towns
>to tear to pieces any who venture out,
for their rebellion is great
>and their backslidings many.

⁷"Why should I forgive you?
>Your children have forsaken me
>and sworn by gods that are not gods.
I supplied all their needs,
>yet they committed adultery
>and thronged to the houses of prostitutes.
⁸They are well-fed, lusty stallions,
>each neighing for another man's wife.
⁹Should I not punish them for this?"
>declares the LORD.
"Should I not avenge^D myself
>on such a nation as this?

¹⁰"Go through her vineyards and ravage them,
>but do not destroy them completely.
Strip off her branches,
>for these people do not belong to the LORD.
¹¹The house of Israel and the house of Judah
>have been utterly unfaithful to me,"
>>>>declares the LORD.

¹²They have lied about the LORD;
>they said, "He will do nothing!
No harm will come to us;

**Wasn't there even one honest person
in Jerusalem? (5:1)**

Yes and more. Besides Jeremiah, the prophets
Zephaniah and Habakkuk also ministered in Jerusalem. Each influenced others to live righteous lives. Ezekiel served in the temple about
this time and Baruch, Jeremiah's scribe, likely
lived in Jerusalem too. This challenge, then,
was a way of saying that Jerusalem was overrun with dishonesty from the top down
(vv. 4–5).

**When had God *struck* and *crushed*
Judah? (5:3)**

This could refer to Josiah's defeat at the hands
of Egypt at Megiddo in 609 B.C., or to the lack
of rain and harvest described in vv. 24–25. Actually the phrase need not be limited to either
event; it could refer to both or perhaps to still
another event unknown to us.

we will never see sword or famine.
¹³The prophets[D] are but wind
and the word is not in them;
so let what they say be done to them."

¹⁴Therefore this is what the LORD God Almighty says:

"Because the people have spoken these words,
I will make my words in your mouth a fire
and these people the wood it consumes.
¹⁵O house of Israel," declares the LORD,
"I am bringing a distant nation against you—
an ancient and enduring nation,
a people whose language you do not know,
whose speech you do not understand.
¹⁶Their quivers are like an open grave;
all of them are mighty warriors.
¹⁷They will devour your harvests and food,
devour your sons and daughters;
they will devour your flocks and herds,
devour your vines and fig trees.
With the sword they will destroy
the fortified cities in which you trust.

¹⁸"Yet even in those days," declares the LORD, "I will not destroy you completely. ¹⁹And when the people ask, 'Why has the LORD our God done all this to us?' you will tell them, 'As you have forsaken me and served foreign gods in your own land, so now you will serve foreigners in a land not your own.'

²⁰"Announce this to the house of Jacob
and proclaim it in Judah:
²¹Hear this, you foolish and senseless people,
who have eyes but do not see,
who have ears but do not hear:
²²Should you not fear me?" declares the LORD.
"Should you not tremble in my presence?
I made the sand a boundary for the sea,
an everlasting barrier it cannot cross.
The waves may roll, but they cannot prevail;
they may roar, but they cannot cross it.
²³But these people have stubborn and rebellious
hearts;
they have turned aside and gone away.
²⁴They do not say to themselves,
'Let us fear the LORD our God,
who gives autumn and spring rains in season,
who assures us of the regular weeks of
harvest.'
²⁵Your wrongdoings have kept these away;
your sins have deprived you of good.

²⁶"Among my people are wicked men
who lie in wait like men who snare birds
and like those who set traps to catch men.
²⁷Like cages full of birds,
their houses are full of deceit;
they have become rich and powerful
²⁸ and have grown fat and sleek.
Their evil deeds have no limit;
they do not plead the case of the fatherless
to win it,
they do not defend the rights of the poor.
²⁹Should I not punish them for this?"
declares the LORD.

Distant nation (5:15)
Babylon. See 1:15; 4:16.

Why was a wicked nation used to punish Israel? (5:15–23)
See article: *Does God use evil to do good?* (Hab. 1:6,13).

Does God cause natural calamities because of people's sin? (5:25)
Since he created all things, God is ultimately behind all natural phenomena—indirectly, if not directly (see Matt. 5:45; John 9:1–3). But every occurrence of a natural disaster can be an occasion for spiritual reflection. In the agricultural society of that time, for example, a great harvest should have prompted the people's thanks and renewed spiritual commitment. When there was famine or drought, the people should have reflected on their spiritual hunger. Also see *Does God use drought to punish?* (3:3).

In what way are *cages full of birds . . . full of deceit?* (5:27)
Jeremiah used a striking image to indict the rich oppressors of the poor. In those days a hunter would lure wild birds by placing several tame birds in a cage. Like hunters cunningly using *cages full of birds* to snare even more birds, so the wicked rich set traps for the poor to accumulate even more wealth for themselves.

"Should I not avenge[D] myself
  on such a nation as this?

30"A horrible and shocking thing
  has happened in the land:
31The prophets[D] prophesy lies,
  the priests[D] rule by their own authority,
and my people love it this way.
  But what will you do in the end?

Jerusalem Under Siege

6 "Flee for safety, people of Benjamin!
  Flee from Jerusalem[D]!
Sound the trumpet in Tekoa!
  Raise the signal over Beth Hakkerem!
For disaster looms out of the north,
  even terrible destruction.
2I will destroy the Daughter of Zion[D],
  so beautiful and delicate.
3Shepherds with their flocks will come against
  her;
they will pitch their tents around her,
  each tending his own portion."

4"Prepare for battle against her!
  Arise, let us attack at noon!
But, alas, the daylight is fading,
  and the shadows of evening grow long.
5So arise, let us attack at night
  and destroy her fortresses!"

6This is what the LORD Almighty says:

"Cut down the trees
  and build siege ramps against Jerusalem.
This city must be punished;
  it is filled with oppression.
7As a well pours out its water,
  so she pours out her wickedness.
Violence and destruction resound in her;
  her sickness and wounds are ever before me.
8Take warning, O Jerusalem,
  or I will turn away from you
and make your land desolate
  so no one can live in it."

9This is what the LORD Almighty says:

"Let them glean the remnant[D] of Israel
  as thoroughly as a vine;
pass your hand over the branches again,
  like one gathering grapes."

10To whom can I speak and give warning?
  Who will listen to me?
Their ears are closed[a]
  so they cannot hear.
The word of the LORD is offensive to them;
  they find no pleasure in it.
11But I am full of the wrath of the LORD,
  and I cannot hold it in.

"Pour it out on the children in the street
  and on the young men gathered together;
both husband and wife will be caught in it,

Why mention these obscure towns? (6:1)

Tekoa and Beth Hakkerem lay south of Jerusalem, twelve and two miles away respectively (see **Map 6** at the back of this Bible). Presumably they were towns in which the people of Jerusalem would seek refuge if they were attacked from the north.

What's so dangerous about shepherds and flocks? (6:3)

Jeremiah described Jerusalem as *beautiful and delicate* (v. 2), words that, in Hebrew, alluded to a green pasture. Just as a peaceful pasture could be overrun with sheep, so Jerusalem was about to be overrun by an invading army.

Who speaks about preparing for battle? (6:4–5)

Jeremiah, to drive home the ferocity of the coming attack, imagined the Babylonian invaders urging each other on with these words. They were so bent on attacking Jerusalem that they would even begin the assault in the middle of the night, a most unusual military procedure at the time.

and the old, those weighed down with years.
¹²Their houses will be turned over to others,
    together with their fields and their wives,
  when I stretch out my hand
    against those who live in the land,"
                       declares the LORD.

¹³"From the least to the greatest,
    all are greedy for gain;
  prophetsᴰ and priestsᴰ alike,
    all practice deceit.
¹⁴They dress the wound of my people
    as though it were not serious.
  'Peaceᴰ, peace,' they say,
    when there is no peace.
¹⁵Are they ashamed of their loathsome conduct?
    No, they have no shame at all;
    they do not even know how to blush.
  So they will fall among the fallen;
    they will be brought down when I punish
      them,"
                       says the LORD.

¹⁶This is what the LORD says:

"Stand at the crossroads and look;
  ask for the ancient paths,
ask where the good way is, and walk in it,
  and you will find rest for your soulsᴰ.
But you said, 'We will not walk in it.'
¹⁷I appointed watchmenᴰ over you and said,
  'Listen to the sound of the trumpet!'
But you said, 'We will not listen.'
¹⁸Therefore hear, O nations;
  observe, O witnesses,
  what will happen to them.
¹⁹Hear, O earth:
I am bringing disaster on this people,
  the fruit of their schemes,
because they have not listened to my words
  and have rejected my law.
²⁰What do I care about incenseᴰ from Sheba
  or sweet calamusᴰ from a distant land?
Your burnt offeringsᴰ are not acceptable;
  your sacrificesᴰ do not please me."

²¹Therefore this is what the LORD says:

"I will put obstacles before this people.
  Fathers and sons alike will stumble over
    them;
  neighbors and friends will perish."

²²This is what the LORD says:

"Look, an army is coming
  from the land of the north;
a great nation is being stirred up
  from the ends of the earth.
²³They are armed with bow and spear;
  they are cruel and show no mercyᴰ.
They sound like the roaring sea
  as they ride on their horses;
they come like men in battle formation
  to attack you, O Daughter of Zionᴰ."

²⁴We have heard reports about them,
  and our hands hang limp.

What was special about *incense from Sheba* and *sweet calamus from a distant land*? (6:20)
The incense was probably frankincense imported from southern Arabia, and the calamus was a type of reed from India, used to manufacture anointing oil for temple use. These were costly goods, showing that people spared no expense to worship God "properly." Nonetheless, God was not pleased with such mere outward symbols—no matter how extravagant—when the hearts of the people were corrupt.

Who is the *great nation from the north*? (6:22)
See *What northern kingdoms would attack Judah?* (1:14–15).

Anguish has gripped us,
　　pain like that of a woman in labor.
²⁵Do not go out to the fields
　　or walk on the roads,
for the enemy has a sword,
　　and there is terror on every side.
²⁶O my people, put on sackcloth ᴰ
　　and roll in ashes;
mourn with bitter wailing
　　as for an only son,
for suddenly the destroyer
　　will come upon us.

²⁷"I have made you a tester of metals
　　and my people the ore,
that you may observe
　　and test their ways.
²⁸They are all hardened rebels,
　　going about to slander.
They are bronze and iron;
　　they all act corruptly.
²⁹The bellows blow fiercely
　　to burn away the lead with fire,
but the refining goes on in vain;
　　the wicked are not purged out.
³⁰They are called rejected silver,
　　because the LORD has rejected them."

How was Jeremiah like a metal tester? (6:27)

A metal tester took samples of silver and melted them, hoping to discover the value of the silver ore by separating out the less valuable metals. When the silver content was too low, it was considered worthless and was rejected. Jeremiah, in testing the "metal" of Judah, concluded that Judah had too many impurities and would likewise be rejected.

Why preach at the temple gate? (7:1–2)

Worshipers had to pass through this gate to get to the activities taking place in the temple court. Possibly Jeremiah informally resumed an ancient practice in which a servant at the gate would greet pilgrims with a reminder to examine their moral lives as they entered the temple.

Why was it deceptive to say *the temple of the LORD?* (7:4)

People believed that because the temple was so important to God and because God was especially present in the temple, he would never allow it or the city it was in to be destroyed. They were deceiving themselves to believe that a religious shrine was more important to God than moral behavior.

What had happened to Shiloh? (7:12)

As the people well knew, this was a place where God had made himself known, especially in raising up the prophet Samuel (1 Samuel 1–4). It lay 30 miles north of Jerusalem, in Israel. It probably had been destroyed in the Assyrian invasion about a hundred years earlier (722 B.C.).

False Religion Worthless

7 This is the word that came to Jeremiah from the LORD: ²"Stand at the gate of the LORD's house and there proclaim this message:

" 'Hear the word of the LORD, all you people of Judah who come through these gates to worship the LORD. ³This is what the LORD Almighty, the God of Israel, says: Reform your ways and your actions, and I will let you live in this place. ⁴Do not trust in deceptive words and say, "This is the temple of the LORD, the temple of the LORD, the temple of the LORD!" ⁵If you really change your ways and your actions and deal with each other justly, ⁶if you do not oppress the alien ᴰ, the fatherless or the widow and do not shed innocent blood in this place, and if you do not follow other gods to your own harm, ⁷then I will let you live in this place, in the land I gave your forefathers for ever and ever. ⁸But look, you are trusting in deceptive words that are worthless.

⁹" 'Will you steal and murder, commit adultery and perjury,ᵃ burn incense ᴰ to Baal ᴰ and follow other gods you have not known, ¹⁰and then come and stand before me in this house, which bears my Name, and say, "We are safe"—safe to do all these detestable things? ¹¹Has this house, which bears my Name, become a den of robbers to you? But I have been watching! declares the LORD.

¹²" 'Go now to the place in Shiloh where I first made a dwelling for my Name, and see what I did to it because of the wickedness of my people Israel. ¹³While you were doing all these things, declares the LORD, I spoke to you again and again, but you did not listen; I called you, but you did not answer. ¹⁴Therefore, what I did to Shiloh I will now do to the house that bears my Name, the temple you trust in, the place I gave to you and your fathers. ¹⁵I will

---

ᵃ9 Or *and swear by false gods*

thrust you from my presence, just as I did all your brothers, the people of Ephraim.'

¹⁶"So do not pray for this people nor offer any plea or petition for them; do not plead with me, for I will not listen to you. ¹⁷Do you not see what they are doing in the towns of Judah and in the streets of JerusalemᴰᎵ ¹⁸The children gather wood, the fathers light the fire, and the women knead the dough and make cakes of bread for the Queen of Heaven. They pour out drink offeringsᴰ to other gods to provoke me to anger. ¹⁹But am I the one they are provoking? declares the LORD. Are they not rather harming themselves, to their own shame?

²⁰" 'Therefore this is what the Sovereign LORD says: My anger and my wrath will be poured out on this place, on man and beast, on the trees of the field and on the fruit of the ground, and it will burn and not be quenched.

²¹" 'This is what the LORD Almighty, the God of Israel, says: Go ahead, add your burnt offeringsᴰ to your other sacrificesᴰ and eat the meat yourselves! ²²For when I brought your forefathers out of Egypt and spoke to them, I did not just give them commands about burnt offerings and sacrifices, ²³but I gave them this command: Obey me, and I will be your God and you will be my people. Walk in all the ways I command you, that it may go well with you. ²⁴But they did not listen or pay attention; instead, they followed the stubborn inclinations of their evil hearts. They went backward and not forward. ²⁵From the time your forefathers left Egypt until now, day after day, again and again I sent you my servants the prophetsᴰ. ²⁶But they did not listen to me or pay attention. They were stiff-necked and did more evil than their forefathers.'

²⁷"When you tell them all this, they will not listen to you; when you call to them, they will not answer. ²⁸Therefore say to them, 'This is the nation that has not obeyed the LORD its God or responded to correction. Truth has perished; it has vanished from their lips. ²⁹Cut off your hair and throw it away; take up a lamentᴰ on the barren heights, for the LORD has rejected and abandoned this generation that is under his wrath.

The Valley of Slaughter

³⁰" 'The people of Judah have done evil in my eyes, declares the LORD. They have set up their detestable idolsᴰ in the house that bears my Name and have defiled it. ³¹They have built the high placesᴰ of TophethᴰᎵ in the Valley of Ben Hinnom to burn their sons and daughters in the fire—something I did not command, nor did it enter my mind. ³²So beware, the days are coming, declares the LORD, when people will no longer call it Topheth or the Valley of Ben Hinnom, but the Valley of Slaughter, for they will bury the dead in Topheth until there is no more room. ³³Then the carcasses of this people will become food for the birds of the air and the beasts of the earth, and there will be no one to frighten them away. ³⁴I will bring an end to the sounds of joy and gladness and to the voices of bride and bridegroom in the towns of Judah and the streets of Jerusalem, for the land will become desolate.

8 " 'At that time, declares the LORD, the bones of the kings and officials of Judah, the bones of the priestsᴰ and prophets, and the bones of the people of Jerusalem will be removed from their graves. ²They will be exposed to the sun and the moon and all the stars of the

Why did God tell Jeremiah not to pray? (7:16)
See *Is it sometimes wrong to pray?* (11:14).

Queen of Heaven (7:18)
See *Queen of Heaven* (44:17).

Why did nature suffer God's judgment? (7:20)
People had been given dominion over the trees, animals and crops (Gen. 1:26). By God's design, our environment is protected most when we live righteous lives. But sinful behavior can wreak havoc, not only in our own lives, but in our environment as well.

Why keep preaching when no one's going to listen? (7:22–27)
Jeremiah had to preach to be obedient to God's call. In fact, he found it impossible to keep God's Word to himself (20:9). Apparently God wanted Jeremiah to speak to unheeding people so they would be without excuse when judgment finally came—unable to say they were not warned. Some speech is designed to *convince*, some to *convict*. A judge can let a first offender off with a stern warning, hoping the speech may persuade a change in behavior. A prosecuting attorney's final argument by contrast, does not aim to change behavior. Its goal is to convict. Jeremiah's early sermons were opportunities for the people to change their ways. His later sermons announced the judgment to come.

What does cutting off hair signify? (7:29)
See *Why shave beards, tear clothes and cut skin?* (41:5).

High places of Topheth in the Valley of Ben Hinnom (7:31)
See *Topheth . . . Valley of Ben Hinnom* (19:6).

Why desecrate graves? (8:1–3)
In some cultures, such as that of ancient Egypt, people were buried with food, tools, supplies and riches—things they believed would help them in the life after death. Perhaps the Babylonians hoped they could retrieve these valuables from the graves. More likely, however, they were trying to humiliate their victims. They weren't satisfied merely to pillage and plunder; they mocked their victims by dishonoring their dead.

heavens, which they have loved and served and which they have followed and consulted and worshiped. They will not be gathered up or buried, but will be like refuse lying on the ground. [3]Wherever I banish them, all the survivors of this evil nation will prefer death[D] to life, declares the LORD Almighty.'

Sin and Punishment

[4]"Say to them, 'This is what the LORD says:

" 'When men fall down, do they not get up?
  When a man turns away, does he not return?
[5]Why then have these people turned away?
  Why does Jerusalem[D] always turn away?
They cling to deceit;
  they refuse to return.
[6]I have listened attentively,
  but they do not say what is right.
No one repents[D] of his wickedness,
  saying, "What have I done?"
Each pursues his own course
  like a horse charging into battle.
[7]Even the stork in the sky
  knows her appointed seasons,
and the dove, the swift and the thrush
  observe the time of their migration.
But my people do not know
  the requirements of the LORD.

[8]" 'How can you say, "We are wise,
  for we have the law of the LORD,"
when actually the lying pen of the scribes
  has handled it falsely?
[9]The wise will be put to shame;
  they will be dismayed and trapped.
Since they have rejected the word of the LORD,
  what kind of wisdom do they have?
[10]Therefore I will give their wives to other men
  and their fields to new owners.
From the least to the greatest,
  all are greedy for gain;
prophets[D] and priests[D] alike,
  all practice deceit.
[11]They dress the wound of my people
  as though it were not serious.
"Peace[D], peace," they say,
  when there is no peace.
[12]Are they ashamed of their loathsome conduct?
No, they have no shame at all;
  they do not even know how to blush.
So they will fall among the fallen;
  they will be brought down when they are
     punished,
                                says the LORD.

[13]" 'I will take away their harvest,
                        declares the LORD.
There will be no grapes on the vine.
There will be no figs on the tree,
  and their leaves will wither.
What I have given them
  will be taken from them.[a]' "

[14]"Why are we sitting here?

What had the scribes done wrong? (8:8)

It seems they had twisted and distorted the law, perhaps misinterpreting it in their commentaries. Somehow they were able to rationalize abhorrent behavior—the worship of other gods and the practice of pagan religion. In the interest of avoiding conflict (peace, peace—v. 11) they seemed willing to tolerate anything. They could have used their considerable influence to teach the truth. Instead they wrote with a lying pen.

Why repeat the same material? (8:10–12; see 6:13–15)

This happens here and elsewhere in Jeremiah. For example, 9:9 repeats 5:9,29 and 39:1–10 repeats 52:4–16. See *Why is this information repeated?* (52:1–24).

Why switch voices? (8:14—9:2)

The use of different voices produced an effect like a drama. In this dialogue, we hear the people's fear about coming judgment (vv. 14–16); God's unrelenting response (v. 17); Jeremiah's lament (vv. 18–19); the Lord's unwavering judgment (v. 19); the people's hopelessness (v. 20) and Jeremiah's deepening despair (8:21–9:2). Jeremiah's "drama" intensified the anguish of Judah's desperate situation.

Poisoned water . . . venomous snakes (8:14,17)

Metaphors for the bitterness and deadliness of the coming judgment.

---

[a]13 The meaning of the Hebrew for this sentence is uncertain.

Gather together!
Let us flee to the fortified cities
    and perish there!
For the LORD our God has doomed us to perish
    and given us poisoned water to drink,
    because we have sinned against him.
¹⁵We hoped for peace[D]
    but no good has come,
for a time of healing
    but there was only terror.
¹⁶The snorting of the enemy's horses
    is heard from Dan;
at the neighing of their stallions
    the whole land trembles.
They have come to devour
    the land and everything in it,
    the city and all who live there."

¹⁷"See, I will send venomous snakes among you,
    vipers that cannot be charmed,
    and they will bite you,"
                        declares the LORD.

¹⁸O my Comforter[a] in sorrow,
    my heart is faint within me.
¹⁹Listen to the cry of my people
    from a land far away:
"Is the LORD not in Zion[D]?
    Is her King no longer there?"

"Why have they provoked me to anger with
        their images,
    with their worthless foreign idols[D]?"

²⁰"The harvest is past,
    the summer has ended,
    and we are not saved."

²¹Since my people are crushed, I am crushed;
    I mourn, and horror grips me.
²²Is there no balm in Gilead?
    Is there no physician there?
Why then is there no healing
    for the wound of my people?

9 ¹Oh, that my head were a spring of water
    and my eyes a fountain of tears!
I would weep day and night
    for the slain of my people.
²Oh, that I had in the desert
    a lodging place for travelers,
so that I might leave my people
    and go away from them;
for they are all adulterers,
    a crowd of unfaithful people.

³"They make ready their tongue
    like a bow, to shoot lies;
it is not by truth
    that they triumph[b] in the land.
They go from one sin to another;
    they do not acknowledge me,"
                        declares the LORD.
⁴"Beware of your friends;
    do not trust your brothers.

Where is Dan? (8:16)
See *Why did a warning come from Dan?*
(4:15–18).

Why did Jeremiah hear cries from a faraway land? (8:19)
Weren't the people still in Judah? Most were.
However, Babylon had already taken a few captives away around 605 and 597 B.C. Perhaps
Jeremiah was thinking of those Jews already
living in Babylon. Or perhaps this was a foreshadowing of the exile yet to come. Another
possibility is that this passage came from a
speech by Jeremiah after Jerusalem was destroyed and still more captives were taken into
exile (586 B.C.).

Did they expect salvation before au-tumn? (8:20)
No. Again, this is a metaphor—perhaps an ancient proverb—about hopelessness. Grains
were harvested from April to June, fruits at the
end of summer. If nothing was reaped by then,
it meant a lean, hard winter with little or no
food.

Gilead (8:22)
A region east of the Jordan River, from which a
medicine famous in the ancient world was exported (see *Conquest of Canaan* on page
301).

If Jeremiah really cared, why did he want to leave? (9:2)
He felt saddened by their plight—judgment—
but was nonetheless repulsed by their sin. He
said it would be better to live in isolation,
alone in the desert and away from such deplor-
able behavior, than to stay with the people he
loved.

What lies were people telling? (9:3–8)
They tried to reassure one another that they
really weren't that bad and that God would never abandon them. But no doubt there was also
the run-of-the-mill hypocrisy, back-stabbing
and deceit that goes on in the business, government and everyday life of many nations.

---

a 18 The meaning of the Hebrew for this word is uncertain.   *b 3* Or
lies; / they are not valiant for truth

For every brother is a deceiver,[a]
and every friend a slanderer.
5Friend deceives friend,
and no one speaks the truth.
They have taught their tongues to lie;
they weary themselves with sinning.
6You[b] live in the midst of deception;
in their deceit they refuse to acknowledge
me,"

> declares the LORD.

7Therefore this is what the LORD Almighty says:

"See, I will refine and test them,
for what else can I do
because of the sin of my people?
8Their tongue is a deadly arrow;
it speaks with deceit.
With his mouth each speaks cordially to his
neighbor,
but in his heart he sets a trap for him.
9Should I not punish them for this?"
declares the LORD.
"Should I not avenge[D] myself
on such a nation as this?"

10I will weep and wail for the mountains
and take up a lament[D] concerning the desert
pastures.
They are desolate and untraveled,
and the lowing of cattle is not heard.
The birds of the air have fled
and the animals are gone.

11"I will make Jerusalem[D] a heap of ruins,
a haunt of jackals;
and I will lay waste the towns of Judah
so no one can live there."

12What man is wise enough to understand this? Who has been instructed by the LORD and can explain it? Why has the land been ruined and laid waste like a desert that no one can cross?

13The LORD said, "It is because they have forsaken my law, which I set before them; they have not obeyed me or followed my law. 14Instead, they have followed the stubbornness of their hearts; they have followed the Baals[D], as their fathers taught them." 15Therefore, this is what the LORD Almighty, the God of Israel, says: "See, I will make this people eat bitter food and drink poisoned water. 16I will scatter them among nations that neither they nor their fathers have known, and I will pursue them with the sword until I have destroyed them."

17This is what the LORD Almighty says:

"Consider now! Call for the wailing women to
come;
send for the most skillful of them.
18Let them come quickly
and wail over us
till our eyes overflow with tears
and water streams from our eyelids.
19The sound of wailing is heard from Zion[D]:

Why punish them when they'd never known any better? (9:13-16)

Weren't they only doing what their parents had taught them? Yes, but the command to honor father and mother does not override the command to remain faithful to God. In fact, the people did know better. Many prophets had warned them about the consequences of their sins. Also, the law had been set before them (v. 13).

Did God plan to completely destroy Israel? (9:16)

Yes, but in only two senses: Israel was destroyed temporarily—the nation ceased to exist as a legitimate nation for a generation or more. It was also destroyed theologically—the old Israel was replaced by the new Israel, the church.

---

a4 Or a deceiving Jacob   b6 That is, Jeremiah (the Hebrew is singular)

'How ruined we are!
　How great is our shame!
We must leave our land
　because our houses are in ruins.' "

20Now, O women, hear the word of the LORD;
　open your ears to the words of his mouth.
Teach your daughters how to wail;
　teach one another a lament^D.
21Death^D has climbed in through our windows
　and has entered our fortresses;
it has cut off the children from the streets
　and the young men from the public squares.

22Say, "This is what the LORD declares:

" 'The dead bodies of men will lie
　like refuse on the open field,
like cut grain behind the reaper,
　with no one to gather them.' "

23This is what the LORD says:

"Let not the wise man boast of his wisdom
　or the strong man boast of his strength
　or the rich man boast of his riches,
24but let him who boasts boast about this:
　that he understands and knows me,
that I am the LORD, who exercises kindness,
　justice and righteousness^D on earth,
　for in these I delight,"

declares the LORD.

25"The days are coming," declares the LORD, "when I
will punish all who are circumcised^D only in the flesh—
26Egypt, Judah, Edom^D, Ammon, Moab and all who live
in the desert in distant places.^a For all these nations are
really uncircumcised^D, and even the whole house of Israel is uncircumcised in heart."

God and Idols

10 Hear what the LORD says to you, O house of Israel.
2This is what the LORD says:

"Do not learn the ways of the nations
　or be terrified by signs in the sky,
　though the nations are terrified by them.
3For the customs of the peoples are worthless;
　they cut a tree out of the forest,
　and a craftsman shapes it with his chisel.
4They adorn it with silver and gold;
　they fasten it with hammer and nails
　so it will not totter.
5Like a scarecrow in a melon patch,
　their idols^D cannot speak;
they must be carried
　because they cannot walk.
Do not fear them;
　they can do no harm
　nor can they do any good."

6No one is like you, O LORD;
　you are great,
　and your name is mighty in power.
7Who should not revere^D you,
　O King of the nations?

Why this judgment against other na-
tions? (9:25–26)

This was a roundabout way of judging Judah.
Jeremiah pointed out that Judah wasn't the
only nation to practice circumcision. It could
not rely merely on this mark of the covenant
(Gen. 17:1–15) to save itself from the coming
judgment. In fact, every nation, including Judah, would one day be judged by a higher standard. Also see *The death of the uncircumcised*
(Ezek. 28:10).

Uncircumcised in heart (9:25–26)

See *What does it mean to circumcise your
hearts?* (4:4).

What were the frightening *signs in the
sky?* (10:1–2)

Eclipses and meteorites, among other celestial
occurrences, were considered signs of good or
evil. People who thought astrology influenced
their lives could easily find bad omens in the
stars. See *What kind of sorceries, spells and
astrology could be found in Babylon?* (Isaiah
47:9).

Why would people believe that wooden
and metal figures had power?
(10:3–16)

See *Why were people attracted to worshiping
idols?* (2:8).

---

^a26 Or *desert and who clip the hair by their foreheads*

This is your due.
Among all the wise men of the nations
    and in all their kingdoms,
    there is no one like you.
[8]They are all senseless and foolish;
    they are taught by worthless wooden idols[D].
[9]Hammered silver is brought from Tarshish
    and gold from Uphaz.
What the craftsman and goldsmith have made
    is then dressed in blue and purple[D]—
    all made by skilled workers.
[10]But the LORD is the true God;
    he is the living God, the eternal King.
When he is angry, the earth trembles;
    the nations cannot endure his wrath.

[11]"Tell them this: 'These gods, who did not make the heavens and the earth, will perish from the earth and from under the heavens.' "[a]

[12]But God made the earth by his power;
    he founded the world by his wisdom
    and stretched out the heavens by his
        understanding.
[13]When he thunders, the waters in the heavens
        roar;
    he makes clouds rise from the ends of the
        earth.
He sends lightning with the rain
    and brings out the wind from his
        storehouses.
[14]Everyone is senseless and without knowledge;
    every goldsmith is shamed by his idols.
His images are a fraud;
    they have no breath in them.
[15]They are worthless, the objects of mockery;
    when their judgment comes, they will perish.
[16]He who is the Portion of Jacob is not like these,
    for he is the Maker of all things,
including Israel, the tribe of his inheritance—
    the LORD Almighty is his name.

Coming Destruction

[17]Gather up your belongings to leave the land,
    you who live under siege.
[18]For this is what the LORD says:
    "At this time I will hurl out
        those who live in this land;
    I will bring distress on them
        so that they may be captured."

[19]Woe to me because of my injury!
    My wound is incurable!
Yet I said to myself,
    "This is my sickness, and I must endure it."
[20]My tent is destroyed;
    all its ropes are snapped.
My sons are gone from me and are no more;
    no one is left now to pitch my tent
    or to set up my shelter.
[21]The shepherds are senseless
    and do not inquire of the LORD;

How is God the Portion of Jacob? (10:16)

As Jacob (meaning all the people of Israel) belonged to God, so did God, in another sense, belong to Jacob. This was an expression for the intimate relationship between God and his people.

How had Jeremiah been injured? (10:19)

He suffered mental torment and spiritual anguish over the sin in the land. He also saw his nation headed for suffering and torment—the unavoidable results of their sinful ways. The coming invaders would injure the nation, taking its sons into captivity (v. 20).

My tent (10:20)

Jeremiah described his people's coming suffering by using the image of a Bedouin family whose home and children are destroyed. Since nomadic tribes owned no real estate, their tents represented all their personal possessions.

Shepherds (10:21)

A metaphor for the leaders of Judah and their followers—their flock. Jeremiah considered the leaders most to blame for Judah's predicament.

[a]11 The text of this verse is in Aramaic.

so they do not prosper
and all their flock is scattered.
²²Listen! The report is coming—
a great commotion from the land of the
north!
It will make the towns of Judah desolate,
a haunt of jackals.

Jeremiah's Prayer

²³I know, O LORD, that a man's life is not his
own;
it is not for man to direct his steps.
²⁴Correct me, LORD, but only with justice—
not in your anger,
lest you reduce me to nothing.
²⁵Pour out your wrath on the nations
that do not acknowledge you,
on the peoples who do not call on your
name.
For they have devoured Jacob;
they have devoured him completely
and destroyed his homeland.

The Covenant Is Broken

11 This is the word that came to Jeremiah from the
LORD: ²"Listen to the terms of this covenantᴰ and
tell them to the people of Judah and to those who live in
JerusalemD. ³Tell them that this is what the LORD, the God
of Israel, says: 'Cursed is the man who does not obey the
terms of this covenant— ⁴the terms I commanded your
forefathers when I brought them out of Egypt, out of the
iron-smelting furnace.' I said, 'Obey me and do everything I command you, and you will be my people, and I
will be your God. ⁵Then I will fulfill the oath I swore to
your forefathers, to give them a land flowing with milk
and honey'—the land you possess today."
I answered, "Amen, LORD."
⁶The LORD said to me, "Proclaim all these words in the
towns of Judah and in the streets of Jerusalem: 'Listen to
the terms of this covenant and follow them. ⁷From the
time I brought your forefathers up from Egypt until today,
I warned them again and again, saying, "Obey me." ⁸But
they did not listen or pay attention; instead, they followed
the stubbornness of their evil hearts. So I brought on
them all the curses of the covenant I had commanded
them to follow but that they did not keep.' "
⁹Then the LORD said to me, "There is a conspiracy
among the people of Judah and those who live in Jerusalem. ¹⁰They have returned to the sins of their forefathers, who refused to listen to my words. They have followed other gods to serve them. Both the house of Israel
and the house of Judah have broken the covenant I
made with their forefathers. ¹¹Therefore this is what the
LORD says: 'I will bring on them a disaster they cannot escape. Although they cry out to me, I will not listen to
them. ¹²The towns of Judah and the people of Jerusalem
will go and cry out to the gods to whom they burn incenseᴰ, but they will not help them at all when disaster
strikes. ¹³You have as many gods as you have towns, O
Judah; and the altars you have set up to burn incense to
that shameful god Baalᴰ are as many as the streets of Jerusalem.'
¹⁴"Do not pray for this people nor offer any plea or peti-

Land of the north (10:22)

See *What northern kingdoms would attack Judah?* (1:14–15).

Why pray so humbly after all the accu-
sations? (10:23–24)

Jeremiah fully identified with his people—he
wanted to be judged by the same standards by
which he had judged them. In spite of all the in-
dications of God's wrath, Jeremiah prayed that
God would finally judge him and Israel with justice, not anger.

Why ask God to judge the nations he
used to punish Judah? (10:25)

Because sin is still sin. True, Babylon's destruction of Judah was put to a holy use by
God; he used Babylon to punish Judah. Nevertheless, rape, murder and pillage were sins for
which Babylon would eventually be judged.

How many gods did Israel serve?
(11:13)

It's impossible to say. They were influenced by
their Canaanite neighbors who had an estimated 2,000 to 3,000 different gods. Pagan
nations at that time typically believed that each
town had its own god to protect and provide for
its people. Perhaps Israel adopted the idea for
their own towns.

Is it sometimes wrong to pray? (11:14)

This was a unique case. Most of our problems
with prayer come from too little prayer rather
than too much. God told Jeremiah not to pray
for the people because they had already been
judged. They had refused to repent while they
had the opportunity. Now it was too late. God
emphasized his resolve by saying, in effect, "I
don't want to hear any more about it. My mind
is made up."

tion for them, because I will not listen when they call to me in the time of their distress.

> 15"What is my beloved doing in my temple
>   as she works out her evil schemes with
>   many?
> Can consecrated[D] meat avert ∟ your
>   punishment⌐?
> When you engage in your wickedness,
>   then you rejoice.[a]"

> 16The LORD called you a thriving olive tree
>   with fruit beautiful in form.
> But with the roar of a mighty storm
>   he will set it on fire,
>   and its branches will be broken.

17The LORD Almighty, who planted you, has decreed disaster for you, because the house of Israel and the house of Judah have done evil and provoked me to anger by burning incense[D] to Baal[D].

Plot Against Jeremiah

18Because the LORD revealed their plot to me, I knew it, for at that time he showed me what they were doing. 19I had been like a gentle lamb led to the slaughter; I did not realize that they had plotted against me, saying,

> "Let us destroy the tree and its fruit;
>   let us cut him off from the land of the living,
>   that his name be remembered no more."
> 20But, O LORD Almighty, you who judge
>   righteously[D]
> and test the heart and mind,
> let me see your vengeance upon them,
>   for to you I have committed my cause.

21"Therefore this is what the LORD says about the men

---

a 15 Or Could consecrated meat avert your punishment? / Then you would rejoice

Is it right to pray for vengeance? (11:20)

Vindictive passages seem troublesome. However, we should realize that Jeremiah was praying, not for his own vengeance, but for God's. It's also important to recognize that God's vengeance does not arise from revenge but from justice. People who oppose God bring judgment upon themselves. See article: *Is it right to pray for revenge?* (Psalm 58:6–8).

What was behind this murder plot? (11:21)

Men from Jeremiah's own hometown wanted to halt his influence, probably because he had been undermining theirs. He supported the king's reforms, including the destruction of altars to their local idol. See *How many gods did Israel serve?* (11:13). He also endorsed the priests at the temple in Jerusalem over the idolatrous priests of Anathoth.

When does God refuse to hear our prayers? (11:11)

God sees, hears and knows everything—including our prayers. Nothing escapes his attention. Why then did God say he would not listen to the people's cries for help? There are several possible reasons.

In this case, God did not respond because judgment was unavoidable. Judah had disobeyed God's laws and ignored his pleas for so long that judgment was, in effect, already on the way. Their cries were too little, too late. God even told Jeremiah *not* to pray for the people (11:14; 14:11–12)—that not even Moses and Samuel could have persuaded him to offer further compassion to them (15:1).

It's also possible that people sometimes sabotage their own prayers. The Bible mentions several attitudes and actions that can short-circuit our prayers: sin (Deut. 1:45; Psalm 66:18; Isaiah 59:2; Jer. 14:10–12), disobedience (Prov. 28:9), hypocrisy and insincerity (Isaiah 29:13; Mal. 1:7–9), wrong motives (Matt. 6:5–6; Luke 18:11–14; James 4:3), lack of faith (Heb. 11:6; James 1:6) and even marital problems (1 Peter 3:7).

Finally, what sometimes appears to be *no* answer to prayer may actually be a *delayed* answer (Daniel 10:12–13). Other times God may deny our request in order to give us something better than what we knew to ask for.

of Anathoth who are seeking your life and saying, 'Do not prophesy in the name of the LORD or you will die by our hands'— ²²therefore this is what the LORD Almighty says: 'I will punish them. Their young men will die by the sword, their sons and daughters by famine. ²³Not even a remnant^D will be left to them, because I will bring disaster on the men of Anathoth in the year of their punishment.' "

Jeremiah's Complaint

12 You are always righteous^D, O LORD,
    when I bring a case before you.
Yet I would speak with you about your justice:
    Why does the way of the wicked prosper?
    Why do all the faithless live at ease?
²You have planted them, and they have taken
      root;
    they grow and bear fruit.
You are always on their lips
    but far from their hearts.
³Yet you know me, O LORD;
    you see me and test my thoughts about you.
Drag them off like sheep to be butchered!
    Set them apart for the day of slaughter!
⁴How long will the land lie parched^a
    and the grass in every field be withered?
Because those who live in it are wicked,
    the animals and birds have perished.
Moreover, the people are saying,
    "He will not see what happens to us."

God's Answer

⁵"If you have raced with men on foot
    and they have worn you out,
    how can you compete with horses?
If you stumble in safe country,^b
    how will you manage in the thickets by^c the
      Jordan?
⁶Your brothers, your own family—
    even they have betrayed you;
    they have raised a loud cry against you.
Do not trust them,
    though they speak well of you.

⁷"I will forsake my house,
    abandon my inheritance;
I will give the one I love
    into the hands of her enemies.
⁸My inheritance has become to me
    like a lion in the forest.
She roars at me;
    therefore I hate her.
⁹Has not my inheritance become to me
    like a speckled bird of prey
    that other birds of prey surround and attack?
Go and gather all the wild beasts;
    bring them to devour.
¹⁰Many shepherds will ruin my vineyard
    and trample down my field;
they will turn my pleasant field
    into a desolate wasteland.

Can we complain when God seems unfair? (12:1)

Many have complained about what seem to be miscarriages of justice. Asaph objected to the prosperity of the wicked (Psalm 73). Habakkuk was upset about the military success of godless Babylon. Jeremiah wondered why the wicked were so well off. God permits such complaints but also hopes in the end we will see his wisdom and righteousness—just as Jeremiah did.

How was God *always on their lips*? (12:2)

Since they had so many gods (11:13), it sounds contradictory to say God was always on their lips. But they thought they could worship both God and Baal. So they "spoke out of both sides of their mouths," forgetting that God would not share his glory with any other. Because Baal was also on their lips, they showed that God was far from their hearts.

Why didn't God answer Jeremiah's question? (12:5-6)

God's answer focused on Jeremiah, not his complaint. His problem with the wicked couldn't compare to the problems and frustrations he was yet going to face. Even his own family would turn against him. So God spoke to Jeremiah's primary need: personal strength of character with the patience, faith and courage to endure future trials. But God didn't ignore Jeremiah's complaints entirely; he later gave a more satisfactory answer (17:11).

How can God hate the one he loves? (12:7-8)

God had warned his people what would happen if they disobeyed him. But they paid no attention and God withdrew his protection—the consequence of their disobedience. Jeremiah described this in vivid terms—he hated them. Surely, though, God must have agonized over what was happening to his people.

---

^a4 Or *land mourn*   ^b5 Or *If you put your trust in a land of safety*
^c5 Or *the flooding of*

11It will be made a wasteland,
  parched and desolate before me;
the whole land will be laid waste
  because there is no one who cares.
12Over all the barren heights in the desert
  destroyers will swarm,
for the sword of the LORD will devour
  from one end of the land to the other;
  no one will be safe.
13They will sow wheat but reap thorns;
  they will wear themselves out but gain
    nothing.
So bear the shame of your harvest
  because of the LORD's fierce anger."

14This is what the LORD says: "As for all my wicked neighbors who seize the inheritance I gave my people Israel, I will uproot them from their lands and I will uproot the house of Judah from among them. 15But after I uproot them, I will again have compassion and will bring each of them back to his own inheritance and his own country. 16And if they learn well the ways of my people and swear by my name, saying, 'As surely as the LORD lives'—even as they once taught my people to swear by BaalD—then they will be established among my people. 17But if any nation does not listen, I will completely uproot and destroy it," declares the LORD.

A Linen Belt

13 This is what the LORD said to me: "Go and buy a linen belt and put it around your waist, but do not let it touch water." 2So I bought a belt, as the LORD directed, and put it around my waist.

3Then the word of the LORD came to me a second time: 4"Take the belt you bought and are wearing around your waist, and go now to Perath*a* and hide it there in a crevice in the rocks." 5So I went and hid it at Perath, as the LORD told me.

6Many days later the LORD said to me, "Go now to Perath and get the belt I told you to hide there." 7So I went to Perath and dug up the belt and took it from the place where I had hidden it, but now it was ruined and completely useless.

8Then the word of the LORD came to me: 9"This is what the LORD says: 'In the same way I will ruin the pride of Judah and the great pride of JerusalemD. 10These wicked people, who refuse to listen to my words, who follow the stubbornness of their hearts and go after other gods to serve and worship them, will be like this belt—completely useless! 11For as a belt is bound around a man's waist, so I bound the whole house of Israel and the whole house of Judah to me,' declares the LORD, 'to be my people for my renown and praise and honor. But they have not listened.'

Wineskins

12"Say to them: 'This is what the LORD, the God of Israel, says: Every wineskinD should be filled with wine.' And if they say to you, 'Don't we know that every wineskin should be filled with wine?' 13then tell them, 'This is what the LORD says: I am going to fill with drunkenness all who live in this land, including the kings who sit on David's

Why offer grace to the heathen oppressors? (12:14–16)

Because God is a merciful God. These verses seem to be a preview of Jeremiah's later prophesying to the nations (chs. 47–49), which God had called him to do (1:10). Like Judah, these nations also were destined to be deported from their lands because of their wickedness. But after their punishment, they could repent and learn the ways of the Lord. God used Israel, whether obedient or not, to show himself to the world. Eventually all nations were blessed through Abraham in Jesus Christ (Gen. 12:3).

Why use an object lesson for a prophecy? (13:1–11)

God often uses symbolic actions to teach important lessons. Symbols dramatize his message in ways words cannot. The linen undergarment, close to the body, symbolized Israel's special relationship with God. But just as linen could easily rot, Israel was prone to corruption. This was a before-and-after picture of Israel: from enjoying a close relationship with God, the nation went to being rotten with sin. God wanted the people to see that idolatry had corrupted them.

Why did the linen belt have to stay dry? (13:1)

So it wouldn't rot too soon. Dry, the linen would have reminded the people of the linen garments worn by the priests. It symbolized purity and holiness—a reminder of Israel's priestly calling and character. Later it was buried among the rocks along the river bank where it would be soiled by mud and water—a picture of the sin that caused Israel's rottenness.

---

a4 Or possibly the Euphrates; also in verses 5-7

throne, the priests^D, the prophets^D and all those living in Jerusalem^D. ¹⁴I will smash them one against the other, fathers and sons alike, declares the LORD. I will allow no pity or mercy^D or compassion to keep me from destroying them.' "

Threat of Captivity

¹⁵Hear and pay attention,
   do not be arrogant,
   for the LORD has spoken.
¹⁶Give glory^D to the LORD your God
   before he brings the darkness,
before your feet stumble
   on the darkening hills.
You hope for light,
   but he will turn it to thick darkness
   and change it to deep gloom.
¹⁷But if you do not listen,
   I will weep in secret
   because of your pride;
my eyes will weep bitterly,
   overflowing with tears,
   because the LORD's flock will be taken
      captive.

¹⁸Say to the king and to the queen mother,
   "Come down from your thrones,
for your glorious crowns
   will fall from your heads."
¹⁹The cities in the Negev^D will be shut up,
   and there will be no one to open them.
All Judah will be carried into exile^D,
   carried completely away.

²⁰Lift up your eyes and see
   those who are coming from the north.
Where is the flock that was entrusted to you,
   the sheep of which you boasted?
²¹What will you say when ⌊the LORD⌋ sets over you
   those you cultivated as your special allies?
Will not pain grip you
   like that of a woman in labor?
²²And if you ask yourself,
   "Why has this happened to me?" —
it is because of your many sins
   that your skirts have been torn off
   and your body mistreated.
²³Can the Ethiopian^a change his skin
   or the leopard its spots?
Neither can you do good
   who are accustomed to doing evil.

²⁴"I will scatter you like chaff^D
   driven by the desert wind.
²⁵This is your lot,
   the portion I have decreed for you,"
              declares the LORD,
   "because you have forgotten me
   and trusted in false gods.
²⁶I will pull up your skirts over your face
   that your shame may be seen—
²⁷your adulteries and lustful neighings,

^a23 Hebrew *Cushite* (probably a person from the upper Nile region)

Who were the king and the queen mother? (13:18)

Jehoiachin and his mother, Nehushta. They were taken captive to Babylon in 597 B.C. (see 2 Kings 24:8,12,15). A king's mother often retained domination over the palace court, especially when the king had many wives who diluted each other's influence. Jehoiachin, who began and ended his reign as an 18-year-old, likely looked to his mother for advice.

North (13:20)

See *What northern kingdoms would attack Judah?* (1:14–15).

Did God ask for the impossible? (13:23)

Jeremiah used a familiar proverb to show how incredibly difficult it would be for Israel to repent. The proverb did not mean it was impossible for the people to change, but that they could not hope to reform on their own. God alone could work such miraculous changes.

Pull up your skirts over your face (13:26)

A picture of public disgrace with *shame* being a synonym for *nakedness*. Promiscuous women were publicly humiliated by being stripped or having their clothing lifted up over their heads (v. 22; Isaiah 47:3; Hosea 2:3,10). Israel—unfaithful to the Lord and yearning for foreign gods—would be disgraced like a prostitute.

Cisterns (14:3)
Covered pits cut into rock or clay to catch and store rain water. Cisterns were a critical part of living in arid regions and sometimes symbolized security.

Why cover heads to show sorrow? (14:3–4)
This cultural expression of grief may have pictured someone trying to shut out a painful sight. It became a custom for people in mourning to cover their heads just as mourners wear black today.

Why pray to protect God's good name? (14:7)
Jewish names often described a person's nature or character and were even changed if someone's life changed dramatically. *Jacob,* for example, became *Israel* (Gen. 32:28). God, however, never changes. Those who blamed God for their problems were attacking the character of his name, saying he was no longer faithful. Jeremiah prayed that God would act, not according to what the people deserved, but according to all that his name said he was. Also see *Why call a city The LORD Our Righteousness?* (33:16).

If God was like *a stranger,* how was he among them? (14:8–9)
Israel's calamities made it seem as though God was unknown. The real problem, however, was not that God had abandoned Israel, but that the people had distanced themselves from him. Their sin had separated them from God even though his presence was among them, in the temple and the ark of the covenant.

Is it sometimes wrong to pray? (14:11)
See *Is it sometimes wrong to pray?* (11:14).

Who were the false prophets? (14:13–14)
Most likely these were the prophets of Baal whose worship was centered in Anathoth, Jeremiah's hometown. See *How can we know who really speaks for God?* (Deut. 18:21).

your shameless prostitution!
I have seen your detestable acts
on the hills and in the fields.
Woe to you, O JerusalemᴰD!
How long will you be uncleanᴰ?"

Drought, Famine, Sword

14 This is the word of the LORD to Jeremiah concerning the drought:

²"Judah mourns,
her cities languish;
they wail for the land,
and a cry goes up from Jerusalem.
³The nobles send their servants for water;
they go to the cisternsᴰ
but find no water.
They return with their jars unfilled;
dismayed and despairing,
they cover their heads.
⁴The ground is cracked
because there is no rain in the land;
the farmers are dismayed
and cover their heads.
⁵Even the doe in the field
deserts her newborn fawn
because there is no grass.
⁶Wild donkeys stand on the barren heights
and pant like jackals;
their eyesight fails
for lack of pasture."

⁷Although our sins testify against us,
O LORD, do something for the sake of your
name.
For our backslidingᴰ is great;
we have sinned against you.
⁸O Hope of Israel,
its Savior in times of distress,
why are you like a stranger in the land,
like a traveler who stays only a night?
⁹Why are you like a man taken by surprise,
like a warrior powerless to save?
You are among us, O LORD,
and we bear your name;
do not forsake us!

¹⁰This is what the LORD says about this people:

"They greatly love to wander;
they do not restrain their feet.
So the LORD does not accept them;
he will now remember their wickedness
and punish them for their sins."

¹¹Then the LORD said to me, "Do not pray for the well-being of this people. ¹²Although they fast, I will not listen to their cry; though they offer burnt offeringsᴰ and grain offeringsᴰ, I will not accept them. Instead, I will destroy them with the sword, famine and plague."

¹³But I said, "Ah, Sovereign LORD, the prophetsᴰ keep telling them, 'You will not see the sword or suffer famine. Indeed, I will give you lasting peaceᴰ in this place.'"

¹⁴Then the LORD said to me, "The prophets are prophesying lies in my name. I have not sent them or appointed them or spoken to them. They are prophesying to you

false visions^D, divinations^D, idolatries^D*a* and the delusions of their own minds. **15**Therefore, this is what the LORD says about the prophets^D who are prophesying in my name: I did not send them, yet they are saying, 'No sword or famine will touch this land.' Those same prophets will perish by sword and famine. **16**And the people they are prophesying to will be thrown out into the streets of Jerusalem^D because of the famine and sword. There will be no one to bury them or their wives, their sons or their daughters. I will pour out on them the calamity they deserve.

17"Speak this word to them:

" 'Let my eyes overflow with tears
   night and day without ceasing;
for my virgin daughter—my people—
   has suffered a grievous wound,
   a crushing blow.
18If I go into the country,
   I see those slain by the sword;
if I go into the city,
   I see the ravages of famine.
Both prophet and priest
   have gone to a land they know not.' "

19Have you rejected Judah completely?
   Do you despise Zion^D?
Why have you afflicted^D us
   so that we cannot be healed?
We hoped for peace^D
   but no good has come,
for a time of healing
   but there is only terror.
20O LORD, we acknowledge our wickedness
   and the guilt of our fathers;
   we have indeed sinned against you.
21For the sake of your name do not despise us;
   do not dishonor your glorious throne.
Remember your covenant^D with us
   and do not break it.
22Do any of the worthless idols^D of the nations
      bring rain?
   Do the skies themselves send down showers?
No, it is you, O LORD our God.
   Therefore our hope is in you,
   for you are the one who does all this.

15 Then the LORD said to me: "Even if Moses and Samuel were to stand before me, my heart would not go out to this people. Send them away from my presence! Let them go! **2**And if they ask you, 'Where shall we go?' tell them, 'This is what the LORD says:

" 'Those destined for death^D, to death;
those for the sword, to the sword;
those for starvation, to starvation;
those for captivity, to captivity.'

3"I will send four kinds of destroyers against them," declares the LORD, "the sword to kill and the dogs to drag away and the birds of the air and the beasts of the earth to devour and destroy. **4**I will make them abhorrent to all the kingdoms of the earth because of what Manasseh son of Hezekiah king of Judah did in Jerusalem.

*a*14 Or *visions, worthless divinations*

Why remind God of his promise? (14:21)

God doesn't forget his promises and he doesn't need reminders. But Jeremiah was desperate. He knew he couldn't ask for God's help on the basis of Judah's faithfulness, for Judah had broken the covenant, leaving it null and void. But he could appeal to God's character which was shown in the covenant. Jeremiah hoped God's faithfulness alone might uphold the broken agreement. See *Why restore unfaithful people?* (16:15).

Do some prayers move God more? (15:1)

Though this verse seems to suggest that the prayers of Moses and Samuel would be more effective than others, God hears all sincere prayers—the sinner's as well as the saint's. God's point was that it is futile for anyone—no matter how well respected—to pray for the wrong thing or for something opposed to God's will. Israel's stubborn unrepentance meant judgment was certain. God would not change his plans. See article: *When does God refuse to hear our prayers?* (11:11). Also see *Is it sometimes wrong to pray?* (11:14).

Why was Manasseh singled out? (15:4)

Jeremiah saw Manasseh's sin as the root reason for Judah's captivity. Manasseh was the instigator of the nation's final moral decline.

SCRIPTURE LINK (15:4)

Read about Manasseh's sins in 2 Kings 21:1–16; 23:26–27; 24:3–4.

Winnowing fork (15:7)
See *Winnowing fork* (Matt. 3:12).

Why destroy the mothers? (15:8–9)
This pictured absolute devastation, totally up-
setting a Hebrew image of complete happiness
—having seven sons. So many sons usually
meant security and comfort for their mother,
but now, Jeremiah said, they could no longer
rely upon such expectations. The coming war
casualties would leave countless women as
childless widows with no means of support.

**Why did Jeremiah wish he'd never been
born? (15:10)**
Jeremiah was in a no-win situation. He knew
judgment was coming to his people, but he
could do nothing about it. God called him to
pronounce judgment, but stopped him from
praying for mercy. The hopelessness of the nation—coupled with his own troubles—made
him lapse into self-pity. Feeling such deep
alienation from the nation he loved, Jeremiah's
human nature caused him to wish he'd never
been born.

⁵"Who will have pity on you, O Jerusalemᴰ?
    Who will mourn for you?
    Who will stop to ask how you are?
⁶You have rejected me," declares the Lᴏʀᴅ.
    "You keep on backslidingᴰ.
So I will lay hands on you and destroy you;
    I can no longer show compassion.
⁷I will winnow them with a winnowing forkᴰ
    at the city gates of the land.
I will bring bereavement and destruction on my
        people,
    for they have not changed their ways.
⁸I will make their widows more numerous
    than the sand of the sea.
At midday I will bring a destroyer
    against the mothers of their young men;
suddenly I will bring down on them
    anguish and terror.
⁹The mother of seven will grow faint
    and breathe her last.
Her sun will set while it is still day;
    she will be disgraced and humiliated.
I will put the survivors to the sword
    before their enemies,"
                        declares the Lᴏʀᴅ.

¹⁰Alas, my mother, that you gave me birth,
    a man with whom the whole land strives and
        contends!
I have neither lent nor borrowed,
    yet everyone curses me.

¹¹The Lᴏʀᴅ said,

"Surely I will deliver you for a good purpose;
    surely I will make your enemies plead with
        you
    in times of disaster and times of distress.

¹²"Can a man break iron—
    iron from the north—or bronze?
¹³Your wealth and your treasures
    I will give as plunderᴰ, without charge,
because of all your sins
    throughout your country.
¹⁴I will enslave you to your enemies
    inᵃ a land you do not know,
for my anger will kindle a fire
    that will burn against you."

¹⁵You understand, O Lᴏʀᴅ;
    remember me and care for me.
    Avengeᴰ me on my persecutors.
You are long-suffering—do not take me away;
    think of how I suffer reproachᴰ for your
        sake.
¹⁶When your words came, I ate them;
    they were my joy and my heart's delight,
for I bear your name,
    O Lᴏʀᴅ God Almighty.
¹⁷I never sat in the company of revelers,
    never made merry with them;

ᵃ 14 Some Hebrew manuscripts, Septuagint and Syriac (see also Jer.
17:4); most Hebrew manuscripts *I will cause your enemies to bring you
/ into*

I sat alone because your hand was on me
  and you had filled me with indignation.
  ¹⁸Why is my pain unending
  and my wound grievous and incurable?
  Will you be to me like a deceptive brook,
  like a spring that fails?

¹⁹Therefore this is what the LORD says:

  "If you repent^D, I will restore you
  that you may serve me;
  if you utter worthy, not worthless, words,
  you will be my spokesman.
  Let this people turn to you,
  but you must not turn to them.
  ²⁰I will make you a wall to this people,
  a fortified wall of bronze;
  they will fight against you
  but will not overcome you,
  for I am with you
  to rescue and save you,"
                                      declares the LORD.
  ²¹"I will save you from the hands of the wicked
  and redeem^D you from the grasp of the
  cruel."

Day of Disaster

16 Then the word of the LORD came to me: **²**"You
must not marry and have sons or daughters in this
place." **³**For this is what the LORD says about the sons and
daughters born in this land and about the women who are
their mothers and the men who are their fathers: **⁴**"They
will die of deadly diseases. They will not be mourned or
buried but will be like refuse lying on the ground. They
will perish by sword and famine, and their dead bodies
will become food for the birds of the air and the beasts of
the earth."

⁵For this is what the LORD says: "Do not enter a house
where there is a funeral meal; do not go to mourn or show
sympathy, because I have withdrawn my blessing, my
love and my pity from this people," declares the LORD.
⁶"Both high and low will die in this land. They will not be
buried or mourned, and no one will cut himself or shave
his head for them. **⁷**No one will offer food to comfort
those who mourn for the dead—not even for a father or
a mother—nor will anyone give them a drink to console
them.

⁸"And do not enter a house where there is feasting and
sit down to eat and drink. **⁹**For this is what the LORD Almighty, the God of Israel, says: Before your eyes and in
your days I will bring an end to the sounds of joy and
gladness and to the voices of bride and bridegroom in this
place.

¹⁰"When you tell these people all this and they ask you,
'Why has the LORD decreed such a great disaster against
us? What wrong have we done? What sin have we committed against the LORD our God?' **¹¹**then say to them, 'It
is because your fathers forsook me,' declares the LORD,
'and followed other gods and served and worshiped them.
They forsook me and did not keep my law. **¹²**But you have
behaved more wickedly than your fathers. See how each
of you is following the stubbornness of his evil heart instead of obeying me. **¹³**So I will throw you out of this land
into a land neither you nor your fathers have known, and

Did Jeremiah fear God might let him down? (15:18)

Despite his close contact with the Lord, Jeremiah was human. With his lack of visible success, he questioned his calling as much as
himself. He feared that he might have missed
God and that he would find nothing from God
to sustain him in his need—like trying to drink
from a dried-up brook.

Of what did Jeremiah need to repent? (15:19)

Jeremiah had indulged in self-pity (v. 10). He
had also been impatient with God and wanted
swift vengeance on his enemies (v. 15). God
considered such complaints *worthless* words
and called Jeremiah to repent and speak *worthy* words. God wanted Jeremiah to lift others
up, not be dragged down to their level.

How could Jeremiah be like a wall? (15:20)

If he would speak the message just as it came
from God, unaltered, God promised to make
him invincible—like a fortified bronze wall. God
didn't promise freedom from trouble or that the
people would never oppose him again. But he
did promise to rescue Jeremiah so his opponents would never be victorious.

Why couldn't Jeremiah get married? (16:2)

A marriage relationship may have required
more than Jeremiah could have given. It could
have distracted him from his single-minded
focus: God's call and claim on his life. Or, perhaps God was saving Jeremiah from overwhelming heartbreak. The next generation of
children would be devastated by disease, war
and famine (vv. 3–4).

Was it unusual to stay single? (16:2)

Celibacy was extremely rare in that culture.
Family life and having children provided not
only a "retirement plan," but also the means to
preserve one's name indefinitely. This reveals
the animosity of Jeremiah's foes when they
said, *Let us cut him off from the land of the living, that his name be remembered no more*
(11:19). By remaining single with no heirs to
remember him, Jeremiah showed his trust in
God and submission to his will.

Cut himself . . . shave his head (16:6)

See *Why shave beards, tear clothes and cut
skin?* (41:5).

Why were the people so naive? (16:10)

Influenced by false prophets over the course of
time, the people had gradually become indifferent to their sin. Unaffected by the gravity of
their sins, they could not see how their troubles had been caused by their own sins.

there you will serve other gods day and night, for I will show you no favor.'

14"However, the days are coming," declares the LORD, "when men will no longer say, 'As surely as the LORD lives, who brought the Israelites up out of Egypt,' **15**but they will say, 'As surely as the LORD lives, who brought the Israelites up out of the land of the north and out of all the countries where he had banished them.' For I will restore them to the land I gave their forefathers.

16"But now I will send for many fishermen," declares the LORD, "and they will catch them. After that I will send for many hunters, and they will hunt them down on every mountain and hill and from the crevices of the rocks. **17**My eyes are on all their ways; they are not hidden from me, nor is their sin concealed from my eyes. **18**I will repay them double for their wickedness and their sin, because they have defiled my land with the lifeless forms of their vile images and have filled my inheritance with their detestable idols^D."

19O LORD, my strength and my fortress,
      my refuge in time of distress,
   to you the nations will come
      from the ends of the earth and say,
   "Our fathers possessed nothing but false gods,
      worthless idols that did them no good.
20Do men make their own gods?
      Yes, but they are not gods!"

21"Therefore I will teach them—
      this time I will teach them
      my power and might.
   Then they will know
      that my name is the LORD.

17 "Judah's sin is engraved with an iron tool,
      inscribed with a flint point,
   on the tablets of their hearts
      and on the horns of their altars.
2Even their children remember
      their altars and Asherah poles^{Da}
   beside the spreading trees
      and on the high hills.
3My mountain in the land
      and your^b wealth and all your treasures
   I will give away as plunder^D,
      together with your high places^D,
      because of sin throughout your country.
4Through your own fault you will lose
      the inheritance I gave you.
   I will enslave you to your enemies
      in a land you do not know,
   for you have kindled my anger,
      and it will burn forever."

5This is what the LORD says:

   "Cursed is the one who trusts in man,
      who depends on flesh for his strength
      and whose heart turns away from the LORD.
6He will be like a bush in the wastelands;
      he will not see prosperity when it comes.

Why restore unfaithful people? (16:15)
Until the *final* judgment, God's discipline is an act of mercy—a means to bring people to a place of repentance and blessing. Though judgment was inescapable, God planned to bring a remnant out of captivity and back to Judah. God remained faithful to his covenant with Abraham, even though the people had been unfaithful (Gen. 12:1–3,7).

Engraved with an iron tool (17:1)
Iron tools were used to chisel inscriptions in stone, the most permanent kind of writing (Job 19:24). Jeremiah's metaphor showed the permanence of their sin. Sin, particularly idolatry, had become unalterably ingrained in their nature.

Is God's anger still burning today? (17:4)
The 70 years in Babylonian exile was only the *physical* penalty for Judah's idolatry. *Spiritual* judgment is eternal, like an unquenchable fire. God's anger has been appeased by the death of Christ for those who belong to him. But for those who reject God's grace, his anger still burns.

Salt land (17:6)
A barren wasteland. Conquering armies would sometimes destroy cities, covering them and surrounding crop lands with salt. Nothing would grow there for years to come, preventing people from living there.

---

^a2 That is, symbols of the goddess Asherah   ^b2,3 Or *hills / 3and the mountains of the land. / Your*

He will dwell in the parched places of the
  desert,
  in a salt land where no one lives.

⁷"But blessed is the man who trusts in the LORD,
  whose confidence is in him.
⁸He will be like a tree planted by the water
  that sends out its roots by the stream.
It does not fear when heat comes;
  its leaves are always green.
It has no worries in a year of drought
  and never fails to bear fruit."

⁹The heart is deceitful above all things
  and beyond cure.
  Who can understand it?

¹⁰"I the LORD search the heart
  and examine the mind,
to reward a man according to his conduct,
  according to what his deeds deserve."

¹¹Like a partridge that hatches eggs it did not lay
  is the man who gains riches by unjust
    means.
When his life is half gone, they will desert him,
  and in the end he will prove to be a fool.

¹²A glorious throne, exalted from the beginning,
  is the place of our sanctuary.
¹³O LORD, the hope of Israel,
  all who forsake you will be put to shame.
Those who turn away from you will be written
    in the dust
because they have forsaken the LORD,
  the spring of living water.

¹⁴Heal me, O LORD, and I will be healed;
  save me and I will be saved,
  for you are the one I praise.
¹⁵They keep saying to me,
  "Where is the word of the LORD?
  Let it now be fulfilled!"
¹⁶I have not run away from being your shepherd;
  you know I have not desired the day of
    despair.
What passes my lips is open before you.
¹⁷Do not be a terror to me;
  you are my refuge in the day of disaster.
¹⁸Let my persecutors be put to shame,
  but keep me from shame;
let them be terrified,
  but keep me from terror.
Bring on them the day of disaster;
  destroy them with double destruction.

Keeping the Sabbath Holy

¹⁹This is what the LORD said to me: "Go and stand at the
gate of the people, through which the kings of Judah go in
and out; stand also at all the other gates of Jerusalem.ᴰ
²⁰Say to them, 'Hear the word of the LORD, O kings of Judah and all people of Judah and everyone living in Jerusalem who come through these gates. ²¹This is what the
LORD says: Be careful not to carry a load on the Sabbathᴰ
day or bring it through the gates of Jerusalem. ²²Do not
bring a load out of your houses or do any work on the
Sabbath, but keep the Sabbath day holy, as I com-

What's the prognosis for a heart *beyond cure*? (17:9)

Sin is terminal. There is no cure. However, God
has a solution: He offers to remove the termi-
nally sinful heart and replace it with a new
heart. The old heart of stone is replaced with a
heart of flesh (Ezek. 11:19). God can write his
laws on this new, pliable heart (31:33). God's
radical solution not only removes sin, it transforms a person so obedience becomes a possibility (Ezek. 11:20).

Does God reward right conduct or right motives? (17:10)

Because God seeks right conduct that stems
from proper motives, good intentions cannot
excuse wrong conduct. On the other hand, righteous living that camouflages ungodly motives
is hypocrisy. God judges both errors. Love for
God and a desire to honor him are the proper
motives for deeds that will be rewarded.

Why did the king use the *gate of the people*? (17:19)

Some think the king, on his way to special occasions, used a gate to the temple where he
could be seen by the most people. Others believe this was a city gate where business was
conducted and judgments were made, again, a
place where the king and people could cross
paths.

Inhabited forever (17:25)

A promise that will be spiritually fulfilled when Christ returns to earth to establish his kingdom.

Wheel (18:3)

This was a potter's wheel, made of either wood or stone and consisting of two discs: a lower disc turned by the potter's foot and an upper disc attached by an axle to the lower disc. Clay placed on the upper disc could be shaped into round bowls or pots as it turned.

Does God still deal with entire nations? (18:7–10)

God rewards and judges individuals today. But nations also can benefit from his blessings or suffer under his judgment. When most citizens are wicked, God considers their nation to be wicked and vice versa. But no simple formula can tell us what to expect. Sometimes a righteous few may prevent God's judgment on a nation (Gen. 18:26; Ezek. 22:30). Perhaps more often, as in Jeremiah's case, the righteous suffer with the nation, though they may be receiving spiritual rewards as individuals.

Why does God seem to change his plans? (18:8)

See articles: *Does God change his plans?* (26:3) and *Can our prayers cause God to change his mind?* (Exodus 32:14).

Virgin Israel (18:13)

This word picture showed how radically Israel had changed. Once pure, chosen by God, Israel had "lost her virginity" by committing prostitution with other lovers (2:20; 3:1–3). Israel was unfaithful to the Lord and worshiped idols. See *Why compare sinful Judah to a virgin?* (Lam. 2:13).

manded your forefathers. ²³Yet they did not listen or pay attention; they were stiff-necked and would not listen or respond to discipline. ²⁴But if you are careful to obey me, declares the LORD, and bring no load through the gates of this city on the Sabbath^D, but keep the Sabbath day holy by not doing any work on it, ²⁵then kings who sit on David's throne will come through the gates of this city with their officials. They and their officials will come riding in chariots and on horses, accompanied by the men of Judah and those living in Jerusalem^D, and this city will be inhabited forever. ²⁶People will come from the towns of Judah and the villages around Jerusalem, from the territory of Benjamin and the western foothills, from the hill country and the Negev^D, bringing burnt offerings^D and sacrifices^D, grain offerings^D, incense^D and thank offerings^D to the house of the LORD. ²⁷But if you do not obey me to keep the Sabbath day holy by not carrying any load as you come through the gates of Jerusalem on the Sabbath day, then I will kindle an unquenchable fire in the gates of Jerusalem that will consume her fortresses.' "

At the Potter's House

18 This is the word that came to Jeremiah from the LORD: ²"Go down to the potter's house, and there I will give you my message." ³So I went down to the potter's house, and I saw him working at the wheel. ⁴But the pot he was shaping from the clay was marred in his hands; so the potter formed it into another pot, shaping it as seemed best to him.

⁵Then the word of the LORD came to me: ⁶"O house of Israel, can I not do with you as this potter does?" declares the LORD. "Like clay in the hand of the potter, so are you in my hand, O house of Israel. ⁷If at any time I announce that a nation or kingdom is to be uprooted, torn down and destroyed, ⁸and if that nation I warned repents^D of its evil, then I will relent and not inflict on it the disaster I had planned. ⁹And if at another time I announce that a nation or kingdom is to be built up and planted, ¹⁰and if it does evil in my sight and does not obey me, then I will reconsider the good I had intended to do for it.

¹¹"Now therefore say to the people of Judah and those living in Jerusalem, 'This is what the LORD says: Look! I am preparing a disaster for you and devising a plan against you. So turn from your evil ways, each one of you, and reform your ways and your actions.' ¹²But they will reply, 'It's no use. We will continue with our own plans; each of us will follow the stubbornness of his evil heart.' "

¹³Therefore this is what the LORD says:

"Inquire among the nations:
　　Who has ever heard anything like this?
A most horrible thing has been done
　　by Virgin Israel.
¹⁴Does the snow of Lebanon
　　ever vanish from its rocky slopes?
Do its cool waters from distant sources
　　ever cease to flow?^a
¹⁵Yet my people have forgotten me;
　　they burn incense to worthless idols,
which made them stumble in their ways
　　and in the ancient paths.

^a14 The meaning of the Hebrew for this sentence is uncertain.

They made them walk in bypaths
    and on roads not built up.
16Their land will be laid waste,
    an object of lasting scorn;
all who pass by will be appalled
    and will shake their heads.
17Like a wind from the east,
    I will scatter them before their enemies;
I will show them my back and not my face
    in the day of their disaster.”

18They said, “Come, let's make plans against Jeremiah; for the teaching of the law by the priest^D will not be lost, nor will counsel from the wise, nor the word from the prophets^D. So come, let's attack him with our tongues and pay no attention to anything he says.”

19Listen to me, O LORD;
    hear what my accusers are saying!
20Should good be repaid with evil?
    Yet they have dug a pit for me.
Remember that I stood before you
    and spoke in their behalf
    to turn your wrath away from them.
21So give their children over to famine;
    hand them over to the power of the sword.
Let their wives be made childless and widows;
    let their men be put to death^D,
    their young men slain by the sword in battle.
22Let a cry be heard from their houses
    when you suddenly bring invaders against
        them,
for they have dug a pit to capture me
    and have hidden snares for my feet.
23But you know, O LORD,
    all their plots to kill me.
Do not forgive their crimes
    or blot out their sins from your sight.
Let them be overthrown before you;
    deal with them in the time of your anger.

19 This is what the LORD says: “Go and buy a clay jar from a potter. Take along some of the elders of the people and of the priests **2**and go out to the Valley of Ben Hinnom, near the entrance of the Potsherd Gate. There proclaim the words I tell you, **3**and say, ‘Hear the word of the LORD, O kings of Judah and people of Jerusalem^D. This is what the LORD Almighty, the God of Israel, says: Listen! I am going to bring a disaster on this place that will make the ears of everyone who hears of it tingle. **4**For they have forsaken me and made this a place of foreign gods; they have burned sacrifices^D in it to gods that neither they nor their fathers nor the kings of Judah ever knew, and they have filled this place with the blood of the innocent. **5**They have built the high places^D of Baal^D to burn their sons in the fire as offerings to Baal—something I did not command or mention, nor did it enter my mind. **6**So beware, the days are coming, declares the LORD, when people will no longer call this place Topheth^D or the Valley of Ben Hinnom, but the Valley of Slaughter.

7“ ‘In this place I will ruin*a* the plans of Judah and Jerusalem. I will make them fall by the sword before their

a7 The Hebrew for *ruin* sounds like the Hebrew for *jar* (see verses 1 and 10).

Why would God show his back? (18:17)

This was a figurative way to say that God would not help the people out of their coming troubles. They would see him walking away instead of toward them—the same treatment they had given him (2:27).

Why was Jeremiah so sensitive to criticism? (18:19–23)

Jeremiah suffered tremendous internal distress because of his accusers. He prayed that God would save them, but they returned his favors with hatred. After all he'd done for them, they did all they could to hurt him. No wonder Jeremiah asked God to punish them. See article: *Is it right to pray for revenge?* (Psalm 58:6–8).

Why would parents sacrifice their children? (19:5)

They probably thought that by appeasing the pagan gods they could improve their quality of life. Life's harsh realities (high infant mortality, for example) may have prompted some to place a lower value on children than adults. Some neighboring cultures abandoned unwanted infants to die. Others didn't name their children until they were older and more likely to survive. The thought of murdering children shocks us, but the Israelites, who were calloused by the pagan views around them, were not as alarmed as we. Also see *Molech* (32:35).

Topheth . . . Valley of Ben Hinnom (19:6,12–13)

Topheth may have come from the word for *fireplace*. Near Jerusalem in the Valley of Ben Hinnom, it was known as the place where people sacrificed their children by fire to Molech. Later, the valley became the city's garbage dump. Its perpetual fires caused it to become a symbol of future judgment. Also see *Hell* (Matt. 5:22).

enemies, at the hands of those who seek their lives, and I will give their carcasses as food to the birds of the air and the beasts of the earth. **8**I will devastate this city and make it an object of scorn; all who pass by will be appalled and will scoff because of all its wounds. **9**I will make them eat the flesh of their sons and daughters, and they will eat one another's flesh during the stress of the siege imposed on them by the enemies who seek their lives.'

10"Then break the jar while those who go with you are watching, **11**and say to them, 'This is what the LORD Almighty says: I will smash this nation and this city just as this potter's jar is smashed and cannot be repaired. They will bury the dead in Topheth^D until there is no more room. **12**This is what I will do to this place and to those who live here, declares the LORD. I will make this city like Topheth. **13**The houses in Jerusalem and those of the kings of Judah will be defiled like this place, Topheth—all the houses where they burned incense^D on the roofs to all the starry hosts^D and poured out drink offerings^D to other gods.' "

14Jeremiah then returned from Topheth, where the LORD had sent him to prophesy, and stood in the court of the LORD's temple and said to all the people, **15**"This is what the LORD Almighty, the God of Israel, says: 'Listen! I am going to bring on this city and the villages around it every disaster I pronounced against them, because they were stiff-necked and would not listen to my words.' "

Jeremiah and Pashhur

20 When the priest^D Pashhur son of Immer, the chief officer in the temple of the LORD, heard Jeremiah prophesying these things, **2**he had Jeremiah the prophet^D beaten and put in the stocks at the Upper Gate of Benjamin at the LORD's temple. **3**The next day, when Pashhur released him from the stocks, Jeremiah said to him, "The LORD's name for you is not Pashhur, but Magor-Missabib.^a **4**For this is what the LORD says: 'I will make you a terror to yourself and to all your friends; with your own eyes you will see them fall by the sword of their enemies. I will hand all Judah over to the king of Babylon, who will carry them away to Babylon or put them to the sword. **5**I will hand over to their enemies all the wealth of this city—all its products, all its valuables and all the treasures of the kings of Judah. They will take it away as plunder^D and carry it off to Babylon. **6**And you, Pashhur, and all who live in your house will go into exile^D to Babylon. There you will die and be buried, you and all your friends to whom you have prophesied lies.' "

Jeremiah's Complaint

7O LORD, you deceived^b me, and I was
    deceived^b;
  you overpowered me and prevailed.
I am ridiculed all day long;
  everyone mocks me.
8Whenever I speak, I cry out
  proclaiming violence and destruction.
So the word of the LORD has brought me
  insult and reproach^D all day long.
9But if I say, "I will not mention him
  or speak any more in his name,"

Why would a priest punish someone? (20:1–2)

Pashhur, *the chief officer*, was an executive priest responsible for maintaining order in the temple area. When he heard Jeremiah, he lost his temper and had him beaten and put in stocks. Some say this was a prison; others, a device for torture that nearly bent the person double. Whatever it was, Pashhur's actions were hardly priestlike.

Pashhur (20:3)

Meant *prosperity everywhere*. Jeremiah played off this and gave him a new name, *Magor-Missabib* or *terror on every side*.

Why did Jeremiah accuse God of deception? (20:7)

Deceived is a strong word. Although it can be translated *persuade* (as in Prov. 25:15), Jeremiah uses it here to complain about being roped into something. (In other places the word is used of seducing a virgin; see Exodus 22:16; 1 Kings 22:20–22.) Jeremiah accused God because he was struggling with his honest emotions that he had been *enticed* or *seduced* to become a prophet. He could not accuse God of lying, however, because God had warned Jeremiah that his message would be ignored (7:27).

Was it impossible for Jeremiah to resist God's call? (20:9)

Jeremiah felt compelled by God to speak for him. Certainly there was no external constraint on the prophet. However, God's inner persuasion would not allow Jeremiah to decline the call. He tried to resist but became so spiritually and emotionally spent that he finally surrendered his will to God's. Also see article: *How can God appoint someone not yet born?* (1:5).

---

^a3 *Magor-Missabib* means *terror on every side.*   ^b7 Or *persuaded*

his word is in my heart like a fire,
    a fire shut up in my bones.
I am weary of holding it in;
    indeed, I cannot.
¹⁰I hear many whispering,
    "Terror on every side!
    Report him! Let's report him!"
All my friends
    are waiting for me to slip, saying,
"Perhaps he will be deceived;
    then we will prevail over him
    and take our revenge on him."

¹¹But the LORD is with me like a mighty warrior;
    so my persecutors will stumble and not
      prevail.
They will fail and be thoroughly disgraced;
    their dishonor will never be forgotten.
¹²O LORD Almighty, you who examine the
      righteousᴰ
    and probe the heart and mind,
let me see your vengeance upon them,
    for to you I have committed my cause.

¹³Sing to the LORD!
    Give praise to the LORD!
He rescues the life of the needy
    from the hands of the wicked.

¹⁴Cursed be the day I was born!
    May the day my mother bore me not be
      blessed!
¹⁵Cursed be the man who brought my father the
      news,
    who made him very glad, saying,
    "A child is born to you—a son!"
¹⁶May that man be like the towns
    the LORD overthrew without pity.
May he hear wailing in the morning,
    a battle cry at noon.
¹⁷For he did not kill me in the womb,
    with my mother as my grave,
    her womb enlarged forever.
¹⁸Why did I ever come out of the womb
    to see trouble and sorrow
    and to end my days in shame?

God Rejects Zedekiah's Request

21 The word came to Jeremiah from the LORD when King Zedekiah sent to him Pashhur son of Malkijah and the priestᴰ Zephaniah son of Maaseiah. They said: ²"Inquire now of the LORD for us because Nebuchadnezzarᵃ king of Babylon is attacking us. Perhaps the LORD will perform wonders for us as in times past so that he will withdraw from us."

³But Jeremiah answered them, "Tell Zedekiah, ⁴'This is what the LORD, the God of Israel, says: I am about to turn against you the weapons of war that are in your hands, which you are using to fight the king of Babylon and the Babyloniansᵇ who are outside the wall besieging you. And I will gather them inside this city. ⁵I myself will fight

ᵃ2 Hebrew *Nebuchadrezzar*, of which *Nebuchadnezzar* is a variant; here and often in Jeremiah and Ezekiel   ᵇ4 Or *Chaldeans*; also in verse 9

Why were they whispering *Terror on every side*? (20:10)
This was the name Jeremiah gave to Pashhur in v. 3. Perhaps some who heard Jeremiah use it now mimicked him by using it as a nickname for him. His message of judgment was so unpopular that the crowds delighted in hounding the prophet. Another view is that Jeremiah described the whispering as the *terror* he heard wherever he went, *on every side.*

What kind of friends were these? (20:10)
Jeremiah's friends were anything but loyal. His message alienated even his allies who now waited to report his unguarded words to the authorities.

Why did Jeremiah wish he'd been aborted? (20:17)
This is not an endorsement of abortion as an escape from life's bitter blows. This is simply a poetic means of expressing Jeremiah's anguish and despair. Because God called him to pronounce judgment on the people he loved, he became extremely unpopular: enemies plotted his death and so-called friends watched for ways to report him.

Why seek advice from a despised prophet? (21:1-2)
Perhaps the proverb "any port in a storm" best describes King Zedekiah's motives in sending an official delegation to Jeremiah. With Nebuchadnezzar approaching the city gates, the panicky king sent emissaries to Jeremiah hoping for an eleventh-hour reprieve. With his back to the wall, Zedekiah was forced to admit what he had tried to deny. If he wanted to hear from God, he knew Jeremiah was the one to turn to.

Nebuchadnezzar (21:2)
King of Babylon from 605 to 562 B.C. His name was literally a prayer to the Babylonian god: "Nabu, protect the crown."

SCRIPTURE LINK (21:2)
The story of Nebuchadnezzar's two sieges of Jerusalem and his deportation of the Jews is found in 2 Kings 24–25.

Why would God fight against his own people? (21:5)
Because: (1) his people had repeatedly sinned, breaking the covenant promises they had made with God; (2) they had continually rejected his calls through the prophets to repent and (3) they now faced certain judgment. God sometimes uses sinful people or nations as his instruments of judgment. See article: *Does God use evil to do good?* (Hab. 1:6,13).

against you with an outstretched hand and a mighty arm in anger and fury and great wrath. **6**I will strike down those who live in this city—both men and animals—and they will die of a terrible plague. **7**After that, declares the LORD, I will hand over Zedekiah king of Judah, his officials and the people in this city who survive the plague, sword and famine, to Nebuchadnezzar king of Babylon and to their enemies who seek their lives. He will put them to the sword; he will show them no mercy^D or pity or compassion.'

8"Furthermore, tell the people, 'This is what the LORD says: See, I am setting before you the way of life and the way of death^D. **9**Whoever stays in this city will die by the sword, famine or plague. But whoever goes out and surrenders to the Babylonians who are besieging you will live; he will escape with his life. **10**I have determined to do this city harm and not good, declares the LORD. It will be given into the hands of the king of Babylon, and he will destroy it with fire.'

11"Moreover, say to the royal house of Judah, 'Hear the word of the LORD; **12**O house of David, this is what the LORD says:

" 'Administer justice every morning;
  rescue from the hand of his oppressor
  the one who has been robbed,
or my wrath will break out and burn like fire
  because of the evil you have done—
  burn with no one to quench it.
13I am against you, ⌞Jerusalem^D,⌟
  you who live above this valley
  on the rocky plateau,
                           declares the LORD—
you who say, "Who can come against us?
  Who can enter our refuge?"
14I will punish you as your deeds deserve,
                           declares the LORD.
I will kindle a fire in your forests
  that will consume everything around you.' "

Judgment Against Evil Kings

22 This is what the LORD says: "Go down to the palace of the king of Judah and proclaim this message there: **2**'Hear the word of the LORD, O king of Judah, you who sit on David's throne—you, your officials and your people who come through these gates. **3**This is what the LORD says: Do what is just and right. Rescue from the hand of his oppressor the one who has been robbed. Do no wrong or violence to the alien^D, the fatherless or the widow, and do not shed innocent blood in this place. **4**For if you are careful to carry out these commands, then kings who sit on David's throne will come through the gates of this palace, riding in chariots and on horses, accompanied by their officials and their people. **5**But if you do not obey these commands, declares the LORD, I swear by myself that this palace will become a ruin.' "

6For this is what the LORD says about the palace of the king of Judah:

"Though you are like Gilead to me,
  like the summit of Lebanon,
I will surely make you like a desert,
  like towns not inhabited.
7I will send destroyers against you,
  each man with his weapons,

Could Jerusalem have been saved? (22:2–5)

It would appear so from these verses. Why then do earlier verses say Jerusalem was beyond hope (7:16; 14:11–12; 15:1)? Perhaps those verses actually came later in time than this passage. See *Why are some of these chapters out of sequence?* (45:1). Or it may be that the earlier verses show that God knew before the people rebelled that they would do just that. See *When does it become impossible to escape judgment?* (Ezek. 14:20).

Why did God swear by himself? (22:5)

Because everything God says is utterly and completely true, he doesn't need oaths to buttress the reliability of his pronouncements. Yet, for greater impact and to underscore the seriousness of his message, it is not uncommon to see this rather human expression used to describe God's words. It reminds us again that God's word cannot be broken.

and they will cut up your fine cedar beams
  and throw them into the fire.

8"People from many nations will pass by this city and will ask one another, 'Why has the LORD done such a thing to this great city?' **9**And the answer will be: 'Because they have forsaken the covenant[D] of the LORD their God and have worshiped and served other gods.' "

10Do not weep for the dead ⌊king⌋ or mourn his
  loss;
rather, weep bitterly for him who is exiled[D],
  because he will never return
  nor see his native land again.

11For this is what the LORD says about Shallum[a] son of Josiah, who succeeded his father as king of Judah but has gone from this place: "He will never return. **12**He will die in the place where they have led him captive; he will not see this land again."

13"Woe to him who builds his palace by
    unrighteousness,
  his upper rooms by injustice,
making his countrymen work for nothing,
  not paying them for their labor.
14He says, 'I will build myself a great palace
  with spacious upper rooms.'
So he makes large windows in it,
  panels it with cedar
  and decorates it in red.

15"Does it make you a king
  to have more and more cedar?
Did not your father have food and drink?
  He did what was right and just,
  so all went well with him.
16He defended the cause of the poor and needy,
  and so all went well.
Is that not what it means to know me?"
  declares the LORD.
17"But your eyes and your heart
  are set only on dishonest gain,
on shedding innocent blood
  and on oppression and extortion[D]."

18Therefore this is what the LORD says about Jehoiakim son of Josiah king of Judah:

"They will not mourn for him:
  'Alas, my brother! Alas, my sister!'
They will not mourn for him:
  'Alas, my master! Alas, his splendor!'
19He will have the burial of a donkey—
  dragged away and thrown
  outside the gates of Jerusalem[D]."

20"Go up to Lebanon and cry out,
  let your voice be heard in Bashan,
cry out from Abarim,
  for all your allies are crushed.
21I warned you when you felt secure,
  but you said, 'I will not listen!'
This has been your way from your youth;
  you have not obeyed me.
22The wind will drive all your shepherds away,

a11 Also called Jehoahaz

Who did they weep for? (22:10)

The dead king was Josiah, who died in battle during his ill-fated encounter with Pharaoh Neco of Egypt (see 2 Kings 23:29–35). He was a good king whose loss was felt keenly. However, his death was not so tragic when compared to the fate awaiting his son. Jeremiah recommended that they save their tears for Josiah's son who would die in exile (v. 12; see 2 Kings 23:34). Sad as it was to die in office, it was worse to be banished to a foreign land and never see Judah again.

What does it take to know the Lord? (22:16)

Is it enough to help the poor and needy? We must not confuse the *evidence* of a relationship with God with the *means* to having that relationship. Throughout Scripture we discover it is by faith alone that we receive forgiveness, salvation and a personal relationship with God. One evidence that a person knows God intimately is the desire to follow God's will. Jeremiah's compassion and justice for the poor demonstrated his love for the Lord.

Why bury a king like a donkey? (22:19)

Then, as now, heads of state were typically given great ceremonial funerals. The dignity of the office demanded that even incompetent and unpopular rulers receive the minimum of burial courtesies. Jehoiakim's depraved and wicked reign, however, ended with the greatest indignity of all—no burial at all. Like a donkey thrown into the field as carrion for the vultures, his body lay exposed and humiliated. The wicked king who brought Jerusalem to its lowest level had no one to mourn his death.

Where were these places? (22:20)

Lebanon, Bashan and Abarim represent the land of Judah in its entirety, from north to northeast to southeast (see **Conquest of Canaan** on page 301). It was the totality of the destruction coming upon Judah that was the point of Jeremiah's statement. The term *allies* probably refers to Egypt and others on whom the kings of Judah had relied for protection from the Babylonians.

and your allies will go into exile.^D
Then you will be ashamed and disgraced
    because of all your wickedness.
23You who live in 'Lebanon,'^a
    who are nestled in cedar buildings,
how you will groan when pangs come upon
        you,
    pain like that of a woman in labor!

24"As surely as I live," declares the LORD, "even if you, Jehoiachin^b son of Jehoiakim king of Judah, were a signet ring^D on my right hand, I would still pull you off. **25**I will hand you over to those who seek your life, those you fear—to Nebuchadnezzar king of Babylon and to the Babylonians.^c **26**I will hurl you and the mother who gave you birth into another country, where neither of you was born, and there you both will die. **27**You will never come back to the land you long to return to."

28Is this man Jehoiachin a despised, broken pot,
    an object no one wants?
Why will he and his children be hurled out,
    cast into a land they do not know?
29O land, land, land,
    hear the word of the LORD!
30This is what the LORD says:
    "Record this man as if childless,
    a man who will not prosper in his lifetime,
for none of his offspring will prosper,
    none will sit on the throne of David
    or rule anymore in Judah."

The Righteous Branch

23 "Woe to the shepherds who are destroying and scattering the sheep of my pasture!" declares the LORD. **2**Therefore this is what the LORD, the God of Israel, says to the shepherds who tend my people: "Because you have scattered my flock and driven them away and have not bestowed care on them, I will bestow punishment on you for the evil you have done," declares the LORD. **3**"I myself will gather the remnant^D of my flock out of all the countries where I have driven them and will bring them back to their pasture, where they will be fruitful and increase in number. **4**I will place shepherds over them who will tend them, and they will no longer be afraid or terrified, nor will any be missing," declares the LORD.

5"The days are coming," declares the LORD,
    "when I will raise up to David^d a righteous^D
        Branch,
a King who will reign wisely
    and do what is just and right in the land.
6In his days Judah will be saved
    and Israel will live in safety.
This is the name by which he will be called:
    The LORD Our Righteousness.^D

7"So then, the days are coming," declares the LORD, "when people will no longer say, 'As surely as the LORD lives, who brought the Israelites up out of Egypt,' **8**but they will say, 'As surely as the LORD lives, who brought the descendants of Israel up out of the land of the north and out of

Signet ring (22:24)

A signet ring was a symbol of a king's authority. Its imprint validated government documents such as laws, treaties, decrees and correspondence in the name of the king. Since it represented his authority, the king would remove it only if he authorized another to act in his behalf. King Jehoiachin was called to validate the Lord's decrees and lead the people in obeying them, as though he were God's signet ring. But since he had failed to represent God, Jehoiachin was a defective ring. He would be judged and removed from his position. For another use of this symbol see *Signet ring* (Haggai 2:23).

Who was destroying the sheep? (23:1)

With leadership comes heavy responsibility. The Lord holds accountable those who have spiritual authority over the people of God. In this case Jeremiah was talking about the priests, the false prophets and the king. They had all failed the people, leading them into idolatry, injustice and unfaithfulness.

How is the Messiah linked to Israel's return from captivity? (23:5–8)

We must be careful to distinguish between the first coming of Christ and his second coming, between the captivity of Babylon and the captivity of sin. The complete promise of restoration will be fulfilled only when Christ establishes his kingdom on earth at the end of the age. More than a political nation, the people of God (all who believe in Christ, both Jew and non-Jew) will then be spiritually restored to the Lord.

---

^a23 That is, the palace in Jerusalem (see 1 Kings 7:2)   ^b24 Hebrew *Coniah,* a variant of *Jehoiachin;* also in verse 28   ^c25 Or *Chaldeans*   ^d5 Or *up from David's line*

all the countries where he had banished them.' Then they will live in their own land."

Lying Prophets

9Concerning the prophetsᴰ:

My heart is broken within me;
  all my bones tremble.
I am like a drunken man,
  like a man overcome by wine,
because of the LORD
  and his holy words.
10The land is full of adulterers;
  because of the curseᵃ the land lies
    parchedᵇ
  and the pastures in the desert are withered.
The ∟ prophets⌟ follow an evil course
  and use their power unjustly.

11"Both prophet and priest are godless;
  even in my temple I find their wickedness,"
                        declares the LORD.

12"Therefore their path will become slippery;
  they will be banished to darkness
  and there they will fall.
I will bring disaster on them
  in the year they are punished,"
                        declares the LORD.

13"Among the prophets of Samaria
  I saw this repulsive thing:
They prophesied by Baalᴰ
  and led my people Israel astray.
14And among the prophets of Jerusalem
  I have seen something horrible:
They commit adultery and live a lie.
They strengthen the hands of evildoers,
  so that no one turns from his wickedness.

ᵃ10 Or because of these things   ᵇ10 Or land mourns

Who were these prophets and what were they doing? (23:9–14)

False prophets and godless priests (v. 11). They were in a position to be spiritual leaders and had actually corrupted the people by introducing idolatry and practicing immorality. Though the spiritual depravity of the northern kingdom was well known (v. 13), Jeremiah was astonished that Judah would go the same way (v. 14). During the reigns of both Ahaz (2 Kings 16:3–4,10–16) and Manasseh (2 Kings 21:2–9) worship to the Lord was compromised by idols being set up in the temple. Most likely, the immoral practices of pagan worship occurred, including temple prostitution and human sacrifice. Some think the people of Judah mixed paganism with worship to the Lord, setting up a repulsive religious hybrid that lasted until Judah fell to the Babylonians.

How much prophecy did Jeremiah understand? (23:5–6)

Did Jeremiah know he was prophesying about the Messiah? Jeremiah was pointing to a future day, to a coming king similar to David who would fulfill all God's covenant promises. Jeremiah must have recognized that this coming king would be someone extraordinary. He may have even connected these promises with his prophecies of a new covenant (31:31–34). But it's also possible his view was limited, allowing him only to see a physical renewal of Israel (30:3).

There is little doubt, however, that Jeremiah could see a coming day when a *righteous Branch* would grow from David's family tree. This Branch would stand in stark contrast to all the wicked and depraved branches—the earlier kings of Judah who had so miserably failed the people.

Jeremiah also knew that the name of this righteous Branch would be *The* LORD *Our Righteousness* (v. 6), although he may have viewed the phrase simply as the name of a man. (*Zedekiah,* for example, king during part of Jeremiah's ministry, meant *the Lord is my righteousness.*) Still, Jeremiah probably saw here at least a hint of the beautiful doctrine of justification: it is not our good works or merit that makes us right with God, but the fact that Jesus is our righteousness (1 Cor. 1:30).

They are all like Sodom to me;
  the people of Jerusalem[D] are like
    Gomorrah."

¹⁵Therefore, this is what the LORD Almighty says concerning the prophets[D]:

"I will make them eat bitter food
  and drink poisoned water,
because from the prophets of Jerusalem
  ungodliness has spread throughout the land."

¹⁶This is what the LORD Almighty says:

"Do not listen to what the prophets are
    prophesying to you;
  they fill you with false hopes.
They speak visions[D] from their own minds,
  not from the mouth of the LORD.
¹⁷They keep saying to those who despise me,
  'The LORD says: You will have peace[D].'
And to all who follow the stubbornness of their
    hearts
  they say, 'No harm will come to you.'
¹⁸But which of them has stood in the council of
    the LORD
  to see or to hear his word?
  Who has listened and heard his word?
¹⁹See, the storm of the LORD
  will burst out in wrath,
a whirlwind swirling down
  on the heads of the wicked.
²⁰The anger of the LORD will not turn back
  until he fully accomplishes
    the purposes of his heart.
In days to come
  you will understand it clearly.
²¹I did not send these prophets,
  yet they have run with their message;
I did not speak to them,
  yet they have prophesied.
²²But if they had stood in my council,
  they would have proclaimed my words to my
    people
and would have turned them from their evil
    ways
  and from their evil deeds.
²³"Am I only a God nearby,"
                   declares the LORD,
  "and not a God far away?
²⁴Can anyone hide in secret places
  so that I cannot see him?"
                   declares the LORD.
"Do not I fill heaven and earth?"
                   declares the LORD.

²⁵"I have heard what the prophets say who prophesy lies in my name. They say, 'I had a dream! I had a dream!' ²⁶How long will this continue in the hearts of these lying prophets, who prophesy the delusions of their own minds? ²⁷They think the dreams they tell one another will make my people forget my name, just as their fathers forgot my name through Baal[D] worship. ²⁸Let the prophet who has a dream tell his dream, but let the one who has my word speak it faithfully. For what has straw to do with grain?" declares the LORD. ²⁹"Is not my word like fire," de-

Stood in the council of the LORD (23:18)

The image of an ancient council of officials gathered about a throne is used here. The false prophets had not stood before the throne of God in prayer and worship, waiting for his word. They had not heard his pronouncement. Instead they created their own prophecies to please the crowds. Events quickly confirmed Jeremiah's authentic prophecy as Babylon crushed Israel, so full of false hopes for security.

clares the LORD, "and like a hammer that breaks a rock in pieces?

30"Therefore," declares the LORD, "I am against the prophets[D] who steal from one another words supposedly from me. **31**Yes," declares the LORD, "I am against the prophets who wag their own tongues and yet declare, 'The LORD declares.' **32**Indeed, I am against those who prophesy false dreams," declares the LORD. "They tell them and lead my people astray with their reckless lies, yet I did not send or appoint them. They do not benefit these people in the least," declares the LORD.

False Oracles and False Prophets

33"When these people, or a prophet or a priest, ask you, 'What is the oracle[Da] of the LORD?' say to them, 'What oracle?[b] I will forsake you, declares the LORD.' **34**If a prophet or a priest or anyone else claims, 'This is the oracle of the LORD,' I will punish that man and his household. **35**This is what each of you keeps on saying to his friend or relative: 'What is the LORD's answer?' or 'What has the LORD spoken?' **36**But you must not mention 'the oracle of the LORD' again, because every man's own word becomes his oracle and so you distort the words of the living God, the LORD Almighty, our God. **37**This is what you keep saying to a prophet: 'What is the LORD's answer to you?' or 'What has the LORD spoken?' **38**Although you claim, 'This is the oracle of the LORD,' this is what the LORD says: You used the words, 'This is the oracle of the LORD,' even though I told you that you must not claim, 'This is the oracle of the LORD.' **39**Therefore, I will surely forget you and cast you out of my presence along with the city I gave to you and your fathers. **40**I will bring upon you everlasting disgrace—everlasting shame that will not be forgotten."

Two Baskets of Figs

24 After Jehoiachin[c] son of Jehoiakim king of Judah and the officials, the craftsmen and the artisans of Judah were carried into exile[D] from Jerusalem[D] to Babylon by Nebuchadnezzar king of Babylon, the LORD showed me two baskets of figs placed in front of the temple of the LORD. **2**One basket had very good figs, like those that ripen early; the other basket had very poor figs, so bad they could not be eaten.

3Then the LORD asked me, "What do you see, Jeremiah?"

"Figs," I answered. "The good ones are very good, but the poor ones are so bad they cannot be eaten."

4Then the word of the LORD came to me: **5**"This is what the LORD, the God of Israel, says: 'Like these good figs, I regard as good the exiles from Judah, whom I sent away from this place to the land of the Babylonians.[d] **6**My eyes will watch over them for their good, and I will bring them back to this land. I will build them up and not tear them down; I will plant them and not uproot them. **7**I will give them a heart to know me, that I am the LORD. They will be my people, and I will be their God, for they will return to me with all their heart.

8"'But like the poor figs, which are so bad they cannot

Nebuchadnezzar (24:1)
See *Nebuchadnezzar* (21:2).

Why do some figs ripen earlier? (24:2)
The long growing season in the land of Israel makes it possible for figs to ripen two times a year. The first figs produce the sweetest crop. These choice figs symbolized the first exiles that had already been carried away into Babylon in 605 and 597 B.C. (v. 5).

Why would God regard the exiles as good? (24:5)
Undoubtedly there were righteous men and women in Judah who had never bowed their knees to idols, yet who became captives in Babylon. Daniel and his friends were taken in the first exile, Ezekiel in the second. Yet, the more likely idea here is that the exiles removed from Judah would be a source for the rebuilding of Israel. The exile served to turn the people back to God.

How did they turn to God? (24:7)
The key to repentance and transformation is found in God's promise: *I will give them a heart to know me.* This verse indicates that God must first work in people's lives for them to escape their sinful condition. It was only because of the Lord's mercy that the exiles could be changed and hope for a return to God. But also see *Must people seek God before he seeks them?* (29:13).

---

a33 Or *burden* (see Septuagint and Vulgate)   *b33* Hebrew; Septuagint and Vulgate *'You are the burden.* (The Hebrew for *oracle* and *burden* is the same.)   *c1* Hebrew *Jeconiah,* a variant of *Jehoiachin*   *d5* Or *Chaldeans*

be eaten,' says the LORD, 'so will I deal with Zedekiah king of Judah, his officials and the survivors from Jerusalem[D], whether they remain in this land or live in Egypt. ⁹I will make them abhorrent and an offense to all the kingdoms of the earth, a reproach[D] and a byword[D], an object of ridicule and cursing, wherever I banish them. ¹⁰I will send the sword, famine and plague against them until they are destroyed from the land I gave to them and their fathers.' "

Seventy Years of Captivity

25 The word came to Jeremiah concerning all the people of Judah in the fourth year of Jehoiakim son of Josiah king of Judah, which was the first year of Nebuchadnezzar king of Babylon. ²So Jeremiah the prophet[D] said to all the people of Judah and to all those living in Jerusalem: ³For twenty-three years—from the thirteenth year of Josiah son of Amon king of Judah until this very day—the word of the LORD has come to me and I have spoken to you again and again, but you have not listened.

⁴And though the LORD has sent all his servants the prophets to you again and again, you have not listened or paid any attention. ⁵They said, "Turn now, each of you, from your evil ways and your evil practices, and you can stay in the land the LORD gave to you and your fathers for ever and ever. ⁶Do not follow other gods to serve and worship them; do not provoke me to anger with what your hands have made. Then I will not harm you."

⁷"But you did not listen to me," declares the LORD, "and you have provoked me with what your hands have made, and you have brought harm to yourselves."

⁸Therefore the LORD Almighty says this: "Because you have not listened to my words, ⁹I will summon all the peoples of the north and my servant Nebuchadnezzar king of Babylon," declares the LORD, "and I will bring them against this land and its inhabitants and against all the surrounding nations. I will completely destroy[a] them and make them an object of horror and scorn, and an everlasting ruin. ¹⁰I will banish from them the sounds of joy and gladness, the voices of bride and bridegroom, the sound of millstones[D] and the light of the lamp. ¹¹This whole country will become a desolate wasteland, and these nations will serve the king of Babylon seventy years.

¹²"But when the seventy years are fulfilled, I will punish the king of Babylon and his nation, the land of the Babylonians,[b] for their guilt," declares the LORD, "and will make it desolate forever. ¹³I will bring upon that land all the things I have spoken against it, all that are written in this book and prophesied by Jeremiah against all the nations. ¹⁴They themselves will be enslaved by many nations and great kings; I will repay them according to their deeds and the work of their hands."

The Cup of God's Wrath

¹⁵This is what the LORD, the God of Israel, said to me: "Take from my hand this cup filled with the wine of my wrath and make all the nations to whom I send you drink it. ¹⁶When they drink it, they will stagger and go mad because of the sword I will send among them."

---

[a]9 The Hebrew term refers to the irrevocable giving over of things or persons to the LORD, often by totally destroying them.   [b]12 Or Chaldeans

---

North (25:9)
See *What northern kingdoms would attack Judah?* (1:14–15).

Why call a pagan king God's servant? (25:9)
See *Why call a pagan king God's servant?* (27:6).

Why 70 years? (25:11–12)
Some suggest that God chose 70 years of captivity because that was a normal life span. A generation of Jews spent a lifetime in exile as punishment for the sins of their fathers. Others say the time represented the number of Sabbath years during which the Israelites had not permitted the land to rest (see 2 Chron. 36:21). The first captives were taken from Jerusalem in 605 B.C.; the first Jews returned from Babylon in 538 B.C. Others count the time from 586 B.C. when the temple was destroyed to 516 B.C. when Zerubbabel's temple was finished.

How could Jeremiah force them to drink God's wrath? (25:15–17)
This is a figurative way of saying that Jeremiah brought the message of divine judgment (the *cup* of God's *wrath*) to the nations.

¹⁷So I took the cup from the Lord's hand and made all the nations to whom he sent me drink it: ¹⁸Jerusalemᴰ and the towns of Judah, its kings and officials, to make them a ruin and an object of horror and scorn and cursing, as they are today; ¹⁹Pharaoh king of Egypt, his attendants, his officials and all his people, ²⁰and all the foreign people there; all the kings of Uz; all the kings of the Philistines (those of Ashkelon, Gaza, Ekron, and the people left at Ashdod); ²¹Edomᴰ, Moab and Ammon; ²²all the kings of Tyre and Sidon; the kings of the coastlands across the sea; ²³Dedan, Tema, Buz and all who are in distant placesᵃ; ²⁴all the kings of Arabia and all the kings of the foreign people who live in the desert; ²⁵all the kings of Zimri, Elam and Media; ²⁶and all the kings of the north, near and far, one after the other—all the kingdoms on the face of the earth. And after all of them, the king of Sheshachᵇ will drink it too.

²⁷"Then tell them, 'This is what the Lord Almighty, the God of Israel, says: Drink, get drunk and vomit, and fall to rise no more because of the sword I will send among you.' ²⁸But if they refuse to take the cup from your hand and drink, tell them, 'This is what the Lord Almighty says: You must drink it! ²⁹See, I am beginning to bring disaster on the city that bears my Name, and will you indeed go unpunished? You will not go unpunished, for I am calling down a sword upon all who live on the earth, declares the Lord Almighty.'

³⁰"Now prophesy all these words against them and say to them:

" 'The Lord will roar from on high;
    he will thunder from his holy dwelling
    and roar mightily against his land.
He will shout like those who tread the grapes,
    shout against all who live on the earth.
³¹The tumult will resound to the ends of the
        earth,
    for the Lord will bring charges against the
        nations;
he will bring judgment on all mankind
    and put the wicked to the sword,' "
                                    declares the Lord.

³²This is what the Lord Almighty says:

"Look! Disaster is spreading
    from nation to nation;
a mighty storm is rising
    from the ends of the earth."

³³At that time those slain by the Lord will be everywhere—from one end of the earth to the other. They will not be mourned or gathered up or buried, but will be like refuse lying on the ground.

³⁴Weep and wail, you shepherds;
    roll in the dust, you leaders of the flock.
For your time to be slaughtered has come;
    you will fall and be shattered like fine
        pottery.
³⁵The shepherds will have nowhere to flee,
    the leaders of the flock no place to escape.

Why give Babylon a code name? (25:26; see NIV text note)

Why say *Sheshach* instead of *Babylon*? It's not entirely clear. Some have suggested that Jeremiah felt it prudent to disguise his prediction that Babylon would one day suffer the same fate as the other nations. Other examples of cryptograms can be found in 51:1,41.

Why did grape treaders shout? (25:30)

Usually those who trod grapes were in a mood to celebrate. They would shout for joy because of the harvest. The ruckus made at such a glad occasion is here compared to the war cry God would shout when he trampled the wicked nations of the world. The noise of the grape treaders, not their mood, however, is the focus of Jeremiah's metaphor.

That time (25:33)

When God would use Babylon as an instrument of destruction. This prophecy was fulfilled in Jeremiah's lifetime, though it may have future implications as well. Several Old Testament prophets speak of God's final judgment on wickedness, sometimes referring to it as the *day of the Lord*.

ᵃ23 Or *who clip the hair by their foreheads*   ᵇ26 *Sheshach* is a cryptogram for Babylon.

³⁶Hear the cry of the shepherds,
    the wailing of the leaders of the flock,
      for the LORD is destroying their pasture.
³⁷The peaceful meadows will be laid waste
    because of the fierce anger of the LORD.
³⁸Like a lion he will leave his lair,
    and their land will become desolate
    because of the sword*ᵃ* of the oppressor
    and because of the LORD's fierce anger.

Jeremiah Threatened With Death

26 Early in the reign of Jehoiakim son of Josiah king of Judah, this word came from the LORD: ²"This is what the LORD says: Stand in the courtyard of the LORD's house and speak to all the people of the towns of Judah who come to worship in the house of the LORD. Tell them everything I command you; do not omit a word. ³Perhaps they will listen and each will turn from his evil way. Then I will relent and not bring on them the disaster I was planning because of the evil they have done. ⁴Say to them, 'This is what the LORD says: If you do not listen to me and follow my law, which I have set before you, ⁵and if you do not listen to the words of my servants the prophets*ᴰ*, whom I have sent to you again and again (though you have not listened), ⁶then I will make this house like Shiloh and this city an object of cursing among all the nations of the earth.'"

⁷The priests*ᴰ*, the prophets and all the people heard Jeremiah speak these words in the house of the LORD. ⁸But as soon as Jeremiah finished telling all the people everything the LORD had commanded him to say, the priests,

ᵃ38 Some Hebrew manuscripts and Septuagint (see also Jer. 46:16 and 50:16); most Hebrew manuscripts *anger*

What was Shiloh like? (26:6)

Shiloh was completely destroyed about 1050 B.C. The terrible irony was that Shiloh was the first place the ark of the covenant had rested in the promised land. It had been the center of worship in the days of Eli, the high priest. The prophet Samuel had received his call from God at Shiloh. Now, the gutted and empty city was a vivid reminder that past spiritual glories were no insurance against God's wrath.

Why were they so upset? (26:8–9)

The people may have suspected Jeremiah was a false prophet. Who else would predict that the temple would be destroyed? That he did so in the name of the Lord made him liable for blasphemy in their minds. Other prophets and religious leaders had assured the people of God's continued blessing and protection. Accustomed to hearing the words they wanted to hear, they could not tolerate Jeremiah's message of calamity and judgment.

Does God change his plans? (26:3)

Since God knows all things, he knew Judah would not repent. Yet his knowledge did not diminish the integrity of his offer. His promise to spare them if they would repent was a legitimate one. A sovereign God can choose when he will or will not execute judgment. God has declared that he chooses to forgive when someone truly repents.

Another example of mercy triumphing over judgment is in Exodus 32:14. When Moses interceded for the people of Israel, God seemed to back away from his original intentions to punish them. But God was not being fickle. He was acting in a manner entirely consistent with his character. He promises to respond when people pray. His mercy, even in the face of Israel's deserved judgment, demonstrated his true character.

The Old Testament never attempts to solve the mysterious tension between God's foreknowledge and human responsibility. The Bible assumes both are at work in the events of history. Yet this much is clear: God never changes so as to mislead or lie. He is never caught by surprise. He knows the decisions each person will make. Yet, in a manner we do not fully understand, his knowledge does not infringe on an individual's freedom before God.

Also see articles: *Can our prayers cause God to change his mind?* (Exodus 32:14) and *Why did God change his mind?* (Isaiah 38:1–5).

the prophets and all the people seized him and said, "You must die! 9Why do you prophesy in the LORD's name that this house will be like Shiloh and this city will be desolate and deserted?" And all the people crowded around Jeremiah in the house of the LORD.

10When the officials of Judah heard about these things, they went up from the royal palace to the house of the LORD and took their places at the entrance of the New Gate of the LORD's house. 11Then the priests[D] and the prophets[D] said to the officials and all the people, "This man should be sentenced to death[D] because he has prophesied against this city. You have heard it with your own ears!"

12Then Jeremiah said to all the officials and all the people: "The LORD sent me to prophesy against this house and this city all the things you have heard. 13Now reform your ways and your actions and obey the LORD your God. Then the LORD will relent and not bring the disaster he has pronounced against you. 14As for me, I am in your hands; do with me whatever you think is good and right. 15Be assured, however, that if you put me to death, you will bring the guilt of innocent blood on yourselves and on this city and on those who live in it, for in truth the LORD has sent me to you to speak all these words in your hearing."

16Then the officials and all the people said to the priests and the prophets, "This man should not be sentenced to death! He has spoken to us in the name of the LORD our God."

17Some of the elders of the land stepped forward and said to the entire assembly of people, 18"Micah of Moresheth prophesied in the days of Hezekiah king of Judah. He told all the people of Judah, 'This is what the LORD Almighty says:

" 'Zion[D] will be plowed like a field,
Jerusalem[D] will become a heap of rubble,
the temple hill a mound overgrown with
thickets.'[a]

19"Did Hezekiah king of Judah or anyone else in Judah put him to death? Did not Hezekiah fear the LORD and seek his favor? And did not the LORD relent, so that he did not bring the disaster he pronounced against them? We are about to bring a terrible disaster on ourselves!"

20(Now Uriah son of Shemaiah from Kiriath Jearim was another man who prophesied in the name of the LORD; he prophesied the same things against this city and this land as Jeremiah did. 21When King Jehoiakim and all his officers and officials heard his words, the king sought to put him to death. But Uriah heard of it and fled in fear to Egypt. 22King Jehoiakim, however, sent Elnathan son of Acbor to Egypt, along with some other men. 23They brought Uriah out of Egypt and took him to King Jehoiakim, who had him struck down with a sword and his body thrown into the burial place of the common people.)

24Furthermore, Ahikam son of Shaphan supported Jeremiah, and so he was not handed over to the people to be put to death.

a18 Micah 3:12

How did Jeremiah talk them out of killing him? (26:10–16)

Jeremiah's words had a ring of truth. While the people and officials recognized this, the priests and false prophets did not. They had apparently become calloused to the true word of the Lord. Jeremiah demonstrated a sincerity his religious rivals did not have and was willing to die for his commitment to truth (vv. 14–15). His attitude stood in stark contrast to those of the self-serving false prophets. God honored Jeremiah for saying what had to be said, regardless of the cost, and intervened to turn the crowd around.

How could a prophet's execution be justified? (26:20–23)

Uriah was likely executed on the grounds of treason. Like Jeremiah, he predicted coming destruction. Then, when he feared for his life and fled to Egypt, he gave the king an excuse to denounce him as a traitor. Labeled a traitor, Uriah was denied a funeral and burial befitting a prophet of the Lord. Jeremiah would have undoubtedly met a similar fate if it had not been for God's protection (see following note).

Why did Ahikam have such political clout? (26:24)

Ahikam had been an official in King Josiah's court during the last reform. Ahikam apparently played the role of an elder statesman, maintaining his influence even after Josiah's reign. His son Gedaliah became governor of Judah after the fall of Jerusalem in 586 B.C. As a result of Ahikam's political connections and prominence, he was able to safeguard Jeremiah's life.

Judah to Serve Nebuchadnezzar

27 Early in the reign of Zedekiah*a* son of Josiah king of Judah, this word came to Jeremiah from the LORD: **2**This is what the LORD said to me: "Make a yokeᴰ out of straps and crossbars and put it on your neck. **3**Then send word to the kings of EdomD, Moab, Ammon, Tyre and Sidon through the envoys who have come to Jerusalemᴰ to Zedekiah king of Judah. **4**Give them a message for their masters and say, 'This is what the LORD Almighty, the God of Israel, says: "Tell this to your masters: **5**With my great power and outstretched arm I made the earth and its people and the animals that are on it, and I give it to anyone I please. **6**Now I will hand all your countries over to my servant Nebuchadnezzar king of Babylon; I will make even the wild animals subject to him. **7**All nations will serve him and his son and his grandson until the time for his land comes; then many nations and great kings will subjugate him.

8 ' "If, however, any nation or kingdom will not serve Nebuchadnezzar king of Babylon or bow its neck under his yoke, I will punish that nation with the sword, famine and plague, declares the LORD, until I destroy it by his hand. **9**So do not listen to your prophetsᴰ, your diviners, your interpreters of dreams, your mediumsᴰ or your sorcerers who tell you, 'You will not serve the king of Babylon.' **10**They prophesy lies to you that will only serve to remove you far from your lands; I will banish you and you will perish. **11**But if any nation will bow its neck under the yoke of the king of Babylon and serve him, I will let that nation remain in its own land to till it and to live there, declares the LORD." ' "

12I gave the same message to Zedekiah king of Judah. I said, "Bow your neck under the yoke of the king of Babylon; serve him and his people, and you will live. **13**Why will you and your people die by the sword, famine and plague with which the LORD has threatened any nation that will not serve the king of Babylon? **14**Do not listen to the words of the prophets who say to you, 'You will not serve the king of Babylon,' for they are prophesying lies to you. **15**'I have not sent them,' declares the LORD. 'They are prophesying lies in my name. Therefore, I will banish you and you will perish, both you and the prophets who prophesy to you.' "

16Then I said to the priestsᴰ and all these people, "This is what the LORD says: Do not listen to the prophets who say, 'Very soon now the articles from the LORD's house will be brought back from Babylon.' They are prophesying lies to you. **17**Do not listen to them. Serve the king of Babylon, and you will live. Why should this city become a ruin? **18**If they are prophets and have the word of the LORD, let them plead with the LORD Almighty that the furnishings remaining in the house of the LORD and in the palace of the king of Judah and in Jerusalem not be taken to Babylon. **19**For this is what the LORD Almighty says about the pillars, the Sea, the movable stands and the other furnishings that are left in this city, **20**which Nebuchadnezzar king of Babylon did not take away when he carried Jehoiachin*b* son of Jehoiakim king of Judah into exileᴰ from Jerusalem to Babylon, along with all the nobles of

Why call a pagan king God's servant? (27:6)

The time had come to punish Judah and the surrounding nations for their wickedness. God chose Nebuchadnezzar and the Babylonians to execute this punishment. They were neither more righteous nor deserving than other nations, but they fit God's purposes. God's choices may sometimes be surprising and perplexing, but we can be sure they are always right. See article: *Does God use evil to do good?* (Hab. 1:6,13).

How did Nebuchadnezzar tame wild animals? (27:6)

See *How did Nebuchadnezzar tame wild animals?* (28:14).

Why help Nebuchadnezzar with plagues and famine? (27:8–15)

This was Jeremiah's warning to the coalition nations that planned to oppose Babylon: in reality, they were opposing God and, as a result, could expect his wrath. Some observe that plagues and famine often accompany war, that rebellion can lead to disease and starvation. Others say famine and plague were God's added punishment against all who resisted his judgment that came through Nebuchadnezzar. The issue was submission to God's will. Those who chose to resist it had nothing but sorrow to look forward to.

When did Babylon confiscate temple articles? (27:16,20)

Nebuchadnezzar attacked Jerusalem in 597 B.C., taking King Jehoiakim and several articles of worship from the temple back to Babylon (2 Chron. 36:5–7). A strange mix of theology and politics in the ancient Middle East caused people to believe a nation was defeated when its gods were defeated. By looting the temple and taking away its furnishings, the Babylonians confirmed that their victory was complete.

---

a1 A few Hebrew manuscripts and Syriac (see also Jer. 27:3, 12 and 28:1); most Hebrew manuscripts *Jehoiakim* (Most Septuagint manuscripts do not have this verse.)   *b20* Hebrew *Jeconiah*, a variant of *Jehoiachin*

Judah and Jerusalem[D]— 21yes, this is what the LORD Almighty, the God of Israel, says about the things that are left in the house of the LORD and in the palace of the king of Judah and in Jerusalem: 22'They will be taken to Babylon and there they will remain until the day I come for them,' declares the LORD. 'Then I will bring them back and restore them to this place.' "

The False Prophet Hananiah

28 In the fifth month of that same year, the fourth year, early in the reign of Zedekiah king of Judah, the prophet[D] Hananiah son of Azzur, who was from Gibeon, said to me in the house of the LORD in the presence of the priests[D] and all the people: 2"This is what the LORD Almighty, the God of Israel, says: 'I will break the yoke[D] of the king of Babylon. 3Within two years I will bring back to this place all the articles of the LORD's house that Nebuchadnezzar king of Babylon removed from here and took to Babylon. 4I will also bring back to this place Jehoiachin[a] son of Jehoiakim king of Judah and all the other exiles[D] from Judah who went to Babylon,' declares the LORD, 'for I will break the yoke of the king of Babylon.' "

5Then the prophet Jeremiah replied to the prophet Hananiah before the priests and all the people who were standing in the house of the LORD. 6He said, "Amen! May the LORD do so! May the LORD fulfill the words you have prophesied by bringing the articles of the LORD's house and all the exiles back to this place from Babylon. 7Nevertheless, listen to what I have to say in your hearing and in the hearing of all the people: 8From early times the prophets who preceded you and me have prophesied war, disaster and plague against many countries and great kingdoms. 9But the prophet who prophesies peace[D] will be recognized as one truly sent by the LORD only if his prediction comes true."

10Then the prophet Hananiah took the yoke off the neck of the prophet Jeremiah and broke it, 11and he said before all the people, "This is what the LORD says: 'In the same way will I break the yoke of Nebuchadnezzar king of Babylon off the neck of all the nations within two years.' " At this, the prophet Jeremiah went on his way.

12Shortly after the prophet Hananiah had broken the yoke off the neck of the prophet Jeremiah, the word of the LORD came to Jeremiah: 13"Go and tell Hananiah, 'This is what the LORD says: You have broken a wooden yoke, but in its place you will get a yoke of iron. 14This is what the LORD Almighty, the God of Israel, says: I will put an iron yoke on the necks of all these nations to make them serve Nebuchadnezzar king of Babylon, and they will serve him. I will even give him control over the wild animals.' "

15Then the prophet Jeremiah said to Hananiah the prophet, "Listen, Hananiah! The LORD has not sent you, yet you have persuaded this nation to trust in lies. 16Therefore, this is what the LORD says: 'I am about to remove you from the face of the earth. This very year you are going to die, because you have preached rebellion against the LORD.' "

17In the seventh month of that same year, Hananiah the prophet died.

a4 Hebrew Jeconiah, a variant of Jehoiachin

Why did God allow the temple to be robbed? (27:21–22)

Probably for several reasons. (1) As part of Judah's punishment: The nation had abandoned God, so he determined to abandon them. (2) To root out all that remained of their superficial worship: Some temple objects had been taken to Babylon earlier (605 and 597 B.C.). But as long as a few objects remained, the people could carry on their empty rituals, feeling a false sense of security. (3) To expose the false prophets as frauds: The false prophets had predicted that the temple items taken earlier would soon be returned (v. 16). Instead, the few items that remained were also taken (586 B.C.).

Was Jeremiah being sarcastic? (28:5–6)

Probably. Some feel Jeremiah genuinely wanted the temple and the nation restored. But it's more likely there was a sarcastic edge to his reply.

Was war so common anyone could predict it? (28:8–9)

Not necessarily. Jeremiah was simply saying that prophets were typically sent to warn people, not comfort them. People could wait and see who was right. Hananiah's assurances of prosperity, while receiving rave reviews, merely restated conventional thinking. Jeremiah's message of doom, by contrast, opposed the tide of popular opinion.

Did Jeremiah always wear the yoke? (28:10)

Undoubtedly Jeremiah had worn it for some time prior to this. It captured the imagination of the people and fulfilled God's instructions (27:2). However, it was not necessary for him to have worn it continually to make his point. Symbolic actions, performed at strategic moments in God's design, often leave an indelible impression on people. The yoke was an effective object lesson.

How did Nebuchadnezzar tame wild animals? (28:14)

This was an overstatement intended to illustrate the absolute dominion Nebuchadnezzar would have over the nations (see 27:6).

Why did Jeremiah bother with false prophets? (28:15–16)

Because they claimed to speak for God, the false prophets held an enormous potential influence. Jeremiah recognized that, left unchecked, they could push the entire nation further away from God. Furthermore, God is jealous about who speaks for him (see 29:21–23,31–32). To claim to be the Lord's spokesman, apart from his calling and his word, is a grievous offense.

A Letter to the Exiles

29 This is the text of the letter that the prophet[D] Jeremiah sent from Jerusalem[D] to the surviving elders among the exiles[D] and to the priests[D], the prophets and all the other people Nebuchadnezzar had carried into exile from Jerusalem to Babylon. ²(This was after King Jehoiachin[a] and the queen mother, the court officials and the leaders of Judah and Jerusalem, the craftsmen and the artisans had gone into exile from Jerusalem.) ³He entrusted the letter to Elasah son of Shaphan and to Gemariah son of Hilkiah, whom Zedekiah king of Judah sent to King Nebuchadnezzar in Babylon. It said:

⁴This is what the LORD Almighty, the God of Israel, says to all those I carried into exile from Jerusalem to Babylon: ⁵"Build houses and settle down; plant gardens and eat what they produce. ⁶Marry and have sons and daughters; find wives for your sons and give your daughters in marriage, so that they too may have sons and daughters. Increase in number there; do not decrease. ⁷Also, seek the peace[D] and prosperity of the city to which I have carried you into exile. Pray to the LORD for it, because if it prospers, you too will prosper." ⁸Yes, this is what the LORD Almighty, the God of Israel, says: "Do not let the prophets and diviners among you deceive you. Do not listen to the dreams you encourage them to have. ⁹They are prophesying lies to you in my name. I have not sent them," declares the LORD.

¹⁰This is what the LORD says: "When seventy years are completed for Babylon, I will come to you and fulfill my gracious promise to bring you back to this place. ¹¹For I know the plans I have for you," declares the LORD, "plans to prosper you and not to harm you, plans to give you hope and a future. ¹²Then you will call upon me and come and pray to me, and I will listen to you. ¹³You will seek me and find me when you seek me with all your heart. ¹⁴I will be found by you," declares the LORD, "and will bring you back from captivity.[b] I will gather you from all the nations and places where I have banished you," declares the LORD, "and will bring you back to the place from which I carried you into exile."

¹⁵You may say, "The LORD has raised up prophets for us in Babylon," ¹⁶but this is what the LORD says about the king who sits on David's throne and all the people who remain in this city, your countrymen who did not go with you into exile— ¹⁷yes, this is what the LORD Almighty says: "I will send the sword, famine and plague against them and I will make them like poor figs that are so bad they cannot be eaten. ¹⁸I will pursue them with the sword, famine and plague and will make them abhorrent to all the kingdoms of the earth and an object of cursing and horror, of scorn and reproach[D], among all the nations where I drive them. ¹⁹For they have not listened to my words," declares the LORD, "words that I sent to them again and again by my servants the prophets. And you exiles have not listened either," declares the LORD.

²⁰Therefore, hear the word of the LORD, all you ex-

Why pray for Babylon? (29:7)

We must remember that God sent Judah into exile. His will was that Babylon defeat the people of Judah, not just to punish them, but so that they could learn once again to submit to his will. Learning to pray for the peace and prosperity of their conquerors was one of their first lessons. Furthermore, the Jews were to bring their faith in God to this strange nation. Perhaps they could influence their captors to serve the Lord as well. Since they would be captive for 70 years (v. 10), it was also wise to pray for peace so they might enjoy their lives.

Seventy years (29:10)

See *Why 70 years?* (25:11–12).

Must people seek God before he seeks them? (29:13)

This has long been debated. One can emphasize either God's sovereign activity in bringing sinners to himself, or the response of the human will to God's grace. Scripture offers both perspectives in what is called an 'antinomy'— two truths, both with Scriptural support, irreconcilable from a human standpoint, yet completely reconcilable from God's viewpoint. Does God seek the lost, or do the lost seek God? The answer is yes to both questions. Also see *How did they turn to God?* (24:7).

---

*a*2 Hebrew *Jeconiah,* a variant of *Jehoiachin*   *b*14 Or *will restore your fortunes*

iles whom I have sent away from Jerusalem[D] to Babylon. **21**This is what the LORD Almighty, the God of Israel, says about Ahab son of Kolaiah and Zedekiah son of Maaseiah, who are prophesying lies to you in my name: "I will hand them over to Nebuchadnezzar king of Babylon, and he will put them to death[D] before your very eyes. **22**Because of them, all the exiles[D] from Judah who are in Babylon will use this curse: 'The LORD treat you like Zedekiah and Ahab, whom the king of Babylon burned in the fire.' **23**For they have done outrageous things in Israel; they have committed adultery with their neighbors' wives and in my name have spoken lies, which I did not tell them to do. I know it and am a witness to it," declares the LORD.

Message to Shemaiah

24Tell Shemaiah the Nehelamite, **25**"This is what the LORD Almighty, the God of Israel, says: You sent letters in your own name to all the people in Jerusalem, to Zephaniah son of Maaseiah the priest[D], and to all the other priests. You said to Zephaniah, **26**'The LORD has appointed you priest in place of Jehoiada to be in charge of the house of the LORD; you should put any madman who acts like a prophet[D] into the stocks and neck-irons. **27**So why have you not reprimanded Jeremiah from Anathoth, who poses as a prophet among you? **28**He has sent this message to us in Babylon: It will be a long time. Therefore build houses and settle down; plant gardens and eat what they produce.' "

29Zephaniah the priest, however, read the letter to Jeremiah the prophet. **30**Then the word of the LORD came to Jeremiah: **31**"Send this message to all the exiles: 'This is what the LORD says about Shemaiah the Nehelamite: Because Shemaiah has prophesied to you, even though I did not send him, and has led you to believe a lie, **32**this is what the LORD says: I will surely punish Shemaiah the Nehelamite and his descendants. He will have no one left among this people, nor will he see the good things I will do for my people, declares the LORD, because he has preached rebellion against me.' "

Restoration of Israel

30 This is the word that came to Jeremiah from the LORD: **2**"This is what the LORD, the God of Israel, says: 'Write in a book all the words I have spoken to you. **3**The days are coming,' declares the LORD, 'when I will bring my people Israel and Judah back from captivity[a] and restore them to the land I gave their forefathers to possess,' says the LORD."

4These are the words the LORD spoke concerning Israel and Judah: **5**"This is what the LORD says:

" 'Cries of fear are heard—
        terror, not peace[D].
    6Ask and see:
        Can a man bear children?
    Then why do I see every strong man
        with his hands on his stomach like a woman
            in labor,
        every face turned deathly pale?
    7How awful that day will be!

Why did people tolerate false prophets? (29:21–23)

The people were so desperate to hear peace and prosperity messages that they apparently were willing to overlook blatant sin. It is a sad commentary on the pathetic spiritual state of the nation that not even their own immoral relationships disqualified the false prophets from receiving a hearing. When spiritual leaders lead wicked lives, they inevitably take people down with them.

Who would confuse madmen and prophets? (29:26)

Because of the dramatic and unusual manner in which some prophets made their points, they were sometimes mistaken for madmen. Jeremiah with his yoke must have been a strange spectacle (27:2). Isaiah went naked for three years (Isaiah 20:3). Ezekiel lay on his left side for 390 days (Ezek. 4:4–5). A young prophet in Jehu's day was called mad because of his strange message (2 Kings 9:11). Eccentric as they often were in their behavior, true prophets were set apart from lunatics by the ultimate fulfillment of their messages.

Why did Jeremiah bother with false prophets? (29:31–32)

See *Why did Jeremiah bother with false prophets? (28:15–16).*

A time of trouble for Jacob (30:7)

"Jacob's trouble," according to some, suggests Israel's defeat and exile. Others say it's a future event, sometimes called *the day of the LORD,* when the nation will undergo severe discipline before final and complete restoration. The ultimate promise, however, is salvation. Such deliverance can only occur when history has run its final course.

---

a3 Or will restore the fortunes of my people Israel and Judah

None will be like it.
It will be a time of trouble for Jacob,
   but he will be saved out of it.
   8" ' In that day,' declares the LORD Almighty,
      'I will break the yoke^D off their necks
   and will tear off their bonds;
      no longer will foreigners enslave them.
   9Instead, they will serve the LORD their God
      and David their king,
      whom I will raise up for them.

10" 'So do not fear, O Jacob my servant;
      do not be dismayed, O Israel,'
                     declares the LORD.
   'I will surely save you out of a distant place,
      your descendants from the land of their
         exile^D.
   Jacob will again have peace^D and security,
      and no one will make him afraid.
   11I am with you and will save you,'
      declares the LORD.
   'Though I completely destroy all the nations
      among which I scatter you,
   I will not completely destroy you.
   I will discipline you but only with justice;
      I will not let you go entirely unpunished.'

12"This is what the LORD says:

   " 'Your wound is incurable,
      your injury beyond healing.
   13There is no one to plead your cause,
      no remedy for your sore,
      no healing for you.
   14All your allies have forgotten you;
      they care nothing for you.
   I have struck you as an enemy would
      and punished you as would the cruel,
   because your guilt is so great
      and your sins so many.
   15Why do you cry out over your wound,
      your pain that has no cure?
   Because of your great guilt and many sins
      I have done these things to you.

16" 'But all who devour you will be devoured;
      all your enemies will go into exile.
   Those who plunder^D you will be plundered;
      all who make spoil of you I will despoil.
   17But I will restore you to health
      and heal your wounds,'
                     declares the LORD,
   'because you are called an outcast,
      Zion^D for whom no one cares.'

18"This is what the LORD says:

   " 'I will restore the fortunes of Jacob's tents
      and have compassion on his dwellings;
   the city will be rebuilt on her ruins,
      and the palace will stand in its proper place.
   19From them will come songs of thanksgiving
      and the sound of rejoicing.
   I will add to their numbers,
      and they will not be decreased;
   I will bring them honor,

Why does God discipline his people? (30:11)

The idea of discipline *with justice* can be found throughout Scripture. Discipline of the people of God brings about their restoration, character and godliness. Discipline for unbelievers results in destruction, banishment and suffering. For the people of God, mercy ultimately triumphs over judgment, because God's justice has been satisfied through the sacrificial atonement of Jesus Christ, the Son of God.

Incurable . . . beyond healing (30:12)

This is a word picture of an individual with a fatal wound. There is no hope for recovery or a cure—an accurate portrayal of our spiritual condition apart from the mercy and restoration of God's grace. We are in a hopeless and dying condition.

and they will not be disdained.
20Their children will be as in days of old,
   and their community will be established
     before me;
  I will punish all who oppress them.
21Their leader will be one of their own;
  their ruler will arise from among them.
I will bring him near and he will come close to
  me,
  for who is he who will devote himself
  to be close to me?'
                 declares the LORD.
22" 'So you will be my people,
  and I will be your God.' "

23See, the storm of the LORD
  will burst out in wrath,
  a driving wind swirling down
  on the heads of the wicked.
24The fierce anger of the LORD will not turn back
  until he fully accomplishes
  the purposes of his heart.
In days to come
  you will understand this.

31 "At that time," declares the LORD, "I will be the God of all the clans of Israel, and they will be my people."

2This is what the LORD says:

"The people who survive the sword
  will find favor in the desert;
  I will come to give rest to Israel."

3The LORD appeared to us in the past,*a* saying:

"I have loved you with an everlasting love;
  I have drawn you with loving-kindness.
4I will build you up again
  and you will be rebuilt, O Virgin Israel.
Again you will take up your tambourines
  and go out to dance with the joyful.
5Again you will plant vineyards
  on the hills of Samaria;
the farmers will plant them
  and enjoy their fruit.
6There will be a day when watchmen*D* cry out
  on the hills of Ephraim,
'Come, let us go up to Zion*D*,
  to the LORD our God.' "

7This is what the LORD says:

"Sing with joy for Jacob;
  shout for the foremost of the nations.
Make your praises heard, and say,
  'O LORD, save your people,
  the remnant*D* of Israel.'
8See, I will bring them from the land of the
  north
  and gather them from the ends of the earth.
Among them will be the blind and the lame,
  expectant mothers and women in labor;
  a great throng will return.
9They will come with weeping;

a3 Or LORD *has appeared to us from afar*

Why couldn't God's love have overcome his wrath? (30:22–24)
Because God's character demands that justice must be satisfied. God does not vent his anger as a tantrum, but to preserve the integrity of his holiness. The ultimate satisfaction of God's wrath toward sin occurred with the death of Christ upon the cross.

Virgin Israel (31:4)
See *Virgin Israel* (18:13) and *Why compare sinful Judah to a virgin?* (Lam. 2:13).

When would Israel be gathered *from the ends of the earth?* (31:8)
To Jeremiah's listeners, Assyria and Babylon seemed like the most remote parts of the world. They understood the prophecy to mean that Jewish captives would return from *those* distant lands—but only if they again became faithful to God. Some see here the migration of Jews to Palestine and the formation of the modern state of Israel after World War II. Others say present-day Israel could not be meant since it has not yet met the conditions of the promise in terms of the new covenant: only through faith in Christ can Jews as well as Gentiles receive God's help.

they will pray as I bring them back.
I will lead them beside streams of water
on a level path where they will not stumble,
because I am Israel's father,
and Ephraim is my firstborn[D] son.

10"Hear the word of the LORD, O nations;
proclaim it in distant coastlands:
'He who scattered Israel will gather them
and will watch over his flock like a
shepherd.'
11For the LORD will ransom Jacob
and redeem[D] them from the hand of those
stronger than they.
12They will come and shout for joy on the
heights of Zion[D];
they will rejoice in the bounty of the LORD—
the grain, the new wine[D] and the oil,
the young of the flocks and herds.
They will be like a well-watered garden,
and they will sorrow no more.
13Then maidens will dance and be glad,
young men and old as well.
I will turn their mourning into gladness;
I will give them comfort and joy instead of
sorrow.
14I will satisfy the priests[D] with abundance,
and my people will be filled with my
bounty,"

declares the LORD.

15This is what the LORD says:

"A voice is heard in Ramah,
mourning and great weeping,
Rachel weeping for her children
and refusing to be comforted,
because her children are no more."

16This is what the LORD says:

"Restrain your voice from weeping
and your eyes from tears,

SCRIPTURE LINK (31:15)
Matthew said this passage was fulfilled when
Herod ordered the massacre of the boys two
years old and under. See Matt. 2:17–18.

Did Matthew misuse this verse? (31:15; see Matt. 2:18)

New Testament writers sometimes quoted the Old Testament to show how a
prophecy had been fulfilled. Other times they quoted it as a previous example,
a parallel situation. When King Herod slaughtered the baby boys in and around Bethlehem, Matthew called that atrocity a "fulfillment" of this passage. It was more of an emotional parallel, however, than a prediction come true. Jeremiah's passage mirrored the
same kind of intense grief that filled Bethlehem after Herod slaughtered the infants.

Jeremiah himself borrowed from Israel's history when he wrote these words. He recalled the experience of Rachel, Jacob's wife, to paint a picture of grief coming to the nation. Dying while in childbirth, Rachel had named her son, *son of my trouble;* Jacob re-
named him Benjamin, *son of my right hand* (Gen. 35:16–20). Jeremiah used this picture
to show that sorrow would come to the tribe of Benjamin. Figuratively, Rachel would weep
again when her descendants were killed and carried into captivity.

Matthew, then, borrowed this imagery again to draw a powerful picture of the terrible
sadness caused by Herod's decree.

for your work will be rewarded,"

> declares the LORD.

"They will return from the land of the
        enemy.
17So there is hope for your future,"

> declares the LORD.

"Your children will return to their own land.

18"I have surely heard Ephraim's moaning:
    'You disciplined me like an unruly calf,
    and I have been disciplined.
Restore me, and I will return,
    because you are the LORD my God.
19After I strayed,
    I repented[D];
after I came to understand,
    I beat my breast.
I was ashamed and humiliated
    because I bore the disgrace of my youth.'
20Is not Ephraim my dear son,
    the child in whom I delight?
Though I often speak against him,
    I still remember him.
Therefore my heart yearns for him;
    I have great compassion for him,"

> declares the LORD.

21"Set up road signs;
    put up guideposts.
Take note of the highway,
    the road that you take.
Return, O Virgin Israel,
    return to your towns.
22How long will you wander,
    O unfaithful daughter?
The LORD will create a new thing on earth—
    a woman will surround[a] a man."

23This is what the LORD Almighty, the God of Israel,
says: "When I bring them back from captivity,[b] the people in the land of Judah and in its towns will once again
use these words: 'The LORD bless you, O righteous[D]
dwelling, O sacred[D] mountain.' **24**People will live together in Judah and all its towns—farmers and those who
move about with their flocks. **25**I will refresh the weary
and satisfy the faint."

26At this I awoke and looked around. My sleep had been
pleasant to me.

27"The days are coming," declares the LORD, "when I
will plant the house of Israel and the house of Judah with
the offspring of men and of animals. **28**Just as I watched
over them to uproot and tear down, and to overthrow, destroy and bring disaster, so I will watch over them to build
and to plant," declares the LORD. **29**"In those days people
will no longer say,

'The fathers have eaten sour grapes,
    and the children's teeth are set on edge.'

30Instead, everyone will die for his own sin; whoever eats
sour grapes—his own teeth will be set on edge.

31"The time is coming," declares the LORD,
    "when I will make a new covenant[D]

**Virgin Israel . . . unfaithful daughter
(31:21–22)**
See *Virgin Israel* (18:13).

A woman will surround a man (31:22)
An alternate meaning of the word *surround* is
to "protect" or "care for" (see NIV text note). In
ancient Israelite culture, the men were expected to love and care for the women. Jeremiah's
new concept—that a woman could protect a
man—was a radical departure from the norm.
Many view this as a hint of what happened in
Christ's birth—when God came to be born of a
virgin. Others think the word simply suggests
the idea of love—that the *unfaithful daughter*
would love the LORD—a fairly novel happening
in Israel's history.

Was this proverb ever true? (31:29)
Not really. It was incorrectly based on the idea
that children do wrong because of their fathers' sins. Though children do suffer for their
parents' bad choices (Exodus 20:5; Num.
14:18), this proverb distorted the truth. Both
Jeremiah and Ezekiel (Ezek. 18:2) wanted the
people to stop using the proverb as an excuse
to avoid responsibility for their own sins. Sour
grapes pucker the mouths of those who eat
them, not those of anyone else (v. 30).

SCRIPTURE LINK (31:31–34)
This is quoted by the writer of Hebrews
(8:8–12; 10:16–17) to show that the new covenant sprang from the old. This is the longest
Old Testament passage quoted in the New Testament.

**Is the new covenant only for Israel and
Judah? (31:31)**
No, it is for all. But Jeremiah used concepts familiar to his audience. God had given the law
to Israel, so the people thought of God's actions on earth only in those terms. With the
law, they could define sin, but they had nothing
with which to cure sin (17:9). In fact, Israel
served as an object lesson to show other nations that something better than the law was
needed.

---

*a*22 Or *will go about ⌊seeking⌋; or will protect
their fortunes   *b*23 Or *I restore*

with the house of Israel
and with the house of Judah.
32It will not be like the covenant^D
I made with their forefathers
when I took them by the hand
to lead them out of Egypt,
because they broke my covenant,
though I was a husband to^a them,^b"
declares the LORD.

When will this promise be fulfilled for Israel? (31:33–34)
God's promises are fulfilled only for those faithful to the conditions of the promises. Just as the old covenant required obedience to the law, the new covenant requires surrender to Christ. Only then can God's laws be written on one's heart and mind. The promise is available for all who turn from sin and give themselves to Christ. Some have redefined *Israel* under the new covenant to mean not the nation or ethnic Jews, but the church of Christ—believers in Jesus (including both Jews and Gentiles).

33"This is the covenant I will make with the
house of Israel
after that time," declares the LORD.
"I will put my law in their minds
and write it on their hearts.
I will be their God,
and they will be my people.
34No longer will a man teach his neighbor,
or a man his brother, saying, 'Know the
LORD,'
because they will all know me,
from the least of them to the greatest,"
declares the LORD.
"For I will forgive their wickedness
and will remember their sins no more."

35This is what the LORD says,

he who appoints the sun
to shine by day,
who decrees the moon and stars
to shine by night,
who stirs up the sea
so that its waves roar—
the LORD Almighty is his name:
36"Only if these decrees vanish from my sight,"
declares the LORD,
"will the descendants of Israel ever cease
to be a nation before me."

Didn't Israel *cease to be a nation*? (31:36,40)
Though Israel was destroyed and taken into captivity, God preserved a remnant of his people. For centuries Jews have lived as foreigners in various places. Yet they have never lost their identity. As a "nation without a homeland" they were not assimilated completely to their host nations. Some believe modern Israel fulfills this promise. Others focus on the fact that God's people are those born spiritually into his kingdom, not those who are natural citizens of a certain country.

37This is what the LORD says:

"Only if the heavens above can be measured
and the foundations of the earth below be
searched out
will I reject all the descendants of Israel
because of all they have done,"
declares the LORD.

38"The days are coming," declares the LORD, "when this city will be rebuilt for me from the Tower of Hananel to the Corner Gate. **39**The measuring line^D will stretch from there straight to the hill of Gareb and then turn to Goah. **40**The whole valley where dead bodies and ashes are thrown, and all the terraces out to the Kidron Valley^D on the east as far as the corner of the Horse Gate, will be holy to the LORD. The city will never again be uprooted or demolished."

How would the garbage dump become holy? (31:40)
Jeremiah used graphic terms to demonstrate the dramatic purification of the nation. The Kidron Valley illustrated total corruption, probably since the time King Josiah dumped and burned idols there (2 Kings 23:6). But idolatry persisted even after Josiah's reform. Jeremiah's prophecy suggests that God would deal with the people and idolatry would finally be wiped out. After the Jews returned from Babylon, they never again became involved in idolatry. Also see *What had they done in the valley?* (2:23).

Jeremiah Buys a Field

32 This is the word that came to Jeremiah from the LORD in the tenth year of Zedekiah king of Judah, which was the eighteenth year of Nebuchadnezzar. **2**The army of the king of Babylon was then besieging Jerusa-

---

^a 32 Hebrew; Septuagint and Syriac / *and I turned away from*
^b 32 Or *was their master*

lem, and Jeremiah the prophet[D] was confined in the courtyard of the guard in the royal palace of Judah.

[3]Now Zedekiah king of Judah had imprisoned him there, saying, "Why do you prophesy as you do? You say, 'This is what the LORD says: I am about to hand this city over to the king of Babylon, and he will capture it. [4]Zedekiah king of Judah will not escape out of the hands of the Babylonians[a] but will certainly be handed over to the king of Babylon, and will speak with him face to face and see him with his own eyes. [5]He will take Zedekiah to Babylon, where he will remain until I deal with him, declares the LORD. If you fight against the Babylonians, you will not succeed.' "

[6]Jeremiah said, "The word of the LORD came to me: [7]Hanamel son of Shallum your uncle is going to come to you and say, 'Buy my field at Anathoth, because as nearest relative it is your right and duty to buy it.'

[8]"Then, just as the LORD had said, my cousin Hanamel came to me in the courtyard of the guard and said, 'Buy my field at Anathoth in the territory of Benjamin. Since it is your right to redeem[D] it and possess it, buy it for yourself.'

"I knew that this was the word of the LORD; [9]so I bought the field at Anathoth from my cousin Hanamel and weighed out for him seventeen shekels[Db] of silver. [10]I signed and sealed the deed, had it witnessed, and weighed out the silver on the scales. [11]I took the deed of purchase—the sealed copy containing the terms and conditions, as well as the unsealed copy— [12]and I gave this deed to Baruch son of Neriah, the son of Mahseiah, in the presence of my cousin Hanamel and of the witnesses who had signed the deed and of all the Jews[D] sitting in the courtyard of the guard.

[13]"In their presence I gave Baruch these instructions: [14]'This is what the LORD Almighty, the God of Israel, says: Take these documents, both the sealed and unsealed copies of the deed of purchase, and put them in a clay jar so they will last a long time. [15]For this is what the LORD Almighty, the God of Israel, says: Houses, fields and vineyards will again be bought in this land.'

[16]"After I had given the deed of purchase to Baruch son of Neriah, I prayed to the LORD:

[17]"Ah, Sovereign LORD, you have made the heavens and the earth by your great power and outstretched arm. Nothing is too hard for you. [18]You show love to thousands but bring the punishment for the fathers' sins into the laps of their children after them. O great and powerful God, whose name is the LORD Almighty, [19]great are your purposes and mighty are your deeds. Your eyes are open to all the ways of men; you reward everyone according to his conduct and as his deeds deserve. [20]You performed miraculous signs and wonders in Egypt and have continued them to this day, both in Israel and among all mankind, and have gained the renown that is still yours. [21]You brought your people Israel out of Egypt with signs and wonders, by a mighty hand and an outstretched arm and with great terror. [22]You gave them this land you had sworn to give their forefathers, a land flowing with milk and honey. [23]They came in and took

Why imprison a prophet? (32:3)

Zedekiah did not believe Jeremiah and punished him for speaking out against the king's policies. God's call on his life was one of hardship, not prosperity or fame. Over the course of his ministry, he was ridiculed, denounced, beaten and imprisoned. But he was absolutely committed to God, willing to pay the price to prophesy faithfully.

Why have two deeds? (32:11)

The sealed deed was perhaps the equivalent of a notarized deed today, the official document that would serve in a similar way to our registry of deeds. Probably the legal system of Jeremiah's day required two documents. One was seen and used more frequently; the other was preserved for safekeeping. Since it was sealed and could not be altered, the document could be used to settle any later disputes.

Why punish the children of sinners? (32:18)

In an imperfect world, many, through no fault of their own, suffer the consequences of others' actions. But affliction in this life does not necessarily mean punishment in eternity. Children are not eternally damned simply because they were born to ungodly parents. Also see *Why accuse innocent grandchildren?* (2:9).

What miracles had God done *among all mankind?* (32:20–33)

We have to understand this in terms of Israel's view of the world. *All mankind* to them meant neighboring nations, who had heard not only about the Egyptian plagues and the exodus, but also about the crossing of the Jordan River, the fall of Jericho and the destruction of Sennacherib's army. These were miracles by anyone's definition and gained the respect of other nations for the God of Israel (vv. 22–23).

[a]4 Or *Chaldeans*; also in verses 5, 24, 25, 28, 29 and 43   [b]9 That is, about 7 ounces (about 200 grams)

possession of it, but they did not obey you or follow your law; they did not do what you commanded them to do. So you brought all this disaster upon them.

24"See how the siege ramps are built up to take the city. Because of the sword, famine and plague, the city will be handed over to the Babylonians who are attacking it. What you said has happened, as you now see. 25And though the city will be handed over to the Babylonians, you, O Sovereign LORD, say to me, 'Buy the field with silver and have the transaction witnessed.' "

26Then the word of the LORD came to Jeremiah: 27"I am the LORD, the God of all mankind. Is anything too hard for me? 28Therefore, this is what the LORD says: I am about to hand this city over to the Babylonians and to Nebuchadnezzar king of Babylon, who will capture it. 29The Babylonians who are attacking this city will come in and set it on fire; they will burn it down, along with the houses where the people provoked me to anger by burning incenseᴰ on the roofs to Baalᴰ and by pouring out drink offeringsᴰ to other gods.

30"The people of Israel and Judah have done nothing but evil in my sight from their youth; indeed, the people of Israel have done nothing but provoke me with what their hands have made, declares the LORD. 31From the day it was built until now, this city has so aroused my anger and wrath that I must remove it from my sight. 32The people of Israel and Judah have provoked me by all the evil they have done—they, their kings and officials, their priestsᴰ and prophetsᴰ, the men of Judah and the people of Jerusalemᴰ. 33They turned their backs to me and not their faces; though I taught them again and again, they would not listen or respond to discipline. 34They set up their abominable idolsᴰ in the house that bears my Name and defiled it. 35They built high placesᴰ for Baal in the Valley of Ben Hinnom to sacrificeᴰ their sons and daughtersᵃ to Molechᴰ, though I never commanded, nor did it enter my mind, that they should do such a detestable thing and so make Judah sin.

36"You are saying about this city, 'By the sword, famine and plague it will be handed over to the king of Babylon'; but this is what the LORD, the God of Israel, says: 37I will surely gather them from all the lands where I banish them in my furious anger and great wrath; I will bring them back to this place and let them live in safety. 38They will be my people, and I will be their God. 39I will give them singleness of heart and action, so that they will always fear me for their own good and the good of their children after them. 40I will make an everlasting covenantᴰ with them: I will never stop doing good to them, and I will inspire them to fear me, so that they will never turn away from me. 41I will rejoice in doing them good and will assuredly plant them in this land with all my heart and soulᴰ.

42"This is what the LORD says: As I have brought all this great calamity on this people, so I will give them all the prosperity I have promised them. 43Once more fields will be bought in this land of which you say, 'It is a desolate waste, without men or animals, for it has been handed over to the Babylonians.' 44Fields will be bought for silver,

Ben Hinnom (32:35)
See *Topheth . . . Valley of Ben Hinnom* (19:6).

Molech (32:35)
One of many pagan gods mentioned in the Old Testament. Baal, meaning *lord* or *master,* was a more generic word. Any god could be called Baal. Some think Molech similarly could mean *the king.* Molech was probably the central Ammonite god, known in Moab as Chemosh. The worship of both Molech and Chemosh often involved child sacrifice (see 7:31). Also see *Why would parents sacrifice their children?* (19:5).

Why make the Israelites into something they weren't? (32:39)
The Israelites needed divine help to break free from their sinful habits. And God used their captivity in Babylon to do just that. There they found themselves surrounded by impotent pagan gods and they began to desire again the God of Israel. After a number of them returned to Israel years later, they never again worshiped idols. Some speculate that synagogue worship, begun during the exile, may have helped them in their devotion to God.

ᵃ35 Or *to make their sons and daughters pass through ⌊the fire⌋*

and deeds will be signed, sealed and witnessed in the territory of Benjamin, in the villages around Jerusalem[D], in
the towns of Judah and in the towns of the hill country,
of the western foothills and of the Negev[D], because I will
restore their fortunes,[a] declares the LORD."

Promise of Restoration

33 While Jeremiah was still confined in the courtyard
of the guard, the word of the LORD came to him a
second time: [2]"This is what the LORD says, he who made
the earth, the LORD who formed it and established it—the
LORD is his name: [3]'Call to me and I will answer you and
tell you great and unsearchable things you do not know.'
[4]For this is what the LORD, the God of Israel, says about
the houses in this city and the royal palaces of Judah that
have been torn down to be used against the siege ramps
and the sword [5]in the fight with the Babylonians[b]: 'They
will be filled with the dead bodies of the men I will slay
in my anger and wrath. I will hide my face from this city
because of all its wickedness.

[6]" 'Nevertheless, I will bring health and healing to it; I
will heal my people and will let them enjoy abundant
peace[D] and security. [7]I will bring Judah and Israel back
from captivity[c] and will rebuild them as they were before. [8]I will cleanse them from all the sin they have committed against me and will forgive all their sins of rebellion against me. [9]Then this city will bring me renown, joy,
praise and honor before all nations on earth that hear of
all the good things I do for it; and they will be in awe and
will tremble at the abundant prosperity and peace I provide for it.'

[10]"This is what the LORD says: 'You say about this place,
"It is a desolate waste, without men or animals." Yet in the
towns of Judah and the streets of Jerusalem that are deserted, inhabited by neither men nor animals, there will
be heard once more [11]the sounds of joy and gladness, the
voices of bride and bridegroom, and the voices of those
who bring thank offerings[D] to the house of the LORD, saying,

> "Give thanks to the LORD Almighty,
>   for the LORD is good;
>   his love endures forever."

For I will restore the fortunes of the land as they were before,' says the LORD.

[12]"This is what the LORD Almighty says: 'In this place,
desolate and without men or animals—in all its towns
there will again be pastures for shepherds to rest their
flocks. [13]In the towns of the hill country, of the western
foothills and of the Negev, in the territory of Benjamin,
in the villages around Jerusalem and in the towns of Judah, flocks will again pass under the hand of the one who
counts them,' says the LORD.

[14]" 'The days are coming,' declares the LORD, 'when I
will fulfill the gracious promise I made to the house of Israel and to the house of Judah.

[15]" 'In those days and at that time
    I will make a righteous[D] Branch sprout from
        David's line;
    he will do what is just and right in the land.

How did shepherds count their flocks under the hand? (33:13)

Accurate counts were probably difficult to obtain. This explains why large numbers of sheep
in the Old Testament often appear to be rounded off (for example, Num. 31:32; Job 1:3). A
good place for counting sheep was the watering hole, where the sheep would be bunched
together at least once per day.

---

[a]44 Or *will bring them back from captivity*   [b]5 Or *Chaldeans*
[c]7 Or *will restore the fortunes of Judah and Israel*

What kind of safety was offered for the city of Jerusalem? (33:16)

This promise, like others in Jeremiah, came with conditions: it was offered to those who would allow the *righteous Branch* (v. 15) to rule over them. This was a prophecy of a future Messiah whose kingdom would not be of this earth. He would offer spiritual safety to all whose hearts belonged to him.

Why call a city *The Lord Our Righteousness?* (33:16)

In Jeremiah's culture names were used to describe someone's characteristics, not just to label or identify a person. See *Why pray to protect God's good name?* (14:7). This prophecy tells of a time when a righteous Jerusalem will honor the name of the Lord by mirroring his characteristics.

Do priests still make sacrifices? (33:18)

This prophecy failed to be fulfilled—in the way the people of Israel expected. But Jeremiah's promise for the future, put in terms they could understand, has been fulfilled in another way. Though the blood of bulls and goats cannot atone for sin (Heb. 10:4), Jesus Christ can. He *offered for all time one sacrifice for sins* (Heb. 10:12; see Heb. 7:27; 10:10–12). He stands continually before God, offering a perpetual sacrifice for sin—the priest and mediator between God and man.

How could there be a countless number of ministering Levites? (33:22)

The Old Testament priesthood called for Levites to stand as intermediaries between God and the people. But the New Testament introduced a new priesthood—believers would be the new Levites. Every believer may enter the presence of God directly because Jesus—the great high priest (Heb. 4:14)—opened the way. Believers enjoy a better priesthood—an intimate and personal relationship with God—than was ever known by the Old Testament priests.

Why did nations conquered by Nebuchadnezzar fight against Jerusalem? (34:1)

Powerful nations demanded both tribute and allegiance of those they conquered. It was advisable for a subjected people to comply with the wishes of their overlord. It was far better to aid the eventual victor than to oppose him. Another reason some were so willing to fight against Jerusalem may have stemmed from Israel's rivalry with her neighbors. With no love lost between them, Israel's neighbors would have been glad to see Israel defeated.

¹⁶In those days Judah will be saved
    and Jerusalem^D will live in safety.
This is the name by which it^a will be called:
    The LORD Our Righteousness^D.'

¹⁷For this is what the LORD says: 'David will never fail to have a man to sit on the throne of the house of Israel, ¹⁸nor will the priests^D, who are Levites^D, ever fail to have a man to stand before me continually to offer burnt offerings^D, to burn grain offerings^D and to present sacrifices^D.' "

¹⁹The word of the LORD came to Jeremiah: ²⁰"This is what the LORD says: 'If you can break my covenant^D with the day and my covenant with the night, so that day and night no longer come at their appointed time, ²¹then my covenant with David my servant—and my covenant with the Levites who are priests ministering before me—can be broken and David will no longer have a descendant to reign on his throne. ²²I will make the descendants of David my servant and the Levites who minister before me as countless as the stars of the sky and as measureless as the sand on the seashore.' "

²³The word of the LORD came to Jeremiah: ²⁴"Have you not noticed that these people are saying, 'The LORD has rejected the two kingdoms^b he chose'? So they despise my people and no longer regard them as a nation. ²⁵This is what the LORD says: 'If I have not established my covenant with day and night and the fixed laws of heaven and earth, ²⁶then I will reject the descendants of Jacob and David my servant and will not choose one of his sons to rule over the descendants of Abraham, Isaac and Jacob. For I will restore their fortunes^c and have compassion on them.' "

Warning to Zedekiah

34 While Nebuchadnezzar king of Babylon and all his army and all the kingdoms and peoples in the empire he ruled were fighting against Jerusalem and all its surrounding towns, this word came to Jeremiah from the LORD: ²"This is what the LORD, the God of Israel, says: Go to Zedekiah king of Judah and tell him, 'This is what the LORD says: I am about to hand this city over to the king of Babylon, and he will burn it down. ³You will not escape from his grasp but will surely be captured and handed over to him. You will see the king of Babylon with your own eyes, and he will speak with you face to face. And you will go to Babylon.

⁴" 'Yet hear the promise of the LORD, O Zedekiah king of Judah. This is what the LORD says concerning you: You will not die by the sword; ⁵you will die peacefully. As people made a funeral fire in honor of your fathers, the former kings who preceded you, so they will make a fire in your honor and lament^D, "Alas, O master!" I myself make this promise, declares the LORD.' "

⁶Then Jeremiah the prophet^D told all this to Zedekiah king of Judah, in Jerusalem, ⁷while the army of the king of Babylon was fighting against Jerusalem and the other cities of Judah that were still holding out—Lachish and Azekah. These were the only fortified cities left in Judah.

---

^a16 Or he   ^b24 Or families   ^c26 Or *will bring them back from captivity*

Freedom for Slaves

8The word came to Jeremiah from the LORD after King Zedekiah had made a covenant^D with all the people in Jerusalem^D to proclaim freedom for the slaves. **9**Everyone was to free his Hebrew^D slaves, both male and female; no one was to hold a fellow Jew^D in bondage. **10**So all the officials and people who entered into this covenant agreed that they would free their male and female slaves and no longer hold them in bondage. They agreed, and set them free. **11**But afterward they changed their minds and took back the slaves they had freed and enslaved them again.

12Then the word of the LORD came to Jeremiah: **13**"This is what the LORD, the God of Israel, says: I made a covenant with your forefathers when I brought them out of Egypt, out of the land of slavery. I said, **14**'Every seventh year each of you must free any fellow Hebrew who has sold himself to you. After he has served you six years, you must let him go free.'*a* Your fathers, however, did not listen to me or pay attention to me. **15**Recently you repented^D and did what is right in my sight: Each of you proclaimed freedom to his countrymen. You even made a covenant before me in the house that bears my Name. **16**But now you have turned around and profaned^D my name; each of you has taken back the male and female slaves you had set free to go where they wished. You have forced them to become your slaves again.

17"Therefore, this is what the LORD says: You have not obeyed me; you have not proclaimed freedom for your fellow countrymen. So I now proclaim 'freedom' for you, declares the LORD—'freedom' to fall by the sword, plague and famine. I will make you abhorrent to all the kingdoms of the earth. **18**The men who have violated my covenant and have not fulfilled the terms of the covenant they made before me, I will treat like the calf they cut in two and then walked between its pieces. **19**The leaders of Judah and Jerusalem, the court officials, the priests and all the people of the land who walked between the pieces of the calf, **20**I will hand over to their enemies who seek their lives. Their dead bodies will become food for the birds of the air and the beasts of the earth.

21"I will hand Zedekiah king of Judah and his officials over to their enemies who seek their lives, to the army of the king of Babylon, which has withdrawn from you. **22**I am going to give the order, declares the LORD, and I will bring them back to this city. They will fight against it, take it and burn it down. And I will lay waste the towns of Judah so no one can live there."

The Recabites

35 This is the word that came to Jeremiah from the LORD during the reign of Jehoiakim son of Josiah king of Judah: **2**"Go to the Recabite family and invite them to come to one of the side rooms of the house of the LORD and give them wine to drink."

3So I went to get Jaazaniah son of Jeremiah, the son of Habazziniah, and his brothers and all his sons—the whole family of the Recabites. **4**I brought them into the house of the LORD, into the room of the sons of Hanan son of Igdaliah the man of God. It was next to the room of the officials, which was over that of Maaseiah son of Shallum the door-

*a*14 Deut. 15:12

How could they repossess their freed slaves? (34:8–11)

By law no Jew was to remain in bondage more than six years. But the wealthy and influential apparently ignored this command after King Josiah's death (609 B.C.). Threatened by Babylon, King Zedekiah freed the slaves in an attempt to gain favor with God. But when the Babylonians lifted their siege to deal with an Egyptian offensive (588 B.C.), the former slave owners felt they could return to life as usual. They probably used their wealth and political clout to put the indentured workers back into bondage.

How did they profane the name of the Lord? (34:16)

God desired to liberate, not enslave his people. His nature is to release captives; sin's nature is to put people in bondage. Since the name of the Lord represents his character, to attack his character, whether by word or deed, was to profane his name. Because Jeremiah's countrymen lived in a way contrary to the nature of God, they profaned his name and corrupted his character.

Why walk between the halves of a slaughtered calf? (34:18)

In ancient times covenants were often made by sacrificing an animal and dividing it along the spine. The parties to the covenant would then walk between the halves and meet in the middle to take their solemn oath. Many think the custom implied that if either party violated the terms of the covenant, then he should be cut in two just as the sacrifice had been. Some believe God was promising judgment because the people had broken their covenant with him. See *Why cut animals in half?* (Gen. 15:10).

Is this chapter out of sequence? (35:1)

It's true that the events of ch. 35 occurred before those in ch. 34. Jehoiakim was king from 609 to 598 B.C. Zedekiah was king from 597 to 587 B.C. The writers and editors of Hebrew Scripture were concerned mainly about their message. They didn't worry about chronology as much as we do. It might help us to view this as a literary technique, a "flashback." See *How did Jeremiah get caught after being released?* (40:1).

Why did Jonadab make these unusual rules? (35:6–7)

Some think Jonadab, who lived nearly three centuries earlier, intended only that his descendants preserve their nomadic lifestyle. They were to live in tents, not houses; they were to travel with their livestock, not plant and care for gardens. Perhaps he thought the allure of wine would cause his descendants to settle down and plant vineyards.

Why were the Recabites so faithful? (35:8–16)

They probably recognized the wisdom of Jonadab's counsel. Their nomadic traditions helped them survive in a dry climate where raising crops on scarce rainfall was risky business. The lack of water kept them on the move, searching for pasture for their flocks. As nomads they lived in tents and lacked many typical elements of other societies, so their traditions became the primary glue that held them together. By contrast, the Israelites had less respect for God's written law than the Recabites had for human traditions.

How could God guarantee that Jonadab's descendants would remain faithful? (35:19)

Many promises that seem absolute actually have unspoken conditions attached to them. Promises are fulfilled when people obey God. With that in mind, it's significant to note that in order to worship the Lord, Jonadab, who was not a Jew, had to convert from paganism. The God of Israel was not Israel's exclusive property. Still, it's likely that the fortunes of the Recabites were hinged to the fortunes of Judah. When Judah was destroyed, the Recabites were also decimated. But, as he had promised Israel, God promised the Recabites that they too would have a surviving remnant.

Is God responsible for disasters? (36:3)

God frequently has used distress or calamity as a means of judgment. But God often judges with redemption in mind; he wants people in trouble to turn to him for help. This does not necessarily mean that God orchestrates disasters. They can occur simply as the result of random events (see Matt. 5:45). Still, even random disasters can be used by God for his own purposes.

What did scribes do in Jeremiah's day? (36:4)

Though much is known about scribes from Ezra's time and following, information on earlier periods is limited. Baruch was apparently Jeremiah's friend and assistant in his work. Much of what he did seemed to be secretarial or administrative work. Baruch remained loyal to Jeremiah, even when Jeremiah was later forced to go to Egypt (43:6).

keeper. **5**Then I set bowls full of wine and some cups before the men of the Recabite family and said to them, "Drink some wine."

6But they replied, "We do not drink wine, because our forefather Jonadab son of Recab gave us this command: 'Neither you nor your descendants must ever drink wine. **7**Also you must never build houses, sow seed or plant vineyards; you must never have any of these things, but must always live in tents. Then you will live a long time in the land where you are nomads.' **8**We have obeyed everything our forefather Jonadab son of Recab commanded us. Neither we nor our wives nor our sons and daughters have ever drunk wine **9**or built houses to live in or had vineyards, fields or crops. **10**We have lived in tents and have fully obeyed everything our forefather Jonadab commanded us. **11**But when Nebuchadnezzar king of Babylon invaded this land, we said, 'Come, we must go to Jerusalem*D* to escape the Babylonian*a* and Aramean armies.' So we have remained in Jerusalem."

12Then the word of the LORD came to Jeremiah, saying: **13**"This is what the LORD Almighty, the God of Israel, says: Go and tell the men of Judah and the people of Jerusalem, 'Will you not learn a lesson and obey my words?' declares the LORD. **14**Jonadab son of Recab ordered his sons not to drink wine and this command has been kept. To this day they do not drink wine, because they obey their forefather's command. But I have spoken to you again and again, yet you have not obeyed me. **15**Again and again I sent all my servants the prophets*D* to you. They said, "Each of you must turn from your wicked ways and reform your actions; do not follow other gods to serve them. Then you will live in the land I have given to you and your fathers." But you have not paid attention or listened to me. **16**The descendants of Jonadab son of Recab have carried out the command their forefather gave them, but these people have not obeyed me.'

17"Therefore, this is what the LORD God Almighty, the God of Israel, says: 'Listen! I am going to bring on Judah and on everyone living in Jerusalem every disaster I pronounced against them. I spoke to them, but they did not listen; I called to them, but they did not answer.' "

18Then Jeremiah said to the family of the Recabites, "This is what the LORD Almighty, the God of Israel, says: 'You have obeyed the command of your forefather Jonadab and have followed all his instructions and have done everything he ordered.' **19**Therefore, this is what the LORD Almighty, the God of Israel, says: 'Jonadab son of Recab will never fail to have a man to serve me.' "

Jehoiakim Burns Jeremiah's Scroll

36 In the fourth year of Jehoiakim son of Josiah king of Judah, this word came to Jeremiah from the LORD: **2**"Take a scroll and write on it all the words I have spoken to you concerning Israel, Judah and all the other nations from the time I began speaking to you in the reign of Josiah till now. **3**Perhaps when the people of Judah hear about every disaster I plan to inflict on them, each of them will turn from his wicked way; then I will forgive their wickedness and their sin."

4So Jeremiah called Baruch son of Neriah, and while Jeremiah dictated all the words the LORD had spoken to him, Baruch wrote them on the scroll. **5**Then Jeremiah

a 11 Or Chaldean

told Baruch, "I am restricted; I cannot go to the LORD's temple. **6**So you go to the house of the LORD on a day of fasting and read to the people from the scroll the words of the LORD that you wrote as I dictated. Read them to all the people of Judah who come in from their towns. **7**Perhaps they will bring their petition before the LORD, and each will turn from his wicked ways, for the anger and wrath pronounced against this people by the LORD are great."

8Baruch son of Neriah did everything Jeremiah the prophet[D] told him to do; at the LORD's temple he read the words of the LORD from the scroll. **9**In the ninth month of the fifth year of Jehoiakim son of Josiah king of Judah, a time of fasting before the LORD was proclaimed for all the people in Jerusalem[D] and those who had come from the towns of Judah. **10**From the room of Gemariah son of Shaphan the secretary, which was in the upper courtyard at the entrance of the New Gate of the temple, Baruch read to all the people at the LORD's temple the words of Jeremiah from the scroll.

11When Micaiah son of Gemariah, the son of Shaphan, heard all the words of the LORD from the scroll, **12**he went down to the secretary's room in the royal palace, where all the officials were sitting: Elishama the secretary, Delaiah son of Shemaiah, Elnathan son of Acbor, Gemariah son of Shaphan, Zedekiah son of Hananiah, and all the other officials. **13**After Micaiah told them everything he had heard Baruch read to the people from the scroll, **14**all the officials sent Jehudi son of Nethaniah, the son of Shelemiah, the son of Cushi, to say to Baruch, "Bring the scroll from which you have read to the people and come." So Baruch son of Neriah went to them with the scroll in his hand. **15**They said to him, "Sit down, please, and read it to us."

So Baruch read it to them. **16**When they heard all these words, they looked at each other in fear and said to Baruch, "We must report all these words to the king." **17**Then they asked Baruch, "Tell us, how did you come to write all this? Did Jeremiah dictate it?"

18"Yes," Baruch replied, "he dictated all these words to me, and I wrote them in ink on the scroll."

19Then the officials said to Baruch, "You and Jeremiah, go and hide. Don't let anyone know where you are."

20After they put the scroll in the room of Elishama the secretary, they went to the king in the courtyard and reported everything to him. **21**The king sent Jehudi to get the scroll, and Jehudi brought it from the room of Elishama the secretary and read it to the king and all the officials standing beside him. **22**It was the ninth month and the king was sitting in the winter apartment, with a fire burning in the firepot in front of him. **23**Whenever Jehudi had read three or four columns of the scroll, the king cut them off with a scribe's knife and threw them into the firepot, until the entire scroll was burned in the fire. **24**The king and all his attendants who heard all these words showed no fear, nor did they tear their clothes. **25**Even though Elnathan, Delaiah and Gemariah urged the king not to burn the scroll, he would not listen to them. **26**Instead, the king commanded Jerahmeel, a son of the king, Seraiah son of Azriel and Shelemiah son of Abdeel to arrest Baruch the scribe and Jeremiah the prophet. But the LORD had hidden them.

27After the king burned the scroll containing the words that Baruch had written at Jeremiah's dictation, the word

How was Jeremiah restricted? (36:5)

The Law of Moses never provided for anyone to be locked up as punishment. In their migrating, nomadic society, some were occasionally banished from the camp or ostracized outside the community. But when Israel settled down in the promised land, some things changed. Prisons and restrictions on activities or travel were introduced. Perhaps Jeremiah was prevented from traveling or speaking publicly. On other occasions, we are told specifically that he was imprisoned (for example, 37:15).

Who proclaimed a fast? (36:9)

Though their commitment to the Lord had been half-hearted at best, the people called out to God for help, apparently sensing that calamity was imminent. Most likely the temple priests made the official proclamation, with the backing of King Jehoiakim. Since judgment came despite their pleas to God, their repentance was probably more self-serving than genuine.

How did all the people fit in one room? (36:10)

There were probably not very many who gathered to hear Baruch. The main part of Solomon's temple was not that large. (Zerubbabel's temple after the exile was about twice as large, Herod's four times.) We don't know whether Baruch spoke from a balcony off a room, or from a platform or a lectern. But the impact of the message caused a ripple effect. Many more heard it second-hand from those who had heard Baruch (see 36:13–15).

Winter apartment . . . firepot (36:22)

Winter in Jerusalem can be cold enough for snow to fall occasionally. Ancient construction generally lacked adequate heating. People in larger houses would typically live in the rooms best protected from the cold. For extra heat, they burned wood or perhaps charcoal in firepots, similar to potbellied stoves without chimneys. Firepots may have been open on top.

Scribe's knife (36:23)

Besides ink, parchment and quills (large feathers), knives were an essential part of a scribe's supplies. Scribes cut the tip of the quill at an angle to form a point, then dipped it in the ink to write on the parchment. When the point wore down or broke, the knife was used to cut a new point on the quill.

of the LORD came to Jeremiah: **28**"Take another scroll and write on it all the words that were on the first scroll, which Jehoiakim king of Judah burned up. **29**Also tell Jehoiakim king of Judah, 'This is what the LORD says: You burned that scroll and said, "Why did you write on it that the king of Babylon would certainly come and destroy this land and cut off both men and animals from it?" **30**Therefore, this is what the LORD says about Jehoiakim king of Judah: He will have no one to sit on the throne of David; his body will be thrown out and exposed to the heat by day and the frost by night. **31**I will punish him and his children and his attendants for their wickedness; I will bring on them and those living in Jerusalem[D] and the people of Judah every disaster I pronounced against them, because they have not listened.' "

32So Jeremiah took another scroll and gave it to the scribe Baruch son of Neriah, and as Jeremiah dictated, Baruch wrote on it all the words of the scroll that Jehoiakim king of Judah had burned in the fire. And many similar words were added to them.

Jeremiah in Prison

37 Zedekiah son of Josiah was made king of Judah by Nebuchadnezzar king of Babylon; he reigned in place of Jehoiachin[a] son of Jehoiakim. **2**Neither he nor his attendants nor the people of the land paid any attention to the words the LORD had spoken through Jeremiah the prophet[D].

3King Zedekiah, however, sent Jehucal son of Shelemiah with the priest[D] Zephaniah son of Maaseiah to Jeremiah the prophet with this message: "Please pray to the LORD our God for us."

4Now Jeremiah was free to come and go among the people, for he had not yet been put in prison. **5**Pharaoh's army had marched out of Egypt, and when the Babylonians[b] who were besieging Jerusalem heard the report about them, they withdrew from Jerusalem.

6Then the word of the LORD came to Jeremiah the prophet: **7**"This is what the LORD, the God of Israel, says: Tell the king of Judah, who sent you to inquire of me, 'Pharaoh's army, which has marched out to support you, will go back to its own land, to Egypt. **8**Then the Babylonians will return and attack this city; they will capture it and burn it down.'

9"This is what the LORD says: Do not deceive yourselves, thinking, 'The Babylonians will surely leave us.' They will not! **10**Even if you were to defeat the entire Babylonian[c] army that is attacking you and only wounded men were left in their tents, they would come out and burn this city down."

11After the Babylonian army had withdrawn from Jerusalem because of Pharaoh's army, **12**Jeremiah started to leave the city to go to the territory of Benjamin to get his share of the property among the people there. **13**But when he reached the Benjamin Gate, the captain of the guard, whose name was Irijah son of Shelemiah, the son of Hananiah, arrested him and said, "You are deserting to the Babylonians!"

14"That's not true!" Jeremiah said. "I am not deserting to the Babylonians." But Irijah would not listen to him; instead, he arrested Jeremiah and brought him to the offi-

---

Why would a wicked king want prayer? (37:3)

He may have considered prayer his last resort. As he saw trouble drawing nearer, King Zedekiah probably panicked. He may have felt it would be better to have Jeremiah, whom he didn't like, praying for him than to have no one praying at all. Zedekiah apparently became more receptive to spiritual matters in the face of looming judgment.

Why did Jeremiah want property in the territory of Benjamin? (37:12)

The Israelites considered it sacrilegious to let a title for land slip into the hands of non-family members. If someone was forced to sell, relatives were given the first option. Jeremiah may have felt obliged to buy land from a financially strapped family member. More likely though, Jeremiah hoped to offer tangible proof that he believed Israel would one day be restored to the land. This incident may be linked to the events in 32:9, but this cannot be shown clearly.

Vaulted cell (37:16)

After being held temporarily in a renovated house (v. 15), Jeremiah was put in a dungeon (literally, *house of the cistern*). It may have been a large underground room that looked similar to a cistern but had been prepared especially to house prisoners. If it had windows, they were too high off the floor to be reached. Later Jeremiah was imprisoned in a literal cistern made to hold water, not prisoners (38:6).

---

*a*1 Hebrew *Coniah*, a variant of *Jehoiachin*   *b*5 Or *Chaldeans*; also in verses 8, 9, 13 and 14   *c*10 Or *Chaldean*; also in verse 11

cials. **15**They were angry with Jeremiah and had him beaten and imprisoned in the house of Jonathan the secretary, which they had made into a prison.

16Jeremiah was put into a vaulted cell in a dungeon, where he remained a long time. **17**Then King Zedekiah sent for him and had him brought to the palace, where he asked him privately, "Is there any word from the LORD?"

"Yes," Jeremiah replied, "you will be handed over to the king of Babylon."

18Then Jeremiah said to King Zedekiah, "What crime have I committed against you or your officials or this people, that you have put me in prison? **19**Where are your prophets^D who prophesied to you, 'The king of Babylon will not attack you or this land'? **20**But now, my lord the king, please listen. Let me bring my petition before you: Do not send me back to the house of Jonathan the secretary, or I will die there."

21King Zedekiah then gave orders for Jeremiah to be placed in the courtyard of the guard and given bread from the street of the bakers each day until all the bread in the city was gone. So Jeremiah remained in the courtyard of the guard.

Jeremiah Thrown Into a Cistern

38 Shephatiah son of Mattan, Gedaliah son of Pashhur, Jehucal^a son of Shelemiah, and Pashhur son of Malkijah heard what Jeremiah was telling all the people when he said, **2**"This is what the LORD says: 'Whoever stays in this city will die by the sword, famine or plague, but whoever goes over to the Babylonians^b will live. He will escape with his life; he will live.' **3**And this is what the LORD says: 'This city will certainly be handed over to the army of the king of Babylon, who will capture it.' "

4Then the officials said to the king, "This man should be put to death^D. He is discouraging the soldiers who are left in this city, as well as all the people, by the things he is saying to them. This man is not seeking the good of these people but their ruin."

5"He is in your hands," King Zedekiah answered. "The king can do nothing to oppose you."

6So they took Jeremiah and put him into the cistern^D of Malkijah, the king's son, which was in the courtyard of the guard. They lowered Jeremiah by ropes into the cistern; it had no water in it, only mud, and Jeremiah sank down into the mud.

7But Ebed-Melech, a Cushite,^c an official^d in the royal palace, heard that they had put Jeremiah into the cistern. While the king was sitting in the Benjamin Gate, **8**Ebed-Melech went out of the palace and said to him, **9**"My lord the king, these men have acted wickedly in all they have done to Jeremiah the prophet. They have thrown him into a cistern, where he will starve to death when there is no longer any bread in the city."

10Then the king commanded Ebed-Melech the Cushite, "Take thirty men from here with you and lift Jeremiah the prophet out of the cistern before he dies."

11So Ebed-Melech took the men with him and went to a room under the treasury in the palace. He took some old rags and worn-out clothes from there and let them down with ropes to Jeremiah in the cistern. **12**Ebed-Melech

---

Courtyard of the guard (37:21)

Shortly before Jerusalem's fall in 586 B.C., the city was in severe difficulty because of the siege imposed by the Babylonians. Everyone was restricted because of the dangerous circumstances. Jeremiah was apparently kept under a type of house arrest, confined to an area policed by the guard. In times of war, this kind of detainment was commonly used by military powers.

How could Jeremiah preach while confined? (38:1)

Jeremiah was probably free to wander throughout the courtyard. Many others may have also been in the courtyard. Some, like Jeremiah, may have been there under detention. Others would have been free to come and go as they pleased. Jeremiah probably spoke to anyone who would listen to him, although not as a pulpit preacher. He simply told people what God was telling him, perhaps talking to one person at a time.

Why sound like a traitor? (38:2–3)

Jeremiah saw correctly that God was using the Babylonians to punish Israel for her spiritual rebellion. If that was true, then simple logic said that anyone who resisted the Babylonians was, in reality, fighting against God. Jeremiah had to speak the truth regardless of the outcome. Unfortunately, the king and his supporters, more concerned about morale than truth, wouldn't listen.

Why surrender to a wicked nation? (38:2–3)

Jeremiah saw the national crisis in simple terms: surrender to the Babylonians meant surrender to God and his method—perplexing though it was—of purifying the nation. He knew the choice was painful, but he also knew it was the best option they had. To resist cruel and wicked Babylon was to resist the holy God of Israel. Jeremiah saw Nebuchadnezzar merely as God's tool to bring about Israel's redemption. Also see *Why call a pagan king God's servant?* (27:6).

Who was in charge here? (38:5)

Zedekiah may have been at least partially receptive to Jeremiah's message. He had asked for Jeremiah's prayers (37:3) and had secretly consulted with him (37:17). But even though he was king, his power depended on the support of close associates. Without them, he had no political future, so he may have felt compelled to maintain the party line. Another view is that Zedekiah, frustrated with Jeremiah, simply was saying he didn't think it really mattered what they might do. No one, not even the king, could get Jeremiah to change.

Cistern (38:6)

See *Cisterns* (14:3).

Why was a foreigner an official in Judah? (38:7)

It was apparently a common practice to recruit foreign advisers. Sometimes it may have been done to reduce the likelihood of a palace coup from the king's relatives. The word *official* may have meant *eunuch* (see NIV text note). Castrated males with no family ambitions were less inclined to initiate political insurrection. Later the word *eunuch* became less specific. It meant *court official* so often that it was not always understood in the technical sense of an emasculated male.

---

^a1 Hebrew *Jucal,* a variant of *Jehucal*   ^b2 Or *Chaldeans;* also in verses 18, 19 and 23   ^c7 Probably from the upper Nile region   ^d7 Or *a eunuch*

Why was a foreigner so concerned about Jeremiah? (38:9)

Many who were not themselves descendants of Jacob feared the God of Israel. Ruth, a Moabitess, is one example, as is Jonadab, the Recabite. See *How could God guarantee that Jonadab's descendants would remain faithful?* (35:19). Ebed-Melech worshiped the Lord and respected Jeremiah as a prophet of the Lord (see 39:18). Unlike others who were afraid to speak up in the face of adversity, Ebed-Melech's concern for justice prompted him to talk to the king on Jeremiah's behalf.

Why did it take 30 men to lift out one? (38:10)

We don't really know. Some think a scribe may have added the sign for "tens" by mistake— changing the number from 3 to 30. Though some translations say *three*, there is no textual evidence to support this idea. Another explanation may be that Jeremiah, sunken deep into the muck on the bottom of the cistern and weighted down with mud, required more effort to be removed than one would expect. More likely, however, the larger number of men was to ensure that their efforts would not be thwarted by Jeremiah's opponents.

Why had some Jews joined the Babylonians? (38:19)

It is quite likely that many Jews surrendered to the Babylonians because of Jeremiah's message. But under such dire circumstances, some may have surrendered because it was the sensible thing to do. It offered hope of eventually being freed; resisting Babylon, though, was hopeless. As it turned out, the descendants of some who surrendered later returned to Israel. The king feared that those who had surrendered might try to take out their anger on him. His policies of holding out against the Babylonians had caused great destruction.

Was Jeremiah involved in a cover-up? (38:27)

It's likely that Jeremiah answered truthfully without divulging everything. He had no obligation to tell everything he'd discussed with the king, so he told only enough to answer their questions (v. 26). For a further discussion on similar ethical dilemmas, see *Is lying ever okay?* (Exodus 1:19–20).

the Cushite said to Jeremiah, "Put these old rags and worn-out clothes under your arms to pad the ropes." Jeremiah did so, **13**and they pulled him up with the ropes and lifted him out of the cistern.D And Jeremiah remained in the courtyard of the guard.

Zedekiah Questions Jeremiah Again

14Then King Zedekiah sent for Jeremiah the prophetD and had him brought to the third entrance to the temple of the LORD. "I am going to ask you something," the king said to Jeremiah. "Do not hide anything from me."

15Jeremiah said to Zedekiah, "If I give you an answer, will you not kill me? Even if I did give you counsel, you would not listen to me."

16But King Zedekiah swore this oath secretly to Jeremiah: "As surely as the LORD lives, who has given us breath, I will neither kill you nor hand you over to those who are seeking your life."

17Then Jeremiah said to Zedekiah, "This is what the LORD God Almighty, the God of Israel, says: 'If you surrender to the officers of the king of Babylon, your life will be spared and this city will not be burned down; you and your family will live. **18**But if you will not surrender to the officers of the king of Babylon, this city will be handed over to the Babylonians and they will burn it down; you yourself will not escape from their hands.' "

19King Zedekiah said to Jeremiah, "I am afraid of the JewsD who have gone over to the Babylonians, for the Babylonians may hand me over to them and they will mistreat me."

20"They will not hand you over," Jeremiah replied. "Obey the LORD by doing what I tell you. Then it will go well with you, and your life will be spared. **21**But if you refuse to surrender, this is what the LORD has revealed to me: **22**All the women left in the palace of the king of Judah will be brought out to the officials of the king of Babylon. Those women will say to you:

> " 'They misled you and overcame you—
> those trusted friends of yours.
> Your feet are sunk in the mud;
> your friends have deserted you.'

23"All your wives and children will be brought out to the Babylonians. You yourself will not escape from their hands but will be captured by the king of Babylon; and this city will*a* be burned down."

24Then Zedekiah said to Jeremiah, "Do not let anyone know about this conversation, or you may die. **25**If the officials hear that I talked with you, and they come to you and say, 'Tell us what you said to the king and what the king said to you; do not hide it from us or we will kill you,' **26**then tell them, 'I was pleading with the king not to send me back to Jonathan's house to die there.' "

27All the officials did come to Jeremiah and question him, and he told them everything the king had ordered him to say. So they said no more to him, for no one had heard his conversation with the king.

28And Jeremiah remained in the courtyard of the guard until the day JerusalemD was captured.

---

a23 Or and you will cause this city to

The Fall of Jerusalem

39 This is how Jerusalem[D] was taken: [1]In the ninth year of Zedekiah king of Judah, in the tenth month, Nebuchadnezzar king of Babylon marched against Jerusalem with his whole army and laid siege to it. [2]And on the ninth day of the fourth month of Zedekiah's eleventh year, the city wall was broken through. [3]Then all the officials of the king of Babylon came and took seats in the Middle Gate: Nergal-Sharezer of Samgar, Nebo-Sarsekim[a] a chief officer, Nergal-Sharezer a high official and all the other officials of the king of Babylon. [4]When Zedekiah king of Judah and all the soldiers saw them, they fled; they left the city at night by way of the king's garden, through the gate between the two walls, and headed toward the Arabah.[b]

[5]But the Babylonian[c] army pursued them and overtook Zedekiah in the plains of Jericho[D]. They captured him and took him to Nebuchadnezzar king of Babylon at Riblah in the land of Hamath, where he pronounced sentence on him. [6]There at Riblah the king of Babylon slaughtered the sons of Zedekiah before his eyes and also killed all the nobles of Judah. [7]Then he put out Zedekiah's eyes and bound him with bronze shackles to take him to Babylon.

[8]The Babylonians[d] set fire to the royal palace and the houses of the people and broke down the walls of Jerusalem. [9]Nebuzaradan commander of the imperial guard carried into exile[D] to Babylon the people who remained in the city, along with those who had gone over to him, and the rest of the people. [10]But Nebuzaradan the commander of the guard left behind in the land of Judah some of the poor people, who owned nothing; and at that time he gave them vineyards and fields.

[11]Now Nebuchadnezzar king of Babylon had given these orders about Jeremiah through Nebuzaradan commander of the imperial guard: [12]"Take him and look after him; don't harm him but do for him whatever he asks." [13]So Nebuzaradan the commander of the guard, Nebushazban a chief officer, Nergal-Sharezer a high official and all the other officers of the king of Babylon [14]sent and had Jeremiah taken out of the courtyard of the guard. They turned him over to Gedaliah son of Ahikam, the son of Shaphan, to take him back to his home. So he remained among his own people.

[15]While Jeremiah had been confined in the courtyard of the guard, the word of the LORD came to him: [16]"Go and tell Ebed-Melech the Cushite, 'This is what the LORD Almighty, the God of Israel, says: I am about to fulfill my words against this city through disaster, not prosperity. At that time they will be fulfilled before your eyes. [17]But I will rescue you on that day, declares the LORD; you will not be handed over to those you fear. [18]I will save you; you will not fall by the sword but will escape with your life, because you trust in me, declares the LORD.' "

Jeremiah Freed

40 The word came to Jeremiah from the LORD after Nebuzaradan commander of the imperial guard had released him at Ramah. He had found Jeremiah bound in chains among all the captives from Jerusalem

Was 18 months typical for a siege? (39:1–2)

Eighteen months was not uncommon. Sieges sometimes lasted a number of years. The Assyrians, for example, laid siege to Samaria for three years (2 Kings 17:5). The city of Ashdod once withstood a siege by the Egyptians for 29 years, the longest known siege. Sieges often lasted until the food supply was exhausted and people began to suffer from starvation and disease.

How did they break through the wall? (39:2)

Armies sometimes used battering rams to break down city gates. Other times they would tunnel under the walls, using wooden beams to keep the walls from falling in on top of them. Later they set fire to the supports, causing the walls to collapse. Sometimes invaders would use ladders or build huge earthen ramps to reach the top of the wall.

Why did foreign officials of the king sit in the city gate? (39:3)

This probably was one place where city business was normally conducted (see 37:8). Conquering armies would typically take control of the existing form of government. The Babylonian officials set up their command center in the Middle Gate, probably strategically located as the most accessible area of the city.

How could they escape when the Babylonians surrounded the city? (39:4)

The king and some soldiers may have prepared an escape as they saw the end approaching. Apparently they were able to make their initial getaway under the cover of darkness. In similar circumstances, others have escaped using bribes or disguises—perhaps as women, since women and children were sometimes permitted to go free.

Why kill all the nobles? (39:6)

About 20 years earlier, Nebuchadnezzar had defeated Jerusalem and deported some of the nobility (see Daniel 1:1–3). But Babylon's patience with the city had apparently run out. So they used brutality to intimidate the Jews. Killing the nobles was intended to teach a lesson to others who might still want to oppose them.

Why didn't Nebuchadnezzar just kill Zedekiah? (39:7)

Nebuchadnezzar was not content to merely conquer Judah. He wanted his barbarous tactics to demoralize and intimidate other nations as well.

How did the king of Babylon know about Jeremiah? (39:11–14)

The Babylonian leaders probably had heard about Jeremiah from those who had defected or were captured. They may have considered him a hero.

Why would a Cushite trust in the God of Israel? (39:18)

Cushite probably meant he was an Ethiopian. Ebed-Melech was a foreigner who had apparently been assimilated into Jewish culture. But while the Israelites were intrigued by false gods, he was disillusioned by them. Perhaps his upbringing in Ethiopia showed him the futility of trusting in idols, causing him to turn instead to the God of Israel. He demonstrated his faith when he saved Jeremiah (38:7–13).

---

[a]3 Or *Nergal-Sharezer, Samgar-Nebo, Sarsekim*   [b]4 Or *the Jordan Valley*   [c]5 Or *Chaldean*   [d]8 Or *Chaldeans*

How did Jeremiah get caught after being released? (40:1; see 39:14)

The events of ch. 40 probably occurred before those in ch. 39. Throughout Jeremiah the sequence of events is difficult to reconstruct. Today's historical approach relies on the calendar to put events in chronological order. Other approaches, however, focus more on the themes and less on the sequence of events. The Hebrews, for example, sometimes used the literary device of arranging narratives with the most important events first. Other times the most important event came last. There is no right or wrong way—just different cultural methods. See *Is this chapter out of sequence?* (35:1).

How did the Babylonians know God was behind Jerusalem's fall? (40:2)

The Babylonians had heard about the God of Israel and his reputation. They also had heard Jeremiah's message from the prisoners they'd captured. With their belief that there were many gods throughout the earth, they could easily believe that the God of Israel was permitting them to punish Jerusalem.

How much of the population had fled? (40:11)

The powerful and influential, a minority, were primarily the ones who would have had the means to escape. Most of the poor, however, would have been unable to flee. Though they would have liked to avoid the dangers of war, they had to take their chances with the invading army.

Mizpah (40:12)

Meant *watchtower* or *lookout point*. There were several locations with this name. This was probably the Mizpah of Joshua 18:26, located in the territory belonging to Benjamin. It was apparently the site of a religious shrine and had been a center for administration or government.

Why did Ishmael work for the Ammonites? (40:14)

Ishmael's rampage was a sad and tragic story of deceit and intrigue. His name suggests he may have been a Jew, but this cannot be proven. He may have been loyal to Zedekiah, the last king of Judah (see 41:1). He may also have been an Ammonite, a Moabite or an Edomite. His actions, apparently prompted by political opportunism, made him a failure in the long run (see 41:15).

Why was Gedaliah so naive? (40:16)

We aren't told why Gedaliah chose to ignore the warnings he received. Nor are we told how Ishmael managed to deceive him so completely. Perhaps Gedaliah assumed that his own standard of behavior, based on the Law of Moses, was the standard others used as well. Gedaliah seemed to be a decent, trusting person—but that made him an easy mark for an unscrupulous person like Ishmael.

and Judah who were being carried into exile[D] to Babylon. [2]When the commander of the guard found Jeremiah, he said to him, "The LORD your God decreed this disaster for this place. [3]And now the LORD has brought it about; he has done just as he said he would. All this happened because you people sinned against the LORD and did not obey him. [4]But today I am freeing you from the chains on your wrists. Come with me to Babylon, if you like, and I will look after you; but if you do not want to, then don't come. Look, the whole country lies before you; go wherever you please." [5]However, before Jeremiah turned to go,[a] Nebuzaradan added, "Go back to Gedaliah son of Ahikam, the son of Shaphan, whom the king of Babylon has appointed over the towns of Judah, and live with him among the people, or go anywhere else you please."

Then the commander gave him provisions and a present and let him go. [6]So Jeremiah went to Gedaliah son of Ahikam at Mizpah and stayed with him among the people who were left behind in the land.

Gedaliah Assassinated

[7]When all the army officers and their men who were still in the open country heard that the king of Babylon had appointed Gedaliah son of Ahikam as governor over the land and had put him in charge of the men, women and children who were the poorest in the land and who had not been carried into exile to Babylon, [8]they came to Gedaliah at Mizpah—Ishmael son of Nethaniah, Johanan and Jonathan the sons of Kareah, Seraiah son of Tanhumeth, the sons of Ephai the Netophathite, and Jaazaniah[b] the son of the Maacathite, and their men. [9]Gedaliah son of Ahikam, the son of Shaphan, took an oath to reassure them and their men. "Do not be afraid to serve the Babylonians,[c]" he said. "Settle down in the land and serve the king of Babylon, and it will go well with you. [10]I myself will stay at Mizpah to represent you before the Babylonians who come to us, but you are to harvest the wine, summer fruit and oil, and put them in your storage jars, and live in the towns you have taken over."

[11]When all the Jews[D] in Moab, Ammon, Edom[D] and all the other countries heard that the king of Babylon had left a remnant[D] in Judah and had appointed Gedaliah son of Ahikam, the son of Shaphan, as governor over them, [12]they all came back to the land of Judah, to Gedaliah at Mizpah, from all the countries where they had been scattered. And they harvested an abundance of wine and summer fruit.

[13]Johanan son of Kareah and all the army officers still in the open country came to Gedaliah at Mizpah [14]and said to him, "Don't you know that Baalis king of the Ammonites has sent Ishmael son of Nethaniah to take your life?" But Gedaliah son of Ahikam did not believe them.

[15]Then Johanan son of Kareah said privately to Gedaliah in Mizpah, "Let me go and kill Ishmael son of Nethaniah, and no one will know it. Why should he take your life and cause all the Jews who are gathered around you to be scattered and the remnant of Judah to perish?"

[16]But Gedaliah son of Ahikam said to Johanan son of Kareah, "Don't do such a thing! What you are saying about Ishmael is not true."

---

[a]5 Or *Jeremiah answered*   [b]8 Hebrew *Jezaniah*, a variant of *Jaazaniah*   [c]9 Or *Chaldeans*; also in verse 10

41 In the seventh month Ishmael son of Nethaniah, the son of Elishama, who was of royal blood and had been one of the king's officers, came with ten men to Gedaliah son of Ahikam at Mizpah. While they were eating together there, ²Ishmael son of Nethaniah and the ten men who were with him got up and struck down Gedaliah son of Ahikam, the son of Shaphan, with the sword, killing the one whom the king of Babylon had appointed as governor over the land. ³Ishmael also killed all the Jews^D who were with Gedaliah at Mizpah, as well as the Babylonian^a soldiers who were there.

⁴The day after Gedaliah's assassination, before anyone knew about it, ⁵eighty men who had shaved off their beards, torn their clothes and cut themselves came from Shechem, Shiloh and Samaria, bringing grain offerings^D and incense^D with them to the house of the LORD. ⁶Ishmael son of Nethaniah went out from Mizpah to meet them, weeping as he went. When he met them, he said, "Come to Gedaliah son of Ahikam." ⁷When they went into the city, Ishmael son of Nethaniah and the men who were with him slaughtered them and threw them into a cistern^D. ⁸But ten of them said to Ishmael, "Don't kill us! We have wheat and barley, oil and honey, hidden in a field." So he let them alone and did not kill them with the others. ⁹Now the cistern where he threw all the bodies of the men he had killed along with Gedaliah was the one King Asa had made as part of his defense against Baasha king of Israel. Ishmael son of Nethaniah filled it with the dead.

¹⁰Ishmael made captives of all the rest of the people who were in Mizpah—the king's daughters along with all the others who were left there, over whom Nebuzaradan commander of the imperial guard had appointed Gedaliah son of Ahikam. Ishmael son of Nethaniah took them captive and set out to cross over to the Ammonites.

¹¹When Johanan son of Kareah and all the army officers who were with him heard about all the crimes Ishmael son of Nethaniah had committed, ¹²they took all their men and went to fight Ishmael son of Nethaniah. They caught up with him near the great pool in Gibeon. ¹³When all the people Ishmael had with him saw Johanan son of Kareah and the army officers who were with him, they were glad. ¹⁴All the people Ishmael had taken captive at Mizpah turned and went over to Johanan son of Kareah. ¹⁵But Ishmael son of Nethaniah and eight of his men escaped from Johanan and fled to the Ammonites.

Flight to Egypt

¹⁶Then Johanan son of Kareah and all the army officers who were with him led away all the survivors from Mizpah whom he had recovered from Ishmael son of Nethaniah after he had assassinated Gedaliah son of Ahikam: the soldiers, women, children and court officials he had brought from Gibeon. ¹⁷And they went on, stopping at Geruth Kimham near Bethlehem on their way to Egypt ¹⁸to escape the Babylonians.^b They were afraid of them because Ishmael son of Nethaniah had killed Gedaliah son of Ahikam, whom the king of Babylon had appointed as governor over the land.

How did only 11 men overpower so many? (41:3)

Ishmael used Gedaliah's trusting nature to his best advantage. He increased his chance for success with a surprise attack. He may also have gained an edge over Gedaliah's forces by attacking during a banquet when some may have put their weapons aside to indulge in food and wine.

Why shave beards, tear clothes and cut skin? (41:5; see 7:29; 16:6; 47:5; 48:37)

While we would dress in black, the culture of the ancient Middle East expressed deep sorrow in other ways. Since a beard signified a man's maturity and dignity, to shave it was to suggest humility and great loss. To tear one's clothing, handmade and more valuable to their culture than ours, demonstrated the depth of a tragedy—greater than mere clothing. Cutting oneself was forbidden by the law (Lev. 19:28; 21:5), but it's not too surprising some adopted this pagan custom—just as others had worshiped idols. For more about mourning customs, see *What did the Israelites do during a 30-day mourning period?* (Deut. 34:8) and *Where did the custom of ashes and torn clothing come from?* (2 Samuel 13:19).

Was the house of the Lord still standing? (41:5)

When Jerusalem fell in 586 B.C., the temple was destroyed with the rest of the city. But the temple site, though covered with debris, was still considered *the house of the LORD* and sacred. Even before the temple had been built, David had offered a sacrifice at that exact spot to halt the plague against Israel (2 Samuel 24:18–25). Some think it was the same location where Abraham prepared to sacrifice his son (Gen. 22:9–14).

Why did Ishmael put on the weeping act? (41:6)

As he had done before (v. 3), Ishmael used deception and surprise to gain the advantage over his unsuspecting victims. By pretending to join the 80 mourners in their sorrow, he was able to win their confidence and catch them off guard.

How were cisterns used as a military defense? (41:9)

Water, typically scarce in Judah, was an even greater necessity during times of war. Cisterns were dug to form pools, collecting the runoff of rainwater or the flow of water from a spring. Cisterns that supplied the army and their animals with water were critical to the defense of the land.

How could captives simply walk away? (41:14)

Ishmael and his men probably recognized that they could not defeat the band of rescuers led by Johanan. Concerned primarily with their own escape, they apparently left their prisoners unguarded. Two of Ishmael's original ten were not able to get away (see vv. 2,15).

^a3 Or *Chaldean*   ^b18 Or *Chaldeans*

Why did they want to escape to Egypt? (41:17)

Egypt, in the minds of the Israelites, had become almost synonymous with security. Sometimes Israel had sought military alliances with Egypt, though God denounced their lack of faith in him (Isaiah 30:1–3; 31:1). The few Jews left in Judah were probably fearful of Babylonian reprisals for the assassination of Gedaliah. They must have felt it safer to go as immigrants to Egypt than to stay and face the wrath of Nebuchadnezzar.

Where was Jeremiah during Ishmael's attack? (42:2)

Jeremiah's whereabouts during Ishmael's violent rampage are not mentioned. Some speculate he may have been one of the captives held by Ishmael and freed by Johanan at Gibeon (41:11–15).

Why ask for divine guidance if the decision was already made? (42:3,6; see 41:17)

Apparently they assumed God wanted them to escape to Egypt. They probably came to Jeremiah to discover not *whether* to go but *how* to go. Perhaps they wanted to be assured God was with them.

What was their *fatal mistake*? (42:20)

Promising to listen to God when they had already decided what they were going to do. They would only obey God if he endorsed their plans. Since his instructions conflicted with their desire to head to Egypt, they changed their tune. They were hypocrites: they said one thing and did another. All along they planned to go to Egypt—with or without God's approval.

How did Jeremiah know their minds were made up? (42:21)

Jeremiah probably sensed the restless mood of the Hebrews. Even though they had not yet responded verbally, he could see their expressions and body language. Or when *the word of the LORD came to Jeremiah* (v. 7) God may have told Jeremiah what their response would be.

42 Then all the army officers, including Johanan son of Kareah and Jezaniah[a] son of Hoshaiah, and all the people from the least to the greatest approached [2]Jeremiah the prophet[D] and said to him, "Please hear our petition and pray to the LORD your God for this entire remnant[D]. For as you now see, though we were once many, now only a few are left. [3]Pray that the LORD your God will tell us where we should go and what we should do."

[4]"I have heard you," replied Jeremiah the prophet. "I will certainly pray to the LORD your God as you have requested; I will tell you everything the LORD says and will keep nothing back from you."

[5]Then they said to Jeremiah, "May the LORD be a true and faithful witness against us if we do not act in accordance with everything the LORD your God sends you to tell us. [6]Whether it is favorable or unfavorable, we will obey the LORD our God, to whom we are sending you, so that it will go well with us, for we will obey the LORD our God."

[7]Ten days later the word of the LORD came to Jeremiah. [8]So he called together Johanan son of Kareah and all the army officers who were with him and all the people from the least to the greatest. [9]He said to them, "This is what the LORD, the God of Israel, to whom you sent me to present your petition, says: [10]'If you stay in this land, I will build you up and not tear you down; I will plant you and not uproot you, for I am grieved over the disaster I have inflicted on you. [11]Do not be afraid of the king of Babylon, whom you now fear. Do not be afraid of him, declares the LORD, for I am with you and will save you and deliver you from his hands. [12]I will show you compassion so that he will have compassion on you and restore you to your land.'

[13]"However, if you say, 'We will not stay in this land,' and so disobey the LORD your God, [14]and if you say, 'No, we will go and live in Egypt, where we will not see war or hear the trumpet or be hungry for bread,' [15]then hear the word of the LORD, O remnant of Judah. This is what the LORD Almighty, the God of Israel, says: 'If you are determined to go to Egypt and you do go to settle there, [16]then the sword you fear will overtake you there, and the famine you dread will follow you into Egypt, and there you will die. [17]Indeed, all who are determined to go to Egypt to settle there will die by the sword, famine and plague; not one of them will survive or escape the disaster I will bring on them.' [18]This is what the LORD Almighty, the God of Israel, says: 'As my anger and wrath have been poured out on those who lived in Jerusalem[D], so will my wrath be poured out on you when you go to Egypt. You will be an object of cursing and horror, of condemnation and reproach[D]; you will never see this place again.'

[19]"O remnant of Judah, the LORD has told you, 'Do not go to Egypt.' Be sure of this: I warn you today [20]that you made a fatal mistake[b] when you sent me to the LORD your God and said, 'Pray to the LORD our God for us; tell us everything he says and we will do it.' [21]I have told you today, but you still have not obeyed the LORD your God in all he sent me to tell you. [22]So now, be sure of this: You will die by the sword, famine and plague in the place where you want to go to settle."

---

[a]1 Hebrew; Septuagint (see also 43:2) *Azariah*   [b]20 Or *you erred in your hearts*

43 When Jeremiah finished telling the people all the words of the LORD their God—everything the LORD had sent him to tell them— [2]Azariah son of Hoshaiah and Johanan son of Kareah and all the arrogant men said to Jeremiah, "You are lying! The LORD our God has not sent you to say, 'You must not go to Egypt to settle there.' [3]But Baruch son of Neriah is inciting you against us to hand us over to the Babylonians,[a] so they may kill us or carry us into exile[D] to Babylon."

[4]So Johanan son of Kareah and all the army officers and all the people disobeyed the LORD's command to stay in the land of Judah. [5]Instead, Johanan son of Kareah and all the army officers led away all the remnant[D] of Judah who had come back to live in the land of Judah from all the nations where they had been scattered. [6]They also led away all the men, women and children and the king's daughters whom Nebuzaradan commander of the imperial guard had left with Gedaliah son of Ahikam, the son of Shaphan, and Jeremiah the prophet[D] and Baruch son of Neriah. [7]So they entered Egypt in disobedience to the LORD and went as far as Tahpanhes.

[8]In Tahpanhes the word of the LORD came to Jeremiah: [9]"While the Jews[D] are watching, take some large stones with you and bury them in clay in the brick pavement at the entrance to Pharaoh's palace in Tahpanhes. [10]Then say to them, 'This is what the LORD Almighty, the God of Israel, says: I will send for my servant Nebuchadnezzar king of Babylon, and I will set his throne over these stones I have buried here; he will spread his royal canopy above them. [11]He will come and attack Egypt, bringing death[D] to those destined for death, captivity to those destined for captivity, and the sword to those destined for the sword. [12]He[b] will set fire to the temples of the gods of Egypt; he will burn their temples and take their gods captive. As a shepherd wraps his garment around him, so will he wrap Egypt around himself and depart from there unscathed. [13]There in the temple of the sun[c] in Egypt he will demolish the sacred[D] pillars and will burn down the temples of the gods of Egypt.'"

Disaster Because of Idolatry

44 This word came to Jeremiah concerning all the Jews living in Lower Egypt—in Migdol, Tahpanhes and Memphis[d]—and in Upper Egypt[e]: [2]"This is what the LORD Almighty, the God of Israel, says: You saw the great disaster I brought on Jerusalem[D] and on all the towns of Judah. Today they lie deserted and in ruins [3]because of the evil they have done. They provoked me to anger by burning incense[D] and by worshiping other gods that neither they nor you nor your fathers ever knew. [4]Again and again I sent my servants the prophets, who said, 'Do not do this detestable thing that I hate!' [5]But they did not listen or pay attention; they did not turn from their wickedness or stop burning incense to other gods. [6]Therefore, my fierce anger was poured out; it raged against the towns of Judah and the streets of Jerusalem and made them the desolate ruins they are today.

[7]"Now this is what the LORD God Almighty, the God of Israel, says: Why bring such great disaster on yourselves by cutting off from Judah the men and women, the children and infants, and so leave yourselves without a rem-

Why ask a liar for advice? (43:2)

They didn't anticipate that Jeremiah actually would give them advice. What they really wanted was some religious reassurance or endorsement of their own plans. When they got advice instead, their human nature rejected it. So they called him a liar and headed to Egypt.

Why were they suspicious of Baruch? (43:3)

Some think the Hebrews suspected that Baruch, Jeremiah's secretary, was an agent of Babylon. If so, they would have thought he was urging Jeremiah to say it was God's will for them to stay and submit to Nebuchadnezzar. Apparently Baruch's personality was strong enough that he was blamed for being a bad influence on Jeremiah.

Flight to Egypt (43:5)

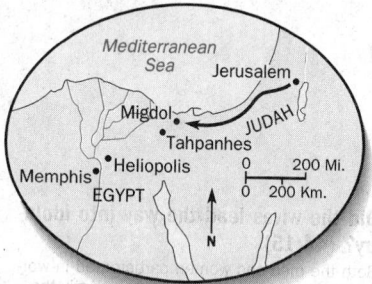

Did Jeremiah and Baruch go willingly? (43:6)

Some feel they were forced to go against their will. Others think they went willingly, seeing the Jews as people in need of divine help. Jeremiah had dedicated his life to serving God. He remained faithful to his commitment even though the people were rebellious.

How did Jeremiah bury stones in the pavement? (43:9)

Details are sketchy, but he may have used farming tools to chisel the clay mortar from between the hardened bricks. In an arid climate, clay bricks would have been nearly like concrete and quite suitable for the main streets.

My servant Nebuchadnezzar (43:10)

See *Why call a pagan king God's servant?* (27:6).

What were the sacred pillars in the temple of the sun? (43:13)

Obelisks—free-standing posts about six feet square at the base and tapering upward 60 feet or more to a pyramid-like top. Some may have been overlaid with gold. Obelisks were erected to honor and worship the Egyptian sun god, Ra. They were located in Heliopolis, called the "temple of the sun."

Lower . . . Upper Egypt (44:1)

Lower Egypt refers to the delta, the broad spreading deposit of soil at the mouth of the Nile. This is where the Nile and its many streams flow north into the Mediterranean Sea. Upper Egypt is the long slender valley south of the delta into which the Nile flows (see *Map 3* at the back of this Bible). This valley is no more than 12 miles wide. Beyond that

is desert. Ancient Pharaohs united the two Egypts into one rule. The modern city of Cairo sits at the junction of these two lands.

Why did the Israelites worship Egyptian gods? (44:8)

The Israelite exiles worshiped pagan gods in Judah which was why God judged Judah by sending Nebuchadnezzar and the Babylonians in the first place. Now as immigrants fitting into a new culture, they took on the gods of that culture as well. People in ancient times often viewed pagan gods as ruling over certain territories or regions, and they thought it was advisable to serve the god on whose land they lived.

Did the wives lead the way into idolatry? (44:15)

Both the men and women participated in worshiping false gods (v. 8). But apparently the Jewish women served the *Queen of Heaven,* a fertility goddess, with a special fervor and devotion (v. 17).

Queen of Heaven (44:17)

Goddess of sexual love and fertility. Many ancient Middle Eastern cultures had similar goddesses, but with different names. The Babylonians called her Ishtar; the Greeks, Aphrodite. Part of the practice of worshiping this goddess included cult prostitution.

Where did they come up with their version of the reasons for their troubles? (44:18)

Typical human nature: they credited good fortune to doing what their preconceived notions said was right, bad fortune to what they thought was wrong. Human pride blinded them from the truth: worshiping the *Queen of Heaven* was the very reason for their troubles.

Were the women trying to defend themselves? (44:19)

Apparently. Jewish culture was male-dominated and the man of the house could override his wife's decisions (Num. 30:8). This seemed like a good excuse to cover their tracks. In such a society, it would be only natural for the women to excuse themselves and place the primary responsibility on their husbands.

nant? **8**Why provoke me to anger with what your hands have made, burning incense[D] to other gods in Egypt, where you have come to live? You will destroy yourselves and make yourselves an object of cursing and reproach[D] among all the nations on earth. **9**Have you forgotten the wickedness committed by your fathers and by the kings and queens of Judah and the wickedness committed by you and your wives in the land of Judah and the streets of Jerusalem[D]? **10**To this day they have not humbled themselves or shown reverence[D], nor have they followed my law and the decrees I set before you and your fathers.

11"Therefore, this is what the LORD Almighty, the God of Israel, says: I am determined to bring disaster on you and to destroy all Judah. **12**I will take away the remnant[D] of Judah who were determined to go to Egypt to settle there. They will all perish in Egypt; they will fall by the sword or die from famine. From the least to the greatest, they will die by sword or famine. They will become an object of cursing and horror, of condemnation and reproach. **13**I will punish those who live in Egypt with the sword, famine and plague, as I punished Jerusalem. **14**None of the remnant of Judah who have gone to live in Egypt will escape or survive to return to the land of Judah, to which they long to return and live; none will return except a few fugitives."

15Then all the men who knew that their wives were burning incense to other gods, along with all the women who were present—a large assembly—and all the people living in Lower and Upper Egypt,[a] said to Jeremiah, **16**"We will not listen to the message you have spoken to us in the name of the LORD! **17**We will certainly do everything we said we would: We will burn incense to the Queen of Heaven and will pour out drink offerings[D] to her just as we and our fathers, our kings and our officials did in the towns of Judah and in the streets of Jerusalem. At that time we had plenty of food and were well off and suffered no harm. **18**But ever since we stopped burning incense to the Queen of Heaven and pouring out drink offerings to her, we have had nothing and have been perishing by sword and famine."

19The women added, "When we burned incense to the Queen of Heaven and poured out drink offerings to her, did not our husbands know that we were making cakes like her image and pouring out drink offerings to her?"

20Then Jeremiah said to all the people, both men and women, who were answering him, **21**"Did not the LORD remember and think about the incense burned in the towns of Judah and the streets of Jerusalem by you and your fathers, your kings and your officials and the people of the land? **22**When the LORD could no longer endure your wicked actions and the detestable things you did, your land became an object of cursing and a desolate waste without inhabitants, as it is today. **23**Because you have burned incense and have sinned against the LORD and have not obeyed him or followed his law or his decrees or his stipulations, this disaster has come upon you, as you now see."

24Then Jeremiah said to all the people, including the women, "Hear the word of the LORD, all you people of Judah in Egypt. **25**This is what the LORD Almighty, the God of Israel, says: You and your wives have shown by your

*a*15 Hebrew *in Egypt and Pathros*

actions what you promised when you said, 'We will certainly carry out the vows[D] we made to burn incense[D] and pour out drink offerings[D] to the Queen of Heaven.'

"Go ahead then, do what you promised! Keep your vows! **26**But hear the word of the LORD, all Jews living in Egypt: 'I swear by my great name,' says the LORD, 'that no one from Judah living anywhere in Egypt will ever again invoke my name or swear, "As surely as the Sovereign LORD lives." **27**For I am watching over them for harm, not for good; the Jews in Egypt will perish by sword and famine until they are all destroyed. **28**Those who escape the sword and return to the land of Judah from Egypt will be very few. Then the whole remnant[D] of Judah who came to live in Egypt will know whose word will stand— mine or theirs.

29" 'This will be the sign to you that I will punish you in this place,' declares the LORD, 'so that you will know that my threats of harm against you will surely stand.' **30**This is what the LORD says: 'I am going to hand Pharaoh Hophra king of Egypt over to his enemies who seek his life, just as I handed Zedekiah king of Judah over to Nebuchadnezzar king of Babylon, the enemy who was seeking his life.' "

A Message to Baruch

45 This is what Jeremiah the prophet[D] told Baruch son of Neriah in the fourth year of Jehoiakim son of Josiah king of Judah, after Baruch had written on a scroll the words Jeremiah was then dictating: **2**"This is what the LORD, the God of Israel, says to you, Baruch: **3**You said, 'Woe to me! The LORD has added sorrow to my pain; I am worn out with groaning and find no rest.' "

4↳The LORD said,↲ "Say this to him: 'This is what the LORD says: I will overthrow what I have built and uproot what I have planted, throughout the land. **5**Should you then seek great things for yourself? Seek them not. For I will bring disaster on all people, declares the LORD, but wherever you go I will let you escape with your life.' "

A Message About Egypt

46 This is the word of the LORD that came to Jeremiah the prophet concerning the nations:

2Concerning Egypt:

This is the message against the army of Pharaoh Neco king of Egypt, which was defeated at Carchemish on the Euphrates River by Nebuchadnezzar king of Babylon in the fourth year of Jehoiakim son of Josiah king of Judah:

3"Prepare your shields, both large and small,
        and march out for battle!
4Harness the horses,
        mount the steeds!
    Take your positions
        with helmets on!
    Polish your spears,
        put on your armor!
5What do I see?
        They are terrified,
    they are retreating,
        their warriors are defeated.
    They flee in haste
        without looking back,

How many fugitives returned from Egypt? (44:28; see v. 14)

No one can say. Some think this refers to fugitive Jews who returned to Palestine down through the centuries. Others believe a small group who witnessed the destruction of Jerusalem and fled to Egypt did return to tell about it.

Pharaoh Hophra (44:30)

A Pharaoh who ruled from 588–569 B.C. and was thought to be strangled to death in a revolt. In the early years of his reign, he allied with King Zedekiah of Judah and assisted his rebellion against Nebuchadnezzar.

Why are some of these chapters out of sequence? (45:1)

At times the stories in Jeremiah appear to be strung together in a random manner. Some think a later editor possibly rearranged the chapters for various reasons. Others think the book was arranged thematically, not chronologically, so that some sections that appear out of place are there intentionally to support a certain theme. Also see *Is this chapter out of sequence?* (35:1) and *How did Jeremiah get caught after being released?* (40:1).

What was Baruch complaining about? (45:3)

Undoubtedly Baruch shared in Jeremiah's sorrows. Baruch may have experienced emotions similar to Jeremiah's: rejection or disappointment because the people would not repent. Or perhaps Baruch had misgivings about his humble lot in life (see following note).

What great things did Baruch want for himself? (45:5)

Baruch's wishes are not revealed. He may have been longing for a quiet life where he could escape the responsibilities of being Jeremiah's helper. Some note that Baruch's brother, Seraiah, enjoyed *great things* (v. 5) for himself as a staff officer under King Zedekiah (see 32:12; 51:59). It may be that Baruch envied his position.

Nations (46:1)

Gentiles or non-Israelites. God commissioned Jeremiah to speak not only to Israel but to non-Jewish people.

Was this a prophecy before the event or a political analysis after the fact? (46:2)

Opinions are divided. Egypt was defeated in 605 B.C. If these words came after Egypt's defeat, they may have been a song expressing Israel's relief. On the other hand, if these words were given before the event, they would have announced Egypt's defeat as God's judgment for their idolatry and past treatment of Israel.

and there is terror on every side,"
                                declares the LORD.

6"The swift cannot flee
  nor the strong escape.
In the north by the River Euphrates
  they stumble and fall.

7"Who is this that rises like the Nile,
  like rivers of surging waters?
8Egypt rises like the Nile,
  like rivers of surging waters.
She says, 'I will rise and cover the earth;
  I will destroy cities and their people.'
9Charge, O horses!
  Drive furiously, O charioteers!
March on, O warriors—
  men of Cush[a] and Put who carry shields,
  men of Lydia who draw the bow.
10But that day belongs to the Lord, the LORD
    Almighty—
  a day of vengeance, for vengeance on his
    foes.
The sword will devour till it is satisfied,
  till it has quenched its thirst with blood.
For the Lord, the LORD Almighty, will offer
    sacrifice[D]
  in the land of the north by the River
    Euphrates.

11"Go up to Gilead and get balm,
  O Virgin Daughter of Egypt.
But you multiply remedies in vain;
  there is no healing for you.
12The nations will hear of your shame;
  your cries will fill the earth.
One warrior will stumble over another;
  both will fall down together."

13This is the message the LORD spoke to Jeremiah the prophet[D] about the coming of Nebuchadnezzar king of Babylon to attack Egypt:

14"Announce this in Egypt, and proclaim it in
    Migdol;
  proclaim it also in Memphis[b] and
    Tahpanhes:
'Take your positions and get ready,
  for the sword devours those around you.'
15Why will your warriors be laid low?
  They cannot stand, for the LORD will push
    them down.
16They will stumble repeatedly;
  they will fall over each other.
They will say, 'Get up, let us go back
  to our own people and our native lands,
  away from the sword of the oppressor.'
17There they will exclaim,
  'Pharaoh king of Egypt is only a loud noise;
  he has missed his opportunity.'

18"As surely as I live," declares the King,
  whose name is the LORD Almighty,

Can vengeance be a godly attribute? (46:10)

Only God can rightfully avenge wrong. His vengeance is equivalent to justice; his wrath against sin is always appropriate. Human vengeance, on the other hand, is almost always distorted by human nature. God desires to balance the scales of justice; people want to get even. God wants to protect the truth; people want to protect themselves. Revenge may be an honest feeling, but it is not a godly attribute. Retaliation should be left to God (Romans 12:17–21).

Lord ... LORD Almighty (46:10)

Two titles for God from the same Hebrew phrase, *Adonai Yahweh*, meaning *the God who runs it all—the master of all things.*

Why would God offer a sacrifice? (46:10)

So that the price of sin would be paid and Israel would be judged for its sin. Jeremiah used human terms in the only way he knew how to describe what God was doing. God's vengeance would be like a sacrifice satisfying his holy wrath.

Virgin Daughter of Egypt (46:11)

An affectionate term applied here to the nation of Egypt. Some think it is used sarcastically, the word *virgin* referring to Egypt being unconquered by other nations. Yet Egypt would soon lose its "virginity"—conquered by King Nebuchadnezzar and put to shame (v. 12).

Announce this in Egypt (46:14)

Announce Nebuchadnezzar's coming destruction of Egypt. This devastation of Egypt probably occurred after Jeremiah's death around 568 B.C.

---

[a]9 That is, the upper Nile region   [b]14 Hebrew *Noph*; also in verse 19

"one will come who is like Tabor among the
        mountains,
    like Carmel by the sea.
¹⁹Pack your belongings for exile[D],
    you who live in Egypt,
for Memphis will be laid waste
    and lie in ruins without inhabitant.

²⁰"Egypt is a beautiful heifer,
    but a gadfly is coming
    against her from the north.
²¹The mercenaries in her ranks
    are like fattened calves.
They too will turn and flee together,
    they will not stand their ground,
for the day of disaster is coming upon them,
    the time for them to be punished.
²²Egypt will hiss like a fleeing serpent
    as the enemy advances in force;
they will come against her with axes,
    like men who cut down trees.
²³They will chop down her forest,"
                        declares the LORD,
    "dense though it be.
They are more numerous than locusts[D],
    they cannot be counted.
²⁴The Daughter of Egypt will be put to shame,
    handed over to the people of the north."

²⁵The LORD Almighty, the God of Israel, says: "I am
about to bring punishment on Amon god of Thebes,[a] on
Pharaoh, on Egypt and her gods and her kings, and on
those who rely on Pharaoh. ²⁶I will hand them over to
those who seek their lives, to Nebuchadnezzar king of
Babylon and his officers. Later, however, Egypt will be inhabited as in times past," declares the LORD.

²⁷"Do not fear, O Jacob my servant;
    do not be dismayed, O Israel.
I will surely save you out of a distant place,
    your descendants from the land of their
        exile.
Jacob will again have peace[D] and security,
    and no one will make him afraid.
²⁸Do not fear, O Jacob my servant,
    for I am with you," declares the LORD.
"Though I completely destroy all the nations
    among which I scatter you,
    I will not completely destroy you.
I will discipline you but only with justice;
    I will not let you go entirely unpunished."

A Message About the Philistines

47 This is the word of the LORD that came to Jeremiah
the prophet[D] concerning the Philistines before
Pharaoh attacked Gaza:

²This is what the LORD says:

"See how the waters are rising in the north;
    they will become an overflowing torrent.
They will overflow the land and everything in
        it,
    the towns and those who live in them.

Gadfly (46:20)
Probably a biting or stinging insect. It depicts
the torment that would be caused by Babylon.

**Why would God want to punish false
gods? (46:25)**
To show that these gods were, in fact, not
gods at all, God punished the cities supposedly being protected by these gods. His judgment
demonstrated his complete sovereignty and
power over all. He is the one true God.

---

[a]25 Hebrew No

The people will cry out;
   all who dwell in the land will wail
³at the sound of the hoofs of galloping steeds,
   at the noise of enemy chariots
   and the rumble of their wheels.
Fathers will not turn to help their children;
   their hands will hang limp.
⁴For the day has come
   to destroy all the Philistines
and to cut off all survivors
   who could help Tyre and Sidon.
The LORD is about to destroy the Philistines,
   the remnant^D from the coasts of Caphtor.ᵃ
⁵Gaza will shave her head in mourning;
   Ashkelon will be silenced.
O remnant on the plain,
   how long will you cut yourselves?

⁶" 'Ah, sword of the LORD,' ⌊you cry,⌋
   'how long till you rest?
Return to your scabbard;
   cease and be still.'
⁷But how can it rest
   when the LORD has commanded it,
when he has ordered it
   to attack Ashkelon and the coast?"

A Message About Moab

48 Concerning Moab:

This is what the LORD Almighty, the God of Israel, says:

"Woe to Nebo, for it will be ruined.
   Kiriathaim will be disgraced and captured;
   the stronghold^{Db} will be disgraced and
      shattered.
²Moab will be praised no more;
   in Heshbonᶜ men will plot her downfall:
   'Come, let us put an end to that nation.'
You too, O Madmen,ᵈ will be silenced;
   the sword will pursue you.
³Listen to the cries from Horonaim,
   cries of great havoc and destruction.
⁴Moab will be broken;
   her little ones will cry out.ᵉ
⁵They go up the way to Luhith,
   weeping bitterly as they go;
on the road down to Horonaim
   anguished cries over the destruction are
      heard.
⁶Flee! Run for your lives;
   become like a bushᶠ in the desert.
⁷Since you trust in your deeds and riches,
   you too will be taken captive,
and Chemosh will go into exile^D,
   together with his priests^D and officials.
⁸The destroyer will come against every town,
   and not a town will escape.
The valley will be ruined
   and the plateau destroyed,

Were all the Philistines destroyed? (47:4)

Apparently. The last Biblical reference to a Philistine city is found in Nehemiah 13:24, 150 years after Jeremiah's time. Most believe the Philistine cities were captured and their people deported by the Babylonian king Nebuchadnezzar. At that point it seems they ceased to exist as a nation. Though the word *Palestine* is linked to the word *Philistine* in the Hebrew, Palestinians today are not related to the Philistines. They merely live on the same land.

Why did they cut themselves? (47:5; see 7:29; 16:6; 41:5; 48:37)

See *Why shave beards, tear clothes and cut skin?* (41:5).

Madmen (48:2)

An otherwise unknown town in Moab which could mean either *be silenced* or *dung*. Jeremiah may have been playing with the Hebrew language, lambasting Moab with a sort of poetic justice.

Why become like a desert bush? (48:6)

It's not clear what this expression meant. The word *bush* comes from a word meaning *to be naked*, suggesting a shrub with tiny, scaly leaves and small cones. But the word may also refer to a Hebrew city named *Aroer* (see NIV text note). Whatever the specific meaning, the general thrust is that those who had known the good life would be stripped of everything and reduced to bare subsistence.

ᵃ4 That is, Crete   ᵇ1 Or / *Misgab*   ᶜ2 The Hebrew for *Heshbon* sounds like the Hebrew for *plot*.   ᵈ2 The name of the Moabite town Madmen sounds like the Hebrew for *be silenced*.   ᵉ4 Hebrew; Septuagint / *proclaim it to Zoar*   ᶠ6 Or *like Aroer*

because the LORD has spoken.
⁹Put salt on Moab,
  for she will be laid waste*a*;
her towns will become desolate,
  with no one to live in them.

¹⁰"A curse on him who is lax in doing the LORD's
      work!
  A curse on him who keeps his sword from
      bloodshed!

¹¹"Moab has been at rest from youth,
  like wine left on its dregsᴰ,
not poured from one jar to another—
  she has not gone into exileᴰ.
So she tastes as she did,
  and her aroma is unchanged.
¹²But days are coming,"
  declares the LORD,
"when I will send men who pour from jars,
  and they will pour her out;
they will empty her jars
  and smash her jugs.
¹³Then Moab will be ashamed of Chemosh,
  as the house of Israel was ashamed
  when they trusted in Bethel.

¹⁴"How can you say, 'We are warriors,
  men valiant in battle'?
¹⁵Moab will be destroyed and her towns
      invaded;
  her finest young men will go down in the
      slaughter,"
  declares the King, whose name is the LORD
      Almighty.
¹⁶"The fall of Moab is at hand;
  her calamity will come quickly.
¹⁷Mourn for her, all who live around her,
  all who know her fame;
say, 'How broken is the mighty scepterᴰ,
  how broken the glorious staff!'

¹⁸"Come down from your gloryᴰ
  and sit on the parched ground,
  O inhabitants of the Daughter of Dibon,
for he who destroys Moab
  will come up against you
  and ruin your fortified cities.
¹⁹Stand by the road and watch,
  you who live in Aroer.
Ask the man fleeing and the woman escaping,
  ask them, 'What has happened?'
²⁰Moab is disgraced, for she is shattered.
  Wail and cry out!
Announce by the Arnon
  that Moab is destroyed.
²¹Judgment has come to the plateau—
  to Holon, Jahzah and Mephaath,
²² to Dibon, Nebo and Beth Diblathaim,
²³ to Kiriathaim, Beth Gamul and Beth Meon,
²⁴ to Kerioth and Bozrah—
  to all the towns of Moab, far and near.

Why salt a nation? (48:9)
Some note that ancient conquerors literally spread salt over defeated cities to prevent crops from growing for years. Others think *put salt* could be translated *give wings* (see NIV text note). If that is the case, then this would instruct Moab to wish for wings so it could fly to safety away from all the destruction. Still others think it could read *set up a grave marker*.

Why would God call his work *bloodshed*? (48:10)
The Old Testament approach to getting rid of sin was to get rid of the sinner, often resulting in men, women and children being slaughtered. Those who picked up the sword to slay the guilty were considered agents of the Lord's wrath and judgment. Those who were killed were not viewed as victims since it was their own sins and hardened hearts that had brought punishment upon them.

What was different about *wine left on its dregs*? (48:11–12)
It became quite bitter—a vivid analogy for Moab. The fermentation process left sediment or *dregs* at the bottom of the wine. The wine had to be carefully poured into other containers from time to time during fermentation in a way that would not disturb the sediment. This procedure, called decanting, kept the wine from becoming bitter.

Why was Israel ashamed when they trusted in Bethel? (48:13)
Bethel was the religious capital of the breakaway northern kingdom of Israel. It became a center for pagan worship. Israel's shame was probably an allusion to the fall of the northern kingdom in 722 B.C., the final consequence of their continual fixation with false gods.

*a*9 Or *Give wings to Moab, / for she will fly away*

²⁵Moab's horn[a] is cut off;
   her arm is broken,"

              declares the LORD.

²⁶"Make her drunk,
   for she has defied the LORD.
Let Moab wallow in her vomit;
   let her be an object of ridicule.
²⁷Was not Israel the object of your ridicule?
   Was she caught among thieves,
that you shake your head in scorn
   whenever you speak of her?
²⁸Abandon your towns and dwell among the rocks,
   you who live in Moab.
Be like a dove that makes its nest
   at the mouth of a cave.

²⁹"We have heard of Moab's pride—
   her overweening pride and conceit,
her pride and arrogance
   and the haughtiness of her heart.
³⁰I know her insolence but it is futile,"

              declares the LORD,
   "and her boasts accomplish nothing.
³¹Therefore I wail over Moab,
   for all Moab I cry out,
   I moan for the men of Kir Hareseth.
³²I weep for you, as Jazer weeps,
   O vines of Sibmah.
Your branches spread as far as the sea;
   they reached as far as the sea of Jazer.
The destroyer has fallen
   on your ripened fruit and grapes.
³³Joy and gladness are gone
   from the orchards and fields of Moab.
I have stopped the flow of wine from the presses;
   no one treads them with shouts of joy.
Although there are shouts,
   they are not shouts of joy.

³⁴"The sound of their cry rises
   from Heshbon to Elealeh and Jahaz,
from Zoar as far as Horonaim and Eglath
     Shelishiyah,
for even the waters of Nimrim are dried up.
³⁵In Moab I will put an end
   to those who make offerings on the high places[D]
   and burn incense[D] to their gods,"

              declares the LORD.
³⁶"So my heart laments[D] for Moab like a flute;
   it laments like a flute for the men of Kir
     Hareseth.
The wealth they acquired is gone.
³⁷Every head is shaved
   and every beard cut off;
every hand is slashed
   and every waist is covered with sackcloth[D].
³⁸On all the roofs in Moab
   and in the public squares
there is nothing but mourning,
   for I have broken Moab
   like a jar that no one wants,"

              declares the LORD.

Why did Jeremiah weep over Moab's impending doom? (48:31–32,36)
Because he was extremely sensitive and felt deeply for others. Though he preached judgment, his heart was tender, causing him to mourn human tragedy—even when it happened to Israel's enemies.

How did shaving, cutting and dressing in sackcloth mean terrible sorrow to that culture? (48:37)
See *Why shave beards, tear clothes and cut skin?* (41:5).

---

[a]25 *Horn* here symbolizes strength.

39"How shattered she is! How they wail!
  How Moab turns her back in shame!
Moab has become an object of ridicule,
  an object of horror to all those around her."

40This is what the LORD says:

"Look! An eagle is swooping down,
  spreading its wings over Moab.
41Kerioth[a] will be captured
  and the strongholds[D] taken.
In that day the hearts of Moab's warriors
  will be like the heart of a woman in labor.
42Moab will be destroyed as a nation
  because she defied the LORD.
43Terror and pit and snare await you,
  O people of Moab,"

                         declares the LORD.

44"Whoever flees from the terror
  will fall into a pit,
whoever climbs out of the pit
  will be caught in a snare;
for I will bring upon Moab
  the year of her punishment,"

                         declares the LORD.

45"In the shadow of Heshbon
  the fugitives stand helpless,
for a fire has gone out from Heshbon,
  a blaze from the midst of Sihon;
it burns the foreheads of Moab,
  the skulls of the noisy boasters.
46Woe to you, O Moab!
  The people of Chemosh are destroyed;
your sons are taken into exile[D]
  and your daughters into captivity.

47"Yet I will restore the fortunes of Moab
  in days to come,"

                         declares the LORD.

Here ends the judgment on Moab.

A Message About Ammon

49 Concerning the Ammonites:

This is what the LORD says:

"Has Israel no sons?
  Has she no heirs?
Why then has Molech[D][b] taken possession of
    Gad?
  Why do his people live in its towns?
2But the days are coming,"
  declares the LORD,
"when I will sound the battle cry
  against Rabbah of the Ammonites;
it will become a mound of ruins,
  and its surrounding villages will be set on
    fire.
Then Israel will drive out
  those who drove her out,"

                           says the LORD.

3"Wail, O Heshbon, for Ai is destroyed!
  Cry out, O inhabitants of Rabbah!

Why this short, unexplained promise of restoration? (48:47; see 49:39)
The proclamation of judgment was frequently coupled with the promise of blessing by the Old Testament prophets. This was Jeremiah's parting shot at Moab and it was a message of hope. God was out to redeem all of humanity, not just the nation of Israel. If repentance followed God's judgment, restoration would follow repentance. God would share his blessings with the Moabites if they would only repent.

How would a small, impotent Israel drive out the Ammonites? (49:2)
Through their highly potent God, the Lord God Almighty. The specific details of when this happened or how God showed his power are not known.

---

a41 Or *The cities*   b1 Or *their king*; Hebrew *malcam*; also in verse 3

Why would God call the pagan Ammonites his *daughter*? (49:4)
Jeremiah may be using this term to show that God had a claim on the entire world. All nations had descended from Noah and all had the opportunity of worshiping the one true God.

Why not wipe them all out like other instances? (49:11)
Some think God was daring the Edomites to leave their children to him. This, then, would be a veiled threat rather than a promise. Others think the writer was contrasting God's concern for the innocent with the hard message of judgment. In any case, God's dealings are not arbitrary. His decisions are steeped in truth, justice and mercy.

Put on sackcloth[D] and mourn;
    rush here and there inside the walls,
for Molech[D] will go into exile[D],
    together with his priests[D] and officials.
4Why do you boast of your valleys,
    boast of your valleys so fruitful?
O unfaithful daughter,
    you trust in your riches and say,
'Who will attack me?'
5I will bring terror on you
    from all those around you,"
            declares the Lord, the LORD Almighty.
"Every one of you will be driven away,
    and no one will gather the fugitives.

6"Yet afterward, I will restore the fortunes of the
    Ammonites,"
            declares the LORD.

A Message About Edom

7Concerning Edom[D]:

This is what the LORD Almighty says:

    "Is there no longer wisdom in Teman?
        Has counsel perished from the prudent?
        Has their wisdom decayed?
8Turn and flee, hide in deep caves,
    you who live in Dedan,
for I will bring disaster on Esau
    at the time I punish him.
9If grape pickers came to you,
    would they not leave a few grapes?
If thieves came during the night,
    would they not steal only as much as they
        wanted?
10But I will strip Esau bare;
    I will uncover his hiding places,
    so that he cannot conceal himself.
His children, relatives and neighbors will
    perish,
    and he will be no more.
11Leave your orphans; I will protect their lives.
    Your widows too can trust in me."

12This is what the LORD says: "If those who do not deserve to drink the cup must drink it, why should you go unpunished? You will not go unpunished, but must drink it. 13I swear by myself," declares the LORD, "that Bozrah will become a ruin and an object of horror, of reproach[D] and of cursing; and all its towns will be in ruins forever."

14I have heard a message from the LORD:
    An envoy was sent to the nations to say,
"Assemble yourselves to attack it!
    Rise up for battle!"

15"Now I will make you small among the nations,
    despised among men.
16The terror you inspire
    and the pride of your heart have deceived
        you,
you who live in the clefts of the rocks,
    who occupy the heights of the hill.
Though you build your nest as high as the
    eagle's,

from there I will bring you down,"
                    declares the LORD.

17"Edom[D] will become an object of horror;
   all who pass by will be appalled and will
      scoff
   because of all its wounds.
18As Sodom and Gomorrah were overthrown,
   along with their neighboring towns,"
                    says the LORD,
  "so no one will live there;
   no man will dwell in it.

19"Like a lion coming up from Jordan's thickets
   to a rich pastureland,
I will chase Edom from its land in an instant.
  Who is the chosen one I will appoint for
     this?
Who is like me and who can challenge me?
  And what shepherd can stand against me?"
20Therefore, hear what the LORD has planned
     against Edom,
  what he has purposed against those who live
     in Teman:
The young of the flock will be dragged away;
  he will completely destroy their pasture
     because of them.
21At the sound of their fall the earth will tremble;
  their cry will resound to the Red Sea.[a]
22Look! An eagle will soar and swoop down,
  spreading its wings over Bozrah.
In that day the hearts of Edom's warriors
  will be like the heart of a woman in labor.

A Message About Damascus

23Concerning Damascus:

"Hamath and Arpad are dismayed,
  for they have heard bad news.
They are disheartened,
  troubled like[b] the restless sea.
24Damascus has become feeble,
  she has turned to flee
  and panic has gripped her;
anguish and pain have seized her,
  pain like that of a woman in labor.
25Why has the city of renown not been
     abandoned,
  the town in which I delight?
26Surely, her young men will fall in the streets;
  all her soldiers will be silenced in that day,"
                    declares the LORD Almighty.
27"I will set fire to the walls of Damascus;
  it will consume the fortresses of Ben-Hadad."

A Message About Kedar and Hazor

28Concerning Kedar and the kingdoms of Hazor, which
Nebuchadnezzar king of Babylon attacked:

This is what the LORD says:

"Arise, and attack Kedar
  and destroy the people of the East.
29Their tents and their flocks will be taken;
  their shelters will be carried off

SCRIPTURE LINK (49:18–26)
Many parts of this passage are repeated almost verbatim in 50:30–46.

What were *Jordan's thickets*? (49:19)
Areas of dense brush along the banks of the river. Lions and other predators lived in the thickets and raided the flocks on the fertile plains and hillsides nearby.

Like the heart of a woman in labor (49:22)
A picture of extreme anxiety, or even panic. Without sedatives or the assistance of techniques known to modern medicine, the pain and danger of childbirth was quite severe. If a baby turned the wrong way and became stuck in the birth canal or if a mother lacked the strength to deliver the child, labor could result in death for either the mother, the baby or both. Jeremiah prophesied that when judgment finally would swoop down upon Edom, the Edomite soldiers would be filled with fear and dread—like a woman struggling with a difficult delivery.

[a]21 Hebrew *Yam Suph*; that is, Sea of Reeds   [b]23 Hebrew *on* or *by*

Why were there no gates on their city walls? (49:31)

This is a picture of a confident, secure people who had no fear of invaders, probably because they lived so far from the center of civilization, in the middle of the desert to the east of Edom. The fact that they had no gates most likely implies that they had no walls either. They seem to be a nomadic tribe, most likely living in villages of tents.

Why would God establish his throne in a foreign land? (49:38)

To show he's in charge of all history and every nation. Elam would be judged for their sins too. Some think *my throne* refers specifically to the instrument God intended to use to judge Elam, that is, Nebuchadnezzar, king of Babylon. He may have invaded Elam, adjacent to Babylon, a year or so after this prophecy was written (see *Nations Descended from Noah's Sons* on page 14). Also see *Why call a pagan king God's servant?* (27:6).

After announcing judgment, why offer hope? (49:39)

See *Why this short, unexplained promise of restoration?* (48:47).

Bel . . . Marduk (50:2)

Bel and Marduk were two names for one of the chief Babylonian gods. This god would be put to shame when destruction would roll over the Babylonians and show their god to be impotent. When compared to the Lord, the Babylonians' god was no god.

---

with all their goods and camels.
Men will shout to them,
　'Terror on every side!'

30"Flee quickly away!
　Stay in deep caves, you who live in Hazor,"
　　　　　　　　declares the LORD.
"Nebuchadnezzar king of Babylon has plotted
　against you;
　he has devised a plan against you.

31"Arise and attack a nation at ease,
　which lives in confidence,"
　　　　　　　　declares the LORD,
"a nation that has neither gates nor bars;
　its people live alone.
32Their camels will become plunderD,
　and their large herds will be booty.
I will scatter to the winds those who are in
　　　distant placesa
　and will bring disaster on them from every
　　　side,"
　　　　　　　　declares the LORD.

33"Hazor will become a haunt of jackals,
　a desolate place forever.
No one will live there;
　no man will dwell in it."

A Message About Elam

34This is the word of the LORD that came to Jeremiah the prophetD concerning Elam, early in the reign of Zedekiah king of Judah:

35This is what the LORD Almighty says:

"See, I will break the bow of Elam,
　the mainstay of their might.
36I will bring against Elam the four winds
　from the four quarters of the heavens;
I will scatter them to the four winds,
　and there will not be a nation
　where Elam's exilesD do not go.
37I will shatter Elam before their foes,
　before those who seek their lives;
I will bring disaster upon them,
　even my fierce anger,"
　　　　　　　　declares the LORD.
"I will pursue them with the sword
　until I have made an end of them.
38I will set my throne in Elam
　and destroy her king and officials,"
　　　　　　　　declares the LORD.

39"Yet I will restore the fortunes of Elam
　in days to come,"
　　　　　　　　declares the LORD.

A Message About Babylon

50 This is the word the LORD spoke through Jeremiah the prophet concerning Babylon and the land of the Babyloniansb:

2"Announce and proclaim among the nations,
　lift up a banner and proclaim it;

---

a32 Or *who clip the hair by their foreheads*　　b1 Or *Chaldeans*; also in verses 8, 25, 35 and 45

keep nothing back, but say,
'Babylon will be captured;
Bel will be put to shame,
Marduk filled with terror.
Her images will be put to shame
and her idols[D] filled with terror.'
[3]A nation from the north will attack her
and lay waste her land.
No one will live in it;
both men and animals will flee away.

[4]"In those days, at that time,"
declares the LORD,
"the people of Israel and the people of Judah
together
will go in tears to seek the LORD their God.
[5]They will ask the way to Zion[D]
and turn their faces toward it.
They will come and bind themselves to the
LORD
in an everlasting covenant[D]
that will not be forgotten.

[6]"My people have been lost sheep;
their shepherds have led them astray
and caused them to roam on the mountains.
They wandered over mountain and hill
and forgot their own resting place.
[7]Whoever found them devoured them;
their enemies said, 'We are not guilty,
for they sinned against the LORD, their true
pasture,
the LORD, the hope of their fathers.'

[8]"Flee out of Babylon;
leave the land of the Babylonians,
and be like the goats that lead the flock.
[9]For I will stir up and bring against Babylon
an alliance of great nations from the land of
the north.
They will take up their positions against her,
and from the north she will be captured.
Their arrows will be like skilled warriors
who do not return empty-handed.
[10]So Babylonia[a] will be plundered[D];
all who plunder her will have their fill,"
declares the LORD.

[11]"Because you rejoice and are glad,
you who pillage my inheritance,
because you frolic like a heifer threshing grain
and neigh like stallions,
[12]your mother will be greatly ashamed;
she who gave you birth will be disgraced.
She will be the least of the nations—
a wilderness, a dry land, a desert.
[13]Because of the LORD's anger she will not be
inhabited
but will be completely desolate.
All who pass Babylon will be horrified and
scoff
because of all her wounds.

Nation from the north (50:3; see vv. 9,41)

Probably Media, to the north of Babylon (see *Setting of Esther* on page 666). Persia, though, was the nation that destroyed Babylon in 539 B.C., not Media. Media was crushed under the Persians even before Babylon. That was, therefore, the route by which Persia came to Babylon. Perhaps Jeremiah was using irony by borrowing the same phrase that had originally been used of Babylon. See *What northern kingdoms would attack Judah?* (1:14–15). Now Babylon, the nation from the north, would itself be judged by another nation from the north.

When did Israel and Judah seek God together? (50:4)

Some think this happened after Cyrus defeated Babylon in 539 B.C. Jews of both captivities—the Assyrian and the Babylonian—filtered back to Palestine and worshiped together in Jerusalem. Others think this is still future and will happen in the thousand-year reign of Christ called the Millennium (Rev. 20:4).

Everlasting covenant (50:5)

The renewed and enlarged promise God originally made to Abraham, Moses and David (Gen. 12:2–3; Exodus 20; 2 Samuel 7:8–16). Here God promises his people a new and improved relationship, which was brought about by Christ. Also called a *new covenant* (31:31).

How could Israel's enemies know so much about Israel's God? (50:7)

Jeremiah may have been putting words in the mouths of Judah's enemies to highlight Judah's guilt. On the other hand, the pagan logic of Judah's enemies would have led them to think Judah's God was either too weak to win or that he had abandoned his own people. See *Why would the king of Assyria claim to have marching orders from the Lord?* (2 Kings 18:25).

*a*10 Or *Chaldea*

Why would God want vengeance against Babylon? (50:15,18,28–29)

See *Why would God punish Babylon for being his instrument of judgment?* (51:24).

When will Israel be blameless? (50:20)

Some think this happened when Israel was restored to Palestine after Babylon was defeated in 539 B.C. God's justice, then, would have been satisfied. Others point to the redemption that comes through Christ. Still others point to a future restoration of Israel they believe will occur after Christ returns.

14"Take up your positions around Babylon,
all you who draw the bow.
Shoot at her! Spare no arrows,
for she has sinned against the LORD.
15Shout against her on every side!
She surrenders, her towers fall,
her walls are torn down.
Since this is the vengeance of the LORD,
take vengeance on her;
do to her as she has done to others.
16Cut off from Babylon the sower,
and the reaper with his sickle at harvest.
Because of the sword of the oppressor
let everyone return to his own people,
let everyone flee to his own land.

17"Israel is a scattered flock
that lions have chased away.
The first to devour him
was the king of Assyria;
the last to crush his bones
was Nebuchadnezzar king of Babylon."

18Therefore this is what the LORD Almighty, the God of Israel, says:

"I will punish the king of Babylon and his land
as I punished the king of Assyria.
19But I will bring Israel back to his own pasture
and he will graze on Carmel and Bashan;
his appetite will be satisfied
on the hills of Ephraim and Gilead.
20In those days, at that time,"
declares the LORD,
"search will be made for Israel's guilt,
but there will be none,
and for the sins of Judah,
but none will be found,
for I will forgive the remnant^b I spare.

21"Attack the land of Merathaim
and those who live in Pekod.
Pursue, kill and completely destroy^a them,"
declares the LORD.
"Do everything I have commanded you.
22The noise of battle is in the land,
the noise of great destruction!
23How broken and shattered
is the hammer of the whole earth!
How desolate is Babylon
among the nations!
24I set a trap for you, O Babylon,
and you were caught before you knew it;
you were found and captured
because you opposed the LORD.
25The LORD has opened his arsenal
and brought out the weapons of his wrath,
for the Sovereign LORD Almighty has work to do
in the land of the Babylonians.
26Come against her from afar.
Break open her granaries;
pile her up like heaps of grain.
Completely destroy her

---

a21 The Hebrew term refers to the irrevocable giving over of things or persons to the LORD, often by totally destroying them; also in verse 26.

and leave her no remnant.^D
²⁷Kill all her young bulls;
   let them go down to the slaughter!
Woe to them! For their day has come,
   the time for them to be punished.
²⁸Listen to the fugitives and refugees from
      Babylon
   declaring in Zion^D
how the LORD our God has taken vengeance,
   vengeance for his temple.

²⁹"Summon archers against Babylon,
   all those who draw the bow.
Encamp all around her;
   let no one escape.
Repay her for her deeds;
   do to her as she has done.
For she has defied the LORD,
   the Holy One of Israel.
³⁰Therefore, her young men will fall in the
      streets;
   all her soldiers will be silenced in that day,"
               declares the LORD.
³¹"See, I am against you, O arrogant one,"
   declares the Lord, the LORD Almighty,
"for your day has come,
   the time for you to be punished.
³²The arrogant one will stumble and fall
   and no one will help her up;
I will kindle a fire in her towns
   that will consume all who are around her."

³³This is what the LORD Almighty says:

"The people of Israel are oppressed,
   and the people of Judah as well.
All their captors hold them fast,
   refusing to let them go.
³⁴Yet their Redeemer^D is strong;
   the LORD Almighty is his name.
He will vigorously defend their cause
   so that he may bring rest to their land,
   but unrest to those who live in Babylon.

³⁵"A sword against the Babylonians!"
   declares the LORD—
"against those who live in Babylon
   and against her officials and wise men!
³⁶A sword against her false prophets^D!
   They will become fools.
A sword against her warriors!
   They will be filled with terror.
³⁷A sword against her horses and chariots
   and all the foreigners in her ranks!
   They will become women.
A sword against her treasures!
   They will be plundered.^D
³⁸A drought on^a her waters!
   They will dry up.
For it is a land of idols^D,
   idols that will go mad with terror.

³⁹"So desert creatures and hyenas will live there,
   and there the owl will dwell.

^a38 Or A sword against

Was Jeremiah really saying that *young bulls* needed to be punished? (50:27)

No. This is figurative language referring to the people of Babylon—particularly the healthy young men of the Babylonian army.

SCRIPTURE LINK (50:31–32)

Though this message of judgment is against Babylon, God delivered a similar message against Jerusalem in 21:13–14.

A sword against (50:35–37)

A symbol of war and devastation. This phrase was like a command uttered by a ruler, ordering that something take place. In this case, the order came from the Lord with the result that the Babylonians were eventually overrun by the Medes and the Persians (539 B.C.).

It will never again be inhabited
   or lived in from generation to generation.
40As God overthrew Sodom and Gomorrah
   along with their neighboring towns,"
                   declares the LORD,
  "so no one will live there;
   no man will dwell in it.

41"Look! An army is coming from the north;
   a great nation and many kings
   are being stirred up from the ends of the
      earth.
42They are armed with bows and spears;
   they are cruel and without mercy.[D]
They sound like the roaring sea
   as they ride on their horses;
they come like men in battle formation
   to attack you, O Daughter of Babylon.
43The king of Babylon has heard reports about
      them,
   and his hands hang limp.
Anguish has gripped him,
   pain like that of a woman in labor.
44Like a lion coming up from Jordan's thickets
   to a rich pastureland,
I will chase Babylon from its land in an instant.
   Who is the chosen one I will appoint for
      this?
Who is like me and who can challenge me?
   And what shepherd can stand against me?"
45Therefore, hear what the LORD has planned
   against Babylon,
   what he has purposed against the land of the
      Babylonians:
The young of the flock will be dragged away;
   he will completely destroy their pasture
      because of them.
46At the sound of Babylon's capture the earth
      will tremble;
   its cry will resound among the nations.

51 This is what the LORD says:

"See, I will stir up the spirit of a destroyer
   against Babylon and the people of Leb
      Kamai.[a]
2I will send foreigners to Babylon
   to winnow her and to devastate her land;
they will oppose her on every side
   in the day of her disaster.
3Let not the archer string his bow,
   nor let him put on his armor.
Do not spare her young men;
   completely destroy[b] her army.
4They will fall down slain in Babylon,[c]
   fatally wounded in her streets.
5For Israel and Judah have not been forsaken
   by their God, the LORD Almighty,
though their land[d] is full of guilt
   before the Holy One of Israel.

What northern army would attack Babylon? (50:41–42)

See *Nation from the north* (50:3).

Leb Kamai (51:1)

Why Jeremiah didn't just use the name *Babylonia* is not clear. (See NIV text note.) The phrase can be literally translated, *the heart of those who rise against me*. See **Why give Babylon a code name?** (25:26).

---

[a]1 *Leb Kamai* is a cryptogram for Chaldea, that is, Babylonia.
[b]3 The Hebrew term refers to the irrevocable giving over of things or persons to the LORD, often by totally destroying them.   [c]4 Or *Chaldea*   [d]5 Or *I and the land ⌊of the Babylonians⌋*

⁶"Flee from Babylon!
　　Run for your lives!
　　Do not be destroyed because of her sins.
It is time for the LORD's vengeance;
　　he will pay her what she deserves.
⁷Babylon was a gold cup in the LORD's hand;
　　she made the whole earth drunk.
The nations drank her wine;
　　therefore they have now gone mad.
⁸Babylon will suddenly fall and be broken.
　　Wail over her!
Get balm for her pain;
　　perhaps she can be healed.

⁹" 'We would have healed Babylon,
　　but she cannot be healed;
let us leave her and each go to his own land,
　　for her judgment reaches to the skies,
　　it rises as high as the clouds.'

¹⁰" 'The LORD has vindicated us;
　　come, let us tell in Zion^D
　　what the LORD our God has done.'

¹¹"Sharpen the arrows,
　　take up the shields!
The LORD has stirred up the kings of the Medes,
　　because his purpose is to destroy Babylon.
The LORD will take vengeance,
　　vengeance for his temple.
¹²Lift up a banner against the walls of Babylon!
　　Reinforce the guard,
station the watchmen^D,
　　prepare an ambush!
The LORD will carry out his purpose,
　　his decree against the people of Babylon.
¹³You who live by many waters
　　and are rich in treasures,
your end has come,
　　the time for you to be cut off.
¹⁴The LORD Almighty has sworn by himself:
　　I will surely fill you with men, as with a
　　　　swarm of locusts^D,
　　and they will shout in triumph over you.

¹⁵"He made the earth by his power;
　　he founded the world by his wisdom
　　and stretched out the heavens by his
　　　　understanding.
¹⁶When he thunders, the waters in the heavens
　　　　roar;
　　he makes clouds rise from the ends of the
　　　　earth.
He sends lightning with the rain
　　and brings out the wind from his
　　　　storehouses.

¹⁷"Every man is senseless and without
　　　　knowledge;
　　every goldsmith is shamed by his idols^D.
His images are a fraud;
　　they have no breath in them.
¹⁸They are worthless, the objects of mockery;
　　when their judgment comes, they will perish.
¹⁹He who is the Portion of Jacob is not like these,
　　for he is the Maker of all things,

Did Babylon deserve to be punished? (51:6)

See *Why would God punish Babylon for being his instrument of judgment?* (51:24).

Why wail for Babylon? (51:8)

See *Why did Jeremiah weep over Moab's impending doom?* (48:31–32).

Why did God swear by himself? (51:14)

See *Why did God swear by himself?* (22:5).

Portion of Jacob (51:19)

God was the inheritance or possession of Israel. The word *portion* has legal implications that tied into the special relationship between God and his chosen people. Jacob was the key patriarch in the history of Israel.

Who was God's *war club*? (51:20-23)

Some say this refers to Israel, used by God to defend his holiness by engaging in the fight against sin and Satan. Others think it may refer to Cyrus who would lead Persia against Babylon. Still others think this meant Babylon itself, used earlier as an instrument of God's judgment. Also see *Why call a pagan king God's servant?* (27:6).

Why would God punish Babylon for being his instrument of judgment? (51:24)

Though the Babylonians unwittingly fulfilled God's purposes, they still had to answer for their excessive methods and ungodly motives. They slaughtered the Israelites and razed Jerusalem for their own interests, not God's. See *Why call a pagan king God's servant?* (27:6) and *Why did God "ordain" Assyria to devastate other nations?* (2 Kings 19:25).

How was Babylon like a *threshing floor*? (51:33)

A threshing floor was a hard surface where grain was separated from the stalk. Bundles of grain stalks were placed on the floor. The farmers would then use a flailing instrument to remove the grain from the heads of grain. Sometimes, instead of beating the grain themselves, they walked their animals across the threshing floor to accomplish the same purpose. In judgment, God would beat and trample Babylon, separating the grain from the chaff.

including the tribe of his inheritance—
the Lord Almighty is his name.

²⁰"You are my war club,
my weapon for battle—
with you I shatter nations,
with you I destroy kingdoms,
²¹with you I shatter horse and rider,
with you I shatter chariot and driver,
²²with you I shatter man and woman,
with you I shatter old man and youth,
with you I shatter young man and maiden,
²³with you I shatter shepherd and flock,
with you I shatter farmer and oxen,
with you I shatter governors and officials.

²⁴"Before your eyes I will repay Babylon and all who live in Babylonia[a] for all the wrong they have done in Zion[D]," declares the Lord.

²⁵"I am against you, O destroying mountain,
you who destroy the whole earth,"
declares the Lord.
"I will stretch out my hand against you,
roll you off the cliffs,
and make you a burned-out mountain.
²⁶No rock will be taken from you for a
cornerstone,
nor any stone for a foundation,
for you will be desolate forever,"
declares the Lord.

²⁷"Lift up a banner in the land!
Blow the trumpet among the nations!
Prepare the nations for battle against her;
summon against her these kingdoms:
Ararat, Minni and Ashkenaz.
Appoint a commander against her;
send up horses like a swarm of locusts[D].
²⁸Prepare the nations for battle against her—
the kings of the Medes,
their governors and all their officials,
and all the countries they rule.
²⁹The land trembles and writhes,
for the Lord's purposes against Babylon
stand—
to lay waste the land of Babylon
so that no one will live there.
³⁰Babylon's warriors have stopped fighting;
they remain in their strongholds[D].
Their strength is exhausted;
they have become like women.
Her dwellings are set on fire;
the bars of her gates are broken.
³¹One courier follows another
and messenger follows messenger
to announce to the king of Babylon
that his entire city is captured,
³²the river crossings seized,
the marshes set on fire,
and the soldiers terrified."

³³This is what the Lord Almighty, the God of Israel, says:

---

a 24 Or *Chaldea*; also in verse 35

"The Daughter of Babylon is like a threshing
        floor
    at the time it is trampled;
    the time to harvest her will soon come."

34"Nebuchadnezzar king of Babylon has devoured
        us,
    he has thrown us into confusion,
    he has made us an empty jar.
Like a serpent he has swallowed us
    and filled his stomach with our delicacies,
    and then has spewed us out.
35May the violence done to our flesh*a* be upon
        Babylon,"
    say the inhabitants of Zion*D*.
"May our blood be on those who live in
        Babylonia,"
    says Jerusalem*D*.

36Therefore, this is what the LORD says:

"See, I will defend your cause
    and avenge*D* you;
I will dry up her sea
    and make her springs dry.
37Babylon will be a heap of ruins,
    a haunt of jackals,
an object of horror and scorn,
    a place where no one lives.
38Her people all roar like young lions,
    they growl like lion cubs.
39But while they are aroused,
    I will set out a feast for them
    and make them drunk,
so that they shout with laughter—
    then sleep forever and not awake,"
                            declares the LORD.
40"I will bring them down
    like lambs to the slaughter,
    like rams and goats.

41"How Sheshach*b* will be captured,
    the boast of the whole earth seized!
What a horror Babylon will be
    among the nations!
42The sea will rise over Babylon;
    its roaring waves will cover her.
43Her towns will be desolate,
    a dry and desert land,
a land where no one lives,
    through which no man travels.
44I will punish Bel in Babylon
    and make him spew out what he has
        swallowed.
The nations will no longer stream to him.
    And the wall of Babylon will fall.

45"Come out of her, my people!
    Run for your lives!
    Run from the fierce anger of the LORD.
46Do not lose heart or be afraid
    when rumors are heard in the land;
    one rumor comes this year, another the next,

Why use a cryptogram? (51:41)
See *Why give Babylon a code name?* (25:26).

The sea will rise over Babylon (51:42)
A metaphor for the way Babylon would be flooded by waves of foreign invaders and swept
away. This is a prophetic image that Jeremiah
has used before (46:7–8). Isaiah described an
invasion using the same figure of speech (Isaiah 8:6–8).

a35 Or *done to us and to our children*   *b41 Sheshach* is a
cryptogram for Babylon.

Where would these northern destroyers come from? (51:48)

See *Nation from the north* (50:3).

Why would God demand retribution of Babylon? (51:56)

See *Why would God punish Babylon for being his instrument of judgment?* (51:24).

Why did King Zedekiah go to Babylon seven years before he was dethroned? (51:59; see 52:5)

Some think he may have been summoned for questioning by Nebuchadnezzar about his loyalty. Others think this could read *from* (instead of *with*) Zedekiah. In that case, Seraiah would have gone to Babylon without the king.

Who was Seraiah and why would he serve as a prophet by proxy? (51:59,61)

Seraiah was the brother of Baruch, Jeremiah's faithful scribe and loyal friend (32:12). His title, *staff officer*, meant *official of the resting place*. He was in charge of food and lodging for the traveling royal party. Why Jeremiah delegated this task to him is not clear. He was apparently sympathetic to Jeremiah's message and was in a position to do something with it. Jeremiah previously had delegated Baruch to read a prophecy at the temple (36:8).

rumors of violence in the land
and of ruler against ruler.
⁴⁷For the time will surely come
when I will punish the idolsᴰ of Babylon;
her whole land will be disgraced
and her slain will all lie fallen within her.
⁴⁸Then heaven and earth and all that is in them
will shout for joy over Babylon,
for out of the north
destroyers will attack her,"
declares the LORD.

⁴⁹"Babylon must fall because of Israel's slain,
just as the slain in all the earth
have fallen because of Babylon.
⁵⁰You who have escaped the sword,
leave and do not linger!
Remember the LORD in a distant land,
and think on Jerusalemᴰ."

⁵¹"We are disgraced,
for we have been insulted
and shame covers our faces,
because foreigners have entered
the holy places of the LORD's house."

⁵²"But days are coming," declares the LORD,
"when I will punish her idols,
and throughout her land
the wounded will groan.
⁵³Even if Babylon reaches the sky
and fortifies her lofty strongholdᴰ,
I will send destroyers against her,"
declares the LORD.

⁵⁴"The sound of a cry comes from Babylon,
the sound of great destruction
from the land of the Babylonians.ᵃ
⁵⁵The LORD will destroy Babylon;
he will silence her noisy din.
Waves ⌞of enemies⌟ will rage like great waters;
the roar of their voices will resound.
⁵⁶A destroyer will come against Babylon;
her warriors will be captured,
and their bows will be broken.
For the LORD is a God of retributionᴰ;
he will repay in full.
⁵⁷I will make her officials and wise men drunk,
her governors, officers and warriors as well;
they will sleep forever and not awake,"
declares the King, whose name is the LORD Almighty.

⁵⁸This is what the LORD Almighty says:

"Babylon's thick wall will be leveled
and her high gates set on fire;
the peoples exhaust themselves for nothing,
the nations' labor is only fuel for the flames."

⁵⁹This is the message Jeremiah gave to the staff officer Seraiah son of Neriah, the son of Mahseiah, when he went to Babylon with Zedekiah king of Judah in the fourth year of his reign. ⁶⁰Jeremiah had written on a scroll about all the disasters that would come upon Babylon—all that had

ᵃ54 Or *Chaldeans*

been recorded concerning Babylon. **61**He said to Seraiah, "When you get to Babylon, see that you read all these words aloud. **62**Then say, 'O Lord, you have said you will destroy this place, so that neither man nor animal will live in it; it will be desolate forever.' **63**When you finish reading this scroll, tie a stone to it and throw it into the Euphrates. **64**Then say, 'So will Babylon sink to rise no more because of the disaster I will bring upon her. And her people will fall.' "

The words of Jeremiah end here.

The Fall of Jerusalem

52 Zedekiah was twenty-one years old when he became king, and he reigned in JerusalemD eleven years. His mother's name was Hamutal daughter of Jeremiah; she was from Libnah. **2**He did evil in the eyes of the Lord, just as Jehoiakim had done. **3**It was because of the Lord's anger that all this happened to Jerusalem and Judah, and in the end he thrust them from his presence.

Now Zedekiah rebelled against the king of Babylon.

4So in the ninth year of Zedekiah's reign, on the tenth day of the tenth month, Nebuchadnezzar king of Babylon marched against Jerusalem with his whole army. They camped outside the city and built siege worksD all around it. **5**The city was kept under siege until the eleventh year of King Zedekiah.

6By the ninth day of the fourth month the famine in the city had become so severe that there was no food for the people to eat. **7**Then the city wall was broken through, and the whole army fled. They left the city at night through the gate between the two walls near the king's garden, though the Babylonians*a* were surrounding the city. They fled toward the Arabah,*b* **8**but the Babylonian*c* army pursued King Zedekiah and overtook him in the plains of JerichoD. All his soldiers were separated from him and scattered, **9**and he was captured.

He was taken to the king of Babylon at Riblah in the land of Hamath, where he pronounced sentence on him. **10**There at Riblah the king of Babylon slaughtered the sons of Zedekiah before his eyes; he also killed all the officials of Judah. **11**Then he put out Zedekiah's eyes, bound him with bronze shackles and took him to Babylon, where he put him in prison till the day of his deathD.

12On the tenth day of the fifth month, in the nineteenth year of Nebuchadnezzar king of Babylon, Nebuzaradan commander of the imperial guard, who served the king of Babylon, came to Jerusalem. **13**He set fire to the temple of the Lord, the royal palace and all the houses of Jerusalem. Every important building he burned down. **14**The whole Babylonian army under the commander of the imperial guard broke down all the walls around Jerusalem. **15**Nebuzaradan the commander of the guard carried into exileD some of the poorest people and those who remained in the city, along with the rest of the craftsmen*d* and those who had gone over to the king of Babylon. **16**But Nebuzaradan left behind the rest of the poorest people of the land to work the vineyards and fields.

17The Babylonians broke up the bronze pillars, the movable stands and the bronze Sea that were at the temple of the Lord and they carried all the bronze to Babylon.

Why is this information repeated? (52:1–24; see 39:1–10)

Some think this chapter is an appendage added by a later editor, suggested by 51:64: *The words of Jeremiah end here.* Others see literary themes that tie this chapter with the rest of the book. In this view, this information was intentionally repeated as a literary device to explain more fully the events surrounding the fall of Jerusalem.

Was 18 months typical for a siege? (52:4)

See *Was 18 months typical for a siege?* (39:1–2).

How did they break through the wall? (52:7)

See *How did they break through the wall?* (39:2).

How could they escape when the Babylonians surrounded the city? (52:7)

See *How could they escape when the Babylonians surrounded the city?* (39:4).

Why didn't Nebuchadnezzar just kill Zedekiah? (52:10–11)

See *Why didn't Nebuchadnezzar just kill Zedekiah?* (39:7).

---

*a*7 Or *Chaldeans*; also in verse 17   *b*7 Or *the Jordan Valley*
*c*8 Or *Chaldean*; also in verse 14   *d*15 Or *populace*

Why were only 4,600 deported? (52:30)
The figures don't add up. This account conflicts with 2 Kings 24:14,16, which states that 10,000 were deported at one time. Some think the discrepancy stems from counts taken at different stages in King Zedekiah's reign. Others think one total included only men, not women and children. Still others say that the figures are approximations and weren't intended to be specific.

Why would an imprisoned king be released after 37 years in prison? (52:31)
Possibly because Nebuchadnezzar was no longer king. The new political regime of Evil-Merodach apparently saw no threat in the aging Jehoiachin, and perhaps to celebrate the coronation of the new king, set Jehoiachin free. Also see *Why release a king after 37 years in prison?* (2 Kings 25:27–30).

18They also took away the pots, shovels, wick trimmers, sprinkling bowls, dishes and all the bronze articles used in the temple service. 19The commander of the imperial guard took away the basins, censers[D], sprinkling bowls, pots, lampstands, dishes and bowls used for drink offerings[D]—all that were made of pure gold or silver.

20The bronze from the two pillars, the Sea and the twelve bronze bulls under it, and the movable stands, which King Solomon had made for the temple of the LORD, was more than could be weighed. 21Each of the pillars was eighteen cubits[D] high and twelve cubits in circumference[a]; each was four fingers thick, and hollow. 22The bronze capital on top of the one pillar was five cubits[b] high and was decorated with a network and pomegranates of bronze all around. The other pillar, with its pomegranates, was similar. 23There were ninety-six pomegranates on the sides; the total number of pomegranates above the surrounding network was a hundred.

24The commander of the guard took as prisoners Seraiah the chief priest[D], Zephaniah the priest next in rank and the three doorkeepers. 25Of those still in the city, he took the officer in charge of the fighting men, and seven royal advisers. He also took the secretary who was chief officer in charge of conscripting the people of the land and sixty of his men who were found in the city. 26Nebuzaradan the commander took them all and brought them to the king of Babylon at Riblah. 27There at Riblah, in the land of Hamath, the king had them executed.

So Judah went into captivity, away from her land. 28This is the number of the people Nebuchadnezzar carried into exile[D]:

in the seventh year, 3,023 Jews[D];
29in Nebuchadnezzar's eighteenth year,
832 people from Jerusalem[D];
30in his twenty-third year,
745 Jews taken into exile by Nebuzaradan the commander of the imperial guard.
There were 4,600 people in all.

Jehoiachin Released

31In the thirty-seventh year of the exile of Jehoiachin king of Judah, in the year Evil-Merodach[c] became king of Babylon, he released Jehoiachin king of Judah and freed him from prison on the twenty-fifth day of the twelfth month. 32He spoke kindly to him and gave him a seat of honor higher than those of the other kings who were with him in Babylon. 33So Jehoiachin put aside his prison clothes and for the rest of his life ate regularly at the king's table. 34Day by day the king of Babylon gave Jehoiachin a regular allowance as long as he lived, till the day of his death[D].

---

a21 That is, about 27 feet (about 8.1 meters) high and 18 feet (about 5.4 meters) in circumference   *b22* That is, about 7 1/2 feet (about 2.3 meters)   *c31* Also called *Amel-Marduk*

LAMENTATIONS

Why read this book?

If you've ever experienced a significant loss, Lamentations is for you. It's a beautiful, though dark book on the pain of injustice and human loss. It's filled with crushing emotions: anger, desperation, fear, loneliness, hopelessness. But in reading Lamentations, those feeling wounded may feel strangely understood. The depths of suffering, well-expressed, can bring comfort and restoration.

Who wrote this book?

Probably Jeremiah.

When and why was it written?

Jeremiah had predicted and witnessed the devastation of his homeland. Moved deeply, he wrote this poem to express his nation's grief. He wrote it soon after Jerusalem's fall to Babylon in 586 B.C., perhaps within a decade.

What to look for in Lamentations:

Look for themes of tragic reversal—despair and hope, repentance and renewal—for individuals, cities and nations. Notice also the book's careful construction. Jeremiah used the alphabet to portray the full extent of his pain and sorrow—as though including everything from A to Z. The 22 Hebrew letters shape the first four chapters, but not the last one. Though we can't say why, perhaps it was Jeremiah's way to express frustration over Jerusalem's slide from order to a final state of chaos.

Why did Judah's friends and lovers become her enemies? (1:2)

When things got tough, Judah's former political allies cut their ties with her. Egypt, Tyre and Sidon failed to come to her rescue when Babylon invaded (see *Judgment on Israel's Neighbors* on page 1257). Some of these former allies even betrayed Judah by joining forces with Babylon.

Does the Lord cause grief? (1:5)

See article: *Why does God send calamity?* (3:38).

Nakedness (1:8)

To have private parts exposed signified total disgrace or ill repute. Because Judah worshiped pagan gods, she was stripped of her dignity and became an object of scorn.

How far did Judah fall? (1:9)

Once a captor, Judah was now a captive. Judah had ruled Moab, Edom and other neighboring areas. Jerusalem had been a regional metropolis but was now only a shadow of her former self. Her riches-to-rags fall was swift.

1 *a* How deserted lies the city,
    once so full of people!
How like a widow is she,
    who once was great among the nations!
She who was queen among the provinces
    has now become a slave.

²Bitterly she weeps at night,
    tears are upon her cheeks.
Among all her lovers
    there is none to comfort her.
All her friends have betrayed her;
    they have become her enemies.

³After affliction ᴰ and harsh labor,
    Judah has gone into exile ᴰ.
She dwells among the nations;
    she finds no resting place.
All who pursue her have overtaken her
    in the midst of her distress.

⁴The roads to Zion ᴰ mourn,
    for no one comes to her appointed feasts.
All her gateways are desolate,
    her priests ᴰ groan,
her maidens grieve,
    and she is in bitter anguish.

⁵Her foes have become her masters;
    her enemies are at ease.
The LORD has brought her grief
    because of her many sins.
Her children have gone into exile,
    captive before the foe.

⁶All the splendor has departed
    from the Daughter of Zion.
Her princes are like deer
    that find no pasture;
in weakness they have fled
    before the pursuer.

⁷In the days of her affliction and wandering
    Jerusalem ᴰ remembers all the treasures
    that were hers in days of old.
When her people fell into enemy hands,
    there was no one to help her.
Her enemies looked at her
    and laughed at her destruction.

⁸Jerusalem has sinned greatly
    and so has become unclean ᴰ.
All who honored her despise her,
    for they have seen her nakedness;
she herself groans
    and turns away.

⁹Her filthiness clung to her skirts;
    she did not consider her future.
Her fall was astounding;
    there was none to comfort her.
"Look, O LORD, on my affliction,
    for the enemy has triumphed."

¹⁰The enemy laid hands

*a*This chapter is an acrostic poem, the verses of which begin with the successive letters of the Hebrew alphabet.

on all her treasures;
she saw pagan nations
    enter her sanctuary—
those you had forbidden
    to enter your assembly.

¹¹All her people groan
    as they search for bread;
they barter their treasures for food
    to keep themselves alive.
"Look, O LORD, and consider,
    for I am despised."

¹²"Is it nothing to you, all you who pass by?
    Look around and see.
Is any suffering like my suffering
    that was inflicted on me,
that the LORD brought on me
    in the day of his fierce anger?

¹³"From on high he sent fire,
    sent it down into my bones.
He spread a net for my feet
    and turned me back.
He made me desolate,
    faint all the day long.

¹⁴"My sins have been bound into a yoke^Da;
    by his hands they were woven together.
They have come upon my neck
    and the Lord has sapped my strength.
He has handed me over
    to those I cannot withstand.

¹⁵"The Lord has rejected
    all the warriors in my midst;
he has summoned an army against me
    to^b crush my young men.
In his winepress^D the Lord has trampled
    the Virgin Daughter of Judah.

¹⁶"This is why I weep
    and my eyes overflow with tears.
No one is near to comfort me,
    no one to restore my spirit.
My children are destitute
    because the enemy has prevailed."

¹⁷Zion^D stretches out her hands,
    but there is no one to comfort her.
The LORD has decreed for Jacob
    that his neighbors become his foes;
Jerusalem^D has become
    an unclean^D thing among them.

¹⁸"The LORD is righteous^D,
    yet I rebelled against his command.
Listen, all you peoples;
    look upon my suffering.
My young men and maidens
    have gone into exile^D.

¹⁹"I called to my allies
    but they betrayed me.
My priests^D and my elders

My suffering (1:12)
Judah's sufferings were Jeremiah's sufferings.
Caught up in their grief, he spoke as an eyewitness and fellow sufferer. His words personified the city of Jerusalem, giving voice to her
suffering and anguish.

---

^a14 Most Hebrew manuscripts; Septuagint *He kept watch over my sins*
^b15 Or *has set a time for me / when he will*

perished in the city
while they searched for food
to keep themselves alive.

20"See, O LORD, how distressed I am!
I am in torment within,
and in my heart I am disturbed,
for I have been most rebellious.
Outside, the sword bereaves;
inside, there is only death.ᴰ

What day was Judah anticipating? (1:21)

The day when God's justice would be reversed, when God would punish the nations inflicting this pain on Judah.

21"People have heard my groaning,
but there is no one to comfort me.
All my enemies have heard of my distress;
they rejoice at what you have done.
May you bring the day you have announced
so they may become like me.

22"Let all their wickedness come before you;
deal with them
as you have dealt with me
because of all my sins.
My groans are many
and my heart is faint."

Footstool (2:1)

God's footstool refers to the ark of the covenant (1 Chron. 28:2; Psalm 99:5), which represented God's presence among them. But the temple where the ark resided now lay in ruins —a tragic reversal of everything God's people had held dear. They were bewildered that God would abandon his dwelling place.

2 ᵃ How the Lord has covered the Daughter of
    Zionᴰ
  with the cloud of his angerᵇ!
He has hurled down the splendor of Israel
  from heaven to earth;
he has not remembered his footstoolᴰ
  in the day of his anger.

²Without pity the Lord has swallowed up
  all the dwellings of Jacob;
in his wrath he has torn down
  the strongholdsᴰ of the Daughter of Judah.
He has brought her kingdom and its princes
  down to the ground in dishonor.

³In fierce anger he has cut off
  every hornᶜ of Israel.
He has withdrawn his right hand
  at the approach of the enemy.
He has burned in Jacob like a flaming fire
  that consumes everything around it.

Withdrawn his right hand (2:3)

God's right hand symbolized his power, protection and security. With it withdrawn, the people lost all of that. See *The years of the right hand of the Most High* (Psalm 77:10).

⁴Like an enemy he has strung his bow;
  his right hand is ready.
Like a foe he has slain
  all who were pleasing to the eye;
he has poured out his wrath like fire
  on the tent of the Daughter of Zion.

How can a loving God be an enemy? (2:4–5)

God was not Judah's enemy. But he couldn't permit her wickedness to go unchecked. Jeremiah was expressing in emotional terms what God's punishment felt like.

⁵The Lord is like an enemy;
  he has swallowed up Israel.
He has swallowed up all her palaces
  and destroyed her strongholds.
He has multiplied mourning and lamentation
  for the Daughter of Judah.

⁶He has laid waste his dwelling like a garden;
  he has destroyed his place of meeting.

ᵃThis chapter is an acrostic poem, the verses of which begin with the successive letters of the Hebrew alphabet.   ᵇ1 Or *How the Lord in his anger / has treated the Daughter of Zion with contempt*   ᶜ3 Or / *all the strength;* or *every king; horn* here symbolizes strength.

The LORD has made Zion^D forget
  her appointed feasts and her Sabbaths^D;
in his fierce anger he has spurned
  both king and priest^D.

⁷The Lord has rejected his altar
  and abandoned his sanctuary.
He has handed over to the enemy
  the walls of her palaces;
they have raised a shout in the house of the
  LORD
    as on the day of an appointed feast.

⁸The LORD determined to tear down
  the wall around the Daughter of Zion.
He stretched out a measuring line^D
  and did not withhold his hand from
    destroying.
He made ramparts and walls lament^D;
  together they wasted away.

⁹Her gates have sunk into the ground;
  their bars he has broken and destroyed.
Her king and her princes are exiled^D among
    the nations,
  the law is no more,
and her prophets^D no longer find
  visions^D from the LORD.

¹⁰The elders of the Daughter of Zion
  sit on the ground in silence;
they have sprinkled dust on their heads
  and put on sackcloth^D.
The young women of Jerusalem^D
  have bowed their heads to the ground.

¹¹My eyes fail from weeping,
  I am in torment within,
my heart is poured out on the ground

Had God made his people forget him? (2:6)

This was a way of saying that God had judged the people and placed them in a situation where they could no longer practice their feasts and Sabbaths. Captives in Babylon where there was no temple to the Lord and where they did not have the freedom to observe their religion, they were cut off from reminders of God's presence. In reality, the people were punished because they had forgotten the Lord by refusing to serve him.

Measuring line (2:8)

This is a metaphor picturing God's thorough and calculated punishment of Judah.

Why does God allow innocent children to suffer? (2:11–12)

Jeremiah's words are laced with emotion. And stewing just beneath his grief was an anguished question: How could God have permitted these children to suffer?

All people—including children—are born into sin (Romans 5:12). The sin of Adam and Eve infected each succeeding generation, leading to the suffering and consequences that sin produces. While these children had not participated in the specific sins that incited God's wrath, they were not themselves sinless.

Unfortunately, children often suffer for their parents' actions—whether they are crack babies, adult children of alcoholics or teens of emotionally absent parents. In the same way, children, as members of a community, share in the benefits or consequences of that community's actions, even though they had nothing to do with the decision. In many countries, children are the victims of the older generation's war and terrorism.

Some insist that no one but God can be ultimately responsible for such suffering, perhaps the feelings behind Jeremiah's honest, but bitter complaints (vv. 19–20). Yet God never wanted anyone to suffer, particularly the children. Death is the natural result of sin (Romans 6:23). Judah could only blame herself.

See article: *Does God punish children for their parents' sins?* (Num. 14:18). Also see *Why punish the children of sinners?* (Jer. 32:18).

because my people are destroyed,
  because children and infants faint
    in the streets of the city.

12They say to their mothers,
    "Where is bread and wine?"
  as they faint like wounded men
    in the streets of the city,
  as their lives ebb away
    in their mothers' arms.

Why compare sinful Judah to a virgin? (2:13)

The writers of the Old Testament often used females metaphorically to describe God's people
(1:1,9; Isaiah 32:9–11). Lamentations frequently refers to Judah as *daughters* (20
times). Sometimes this figure of speech is
combined with *virgin* (see Jer. 18:13; 31:4,21;
46:11), perhaps to accent Judah's fall from purity and grace. The original word for *virgin* did
not always imply sexual purity, however, and
sometimes simply meant *young woman*.

13What can I say for you?
    With what can I compare you,
    O Daughter of Jerusalem D?
  To what can I liken you,
    that I may comfort you,
    O Virgin Daughter of Zion D?
  Your wound is as deep as the sea.
    Who can heal you?

14The visions D of your prophets D
    were false and worthless;
  they did not expose your sin
    to ward off your captivity.
  The oracles D they gave you
    were false and misleading.

Clap their hands (2:15)

An expression of scorn, as were scoffing and
shaking heads. Others delighted in Jerusalem's pain and loss (see Job 27:23; Jer.
18:16; 19:8).

15All who pass your way
    clap their hands at you;
  they scoff and shake their heads
    at the Daughter of Jerusalem:
  "Is this the city that was called
    the perfection of beauty,
    the joy of the whole earth?"

16All your enemies open their mouths
    wide against you;
  they scoff and gnash their teeth
    and say, "We have swallowed her up.
  This is the day we have waited for;
    we have lived to see it."

17The LORD has done what he planned;
    he has fulfilled his word,
    which he decreed long ago.
  He has overthrown you without pity,
    he has let the enemy gloat over you,
    he has exalted the horn a of your foes.

18The hearts of the people
    cry out to the Lord.
  O wall of the Daughter of Zion,
    let your tears flow like a river
    day and night;
  give yourself no relief,
    your eyes no rest.

19Arise, cry out in the night,
    as the watches of the night begin;
  pour out your heart like water
    in the presence of the Lord.
  Lift up your hands to him
    for the lives of your children,
  who faint from hunger
    at the head of every street.

---

a17 *Horn* here symbolizes strength.

²⁰"Look, O LORD, and consider:
  Whom have you ever treated like this?
Should women eat their offspring,
  the children they have cared for?
Should priest^D and prophet^D be killed
  in the sanctuary of the Lord?

²¹"Young and old lie together
  in the dust of the streets;
my young men and maidens
  have fallen by the sword.
You have slain them in the day of your anger;
  you have slaughtered them without pity.

²²"As you summon to a feast day,
  so you summoned against me terrors on
    every side.
In the day of the LORD's^D anger
  no one escaped or survived;
those I cared for and reared,
  my enemy has destroyed."

3 ^a I am the man who has seen affliction^D
  by the rod of his wrath.
²He has driven me away and made me walk
  in darkness rather than light;
³indeed, he has turned his hand against me
  again and again, all day long.

⁴He has made my skin and my flesh grow old
  and has broken my bones.
⁵He has besieged me and surrounded me
  with bitterness and hardship.
⁶He has made me dwell in darkness
  like those long dead.

⁷He has walled me in so I cannot escape;
  he has weighed me down with chains.
⁸Even when I call out or cry for help,
  he shuts out my prayer.
⁹He has barred my way with blocks of stone;
  he has made my paths crooked.

¹⁰Like a bear lying in wait,
  like a lion in hiding,
¹¹he dragged me from the path and mangled me
  and left me without help.
¹²He drew his bow
  and made me the target for his arrows.

¹³He pierced my heart
  with arrows from his quiver.
¹⁴I became the laughingstock of all my people;
  they mock me in song all day long.
¹⁵He has filled me with bitter herbs
  and sated me with gall.

¹⁶He has broken my teeth with gravel;
  he has trampled me in the dust.
¹⁷I have been deprived of peace^D;
  I have forgotten what prosperity is.
¹⁸So I say, "My splendor is gone
  and all that I had hoped from the LORD."

Why would God turn against his faithful prophet? (3:3)

God was not unfaithful to Jeremiah, even though Jeremiah often felt abandoned. However, Jeremiah was probably not speaking about himself, but on behalf of the whole nation of Judah. See *My suffering* (1:12).

Why would God dismiss prayers? (3:8)

Feeling completely isolated, Jeremiah felt God's judgment personally. It felt to him as if God wasn't listening. However, God still cared for Jeremiah and Judah. He still heard their prayers. But part of the price of willful disobedience is that prayer becomes ineffective. See article: *When does God refuse to answer our prayers?* (Jer. 11:11).

---

^aThis chapter is an acrostic poem; the verses of each stanza begin with the successive letters of the Hebrew alphabet, and the verses within each stanza begin with the same letter.

Where did Jeremiah find optimism in such bleak times? (3:21-24)
These verses are a lighted match in a dark room. Their hopefulness, contrasted sharply with the surrounding dismal verses, points to Jeremiah's underlying faith which—despite his desperation—was rooted in God's unchanging character.

¹⁹I remember my affliction^D and my wandering,
the bitterness and the gall.
²⁰I well remember them,
and my soul^D is downcast within me.
²¹Yet this I call to mind
and therefore I have hope:

²²Because of the LORD's great love we are not
consumed,
for his compassions never fail.
²³They are new every morning;
great is your faithfulness.
²⁴I say to myself, "The LORD is my portion;
therefore I will wait for him."

²⁵The LORD is good to those whose hope is in
him,
to the one who seeks him;
²⁶it is good to wait quietly
for the salvation^D of the LORD.
²⁷It is good for a man to bear the yoke^D
while he is young.

²⁸Let him sit alone in silence,
for the LORD has laid it on him.
²⁹Let him bury his face in the dust—
there may yet be hope.
³⁰Let him offer his cheek to one who would
strike him,
and let him be filled with disgrace.

³¹For men are not cast off
by the Lord forever.
³²Though he brings grief, he will show
compassion,
so great is his unfailing love.
³³For he does not willingly bring affliction
or grief to the children of men.

³⁴To crush underfoot
all prisoners in the land,
³⁵to deny a man his rights
before the Most High,
³⁶to deprive a man of justice—
would not the Lord see such things?

³⁷Who can speak and have it happen
if the Lord has not decreed it?
³⁸Is it not from the mouth of the Most High
that both calamities and good things come?
³⁹Why should any living man complain
when punished for his sins?

⁴⁰Let us examine our ways and test them,
and let us return to the LORD.
⁴¹Let us lift up our hearts and our hands
to God in heaven, and say:
⁴²"We have sinned and rebelled
and you have not forgiven.

⁴³"You have covered yourself with anger and
pursued us;
you have slain without pity.
⁴⁴You have covered yourself with a cloud
so that no prayer can get through.
⁴⁵You have made us scum and refuse
among the nations.

⁴⁶"All our enemies have opened their mouths
    wide against us.
⁴⁷We have suffered terror and pitfalls,
    ruin and destruction."
⁴⁸Streams of tears flow from my eyes
    because my people are destroyed.

⁴⁹My eyes will flow unceasingly,
    without relief,
⁵⁰until the LORD looks down
    from heaven and sees.
⁵¹What I see brings grief to my soulᴰ
    because of all the women of my city.

⁵²Those who were my enemies without cause
    hunted me like a bird.
⁵³They tried to end my life in a pit
    and threw stones at me;
⁵⁴the waters closed over my head,
    and I thought I was about to be cut off.

⁵⁵I called on your name, O LORD,
    from the depths of the pit.
⁵⁶You heard my plea: "Do not close your ears
    to my cry for relief."
⁵⁷You came near when I called you,
    and you said, "Do not fear."

⁵⁸O Lord, you took up my case;
    you redeemedᴰ my life.
⁵⁹You have seen, O LORD, the wrong done to me.
    Uphold my cause!
⁶⁰You have seen the depth of their vengeance,
    all their plots against me.

⁶¹O LORD, you have heard their insults,
    all their plots against me—
⁶²what my enemies whisper and mutter
    against me all day long.
⁶³Look at them! Sitting or standing,
    they mock me in their songs.

Opened their mouths wide against us (3:46)

This is a picture of Jerusalem being devoured by Babylon. Like wild animals, Judah's enemies opened their mouths wide and swallowed up the nation. Also see 2:16.

SCRIPTURE LINK (3:52–57)

Jeremiah recalls his imprisonment in the bottom of a cistern. See Jer. 38:6–13.

Why does God send calamity? (3:38)

All of this world's suffering can be traced back to one tragic event—the disobedience of Adam and Eve (Gen. 3:6–7). Consequently, sin and its result—suffering and evil—entered the world. But God's hands were not tied as a result.

In working out his purposes, God often uses suffering to discipline us. When the people sinned defiantly, God wreaked havoc by raining catastrophe upon them. God was not capricious or whimsical. Their sin had to be punished; God's holiness demanded it. When they refused to repent, only suffering remained as a way to bring them to repentance.

Not all suffering, though, can be traced to specific sin. Some disasters are the indirect results of a broken world. Certain weather patterns can form a tornado that strikes a city—destroying the property and lives of believers and nonbelievers alike. Highs and lows are a part of the atmosphere; when they collide, destruction is inevitable.

While appearing to be senseless, disasters can have meaning. Suffering can pry our attention away from the trivial to the eternal, from making money and acquiring possessions to our relationship with God. Pain can be an effective tool to raise our sights to God's level and cause us to live more like Christ.

Should we ask for revenge? (3:64)

In his exasperation, Jeremiah implored God to retaliate. Yet even in the Old Testament, vengeance was solely God's prerogative, executed in his timing (Deut. 32:35; Romans 12:19–20). Modern believers should expect, work towards and pray for justice on earth (Matt. 16:27; 2 Tim. 4:14). But we're also commanded to love our enemies (Luke 23:34; Acts 7:60). God will ultimately right every wrong. See article: *Is it right to pray for revenge?* (Psalm 58:6–8).

Why compare God's people to jackals and ostriches? (4:3)

It seemed to Jeremiah that God's people had less character even than jackals. Jackals nursed their cubs, but the women of Jerusalem, themselves starving, could not provide for their children. Worse, like the proverbial ostrich with eggs abandoned in the sand, the people had become self-centered. Their personal hardships caused them to become more and more unconcerned about the suffering of others. Each one looked out only for himself or herself.

Purple (4:5)

The color purple symbolized wealth and royalty (Exodus 25:4; Song 3:10; 7:5). Purple dye was derived from various shellfish common to Canaan or Phoenicia (names which mean *land of purple*).

How was Judah's punishment worse than Sodom's? (4:6)

Sodom's sudden destruction seemed more tolerable to Jeremiah than Judah's slow, agonizing ordeal. Death and destruction were the results in each case, but Jerusalem's siege and starvation seemed more torturous than God's overnight annihilation of Sodom. Crazed with hunger, Jerusalem's women sold off—and even cannibalized—their own children (1:11; 4:10).

Why was Jerusalem considered invincible? (4:12)

Some think Jeremiah was describing the false confidence of Jerusalem's people: God would never allow the city where his presence dwelt to be destroyed, they thought. Others, though, say Jerusalem did have a reputation for being impregnable. Around 700 b.c., Sennacherib, an Assyrian king, lay siege to Jerusalem but failed to capture it.

64Pay them back what they deserve, O LORD,
for what their hands have done.
65Put a veil over their hearts,
and may your curse be on them!
66Pursue them in anger and destroy them
from under the heavens of the LORD.

4 ^*a* How the gold has lost its luster,
the fine gold become dull!
The sacred^D gems are scattered
at the head of every street.

2How the precious sons of Zion^D,
once worth their weight in gold,
are now considered as pots of clay,
the work of a potter's hands!

3Even jackals offer their breasts
to nurse their young,
but my people have become heartless
like ostriches in the desert.

4Because of thirst the infant's tongue
sticks to the roof of its mouth;
the children beg for bread,
but no one gives it to them.

5Those who once ate delicacies
are destitute in the streets.
Those nurtured in purple^D
now lie on ash heaps.

6The punishment of my people
is greater than that of Sodom,
which was overthrown in a moment
without a hand turned to help her.

7Their princes were brighter than snow
and whiter than milk,
their bodies more ruddy than rubies,
their appearance like sapphires.^*b*

8But now they are blacker than soot;
they are not recognized in the streets.
Their skin has shriveled on their bones;
it has become as dry as a stick.

9Those killed by the sword are better off
than those who die of famine;
racked with hunger, they waste away
for lack of food from the field.

10With their own hands compassionate women
have cooked their own children,
who became their food
when my people were destroyed.

11The LORD has given full vent to his wrath;
he has poured out his fierce anger.
He kindled a fire in Zion
that consumed her foundations.

12The kings of the earth did not believe,
nor did any of the world's people,
that enemies and foes could enter
the gates of Jerusalem^D.

---

^*a*This chapter is an acrostic poem, the verses of which begin with the successive letters of the Hebrew alphabet.   ^*b*7 Or *lapis lazuli*

¹³But it happened because of the sins of her
        prophets^D
    and the iniquities of her priests^D,
who shed within her
    the blood of the righteous^D.

¹⁴Now they grope through the streets
    like men who are blind.
They are so defiled with blood
    that no one dares to touch their garments.

¹⁵"Go away! You are unclean^D!" men cry to
        them.
    "Away! Away! Don't touch us!"
When they flee and wander about,
    people among the nations say,
    "They can stay here no longer."

¹⁶The LORD himself has scattered them;
    he no longer watches over them.
The priests are shown no honor,
    the elders no favor.

¹⁷Moreover, our eyes failed,
    looking in vain for help;
from our towers we watched
    for a nation that could not save us.

¹⁸Men stalked us at every step,
    so we could not walk in our streets.
Our end was near, our days were numbered,
    for our end had come.

¹⁹Our pursuers were swifter
    than eagles in the sky;
they chased us over the mountains
    and lay in wait for us in the desert.

²⁰The LORD's anointed^D, our very life breath,
    was caught in their traps.
We thought that under his shadow
    we would live among the nations.

²¹Rejoice and be glad, O Daughter of Edom^D,
    you who live in the land of Uz.
But to you also the cup will be passed;
    you will be drunk and stripped naked.

²²O Daughter of Zion^D, your punishment will
        end;
    he will not prolong your exile^D.
But, O Daughter of Edom, he will punish
        your sin
    and expose your wickedness.

5 Remember, O LORD, what has happened to us;
        look, and see our disgrace.
²Our inheritance has been turned over to
        aliens^D,
    our homes to foreigners.
³We have become orphans and fatherless,
    our mothers like widows.
⁴We must buy the water we drink;
    our wood can be had only at a price.
⁵Those who pursue us are at our heels;
    we are weary and find no rest.
⁶We submitted to Egypt and Assyria
    to get enough bread.

The LORD's anointed (4:20)

An Old Testament expression synonymous with
king—in this case, Zedekiah. The sacred rite of
anointing imparted God's authority on a chosen leader.

Daughter of Edom (4:22)

The Edomites were the descendants of Esau.
They had a long-standing rivalry with the Israelites, the descendants of Esau's brother Jacob.
The contrast between the futures of Edom and
Judah show that the tide would turn. Violence
against Judah would end, but not the violence
against treacherous Edom (see also Ezek.
25:12–14; Obad. 10–16).

When did Judah submit to Egypt and Assyria? (5:6)

Some think Egypt and Assyria refer to two geographical locations (west and east) where Jerusalem's refugees fled to find food. Others,
though, believe this refers to a historical, political alliance made during the eighth century B.C.
(Hosea 7:11; 12:1). Still others think this
points to Judah's spiritual idolatry when she
pursued the gods of Egypt and Assyria (Jer.
2:13,18).

What atrocities had occurred? (5:10-13)

The Babylonians were notorious for their fiendish tortures. See article: **Does God use evil to do good?** (Hab. 1:6,13). Turning Judah's society upside down, they raped the women, hanged the nobles and left their bodies to twist in the sun, forced children into hard labor and murdered citizens at random. The siege itself caused unthinkable horrors: mothers, insane from hunger, slaughtered their children for food (2:20).

Why couldn't Judah return unless God restored her first? (5:21)

Judah couldn't even repent without God's approval. Recognizing God's absolute authority was the first step towards reconciliation. Only through God's grace would Judah survive to make things right with him.

Is there a point of no return? (5:22)

In an emotional finish, Jeremiah wavers in his confidence: What if God doesn't give Judah another chance? But God specializes in second chances. No sin is too great for God. Only if we reject God and his provision for our sin, Jesus Christ, will we go beyond the point of no return (Romans 8:35-39).

[7]Our fathers sinned and are no more,
and we bear their punishment.
[8]Slaves rule over us,
and there is none to free us from their hands.
[9]We get our bread at the risk of our lives
because of the sword in the desert.
[10]Our skin is hot as an oven,
feverish from hunger.
[11]Women have been ravished in Zion[D],
and virgins in the towns of Judah.
[12]Princes have been hung up by their hands;
elders are shown no respect.
[13]Young men toil at the millstones[D];
boys stagger under loads of wood.
[14]The elders are gone from the city gate;
the young men have stopped their music.
[15]Joy is gone from our hearts;
our dancing has turned to mourning.
[16]The crown has fallen from our head.
Woe to us, for we have sinned!
[17]Because of this our hearts are faint,
because of these things our eyes grow dim
[18]for Mount Zion, which lies desolate,
with jackals prowling over it.

[19]You, O LORD, reign forever;
your throne endures from generation to generation.
[20]Why do you always forget us?
Why do you forsake us so long?
[21]Restore us to yourself, O LORD, that we may return;
renew our days as of old
[22]unless you have utterly rejected us
and are angry with us beyond measure.

EZEKIEL

Why read this book?

Filled with bizarre visions and puzzling revelations, this book might intimidate some readers today. But it shouldn't. If you dig beneath the surface of this book you'll find timeless lessons about God and his relationship with his people: He'd rather forgive us than judge us; he remains faithful even if we don't; he can use anything—even something bad—to accomplish his greater good.

Who wrote this book and when was it written?

Ezekiel, a priest who was taken captive from Jerusalem to Babylon where his prophetic visions began, wrote it between 593 and 571 B.C.

Why and to whom was it written?

Ezekiel wrote to the Israelites living in exile. They needed to know that the God of Israel was God even in pagan Babylon. Ezekiel warned the people that their idolatry would be judged. Later, after Jerusalem's destruction, he wrote to encourage them that God would bring them back.

What was happening during this time?

More than a century after Assyria had conquered the northern kingdom of Israel (722 B.C.), Babylon ascended on the world scene as the dominant power. Judah was defeated and hostages were taken to Babylon in three stages: first in 605 B.C., again in 597 B.C. and finally in 586 B.C., when Jerusalem was destroyed.

What to look for in Ezekiel:

Beyond the fantastic visions of Almighty God, look for four themes: (1) warnings of judgment to come on unrepentant Jerusalem (chs. 1–24); (2) promise of judgment on other nations (chs. 25–32); (3) words of hope for Israel's future (chs. 33–39); (4) a vision of the new temple and renewed land (chs. 40–48). Throughout the book watch for the message of God's majesty and glory: all this would happen, God says, so that *they will know that I am the* Lord (6:10).

When did these things happen?

TIME LINE	1300 B.C.	1200	1100	1000	900	800	700	600	500	400
Division of the kingdom (930 B.C.)					■					
Ministries of Micah and Isaiah in Judah (c.742-681 B.C.)							■			
Jeremiah's ministry in Judah (c.626-585 B.C.)								■		
Daniel's exile in Babylon (c.605-536 B.C.)								■		
Ezekiel's ministry (c.593-571 B.C.)								■		
Fall of Jerusalem (586 B.C.)								▪		
Book of Ezekiel written (c.571 B.C.)								▪		
First return of exiles to Jerusalem (538 B.C.)									▪	

Ezekiel in Babylon (1:1)

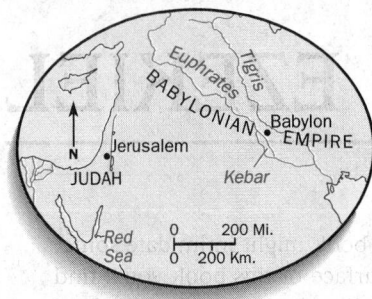

In the thirtieth year (1:1)
This is probably Ezekiel's thirtieth year of life, placing his birth in 623 B.C. This was significant because he would normally have begun performing his priestly duties at the temple in Jerusalem at age 30 (Num. 4:3).

Where was the Kebar River? (1:1)
The Kebar River was actually a large irrigation canal which took water from the Euphrates River north of Babylon and rejoined it south of the city of Uruk. The canal's modern name is Shatt en-Nil in southern Iraq.

Visions of God (1:1)
God reveals his will in many ways. Prophetic words, parables, analogies and poetry are some examples. In Ezekiel's case, God caused him to see vivid mental pictures—visions of what God was going to do.

The hand of the LORD (1:3)
An expression of God's commission of Ezekiel as a prophet—one who speaks for God. It may also have indicated the presence of God's Spirit in Ezekiel.

Why this bizarre vision? (1:4–28)
God intended these unearthly shapes and sounds to get Ezekiel's attention. Some have guessed at the underlying meanings: the intersecting wheels (v. 16) may have suggested God was on the move. His sovereign power appeared in the vision (for example, in the *expanse* described as a platform for God's throne; v. 26). The vision seems bizarre only because it describes things far beyond human experience. Ezekiel said it *was the appearance of the likeness of the glory of the LORD* (v. 28).

What special meaning did the four faces of each *living creature* have? (1:5–6)
Most believe these creatures were cherubim. The four faces probably represent supremacy over the earth and air: *man,* declared ruler over creation; the *lion,* "king of the beasts"; the *ox,* most powerful of the domesticated animals; the *eagle,* greatest of the birds. The greatest of this world are but "beasts of burden" to God—a marvelous image of God's glory and sovereignty.

The Living Creatures and the Glory of the LORD

1 In the[a] thirtieth year, in the fourth month on the fifth day, while I was among the exiles[D] by the Kebar River, the heavens were opened and I saw visions[D] of God.

2On the fifth of the month—it was the fifth year of the exile of King Jehoiachin— 3the word of the LORD came to Ezekiel the priest[D], the son of Buzi,[b] by the Kebar River in the land of the Babylonians.[c] There the hand of the LORD was upon him.

4I looked, and I saw a windstorm coming out of the north—an immense cloud with flashing lightning and surrounded by brilliant light. The center of the fire looked like glowing metal, 5and in the fire was what looked like four living creatures. In appearance their form was that of a man, 6but each of them had four faces and four wings. 7Their legs were straight; their feet were like those of a calf and gleamed like burnished bronze. 8Under their wings on their four sides they had the hands of a man. All four of them had faces and wings, 9and their wings touched one another. Each one went straight ahead; they did not turn as they moved.

10Their faces looked like this: Each of the four had the face of a man, and on the right side each had the face of a lion, and on the left the face of an ox; each also had the face of an eagle. 11Such were their faces. Their wings were spread out upward; each had two wings, one touching the wing of another creature on either side, and two wings covering its body. 12Each one went straight ahead. Wherever the spirit would go, they would go, without turning as they went. 13The appearance of the living creatures was like burning coals of fire or like torches. Fire moved back and forth among the creatures; it was bright, and lightning flashed out of it. 14The creatures sped back and forth like flashes of lightning.

15As I looked at the living creatures, I saw a wheel on the ground beside each creature with its four faces. 16This was the appearance and structure of the wheels: They sparkled like chrysolite, and all four looked alike. Each appeared to be made like a wheel intersecting a wheel. 17As they moved, they would go in any one of the four directions the creatures faced; the wheels did not turn about[d] as the creatures went. 18Their rims were high and awesome, and all four rims were full of eyes all around.

19When the living creatures moved, the wheels beside them moved; and when the living creatures rose from the ground, the wheels also rose. 20Wherever the spirit would go, they would go, and the wheels would rise along with them, because the spirit of the living creatures was in the wheels. 21When the creatures moved, they also moved; when the creatures stood still, they also stood still; and when the creatures rose from the ground, the wheels rose along with them, because the spirit of the living creatures was in the wheels.

22Spread out above the heads of the living creatures was what looked like an expanse, sparkling like ice, and awesome. 23Under the expanse their wings were stretched out one toward the other, and each had two wings covering its body. 24When the creatures moved, I heard the sound of their wings, like the roar of rushing

---

a1 Or ⌊my⌋   b3 Or *Ezekiel son of Buzi the priest*   c3 Or *Chaldeans*   d17 Or *aside*

waters, like the voice of the Almighty,*a* like the tumult of an army. When they stood still, they lowered their wings.

²⁵Then there came a voice from above the expanse over their heads as they stood with lowered wings. ²⁶Above the expanse over their heads was what looked like a throne of sapphire,*b* and high above on the throne was a figure like that of a man. ²⁷I saw that from what appeared to be his waist up he looked like glowing metal, as if full of fire, and that from there down he looked like fire; and brilliant light surrounded him. ²⁸Like the appearance of a rainbow in the clouds on a rainy day, so was the radiance around him.

This was the appearance of the likeness of the gloryᴰ of the LORD. When I saw it, I fell facedown, and I heard the voice of one speaking.

Ezekiel's Call

2 He said to me, "Son of manᴰ, stand up on your feet and I will speak to you." ²As he spoke, the Spirit came into me and raised me to my feet, and I heard him speaking to me.

³He said: "Son of man, I am sending you to the Israelites, to a rebellious nation that has rebelled against me; they and their fathers have been in revolt against me to this very day. ⁴The people to whom I am sending you are obstinate and stubborn. Say to them, 'This is what the Sovereign LORD says.' ⁵And whether they listen or fail to listen—for they are a rebellious house—they will know that a prophetᴰ has been among them. ⁶And you, son of man, do not be afraid of them or their words. Do not be afraid, though briers and thorns are all around you and you live among scorpions. Do not be afraid of what they say or terrified by them, though they are a rebellious house. ⁷You must speak my words to them, whether they listen or fail to listen, for they are rebellious. ⁸But you, son of man, listen to what I say to you. Do not rebel like that rebellious house; open your mouth and eat what I give you."

⁹Then I looked, and I saw a hand stretched out to me. In it was a scroll, ¹⁰which he unrolled before me. On both sides of it were written words of lamentᴰ and mourning and woe.

3 And he said to me, "Son of man, eat what is before you, eat this scroll; then go and speak to the house of Israel." ²So I opened my mouth, and he gave me the scroll to eat.

³Then he said to me, "Son of man, eat this scroll I am giving you and fill your stomach with it." So I ate it, and it tasted as sweet as honey in my mouth.

⁴He then said to me: "Son of man, go now to the house of Israel and speak my words to them. ⁵You are not being sent to a people of obscure speech and difficult language, but to the house of Israel— ⁶not to many peoples of obscure speech and difficult language, whose words you cannot understand. Surely if I had sent you to them, they would have listened to you. ⁷But the house of Israel is not willing to listen to you because they are not willing to listen to me, for the whole house of Israel is hardened and obstinate. ⁸But I will make you as unyielding and hardened as they are. ⁹I will make your forehead like the hardest stone, harder than flint. Do not be afraid of them or terrified by them, though they are a rebellious house."

Son of man (2:1)
Used some 90 times in the book of Ezekiel, this label underscores Ezekiel's humanity and his dependence on God's supernatural power. It may also have reminded Ezekiel that his job was to convey, not create, the message.

How had Israel rebelled against God? (2:3)
The Israelites had a long history of being unfaithful to the Lord. Often they had followed the examples of their pagan neighbors and worshiped their idols. Jeremiah, a contemporary of Ezekiel, spent years warning the people to stop trusting in their human wisdom, riches and power (Jer. 9:23-24).

Son of man (3:1)
See *Son of man* (2:1).

Why did God tell Ezekiel to eat the scroll? (3:1)
Eating the scroll was a graphic way of saying Ezekiel was to preach only the words God gave him and nothing else. He could not fulfill God's commission in his own strength, only in God's. Remember that this was a spiritual vision, not a natural incident.

Why bother speaking to people who refuse to listen? (3:7)
Because God's offer of mercy always precedes judgment. Although he knows their response beforehand, God consistently warns sinners—whether they will listen or not. Being warned, however, means there can be no excuse when judgment comes.

*a*24 Hebrew *Shaddai*   *b*26 Or *lapis lazuli*

Did the Spirit physically transport Ezekiel? (3:14)
Although it's entirely possible, it's unlikely. Probably God caused Ezekiel to see and experience these things in visions (8:3; 11:24–25).

Watchman (3:17)
Usually someone on a tower or a high point entrusted to watch for approaching messengers or enemies. God wanted to impress Ezekiel with the critical responsibility of being alert and warning people of coming judgment. In a sense, Ezekiel was accountable for their fate.

Are all those who speak for God held accountable like Ezekiel? (3:18)
None of us is free to leave God's call on our lives unfulfilled. We are obliged to obey God and will be judged on the basis of our faithfulness to his call, not the results of our labors. Compare Paul's sense of responsibility in 1 Cor. 9:16.

Why was Ezekiel tied up? (3:25)
This was probably an "enactment" prophecy—God's use of drama to deliver a message. If so, this message seems primarily for Ezekiel's benefit. It was perhaps a sign that he was restricted to God's purposes only. It is not clear, however, who tied him up or even if this is to be taken literally. Certainly Ezekiel was called to be God's prisoner, subject to God's will.

Son of man (4:1)
See *Son of man* (2:1).

¹⁰And he said to me, "Son of man^D, listen carefully and take to heart all the words I speak to you. ¹¹Go now to your countrymen in exile^D and speak to them. Say to them, 'This is what the Sovereign LORD says,' whether they listen or fail to listen."

¹²Then the Spirit lifted me up, and I heard behind me a loud rumbling sound—May the glory^D of the LORD be praised in his dwelling place!— ¹³the sound of the wings of the living creatures brushing against each other and the sound of the wheels beside them, a loud rumbling sound. ¹⁴The Spirit then lifted me up and took me away, and I went in bitterness and in the anger of my spirit, with the strong hand of the LORD upon me. ¹⁵I came to the exiles who lived at Tel Abib near the Kebar River. And there, where they were living, I sat among them for seven days—overwhelmed.

Warning to Israel

¹⁶At the end of seven days the word of the LORD came to me: ¹⁷"Son of man, I have made you a watchman for the house of Israel; so hear the word I speak and give them warning from me. ¹⁸When I say to a wicked man, 'You will surely die,' and you do not warn him or speak out to dissuade him from his evil ways in order to save his life, that wicked man will die for[a] his sin, and I will hold you accountable for his blood. ¹⁹But if you do warn the wicked man and he does not turn from his wickedness or from his evil ways, he will die for his sin; but you will have saved yourself.

²⁰"Again, when a righteous^D man turns from his righteousness^D and does evil, and I put a stumbling block^D before him, he will die. Since you did not warn him, he will die for his sin. The righteous things he did will not be remembered, and I will hold you accountable for his blood. ²¹But if you do warn the righteous man not to sin and he does not sin, he will surely live because he took warning, and you will have saved yourself."

²²The hand of the LORD was upon me there, and he said to me, "Get up and go out to the plain, and there I will speak to you." ²³So I got up and went out to the plain. And the glory of the LORD was standing there, like the glory I had seen by the Kebar River, and I fell facedown. ²⁴Then the Spirit came into me and raised me to my feet. He spoke to me and said: "Go, shut yourself inside your house. ²⁵And you, son of man, they will tie with ropes; you will be bound so that you cannot go out among the people. ²⁶I will make your tongue stick to the roof of your mouth so that you will be silent and unable to rebuke them, though they are a rebellious house. ²⁷But when I speak to you, I will open your mouth and you shall say to them, 'This is what the Sovereign LORD says.' Whoever will listen let him listen, and whoever will refuse let him refuse; for they are a rebellious house.

Siege of Jerusalem Symbolized

4 "Now, son of man, take a clay tablet, put it in front of you and draw the city of Jerusalem^D on it. ²Then lay siege to it: Erect siege works^D against it, build a ramp up to it, set up camps against it and put battering rams

---

[a]*18 Or in;* also in verses 19 and 20

around it. ³Then take an iron pan, place it as an iron wall between you and the city and turn your face toward it. It will be under siege, and you shall besiege it. This will be a sign to the house of Israel.

⁴"Then lie on your left side and put the sin of the house of Israel upon yourself.ᵃ You are to bear their sin for the number of days you lie on your side. ⁵I have assigned you the same number of days as the years of their sin. So for 390 days you will bear the sin of the house of Israel.

⁶"After you have finished this, lie down again, this time on your right side, and bear the sin of the house of Judah. I have assigned you 40 days, a day for each year. ⁷Turn your face toward the siege of Jerusalemᴰ and with bared arm prophesy against her. ⁸I will tie you up with ropes so that you cannot turn from one side to the other until you have finished the days of your siege.

⁹"Take wheat and barley, beans and lentils, millet and spelt; put them in a storage jar and use them to make bread for yourself. You are to eat it during the 390 days you lie on your side. ¹⁰Weigh out twenty shekelsᴰᵇ of food to eat each day and eat it at set times. ¹¹Also measure out a sixth of a hinᶜ of water and drink it at set times. ¹²Eat the food as you would a barley cake; bake it in the sight of the people, using human excrement for fuel." ¹³The LORD said, "In this way the people of Israel will eat defiled food among the nations where I will drive them."

¹⁴Then I said, "Not so, Sovereign LORD! I have never defiled myself. From my youth until now I have never eaten anything found dead or torn by wild animals. No uncleanᴰ meat has ever entered my mouth."

¹⁵"Very well," he said, "I will let you bake your bread over cow manure instead of human excrement."

¹⁶He then said to me: "Son of man,ᴰ I will cut off the supply of food in Jerusalem. The people will eat ra-

---

ᵃ4 Or your side   ᵇ10 That is, about 8 ounces (about 0.2 kilogram)
ᶜ11 That is, about 2/3 quart (about 0.6 liter)

How did Ezekiel put others' sins on himself? (4:4–6)

What Ezekiel did represented punishment he endured for the sins of the people, but only as an example, not as a substitute. His actions did not *remove* Israel's sins, they only represented the weight of their sins, first the sins of Samaria to the north (390 days) and then of Judah to the south (40 days).

Why did Ezekiel think cow manure was any better? (4:14–15)

God knew human excrement would offend Ezekiel since he observed strict laws regarding cleanliness (vv. 12–13). The object lesson originally called for Ezekiel to eat something unclean (by being cooked over human excrement) to show the extent of the exiles' defilement in captivity. Living in a pagan culture, they could not easily maintain their ceremonial purity. On the other hand, dried cow manure was and still is, a common source of fuel in the Middle East. It was probably not considered unclean by the Israelites.

Why such bizarre behavior? (4:3–6)

Ezekiel's outlandish prophecies were designed to make the largest impact possible on the people. The Israelites could not comprehend his message that Jerusalem and the temple—where God dwelt—might ever be destroyed. The force of his role-playing, however, insured that they would at least pay attention, even if they couldn't understand.

The people thought their exile alone was bad enough and should be the extent of their punishment. Ezekiel wanted them to see more: that they had underestimated the gravity of their persistent sins; that they had not realized the depth of God's anger with them; that they needed to see and revere God's holiness.

Ezekiel laid on his side a total of 430 days, significant because the Israelites had been enslaved in Egypt for 430 years. This picture of bondage and captivity said that God was punishing his people with still more captivity. Ezekiel probably did not lay on his side around the clock; he still cooked, ate and preached (4:9–17).

The strange drama performed by Ezekiel failed to win his audience. But the lessons he taught are still appropriate for us: we must not underestimate either our sin or God's holiness. We will reap what we sow—God will not be mocked by sin.

tioned food in anxiety and drink rationed water in despair, [17]for food and water will be scarce. They will be appalled at the sight of each other and will waste away because of[a] their sin.

5 "Now, son of man[D], take a sharp sword and use it as a barber's razor to shave your head and your beard. Then take a set of scales and divide up the hair. [2]When the days of your siege come to an end, burn a third of the hair with fire inside the city. Take a third and strike it with the sword all around the city. And scatter a third to the wind. For I will pursue them with drawn sword. [3]But take a few strands of hair and tuck them away in the folds of your garment. [4]Again, take a few of these and throw them into the fire and burn them up. A fire will spread from there to the whole house of Israel.

[5]"This is what the Sovereign LORD says: This is Jerusalem[D], which I have set in the center of the nations, with countries all around her. [6]Yet in her wickedness she has rebelled against my laws and decrees more than the nations and countries around her. She has rejected my laws and has not followed my decrees.

[7]"Therefore this is what the Sovereign LORD says: You have been more unruly than the nations around you and have not followed my decrees or kept my laws. You have not even[b] conformed to the standards of the nations around you.

[8]"Therefore this is what the Sovereign LORD says: I myself am against you, Jerusalem, and I will inflict punishment on you in the sight of the nations. [9]Because of all your detestable idols[D], I will do to you what I have never done before and will never do again. [10]Therefore in your midst fathers will eat their children, and children will eat their fathers. I will inflict punishment on you and will scatter all your survivors to the winds. [11]Therefore as surely as I live, declares the Sovereign LORD, because you have defiled my sanctuary with all your vile images and detestable practices, I myself will withdraw my favor; I will not look on you with pity or spare you. [12]A third of your people will die of the plague or perish by famine inside you; a third will fall by the sword outside your walls; and a third I will scatter to the winds and pursue with drawn sword.

[13]"Then my anger will cease and my wrath against them will subside, and I will be avenged[D]. And when I have spent my wrath upon them, they will know that I the LORD have spoken in my zeal[D].

[14]"I will make you a ruin and a reproach[D] among the nations around you, in the sight of all who pass by. [15]You will be a reproach and a taunt, a warning and an object of horror to the nations around you when I inflict punishment on you in anger and in wrath and with stinging rebuke. I the LORD have spoken. [16]When I shoot at you with my deadly and destructive arrows of famine, I will shoot to destroy you. I will bring more and more famine upon you and cut off your supply of food. [17]I will send famine and wild beasts against you, and they will leave you childless. Plague and bloodshed will sweep through you, and I will bring the sword against you. I the LORD have spoken."

Son of man (5:1)

See *Son of man* (2:1).

Why tell Ezekiel to shave his *head* with a sword? (5:1)

The sword, symbol of warfare and death, was often used to poetically depict God's justice when his laws were violated (see Lev. 26:25; Deut. 32:41). For Ezekiel, to shave his head (a sign of shame in that culture) with a sword left no doubt that he was predicting a shameful death for the people of Jerusalem. See *Faces ... covered with shame and their heads ... shaved* (7:18).

Why save a few strands of hair? (5:3)

The hair represented people, some killed in the destruction of Jerusalem, others killed as they tried to flee. The hair scattered to the wind (v. 2)—virtually impossible to reclaim—represented those taken into captivity to foreign lands. They were scattered and left with little hope. Yet, when Ezekiel tucked a few strands of hair into his clothing, he pictured God's plan to keep a few people safe through the time of judgment. He would bring back a remnant so they could serve him again.

SCRIPTURE LINK (5:9,11) *Detestable idols ... vile images and detestable practices*

See 2 Kings 21:2–9.

How would plague, famine and death cause them to acknowledge God? (5:12–13)

The phrase *they will know that I the LORD have spoken* occurs 65 times in Ezekiel. If the people would not respond to his invitation to repent, they would be taught by his actions. God reveals himself by acts of judgment as well as salvation.

Did God punish out of anger? (5:13)

Yes, but God's wrath was a righteous and appropriate response to the people's lack of faith. When they abandoned God to trust their own schemes or the gods of other nations, God became angry with them. God's *love* for his people and his desire that they trust Him remained the basis for his wrath.

[a]17 Or *away in*   [b]7 Most Hebrew manuscripts; some Hebrew manuscripts and Syriac *You have*

A Prophecy Against the Mountains of Israel

6 The word of the LORD came to me: **2**"Son of man,D set your face against the mountains of Israel; prophesy against them **3**and say: 'O mountains of Israel, hear the word of the Sovereign LORD. This is what the Sovereign LORD says to the mountains and hills, to the ravines and valleys: I am about to bring a sword against you, and I will destroy your high places.D **4**Your altars will be demolished and your incenseD altars will be smashed; and I will slay your people in front of your idols.D **5**I will lay the dead bodies of the Israelites in front of their idols, and I will scatter your bones around your altars. **6**Wherever you live, the towns will be laid waste and the high places demolished, so that your altars will be laid waste and devastated, your idols smashed and ruined, your incense altars broken down, and what you have made wiped out. **7**Your people will fall slain among you, and you will know that I am the LORD.

8" 'But I will spare some, for some of you will escape the sword when you are scattered among the lands and nations. **9**Then in the nations where they have been carried captive, those who escape will remember me—how I have been grieved by their adulterous hearts, which have turned away from me, and by their eyes, which have lusted after their idols. They will loathe themselves for the evil they have done and for all their detestable practices. **10**And they will know that I am the LORD; I did not threaten in vain to bring this calamity on them.

11" 'This is what the Sovereign LORD says: Strike your hands together and stamp your feet and cry out "Alas!" because of all the wicked and detestable practices of the house of Israel, for they will fall by the sword, famine and plague. **12**He that is far away will die of the plague, and he that is near will fall by the sword, and he that survives and is spared will die of famine. So will I spend my wrath upon them. **13**And they will know that I am the LORD, when their people lie slain among their idols around their altars, on every high hill and on all the mountaintops, under every spreading tree and every leafy oak— places where they offered fragrant incense to all their idols. **14**And I will stretch out my hand against them and make the land a desolate waste from the desert to Diblah*a*—wherever they live. Then they will know that I am the LORD.' "

a14 Most Hebrew manuscripts; a few Hebrew manuscripts Riblah

Son of man (6:2)
See *Son of man* (2:1).

Why prophesy against the mountains? (6:2)
Idolatry, the standard form of worship in ancient cultures, was practiced mostly on hilltop shrines or *high places* (see 1 Kings 14:23). Speaking toward the mountains was a symbolic condemnation of Israel's idolatry.

Why did God call the people *adulterous*? (6:9)
Because they were unfaithful to him just as an adulterer is unfaithful to a spouse and the marriage vow. They violated the covenant they had made with God when they walked out on him to worship idols. The charge of adultery fit what they had done.

Why clap, stamp and shout? (6:11)
Usually this kind of behavior shows great pleasure (like applause; see 25:6). But God was not happy about their *wicked and detestable practices*. It may be that Ezekiel was enacting the taunts of enemies who would later cheer Israel's defeat. His shouts of anguish, however, suggest that clapping, stamping and shouting could represent *any* intense emotional outburst—joyful or distressed.

Why use Diblah to describe *a desolate waste*? (6:14)
This probably refers to *Riblah* (see NIV text note), a city in northern Syria (see *Map 7* at the back of this Bible). God used this familiar image of the barren desert to describe in exaggerated language the desolation that would come to Israel.

Why were the Israelites so slow to learn? (6:14)

People are often slow to understand. Sinful tendencies and human nature become roadblocks to learning of God. In Israel's case, it took repeated disasters—plagues, famines, death and exile before they repented of their sins (5:12–13).

God's judgment of sin is certain. But this Ezekiel passage shows that God's purpose for judgment was not to punish so much as it was to bring the people back to himself. God wanted them to acknowledge that he is the Lord.

God still desires all people everywhere to know him as the only true God. He has sent warnings of judgment so people might have an opportunity to turn to him. And he has provided forgiveness through the sacrifice of Christ.

Son of man (7:1)

See *Son of man* (2:1).

The end! (7:2)

These words carry a sense of urgency; they were designed to shake the hearers out of their complacency. It was time for Jerusalem to be judged and destroyed. *The end* meant this was the culmination of centuries of rebellion against God: the time of judgment had finally arrived.

The four corners of the land (7:2)

This was a colloquial expression not meant to be understood literally. It is a way of saying "the whole land" of Israel.

Why didn't God show them any mercy? (7:4)

See *Why judge without pity or compassion?* (9:5).

How would a budding staff be a sign of judgment? (7:10)

The rod was a symbol of the pride of the Israelites, a picture of their presumed authority. A rod that had budded indicated that their arrogance had blossomed. It was a sign of judgment in the same way that Aaron's staff was meant to be a *sign to the rebellious* (Num. 17:10).

When could a seller normally recover land he had sold? (7:13)

The law mandated that every 50 years all land that had changed hands was to be returned to the original owner. It was called the *Year of Jubilee* and was intended to be a way of maintaining equity among God's people. But since the Israelites at this time were facing commercial collapse and the destruction of their society, the restitution of Jubilee was impossible. See Lev. 25:10–13.

Faces . . . covered with shame and their heads . . . shaved (7:18)

This was common practice for those in mourning. Wearing rough, itchy clothing and shaving off hair (see 27:31), as well as other customs, were ways of heightening their misery. It was considered inappropriate for those in mourning to indulge their own comforts. Loss of hair also was considered to be a great humiliation (2 Samuel 10:4–5); shaving their heads left nothing with which to cover their shame.

My treasured place (7:22)

The temple in Jerusalem. The strong emotional language shows that when God judges his people he himself suffers pain as well.

The End Has Come

7 The word of the LORD came to me: **2**"Son of man,D this is what the Sovereign LORD says to the land of Israel: The end! The end has come upon the four corners of the land. **3**The end is now upon you and I will unleash my anger against you. I will judge you according to your conduct and repay you for all your detestable practices. **4**I will not look on you with pity or spare you; I will surely repay you for your conduct and the detestable practices among you. Then you will know that I am the LORD.

5"This is what the Sovereign LORD says: Disaster! An unheard-of[a] disaster is coming. **6**The end has come! The end has come! It has roused itself against you. It has come! **7**Doom has come upon you—you who dwell in the land. The time has come, the day is near; there is panic, not joy, upon the mountains. **8**I am about to pour out my wrath on you and spend my anger against you; I will judge you according to your conduct and repay you for all your detestable practices. **9**I will not look on you with pity or spare you; I will repay you in accordance with your conduct and the detestable practices among you. Then you will know that it is I the LORD who strikes the blow.

10"The day is here! It has come! Doom has burst forth, the rod has budded, arrogance has blossomed! **11**Violence has grown into[b] a rod to punish wickedness; none of the people will be left, none of that crowd—no wealth, nothing of value. **12**The time has come, the day has arrived. Let not the buyer rejoice nor the seller grieve, for wrath is upon the whole crowd. **13**The seller will not recover the land he has sold as long as both of them live, for the visionD concerning the whole crowd will not be reversed. Because of their sins, not one of them will preserve his life. **14**Though they blow the trumpet and get everything ready, no one will go into battle, for my wrath is upon the whole crowd.

15"Outside is the sword, inside are plague and famine; those in the country will die by the sword, and those in the city will be devoured by famine and plague. **16**All who survive and escape will be in the mountains, moaning like doves of the valleys, each because of his sins. **17**Every hand will go limp, and every knee will become as weak as water. **18**They will put on sackclothD and be clothed with terror. Their faces will be covered with shame and their heads will be shaved. **19**They will throw their silver into the streets, and their gold will be an uncleanD thing. Their silver and gold will not be able to save them in the day of the LORD'sD wrath. They will not satisfy their hunger or fill their stomachs with it, for it has made them stumble into sin. **20**They were proud of their beautiful jewelry and used it to make their detestable idolsD and vile images. Therefore I will turn these into an unclean thing for them. **21**I will hand it all over as plunderD to foreigners and as loot to the wicked of the earth, and they will defile it. **22**I will turn my face away from them, and they will desecrateD my treasured place; robbers will enter it and desecrate it.

23"Prepare chains, because the land is full of bloodshed and the city is full of violence. **24**I will bring the most wicked of the nations to take possession of their houses; I will put an end to the pride of the mighty, and their sanc-

---

a5 Most Hebrew manuscripts; some Hebrew manuscripts and Syriac *Disaster after*   *b11* Or *The violent one has become*

tuaries will be desecrated^D. **25**When terror comes, they will seek peace^D, but there will be none. **26**Calamity upon calamity will come, and rumor upon rumor. They will try to get a vision^D from the prophet^D; the teaching of the law by the priest^D will be lost, as will the counsel of the elders. **27**The king will mourn, the prince will be clothed with despair, and the hands of the people of the land will tremble. I will deal with them according to their conduct, and by their own standards I will judge them. Then they will know that I am the LORD."

Idolatry in the Temple

8 In the sixth year, in the sixth month on the fifth day, while I was sitting in my house and the elders of Judah were sitting before me, the hand of the Sovereign LORD came upon me there. **2**I looked, and I saw a figure like that of a man.^a From what appeared to be his waist down he was like fire, and from there up his appearance was as bright as glowing metal. **3**He stretched out what looked like a hand and took me by the hair of my head. The Spirit lifted me up between earth and heaven and in visions of God he took me to Jerusalem, to the entrance to the north gate of the inner court, where the idol^D that provokes to jealousy stood. **4**And there before me was the glory^D of the God of Israel, as in the vision I had seen in the plain.

5Then he said to me, "Son of man^D, look toward the north." So I looked, and in the entrance north of the gate of the altar I saw this idol of jealousy.

6And he said to me, "Son of man, do you see what they are doing—the utterly detestable things the house of Israel is doing here, things that will drive me far from my sanctuary? But you will see things that are even more detestable."

7Then he brought me to the entrance to the court. I looked, and I saw a hole in the wall. **8**He said to me, "Son of man, now dig into the wall." So I dug into the wall and saw a doorway there.

9And he said to me, "Go in and see the wicked and detestable things they are doing here." **10**So I went in and looked, and I saw portrayed all over the walls all kinds of crawling things and detestable animals and all the idols of the house of Israel. **11**In front of them stood seventy elders of the house of Israel, and Jaazaniah son of Shaphan was standing among them. Each had a censer^D in his hand, and a fragrant cloud of incense^D was rising.

12He said to me, "Son of man, have you seen what the elders of the house of Israel are doing in the darkness, each at the shrine of his own idol? They say, 'The LORD does not see us; the LORD has forsaken the land.'" **13**Again, he said, "You will see them doing things that are even more detestable."

14Then he brought me to the entrance to the north gate of the house of the LORD, and I saw women sitting there, mourning for Tammuz. **15**He said to me, "Do you see this, son of man? You will see things that are even more detestable than this."

16He then brought me into the inner court of the house of the LORD, and there at the entrance to the temple, between the portico and the altar, were about twenty-five men. With their backs toward the temple of the LORD and

^a2 Or *saw a fiery figure*

The counsel of the elders (7:26)
Prompted by their suffering, the people would seek help from their leaders. But it would be too little, too late. Since God had already withdrawn his presence, there would be no way to hear from him. Elders, along with prophets and priests, usually helped set national policy. Prophets received visions and specific words from the Lord; priests could instruct in matters of the law and elders drew from their vast experience to advise political leaders.

How would they be judged *by their own standards?* (7:27)
The people had failed to live up to their covenant with the Lord. They had failed to uphold their pledge of complete devotion and allegiance to him. God was, in effect, saying they were their own worst enemy. It was their own sinfulness that had destroyed them. Failure to follow God comes from disobedience—our lack of discipline or will. God, for his part, is always faithful to keep the bargain.

Hand of the Sovereign LORD (8:1)
See *The hand of the LORD* (1:3).

How had an idol been allowed in the temple? (8:3)
This may have been the goddess Asherah, installed during the decadent days of King Manasseh (2 Kings 21:7). Any idol, whether in the temple or not, undermined the loyalty God's people had for the Lord, and would provoke God to righteous jealousy. See *Is God wrong to be jealous?* (Nahum 1:2).

Son of man (8:5)
See *Son of man* (2:1).

What detestable things were done in the temple? (8:6)
They had placed pictures of crawling things and detestable animals on the temple walls, along with many different idols (v. 10). How repugnant to allow into the temple even pictures of animals designated as unclean, off-limits to God's people! See article: *Why did God keep some meats off the menu?* (Lev. 11:4–41). Serpent deities associated with neighboring Egyptian, Canaanite and Babylonian religions had corrupted the sanctuary of the Lord.

Jaazaniah son of Shaphan (8:11)
From a prominent Jerusalem family (see 2 Kings 22:3), he presided over the idolatrous worship. He is not the same as the Jaazaniah mentioned in 11:1.

Why were women mourning for Tammuz? (8:14)
Tammuz was the Hebrew name for the Sumerian-Babylonian god of plant life. Every fall, when the crops died and the trees shed their leaves, women would ceremonially mourn his death. Every spring, when the plants began to sprout, they would celebrate his coming back to life.

Putting the branch to their nose (8:17)

This obscure phrase is not found elsewhere in the Bible. It could perhaps be rendered "are a stench to my nose," illustrating how offensive the people's idolatry was to God. Or it may be part of a pagan ceremony involving the worship of nature.

Wouldn't it take more than six men to guard the city? (9:1–2)

The language and description of these men suggest that they were actually angels rather than human. Not only do people have guardian angels (Heb. 1:14), but nations (Daniel 10) and cities can have them as well. These angels operate in spiritual realms with the authority given to them by God.

Writing kit (9:2)

This was a small case hung from the belt to carry the scribe's writing equipment—items such as reed pens, a knife (to sharpen the pens) and ink. Some think it may be related to the Egyptian writer's palette, a wax writing tablet that included receptacles for pens and ink.

Why did God's glory move to the threshold of the temple? (9:3)

Grieved and angry over his people's rejection, God fulfilled his promise to leave the temple if they turned away from him (1 Kings 9:6–9). But rather than leave all at once, the glory of the Lord departed in stages: (1) from the cherubim in the Most Holy Place to the door, (2) from the door to the cherubim of Ezekiel's vision (10:18,20), (3) to the east gate of the temple (10:19) and (4) to the Mount of Olives just outside Jerusalem (11:23).

SCRIPTURE LINK (9:4) *Put a mark on the foreheads*

God is not unfair; each individual will be held personally responsible to him. Compare another time when God marked those who belonged to him in Rev. 7:3.

Why judge without pity or compassion? (9:5)

Mercy had earlier been offered. But now it was time for judgment, not mercy. In the Old Testament, judgment upon those so rebellious that they would never repent was total annihilation. There could be no cure or reform for such cases, only destruction. See articles: *Why would God annihilate an entire nation?* (Deut. 2:34) and *Why kill everything?* (Joshua 6:21).

Why did God want burning coals scattered over the city? (10:2)

Fire is usually a symbol of God's judgment against evil (see Gen. 19:24; Deut. 32:22; Amos 1–2). Burning coals represented divine judgment against Jerusalem.

their faces toward the east, they were bowing down to the sun in the east.

¹⁷He said to me, "Have you seen this, son of manᴰ? Is it a trivial matter for the house of Judah to do the detestable things they are doing here? Must they also fill the land with violence and continually provoke me to anger? Look at them putting the branch to their nose! ¹⁸Therefore I will deal with them in anger; I will not look on them with pity or spare them. Although they shout in my ears, I will not listen to them."

Idolaters Killed

9 Then I heard him call out in a loud voice, "Bring the guards of the city here, each with a weapon in his hand." ²And I saw six men coming from the direction of the upper gate, which faces north, each with a deadly weapon in his hand. With them was a man clothed in linen who had a writing kit at his side. They came in and stood beside the bronze altar.

³Now the gloryᴰ of the God of Israel went up from above the cherubimᴰ, where it had been, and moved to the threshold of the temple. Then the LORD called to the man clothed in linen who had the writing kit at his side ⁴and said to him, "Go throughout the city of Jerusalemᴰ and put a mark on the foreheads of those who grieve and lamentᴰ over all the detestable things that are done in it."

⁵As I listened, he said to the others, "Follow him through the city and kill, without showing pity or compassion. ⁶Slaughter old men, young men and maidens, women and children, but do not touch anyone who has the mark. Begin at my sanctuary." So they began with the elders who were in front of the temple.

⁷Then he said to them, "Defile the temple and fill the courts with the slain. Go!" So they went out and began killing throughout the city. ⁸While they were killing and I was left alone, I fell facedown, crying out, "Ah, Sovereign LORD! Are you going to destroy the entire remnantᴰ of Israel in this outpouring of your wrath on Jerusalem?"

⁹He answered me, "The sin of the house of Israel and Judah is exceedingly great; the land is full of bloodshed and the city is full of injustice. They say, 'The LORD has forsaken the land; the LORD does not see.' ¹⁰So I will not look on them with pity or spare them, but I will bring down on their own heads what they have done."

¹¹Then the man in linen with the writing kit at his side brought back word, saying, "I have done as you commanded."

The Glory Departs From the Temple

10 I looked, and I saw the likeness of a throne of sapphireᵃ above the expanse that was over the heads of the cherubim. ²The LORD said to the man clothed in linen, "Go in among the wheels beneath the cherubim. Fill your hands with burning coals from among the cherubim and scatter them over the city." And as I watched, he went in.

³Now the cherubim were standing on the south side of the temple when the man went in, and a cloud filled the inner court. ⁴Then the glory of the LORD rose from above the cherubim and moved to the threshold of the temple. The cloud filled the temple, and the court was full

---

ᵃ1 Or lapis lazuli

of the radiance of the glory^D of the LORD. **⁵**The sound of the wings of the cherubim^D could be heard as far away as the outer court, like the voice of God Almighty^a when he speaks.

⁶When the LORD commanded the man in linen, "Take fire from among the wheels, from among the cherubim," the man went in and stood beside a wheel. **⁷**Then one of the cherubim reached out his hand to the fire that was among them. He took up some of it and put it into the hands of the man in linen, who took it and went out. **⁸**(Under the wings of the cherubim could be seen what looked like the hands of a man.)

⁹I looked, and I saw beside the cherubim four wheels, one beside each of the cherubim; the wheels sparkled like chrysolite. **¹⁰**As for their appearance, the four of them looked alike; each was like a wheel intersecting a wheel. **¹¹**As they moved, they would go in any one of the four directions the cherubim faced; the wheels did not turn about^b as the cherubim went. The cherubim went in whatever direction the head faced, without turning as they went. **¹²**Their entire bodies, including their backs, their hands and their wings, were completely full of eyes, as were their four wheels. **¹³**I heard the wheels being called "the whirling wheels." **¹⁴**Each of the cherubim had four faces: One face was that of a cherub, the second the face of a man, the third the face of a lion, and the fourth the face of an eagle.

¹⁵Then the cherubim rose upward. These were the living creatures I had seen by the Kebar River. **¹⁶**When the cherubim moved, the wheels beside them moved; and when the cherubim spread their wings to rise from the ground, the wheels did not leave their side. **¹⁷**When the cherubim stood still, they also stood still; and when the cherubim rose, they rose with them, because the spirit of the living creatures was in them.

¹⁸Then the glory of the LORD departed from over the threshold of the temple and stopped above the cherubim. **¹⁹**While I watched, the cherubim spread their wings and rose from the ground, and as they went, the wheels went with them. They stopped at the entrance to the east gate of the LORD's house, and the glory of the God of Israel was above them.

²⁰These were the living creatures I had seen beneath the God of Israel by the Kebar River, and I realized that they were cherubim. **²¹**Each had four faces and four wings, and under their wings was what looked like the hands of a man. **²²**Their faces had the same appearance as those I had seen by the Kebar River. Each one went straight ahead.

Judgment on Israel's Leaders

11 Then the Spirit lifted me up and brought me to the gate of the house of the LORD that faces east. There at the entrance to the gate were twenty-five men, and I saw among them Jaazaniah son of Azzur and Pelatiah son of Benaiah, leaders of the people. **²**The LORD said to me, "Son of man^D, these are the men who are plotting evil and giving wicked advice in this city. **³**They say, 'Will it not soon be time to build houses?^c This city is a cooking pot, and we are the meat.' **⁴**Therefore prophesy against them; prophesy, son of man."

---

^a5 Hebrew *El-Shaddai*   ^b11 Or *aside*   ^c3 Or *This is not the time to build houses.*

Why were the cherubim covered with eyes? (10:12)

As with the first vision (1:18), the numerous eyes represent the all-seeing nature of God. Nothing, even those things done in secret, can be hidden from God.

Why were the wheels called *the whirling wheels*? (10:13)

This name, as well as the description of *a wheel intersecting a wheel* (1:16; 10:10), suggest God's constant motion. He is active and moving.

How did Ezekiel recognize these cherubim? (10:14)

Ezekiel called the creatures *cherubim* to draw the association between them and the presence of God: God's throne was between the cherubim on the ark (Exodus 25:22); the temple was filled with carvings of cherubim (1 Kings 6:29); and God is frequently seen in the Old Testament being carried by cherubim (Psalm 18:10). The message is: God is on the move.

Jaazaniah son of Azzur . . . Pelatiah son of Benaiah (11:1)

This is not the same Jaazaniah mentioned in 8:11. All that is known of these men is that they wielded considerable power and they led the people to defy the Lord, proclaiming peace and safety (11:2–3) when God's word to the people was one of judgment and destruction.

Son of man (11:2)

See *Son of man* (2:1).

What did they mean by talking about a cooking pot and meat? (11:3)

The wicked leaders, perhaps using a familiar proverb, suggested that they belonged in Jerusalem just as meat belongs in a pot. They may have been urging people to make long-term plans to live there. Or they may have thought their buildings could offer protection from the Babylonians. Either way, their counsel was opposed to God's purposes and would bring even greater disaster.

Who killed whom in Jerusalem? (11:6)

This was a prediction of what would happen in the future because of the corruption of the city's leaders. Though the rulers would execute many—Manasseh *filled Jerusalem with innocent blood* (2 Kings 24:4)—God would avenge the deaths of the innocent with the lives of the disobedient rulers (2 Kings 25:18–21).

What were the standards of the nations around them? (11:12)

Some of the things the surrounding nations practiced were materialistic idolatry, exploitation of the poor, ritual sex, astrology and human sacrifice—all as part of their worship (2 Kings 23:4–10).

Who were those *far away from the* Lord? (11:15)

Those in Jerusalem who initially escaped exile and death thought they were more favored by God than those who had been carried off to faraway lands. Didn't they still have the temple? But the Lord promised to be a sanctuary for those exiled in foreign countries (v. 16). Ironically, the surviving remnant would not come from those in Jerusalem, for they would ultimately be destroyed.

How was the Lord a *sanctuary*? (11:16)

This is a critical verse for understanding the book of Ezekiel. Before the time of the exile, God's people associated Jerusalem and the temple with God's presence among them. Now God showed his people that he himself could be their sanctuary: he cannot be confined geographically. God was with them in their exile, even in pagan Babylon. Later Christ came to replace the temple (John 2:19–21).

How did the returning people do away with idolatry that had been practiced for centuries? (11:18–20)

When the Jews began to return to Israel in 538 b.c. (Ezra 1,3), Jerusalem was still practicing false religions. Although it required more than a hundred years after their return to correct the abuses and promote true worship and obedience to God's law, the tide was turned. By the time of Christ the Jews no longer became involved with idol worship.

New spirit . . . heart of flesh (11:19)

This is a recurring theme in Ezekiel and Jeremiah (18:31; 36:26; Jer. 32:39). It describes the radical spiritual change that leads to genuine obedience of God's laws. As the exiles repented and took steps to demonstrate their repentance, such as cleaning out the tangible signs of idolatry (v. 18), God gave them new hearts that were open to him. When they removed the external problems, God removed the internal problems.

5Then the Spirit of the Lord came upon me, and he told me to say: "This is what the Lord says: That is what you are saying, O house of Israel, but I know what is going through your mind. 6You have killed many people in this city and filled its streets with the dead.

7"Therefore this is what the Sovereign Lord says: The bodies you have thrown there are the meat and this city is the pot, but I will drive you out of it. 8You fear the sword, and the sword is what I will bring against you, declares the Sovereign Lord. 9I will drive you out of the city and hand you over to foreigners and inflict punishment on you. 10You will fall by the sword, and I will execute judgment on you at the borders of Israel. Then you will know that I am the Lord. 11This city will not be a pot for you, nor will you be the meat in it; I will execute judgment on you at the borders of Israel. 12And you will know that I am the Lord, for you have not followed my decrees or kept my laws but have conformed to the standards of the nations around you."

13Now as I was prophesying, Pelatiah son of Benaiah died. Then I fell facedown and cried out in a loud voice, "Ah, Sovereign Lord! Will you completely destroy the remnantD of Israel?"

14The word of the Lord came to me: 15"Son of manD, your brothers—your brothers who are your blood relatives*a* and the whole house of Israel—are those of whom the people of JerusalemD have said, 'They are*b* far away from the Lord; this land was given to us as our possession.'

Promised Return of Israel

16"Therefore say: 'This is what the Sovereign Lord says: Although I sent them far away among the nations and scattered them among the countries, yet for a little while I have been a sanctuary for them in the countries where they have gone.'

17"Therefore say: 'This is what the Sovereign Lord says: I will gather you from the nations and bring you back from the countries where you have been scattered, and I will give you back the land of Israel again.'

18"They will return to it and remove all its vile images and detestable idolsD. 19I will give them an undivided heart and put a new spirit in them; I will remove from them their heart of stone and give them a heart of flesh. 20Then they will follow my decrees and be careful to keep my laws. They will be my people, and I will be their God. 21But as for those whose hearts are devoted to their vile images and detestable idols, I will bring down on their own heads what they have done, declares the Sovereign Lord."

22Then the cherubimD, with the wheels beside them, spread their wings, and the gloryD of the God of Israel was above them. 23The glory of the Lord went up from within the city and stopped above the mountain east of it. 24The Spirit lifted me up and brought me to the exilesD in Babylonia*c* in the visionD given by the Spirit of God. Then the vision I had seen went up from me, 25and I told the exiles everything the Lord had shown me.

---

*a*15 Or *are in exile with you* (see Septuagint and Syriac) *b*15 Or *those to whom the people of Jerusalem have said, 'Stay* *c*24 Or *Chaldea*

The Exile Symbolized

12 The word of the LORD came to me: ²"Son of manᴰ, you are living among a rebellious people. They have eyes to see but do not see and ears to hear but do not hear, for they are a rebellious people.

³"Therefore, son of man, pack your belongings for exileᴰ and in the daytime, as they watch, set out and go from where you are to another place. Perhaps they will understand, though they are a rebellious house. ⁴During the daytime, while they watch, bring out your belongings packed for exile. Then in the evening, while they are watching, go out like those who go into exile. ⁵While they watch, dig through the wall and take your belongings out through it. ⁶Put them on your shoulder as they are watching and carry them out at dusk. Cover your face so that you cannot see the land, for I have made you a sign to the house of Israel."

⁷So I did as I was commanded. During the day I brought out my things packed for exile. Then in the evening I dug through the wall with my hands. I took my belongings out at dusk, carrying them on my shoulders while they watched.

⁸In the morning the word of the LORD came to me: ⁹"Son of man, did not that rebellious house of Israel ask you, 'What are you doing?'

¹⁰"Say to them, 'This is what the Sovereign LORD says: This oracleᴰ concerns the prince in Jerusalemᴰ and the whole house of Israel who are there.' ¹¹Say to them, 'I am a sign to you.'

"As I have done, so it will be done to them. They will go into exile as captives.

¹²"The prince among them will put his things on his shoulder at dusk and leave, and a hole will be dug in the wall for him to go through. He will cover his face so that he cannot see the land. ¹³I will spread my net for him, and he will be caught in my snare; I will bring him to Babylonia, the land of the Chaldeans, but he will not see it, and there he will die. ¹⁴I will scatter to the winds all those around him—his staff and all his troops—and I will pursue them with drawn sword.

¹⁵"They will know that I am the LORD, when I disperse them among the nations and scatter them through the countries. ¹⁶But I will spare a few of them from the sword, famine and plague, so that in the nations where they go they may acknowledge all their detestable practices. Then they will know that I am the LORD."

¹⁷The word of the LORD came to me: ¹⁸"Son of man, tremble as you eat your food, and shudder in fear as you drink your water. ¹⁹Say to the people of the land: 'This is what the Sovereign LORD says about those living in Jerusalem and in the land of Israel: They will eat their food in anxiety and drink their water in despair, for their land will be stripped of everything in it because of the violence of all who live there. ²⁰The inhabited towns will be laid waste and the land will be desolate. Then you will know that I am the LORD.' "

²¹The word of the LORD came to me: ²²"Son of man, what is this proverb you have in the land of Israel: 'The days go by and every visionᴰ comes to nothing'? ²³Say to them, 'This is what the Sovereign LORD says: I am going to put an end to this proverb, and they will no longer quote it in Israel.' Say to them, 'The days are near when every vision will be fulfilled. ²⁴For there will be no more false

How did digging through a wall symbolize exile? (12:5)
Ezekiel's action reminded the people of the way a conquering army would systematically break through the various walls protecting a city. See Amos 4:3 for a similar prediction.

The prince among them (12:12)
This was Zedekiah, the king of Jerusalem, who tried but failed to escape capture by the Babylonians. See 2 Kings 25:1–7.

Why did the prince *cover his face*? (12:12)
Covering one's face was a sign of grief and humiliation. But in this case, the covering might mean something Zedekiah wore to disguise himself during his escape attempt. It's also possible, since the Babylonians put out his eyes, that this was a metaphor for his blindness. See 2 Kings 25:1–7.

Why wouldn't he see the place where they took him? (12:13)
Though the Babylonians took the king as a captive to their own country, they blinded him before he made the journey. See 2 Kings 25:1–7.

What were the *false visions* and *flattering divinations*? (12:24)
These were reassuring prophecies given by false prophets and leaders. Though God's true prophets warned of judgment and destruction, others insisted all would be well. See *Jaazaniah son of Azzur . . . Pelatiah son of Benaiah* (11:1).

visions[D] or flattering divinations[D] among the people of Israel. **25**But I the LORD will speak what I will, and it shall be fulfilled without delay. For in your days, you rebellious house, I will fulfill whatever I say, declares the Sovereign LORD.' "

26The word of the LORD came to me: **27**"Son of man[D], the house of Israel is saying, 'The vision he sees is for many years from now, and he prophesies about the distant future.'

28"Therefore say to them, 'This is what the Sovereign LORD says: None of my words will be delayed any longer; whatever I say will be fulfilled, declares the Sovereign LORD.' "

False Prophets Condemned

13 The word of the LORD came to me: **2**"Son of man, prophesy against the prophets[D] of Israel who are now prophesying. Say to those who prophesy out of their own imagination: 'Hear the word of the LORD! **3**This is what the Sovereign LORD says: Woe to the foolish[a] prophets who follow their own spirit and have seen nothing! **4**Your prophets, O Israel, are like jackals among ruins. **5**You have not gone up to the breaks in the wall to repair it for the house of Israel so that it will stand firm in the battle on the day of the LORD[D]. **6**Their visions are false and their divinations a lie. They say, "The LORD declares," when the LORD has not sent them; yet they expect their words to be fulfilled. **7**Have you not seen false visions and uttered lying divinations when you say, "The LORD declares," though I have not spoken?

8" 'Therefore this is what the Sovereign LORD says: Because of your false words and lying visions, I am against you, declares the Sovereign LORD. **9**My hand will be against the prophets who see false visions and utter lying divinations. They will not belong to the council of my people or be listed in the records of the house of Israel, nor will they enter the land of Israel. Then you will know that I am the Sovereign LORD.

10" 'Because they lead my people astray, saying, "Peace[D]," when there is no peace, and because, when a flimsy wall is built, they cover it with whitewash, **11**therefore tell those who cover it with whitewash that it is going to fall. Rain will come in torrents, and I will send hailstones hurtling down, and violent winds will burst forth. **12**When the wall collapses, will people not ask you, "Where is the whitewash you covered it with?"

13" 'Therefore this is what the Sovereign LORD says: In my wrath I will unleash a violent wind, and in my anger hailstones and torrents of rain will fall with destructive fury. **14**I will tear down the wall you have covered with whitewash and will level it to the ground so that its foundation will be laid bare. When it[b] falls, you will be destroyed in it; and you will know that I am the LORD. **15**So I will spend my wrath against the wall and against those who covered it with whitewash. I will say to you, "The wall is gone and so are those who whitewashed it, **16**those prophets of Israel who prophesied to Jerusalem and saw visions of peace for her when there was no peace, declares the Sovereign LORD." '

17"Now, son of man, set your face against the daughters of your people who prophesy out of their own imagination. Prophesy against them **18**and say, 'This is what the

---

SCRIPTURE LINK (13:2–9) *False words and lying visions*

See what the law said about false prophets in Deut. 18:20–22.

How were these prophets like jackals? (13:4)

Jackals are doglike scavengers that often live among ruins with no concern for the debris and decay all around them. Like jackals, these false prophets were content to live in a disintegrating environment, oblivious to the judgment that was falling upon the nation. They promised prosperity, rather than denouncing sin and warning of impending doom.

Why expect a prophet to repair the wall? (13:5)

The language is figurative. The image of a deteriorating wall pictures Israel's vulnerability before invading armies, enemies which God raised up against the nation. The prophets were to *repair* the walls by exposing Israel's sins and calling the people to repentance. Instead, the false prophets' promises of prosperity were like *whitewash* (v. 10) in that they covered the flaws in the people's thinking and confirmed their false hopes.

How would the false prophets be kept from entering the land? (13:9)

The false prophets would have no place in this future restoration of the nation. Their names would be expunged from the register of citizens and their descendants would be cut off from Israel through God's judgment. God's judgment would not totally destroy his people. Someday he would bring the exiled nation back to the land and fulfill his promise to Abraham.

Flimsy wall (13:10–16)

See *Why expect a prophet to repair the wall?* (13:5).

How common were women prophets? (13:17)

The Old Testament refers to several women prophets, including Miriam (Exodus 15:20), Deborah (Judges 4:4) and Huldah (2 Kings 22:14). Noadiah (Neh. 6:14) was condemned by Nehemiah as a false prophetess. The women *prophets* denounced by Ezekiel were not true spokespersons for God, but rather diviners who employed witchcraft and other pagan methods for personal profit.

What kind of magic charms and snares were these? (13:18)

These *magic charms* may refer to strips of cloth tied around the wrists or lower arms, perhaps to illustrate their binding character. These charms were dedicated with incantations, curses and spells. The meaning of the word translated *veils* is unclear, but it may refer to head coverings or shrouds which were viewed as a source of supernatural power.

---

*a*3 Or *wicked*   *b*14 Or *the city*

Sovereign LORD says: Woe to the women who sew magic charms on all their wrists and make veils of various lengths for their heads in order to ensnare people. Will you ensnare the lives of my people but preserve your own? **19**You have profaned[D] me among my people for a few handfuls of barley and scraps of bread. By lying to my people, who listen to lies, you have killed those who should not have died and have spared those who should not live.

20" 'Therefore this is what the Sovereign LORD says: I am against your magic charms with which you ensnare people like birds and I will tear them from your arms; I will set free the people that you ensnare like birds. **21**I will tear off your veils and save my people from your hands, and they will no longer fall prey to your power. Then you will know that I am the LORD. **22**Because you disheartened the righteous[D] with your lies, when I had brought them no grief, and because you encouraged the wicked not to turn from their evil ways and so save their lives, **23**therefore you will no longer see false visions[D] or practice divination[D]. I will save my people from your hands. And then you will know that I am the LORD.' "

Idolaters Condemned

14 Some of the elders of Israel came to me and sat down in front of me. **2**Then the word of the LORD came to me: **3**"Son of man[D], these men have set up idols[D] in their hearts and put wicked stumbling blocks before their faces. Should I let them inquire of me at all? **4**Therefore speak to them and tell them, 'This is what the Sovereign LORD says: When any Israelite sets up idols in his heart and puts a wicked stumbling block[D] before his face and then goes to a prophet[D], I the LORD will answer him myself in keeping with his great idolatry[D]. **5**I will do this to recapture the hearts of the people of Israel, who have all deserted me for their idols.'

6"Therefore say to the house of Israel, 'This is what the Sovereign LORD says: Repent[D]! Turn from your idols and renounce all your detestable practices!

7" 'When any Israelite or any alien[D] living in Israel separates himself from me and sets up idols in his heart and puts a wicked stumbling block before his face and then goes to a prophet to inquire of me, I the LORD will answer him myself. **8**I will set my face against that man and make him an example and a byword[D]. I will cut him off from my people. Then you will know that I am the LORD.

9" 'And if the prophet is enticed to utter a prophecy, I the LORD have enticed that prophet, and I will stretch out my hand against him and destroy him from among my people Israel. **10**They will bear their guilt—the prophet will be as guilty as the one who consults him. **11**Then the people of Israel will no longer stray from me, nor will they defile themselves anymore with all their sins. They will be my people, and I will be their God, declares the Sovereign LORD.' "

Judgment Inescapable

12The word of the LORD came to me: **13**"Son of man, if a country sins against me by being unfaithful and I stretch out my hand against it to cut off its food supply and send famine upon it and kill its men and their ani-

Detestable practices (14:6)
One of Ezekiel's favorite ways of referring to Israel's idolatry and pagan religious practices. These practices included child sacrifice, as well as the worship of animal images, the Babylonian god Tammuz and the sun.

How did God cut someone off? (14:8)
See *Cut off from my presence* (Lev. 22:3) and *Cut off* (Psalm 37:9).

Why would God entice a false prophet to prophesy? (14:9)
Sometimes God hastens the destruction of a rebellious person through influences which cause them to fall deeper into depravity. Such is the case here, where the Lord warns that he will judge a prophet for cooperating with an idolater. The passage does not say that God will overpower the prophet and force him to sin against his will. Rather it assumes that the prophet is aware of the inquirer's idolatry but minimizes it, perhaps for financial gain.

Why were Noah, Daniel and Job singled out as special examples? (14:14)

Many Biblical figures could have been listed as examples of godliness. It is not clear why the Lord specifically mentioned these men, but righteousness (the character quality emphasized in vv. 14,20) was a prominent virtue of all three. Noah is an especially appropriate choice because his righteousness spared his immediate family from destruction. The point here is that not even Noah could effectively intercede for Ezekiel's sinful generation.

When does it become impossible to escape judgment? (14:20)

God is patient with rebellious people and usually gives them ample opportunity to turn from their wicked ways. His patience, however, does not last forever. After sufficient time, he decrees judgment against incorrigible sinners because of their refusal to repent. At that point their destiny is sealed and nothing can prevent his judgment from falling.

What consolation could a few survivors give? (14:22–23)

God would allow a few of Jerusalem's godless people to survive the coming judgment and go into exile. When the Babylonian exiles saw firsthand the wickedness of this later group of exiles, they would be convinced that God's judgment of the city was well-deserved and necessary. This would reassure the exiles, because they would realize that Jerusalem's tragic fall was the outworking of God's justice, not an indiscriminate divine action or a sign of weakness on his part.

How had they *come out of the fire?* (15:7)

Jerusalem escaped physical destruction in 597 B.C., when Nebuchadnezzar plundered the temple treasuries and carried away thousands, including King Jehoiachin. However, this narrow escape from the Babylonians did not mean the sinful city would be spared. The Babylonians soon returned and finished what they had started, breaking down the city's walls and setting afire its houses and important buildings, including the temple.

Amorite . . . Hittite (16:3)

Sinful Jerusalem is personified here as a woman born of pagan parents. The imagery accurately reflects the city's pagan origin and early history. Prior to Israel's conquest of the land, Jerusalem was controlled by Canaanite peoples, including the Amorites and Jebusites. Though no other texts mention the Hittites as possessing Jerusalem, they are closely associated with the Amorites in many texts (Gen. 10:15–16; Joshua 12:8).

mals, **14**even if these three men—Noah, Daniel*a* and Job—were in it, they could save only themselves by their righteousness*D*, declares the Sovereign LORD.

15"Or if I send wild beasts through that country and they leave it childless and it becomes desolate so that no one can pass through it because of the beasts, **16**as surely as I live, declares the Sovereign LORD, even if these three men were in it, they could not save their own sons or daughters. They alone would be saved, but the land would be desolate.

17"Or if I bring a sword against that country and say, 'Let the sword pass throughout the land,' and I kill its men and their animals, **18**as surely as I live, declares the Sovereign LORD, even if these three men were in it, they could not save their own sons or daughters. They alone would be saved.

19"Or if I send a plague into that land and pour out my wrath upon it through bloodshed, killing its men and their animals, **20**as surely as I live, declares the Sovereign LORD, even if Noah, Daniel and Job were in it, they could save neither son nor daughter. They would save only themselves by their righteousness.

21"For this is what the Sovereign LORD says: How much worse will it be when I send against Jerusalem*D* my four dreadful judgments—sword and famine and wild beasts and plague—to kill its men and their animals! **22**Yet there will be some survivors—sons and daughters who will be brought out of it. They will come to you, and when you see their conduct and their actions, you will be consoled regarding the disaster I have brought upon Jerusalem—every disaster I have brought upon it. **23**You will be consoled when you see their conduct and their actions, for you will know that I have done nothing in it without cause, declares the Sovereign LORD."

Jerusalem, A Useless Vine

15 The word of the LORD came to me: **2**"Son of man*D*, how is the wood of a vine better than that of a branch on any of the trees in the forest? **3**Is wood ever taken from it to make anything useful? Do they make pegs from it to hang things on? **4**And after it is thrown on the fire as fuel and the fire burns both ends and chars the middle, is it then useful for anything? **5**If it was not useful for anything when it was whole, how much less can it be made into something useful when the fire has burned it and it is charred?

6"Therefore this is what the Sovereign LORD says: As I have given the wood of the vine among the trees of the forest as fuel for the fire, so will I treat the people living in Jerusalem. **7**I will set my face against them. Although they have come out of the fire, the fire will yet consume them. And when I set my face against them, you will know that I am the LORD. **8**I will make the land desolate because they have been unfaithful, declares the Sovereign LORD."

An Allegory of Unfaithful Jerusalem

16 The word of the LORD came to me: **2**"Son of man, confront Jerusalem with her detestable practices **3**and say, 'This is what the Sovereign LORD says to Jerusalem: Your ancestry and birth were in the land of the Ca-

a 14 Or Danel; the Hebrew spelling may suggest a person other than the prophet Daniel; also in verse 20.

naanites; your father was an Amorite and your mother a Hittite. **4**On the day you were born your cord was not cut, nor were you washed with water to make you clean, nor were you rubbed with salt or wrapped in cloths. **5**No one looked on you with pity or had compassion enough to do any of these things for you. Rather, you were thrown out into the open field, for on the day you were born you were despised.

6" 'Then I passed by and saw you kicking about in your blood, and as you lay there in your blood I said to you, "Live!"*a* **7**I made you grow like a plant of the field. You grew up and developed and became the most beautiful of jewels.*b* Your breasts were formed and your hair grew, you who were naked and bare.

8" 'Later I passed by, and when I looked at you and saw that you were old enough for love, I spread the corner of my garment over you and covered your nakedness. I gave you my solemn oath and entered into a covenant**D** with you, declares the Sovereign LORD, and you became mine.

9" 'I bathed*c* you with water and washed the blood from you and put ointments on you. **10**I clothed you with an embroidered dress and put leather sandals on you. I dressed you in fine linen and covered you with costly garments. **11**I adorned you with jewelry: I put bracelets on your arms and a necklace around your neck, **12**and I put a ring on your nose, earrings on your ears and a beautiful crown on your head. **13**So you were adorned with gold and silver; your clothes were of fine linen and costly fabric and embroidered cloth. Your food was fine flour, honey and olive oil. You became very beautiful and rose to be a queen. **14**And your fame spread among the nations on account of your beauty, because the splendor I had given you made your beauty perfect, declares the Sovereign LORD.

15" 'But you trusted in your beauty and used your fame to become a prostitute. You lavished your favors on anyone who passed by and your beauty became his.*d* **16**You took some of your garments to make gaudy high places**D**, where you carried on your prostitution. Such things should not happen, nor should they ever occur. **17**You also took the fine jewelry I gave you, the jewelry made of my gold and silver, and you made for yourself male idols**D** and engaged in prostitution with them. **18**And you took your embroidered clothes to put on them, and you offered my oil and incense**D** before them. **19**Also the food I provided for you—the fine flour, olive oil and honey I gave you to eat—you offered as fragrant incense before them. That is what happened, declares the Sovereign LORD.

20" 'And you took your sons and daughters whom you bore to me and sacrificed them as food to the idols. Was your prostitution not enough? **21**You slaughtered my children and sacrificed them*e* to the idols. **22**In all your detestable practices and your prostitution you did not remember the days of your youth, when you were naked and bare, kicking about in your blood.

23" 'Woe! Woe to you, declares the Sovereign LORD. In

What did it mean to cover with the corner of a garment? (16:8)

The personification of Jerusalem continues as God compares the city to a young woman whom he graciously chose for a wife once she reached childbearing age. Covering a woman with the corner of a garment symbolized one's intent to acquire her as a wife. See *What did it mean to spread the corner of your garment over someone?* (Ruth 3:9). By covering her with his garment, the Lord shielded her from public humiliation until he could marry her and clothe her in appropriate attire.

How was Israel like a prostitute? (16:15)

See article: *What was the spirit of prostitution?* (Hosea 4:12). Also see *Pull up your skirts over your face* (Jer. 13:26).

Why would parents sacrifice their children? (16:20–21)

See *Why would parents sacrifice their children?* (Jer. 19:5).

---

*a*6 A few Hebrew manuscripts, Septuagint and Syriac; most Hebrew manuscripts *"Live!" And as you lay there in your blood I said to you, "Live!"*   *b*7 Or *became mature*   *c*9 Or *I had bathed*
*d*15 Most Hebrew manuscripts; one Hebrew manuscript (see some Septuagint manuscripts) *by. Such a thing should not happen*   *e*21 Or *and made them pass through ⌊the fire⌋*

Mound (16:24)

The precise meaning of the Hebrew word is uncertain. The word may refer to an elevated idolatrous shrine or platform; others have suggested that a harlot's bed or a brothel is in view. In any case, the passage is emphasizing that Jerusalem's unfaithfulness was obvious to everyone.

How did Judah prostitute itself to Egypt, Assyria and Babylon? (16:26–29)

Rather than trusting in God alone for national security, Judah formed alliances with these foreign powers.

Why yield Israel to the Philistine daughters? (16:27)

Within the extended metaphor of this chapter, Judah is compared to a young woman who has been unfaithful to her husband, the Lord. The neighboring Philistines are pictured as jealous young women who greedily steal Israel's wealth when given the opportunity. The historical reality behind the figurative language is the Assyrian Sennacherib's transferal of Judah's land to three Philistine kings following Hezekiah's rebellion in 701 B.C.

Were women punished differently than men for adultery and murder? (16:37–38)

According to the Old Testament law, both adulterous men and women were to be executed by stoning. It is uncertain if this law was consistently applied in ancient Israel. In ch. 16 the situation is complicated by the fact that God's adulterous wife (Israel) has acted like a common prostitute and had sexual relations with countless men, many of them foreigners.

addition to all your other wickedness, **24**you built a mound for yourself and made a lofty shrine in every public square. **25**At the head of every street you built your lofty shrines and degraded your beauty, offering your body with increasing promiscuity to anyone who passed by. **26**You engaged in prostitution with the Egyptians, your lustful neighbors, and provoked me to anger with your increasing promiscuity. **27**So I stretched out my hand against you and reduced your territory; I gave you over to the greed of your enemies, the daughters of the Philistines, who were shocked by your lewd conduct. **28**You engaged in prostitution with the Assyrians too, because you were insatiable; and even after that, you still were not satisfied. **29**Then you increased your promiscuity to include Babylonia,*a* a land of merchants, but even with this you were not satisfied.

30" 'How weak-willed you are, declares the Sovereign LORD, when you do all these things, acting like a brazen prostitute! **31**When you built your mounds at the head of every street and made your lofty shrines in every public square, you were unlike a prostitute, because you scorned payment.

32" 'You adulterous wife! You prefer strangers to your own husband! **33**Every prostitute receives a fee, but you give gifts to all your lovers, bribing them to come to you from everywhere for your illicit favors. **34**So in your prostitution you are the opposite of others; no one runs after you for your favors. You are the very opposite, for you give payment and none is given to you.

35" 'Therefore, you prostitute, hear the word of the LORD! **36**This is what the Sovereign LORD says: Because you poured out your wealth*b* and exposed your nakedness in your promiscuity with your lovers, and because of all your detestable idols, and because you gave them your children's blood, **37**therefore I am going to gather all your lovers, with whom you found pleasure, those you loved as well as those you hated. I will gather them against you from all around and will strip you in front of them, and they will see all your nakedness. **38**I will sentence you to the punishment of women who commit adultery and who shed blood; I will bring upon you the blood vengeance of my wrath and jealous anger. **39**Then I will hand you over to your lovers, and they will tear down your mounds and destroy your lofty shrines. They will strip you of your clothes and take your fine jewelry and leave you naked and bare. **40**They will bring a mob against you, who will stone you and hack you to pieces with their swords. **41**They will burn down your houses and inflict punishment on you in the sight of many women. I will put a stop to your prostitution, and you will no longer pay your lovers. **42**Then my wrath against you will subside and my jealous anger will turn away from you; I will be calm and no longer angry.

43" 'Because you did not remember the days of your youth but enraged me with all these things, I will surely bring down on your head what you have done, declares the Sovereign LORD. Did you not add lewdness to all your other detestable practices?

44" 'Everyone who quotes proverbs will quote this proverb about you: "Like mother, like daughter." **45**You are a true daughter of your mother, who despised her husband and her children; and you are a true sister of your sisters,

a29 Or Chaldea　　*b36 Or lust*

who despised their husbands and their children. Your mother was a Hittite and your father an Amorite. **46**Your older sister was Samaria, who lived to the north of you with her daughters; and your younger sister, who lived to the south of you with her daughters, was Sodom. **47**You not only walked in their ways and copied their detestable practices, but in all your ways you soon became more depraved than they. **48**As surely as I live, declares the Sovereign LORD, your sister Sodom and her daughters never did what you and your daughters have done.

49" 'Now this was the sin of your sister Sodom: She and her daughters were arrogant, overfed and unconcerned; they did not help the poor and needy. **50**They were haughty and did detestable things before me. Therefore I did away with them as you have seen. **51**Samaria did not commit half the sins you did. You have done more detestable things than they, and have made your sisters seem righteousᴰ by all these things you have done. **52**Bear your disgrace, for you have furnished some justificationᴰ for your sisters. Because your sins were more vile than theirs, they appear more righteous than you. So then, be ashamed and bear your disgrace, for you have made your sisters appear righteous.

53" 'However, I will restore the fortunes of Sodom and her daughters and of Samaria and her daughters, and your fortunes along with them, **54**so that you may bear your disgrace and be ashamed of all you have done in giving them comfort. **55**And your sisters, Sodom with her daughters and Samaria with her daughters, will return to what they were before; and you and your daughters will return to what you were before. **56**You would not even mention your sister Sodom in the day of your pride, **57**before your wickedness was uncovered. Even so, you are now scorned by the daughters of Edomᴰᵃ and all her neighbors and the daughters of the Philistines—all those around you who despise you. **58**You will bear the consequences of your lewdness and your detestable practices, declares the LORD.

59" 'This is what the Sovereign LORD says: I will deal with you as you deserve, because you have despised my oath by breaking the covenantᴰ. **60**Yet I will remember the covenant I made with you in the days of your youth, and I will establish an everlasting covenant with you. **61**Then you will remember your ways and be ashamed when you receive your sisters, both those who are older than you and those who are younger. I will give them to you as daughters, but not on the basis of my covenant with you. **62**So I will establish my covenant with you, and you will know that I am the LORD. **63**Then, when I make atonementᴰ for you for all you have done, you will remember and be ashamed and never again open your mouth because of your humiliation, declares the Sovereign LORD.' "

Two Eagles and a Vine

17 The word of the LORD came to me: **2**"Son of manᴰ, set forth an allegory and tell the house of Israel a parableᴰ. **3**Say to them, 'This is what the Sovereign LORD says: A great eagle with powerful wings, long feathers and full plumage of varied colors came to Lebanon. Taking hold of the top of a cedar, **4**he broke off its topmost shoot

---

How was Israel's behavior worse than Sodom's? (16:47–48)

The context emphasizes Sodom's pride, materialism and social injustice, not the sexual perversities highlighted in Genesis 18–19. It is possible that Jerusalem surpassed Sodom in these specific areas. Another possibility is that the language is exaggerated for its shock effect. Perhaps Jerusalem's sins, though not actually as perverse as Sodom's, were more offensive to God because she had received such a clear revelation of his moral will.

SCRIPTURE LINK (16:49) *Sin of your sister Sodom*

More is said about Sodom's sexual sins in Gen. 19. Ezekiel's emphasis on social injustice indicates he was more influenced by contemporary extrabiblical traditions about Sodom than by the Genesis account.

Why would God restore Sodom and Samaria? (16:53)

Jerusalem was even more sinful than Samaria and Sodom, so much so that they almost looked righteous in comparison to her. Though self-righteous Jerusalem refused to admit this, the Lord would force the proud city to recognize the magnitude of her sin. Jerusalem would suffer judgment like Samaria and Sodom and then God would eventually restore all three *sisters* (v. 55).

Everlasting covenant (16:60)

A new covenant which God will institute with Jerusalem in the day of her restoration. God will forgive the city and reestablish his *marriage* relationship with her. At that time he will revive the Davidic kingship and once more live among his people (37:24–28).

Atonement (16:63)

The background for the language is the Old Testament sacrificial system. In this system, God's wrath was appeased by sacrifices which *covered over* the sins of the offender. Here God assures Jerusalem (representative of its people) that he will make adequate provision for her sins, allowing him to reestablish his relationship with her. In the progress of revelation and history, we discover that God views Jesus' death as the sacrifice which enables him to make peace with sinners and restore them to his favor.

What do the eagles represent? (17:3)

The Lord explains this parable in vv. 11–15. The first eagle stands for the Babylonian king Nebuchadnezzar, who deported Judah's king Jehoiachin (*the top of a cedar*) in 597 B.C. The seed and vine stand for the remnant left by Nebuchadnezzar in the land under the authority of King Zedekiah. This vine sent out roots toward a second eagle, which represents Egypt, to whom Zedekiah looked for help in his effort to free Judah from Babylonian rule.

ᵃ57 Many Hebrew manuscripts and Syriac; most Hebrew manuscripts, Septuagint and Vulgate *Aram*

and carried it away to a land of merchants, where he planted it in a city of traders.

5" 'He took some of the seed of your land and put it in fertile soil. He planted it like a willow by abundant water, 6and it sprouted and became a low, spreading vine. Its branches turned toward him, but its roots remained under it. So it became a vine and produced branches and put out leafy boughs.

7" 'But there was another great eagle with powerful wings and full plumage. The vine now sent out its roots toward him from the plot where it was planted and stretched out its branches to him for water. 8It had been planted in good soil by abundant water so that it would produce branches, bear fruit and become a splendid vine.'

9"Say to them, 'This is what the Sovereign LORD says: Will it thrive? Will it not be uprooted and stripped of its fruit so that it withers? All its new growth will wither. It will not take a strong arm or many people to pull it up by the roots. 10Even if it is transplanted, will it thrive? Will it not wither completely when the east wind strikes it—wither away in the plot where it grew?' "

11Then the word of the LORD came to me: 12"Say to this rebellious house, 'Do you not know what these things mean?' Say to them: 'The king of Babylon went to Jerusalem^D and carried off her king and her nobles, bringing them back with him to Babylon. 13Then he took a member of the royal family and made a treaty with him, putting him under oath. He also carried away the leading men of the land, 14so that the kingdom would be brought low, unable to rise again, surviving only by keeping his treaty. 15But the king rebelled against him by sending his envoys to Egypt to get horses and a large army. Will he succeed? Will he who does such things escape? Will he break the treaty and yet escape?

16" 'As surely as I live, declares the Sovereign LORD, he shall die in Babylon, in the land of the king who put him on the throne, whose oath he despised and whose treaty he broke. 17Pharaoh with his mighty army and great horde will be of no help to him in war, when ramps are built and siege works^D erected to destroy many lives. 18He despised the oath by breaking the covenant^D. Because he had given his hand in pledge and yet did all these things, he shall not escape.

19" 'Therefore this is what the Sovereign LORD says: As surely as I live, I will bring down on his head my oath that he despised and my covenant that he broke. 20I will spread my net for him, and he will be caught in my snare. I will bring him to Babylon and execute judgment upon him there because he was unfaithful to me. 21All his fleeing troops will fall by the sword, and the survivors will be scattered to the winds. Then you will know that I the LORD have spoken.

22" 'This is what the Sovereign LORD says: I myself will take a shoot from the very top of a cedar and plant it; I will break off a tender sprig from its topmost shoots and plant it on a high and lofty mountain. 23On the mountain heights of Israel I will plant it; it will produce branches and bear fruit and become a splendid cedar. Birds of every kind will nest in it; they will find shelter in the shade of its branches. 24All the trees of the field will know that I the LORD bring down the tall tree and make the low tree grow tall. I dry up the green tree and make the dry tree flourish.

" 'I the LORD have spoken, and I will do it.' "

SCRIPTURE LINK (17:12–13)

The account of this Babylonian victory over Judah and the captivity of its king can be found in 2 Kings 24:10–16 and 2 Chron. 36:9–10. These events took place in 597 B.C.

SCRIPTURE LINK (17:15) *But the king rebelled*

Read what happened in 2 Kings 24:20–25:21; 2 Chron. 36:11–21; Jer. 39:1–10.

Ramps . . . siege works (17:17)

During siege warfare, the attackers sometimes erected earthen mounds and ramps against the city walls. Siege engines were wheeled up these ramps. From inside the engines, archers fired arrows at the city's defenders, while others smashed the walls with battering rams.

What new shoot will the Lord plant? (17:22–24)

The new shoot from the cedar (which symbolizes Judah's king) stands for a future king through whom the Lord would restore the glory of the Davidic dynasty and the nation. Jesus the Messiah fulfilled this prophecy.

The Soul Who Sins Will Die

18 The word of the LORD came to me: **2**"What do you people mean by quoting this proverb about the land of Israel:

" 'The fathers eat sour grapes,
and the children's teeth are set on edge'?

3"As surely as I live, declares the Sovereign LORD, you will no longer quote this proverb in Israel. **4**For every living soul[D] belongs to me, the father as well as the son—both alike belong to me. The soul who sins is the one who will die.

5"Suppose there is a righteous[D] man
who does what is just and right.
6He does not eat at the mountain shrines
or look to the idols[D] of the house of Israel.
He does not defile his neighbor's wife
or lie with a woman during her period.
7He does not oppress anyone,
but returns what he took in pledge for a
loan.
He does not commit robbery
but gives his food to the hungry
and provides clothing for the naked.
8He does not lend at usury[D]
or take excessive interest.[a]
He withholds his hand from doing wrong
and judges fairly between man and man.
9He follows my decrees
and faithfully keeps my laws.
That man is righteous;
he will surely live,
declares the Sovereign LORD.

10"Suppose he has a violent son, who sheds blood or does any of these other things[b] **11**(though the father has done none of them):

"He eats at the mountain shrines.
He defiles his neighbor's wife.
12He oppresses the poor and needy.
He commits robbery.
He does not return what he took in pledge.
He looks to the idols.
He does detestable things.
13He lends at usury and takes excessive
interest.

Will such a man live? He will not! Because he has done all these detestable things, he will surely be put to death[D] and his blood will be on his own head.

14"But suppose this son has a son who sees all the sins his father commits, and though he sees them, he does not do such things:

15"He does not eat at the mountain shrines
or look to the idols of the house of Israel.
He does not defile his neighbor's wife.
16He does not oppress anyone
or require a pledge for a loan.
He does not commit robbery
but gives his food to the hungry

What did the people mean by this proverb? (18:2)

Eating unripe grapes leaves an unpleasant aftertaste. The point of the proverb is that Israel claims that the children are unfairly enduring the consequences of their fathers' deeds. Their thinking was wrong, for they had followed in the footsteps of their fathers and were receiving the just punishment for their own sins. See *Was this proverb ever true?* (Jer. 31:29).

SCRIPTURE LINK (18:6)

See Lev. 15:24; 18:19.

---

a8 Or take interest; similarly in verses 13 and 17   *b10 Or things to a brother*

SCRIPTURE LINK (18:19–20)

The Old Testament teaches that individuals sometimes suffer the consequences of their parents' deeds. The Lord warned his enemies that their sin would have an adverse effect on their families throughout their lifetimes (Exodus 20:5). Korah's and Achan's innocent children died along with their sinful parents (Num. 16:27,32; Joshua 7:24–25). Whenever children were punished for their parents' sins, direct rebellion against God was involved. It would seem, then, that God, who is sovereign and just, judges someone's children when his authority has been violated. See Deut. 24:16; 2 Kings 14:6; Jer. 31:29–30.

SCRIPTURE LINK (18:23)

Also see v. 32; Micah 7:18; 1 Tim. 2:3–4; 2 Peter 3:9.

and provides clothing for the naked. [17]He withholds his hand from sin[a] and takes no usury[D] or excessive interest. He keeps my laws and follows my decrees.

He will not die for his father's sin; he will surely live. [18]But his father will die for his own sin, because he practiced extortion[D], robbed his brother and did what was wrong among his people.

[19]"Yet you ask, 'Why does the son not share the guilt of his father?' Since the son has done what is just and right and has been careful to keep all my decrees, he will surely live. [20]The soul[D] who sins is the one who will die. The son will not share the guilt of the father, nor will the father share the guilt of the son. The righteousness[D] of the righteous[D] man will be credited to him, and the wickedness of the wicked will be charged against him.

[21]"But if a wicked man turns away from all the sins he has committed and keeps all my decrees and does what is just and right, he will surely live; he will not die. [22]None of the offenses he has committed will be remembered against him. Because of the righteous things he has done, he will live. [23]Do I take any pleasure in the death[D] of the wicked? declares the Sovereign LORD. Rather, am I not pleased when they turn from their ways and live?

[24]"But if a righteous man turns from his righteousness and commits sin and does the same detestable things the wicked man does, will he live? None of the righteous things he has done will be remembered. Because of the unfaithfulness he is guilty of and because of the sins he has committed, he will die.

[25]"Yet you say, 'The way of the Lord is not just.' Hear, O house of Israel: Is my way unjust? Is it not your ways that are unjust? [26]If a righteous man turns from his righteousness and commits sin, he will die for it; because of the sin he has committed he will die. [27]But if a wicked man turns away from the wickedness he has committed and does what is just and right, he will save his life. [28]Because he considers all the offenses he has committed and

[a]17 Septuagint (see also verse 8); Hebrew *from the poor*

How does sin undo the good we have done? (18:24)

The verse describes a radical change in lifestyle, not isolated misdeeds that stain an otherwise godly record. The passage does not refer to one's eternal destiny, but rather to the effects of sin in this life. Note Ezekiel's appeal to the house of Israel (18:30–32) to escape death by repenting. This exhortation must be understood in light of the threatened Babylonian invasion which would result in the nation's loss of political independence and the slaughter or exile of its people.

God's warning to Judah reminds us of an important Biblical principle. In addition to a profession of allegiance to God and righteous acts, God expects believers to persevere in good works and finish well. Failure to do so can result in divine discipline and can negate, at least in a practical and temporal sense, our former good works. This is illustrated in the life of David. During his youth and early reign he was loyal to God and richly rewarded for his good deeds. When he abandoned righteousness and pursued a wicked course, he suffered God's discipline. Though God forgave David and gave a positive final assessment of his life, the king's sin brought him and his family great pain.

turns away from them, he will surely live; he will not die. **29**Yet the house of Israel says, 'The way of the Lord is not just.' Are my ways unjust, O house of Israel? Is it not your ways that are unjust?

30"Therefore, O house of Israel, I will judge you, each one according to his ways, declares the Sovereign LORD. Repent^D! Turn away from all your offenses; then sin will not be your downfall. **31**Rid yourselves of all the offenses you have committed, and get a new heart and a new spirit. Why will you die, O house of Israel? **32**For I take no pleasure in the death^D of anyone, declares the Sovereign LORD. Repent and live!

A Lament for Israel's Princes

19 "Take up a lament^D concerning the princes of Israel **2**and say:

" 'What a lioness was your mother
    among the lions!
She lay down among the young lions
    and reared her cubs.
3She brought up one of her cubs,
    and he became a strong lion.
He learned to tear the prey
    and he devoured men.
4The nations heard about him,
    and he was trapped in their pit.
They led him with hooks
    to the land of Egypt.

5" 'When she saw her hope unfulfilled,
    her expectation gone,
she took another of her cubs
    and made him a strong lion.
6He prowled among the lions,
    for he was now a strong lion.
He learned to tear the prey
    and he devoured men.
7He broke down^a their strongholds^D
    and devastated their towns.
The land and all who were in it
    were terrified by his roaring.
8Then the nations came against him,
    those from regions round about.
They spread their net for him,
    and he was trapped in their pit.
9With hooks they pulled him into a cage
    and brought him to the king of Babylon.
They put him in prison,
    so his roar was heard no longer
    on the mountains of Israel.

10" 'Your mother was like a vine in your
    vineyard^b
    planted by the water;
it was fruitful and full of branches
    because of abundant water.
11Its branches were strong,
    fit for a ruler's scepter^D.
It towered high
    above the thick foliage,
conspicuous for its height

SCRIPTURE LINK (18:31) *A new heart and a new spirit*
See Psalm 51:10.

Lament (19:1)
See *Lament* (26:17).

Mother . . . cubs (19:2–9)
The mother lioness is either the nation of Judah or its capital city Jerusalem. The first cub, or lion, mentioned was King Jehoahaz, whom the Egyptian Pharaoh took captive in 609 B.C. The second was either King Jehoiachin or his successor Zedekiah, both of whom were taken into Babylonian exile.

How were captives led away by hooks? (19:4,9)
Conquerors would sometimes humiliate defeated kings by putting hooks or rings attached to a leash through the victim's nose, jaw or lip. Apparently the same technique was used with wild animals. 2 Kings 19:28, as well as Assyrian inscriptions and artwork, give evidence of the practice in the Middle East.

How was the mother like a fruitful vine? (19:10)
The vine probably stands for Judah or Jerusalem, rather than a literal queen mother. In light of the context, the fruitfulness of the vine probably refers to the glory and strength of the Davidic dynasty, which never lacked a ruler.

---

^a7 Targum (see Septuagint); Hebrew *He knew*   ^b10 Two Hebrew manuscripts; most Hebrew manuscripts *your blood*

and for its many branches.
¹²But it was uprooted in fury
    and thrown to the ground.
The east wind made it shrivel,
    it was stripped of its fruit;
its strong branches withered
    and fire consumed them.
¹³Now it is planted in the desert,
    in a dry and thirsty land.
¹⁴Fire spread from one of its main*ᵃ* branches
    and consumed its fruit.
No strong branch is left on it
    fit for a ruler's scepterᴰ.'

This is a lamentᴰ and is to be used as a lament."

Rebellious Israel

20 In the seventh year, in the fifth month on the tenth day, some of the elders of Israel came to inquire of the LORD, and they sat down in front of me.

²Then the word of the LORD came to me: ³"Son of manᴰ, speak to the elders of Israel and say to them, 'This is what the Sovereign LORD says: Have you come to inquire of me? As surely as I live, I will not let you inquire of me, declares the Sovereign LORD.'

⁴"Will you judge them? Will you judge them, son of man? Then confront them with the detestable practices of their fathers ⁵and say to them: 'This is what the Sovereign LORD says: On the day I chose Israel, I swore with uplifted hand to the descendants of the house of Jacob and revealed myself to them in Egypt. With uplifted hand I said to them, "I am the LORD your God." ⁶On that day I swore to them that I would bring them out of Egypt into a land I had searched out for them, a land flowing with milk and honey, the most beautiful of all lands. ⁷And I said to them, "Each of you, get rid of the vile images you have set your eyes on, and do not defile yourselves with the idolsᴰ of Egypt. I am the LORD your God."

⁸" 'But they rebelled against me and would not listen to me; they did not get rid of the vile images they had set their eyes on, nor did they forsake the idols of Egypt. So I said I would pour out my wrath on them and spend my anger against them in Egypt. ⁹But for the sake of my name I did what would keep it from being profanedᴰ in the eyes of the nations they lived among and in whose sight I had revealed myself to the Israelites by bringing them out of Egypt. ¹⁰Therefore I led them out of Egypt and brought them into the desert. ¹¹I gave them my decrees and made known to them my laws, for the man who obeys them will live by them. ¹²Also I gave them my Sabbathsᴰ as a sign between us, so they would know that I the LORD made them holy.

¹³" 'Yet the people of Israel rebelled against me in the desert. They did not follow my decrees but rejected my laws—although the man who obeys them will live by them—and they utterly desecratedᴰ my Sabbaths. So I said I would pour out my wrath on them and destroy them in the desert. ¹⁴But for the sake of my name I did what would keep it from being profaned in the eyes of the nations in whose sight I had brought them out. ¹⁵Also with uplifted hand I swore to them in the desert that I would not bring them into the land I had given them—a

---

Seventh year (20:1)
The seventh year of King Jehoiachin's exile. Ezekiel had been taken to Babylon that same year. The precise dating gives the message a formal quality and suggests it had special significance.

Why would God turn away from those seeking him? (20:3)
These leaders and the people they represented were not genuinely seeking the Lord with remorseful hearts. In their eyes, the Lord was just one of several gods to placate and worship. The Lord demanded uncompromising allegiance and refused to tolerate such pluralism.

Uplifted hand (20:5)
A solemn gesture which often accompanied oaths, similar to what is done in modern day court systems.

Why would God be concerned about what others think of him? (20:9)
God is concerned that human beings correctly understand him—for their own good, not to protect his reputation. He takes into consideration how his decisions will affect their perception of his character. Such was the case at the time of the exodus. Though Israel worshiped idols in Egypt and angered the Lord, he still delivered them from their bondage so that observers would not question his faithfulness or conclude that he was too weak to rescue his people.

How were Sabbaths a *sign* to Israel? (20:12)
The Sabbath observance would serve as an ongoing reminder that Israel was the Lord's chosen, covenant people, set aside to serve him in a special way.

ᵃ14 Or from under its

land flowing with milk and honey, most beautiful of all lands— [16]because they rejected my laws and did not follow my decrees and desecrated[D] my Sabbaths[D]. For their hearts were devoted to their idols[D]. [17]Yet I looked on them with pity and did not destroy them or put an end to them in the desert. [18]I said to their children in the desert, "Do not follow the statutes of your fathers or keep their laws or defile yourselves with their idols. [19]I am the LORD your God; follow my decrees and be careful to keep my laws. [20]Keep my Sabbaths holy, that they may be a sign between us. Then you will know that I am the LORD your God."

[21]" 'But the children rebelled against me: They did not follow my decrees, they were not careful to keep my laws—although the man who obeys them will live by them—and they desecrated my Sabbaths. So I said I would pour out my wrath on them and spend my anger against them in the desert. [22]But I withheld my hand, and for the sake of my name I did what would keep it from being profaned[D] in the eyes of the nations in whose sight I had brought them out. [23]Also with uplifted hand I swore to them in the desert that I would disperse them among the nations and scatter them through the countries, [24]because they had not obeyed my laws but had rejected my decrees and desecrated my Sabbaths, and their eyes ⌞lusted⌟ after their fathers' idols. [25]I also gave them over to statutes that were not good and laws they could not live by; [26]I let them become defiled through their gifts—the sacrifice[D] of every firstborn[D][a]—that I might fill them with horror so they would know that I am the LORD.'

[27]"Therefore, son of man[D], speak to the people of Israel and say to them, 'This is what the Sovereign LORD says: In this also your fathers blasphemed[D] me by forsaking me: [28]When I brought them into the land I had sworn to give them and they saw any high hill or any leafy tree, there they offered their sacrifices, made offerings that provoked me to anger, presented their fragrant incense[D] and poured out their drink offerings[D]. [29]Then I said to them: What is this high place you go to?' " (It is called Bamah[b] to this day.)

Judgment and Restoration

[30]"Therefore say to the house of Israel: 'This is what the Sovereign LORD says: Will you defile yourselves the way your fathers did and lust after their vile images? [31]When you offer your gifts—the sacrifice of your sons in[c] the fire—you continue to defile yourselves with all your idols to this day. Am I to let you inquire of me, O house of Israel? As surely as I live, declares the Sovereign LORD, I will not let you inquire of me.

[32]" 'You say, "We want to be like the nations, like the peoples of the world, who serve wood and stone." But what you have in mind will never happen. [33]As surely as I live, declares the Sovereign LORD, I will rule over you with a mighty hand and an outstretched arm and with outpoured wrath. [34]I will bring you from the nations and gather you from the countries where you have been scattered—with a mighty hand and an outstretched arm and with outpoured wrath. [35]I will bring you into the desert of the nations and there, face to face, I will execute judgment upon you. [36]As I judged your fathers in the desert of

SCRIPTURE LINK (20:23-24)
This warning appeared in Deut. 28:64-67.

Where did the bad commandments come from? (20:25)
Many of these statutes were probably borrowed from or influenced by the civil and religious practices of the surrounding pagan nations. Verse 26, which denounces child sacrifice, suggests this. Micah 6:16 refers to the oppressive social policies and statutes of the Israelite kings Omri and Ahab. Such practices may have been influenced by pagan patterns, but they also derive from the desire for power and self-aggrandizement that characterizes fallen humankind.

Why would parents sacrifice their children? (20:26)
See *Why would parents sacrifice their children?* (Jer. 19:5).

What attracted people to worship high hills and leafy trees? (20:28)
Baal, the most powerful of the Canaanite gods, was a god of fertility who promised his devotees good crops and an abundance of children. Both of these promises were highly valued in ancient Israel's agrarian society, causing them to be tempted into local pagan religions. One of the ways people worshiped this fertility god was to engage in ritual sex with priests or priestesses of the Baal cult. In this way they hoped to gain the god's favor and ensure his blessing.

Drink offerings (20:28)
See *Drink offering* (Gen. 35:14).

[a]26 Or —making every firstborn pass through ⌞the fire⌟   [b]29 Bamah means high place.   [c]31 Or —making your sons pass through

Pass under my rod (20:37)
Shepherds used their staffs to count their sheep, often for the purpose of separating a specified number from the flock. Through the judgment of exile the Lord would remove the rebels from his flock. They would not return to the land or be a part of the new covenant community.

Why prophesy against the south? (20:46)
This is a prophecy against Jerusalem and Judah. Though an exile in Babylon, Ezekiel speaks rhetorically here, as if he were standing on the northern border of Judah. God's fire of judgment, in the form of the Babylonian army, would sweep through Judah from north to south.

Parables (20:49)
See *What do the eagles represent?* (17:3).

the land of Egypt, so I will judge you, declares the Sovereign LORD. **37**I will take note of you as you pass under my rod, and I will bring you into the bond of the covenant^D. **38**I will purge you of those who revolt and rebel against me. Although I will bring them out of the land where they are living, yet they will not enter the land of Israel. Then you will know that I am the LORD.

39" 'As for you, O house of Israel, this is what the Sovereign LORD says: Go and serve your idols^D, every one of you! But afterward you will surely listen to me and no longer profane^D my holy name with your gifts and idols. **40**For on my holy mountain, the high mountain of Israel, declares the Sovereign LORD, there in the land the entire house of Israel will serve me, and there I will accept them. There I will require your offerings and your choice gifts,^a along with all your holy sacrifices^D. **41**I will accept you as fragrant incense^D when I bring you out from the nations and gather you from the countries where you have been scattered, and I will show myself holy among you in the sight of the nations. **42**Then you will know that I am the LORD, when I bring you into the land of Israel, the land I had sworn with uplifted hand to give to your fathers. **43**There you will remember your conduct and all the actions by which you have defiled yourselves, and you will loathe yourselves for all the evil you have done. **44**You will know that I am the LORD, when I deal with you for my name's sake and not according to your evil ways and your corrupt practices, O house of Israel, declares the Sovereign LORD.' "

Prophecy Against the South

45The word of the LORD came to me: **46**"Son of man^D, set your face toward the south; preach against the south and prophesy against the forest of the southland. **47**Say to the southern forest: 'Hear the word of the LORD. This is what the Sovereign LORD says: I am about to set fire to you, and it will consume all your trees, both green and dry. The blazing flame will not be quenched, and every face from south to north will be scorched by it. **48**Everyone will see that I the LORD have kindled it; it will not be quenched.' "

49Then I said, "Ah, Sovereign LORD! They are saying of me, 'Isn't he just telling parables^D?' "

Babylon, God's Sword of Judgment

21 The word of the LORD came to me: **2**"Son of man, set your face against Jerusalem^D and preach against the sanctuary. Prophesy against the land of Israel **3**and say to her: 'This is what the LORD says: I am against you. I will draw my sword from its scabbard and cut off from you both the righteous^D and the wicked. **4**Because I am going to cut off the righteous and the wicked, my sword will be unsheathed against everyone from south to north. **5**Then all people will know that I the LORD have drawn my sword from its scabbard; it will not return again.'

6"Therefore groan, son of man! Groan before them with broken heart and bitter grief. **7**And when they ask you, 'Why are you groaning?' you shall say, 'Because of the news that is coming. Every heart will melt and every hand go limp; every spirit will become faint and every

---

^a 40 Or *and the gifts of your firstfruits*

knee become as weak as water.' It is coming! It will surely take place, declares the Sovereign LORD."

[8]The word of the LORD came to me: [9]"Son of man[D], prophesy and say, 'This is what the Lord says:

" 'A sword, a sword,
    sharpened and polished—
[10]sharpened for the slaughter,
    polished to flash like lightning!

" 'Shall we rejoice in the scepter[D] of my son ⌞Judah⌟? The sword despises every such stick.'

[11]" 'The sword is appointed to be polished,
    to be grasped with the hand;
it is sharpened and polished,
    made ready for the hand of the slayer.
[12]Cry out and wail, son of man,
    for it is against my people;
    it is against all the princes of Israel.
They are thrown to the sword
    along with my people.
Therefore beat your breast.

[13]" 'Testing will surely come. And what if the scepter ⌞of Judah⌟, which the sword despises, does not continue? declares the Sovereign LORD.'

[14]"So then, son of man, prophesy
    and strike your hands together.
Let the sword strike twice,
    even three times.
It is a sword for slaughter—
    a sword for great slaughter,
    closing in on them from every side.
[15]So that hearts may melt
    and the fallen be many,
I have stationed the sword for slaughter[a]
    at all their gates.
Oh! It is made to flash like lightning,

[a]15 Septuagint; the meaning of the Hebrew for this word is uncertain.

Scepter of my son (21:10)

The precise meaning of the phrase is not clear. It is possible that the scepter is a royal symbol here and that *my son* refers to the Davidic king (2 Samuel 7:14). God may be quoting the people who wondered if the Davidic king was still a legitimate source of hope. The Lord makes it clear that not even the king would be protected from God's sword of judgment.

Strike your hands together (21:14)

A gesture of anger or sorrow, which may mimic the suddenness of the coming judgment.

Why punish everyone? (21:4)

Punishing the righteous along with the wicked emphasizes the degree of God's anger, as well as the corporate solidarity of the covenant community in God's sight. Sin has adverse consequences and frequently the innocent suffer because of the misdeeds of the wicked.

This warning seems to contradict earlier passages in Ezekiel's prophecy where the Lord assured the righteous special consideration on the day of judgment. According to 9:4–6, the Lord would spare the repentant when he poured out his anger on Jerusalem. In ch. 18 he emphasizes that the righteous person would *live* because of his devotion to God, even though his father may have been a vile sinner.

Interpreters have struggled to harmonize these apparently contradictory passages. One possibility is that 21:3–4 is talking about the exile of the city's residents, not the death of individuals. With his sword (a symbol here of the Babylonians) God would *cut off* all citizens from Jerusalem. Both the righteous (like Ezekiel) and the wicked would go into exile. At the same time, in the midst of this seemingly indiscriminate judgment, God would take special note of righteous individuals and protect their lives.

it is grasped for slaughter.
16O sword, slash to the right,
    then to the left,
    wherever your blade is turned.
17I too will strike my hands together,
    and my wrath will subside.
I the LORD have spoken."

18The word of the LORD came to me: **19**"Son of man[D], mark out two roads for the sword of the king of Babylon to take, both starting from the same country. Make a signpost where the road branches off to the city. **20**Mark out one road for the sword to come against Rabbah of the Ammonites and another against Judah and fortified Jerusalem[D]. **21**For the king of Babylon will stop at the fork in the road, at the junction of the two roads, to seek an omen: He will cast lots with arrows, he will consult his idols[D], he will examine the liver. **22**Into his right hand will come the lot for Jerusalem, where he is to set up battering rams, to give the command to slaughter, to sound the battle cry, to set battering rams against the gates, to build a ramp and to erect siege works[D]. **23**It will seem like a false omen to those who have sworn allegiance to him, but he will remind them of their guilt and take them captive.

24"Therefore this is what the Sovereign LORD says: 'Because you people have brought to mind your guilt by your open rebellion, revealing your sins in all that you do—because you have done this, you will be taken captive.

25" 'O profane[D] and wicked prince of Israel, whose day has come, whose time of punishment has reached its climax, **26**this is what the Sovereign LORD says: Take off the turban, remove the crown. It will not be as it was: The lowly will be exalted and the exalted will be brought low. **27**A ruin! A ruin! I will make it a ruin! It will not be restored until he comes to whom it rightfully belongs; to him I will give it.'

28"And you, son of man, prophesy and say, 'This is what the Sovereign LORD says about the Ammonites and their insults:

    " 'A sword, a sword,
        drawn for the slaughter,
    polished to consume
        and to flash like lightning!
    29Despite false visions[D] concerning you
        and lying divinations[D] about you,
    it will be laid on the necks
        of the wicked who are to be slain,
    whose day has come,
        whose time of punishment has reached its
            climax.
    30Return the sword to its scabbard.
        In the place where you were created,
    in the land of your ancestry,
        I will judge you.
    31I will pour out my wrath upon you
        and breathe out my fiery anger against you;
    I will hand you over to brutal men,
        men skilled in destruction.
    32You will be fuel for the fire,
        your blood will be shed in your land,
    you will be remembered no more;
        for I the LORD have spoken.' "

Ammonites (21:20)
The descendants of Ammon (one of Lot's grandsons through incest: Gen. 19:36–38), who lived east of central Israel on the east side of the Jordan River (see *Judah's Enemies* on page 1172).

Why examine a liver before making a decision? (21:21)
The Babylonians believed that the gods revealed the future through omens. One of the most popular divination techniques was to study animal livers for abnormal physical characteristics. One such ancient omen says: "If the right lobe is in the area of the left, the king will capture a land not his own." The Babylonian king would also consult his idols, or gods, by seeking an oracle from prophet-priests of the respective deities.

Wicked prince of Israel (21:25)
Judah's last king, Zedekiah, who was humiliated by the Babylonians and taken into exile.

SCRIPTURE LINK (21:26) *The lowly will be exalted and the exalted will be brought low*
A recurring theme in the Bible. Some examples include 17:24; Matt. 23:12; and 1 Peter 5:6.

What would remain a ruin? (21:27)
The turban or crown, a symbol of rulership, would be *ruined* as Zedekiah was taken into exile. The dynasty would not be restored until the rightful ruler arrived on the scene. Ezekiel later calls this ideal Messianic prince *David* (34:23–24; 37:24–25), for he would reunite the divided nation and restore the glory of the Davidic era.

Jerusalem's Sins

22 The word of the LORD came to me: ²"Son of manᴰ, will you judge her? Will you judge this city of bloodshed? Then confront her with all her detestable practices ³and say: 'This is what the Sovereign LORD says: O city that brings on herself doom by shedding blood in her midst and defiles herself by making idolsᴰ, ⁴you have become guilty because of the blood you have shed and have become defiled by the idols you have made. You have brought your days to a close, and the end of your years has come. Therefore I will make you an object of scorn to the nations and a laughingstock to all the countries. ⁵Those who are near and those who are far away will mock you, O infamous city, full of turmoil.

⁶" 'See how each of the princes of Israel who are in you uses his power to shed blood. ⁷In you they have treated father and mother with contempt; in you they have oppressed the alienᴰ and mistreated the fatherless and the widow. ⁸You have despised my holy things and desecratedᴰ my Sabbathsᴰ. ⁹In you are slanderous men bent on shedding blood; in you are those who eat at the mountain shrines and commit lewd acts. ¹⁰In you are those who dishonor their fathers' bed; in you are those who violate women during their period, when they are ceremonially uncleanᴰ. ¹¹In you one man commits a detestable offense with his neighbor's wife, another shamefully defiles his daughter-in-law, and another violates his sister, his own father's daughter. ¹²In you men accept bribes to shed blood; you take usuryᴰ and excessive interestᵃ and make unjust gain from your neighbors by extortionᴰ. And you have forgotten me, declares the Sovereign LORD.

¹³" 'I will surely strike my hands together at the unjust gain you have made and at the blood you have shed in your midst. ¹⁴Will your courage endure or your hands be strong in the day I deal with you? I the LORD have spoken, and I will do it. ¹⁵I will disperse you among the nations and scatter you through the countries; and I will put an end to your uncleannessᴰ. ¹⁶When you have been defiledᵇ in the eyes of the nations, you will know that I am the LORD.' "

¹⁷Then the word of the LORD came to me: ¹⁸"Son of man, the house of Israel has become dross to me; all of them are the copper, tin, iron and lead left inside a furnace. They are but the dross of silver. ¹⁹Therefore this is what the Sovereign LORD says: 'Because you have all become dross, I will gather you into Jerusalem. ²⁰As men gather silver, copper, iron, lead and tin into a furnace to melt it with a fiery blast, so will I gather you in my anger and my wrath and put you inside the city and melt you. ²¹I will gather you and I will blow on you with my fiery wrath, and you will be melted inside her. ²²As silver is melted in a furnace, so you will be melted inside her, and you will know that I the LORD have poured out my wrath upon you.' "

²³Again the word of the LORD came to me: ²⁴"Son of man, say to the land, 'You are a land that has had no rain or showersᶜ in the day of wrath.' ²⁵There is a conspiracy of her princesᵈ within her like a roaring lion tearing its prey; they devour people, take treasures and pre-

Eat at the mountain shrines (22:9)
The Canaanites worshiped at sanctuaries built atop hills and mountains. Animals would be sacrificed to idols there, and the worshipers would then eat the meat of the offerings. Some unfaithful Israelites joined in this worship.

SCRIPTURE LINK (22:10)
See Lev. 15:24; 18:19.

Strike my hands together (22:13)
See *Strike your hands together* (21:14).

ᵃ12 Or *usury and interest*   ᵇ16 Or *When I have allotted you your inheritance*   ᶜ24 Septuagint; Hebrew *has not been cleansed or rained on*   ᵈ25 Septuagint; Hebrew *prophets*

How could they miss the difference between holy and common things? (22:26)

The priests, who were supposed to instruct the people concerning ritual holiness, no longer took their duties seriously. The Mosaic Law clearly spelled out the guidelines for Israel's formal worship and religious practices. The text does not specifically identify the reasons for their neglect, but the context suggests it was more convenient and economically profitable for them to blur the proper distinctions.

Oholah . . . Oholibah (23:4)

It is not entirely clear why these names were chosen for the parable. Both names are derived from the Hebrew word for *tent*, which is often used in *tent* of worship. The name Oholah (used for Samaria) means *her tent* and might be paraphrased *she who has her own tent*. This would allude to the idolatrous northern kingdom's religious independence and rejection of the Jerusalem temple. The name Oholibah (used for Jerusalem) means *my tent is in her*, which may allude to the Jerusalem temple, God's special dwelling place among his covenant people.

cious things and make many widows within her. [26]Her priests[D] do violence to my law and profane[D] my holy things; they do not distinguish between the holy and the common; they teach that there is no difference between the unclean[D] and the clean; and they shut their eyes to the keeping of my Sabbaths[D], so that I am profaned among them. [27]Her officials within her are like wolves tearing their prey; they shed blood and kill people to make unjust gain. [28]Her prophets[D] whitewash these deeds for them by false visions[D] and lying divinations[D]. They say, 'This is what the Sovereign LORD says'—when the LORD has not spoken. [29]The people of the land practice extortion[D] and commit robbery; they oppress the poor and needy and mistreat the alien[D], denying them justice.

[30]"I looked for a man among them who would build up the wall and stand before me in the gap on behalf of the land so I would not have to destroy it, but I found none. [31]So I will pour out my wrath on them and consume them with my fiery anger, bringing down on their own heads all they have done, declares the Sovereign LORD."

Two Adulterous Sisters

23 The word of the LORD came to me: [2]"Son of man[D], there were two women, daughters of the same mother. [3]They became prostitutes in Egypt, engaging in prostitution from their youth. In that land their breasts were fondled and their virgin bosoms caressed. [4]The older was named Oholah, and her sister was Oholibah. They were mine and gave birth to sons and daughters. Oholah is Samaria, and Oholibah is Jerusalem[D].

[5]"Oholah engaged in prostitution while she was still mine; and she lusted after her lovers, the Assyrians—warriors [6]clothed in blue, governors and commanders, all of them handsome young men, and mounted horsemen. [7]She gave herself as a prostitute to all the elite of the Assyrians and defiled herself with all the idols[D] of everyone she lusted after. [8]She did not give up the prostitution she began in Egypt, when during her youth men slept with her, caressed her virgin bosom and poured out their lust upon her.

[9]"Therefore I handed her over to her lovers, the Assyrians, for whom she lusted. [10]They stripped her naked, took away her sons and daughters and killed her with the

Why did God need someone to *stand in the gap?* (22:30)

God is sovereign over the affairs of this world. However, he also holds human beings accountable for their actions and often even accommodates his decrees and actions to their responses. In Judah's case, God determined that the nation's response to his warnings and disciplinary actions would decide its destiny. Genuine repentance would bring renewed blessing; persistence in sin would bring invasion and exile.

God was very patient with the rebellious nation. Up to a point, he was willing to postpone judgment if a righteous leader would intercede on behalf of the nation and lead it back to God. No such intercessor arose from Judah's corrupt leadership, which left God no alternative but to judge the nation. Once this judgment was decreed and set in motion, it would be too late. They would have to suffer the just punishment for their sins.

sword. She became a byword[D] among women, and punishment was inflicted on her.

11"Her sister Oholibah saw this, yet in her lust and prostitution she was more depraved than her sister. **12**She too lusted after the Assyrians—governors and commanders, warriors in full dress, mounted horsemen, all handsome young men. **13**I saw that she too defiled herself; both of them went the same way.

14"But she carried her prostitution still further. She saw men portrayed on a wall, figures of Chaldeans[a] portrayed in red, **15**with belts around their waists and flowing turbans on their heads; all of them looked like Babylonian chariot officers, natives of Chaldea.[b] **16**As soon as she saw them, she lusted after them and sent messengers to them in Chaldea. **17**Then the Babylonians came to her, to the bed of love, and in their lust they defiled her. After she had been defiled by them, she turned away from them in disgust. **18**When she carried on her prostitution openly and exposed her nakedness, I turned away from her in disgust, just as I had turned away from her sister. **19**Yet she became more and more promiscuous as she recalled the days of her youth, when she was a prostitute in Egypt. **20**There she lusted after her lovers, whose genitals were like those of donkeys and whose emission was like that of horses. **21**So you longed for the lewdness of your youth, when in Egypt your bosom was caressed and your young breasts fondled.[c]

22"Therefore, Oholibah, this is what the Sovereign LORD says: I will stir up your lovers against you, those you turned away from in disgust, and I will bring them against you from every side— **23**the Babylonians and all the Chaldeans, the men of Pekod and Shoa and Koa, and all the Assyrians with them, handsome young men, all of them governors and commanders, chariot officers and men of high rank, all mounted on horses. **24**They will come against you with weapons,[d] chariots and wagons and with a throng of people; they will take up positions against you on every side with large and small shields and with helmets. I will turn you over to them for punishment, and they will punish you according to their standards. **25**I will direct my jealous anger against you, and they will deal with you in fury. They will cut off your noses and your ears, and those of you who are left will fall by the sword. They will take away your sons and daughters, and those of you who are left will be consumed by fire. **26**They will also strip you of your clothes and take your fine jewelry. **27**So I will put a stop to the lewdness and prostitution you began in Egypt. You will not look on these things with longing or remember Egypt anymore.

28"For this is what the Sovereign LORD says: I am about to hand you over to those you hate, to those you turned away from in disgust. **29**They will deal with you in hatred and take away everything you have worked for. They will leave you naked and bare, and the shame of your prostitution will be exposed. Your lewdness and promiscuity **30**have brought this upon you, because you lusted after the nations and defiled yourself with their idols[D]. **31**You

After courting the Babylonians, why did Jerusalem become disgusted with them? (23:17)

Judah allied with the Babylonians against their once powerful oppressors, the Assyrians. The Babylonians conquered Assyria, defeated the Egyptians at Carchemish in 605 B.C. and emerged as the most powerful empire in the Middle East. At that point, Judah realized that the Babylonians were just as imperialistic and oppressive as the Assyrians. Judah then embarked on an anti-Babylonian policy that eventually led to her demise.

Why use such repulsive imagery? (23:20)

The graphic imagery depicts Egypt as a lusty male with whom the promiscuous female, Jerusalem, desired intercourse. The reality behind the repulsive imagery was Judah's obsession for a political alliance with Egypt which God considered indecent. When Judah looked to Egypt for help, it was more than happy to oblige. Egypt wanted to establish a buffer state in Palestine to challenge Babylonian dominance in the Near East.

What was the difference between Babylonians and Chaldeans? (23:23)

The Chaldeans were a group of southern Mesopotamian tribes who took control of Babylon in the late seventh century B.C., and defeated the Assyrians. They established the neo-Babylonian empire which included the native Babylonian population and some Aramean tribes. This verse makes a distinction between the *Chaldeans*, the dominant ethnic group, and the *Babylonians*, perhaps a reference to non-Chaldean residents of Babylon.

Why mutilate victims? (23:25)

Mutilating the face of an adulteress was a common ancient Mesopotamian practice. An Assyrian law allowed a man to cut off his adulterous wife's nose. If he did, he also had to castrate her lover. Jerusalem, personified as an adulterous woman, would be punished for her unfaithfulness in this way.

Why would parents sacrifice their children? (23:27)

See *Why would parents sacrifice their children?* (Jer. 19:5).

---

[a]14 Or *Babylonians*   [b]15 Or *Babylonia*; also in verse 16
[c]21 Syriac (see also verse 3); Hebrew *caressed because of your young breasts*   [d]24 The meaning of the Hebrew for this word is uncertain.

have gone the way of your sister; so I will put her cup into your hand.

32"This is what the Sovereign LORD says:

> "You will drink your sister's cup,
>> a cup large and deep;
> it will bring scorn and derision,
>> for it holds so much.
> **33**You will be filled with drunkenness and
>> sorrow,
> the cup of ruin and desolation,
>> the cup of your sister Samaria.
> **34**You will drink it and drain it dry;
>> you will dash it to pieces
>> and tear your breasts.

I have spoken, declares the Sovereign LORD.

35"Therefore this is what the Sovereign LORD says: Since you have forgotten me and thrust me behind your back, you must bear the consequences of your lewdness and prostitution."

36The LORD said to me: "Son of man^D, will you judge Oholah and Oholibah? Then confront them with their detestable practices, **37**for they have committed adultery and blood is on their hands. They committed adultery with their idols^D; they even sacrificed their children, whom they bore to me,^a as food for them. **38**They have also done this to me: At that same time they defiled my sanctuary and desecrated^D my Sabbaths^D. **39**On the very day they sacrificed their children to their idols, they entered my sanctuary and desecrated it. That is what they did in my house.

40"They even sent messengers for men who came from far away, and when they arrived you bathed yourself for them, painted your eyes and put on your jewelry. **41**You sat on an elegant couch, with a table spread before it on which you had placed the incense^D and oil that belonged to me.

42"The noise of a carefree crowd was around her; Sabeans^b were brought from the desert along with men from the rabble, and they put bracelets on the arms of the woman and her sister and beautiful crowns on their heads. **43**Then I said about the one worn out by adultery, 'Now let them use her as a prostitute, for that is all she is.' **44**And they slept with her. As men sleep with a prostitute, so they slept with those lewd women, Oholah and Oholibah. **45**But righteous^D men will sentence them to the punishment of women who commit adultery and shed blood, because they are adulterous and blood is on their hands.

46"This is what the Sovereign LORD says: Bring a mob against them and give them over to terror and plunder^D. **47**The mob will stone them and cut them down with their swords; they will kill their sons and daughters and burn down their houses.

48"So I will put an end to lewdness in the land, that all women may take warning and not imitate you. **49**You will suffer the penalty for your lewdness and bear the consequences of your sins of idolatry^D. Then you will know that I am the Sovereign LORD."

In what sense had children been born to the Lord? (23:37)

Within the allegorical framework of the chapter, Samaria and Jerusalem were viewed as the Lord's wives who had borne him children. These children belonged to him, but his wives had the audacity to sacrifice them to idols.

Sabeans (23:42)

Descendants of Seba, son of Cush (Gen. 10:7). Known for their height, they lived either on the Arabian Peninsula or in Africa. There is a close association of the Sabeans with Egypt and Ethiopia in Isaiah 43:3 and 45:14.

Were women punished differently than men for adultery and murder? (23:45)

See *Were women punished differently than men for adultery and murder?* (16:37–38).

---

^a37 Or *even made the children they bore to me pass through ⌊the fire⌋*
^b42 Or *drunkards*

The Cooking Pot

24 In the ninth year, in the tenth month on the tenth day, the word of the LORD came to me: ²"Son of man^D, record this date, this very date, because the king of Babylon has laid siege to Jerusalem^D this very day. ³Tell this rebellious house a parable^D and say to them: 'This is what the Sovereign LORD says:

" 'Put on the cooking pot; put it on
    and pour water into it.
⁴Put into it the pieces of meat,
    all the choice pieces—the leg and the
        shoulder.
Fill it with the best of these bones;
⁵   take the pick of the flock.
Pile wood beneath it for the bones;
    bring it to a boil
    and cook the bones in it.

⁶" 'For this is what the Sovereign LORD says:

" 'Woe to the city of bloodshed,
    to the pot now encrusted,
    whose deposit will not go away!
Empty it piece by piece
    without casting lots for them.

⁷" 'For the blood she shed is in her midst:
    She poured it on the bare rock;
she did not pour it on the ground,
    where the dust would cover it.
⁸To stir up wrath and take revenge
    I put her blood on the bare rock,
    so that it would not be covered.

⁹" 'Therefore this is what the Sovereign LORD says:

" 'Woe to the city of bloodshed!
    I, too, will pile the wood high.
¹⁰So heap on the wood
    and kindle the fire.
Cook the meat well,
    mixing in the spices;
    and let the bones be charred.
¹¹Then set the empty pot on the coals
    till it becomes hot and its copper glows
so its impurities may be melted
    and its deposit burned away.
¹²It has frustrated all efforts;
    its heavy deposit has not been removed,
        not even by fire.

¹³" 'Now your impurity is lewdness. Because I tried to cleanse you but you would not be cleansed from your impurity, you will not be clean again until my wrath against you has subsided.

¹⁴" 'I the LORD have spoken. The time has come for me to act. I will not hold back; I will not have pity, nor will I relent. You will be judged according to your conduct and your actions, declares the Sovereign LORD.' "

Ezekiel's Wife Dies

¹⁵The word of the LORD came to me: ¹⁶"Son of man, with one blow I am about to take away from you the delight of your eyes. Yet do not lament^D or weep or shed any tears. ¹⁷Groan quietly; do not mourn for the dead.

Ninth year (24:1)
See *Seventh year* (20:1).

Parable (24:3)
See *What do the eagles represent?* (17:3).

Why compare the city to a cooking pot? (24:4–6)
The evil leaders of Jerusalem compared themselves to choice meat in a cooking pot and were confident that they would not be charred by the flames of divine judgment (11:3). The Lord challenged their false confidence and warned that they would not escape judgment. The fire under the pot (the Babylonians) would cook the meat and each piece would then be removed (a reference to the exile).

Why cover up blood with dust? (24:7)
One would expect a murderer to try to cover up his crime, but Jerusalem's citizens made no effort to hide the evidence of their misdeeds. The Lord refers here to crimes against the poor which resulted, whether directly or indirectly, in their death.

Why would God cause the death of Ezekiel's wife simply for an object lesson? (24:16–18)
God often required his prophets to perform difficult tasks or endure an extra measure of suffering (Heb. 11:35–38). Ezekiel's suffering was an attention-getting device by which God forced his people to confront the realities of their sin. His experience foreshadowed the emotional trauma the exiles would endure and served as an example of how they should acknowledge God's sovereignty at that time.

How did Ezekiel's lack of mourning affect the people? (24:17–19)
In ancient Israel, it was socially proper to publicly mourn the death of a loved one. Customs of grief included loud weeping, tearing clothes and wearing sackcloth. When people noticed that Ezekiel was not mourning his wife's death in the normal way, they asked why. At that point he explained the symbolic significance of his actions.

Keep your turban fastened and your sandals on your feet; do not cover the lower part of your face or eat the customary food ⌊of mourners⌋."

18So I spoke to the people in the morning, and in the evening my wife died. The next morning I did as I had been commanded.

19Then the people asked me, "Won't you tell us what these things have to do with us?"

20So I said to them, "The word of the LORD came to me: 21Say to the house of Israel, 'This is what the Sovereign LORD says: I am about to desecrateᴰ my sanctuary—the strongholdᴰ in which you take pride, the delight of your eyes, the object of your affection. The sons and daughters you left behind will fall by the sword. 22And you will do as I have done. You will not cover the lower part of your face or eat the customary food ⌊of mourners⌋. 23You will keep your turbans on your heads and your sandals on your feet. You will not mourn or weep but will waste away because of[a] your sins and groan among yourselves. 24Ezekiel will be a sign to you; you will do just as he has done. When this happens, you will know that I am the Sovereign LORD.'

25"And you, son of manᴰ, on the day I take away their stronghold, their joy and glory, the delight of their eyes, their heart's desire, and their sons and daughters as well— 26on that day a fugitive will come to tell you the news. 27At that time your mouth will be opened; you will speak with him and will no longer be silent. So you will be a sign to them, and they will know that I am the LORD."

A Prophecy Against Ammon

25 The word of the LORD came to me: 2"Son of man, set your face against the Ammonites and prophesy against them. 3Say to them, 'Hear the word of the Sovereign LORD. This is what the Sovereign LORD says: Because you said "Aha!" over my sanctuary when it was desecrated and over the land of Israel when it was laid waste and over the people of Judah when they went into exileᴰ, 4therefore I am going to give you to the people of the East as a possession. They will set up their camps and pitch their tents among you; they will eat your fruit and drink

---

How long was Ezekiel silent? (24:26–27)

See *Why and for how long had Ezekiel been silent?* (33:22).

Judah's Enemies (25:2)

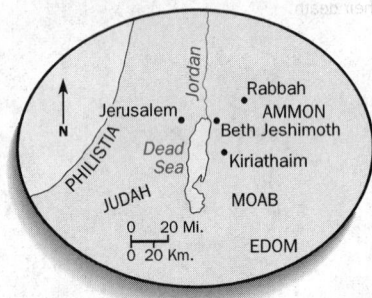

---

[a]23 Or *away in*

Did God want to get even? (25:3–7)

Think of judgment, not revenge. Revenge contradicts God's nature; judgment does not. In fact, the holiness of God requires that he pronounce justice. If he neglected justice by overlooking sin, he would not be a holy God. No, God did not want to get even; he was simply being holy by punishing sin.

But even God's punishment can be considered an expression of his mercy. His Old Testament judgment typically halted the slide into further sin. Left unchecked, sin violates the order God planned for creation and would eventually cause the destruction of the world and humanity. Judgment mercifully halts the process.

Before Christ took the punishment for sin by dying on the cross, judgment fell upon sinners. Old Testament sacrifices provided pardon, but no sacrifice was sufficient to completely and permanently satisfy the requirements of holiness. Only through the cross of Christ did mercy triumph completely over judgment.

your milk. **5**I will turn Rabbah into a pasture for camels and Ammon into a resting place for sheep. Then you will know that I am the LORD. **6**For this is what the Sovereign LORD says: Because you have clapped your hands and stamped your feet, rejoicing with all the malice of your heart against the land of Israel, **7**therefore I will stretch out my hand against you and give you as plunderD to the nations. I will cut you off from the nations and exterminate you from the countries. I will destroy you, and you will know that I am the LORD.' "

A Prophecy Against Moab

8"This is what the Sovereign LORD says: 'Because Moab and Seir said, "Look, the house of Judah has become like all the other nations," **9**therefore I will expose the flank of Moab, beginning at its frontier towns—Beth Jeshimoth, Baal Meon and Kiriathaim—the gloryD of that land. **10**I will give Moab along with the Ammonites to the people of the East as a possession, so that the Ammonites will not be remembered among the nations; **11**and I will inflict punishment on Moab. Then they will know that I am the LORD.' "

A Prophecy Against Edom

12"This is what the Sovereign LORD says: 'Because EdomD took revenge on the house of Judah and became very guilty by doing so, **13**therefore this is what the Sovereign LORD says: I will stretch out my hand against Edom and kill its men and their animals. I will lay it waste, and from Teman to Dedan they will fall by the sword. **14**I will take vengeance on Edom by the hand of my people Israel, and they will deal with Edom in accordance with my anger and my wrath; they will know my vengeance, declares the Sovereign LORD.' "

A Prophecy Against Philistia

15"This is what the Sovereign LORD says: 'Because the Philistines acted in vengeance and took revenge with malice in their hearts, and with ancient hostility sought to destroy Judah, **16**therefore this is what the Sovereign LORD says: I am about to stretch out my hand against the Philistines, and I will cut off the Kerethites and destroy those remaining along the coast. **17**I will carry out great vengeance on them and punish them in my wrath. Then they will know that I am the LORD, when I take vengeance on them.' "

A Prophecy Against Tyre

26 In the eleventh year, on the first day of the month, the word of the LORD came to me: **2**"Son of manD, because Tyre has said of JerusalemD, 'Aha! The gate to the nations is broken, and its doors have swung open to me; now that she lies in ruins I will prosper,' **3**therefore this is what the Sovereign LORD says: I am against you, O Tyre, and I will bring many nations against you, like the sea casting up its waves. **4**They will destroy the walls of Tyre and pull down her towers; I will scrape away her rubble and make her a bare rock. **5**Out in the sea she will become a place to spread fishnets, for I have spoken, declares the Sovereign LORD. She will become plunder for the nations, **6**and her settlements on the mainland will be ravaged by the sword. Then they will know that I am the LORD.

7"For this is what the Sovereign LORD says: From the

What good did God's vengeance do? (25:17)
The Philistines learned that God was holy and would not tolerate sin. They learned that his judgment falls on those who violate others, especially those who violate God's own people. They may not have understood much of the Old Testament law, but the Philistines came to see in God's vengeance his great displeasure for their sin.

Why call Nebuchadnezzar *king of kings*? (26:7)
Because God wanted to speak in terms the people could understand, he took the human limitations of his listeners into account. Since Nebuchadnezzar was the greatest king the people then had ever known and since other kings served him, Nebuchadnezzar was viewed by the people of that day as the *king of kings*. Of course, we know that God alone is the King of kings (see 1 Tim. 6:15).

north I am going to bring against Tyre Nebuchadnezzar[a] king of Babylon, king of kings, with horses and chariots, with horsemen and a great army. [8]He will ravage your settlements on the mainland with the sword; he will set up siege works[D] against you, build a ramp up to your walls and raise his shields against you. [9]He will direct the blows of his battering rams against your walls and demolish your towers with his weapons. [10]His horses will be so many that they will cover you with dust. Your walls will tremble at the noise of the war horses, wagons and chariots when he enters your gates as men enter a city whose walls have been broken through. [11]The hoofs of his horses will trample all your streets; he will kill your people with the sword, and your strong pillars will fall to the ground. [12]They will plunder[D] your wealth and loot your merchandise; they will break down your walls and demolish your fine houses and throw your stones, timber and rubble into the sea. [13]I will put an end to your noisy songs, and the music of your harps will be heard no more. [14]I will make you a bare rock, and you will become a place to spread fishnets. You will never be rebuilt, for I the Lord have spoken, declares the Sovereign Lord.

[15]"This is what the Sovereign Lord says to Tyre: Will not the coastlands tremble at the sound of your fall, when the wounded groan and the slaughter takes place in you? [16]Then all the princes of the coast will step down from their thrones and lay aside their robes and take off their embroidered garments. Clothed with terror, they will sit on the ground, trembling every moment, appalled at you. [17]Then they will take up a lament[D] concerning you and say to you:

> " 'How you are destroyed, O city of renown,
>   peopled by men of the sea!
> You were a power on the seas,
>   you and your citizens;
> you put your terror
>   on all who lived there.
> [18]Now the coastlands tremble
>   on the day of your fall;
> the islands in the sea
>   are terrified at your collapse.'

[19]"This is what the Sovereign Lord says: When I make you a desolate city, like cities no longer inhabited, and when I bring the ocean depths over you and its vast waters cover you, [20]then I will bring you down with those who go down to the pit, to the people of long ago. I will make you dwell in the earth below, as in ancient ruins, with those who go down to the pit, and you will not return or take your place[b] in the land of the living. [21]I will bring you to a horrible end and you will be no more. You will be sought, but you will never again be found, declares the Sovereign Lord."

A Lament for Tyre

27 The word of the Lord came to me: [2]"Son of man[D], take up a lament concerning Tyre. [3]Say to Tyre, situated at the gateway to the sea, merchant of peoples on many coasts, 'This is what the Sovereign Lord says:

What's left in place of Tyre today? (26:14)

Never be rebuilt is best understood to mean that Tyre's glory and prestige would never be restored. It took Nebuchadnezzar 13 years to conquer Tyre (598 to 585 B.C.); it is not known for certain that the island portion of the city fell at that time. For the next two and a half centuries the city endured continuous hardship, until Alexander the Great devastated it in 332 B.C. Today Tyre exists as a small town of 5,000 (see *Map 10* at the back of this Bible). Also see *How was Tyre destroyed?* (Isaiah 23:1–5).

Did these princes abdicate their thrones? (26:16)

In essence, yes. But this is really a picture of surrender, not abdication—surrender being the only way to survive the invasion. Ezekiel prophesied that the king of Babylon would completely humiliate the area's leading men. Biblical prophets often painted vivid word pictures like this.

Lament (26:17)

Suggests two ideas: (1) a musical or poetic dirge—a song of sorrow; (2) a recognition of judgment, which seems to be primarily implied here.

The pit (26:20)

This suggests an end to life, perhaps referring to hell (although our concepts of hell generally stem from the New Testament and contain the idea of perpetual punishment). *The pit* may be better understood to mean the final destruction of the city—not the personal fate of its citizens.

---

[a]7 Hebrew *Nebuchadrezzar*, of which *Nebuchadnezzar* is a variant; here and often in Ezekiel and Jeremiah   [b]20 Septuagint; Hebrew *return, and I will give glory*

" 'You say, O Tyre,
    "I am perfect in beauty."
4Your domain was on the high seas;
    your builders brought your beauty to
        perfection.
5They made all your timbers
    of pine trees from Senir*a*;
they took a cedar from Lebanon
    to make a mast for you.
6Of oaks from Bashan
    they made your oars;
of cypress wood*b* from the coasts of Cyprus*c*
    they made your deck, inlaid with ivory.
7Fine embroidered linen from Egypt was your
        sail
    and served as your banner;
your awnings were of blue and purple*D*
    from the coasts of Elishah.
8Men of Sidon and Arvad were your oarsmen;
    your skilled men, O Tyre, were aboard as
        your seamen.
9Veteran craftsmen of Gebal*d* were on board
    as shipwrights to caulk your seams.
All the ships of the sea and their sailors
    came alongside to trade for your wares.

10" 'Men of Persia, Lydia and Put
    served as soldiers in your army.
They hung their shields and helmets on your
        walls,
    bringing you splendor.
11Men of Arvad and Helech
    manned your walls on every side;
men of Gammad
    were in your towers.
They hung their shields around your walls;
    they brought your beauty to perfection.

12" 'Tarshish did business with you because of your great wealth of goods; they exchanged silver, iron, tin and lead for your merchandise.

13" 'Greece, Tubal and Meshech traded with you; they exchanged slaves and articles of bronze for your wares.

14" 'Men of Beth Togarmah exchanged work horses, war horses and mules for your merchandise.

15" 'The men of Rhodes*e* traded with you, and many coastlands were your customers; they paid you with ivory tusks and ebony.

16" 'Aram*f* did business with you because of your many products; they exchanged turquoise, purple fabric, embroidered work, fine linen, coral and rubies for your merchandise.

17" 'Judah and Israel traded with you; they exchanged wheat from Minnith and confections,*g* honey, oil and balm for your wares.

18" 'Damascus, because of your many products and great wealth of goods, did business with you in wine from Helbon and wool from Zahar.

19" 'Danites and Greeks from Uzal bought your mer-

Why would foreigners fight for Tyre? (27:10–11)

These were mercenaries—soldiers for hire. Hiring armies has been a common practice throughout history. Such soldiers were generally well-trained, ruthless and well-paid. Even David used mercenaries (2 Samuel 15:18).

Why list all of Tyre's trading partners? (27:12–24)

To fully understand the dimensions of the destruction coming to Tyre, it's necessary first to see its influence at the height of its glory days. Seeing the extent of Tyre's wealth and power enable us to recognize how far it fell and how severely it was judged. The list of trading partners stood in stark contrast to what history would later write—a list of those who conquered Tyre: Babylonians, Persians, Greeks, Romans and Turks.

---

*a*5 That is, Hermon   *b*6 Targum; the Masoretic Text has a different division of the consonants.   *c*6 Hebrew *Kittim*   *d*9 That is, Byblos   *e*15 Septuagint; Hebrew *Dedan*   *f*16 Most Hebrew manuscripts; some Hebrew manuscripts and Syriac *Edom*   *g*17 The meaning of the Hebrew for this word is uncertain.

chandise; they exchanged wrought iron, cassia and calamusᴰ for your wares.

20" 'Dedan traded in saddle blankets with you.

21" 'Arabia and all the princes of Kedar were your customers; they did business with you in lambs, rams and goats.

22" 'The merchants of Sheba and Raamah traded with you; for your merchandise they exchanged the finest of all kinds of spices and precious stones, and gold.

23" 'Haran, Canneh and Eden and merchants of Sheba, Asshur and Kilmad traded with you. 24In your marketplace they traded with you beautiful garments, blue fabric, embroidered work and multicolored rugs with cords twisted and tightly knotted.

25" 'The ships of Tarshish serve
  as carriers for your wares.
You are filled with heavy cargo
  in the heart of the sea.
26Your oarsmen take you
  out to the high seas.
But the east wind will break you to pieces
  in the heart of the sea.
27Your wealth, merchandise and wares,
  your mariners, seamen and shipwrights,
your merchants and all your soldiers,
  and everyone else on board
will sink into the heart of the sea
  on the day of your shipwreck.
28The shorelands will quake
  when your seamen cry out.
29All who handle the oars
  will abandon their ships;
the mariners and all the seamen
  will stand on the shore.
30They will raise their voice
  and cry bitterly over you;
they will sprinkle dust on their heads
  and roll in ashes.
31They will shave their heads because of you
  and will put on sackclothᴰ.
They will weep over you with anguish of
    soulᴰ
  and with bitter mourning.
32As they wail and mourn over you,
  they will take up a lamentᴰ concerning you:
"Who was ever silenced like Tyre,
  surrounded by the sea?"
33When your merchandise went out on the
    seas,
  you satisfied many nations;
with your great wealth and your wares
  you enriched the kings of the earth.
34Now you are shattered by the sea
  in the depths of the waters;
your wares and all your company
  have gone down with you.
35All who live in the coastlands
  are appalled at you;
their kings shudder with horror
  and their faces are distorted with fear.
36The merchants among the nations hiss at you;
  you have come to a horrible end
  and will be no more.' "

Why would other nations grieve over Tyre's downfall? (27:28–32)
Because it had made so many wealthy. If Tyre, which trusted in power and wealth, could fall, then all who profited because of Tyre must have felt their own vulnerability.

Why would dusty heads and sooty clothes be a sign of mourning? (27:30)
Deep inner sorrow in Ezekiel's time was expressed openly and outwardly. Dust and ashes may have become symbols of mourning because ashes were all that remained following a devastating fire, while dust followed the death of a body. "Ashes to ashes and dust to dust" continues to this day as a statement of grief and death.

What were these kings afraid of? (27:35)
They were afraid that what happened to Tyre could happen to them. The news of Tyre's destruction *appalled* them because they realized Babylon could do the same to them. They also feared that Tyre's fall would cause severe economic depression in the region.

Hiss (27:36)
Hissing—throughout the world—implies both contempt and the threat of harm. Those who once honored the merchants and leaders of Tyre now wanted nothing to do with them.

A Prophecy Against the King of Tyre

28 The word of the LORD came to me: **2**"Son of man,[D] say to the ruler of Tyre, 'This is what the Sovereign LORD says:

" 'In the pride of your heart
 you say, "I am a god;
I sit on the throne of a god
 in the heart of the seas."
But you are a man and not a god,
 though you think you are as wise as a god.
3Are you wiser than Daniel[a]?
 Is no secret hidden from you?
4By your wisdom and understanding
 you have gained wealth for yourself
and amassed gold and silver
 in your treasuries.
5By your great skill in trading
 you have increased your wealth,
and because of your wealth
 your heart has grown proud.

6" 'Therefore this is what the Sovereign LORD says:

" 'Because you think you are wise,
 as wise as a god,
7I am going to bring foreigners against you,
 the most ruthless of nations;
they will draw their swords against your beauty
 and wisdom
 and pierce your shining splendor.
8They will bring you down to the pit,
 and you will die a violent death[D]
 in the heart of the seas.
9Will you then say, "I am a god,"
 in the presence of those who kill you?
You will be but a man, not a god,
 in the hands of those who slay you.
10You will die the death of the uncircumcised
 at the hands of foreigners.

I have spoken, declares the Sovereign LORD.' "

11The word of the LORD came to me: **12**"Son of man, take up a lament[D] concerning the king of Tyre and say to him: 'This is what the Sovereign LORD says:

" 'You were the model of perfection,
 full of wisdom and perfect in beauty.
13You were in Eden,
 the garden of God;
every precious stone adorned you:
 ruby, topaz and emerald,
 chrysolite, onyx and jasper,
 sapphire,[b] turquoise and beryl.[c]
Your settings and mountings[d] were made of
 gold;
 on the day you were created they were
 prepared.
14You were anointed[D] as a guardian cherub,[D]
 for so I ordained you.
You were on the holy mount of God;

---
a3 Or *Danel*; the Hebrew spelling may suggest a person other than the prophet Daniel.   **b**13 Or *lapis lazuli*   **c**13 The precise identification of some of these precious stones is uncertain.   **d**13 The meaning of the Hebrew for this phrase is uncertain.

Why would a human call himself a god? (28:2)
The Phoenicians, like most who believed in many different gods, believed in a hierarchy of gods—some having more power, some less. Apparently the king of Tyre, in an arrogant mood, viewed himself as equal to at least some of the gods. The worship of kings and emperors as gods was common in such cultures (see Daniel 3).

The pit (28:8)
See *The pit* (26:20).

The death of the uncircumcised (28:10)
Uncircumcised was a typical Jewish way of speaking about those outside their covenant relationship with God. To *die the death of the uncircumcised* was to die separated from God, cut off for eternity. He who thought himself to be a god would die without God. Ironically, the king of Tyre may have been circumcised. See article: **Why did God command circumcision?** (Gen. 17:10). Also see **Why this judgment against other nations?** (Jer. 9:25–26).

Lament (28:12)
See *Lament* (26:17).

Is this a picture of Satan? (28:13)
This was a description of the king of Tyre, a human being. Nonetheless, the poetic language used by Ezekiel goes far beyond the scope of the king of Tyre. When was this man ever in Eden? When was he anointed as a cherub? When was he on the holy mount of God (v. 14)? These extreme statements lead some to believe that the fall of the wicked king of Tyre paralleled the fall of Satan from the heavenly realms. Others think this figurative language should not be used in a literal sense to discover Satan's past. Also see **Does this describe the fall of Satan?** (Isaiah 14:12–15).

Fiery stones (28:14)
There are at least three views: (1) *Fiery stones* could be an image for angels called *flames of fire* (Heb. 1:7), among whom the *guardian cherub* walked. (2) These *stones* were brilliant, sparkling jewels of heaven (Rev. 21:18–21). (3) They were fiery coals, illustrating the pride of the king of Tyre who thought himself able to walk on them without being burned.

you walked among the fiery stones.
¹⁵You were blameless in your ways
  from the day you were created
  till wickedness was found in you.
¹⁶Through your widespread trade
  you were filled with violence,
  and you sinned.
So I drove you in disgrace from the mount of
    God,
  and I expelled you, O guardian cherub^D,
  from among the fiery stones.
¹⁷Your heart became proud
  on account of your beauty,
and you corrupted your wisdom
  because of your splendor.
So I threw you to the earth;
  I made a spectacle of you before kings.
¹⁸By your many sins and dishonest trade
  you have desecrated^D your sanctuaries.
So I made a fire come out from you,
  and it consumed you,
and I reduced you to ashes on the ground
  in the sight of all who were watching.
¹⁹All the nations who knew you
  are appalled at you;
you have come to a horrible end
  and will be no more.' "

A Prophecy Against Sidon

²⁰The word of the LORD came to me: ²¹"Son of man^D, set your face against Sidon; prophesy against her ²²and say: 'This is what the Sovereign LORD says:

" 'I am against you, O Sidon,
  and I will gain glory^D within you.
They will know that I am the LORD,
  when I inflict punishment on her
  and show myself holy within her.
²³I will send a plague upon her
  and make blood flow in her streets.
The slain will fall within her,
  with the sword against her on every side.
Then they will know that I am the LORD.

²⁴" 'No longer will the people of Israel have malicious neighbors who are painful briers and sharp thorns. Then they will know that I am the Sovereign LORD.
²⁵" 'This is what the Sovereign LORD says: When I gather the people of Israel from the nations where they have been scattered, I will show myself holy among them in the sight of the nations. Then they will live in their own land, which I gave to my servant Jacob. ²⁶They will live there in safety and will build houses and plant vineyards; they will live in safety when I inflict punishment on all their neighbors who maligned them. Then they will know that I am the LORD their God.' "

A Prophecy Against Egypt

29 In the tenth year, in the tenth month on the twelfth day, the word of the LORD came to me: ²"Son of man, set your face against Pharaoh king of Egypt and prophesy against him and against all Egypt. ³Speak to him and say: 'This is what the Sovereign LORD says:

What kind of glory comes from punishment? (28:22)
When God punishes sin, he is shown to be holy, far above all who tolerate sin. God's glory is revealed when he deals with evil and removes it. He is shown to be holy, righteous and just. Also see article: *Did God want to get even?* (25:3–7).

How does God show himself holy? (28:25)
God can show his holiness in many ways. Punishment for sin, for example, shows God's holy, righteous nature. We can also see his holiness when we experience his blessings for obedience.

Tenth year (29:1)
Probably a reference either to the tenth year of the exile or the tenth year of Ezekiel's prophetic ministry. It was typical at that time to date events by linking them to the reign of a king or to an incident of major proportion. Also see *In the thirtieth year* (1:1).

Great monster (29:3)
Ezekiel borrowed the image of a crocodile sunning on the banks of the Nile to describe Pharaoh's self-assurance. Surrounded by water and desert, Egypt seemed safe from foreign invasion. Pharaoh, the powerful leader of a powerful country, was like a confident crocodile—a great monster.

" 'I am against you, Pharaoh king of Egypt,
  you great monster lying among your streams.
You say, "The Nile is mine;
  I made it for myself."
4But I will put hooks in your jaws
  and make the fish of your streams stick to
    your scales.
I will pull you out from among your streams,
  with all the fish sticking to your scales.
5I will leave you in the desert,
  you and all the fish of your streams.
You will fall on the open field
  and not be gathered or picked up.
I will give you as food
  to the beasts of the earth and the birds of the
    air.

6Then all who live in Egypt will know that I am the LORD.

" 'You have been a staff of reed for the house of Israel.
7When they grasped you with their hands, you splintered
and you tore open their shoulders; when they leaned on
you, you broke and their backs were wrenched.*a*

8" 'Therefore this is what the Sovereign LORD says: I will
bring a sword against you and kill your men and their animals. **9**Egypt will become a desolate wasteland. Then they
will know that I am the LORD.

" 'Because you said, "The Nile is mine; I made it,"
10therefore I am against you and against your streams,
and I will make the land of Egypt a ruin and a desolate
waste from Migdol to Aswan, as far as the border of
Cush.*b* **11**No foot of man or animal will pass through it;
no one will live there for forty years. **12**I will make the
land of Egypt desolate among devastated lands, and her
cities will lie desolate forty years among ruined cities. And
I will disperse the Egyptians among the nations and scatter them through the countries.

13" 'Yet this is what the Sovereign LORD says: At the end
of forty years I will gather the Egyptians from the nations
where they were scattered. **14**I will bring them back from
captivity and return them to Upper Egypt,*c* the land of
their ancestry. There they will be a lowly kingdom. **15**It
will be the lowliest of kingdoms and will never again exalt
itself above the other nations. I will make it so weak that
it will never again rule over the nations. **16**Egypt will no
longer be a source of confidence for the people of Israel
but will be a reminder of their sin in turning to her for
help. Then they will know that I am the Sovereign LORD.' "

17In the twenty-seventh year, in the first month on the
first day, the word of the LORD came to me: **18**"Son of
man*D*, Nebuchadnezzar king of Babylon drove his army
in a hard campaign against Tyre; every head was rubbed
bare and every shoulder made raw. Yet he and his army
got no reward from the campaign he led against Tyre.
19Therefore this is what the Sovereign LORD says: I am going to give Egypt to Nebuchadnezzar king of Babylon, and
he will carry off its wealth. He will loot and plunder*D* the
land as pay for his army. **20**I have given him Egypt as a
reward for his efforts because he and his army did it for
me, declares the Sovereign LORD.

a7 Syriac (see also Septuagint and Vulgate); Hebrew *and you caused
their backs to stand*   *b10* That is, the upper Nile region
c14 Hebrew *to Pathros*

Hooks in your jaws (29:4)

Fish hooks were literally used in ancient times
to lead prisoners into captivity. By inserting
fish hooks into their jaws or noses and attaching them to strong lines, one soldier could lead
many prisoners into captivity.

What had Pharaoh done to Israel? (29:6–7)

It was on the strength of Egypt's promise of
military aid that Israel had rebelled against
Babylon. But Egypt failed to deliver. Ezekiel described Pharaoh's treachery as a *staff of reed*.
One could trust a wooden staff, but not a reed
from the Egyptian marsh lands. Put your weight
on a reed and it will break, either poking your
skin or wrenching your back. Israel leaned on
Egypt—only to regret it later.

Why give the Egyptians special treat-ment? (29:13–14)

We can't be certain why God spared Egypt from
the destruction he brought upon other nations.
Perhaps he was lenient with Egypt because it
had spared Israel in Joseph's day, or because
it had offered refuge to Israelites fleeing from
the Babylonian invasion. Though he spared
Egypt, he nonetheless judged Egypt, removing
its power and grandeur.

Every head was rubbed bare and every shoulder made raw (29:18)

This may refer to the extended rubbing of the
helmets on their heads and the weight of military equipment on their shoulders over the
13-year campaign against Tyre. Or it may have
been an idiom of that age used to express absolute exhaustion, similar to someone today
saying "worn to a frazzle."

Why didn't Nebuchadnezzar get any-thing from Tyre? (29:18)

After a 13-year siege, there seems to have
been nothing left in Tyre worth taking. Possibly
the people of Tyre, in the end recognizing it
was going to fall, had even set fire to their own
city, to keep its wealth from going to foreigners. The exhausted Babylonian army had invested 13 years for nothing.

Why did God say Nebuchadnezzar had conquered lands for him? (29:20)

God used the wicked Nebuchadnezzar as his
unwitting servant. God used Nebuchadnezzar
and his army to punish Judah, taking God's
people into exile to purge them from their wicked ways.

What kind of horn would God grow in Israel? (29:21)

Horns symbolized strength and power (see NIV text note). Mature, strong animals were ranked according to the size of their horns. This promise reassured Ezekiel that his prophecy was strong and would be fulfilled; strength and honor would be restored to Israel.

People of the covenant land (30:5)

Jews who were not serving the Lord and lived in the foreign lands listed here. Also see Jer. 44:27–28.

Why would God use *the most ruthless* to do his work? (30:11)

Because this was a time of judgment; the time for patience and mercy had passed. It was now God's will that wrath should be administered without hesitation or compromise.

21"On that day I will make a horn[a] grow for the house of Israel, and I will open your mouth among them. Then they will know that I am the LORD."

A Lament for Egypt

30 The word of the LORD came to me: 2"Son of man,[D] prophesy and say: 'This is what the Sovereign LORD says:

" 'Wail and say,
    "Alas for that day!"
3For the day is near,
    the day of the LORD[D] is near—
a day of clouds,
    a time of doom for the nations.
4A sword will come against Egypt,
    and anguish will come upon Cush.[b]
When the slain fall in Egypt,
    her wealth will be carried away
    and her foundations torn down.

5Cush and Put, Lydia and all Arabia, Libya[c] and the people of the covenant[D] land will fall by the sword along with Egypt.

6" 'This is what the LORD says:

" 'The allies of Egypt will fall
    and her proud strength will fail.
From Migdol to Aswan
    they will fall by the sword within her,
                declares the Sovereign LORD.
7" 'They will be desolate
    among desolate lands,
and their cities will lie
    among ruined cities.
8Then they will know that I am the LORD,
    when I set fire to Egypt
    and all her helpers are crushed.

9" 'On that day messengers will go out from me in ships to frighten Cush out of her complacency. Anguish will take hold of them on the day of Egypt's doom, for it is sure to come.

10" 'This is what the Sovereign LORD says:

" 'I will put an end to the hordes of Egypt
    by the hand of Nebuchadnezzar king of
        Babylon.
11He and his army—the most ruthless of
        nations—
    will be brought in to destroy the land.
They will draw their swords against Egypt
    and fill the land with the slain.
12I will dry up the streams of the Nile
    and sell the land to evil men;
by the hand of foreigners
    I will lay waste the land and everything in it.

I the LORD have spoken.

13" 'This is what the Sovereign LORD says:

---

a21 Horn here symbolizes strength.   b4 That is, the upper Nile region; also in verses 5 and 9   c5 Hebrew Cub

" 'I will destroy the idols[D]
    and put an end to the images in Memphis.[a]
No longer will there be a prince in Egypt,
    and I will spread fear throughout the land.
14I will lay waste Upper Egypt,[b]
    set fire to Zoan
    and inflict punishment on Thebes.[c]
15I will pour out my wrath on Pelusium,[d]
    the stronghold[D] of Egypt,
    and cut off the hordes of Thebes.
16I will set fire to Egypt;
    Pelusium will writhe in agony.
Thebes will be taken by storm;
    Memphis will be in constant distress.
17The young men of Heliopolis[e] and Bubastis[f]
    will fall by the sword,
    and the cities themselves will go into
        captivity.
18Dark will be the day at Tahpanhes
    when I break the yoke[D] of Egypt;
    there her proud strength will come to an end.
She will be covered with clouds,
    and her villages will go into captivity.
19So I will inflict punishment on Egypt,
    and they will know that I am the LORD.' "

20In the eleventh year, in the first month on the seventh day, the word of the LORD came to me: **21**"Son of man[D], I have broken the arm of Pharaoh king of Egypt. It has not been bound up for healing or put in a splint so as to become strong enough to hold a sword. **22**Therefore this is what the Sovereign LORD says: I am against Pharaoh king of Egypt. I will break both his arms, the good arm as well as the broken one, and make the sword fall from his hand. **23**I will disperse the Egyptians among the nations and scatter them through the countries. **24**I will strengthen the arms of the king of Babylon and put my sword in his hand, but I will break the arms of Pharaoh, and he will groan before him like a mortally wounded man. **25**I will strengthen the arms of the king of Babylon, but the arms of Pharaoh will fall limp. Then they will know that I am the LORD, when I put my sword into the hand of the king of Babylon and he brandishes it against Egypt. **26**I will disperse the Egyptians among the nations and scatter them through the countries. Then they will know that I am the LORD."

A Cedar in Lebanon

31 In the eleventh year, in the third month on the first day, the word of the LORD came to me: **2**"Son of man, say to Pharaoh king of Egypt and to his hordes:

" 'Who can be compared with you in majesty?
3Consider Assyria, once a cedar in Lebanon,
    with beautiful branches overshadowing the
        forest;
    it towered on high,
        its top above the thick foliage.
4The waters nourished it,
    deep springs made it grow tall;
    their streams flowed

My sword (30:24)
The sword of the Lord represents judgment and destruction as well as authority.

Why call Assyria *a cedar in Lebanon*? (31:3)
Many trees remain small in Lebanon due to its arid climate. But certain cedar-like trees grow larger by sending their roots down deep, tapping into underground springs. Like the cedar, God had caused Assyria to grow larger and more powerful than other nations around it.

---

*a*13 Hebrew *Noph*; also in verse 16   *b*14 Hebrew *waste Pathros*
*c*14 Hebrew *No*; also in verses 15 and 16   *d*15 Hebrew *Sin*; also in
verse 16   *e*17 Hebrew *Awen* (or *On*)   *f*17 Hebrew *Pi Beseth*

all around its base
and sent their channels
to all the trees of the field.
5So it towered higher
than all the trees of the field;
its boughs increased
and its branches grew long,
spreading because of abundant waters.
6All the birds of the air
nested in its boughs,
all the beasts of the field
gave birth under its branches;
all the great nations
lived in its shade.
7It was majestic in beauty,
with its spreading boughs,
for its roots went down
to abundant waters.
8The cedars in the garden of God
could not rival it,
nor could the pine trees
equal its boughs,
nor could the plane trees
compare with its branches—
no tree in the garden of God
could match its beauty.
9I made it beautiful
with abundant branches,
the envy of all the trees of Eden
in the garden of God.

10" 'Therefore this is what the Sovereign LORD says: Because it towered on high, lifting its top above the thick foliage, and because it was proud of its height, 11I handed it over to the ruler of the nations, for him to deal with according to its wickedness. I cast it aside, 12and the most ruthless of foreign nations cut it down and left it. Its boughs fell on the mountains and in all the valleys; its branches lay broken in all the ravines of the land. All the nations of the earth came out from under its shade and left it. 13All the birds of the air settled on the fallen tree, and all the beasts of the field were among its branches. 14Therefore no other trees by the waters are ever to tower proudly on high, lifting their tops above the thick foliage. No other trees so well-watered are ever to reach such a height; they are all destined for deathD, for the earth below, among mortal men, with those who go down to the pit.

15" 'This is what the Sovereign LORD says: On the day it was brought down to the gravea I covered the deep springs with mourning for it; I held back its streams, and its abundant waters were restrained. Because of it I clothed Lebanon with gloom, and all the trees of the field withered away. 16I made the nations tremble at the sound of its fall when I brought it down to the grave with those who go down to the pit. Then all the trees of Eden, the choicest and best of Lebanon, all the trees that were well-watered, were consoled in the earth below. 17Those who lived in its shade, its allies among the nations, had also gone down to the grave with it, joining those killed by the sword.

18" 'Which of the trees of Eden can be compared with

a15 Hebrew Sheol; also in verses 16 and 17

Why did God help wicked Assyria? (31:9)
God aided Assyria not because he wanted to reward its evil ways, but because he wanted to punish Israel for its sin. God often used nations more wicked than Israel to punish his people when they rejected him.

Ruler of the nations (31:11)
The increasingly powerful ruler of Babylon who conquered Assyria. Until that happened, Assyria had itself been a superpower.

Why would God lift no other tree as high as he did Assyria? (31:14)
God probably refrained from exalting another nation because Assyria had become so extremely arrogant and wicked. While God raised Assyria up to judge his own people, Assyria later faced judgment for the excessive cruelty they used (Isaiah 10:12; Zeph. 2:15). See **Why did God "ordain" Assyria to devastate other nations?** (2 Kings 19:25). This was not a perpetual, worldwide prophecy. Later, other nations from other regions of the globe would achieve greater accomplishments than Assyria.

The pit (31:14)
See **The pit** (26:20).

Why give Pharaoh a history lesson? (31:16–18)
God warned Pharaoh by reminding him of Assyria's fate. Since Egypt had not turned from its wicked ways, judgment would come against Egypt—just as it had against Assyria. Assyria had surpassed Egypt in power and prominence but had not been able to escape destruction. The lesson for Pharaoh? He could expect nothing less than what happened to Assyria.

What other nations went down with Assyria? (31:17)
Archaeology has not yet revealed which nations might have been Assyria's allies. However, Assyria's ruthless ways caused many to have an intense hatred toward it (see the book of Nahum). As a result, it's doubtful there would have been many allies.

you in splendor and majesty? Yet you, too, will be brought down with the trees of Eden to the earth below; you will lie among the uncircumcised[D], with those killed by the sword.

" 'This is Pharaoh and all his hordes, declares the Sovereign LORD.' "

A Lament for Pharaoh

32 In the twelfth year, in the twelfth month on the first day, the word of the LORD came to me: [2]"Son of man[D], take up a lament[D] concerning Pharaoh king of Egypt and say to him:

" 'You are like a lion among the nations;
   you are like a monster in the seas
thrashing about in your streams,
   churning the water with your feet
   and muddying the streams.

[3]" 'This is what the Sovereign LORD says:

" 'With a great throng of people
   I will cast my net over you,
   and they will haul you up in my net.
[4]I will throw you on the land
   and hurl you on the open field.
I will let all the birds of the air settle on you
   and all the beasts of the earth gorge
     themselves on you.
[5]I will spread your flesh on the mountains
   and fill the valleys with your remains.
[6]I will drench the land with your flowing blood
   all the way to the mountains,
   and the ravines will be filled with your flesh.
[7]When I snuff you out, I will cover the heavens
   and darken their stars;
 I will cover the sun with a cloud,
   and the moon will not give its light.
[8]All the shining lights in the heavens
   I will darken over you;
 I will bring darkness over your land,
        declares the Sovereign LORD.
[9]I will trouble the hearts of many peoples
   when I bring about your destruction among
     the nations,
   among[a] lands you have not known.
[10]I will cause many peoples to be appalled at
     you,
   and their kings will shudder with horror
     because of you
   when I brandish my sword before them.
On the day of your downfall
   each of them will tremble
   every moment for his life.

[11]" 'For this is what the Sovereign LORD says:

" 'The sword of the king of Babylon
   will come against you.
[12]I will cause your hordes to fall
   by the swords of mighty men—
   the most ruthless of all nations.
They will shatter the pride of Egypt,
   and all her hordes will be overthrown.

---

a9 Hebrew; Septuagint *bring you into captivity among the nations, / to*

Twelfth year (32:1)
See *Tenth year* (29:1).

Lament (32:2)
See *Lament* (26:17).

Monster (32:2)
See *Great monster* (29:3).

What kind of darkness was coming? (32:7–8)
Darkness, in this case, symbolized God's severe wrath—the absence of his light. Hidden terrors lurk in the dark, causing it to be almost universally associated with danger and judgment.

Why would *streams flow like oil?*
(32:14)

This suggests the picture of a coming drought
in which streams would be reduced to only a
slow trickle. Water would ooze like oil instead
of flowing freely.

The pit (32:18)
See *The pit* (26:20).

13I will destroy all her cattle
　　from beside abundant waters
　no longer to be stirred by the foot of man
　　or muddied by the hoofs of cattle.
14Then I will let her waters settle
　　and make her streams flow like oil,
　　　　declares the Sovereign LORD.
15When I make Egypt desolate
　　and strip the land of everything in it,
　when I strike down all who live there,
　　then they will know that I am the LORD.'

16"This is the lamentD they will chant for her. The
daughters of the nations will chant it; for Egypt and all her
hordes they will chant it, declares the Sovereign LORD."

17In the twelfth year, on the fifteenth day of the month,
the word of the LORD came to me: 18"Son of manD, wail
for the hordes of Egypt and consign to the earth below
both her and the daughters of mighty nations, with those
who go down to the pit. 19Say to them, 'Are you more favored than others? Go down and be laid among the uncircumcisedD.' 20They will fall among those killed by the
sword. The sword is drawn; let her be dragged off with all
her hordes. 21From within the gravea the mighty leaders
will say of Egypt and her allies, 'They have come down
and they lie with the uncircumcised, with those killed
by the sword.'.
22"Assyria is there with her whole army; she is surrounded by the graves of all her slain, all who have fallen
by the sword. 23Their graves are in the depths of the pit
and her army lies around her grave. All who had spread
terror in the land of the living are slain, fallen by the
sword.
24"Elam is there, with all her hordes around her grave.
All of them are slain, fallen by the sword. All who had
spread terror in the land of the living went down uncircumcised to the earth below. They bear their shame
with those who go down to the pit. 25A bed is made for
her among the slain, with all her hordes around her grave.
All of them are uncircumcised, killed by the sword. Because their terror had spread in the land of the living, they
bear their shame with those who go down to the pit; they
are laid among the slain.
26"Meshech and Tubal are there, with all their hordes
around their graves. All of them are uncircumcised,
killed by the sword because they spread their terror in the
land of the living. 27Do they not lie with the other uncircumcised warriors who have fallen, who went down to
the grave with their weapons of war, whose swords were
placed under their heads? The punishment for their sins
rested on their bones, though the terror of these warriors
had stalked through the land of the living.
28"You too, O Pharaoh, will be broken and will lie
among the uncircumcised, with those killed by the
sword.
29"EdomD is there, her kings and all her princes; despite their power, they are laid with those killed by the
sword. They lie with the uncircumcised, with those who
go down to the pit.
30"All the princes of the north and all the Sidonians are
there; they went down with the slain in disgrace despite
the terror caused by their power. They lie uncircum-

a21 Hebrew *Sheol*; also in verse 27

cised with those killed by the sword and bear their shame with those who go down to the pit. ³¹"Pharaoh—he and all his army—will see them and he will be consoled for all his hordes that were killed by the sword, declares the Sovereign LORD. ³²Although I had him spread terror in the land of the living, Pharaoh and all his hordes will be laid among the uncircumcised^D, with those killed by the sword, declares the Sovereign LORD."

Ezekiel a Watchman

33 The word of the LORD came to me: ²"Son of man^D, speak to your countrymen and say to them: 'When I bring the sword against a land, and the people of the land choose one of their men and make him their watchman^D, ³and he sees the sword coming against the land and blows the trumpet to warn the people, ⁴then if anyone hears the trumpet but does not take warning and the sword comes and takes his life, his blood will be on his own head. ⁵Since he heard the sound of the trumpet but did not take warning, his blood will be on his own head. If he had taken warning, he would have saved himself. ⁶But if the watchman sees the sword coming and does not blow the trumpet to warn the people and the sword comes and takes the life of one of them, that man will be taken away because of his sin, but I will hold the watchman accountable for his blood.'

⁷"Son of man, I have made you a watchman for the house of Israel; so hear the word I speak and give them warning from me. ⁸When I say to the wicked, 'O wicked man, you will surely die,' and you do not speak out to dissuade him from his ways, that wicked man will die for^a his sin, and I will hold you accountable for his blood. ⁹But if you do warn the wicked man to turn from his ways and he does not do so, he will die for his sin, but you will have saved yourself.

¹⁰"Son of man, say to the house of Israel, 'This is what you are saying: "Our offenses and sins weigh us down, and we are wasting away because of^b them. How then can we live?" ' ¹¹Say to them, 'As surely as I live, declares the Sovereign LORD, I take no pleasure in the death^D of the wicked, but rather that they turn from their ways and live. Turn! Turn from your evil ways! Why will you die, O house of Israel?'

¹²"Therefore, son of man, say to your countrymen, 'The righteousness^D of the righteous^D man will not save him when he disobeys, and the wickedness of the wicked man will not cause him to fall when he turns from it. The righteous man, if he sins, will not be allowed to live because of his former righteousness.' ¹³If I tell the righteous man that he will surely live, but then he trusts in his righteousness and does evil, none of the righteous things he has done will be remembered; he will die for the evil he has done. ¹⁴And if I say to the wicked man, 'You will surely die,' but he then turns away from his sin and does what is just and right— ¹⁵if he gives back what he took in pledge for a loan, returns what he has stolen, follows the decrees that give life, and does no evil, he will surely live; he will not die. ¹⁶None of the sins he has committed will be remembered against him. He has done what is just and right; he will surely live.

¹⁷"Yet your countrymen say, 'The way of the Lord is not just.' But it is their way that is not just. ¹⁸If a righ-

^a8 Or in; also in verse 9   ^b10 Or away in

Watchman (33:2)
See *Watchman* (3:17).

How was a negligent watchman held accountable? (33:6–9)
A sentry who fell asleep, allowing an enemy to invade the land, would be executed. Ezekiel saw that, in the same way, he was responsible to warn the people of coming judgment. If he failed to fulfill his duty, he would be held accountable for what happened to them. He would face a stricter judgment himself because he knew the truth and failed to sound the alarm.

Why isn't God pleased to see the wicked die? (33:11)
Sin and its consequences grieve God, who created the world in order to provide grace, not judgment. Why then doesn't he just let the wicked off the hook? Why do they have to die? Though God does not delight in destroying the wicked, he cannot allow sin to go unchecked. If he did, sin would eventually destroy all people and all creation. So, for the one who persists in sin, punishment is the final result. But if someone abandons a life of sin, that one can escape punishment. The choice for judgment or mercy, for death or life, belongs to the wicked. Also see article: *Did God want to get even?* (25:3–7).

When the righteous do wrong, do they lose their salvation? (33:13)
Christians disagree on this question. Some believe that once one is chosen by God he or she can never lose salvation. Others say that sin can cause a person to lose a relationship with God. The risk of the former view is a life of spiritual complacency; the risk of the latter is a life of anxious insecurity. A middle view suggests that a person is secure as long as he or she lives by faith—neither complacent nor anxious, but trusting in God's grace.

teous man turns from his righteousness[D] and does evil, he will die for it. **19**And if a wicked man turns away from his wickedness and does what is just and right, he will live by doing so. **20**Yet, O house of Israel, you say, 'The way of the Lord is not just.' But I will judge each of you according to his own ways."

Jerusalem's Fall Explained

21In the twelfth year of our exile[D], in the tenth month on the fifth day, a man who had escaped from Jerusalem[D] came to me and said, "The city has fallen!" **22**Now the evening before the man arrived, the hand of the Lord was upon me, and he opened my mouth before the man came to me in the morning. So my mouth was opened and I was no longer silent.

23Then the word of the Lord came to me: **24**"Son of man[D], the people living in those ruins in the land of Israel are saying, 'Abraham was only one man, yet he possessed the land. But we are many; surely the land has been given to us as our possession.' **25**Therefore say to them, 'This is what the Sovereign Lord says: Since you eat meat with the blood still in it and look to your idols[D] and shed blood, should you then possess the land? **26**You rely on your sword, you do detestable things, and each of you defiles his neighbor's wife. Should you then possess the land?'

27"Say this to them: 'This is what the Sovereign Lord says: As surely as I live, those who are left in the ruins will fall by the sword, those out in the country I will give to the wild animals to be devoured, and those in strongholds[D] and caves will die of a plague. **28**I will make the land a desolate waste, and her proud strength will come to an end, and the mountains of Israel will become desolate so that no one will cross them. **29**Then they will know that I am the Lord, when I have made the land a desolate waste because of all the detestable things they have done.'

30"As for you, son of man, your countrymen are talking together about you by the walls and at the doors of the houses, saying to each other, 'Come and hear the message that has come from the Lord.' **31**My people come to you, as they usually do, and sit before you to listen to your words, but they do not put them into practice. With their mouths they express devotion, but their hearts are greedy for unjust gain. **32**Indeed, to them you are nothing more than one who sings love songs with a beautiful voice and plays an instrument well, for they hear your words but do not put them into practice.

33"When all this comes true—and it surely will—then they will know that a prophet[D] has been among them."

Shepherds and Sheep

34 The word of the Lord came to me: **2**"Son of man, prophesy against the shepherds of Israel; prophesy and say to them: 'This is what the Sovereign Lord says: Woe to the shepherds of Israel who only take care of themselves! Should not shepherds take care of the flock? **3**You eat the curds, clothe yourselves with the wool and slaughter the choice animals, but you do not take care of the flock. **4**You have not strengthened the weak or healed the sick or bound up the injured. You have not brought back the strays or searched for the lost. You have ruled them harshly and brutally. **5**So they were scattered because there was no shepherd, and when they were scattered they became food for all the wild animals. **6**My

---

Why and for how long had Ezekiel been silent? (33:22)

It's not entirely clear. It seems that from early on in his ministry, perhaps as a sign of his calling, Ezekiel could not speak unless he gave a direct word from God (3:26–27). Around 588 B.C., when Babylon laid siege to Jerusalem (24:1–2), God let Ezekiel know that he would once again be able to speak when a fugitive came to Babylon with news of Jerusalem's fall (24:25–27). The news arrived about three years later, in 585 B.C.

Why would people enjoy a prophecy and not obey it? (33:32)

Probably because the people were in denial, unable to admit that they had any problem with sin. Outwardly, they looked good enough; they said all the right things. They probably enjoyed Ezekiel's messages because they thought his words were meant for others—those with problems. It was easier to listen to Ezekiel's words than it was to take them personally and obey them.

Shepherds of Israel (34:2)

Included both Israel's spiritual and political leaders. A shepherd, responsible for a flock of sheep, was a common sight in Ezekiel's time, an image the people associate with leadership.

sheep wandered over all the mountains and on every high hill. They were scattered over the whole earth, and no one searched or looked for them.

⁷" 'Therefore, you shepherds, hear the word of the LORD: ⁸As surely as I live, declares the Sovereign LORD, because my flock lacks a shepherd and so has been plundered^D and has become food for all the wild animals, and because my shepherds did not search for my flock but cared for themselves rather than for my flock, ⁹therefore, O shepherds, hear the word of the LORD: ¹⁰This is what the Sovereign LORD says: I am against the shepherds and will hold them accountable for my flock. I will remove them from tending the flock so that the shepherds can no longer feed themselves. I will rescue my flock from their mouths, and it will no longer be food for them.

¹¹" 'For this is what the Sovereign LORD says: I myself will search for my sheep and look after them. ¹²As a shepherd looks after his scattered flock when he is with them, so will I look after my sheep. I will rescue them from all the places where they were scattered on a day of clouds and darkness. ¹³I will bring them out from the nations and gather them from the countries, and I will bring them into their own land. I will pasture them on the mountains of Israel, in the ravines and in all the settlements in the land. ¹⁴I will tend them in a good pasture, and the mountain heights of Israel will be their grazing land. There they will lie down in good grazing land, and there they will feed in a rich pasture on the mountains of Israel. ¹⁵I myself will tend my sheep and have them lie down, declares the Sovereign LORD. ¹⁶I will search for the lost and bring back the strays. I will bind up the injured and strengthen the weak, but the sleek and the strong I will destroy. I will shepherd the flock with justice.

¹⁷" 'As for you, my flock, this is what the Sovereign LORD says: I will judge between one sheep and another, and between rams and goats. ¹⁸Is it not enough for you to feed on the good pasture? Must you also trample the rest of your pasture with your feet? Is it not enough for you to drink clear water? Must you also muddy the rest with your feet? ¹⁹Must my flock feed on what you have trampled and drink what you have muddied with your feet?

²⁰" 'Therefore this is what the Sovereign LORD says to them: See, I myself will judge between the fat sheep and the lean sheep. ²¹Because you shove with flank and shoulder, butting all the weak sheep with your horns until you have driven them away, ²²I will save my flock, and they will no longer be plundered. I will judge between one sheep and another. ²³I will place over them one shepherd, my servant David, and he will tend them; he will tend them and be their shepherd. ²⁴I the LORD will be their God, and my servant David will be prince among them. I the LORD have spoken.

²⁵" 'I will make a covenant^D of peace^D with them and rid the land of wild beasts so that they may live in the desert and sleep in the forests in safety. ²⁶I will bless them and the places surrounding my hill.^a I will send down showers in season; there will be showers of blessing. ²⁷The trees of the field will yield their fruit and the ground will yield its crops; the people will be secure in their land. They will know that I am the LORD, when I break the bars of their yoke^D and rescue them from the hands of those who enslaved them. ²⁸They will no longer be plundered

^a26 Or I will make them and the places surrounding my hill a blessing

How did the Lord intend to be Israel's shepherd? (34:11)
Since Israel's leaders had failed to care for the people, God declared he would again lead them himself. Earlier Israel had been ruled by God's direct decree, not by kings. Following their return from Babylonian captivity, the Israelites again would have no king but only leaders raised up by God. This prophetic word would also find fulfillment in the coming of the Messiah—the Good Shepherd (John 10) for each individual to follow as Savior.

How could David, long dead, lead Israel again? (34:23–24)
The people of Ezekiel's day had no trouble recognizing that this was not a promise that King David himself would return from the dead. It was clear to them that this was a promise of the coming Messiah—a descendant of David. To them a person's name was an expression of character, perhaps more so than identity. David's name in this prophecy not only indicated his descendant, but it also indicated someone who would be like David—a man after God's own heart.

by the nations, nor will wild animals devour them. They will live in safety, and no one will make them afraid. ²⁹I will provide for them a land renowned for its crops, and they will no longer be victims of famine in the land or bear the scorn of the nations. ³⁰Then they will know that I, the LORD their God, am with them and that they, the house of Israel, are my people, declares the Sovereign LORD. ³¹You my sheep, the sheep of my pasture, are people, and I am your God, declares the Sovereign LORD.' "

A Prophecy Against Edom

35 The word of the LORD came to me: ²"Son of man D, set your face against Mount Seir; prophesy against it ³and say: 'This is what the Sovereign LORD says: I am against you, Mount Seir, and I will stretch out my hand against you and make you a desolate waste. ⁴I will turn your towns into ruins and you will be desolate. Then you will know that I am the LORD.

⁵" 'Because you harbored an ancient hostility and delivered the Israelites over to the sword at the time of their calamity, the time their punishment reached its climax, ⁶therefore as surely as I live, declares the Sovereign LORD, I will give you over to bloodshed and it will pursue you. Since you did not hate bloodshed, bloodshed will pursue you. ⁷I will make Mount Seir a desolate waste and cut off from it all who come and go. ⁸I will fill your mountains with the slain; those killed by the sword will fall on your hills and in your valleys and in all your ravines. ⁹I will make you desolate forever; your towns will not be inhabited. Then you will know that I am the LORD.

¹⁰" 'Because you have said, "These two nations and countries will be ours and we will take possession of them," even though I the LORD was there, ¹¹therefore as surely as I live, declares the Sovereign LORD, I will treat you in accordance with the anger and jealousy you showed in your hatred of them and I will make myself known among them when I judge you. ¹²Then you will know that I the LORD have heard all the contemptible things you have said against the mountains of Israel. You said, "They have been laid waste and have been given over to us to devour." ¹³You boasted against me and spoke against me without restraint, and I heard it. ¹⁴This is what the Sovereign LORD says: While the whole earth rejoices, I will make you desolate. ¹⁵Because you rejoiced when the inheritance of the house of Israel became desolate, that is how I will treat you. You will be desolate, O Mount Seir, you and all of Edom D. Then they will know that I am the LORD.' "

A Prophecy to the Mountains of Israel

36 "Son of man, prophesy to the mountains of Israel and say, 'O mountains of Israel, hear the word of the LORD. ²This is what the Sovereign LORD says: The enemy said of you, "Aha! The ancient heights have become our possession." ' ³Therefore prophesy and say, 'This is what the Sovereign LORD says: Because they ravaged and hounded you from every side so that you became the possession of the rest of the nations and the object of people's malicious talk and slander, ⁴therefore, O mountains of Israel, hear the word of the Sovereign LORD: This is what the Sovereign LORD says to the mountains and hills, to the ravines and valleys, to the desolate ruins and the deserted towns that have been plundered D and ridiculed by the rest of the nations around you—

Mount Seir (35:2)
Mount Seir is the country of Edom where the descendants of Esau lived. See *Seir* (Gen. 36:8).

What caused their grudge against Israel? (35:5)
It started when Jacob tricked his brother Esau out of his birthright (Gen. 25:29–34) and then cheated him out of his blessing as the firstborn (Gen. 27:35–36). Since that time their descendants had been at odds. This ancient hostility kept the Edomites from coming to Israel's aid during the Babylonian invasion.

⁵this is what the Sovereign LORD says: In my burning zealᴰ I have spoken against the rest of the nations, and against all Edomᴰ, for with glee and with malice in their hearts they made my land their own possession so that they might plunderᴰ its pastureland.' ⁶Therefore prophesy concerning the land of Israel and say to the mountains and hills, to the ravines and valleys: 'This is what the Sovereign LORD says: I speak in my jealous wrath because you have suffered the scorn of the nations. ⁷Therefore this is what the Sovereign LORD says: I swear with uplifted hand that the nations around you will also suffer scorn.

⁸" 'But you, O mountains of Israel, will produce branches and fruit for my people Israel, for they will soon come home. ⁹I am concerned for you and will look on you with favor; you will be plowed and sown, ¹⁰and I will multiply the number of people upon you, even the whole house of Israel. The towns will be inhabited and the ruins rebuilt. ¹¹I will increase the number of men and animals upon you, and they will be fruitful and become numerous. I will settle people on you as in the past and will make you prosper more than before. Then you will know that I am the LORD. ¹²I will cause people, my people Israel, to walk upon you. They will possess you, and you will be their inheritance; you will never again deprive them of their children.

¹³" 'This is what the Sovereign LORD says: Because people say to you, "You devour men and deprive your nation of its children," ¹⁴therefore you will no longer devour men or make your nation childless, declares the Sovereign LORD. ¹⁵No longer will I make you hear the taunts of the nations, and no longer will you suffer the scorn of the peoples or cause your nation to fall, declares the Sovereign LORD.' "

¹⁶Again the word of the LORD came to me: ¹⁷"Son of manᴰ, when the people of Israel were living in their own land, they defiled it by their conduct and their actions. Their conduct was like a woman's monthly uncleannessᴰ in my sight. ¹⁸So I poured out my wrath on them because they had shed blood in the land and because they had defiled it with their idolsᴰ. ¹⁹I dispersed them among the nations, and they were scattered through the countries; I judged them according to their conduct and their actions. ²⁰And wherever they went among the nations they profanedᴰ my holy name, for it was said of them, 'These are the LORD's people, and yet they had to leave his land.' ²¹I had concern for my holy name, which the house of Israel profaned among the nations where they had gone.

²²"Therefore say to the house of Israel, 'This is what the Sovereign LORD says: It is not for your sake, O house of Israel, that I am going to do these things, but for the sake of my holy name, which you have profaned among the nations where you have gone. ²³I will show the holiness of my great name, which has been profaned among the nations, the name you have profaned among them. Then the nations will know that I am the LORD, declares the Sovereign LORD, when I show myself holy through you before their eyes.

²⁴" 'For I will take you out of the nations; I will gather you from all the countries and bring you back into your own land. ²⁵I will sprinkle clean water on you, and you will be clean; I will cleanse you from all your impurities and from all your idols. ²⁶I will give you a new heart and put a new spirit in you; I will remove from you your heart

How had the mountains deprived the Israelites of their children? (36:12)

This is not simply a literal prophecy about mountains. It is a prophecy about the people who lived on them. In Middle Eastern culture, the people were seen as part of the land, inseparable from it. (The concept of "Holy Land" shows how fully a nation can be identified with its locale.) Thus, the deeds of a nation or people could be described as the deeds of the mountain on which they lived. To say the mountains had displaced the Israelites and their descendants was to say that the foreigners who had moved up into Israel during the exile had done it.

How did the people of Israel profane the name of the Lord? (36:20)

The people of other lands formed their opinion of God based on the conduct of his people. When they sinned, their behavior stood in stark contrast to the holy God they claimed to serve. To defend his own reputation, he was forced to send them out of the land. Still, wherever they went, they were a blight on his name because foreigners would interpret their defeat as a sign that their God was weak and inept.

How did God finally break his people of their addiction to idols? (36:25–26)

God purified his people by putting them through a time of exile in Babylon. Away from their homeland, separated from both the temple of the Lord and their idols, the Israelites came to realize what was real and what was not. They saw that the prophets of the Lord had been right—their idols had been impotent to save them from the judgment they deserved. Captivity in a foreign land caused the Israelites to abandon idolatry for good.

In what way would God give them a new heart? (36:26)

God not only promised to bring the people back, he promised to completely change their hearts. It's figurative language: their hearts of stone had been cold and unfeeling, unable to respond to God's love. But God performed a radical transformation and gave them hearts of flesh—hearts that were spiritually alive and open to him.

How did God *move* them to obey him? (36:27)

Through difficult circumstances God brought the people to a place of decision. While he did not coerce or force their obedience, he used their hardships to help them see that it would be to their own benefit to obey him.

of stone and give you a heart of flesh. **27**And I will put my Spirit in you and move you to follow my decrees and be careful to keep my laws. **28**You will live in the land I gave your forefathers; you will be my people, and I will be your God. **29**I will save you from all your uncleanness^D. I will call for the grain and make it plentiful and will not bring famine upon you. **30**I will increase the fruit of the trees and the crops of the field, so that you will no longer suffer disgrace among the nations because of famine. **31**Then you will remember your evil ways and wicked deeds, and you will loathe yourselves for your sins and detestable practices. **32**I want you to know that I am not doing this for your sake, declares the Sovereign LORD. Be ashamed and disgraced for your conduct, O house of Israel!

33" 'This is what the Sovereign LORD says: On the day I cleanse you from all your sins, I will resettle your towns, and the ruins will be rebuilt. **34**The desolate land will be cultivated instead of lying desolate in the sight of all who pass through it. **35**They will say, "This land that was laid waste has become like the garden of Eden; the cities that were lying in ruins, desolate and destroyed, are now fortified and inhabited." **36**Then the nations around you that remain will know that I the LORD have rebuilt what was destroyed and have replanted what was desolate. I the LORD have spoken, and I will do it.'

37"This is what the Sovereign LORD says: Once again I will yield to the plea of the house of Israel and do this for them: I will make their people as numerous as sheep, **38**as numerous as the flocks for offerings at Jerusalem^D during her appointed feasts. So will the ruined cities be filled with flocks of people. Then they will know that I am the LORD."

How did the Lord put his hand on Ezekiel? (37:1)

See *The hand of the LORD* (1:3).

Where is the valley of bones? (37:1)

This may have been the large, flat valley through which the Kebar River flowed (1:1). (The Hebrew word for *valley* is also translated *plain* in 3:22.) Earlier Ezekiel had seen the glory of God in this place.

The Valley of Dry Bones

37 The hand of the LORD was upon me, and he brought me out by the Spirit of the LORD and set me in the middle of a valley; it was full of bones. **2**He led me back and forth among them, and I saw a great many

Did Ezekiel foresee the modern Israel? (36:35–38)

Ezekiel recognized that God had a plan in mind for the future of his people as a nation. He had promised a homeland for his people Israel and had affirmed his promise to Abraham and David.

Many believe that the Jewish nation continues to figure prominently in God's prophetic plan. They note that though the Israelites were forced to leave their land several times throughout history, God always brought them back. They see the re-establishment of Israel as another indication of God's work among his chosen people.

Some are careful to point to God's promise to restore Israel spiritually. They interpret the future glory of Israel as an indication of spiritual blessings poured out on a spiritual Israel—the church of Jesus Christ. The foundation of the restoration is Christ (Heb. 8:6). Salvation—for both Jew and Gentile—is by grace through faith in Christ (Eph. 2:8–9).

There are others who see this prophecy primarily fulfilled in the return of Israel from captivity in Babylon. They believe modern parallels of the Jews returning to their homeland are mostly coincidental.

bones on the floor of the valley, bones that were very dry. ³He asked me, "Son of man,ᴰ can these bones live?"

I said, "O Sovereign Lᴏʀᴅ, you alone know."

⁴Then he said to me, "Prophesy to these bones and say to them, 'Dry bones, hear the word of the Lᴏʀᴅ! ⁵This is what the Sovereign Lᴏʀᴅ says to these bones: I will make breathᵃ enter you, and you will come to life. ⁶I will attach tendons to you and make flesh come upon you and cover you with skin; I will put breath in you, and you will come to life. Then you will know that I am the Lᴏʀᴅ.' "

⁷So I prophesied as I was commanded. And as I was prophesying, there was a noise, a rattling sound, and the bones came together, bone to bone. ⁸I looked, and tendons and flesh appeared on them and skin covered them, but there was no breath in them.

⁹Then he said to me, "Prophesy to the breath; prophesy, son of man, and say to it, 'This is what the Sovereign Lᴏʀᴅ says: Come from the four winds, O breath, and breathe into these slain, that they may live.' " ¹⁰So I prophesied as he commanded me, and breath entered them; they came to life and stood up on their feet—a vast army.

¹¹Then he said to me: "Son of man, these bones are the whole house of Israel. They say, 'Our bones are dried up and our hope is gone; we are cut off.' ¹²Therefore prophesy and say to them: 'This is what the Sovereign Lᴏʀᴅ says: O my people, I am going to open your graves and bring you up from them; I will bring you back to the land of Israel. ¹³Then you, my people, will know that I am the Lᴏʀᴅ, when I open your graves and bring you up from them. ¹⁴I will put my Spirit in you and you will live, and I will settle you in your own land. Then you will know that I the Lᴏʀᴅ have spoken, and I have done it, declares the Lᴏʀᴅ.' "

One Nation Under One King

¹⁵The word of the Lᴏʀᴅ came to me: ¹⁶"Son of man, take a stick of wood and write on it, 'Belonging to Judah and the Israelites associated with him.' Then take another stick of wood, and write on it, 'Ephraim's stick, belonging to Joseph and all the house of Israel associated with him.' ¹⁷Join them together into one stick so that they will become one in your hand.

¹⁸"When your countrymen ask you, 'Won't you tell us what you mean by this?' ¹⁹say to them, 'This is what the Sovereign Lᴏʀᴅ says: I am going to take the stick of Joseph—which is in Ephraim's hand—and of the Israelite tribes associated with him, and join it to Judah's stick, making them a single stick of wood, and they will become one in my hand.' ²⁰Hold before their eyes the sticks you have written on ²¹and say to them, 'This is what the Sovereign Lᴏʀᴅ says: I will take the Israelites out of the nations where they have gone. I will gather them from all around and bring them back into their own land. ²²I will make them one nation in the land, on the mountains of Israel. There will be one king over all of them and they will never again be two nations or be divided into two kingdoms. ²³They will no longer defile themselves with their idolsᴰ and vile images or with any of their offenses, for I will save them from all their sinful backslidingᴰ,ᵇ

ᵃ5 The Hebrew for this word can also mean *wind* or *spirit* (see verses 6-14).   ᵇ23 Many Hebrew manuscripts (see also Septuagint); most Hebrew manuscripts *all their dwelling places where they sinned*

Son of man (37:3)
See *Son of man* (2:1).

Why raise an army of the living dead? (37:10)
God was illustrating what he intended to do with the exiled Jews. Though their nation was "dead," God would raise it to life again. Ezekiel was speaking of a spiritual resurrection, not a physical one. This was to be a revival restoring Israel to spiritual life. By the prophet's word the valley of bones is transformed into a battlefield covered by God's mighty army.

Why prophesy to bones instead of people? (37:11)
Speaking to dead, dry bones was a metaphor for prophesying to people who were spiritually dead—*the whole house of Israel.* The exiles had no hope, no spark of faith. On another level, it may also illustrate the spiritual needs of Israel just before the return of Christ.

Why was Israel hopeless? (37:11)
During Ezekiel's day the northern kingdom was destroyed and taken into captivity by Assyria. Later, Judah was crushed by Babylon. The temple of the Lord was destroyed, the city of Jerusalem was burned and left in ruins and the people were taken into exile. After such devastation, the Israelites could not imagine that God would restore them again as a nation.

Where were the Israelites? (37:21)
See previous note.

When was this fulfilled? (37:22–27)
Some think this was fulfilled, at least partially, when the Jews were released from captivity to return to the land of Israel. Others see the act of joining sticks (v. 17) as a symbol of the future Messianic kingdom when the northern and southern kingdoms (Ephraim and Judah) will be reunited. The Messiah will come, establish his kingdom and restore Israel to the land forever (vv. 21,25), so that God can live among them (v. 27).

Backsliding (37:23)
Means *to turn away* or *to move away.* A backslider is one who turns away or moves away from God.

How can a dead king rule? (37:24–25)

This does not mean David would literally return from the grave to rule over Israel. Instead, *David* was used to picture the type of ruler to come—one who would rule on behalf of the Lord. This is a reference to Jesus Christ who is from the line of David (Matt. 1:1–17). The phrase could also mean some future, human representative of David's line, though there has never been a human ruler on the throne of David since the time of Ezekiel.

Was this a curse? (38:2)

It may be better to think of the phrase *set your face against* as a prophetic judgment rather than a curse. Because of their sin and hatred for Israel, the nations received a word about the judgment God would send against them as he defended his people.

Who were all these nations? (38:2–6)

Some identify *Gog* as one or another historical figure; others think he symbolizes the leader of the forces of evil. *Magog* (as well as *Meshech and Tubal*) may refer to peoples he ruled rather than a geographical area (Gen. 10:2). Some see links to modern Russia, partly because they are *from the far north* (39:2). Others think this unlikely and point out that *far* is a non-specific term. While it is true that Ezekiel used names of nations and peoples from his time, his prophecy seems to fit the end times. Nothing in history corresponds to the severity of this judgment, suggesting it remains yet to be fulfilled.

Hooks in your jaws (38:4)

See *How were captives led away by hooks?* (19:4,9) and *Hooks in your jaws* (29:4).

and I will cleanse them. They will be my people, and I will be their God.

24 " 'My servant David will be king over them, and they will all have one shepherd. They will follow my laws and be careful to keep my decrees. 25They will live in the land I gave to my servant Jacob, the land where your fathers lived. They and their children and their children's children will live there forever, and David my servant will be their prince forever. 26I will make a covenant[D] of peace[D] with them; it will be an everlasting covenant. I will establish them and increase their numbers, and I will put my sanctuary among them forever. 27My dwelling place will be with them; I will be their God, and they will be my people. 28Then the nations will know that I the LORD make Israel holy, when my sanctuary is among them forever.' "

A Prophecy Against Gog

38 The word of the LORD came to me: 2"Son of man[D], set your face against Gog, of the land of Magog, the chief prince of[a] Meshech and Tubal; prophesy against him 3and say: 'This is what the Sovereign LORD says: I am against you, O Gog, chief prince of[b] Meshech and Tubal. 4I will turn you around, put hooks in your jaws and bring you out with your whole army—your horses, your horsemen fully armed, and a great horde with large and small shields, all of them brandishing their swords. 5Persia, Cush[c] and Put will be with them, all with shields and helmets, 6also Gomer with all its troops, and Beth Togarmah from the far north with all its troops—the many nations with you.

7 " 'Get ready; be prepared, you and all the hordes gathered about you, and take command of them. 8After many days you will be called to arms. In future years you will invade a land that has recovered from war, whose people were gathered from many nations to the mountains of Israel, which had long been desolate. They had been brought out from the nations, and now all of them live in safety. 9You and all your troops and the many nations with you will go up, advancing like a storm; you will be like a cloud covering the land.

10 " 'This is what the Sovereign LORD says: On that day

[a]2 Or *the prince of Rosh,*   [b]3 Or *Gog, prince of Rosh,*   [c]5 That is, the upper Nile region

When will peace come to the Middle East? (37:26–28)

Some believe that the national or political elements of this prophecy were fulfilled in the time of Ezekiel the prophet. They further understand the *covenant of peace* to mean the new covenant in which all are now invited to participate (Heb. 10:16–17). They say God's *sanctuary* means God's presence among his people (Rev. 21:3).

Others think this can also refer to the physical peace to be ushered in by the Messianic kingdom. They believe Israel's Messiah brought spiritual peace (Romans 5:1), but they also expect him to bring literal peace to the earth one day. They say that a temple to the Lord literally will be built and filled with God's glory (43:1–12).

Though this prophecy is addressed first to Israel, the New Testament suggests that this *covenant of peace* looks to the final peace that will characterize life in the new heaven and the new earth (Rev. 21:1–4).

thoughts will come into your mind and you will devise an evil scheme. **11**You will say, "I will invade a land of un-walled villages; I will attack a peaceful and unsuspecting people—all of them living without walls and without gates and bars. **12**I will plunderᴰ and loot and turn my hand against the resettled ruins and the people gathered from the nations, rich in livestock and goods, living at the center of the land." **13**Sheba and Dedan and the merchants of Tarshish and all her villagesᵃ will say to you, "Have you come to plunder? Have you gathered your hordes to loot, to carry off silver and gold, to take away livestock and goods and to seize much plunder?" '

14"Therefore, son of manᴰ, prophesy and say to Gog: 'This is what the Sovereign LORD says: In that day, when my people Israel are living in safety, will you not take notice of it? **15**You will come from your place in the far north, you and many nations with you, all of them riding on horses, a great horde, a mighty army. **16**You will advance against my people Israel like a cloud that covers the land. In days to come, O Gog, I will bring you against my land, so that the nations may know me when I show myself holy through you before their eyes.

17" 'This is what the Sovereign LORD says: Are you not the one I spoke of in former days by my servants the prophetsᴰ of Israel? At that time they prophesied for years that I would bring you against them. **18**This is what will happen in that day: When Gog attacks the land of Israel, my hot anger will be aroused, declares the Sovereign LORD. **19**In my zealᴰ and fiery wrath I declare that at that time there shall be a great earthquake in the land of Israel. **20**The fish of the sea, the birds of the air, the beasts of the field, every creature that moves along the ground, and all the people on the face of the earth will tremble at my presence. The mountains will be overturned, the cliffs will crumble and every wall will fall to the ground. **21**I will summon a sword against Gog on all my mountains, declares the Sovereign LORD. Every man's sword will be against his brother. **22**I will execute judgment upon him with plague and bloodshed; I will pour down torrents of rain, hailstones and burning sulfur on him and on his troops and on the many nations with him. **23**And so I will show my greatness and my holiness, and I will make myself known in the sight of many nations. Then they will know that I am the LORD.'

39 "Son of man, prophesy against Gog and say: 'This is what the Sovereign LORD says: I am against you, O Gog, chief prince ofᵇ Meshech and Tubal. **2**I will turn you around and drag you along. I will bring you from the far north and send you against the mountains of Israel. **3**Then I will strike your bow from your left hand and make your arrows drop from your right hand. **4**On the mountains of Israel you will fall, you and all your troops and the nations with you. I will give you as food to all kinds of carrion birds and to the wild animals. **5**You will fall in the open field, for I have spoken, declares the Sovereign LORD. **6**I will send fire on Magog and on those who live in safety in the coastlands, and they will know that I am the LORD.

7" 'I will make known my holy name among my people Israel. I will no longer let my holy name be profanedᴰ, and the nations will know that I the LORD am the Holy One

Does God sometimes cause war? (38:16)

God can use anything to accomplish his purposes—even those things that humans intend for evil. God used war to punish the wicked; he also engaged in battle to defend the righteous and the honor of his name. God is sovereign and uses all human affairs to bring glory to himself. Also see article: *Does God use evil to do good?* (Hab. 1:6,13).

What had earlier prophets said about Gog? (38:17)

Some suggest Gog was the leader of Assyria. They say that the prophets Isaiah (10:5–16) and Micah (5:5) had spoken earlier about him. Another view is that earlier prophets had never prophesied specifically about Gog but had foretold God's judgment on the ungodly nations of the north (for example, Joel 3:1–16; Zeph. 3:8). Those who hold this view say these prophecies are fulfilled in God's judgment on Gog.

Are earthquakes acts of God? (38:19–20)

Earthquakes are just one means God uses to bring about his judgment. Gog will also be judged by anarchy, pestilence and other natural disasters (vv. 21–22). It may be hard to accept earthquakes as acts of God, particularly when they bring indiscriminate suffering upon both the wicked and the righteous. Yet God established the laws of nature. As a result, though he may not be the immediate cause of a disaster, he allows it. See *Does God cause natural calamities because of people's sin?* (Jer. 5:25). Also see article: *Why does God send calamity?* (Lam. 3:38).

ᵃ13 Or *her strong lions*   ᵇ1 Or *Gog, prince of Rosh,*

SCRIPTURE LINK (39:8) *The day*
See *The day of the LORD* (Zeph. 1:7).

What weapons would take seven years to burn? (39:9–10)

Made of wood or leather, these weapons would burn. Though it's hard to imagine these weapons supplying fuel for seven years, it is possible. Another view is that the number *seven*, important in apocalyptic or prophetic literature, conveys the idea of complete destruction. Some suggest that Ezekiel was describing nuclear energy but was limited to using words from his own time.

How could a graveyard be a roadblock? (39:11)

This prophecy could be fulfilled literally. Travelers could find the way impassable if the valley was filled with the corpses of Gog's army. Such overwhelming and graphic images of death might also be a psychological barrier for travelers who would avoid the valley if at all possible.

Why would it take so long to bury the dead? (39:12)

It is impossible to know whether *seven* is strictly symbolic—or literal and symbolic. Ezekiel paints a picture of absolute and total destruction (see previous note). Since the whole nation would be occupied for so long with burying the dead, it would be a lingering and vivid reminder of God's great victory.

Why would God endorse human sacrifices? (39:17–19)

He doesn't. But the sacrificial feast offers a vivid word picture that shows judgment, great carnage and irrevocable doom. This metaphor for God's judgment is found in other prophets as well (Isaiah 34:6; Jer. 46:10; Zeph. 1:7–8). The various animals represent the different

in Israel. ⁸It is coming! It will surely take place, declares the Sovereign LORD. This is the day I have spoken of.

⁹" 'Then those who live in the towns of Israel will go out and use the weapons for fuel and burn them up—the small and large shields, the bows and arrows, the war clubs and spears. For seven years they will use them for fuel. ¹⁰They will not need to gather wood from the fields or cut it from the forests, because they will use the weapons for fuel. And they will plunderᴰ those who plundered them and loot those who looted them, declares the Sovereign LORD.

¹¹" 'On that day I will give Gog a burial place in Israel, in the valley of those who travel east towardᵃ the Sea.ᵇ It will block the way of travelers, because Gog and all his hordes will be buried there. So it will be called the Valley of Hamon Gog.ᶜ

¹²" 'For seven months the house of Israel will be burying them in order to cleanse the land. ¹³All the people of the land will bury them, and the day I am glorified will be a memorable day for them, declares the Sovereign LORD.

¹⁴" 'Men will be regularly employed to cleanse the land. Some will go throughout the land and, in addition to them, others will bury those that remain on the ground. At the end of the seven months they will begin their search. ¹⁵As they go through the land and one of them sees a human bone, he will set up a marker beside it until the gravediggers have buried it in the Valley of Hamon Gog. ¹⁶(Also a town called Hamonahᵈ will be there.) And so they will cleanse the land.'

¹⁷"Son of manᴰ, this is what the Sovereign LORD says: Call out to every kind of bird and all the wild animals: 'Assemble and come together from all around to the sacrificeᴰ I am preparing for you, the great sacrifice on the

---

ᵃ11 Or of   ᵇ11 That is, the Dead Sea   ᶜ11 *Hamon Gog* means *hordes of Gog.*   ᵈ16 *Hamonah* means *horde.*

What is holy about wiping out a nation? (38:22–23)

Simply put, wiping out a nation can be holy if it is *just*. Such justice must include the authority to impose standards of behavior, consistent moral standards, an awareness of the requirements and true guilt. Only God can administer these standards of justice.

(1) God has the right to require certain behavior of people because he is the Creator of heaven and earth. He expects certain behavior from those he made.

(2) God's requirements are not arbitrary or inconsistent. His laws are moral and just, rooted in his holy and righteous character.

(3) People know about God's requirements—most clearly through his Word, but also through their consciences. Even those who have never heard God's written revelation have had moral truth imprinted upon their hearts (Romans 2:14–16).

(4) All who are judged have broken God's law. Often judgment comes only after a nation has long spurned God's mercy and patience. God gave the Amorites more than 400 years to abandon their wicked ways (Gen. 15:13–16), but removed them like a cancer from humanity when they refused to change. Later it was Israel's turn to be judged for disobeying God's commands.

God's justice, then, is holy and righteous. Also see article: *Why kill everything?* (Joshua 6:21).

mountains of Israel. There you will eat flesh and drink blood. **18**You will eat the flesh of mighty men and drink the blood of the princes of the earth as if they were rams and lambs, goats and bulls—all of them fattened animals from Bashan. **19**At the sacrifice^D I am preparing for you, you will eat fat till you are glutted and drink blood till you are drunk. **20**At my table you will eat your fill of horses and riders, mighty men and soldiers of every kind,' declares the Sovereign LORD.

21"I will display my glory^D among the nations, and all the nations will see the punishment I inflict and the hand I lay upon them. **22**From that day forward the house of Israel will know that I am the LORD their God. **23**And the nations will know that the people of Israel went into exile^D for their sin, because they were unfaithful to me. So I hid my face from them and handed them over to their enemies, and they all fell by the sword. **24**I dealt with them according to their uncleanness^D and their offenses, and I hid my face from them.

25"Therefore this is what the Sovereign LORD says: I will now bring Jacob back from captivity^a and will have compassion on all the people of Israel, and I will be zealous for my holy name. **26**They will forget their shame and all the unfaithfulness they showed toward me when they lived in safety in their land with no one to make them afraid. **27**When I have brought them back from the nations and have gathered them from the countries of their enemies, I will show myself holy through them in the sight of many nations. **28**Then they will know that I am the LORD their God, for though I sent them into exile among the nations, I will gather them to their own land, not leaving any behind. **29**I will no longer hide my face from them, for I will pour out my Spirit on the house of Israel, declares the Sovereign LORD."

The New Temple Area

40 In the twenty-fifth year of our exile, at the beginning of the year, on the tenth of the month, in the fourteenth year after the fall of the city—on that very day the hand of the LORD was upon me and he took me there. **2**In visions^D of God he took me to the land of Israel and set me on a very high mountain, on whose south side were some buildings that looked like a city. **3**He took me there, and I saw a man whose appearance was like bronze; he was standing in the gateway with a linen cord and a measuring rod in his hand. **4**The man said to me, "Son of man^D, look with your eyes and hear with your ears and pay attention to everything I am going to show you, for that is why you have been brought here. Tell the house of Israel everything you see."

The East Gate to the Outer Court

5I saw a wall completely surrounding the temple area. The length of the measuring rod in the man's hand was six long cubits^D, each of which was a cubit^b and a handbreadth.^c He measured the wall; it was one measuring rod thick and one rod high. **6**Then he went to the gate facing east. He climbed its steps and measured the threshold of the gate; it was one

ranks of men who disobeyed God's commands and tried to destroy God's people.

Why all this gore? (39:17–20)
The consequences of sin and wickedness are never a pretty sight. God does not sanitize this scene out of respect for our sensitivities. Instead, these gory details demonstrate the large scale of the attack against God's people and the completeness of the slaughter at the hand of the Lord. We may think God's actions excessive, but we cannot forget that his patience precedes judgment. Nor can we forget that his holiness and justice demand retribution.

Why free Jacob now? (39:25)
Jacob, another name for the nation of Israel, was freed because God's promises of mercy, hope and restoration are to be fulfilled. God's judgment of Israel was not to destroy them but to chasten them. Because of their disobedience God allowed them to go into captivity. But because of God's mercy, he intended to regather them to the land, bless them and make them a channel of blessing to all the nations of the world.

Weren't some left behind? (39:28)
Technically, yes—if this is talking about the return of exiles from Babylon. But some suggest this refers to a future return of Jews to their land in the Messianic age when all will repent and none will be left behind. Others see a spiritual fulfillment when all believers will join together as part of Christ's kingdom.

How did God pour out his Spirit? (39:29)
Part of the promise of the new covenant is an outpouring of God's Spirit upon *everyone who calls on the name of the LORD* (Joel 2:28–32). It is through the power of the Holy Spirit that Israel will finally obey God wholeheartedly. These promises are amplified in the New Testament through the death of Christ and the coming of the Holy Spirit on the day of Pentecost. Many anticipate that Israel will experience this as a nation when Christ returns and they accept him as their Messiah.

Why is *the city* nameless? (40:1)
We can't be sure. Some suggest no name was necessary because the description left no doubt that this was Jerusalem. Others think it may be simply a matter of style—perhaps implying that mentioning the name Jerusalem would only add to the despair of the exiles.

Who was the bronze man? (40:3)
Some think the bronze man was an angel like the one who interpreted Zechariah (Zech. 1:9) and Revelation (Rev. 17:7). Others think it better to see him as the angel of the Lord, since later he was called *the LORD* (44:2,5). The angel of the Lord appears throughout the Old Testament and is sometimes called God (Gen. 16:7–13; Zech. 1:7–17).

Why measure a vision? (40:5)
The temple area in the vision is measured to mark off the temple from its surroundings by building a wall. It's a picture of separating the sacred from the secular. God's presence is not to be profaned.

---

^a25 Or *now restore the fortunes of Jacob*   ^b5 The common cubit was about 1 1/2 feet (about 0.5 meter).   ^c5 That is, about 3 inches (about 8 centimeters)

rod deep.^a ⁷The alcoves for the guards were one rod long and one rod wide, and the projecting walls between the alcoves were five cubits^b thick. And the threshold of the gate next to the portico facing the temple was one rod deep.

⁸Then he measured the portico of the gateway; ⁹it^b was eight cubits deep and its jambs were two cubits thick. The portico of the gateway faced the temple.

¹⁰Inside the east gate were three alcoves on each side; the three had the same measurements, and the faces of the projecting walls on each side had the same measurements. ¹¹Then he measured the width of the entrance to the gateway; it was ten cubits and its length was thirteen cubits. ¹²In front of each alcove was a wall one cubit high, and the alcoves were six cubits square. ¹³Then he measured the gateway from the top of the rear wall of one alcove to the top of the opposite one; the distance was twenty-five cubits from one parapet opening to the opposite one. ¹⁴He measured along the faces of the projecting walls all around the inside of the gateway—sixty cubits. The measurement was up to the portico^c facing the courtyard.^d ¹⁵The distance from the entrance of the gateway to the far end of its portico was fifty cubits. ¹⁶The alcoves and the projecting walls inside the gateway were surmounted by narrow parapet openings all around, as was the portico; the openings all around faced inward. The faces of the projecting walls were decorated with palm trees.

The Outer Court

¹⁷Then he brought me into the outer court. There I saw some rooms and a pavement that had been constructed all around the court; there were thirty rooms along the

Why provide such detail about the various parts of the temple? (40:10–16)

It may be that Ezekiel was recalling the details of the temple he had known before being taken captive to Babylon. Some say that he had a vivid picture of the temple that was to be rebuilt once they returned to Jerusalem. See article: *What temple is this?* (40:5—42:20). Either way, the precise measurements and concrete details served to underscore that Ezekiel's vision was something real. This was not an abstract concept; his prophecy—whether literal or figurative—would be fulfilled.

^a6 Septuagint; Hebrew *deep, the first threshold, one rod deep* ^b8,9 Many Hebrew manuscripts, Septuagint, Vulgate and Syriac; most Hebrew manuscripts *gateway facing the temple; it was one rod deep.* ⁹*Then he measured the portico of the gateway; it* ^c14 Septuagint; Hebrew *projecting wall* ^d14 The meaning of the Hebrew for this verse is uncertain.

What temple is this? (40:5—42:20)

People disagree about the significance of these chapters. Some insist that this is a description of Solomon's temple. There are, however, a number of important differences between this temple and Solomon's. Consequently, others suggest that these are plans for a temple Ezekiel intended the exiles to build when they returned to Jerusalem.

A third view says that since Ezekiel was a prophet, not an architect, these chapters should be interpreted in a symbolic manner. This view sees these chapters fulfilled figuratively in the church or in a future Messianic age. In the former case this "temple" predicts the blessings that God has for the church. In the latter case the perfect symmetry of the "temple" would express symbolically the perfection of God's plan for his restored people.

Still another view expects a future, literal fulfillment of this prophecy when Christ returns to set up his Messianic kingdom. Some object to this interpretation and say that to reinstitute Old Testament sacrifices seems contrary to the New Testament (Heb. 10:1–18). Those who look for a literal temple in the Messianic age, however, see its ceremonies simply as memorials of the Messiah's death, burial and resurrection.

pavement. [18]It abutted the sides of the gateways and was as wide as they were long; this was the lower pavement. [19]Then he measured the distance from the inside of the lower gateway to the outside of the inner court; it was a hundred cubits[D] on the east side as well as on the north.

The North Gate

[20]Then he measured the length and width of the gate facing north, leading into the outer court. [21]Its alcoves— three on each side—its projecting walls and its portico had the same measurements as those of the first gateway. It was fifty cubits long and twenty-five cubits wide. [22]Its openings, its portico and its palm tree decorations had the same measurements as those of the gate facing east. Seven steps led up to it, with its portico opposite them. [23]There was a gate to the inner court facing the north gate, just as there was on the east. He measured from one gate to the opposite one; it was a hundred cubits.

The South Gate

[24]Then he led me to the south side and I saw a gate facing south. He measured its jambs and its portico, and they had the same measurements as the others. [25]The gateway and its portico had narrow openings all around, like the openings of the others. It was fifty cubits long and twenty-five cubits wide. [26]Seven steps led up to it, with its portico opposite them; it had palm tree decorations on the faces of the projecting walls on each side. [27]The inner court also had a gate facing south, and he measured from this gate to the outer gate on the south side; it was a hundred cubits.

Gates to the Inner Court

[28]Then he brought me into the inner court through the south gate, and he measured the south gate; it had the same measurements as the others. [29]Its alcoves, its projecting walls and its portico had the same measurements as the others. The gateway and its portico had openings all around. It was fifty cubits long and twenty-five cubits wide. [30](The porticoes of the gateways around the inner court were twenty-five cubits wide and five cubits deep.) [31]Its portico faced the outer court; palm trees decorated its jambs, and eight steps led up to it.

[32]Then he brought me to the inner court on the east side, and he measured the gateway; it had the same measurements as the others. [33]Its alcoves, its projecting walls and its portico had the same measurements as the others. The gateway and its portico had openings all around. It was fifty cubits long and twenty-five cubits wide. [34]Its portico faced the outer court; palm trees decorated the jambs on either side, and eight steps led up to it.

[35]Then he brought me to the north gate and measured it. It had the same measurements as the others, [36]as did its alcoves, its projecting walls and its portico, and it had openings all around. It was fifty cubits long and twenty-five cubits wide. [37]Its portico[a] faced the outer court; palm trees decorated the jambs on either side, and eight steps led up to it.

Why have seven steps in some places and eight steps in others? (40:22,26,34,37)

It's not entirely clear. Seven was typically used as a symbol of completion or perfection. See *Why sprinkle blood seven times?* (Lev. 4:5–7) and *What was so special about the number seven?* (2 Chron. 29:21). It may be that seven steps were used to remind people of the need for holiness when entering the temple precincts. Then, to enter the inner court, an additional step may have been used to raise it one step higher above the outer court—a tangible sign for the priests climbing the steps that they were approaching the presence of God. Note that the temple itself was reached from the inner court by *a flight of stairs*, perhaps ten steps (v. 49; see NIV text note). Some have pointed out that in later times, there were 15 steps (7 plus 8) that led from the court of the women to the court of Israel. On those steps the Levites would stand to chant the 15 psalms (Psalms 120–134) which are called "songs of ascents."

Were these real palm trees? (40:31)

Probably not. Like the 200 pomegranates Solomon had carved on the capitals of each temple pillar (1 Kings 7:18,20), these palm trees were carved for decoration. Details given later show that palm trees were also carved on the upper part of the walls all around the inner and outer sanctuary, alternating with carved cherubim (41:18).

[a]37 Septuagint (see also verses 31 and 34); Hebrew *jambs*

The Rooms for Preparing Sacrifices

38A room with a doorway was by the portico in each of the inner gateways, where the burnt offerings[D] were washed. **39**In the portico of the gateway were two tables on each side, on which the burnt offerings, sin offerings[D] and guilt offerings[D] were slaughtered. **40**By the outside wall of the portico of the gateway, near the steps at the entrance to the north gateway were two tables, and on the other side of the steps were two tables. **41**So there were four tables on one side of the gateway and four on the other—eight tables in all—on which the sacrifices[D] were slaughtered. **42**There were also four tables of dressed stone for the burnt offerings, each a cubit and a half long, a cubit and a half wide and a cubit high. On them were placed the utensils for slaughtering the burnt offerings and the other sacrifices. **43**And double-pronged hooks, each a handbreadth long, were attached to the wall all around. The tables were for the flesh of the offerings.

Rooms for the Priests

44Outside the inner gate, within the inner court, were two rooms, one[a] at the side of the north gate and facing south, and another at the side of the south[b] gate and facing north. **45**He said to me, "The room facing south is for the priests[D] who have charge of the temple, **46**and the room facing north is for the priests who have charge of the altar. These are the sons of Zadok, who are the only Levites[D] who may draw near to the LORD to minister before him."

47Then he measured the court: It was square—a hundred cubits long and a hundred cubits wide. And the altar was in front of the temple.

The Temple

48He brought me to the portico of the temple and measured the jambs of the portico; they were five cubits wide on either side. The width of the entrance was fourteen cubits and its projecting walls were[c] three cubits wide on either side. **49**The portico was twenty cubits wide, and twelve[d] cubits from front to back. It was reached by a flight of stairs,[e] and there were pillars on each side of the jambs.

41 Then the man brought me to the outer sanctuary and measured the jambs; the width of the jambs was six cubits[f] on each side.[g] **2**The entrance was ten cubits wide, and the projecting walls on each side of it were five cubits wide. He also measured the outer sanctuary; it was forty cubits long and twenty cubits wide. **3**Then he went into the inner sanctuary and measured the jambs of the entrance; each was two cubits wide. The entrance was six cubits wide, and the projecting walls on each side of it were seven cubits wide. **4**And he measured the length of the inner sanctuary; it was twenty cubits, and its width was twenty cubits across the end of the outer sanctuary. He said to me, "This is the Most Holy Place."

Who was Zadok? (40:46)
Zadok was a priest during David's and Solomon's time. God chose Zadok to minister in the temple when Abiathar was removed as priest for supporting Adonijah as David's successor (1 Kings 1:7–8; 2:26–27).

Most Holy Place (41:4)
The inner sanctuary of the temple, within the holy place, which was within the outer court. It contained the ark of the covenant, the symbol of God's presence. The high priest alone was allowed to enter *the Most Holy Place,* and then only once each year on the Day of Atonement.

---

*a*44 Septuagint; Hebrew *were rooms for singers, which were*
*b*44 Septuagint; Hebrew *east*   *c*48 Septuagint; Hebrew *entrance was*
*d*49 Septuagint; Hebrew *eleven*   *e*49 Hebrew; Septuagint *Ten steps led up to it*   *f*1 The common cubit was about 1 1/2 feet (about 0.5 meter).   *g*1 One Hebrew manuscript and Septuagint; most Hebrew manuscripts *side, the width of the tent*

5Then he measured the wall of the temple; it was six cubits^D thick, and each side room around the temple was four cubits wide. **6**The side rooms were on three levels, one above another, thirty on each level. There were ledges all around the wall of the temple to serve as supports for the side rooms, so that the supports were not inserted into the wall of the temple. **7**The side rooms all around the temple were wider at each successive level. The structure surrounding the temple was built in ascending stages, so that the rooms widened as one went upward. A stairway went up from the lowest floor to the top floor through the middle floor.

8I saw that the temple had a raised base all around it, forming the foundation of the side rooms. It was the length of the rod, six long cubits. **9**The outer wall of the side rooms was five cubits thick. The open area between the side rooms of the temple **10**and the ∟ priests'^D⌐ rooms was twenty cubits wide all around the temple. **11**There were entrances to the side rooms from the open area, one on the north and another on the south; and the base adjoining the open area was five cubits wide all around.

12The building facing the temple courtyard on the west side was seventy cubits wide. The wall of the building was five cubits thick all around, and its length was ninety cubits.

13Then he measured the temple; it was a hundred cubits long, and the temple courtyard and the building with its walls were also a hundred cubits long. **14**The width of the temple courtyard on the east, including the front of the temple, was a hundred cubits.

15Then he measured the length of the building facing the courtyard at the rear of the temple, including its galleries on each side; it was a hundred cubits.

The outer sanctuary, the inner sanctuary and the portico facing the court, **16**as well as the thresholds and the narrow windows and galleries around the three of them—everything beyond and including the threshold was covered with wood. The floor, the wall up to the windows, and the windows were covered. **17**In the space above the outside of the entrance to the inner sanctuary and on the walls at regular intervals all around the inner and outer sanctuary **18**were carved cherubim^D and palm trees. Palm trees alternated with cherubim. Each cherub had two faces: **19**the face of a man toward the palm tree on one side and the face of a lion toward the palm tree on the other. They were carved all around the whole temple. **20**From the floor to the area above the entrance, cherubim and palm trees were carved on the wall of the outer sanctuary.

21The outer sanctuary had a rectangular doorframe, and the one at the front of the Most Holy Place^D was similar. **22**There was a wooden altar three cubits high and two cubits square^a; its corners, its base^b and its sides were of wood. The man said to me, "This is the table that is before the LORD." **23**Both the outer sanctuary and the Most Holy Place had double doors. **24**Each door had two leaves—two hinged leaves for each door. **25**And on the doors of the outer sanctuary were carved cherubim and palm trees like those carved on the walls, and there was a wooden overhang on the front of the portico. **26**On the sidewalls of the portico were narrow windows with palm

Cherubim (41:18)
Plural of *cherub*, which was a specific type of angel. Here cherubim are carved on the walls of the temple with two faces, a man's and a young lion's. These may be different from the *cherubim* with four faces (10:14) simply because the carving showed only a one-sided view.

^a22 Septuagint; Hebrew *long*   ^b22 Septuagint; Hebrew *length*

trees carved on each side. The side rooms of the temple also had overhangs.

Rooms for the Priests

42 Then the man led me northward into the outer court and brought me to the rooms opposite the temple courtyard and opposite the outer wall on the north side. ²The building whose door faced north was a hundred cubits[D][a] long and fifty cubits wide. ³Both in the section twenty cubits from the inner court and in the section opposite the pavement of the outer court, gallery faced gallery at the three levels. ⁴In front of the rooms was an inner passageway ten cubits wide and a hundred cubits[b] long. Their doors were on the north. ⁵Now the upper rooms were narrower, for the galleries took more space from them than from the rooms on the lower and middle floors of the building. ⁶The rooms on the third floor had no pillars, as the courts had; so they were smaller in floor space than those on the lower and middle floors. ⁷There was an outer wall parallel to the rooms and the outer court; it extended in front of the rooms for fifty cubits. ⁸While the row of rooms on the side next to the outer court was fifty cubits long, the row on the side nearest the sanctuary was a hundred cubits long. ⁹The lower rooms had an entrance on the east side as one enters them from the outer court.

¹⁰On the south side[c] along the length of the wall of the outer court, adjoining the temple courtyard and opposite the outer wall, were rooms ¹¹with a passageway in front of them. These were like the rooms on the north; they had the same length and width, with similar exits and dimensions. Similar to the doorways on the north ¹²were the doorways of the rooms on the south. There was a doorway at the beginning of the passageway that was parallel to the corresponding wall extending eastward, by which one enters the rooms.

¹³Then he said to me, "The north and south rooms facing the temple courtyard are the priests'[D] rooms, where the priests who approach the LORD will eat the most holy offerings. There they will put the most holy offerings—the grain offerings[D], the sin offerings[D] and the guilt offerings[D]—for the place is holy. ¹⁴Once the priests enter the holy precincts, they are not to go into the outer court until they leave behind the garments in which they minister, for these are holy. They are to put on other clothes before they go near the places that are for the people."

¹⁵When he had finished measuring what was inside the temple area, he led me out by the east gate and measured the area all around: ¹⁶He measured the east side with the measuring rod; it was five hundred cubits.[d] ¹⁷He measured the north side; it was five hundred cubits[e] by the measuring rod. ¹⁸He measured the south side; it was five hundred cubits by the measuring rod. ¹⁹Then he turned to the west side and measured; it was five hundred cubits by the measuring rod. ²⁰So he measured the area on all four sides. It had a wall around it, five hundred cubits long and five hundred cubits wide, to separate the holy from the common.

Why did the priests eat the offerings? (42:13)
See *Why did God want the priests to eat some offerings and not others?* (Lev. 6:23).

What was holy and what was common? (42:20)
The temple and everything within it was reserved for God alone. Those things dedicated for use in honoring God were holy and used only by designated priests. Common things, on the other hand, could be used in everyday life by anyone. The wall that distinguished the boundary between the two categories was important so that the people would maintain respect for God's holiness.

---

[a]2 The common cubit was about 1 1/2 feet (about 0.5 meter).
[b]4 Septuagint and Syriac; Hebrew *and one cubit*   [c]10 Septuagint; Hebrew *Eastward*   [d]16 See Septuagint of verse 17; Hebrew *rods*; also in verses 18 and 19.   [e]17 Septuagint; Hebrew *rods*

The Glory Returns to the Temple

43 Then the man brought me to the gate facing east, ²and I saw the glory[D] of the God of Israel coming from the east. His voice was like the roar of rushing waters, and the land was radiant with his glory. ³The vision[D] I saw was like the vision I had seen when he[a] came to destroy the city and like the visions I had seen by the Kebar River, and I fell facedown. ⁴The glory of the LORD entered the temple through the gate facing east. ⁵Then the Spirit lifted me up and brought me into the inner court, and the glory of the LORD filled the temple.

⁶While the man was standing beside me, I heard someone speaking to me from inside the temple. ⁷He said: "Son of man[D], this is the place of my throne and the place for the soles of my feet. This is where I will live among the Israelites forever. The house of Israel will never again defile my holy name—neither they nor their kings—by their prostitution[b] and the lifeless idols[D c] of their kings at their high places[D]. ⁸When they placed their threshold next to my threshold and their doorposts beside my doorposts, with only a wall between me and them, they defiled my holy name by their detestable practices. So I destroyed them in my anger. ⁹Now let them put away from me their prostitution and the lifeless idols of their kings, and I will live among them forever.

¹⁰"Son of man, describe the temple to the people of Israel, that they may be ashamed of their sins. Let them consider the plan, ¹¹and if they are ashamed of all they have done, make known to them the design of the temple—its arrangement, its exits and entrances—its whole design and all its regulations[d] and laws. Write these down before them so that they may be faithful to its design and follow all its regulations.

¹²"This is the law of the temple: All the surrounding area on top of the mountain will be most holy. Such is the law of the temple.

The Altar

¹³"These are the measurements of the altar in long cubits[D], that cubit being a cubit[e] and a handbreadth[f]: Its gutter is a cubit deep and a cubit wide, with a rim of one span[g] around the edge. And this is the height of the altar: ¹⁴From the gutter on the ground up to the lower ledge it is two cubits high and a cubit wide, and from the smaller ledge up to the larger ledge it is four cubits high and a cubit wide. ¹⁵The altar hearth is four cubits high, and four horns project upward from the hearth. ¹⁶The altar hearth is square, twelve cubits long and twelve cubits wide. ¹⁷The upper ledge also is square, fourteen cubits long and fourteen cubits wide, with a rim of half a cubit and a gutter of a cubit all around. The steps of the altar face east."

¹⁸Then he said to me, "Son of man, this is what the Sovereign LORD says: These will be the regulations for sacrificing burnt offerings[D] and sprinkling blood upon the altar when it is built: ¹⁹You are to give a young bull as a

Glory of the LORD (43:4–5)

A physical manifestation of God's presence and power. Prior to the time God appeared in the flesh through Jesus Christ, he occasionally revealed his glory in the tabernacle, the temple and so on. Also see *How did the people see the glory of the LORD?* (Lev. 9:23).

What were the *lifeless idols of their kings?* (43:7,9)

This may refer to the pagan idols to which various kings had erected altars. Another view is that this refers to the *corpses* of the kings (see NIV text note). Fourteen kings of Judah were buried in royal sepulchers next to the sanctuary. It may be that God wanted their graves removed so that the temple and God's holy name would not be defiled.

Did God promise to live in the temple forever? (43:9)

This promise of God's continual presence does not have to be tied to any historical temple. The temple in Jerusalem was destroyed by the Babylonians in the sixth century B.C.—after God's glory departed from it (10:4,18; 11:22–23). Rebuilt after the exile and later enlarged by Herod, the temple was again destroyed in A.D. 70. This promise, therefore, probably refers to the millennial temple where God will dwell forever with his people.

How would a blueprint shame Israel? (43:10)

Describing the details of the temple reminded the people of God's holiness—and how much they had lost. If they could once again see the difference between what was holy and what was ordinary, they would perhaps be moved to repent. Ezekiel hoped to rekindle within the people a desire for the fellowship with God that they had lost because of sin.

Was this temple ever built? (43:11)

Though a temple was built when the exiles returned from Babylon (Ezra 6:14–15), there is no evidence to show that it was this particular one. Some think these plans were at least consulted at that time; others say these plans are for a temple to be rebuilt after Christ returns.

What makes land holy? (43:12)

See *What was holy and what was common?* (42:20).

Burnt offering (43:18)

See *What did the guilt offerings do that other offerings couldn't?* (Lev. 5:15).

---

a3 Some Hebrew manuscripts and Vulgate; most Hebrew manuscripts *I*
b7 Or *their spiritual adultery*; also in verse 9   *c7* Or *the corpses*;
also in verse 9   *d11* Some Hebrew manuscripts and Septuagint;
most Hebrew manuscripts *regulations and its whole design*
e13 The common cubit was about 1 1/2 feet (about 0.5 meter).
f13 That is, about 3 inches (about 8 centimeters)   *g13* That is,
about 9 inches (about 22 centimeters)

Fellowship offerings (43:27)

See *How were some offerings for fellowship?* (Lev. 3:1).

Who was the prince? (44:3)

The prince, mentioned prominently throughout the remainder of Ezekiel, was thought by the rabbis to be a prediction of the coming Messiah. This seems unlikely since he would have no priestly rights, would need a sin offering (45:22) and would have sons (46:16)—none of which would be true of the Messiah. Some think the prince will be a descendant of David —a head of state responsible for the administration of government and accountable to the Messiah.

Why pay special attention to the entrances and exits? (44:5)

Ezekiel is to watch the temple gates so that the purity of God's house would not be compromised by allowing in people and practices that would defile. Ezekiel's strong words to *the rebellious house of Israel* (v. 6) were intended to bring them to the place of repentance.

How do you circumcise a heart? (44:7,9)

See *What does it mean to circumcise your hearts?* (Jer. 4:4).

Could non-Jews worship God? (44:7–9)

Yes, but only with certain prerequisites. Foreigners were allowed to bring offerings (Lev. 17:8; Num. 15:14) but not enter the sanctuary. Foreigners could be circumcised, however and enter the temple courts after having accepted God's covenant.

Why could the priests *alone* serve God? (44:16)

The priests inherited their responsibility for temple service because God wanted his worship led by those prepared for the task. However, mere heredity was not enough. Anyone with physical flaws or disabilities was exempted from service. So were those who were disobedient. All of these restrictions helped the people respect and fear their holy God. Now believers can present themselves as *living sacrifices, holy and pleasing to God* (Romans 12:1).

sin offering[D] to the priests[D], who are Levites[D], of the family of Zadok, who come near to minister before me, declares the Sovereign LORD. **20**You are to take some of its blood and put it on the four horns of the altar and on the four corners of the upper ledge and all around the rim, and so purify[D] the altar and make atonement[D] for it. **21**You are to take the bull for the sin offering and burn it in the designated part of the temple area outside the sanctuary.

22"On the second day you are to offer a male goat without defect for a sin offering, and the altar is to be purified as it was purified with the bull. **23**When you have finished purifying it, you are to offer a young bull and a ram from the flock, both without defect. **24**You are to offer them before the LORD, and the priests are to sprinkle salt on them and sacrifice[D] them as a burnt offering[D] to the LORD.

25"For seven days you are to provide a male goat daily for a sin offering; you are also to provide a young bull and a ram from the flock, both without defect. **26**For seven days they are to make atonement for the altar and cleanse it; thus they will dedicate it. **27**At the end of these days, from the eighth day on, the priests are to present your burnt offerings and fellowship offerings[a] on the altar. Then I will accept you, declares the Sovereign LORD."

The Prince, the Levites, the Priests

44 Then the man brought me back to the outer gate of the sanctuary, the one facing east, and it was shut. **2**The LORD said to me, "This gate is to remain shut. It must not be opened; no one may enter through it. It is to remain shut because the LORD, the God of Israel, has entered through it. **3**The prince himself is the only one who may sit inside the gateway to eat in the presence of the LORD. He is to enter by way of the portico of the gateway and go out the same way."

4Then the man brought me by way of the north gate to the front of the temple. I looked and saw the glory[D] of the LORD filling the temple of the LORD, and I fell facedown.

5The LORD said to me, "Son of man[D], look carefully, listen closely and give attention to everything I tell you concerning all the regulations regarding the temple of the LORD. Give attention to the entrance of the temple and all the exits of the sanctuary. **6**Say to the rebellious house of Israel, 'This is what the Sovereign LORD says: Enough of your detestable practices, O house of Israel! **7**In addition to all your other detestable practices, you brought foreigners uncircumcised[D] in heart and flesh into my sanctuary, desecrating[D] my temple while you offered me food, fat and blood, and you broke my covenant[D]. **8**Instead of carrying out your duty in regard to my holy things, you put others in charge of my sanctuary. **9**This is what the Sovereign LORD says: No foreigner uncircumcised in heart and flesh is to enter my sanctuary, not even the foreigners who live among the Israelites.

10" 'The Levites who went far from me when Israel went astray and who wandered from me after their idols[D] must bear the consequences of their sin. **11**They may serve in my sanctuary, having charge of the gates of the temple and serving in it; they may slaughter the burnt

a27 Traditionally *peace offerings*

offerings^D and sacrifices^D for the people and stand before the people and serve them. 12But because they served them in the presence of their idols^D and made the house of Israel fall into sin, therefore I have sworn with uplifted hand that they must bear the consequences of their sin, declares the Sovereign LORD. 13They are not to come near to serve me as priests^D or come near any of my holy things or my most holy offerings; they must bear the shame of their detestable practices. 14Yet I will put them in charge of the duties of the temple and all the work that is to be done in it.

15" 'But the priests, who are Levites and descendants of Zadok and who faithfully carried out the duties of my sanctuary when the Israelites went astray from me, are to come near to minister before me; they are to stand before me to offer sacrifices of fat and blood, declares the Sovereign LORD. 16They alone are to enter my sanctuary; they alone are to come near my table to minister before me and perform my service.

17" 'When they enter the gates of the inner court, they are to wear linen clothes; they must not wear any woolen garment while ministering at the gates of the inner court or inside the temple. 18They are to wear linen turbans on their heads and linen undergarments around their waists. They must not wear anything that makes them perspire. 19When they go out into the outer court where the people are, they are to take off the clothes they have been ministering in and are to leave them in the sacred^D rooms, and put on other clothes, so that they do not consecrate^D the people by means of their garments.

20" 'They must not shave their heads or let their hair grow long, but they are to keep the hair of their heads trimmed. 21No priest is to drink wine when he enters the inner court. 22They must not marry widows or divorced women; they may marry only virgins of Israelite descent or widows of priests. 23They are to teach my people the difference between the holy and the common and show them how to distinguish between the unclean^D and the clean.

24" 'In any dispute, the priests are to serve as judges and decide it according to my ordinances. They are to keep my laws and my decrees for all my appointed feasts, and they are to keep my Sabbaths^D holy.

25" 'A priest must not defile himself by going near a dead person; however, if the dead person was his father or mother, son or daughter, brother or unmarried sister, then he may defile himself. 26After he is cleansed, he must wait seven days. 27On the day he goes into the inner court of the sanctuary to minister in the sanctuary, he is to offer a sin offering^D for himself, declares the Sovereign LORD.

28" 'I am to be the only inheritance the priests have. You are to give them no possession in Israel; I will be their possession. 29They will eat the grain offerings^D, the sin offerings and the guilt offerings; and everything in Israel devoted^a to the LORD will belong to them. 30The best of all the firstfruits^D and of all your special gifts will belong to the priests. You are to give them the first portion of your ground meal so that a blessing may rest on your household. 31The priests must not eat anything, bird or animal, found dead or torn by wild animals.

---

^a29 The Hebrew term refers to the irrevocable giving over of things or persons to the LORD.

What was wrong with wool? (44:17)

God instructed the priests to wear linen (Exodus 39:27–29), apparently to prevent perspiration caused by woolen garments (v. 18). Apparently sweat was associated with uncleanness.

What if a priest started to sweat? (44:18)

Perspiration would make a priest ceremonially unclean. Though this may seem excessive to us today, it was another illustration of how seriously they were to take approaching the holy God. In their dress, appearance and personal hygiene, priests were to be clean.

Why wouldn't God want the people consecrated? (44:19)

It would have been good to have a consecrated people. The problem was that it would have meant that the priests' garments would become contaminated—unusable in the service of the Lord. They were to separate their priestly functions and clothing from their common activities. As with the temple itself, God wanted a clear distinction between the holy and the common. In addition, it may have been that if the people became ceremonially consecrated, they would have been required to interrupt their lives with further ritual obligations.

How should we apply these instructions today? (44:20–23)

The priests were to live for God alone. They were to be examples of actual and ritual purity, in every area of life—from haircuts to marriages. Regulations that seem meaningless to our culture today taught the Israelites something about God's holiness. Still, they remind us that leaders, no matter what era they live in, bear greater responsibilities than those they lead.

Does God have double standards? (44:20–25)

In a certain sense, yes. God requires more of those who minister on his behalf or hold places of spiritual leadership. However, this must be qualified in two ways: (1) This does not mean that failures cannot be forgiven. They can. (2) Though only certain members of the Levites could be priests in the Old Testament, today God calls all believers to serve him as priests (1 Peter 2:5; Rev. 1:6). Though church leaders are to meet certain qualifications (1 Tim. 3:1–13) and more is expected of them (James 3:1), all believers are called to live holy lives (1 Peter 1:15).

How would death defile someone? (44:25)

It may seem unrealistic for God to insulate priests from death, a natural part of life. But death was linked closely with sin, the consequence for Adam's sin (Gen. 2:17). To remain ritually clean, priests could not come into contact with anything that directly resulted from sin. Still, a priest could temporarily defile himself to make funeral preparations for the members of his own family.

Why couldn't the priests own land? (44:28)

There was nothing inherently wrong with owning land. But three factors may have been behind this requirement for the priests: (1) It taught absolute dependence on God. (2) It allowed people to show their generosity to God by caring for his servants. (3) It freed the priests of materialistic responsibilities so they could serve the Lord more completely.

How had princes cheated the people? (45:8–12)

The people often had been cheated and oppressed in the past by their rulers. Some lost land, others were impoverished by excessive taxes or exorbitant lending rates, still others even lost their freedom. See *Why were some Jews selling their sons and daughters into slavery?* (Neh. 5:5) and *Were the powerful and elite the cause behind the nation's problems?* (Micah 2:1–2).

Why not just say 60 shekels? (45:12)

It's not entirely clear. Perhaps these different amounts represented various weights commonly used on scales at the time; this would have been Ezekiel's call for honest, exacting standards. It's possible this may have had something to do with a devaluation of the shekel (from 50 to 60 per minas; see NIV text note) to correlate more closely to Babylonian values.

What do these offerings have to do with us? (45:13–25)

Though we do not live under the conditions described here, we would be wrong to conclude that there is nothing of value in this text for us today. These instructions give us insight into the character and holiness of God, principles that never change. We are still to honor God with all our being and with the best of what we have to offer (Romans 12:1).

Division of the Land

45 " 'When you allot the land as an inheritance, you are to present to the LORD a portion of the land as a sacred^D district, 25,000 cubits^D long and 20,000^a cubits wide; the entire area will be holy. ²Of this, a section 500 cubits square is to be for the sanctuary, with 50 cubits around it for open land. ³In the sacred district, measure off a section 25,000 cubits^b long and 10,000 cubits^c wide. In it will be the sanctuary, the Most Holy Place^D. ⁴It will be the sacred portion of the land for the priests^D, who minister in the sanctuary and who draw near to minister before the LORD. It will be a place for their houses as well as a holy place for the sanctuary. ⁵An area 25,000 cubits long and 10,000 cubits wide will belong to the Levites^D, who serve in the temple, as their possession for towns to live in.^d

⁶" 'You are to give the city as its property an area 5,000 cubits wide and 25,000 cubits long, adjoining the sacred portion; it will belong to the whole house of Israel.

⁷" 'The prince will have the land bordering each side of the area formed by the sacred district and the property of the city. It will extend westward from the west side and eastward from the east side, running lengthwise from the western to the eastern border parallel to one of the tribal portions. ⁸This land will be his possession in Israel. And my princes will no longer oppress my people but will allow the house of Israel to possess the land according to their tribes.

⁹" 'This is what the Sovereign LORD says: You have gone far enough, O princes of Israel! Give up your violence and oppression and do what is just and right. Stop dispossessing my people, declares the Sovereign LORD. ¹⁰You are to use accurate scales, an accurate ephah^e and an accurate bath.^f ¹¹The ephah and the bath are to be the same size, the bath containing a tenth of a homer^g and the ephah a tenth of a homer; the homer is to be the standard measure for both. ¹²The shekel^Dh is to consist of twenty gerahs. Twenty shekels plus twenty-five shekels plus fifteen shekels equal one mina.^i

Offerings and Holy Days

¹³" 'This is the special gift you are to offer: a sixth of an ephah from each homer of wheat and a sixth of an ephah from each homer of barley. ¹⁴The prescribed portion of oil, measured by the bath, is a tenth of a bath from each cor (which consists of ten baths or one homer, for ten baths are equivalent to a homer). ¹⁵Also one sheep is to be taken from every flock of two hundred from the well-watered pastures of Israel. These will be used for the grain offerings^D, burnt offerings^D and fellowship offerings^Dj to make atonement^D for the people, declares the Sovereign LORD. ¹⁶All the people of the land will participate in this special gift for the use of the prince in Israel. ¹⁷It will be the duty of the prince to provide the burnt offerings, grain offerings and drink offerings at the festivals, the

---

a1 Septuagint (see also verses 3 and 5 and 48:9); Hebrew *10,000*
b3 That is, about 7 miles (about 12 kilometers)   *c3* That is, about 3 miles (about 5 kilometers)   *d5* Septuagint; Hebrew *temple; they will have as their possession 20 rooms*   *e10* An ephah was a dry measure.   *f10* A bath was a liquid measure.   *g11* A homer was a dry measure.   *h12* A shekel weighed about 2/5 ounce (about 11.5 grams).   *i12* That is, 60 shekels; the common mina was 50 shekels.   *j15* Traditionally *peace offerings*; also in verse 17

New Moons and the Sabbaths[D]—at all the appointed feasts of the house of Israel. He will provide the sin offerings[D], grain offerings[D], burnt offerings[D] and fellowship offerings[D] to make atonement[D] for the house of Israel.

18" 'This is what the Sovereign LORD says: In the first month on the first day you are to take a young bull without defect and purify[D] the sanctuary. **19**The priest[D] is to take some of the blood of the sin offering and put it on the doorposts of the temple, on the four corners of the upper ledge of the altar and on the gateposts of the inner court. **20**You are to do the same on the seventh day of the month for anyone who sins unintentionally or through ignorance; so you are to make atonement for the temple.

21" 'In the first month on the fourteenth day you are to observe the Passover, a feast lasting seven days, during which you shall eat bread made without yeast[D]. **22**On that day the prince is to provide a bull as a sin offering for himself and for all the people of the land. **23**Every day during the seven days of the Feast he is to provide seven bulls and seven rams without defect as a burnt offering to the LORD, and a male goat for a sin offering. **24**He is to provide as a grain offering an ephah for each bull and an ephah for each ram, along with a hin[a] of oil for each ephah.

25" 'During the seven days of the Feast, which begins in the seventh month on the fifteenth day, he is to make the same provision for sin offerings, burnt offerings, grain offerings and oil.

46 " 'This is what the Sovereign LORD says: The gate of the inner court facing east is to be shut on the six working days, but on the Sabbath day and on the day of the New Moon it is to be opened. **2**The prince is to enter from the outside through the portico of the gateway and stand by the gatepost. The priests are to sacrifice his burnt offering and his fellowship offerings.[b] He is to worship at the threshold of the gateway and then go out, but the gate will not be shut until evening. **3**On the Sabbaths and New Moons the people of the land are to worship in the presence of the LORD at the entrance to that gateway. **4**The burnt offering the prince brings to the LORD on the Sabbath day is to be six male lambs and a ram, all without defect. **5**The grain offering given with the ram is to be an ephah,[c] and the grain offering with the lambs is to be as much as he pleases, along with a hin[a] of oil for each ephah. **6**On the day of the New Moon he is to offer a young bull, six lambs and a ram, all without defect. **7**He is to provide as a grain offering one ephah with the bull, one ephah with the ram, and with the lambs as much as he wants to give, along with a hin of oil with each ephah. **8**When the prince enters, he is to go in through the portico of the gateway, and he is to come out the same way.

9" 'When the people of the land come before the LORD at the appointed feasts, whoever enters by the north gate to worship is to go out the south gate; and whoever enters by the south gate is to go out the north gate. No one is to return through the gate by which he entered, but each is to go out the opposite gate. **10**The prince is to be among them, going in when they go in and going out when they go out.

---

[a]24,5 That is, probably about 4 quarts (about 4 liters)
[b]2 Traditionally *peace offerings*; also in verse 12   [c]5 That is, probably about 3/5 bushel (about 22 liters)

SCRIPTURE LINK (45:21) *Passover*
See Exodus 12:1–30.

What made the eastern gate unique from the others? (46:1–3)

The eastern gate was the one through which the glory of the Lord entered (43:4). No human would be allowed to enter the east gate since that would contaminate it. The outer gate facing east was permanently closed (44:2). The inner gate facing east was opened only on the Sabbath to allow the prince to enter it for worship.

New moon (46:1)

See *New Moon festival* (1 Samuel 20:5).

Why exit by a different gate? (46:9)

Perhaps simply to prevent congestion and confusion among the huge crowds gathered for festivals. Such instructions would keep the pedestrian traffic moving along.

11" 'At the festivals and the appointed feasts, the grain offeringᴰ is to be an ephah with a bull, an ephah with a ram, and with the lambs as much as one pleases, along with a hin of oil for each ephah. 12When the prince provides a freewill offering to the LORD—whether a burnt offeringᴰ or fellowship offeringsᴰ—the gate facing east is to be opened for him. He shall offer his burnt offering or his fellowship offerings as he does on the Sabbath day. Then he shall go out, and after he has gone out, the gate will be shut.

13" 'Every day you are to provide a year-old lamb without defect for a burnt offering to the LORD; morning by morning you shall provide it. 14You are also to provide with it morning by morning a grain offering, consisting of a sixth of an ephah with a third of a hin of oil to moisten the flour. The presenting of this grain offering to the LORD is a lasting ordinance. 15So the lamb and the grain offering and the oil shall be provided morning by morning for a regular burnt offering.

16" 'This is what the Sovereign LORD says: If the prince makes a gift from his inheritance to one of his sons, it will also belong to his descendants; it is to be their property by inheritance. 17If, however, he makes a gift from his inheritance to one of his servants, the servant may keep it until the year of freedom; then it will revert to the prince. His inheritance belongs to his sons only; it is theirs. 18The prince must not take any of the inheritance of the people, driving them off their property. He is to give his sons their inheritance out of his own property, so that none of my people will be separated from his property.' "

19Then the man brought me through the entrance at the side of the gate to the sacredᴰ rooms facing north, which belonged to the priestsᴰ, and showed me a place at the western end. 20He said to me, "This is the place where the priests will cook the guilt offering and the sin offeringᴰ and bake the grain offering, to avoid bringing them into the outer court and consecratingᴰ the people."

21He then brought me to the outer court and led me around to its four corners, and I saw in each corner another court. 22In the four corners of the outer court were enclosedᵃ courts, forty cubitsᴰ long and thirty cubits wide; each of the courts in the four corners was the same size. 23Around the inside of each of the four courts was a ledge of stone, with places for fire built all around under the ledge. 24He said to me, "These are the kitchens where those who minister at the temple will cook the sacrificesᴰ of the people."

The River From the Temple

47 The man brought me back to the entrance of the temple, and I saw water coming out from under the threshold of the temple toward the east (for the temple faced east). The water was coming down from under the south side of the temple, south of the altar. 2He then brought me out through the north gate and led me around the outside to the outer gate facing east, and the water was flowing from the south side.

3As the man went eastward with a measuring lineᴰ in his hand, he measured off a thousand cubitsᵇ and then led me through water that was ankle-deep. 4He measured

---

Lasting ordinance (46:14)
May mean an ordinance of *long duration*, not necessarily a never-ending law. Some say this ordinance is intended for the Messianic age—the Millennium. Also see **Lasting ordinance** (Lev. 3:17).

Year of freedom (46:17)
Also known as the Year of Jubilee. Every 50th year—to recognize God's ownership of the land—all slaves were freed and all property reverted to its original owner (Lev. 25:23). Some expect 20 jubilees during the Millennium. Others see here simply an allusion to God's people once again living by God's ways in the promised land. Still others think the *year of freedom* may symbolize spiritual freedom from Satan and sin. Also see **Jubilee** (Lev. 25:10).

Why wouldn't God want the people consecrated? (46:20)
See *Why wouldn't God want the people consecrated?* (44:19).

Why were sacrifices cooked in separate kitchens? (46:24)
Fellowship offerings were eaten by both the priests (as God's representatives) and by those who offered the sacrifices. This seems to suggest that the portions for the people were to be cooked separately from the portions for the priests, perhaps another way that God made a distinction between holy things and common things. See *What was holy and what was common?* (42:20). Keeping the people separate from the cooking sacrifices kept them from becoming consecrated in a ceremonial sense. See *Why wouldn't God want the people consecrated?* (44:19).

What did this river symbolize? (47:1–12)
Some think these waters symbolized the blessings of God that flowed from the temple. One view is that they parallel the eternal blessings described by John (Rev. 22:1–5). Another view is that these waters represent both physical prosperity and spiritual blessings that God will send during the 1,000-year millennial period. Still others see a spiritual interpretation similar to the living waters that flow within believers (John 7:38).

Why wade in the river? (47:3–6)
The description of this river defies all natural explanation. The river begins as a trickle, but before it reaches the Dead Sea, it is a deep river. Without any tributaries and in such a short distance, this river is clearly seen to be a miraculous stream. By wading in the river, Ezekiel demonstrated the greatness of God's coming blessings when they would be returned to the land and the Messiah would be with them.

ᵃ22 The meaning of the Hebrew for this word is uncertain.
ᵇ3 That is, about 1,500 feet (about 450 meters)

off another thousand cubits[D] and led me through water that was knee-deep. He measured off another thousand and led me through water that was up to the waist. **5**He measured off another thousand, but now it was a river that I could not cross, because the water had risen and was deep enough to swim in—a river that no one could cross. **6**He asked me, "Son of man[D], do you see this?"

Then he led me back to the bank of the river. **7**When I arrived there, I saw a great number of trees on each side of the river. **8**He said to me, "This water flows toward the eastern region and goes down into the Arabah,[a] where it enters the Sea.[b] When it empties into the Sea,[b] the water there becomes fresh. **9**Swarms of living creatures will live wherever the river flows. There will be large numbers of fish, because this water flows there and makes the salt water fresh; so where the river flows everything will live. **10**Fishermen will stand along the shore; from En Gedi to En Eglaim there will be places for spreading nets. The fish will be of many kinds—like the fish of the Great Sea.[c] **11**But the swamps and marshes will not become fresh; they will be left for salt. **12**Fruit trees of all kinds will grow on both banks of the river. Their leaves will not wither, nor will their fruit fail. Every month they will bear, because the water from the sanctuary flows to them. Their fruit will serve for food and their leaves for healing."

The Boundaries of the Land

13This is what the Sovereign LORD says: "These are the boundaries by which you are to divide the land for an inheritance among the twelve tribes of Israel, with two portions for Joseph. **14**You are to divide it equally among them. Because I swore with uplifted hand to give it to your forefathers, this land will become your inheritance.

15"This is to be the boundary of the land:

"On the north side it will run from the Great Sea by the Hethlon road past Lebo[d] Hamath to Zedad, **16**Berothah[e] and Sibraim (which lies on the border between Damascus and Hamath), as far as Hazer Hatticon, which is on the border of Hauran. **17**The boundary will extend from the sea to Hazar Enan,[f] along the northern border of Damascus, with the border of Hamath to the north. This will be the north boundary.
18"On the east side the boundary will run between Hauran and Damascus, along the Jordan between Gilead and the land of Israel, to the eastern sea and as far as Tamar.[g] This will be the east boundary.
19"On the south side it will run from Tamar as far as the waters of Meribah Kadesh, then along the Wadi ˩of Egypt˩ to the Great Sea. This will be the south boundary.
20"On the west side, the Great Sea will be the boundary to a point opposite Lebo[h] Hamath. This will be the west boundary.

21"You are to distribute this land among yourselves according to the tribes of Israel. **22**You are to allot it as an inheritance for yourselves and for the aliens[D] who have

---

a8 Or the Jordan Valley   b8 That is, the Dead Sea   c10 That is, the Mediterranean; also in verses 15, 19 and 20   d15 Or past the entrance to   e15,16 See Septuagint and Ezekiel 48:1; Hebrew road to go into Zedad, 16Hamath, Berothah   f17 Hebrew Enon, a variant of Enan   g18 Septuagint and Syriac; Hebrew Israel. You will measure to the eastern sea   h20 Or opposite the entrance to

Why should the tribe of Joseph get twice as much? (47:13)
Typically, the oldest son received the birthright which consisted of double the amount of inheritance received by the other sons. Originally, the birthright belonged to Reuben but he lost it by defiling his father's bed (Gen. 35:22; 49:3–4). So Jacob promised the birthright to his favorite son, Joseph (Gen. 48:5–6,22; 49:22–26).

Is Israel within these borders today? (47:15–20)
No. But people disagree as to whether this means that Israel has a divine right to this land and will some day possess it. Some say that the promise of the land required their obedience and has thus been forfeited because of their disobedience. Others say that the promise will be fulfilled when the Messiah returns and the nation of Israel is given a new heart.

Were these instructions to help the returning captives resettle in Israel? (47:21–23)
The resettlement of the exiles in the land of Israel is similar to that commanded in Numbers 34:1–12. However, many believe this was intended to guide those from all over the earth who would be joining the Messianic kingdom. There were some key differences from the law prior to the exile—most notably, foreigners would be able to own land and have the right of full inheritance.

How could foreigners become citizens of Israel? (47:22–23)
God had always been concerned for the foreigner (Lev. 19:34). Many of them had joined God's people and agreed to the covenant of circumcision. Here God expanded his concern to make it clear that non-Israelites could participate in the blessings of the Millennium—symbolized by the right to acquire land.

settled among you and who have children. You are to consider them as native-born Israelites; along with you they are to be allotted an inheritance among the tribes of Israel. 23In whatever tribe the alienD settles, there you are to give him his inheritance," declares the Sovereign LORD.

The Division of the Land

48 "These are the tribes, listed by name: At the northern frontier, Dan will have one portion; it will follow the Hethlon road to Leboª Hamath; Hazar Enan and the northern border of Damascus next to Hamath will be part of its border from the east side to the west side.

2"Asher will have one portion; it will border the territory of Dan from east to west.

3"Naphtali will have one portion; it will border the territory of Asher from east to west.

4"Manasseh will have one portion; it will border the territory of Naphtali from east to west.

5"Ephraim will have one portion; it will border the territory of Manasseh from east to west.

6"Reuben will have one portion; it will border the territory of Ephraim from east to west.

7"Judah will have one portion; it will border the territory of Reuben from east to west.

8"Bordering the territory of Judah from east to west will be the portion you are to present as a special gift. It will be 25,000 cubitsDb wide, and its length from east to west will equal one of the tribal portions; the sanctuary will be in the center of it.

9"The special portion you are to offer to the LORD will be 25,000 cubits long and 10,000 cubitsc wide. 10This will be the sacredD portion for the priestsD. It will be 25,000 cubits long on the north side, 10,000 cubits wide on the west side, 10,000 cubits wide on the east side and 25,000 cubits long on the south side. In the center of it will be the sanctuary of the LORD. 11This will be for the consecratedD priests, the Zadokites, who were faithful in serving me and did not go astray as the LevitesD did when the Israelites went astray. 12It will be a special gift to them from the sacred portion of the land, a most holy portion, bordering the territory of the Levites.

13"Alongside the territory of the priests, the Levites will have an allotment 25,000 cubits long and 10,000 cubits wide. Its total length will be 25,000 cubits and its width 10,000 cubits. 14They must not sell or exchange any of it. This is the best of the land and must not pass into other hands, because it is holy to the LORD.

15"The remaining area, 5,000 cubits wide and 25,000 cubits long, will be for the common use of the city, for houses and for pastureland. The city will be in the center of it 16and will have these measurements: the north side 4,500 cubits, the south side 4,500 cubits, the east side 4,500 cubits, and the west side 4,500 cubits. 17The pastureland for the city will be 250 cubits on the north, 250 cubits on the south, 250 cubits on the east, and 250 cubits on the west. 18What remains of the area, bordering on the sacred portion and running the length of it, will be 10,000 cubits on the east side and 10,000 cubits on the west side. Its produce will supply food for the workers of the city. 19The workers from the city who

---

Is this some sort of commune?
(48:18–19)
This is figurative, prophetic language. It pictures people who are connected both by their relationship to the Lord and by their work responsibilities. Some see this as the ideal community to be established in the Messianic age —a city near the temple.

ª1 Or to the entrance to   b8 That is, about 7 miles (about 12 kilometers)   c9 That is, about 3 miles (about 5 kilometers)

farm it will come from all the tribes of Israel. **20**The entire portion will be a square, 25,000 cubits[D] on each side. As a special gift you will set aside the sacred[D] portion, along with the property of the city.

21"What remains on both sides of the area formed by the sacred portion and the city property will belong to the prince. It will extend eastward from the 25,000 cubits of the sacred portion to the eastern border, and westward from the 25,000 cubits to the western border. Both these areas running the length of the tribal portions will belong to the prince, and the sacred portion with the temple sanctuary will be in the center of them. **22**So the property of the Levites[D] and the property of the city will lie in the center of the area that belongs to the prince. The area belonging to the prince will lie between the border of Judah and the border of Benjamin.

23"As for the rest of the tribes: Benjamin will have one portion; it will extend from the east side to the west side.

24"Simeon will have one portion; it will border the territory of Benjamin from east to west.

25"Issachar will have one portion; it will border the territory of Simeon from east to west.

26"Zebulun will have one portion; it will border the territory of Issachar from east to west.

27"Gad will have one portion; it will border the territory of Zebulun from east to west.

28"The southern boundary of Gad will run south from Tamar to the waters of Meribah Kadesh, then along the Wadi ⌊of Egypt⌋ to the Great Sea.[a]

29"This is the land you are to allot as an inheritance to the tribes of Israel, and these will be their portions," declares the Sovereign LORD.

The Gates of the City

30"These will be the exits of the city: Beginning on the north side, which is 4,500 cubits long, **31**the gates of the city will be named after the tribes of Israel. The three gates on the north side will be the gate of Reuben, the gate of Judah and the gate of Levi.

32"On the east side, which is 4,500 cubits long, will be three gates: the gate of Joseph, the gate of Benjamin and the gate of Dan.

33"On the south side, which measures 4,500 cubits, will be three gates: the gate of Simeon, the gate of Issachar and the gate of Zebulun.

34"On the west side, which is 4,500 cubits long, will be three gates: the gate of Gad, the gate of Asher and the gate of Naphtali.

35"The distance all around will be 18,000 cubits.

"And the name of the city from that time on will be:

THE LORD IS THERE."

SCRIPTURE LINK (48:30–34)
Twelve gates appear again in Rev. 21:12–13.

Was this Jerusalem? (48:35)
Yes. But Jerusalem is given a new name to demonstrate that the city has been changed. Hebrew culture would often indicate a shift in one's character or circumstance by a name change. Jerusalem's new name announces that God once again lives within it.

---

*a*28 That is, the Mediterranean

DANIEL

Why read this book?

If you've ever wished God would come right out and show himself, boosting your faith and striking awe into the hearts of unbelievers, you'll appreciate this book. The miraculous rescues, the humbling of pagan kings, the amazing predictions of how God would depose tyrants—all display God's power and his willingness to use it.

Who wrote this book?

Daniel—whose name means *God's judge, God's judgment* or *God is my judge.* Possibly a member of Judah's royal family, he was taken captive to Babylon around 605 B.C.

To whom was it written and why?

The people of Judah, who were exiles in Babylon. Daniel encouraged them by reminding them of God's ultimate control over events—God would soon restore his people and his temple.

When was it written?

Critics contend it was written after many of the predicted events it describes had occurred. But others, who believe God can supernaturally reveal future events, place it between 536 and 530 B.C.—soon after Cyrus captured Babylon in 539 B.C.

What was happening in the world at this time?

The Babylonian empire (626–539 B.C.) had replaced Assyria as the world's superpower. Nebuchadnezzar's Babylonian army had conquered Judah, taking thousands of God's people to Babylon, while others fled to Egypt. Jerusalem and the temple had been looted and burned.

What to look for in Daniel:

God's faithfulness and power. See how he kept his promise to punish his disobedient people, but he also kept his promise never to desert them. Note how God turned leaders and empires upside down at will, continually proving his superiority over all other gods.

When did these things happen?

TIME LINE	1400BC	1300	1200	1100	1000	900	800	700	600	500	400
Jeremiah's ministry in Judah (c.626–585 B.C.)											
Daniel's exile in Babylon (c.605–536 B.C.)											
Fall of Jerusalem (586 B.C.)											
Daniel in the lions' den (c.539 B.C.)											
First return of exiles to Jerusalem (538 B.C.)											
Book of Daniel written (c.536–530 B.C.)											
End of Daniel's ministry (c.536 B.C.)											

Daniel's Training in Babylon

1 In the third year of the reign of Jehoiakim king of Judah, Nebuchadnezzar king of Babylon came to Jerusalemᴰ and besieged it. ²And the Lord delivered Jehoiakim king of Judah into his hand, along with some of the articles from the temple of God. These he carried off to the temple of his god in Babyloniaª and put in the treasure house of his god.

³Then the king ordered Ashpenaz, chief of his court officials, to bring in some of the Israelites from the royal family and the nobility— ⁴young men without any physical defect, handsome, showing aptitude for every kind of learning, well informed, quick to understand, and qualified to serve in the king's palace. He was to teach them the language and literature of the Babylonians.ᵇ ⁵The king assigned them a daily amount of food and wine from the king's table. They were to be trained for three years, and after that they were to enter the king's service.

⁶Among these were some from Judah: Daniel, Hananiah, Mishael and Azariah. ⁷The chief official gave them new names: to Daniel, the name Belteshazzar; to Hananiah, Shadrach; to Mishael, Meshach; and to Azariah, Abednego.

⁸But Daniel resolved not to defile himself with the royal food and wine, and he asked the chief official for permission not to defile himself this way. ⁹Now God had caused the official to show favor and sympathy to Daniel, ¹⁰but the official told Daniel, "I am afraid of my lord the king, who has assigned yourᶜ food and drink. Why should he see you looking worse than the other young men your age? The king would then have my head because of you."

¹¹Daniel then said to the guard whom the chief official had appointed over Daniel, Hananiah, Mishael and Azariah, ¹²"Please test your servants for ten days: Give us nothing but vegetables to eat and water to drink. ¹³Then compare our appearance with that of the young men who eat the royal food, and treat your servants in accordance with what you see." ¹⁴So he agreed to this and tested them for ten days.

¹⁵At the end of the ten days they looked healthier and better nourished than any of the young men who ate the royal food. ¹⁶So the guard took away their choice food and the wine they were to drink and gave them vegetables instead.

¹⁷To these four young men God gave knowledge and understanding of all kinds of literature and learning. And Daniel could understand visionsᴰ and dreams of all kinds.

¹⁸At the end of the time set by the king to bring them in, the chief official presented them to Nebuchadnezzar. ¹⁹The king talked with them, and he found none equal to Daniel, Hananiah, Mishael and Azariah; so they entered the king's service. ²⁰In every matter of wisdom and understanding about which the king questioned them, he found them ten times better than all the magiciansᴰ and enchanters in his whole kingdom.

²¹And Daniel remained there until the first year of King Cyrusᴰ.

Why would God abandon his people? (1:2)

It may seem that God was betraying Judah, but he was actually keeping a promise. God's covenant with his people (Deut. 28–30) had promised blessing if they obeyed him—and punishment if they didn't. As he had allowed the disobedient northern kingdom of Israel to be captured by Assyria in 722 B.C., God let the idol-worshiping southern kingdom of Judah fall victim to Babylon. Instead of abandoning his people, God made sure the nation survived the exile and learned from it.

What god did Nebuchadnezzar serve? (1:2)

The Babylonians had many gods; the chief deity was Bel, also called Marduk. This is probably the god referred to here, since the king later described Daniel as *Belteshazzar, after the name of my god* (4:8).

Why did the young men cooperate with their captors? (1:3–7)

Even though they were given new names that honored the false gods of Babylon, the young men appear not to have protested. Why? First, these young teenagers probably were hostages, held by Nebuchadnezzar to prevent a revolt by those who remained in Judah. Resistance could have meant death to the young men and to their relatives back home. Second, the prophet Jeremiah, warning of Babylon's invasion, had told the people not to fight back (Jer. 21:9)—and most hadn't.

Daniel in Babylon (1:6)

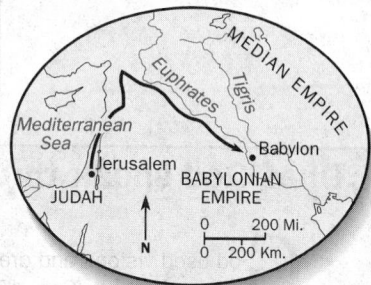

How would the king's food and wine have "defiled" Daniel? (1:8,12)

At least part of it probably had been offered to idols, which prohibited faithful Jews from eating it (Exodus 34:15). Also, Gentiles had prepared the food without attention to Jewish dietary laws, without which it would be unclean. The food probably included certain meats forbidden by the Law of Moses. Since there were no "unclean" vegetables, the young men switched to a vegetarian diet.

ª2 Hebrew *Shinar*   ᵇ4 Or *Chaldeans*   ᶜ10 The Hebrew for *your* and *you* in this verse is plural.

Nebuchadnezzar's Dream

2 In the second year of his reign, Nebuchadnezzar had dreams; his mind was troubled and he could not sleep. ²So the king summoned the magiciansᴰ, enchanters, sorcerers and astrologersᵃ to tell him what he had dreamed. When they came in and stood before the king, ³he said to them, "I have had a dream that troubles me and I want to know what it means.ᵇ"

⁴Then the astrologers answered the king in Aramaicᴰ,ᶜ "O king, live forever! Tell your servants the dream, and we will interpret it."

⁵The king replied to the astrologers, "This is what I have firmly decided: If you do not tell me what my dream was and interpret it, I will have you cut into pieces and your houses turned into piles of rubble. ⁶But if you tell me the dream and explain it, you will receive from me gifts and rewards and great honor. So tell me the dream and interpret it for me."

⁷Once more they replied, "Let the king tell his servants the dream, and we will interpret it."

⁸Then the king answered, "I am certain that you are trying to gain time, because you realize that this is what I have firmly decided: ⁹If you do not tell me the dream, there is just one penalty for you. You have conspired to tell me misleading and wicked things, hoping the situation will change. So then, tell me the dream, and I will know that you can interpret it for me."

¹⁰The astrologers answered the king, "There is not a man on earth who can do what the king asks! No king, however great and mighty, has ever asked such a thing of any magician or enchanter or astrologer. ¹¹What the king asks is too difficult. No one can reveal it to the king except the gods, and they do not live among men."

Magicians, enchanters, sorcerers and astrologers (2:2)

These were the various types of *wise men* (v. 12) Babylon relied on to foretell the future and influence such events as harvests, droughts and battles. *Magicians* could have been anyone involved in occult practices. *Enchanters* may have been "experts" in exorcisms. *Sorcerers* cast spells. *Astrologers* were a class of priests who claimed to receive special knowledge through the stars. It's possible that some of these practitioners had demonic powers, but they seem ineffective in the story of Daniel (2:1–12). Also see *How could Daniel be in charge of things God abhors?* (5:11).

Why was the king so hard on the astrologers? (2:5)

He may have sensed this dream was more important than others he'd had—and wanted to test the interpreters' powers before accepting the results. He may also have inherited these fortune-tellers from the days when his father was king and doubted their abilities. In any case, Nebuchadnezzar's personality seemed to dispose him to sudden rages and harsh punishments (3:19–20; 6:24).

ᵃ2 Or *Chaldeans*; also in verses 4, 5 and 10   ᵇ3 Or *was*
ᶜ4 The text from here through chapter 7 is in Aramaic.

Does God speak through visions and dreams? (1:17)

God used visions and dreams to communicate with many throughout the Bible, from Abraham (Gen. 15:1) to John (Rev. 1:9–11). But there was no regularity to these events. Apparently God communicated through whatever means served his purposes—including visions, angels, prophets, the written Word and even a talking animal (Num. 22:21–31).

God still can communicate in any way he chooses. Some believe he continues to send special revelations, especially to those with the gift of prophecy and that these must be interpreted within strict guidelines (1 Cor. 14:26–33). Others believe that the need for such revelations stopped after the early days of the church, when every Christian began to be guided personally by the Holy Spirit and the written Scriptures (John 16:13).

Evaluating people's claims that they have had dreams or visions from God must be done carefully. The Law of Moses demanded the death penalty for false interpreters of dreams who tried to mislead God's people (Deut. 13:1–5). Even Daniel knew his abilities were limited; he had to ask God for the meaning of Nebuchadnezzar's dream (2:18–19) and needed help to interpret his own visions (7:15–16; 8:15–16). Also see article: *What do ancient visions mean to us today?* (Zech. 1:8).

12This made the king so angry and furious that he ordered the execution of all the wise men of Babylon. **13**So the decree was issued to put the wise men to death[D], and men were sent to look for Daniel and his friends to put them to death.

14When Arioch, the commander of the king's guard, had gone out to put to death the wise men of Babylon, Daniel spoke to him with wisdom and tact. **15**He asked the king's officer, "Why did the king issue such a harsh decree?" Arioch then explained the matter to Daniel. **16**At this, Daniel went in to the king and asked for time, so that he might interpret the dream for him.

17Then Daniel returned to his house and explained the matter to his friends Hananiah, Mishael and Azariah. **18**He urged them to plead for mercy[D] from the God of heaven concerning this mystery[D], so that he and his friends might not be executed with the rest of the wise men of Babylon. **19**During the night the mystery was revealed to Daniel in a vision[D]. Then Daniel praised the God of heaven **20**and said:

> "Praise be to the name of God for ever
>   and ever;
> wisdom and power are his.
> **21**He changes times and seasons;
>   he sets up kings and deposes them.
> He gives wisdom to the wise
>   and knowledge to the discerning.
> **22**He reveals deep and hidden things;
>   he knows what lies in darkness,
>   and light dwells with him.
> **23**I thank and praise you, O God of my
>   fathers:
> You have given me wisdom and
>   power,
> you have made known to me what we
>   asked of you,
>   you have made known to us the dream of
>   the king."

Daniel Interprets the Dream

24Then Daniel went to Arioch, whom the king had appointed to execute the wise men of Babylon, and said to him, "Do not execute the wise men of Babylon. Take me to the king, and I will interpret his dream for him."

25Arioch took Daniel to the king at once and said, "I have found a man among the exiles[D] from Judah who can tell the king what his dream means."

26The king asked Daniel (also called Belteshazzar), "Are you able to tell me what I saw in my dream and interpret it?"

27Daniel replied, "No wise man, enchanter, magician[D] or diviner can explain to the king the mystery he has asked about, **28**but there is a God in heaven who reveals mysteries. He has shown King Nebuchadnezzar what will happen in days to come. Your dream and the visions that passed through your mind as you lay on your bed are these:

29"As you were lying there, O king, your mind turned to things to come, and the revealer of mysteries showed you what is going to happen. **30**As for me, this mystery

Wise men (2:12)
See *Magicians, enchanters, sorcerers and astrologers* (2:2).

Is God responsible for bad government? (2:21)
See *Is God responsible for bad government?* (5:18).

What kingdoms did the statue represent? (2:31–45)

Most likely the head stood for the Babylonian empire (626–539 B.C.), the chest and arms for the Medo-Persian empire (539–331 B.C.), the belly and thighs for the Greek empire (331–146 B.C.) and the legs and feet for the Roman empire (146 B.C.—A.D. 476). Some distinguish between the Medes and the Persians, omitting the Romans. Some think the ten toes might suggest Rome's fall into the hands of ten kingdoms. But others believe they represent a ten-nation alliance yet to rule the world under the leadership of a God-opposing dictator (see 7:24–25; Rev. 17:12–14). The last kingdom (v. 44) is the kingdom of God, established by Christ (the rock in v. 45).

Was Nebuchadnezzar a "believer"? (2:47)

The king was impressed enough with Daniel's abilities to declare God the top deity. But Nebuchadnezzar still believed in many gods (3:14). The king's growing recognition of the Most High God (4:2) was an amazing declaration coming from the most powerful pagan on earth. But there is no evidence that the king abandoned Babylonian religion.

SCRIPTURE LINK (2:48) The king placed Daniel in a high position

See Gen. 39–41 for the story of Joseph, another godly captive who was rewarded for interpreting a ruler's dreams.

has been revealed to me, not because I have greater wisdom than other living men, but so that you, O king, may know the interpretation and that you may understand what went through your mind.

31"You looked, O king, and there before you stood a large statue—an enormous, dazzling statue, awesome in appearance. 32The head of the statue was made of pure gold, its chest and arms of silver, its belly and thighs of bronze, 33its legs of iron, its feet partly of iron and partly of baked clay. 34While you were watching, a rock was cut out, but not by human hands. It struck the statue on its feet of iron and clay and smashed them. 35Then the iron, the clay, the bronze, the silver and the gold were broken to pieces at the same time and became like chaffD on a threshing floor in the summer. The wind swept them away without leaving a trace. But the rock that struck the statue became a huge mountain and filled the whole earth.

36"This was the dream, and now we will interpret it to the king. 37You, O king, are the king of kings. The God of heaven has given you dominion and power and might and gloryD; 38in your hands he has placed mankind and the beasts of the field and the birds of the air. Wherever they live, he has made you ruler over them all. You are that head of gold.

39"After you, another kingdom will rise, inferior to yours. Next, a third kingdom, one of bronze, will rule over the whole earth. 40Finally, there will be a fourth kingdom, strong as iron—for iron breaks and smashes everything—and as iron breaks things to pieces, so it will crush and break all the others. 41Just as you saw that the feet and toes were partly of baked clay and partly of iron, so this will be a divided kingdom; yet it will have some of the strength of iron in it, even as you saw iron mixed with clay. 42As the toes were partly iron and partly clay, so this kingdom will be partly strong and partly brittle. 43And just as you saw the iron mixed with baked clay, so the people will be a mixture and will not remain united, any more than iron mixes with clay.

44"In the time of those kings, the God of heaven will set up a kingdom that will never be destroyed, nor will it be left to another people. It will crush all those kingdoms and bring them to an end, but it will itself endure forever. 45This is the meaning of the visionD of the rock cut out of a mountain, but not by human hands—a rock that broke the iron, the bronze, the clay, the silver and the gold to pieces.

"The great God has shown the king what will take place in the future. The dream is true and the interpretation is trustworthy."

46Then King Nebuchadnezzar fell prostrate before Daniel and paid him honor and ordered that an offering and incenseD be presented to him. 47The king said to Daniel, "Surely your God is the God of gods and the Lord of kings and a revealer of mysteriesD, for you were able to reveal this mystery."

48Then the king placed Daniel in a high position and lavished many gifts on him. He made him ruler over the entire province of Babylon and placed him in charge of all its wise men. 49Moreover, at Daniel's request the king appointed Shadrach, Meshach and Abednego administrators over the province of Babylon, while Daniel himself remained at the royal court.

The Image of Gold and the Fiery Furnace

3 King Nebuchadnezzar made an image of gold, ninety feet high and nine feet[a] wide, and set it up on the plain of Dura in the province of Babylon. ²He then summoned the satraps[D], prefects, governors, advisers, treasurers, judges, magistrates and all the other provincial officials to come to the dedication of the image he had set up. ³So the satraps, prefects, governors, advisers, treasurers, judges, magistrates and all the other provincial officials assembled for the dedication of the image that King Nebuchadnezzar had set up, and they stood before it.

⁴Then the herald loudly proclaimed, "This is what you are commanded to do, O peoples, nations and men of every language: ⁵As soon as you hear the sound of the horn, flute, zither, lyre[D], harp, pipes and all kinds of music, you must fall down and worship the image of gold that King Nebuchadnezzar has set up. ⁶Whoever does not fall down and worship will immediately be thrown into a blazing furnace."

⁷Therefore, as soon as they heard the sound of the horn, flute, zither, lyre, harp and all kinds of music, all the peoples, nations and men of every language fell down and worshiped the image of gold that King Nebuchadnezzar had set up.

⁸At this time some astrologers[b] came forward and denounced the Jews[D]. ⁹They said to King Nebuchadnezzar, "O king, live forever! ¹⁰You have issued a decree, O king, that everyone who hears the sound of the horn, flute, zither, lyre, harp, pipes and all kinds of music must fall down and worship the image of gold, ¹¹and that whoever does not fall down and worship will be thrown into a blazing furnace. ¹²But there are some Jews whom you have set over the affairs of the province of Babylon—Shadrach, Meshach and Abednego—who pay no attention to you, O king. They neither serve your gods nor worship the image of gold you have set up."

¹³Furious with rage, Nebuchadnezzar summoned Shadrach, Meshach and Abednego. So these men were brought before the king, ¹⁴and Nebuchadnezzar said to them, "Is it true, Shadrach, Meshach and Abednego, that you do not serve my gods or worship the image of gold I have set up? ¹⁵Now when you hear the sound of the horn, flute, zither, lyre, harp, pipes and all kinds of music, if you are ready to fall down and worship the image I made, very good. But if you do not worship it, you will be thrown immediately into a blazing furnace. Then what god will be able to rescue you from my hand?"

¹⁶Shadrach, Meshach and Abednego replied to the king, "O Nebuchadnezzar, we do not need to defend ourselves before you in this matter. ¹⁷If we are thrown into the blazing furnace, the God we serve is able to save us from it, and he will rescue us from your hand, O king. ¹⁸But even if he does not, we want you to know, O king, that we will not serve your gods or worship the image of gold you have set up."

¹⁹Then Nebuchadnezzar was furious with Shadrach, Meshach and Abednego, and his attitude toward them changed. He ordered the furnace heated seven times hotter than usual ²⁰and commanded some of the strongest soldiers in his army to tie up Shadrach, Meshach and

---

What kind of image was this? (3:1)

Probably a gold-plated statue with a tall pedestal that brought its total height to 90 feet. It may have depicted the god Nabu, to whom Nebuchadnezzar's own name paid tribute. Or the image might not have been human in form, but an Egyptian-style monument symbolizing the power of the Babylonian empire.

Satraps, prefects (3:2)

Satraps were chief representatives of the king. Prefects were military commanders.

Where was Daniel? (3:12)

His whereabouts aren't mentioned. But his high governmental position (2:48) may have kept the astrologers from accusing him. Or his position may have required him to travel throughout the empire, which could explain why he wasn't at the plain of Dura or at the palace to defend his friends.

Why was the king so angry? (3:13–14)

Nebuchadnezzar was the ruler of the most powerful empire the world had ever seen. Though he had acknowledged God (2:47), he still considered himself the top political and spiritual authority (3:15). Rebellion of any kind was intolerable to him. And if he had made an exception to his own rule, his authority would have been undermined.

How hot was the furnace? (3:19)

The furnace probably was the type used as a kiln for firing bricks—though this one might have been used exclusively for executions, since burning people alive was a traditional Babylonian punishment. Kilns today are heated to 1,600–2,300 degrees Fahrenheit to fire bricks. The order to heat the furnace *seven times hotter than usual* may have meant *to the maximum*, since seven symbolized completeness.

---

a 1 Aramaic sixty cubits high and six cubits wide (about 27 meters high and 2.7 meters wide)   *b 8 Or Chaldeans*

Who was the fourth man in the furnace? (3:25)

Nebuchadnezzar knew he was looking at a supernatural being, though his *son of the gods* description reflected his belief in many gods. Later the king described the man as an angel (3:28). Some believe the figure *was* an angel; others feel he was literally the Son of God—Christ making an appearance more than five centuries before his earthly birth.

Why was the king's change of mind so extreme? (3:29)

Mood swings and deadly threats were typical of Nebuchadnezzar (2:12; 3:19–20). Simply allowing the Jews to worship their God could have made the king seem indecisive, given his earlier decree. Vowing to kill any who opposed the Lord helped to maintain the king's image as ultimate authority.

Did Nebuchadnezzar write this part of the Bible? (4:1)

Chapter 4 appears to be an official proclamation from the king. But does it belong in the Bible, since it reflects the king's belief in many gods? Yes, because it exalts the true God—a remarkable statement coming from a pagan ruler. Surely that's why Daniel was inspired to quote it—as Paul was later inspired to quote a Cretan writer (Titus 1:12–13).

Abednego and throw them into the blazing furnace. ²¹So these men, wearing their robes, trousers, turbans and other clothes, were bound and thrown into the blazing furnace. ²²The king's command was so urgent and the furnace so hot that the flames of the fire killed the soldiers who took up Shadrach, Meshach and Abednego, ²³and these three men, firmly tied, fell into the blazing furnace.

²⁴Then King Nebuchadnezzar leaped to his feet in amazement and asked his advisers, "Weren't there three men that we tied up and threw into the fire?"

They replied, "Certainly, O king."

²⁵He said, "Look! I see four men walking around in the fire, unbound and unharmed, and the fourth looks like a son of the gods."

²⁶Nebuchadnezzar then approached the opening of the blazing furnace and shouted, "Shadrach, Meshach and Abednego, servants of the Most High God, come out! Come here!"

So Shadrach, Meshach and Abednego came out of the fire, ²⁷and the satraps[D], prefects, governors and royal advisers crowded around them. They saw that the fire had not harmed their bodies, nor was a hair of their heads singed; their robes were not scorched, and there was no smell of fire on them.

²⁸Then Nebuchadnezzar said, "Praise be to the God of Shadrach, Meshach and Abednego, who has sent his angel and rescued his servants! They trusted in him and defied the king's command and were willing to give up their lives rather than serve or worship any god except their own God. ²⁹Therefore I decree that the people of any nation or language who say anything against the God of Shadrach, Meshach and Abednego be cut into pieces and their houses be turned into piles of rubble, for no other god can save in this way."

³⁰Then the king promoted Shadrach, Meshach and Abednego in the province of Babylon.

Nebuchadnezzar's Dream of a Tree

4 King Nebuchadnezzar,

To the peoples, nations and men of every language, who live in all the world:

May you prosper greatly!

²It is my pleasure to tell you about the miraculous signs and wonders that the Most High God has performed for me.

³How great are his signs,
    how mighty his wonders!
His kingdom is an eternal kingdom;
    his dominion endures from generation to
        generation.

⁴I, Nebuchadnezzar, was at home in my palace, contented and prosperous. ⁵I had a dream that made me afraid. As I was lying in my bed, the images and visions[D] that passed through my mind terrified me. ⁶So I commanded that all the wise men of Babylon be brought before me to interpret the dream for me. ⁷When the magicians[D], enchanters, astrologers[a] and diviners came, I told them the dream, but they could not interpret it for me. ⁸Finally, Daniel came

---

a 7 Or Chaldeans

into my presence and I told him the dream. (He is called Belteshazzar, after the name of my god, and the spirit of the holy gods is in him.)

⁹I said, "Belteshazzar, chief of the magicians,ᴰ I know that the spirit of the holy gods is in you, and no mysteryᴰ is too difficult for you. Here is my dream; interpret it for me. ¹⁰These are the visionsᴰ I saw while lying in my bed: I looked, and there before me stood a tree in the middle of the land. Its height was enormous. ¹¹The tree grew large and strong and its top touched the sky; it was visible to the ends of the earth. ¹²Its leaves were beautiful, its fruit abundant, and on it was food for all. Under it the beasts of the field found shelter, and the birds of the air lived in its branches; from it every creature was fed.

¹³"In the visions I saw while lying in my bed, I looked, and there before me was a messenger,ᵃ a holy one, coming down from heaven. ¹⁴He called in a loud voice: 'Cut down the tree and trim off its branches; strip off its leaves and scatter its fruit. Let the animals flee from under it and the birds from its branches. ¹⁵But let the stump and its roots, bound with iron and bronze, remain in the ground, in the grass of the field.

" 'Let him be drenched with the dew of heaven, and let him live with the animals among the plants of the earth. ¹⁶Let his mind be changed from that of a man and let him be given the mind of an animal, till seven timesᵇ pass by for him.

¹⁷" 'The decision is announced by messengers, the holy ones declare the verdict, so that the living may know that the Most High is sovereign over the kingdoms of men and gives them to anyone he wishes and sets over them the lowliest of men.'

¹⁸"This is the dream that I, King Nebuchadnezzar, had. Now, Belteshazzar, tell me what it means, for none of the wise men in my kingdom can interpret it for me. But you can, because the spirit of the holy gods is in you."

Daniel Interprets the Dream

¹⁹Then Daniel (also called Belteshazzar) was greatly perplexed for a time, and his thoughts terrified him. So the king said, "Belteshazzar, do not let the dream or its meaning alarm you."

Belteshazzar answered, "My lord, if only the dream applied to your enemies and its meaning to your adversaries! ²⁰The tree you saw, which grew large and strong, with its top touching the sky, visible to the whole earth, ²¹with beautiful leaves and abundant fruit, providing food for all, giving shelter to the beasts of the field, and having nesting places in its branches for the birds of the air— ²²you, O king, are that tree! You have become great and strong; your greatness has grown until it reaches the sky, and your dominion extends to distant parts of the earth.

²³"You, O king, saw a messenger, a holy one, coming down from heaven and saying, 'Cut down the tree and destroy it, but leave the stump, bound with iron and bronze, in the grass of the field, while its roots remain in the ground. Let him be drenched with the

A messenger, a holy one (4:13)
The word translated *messenger* can also mean *watchman*. This was apparently an angel (see vv. 17,23).

ᵃ13 Or *watchman*; also in verses 17 and 23   ᵇ16 Or *years*; also in verses 23, 25 and 32

dew of heaven; let him live like the wild animals, until seven times pass by for him.'

²⁴"This is the interpretation, O king, and this is the decree the Most High has issued against my lord the king: ²⁵You will be driven away from people and will live with the wild animals; you will eat grass like cattle and be drenched with the dew of heaven. Seven times will pass by for you until you acknowledge that the Most High is sovereign over the kingdoms of men and gives them to anyone he wishes. ²⁶The command to leave the stump of the tree with its roots means that your kingdom will be restored to you when you acknowledge that Heaven rules. ²⁷Therefore, O king, be pleased to accept my advice: Renounce your sins by doing what is right, and your wickedness by being kind to the oppressed. It may be that then your prosperity will continue."

The Dream Is Fulfilled

²⁸All this happened to King Nebuchadnezzar. ²⁹Twelve months later, as the king was walking on the roof of the royal palace of Babylon, ³⁰he said, "Is not this the great Babylon I have built as the royal residence, by my mighty power and for the glory^D of my majesty?"

³¹The words were still on his lips when a voice came from heaven, "This is what is decreed for you, King Nebuchadnezzar: Your royal authority has been taken from you. ³²You will be driven away from people and will live with the wild animals; you will eat grass like cattle. Seven times will pass by for you until you acknowledge that the Most High is sovereign over the kingdoms of men and gives them to anyone he wishes."

³³Immediately what had been said about Nebuchadnezzar was fulfilled. He was driven away from people and ate grass like cattle. His body was drenched with the dew of heaven until his hair grew like the feathers of an eagle and his nails like the claws of a bird.

³⁴At the end of that time, I, Nebuchadnezzar, raised my eyes toward heaven, and my sanity was restored. Then I praised the Most High; I honored and glorified him who lives forever.

> His dominion is an eternal dominion;
>   his kingdom endures from generation to
>   generation.
> ³⁵All the peoples of the earth
>   are regarded as nothing.
> He does as he pleases
>   with the powers of heaven
>   and the peoples of the earth.
> No one can hold back his hand
>   or say to him: "What have you done?"

³⁶At the same time that my sanity was restored, my honor and splendor were returned to me for the glory of my kingdom. My advisers and nobles sought me out, and I was restored to my throne and became even greater than before. ³⁷Now I, Nebuchadnezzar, praise and exalt and glorify the King of heaven, because everything he does is right and all his ways are

What were Nebuchadnezzar's sins? (4:27)

In addition to attacking other nations and killing, torturing or deporting their people, the king kept his own citizens in relative poverty. He spent huge sums on elaborate building projects—including, according to tradition, the famed Hanging Gardens of Babylon. Excavations have shown that the king's palace was enormous, surrounded by a series of thickly fortified walls, while most of the populace lived in one-story mud brick houses.

Who would dare drive away the king? (4:33)

No palace coup was needed, since Nebuchadnezzar's mental state probably kept him from putting up a struggle. The king's humiliation may have been kept a secret from the public. There were parks that contained animals on the vast palace grounds, and it may have been that the king lived out his time as a beast in those parks. Daniel probably helped run the government in the king's absence and kept the king from being killed.

Does God really regard everyone *as* nothing? (4:35)

Nebuchadnezzar, having learned a humbling lesson, is contrasting God's power with human power. His emphasis seems to be on kingdoms—God's (v. 34) versus the nations (v. 36). God makes it clear in other passages that he values and loves people (John 3:16) and has given them a position of honor (Psalm 8:4–5).

just. And those who walk in pride he is able to humble.

The Writing on the Wall

5 King Belshazzar gave a great banquet for a thousand of his nobles and drank wine with them. ²While Belshazzar was drinking his wine, he gave orders to bring in the gold and silver goblets that Nebuchadnezzar his father[a] had taken from the temple in Jerusalem[D], so that the king and his nobles, his wives and his concubines[D] might drink from them. ³So they brought in the gold goblets that had been taken from the temple of God in Jerusalem, and the king and his nobles, his wives and his concubines drank from them. ⁴As they drank the wine, they praised the gods of gold and silver, of bronze, iron, wood and stone.

⁵Suddenly the fingers of a human hand appeared and wrote on the plaster of the wall, near the lampstand in the royal palace. The king watched the hand as it wrote. ⁶His face turned pale and he was so frightened that his knees knocked together and his legs gave way.

⁷The king called out for the enchanters, astrologers[b] and diviners to be brought and said to these wise men of Babylon, "Whoever reads this writing and tells me what it means will be clothed in purple[D] and have a gold chain placed around his neck, and he will be made the third highest ruler in the kingdom."

⁸Then all the king's wise men came in, but they could not read the writing or tell the king what it meant. ⁹So King Belshazzar became even more terrified and his face grew more pale. His nobles were baffled.

¹⁰The queen,[c] hearing the voices of the king and his nobles, came into the banquet hall. "O king, live forever!" she said. "Don't be alarmed! Don't look so pale! ¹¹There is a man in your kingdom who has the spirit of the holy gods in him. In the time of your father he was found to have insight and intelligence and wisdom like that of the gods. King Nebuchadnezzar your father—your father the king, I say—appointed him chief of the magicians[D], enchanters, astrologers and diviners. ¹²This man Daniel, whom the king called Belteshazzar, was found to have a keen mind and knowledge and understanding, and also the ability to interpret dreams, explain riddles and solve difficult problems. Call for Daniel, and he will tell you what the writing means."

¹³So Daniel was brought before the king, and the king said to him, "Are you Daniel, one of the exiles[D] my father the king brought from Judah? ¹⁴I have heard that the spirit of the gods is in you and that you have insight, intelligence and outstanding wisdom. ¹⁵The wise men and enchanters were brought before me to read this writing and tell me what it means, but they could not explain it. ¹⁶Now I have heard that you are able to give interpretations and to solve difficult problems. If you can read this writing and tell me what it means, you will be clothed in purple and have a gold chain placed around your neck, and you will be made the third highest ruler in the kingdom."

¹⁷Then Daniel answered the king, "You may keep your gifts for yourself and give your rewards to someone else.

How and when had Belshazzar become king? (5:1)

After ruling for nearly 45 years, Nebuchadnezzar died in 562 B.C. Three weak kings followed before Nabonidas came to power in 555 B.C. His oldest son, Belshazzar, became co-regent with his father about 550 B.C. He controlled the army and government alone for about ten years while his father was away. Calling Nebuchadnezzar his father (5:2) probably meant simply that Belshazzar was a successor of Nebuchadnezzar.

Why was using temple goblets so offensive to God? (5:2–3)

These cups, dedicated for worship in God's temple, had been stored in the temple of Bel as trophies of war (1:2). When Belshazzar's revelers used the goblets to "toast" their idols, they were declaring in effect that God, if he existed at all, was subordinate to the idols of Babylon.

Who were these gods? (5:4)

These idols are not identified, but people of the region worshiped hundreds of gods—some estimates run as high as 2,500 deities. One Babylonian inscription reveals that in Babylon there were 53 temples of the "chief gods," 55 chapels of Marduk (the chief deity), 900 chapels for other gods and more than 370 additional altars.

How could Daniel be in charge of things God abhors? (5:11)

Being chief of the magicians and others (4:9) didn't necessarily mean Daniel had authority over them. This phrase may simply have acknowledged Daniel's superior wisdom and ability to interpret dreams. Even if this was an official position, there is no evidence that Daniel was involved in occult activities—all of which had been declared by God to be off-limits (Deut. 18:9–12).

---

a2 Or ancestor; or predecessor; also in verses 11, 13 and 18   b7 Or Chaldeans; also in verse 11   c10 Or queen mother

Is God responsible for bad government? (5:18)

We might expect an all-powerful God to place only righteous leaders in office, but he has used both good and bad rulers to achieve his goals. Nebuchadnezzar (see also 2:21) carried out God's plan to discipline Judah, just as Roman persecution (see Romans 13:1–7) would later strengthen the church and advance the spread of the gospel. God will judge evil rulers (7:26–27). But for his own reasons, he allows sinful leaders—and sinful followers, which includes all of us—to live and even prosper.

In what language was the handwriting on the wall? (5:25)

The words were Aramaic, a language widely known in the Gentile world. It isn't clear why Belshazzar's wise men couldn't read them, but it is obvious why Daniel's explanation (vv. 26–28) was needed. *Mene* could mean *numbered* or could refer to a 1 ¼-pound weight called a mina. *Tekel* could mean *weighed* or could refer to a ⅖-ounce weight called a shekel. *Peres* (the singular of *Parsin*) could mean *divided* or *Persia* or a *half shekel* or a *half mina*. Without a context, the words seemed meaningless.

Darius the Mede (5:30)

Possibly a local name for Cyrus II, the Great, ruler of the Medo-Persian empire that conquered Babylon in 539 B.C. (see NIV text note at 6:28). Some have suggested that Darius is another name for Gubaru, the governor Cyrus installed in Babylon, or for Ugbaru, who led the Persian army's assault. Still others think Darius was another name for Cyrus's son Cambyses, who ruled Persia several years later.

Satraps (6:1)

See *Satraps, prefects* (3:2).

Why would Darius want advice from someone on the losing side? (6:2)

No doubt the reputation of Daniel, who had been respected in Babylonian government for most of his life, had preceded him. Darius would need Daniel's help to run the empire—and Daniel, probably now in his nineties, posed little threat to the position of Darius. Darius also may have been impressed by the fact that Daniel predicted the victory of the Medes (5:28).

What kind of loss was the king trying to avoid? (6:2)

By having the satraps (the king's representatives) report to the administrators, Darius was steering clear of political battles that could have undermined his rule. Daniel and the other administrators would have to listen to the satraps' complaints and take the heat when those officials were dissatisfied.

Nevertheless, I will read the writing for the king and tell him what it means.

¹⁸"O king, the Most High God gave your father Nebuchadnezzar sovereignty and greatness and glory[D] and splendor. ¹⁹Because of the high position he gave him, all the peoples and nations and men of every language dreaded and feared him. Those the king wanted to put to death[D], he put to death; those he wanted to spare, he spared; those he wanted to promote, he promoted; and those he wanted to humble, he humbled. ²⁰But when his heart became arrogant and hardened with pride, he was deposed from his royal throne and stripped of his glory. ²¹He was driven away from people and given the mind of an animal; he lived with the wild donkeys and ate grass like cattle; and his body was drenched with the dew of heaven, until he acknowledged that the Most High God is sovereign over the kingdoms of men and sets over them anyone he wishes.

²²"But you his son,[a] O Belshazzar, have not humbled yourself, though you knew all this. ²³Instead, you have set yourself up against the Lord of heaven. You had the goblets from his temple brought to you, and you and your nobles, your wives and your concubines[D] drank wine from them. You praised the gods of silver and gold, of bronze, iron, wood and stone, which cannot see or hear or understand. But you did not honor the God who holds in his hand your life and all your ways. ²⁴Therefore he sent the hand that wrote the inscription.

²⁵"This is the inscription that was written:

MENE, MENE, TEKEL, PARSIN[b]

²⁶"This is what these words mean:

Mene[c]: God has numbered the days of your reign and brought it to an end.
²⁷*Tekel*[d]: You have been weighed on the scales and found wanting.
²⁸*Peres*[e]: Your kingdom is divided and given to the Medes and Persians."

²⁹Then at Belshazzar's command, Daniel was clothed in purple[D], a gold chain was placed around his neck, and he was proclaimed the third highest ruler in the kingdom.

³⁰That very night Belshazzar, king of the Babylonians,[f] was slain, ³¹and Darius the Mede took over the kingdom, at the age of sixty-two.

Daniel in the Den of Lions

6 It pleased Darius to appoint 120 satraps[D] to rule throughout the kingdom, ²with three administrators over them, one of whom was Daniel. The satraps were made accountable to them so that the king might not suffer loss. ³Now Daniel so distinguished himself among the administrators and the satraps by his exceptional qualities that the king planned to set him over the whole kingdom. ⁴At this, the administrators and the satraps tried to find grounds for charges against Daniel in his conduct of government affairs, but they were unable to do so. They could find no corruption in him, because he was trust-

---

a22 Or *descendant*; or *successor*   *b25* Aramaic *UPARSIN* (that is, *AND PARSIN*)   *c26 Mene* can mean *numbered* or *mina* (a unit of money).   *d27 Tekel* can mean *weighed* or *shekel*.   *e28 Peres* (the singular of *Parsin*) can mean *divided* or *Persia* or a *half mina* or a *half shekel*.   *f30* Or *Chaldeans*

worthy and neither corrupt nor negligent. **5**Finally these men said, "We will never find any basis for charges against this man Daniel unless it has something to do with the law of his God."

6So the administrators and the satraps[D] went as a group to the king and said: "O King Darius, live forever! **7**The royal administrators, prefects, satraps, advisers and governors have all agreed that the king should issue an edict[D] and enforce the decree that anyone who prays to any god or man during the next thirty days, except to you, O king, shall be thrown into the lions' den. **8**Now, O king, issue the decree and put it in writing so that it cannot be altered—in accordance with the laws of the Medes and Persians, which cannot be repealed." **9**So King Darius put the decree in writing.

10Now when Daniel learned that the decree had been published, he went home to his upstairs room where the windows opened toward Jerusalem[D]. Three times a day he got down on his knees and prayed, giving thanks to his God, just as he had done before. **11**Then these men went as a group and found Daniel praying and asking God for help. **12**So they went to the king and spoke to him about his royal decree: "Did you not publish a decree that during the next thirty days anyone who prays to any god or man except to you, O king, would be thrown into the lions' den?"

The king answered, "The decree stands—in accordance with the laws of the Medes and Persians, which cannot be repealed."

13Then they said to the king, "Daniel, who is one of the exiles[D] from Judah, pays no attention to you, O king, or to the decree you put in writing. He still prays three times a day." **14**When the king heard this, he was greatly distressed; he was determined to rescue Daniel and made every effort until sundown to save him.

15Then the men went as a group to the king and said to him, "Remember, O king, that according to the law of the Medes and Persians no decree or edict that the king issues can be changed."

16So the king gave the order, and they brought Daniel and threw him into the lions' den. The king said to Daniel, "May your God, whom you serve continually, rescue you!"

17A stone was brought and placed over the mouth of the den, and the king sealed it with his own signet ring[D] and with the rings of his nobles, so that Daniel's situation might not be changed. **18**Then the king returned to his palace and spent the night without eating and without any entertainment being brought to him. And he could not sleep.

19At the first light of dawn, the king got up and hurried to the lions' den. **20**When he came near the den, he called to Daniel in an anguished voice, "Daniel, servant of the living God, has your God, whom you serve continually, been able to rescue you from the lions?"

21Daniel answered, "O king, live forever! **22**My God sent his angel, and he shut the mouths of the lions. They have not hurt me, because I was found innocent in his sight. Nor have I ever done any wrong before you, O king."

23The king was overjoyed and gave orders to lift Daniel out of the den. And when Daniel was lifted from the den, no wound was found on him, because he had trusted in his God.

24At the king's command, the men who had falsely ac-

Why couldn't the laws of the Medes and Persians be repealed? (6:8)

According to the Medo-Persian way of thinking, it was impossible for the law to contradict itself. Since a reigning monarch was the law, revoking a bad decree was more than a personal embarrassment; it was like a constitutional crisis. This led to some carefully worded non-reversals, like the one Xerxes used to neutralize his own genocidal decree (Esther 3:13; 8:5,11).

Why did Daniel face Jerusalem to pray? (6:10)

While not commanded in Scripture, this appears to have been a customary way for Jews who were away from Jerusalem to express devotion for God. Despite the destruction of Jerusalem, it was still the holy city and the site of God's temple. See *Exactly what had happened to Jerusalem?* (9:12).

Why wasn't Daniel martyred? (6:22–23)

Daniel was protected from the lions because he was innocent of wrongdoing (v. 22) and because he trusted in God (v. 23). Yet relatively few of God's people have been rescued from imminent martyrdom, despite their faith. Perhaps Daniel as well as his three friends (3:19–27) were exceptions because God wanted to show their pagan captors—as well as the discouraged exiles—who the true God was.

cused Daniel were brought in and thrown into the lions' den, along with their wives and children. And before they reached the floor of the den, the lions overpowered them and crushed all their bones.

²⁵Then King Darius wrote to all the peoples, nations and men of every language throughout the land:

"May you prosper greatly!

²⁶"I issue a decree that in every part of my kingdom people must fear and reverence[D] the God of Daniel.

> "For he is the living God
>   and he endures forever;
> his kingdom will not be destroyed,
>   his dominion will never end.
> ²⁷He rescues and he saves;
>   he performs signs and wonders
>   in the heavens and on the earth.
> He has rescued Daniel
>   from the power of the lions."

²⁸So Daniel prospered during the reign of Darius and the reign of Cyrus[Da] the Persian.

Daniel's Dream of Four Beasts

7 In the first year of Belshazzar king of Babylon, Daniel had a dream, and visions[D] passed through his mind as he was lying on his bed. He wrote down the substance of his dream.

²Daniel said: "In my vision at night I looked, and there before me were the four winds of heaven churning up the great sea. ³Four great beasts, each different from the others, came up out of the sea.

⁴"The first was like a lion, and it had the wings of an eagle. I watched until its wings were torn off and it was lifted from the ground so that it stood on two feet like a man, and the heart of a man was given to it.

---

*a*28 Or *Darius, that is, the reign of Cyrus*

Did Darius make Judaism the national religion? (6:26)

No. Like Nebuchadnezzar before him, Darius was awestruck by the power of God. But also like Nebuchadnezzar, Darius was adding God to a list of gods rather than tearing up the list. Darius acknowledged the living God's immortality and strength, but not God's exclusive right to be worshiped (Exodus 20:3–6).

Why does this book use such obscure symbols? (7:1)

Though it may seem Daniel used riddles to reveal the future, the fact is that in Daniel's day, some of the symbols may have been easily understood. For example, Daniel's contemporaries would have known that horns (7:8; 8:3–12) were often used to represent power. Some symbols may have been used because they had dual meanings, referring to near-future and distant-future events simultaneously (7:4–27). Daniel may have used other symbols as a barrier to keep *the wicked* (12:10) from understanding.

The symbolism is difficult to understand, but these predictions weren't meant to be digested in a single reading, then or now. And how could anyone describe future technology (as some interpret the images of 7:19) or the appearance of God (7:9–10) without using analogies?

The most important message of these prophecies is the easiest to understand: that nothing can stand in the way of God's promises to restore his people and to set up his perfect, everlasting kingdom. Our response should be to prepare for it by letting God refine and purify us (12:10).

⁵"And there before me was a second beast, which looked like a bear. It was raised up on one of its sides, and it had three ribs in its mouth between its teeth. It was told, 'Get up and eat your fill of flesh!'

⁶"After that, I looked, and there before me was another beast, one that looked like a leopard. And on its back it had four wings like those of a bird. This beast had four heads, and it was given authority to rule.

⁷"After that, in my vision^D at night I looked, and there before me was a fourth beast—terrifying and frightening and very powerful. It had large iron teeth; it crushed and devoured its victims and trampled underfoot whatever was left. It was different from all the former beasts, and it had ten horns.

⁸"While I was thinking about the horns, there before me was another horn, a little one, which came up among them; and three of the first horns were uprooted before it. This horn had eyes like the eyes of a man and a mouth that spoke boastfully.

⁹"As I looked,

"thrones were set in place,
    and the Ancient of Days took his seat.
His clothing was as white as snow;
    the hair of his head was white like wool.
His throne was flaming with fire,
    and its wheels were all ablaze.
¹⁰A river of fire was flowing,
    coming out from before him.
Thousands upon thousands attended him;
    ten thousand times ten thousand stood
        before him.
The court was seated,
    and the books were opened.

¹¹"Then I continued to watch because of the boastful words the horn was speaking. I kept looking until the beast was slain and its body destroyed and thrown into the blazing fire. ¹²(The other beasts had been stripped of their authority, but were allowed to live for a period of time.)

¹³"In my vision at night I looked, and there before me was one like a son of man^D, coming with the clouds of heaven. He approached the Ancient of Days and was led into his presence. ¹⁴He was given authority, glory^D and sovereign power; all peoples, nations and men of every language worshiped him. His dominion is an everlasting dominion that will not pass away, and his kingdom is one that will never be destroyed.

The Interpretation of the Dream

¹⁵"I, Daniel, was troubled in spirit, and the visions that passed through my mind disturbed me. ¹⁶I approached one of those standing there and asked him the true meaning of all this.

"So he told me and gave me the interpretation of these things: ¹⁷'The four great beasts are four kingdoms that will rise from the earth. ¹⁸But the saints^D of the Most High will receive the kingdom and will possess it forever—yes, for ever and ever.'

¹⁹"Then I wanted to know the true meaning of the fourth beast, which was different from all the others and most terrifying, with its iron teeth and bronze claws—the beast that crushed and devoured its victims and trampled underfoot whatever was left. ²⁰I also wanted to know

Ancient of Days (7:9)
A name for God that emphasizes his eternal existence (see Isaiah 43:13). His white hair symbolizes purity, not age. His flaming throne and the river of fire probably represent his role as powerful judge. Even though God is Spirit, symbolic physical descriptions like this one are used often in the Bible to tell us important things about God's nature.

SCRIPTURE LINK (7:9) *His throne was flaming with fire and its wheels were all ablaze*
For a similar description of God from one of Daniel's contemporaries, see Ezek. 1:15–21, 26–27.

What kind of court was this? (7:10)
This was apparently God's judging of nations and individuals, especially those symbolized in vv. 1–8,11–12. The books that were opened represent a record of what the "defendants" had done. Opening the books meant that the evidence was reviewed.

Son of man (7:13)
This expression usually meant a human being (or all humans), emphasizing their distinction from God. Here it could stand for the people of Israel, or for Israel's angelic representation in heaven. But many believe this refers to Christ, stressing his humanity as well as the authority and power given him (see Matt. 28:18). Jesus frequently applied this title to himself (Mark 8:31; John 1:51). Since Christ is not yet worshiped by every people and nation (v. 14), these events apparently are still to come. See *Son of man* (Ezek. 2:1).

What four kingdoms do these beasts represent? (7:17)
This vision seems to parallel the one in ch. 2. See *What kingdoms did the statue represent?* (2:31–45). Many think the lion is the Babylonian empire; the bear, the Medo-Persian empire; the leopard, the Greek empire; the frightening and powerful beast, the Roman empire. Others believe the bear stands for the Medes, the leopard for the Persians and the fourth beast for the Greeks.

about the ten horns on its head and about the other horn that came up, before which three of them fell—the horn that looked more imposing than the others and that had eyes and a mouth that spoke boastfully. **21**As I watched, this horn was waging war against the saints[D] and defeating them, **22**until the Ancient of Days came and pronounced judgment in favor of the saints of the Most High, and the time came when they possessed the kingdom.

23"He gave me this explanation: 'The fourth beast is a fourth kingdom that will appear on earth. It will be different from all the other kingdoms and will devour the whole earth, trampling it down and crushing it. **24**The ten horns are ten kings who will come from this kingdom. After them another king will arise, different from the earlier ones; he will subdue three kings. **25**He will speak against the Most High and oppress his saints and try to change the set times and the laws. The saints will be handed over to him for a time, times and half a time.[a]

26" 'But the court will sit, and his power will be taken away and completely destroyed forever. **27**Then the sovereignty, power and greatness of the kingdoms under the whole heaven will be handed over to the saints, the people of the Most High. His kingdom will be an everlasting kingdom, and all rulers will worship and obey him.'

28"This is the end of the matter. I, Daniel, was deeply

[a]25 Or *for a year, two years and half a year*

SCRIPTURE LINK (7:21–22) *War against the saints*

For another look at war on the saints and God's ultimate judgment and victory, see Rev. 13,19–21.

What eleven kings do these horns represent? (7:24)

The first ten horns are nations or leaders arising from the fourth kingdom. See *What four kingdoms do these beasts represent?* (7:17). If the fourth kingdom is Rome, the ten horns could be the nations that were formed by the breakup of the Roman empire. Others believe the ten horns won't arise until the future, when a ten-nation bloc—perhaps a revival of the Roman empire—challenges God's authority. See *What kingdoms did the statue represent?* (2:31–35). If this is the case, the eleventh horn could be the leader of that confederacy, usually thought to be the *beast* (Rev. 19:19). Another view is that the fourth kingdom is Greece and the ten horns are rulers deposed by the king of Greece—the eleventh horn. See *Prince of the host* (8:11).

Identification of the Four Kingdoms

Vision in Daniel ch. 2	Vision in Daniel ch. 7	Vision in Daniel ch. 8	Empire	Period of Domination
HEAD OF GOLD	LION		BABYLONIAN	626 B.C.–539 B.C.
CHEST AND ARMS OF SILVER	BEAR	RAM	MEDO-PERSIAN	539 B.C.–331 B.C.
BELLY AND THIGHS OF BRONZE	LEOPARD	GOAT	GRECIAN	331 B.C.–146 B.C.
LEGS OF IRON / FEET OF CLAY	TERRIFYING AND FRIGHTENING BEAST		ROMAN	146 B.C.–A.D.476

troubled by my thoughts, and my face turned pale, but I kept the matter to myself."

Daniel's Vision of a Ram and a Goat

8 In the third year of King Belshazzar's reign, I, Daniel, had a vision[D], after the one that had already appeared to me. [2]In my vision I saw myself in the citadel of Susa in the province of Elam; in the vision I was beside the Ulai Canal. [3]I looked up, and there before me was a ram with two horns, standing beside the canal, and the horns were long. One of the horns was longer than the other but grew up later. [4]I watched the ram as he charged toward the west and the north and the south. No animal could stand against him, and none could rescue from his power. He did as he pleased and became great.

[5]As I was thinking about this, suddenly a goat with a prominent horn between his eyes came from the west, crossing the whole earth without touching the ground. [6]He came toward the two-horned ram I had seen standing beside the canal and charged at him in great rage. [7]I saw him attack the ram furiously, striking the ram and shattering his two horns. The ram was powerless to stand against him; the goat knocked him to the ground and trampled on him, and none could rescue the ram from his power. [8]The goat became very great, but at the height of his power his large horn was broken off, and in its place four prominent horns grew up toward the four winds of heaven.

[9]Out of one of them came another horn, which started small but grew in power to the south and to the east and toward the Beautiful Land. [10]It grew until it reached the host of the heavens, and it threw some of the starry host[D] down to the earth and trampled on them. [11]It set itself up to be as great as the Prince of the host; it took away the daily sacrifice[D] from him, and the place of his sanctuary was brought low. [12]Because of rebellion, the host ⌊of the saints[D]⌋[a] and the daily sacrifice were given over to it. It prospered in everything it did, and truth was thrown to the ground.

[13]Then I heard a holy one speaking, and another holy one said to him, "How long will it take for the vision to be fulfilled—the vision concerning the daily sacrifice, the rebellion that causes desolation, and the surrender of the sanctuary and of the host that will be trampled underfoot?"

[14]He said to me, "It will take 2,300 evenings and mornings; then the sanctuary will be reconsecrated."

The Interpretation of the Vision

[15]While I, Daniel, was watching the vision and trying to understand it, there before me stood one who looked like a man. [16]And I heard a man's voice from the Ulai calling, "Gabriel[D], tell this man the meaning of the vision."

[17]As he came near the place where I was standing, I was terrified and fell prostrate. "Son of man[D]," he said to me, "understand that the vision concerns the time of the end."

[18]While he was speaking to me, I was in a deep sleep, with my face to the ground. Then he touched me and raised me to my feet.

[19]He said: "I am going to tell you what will happen later in the time of wrath, because the vision concerns the

[a]12 Or *rebellion, the armies*

Beautiful Land (8:9)

Israel. The term sounds almost wistful here, since the Jewish people longed for the land from which they'd been exiled.

Prince of the host (8:11)

God, the ruler of a host of faithful believers (v. 10). The small *horn* was the king of Greece, Antiochus IV Epiphanes. In 169 B.C. he began a four-year attempt to wipe out Judaism. One Sabbath he led 22,000 soldiers against Jerusalem, massacring many and making slaves of women and children. Later he banned Jewish sacrifices and desecrated the temple with an altar to Zeus Olympius.

Why talk about sacrifices? (8:11–14)

The exiled Jews, cut off from the temple, had stopped making sacrifices while in Babylon. Perhaps they were encouraged to know that sacrifices would someday resume, in spite of further persecution. The 2,300 evenings and mornings (v. 14) probably refer to the evening and morning sacrifices that would have been offered between the desecration of the altar by Antiochus IV (168 B.C.) and its reconsecration (164 B.C.).

Gabriel (8:16)

An angel whose name means *man of God* or *God is powerful*. He also heralded the coming births of John the Baptist (Luke 1:11–20) and Jesus (Luke 1:26–28). Gabriel and Michael are the only two angels mentioned by name in Scripture.

Why was Daniel called the *son of man*? (8:17)

Though we've come to associate this term with Jesus (Matt. 8:20), it was used earlier to emphasize the difference between any person (or people) and God (Psalm 8:4; Ezek. 2:1–2). Gabriel probably was contrasting Daniel's humanity with his own angelic nature. Also see *Son of man* (7:13).

If this vision was sealed, how did it come to us? (8:26)

The command to seal up the vision apparently meant that Daniel should conclude it. The point was to preserve it for the future, not to keep it a secret.

If Daniel couldn't understand, how can we? (8:27)

While our interpretations may be flawed, we do have the advantage of hindsight; some of Daniel's future is history to us. We also have prophetic New Testament passages (such as Matthew 24 and the book of Revelation) for comparison. Yet we would do well to respond with awe and humility to these mysteries, as Daniel did.

Where did Daniel read Jeremiah's prophecies? (9:2)

After most of Judah's people were deported to Babylon in 586 B.C., Jeremiah and many other remaining Jews fled to Egypt. His letter to the exiles in Babylon (Jer. 29) must have made its way to Daniel, along with all or part of the rest of the book of Jeremiah. While Jeremiah's writings had not yet been adopted officially as Scripture, their accurate prediction of Judah's fall probably led Daniel to accept them as such.

SCRIPTURE LINK (9:2) Seventy years

See Jer. 25:11–14.

Why did Jeremiah's prophecy prompt Daniel to pray? (9:3)

Jeremiah had assured the people that the captivity would end after 70 years. Since the first captives had been taken from Jerusalem around 605 B.C. and it was now about 538 B.C., Daniel realized the 70 years were nearly over. Since repentance was required before God would return his people to their home (Deut. 30:1–3), Daniel repented as if every one of Judah's sins had been his own. See *Why did Daniel consider himself guilty for the nation's sins?* (9:5).

Do fasting, sackcloth and ashes help to change God's mind? (9:3)

These practices had long been signs of mourning in Middle Eastern culture (Gen. 37:34). Daniel was expressing his grief and shame over the sins of his people—not trying to impress God with self-denial. Expressing sincere grief for sin is still appropriate, whether or not it's done with fasting, sackcloth and ashes. When sin is not an issue, effective prayer seems to be based on faith (Matt. 17:20) and praying in harmony with God's will (Matt. 6:10).

Why did Daniel consider himself guilty for the nation's sins? (9:5)

Confessing on behalf of the Jewish nation was a long-standing practice for priests, prophets and kings (Lev. 16:21; Ezra 10:1; Neh. 1:6). The New Testament emphasizes confession of individual sin (1 John 1:9; 2:1), but many Christians believe repentance on behalf of a nation (2 Chron. 7:14) still applies today. In any case, we can acknowledge our own dependence on God by humbly identifying with the sins of those around us—as Daniel did.

appointed time of the end.[a] 20The two-horned ram that you saw represents the kings of Media and Persia. 21The shaggy goat is the king of Greece, and the large horn between his eyes is the first king. 22The four horns that replaced the one that was broken off represent four kingdoms that will emerge from his nation but will not have the same power.

23"In the latter part of their reign, when rebels have become completely wicked, a stern-faced king, a master of intrigue, will arise. 24He will become very strong, but not by his own power. He will cause astounding devastation and will succeed in whatever he does. He will destroy the mighty men and the holy people. 25He will cause deceit to prosper, and he will consider himself superior. When they feel secure, he will destroy many and take his stand against the Prince of princes. Yet he will be destroyed, but not by human power.

26"The vision[D] of the evenings and mornings that has been given you is true, but seal up the vision, for it concerns the distant future."

27I, Daniel, was exhausted and lay ill for several days. Then I got up and went about the king's business. I was appalled by the vision; it was beyond understanding.

Daniel's Prayer

9 In the first year of Darius son of Xerxes[b] (a Mede by descent), who was made ruler over the Babylonian[c] kingdom— 2in the first year of his reign, I, Daniel, understood from the Scriptures, according to the word of the LORD given to Jeremiah the prophet[D], that the desolation of Jerusalem[D] would last seventy years. 3So I turned to the Lord God and pleaded with him in prayer and petition, in fasting, and in sackcloth[D] and ashes.

4I prayed to the LORD my God and confessed:

"O Lord, the great and awesome God, who keeps his covenant[D] of love with all who love him and obey his commands, 5we have sinned and done wrong. We have been wicked and have rebelled; we have turned away from your commands and laws. 6We have not listened to your servants the prophets, who spoke in your name to our kings, our princes and our fathers, and to all the people of the land.

7"Lord, you are righteous[D], but this day we are covered with shame—the men of Judah and people of Jerusalem and all Israel, both near and far, in all the countries where you have scattered us because of our unfaithfulness to you. 8O LORD, we and our kings, our princes and our fathers are covered with shame because we have sinned against you. 9The Lord our God is merciful and forgiving, even though we have rebelled against him; 10we have not obeyed the LORD our God or kept the laws he gave us through his servants the prophets. 11All Israel has transgressed your law and turned away, refusing to obey you.

"Therefore the curses and sworn judgments written in the Law of Moses, the servant of God, have been poured out on us, because we have sinned against you. 12You have fulfilled the words spoken against us and against our rulers by bringing upon us

---

[a]19 Or *because the end will be at the appointed time*   [b]1 Hebrew *Ahasuerus*   [c]1 Or *Chaldean*

great disaster. Under the whole heaven nothing has ever been done like what has been done to Jerusalem[D]. [13]Just as it is written in the Law of Moses, all this disaster has come upon us, yet we have not sought the favor of the LORD our God by turning from our sins and giving attention to your truth. [14]The LORD did not hesitate to bring the disaster upon us, for the LORD our God is righteous[D] in everything he does; yet we have not obeyed him.

[15]"Now, O Lord our God, who brought your people out of Egypt with a mighty hand and who made for yourself a name that endures to this day, we have sinned, we have done wrong. [16]O Lord, in keeping with all your righteous acts, turn away your anger and your wrath from Jerusalem, your city, your holy hill. Our sins and the iniquities of our fathers have made Jerusalem and your people an object of scorn to all those around us.

[17]"Now, our God, hear the prayers and petitions of your servant. For your sake, O Lord, look with favor on your desolate sanctuary. [18]Give ear, O God, and hear; open your eyes and see the desolation of the city that bears your Name. We do not make requests of you because we are righteous, but because of your great mercy[D]. [19]O Lord, listen! O Lord, forgive! O Lord, hear and act! For your sake, O my God, do not delay, because your city and your people bear your Name."

The Seventy "Sevens"

[20]While I was speaking and praying, confessing my sin and the sin of my people Israel and making my request to the LORD my God for his holy hill— [21]while I was still in prayer, Gabriel[D], the man I had seen in the earlier vision[D], came to me in swift flight about the time of the evening sacrifice[D]. [22]He instructed me and said to me, "Daniel, I have now come to give you insight and understanding. [23]As soon as you began to pray, an answer was given, which I have come to tell you, for you are highly esteemed. Therefore, consider the message and understand the vision:

[24]"Seventy 'sevens'[a] are decreed for your people and your holy city to finish[b] transgression, to put an end to sin, to atone for wickedness, to bring in everlasting righteousness[D], to seal up vision and prophecy and to anoint[D] the most holy.[c]

[25]"Know and understand this: From the issuing of the decree[d] to restore and rebuild Jerusalem until the Anointed One,[e] the ruler, comes, there will be seven 'sevens,' and sixty-two 'sevens.' It will be rebuilt with streets and a trench, but in times of trouble. [26]After the sixty-two 'sevens,' the Anointed One will be cut off and will have nothing.[f] The people of the ruler who will come will destroy the city and the sanctuary. The end will come like a flood: War will continue until the end, and desolations have been decreed. [27]He will confirm a covenant[D] with many for one 'seven.'[g] In the middle of the 'seven'[g] he will put an end to sacrifice and offering. And on a wing ⌊of the temple⌋ he will set up an abomina-

---

[a]24 Or 'weeks'; also in verses 25 and 26   [b]24 Or restrain
[c]24 Or Most Holy Place; or most holy One   [d]25 Or word
[e]25 Or an anointed one; also in verse 26   [f]26 Or off and will have
no one; or off, but not for himself   [g]27 Or 'week'

SCRIPTURE LINK (9:11) *Curses and sworn judgments*
See Lev. 26:33; Deut. 28:63–67.

Exactly what had happened to Jerusalem? (9:12; also v. 2)

After attacking Jerusalem in 605 B.C., the Babylonians returned in 597 B.C. and took an estimated 10,000 captives. In 588 B.C. Nebuchadnezzar's army undertook an 18-month siege of the city. Jerusalem was eventually looted and the palace and temple were burned along with the city walls and fortifications. While Jerusalem and the temple were not literally leveled, the destruction was complete enough that most were cut off from their homeland and center of worship for about 70 years.

What does this prophecy mean? (9:24–27)

The 70 "sevens" (v. 24) could be 70 weeks, but many think they are 70 seven-year periods, or 490 years. Some believe the six goals in v. 24 were met during and shortly after Jesus' earthly ministry, which occurred about 490 years after the rebuilding of Jerusalem was decreed. Others think the goals *began* to be met in the first 69 sevens, or 483 years—but that complete achievement of these goals will not happen until the 70th seven-year period, which they say has been delayed until the end of history (Rev. 21). The *Anointed One* (v. 25) is the Christ Messiah, and his being *cut off* (v. 26) is his crucifixion. Jerusalem's destruction (v. 26) came at the hands of the Roman emperor Titus in A.D. 70; some think *ruler* (v. 26) also refers to a future leader who will make a peace treaty with Israel, only to turn against that nation and demand worship himself (Rev. 13:8).

Abomination that causes desolation (9:27)

This first happened in 168 B.C. when Antiochus IV Epiphanes desecrated the temple with a pagan altar. See *Prince of the host* (8:11). Some believe it happened again around A.D. 40 when Emperor Caligula tried to desecrate the temple and in A.D. 70 when the Romans finally destroyed Jerusalem. Jesus predicted a similar desecration, apparently yet to come (Matt. 24:15), which many believe will be engineered in the end times by a powerful rebel against God (2 Thes. 2:3–4), often identified as the antichrist. Also see *Abomination that causes desolation* (Matt. 24:15).

tion[D] that causes desolation, until the end that is decreed is poured out on him.[a][b]

Daniel's Vision of a Man

10 In the third year of Cyrus[D] king of Persia, a revelation[D] was given to Daniel (who was called Belteshazzar). Its message was true and it concerned a great war.[c] The understanding of the message came to him in a vision[D].

[2]At that time I, Daniel, mourned for three weeks. [3]I ate no choice food; no meat or wine touched my lips; and I used no lotions at all until the three weeks were over.

[4]On the twenty-fourth day of the first month, as I was standing on the bank of the great river, the Tigris, [5]I looked up and there before me was a man dressed in linen, with a belt of the finest gold around his waist. [6]His body was like chrysolite, his face like lightning, his eyes like flaming torches, his arms and legs like the gleam of burnished bronze, and his voice like the sound of a multitude.

[7]I, Daniel, was the only one who saw the vision; the men with me did not see it, but such terror overwhelmed them that they fled and hid themselves. [8]So I was left alone, gazing at this great vision; I had no strength left, my face turned deathly pale and I was helpless. [9]Then I heard him speaking, and as I listened to him, I fell into a deep sleep, my face to the ground.

[10]A hand touched me and set me trembling on my hands and knees. [11]He said, "Daniel, you who are highly esteemed, consider carefully the words I am about to speak to you, and stand up, for I have now been sent to you." And when he said this to me, I stood up trembling.

[12]Then he continued, "Do not be afraid, Daniel. Since the first day that you set your mind to gain understanding and to humble yourself before your God, your words were heard, and I have come in response to them. [13]But the prince of the Persian kingdom resisted me twenty-one days. Then Michael, one of the chief princes, came to help me, because I was detained there with the king of Persia. [14]Now I have come to explain to you what will happen to your people in the future, for the vision concerns a time yet to come."

[15]While he was saying this to me, I bowed with my face toward the ground and was speechless. [16]Then one who looked like a man[d] touched my lips, and I opened my mouth and began to speak. I said to the one standing before me, "I am overcome with anguish because of the vision, my lord, and I am helpless. [17]How can I, your servant, talk with you, my lord? My strength is gone and I can hardly breathe."

[18]Again the one who looked like a man touched me and gave me strength. [19]"Do not be afraid, O man highly esteemed," he said. "Peace[D]! Be strong now; be strong."

When he spoke to me, I was strengthened and said, "Speak, my lord, since you have given me strength."

[20]So he said, "Do you know why I have come to you? Soon I will return to fight against the prince of Persia, and

Had Daniel abandoned his vegetarian diet? (10:3)

As a new captive, Daniel had preferred a vegetable-and-water diet. See *How would the king's food and wine have "defiled" Daniel?* (1:8). But it's unlikely he maintained that diet after he'd received his official appointment to serve the king. No doubt Daniel, who had been a top Babylonian official for decades, was allowed to have his food prepared in keeping with his faith. This then would have been a partial fast —eliminating the best foods from his Jewish diet as an expression of mourning.

Who was this *man*? (10:5)

Probably an angel—perhaps Gabriel, who had visited Daniel before (8:16). Some suggest the man was Christ, given the similar description in Rev. 1:13–16. But it seems unlikely that Christ would need help from the angel Michael (10:13) in a spiritual battle.

SCRIPTURE LINK (10:5–6)

A similar description of Christ is found in Rev. 1:12–16.

Why was the answer to Daniel's prayer delayed? (10:12)

Gabriel was detained by a stubborn Persian ruler who was either demonic or human (see following note). Angels, not God himself, were fighting this battle—and, unlike God, angels are not all-powerful. The Bible doesn't say why God allowed Gabriel to be hindered, but it does state clearly that God's enemies will suffer a crushing, final defeat when he decides the time is right (Rev. 20:10).

Why would the prince of Persia battle an angel? (10:13)

Some think this was a spiritual fight in which a demon assigned to Persia was trying to keep Gabriel from getting his message to Daniel. Some speculate that God assigned each nation a guardian angel, that Satan countered with a high-ranking demon and that clashes between these forces are part of the battle Paul describes in Ephesians 6:12. Others believe that this refers to human rulers of Persia and Greece who opposed Israel.

---

[a]27 Or *it*   [b]27 Or *And one who causes desolation will come upon the pinnacle of the abominable ⌞temple⌟, until the end that is decreed is poured out on the desolated ⌞city⌟*   [c]1 Or *true and burdensome*
[d]16 Most manuscripts of the Masoretic Text; one manuscript of the Masoretic Text, Dead Sea Scrolls and Septuagint *Then something that looked like a man's hand*

when I go, the prince of Greece will come; **21**but first I will tell you what is written in the Book of Truth. (No one supports me against them except Michael, your prince.

11 **1**And in the first year of Darius the Mede, I took my stand to support and protect him.)

The Kings of the South and the North

2"Now then, I tell you the truth: Three more kings will appear in Persia, and then a fourth, who will be far richer than all the others. When he has gained power by his wealth, he will stir up everyone against the kingdom of Greece. **3**Then a mighty king will appear, who will rule with great power and do as he pleases. **4**After he has appeared, his empire will be broken up and parceled out toward the four winds of heaven. It will not go to his descendants, nor will it have the power he exercised, because his empire will be uprooted and given to others.

5"The king of the South will become strong, but one of his commanders will become even stronger than he and will rule his own kingdom with great power. **6**After some years, they will become allies. The daughter of the king of the South will go to the king of the North to make an alliance, but she will not retain her power, and he and his power*a* will not last. In those days she will be handed over, together with her royal escort and her father*b* and the one who supported her.

7"One from her family line will arise to take her place. He will attack the forces of the king of the North and enter his fortress; he will fight against them and be victorious. **8**He will also seize their gods, their metal images and their valuable articles of silver and gold and carry them off to Egypt. For some years he will leave the king of the North alone. **9**Then the king of the North will invade the realm of the king of the South but will retreat to his own country. **10**His sons will prepare for war and assemble a great army, which will sweep on like an irresistible flood and carry the battle as far as his fortress.

*a*6 Or *offspring*   *b*6 Or *child* (see Vulgate and Syriac)

Book of Truth (10:21)

This may be God's account of the destiny of every person and nation. Or it could be his general record of truth, which would include the Bible.

How were these prophecies fulfilled? (11:2–45)

After three more Persian kings reigned (v. 2), Xerxes came to the throne and tried unsuccessfully to conquer Greece in 480 B.C. Daniel predicted the reign of Alexander the Great (v. 3) and, after his death, the disputes between his four generals (v. 4).

The kings *of the South* (v. 5) were the Ptolemies; the kings *of the North* (v. 6) were the Seleucids. Six Ptolemies and seven Seleucids are mentioned here; the predictions of their battles, marriages and intrigues came true, down to the last detail. Antiochus III (223 to 187 B.C.) took control of Palestine from the Ptolemies by 197 B.C. (v. 16).

Most of the remaining prophecies in this section focus on Israel. Attacks on Israel mounted until Antiochus IV—the *contemptible person* (v. 21)—profaned the temple. See **Prince of the host** (8:11).

Many assume the prophecies after v. 35 point to events and persons yet to come. The self-exalting king is thought by some to be the *beast* (Rev. 13:5–8), whose battles with other nations (vv. 40–45) apparently will end at Jerusalem's temple mount (v. 45), perhaps in connection with the battle of Armageddon (Rev. 16:13–16).

Beautiful Land (11:16)
See *Beautiful Land* (8:9).

Prince of the covenant (11:22)
Perhaps the high priest Onias III, murdered in 170 B.C. This phrase could also be translated *confederate prince*, in which case it could be Egypt's Ptolemy VI Philometor (181–146 B.C.).

11"Then the king of the South will march out in a rage and fight against the king of the North, who will raise a large army, but it will be defeated. 12When the army is carried off, the king of the South will be filled with pride and will slaughter many thousands, yet he will not remain triumphant. 13For the king of the North will muster another army, larger than the first; and after several years, he will advance with a huge army fully equipped.

14"In those times many will rise against the king of the South. The violent men among your own people will rebel in fulfillment of the vision[D], but without success. 15Then the king of the North will come and build up siege ramps and will capture a fortified city. The forces of the South will be powerless to resist; even their best troops will not have the strength to stand. 16The invader will do as he pleases; no one will be able to stand against him. He will establish himself in the Beautiful Land and will have the power to destroy it. 17He will determine to come with the might of his entire kingdom and will make an alliance with the king of the South. And he will give him a daughter in marriage in order to overthrow the kingdom, but his plans[a] will not succeed or help him. 18Then he will turn his attention to the coastlands and will take many of them, but a commander will put an end to his insolence and will turn his insolence back upon him. 19After this, he will turn back toward the fortresses of his own country but will stumble and fall, to be seen no more.

20"His successor will send out a tax collector[D] to maintain the royal splendor. In a few years, however, he will be destroyed, yet not in anger or in battle.

21"He will be succeeded by a contemptible person who has not been given the honor of royalty. He will invade the kingdom when its people feel secure, and he will seize it through intrigue. 22Then an overwhelming army will be swept away before him; both it and a prince of the covenant[D] will be destroyed. 23After coming to an agreement with him, he will act deceitfully, and with only a few people he will rise to power. 24When the richest provinces feel secure, he will invade them and will achieve what neither his fathers nor his forefathers did. He will distribute plunder[D], loot and wealth among his followers. He will plot the overthrow of fortresses—but only for a time.

25"With a large army he will stir up his strength and courage against the king of the South. The king of the South will wage war with a large and very powerful army, but he will not be able to stand because of the plots devised against him. 26Those who eat from the king's provisions will try to destroy him; his army will be swept away, and many will fall in battle. 27The two kings, with their hearts bent on evil, will sit at the same table and lie to each other, but to no avail, because an end will still come at the appointed time. 28The king of the North will return to his own country with great wealth, but his heart will be set against the holy covenant. He will take action against it and then return to his own country.

29"At the appointed time he will invade the South again, but this time the outcome will be different from what it was before. 30Ships of the western coastlands[b] will oppose him, and he will lose heart. Then he will turn back and vent his fury against the holy covenant. He will re-

a17 Or but she   *b30 Hebrew of Kittim*

turn and show favor to those who forsake the holy covenant[D].

31"His armed forces will rise up to desecrate[D] the temple fortress and will abolish the daily sacrifice[D]. Then they will set up the abomination[D] that causes desolation. **32**With flattery he will corrupt those who have violated the covenant, but the people who know their God will firmly resist him.

33"Those who are wise will instruct many, though for a time they will fall by the sword or be burned or captured or plundered[D]. **34**When they fall, they will receive a little help, and many who are not sincere will join them. **35**Some of the wise will stumble, so that they may be refined, purified[D] and made spotless until the time of the end, for it will still come at the appointed time.

The King Who Exalts Himself

36"The king will do as he pleases. He will exalt and magnify himself above every god and will say unheard-of things against the God of gods. He will be successful until the time of wrath is completed, for what has been determined must take place. **37**He will show no regard for the gods of his fathers or for the one desired by women, nor will he regard any god, but will exalt himself above them all. **38**Instead of them, he will honor a god of fortresses; a god unknown to his fathers he will honor with gold and silver, with precious stones and costly gifts. **39**He will attack the mightiest fortresses with the help of a foreign god and will greatly honor those who acknowledge him. He will make them rulers over many people and will distribute the land at a price.[a]

40"At the time of the end the king of the South will engage him in battle, and the king of the North will storm out against him with chariots and cavalry and a great fleet of ships. He will invade many countries and sweep through them like a flood. **41**He will also invade the Beautiful Land. Many countries will fall, but Edom[D], Moab and the leaders of Ammon will be delivered from his hand. **42**He will extend his power over many countries; Egypt will not escape. **43**He will gain control of the treasures of gold and silver and all the riches of Egypt, with the Libyans and Nubians in submission. **44**But reports from the east and the north will alarm him, and he will set out in a great rage to destroy and annihilate many. **45**He will pitch his royal tents between the seas at[b] the beautiful holy mountain. Yet he will come to his end, and no one will help him.

The End Times

12 "At that time Michael, the great prince who protects your people, will arise. There will be a time of distress such as has not happened from the beginning of nations until then. But at that time your people—everyone whose name is found written in the book—will be delivered. **2**Multitudes who sleep in the dust of the earth will awake: some to everlasting life, others to shame and everlasting contempt. **3**Those who are wise[c] will shine like the brightness of the heavens, and those who lead many to righteousness[D], like the stars for ever and ever. **4**But you, Daniel, close up and seal the words of the scroll

[a]39 Or *land for a reward*   [b]45 Or *the sea and*   [c]3 Or *who impart wisdom*

How was the temple a fortress? (11:31)

Temple fortress may mean *sanctuary of strength.* While the temple was not the kind of fortress that would repel an army, it represented the earthly "headquarters" of the Lord, a tangible source of strength for the Jewish people and a central focus for their faith.

Abomination that causes desolation (11:31)

See *Abomination that causes desolation* (9:27).

How can stumbling purify someone? (11:35)

Unlike other Biblical references to stumbling that mean sinning (James 2:10), this word refers to suffering. Like *fall* (vv. 33–34), *stumble* describes the difficulties that faithful Jews would face under the rule of Antiochus IV. See *Prince of the host* (8:11). Many Jews, refusing to abandon the true God for the false one Antiochus had set up, were tortured and killed. The result was a refining of Israel's faith. We should avoid stumbling into sin, but can welcome persecution for our faith—which promises to strengthen us (James 1:2–4).

One desired by women (11:37)

Perhaps Tammuz, a Babylonian fertility god (see Ezek. 8:14), mentioned here as an example of a false deity. Or this might refer to the Messiah. Some suggest that many Israelite women, hoping for the nation's rescuer, might have wondered whether they would have the honor of being his mother.

SCRIPTURE LINK (12:1) *The book*

For an explanation of what this book was, see Rev. 20:11–15.

How did the Old Testament view resurrection? (12:2,13)

The Hebrew word for the place of the dead offers few details about what it was like. Yet there are hints that the dead would be raised (Job 19:25–27; Psalm 49:15; Isaiah 25:8; 26:19). Daniel 12:2 is the first obvious mention of resurrection for both the righteous and the wicked.

When would the power of the holy people be broken? (12:7)

This verse seems to refer to a military conquest of Israel (11:40–41), which many believe will happen in the end times, perhaps as part of the battle of Armageddon (Rev. 16:13–16). The word *finally* seems to reflect the passage of time before the event—not its desirability.

How did Daniel's prophecies help? (12:9–10)

They made it clear that suffering would be followed by justice and God's eternal reign. For the exiles in Babylon, that meant new motivation to stay true to their faith. For those who would later suffer at the hands of Antiochus IV, it meant hope for a time when the Messiah would come. For the early Christians and oppressed believers today, it means a glimpse at the end of the story—when Christ will return.

What's been sealed until the time of the end? (12:9)

The prophecy was to be safeguarded so that current and future believers could benefit from it. See *If this vision was sealed, how did it come to us?* (8:26). The heavenly messenger also seemed to be saying that the prophecy was complete and further information would not be given (see Rev. 22:18–19).

Abomination that causes desolation (12:11)

See *Abomination that causes desolation* (9:27).

What happened when these two time periods had passed? (12:11–12)

The persecution by Antiochus IV Epiphanes was followed by the rededication of the temple in 165 B.C. If this is what the times stand for, it's not certain why one is longer than the other. Some think the times involve the great tribulation described in the book of Revelation (see Rev. 11:2–3). If so, the 45-day difference might be a gap between the end of the tribulation and the beginning of a 1,000-year reign by Jesus Christ.

until the time of the end. Many will go here and there to increase knowledge."

5Then I, Daniel, looked, and there before me stood two others, one on this bank of the river and one on the opposite bank. **6**One of them said to the man clothed in linen, who was above the waters of the river, "How long will it be before these astonishing things are fulfilled?"

7The man clothed in linen, who was above the waters of the river, lifted his right hand and his left hand toward heaven, and I heard him swear by him who lives forever, saying, "It will be for a time, times and half a time.[a] When the power of the holy people has been finally broken, all these things will be completed."

8I heard, but I did not understand. So I asked, "My lord, what will the outcome of all this be?"

9He replied, "Go your way, Daniel, because the words are closed up and sealed until the time of the end. **10**Many will be purified[D], made spotless and refined, but the wicked will continue to be wicked. None of the wicked will understand, but those who are wise will understand.

11"From the time that the daily sacrifice[D] is abolished and the abomination[D] that causes desolation is set up, there will be 1,290 days. **12**Blessed is the one who waits for and reaches the end of the 1,335 days.

13"As for you, go your way till the end. You will rest, and then at the end of the days you will rise to receive your allotted inheritance."

HOSEA

Why read this book?

This book tells a story as contemporary as today's talk shows—that of a man's love for his unfaithful spouse. But the story of the prophet Hosea and his wife Gomer illustrates another love story—that God loves us, even when our sins have broken his heart. Here is a picture of a God who longs to forgive us when we turn to him.

Who wrote this book?

Hosea, a prophet to the northern kingdom of Israel.

To whom was it written?

Hosea originally delivered his prophecies to the northern kingdom of Israel. After Assyria conquered Israel, the words were transcribed to scrolls as a record of prophecy fulfilled and as a warning—possibly to the remnant left behind in Israel, or possibly to the people of Judah.

When was it written?

Approximately 715 B.C. But Hosea first prophesied around 753 B.C. and continued to speak to the people until Samaria and the northern kingdom fell in 722 B.C.

What was happening at this time?

Jeroboam II was a wicked king whose leadership had produced a materialistic, immoral, unjust society. Six kings ruled Israel within 25 years. This was the twilight of the northern kingdom.

What to look for in Hosea:

Don't be shocked by the prostitution, unfaithfulness and sorrow in this book. Notice the stark consequences of sin as God states his case against his people. But then, look beyond Hosea's suffering (and God's pain) to see an example of love that will not quit—first, in God's love for his people Israel, and second, in God's love for us. Look for ways that Hosea loved his undeserving wife and consider how God does the same for us.

When did these things happen?

TIME LINE

	1300 BC	1200	1100	1000	900	800	700	600	500	400
Division of the kingdom (930 B.C.)										
Ministries of Elijah and Elisha in Israel (c.875-797 B.C.)										
Amos's ministry in Israel (c.760-750 B.C.)										
Hosea's ministry in Israel (c.753-715 B.C.)										
Ministries of Micah and Isaiah in Judah (c.742-681 B.C.)										
Exile of Israel (722 B.C.)										
Book of Hosea written (c.715 B.C.)										
Fall of Jerusalem (586 B.C.)										

1 The word of the LORD that came to Hosea son of Beeri during the reigns of Uzziah, Jotham, Ahaz and Hezekiah, kings of Judah, and during the reign of Jeroboam son of Jehoash*a* king of Israel:

Hosea's Wife and Children

2When the LORD began to speak through Hosea, the LORD said to him, "Go, take to yourself an adulterous wife and children of unfaithfulness, because the land is guilty of the vilest adultery in departing from the LORD." **3**So he married Gomer daughter of Diblaim, and she conceived and bore him a son.

4Then the LORD said to Hosea, "Call him Jezreel, because I will soon punish the house of Jehu for the massacre at Jezreel, and I will put an end to the kingdom of Israel. **5**In that day I will break Israel's bow in the Valley of Jezreel."

6Gomer conceived again and gave birth to a daughter. Then the LORD said to Hosea, "Call her Lo-Ruhamah,*b* for I will no longer show love to the house of Israel, that I should at all forgive them. **7**Yet I will show love to the house of Judah; and I will save them—not by bow, sword or battle, or by horses and horsemen, but by the LORD their God."

8After she had weaned Lo-Ruhamah, Gomer had another son. **9**Then the LORD said, "Call him Lo-Ammi,*c* for you are not my people, and I am not your God.

10"Yet the Israelites will be like the sand on the seashore, which cannot be measured or counted. In the place where it was said to them, 'You are not my people,' they will be called 'sons of the living God.' **11**The people of Judah and the people of Israel will be reunited, and they will appoint one leader and will come up out of the land, for great will be the day of Jezreel.

2 "Say of your brothers, 'My people,' and of your sisters, 'My loved one.'

Israel Punished and Restored

2"Rebuke your mother, rebuke her,
   for she is not my wife,
   and I am not her husband.
Let her remove the adulterous look from her
      face
   and the unfaithfulness from between her
      breasts.
3Otherwise I will strip her naked
   and make her as bare as on the day she was
      born;
I will make her like a desert,
   turn her into a parched land,
   and slay her with thirst.
4I will not show my love to her children,
   because they are the children of adultery.
5Their mother has been unfaithful
   and has conceived them in disgrace.
She said, 'I will go after my lovers,
   who give me my food and my water,
   my wool and my linen, my oil and my
      drink.'

Why would God tell a godly man to marry an adulteress? (1:2)

Hosea risked losing everything—family, friends, reputation and self-respect. Yet God was saying through Hosea's marriage, "Wake up, Israel!" God wanted Hosea to demonstrate God's own love for his unfaithful people.

Did Hosea's wife already have children when he married her? (1:2)

There is the strong possibility that Gomer was a prostitute who had borne children out of wedlock with unknown fathers. These children might also be the offspring of an adulterous relationship after Hosea married Gomer.

Why call Israel *Jezreel?* (1:4)

Jehu had engineered the slaughter of the descendants of Ahab at Jezreel in fulfillment of the prophecies of Elijah (1 Kings 21:21; 2 Kings 10:1–11). So *Jezreel* became a picture of judgment as well as a warning to heed God's prophet.

Why choose such odd names for children? (1:4,6,9)

The Israelites often named children to reflect the circumstances surrounding their conception and birth. But the names Hosea selected were unusual even by the standards of his Jewish culture. He gave these names to send a message about the consequences of sin.

Wouldn't a name that means *not loved* harm a child's self-esteem? (1:6)

Perhaps. But probably not any more than the pain of having a mother like Gomer who would abandon her husband and children to live with another man (3:1). Since Hosea was committed to demonstrate God's unconditional love, he probably showed more love to Lo-Ruhamah than Gomer did. But see **Why refuse to love children of adultery?** (2:4–5).

What was meant by the promise of a reunited Judah and Israel? (1:11)

This common prophetic theme spoke of restoring Israel as a political and spiritual power. It's a reminder to us that God will accomplish his purposes despite humanity's failures.

How could *Jezreel* be a picture of something good? (1:11)

The *events* at Jezreel pictured judgment; see **Why call Israel *Jezreel?*** (1:4). However, the word *Jezreel* literally means *God scatters*—a picture of scattering seed for planting. Planting was a positive image because it anticipated a harvest.

Why refuse to love *children* of adultery? (2:4–5)

This continues the metaphor for the terrible consequences of unfaithfulness to God. It contrasts with God's promise to call the Israelites 'sons of the living God' (1:10).

a1 Hebrew *Joash,* a variant of *Jehoash*   *b6 Lo-Ruhamah* means *not loved.*   *c9 Lo-Ammi* means *not my people.*

⁶Therefore I will block her path with
        thornbushes;
    I will wall her in so that she cannot find her
        way.
⁷She will chase after her lovers but not catch
        them;
    she will look for them but not find them.
Then she will say,
    'I will go back to my husband as at first,
    for then I was better off than now.'
⁸She has not acknowledged that I was the one
    who gave her the grain, the new wineᴰ and
        oil,
    who lavished on her the silver and gold—
    which they used for Baalᴰ.

⁹"Therefore I will take away my grain when it
        ripens,
    and my new wine when it is ready.
    I will take back my wool and my linen,
        intended to cover her nakedness.
¹⁰So now I will expose her lewdness
    before the eyes of her lovers;
    no one will take her out of my hands.
¹¹I will stop all her celebrations:
    her yearly festivals, her New Moons,
    her Sabbathᴰ days—all her appointed feasts.
¹²I will ruin her vines and her fig trees,
    which she said were her pay from her lovers;
    I will make them a thicket,
    and wild animals will devour them.
¹³I will punish her for the days
    she burned incenseᴰ to the Baals;
    she decked herself with rings and jewelry,
    and went after her lovers,
    but me she forgot,"
                                    declares the LORD.

¹⁴"Therefore I am now going to allure her;
    I will lead her into the desert
    and speak tenderly to her.
¹⁵There I will give her back her vineyards,
    and will make the Valley of Achorᵃ a door
        of hope.
    There she will singᵇ as in the days of her
        youth,
    as in the day she came up out of Egypt.
¹⁶"In that day," declares the LORD,
    "you will call me 'my husband';
    you will no longer call me 'my master.ᶜ'
¹⁷I will remove the names of the Baals from
        her lips;
    no longer will their names be invoked.
¹⁸In that day I will make a covenantᴰ for them
    with the beasts of the field and the birds of
        the air
    and the creatures that move along the
        ground.
    Bow and sword and battle
    I will abolish from the land,
    so that all may lie down in safety.
¹⁹I will betroth you to me forever;

Why stop God-appointed celebrations? (2:11)

This was actually a picture of the destruction that could come to Israel—a destruction so complete that the people would be forbidden to practice their religious customs. Their religion had become empty ritual. God hates insincere religious rituals accompanied by disobedience (see Amos 5:21–24).

Why does God act like a jealous lover? (2:13–14)

Though God is sovereign and in need of nothing, he has chosen to reveal himself as a God deeply in love with his creation. Hosea shows that God is not merely a business-like overseer of the world who methodically dispenses appropriate judgment: He also is a God with feelings. He can be grieved, angered, frustrated or delighted by our behavior. He illustrates this side of his nature by describing a spouse who has been betrayed and who swings from emotion to emotion. Nevertheless, throughout the Bible, the threat of punishment is consistently followed by tender promises of intimacy.

ᵃ15 Achor means trouble.   ᵇ15 Or respond   ᶜ16 Hebrew baal

I will betroth you in^a righteousness^D and
  justice,
  in^b love and compassion.
20I will betroth you in faithfulness,
  and you will acknowledge the LORD.

21"In that day I will respond,"
  declares the LORD—
  "I will respond to the skies,
    and they will respond to the earth;
22and the earth will respond to the grain,
  the new wine^D and oil,
    and they will respond to Jezreel.^{c}
23I will plant her for myself in the land;
  I will show my love to the one I called 'Not
    my loved one.^{d}'
I will say to those called 'Not my people,^{e}'
  'You are my people';
  and they will say, 'You are my God.'"

Hosea's Reconciliation With His Wife

3 The LORD said to me, "Go, show your love to your
wife again, though she is loved by another and is an
adulteress. Love her as the LORD loves the Israelites,
though they turn to other gods and love the sacred^D raisin cakes." 2So I bought her for fifteen shekels$^{D\!f}$ of silver and
about a homer and a lethek^g of barley. 3Then I told her,
"You are to live with^h me many days; you must not be a
prostitute or be intimate with any man, and I will live
with^h you."

4For the Israelites will live many days without king or
prince, without sacrifice^D or sacred stones^D, without
ephod^D or idol^D. 5Afterward the Israelites will return
and seek the LORD their God and David their king. They
will come trembling to the LORD and to his blessings in the
last days.

The Charge Against Israel

4 Hear the word of the LORD, you Israelites,
    because the LORD has a charge to bring
    against you who live in the land:
  "There is no faithfulness, no love,
    no acknowledgment of God in the land.
2There is only cursing,^{i} lying and murder,
    stealing and adultery;
  they break all bounds,
    and bloodshed follows bloodshed.
3Because of this the land mourns,^{j}
    and all who live in it waste away;
  the beasts of the field and the birds of the air
    and the fish of the sea are dying.

4"But let no man bring a charge,
    let no man accuse another,
  for your people are like those
    who bring charges against a priest^D.
5You stumble day and night,
    and the prophets^D stumble with you.

Sacred raisin cakes (3:1)
Used in the worship of Baal. The implication
was that Israel had turned to idolatry to enjoy
the sensuality of pagan rituals.

**Why did Hosea have to pay to buy back
his wife? (3:2)**
Gomer had apparently sold herself into prostitution, possibly with one of the pagan sects
that engaged prostitutes as part of its worship
practices. Hosea had to reimburse the man at
least what he had paid for her services—six
ounces of silver (see NIV text note), worth
about half the value of a slave (Exodus 21:32)
plus nearly ten bushels of barley.

**What does this prediction refer
to? (3:4)**
This is the eventual destruction of Israel which
occurred in 722 B.C. The Assyrians under Shalmaneser invaded the land, laid siege to Samaria, finally capturing the city and carrying its residents off to exile in Nineveh. See 2 Kings
17:3–6.

Was Hosea exaggerating? (4:1–2)
Perhaps. The prophets often used exaggeration to emphasize a point. From Hosea's perspective, it probably seemed that there was no
faithfulness, no love and no acknowledgment
of God. In reality, there were likely others who,
like Hosea himself, remained faithful to the
Lord.

**What's wrong with bringing a charge
against a priest? (4:4)**
Hosea was accusing the people of blaming the
priests without accepting responsibility for
their own sins. Their lack of respect for the
priesthood was also an expression of their rebellion against God's authority. On the other
hand, Hosea himself leveled charges against
the priests because they too were guilty of ignoring God's law (v. 6).

---

^{a}19 Or with; also in verse 20 ^{b}19 Or with ^{c}22 Jezreel means
God plants. ^{d}23 Hebrew Lo-Ruhamah ^{e}23 Hebrew Lo-Ammi
^{f}2 That is, about 6 ounces (about 170 grams) ^{g}2 That is, probably
about 10 bushels (about 330 liters) ^{h}3 Or wait for ^{i}2 That is,
to pronounce a curse upon ^{j}3 Or dries up

So I will destroy your mother—
6 my people are destroyed from lack of
        knowledge.

"Because you have rejected knowledge,
    I also reject you as my priests[D];
because you have ignored the law of your God,
    I also will ignore your children.
7The more the priests increased,
    the more they sinned against me;
they exchanged[a] their[b] Glory[D] for
        something disgraceful.
8They feed on the sins of my people
    and relish their wickedness.
9And it will be: Like people, like priests.
    I will punish both of them for their ways
    and repay them for their deeds.

10"They will eat but not have enough;
    they will engage in prostitution but not
        increase,
because they have deserted the LORD
    to give themselves 11to prostitution,
to old wine and new,
    which take away the understanding 12of my
        people.
They consult a wooden idol[D]
    and are answered by a stick of wood.
A spirit of prostitution leads them astray;
    they are unfaithful to their God.
13They sacrifice[D] on the mountaintops
    and burn offerings on the hills,
under oak, poplar and terebinth,
    where the shade is pleasant.
Therefore your daughters turn to prostitution
    and your daughters-in-law to adultery.

14"I will not punish your daughters
    when they turn to prostitution,

a7 Syriac and an ancient Hebrew scribal tradition; Masoretic Text
I will exchange   *b7* Masoretic Text; an ancient Hebrew scribal
tradition *my*

What's the difference between old wine and new wine? (4:11)

Some believe that new wine was not yet fermented. Others think it simply meant wine not fully aged but still intoxicating since it would *take away the understanding.* Hosea's point may have been that those addicted to wine were impatient and drank the wine before its time. Or he may have meant they did not bother to discriminate between fine and poor wine.

How did men sacrifice with shrine prostitutes? (4:14)

Many pagan religions have been heavily subsidized by proceeds from prostitution. Shrine prostitutes were purchased as a religious rite in various temples and ceremonies in cultures surrounding Israel. A sacrifice was normally paid for the right of sexual intercourse with a prostitute. These sexual acts were committed under the thin veneer of imitating the gods through "dramas." They were also used in fertility rites to symbolically express gratitude for the changing of the seasons or to request bountiful crops.

What was the *spirit of prostitution?* (4:12)

This was a figurative way to describe Israel's unfaithfulness to God. The Hebrew language used words like *spirit* to describe a person's inner characteristics or disposition. Israel's tendency was to commit spiritual "prostitution"—being unfaithful to God and chasing after other gods, just as a prostitute solicits customers to buy sexual favors.

Such a description was doubly appropriate since the worship of foreign gods frequently involved literal prostitution (vv. 13–14). See *How did men sacrifice with shrine prostitutes?* (4:14).

The ancient Israelites were not the only people to become involved in a *spirit of prostitution.* Today people can be tempted to be unfaithful toward God by abandoning their commitment to him. Whenever people desire the ways of the culture around them, including its pleasures and forms of instant gratification, we see the *spirit of prostitution.* Those who are disobedient to God are guilty of spiritual adultery.

nor your daughters-in-law
  when they commit adultery,
because the men themselves consort with
    harlots
  and sacrifice[D] with shrine prostitutes[D]—
  a people without understanding will come to
    ruin!

15"Though you commit adultery, O Israel,
  let not Judah become guilty.

"Do not go to Gilgal;
  do not go up to Beth Aven.[a]
  And do not swear, 'As surely as the LORD
    lives!'
16The Israelites are stubborn,
  like a stubborn heifer.
How then can the LORD pasture them
  like lambs in a meadow?
17Ephraim is joined to idols[D];
  leave him alone!
18Even when their drinks are gone,
  they continue their prostitution;
  their rulers dearly love shameful ways.
19A whirlwind will sweep them away,
  and their sacrifices will bring them shame.

Judgment Against Israel

5 "Hear this, you priests[D]!
  Pay attention, you Israelites!
Listen, O royal house!
  This judgment is against you:
You have been a snare at Mizpah,
  a net spread out on Tabor.
2The rebels are deep in slaughter.
  I will discipline all of them.
3I know all about Ephraim;
  Israel is not hidden from me.
Ephraim, you have now turned to prostitution;
  Israel is corrupt.

4"Their deeds do not permit them
  to return to their God.
A spirit of prostitution is in their heart;
  they do not acknowledge the LORD.
5Israel's arrogance testifies against them;
  the Israelites, even Ephraim, stumble in their
    sin;
  Judah also stumbles with them.
6When they go with their flocks and herds
  to seek the LORD,
they will not find him;
  he has withdrawn himself from them.
7They are unfaithful to the LORD;
  they give birth to illegitimate children.
Now their New Moon festivals[D]
  will devour them and their fields.

8"Sound the trumpet in Gibeah,
  the horn in Ramah.
Raise the battle cry in Beth Aven[a];
  lead on, O Benjamin.
9Ephraim will be laid waste

What did Hosea mean by Judah not becoming guilty? (4:15)

He was using the example of the northern kingdom of Israel to warn the southern kingdom of Judah. Hosea probably wrote down the warnings he had given Israel shortly after it fell to Assyria (see Introduction: *To whom was it written?*). His hope was that Judah would avoid the guilt—and the consequences—of turning away from God as Israel had. Judah, however, encountered its own problems with idolatry and only survived Israel by 136 years.

Does God ever hide from us? (5:6)

Our sinful deeds (v. 4) and our arrogance (v. 5) can become like a wall separating us from God. Until we repent of such sinful attitudes and behavior, fellowship with God will be impossible. But when we seek God with repentant hearts, we will find him (Deut. 4:29).

---

a 15,8 *Beth Aven* means *house of wickedness* (a name for Bethel, which means *house of God*).

on the day of reckoning.
Among the tribes of Israel
    I proclaim what is certain.
[10]Judah's leaders are like those
    who move boundary stones.
I will pour out my wrath on them
    like a flood of water.
[11]Ephraim is oppressed,
    trampled in judgment,
    intent on pursuing idols[D, a]
[12]I am like a moth to Ephraim,
    like rot to the people of Judah.

[13]"When Ephraim saw his sickness,
    and Judah his sores,
then Ephraim turned to Assyria,
    and sent to the great king for help.
But he is not able to cure you,
    not able to heal your sores.
[14]For I will be like a lion to Ephraim,
    like a great lion to Judah.
I will tear them to pieces and go away;
    I will carry them off, with no one to rescue
        them.
[15]Then I will go back to my place
    until they admit their guilt.
And they will seek my face;
    in their misery they will earnestly seek me."

Israel Unrepentant

6   "Come, let us return to the LORD.
    He has torn us to pieces
      but he will heal us;
    he has injured us
      but he will bind up our wounds.
[2]After two days he will revive us;
    on the third day he will restore us,
    that we may live in his presence.
[3]Let us acknowledge the LORD;
    let us press on to acknowledge him.
As surely as the sun rises,
    he will appear;
he will come to us like the winter rains,
    like the spring rains that water the earth."

[4]"What can I do with you, Ephraim?
    What can I do with you, Judah?
Your love is like the morning mist,
    like the early dew that disappears.
[5]Therefore I cut you in pieces with my
        prophets[D],
    I killed you with the words of my mouth;
    my judgments flashed like lightning upon
        you.
[6]For I desire mercy[D], not sacrifice[D],
    and acknowledgment of God rather than
        burnt offerings[D].
[7]Like Adam,[b] they have broken the
      covenant[D]—
    they were unfaithful to me there.
[8]Gilead is a city of wicked men,
    stained with footprints of blood.

What was meant by moving boundary stones? (5:10)

Judah's legal system had become thoroughly corrupt, just like that of Israel. Hosea accused the leaders of cheating others and stealing their land by changing the boundary lines. Their actions would have been like someone today altering a deed or purchase agreement deceptively, in order to get more property. But Hosea's implications were even broader. These leaders were ignoring their civic responsibilities and forgetting their ultimate accountability to God.

When did Ephraim turn to Assyria? (5:13)

When Pul, king of Assyria, invaded Israel (*Ephraim*, a dominant tribe in the northern kingdom, was often used to describe the whole nation), King Menahem sought to pay him off with tribute. In a sense he bought protection from the very nation that was invading Israel. Though Assyria withdrew temporarily, Israel was left with a horrendous tax burden. See 2 Kings 15:19–20.

Was Israel's repentance genuine or fake? (6:1–3)

If genuine, these beautiful words of repentance were extremely short-lived (v. 4). It may be that Hosea recalled Israel's pattern throughout history: when in trouble, the people would cry out to God for help; when help came, the people would quickly revert to their old ways.

Why didn't God want the people to offer sacrifices anymore? (6:6)

God preferred to see the practical results of a repentant lifestyle. He wanted them to do what was right and just (2:19–20; Micah 6:8); he wanted them to turn away from sin. What God did not want was empty religious ritual. The people were simply going through the motions; they were following his instructions, but their hearts were not in their religious deeds.

---

[a]11 The meaning of the Hebrew for this word is uncertain.   [b]7 Or *As at Adam;* or *Like men*

How could priests become a murdering, marauding mob? (6:9)

The priests were destroying the people by leading them into idolatry and failing to provide genuine spiritual leadership. The results of the priests' actions would be just as devastating and destructive as if they were a hostile army invading the land.

What exactly did the people do to provoke God's anger? (7:1–4)

Israel was a society in turmoil. Six kings had reigned in 25 years. The nation had been seduced by foreign religions. It now wallowed in widespread immorality characterized by deceit, violence, robbery, adultery and drunkenness.

Why were the leaders' *hearts like an oven*? (7:6)

The princes of the land were leaders who burned within, full of hatred and lust for power. As the fire of an oven cannot always be seen from the outside, these princes secretly plotted against the king while entertaining him with their lies (v. 3). They apparently hoped to organize a rebellion, kill the king and assume power.

What was wrong with calling other nations for help? (7:11)

While international treaties are not forbidden in the Bible, the people of Israel were to never depend upon any source other than God for their survival and security. The primary reason they turned to Egypt and Assyria for help was because they did not want to turn to God in repentance.

⁹As marauders lie in ambush for a man,
　　so do bands of priests[D];
they murder on the road to Shechem,
　　committing shameful crimes.
¹⁰I have seen a horrible thing
　　in the house of Israel.
There Ephraim is given to prostitution
　　and Israel is defiled.

¹¹"Also for you, Judah,
　　a harvest is appointed.

"Whenever I would restore the fortunes of my
　　people,
7 ¹whenever I would heal Israel,
the sins of Ephraim are exposed
　　and the crimes of Samaria revealed.
They practice deceit,
　　thieves break into houses,
　　bandits rob in the streets;
²but they do not realize
　　that I remember all their evil deeds.
Their sins engulf them;
　　they are always before me.

³"They delight the king with their wickedness,
　　the princes with their lies.
⁴They are all adulterers,
　　burning like an oven
whose fire the baker need not stir
　　from the kneading of the dough till it rises.
⁵On the day of the festival of our king
　　the princes become inflamed with wine,
　　and he joins hands with the mockers.
⁶Their hearts are like an oven;
　　they approach him with intrigue.
Their passion smolders all night;
　　in the morning it blazes like a flaming fire.
⁷All of them are hot as an oven;
　　they devour their rulers.
All their kings fall,
　　and none of them calls on me.

⁸"Ephraim mixes with the nations;
　　Ephraim is a flat cake not turned over.
⁹Foreigners sap his strength,
　　but he does not realize it.
His hair is sprinkled with gray,
　　but he does not notice.
¹⁰Israel's arrogance testifies against him,
　　but despite all this
he does not return to the LORD his God
　　or search for him.

¹¹"Ephraim is like a dove,
　　easily deceived and senseless—
now calling to Egypt,
　　now turning to Assyria.
¹²When they go, I will throw my net over them;
　　I will pull them down like birds of the air.
When I hear them flocking together,
　　I will catch them.
¹³Woe to them,
　　because they have strayed from me!
Destruction to them,
　　because they have rebelled against me!

I long to redeem^D them
    but they speak lies against me.
14They do not cry out to me from their hearts
    but wail upon their beds.
They gather together^a for grain and new
    wine^D
    but turn away from me.
15I trained them and strengthened them,
    but they plot evil against me.
16They do not turn to the Most High;
    they are like a faulty bow.
Their leaders will fall by the sword
    because of their insolent words.
For this they will be ridiculed
    in the land of Egypt.

Israel to Reap the Whirlwind

8 "Put the trumpet to your lips!
    An eagle is over the house of the Lord
because the people have broken my covenant^D
    and rebelled against my law.
2Israel cries out to me,
    'O our God, we acknowledge you!'
3But Israel has rejected what is good;
    an enemy will pursue him.
4They set up kings without my consent;
    they choose princes without my approval.
With their silver and gold
    they make idols^D for themselves
    to their own destruction.
5Throw out your calf-idol, O Samaria!
    My anger burns against them.
How long will they be incapable of purity?
6 They are from Israel!
This calf—a craftsman has made it;
    it is not God.
It will be broken in pieces,
    that calf of Samaria.

7"They sow the wind
    and reap the whirlwind.
The stalk has no head;
    it will produce no flour.
Were it to yield grain,
    foreigners would swallow it up.
8Israel is swallowed up;
    now she is among the nations
    like a worthless thing.
9For they have gone up to Assyria
    like a wild donkey wandering alone.
Ephraim has sold herself to lovers.
10Although they have sold themselves among the
    nations,
    I will now gather them together.
They will begin to waste away
    under the oppression of the mighty king.

11"Though Ephraim built many altars for sin
    offerings^D,
    these have become altars for sinning.
12I wrote for them the many things of my law,
    but they regarded them as something alien^D.

How were the people of Israel like a faulty bow? (7:16)
God could not depend upon Israel, just as an archer cannot depend upon a faulty bow. A bow that is warped or strung incorrectly will cause the arrow to miss its target—just as Israel had missed the mark.

What did an eagle over the house signify? (8:1)
This was a picture of a vulture circling over a dying animal or a corpse. The image signified God's coming judgment—Assyria would invade and destroy Israel, the house of the Lord.

How were the people supposed to choose their leaders? (8:4)
They were supposed to support leaders who would obey the law, destroy idols, care for the poor, provide justice and seek God. As it was, violent coups and assassinations often deposed the kings. Power-hungry men and their cohorts competed for the throne. Conditions worsened because those who ruled by the sword became more paranoid of others with power and less sensitive to issues that concerned God.

---

^a14 Most Hebrew manuscripts; some Hebrew manuscripts and Septuagint *They slash themselves*

How and when did God send fire upon their cities? (8:14)

Shalmaneser, king of Assyria, invaded and conquered Israel in 722 B.C., after laying siege for three years to the capital city of Samaria. This reference to fire was fulfilled in two ways: (1) literally, because much of the city was burned when conquered by the Assyrians; (2) figuratively, because the invasion consumed the nation politically and geographically, just as fire consumes fuel.

What is the *bread of mourners*? (9:4)

The bread in a home where someone had died was unclean and therefore forbidden to Israel. The phrase *bread of mourners* seems to point to a time when God would not accept their sacrifices. They would be able to do nothing to reverse the judgment they would experience.

Why did they think the prophet was a *fool* or a *maniac*? (9:7)

First, Hosea was considered a fool because of his faithful allegiance to his adulterous wife. See *Why would God tell a godly man to marry an adulteress?* (1:2). Second, Hosea was thought to be weird because he persisted in hardline pronouncements about God's coming judgment. The uncompromising messages of the prophets, coupled with their unconventional ways and anti-social behavior, often caused them to be labeled as crazy misfits. See also *Why did they call the prophet a madman?* (2 Kings 9:11).

Was Hosea in physical danger? (9:8)

There's nothing to indicate that Hosea was in physical danger. It's possible that the *hostility* against him suggests a general sentiment, and the *snares* may have been things such as character assassination, threats, fatigue, loss of reputation and a sense of rejection. He undoubtedly was frequently challenged, his influence was constantly thwarted and the people hated him for continually denouncing their lifestyle.

---

¹³They offer sacrifices^D given to me
    and they eat the meat,
      but the LORD is not pleased with them.
Now he will remember their wickedness
    and punish their sins:
      They will return to Egypt.
¹⁴Israel has forgotten his Maker
    and built palaces;
    Judah has fortified many towns.
But I will send fire upon their cities
    that will consume their fortresses."

Punishment for Israel

9 Do not rejoice, O Israel;
    do not be jubilant like the other nations.
For you have been unfaithful to your God;
    you love the wages of a prostitute
      at every threshing floor.
²Threshing floors and winepresses^D will not
      feed the people;
    the new wine^D will fail them.
³They will not remain in the LORD's land;
    Ephraim will return to Egypt
    and eat unclean^{Da} food in Assyria.
⁴They will not pour out wine offerings to the
    LORD,
    nor will their sacrifices please him.
Such sacrifices will be to them like the bread
      of mourners;
    all who eat them will be unclean.
This food will be for themselves;
    it will not come into the temple of the LORD.

⁵What will you do on the day of your appointed
      feasts,
    on the festival days of the LORD?
⁶Even if they escape from destruction,
    Egypt will gather them,
    and Memphis will bury them.
Their treasures of silver will be taken over by
      briers,
    and thorns will overrun their tents.
⁷The days of punishment are coming,
    the days of reckoning are at hand.
    Let Israel know this.
Because your sins are so many
    and your hostility so great,
the prophet^D is considered a fool,
    the inspired man a maniac.
⁸The prophet, along with my God,
    is the watchman^D over Ephraim,^{b}
yet snares await him on all his paths,
    and hostility in the house of his God.
⁹They have sunk deep into corruption,
    as in the days of Gibeah.
God will remember their wickedness
    and punish them for their sins.

¹⁰"When I found Israel,
    it was like finding grapes in the desert;
when I saw your fathers,

---

^{a}3 That is, ceremonially unclean ^{b}8 Or *The prophet is the watchman over Ephraim, / the people of my God*

it was like seeing the early fruit on the fig
    tree.
But when they came to Baal Peor,
    they consecrated^D themselves to that
      shameful idol^D
and became as vile as the thing they loved.
¹¹Ephraim's glory^D will fly away like a bird—
    no birth, no pregnancy, no conception.
¹²Even if they rear children,
    I will bereave them of every one.
Woe to them
    when I turn away from them!
¹³I have seen Ephraim, like Tyre,
    planted in a pleasant place.
But Ephraim will bring out
    their children to the slayer."

¹⁴Give them, O LORD—
    what will you give them?
Give them wombs that miscarry
    and breasts that are dry.

¹⁵"Because of all their wickedness in Gilgal,
    I hated them there.
Because of their sinful deeds,
    I will drive them out of my house.
I will no longer love them;
    all their leaders are rebellious.
¹⁶Ephraim is blighted,
    their root is withered,
    they yield no fruit.
Even if they bear children,
    I will slay their cherished offspring."

¹⁷My God will reject them
    because they have not obeyed him;
    they will be wanderers among the nations.

10 Israel was a spreading vine;
    he brought forth fruit for himself.
As his fruit increased,
    he built more altars;
as his land prospered,
    he adorned his sacred stones^D.
²Their heart is deceitful,
    and now they must bear their guilt.
The LORD will demolish their altars
    and destroy their sacred stones.

³Then they will say, "We have no king
    because we did not revere^D the LORD.
But even if we had a king,
    what could he do for us?"
⁴They make many promises,
    take false oaths
    and make agreements;
therefore lawsuits spring up
    like poisonous weeds in a plowed field.
⁵The people who live in Samaria fear
    for the calf-idol of Beth Aven.^a
Its people will mourn over it,
    and so will its idolatrous priests^D,

---

^a5 *Beth Aven* means *house of wickedness* (a name for Bethel, which means *house of God*).

Early fruit on the fig tree (9:10)
This *early fruit* is considered especially delicious. Hosea used this poignant imagery to picture God's delight in his chosen people in Israel's earliest days as a nation. When God first found Israel in the desert (Deut. 32:10), it was like finding and savoring a mouthwatering delicacy like the early fig.

Ephraim's glory will fly away (9:11)
A poetic and powerful way of saying that the nation will not grow. God had turned away from them (v. 12), and there could be no blessing where he was not present.

Is this hateful vengeance? (9:14)
See *Can we praise God while inflicting vengeance?* (Psalm 149:6–9).

Calf-idol (10:5)
A huge calf-idol had been erected by Jeroboam II at Bethel, or *Beth Aven* (see NIV text note). See *Sins of Jeroboam* (1 Kings 16:31).

those who had rejoiced over its splendor,
  because it is taken from them into
    exile.D
6It will be carried to Assyria
  as tribute for the great king.
Ephraim will be disgraced;
  Israel will be ashamed of its wooden
    idols.D, a
7Samaria and its king will float away
  like a twig on the surface of the
    waters.
8The high placesD of wicknessb will be
    destroyed—
  it is the sin of Israel.
Thorns and thistles will grow up
  and cover their altars.
Then they will say to the mountains, "Cover
    us!"
  and to the hills, "Fall on us!"

9"Since the days of Gibeah, you have sinned,
    O Israel,
  and there you have remained.c
Did not war overtake
  the evildoers in Gibeah?
10When I please, I will punish them;
  nations will be gathered against them
  to put them in bonds for their double
    sin.
11Ephraim is a trained heifer
  that loves to thresh;
so I will put a yokeD
  on her fair neck.
I will drive Ephraim,
  Judah must plow,
  and Jacob must break up the ground.
12Sow for yourselves righteousness,D
  reap the fruit of unfailing love,
and break up your unplowed ground;
  for it is time to seek the LORD,
until he comes
  and showers righteousness on you.
13But you have planted wickedness,
  you have reaped evil,
  you have eaten the fruit of deception.
Because you have depended on your own
    strength
  and on your many warriors,
14the roar of battle will rise against your people,
  so that all your fortresses will be
    devastated—
as Shalman devastated Beth Arbel on the day
    of battle,
  when mothers were dashed to the ground
    with their children.
15Thus will it happen to you, O Bethel,
  because your wickedness is great.
When that day dawns,
  the king of Israel will be completely
    destroyed.

What happened in the *days of Gibeah?* (10:9)

A traveling Levite, spending the night in Gibe-ah, yielded to a gang of sexual perverts who raped, beat and murdered his concubine (Judges 19:20–30). Hosea declared that the entire nation had sunk to the same depths of depravity. He also implied that their punishment would be certain and just.

What was Israel's *double sin?* (10:10)

Israel sinned doubly in that the people turned *from* God and turned *to* idol worship.

Who was *Shalman* and where was *Beth Arbel?* (10:14)

Shalman (usually known as Shalmaneser) was the king of Assyria who attacked Samaria in 722 B.C. *Beth Arbel* may be another name for Beth-El. As one of the centers for the idolatry established to rival worship in Jerusalem, its destruction by the Assyrians signaled the death blow to the northern kingdom. Hosea used the same term (*Bethel*, meaning *House of God*, v. 15) to refer to the entire nation of Isra-el (see *Map 6* at the back of this Bible).

a6 Or *its counsel*   b8 Hebrew *aven*, a reference to Beth Aven (a derogatory name for Bethel)   c9 Or *there a stand was taken*

God's Love for Israel

11 "When Israel was a child, I loved him,
and out of Egypt I called my son.
[2]But the more I[a] called Israel,
the further they went from me.[b]
They sacrificed to the Baals[D]
and they burned incense[D] to images.
[3]It was I who taught Ephraim to walk,
taking them by the arms;
but they did not realize
it was I who healed them.
[4]I led them with cords of human kindness,
with ties of love;
I lifted the yoke[D] from their neck
and bent down to feed them.

[5]"Will they not return to Egypt
and will not Assyria rule over them
because they refuse to repent[D]?
[6]Swords will flash in their cities,
will destroy the bars of their gates
and put an end to their plans.
[7]My people are determined to turn from me.
Even if they call to the Most High,
he will by no means exalt them.

[8]"How can I give you up, Ephraim?
How can I hand you over, Israel?
How can I treat you like Admah?
How can I make you like Zeboiim?
My heart is changed within me;
all my compassion is aroused.
[9]I will not carry out my fierce anger,
nor will I turn and devastate Ephraim.
For I am God, and not man—
the Holy One among you.
I will not come in wrath.[c]
[10]They will follow the LORD;
he will roar like a lion.
When he roars,
his children will come trembling from the
west.
[11]They will come trembling

[a]2 Some Septuagint manuscripts; Hebrew *they*   [b]2 Septuagint;
Hebrew *them*   [c]9 Or *come against any city*

Why switch the love analogy from husband-wife to father-son? (11:1)

Hosea did not limit himself to one level of communication. Since Israel had not responded to his analogy of an unfaithful wife, he shifted his message to try to reach the people by appealing to history. Just as a father cares for and nurtures his son, God had taken care of the people Israel, bringing them out of Egypt and establishing them in a land of promise.

SCRIPTURE LINK (11:1) *Out of Egypt I called my son*

Matthew saw this as a picture of God's protection of Jesus, when he led Joseph to take Jesus to Egypt to escape from King Herod. See Matt. 2:15.

Cords of human kindness (11:4)

The exact meaning is unknown. Some think it pictures a farmer using ropes to lift the yoke off his oxen so they can eat. Others suggest these cords were used to help young children learn to walk—certainly much kinder cords than those that hitched oxen to the plow. Still others see here a picture of God as a father bending over to lift or perhaps to help or feed a small child.

Does God change his mind? (11:8)

Many would say that since God knows all things, he does not change his mind. Yet the Bible frequently speaks of God's mercy in terms of God changing his mind about judgment. The intentions of God—both for blessings and punishment—are often tied to our response. God's promises are often conditional, dependent upon the obedient response of his people. God's judgments also are often conditional, dependent on the continued refusal of his people to repent.

God wants us to see him as a God who cares passionately for his people and longs to have a loving relationship with us. To dramatize the depths of God's love for Israel, Hosea spoke of him changing his mind, still looking for some glimmer of response from the people. See article: *Why did God change his mind?* (Isaiah 38:1–5).

like birds from Egypt,
  like doves from Assyria.
I will settle them in their homes,"
  declares the LORD.

Israel's Sin

¹²Ephraim has surrounded me with lies,
  the house of Israel with deceit.
And Judah is unruly against God,
  even against the faithful Holy One.

12 ¹Ephraim feeds on the wind;
  he pursues the east wind all day
  and multiplies lies and violence.
He makes a treaty with Assyria
  and sends olive oil to Egypt.
²The LORD has a charge to bring against Judah;
  he will punish Jacob*a* according to his ways
  and repay him according to his deeds.
³In the womb he grasped his brother's heel;
  as a man he struggled with God.
⁴He struggled with the angel and overcame him;
  he wept and begged for his favor.
 He found him at Bethel
  and talked with him there—
⁵the LORD God Almighty,
  the LORD is his name of renown!
⁶But you must return to your God;
  maintain love and justice,
  and wait for your God always.

⁷The merchant uses dishonest scales;
  he loves to defraud.
⁸Ephraim boasts,
  "I am very rich; I have become wealthy.
With all my wealth they will not find in me
  any iniquity or sin."

⁹"I am the LORD your God,
  ⌞who brought you⌟ out of*b* Egypt;
I will make you live in tents again,
  as in the days of your appointed feasts.
¹⁰I spoke to the prophets*D*,
  gave them many visions*D*
  and told parables*D* through them."

¹¹Is Gilead wicked?
  Its people are worthless!
Do they sacrifice*D* bulls in Gilgal?
  Their altars will be like piles of stones
  on a plowed field.
¹²Jacob fled to the country of Aram*c*;
  Israel served to get a wife,
  and to pay for her he tended sheep.
¹³The LORD used a prophet to bring Israel up
    from Egypt,
  by a prophet he cared for him.
¹⁴But Ephraim has bitterly provoked him to
    anger;
  his Lord will leave upon him the guilt of his
    bloodshed
  and will repay him for his contempt.

Why did Hosea use Jacob as an example? (12:2–5)

Jacob, known for his deceit (see NIV text note), was the father of Israel's 12 tribes. Like their ancestor, the people of Hosea's day also were deceitful. But Hosea wanted them to follow Jacob's further example: Jacob had searched for God and allowed God to transform him, he had cleansed himself and his household of idol worship, and he had received God's blessings.

---

a2 Jacob means *he grasps the heel* (figuratively, *he deceives*).   *b9* Or
God / ever since you were in   *c12* That is, Northwest Mesopotamia

The LORD's Anger Against Israel

13

When Ephraim spoke, men trembled;
  he was exalted in Israel.
But he became guilty of Baal[D] worship and
    died.
2Now they sin more and more;
  they make idols[D] for themselves from their
      silver,
cleverly fashioned images,
  all of them the work of craftsmen.
It is said of these people,
  "They offer human sacrifice[D]
  and kiss[a] the calf-idols."
3Therefore they will be like the morning mist,
  like the early dew that disappears,
  like chaff[D] swirling from a threshing floor,
  like smoke escaping through a window.

4"But I am the LORD your God,
  ⌞who brought you⌟ out of[b] Egypt.
You shall acknowledge no God but me,
  no Savior except me.
5I cared for you in the desert,
  in the land of burning heat.
6When I fed them, they were satisfied;
  when they were satisfied, they became
      proud;
  then they forgot me.
7So I will come upon them like a lion,
  like a leopard I will lurk by the path.
8Like a bear robbed of her cubs,
  I will attack them and rip them open.
Like a lion I will devour them;
  a wild animal will tear them apart.

9"You are destroyed, O Israel,
  because you are against me, against your
      helper.
10Where is your king, that he may save you?
  Where are your rulers in all your towns,
of whom you said,
  'Give me a king and princes'?
11So in my anger I gave you a king,
  and in my wrath I took him away.
12The guilt of Ephraim is stored up,
  his sins are kept on record.
13Pains as of a woman in childbirth come to him,
  but he is a child without wisdom;
when the time arrives,
  he does not come to the opening of the
      womb.

14"I will ransom them from the power of the
      grave[c];
  I will redeem[D] them from death[D].
Where, O death, are your plagues?
  Where, O grave,[c] is your destruction?

  "I will have no compassion,
15 even though he thrives among his brothers.
An east wind from the LORD will come,
  blowing in from the desert;

Did Israel really offer human sacrifices? (13:2)

The Israelites had adopted forms of pagan worship and had even *sacrificed their sons and daughters in the fire* (2 Kings 17:17). Some think the practice was not literal sacrifice, but a ritual intended to give children extra vitality and strength from the gods. The extraordinarily strong language used to denounce these pagan rites, however, lead most to believe it referred to actual human sacrifice. See *Why would parents sacrifice their children?* (Jer. 19:5).

Calf-idols (13:2)
See *Calf-idol* (10:5).

Why did God still say he *will have no compassion?* (13:14)
This promise of blessing appeared within the larger context of judgment. *Death* and the *grave,* in fact, spoke of the nation's ultimate demise. But in spite of all that, Hosea offered a glimmer of God's love in God's promise to ransom and redeem the people. The nation, after being judged and destroyed, would be restored. But for the moment, God would show no compassion.

---

a2 Or *"Men who sacrifice / kiss*   *b4* Or *God / ever since you were in*
c14 Hebrew *Sheol*

How could such brutality be part of God's plan? (13:16)

We must understand these atrocities as consequences of Israel's rebellion rather than the fulfillment of God's plan. God's plan was to forgive and restore. But the tragic consequences of unrepented sin can result in appalling calamities. Also see *Why does God permit the innocent to suffer?* (Isaiah 13:16) and *Who dashed infants to pieces?* (Nahum 3:10).

What was *the fruit of our lips?* (14:2)

Earlier Hosea had denounced the empty religious rituals of the people (6:6; 7:14). Here he elaborated further by describing a genuine sacrifice—lips that sincerely offered one's whole being to God. *The fruit of our lips* is a phrase used to describe human praise and thanksgiving in worship (see Heb. 13:15).

Have God's promises to Israel been fulfilled? (14:5-7)

While some point to certain aspects of these promises that have been fulfilled at various stages of Israel's history, the ultimate fulfillment is yet to come, at the second coming of Christ.

his spring will fail
　　and his well dry up.
His storehouse will be plundered[D]
　　of all its treasures.
16The people of Samaria must bear their guilt,
　　because they have rebelled against their God.
They will fall by the sword;
　　their little ones will be dashed to the ground,
　　their pregnant women ripped open."

Repentance to Bring Blessing

14 Return, O Israel, to the LORD your God.
　　Your sins have been your downfall!
2Take words with you
　　and return to the LORD.
Say to him:
　　"Forgive all our sins
and receive us graciously,
　　that we may offer the fruit of our lips.[a]
3Assyria cannot save us;
　　we will not mount war-horses.
We will never again say 'Our gods'
　　to what our own hands have made,
　　for in you the fatherless find compassion."

4"I will heal their waywardness
　　and love them freely,
　　for my anger has turned away from them.
5I will be like the dew to Israel;
　　he will blossom like a lily.
Like a cedar of Lebanon
　　he will send down his roots;
6　his young shoots will grow.
His splendor will be like an olive tree,
　　his fragrance like a cedar of Lebanon.
7Men will dwell again in his shade.
　　He will flourish like the grain.
He will blossom like a vine,
　　and his fame will be like the wine from
　　　　Lebanon.
8O Ephraim, what more have I[b] to do with
　　　　idols[D]?
　　I will answer him and care for him.
I am like a green pine tree;
　　your fruitfulness comes from me."

9Who is wise? He will realize these things.
　　Who is discerning? He will understand them.
The ways of the LORD are right;
　　the righteous[D] walk in them,
　　but the rebellious stumble in them.

---

a2 Or offer our lips as sacrifices of bulls　　*b8 Or What more has Ephraim*

JOEL

Why read this book?

If you long to personally experience God's work and power, you'll find Joel's prophecies right on target. His predictions, though frightening at times, will also inspire you. In fact, Joel prophesies the coming of the Holy Spirit, linking God's work in the Old Testament with the birth of the church in the New Testament (compare 2:28; Acts 2:17–21). Reading Joel will show you God's intense desire for intimacy with all his people.

Who wrote this book?

Joel, a prophet of God.

When was it written?

Some think Joel wrote during Jeremiah's lifetime, around 609 B.C. Others say he could have written later, after the Jews returned from exile in Babylon (538 B.C.). But because Joel mentions no king and speaks of elders as leaders (1:2), still others suggest a much earlier date—perhaps around 835 B.C., when Judah's king was a child (2 Kings 11:21).

What was happening at this time?

Assuming the earlier date, seven-year-old Joash had just been crowned king over Judah, though Jehoiada, the high priest, was the power behind the throne. Under Joash's wicked father and grandmother, pagan idol worship had flourished in Judah (see 2 Kings 8:25—11:21).

To whom was it written and why?

The prophet Joel urged the people of Judah to turn again to God. With Joash's wicked father and grandmother out of the way, Joel saw tremendous opportunity for renewal in the land. But he also warned Judah that judgment—in the form of an agricultural disaster of major consequence—would come if they did not repent.

What to look for in Joel:

Watch for God's double-barreled plan for his people: a specific plan of punishment for sin, but also a promise to defend his people zealously (2:1,18). In both modes, look for God's passionate concern for his people.

1 The word of the LORD that came to Joel son of Pethuel.

An Invasion of Locusts

Elders (1:2)

During this time, each community in Judah was administered locally by a group of respected elders. This type of government was known as a regency. Joel appealed to these community leaders rather than to the king. See Introduction: *When was it written?*

When were these predictions fulfilled? (1:2,4,15)

The plague of locusts probably occurred not long after the writing of Joel. Some also think that, in addition to the locust plague, Joel was predicting a military invasion. It is believed that the Cythians, a tribe from the Black Sea region, were the vehicle by which God punished Judah. Several centuries later, the Cythians put an end to the great career of Alexander the Great.

Locust (1:4)

The locust is an aggressive type of grasshopper. An army of these insects can devastate entire fields of crops within minutes, bringing economic ruin and destroying food supplies. A locust can consume every green thing in its path, all the while making a loud, terrifying noise with its wings.

Was drunkenness a problem in Judah? (1:5)

Yes. Apparently the upper classes of Judah consumed great quantities of wine. Times were prosperous and, perhaps out of boredom or a twisted sense of competition to out-drink each other, they shamelessly drank themselves into oblivion.

New wine (1:5)

The newly pressed juice of the grape. It contains less flavor and less alcohol because of the short aging process. Also see *What's the difference between old wine and new wine?* (Hosea 4:11).

Nation (1:6)

A metaphor for the swarms of insects that would invade Judah. Some believe it also refers, in a secondary sense, to the Cythians, a tribe from the Black Sea region, who would invade from the north (2:20). See *Map 7* at the back of this Bible.

How could a virgin have a husband? (1:8)

This was a picture of a virgin pledged to be married. Her husband-to-be was called her husband. It could also refer to a newly married couple, who, because of the tragic death of the groom, never got the chance to consummate their marriage.

²Hear this, you elders;
   listen, all who live in the land.
Has anything like this ever happened in your
         days
   or in the days of your forefathers?
³Tell it to your children,
   and let your children tell it to their children,
   and their children to the next generation.
⁴What the locust[D] swarm has left
   the great locusts have eaten;
what the great locusts have left
   the young locusts have eaten;
what the young locusts have left
   other locusts[a] have eaten.

⁵Wake up, you drunkards, and weep!
   Wail, all you drinkers of wine;
wail because of the new wine[D],
   for it has been snatched from your lips.
⁶A nation has invaded my land,
   powerful and without number;
it has the teeth of a lion,
   the fangs of a lioness.
⁷It has laid waste my vines
   and ruined my fig trees.
It has stripped off their bark
   and thrown it away,
   leaving their branches white.

⁸Mourn like a virgin[b] in sackcloth[D]
   grieving for the husband[c] of her youth.
⁹Grain offerings and drink offerings[D]
   are cut off from the house of the LORD.
The priests[D] are in mourning,
   those who minister before the LORD.
¹⁰The fields are ruined,
   the ground is dried up[d];
the grain is destroyed,
   the new wine is dried up,
   the oil fails.
¹¹Despair, you farmers,
   wail, you vine growers;
grieve for the wheat and the barley,
   because the harvest of the field is destroyed.
¹²The vine is dried up
   and the fig tree is withered;
the pomegranate, the palm and the apple
         tree—
   all the trees of the field—are dried up.
Surely the joy of mankind
   is withered away.

A Call to Repentance

¹³Put on sackcloth, O priests, and mourn;
   wail, you who minister before the altar.
Come, spend the night in sackcloth,

---

a4 The precise meaning of the four Hebrew words used here for locusts is uncertain.   *b8* Or *young woman*   *c8* Or *betrothed*   *d10* Or *ground mourns*

you who minister before my God;
for the grain offerings^D and drink offerings^D
   are withheld from the house of your God.
14Declare a holy fast;
   call a sacred assembly.^D
Summon the elders
   and all who live in the land
to the house of the LORD your God,
   and cry out to the LORD.

15Alas for that day!
   For the day of the LORD^D is near;
it will come like destruction from the
     Almighty.^a

16Has not the food been cut off
   before our very eyes—
joy and gladness
   from the house of our God?
17The seeds are shriveled
   beneath the clods.^b
The storehouses are in ruins,
   the granaries have been broken down,
for the grain has dried up.
18How the cattle moan!
   The herds mill about
because they have no pasture;
   even the flocks of sheep are suffering.

19To you, O LORD, I call,
   for fire has devoured the open pastures
and flames have burned up all the trees of
     the field.
20Even the wild animals pant for you;
   the streams of water have dried up
and fire has devoured the open pastures.

An Army of Locusts

2 Blow the trumpet in Zion^D;
   sound the alarm on my holy hill.
Let all who live in the land tremble,
   for the day of the LORD is coming.
It is close at hand—
2 a day of darkness and gloom,
   a day of clouds and blackness.
Like dawn spreading across the mountains
   a large and mighty army comes,
such as never was of old
   nor ever will be in ages to come.

3Before them fire devours,
   behind them a flame blazes.
Before them the land is like the garden of
     Eden,
   behind them, a desert waste—
nothing escapes them.
4They have the appearance of horses;
   they gallop along like cavalry.
5With a noise like that of chariots
   they leap over the mountaintops,
like a crackling fire consuming stubble,
   like a mighty army drawn up for battle.

Holy fast . . . sacred assembly (1:14)
A general call to fast and pray because of impending doom. Joel told Judah to show God they meant business by declaring a national day of fasting and prayer.

The day of the LORD (1:15)
This refers to any time God deals with a nation or generation so that it will return to its spiritual senses. The final day of reckoning, however, will be when Christ returns the second time. See *The day of the LORD* (Zeph. 1:7).

Holy hill (2:1)
Mount Zion or the mountain where Solomon built the temple. Today, it lies south of Jerusalem's city walls.

The day of the LORD (2:1)
See *The day of the LORD* (1:15).

Army (2:2)
See *Nation* (1:6).

---

^a15 Hebrew *Shaddai*   ^b17 The meaning of the Hebrew for this word is uncertain.

⁶At the sight of them, nations are in anguish;
  every face turns pale.
⁷They charge like warriors;
  they scale walls like soldiers.
They all march in line,
  not swerving from their course.
⁸They do not jostle each other;
  each marches straight ahead.
They plunge through defenses
  without breaking ranks.
⁹They rush upon the city;
  they run along the wall.
They climb into the houses;
  like thieves they enter through the windows.

¹⁰Before them the earth shakes,
  the sky trembles,
the sun and moon are darkened,
  and the stars no longer shine.
¹¹The LORD thunders
  at the head of his army;
his forces are beyond number,
  and mighty are those who obey his
    command.
The day of the LORDᴰ is great;
  it is dreadful.
Who can endure it?

Rend Your Heart

¹²"Even now," declares the LORD,
  "return to me with all your heart,
  with fasting and weeping and mourning."

¹³Rend your heart
  and not your garments.
Return to the LORD your God,
  for he is gracious and compassionate,
slow to anger and abounding in love,
  and he relents from sending calamity.
¹⁴Who knows? He may turn and have pity
  and leave behind a blessing—
grain offeringsᴰ and drink offeringsᴰ
  for the LORD your God.

¹⁵Blow the trumpet in Zionᴰ,
  declare a holy fast,
  call a sacred assemblyᴰ.
¹⁶Gather the people,
  consecrateᴰ the assembly;
bring together the elders,
  gather the children,
  those nursing at the breast.
Let the bridegroom leave his room
  and the bride her chamber.
¹⁷Let the priestsᴰ, who minister before the LORD,
  weep between the temple porch and the
    altar.
Let them say, "Spare your people, O LORD.
  Do not make your inheritance an object of
    scorn,
  a bywordᴰ among the nations.
Why should they say among the peoples,
  'Where is their God?' "

Does repentance prevent catastrophes? (2:12–14)

Like removing a cancerous growth from the body, God uses catastrophes to practice spiritual surgery. If repentance does not follow sin, judgment will. With repentance, however, the full weight of God's wrath is restrained or sometimes averted altogether. Natural consequences of sin may still follow, but repentance restores the relationship with God. Also see article: *Why does God send calamity?* (Lam. 3:38).

Why broken hearts instead of torn clothes? (2:13)

A traditional sign of sorrow was to tear one's clothes. See *Where did the custom of ashes and torn clothing come from?* (2 Samuel 13:19). However, outward actions don't always correspond to the heart's condition. What matters most to God is not outward show but an inner reality that consists of sincere grief and loathing of sin.

Holy fast . . . sacred assembly (2:15)

See *Holy fast . . . sacred assembly* (1:14).

The LORD's Answer

18Then the LORD will be jealous for his land
and take pity on his people.

19The LORD will reply*a* to them:

"I am sending you grain, new wine*D* and oil,
enough to satisfy you fully;
never again will I make you
an object of scorn to the nations.

20"I will drive the northern army far from you,
pushing it into a parched and barren land,
with its front columns going into the eastern
sea*b*
and those in the rear into the western sea.*c*
And its stench will go up;
its smell will rise."

Surely he has done great things.*d*
21 Be not afraid, O land;
be glad and rejoice.
Surely the LORD has done great things.
22 Be not afraid, O wild animals,
for the open pastures are becoming green.
The trees are bearing their fruit;
the fig tree and the vine yield their riches.
23Be glad, O people of Zion*D*,
rejoice in the LORD your God,
for he has given you
the autumn rains in righteousness*D*.*e*
He sends you abundant showers,
both autumn and spring rains, as before.
24The threshing floors will be filled with grain;
the vats will overflow with new wine and
oil.

25"I will repay you for the years the locusts*D*
have eaten—
the great locust and the young locust,
the other locusts and the locust
swarm*f*—
my great army that I sent among you.
26You will have plenty to eat, until you are full,
and you will praise the name of the LORD
your God,
who has worked wonders for you;
never again will my people be shamed.
27Then you will know that I am in Israel,
that I am the LORD your God,
and that there is no other;
never again will my people be shamed.

The Day of the LORD

28"And afterward,
I will pour out my Spirit on all people.
Your sons and daughters will prophesy,
your old men will dream dreams,
your young men will see visions*D*.
29Even on my servants, both men and women,

---

*a*18,19 Or LORD *was jealous . . . / and took pity . . . / *19*The LORD replied*
*b*20 That is, the Dead Sea   *c*20 That is, the Mediterranean
*d*20 Or *rise. / Surely it has done great things."*   *e*23 Or *l the teacher*
for righteousness: *f*25 The precise meaning of the four Hebrew
words used here for locusts is uncertain.

How was God *jealous for his land?* (2:18)

God's jealousy is an expression of his deep love for and commitment to his people. It stems from a love that claims a special relationship with the beloved. If a wife turns her attention to another man, the husband, because he cares about her, acts to recover her. God could have wiped his hands of Israel, but instead he used a foreign oppressor to convince his beloved to return. Also see *Burning with jealousy* (Zech. 8:2).

Object of scorn (2:19)

Israel would be humiliated as a result of the famine caused by the invasion of locusts. The surrounding enemies would look on with scorn and satisfaction.

How would this work of the Spirit be different from before? (2:28)

In the Old Testament, access to God was restricted to priests and specially selected individuals such as the 70 elders of Moses' time (Num. 11:16–17). But Joel predicted a fresh work of God's Spirit, available to everyone regardless of position or status. Men and women, servants and free, young and old—all would be given equal access to God's power.

SCRIPTURE LINK (2:28–32)

Peter said this passage was fulfilled in the events that occurred on the day of Pentecost. See Acts 2:16–21.

When will the moon turn to blood? (2:30–32)

At the final judgment when Christ returns. With the coming of the Holy Spirit on all believers, the last days began (Acts 2:14–21). At the end of the *last days,* God will judge the earth. The moon will appear blood red, signaling the end of human rule on earth and the subsequent rule of Christ (Matt. 24:29–30).

In those days (3:1)

Points to the final, cosmic struggle between good and evil when Christ returns.

The Valley of Jehoshaphat (3:2)

The city of Jerusalem overlooks this valley. It cuts a swath north of the Mount of Olives southward past the old, dug-down city of Zion. It eventually joins the Valley of the Hinnom, on the western side of the city.

The Nations Judged (3:2)

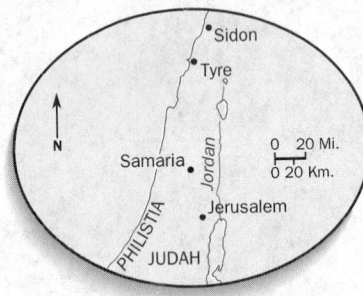

What had Tyre and Sidon done? (3:4–8)

They had invaded and plundered Judah repeatedly, taking Israelites to be sold in the Greek slave markets across the Aegean Sea. They treated their captives inhumanely, holding them in the bellies of overcrowded ships and selling them like cattle to the highest bidder.

Did God challenge the nations to battle? (3:9–11)

In a sense, yes. The theme is still judgment, but now Joel's prophecy extends far into the future. At the great final battle, all the armies of darkness, under control of the beast (Rev. 19:19), will march against God and his armies of righteousness. The beast and his legions will be utterly crushed by God's total victory.

I will pour out my Spirit in those days.
30 I will show wonders in the heavens
    and on the earth,
       blood and fire and billows of smoke.
31 The sun will be turned to darkness
    and the moon to blood
       before the coming of the great and dreadful
          day of the LORD.
32 And everyone who calls
    on the name of the LORD will be saved;
for on Mount Zion D and in Jerusalem D
    there will be deliverance,
       as the LORD has said,
among the survivors
    whom the LORD calls.

The Nations Judged

3 "In those days and at that time,
    when I restore the fortunes of Judah and
       Jerusalem,
2 I will gather all nations
    and bring them down to the Valley of
       Jehoshaphat.*a*
There I will enter into judgment against them
    concerning my inheritance, my people Israel,
for they scattered my people among the
       nations
    and divided up my land.
3 They cast lots for my people
    and traded boys for prostitutes;
they sold girls for wine
    that they might drink.

4 "Now what have you against me, O Tyre and Sidon and all you regions of Philistia? Are you repaying me for something I have done? If you are paying me back, I will swiftly and speedily return on your own heads what you have done. 5 For you took my silver and my gold and carried off my finest treasures to your temples. 6 You sold the people of Judah and Jerusalem to the Greeks, that you might send them far from their homeland.

7 "See, I am going to rouse them out of the places to which you sold them, and I will return on your own heads what you have done. 8 I will sell your sons and daughters to the people of Judah, and they will sell them to the Sabeans, a nation far away." The LORD has spoken.

9 Proclaim this among the nations:
    Prepare for war!
Rouse the warriors!
    Let all the fighting men draw near and
       attack.
10 Beat your plowshares into swords
    and your pruning hooks into spears.
Let the weakling say,
    "I am strong!"
11 Come quickly, all you nations from every
       side,
    and assemble there.

Bring down your warriors, O LORD!

---

*a*2 *Jehoshaphat* means *the* LORD *judges*; also in verse 12.

¹²"Let the nations be roused;
    let them advance into the Valley of
        Jehoshaphat,
    for there I will sit
        to judge all the nations on every side.
¹³Swing the sickle,
    for the harvest is ripe.
Come, trample the grapes,
    for the winepress^D is full
    and the vats overflow—
    so great is their wickedness!"

¹⁴Multitudes, multitudes
    in the valley of decision!
For the day of the LORD^D is near
    in the valley of decision.
¹⁵The sun and moon will be darkened,
    and the stars no longer shine.
¹⁶The LORD will roar from Zion^D
    and thunder from Jerusalem^D;
    the earth and the sky will tremble.
But the LORD will be a refuge for his people,
    a stronghold^D for the people of Israel.

Blessings for God's People

¹⁷"Then you will know that I, the LORD your God,
    dwell in Zion, my holy hill.
Jerusalem will be holy;
    never again will foreigners invade her.

¹⁸"In that day the mountains will drip new
        wine^D,
    and the hills will flow with milk;
    all the ravines of Judah will run with water.
A fountain will flow out of the LORD's house
    and will water the valley of acacias^D.^a
¹⁹But Egypt will be desolate,
    Edom^D a desert waste,
because of violence done to the people of
        Judah,
    in whose land they shed innocent blood.
²⁰Judah will be inhabited forever
    and Jerusalem through all generations.
²¹Their bloodguilt^D, which I have not pardoned,
    I will pardon."

        The LORD dwells in Zion!

What kind of *harvest* did God intend to take? (3:13)

Soldiers or perhaps, nations—mowed down as grain is cut down by the sickle. The *harvest* is the slaughter—those cut down by God's judgment—in the final battle between good and evil.

The valley of decision (3:14)

The Valley of Jehoshaphat, where the final battle will take place. See *The Valley of Jehoshaphat* (3:2). The *decision* may reflect the outcome of the battle: God will win decisively. On the other hand, this may speak of God's judgment as a *decision* handed down by a judge.

The day of the LORD (3:14)

See *The day of the LORD* (1:15).

How will the sun, moon and stars be darkened? (3:15)

We can only guess, but it seems that Joel was describing a cataclysmic event that produced heavy clouds of ash or pollution. Whatever the cause, the effect would be to obscure the skies and contaminate the atmosphere. Also see *When will the moon turn to blood?* (2:30–32).

When will Jerusalem finally be holy and safe? (3:17)

Some say Jerusalem's security will occur as soon as Christ returns to rout Satan and his evil armies (Matt. 24:30–31). Others, believing in a literal thousand-year peaceful reign of Christ on earth (Rev. 20:4), think Jerusalem will be secure in the end. Also see article: *When will the Lord be the king over the whole earth?* (Zech. 14:9).

A fountain will flow (3:18)

A picture of a fresh, flowing source of water that washes away filth and contamination. It also depicts a fresh water spring invigorating all who dwell by it and drink from it (see Ezek. 47:1–12).

Bloodguilt (3:21)

Probably the verdict on Egypt and Edom for crimes deserving the death penalty (v. 19). Their vicious hostilities would be avenged and justice would finally be done. Also see *Save me from bloodguilt* (Psalm 51:14).

---

^a18 Or *Valley of Shittim*

AMOS

Why read this book?

This book gives us God's perspective on some volatile social issues. It takes a hard look at injustice and gives a call to righteousness. Amos tells us how God feels when the wealthy and the powerful exploit the poor and the defenseless. Whether you're well-off or struggling to make ends meet—or even if you're middle-class—you'll find these words hitting close to home.

Who wrote this book and when was it written?

Amos wrote this book between 760 and 750 B.C., a time of economic growth and prosperity. He was a shepherd from Judah with no known ministry credentials—except a word from God.

What was happening at this time?

The leadership and military conquests of Jeroboam II had enabled Israel to flourish. But while everything appeared fine on the surface, the moral fiber of the nation was disintegrating.

To whom was it written and why?

This message was for the people of Israel, the northern kingdom. Amos, from the southern kingdom, challenged their materialism and low morality, which they learned from their pagan neighbors. Many were exploiting the poor. Amos wrote to remind them that God has a special interest in the disadvantaged. His prophecy was God's last appeal to Israel, warning them to repent before it was too late.

What to look for in Amos:

With strong, poetic imagery, Amos speaks passionately about God's concern for the poor. He urges a return to righteousness and justice by returning to the Lord. Watch for parallels between Amos's time and ours. When he speaks of the poor, think of the homeless, racial minorities, single parents, the elderly and others who are often exploited.

When did these things happen?

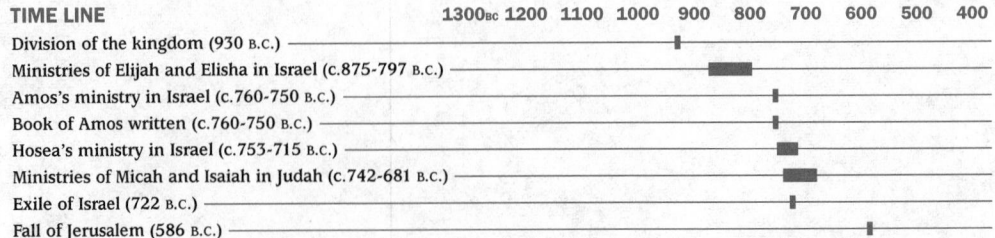

TIME LINE	1300BC	1200	1100	1000	900	800	700	600	500	400
Division of the kingdom (930 B.C.)										
Ministries of Elijah and Elisha in Israel (c.875-797 B.C.)										
Amos's ministry in Israel (c.760-750 B.C.)										
Book of Amos written (c.760-750 B.C.)										
Hosea's ministry in Israel (c.753-715 B.C.)										
Ministries of Micah and Isaiah in Judah (c.742-681 B.C.)										
Exile of Israel (722 B.C.)										
Fall of Jerusalem (586 B.C.)										

1 The words of Amos, one of the shepherds of Tekoa—
what he saw concerning Israel two years before the
earthquake, when Uzziah was king of Judah and Jeroboam son of Jehoash[a] was king of Israel.

²He said:

"The LORD roars from Zion[D]
    and thunders from Jerusalem[D];
the pastures of the shepherds dry up,[b]
    and the top of Carmel withers."

Judgment on Israel's Neighbors

³This is what the LORD says:

"For three sins of Damascus,
    even for four, I will not turn back ⌊my
        wrath⌋.
Because she threshed Gilead
    with sledges having iron teeth,
⁴I will send fire upon the house of Hazael
    that will consume the fortresses of
        Ben-Hadad.
⁵I will break down the gate of Damascus;
    I will destroy the king who is in[c] the Valley
        of Aven[d]
and the one who holds the scepter[D] in Beth
    Eden.
The people of Aram will go into exile[D] to
    Kir,"
                                    says the LORD.

⁶This is what the LORD says:

"For three sins of Gaza,
    even for four, I will not turn back ⌊my
        wrath⌋.
Because she took captive whole communities
    and sold them to Edom[D],
⁷I will send fire upon the walls of Gaza
    that will consume her fortresses.
⁸I will destroy the king[e] of Ashdod
    and the one who holds the scepter in
        Ashkelon.
I will turn my hand against Ekron,
    till the last of the Philistines is dead,"
                            says the Sovereign LORD.

⁹This is what the LORD says:

"For three sins of Tyre,
    even for four, I will not turn back ⌊my
        wrath⌋.
Because she sold whole communities of
    captives to Edom,
disregarding a treaty of brotherhood,
¹⁰I will send fire upon the walls of Tyre
    that will consume her fortresses."

¹¹This is what the LORD says:

"For three sins of Edom,
    even for four, I will not turn back ⌊my
        wrath⌋.
Because he pursued his brother with a sword,

---

a 1 Hebrew Joash, a variant of Jehoash   b 2 Or shepherds mourn
c 5 Or the inhabitants of   d 5 Aven means wickedness.   e 8 Or
inhabitants

What credentials did Amos have? (1:1)
Amos, a shepherd by profession, had only a vision from God. He was confident that God had
given him a mission to warn Israel of coming
judgment. See 7:14–15.

The earthquake (1:1)
Zechariah also tells of an earthquake during
Uzziah's reign (Zech. 14:5). Information about
it is sketchy, but it probably occurred during
the ministry of Amos, between 760 and 750
B.C. It must have been severe.

For three sins . . . even for four (1:3)
This is a literary device used to express the
concept of many. The formula describing the
sins of Damascus is repeated with each of the
other nations indicted by Amos, including Judah and Israel (vv. 6,9,11,13; 2:1,4,6).

Sledges having iron teeth (1:3)
A picture of extreme violence. Farmers
threshed their grain by pulling wooden sledges
over it. The sharp teeth on the bottom separated the kernels from the stalks. Sledges were
also used to cut furrows in the ground. In battle they were sometimes dragged behind chariots. Although this may be a figure of speech to
describe war atrocities, some think Amos was
denouncing a literal method of torture—dragging sledges over prisoners of war who were
staked to the ground.

What has happened to these nations?
(1:3–5)
Down through the centuries, each of these nations met its end. Some, such as the Moabites, Edomites and Philistines, were annihilated by Nebuchadnezzar, king of the great
Babylonian empire in the late seventh and
early sixth centuries B.C. Ancient inscriptions
say he exterminated them because he found
them troublesome. None of these tribes survived intact after Alexander the Great conquered the region in the early 300s B.C.

Judgment on Israel's Neighbors (1:3)

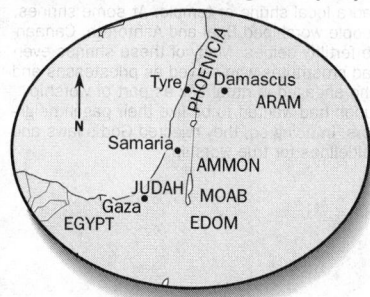

Fire (1:4)
Captured cities were often torched, especially
those that had resisted surrender. If a city did
surrender, however, it was often spared,
though its nobility, intelligentsia and craftsmen
could be whisked away into captivity.

stifling all compassion,[a]
because his anger raged continually
and his fury flamed unchecked,
12I will send fire upon Teman
that will consume the fortresses of Bozrah."

13This is what the LORD says:

"For three sins of Ammon,
even for four, I will not turn back ⌐my
wrath⌐.
Because he ripped open the pregnant women
of Gilead
in order to extend his borders,
14I will set fire to the walls of Rabbah
that will consume her fortresses
amid war cries on the day of battle,
amid violent winds on a stormy day.
15Her king[b] will go into exile[D],
he and his officials together,"
says the LORD.

2 This is what the LORD says:

"For three sins of Moab,
even for four, I will not turn back ⌐my
wrath⌐.
Because he burned, as if to lime,
the bones of Edom's[D] king,
2I will send fire upon Moab
that will consume the fortresses of Kerioth.[c]
Moab will go down in great tumult
amid war cries and the blast of the trumpet.
3I will destroy her ruler
and kill all her officials with him,"
says the LORD.

4This is what the LORD says:

"For three sins of Judah,
even for four, I will not turn back ⌐my
wrath⌐.
Because they have rejected the law of the LORD
and have not kept his decrees,
because they have been led astray by false
gods,[d]
the gods[e] their ancestors followed,
5I will send fire upon Judah
that will consume the fortresses of
Jerusalem[D]."

Judgment on Israel

6This is what the LORD says:

"For three sins of Israel,
even for four, I will not turn back ⌐my
wrath⌐.
They sell the righteous[D] for silver,
and the needy for a pair of sandals.
7They trample on the heads of the poor
as upon the dust of the ground
and deny justice to the oppressed.
Father and son use the same girl
and so profane[D] my holy name.

Why did Ammon rip open pregnant women? (1:13)

Killing a pregnant woman was seen as a way to destroy two enemies with one thrust of the sword. This was not a strategic method for winning a war. This was bloodthirsty madness—an insane hatred for those of a different ethnic group.

What's so terrible about burning bones? (2:1)

Burning the bones of the king showed how much the Moabites hated the people of Edom. They believed they were preventing the dead king from resting in peace—perhaps even denying him eternal life. And by desecrating a burial ground, they probably thought they were desecrating a sacred place.

To lime (2:1)

Lime is a caustic substance that can disintegrate the bones of a human. But the reference here may describe the result of the burning: all that would remain would be a pile of white ashes that looked like lime.

Fire (2:2,5)

See *Fire* (1:4).

What false gods led Judah astray? (2:4)

By Amos's time, almost every town in Judah had a local shrine or temple. At some shrines, people worshiped Baal and Ashtoreth, Canaanite fertility deities. Many of these shrines even had prostitutes who served as priestesses and who engaged in ritual sex as part of worship. Judah had wanted to be like their pagan neighbors. In doing so, they rejected God's laws and guidelines for true worship.

Use the same girl (2:7)

A father and son worshiping at a pagan shrine had sex with the same temple prostitute. Prostitution was a sin, but this made it even more outrageous. It amounted to a kind of secondary incest, a perversion between the father and son (see Lev. 20:12).

---

a11 Or *sword / and destroyed his allies*   *b15* Or *Molech*; Hebrew *malcam*   *c2* Or *of her cities*   *d4* Or *by lies*   *e4* Or *lies*

8They lie down beside every altar
  on garments taken in pledge.
In the house of their god
  they drink wine taken as fines.

9"I destroyed the Amorite before them,
  though he was tall as the cedars
  and strong as the oaks.
I destroyed his fruit above
  and his roots below.

10"I brought you up out of Egypt,
  and I led you forty years in the desert
  to give you the land of the Amorites.
11I also raised up prophetsᴰ from among your
    sons
  and Naziritesᴰ from among your young
    men.
Is this not true, people of Israel?"
                        declares the LORD.

12"But you made the Nazirites drink wine
  and commanded the prophets not to
    prophesy.

13"Now then, I will crush you
  as a cart crushes when loaded with grain.
14The swift will not escape,
  the strong will not muster their strength,
  and the warrior will not save his life.
15The archer will not stand his ground,
  the fleet-footed soldier will not get away,
  and the horseman will not save his life.
16Even the bravest warriors
  will flee naked on that day,"
                        declares the LORD.

Witnesses Summoned Against Israel

3 Hear this word the LORD has spoken against you, O people of Israel—against the whole family I brought up out of Egypt:

2"You only have I chosen
  of all the families of the earth;
therefore I will punish you
  for all your sins."

3Do two walk together
  unless they have agreed to do so?
4Does a lion roar in the thicket
  when he has no prey?
Does he growl in his den
  when he has caught nothing?
5Does a bird fall into a trap on the ground
  where no snare has been set?
Does a trap spring up from the earth
  when there is nothing to catch?
6When a trumpet sounds in a city,
  do not the people tremble?
When disaster comes to a city,
  has not the LORD caused it?

7Surely the Sovereign LORD does nothing
  without revealing his plan
  to his servants the prophets.

8The lion has roared—
  who will not fear?

Fruit above . . . roots below (2:9)
Destroying the crop was one thing. Destroying the root system was something more devastating. The point of this agricultural metaphor is to show total destruction. Ancient armies would sometimes ruin their victims' fields by covering them with salt so they would not grow crops for years to come.

Why force the Nazirites to drink wine? (2:12)
Nazirites were Hebrews who made extraordinary lifestyle sacrifices to God, usually for a limited time (Num. 6:1–21). One such sacrifice was to abstain from alcohol. Forcing Nazirites to abandon their vows to God was an act of defiance, an intentional destruction of something sacred.

Why did God punish his chosen people? (3:2)
Though Israel had a special relationship with God because of his covenant with Abraham, the people had grown complacent about their responsibilities in the covenant. They knew from the law how to live a godly life and what God expected from them. Yet they ignored it. It seems that God expected more of them because he had blessed them with so much: *You only have I chosen . . . therefore I will punish you . . .*

What did these questions mean? (3:3–8)
Through the use of rhetorical questions, Amos was saying, "Wake up, Israel. The signs of imminent disaster are all around you." Sadly, Israel slept through this wake-up call.

Are disasters acts of God? (3:6)
See article: *What sort of evil did the Lord intend to do?* (9:4).

What do these body parts represent? (3:12)

A lion, after killing a lamb, will not eat every part of the carcass. It may leave, for example, the hooves or a bone from the leg. Amos was saying that these leftovers would be all that remained of Israel after God judged them. This occurred when Sargon II, an Assyrian king, led the inhabitants of Samaria and the rest of the northern kingdom into exile a thousand miles away, to the eastern regions of his empire. Only the poorest were left behind.

Who are those on beds and couches? (3:12)

These are the wealthy elite of Israel who lived in luxury with no thought of the future. They refused to worry about God and his warnings, or to believe there would come a day of reckoning.

Why cut off the horns of the altar? (3:14)

It was part of the process of destroying pagan altars. Jeroboam was the first king of Israel to violate God's command to worship only in Jerusalem. He built altars in Bethel and Dan to keep his people from returning to Jerusalem for worship in the rival southern kingdom. At each altar he placed a golden calf. Similar altars to pagan gods quickly sprung up across the countryside. Traditionally altars had horns on the four corners. The meat was tied to the horns with a rope or a slow-burning cable. As the kindling and logs crumbled and burned away, the sacrifice remained in place.

Who needed a summer house in Palestine? (3:15)

The Mediterranean climate varied tremendously depending on the altitude and proximity to water. During the hottest days of summer, the kings of Israel would retreat to a summer palace in a cooler altitude, located in the hilltop city of Jezreel, near Mount Gilboa. The regular palace was about 20 miles south, in Samaria.

Why call these women *cows*? (4:1)

It's not certain. It could have been sarcastic flattery. Cows raised in Bashan (see **Map 3** at the back of this Bible), in what is now southern Syria, were some of the finest bred cattle in the region. On the other hand, cows are not considered intelligent animals. All they seem to care about is filling their bellies. The implication here may be that these materialistic women, though they were of the noble class, were considered stupid in the eyes of the Lord.

Taken away with hooks (4:2)

Assyrian pictures chiseled into stone show this very image. This empire, which eventually conquered Israel, led their prisoners single-file on ropes attached to hooks. The hooks, in turn, punctured the captives' noses or lips.

What sins occurred at Bethel and Gilgal? (4:4)

The worship of Baal and Ashtoreth, pagan Canaanite gods. The Hebrews apparently worshiped the Lord there as well, instead of following God's instructions to worship at the temple in Jerusalem. King Jeroboam, who reigned from 931 to 910 B.C., prohibited his subjects from worshiping in Jerusalem. He feared his people would want to merge again with the southern kingdom, Judah. So he built new wor-

The Sovereign LORD has spoken—
who can but prophesy?

⁹Proclaim to the fortresses of Ashdod
and to the fortresses of Egypt:
"Assemble yourselves on the mountains of
Samaria;
see the great unrest within her
and the oppression among her people."

¹⁰"They do not know how to do right," declares
the LORD,
"who hoard plunderᴰ and loot in their
fortresses."

¹¹Therefore this is what the Sovereign LORD says:

"An enemy will overrun the land;
he will pull down your strongholdsᴰ
and plunder your fortresses."

¹²This is what the LORD says:

"As a shepherd saves from the lion's mouth
only two leg bones or a piece of an ear,
so will the Israelites be saved,
those who sit in Samaria
on the edge of their beds
and in Damascus on their couches.ᵃ"

¹³"Hear this and testify against the house of Jacob," declares the Lord, the LORD God Almighty.

¹⁴"On the day I punish Israel for her sins,
I will destroy the altars of Bethel;
the horns of the altar will be cut off
and fall to the ground.
¹⁵I will tear down the winter house
along with the summer house;
the houses adorned with ivory will be
destroyed
and the mansions will be demolished,"
declares the LORD.

Israel Has Not Returned to God

4 Hear this word, you cows of Bashan on Mount
Samaria,
you women who oppress the poor and crush
the needy
and say to your husbands, "Bring us some
drinks!"
²The Sovereign LORD has sworn by his holiness:
"The time will surely come
when you will be taken away with hooks,
the last of you with fishhooks.
³You will each go straight out
through breaks in the wall,
and you will be cast out toward Harmon,ᵇ"
declares the LORD.

⁴"Go to Bethel and sin;
go to Gilgal and sin yet more.
Bring your sacrificesᴰ every morning,
your tithesᴰ every three years.ᶜ

ᵃ12 The meaning of the Hebrew for this line is uncertain. ᵇ3 Masoretic Text; with a different word division of the Hebrew (see Septuagint) *out, O mountain of oppression* ᶜ4 Or *tithes on the third day*

[5]Burn leavened bread as a thank offering[D]
    and brag about your freewill offerings—
boast about them, you Israelites,
    for this is what you love to do,"
                        declares the Sovereign LORD.

[6]"I gave you empty stomachs[a] in every city
    and lack of bread in every town,
    yet you have not returned to me,"
                        declares the LORD.

[7]"I also withheld rain from you
    when the harvest was still three months
        away.
I sent rain on one town,
    but withheld it from another.
One field had rain;
    another had none and dried up.
[8]People staggered from town to town for water
    but did not get enough to drink,
    yet you have not returned to me,"
                        declares the LORD.

[9]"Many times I struck your gardens and
        vineyards,
    I struck them with blight and mildew.
Locusts[D] devoured your fig and olive trees,
    yet you have not returned to me,"
                        declares the LORD.

[10]"I sent plagues among you
    as I did to Egypt.
I killed your young men with the sword,
    along with your captured horses.
I filled your nostrils with the stench of your
        camps,
    yet you have not returned to me,"
                        declares the LORD.

[11]"I overthrew some of you
    as I[b] overthrew Sodom and Gomorrah.
You were like a burning stick snatched from
        the fire,
    yet you have not returned to me,"
                        declares the LORD.

[12]"Therefore this is what I will do to you, Israel,
    and because I will do this to you,
    prepare to meet your God, O Israel."

[13]He who forms the mountains,
    creates the wind,
    and reveals his thoughts to man,
he who turns dawn to darkness,
    and treads the high places[D] of the earth—
    the LORD God Almighty is his name.

A Lament and Call to Repentance

5 Hear this word, O house of Israel, this lament[D] I take
up concerning you:

[2]"Fallen is Virgin Israel,
    never to rise again,
deserted in her own land,
    with no one to lift her up."

[a]6 Hebrew *you cleanness of teeth*   [b]11 Hebrew *God*

ship centers at Bethel and Gilgal and elsewhere (see *Map 4* at the back of this Bible).
This was a clear breach of God's command.

Does God still try to get our attention through droughts and plagues? (4:6–11)

Some are probably a direct punishment from
God; others cannot be directly attributed to
him or easily explained. In Amos's time, God
was teaching his covenant people their responsibilities in the agreement. The training was
painful for them because they didn't respond
to him. Also see *Does God use drought to punish?* (Jer. 3:3).

SCRIPTURE LINK (4:11) *Sodom and Gomorrah*

See Gen. 19:24.

Burning stick snatched from the fire (4:11)

As a result of God's judgment, Israel would be
burnt, but not completely destroyed. And the
salvation they would experience would be only
because of the grace of God.

Prepare to meet your God (4:12)

God had warned Israel repeatedly, but to no
avail. Israel would now have the unenviable position of meeting God face to face—in judgment. For this generation of Israelites, the
judgment would be final and complete. The
specific way they would meet God through judgment is not revealed.

How does God reveal his thoughts? (4:13)

One way is through calamity. When people are
devastated by a flood, hurricane or war, they
start thinking about the important issues of
life. In that frame of mind they are often better
able to hear what God has to say to them. Also
see article: *Why does God send calamity?*
(Lam. 3:38).

The high places of the earth (4:13)

This phrase is wedged into a series of statements about God's control over all the earth,
so it may refer to his presence as revealed in
the sky. Countless stars, mile-high clouds and
lightning storms are just a few of the dazzling
reminders of humanity's transiency and God's
awesome power.

Lament (5:1)

See *Lament* (Ezek. 26:17).

Virgin Israel (5:2)

See *Virgin Israel* (Jer. 18:13).

³This is what the Sovereign LORD says:

"The city that marches out a thousand strong
 for Israel
   will have only a hundred left;
 the town that marches out a hundred strong
   will have only ten left."

⁴This is what the LORD says to the house of Israel:

"Seek me and live;
 ⁵ do not seek Bethel,
 do not go to Gilgal,
   do not journey to Beersheba.
 For Gilgal will surely go into exile^D,
   and Bethel will be reduced to nothing. ^a"
⁶Seek the LORD and live,
 or he will sweep through the house of Joseph
   like a fire;
 it will devour,
   and Bethel will have no one to quench it.

⁷You who turn justice into bitterness
   and cast righteousness^D to the ground
⁸(he who made the Pleiades and Orion,
   who turns blackness into dawn
   and darkens day into night,
 who calls for the waters of the sea
   and pours them out over the face of the
     land—
   the LORD is his name—
⁹he flashes destruction on the stronghold^D
   and brings the fortified city to ruin),
¹⁰you hate the one who reproves in court
   and despise him who tells the truth.

¹¹You trample on the poor
   and force him to give you grain.
 Therefore, though you have built stone
     mansions,
   you will not live in them;
 though you have planted lush vineyards,
   you will not drink their wine.
¹²For I know how many are your offenses
   and how great your sins.

 You oppress the righteous^D and take bribes
   and you deprive the poor of justice in the
     courts.
¹³Therefore the prudent man keeps quiet in such
     times,
   for the times are evil.

¹⁴Seek good, not evil,
   that you may live.
 Then the LORD God Almighty will be with you,
   just as you say he is.
¹⁵Hate evil, love good;
   maintain justice in the courts.
 Perhaps the LORD God Almighty will have
     mercy^D
   on the remnant^D of Joseph.

¹⁶Therefore this is what the Lord, the LORD God Almighty, says:

What attracted people to these places? (5:5)

Each of these places had historical significance. It was at Bethel that Israel's ancestor Abraham built his first altar in Palestine. Gilgal was where Israel first set up camp after Joshua led them across the Jordan River. And Beersheba was the place where Abraham had found a deep well and where the Lord had appeared to Isaac and Jacob. Despite God's command to worship only in Jerusalem, the people of Israel traveled to these places to worship. Worse, they worshiped pagan gods there as well as the Lord.

Why keep silent? (5:13)

Nobody would listen anyway. There is a time for silence—a time when speaking up is futile. At such times the only thing to do is to wait for God to move in to judge.

---

^a5 Or *grief*; or *wickedness*; Hebrew *aven*, a reference to Beth Aven (a derogatory name for Bethel)

"There will be wailing in all the streets
  and cries of anguish in every public square.
The farmers will be summoned to weep
  and the mourners to wail.
¹⁷There will be wailing in all the vineyards,
  for I will pass through your midst,"
                                    says the LORD.

The Day of the LORD

¹⁸Woe to you who long
  for the day of the LORDᴰ!
Why do you long for the day of the LORD?
  That day will be darkness, not light.
¹⁹It will be as though a man fled from a lion
  only to meet a bear,
as though he entered his house
  and rested his hand on the wall
  only to have a snake bite him.
²⁰Will not the day of the LORD be darkness, not
    light—
  pitch-dark, without a ray of brightness?

²¹"I hate, I despise your religious feasts;
  I cannot stand your assemblies.
²²Even though you bring me burnt offeringsᴰ
    and grain offeringsᴰ,
  I will not accept them.
Though you bring choice fellowship
    offeringsᴰ,ᵃ
  I will have no regard for them.
²³Away with the noise of your songs!
  I will not listen to the music of your harps.
²⁴But let justice roll on like a river,
  righteousnessᴰ like a never-failing stream!

²⁵"Did you bring me sacrificesᴰ and offerings
  forty years in the desert, O house of Israel?
²⁶You have lifted up the shrine of your king,
  the pedestal of your idolsᴰ,
  the star of your godᵇ—
  which you made for yourselves.
²⁷Therefore I will send you into exileᴰ beyond
    Damascus,"
  says the LORD, whose name is God Almighty.

Woe to the Complacent

6 Woe to you who are complacent in Zionᴰ,
  and to you who feel secure on Mount
    Samaria,
you notable men of the foremost nation,
  to whom the people of Israel come!
²Go to Calneh and look at it;
  go from there to great Hamath,
  and then go down to Gath in Philistia.
Are they better off than your two kingdoms?
  Is their land larger than yours?
³You put off the evil day
  and bring near a reign of terror.
⁴You lie on beds inlaid with ivory
  and lounge on your couches.
You dine on choice lambs

ᵃ22 Traditionally *peace offerings*   ᵇ26 Or *lifted up Sakkuth your
king / and Kaiwan your idols, / your star-gods*; Septuagint *lifted up the
shrine of Molech / and the star of your god Rephan, / their idols*

Why wail and mourn when the Lord passed through? (5:17)

Perhaps because the lack of rain or the armed invaders would destroy their grape vineyards, a symbol of their affluence. The drought (4:7–8) devastated the agricultural landscape, causing famine and starvation.

Why did they want the *day of the Lord* to come? (5:18)

During Amos's time, a popular sort of preaching arose throughout the land, denying the problems Amos denounced. The essence of this preaching was that everything was all right and that prosperity lay just ahead. It went on to say that God would deliver them from their enemies on *the day of the Lord*. What they thought would be a day of reckoning for their enemies, however, actually turned out to be a day of reckoning for them.

Why did God hate religious customs he himself had established? (5:21–23)

God set up the customs as tangible, outward expressions to be practiced by his people who wanted to demonstrate their faith and the love they felt for God. But the Israelites of Amos's day were hypocrites. They attended feasts and offered sacrifices, but their love for God had died out long before. They went to worship to appear respectable, but their hearts had grown cold and empty. Their religion was insincere; it had form but no substance. And this religion was even used to worship idols (vv. 25–26). It wasn't the customs that God hated; it was hypocrisy.

How could a thinking person deny the problems? (6:1)

They were suppressing the evidence, saying in effect, "Perhaps there will be some difficulty sometime in the future, but it's not going to happen to us." Their optimism was worldly and naive. The *evil day* (v. 3) refers to the day of God's judgment, which came upon all of these cities.

What would they see at Calneh, Hamath and Gath? (6:2)

Some say the Israelites would see the destruction caused by God's judgment of these foreign cities (see **Map 5** at the back of this Bible). Others suggest Israel would see that they were better off and possessed larger tracts of land than these pagan cities, yet had sunk to the same immoral level.

How could the people live in such ease with ruin all around? (6:4–6)

The *ruin of Joseph* refers to the devastation of the rank and file Israelites. Jeroboam II had won many military victories. He and his royal court enjoyed the spoils of war and could afford excessive carousing and first-class living. They ignored the poor city dwellers and cared nothing for the peasants. The social set lived as if they were the only ones that mattered.

and fattened calves.
[5]You strum away on your harps like David
    and improvise on musical instruments.
[6]You drink wine by the bowlful
    and use the finest lotions,
but you do not grieve over the ruin of
    Joseph.
[7]Therefore you will be among the first to go
    into exile[D];
your feasting and lounging will end.

The LORD Abhors the Pride of Israel

[8]The Sovereign LORD has sworn by himself—the LORD
God Almighty declares:

> "I abhor the pride of Jacob
>   and detest his fortresses;
> I will deliver up the city
>   and everything in it."

[9]If ten men are left in one house, they too will die. [10]And if a relative who is to burn the bodies comes to carry them out of the house and asks anyone still hiding there, "Is anyone with you?" and he says, "No," then he will say, "Hush! We must not mention the name of the LORD."

[11]For the LORD has given the command,
    and he will smash the great house into
        pieces
    and the small house into bits.

[12]Do horses run on the rocky crags?
    Does one plow there with oxen?
But you have turned justice into poison
    and the fruit of righteousness[D] into
        bitterness—
[13]you who rejoice in the conquest of Lo Debar[a]
    and say, "Did we not take Karnaim[b] by our
        own strength?"

[14]For the LORD God Almighty declares,
    "I will stir up a nation against you, O house
        of Israel,
that will oppress you all the way
    from Lebo[c] Hamath to the valley of the
        Arabah."

Locusts, Fire and a Plumb Line

7 This is what the Sovereign LORD showed me: He was preparing swarms of locusts[D] after the king's share had been harvested and just as the second crop was coming up. [2]When they had stripped the land clean, I cried out, "Sovereign LORD, forgive! How can Jacob survive? He is so small!"

[3]So the LORD relented.

"This will not happen," the LORD said.

[4]This is what the Sovereign LORD showed me: The Sovereign LORD was calling for judgment by fire; it dried up the great deep and devoured the land. [5]Then I cried out, "Sovereign LORD, I beg you, stop! How can Jacob survive? He is so small!"

[6]So the LORD relented.

Why cremate the dead? (6:10)

When an ancient city was being sacked, the corpses piled up quickly. And in that hot Mediterranean climate, a corpse would begin to decompose quickly. The custom was to bury the body within a day of the death. But in times of war, cremation was more practical. Also see *Why did they burn the bodies before they buried them?* (1 Samuel 31:12–13) and *Why have a bonfire at a funeral?* (2 Chron. 16:14).

Why were they afraid to mention the name of the Lord? (6:10)

Some, recognizing that their devastating punishment came from the Lord, may have feared that mentioning his name would call his attention to the fact that there were still survivors. Or it's possible others were afraid they might accuse or curse God for failing to protect them. Aware by now of his wrath, they wanted to guard themselves against more of it.

Does God change his mind? (7:3,6)

Prayer does affect God's actions. Repentance and brokenness can chart a new course for a nation or an individual. Amos took the role of an intercessor on behalf of Israel. Also see article: *Can our prayers cause God to change his mind?* (Exodus 32:14).

---

[a]13 *Lo Debar* means *nothing.*   [b]13 *Karnaim* means *horns; horn* here symbolizes strength.   [c]14 Or *from the entrance to*

"This will not happen either," the Sovereign LORD said.

7This is what he showed me: The Lord was standing by a wall that had been built true to plumb, with a plumb line in his hand. **8**And the LORD asked me, "What do you see, Amos?"

"A plumb line," I replied.

Then the Lord said, "Look, I am setting a plumb line among my people Israel; I will spare them no longer.

9"The high places[D] of Isaac will be destroyed
and the sanctuaries of Israel will be ruined;
with my sword I will rise against the house
of Jeroboam."

Amos and Amaziah

10Then Amaziah the priest[D] of Bethel sent a message to Jeroboam king of Israel: "Amos is raising a conspiracy against you in the very heart of Israel. The land cannot bear all his words. **11**For this is what Amos is saying:

" 'Jeroboam will die by the sword,
and Israel will surely go into exile[D],
away from their native land.' "

12Then Amaziah said to Amos, "Get out, you seer[D]! Go back to the land of Judah. Earn your bread there and do your prophesying there. **13**Don't prophesy anymore at Bethel, because this is the king's sanctuary and the temple of the kingdom."

14Amos answered Amaziah, "I was neither a prophet[D] nor a prophet's son, but I was a shepherd, and I also took care of sycamore-fig trees. **15**But the LORD took me from tending the flock and said to me, 'Go, prophesy to my people Israel.' **16**Now then, hear the word of the LORD. You say,

" 'Do not prophesy against Israel,
and stop preaching against the house of
Isaac.'

17"Therefore this is what the LORD says:

" 'Your wife will become a prostitute in the
city,
and your sons and daughters will fall by the
sword.
Your land will be measured and divided up,
and you yourself will die in a pagan[a]
country.
And Israel will certainly go into exile,
away from their native land.' "

A Basket of Ripe Fruit

8 This is what the Sovereign LORD showed me: a basket of ripe fruit. **2**"What do you see, Amos?" he asked.

"A basket of ripe fruit," I answered.

Then the LORD said to me, "The time is ripe for my people Israel; I will spare them no longer.

3"In that day," declares the Sovereign LORD, "the songs in the temple will turn to wailing.[b] Many, many bodies— flung everywhere! Silence!"

4Hear this, you who trample the needy
and do away with the poor of the land,

What did the plumb line show? (7:7–8)

It showed that Israel was crooked. The plumb line was a cord with a weight tied on the end. Ancient builders, like those today, held it beside buildings under construction, to make sure the walls were being built straight. When God put the plumb line to Israel, they didn't meet his standards. He had to tear them down and start over.

High places of Isaac (7:9)

These were places where Isaac had offered sacrifices centuries before. But Jeroboam had erected sanctuaries there. See **What sins occurred at Bethel and Gilgal?** (4:4).

Why was Amos seen as a political conspirator? (7:10)

Because his message of impending judgment threatened the political and religious establishment. Amaziah, one of Jeroboam's priests, stood to lose his job if people accepted Amos's prophecy against the status quo. So Amaziah tried to discredit Amos and run him out of town.

What happened to Amaziah? (7:17)

The prophecy said that he would be carried off into exile with the other prisoners of war. But there is no further mention of how and when he died.

---

a17 Hebrew *an unclean*   *b3* Or *"the temple singers will wail*

New Moon (8:5)

See *New Moon festival* (1 Samuel 20:5).

Sweepings (8:6)

Chaff that fell to the floor when grain was threshed. It was inedible and thrown away. Wealthy and dishonest merchants, though, mixed the *sweepings* with the grain and sold it as pure grain to the poor.

The Pride of Jacob (8:7)

Some say that God made an oath, swearing not by his holy name but by the land of Israel, *the Pride of Jacob.* This was his solemn vow to judge the people to whom the land had been promised in his covenant with Abraham. Others suggest that the Lord was *the Pride of Jacob* and that he was swearing by himself as he had done before (6:8).

Shave your heads (8:10)

This was one of the cultural expressions of mourning the loss of a loved one. Even women, especially the widowed, would shave their heads and put ashes on them. They would also tear their clothes and put on sackcloth. Also see *Why shave beards, tear clothes and cut skin?* (Jer. 41:5).

Why would God starve his people spiritually? (8:11–12)

God's people had starved themselves by chasing after other gods, worldliness and materialism, so God would judge them. Part of their judgment would be God's absence.

The shame of Samaria (8:14)

The worship of idols. Idols to Baal had sprung up across the northern kingdom of Israel. Jeroboam initiated the worship of golden calves at Dan and at Bethel. His rationale may have been that they could represent the presence of the invisible God standing on the back of each calf, just as Baal has been depicted on the back of a bull in stone pictures found by archaeologists.

---

⁵saying,

"When will the New Moon be over
    that we may sell grain,
and the Sabbathᴰ be ended
    that we may market wheat?"—
skimping the measure,
    boosting the price
    and cheating with dishonest scales,
⁶buying the poor with silver
    and the needy for a pair of sandals,
    selling even the sweepings with the wheat.

⁷The LORD has sworn by the Pride of Jacob: "I will never forget anything they have done.

⁸"Will not the land tremble for this,
    and all who live in it mourn?
The whole land will rise like the Nile;
    it will be stirred up and then sink
    like the river of Egypt.

⁹"In that day," declares the Sovereign LORD,

"I will make the sun go down at noon
    and darken the earth in broad daylight.
¹⁰I will turn your religious feasts into mourning
    and all your singing into weeping.
I will make all of you wear sackclothᴰ
    and shave your heads.
I will make that time like mourning for an only
        son
    and the end of it like a bitter day.

¹¹"The days are coming," declares the Sovereign
        LORD,
    "when I will send a famine through the
        land—
not a famine of food or a thirst for water,
    but a famine of hearing the words of the
        LORD.
¹²Men will stagger from sea to sea
    and wander from north to east,
searching for the word of the LORD,
    but they will not find it.

¹³"In that day

"the lovely young women and strong young
        men
    will faint because of thirst.
¹⁴They who swear by the shameᵃ of Samaria,
    or say, 'As surely as your god lives, O Dan,'
    or, 'As surely as the godᵇ of Beersheba
        lives'—
they will fall,
    never to rise again."

Israel to Be Destroyed

9 I saw the Lord standing by the altar, and he said:

"Strike the tops of the pillars
    so that the thresholds shake.
Bring them down on the heads of all the
        people;
    those who are left I will kill with the sword.

ᵃ14 Or *by Ashima; or by the idol*   ᵇ14 Or *power*

Not one will get away,
    none will escape.
2Though they dig down to the depths of the
        grave,*a*
    from there my hand will take them.
Though they climb up to the heavens,
    from there I will bring them down.
3Though they hide themselves on the top of
        Carmel,
    there I will hunt them down and seize them.
Though they hide from me at the bottom of
        the sea,
    there I will command the serpent to bite
        them.
4Though they are driven into exile*b* by their
        enemies,
    there I will command the sword to slay
        them.
I will fix my eyes upon them
    for evil and not for good."

5The Lord, the LORD Almighty,
    he who touches the earth and it melts,
    and all who live in it mourn—
the whole land rises like the Nile,
    then sinks like the river of Egypt—
6he who builds his lofty palace*b* in the heavens
    and sets its foundation*c* on the earth,
who calls for the waters of the sea
    and pours them out over the face of the
        land—
    the LORD is his name.

7"Are not you Israelites
    the same to me as the Cushites*d*?"
                    declares the LORD.
"Did I not bring Israel up from Egypt,
    the Philistines from Caphtor*e*
    and the Arameans from Kir?

*a*2 Hebrew *to Sheol*   *b*6 The meaning of the Hebrew for this
phrase is uncertain.   *c*6 The meaning of the Hebrew for this word
is uncertain.   *d*7 That is, people from the upper Nile region
*e*7 That is, Crete

Were God's chosen people not that special after all? (9:7)

Not any more. The only difference between Israel and these other nations had been Israel's covenant relationship with God. But Israel broke the covenant and as a result sacrificed the relationship with God. The Israelites were no better off than any other pagan nation.

What sort of *evil* did the Lord intend to do? (9:4)

God cannot be accused of doing evil, but he may allow evil to take place. In this case, he simply permitted Israel to suffer the consequences of its own evil actions. The consequences themselves would be called evil.

What God did was to strip away Israel's national identity. He allowed Assyria to carry the nation off into captivity and resettle the people in a foreign country. Their punishment was that they would be absorbed into the pagan world—so absorbed, in fact, that they never regained their identity as a nation. They never returned, as Judah would do a century and a half later after their own exile.

The Israelites had wanted to adopt the lifestyle and customs of their neighbors, so God punished them by granting their wish. Their idolatry, immorality and exploitation of the poor had polluted their faith in God. So God judged them by allowing them to become totally immersed in their paganism.

Why shake Israel like grain in a sieve? (9:9)

As part of God's judgment, Israel would be shaken all over the landscape. This refers to a scattering of the Israelite race—a scattering known as the Diaspora—that would take place over the next few centuries.

How could Amos change his tone so abruptly? (9:11)

Prophecy usually included both doom and promise. The warnings of impending judgment were meant to jar people into a state of alarm and give them one last chance to repent. But offering hope was also part of being a prophet of the God of grace. This double-barreled approach to prophecy—judgment and mercy—is consistent throughout the Bible.

Edom (9:12)

This may refer to the nation descended from Esau, long an enemy of Israel. Some think *Edom* could mean Adam, referring to all humanity (see NIV text note). The two words are quite similar in the Hebrew language. Or this could simply mean the remnant of all nations —the Gentiles—will one day come to faith in God, which is how it is quoted in the New Testament (Acts 15:17).

What other nations will *bear my name*? (9:12)

Every nation whose people turn to faith in Christ. This is a prophecy that began to be fulfilled shortly after Christ's death and continues to be fulfilled today. Through Christ's death, all are invited into a relationship with God. Those who follow Christ bear God's name.

When will God establish Israel permanently? (9:15)

Some believe God plans to do this for the Jews some time in the future. This would take place in the Millennium, the thousand-year earthly reign of Christ after he returns. There the nation of Israel would finally be restored. Others, though, think this refers to Christ's return, when God's people—those who believe in Christ, Jews and non-Jews—will be permanently settled in heaven.

8"Surely the eyes of the Sovereign LORD
　　are on the sinful kingdom.
I will destroy it
　　from the face of the earth—
yet I will not totally destroy
　　the house of Jacob,"
　　　　　　　　　　　　　declares the LORD.
9"For I will give the command,
　　and I will shake the house of Israel
　　among all the nations
as grain is shaken in a sieve,
　　and not a pebble will reach the ground.
10All the sinners among my people
　　will die by the sword,
all those who say,
　　'Disaster will not overtake or meet us.'

Israel's Restoration

11"In that day I will restore
　　David's fallen tent.
I will repair its broken places,
　　restore its ruins,
　　and build it as it used to be,
12so that they may possess the remnantᴰ of
　　Edomᴰ
　　and all the nations that bear my name,ᵃ"
　　　　　　　　　　　　declares the LORD, who will
　　　　　　　　　　　　　　　do these things.

13"The days are coming," declares the LORD,

　　"when the reaper will be overtaken by the
　　　　plowman
　　and the planter by the one treading grapes.
New wine will drip from the mountains
　　and flow from all the hills.
14I will bring back my exiledᴰᵇ people Israel;
　　they will rebuild the ruined cities and live in
　　　　them.
They will plant vineyards and drink their wine;
　　they will make gardens and eat their fruit.
15I will plant Israel in their own land,
　　never again to be uprooted
　　from the land I have given them,"

　　　　　　　　　　　　　says the LORD your God.

ᵃ12 Hebrew; Septuagint *so that the remnant of men / and all the nations that bear my name may seek ⌞the Lord⌟*　　ᵇ14 Or *will restore the fortunes of my*

OBADIAH

Why read this book?

Has anyone ever taken advantage of you—and gotten away with it? Perhaps a friend or maybe even a family member turned on you when you needed them. Obadiah tells us that God will take care of such injustices.

Who wrote this book?

Obadiah, an otherwise unknown prophet, whose name means *servant of the Lord.*

When was it written?

Perhaps between 850 and 732 B.C., but more likely between 605 and 587 B.C.

What was happening in the world at this time?

God's people had a longstanding feud with Edom, a neighboring nation of distant blood relatives. When Judah was invaded and conquered by Babylon, Edom not only cheered and gloated, they also looted Judah in the aftermath. They even captured those who tried to escape and turned them over to the enemy.

Why was it written?

To condemn the Edomites' treachery and arrogance and declare God's eventual punishment for their crimes against his people.

What to look for in Obadiah:

Watch for God's loyalty to his people—evidenced by the judgment he pronounces against those who defy him by opposing his people.

Edom (v. 1)

The descendants of Esau, the twin brother of Jacob (see Gen. 25:23–27). Jacob and Esau had always competed as brothers and their descendants continued to compete as nations. Edom occupied the mountainous region southeast of the Dead Sea (see *Map 6* at the back of this Bible). Also see *Why did the Israelites call themselves the brother of Edom?* (Num. 20:14).

What kind of envoy would God send to recruit armies against Edom? (v. 1)

This special messenger may have been human or angelic. It isn't clear which God used in this case. The result, however, was the same. International events would somehow engulf Edom in a major war.

Why would people live among the rocks? (v. 3)

Edom was famous for its capital, Petra, a city of caves high in a solid rock cliff. Though living among the rocks had its disadvantages, it also had its benefits. The rocks were considered a place of safety from attack.

Esau . . . Teman (vv. 6,9)

Esau was the father of the nation of Edom; Teman was an Edomite city famous for its wise men.

Who ate Edom's bread? (v. 7)

Edom's unnamed allies. In a culture where hospitality and eating together were considered basic virtues, having *those who eat your bread* turn against you was a graphic picture of the worst kind of betrayal. God said the Edomites' so-called friends would turn on them and exploit them, just as they had done to the people of Judah.

Why was God so angry with Edom? (vv. 10–11)

The Edomites were guilty of gross cruelty against God's people. They didn't just stand by passively as Judah was conquered. They looted Jerusalem and even captured Judah's fleeing citizens to return them to the Babylonian army. In addition to these crimes, Edom was guilty of arrogance, boasting against God himself. God's wrath came as a righteous response to the nation's blatant defiance (see Ezek. 35:1–15).

---

[1]The vision[D] of Obadiah.

This is what the Sovereign LORD says about Edom[D]—

We have heard a message from the LORD:
   An envoy was sent to the nations to say,
"Rise, and let us go against her for battle"—

[2]"See, I will make you small among the nations;
   you will be utterly despised.
[3]The pride of your heart has deceived you,
   you who live in the clefts of the rocks[a]
   and make your home on the heights,
you who say to yourself,
   'Who can bring me down to the ground?'
[4]Though you soar like the eagle
   and make your nest among the stars,
   from there I will bring you down,"
                              declares the LORD.
[5]"If thieves came to you,
   if robbers in the night—
Oh, what a disaster awaits you—
   would they not steal only as much as they
      wanted?
If grape pickers came to you,
   would they not leave a few grapes?
[6]But how Esau will be ransacked,
   his hidden treasures pillaged!
[7]All your allies will force you to the border;
   your friends will deceive and overpower you;
those who eat your bread will set a trap for
      you,[b]
   but you will not detect it.

[8]"In that day," declares the LORD,
   "will I not destroy the wise men of Edom,
   men of understanding in the mountains of
      Esau?
[9]Your warriors, O Teman, will be terrified,
   and everyone in Esau's mountains
   will be cut down in the slaughter.
[10]Because of the violence against your brother
      Jacob,
   you will be covered with shame;
   you will be destroyed forever.
[11]On the day you stood aloof
   while strangers carried off his wealth
and foreigners entered his gates
   and cast lots for Jerusalem[D],
   you were like one of them.
[12]You should not look down on your brother
   in the day of his misfortune,
nor rejoice over the people of Judah
   in the day of their destruction,
nor boast so much
   in the day of their trouble.
[13]You should not march through the gates of my
      people
   in the day of their disaster,
nor look down on them in their calamity
   in the day of their disaster,
nor seize their wealth

---

[a]3 Or *of Sela*   [b]7 The meaning of the Hebrew for this clause is uncertain.

in the day of their disaster.
¹⁴You should not wait at the crossroads
    to cut down their fugitives,
nor hand over their survivors
    in the day of their trouble.

¹⁵"The day of the LORD ᴰ is near
    for all nations.
As you have done, it will be done to you;
    your deeds will return upon your own head.
¹⁶Just as you drank on my holy hill,
    so all the nations will drink continually;
they will drink and drink
    and be as if they had never been.
¹⁷But on Mount Zion ᴰ will be deliverance;
    it will be holy,
and the house of Jacob
    will possess its inheritance.
¹⁸The house of Jacob will be a fire
    and the house of Joseph a flame;
the house of Esau will be stubble,
    and they will set it on fire and consume it.
There will be no survivors
    from the house of Esau."
                    The LORD has spoken.

¹⁹People from the Negev ᴰ will occupy
    the mountains of Esau,
and people from the foothills will possess
    the land of the Philistines.
They will occupy the fields of Ephraim and
        Samaria,
    and Benjamin will possess Gilead.
²⁰This company of Israelite exiles ᴰ who are in
        Canaan
    will possess ⌊the land⌋ as far as Zarephath;
the exiles from Jerusalem who are in
        Sepharad
    will possess the towns of the Negev.
²¹Deliverers will go up on ᵃ Mount Zion
    to govern the mountains of Esau.
And the kingdom will be the LORD's.

The day of the LORD (v. 15)
See *The day of the LORD* (Joel 1:15).

Drank on my holy hill (v. 16)
The Edomites had apparently joined the drunken orgies of the Babylonians as they celebrated the destruction of the temple on Mount Zion. Now the Edomites and others that had desecrated God's holy place would have to drink a different beverage—the full cup of God's wrath. In fact, they would drink themselves into oblivion and disappear as a nation —as if they had never existed.

When were these prophecies against Edom fulfilled? (vv. 18–20)
Arab invaders soon began driving the Edomites from their mountain strongholds. By the first century A.D., Edom no longer existed as a nation. In Jesus' day, the family of King Herod was recognized to be of Edomite descent. But following the fall of Jerusalem in A.D. 70 Edomites totally disappeared from history.

Deliverers (v. 21)
Future leaders that would restore God's people as a nation. Edom would vanish and Judah would rise from the ashes, demonstrating God's faithfulness to his people. Some think this may allude to the Messiah who one day would deliver his people from sin.

ᵃ21 Or *from*

JONAH

Why read this book?

If you've ever thought that some people are beyond hope—so evil that they are incapable of change—the book of Jonah may upset your thinking. Consider serial killers, rapists, drug kingpins or terrorists; it's not unnatural to wish such violent, hate-filled individuals would be punished. But this book shows us that God wants to extend his grace and mercy to even the worst of people. It also challenges us to see that God may want to use us to reach out to the very people we tend to despise and see as beyond redemption.

Who wrote this book?

Most likely the prophet Jonah wrote autobiographically about what had happened to him.

When was it written?

Probably sometime between 785 and 750 B.C., during the reign of Jeroboam II, the king of Israel (see 2 Kings 14:25).

What was happening at this time?

Israel's northern kingdom regained its influence and was restored by Jeroboam II. But the Assyrians, whose capital city was Nineveh, were asserting themselves in increasingly menacing ways.

Why was it written?

To tell the story of God's concern even for the enemies of his people. This book also shows how God used a reluctant prophet as a vehicle of his grace.

What to look for in Jonah:

God's compassion for all people, his desire for earnest repentance regardless of what someone has done, and the extraordinary lengths to which he will sometimes go to get our attention.

When did these things happen?

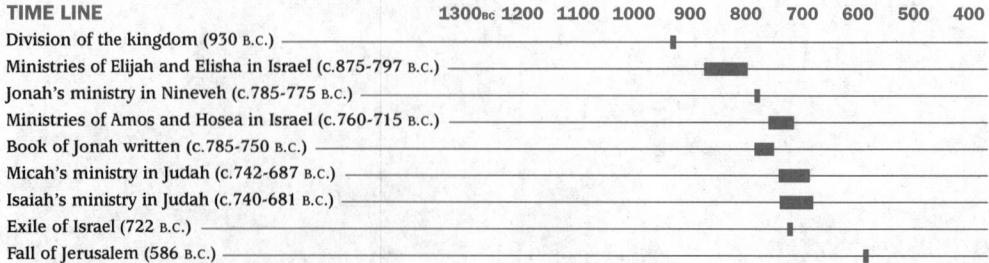

TIME LINE	1300BC 1200 1100 1000 900 800 700 600 500 400
Division of the kingdom (930 B.C.)	
Ministries of Elijah and Elisha in Israel (c.875-797 B.C.)	
Jonah's ministry in Nineveh (c.785-775 B.C.)	
Ministries of Amos and Hosea in Israel (c.760-715 B.C.)	
Book of Jonah written (c.785-750 B.C.)	
Micah's ministry in Judah (c.742-687 B.C.)	
Isaiah's ministry in Judah (c.740-681 B.C.)	
Exile of Israel (722 B.C.)	
Fall of Jerusalem (586 B.C.)	

Jonah Flees From the LORD

1 The word of the LORD came to Jonah son of Amittai: **2**"Go to the great city of Nineveh and preach against it, because its wickedness has come up before me."

3But Jonah ran away from the LORD and headed for Tarshish. He went down to Joppa^D, where he found a ship bound for that port. After paying the fare, he went aboard and sailed for Tarshish to flee from the LORD.

4Then the LORD sent a great wind on the sea, and such a violent storm arose that the ship threatened to break up. **5**All the sailors were afraid and each cried out to his own god. And they threw the cargo into the sea to lighten the ship.

But Jonah had gone below deck, where he lay down and fell into a deep sleep. **6**The captain went to him and said, "How can you sleep? Get up and call on your god! Maybe he will take notice of us, and we will not perish."

7Then the sailors said to each other, "Come, let us cast lots to find out who is responsible for this calamity." They cast lots and the lot fell on Jonah.

8So they asked him, "Tell us, who is responsible for making all this trouble for us? What do you do? Where do you come from? What is your country? From what people are you?"

9He answered, "I am a Hebrew^D and I worship the LORD, the God of heaven, who made the sea and the land."

10This terrified them and they asked, "What have you done?" (They knew he was running away from the LORD, because he had already told them so.)

11The sea was getting rougher and rougher. So they asked him, "What should we do to you to make the sea calm down for us?"

12"Pick me up and throw me into the sea," he replied, "and it will become calm. I know that it is my fault that this great storm has come upon you."

13Instead, the men did their best to row back to land. But they could not, for the sea grew even wilder than before. **14**Then they cried to the LORD, "O LORD, please do not let us die for taking this man's life. Do not hold us accountable for killing an innocent man, for you, O LORD, have done as you pleased." **15**Then they took Jonah and threw him overboard, and the raging sea grew calm. **16**At this the men greatly feared the LORD, and they offered a sacrifice^D to the LORD and made vows^D to him.

17But the LORD provided a great fish to swallow Jonah, and Jonah was inside the fish three days and three nights.

How did God send his *word* to Jonah? (1:1)

God could have used visions, dreams, signs in nature or spoken to him directly.

Why did Jonah run from God? (1:3)

First, he was probably afraid of the wicked Ninevites—international terrorists who fueled the Assyrian war machine. But he may also have been influenced by nationalistic prejudice and wanted God to favor Israel alone. See Jonah's own explanation in 4:2.

Tarshish (1:3)

A city in Spain in the opposite direction from Nineveh and about as far away as possible.

Joppa (1:3)

A seaport northwest of Jerusalem, known today as Jaffa.

Jonah on the Run (1:3)

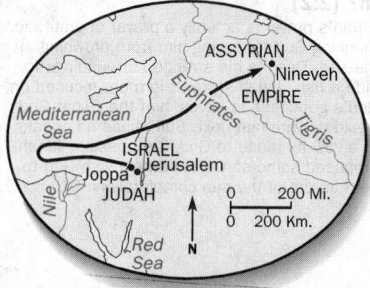

How did the lots expose Jonah? (1:7)

He may have drawn a marked pebble or the short straw. Whatever the method, it was no coincidence: God was in control, confronting Jonah's stubbornness. See Prov. 16:33.

What frightened the sailors? (1:10)

These pagan sailors believed in many gods, each restricted to certain domains or limited to certain abilities. Yet they were suddenly confronted with an unfamiliar concept: that one God who ruled over heaven was Creator of the sea and land. And they were caught in the middle of a storm caused by this awesome God's anger. They may also have been afraid of Jonah, who, in their minds, must have been a wicked man to have caused such divine wrath.

Does God always pursue those who run from him? (1:10)

No. Apparently in Jonah's case, God had a particular mission in mind for a particular person.

In other cases, God may not pursue those who run, perhaps because he knows that running away will result eventually in their coming back to him. For instance, in Jesus' parable of the prodigal son, the father allowed the son to leave home. Though the father did not chase after his son, the hardships of his son's own choices later brought him to his senses and caused him to return home to his father (Luke 15:11–32).

Whether by pursuing someone or choosing not to, God's goal is the same: he works to firmly, lovingly reach out to those who run from him.

Why does God use such unusual methods? (1:17)

God can use what is unusual in our eyes to get our attention and build our faith in him. Unusual or miraculous events tend to be more impressive and harder to explain away as coincidence. When God used the great fish in Jonah's life, he got Jonah's attention in a dramatic way and caused Jonah's stubborn attitude to change.

What kind of fish swallowed Jonah? (1:17)

We don't have enough information to say for sure. Since the Bible uses language that spoke to people in ancient times in terms they knew, the word *fish* could refer to a whale, but the Hebrew is not specific. All we know for certain is that the creature was big enough to swallow Jonah whole and house him in its belly for three days and nights.

Did Jonah pray to be rescued or forgiven? (2:2)

Jonah's prayer is actually a prayer of gratitude, thanking God for saving him from drowning in the sea. Despite his strange surroundings inside a fish, Jonah's prayer is more focused on God's goodness in saving him than what God would do with him next. Still, since he speaks of a vow he made to God, it's possible Jonah proposed some sort of a bargain with God to get him out of the sea completely (v. 9).

Was Jonah's message of doom untrue? (3:4)

Not at all. Jonah had only told what would happen if Nineveh didn't repent. The truth of his message prompted the Ninevites to avert the promised judgment by changing their ways.

Jonah's Prayer

2 From inside the fish Jonah prayed to the LORD his God. ²He said:

"In my distress I called to the LORD,
  and he answered me.
From the depths of the grave*a* I called for
    help,
  and you listened to my cry.
³You hurled me into the deep,
  into the very heart of the seas,
  and the currents swirled about me;
all your waves and breakers
  swept over me.
⁴I said, 'I have been banished
  from your sight;
yet I will look again
  toward your holy temple.'
⁵The engulfing waters threatened me,*b*
  the deep surrounded me;
  seaweed was wrapped around my head.
⁶To the roots of the mountains I sank down;
  the earth beneath barred me in forever.
But you brought my life up from the pit,
  O LORD my God.

⁷"When my life was ebbing away,
  I remembered you, LORD,
and my prayer rose to you,
  to your holy temple.

⁸"Those who cling to worthless idols*D*
  forfeit the grace*D* that could be theirs.
⁹But I, with a song of thanksgiving,
  will sacrifice*D* to you.
What I have vowed*D* I will make good.
  Salvation*D* comes from the LORD."

¹⁰And the LORD commanded the fish, and it vomited Jonah onto dry land.

*a*2 Hebrew *Sheol*   *b*5 Or *waters were at my throat*

What was Jonah's view of the Lord? (2:7–9)

Jonah had a somewhat restricted view of God and his presence. The prevailing opinion in Israel in Jonah's time was that God was limited to the temple in Jerusalem or, at most, to the soil of Israel. That's why Jonah thought he could flee from God.

At the same time, however, Jonah had begun to envision a broader scope to God's power: he knew God's grace was available to idol worshipers who turned from their idols (v. 8); he knew that *salvation comes from the* LORD (v. 9).

This is the central message of this book. Though the Jews had a keen sense of being God's chosen people and wanted to keep God all to themselves, Jonah discovered that God is the God of all humanity. *Salvation comes from the* LORD, not from belonging to a particular ethnic background or nationality.

Jonah found God in the belly of a great fish and again later in a wicked, pagan city—in both cases far from the "holy land." Jonah learned that God wanted to make himself known to all people everywhere.

Jonah Goes to Nineveh

3 Then the word of the LORD came to Jonah a second time: **2**"Go to the great city of Nineveh and proclaim to it the message I give you."

3Jonah obeyed the word of the LORD and went to Nineveh. Now Nineveh was a very important city—a visit required three days. **4**On the first day, Jonah started into the city. He proclaimed: "Forty more days and Nineveh will be overturned." **5**The Ninevites believed God. They declared a fast, and all of them, from the greatest to the least, put on sackcloth^D.

6When the news reached the king of Nineveh, he rose from his throne, took off his royal robes, covered himself with sackcloth and sat down in the dust. **7**Then he issued a proclamation in Nineveh:

"By the decree of the king and his nobles:

Do not let any man or beast, herd or flock, taste anything; do not let them eat or drink. **8**But let man and beast be covered with sackcloth. Let everyone call urgently on God. Let them give up their evil ways and their violence. **9**Who knows? God may yet relent and with compassion turn from his fierce anger so that we will not perish."

10When God saw what they did and how they turned from their evil ways, he had compassion and did not bring upon them the destruction he had threatened.

Jonah's Anger at the LORD's Compassion

4 But Jonah was greatly displeased and became angry. **2**He prayed to the LORD, "O LORD, is this not what I said when I was still at home? That is why I was so quick to flee to Tarshish. I knew that you are a gracious and compassionate God, slow to anger and abounding in love, a God who relents from sending calamity. **3**Now, O LORD, take away my life, for it is better for me to die than to live."

4But the LORD replied, "Have you any right to be angry?"

5Jonah went out and sat down at a place east of the city. There he made himself a shelter, sat in its shade and waited to see what would happen to the city. **6**Then the LORD God provided a vine and made it grow up over Jonah to give shade for his head to ease his discomfort, and Jonah was very happy about the vine. **7**But at dawn the next day God provided a worm, which chewed the vine so that it withered. **8**When the sun rose, God provided a scorching east wind, and the sun blazed on Jonah's head so that he grew faint. He wanted to die, and said, "It would be better for me to die than to live."

9But God said to Jonah, "Do you have a right to be angry about the vine?"

"I do," he said. "I am angry enough to die."

10But the LORD said, "You have been concerned about this vine, though you did not tend it or make it grow. It sprang up overnight and died overnight. **11**But Nineveh has more than a hundred and twenty thousand people who cannot tell their right hand from their left, and many cattle as well. Should I not be concerned about that great city?"

Why would idol worshipers listen to a foreign prophet? (3:5)

Jonah may have looked peculiar, perhaps bearing the acidic effects of three days inside the digestive system of a large fish. Whatever captured their attention, Jonah's news of coming judgment was more important to them than who he was or where he came from.

Can a ruler decree a revival? (3:7–9)

The royal decree set the stage for repentance among the Ninevites. The people had to obey the king's decree, but in their hearts they could still choose whether they were sincere.

Why force animals to be religious? (3:8)

The animals were used to express the sincerity and depth of repentance in the city. Causing the animals to go without food and to wear sackcloth was a symbolic gesture of mourning.

How long did Nineveh's repentance last? (3:10)

The people eventually returned to their wicked ways. God judged the city in 612 B.C.—about 150 years after Jonah's ministry.

Why was Jonah upset that people turned to God? (4:1–2)

The Ninevites were known far and wide for their savage cruelty. Jonah wished that they would be destroyed rather than saved.

Why would a successful preacher want to die? (4:3)

As a Jew, Jonah would rather die than help the enemies of his people. He wanted to see judgment fall upon the people of Nineveh.

Vine (4:6)

Perhaps a castor oil plant, which can reach a height of over 12 feet. God caused its astonishing, rapid growth.

Why did God take away what he had just given? (4:6–7)

God was using the vine to teach Jonah an important lesson, not to provide him shade. He took away a source of Jonah's comfort to expand his understanding of God's goodness and concern for all people.

What made Jonah so angry? (4:9)

Along with emotional and spiritual distress, Jonah felt physical discomfort from the sun and harsh wind.

Why couldn't they tell their right hand from their left? (4:11)

This was an expression used to show that they were spiritually ignorant. No one had ever told them about the one true God, so they knew nothing about him.

How does God show his concern for people who don't worship him? (4:11)

If not for God's patience and mercy, the world would have been judged for its sins long ago. But beyond that, God sustains all physical life, provides life's pleasures, demonstrates his power and existence in nature and sends prophets and missionaries. Most important, he shows his concern by offering forgiveness in Jesus.

MICAH

Why read this book?

If you've ever wondered how faith fits in an increasingly corrupt and violent society, you'll be able to identify with the message in this book. When God seems distant and uninvolved, Micah reminds us that he still cares and offers hope for those who choose to remain faithful to him. Reading this book reminds us that God is still active in this world and will not allow sin to hinder his purposes.

Who wrote this book and when was it written?

The prophet Micah, whose name means *Who is like the Lord?*, wrote it during the reigns of Jotham (750–735 B.C.), Ahaz (735–715 B.C.) and Hezekiah (715–686 B.C.), kings of Judah.

What was happening in the world at this time?

The powerful Assyrian empire was expanding westward, demanding surrender and tribute. When the northern kingdom of Israel rebelled, the Assyrians destroyed its capital city of Samaria and took many Israelites into exile. Later King Hezekiah of Judah, the southern kingdom, rebelled. The Assyrians invaded Palestine in 701 B.C., devastated Judah and carried many into captivity. Though they besieged Jerusalem, God delivered the city in answer to Hezekiah's prayer.

To whom was it written and why?

Micah wrote to the people of Judah to warn them that God's judgment was approaching because they had rejected God and his law. Micah also encouraged the godly few, assuring them that judgment would not permanently destroy Israel. The nation would eventually be restored.

What to look for in Micah:

Pay close attention to how Micah portrays God, balancing his divine attributes of justice and mercy. Remember that Micah uses poetry. Many figures of speech make his messages more vivid and create a profound emotional impact.

When did these things happen?

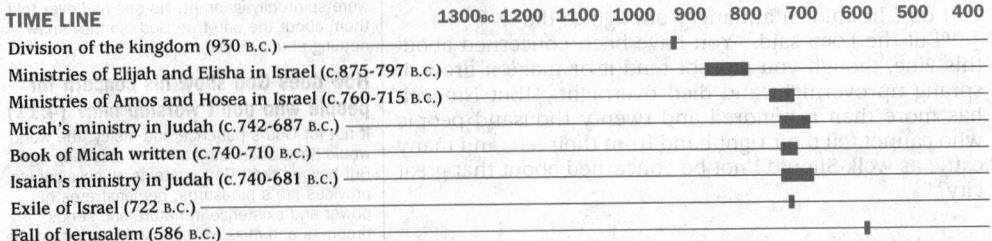

TIME LINE	1300BC 1200 1100 1000 900 800 700 600 500 400
Division of the kingdom (930 B.C.)	
Ministries of Elijah and Elisha in Israel (c.875–797 B.C.)	
Ministries of Amos and Hosea in Israel (c.760–715 B.C.)	
Micah's ministry in Judah (c.742–687 B.C.)	
Book of Micah written (c.740–710 B.C.)	
Isaiah's ministry in Judah (c.740–681 B.C.)	
Exile of Israel (722 B.C.)	
Fall of Jerusalem (586 B.C.)	

1 The word of the LORD that came to Micah of Moresheth during the reigns of Jotham, Ahaz and Hezekiah, kings of Judah—the vision[D] he saw concerning Samaria and Jerusalem[D].

2Hear, O peoples, all of you,
    listen, O earth and all who are in it,
that the Sovereign LORD may witness against
        you,
    the Lord from his holy temple.

Judgment Against Samaria and Jerusalem

3Look! The LORD is coming from his dwelling
        place;
    he comes down and treads the high places[D]
        of the earth.
4The mountains melt beneath him
    and the valleys split apart,
like wax before the fire,
    like water rushing down a slope.
5All this is because of Jacob's transgression,
    because of the sins of the house of Israel.
What is Jacob's transgression?
    Is it not Samaria?
What is Judah's high place?
    Is it not Jerusalem?

6"Therefore I will make Samaria a heap of
        rubble,
    a place for planting vineyards.
I will pour her stones into the valley
    and lay bare her foundations.
7All her idols[D] will be broken to pieces;
    all her temple gifts will be burned with fire;
    I will destroy all her images.
Since she gathered her gifts from the wages of
        prostitutes,
    as the wages of prostitutes they will again be
        used."

Weeping and Mourning

8Because of this I will weep and wail;
    I will go about barefoot and naked.
I will howl like a jackal
    and moan like an owl.
9For her wound is incurable;
    it has come to Judah.
It[a] has reached the very gate of my people,
    even to Jerusalem itself.
10Tell it not in Gath[b];
    weep not at all.[c]
In Beth Ophrah[d]
    roll in the dust.
11Pass on in nakedness and shame,
    you who live in Shaphir.[e]
Those who live in Zaanan[f]
    will not come out.
Beth Ezel is in mourning;
    its protection is taken from you.

---

a9 Or He   b10 Gath sounds like the Hebrew for tell.
c10 Hebrew; Septuagint may suggest not in Acco. The Hebrew for in Acco sounds like the Hebrew for weep.   d10 Beth Ophrah means house of dust.   e11 Shaphir means pleasant.   f11 Zaanan sounds like the Hebrew for come out.

Moresheth (1:1)

Micah's hometown, probably the same as Moresheth Gath (v. 14), located about 25 miles southwest of Jerusalem (see Map 6 at the back of this Bible).

Where does God live? (1:3)

This Old Testament poetry pictures God as living in a heavenly palace from which he sometimes descends to intervene in the affairs of nations. Some take the language literally, while others say it reflects ancient Israel's figurative view of the universe which vividly affirms God's sovereignty over his creation.

Judgment on Samaria and Jerusalem (1:5)

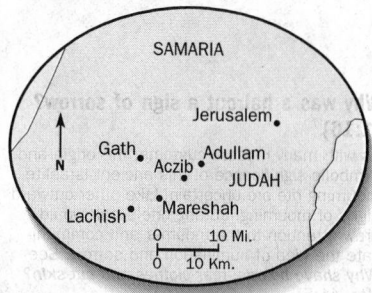

How was Samaria Jacob's transgression? (1:5)

Samaria, the capital of Israel, was a center for the idol worship that was so widespread in the land (2 Kings 17:7–17). Micah used Jacob, an earlier name for Israel (see Gen. 32:28).

What idols did the people worship? (1:7)

Citizens of the northern kingdom worshiped two golden calves in Bethel and Dan (see Map 4 at the back of this Bible). They also served the Canaanite fertility god, Baal, at a temple built by King Ahab in Samaria. The people also revered images of the goddess Asherah, worshiped the stars, sacrificed children to the god Molech, and practiced divination and sorcery (2 Kings 17:16–17). The citizens of Judah followed the example of their northern relatives in idolatry.

Why would Micah go nude? (1:8)

Probably to be a living, breathing object lesson. It was a picture of the future prisoners taken into captivity following the coming Assyrian invasion (see Isaiah 20:2–4). It may also have been his way of mourning his country's coming destruction. Walking about barefoot was a sign of mourning in his culture, where outward displays of sorrow were typical. Also see Where did the custom of ashes and torn clothing come from? (2 Samuel 13:19) and Why shave beards, tear clothes and cut skin? (Jer. 41:5).

What happened to cause such overwhelming grief? (1:8–16)

The coming Assyrian invasion would devastate Judah's crops, cities and people. An inscription records the boasts of the Assyrian king Sennacherib about his invasion of Judah (701 B.C.), that he took "200,150 people, young and old, male and female, horses, mules, donkeys, camels, big and small cattle beyond counting and considered them booty."

Daughter of Zion (1:13)

A poetic name representing Jerusalem and its residents as a woman. This image sometimes portrays the city as tender and desirable, but it also could be seen as weak and vulnerable to pain and suffering.

Why was a haircut a sign of sorrow? (1:16)

As with many modern customs, the origin and symbolic significance of this ancient Israelite mourning rite are uncertain. Like other outward signs of mourning, cutting one's hair would draw attention to the mourner and communicate the idea of humiliation and sorrow. See *Why shave beards, tear clothes and cut skin?* (Jer. 41:5).

Where would they be exiled? (1:16)

To Assyria, several hundred miles to the northeast of Judah (see *Map 7* at the back of this Bible).

Were the powerful and elite the cause behind the nation's problems? (2:1–2)

Yes, although they were not the sole problem. Their injustice roused the Lord's anger and prompted his judgment. Many in Judah's upper class, some of whom were apparently government administrators, disregarded God's law. They used deception and fraud to greedily acquire land belonging to others. See *How could people steal God's blessing?* (2:9).

Why would God reward traitors? (2:4)

The *traitors*—the Assyrians—would take away the property of the rich when they invaded the land. It wasn't so much that God was rewarding the traitors as he was punishing the wealthy who had robbed others of their fields and houses (v. 2). The rich would find out how it feels to be mistreated and plundered by someone more powerful.

¹²Those who live in Maroth*ᵃ* writhe in pain,
    waiting for relief,
because disaster has come from the LORD,
    even to the gate of Jerusalem*ᴰ*.
¹³You who live in Lachish,*ᵇ*
    harness the team to the chariot.
You were the beginning of sin
    to the Daughter of Zion*ᴰ*,
for the transgressions of Israel
    were found in you.
¹⁴Therefore you will give parting gifts
    to Moresheth Gath.
The town of Aczib*ᶜ* will prove deceptive
    to the kings of Israel.
¹⁵I will bring a conqueror against you
    who live in Mareshah.*ᵈ*
He who is the glory*ᴰ* of Israel
    will come to Adullam.
¹⁶Shave your heads in mourning
    for the children in whom you delight;
make yourselves as bald as the vulture,
    for they will go from you into exile*ᴰ*.

Man's Plans and God's

2 Woe to those who plan iniquity,
    to those who plot evil on their beds!
At morning's light they carry it out
    because it is in their power to do it.
²They covet fields and seize them,
    and houses, and take them.
They defraud a man of his home,
    a fellowman of his inheritance.

³Therefore, the LORD says:

"I am planning disaster against this people,
    from which you cannot save yourselves.
You will no longer walk proudly,
    for it will be a time of calamity.
⁴In that day men will ridicule you;
    they will taunt you with this mournful song:
'We are utterly ruined;
    my people's possession is divided up.
He takes it from me!
    He assigns our fields to traitors.' "

⁵Therefore you will have no one in the
        assembly of the LORD
    to divide the land by lot.

False Prophets

⁶"Do not prophesy," their prophets*ᴰ* say.
    "Do not prophesy about these things;
    disgrace will not overtake us."
⁷Should it be said, O house of Jacob:
    "Is the Spirit of the LORD angry?
    Does he do such things?"

"Do not my words do good
    to him whose ways are upright?
⁸Lately my people have risen up
    like an enemy.

ᵃ12 Maroth sounds like the Hebrew for *bitter.*   *ᵇ13 Lachish* sounds like the Hebrew for *team.*   *ᶜ14 Aczib* means *deception.*
ᵈ15 Mareshah sounds like the Hebrew for *conqueror.*

You strip off the rich robe
   from those who pass by without a care,
   like men returning from battle.
⁹You drive the women of my people
   from their pleasant homes.
You take away my blessing
   from their children forever.
¹⁰Get up, go away!
   For this is not your resting place,
because it is defiled,
   it is ruined, beyond all remedy.
¹¹If a liar and deceiver comes and says,
   'I will prophesy for you plenty of wine and
      beer,'
   he would be just the prophetᴰ for this
      people!

Deliverance Promised

¹²"I will surely gather all of you, O Jacob;
   I will surely bring together the remnantᴰ of
      Israel.
I will bring them together like sheep in a pen,
   like a flock in its pasture;
   the place will throng with people.
¹³One who breaks open the way will go up
      before them;
   they will break through the gate and go out.
Their king will pass through before them,
   the LORD at their head."

Leaders and Prophets Rebuked

3 Then I said,

"Listen, you leaders of Jacob,
   you rulers of the house of Israel.
Should you not know justice,
² you who hate good and love evil;
who tear the skin from my people
   and the flesh from their bones;
³who eat my people's flesh,
   strip off their skin
   and break their bones in pieces;
who chop them up like meat for the pan,
   like flesh for the pot?"

⁴Then they will cry out to the LORD,
   but he will not answer them.
At that time he will hide his face from them
   because of the evil they have done.

⁵This is what the LORD says:

"As for the prophets
   who lead my people astray,
if one feeds them,
   they proclaim 'peaceᴰ';
if he does not,
   they prepare to wage war against him.
⁶Therefore night will come over you, without
      visionsᴰ,
   and darkness, without divinationᴰ.
The sun will set for the prophets,
   and the day will go dark for them.
⁷The seersᴰ will be ashamed
   and the diviners disgraced.

How could people steal God's blessing? (2:9)

Each family in the nation had a *blessing* from God—an inheritance of land. But the rich had stolen the *blessing* of many families by evicting them from their land through a combination of exorbitant interest rates, debt slavery, excessive taxation, oppressive economic regulations and unfair judicial decisions (sometimes secured by bribery). Widows and orphans were especially vulnerable to such injustice because they lacked clout in the economic and legal system.

Why would a liar be *just the prophet* for them? (2:11)

This is a sarcastic statement. Most of the people resented being called sinners and were not interested in Micah's warning of judgment. Instead they preferred to think that God was going to bless them with good crops. False prophets told the people what they wanted to hear and gave them a false sense of security.

What changed? (2:12–13)

Like a sudden scene change in a movie, prophetic books often shift abruptly from judgment to salvation. Even in the worst of times God had a group of faithful and obedient people. He wanted them to know that judgment would not totally destroy the nation. Out of the rubble and smoke of judgment, God would restore and rebuild the nation.

Were they cannibals? (3:3)

No. This language is figurative and sarcastic. Micah compares social injustice to cannibalism in order to emphasize the insatiable greed of the rich and their cruel, insensitive treatment of the poor.

Seers (3:7)

Prophets who foretell future events. See *What was the difference between a prophet and a seer?* (2 Kings 17:13) and *Seer* (1 Chron. 21:9).

They will all cover their faces
   because there is no answer from God."

8But as for me, I am filled with power,
   with the Spirit of the LORD,
   and with justice and might,
to declare to Jacob his transgression,
   to Israel his sin.
9Hear this, you leaders of the house of Jacob,
   you rulers of the house of Israel,
who despise justice
   and distort all that is right;
10who build ZionD with bloodshed,
   and JerusalemD with wickedness.
11Her leaders judge for a bribe,
   her priestsD teach for a price,
   and her prophetsD tell fortunes for money.
Yet they lean upon the LORD and say,
   "Is not the LORD among us?
   No disaster will come upon us."
12Therefore because of you,
Zion will be plowed like a field,
Jerusalem will become a heap of rubble,
   the temple hill a mound overgrown with
      thickets.

The Mountain of the LORD

4 In the last days

the mountain of the LORD's temple will be
      established
   as chief among the mountains;
it will be raised above the hills,
   and peoples will stream to it.

2Many nations will come and say,

"Come, let us go up to the mountain of the
   LORD,
to the house of the God of Jacob.
He will teach us his ways,

Last days (4:1)
A phrase that sometimes refers to the future in general (rendered as *in days to come*, Gen. 49:1), to the course of human history (Daniel 2:28) or, as here, to the time when God will restore Israel and establish his kingdom on earth.

Will people have to visit Jerusalem to worship God? (4:2)
Micah is not talking about worship per se, but about the whole world submitting to God during the kingdom age. His decisions will defuse potential international conflicts and establish an era of peace (v. 3). But nations will also come to Jerusalem during those days for religious celebrations and festivals. See *Will temple worship in Jerusalem be reestablished someday?* (Zech. 14:16).

Does God refuse to listen to sinners? (3:4)

Normally God responds when people genuinely repent. When a change in heart and attitude is demonstrated by changed behavior, God listens and often cancels the judgment he had announced (see, for example, Jer. 18:7–8; Jonah 3:10; also compare 3:12 with Jer. 26:17–19).

Sometimes, however, with repeat offenders, God's mercy is cut off. God sees that they have crossed a line and degraded his compassion and forgiveness. So for them he withdraws his offer for repentance and unconditionally decrees judgment and destruction.

Such a time had come for the rich oppressors in the land of Judah. When the Assyrians invaded the land, the wealthy Israelites cried out to God for help, but the Lord turned a deaf ear to them—just as they had mercilessly ignored the cries of the poor people they had mistreated.

Though all who repent and trust in Jesus can be saved, God's patience will not last forever. He has ordained a day of judgment for everyone. At that time it will be too late to repent and one's eternal fate will be sealed (Heb. 9:27; Rev. 20:11–15).

Also see article: *When does God refuse to hear our prayers?* (Jer. 11:11).

so that we may walk in his paths."
The law will go out from Zion[D],
   the word of the LORD from Jerusalem[D].
³He will judge between many peoples
   and will settle disputes for strong nations far
      and wide.
They will beat their swords into plowshares
   and their spears into pruning hooks.
Nation will not take up sword against nation,
   nor will they train for war anymore.
⁴Every man will sit under his own vine
   and under his own fig tree,
and no one will make them afraid,
   for the LORD Almighty has spoken.
⁵All the nations may walk
   in the name of their gods;
we will walk in the name of the LORD
   our God for ever and ever.

The LORD's Plan

⁶"In that day," declares the LORD,

"I will gather the lame;
   I will assemble the exiles[D]
   and those I have brought to grief.
⁷I will make the lame a remnant[D],
   those driven away a strong nation.
The LORD will rule over them in Mount Zion
   from that day and forever.
⁸As for you, O watchtower[D] of the flock,
   O stronghold[Da] of the Daughter of Zion,
the former dominion will be restored to you;
   kingship will come to the Daughter of
      Jerusalem."

⁹Why do you now cry aloud—
   have you no king?
Has your counselor perished,
   that pain seizes you like that of a woman in
      labor?
¹⁰Writhe in agony, O Daughter of Zion,
   like a woman in labor,
for now you must leave the city
   to camp in the open field.
You will go to Babylon;
   there you will be rescued.
There the LORD will redeem[D] you
   out of the hand of your enemies.

¹¹But now many nations
   are gathered against you.
They say, "Let her be defiled,
   let our eyes gloat over Zion!"
¹²But they do not know
   the thoughts of the LORD;
they do not understand his plan,
   he who gathers them like sheaves to the
      threshing floor.
¹³"Rise and thresh, O Daughter of Zion,
   for I will give you horns of iron;
I will give you hoofs of bronze
   and you will break to pieces many nations."

ᵃ8 Or hill

How will God govern? (4:3)

Micah seems to indicate that God will resolve these potential conflicts directly. Other passages, however, suggest the Messiah will rule on his behalf (Isaiah 11:1–10).

When will nations finally disarm themselves? (4:3)

This will happen during the kingdom age, after God has destroyed his enemies and established his rule from Jerusalem (v. 2). In an age of peace, weapons will become obsolete and nations will devote their energies to more productive endeavors.

Whom will God gather together in that day? (4:6)

God will restore his exiled people Israel to their land and reverse the judgment brought about by the Assyrian invasion. The image of bringing back lame, grieving exiles also pictures the spiritual work to be done when God draws people to him during the kingdom age.

Watchtower . . . stronghold (4:8)

A tower where guards could watch for danger or where a group of people could find protection from invaders. Watchtower of the flock probably means Jerusalem, the fortress for God's people. The stronghold of the Daughter of Zion may mean the hill within Jerusalem where David's ancient fortified city was located.

Daughter of Zion (4:8)

See Daughter of Zion (1:13).

When will Israel break many nations to pieces? (4:13)

This most likely is a description of God's end time destruction of hostile nations (Zech. 12:1–9; 14:1–4). But the defeat of Sennacherib's army outside Jerusalem (701 B.C.) also may have inspired this language (Isaiah 37:36–37). The Lord's miraculous deliverance of the city from the Assyrian hordes foreshadows a future time when he will deliver his people from their fierce enemies once and for all.

City of troops (5:1)

An ironic title for Jerusalem, a picture of a city besieged by enemy troops. It could be paraphrased as "city surrounded by troops."

Ephrathah (5:2)

Either an alternate name for Bethlehem or the name of the district in which Bethlehem was located (Gen. 35:19).

SCRIPTURE LINK (5:2)

Centuries later the religious leaders used this verse to tell King Herod where the Messiah would be born. See Matt. 2:6.

Did Micah know he was predicting the Messiah? (5:2–4)

Yes, though he may not have known that his vision would not be fulfilled for centuries. He describes the coming ideal ruler in terms meaningful to the people of his day.

Will Assyria again be a power in the last days? (5:5)

Probably only in a figurative sense. *Assyria* serves as a model to represent all God's enemies. When God rules through his Messianic king, his people will no longer need to fear cruel, would-be oppressors like the Assyrians, for the Messiah will protect God's people.

Nimrod (5:6)

The traditional founder of Assyria, a famed hunter and warrior (Gen. 10:8–12).

You will devote their ill-gotten gains to the
LORD,
their wealth to the Lord of all the earth.

A Promised Ruler From Bethlehem

5 Marshal your troops, O city of troops,[a]
for a siege is laid against us.
They will strike Israel's ruler
on the cheek with a rod.

2"But you, Bethlehem Ephrathah,
though you are small among the clans[b] of
Judah,
out of you will come for me
one who will be ruler over Israel,
whose origins[c] are from of old,
from ancient times.[d]"

3Therefore Israel will be abandoned
until the time when she who is in labor gives
birth
and the rest of his brothers return
to join the Israelites.

4He will stand and shepherd his flock
in the strength of the LORD,
in the majesty of the name of the LORD his
God.
And they will live securely, for then his
greatness
will reach to the ends of the earth.
5   And he will be their peace[D].

Deliverance and Destruction

When the Assyrian invades our land
and marches through our fortresses,
we will raise against him seven shepherds,
even eight leaders of men.
6They will rule[e] the land of Assyria with the
sword,
the land of Nimrod with drawn sword.[f]
He will deliver us from the Assyrian
when he invades our land
and marches into our borders.

7The remnant[D] of Jacob will be
in the midst of many peoples
like dew from the LORD,
like showers on the grass,
which do not wait for man
or linger for mankind.
8The remnant of Jacob will be among the
nations,
in the midst of many peoples,
like a lion among the beasts of the forest,
like a young lion among flocks of sheep,
which mauls and mangles as it goes,
and no one can rescue.
9Your hand will be lifted up in triumph over
your enemies,
and all your foes will be destroyed.

---

*a*1 Or *Strengthen your walls, O walled city*   *b*2 Or *rulers*
*c*2 Hebrew *goings out*   *d*2 Or *from days of eternity*   *e*6 Or
crush   *f*6 Or *Nimrod in its gates*

[10]"In that day," declares the LORD,

"I will destroy your horses from among you
and demolish your chariots.
[11]I will destroy the cities of your land
and tear down all your strongholds[D].
[12]I will destroy your witchcraft[D]
and you will no longer cast spells.
[13]I will destroy your carved images
and your sacred stones[D] from among you;
you will no longer bow down
to the work of your hands.
[14]I will uproot from among you your Asherah
poles[Da]
and demolish your cities.
[15]I will take vengeance in anger and wrath
upon the nations that have not obeyed
me."

The LORD's Case Against Israel

6 Listen to what the LORD says:

"Stand up, plead your case before the
mountains;
let the hills hear what you have to say.
[2]Hear, O mountains, the LORD's accusation;
listen, you everlasting foundations of the
earth.
For the LORD has a case against his people;
he is lodging a charge against Israel.

[3]"My people, what have I done to you?
How have I burdened you? Answer me.
[4]I brought you up out of Egypt
and redeemed[D] you from the land of
slavery.
I sent Moses to lead you,
also Aaron and Miriam.
[5]My people, remember
what Balak king of Moab counseled
and what Balaam son of Beor answered.
Remember ⌊your journey⌋ from Shittim to
Gilgal,
that you may know the righteous[D] acts of
the LORD."

[6]With what shall I come before the LORD
and bow down before the exalted God?
Shall I come before him with burnt
offerings[D],
with calves a year old?
[7]Will the LORD be pleased with thousands of
rams,
with ten thousand rivers of oil?
Shall I offer my firstborn[D] for my
transgression,
the fruit of my body for the sin of my
soul[D]?
[8]He has showed you, O man, what is good.
And what does the LORD require of you?
To act justly and to love mercy[D]
and to walk humbly with your God.

---

a14 That is, symbols of the goddess Asherah

Witchcraft . . . spells (5:12)

Ancient peoples were obsessed with gaining special insight from the gods and finding out what would happen in the future. To get this kind of information they would consult "experts" of divination who claimed they could tell the future by interpreting omens, examining livers of sacrificed animals and contacting the dead—among other techniques. The Old Testament law prohibited these occultic and magical practices (Deut. 18:9–12).

How could mountains judge the Lord's complaint? (6:1–2)

Micah personifies the mountains and casts them in the role of a witness at a trial. (Mountains assume a similar role in some ancient Middle Eastern treaties.) The mountains seem immovable and eternal, towering above the world. If alive, they would be able to see all that goes on and could testify whether one's claims were true or false. By appealing to the mountains in his lawsuit against God's disobedient people, Micah adds drama and emotion to his accusations. Also see *How could God call heaven and earth as witnesses?* (Deut. 4:26).

SCRIPTURE LINK (6:4)

I brought you up out of Egypt (see Exodus 12:40–41); *I sent Moses to lead you* (see Exodus 3:10); *Aaron and Miriam* (see Exodus 4:27; 15:20).

Why recall these events? (6:4–5)

God's people had accused him of mistreating them (v. 3). God defends himself against this charge by recalling how he had delivered them from slavery, given them leaders and protected them on their journey to the promised land. History defended God's actions, but it also indicted the people for their lack of gratitude.

SCRIPTURE LINK (6:5) Balak . . . Balaam

See Num. 22:4–5.

Why was Micah so unsure of how to worship God? (6:6–7)

He wasn't. He knew God required pure, sincere worship—not just in words or ritual, but in lifestyle (v. 8). But with a bit of drama, Micah put himself in the place of his listeners to ask these rhetorical questions. Many thought God desired sacrifice and ritual above all else. But Micah's questions—followed by his straightforward declaration (v. 8)—made it clear that ethical living is what God wants.

Israel's Guilt and Punishment

⁹Listen! The LORD is calling to the city—
  and to fear your name is wisdom—
"Heed the rod and the One who
  appointed it.ᵃ
¹⁰Am I still to forget, O wicked house,
  your ill-gotten treasures
  and the short ephah,ᵇ which is
    accursed?
¹¹Shall I acquit a man with dishonest
    scales,
  with a bag of false weights?
¹²Her rich men are violent;
  her people are liars
  and their tongues speak deceitfully.
¹³Therefore, I have begun to destroy you,
  to ruin you because of your sins.
¹⁴You will eat but not be satisfied;
  your stomach will still be empty.ᶜ
You will store up but save nothing,
  because what you save I will give to the
    sword.
¹⁵You will plant but not harvest;
  you will press olives but not use the oil on
    yourselves,
  you will crush grapes but not drink the
    wine.
¹⁶You have observed the statutes of Omri
  and all the practices of Ahab's house,
  and you have followed their traditions.
Therefore I will give you over to ruin
  and your people to derision;
  you will bear the scorn of the nations.ᵈ"

SCRIPTURE LINK (6:13-15)

Micah echoed the curses Moses said would come if the people disobeyed. See Deut. 28:38–42.

Statutes of Omri (6:16)

Probably a reference to a perverted legal system under one of Israel's most wicked kings (1 Kings 16:15–28). Short measures, dishonest scales and false weights (vv. 10–11) were used by the rich and powerful to cheat the poor. Unjust laws were yet another means used by unscrupulous men to take advantage of others.

What had Ahab done? (6:16)

Besides worshiping idols, Ahab was greedy and cruel. With the help of his wife, Jezebel, he cheated Naboth out of his ancestral vineyard. With bribes, trumped up charges and a miscarriage of justice, Naboth was condemned and executed for blasphemy and treason (1 Kings 21:1–16). From the king on down, greed and dishonesty became commonplace in Israel and Judah.

ᵃ9 The meaning of the Hebrew for this line is uncertain.   ᵇ10 An ephah was a dry measure.   ᶜ14 The meaning of the Hebrew for this word is uncertain.   ᵈ16 Septuagint; Hebrew *scorn due my people*

What does God require from us? (6:8)

God wants his people to live lives that measure up to his moral and ethical standards. Through faith in Christ's death, not good works, God graciously saves us from the penalty of sin and makes peace with us. But that's not the end of the story. He saves us so that we might do good deeds which mirror God's character (Eph. 2:8–10). He wants us to treat others fairly and compassionately; he wants us to live humble, obedient lives.

Many of God's people failed to live up to God's high standards in Micah's time. God had delivered the Israelites from Egypt and established them as a nation. He called them to be a model society that would attract other nations to him (Deut. 4:5–6). Instead they exploited the poor, selfishly pursuing their own interests. They rebelled against God's authority and rejected his prophets.

Despite their crimes, many Israelites actually thought their sacrifices made them pleasing to God. Micah attacked their faulty thinking. Empty ritual (vv. 6–7) means nothing to God, Micah said. God wants lives of genuine ethical and moral integrity.

Israel's Misery

7 What misery is mine!
I am like one who gathers summer fruit
at the gleaning of the vineyard;
there is no cluster of grapes to eat,
none of the early figs that I crave.
²The godly have been swept from the land;
not one upright man remains.
All men lie in wait to shed blood;
each hunts his brother with a net.
³Both hands are skilled in doing evil;
the ruler demands gifts,
the judge accepts bribes,
the powerful dictate what they desire—
they all conspire together.
⁴The best of them is like a brier,
the most upright worse than a thorn hedge.
The day of your watchmenᴰ has come,
the day God visits you.
Now is the time of their confusion.
⁵Do not trust a neighbor;
put no confidence in a friend.
Even with her who lies in your embrace
be careful of your words.
⁶For a son dishonors his father,
a daughter rises up against her mother,
a daughter-in-law against her mother-in-law—
a man's enemies are the members of his
own household.

⁷But as for me, I watch in hope for the LORD,
I wait for God my Savior;
my God will hear me.

Israel Will Rise

⁸Do not gloat over me, my enemy!
Though I have fallen, I will rise.
Though I sit in darkness,
the LORD will be my light.
⁹Because I have sinned against him,
I will bear the LORD's wrath,
until he pleads my case
and establishes my right.
He will bring me out into the light;
I will see his righteousnessᴰ.
¹⁰Then my enemy will see it
and will be covered with shame,
she who said to me,
"Where is the LORD your God?"
My eyes will see her downfall;
even now she will be trampled underfoot
like mire in the streets.

¹¹The day for building your walls will come,
the day for extending your boundaries.
¹²In that day people will come to you
from Assyria and the cities of Egypt,
even from Egypt to the Euphrates
and from sea to sea
and from mountain to mountain.
¹³The earth will become desolate because of its
inhabitants,
as the result of their deeds.

What kind of *summer fruit* could a person gather? (7:1)
Summer fruit was rare—figs or grapes that ripened late, after the regular harvest was over. Occasionally, someone walking through the trees or vineyard could find such fruit. Micah uses this image as a picture of his search for any godly people who might yet remain faithful to the Lord. He was disappointed to find *not one upright man* (v. 2). All he finds are weeds —briers and thorns—a generation of violent, dishonest and greedy men (vv. 2–4).

Early figs (7:1)
In ancient Israel there were two fig crops each year. The early figs ripened in June and were considered a delicacy. The second crop ripened in August or September and was dried and stored for the winter.

Day of your watchmen (7:4)
The coming day of judgment. Some see the *watchmen* as prophets who warned of judgment if the people did not repent. Others see them as the guards on the cities' walls who would be the first to spot the Assyrian invaders on the day of judgment.

What did Micah expect from God? (7:7)
In spite of coming judgment, Micah anticipated a day when God would vindicate the righteous and restore Israel. He expected the reborn nation to be a righteous one, characterized by justice. Micah essentially spoke on behalf of the few righteous people who remained, those who were trusting God no matter how bleak the circumstances (Hab. 3:16–19).

How did Micah fall? (7:8)
Micah was playing the role of Jerusalem (which, in turn, represented the entire nation of Israel). It was Jerusalem, not Micah, that faced its downfall when it would be defeated and its citizens carried away into exile. Still, in spite of the impending judgment, Micah could offer hope. God would eventually lift Jerusalem up; he would bring light in dark times.

SCRIPTURE LINK (7:9) *Until he pleads my case . . .*
Earlier God had brought charges against Israel. See 6:2.

Why would God plead on behalf of the one he had charged? (7:9)
Though his people may be unfaithful, God never is. Because of his promises to Abraham, Isaac and Jacob (v. 20), God was committed to his people. Though for a time he was forced to discipline his people for their sins, he promised that he would vindicate them before the hostile nations who had taken advantage of their weakness.

Bashan and Gilead (7:14)

Located east of the Jordan River and well-known for their grazing lands and fine cattle (see **Conquest of Canaan** on page 301). Micah prayed that God might provide for Israel's needs as he had in earlier times. He compared God to a shepherd and exiled Israel to a flock of sheep. Micah asked God to lead his sheep to the bountiful feeding grounds of Bashan and Gilead.

How did Micah view God? (7:18–20)

Micah saw not only God's judgment, but also his mercy. He prophesied that God would eventually restore Israel even though judgment would come first. Here Micah praises God for his compassion and willingness to forgive. He saw how God's great mercy and faithfulness set him apart from the other so-called gods of the surrounding nations. *Who is a God like you?* Micah asks, perhaps a deliberate pun on his name, which meant *Who is like the Lord?*

Prayer and Praise

14Shepherd your people with your staff,
    the flock of your inheritance,
which lives by itself in a forest,
    in fertile pasturelands. *a*
Let them feed in Bashan and Gilead
    as in days long ago.

15"As in the days when you came out of Egypt,
    I will show them my wonders."

16Nations will see and be ashamed,
    deprived of all their power.
They will lay their hands on their mouths
    and their ears will become deaf.
17They will lick dust like a snake,
    like creatures that crawl on the ground.
They will come trembling out of their dens;
    they will turn in fear to the Lord our God
    and will be afraid of you.
18Who is a God like you,
    who pardons sin and forgives the
        transgression
    of the remnant*D* of his inheritance?
You do not stay angry forever
    but delight to show mercy*D*.
19You will again have compassion on us;
    you will tread our sins underfoot
    and hurl all our iniquities into the depths of
        the sea.
20You will be true to Jacob,
    and show mercy to Abraham,
as you pledged on oath to our fathers
    in days long ago.

---

a 14 Or in the middle of Carmel

NAHUM

Why read this book?

Have you ever been angry? Not just annoyed, but deeply angry? Perhaps a friend has been victimized by gang cruelty. Perhaps you've worked for a boss who puts people down to make himself look good. Perhaps you've been the victim of racial slurs. Nahum reminds us that God is in control of history and will not allow evil to persist forever.

Who wrote this book?

Nahum, an otherwise unknown prophet, whose name means *comfort*.

To whom was it written?

Although the book seems to be addressed to the Assyrians, Nahum's message is actually for God's people, the nation of Judah.

When was it written?

Between 663 B.C., when Assyria conquered Egypt, and 609 B.C., when Assyria was defeated by Babylon. This was perhaps 100 years after Jonah had delivered God's message to Nineveh, the capital of Assyria.

What was happening in the world at this time?

In 722 B.C. Assyria defeated the northern kingdom of Israel. Now, almost 100 years later, the southern kingdom of Judah was ruled by Manasseh, a puppet king of the Assyrians.

Why was it written?

To assure people that evil does not endure forever and that God will one day fulfill his plan to restore good permanently.

What to look for in Nahum:

Mercy and judgment, both of which reveal the character of God (see 1:2,7). Look for ways these seemingly opposite traits actually reflect God's consistent stance toward his people.

When did these things happen?

TIME LINE   1300ʙᴄ 1200 1100 1000 900 800 700 600 500 400

Ministries of Micah and Isaiah in Judah (c.742-681 B.C.) ————————————————————————

Exile of Israel (722 B.C.) ——

Nahum's ministry (c.663-612 B.C.) ————————————————————————————————————

Zephaniah's ministry in Judah (c.640-621 B.C.) ——————————————————————————

Book of Nahum written (c.663-609 B.C.) ——————————————————————————————

Jeremiah's ministry in Judah (c.626-585 B.C.) ———————————————————————————

Habakkuk's ministry in Judah (c.612-588 B.C.) ——————————————————————————

Fall of Jerusalem (586 B.C.) ————————————————————————————————————

Ministries of Haggai and Zechariah (c.520-480 B.C.) ————————————————————————

Oracle (1:1)

A message from God; in some cases the word suggests unwelcome news or judgment.

Is God wrong to be jealous? (1:2)

Jealousy is in its usual sense a sinful trait (Gal. 5:20), but the word can also denote a godly quality (2 Cor. 11:2). In this way God is "jealous" (the word is related to the word *zealous*) for people's faithfulness. God's jealousy shows his love, not a selfishness or lack of control. This righteous jealousy takes vengeance on those who hurt his children.

Does God have mood swings? (1:7)

No, although here it seems that he does abruptly shift from wrath (v. 6) to comfort (v. 7). It might be difficult at times to see how God's love can be compatible with his judgment. But God never changes. His character and actions are consistent throughout human history. He loves people—and hates injustice.

Who would plot against God? (1:11)

Perhaps Sennacherib (705–681 B.C.), the Assyrian king who defied God and threatened Judah during Hezekiah's reign (2 Kings 18:13–35). Another possibility was Ashurbanipal (669–627 B.C.), a later Assyrian king who conquered Egypt and subdued Judah's King Manasseh (2 Chron. 33:11–13). Or the verse could refer generally to the nation of Assyria itself—with all its brutally ambitious kings. Some think the phrase suggests an evil spiritual power behind Assyria's aggression.

How did God hurt Judah? (1:12)

God put his people into the hands of a cruel foreign army. Assyria became God's tool to cleanse Judah, thus fulfilling the prediction that foreigners would dominate those who became unfaithful (see Lev. 26:17–39; Deut. 28:25–37,43–68; 29:28).

---

1 An oracle[D] concerning Nineveh. The book of the vision[D] of Nahum the Elkoshite.

The LORD's Anger Against Nineveh

²The LORD is a jealous and avenging[D] God;
    the LORD takes vengeance and is filled with
        wrath.
The LORD takes vengeance on his foes
    and maintains his wrath against his enemies.
³The LORD is slow to anger and great in power;
    the LORD will not leave the guilty
        unpunished.
His way is in the whirlwind and the storm,
    and clouds are the dust of his feet.
⁴He rebukes the sea and dries it up;
    he makes all the rivers run dry.
Bashan and Carmel wither
    and the blossoms of Lebanon fade.
⁵The mountains quake before him
    and the hills melt away.
The earth trembles at his presence,
    the world and all who live in it.
⁶Who can withstand his indignation?
    Who can endure his fierce anger?
His wrath is poured out like fire;
    the rocks are shattered before him.

⁷The LORD is good,
    a refuge in times of trouble.
He cares for those who trust in him,
⁸ but with an overwhelming flood
he will make an end of ⌊Nineveh⌋;
    he will pursue his foes into darkness.

⁹Whatever they plot against the LORD
    he[a] will bring to an end;
    trouble will not come a second time.
¹⁰They will be entangled among thorns
    and drunk from their wine;
    they will be consumed like dry stubble.[b]
¹¹From you, ⌊O Nineveh,⌋ has one come forth
    who plots evil against the LORD
    and counsels wickedness.

¹²This is what the LORD says:

"Although[D] they have allies and are numerous,
    they will be cut off and pass away.
Although I have afflicted[D] you, ⌊O Judah,⌋
    I will afflict you no more.
¹³Now I will break their yoke[D] from your neck
    and tear your shackles away."

¹⁴The LORD has given a command concerning
    you, ⌊Nineveh⌋:

"You will have no descendants to bear your
    name.
I will destroy the carved images and cast
    idols[D]
that are in the temple of your gods.
I will prepare your grave,
    for you are vile."

---

a 9 Or *What do you foes plot against the LORD? / He*   *b* 10 The meaning of the Hebrew for this verse is uncertain.

[15]Look, there on the mountains,
    the feet of one who brings good news,
    who proclaims peace[D]!
Celebrate your festivals, O Judah,
    and fulfill your vows[D].
No more will the wicked invade you;
    they will be completely destroyed.

Nineveh to Fall

2 An attacker advances against you, ⌊Nineveh⌋.
    Guard the fortress,
    watch the road,
    brace yourselves,
    marshal all your strength!

[2]The Lord will restore the splendor of Jacob
    like the splendor of Israel,
though destroyers have laid them waste
    and have ruined their vines.

[3]The shields of his soldiers are red;
    the warriors are clad in scarlet.
The metal on the chariots flashes
    on the day they are made ready;
    the spears of pine are brandished.[a]
[4]The chariots storm through the streets,
    rushing back and forth through the squares.
They look like flaming torches;
    they dart about like lightning.

[5]He summons his picked troops,
    yet they stumble on their way.
They dash to the city wall;
    the protective shield is put in place.
[6]The river gates are thrown open
    and the palace collapses.
[7]It is decreed[b] that ⌊the city⌋
    be exiled[D] and carried away.
Its slave girls moan like doves
    and beat upon their breasts.
[8]Nineveh is like a pool,
    and its water is draining away.
"Stop! Stop!" they cry,
    but no one turns back.
[9]Plunder the silver!
    Plunder the gold!
The supply is endless,
    the wealth from all its treasures!
[10]She is pillaged, plundered[D], stripped!
    Hearts melt, knees give way,
    bodies tremble, every face grows pale.

[11]Where now is the lions' den,
    the place where they fed their young,
where the lion and lioness went,
    and the cubs, with nothing to fear?
[12]The lion killed enough for his cubs
    and strangled the prey for his mate,
filling his lairs with the kill
    and his dens with the prey.

[13]"I am against you,"
    declares the Lord Almighty.

---

[a]3 Hebrew; Septuagint and Syriac / the horsemen rush to and fro
[b]7 The meaning of the Hebrew for this word is uncertain.

When will this peace come? (1:15)

Some see two ways that this promise could be fulfilled. First, the people of Judah heard great news: Nineveh had been destroyed (612 b.c.) and, soon after, Assyrian forces suffered their final defeat (609 b.c.). Nineveh was so completely destroyed that its ruins were not identified until 1845. The second promise of peace tells the good news of the Messiah: he breaks the power of evil and will achieve final victory at his second coming.

SCRIPTURE LINK (1:15) The feet of one who brings good news

See Isaiah 52:7 and Romans 10:15 for other examples of feet that bring good news.

Attacker (2:1)

May refer to the king of Babylon, or more likely, the alliance of nations that joined forces to destroy Nineveh (see **Map 7** at the back of this Bible).

Did God keep this promise? (2:2)

The *splendor* promised here may not be earthly fame for Judah so much as eternal rewards for the faithful and the honor of being the homeland of the Messiah. Compared to Nineveh, which was destroyed and never rebuilt, Judah's honored place in history was forever assured by the birth of Christ.

Protective shield (2:5)

This could refer to a framework covered with hides and used by defenders on the top of the city wall to deflect the arrows of the invaders. But the exact meaning is uncertain.

Why such graphic violence? (2:5–10)

People oppressed by this cruel nation would undoubtedly cheer this scene—the vicious Assyrians would soon get what they deserved! Their atrocities were well-known—pillaging and plundering, impaling victims on poles, even heaping the bodies of their unfortunate victims in huge mounds. Now Nahum promised in terms as graphic as Nineveh's own reputation that it would be plundered and its own people victimized.

River gates (2:6)

Perhaps Nineveh's main gates, which faced the Tigris River. Some, however, think *thrown open* suggests that dams above the city were opened suddenly, flooding the city and eroding parts of the walls. One ancient source reports that a flood helped the invaders breach Nineveh's defenses.

"I will burn up your chariots in smoke,
    and the sword will devour your young lions.
I will leave you no prey on the earth.
The voices of your messengers
    will no longer be heard."

Woe to Nineveh

3   Woe to the city of blood,
        full of lies,
    full of plunder[D],
        never without victims!
²The crack of whips,
    the clatter of wheels,
galloping horses
    and jolting chariots!
³Charging cavalry,
    flashing swords
    and glittering spears!
Many casualties,
    piles of dead,
bodies without number,
    people stumbling over the corpses—
⁴all because of the wanton lust of a harlot,
    alluring, the mistress of sorceries[D],
who enslaved nations by her prostitution
    and peoples by her witchcraft[D].

⁵"I am against you," declares the LORD Almighty.
    "I will lift your skirts over your face.
I will show the nations your nakedness
    and the kingdoms your shame.
⁶I will pelt you with filth,
    I will treat you with contempt
    and make you a spectacle.
⁷All who see you will flee from you and say,
    'Nineveh is in ruins—who will mourn for
        her?'
    Where can I find anyone to comfort you?"

⁸Are you better than Thebes,[a]
    situated on the Nile,
    with water around her?
The river was her defense,

---

a8 Hebrew No Amon

How was Nineveh like a prostitute? (3:1–4)

In the ancient world the term *harlot* was a standard insult leveled at anyone who broke a promise or violated treaties, something Assyria did regularly. Nahum implies that all nations, even Assyria, have some kind of covenant with God (see Amos 1–2). Nineveh had, in fact, repented and humbled itself in the days of Jonah. But the city had long since rebelled against God.

Why would a holy God do such humiliating things? (3:5–6)

Prostitutes and adulteresses were sometimes publicly humiliated in this manner (Ezek. 16:37–39). Nahum refers to this practice to illustrate the degree of humiliation God would bring to those who defy him. This description of Assyria's humiliation could also be a play on words since the Hebrew term for *nakedness* also means *exile*.

SCRIPTURE LINK (3:5) *I will show the nations your nakedness*

The picture of another embarrassed harlot nation—this time Israel—is found in Hosea 2:10.

Why compare Nineveh to Thebes? (3:8)

Both were capitals of superpowers in the Middle East: Thebes of Egypt and Nineveh of Assyria. Assyria sacked Thebes in 663 B.C. Half a century later, Nineveh was crushed by Babylon. Both were mighty. Both were utterly destroyed.

Why does a merciful God punish anyone? (2:13)

G od blends his mercy with his justice. Though God had extended mercy to Nineveh through Jonah a century or so earlier, Nineveh had abandoned the mercy God offered. Justice now required payment for the nation's crimes against humanity.

The Assyrian empire exploited much of the world with its brutal army. It was notorious for its wartime atrocities. One of the kings of Assyria boasted how he conquered cities, chopped off the heads of the inhabitants and piled the heads like a gruesome monument outside the city gates.

Assyria's day for mercy was over; since they had rejected God's mercy they could expect his judgment. They would receive what they had given others. Sometimes mercy means punishing cruelty.

the waters her wall.
⁹Cush* and Egypt were her boundless strength;
   Put and Libya were among her allies.
¹⁰Yet she was taken captive
   and went into exileᴰ.
Her infants were dashed to pieces
   at the head of every street.
Lots were cast for her nobles,
   and all her great men were put in chains.
¹¹You too will become drunk;
   you will go into hiding
   and seek refuge from the enemy.

¹²All your fortresses are like fig trees
   with their first ripe fruit;
when they are shaken,
   the figs fall into the mouth of the eater.
¹³Look at your troops—
   they are all women!
The gates of your land
   are wide open to your enemies;
   fire has consumed their bars.

¹⁴Draw water for the siege,
   strengthen your defenses!
Work the clay,
   tread the mortar,
   repair the brickwork!
¹⁵There the fire will devour you;
   the sword will cut you down
   and, like grasshoppers, consume you.
Multiply like grasshoppers,
   multiply like locustsᴰ!
¹⁶You have increased the number of your
     merchants
   till they are more than the stars of the sky,
but like locusts they strip the land
   and then fly away.
¹⁷Your guards are like locusts,
   your officials like swarms of locusts

*9 That is, the upper Nile region

Who dashed infants to pieces? (3:10)

In the ancient world it was not uncommon for an invading army to punish resistant cities by killing their babies. Assyria had killed Egyptian babies in Thebes. Also see *Why does God permit the innocent to suffer?* (Isaiah 13:16) and *How could such brutality be part of God's plan?* (Hosea 13:16).

Can we pass the point of forgiveness? (3:19)

If nothing could be done for Assyria, is there danger for us of passing the point of forgiveness? Nahum's intent was not to say how far God could be pushed before punishment becomes certain. Sin is sin; we cannot think in terms of minor or major sins. Yet the Bible does indicate that persistent refusal to respond to God will result in punishment.

When people continue to rebel, they can become numb to God's spirit. At some point, God declares, "Enough!" Persistent, repeat offenders in this situation cannot escape the consequences of their rebellion against God. When judgment comes to such sinners, it is too little, too late for them to beg for mercy. See article: *Does God refuse to listen to sinners?* (Micah 3:4).

Nevertheless, we can be confident that when it comes to our eternal destiny, God deeply desires to forgive our sins when we turn to him in repentance. Only those who persist in their rebellion against God are incapable of finding forgiveness. See article: *What is blasphemy against the Holy Spirit?* (Matt. 12:31–32).

How were Nineveh's guards *like locusts?* (3:17)

Locusts, which traveled in huge swarms, could swoop in and destroy acres of crops within minutes. They would devour everything in their path, and then disappear as quickly as they had come. So too Assyria's leaders left devastation in their wake as they invaded enemy cities, committed unspeakable horrors and moved on to wreak further havoc. Yet, as Nahum prophesied, Nineveh would *fly away* disappearing without a trace. God's word through Nahum was fulfilled when Nineveh fell to the Babylonians in 612 B.C., so totally destroyed that it was never rebuilt.

that settle in the walls on a cold day—
but when the sun appears they fly away,
   and no one knows where.

[18]O king of Assyria, your shepherds[a] slumber;
   your nobles lie down to rest.
Your people are scattered on the mountains
   with no one to gather them.
[19]Nothing can heal your wound;
   your injury is fatal.
Everyone who hears the news about you
   claps his hands at your fall,
for who has not felt
   your endless cruelty?

HABAKKUK

Why read this book?

Have you ever wanted to ask God, "If you're in control, why does evil so often win?" If so, you'll identify with Habakkuk, who entered into a great debate with God. Habakkuk, whose name may mean *wrestler,* grappled with God about questions still relevant today: How can a just God ignore injustice? Why does God allow the wicked to prosper? And how can a good God use evil to accomplish his purposes? Habakkuk struggled to understand how God works, but in the end he became convinced that he could trust God no matter how bleak or confusing the present circumstances appeared to be.

Who wrote this book?

Habakkuk, a prophet in the nation of Judah.

When was it written?

Around 610 to 605 B.C.

What was happening during this time?

Sin was rampant in Judah. The people worshiped idols, sacrificed their children to pagan gods and ignored God. The wicked King Jehoiakim not only refused to listen to God's prophets, but he also burned their writings, arrested several of them and even murdered one. Jehoiakim foolishly aligned Judah between two warring superpowers—the declining Assyrian empire and the rising Babylonian empire. The historical background to the book of Habakkuk is found in 2 Kings 23:31—24:7 and 2 Chron. 36:1–8.

What to look for in Habakkuk:

Most prophets speak to the people on God's behalf. Habakkuk was unique in that he spoke to God on behalf of the people. As you read, notice his complaints to God, God's unexpected (and unwelcome!) answer, and the hope Habakkuk finally discovered.

When did these things happen?

TIME LINE	1300BC	1200	1100	1000	900	800	700	600	500	400
Ministries of Micah and Isaiah in Judah (c.742-681 B.C.)										
Exile of Israel (722 B.C.)										
Nahum's ministry (c.663-612 B.C.)										
Zephaniah's ministry in Judah (c.640-621 B.C.)										
Jeremiah's ministry in Judah (c.626-585 B.C.)										
Habakkuk's ministry in Judah (c.612-588 B.C.)										
Book of Habakkuk written (c.610-605 B.C.)										
Fall of Jerusalem (586 B.C.)										

Oracle (1:1)

An announcement from God. The word often suggests unwelcome news or judgment.

Was God ignoring Habakkuk's prayers? (1:2)

Habakkuk may have prayed as long as 12 years for justice without any response. During his wait Habakkuk learned something about God's timing: God wasn't ignoring his prayer, but God answered it by working behind the scenes, where Habakkuk could not see his action.

SCRIPTURE LINK (1:5) Be utterly amazed

Centuries later, the apostle Paul quoted Habakkuk to support his point that God will judge those who reject Christ (Acts 13:41).

Babylonians (1:6)

Babylon was a nation northwest of the Persian Gulf, in modern Iraq. The Babylonians rose to power between 612 and 605 B.C., conquering both the Assyrian and Egyptian empires in the process. They were ruthless in their quest for power. Still, as bad as they were, God used them to correct Judah. In 597 B.C. they conquered Jerusalem, destroyed the temple and took the people into captivity.

1 The oracle[D] that Habakkuk the prophet[D] received.

Habakkuk's Complaint

2How long, O LORD, must I call for help,
    but you do not listen?
Or cry out to you, "Violence!"
    but you do not save?
3Why do you make me look at injustice?
    Why do you tolerate wrong?
Destruction and violence are before me;
    there is strife, and conflict abounds.
4Therefore the law is paralyzed,
    and justice never prevails.
The wicked hem in the righteous[D],
    so that justice is perverted.

The LORD's Answer

5"Look at the nations and watch—
    and be utterly amazed.
For I am going to do something in your days
    that you would not believe,
    even if you were told.
6I am raising up the Babylonians,[a]
    that ruthless and impetuous people,
who sweep across the whole earth
    to seize dwelling places not their own.
7They are a feared and dreaded people;
    they are a law to themselves
    and promote their own honor.
8Their horses are swifter than leopards,
    fiercer than wolves at dusk.
Their cavalry gallops headlong;
    their horsemen come from afar.
They fly like a vulture swooping to devour;

---

[a]6 Or Chaldeans

Does God use evil to do good? (1:6,13)

When Habakkuk asked God to end the corruption in Judah, he didn't expect God to do it so severely. True, King Jehoiakim and his cronies had grown wealthy by injustice and extortion. They had even enslaved their own people (Jer. 22:13,17) and arrogantly burned the writings of Jeremiah, another prophet who pled for justice (Jer. 36:23–27).

But if Judah was bad, the Babylonians were worse! Habakkuk knew about their sadistic reputation—chariots and horsemen trampling defenders; armies laying siege and starving cities into submission; soldiers raping their victims, even torturing pregnant women and infants. Now this army of destruction was coming toward Judah. This was God's justice?

Eventually God enlarged Habakkuk's vision. He saw that God is in control even when it appears he is not. God uses people and nations, often without their knowledge, for his good purposes. At times the events seem evil, but God's severity, like a surgeon's scalpel, is working not to hurt but to heal.

In a word, yes, God does use evil to do good. But the reason he does is that he's working to transform the tragic circumstances of a fallen world so that good ultimately prevails.

9 they all come bent on violence.
  Their hordes*ᵃ* advance like a desert wind
    and gather prisoners like sand.
10They deride kings
    and scoff at rulers.
  They laugh at all fortified cities;
    they build earthen ramps and capture them.
11Then they sweep past like the wind and go
      on—
    guilty men, whose own strength is their
      god."

Habakkuk's Second Complaint

12O Lord, are you not from everlasting?
  My God, my Holy One, we will not die.
  O Lord, you have appointed them to execute
      judgment;
  O Rock, you have ordained them to punish.
13Your eyes are too pure to look on evil;
    you cannot tolerate wrong.
  Why then do you tolerate the treacherous?
  Why are you silent while the wicked
    swallow up those more righteousᴰ than
      themselves?
14You have made men like fish in the sea,
    like sea creatures that have no ruler.
15The wicked foe pulls all of them up with
      hooks,
    he catches them in his net,
  he gathers them up in his dragnet;
    and so he rejoices and is glad.
16Therefore he sacrificesᴰ to his net
    and burns incenseᴰ to his dragnet,
  for by his net he lives in luxury
    and enjoys the choicest food.
17Is he to keep on emptying his net,
    destroying nations without mercyᴰ?

2 I will stand at my watch
    and station myself on the ramparts;
  I will look to see what he will say to me,
    and what answer I am to give to this
      complaint.*ᵇ*

The Lord's Answer

2Then the Lord replied:

  "Write down the revelationᴰ
    and make it plain on tablets
    so that a heraldᶜ may run with it.
3For the revelation awaits an appointed time;
    it speaks of the end
    and will not prove false.
  Though it linger, wait for it;
    it*ᵈ* will certainly come and will not delay.

4"See, he is puffed up;
    his desires are not upright—
    but the righteous will live by his faith*ᵉ*—
5indeed, wine betrays him;

The Babylonian Empire (1:6)

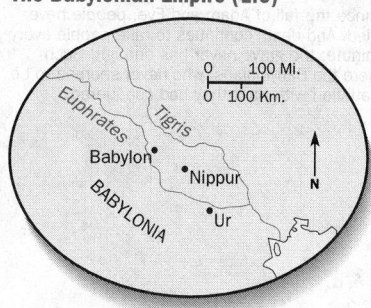

Why would anyone worship a net? (1:16)
The net symbolized power. Fishermen used a net to encircle an area so no fish could escape. Since no nation could escape Babylon, some ancient artwork pictures Babylon's enemies captured in fish nets. The proud Babylonians worshiped their *own strength* (v. 11); military power became their god.

***Stand at my watch . . . on the ramparts* (2:1)**
Around the clock watchmen stood in watchtowers to guard against possible invasion or to watch for messengers. *Ramparts,* embankments of earth beyond the city walls, were the first lines of defense. Habakkuk, like a watchman, was waiting and ready for God's answer to his question.

***Will not delay* (2:3)**
This phrase may refer more to the certainty of God's promise than to its immediacy. God's promise—to punish the Babylonians—wasn't fulfilled for nearly 80 years. This may seem like a lifetime to us, but it's not long from God's perspective. To believe God will act, even when circumstances look like he's forgotten—that's what faith is all about.

SCRIPTURE LINK (2:4) *The righteous will live by his faith*
This idea of trusting God even when everything is going wrong is expanded in the New Testament to include trusting Christ for spiritual life (Romans 1:17; Gal. 3:11; Heb. 10:37–38).

ᵃ9 The meaning of the Hebrew for this word is uncertain.   *ᵇ1 Or and what to answer when I am rebuked*   *ᶜ2 Or so that whoever reads it*   *ᵈ3 Or Though he linger, wait for him; / he*   *ᵉ4 Or faithfulness*

Greedy as the grave (2:5)

Since the fall of Adam and Eve, people have died. And death continues to take people every minute: the grave never has enough. Such were the Babylonians, who never seemed to be satisfied with what they had conquered.

he is arrogant and never at rest.
Because he is as greedy as the grave[a]
    and like death[D] is never satisfied,
he gathers to himself all the nations
    and takes captive all the peoples.

6"Will not all of them taunt him with ridicule and scorn, saying,

" 'Woe to him who piles up stolen goods
    and makes himself wealthy by extortion[D]!
    How long must this go on?'
7Will not your debtors[b] suddenly arise?
    Will they not wake up and make you
        tremble?
    Then you will become their victim.
8Because you have plundered[D] many nations,
    the peoples who are left will plunder you.
For you have shed man's blood;
    you have destroyed lands and cities and
        everyone in them.

9"Woe to him who builds his realm by unjust
        gain
    to set his nest on high,
    to escape the clutches of ruin!
10You have plotted the ruin of many peoples,
    shaming your own house and forfeiting your
        life.
11The stones of the wall will cry out,
    and the beams of the woodwork will echo it.

12"Woe to him who builds a city with bloodshed
    and establishes a town by crime!
13Has not the LORD Almighty determined
    that the people's labor is only fuel for the
        fire,
    that the nations exhaust themselves for
        nothing?

a5 Hebrew Sheol   b7 Or creditors

Is it okay to argue with God? (2:1)

Passionate, honest, even angry prayers were expressed by many people in the Bible. Habakkuk wasn't the only one to give voice to his complaints. Moses, Gideon, Elijah and Job, among others, also questioned and argued with God.

God listens with a sympathetic ear when we complain about injustice. Whenever we are jolted by life's unfairness, we should realize that God was bothered by such things long before we were. In fact, injustice would not upset us at all if God had not given us a sense of justice. Where else could we get a sense of right and wrong if not from God?

Because God knows our deepest thoughts, we might as well be honest with him (and ourselves) and admit our feelings of outrage or confusion. But watch out! God's "answer" may be as perplexing as the problem. God isn't obligated to answer our questions as we'd expect.

As Habakkuk, Job and the others discovered, God seldom explains himself or his ways completely. When he does, people don't have the capacity to comprehend his answers, but they are overwhelmed with his power and love. In the end, though we may not know the answers to our questions, we come to know God better.

¹⁴For the earth will be filled with the knowledge
of the glory^D of the LORD,
as the waters cover the sea.

¹⁵"Woe to him who gives drink to his neighbors,
pouring it from the wineskin^D till they are
drunk,
so that he can gaze on their naked bodies.
¹⁶You will be filled with shame instead of
glory.
Now it is your turn! Drink and be exposed^a!
The cup from the LORD's right hand is coming
around to you,
and disgrace will cover your glory.
¹⁷The violence you have done to Lebanon will
overwhelm you,
and your destruction of animals will terrify
you.
For you have shed man's blood;
you have destroyed lands and cities and
everyone in them.

¹⁸"Of what value is an idol^D, since a man has
carved it?
Or an image that teaches lies?
For he who makes it trusts in his own creation;
he makes idols that cannot speak.
¹⁹Woe to him who says to wood, 'Come to life!'
Or to lifeless stone, 'Wake up!'
Can it give guidance?
It is covered with gold and silver;
there is no breath in it.
²⁰But the LORD is in his holy temple;
let all the earth be silent before him."

Habakkuk's Prayer

3 A prayer of Habakkuk the prophet^D. On *shigionoth.*^b

²LORD, I have heard of your fame;
I stand in awe of your deeds, O LORD.
Renew them in our day,
in our time make them known;
in wrath remember mercy^D.

³God came from Teman,
the Holy One from Mount Paran.   *Selah*^{Dc}
His glory covered the heavens
and his praise filled the earth.
⁴His splendor was like the sunrise;
rays flashed from his hand,
where his power was hidden.
⁵Plague went before him;
pestilence followed his steps.
⁶He stood, and shook the earth;
he looked, and made the nations tremble.
The ancient mountains crumbled
and the age-old hills collapsed.
His ways are eternal.
⁷I saw the tents of Cushan in distress,
the dwellings of Midian in anguish.

**Who's getting drunk and naked?
(2:15)**
This verse describes the rape of a nation. Pouring alcohol into someone in order to take advantage of them is nothing new. The Babylonians exploited other nations, doing what they wanted with them. But the shame they caused others would soon be their own (v. 16).

In his holy temple (2:20)
This phrase suggests that even though everything on earth is in shambles, God still reigns. All things are under his control and in his power.

Teman (3:3)
Means *southland*, a poetic description of the Sinai Desert through which the Israelites traveled out of Egypt and where God gave them the law (see *Map 2* at the back of this Bible). From there God led them north past *Mount Paran* to the promised land.

Why boast about plague and pestilence? (3:5)
Egypt enslaved and oppressed Israel. Eventually God used plagues and pestilence to free the Israelites. Habakkuk praised God for the plagues that overpowered the ironfisted Egyptians (Exodus 7:17). In this case plague and pestilence meant freedom and deliverance.

---

^a16 Masoretic Text; Dead Sea Scrolls, Aquila, Vulgate and Syriac (see also Septuagint) *and stagger*   ^b1 Probably a literary or musical term   ^c3 A word of uncertain meaning; possibly a musical term; also in verses 9 and 13

[8]Were you angry with the rivers, O LORD?
　　Was your wrath against the streams?
　Did you rage against the sea
　　when you rode with your horses
　　and your victorious chariots?
[9]You uncovered your bow,
　　you called for many arrows.   *Selah*[D]
　You split the earth with rivers;
[10]　the mountains saw you and writhed.
　Torrents of water swept by;
　　the deep roared
　　and lifted its waves on high.

[11]Sun and moon stood still in the heavens
　　at the glint of your flying arrows,
　　at the lightning of your flashing spear.
[12]In wrath you strode through the earth
　　and in anger you threshed the nations.
[13]You came out to deliver your people,
　　to save your anointed[D] one.
　You crushed the leader of the land of
　　　wickedness,
　　you stripped him from head to foot.   *Selah*
[14]With his own spear you pierced his head
　　when his warriors stormed out to scatter us,
　gloating as though about to devour
　　the wretched who were in hiding.
[15]You trampled the sea with your horses,
　　churning the great waters.

[16]I heard and my heart pounded,
　　my lips quivered at the sound;
　decay crept into my bones,
　　and my legs trembled.
　Yet I will wait patiently for the day of calamity
　　to come on the nation invading us.
[17]Though the fig tree does not bud
　　and there are no grapes on the vines,
　though the olive crop fails
　　and the fields produce no food,
　though there are no sheep in the pen
　　and no cattle in the stalls,
[18]yet I will rejoice in the LORD,
　　I will be joyful in God my Savior.

[19]The Sovereign LORD is my strength;
　　he makes my feet like the feet of a deer,
　　he enables me to go on the heights.

For the director of music. On my stringed
　　instruments.

What did buds signify? (3:17)

With no buds on the trees, there was no hope
for a harvest, no prospects for better times to
come. Figs were such a valuable food source
in ancient Israel that a failed crop impacted
the whole economy. Despite such a dismal
forecast, Habakkuk decided to find hope in
trusting God.

Was Habakkuk kidding himself? (3:17–18)

To rejoice during disaster seems like denial—
and totally inappropriate if you look only at
present circumstances. But faith in God adds a
new ingredient. Habakkuk learned to look beyond his present troubles to a larger perspective. Faith assures us, just as it did Habakkuk,
that even when things seem hopeless, our all-
powerful God will eventually restore us.

SCRIPTURE LINK (3:18) *Yet I will rejoice in the LORD*

Paul echoes this verse when he writes of joy
regardless of circumstances (Phil. 4:4).

ZEPHANIAH

Why read this book?

To reinforce your confidence that God will make everything right. When justice is distorted, when the line between right and wrong is blurred, when leaders become corrupt, it's easy to become discouraged. And when religious leaders fail, discouragement can turn to cynicism. Zephaniah reassures us that we can still trust God—that even in dark times our faith can still burn brightly.

Who wrote this book?

Zephaniah, whose name may mean *the Lord hides* or *the Lord protects*.

When was it written?

During the reign of King Josiah of Judah (640–609 B.C.), but before the city of Nineveh was destroyed (612 B.C.).

What was happening at this time?

Despite King Josiah's well-intended civil and religious reforms, leaders were corrupt and idolatry was widespread. The Assyrian empire, the superpower which had ruled over Judah for more than a century, was disintegrating. Shortly after Josiah's death and Zephaniah's ministry, the Babylonians conquered Judah, destroyed the temple and took many into exile.

To whom was it written and why?

Zephaniah wrote to the people of Judah, warning them of impending judgment for their sins. He hoped to stir them to repentance before it was too late. But he also assured them that God's judgment would pave the way for a new society in which justice would prevail and all humankind would worship the Lord.

What to look for in Zephaniah:

The balance between judgment and salvation, between God's anger and his compassion. Like most prophets, Zephaniah writes in a poetic form marked by vivid figures of speech and emotionally charged language.

When did these things happen?

TIME LINE	1300 B.C.	1200	1100	1000	900	800	700	600	500	400
Ministries of Micah and Isaiah in Judah (c.742-681 B.C.)										
Exile of Israel (722 B.C.)										
Nahum's ministry (c.663-612 B.C.)										
Zephaniah's ministry in Judah (c.640-621 B.C.)										
Book of Zephaniah written (c.635-630 B.C.)										
Jeremiah's ministry in Judah (c.626-585 B.C.)										
Habakkuk's ministry in Judah (c.612-588 B.C.)										
Fall of Jerusalem (586 B.C.)										

Why give a prophet's genealogy? (1:1)

This genealogy of four generations seems significant since it was more typical to list only a prophet's father. Zephaniah is traced back to Hezekiah, perhaps the famous king who died about 60 years earlier (698 B.C.). This could mean that Zephaniah was a member of the extended royal family. Some note, however, that Hezekiah was a common name and that the verse stops short of identifying him as the king —seemingly a major oversight if he was.

Is this the end of the world? (1:2)

Yes, but not only that. Zephaniah describes Judah's coming judgment (1:4–13) against the backdrop of a final, worldwide judgment (1:2–3,14–18). Old Testament prophecies sometimes had two meanings: one involved the immediate future and the other foreshadowed events of the end times.

What all did Jerusalem worship? (1:4–5)

Baal was the Canaanite storm god who supposedly enabled crops to grow and human beings to have children. Molech was likely Milcom, the Ammonites' chief god. See Molech (Jer. 32:35). The starry host included the sun, moon and stars, all of which were objects of worship in Zephaniah's day (2 Kings 23:5).

The day of the Lord (1:7)

A phrase referring to times when God decisively defeats his enemies in battle. The phrase has its origin in ancient Middle Eastern culture, where kings would sometimes boast that they had won a war in a single day. The Old Testament applies the phrase to several different historical events, including God's judgments on Israel (Amos 5:18,20), Judah (2:2–3), Babylon (Isaiah 13:6), Egypt (Ezek. 30:3) and Edom (Isaiah 34:8–9). Several passages also associate the Lord's day with his final, culminating judgment upon the earth.

Those clad in foreign clothes (1:8)

Probably the wealthy princes who had become enamored with foreign customs. Their behavior was a telltale sign that they had lost their sense of being God's distinct people among the surrounding nations.

Why would it anger God for someone to step over a threshold? (1:9)

This verse perhaps refers to a practice associated with the Philistine god Dagon (1 Samuel 5:5) or to a superstitious belief that demons lived at the entrance of a house. In either case the practice illustrates the pagan thinking of some of God's people.

Fish Gate . . . New Quarter (1:10)

The Fish Gate was probably on the northern side of the city, named for the fish brought by merchants from Tyre and the Sea of Galilee. The New Quarter had apparently developed as the number of merchants increased, expanding into a newer market area, probably near the Fish Gate.

Wine left on its dregs (1:12)

When fermenting wine is not separated from its sediment (dregs) at the right time, it gets thick, loses its strength, becomes bitter and is of little use. Like such congealed wine, Jerusalem's complacent and spiritually insensitive leaders were no longer effective and useful.

1 The word of the LORD that came to Zephaniah son of Cushi, the son of Gedaliah, the son of Amariah, the son of Hezekiah, during the reign of Josiah son of Amon king of Judah:

Warning of Coming Destruction

2"I will sweep away everything
  from the face of the earth,"
                                    declares the LORD.
3"I will sweep away both men and animals;
  I will sweep away the birds of the air
  and the fish of the sea.
The wicked will have only heaps of rubble[a]
  when I cut off man from the face of the
    earth,"
                                    declares the LORD.

Against Judah

4"I will stretch out my hand against Judah
  and against all who live in Jerusalem[D].
I will cut off from this place every remnant[D]
    of Baal[D],
  the names of the pagan and the idolatrous
    priests[D]—
5those who bow down on the roofs
  to worship the starry host[D],
  those who bow down and swear by the LORD
  and who also swear by Molech[D],[b]
6those who turn back from following the LORD
  and neither seek the LORD nor inquire of
    him.
7Be silent before the Sovereign LORD,
  for the day of the LORD[D] is near.
The LORD has prepared a sacrifice[D];
  he has consecrated[D] those he has invited.
8On the day of the LORD's sacrifice
  I will punish the princes
  and the king's sons
and all those clad
  in foreign clothes.
9On that day I will punish
  all who avoid stepping on the threshold,[c]
  who fill the temple of their gods
  with violence and deceit.

10"On that day," declares the LORD,
  "a cry will go up from the Fish Gate,
  wailing from the New Quarter,
  and a loud crash from the hills.
11Wail, you who live in the market district[d];
  all your merchants will be wiped out,
  all who trade with[e] silver will be ruined.
12At that time I will search Jerusalem with
    lamps
  and punish those who are complacent,
  who are like wine left on its dregs[D],
  who think, 'The LORD will do nothing,
    either good or bad.'
13Their wealth will be plundered[D],
  their houses demolished.

---

[a]3 The meaning of the Hebrew for this line is uncertain.   [c]9 See 1 Samuel 5:5.
[b]5 Hebrew Malcam, that is, Milcom
[d]11 Or the Mortar   [e]11 Or in

They will build houses
  but not live in them;
they will plant vineyards
  but not drink the wine.

The Great Day of the LORD

14"The great day of the LORD[D] is near—
  near and coming quickly.
Listen! The cry on the day of the LORD will be
    bitter,
  the shouting of the warrior there.
15That day will be a day of wrath,
  a day of distress and anguish,
  a day of trouble and ruin,
  a day of darkness and gloom,
  a day of clouds and blackness,
16a day of trumpet and battle cry
  against the fortified cities
  and against the corner towers.
17I will bring distress on the people
  and they will walk like blind men,
  because they have sinned against the LORD.
Their blood will be poured out like dust
  and their entrails like filth.
18Neither their silver nor their gold
  will be able to save them
  on the day of the LORD's wrath.
In the fire of his jealousy
  the whole world will be consumed,
for he will make a sudden end
  of all who live in the earth."

2 Gather together, gather together,
  O shameful nation,
2before the appointed time arrives
  and that day sweeps on like chaff[D],
before the fierce anger of the LORD comes upon
    you,
  before the day of the LORD's wrath comes
    upon you.
3Seek the LORD, all you humble of the land,
  you who do what he commands.
Seek righteousness[D], seek humility;
  perhaps you will be sheltered
  on the day of the LORD's anger.

Against Philistia

4Gaza will be abandoned
  and Ashkelon left in ruins.
At midday Ashdod will be emptied
  and Ekron uprooted.
5Woe to you who live by the sea,
  O Kerethite people;
the word of the LORD is against you,
  O Canaan, land of the Philistines.
"I will destroy you,
  and none will be left."

6The land by the sea, where the Kerethites[a]
    dwell,
  will be a place for shepherds and sheep
    pens.

Why was God against the Philistines? (2:5)
God regarded the Philistines as enemies because they had oppressed and opposed his people for hundreds of years. Like other nations of the earth, they had abandoned the faith of their forefather Noah. Also they had rejected God's self-revelation made obvious through creation and had worshiped false gods and idols (Romans 1:20–23).

---

a6 The meaning of the Hebrew for this word is uncertain.

Why reward Judah? (2:7)

Judah had broken its covenant with God and deserved nothing but punishment. But after the judgment, God would fulfill his promise to make his people into a great nation and give them all of Palestine as an eternal possession.

SCRIPTURE LINK (2:9) Sodom . . . Gomorrah

Destroyed when burning sulfur rained down on them. See Gen. 19:24–25.

When did Moab and Ammon eventually worship the Lord? (2:11)

Moab and Ammon are not necessarily the nations in view here. The nations mentioned may symbolize the four points of the compass: Moab and Ammon to the east of Judah, Philistia to the west, Cush to the south and Assyria to the north (see *Judah's Enemies* on page 1172). This speaks of a time when, because of God's judgment, all the people of the earth will recognize God's power and will worship him as the only true God (3:9; Rev. 21:24).

The Assyrian Empire (2:13)

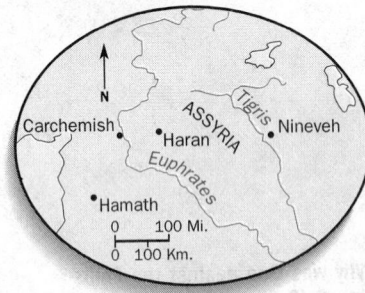

Shake their fists (2:15)

This gesture of contempt expresses satisfaction that vengeance has been accomplished against the hated Assyrians.

7It will belong to the remnant[D] of the house of Judah;
    there they will find pasture.
In the evening they will lie down
    in the houses of Ashkelon.
The LORD their God will care for them;
    he will restore their fortunes.[a]

Against Moab and Ammon

8"I have heard the insults of Moab
    and the taunts of the Ammonites,
who insulted my people
    and made threats against their land.
9Therefore, as surely as I live,"
    declares the LORD Almighty, the God of Israel,
"surely Moab will become like Sodom,
    the Ammonites like Gomorrah—
a place of weeds and salt pits,
    a wasteland forever.
The remnant of my people will plunder them;
    the survivors of my nation will inherit their land."

10This is what they will get in return for their pride,
    for insulting and mocking the people of the LORD Almighty.
11The LORD will be awesome to them
    when he destroys all the gods of the land.
The nations on every shore will worship him,
    every one in its own land.

Against Cush

12"You too, O Cushites,[b]
    will be slain by my sword."

Against Assyria

13He will stretch out his hand against the north
    and destroy Assyria,
leaving Nineveh utterly desolate
    and dry as the desert.
14Flocks and herds will lie down there,
    creatures of every kind.
The desert owl and the screech owl
    will roost on her columns.
Their calls will echo through the windows,
    rubble will be in the doorways,
    the beams of cedar will be exposed.
15This is the carefree city
    that lived in safety.
She said to herself,
    "I am, and there is none besides me."
What a ruin she has become,
    a lair for wild beasts!
All who pass by her scoff
    and shake their fists.

a 7 Or will bring back their captives   b 12 That is, people from the upper Nile region

The Future of Jerusalem

3 Woe to the city of oppressors,
  rebellious and defiled!
²She obeys no one,
  she accepts no correction.
She does not trust in the LORD,
  she does not draw near to her God.
³Her officials are roaring lions,
  her rulers are evening wolves,
  who leave nothing for the morning.
⁴Her prophetsᴰ are arrogant;
  they are treacherous men.
Her priestsᴰ profaneᴰ the sanctuary
  and do violence to the law.
⁵The LORD within her is righteousᴰ;
  he does no wrong.
Morning by morning he dispenses his justice,
  and every new day he does not fail,
  yet the unrighteous know no shame.

⁶"I have cut off nations;
  their strongholdsᴰ are demolished.
I have left their streets deserted,
  with no one passing through.
Their cities are destroyed;
  no one will be left—no one at all.
⁷I said to the city,
  'Surely you will fear me
  and accept correction!'
Then her dwelling would not be cut off,
  nor all my punishments come upon her.
But they were still eager
  to act corruptly in all they did.
⁸Therefore wait for me," declares the LORD,
  "for the day I will stand up to testify.ᵃ
I have decided to assemble the nations,
  to gather the kingdoms
and to pour out my wrath on them—
  all my fierce anger.
The whole world will be consumed
  by the fire of my jealous anger.

⁹"Then will I purifyᴰ the lips of the peoples,
  that all of them may call on the name of the
    LORD
and serve him shoulder to shoulder.
¹⁰From beyond the rivers of Cushᵇ
  my worshipers, my scattered people,
  will bring me offerings.
¹¹On that day you will not be put to shame
  for all the wrongs you have done to me,
because I will remove from this city
  those who rejoice in their pride.
Never again will you be haughty
  on my holy hill.
¹²But I will leave within you
  the meek and humble,
  who trust in the name of the LORD.
¹³The remnantᴰ of Israel will do no wrong;
  they will speak no lies,
  nor will deceit be found in their mouths.

City of oppressors (3:1)

Verses 2 and 5 indicate that Jerusalem is in view. Verse 2 identifies the city's God as *the LORD,* the special name for Israel's God. Verse 5 speaks of the Lord dwelling *within her,* a reference to God's presence in the Jerusalem temple.

What were the religious leaders doing wrong? (3:4)

These prophets, who claimed to be God's spokespersons, refused to expose the social injustice of Judah's civil leaders. Instead, they proudly claimed that their false assurances of a bright future for Judah were messages from God. The priests, who were supposed to teach God's law to the people, did not follow the proper standards for ritual purity and neglected Sabbath observations.

Does God balance the scales of justice daily? (3:5)

God often allows injustice to sweep through and even temporarily dominate a society. But the point of the verse is not that God provides immediate justice for everyone, but that he regularly promotes justice in the world. Sooner or later he will reward righteousness and pay back all evildoers in full.

Is this the end of the world? (3:8)

See *Is this the end of the world?* (1:2).

ᵃ8 Septuagint and Syriac; Hebrew *will rise up to plunder*   ᵇ10 That is, the upper Nile region

They will eat and lie down
    and no one will make them afraid."

14Sing, O Daughter of Zion^D;
    shout aloud, O Israel!
Be glad and rejoice with all your heart,
    O Daughter of Jerusalem^D!
15The LORD has taken away your punishment,
    he has turned back your enemy.
The LORD, the King of Israel, is with you;
    never again will you fear any harm.
16On that day they will say to Jerusalem,
    "Do not fear, O Zion;
    do not let your hands hang limp.
17The LORD your God is with you,
    he is mighty to save.
He will take great delight in you,
    he will quiet you with his love,
    he will rejoice over you with singing."

18"The sorrows for the appointed feasts
    I will remove from you;
    they are a burden and a reproach^D to
        you.^a
19At that time I will deal
    with all who oppressed you;
I will rescue the lame
    and gather those who have been scattered.
I will give them praise and honor
    in every land where they were put to
        shame.
20At that time I will gather you;
    at that time I will bring you home.
I will give you honor and praise
    among all the peoples of the earth
when I restore your fortunes^b
    before your very eyes,"
                                says the LORD.

---

*a*18 Or *"I will gather you who mourn for the appointed feasts; / your
reproach is a burden to you*   *b*20 Or *I bring back your captives*

Daughter of Zion (3:14)

See *Daughter of Zion* (Isaiah 1:8).

Does God sing? (3:17)

It would seem so, although this also may be a
way of describing God's feelings in terms we
can understand. Still, God can express emotions, including joy, in a variety of ways. The
Hebrew word translated *singing* may even refer
to a shout of delight or happy laughter. This
shows the great joy the Lord will feel when Jerusalem, his chosen city, is repopulated by his
exiled people and the pain of past judgment
has passed once and for all.

How were their feasts a burden and a reproach? (3:18)

Some think this means that during the exile,
while the temple lay in ruins, God's people
would mourn for the feasts they were missing
(see NIV text note). Others believe this indicates the possibility of a closer fellowship with
God once the traditional feasts are replaced by
the reality of God's coming kingdom in Christ.
Some also see this as a picture of the millennial age after the second coming of Christ.

Is this book a warning or an encouragement? (3:15)

Both, as is the case with most Old Testament prophetic books. A prophet's typical audience consisted of a wide variety of people, including both hardened
sinners and faithful followers of the Lord.

The prophets aimed their accusations and warnings at the civil and spiritual leaders
who were violating God's standards and jeopardizing the well-being and future of the nation. Though God intended these hard-hitting messages to shock sinners and drive them
to repentance, the prophets' words often fell on deaf ears.

The positive messages described how God would someday reverse the effects of judgment and restore his people. Zephaniah intended to encourage the followers of the Lord
by assuring them that God would preserve a remnant and ultimately fulfill his promises to
their forefathers. Assured of eventual vindication, the faithful could persevere through
hard times and look past the coming judgment with anticipation (3:16–20).

HAGGAI

Why read this book?

Read Haggai to escape—or, better yet, to avoid—the spiritual doldrums. If you've ever felt discouraged or complacent about your spiritual life, Haggai has encouraging words for you. Though aimed at correcting a particular situation long ago, the lessons of this prophetic book remain relevant for today. When spiritual vitality seems to be ebbing away, Haggai meets the problem head-on.

Who wrote this book?

The prophet Haggai. His name means *my feast,* suggesting that he may have been born during a temple feast.

When was it written?

Haggai delivered his messages in 520 B.C.

What was happening at this time?

Eighteen years before Haggai's prophecy, the Persian king Cyrus had allowed thousands of Jews to return from Babylon to Judah (538 B.C.). Though the Jews had begun rebuilding the temple 16 years earlier, the opposition of neighboring peoples had intimidated them and caused them to abandon their work on the temple.

To whom was it written and why?

Haggai directed his messages specifically to Zerubbabel, the governor of Judah, and to Joshua, the high priest. But since they were the civil and religious leaders, they represented all the Jews who had returned from exile and needed Haggai's message. His purpose was simple and direct: he wanted them to see that they had deprived themselves of God's blessings by allowing the temple building project to lie dormant.

What to look for in Haggai:

Look for the ways in which God rebukes, challenges and encourages his people. Also note how closely connected obedience and blessing are. You will also find prophecies regarding God's coming Messianic kingdom.

When did these things happen?

TIME LINE

	1300BC	1200	1100	1000	900	800	700	600	500	400
Fall of Jerusalem (586 B.C.)										
First return of exiles to Jerusalem (538 B.C.)										
Ministries of Haggai and Zechariah (c.520-480 B.C.)										
Book of Haggai written (c.520 B.C.)										
Completion of temple (516 B.C.)										
Second return to Jerusalem under Ezra (458 B.C.)										
Third return to Jerusalem under Nehemiah (445 B.C.)										
Malachi's ministry (c.440-430 B.C.)										

King Darius (1:1)
One of three rulers with this name mentioned in the Bible. This was Darius I Hystaspes who ruled Persia from 522 to 486 B.C.

First day of the sixth month (1:1)
Each of Haggai's major messages is precisely dated by month and day, perhaps to give the prophecies an official aura. This would have been August 29, 520 B.C.

Zerubbabel . . . and to Joshua (1:1)
See Introduction: *To whom was it written and why?*

Why were the people reluctant to build the temple? (1:2)
When the Jews first returned from exile in Babylon, they had started rebuilding the temple. But they grew discouraged when people in the area opposed their work. They suspended the project and concentrated on building their homes and growing their crops during the following years. By this time, discouragement had turned into complacency and procrastination.

Paneled houses (1:4)
Though royal dwellings sometimes had cedar paneling, these were homes of rank-and-file citizens. Some think *paneled* means *finished* or, more literally, *roofed over*. The NIV also translates this word as *roofing* (1 Kings 6:9), *roofed* (1 Kings 7:3) and *covered* (1 Kings 7:7). The main point does not seem to be that their homes were luxurious, but that they were completed, while the temple of the Lord was not.

Are frustrations God's punishment? (1:6,9)
Frustrations can be part of anyone's life, deserved or not. Sometimes God allows the righteous to suffer in order to test and mature their faith (James 1:2–4). Other times he may discipline people to bring them to repentance. In this case, God's withholding of agricultural and economic blessings signaled his displeasure with their selfish priorities.

Why does God find pleasure in our praise? (1:8)
God desires praise because he desires a relationship with people. He expects his creation to recognize his authority as the Creator. The absence of genuine praise is a sign of a neglected relationship with God.

Twenty-first day of the seventh month (2:1)
October 17, 520 B.C. See *First day of the sixth month* (1:1).

How many people still survived who had seen the former temple? (2:3)
Since the temple had been destroyed in 586 B.C., 66 years before, only a small number of those present could have recalled its glory. Some speculate that Haggai may have been one who remembered the original temple.

A Call to Build the House of the LORD

1 In the second year of King Darius, on the first day of the sixth month, the word of the LORD came through the prophet^D Haggai to Zerubbabel son of Shealtiel, governor of Judah, and to Joshua^a son of Jehozadak, the high priest^D:

2 This is what the LORD Almighty says: "These people say, 'The time has not yet come for the LORD's house to be built.'"

3 Then the word of the LORD came through the prophet Haggai: 4"Is it a time for you yourselves to be living in your paneled houses, while this house remains a ruin?"

5 Now this is what the LORD Almighty says: "Give careful thought to your ways. 6You have planted much, but have harvested little. You eat, but never have enough. You drink, but never have your fill. You put on clothes, but are not warm. You earn wages, only to put them in a purse with holes in it."

7 This is what the LORD Almighty says: "Give careful thought to your ways. 8Go up into the mountains and bring down timber and build the house, so that I may take pleasure in it and be honored," says the LORD. 9"You expected much, but see, it turned out to be little. What you brought home, I blew away. Why?" declares the LORD Almighty. "Because of my house, which remains a ruin, while each of you is busy with his own house. 10Therefore, because of you the heavens have withheld their dew and the earth its crops. 11I called for a drought on the fields and the mountains, on the grain, the new wine^D, the oil and whatever the ground produces, on men and cattle, and on the labor of your hands."

12 Then Zerubbabel son of Shealtiel, Joshua son of Jehozadak, the high priest, and the whole remnant of the people obeyed the voice of the LORD their God and the message of the prophet Haggai, because the LORD their God had sent him. And the people feared the LORD. 13Then Haggai, the LORD's messenger, gave this message of the LORD to the people: "I am with you," declares the LORD. 14So the LORD stirred up the spirit of Zerubbabel son of Shealtiel, governor of Judah, and the spirit of Joshua son of Jehozadak, the high priest, and the spirit of the whole remnant of the people. They came and began to work on the house of the LORD Almighty, their God, 15on the twenty-fourth day of the sixth month in the second year of King Darius.

The Promised Glory of the New House

2 On the twenty-first day of the seventh month, the word of the LORD came through the prophet Haggai: 2"Speak to Zerubbabel son of Shealtiel, governor of Judah, to Joshua son of Jehozadak, the high priest, and to the remnant of the people. Ask them, 3'Who of you is left who saw this house in its former glory^D? How does it look to you now? Does it not seem to you like nothing? 4But now be strong, O Zerubbabel,' declares the LORD. 'Be strong, O Joshua son of Jehozadak, the high priest. Be strong, all you people of the land,' declares the LORD, 'and work. For I am with you,' declares the LORD Almighty. 5'This is what I covenanted^D with you when you came

---

^a1 A variant of *Jeshua*; here and elsewhere in Haggai

out of Egypt. And my Spirit remains among you. Do not fear.'

6"This is what the LORD Almighty says: 'In a little while I will once more shake the heavens and the earth, the sea and the dry land. 7I will shake all nations, and the desired of all nations will come, and I will fill this house with glory^D,' says the LORD Almighty. 8'The silver is mine and the gold is mine,' declares the LORD Almighty. 9'The glory of this present house will be greater than the glory of the former house,' says the LORD Almighty. 'And in this place I will grant peace^D,' declares the LORD Almighty."

Blessings for a Defiled People

10On the twenty-fourth day of the ninth month, in the second year of Darius, the word of the LORD came to the prophet^D Haggai: 11"This is what the LORD Almighty says: 'Ask the priests^D what the law says: 12If a person carries consecrated^D meat in the fold of his garment, and that fold touches some bread or stew, some wine, oil or other food, does it become consecrated?' "

The priests answered, "No."

13Then Haggai said, "If a person defiled by contact with a dead body touches one of these things, does it become defiled?"

"Yes," the priests replied, "it becomes defiled."

14Then Haggai said, " 'So it is with this people and this nation in my sight,' declares the LORD. 'Whatever they do and whatever they offer there is defiled.

15" 'Now give careful thought to this from this day on^a—consider how things were before one stone was laid on another in the LORD's temple. 16When anyone came to a heap of twenty measures, there were only ten. When anyone went to a wine vat to draw fifty measures, there were only twenty. 17I struck all the work of your hands with blight, mildew and hail, yet you did not turn to me,' declares the LORD. 18'From this day on, from this twenty-fourth day of the ninth month, give careful thought to the day when the foundation of the LORD's temple was laid. Give careful thought: 19Is there yet any seed left in the barn? Until now, the vine and the fig tree, the pomegranate and the olive tree have not borne fruit.

" 'From this day on I will bless you.' "

Zerubbabel the LORD's Signet Ring

20The word of the LORD came to Haggai a second time on the twenty-fourth day of the month: 21"Tell Zerubbabel governor of Judah that I will shake the heavens and the earth. 22I will overturn royal thrones and shatter the power of the foreign kingdoms. I will overthrow chariots and their drivers; horses and their riders will fall, each by the sword of his brother.

23" 'On that day,' declares the LORD Almighty, 'I will take you, my servant Zerubbabel son of Shealtiel,' declares the LORD, 'and I will make you like my signet ring^D, for I have chosen you,' declares the LORD Almighty."

How would God *shake the heavens and the earth*? (2:6-7)

This is a picture of judgment, probably describing political and military turmoil which would alter the structure of the world order. Some suggest that Alexander's conquests almost 200 years later were an initial fulfillment of this prophecy. Haggai tells of a final judgment before a Messianic kingdom is established (vv. 20–23).

Why has *a little while* taken so long? (2:6)

Some explain this puzzling phrase by remembering that God's perspective on time is quite different from ours. Others say it refers to the period of time about five centuries prior to the Messianic age. Still others think the phrase was an expression that simply referred to the future in general.

Desired of all nations (2:7)

Many believe this refers to the Messiah, Jesus Christ. Others think it means desirable things (wealth, including silver and gold, v. 8) sent by the nations as tribute to the Lord when he reigns in Jerusalem. See Isaiah 60:5–9 and Zech. 14:14.

Why was defilement contagious? (2:13-14)

According to priestly principles found in the Old Testament law, defilement could be transmitted by both direct and indirect contact (Num. 19:22). This ritual law was apparently an object lesson to teach God's people about the terrible consequences of moral defilement and the harmful effects of sin.

Does God send failure and destruction to get our attention? (2:15-17)

See *Are frustrations God's punishment?* (1:6,9).

Was this a promise that their fortunes would turn? (2:18-19)

Yes. Haggai's audience responded to his message with wholehearted approval (1:12,14) and started to work on the temple again. The Lord here urged them to observe carefully what was about to happen in the coming months, for he would prove his word by blessing them agriculturally as a sign of his restored favor.

What political changes were about to happen? (2:21-22)

These verses actually refer to the final downfall of the earth's kingdoms prior to the establishment of God's Messianic kingdom. Some see power shifts that happened over the next two centuries as a hint of the major changes that would occur in the end times. See **How would God shake the heavens and the earth?** (2:6-7).

Signet ring (2:23)

A ring containing a king's seal or name, with which he authorized documents. The signet ring thus symbolized the king's authority. Zerubbabel, the governor of Judah and a descendant of David, would be God's *signet ring*—his official representative on earth. The prophecy looks beyond Zerubbabel, however, to the coming Messiah. Also see **Signet ring** (Jer. 22:24).

---

^a15 Or *to the days past*

ZECHARIAH

Why read this book?

This book offers spiritual strength and encouragement. Have you ever struggled with your own significance? Perhaps you've felt unappreciated or that your efforts weren't worth much. At times you may have been tempted to quit. Zechariah found a city full of people who felt like this. So he spoke words of encouragement and motivation to them and they picked up the pieces and kept on going. Zechariah's words can do the same for us today.

Who wrote this book?

Zechariah, whose name means *Yahweh remembers*, was a prophet and a priest. He was born in exile; as a young man he returned from Babylon to Jerusalem.

When was it written?

In the eighth month of the second year of Darius (1:1), that is, in October/November, 520 B.C.

What was happening at this time?

God's people had been in captivity in Babylon for 70 years. But when Cyrus came to power he gave permission for people to return to Jerusalem and rebuild the temple. Many chose to stay, but those who returned set about their task with great enthusiasm. They soon encountered many obstacles, however, and became discouraged. Zechariah not only motivated them to finish what they had begun, but he also gave them a vision of God's purposes beyond the restored temple.

What to look for in Zechariah:

Notice the brief history lesson Zechariah gave. It showed the people how God had been working in their lives even when they hadn't realized it. Also watch for Zechariah's insights into what God intended to do for and through the Jews. Though many words and phrases in Zechariah seem obscure, be on the lookout for its many predictions concerning the coming Messiah.

When did these things happen?

TIME LINE	1300вс	1200	1100	1000	900	800	700	600	500	400
Fall of Jerusalem (586 B.C.)										
First return of exiles to Jerusalem (538 B.C.)										
Ministries of Haggai and Zechariah (c.520–480 B.C.)										
Book of Zechariah written (c.520 B.C.)										
Completion of temple (516 B.C.)										
Second return to Jerusalem under Ezra (458 B.C.)										
Third return to Jerusalem under Nehemiah (445 B.C.)										
Malachi's ministry (c.440–430 B.C.)										

A Call to Return to the LORD

1 In the eighth month of the second year of Darius, the word of the LORD came to the prophet[D] Zechariah son of Berekiah, the son of Iddo:

2"The LORD was very angry with your forefathers. 3Therefore tell the people: This is what the LORD Almighty says: 'Return to me,' declares the LORD Almighty, 'and I will return to you,' says the LORD Almighty. 4Do not be like your forefathers, to whom the earlier prophets proclaimed: This is what the LORD Almighty says: 'Turn from your evil ways and your evil practices.' But they would not listen or pay attention to me, declares the LORD. 5Where are your forefathers now? And the prophets, do they live forever? 6But did not my words and my decrees, which I commanded my servants the prophets, overtake your forefathers?

"Then they repented[D] and said, 'The LORD Almighty has done to us what our ways and practices deserve, just as he determined to do.' "

The Man Among the Myrtle Trees

7On the twenty-fourth day of the eleventh month, the month of Shebat, in the second year of Darius, the word of the LORD came to the prophet Zechariah son of Berekiah, the son of Iddo.

8During the night I had a vision[D]—and there before me was a man riding a red horse! He was standing among the myrtle trees in a ravine. Behind him were red, brown and white horses.

9I asked, "What are these, my lord?"

The angel who was talking with me answered, "I will show you what they are."

10Then the man standing among the myrtle trees explained, "They are the ones the LORD has sent to go throughout the earth."

11And they reported to the angel of the LORD, who was standing among the myrtle trees, "We have gone throughout the earth and found the whole world at rest and in peace[D]."

12Then the angel of the LORD said, "LORD Almighty, how long will you withhold mercy[D] from Jerusalem[D] and from the towns of Judah, which you have been angry with these seventy years?" 13So the LORD spoke kind and comforting words to the angel who talked with me.

How did the word of the Lord come to Zechariah? (1:1)
We don't know for sure. Perhaps it came through a vision (see Ezek. 1:1–3), an angel (see Luke 1:28) or an audible voice (see Deut. 4:12,13).

What made God angry? (1:2,15)
The unfaithfulness and disobedience of his chosen people. We should not assume because Zechariah speaks of God being *very angry* after first being only *a little angry* (v. 15), that his anger is vindictive or gets out of control. His anger, like everything else about him, is holy and is never divorced from his grace (1:3).

How do we return to God? (1:3)
This is another way of saying *repent*. To repent means more than being sorry: sometimes we are sorry only because we have been caught or because we dislike the painful consequences of our actions. True repentance means a change of mind which leads to a change of behavior.

Shebat (1:7)
The 11th month in the Hebrew lunar calendar corresponding to our January/February.

Who was the man on the horse? (1:8)
An angel in human form—some say any angel or *the angel of the LORD* (v. 11), others say he may have been Michael.

How did the nations add to the calamity? (1:15)
God had no option but to punish his disobedient, unrepentant people. He had repeatedly warned them of impending judgment and urged them to repent. Judgment eventually came through the Assyrians and the Babylonians. But those nations had gone far beyond what was necessary to punish God's people. Though instruments of God's judgment, they inflicted their own vicious and excessive brand of violence on their unfortunate victims.

Measuring line (1:16)
See *Why measure Jerusalem?* (2:1–2).

What do ancient visions mean to us today? (1:8)

The visions of the Old Testament prophets often were the means by which they received the word of the Lord. Because visions were revelations from God, they can benefit us centuries after they were first given.

First, we can observe what the visions did for the people who originally received them. As they were inspired or challenged, so can we be. Often God reveals principles that apply to many different situations even though specific details may change.

Second, many visions contained revelation from God that transcended immediate circumstances. Prophecy about a coming glorious age, for example, was understood by the original listeners to mean a prosperous future for Israel. But it may also refer to God's eternal plans for his people, and is thus relevant to us today.

How did God intend to *choose Jerusalem*? (1:17)

Some say the language in this verse is symbolic of God's spiritual blessings for his people. Jerusalem never attained the prominence it had once possessed during its glory days. Others suggest that this language hints at future eternal blessings for all those who follow the Lord. God earlier had made it clear to Abraham and David that he had chosen their descendants as his people (Gen. 12:2–3; 2 Samuel 7:9–11). But now, after their descendants' dismal failure to keep the covenant, God reaffirmed his calling and promised his blessing.

Horns that scattered (1:19)

It cannot be stated with certainty who or what the horns are. *Horns* could mean individual rulers or perhaps their nations, maybe Assyria and Babylon. These horns scattered God's people, forcing them to flee and removing them from their homeland. Eventually these horns received similar treatment themselves. The enemies of God's people will never prevail.

Craftsmen (1:20–21)

A peculiar word choice to describe those whose task it is to terrify and defeat. Perhaps Zechariah was thinking of the skill they used in such violent activities. More likely he was completing his analogy: a skilled *craftsman* could remove the horns of an angry bull. God planned to remove the power of those who had terrorized his people.

Why measure Jerusalem? (2:1–2)

Zechariah, like John (in Rev. 21:15–17) was using symbolism to describe the extent of the blessings God's people could expect in the coming kingdom.

Why did the city have no walls? (2:4)

Because the blessing of God would overflow beyond all expectations, and the resulting growth would push the city beyond its limits. But walls would not be needed for protection since the power of God would protect his people (v. 5).

Why did God want them to flee? (2:6)

Some of God's people had remained in Babylon. God challenged them to escape their comfortable lives in a foreign land to return to the promised land. The returning Jews would have traveled around the desert and entered Jerusalem from the north (see *Map 7* at the back of this Bible).

After he has honored me (2:8)

The *he* who will honor God may refer to Zechariah, the angel (v. 3) or to the Messiah.

Why were the people of Israel the *apple of his eye*? (2:8)

This does not imply favoritism on God's part. Rather it reminds us that God chose to work out his purposes for the whole world through this particular people. See *If God doesn't show favoritism, why were the Jews the chosen people?* (Romans 2:10–11) and *Apple of your eye* (Prov. 7:2).

Choose Jerusalem (2:12)

See *How did God intend to choose Jerusalem?* (1:17).

[14]Then the angel who was speaking to me said, "Proclaim this word: This is what the LORD Almighty says: 'I am very jealous for Jerusalem[D] and Zion[D], [15]but I am very angry with the nations that feel secure. I was only a little angry, but they added to the calamity.'

[16]"Therefore, this is what the LORD says: 'I will return to Jerusalem with mercy, and there my house will be rebuilt. And the measuring line[D] will be stretched out over Jerusalem,' declares the LORD Almighty.

[17]"Proclaim further: This is what the LORD Almighty says: 'My towns will again overflow with prosperity, and the LORD will again comfort Zion and choose Jerusalem.'"

Four Horns and Four Craftsmen

[18]Then I looked up—and there before me were four horns! [19]I asked the angel who was speaking to me, "What are these?"

He answered me, "These are the horns that scattered Judah, Israel and Jerusalem."

[20]Then the LORD showed me four craftsmen. [21]I asked, "What are these coming to do?"

He answered, "These are the horns that scattered Judah so that no one could raise his head, but the craftsmen have come to terrify them and throw down these horns of the nations who lifted up their horns against the land of Judah to scatter its people."

A Man With a Measuring Line

2 Then I looked up—and there before me was a man with a measuring line in his hand! [2]I asked, "Where are you going?"

He answered me, "To measure Jerusalem, to find out how wide and how long it is."

[3]Then the angel who was speaking to me left, and another angel came to meet him [4]and said to him: "Run, tell that young man, 'Jerusalem will be a city without walls because of the great number of men and livestock in it. [5]And I myself will be a wall of fire around it,' declares the LORD, 'and I will be its glory[D] within.'

[6]"Come! Come! Flee from the land of the north," declares the LORD, "for I have scattered you to the four winds of heaven," declares the LORD.

[7]"Come, O Zion! Escape, you who live in the Daughter of Babylon!" [8]For this is what the LORD Almighty says: "After he has honored me and has sent me against the nations that have plundered[D] you—for whoever touches you touches the apple of his eye— [9]I will surely raise my hand against them so that their slaves will plunder them.[a] Then you will know that the LORD Almighty has sent me.

[10]"Shout and be glad, O Daughter of Zion. For I am coming, and I will live among you," declares the LORD. [11]"Many nations will be joined with the LORD in that day and will become my people. I will live among you and you will know that the LORD Almighty has sent me to you. [12]The LORD will inherit Judah as his portion in the holy land and will again choose Jerusalem. [13]Be still before the LORD, all mankind, because he has roused himself from his holy dwelling."

---

[a]8,9 Or *says after . . . eye:* [9]"*I . . . plunder them.*"

Clean Garments for the High Priest

3 Then he showed me Joshua*a* the high priest*D* standing before the angel of the LORD, and Satan*b* standing at his right side to accuse him. **2**The LORD said to Satan, "The LORD rebuke you, Satan! The LORD, who has chosen Jerusalem*D*, rebuke you! Is not this man a burning stick snatched from the fire?"

3Now Joshua was dressed in filthy clothes as he stood before the angel. **4**The angel said to those who were standing before him, "Take off his filthy clothes."

Then he said to Joshua, "See, I have taken away your sin, and I will put rich garments on you."

5Then I said, "Put a clean turban on his head." So they put a clean turban on his head and clothed him, while the angel of the LORD stood by.

6The angel of the LORD gave this charge to Joshua: **7**"This is what the LORD Almighty says: 'If you will walk in my ways and keep my requirements, then you will govern my house and have charge of my courts, and I will give you a place among these standing here.

8" 'Listen, O high priest Joshua and your associates seated before you, who are men symbolic of things to come: I am going to bring my servant, the Branch. **9**See, the stone I have set in front of Joshua! There are seven eyes*c* on that one stone, and I will engrave an inscription on it,' says the LORD Almighty, 'and I will remove the sin of this land in a single day.

10" 'In that day each of you will invite his neighbor to sit under his vine and fig tree,' declares the LORD Almighty."

The Gold Lampstand and the Two Olive Trees

4 Then the angel who talked with me returned and wakened me, as a man is wakened from his sleep. **2**He asked me, "What do you see?"

I answered, "I see a solid gold lampstand with a bowl at the top and seven lights on it, with seven channels to the lights. **3**Also there are two olive trees by it, one on the right of the bowl and the other on its left."

4I asked the angel who talked with me, "What are these, my lord?"

5He answered, "Do you not know what these are?"

"No, my lord," I replied.

6So he said to me, "This is the word of the LORD to Zerubbabel: 'Not by might nor by power, but by my Spirit,' says the LORD Almighty.

7"What*d* are you, O mighty mountain? Before Zerubbabel you will become level ground. Then he will bring out the capstone*D* to shouts of 'God bless it! God bless it!' "

8Then the word of the LORD came to me: **9**"The hands of Zerubbabel have laid the foundation of this temple; his hands will also complete it. Then you will know that the LORD Almighty has sent me to you.

10"Who despises the day of small things? Men will rejoice when they see the plumb line in the hand of Zerubbabel.

"(These seven are the eyes of the LORD, which range throughout the earth.)"

11Then I asked the angel, "What are these two olive trees on the right and the left of the lampstand?"

12Again I asked him, "What are these two olive

Be still (2:13)
People should enter God's presence with a great sense of awe, respect and wonder. This means much more than merely being quiet.

Joshua the high priest (3:1)
Satan probably accused Joshua as the representative of the entire nation.

Why is Satan allowed to come before God? (3:1)
Satan is the accuser and confronts God about the behavior and spiritual condition of God's people. Also see *Why did Satan mingle with God's angels?* (Job 2:1).

A burning stick (3:2)
Israel—like a stick pulled out of the fire—had been snatched from the judgment of God which was accomplished through their years of captivity in Babylon.

Why the filthy clothes? (3:3)
The filthy clothes represented the sins of the people. In place of the filthy clothes, Joshua (representing the nation) would be clothed in splendid garments—a picture of righteousness (v. 4). Also see Isaiah 64:6.

What would Joshua govern? (3:7)
The high priest was responsible for overseeing the orderly activities of the temple. In the same way, the cleansed and restored people of God would oversee the life of the redeemed and even judge the nations.

The Branch (3:8)
The Servant of God, called a *Branch* to suggest the fruitfulness of his life. This same analogy for the Messiah was used by others as well (see Isaiah 4:2; Jer. 23:5).

Why sit under a vine and fig tree? (3:10)
In ancient Israel this was a picture of the good life. It was their idea of heaven on earth and therefore spoke of abundant blessing.

What does the lampstand symbolize? (4:2–3)
The lampstand symbolized the bright shining testimony of the people of God, giving glory to God. The repetition of the number *seven* and the fact that the lampstand was connected to living olive trees suggest the idea of completeness. Also see Exodus 25:31–40.

Zerubbabel (4:6)
The governor of Jerusalem. He returned with the exiles and was leading a disheartened people. Also see Ezra 3:2,8.

My Spirit (4:6)
The overburdened governor needed to be reminded that God's work must flow from the Spirit of God.

Which mountain was going to be leveled? (4:7)
Most think the mountain referred to some kind of opposition to Zerubbabel's work—perhaps human enemies such as Tobiah and Sanballat, or perhaps Satan, the Persians or the antichrist.

---

a1 A variant of *Jeshua*; here and elsewhere in Zechariah   *b1* *Satan* means *accuser.*   *c9* Or *facets*   *d7* Or *Who*

The day of small things (4:10)

The rebuilders of Jerusalem had been thoroughly discouraged and had come to the conclusion that their best efforts amounted to nothing significant. They were overlooking the fact that the Lord was still at work.

Does the Lord have seven eyes? (4:10)

God is sometimes revealed with human features and characteristics. On other occasions he is spoken about in symbolic terms. Here the seven eyes of the Lord suggest he watches all things.

Who were the two anointed ones? (4:14)

Joshua and Zerubbabel (symbolized by the two olive trees). They represented the priestly and kingly branches of Israel through whom God's purposes were being worked out.

A flying scroll (5:1)

This vision to Zechariah suggests that news of God's coming judgment was for all to see and hear. Like a huge billboard in the sky, God was announcing swift and certain judgment.

Which land did God curse? (5:3)

It's possible to see this not only as judgment against Zechariah's contemporaries but also as judgment against all who break God's law. Also see Gal. 3:10.

Why picture wickedness as a woman? (5:7–8)

The people of God are often portrayed in the feminine gender, particularly in their relationship to God. So it is not surprising for their unrighteousness to be described in feminine terms. This was a literary tool meant simply to illustrate the wickedness of the people—men as well as women.

Why have a lead cover on a basket? (5:7–8)

Perhaps to show the immensity of sin and the power necessary to restrain it.

Who were these two women? (5:9)

These women with wings suggest angelic beings. Human agents such as the Babylonians (v. 11) were not the only ones carrying out God's purposes. There were also spiritual agents.

Why set the basket down in Babylonia? (5:11)

The Hebrew word translated *Babylonia* is *Shinar*, the area where, at the tower of Babel, the human race had proudly rebelled against God (see Gen. 11:2). Taking the wickedness back to these roots may suggest that sin will finally be banished so righteousness can reign.

Do the colors of these horses mean anything? (6:2–3)

The colored horses pulling the chariots (which are symbols of power) suggest the powerful forces through which judgment comes: red for war, black for famine, white for triumph and dappled for plagues (see also Rev. 6:1–8).

Spirits of heaven (6:5)

The word translated *spirits* also means *winds* —perhaps suggesting God's judgment will cover the whole world.

branches beside the two gold pipes that pour out golden oil?"

¹³He replied, "Do you not know what these are?"

"No, my lord," I said.

¹⁴So he said, "These are the two who are anointed[D] to[a] serve the Lord of all the earth."

The Flying Scroll

5 I looked again—and there before me was a flying scroll!

²He asked me, "What do you see?"

I answered, "I see a flying scroll, thirty feet long and fifteen feet wide.[b]"

³And he said to me, "This is the curse that is going out over the whole land; for according to what it says on one side, every thief will be banished, and according to what it says on the other, everyone who swears falsely will be banished. ⁴The LORD Almighty declares, 'I will send it out, and it will enter the house of the thief and the house of him who swears falsely by my name. It will remain in his house and destroy it, both its timbers and its stones.'"

The Woman in a Basket

⁵Then the angel who was speaking to me came forward and said to me, "Look up and see what this is that is appearing."

⁶I asked, "What is it?"

He replied, "It is a measuring basket.[c]" And he added, "This is the iniquity[d] of the people throughout the land."

⁷Then the cover of lead was raised, and there in the basket sat a woman! ⁸He said, "This is wickedness," and he pushed her back into the basket and pushed the lead cover down over its mouth.

⁹Then I looked up—and there before me were two women, with the wind in their wings! They had wings like those of a stork, and they lifted up the basket between heaven and earth.

¹⁰"Where are they taking the basket?" I asked the angel who was speaking to me.

¹¹He replied, "To the country of Babylonia[e] to build a house for it. When it is ready, the basket will be set there in its place."

Four Chariots

6 I looked up again—and there before me were four chariots coming out from between two mountains—mountains of bronze! ²The first chariot had red horses, the second black, ³the third white, and the fourth dappled—all of them powerful. ⁴I asked the angel who was speaking to me, "What are these, my lord?"

⁵The angel answered me, "These are the four spirits[f] of heaven, going out from standing in the presence of the Lord of the whole world. ⁶The one with the black horses is going toward the north country, the one with the white horses toward the west,[g] and the one with the dappled horses toward the south."

⁷When the powerful horses went out, they were straining to go throughout the earth. And he said, "Go throughout the earth!" So they went throughout the earth.

a14 Or *two who bring oil and*   b2 Hebrew *twenty cubits long and ten cubits wide* (about 9 meters long and 4.5 meters wide)
c6 Hebrew *an ephah*; also in verses 7-11   d6 Or *appearance*
e11 Hebrew *Shinar*   f5 Or *winds*   g6 Or *horses after them*

8Then he called to me, "Look, those going toward the north country have given my Spirit*a* rest in the land of the north."

A Crown for Joshua

9The word of the LORD came to me: **10**"Take ⌐silver and gold¬ from the exiles*D* Heldai, Tobijah and Jedaiah, who have arrived from Babylon. Go the same day to the house of Josiah son of Zephaniah. **11**Take the silver and gold and make a crown, and set it on the head of the high priest*D*, Joshua son of Jehozadak. **12**Tell him this is what the LORD Almighty says: 'Here is the man whose name is the Branch, and he will branch out from his place and build the temple of the LORD. **13**It is he who will build the temple of the LORD, and he will be clothed with majesty and will sit and rule on his throne. And he will be a priest on his throne. And there will be harmony between the two.' **14**The crown will be given to Heldai,*b* Tobijah, Jedaiah and Hen*c* son of Zephaniah as a memorial in the temple of the LORD. **15**Those who are far away will come and help to build the temple of the LORD, and you will know that the LORD Almighty has sent me to you. This will happen if you diligently obey the LORD your God."

Justice and Mercy, Not Fasting

7 In the fourth year of King Darius, the word of the LORD came to Zechariah on the fourth day of the ninth month, the month of Kislev. **2**The people of Bethel had sent Sharezer and Regem-Melech, together with their men, to entreat the LORD **3**by asking the priests of the house of the LORD Almighty and the prophets*D*, "Should I mourn and fast in the fifth month, as I have done for so many years?"

4Then the word of the LORD Almighty came to me: **5**"Ask all the people of the land and the priests, 'When you fasted and mourned in the fifth and seventh months for the past seventy years, was it really for me that you fasted? **6**And when you were eating and drinking, were you not just feasting for yourselves? **7**Are these not the

---

*a*8 Or spirit   *b*14 Syriac; Hebrew *Helem*   *c*14 Or and the gracious one, the

---

What happened to the red horse? (6:6)
We don't know. It may be that God is holding some judgment in reserve. Or it could be that when symbolism is used, all details do not necessarily have to fit logically together.

How did God's Spirit find rest in the north? (6:8)
The *north country* speaks of Babylon. See **Why did God want them to flee?** (2:6). In the Bible Babylon often represents the rule of evil. This may mean that God's Spirit found peace because Babylon was finally judged.

Heldai, Tobijah and Jedaiah (6:10)
These men were presumably envoys from the Jews who had remained in Babylon. We have no further knowledge of them.

The Branch (6:12)
See **The Branch** (3:8).

Could a priest also be a king in Israel? (6:13)
Priests had to belong to the tribe of Levi; kings were to come from the line of David (from the tribe of Judah). A priest, therefore, could not also be a king. This was apparently a symbolic statement that pointed to the Messiah. Also see **The order of Melchizedek** (Heb. 5:6,10).

What harmony is meant? (6:13)
The harmony between the priest and the king or perhaps between the two functions. The Messiah would bring both offices together.

Why give the crown to four men? (6:14)
This was a symbolic action. The crown was given in their name to be put on display as a memorial in the temple—a sign of their alliance with the Jews in Jerusalem (v. 15). Perhaps this also implies that everyone, near and far, can participate in the blessings of the Messiah. See Gen. 12:3; Matt. 28:19.

Kislev (7:1)
A month in the Hebrew calendar corresponding to December.

When does worship become insincere ritual? (7:5–6)

Traditions have great value because they preserve the lessons of the past. They remind us of things we might otherwise forget. While living in a foreign land, surrounded by foreign culture and language, the Jews could have easily forgotten the important events of their history. Future generations could have missed out on how significantly God had dealt with their ancestors. But they used rituals and traditions to avoid historical ignorance. They commemorated the past so they could remember the lessons learned.

Unfortunately, the rituals "fossilized" over time. Eventually, people were celebrating only the form and forgetting the reality behind it. Their fasting appeared meaningful but had no inner substance.

When this, or something similar happens, a worship activity becomes an empty ritual, or worse, a ritual with the wrong meaning attached to it. Often this can occur as a slow erosion of values.

Why fast year after year? (7:3-5)

Because the annual fast memorialized significant events in Israel's history—just as our national holidays do today. The fifth month recalled the burning of the temple (2 Kings
25:8-10). The seventh month marked the assassination of Gedaliah (2 Kings 25:22-25).

Who refused to pay attention? (7:11-12)

God's people. This had been an ongoing problem throughout their history. Now, after their
return from exile to Jerusalem, Zechariah reminded the people of their ancestors' religious
decline. Perhaps they would heed the warning
and avoid repeating history.

At what point does God stop listening? (7:13)

There comes a point when God allows those
who refuse to listen to him to be handed over
to the consequences of their own actions. If
they repent of their ways and are ready to listen to God, then he will listen to them. If they
go without repenting long enough, however,
judgment may become irrevocable. Also see article: *When does God refuse to hear our
prayers?* (Jer. 11:11).

Why couldn't anyone come or go? (7:14)

Their land had become so devastated that the
necessities for travel were missing. There was
no place to stay and no food to eat. Everywhere people were vulnerable to the elements
and to robbers. No one traveled because their
civilization had disintegrated.

Burning with jealousy (8:2)

When we are jealous, we are usually envious.
When God is jealous, he is zealous; to put it
another way, God feels deeply and intensely
about something. In this instance, he is zealously committed to Israel. He will allow nothing
to interfere with his plans for his people, whatever it takes to get them where he wants them.

Has God returned to dwell in Jerusa-lem? (8:3-5)

Some believe this happened when the temple
was rebuilt. But others point out that Jerusalem could hardly be called *the City of Truth* at
that time. They anticipate a future millennial
age when yet another temple will be built and
the descriptions of Jerusalem will be literally
fulfilled. Still others see a figurative fulfillment
in Paul's analogy of the church—God is
present in his temple because his Spirit dwells
in the church (1 Cor. 3:16).

The east and the west (8:7)

Since Babylon is represented in this prophecy
as *the north country* (6:8), this probably refers
to a worldwide gathering, something other than
the return from exile in Babylon.

How long had it been since the foun-dations were laid? (8:9)

The work of restoration began in *the first year
of Cyrus* (Ezra 1:1), around 535 B.C. After a
long delay due to various discouragements,
the work was restarted in the *second year of
Darius* (1:1), around 521 B.C. It had been about
14 years since the foundations had been laid.

words the LORD proclaimed through the earlier prophets[D] when Jerusalem[D] and its surrounding towns were
at rest and prosperous, and the Negev[D] and the western
foothills were settled?' "

8And the word of the LORD came again to Zechariah:
9"This is what the LORD Almighty says: 'Administer true
justice; show mercy[D] and compassion to one another.
10Do not oppress the widow or the fatherless, the alien[D]
or the poor. In your hearts do not think evil of each other.'

11"But they refused to pay attention; stubbornly they
turned their backs and stopped up their ears. **12**They
made their hearts as hard as flint and would not listen to
the law or to the words that the LORD Almighty had sent
by his Spirit through the earlier prophets. So the LORD
Almighty was very angry.

13" 'When I called, they did not listen; so when they
called, I would not listen,' says the LORD Almighty. **14**'I
scattered them with a whirlwind among all the nations,
where they were strangers. The land was left so desolate
behind them that no one could come or go. This is how
they made the pleasant land desolate.' "

The LORD Promises to Bless Jerusalem

8 Again the word of the LORD Almighty came to me.
2This is what the LORD Almighty says: "I am very jealous for Zion[D]; I am burning with jealousy for her."

3This is what the LORD says: "I will return to Zion and
dwell in Jerusalem. Then Jerusalem will be called the
City of Truth, and the mountain of the LORD Almighty will
be called the Holy Mountain."

4This is what the LORD Almighty says: "Once again men
and women of ripe old age will sit in the streets of Jerusalem, each with cane in hand because of his age. **5**The
city streets will be filled with boys and girls playing
there."

6This is what the LORD Almighty says: "It may seem
marvelous to the remnant[D] of this people at that time,
but will it seem marvelous to me?" declares the LORD Almighty.

7This is what the LORD Almighty says: "I will save my
people from the countries of the east and the west. **8**I will
bring them back to live in Jerusalem; they will be my
people, and I will be faithful and righteous[D] to them as
their God."

9This is what the LORD Almighty says: "You who now
hear these words spoken by the prophets who were
there when the foundation was laid for the house of the
LORD Almighty, let your hands be strong so that the temple may be built. **10**Before that time there were no wages
for man or beast. No one could go about his business safely because of his enemy, for I had turned every man
against his neighbor. **11**But now I will not deal with the
remnant of this people as I did in the past," declares the
LORD Almighty.

12"The seed will grow well, the vine will yield its fruit,
the ground will produce its crops, and the heavens will
drop their dew. I will give all these things as an inheritance to the remnant of this people. **13**As you have been
an object of cursing among the nations, O Judah and Israel, so will I save you, and you will be a blessing. Do not
be afraid, but let your hands be strong."

14This is what the LORD Almighty says: "Just as I had determined to bring disaster upon you and showed no pity
when your fathers angered me," says the LORD Almighty,

15"so now I have determined to do good again to Jerusalem^D and Judah. Do not be afraid. 16These are the things you are to do: Speak the truth to each other, and render true and sound judgment in your courts; 17do not plot evil against your neighbor, and do not love to swear falsely. I hate all this," declares the LORD.

18Again the word of the LORD Almighty came to me. 19This is what the LORD Almighty says: "The fasts of the fourth, fifth, seventh and tenth months will become joyful and glad occasions and happy festivals for Judah. Therefore love truth and peace^D."

20This is what the LORD Almighty says: "Many peoples and the inhabitants of many cities will yet come, 21and the inhabitants of one city will go to another and say, 'Let us go at once to entreat the LORD and seek the LORD Almighty. I myself am going.' 22And many peoples and powerful nations will come to Jerusalem to seek the LORD Almighty and to entreat him."

23This is what the LORD Almighty says: "In those days ten men from all languages and nations will take firm hold of one Jew^D by the hem of his robe and say, 'Let us go with you, because we have heard that God is with you.' "

Judgment on Israel's Enemies
An Oracle^D

9 The word of the LORD is against the land of Hadrach
and will rest upon Damascus—
for the eyes of men and all the tribes of Israel
are on the LORD—^a
2and upon Hamath too, which borders on it,
and upon Tyre and Sidon, though they are
very skillful.
3Tyre has built herself a stronghold^D;
she has heaped up silver like dust,
and gold like the dirt of the streets.
4But the Lord will take away her possessions
and destroy her power on the sea,
and she will be consumed by fire.
5Ashkelon will see it and fear;
Gaza will writhe in agony,
and Ekron too, for her hope will wither.
Gaza will lose her king
and Ashkelon will be deserted.
6Foreigners will occupy Ashdod,
and I will cut off the pride of the
Philistines.
7I will take the blood from their mouths,
the forbidden food from between their
teeth.
Those who are left will belong to our God
and become leaders in Judah,
and Ekron will be like the Jebusites.
8But I will defend my house
against marauding forces.
Never again will an oppressor overrun my
people,
for now I am keeping watch.

^a1 Or Damascus. / For the eye of the LORD is on all mankind, / as well as on the tribes of Israel,

Why schedule so many fasts? (8:19)
Each fast commemorated days of national mourning. There were many fasts because the people of Israel had much to mourn in their history. In the fourth month they remembered when the Babylonians broke through the walls of Jerusalem. The tenth month reminded them of the start of the siege against the city. See article: *When does worship become insincere ritual?* (7:5–6).

How could fasts be turned into feasts? (8:19)
Amos had predicted that feasts would be turned into fasts because of the nation's sin (Amos 8:10). But God's judgment would be replaced by his grace. Fasts became feasts by his divine power. Likewise, Isaiah had promised *the oil of gladness instead of mourning, and a garment of praise instead of a spirit of despair* (Isaiah 61:3).

When will people turn to the Jews for spiritual blessings? (8:23)
A literal understanding of this prophecy would look for a future fulfillment in a millennial kingdom. Another interpretation, however, sees this as a picture of the church, as the *Israel of God* (Gal. 6:16), bringing people to God.

Oracle (9:1)
An announcement from God. The word often suggests unwelcome news or judgment.

Why were the nations judged? (9:1–6)
God holds people accountable for their sin— no matter what it might be. In this case, Israel's enemies had taken advantage of God's people when they were down. Though God allowed his people to be vulnerable, he did not approve of the vicious and arrogant attitudes and actions of their enemies. They would have to answer for their pride.

Why were they eating bloody meat? (9:7)
This probably refers to their idolatrous practices. The Old Testament law prohibited God's people from eating blood (Lev. 3:17). But this phrase may be a figure of speech to describe the way they "devoured" God's people.

Who are *those . . . left*, who would become leaders? (9:7)
Even in judgment God remembers to be merciful. Even the idolatrous tribal groups of Canaan would be given the opportunity to repent of their ways and become part of the people of God. Because God's people would rise again, Ekron, a Philistine city, would be conquered like the Jebusites—the former inhabitants of Jerusalem—had been.

Never again (9:8)
Jerusalem has been overrun often since the days of Zechariah. Some therefore understand the prophecy to mean the security of Jerusalem in a future millennial age. Others think it may suggest the impregnability of the church (Matt. 16:18).

SCRIPTURE LINK (9:9) *Your King comes . . . riding on a donkey*

Quoted by the writers of the Gospels when Christ fulfilled this prophecy literally. See Matt. 21:5; John 12:15.

Why have a king on a donkey? (9:9–10)

Why not have a king on a war-horse? Because this would be a completely different kind of king from any the world had ever known. Zechariah paints a picture of the coming king's humility and grace. By contrast, the arrival of a foreign dignitary in those days often presented arrogance and terror.

Waterless pit (9:11)

Dry cisterns were customarily used as places of imprisonment—as Joseph, to name one, discovered (Gen. 37:22).

Prisoners of hope (9:12)

The people of God have always been and must continue to be people of *hope*, confident that God will ultimately triumph. Even in difficult circumstances believers should always affirm that their hope is in the Lord (Psalm 39:7).

When will the Lord appear over them? (9:14)

The Lord's defense of his people is spelled out in poetically dramatic language. While it makes for a vivid picture, it doesn't really give us much to determine a specific time. We can say, however, that God is always ready to protect his loved ones.

How could a battle be won with slingshots? (9:15)

With God all things are possible. With God's help even primitive weapons could overcome swords and spears. Some think this means that the Lord's people would "overcome the slingstones"—meaning they would be protected from the slingshots of the enemy.

SCRIPTURE LINK (9:15) *Bowl used for sprinkling*

See tabernacle customs in Exodus 27:1–3.

Is God to blame for storms? (10:1)

God certainly *makes the storm clouds*—he has created all things, including weather patterns. If we accept the blessings of a needed downpour, we have to face the fierceness unleashed by a storm. It's difficult, however, to understand why God allows suffering and damage to be caused by storms that he created. All we can say is that though God created all things good (Gen. 1:31), suffering and sin have marred God's creation. Also see article: **Why does God send calamity?** (Lam. 3:38).

What idols and diviners were tempting God's people? (10:2)

Israel had an apparent weakness for idols (probably household gods) and the smooth talk of diviners, despite God's continual rebukes. Abraham had come from a family of idol worshipers and his descendants frequently seemed to revert to those old ways. It didn't much matter which specific idols they looked to. They adopted idols depending on what gods were currently popular. Human nature has remained pretty much the same down through the ages.

The Coming of Zion's King

[9]Rejoice greatly, O Daughter of Zion[D]!
    Shout, Daughter of Jerusalem[D]!
  See, your king[a] comes to you,
    righteous[D] and having salvation[D],
    gentle and riding on a donkey,
    on a colt, the foal of a donkey.
[10]I will take away the chariots from Ephraim
    and the war-horses from Jerusalem,
    and the battle bow will be broken.
  He will proclaim peace[D] to the nations.
    His rule will extend from sea to sea
    and from the River[b] to the ends of the
      earth.[c]
[11]As for you, because of the blood of my
    covenant[D] with you,
  I will free your prisoners from the waterless
    pit.
[12]Return to your fortress, O prisoners of hope;
    even now I announce that I will restore twice
      as much to you.
[13]I will bend Judah as I bend my bow
    and fill it with Ephraim.
  I will rouse your sons, O Zion,
    against your sons, O Greece,
    and make you like a warrior's sword.

The LORD Will Appear

[14]Then the LORD will appear over them;
    his arrow will flash like lightning.
  The Sovereign LORD will sound the trumpet;
    he will march in the storms of the south,
[15] and the LORD Almighty will shield them.
  They will destroy
    and overcome with slingstones.
  They will drink and roar as with wine;
    they will be full like a bowl
    used for sprinkling[d] the corners of the altar.
[16]The LORD their God will save them on that day
    as the flock of his people.
  They will sparkle in his land
    like jewels in a crown.
[17]How attractive and beautiful they will be!
    Grain will make the young men thrive,
    and new wine[D] the young women.

The LORD Will Care for Judah

10 Ask the LORD for rain in the springtime;
    it is the LORD who makes the storm clouds.
  He gives showers of rain to men,
    and plants of the field to everyone.
[2]The idols[D] speak deceit,
    diviners see visions[D] that lie;
  they tell dreams that are false,
    they give comfort in vain.
  Therefore the people wander like sheep
    oppressed for lack of a shepherd.

[3]"My anger burns against the shepherds,
    and I will punish the leaders;

---

[a]9 Or *King*   [b]10 That is, the Euphrates   [c]10 Or *the end of the land*   [d]15 Or *bowl, / like*

for the LORD Almighty will care
   for his flock, the house of Judah,
   and make them like a proud horse in battle.
⁴From Judah will come the cornerstone,
   from him the tent peg,
   from him the battle bow,
   from him every ruler.
⁵Together they*ᵃ* will be like mighty men
   trampling the muddy streets in battle.
Because the LORD is with them,
   they will fight and overthrow the horsemen.

⁶"I will strengthen the house of Judah
   and save the house of Joseph.
I will restore them
   because I have compassion on them.
They will be as though
   I had not rejected them,
for I am the LORD their God
   and I will answer them.
⁷The Ephraimites will become like mighty men,
   and their hearts will be glad as with wine.
Their children will see it and be joyful;
   their hearts will rejoice in the LORD.
⁸I will signal for them
   and gather them in.
Surely I will redeemᴰ them;
   they will be as numerous as before.
⁹Though I scatter them among the peoples,
   yet in distant lands they will remember me.
They and their children will survive,
   and they will return.
¹⁰I will bring them back from Egypt
   and gather them from Assyria.
I will bring them to Gilead and Lebanon,
   and there will not be room enough for them.
¹¹They will pass through the sea of trouble;
   the surging sea will be subdued
   and all the depths of the Nile will dry up.
Assyria's pride will be brought down

ᵃ4,5 Or ruler, all of them together. / ⁵They

Cornerstone (10:4)

A name for the Messiah that suggests his key role in the construction of God's plan of salvation (1 Peter 2:6). He is also the *nail*, the one on whom God's glory hangs, as well as the *battle bow* through whom God will ultimately triumph.

Ephraimites (10:7)

Ephraim was a son of Joseph and later became a tribe in Israel (Gen. 48:5). It became a synonym for the northern kingdom of Israel, distinct from the southern kingdom (v. 6).

Should wine make our hearts glad? (10:7)

See *Does Proverbs teach abstinence from alcohol?* (Prov. 20:1).

What *signal* will God send to gather his people? (10:8)

The word literally meant to *whistle* (see, for example, Isaiah 5:26). It may also have been used to speak of hissing or buzzing—perhaps like swarming bees. Shepherds would whistle and call for their flocks, gathering them in as the Lord intended to do with his people.

Sea of trouble (10:11)

Probably a reminder that, just as the Lord had brought the Israelites out of Egypt through the Red Sea, still he would allow nothing to interfere with his plans for his people.

Why destroy Lebanon? (11:1-3)

Lebanon, Bashan and Jordan represented the areas at the extremities of Israel (see *Conquest of Canaan* on page 301). Some think this was figurative language to describe God's punishment of Israel's enemies—from far away Assyria and Egypt (10:11) right up to Israel's borders. Others think this may have had a more literal fulfillment when Palestine rejected the Messiah and was subsequently devastated by Rome (A.D. 70).

Who was marked for slaughter? (11:4)

Israel was often referred to as a flock (Isaiah 40:11; Ezek. 34:2, for instance). But for the last number of years, God's flock had been singled out for slaughter by its enemies.

Why pray for rain? (10:1)

Zechariah urged the people of Israel to declare their total dependence upon the Lord. Surrounding them were people who counted on false gods for their daily needs—crops, harvest and food at the top of the list. But by depending on the Lord to provide for them, the Israelites proved their independence from the idols of the other nations (v. 2).

Israel had learned to recognize that a fruitful harvest was evidence of God's blessing; a poor crop was sign of his judgment. Since the Jews had just returned from exile in Babylon, Zechariah was intent on establishing their allegiance to the Lord from the beginning by teaching them to trust in him for everything in their lives.

This does not imply that they thought he would withhold rain if they did not pray. It was simply their way of showing that they relied totally on God. Though God sends rain on both the righteous and the unrighteous (Matt. 5:45), acknowledging him as our provider is one of the basic ways of honoring God as Lord.

Why give names to pieces of wood? (11:7)

These were tools used by the shepherd to lead the flock. The shepherd would lead the people with *favor* and *unity*—gently, with grace to bring them together with God. This is most likely a picture of the ministry of the coming Messiah, the Good Shepherd. Others, however, think this spoke primarily of the way God would care for his people in Zechariah's day.

Which three shepherds lost their jobs? (11:8)

At least 40 different suggestions have been made concerning the identity of these shepherds. It's possible that they represented the prophets, priests and kings who were the leaders—shepherds of Israel.

Was this cannibalism? (11:9)

With his experience perhaps paralleling that of the coming Messiah, Zechariah seems to have lost his patience with the leaders of the people. Possibly the language is figurative: disputes and fighting can be characterized as backbiting—"eating one another up."

What covenant had been made with all the nations? (11:10)

If the staff *Favor* was designed to protect the flock from external attack, breaking it would have signaled that they were now left vulnerable. This suggests that the covenant was perhaps designed to protect Israel from attack.

SCRIPTURE LINK (11:12–13) *Thirty pieces of silver*

Matthew borrowed these words, crediting them to Jeremiah, to describe what Judas did to Jesus. See Matt. 26:15; 27:9–10.

How was the brotherhood between Israel and Judah broken? (11:14)

This was likely a prediction of the breakdown and dispersion of the Jews during the era of the second temple when the Romans finally decimated the land (A.D. 70).

Worthless shepherd (11:17)

Variously identified as Herod, Agrippa or the antichrist. Others see this as a false Messiah—one whose promises for God's people amount to nothing.

Oracle (12:1)

See *Oracle* (9:1).

Cup that sends ... peoples reeling (12:2)

Drinking from a cup was a metaphor in Zechariah's time similar to our expression, "Take your medicine" (see Isaiah 51:17). In this case, the nations opposed to Jerusalem would be sent *reeling* when they drank the concoction prepared for them in Jerusalem.

Why would all the nations of the world attack Jerusalem? (12:3)

Some think this is a prediction concerning Armageddon, the last major battle of history. See article: *Armageddon* (Rev. 16:16). Others see this in a figurative sense, referring to the church, which is constantly besieged by enemies but never overthrown.

and Egypt's scepter[D] will pass away.
¹²I will strengthen them in the LORD
    and in his name they will walk,"
                        declares the LORD.

11 Open your doors, O Lebanon,
    so that fire may devour your cedars!
²Wail, O pine tree, for the cedar has fallen;
    the stately trees are ruined!
Wail, oaks of Bashan;
    the dense forest has been cut down!
³Listen to the wail of the shepherds;
    their rich pastures are destroyed!
Listen to the roar of the lions;
    the lush thicket of the Jordan is ruined!

Two Shepherds

⁴This is what the LORD my God says: "Pasture the flock marked for slaughter. ⁵Their buyers slaughter them and go unpunished. Those who sell them say, 'Praise the LORD, I am rich!' Their own shepherds do not spare them. ⁶For I will no longer have pity on the people of the land," declares the LORD. "I will hand everyone over to his neighbor and his king. They will oppress the land, and I will not rescue them from their hands."

⁷So I pastured the flock marked for slaughter, particularly the oppressed of the flock. Then I took two staffs and called one Favor and the other Union, and I pastured the flock. ⁸In one month I got rid of the three shepherds.

The flock detested me, and I grew weary of them ⁹and said, "I will not be your shepherd. Let the dying die, and the perishing perish. Let those who are left eat one another's flesh."

¹⁰Then I took my staff called Favor and broke it, revoking the covenant[D] I had made with all the nations. ¹¹It was revoked on that day, and so the afflicted[D] of the flock who were watching me knew it was the word of the LORD.

¹²I told them, "If you think it best, give me my pay; but if not, keep it." So they paid me thirty pieces of silver. ¹³And the LORD said to me, "Throw it to the potter"—the handsome price at which they priced me! So I took the thirty pieces of silver and threw them into the house of the LORD to the potter. ¹⁴Then I broke my second staff called Union, breaking the brotherhood between Judah and Israel.

¹⁵Then the LORD said to me, "Take again the equipment of a foolish shepherd. ¹⁶For I am going to raise up a shepherd over the land who will not care for the lost, or seek the young, or heal the injured, or feed the healthy, but will eat the meat of the choice sheep, tearing off their hoofs.

¹⁷"Woe to the worthless shepherd,
    who deserts the flock!
May the sword strike his arm and his right eye!
    May his arm be completely withered,
    his right eye totally blinded!"

Jerusalem's Enemies to Be Destroyed

An Oracle[D]

12 This is the word of the LORD concerning Israel. The LORD, who stretches out the heavens, who lays the foundation of the earth, and who forms the spirit of man

within him, declares: 2"I am going to make Jerusalem⁰ a cup that sends all the surrounding peoples reeling. Judah will be besieged as well as Jerusalem. 3On that day, when all the nations of the earth are gathered against her, I will make Jerusalem an immovable rock for all the nations. All who try to move it will injure themselves. 4On that day I will strike every horse with panic and its rider with madness," declares the LORD. "I will keep a watchful eye over the house of Judah, but I will blind all the horses of the nations. 5Then the leaders of Judah will say in their hearts, 'The people of Jerusalem are strong, because the LORD Almighty is their God.'

6"On that day I will make the leaders of Judah like a firepot in a woodpile, like a flaming torch among sheaves. They will consume right and left all the surrounding peoples, but Jerusalem will remain intact in her place.

7"The LORD will save the dwellings of Judah first, so that the honor of the house of David and of Jerusalem's inhabitants may not be greater than that of Judah. 8On that day the LORD will shield those who live in Jerusalem, so that the feeblest among them will be like David, and the house of David will be like God, like the Angel of the LORD going before them. 9On that day I will set out to destroy all the nations that attack Jerusalem.

Mourning for the One They Pierced

10"And I will pour out on the house of David and the inhabitants of Jerusalem a spirit* of grace and supplication. They will look on* me, the one they have pierced, and they will mourn for him as one mourns for an only child, and grieve bitterly for him as one grieves for a firstborn⁰ son. 11On that day the weeping in Jerusalem will be great, like the weeping of Hadad Rimmon in the plain of Megiddo. 12The land will mourn, each clan by itself, with their wives by themselves: the clan of the house of David and their wives, the clan of the house of Nathan and their wives, 13the clan of the house of Levi and their wives, the clan of Shimei and their wives, 14and all the rest of the clans and their wives.

Cleansing From Sin

13 "On that day a fountain will be opened to the house of David and the inhabitants of Jerusalem, to cleanse them from sin and impurity.

2"On that day, I will banish the names of the idols⁰ from the land, and they will be remembered no more," declares the LORD Almighty. "I will remove both the prophets⁰ and the spirit of impurity from the land. 3And if anyone still prophesies, his father and mother, to whom he was born, will say to him, 'You must die, because you have told lies in the LORD's name.' When he prophesies, his own parents will stab him.

4"On that day every prophet will be ashamed of his prophetic vision⁰. He will not put on a prophet's garment of hair in order to deceive. 5He will say, 'I am not a prophet. I am a farmer; the land has been my livelihood since my youth.* 6If someone asks him, 'What are these wounds on your body*?' he will answer, 'The wounds I was given at the house of my friends.'

What kind of battle is this? (12:4)

Since cavalries no longer play a major role in war, the horses here must refer either to an event in the past or, in a symbolic way, to some future event, perhaps Armageddon.

Why prioritize who would be saved? (12:7)

The *dwellings of Judah* probably refer to the undefended areas of the land as opposed to the fortress city of David, Jerusalem. The point is the Lord will not allow those who live in the city to think they are more safe than those outside.

Angel of the LORD (12:8)

Perhaps a reference to the way the Lord led the people of Israel in the desert—as a cloud by day and fire by night (Exodus 14:19–20).

The one they have pierced (12:10)

This is a prophecy of the Messiah—this time shown as one who suffers undeservedly. This predicted the anguish of those in Jerusalem who saw Jesus nailed to the cross. See John 19:37; Rev. 1:7.

Hadad Rimmon (12:11)

The place where the people mourned for King Josiah (2 Chron. 35:22–27). It may also have been a comparison to a type of worship to a false god (see, for example, Ezek. 8:14).

What did the weeping mean? (12:11–14)

The depth and breadth of the grief expressed suggest individual and national repentance. If their grief was created by the sight of Christ, it presumably led to faith in him.

Why name these particular clans? (12:12–13)

Some suggest *David* stood for the kings, *Nathan* for the prophets and *Levi* for the priests. If so, it is unclear why *Shimei*, a descendant of Levi, would be listed separately. Others think *Nathan* was not the prophet, but David's son (2 Samuel 5:14). Along with *Shimei*, Levi's son, then, both the royal and the priestly branches of government would grieve for the one who was pierced.

Fountain (13:1)

In the Old Testament water was necessary for ceremonial cleansing from sin. In the New Testament the cleansing comes through the blood of Christ.

Why should parents have to execute their own son? (13:3)

Under the new covenant, people would be transformed so their allegiance would be first and foremost to the Lord. Still, it is hard to imagine how concern for the truth will supersede even the most intimate human concerns. See article: *Does Jesus really want us to hate our families?* (Luke 14:26).

Prophet's garment of hair (13:4)

See *Why did prophets wear eccentric clothes?* (2 Kings 1:8).

Were prophets sometimes wounded? (13:6)

Yes. It was not uncommon in those days for false prophets, seeking to work themselves into some sort of ecstatic frenzy, to cut themselves (see 1 Kings 18:28).

---

*a*10 Or *the Spirit*   *b*10 Or *to*   *c*5 Or *farmer; a man sold me in my youth*   *d*6 Or *wounds between your hands*

SCRIPTURE LINK (13:7) *Strike the shepherd, and the sheep will be scattered*

Quoted by Jesus to describe what would happen to him and his disciples. See Matt. 26:31; Mark 14:27.

What catastrophe was Zechariah describing? (13:8-9)

This may predict the attack against Jerusalem that actually came about in A.D. 70. Or it may refer symbolically to the persecution of the church.

Bring into the fire (13:9)

The catastrophe (see previous question) would bring suffering against *the little ones* (v. 7). Nonetheless, like metal refined in a crucible, this fire would purify God's remnant.

Day of the LORD (14:1)

A time when the Lord will be vindicated. His wrath will be unleashed against those opposed to him. At the same time, his grace will be poured out upon those who belong to him. See *The day of the LORD* (Zeph. 1:7).

Why would God cause an attack against Jerusalem only to defend against it? (14:2-3)

Though God may use the heathen as instruments of his wrath, they are not exempt from judgment themselves. So he brings the nations in judgment against Jerusalem but also turns judgment back on the unrighteousness of those nations.

Will the Mount of Olives be split literally in two? (14:4)

Some envision a monumental earthquake that would split the Mount of Olives from east to west. This would make escape from Jerusalem much more accessible—through a valley rather than over a mountain. Others take a figurative approach and see here a picture of God providing a way of escape for his people.

Earthquake in the days of Uzziah king of Judah (14:5)

We have no details of the earthquake except that it occurred during Uzziah's reign (Amos 1:1). The fact that it was remembered approximately 200 years later suggests it was no small event.

Who are the holy ones who will come with God? (14:5)

This may mean angels or the righteous dead brought back to life, or both (1 Thes. 3:13).

Living water (14:8)

Since water in Israel was in short supply, the inhabitants would have had a sharpened awareness of how essential water is to life. *Living water* referred to fresh spring water, in contrast to water collected and held in cisterns.

Arabah (14:10)

A low-lying dry region (including the lowest elevation on earth, the Dead Sea, which has a surface about 1,300 feet below sea level). It stretches from Mount Hermon to the Red Sea. See also *Arabah* (Deut. 1:1).

The Shepherd Struck, the Sheep Scattered

⁷"Awake, O sword, against my shepherd,
    against the man who is close to me!"
    declares the LORD Almighty.
"Strike the shepherd,
    and the sheep will be scattered,
    and I will turn my hand against the little
      ones.
⁸In the whole land," declares the LORD,
    "two-thirds will be struck down and perish;
    yet one-third will be left in it.
⁹This third I will bring into the fire;
    I will refine them like silver
    and test them like gold.
They will call on my name
    and I will answer them;
I will say, 'They are my people,'
    and they will say, 'The LORD is our God.' "

The LORD Comes and Reigns

14 A day of the LORD^D is coming when your plunder^D will be divided among you.

²I will gather all the nations to Jerusalem^D to fight against it; the city will be captured, the houses ransacked, and the women raped. Half of the city will go into exile^D, but the rest of the people will not be taken from the city. ³Then the LORD will go out and fight against those nations, as he fights in the day of battle. ⁴On that day his feet will stand on the Mount of Olives, east of Jerusalem, and the Mount of Olives will be split in two from east to west, forming a great valley, with half of the mountain moving north and half moving south. ⁵You will flee by my mountain valley, for it will extend to Azel. You will flee as you fled from the earthquake^a in the days of Uzziah king of Judah. Then the LORD my God will come, and all the holy ones with him.

⁶On that day there will be no light, no cold or frost. ⁷It will be a unique day, without daytime or nighttime—a day known to the LORD. When evening comes, there will be light.

⁸On that day living water will flow out from Jerusalem, half to the eastern sea^b and half to the western sea,^c in summer and in winter.

⁹The LORD will be king over the whole earth. On that day there will be one LORD, and his name the only name.

¹⁰The whole land, from Geba to Rimmon, south of Jerusalem, will become like the Arabah. But Jerusalem will be raised up and remain in its place, from the Benjamin Gate to the site of the First Gate, to the Corner Gate, and from the Tower of Hananel to the royal winepresses^D. ¹¹It will be inhabited; never again will it be destroyed. Jerusalem will be secure.

¹²This is the plague with which the LORD will strike all the nations that fought against Jerusalem: Their flesh will rot while they are still standing on their feet, their eyes will rot in their sockets, and their tongues will rot in their mouths. ¹³On that day men will be stricken by the LORD with great panic. Each man will seize the hand of another, and they will attack each other. ¹⁴Judah too will

---

^a 5 Or ⁵*My mountain valley will be blocked and will extend to Azel. It will be blocked as it was blocked because of the earthquake*   ^b 8 That is, the Dead Sea   ^c 8 That is, the Mediterranean

fight at Jerusalem^D. The wealth of all the surrounding nations will be collected—great quantities of gold and silver and clothing. ¹⁵A similar plague will strike the horses and mules, the camels and donkeys, and all the animals in those camps.

¹⁶Then the survivors from all the nations that have attacked Jerusalem will go up year after year to worship the King, the LORD Almighty, and to celebrate the Feast of Tabernacles. ¹⁷If any of the peoples of the earth do not go up to Jerusalem to worship the King, the LORD Almighty, they will have no rain. ¹⁸If the Egyptian people do not go up and take part, they will have no rain. The LORD^a will bring on them the plague he inflicts on the nations that do not go up to celebrate the Feast of Tabernacles. ¹⁹This will be the punishment of Egypt and the punishment of all the nations that do not go up to celebrate the Feast of Tabernacles.

²⁰On that day HOLY TO THE LORD will be inscribed on the bells of the horses, and the cooking pots in the LORD's house will be like the sacred^D bowls in front of the altar. ²¹Every pot in Jerusalem and Judah will be holy to the LORD Almighty, and all who come to sacrifice^D will take some of the pots and cook in them. And on that day there will no longer be a Canaanite^b in the house of the LORD Almighty.

^a18 Or part, then the LORD   ^b21 Or merchant

What kind of plague will God send? (14:12)

Those who look for a literal fulfillment see in this horrible description the results of modern mass warfare—perhaps a nuclear holocaust.

Feast of Tabernacles (14:16)

See *Feast of Tabernacles* (John 7:2).

Will temple worship in Jerusalem be reestablished someday? (14:16)

Some think it will be, others do not. Those who do point out that the Feast of Tabernacles was a time for celebrating the harvest. What better way to celebrate those gathered from the nations into God's kingdom? Those who do not think it will be reestablished say that there is no reason to turn the clock back before the sacrifice of Christ.

When were the Canaanites ever in the temple? (14:21)

They probably weren't. Canaanites were notorious for their deceitful business practices and the term *Canaanite* came to mean a deceitful person. Conniving merchants worked the temple precincts during the time of Christ (John 2:13–16).

When will the Lord be king over the whole earth? (14:9)

Many believers are convinced that the risen Lord will return to Jerusalem to reign for a thousand years (Rev. 20:1–6)—a period called the Millennium (from the Latin word for *thousand*). In this view, Christ will come to take believers out of this world, then return with them to establish his millennial reign. The term *premillennial* indicates that the first part of Christ's return will happen *before* the Millennium.

Another view sees the ideal reign of Christ coming about through the increasing impact of the church upon the world. In this *postmillennial* scenario, Christ would return *after* the Millennium. In both of these views a definite thousand year period is in view, the former preceded by the Rapture, the latter terminated by Christ's triumphant return.

In contrast, the *amillennial* view sees the promised reign of Christ fulfilled through the church rather than through a literal reign from Jerusalem. These wide-ranging opinions demonstrate the uncertainty of how it will happen, even though all believers are convinced Christ will reign as King of kings and Lord of lords.

MALACHI

Why read this book?

Malachi holds a mirror before us, helping us assess our relationship with the living God. Do we believe he loves us? Does he have our wholehearted love and obedience? Or are we only going through the motions? God's questions to Israel sneak behind our defenses and shake us out of mere routine, igniting new affection for him.

Who wrote this book?

The name Malachi means *my message*. It is uncertain whether this was actually the author's name, or whether it was used as a title, since prophets in general were called messengers of the Lord. Either way, this prophet clearly sensed God was speaking through him.

When was it written?

Sometime after 460 B.C., after Israel returned from captivity in Babylon, after the temple in Jerusalem had been rebuilt (516 B.C.) and after worship there had lapsed into mere routine.

Why was it written?

To confront the spirit of complacency and indifference that so easily overcomes the people of God.

What to look for in Malachi:

Malachi presents a word from God, followed by a complaint from the people, followed in turn by an answer from God. Look for God's passion in this exchange. God loves us with a passionate love and wants us to return that love by faithfulness in human relationships, integrity, purity, and justice for the powerless of society.

When did these things happen?

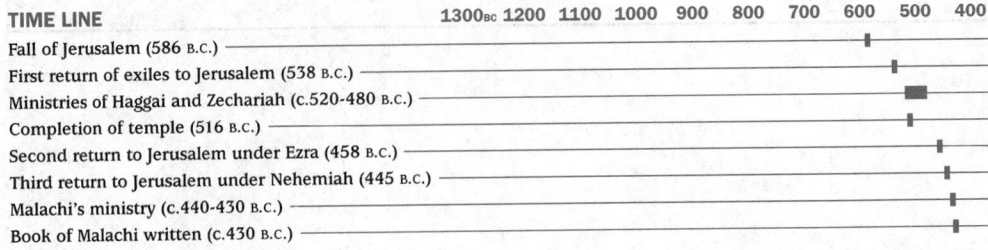

TIME LINE	1300BC 1200 1100 1000 900 800 700 600 500 400
Fall of Jerusalem (586 B.C.)	
First return of exiles to Jerusalem (538 B.C.)	
Ministries of Haggai and Zechariah (c.520-480 B.C.)	
Completion of temple (516 B.C.)	
Second return to Jerusalem under Ezra (458 B.C.)	
Third return to Jerusalem under Nehemiah (445 B.C.)	
Malachi's ministry (c.440-430 B.C.)	
Book of Malachi written (c.430 B.C.)	

1 An oracle[D]: The word of the LORD to Israel through Malachi.*a*

Jacob Loved, Esau Hated

2"I have loved you," says the LORD.

"But you ask, 'How have you loved us?'

"Was not Esau Jacob's brother?" the LORD says. "Yet I have loved Jacob, **3**but Esau I have hated, and I have turned his mountains into a wasteland and left his inheritance to the desert jackals."

4Edom[D] may say, "Though we have been crushed, we will rebuild the ruins."

But this is what the LORD Almighty says: "They may build, but I will demolish. They will be called the Wicked Land, a people always under the wrath of the LORD. **5**You will see it with your own eyes and say, 'Great is the LORD—even beyond the borders of Israel!'

Blemished Sacrifices

6"A son honors his father, and a servant his master. If I am a father, where is the honor due me? If I am a master, where is the respect due me?" says the LORD Almighty. "It is you, O priests[D], who show contempt for my name.

"But you ask, 'How have we shown contempt for your name?'

7"You place defiled food on my altar.

"But you ask, 'How have we defiled you?'

"By saying that the LORD's table is contemptible. **8**When you bring blind animals for sacrifice[D], is that not wrong? When you sacrifice crippled or diseased animals, is that not wrong? Try offering them to your governor! Would he be pleased with you? Would he accept you?" says the LORD Almighty.

9"Now implore God to be gracious to us. With such offerings from your hands, will he accept you?"—says the LORD Almighty.

10"Oh, that one of you would shut the temple doors, so that you would not light useless fires on my altar! I am not pleased with you," says the LORD Almighty, "and I will accept no offering from your hands. **11**My name will be great among the nations, from the rising to the setting of the sun. In every place incense[D] and pure offerings will be brought to my name, because my name will be great among the nations," says the LORD Almighty.

12"But you profane[D] it by saying of the Lord's table, 'It is defiled,' and of its food, 'It is contemptible.' **13**And you say, 'What a burden!' and you sniff at it contemptuously," says the LORD Almighty.

"When you bring injured, crippled or diseased animals and offer them as sacrifices, should I accept them from your hands?" says the LORD. **14**"Cursed is the cheat who has an acceptable male in his flock and vows[D] to give it, but then sacrifices a blemished animal to the Lord. For I am a great king," says the LORD Almighty, "and my name is to be feared among the nations.

Admonition for the Priests

2 "And now this admonition is for you, O priests. **2**If you do not listen, and if you do not set your heart to

a1 Malachi means my messenger.

How can God hate? (1:2–3)

"Hatred," used here is in contrast with God's special love for Jacob, chosen to be the instrument of redemption. Esau and Jacob were twin sons of Isaac, grandsons of Abraham. Only one of them could provide the family line through which the Messiah would come. The point of this verse is primarily that God chose Jacob and not Esau for that special role.

Edom (1:4)

Edom is the nation of Esau's line (see **Map 6** at the back of this Bible). Edom and Israel were often in conflict.

Why would God destroy Edom? (1:4)

Even a God of love will act in judgment against an evil nation. When people, like the Edomites, deliberately keep on rejecting God's ways, they inevitably end up in ruins.

Was Edom's behavior any worse than Israel's? (1:4)

At times, Israel behaved as badly as Edom, but the nation also periodically repented and turned to God. Malachi wanted Israel to grasp the undeserved love of God that the nation was experiencing. Other nations, just as bad, were being destroyed and Israel considered that just. Malachi wanted Israel to come to its senses and follow the Lord in faithful obedience.

Why would God prefer no offering to a blemished one? (1:10)

Your offering reveals your attitude toward God. Offering God second-rate goods (when you have first-rate goods to offer) indicates you don't think much of God.

Has this prophecy been fulfilled? (1:11)

Yes and no. Yes, because even in Malachi's day, some Gentiles (who weren't expected to) offered more sincere worship than apathetic Israel. No, because we still wait for the worldwide worship of the living God.

How does God curse? (1:14; 2:2)

At times God brings catastrophe, while at other times he lets disobedient people experience the consequences of their ungodly choices. We reap what we sow (Gal. 6:7–8).

Why should the descendants be rebuked for the wrong their ancestors did? (2:3)

This word is addressed to the priests who were failing to fulfill their duties. The generation to come, having only seen the corrupt model, will likely continue in corrupt worship. Therefore, they too will be guilty, in need of rebuke. Spiritual leadership has greater responsibilities than we imagine. If leaders carry out their responsibilities faithfully, the people of God grow in their relationship to God; if leaders serve half-heartedly and unfaithfully, the people of God suffer.

Offal (2:3)

The dung of the animals to be sacrificed. It was supposed to be removed from the sacred place and burned (Exodus 29:14). The point is that if the priests showed disrespect for God, they themselves would come to be treated with disrespect (2:9).

Covenant with Levi (2:4)

Levi was the first official priest called by God. God made a "covenant," a binding agreement, with Levi and his descendants (Num. 3:11–13). They were set apart to carry out the worship duties.

How had Judah married the daughter of a foreign god? (2:11)

The men of Judah were divorcing their wives in order to marry pagan women. Not only were the men unfaithful to their marriage vows, they also treated just as lightly their faithfulness to God and worshiped the gods of their pagan wives, thus provoking the Lord.

Broken faith with her (2:14)

Malachi is referring to divorce, breaking the vows of faithfulness. Although divorce is a personal matter, it affects the larger community and is therefore also a public matter.

How were they "covering themselves with violence"? (2:16)

This doesn't necessarily refer to physical violence. It's God's way of saying that divorce, no matter how calmly and reasonably it's done, does violence to human relationships.

When do our words push God too far? (2:17)

Other places in the Bible, especially the book of Job, show that the living God welcomes our words (even words of doubt, frustration and need) when they emerge from our trying to be faithful and obedient. But some words come out of cold indifference to the will and glory of God. People try to justify themselves by saying, "Everyone does it, so my sin can't be that serious a problem." Such rationalizations provoke God's wrath.

honor my name," says the LORD Almighty, "I will send a curse upon you, and I will curse your blessings. Yes, I have already cursed them, because you have not set your heart to honor me.

³"Because of you I will rebuke*a* your descendants*b*; I will spread on your faces the offal*D* from your festival sacrifices*D*, and you will be carried off with it. ⁴And you will know that I have sent you this admonition so that my covenant*D* with Levi may continue," says the LORD Almighty. ⁵"My covenant was with him, a covenant of life and peace*D*, and I gave them to him; this called for reverence*D* and he revered me and stood in awe of my name. ⁶True instruction was in his mouth and nothing false was found on his lips. He walked with me in peace and uprightness, and turned many from sin.

⁷"For the lips of a priest*D* ought to preserve knowledge, and from his mouth men should seek instruction—because he is the messenger of the LORD Almighty. ⁸But you have turned from the way and by your teaching have caused many to stumble; you have violated the covenant with Levi," says the LORD Almighty. ⁹"So I have caused you to be despised and humiliated before all the people, because you have not followed my ways but have shown partiality in matters of the law."

Judah Unfaithful

¹⁰Have we not all one Father*c*? Did not one God create us? Why do we profane*D* the covenant of our fathers by breaking faith with one another?

¹¹Judah has broken faith. A detestable thing has been committed in Israel and in Jerusalem*D*: Judah has desecrated*D* the sanctuary the LORD loves, by marrying the daughter of a foreign god. ¹²As for the man who does this, whoever he may be, may the LORD cut him off from the tents of Jacob*d*—even though he brings offerings to the LORD Almighty.

¹³Another thing you do: You flood the LORD's altar with tears. You weep and wail because he no longer pays attention to your offerings or accepts them with pleasure from your hands. ¹⁴You ask, "Why?" It is because the LORD is acting as the witness between you and the wife of your youth, because you have broken faith with her, though she is your partner, the wife of your marriage covenant.

¹⁵Has not ⌊the LORD⌋ made them one? In flesh and spirit they are his. And why one? Because he was seeking godly offspring.*e* So guard yourself in your spirit, and do not break faith with the wife of your youth.

¹⁶"I hate divorce," says the LORD God of Israel, "and I hate a man's covering himself*f* with violence as well as with his garment," says the LORD Almighty.

So guard yourself in your spirit, and do not break faith.

The Day of Judgment

¹⁷You have wearied the LORD with your words.
"How have we wearied him?" you ask.

---

*a*3 Or *cut off* (see Septuagint)   *b*3 Or *will blight your grain*
*c*10 Or *father*   *d*12 Or *¹²May the LORD cut off from the tents of Jacob anyone who gives testimony in behalf of the man who does this*
*e*15 Or *¹⁵But the one ⌊who is our father⌋ did not do this, not as long as life remained in him. And what was he seeking? An offspring from God*
*f*16 Or *his wife*

By saying, "All who do evil are good in the eyes of the LORD, and he is pleased with them" or "Where is the God of justice?"

3 "See, I will send my messenger, who will prepare the way before me. Then suddenly the Lord you are seeking will come to his temple; the messenger of the covenant^D, whom you desire, will come," says the LORD Almighty.

²But who can endure the day of his coming? Who can stand when he appears? For he will be like a refiner's fire or a launderer's soap. ³He will sit as a refiner and purifier of silver; he will purify^D the Levites^D and refine them like gold and silver. Then the LORD will have men who will bring offerings in righteousness^D, ⁴and the offerings of Judah and Jerusalem^D will be acceptable to the LORD, as in days gone by, as in former years.

⁵"So I will come near to you for judgment. I will be quick to testify against sorcerers, adulterers and perjurers, against those who defraud laborers of their wages, who oppress the widows and the fatherless, and deprive aliens^D of justice, but do not fear me," says the LORD Almighty.

Robbing God

⁶"I the LORD do not change. So you, O descendants of Jacob, are not destroyed. ⁷Ever since the time of your forefathers you have turned away from my decrees and have not kept them. Return to me, and I will return to you," says the LORD Almighty.

"But you ask, 'How are we to return?'

⁸"Will a man rob God? Yet you rob me.

"But you ask, 'How do we rob you?'

"In tithes^D and offerings. ⁹You are under a curse—the whole nation of you—because you are robbing me. ¹⁰Bring the whole tithe into the storehouse, that there may be food in my house. Test me in this," says the LORD Almighty, "and see if I will not throw open the floodgates of heaven and pour out so much blessing that you will not have room enough for it. ¹¹I will prevent pests from devouring your crops, and the vines in your fields will not cast their fruit," says the LORD Almighty. ¹²"Then all the nations will call you blessed, for yours will be a delightful land," says the LORD Almighty.

¹³"You have said harsh things against me," says the LORD.

"Yet you ask, 'What have we said against you?'

¹⁴"You have said, 'It is futile to serve God. What did we gain by carrying out his requirements and going about like mourners before the LORD Almighty? ¹⁵But now we call the arrogant blessed. Certainly the evildoers prosper, and even those who challenge God escape.' "

¹⁶Then those who feared the LORD talked with each other, and the LORD listened and heard. A scroll of remembrance was written in his presence concerning those who feared the LORD and honored his name.

¹⁷"They will be mine," says the LORD Almighty, "in the day when I make up my treasured possession.ᵃ I will spare them, just as in compassion a man spares his son who serves him. ¹⁸And you will again see the distinction between the righteous^D and the wicked, between those who serve God and those who do not.

ᵃ17 Or Almighty, "my treasured possession, in the day when I act

Who is the promised messenger? (3:1)

This may refer to John the Baptist, the one sent to prepare the way for Christ. See *How would Elijah return?* (4:5–6). But the messenger may be the Lord himself, the living God! If so, this is the only place in the Bible where God speaks of himself this way: God confronting his people in person!

Refiner's fire (3:2)

The process by which precious metals are shaped. The goldsmith stokes up the fire until it's hot enough to burn away all impurities. When the living God comes, he burns away everything in us that displeases him.

Launderer's soap (3:2)

The alkaline lye used to bleach dirty garments white. Only because God comes as fire and soap can the promise of 1:11 be fulfilled: that we will be able to offer pure worship to the Holy One.

Do we have to tithe? (3:9–10)

The word tithe simply means *tenth*. To tithe means to offer to God the first tenth of whatever God gives us. Abraham offered it (Gen. 14:1–24) and the Mosaic Law required it (Lev. 27:30–33; Deut. 14:22) as an act of gratitude and allegiance. The New Testament does not teach the tithe, possibly because it's assumed, not as the goal but as the starting place. The New Testament teaches us to use *all* we are for the glory of God (Mark 8:34–37; Romans 12:1).

Should we give in order to get? (3:10)

God is saying that if we choose to be generous, he will keep giving to us so that we can continue our lifestyle of giving (2 Cor. 9:8–11). Giving the tithe does not require God to give. Giving the tithe is our way of telling God, "I'm trusting you to give me all I need to follow you in a life of generosity" (2 Cor. 9:6).

Was God offended by doubts? (3:14–15)

Expressing doubts was not the problem. Many of God's people expressed doubts forcefully: David (Psalm 73:2–14), Job (Job 21:4–15), Jeremiah (Jer. 12:1) and Habakkuk (Hab. 1:13–17). The problem here was that the people weren't serious about serving God.

What's a *scroll of remembrance*? (3:16)

God remembers those who honor him. Even if faithful people feel forgotten, acts of loyalty to God—which indifferent people treat with cynicism—will be rewarded in due time.

How can you tell good people from bad? (3:18)

You can't, though in the previous verses of this chapter God does provide insight into what pleases him. However, this verse speaks of a coming judgment, when God will reveal the righteous and unrighteous.

Will evildoers literally burn? (4:1)

The picture is of the good grain having been harvested and the remaining stubble set on fire, so that the field can be used again. This may be a figurative description of judgment, not necessarily a literal one.

The sun of righteousness (4:2)

After the firestorm sweeps through, a new day will dawn. The sunrise Malachi has in mind is the coming of God's Son, Jesus Christ.

How do wings heal? (4:2)

Just as the sun rises and spreads its rays (wings) in every direction, bringing light and warmth, so Jesus Christ, when he appears in human lives, brings light and warmth that are totally healing.

How would Elijah return? (4:5–6)

Jesus said that John the Baptist fulfilled that great expectation, preparing the way for Christ himself (Matt. 11:7–14).

How will Elijah turn the hearts of fathers and children? (4:6)

"Elijah's" message is a call to righteousness or "right-relatedness." Specifically he mentions the family and especially parent-child relationships.

How would God curse the land? (4:6)

This was a figurative way of describing the negative consequences of sin in the land. When people rebel against God, the fallout affects many others besides themselves. In this case, Malachi alludes to the curse of breakdowns in family relationships. If parents and children would not turn to God, they would be unable to turn to each other.

The Day of the LORD

4 "Surely the day is coming; it will burn like a furnace. All the arrogant and every evildoer will be stubble, and that day that is coming will set them on fire," says the LORD Almighty. "Not a root or a branch will be left to them. ²But for you who revere^D my name, the sun of righteousness^D will rise with healing in its wings. And you will go out and leap like calves released from the stall. ³Then you will trample down the wicked; they will be ashes under the soles of your feet on the day when I do these things," says the LORD Almighty.

⁴"Remember the law of my servant Moses, the decrees and laws I gave him at Horeb for all Israel.

⁵"See, I will send you the prophet^D Elijah before that great and dreadful day of the LORD^D comes. ⁶He will turn the hearts of the fathers to their children, and the hearts of the children to their fathers; or else I will come and strike the land with a curse."

From Malachi to Christ

	450 B.C.
	440
THE PERSIAN PERIOD	430
450-330 B.C.	420
	410
For about 100 years after Nehemiah's time the	400
Persians controlled Judah, but the Jews were	390
allowed to carry on their religious observances	380
and were not interfered with. During this time	370
Judah was ruled by high priests who were respon-	360
sible to the Jewish government.	350
	340
	330

THE HELLENISTIC PERIOD
330-166 B.C.

Rule of Alexander the Great — 320

In 333 B.C. the Persian armies stationed in
Macedonia were defeated by Alexander the
Great. He was convinced that Greek culture was
the one force that could unify the world. Alexander permitted the Jews to observe their laws
and even granted them exemption from tribute
or tax during their sabbath years. The Greek
conquest prepared the way for the translation
of the Old Testament into Greek (Septuagint
version) c.250 B.C.

Rule of the Ptolemies of Egypt —

Rule of the Seleucids of Syria —

310
300
290
280
270
260
250
240
230
220
210
200
190
180
170
160

THE HASMONEAN PERIOD
166-63 B.C.

When this historical period began, the Jews were
being greatly oppressed. The Ptolemies had been
tolerant of the Jews and their religious practices,
but the Seleucid rulers were determined to force
Hellenism on them. Copies of the Scriptures
were ordered destroyed and laws were enforced
with extreme cruelty. The oppressed Jews
revolted, led by Judas the Maccabee.

Hasmonean Dynasty —

150
140
130
120
110
100
90
80
70
60

THE ROMAN PERIOD
63 B.C. . . .

In the year 63 B.C. Pompey, the Roman general,
captured Jerusalem, and the provinces of Palestine became subject to Rome. The local government was entrusted part of the time to princes
and the rest of the time to procurators who were
appointed by the emperors. Herod the Great was
ruler of all Palestine at the time of Christ's birth.

Herod the Great rules as king;
subject to Rome

50
40
30
20
10
1
10
20
A.D.30

THE PERSIAN PERIOD
450-330 B.C.

For about 100 years after Nehemiah's time, the Persians controlled Judah, but the Jews were allowed to carry on their religious observances and were not interfered with. During this time Judah was ruled by high priests who were responsible to the Jewish government.

THE HELLENISTIC PERIOD
330-166 B.C.

In 333 B.C. the Persian armies stationed in Macedonia were defeated by Alexander the Great. He was convinced that Greek culture was the one force that could unify the world. Alexander permitted the Jews to observe their laws and even granted them exemption from tribute or tax during their sabbath years. The Greek conquest prepared the way for the translation of the Old Testament into Greek (Septuagint version), c. 250 B.C.

Rule of Alexander the Great

Rule of the Ptolemies of Egypt

Rule of the Seleucids of Syria

THE HASMONEAN PERIOD
166-63 B.C.

When this historical period began, the Jews were being greatly oppressed. The Ptolemies had been tolerant of the Jews and their religious practices, but the Seleucid rulers were determined to force Hellenism on their people of the Scriptures were ordered destroyed and laws were enacted with extreme cruelty. The oppressed Jews revolted, led by Judas the Maccabee.

Hasmonean dynasty

THE ROMAN PERIOD
63 B.C.–

In the year 63 B.C. Pompey, the Roman general, captured Jerusalem, and the provinces of Palestine became subject to Rome. The local government was entrusted during this time to princes and the rest of the area to procurators who were appointed by the emperor. Herod the Great was ruler of all Palestine at the time of Christ's birth.

Herod the Great rules as king, subject to Rome

THE **NEW** TESTAMENT

MATTHEW

Why read this book?

Have you ever read a sequel to a novel without having read the original story? Trying to pick up the story line without a transition can be difficult. The Gospel of Matthew serves as such a transition. It connects the story of the Old Testament with the story of the New Testament, helping us understand how the life and teaching of Jesus built upon what had come before.

Who wrote this book?

Matthew, a tax collector who became one of Christ's twelve disciples.

Why was it written?

To offer irrefutable proof that the long-awaited Jewish Messiah had come to inaugurate God's kingdom on earth.

When and to whom was it written?

Matthew possibly wrote this book in the A.D. 70s (though some believe he may have written it in the 50s or 60s), primarily for Jewish readers. He offered a persuasive account of the Good News of Jesus, citing Old Testament evidence that supported the claims believers had been making about Jesus.

What to look for in Matthew:

Notice Matthew's frequent use of the Old Testament and how his Jewish bias flavors his descriptions. For example, he uses *Son of David* instead of *Son of God* (as in the Gospel of John). One of Matthew's major themes is the kingdom of heaven. Note Jesus' teachings about what it means to be a citizen of that kingdom.

When did these things happen?

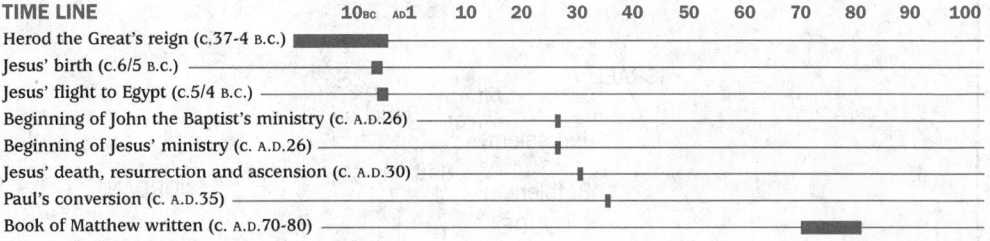

TIME LINE	10 B.C.	A.D. 1	10	20	30	40	50	60	70	80	90	100
Herod the Great's reign (c. 37-4 B.C.)												
Jesus' birth (c. 6/5 B.C.)												
Jesus' flight to Egypt (c. 5/4 B.C.)												
Beginning of John the Baptist's ministry (c. A.D. 26)												
Beginning of Jesus' ministry (c. A.D. 26)												
Jesus' death, resurrection and ascension (c. A.D. 30)												
Paul's conversion (c. A.D. 35)												
Book of Matthew written (c. A.D. 70-80)												

Why give Christ's genealogy? (1:1)

Matthew wanted to underscore Jesus' human birth into a family with traceable roots. A Jewish male always traced his lineage through his father—and Joseph was Jesus' legal father. The genealogy also introduces a major theme in this book: since he was considered a descendant of both David and Abraham, Jesus became the fulfillment of prophecies and of covenants God had made with them.

SCRIPTURE LINK (1:1–17)

Luke also lists a genealogy of Christ, with some differences. See Luke 3:23–38. Matthew traces Jesus' ancestry through the royal line of David and Solomon, being concerned with Israel's heritage and hopes. Luke's concern is Jesus' relation to the broader human race. See *Why aren't the genealogies of Matthew and Luke the same?* (Luke 3:23–38).

Why list Uriah in the genealogy of Christ? (1:6)

Including Uriah's name shows us a remarkable glimpse of God's grace: Jesus was willing to be identified with sinful humanity; his ancestry was not untainted. Jewish readers of Matthew would remember that Uriah had been cheated by David: first of his wife Bathsheba, and then of his life (see 2 Samuel 11).

The Genealogy of Jesus

1 A record of the genealogy[D] of Jesus Christ the son of David, the son of Abraham:

²Abraham was the father of Isaac,
    Isaac the father of Jacob,
    Jacob the father of Judah and his brothers,
    ³Judah the father of Perez and Zerah, whose mother was Tamar,
    Perez the father of Hezron,
    Hezron the father of Ram,
    ⁴Ram the father of Amminadab,
    Amminadab the father of Nahshon,
    Nahshon the father of Salmon,
    ⁵Salmon the father of Boaz, whose mother was Rahab[D],
    Boaz the father of Obed, whose mother was Ruth,
    Obed the father of Jesse,
    ⁶and Jesse the father of King David.

David was the father of Solomon, whose mother had been Uriah's wife,
    ⁷Solomon the father of Rehoboam,

Setting of the Gospels (1:1)

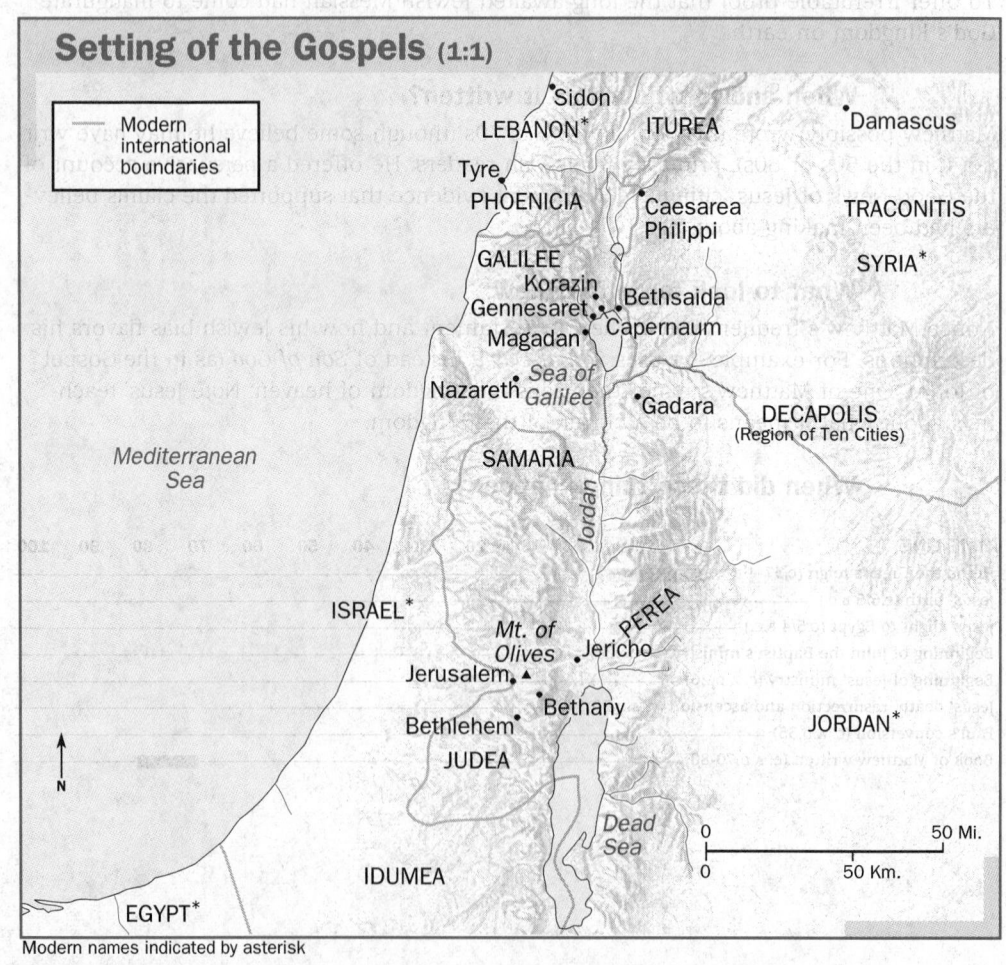

Modern international boundaries

Sidon
LEBANON*
ITUREA
Damascus
Tyre
PHOENICIA
Caesarea Philippi
TRACONITIS
GALILEE
Korazin
Bethsaida
SYRIA*
Gennesaret
Capernaum
Magadan
Sea of Galilee
Nazareth
Gadara
DECAPOLIS
(Region of Ten Cities)
Mediterranean Sea
SAMARIA
Jordan
ISRAEL*
PEREA
Mt. of Olives
Jericho
Jerusalem
Bethany
JORDAN*
Bethlehem
JUDEA
Dead Sea
0   50 Mi.
0   50 Km.
IDUMEA
EGYPT*
N

Modern names indicated by asterisk

Rehoboam the father of Abijah,
Abijah the father of Asa,
8Asa the father of Jehoshaphat,
Jehoshaphat the father of Jehoram,
Jehoram the father of Uzziah,
9Uzziah the father of Jotham,
Jotham the father of Ahaz,
Ahaz the father of Hezekiah,
10Hezekiah the father of Manasseh,
Manasseh the father of Amon,
Amon the father of Josiah,
11and Josiah the father of Jeconiah*a* and his brothers
at the time of the exile*D* to Babylon.

12After the exile to Babylon:
Jeconiah was the father of Shealtiel,
Shealtiel the father of Zerubbabel,
13Zerubbabel the father of Abiud,
Abiud the father of Eliakim,
Eliakim the father of Azor,
14Azor the father of Zadok,
Zadok the father of Akim,
Akim the father of Eliud,
15Eliud the father of Eleazar,
Eleazar the father of Matthan,
Matthan the father of Jacob,
16and Jacob the father of Joseph, the husband of
Mary, of whom was born Jesus, who is called
Christ.

17Thus there were fourteen generations in all from
Abraham to David, fourteen from David to the exile to
Babylon, and fourteen from the exile to the Christ.*b*

The Birth of Jesus Christ

18This is how the birth of Jesus Christ came about:
His mother Mary was pledged to be married to Joseph, but
before they came together, she was found to be with
child through the Holy Spirit. **19**Because Joseph her husband was a righteous*D* man and did not want to expose
her to public disgrace, he had in mind to divorce her
quietly.

20But after he had considered this, an angel of the Lord
appeared to him in a dream and said, "Joseph son of David, do not be afraid to take Mary home as your wife, because what is conceived in her is from the Holy Spirit.
21She will give birth to a son, and you are to give him the
name Jesus,*c* because he will save his people from their
sins."

22All this took place to fulfill what the Lord had said
through the prophet*D*: **23**"The virgin will be with child
and will give birth to a son, and they will call him Immanuel"*d*—which means, "God with us."

24When Joseph woke up, he did what the angel of the
Lord had commanded him and took Mary home as his
wife. **25**But he had no union with her until she gave birth
to a son. And he gave him the name Jesus.

Jesus, who is called Christ (1:16)
For the significance of the word *Christ* to Jew-
ish readers, see NIV note at v. 17; also see
Anointed one (Psalm 2:2).

What's so special about the number fourteen? (1:17)
Perhaps Matthew used it because it is a multiple of seven—a number that symbolized completeness. He skipped over some generations
in order to achieve this literary order.

Why did Joseph consider divorce? (1:19)
His wife-to-be was pregnant and her child
wasn't his—a disgrace in any era! Unlike today, first-century engagements were binding
premarital contracts leading to marriage. During the year of engagement, the couple behaved like husband and wife (except that they
did not live together or have sex). To break off
such an engagement, a divorce was required.

Why a virgin birth? (1:23)
Some think it was because Adam's original sin
has been passed down to humanity through
sinful parents. They say Jesus, to be free of sin,
needed to circumvent the natural method and be
conceived in a supernatural way. More likely,
Jesus' birth, a miraculous birth to a sexually
pure young woman, served to underscore his
supernatural beginning—a sign of his divinity.

a 11 That is, Jehoiachin; also in verse 12   *b 17* Or *Messiah.* "The
Christ" (Greek) and "the Messiah" (Hebrew) both mean "the Anointed
One."   *c 21 Jesus* is the Greek form of *Joshua,* which means *the
Lord saves.*   *d 23* Isaiah 7:14

King Herod (2:1)

Herod the Great reigned over Judea from 37 to 4 B.C. A bloodthirsty tyrant who murdered, among others, his wife, mother-in-law and three sons, Herod was part Jew and part Gentile. The Roman empire gave Herod his authority to rule the Jews, but most Jews hated him even though he referred to himself as the king of the Jews.

Magi (2:1)

Some have suggested that the *Magi* were a priestly tribe of Medes. Others say they were Persian elders from Babylon, schooled in philosophy, medicine and science. They may have belonged to the same order of astrologers as those in Daniel's day (see Daniel 1:20; 2:2; 4:7; 5:7).

Why would God give special revelation to astrologers? (2:2)

These would not be astrologers as we think of them today. In the New Testament, the word *Magi* can mean two different things: those who study the stars, or sorcerers who practice magical arts. Here we find the first sense: experts of the stars who are searching for the god of the stars. The Magi symbolize the non-Jewish world and all who search for ultimate truth. By including this story, Matthew shows that God's salvation is intended for Jews and Gentiles alike.

Why would God warn only Joseph? (2:13,16)

The Bible doesn't tell us. Matthew includes this episode to show God's protection of his Son. Herod's sinister plans could not thwart God's purpose. The salvation of humanity was at stake.

Escape to Egypt (2:13)

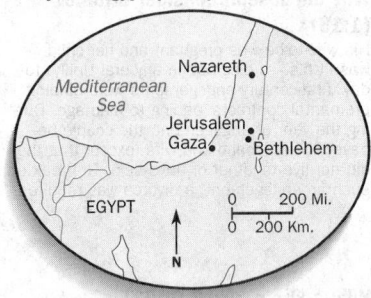

Did Matthew take this prophecy out of context? (2:15)

No. Inspired by the Holy Spirit to write, Matthew, like other New Testament writers, sometimes saw a theme or a symbol in the Old Testament that illustrated what Jesus accomplished or experienced. The prophet Hosea's words, *Out of Egypt I called my son* (Hosea 11:1), originally referred to the nation of Israel as God's son, set free from Pharaoh's bondage. But they were also a parallel to what happened to Jesus, God's son, when he was taken to Egypt to escape Herod's evil ambitions.

The Visit of the Magi

2 After Jesus was born in Bethlehem in Judea, during the time of King Herod, Magi[a] from the east came to Jerusalem[D] [2]and asked, "Where is the one who has been born king of the Jews[D]? We saw his star in the east[b] and have come to worship him."

[3]When King Herod heard this he was disturbed, and all Jerusalem with him. [4]When he had called together all the people's chief priests[D] and teachers of the law, he asked them where the Christ[c] was to be born. [5]"In Bethlehem in Judea," they replied, "for this is what the prophet[D] has written:

[6]" 'But you, Bethlehem, in the land of Judah,
    are by no means least among the rulers of Judah;
for out of you will come a ruler
    who will be the shepherd of my people Israel.'[d] "

[7]Then Herod called the Magi secretly and found out from them the exact time the star had appeared. [8]He sent them to Bethlehem and said, "Go and make a careful search for the child. As soon as you find him, report to me, so that I too may go and worship him."

[9]After they had heard the king, they went on their way, and the star they had seen in the east[e] went ahead of them until it stopped over the place where the child was. [10]When they saw the star, they were overjoyed. [11]On coming to the house, they saw the child with his mother Mary, and they bowed down and worshiped him. Then they opened their treasures and presented him with gifts of gold and of incense[D] and of myrrh[D]. [12]And having been warned in a dream not to go back to Herod, they returned to their country by another route.

The Escape to Egypt

[13]When they had gone, an angel of the Lord appeared to Joseph in a dream. "Get up," he said, "take the child and his mother and escape to Egypt. Stay there until I tell you, for Herod is going to search for the child to kill him."

[14]So he got up, took the child and his mother during the night and left for Egypt, [15]where he stayed until the death[D] of Herod. And so was fulfilled what the Lord had said through the prophet: "Out of Egypt I called my son."[f]

[16]When Herod realized that he had been outwitted by the Magi, he was furious, and he gave orders to kill all the boys in Bethlehem and its vicinity who were two years old and under, in accordance with the time he had learned from the Magi. [17]Then what was said through the prophet Jeremiah was fulfilled:

[18]"A voice is heard in Ramah,
    weeping and great mourning,
Rachel weeping for her children
    and refusing to be comforted,
    because they are no more."[g]

[a]1 Traditionally *Wise Men*   [b]2 Or *star when it rose*   [c]4 Or *Messiah*   [d]6 Micah 5:2   [e]9 Or *seen when it rose*   [f]15 Hosea 11:1   [g]18 Jer. 31:15

The Return to Nazareth

[19]After Herod died, an angel of the Lord appeared in a dream to Joseph in Egypt [20]and said, "Get up, take the child and his mother and go to the land of Israel, for those who were trying to take the child's life are dead."

[21]So he got up, took the child and his mother and went to the land of Israel. [22]But when he heard that Archelaus was reigning in Judea in place of his father Herod, he was afraid to go there. Having been warned in a dream, he withdrew to the district of Galilee, [23]and he went and lived in a town called Nazareth. So was fulfilled what was said through the prophets[D]: "He will be called a Nazarene."

John the Baptist Prepares the Way

3 In those days John the Baptist came, preaching in the Desert of Judea [2]and saying, "Repent[D], for the kingdom of heaven is near." [3]This is he who was spoken of through the prophet Isaiah:

"A voice of one calling in the desert,
'Prepare the way for the Lord,
      make straight paths for him.' "[a]

[4]John's clothes were made of camel's hair, and he had a leather belt around his waist. His food was locusts[D] and wild honey. [5]People went out to him from Jerusalem[D] and all Judea and the whole region of the Jordan. [6]Confessing their sins, they were baptized by him in the Jordan River.

[7]But when he saw many of the Pharisees[D] and Sadducees[D] coming to where he was baptizing, he said to them: "You brood of vipers! Who warned you to flee from the coming wrath? [8]Produce fruit in keeping with repentance[D]. [9]And do not think you can say to yourselves, 'We have Abraham as our father.' I tell you that out of these stones God can raise up children for Abraham. [10]The ax is already at the root of the trees, and every tree that does not produce good fruit will be cut down and thrown into the fire.

[11]"I baptize you with[b] water for repentance. But after me will come one who is more powerful than I, whose sandals I am not fit to carry. He will baptize you with the Holy Spirit and with fire. [12]His winnowing fork[D] is in his hand, and he will clear his threshing floor, gathering his wheat into the barn and burning up the chaff[D] with unquenchable fire."

The Baptism of Jesus

[13]Then Jesus came from Galilee to the Jordan to be baptized by John. [14]But John tried to deter him, saying, "I need to be baptized by you, and do you come to me?"

[15]Jesus replied, "Let it be so now; it is proper for us to do this to fulfill all righteousness[D]." Then John consented.

[16]As soon as Jesus was baptized, he went up out of the water. At that moment heaven was opened, and he saw the Spirit of God descending like a dove and lighting on him. [17]And a voice from heaven said, "This is my Son, whom I love; with him I am well pleased."

[a]3 Isaiah 40:3   [b]11 Or in

Who prophesied that Christ would be called a Nazarene? (2:23)

Matthew was using a contemporary idiom to describe what the ancient writers had foretold. The word *Nazarene* was a derogatory term— those who lived in Nazareth (or anywhere else in Galilee) were viewed as second-class citizens. Matthew was saying that several prophets had predicted the Holy One of God would be despised and rejected—a victim of prejudice.

SCRIPTURE LINK (3:1-12)

Mark talks about the coming of John the Baptist in Mark 1:3–8. Luke covers it in Luke 3:2–17.

Was John the Baptist eccentric? (3:4)

John's appearance was certainly unusual, but it may not have been unique. Poor people of his day also wore camel hair clothing and leather belts; they too may have eaten grasshoppers and wild honey, more out of necessity than choice. What attracted the crowds was not so much what John ate and wore, but his dynamic preaching in the desert. All these things, taken together, reminded them of the Old Testament prophets. See *Why did prophets wear eccentric clothes?* (2 Kings 1:8).

Did John preach that sins were forgiven by baptism? (3:6)

This baptism did not bring about salvation any more than sacrifices did in the Old Testament. The ritual served only to illustrate what was occurring within the hearts of people. The faith expressed in baptism indicated a readiness for the Messiah who would bring forgiveness. Also see *Does baptism save us?* (1 Peter 3:21).

Did John invent baptism? (3:11)

No, John was not the first one to baptize. His baptism, however, was unlike any previous cleansing rite. After Judah's exile to Babylon in 586 B.C., Jewish rabbis used baptism, in addition to circumcision, as a rite of cleansing when bringing Gentile converts into Judaism. Jews were not baptized though. A later sect of Jews (the Essenes) used baptism as frequent, repeated washings to deal with ceremonial uncleanliness. John redefined this sacred use of water as a one-time public sign of repentance —turning away from sin and turning to God.

Baptize . . . with the Holy Spirit and with fire (3:11)

The precise meaning of this phrase is difficult to specify since *fire* is used Biblically to symbolize both God's presence and God's judgment. God's presence was revealed in fire at the burning bush (Exodus 3:2), on Mount Sinai (Exodus 19:18), in chariots of fire (2 Kings 6:17) and on the day of Pentecost (Acts 2:3), to name just a few examples. However, the phrase also suggests a figurative baptism, one where believers would be baptized with the Holy Spirit and non-believers would be baptized with the fire of judgment.

Winnowing fork (3:12)

Ancient farmers would toss the threshed grain into the air with a large, wooden fork so the wind would blow away the lighter chaff while the grain dropped back to the ground. John used this image to illustrate the dual nature of Jesus' ministry: he would separate humanity, some to judgment and some to reward.

SCRIPTURE LINK (3:13–17)
Mark tells about Jesus' baptism in Mark 1:9–11. You'll also find it in Luke 3:21–22 and John 1:31–34.

SCRIPTURE LINK (4:1–11)
Mark records Jesus' temptation in Mark 1:12–13. Luke gives an account of it in Luke 4:1–13.

Did the Spirit lead Jesus into temptation? (4:1)
For Christ to accomplish God's will, he had to face Satan and prevail. This was the first major confrontation. Matthew presents Christ as one who served faithfully despite enormous opposition. The Holy Spirit led Jesus into the desert to be tempted by Satan to show that temptation doesn't need to end in failure. That's an encouragement to all believers who find themselves the objects of Satan's schemes (Eph. 6:11).

Temptation of Jesus (4:1)

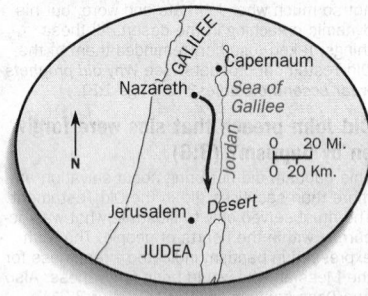

What was wrong with turning a stone into bread? (4:3–4)
The issue was not what the temptation was, but the motive behind it. The devil often appeals to our pride, hoping that we will take matters into our own hands rather than trust in God. If Jesus had turned the stone into bread, he wouldn't have been depending on his Father in heaven. He resisted these temptations by quoting Scripture to reaffirm his trust in God.

The Temptation of Jesus

4 Then Jesus was led by the Spirit into the desert to be tempted by the devil. ²After fasting forty days and forty nights, he was hungry. ³The tempter came to him and said, "If you are the Son of God, tell these stones to become bread."

⁴Jesus answered, "It is written: 'Man does not live on bread alone, but on every word that comes from the mouth of God.'ᵃ"

⁵Then the devil took him to the holy city and had him stand on the highest point of the temple. ⁶"If you are the Son of God," he said, "throw yourself down. For it is written:

" 'He will command his angels concerning you,
    and they will lift you up in their hands,
so that you will not strike your foot against a
    stone.'ᵇ"

⁷Jesus answered him, "It is also written: 'Do not put the Lord your God to the test.'ᶜ"

⁸Again, the devil took him to a very high mountain and showed him all the kingdoms of the world and their splendor. ⁹"All this I will give you," he said, "if you will bow down and worship me."

¹⁰Jesus said to him, "Away from me, Satan! For it is written: 'Worship the Lord your God, and serve him only.'ᵈ"

¹¹Then the devil left him, and angels came and attended him.

Jesus Begins to Preach

¹²When Jesus heard that John had been put in prison, he returned to Galilee. ¹³Leaving Nazareth, he went and lived in Capernaum, which was by the lake in the area of Zebulun and Naphtali— ¹⁴to fulfill what was said through the prophetᴰ Isaiah:

¹⁵"Land of Zebulun and land of Naphtali,
    the way to the sea, along the Jordan,

ᵃ4 Deut. 8:3   ᵇ6 Psalm 91:11,12   ᶜ7 Deut. 6:16   ᵈ10 Deut. 6:13

Does the Spirit lead us into temptation? (4:1)

G od does not tempt us to sin—that's Satan's specialty. But God does test us at times, though the difference might seem subtle. See *How are temptations different from trials?* (James 1:13). On occasion God may test us by putting us directly into the line of Satan's fire.

In this case, the Spirit put Jesus to the test by allowing Satan to tempt him to sin. Before his divine mission on earth could succeed, Jesus had to first overcome this encounter with the enemy. Similarly, we will have to win numerous small battles over temptation if we're to fulfill the purpose or call God has given us. God may allow our faith to be tested so that, as he helps us, initial skirmishes can bring us small victories and prepare us to fight and win even bigger battles.

God tests us, not that we might fall into sin, but that we might become victorious. Also see *How does the Lord discipline?* (Heb. 12:5) and *Why does God allow our faith to be tested?* (1 Peter 1:7).

Galilee of the Gentiles[D]—
   [16]the people living in darkness
      have seen a great light;
   on those living in the land of the shadow of
      death[D]
      a light has dawned."[a]

[17]From that time on Jesus began to preach, "Repent[D],
for the kingdom of heaven is near."

The Calling of the First Disciples

[18]As Jesus was walking beside the Sea of Galilee, he saw
two brothers, Simon called Peter and his brother Andrew.
They were casting a net into the lake, for they were fishermen. [19]"Come, follow me," Jesus said, "and I will make
you fishers of men." [20]At once they left their nets and followed him.
   [21]Going on from there, he saw two other brothers,
James son of Zebedee and his brother John. They were in
a boat with their father Zebedee, preparing their nets.
Jesus called them, [22]and immediately they left the boat
and their father and followed him.

Jesus Heals the Sick

[23]Jesus went throughout Galilee, teaching in their synagogues, preaching the good news of the kingdom, and
healing every disease and sickness among the people.
[24]News about him spread all over Syria, and people
brought to him all who were ill with various diseases,
those suffering severe pain, the demon-possessed, those
having seizures, and the paralyzed, and he healed them.
[25]Large crowds from Galilee, the Decapolis[D],[b] Jerusalem[D], Judea and the region across the Jordan followed
him.

The Beatitudes

5 Now when he saw the crowds, he went up on a
   mountainside and sat down. His disciples[D] came to
him, [2]and he began to teach them, saying:

   [3]"Blessed are the poor in spirit,
      for theirs is the kingdom of heaven.
   [4]Blessed are those who mourn,
      for they will be comforted.
   [5]Blessed are the meek,
      for they will inherit the earth.
   [6]Blessed are those who hunger and thirst for
         righteousness[D],
      for they will be filled.
   [7]Blessed are the merciful,
      for they will be shown mercy[D].
   [8]Blessed are the pure in heart,
      for they will see God.
   [9]Blessed are the peacemakers,
      for they will be called sons of God.
   [10]Blessed are those who are persecuted because
         of righteousness,
      for theirs is the kingdom of heaven.

[11]"Blessed are you when people insult you, persecute
you and falsely say all kinds of evil against you because
of me. [12]Rejoice and be glad, because great is your reward

[a]16 Isaiah 9:1,2   [b]25 That is, the Ten Cities

Was there any risk Jesus might yield to Satan's temptations? (4:3–11)

Some say the Spirit could never have put Jesus at risk since his divine nature would nev-er succumb to temptation. Others say that be-cause Jesus was human his temptations were legitimate. If this had been merely a mock spir-itual battle, they say, then our salvation could not be legitimate. See Heb. 2:14–18; 4:15.

Was the devil right to claim that the world belonged to him? (4:8–9)

Only partially right—this was a half-truth. The Bible speaks of Satan's power in the world (Eph. 2:1–2). But it was an exaggeration to present himself as sovereign over all of the earth's kingdoms.

In what sense was the kingdom of heaven near? (4:17)

The kingdom was near because the King was near. Jesus was introducing God's plan of sal-vation, of which he was the central figure. Through the life, death and resurrection of Jesus, God could regain a world in rebellion to his spiritual authority. When men and women repent, they leave the kingdom of the world and enter the kingdom of heaven. Not until Christ returns, though, will God's rule be fully realized on earth.

SCRIPTURE LINK (4:18–22)

The other Gospel writers also record Jesus' calling of his first disciples. See Mark 1:16–20; Luke 5:2–11 and John 1:35–42.

Were Simon and Andrew acting on impulse? (4:20)

Some see their immediate response as a mod-el of Christian discipleship. Others, with clues from John's Gospel (John 1:35–51), think Si-mon and Andrew may have followed Jesus in a limited sense before this incident. Having al-ready seen Jesus' power, they were ready when he asked for a more complete commit-ment.

Why do Matthew and Luke disagree about where the sermon was preached? (5:1)

Most likely Jesus spoke from a plateau that was part way down the mountain, making both Luke's description (Luke 6:17) and Matthew's correct. The two accounts are parallel in other respects, although Luke reduces Matthew's longer account to its basic core. It's also pos-sible that Luke records a different sermon from the one Matthew records.

SCRIPTURE LINK (5:3–12)

The Beatitudes can also be found in Luke 6:20–23.

Why did Jesus teach reversed values? (5:3–12)

He wanted to dispute the conventional wisdom of that time which said the wealthy and influen-tial enjoyed more of God's blessings. Jesus wanted his followers to see that material things are only temporary and certainly not the only reality. He didn't want them to think of their current situations as signs of God's blessing or judgment. Instead, he wanted them to see that the poor can be spiritually wealthy (James 2:5).

Why rejoice and be glad about persecution? (5:11–12)

Because it reinforces our identity with what is right—with Christ and the prophets. We can also be glad because, though righteousness has a price, it also has a reward. Persecution reminds us that we can anticipate something better in heaven. Matthew is not encouraging a martyr complex; there's no glory in pain. Joy comes not from the physical suffering itself but from the *reason* for the suffering: Jesus Christ.

How is the law fulfilled? (5:17–18)

With his sin-free life and sacrificial death, Christ perfectly kept both the letter *and* the spirit of the law. Other than Jesus, no one can perfectly obey God's law. But when God looks at believers in Christ, he sees Christ's righteousness instead of their sins. Christ, with his perfect life, paid our penalty for breaking God's law. Consequently God credits us with the righteousness from Christ's account. Also see *Did Jesus abolish the Old Testament law or fulfill it?* (Eph. 2:15).

Is there a class system in heaven? (5:19)

No. The terms *least* and *great* show those things which are valued in God's spiritual kingdom. The principles of the kingdom are found in values such as obedience and faithfulness to God's ways. Those who live according to God's ways will be rewarded. There will be no elitism in heaven, though some may receive greater rewards.

How can we do better than the Pharisees? (5:20)

By openly and honestly checking the spiritual condition of our hearts. The Pharisees, proud of their zealous efforts to follow every detail of Jewish law, could never admit they were *poor in spirit* (v. 3). Their outward religious legalism covered up their inner spiritual poverty. When we confess our need, God makes us righteous where our own efforts could not.

in heaven, for in the same way they persecuted the prophets[D] who were before you.

Salt and Light

13"You are the salt of the earth. But if the salt loses its saltiness, how can it be made salty again? It is no longer good for anything, except to be thrown out and trampled by men.

14"You are the light of the world. A city on a hill cannot be hidden. **15**Neither do people light a lamp and put it under a bowl. Instead they put it on its stand, and it gives light to everyone in the house. **16**In the same way, let your light shine before men, that they may see your good deeds and praise your Father in heaven.

The Fulfillment of the Law

17"Do not think that I have come to abolish the Law or the Prophets; I have not come to abolish them but to fulfill them. **18**I tell you the truth, until heaven and earth disappear, not the smallest letter, not the least stroke of a pen, will by any means disappear from the Law until everything is accomplished. **19**Anyone who breaks one of the least of these commandments and teaches others to do the same will be called least in the kingdom of heaven, but whoever practices and teaches these commands will be called great in the kingdom of heaven. **20**For I tell you that unless your righteousness[D] surpasses that of the Pharisees[D] and the teachers of the law, you will certainly not enter the kingdom of heaven.

Murder

21"You have heard that it was said to the people long ago, 'Do not murder,[a] and anyone who murders will be subject to judgment.' **22**But I tell you that anyone who is angry with his brother[b] will be subject to judgment. Again, anyone who says to his brother, 'Raca,[c]' is an-

a21 Exodus 20:13   *b22* Some manuscripts *brother without cause*
c22 An Aramaic term of contempt

Is it possible to live up to these standards? (5:3–10)

Even though the Sermon on the Mount has been called the constitution for citizens of the kingdom of God, we will never see flawed human beings, though they are Christians, reach this level of perfection. Jesus begins the Beatitudes, the preamble to this constitution, with our inability in mind—*Blessed are the poor in spirit, for theirs is the kingdom of heaven*. Those who begin by admitting their shortcomings are in the best position to experience God's blessing and enjoy his kingdom.

Nevertheless, we cannot escape the fact that Jesus gave his followers these lifestyle goals. Those who respond out of love for the Lord, grateful for his grace in their lives, will better approach these ideals. The Beatitudes are a model of perfection requiring our declaration of dependence on God: we can't, but God can. Even when doing so involves failure to follow perfectly, we're to press on in obedience.

The Beatitudes describe the quality of life God intended for humanity from the beginning—a life of blessing. The word *blessed* can also be translated *happy,* but it is something more than an emotion. The closer we come to Jesus' standards, the more we experience the blessing of God.

swerable to the Sanhedrin.^D But anyone who says, 'You fool!' will be in danger of the fire of hell.^D

23"Therefore, if you are offering your gift at the altar and there remember that your brother has something against you, **24**leave your gift there in front of the altar. First go and be reconciled to your brother; then come and offer your gift.

25"Settle matters quickly with your adversary who is taking you to court. Do it while you are still with him on the way, or he may hand you over to the judge, and the judge may hand you over to the officer, and you may be thrown into prison. **26**I tell you the truth, you will not get out until you have paid the last penny.^a

Adultery

27"You have heard that it was said, 'Do not commit adultery.'^b **28**But I tell you that anyone who looks at a woman lustfully has already committed adultery with her in his heart. **29**If your right eye causes you to sin, gouge it out and throw it away. It is better for you to lose one part of your body than for your whole body to be thrown into hell. **30**And if your right hand causes you to sin, cut it off and throw it away. It is better for you to lose one part of your body than for your whole body to go into hell.

Divorce

31"It has been said, 'Anyone who divorces his wife must give her a certificate of divorce.'^c **32**But I tell you that anyone who divorces his wife, except for marital unfaithfulness, causes her to become an adulteress, and anyone who marries the divorced woman commits adultery.

Oaths

33"Again, you have heard that it was said to the people long ago, 'Do not break your oath, but keep the oaths you have made to the Lord.' **34**But I tell you, Do not swear at all: either by heaven, for it is God's throne; **35**or by the earth, for it is his footstool^D; or by Jerusalem,^D for it is the city of the Great King. **36**And do not swear by your head, for you cannot make even one hair white or black. **37**Simply let your 'Yes' be 'Yes,' and your 'No,' 'No'; anything beyond this comes from the evil one.

An Eye for an Eye

38"You have heard that it was said, 'Eye for eye, and tooth for tooth.'^d **39**But I tell you, Do not resist an evil person. If someone strikes you on the right cheek, turn to him the other also. **40**And if someone wants to sue you and take your tunic, let him have your cloak as well. **41**If someone forces you to go one mile, go with him two miles. **42**Give to the one who asks you, and do not turn away from the one who wants to borrow from you.

Love for Enemies

43"You have heard that it was said, 'Love your neighbor^e and hate your enemy.' **44**But I tell you: Love your enemies^f and pray for those who persecute you, **45**that you may be sons of your Father in heaven. He causes his sun to rise on the evil and the good, and sends rain on the

---

What's so bad about name-calling? (5:22)

Sticks and stones and, yes, words can harm others. Jesus traces sin to its inner source: the condition of the human heart. Murder begins with a murderous attitude, wishing harm to another person. Jesus considers the intent as dangerous as the act. Angry words can harm the person uttering them as much as their intended target.

Hell (5:22)

Derived from *gehenna*, a word that refers to the Valley of Hinnom, a deep ravine outside of Jerusalem (see **Map 8** at the back of this Bible). During the regimes of Ahaz and Manasseh, two of Judah's evil kings in the Old Testament, human sacrifices had been offered to the pagan god Molech in this ravine. It subsequently became a dumping ground of smoldering garbage and a place where the corpses of criminals were discarded. Jews in Christ's time used it as a metaphor for the place of final punishment.

SCRIPTURE LINK (5:25–26)

Luke records Jesus' instruction for handling matters with one's adversary in Luke 12:58–59.

Gouge it out . . . cut it off (5:29–30)

This is hyperbole, a figure of speech in which exaggeration is used to emphasize a point. Jesus used hyperbole here to get his listeners' attention: Sin is deadly serious; radical measures are required to eradicate it. Persistent or recurring sin jeopardizes spiritual life much as a gangrenous infection threatens physical health.

Is divorce never an option for Christians? (5:32)

See *Is divorce always wrong?* (Mark 10:1–12).

Is it wrong to swear to tell the truth in court? (5:34–37)

Jesus was talking about the misuse of oaths common in Jewish culture (the equivalent of someone today saying, "I swear to God"). He was not prohibiting solemn vows. Jesus' point is that truth-telling is essential, no matter how costly. At times it may be appropriate to commit ourselves to the truthfulness of our words. Even God set an example of swearing by himself to prove his word trustworthy. See *If God swore an oath, should we?* (Heb. 6:13).

Should evil people never be resisted? (5:39)

Jesus is setting forth the way to break the vicious cycle of retaliation. God's people are to work for justice but not take personal revenge. Elsewhere the Bible makes it clear that Christians are to resist the devil (James 4:7) and the forces of evil that are in society (Eph. 6:13).

---

^a26 Greek *kodrantes*   ^b27 Exodus 20:14   ^c31 Deut. 24:1
^d38 Exodus 21:24; Lev. 24:20; Deut. 19:21   ^e43 Lev. 19:18
^f44 Some late manuscripts *enemies, bless those who curse you, do good to those who hate you*

Who can be as perfect as God? (5:48)

No one can be as perfect as God. But Jesus does not call us to an exercise in futility. The word *perfect* implies completion or maturity, something more than sinless perfection. Later Jesus summarized the whole law with two basic principles—the laws of love for God and for neighbor (22:37–40). Here, in the same way, Jesus says that the law of love (vv. 43–44) represents the full and mature expression of the law. To live in a *perfect* way, God's love must flow through our lives to others—even to our enemies.

Can we hide our *acts of righteousness* and still let our light shine? (6:1; see 5:16)

It depends on our motivation. Doing the right things for the wrong reasons (to gain the honor and recognition of others, for example) undermines the purity of our good works. Jesus encourages us to let our deeds be seen so that onlookers will glorify God, not so they will be impressed with us.

Why are some prayers wrong? (6:7)

When prayers are reduced to techniques or formulas as a means to manipulate God, they are wrong. In the first century, some had developed long lists with the names of pagan gods. They would recite their lists hoping to correctly pronounce the names of the true gods and thereby harness their power to grant their wishes. Others would endlessly repeat phrases or syllables in an attempt to earn the favor of the gods. Jesus recalled such pagan practices to show that true prayer depends on what is in the heart more than what is on the tongue.

If God knows what we need before we ask, why ask? (6:8)

Prayer was never intended to inform God of something he doesn't know. The point of prayer isn't merely to get what we want but to nurture our relationship with God. As a result, prayer can change us rather than the situation, reinforcing our confidence in our God's sufficiency and realigning our will with his will. On the other hand, God invites us to involve ourselves in his work by praying. He tells us that we lack what we need because we fail to pray: *You do not have, because you do not ask God* (James 4:2). When it seems that answers to prayer are slow in coming, Jesus urges us to keep on praying and not give up (Luke 18:1–8).

SCRIPTURE LINK (6:9–13)

Luke shares Jesus' prayer in Luke 11:2–4.

Why pray for God's will to be done? (6:10)

Because when we do, we yield to God's authority, giving him permission to fulfill his best purposes in our lives. It is a humble admission that he knows better than we what is right. It also announces our intentions to obey him, so we will not obstruct his purposes or hinder the advancement of the kingdom of God.

What are the benefits of sincere fasting? (6:18)

The purpose of fasting is to attract the attention of God, not the attention of others. As a spiritual discipline, fasting can help us focus more intently on God, increasing our ability to concentrate mentally and increasing our sensi-

righteous[D] and the unrighteous. **46**If you love those who love you, what reward will you get? Are not even the tax collectors[D] doing that? **47**And if you greet only your brothers, what are you doing more than others? Do not even pagans do that? **48**Be perfect, therefore, as your heavenly Father is perfect.

Giving to the Needy

6 "Be careful not to do your 'acts of righteousness[D]' before men, to be seen by them. If you do, you will have no reward from your Father in heaven.

2"So when you give to the needy, do not announce it with trumpets, as the hypocrites do in the synagogues and on the streets, to be honored by men. I tell you the truth, they have received their reward in full. **3**But when you give to the needy, do not let your left hand know what your right hand is doing, **4**so that your giving may be in secret. Then your Father, who sees what is done in secret, will reward you.

Prayer

5"And when you pray, do not be like the hypocrites, for they love to pray standing in the synagogues and on the street corners to be seen by men. I tell you the truth, they have received their reward in full. **6**But when you pray, go into your room, close the door and pray to your Father, who is unseen. Then your Father, who sees what is done in secret, will reward you. **7**And when you pray, do not keep on babbling like pagans, for they think they will be heard because of their many words. **8**Do not be like them, for your Father knows what you need before you ask him.

9"This, then, is how you should pray:

" 'Our Father in heaven,
hallowed be your name,
10your kingdom come,
your will be done
on earth as it is in heaven.
11Give us today our daily bread.
12Forgive us our debts,
as we also have forgiven our debtors.
13And lead us not into temptation,
but deliver us from the evil one.[a] '

14For if you forgive men when they sin against you, your heavenly Father will also forgive you. **15**But if you do not forgive men their sins, your Father will not forgive your sins.

Fasting

16"When you fast, do not look somber as the hypocrites do, for they disfigure their faces to show men they are fasting. I tell you the truth, they have received their reward in full. **17**But when you fast, put oil on your head and wash your face, **18**so that it will not be obvious to men that you are fasting, but only to your Father, who is unseen; and your Father, who sees what is done in secret, will reward you.

Treasures in Heaven

19"Do not store up for yourselves treasures on earth, where moth and rust destroy, and where thieves break in

---

a13 Or *from evil*; some late manuscripts *one, / for yours is the kingdom and the power and the glory forever. Amen.*

and steal. **20**But store up for yourselves treasures in heaven, where moth and rust do not destroy, and where thieves do not break in and steal. **21**For where your treasure is, there your heart will be also.

22"The eye is the lamp of the body. If your eyes are good, your whole body will be full of light. **23**But if your eyes are bad, your whole body will be full of darkness. If then the light within you is darkness, how great is that darkness!

24"No one can serve two masters. Either he will hate the one and love the other, or he will be devoted to the one and despise the other. You cannot serve both God and Money.

Do Not Worry

25"Therefore I tell you, do not worry about your life, what you will eat or drink; or about your body, what you will wear. Is not life more important than food, and the body more important than clothes? **26**Look at the birds of the air; they do not sow or reap or store away in barns, and yet your heavenly Father feeds them. Are you not much more valuable than they? **27**Who of you by worrying can add a single hour to his life*a*?

28"And why do you worry about clothes? See how the lilies of the field grow. They do not labor or spin. **29**Yet I tell you that not even Solomon in all his splendor was dressed like one of these. **30**If that is how God clothes the grass of the field, which is here today and tomorrow is thrown into the fire, will he not much more clothe you, O you of little faith? **31**So do not worry, saying, 'What shall we eat?' or 'What shall we drink?' or 'What shall we wear?' **32**For the pagans run after all these things, and your heavenly Father knows that you need them. **33**But seek first his kingdom and his righteousness**D**, and all these things will be given to you as well. **34**Therefore do not worry about tomorrow, for tomorrow will worry about itself. Each day has enough trouble of its own.

Judging Others

7 "Do not judge, or you too will be judged. **2**For in the same way you judge others, you will be judged, and with the measure you use, it will be measured to you.

3"Why do you look at the speck of sawdust in your brother's eye and pay no attention to the plank in your own eye? **4**How can you say to your brother, 'Let me take the speck out of your eye,' when all the time there is a plank in your own eye? **5**You hypocrite, first take the plank out of your own eye, and then you will see clearly to remove the speck from your brother's eye.

6"Do not give dogs what is sacred**D**; do not throw your pearls to pigs. If you do, they may trample them under their feet, and then turn and tear you to pieces.

Ask, Seek, Knock

7"Ask and it will be given to you; seek and you will find; knock and the door will be opened to you. **8**For everyone who asks receives; he who seeks finds; and to him who knocks, the door will be opened. **9**"Which of you, if his son asks for bread, will give him a stone? **10**Or if he asks for a fish, will give him a snake? **11**If you, then, though you are evil, know how to give good gifts to your children, how much more will your Father in

a27 Or single cubit to his height

---

tivity to the things of the Spirit. Some suggest that fasting also cleanses the body of toxins and, by extension, cleanses the spirit of preoccupations. Also see *Should Christians fast?* (9:14–15).

Eye . . . the lamp of the body (6:22)
In Jesus' day, the eye was thought to be like a window that carried light into the body. An eye could be either good or bad. Because the surrounding verses focus on wealth, the meaning of the word *good* seems to imply *generous*, and the word *bad* means *greedy*. A generous eye brings moral health, and a greedy eye corrupts one's entire perspective.

SCRIPTURE LINK (6:22,23)
Luke talks about the eye being the lamp of the body in Luke 11:34–36.

How can light be darkness? (6:23)
This is a figure of speech that's explained from the context of this verse. Jesus was speaking about the light we take into our minds. We can take in so-called "light" that is actually darkness—something false or evil masquerading as something true or good. If a person is open to this kind of "light," soon that person will be filled with darkness. So Jesus warns us to be careful about what ideas and thoughts we entertain.

Does Jesus command us not to worry? (6:25)
Jesus does not give a command so much as an invitation to rest in the arms of a loving Father. As humans, we will at times cross the line and fret when we should trust. But only when we allow ourselves to constantly focus on ourselves instead of on God do we violate Jesus' principle. He gave it to us as a liberating principle, not as another law to worry about.

SCRIPTURE LINK (6:25–33)
Luke covers Jesus' admonition against worry in Luke 12:22–31.

SCRIPTURE LINK (7:3–5)
Jesus' teaching about judging others can also be found in Luke 6:41–42.

What is so sacred? (7:6)
Some think this verse refers to evangelism: Christians who dispense the priceless pearls of God's redemptive plan should be careful about giving ammunition to those who would enjoy denouncing the truth. Instead they should preach to those who are prepared by the Spirit of God to receive the truth. Others, however, believe this is common sense advice to preserve the lives of believers in a hostile world: they should guard themselves from being trampled underfoot by scoffers.

What can we expect when we pray? (7:7–8)
What Jesus promises here is insight and direction through the work of the Spirit within us. Jesus does not promise that we will receive whatever we might think we need. As the Holy Spirit directs our hearts, we will desire those things that will benefit us spiritually. We can have faith to see those things accomplished as the fulfillment of his promise.

Narrow gate . . . narrow the road (7:13–14)

The narrow road and narrow gate symbolize the challenge presented by the way of the kingdom. It's a road of suffering and self-denial, not the path taken by the majority.

How do we guard against false prophets without judging? (7:15–16)

Jesus tells us *Do not judge* (v. 1), a caution against being judgmental about people's intentions. Pointing out heresy, however, is not judging the motives of others, but merely identifying the obvious. In this case Jesus urges us to be on the lookout for those whose lifestyles and teachings stand as an indictment against them.

How can evildoers do miracles in Jesus' name? (7:22–23)

Some think this means that God occasionally works through flawed instruments—unregenerated ministers, for example. His work is accomplished in spite of such people, not because of them. Others say that miracles may come from sources other than God: Satan can produce counterfeit miracles. Psychological delusions or hypnotic suggestions may explain others. Some impostors, claiming their supernatural abilities come from the Lord, may fool others and sometimes even themselves.

SCRIPTURE LINK (7:24–27)

Jesus' story of the wise and foolish builders can also be found in Luke 6:46–49.

SCRIPTURE LINK (8:2–4)

In Mark 1:40–44, Mark tells about Jesus healing the man with leprosy. Luke gives the account in Luke 5:12–14.

Why did Jesus touch the leper? (8:3)

Though he upheld the spirit of the law, Jesus could be accused by his critics of breaking the letter of the Old Testament law about lepers: to touch anything ceremonially unclean was forbidden (Lev. 5:2). Since lepers were unclean, they were banished from the community and dressed as mourners grieving their own death (Lev. 13:45–46). By touching an "untouchable," Jesus demonstrated his authority over the law. He cared more about people's needs than about religious ritual.

Why didn't Jesus want anyone to hear of his miracles? (8:4)

See *Why didn't Jesus want anyone to know he was the Christ?* (16:20).

SCRIPTURE LINK (8:5–13)

Read about the centurion's faith in Luke 7:1–10.

Why was Jesus amazed? (8:10)

Jesus was amazed that this Gentile seemed more spiritually aware than most Jews. His amazement was two-sided: (1) that a Gentile understood spiritual authority; and (2) that God's chosen people did not. The only other time Jesus was amazed like this was over the Jews' lack of faith (Mark 6:6).

Subjects of the kingdom (8:12)

These *subjects* were Jews, in contrast to the *many* (Gentiles) in the previous verse. Though they were native to God's promises, the Jews also needed faith. Faith is the prerequisite of eternal life regardless of nationality.

---

heaven give good gifts to those who ask him! [12]So in everything, do to others what you would have them do to you, for this sums up the Law and the Prophets[D].

The Narrow and Wide Gates

[13]"Enter through the narrow gate. For wide is the gate and broad is the road that leads to destruction, and many enter through it. [14]But small is the gate and narrow the road that leads to life, and only a few find it.

A Tree and Its Fruit

[15]"Watch out for false prophets. They come to you in sheep's clothing, but inwardly they are ferocious wolves. [16]By their fruit you will recognize them. Do people pick grapes from thornbushes, or figs from thistles? [17]Likewise every good tree bears good fruit, but a bad tree bears bad fruit. [18]A good tree cannot bear bad fruit, and a bad tree cannot bear good fruit. [19]Every tree that does not bear good fruit is cut down and thrown into the fire. [20]Thus, by their fruit you will recognize them.

[21]"Not everyone who says to me, 'Lord, Lord,' will enter the kingdom of heaven, but only he who does the will of my Father who is in heaven. [22]Many will say to me on that day, 'Lord, Lord, did we not prophesy in your name, and in your name drive out demons and perform many miracles?' [23]Then I will tell them plainly, 'I never knew you. Away from me, you evildoers!'

The Wise and Foolish Builders

[24]"Therefore everyone who hears these words of mine and puts them into practice is like a wise man who built his house on the rock. [25]The rain came down, the streams rose, and the winds blew and beat against that house; yet it did not fall, because it had its foundation on the rock. [26]But everyone who hears these words of mine and does not put them into practice is like a foolish man who built his house on sand. [27]The rain came down, the streams rose, and the winds blew and beat against that house, and it fell with a great crash."

[28]When Jesus had finished saying these things, the crowds were amazed at his teaching, [29]because he taught as one who had authority, and not as their teachers of the law.

The Man With Leprosy

8 When he came down from the mountainside, large crowds followed him. [2]A man with leprosy[D][a] came and knelt before him and said, "Lord, if you are willing, you can make me clean."

[3]Jesus reached out his hand and touched the man. "I am willing," he said. "Be clean!" Immediately he was cured[b] of his leprosy. [4]Then Jesus said to him, "See that you don't tell anyone. But go, show yourself to the priest[D] and offer the gift Moses commanded, as a testimony to them."

The Faith of the Centurion

[5]When Jesus had entered Capernaum, a centurion[D] came to him, asking for help. [6]"Lord," he said, "my servant lies at home paralyzed and in terrible suffering."

---

a2 The Greek word was used for various diseases affecting the skin—not necessarily leprosy.   *b3* Greek *made clean*

7Jesus said to him, "I will go and heal him."

8The centurion[D] replied, "Lord, I do not deserve to have you come under my roof. But just say the word, and my servant will be healed. 9For I myself am a man under authority, with soldiers under me. I tell this one, 'Go,' and he goes; and that one, 'Come,' and he comes. I say to my servant, 'Do this,' and he does it."

10When Jesus heard this, he was astonished and said to those following him, "I tell you the truth, I have not found anyone in Israel with such great faith. 11I say to you that many will come from the east and the west, and will take their places at the feast with Abraham, Isaac and Jacob in the kingdom of heaven. 12But the subjects of the kingdom will be thrown outside, into the darkness, where there will be weeping and gnashing of teeth."

13Then Jesus said to the centurion, "Go! It will be done just as you believed it would." And his servant was healed at that very hour.

Jesus Heals Many

14When Jesus came into Peter's house, he saw Peter's mother-in-law lying in bed with a fever. 15He touched her hand and the fever left her, and she got up and began to wait on him.

16When evening came, many who were demon-possessed were brought to him, and he drove out the spirits with a word and healed all the sick. 17This was to fulfill what was spoken through the prophet[D] Isaiah:

"He took up our infirmities
and carried our diseases."[a]

The Cost of Following Jesus

18When Jesus saw the crowd around him, he gave orders to cross to the other side of the lake. 19Then a teacher of the law came to him and said, "Teacher, I will follow you wherever you go."

20Jesus replied, "Foxes have holes and birds of the air have nests, but the Son of Man[D] has no place to lay his head."

21Another disciple[D] said to him, "Lord, first let me go and bury my father."

22But Jesus told him, "Follow me, and let the dead bury their own dead."

Jesus Calms the Storm

23Then he got into the boat and his disciples followed him. 24Without warning, a furious storm came up on the lake, so that the waves swept over the boat. But Jesus was sleeping. 25The disciples went and woke him, saying, "Lord, save us! We're going to drown!"

26He replied, "You of little faith, why are you so afraid?" Then he got up and rebuked the winds and the waves, and it was completely calm.

27The men were amazed and asked, "What kind of man is this? Even the winds and the waves obey him!"

The Healing of Two Demon-possessed Men

28When he arrived at the other side in the region of the Gadarenes,[b] two demon-possessed men coming from the tombs met him. They were so violent that no one

---

Darkness . . . weeping . . . gnashing (8:12)

Jesus uses the word *darkness* to illustrate an existence apart from the light of God's presence. The idea is expanded with other graphic words: *weeping* implies suffering; *gnashing of teeth* signifies despair.

Did healing depend on the centurion's belief? (8:13)

See *Why did Jesus require people's faith to do miracles?* (13:58).

SCRIPTURE LINK (8:14–16)

Mark and Luke both tell about the healing of Peter's mother-in-law and others. See Mark 1:29–34 and Luke 4:38–41.

SCRIPTURE LINK (8:19–22)

Luke talks about the cost of following Jesus in Luke 9:57–60.

Why did Jesus discourage those who were at least going in the right direction? (8:20)

He wanted them to know it would cost them something to follow him, and not to discover later that there were additional requirements to being his disciples. As the Jewish religious leaders became increasingly hostile toward Jesus, he wanted his disciples to be prepared for the worst (John 15:18).

What was wrong with a disciple burying his father? (8:22)

Most likely the problem was that his father was still quite alive. Jews understood the command to honor father and mother to mean caring for their elderly parents and giving them a proper burial. Apparently this man had not yet put his commitment to Christ above these cultural expectations. Some suggest he may have used an expression for putting things off: "Let me wait until my father reaches the end of his life (which, by the way, could be years from now)." Either way, he was insincere about devoting himself to Jesus.

SCRIPTURE LINK (8:23–27)

For Mark's and Luke's accounts of Jesus calming the storm, see Mark 4:36–41 and Luke 8:22–25. Matthew tells about Jesus calming another storm in 14:22–33.

Does having faith mean we'll never be afraid? (8:26)

Jesus doesn't promise we'll never face fearful circumstances. Instead, he teaches that God is greater than whatever we are facing and he is in control. Faith means trusting that we never face dangers alone. Knowing God is present keeps fear from paralyzing us.

SCRIPTURE LINK (8:28–34)

Mark tells about Jesus healing the demon possessed in Mark 5:1–17 and Luke covers it in Luke 8:26–37.

Why doesn't Matthew agree with Mark and Luke? (8:28; see Mark 5:2; Luke 8:27)

Whenever there is more than one witness to an event, there will be more than one account of it. It's not necessarily that the witnesses disagree; it's that they stress different aspects of the story. Many think that while Matthew

---

[a]17 Isaiah 53:4   [b]28 Some manuscripts *Gergesenes*; others *Gerasenes*

had the number of demoniacs right, Mark and Luke chose to focus on only one of the men—probably the one who was most notorious and feared for the extreme degree to which he was demon possessed. Also see *Why does Matthew mention two blind men while Mark and Luke mention only one?* (20:30).

Why would demons beg to go into a herd of pigs? (8:31)

The reason is unclear. Some think demons, as spiritual beings, desire a physical body of some sort to inhabit. But when these demons drove the crazed pigs to their death, they were left without a material body. Though a satisfactory answer may not be found, the point here is to see Jesus' power over the demons, not to explain demon possession.

What happened to the demons after the pigs drowned? (8:32)

The evil spirits, left without a living body to inhabit, probably searched for others they could enter (see 12:45). It was not yet the time for Jesus to execute final judgment upon Satan, but the slaughter of the pigs served as a sign of coming judgment on Satan, his demons and everyone who opposes Christ.

SCRIPTURE LINK (9:2–8)

You can find Mark's and Luke's accounts of Jesus healing the paralytic in Mark 2:3–12 and Luke 5:18–26.

Tax collectors (9:9–10)

A group of Jews despised by other Jews for collaborating with the Roman government that ruled over them. Tax collectors paid the authorities for the privilege of collecting taxes, then would overcharge the people, skimming off the top to line their own pockets.

SCRIPTURE LINK (9:9–13)

Mark recounts the calling of Matthew in Mark 2:14–17. Luke describes it in Luke 5:27–32.

Should Christians fast? (9:14–15)

Jesus compared his time with his disciples to a wedding feast. Since he is no longer physically among us, it is appropriate to fast—not because it is commanded as in the Old Testament, but because it is beneficial to our spiritual development. Fasting helps us concentrate in prayer. It heightens our spiritual awareness, lends intensity to our communion with God and reminds us of our weaknesses and complete dependence on God. Also see *What are the benefits of sincere fasting?* (6:18).

SCRIPTURE LINK (9:14–17)

Mark and Luke also cover Jesus' teaching on fasting. See Mark 2:18–22 and Luke 5:33–39.

New wine . . . old wineskins (9:17)

Wineskins were the bottles of the first century. They were made of animal skins sewn in the shape of a flexible bag. At first they were soft and pliable, but with age they became brittle. Since wine gives off gases and expands as it undergoes the process of fermentation, a wineskin would have to stretch to accommodate the expanding wine. Non-elastic, old skins would burst during fermentation. Jesus used this as a metaphor: *old wineskins* represented the Jewish system, which was unable to accommodate the *new wine* of the kingdom of God.

could pass that way. [29]"What do you want with us, Son of God?" they shouted. "Have you come here to torture us before the appointed time?"

[30]Some distance from them a large herd of pigs was feeding. [31]The demons begged Jesus, "If you drive us out, send us into the herd of pigs."

[32]He said to them, "Go!" So they came out and went into the pigs, and the whole herd rushed down the steep bank into the lake and died in the water. [33]Those tending the pigs ran off, went into the town and reported all this, including what had happened to the demon-possessed men. [34]Then the whole town went out to meet Jesus. And when they saw him, they pleaded with him to leave their region.

Jesus Heals a Paralytic

9 Jesus stepped into a boat, crossed over and came to his own town. [2]Some men brought to him a paralytic, lying on a mat. When Jesus saw their faith, he said to the paralytic, "Take heart, son; your sins are forgiven."

[3]At this, some of the teachers of the law said to themselves, "This fellow is blaspheming!"

[4]Knowing their thoughts, Jesus said, "Why do you entertain evil thoughts in your hearts? [5]Which is easier: to say, 'Your sins are forgiven,' or to say, 'Get up and walk'? [6]But so that you may know that the Son of Man[D] has authority on earth to forgive sins. . . ." Then he said to the paralytic, "Get up, take your mat and go home." [7]And the man got up and went home. [8]When the crowd saw this, they were filled with awe; and they praised God, who had given such authority to men.

The Calling of Matthew

[9]As Jesus went on from there, he saw a man named Matthew sitting at the tax collector's[D] booth. "Follow me," he told him, and Matthew got up and followed him.

[10]While Jesus was having dinner at Matthew's house, many tax collectors and "sinners" came and ate with him and his disciples[D]. [11]When the Pharisees[D] saw this, they asked his disciples, "Why does your teacher eat with tax collectors and 'sinners'?"

[12]On hearing this, Jesus said, "It is not the healthy who need a doctor, but the sick. [13]But go and learn what this means: 'I desire mercy[D], not sacrifice[D].'[a] For I have not come to call the righteous[D], but sinners."

Jesus Questioned About Fasting

[14]Then John's disciples came and asked him, "How is it that we and the Pharisees fast, but your disciples do not fast?"

[15]Jesus answered, "How can the guests of the bridegroom mourn while he is with them? The time will come when the bridegroom will be taken from them; then they will fast.

[16]"No one sews a patch of unshrunk cloth on an old garment, for the patch will pull away from the garment, making the tear worse. [17]Neither do men pour new wine[D] into old wineskins[D]. If they do, the skins will burst, the wine will run out and the wineskins will be ruined. No, they pour new wine into new wineskins, and both are preserved."

a13 Hosea 6:6

A Dead Girl and a Sick Woman

18While he was saying this, a ruler came and knelt before him and said, "My daughter has just died. But come and put your hand on her, and she will live." **19**Jesus got up and went with him, and so did his disciples^D.

20Just then a woman who had been subject to bleeding for twelve years came up behind him and touched the edge of his cloak. **21**She said to herself, "If I only touch his cloak, I will be healed."

22Jesus turned and saw her. "Take heart, daughter," he said, "your faith has healed you." And the woman was healed from that moment.

23When Jesus entered the ruler's house and saw the flute players and the noisy crowd, **24**he said, "Go away. The girl is not dead but asleep." But they laughed at him. **25**After the crowd had been put outside, he went in and took the girl by the hand, and she got up. **26**News of this spread through all that region.

Jesus Heals the Blind and Mute

27As Jesus went on from there, two blind men followed him, calling out, "Have mercy^D on us, Son of David!"

28When he had gone indoors, the blind men came to him, and he asked them, "Do you believe that I am able to do this?"

"Yes, Lord," they replied.

29Then he touched their eyes and said, "According to your faith will it be done to you"; **30**and their sight was restored. Jesus warned them sternly, "See that no one knows about this." **31**But they went out and spread the news about him all over that region.

32While they were going out, a man who was demon-possessed and could not talk was brought to Jesus. **33**And when the demon was driven out, the man who had been mute spoke. The crowd was amazed and said, "Nothing like this has ever been seen in Israel."

34But the Pharisees^D said, "It is by the prince of demons that he drives out demons."

The Workers Are Few

35Jesus went through all the towns and villages, teaching in their synagogues, preaching the good news of the kingdom and healing every disease and sickness. **36**When he saw the crowds, he had compassion on them, because they were harassed and helpless, like sheep without a shepherd. **37**Then he said to his disciples, "The harvest is plentiful but the workers are few. **38**Ask the Lord of the harvest, therefore, to send out workers into his harvest field."

Jesus Sends Out the Twelve

10 He called his twelve disciples to him and gave them authority to drive out evil^a spirits and to heal every disease and sickness.

2These are the names of the twelve apostles^D: first, Simon (who is called Peter) and his brother Andrew; James son of Zebedee, and his brother John; **3**Philip and Bartholomew; Thomas and Matthew the tax collector^D; James son of Alphaeus, and Thaddaeus; **4**Simon the Zealot and Judas Iscariot, who betrayed him.

5These twelve Jesus sent out with the following instruc-

a1 Greek *unclean*

SCRIPTURE LINK (9:18-26)

Mark reports on Jesus' healing of the sick woman and raising of the dead girl in Mark 5:22-43. Luke gives an account in Luke 8:41-56.

Will I be healed if I have faith? (9:22)

Jesus teaches that faith prompts God to respond to our need. Sometimes, it is the faith of friends or family that God rewards. Occasionally, God's healing work seems unrelated to anyone's faith—the only explanation is God's sovereign choice. But Jesus never teaches that faith automatically brings healing. In Christ's 35 miracles recorded in the Gospels, no formula to guarantee healing can be found. Also see **Does God guarantee healing from any disease?** (Psalm 103:3) and **Is healing guaranteed?** (James 5:15-16).

Why have flutes and noise at a funeral? (9:23)

At ancient Middle Eastern funerals, mourners vented their sorrow without reservation. In fact, more noise expressed greater grief, so the culture expected professional wailers to be hired to better help a family grieve. Music then, as now, was commonly used to enhance the emotions during either festive celebrations or times of sorrow.

Why say the dead are only *asleep*? (9:24)

Just as many people today use "passed away," the Bible uses "asleep" as a euphemism for death (John 11:11-14; 1 Cor. 11:30; 15:51; 1 Thes. 4:13-15). Jesus speaks of death as sleep only because it is no more serious than slumber for believers, whom Christ will raise when he returns.

Why ask the blind men if they believed? (9:28-29)

See **Why did Jesus require people's faith to do miracles?** (13:58).

Why not tell? (9:30)

See **Why didn't Jesus want anyone to know he was the Christ?** (16:20).

SCRIPTURE LINK (10:2-4)

Mark gives the names of the disciples in Mark 3:16-19. Luke names them in Luke 6:14-16.

Why hide the message from Gentiles and Samaritans? (10:5)

Jesus' intent was not to exclude but to prioritize. God's plan of salvation originated with the Jewish people, and Jesus, the Messiah, was a Jew. Later Jesus would commission his disciples to go to the entire world (28:19).

Leprosy (10:8)

See *Leprosy* (Mark 1:40).

Why did Jesus say to take nothing? (10:9–10)

Jesus wanted the Twelve to be completely dependent on God for their provision. He wanted them to see how God would provide for them. He was not setting a precedent, however, that all ministries must follow. The New Testament churches were encouraged to support those who ministered to them (Phil. 4:14; 1 Tim. 5:17–18; 3 John 5–8).

SCRIPTURE LINK (10:9–15)

Mark details Jesus' instructions to his disciples in Mark 6:8–11. Luke does so in Luke 9:3–5; 10:4–12.

Why *shake the dust off your feet*? (10:14)

Jews returning to Israel from a foreign land would shake the dust from their sandals and clothing to avoid defiling the land they considered holy. The disciples were delivering a similar warning to the people of Israel. If they rejected the message of Christ, they would face the same future judgment as unbelieving foreigners.

Sheep among wolves (10:16)

Some think this illustrates the danger to which the disciples would be exposed. Others place the emphasis on the character qualities of the two animals: the sheep-like response of the disciples and the ferocious reactions of the religious and political leaders.

How shrewd are snakes? (10:16)

In the ancient Middle East, the serpent was a symbol of cunning whose wisdom was worth emulating. Most likely Jesus was quoting a proverb familiar to his listeners.

What's wrong with preparing a legal defense? (10:19)

Nothing. Jesus is simply saying that when we face legal battles because of our stand for him, we won't have to *worry*. Though we may have legal counsel and a prepared defense, our trust ultimately must be in God. Jesus, anticipating his disciples' future troubles, was simply assuring them that they need not panic. The Spirit would be with them to assist them during such times.

SCRIPTURE LINK (10:19–22)

In Mark 13:11–13, Mark relates Jesus' words about persecution. Luke records them in Luke 21:12–17.

Beelzebub (10:25)

The prince of demons, that is, Satan (12:24). In the Old Testament, *Baal* was a Canaanite deity, expanded to *Beelzebul* (meaning *Exalted* or *Prince Baal*). The Jews may have mocked Baal by adding *-zebub* (meaning *Lord of the Flies*). See **Was the king involved in Satan worship?** (2 Kings 1:2).

SCRIPTURE LINK (10:26–33)

Jesus' words about his Father's care can also be found in Luke 12:2–9.

---

tions: "Do not go among the Gentiles[D] or enter any town of the Samaritans. **6**Go rather to the lost sheep of Israel. **7**As you go, preach this message: 'The kingdom of heaven is near.' **8**Heal the sick, raise the dead, cleanse those who have leprosy[D],[a] drive out demons. Freely you have received, freely give. **9**Do not take along any gold or silver or copper in your belts; **10**take no bag for the journey, or extra tunic, or sandals or a staff; for the worker is worth his keep.

11"Whatever town or village you enter, search for some worthy person there and stay at his house until you leave. **12**As you enter the home, give it your greeting. **13**If the home is deserving, let your peace[D] rest on it; if it is not, let your peace return to you. **14**If anyone will not welcome you or listen to your words, shake the dust off your feet when you leave that home or town. **15**I tell you the truth, it will be more bearable for Sodom and Gomorrah on the day of judgment than for that town. **16**I am sending you out like sheep among wolves. Therefore be as shrewd as snakes and as innocent as doves.

17"Be on your guard against men; they will hand you over to the local councils and flog you in their synagogues. **18**On my account you will be brought before governors and kings as witnesses to them and to the Gentiles. **19**But when they arrest you, do not worry about what to say or how to say it. At that time you will be given what to say, **20**for it will not be you speaking, but the Spirit of your Father speaking through you.

21"Brother will betray brother to death[D], and a father his child; children will rebel against their parents and have them put to death. **22**All men will hate you because of me, but he who stands firm to the end will be saved. **23**When you are persecuted in one place, flee to another. I tell you the truth, you will not finish going through the cities of Israel before the Son of Man[D] comes.

24"A student is not above his teacher, nor a servant above his master. **25**It is enough for the student to be like his teacher, and the servant like his master. If the head of the house has been called Beelzebub[D],[b] how much more the members of his household!

26"So do not be afraid of them. There is nothing concealed that will not be disclosed, or hidden that will not be made known. **27**What I tell you in the dark, speak in the daylight; what is whispered in your ear, proclaim from the roofs. **28**Do not be afraid of those who kill the body but cannot kill the soul[D]. Rather, be afraid of the One who can destroy both soul and body in hell. **29**Are not two sparrows sold for a penny[c]? Yet not one of them will fall to the ground apart from the will of your Father. **30**And even the very hairs of your head are all numbered. **31**So don't be afraid; you are worth more than many sparrows.

32"Whoever acknowledges me before men, I will also acknowledge him before my Father in heaven. **33**But whoever disowns me before men, I will disown him before my Father in heaven.

34"Do not suppose that I have come to bring peace to the earth. I did not come to bring peace, but a sword. **35**For I have come to turn

---

[a]8 The Greek word was used for various diseases affecting the skin—not necessarily leprosy.   [b]25 Greek *Beezeboul* or *Beelzeboul*
[c]29 Greek *an assarion*

" 'a man against his father,
  a daughter against her mother,
  a daughter-in-law against her mother-in-law—
  36 a man's enemies will be the members of his
  own household.'*a*

37"Anyone who loves his father or mother more than
me is not worthy of me; anyone who loves his son or
daughter more than me is not worthy of me; **38**and anyone who does not take his cross and follow me is not worthy of me. **39**Whoever finds his life will lose it, and whoever loses his life for my sake will find it.

40"He who receives you receives me, and he who receives me receives the one who sent me. **41**Anyone who
receives a prophetᴰ because he is a prophet will receive a prophet's reward, and anyone who receives a
righteousᴰ man because he is a righteous man will receive a righteous man's reward. **42**And if anyone gives
even a cup of cold water to one of these little ones because he is my discipleᴰ, I tell you the truth, he will certainly not lose his reward."

Jesus and John the Baptist

11 After Jesus had finished instructing his twelve disciples, he went on from there to teach and
preach in the towns of Galilee.*b*

2When John heard in prison what Christ was doing, he
sent his disciples **3**to ask him, "Are you the one who was
to come, or should we expect someone else?"

4Jesus replied, "Go back and report to John what you
hear and see: **5**The blind receive sight, the lame walk,
those who have leprosyᴰc are cured, the deaf hear, the
dead are raised, and the good news is preached to the
poor. **6**Blessed is the man who does not fall away on account of me."

7As John's disciples were leaving, Jesus began to
speak to the crowd about John: "What did you go out into
the desert to see? A reed swayed by the wind? **8**If not,
what did you go out to see? A man dressed in fine clothes?
No, those who wear fine clothes are in kings' palaces.
9Then what did you go out to see? A prophet? Yes, I tell
you, and more than a prophet. **10**This is the one about
whom it is written:

" 'I will send my messenger ahead of you,
  who will prepare your way before you.'*d*

11I tell you the truth: Among those born of women there
has not risen anyone greater than John the Baptist; yet he
who is least in the kingdom of heaven is greater than he.
12From the days of John the Baptist until now, the kingdom of heaven has been forcefully advancing, and forceful men lay hold of it. **13**For all the Prophets and the Law
prophesied until John. **14**And if you are willing to accept
it, he is the Elijah who was to come. **15**He who has ears,
let him hear.

16"To what can I compare this generation? They are like
children sitting in the marketplaces and calling out to others:

17" 'We played the flute for you,
  and you did not dance;

a36 Micah 7:6   *b1* Greek *in their towns*   *c5* The Greek word
was used for various diseases affecting the skin—not necessarily
leprosy.   *d10* Mal. 3:1

Why did Jesus bring a sword, if he is the Prince of Peace? (10:34; see Isaiah 9:6)

The peace that Jesus brings is the result of
people being "made right" with God. It is an inner peace that resolves all barriers between
one's soul and one's Creator. However, not all
people experience this peace from Christ, and
the result is sometimes conflict in relationships. See *Does Jesus break up families?*
(10:35–37).

SCRIPTURE LINK (10:34,35)

Luke recounts Jesus' words about conflict
among family members in Luke 12:51–53.

Does Jesus break up families? (10:35–37)

These verses illustrate one of the harsher
truths of God's kingdom: not everyone will respond to the gospel. Hearts full of prejudice,
hate and pride will resist Christ's offer of
peace. Because many will reject it, the message will divide people, families and nations.

SCRIPTURE LINK (11:2–19)

Luke reports on Jesus' assurance to John the
Baptist in Luke 7:18–35.

Why did John doubt? (11:3)

Even people with strong faith ask tough questions during stressful times. John was suffering unjustly, so it is not surprising that he
sought answers from Jesus. Further, since
Jesus' actions as Messiah differed from what
many of the Jews expected, reports of Jesus'
activities must have puzzled John. Jesus' answer brought reassurance: the miracles he performed provided convincing evidence that he
was indeed *the one who was to come.*

How can those *least in the kingdom of heaven* be greater than John? (11:11)

Jesus affirmed both the greatness of John the
Baptist and the greater privileges kingdom citizens enjoy. Great as he was, John served only
as a forerunner who announced that the kingdom was near. Under Christ's new covenant,
we enjoy the fuller benefits of kingdom life
(Col. 1:13–14).

Must we force our way into the kingdom? (11:12)

The *forceful men* Jesus mentioned may refer to
the corrupt people like the Pharisees and Herodians who tried to control the kingdom through
violence or political force. However, Jesus may
have meant that it takes courageous dedication to be part of his advancing kingdom. The
poor in spirit will possess the kingdom, but
Christ-like meekness includes bold, aggressive
obedience (Luke 6:46; 9:57–62).

Why were Jesus and John so different? (11:18–19)

They were not really as different as their detractors made them appear. John's simple lifestyle fit his message of repentance and self-denial, while Jesus' attendance at public dinners expressed his gracious willingness to mingle with those who needed him. John and Jesus were neither demon-possessed nor overindulgent, as their opponents charged; they simply refused to play along with their critics' childish games.

SCRIPTURE LINK (11:21–23)

Jesus' pronouncement of woe on unrepentant cities can also be found in Luke 10:13–15.

Will judgment be easier for some than others? (11:22)

Some sins may deserve more severe punishment because greater knowledge implies greater accountability. According to Jesus, a servant who knowingly disobeys his master deserves more punishment than one who disobeys in ignorance (Luke 12:47–48). God's judgment will be completely just. Sometimes he has extended special mercy to those who act in ignorance, but now he calls everyone to repent (see Romans 2:4–11).

SCRIPTURE LINK (11:25–27)

Luke records Jesus' praise to the Father in Luke 10:21–22.

Why use a yoke to symbolize rest? (11:29)

Farmers used yokes to bind their oxen together, so yokes came to represent labor, service and submission to authority. Yokes are oppressive when the ones in charge are harsh and cruel, but the Lord's commands *are not burdensome* (1 John 5:3). Christ's servants can find rest and refreshment in fellowship with him even when their work is difficult and stressful.

As Lord of the Sabbath, did Jesus change the rules? (12:1–8)

No, but he insisted that some principles took precedence over others. The Pharisees were so particular about nonessentials that they failed to see the deeper truths: Minimal food preparation on the Sabbath did not offend God. Doing good on the Sabbath did not violate the spirit of the law. Ultimately, Jesus offered himself as the central overriding principle: The Lord of the Sabbath was qualified to say what honored God and what did not.

SCRIPTURE LINK (12:1–8)

Mark records Jesus' declaration of being the Lord of the Sabbath in Mark 2:23–28. Luke's account can be found in Luke 6:1–5.

What was so bad about getting food on the Sabbath? (12:2)

Jesus' disciples were violating the Pharisees' detailed rules regarding Sabbath rest. God's law did forbid working on the Sabbath, but Jewish traditions defined work with stifling legalism. The Pharisees considered it wrong even to pluck a bit of grain and rub it in one's hand before eating it. In their opinion, these actions constituted reaping and threshing. Yet God intended Sabbath-keeping to be a blessing, not a burden. (See Mark 2:27–28.)

we sang a dirge,
    and you did not mourn.'

18For John came neither eating nor drinking, and they say, 'He has a demon.' **19**The Son of Man[D] came eating and drinking, and they say, 'Here is a glutton[D] and a drunkard, a friend of tax collectors[D] and "sinners." ' But wisdom is proved right by her actions."

Woe on Unrepentant Cities

20Then Jesus began to denounce the cities in which most of his miracles had been performed, because they did not repent[D]. **21**"Woe to you, Korazin! Woe to you, Bethsaida! If the miracles that were performed in you had been performed in Tyre and Sidon, they would have repented long ago in sackcloth and ashes. **22**But I tell you, it will be more bearable for Tyre and Sidon on the day of judgment than for you. **23**And you, Capernaum, will you be lifted up to the skies? No, you will go down to the depths.[a] If the miracles that were performed in you had been performed in Sodom, it would have remained to this day. **24**But I tell you that it will be more bearable for Sodom on the day of judgment than for you."

Rest for the Weary

25At that time Jesus said, "I praise you, Father, Lord of heaven and earth, because you have hidden these things from the wise and learned, and revealed them to little children. **26**Yes, Father, for this was your good pleasure.

27"All things have been committed to me by my Father. No one knows the Son except the Father, and no one knows the Father except the Son and those to whom the Son chooses to reveal him.

28"Come to me, all you who are weary and burdened, and I will give you rest. **29**Take my yoke[D] upon you and learn from me, for I am gentle and humble in heart, and you will find rest for your souls[D]. **30**For my yoke is easy and my burden is light."

Lord of the Sabbath

12 At that time Jesus went through the grainfields on the Sabbath[D]. His disciples[D] were hungry and began to pick some heads of grain and eat them. **2**When the Pharisees[D] saw this, they said to him, "Look! Your disciples are doing what is unlawful on the Sabbath."

3He answered, "Haven't you read what David did when he and his companions were hungry? **4**He entered the house of God, and he and his companions ate the consecrated[D] bread—which was not lawful for them to do, but only for the priests[D]. **5**Or haven't you read in the Law that on the Sabbath the priests in the temple desecrate[D] the day and yet are innocent? **6**I tell you that one[b] greater than the temple is here. **7**If you had known what these words mean, 'I desire mercy[D], not sacrifice[D],'[c] you would not have condemned the innocent. **8**For the Son of Man is Lord of the Sabbath."

9Going on from that place, he went into their synagogue, **10**and a man with a shriveled hand was there. Looking for a reason to accuse Jesus, they asked him, "Is it lawful to heal on the Sabbath?"

11He said to them, "If any of you has a sheep and it falls

---

*a*23 Greek *Hades*   *b*6 Or *something*; also in verses 41 and 42
*c*7 Hosea 6:6

into a pit on the Sabbath^D, will you not take hold of it and lift it out? ¹²How much more valuable is a man than a sheep! Therefore it is lawful to do good on the Sabbath."

¹³Then he said to the man, "Stretch out your hand." So he stretched it out and it was completely restored, just as sound as the other. ¹⁴But the Pharisees^D went out and plotted how they might kill Jesus.

God's Chosen Servant

¹⁵Aware of this, Jesus withdrew from that place. Many followed him, and he healed all their sick, ¹⁶warning them not to tell who he was. ¹⁷This was to fulfill what was spoken through the prophet^D Isaiah:

¹⁸"Here is my servant whom I have chosen,
  the one I love, in whom I delight;
I will put my Spirit on him,
  and he will proclaim justice to the nations.
¹⁹He will not quarrel or cry out;
  no one will hear his voice in the streets.
²⁰A bruised reed he will not break,
  and a smoldering wick he will not snuff out,
  till he leads justice to victory.
²¹ In his name the nations will put their
      hope."^a

Jesus and Beelzebub

²²Then they brought him a demon-possessed man who was blind and mute, and Jesus healed him, so that he could both talk and see. ²³All the people were astonished and said, "Could this be the Son of David?"

²⁴But when the Pharisees heard this, they said, "It is only by Beelzebub^D,^b the prince of demons, that this fellow drives out demons."

²⁵Jesus knew their thoughts and said to them, "Every kingdom divided against itself will be ruined, and every city or household divided against itself will not stand. ²⁶If Satan drives out Satan, he is divided against himself. How then can his kingdom stand? ²⁷And if I drive out demons by Beelzebub, by whom do your people drive them out? So then, they will be your judges. ²⁸But if I drive out demons by the Spirit of God, then the kingdom of God^D has come upon you.

²⁹"Or again, how can anyone enter a strong man's house and carry off his possessions unless he first ties up the strong man? Then he can rob his house.

³⁰"He who is not with me is against me, and he who does not gather with me scatters. ³¹And so I tell you, every sin and blasphemy^D will be forgiven men, but the blasphemy against the Spirit will not be forgiven. ³²Anyone who speaks a word against the Son of Man^D will be forgiven, but anyone who speaks against the Holy Spirit will not be forgiven, either in this age or in the age to come.

³³"Make a tree good and its fruit will be good, or make a tree bad and its fruit will be bad, for a tree is recognized by its fruit. ³⁴You brood of vipers, how can you who are evil say anything good? For out of the overflow of the heart the mouth speaks. ³⁵The good man brings good things out of the good stored up in him, and the evil man brings evil things out of the evil stored up in him. ³⁶But I

^a21 Isaiah 42:1-4   ^b24 Greek *Beezeboul* or *Beelzeboul*; also in verse 27

SCRIPTURE LINK (12:9–14)

Mark tells about Jesus healing the man with a shriveled hand in Mark 3:1–6. Luke reports on it in Luke 6:6–11.

SCRIPTURE LINK (12:25–29)

Jesus' words about Satan can also be found in Mark 3:23–27 and Luke 11:17–22.

Who, besides Jesus and his disciples, could drive out demons? (12:27)

Evidently some of the Pharisees drove out demons, or at least claimed to do so. Acts 19:13 mentions a group of Jews who *went around driving out evil spirits*. Others cast out demons in Jesus' name, even though these people ordinarily were not associated with the apostles (Luke 9:49–50).

Can some sins be forgiven *in the age to come*? (12:32)

This does not imply there will be a "second chance" to receive forgiveness after death. The statement simply means that some sins will be forgiven neither now nor in the future. By *the age to come,* Jesus may have meant the time of the new covenant, which began with his death and resurrection (Heb. 9:27–28).

What will our careless words cost us? (12:36–37)

Words are important because they reveal the inner attitude of our hearts. Just as saving faith must be confessed with boldness and truth, careless words (which in this context may mean *blasphemous* words—see vv. 31–32) bring tragic consequences because they spring from a faithless heart.

tell you that men will have to give account on the day of judgment for every careless word they have spoken. **37**For by your words you will be acquitted, and by your words you will be condemned."

The Sign of Jonah

38Then some of the Pharisees[D] and teachers of the law said to him, "Teacher, we want to see a miraculous sign from you."

39He answered, "A wicked and adulterous generation asks for a miraculous sign! But none will be given it except the sign of the prophet[D] Jonah. **40**For as Jonah was three days and three nights in the belly of a huge fish, so the Son of Man[D] will be three days and three nights in the heart of the earth. **41**The men of Nineveh will stand up at the judgment with this generation and condemn it; for they repented[D] at the preaching of Jonah, and now one*a* greater than Jonah is here. **42**The Queen of the South will rise at the judgment with this generation and condemn it; for she came from the ends of the earth to listen to Solomon's wisdom, and now one greater than Solomon is here.

43"When an evil*b* spirit comes out of a man, it goes through arid places seeking rest and does not find it. **44**Then it says, 'I will return to the house I left.' When it arrives, it finds the house unoccupied, swept clean and put in order. **45**Then it goes and takes with it seven other spirits more wicked than itself, and they go in and live there. And the final condition of that man is worse than the first. That is how it will be with this wicked generation."

a41 Or *something*; also in verse 42   *b43* Greek *unclean*

What's wrong with wanting hard evidence? (12:39)

Nothing, but we must be willing to accept the evidence once it is presented. Jesus repeatedly offered miraculous evidence to substantiate his claims but refused to perform miracles just for show. Some Pharisees and teachers of the law refused to believe despite all the evidence Jesus had already given them (John 12:37). Therefore, Jesus pointed them to the one, climactic sign of his identity: his own resurrection from the dead (v. 40).

SCRIPTURE LINK (12:39-42)

You can also read about the sign of Jonah in Luke 11:29-32.

Arid places (12:43)

Evil spirits evidently prefer to live in bodies (see 8:31-32). Since few houses exist in a desert, Jesus used *arid places* to picture the restless discomfort of a disembodied evil spirit seeking a dwelling place.

SCRIPTURE LINK (12:43-45)

Luke records Jesus' saying about evil spirits in Luke 11:24-26.

What is blasphemy against the Holy Spirit? (12:31-32)

Jesus gave the solemn warning in these verses to people whose hard-heartedness placed them on the brink of disaster. *Blasphemy against the Spirit* evidently is not just a one-time offense; rather, it is an ongoing attitude of rebellion—a stubborn way of life that continually resists, rejects and insults the Holy Spirit. This is what makes it, in effect, an *eternal sin* (Mark 3:29).

Some other helpful points to keep in mind:

(1) Mark specifically notes that Jesus gave this teaching because his opponents claimed he had an evil spirit (Mark 3:30). The Pharisees were so hard-hearted that they could observe the miraculous works of God's Son and then accuse him of being Satan's co-worker—a tragic contradiction of the truth.

(2) Many people expressed honest uncertainty about Jesus during his earthly ministry because his identity as the Messiah only gradually dawned on them. Words spoken against the Son of Man could therefore be forgiven. Since the day of Pentecost however, the Holy Spirit's ongoing ministry through the revealed Word offers people the opportunity to repent and accept the gospel. Thus, to blaspheme the Holy Spirit is to reject all that God is doing to bring us to salvation through Christ.

(3) *Blasphemy against the Spirit* is not unforgivable because of something done unintentionally in the past, but because of something being done deliberately and unrelentingly in the present. Jesus' warning was motivated by love. If we are willing to repent, God is willing to forgive (1 John 1:9).

Jesus' Mother and Brothers

46While Jesus was still talking to the crowd, his mother and brothers stood outside, wanting to speak to him. **47**Someone told him, "Your mother and brothers are standing outside, wanting to speak to you."*a*

48He replied to him, "Who is my mother, and who are my brothers?" **49**Pointing to his disciplesᴰ, he said, "Here are my mother and my brothers. **50**For whoever does the will of my Father in heaven is my brother and sister and mother."

The Parable of the Sower

13 That same day Jesus went out of the house and sat by the lake. **2**Such large crowds gathered around him that he got into a boat and sat in it, while all the people stood on the shore. **3**Then he told them many things in parablesᴰ, saying: "A farmer went out to sow his seed. **4**As he was scattering the seed, some fell along the path, and the birds came and ate it up. **5**Some fell on rocky places, where it did not have much soil. It sprang up quickly, because the soil was shallow. **6**But when the sun came up, the plants were scorched, and they withered because they had no root. **7**Other seed fell among thorns, which grew up and choked the plants. **8**Still other seed fell on good soil, where it produced a crop—a hundred, sixty or thirty times what was sown. **9**He who has ears, let him hear."

10The disciples came to him and asked, "Why do you speak to the people in parables?"

11He replied, "The knowledge of the secrets of the kingdom of heaven has been given to you, but not to them. **12**Whoever has will be given more, and he will have an abundance. Whoever does not have, even what he has will be taken from him. **13**This is why I speak to them in parables:

a47 Some manuscripts do not have verse 47.

Was Jesus rude to his family? (12:46–50)

Jesus emphasized that following God, not family heritage, is what really counts. He wasn't denying his love for his family, but he used their presence to contrast earthly loyalties with the more important eternal allegiance.

SCRIPTURE LINK (12:46–50)

Mark gives Jesus' declaration about his mother and brothers in Mark 3:31–35. Luke recounts it in Luke 8:19–21.

SCRIPTURE LINK (13:1–15)

Jesus' parable of the sower is also recorded in Mark 4:1–12 and Luke 8:4–10.

What can we learn from soil? (13:3–23)

The parable of the soils teaches that the gospel won't be received with equal effect. At least three things can interfere: satanic opposition, outside persecution and peer pressure, and the attraction of the world's pleasures. But if it does take root, God's Word can produce a fruitful life.

Why did Jesus speak in parables? (13:11–13)

On one level, parables were not difficult to understand. Jesus masterfully taught moral principles by using simple, down-to-earth illustrations about everyday objects familiar to farmers, fishermen, merchants and others in his audience. At the same time, the deeper meanings of Jesus' parables seemed obscure (or even incomprehensible) to those who opposed Jesus or who simply were not attuned to his mission and message.

People with *ears to hear* (those seriously seeking the truth) could dig deeper and find profound spiritual insight. For others, Jesus' parables were little more than fascinating but puzzling riddles. Those who were resistant to his message would not have the interest or the energy to pursue deeper truths.

Jesus frequently used parables when speaking to large crowds, but in private he provided his disciples with more detailed explanations (Mark 4:33–34). At this point in Jesus' ministry, to keep the cross from approaching too quickly, it was best for certain secrets of the kingdom to be kept somewhat hidden from his many casual observers, from overzealous but poorly-informed supporters and from outright opponents. Sometimes Jesus did use more direct, non-figurative teaching methods (compare Matthew 5–7).

"Though seeing, they do not see;
>   though hearing, they do not hear or
>   understand.

14In them is fulfilled the prophecy[D] of Isaiah:

> " 'You will be ever hearing but never
>   understanding;
>   you will be ever seeing but never perceiving.
> **15**For this people's heart has become calloused;
>   they hardly hear with their ears,
>   and they have closed their eyes.
> Otherwise they might see with their eyes,
>   hear with their ears,
>   understand with their hearts
> and turn, and I would heal them.'[a]

16But blessed are your eyes because they see, and your ears because they hear. **17**For I tell you the truth, many prophets[D] and righteous[D] men longed to see what you see but did not see it, and to hear what you hear but did not hear it.

18"Listen then to what the parable[D] of the sower means: **19**When anyone hears the message about the kingdom and does not understand it, the evil one comes and snatches away what was sown in his heart. This is the seed sown along the path. **20**The one who received the seed that fell on rocky places is the man who hears the word and at once receives it with joy. **21**But since he has no root, he lasts only a short time. When trouble or persecution comes because of the word, he quickly falls away. **22**The one who received the seed that fell among the thorns is the man who hears the word, but the worries of this life and the deceitfulness of wealth choke it, making it unfruitful. **23**But the one who received the seed that fell on good soil is the man who hears the word and understands it. He produces a crop, yielding a hundred, sixty or thirty times what was sown."

The Parable of the Weeds

24Jesus told them another parable: "The kingdom of heaven is like a man who sowed good seed in his field. **25**But while everyone was sleeping, his enemy came and sowed weeds among the wheat, and went away. **26**When the wheat sprouted and formed heads, then the weeds also appeared.

27"The owner's servants came to him and said, 'Sir, didn't you sow good seed in your field? Where then did the weeds come from?'

28" 'An enemy did this,' he replied.

"The servants asked him, 'Do you want us to go and pull them up?'

29" 'No,' he answered, 'because while you are pulling the weeds, you may root up the wheat with them. **30**Let both grow together until the harvest. At that time I will tell the harvesters: First collect the weeds and tie them in bundles to be burned; then gather the wheat and bring it into my barn.' "

The Parables of the Mustard Seed and the Yeast

31He told them another parable: "The kingdom of heaven is like a mustard seed, which a man took and planted in his field. **32**Though it is the smallest of all your

---

SCRIPTURE LINK (13:16–17)

Parallel verses are found in Luke 10:23–24.

SCRIPTURE LINK (13:18–23)

Jesus makes plain the meaning of the parable of the sower in Mark 4:13–20 and Luke 8:11–15.

The kingdom of heaven (13:24)

Refers to the Lord's reign over his people, a realm in which God's will is done. The other Gospel writers ordinarily use the synonymous phrase *kingdom of God,* but Matthew repeatedly uses *kingdom of heaven.* Perhaps because of his Jewish background Matthew avoided writing the name of God.

Why did Jesus tell these stories about seeds? (13:31–32)

Seeds grow quietly but persistently. Like seeds, the growth of God's kingdom is the result of divine power, not human effort. The mustard seed illustrates the amazing growth of God's kingdom, which will reach across international boundaries and nations before it is finished (Daniel 4:10–12; Ezek. 17:22–24; 31:3–14).

SCRIPTURE LINK (13:31–32)

Mark records the parable of the mustard seed in Mark 4:30–32.

SCRIPTURE LINK (13:31–33)

Luke records Jesus' parables of the mustard seed and the yeast in Luke 13:18–21.

---

a15 Isaiah 6:9,10

seeds, yet when it grows, it is the largest of garden plants and becomes a tree, so that the birds of the air come and perch in its branches."

33He told them still another parableD: "The kingdom of heaven is like yeastD that a woman took and mixed into a large amount*a* of flour until it worked all through the dough."

34Jesus spoke all these things to the crowd in parables; he did not say anything to them without using a parable. 35So was fulfilled what was spoken through the prophetD:

> "I will open my mouth in parables,
> I will utter things hidden since the creation
>   of the world."*b*

The Parable of the Weeds Explained

36Then he left the crowd and went into the house. His disciplesD came to him and said, "Explain to us the parable of the weeds in the field."

37He answered, "The one who sowed the good seed is the Son of ManD. 38The field is the world, and the good seed stands for the sons of the kingdom. The weeds are the sons of the evil one, 39and the enemy who sows them is the devil. The harvest is the end of the age, and the harvesters are angels.

40"As the weeds are pulled up and burned in the fire, so it will be at the end of the age. 41The Son of Man will send out his angels, and they will weed out of his kingdom everything that causes sin and all who do evil. 42They will throw them into the fiery furnace, where there will be weeping and gnashing of teeth. 43Then the righteousD will shine like the sun in the kingdom of their Father. He who has ears, let him hear.

The Parables of the Hidden Treasure and the Pearl

44"The kingdom of heaven is like treasure hidden in a field. When a man found it, he hid it again, and then in his joy went and sold all he had and bought that field.

45"Again, the kingdom of heaven is like a merchant looking for fine pearls. 46When he found one of great value, he went away and sold everything he had and bought it.

The Parable of the Net

47"Once again, the kingdom of heaven is like a net that was let down into the lake and caught all kinds of fish. 48When it was full, the fishermen pulled it up on the shore. Then they sat down and collected the good fish in baskets, but threw the bad away. 49This is how it will be at the end of the age. The angels will come and separate the wicked from the righteous 50and throw them into the fiery furnace, where there will be weeping and gnashing of teeth.

51"Have you understood all these things?" Jesus asked.
"Yes," they replied.

52He said to them, "Therefore every teacher of the law who has been instructed about the kingdom of heaven is like the owner of a house who brings out of his storeroom new treasures as well as old."

a33 Greek *three satas* (probably about 1/2 bushel or 22 liters)
b35 Psalm 78:2

New treasures (13:52)

People who have been *instructed about the kingdom of heaven* have in their hearts a *storeroom* of fresh new insights as well as the time-tested wisdom of the ages. Like hospitable homeowners who share their belongings, both old and new, effective teachers refresh others both with wisdom gained in the past and lessons gained through current study and experience.

SCRIPTURE LINK (13:54–58)

Mark tells of Jesus' rejection in his hometown in Mark 6:1–6.

Why did Jesus require people's faith to do miracles? (13:58)

God has unlimited power, but it pleases him to exercise his power through our faithful cooperation. Jesus did not force divine blessings upon people who openly rejected him. He often performed miracles for those who already believed, and sometimes his miracles led to faith in those who did *not* previously believe (John 11:45; 12:9–11; 14:11). But Jesus would not perform miracles simply for his own personal benefit.

Herod the tetrarch (14:1)

This is Herod Antipas, before whom Jesus eventually appeared during part of his trial (Luke 13:31–32; 23:6–12). His father, Herod the Great, ruled during the time of Jesus' birth. Technically, the term *tetrarch* meant someone who governed one-fourth of a country, but sometimes the title was used simply as a synonym for "prince" or "king." Herod Antipas reigned over the regions of Galilee and Perea (see **Setting of the Gospels** on page 1332) from approximately 4 B.C. to A.D. 39.

SCRIPTURE LINK (14:1–12)

Mark gives an account of the beheading of John the Baptist in Mark 6:14–29.

SCRIPTURE LINK (14:13–21)

Accounts of Jesus feeding the five thousand can be found in Mark 6:32–44; Luke 9:10–17 and John 6:1–13. Matthew tells about Jesus feeding the four thousand in 15:32–38.

A Prophet Without Honor

53When Jesus had finished these parables[D], he moved on from there. **54**Coming to his hometown, he began teaching the people in their synagogue, and they were amazed. "Where did this man get this wisdom and these miraculous powers?" they asked. **55**"Isn't this the carpenter's son? Isn't his mother's name Mary, and aren't his brothers James, Joseph, Simon and Judas? **56**Aren't all his sisters with us? Where then did this man get all these things?" **57**And they took offense at him.

But Jesus said to them, "Only in his hometown and in his own house is a prophet[D] without honor."

58And he did not do many miracles there because of their lack of faith.

John the Baptist Beheaded

14 At that time Herod the tetrarch[D] heard the reports about Jesus, **2**and he said to his attendants, "This is John the Baptist; he has risen from the dead! That is why miraculous powers are at work in him."

3Now Herod had arrested John and bound him and put him in prison because of Herodias, his brother Philip's wife, **4**for John had been saying to him: "It is not lawful for you to have her." **5**Herod wanted to kill John, but he was afraid of the people, because they considered him a prophet.

6On Herod's birthday the daughter of Herodias danced for them and pleased Herod so much **7**that he promised with an oath to give her whatever she asked. **8**Prompted by her mother, she said, "Give me here on a platter the head of John the Baptist." **9**The king was distressed, but because of his oaths and his dinner guests, he ordered that her request be granted **10**and had John beheaded in the prison. **11**His head was brought in on a platter and given to the girl, who carried it to her mother. **12**John's disciples[D] came and took his body and buried it. Then they went and told Jesus.

Jesus Feeds the Five Thousand

13When Jesus heard what had happened, he withdrew by boat privately to a solitary place. Hearing of this, the crowds followed him on foot from the towns. **14**When Jesus landed and saw a large crowd, he had compassion on them and healed their sick.

15As evening approached, the disciples came to him and said, "This is a remote place, and it's already getting late. Send the crowds away, so they can go to the villages and buy themselves some food."

16Jesus replied, "They do not need to go away. You give them something to eat."

17"We have here only five loaves of bread and two fish," they answered.

18"Bring them here to me," he said. **19**And he directed the people to sit down on the grass. Taking the five loaves and the two fish and looking up to heaven, he gave thanks and broke the loaves. Then he gave them to the disciples, and the disciples gave them to the people. **20**They all ate and were satisfied, and the disciples picked up twelve basketfuls of broken pieces that were left over. **21**The number of those who ate was about five thousand men, besides women and children.

Jesus Walks on the Water

22Immediately Jesus made the disciples[D] get into the boat and go on ahead of him to the other side, while he dismissed the crowd. **23**After he had dismissed them, he went up on a mountainside by himself to pray. When evening came, he was there alone, **24**but the boat was already a considerable distance[a] from land, buffeted by the waves because the wind was against it.

25During the fourth watch of the night Jesus went out to them, walking on the lake. **26**When the disciples saw him walking on the lake, they were terrified. "It's a ghost," they said, and cried out in fear.

27But Jesus immediately said to them: "Take courage! It is I. Don't be afraid."

28"Lord, if it's you," Peter replied, "tell me to come to you on the water."

29"Come," he said.

Then Peter got down out of the boat, walked on the water and came toward Jesus. **30**But when he saw the wind, he was afraid, and beginning to sink, cried out, "Lord, save me!"

31Immediately Jesus reached out his hand and caught him. "You of little faith," he said, "why did you doubt?"

32And when they climbed into the boat, the wind died down. **33**Then those who were in the boat worshiped him, saying, "Truly you are the Son of God."

34When they had crossed over, they landed at Gennesaret. **35**And when the men of that place recognized Jesus, they sent word to all the surrounding country. People brought all their sick to him **36**and begged him to let the sick just touch the edge of his cloak, and all who touched him were healed.

Clean and Unclean

15 Then some Pharisees[D] and teachers of the law came to Jesus from Jerusalem[D] and asked, **2**"Why do your disciples break the tradition of the elders? They don't wash their hands before they eat!"

3Jesus replied, "And why do you break the command of God for the sake of your tradition? **4**For God said, 'Honor your father and mother'[b] and 'Anyone who curses his father or mother must be put to death[D].'[c] **5**But you say that if a man says to his father or mother, 'Whatever help you might otherwise have received from me is a gift devoted to God,' **6**he is not to 'honor his father[d]' with it. Thus you nullify the word of God for the sake of your tradition. **7**You hypocrites! Isaiah was right when he prophesied about you:

8" 'These people honor me with their lips,
>   but their hearts are far from me.
9They worship me in vain;
>   their teachings are but rules taught by men.'[e]"

10Jesus called the crowd to him and said, "Listen and understand. **11**What goes into a man's mouth does not make him 'unclean[D],' but what comes out of his mouth, that is what makes him 'unclean.' "

12Then the disciples came to him and asked, "Do you

SCRIPTURE LINK (14:22–23)

Mark tells about Jesus walking on the water in Mark 6:45–51. John talks about it in John 6:15–21.

Why did Jesus need to pray? (14:23)

Jesus himself is God, but he is not God the Father. Because he lived in constant communication with the heavenly Father, Jesus' consistent prayer life provided a living example for his disciples and enabled him to identify with our humanity (Heb. 4:14–16). He demonstrated what it means to live in complete harmony with the Father's will and to *pray continually* (1 Thes. 5:17).

Fourth watch (14:25)

In ancient times, the hours of the night were divided into military watches, which designated the length of time sentinels remained on duty. Originally the Jews divided the night into three sections (Judges 7:19). The Romans divided the night into four watches, which ended at 9 p.m., 12 a.m., 3 a.m. and 6 a.m. Thus, Jesus' appearance occurred sometime between 3 and 6 a.m.

Why did Jesus walk on the water? (14:25)

This incident served to strengthen the disciples' trust in Jesus at a time when they probably felt disappointed and confused by his refusal to be made king the day before (John 6:14–15). It also provides powerful evidence of Jesus' ability to help us in the storms and troubles we face.

Why did Peter want to come to Jesus on the water? (14:28)

Perhaps he sought further confirmation of the Lord's identity and power. Peter's struggling faith led him to do things that seem impulsive and even reckless. On other occasions, too, he willingly risked his own safety and comfort to be near Jesus (see 26:35; John 18:10–11, 15–27; 21:7).

Why was washing before meals so important? (15:2)

As a matter of religious custom, the Pharisees insisted on special hand-washing ceremonies to remove the contaminating effects of any possible contact with "unclean" persons or objects. This practice probably was derived from Old Testament teachings that prohibited contact with "unclean" things (Lev. 5:2–3) and prescribed special washings for the priests (Exodus 30:17–21). Jesus followed God's law, but he felt no obligation to observe all the traditions of the elders (Luke 11:37–39).

How can worship be *in vain*? (15:9)

Empty ritual strips worship of its meaning and power, for God desires worshipers who come to him in *spirit and truth* (John 4:23–24). Naturally, worship is vain if it is directed toward a false god. Worship can also be vain when it consists of a rote adherence to human rules and teachings—without honest, thoughtful, heartfelt praise to God.

---

a24 Greek *many stadia*   *b4* Exodus 20:12; Deut. 5:16
c4 Exodus 21:17; Lev. 20:9   *d6* Some manuscripts *father or his mother*   *e9* Isaiah 29:13

know that the Pharisees[D] were offended when they heard this?"

[13]He replied, "Every plant that my heavenly Father has not planted will be pulled up by the roots. [14]Leave them; they are blind guides.[a] If a blind man leads a blind man, both will fall into a pit."

[15]Peter said, "Explain the parable[D] to us."

[16]"Are you still so dull?" Jesus asked them. [17]"Don't you see that whatever enters the mouth goes into the stomach and then out of the body? [18]But the things that come out of the mouth come from the heart, and these make a man 'unclean[D].' [19]For out of the heart come evil thoughts, murder, adultery, sexual immorality, theft, false testimony, slander. [20]These are what make a man 'unclean'; but eating with unwashed hands does not make him 'unclean.' "

The Faith of the Canaanite Woman

[21]Leaving that place, Jesus withdrew to the region of Tyre and Sidon. [22]A Canaanite woman from that vicinity came to him, crying out, "Lord, Son of David, have mercy[D] on me! My daughter is suffering terribly from demon-possession."

[23]Jesus did not answer a word. So his disciples[D] came to him and urged him, "Send her away, for she keeps crying out after us."

[24]He answered, "I was sent only to the lost sheep of Israel."

[25]The woman came and knelt before him. "Lord, help me!" she said.

[26]He replied, "It is not right to take the children's bread and toss it to their dogs."

[27]"Yes, Lord," she said, "but even the dogs eat the crumbs that fall from their masters' table."

[28]Then Jesus answered, "Woman, you have great faith! Your request is granted." And her daughter was healed from that very hour.

Jesus Feeds the Four Thousand

[29]Jesus left there and went along the Sea of Galilee. Then he went up on a mountainside and sat down. [30]Great crowds came to him, bringing the lame, the blind, the crippled, the mute and many others, and laid them at his feet; and he healed them. [31]The people were amazed when they saw the mute speaking, the crippled made well, the lame walking and the blind seeing. And they praised the God of Israel.

[32]Jesus called his disciples to him and said, "I have compassion for these people; they have already been with me three days and have nothing to eat. I do not want to send them away hungry, or they may collapse on the way."

[33]His disciples answered, "Where could we get enough bread in this remote place to feed such a crowd?"

[34]"How many loaves do you have?" Jesus asked.

"Seven," they replied, "and a few small fish."

[35]He told the crowd to sit down on the ground. [36]Then he took the seven loaves and the fish, and when he had given thanks, he broke them and gave them to the disciples, and they in turn to the people. [37]They all ate and were satisfied. Afterward the disciples picked up seven basketfuls of broken pieces that were left over. [38]The

---

Why did Jesus go into Gentile territory? (15:21)

Jesus may have gone to Tyre and Sidon because he was interested in ministering to non-Jews (see **Jesus Visits Phoenicia** on page 1393); however, he clearly saw the *lost sheep of Israel* (15:24) as his main focus at this point in his ministry. Eventually he sent his disciples to the whole world.

SCRIPTURE LINK (15:21–28)

In Mark 7:24–30, Mark tells about the faith of the Syrophoenician woman.

Why did Jesus resist helping the woman? (15:23–26)

Jesus was not forcing the Gentile woman to beg, but was perhaps probing the depth of her faith in the God of Israel. Or, he may have been teaching his disciples a lesson in the universal love of God. The woman's persistence indicates she sensed something from Jesus that encouraged her to continue asking—perhaps a twinkle in his eye or a warmth in his tone of voice. Using the word *dogs*, commonly used by Jews to describe Gentiles, may have been sarcasm—his way to make the point that demeaning others is alien to the heart of God.

SCRIPTURE LINK (15:29–31)

Mark tells in Mark 7:31–37 about the great crowds of people who came to Jesus for healing.

SCRIPTURE LINK (15:32–39)

You can also read about Jesus feeding the four thousand in Mark 8:1–10. And Matthew tells about Jesus feeding the five thousand in 14:13–21.

Why didn't the disciples feel a sense of déjà vu? (15:33)

No doubt they did remember Jesus' previous miracle when he fed the five thousand. Their question probably reflected their usual custom of asking Jesus for help when problems arose. They could count on Jesus to deal with the hungry crowd, whether by performing another miracle or by some other means.

SCRIPTURE LINK (16:1–12)

Mark writes about the Pharisees' demand for a sign in Mark 8:11–21.

Why did Jesus compare the teaching of the Pharisees and Sadducees to yeast? (16:11–12)

Yeast symbolized a quiet, but potent, rapidly spreading influence. Earlier Jesus used yeast in a positive way to picture how the kingdom of heaven spreads its influence (13:33). Here he referred to the negative way corrupt or hypocritical teachings can spread and weaken Christ's followers from within.

---

a 14 Some manuscripts *guides of the blind*

number of those who ate was four thousand, besides women and children. **39**After Jesus had sent the crowd away, he got into the boat and went to the vicinity of Magadan.

The Demand for a Sign

16 The Pharisees[D] and Sadducees[D] came to Jesus and tested him by asking him to show them a sign from heaven.

2He replied,[a] "When evening comes, you say, 'It will be fair weather, for the sky is red,' **3**and in the morning, 'Today it will be stormy, for the sky is red and overcast.' You know how to interpret the appearance of the sky, but you cannot interpret the signs of the times. **4**A wicked and adulterous generation looks for a miraculous sign, but none will be given it except the sign of Jonah." Jesus then left them and went away.

The Yeast of the Pharisees and Sadducees

5When they went across the lake, the disciples[D] forgot to take bread. **6**"Be careful," Jesus said to them. "Be on your guard against the yeast[D] of the Pharisees and Sadducees."

7They discussed this among themselves and said, "It is because we didn't bring any bread."

8Aware of their discussion, Jesus asked, "You of little faith, why are you talking among yourselves about having no bread? **9**Do you still not understand? Don't you remember the five loaves for the five thousand, and how many basketfuls you gathered? **10**Or the seven loaves for the four thousand, and how many basketfuls you gathered? **11**How is it you don't understand that I was not talking to you about bread? But be on your guard against the yeast of the Pharisees and Sadducees." **12**Then they understood that he was not telling them to guard against the yeast used in bread, but against the teaching of the Pharisees and Sadducees.

Peter's Confession of Christ

13When Jesus came to the region of Caesarea Philippi, he asked his disciples, "Who do people say the Son of Man[D] is?"

14They replied, "Some say John the Baptist; others say Elijah; and still others, Jeremiah or one of the prophets[D]."

15"But what about you?" he asked. "Who do you say I am?"

16Simon Peter answered, "You are the Christ,[b] the Son of the living God."

17Jesus replied, "Blessed are you, Simon son of Jonah, for this was not revealed to you by man, but by my Father in heaven. **18**And I tell you that you are Peter,[c] and on this rock I will build my church, and the gates of Hades[D][d] will not overcome it.[e] **19**I will give you the keys of the kingdom of heaven; whatever you bind on earth will be[f] bound in heaven, and whatever you loose on earth will be[f] loosed in heaven." **20**Then he warned his disciples not to tell anyone that he was the Christ.

---

a2 Some early manuscripts do not have the rest of verse 2 and all of verse 3.   b16 Or Messiah; also in verse 20   c18 Peter means rock.   d18 Or hell   e18 Or not prove stronger than it   f19 Or have been

SCRIPTURE LINK (16:13–16)

Peter's declaration that Jesus is the Christ can also be found in Mark 8:27–29 and Luke 9:18–20.

Jesus Visits Caesarea Philippi (16:13)

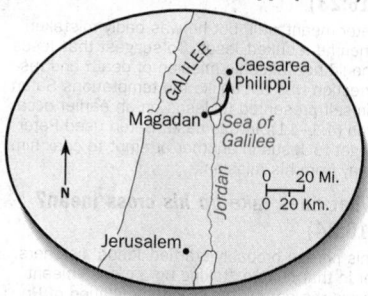

Upon what rock did Jesus build his church? (16:18)

Jesus likely meant that he would build his church on the rock-solid truth of his own identity as the Son of God, which Peter had just acknowledged. Yet the apostles played a crucial role in establishing the church's foundation (Eph. 2:20). Peter may very well have been the first person to grasp the true identity of Jesus. As such he was the first member of a church that would continue to grow, stone by stone (1 Peter 2:4–8).

Gates of Hades (16:18)

Hades was the Greeks' designation for the dwelling place of departed spirits. Gates were more than entryways; they were symbols of power and authority. City gates served as reinforced defense structures and as gathering places where Hebrew community leaders handled important legal matters (Deut. 25:7).

What authority did Jesus give to Peter? (16:19)

Jesus gave Peter and the other apostles spiritual authority to preach the gospel and thus open the door of his kingdom both to Jews and Gentiles (Acts 2:14–41; 10:22–48).

What can we *bind* and *loose* today? (16:19)

We can *bind* and *loose* what the Lord has prohibited or permitted in Scripture (2 Tim. 3:16–17). To *bind* meant to forbid, refuse or prohibit; to *loose* meant to permit or allow. Christ intended that the apostles' inspired teaching should become the standard for our faith and practice. God also gives special wisdom and power to the church during times of earnest prayer (18:17–20).

Why didn't Jesus want anyone to know he was the Christ? (16:20)

Before they could tell the news accurately, the disciples first needed to learn more about what it *meant* to say that Jesus was the Christ. Faulty ideas about the Messiah were common among the people who expected an earthly or militaristic kingdom. It's obvious the disciples did not understand Jesus well enough yet, for at this time even Peter (who stated his belief in v. 16) found it difficult to accept Jesus' coming suffering (v. 22).

SCRIPTURE LINK (16:21–28)

Both Mark and Luke record Jesus' prediction of his death and Peter's response. See Mark 8:31—9:1 and Luke 9:22–27.

Why did Jesus call Peter *Satan?* (16:23)

Peter meant well, but he was badly mistaken when he rebuked Jesus. To suggest that Jesus should not fulfill his mission of death and resurrection was not unlike the temptations Satan himself presented to Jesus on an earlier occasion (4:1–11). In this case, Satan used Peter to get to Jesus in another attempt to coax him away from his mission.

What does *take up his cross* mean? (16:24)

This phrase probably startled Jesus' listeners, for in that culture "taking up a cross" meant facing the horrible pain and humiliation of Roman crucifixion. Usually condemned criminals were *forced* to carry crosses, but Jesus laid down his life *voluntarily.* He asks us to do the same—to commit our lives wholeheartedly to him, accepting any hardship this choice may bring.

How has the kingdom come? (16:28)

In one view, the kingdom came when the Holy Spirit came on the day of Pentecost and thousands accepted Christ (Acts 2:1–47). Another view is that Jesus here referred to his transfiguration, which served as a glimpse of his heavenly glory (17:1–8). Still another view holds that Jesus was describing the destruction of Jerusalem in A.D. 70.

SCRIPTURE LINK (17:1–8)

Luke tells about Jesus' transfiguration in Luke 9:28–36.

Why was Jesus transfigured? (17:2)

Perhaps the disciples were still upset and confused because Jesus had predicted his death just a few days before. When he was transfigured, the disciples received a reassuring glimpse of Jesus' heavenly splendor and God's spoken words powerfully reinforced Jesus' identity as the Messiah. What the disciples saw and heard must have made an indelible impression on their minds, preparing them to proclaim unique, eyewitness testimony about the Lord (2 Peter 1:16–18).

How could Moses and Elijah return from the dead? (17:3)

God briefly brought them from the spiritual realm (presumably Paradise—see Luke 23:43; 2 Cor. 12:2–4) to appear with Jesus on this special occasion. This should not be confused with spiritualist practices; this was not a séance or an example of reincarnation. Evidently this event linked Jesus to the religious heritage of the Jews. Moses (representing the law) and Elijah (representing the prophets) demonstrated their approval for Jesus and his new covenant which was superior to their earlier covenant with God (Heb. 8:6).

How did they recognize Moses and Elijah? (17:3)

The Bible doesn't tell us. If this was a vision, God could also have given them divine insight to recognize Moses and Elijah.

Jesus Predicts His Death

21From that time on Jesus began to explain to his disciplesᴰ that he must go to Jerusalemᴰ and suffer many things at the hands of the elders, chief priestsᴰ and teachers of the law, and that he must be killed and on the third day be raised to life.

22Peter took him aside and began to rebuke him. "Never, Lord!" he said. "This shall never happen to you!"

23Jesus turned and said to Peter, "Get behind me, Satan! You are a stumbling blockᴰ to me; you do not have in mind the things of God, but the things of men."

24Then Jesus said to his disciples, "If anyone would come after me, he must deny himself and take up his cross and follow me. **25**For whoever wants to save his life*ᵃ* will lose it, but whoever loses his life for me will find it. **26**What good will it be for a man if he gains the whole world, yet forfeits his soulᴰ? Or what can a man give in exchange for his soul? **27**For the Son of Man is going to come in his Father's gloryᴰ with his angels, and then he will reward each person according to what he has done. **28**I tell you the truth, some who are standing here will not taste deathᴰ before they see the Son of Man coming in his kingdom."

The Transfiguration

17 After six days Jesus took with him Peter, James and John the brother of James, and led them up a high mountain by themselves. **2**There he was transfigured before them. His face shone like the sun, and his clothes became as white as the light. **3**Just then there appeared before them Moses and Elijah, talking with Jesus.

4Peter said to Jesus, "Lord, it is good for us to be here. If you wish, I will put up three shelters—one for you, one for Moses and one for Elijah."

5While he was still speaking, a bright cloud enveloped them, and a voice from the cloud said, "This is my Son, whom I love; with him I am well pleased. Listen to him!"

6When the disciples heard this, they fell facedown to the ground, terrified. **7**But Jesus came and touched them. "Get up," he said. "Don't be afraid." **8**When they looked up, they saw no one except Jesus.

9As they were coming down the mountain, Jesus instructed them, "Don't tell anyone what you have seen, until the Son of Man has been raised from the dead."

10The disciples asked him, "Why then do the teachers of the law say that Elijah must come first?"

11Jesus replied, "To be sure, Elijah comes and will restore all things. **12**But I tell you, Elijah has already come, and they did not recognize him, but have done to him everything they wished. In the same way the Son of Man is going to suffer at their hands." **13**Then the disciples understood that he was talking to them about John the Baptist.

The Healing of a Boy With a Demon

14When they came to the crowd, a man approached Jesus and knelt before him. **15**"Lord, have mercyᴰ on my son," he said. "He has seizures and is suffering greatly. He often falls into the fire or into the water. **16**I brought him to your disciples, but they could not heal him."

17"O unbelieving and perverse generation," Jesus re-

---

*ᵃ25 The Greek word means either *life* or *soul*; also in verse 26.*

plied, "how long shall I stay with you? How long shall I put up with you? Bring the boy here to me." **18**Jesus rebuked the demon, and it came out of the boy, and he was healed from that moment.

19Then the disciples[D] came to Jesus in private and asked, "Why couldn't we drive it out?"

20He replied, "Because you have so little faith. I tell you the truth, if you have faith as small as a mustard seed, you can say to this mountain, 'Move from here to there' and it will move. Nothing will be impossible for you.*a*"

22When they came together in Galilee, he said to them, "The Son of Man[D] is going to be betrayed into the hands of men. **23**They will kill him, and on the third day he will be raised to life." And the disciples were filled with grief.

The Temple Tax

24After Jesus and his disciples arrived in Capernaum, the collectors of the two-drachma tax came to Peter and asked, "Doesn't your teacher pay the temple tax*b*?"

25"Yes, he does," he replied.

When Peter came into the house, Jesus was the first to speak. "What do you think, Simon?" he asked. "From whom do the kings of the earth collect duty and taxes— from their own sons or from others?"

26"From others," Peter answered.

"Then the sons are exempt," Jesus said to him. **27**"But so that we may not offend them, go to the lake and throw out your line. Take the first fish you catch; open its mouth and you will find a four-drachma coin. Take it and give it to them for my tax and yours."

The Greatest in the Kingdom of Heaven

18 At that time the disciples came to Jesus and asked, "Who is the greatest in the kingdom of heaven?"

2He called a little child and had him stand among them. **3**And he said: "I tell you the truth, unless you change and become like little children, you will never enter the kingdom of heaven. **4**Therefore, whoever humbles himself like this child is the greatest in the kingdom of heaven.

5"And whoever welcomes a little child like this in my name welcomes me. **6**But if anyone causes one of these little ones who believe in me to sin, it would be better for him to have a large millstone[D] hung around his neck and to be drowned in the depths of the sea.

7"Woe to the world because of the things that cause people to sin! Such things must come, but woe to the man through whom they come! **8**If your hand or your foot causes you to sin, cut it off and throw it away. It is better for you to enter life maimed or crippled than to have two hands or two feet and be thrown into eternal fire. **9**And if your eye causes you to sin, gouge it out and throw it away. It is better for you to enter life with one eye than to have two eyes and be thrown into the fire of hell[D].

The Parable of the Lost Sheep

10"See that you do not look down on one of these little ones. For I tell you that their angels in heaven always see the face of my Father in heaven.*c*

Why did the disciples ask about Elijah? (17:10)

Elijah's appearance with Jesus on the mountain may have reminded them of a familiar prophecy in Mal. 4:5, which said Elijah would come *before that great and dreadful day of the* LORD *comes* (that is, before the coming of the Messiah). The *teachers of the law* evidently used the idea that *Elijah must come first* to argue against Jesus' identity as the Messiah. Jesus would help his followers understand that John the Baptist fulfilled Malachi's prophecy (vv. 11–13).

SCRIPTURE LINK (17:11–13)

Jesus' explanation of Elijah's coming can also be found in Mark 9:2–13.

SCRIPTURE LINK (17:14–19)

Mark and Luke give accounts of Jesus healing the boy possessed by a demon. See Mark 9:14–28 and Luke 9:37–42.

Why didn't the disciples have enough faith? (17:20)

Faith was a struggle for them, just as it is for us today. Yet lack of faith creates obstacles to God's work, so Jesus urged his disciples not to wallow in unbelief but to recognize how God can use even a tiny amount of faith. Our faith may seem small and insignificant (especially in times of hardship and testing), but as our faith grows, so does our potential to overcome great obstacles and achieve noble goals.

Two-drachma tax (17:24)

Jewish leaders collected taxes to pay for the upkeep of the temple and its services. "Drachmas" were Greek silver coins, each worth about a day's wages. Two of them were equivalent to the half-shekel required under the Hebrew monetary system (see Exodus 30:13–15; 2 Chron. 24:5–6).

SCRIPTURE LINK (18:1–5)

Jesus also addresses the disciples' question of who is the greatest in the kingdom of God in Mark 9:33–37 and Luke 9:46–48.

Should we really amputate body parts? (18:8)

Jesus was not advocating self-mutilation, since he made it plain that the root of our sin problem is spiritual, not physical. This somewhat extreme example shows not only that we must avoid causing *others* to sin, but also that we must get rid of anything that causes evil in our *own* lives, even at the cost of painful sacrifice. Things we may consider indispensable cannot compare with the greater value of eternal life (1 John 2:16–17).

Do children have personal, guardian angels? (18:10)

God may assign particular angels to watch over specific individuals, although the exact details are not clear to us (see Psalm 34:7; Heb. 1:14). Jesus was making the point that every person matters greatly to God, and that his kingdom gives special honor to the *little ones* (young children, or perhaps new Christians who need our help—see vv. 1–6). No one is too insignificant to be noticed in heaven.

---

a20 Some manuscripts *you.* *21But this kind does not go out except by prayer and fasting.*   *b24* Greek *the two drachmas*   *c10* Some manuscripts *heaven.* *11The Son of Man came to save what was lost.*

Why so little concern for the 99 sheep left in the open country? (18:12)

They were not left unattended. We tend to assume there was only one shepherd, but a Middle Eastern shepherd would rarely go out alone with 100 sheep. If a sheep was lost, the head shepherd would leave the rest of the flock safe and content with hired helpers and go search for it. God does not abandon his followers, but he zealously seeks the lost.

SCRIPTURE LINK (18:12–14)

Luke relates the parable of the lost sheep in Luke 15:4–7.

Can we set people free from their sins? (18:18)

In the highest sense, God alone can forgive sins, for he is the absolute standard of justice and the perfect giver of grace. Yet Christ's church plays an important role in extending God's love to sinners, through administering corrective discipline, through extending sincere friendship and through announcing God's forgiveness. The decisions we make, the correction we give and the forgiveness we offer must harmonize with God's revealed truth in order to be binding (John 16:13).

Does this guarantee God will answer prayers made in agreement? (18:19–20)

Whether we pray with others or alone, God promises to hear and answer requests made in line with his will (1 John 5:14–15). According to Jesus, though, we can find a special sense of his presence and power during times of united prayer. This is especially reassuring when we must deal with problems of discipline and forgiveness, as the context suggests. However, God does not guarantee he will grant requests offered selfishly or foolishly.

How large were these debts? (18:24–28)

Estimates vary about the exact value of a talent, but it is clear that even one talent represented a sizeable sum of money—probably thousands of dollars (see 25:14–30). So ten thousand talents would be an enormous and hopelessly insurmountable debt, equivalent to several million dollars. By contrast, the fellow servant in Jesus' example owed a hundred denarii—a much more manageable debt, equivalent to perhaps three or four months' wages.

What was the cultural rationale behind debtors' prisons? (18:34)

The imprisonment of debtors served both as a punishment for dishonesty and as a warning to others. Sometimes debtors performed forced labor to repay their creditors (2 Kings 4:1). Other times they were thrown into prison and their property confiscated. The threat of imprisonment was also used to compel debtors to acknowledge openly any hidden property they possessed so this could be used to pay off their debts.

---

[12]"What do you think? If a man owns a hundred sheep, and one of them wanders away, will he not leave the ninety-nine on the hills and go to look for the one that wandered off? [13]And if he finds it, I tell you the truth, he is happier about that one sheep than about the ninety-nine that did not wander off. [14]In the same way your Father in heaven is not willing that any of these little ones should be lost.

A Brother Who Sins Against You

[15]"If your brother sins against you,[a] go and show him his fault, just between the two of you. If he listens to you, you have won your brother over. [16]But if he will not listen, take one or two others along, so that 'every matter may be established by the testimony of two or three witnesses.'[b] [17]If he refuses to listen to them, tell it to the church; and if he refuses to listen even to the church, treat him as you would a pagan or a tax collector.

[18]"I tell you the truth, whatever you bind on earth will be[c] bound in heaven, and whatever you loose on earth will be[c] loosed in heaven.

[19]"Again, I tell you that if two of you on earth agree about anything you ask for, it will be done for you by my Father in heaven. [20]For where two or three come together in my name, there am I with them."

The Parable of the Unmerciful Servant

[21]Then Peter came to Jesus and asked, "Lord, how many times shall I forgive my brother when he sins against me? Up to seven times?"

[22]Jesus answered, "I tell you, not seven times, but seventy-seven times.[d]

[23]"Therefore, the kingdom of heaven is like a king who wanted to settle accounts with his servants. [24]As he began the settlement, a man who owed him ten thousand talents[e] was brought to him. [25]Since he was not able to pay, the master ordered that he and his wife and his children and all that he had be sold to repay the debt.

[26]"The servant fell on his knees before him. 'Be patient with me,' he begged, 'and I will pay back everything.' [27]The servant's master took pity on him, canceled the debt and let him go.

[28]"But when that servant went out, he found one of his fellow servants who owed him a hundred denarii.[f] He grabbed him and began to choke him. 'Pay back what you owe me!' he demanded.

[29]"His fellow servant fell to his knees and begged him, 'Be patient with me, and I will pay you back.'

[30]"But he refused. Instead, he went off and had the man thrown into prison until he could pay the debt. [31]When the other servants saw what had happened, they were greatly distressed and went and told their master everything that had happened.

[32]"Then the master called the servant in. 'You wicked servant,' he said, 'I canceled all that debt of yours because you begged me to. [33]Shouldn't you have had mercy[D] on your fellow servant just as I had on you?' [34]In anger his master turned him over to the jailers to be tortured, until he should pay back all he owed.

---

[a]15 Some manuscripts do not have *against you*.   [b]16 Deut. 19:15
[c]18 Or *have been*   [d]22 Or *seventy times seven*   [e]24 That is, millions of dollars   [f]28 That is, a few dollars

35"This is how my heavenly Father will treat each of you unless you forgive your brother from your heart."

Divorce

19 When Jesus had finished saying these things, he left Galilee and went into the region of Judea to the other side of the Jordan. **2**Large crowds followed him, and he healed them there.

3Some Pharisees^D came to him to test him. They asked, "Is it lawful for a man to divorce his wife for any and every reason?"

4"Haven't you read," he replied, "that at the beginning the Creator 'made them male and female,'^a **5**and said, 'For this reason a man will leave his father and mother and be united to his wife, and the two will become one flesh'^b? **6**So they are no longer two, but one. Therefore what God has joined together, let man not separate."

7"Why then," they asked, "did Moses command that a man give his wife a certificate of divorce and send her away?"

8Jesus replied, "Moses permitted you to divorce your wives because your hearts were hard. But it was not this way from the beginning. **9**I tell you that anyone who divorces his wife, except for marital unfaithfulness, and marries another woman commits adultery."

10The disciples^D said to him, "If this is the situation between a husband and wife, it is better not to marry."

11Jesus replied, "Not everyone can accept this word, but only those to whom it has been given. **12**For some are eunuchs^D because they were born that way; others were made that way by men; and others have renounced marriage^c because of the kingdom of heaven. The one who can accept this should accept it."

The Little Children and Jesus

13Then little children were brought to Jesus for him to place his hands on them and pray for them. But the disciples rebuked those who brought them. **14**Jesus said, "Let the little children come to me, and do not hinder them, for the kingdom of heaven belongs to such as these." **15**When he had placed his hands on them, he went on from there.

The Rich Young Man

16Now a man came up to Jesus and asked, "Teacher, what good thing must I do to get eternal life?"

17"Why do you ask me about what is good?" Jesus replied. "There is only One who is good. If you want to enter life, obey the commandments."

18"Which ones?" the man inquired.

Jesus replied, " 'Do not murder, do not commit adultery, do not steal, do not give false testimony, **19**honor your father and mother,'^d and 'love your neighbor as yourself.'^e "

20"All these I have kept," the young man said. "What do I still lack?"

21Jesus answered, "If you want to be perfect, go, sell your possessions and give to the poor, and you will have treasure in heaven. Then come, follow me."

22When the young man heard this, he went away sad, because he had great wealth.

Is divorce always wrong? (19:1–9)
Women in the days of Jesus had little legal protection. They could be divorced simply for displeasing their husbands. Jesus teaches that divorce is contrary to the will of God and it's his intention that marriages last a lifetime. This is not the Bible's last word on divorce, however. Jesus acknowledges that in the case of adultery, divorce may be a sad necessity when one partner refuses to stop his or her unfaithfulness. Later, Paul suggests another such situation, when a believer is deserted by an unbelieving spouse (1 Cor. 7:15).

SCRIPTURE LINK (19:1–9)
Mark records Jesus' teaching on divorce in Mark 10:1–12.

Are those in a second or third marriage committing adultery? (19:9)
Jesus reaffirmed God's ideal for marriage as one man and one woman together for life. He also acknowledged divorce as a less-than-ideal concession to hard human hearts. Some argue that Jesus forbade remarriage under any circumstances, in light of stark passages like Mark 10:11–12. Others believe remarriage is allowable only when marital unfaithfulness or desertion have occurred (see 1 Cor. 7:10–17). See *Have all those who are divorced and remarried committed adultery?* (Luke 16:18).

Was this principle intended only for a select few? (19:11–12)
Everyone needs to understand this Scriptural teaching, but the way we apply it varies according to our different circumstances and gifts. Jesus recognized that in some situations it is better for a person to remain unmarried. Singleness can provide God-given opportunities for undistracted and fruitful Christian service; for others, however, it is better to marry (1 Cor. 7:1–9,25–40).

Born that way (19:12)
They cannot engage in sexual intercourse because of congenital physical deformities. Or perhaps they are born with a special God-given ability to remain unmarried without sexual sin. Jesus noted two other reasons for celibacy: castration by others (see Esther 2:3; Acts 8:27) or a voluntary choice to serve in Christ's kingdom without the encumbrances of married life.

SCRIPTURE LINK (19:13–15)
Both Mark and Luke tell about the little children and Jesus. See Mark 10:13–16 and Luke 18:15–17.

Should adults act like children? (19:14)
Jesus doesn't call people to childish behavior but to childlike faith. The qualities of humility, trust, receptivity and a lack of self-sufficiency all characterize the person of faith. The kingdom of God is not earned by human effort, but received in childlike trust as a gift of the mercy and grace of God.

SCRIPTURE LINK (19:16–29)
The story of the rich young man can also be found in Mark 10:17–30 and Luke 18:18–30.

---

a4 Gen. 1:27   *b5* Gen. 2:24   *c12 Or have made themselves eunuchs*   *d19* Exodus 20:12-16; Deut. 5:16-20   *e19* Lev. 19:18

Did Jesus say salvation comes by obeying the commandments? (19:17)

If this were the only thing Jesus said about salvation, it might sound as though strict adherence to the commandments could earn us a place in heaven. But Jesus said much more that helps explain this verse. For instance, he spoke of outward obedience as an indicator of the condition of a person's heart (7:17–21). He stressed that our relationship with God must be our primary focus; but he also expected obedience to grow out of our relationship with God (22:37–40; John 14:15).

What do we have to give up to gain eternal life? (19:21)

Jesus was not saying we have to become poor to gain eternal life. He was saying that it only takes one thing to block a relationship with God. Some, like the ruler, may be spiritually hindered because they depend on material possessions. But others may have to surrender to God such things as fame, extraordinary talent, good looks or intellectualism.

Camel . . . through the eye of a needle (19:24)

Jesus' analogy painted an amusing picture of something impossible or absurd by human standards. The disciples probably saw material wealth as a certain sign of God's favor—but Jesus recognized how the love of money creates temptations many cannot resist. No sinner, whether rich or poor, *deserves* to enter the kingdom of heaven. But God's grace can overcome seemingly impossible obstacles. See also *What did Jesus mean by a camel going through the eye of a needle?* (Luke 18:25).

The renewal of all things (19:28)

Some interpret this to mean the church age, in which the apostles would exercise spiritual authority and proclaim the gospel that brings renewal or new birth (Titus 3:5; 2 Peter 3:2). Others believe this refers to the end of time when heaven and earth will be renewed (Romans 8:19–21; Rev. 21:1–5). According to the latter view, the apostles will receive special honor and responsibility when God's final judgment occurs (1 Cor. 6:2).

SCRIPTURE LINK (20:17–19)

In Mark 10:32–34 and Luke 18:31–33 you can also read about Jesus' prediction of his death.

What was this mother's ambition for her sons? (20:20–21)

She wanted them to occupy important positions of honor and influence as Jesus' closest advisers in his new kingdom. For us today, sitting at the king's right and left might compare to serving as key members of a presidential cabinet.

SCRIPTURE LINK (20:20–28)

Mark relates this request for a position of honor in Mark 10:35–45.

Is Jesus advocating slavery? (20:26–28)

Jesus isn't endorsing the institution of slavery, but he uses it as an object lesson in humility. His own willingness to submit to the Father's will, even to the point of death, is an example of servanthood lived out to its fullest. It is an example that he asks us to imitate. See article:

23Then Jesus said to his disciples^D, "I tell you the truth, it is hard for a rich man to enter the kingdom of heaven. 24Again I tell you, it is easier for a camel to go through the eye of a needle than for a rich man to enter the kingdom of God."

25When the disciples heard this, they were greatly astonished and asked, "Who then can be saved?"

26Jesus looked at them and said, "With man this is impossible, but with God all things are possible."

27Peter answered him, "We have left everything to follow you! What then will there be for us?"

28Jesus said to them, "I tell you the truth, at the renewal of all things, when the Son of Man^D sits on his glorious throne, you who have followed me will also sit on twelve thrones, judging the twelve tribes of Israel. 29And everyone who has left houses or brothers or sisters or father or mother*a* or children or fields for my sake will receive a hundred times as much and will inherit eternal life^D. 30But many who are first will be last, and many who are last will be first.

The Parable of the Workers in the Vineyard

20 "For the kingdom of heaven is like a landowner who went out early in the morning to hire men to work in his vineyard. 2He agreed to pay them a denarius for the day and sent them into his vineyard.

3"About the third hour he went out and saw others standing in the marketplace doing nothing. 4He told them, 'You also go and work in my vineyard, and I will pay you whatever is right.' 5So they went.

"He went out again about the sixth hour and the ninth hour and did the same thing. 6About the eleventh hour he went out and found still others standing around. He asked them, 'Why have you been standing here all day long doing nothing?'

7" 'Because no one has hired us,' they answered.

"He said to them, 'You also go and work in my vineyard.'

8"When evening came, the owner of the vineyard said to his foreman, 'Call the workers and pay them their wages, beginning with the last ones hired and going on to the first.'

9"The workers who were hired about the eleventh hour came and each received a denarius. 10So when those came who were hired first, they expected to receive more. But each one of them also received a denarius. 11When they received it, they began to grumble against the landowner. 12'These men who were hired last worked only one hour,' they said, 'and you have made them equal to us who have borne the burden of the work and the heat of the day.'

13"But he answered one of them, 'Friend, I am not being unfair to you. Didn't you agree to work for a denarius? 14Take your pay and go. I want to give the man who was hired last the same as I gave you. 15Don't I have the right to do what I want with my own money? Or are you envious because I am generous?'

16"So the last will be first, and the first will be last."

Jesus Again Predicts His Death

17Now as Jesus was going up to Jerusalem^D, he took the twelve disciples aside and said to them, 18"We are going

---

*a*29 Some manuscripts *mother or wife*

up to Jerusalem[D], and the Son of Man[D] will be betrayed to the chief priests[D] and the teachers of the law. They will condemn him to death[D] [19]and will turn him over to the Gentiles[D] to be mocked and flogged and crucified. On the third day he will be raised to life!"

A Mother's Request

[20]Then the mother of Zebedee's sons came to Jesus with her sons and, kneeling down, asked a favor of him. [21]"What is it you want?" he asked.

She said, "Grant that one of these two sons of mine may sit at your right and the other at your left in your kingdom."

[22]"You don't know what you are asking," Jesus said to them. "Can you drink the cup I am going to drink?"

"We can," they answered.

[23]Jesus said to them, "You will indeed drink from my cup, but to sit at my right or left is not for me to grant. These places belong to those for whom they have been prepared by my Father."

[24]When the ten heard about this, they were indignant with the two brothers. [25]Jesus called them together and said, "You know that the rulers of the Gentiles lord it over them, and their high officials exercise authority over them. [26]Not so with you. Instead, whoever wants to become great among you must be your servant, [27]and whoever wants to be first must be your slave— [28]just as the Son of Man did not come to be served, but to serve, and to give his life as a ransom for many."

Two Blind Men Receive Sight

[29]As Jesus and his disciples[D] were leaving Jericho[D], a large crowd followed him. [30]Two blind men were sitting by the roadside, and when they heard that Jesus was going by, they shouted, "Lord, Son of David, have mercy[D] on us!"

[31]The crowd rebuked them and told them to be quiet, but they shouted all the louder, "Lord, Son of David, have mercy on us!"

[32]Jesus stopped and called them. "What do you want me to do for you?" he asked.

[33]"Lord," they answered, "we want our sight."

[34]Jesus had compassion on them and touched their eyes. Immediately they received their sight and followed him.

The Triumphal Entry

21 As they approached Jerusalem and came to Bethphage on the Mount of Olives, Jesus sent two disciples, [2]saying to them, "Go to the village ahead of you, and at once you will find a donkey tied there, with her colt by her. Untie them and bring them to me. [3]If anyone says anything to you, tell him that the Lord needs them, and he will send them right away."

[4]This took place to fulfill what was spoken through the prophet[D]:

[5]"Say to the Daughter of Zion[D],
  'See, your king comes to you,
gentle and riding on a donkey,
  on a colt, the foal of a donkey.' "[a]

[6]The disciples went and did as Jesus had instructed

[a]5 Zech. 9:9

Why doesn't the Bible condemn slavery? (1 Peter 2:18–20).

If ministers are servants, how can they lead? (20:26–28)

Jesus was not putting down the importance of leadership; he was highlighting the proper *motives* for leadership. All of us must be servants, and some serve by leading. Following Christ's example, godly leaders choose the way of humility. They are driven not by selfish ambition but by a burning desire to care for God's people and accomplish his purposes (1 Peter 5:2–6).

SCRIPTURE LINK (20:29–34)

Mark tells about the blind receiving their sight in Mark 10:46–52. Luke talks about it in Luke 18:35–43.

Why does Matthew mention two blind men while Mark and Luke mention only one? (20:30; see Mark 10:46; Luke 18:35)

This is not a contradiction. By saying Jesus healed a blind man, Mark and Luke did not insist that Jesus healed *only* one. It's likely they just focused their account on the one blind man (named Bartimaeus) who was the more prominent of the two. Also see *Why doesn't Matthew agree with Mark and Luke?* (8:28).

Why did the blind man call Jesus the Son of David? (20:30)

The blind man recognized Jesus as the prophesied Messiah. It is ironic that a man without physical sight was able to see things that others had missed.

SCRIPTURE LINK (21:1–9)

You can read about Jesus' triumphal entry into Jerusalem in Mark 11:1–10 and Luke 19:29–38.

The Triumphal Entry (21:1)

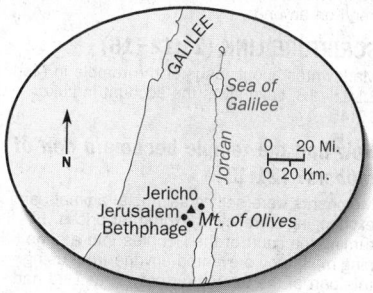

Why did Jesus "borrow" without asking? (21:2–6)

It's possible that Jesus had prearranged with the owner to use the donkey and her colt, especially since Jesus knew in advance what would happen when he arrived in Jerusalem (16:21). Even if the request was spontaneous, Jesus undoubtedly knew the owner (probably a disciple or at least a sympathizer) would gladly lend the animals once he learned that the Lord needed them (v. 3).

SCRIPTURE LINK (21:4–9)

John relates the prophecy about Jesus riding on a donkey's colt. See John 12:12–15.

How did Jesus sit on *them*—on a donkey and on a colt? (21:7)

He didn't literally sit on both. Jesus sat on the colt while its mother apparently walked alongside (see Luke 19:35), perhaps to help calm the unbroken colt. The disciples may have prepared both animals because they did not know which Jesus would use.

Why did Jesus ride a donkey? (21:7)

Donkeys or mules were often associated with leaders (Judges 10:4; 1 Kings 1:33). By riding this young colt, however, Jesus demonstrated his humility and gentleness. He also fulfilled one of the prophecies of the Messiah (Zech. 9:9). See *Why have a king on a donkey?* (Zech. 9:9–10).

Why did Jesus participate in this procession? (21:7–10)

Jesus, at the climax of his ministry, was making a statement. This was an object lesson that proclaimed who he was—the Son of David, the King of kings, the one who conquered sin and sickness. Conquering generals at that time were given a "triumphal entry" upon their return to their home city. Palm branches were often waved during times of celebration and victory (Lev. 23:40; Psalm 118:25–27). The procession caused the city, crowded with people for Passover, to consider Jesus' claims. Also see *Why carpet the road with cloaks?* (Luke 19:36).

Why did Jesus resort to violence? (21:12)

It would seem strange if Jesus had not expressed anger over the corruption in God's house. Jesus asserted his authority and created an environment for healing instead of stealing (vv. 13–14). Though Jesus tells us to turn the other cheek (5:39), his example showed there are also times when anger is the right response (see Mark 3:5). But notice that Jesus controlled his anger; this was not a temper tantrum. Nor is there any indication that he laid a hand on anyone.

SCRIPTURE LINK (21:12–16)

Mark writes about Jesus at the temple in Mark 11:15–18. Luke gives the account in Luke 19:45–47.

How had the temple become *a den of robbers?* (21:13)

Merchants were selling sacrificial animals and exchanging currency at exorbitant prices. By turning the court of the Gentiles into a shopping mall, they prevented anyone from using this part of the temple for prayer, as God had intended (Jer. 7:11).

SCRIPTURE LINK (21:18–22)

Mark tells about the fig tree withering in Mark 11:12–14,20–24.

Why did Jesus ruin the fig tree? (21:19)

Though it was not the season for figs (Mark 11:13), the tree seemed to indicate that it had something to give. (It was not the season for leaves, either, since a fig tree full of leaves was usually a place to find food.) The leaves were an empty promise, so Jesus cursed the unfruitful tree as a visual aid—a warning that God's judgment will come to those who appear fruitful but are not.

them. **7**They brought the donkey and the colt, placed their cloaks on them, and Jesus sat on them. **8**A very large crowd spread their cloaks on the road, while others cut branches from the trees and spread them on the road. **9**The crowds that went ahead of him and those that followed shouted,

> "Hosanna[a] to the Son of David!"

> "Blessed is he who comes in the name of the Lord!"[b]

> "Hosanna[a] in the highest!"

10When Jesus entered Jerusalem[D], the whole city was stirred and asked, "Who is this?" **11**The crowds answered, "This is Jesus, the prophet[D] from Nazareth in Galilee."

Jesus at the Temple

12Jesus entered the temple area and drove out all who were buying and selling there. He overturned the tables of the money changers and the benches of those selling doves. **13**"It is written," he said to them, " 'My house will be called a house of prayer,'[c] but you are making it a 'den of robbers.'[d]

14The blind and the lame came to him at the temple, and he healed them. **15**But when the chief priests[D] and the teachers of the law saw the wonderful things he did and the children shouting in the temple area, "Hosanna to the Son of David," they were indignant.

16"Do you hear what these children are saying?" they asked him.

"Yes," replied Jesus, "have you never read,

> " 'From the lips of children and infants
> you have ordained praise'[e]?"

17And he left them and went out of the city to Bethany, where he spent the night.

The Fig Tree Withers

18Early in the morning, as he was on his way back to the city, he was hungry. **19**Seeing a fig tree by the road, he went up to it but found nothing on it except leaves. Then he said to it, "May you never bear fruit again!" Immediately the tree withered.

20When the disciples[D] saw this, they were amazed. "How did the fig tree wither so quickly?" they asked.

21Jesus replied, "I tell you the truth, if you have faith and do not doubt, not only can you do what was done to the fig tree, but also you can say to this mountain, 'Go, throw yourself into the sea,' and it will be done. **22**If you believe, you will receive whatever you ask for in prayer."

The Authority of Jesus Questioned

23Jesus entered the temple courts, and, while he was teaching, the chief priests and the elders of the people came to him. "By what authority are you doing these things?" they asked. "And who gave you this authority?"

24Jesus replied, "I will also ask you one question. If you answer me, I will tell you by what authority I am doing

a9 A Hebrew expression meaning "Save!" which became an exclamation of praise; also in verse 15   *b9 Psalm 118:26*   *c13 Isaiah 56:7*   *d13 Jer. 7:11*   *e16 Psalm 8:2*

these things. **25**John's baptism^D—where did it come from? Was it from heaven, or from men?"

They discussed it among themselves and said, "If we say, 'From heaven,' he will ask, 'Then why didn't you believe him?' **26**But if we say, 'From men'—we are afraid of the people, for they all hold that John was a prophet^D."

27So they answered Jesus, "We don't know."

Then he said, "Neither will I tell you by what authority I am doing these things.

The Parable of the Two Sons

28"What do you think? There was a man who had two sons. He went to the first and said, 'Son, go and work today in the vineyard.'

29" 'I will not,' he answered, but later he changed his mind and went.

30"Then the father went to the other son and said the same thing. He answered, 'I will, sir,' but he did not go.

31"Which of the two did what his father wanted?"

"The first," they answered.

Jesus said to them, "I tell you the truth, the tax collectors^D and the prostitutes are entering the kingdom of God^D ahead of you. **32**For John came to you to show you the way of righteousness^D, and you did not believe him, but the tax collectors and the prostitutes did. And even after you saw this, you did not repent^D and believe him.

The Parable of the Tenants

33"Listen to another parable^D: There was a landowner who planted a vineyard. He put a wall around it, dug a winepress^D in it and built a watchtower^D. Then he rented the vineyard to some farmers and went away on a journey. **34**When the harvest time approached, he sent his servants to the tenants to collect his fruit.

35"The tenants seized his servants; they beat one, killed another, and stoned a third. **36**Then he sent other servants to them, more than the first time, and the tenants treated them the same way. **37**Last of all, he sent his son to them. 'They will respect my son,' he said.

38"But when the tenants saw the son, they said to each other, 'This is the heir. Come, let's kill him and take his inheritance.' **39**So they took him and threw him out of the vineyard and killed him.

40"Therefore, when the owner of the vineyard comes, what will he do to those tenants?"

41"He will bring those wretches to a wretched end," they replied, "and he will rent the vineyard to other tenants, who will give him his share of the crop at harvest time."

42Jesus said to them, "Have you never read in the Scriptures:

" 'The stone the builders rejected
has become the capstone^D^a;
the Lord has done this,
and it is marvelous in our eyes'^b?

43"Therefore I tell you that the kingdom of God will be taken away from you and given to a people who will produce its fruit. **44**He who falls on this stone will be broken to pieces, but he on whom it falls will be crushed."^c

45When the chief priests^D and the Pharisees^D heard

^a42 Or *cornerstone*   ^b42 Psalm 118:22,23   ^c44 Some manuscripts do not have verse 44.

Why give the disciples power to wither trees? (21:21)
Jesus wanted his disciples to be confident that God's power was available to them. The withered tree served as an example of the kind of authority they would have. Jesus knew he would soon be sending his disciples out with the daunting task of bringing the world to him (Acts 1:8). The fig tree would remind them that God's power could help them overcome any obstacle.

Will we receive *whatever* we ask for in prayer? (21:21-22)
Jesus' promise is faith-stretching. We can pray with the conviction that God is able (Eph. 3:20; James 5:16). But while Jesus intended to expand our confidence in the possibilities of prayer, he was not encouraging us to use prayer to manipulate God. The Bible tells us that answers to prayer depend on meeting certain conditions (see, for example, James 4:2-3; 1 Peter 3:7; 1 John 5:14-15). Sometimes God will say "No" to a request (2 Cor. 12:8-9) because he has a better plan than we do (Isaiah 55:8-9; Phil. 4:6-7). Also see *How much can faith do?* (Mark 11:22-24).

SCRIPTURE LINK (21:23-27)
Both Mark and Luke give accounts about Jesus' authority being questioned. See Mark 11:27-33 and Luke 20:1-8.

The kingdom of God (21:31,43)
See *The kingdom of heaven* (13:24).

SCRIPTURE LINK (21:33-46)
The parable of the tenants can also be found in Mark 12:1-12 and Luke 20:9-19.

Capstone (21:42)
Literally "head of the corner." Used to describe either the bottom corner of the building (a foundation stone) or the keystone of an archway. It can either cause a person to stumble, or it can fall on someone. Either way, the stone is essential for holding the building together.

Jesus' parables[D], they knew he was talking about them. **46**They looked for a way to arrest him, but they were afraid of the crowd because the people held that he was a prophet[D].

The Parable of the Wedding Banquet

22 Jesus spoke to them again in parables, saying: **2**"The kingdom of heaven is like a king who prepared a wedding banquet for his son. **3**He sent his servants to those who had been invited to the banquet to tell them to come, but they refused to come.

4"Then he sent some more servants and said, 'Tell those who have been invited that I have prepared my dinner: My oxen and fattened cattle have been butchered, and everything is ready. Come to the wedding banquet.'

5"But they paid no attention and went off—one to his field, another to his business. **6**The rest seized his servants, mistreated them and killed them. **7**The king was enraged. He sent his army and destroyed those murderers and burned their city.

8"Then he said to his servants, 'The wedding banquet is ready, but those I invited did not deserve to come. **9**Go to the street corners and invite to the banquet anyone you find.' **10**So the servants went out into the streets and gathered all the people they could find, both good and bad, and the wedding hall was filled with guests.

11"But when the king came in to see the guests, he noticed a man there who was not wearing wedding clothes. **12**'Friend,' he asked, 'how did you get in here without wedding clothes?' The man was speechless.

13"Then the king told the attendants, 'Tie him hand and foot, and throw him outside, into the darkness, where there will be weeping and gnashing of teeth.'

14"For many are invited, but few are chosen."

Paying Taxes to Caesar

15Then the Pharisees[D] went out and laid plans to trap him in his words. **16**They sent their disciples[D] to him along with the Herodians[D]. "Teacher," they said, "we know you are a man of integrity and that you teach the way of God in accordance with the truth. You aren't swayed by men, because you pay no attention to who they are. **17**Tell us then, what is your opinion? Is it right to pay taxes to Caesar or not?"

18But Jesus, knowing their evil intent, said, "You hypocrites, why are you trying to trap me? **19**Show me the coin used for paying the tax." They brought him a denarius, **20**and he asked them, "Whose portrait is this? And whose inscription?"

21"Caesar's," they replied.

Then he said to them, "Give to Caesar what is Caesar's, and to God what is God's."

22When they heard this, they were amazed. So they left him and went away.

Marriage at the Resurrection

23That same day the Sadducees[D], who say there is no resurrection[D], came to him with a question. **24**"Teacher," they said, "Moses told us that if a man dies without having children, his brother must marry the widow and have children for him. **25**Now there were seven brothers among us. The first one married and died, and since he had no children, he left his wife to his brother. **26**The same thing happened to the second and third brother, right on down

---

SCRIPTURE LINK (22:2–14)

In Luke 14:16–24, Luke records a similar parable.

Why was the king so upset about his guest's clothes? (22:12)

Even among the lower class, first-century weddings often included several days of joyful feasting. The bride and groom wore their best clothes; their guests enjoyed the best food and drink they could provide (Isaiah 61:10; John 2:1–11). A royal wedding would be even more elaborate. If a guest of the king was unable to find suitable attire, the king himself could provide something to wear (1 Samuel 18:4; Esther 6:8; Rev. 19:7–9). Of all the guests brought to this wedding—good and bad, worthy and unworthy—this particular guest had apparently rejected the garments provided by the king.

SCRIPTURE LINK (22:15–22)

Jesus' teaching on paying taxes can also be found in Mark 12:13–17 and Luke 20:20–26.

What is *Caesar's* and what is *God's*? (22:21)

God is over all things, but he entrusts some of those things to people. The things that belong to Caesar—that is, government authorities—are responsibilities to maintain civil order, to punish wrongdoers, to protect the helpless and to collect taxes to administer these assignments. See Romans 13:1–7 and 1 Peter 2:13–17. God, however, deserves our highest allegiance. Only he deserves our worship. All human government is subject to his higher authority and purpose (Daniel 3:17–18; 6:1–28; Acts 4:19–20; 5:29).

Did Jews still marry their brothers' widows? (22:24)

Some Jews probably still practiced this law (Gen. 38:8; Deut. 25:5). Yet polygamy had not been practiced for nearly five centuries, since the end of the exile in Babylon. The Sadducees' interest was not polygamy, however. They simply invented a hypothetical case in an attempt to lampoon the idea of resurrection.

SCRIPTURE LINK (22:25) *He left his wife to his brother*

By Jewish law, a man was supposed to marry his brother's widow, providing for her and raising their firstborn son in his brother's name. See *Why was a man required to marry his brother's widow?* (Deut. 25:5–9).

to the seventh. **27**Finally, the woman died. **28**Now then, at the resurrection[D], whose wife will she be of the seven, since all of them were married to her?"

29Jesus replied, "You are in error because you do not know the Scriptures or the power of God. **30**At the resurrection people will neither marry nor be given in marriage; they will be like the angels in heaven. **31**But about the resurrection of the dead—have you not read what God said to you, **32**'I am the God of Abraham, the God of Isaac, and the God of Jacob'[a]? He is not the God of the dead but of the living."

33When the crowds heard this, they were astonished at his teaching.

The Greatest Commandment

34Hearing that Jesus had silenced the Sadducees[D], the Pharisees[D] got together. **35**One of them, an expert in the law, tested him with this question: **36**"Teacher, which is the greatest commandment in the Law?"

37Jesus replied: " 'Love the Lord your God with all your heart and with all your soul[D] and with all your mind.'[b] **38**This is the first and greatest commandment. **39**And the second is like it: 'Love your neighbor as yourself.'[c] **40**All the Law and the Prophets[D] hang on these two commandments."

Whose Son Is the Christ?

41While the Pharisees were gathered together, Jesus asked them, **42**"What do you think about the Christ[d]? Whose son is he?"

"The son of David," they replied.

43He said to them, "How is it then that David, speaking by the Spirit, calls him 'Lord'? For he says,

44" 'The Lord said to my Lord:
  "Sit at my right hand
   until I put your enemies
       under your feet." '[e]

45If then David calls him 'Lord,' how can he be his son?" **46**No one could say a word in reply, and from that day on no one dared to ask him any more questions.

Seven Woes

23 Then Jesus said to the crowds and to his disciples[D]: **2**"The teachers of the law and the Pharisees sit in Moses' seat. **3**So you must obey them and do everything they tell you. But do not do what they do, for they do not practice what they preach. **4**They tie up heavy loads and put them on men's shoulders, but they themselves are not willing to lift a finger to move them.

5"Everything they do is done for men to see: They make their phylacteries[f] wide and the tassels on their garments long; **6**they love the place of honor at banquets and the most important seats in the synagogues; **7**they love to be greeted in the marketplaces and to have men call them 'Rabbi[D].'

8"But you are not to be called 'Rabbi,' for you have only one Master and you are all brothers. **9**And do not call anyone on earth 'father,' for you have one Father, and he is in heaven. **10**Nor are you to be called 'teacher,' for you

---

a32 Exodus 3:6   *b37* Deut. 6:5   *c39* Lev. 19:18   *d42* Or *Messiah*   *e44* Psalm 110:1   *f5* That is, boxes containing Scripture verses, worn on forehead and arm

---

Is heaven sexless? (22:30)

We really don't know. The Sadducees were attempting to show that the concept of the resurrection was absurd. Jesus' point was the reality of resurrection, not the lifestyle of heaven. It would appear, however, that we will not have sexual relations in heaven. Still, Paul says that heaven's pleasures will be infinitely better than the best this life offers (1 Cor. 15:35–57). See article: *What do we have to look forward to?* (1 Cor. 15:35–57).

What kind of logic did Jesus use? (22:31–33)

We might think this phrase could have meant, "I *am* the God of the one who *was* Abraham." But most Jews didn't reason that way. To speak of "Yahweh (I AM), the God of Abraham," was to imply not only a past but a present relationship. Thus, they reasoned, "If we believe there is a God, then we can also believe Abraham still is." Because the Sadducees based their doctrine on only the five books of Moses (Genesis to Deuteronomy), Jesus made his case from Exodus 3:6.

SCRIPTURE LINK (22:34–40)

Mark records Jesus giving the greatest commandment in Mark 12:28–31.

SCRIPTURE LINK (22:41–46)

Both Mark and Luke report Jesus asking whose Son is the Christ. See Mark 12:35–37 and Luke 20:41–44.

Why did Jesus' question stump the Pharisees? (22:45)

The Pharisees correctly believed that the Messiah would be the son—that is, the descendant—of David (2 Samuel 7:8–16; Jer. 33:14–17; Matt. 1:1). But by quoting from David's own writings (Psalm 110:1), Jesus showed that David himself spoke of the Messiah as Lord—a title of profound respect and honor. Because they knew a father would not call his son "Lord," the Pharisees could not answer Jesus' question.

SCRIPTURE LINK (23:1–7)

Jesus' warning against following the ways of the Pharisees can also be found in Mark 12:38–39 and Luke 20:45–46.

Phylacteries (23:5)

Small leather boxes containing portions of God's Word. They were worn by Jews who interpreted literally the instructions to fasten God's Word on their hands and foreheads. See *A sign on your hand and a symbol on your forehead* (Exodus 13:9).

Why can't we call our fathers father? (23:9)

We can. Jesus was not removing the word from our vocabulary. He was simply telling us not to misuse the term to inflate the egos of those who want honor from special titles or positions. Jesus himself used the word *father* in its ordinary sense (21:31; Luke 15:12–28).

have one Teacher, the Christ.[a] **11**The greatest among you will be your servant. **12**For whoever exalts himself will be humbled, and whoever humbles himself will be exalted.

13"Woe to you, teachers of the law and Pharisees[D], you hypocrites! You shut the kingdom of heaven in men's faces. You yourselves do not enter, nor will you let those enter who are trying to.[b]

15"Woe to you, teachers of the law and Pharisees, you hypocrites! You travel over land and sea to win a single convert, and when he becomes one, you make him twice as much a son of hell[D] as you are.

16"Woe to you, blind guides! You say, 'If anyone swears by the temple, it means nothing; but if anyone swears by the gold of the temple, he is bound by his oath.' **17**You blind fools! Which is greater: the gold, or the temple that makes the gold sacred[D]? **18**You also say, 'If anyone swears by the altar, it means nothing; but if anyone swears by the gift on it, he is bound by his oath.' **19**You blind men! Which is greater: the gift, or the altar that makes the gift sacred? **20**Therefore, he who swears by the altar swears by it and by everything on it. **21**And he who swears by the temple swears by it and by the one who dwells in it. **22**And he who swears by heaven swears by God's throne and by the one who sits on it.

23"Woe to you, teachers of the law and Pharisees, you hypocrites! You give a tenth of your spices—mint, dill and cummin. But you have neglected the more important matters of the law—justice, mercy[D] and faithfulness. You should have practiced the latter, without neglecting the former. **24**You blind guides! You strain out a gnat but swallow a camel.

25"Woe to you, teachers of the law and Pharisees, you hypocrites! You clean the outside of the cup and dish, but inside they are full of greed and self-indulgence. **26**Blind Pharisee! First clean the inside of the cup and dish, and then the outside also will be clean.

27"Woe to you, teachers of the law and Pharisees, you hypocrites! You are like whitewashed tombs, which look beautiful on the outside but on the inside are full of dead men's bones and everything unclean[D]. **28**In the same way, on the outside you appear to people as righteous[D] but on the inside you are full of hypocrisy and wickedness.

29"Woe to you, teachers of the law and Pharisees, you hypocrites! You build tombs for the prophets[D] and decorate the graves of the righteous. **30**And you say, 'If we had lived in the days of our forefathers, we would not have taken part with them in shedding the blood of the prophets.' **31**So you testify against yourselves that you are the descendants of those who murdered the prophets. **32**Fill up, then, the measure of the sin of your forefathers!

33"You snakes! You brood of vipers! How will you escape being condemned to hell? **34**Therefore I am sending you prophets and wise men and teachers. Some of them you will kill and crucify; others you will flog in your synagogues and pursue from town to town. **35**And so upon you will come all the righteous blood that has been shed on earth, from the blood of righteous Abel to

---

How did Pharisees turn others into sons of hell? (23:15)

The phrase *son of hell,* was likely a Hebrew expression that meant a particularly wicked person—in contrast to the *sons of the kingdom* (13:38). Jesus bluntly accused the Pharisees —who bragged about being righteous—of being blatant sinners and hypocrites. Worse, they spread their false teaching and legalistic ways to those they recruited. They led people further away from God's truth by taking them deeper into human tradition.

What did it mean to swear by the altar, the temple or heaven? (23:16–22)

The Pharisees thought they could strengthen their words by reinforcing them with oaths. It was thought that words carried more weight when they were backed by objects of value (such as the altar in the temple) or persons of authority. People thought a person who invited some sort of curse upon himself if he lied or failed to keep his promise could be trusted more than one who did not.

Why are some matters of the law more important than others? (23:23)

Because some parts of the law are foundational principles that undergird the rest of the law. Though all of God's law is important (5:17–20; James 2:10), Jesus asserted that all the Law and the Prophets hang on the commandments to love God and to love your neighbor (22:35–40). Jesus accused the Pharisees of focusing on minor details while neglecting the main point of the law.

Whitewashed tombs (23:27)

Tombs were whitewashed once a year, perhaps to show respect for the dead, but primarily to make the tombs easier to see. The Jews believed that touching or walking over a grave caused a person to become ceremonially unclean (Num. 19:16). Whitewashing the tombs helped prevent accidental contact.

What was it about the religious leaders that bothered Jesus so much? (23:33)

Their hypocrisy—six times in this chapter Jesus called them hypocrites. The religious leaders had exchanged the holy for the hollow. They were concerned with appearance rather than substance. They pretended to obey God's Word but consistently violated the spirit of the law. Jesus, by contrast, desired genuine spiritual commitment (22:37–39; Mark 7:14–23).

---

[a]10 Or *Messiah*   [b]13 Some manuscripts *to.* [14]*Woe to you, teachers of the law and Pharisees, you hypocrites! You devour widows' houses and for a show make lengthy prayers. Therefore you will be punished more severely.*

the blood of Zechariah son of Berekiah, whom you murdered between the temple and the altar. **36**I tell you the truth, all this will come upon this generation.

37"O Jerusalem^D, Jerusalem, you who kill the prophets^D and stone those sent to you, how often I have longed to gather your children together, as a hen gathers her chicks under her wings, but you were not willing. **38**Look, your house is left to you desolate. **39**For I tell you, you will not see me again until you say, 'Blessed is he who comes in the name of the Lord.'*a*"

Signs of the End of the Age

24 Jesus left the temple and was walking away when his disciples^D came up to him to call his attention to its buildings. **2**"Do you see all these things?" he asked. "I tell you the truth, not one stone here will be left on another; every one will be thrown down."

3As Jesus was sitting on the Mount of Olives, the disciples came to him privately. "Tell us," they said, "when will this happen, and what will be the sign of your coming and of the end of the age?"

4Jesus answered: "Watch out that no one deceives you. **5**For many will come in my name, claiming, 'I am the Christ,*b*' and will deceive many. **6**You will hear of wars and rumors of wars, but see to it that you are not alarmed. Such things must happen, but the end is still to come. **7**Nation will rise against nation, and kingdom against kingdom. There will be famines and earthquakes in various places. **8**All these are the beginning of birth pains.

9"Then you will be handed over to be persecuted and put to death^D, and you will be hated by all nations because of me. **10**At that time many will turn away from the faith and will betray and hate each other, **11**and many false prophets will appear and deceive many people.

*a*39 Psalm 118:26   *b*5 Or *Messiah*; also in verse 23

Why couldn't a sovereign God overrule an unwilling city? (23:37)

He could have, but he wanted people to accept his love because they *wanted* to, not because they *had* to. Jesus did not force his love upon Jerusalem; instead, he sought the allegiance and acceptance of willing hearts. God longs for people to turn to him in faith (1 Tim. 2:3–4; 2 Peter 3:9), so he leaves our personal choice as part of the equation. God's sovereignty does not diminish human responsibility.

SCRIPTURE LINK (23:37–39)

Luke writes of Jesus' sorrowing over Jerusalem in Luke 13:34–35.

SCRIPTURE LINK (24:1–51)

Mark talks about the signs of the end of the age in Mark 13:1–37. Luke takes up the topic in Luke 21:5–36.

What events did Jesus include in his answer? (24:4–14)

The disciples actually asked more than one question, although they were linked (see previous note). Jesus answered their questions by describing the fall of Jerusalem (which occurred in A.D. 70). But he also revealed some events that will occur at the time of his return or at the end of the world.

Why ask about the end of the age? (24:2–3)

Why, when Jesus said the temple would be destroyed, did the disciples ask about the end of the age? It is quite possible they believed the destruction of the temple would usher in the end of the age. Perhaps their curiosity about Jesus' role in all this was stirred even more because Jesus answered their questions while sitting on the Mount of Olives, a location with prophetic significance (Zech. 14:4).

What might have led them to think this way? One factor may have been the prominent place of the temple in the life of the people. It was the focal point for worship, religious instruction and sacrifice.

Another thing that may have contributed to their thinking was the awe-inspiring, impressive sight created by the temple. Thousands of craftsmen had worked for years to build its towering walls, some gleaming with white marble. Its gates were decorated with gold and silver. The Beautiful Gate (named because it was covered with polished brass) was about 75 feet high and 60 feet wide. Such splendor would have made it difficult for the disciples to imagine the temple's ruin unless the world itself was coming to an end.

Enormous stones from the temple wall can still be seen in Jerusalem. One, for example, is 27 feet long and weighs at least 200 tons. No wonder the disciples were so impressed by the stones (Mark 13:1). In their minds, the destruction of the temple would be both a physical and a spiritual calamity.

How much did Jesus teach here about the end times? (24:15–28)

These predictions accurately describe the terrible conditions leading to the fall of Jerusalem in A.D. 70. Many also see a parallel to the dangerous conditions and spiritual decline to come in the last days (2 Tim. 3:1–5). He was apparently talking about both events, underscoring the need for faithfulness, discernment and patience.

Abomination that causes desolation (24:15)

See *What is the abomination that causes desolation?* (Mark 13:14).

Why did Jesus say *let the reader understand?* (24:15)

Jesus was probably urging his listeners to read and understand Daniel's prophecy (see Daniel 9:27). In the same context, Daniel wrote similar words, to *know and understand* (Daniel 9:25; 12:10). But some think these are Matthew's words, added to urge his readers to carefully consider what Jesus said.

Does this describe the "Great Tribulation"? (24:21)

Maybe. Some think this describes a future time of unprecedented disaster—judgment to come upon the world at the end of the age (Rev. 6:15–17; 7:14). Others believe this refers to the terrible suffering that occurred when Jerusalem was destroyed in A.D. 70. People died at the hands of Roman troops or by starvation, fire and disease. To a certain extent, God's people can expect to face tribulation in every age (John 16:33).

Will the sun be literally darkened? (24:29)

Since Jesus' first coming was accompanied by unusual signs on earth and in the sky (28:2–4; Luke 2:8–14; 23:44–45), it does not seem unreasonable to believe these signs will occur literally when Jesus returns. Other passages also tell of dramatic events that will take place at the return of Christ (1 Thes. 4:16–17), including a worldwide holocaust (2 Peter 3:10–13).

Did all these things happen while that generation was still alive? (24:34)

Some think so. They believe this verse limits the timing of the events in this chapter to a literal generation, that is, to the destruction of Jerusalem in A.D. 70. Others think *this generation* refers to the generation that learns the lesson of the fig tree (vv. 32–33) and recognizes the signs of Jesus' impending return. Still others say *generation* means the Jewish race—a promise that Jews would survive until the end.

SCRIPTURE LINK (24:37–39)

Jesus also discusses the question of the time of his return in Luke 17:26–27.

12Because of the increase of wickedness, the love of most will grow cold, **13**but he who stands firm to the end will be saved. **14**And this gospel[D] of the kingdom will be preached in the whole world as a testimony to all nations, and then the end will come.

15"So when you see standing in the holy place 'the abomination[D] that causes desolation,'[a] spoken of through the prophet[D] Daniel—let the reader understand— **16**then let those who are in Judea flee to the mountains. **17**Let no one on the roof of his house go down to take anything out of the house. **18**Let no one in the field go back to get his cloak. **19**How dreadful it will be in those days for pregnant women and nursing mothers! **20**Pray that your flight will not take place in winter or on the Sabbath[D]. **21**For then there will be great distress, unequaled from the beginning of the world until now—and never to be equaled again. **22**If those days had not been cut short, no one would survive, but for the sake of the elect[D] those days will be shortened. **23**At that time if anyone says to you, 'Look, here is the Christ!' or, 'There he is!' do not believe it. **24**For false Christs and false prophets will appear and perform great signs and miracles to deceive even the elect—if that were possible. **25**See, I have told you ahead of time.

26"So if anyone tells you, 'There he is, out in the desert,' do not go out; or, 'Here he is, in the inner rooms,' do not believe it. **27**For as lightning that comes from the east is visible even in the west, so will be the coming of the Son of Man[D]. **28**Wherever there is a carcass, there the vultures will gather.

29"Immediately after the distress of those days

" 'the sun will be darkened,
    and the moon will not give its light;
  the stars will fall from the sky,
    and the heavenly bodies will be shaken.'[b]

30"At that time the sign of the Son of Man will appear in the sky, and all the nations of the earth will mourn. They will see the Son of Man coming on the clouds of the sky, with power and great glory[D]. **31**And he will send his angels with a loud trumpet call, and they will gather his elect from the four winds, from one end of the heavens to the other.

32"Now learn this lesson from the fig tree: As soon as its twigs get tender and its leaves come out, you know that summer is near. **33**Even so, when you see all these things, you know that it[c] is near, right at the door. **34**I tell you the truth, this generation[d] will certainly not pass away until all these things have happened. **35**Heaven and earth will pass away, but my words will never pass away.

The Day and Hour Unknown

36"No one knows about that day or hour, not even the angels in heaven, nor the Son,[e] but only the Father. **37**As it was in the days of Noah, so it will be at the coming of the Son of Man. **38**For in the days before the flood, people were eating and drinking, marrying and giving in marriage, up to the day Noah entered the ark; **39**and they knew nothing about what would happen until the flood came and took them all away. That is how it will be at the

---

*a*15 Daniel 9:27; 11:31; 12:11   *b*29 Isaiah 13:10; 34:4
*c*33 Or he   *d*34 Or race   *e*36 Some manuscripts do not have nor the Son.

coming of the Son of Man[D]. **40**Two men will be in the field; one will be taken and the other left. **41**Two women will be grinding with a hand mill; one will be taken and the other left.

42"Therefore keep watch, because you do not know on what day your Lord will come. **43**But understand this: If the owner of the house had known at what time of night the thief was coming, he would have kept watch and would not have let his house be broken into. **44**So you also must be ready, because the Son of Man will come at an hour when you do not expect him.

45"Who then is the faithful and wise servant, whom the master has put in charge of the servants in his household to give them their food at the proper time? **46**It will be good for that servant whose master finds him doing so when he returns. **47**I tell you the truth, he will put him in charge of all his possessions. **48**But suppose that servant is wicked and says to himself, 'My master is staying away a long time,' **49**and he then begins to beat his fellow servants and to eat and drink with drunkards. **50**The master of that servant will come on a day when he does not expect him and at an hour he is not aware of. **51**He will cut him to pieces and assign him a place with the hypocrites, where there will be weeping and gnashing of teeth.

The Parable of the Ten Virgins

25 "At that time the kingdom of heaven will be like ten virgins who took their lamps and went out to meet the bridegroom. **2**Five of them were foolish and five were wise. **3**The foolish ones took their lamps but did not take any oil with them. **4**The wise, however, took oil in jars along with their lamps. **5**The bridegroom was a long time in coming, and they all became drowsy and fell asleep.

6"At midnight the cry rang out: 'Here's the bridegroom! Come out to meet him!'

7"Then all the virgins woke up and trimmed their lamps. **8**The foolish ones said to the wise, 'Give us some of your oil; our lamps are going out.'

9" 'No,' they replied, 'there may not be enough for both us and you. Instead, go to those who sell oil and buy some for yourselves.'

10"But while they were on their way to buy the oil, the bridegroom arrived. The virgins who were ready went in with him to the wedding banquet. And the door was shut.

11"Later the others also came. 'Sir! Sir!' they said. 'Open the door for us!'

12"But he replied, 'I tell you the truth, I don't know you.'

13"Therefore keep watch, because you do not know the day or the hour.

The Parable of the Talents

14"Again, it will be like a man going on a journey, who called his servants and entrusted his property to them. **15**To one he gave five talents[a] of money, to another two talents, and to another one talent, each according to his ability. Then he went on his journey. **16**The man who had received the five talents went at once and put his money to work and gained five more. **17**So also, the one with the two talents gained two more. **18**But the man who had received the one talent went off, dug a hole in the ground and hid his master's money.

---

[a]15 A talent was worth more than a thousand dollars.

SCRIPTURE LINK (24:45–51)
Luke records Jesus' parable of the faithful and wise servant in Luke 12:42–46.

Why would a master cut his servant to pieces? (24:51)
In ancient times, those who owned slaves held complete mastery over them. Slaves were considered as property and one who displeased his master could be severely punished, even killed. Such deeds were within the master's legal rights. Jesus may have used this particularly gruesome punishment to illustrate the spiritual truth of his example: that a hypocritical leader will be cut off from any life with God.

A place with the hypocrites (24:51)
Hell is frequently described by Jesus as a place *where there will be weeping and gnashing of teeth.* The phrase is connected with (1) a place *outside in darkness* (8:12; 22:13; 25:30) and (2) a *fiery furnace* (13:42,50).

Kingdom of heaven (25:1)
Just as an earthly kingdom identifies the domain of an earthly ruler, the *kingdom of heaven* (also called the *kingdom of God*) signifies everything over which God rules. It means more than mere territory, however; God's kingdom is spiritual and is in the hearts of people who have submitted to him (Luke 18:36; John 18:36). It can also refer to the coming age when God will again rule over all creation.

How is the kingdom like ten virgins? (25:1)
Jesus compared the kingdom to ten virgins who were part of a wedding party, waiting for the bridegroom to arrive. Some were prepared to meet him; others were not. The kingdom is characterized by anticipation—people are to be waiting and ready for Christ to return.

Why start a wedding at midnight? (25:6)
Although this was a common custom, it's not known exactly why weddings began so late at night. Weddings typically lasted several days. The groom and his friends often began the feast at the groom's house while the bride and her attendants waited at her house. Eventually, the groom and his friends came unannounced to claim the bride. Then the whole group formed a joyful procession back to the groom's house.

SCRIPTURE LINK (25:14–30)
In Luke 19:12–17, Jesus tells a parable similar to the parable of the talents.

19"After a long time the master of those servants returned and settled accounts with them. **20**The man who had received the five talents brought the other five. 'Master,' he said, 'you entrusted me with five talents. See, I have gained five more.'

21"His master replied, 'Well done, good and faithful servant! You have been faithful with a few things; I will put you in charge of many things. Come and share your master's happiness!'

22"The man with the two talents also came. 'Master,' he said, 'you entrusted me with two talents; see, I have gained two more.'

23"His master replied, 'Well done, good and faithful servant! You have been faithful with a few things; I will put you in charge of many things. Come and share your master's happiness!'

24"Then the man who had received the one talent came. 'Master,' he said, 'I knew that you are a hard man, harvesting where you have not sown and gathering where you have not scattered seed. **25**So I was afraid and went out and hid your talent in the ground. See, here is what belongs to you.'

26"His master replied, 'You wicked, lazy servant! So you knew that I harvest where I have not sown and gather where I have not scattered seed? **27**Well then, you should have put my money on deposit with the bankers, so that when I returned I would have received it back with interest.

28" 'Take the talent from him and give it to the one who has the ten talents. **29**For everyone who has will be given more, and he will have an abundance. Whoever does not have, even what he has will be taken from him. **30**And throw that worthless servant outside, into the darkness, where there will be weeping and gnashing of teeth.'

The Sheep and the Goats

31"When the Son of Man^D comes in his glory^D, and all the angels with him, he will sit on his throne in heavenly glory. **32**All the nations will be gathered before him, and he will separate the people one from another as a shepherd separates the sheep from the goats. **33**He will put the sheep on his right and the goats on his left.

34"Then the King will say to those on his right, 'Come, you who are blessed by my Father; take your inheritance, the kingdom prepared for you since the creation of the world. **35**For I was hungry and you gave me something to

---

**What does God expect of us?
(25:26–27)**
God wants us to use whatever opportunities he gives us. By some standards, the third servant did well. He didn't steal, waste or lose the money—he guarded and preserved it. Nevertheless, he was judged unfaithful because he did nothing productive. Faithful service requires some risk. We must make the most of our opportunities (Eph. 5:16) and use our gifts productively (1 Peter 4:10–12).

Are good works necessary for eternal life? (25:35–36)

Jesus did not teach that good deeds form the basis of our salvation. The Bible shows clearly that eternal life results from what God does, not what we do (Titus 3:4–5). We are saved by God's grace, not by our works. Still, God intends that those who receive his grace will also do good works (Eph. 2:8–10).

True faith is more than just claiming to have faith. Genuine love for God will be expressed through service to others (1 John 3:16–18)—not to earn salvation, but because a heart that truly loves God will be filled with compassion for people. Jesus wanted his followers to set the pace by helping those who were hurting. Good works that come from people grateful for God's grace are at the heart of true religion (James 1:27).

eat, I was thirsty and you gave me something to drink, I was a stranger and you invited me in, **36**I needed clothes and you clothed me, I was sick and you looked after me, I was in prison and you came to visit me.'

37"Then the righteous^D will answer him, 'Lord, when did we see you hungry and feed you, or thirsty and give you something to drink? **38**When did we see you a stranger and invite you in, or needing clothes and clothe you? **39**When did we see you sick or in prison and go to visit you?'

40"The King will reply, 'I tell you the truth, whatever you did for one of the least of these brothers of mine, you did for me.'

41"Then he will say to those on his left, 'Depart from me, you who are cursed, into the eternal fire prepared for the devil and his angels. **42**For I was hungry and you gave me nothing to eat, I was thirsty and you gave me nothing to drink, **43**I was a stranger and you did not invite me in, I needed clothes and you did not clothe me, I was sick and in prison and you did not look after me.'

44"They also will answer, 'Lord, when did we see you hungry or thirsty or a stranger or needing clothes or sick or in prison, and did not help you?'

45"He will reply, 'I tell you the truth, whatever you did not do for one of the least of these, you did not do for me.'

46"Then they will go away to eternal punishment, but the righteous to eternal life."

The Plot Against Jesus

26 When Jesus had finished saying all these things, he said to his disciples^D, **2**"As you know, the Passover is two days away—and the Son of Man^D will be handed over to be crucified."

3Then the chief priests^D and the elders of the people assembled in the palace of the high priest, whose name was Caiaphas, **4**and they plotted to arrest Jesus in some sly way and kill him. **5**"But not during the Feast," they said, "or there may be a riot among the people."

Jesus Anointed at Bethany

6While Jesus was in Bethany in the home of a man known as Simon the Leper, **7**a woman came to him with an alabaster jar of very expensive perfume, which she poured on his head as he was reclining at the table.

8When the disciples saw this, they were indignant. "Why this waste?" they asked. **9**"This perfume could have been sold at a high price and the money given to the poor."

10Aware of this, Jesus said to them, "Why are you bothering this woman? She has done a beautiful thing to me. **11**The poor you will always have with you, but you will not always have me. **12**When she poured this perfume on my body, she did it to prepare me for burial. **13**I tell you the truth, wherever this gospel^D is preached throughout the world, what she has done will also be told, in memory of her."

Judas Agrees to Betray Jesus

14Then one of the Twelve—the one called Judas Iscariot—went to the chief priests **15**and asked, "What are you willing to give me if I hand him over to you?" So they counted out for him thirty silver coins. **16**From then on Judas watched for an opportunity to hand him over.

SCRIPTURE LINK (26:1-5)
The plot against Jesus is also exposed in Mark 14:1-2 and Luke 22:1-2.

SCRIPTURE LINK (26:6-13)
Mark tells about the anointing of Jesus at Bethany in Mark 14:3-9. Luke and John give similar accounts in Luke 7:37-38 and John 12:1-8.

Is Matthew telling the same story as Mark, Luke and John? (26:6-13)
See *Is this the same story as in Matthew, Luke and John?* (Mark 14:3-9).

Why were the disciples indignant? (26:8-9)
They thought the woman's actions were extravagant and wasteful because the perfume she poured out was so valuable. It could have been sold and the money used for benevolent purposes. However, it seems that the major complainer was Judas, whose real motive was not concern for the poor but personal greed (John 12:4-6).

Why did Jesus endorse such extravagance? (26:10)
This was a special occasion—he knew that he soon would be crucified. In this impulsive act of sacrifice, the woman symbolically prepared his body for burial. It was a custom in those days to anoint the bodies of the dead with sweet-smelling oil or spices. Jesus had already emphasized the ongoing need to help the poor (25:35-36). Now he affirmed another important principle: it is never a waste to give one's best to honor Jesus.

What prompted Judas to turn Jesus in? (26:14-16)
Judas was undoubtedly annoyed when Jesus rebuked him for his comments about the waste of the expensive perfume (John 12:4-8). His greed may have been a factor in his accepting 30 silver coins to betray Jesus. Some speculate that Jesus' talk of burial (v. 12) disillusioned Judas, who may have been put off or confused by the idea that a real Messiah could die (see 16:21-25; Mark 9:9-10). Others think Judas was disappointed because Jesus seemed unwilling to establish the earthly kingdom many expected. Whatever the cause, Satan was behind Judas's deed (John 13:27).

SCRIPTURE LINK (26:14-16)
In Mark 14:17-21, Mark tells that Judas would be the one to betray Jesus.

SCRIPTURE LINK (26:14-16)
Judas's agreement to betray Jesus can also be found in Mark 14:10-11 and Luke 22:3-6.

SCRIPTURE LINK (26:17–19)

Details of the Passover preparations are also recorded in Mark 14:12–16 and Luke 22:7–13.

How did the disciples prepare for the Passover? (26:19)

Most importantly, they needed to acquire a lamb, take it to the temple for slaughter and then roast it whole as prescribed by Jewish law (Exodus 12:8–9). They also would have had to purchase specific items required for the Passover meal, prepare the food and set the table.

SCRIPTURE LINK (26:26–29)

Jesus' use of bread and the cup to symbolize his body and blood can also be seen in Mark 14:22–25 and Luke 22:17–20.

How did Jesus change Passover? (26:26–29)

Rather than change Passover, Christ fulfilled it (1 Cor. 5:7), infusing a time-honored practice with profound new meaning. For centuries, the unleavened bread had reminded God's people of their hasty exit from Egypt (see Exodus 12:14–20,39). Now the bread would remind Jesus' followers of his body, given as a sacrifice for their sins. The lamb had recalled the blood that spared the Israelites from death (Exodus 12:3–13). Now the cup would remind Jesus' followers of his blood and its saving effects.

Why did Jesus say he would not drink again? (26:29)

Because Jesus was going to die, he wouldn't be here on earth to eat or drink anything. But when he returns, he will celebrate again in perfect fellowship with all his followers. Even now when Christians celebrate the Lord's Supper, they are not only remembering his crucifixion but also looking ahead to his second coming.

SCRIPTURE LINK (26:31–35)

Mark writes about Jesus' prediction of Peter's denial in Mark 14:27–31. Luke tells about it in Luke 22:31–34.

SCRIPTURE LINK (26:36–46)

Jesus' suffering in Gethsemane is also recorded in Mark 14:32–42 and Luke 22:40–46.

Did Jesus resist his mission? (26:38–39)

No, but he did wonder if there might not be a less painful alternative. Though Jesus was fully God, he was also fully human—revealed in this vulnerable moment. Jesus was still committed to his purpose to be the Savior of the world (John 12:27). However, the intense suffering he faced caused him to turn to his Father for help—just as we might pray when confronted with overwhelming emotional or physical pain.

The Lord's Supper

17 On the first day of the Feast of Unleavened Bread, the disciples[D] came to Jesus and asked, "Where do you want us to make preparations for you to eat the Passover?"

18 He replied, "Go into the city to a certain man and tell him, 'The Teacher says: My appointed time is near. I am going to celebrate the Passover with my disciples at your house.'" **19** So the disciples did as Jesus had directed them and prepared the Passover.

20 When evening came, Jesus was reclining at the table with the Twelve. **21** And while they were eating, he said, "I tell you the truth, one of you will betray me."

22 They were very sad and began to say to him one after the other, "Surely not I, Lord?"

23 Jesus replied, "The one who has dipped his hand into the bowl with me will betray me. **24** The Son of Man[D] will go just as it is written about him. But woe to that man who betrays the Son of Man! It would be better for him if he had not been born."

25 Then Judas, the one who would betray him, said, "Surely not I, Rabbi[D]?"

Jesus answered, "Yes, it is you."[a]

26 While they were eating, Jesus took bread, gave thanks and broke it, and gave it to his disciples, saying, "Take and eat; this is my body."

27 Then he took the cup, gave thanks and offered it to them, saying, "Drink from it, all of you. **28** This is my blood of the[b] covenant[D], which is poured out for many for the forgiveness of sins. **29** I tell you, I will not drink of this fruit of the vine from now on until that day when I drink it anew with you in my Father's kingdom."

30 When they had sung a hymn, they went out to the Mount of Olives.

Jesus Predicts Peter's Denial

31 Then Jesus told them, "This very night you will all fall away on account of me, for it is written:

"'I will strike the shepherd,
and the sheep of the flock will be scattered.'[c]

32 But after I have risen, I will go ahead of you into Galilee."

33 Peter replied, "Even if all fall away on account of you, I never will."

34 "I tell you the truth," Jesus answered, "this very night, before the rooster crows, you will disown me three times."

35 But Peter declared, "Even if I have to die with you, I will never disown you." And all the other disciples said the same.

Gethsemane

36 Then Jesus went with his disciples to a place called Gethsemane, and he said to them, "Sit here while I go over there and pray." **37** He took Peter and the two sons of Zebedee along with him, and he began to be sorrowful and troubled. **38** Then he said to them, "My soul[D] is overwhelmed with sorrow to the point of death[D]. Stay here and keep watch with me."

[a]25 Or "You yourself have said it" [b]28 Some manuscripts the new [c]31 Zech. 13:7

³⁹Going a little farther, he fell with his face to the ground and prayed, "My Father, if it is possible, may this cup be taken from me. Yet not as I will, but as you will."

⁴⁰Then he returned to his disciples⁰ and found them sleeping. "Could you men not keep watch with me for one hour?" he asked Peter. ⁴¹"Watch and pray so that you will not fall into temptation. The spirit is willing, but the body is weak."

⁴²He went away a second time and prayed, "My Father, if it is not possible for this cup to be taken away unless I drink it, may your will be done."

⁴³When he came back, he again found them sleeping, because their eyes were heavy. ⁴⁴So he left them and went away once more and prayed the third time, saying the same thing.

⁴⁵Then he returned to the disciples and said to them, "Are you still sleeping and resting? Look, the hour is near, and the Son of Man⁰ is betrayed into the hands of sinners. ⁴⁶Rise, let us go! Here comes my betrayer!"

Jesus Arrested

⁴⁷While he was still speaking, Judas, one of the Twelve, arrived. With him was a large crowd armed with swords and clubs, sent from the chief priests⁰ and the elders of the people. ⁴⁸Now the betrayer had arranged a signal with them: "The one I kiss is the man; arrest him." ⁴⁹Going at once to Jesus, Judas said, "Greetings, Rabbi⁰!" and kissed him.

⁵⁰Jesus replied, "Friend, do what you came for."ᵃ

Then the men stepped forward, seized Jesus and arrested him. ⁵¹With that, one of Jesus' companions reached for his sword, drew it out and struck the servant of the high priest, cutting off his ear.

⁵²"Put your sword back in its place," Jesus said to him, "for all who draw the sword will die by the sword. ⁵³Do you think I cannot call on my Father, and he will at once put at my disposal more than twelve legions⁰ of angels? ⁵⁴But how then would the Scriptures be fulfilled that say it must happen in this way?"

⁵⁵At that time Jesus said to the crowd, "Am I leading a rebellion, that you have come out with swords and clubs to capture me? Every day I sat in the temple courts teaching, and you did not arrest me. ⁵⁶But this has all taken place that the writings of the prophets⁰ might be fulfilled." Then all the disciples deserted him and fled.

Before the Sanhedrin

⁵⁷Those who had arrested Jesus took him to Caiaphas, the high priest, where the teachers of the law and the elders had assembled. ⁵⁸But Peter followed him at a distance, right up to the courtyard of the high priest. He entered and sat down with the guards to see the outcome.

⁵⁹The chief priests and the whole Sanhedrin were looking for false evidence against Jesus so that they could put him to death⁰. ⁶⁰But they did not find any, though many false witnesses came forward.

Finally two came forward ⁶¹and declared, "This fellow said, 'I am able to destroy the temple of God and rebuild it in three days.'"

⁶²Then the high priest stood up and said to Jesus, "Are you not going to answer? What is this testimony that

Why did Jesus ask the disciples to watch and pray? (26:41)

In the loneliness that comes while awaiting death, Jesus longed for the presence of friends who would pray with him. In addition, the disciples needed to pray for their own benefit, considering their predicted denial, cowardice and abandonment of Jesus. Their boasts of allegiance (v. 35) appear pathetic in light of their behavior as the night wore on. Their failure to pray would make them an easy mark when assaulted by fear and temptation.

SCRIPTURE LINK (26:47–56)

Mark gives the details of Jesus' arrest in Mark 14:43–50. Luke gives them in Luke 22:47–53.

Why did Judas kiss Jesus? (26:49)

A kiss was a traditional greeting. A disciple would greet his teacher with a kiss on the cheek or beard to show honor and submission. The less important person initiated the kiss. This is the irony in this passage, that Judas would use something meant to give honor to instead betray.

SCRIPTURE LINK (26:57–68)

Mark tells about Jesus' trial before the Sanhedrin in Mark 14:53–65. John tells about it in John 18:12–13,19–24.

ᵃ50 Or "Friend, why have you come?"

Why did Jesus refuse to answer the false charges? (26:63)

These same men had resisted and twisted Jesus' words before. Why should he speak to them now? This was a biased, hostile trial—not an impartial hearing. The unfair and contradictory charges did not deserve a response. Jesus did answer, however, when the high priest pressured him further and charged him under oath to repeat the claims Jesus had made throughout his ministry (vv. 63–64).

SCRIPTURE LINK (26:69–75)

You can also read about Peter disowning Jesus in Mark 14:66–72; Luke 22:54–62 and John 18:16–18,25–27.

Why did Peter weep? (26:75)

Because he suddenly felt the weight of his own failure. Though he had earlier wanted to fight for Jesus, now his courage had melted into confusion. He'd been bewildered and disheartened when Jesus had rejected his rescue attempt in the garden (John 18:10–11). But the crowing rooster brought things back into perspective again with a shocking realization: he had betrayed the one he loved just as Jesus had foretold.

Why did Matthew credit Jeremiah with something Zechariah said? (27:9–10)

Some say that Matthew made a mistake. Others say some later scribe did. Other solutions suggest that Matthew combined Jeremiah's material (see Jer. 18:2; 19:1,11) with Zechariah's statement (see Zech. 11:12–13) but attributed it to Jeremiah because he was the major prophet. Also it was customary to allude to an entire section of the Bible by the name of the first book in that section. It may be that in Matthew's day Jeremiah was the first of the prophetic books.

these men are bringing against you?" **63**But Jesus remained silent.

The high priest[D] said to him, "I charge you under oath by the living God: Tell us if you are the Christ,[a] the Son of God."

64"Yes, it is as you say," Jesus replied. "But I say to all of you: In the future you will see the Son of Man[D] sitting at the right hand of the Mighty One and coming on the clouds of heaven."

65Then the high priest tore his clothes and said, "He has spoken blasphemy[D]! Why do we need any more witnesses? Look, now you have heard the blasphemy. **66**What do you think?"

"He is worthy of death[D]," they answered.

67Then they spit in his face and struck him with their fists. Others slapped him **68**and said, "Prophesy to us, Christ. Who hit you?"

Peter Disowns Jesus

69Now Peter was sitting out in the courtyard, and a servant girl came to him. "You also were with Jesus of Galilee," she said.

70But he denied it before them all. "I don't know what you're talking about," he said.

71Then he went out to the gateway, where another girl saw him and said to the people there, "This fellow was with Jesus of Nazareth."

72He denied it again, with an oath: "I don't know the man!"

73After a little while, those standing there went up to Peter and said, "Surely you are one of them, for your accent gives you away."

74Then he began to call down curses on himself and he swore to them, "I don't know the man!"

Immediately a rooster crowed. **75**Then Peter remembered the word Jesus had spoken: "Before the rooster crows, you will disown me three times." And he went outside and wept bitterly.

Judas Hangs Himself

27 Early in the morning, all the chief priests and the elders of the people came to the decision to put Jesus to death. **2**They bound him, led him away and handed him over to Pilate, the governor.

3When Judas, who had betrayed him, saw that Jesus was condemned, he was seized with remorse and returned the thirty silver coins to the chief priests and the elders. **4**"I have sinned," he said, "for I have betrayed innocent blood."

"What is that to us?" they replied. "That's your responsibility."

5So Judas threw the money into the temple and left. Then he went away and hanged himself.

6The chief priests picked up the coins and said, "It is against the law to put this into the treasury, since it is blood money." **7**So they decided to use the money to buy the potter's field as a burial place for foreigners. **8**That is why it has been called the Field of Blood to this day. **9**Then what was spoken by Jeremiah the prophet[D] was fulfilled: "They took the thirty silver coins, the price set on

a63 Or Messiah; also in verse 68

him by the people of Israel, [10]and they used them to buy the potter's field, as the Lord commanded me."[a]

Jesus Before Pilate

[11]Meanwhile Jesus stood before the governor, and the governor asked him, "Are you the king of the Jews[D]?"

"Yes, it is as you say," Jesus replied.

[12]When he was accused by the chief priests[D] and the elders, he gave no answer. [13]Then Pilate asked him, "Don't you hear the testimony they are bringing against you?" [14]But Jesus made no reply, not even to a single charge—to the great amazement of the governor.

[15]Now it was the governor's custom at the Feast to release a prisoner chosen by the crowd. [16]At that time they had a notorious prisoner, called Barabbas. [17]So when the crowd had gathered, Pilate asked them, "Which one do you want me to release to you: Barabbas, or Jesus who is called Christ?" [18]For he knew it was out of envy that they had handed Jesus over to him.

[19]While Pilate was sitting on the judge's seat, his wife sent him this message: "Don't have anything to do with that innocent man, for I have suffered a great deal today in a dream because of him."

[20]But the chief priests and the elders persuaded the crowd to ask for Barabbas and to have Jesus executed.

[21]"Which of the two do you want me to release to you?" asked the governor.

"Barabbas," they answered.

[22]"What shall I do, then, with Jesus who is called Christ?" Pilate asked.

They all answered, "Crucify him!"

[23]"Why? What crime has he committed?" asked Pilate.

But they shouted all the louder, "Crucify him!"

[24]When Pilate saw that he was getting nowhere, but that instead an uproar was starting, he took water and washed his hands in front of the crowd. "I am innocent of this man's blood," he said. "It is your responsibility!"

[25]All the people answered, "Let his blood be on us and on our children!"

[26]Then he released Barabbas to them. But he had Jesus flogged, and handed him over to be crucified.

The Soldiers Mock Jesus

[27]Then the governor's soldiers took Jesus into the Praetorium and gathered the whole company of soldiers around him. [28]They stripped him and put a scarlet robe on him, [29]and then twisted together a crown of thorns and set it on his head. They put a staff in his right hand and knelt in front of him and mocked him. "Hail, king of the Jews!" they said. [30]They spit on him, and took the staff and struck him on the head again and again. [31]After they had mocked him, they took off the robe and put his own clothes on him. Then they led him away to crucify him.

The Crucifixion

[32]As they were going out, they met a man from Cyrene, named Simon, and they forced him to carry the cross. [33]They came to a place called Golgotha (which means The Place of the Skull). [34]There they offered Jesus wine to

[a]10 See Zech. 11:12,13; Jer. 19:1-13; 32:6-9.

What did the title the king of the Jews mean to Pilate? (27:11)

The Roman government was particularly sensitive to subversive elements in society that would undermine their base of power. Any who claimed to be a leader or a king could be a potential threat. Jesus had been accused of rebelling against Rome and opposing payment of taxes to Caesar (Luke 23:1–2). It was only natural for Pilate to probe Jesus' political aspirations. In Jesus' case, the title carried a deeper spiritual meaning. Since the charge against Jesus carried no real weight, Pilate did not put any stock in it. See *Why wasn't Pilate bothered by Jesus' claim to be king of the Jews?* (Luke 23:3–4).

SCRIPTURE LINK (27:11–26)

Jesus' trial and sentencing before Pilate can also be found in Mark 15:2–15; Luke 23:2–3,18–25 and John 18:29—19:16.

Who was most guilty for Christ's death? (27:24–25)

Pilate was guilty of cowardice and the unjust use of his authority. Caiaphas, who should have been the spiritual leader and thus should have understood how Jesus fulfilled the prophecies of the Messiah, bore the greater guilt. Though he knew about Jesus' miracles and ministry, his hatred and envy caused him to condemn Jesus (see John 11:49–50). He saw Jesus' popularity with the people as a threat to the political power given by the Romans that he and other Jewish leaders enjoyed.

How was Jesus flogged? (27:26)

Flogging was a ruthless punishment that used a leather whip with multiple ends and sharp bits of bone or metal embedded in the ends. It could leave the back raw and bleeding, sometimes exposing bones and organs. Floggings occasionally caused death.

Was Jesus singled out for special brutality? (27:26–31)

Flogging and crucifixion were common in the Roman empire. Death on a cross, however, was usually reserved for criminals and slaves (non-Roman citizens). Soldiers commonly mocked their powerless prisoners, but they took special delight in taunting a man alleged to be a Jewish king.

SCRIPTURE LINK (27:27–31)

Mark tells how the soldiers mocked Jesus in Mark 15:16–20.

SCRIPTURE LINK (27:33–44)

All of the Gospel writers tell of Jesus' crucifixion. See Mark 15:22–32; Luke 23:33–43 and John 19:17–24.

Why did the soldiers offer Jesus a drink of wine and gall? (27:34)

Sometimes gall was mixed with wine and offered to victims of crucifixion as an anesthetic to reduce suffering—but Jesus rejected this crude painkiller. The term *gall* was used for a variety of bitter-tasting substances derived from plants or tree bark. It probably means the same thing as the myrrh mentioned in Mark 15:23. Or it may be that both gall and myrrh were added to the wine.

Did one thief repent or not? (27:44; see Luke 23:40–42)

According to Luke, one robber had a change of heart. The apparent difference between Matthew's and Luke's accounts seems to stem from the timing of events. Matthew records earlier events when both robbers hurled insults at Jesus. Luke picks up the story, when one of them, seeing Jesus forgive his executioners (Luke 23:34), determined that Jesus could be trusted.

SCRIPTURE LINK (27:45–56)

Mark tells of Jesus' death in Mark 15:33–41, and Luke writes about it in Luke 23:44–49.

Did God actually forsake Jesus? (27:46)

The divine and human natures of Jesus were never separated, even during the crucifixion. Yet it is clear, difficult as it is to explain, that Jesus' intimate fellowship with God the Father was temporarily broken as he took the sin of the entire world on himself. Jesus used the words of Psalm 22, which begins with despair but ends with renewed trust in God. By quoting that psalm, Jesus may have hinted that he knew the broken relationship with his Father would soon be restored.

Why did the curtain in the temple tear? (27:51)

This large blue, purple and scarlet curtain separated the Holy Place from the Most Holy Place, an inner room which symbolized God's presence (Exodus 26:31–33). It was, in effect, the barrier that separated people from God. When God supernaturally tore the curtain (perhaps by earthquake) he showed dramatically that Christ's death had given people access to God (Heb. 9:1–15; 10:19–22).

Why did God bring some dead people back to life at this time? (27:52–53)

The unusual events that accompanied Jesus' death and resurrection marked an unprecedented crossroads in history. Some say that Jesus went to the place of dead spirits, awakened the righteous dead and led them to paradise. Apparently many of these dead were seen in Jerusalem while on their way. The resurrection of these holy people gave additional evidence that death was not the final victor. It also foreshadowed a time when all the faithful will be raised to life (1 Cor. 15:20,50–57; 1 Thes. 4:13–18).

SCRIPTURE LINK (27:57–61)

See also Mark 15:42–47; Luke 23:50–56 and John 19:38–42 for other accounts of Jesus' burial.

---

drink, mixed with gall; but after tasting it, he refused to drink it. [35]When they had crucified him, they divided up his clothes by casting lots.[a] [36]And sitting down, they kept watch over him there. [37]Above his head they placed the written charge against him: THIS IS JESUS, THE KING OF THE JEWS. [38]Two robbers were crucified with him, one on his right and one on his left. [39]Those who passed by hurled insults at him, shaking their heads [40]and saying, "You who are going to destroy the temple and build it in three days, save yourself! Come down from the cross, if you are the Son of God!"

[41]In the same way the chief priests[D], the teachers of the law and the elders mocked him. [42]"He saved others," they said, "but he can't save himself! He's the King of Israel! Let him come down now from the cross, and we will believe in him. [43]He trusts in God. Let God rescue him now if he wants him, for he said, 'I am the Son of God.'" [44]In the same way the robbers who were crucified with him also heaped insults on him.

The Death of Jesus

[45]From the sixth hour until the ninth hour darkness came over all the land. [46]About the ninth hour Jesus cried out in a loud voice, "Eloi, Eloi,[b] lama sabachthani?"—which means, "My God, my God, why have you forsaken me?"[c]

[47]When some of those standing there heard this, they said, "He's calling Elijah."

[48]Immediately one of them ran and got a sponge. He filled it with wine vinegar, put it on a stick, and offered it to Jesus to drink. [49]The rest said, "Now leave him alone. Let's see if Elijah comes to save him."

[50]And when Jesus had cried out again in a loud voice, he gave up his spirit.

[51]At that moment the curtain of the temple was torn in two from top to bottom. The earth shook and the rocks split. [52]The tombs broke open and the bodies of many holy people who had died were raised to life. [53]They came out of the tombs, and after Jesus' resurrection[D] they went into the holy city and appeared to many people.

[54]When the centurion[D] and those with him who were guarding Jesus saw the earthquake and all that had happened, they were terrified, and exclaimed, "Surely he was the Son[d] of God!"

[55]Many women were there, watching from a distance. They had followed Jesus from Galilee to care for his needs. [56]Among them were Mary Magdalene, Mary the mother of James and Joses, and the mother of Zebedee's sons.

The Burial of Jesus

[57]As evening approached, there came a rich man from Arimathea, named Joseph, who had himself become a disciple[D] of Jesus. [58]Going to Pilate, he asked for Jesus' body, and Pilate ordered that it be given to him. [59]Joseph took the body, wrapped it in a clean linen cloth, [60]and placed it in his own new tomb that he had cut out of the

---

[a]35 A few late manuscripts lots that the word spoken by the prophet might be fulfilled: "They divided my garments among themselves and cast lots for my clothing" (Psalm 22:18)　　[b]46 Some manuscripts Eli, Eli
[c]46 Psalm 22:1　　[d]54 Or a son

rock. He rolled a big stone in front of the entrance to the tomb and went away. **61**Mary Magdalene and the other Mary were sitting there opposite the tomb.

The Guard at the Tomb

62The next day, the one after Preparation Day, the chief priestsD and the PhariseesD went to Pilate. **63**"Sir," they said, "we remember that while he was still alive that deceiver said, 'After three days I will rise again.' **64**So give the order for the tomb to be made secure until the third day. Otherwise, his disciplesD may come and steal the body and tell the people that he has been raised from the dead. This last deception will be worse than the first."

65"Take a guard," Pilate answered. "Go, make the tomb as secure as you know how." **66**So they went and made the tomb secure by putting a seal on the stone and posting the guard.

The Resurrection

28 After the SabbathD, at dawn on the first day of the week, Mary Magdalene and the other Mary went to look at the tomb.

2There was a violent earthquake, for an angel of the Lord came down from heaven and, going to the tomb, rolled back the stone and sat on it. **3**His appearance was like lightning, and his clothes were white as snow. **4**The guards were so afraid of him that they shook and became like dead men.

5The angel said to the women, "Do not be afraid, for I know that you are looking for Jesus, who was crucified. **6**He is not here; he has risen, just as he said. Come and see the place where he lay. **7**Then go quickly and tell his disciples: 'He has risen from the dead and is going ahead of you into Galilee. There you will see him.' Now I have told you."

8So the women hurried away from the tomb, afraid yet filled with joy, and ran to tell his disciples. **9**Suddenly Jesus met them. "Greetings," he said. They came to him, clasped his feet and worshiped him. **10**Then Jesus said to them, "Do not be afraid. Go and tell my brothers to go to Galilee; there they will see me."

The Guards' Report

11While the women were on their way, some of the guards went into the city and reported to the chief priests everything that had happened. **12**When the chief priests had met with the elders and devised a plan, they gave the soldiers a large sum of money, **13**telling them, "You are to say, 'His disciples came during the night and stole him away while we were asleep.' **14**If this report gets to the governor, we will satisfy him and keep you out of trouble." **15**So the soldiers took the money and did as they were instructed. And this story has been widely circulated among the JewsD to this very day.

The Great Commission

16Then the eleven disciples went to Galilee, to the mountain where Jesus had told them to go. **17**When they saw him, they worshiped him; but some doubted. **18**Then Jesus came to them and said, "All authority in heaven and

What kind of seal would make the tomb secure? (27:66)

The stone covering the tomb's entrance probably had a rope or cord wrapped across it. The cord was then sealed in wax or clay at each end, so that no one could move the stone without breaking the seal or cutting the cord. It is possible that the seal included the official imprint of the Roman empire, so anyone who broke the seal would be violating imperial law. Of course, the detachment of soldiers stationed by the tomb added force to the seal.

SCRIPTURE LINK (28:1–8)

Mark and Luke both report on the events surrounding Jesus' resurrection. Check out Mark 16:1–8 and Luke 24:1–10.

Why did some disciples doubt what they saw? (28:17)

The resurrection was so startling at first that many of the disciples found it hard to believe. For more than a month, therefore, Jesus supplied his disciples with many convincing proofs that he was alive (Acts 1:3; 10:40–41). It is possible that on this occasion some were seeing the risen Christ for the first time.

Why doesn't Jesus use his authority to right earth's wrongs? (28:18)

The earth's wrongs do not result from a lack of power or concern on the Lord's part, but from human rebellion against his authority. Eventually Jesus will bring a full and final end to life's injustice. Eventually everyone will acknowledge his authority (Phil. 2:9–11).

Who should go and make disciples? (28:19)

Jesus' command was intended not only for his first disciples, but also for us today. By sharing in the ministry of disciple-making, we submit to the authority of Christ (v. 18). Individuals may have different roles and abilities, but all of Jesus' disciples can have a part in calling others to follow Christ.

Is the method of baptism important? (28:19)

Throughout church history Christians have often been divided over this question. The original word translated *baptize* meant *to dip, immerse or wash*, so some insist that immersion is the required method for Christian baptism. Others think the word is used as a metaphor (Luke 12:50; 1 Cor. 10:2) and emphasize the significance rather than the method. For them, pouring or sprinkling can identify one's commitment with Christ. All essentially agree, however, that baptism must be a matter of the heart—a spiritual immersion into Christ's body (1 Cor. 12:13). For other matters concerning baptism, see *Why didn't Paul baptize in the way Jesus had instructed?* (Acts 19:5) and *Does baptism save us?* (1 Peter 3:21).

In what sense is Jesus always with us? (28:20)

Soon after saying these words, Jesus left this earth and ascended into heaven (Luke 24:50–51). Though physically absent, he remains with believers in a spiritual sense. It is his spiritual presence within that strengthens and encourages believers (John 14:16–20; Romans 8:9–11). Those who trust in Jesus will find him with them no matter where they go or what problems they face.

To the very end of the age (28:20)
Though this could be an expression of speech that conveys the idea of "forever," the phrase is better understood to mean "until Christ returns again." Then a new era will begin when we shall be with Jesus and see him in his physical form.

on earth has been given to me. [19]Therefore go and make disciples of all nations, baptizing them in[a] the name of the Father and of the Son and of the Holy Spirit, [20]and teaching them to obey everything I have commanded you. And surely I am with you always, to the very end of the age."

---

[a]19 Or *into*; see Acts 8:16; 19:5; Romans 6:3; 1 Cor. 1:13; 10:2 and Gal. 3:27.

MARK

Why read this book?

All-news radio stations give you highlights of all the news in the world—in 30 minutes or less. The Gospel of Mark follows a similar fast-paced approach while introducing Jesus Christ, the Son of God. Readers see highlights of the ministry, death and resurrection of Jesus. Coming out of obscurity, this unique God-man preaches, performs miracles and encounters both great popularity and deadly opposition. It's the greatest news story of all time.

Who wrote this book?

John Mark, the son of a Jerusalem widow whose home was a meeting place for early believers (see Acts 12:12). Mark most likely recorded the events as he heard them firsthand from the disciple Peter.

When was it written?

Possibly as early as A.D. 50. Others place it around A.D. 65, closer to the time Peter was executed, but before Jerusalem was destroyed by Roman armies in A.D. 70.

To whom was it written?

The book's distinctly non-Jewish flavor suggests it may have been written to believers in Rome.

Why was it written?

The Roman empire, the dominant world power, had begun to persecute Christians. Mark wanted to encourage suffering believers. He showed Jesus as the suffering servant who came to die. He also portrayed him as the Savior of the entire world, including Romans as well as Jews.

What to look for in Mark:

The humanity of Jesus, who was both the Son of God and the Son of Man. Watch for the emotional impact of this action-packed Gospel. More than 40 percent of Mark focuses on the suffering and sacrifice of Christ's final week on earth.

When did these things happen?

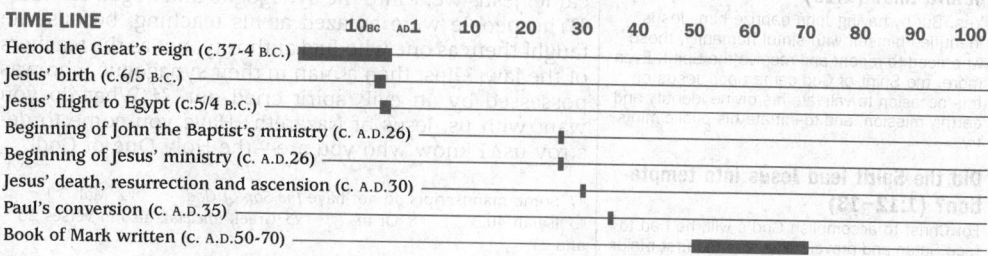

TIME LINE	10 BC	AD 1	10	20	30	40	50	60	70	80	90	100
Herod the Great's reign (c.37-4 B.C.)												
Jesus' birth (c.6/5 B.C.)												
Jesus' flight to Egypt (c.5/4 B.C.)												
Beginning of John the Baptist's ministry (c. A.D.26)												
Beginning of Jesus' ministry (c. A.D.26)												
Jesus' death, resurrection and ascension (c. A.D.30)												
Paul's conversion (c. A.D.35)												
Book of Mark written (c. A.D.50-70)												

SCRIPTURE LINK (1:2–8)

Matthew talks about the coming of John the Baptist in Matt. 3:1–11. Luke covers it in Luke 3:2–16.

Why did John baptize? (1:4)

Jews had a ritual washing for converts to Judaism. John used baptism to symbolize the washing and freshness that comes when someone repents from sin. John's baptism was a visual message that just being Jewish was not enough: repentance, a radical change of heart, was essential for entering God's kingdom. Later, Christians used baptism as a reenactment of Christ's death and resurrection (Romans 6:3–4), which makes forgiveness possible.

Was John eccentric? (1:6)

He appeared to be, dressed in camel hair and dieting on locusts. He was following the lifestyle of an earlier prophet, Elijah (2 Kings 1:8), whom Malachi the prophet said would appear before the Messiah came (Mal. 4:5–6). John, like Elijah, devoted his life to calling people back to God. John may have also stayed in the desert to protect himself from the corrupt religious establishment of his day.

What is baptism *with the Holy Spirit*? (1:8)

This phrase refers to the Spirit coming to dwell within believers, empowering them to be witnesses for the Lord and to live holy lives (Luke 24:48–49; Acts 1:8; 2:1–21). There are basically two views: (1) Some say we are baptized with the Holy Spirit when by faith we accept Christ as Savior and become members of his body (1 Cor. 6:19–20; 12:13). (2) Others say believers can be filled with the Spirit in a deeper, more powerful sense following salvation (Acts 8:14–17).

SCRIPTURE LINK (1:9–11)

Matthew tells about Jesus' baptism in Matt. 3:13–17. You'll also find it in Luke 3:21–22.

John Baptizes Jesus (1:9)

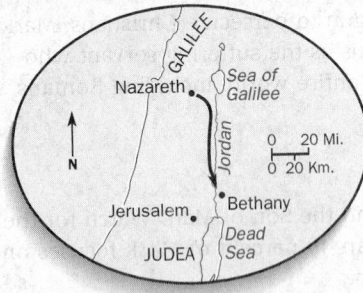

Didn't Jesus possess the Spirit of God before this? (1:10)

Yes. But by having John baptize him, Jesus identified himself with sinful humanity, those who need to repent and receive the Spirit. Even more, the Spirit of God came upon Jesus on this occasion to validate his divine identity and earthly mission, and to initiate his public ministry.

Did the Spirit lead Jesus into temptation? (1:12–13)

For Christ to accomplish God's will, he had to face Satan and prevail. This was the first major

John the Baptist Prepares the Way

1 The beginning of the gospel[D] about Jesus Christ, the Son of God.[a]

[2]It is written in Isaiah the prophet[D]:

> "I will send my messenger ahead of you,
> who will prepare your way"[b]—
> [3]"a voice of one calling in the desert,
> 'Prepare the way for the Lord,
> make straight paths for him.' "[c]

[4]And so John came, baptizing in the desert region and preaching a baptism[D] of repentance[D] for the forgiveness of sins. [5]The whole Judean countryside and all the people of Jerusalem[D] went out to him. Confessing their sins, they were baptized by him in the Jordan River. [6]John wore clothing made of camel's hair, with a leather belt around his waist, and he ate locusts[D] and wild honey. [7]And this was his message: "After me will come one more powerful than I, the thongs of whose sandals I am not worthy to stoop down and untie. [8]I baptize you with[d] water, but he will baptize you with the Holy Spirit."

The Baptism and Temptation of Jesus

[9]At that time Jesus came from Nazareth in Galilee and was baptized by John in the Jordan. [10]As Jesus was coming up out of the water, he saw heaven being torn open and the Spirit descending on him like a dove. [11]And a voice came from heaven: "You are my Son, whom I love; with you I am well pleased."

[12]At once the Spirit sent him out into the desert, [13]and he was in the desert forty days, being tempted by Satan. He was with the wild animals, and angels attended him.

The Calling of the First Disciples

[14]After John was put in prison, Jesus went into Galilee, proclaiming the good news of God. [15]"The time has come," he said. "The kingdom of God[D] is near. Repent[D] and believe the good news!"

[16]As Jesus walked beside the Sea of Galilee, he saw Simon and his brother Andrew casting a net into the lake, for they were fishermen. [17]"Come, follow me," Jesus said, "and I will make you fishers of men." [18]At once they left their nets and followed him.

[19]When he had gone a little farther, he saw James son of Zebedee and his brother John in a boat, preparing their nets. [20]Without delay he called them, and they left their father Zebedee in the boat with the hired men and followed him.

Jesus Drives Out an Evil Spirit

[21]They went to Capernaum, and when the Sabbath[D] came, Jesus went into the synagogue and began to teach. [22]The people were amazed at his teaching, because he taught them as one who had authority, not as the teachers of the law. [23]Just then a man in their synagogue who was possessed by an evil[e] spirit cried out, [24]"What do you want with us, Jesus of Nazareth? Have you come to destroy us? I know who you are—the Holy One of God!"

---

[a]1 Some manuscripts do not have *the Son of God.*   [b]2 Mal. 3:1
[c]3 Isaiah 40:3   [d]8 Or *in*   [e]23 Greek *unclean;* also in verses 26 and 27

25"Be quiet!" said Jesus sternly. "Come out of him!" 26The evil spirit shook the man violently and came out of him with a shriek.

27The people were all so amazed that they asked each other, "What is this? A new teaching—and with authority! He even gives orders to evil spirits and they obey him." 28News about him spread quickly over the whole region of Galilee.

Jesus Heals Many

29As soon as they left the synagogue, they went with James and John to the home of Simon and Andrew. 30Simon's mother-in-law was in bed with a fever, and they told Jesus about her. 31So he went to her, took her hand and helped her up. The fever left her and she began to wait on them.

32That evening after sunset the people brought to Jesus all the sick and demon-possessed. 33The whole town gathered at the door, 34and Jesus healed many who had various diseases. He also drove out many demons, but he would not let the demons speak because they knew who he was.

Jesus Prays in a Solitary Place

35Very early in the morning, while it was still dark, Jesus got up, left the house and went off to a solitary place, where he prayed. 36Simon and his companions went to look for him, 37and when they found him, they exclaimed: "Everyone is looking for you!"

38Jesus replied, "Let us go somewhere else—to the nearby villages—so I can preach there also. That is why I have come." 39So he traveled throughout Galilee, preaching in their synagogues and driving out demons.

A Man With Leprosy

40A man with leprosy[D][a] came to him and begged him on his knees, "If you are willing, you can make me clean."

41Filled with compassion, Jesus reached out his hand and touched the man. "I am willing," he said. "Be clean!" 42Immediately the leprosy left him and he was cured.

43Jesus sent him away at once with a strong warning: 44"See that you don't tell this to anyone. But go, show yourself to the priest[D] and offer the sacrifices[D] that Moses commanded for your cleansing, as a testimony to them." 45Instead he went out and began to talk freely, spreading the news. As a result, Jesus could no longer enter a town openly but stayed outside in lonely places. Yet the people still came to him from everywhere.

Jesus Heals a Paralytic

2 A few days later, when Jesus again entered Capernaum, the people heard that he had come home. 2So many gathered that there was no room left, not even outside the door, and he preached the word to them. 3Some men came, bringing to him a paralytic, carried by four of them. 4Since they could not get him to Jesus because of the crowd, they made an opening in the roof above Jesus and, after digging through it, lowered the mat the paralyzed man was lying on. 5When Jesus saw their faith, he said to the paralytic, "Son, your sins are forgiven."

6Now some teachers of the law were sitting there,

---

[a]40 The Greek word was used for various diseases affecting the skin—not necessarily leprosy.

confrontation. Mark presents Christ as one who served faithfully despite enormous opposition. The Holy Spirit led Jesus into the desert to be tempted by Satan to show that temptation doesn't need to end in failure. That's an encouragement to all believers who find themselves the objects of Satan's schemes (Eph. 6:11). For a fuller account of the temptation, see Matt. 4:1–11 and Luke 4:1–13.

SCRIPTURE LINK (1:12–13)
Matthew records Jesus' temptation in Matt. 4:1–11. Luke gives an account in Luke 4:1–13.

Were Simon and Andrew acting on impulse? (1:16–17)
Some see their immediate response as a model of Christian discipleship. Others, with clues from John's Gospel (John 1:35–51), think Simon and Andrew may have followed Jesus in a limited sense before this incident. Having already seen Jesus' power, they were ready when he asked for a more complete commitment.

SCRIPTURE LINK (1:16–20)
The calling of the first disciples can also be found in Matt. 4:18–22; Luke 5:2–11 and John 1:35–42.

How do demons possess someone? (1:23)
A person can be "demonized" by a wicked spirit that poses as a sickness (physical or emotional) or unusual behavior beyond the control of the person involved. Such symptoms alone do not indicate demonization. In Scripture, the appearance of evil spirits reached a climax during the earthly ministry of Jesus, perhaps as part of Satan's effort to discredit Jesus.

Why would demons publicize Jesus' true identity? (1:24)
Their confession was true but was likely motivated by fear. They knew Jesus would one day execute their final judgment and they feared that day had arrived. Ironically, those who deny Jesus' deity and authority show less knowledge than the demons who acknowledge it. Their open admission of his deity, while true, may have been an attempt to incriminate him as one who had enjoyed Satan's cooperation. This would have been similar to the charge the teachers of the law made later (3:22).

SCRIPTURE LINK (1:29–31)
Matthew and Luke also tell about Jesus healing Peter's mother-in-law. See Matt. 8:14–15 and Luke 4:38–39.

SCRIPTURE LINK (1:32–34)
Matthew reports that Jesus healed many in Matt. 8:16–17. Luke gives a similar report in Luke 4:40–41.

Leprosy (1:40)
Known today as *Hansen's disease,* although the Biblical term may have also included other types of skin ailments. Some forms are more contagious, some effects more tragic: paralysis and gangrene, for example. Ceremonial Old Testament law declared lepers to be unclean (Lev. 13–14). The Jews saw leprosy as a sign of God's curse and, as a result, often treated lepers inhumanely. See *Why treat someone with a disease in such a callous manner?* (Lev. 13:46).

Why keep this miracle a secret? (1:40–44)

Jesus, though he cared deeply for people in need, did not want the emphasis of his work to focus merely on miracles. Many were already flocking to him because of their fascination for the sensational. More publicity could have increased the crowds, causing them to interfere with his teaching. It's also possible Jesus wanted to avoid too much attention, which could solidify his opponents before he was finished with his ministry. Also see *Why use stories people don't understand?* (4:10–12).

SCRIPTURE LINK (1:40–44)

Read about Jesus healing a man with leprosy in Matt. 8:2–4 and Luke 5:12–14.

SCRIPTURE LINK (2:3–12)

See Matt. 9:2–8 and Luke 5:18–26 for the story of Jesus healing the paralytic.

Did these men destroy the roof? (2:4)

The damage wasn't as serious as it sounds. Often homes were built with outside staircases to the roof. The roof itself was flat and made of tile sandwiched around brush or branch insulation. To lift a section of the roof, then dig through the insulation and remove a tile from the ceiling, was not a drastic measure. The opening could easily be repaired. Jesus rightly focused on the compassion of these men for their sick friend, rather than the minor structural damage which occurred.

SCRIPTURE LINK (2:14–17)

The calling of Levi can also be found in Matt. 9:9–13 and Luke 5:27–32.

Tax collectors (2:15)

A group of Jews despised by other Jews for collaborating with the Roman government that ruled over them. Tax collectors paid the authorities for the privilege of collecting taxes, then overcharged the people for personal gain.

thinking to themselves, **7**"Why does this fellow talk like that? He's blaspheming! Who can forgive sins but God alone?"

8Immediately Jesus knew in his spirit that this was what they were thinking in their hearts, and he said to them, "Why are you thinking these things? **9**Which is easier: to say to the paralytic, 'Your sins are forgiven,' or to say, 'Get up, take your mat and walk'? **10**But that you may know that the Son of Man[D] has authority on earth to forgive sins . . . ." He said to the paralytic, **11**"I tell you, get up, take your mat and go home." **12**He got up, took his mat and walked out in full view of them all. This amazed everyone and they praised God, saying, "We have never seen anything like this!"

The Calling of Levi

13Once again Jesus went out beside the lake. A large crowd came to him, and he began to teach them. **14**As he walked along, he saw Levi son of Alphaeus sitting at the tax collector's[D] booth. "Follow me," Jesus told him, and Levi got up and followed him.

15While Jesus was having dinner at Levi's house, many tax collectors and "sinners" were eating with him and his disciples[D], for there were many who followed him. **16**When the teachers of the law who were Pharisees[D] saw him eating with the "sinners" and tax collectors, they asked his disciples: "Why does he eat with tax collectors and 'sinners'?"

17On hearing this, Jesus said to them, "It is not the healthy who need a doctor, but the sick. I have not come to call the righteous[D], but sinners."

Jesus Questioned About Fasting

18Now John's disciples and the Pharisees were fasting. Some people came and asked Jesus, "How is it that John's disciples and the disciples of the Pharisees are fasting, but yours are not?"

Why did Jesus call himself the Son of Man? (2:10)

Jesus revealed and concealed himself by using this somewhat mysterious phrase. He was clearly human, but he was divine as well. His ministry progressively revealed this fact. To those who would oppose him, he chose to conceal his identity. To those who would accept him as the Messiah destined to give his life for humanity, the term revealed his identity.

Son of Man is used 14 times in Mark and was Jesus' favorite term for himself. It describes the servant role he willingly assumed. Sometimes the term is used to describe his divine authority, his sacrificial role and his future glory when he returns. By taking on this title in Mark 13:26 and 14:62, Jesus established himself as the fulfillment of the heavenly authority figure of Daniel 7 who is granted the right to come to earth, rule and judge on behalf of God.

The term blends the heavenly and earthly aspects of Christ. Because of his divine nature, God grants authority to Jesus to forgive sin. Because of his earthly purpose to be a ransom for many, he must suffer, be rejected, betrayed and killed, finally to rise again. While others may not have immediately grasped what Jesus meant by this title, Jesus used it to claim authority, demonstrate power and assume responsibilities no other man could.

[19]Jesus answered, "How can the guests of the bridegroom fast while he is with them? They cannot, so long as they have him with them. [20]But the time will come when the bridegroom will be taken from them, and on that day they will fast.

[21]"No one sews a patch of unshrunk cloth on an old garment. If he does, the new piece will pull away from the old, making the tear worse. [22]And no one pours new wine[D] into old wineskins[D]. If he does, the wine will burst the skins, and both the wine and the wineskins will be ruined. No, he pours new wine into new wineskins."

Lord of the Sabbath

[23]One Sabbath[D] Jesus was going through the grainfields, and as his disciples[D] walked along, they began to pick some heads of grain. [24]The Pharisees[D] said to him, "Look, why are they doing what is unlawful on the Sabbath?"

[25]He answered, "Have you never read what David did when he and his companions were hungry and in need? [26]In the days of Abiathar the high priest[D], he entered the house of God and ate the consecrated[D] bread, which is lawful only for priests to eat. And he also gave some to his companions."

[27]Then he said to them, "The Sabbath was made for man, not man for the Sabbath. [28]So the Son of Man is Lord even of the Sabbath."

3 Another time he went into the synagogue, and a man with a shriveled hand was there. [2]Some of them were looking for a reason to accuse Jesus, so they watched him closely to see if he would heal him on the Sabbath. [3]Jesus said to the man with the shriveled hand, "Stand up in front of everyone."

[4]Then Jesus asked them, "Which is lawful on the Sabbath: to do good or to do evil, to save life or to kill?" But they remained silent.

[5]He looked around at them in anger and, deeply distressed at their stubborn hearts, said to the man, "Stretch out your hand." He stretched it out, and his hand was completely restored. [6]Then the Pharisees went out and began to plot with the Herodians[D] how they might kill Jesus.

Crowds Follow Jesus

[7]Jesus withdrew with his disciples to the lake, and a large crowd from Galilee followed. [8]When they heard all he was doing, many people came to him from Judea, Jerusalem[D], Idumea, and the regions across the Jordan and around Tyre and Sidon. [9]Because of the crowd he told his disciples to have a small boat ready for him, to keep the people from crowding him. [10]For he had healed many, so that those with diseases were pushing forward to touch him. [11]Whenever the evil[a] spirits saw him, they fell down before him and cried out, "You are the Son of God." [12]But he gave them strict orders not to tell who he was.

The Appointing of the Twelve Apostles

[13]Jesus went up on a mountainside and called to him those he wanted, and they came to him. [14]He appointed twelve—designating them apostles[D][b]—that they might

Should Christians fast? (2:18–20)
Jesus compared his time with his disciples to a wedding feast. Since there is no longer physically among us, it is appropriate to fast—not because it is commanded as in the Old Testament, but because it is beneficial to our spiritual development. Fasting helps us concentrate in prayer. It heightens our spiritual awareness, lends intensity to our communion with God and reminds us of our weakness and complete dependence on God. Also see **What are the benefits of sincere fasting?** (Matt. 6:18).

Why did Jesus talk about new patches and old wineskins? (2:21–22)
Jesus was making the point that rigid forms of religion (like those of the Pharisees) were incompatible with the living faith he taught. Just as new patches shrink, ruining old clothing, and new wine expands, ruining unpliable wineskins, it's useless to try to merge the two faiths. God is doing something new in the lives of people through Christ.

What was so bad about getting food on the Sabbath? (2:23–24)
Jesus' disciples were violating the Pharisees' detailed rules regarding Sabbath rest. God's law did forbid working on the Sabbath, but Jewish traditions defined work with stifling legalism. The Pharisees considered it wrong even to pluck a bit of grain and rub it in one's hand before eating it. In their opinion, these actions constituted reaping and threshing. Yet God intended Sabbath-keeping to be a blessing, not a burden (vv. 27–28).

SCRIPTURE LINK (2:23–28)
To find Jesus' declaration that he is Lord of the Sabbath look also at Matt. 12:1–8 and Luke 6:1–5.

Did Jesus break the law? (2:27)
Jesus didn't violate one of the Ten Commandments, but he refused to obey the man-made laws that violated what God intended for the Sabbath. Instead of the Sabbath being seen as a welcomed rest in remembrance of God, it had become a joyless ritual because of the Pharisees' regulations. Jesus insisted on observing the Sabbath as it was originally intended, not as the caricature it had become. Rather than discarding the commandment to "keep the Sabbath day holy," Jesus instead demonstrated that one way to obey God's directive for the day was by feeding the hungry.

SCRIPTURE LINK (3:1–6)
You can also read the account of Jesus healing on the Sabbath in Matt. 12:9–14 and Luke 6:6–11.

Why did the Pharisees and the Herodians dislike Jesus? (3:6)
The Herodians were supporters of Herod Antipas, the ruler of Galilee. They perceived Jesus as a political threat. The Pharisees, a religious group, were nervous about Jesus' spiritual influence. Normally bitter political opponents, the Herodians and Pharisees both saw Jesus as an enemy. This unholy Jewish and Roman alliance shared a common objective: to eliminate Jesus.

SCRIPTURE LINK (3:7–12)
Matthew and Luke also tell about the great crowds that followed Jesus. See Matt. 12:15–16 and Luke 6:17–19.

---

[a] 11 Greek *unclean*; also in verse 30   [b] 14 Some manuscripts do not have *designating them apostles*.

SCRIPTURE LINK (3:16-19)

Matthew lists the apostles in Matt. 10:2-4 and Luke names them in Luke 6:14-16.

Did Jesus' family think he was crazy? (3:21)

His incredible claims, mass popularity and unusual behavior worried his brothers and sisters, who didn't yet believe he was the Son of God. They probably feared he was going mad because of his hectic schedule of teaching, performing miracles and traveling. Most likely embarrassment and fear motivated them to confront Jesus with their concerns.

Why accuse Jesus of demon possession? (3:22)

The religious leaders accused Jesus of being possessed by Beelzebub, the Philistine "Lord of the Flies" (2 Kings 1:2-17), another name for Satan. This ultimate insult, though completely false, was their attempt to discredit the power behind the miracles of Jesus.

SCRIPTURE LINK (3:23-27)

Jesus' talk about Satan can also be found in Matt. 12:25-29 and Luke 11:17-22.

What sin is unforgivable? (3:29)

Jesus says that attributing to Satan the work performed through the power of the Holy Spirit is blasphemy of the worst kind. The teachers' stubborn refusal to accept the work of the Holy Spirit led Jesus to announce the eternal consequences of judgment. We should always be careful to avoid speaking wrongly about what God may be doing and not to resist the Holy Spirit's work in our lives. See article: **What is blasphemy against the Holy Spirit?** (Matt. 12:31-32).

SCRIPTURE LINK (3:31-35)

You can also find Jesus' proclamation of who his mother and brothers are in Matt. 12:46-50 and Luke 8:19-21.

Was Jesus rude to his family? (3:31-35)

Jesus emphasized that following God, not family heritage, is what really counts. He wasn't denying his love for his family, but he used their presence to contrast earthly loyalties with the more important eternal allegiance.

SCRIPTURE LINK (4:1-12)

Matthew gives the parable of the sower in Matt. 13:1-15. Luke shares it in Luke 8:4-10.

Why use stories people don't understand? (4:10-12,21-25)

Parables were used to reveal as well as to conceal truth (Isaiah 6:9-10). Jesus concealed truth from those who would reject his message —a judgment on their hard-heartedness. Also, Jesus may have recognized that his teachings could cause casual observers, opponents and overzealous supporters to steer his ministry toward a premature conclusion. Perhaps he obscured some teaching to prevent that from happening. To people willing to receive his message, however, Jesus' stories communicate further truth about the nature of God's kingdom.

be with him and that he might send them out to preach [15]and to have authority to drive out demons. [16]These are the twelve he appointed: Simon (to whom he gave the name Peter); [17]James son of Zebedee and his brother John (to whom he gave the name Boanerges, which means Sons of Thunder); [18]Andrew, Philip, Bartholomew, Matthew, Thomas, James son of Alphaeus, Thaddaeus, Simon the Zealot [19]and Judas Iscariot, who betrayed him.

Jesus and Beelzebub

[20]Then Jesus entered a house, and again a crowd gathered, so that he and his disciples[D] were not even able to eat. [21]When his family heard about this, they went to take charge of him, for they said, "He is out of his mind." [22]And the teachers of the law who came down from Jerusalem[D] said, "He is possessed by Beelzebub[D a]! By the prince of demons he is driving out demons."

[23]So Jesus called them and spoke to them in parables[D]: "How can Satan drive out Satan? [24]If a kingdom is divided against itself, that kingdom cannot stand. [25]If a house is divided against itself, that house cannot stand. [26]And if Satan opposes himself and is divided, he cannot stand; his end has come. [27]In fact, no one can enter a strong man's house and carry off his possessions unless he first ties up the strong man. Then he can rob his house. [28]I tell you the truth, all the sins and blasphemies[D] of men will be forgiven them. [29]But whoever blasphemes[D] against the Holy Spirit will never be forgiven; he is guilty of an eternal sin."

[30]He said this because they were saying, "He has an evil spirit."

Jesus' Mother and Brothers

[31]Then Jesus' mother and brothers arrived. Standing outside, they sent someone in to call him. [32]A crowd was sitting around him, and they told him, "Your mother and brothers are outside looking for you."

[33]"Who are my mother and my brothers?" he asked.

[34]Then he looked at those seated in a circle around him and said, "Here are my mother and my brothers! [35]Whoever does God's will is my brother and sister and mother."

The Parable of the Sower

4 Again Jesus began to teach by the lake. The crowd that gathered around him was so large that he got into a boat and sat in it out on the lake, while all the people were along the shore at the water's edge. [2]He taught them many things by parables, and in his teaching said: [3]"Listen! A farmer went out to sow his seed. [4]As he was scattering the seed, some fell along the path, and the birds came and ate it up. [5]Some fell on rocky places, where it did not have much soil. It sprang up quickly, because the soil was shallow. [6]But when the sun came up, the plants were scorched, and they withered because they had no root. [7]Other seed fell among thorns, which grew up and choked the plants, so that they did not bear grain. [8]Still other seed fell on good soil. It came up, grew and produced a crop, multiplying thirty, sixty, or even a hundred times."

[9]Then Jesus said, "He who has ears to hear, let him hear."

[10]When he was alone, the Twelve and the others around him asked him about the parables. [11]He told

a 22 Greek Beezeboul or Beelzeboul

them, "The secret of the kingdom of God^D has been given to you. But to those on the outside everything is said in parables^D ¹²so that,

> " 'they may be ever seeing but never
>   perceiving,
>   and ever hearing but never understanding;
>   otherwise they might turn and be forgiven!' ^a "

¹³Then Jesus said to them, "Don't you understand this parable? How then will you understand any parable? ¹⁴The farmer sows the word. ¹⁵Some people are like seed along the path, where the word is sown. As soon as they hear it, Satan comes and takes away the word that was sown in them. ¹⁶Others, like seed sown on rocky places, hear the word and at once receive it with joy. ¹⁷But since they have no root, they last only a short time. When trouble or persecution comes because of the word, they quickly fall away. ¹⁸Still others, like seed sown among thorns, hear the word; ¹⁹but the worries of this life, the deceitfulness of wealth and the desires for other things come in and choke the word, making it unfruitful. ²⁰Others, like seed sown on good soil, hear the word, accept it, and produce a crop—thirty, sixty or even a hundred times what was sown."

A Lamp on a Stand

²¹He said to them, "Do you bring in a lamp to put it under a bowl or a bed? Instead, don't you put it on its stand? ²²For whatever is hidden is meant to be disclosed, and whatever is concealed is meant to be brought out into the open. ²³If anyone has ears to hear, let him hear."

²⁴"Consider carefully what you hear," he continued. "With the measure you use, it will be measured to you—and even more. ²⁵Whoever has will be given more; whoever does not have, even what he has will be taken from him."

The Parable of the Growing Seed

²⁶He also said, "This is what the kingdom of God is like. A man scatters seed on the ground. ²⁷Night and day, whether he sleeps or gets up, the seed sprouts and grows, though he does not know how. ²⁸All by itself the soil produces grain—first the stalk, then the head, then the full kernel in the head. ²⁹As soon as the grain is ripe, he puts the sickle to it, because the harvest has come."

The Parable of the Mustard Seed

³⁰Again he said, "What shall we say the kingdom of God is like, or what parable shall we use to describe it? ³¹It is like a mustard seed, which is the smallest seed you plant in the ground. ³²Yet when planted, it grows and becomes the largest of all garden plants, with such big branches that the birds of the air can perch in its shade."

³³With many similar parables Jesus spoke the word to them, as much as they could understand. ³⁴He did not say anything to them without using a parable. But when he was alone with his own disciples^D, he explained everything.

Jesus Calms the Storm

³⁵That day when evening came, he said to his disciples, "Let us go over to the other side." ³⁶Leaving the

^a12 Isaiah 6:9,10

SCRIPTURE LINK (4:13-20)
Jesus also makes plain the meaning of the sower in Matt. 13:18–23 as well as in Luke 8:11–15.

What can we learn from soil? (4:13-20)
The parable of the sower teaches that the gospel won't be received with equal effect. At least three things can interfere: satanic opposition, outside persecution and peer pressure, and the attraction of the world's pleasures. But if it does take root, God's Word can produce a fruitful life.

Why did Jesus tell these stories about seeds? (4:26-32)
Seeds grow quietly but persistently. Like seeds, the growth of God's kingdom is the result of divine power, not human effort. The mustard seed illustration portrays the amazing growth of God's kingdom, which will reach across international boundaries and nations before it is finished (Ezek. 17:22–24; 31:3–14; Daniel 4:10–12).

SCRIPTURE LINK (4:30-32)
The parable of the mustard seed can also be found in Matt. 13:31–32 and Luke 13:18–19.

SCRIPTURE LINK (4:35-41)
Matthew tells about Jesus calming the storm in Matt. 8:18,23–27. Luke talks about it in Luke 8:22–25.

Does having faith mean we'll never be afraid? (4:40)

Jesus doesn't promise we'll never face fearful circumstances. Instead, he teaches that God is greater than whatever we are facing and he is in control. Faith means trusting that we never face dangers alone. Knowing God is present keeps fear from paralyzing us.

SCRIPTURE LINK (5:1–17)

Matthew relates Jesus' healing of a demon-possessed man in Matt. 8:28–34. Luke gives the account in Luke 8:26–37.

Jesus Heals a Possessed Man (5:2)

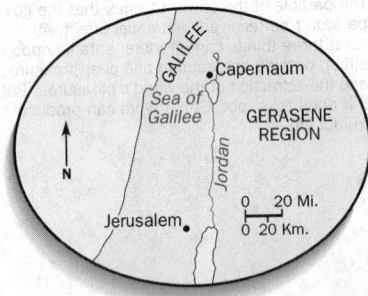

Why did Jesus send the demons into pigs? (5:11–13)

Perhaps Jesus wanted a visible way to demonstrate to the man and his neighbors that the demons had left him. This dramatic exit would convince onlookers that Jesus had power over this destructive force and that the man was truly free. Pigs, according to Lev. 11:7, were *unclean*, not to be eaten by Jews.

What happened to the demons after the pigs drowned? (5:13)

The evil spirits, left without a living body to inhabit, probably searched for others they could enter (see Matt. 12:43). It was not yet the time for Jesus to execute final judgment upon Satan, but the slaughter of the pigs served as a sign of coming judgment on Satan, his demons and everyone who opposes Christ.

What were the people afraid of? (5:17)

They seemed to fear the awesome power of God displayed in their midst. Such supernatural power would have been unnerving to people who had not shown any interest in honoring God. They may have seen the loss of their herd as God's judgment and perhaps feared further judgment.

SCRIPTURE LINK (5:18–20)

Luke also tells how the restored man begged to go with Jesus. See Luke 8:38–39.

Decapolis (5:20)

The name of ten Gentile cities taken from Jewish control by the Roman general Pompey in 65 B.C. All of the cities were located east of the Jordan River except Scythopolis (see *Map 9* at the back of this Bible). The other nine included Damascus, Canatha, Abila, Raphana, Gadara, Pella, Dion, Philadelphia and Gerasa. The fact that Jesus commands the man delivered from demonic torment to go and share his good

crowd behind, they took him along, just as he was, in the boat. There were also other boats with him. **37**A furious squall came up, and the waves broke over the boat, so that it was nearly swamped. **38**Jesus was in the stern, sleeping on a cushion. The disciples**D** woke him and said to him, "Teacher, don't you care if we drown?"

39He got up, rebuked the wind and said to the waves, "Quiet! Be still!" Then the wind died down and it was completely calm.

40He said to his disciples, "Why are you so afraid? Do you still have no faith?"

41They were terrified and asked each other, "Who is this? Even the wind and the waves obey him!"

The Healing of a Demon-possessed Man

5 They went across the lake to the region of the Gerasenes.*a* **2**When Jesus got out of the boat, a man with an evil*b* spirit came from the tombs to meet him. **3**This man lived in the tombs, and no one could bind him any more, not even with a chain. **4**For he had often been chained hand and foot, but he tore the chains apart and broke the irons on his feet. No one was strong enough to subdue him. **5**Night and day among the tombs and in the hills he would cry out and cut himself with stones.

6When he saw Jesus from a distance, he ran and fell on his knees in front of him. **7**He shouted at the top of his voice, "What do you want with me, Jesus, Son of the Most High God? Swear to God that you won't torture me!" **8**For Jesus had said to him, "Come out of this man, you evil spirit!"

9Then Jesus asked him, "What is your name?"

"My name is Legion**D**," he replied, "for we are many." **10**And he begged Jesus again and again not to send them out of the area.

11A large herd of pigs was feeding on the nearby hillside. **12**The demons begged Jesus, "Send us among the pigs; allow us to go into them." **13**He gave them permission, and the evil spirits came out and went into the pigs. The herd, about two thousand in number, rushed down the steep bank into the lake and were drowned.

14Those tending the pigs ran off and reported this in the town and countryside, and the people went out to see what had happened. **15**When they came to Jesus, they saw the man who had been possessed by the legion of demons, sitting there, dressed and in his right mind; and they were afraid. **16**Those who had seen it told the people what had happened to the demon-possessed man—and told about the pigs as well. **17**Then the people began to plead with Jesus to leave their region.

18As Jesus was getting into the boat, the man who had been demon-possessed begged to go with him. **19**Jesus did not let him, but said, "Go home to your family and tell them how much the Lord has done for you, and how he has had mercy**D** on you." **20**So the man went away and began to tell in the Decapolis**Dc** how much Jesus had done for him. And all the people were amazed.

A Dead Girl and a Sick Woman

21When Jesus had again crossed over by boat to the other side of the lake, a large crowd gathered around him

---

*a*1 Some manuscripts *Gadarenes*; other manuscripts *Gergesenes*   *b*2 Greek *unclean*; also in verses 8 and 13   *c*20 That is, the Ten Cities

while he was by the lake. **22**Then one of the synagogue rulers, named Jairus, came there. Seeing Jesus, he fell at his feet **23**and pleaded earnestly with him, "My little daughter is dying. Please come and put your hands on her so that she will be healed and live." **24**So Jesus went with him.

A large crowd followed and pressed around him. **25**And a woman was there who had been subject to bleeding for twelve years. **26**She had suffered a great deal under the care of many doctors and had spent all she had, yet instead of getting better she grew worse. **27**When she heard about Jesus, she came up behind him in the crowd and touched his cloak, **28**because she thought, "If I just touch his clothes, I will be healed." **29**Immediately her bleeding stopped and she felt in her body that she was freed from her suffering.

30At once Jesus realized that power had gone out from him. He turned around in the crowd and asked, "Who touched my clothes?"

31"You see the people crowding against you," his disciplesᴰ answered, "and yet you can ask, 'Who touched me?' "

32But Jesus kept looking around to see who had done it. **33**Then the woman, knowing what had happened to her, came and fell at his feet and, trembling with fear, told him the whole truth. **34**He said to her, "Daughter, your faith has healed you. Go in peaceᴰ and be freed from your suffering."

35While Jesus was still speaking, some men came from the house of Jairus, the synagogue ruler. "Your daughter is dead," they said. "Why bother the teacher any more?"

36Ignoring what they said, Jesus told the synagogue ruler, "Don't be afraid; just believe."

37He did not let anyone follow him except Peter, James and John the brother of James. **38**When they came to the home of the synagogue ruler, Jesus saw a commotion, with people crying and wailing loudly. **39**He went in and said to them, "Why all this commotion and wailing? The child is not dead but asleep." **40**But they laughed at him.

After he put them all out, he took the child's father and mother and the disciples who were with him, and went in where the child was. **41**He took her by the hand and said to her, *"Talitha koum!"* (which means, "Little girl, I say to you, get up!"). **42**Immediately the girl stood up and walked around (she was twelve years old). At this they were completely astonished. **43**He gave strict orders not to let anyone know about this, and told them to give her something to eat.

A Prophet Without Honor

6 Jesus left there and went to his hometown, accompanied by his disciples. **2**When the Sabbath came, he began to teach in the synagogue, and many who heard him were amazed.

"Where did this man get these things?" they asked. "What's this wisdom that has been given him, that he even does miracles! **3**Isn't this the carpenter? Isn't this Mary's son and the brother of James, Joseph,ᵃ Judas and Simon? Aren't his sisters here with us?" And they took offense at him.

4Jesus said to them, "Only in his hometown, among his relatives and in his own house is a prophetᴰ without

---

news throughout the Decapolis is evidence that God has deep love and mercy for Gentiles as well as Jews.

SCRIPTURE LINK (5:22–43)
You can also find the accounts of the dead girl and the sick woman in Matt. 9:18–26 and Luke 8:41–56.

Could others tap Jesus' power without his permission? (5:25–29)
Jesus was always in control; his power was never released without his consent. Why, then, did he ask who had touched him? Possibly he did it to make the woman go public. It would have been in her own best interest—not to mention the crowd's—to tell others what had happened to her. Thus a person of timid faith became a faithful witness.

Will I be healed if I have faith? (5:34–36)
Jesus teaches that faith prompts God to respond to our need. Sometimes it is the faith of friends or family that God rewards. Occasionally, God's healing work seems unrelated to anyone's faith—the only explanation is God's sovereign choice. But Jesus never teaches that faith automatically brings healing. In Christ's 35 miracles recorded in the Gospels, no formula to guarantee healing can be found. Also see *Does God guarantee healing from any disease?* (Psalm 103:3) and *Is healing guaranteed?* (James 5:15–16).

Why say the dead are only *asleep*? (5:39)
Just as many people today use "passed away," the Bible uses *asleep* as a euphemism for death (John 11:11–14; 1 Cor. 11:30; 15:51; 1 Thes. 4:13–15). Jesus speaks of death as sleep only because it is no more serious than slumber for believers, whom Christ will raise when he returns.

Why did Jesus insist the witnesses keep quiet? (5:43)
See *Why couldn't the disciples tell anyone?* (8:30).

SCRIPTURE LINK (6:1–6)
In Matt. 13:54–58, Matthew says that Jesus was without honor in his hometown.

ᵃ3 Greek *Joses*, a variant of *Joseph*

Does unbelief diminish Jesus' power? (6:5-6)

The issue was not power but effectiveness. The reason Jesus could not perform miracles in the region was due to the fact that they would have been a waste of time. Miracles serve a greater purpose than simply a raw display of power. The moral climate of Nazareth was polluted with unbelief and opposition. Miracles, which are designed to prompt faith, would not have accomplished their purpose in this hard-hearted region. While Jesus did perform a few miracles, the people's attitude forfeited the opportunity for the miracles to increase their faith.

Were the disciples exorcists? (6:7)

The issue was authority, not power, over the kingdom of darkness. The disciples, as believers in Christ, shared in his authority. As the demons fled before the disciples, the authority of the gospel message was unmistakably apparent. Jesus and his followers will ultimately defeat Satan.

SCRIPTURE LINK (6:7-11)

Matthew describes how Jesus sent out the Twelve in Matt. 10:1,9-14. Luke covers it in Luke 9:1,3-5.

Why did Jesus say to take nothing? (6:8)

Jesus wanted the Twelve to be completely dependent on God for their provision. He wanted them to see how God would provide for them. He was not setting a precedent, however, that ministries should be without regular support. The New Testament churches were encouraged to support those who ministered to them (Phil. 4:14; 1 Tim. 5:17-18; 3 John 5-8).

Why *shake the dust off your feet?* (6:11)

Jews returning to Israel from a foreign land would shake the dust from their sandals and clothing to avoid defiling the land they considered holy. The disciples were delivering a similar warning to the people of Israel. If they rejected the message of Christ, they would face the same future judgment as unbelieving foreigners.

Does oil cure sickness? (6:13)

While olive oil was used for medicinal purposes in ancient Palestine, it isn't a cure for disease or illness. The disciples used it as a symbolic act to seek God's healing and blessing. Anointing with oil is a common Biblical metaphor for the pouring out of God's Spirit on an individual. It is the Spirit of God, not crushed olives, that heals the sick.

SCRIPTURE LINK (6:14-29)

Matthew tells about the beheading of John the Baptist in Matt. 14:1-12.

SCRIPTURE LINK (6:14-16)

Luke talks about Herod's confusion over Jesus' identity in Luke 9:7-9.

Was John trying to confuse Herod? (6:20)

No. Herod was *puzzled* because he was torn between the voice of his conscience and the desire of his lover, Herodias, to see John killed. His conflict of interests prevented him from accepting John's clear message to re-

honor." [5]He could not do any miracles there, except lay his hands on a few sick people and heal them. [6]And he was amazed at their lack of faith.

Jesus Sends Out the Twelve

Then Jesus went around teaching from village to village. [7]Calling the Twelve to him, he sent them out two by two and gave them authority over evil[a] spirits.

[8]These were his instructions: "Take nothing for the journey except a staff—no bread, no bag, no money in your belts. [9]Wear sandals but not an extra tunic. [10]Whenever you enter a house, stay there until you leave that town. [11]And if any place will not welcome you or listen to you, shake the dust off your feet when you leave, as a testimony against them."

[12]They went out and preached that people should repent[D]. [13]They drove out many demons and anointed[D] many sick people with oil and healed them.

John the Baptist Beheaded

[14]King Herod heard about this, for Jesus' name had become well known. Some were saying,[b] "John the Baptist has been raised from the dead, and that is why miraculous powers are at work in him."

[15]Others said, "He is Elijah."

And still others claimed, "He is a prophet[D], like one of the prophets of long ago."

[16]But when Herod heard this, he said, "John, the man I beheaded, has been raised from the dead!"

[17]For Herod himself had given orders to have John arrested, and he had him bound and put in prison. He did this because of Herodias, his brother Philip's wife, whom he had married. [18]For John had been saying to Herod, "It is not lawful for you to have your brother's wife." [19]So Herodias nursed a grudge against John and wanted to kill him. But she was not able to, [20]because Herod feared John and protected him, knowing him to be a righteous[D] and holy man. When Herod heard John, he was greatly puzzled[c]; yet he liked to listen to him.

[21]Finally the opportune time came. On his birthday Herod gave a banquet for his high officials and military commanders and the leading men of Galilee. [22]When the daughter of Herodias came in and danced, she pleased Herod and his dinner guests.

The king said to the girl, "Ask me for anything you want, and I'll give it to you." [23]And he promised her with an oath, "Whatever you ask I will give you, up to half my kingdom."

[24]She went out and said to her mother, "What shall I ask for?"

"The head of John the Baptist," she answered.

[25]At once the girl hurried in to the king with the request: "I want you to give me right now the head of John the Baptist on a platter."

[26]The king was greatly distressed, but because of his oaths and his dinner guests, he did not want to refuse her. [27]So he immediately sent an executioner with orders to bring John's head. The man went, beheaded John in the prison, [28]and brought back his head on a platter. He presented it to the girl, and she gave it to her mother. [29]On

---

[a]7 Greek *unclean*   [b]14 Some early manuscripts *He was saying*
[c]20 Some early manuscripts *he did many things*

hearing of this, John's disciples^D came and took his body and laid it in a tomb.

Jesus Feeds the Five Thousand

30The apostles^D gathered around Jesus and reported to him all they had done and taught. **31**Then, because so many people were coming and going that they did not even have a chance to eat, he said to them, "Come with me by yourselves to a quiet place and get some rest."

32So they went away by themselves in a boat to a solitary place. **33**But many who saw them leaving recognized them and ran on foot from all the towns and got there ahead of them. **34**When Jesus landed and saw a large crowd, he had compassion on them, because they were like sheep without a shepherd. So he began teaching them many things.

35By this time it was late in the day, so his disciples came to him. "This is a remote place," they said, "and it's already very late. **36**Send the people away so they can go to the surrounding countryside and villages and buy themselves something to eat."

37But he answered, "You give them something to eat." They said to him, "That would take eight months of a man's wages^a! Are we to go and spend that much on bread and give it to them to eat?"

38"How many loaves do you have?" he asked. "Go and see."

When they found out, they said, "Five—and two fish."

39Then Jesus directed them to have all the people sit down in groups on the green grass. **40**So they sat down in groups of hundreds and fifties. **41**Taking the five loaves and the two fish and looking up to heaven, he gave thanks and broke the loaves. Then he gave them to his disciples to set before the people. He also divided the two fish among them all. **42**They all ate and were satisfied, **43**and the disciples picked up twelve basketfuls of broken pieces of bread and fish. **44**The number of the men who had eaten was five thousand.

Jesus Walks on the Water

45Immediately Jesus made his disciples get into the boat and go on ahead of him to Bethsaida, while he dismissed the crowd. **46**After leaving them, he went up on a mountainside to pray.

47When evening came, the boat was in the middle of the lake, and he was alone on land. **48**He saw the disciples straining at the oars, because the wind was against them. About the fourth watch of the night he went out to them, walking on the lake. He was about to pass by them, **49**but when they saw him walking on the lake, they thought he was a ghost. They cried out, **50**because they all saw him and were terrified.

Immediately he spoke to them and said, "Take courage! It is I. Don't be afraid." **51**Then he climbed into the boat with them, and the wind died down. They were completely amazed, **52**for they had not understood about the loaves; their hearts were hardened.

53When they had crossed over, they landed at Gennesaret and anchored there. **54**As soon as they got out of the boat, people recognized Jesus. **55**They ran throughout that whole region and carried the sick on mats to wherever they heard he was. **56**And wherever he went—into vil-

^a37 Greek *take two hundred denarii*

pent. He liked listening to the prophet, but he wasn't prepared to give up his adulterous affair with his brother's wife.

Would Herod really give half his kingdom to this girl? (6:23)
See *Was the king literally promising half his kingdom to Esther?* (Esther 5:3).

SCRIPTURE LINK (6:32–44)
Matt. 14:13–21; Luke 9:10–17 and John 6:5–13 all document Jesus' feeding of the five thousand. In Mark 8:2–9 Mark tells how Jesus also fed four thousand.

SCRIPTURE LINK (6:45–51)
In Matt. 6:45–51, Matthew tells about Jesus walking on the water. John talks about it in John 6:15–21.

Why did Jesus need to pray? (6:46)
Jesus himself is God, but he is not God the Father. Because he lived in constant communication with the heavenly Father, Jesus' consistent prayer life provided a living example for his disciples and enabled him to identify with our humanity (Heb. 4:14–16). He demonstrated what it means to live in complete harmony with the Father's will and to *pray continually* (1 Thes. 5:17).

Fourth watch (6:48)
In ancient times, the hours of the night were divided into military watches, which designated the length of time sentinels remained on duty. Originally the Jews divided the night into three sections (Judges 7:19). The Romans divided the night into four watches, which ended at 9 p.m., 12 a.m., 3 a.m. and 6 a.m. Thus, Jesus' appearance occurred sometime between 3 and 6 a.m.

Why did Jesus walk on the water? (6:48)
This incident served to strengthen the disciples' trust in Jesus at a time when they probably felt disappointed and confused by his refusal to be made king the day before (John 6:14–15). It also provides powerful evidence of Jesus' ability to help us in the storms and troubles we face.

How were their hearts hardened? (6:51–52)
The disciples missed the point of the feeding of the five thousand people with a few loaves of bread. They focused on Jesus' ability to do miracles rather than considering that he was the Son of God. When the storm arose, they were still doubting if he could protect them from drowning, because they hadn't yet acknowledged who he was.

SCRIPTURE LINK (6:53–56)
Matthew relates in Matt. 14:34–36 how the sick flocked to Jesus and were healed by touching him.

lages, towns or countryside—they placed the sick in the marketplaces. They begged him to let them touch even the edge of his cloak, and all who touched him were healed.

Clean and Unclean

7 The Pharisees[D] and some of the teachers of the law who had come from Jerusalem[D] gathered around Jesus and [2]saw some of his disciples[D] eating food with hands that were "unclean[D]," that is, unwashed. [3](The Pharisees and all the Jews do not eat unless they give their hands a ceremonial washing, holding to the tradition of the elders. [4]When they come from the marketplace they do not eat unless they wash. And they observe many other traditions, such as the washing of cups, pitchers and kettles.[a])

[5]So the Pharisees and teachers of the law asked Jesus, "Why don't your disciples live according to the tradition of the elders instead of eating their food with 'unclean' hands?"

[6]He replied, "Isaiah was right when he prophesied about you hypocrites; as it is written:

" 'These people honor me with their lips,
    but their hearts are far from me.
[7]They worship me in vain;
    their teachings are but rules taught by
        men.'[b]

[8]You have let go of the commands of God and are holding on to the traditions of men."

[9]And he said to them: "You have a fine way of setting aside the commands of God in order to observe[c] your own traditions! [10]For Moses said, 'Honor your father and your mother,'[d] and, 'Anyone who curses his father or mother must be put to death[D].'[e] [11]But you say that if a man says to his father or mother: 'Whatever help you might otherwise have received from me is Corban' (that is, a gift devoted to God), [12]then you no longer let him do anything for his father or mother. [13]Thus you nullify the word of God by your tradition that you have handed down. And you do many things like that."

[14]Again Jesus called the crowd to him and said, "Listen to me, everyone, and understand this. [15]Nothing outside a man can make him 'unclean' by going into him. Rather, it is what comes out of a man that makes him 'unclean.'[f]"

[17]After he had left the crowd and entered the house, his disciples asked him about this parable. [18]"Are you so dull?" he asked. "Don't you see that nothing that enters a man from the outside can make him 'unclean'? [19]For it doesn't go into his heart but into his stomach, and then out of his body." (In saying this, Jesus declared all foods "clean.")

[20]He went on: "What comes out of a man is what makes him 'unclean.' [21]For from within, out of men's hearts, come evil thoughts, sexual immorality, theft, murder, adultery, [22]greed, malice, deceit, lewdness, envy, slander, arrogance and folly. [23]All these evils come from inside and make a man 'unclean.' "

Why was washing before meals so important? (7:1–3)

As a matter of religious custom, the Pharisees insisted on special hand-washing ceremonies to remove the contaminating effects of any possible contact with "unclean" persons or objects. This practice probably was derived from Old Testament teachings that prohibited contact with "unclean" things (Lev. 5:2–3) and prescribed special washings for the priests (Exodus 30:17–21). Jesus followed God's law, but he felt no obligation to observe all the traditions of the elders (Luke 11:37–39).

SCRIPTURE LINK (7:1–23)

Matthew records Jesus' teaching on the clean and unclean in Matt. 15:1–20.

How can worship be *in vain*? (7:7)

Empty ritual strips worship of its meaning and power, for God desires worshipers to come to him in *spirit and truth* (John 4:23–24). Naturally, worship is vain if it is directed toward a false god. Worship can also be vain when it consists of a rote adherence to human rules and teachings—without honest, thoughtful, heartfelt praise to God.

Corban (7:11)

Corban is a Hebrew word that means *a gift devoted to God*. Once something was declared *devoted* it could never be used for any other purpose. The scam mentioned here was simple: people could protect their assets until after their death by simply putting them under a vow. Even needy elderly parents were excluded from help once something was *Corban*. This was a clear example of hypocrisy as defined by Jesus.

---

[a]4 Some early manuscripts *pitchers, kettles and dining couches*   [b]6,7 Isaiah 29:13   [c]9 Some manuscripts *set up*   [d]10 Exodus 20:12; Deut. 5:16   [e]10 Exodus 21:17; Lev. 20:9   [f]15 Some early manuscripts *'unclean.'* [16]*If anyone has ears to hear, let him hear*.

The Faith of a Syrophoenician Woman

24Jesus left that place and went to the vicinity of Tyre.[a] He entered a house and did not want anyone to know it; yet he could not keep his presence secret. **25**In fact, as soon as she heard about him, a woman whose little daughter was possessed by an evil[b] spirit came and fell at his feet. **26**The woman was a Greek, born in Syrian Phoenicia. She begged Jesus to drive the demon out of her daughter.

27"First let the children eat all they want," he told her, "for it is not right to take the children's bread and toss it to their dogs."

28"Yes, Lord," she replied, "but even the dogs under the table eat the children's crumbs."

29Then he told her, "For such a reply, you may go; the demon has left your daughter."

30She went home and found her child lying on the bed, and the demon gone.

The Healing of a Deaf and Mute Man

31Then Jesus left the vicinity of Tyre and went through Sidon, down to the Sea of Galilee and into the region of the Decapolis.[D][c] **32**There some people brought to him a man who was deaf and could hardly talk, and they begged him to place his hand on the man.

33After he took him aside, away from the crowd, Jesus put his fingers into the man's ears. Then he spit and touched the man's tongue. **34**He looked up to heaven and with a deep sigh said to him, *"Ephphatha!"* (which means, "Be opened!"). **35**At this, the man's ears were opened, his tongue was loosened and he began to speak plainly.

36Jesus commanded them not to tell anyone. But the more he did so, the more they kept talking about it. **37**People were overwhelmed with amazement. "He has done everything well," they said. "He even makes the deaf hear and the mute speak."

Jesus Feeds the Four Thousand

8 During those days another large crowd gathered. Since they had nothing to eat, Jesus called his disciples[D] to him and said, **2**"I have compassion for these people; they have already been with me three days and have nothing to eat. **3**If I send them home hungry, they will collapse on the way, because some of them have come a long distance."

4His disciples answered, "But where in this remote place can anyone get enough bread to feed them?"

5"How many loaves do you have?" Jesus asked.

"Seven," they replied.

6He told the crowd to sit down on the ground. When he had taken the seven loaves and given thanks, he broke them and gave them to his disciples to set before the people, and they did so. **7**They had a few small fish as well; he gave thanks for them also and told the disciples to distribute them. **8**The people ate and were satisfied. Afterward the disciples picked up seven basketfuls of broken pieces that were left over. **9**About four thousand men were present. And having sent them away, **10**he got into the boat with his disciples and went to the region of Dalmanutha.

---

a24 Many early manuscripts *Tyre and Sidon*   *b25* Greek *unclean*
c31 That is, the Ten Cities

Why did Jesus go into Gentile territory? (7:24–28)

Jesus may have gone to Tyre and Sidon because he was interested in ministering to non-Jews; however, he clearly saw the *lost sheep of Israel* as his main focus at this point in his ministry. Eventually he sent his disciples to the whole world.

SCRIPTURE LINK (7:24–30)

Matthew writes about the faith of the Canaanite woman in Matt. 15:21–28.

Jesus Visits Phoenicia (7:24)

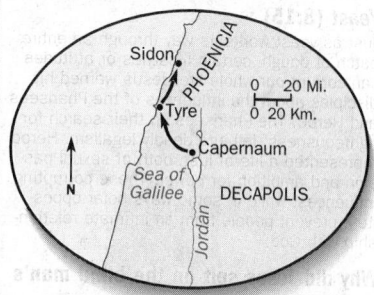

Why did Jesus resist helping the woman? (7:26–27)

Jesus was not forcing the Gentile woman to beg, but was perhaps probing the depth of her faith in the God of Israel. Or, he may have been teaching his disciples a lesson in the universal love of God. The woman's persistence indicates she sensed something from Jesus that encouraged her to continue asking—perhaps a twinkle in his eye or a warmth in his tone of voice. Using the word *dogs*, commonly used by Jews to describe Gentiles, may have been sarcasm—his way to make the point that demeaning others is alien to the heart of God.

SCRIPTURE LINK (7:31–37)

The healing of the deaf and mute man can also be found in Matt. 15:29–31.

Why did Jesus spit? (7:33)

Because the man could neither hear nor speak, Jesus showed, rather than told, what he was about to do to him. By touching the man's ears, it was obvious that he was going to deal with his deafness. By spitting and touching the man's tongue, he communicated through sign language his intention to give him speech. Also see *Why did Jesus spit on the blind man's eyes?* (8:23).

Why didn't the disciples feel a sense of déjà vu? (8:1–9)

No doubt they did remember Jesus' previous miracle when he fed the five thousand. Their question probably reflected their usual custom of asking Jesus for help when problems arose. They could count on Jesus to deal with the hungry crowd, whether by performing another miracle or by some other means.

SCRIPTURE LINK (8:1–9)

Matthew tells about the feeding of the four thousand in Matt. 15:32–39. Mark also gives an account of Jesus feeding five thousand in Mark 6:32–44.

SCRIPTURE LINK (8:11–21)

Jesus' warning about the yeast of the Pharisees can also be found in Matt. 16:1–12.

Is it wrong to want a miracle? (8:12)

Miracles have a very specific purpose. They are intended to glorify God and bring people to faith. Jesus wasn't condemning a desire to see that happen. Rather, he was rejecting the demand for a supernatural sideshow by those who doubted his divine authority. He knew that even if he performed the miraculous, his critics still wouldn't accept his divine identity and message.

Yeast (8:15)

Just as yeast works its way through an entire batch of dough, certain lifestyles or attitudes can corrupt our whole life. Jesus warned his disciples about the influences of the Pharisees and Herod. The Pharisees, in their search for righteousness, fell into deadly legalism. Herod represented a life of lust, both of sexual passion and ambition for power. These corrupting influences, while in some ways polar opposites, prevent people from an intimate relationship with God.

Why did Jesus spit on the blind man's eyes? (8:23)

Certainly Jesus, with his divine powers, did not need to spit in order to heal blindness. Several Roman writers as well as Jewish rabbis considered saliva to be a valid treatment for blindness. It may be, in this case, that Jesus recognized the man's need for increased faith and offered his physical action to raise his expectations. If so, the man's spiritual sight was strengthened as physical sight was imparted to him.

Did Jesus fail to heal the first time? (8:25)

This story appears to teach two lessons. First, Jesus heals people in a variety of ways. In this case, he used a two-step process. Second, and more importantly, achieving spiritual insight may be a gradual process rather than a dramatic event. The disciples, like the blind man, had a measure of insight, but still needed the help of Jesus for further understanding.

SCRIPTURE LINK (8:27–29)

For other accounts of Peter's confession of Christ, see Matt. 16:13–16 and Luke 9:18–20.

Why couldn't the disciples tell anyone? (8:30)

Several times Jesus tried to remain anonymous. Why? Probably for several reasons. First, Jesus was on his own timetable in revealing to the world who he was and what his future held. Second, his disciples and others had a false idea about the Messiah, thinking he would expel the Romans and establish a politically independent Israel. Finally, he was more concerned about fulfilling his mission of dying and rising from the dead than he was in promoting his rights to the title of Messiah (8:31).

SCRIPTURE LINK (8:31–9:1)

Matt. 16:21–28 and Luke 9:22–27 also record Jesus' prediction of his death.

Why call Peter *Satan*? (8:33)

Peter failed to see that God's plan was for Jesus to die in order to offer salvation to the

---

[11]The Pharisees[D] came and began to question Jesus. To test him, they asked him for a sign from heaven. [12]He sighed deeply and said, "Why does this generation ask for a miraculous sign? I tell you the truth, no sign will be given to it." [13]Then he left them, got back into the boat and crossed to the other side.

The Yeast of the Pharisees and Herod

[14]The disciples[D] had forgotten to bring bread, except for one loaf they had with them in the boat. [15]"Be careful," Jesus warned them. "Watch out for the yeast[D] of the Pharisees and that of Herod."

[16]They discussed this with one another and said, "It is because we have no bread."

[17]Aware of their discussion, Jesus asked them: "Why are you talking about having no bread? Do you still not see or understand? Are your hearts hardened? [18]Do you have eyes but fail to see, and ears but fail to hear? And don't you remember? [19]When I broke the five loaves for the five thousand, how many basketfuls of pieces did you pick up?"

"Twelve," they replied.

[20]"And when I broke the seven loaves for the four thousand, how many basketfuls of pieces did you pick up?"

They answered, "Seven."

[21]He said to them, "Do you still not understand?"

The Healing of a Blind Man at Bethsaida

[22]They came to Bethsaida, and some people brought a blind man and begged Jesus to touch him. [23]He took the blind man by the hand and led him outside the village. When he had spit on the man's eyes and put his hands on him, Jesus asked, "Do you see anything?"

[24]He looked up and said, "I see people; they look like trees walking around."

[25]Once more Jesus put his hands on the man's eyes. Then his eyes were opened, his sight was restored, and he saw everything clearly. [26]Jesus sent him home, saying, "Don't go into the village.[a]"

Peter's Confession of Christ

[27]Jesus and his disciples went on to the villages around Caesarea Philippi. On the way he asked them, "Who do people say I am?"

[28]They replied, "Some say John the Baptist; others say Elijah; and still others, one of the prophets[D]."

[29]"But what about you?" he asked. "Who do you say I am?"

Peter answered, "You are the Christ.[b]"

[30]Jesus warned them not to tell anyone about him.

Jesus Predicts His Death

[31]He then began to teach them that the Son of Man[D] must suffer many things and be rejected by the elders, chief priests[D] and teachers of the law, and that he must be killed and after three days rise again. [32]He spoke plainly about this, and Peter took him aside and began to rebuke him.

[33]But when Jesus turned and looked at his disciples, he rebuked Peter. "Get behind me, Satan!" he said. "You

---

[a]26 Some manuscripts *Don't go and tell anyone in the village*
[b]29 Or *Messiah.* "The Christ" (Greek) and "the Messiah" (Hebrew) both mean "the Anointed One."

do not have in mind the things of God, but the things of men."

34Then he called the crowd to him along with his disciplesᴰ and said: "If anyone would come after me, he must deny himself and take up his cross and follow me. **35**For whoever wants to save his lifeᵃ will lose it, but whoever loses his life for me and for the gospelᴰ will save it. **36**What good is it for a man to gain the whole world, yet forfeit his soulᴰ? **37**Or what can a man give in exchange for his soul? **38**If anyone is ashamed of me and my words in this adulterous and sinful generation, the Son of Manᴰ will be ashamed of him when he comes in his Father's gloryᴰ with the holy angels."

9 And he said to them, "I tell you the truth, some who are standing here will not taste deathᴰ before they see the kingdom of Godᴰ come with power."

The Transfiguration

2After six days Jesus took Peter, James and John with him and led them up a high mountain, where they were all alone. There he was transfigured before them. **3**His clothes became dazzling white, whiter than anyone in the world could bleach them. **4**And there appeared before them Elijah and Moses, who were talking with Jesus.

5Peter said to Jesus, "Rabbiᴰ, it is good for us to be here. Let us put up three shelters—one for you, one for Moses and one for Elijah." **6**(He did not know what to say, they were so frightened.)

7Then a cloud appeared and enveloped them, and a voice came from the cloud: "This is my Son, whom I love. Listen to him!"

8Suddenly, when they looked around, they no longer saw anyone with them except Jesus.

9As they were coming down the mountain, Jesus gave them orders not to tell anyone what they had seen until the Son of Man had risen from the dead. **10**They kept the matter to themselves, discussing what "rising from the dead" meant.

11And they asked him, "Why do the teachers of the law say that Elijah must come first?"

12Jesus replied, "To be sure, Elijah does come first, and restores all things. Why then is it written that the Son of Man must suffer much and be rejected? **13**But I tell you, Elijah has come, and they have done to him everything they wished, just as it is written about him."

The Healing of a Boy With an Evil Spirit

14When they came to the other disciples, they saw a large crowd around them and the teachers of the law arguing with them. **15**As soon as all the people saw Jesus, they were overwhelmed with wonder and ran to greet him.

16"What are you arguing with them about?" he asked.

17A man in the crowd answered, "Teacher, I brought you my son, who is possessed by a spirit that has robbed him of speech. **18**Whenever it seizes him, it throws him to the ground. He foams at the mouth, gnashes his teeth and becomes rigid. I asked your disciples to drive out the spirit, but they could not."

19"O unbelieving generation," Jesus replied, "how long shall I stay with you? How long shall I put up with you? Bring the boy to me."

ᵃ35 The Greek word means either *life* or *soul*; also in verse 36.

world. Peter scolded Jesus, thinking he knew better than Christ what was good for him and the others. When Jesus called Peter *Satan*, he was identifying the source of Peter's false assumptions, rather than labeling Peter as the devil himself. In another sense, Peter's objection to the cross was a temptation for Jesus, who, humanly speaking, would rather not have faced that terrible agony. Jesus knew all temptation ultimately comes from Satan, even if it's communicated by a close friend.

Why is self-denial a prerequisite to being a Christian? (8:34)

The kingdom of heaven belongs to those who are *poor in spirit* (5:3)—those who recognize their spiritual poverty and see their need for God's help. We must say no to any selfishness or unhealthy pride that could inhibit the genuine humility and faith God desires (James 4:6–10; 1 Peter 5:6). Without denying our self-worth, Jesus asks us to deny our self-centeredness so that his priorities become ours.

What does it mean to take up a cross? (8:34)

As a means of inflicting the ultimate punishment, the Romans required a criminal to carry his own cross to the place of execution. The prisoner was shamed and humiliated. Jesus used this powerful image, hated as it was by the people, to illustrate the price of following him as a disciple. It symbolizes the suffering a person may have to endure who chooses to put Christ and his kingdom first.

Why did Jesus' appearance change? (9:2–3)

Jesus had already told the disciples who he was; now God verified it. For the disciples' benefit and not his own, Jesus took on incredible brilliance, Moses and Elijah appeared and God himself spoke. The cloud that surrounded them signified that they were in the presence of the Lord. The message was clear: Jesus is the Messiah, the Son of God.

SCRIPTURE LINK (9:2–8)

Luke tells about Jesus' transfiguration in Luke 9:28–36.

SCRIPTURE LINK (9:2–13)

Check out Matt. 17:1–13 for another account of the transfiguration of Jesus and for Jesus' words about Elijah.

How did they recognize Moses and Elijah? (9:4)

The Bible doesn't tell us. If this was a vision, God could also have given them divine insight to recognize Moses and Elijah.

What does Elijah restore? (9:12)

The final words of the Old Testament (Mal. 4:5–6) predict that, before God judges the world, a man like Elijah the prophet will appear with a dramatic ministry of reconciliation. As people are reunited to the Lord, family relationships will be healed as well. Jesus identifies this person as John the Baptist, who prepared the people for the life and ministry of Jesus (Luke 1:17).

SCRIPTURE LINK (9:14–28,30–32)

Matthew and Luke also report Jesus' healing of the boy with an evil spirit. See Matt. 17:14–19,22–23 and Luke 9:37–45.

Are evil spirits the cause of convulsions? (9:18)

They may be the cause of some convulsions. Passages like this indicate that sometimes possession manifests itself in visible physical signs. But this is not automatically the case; physical causes may also lie behind such symptoms.

What does welcoming a child have to do with spiritual greatness? (9:33–37)

People often ignore those who have no influence and play up to those who do. We rub shoulders with the great in order to boost our own egos and status in the eyes of others. Jesus calls for us to humble ourselves. We should care nothing about the world's status symbols because the true way to greatness is humility (1 Peter 5:5–6). One sign of this humility is to welcome those the world would consider insignificant.

SCRIPTURE LINK (9:33–37)

Both Matt. 18:1–5 and Luke 9:46–48 cover the disciples' question of who is the greatest.

SCRIPTURE LINK (9:38–40)

Luke relates Jesus' teaching that whoever is not against us is for us in Luke 9:49–50.

Is Jesus suggesting amputation? (9:43–47)

No one should take these phrases literally, nor should we ignore them. Jesus is using overstatement, a figure of speech called *hyperbole*, to make a point. We need to get rid of whatever harms us spiritually. If something is hindering our intimate relationship with God, we need to get rid of it. Pornography, bad habits, illicit relationships and many other self-destructive behaviors fall into this category.

---

²⁰So they brought him. When the spirit saw Jesus, it immediately threw the boy into a convulsion. He fell to the ground and rolled around, foaming at the mouth.

²¹Jesus asked the boy's father, "How long has he been like this?"

"From childhood," he answered. ²²"It has often thrown him into fire or water to kill him. But if you can do anything, take pity on us and help us."

²³" 'If you can'?" said Jesus. "Everything is possible for him who believes."

²⁴Immediately the boy's father exclaimed, "I do believe; help me overcome my unbelief!"

²⁵When Jesus saw that a crowd was running to the scene, he rebuked the evil*ᵃ* spirit. "You deaf and mute spirit," he said, "I command you, come out of him and never enter him again."

²⁶The spirit shrieked, convulsed him violently and came out. The boy looked so much like a corpse that many said, "He's dead." ²⁷But Jesus took him by the hand and lifted him to his feet, and he stood up.

²⁸After Jesus had gone indoors, his disciples*ᴰ* asked him privately, "Why couldn't we drive it out?"

²⁹He replied, "This kind can come out only by prayer.*ᵇ*"

³⁰They left that place and passed through Galilee. Jesus did not want anyone to know where they were, ³¹because he was teaching his disciples. He said to them, "The Son of Man*ᴰ* is going to be betrayed into the hands of men. They will kill him, and after three days he will rise." ³²But they did not understand what he meant and were afraid to ask him about it.

Who Is the Greatest?

³³They came to Capernaum. When he was in the house, he asked them, "What were you arguing about on the road?" ³⁴But they kept quiet because on the way they had argued about who was the greatest.

³⁵Sitting down, Jesus called the Twelve and said, "If anyone wants to be first, he must be the very last, and the servant of all."

³⁶He took a little child and had him stand among them. Taking him in his arms, he said to them, ³⁷"Whoever welcomes one of these little children in my name welcomes me; and whoever welcomes me does not welcome me but the one who sent me."

Whoever Is Not Against Us Is for Us

³⁸"Teacher," said John, "we saw a man driving out demons in your name and we told him to stop, because he was not one of us."

³⁹"Do not stop him," Jesus said. "No one who does a miracle in my name can in the next moment say anything bad about me, ⁴⁰for whoever is not against us is for us. ⁴¹I tell you the truth, anyone who gives you a cup of water in my name because you belong to Christ will certainly not lose his reward.

Causing to Sin

⁴²"And if anyone causes one of these little ones who believe in me to sin, it would be better for him to be thrown into the sea with a large millstone*ᴰ* tied around his neck. ⁴³If your hand causes you to sin, cut it off. It is better for

---

*ᵃ*25 Greek *unclean*   *ᵇ*29 Some manuscripts *prayer and fasting*

you to enter life maimed than with two hands to go into hell[D], where the fire never goes out.[a] **45**And if your foot causes you to sin, cut it off. It is better for you to enter life crippled than to have two feet and be thrown into hell.[b] **47**And if your eye causes you to sin, pluck it out. It is better for you to enter the kingdom of God[D] with one eye than to have two eyes and be thrown into hell, **48**where

> " 'their worm does not die,
>   and the fire is not quenched.'[c]

49Everyone will be salted with fire.

50"Salt is good, but if it loses its saltiness, how can you make it salty again? Have salt in yourselves, and be at peace[D] with each other."

Divorce

10 Jesus then left that place and went into the region of Judea and across the Jordan. Again crowds of people came to him, and as was his custom, he taught them.

2Some Pharisees[D] came and tested him by asking, "Is it lawful for a man to divorce his wife?"

3"What did Moses command you?" he replied.

4They said, "Moses permitted a man to write a certificate of divorce and send her away."

5"It was because your hearts were hard that Moses wrote you this law," Jesus replied. **6**"But at the beginning of creation God 'made them male and female.'[d] **7**For this reason a man will leave his father and mother and be united to his wife,[e] **8**and the two will become one flesh.'[f] So they are no longer two, but one. **9**Therefore what God has joined together, let man not separate."

10When they were in the house again, the disciples[D] asked Jesus about this. **11**He answered, "Anyone who divorces his wife and marries another woman commits adultery against her. **12**And if she divorces her husband and marries another man, she commits adultery."

The Little Children and Jesus

13People were bringing little children to Jesus to have him touch them, but the disciples rebuked them. **14**When Jesus saw this, he was indignant. He said to them, "Let the little children come to me, and do not hinder them, for the kingdom of God belongs to such as these. **15**I tell you the truth, anyone who will not receive the kingdom of God like a little child will never enter it." **16**And he took the children in his arms, put his hands on them and blessed them.

The Rich Young Man

17As Jesus started on his way, a man ran up to him and fell on his knees before him. "Good teacher," he asked, "what must I do to inherit eternal life?"

18"Why do you call me good?" Jesus answered. "No one is good—except God alone. **19**You know the commandments: 'Do not murder, do not commit adultery, do not

---

Is divorce always wrong? (10:1–12)
Women in the days of Jesus had little legal protection. They could be divorced simply for displeasing their husbands. Jesus teaches that divorce is contrary to the will of God and it's his intention that marriages last a lifetime. This is not the Bible's last word on divorce, however. Jesus acknowledges that in the case of adultery, divorce may be a sad necessity when one partner refuses to stop his or her unfaithfulness. Later, Paul suggests another such situation, when a believer is deserted by an unbelieving spouse (1 Cor. 7:15).

SCRIPTURE LINK (10:1–12)
Jesus' teaching on divorce can also be found in Matt. 19:1–9.

In what sense do two become one in marriage? (10:8)
God designed marriage as a living illustration of harmony and interdependence. *One flesh* underscores the sexual union, but the marriage bond also signifies a profound spiritual merger as two individuals blend their time, resources, emotions and goals. Just as Christ binds together many individuals with unique personalities and gifts (1 Cor. 12:12–13), marriage combines two persons in a common bond of committed and lasting faithfulness (Eph. 5:21–33).

Why were the disciples so upset? (10:13)
No doubt the disciples meant well. Jesus was under great pressure from the constant crowds and a demanding schedule that sometimes left no time even to eat. Like a receptionist for a busy executive, the disciples apparently thought their role was to protect the Lord from their idea of annoying interruptions and petty distractions. Jesus, however, always had time for children, seeing them as models of innocence, humility and trust.

SCRIPTURE LINK (10:13–16)
Matthew tells about Jesus and the children in Matt. 19:13–15. Luke covers it in Luke 18:15–17.

Should adults act like children? (10:14–15)
Jesus doesn't call people to childish behavior but to childlike faith. The qualities of humility, trust, receptivity and a lack of self-sufficiency all characterize the person of faith. The kingdom of God is not earned by human effort, but received in childlike trust as a gift of the mercy and grace of God.

SCRIPTURE LINK (10:17–31)
Jesus' story of the rich young man is recounted by Matthew in Matt. 19:16–30 and by Luke in Luke 18:18–30.

Did Jesus say salvation comes by obeying the commandments? (10:19)
No. Jesus' response focused on obedience to God's law because this provided a familiar starting point for all who lived under God's old covenant. This young man was badly mistaken, however, if he assumed eternal life could be gained by his superior ethical performance, for none of us are good enough to earn salvation by our own good works (Gal. 3:23–29).

---

[a]43 Some manuscripts *out,* *44where / " 'their worm does not die, / and the fire is not quenched.'* [b]45 Some manuscripts *hell, 46where /* " 'their worm does not die, / and the fire is not quenched.' [c]48 Isaiah 66:24   [d]6 Gen. 1:27   [e]7 Some early manuscripts do not have *and be united to his wife.* [f]8 Gen. 2:24

steal, do not give false testimony, do not defraud, honor your father and mother.'ᵃ"

²⁰"Teacher," he declared, "all these I have kept since I was a boy."

²¹Jesus looked at him and loved him. "One thing you lack," he said. "Go, sell everything you have and give to the poor, and you will have treasure in heaven. Then come, follow me."

²²At this the man's face fell. He went away sad, because he had great wealth.

²³Jesus looked around and said to his disciplesᴰ, "How hard it is for the rich to enter the kingdom of God!"

²⁴The disciples were amazed at his words. But Jesus said again, "Children, how hard it isᵇ to enter the kingdom of Godᴰ! ²⁵It is easier for a camel to go through the eye of a needle than for a rich man to enter the kingdom of God."

²⁶The disciples were even more amazed, and said to each other, "Who then can be saved?"

²⁷Jesus looked at them and said, "With man this is impossible, but not with God; all things are possible with God."

²⁸Peter said to him, "We have left everything to follow you!"

²⁹"I tell you the truth," Jesus replied, "no one who has left home or brothers or sisters or mother or father or children or fields for me and the gospelᴰ ³⁰will fail to receive a hundred times as much in this present age (homes, brothers, sisters, mothers, children and fields—and with them, persecutions) and in the age to come, eternal lifeᴰ. ³¹But many who are first will be last, and the last first."

Jesus Again Predicts His Death

³²They were on their way up to Jerusalemᴰ, with Jesus leading the way, and the disciples were astonished, while those who followed were afraid. Again he took the Twelve aside and told them what was going to happen to him. ³³"We are going up to Jerusalem," he said, "and the Son of Manᴰ will be betrayed to the chief priestsᴰ and teachers of the law. They will condemn him to deathᴰ and will hand him over to the Gentilesᴰ, ³⁴who will mock him and spit on him, flog him and kill him. Three days later he will rise."

The Request of James and John

³⁵Then James and John, the sons of Zebedee, came to him. "Teacher," they said, "we want you to do for us whatever we ask."

³⁶"What do you want me to do for you?" he asked.

³⁷They replied, "Let one of us sit at your right and the other at your left in your gloryᴰ."

³⁸"You don't know what you are asking," Jesus said. "Can you drink the cup I drink or be baptized with the baptismᴰ I am baptized with?"

³⁹"We can," they answered.

Jesus said to them, "You will drink the cup I drink and be baptized with the baptism I am baptized with, ⁴⁰but to sit at my right or left is not for me to grant. These places belong to those for whom they have been prepared."

⁴¹When the ten heard about this, they became indig-

Should Christians sell their possessions and give to the poor? (10:21)

This young man was overly attached to his possessions, so Jesus challenged him to sacrifice in the one crucial area that kept him from following Christ. Yet there is great value in living a simple and contented life and at times we do need to sell or share our belongings in order to help others.

Camel . . . through the eye of a needle (10:25)

Jesus' analogy painted an amusing picture of something impossible or absurd by human standards. The disciples probably saw material wealth as a certain sign of God's favor—but Jesus recognized how the love of money creates temptations many cannot resist. No sinner, whether rich or poor, *deserves* to enter the kingdom of heaven. But God's grace can overcome seemingly impossible obstacles. Also see *What did Jesus mean by a camel going through the eye of a needle?* (Luke 18:25).

Does Christ want his followers to abandon their families? (10:29)

As he did in 9:43–47, Jesus uses overstatement to make his point. The love Jesus asks of his followers cannot compare to other earthly relationships (see Matt. 10:37,39; Luke 14:26–33). It takes first priority. Yet, putting Christ at the center of our lives does not compromise our other relationships; it enhances them. The Bible clearly teaches us to love our families even as Christ loves the church. The most solid foundation a family can establish is putting Christ first in everything.

Are we promised a return on our life investment? (10:30)

We aren't guaranteed prosperity, nor do we gain a hefty spiritual stock portfolio with guaranteed returns when we serve God. Realistically, there will be problems and perhaps a high price to pay. No one follows Jesus without experiencing persecutions and loss. But we are promised a priceless relationship, better than the love of a family, if we choose to follow him.

SCRIPTURE LINK (10:32–34)

Jesus' prediction of his death can also be found in Matt. 20:17–19 and Luke 18:31–33. In addition, the writers of the Old Testament foretold these events many years earlier. For Christ's betrayal, see Psalm 41:5–9. The crucifixion is foretold in Psalm 22:16–18 and Isaiah 53:4–7. The resurrection is foretold in Psalm 16:10. In Matt. 20:20–28, Matthew tells how the mother of James and John came to request positions of honor for her sons.

ᵃ19 Exodus 20:12-16; Deut. 5:16-20   ᵇ24 Some manuscripts *is for those who trust in riches*

nant with James and John. **42**Jesus called them together and said, "You know that those who are regarded as rulers of the Gentiles^D lord it over them, and their high officials exercise authority over them. **43**Not so with you. Instead, whoever wants to become great among you must be your servant, **44**and whoever wants to be first must be slave of all. **45**For even the Son of Man^D did not come to be served, but to serve, and to give his life as a ransom for many."

Blind Bartimaeus Receives His Sight

46Then they came to Jericho^D. As Jesus and his disciples^D, together with a large crowd, were leaving the city, a blind man, Bartimaeus (that is, the Son of Timaeus), was sitting by the roadside begging. **47**When he heard that it was Jesus of Nazareth, he began to shout, "Jesus, Son of David, have mercy^D on me!"

48Many rebuked him and told him to be quiet, but he shouted all the more, "Son of David, have mercy on me!"

49Jesus stopped and said, "Call him."

So they called to the blind man, "Cheer up! On your feet! He's calling you." **50**Throwing his cloak aside, he jumped to his feet and came to Jesus.

51"What do you want me to do for you?" Jesus asked him.

The blind man said, "Rabbi^D, I want to see."

52"Go," said Jesus, "your faith has healed you." Immediately he received his sight and followed Jesus along the road.

The Triumphal Entry

11 As they approached Jerusalem^D and came to Bethphage and Bethany at the Mount of Olives, Jesus sent two of his disciples, **2**saying to them, "Go to the village ahead of you, and just as you enter it, you will find a colt tied there, which no one has ever ridden. Untie it and bring it here. **3**If anyone asks you, 'Why are you doing this?' tell him, 'The Lord needs it and will send it back here shortly.'"

4They went and found a colt outside in the street, tied at a doorway. As they untied it, **5**some people standing there asked, "What are you doing, untying that colt?" **6**They answered as Jesus had told them to, and the people let them go. **7**When they brought the colt to Jesus and threw their cloaks over it, he sat on it. **8**Many people spread their cloaks on the road, while others spread branches they had cut in the fields. **9**Those who went ahead and those who followed shouted,

"Hosanna!^a"

"Blessed is he who comes in the name of the Lord!"^b

10"Blessed is the coming kingdom of our father David!"

"Hosanna in the highest!"

11Jesus entered Jerusalem and went to the temple. He looked around at everything, but since it was already late, he went out to Bethany with the Twelve.

---

^a9 A Hebrew expression meaning "Save!" which became an exclamation of praise; also in verse 10   ^b9 Psalm 118:25,26

Is Jesus advocating slavery? (10:43–45)

Jesus isn't endorsing the institution of slavery, but he uses it as an object lesson in humility. His own willingness to submit to the Father's will, even to the point of death, is an example of servanthood lived out to its fullest. It is an example that he asks us to imitate.

SCRIPTURE LINK (10:46–52)

Matthew describes how Bartimaeus received his sight in Matt. 20:29–34. Luke gives an account in Luke 18:35–43.

Why do Mark and Luke mention one man while Matthew mentions two? (10:46; see Matt. 20:30; Luke 18:35)

This is not a contradiction. By saying Jesus healed a blind man, Mark and Luke did not insist that Jesus healed *only* one. It's likely they just focused their account on the one blind man (named Bartimaeus) who was the more prominent of the two.

Why did the blind man call Jesus the Son of David? (10:47)

The blind man recognized Jesus as the prophesied Messiah. It is ironic that a man without physical sight was able to see things that others had missed.

SCRIPTURE LINK (11:1–10)

Check out Matt. 21:1–9 and Luke 19:29–38 for other accounts of Jesus' triumphal entry into Jerusalem.

Did Jesus borrow the colt without permission? (11:3)

We don't know for sure. It may have been prearranged (as perhaps was the case in 14:14 when he secured the room). The disciples, however, knew Jesus was the Master of all creation and had an owner's authority to use whatever he wished. Also see *Why did Jesus "borrow" without asking?* (Matt. 21:2–6).

Why did Jesus participate in this procession? (11:7–10)

Jesus, at the climax of his ministry, was making a statement. This was an object lesson that proclaimed who he was—the Son of David, the King of kings, the one who conquered sin and sickness. Conquering generals at that time were given a "triumphal entry" upon their return to their home city. Palm branches were often waved during times of celebration and victory (Lev. 23:40; Psalm 118:25–27). The procession caused the city, crowded with people for Passover, to consider Jesus' claims. Also see *Why carpet the road with cloaks?* (Luke 19:36).

SCRIPTURE LINK (11:7–10)

John tells how Jesus rode into Jerusalem on a colt in John 12:12–15.

Why put coats and branches on the roadway? (11:8)

This was a customary way for a crowd to welcome a triumphant king returning home in victory; see 2 Kings 9:13. This crowd was primarily looking for a political Messiah to lead them to independence from the Roman empire. They did not understand that Christ's mission was to free them from the tyranny of sin rather than that of political domination.

SCRIPTURE LINK (11:12–14)

Matthew also reports that Jesus cursed a fig tree. See Matt. 21:18–22.

Why was Jesus angry at a tree? (11:13–14)

The problem may have been that the fig tree had leaves but no fruit, like a person who promises to do good but does not. (Though it was not the season for figs, neither was it the season for leaves. Since this tree had produced its leaves, one could expect that it had also produced figs.) Jesus' anger can be viewed as a vivid object lesson. Fig trees often stood for the nation of Israel (Micah 7:1–6; Jer. 8:13). So the *story* of the unproductive fig tree (Luke 13:6–9) and the *incident* both convey the same lesson: Israel will be judged for its spiritual unfruitfulness unless it repents and acknowledges Jesus as the true Messiah.

SCRIPTURE LINK (11:15–18)

All of the Gospel writers give details of Jesus' clearing the temple. See Matt. 21:12–16; Luke 19:45–47 and John 2:13–16.

How had the temple become *a den of robbers*? (11:17)

Merchants were selling sacrificial animals and exchanging currency at exorbitant prices. By turning the court of the Gentiles into a shopping mall, they prevented anyone from using this part of the temple for prayer, as God had intended (Jer. 7:11).

SCRIPTURE LINK (11:20–24)

Matthew tells about the withering of the fig tree in Matt. 21:19–22.

How much can faith do? (11:22–24)

Faith in God is all-powerful because God is omnipotent. The one who prays correctly will leave room for God's will to overrule any request (Matt. 6:10). In this case, Jesus may have had the Mount of Olives in mind. Christ's return will upset the mountain, splitting it in two when he descends from heaven. See *Will the Mount of Olives be split literally in two?* (Zech. 14:4).

SCRIPTURE LINK (11:27–33)

In Matt. 21:23–27, Matthew tells about the religious leaders questioning Jesus' authority. Luke covers it in Luke 20:1–8.

Jesus Clears the Temple

¹²The next day as they were leaving Bethany, Jesus was hungry. ¹³Seeing in the distance a fig tree in leaf, he went to find out if it had any fruit. When he reached it, he found nothing but leaves, because it was not the season for figs. ¹⁴Then he said to the tree, "May no one ever eat fruit from you again." And his disciples[D] heard him say it.

¹⁵On reaching Jerusalem,[D] Jesus entered the temple area and began driving out those who were buying and selling there. He overturned the tables of the money changers and the benches of those selling doves, ¹⁶and would not allow anyone to carry merchandise through the temple courts. ¹⁷And as he taught them, he said, "Is it not written:

" 'My house will be called
        a house of prayer for all nations'[a]?

But you have made it 'a den of robbers.'[b]"

¹⁸The chief priests[D] and the teachers of the law heard this and began looking for a way to kill him, for they feared him, because the whole crowd was amazed at his teaching.

¹⁹When evening came, they[c] went out of the city.

The Withered Fig Tree

²⁰In the morning, as they went along, they saw the fig tree withered from the roots. ²¹Peter remembered and said to Jesus, "Rabbi,[D] look! The fig tree you cursed has withered!"

²²"Have[d] faith in God," Jesus answered. ²³"I tell you the truth, if anyone says to this mountain, 'Go, throw yourself into the sea,' and does not doubt in his heart but believes that what he says will happen, it will be done for him. ²⁴Therefore I tell you, whatever you ask for in prayer, believe that you have received it, and it will be yours. ²⁵And when you stand praying, if you hold anything against anyone, forgive him, so that your Father in heaven may forgive you your sins.[e]"

The Authority of Jesus Questioned

²⁷They arrived again in Jerusalem, and while Jesus was walking in the temple courts, the chief priests, the teachers of the law and the elders came to him. ²⁸"By what authority are you doing these things?" they asked. "And who gave you authority to do this?"

²⁹Jesus replied, "I will ask you one question. Answer me, and I will tell you by what authority I am doing these things. ³⁰John's baptism[D]—was it from heaven, or from men? Tell me!"

³¹They discussed it among themselves and said, "If we say, 'From heaven,' he will ask, 'Then why didn't you believe him?' ³²But if we say, 'From men' . . . ." (They feared the people, for everyone held that John really was a prophet[D].)

³³So they answered Jesus, "We don't know."

Jesus said, "Neither will I tell you by what authority I am doing these things."

---

[a]17 Isaiah 56:7   [b]17 Jer. 7:11   [c]19 Some early manuscripts *he*
[d]22 Some early manuscripts *If you have*   [e]25 Some manuscripts *sins.* [26]*But if you do not forgive, neither will your Father who is in heaven forgive your sins.*

The Parable of the Tenants

12 He then began to speak to them in parables^D: "A man planted a vineyard. He put a wall around it, dug a pit for the winepress^D and built a watchtower^D. Then he rented the vineyard to some farmers and went away on a journey. **2**At harvest time he sent a servant to the tenants to collect from them some of the fruit of the vineyard. **3**But they seized him, beat him and sent him away empty-handed. **4**Then he sent another servant to them; they struck this man on the head and treated him shamefully. **5**He sent still another, and that one they killed. He sent many others; some of them they beat, others they killed.

6"He had one left to send, a son, whom he loved. He sent him last of all, saying, 'They will respect my son.'

7"But the tenants said to one another, 'This is the heir. Come, let's kill him, and the inheritance will be ours.' **8**So they took him and killed him, and threw him out of the vineyard.

9"What then will the owner of the vineyard do? He will come and kill those tenants and give the vineyard to others. **10**Haven't you read this scripture:

" 'The stone the builders rejected
　　has become the capstone^D*a*;
11the Lord has done this,
　　and it is marvelous in our eyes'*b*?"

12Then they looked for a way to arrest him because they knew he had spoken the parable against them. But they were afraid of the crowd; so they left him and went away.

Paying Taxes to Caesar

13Later they sent some of the Pharisees^D and Herodians^D to Jesus to catch him in his words. **14**They came to him and said, "Teacher, we know you are a man of integrity. You aren't swayed by men, because you pay no attention to who they are; but you teach the way of God in accordance with the truth. Is it right to pay taxes to Caesar or not? **15**Should we pay or shouldn't we?"

But Jesus knew their hypocrisy. "Why are you trying to trap me?" he asked. "Bring me a denarius and let me look at it." **16**They brought the coin, and he asked them, "Whose portrait is this? And whose inscription?"

"Caesar's," they replied.

17Then Jesus said to them, "Give to Caesar what is Caesar's and to God what is God's."

And they were amazed at him.

Marriage at the Resurrection

18Then the Sadducees^D, who say there is no resurrection^D, came to him with a question. **19**"Teacher," they said, "Moses wrote for us that if a man's brother dies and leaves a wife but no children, the man must marry the widow and have children for his brother. **20**Now there were seven brothers. The first one married and died without leaving any children. **21**The second one married the widow, but he also died, leaving no child. It was the same with the third. **22**In fact, none of the seven left any children. Last of all, the woman died too. **23**At the resurrec-

*a*10 Or *cornerstone*　　*b*11 Psalm 118:22,23

Parables (12:1)
See article: *Why did Jesus speak in parables?* (Matt. 13:11–13).

SCRIPTURE LINK (12:1–12)
To read Matthew's and Luke's accounts of the parable of the tenants, turn to Matt. 21:33–46 and Luke 20:9–19.

Capstone (12:10)
Literally "head of the corner." Used to describe either the bottom corner of the building (a foundation stone) or the keystone of an archway. It can either cause a person to stumble, or it can fall on someone (Matt. 21:44). Either way, the stone is essential for holding the building together.

SCRIPTURE LINK (12:13–17)
You'll also find Jesus' teaching on paying taxes in Matt. 22:15–22 and Luke 20:20–26.

Did Jesus support paying taxes? (12:16–17)
The Pharisees resented the idea of paying taxes to Rome; the Herodians supported it. These two opposing groups joined forces to try to make Jesus say something politically offensive. But neither side could refute his answer: acknowledge God's rule, but recognize human government as well (Romans 13:1–7). If legitimate taxes are owed, pay them. See *When is it right to disobey authority?* (Acts 4:19) for a note about what to do if God and government clash.

SCRIPTURE LINK (12:18–27)
Jesus' teaching on marriage at the resurrection can also be found in Matt. 22:23–33 and Luke 20:27–38.

Did Jews still marry their brothers' widows? (12:19)
Some Jews probably still practiced this law. See *Why was a man required to marry his brother's widow?* (Deut. 25:5). Yet polygamy had not been practiced for nearly five centuries, since the end of the exile in Babylon. The Sadducees' interest was not polygamy, however. They simply invented a hypothetical case in an attempt to lampoon the idea of resurrection.

tion[D][a] whose wife will she be, since the seven were married to her?"

24Jesus replied, "Are you not in error because you do not know the Scriptures or the power of God? **25**When the dead rise, they will neither marry nor be given in marriage; they will be like the angels in heaven. **26**Now about the dead rising—have you not read in the book of Moses, in the account of the bush, how God said to him, 'I am the God of Abraham, the God of Isaac, and the God of Jacob'[b]? **27**He is not the God of the dead, but of the living. You are badly mistaken!"

The Greatest Commandment

28One of the teachers of the law came and heard them debating. Noticing that Jesus had given them a good answer, he asked him, "Of all the commandments, which is the most important?"

29"The most important one," answered Jesus, "is this: 'Hear, O Israel, the Lord our God, the Lord is one.[c] **30**Love the Lord your God with all your heart and with all your soul[D] and with all your mind and with all your strength.'[d] **31**The second is this: 'Love your neighbor as yourself.'[e] There is no commandment greater than these."

32"Well said, teacher," the man replied. "You are right in saying that God is one and there is no other but him. **33**To love him with all your heart, with all your understanding and with all your strength, and to love your neighbor as yourself is more important than all burnt offerings[D] and sacrifices[D]."

34When Jesus saw that he had answered wisely, he said to him, "You are not far from the kingdom of God[D]." And from then on no one dared ask him any more questions.

Whose Son Is the Christ?

35While Jesus was teaching in the temple courts, he asked, "How is it that the teachers of the law say that the Christ[f] is the son of David? **36**David himself, speaking by the Holy Spirit, declared:

" 'The Lord said to my Lord:
"Sit at my right hand
until I put your enemies
under your feet." '[g]

37David himself calls him 'Lord.' How then can he be his son?"

The large crowd listened to him with delight.

38As he taught, Jesus said, "Watch out for the teachers of the law. They like to walk around in flowing robes and be greeted in the marketplaces, **39**and have the most important seats in the synagogues and the places of honor at banquets. **40**They devour widows' houses and for a show make lengthy prayers. Such men will be punished most severely."

The Widow's Offering

41Jesus sat down opposite the place where the offerings were put and watched the crowd putting their money into the temple treasury. Many rich people threw in large

Is heaven sexless? (12:25)
We really don't know. The Sadducees were attempting to show that the concept of the resurrection was absurd. Jesus' point was the reality of resurrection, not the lifestyle of heaven. It would appear, however, that we will not have sexual relations in heaven. Still, Paul says that heaven's pleasures will be infinitely better than the best this life offers (1 Cor. 15:35–57). See article: *What do we have to look forward to?* (1 Cor. 15:35–57).

What kind of logic did Jesus use? (12:26)
How could Jesus use a title for God to prove that there is a resurrection? We might think the phrase he used could have meant, "I *am* the God of the one who *was* Abraham." But most Jews didn't reason that way. To speak of "Yahweh (I AM), the God of Abraham," was to imply not only a past relationship with Abraham but also a continuing relationship in the present. Jesus was saying, in effect, "If you believe there is a God, then, since he *is* (not *was*) Abraham's God, you should believe Abraham still exists." Jesus could have quoted more obvious Old Testament texts to prove the resurrection. But because the Sadducees did not base their doctrine on any Old Testament books except the five books of Moses (Genesis—Deuteronomy), Jesus made his case by quoting from one of those books (Exodus 3:6).

SCRIPTURE LINK (12:28–34)
Jesus can also be found giving the greatest commandment in Matt. 22:34–40.

SCRIPTURE LINK (12:35–37)
In Matt. 22:41–46, Matthew tells about Jesus addressing the question of whose Son is the Christ. Luke covers it in Luke 20:41–44.

What clue is Jesus giving about the Messiah? (12:35–37)
Jesus cited Psalm 110:1, which speaks of two "Lords" above Israel's king. The first is clearly God (Yahweh), but who is the second? Since no person reigned over David, many first-century Jews believed this Psalm spoke of the Messiah. Jesus pointed out, then, that this Messiah had to be more than a descendant of David—the political liberator they expected. He also had to be a heavenly or supernatural being.

SCRIPTURE LINK (12:38–40)
Jesus' warning about following the ways of the teachers of the law can also be found in Matt. 23:1–7 and Luke 20:45–47.

Temple treasury (12:41)
The temple treasury was located either in the outermost court of the temple, called the court of women, or in a nearby hallway. There were seven boxes for the temple tax and six boxes for freewill offerings. The poor widow gave to the latter.

SCRIPTURE LINK (12:41–44)
Luke talks about the widow's offering in Luke 21:1–4.

[a]23 Some manuscripts *resurrection, when men rise from the dead,* [b]26 Exodus 3:6 [c]29 Or *the Lord our God is one Lord* [d]30 Deut. 6:4,5 [e]31 Lev. 19:18 [f]35 Or *Messiah* [g]36 Psalm 110:1

amounts. **42**But a poor widow came and put in two very small copper coins,*a* worth only a fraction of a penny.*b*

43Calling his disciples**D** to him, Jesus said, "I tell you the truth, this poor widow has put more into the treasury than all the others. **44**They all gave out of their wealth; but she, out of her poverty, put in everything—all she had to live on."

Signs of the End of the Age

13 As he was leaving the temple, one of his disciples said to him, "Look, Teacher! What massive stones! What magnificent buildings!"

2"Do you see all these great buildings?" replied Jesus. "Not one stone here will be left on another; every one will be thrown down."

3As Jesus was sitting on the Mount of Olives opposite the temple, Peter, James, John and Andrew asked him privately, **4**"Tell us, when will these things happen? And what will be the sign that they are all about to be fulfilled?"

5Jesus said to them: "Watch out that no one deceives you. **6**Many will come in my name, claiming, 'I am he,' and will deceive many. **7**When you hear of wars and rumors of wars, do not be alarmed. Such things must happen, but the end is still to come. **8**Nation will rise against nation, and kingdom against kingdom. There will be earthquakes in various places, and famines. These are the beginning of birth pains.

9"You must be on your guard. You will be handed over to the local councils and flogged in the synagogues. On account of me you will stand before governors and kings as witnesses to them. **10**And the gospel**D** must first be preached to all nations. **11**Whenever you are arrested and brought to trial, do not worry beforehand about what to say. Just say whatever is given you at the time, for it is not you speaking, but the Holy Spirit.

12"Brother will betray brother to death**D**, and a father his child. Children will rebel against their parents and have them put to death. **13**All men will hate you because of me, but he who stands firm to the end will be saved.

14"When you see 'the abomination**D** that causes desolation'*c* standing where it*d* does not belong—let the reader understand—then let those who are in Judea flee to the mountains. **15**Let no one on the roof of his house go down or enter the house to take anything out. **16**Let no one in the field go back to get his cloak. **17**How dreadful it will be in those days for pregnant women and nursing mothers! **18**Pray that this will not take place in winter, **19**because those will be days of distress unequaled from the beginning, when God created the world, until now—and never to be equaled again. **20**If the Lord had not cut short those days, no one would survive. But for the sake of the elect**D**, whom he has chosen, he has shortened them. **21**At that time if anyone says to you, 'Look, here is the Christ*e*!' or, 'Look, there he is!' do not believe it. **22**For false Christs and false prophets**D** will appear and perform signs and miracles to deceive the elect—if that were possible. **23**So be on your guard; I have told you everything ahead of time.

24"But in those days, following that distress,

SCRIPTURE LINK (13:1–37)
Matthew and Luke both carry Jesus' discussion of the signs of the end of the age. See Matt. 24:1–51 and Luke 21:5–36.

What was the disciples' real agenda? (13:4)
Matthew makes it clear they not only wanted to know when the temple would be destroyed, but what would be the signs of Christ's return and the end of human history (Matt. 24:3). Human nature seems to desire inside information. Jesus addressed all these questions together (13:5–37), but did not offer the definitive answer they, and Christians through the ages, have wished for.

Has this prophecy already been fulfilled? (13:5–25)
Christians disagree. Deceivers, wars, earthquakes, famine and persecution (vv. 5–13) occurred in the first generation of the church—and have recurred in most generations since. But the gospel has yet to be preached to all nations. While some prophecies have been fulfilled, such as Jerusalem's destruction at the hands of Rome in A.D. 70, their complete fulfillment awaits the final return of Christ.

What is *the abomination that causes desolation?* (13:14)
The phrase (from Daniel 9:27) refers to an act of sacrilege in the temple. One example from Jewish history occurred in 167 B.C. when an invader, Antiochus IV, slaughtered a pig (an unclean animal) on the temple altar. Jesus apparently was referring to the temple's coming destruction by the Romans, which occurred in A.D. 70. Some think 2 Thes. 2:4 and Rev. 13:5–7 teach that an antichrist will commit a similar sacrilege just before Christ returns.

Is Jesus predicting a future tribulation? (13:19)
Jesus predicts that a time of unequalled distress will occur on earth between the temple's desolation (vv. 4–18) and Christ's return (vv. 24–27). During this extended period of time, Gentiles will overrun Jerusalem. The distress, sometimes referred to as the tribulation, may become particularly intense just before Christ's return.

Is it wrong to ask for signs and miracles? (13:22)
See *What's wrong with wanting hard evidence?* (Matt. 12:39) and *Was Jesus reluctant to perform signs and wonders?* (John 4:48).

Will the sun be literally darkened? (13:24)
Since Jesus' first coming was accompanied by unusual signs on earth and in the sky (Matt. 28:2–4; Luke 2:8–14; 23:44–45), it does not seem unreasonable to believe these signs will occur literally when Jesus returns. Other passages also tell of dramatic events that will take place at the return of Christ (1 Thes. 4:16–17), including a worldwide holocaust (2 Peter 3:10–13).

---

a42 Greek *two lepta*   *b42* Greek *kodrantes*   *c14* Daniel 9:27; 11:31; 12:11   *d14* Or *he*; also in verse 29   *e21* Or *Messiah*

" 'the sun will be darkened,
and the moon will not give its light;
25the stars will fall from the sky,
and the heavenly bodies will be shaken.'ᵃ

26"At that time men will see the Son of Manᴰ coming in clouds with great power and gloryᴰ. 27And he will send his angels and gather his electᴰ from the four winds, from the ends of the earth to the ends of the heavens.

28"Now learn this lesson from the fig tree: As soon as its twigs get tender and its leaves come out, you know that summer is near. 29Even so, when you see these things happening, you know that it is near, right at the door. 30I tell you the truth, this generationᵇ will certainly not pass away until all these things have happened. 31Heaven and earth will pass away, but my words will never pass away.

The Day and Hour Unknown

32"No one knows about that day or hour, not even the angels in heaven, nor the Son, but only the Father. 33Be on guard! Be alertᶜ! You do not know when that time will come. 34It's like a man going away: He leaves his house and puts his servants in charge, each with his assigned task, and tells the one at the door to keep watch.

35"Therefore keep watch because you do not know when the owner of the house will come back—whether in the evening, or at midnight, or when the rooster crows, or at dawn. 36If he comes suddenly, do not let him find you sleeping. 37What I say to you, I say to everyone: 'Watch!' "

Jesus Anointed at Bethany

14 Now the Passover and the Feast of Unleavened Bread were only two days away, and the chief priestsᴰ and the teachers of the law were looking for some sly way to arrest Jesus and kill him. 2"But not during the Feast," they said, "or the people may riot."

3While he was in Bethany, reclining at the table in the home of a man known as Simon the Leper, a woman came with an alabaster jar of very expensive perfume, made of pure nard. She broke the jar and poured the perfume on his head.

4Some of those present were saying indignantly to one another, "Why this waste of perfume? 5It could have been sold for more than a year's wagesᵈ and the money given to the poor." And they rebuked her harshly.

6"Leave her alone," said Jesus. "Why are you bothering her? She has done a beautiful thing to me. 7The poor you will always have with you, and you can help them any time you want. But you will not always have me. 8She did what she could. She poured perfume on my body beforehand to prepare for my burial. 9I tell you the truth, wherever the gospelᴰ is preached throughout the world, what she has done will also be told, in memory of her."

10Then Judas Iscariot, one of the Twelve, went to the chief priests to betray Jesus to them. 11They were delighted to hear this and promised to give him money. So he watched for an opportunity to hand him over.

How long is a generation? (13:30)
A generation was considered to span about 40 years. But the word *generation* may also mean a race of people. Since many of the signs of Christ's coming occurred in the first century, the word may refer to the final generation alive when the last of the signs are fulfilled. Or perhaps it refers to the Jewish race itself, which has survived against all odds, and which will live to see Christ's return.

Why didn't Jesus know when he was returning? (13:32)
When Christ became human, he gave up the right to use his divine abilities for his own purposes (Phil. 2:6–8). Because Jesus submitted to the Father in everything, he left the matter of the timing of his return to the Father, too. People today who claim to know the day of Christ's return are claiming to know more than Jesus did, and are false prophets.

SCRIPTURE LINK (14:1–11)
Matthew tells about Jesus' anointing at Bethany in Matt. 26:2–16. John carries a similar account in John 12:1–8.

SCRIPTURE LINK (14:1–2,10–11)
Luke reveals the plot to arrest and kill Jesus in Luke 22:1–6.

Is this the same story as in Matthew, Luke and John? (14:3–9; see Matt. 26:6–13; Luke 7:37–38; John 12:1–8)
This story occurs in Matthew and John. The incident in Luke is an entirely different event. The point of this story is that Jesus is being prepared for his death by being anointed with perfume (a Jewish burial custom). The others present completely miss the point of this incident.

Did Jesus downplay the needs of the poor? (14:7)
No. Jesus' point is that we should never criticize generosity aimed at honoring God, regardless of how the money might otherwise have been used. No human pretext, however noble (as in caring for the poor), should be used to prevent true worship. At the same time, it's clear by his life and teaching that showing compassion toward the needy is a high priority to Jesus.

Why did Judas turn traitor? (14:10–11)
Some think he was trying to force Jesus into using his miraculous powers to overthrow the Romans. He may have become impatient with Jesus' concern for spiritual rather than political matters. Others think he simply sold out for the money. God used Judas's betrayal to make forgiveness available to anyone who would accept it, though, tragically, Judas died apparently without ever asking for it (Matt. 27:3–10).

ᵃ25 Isaiah 13:10; 34:4   ᵇ30 Or race   ᶜ33 Some manuscripts alert and pray   ᵈ5 Greek than three hundred denarii

The Lord's Supper

¹²On the first day of the Feast of Unleavened Bread, when it was customary to sacrifice[D] the Passover lamb, Jesus' disciples[D] asked him, "Where do you want us to go and make preparations for you to eat the Passover?"

¹³So he sent two of his disciples, telling them, "Go into the city, and a man carrying a jar of water will meet you. Follow him. ¹⁴Say to the owner of the house he enters, 'The Teacher asks: Where is my guest room, where I may eat the Passover with my disciples?' ¹⁵He will show you a large upper room, furnished and ready. Make preparations for us there."

¹⁶The disciples left, went into the city and found things just as Jesus had told them. So they prepared the Passover.

¹⁷When evening came, Jesus arrived with the Twelve. ¹⁸While they were reclining at the table eating, he said, "I tell you the truth, one of you will betray me—one who is eating with me."

¹⁹They were saddened, and one by one they said to him, "Surely not I?"

²⁰"It is one of the Twelve," he replied, "one who dips bread into the bowl with me. ²¹The Son of Man[D] will go just as it is written about him. But woe to that man who betrays the Son of Man! It would be better for him if he had not been born."

²²While they were eating, Jesus took bread, gave thanks and broke it, and gave it to his disciples, saying, "Take it; this is my body."

²³Then he took the cup, gave thanks and offered it to them, and they all drank from it.

²⁴"This is my blood of the[a] covenant[D], which is poured out for many," he said to them. ²⁵"I tell you the truth, I will not drink again of the fruit of the vine until that day when I drink it anew in the kingdom of God."

²⁶When they had sung a hymn, they went out to the Mount of Olives.

Jesus Predicts Peter's Denial

²⁷"You will all fall away," Jesus told them, "for it is written:

" 'I will strike the shepherd,
    and the sheep will be scattered.'[b]

²⁸But after I have risen, I will go ahead of you into Galilee."

²⁹Peter declared, "Even if all fall away, I will not."

³⁰"I tell you the truth," Jesus answered, "today—yes, tonight—before the rooster crows twice[c] you yourself will disown me three times."

³¹But Peter insisted emphatically, "Even if I have to die with you, I will never disown you." And all the others said the same.

Gethsemane

³²They went to a place called Gethsemane, and Jesus said to his disciples, "Sit here while I pray." ³³He took Peter, James and John along with him, and he began to be deeply distressed and troubled. ³⁴"My soul[D] is over-

---

*a*24 Some manuscripts *the new*   *b*27 Zech. 13:7   *c*30 Some early manuscripts do not have *twice.*

Abba (14:36)

An Aramaic word, it is a small child's way of saying "Daddy." It was an intimate word, one which Jews of that day would never dream of using toward God. Jesus astounded his listeners by claiming this kind of close relationship with his heavenly Father. Although Mark wrote his Gospel in the Greek language, the Jews spoke Aramaic. Mark quotes the Aramaic word because the Greek word for father (*Pater*) is far less personal.

Why did Jesus ask the disciples to watch and pray? (14:38)

In the loneliness that comes while awaiting death, Jesus longed for the presence of friends who would pray with him. In addition, the disciples needed to pray for their own benefit, considering their predicted denial, cowardice and abandonment of Jesus. Their boasts of allegiance (v. 31) appear pathetic in light of their behavior as the night wore on. Their failure to pray would make them an easy mark when assaulted by fear and temptation.

SCRIPTURE LINK (14:43–50)

All of the Gospel writers give details of Jesus' arrest. See Matt. 26:47–56; Luke 22:47–50 and John 18:3–11.

Why did Judas kiss Jesus? (14:45)

A kiss was a traditional greeting. A disciple would greet his teacher with a kiss on the cheek or beard to show honor and submission. The less important person initiated the kiss. This is the irony in this passage, that Judas would use something meant to give honor to instead betray.

Who was the naked young man? (14:51–52)

Nobody knows for sure. Early in church history it was suggested that this was Mark, the Gospel writer himself. Perhaps he—in his night clothes—had followed the disciples from his home where Jesus and the Twelve had earlier celebrated the Last Supper (inferred from Acts 12:12). He may be including a bit of his own biography, however shameful, right in the middle of this dramatic story. Whether or not this was Mark, the story documents how Jesus' followers completely abandoned him.

SCRIPTURE LINK (14:53–65)

You can also read about Jesus' trial before the Sanhedrin in Matt. 26:57–68 and John 18:12,13,19–24.

Why did Jesus refuse to answer the false charges? (14:61)

These same men had resisted and twisted Jesus' words before. Why should he speak to them now? This was a biased, hostile trial—not an impartial hearing. The unfair and contradictory charges did not deserve a response. Jesus did answer, however, when the high priest pressured him further and charged him under oath to repeat the claims Jesus had made throughout his ministry (Matt. 26:63–64).

SCRIPTURE LINK (14:61–63)

Luke tells about the high priest's questioning of Jesus in Luke 22:67–71.

whelmed with sorrow to the point of death[D]," he said to them. "Stay here and keep watch."

[35]Going a little farther, he fell to the ground and prayed that if possible the hour might pass from him. [36]"Abba[D],[a] Father," he said, "everything is possible for you. Take this cup from me. Yet not what I will, but what you will."

[37]Then he returned to his disciples[D] and found them sleeping. "Simon," he said to Peter, "are you asleep? Could you not keep watch for one hour? [38]Watch and pray so that you will not fall into temptation. The spirit is willing, but the body is weak."

[39]Once more he went away and prayed the same thing. [40]When he came back, he again found them sleeping, because their eyes were heavy. They did not know what to say to him.

[41]Returning the third time, he said to them, "Are you still sleeping and resting? Enough! The hour has come. Look, the Son of Man[D] is betrayed into the hands of sinners. [42]Rise! Let us go! Here comes my betrayer!"

Jesus Arrested

[43]Just as he was speaking, Judas, one of the Twelve, appeared. With him was a crowd armed with swords and clubs, sent from the chief priests[D], the teachers of the law, and the elders.

[44]Now the betrayer had arranged a signal with them: "The one I kiss is the man; arrest him and lead him away under guard." [45]Going at once to Jesus, Judas said, "Rabbi[D]!" and kissed him. [46]The men seized Jesus and arrested him. [47]Then one of those standing near drew his sword and struck the servant of the high priest, cutting off his ear.

[48]"Am I leading a rebellion," said Jesus, "that you have come out with swords and clubs to capture me? [49]Every day I was with you, teaching in the temple courts, and you did not arrest me. But the Scriptures must be fulfilled." [50]Then everyone deserted him and fled.

[51]A young man, wearing nothing but a linen garment, was following Jesus. When they seized him, [52]he fled naked, leaving his garment behind.

Before the Sanhedrin

[53]They took Jesus to the high priest, and all the chief priests, elders and teachers of the law came together. [54]Peter followed him at a distance, right into the courtyard of the high priest. There he sat with the guards and warmed himself at the fire.

[55]The chief priests and the whole Sanhedrin were looking for evidence against Jesus so that they could put him to death, but they did not find any. [56]Many testified falsely against him, but their statements did not agree.

[57]Then some stood up and gave this false testimony against him: [58]"We heard him say, 'I will destroy this man-made temple and in three days will build another, not made by man.' " [59]Yet even then their testimony did not agree.

[60]Then the high priest stood up before them and asked Jesus, "Are you not going to answer? What is this testimony that these men are bringing against you?" [61]But Jesus remained silent and gave no answer.

[a]36 Aramaic for *Father*

Again the high priest[D] asked him, "Are you the Christ,[a] the Son of the Blessed One?"

62"I am," said Jesus. "And you will see the Son of Man[D] sitting at the right hand of the Mighty One and coming on the clouds of heaven."

63The high priest tore his clothes. "Why do we need any more witnesses?" he asked. **64**"You have heard the blasphemy[D]. What do you think?"

They all condemned him as worthy of death[D]. **65**Then some began to spit at him; they blindfolded him, struck him with their fists, and said, "Prophesy!" And the guards took him and beat him.

Peter Disowns Jesus

66While Peter was below in the courtyard, one of the servant girls of the high priest came by. **67**When she saw Peter warming himself, she looked closely at him.

"You also were with that Nazarene, Jesus," she said.

68But he denied it. "I don't know or understand what you're talking about," he said, and went out into the entryway.[b]

69When the servant girl saw him there, she said again to those standing around, "This fellow is one of them." **70**Again he denied it.

After a little while, those standing near said to Peter, "Surely you are one of them, for you are a Galilean."

71He began to call down curses on himself, and he swore to them, "I don't know this man you're talking about."

72Immediately the rooster crowed the second time.[c] Then Peter remembered the word Jesus had spoken to him: "Before the rooster crows twice[d] you will disown me three times." And he broke down and wept.

Jesus Before Pilate

15 Very early in the morning, the chief priests, with the elders, the teachers of the law and the whole Sanhedrin[D], reached a decision. They bound Jesus, led him away and handed him over to Pilate.

2"Are you the king of the Jews[D]?" asked Pilate.

"Yes, it is as you say," Jesus replied.

3The chief priests accused him of many things. **4**So again Pilate asked him, "Aren't you going to answer? See how many things they are accusing you of."

5But Jesus still made no reply, and Pilate was amazed.

6Now it was the custom at the Feast to release a prisoner whom the people requested. **7**A man called Barabbas was in prison with the insurrectionists who had committed murder in the uprising. **8**The crowd came up and asked Pilate to do for them what he usually did.

9"Do you want me to release to you the king of the Jews?" asked Pilate, **10**knowing it was out of envy that the chief priests had handed Jesus over to him. **11**But the chief priests stirred up the crowd to have Pilate release Barabbas instead.

12"What shall I do, then, with the one you call the king of the Jews?" Pilate asked them.

13"Crucify him!" they shouted.

14"Why? What crime has he committed?" asked Pilate.

But they shouted all the louder, "Crucify him!"

---

*a*61 Or *Messiah*   *b*68 Some early manuscripts *entryway and the rooster crowed*   *c*72 Some early manuscripts do not have *the second time.*   *d*72 Some early manuscripts do not have *twice.*

SCRIPTURE LINK (14:66–72)

All of the Gospel writers give accounts of Peter's denial of Jesus. See Matt. 26:69–75; Luke 22:56–62 and John 18:16–18,25–27.

Why did Peter weep? (14:72)

Because he suddenly felt the weight of his own failure. Though he had earlier wanted to fight for Jesus, now his courage had melted into confusion. He'd been bewildered and disheartened when Jesus had rejected his rescue attempt in the garden (John 18:10–11). But the crowing rooster brought things back into perspective again with a shocking realization: he had betrayed the one he loved just as Jesus had foretold.

Why did Jewish leaders seek a Roman judge? (15:1)

The Jewish leaders believed that, according to their law, Jesus was guilty of a capital offense —blasphemy. He, a mere man in their eyes, had claimed to be God (14:62). Because Roman troops occupied their country, Jews were denied the right to carry out capital sentences themselves except for religious offenses. See *Why would the Jews' lack of authority to execute indicate how Jesus would die?* (John 18:31–32). Since Romans cared little about religious squabbles, the Jewish leaders changed the charges from blasphemy to treason, which they knew would bring death in a Roman court and would deflect blame for Jesus' death away from themselves.

What did the title *the king of the Jews* mean to Pilate? (15:2)

The Roman government was particularly sensitive to subversive elements in society that would undermine their base of power. Any who claimed to be a leader or a king could be a potential threat. Jesus had been accused of rebelling against Rome and opposing payment of taxes to Caesar (Luke 23:1–2). It was only natural for Pilate to probe Jesus' political aspirations. In Jesus' case, the title carried a deeper spiritual meaning. Since the charge against Jesus carried no real weight, Pilate did not put any stock in it. See *Why wasn't Pilate bothered by Jesus' claim to be king of the Jews?* (Luke 23:3–4).

SCRIPTURE LINK (15:2–15)

Jesus' trial before Pilate can also be found in Matt. 27:11–26; Luke 23:2–3,18–25 and John 18:29—19:16.

Why did the people want a criminal released? (15:6–11)

Pilate offered the crowd a choice between Jesus and Barabbas (Matt. 27:16–18). Since Barabbas was a killer, Pilate may have thought the people would come to their senses at the thought of letting a dangerous criminal back on the streets. But the rulers had whipped the crowd into such an irrational frenzy against Jesus that they chose a murderer over Jesus.

Was Jesus singled out for special brutality? (15:15–20)

Flogging and crucifixion were common in the Roman empire. Death on a cross, however, was usually reserved for criminals and slaves (non-Roman citizens). Soldiers commonly mocked their powerless prisoners, but they took special delight in taunting a man alleged to be a Jewish king.

SCRIPTURE LINK (15:16–20)

In Matt. 27:27–31, Matthew tells about the soldiers mocking Jesus.

SCRIPTURE LINK (15:22–32)

Other Gospel accounts of Jesus' crucifixion can be found in Matt. 27:33–44; Luke 23:33–43 and John 19:17–24.

Why did the soldiers offer Jesus *wine mixed with myrrh*? (15:23)

It may have been a kind of poison, adding to his torture—but also speeding his death. More likely it was a kind of narcotic, designed to deaden his senses and relieve some of his suffering. But Jesus refused to avoid any of the agony God had called him to endure. So, after tasting the concoction (Matt. 27:34), he refused to drink any more of it.

Did one thief repent or not? (15:27,32; see Luke 23:40–42)

According to Luke, one robber had a change of heart. The apparent difference between Mark's and Luke's accounts seems to stem from the timing of events. Mark records earlier events when both robbers hurled insults at Jesus. Luke picks up the story, when one of them, seeing Jesus forgive his executioners (Luke 23:34), determined that Jesus could be trusted.

SCRIPTURE LINK (15:33–41)

Matthew writes about Jesus' death in Matt. 27:45–56. Luke covers it in Luke 23:44–49.

Did God actually forsake Jesus? (15:34)

The divine and human natures of Jesus were never separated, even during the crucifixion. Yet it is clear, difficult as it is to explain, that Jesus' intimate fellowship with God the Father was temporarily broken as he took the sin of the entire world on himself. Jesus used the words of Psalm 22, which begins with despair but ends with renewed trust in God. By quoting that psalm, Jesus may have hinted that he knew the broken relationship with his Father would soon be restored.

Why did the curtain in the temple tear? (15:38)

This large blue, purple and scarlet curtain separated the Holy Place from the Most Holy Place, an inner room which symbolized God's presence (Exodus 26:31–33). It was, in effect, the barrier that separated people from God. When God supernaturally tore the curtain (perhaps by earthquake) he showed dramatically that Christ's death had given people access to God (Heb. 9:1–15; 10:19–22).

15Wanting to satisfy the crowd, Pilate released Barabbas to them. He had Jesus flogged, and handed him over to be crucified.

The Soldiers Mock Jesus

16The soldiers led Jesus away into the palace (that is, the Praetorium) and called together the whole company of soldiers. **17**They put a purpleᴰ robe on him, then twisted together a crown of thorns and set it on him. **18**And they began to call out to him, "Hail, king of the Jewsᴰ!" **19**Again and again they struck him on the head with a staff and spit on him. Falling on their knees, they paid homage to him. **20**And when they had mocked him, they took off the purple robe and put his own clothes on him. Then they led him out to crucify him.

The Crucifixion

21A certain man from Cyrene, Simon, the father of Alexander and Rufus, was passing by on his way in from the country, and they forced him to carry the cross. **22**They brought Jesus to the place called Golgotha (which means The Place of the Skull). **23**Then they offered him wine mixed with myrrhᴰ, but he did not take it. **24**And they crucified him. Dividing up his clothes, they cast lots to see what each would get.

25It was the third hour when they crucified him. **26**The written notice of the charge against him read: THE KING OF THE JEWS. **27**They crucified two robbers with him, one on his right and one on his left.ᵃ **29**Those who passed by hurled insults at him, shaking their heads and saying, "So! You who are going to destroy the temple and build it in three days, **30**come down from the cross and save yourself!"

31In the same way the chief priestsᴰ and the teachers of the law mocked him among themselves. "He saved others," they said, "but he can't save himself! **32**Let this Christ,ᵇ this King of Israel, come down now from the cross, that we may see and believe." Those crucified with him also heaped insults on him.

The Death of Jesus

33At the sixth hour darkness came over the whole land until the ninth hour. **34**And at the ninth hour Jesus cried out in a loud voice, *"Eloi, Eloi, lama sabachthani?"* —which means, "My God, my God, why have you forsaken me?"ᶜ

35When some of those standing near heard this, they said, "Listen, he's calling Elijah."

36One man ran, filled a sponge with wine vinegar, put it on a stick, and offered it to Jesus to drink. "Now leave him alone. Let's see if Elijah comes to take him down," he said.

37With a loud cry, Jesus breathed his last.

38The curtain of the temple was torn in two from top to bottom. **39**And when the centurionᴰ, who stood there in front of Jesus, heard his cry andᵈ saw how he died, he said, "Surely this man was the Sonᵉ of God!"

40Some women were watching from a distance. Among them were Mary Magdalene, Mary the mother of James the younger and of Joses, and Salome. **41**In Galilee these

---

ᵃ27 Some manuscripts *left,* ²⁸*and the scripture was fulfilled which says,* "He was counted with the lawless ones" (Isaiah 53:12)   ᵇ32 Or *Messiah*   ᶜ34 Psalm 22:1   ᵈ39 Some manuscripts do not have *heard his cry and*   ᵉ39 Or *a son*

women had followed him and cared for his needs. Many other women who had come up with him to Jerusalem[D] were also there.

The Burial of Jesus

42It was Preparation Day (that is, the day before the Sabbath[D]). So as evening approached, **43**Joseph of Arimathea, a prominent member of the Council, who was himself waiting for the kingdom of God[D], went boldly to Pilate and asked for Jesus' body. **44**Pilate was surprised to hear that he was already dead. Summoning the centurion[D], he asked him if Jesus had already died. **45**When he learned from the centurion that it was so, he gave the body to Joseph. **46**So Joseph bought some linen cloth, took down the body, wrapped it in the linen, and placed it in a tomb cut out of rock. Then he rolled a stone against the entrance of the tomb. **47**Mary Magdalene and Mary the mother of Joses saw where he was laid.

The Resurrection

16 When the Sabbath was over, Mary Magdalene, Mary the mother of James, and Salome bought spices so that they might go to anoint[D] Jesus' body. **2**Very early on the first day of the week, just after sunrise, they were on their way to the tomb **3**and they asked each other, "Who will roll the stone away from the entrance of the tomb?"

4But when they looked up, they saw that the stone, which was very large, had been rolled away. **5**As they entered the tomb, they saw a young man dressed in a white robe sitting on the right side, and they were alarmed.

6"Don't be alarmed," he said. "You are looking for Jesus the Nazarene, who was crucified. He has risen! He is not here. See the place where they laid him. **7**But go, tell his disciples[D] and Peter, 'He is going ahead of you into Galilee. There you will see him, just as he told you.' "

8Trembling and bewildered, the women went out and fled from the tomb. They said nothing to anyone, because they were afraid.

[The earliest manuscripts and some other ancient witnesses do not have Mark 16:9–20.]

9When Jesus rose early on the first day of the week, he appeared first to Mary Magdalene, out of whom he had driven seven demons. **10**She went and told those who had been with him and who were mourning and weeping. **11**When they heard that Jesus was alive and that she had seen him, they did not believe it.

12Afterward Jesus appeared in a different form to two of them while they were walking in the country. **13**These returned and reported it to the rest; but they did not believe them either.

14Later Jesus appeared to the Eleven as they were eating; he rebuked them for their lack of faith and their stubborn refusal to believe those who had seen him after he had risen.

15He said to them, "Go into all the world and preach the good news to all creation. **16**Whoever believes and is baptized will be saved, but whoever does not believe will be condemned. **17**And these signs will accompany those who believe: In my name they will drive out demons; they will

Council (15:43)

See *Sanhedrin* in the Dictionary.

Why did this secret disciple risk discovery after Jesus was dead? (15:43)

During Christ's life, he apparently kept quiet about his convictions. He probably feared being thrown out of the synagogue (see 7:13; 9:22; 20:19). Now, with Jesus dead, the threat of reprisal seemed remote. Still, to openly ask for the body required tremendous courage. Perhaps the miraculous events accompanying Christ's death on the cross had changed him and given him the boldness to identify with Jesus (see John 12:32).

SCRIPTURE LINK (16:1–8)

Matthew tells about Jesus' resurrection in Matt. 28:1–8. Luke talks about it in Luke 24:1–10.

Why do the four Gospels describe the Easter events differently? (16:1)

Like any four witnesses to one event, the writers of the Gospels each offer a different perspective. The appearances of the Christ that first day may have occurred as follows: (1) To the women at the empty tomb early Sunday morning (Matt. 28:1–10; Mark 16:1–8; Luke 24:1–12; John 20:1–9); (2) To Mary Magdalene at the tomb early Sunday morning (Mark 16:9–11; John 20:11–18); (3) To Peter in Jerusalem during the day on Sunday (Luke 24:34); (4) To the two travelers on the road to Emmaus Sunday afternoon (Luke 24:13–32); (5) To the ten disciples in the upper room Sunday evening (Mark 16:14; Luke 24:36–43; John 20:19–25).

Why was Peter given special notice? (16:7)

Peter was often the spokesman for the 12 apostles. Jesus had promised to build his church on Peter's confession of faith (Matt. 16:16–19). Because Peter had recently denied Jesus three times, Jesus was preparing the way for Peter's restoration. Peter's rehabilitation gives disciples in every age hope for forgiveness regardless of how badly they have sinned.

Why would Jesus tell believers to *pick up snakes* and *drink deadly poison*? (16:18)

He didn't. This was Jesus' promise to his followers that they would be protected while taking the gospel throughout the world. Some see snakes, poison and scorpions as symbols of spiritual attacks from the enemy—attacks which cannot defeat those who trust in Christ (see Luke 10:19). Although the New Testament has no record of any believer accidently drinking poison, there were many accounts of healings in the early church and one incident where a poisonous snake had no effect on Paul (Acts 28:3–6).

speak in new tongues; **18**they will pick up snakes with their hands; and when they drink deadly poison, it will not hurt them at all; they will place their hands on sick people, and they will get well."

19After the Lord Jesus had spoken to them, he was taken up into heaven and he sat at the right hand of God. **20**Then the disciples^D went out and preached everywhere, and the Lord worked with them and confirmed his word by the signs that accompanied it.

Do these verses belong in the Bible? (16:9–20)

The translators of the earliest English versions of the Bible, such as the King James Version, did not have access to nearly as many ancient Greek and Hebrew manuscripts as we now have. The older manuscripts, discovered since 1611, do not include these verses. In them Mark's Gospel ends abruptly at v. 8.

It is possible that the original ending of Mark was lost, perhaps torn off the end of a scroll. It's also possible that Mark ended his story with v. 8, showing that the disciples were still afraid and confused, unable to grasp the truth of the resurrection.

But since that ending seems to leave the Gospel hanging, without describing any actual resurrection appearance of Jesus, by the middle of the second century A.D. someone apparently added a more complete conclusion with information drawn from accounts other than Mark's. Because vv. 9–20 have been included in so many Bibles for so many years, they are often included along with a disclaimer about the older manuscript. But they may not be inspired or authoritative.

This does not, however, discredit the infallibility or inerrancy of God's Word. Christians stress that only what the Biblical authors (which in this case may include another writer besides Mark) wrote which is confirmed by the early church's acceptance of its authority, should be accepted as Scripture. Careful research has allowed us to determine with great precision what those inspired authors actually wrote.

The Ministry of Jesus

Event	Place	Matthew	Mark	Luke	John
Jesus baptized	Jordan River	3:13-17	1:9-11	3:21-22	1:29-34
Jesus tempted by Satan	Desert	4:1-11	1:12-13	4:1-13	
Jesus' first miracle	Cana				2:1-11
Jesus and Nicodemus	Judea				3:1-21
Jesus talks to a Samaritan woman	Samaria				4:5-42
Jesus heals an official's son	Cana				4:46-54
The people of Nazareth try to kill Jesus	Nazareth			4:16-30	
Jesus calls four fishermen	Sea of Galilee	4:18-22	1:16-20	5:1-11	
Jesus heals Peter's mother-in-law	Capernaum	8:14-15	1:29-31	4:38-39	
Jesus begins preaching in Galilee	Galilee	4:23-25	1:35-39	4:42-44	
Matthew decides to follow Jesus	Capernaum	9:9-13	2:13-17	5:27-32	
Jesus chooses twelve disciples	Galilee	10:2-4	3:13-19	6:12-15	
Jesus preaches the Sermon on the Mount	Galilee	5:1–7:29		6:20-49	
A sinful woman anoints Jesus	Capernaum			7:36-50	
Jesus travels again through Galilee	Galilee			8:1-3	
Jesus tells kingdom parables	Galilee	13:1-52	4:1-34	8:4-18	
Jesus quiets the storm	Sea of Galilee	8:23-27	4:35-41	8:22-25	
Jairus's daughter raised to life	Capernaum	9:18-26	5:21-43	8:40-56	
Jesus sends out the twelve	Galilee	9:35–11:1	6:6-13	9:1-6	
John the Baptist killed by Herod	Machaerus in Judea	14:1-12	6:14-29	9:7-9	
Jesus feeds the 5,000	Bethsaida	14:13-21	6:30-44	9:10-17	6:1-14
Jesus walks on water	Sea of Galilee	14:22-32	6:47-52		6:16-21
Jesus feeds the 4,000	Sea of Galilee	15:32-39	8:1-10		
Peter confesses Jesus as the Son of God	Caesarea Philippi	16:13-20	8:27-30	9:18-21	
Jesus predicts his death	Caesarea Philippi	16:21-26	8:31-37	9:22-25	
Jesus is transfigured	Mount Hermon	17:1-13	9:2-13	9:28-36	
Jesus pays his temple taxes	Capernaum	17:24-27			
Jesus attends the Feast of Tabernacles	Jerusalem				7:10-52
Jesus heals a man born blind	Jerusalem				9:1-41
Jesus visits Mary and Martha	Bethany			10:38-42	
Jesus raises Lazarus from the dead	Bethany				11:1-44
Jesus begins his last trip to Jerusalem	Border road			17:11	
Jesus blesses the little children	Transjordan	19:13-15	10:13-16	18:15-17	
Jesus talks to the rich young man	Transjordan	19:16-30	10:17-31	18:18-30	
Jesus again predicts his death	Near the Jordan	20:17-19	10:32-34	18:31-34	
Jesus heals blind Bartimaeus	Jericho	20:29-34	10:46-52	18:35-43	
Jesus talks to Zacchaeus	Jericho			19:1-10	
Jesus visits Mary and Martha again	Bethany				12:1-11

The Last Week

Event	Place	Day of the Week	Matthew	Mark	Luke	John
The triumphal entry	Jerusalem	Sunday	21:1-11	11:1-11	19:29-44	12:12-19
Jesus curses the fig tree	Jerusalem	Monday	21:18-22	11:12-14		
Jesus clears the temple	Jerusalem	Monday	21:12-13	11:15-18	19:45-48	
The authority of Jesus questioned	Jerusalem	Tuesday	21:23-27	11:27-33	20:1-8	
Jesus teaches in the temple	Jerusalem	Tuesday	21:28–23:39	12:1-44	20:9–21:4	
Jesus' feet anointed	Bethany	Tuesday	26:6-13	14:3-9		12:2-11
The plot against Jesus	Jerusalem	Wednesday	26:14-16	14:10-11	22:3-6	
The Last Supper	Jerusalem	Thursday	26:17-29	14:12-25	22:7-38	13:1-38
Jesus comforts his disciples	Jerusalem	Thursday				14:1–16:33
Jesus' high priestly prayer	Jerusalem	Thursday				17:1-26
Gethsemane	Jerusalem	Thursday	26:36-46	14:32-42	22:40-46	
Jesus' arrest and trial	Jerusalem	Friday	26:47–27:26	14:43–15:15	22:47–23:25	18:2–19:16
Jesus' crucifixion and death	Golgotha	Friday	27:27-56	15:16-41	23:26-49	19:17-37
The burial of Jesus	Garden tomb	Friday	27:57-66	15:42-47	23:50-56	19:38-42

Resurrection Appearances

Event	Place	Day of the Week	Matthew	Mark	Luke	John	Acts	1Cor
The empty tomb	Jerusalem	Resurrection Sunday	28:1-8	16:1-8	24:1-12	20:1-10		
To Mary Magdalene in the garden	Jerusalem	Resurrection Sunday		16:9-11		20:11-18		
To other women	Jerusalem	Resurrection Sunday	28:9-10					
To two people going to Emmaus	Road to Emmaus	Resurrection Sunday		16:12-13	24:13-32			
To Peter	Jerusalem	Resurrection Sunday			24:34			15:5
To the ten disciples in the upper room	Jerusalem	Resurrection Sunday			24:36-43	20:19-25		
To the eleven disciples in the upper room	Jerusalem	Following Sunday		16:14		20:26-31		15:5
To seven disciples fishing	Sea of Galilee	Some time later				21:1-14		
To the eleven disciples on a mountain	Galilee	Some time later	28:16-20	16:15-18				
To more than five hundred	Unknown	Some time later						15:6
To James	Unknown	Some time later						15:7
To his disciples at his ascension	Mount of Olives	Forty days after Jesus' resurrection			24:36-51		1:3-9	15:7
To Paul	Damascus	Several years later					9:1-19 22:3-16 26:9-18	9:1

LUKE

Why read this book?

Does this book offer anything that can't be found in the other Gospels? Yes, it offers plenty. Just as a witness at a trial does more than confirm the story of another witness, Luke enlarges the story of Jesus. You'll gain new information from Luke and see Jesus from a new angle. Of all the Gospel writers, Luke gives us the greatest variety of teaching, parables and events from the life of Jesus.

Who wrote this book?

Luke, a companion of Paul the apostle. Luke, who also wrote Acts, was probably a Gentile medical doctor.

To whom was it written and why?

Luke wrote to Theophilus, probably a Gentile who was likely either a new believer or someone seeking to learn about Christ. Theophilus means *lover of God,* leading some to think the book was written in general to people who loved God. Luke hoped Theophilus and other readers would learn that God's love reaches beyond the Jews to the entire world.

When was it written?

Possibly A.D. 59 to 63, although some think it may have been 15 to 20 years later.

What to look for in Luke:

Watch for ways that Luke elaborates on the accounts of Matthew and Mark. You'll find new information here—more stories about Jesus' birth, for example, and the parable of the Good Samaritan. You'll also see Luke's personal perspective in the incidents he included—stories, for instance, that demonstrate Jesus' interest in the non-Jewish world and the poor.

When did these things happen?

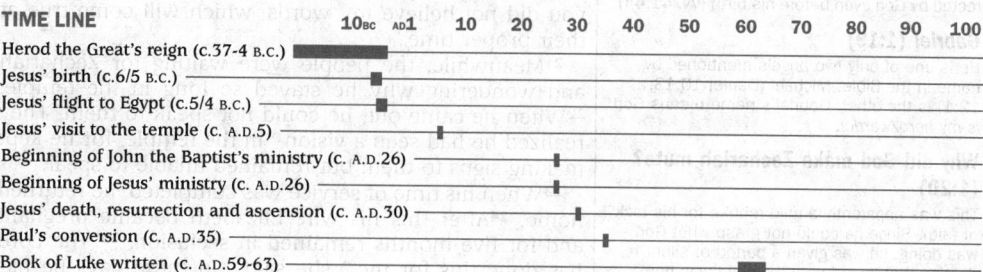

TIME LINE	10 B.C.	A.D.1	10	20	30	40	50	60	70	80	90	100
Herod the Great's reign (c.37-4 B.C.)												
Jesus' birth (c.6/5 B.C.)												
Jesus' flight to Egypt (c.5/4 B.C.)												
Jesus' visit to the temple (c. A.D.5)												
Beginning of John the Baptist's ministry (c. A.D.26)												
Beginning of Jesus' ministry (c. A.D.26)												
Jesus' death, resurrection and ascension (c. A.D.30)												
Paul's conversion (c. A.D.35)												
Book of Luke written (c. A.D.59-63)												

Introduction

1 Many have undertaken to draw up an account of the things that have been fulfilled[a] among us, [2]just as they were handed down to us by those who from the first were eyewitnesses and servants of the word. [3]Therefore, since I myself have carefully investigated everything from the beginning, it seemed good also to me to write an orderly account for you, most excellent Theophilus, [4]so that you may know the certainty of the things you have been taught.

The Birth of John the Baptist Foretold

[5]In the time of Herod king of Judea there was a priest[D] named Zechariah, who belonged to the priestly division of Abijah; his wife Elizabeth was also a descendant of Aaron. [6]Both of them were upright in the sight of God, observing all the Lord's commandments and regulations blamelessly. [7]But they had no children, because Elizabeth was barren; and they were both well along in years.

[8]Once when Zechariah's division was on duty and he was serving as priest before God, [9]he was chosen by lot, according to the custom of the priesthood, to go into the temple of the Lord and burn incense[D]. [10]And when the time for the burning of incense came, all the assembled worshipers were praying outside.

[11]Then an angel of the Lord appeared to him, standing at the right side of the altar of incense. [12]When Zechariah saw him, he was startled and was gripped with fear. [13]But the angel said to him: "Do not be afraid, Zechariah; your prayer has been heard. Your wife Elizabeth will bear you a son, and you are to give him the name John. [14]He will be a joy and delight to you, and many will rejoice because of his birth, [15]for he will be great in the sight of the Lord. He is never to take wine or other fermented drink, and he will be filled with the Holy Spirit even from birth.[b] [16]Many of the people of Israel will he bring back to the Lord their God. [17]And he will go on before the Lord, in the spirit and power of Elijah, to turn the hearts of the fathers to their children and the disobedient to the wisdom of the righteous[D]—to make ready a people prepared for the Lord."

[18]Zechariah asked the angel, "How can I be sure of this? I am an old man and my wife is well along in years."

[19]The angel answered, "I am Gabriel[D]. I stand in the presence of God, and I have been sent to speak to you and to tell you this good news. [20]And now you will be silent and not able to speak until the day this happens, because you did not believe my words, which will come true at their proper time."

[21]Meanwhile, the people were waiting for Zechariah and wondering why he stayed so long in the temple. [22]When he came out, he could not speak to them. They realized he had seen a vision[D] in the temple, for he kept making signs to them but remained unable to speak.

[23]When his time of service was completed, he returned home. [24]After this his wife Elizabeth became pregnant and for five months remained in seclusion. [25]"The Lord has done this for me," she said. "In these days he has shown his favor and taken away my disgrace among the people."

Theophilus (1:3)
See Introduction: *To whom was it written and why?*

Herod king of Judea (1:5)
This is Herod the Great, who ruled Judea (Palestine) from 40 to 4 B.C. See *King Herod* (Matt. 2:1).

Priestly division (1:5)
There were 24 divisions of priests (1 Chron. 24:1–4). They served twice a year at the temple for a week at a time. With the distribution of labor, a priest like Zechariah would likely prepare the sacrifice only once in his career.

Why was John supposed to abstain from wine? (1:15)
This act showed his special dedication to God. It did not make him more spiritual or holy, but was rather a sign that he was totally focused on God. See *What was a Nazirite?* (Num. 6:2).

How could a baby be filled with the Holy Spirit? (1:15)
Zechariah would have understood this promise from the Jewish point of view, not as we understand it from a New Testament point of view. We know that the Spirit is offered to those who repent and turn to the Lord (Acts 2:38), and we wonder how this could be the case for a newborn baby. But Zechariah saw this as an announcement that the Spirit would come as God's call to his son, anointing him for a prophetic assignment. As with that of Jeremiah (Jer. 1:5), John's ministry was sovereignly directed by God even before his birth (vv. 41,44).

Gabriel (1:19)
He is one of only two angels mentioned by name in the Bible. Michael (Daniel 10:13; 12:1) is the other. Gabriel's name means *God is my hero/warrior*.

Why did God make Zechariah mute? (1:20)
This was apparently a mild rebuke for his lack of faith. Since he could not grasp what God was doing, he was given a period of silent reflection that lasted until the child was born. Zechariah, though a righteous man, still needed to learn to trust God more. His inability to speak, a supernatural sign, undoubtedly increased his faith, causing him to believe that God's promise for a child would come to pass.

---

a 1 Or been surely believed   *b 15 Or from his mother's womb*

The Birth of Jesus Foretold

26In the sixth month, God sent the angel Gabriel^D to Nazareth, a town in Galilee, **27**to a virgin pledged to be married to a man named Joseph, a descendant of David. The virgin's name was Mary. **28**The angel went to her and said, "Greetings, you who are highly favored! The Lord is with you."

29Mary was greatly troubled at his words and wondered what kind of greeting this might be. **30**But the angel said to her, "Do not be afraid, Mary, you have found favor with God. **31**You will be with child and give birth to a son, and you are to give him the name Jesus. **32**He will be great and will be called the Son of the Most High. The Lord God will give him the throne of his father David, **33**and he will reign over the house of Jacob forever; his kingdom will never end."

34"How will this be," Mary asked the angel, "since I am a virgin?"

35The angel answered, "The Holy Spirit will come upon you, and the power of the Most High will overshadow you. So the holy one to be born will be called*a* the Son of God. **36**Even Elizabeth your relative is going to have a child in her old age, and she who was said to be barren is in her sixth month. **37**For nothing is impossible with God."

38"I am the Lord's servant," Mary answered. "May it be to me as you have said." Then the angel left her.

Mary Visits Elizabeth

39At that time Mary got ready and hurried to a town in the hill country of Judea, **40**where she entered Zechariah's home and greeted Elizabeth. **41**When Elizabeth heard Mary's greeting, the baby leaped in her womb, and Elizabeth was filled with the Holy Spirit. **42**In a loud voice she exclaimed: "Blessed are you among women, and blessed is the child you will bear! **43**But why am I so favored, that the mother of my Lord should come to me? **44**As soon as the sound of your greeting reached my ears, the baby in my womb leaped for joy. **45**Blessed is she who has believed that what the Lord has said to her will be accomplished!"

Mary's Song

46And Mary said:

"My soul^D glorifies the Lord
47 and my spirit rejoices in God my Savior,
48for he has been mindful
    of the humble state of his servant.
From now on all generations will call me
    blessed,
49 for the Mighty One has done great things for
    me—
  holy is his name.
50His mercy^D extends to those who fear him,
    from generation to generation.
51He has performed mighty deeds with his arm;
    he has scattered those who are proud in
    their inmost thoughts.
52He has brought down rulers from their thrones
    but has lifted up the humble.
53He has filled the hungry with good things
    but has sent the rich away empty.

Why name him Jesus? (1:31)
The name was a sign that God would save his people (Matt. 1:21). Its Old Testament form was *Yeshua* or *Joshua,* meaning, *Yahweh is salvation.*

How much did Mary know about Jesus? (1:46–55)
Mary realized that Jesus was a promised gift of God, the Messiah (vv. 31–35). But the incident recorded in 2:41–52 indicates that she didn't realize Jesus was God in human flesh.

Was Mary boasting? (1:48)
No. She was filled with wonder that she—poor, young and female—could be used by God for an eternal purpose. Sinful pride would have caused her to refuse God's call to serve or to claim credit for what God had done. Mary joyfully and gratefully praised God.

a35 Or So the child to be born will be called holy,

⁵⁴He has helped his servant Israel,
    remembering to be merciful
⁵⁵to Abraham and his descendants forever,
    even as he said to our fathers."

⁵⁶Mary stayed with Elizabeth for about three months and then returned home.

The Birth of John the Baptist

⁵⁷When it was time for Elizabeth to have her baby, she gave birth to a son. ⁵⁸Her neighbors and relatives heard that the Lord had shown her great mercy^D, and they shared her joy.

⁵⁹On the eighth day they came to circumcise^D the child, and they were going to name him after his father Zechariah, ⁶⁰but his mother spoke up and said, "No! He is to be called John."

⁶¹They said to her, "There is no one among your relatives who has that name."

⁶²Then they made signs to his father, to find out what he would like to name the child. ⁶³He asked for a writing tablet, and to everyone's astonishment he wrote, "His name is John." ⁶⁴Immediately his mouth was opened and his tongue was loosed, and he began to speak, praising God. ⁶⁵The neighbors were all filled with awe, and throughout the hill country of Judea people were talking about all these things. ⁶⁶Everyone who heard this wondered about it, asking, "What then is this child going to be?" For the Lord's hand was with him.

Zechariah's Song

⁶⁷His father Zechariah was filled with the Holy Spirit and prophesied:

⁶⁸"Praise be to the Lord, the God of Israel,
    because he has come and has redeemed^D
        his people.
⁶⁹He has raised up a horn^a of salvation^D for us
    in the house of his servant David
⁷⁰(as he said through his holy prophets^D of long
        ago),
⁷¹salvation from our enemies
    and from the hand of all who hate us—
⁷²to show mercy to our fathers
    and to remember his holy covenant^D,
⁷³ the oath he swore to our father Abraham:
⁷⁴to rescue us from the hand of our enemies,
    and to enable us to serve him without fear
⁷⁵ in holiness and righteousness^D before him
        all our days.

⁷⁶And you, my child, will be called a prophet
    of the Most High;
    for you will go on before the Lord to prepare
        the way for him,
⁷⁷to give his people the knowledge of salvation
    through the forgiveness of their sins,
⁷⁸because of the tender mercy of our God,
    by which the rising sun will come to us from
        heaven
⁷⁹to shine on those living in darkness
    and in the shadow of death^D,
    to guide our feet into the path of peace^D."

---

a69 Horn here symbolizes strength.

Circumcise the child (1:59)
See article: *Why did God command circumcision?* (Gen. 17:10).

80And the child grew and became strong in spirit; and he lived in the desert until he appeared publicly to Israel.

The Birth of Jesus

2 In those days Caesar Augustus issued a decree that a census should be taken of the entire Roman world. **2**(This was the first census that took place while Quirinius was governor of Syria.) **3**And everyone went to his own town to register.

4So Joseph also went up from the town of Nazareth in Galilee to Judea, to Bethlehem the town of David, because he belonged to the house and line of David. **5**He went there to register with Mary, who was pledged to be married to him and was expecting a child. **6**While they were there, the time came for the baby to be born, **7**and she gave birth to her firstbornᴰ, a son. She wrapped him in cloths and placed him in a manger, because there was no room for them in the inn.

The Shepherds and the Angels

8And there were shepherds living out in the fields nearby, keeping watch over their flocks at night. **9**An angel of the Lord appeared to them, and the gloryᴰ of the Lord shone around them, and they were terrified. **10**But the angel said to them, "Do not be afraid. I bring you good news of great joy that will be for all the people. **11**Today in the town of David a Savior has been born to you; he is Christᵃ the Lord. **12**This will be a sign to you: You will find a baby wrapped in cloths and lying in a manger."

13Suddenly a great company of the heavenly host appeared with the angel, praising God and saying,

14"Glory to God in the highest,
    and on earth peaceᴰ to men on whom his
        favor rests."

15When the angels had left them and gone into heaven, the shepherds said to one another, "Let's go to Bethlehem and see this thing that has happened, which the Lord has told us about."

16So they hurried off and found Mary and Joseph, and the baby, who was lying in the manger. **17**When they had seen him, they spread the word concerning what had been told them about this child, **18**and all who heard it were amazed at what the shepherds said to them. **19**But Mary treasured up all these things and pondered them in her heart. **20**The shepherds returned, glorifying and praising God for all the things they had heard and seen, which were just as they had been told.

Jesus Presented in the Temple

21On the eighth day, when it was time to circumciseᴰ him, he was named Jesus, the name the angel had given him before he had been conceived.

22When the time of their purification according to the Law of Moses had been completed, Joseph and Mary took him to Jerusalemᴰ to present him to the Lord **23**(as it is written in the Law of the Lord, "Every firstborn male is to be consecratedᴰ to the Lord"ᵇ), **24**and to offer a sacrificeᴰ in keeping with what is said in the Law of the Lord: "a pair of doves or two young pigeons."ᶜ

ᵃ11 Or *Messiah*. "The Christ" (Greek) and "the Messiah" (Hebrew) both mean "the Anointed One"; also in verse 26. ᵇ23 Exodus 13:2,12
ᶜ24 Lev. 12:8

Why did John live in the desert? (1:80)
The harsh climate may have helped to focus his attention on God. Being separated from the economic and political powers of his day allowed him to speak his words of judgment more freely. His chosen lifestyle also clearly distinguished him from other religious leaders who enjoyed living near the halls of power.

When was Jesus born? (2:1–2)
Perhaps a year or so before Herod the Great's death in 4 B.C. (Matt. 2:19). The actual date of Jesus' birth was not discussed until the fourth century, the delay leading to some uncertainty. The Italian monk who devised the Christian calendar complicated matters by making a miscalculation. Confusion also exists because the only census by Quirinius as yet found in other historical sources occurred too late (A.D. 6) to be the first one Luke mentions here.

The house and line of David (2:4)
The Old Testament prophets foretold that the Messiah would be a descendant of King David's royal family (Isaiah 11:1; Ezek. 37:24; Hosea 3:5). Also see *How has David's house and kingdom endured forever?* (2 Samuel 7:16).

Jesus Is Born (2:4)

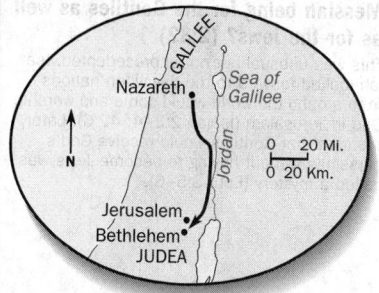

Why announce the birth of Jesus to shepherds? (2:9–12)
Perhaps the common shepherds were more receptive to God's plan than, say, the religious leaders in Jerusalem. The more orthodox members of society despised shepherds for being unclean by strict ceremonial standards. Their reputation was that they were untrustworthy—a shepherd's testimony was not valid for legal matters. Yet God chose them to be the first witnesses to the birth of Christ (vv. 17–18)! Shepherds may have been chosen because they represented all who needed cleansing. Jesus was a king for all those humble enough to see their need for a Savior.

Why these ceremonies for parents and infants? (2:21-24)

To fulfill *the Law of the Lord* (v. 39). Jewish families went through at least three ceremonies after the birth of a firstborn son: (1) Circumcision. As a sign of the Jews' covenant with God, each Hebrew boy was circumcised on the eighth day after his birth (Lev. 12:3). (2) Redemption of the firstborn. Each firstborn son was presented to God a month after his birth, a dedication acknowledging that he belonged to God. The child would be "redeemed," that is, repurchased, by giving a sacrificial offering in his place (Exodus 13:2,11-16). (3) Purification of the mother. For 40 days following the birth of a son (80 days following the birth of a daughter), a mother was considered unclean. At the end of this ritual impurity, a sacrifice was offered as part of her cleansing process. See *Why would a good thing like giving birth require purification?* (Lev. 12:4).

The consolation of Israel (2:25)

This phrase refers to the Old Testament hope in a Messiah that would finally and decisively deliver Israel from the political bondage of other nations. Zechariah had earlier expressed this same hope (1:68-75).

How common was it to think of the Messiah being for the Gentiles as well as for the Jews? (2:32)

This was unusual but not unprecedented. Isaiah looked forward to the day when nations from around the world would come and worship God in Jerusalem (Isaiah 2:2-4; 42:6). Later, the idea that Gentiles would receive God's blessings without having to become Jews was called a *mystery* (Eph. 3:5-6).

Were Joseph and Mary careless parents? (2:44)

Probably not, given the expectations of their society. They were apparently trusting a normally responsible Jesus to be with friends or relatives. Some, observing later customs of the Middle East, suggest that the women and children traveled separately from the men. If so, each parent could have assumed that their 12-year-old was with the other.

Why did Mary call Joseph Jesus' father? (2:48)

Joseph functioned as a father to Jesus, so the title was appropriate on a human level. The contrast Jesus made in speaking about his involvement with the things of his heavenly Father shows how clearly Jesus saw his mission and his unique relationship to God.

25Now there was a man in Jerusalem^D called Simeon, who was righteous^D and devout. He was waiting for the consolation of Israel, and the Holy Spirit was upon him. **26**It had been revealed to him by the Holy Spirit that he would not die before he had seen the Lord's Christ. **27**Moved by the Spirit, he went into the temple courts. When the parents brought in the child Jesus to do for him what the custom of the Law required, **28**Simeon took him in his arms and praised God, saying:

> **29**"Sovereign Lord, as you have promised,
>   you now dismiss^a your servant in peace^D.
> **30**For my eyes have seen your salvation^D,
> **31**   which you have prepared in the sight of all
>   people,
> **32**a light for revelation^D to the Gentiles^D
>   and for glory^D to your people Israel."

33The child's father and mother marveled at what was said about him. **34**Then Simeon blessed them and said to Mary, his mother: "This child is destined to cause the falling and rising of many in Israel, and to be a sign that will be spoken against, **35**so that the thoughts of many hearts will be revealed. And a sword will pierce your own soul^D too."

36There was also a prophetess^D, Anna, the daughter of Phanuel, of the tribe of Asher. She was very old; she had lived with her husband seven years after her marriage, **37**and then was a widow until she was eighty-four.^b She never left the temple but worshiped night and day, fasting and praying. **38**Coming up to them at that very moment, she gave thanks to God and spoke about the child to all who were looking forward to the redemption^D of Jerusalem.

39When Joseph and Mary had done everything required by the Law of the Lord, they returned to Galilee to their own town of Nazareth. **40**And the child grew and became strong; he was filled with wisdom, and the grace^D of God was upon him.

The Boy Jesus at the Temple

41Every year his parents went to Jerusalem for the Feast of the Passover. **42**When he was twelve years old, they went up to the Feast, according to the custom. **43**After the Feast was over, while his parents were returning home, the boy Jesus stayed behind in Jerusalem, but they were unaware of it. **44**Thinking he was in their company, they traveled on for a day. Then they began looking for him among their relatives and friends. **45**When they did not find him, they went back to Jerusalem to look for him. **46**After three days they found him in the temple courts, sitting among the teachers, listening to them and asking them questions. **47**Everyone who heard him was amazed at his understanding and his answers. **48**When his parents saw him, they were astonished. His mother said to him, "Son, why have you treated us like this? Your father and I have been anxiously searching for you."

49"Why were you searching for me?" he asked. "Didn't you know I had to be in my Father's house?" **50**But they did not understand what he was saying to them.

51Then he went down to Nazareth with them and was obedient to them. But his mother treasured all these

---

a 29 Or *promised, / now dismiss*   b 37 Or *widow for eighty-four years*

things in her heart. **52**And Jesus grew in wisdom and stature, and in favor with God and men.

John the Baptist Prepares the Way

3 In the fifteenth year of the reign of Tiberius Caesar— when Pontius Pilate was governor of Judea, Herod tetrarchᴰ of Galilee, his brother Philip tetrarch of Iturea and Traconitis, and Lysanias tetrarch of Abilene— **2**during the high priesthood of Annas and Caiaphas, the word of God came to John son of Zechariah in the desert. **3**He went into all the country around the Jordan, preaching a baptismᴰ of repentanceᴰ for the forgiveness of sins. **4**As is written in the book of the words of Isaiah the prophetᴰ:

> "A voice of one calling in the desert,
> 'Prepare the way for the Lord,
>   make straight paths for him.
> **5**Every valley shall be filled in,
>   every mountain and hill made low.
> The crooked roads shall become straight,
>   the rough ways smooth.
> **6**And all mankind will see God's salvationᴰ.' " *a*

7John said to the crowds coming out to be baptized by him, "You brood of vipers! Who warned you to flee from the coming wrath? **8**Produce fruit in keeping with repentance. And do not begin to say to yourselves, 'We have Abraham as our father.' For I tell you that out of these stones God can raise up children for Abraham. **9**The ax is already at the root of the trees, and every tree that does not produce good fruit will be cut down and thrown into the fire."

10"What should we do then?" the crowd asked.

11John answered, "The man with two tunics should share with him who has none, and the one who has food should do the same."

12Tax collectors also came to be baptized. "Teacher," they asked, "what should we do?"

13"Don't collect any more than you are required to," he told them.

14Then some soldiers asked him, "And what should we do?"

He replied, "Don't extort money and don't accuse people falsely—be content with your pay."

15The people were waiting expectantly and were all wondering in their hearts if John might possibly be the Christ.*b* **16**John answered them all, "I baptize you with*c* water. But one more powerful than I will come, the thongs of whose sandals I am not worthy to untie. He will baptize you with the Holy Spirit and with fire. **17**His winnowing forkᴰ is in his hand to clear his threshing floor and to gather the wheat into his barn, but he will burn up the chaffᴰ with unquenchable fire." **18**And with many other words John exhorted the people and preached the good news to them.

19But when John rebuked Herod the tetrarch because of Herodias, his brother's wife, and all the other evil things he had done, **20**Herod added this to them all: He locked John up in prison.

What year was this? (3:1–2)
Opinions vary, but a good case can be made for A.D. 25 to 26. If Jesus was crucified in A.D. 30, this would allow time for his ministry of a little over three years and still allow enough time for John to precede Jesus with his own ministry.

SCRIPTURE LINK (3:2–10)
Matthew tells about John the Baptist preparing the way for Jesus in Matt. 3:1–10. Mark talks about it in Mark 1:3–5.

Did John preach that sins were forgiven by baptism? (3:3)
This baptism did not bring about salvation any more than sacrifices did in the Old Testament. The ritual served only to illustrate what was occurring within the hearts of people. The faith expressed in baptism indicated a readiness for the Messiah who would bring forgiveness (1:76–79). Also see **Does baptism save us?** (1 Peter 3:21).

How did John fulfill Isaiah's prophecy? (3:4–6)
Isaiah prophesied about God's *pattern* for saving his people, covering both the deliverance of Israel from Old Testament exile and the deliverance from sin through the Messiah. John the Baptist "prepared the way" for the coming Messiah much as citizens of his day would prepare for the coming of a great leader, repairing the roads and cleaning up the towns in anticipation of their royal guest. John prepared the hearts of the people, removing obstacles or barriers to the coming Messiah and his message of the kingdom of God. See Isaiah 57:14–15.

Tax collectors (3:12)
See *Tax collectors* (5:29).

What is baptism *with the Holy Spirit?* (3:16)
This phrase refers to the Spirit coming to dwell within believers, empowering them to be witnesses for the Lord and to live holy lives (24:48–49; Acts 1:8; 2:1–21). There are basically two views: (1) Some say we are baptized with the Holy Spirit when by faith we accept Christ as Savior and become members of his body (1 Cor. 12:13; 6:19–20). (2) Others say believers can be filled with the Spirit in a deeper, more powerful sense following salvation (Acts 8:14–17).

What is baptism *with fire?* (3:16)
Fire, frequently a Biblical picture of judgment, here suggests a work of purification and cleansing connected with the baptism of the Spirit. The Spirit's fire accomplishes two things simultaneously, causing some to be cleansed and others to be judged—just as a refiner's fire purifies gold as well as separates dross. This is why the following verse uses the image of wheat and chaff, to indicate the separation God makes between people as they respond— one way or the other—to Christ.

SCRIPTURE LINK (3:16–17)
In Matt. 3:11–12, Matthew records John's words about Jesus baptizing with the Holy Spirit. Mark records them in Mark 1:7–8.

Winnowing fork (3:17)
Ancient farmers would toss the threshed grain into the air with a large, wooden fork so the

---

*a*6 Isaiah 40:3-5   *b*15 Or *Messiah*   *c*16 Or *in*

wind would blow away the lighter chaff while the grain dropped back to the ground. John used this image to illustrate the dual nature of Jesus' ministry: he would separate humanity, some to judgment and some to reward.

SCRIPTURE LINK (3:21–22)

Matthew writes about Jesus' baptism in Matt. 3:13–17. Mark covers it in Mark 1:9–11.

SCRIPTURE LINK (3:23–38)

Matthew provides a similar genealogy in Matt. 1:1–17.

Why aren't the genealogies of Matthew and Luke the same? (3:23–38)

Some say Matthew gave Joseph's line, while Luke gave Mary's. Others think the difference was between a royal line (that of Joseph) and a physical line (that of Mary). Still others see the variation as the result of at least two levirate marriages (where a man without sons was included in the list because his widow had children in his name by his brother). Probably a combination of factors is at work. The unique thing about Luke's list is that it goes back to Adam, showing that Jesus came for all humanity.

SCRIPTURE LINK (4:1–13)

Matthew's coverage of Jesus' temptation can be found in Matt. 4:1–11. Mark's account is in Mark 1:12–13.

What was wrong with turning a stone into bread? (4:3)

The issue was not what the temptation was, but the motive behind it. The devil often appeals to our pride, hoping that we will take matters into our own hands rather than trusting in God. If Jesus had turned the stone into bread, he wouldn't have been depending on his Father in heaven. He resisted these temptations by quoting Scripture to reaffirm his trust in God.

What did the devil hope to accomplish by tempting Jesus? (4:3–13)

Perhaps he hoped to replay the fall of humankind, this time through the one descended from Adam (3:38). See Gen. 3:1–6 and Romans 5:14–15,18–19. But Jesus did not fall prey to Satan's schemes as Adam had done. Satan no doubt hoped to engineer a second great defection and remove Jesus as a viable redeemer for humankind.

Was there any risk Jesus might yield to Satan's temptations? (4:3–13)

Some say the Spirit could never have put Jesus at risk since his divine nature would never succumb to temptation. Others say that because Jesus was human his temptations were legitimate. If this had been merely a mock spiritual battle, they say, then our salvation could not be legitimate. See Heb. 2:14–18; 4:15.

Was the devil right to claim that the world belonged to him? (4:6)

Only partially right—this was a half-truth. The Bible speaks of Satan's power in the world (Eph. 2:1–2). But it was an exaggeration to present himself as sovereign over all of the earth's kingdoms.

The Baptism and Genealogy of Jesus

21When all the people were being baptized, Jesus was baptized too. And as he was praying, heaven was opened **22**and the Holy Spirit descended on him in bodily form like a dove. And a voice came from heaven: "You are my Son, whom I love; with you I am well pleased."

23Now Jesus himself was about thirty years old when he began his ministry. He was the son, so it was thought, of Joseph,

the son of Heli, **24**the son of Matthat,
the son of Levi, the son of Melki,
the son of Jannai, the son of Joseph,
25the son of Mattathias, the son of Amos,
the son of Nahum, the son of Esli,
the son of Naggai, **26**the son of Maath,
the son of Mattathias, the son of Semein,
the son of Josech, the son of Joda,
27the son of Joanan, the son of Rhesa,
the son of Zerubbabel, the son of Shealtiel,
the son of Neri, **28**the son of Melki,
the son of Addi, the son of Cosam,
the son of Elmadam, the son of Er,
29the son of Joshua, the son of Eliezer,
the son of Jorim, the son of Matthat,
the son of Levi, **30**the son of Simeon,
the son of Judah, the son of Joseph,
the son of Jonam, the son of Eliakim,
31the son of Melea, the son of Menna,
the son of Mattatha, the son of Nathan,
the son of David, **32**the son of Jesse,
the son of Obed, the son of Boaz,
the son of Salmon, *a* the son of Nahshon,
33the son of Amminadab, the son of Ram, *b*
the son of Hezron, the son of Perez,
the son of Judah, **34**the son of Jacob,
the son of Isaac, the son of Abraham,
the son of Terah, the son of Nahor,
35the son of Serug, the son of Reu,
the son of Peleg, the son of Eber,
the son of Shelah, **36**the son of Cainan,
the son of Arphaxad, the son of Shem,
the son of Noah, the son of Lamech,
37the son of Methuselah, the son of Enoch,
the son of Jared, the son of Mahalalel,
the son of Kenan, **38**the son of Enosh,
the son of Seth, the son of Adam,
the son of God.

The Temptation of Jesus

4 Jesus, full of the Holy Spirit, returned from the Jordan and was led by the Spirit in the desert, **2**where for forty days he was tempted by the devil. He ate nothing during those days, and at the end of them he was hungry.

3The devil said to him, "If you are the Son of God, tell this stone to become bread."

4Jesus answered, "It is written: 'Man does not live on bread alone.' *c*"

5The devil led him up to a high place and showed him in an instant all the kingdoms of the world. **6**And he said

*a*32 Some early manuscripts *Sala*   *b*33 Some manuscripts *Amminadab, the son of Admin, the son of Arni*; other manuscripts vary widely.   *c*4 Deut. 8:3

to him, "I will give you all their authority and splendor, for it has been given to me, and I can give it to anyone I want to. ⁷So if you worship me, it will all be yours."

⁸Jesus answered, "It is written: 'Worship the Lord your God and serve him only.'ᵃ"

⁹The devil led him to JerusalemD and had him stand on the highest point of the temple. "If you are the Son of God," he said, "throw yourself down from here. ¹⁰For it is written:

" 'He will command his angels concerning you
        to guard you carefully;
¹¹they will lift you up in their hands,
        so that you will not strike your foot against a
        stone.'ᵇ"

¹²Jesus answered, "It says: 'Do not put the Lord your God to the test.'ᶜ"

¹³When the devil had finished all this tempting, he left him until an opportune time.

Jesus Rejected at Nazareth

¹⁴Jesus returned to Galilee in the power of the Spirit, and news about him spread through the whole countryside. ¹⁵He taught in their synagogues, and everyone praised him.

¹⁶He went to Nazareth, where he had been brought up, and on the SabbathD day he went into the synagogue, as was his custom. And he stood up to read. ¹⁷The scroll of the prophetD Isaiah was handed to him. Unrolling it, he found the place where it is written:

¹⁸"The Spirit of the Lord is on me,
        because he has anointedD me
        to preach good news to the poor.
    He has sent me to proclaim freedom for the
        prisoners
    and recovery of sight for the blind,
        to release the oppressed,
¹⁹   to proclaim the year of the Lord's favor."ᵈ

²⁰Then he rolled up the scroll, gave it back to the attendant and sat down. The eyes of everyone in the synagogue were fastened on him, ²¹and he began by saying to them, "Today this scripture is fulfilled in your hearing."

²²All spoke well of him and were amazed at the gracious words that came from his lips. "Isn't this Joseph's son?" they asked.

²³Jesus said to them, "Surely you will quote this proverb to me: 'Physician, heal yourself! Do here in your hometown what we have heard that you did in Capernaum.' "

²⁴"I tell you the truth," he continued, "no prophet is accepted in his hometown. ²⁵I assure you that there were many widows in Israel in Elijah's time, when the sky was shut for three and a half years and there was a severe famine throughout the land. ²⁶Yet Elijah was not sent to any of them, but to a widow in Zarephath in the region of Sidon. ²⁷And there were many in Israel with leprosyDe in the time of Elisha the prophet, yet not one of them was cleansed—only Naaman the Syrian."

²⁸All the people in the synagogue were furious when they heard this. ²⁹They got up, drove him out of the town,

How did Jesus get permission to speak in the synagogue? (4:15–20)
In any synagogue service, any man who wished to speak could do so by notifying the one in charge. Usually the speaker linked the weekly reading of the Law and the Prophets with various other texts.

He stood up to read (4:16)
Men stood to read the Scripture to show their reverence for it. But they sat to teach, distinguishing their commentary from the Scripture itself.

Why did Jesus antagonize these people? (4:28)
Jesus' barbed words succeeded in getting their full attention, which was apparently part of his strategy to warn them of their sins. They were offended not only that he would compare them to the faithless Jews of Elijah and Elisha's time, but also that he suggested that Gentiles could enjoy the blessings of God missed by the Jews—an unthinkable violation of their cultural bias. At other times, Jesus dealt gently with people who were aware of their guilt and wanted to find forgiveness.

ᵃ8 Deut. 6:13   ᵇ11 Psalm 91:11,12   ᶜ12 Deut. 6:16
ᵈ19 Isaiah 61:1,2   ᵉ27 The Greek word was used for various diseases affecting the skin—not necessarily leprosy.

and took him to the brow of the hill on which the town was built, in order to throw him down the cliff. **30**But he walked right through the crowd and went on his way.

Jesus Drives Out an Evil Spirit

31Then he went down to Capernaum, a town in Galilee, and on the Sabbath[D] began to teach the people. **32**They were amazed at his teaching, because his message had authority.

33In the synagogue there was a man possessed by a demon, an evil[a] spirit. He cried out at the top of his voice, **34**"Ha! What do you want with us, Jesus of Nazareth? Have you come to destroy us? I know who you are—the Holy One of God!"

35"Be quiet!" Jesus said sternly. "Come out of him!" Then the demon threw the man down before them all and came out without injuring him.

36All the people were amazed and said to each other, "What is this teaching? With authority and power he gives orders to evil spirits and they come out!" **37**And the news about him spread throughout the surrounding area.

Jesus Heals Many

38Jesus left the synagogue and went to the home of Simon. Now Simon's mother-in-law was suffering from a high fever, and they asked Jesus to help her. **39**So he bent over her and rebuked the fever, and it left her. She got up at once and began to wait on them.

40When the sun was setting, the people brought to Jesus all who had various kinds of sickness, and laying his hands on each one, he healed them. **41**Moreover, demons came out of many people, shouting, "You are the Son of God!" But he rebuked them and would not allow them to speak, because they knew he was the Christ.[b]

42At daybreak Jesus went out to a solitary place. The people were looking for him and when they came to where he was, they tried to keep him from leaving them. **43**But he said, "I must preach the good news of the kingdom of God[D] to the other towns also, because that is why I was sent." **44**And he kept on preaching in the synagogues of Judea.[c]

The Calling of the First Disciples

5 One day as Jesus was standing by the Lake of Gennesaret,[d] with the people crowding around him and listening to the word of God, **2**he saw at the water's edge two boats, left there by the fishermen, who were washing their nets. **3**He got into one of the boats, the one belonging to Simon, and asked him to put out a little from shore. Then he sat down and taught the people from the boat.

4When he had finished speaking, he said to Simon, "Put out into deep water, and let down[e] the nets for a catch."

5Simon answered, "Master, we've worked hard all night and haven't caught anything. But because you say so, I will let down the nets."

6When they had done so, they caught such a large number of fish that their nets began to break. **7**So they signaled their partners in the other boat to come and help them, and they came and filled both boats so full that they began to sink.

SCRIPTURE LINK (4:31–37)

Mark tells about Jesus driving out an evil spirit in Mark 1:21–28.

How do demons possess someone? (4:33)

A person can be "demonized" by a wicked spirit that poses as a sickness (physical or emotional) or unusual behavior beyond the control of the person involved. Such symptoms alone do not indicate demon possession. In Scripture, the appearance of evil spirits reached a climax during the earthly ministry of Jesus, perhaps as part of Satan's effort to discredit Jesus.

Why would demons publicize Jesus' true identity? (4:34)

Their confession was true but was likely motivated by fear. They knew Jesus would one day execute their final judgment and they feared that day had arrived. Ironically, those who deny Jesus' deity and authority show less knowledge than the demons who acknowledge it. Their open admission of his deity, while true, may have been an attempt to incriminate him as one who had cooperated with Satan. This would have been similar to the charge the teachers of the law made later (Mark 3:22).

SCRIPTURE LINK (4:38–43)

Similar accounts of the healing of Peter's mother-in-law and others can be found in Matt. 8:14–17 and Mark 1:29–38.

Why rebuke a fever? (4:39)

This is a figure of speech, not a formula for healing. It is a dramatic way to show that all nature is subject to the authority of God. The fever is personified to demonstrate Jesus' healing power. Some see this as a type of exorcism, but the view seems unlikely because elsewhere Luke writes about casting out evil spirits in straightforward language.

SCRIPTURE LINK (5:1–11)

You'll find other accounts of Jesus calling his first disciples in Matt. 4:18–22; Mark 1:16–20 and John 1:40–42.

Why did Jesus tell Peter where to fish? (5:4)

This miracle, like many of Jesus' miracles, was intended to demonstrate his power and to give a picture of a deeper reality. *Even though you do not believe me,* Jesus said, *believe the miracles* (John 10:38). When Jesus told these fishermen that in the future they would *catch men* (5:10), he showed them that their miraculous catch was descriptive of their future ministry of evangelism.

---

a33 Greek *unclean*; also in verse 36   *b41* Or *Messiah*   *c44* Or *the land of the Jews*; some manuscripts *Galilee*   *d1* That is, Sea of Galilee   *e4* The Greek verb is plural.

The Miracles of Jesus

Healing Miracles	Matthew	Mark	Luke	John
Man with leprosy	8:2-4	1:40-44	5:12-14	
Roman centurion's servant	8:5-13		7:1-10	
Peter's mother-in-law	8:14-15	1:30-31	4:38-39	
Two men from Gadara	8:28-34	5:1-15	8:27-39	
Paralyzed man	9:2-7	2:3-12	5:18-26	
Woman with bleeding	9:20-22	5:25-34	8:43-48	
Two blind men	9:27-31			
Mute, demon-possessed man	9:32-33			
Man with a shriveled hand	12:10-13	3:1-5	6:6-11	
Blind, mute, demon-possessed man	12:22-23		11:14	
Canaanite woman's daughter	15:21-28	7:24-30		
Boy with a demon	17:14-21	9:17-29	9:38-43	
Two blind men (including Bartimaeus)	20:29-34	10:46-52	18:35-43	
Deaf mute		7:31-37		
Possessed man in synagogue		1:21-28	4:31-37	
Blind man at Bethsaida		8:22-26		
Crippled woman			13:10-17	
Man with dropsy			14:1-4	
Ten men with leprosy			17:11-19	
The high priest's servant			22:50-51	
Official's son at Capernaum				4:46-54
Sick man at pool of Bethesda				5:1-15
Man born blind				9:1-41

Miracles showing power over nature

	Matthew	Mark	Luke	John
Calming the storm	8:23-27	4:37-41	8:22-25	
Walking on water	14:22-32	6:47-52		6:16-21
Feeding of the 5,000	14:13-21	6:30-44	9:10-17	6:1-14
Feeding of the 4,000	15:32-39	8:1-10		
Coin in fish	17:24-27			
Fig tree withered	21:18-22	11:12-14, 20-25		
Large catch of fish			5:4-11	
Water turned into wine				2:1-11
Another large catch of fish				21:1-11

Miracles of raising the dead

	Matthew	Mark	Luke	John
Jairus's daughter	9:18-26	5:21-43	8:40-56	
Widow's son at Nain			7:11-17	
Lazarus				11:1-44

[8]When Simon Peter saw this, he fell at Jesus' knees and said, "Go away from me, Lord; I am a sinful man!" [9]For he and all his companions were astonished at the catch of fish they had taken, [10]and so were James and John, the sons of Zebedee, Simon's partners.

Then Jesus said to Simon, "Don't be afraid; from now on you will catch men." [11]So they pulled their boats up on shore, left everything and followed him.

The Man With Leprosy

[12]While Jesus was in one of the towns, a man came along who was covered with leprosy[D].[a] When he saw Jesus, he fell with his face to the ground and begged him, "Lord, if you are willing, you can make me clean."

[13]Jesus reached out his hand and touched the man. "I am willing," he said. "Be clean!" And immediately the leprosy left him.

[14]Then Jesus ordered him, "Don't tell anyone, but go, show yourself to the priest[D] and offer the sacrifices[D] that Moses commanded for your cleansing, as a testimony to them."

[15]Yet the news about him spread all the more, so that crowds of people came to hear him and to be healed of their sicknesses. [16]But Jesus often withdrew to lonely places and prayed.

Jesus Heals a Paralytic

[17]One day as he was teaching, Pharisees[D] and teachers of the law, who had come from every village of Galilee and from Judea and Jerusalem[D], were sitting there. And the power of the Lord was present for him to heal the sick. [18]Some men came carrying a paralytic on a mat and tried to take him into the house to lay him before Jesus. [19]When they could not find a way to do this because of the crowd, they went up on the roof and lowered him on his mat through the tiles into the middle of the crowd, right in front of Jesus.

[20]When Jesus saw their faith, he said, "Friend, your sins are forgiven."

[21]The Pharisees and the teachers of the law began thinking to themselves, "Who is this fellow who speaks blasphemy[D]? Who can forgive sins but God alone?"

[22]Jesus knew what they were thinking and asked, "Why are you thinking these things in your hearts? [23]Which is easier: to say, 'Your sins are forgiven,' or to say, 'Get up and walk'? [24]But that you may know that the Son of Man[D] has authority on earth to forgive sins. . . ." He said to the paralyzed man, "I tell you, get up, take your mat and go home." [25]Immediately he stood up in front of them, took what he had been lying on and went home praising God. [26]Everyone was amazed and gave praise to God. They were filled with awe and said, "We have seen remarkable things today."

The Calling of Levi

[27]After this, Jesus went out and saw a tax collector[D] by the name of Levi sitting at his tax booth. "Follow me," Jesus said to him, [28]and Levi got up, left everything and followed him.

[29]Then Levi held a great banquet for Jesus at his house, and a large crowd of tax collectors and others were eat-

---

[a]12 The Greek word was used for various diseases affecting the skin—not necessarily leprosy.

ing with them. **30**But the Pharisees[D] and the teachers of the law who belonged to their sect complained to his disciples[D], "Why do you eat and drink with tax collectors[D] and 'sinners'?"

31Jesus answered them, "It is not the healthy who need a doctor, but the sick. **32**I have not come to call the righteous[D], but sinners to repentance[D]."

Jesus Questioned About Fasting

33They said to him, "John's disciples often fast and pray, and so do the disciples of the Pharisees, but yours go on eating and drinking."

34Jesus answered, "Can you make the guests of the bridegroom fast while he is with them? **35**But the time will come when the bridegroom will be taken from them; in those days they will fast."

36He told them this parable[D]: "No one tears a patch from a new garment and sews it on an old one. If he does, he will have torn the new garment, and the patch from the new will not match the old. **37**And no one pours new wine[D] into old wineskins[D]. If he does, the new wine will burst the skins, the wine will run out and the wineskins will be ruined. **38**No, new wine must be poured into new wineskins. **39**And no one after drinking old wine wants the new, for he says, 'The old is better.' "

Lord of the Sabbath

6 One Sabbath[D] Jesus was going through the grainfields, and his disciples began to pick some heads of grain, rub them in their hands and eat the kernels. **2**Some of the Pharisees asked, "Why are you doing what is unlawful on the Sabbath?"

3Jesus answered them, "Have you never read what David did when he and his companions were hungry? **4**He entered the house of God, and taking the consecrated[D] bread, he ate what is lawful only for priests[D] to eat. And he also gave some to his companions." **5**Then Jesus said to them, "The Son of Man[D] is Lord of the Sabbath."

6On another Sabbath he went into the synagogue and was teaching, and a man was there whose right hand was shriveled. **7**The Pharisees and the teachers of the law were looking for a reason to accuse Jesus, so they watched him closely to see if he would heal on the Sabbath. **8**But Jesus knew what they were thinking and said to the man with the shriveled hand, "Get up and stand in front of everyone." So he got up and stood there.

9Then Jesus said to them, "I ask you, which is lawful on the Sabbath: to do good or to do evil, to save life or to destroy it?"

10He looked around at them all, and then said to the man, "Stretch out your hand." He did so, and his hand was completely restored. **11**But they were furious and began to discuss with one another what they might do to Jesus.

The Twelve Apostles

12One of those days Jesus went out to a mountainside to pray, and spent the night praying to God. **13**When morning came, he called his disciples to him and chose twelve of them, whom he also designated apostles[D]: **14**Simon (whom he named Peter), his brother Andrew, James, John, Philip, Bartholomew, **15**Matthew, Thomas, James son of Alphaeus, Simon who was called the Zealot, **16**Ju-

SCRIPTURE LINK (5:33–39)

Jesus' reply to the Pharisees' question about fasting can also be found in Matt. 9:14–17 and Mark 2:18–22.

Should Christians fast? (5:35)

Jesus compared his time with his disciples to a wedding feast. Since he is no longer physically among us, it is appropriate to fast—not because it is commanded, as in the Old Testament, but because it is beneficial to our spiritual development. Fasting helps us concentrate in prayer. It heightens our spiritual awareness, lends intensity to our communion with God, and reminds us of our weakness and complete dependence on God. Also see *What are the benefits of sincere fasting?* (Matt. 6:18).

New wine . . . old wineskins (5:37)

Wineskins were the bottles of the first century. They were made of animal skins sewn in the shape of a flexible bag. At first they were soft and pliable, but with age they became brittle. Since wine gives off gases and expands as it undergoes the process of fermentation, a wineskin would have to stretch to accommodate the expanding wine. Non-elastic, old skins would burst during fermentation. Jesus used this as a metaphor: old wineskins represented the Jewish system, which was unable to accommodate the new wine of the kingdom of God.

SCRIPTURE LINK (6:1–11)

You'll also find Jesus' declaration that he is Lord of the Sabbath in Matt. 12:1–14 and Mark 2:23—3:6.

As *Lord of the Sabbath*, did Jesus change the rules? (6:2–5)

No, but he insisted that some principles took precedence over others. The Pharisees were so particular about nonessentials that they failed to see the deeper truths: Minimal food preparation on the Sabbath (vv. 1–2) did not offend God. Doing good on the Sabbath did not violate the spirit of the law (v. 9). Ultimately, Jesus offered himself as the central overriding principle: the Lord of the Sabbath was qualified to say what honored God and what did not.

What was the difference between a disciple and an apostle? (6:13)

A disciple was one who learned from Jesus. An apostle was commissioned as his representative. These twelve disciples were men who were also commissioned as his special representatives. Later, as Jesus' agents, they became leaders in the church (Acts 1–12).

SCRIPTURE LINK (6:13–16)

Matthew lists the twelve apostles in Matt. 10:2–4. Mark names them in Mark 3:16–19.

das son of James, and Judas Iscariot, who became a traitor.

Blessings and Woes

17He went down with them and stood on a level place. A large crowd of his disciples[D] was there and a great number of people from all over Judea, from Jerusalem[D], and from the coast of Tyre and Sidon, **18**who had come to hear him and to be healed of their diseases. Those troubled by evil[a] spirits were cured, **19**and the people all tried to touch him, because power was coming from him and healing them all.

20Looking at his disciples, he said:

"Blessed are you who are poor,
     for yours is the kingdom of God[D].
21Blessed are you who hunger now,
     for you will be satisfied.
Blessed are you who weep now,
     for you will laugh.
22Blessed are you when men hate you,
     when they exclude you and insult you
     and reject your name as evil,
         because of the Son of Man[D].

23"Rejoice in that day and leap for joy, because great is your reward in heaven. For that is how their fathers treated the prophets[D].

24"But woe to you who are rich,
     for you have already received your
         comfort.
25Woe to you who are well fed now,
     for you will go hungry.
Woe to you who laugh now,
     for you will mourn and weep.
26Woe to you when all men speak well of
         you,
     for that is how their fathers treated the
         false prophets.

Love for Enemies

27"But I tell you who hear me: Love your enemies, do good to those who hate you, **28**bless those who curse you, pray for those who mistreat you. **29**If someone strikes you on one cheek, turn to him the other also. If someone takes your cloak, do not stop him from taking your tunic. **30**Give to everyone who asks you, and if anyone takes what belongs to you, do not demand it back. **31**Do to others as you would have them do to you.

32"If you love those who love you, what credit is that to you? Even 'sinners' love those who love them. **33**And if you do good to those who are good to you, what credit is that to you? Even 'sinners' do that. **34**And if you lend to those from whom you expect repayment, what credit is that to you? Even 'sinners' lend to 'sinners,' expecting to be repaid in full. **35**But love your enemies, do good to them, and lend to them without expecting to get anything back. Then your reward will be great, and you will be sons of the Most High, because he is kind to the ungrateful and wicked. **36**Be merciful, just as your Father is merciful.

a 18 Greek *unclean*

SCRIPTURE LINK (6:17–49)

Matthew gives this account as the Sermon on the Mount. See Matt. 5:1—7:27.

Why does Matthew say Jesus gave this sermon on the mountainside, while Luke says *he went down . . . on a level place?* (6:17)

Most likely Jesus spoke from a plateau that was partway down the mountain (see **Map 9** at the back of this Bible), making both Luke's description and Matthew's (Matt. 5:1) correct. The two accounts are parallel in other respects, although Luke reduces Matthew's longer account to its basic core. It's also possible that this is a different sermon from the one Matthew records.

Why did Jesus teach reversed values? (6:20–22)

He wanted to dispute the conventional wisdom of that time which said the wealthy and influential enjoyed more of God's blessings. Jesus wanted his followers to see that material things are only temporary and certainly not the only reality. He didn't want them to think of their current situations as signs of God's blessing or judgment. Instead, he wanted them to see that the poor can be spiritually wealthy (James 2:5).

SCRIPTURE LINK (6:20–23)

Matthew records the Beatitudes in Matt. 5:3–12.

Is it wrong to be financially well-off? (6:24–26)

No, but it can be dangerous. Those who enjoy the "good life" may be more easily tempted to neglect the godly life. Also they may never learn to depend upon God. A Biblical principle says that those entrusted with something are held responsible for it (Matt. 25:19–23; Luke 12:48; 1 Cor. 4:2; 2 Cor. 9:11). The wealthy are to be generous and not take advantage of others (see 1 Tim. 6:17–19).

SCRIPTURE LINK (6:29–30)

You can also find Jesus' teaching on turning the other cheek in Matt. 5:39–42.

How does God show kindness to the ungrateful and wicked? (6:35)

The creation and environment in which we live show the signs of God's universal care—he sends rain, for example, both to those who deserve it and to those who don't (Matt. 5:45). The wicked also can enjoy God's creation, good health and physical sustenance. On the spiritual level, God extends his grace for salvation to all humankind, none of whom are righteous or free from sin.

Judging Others

37"Do not judge, and you will not be judged. Do not condemn, and you will not be condemned. Forgive, and you will be forgiven. **38**Give, and it will be given to you. A good measure, pressed down, shaken together and running over, will be poured into your lap. For with the measure you use, it will be measured to you."

39He also told them this parableD: "Can a blind man lead a blind man? Will they not both fall into a pit? **40**A student is not above his teacher, but everyone who is fully trained will be like his teacher.

41"Why do you look at the speck of sawdust in your brother's eye and pay no attention to the plank in your own eye? **42**How can you say to your brother, 'Brother, let me take the speck out of your eye,' when you yourself fail to see the plank in your own eye? You hypocrite, first take the plank out of your eye, and then you will see clearly to remove the speck from your brother's eye.

A Tree and Its Fruit

43"No good tree bears bad fruit, nor does a bad tree bear good fruit. **44**Each tree is recognized by its own fruit. People do not pick figs from thornbushes, or grapes from briers. **45**The good man brings good things out of the good stored up in his heart, and the evil man brings evil things out of the evil stored up in his heart. For out of the overflow of his heart his mouth speaks.

The Wise and Foolish Builders

46"Why do you call me, 'Lord, Lord,' and do not do what I say? **47**I will show you what he is like who comes to me and hears my words and puts them into practice. **48**He is like a man building a house, who dug down deep and laid the foundation on rock. When a flood came, the torrent struck that house but could not shake it, because it was well built. **49**But the one who hears my words and does not put them into practice is like a man who built a house on the ground without a foundation. The moment the torrent struck that house, it collapsed and its destruction was complete."

SCRIPTURE LINK (6:37–42)
Matthew relates Jesus' teaching about judging others in Matt. 7:1–5.

SCRIPTURE LINK (6:43–44)
Jesus' teaching about a tree and its fruit can be found in Matt. 7:16,18,20.

Isn't there a little good in the worst— and a little bad in the best? (6:43–45)
Yes, but Jesus was speaking in broad general terms, not in specifics. He looked at life as a whole and said that one's basic character reveals itself in the basic product. An evil person who ignores God will reveal his own evil nature; a good person who follows God will reveal his own goodness. Jesus used the analogy of a fruit tree to illustrate his point. But analogies are limited and cannot be expected to parallel every detail exactly.

SCRIPTURE LINK (6:47–49)
Matthew shares Jesus' parable of the wise and foolish builders in Matt. 7:24–27.

Should we not resist oppression? (6:29–30)

In this context, Jesus was talking primarily about religious intolerance. When we are persecuted because of righteousness, we should not strike back (Matt. 5:10–12). The early believers went peacefully to jail when arrested for preaching about Christ. At other times they fled in order to avoid persecution. But we never see armed resistance from the New Testament church. In fact, when Jesus was arrested, Peter was told to put his sword away (John 18:10–11).

On the other hand, Christians with convictions about right and wrong will not idly stand by, blind to injustices against humanity. Some say prayer alone is a sufficient response to injustice. Others say a voice of reason should be raised in opposition to persuade society to do what is right. Some go further and suggest that civil protests or civil disobedience are in order. Still others say that in a fallen world, force (either police or military) may be required to confront evil (Romans 13:4). Though believers may disagree about the best response, they agree some response against injustice is necessary. Also see article: *Does God support bad government?* (Romans 13:1–7).

SCRIPTURE LINK (7:1–10)

Matthew tells about the faith of the centurion in Matt. 8:5–13.

Why would a Gentile build a synagogue for the Jews? (7:5)

This Roman centurion was probably a "God-fearer" (a Gentile interested in the God of the Jews). If so, giving funds for a synagogue was one way he could express his devotion to God. It's also possible he was encouraged by his superiors to do whatever might contribute to the political stability of the area. Making the Jews happy would have helped defuse civil strife.

Why was Jesus amazed? (7:9)

Jesus was amazed that this Gentile seemed more spiritually aware than most Jews. His amazement was two-sided: (1) that a Gentile understood spiritual authority; (2) that God's chosen people did not. The only other time Jesus was amazed like this was over the Jews' lack of faith (Mark 6:6).

SCRIPTURE LINK (7:11–16)

Similar accounts can be found in Mark 5:21–24,35–43 and John 11:1–44. See also 1 Kings 17:17–24; 2 Kings 4:32–37.

Jesus Visits Nain (7:11)

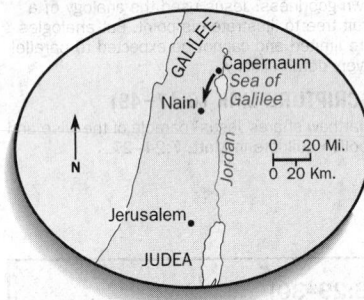

SCRIPTURE LINK (7:18–35)

In Matt. 11:2–19, Matthew also tells how Jesus reassured John the Baptist.

Why did John doubt? (7:19–23)

John probably had doubts because Jesus did not exercise the kind of coercive power John had anticipated from the Messiah. Unlike skeptics, however, John was honest enough to admit his doubts and deal directly with them.

The Faith of the Centurion

7 When Jesus had finished saying all this in the hearing of the people, he entered Capernaum. ²There a centurion'sᴰ servant, whom his master valued highly, was sick and about to die. ³The centurion heard of Jesus and sent some elders of the Jewsᴰ to him, asking him to come and heal his servant. ⁴When they came to Jesus, they pleaded earnestly with him, "This man deserves to have you do this, ⁵because he loves our nation and has built our synagogue." ⁶So Jesus went with them.

He was not far from the house when the centurion sent friends to say to him: "Lord, don't trouble yourself, for I do not deserve to have you come under my roof. ⁷That is why I did not even consider myself worthy to come to you. But say the word, and my servant will be healed. ⁸For I myself am a man under authority, with soldiers under me. I tell this one, 'Go,' and he goes; and that one, 'Come,' and he comes. I say to my servant, 'Do this,' and he does it."

⁹When Jesus heard this, he was amazed at him, and turning to the crowd following him, he said, "I tell you, I have not found such great faith even in Israel." ¹⁰Then the men who had been sent returned to the house and found the servant well.

Jesus Raises a Widow's Son

¹¹Soon afterward, Jesus went to a town called Nain, and his disciplesᴰ and a large crowd went along with him. ¹²As he approached the town gate, a dead person was being carried out—the only son of his mother, and she was a widow. And a large crowd from the town was with her. ¹³When the Lord saw her, his heart went out to her and he said, "Don't cry."

¹⁴Then he went up and touched the coffin, and those carrying it stood still. He said, "Young man, I say to you, get up!" ¹⁵The dead man sat up and began to talk, and Jesus gave him back to his mother.

¹⁶They were all filled with awe and praised God. "A great prophetᴰ has appeared among us," they said. "God has come to help his people." ¹⁷This news about Jesus spread throughout Judeaᵃ and the surrounding country.

Jesus and John the Baptist

¹⁸John's disciples told him about all these things. Calling two of them, ¹⁹he sent them to the Lord to ask, "Are you the one who was to come, or should we expect someone else?"

²⁰When the men came to Jesus, they said, "John the Baptist sent us to you to ask, 'Are you the one who was to come, or should we expect someone else?' "

²¹At that very time Jesus cured many who had diseases, sicknesses and evil spirits, and gave sight to many who were blind. ²²So he replied to the messengers, "Go back and report to John what you have seen and heard: The blind receive sight, the lame walk, those who have leprosyᴰᵇ are cured, the deaf hear, the dead are raised, and the good news is preached to the poor. ²³Blessed is the man who does not fall away on account of me."

²⁴After John's messengers left, Jesus began to speak to the crowd about John: "What did you go out into the

desert to see? A reed swayed by the wind? **25**If not, what did you go out to see? A man dressed in fine clothes? No, those who wear expensive clothes and indulge in luxury are in palaces. **26**But what did you go out to see? A prophet**D**? Yes, I tell you, and more than a prophet. **27**This is the one about whom it is written:

> " 'I will send my messenger ahead of you,
>   who will prepare your way before you.'*a*

28I tell you, among those born of women there is no one greater than John; yet the one who is least in the kingdom of God**D** is greater than he."

29(All the people, even the tax collectors**D**, when they heard Jesus' words, acknowledged that God's way was right, because they had been baptized by John. **30**But the Pharisees**D** and experts in the law rejected God's purpose for themselves, because they had not been baptized by John.)

31"To what, then, can I compare the people of this generation? What are they like? **32**They are like children sitting in the marketplace and calling out to each other:

> " 'We played the flute for you,
>   and you did not dance;
>   we sang a dirge,
>   and you did not cry.'

33For John the Baptist came neither eating bread nor drinking wine, and you say, 'He has a demon.' **34**The Son of Man**D** came eating and drinking, and you say, 'Here is a glutton**D** and a drunkard, a friend of tax collectors and "sinners." ' **35**But wisdom is proved right by all her children."

Jesus Anointed by a Sinful Woman

36Now one of the Pharisees invited Jesus to have dinner with him, so he went to the Pharisee's house and reclined at the table. **37**When a woman who had lived a sinful life in that town learned that Jesus was eating at the Pharisee's house, she brought an alabaster jar of perfume, **38**and as she stood behind him at his feet weeping, she began to wet his feet with her tears. Then she wiped them with her hair, kissed them and poured perfume on them.

39When the Pharisee who had invited him saw this, he said to himself, "If this man were a prophet, he would know who is touching him and what kind of woman she is—that she is a sinner."

40Jesus answered him, "Simon, I have something to tell you."

"Tell me, teacher," he said.

41"Two men owed money to a certain moneylender. One owed him five hundred denarii,*b* and the other fifty. **42**Neither of them had the money to pay him back, so he canceled the debts of both. Now which of them will love him more?"

43Simon replied, "I suppose the one who had the bigger debt canceled."

"You have judged correctly," Jesus said.

44Then he turned toward the woman and said to Simon, "Do you see this woman? I came into your house. You did not give me any water for my feet, but she wet my feet

---

How can those *least in the kingdom of God* be greater than John? (7:28)

Jesus affirmed both the greatness of John the Baptist and the greater privileges kingdom citizens enjoy. Great as he was, John served only as a forerunner who announced that the kingdom was near. Under Christ's new covenant, we enjoy the fuller benefits of kingdom life (Col. 1:13–14).

How did John's baptism prepare people to accept Jesus? (7:29–30)

Before people could appreciate God's offer of salvation through Jesus, they needed to see their need of salvation. John's ministry caused people to see themselves as sinners who needed to change their ways. Humbled by their overwhelming spiritual needs, they repented and became receptive to forgiveness made possible by Jesus' sacrifice.

Why were Jesus and John so different? (7:33–34)

They were not really as different as their detractors made them appear. John's simple lifestyle fit his message of repentance and self-denial, while Jesus' attendance at public dinners expressed his gracious willingness to mingle with those who needed him. John and Jesus were neither demon-possessed nor overindulgent, as their opponents charged; they simply refused to play along with their critics' childish games.

SCRIPTURE LINK (7:37–39)

Similar accounts of the anointing of Jesus can be found in Matt. 26:6–13; Mark 14:3–9 and John 12:1–8.

SCRIPTURE LINK (7:41–42)

Matthew records a similar parable in Matt. 18:23–34.

Did Simon neglect common courtesies? (7:44–46)

Many suggest that Simon, by failing to provide water for his guest's feet, did not follow typical customs of hospitality. Others say such practices were optional. But Jesus may not have been criticizing Simon so much as commending the woman and using her actions to make a point. Her special attention to Jesus showed her devotion and dedication to him. The measure of her forgiveness was demonstrated by her expressions of love.

---

*a*27 Mal. 3:1   *b*41 A denarius was a coin worth about a day's wages.

with her tears and wiped them with her hair. **45**You did not give me a kiss, but this woman, from the time I entered, has not stopped kissing my feet. **46**You did not put oil on my head, but she has poured perfume on my feet. **47**Therefore, I tell you, her many sins have been forgiven—for she loved much. But he who has been forgiven little loves little."

48Then Jesus said to her, "Your sins are forgiven."

49The other guests began to say among themselves, "Who is this who even forgives sins?"

50Jesus said to the woman, "Your faith has saved you; go in peace[D]."

The Parable of the Sower

8 After this, Jesus traveled about from one town and village to another, proclaiming the good news of the kingdom of God[D]. The Twelve were with him, **2**and also some women who had been cured of evil spirits and diseases: Mary (called Magdalene) from whom seven demons had come out; **3**Joanna the wife of Cuza, the manager of Herod's household; Susanna; and many others. These women were helping to support them out of their own means.

4While a large crowd was gathering and people were coming to Jesus from town after town, he told this parable[D]: **5**"A farmer went out to sow his seed. As he was scattering the seed, some fell along the path; it was trampled on, and the birds of the air ate it up. **6**Some fell on rock, and when it came up, the plants withered because they had no moisture. **7**Other seed fell among thorns, which grew up with it and choked the plants. **8**Still other seed fell on good soil. It came up and yielded a crop, a hundred times more than was sown."

When he said this, he called out, "He who has ears to hear, let him hear."

9His disciples[D] asked him what this parable meant. **10**He said, "The knowledge of the secrets of the kingdom of God has been given to you, but to others I speak in parables, so that,

> " 'though seeing, they may not see;
>   though hearing, they may not understand.'[a]

11"This is the meaning of the parable: The seed is the word of God. **12**Those along the path are the ones who hear, and then the devil comes and takes away the word from their hearts, so that they may not believe and be saved. **13**Those on the rock are the ones who receive the word with joy when they hear it, but they have no root. They believe for a while, but in the time of testing they fall away. **14**The seed that fell among thorns stands for those who hear, but as they go on their way they are choked by life's worries, riches and pleasures, and they do not mature. **15**But the seed on good soil stands for those with a noble and good heart, who hear the word, retain it, and by persevering produce a crop.

A Lamp on a Stand

16"No one lights a lamp and hides it in a jar or puts it under a bed. Instead, he puts it on a stand, so that those who come in can see the light. **17**For there is nothing hidden that will not be disclosed, and nothing concealed that will not be known or brought out into the open. **18**There-

---

How could these women help support Jesus and all his disciples? (8:3)
It is unknown. Perhaps these women came from wealthy backgrounds, as suggested by the fact that one of them was the wife of a government official.

Why use stories people don't understand? (8:4–10)
Parables were used to reveal as well as to conceal truth. Jesus concealed truth from those who would reject his message—a judgment on their hard-heartedness. Also, Jesus may have recognized that his teachings could cause casual observers, opponents, and overzealous supporters to steer his ministry toward a premature conclusion. Perhaps he obscured some teaching to prevent that from happening. To people willing to receive his message, however, Jesus' stories communicate further truth about the nature of God's kingdom.

SCRIPTURE LINK (8:4–15)
You can also find the parable of the sower in Matt. 13:2–23 and Mark 4:1–20.

What does it mean to *produce a crop*? (8:15)
Elsewhere the Bible speaks of *the fruit of the Spirit*—the godly characteristics that are products of a Christian's relationship with God and others (Gal. 5:22–25). In this verse, *produce a crop* may also suggest Christians who share their faith with others and urge them to accept salvation in Christ.

Is it fair to give more to one who already has? (8:18)
Fairness is not the issue. If it were, no one could expect anything from God except judgment. The point here is that God, in his mercy, rewards those who are faithful. The one who lives a righteous life will enjoy the best life has to offer, though rewards may often seem intangible. The more closely that one lines up with God's purposes, the greater the benefits—in this life as well as in the next.

---

a 10 Isaiah 6:9

fore consider carefully how you listen. Whoever has will be given more; whoever does not have, even what he thinks he has will be taken from him."

Jesus' Mother and Brothers

19Now Jesus' mother and brothers came to see him, but they were not able to get near him because of the crowd. 20Someone told him, "Your mother and brothers are standing outside, wanting to see you."

21He replied, "My mother and brothers are those who hear God's word and put it into practice."

Jesus Calms the Storm

22One day Jesus said to his disciples,ᴰ "Let's go over to the other side of the lake." So they got into a boat and set out. 23As they sailed, he fell asleep. A squall came down on the lake, so that the boat was being swamped, and they were in great danger.

24The disciples went and woke him, saying, "Master, Master, we're going to drown!"

He got up and rebuked the wind and the raging waters; the storm subsided, and all was calm. 25"Where is your faith?" he asked his disciples.

In fear and amazement they asked one another, "Who is this? He commands even the winds and the water, and they obey him."

The Healing of a Demon-possessed Man

26They sailed to the region of the Gerasenes,ᵃ which is across the lake from Galilee. 27When Jesus stepped ashore, he was met by a demon-possessed man from the town. For a long time this man had not worn clothes or lived in a house, but had lived in the tombs. 28When he saw Jesus, he cried out and fell at his feet, shouting at the top of his voice, "What do you want with me, Jesus, Son of the Most High God? I beg you, don't torture me!" 29For Jesus had commanded the evilᵇ spirit to come out of the man. Many times it had seized him, and though he was chained hand and foot and kept under guard, he had bro-

ᵃ26 Some manuscripts *Gadarenes*; other manuscripts *Gergesenes*; also in verse 37   ᵇ29 Greek *unclean*

SCRIPTURE LINK (8:19–21)

Jesus also tells who his mother and brothers are in Matt. 12:46–50 and Mark 3:31–35.

Did Jesus reject his own family? (8:20–21)

No. He simply used this incident to make a point: if one has to choose between one's family and the will of God, the will of God must come first. Also see 18:29–30.

SCRIPTURE LINK (8:22–25)

You can also read about Jesus calming the storm in Matt. 8:23–27 and Mark 4:36–41. Similar stories appear in Mark 6:47–52 and John 6:16–21.

SCRIPTURE LINK (8:26–39)

Matthew tells about Jesus healing the demon-possessed man in Matt. 8:28–34. Mark gives the account in Mark 5:1–20.

Can believers fall away? (8:13)

It would seem so, according to this verse. But some see another possibility: that this verse looks at how people *appear,* rather than their true spiritual condition. They suggest the *appearance* of falling away (that is, turning away from the faith entirely and decisively) reveals that the person never had true faith.

Others, however, say it's possible to *believe for a while.* They say the New Testament warns believers to *persevere* in their faith—a warning different from that given to unbelievers. They say God gives people a free will—something they still have when they accept Christ.

The debate goes on, so it is perhaps best to emphasize what both sides agree on: that in the end those who believe will be saved and that only the seed that bears fruit will reach its goal.

Also see article: *Should we fear falling?* (Heb. 6:6).

Abyss (8:31)

The Greeks used this word to describe the underworld of spirits, suggesting a place that cannot be seen—a place so deep it is unfathomable. The New Testament uses this word once for the place of the dead (*the deep*, Romans 10:7). More often it describes what traditionally was known as the "bottomless pit" where Satan will be banished for a time (Rev. 20:3).

What were the people afraid of? (8:37)

They seemed to fear the awesome power of God displayed in their midst. Such supernatural power would have been unnerving to people who had not shown any interest in honoring God. They may have seen the loss of their herd as God's judgment and perhaps feared further judgment.

SCRIPTURE LINK (8:40–56)

Matthew carries the accounts of the dead girl and sick woman in Matt. 9:18–26 as does Mark in Mark 5:22–43.

Could others tap Jesus' power without his permission? (8:46)

Jesus was always in control; his power was never released without his consent. Why then did he ask who had touched him? Possibly he did it to make the woman go public. It would have been in her own best interest—not to mention the crowd's—to tell others what had happened to her. Thus a person of timid faith became a faithful witness.

Will I be healed if I have faith? (8:48)

Jesus teaches that faith prompts God to respond to our need. Sometimes, it is the faith of friends or family that God rewards. Occasionally, God's healing work seems unrelated to anyone's faith—the only explanation is God's sovereign choice. But Jesus never teaches that faith automatically brings healing. In Christ's 35 miracles recorded in the Gospels, no formula to guarantee healing can be found. Also see *Does God guarantee healing from any disease?* (Psalm 103:3) and *Is healing guaranteed?* (James 5:15–16).

Why did Jesus insist the girl was not dead? (8:52)

Jesus used sleep as a picture of death on more than one occasion (John 11:11–14). Perhaps he spoke this way to show that when he is involved, death is not final. He could bring this girl back from death. See also *Fall asleep* (1 Thes. 4:13).

ken his chains and had been driven by the demon into solitary places.

[30]Jesus asked him, "What is your name?"

"Legion[D]," he replied, because many demons had gone into him. [31]And they begged him repeatedly not to order them to go into the Abyss[D].

[32]A large herd of pigs was feeding there on the hillside. The demons begged Jesus to let them go into them, and he gave them permission. [33]When the demons came out of the man, they went into the pigs, and the herd rushed down the steep bank into the lake and was drowned.

[34]When those tending the pigs saw what had happened, they ran off and reported this in the town and countryside, [35]and the people went out to see what had happened. When they came to Jesus, they found the man from whom the demons had gone out, sitting at Jesus' feet, dressed and in his right mind; and they were afraid. [36]Those who had seen it told the people how the demon-possessed man had been cured. [37]Then all the people of the region of the Gerasenes asked Jesus to leave them, because they were overcome with fear. So he got into the boat and left.

[38]The man from whom the demons had gone out begged to go with him, but Jesus sent him away, saying, [39]"Return home and tell how much God has done for you." So the man went away and told all over town how much Jesus had done for him.

A Dead Girl and a Sick Woman

[40]Now when Jesus returned, a crowd welcomed him, for they were all expecting him. [41]Then a man named Jairus, a ruler of the synagogue, came and fell at Jesus' feet, pleading with him to come to his house [42]because his only daughter, a girl of about twelve, was dying.

As Jesus was on his way, the crowds almost crushed him. [43]And a woman was there who had been subject to bleeding for twelve years,[a] but no one could heal her. [44]She came up behind him and touched the edge of his cloak, and immediately her bleeding stopped.

[45]"Who touched me?" Jesus asked.

When they all denied it, Peter said, "Master, the people are crowding and pressing against you."

[46]But Jesus said, "Someone touched me; I know that power has gone out from me."

[47]Then the woman, seeing that she could not go unnoticed, came trembling and fell at his feet. In the presence of all the people, she told why she had touched him and how she had been instantly healed. [48]Then he said to her, "Daughter, your faith has healed you. Go in peace[D]."

[49]While Jesus was still speaking, someone came from the house of Jairus, the synagogue ruler. "Your daughter is dead," he said. "Don't bother the teacher any more."

[50]Hearing this, Jesus said to Jairus, "Don't be afraid; just believe, and she will be healed."

[51]When he arrived at the house of Jairus, he did not let anyone go in with him except Peter, John and James, and the child's father and mother. [52]Meanwhile, all the people were wailing and mourning for her. "Stop wailing," Jesus said. "She is not dead but asleep."

[53]They laughed at him, knowing that she was dead. [54]But he took her by the hand and said, "My child, get up!" [55]Her spirit returned, and at once she stood up. Then

[a]43 Many manuscripts *years, and she had spent all she had on doctors*

Jesus told them to give her something to eat. **56**Her parents were astonished, but he ordered them not to tell anyone what had happened.

Jesus Sends Out the Twelve

9 When Jesus had called the Twelve together, he gave them power and authority to drive out all demons and to cure diseases, **2**and he sent them out to preach the kingdom of God[D] and to heal the sick. **3**He told them: "Take nothing for the journey—no staff, no bag, no bread, no money, no extra tunic. **4**Whatever house you enter, stay there until you leave that town. **5**If people do not welcome you, shake the dust off your feet when you leave their town, as a testimony against them." **6**So they set out and went from village to village, preaching the gospel[D] and healing people everywhere.

7Now Herod the tetrarch[D] heard about all that was going on. And he was perplexed, because some were saying that John had been raised from the dead, **8**others that Elijah had appeared, and still others that one of the prophets[D] of long ago had come back to life. **9**But Herod said, "I beheaded John. Who, then, is this I hear such things about?" And he tried to see him.

Jesus Feeds the Five Thousand

10When the apostles[D] returned, they reported to Jesus what they had done. Then he took them with him and they withdrew by themselves to a town called Bethsaida, **11**but the crowds learned about it and followed him. He welcomed them and spoke to them about the kingdom of God, and healed those who needed healing.

12Late in the afternoon the Twelve came to him and said, "Send the crowd away so they can go to the surrounding villages and countryside and find food and lodging, because we are in a remote place here."

13He replied, "You give them something to eat."

They answered, "We have only five loaves of bread and two fish—unless we go and buy food for all this crowd." **14**(About five thousand men were there.)

But he said to his disciples[D], "Have them sit down in groups of about fifty each." **15**The disciples did so, and everybody sat down. **16**Taking the five loaves and the two fish and looking up to heaven, he gave thanks and broke them. Then he gave them to the disciples to set before the people. **17**They all ate and were satisfied, and the disciples picked up twelve basketfuls of broken pieces that were left over.

Peter's Confession of Christ

18Once when Jesus was praying in private and his disciples were with him, he asked them, "Who do the crowds say I am?"

19They replied, "Some say John the Baptist; others Elijah; and still others, that one of the prophets of long ago has come back to life."

20"But what about you?" he asked. "Who do you say I am?"

Peter answered, "The Christ[a] of God."

21Jesus strictly warned them not to tell this to anyone. **22**And he said, "The Son of Man[D] must suffer many things and be rejected by the elders, chief priests[D] and

[a]20 Or *Messiah*

Why did Jesus say to take nothing? (9:3)

Jesus wanted the Twelve to be completely dependent on God for their provision. He wanted them to see how God would provide for them. He was not setting a precedent, however, that all ministries must follow. The New Testament churches were encouraged to support those who ministered to them (Phil. 4:14; 1 Tim. 5:17–18; 3 John 5–8).

SCRIPTURE LINK (9:3–5)

Jesus also gives the disciples instructions about dealing with rejection in Matt. 10:9–15 and Mark 6:8–11.

Why shake the dust off your feet? (9:5)

Jews returning to Israel from a foreign land would shake the dust from their sandals and clothing to avoid defiling the land they considered holy. The disciples were delivering a similar warning to the people of Israel. If they rejected the message of Christ, they would face the same future judgment as unbelieving foreigners.

Herod the tetrarch (9:7)

This is Herod Antipas, before whom Jesus eventually appeared during part of his trial (13:31–32; 23:6–12). His father, Herod the Great, ruled during the time of Jesus' birth. Technically, the term *tetrarch* meant someone who governed one-fourth of a country, but sometimes the title was used simply as a synonym for "prince" or "king." Herod Antipas reigned over the regions of Galilee and Perea from approximately 4 B.C. to A.D. 39.

SCRIPTURE LINK (9:7–9)

Both Matthew and Mark also relate Herod's confusion over Jesus' identity. See Matt. 14:1–2 and Mark 6:14–16.

SCRIPTURE LINK (9:10–17)

Accounts of Jesus feeding the five thousand can also be found in Matt. 14:13–21; Mark 6:32–44 and John 6:5–13.

SCRIPTURE LINK (9:18–20)

Matthew tells of Peter's confession of Christ in Matt. 16:13–16. You'll also find it in Mark 8:27–29.

SCRIPTURE LINK (9:22–27)

Jesus predicts his death and resurrection in Matt. 16:21–28 and Mark 8:31—9:1.

Why is self-denial a prerequisite to being a Christian? (9:23)

The kingdom of heaven belongs to those who are *poor in spirit* (Matt. 5:3)—those who recognize their spiritual poverty and see their need for God's help. We must say no to any selfishness or unhealthy pride that could inhibit the genuine humility and faith God desires (James 4:6–10; 1 Peter 5:6). Without denying our self-worth, Jesus asks us to deny our self-centeredness so that his priorities become ours.

What does *take up his cross* mean? (9:23)

This phrase probably startled Jesus' listeners, for in that culture "taking up a cross" meant facing the horrible pain and humiliation of Roman crucifixion. Usually condemned criminals were *forced* to carry crosses, but Jesus laid down his life voluntarily. He asks us to do the same—to commit our lives wholeheartedly to him, accepting any hardship this choice may bring.

SCRIPTURE LINK (9:28–36)

Matthew gives the account of Jesus' transfiguration in Matt. 17:1–8. Mark covers it in Mark 9:2–8.

How could Moses and Elijah return from the dead? (9:30)

God briefly brought them from the spiritual realm (presumably Paradise—see 23:43; 2 Cor. 12:2–4) to appear with Jesus on this special occasion. This should not be confused with spiritualist practices; this was not a séance or an example of reincarnation. Evidently this event linked Jesus to the religious heritage of the Jews. Moses (representing the law) and Elijah (representing the prophets) demonstrated their approval for Jesus and his new covenant which was superior to their earlier covenant with God (Heb. 8:6).

SCRIPTURE LINK (9:37–42,43–45)

Matthew's account of the healing of a boy with an evil spirit can be found in Matt. 17:14–18,22–23 and Mark wrote about it in Mark 9:14–27,30–32.

Are evil spirits the cause of convulsions? (9:39)

They may be the cause of some convulsions. Passages like this indicate that sometimes demon possession manifests itself in visible physical signs. But this is not automatically the case; physical causes may also lie behind such symptoms.

teachers of the law, and he must be killed and on the third day be raised to life."

²³Then he said to them all: "If anyone would come after me, he must deny himself and take up his cross daily and follow me. ²⁴For whoever wants to save his life will lose it, but whoever loses his life for me will save it. ²⁵What good is it for a man to gain the whole world, and yet lose or forfeit his very self? ²⁶If anyone is ashamed of me and my words, the Son of Man[D] will be ashamed of him when he comes in his glory[D] and in the glory of the Father and of the holy angels. ²⁷I tell you the truth, some who are standing here will not taste death[D] before they see the kingdom of God."

The Transfiguration

²⁸About eight days after Jesus said this, he took Peter, John and James with him and went up onto a mountain to pray. ²⁹As he was praying, the appearance of his face changed, and his clothes became as bright as a flash of lightning. ³⁰Two men, Moses and Elijah, ³¹appeared in glorious splendor, talking with Jesus. They spoke about his departure, which he was about to bring to fulfillment at Jerusalem[D]. ³²Peter and his companions were very sleepy, but when they became fully awake, they saw his glory and the two men standing with him. ³³As the men were leaving Jesus, Peter said to him, "Master, it is good for us to be here. Let us put up three shelters—one for you, one for Moses and one for Elijah." (He did not know what he was saying.)

³⁴While he was speaking, a cloud appeared and enveloped them, and they were afraid as they entered the cloud. ³⁵A voice came from the cloud, saying, "This is my Son, whom I have chosen; listen to him." ³⁶When the voice had spoken, they found that Jesus was alone. The disciples[D] kept this to themselves, and told no one at that time what they had seen.

The Healing of a Boy With an Evil Spirit

³⁷The next day, when they came down from the mountain, a large crowd met him. ³⁸A man in the crowd called out, "Teacher, I beg you to look at my son, for he is my only child. ³⁹A spirit seizes him and he suddenly screams; it throws him into convulsions so that he foams at the mouth. It scarcely ever leaves him and is destroying him. ⁴⁰I begged your disciples to drive it out, but they could not."

⁴¹"O unbelieving and perverse generation," Jesus replied, "how long shall I stay with you and put up with you? Bring your son here."

⁴²Even while the boy was coming, the demon threw him to the ground in a convulsion. But Jesus rebuked the evil[a] spirit, healed the boy and gave him back to his father. ⁴³And they were all amazed at the greatness of God.

While everyone was marveling at all that Jesus did, he said to his disciples, ⁴⁴"Listen carefully to what I am about to tell you: The Son of Man is going to be betrayed into the hands of men." ⁴⁵But they did not understand what this meant. It was hidden from them, so that they did not grasp it, and they were afraid to ask him about it.

*a*42 Greek *unclean*

Who Will Be the Greatest?

46An argument started among the disciples[D] as to which of them would be the greatest. **47**Jesus, knowing their thoughts, took a little child and had him stand beside him. **48**Then he said to them, "Whoever welcomes this little child in my name welcomes me; and whoever welcomes me welcomes the one who sent me. For he who is least among you all—he is the greatest."

49"Master," said John, "we saw a man driving out demons in your name and we tried to stop him, because he is not one of us."

50"Do not stop him," Jesus said, "for whoever is not against you is for you."

Samaritan Opposition

51As the time approached for him to be taken up to heaven, Jesus resolutely set out for Jerusalem[D]. **52**And he sent messengers on ahead, who went into a Samaritan village to get things ready for him; **53**but the people there did not welcome him, because he was heading for Jerusalem. **54**When the disciples James and John saw this, they asked, "Lord, do you want us to call fire down from heaven to destroy them[a]?" **55**But Jesus turned and rebuked them, **56**and[b] they went to another village.

The Cost of Following Jesus

57As they were walking along the road, a man said to him, "I will follow you wherever you go."

58Jesus replied, "Foxes have holes and birds of the air have nests, but the Son of Man[D] has no place to lay his head."

59He said to another man, "Follow me."

But the man replied, "Lord, first let me go and bury my father."

60Jesus said to him, "Let the dead bury their own dead, but you go and proclaim the kingdom of God."

61Still another said, "I will follow you, Lord; but first let me go back and say good-by to my family."

62Jesus replied, "No one who puts his hand to the plow and looks back is fit for service in the kingdom of God."

Jesus Sends Out the Seventy-two

10 After this the Lord appointed seventy-two[c] others and sent them two by two ahead of him to every town and place where he was about to go. **2**He told them, "The harvest is plentiful, but the workers are few. Ask the Lord of the harvest, therefore, to send out workers into his harvest field. **3**Go! I am sending you out like lambs among wolves. **4**Do not take a purse or bag or sandals; and do not greet anyone on the road.

5"When you enter a house, first say, 'Peace[D] to this house.' **6**If a man of peace is there, your peace will rest on him; if not, it will return to you. **7**Stay in that house, eating and drinking whatever they give you, for the worker deserves his wages. Do not move around from house to house.

8"When you enter a town and are welcomed, eat what is set before you. **9**Heal the sick who are there and tell

SCRIPTURE LINK (9:46–50)

Jesus also answers the question of who will be the greatest in Matt. 18:1–5 and Mark 9:33–40.

What does *welcoming* a child have to do with spiritual greatness? (9:48)

Human nature generally ignores those who have no influence and plays up to those who do. Human nature rubs shoulders with the great in order to boost one's own ego and status in the eyes of others. Jesus calls for us to humble ourselves. We should care nothing about the world's status symbols because the true way to greatness is humility (1 Peter 5:5–6). One sign of this humility is to enjoy those the world would consider insignificant.

Why did the Samaritans care where Jesus was going? (9:53)

The Samaritans were disturbed about anybody worshiping in Jerusalem. They believed that Mount Gerizim was the place to meet with God (see **Map 9** at the back of this Bible). Deep hostilities had existed between the Samaritans and the Jews for centuries because of ethnic as well as religious differences. See **Why the tension between Jews and Samaritans?** (John 4:9).

SCRIPTURE LINK (9:57–60)

Matthew talks about the cost of following Jesus in Matt. 8:19–22.

Why did Jesus discourage those who were at least going in the right direction? (9:57–62)

He wanted them to know it would cost them something to follow him, not to discover later that there were additional requirements for being his disciples. As the Jewish religious leaders became increasingly hostile toward Jesus, he wanted his disciples to be prepared for the worst (John 15:18).

Lambs among wolves (10:3)

Jesus wanted his 72 disciples to understand what they were getting into. Their task would be dangerous. Often they would be rejected. Jesus was up front about what would happen if they worked for him.

SCRIPTURE LINK (10:4–12)

Jesus gives the same instructions to the Twelve in Luke 9:3–5.

---

a54 Some manuscripts them, even as Elijah did   *b55,56 Some manuscripts them. And he said, "You do not know what kind of spirit you are of, for the Son of Man did not come to destroy men's lives, but to save them." 56And*   *c1 Some manuscripts seventy; also in verse 17*

SCRIPTURE LINK (10:13–15,21,22)
Matthew records Jesus' pronouncement of woe on unrepentant cities in Matt. 11:21–23 and Jesus' praise to the Father in Matt. 11:25–27.

Will judgment be easier for some than others? (10:14)

Some sins may deserve more severe punishment because greater knowledge implies greater accountability. According to Jesus, a servant who knowingly disobeys his master deserves more punishment than one who disobeys in ignorance (12:47–48). God's judgment will be completely just. Sometimes he has extended special mercy to those who act in ignorance, but now he calls everyone to repent (see Romans 2:4–11).

How did Satan fall from heaven? (10:18)

Satan fell in the sense that he was defeated when confronted with the power of Christ: the disciples were in charge, not Satan's demons (v. 17). The disciples preached the message of the kingdom, healed the sick, raised the dead, cleansed lepers and drove out demons (Matt. 10:7–8). The miraculous ministry of Jesus proved God's power to be far greater than Satan's. When Jesus ushered in the kingdom of God, Satan's demise began. Some tie this verse to Isaiah 14 and Revelation 12, but both of those contexts are different. There may be a parallel, but that similarity does not make the events identical. See *Does this describe the fall of Satan?* (Isaiah 14:12–15).

In what sense are snakes and scorpions used by the enemy? (10:19)

These parts of the creation were symbols of the presence of evil (Rev. 20:2). This was, then, a figurative way to speak of trampling over evil. Nonetheless, some see this as a literal promise of physical protection.

SCRIPTURE LINK (10:23–24)
Jesus' words of blessing to his disciples can also be found in Matt. 13:16–17.

SCRIPTURE LINK (10:25–28)
You'll also find the greatest commandment in Matt. 22:34–40 and Mark 12:28–31.

Priest . . . Levite . . . Samaritan (10:31–33)

Jesus included three kinds of individuals in his story, raising three kinds of expectations among his listeners. A priest was God's representative, a Levite his assistant—so-called examples of righteousness. Jesus' listeners would have expected them to help. Samaritans, on the other hand, despised for their ethnic and religious impurities, would have been expected to walk on by. See *Why the tension between Jews and Samaritans?* (John 4:9).

---

them, 'The kingdom of God[D] is near you.' **10**But when you enter a town and are not welcomed, go into its streets and say, **11**'Even the dust of your town that sticks to our feet we wipe off against you. Yet be sure of this: The kingdom of God is near.' **12**I tell you, it will be more bearable on that day for Sodom than for that town.

13"Woe to you, Korazin! Woe to you, Bethsaida! For if the miracles that were performed in you had been performed in Tyre and Sidon, they would have repented[D] long ago, sitting in sackcloth[D] and ashes. **14**But it will be more bearable for Tyre and Sidon at the judgment than for you. **15**And you, Capernaum, will you be lifted up to the skies? No, you will go down to the depths.[a]

16"He who listens to you listens to me; he who rejects you rejects me; but he who rejects me rejects him who sent me."

17The seventy-two returned with joy and said, "Lord, even the demons submit to us in your name."

18He replied, "I saw Satan fall like lightning from heaven. **19**I have given you authority to trample on snakes and scorpions and to overcome all the power of the enemy; nothing will harm you. **20**However, do not rejoice that the spirits submit to you, but rejoice that your names are written in heaven."

21At that time Jesus, full of joy through the Holy Spirit, said, "I praise you, Father, Lord of heaven and earth, because you have hidden these things from the wise and learned, and revealed them to little children. Yes, Father, for this was your good pleasure.

22"All things have been committed to me by my Father. No one knows who the Son is except the Father, and no one knows who the Father is except the Son and those to whom the Son chooses to reveal him."

23Then he turned to his disciples[D] and said privately, "Blessed are the eyes that see what you see. **24**For I tell you that many prophets[D] and kings wanted to see what you see but did not see it, and to hear what you hear but did not hear it."

The Parable of the Good Samaritan

25On one occasion an expert in the law stood up to test Jesus. "Teacher," he asked, "what must I do to inherit eternal life?"

26"What is written in the Law?" he replied. "How do you read it?"

27He answered: " 'Love the Lord your God with all your heart and with all your soul[D] and with all your strength and with all your mind'[b]; and, 'Love your neighbor as yourself.'[c]"

28"You have answered correctly," Jesus replied. "Do this and you will live."

29But he wanted to justify[D] himself, so he asked Jesus, "And who is my neighbor?"

30In reply Jesus said: "A man was going down from Jerusalem[D] to Jericho[D], when he fell into the hands of robbers. They stripped him of his clothes, beat him and went away, leaving him half dead. **31**A priest[D] happened to be going down the same road, and when he saw the man, he passed by on the other side. **32**So too, a Levite[D], when he came to the place and saw him, passed by on the other side. **33**But a Samaritan, as he traveled, came where the man was; and when he saw him, he took pity on him.

a 15 Greek *Hades*   b 27 Deut. 6:5   c 27 Lev. 19:18

34He went to him and bandaged his wounds, pouring on oil and wine. Then he put the man on his own donkey, took him to an inn and took care of him. **35**The next day he took out two silver coins*a* and gave them to the innkeeper. 'Look after him,' he said, 'and when I return, I will reimburse you for any extra expense you may have.'

36"Which of these three do you think was a neighbor to the man who fell into the hands of robbers?"

37The expert in the law replied, "The one who had mercy*D* on him."

Jesus told him, "Go and do likewise."

At the Home of Martha and Mary

38As Jesus and his disciples*D* were on their way, he came to a village where a woman named Martha opened her home to him. **39**She had a sister called Mary, who sat at the Lord's feet listening to what he said. **40**But Martha was distracted by all the preparations that had to be made. She came to him and asked, "Lord, don't you care that my sister has left me to do the work by myself? Tell her to help me!"

41"Martha, Martha," the Lord answered, "you are worried and upset about many things, **42**but only one thing is needed.*b* Mary has chosen what is better, and it will not be taken away from her."

Jesus' Teaching on Prayer

11 One day Jesus was praying in a certain place. When he finished, one of his disciples said to him, "Lord, teach us to pray, just as John taught his disciples."

2He said to them, "When you pray, say:

" 'Father,*c*
hallowed be your name,
your kingdom come.*d*
3Give us each day our daily bread.
4Forgive us our sins,
    for we also forgive everyone who sins against
        us.*e*
And lead us not into temptation.*f* ' "

5Then he said to them, "Suppose one of you has a friend, and he goes to him at midnight and says, 'Friend, lend me three loaves of bread, **6**because a friend of mine on a journey has come to me, and I have nothing to set before him.'

7"Then the one inside answers, 'Don't bother me. The door is already locked, and my children are with me in bed. I can't get up and give you anything.' **8**I tell you, though he will not get up and give him the bread because he is his friend, yet because of the man's boldness*g* he will get up and give him as much as he needs.

9"So I say to you: Ask and it will be given to you; seek and you will find; knock and the door will be opened to you. **10**For everyone who asks receives; he who seeks finds; and to him who knocks, the door will be opened.

a35 Greek two denarii   b42 Some manuscripts but few things are needed—or only one   c2 Some manuscripts Our Father in heaven   d2 Some manuscripts come. May your will be done on earth as it is in heaven.   e4 Greek everyone who is indebted to us   f4 Some manuscripts temptation but deliver us from the evil one   g8 Or persistence

---

What was wrong with Martha's hospitality? (10:38-41)

Nothing was wrong with her hospitality. However, her priorities were out of order. She was so concerned with the task of serving that she missed the greater importance of taking time to sit at Jesus' feet. Life's greatest priority should be to take in and reflect upon what God would have us do.

SCRIPTURE LINK (11:2-4)

Matthew records Jesus' prayer in Matt. 6:9-13.

Did people in New Testament times have only one bed per family? (11:7)

Common homes, particularly those belonging to poorer families, usually had only one room. The whole family typically would have slept in that single room, on mats spread out on the floor. Some suggest this bed may have been a divan, a large platform set against the wall. During the day it would be used for sitting, at night for sleeping. Either way, any disturbance would have likely awakened the whole family.

SCRIPTURE LINK (11:9-13)

Jesus' admonition to ask, seek and knock can also be found in Matt. 7:7-11.

What can we expect when we pray? (11:9-13)

What Jesus promises here is insight and direction through the work of the Spirit within us (v. 13). Jesus does not promise that we will receive whatever we might think we need. As the Holy Spirit directs our hearts, we will desire those things that will benefit us spiritually. We can have faith to see those things accomplished as the fulfillment of his promise.

11"Which of you fathers, if your son asks for[a] a fish, will give him a snake instead? **12**Or if he asks for an egg, will give him a scorpion? **13**If you then, though you are evil, know how to give good gifts to your children, how much more will your Father in heaven give the Holy Spirit to those who ask him!"

Jesus and Beelzebub

14Jesus was driving out a demon that was mute. When the demon left, the man who had been mute spoke, and the crowd was amazed. **15**But some of them said, "By Beelzebub[D,][b] the prince of demons, he is driving out demons." **16**Others tested him by asking for a sign from heaven.

17Jesus knew their thoughts and said to them: "Any kingdom divided against itself will be ruined, and a house divided against itself will fall. **18**If Satan is divided against himself, how can his kingdom stand? I say this because you claim that I drive out demons by Beelzebub. **19**Now if I drive out demons by Beelzebub, by whom do your followers drive them out? So then, they will be your judges. **20**But if I drive out demons by the finger of God, then the kingdom of God[D] has come to you.

21"When a strong man, fully armed, guards his own house, his possessions are safe. **22**But when someone stronger attacks and overpowers him, he takes away the armor in which the man trusted and divides up the spoils.

23"He who is not with me is against me, and he who does not gather with me, scatters.

24"When an evil[c] spirit comes out of a man, it goes through arid places seeking rest and does not find it. Then it says, 'I will return to the house I left.' **25**When it arrives, it finds the house swept clean and put in order. **26**Then it goes and takes seven other spirits more wicked than itself, and they go in and live there. And the final condition of that man is worse than the first."

27As Jesus was saying these things, a woman in the crowd called out, "Blessed is the mother who gave you birth and nursed you."

28He replied, "Blessed rather are those who hear the word of God and obey it."

The Sign of Jonah

29As the crowds increased, Jesus said, "This is a wicked generation. It asks for a miraculous sign, but none will be given it except the sign of Jonah. **30**For as Jonah was a sign to the Ninevites, so also will the Son of Man[D] be to this generation. **31**The Queen of the South will rise at the judgment with the men of this generation and condemn them; for she came from the ends of the earth to listen to Solomon's wisdom, and now one[d] greater than Solomon is here. **32**The men of Nineveh will stand up at the judgment with this generation and condemn it; for they repented[D] at the preaching of Jonah, and now one greater than Jonah is here.

The Lamp of the Body

33"No one lights a lamp and puts it in a place where it will be hidden, or under a bowl. Instead he puts it on its stand, so that those who come in may see the light.

SCRIPTURE LINK (11:14–22)
Similar accounts are given in Matt. 12:22–45 and Mark 3:23–27.

Who, besides Jesus and his disciples, could drive out demons? (11:19)
Evidently some of the Pharisees drove out demons, or at least claimed to do so. Acts 19:13 mentions a group of Jews who *went around driving out evil spirits.* Others cast out demons in Jesus' name, even though these people ordinarily were not associated with the apostles (9:49–50).

Arid places (11:24)
Evil spirits evidently prefer to live in bodies (see Matt. 8:31–32). Since few houses exist in a desert, Jesus used *arid places* to picture the restless discomfort of a disembodied evil spirit seeking a dwelling place.

What's wrong with wanting hard evidence? (11:29)
Nothing, but we must be willing to accept the evidence once it is presented. Jesus repeatedly offered miraculous evidence to substantiate his claims but refused to perform miracles just for show. Some Pharisees and teachers of the law refused to believe despite all the evidence Jesus had already given them (John 12:37). Therefore, Jesus pointed them to the one, climactic sign of his identity: his own resurrection from the dead (v. 30).

SCRIPTURE LINK (11:29–32)
You can also find Jesus telling about the sign of Jonah in Matt. 12:39–42.

[a]11 Some manuscripts *for bread, will give him a stone; or if he asks for*
[b]15 Greek *Beezeboul* or *Beelzeboul*; also in verses 18 and 19
[c]24 Greek *unclean*   [d]31 Or *something*; also in verse 32

³⁴Your eye is the lamp of your body. When your eyes are good, your whole body also is full of light. But when they are bad, your body also is full of darkness. ³⁵See to it, then, that the light within you is not darkness. ³⁶Therefore, if your whole body is full of light, and no part of it dark, it will be completely lighted, as when the light of a lamp shines on you."

Six Woes

³⁷When Jesus had finished speaking, a Pharisee^D invited him to eat with him; so he went in and reclined at the table. ³⁸But the Pharisee, noticing that Jesus did not first wash before the meal, was surprised.

³⁹Then the Lord said to him, "Now then, you Pharisees clean the outside of the cup and dish, but inside you are full of greed and wickedness. ⁴⁰You foolish people! Did not the one who made the outside make the inside also? ⁴¹But give what is inside ⌊the dish⌋^a to the poor, and everything will be clean for you.

⁴²"Woe to you Pharisees, because you give God a tenth of your mint, rue and all other kinds of garden herbs, but you neglect justice and the love of God. You should have practiced the latter without leaving the former undone.

⁴³"Woe to you Pharisees, because you love the most important seats in the synagogues and greetings in the marketplaces.

⁴⁴"Woe to you, because you are like unmarked graves, which men walk over without knowing it."

⁴⁵One of the experts in the law answered him, "Teacher, when you say these things, you insult us also."

⁴⁶Jesus replied, "And you experts in the law, woe to you, because you load people down with burdens they can hardly carry, and you yourselves will not lift one finger to help them.

⁴⁷"Woe to you, because you build tombs for the prophets^D, and it was your forefathers who killed them. ⁴⁸So you testify that you approve of what your forefathers did;

^a41 Or what you have

SCRIPTURE LINK (11:34–35)
Jesus also talks about the lamp of the body in Matt. 6:22–23.

Didn't they use grave markers in those days? (11:44)
Graves, usually cave-like tombs, were not marked the way we might expect. Because Old Testament law warned that contact with the dead would make a person ceremonially unclean, the Jews frequently whitewashed their tombs so no one would accidently touch a grave site and thereby defile himself. See **Whitewashed tombs** (Matt. 23:27).

Why were the Pharisees *like unmarked graves*? (11:44)
Though the Pharisees pretended to be righteous, they were really full of unrighteousness. Jesus was saying that just as someone could, in their view, be defiled by accidently touching an unmarked grave, in the same way a person could be defiled by associating with the Pharisees. They were hardly the models of purity they pretended to be.

Why did Jesus do miracles? (11:29)

If miracles satisfied people's craving for sensationalism, why did Jesus do them? Because, like many things, miracles produced both good and negative results.

Jesus' miracles provided proof that he was sent from God (Acts 2:22–24). Though they gave evidence of God's victory over Satan (vv. 14–23), they were never designed to be the primary focus of Jesus' activity (1 Cor. 1:21–25). Jesus pointed to miracles as signs of something deeper and more significant (John 10:24–25,38).

Jesus' miracles were like object lessons demonstrating the vast scope of his power. They showed his authority over nature, demons, disease and death (8:22–56). Miracles occurred ultimately to reveal Christ as Savior, the one who came to perform the greatest miracle of all.

Jesus' miracles provided a spiritual starting point to those whose hearts were open to the things of God. But for those who resisted God, miracles were an end in themselves. That's why Jesus refused to devalue his ministry to a kind of spiritual sideshow just to satisfy the curious who wanted to see something sensational.

they killed the prophets[D], and you build their tombs. [49]Because of this, God in his wisdom said, 'I will send them prophets and apostles, some of whom they will kill and others they will persecute.' [50]Therefore this generation will be held responsible for the blood of all the prophets that has been shed since the beginning of the world, [51]from the blood of Abel to the blood of Zechariah, who was killed between the altar and the sanctuary. Yes, I tell you, this generation will be held responsible for it all.

[52]"Woe to you experts in the law, because you have taken away the key to knowledge. You yourselves have not entered, and you have hindered those who were entering."

[53]When Jesus left there, the Pharisees[D] and the teachers of the law began to oppose him fiercely and to besiege him with questions, [54]waiting to catch him in something he might say.

Warnings and Encouragements

12 Meanwhile, when a crowd of many thousands had gathered, so that they were trampling on one another, Jesus began to speak first to his disciples[D], saying: "Be on your guard against the yeast[D] of the Pharisees, which is hypocrisy. [2]There is nothing concealed that will not be disclosed, or hidden that will not be made known. [3]What you have said in the dark will be heard in the daylight, and what you have whispered in the ear in the inner rooms will be proclaimed from the roofs.

[4]"I tell you, my friends, do not be afraid of those who kill the body and after that can do no more. [5]But I will show you whom you should fear: Fear him who, after the killing of the body, has power to throw you into hell[D]. Yes, I tell you, fear him. [6]Are not five sparrows sold for two pennies[a]? Yet not one of them is forgotten by God. [7]Indeed, the very hairs of your head are all numbered. Don't be afraid; you are worth more than many sparrows.

[8]"I tell you, whoever acknowledges me before men, the Son of Man[D] will also acknowledge him before the angels of God. [9]But he who disowns me before men will be disowned before the angels of God. [10]And everyone who speaks a word against the Son of Man will be forgiven, but anyone who blasphemes[D] against the Holy Spirit will not be forgiven.

[11]"When you are brought before synagogues, rulers and authorities, do not worry about how you will defend yourselves or what you will say, [12]for the Holy Spirit will teach you at that time what you should say."

The Parable of the Rich Fool

[13]Someone in the crowd said to him, "Teacher, tell my brother to divide the inheritance with me."

[14]Jesus replied, "Man, who appointed me a judge or an arbiter between you?" [15]Then he said to them, "Watch out! Be on your guard against all kinds of greed; a man's life does not consist in the abundance of his possessions."

[16]And he told them this parable[D]: "The ground of a certain rich man produced a good crop. [17]He thought to himself, 'What shall I do? I have no place to store my crops.' [18]"Then he said, 'This is what I'll do. I will tear down my barns and build bigger ones, and there I will store all my grain and my goods. [19]And I'll say to myself, "You have

Why did Jesus compare hypocrisy to yeast? (12:1)

Yeast was a Biblical symbol of corruption since its nature was to expand, spreading throughout and "corrupting" the entire batch of bread dough (Exodus 12:14–20; 1 Cor. 5:6–7). We might say, "A rotten apple spoils the whole barrel." In the same way, a little hypocrisy can spread through a person, contaminating his or her spiritual integrity.

SCRIPTURE LINK (12:2–9)

Matthew gives Jesus' warnings and encouragements in Matt. 10:26–33.

---

[a]6 Greek two assaria

plenty of good things laid up for many years. Take life easy; eat, drink and be merry." '

²⁰"But God said to him, 'You fool! This very night your life will be demanded from you. Then who will get what you have prepared for yourself?'

²¹"This is how it will be with anyone who stores up things for himself but is not rich toward God."

Do Not Worry

²²Then Jesus said to his disciples[D]: "Therefore I tell you, do not worry about your life, what you will eat; or about your body, what you will wear. ²³Life is more than food, and the body more than clothes. ²⁴Consider the ravens: They do not sow or reap, they have no storeroom or barn; yet God feeds them. And how much more valuable you are than birds! ²⁵Who of you by worrying can add a single hour to his life[a]? ²⁶Since you cannot do this very little thing, why do you worry about the rest?

²⁷"Consider how the lilies grow. They do not labor or spin. Yet I tell you, not even Solomon in all his splendor was dressed like one of these. ²⁸If that is how God clothes the grass of the field, which is here today, and tomorrow is thrown into the fire, how much more will he clothe you, O you of little faith! ²⁹And do not set your heart on what you will eat or drink; do not worry about it. ³⁰For the pagan world runs after all such things, and your Father knows that you need them. ³¹But seek his kingdom, and these things will be given to you as well.

³²"Do not be afraid, little flock, for your Father has been pleased to give you the kingdom. ³³Sell your possessions and give to the poor. Provide purses for yourselves that will not wear out, a treasure in heaven that will not be exhausted, where no thief comes near and no moth destroys. ³⁴For where your treasure is, there your heart will be also.

Watchfulness

³⁵"Be dressed ready for service and keep your lamps burning, ³⁶like men waiting for their master to return from a wedding banquet, so that when he comes and knocks they can immediately open the door for him. ³⁷It will be good for those servants whose master finds them watching when he comes. I tell you the truth, he will dress himself to serve, will have them recline at the table and will come and wait on them. ³⁸It will be good for those servants whose master finds them ready, even if he comes in the second or third watch of the night. ³⁹But understand this: If the owner of the house had known at what hour the thief was coming, he would not have let his house be broken into. ⁴⁰You also must be ready, because the Son of Man[D] will come at an hour when you do not expect him."

⁴¹Peter asked, "Lord, are you telling this parable[D] to us, or to everyone?"

⁴²The Lord answered, "Who then is the faithful and wise manager, whom the master puts in charge of his servants to give them their food allowance at the proper time? ⁴³It will be good for that servant whom the master finds doing so when he returns. ⁴⁴I tell you the truth, he will put him in charge of all his possessions. ⁴⁵But suppose the servant says to himself, 'My master is taking a long time in coming,' and he then begins to beat the men-

Does Jesus command us not to worry? (12:22)
Jesus does not give a command so much as an invitation to rest in the arms of a loving Father. As humans, we will at times cross the line and fret when we should trust. But only when we allow ourselves to constantly focus on ourselves instead of God do we violate Jesus' principle. He gave it to us as a liberating principle, not as another law to worry about.

SCRIPTURE LINK (12:22–31)
Jesus' admonition against worrying can be found in Matt. 6:25–33.

Does Christ really want us to sell all our possessions? (12:33–34)
Jesus' concern is that our possessions do not possess us. Some have felt that God wanted them to take a vow of poverty, learning to trust him by giving away everything they owned to help the poor. Others look to other verses in the Bible to help interpret this one. They believe the point here is that all we have belongs to God. But he gives us the responsibility to manage those possessions in ways that will honor him and accomplish his will. Also see *Is it wrong to be financially well-off?* (6:24–26).

SCRIPTURE LINK (12:35–36)
Matthew writes about Jesus' exhortation to be watchful in Matt. 25:1–13. Mark carries it in Mark 13:33–37.

SCRIPTURE LINK (12:39–46)
A similar passage can be found in Matt. 24:43–51.

---

a25 Or *single cubit to his height*

Why would a master cut his servant to pieces? (12:46)

In ancient times, those who owned slaves held complete mastery over them. Slaves were considered as property and one who displeased his master could be severely punished, even killed. Such deeds were within the master's legal rights. Jesus may have used this particularly gruesome punishment to illustrate the spiritual truth of his example: that a hypocritical leader will be cut off from any life with God.

What kind of baptism did Jesus expect? (12:50)

This was Jesus' way of talking about his approaching death. The word *baptism* was not just describing a ceremony or ritual with water. It was used to describe being overwhelmed by something—even trials or judgment. See **Baptized into Moses** (1 Cor. 10:2).

Does Jesus break up families? (12:51–53)

These verses illustrate one of the harsher truths of God's kingdom: not everyone will respond to the gospel. Hearts full of prejudice, hate and pride will resist Christ's offer of peace. Because many will reject it, the message will divide people, families and nations.

SCRIPTURE LINK (12:51–53)

Jesus' declaration that he came not to bring peace but division can also be found in Matt. 10:34–36.

What did Pilate do to the Galileans? (13:1)

The Galileans, in Jerusalem to sacrifice at the temple, suffered the random violence commonplace under Roman occupation. The Roman army maintained a fortress on the northwest corner of the temple grounds. The Roman officials sometimes raided the groups of worshipers there, even for minor or contrived infractions.

What was Jesus warning them about? (13:3–5)

The cause of a person's death is not an indication of how that person lived. All people will die, but Jesus was saying that no one has to perish eternally. He warned the people not to make judgments about others' lives but to repent in order to ensure their own eternal life.

Tower of Siloam (13:4)

It was made of stone and was part of the southern wall of Jerusalem (see **Map 8** at the back of this Bible). Construction was reliable at this time; much of the Jerusalem wall still stands today. No one knows what caused the tower to collapse, but frequent earthquakes in the area suggest one possibility.

How does this parable end? (13:6–9)

The point of Jesus' parable is that everyone is going to die, just like the Galileans and those at the tower of Siloam (vv. 1–5). Judgment is coming. What will we do with our lives before it does? What fruit are we going to bear in the meantime? The open ending of the parable suggests that Jesus may have wanted his listeners to finish it for themselves.

servants and maidservants and to eat and drink and get drunk. **46**The master of that servant will come on a day when he does not expect him and at an hour he is not aware of. He will cut him to pieces and assign him a place with the unbelievers.

47"That servant who knows his master's will and does not get ready or does not do what his master wants will be beaten with many blows. **48**But the one who does not know and does things deserving punishment will be beaten with few blows. From everyone who has been given much, much will be demanded; and from the one who has been entrusted with much, much more will be asked.

Not Peace but Division

49"I have come to bring fire on the earth, and how I wish it were already kindled! **50**But I have a baptismᴰ to undergo, and how distressed I am until it is completed! **51**Do you think I came to bring peaceᴰ on earth? No, I tell you, but division. **52**From now on there will be five in one family divided against each other, three against two and two against three. **53**They will be divided, father against son and son against father, mother against daughter and daughter against mother, mother-in-law against daughter-in-law and daughter-in-law against mother-in-law."

Interpreting the Times

54He said to the crowd: "When you see a cloud rising in the west, immediately you say, 'It's going to rain,' and it does. **55**And when the south wind blows, you say, 'It's going to be hot,' and it is. **56**Hypocrites! You know how to interpret the appearance of the earth and the sky. How is it that you don't know how to interpret this present time?

57"Why don't you judge for yourselves what is right? **58**As you are going with your adversary to the magistrate, try hard to be reconciled to him on the way, or he may drag you off to the judge, and the judge turn you over to the officer, and the officer throw you into prison. **59**I tell you, you will not get out until you have paid the last penny.ᵃ"

Repent or Perish

13 Now there were some present at that time who told Jesus about the Galileans whose blood Pilate had mixed with their sacrificesᴰ. **2**Jesus answered, "Do you think that these Galileans were worse sinners than all the other Galileans because they suffered this way? **3**I tell you, no! But unless you repentᴰ, you too will all perish. **4**Or those eighteen who died when the tower in Siloam fell on them—do you think they were more guilty than all the others living in Jerusalemᴰ? **5**I tell you, no! But unless you repent, you too will all perish."

6Then he told this parableᴰ: "A man had a fig tree, planted in his vineyard, and he went to look for fruit on it, but did not find any. **7**So he said to the man who took care of the vineyard, 'For three years now I've been coming to look for fruit on this fig tree and haven't found any. Cut it down! Why should it use up the soil?'

8" 'Sir,' the man replied, 'leave it alone for one more year, and I'll dig around it and fertilize it. **9**If it bears fruit next year, fine! If not, then cut it down.' "

ᵃ59 Greek *lepton*

A Crippled Woman Healed on the Sabbath

10On a Sabbath^D Jesus was teaching in one of the synagogues, **11**and a woman was there who had been crippled by a spirit for eighteen years. She was bent over and could not straighten up at all. **12**When Jesus saw her, he called her forward and said to her, "Woman, you are set free from your infirmity." **13**Then he put his hands on her, and immediately she straightened up and praised God.

14Indignant because Jesus had healed on the Sabbath, the synagogue ruler said to the people, "There are six days for work. So come and be healed on those days, not on the Sabbath."

15The Lord answered him, "You hypocrites! Doesn't each of you on the Sabbath untie his ox or donkey from the stall and lead it out to give it water? **16**Then should not this woman, a daughter of Abraham, whom Satan has kept bound for eighteen long years, be set free on the Sabbath day from what bound her?"

17When he said this, all his opponents were humiliated, but the people were delighted with all the wonderful things he was doing.

The Parables of the Mustard Seed and the Yeast

18Then Jesus asked, "What is the kingdom of God^D like? What shall I compare it to? **19**It is like a mustard seed, which a man took and planted in his garden. It grew and became a tree, and the birds of the air perched in its branches."

20Again he asked, "What shall I compare the kingdom of God to? **21**It is like yeast that a woman took and mixed into a large amount*a* of flour until it worked all through the dough."

The Narrow Door

22Then Jesus went through the towns and villages, teaching as he made his way to Jerusalem^D. **23**Someone asked him, "Lord, are only a few people going to be saved?"

He said to them, **24**"Make every effort to enter through the narrow door, because many, I tell you, will try to enter and will not be able to. **25**Once the owner of the house gets up and closes the door, you will stand outside knocking and pleading, 'Sir, open the door for us.'

"But he will answer, 'I don't know you or where you come from.'

26"Then you will say, 'We ate and drank with you, and you taught in our streets.'

27"But he will reply, 'I don't know you or where you come from. Away from me, all you evildoers!'

28"There will be weeping there, and gnashing of teeth, when you see Abraham, Isaac and Jacob and all the prophets^D in the kingdom of God, but you yourselves thrown out. **29**People will come from east and west and north and south, and will take their places at the feast in the kingdom of God. **30**Indeed there are those who are last who will be first, and first who will be last."

Jesus' Sorrow for Jerusalem

31At that time some Pharisees^D came to Jesus and said to him, "Leave this place and go somewhere else. Herod wants to kill you."

a21 Greek three satas (probably about 1/2 bushel or 22 liters)

How do spirits cripple people? (13:11)

Evil spirits have spiritual powers that can affect the physical world. Though medical technology has discovered various other causes of disease, it has not discounted the effect the spiritual has on the physical. It's possible some psychosomatic illnesses—those caused, psychiatrists say, by mental or emotional problems—have a spiritual explanation. Jesus himself recognized that demons had the power to cause physical maladies (v. 16; 9:42).

Why was healing considered *work* instead of a miracle of God? (13:14)

Sabbath laws and traditions included rigid details defining work. But the synagogue leaders had to acknowledge that God "worked" on the Sabbath whenever babies were born or people died. So they concluded it was permissible for people also to save someone's life on the Sabbath. Jesus argued in true rabbinic form that if it was permissible to save a life, then it would also be permissible to heal on the Sabbath.

SCRIPTURE LINK (13:18–19)

Matthew tells the parable of the mustard seed in Matt. 13:31–33. Mark gives it in Mark 4:30–32.

What shall I compare it to? (13:18)

See article: *Why did Jesus speak in parables?* (Matt. 13:11–13).

SCRIPTURE LINK (13:20–21)

Matthew records the parable of the yeast in Matt. 13:31–33.

The narrow door (13:24)

See *Narrow gate . . . narrow the road* (Matt. 7:13–14).

Gnashing of teeth (13:28)

Grinding the teeth in anguish.

What was Jesus' goal? (13:32)

Jesus' goal was to complete his mission of redemption which would be accomplished by his death and resurrection. Jesus came to earth to die for the sins of the world. He alluded to his sacrificial death by reciting a proverb that spoke of Jerusalem as the place where God's prophets frequently met their end (v. 33). But his language was figurative: *Today and tomorrow* was a phrase his listeners understood to mean "for now and soon after"; *the third day* carried the idea of "in the near future."

Why did Jesus say that no prophet could die outside Jerusalem? (13:33)

Jesus quoted a proverbial saying—one that conveyed a general truth, even though it was not precisely accurate. (There were prophets who died in other places than Jersualem.) The idea behind the saying seemed to be that the prophets who spoke for God frequently encountered their harshest critics amid the religious and political establishment in Jersualem, the hub of the Jewish nation. Though Herod may have been a threat to him, Jesus was saying his real opponents were those Jews who merely pretended to serve God.

SCRIPTURE LINK (13:34-35)

Matthew writes about Jesus' sorrow for Jerusalem in Matt. 23:37-39. Luke gives a similar account in Luke 19:41.

Was Jesus trying to trap the Pharisees? (14:3)

In a sense, yes. Jesus knew the Pharisees were trying to trap him. So he turned the tables on them and took the initiative, shifting the burden of proof to them.

Does false humility count? (14:11)

No. Humility is more than what shows outwardly. Humility means seeing what God has done to overcome faults and sins. Those who role-play at humility to impress others, those who compare themselves to people instead of God, and those who put themselves down to gain God's favor have missed true humility. Outward humility alone often masks inner pride.

Does Jesus want us to deliberately avoid earthly rewards? (14:12-14)

No. His point is that if we serve the poor earnestly and gain no reward on earth, we shouldn't worry about it. We will be rewarded in heaven. Jesus' focus here is on motives. A good deed is not good if it is done to get a reward. But if rewards come, they don't have to be spurned.

SCRIPTURE LINK (14:16-24)

You'll find a similar parable about a banquet in Matt. 22:2-14.

Why were these lame excuses? (14:18-20)

Because the field and oxen could be examined any time, and because the newlywed longed merely for privacy. These flimsy reasons for not coming showed these had been insincere. In Biblical times it was common for a host to give two invitations: the first required a response; the second informed those who had responded that the banquet was ready (Esther 6:14). Apparently, these guests had accepted the first invitation only to change their minds for the second.

³²He replied, "Go tell that fox, 'I will drive out demons and heal people today and tomorrow, and on the third day I will reach my goal.' ³³In any case, I must keep going today and tomorrow and the next day—for surely no prophet D can die outside Jerusalem D!

³⁴"O Jerusalem, Jerusalem, you who kill the prophets and stone those sent to you, how often I have longed to gather your children together, as a hen gathers her chicks under her wings, but you were not willing! ³⁵Look, your house is left to you desolate. I tell you, you will not see me again until you say, 'Blessed is he who comes in the name of the Lord.'ᵃ"

Jesus at a Pharisee's House

14 One Sabbath D, when Jesus went to eat in the house of a prominent Pharisee D, he was being carefully watched. ²There in front of him was a man suffering from dropsy. ³Jesus asked the Pharisees and experts in the law, "Is it lawful to heal on the Sabbath or not?" ⁴But they remained silent. So taking hold of the man, he healed him and sent him away.

⁵Then he asked them, "If one of you has a sonᵇ or an ox that falls into a well on the Sabbath day, will you not immediately pull him out?" ⁶And they had nothing to say.

⁷When he noticed how the guests picked the places of honor at the table, he told them this parable D: ⁸"When someone invites you to a wedding feast, do not take the place of honor, for a person more distinguished than you may have been invited. ⁹If so, the host who invited both of you will come and say to you, 'Give this man your seat.' Then, humiliated, you will have to take the least important place. ¹⁰But when you are invited, take the lowest place, so that when your host comes, he will say to you, 'Friend, move up to a better place.' Then you will be honored in the presence of all your fellow guests. ¹¹For everyone who exalts himself will be humbled, and he who humbles himself will be exalted."

¹²Then Jesus said to his host, "When you give a luncheon or dinner, do not invite your friends, your brothers or relatives, or your rich neighbors; if you do, they may invite you back and so you will be repaid. ¹³But when you give a banquet, invite the poor, the crippled, the lame, the blind, ¹⁴and you will be blessed. Although they cannot repay you, you will be repaid at the resurrection D of the righteous D."

The Parable of the Great Banquet

¹⁵When one of those at the table with him heard this, he said to Jesus, "Blessed is the man who will eat at the feast in the kingdom of God."

¹⁶Jesus replied: "A certain man was preparing a great banquet and invited many guests. ¹⁷At the time of the banquet he sent his servant to tell those who had been invited, 'Come, for everything is now ready.'

¹⁸"But they all alike began to make excuses. The first said, 'I have just bought a field, and I must go and see it. Please excuse me.'

¹⁹"Another said, 'I have just bought five yoke D of oxen, and I'm on my way to try them out. Please excuse me.'

²⁰"Still another said, 'I just got married, so I can't come.'

²¹"The servant came back and reported this to his master. Then the owner of the house became angry and or-

---

ᵃ35 Psalm 118:26   ᵇ5 Some manuscripts *donkey*

dered his servant, 'Go out quickly into the streets and alleys of the town and bring in the poor, the crippled, the blind and the lame.'

22" 'Sir,' the servant said, 'what you ordered has been done, but there is still room.'

23"Then the master told his servant, 'Go out to the roads and country lanes and make them come in, so that my house will be full. **24**I tell you, not one of those men who were invited will get a taste of my banquet.' "

The Cost of Being a Disciple

25Large crowds were traveling with Jesus, and turning to them he said: **26**"If anyone comes to me and does not hate his father and mother, his wife and children, his brothers and sisters—yes, even his own life—he cannot be my disciple^D. **27**And anyone who does not carry his cross and follow me cannot be my disciple.

28"Suppose one of you wants to build a tower. Will he not first sit down and estimate the cost to see if he has enough money to complete it? **29**For if he lays the foundation and is not able to finish it, everyone who sees it will ridicule him, **30**saying, 'This fellow began to build and was not able to finish.'

31"Or suppose a king is about to go to war against another king. Will he not first sit down and consider whether he is able with ten thousand men to oppose the one coming against him with twenty thousand? **32**If he is not able, he will send a delegation while the other is still a long way off and will ask for terms of peace^D. **33**In the same way, any of you who does not give up everything he has cannot be my disciple.

34"Salt is good, but if it loses its saltiness, how can it be made salty again? **35**It is fit neither for the soil nor for the manure pile; it is thrown out.

"He who has ears to hear, let him hear."

The Parable of the Lost Sheep

15 Now the tax collectors^D and "sinners" were all gathering around to hear him. **2**But the Pharisees^D and the teachers of the law muttered, "This man welcomes sinners and eats with them."

3Then Jesus told them this parable^D: **4**"Suppose one of you has a hundred sheep and loses one of them. Does he not leave the ninety-nine in the open country and go after the lost sheep until he finds it? **5**And when he finds it, he

Carry his cross (14:27)
See *What does take up his cross mean?* (Matt. 16:24).

What does salt have to do with counting the cost? (14:34–35)
Pure salt was not something to be taken for granted in New Testament times. It required considerable commitment to separate the sand and other impurities from the salt obtained from the Dead Sea. In the same way, Christians must count the cost of purity so they will retain the full flavor of Christ and his teachings. Anything less may cause Christians to become "unsalty"—no different than the world. If we count the cost, we won't let our "salt" become mixed with the world's "sand."

Tax collectors (15:1)
See *Tax collectors (5:29).*

Why so little concern for the 99 sheep left in the open country? (15:3–7)
They were not left unattended. We tend to assume there was only one shepherd, but a Middle Eastern shepherd would rarely go out alone with 100 sheep. If a sheep was lost, the head shepherd would leave the rest of the flock, safe and content with hired helpers, and go search for it. God does not abandon his followers, but he zealously seeks the lost.

SCRIPTURE LINK (15:4–7)
Matthew shares the parable of the lost sheep in Matt. 18:12–14.

Does Jesus really want us to hate our families? (14:26)

Jesus' comments here are an example of hyperbole, a figure of speech that exaggerates for emphasis. Jesus was setting up an extreme contrast to make a point: our passion for Jesus should be so strong and so committed that our affection for our families could, by comparison, be considered hatred.

By setting up such an exaggerated contrast, Jesus was describing the total commitment required from his disciples. We know Jesus was not literally calling us to hate our families. The balance of Biblical teaching tells us to honor our parents and love others (for example, Exodus 20:12; Luke 10:26–28). Jesus was establishing priorities. We owe an unqualified loyalty and love to God. Then, because we put him first, we are to love others. The two actually go hand in hand.

The Parables of Jesus

Parable	Matthew	Mark	Luke
Lamp under a bowl	5:14-16	4:21-22	8:16; 11:33-36
Wise and foolish builders	7:24-27		6:46-49
New cloth on an old garment	9:16	2:21	5:36
New wine in old wineskins	9:17	2:22	5:37-38
Sower and the soils	13:3-8, 18-23	4:3-8, 14-20	8:5-8, 11-15
Weeds	13:24-30, 36-43		
Mustard seed	13:31-32	4:30-32	13:18-19
Yeast	13:33		13:20-21
Hidden treasure	13:44		
Valuable pearl	13:45-46		
Net	13:47-50		
Owner of a house	13:52		
Lost sheep	18:12-14		15:4-7
Unmerciful servant	18:23-35		
Workers in the vineyard	20:1-16		
Two sons	21:28-32		
Tenants	21:33-44	12:1-11	20:9-18
Wedding banquet	22:2-14		
Fig tree	24:32-35	13:28-31	21:29-33
Faithful and wise servant	24:45-51		12:42-48
Ten virgins	25:1-13		
Talents (minas)	25:14-30		19:12-27
Sheep and goats	25:31-46		
Growing seed		4:26-29	
Watchful servants		13:34-37	12:35-40
Moneylender			7:41-43
Good Samaritan			10:30-37
Friend in need			11:5-8
Rich fool			12:16-21
Unfruitful fig tree			13:6-9
Lowest seat at the feast			14:7-14
Great banquet			14:16-24
Cost of discipleship			14:28-33
Lost coin			15:8-10
Lost (prodigal) son			15:11-32
Shrewd manager			16:1-8
Rich man and Lazarus			16:19-31
Master and his servant			17:7-10
Persistent widow			18:2-8

joyfully puts it on his shoulders **6**and goes home. Then he calls his friends and neighbors together and says, 'Rejoice with me; I have found my lost sheep.' **7**I tell you that in the same way there will be more rejoicing in heaven over one sinner who repents^D than over ninety-nine righteous^D persons who do not need to repent.

The Parable of the Lost Coin

8"Or suppose a woman has ten silver coins*a* and loses one. Does she not light a lamp, sweep the house and search carefully until she finds it? **9**And when she finds it, she calls her friends and neighbors together and says, 'Rejoice with me; I have found my lost coin.' **10**In the same way, I tell you, there is rejoicing in the presence of the angels of God over one sinner who repents."

The Parable of the Lost Son

11Jesus continued: "There was a man who had two sons. **12**The younger one said to his father, 'Father, give me my share of the estate.' So he divided his property between them.

13"Not long after that, the younger son got together all he had, set off for a distant country and there squandered his wealth in wild living. **14**After he had spent everything, there was a severe famine in that whole country, and he began to be in need. **15**So he went and hired himself out to a citizen of that country, who sent him to his fields to feed pigs. **16**He longed to fill his stomach with the pods that the pigs were eating, but no one gave him anything.

17"When he came to his senses, he said, 'How many of my father's hired men have food to spare, and here I am starving to death^D! **18**I will set out and go back to my father and say to him: Father, I have sinned against heaven and against you. **19**I am no longer worthy to be called your son; make me like one of your hired men.' **20**So he got up and went to his father.

"But while he was still a long way off, his father saw him and was filled with compassion for him; he ran to his son, threw his arms around him and kissed him.

21"The son said to him, 'Father, I have sinned against heaven and against you. I am no longer worthy to be called your son.*b*'

22"But the father said to his servants, 'Quick! Bring the best robe and put it on him. Put a ring on his finger and sandals on his feet. **23**Bring the fattened calf and kill it. Let's have a feast and celebrate. **24**For this son of mine was dead and is alive again; he was lost and is found.' So they began to celebrate.

25"Meanwhile, the older son was in the field. When he came near the house, he heard music and dancing. **26**So he called one of the servants and asked him what was going on. **27**'Your brother has come,' he replied, 'and your father has killed the fattened calf because he has him back safe and sound.'

28"The older brother became angry and refused to go in. So his father went out and pleaded with him. **29**But he answered his father, 'Look! All these years I've been slaving for you and never disobeyed your orders. Yet you never gave me even a young goat so I could celebrate with my friends. **30**But when this son of yours who has squandered

Why throw a party because of a coin? (15:8–9)
This coin was probably part of the woman's dowry of ten coins, perhaps worn on a chain as jewelry or kept in a small purse. If so, it would have been a sign that the woman was married, like a wedding ring signifies today. Losing it would have had more sentimental value than merely its face value. The coin itself, a drachma, was worth about a day's wage.

Why didn't the father search for the lost son? (15:11–32)
The younger son had to find his own way home, though diligent searches were made in the two preceding parables. Why the difference? Because analogies only go so far; parallels are seldom complete. The coin and the sheep, for example, were unable to return without help. People, on the other hand, have a free will to decide to return or not. Still, the father saw his son while he was far away and ran eagerly to meet him, showing how much he had been longing for his return.

Was it common to claim an inheritance early? (15:12)
No. It was highly irregular for a son to claim his inheritance before his father's death. A less loving father could have had his son stoned to death for such a rebellious attitude (Deut. 21:18–21). The son's terrible offense to his father illustrates the depth of the offense sinners give God.

How much did the younger son inherit? (15:12)
According to Jewish law, the firstborn son received a double share of the inheritance, twice as much as any of his brothers. The younger son would have gotten 1/3 of the estate and the older son 2/3 (Deut. 21:17).

What was behind the older son's actions? (15:25–32)
Jesus told about the older son to describe the actions of the Pharisees. The older son, thinking himself far more worthy than his brother, refused to join the party. His actions showed he did not understand his father's love either toward his brother or himself. In the same way, the hollow religion of the self-righteous Pharisees showed that they didn't really understand God at all. They continually compared themselves to others and took great pride in proving how much better they were.

*a*8 Greek *ten drachmas*, each worth about a day's wages
*b*21 Some early manuscripts *son. Make me like one of your hired men.*

Why commend someone who was dishonest? (16:8)

This passage is one of the most difficult in the Gospels to interpret. It's important to notice that the manager was not commended for his *dishonesty;* he was commended for his *shrewdness.* Jesus was not urging us to cheat. He was encouraging his disciples to be savvy about the use of money and other worldly matters. Some think Jesus' statement was originally a question—"Would the master commend the dishonest manager because he had acted shrewdly?"—with "No" as the implied answer. His following comments, then, would be simply an observation about life—that though his disciples should live ethically, they could, nonetheless, learn to be more shrewd about using material things to make an impact for eternity.

Why use money to buy friendships? (16:9)

This is not the same as bribing people to win recognition or favors on earth. Jesus was encouraging his disciples to use their money generously whenever and wherever they could to help others. Good deeds cannot buy eternal rewards, but those who do good because Christ has changed them will be rewarded in heaven.

What do financial abilities have to do with spiritual responsibilities? (16:10–11)

It's a matter of increasing responsibilities. Mailroom to CEO promotions don't happen in one giant step. It's the same with spiritual promotions. Since spiritual wealth is far more valuable than worldly wealth, we will not be trusted to manage heavenly riches if we have proved ourselves untrustworthy with money on earth. Those who are selfish and materialistic, failing to honor God with their money and possessions, demonstrate that they do not value true spiritual wealth. The primary focus is to use money responsibly and with integrity.

Who forces their way into God's kingdom? (16:16)

This difficult passage has been interpreted several ways: (1) Those who wish to enter the kingdom can only enter it if they are decisive and earnest. (2) When the good news is preached, the kingdom will suffer violence or attacks from Satan. (3) Those who force their way into the kingdom are those who believe it must come through politics or even revolt. (4) Those who were shocked to think the law was annulled by the gospel feel that lawless people can now force their way into the kingdom.

Did the *good news* replace *the Law and Prophets?* (16:16–17)

Why did Jesus say the law was no longer proclaimed—and then say nothing in it had changed? The gospel Jesus preached did not cancel the Old Testament law; it fulfilled it. The law was given new depth and meaning when Christ came. Now it can be seen that the law paved the way for God to show his love for people through Jesus Christ. Also see *Did Jesus abolish the Old Testament law or fulfill it?* (Eph. 2:15).

your property with prostitutes comes home, you kill the fattened calf for him!'

³¹" 'My son,' the father said, 'you are always with me, and everything I have is yours. ³²But we had to celebrate and be glad, because this brother of yours was dead and is alive again; he was lost and is found.' "

The Parable of the Shrewd Manager

16 Jesus told his disciples[D]: "There was a rich man whose manager was accused of wasting his possessions. ²So he called him in and asked him, 'What is this I hear about you? Give an account of your management, because you cannot be manager any longer.'

³"The manager said to himself, 'What shall I do now? My master is taking away my job. I'm not strong enough to dig, and I'm ashamed to beg— ⁴I know what I'll do so that, when I lose my job here, people will welcome me into their houses.'

⁵"So he called in each one of his master's debtors. He asked the first, 'How much do you owe my master?'

⁶" 'Eight hundred gallons[a] of olive oil,' he replied.

"The manager told him, 'Take your bill, sit down quickly, and make it four hundred.'

⁷"Then he asked the second, 'And how much do you owe?'

" 'A thousand bushels[b] of wheat,' he replied.

"He told him, 'Take your bill and make it eight hundred.'

⁸"The master commended the dishonest manager because he had acted shrewdly. For the people of this world are more shrewd in dealing with their own kind than are the people of the light. ⁹I tell you, use worldly wealth to gain friends for yourselves, so that when it is gone, you will be welcomed into eternal dwellings.

¹⁰"Whoever can be trusted with very little can also be trusted with much, and whoever is dishonest with very little will also be dishonest with much. ¹¹So if you have not been trustworthy in handling worldly wealth, who will trust you with true riches? ¹²And if you have not been trustworthy with someone else's property, who will give you property of your own?

¹³"No servant can serve two masters. Either he will hate the one and love the other, or he will be devoted to the one and despise the other. You cannot serve both God and Money."

¹⁴The Pharisees[D], who loved money, heard all this and were sneering at Jesus. ¹⁵He said to them, "You are the ones who justify[D] yourselves in the eyes of men, but God knows your hearts. What is highly valued among men is detestable in God's sight.

Additional Teachings

¹⁶"The Law and the Prophets[D] were proclaimed until John. Since that time, the good news of the kingdom of God[D] is being preached, and everyone is forcing his way into it. ¹⁷It is easier for heaven and earth to disappear than for the least stroke of a pen to drop out of the Law.

¹⁸"Anyone who divorces his wife and marries another

ᵃ6 Greek *one hundred batous* (probably about 3 kiloliters)
ᵇ7 Greek *one hundred korous* (probably about 35 kiloliters)

woman commits adultery, and the man who marries a divorced woman commits adultery.

The Rich Man and Lazarus

19"There was a rich man who was dressed in purple[D] and fine linen and lived in luxury every day. **20**At his gate was laid a beggar named Lazarus, covered with sores **21**and longing to eat what fell from the rich man's table. Even the dogs came and licked his sores.

22"The time came when the beggar died and the angels carried him to Abraham's side. The rich man also died and was buried. **23**In hell[D],*a* where he was in torment, he looked up and saw Abraham far away, with Lazarus by his side. **24**So he called to him, 'Father Abraham, have pity on me and send Lazarus to dip the tip of his finger in water and cool my tongue, because I am in agony in this fire.'

25"But Abraham replied, 'Son, remember that in your lifetime you received your good things, while Lazarus received bad things, but now he is comforted here and you are in agony. **26**And besides all this, between us and you a great chasm has been fixed, so that those who want to go from here to you cannot, nor can anyone cross over from there to us.'

27"He answered, 'Then I beg you, father, send Lazarus to my father's house, **28**for I have five brothers. Let him warn them, so that they will not also come to this place of torment.'

29"Abraham replied, 'They have Moses and the Prophets[D]; let them listen to them.'

30" 'No, father Abraham,' he said, 'but if someone from the dead goes to them, they will repent[D].'

31"He said to him, 'If they do not listen to Moses and the Prophets, they will not be convinced even if someone rises from the dead.' "

Sin, Faith, Duty

17 Jesus said to his disciples[D]: "Things that cause people to sin are bound to come, but woe to that person through whom they come. **2**It would be better for him to be thrown into the sea with a millstone[D] tied around his neck than for him to cause one of these little ones to sin. **3**So watch yourselves.

"If your brother sins, rebuke him, and if he repents, forgive him. **4**If he sins against you seven times in a day, and seven times comes back to you and says, 'I repent,' forgive him."

5The apostles[D] said to the Lord, "Increase our faith!"

6He replied, "If you have faith as small as a mustard seed, you can say to this mulberry tree, 'Be uprooted and planted in the sea,' and it will obey you.

7"Suppose one of you had a servant plowing or looking after the sheep. Would he say to the servant when he comes in from the field, 'Come along now and sit down to eat'? **8**Would he not rather say, 'Prepare my supper, get yourself ready and wait on me while I eat and drink; after that you may eat and drink'? **9**Would he thank the servant because he did what he was told to do? **10**So you also, when you have done everything you were told to do, should say, 'We are unworthy servants; we have only done our duty.' "

a23 Greek *Hades*

Have all those who are divorced and remarried committed adultery? (16:18)

Jesus used this example to show the necessity of the law (vv. 16–17), not to make a definitive statement about divorce and remarriage. The rabbis, concerned only about the letter of the law, provided many conditions that permitted divorce. Jesus, concerned with the spirit of the law, recalled God's original intent for marriage.

What does this story teach us? (16:19–31)

Although Jesus hinted about some fascinating details of life after death, that was not his reason for telling this story. His point was that, contrary to popular opinion, money is not evidence of favor with God, nor does poverty indicate God's displeasure.

Little ones (17:2)

Jesus may have been referring to the people taught by the Pharisees—disciples who were still young in their faith or to those who were young in years—children.

Why did the disciples think their faith was so inadequate? (17:5)

Probably because they saw how impossible it would be to do on their own what Jesus told them about forgiveness (vv. 3–4). Who could forgive such chronic sinful behavior? The disciples most likely recognized that there was a link between their substandard actions and a shortfall in their faith.

How much faith do we need? (17:6)

Not much, according to Jesus. This is an example of hyperbole, a figure of speech not restricted to its literal meaning. Rather than give his disciples a formula for increasing their faith, he pictured faith as a seed. Plant a seed and it grows; use a little faith and it will grow too. We don't need to pray that God will increase our faith; we need to ask him to help us use the faith we have.

Why didn't the master appreciate good service? (17:7–10)

Jesus used an example familiar to the people from their own culture. He wasn't saying that the master was right to be so unappreciative. He was simply using the example of a servant's attitude: a servant merely did what he had to do. Jesus wanted his disciples to see that strong faith should not lead to spiritual pride. Our prayers should not be based on an attitude that says, "If I do this, then God will give me that." God gives out of his grace, not as a reward for good behavior.

Ten Healed of Leprosy

[11]Now on his way to Jerusalem[D], Jesus traveled along the border between Samaria and Galilee. [12]As he was going into a village, ten men who had leprosy[Da] met him. They stood at a distance [13]and called out in a loud voice, "Jesus, Master, have pity on us!"

[14]When he saw them, he said, "Go, show yourselves to the priests[D]." And as they went, they were cleansed.

[15]One of them, when he saw he was healed, came back, praising God in a loud voice. [16]He threw himself at Jesus' feet and thanked him—and he was a Samaritan.

[17]Jesus asked, "Were not all ten cleansed? Where are the other nine? [18]Was no one found to return and give praise to God except this foreigner?" [19]Then he said to him, "Rise and go; your faith has made you well."

The Coming of the Kingdom of God

[20]Once, having been asked by the Pharisees[D] when the kingdom of God[D] would come, Jesus replied, "The kingdom of God does not come with your careful observation, [21]nor will people say, 'Here it is,' or 'There it is,' because the kingdom of God is within[b] you."

[22]Then he said to his disciples[D], "The time is coming when you will long to see one of the days of the Son of Man[D], but you will not see it. [23]Men will tell you, 'There he is!' or 'Here he is!' Do not go running off after them. [24]For the Son of Man in his day[c] will be like the lightning, which flashes and lights up the sky from one end to the other. [25]But first he must suffer many things and be rejected by this generation.

[26]"Just as it was in the days of Noah, so also will it be in the days of the Son of Man. [27]People were eating, drinking, marrying and being given in marriage up to the day Noah entered the ark. Then the flood came and destroyed them all.

[28]"It was the same in the days of Lot. People were eating and drinking, buying and selling, planting and building. [29]But the day Lot left Sodom, fire and sulfur rained down from heaven and destroyed them all.

[30]"It will be just like this on the day the Son of Man is revealed. [31]On that day no one who is on the roof of his house, with his goods inside, should go down to get them. Likewise, no one in the field should go back for anything. [32]Remember Lot's wife! [33]Whoever tries to keep his life will lose it, and whoever loses his life will preserve it. [34]I tell you, on that night two people will be in one bed; one will be taken and the other left. [35]Two women will be grinding grain together; one will be taken and the other left.[d]"

[37]"Where, Lord?" they asked.

He replied, "Where there is a dead body, there the vultures will gather."

The Parable of the Persistent Widow

18 Then Jesus told his disciples a parable to show them that they should always pray and not give up. [2]He said: "In a certain town there was a judge who neither feared God nor cared about men. [3]And there was

---

In what way was the kingdom of God *within* the Pharisees? (17:20–21)
If Jesus was speaking about an inner, spiritual kingdom, he was speaking generically, not about the condition of the Pharisees' hearts. But the word *within* may be translated *among* (see NIV text note), in which case Jesus would have been saying he was with them—the King was among them. Jesus taught that the kingdom of God is more than a political solution, more than a future event, and even more than an individual, personal relationship. Jesus' arrival on earth meant that the kingdom itself had arrived and was present.

What event was Jesus predicting? (17:22–37)
Jesus was predicting his return to the earth to gather believers everywhere. This event is known as the second coming. See 1 Thes. 4–5 for more about Christ's return.

SCRIPTURE LINK (17:26–27)
Jesus also likens the time of his coming to the days of Noah in Matt. 24:37–39.

What does this proverb mean? (17:37)
This proverb seems to say: if these signs are all visible, then the end is near. But it also means where there is spiritual death, there will be judgment.

Why compare God to an uncaring, unjust judge? (18:2–7)
Jesus was not comparing but contrasting: if an unjust judge eventually listens to the widow, how much more quickly will a caring, loving God respond to one of his children?

---

[a]12 The Greek word was used for various diseases affecting the skin—not necessarily leprosy.   [b]21 Or *among*   [c]24 Some manuscripts do not have *in his day.*   [d]35 Some manuscripts *left.* [36]*Two men will be in the field; one will be taken and the other left.*

a widow in that town who kept coming to him with the plea, 'Grant me justice against my adversary.'

4"For some time he refused. But finally he said to himself, 'Even though I don't fear God or care about men, **5**yet because this widow keeps bothering me, I will see that she gets justice, so that she won't eventually wear me out with her coming!' "

6And the Lord said, "Listen to what the unjust judge says. **7**And will not God bring about justice for his chosen ones, who cry out to him day and night? Will he keep putting them off? **8**I tell you, he will see that they get justice, and quickly. However, when the Son of Man^D comes, will he find faith on the earth?"

The Parable of the Pharisee and the Tax Collector

9To some who were confident of their own righteousness^D and looked down on everybody else, Jesus told this parable^D: **10**"Two men went up to the temple to pray, one a Pharisee^D and the other a tax collector^D. **11**The Pharisee stood up and prayed about^a himself: 'God, I thank you that I am not like other men—robbers, evildoers, adulterers—or even like this tax collector. **12**I fast twice a week and give a tenth of all I get.'

13"But the tax collector stood at a distance. He would not even look up to heaven, but beat his breast and said, 'God, have mercy^D on me, a sinner.'

14"I tell you that this man, rather than the other, went home justified^D before God. For everyone who exalts himself will be humbled, and he who humbles himself will be exalted."

The Little Children and Jesus

15People were also bringing babies to Jesus to have him touch them. When the disciples^D saw this, they rebuked them. **16**But Jesus called the children to him and said, "Let the little children come to me, and do not hinder them, for the kingdom of God^D belongs to such as these. **17**I tell you the truth, anyone who will not receive the kingdom of God like a little child will never enter it."

The Rich Ruler

18A certain ruler asked him, "Good teacher, what must I do to inherit eternal life?"

19"Why do you call me good?" Jesus answered. "No one is good—except God alone. **20**You know the commandments: 'Do not commit adultery, do not murder, do not steal, do not give false testimony, honor your father and mother.'^b "

21"All these I have kept since I was a boy," he said.

22When Jesus heard this, he said to him, "You still lack one thing. Sell everything you have and give to the poor, and you will have treasure in heaven. Then come, follow me."

23When he heard this, he became very sad, because he was a man of great wealth. **24**Jesus looked at him and said, "How hard it is for the rich to enter the kingdom of God! **25**Indeed, it is easier for a camel to go through the eye of a needle than for a rich man to enter the kingdom of God."

26Those who heard this asked, "Who then can be saved?"

^a11 Or to   ^b20 Exodus 20:12-16; Deut. 5:16-20

Tax collector (18:10)
See *Tax collectors* (5:29).

Why were the disciples opposed to people bringing babies to Jesus? (18:15)

It wasn't that they thought children had no value. Families at that time placed great value on having children, but in this patriarchal system women and children took a back seat to men. At the same time, important and busy rabbis had time only for the best students. The disciples were probably trying to protect Jesus' public image. They thought it was inappropriate for him to waste his time with young children.

SCRIPTURE LINK (18:15–17)

Matthew tells about Jesus and the children in Matt. 19:13–15. Mark talks about it in Mark 10:13–16.

SCRIPTURE LINK (18:18–30)

Matthew and Mark also carry Jesus' story of the rich young ruler. See Matt. 19:16–29 and Mark 10:17–30.

What do we have to give up to gain eternal life? (18:22–30)

Jesus was not saying we have to become poor to gain eternal life. He was saying that it only takes one thing to block a relationship with God. Some, like the ruler, may be spiritually hindered because they depend on material possessions. But others may have to surrender to God such things as fame, extraordinary talent, good looks or intellectualism.

What did Jesus mean by a camel going through the eye of a needle? (18:25)

Some have dealt with this verse in ingenious ways: they suggest that the word *camel* should have been translated *rope* or that *the eye of the needle* was a nickname for a low, after-hours gate in the wall of Jerusalem. It's probably better, however, to see this as a hyperbole, a figure of speech that exaggerates for emphasis. Jesus' point was that some things on earth can prevent us from entering the kingdom of God. His impossible example was meant to raise a note of alarm: wealth can be dangerous to our spiritual lives.

SCRIPTURE LINK (18:31–33)

Jesus' prediction of his death can also be found in Matt. 20:17–19 and Mark 10:32–34. In addition, the writers of the Old Testament foretold these events many years earlier. For Christ's betrayal, see Psalm 41:5–9. The crucifixion is foretold in Psalm 22:16–18 and Isaiah 53:4–7. The resurrection is foretold in Psalm 16:10.

Why couldn't the disciples understand? (18:34)

We have the benefit of hindsight. We can read the things *written by the prophets* (v. 31) in light of the Gospels, but the disciples had never heard such things. In fact, Jesus' announcement flew in the face of conventional wisdom: the Jews anticipated a triumphant Messiah—not one who would suffer and die. God could have given the disciples spiritual insight into Jesus' words, but for reasons unknown to us, God hid the meaning from them until they saw the resurrected Christ (24:15).

SCRIPTURE LINK (18:35–43)

You'll also find accounts of the blind beggar receiving his sight in Matt. 20:29–34 and Mark 10:46–52.

Why did the blind man call Jesus the Son of David? (18:38)

The blind man recognized Jesus as the prophesied Messiah. It is ironic that a man without physical sight was able to see things that others had missed.

How did Zacchaeus gain salvation? (19:9)

Jesus implied that the sons of Abraham (Jews) were lost and in need of salvation just like everyone else (vv. 9–10). Though Zacchaeus was a son of Abraham, he was not saved by his ethnic background or by doing good deeds. He was saved by trusting in God's grace and then acting on his faith. Zacchaeus's desire to repay those he had cheated proved that he had undergone a change of heart.

27Jesus replied, "What is impossible with men is possible with God."

28Peter said to him, "We have left all we had to follow you!"

29"I tell you the truth," Jesus said to them, "no one who has left home or wife or brothers or parents or children for the sake of the kingdom of GodD 30will fail to receive many times as much in this age and, in the age to come, eternal life."

Jesus Again Predicts His Death

31Jesus took the Twelve aside and told them, "We are going up to JerusalemD, and everything that is written by the prophetsD about the Son of ManD will be fulfilled. 32He will be handed over to the GentilesD. They will mock him, insult him, spit on him, flog him and kill him. 33On the third day he will rise again."

34The disciplesD did not understand any of this. Its meaning was hidden from them, and they did not know what he was talking about.

A Blind Beggar Receives His Sight

35As Jesus approached JerichoD, a blind man was sitting by the roadside begging. 36When he heard the crowd going by, he asked what was happening. 37They told him, "Jesus of Nazareth is passing by."

38He called out, "Jesus, Son of David, have mercyD on me!"

39Those who led the way rebuked him and told him to be quiet, but he shouted all the more, "Son of David, have mercy on me!"

40Jesus stopped and ordered the man to be brought to him. When he came near, Jesus asked him, 41"What do you want me to do for you?"

"Lord, I want to see," he replied.

42Jesus said to him, "Receive your sight; your faith has healed you." 43Immediately he received his sight and followed Jesus, praising God. When all the people saw it, they also praised God.

Zacchaeus the Tax Collector

19 Jesus entered Jericho and was passing through. 2A man was there by the name of Zacchaeus; he was a chief tax collectorD and was wealthy. 3He wanted to see who Jesus was, but being a short man he could not, because of the crowd. 4So he ran ahead and climbed a sycamore-fig tree to see him, since Jesus was coming that way.

5When Jesus reached the spot, he looked up and said to him, "Zacchaeus, come down immediately. I must stay at your house today." 6So he came down at once and welcomed him gladly.

7All the people saw this and began to mutter, "He has gone to be the guest of a 'sinner.'"

8But Zacchaeus stood up and said to the Lord, "Look, Lord! Here and now I give half of my possessions to the poor, and if I have cheated anybody out of anything, I will pay back four times the amount."

9Jesus said to him, "Today salvationD has come to this house, because this man, too, is a son of Abraham. 10For the Son of Man came to seek and to save what was lost."

The Parable of the Ten Minas

11While they were listening to this, he went on to tell them a parable[D], because he was near Jerusalem[D] and the people thought that the kingdom of God[D] was going to appear at once. **12**He said: "A man of noble birth went to a distant country to have himself appointed king and then to return. **13**So he called ten of his servants and gave them ten minas.[a] 'Put this money to work,' he said, 'until I come back.'

14"But his subjects hated him and sent a delegation after him to say, 'We don't want this man to be our king.'

15"He was made king, however, and returned home. Then he sent for the servants to whom he had given the money, in order to find out what they had gained with it.

16"The first one came and said, 'Sir, your mina has earned ten more.'

17" 'Well done, my good servant!' his master replied. 'Because you have been trustworthy in a very small matter, take charge of ten cities.'

18"The second came and said, 'Sir, your mina has earned five more.'

19"His master answered, 'You take charge of five cities.'

20"Then another servant came and said, 'Sir, here is your mina; I have kept it laid away in a piece of cloth. **21**I was afraid of you, because you are a hard man. You take out what you did not put in and reap what you did not sow.'

22"His master replied, 'I will judge you by your own words, you wicked servant! You knew, did you, that I am a hard man, taking out what I did not put in, and reaping what I did not sow? **23**Why then didn't you put my money on deposit, so that when I came back, I could have collected it with interest?'

24"Then he said to those standing by, 'Take his mina away from him and give it to the one who has ten minas.'

25" 'Sir,' they said, 'he already has ten!'

26"He replied, 'I tell you that to everyone who has, more will be given, but as for the one who has nothing, even what he has will be taken away. **27**But those enemies of mine who did not want me to be king over them—bring them here and kill them in front of me.' "

The Triumphal Entry

28After Jesus had said this, he went on ahead, going up to Jerusalem. **29**As he approached Bethphage and Bethany at the hill called the Mount of Olives, he sent two of his disciples[D], saying to them, **30**"Go to the village ahead of you, and as you enter it, you will find a colt tied there, which no one has ever ridden. Untie it and bring it here. **31**If anyone asks you, 'Why are you untying it?' tell him, 'The Lord needs it.' "

32Those who were sent ahead went and found it just as he had told them. **33**As they were untying the colt, its owners asked them, "Why are you untying the colt?"

34They replied, "The Lord needs it."

35They brought it to Jesus, threw their cloaks on the colt and put Jesus on it. **36**As he went along, people spread their cloaks on the road.

37When he came near the place where the road goes down the Mount of Olives, the whole crowd of disciples

_a13_ A mina was about three months' wages.

Why did Jesus tell this story? (19:11–27)

The people hoped Jesus would establish an immediate earthly kingdom. Jesus wanted them to see that they should expect something else. His kingdom would be spiritual, not physical. Though present (17:21), it would not be fully established until he returned. Jesus was encouraging the people to remain faithful until the kingdom had fully come.

SCRIPTURE LINK (19:12–27)

In Matt. 25:14–30, Matthew records a parable similar to this one.

SCRIPTURE LINK (19:29–38)

Matthew and Mark also give detailed accounts of Jesus' triumphal entry into Jerusalem. See Matt. 21:1–9 and Mark 11:1–10. Also see John 12:12–15.

Did Jesus borrow the colt without permission? (19:30)

We don't know for sure. It may have been prearranged. The disciples, however, knew Jesus was the Master of all creation and had an owner's authority to use whatever he wished. Also see *Why did Jesus "borrow" without asking?* (Matt. 2:2–6).

Why carpet the road with cloaks? (19:36)

This was a common custom to show respect and honor for conquerors or royalty. Their adoring subjects would cover their way with flowers, branches or garments. When Jehu was named king, his followers laid their cloaks before him to walk upon (2 Kings 9:13). Even today we see remnants of the custom in the phrase "roll out the red carpet" or when people strew flower petals down the aisle at a wedding. Also see *Why did Jesus participate in this procession?* (Matt. 21:7–10).

began joyfully to praise God in loud voices for all the miracles they had seen:

> 38"Blessed is the king who comes in the name of
> the Lord!"ᵃ

> "Peaceᴰ in heaven and gloryᴰ in the highest!"

39Some of the Phariseesᴰ in the crowd said to Jesus, "Teacher, rebuke your disciplesᴰ!"

40"I tell you," he replied, "if they keep quiet, the stones will cry out."

41As he approached Jerusalemᴰ and saw the city, he wept over it 42and said, "If you, even you, had only known on this day what would bring you peace—but now it is hidden from your eyes. 43The days will come upon you when your enemies will build an embankment against you and encircle you and hem you in on every side. 44They will dash you to the ground, you and the children within your walls. They will not leave one stone on another, because you did not recognize the time of God's coming to you."

Jesus at the Temple

45Then he entered the temple area and began driving out those who were selling. 46"It is written," he said to them, " 'My house will be a house of prayer'ᵇ; but you have made it 'a den of robbers.'ᶜ"

47Every day he was teaching at the temple. But the chief priestsᴰ, the teachers of the law and the leaders among the people were trying to kill him. 48Yet they could not find any way to do it, because all the people hung on his words.

The Authority of Jesus Questioned

20 One day as he was teaching the people in the temple courts and preaching the gospelᴰ, the chief priests and the teachers of the law, together with the elders, came up to him. 2"Tell us by what authority you are doing these things," they said. "Who gave you this authority?"

3He replied, "I will also ask you a question. Tell me, 4John's baptismᴰ—was it from heaven, or from men?"

5They discussed it among themselves and said, "If we say, 'From heaven,' he will ask, 'Why didn't you believe him?' 6But if we say, 'From men,' all the people will stone us, because they are persuaded that John was a prophetᴰ."

7So they answered, "We don't know where it was from."

8Jesus said, "Neither will I tell you by what authority I am doing these things."

The Parable of the Tenants

9He went on to tell the people this parableᴰ: "A man planted a vineyard, rented it to some farmers and went away for a long time. 10At harvest time he sent a servant to the tenants so they would give him some of the fruit of the vineyard. But the tenants beat him and sent him away empty-handed. 11He sent another servant, but that one also they beat and treated shamefully and sent away empty-handed. 12He sent still a third, and they wounded him and threw him out.

Did Jesus' prediction about Jerusalem come true? (19:41–44)

Yes. In A.D. 66, forty years after this prediction, the Jews revolted against Rome. After three years the rebellion was put down by Titus, the son of the emperor Vespasian. The Roman soldiers attacked Jerusalem but didn't capture it until A.D. 70 when thousands were killed and the city was burned to the ground.

Why did Jesus resort to violence? (19:45)

See *Why did Jesus resort to violence?* (Matt. 21:12).

SCRIPTURE LINK (19:45–46)

Accounts of Jesus clearing the temple can also be found in Matt. 21:12–16; Mark 11:15–18 and John 2:13–16.

SCRIPTURE LINK (20:1–8)

In Matt. 21:23–27, Matthew also writes of the religious leaders questioning Jesus' authority. Mark tells the story in Mark 11:27–33.

Parable (20:9)

See article: *Why did Jesus speak in parables?* (Matt. 13:11–13).

SCRIPTURE LINK (20:9–19)

Jesus' parable of the tenants also appears in Matt. 21:33–46 and Mark 12:1–12.

ᵃ38 Psalm 118:26   ᵇ46 Isaiah 56:7   ᶜ46 Jer. 7:11

13"Then the owner of the vineyard said, 'What shall I do? I will send my son, whom I love; perhaps they will respect him.'

14"But when the tenants saw him, they talked the matter over. 'This is the heir,' they said. 'Let's kill him, and the inheritance will be ours.' **15**So they threw him out of the vineyard and killed him.

"What then will the owner of the vineyard do to them? **16**He will come and kill those tenants and give the vineyard to others."

When the people heard this, they said, "May this never be!"

17Jesus looked directly at them and asked, "Then what is the meaning of that which is written:

" 'The stone the builders rejected
    has become the capstone$^{Da'b}$?

18Everyone who falls on that stone will be broken to pieces, but he on whom it falls will be crushed."

19The teachers of the law and the chief priests^D looked for a way to arrest him immediately, because they knew he had spoken this parable^D against them. But they were afraid of the people.

Paying Taxes to Caesar

20Keeping a close watch on him, they sent spies, who pretended to be honest. They hoped to catch Jesus in something he said so that they might hand him over to the power and authority of the governor. **21**So the spies questioned him: "Teacher, we know that you speak and teach what is right, and that you do not show partiality but teach the way of God in accordance with the truth. **22**Is it right for us to pay taxes to Caesar or not?"

23He saw through their duplicity and said to them, **24**"Show me a denarius. Whose portrait and inscription are on it?"

25"Caesar's," they replied.

He said to them, "Then give to Caesar what is Caesar's, and to God what is God's."

26They were unable to trap him in what he had said there in public. And astonished by his answer, they became silent.

The Resurrection and Marriage

27Some of the Sadducees^D, who say there is no resurrection^D, came to Jesus with a question. **28**"Teacher," they said, "Moses wrote for us that if a man's brother dies and leaves a wife but no children, the man must marry the widow and have children for his brother. **29**Now there were seven brothers. The first one married a woman and died childless. **30**The second **31**and then the third married her, and in the same way the seven died, leaving no children. **32**Finally, the woman died too. **33**Now then, at the resurrection whose wife will she be, since the seven were married to her?"

34Jesus replied, "The people of this age marry and are given in marriage. **35**But those who are considered worthy of taking part in that age and in the resurrection from the dead will neither marry nor be given in marriage, **36**and they can no longer die; for they are like the angels. They are God's children, since they are children of the resurrection. **37**But in the account of the bush, even Mo-

a 17 Or *cornerstone*   *b* 17 Psalm 118:22

What so shocked the people about Jesus' parable? (20:16)
Being familiar with parables (see, for example, Isaiah 5:1–7), the people quickly saw the implications of this one. They probably realized that the owner represented God, the vineyard was Israel, the tenant farmers were the religious leaders, the servants were prophets and priests, the son was the Messiah and the others were the Gentiles. Though both the killing of the son and the judgment on the tenants were shocking, the priests and teachers were even more aghast that God would give Israel's vineyard to Gentiles.

Capstone (20:17)
See *Capstone* (Mark 12:10).

SCRIPTURE LINK (20:20–26)
Matt. 22:15–22 and Mark 12:13–17 also record Jesus' teaching on paying taxes.

What is *Caesar's* and what is *God's*? (20:22–25)
God is over all things, but he entrusts some of those things to people. The things that belong to Caesar—that is, government authorities—are responsibilities to maintain civil order, to punish wrongdoers, to protect the helpless and to collect taxes to administer these assignments. See Romans 13:1–7 and 1 Peter 2:13–17. God, however, deserves our highest allegiance. Only he deserves our worship. All human government is subject to his higher authority and purpose (Daniel 3:17–18; 6:1–28; Acts 4:19–20; 5:29).

SCRIPTURE LINK (20:27–40)
Jesus' words to the Sadducees about marriage and the resurrection can also be found in Matt. 22:23–33 and Mark 12:18–27.

Would a first-century Jew marry his brother's widow? (20:28)
See *Did Jews still marry their brothers' widows?* (Mark 12:19).

Is heaven sexless? (20:35)
See *Is heaven sexless?* (Mark 12:25).

ses showed that the dead rise, for he calls the Lord 'the God of Abraham, and the God of Isaac, and the God of Jacob.'[a] **38**He is not the God of the dead, but of the living, for to him all are alive."

39Some of the teachers of the law responded, "Well said, teacher!" **40**And no one dared to ask him any more questions.

Whose Son Is the Christ?

41Then Jesus said to them, "How is it that they say the Christ[b] is the Son of David? **42**David himself declares in the Book of Psalms:

" 'The Lord said to my Lord:
   "Sit at my right hand
43until I make your enemies
   a footstool[D] for your feet." '[c]

44David calls him 'Lord.' How then can he be his son?"

45While all the people were listening, Jesus said to his disciples[D], **46**"Beware of the teachers of the law. They like to walk around in flowing robes and love to be greeted in the marketplaces and have the most important seats in the synagogues and the places of honor at banquets. **47**They devour widows' houses and for a show make lengthy prayers. Such men will be punished most severely."

The Widow's Offering

21 As he looked up, Jesus saw the rich putting their gifts into the temple treasury. **2**He also saw a poor widow put in two very small copper coins.[d] **3**"I tell you the truth," he said, "this poor widow has put in more than all the others. **4**All these people gave their gifts out of their wealth; but she out of her poverty put in all she had to live on."

Signs of the End of the Age

5Some of his disciples were remarking about how the temple was adorned with beautiful stones and with gifts dedicated to God. But Jesus said, **6**"As for what you see here, the time will come when not one stone will be left on another; every one of them will be thrown down."

7"Teacher," they asked, "when will these things happen? And what will be the sign that they are about to take place?"

8He replied: "Watch out that you are not deceived. For many will come in my name, claiming, 'I am he,' and, 'The time is near.' Do not follow them. **9**When you hear of wars and revolutions, do not be frightened. These things must happen first, but the end will not come right away."

10Then he said to them: "Nation will rise against nation, and kingdom against kingdom. **11**There will be great earthquakes, famines and pestilences in various places, and fearful events and great signs from heaven.

12"But before all this, they will lay hands on you and persecute you. They will deliver you to synagogues and prisons, and you will be brought before kings and governors, and all on account of my name. **13**This will result in your being witnesses to them. **14**But make up your mind not to worry beforehand how you will defend yourselves.

What did Jesus want to teach about the Messiah? (20:41–44)

Jesus challenged the Pharisees' concept of the Messiah. They believed the Messiah would be a human descendant of David—a political leader. Jesus wanted them to see that the Son of David was also the Son of God. So he quoted Psalm 110:1 where David spoke of two *Lords:* God and the Messiah. Jesus' question pointedly showed the Pharisees that the one they called the Son of David was to be seated at the right hand of the Almighty God. Also see *What clue is Jesus giving about the Messiah?* (Mark 12:35–37).

SCRIPTURE LINK (20:41–47)

Jesus also addresses the question of whose Son is the Christ in Matt. 22:41—23:7 and Mark 12:35–40.

Temple treasury (21:1)

The temple treasury was located either in the outermost court of the temple, called the court of women, or in a nearby hallway (see *Map 8* at the back of this Bible). There were seven boxes for the temple tax and six boxes for free-will offerings. The poor widow gave to the latter (v. 2).

SCRIPTURE LINK (21:1–4)

Mark tells about the widow's offering in Mark 12:41–44.

SCRIPTURE LINK (21:5–36)

Jesus also gives the signs of the end of the age in Matt. 24 and Mark 13.

What was the disciples' real agenda? (21:7)

Matthew makes it clear they not only wanted to know when the temple would be destroyed, but what would be the signs of Christ's return and the end of human history (Matt. 24:3). Human nature seems to desire inside information. Jesus addressed all these questions together (21:8–32), but did not offer the definitive answer they, and Christians through the ages, have wished for.

What's wrong with preparing a legal defense? (21:14)

Nothing. Jesus is simply saying that when we face legal battles because of our stand for him, we won't have to *worry*. Though we may have legal counsel and a prepared defense, our trust ultimately must be in God. Jesus, anticipating his disciples' future troubles, was simply assuring them that they need not panic. The Spirit would be with them to assist them during such times.

---

a37 Exodus 3:6   *b41* Or *Messiah*   *c43* Psalm 110:1
d2 Greek *two lepta*

¹⁵For I will give you words and wisdom that none of your adversaries will be able to resist or contradict. ¹⁶You will be betrayed even by parents, brothers, relatives and friends, and they will put some of you to death[D]. ¹⁷All men will hate you because of me. ¹⁸But not a hair of your head will perish. ¹⁹By standing firm you will gain life.

²⁰"When you see Jerusalem[D] being surrounded by armies, you will know that its desolation is near. ²¹Then let those who are in Judea flee to the mountains, let those in the city get out, and let those in the country not enter the city. ²²For this is the time of punishment in fulfillment of all that has been written. ²³How dreadful it will be in those days for pregnant women and nursing mothers! There will be great distress in the land and wrath against this people. ²⁴They will fall by the sword and will be taken as prisoners to all the nations. Jerusalem will be trampled on by the Gentiles[D] until the times of the Gentiles are fulfilled.

²⁵"There will be signs in the sun, moon and stars. On the earth, nations will be in anguish and perplexity at the roaring and tossing of the sea. ²⁶Men will faint from terror, apprehensive of what is coming on the world, for the heavenly bodies will be shaken. ²⁷At that time they will see the Son of Man[D] coming in a cloud with power and great glory[D]. ²⁸When these things begin to take place, stand up and lift up your heads, because your redemption[D] is drawing near."

²⁹He told them this parable[D]: "Look at the fig tree and all the trees. ³⁰When they sprout leaves, you can see for yourselves and know that summer is near. ³¹Even so, when you see these things happening, you know that the kingdom of God[D] is near.

³²"I tell you the truth, this generation[a] will certainly not pass away until all these things have happened. ³³Heaven and earth will pass away, but my words will never pass away.

³⁴"Be careful, or your hearts will be weighed down with dissipation[D], drunkenness and the anxieties of life, and that day will close on you unexpectedly like a trap. ³⁵For it will come upon all those who live on the face of the

[a]32 Or *race*

What events did Jesus predict here? (21:20–24)

Jesus predicted two things: the end of Jerusalem and the end of the world. The descriptions of these two events were intertwined, probably because the catastrophic first-century events in Jerusalem foreshadowed the even greater events to come at the end of the world.

Does this describe the "Great Tribulation"? (21:23–26)

Maybe. Some think this describes a future time of unprecedented disaster—judgment to come upon the world at the end of the age (Rev. 6:15–17; 7:14). Others believe this refers to the terrible suffering that occurred when Jerusalem was destroyed in A.D. 70. People died at the hands of Roman troops or by starvation, fire and disease. To a certain extent, God's people can expect to face tribulation in every age (John 16:33).

Times of the Gentiles (21:24)

This refers to a period after Jerusalem's fall, either at the hands of the Babylonians (586 B.C.) or the Romans (A.D. 70). Some believe it means a time during which the Gentiles carry out God's judgments. Others say it is a time when the Gentiles enjoy privileges God originally promised to Israel. Still others feel it is a time during which the gospel is preached to the Gentiles—in other words, lasting up to the time Christ returns. Whatever the phrase means, God is behind it all, working his purpose and bringing the times to their fulfillment.

Did all this happen within the lifespan of that generation? (21:32)

The destruction of Jerusalem took place in A.D. 70, within the lifespan of those Jesus spoke to. Some feel this is what Jesus was referring to. Others say that the word *generation* can mean the Jewish race, not a literal 40-year period. Still others say that *generation* means humankind and that those who see the beginning of the end time events will also see their culmination in the coming of Christ. Whatever the meaning, Jesus affirmed the certainty of coming judgment upon both Jerusalem and the world. He did not give a timetable for these events.

Did Jesus promise complete physical protection? (21:18)

No. In fact, he told of coming persecutions: believers would be hated, persecuted by religious and political leaders, betrayed by family and friends and some would even be killed (vv. 12–17). James (Acts 12:1–2), Peter (Acts 12:3–5), Stephen (Acts 6:8–15; 7:54–60) and many other apostles (Acts 4:1–3; 5:17–18,40) suffered beatings, imprisonment and death because of their faith.

But at the same time Jesus promised that *not a hair of your head will perish*. How does that square with the promise of persecution? It was a figurative way of saying that though their earthly bodies could be killed, their spirits would live forever. If they remained true to the faith, they would be ensured of life everlasting (v. 19). Furthermore, God would assist them in times of persecution, giving them the right words to say and the wisdom to know how to respond (v. 15).

Jesus' primary focus was on the spiritual results, not the physical outcome. That's why, though Christian martyrs have been beheaded, "not a hair of their heads perished."

SCRIPTURE LINK (22:1–6)

You can read about Judas's agreement to betray Jesus in Matt. 26:2–5,14–16 and Mark 14:1–2,10–11.

How did Satan enter Judas? (22:3)

A few have speculated that Judas may have been possessed by Satan. But most disagree, saying that Judas put himself in a position where he could be influenced by Satan. Perhaps he had given up on Jesus and was trying to force him into making a political move. Perhaps he was motivated solely by greed (v. 5). Whatever the case, Satan was able to target Judas because he had opened himself up to temptation.

SCRIPTURE LINK (22:7–13)

Matthew and Mark both tell about the preparations for the Last Supper. See Matt. 26:17–19 and Mark 14:12–16.

How did the disciples prepare for the Passover? (22:13)

Most importantly, they needed to acquire a lamb, take it to the temple for slaughter and then roast it whole as prescribed by Jewish law (Exodus 12:8–9). They also had to purchase specific items required for the Passover meal, prepare the food and set the table.

SCRIPTURE LINK (22:17–20)

You will find additional passages on the symbolism of the bread and the cup in Matt. 26:26–29 and Mark 14:22–25.

How did Jesus change the Passover? (22:19–20)

The Jewish Feast of Passover celebrated how God delivered his people out of Egyptian slavery; the Lord's Supper celebrates how God delivers us from slavery to sin. The Passover sacrificial lamb appeased the death angel; the bread of Communion signifies Christ's body, broken in judgment for our sin. The Passover wine symbolized the lamb's blood on the doorframe; Communion wine symbolizes Christ's blood given for us, his death purchasing our eternal life. The Passover represented God's former covenant with his people; the Lord's Supper reminds us of his new covenant. See Exodus 12:1–17 for details about the original Passover.

SCRIPTURE LINK (22:21–23)

Jesus also indicates who his betrayer will be in Matt. 26:21–24; Mark 14:18–21 and John 13:21–30.

If ministers are servants, how can they lead? (22:24–26)

Jesus was not putting down the importance of leadership; he was highlighting the proper *motives* for leadership. All of us must be servants, and some serve by leading. Following Christ's example, godly leaders choose the way of humility. They are driven not by selfish ambition but by a burning desire to care for God's people and accomplish his purposes (1 Peter 5:2–6).

SCRIPTURE LINK (22:25–27)

Jesus' words about who will be the greatest can also be found in Matt. 20:25–28 and Mark 10:42–45.

whole earth. ³⁶Be always on the watch, and pray that you may be able to escape all that is about to happen, and that you may be able to stand before the Son of Man."

³⁷Each day Jesus was teaching at the temple, and each evening he went out to spend the night on the hill called the Mount of Olives, ³⁸and all the people came early in the morning to hear him at the temple.

Judas Agrees to Betray Jesus

22 Now the Feast of Unleavened Bread, called the Passover, was approaching, ²and the chief priests^D and the teachers of the law were looking for some way to get rid of Jesus, for they were afraid of the people. ³Then Satan entered Judas, called Iscariot, one of the Twelve. ⁴And Judas went to the chief priests and the officers of the temple guard and discussed with them how he might betray Jesus. ⁵They were delighted and agreed to give him money. ⁶He consented, and watched for an opportunity to hand Jesus over to them when no crowd was present.

The Last Supper

⁷Then came the day of Unleavened Bread on which the Passover lamb had to be sacrificed. ⁸Jesus sent Peter and John, saying, "Go and make preparations for us to eat the Passover."

⁹"Where do you want us to prepare for it?" they asked.

¹⁰He replied, "As you enter the city, a man carrying a jar of water will meet you. Follow him to the house that he enters, ¹¹and say to the owner of the house, 'The Teacher asks: Where is the guest room, where I may eat the Passover with my disciples^D?' ¹²He will show you a large upper room, all furnished. Make preparations there."

¹³They left and found things just as Jesus had told them. So they prepared the Passover.

¹⁴When the hour came, Jesus and his apostles^D reclined at the table. ¹⁵And he said to them, "I have eagerly desired to eat this Passover with you before I suffer. ¹⁶For I tell you, I will not eat it again until it finds fulfillment in the kingdom of God."

¹⁷After taking the cup, he gave thanks and said, "Take this and divide it among you. ¹⁸For I tell you I will not drink again of the fruit of the vine until the kingdom of God^D comes."

¹⁹And he took bread, gave thanks and broke it, and gave it to them, saying, "This is my body given for you; do this in remembrance of me."

²⁰In the same way, after the supper he took the cup, saying, "This cup is the new covenant^D in my blood, which is poured out for you. ²¹But the hand of him who is going to betray me is with mine on the table. ²²The Son of Man^D will go as it has been decreed, but woe to that man who betrays him." ²³They began to question among themselves which of them it might be who would do this.

²⁴Also a dispute arose among them as to which of them was considered to be greatest. ²⁵Jesus said to them, "The kings of the Gentiles^D lord it over them; and those who exercise authority over them call themselves Benefactors. ²⁶But you are not to be like that. Instead, the greatest among you should be like the youngest, and the one who rules like the one who serves. ²⁷For who is greater, the one who is at the table or the one who serves? Is it not the one who is at the table? But I am among you as one who serves. ²⁸You are those who have stood by me in my tri-

als. **29**And I confer on you a kingdom, just as my Father conferred one on me, **30**so that you may eat and drink at my table in my kingdom and sit on thrones, judging the twelve tribes of Israel.

31"Simon, Simon, Satan has asked to sift you*a* as wheat. **32**But I have prayed for you, Simon, that your faith may not fail. And when you have turned back, strengthen your brothers."

33But he replied, "Lord, I am ready to go with you to prison and to death*D*."

34Jesus answered, "I tell you, Peter, before the rooster crows today, you will deny three times that you know me."

35Then Jesus asked them, "When I sent you without purse, bag or sandals, did you lack anything?"

"Nothing," they answered.

36He said to them, "But now if you have a purse, take it, and also a bag; and if you don't have a sword, sell your cloak and buy one. **37**It is written: 'And he was numbered with the transgressors'*b*; and I tell you that this must be fulfilled in me. Yes, what is written about me is reaching its fulfillment."

38The disciples*D* said, "See, Lord, here are two swords."

"That is enough," he replied.

Jesus Prays on the Mount of Olives

39Jesus went out as usual to the Mount of Olives, and his disciples followed him. **40**On reaching the place, he said to them, "Pray that you will not fall into temptation." **41**He withdrew about a stone's throw beyond them, knelt down and prayed, **42**"Father, if you are willing, take this cup from me; yet not my will, but yours be done." **43**An angel from heaven appeared to him and strengthened him. **44**And being in anguish, he prayed more earnestly, and his sweat was like drops of blood falling to the ground.*c*

45When he rose from prayer and went back to the disciples, he found them asleep, exhausted from sorrow. **46**"Why are you sleeping?" he asked them. "Get up and pray so that you will not fall into temptation."

Jesus Arrested

47While he was still speaking a crowd came up, and the man who was called Judas, one of the Twelve, was leading them. He approached Jesus to kiss him, **48**but Jesus asked him, "Judas, are you betraying the Son of Man*D* with a kiss?"

49When Jesus' followers saw what was going to happen, they said, "Lord, should we strike with our swords?" **50**And one of them struck the servant of the high priest*D*, cutting off his right ear.

51But Jesus answered, "No more of this!" And he touched the man's ear and healed him.

52Then Jesus said to the chief priests, the officers of the temple guard, and the elders, who had come for him, "Am I leading a rebellion, that you have come with swords and clubs? **53**Every day I was with you in the temple courts, and you did not lay a hand on me. But this is your hour—when darkness reigns."

*a*31 The Greek is plural.   *b*37 Isaiah 53:12   *c*44 Some early manuscripts do not have verses 43 and 44.

SCRIPTURE LINK (22:33–34)

In Matt. 26:33–35; Mark 14:29–31 and John 13:37–38, Jesus also predicts Peter's betrayal.

Why did Jesus tell the disciples to buy a sword? (22:36–38)

As he had often done before, Jesus was speaking figuratively here. He knew persecution was coming and was urging his disciples to be prepared to suffer because of it. Some think Jesus' words *That is enough* (v. 38) were uttered in exasperation. The disciples had understood him literally when he meant to be understood figuratively.

Why did Jesus ask the disciples to pray? (22:40)

In the loneliness that comes while awaiting death, Jesus longed for the presence of friends who would pray with him. In addition, the disciples needed to pray for their own benefit, considering their predicted denial, cowardice and abandonment of Jesus. Their boasts of allegiance (Mark 14:31) appear pathetic in light of their behavior as the night wore on. Their failure to pray would make them an easy mark when assaulted by fear and temptation.

SCRIPTURE LINK (22:40–46)

Matthew writes about Jesus' sorrowing in Gethsemane in Matt. 26:36–46. Mark covers it in Mark 14:32–42.

Did Jesus resist his mission? (22:42–44)

No, but he did wonder if there might not be a less painful alternative. Though Jesus was fully God, he was also fully human—revealed in this vulnerable moment. Jesus was still committed to his purpose to be the Savior of the world (John 12:27). However, the intense suffering he faced caused him to turn to his Father for help—just as we might pray when confronted with overwhelming emotional or physical pain.

SCRIPTURE LINK (22:47–53)

All of the Gospel writers give details of Jesus' arrest. See Matt. 26:47–56; Mark 14:43–50 and John 18:3–11.

Why did Judas kiss Jesus? (22:47–48)

A kiss was a traditional greeting. A disciple would greet his teacher with a kiss on the cheek or beard to show honor and submission. The less important person initiated the kiss. This is the irony in this passage, that Judas would use something meant to give honor to betray instead.

Why did Peter weep? (22:61–62)
Because he suddenly felt the weight of his own
failure. Though he had earlier wanted to fight
for Jesus, now his courage had melted into
confusion. He'd been bewildered and disheartened when Jesus had rejected his rescue attempt in the garden (John 18:10–11). But the
crowing rooster brought things back into perspective again with a shocking realization: he
had betrayed the one he loved just as Jesus
had foretold.

**What was criminal about Jesus' saying
that he was the Son of God?
(22:70–71)**
Jesus used the same *I AM* that God used to describe himself to Moses: *I AM WHO I AM* (Exodus
3:14). The priests recognized immediately
what Jesus was claiming. From their perspective, this was the highest form of blasphemy, a
crime punishable by death. They didn't know
that the Messiah would be God himself.

**Why wasn't Pilate bothered by Jesus'
claim to be king of the Jews?
(23:3–4)**
If Jesus had been leading a militant band and
claiming to be their king, Pilate could have condemned him for treason against Rome. But
Jesus' reply to Pilate suggested no such rebellion. Jesus' literal answer was, *You say.* He
merely echoed Pilate's own words. Jesus
didn't deny the charge but was so vague that
Pilate had nothing to go on.

Peter Disowns Jesus

54Then seizing him, they led him away and took him
into the house of the high priest[D]. Peter followed at a distance. **55**But when they had kindled a fire in the middle of
the courtyard and had sat down together, Peter sat down
with them. **56**A servant girl saw him seated there in the
firelight. She looked closely at him and said, "This man
was with him."

57But he denied it. "Woman, I don't know him," he said.

58A little later someone else saw him and said, "You
also are one of them."

"Man, I am not!" Peter replied.

59About an hour later another asserted, "Certainly this
fellow was with him, for he is a Galilean."

60Peter replied, "Man, I don't know what you're talking
about!" Just as he was speaking, the rooster crowed. **61**The
Lord turned and looked straight at Peter. Then Peter remembered the word the Lord had spoken to him: "Before
the rooster crows today, you will disown me three times."
62And he went outside and wept bitterly.

The Guards Mock Jesus

63The men who were guarding Jesus began mocking
and beating him. **64**They blindfolded him and demanded,
"Prophesy! Who hit you?" **65**And they said many other insulting things to him.

Jesus Before Pilate and Herod

66At daybreak the council of the elders of the people,
both the chief priests and teachers of the law, met together, and Jesus was led before them. **67**"If you are the
Christ,[a]" they said, "tell us."

Jesus answered, "If I tell you, you will not believe me,
68and if I asked you, you would not answer. **69**But from
now on, the Son of Man[D] will be seated at the right hand
of the mighty God."

70They all asked, "Are you then the Son of God?"

He replied, "You are right in saying I am."

71Then they said, "Why do we need any more testimony? We have heard it from his own lips."

23 Then the whole assembly rose and led him off to
Pilate. **2**And they began to accuse him, saying,
"We have found this man subverting our nation. He op-
poses payment of taxes to Caesar and claims to be
Christ,[b] a king."

3So Pilate asked Jesus, "Are you the king of the Jews[D]?"

"Yes, it is as you say," Jesus replied.

4Then Pilate announced to the chief priests and the
crowd, "I find no basis for a charge against this man."

5But they insisted, "He stirs up the people all over Judea[c] by his teaching. He started in Galilee and has come
all the way here."

6On hearing this, Pilate asked if the man was a Galilean.
7When he learned that Jesus was under Herod's jurisdiction, he sent him to Herod, who was also in Jerusalem[D]
at that time.

8When Herod saw Jesus, he was greatly pleased, because for a long time he had been wanting to see him.
From what he had heard about him, he hoped to see him
perform some miracle. **9**He plied him with many ques-

[a]67 Or *Messiah*   [b]2 Or *Messiah*; also in verses 35 and 39
[c]5 Or *over the land of the Jews*

tions, but Jesus gave him no answer. **10**The chief priests[D] and the teachers of the law were standing there, vehemently accusing him. **11**Then Herod and his soldiers ridiculed and mocked him. Dressing him in an elegant robe, they sent him back to Pilate. **12**That day Herod and Pilate became friends—before this they had been enemies.

13Pilate called together the chief priests, the rulers and the people, **14**and said to them, "You brought me this man as one who was inciting the people to rebellion. I have examined him in your presence and have found no basis for your charges against him. **15**Neither has Herod, for he sent him back to us; as you can see, he has done nothing to deserve death[D]. **16**Therefore, I will punish him and then release him.[a]"

18With one voice they cried out, "Away with this man! Release Barabbas to us!" **19**(Barabbas had been thrown into prison for an insurrection in the city, and for murder.)

20Wanting to release Jesus, Pilate appealed to them again. **21**But they kept shouting, "Crucify him! Crucify him!"

22For the third time he spoke to them: "Why? What crime has this man committed? I have found in him no grounds for the death penalty. Therefore I will have him punished and then release him."

23But with loud shouts they insistently demanded that he be crucified, and their shouts prevailed. **24**So Pilate decided to grant their demand. **25**He released the man who had been thrown into prison for insurrection and murder, the one they asked for, and surrendered Jesus to their will.

The Crucifixion

26As they led him away, they seized Simon from Cyrene, who was on his way in from the country, and put the cross on him and made him carry it behind Jesus. **27**A large number of people followed him, including women who mourned and wailed for him. **28**Jesus turned and said to them, "Daughters of Jerusalem[D], do not weep for me; weep for yourselves and for your children. **29**For the time will come when you will say, 'Blessed are the barren women, the wombs that never bore and the breasts that never nursed!' **30**Then

" 'they will say to the mountains, "Fall on us!"
and to the hills, "Cover us!" '[b]

31For if men do these things when the tree is green, what will happen when it is dry?"

32Two other men, both criminals, were also led out with him to be executed. **33**When they came to the place called the Skull, there they crucified him, along with the criminals—one on his right, the other on his left. **34**Jesus said, "Father, forgive them, for they do not know what they are doing."[c] And they divided up his clothes by casting lots.

35The people stood watching, and the rulers even sneered at him. They said, "He saved others; let him save himself if he is the Christ of God, the Chosen One."

36The soldiers also came up and mocked him. They of-

a16 Some manuscripts him." 17Now he was obliged to release one man to them at the Feast. b30 Hosea 10:8 c34 Some early manuscripts do not have this sentence.

What made Herod and Pilate become friends? (23:12)

Pilate ruled over Judea and Samaria, land that had once belonged to Herod Antipas's father, Herod the Great (Matt. 2:1,19; see *Setting of the Gospels* on page 1332). The Romans had wrested control of the land from Herod Antipas's half-brother, who was an ineffective ruler. So Herod would have viewed Pilate with suspicion; Pilate represented a Roman threat to his own rule. But when Pilate sent Jesus to Herod Antipas, he was publicly recognizing Herod's position, putting his mind at ease.

Why did the people want a criminal released? (23:18–19)

Pilate offered the crowd a choice between Jesus and Barabbas (Matt. 27:16–18). Since Barabbas was a killer, Pilate may have thought the people would come to their senses at the thought of letting a dangerous criminal back on the streets. But the rulers had whipped the crowd into such an irrational frenzy against Jesus, that they chose a murderer over Jesus.

SCRIPTURE LINK (23:18–25)

All of the Gospel writers tell of the crowd's demand to crucify Jesus. See Matt. 27:15–26; Mark 15:6–15 and John 18:39—19:16.

Why was a foreigner pressed into service? (23:26)

We might say Simon was in the wrong place at the wrong time. Jesus began the journey to Golgotha carrying his own cross (John 19:17). But it seems he was unable to carry it the whole way, probably because he had been weakened by a Roman beating (John 19:1–3). Simon was most likely a Jew from a city now in Libya, visiting Jerusalem for Passover, who was singled out of the crowd at random. Roman law permitted soldiers to press any Roman subject into immediate service.

SCRIPTURE LINK (23:33–43)

Detailed accounts of Jesus' crucifixion can be found in Matt. 27:33–44; Mark 15:22–32 and John 19:17–24.

Why did Jesus pray for his captors' forgiveness? (23:34)

Jesus desired forgiveness, not only for those who crucified him, but for everyone. Jesus' death was caused by the sins of the world, so in a sense we are all responsible. God's forgiveness is extended to everyone, even those who were responsible for the crucifixion. Still, no one is forgiven against his or her own will, for each one must respond to God's call to repent and turn to him to be forgiven. Also see *Why should God forgive those who don't repent?* (Acts 7:60).

Why is Luke the only writer who tells of the thief's repentance? (23:40–42)
According to Luke, one robber had a change of heart. The apparent difference between Luke's account and that of Matthew and Mark seems to stem from the timing of events. Matthew and Mark record earlier events when both robbers hurled insults at Jesus (Matt. 27:41–44; Mark 15:27–32). Luke picks up the story when one of them, seeing Jesus forgive his executioners (23:34), determined that Jesus could be trusted.

Paradise (23:43)
Some say that when Jesus died, his spirit went to the place of dead spirits (usually called the *grave* in the Old Testament). There it awakened the righteous dead and led them to a newly-opened heaven, or paradise (Matt. 27:51–53). Apparently many of these dead were seen in Jerusalem while on their way.

SCRIPTURE LINK (23:44–49)
Matthew tells about Jesus' death in Matt. 27:45–56. Mark writes about it in Mark 15:33–41.

Why did the curtain in the temple tear? (23:45)
See *Why did the curtain in the temple tear?* (Matt. 27:51).

Centurion (23:47)
See *What would be a centurion's equivalent rank in today's military?* (Acts 10:1).

Council (23:50)
See *Sanhedrin* in the Dictionary.

Why did this secret disciple risk discovery after Jesus was dead? (23:50–53)
During Christ's life, he apparently kept quiet about his convictions. He probably feared being thrown out of the synagogue (see John 7:13; 9:22; 20:19). Now, with Jesus dead, the threat of reprisal seemed remote. Still, to openly ask for the body required tremendous courage. Perhaps the miraculous events accompanying Christ's death on the cross had changed him and given him the boldness to identify with Jesus (see John 12:32).

SCRIPTURE LINK (23:50–56)
Matt. 27:57–61; Mark 15:42–47 and John 19:38–42 give other accounts of Jesus' burial.

SCRIPTURE LINK (24:1–10)
You'll also find the account of Jesus' resurrection in Matt. 28:1–8; Mark 16:1–8 and John 20:1–8.

SCRIPTURE LINK (24:6–8)
Jesus had told the disciples several times that he would suffer death and be raised to life again, but they had no idea what he was talking about. See 9:22–27,43–45; 18:31–34.

fered him wine vinegar **37**and said, "If you are the king of the Jews[D], save yourself."

38There was a written notice above him, which read: THIS IS THE KING OF THE JEWS.

39One of the criminals who hung there hurled insults at him: "Aren't you the Christ? Save yourself and us!"

40But the other criminal rebuked him. "Don't you fear God," he said, "since you are under the same sentence? **41**We are punished justly, for we are getting what our deeds deserve. But this man has done nothing wrong."

42Then he said, "Jesus, remember me when you come into your kingdom.[a]"

43Jesus answered him, "I tell you the truth, today you will be with me in paradise."

Jesus' Death

44It was now about the sixth hour, and darkness came over the whole land until the ninth hour, **45**for the sun stopped shining. And the curtain of the temple was torn in two. **46**Jesus called out with a loud voice, "Father, into your hands I commit my spirit." When he had said this, he breathed his last.

47The centurion[D], seeing what had happened, praised God and said, "Surely this was a righteous[D] man." **48**When all the people who had gathered to witness this sight saw what took place, they beat their breasts and went away. **49**But all those who knew him, including the women who had followed him from Galilee, stood at a distance, watching these things.

Jesus' Burial

50Now there was a man named Joseph, a member of the Council, a good and upright man, **51**who had not consented to their decision and action. He came from the Judean town of Arimathea and he was waiting for the kingdom of God[D]. **52**Going to Pilate, he asked for Jesus' body. **53**Then he took it down, wrapped it in linen cloth and placed it in a tomb cut in the rock, one in which no one had yet been laid. **54**It was Preparation Day, and the Sabbath[D] was about to begin.

55The women who had come with Jesus from Galilee followed Joseph and saw the tomb and how his body was laid in it. **56**Then they went home and prepared spices and perfumes. But they rested on the Sabbath in obedience to the commandment.

The Resurrection

24 On the first day of the week, very early in the morning, the women took the spices they had prepared and went to the tomb. **2**They found the stone rolled away from the tomb, **3**but when they entered, they did not find the body of the Lord Jesus. **4**While they were wondering about this, suddenly two men in clothes that gleamed like lightning stood beside them. **5**In their fright the women bowed down with their faces to the ground, but the men said to them, "Why do you look for the living among the dead? **6**He is not here; he has risen! Remember how he told you, while he was still with you in Galilee: **7**'The Son of Man[D] must be delivered into the hands of sinful men, be crucified and on the third day be raised again.' " **8**Then they remembered his words.

9When they came back from the tomb, they told all

a42 Some manuscripts *come with your kingly power*

these things to the Eleven and to all the others. ¹⁰It was Mary Magdalene, Joanna, Mary the mother of James, and the others with them who told this to the apostles ᴰ. ¹¹But they did not believe the women, because their words seemed to them like nonsense. ¹²Peter, however, got up and ran to the tomb. Bending over, he saw the strips of linen lying by themselves, and he went away, wondering to himself what had happened.

On the Road to Emmaus

¹³Now that same day two of them were going to a village called Emmaus, about seven miles ᵃ from Jerusalem ᴰ. ¹⁴They were talking with each other about everything that had happened. ¹⁵As they talked and discussed these things with each other, Jesus himself came up and walked along with them; ¹⁶but they were kept from recognizing him.

¹⁷He asked them, "What are you discussing together as you walk along?"

They stood still, their faces downcast. ¹⁸One of them, named Cleopas, asked him, "Are you only a visitor to Jerusalem and do not know the things that have happened there in these days?"

¹⁹"What things?" he asked.

"About Jesus of Nazareth," they replied. "He was a prophet ᴰ, powerful in word and deed before God and all the people. ²⁰The chief priests ᴰ and our rulers handed him over to be sentenced to death ᴰ, and they crucified him; ²¹but we had hoped that he was the one who was going to redeem ᴰ Israel. And what is more, it is the third day since all this took place. ²²In addition, some of our women amazed us. They went to the tomb early this morning ²³but didn't find his body. They came and told us that they had seen a vision ᴰ of angels, who said he was alive. ²⁴Then some of our companions went to the tomb and found it just as the women had said, but him they did not see."

ᵃ13 Greek *sixty stadia* (about 11 kilometers)

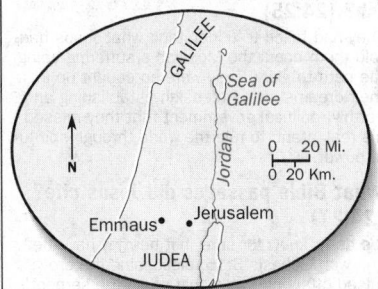

On the Road to Emmaus (24:13)

Kept from recognizing him (24:16)
We don't know how or why this happened, but this verse indicates that *God* did not allow these followers to recognize Jesus. Perhaps had they recognized Jesus immediately they would have been so excited and awe-stricken they might not have heard the important things he wanted to explain to them (vv. 25–27).

What changed at this pivotal point in history? (24:5–6)

The resurrection vindicated Jesus' claims about himself, that he was the Son of God in the flesh, the fulfillment of God's dealings with humankind. No longer would people have to follow rules and traditions to find salvation (Col. 2:20–23). The old covenant had been superseded by the new and the proof was in the resurrection. Because Jesus lives, he is the Messiah, the one to trust.

Another way to look at this question is to ask what would be different if Jesus had not risen from the dead. If there had been no resurrection, Christianity as we know it would not exist. At most, Christians would be following the teachings of just another popular rabbi. His words merely would have joined the countless words of other religious writings. People would be left with no other option for salvation than to strive for absolute obedience.

But the resurrection changed everything. People follow Christ's teachings, not to *become* saved, but because they *are* saved. They've discovered something even better than knowing *words;* they've found what it means to know *him!* Because *he* was raised from the dead, *we* can be too. We can live—really live—both now and through all eternity.

Why did Jesus call these disciples foolish? (24:25)

They had failed to understand what Jesus had told them about the Messiah's suffering being the path to glory. They were so caught up in their dreams of the Messiah establishing an earthly, political government that they missed his real intent: to rule the world through spiritual power.

What Bible passages did Jesus cite? (24:27)

We don't know for sure, but he may have begun with Genesis 3:15, discussing the promised offspring who would crush the serpent's head—just as he had defeated Satan through his death on the cross. Jesus may have then continued by reminding them of the suffering servant in Isaiah 53, the pierced one in Zecheriah 12:10 and the messenger of the covenant in Malachi 3:1—all prophecies fulfilled in Christ. The theme of the Messiah and God's redemption occurs throughout the Bible.

How is a resurrected body different from that of a ghost? (24:31,37–39)

When Jesus was resurrected, he received a new kind of body, quite different from the bodies we know. This new spiritual body had different properties that made it possible for Jesus to defy natural laws, appearing and disappearing at will. The disciples could think of only one explanation: this was a ghost. But Jesus emphatically declared that since he had a body of flesh and bones he was not a ghost. See article: *What do we have to look forward to?* (1 Cor. 15:35–57).

Why did Jesus come and go in supernatural ways after the resurrection? (24:31)

When he took on the form of human flesh, Jesus usually restricted himself to the laws of nature: he had to eat, drink and rest. To get somewhere he walked. But with his resurrected body his self-imposed limitations were lifted. It was as normal for Jesus to use the characteristics of his spiritual body as it is for a bird to fly or for a fish to breathe water.

What did the disciples understand now that they hadn't understood before? (24:45)

Seeing the resurrected Christ before them, the disciples saw the Old Testament writings in a whole new light. The Spirit gave them insight from what they had seen and experienced so that what had been foretold by the prophets took on a whole new meaning. Now they could read the Old Testament with the benefit of hindsight and discover Christ as its fulfillment.

What did the Father promise? (24:49)

He promised the outpouring of the Holy Spirit (Ezek. 36:26–27; Joel 2:28–29). Luke expands on this scene and adds details about the promise in his sequel to the Gospel of Luke—the Acts of the Apostles (Acts 1:4–5).

²⁵He said to them, "How foolish you are, and how slow of heart to believe all that the prophets^D have spoken! ²⁶Did not the Christ*ᵃ* have to suffer these things and then enter his glory^D?" ²⁷And beginning with Moses and all the Prophets, he explained to them what was said in all the Scriptures concerning himself.

²⁸As they approached the village to which they were going, Jesus acted as if he were going farther. ²⁹But they urged him strongly, "Stay with us, for it is nearly evening; the day is almost over." So he went in to stay with them.

³⁰When he was at the table with them, he took bread, gave thanks, broke it and began to give it to them. ³¹Then their eyes were opened and they recognized him, and he disappeared from their sight. ³²They asked each other, "Were not our hearts burning within us while he talked with us on the road and opened the Scriptures to us?"

³³They got up and returned at once to Jerusalem^D. There they found the Eleven and those with them, assembled together ³⁴and saying, "It is true! The Lord has risen and has appeared to Simon." ³⁵Then the two told what had happened on the way, and how Jesus was recognized by them when he broke the bread.

Jesus Appears to the Disciples

³⁶While they were still talking about this, Jesus himself stood among them and said to them, "Peace^D be with you."

³⁷They were startled and frightened, thinking they saw a ghost. ³⁸He said to them, "Why are you troubled, and why do doubts rise in your minds? ³⁹Look at my hands and my feet. It is I myself! Touch me and see; a ghost does not have flesh and bones, as you see I have."

⁴⁰When he had said this, he showed them his hands and feet. ⁴¹And while they still did not believe it because of joy and amazement, he asked them, "Do you have anything here to eat?" ⁴²They gave him a piece of broiled fish, ⁴³and he took it and ate it in their presence.

⁴⁴He said to them, "This is what I told you while I was still with you: Everything must be fulfilled that is written about me in the Law of Moses, the Prophets and the Psalms."

⁴⁵Then he opened their minds so they could understand the Scriptures. ⁴⁶He told them, "This is what is written: The Christ will suffer and rise from the dead on the third day, ⁴⁷and repentance^D and forgiveness of sins will be preached in his name to all nations, beginning at Jerusalem. ⁴⁸You are witnesses of these things. ⁴⁹I am going to send you what my Father has promised; but stay in the city until you have been clothed with power from on high."

The Ascension

⁵⁰When he had led them out to the vicinity of Bethany, he lifted up his hands and blessed them. ⁵¹While he was blessing them, he left them and was taken up into heaven. ⁵²Then they worshiped him and returned to Jerusalem with great joy. ⁵³And they stayed continually at the temple, praising God.

ᵃ26 Or Messiah; also in verse 46

JOHN

Why read this book?

Our world offers a variety of gods to worship. One major religion features a god of power and revenge; another worships one that is silent and indifferent to the suffering of people; still another offers a god that is mysterious and unknowable, absorbing all of humanity into a great cosmic ocean of oneness. Some people worship *gods* of possessions, fame and entertainment. Only one faith worships a person known primarily for his sacrificial love. This book profiles that God, revealed in the person of Jesus Christ.

Who wrote this book?

John, the apostle—one of the twelve original disciples of Christ.

When and where was it written?

Sometime between A.D. 80 and 95 (though some scholars argue that the book can be dated as early as the 50s and no later than 70). John was probably in Ephesus, a city located in modern-day Turkey (see *Setting of Acts* on page 1504).

Why was it written?

John himself explains his goal: *that you may believe that Jesus is the Christ, the Son of God and that by believing you may have life in his name* (20:31).

To whom was it written?

Non-Jewish followers of Jesus, particularly those struggling with predominant Greek philosophies of the day. These taught that salvation comes through special knowledge and that Jesus was divine but not truly human.

What to look for in John:

The images of light and life to describe God's activity in the world. John records seven miracles, climaxing in Jesus' resurrection, which he sees as proof that Jesus is the Son of God. John also includes several sermons of Christ not found in the other Gospels (chs. 6, 10,13–16), which explain the purpose of Jesus' life.

When did these things happen?

TIME LINE	10 BC	AD 1	10	20	30	40	50	60	70	80	90	100
Herod the Great's reign (c.37-4 B.C.)												
Jesus' birth (c.6/5 B.C.)												
Jesus' flight to Egypt (c.5/4 B.C.)												
Beginning of John the Baptist's ministry (c. A.D.26)												
Beginning of Jesus' ministry (c. A.D.26)												
Jesus' death, resurrection and ascension (c. A.D.30)												
Paul's conversion (c. A.D.35)												
Book of John written (c. A.D.80-95)												
John's exile on Patmos (c. A.D.90-95)												

Word (1:1)

This term had special meaning to both Greeks and Jews. Plato and other Greek philosophers used *word* (*logos*) to mean the divine mind. To Jews, *word* refers to God's active and personal involvement in the world. The creation is one example, when God spoke the *word* and the earth came into existence. In this verse, it refers to Jesus Christ, who is the personal presence of God.

Why is John the Baptist so important? (1:6)

John the Baptist was sent for two reasons: to call the world to repentance (Mark 1:4) and to prepare the way for the coming Messiah (1:23). In the Old Testament, God often prepared people for some mighty action on his part by sending a prophet to call the people to repentance. John was the last of these prophets. Just as an "advance man" goes ahead of a king or president to clear the roads, arrange housing and prepare meals, John called people to prepare for the arrival of Jesus Christ.

The One and Only (1:18)

John uses this term to describe the unique character of Jesus. He isn't like other people; he is the divine Son of God. Because he is God, Jesus reveals to us what God is like (see Heb. 1:3).

What did John's baptism mean? (1:24–28)

Jewish ceremonies included ritual washings, but normally only non-Jews were baptized when they converted to Judaism. The Pharisees questioned John's practice because he was baptizing Jews. In effect, he was treating Jews like Gentiles. His baptism symbolized repentance, in preparation for the one to come who would forgive sins. John's baptism prepared people to meet the Messiah. See *Did John invent baptism?* (Matt. 3:11).

The Word Became Flesh

1 In the beginning was the Word, and the Word was with God, and the Word was God. ²He was with God in the beginning.

³Through him all things were made; without him nothing was made that has been made. ⁴In him was life, and that life was the light of men. ⁵The light shines in the darkness, but the darkness has not understood*ᵃ* it.

⁶There came a man who was sent from God; his name was John. ⁷He came as a witness to testify concerning that light, so that through him all men might believe. ⁸He himself was not the light; he came only as a witness to the light. ⁹The true light that gives light to every man was coming into the world.*ᵇ*

¹⁰He was in the world, and though the world was made through him, the world did not recognize him. ¹¹He came to that which was his own, but his own did not receive him. ¹²Yet to all who received him, to those who believed in his name, he gave the right to become children of God— ¹³children born not of natural descent,*ᶜ* nor of human decision or a husband's will, but born of God.

¹⁴The Word became flesh and made his dwelling among us. We have seen his glory*ᴰ*, the glory of the One and Only,*ᵈ* who came from the Father, full of grace*ᴰ* and truth.

¹⁵John testifies concerning him. He cries out, saying, "This was he of whom I said, 'He who comes after me has surpassed me because he was before me.' " ¹⁶From the fullness of his grace we have all received one blessing after another. ¹⁷For the law was given through Moses; grace and truth came through Jesus Christ. ¹⁸No one has ever seen God, but God the One and Only,*ᵈ,ᵉ* who is at the Father's side, has made him known.

John the Baptist Denies Being the Christ

¹⁹Now this was John's testimony when the Jews*ᴰ* of Jerusalem*ᴰ* sent priests*ᴰ* and Levites*ᴰ* to ask him who he was. ²⁰He did not fail to confess, but confessed freely, "I am not the Christ.*ᶠ*"

²¹They asked him, "Then who are you? Are you Elijah?"

He said, "I am not."

"Are you the Prophet*ᴰ*?"

He answered, "No."

²²Finally they said, "Who are you? Give us an answer to take back to those who sent us. What do you say about yourself?"

²³John replied in the words of Isaiah the prophet, "I am the voice of one calling in the desert, 'Make straight the way for the Lord.' "*ᵍ*

²⁴Now some Pharisees*ᴰ* who had been sent ²⁵questioned him, "Why then do you baptize if you are not the Christ, nor Elijah, nor the Prophet?"

²⁶"I baptize with*ʰ* water," John replied, "but among you stands one you do not know. ²⁷He is the one who comes after me, the thongs of whose sandals I am not worthy to untie."

ᵃ5 Or darkness, and the darkness has not overcome   *ᵇ9 Or This was the true light that gives light to every man who comes into the world* *ᶜ13 Greek of bloods*   *ᵈ14,18 Or the Only Begotten*   *ᵉ18 Some manuscripts but the only (or only begotten) Son*   *ᶠ20 Or Messiah.* "The Christ" (Greek) and "the Messiah" (Hebrew) both mean "the Anointed One"; also in verse 25.   *ᵍ23 Isaiah 40:3*   *ʰ26 Or in; also in verses 31 and 33*

28This all happened at Bethany on the other side of the Jordan, where John was baptizing.

Jesus the Lamb of God

29The next day John saw Jesus coming toward him and said, "Look, the Lamb of God, who takes away the sin of the world! **30**This is the one I meant when I said, 'A man who comes after me has surpassed me because he was before me.' **31**I myself did not know him, but the reason I came baptizing with water was that he might be revealed to Israel."

32Then John gave this testimony: "I saw the Spirit come down from heaven as a dove and remain on him. **33**I would not have known him, except that the one who sent me to baptize with water told me, 'The man on whom you see the Spirit come down and remain is he who will baptize with the Holy Spirit.' **34**I have seen and I testify that this is the Son of God."

Jesus' First Disciples

35The next day John was there again with two of his disciples[D]. **36**When he saw Jesus passing by, he said, "Look, the Lamb of God!"

37When the two disciples heard him say this, they followed Jesus. **38**Turning around, Jesus saw them following and asked, "What do you want?"

They said, "Rabbi[D]" (which means Teacher), "where are you staying?"

39"Come," he replied, "and you will see."

So they went and saw where he was staying, and spent that day with him. It was about the tenth hour.

40Andrew, Simon Peter's brother, was one of the two who heard what John had said and who had followed Jesus. **41**The first thing Andrew did was to find his brother Simon and tell him, "We have found the Messiah" (that is, the Christ). **42**And he brought him to Jesus.

Jesus looked at him and said, "You are Simon son of John. You will be called Cephas" (which, when translated, is Peter[a]).

Jesus Calls Philip and Nathanael

43The next day Jesus decided to leave for Galilee. Finding Philip, he said to him, "Follow me."

44Philip, like Andrew and Peter, was from the town of Bethsaida. **45**Philip found Nathanael and told him, "We have found the one Moses wrote about in the Law, and about whom the prophets[D] also wrote—Jesus of Nazareth, the son of Joseph."

46"Nazareth! Can anything good come from there?" Nathanael asked.

"Come and see," said Philip.

47When Jesus saw Nathanael approaching, he said of him, "Here is a true Israelite, in whom there is nothing false."

48"How do you know me?" Nathanael asked.

Jesus answered, "I saw you while you were still under the fig tree before Philip called you."

49Then Nathanael declared, "Rabbi, you are the Son of God; you are the King of Israel."

50Jesus said, "You believe[b] because I told you I saw you under the fig tree. You shall see greater things than that."

How is Jesus the Lamb of God? (1:29)

Lambs were used in the temple as a daily sacrifice to remove the sins of the people. A symbol of innocence, they bore the people's guilt as a substitutionary offering. Seven hundred years earlier, Isaiah had predicted the Messiah who would offer his life, *led like a lamb to the slaughter* (Isaiah 53:7), to atone for the sins of the world.

SCRIPTURE LINK (1:40–42)

For the other Gospel writers' accounts of Jesus calling his first disciples, see Matt. 4:18–22; Mark 1:16–20 and Luke 5:2–11.

Were Simon and Andrew acting on impulse? (1:40–42)

Some see their immediate response as a model of Christian discipleship. Others think Simon and Andrew may have followed Jesus in a limited sense before this incident. Having already seen Jesus' power, they were ready when he asked for a more complete commitment.

Why did Nathanael disdain Nazareth? (1:46)

Nathanael had good reasons to question the credentials of someone from Nazareth touted as the Messiah. It was an obscure town never mentioned in the Old Testament. It also had become a barracks for Roman troops who brought with them their gods, their sins and their oppression of the Jews. These factors made it seem improbable that it could be the hometown of the Messiah (see *Map 9* at the back of this Bible).

---

*a*42 Both *Cephas* (Aramaic) and *Peter* (Greek) mean *rock*.　　*b*50 Or *Do you believe . . . ?*

Jesus Visits Cana (2:1)

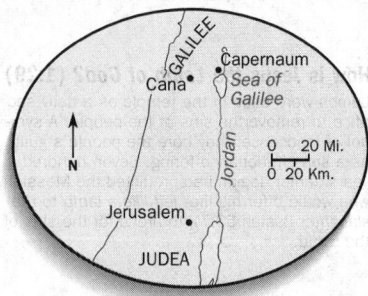

Was Jesus being rude to his mother? (2:4)

No, his words *dear woman* showed his love and respect. Jesus was reminding her that it was not yet time for people to know his true identity. Her reply and her directions to the servants indicate she understood his desire to keep his identity secret and that she trusted his sense of timing.

What moment was Jesus waiting for? (2:4)

My time refers to Jesus' coming death. Both here and later in John, Jesus clearly states that his time to be revealed as the Messiah and crucified as the sacrificial Lamb has not yet arrived. Completely in tune with the will of God, Jesus was waiting for the right moment to fulfill the purpose for which God had sent him into the world.

SCRIPTURE LINK (2:14–16)

Matt. 21:12–13; Mark 11:15–17 and Luke 19:45–46 also tell about Jesus clearing the temple.

What made Jesus so angry? (2:15)

Everyone who worshiped in the temple at Jerusalem was required to present a sacrifice accepted as unblemished by a priest and to pay the annual head tax using temple currency. The priests refused to accept foreign currency and so exchanged travelers' money at exorbitant rates. They also regularly rejected any animal that wasn't purchased at the temple (at inflated prices). Such exploitation under the guise of proper worship of God made Jesus angry.

Why did the people demand a miracle? (2:18; see 6:30)

It was common in the Old Testament for prophets to prove their authenticity by performing a miracle. This established that they were sent by God. Yet Jesus was reluctant to perform signs for skeptics. Instead he offered a riddle about raising the temple, which referred to his future death and resurrection, as the only miracle they needed to see to believe in him as Messiah.

51He then added, "I tell you[a] the truth, you[a] shall see heaven open, and the angels of God ascending and descending on the Son of Man."

Jesus Changes Water to Wine

2 On the third day a wedding took place at Cana in Galilee. Jesus' mother was there, **2**and Jesus and his disciples[D] had also been invited to the wedding. **3**When the wine was gone, Jesus' mother said to him, "They have no more wine."

4"Dear woman, why do you involve me?" Jesus replied. "My time has not yet come."

5His mother said to the servants, "Do whatever he tells you."

6Nearby stood six stone water jars, the kind used by the Jews[D] for ceremonial washing, each holding from twenty to thirty gallons.[b]

7Jesus said to the servants, "Fill the jars with water"; so they filled them to the brim.

8Then he told them, "Now draw some out and take it to the master of the banquet."

They did so, **9**and the master of the banquet tasted the water that had been turned into wine. He did not realize where it had come from, though the servants who had drawn the water knew. Then he called the bridegroom aside **10**and said, "Everyone brings out the choice wine first and then the cheaper wine after the guests have had too much to drink; but you have saved the best till now."

11This, the first of his miraculous signs, Jesus performed at Cana in Galilee. He thus revealed his glory[D], and his disciples put their faith in him.

Jesus Clears the Temple

12After this he went down to Capernaum with his mother and brothers and his disciples. There they stayed for a few days.

13When it was almost time for the Jewish Passover, Jesus went up to Jerusalem[D]. **14**In the temple courts he found men selling cattle, sheep and doves, and others sitting at tables exchanging money. **15**So he made a whip out of cords, and drove all from the temple area, both sheep and cattle; he scattered the coins of the money changers and overturned their tables. **16**To those who sold doves he said, "Get these out of here! How dare you turn my Father's house into a market!"

17His disciples remembered that it is written: "Zeal for your house will consume me."[c]

18Then the Jews demanded of him, "What miraculous sign can you show us to prove your authority to do all this?"

19Jesus answered them, "Destroy this temple, and I will raise it again in three days."

20The Jews replied, "It has taken forty-six years to build this temple, and you are going to raise it in three days?" **21**But the temple he had spoken of was his body. **22**After he was raised from the dead, his disciples recalled what he had said. Then they believed the Scripture and the words that Jesus had spoken.

23Now while he was in Jerusalem at the Passover Feast, many people saw the miraculous signs he was do-

---

a51 The Greek is plural.   *b6* Greek *two to three metretes* (probably about 75 to 115 liters)   *c17* Psalm 69:9

ing and believed in his name.ᵃ **24**But Jesus would not entrust himself to them, for he knew all men. **25**He did not need man's testimony about man, for he knew what was in a man.

Jesus Teaches Nicodemus

3 Now there was a man of the PhariseesᴰᴅÂᴰ named Nicodemus, a member of the Jewish ruling council. **2**He came to Jesus at night and said, "Rabbiᴰ, we know you are a teacher who has come from God. For no one could perform the miraculous signs you are doing if God were not with him."

3In reply Jesus declared, "I tell you the truth, no one can see the kingdom of Godᴰ unless he is born again.ᵇ"

4"How can a man be born when he is old?" Nicodemus asked. "Surely he cannot enter a second time into his mother's womb to be born!"

5Jesus answered, "I tell you the truth, no one can enter the kingdom of God unless he is born of water and the Spirit. **6**Flesh gives birth to flesh, but the Spiritᶜ gives birth to spirit. **7**You should not be surprised at my saying, 'Youᵈ must be born again.' **8**The wind blows wherever it pleases. You hear its sound, but you cannot tell where it comes from or where it is going. So it is with everyone born of the Spirit."

9"How can this be?" Nicodemus asked.

10"You are Israel's teacher," said Jesus, "and do you not understand these things? **11**I tell you the truth, we speak of what we know, and we testify to what we have seen, but still you people do not accept our testimony. **12**I have spoken to you of earthly things and you do not believe; how then will you believe if I speak of heavenly things? **13**No one has ever gone into heaven except the one who came from heaven—the Son of Manᴰ·ᵉ **14**Just as Moses lifted up the snake in the desert, so the Son of Man must be lifted up, **15**that everyone who believes in him may have eternal life.ᶠ

16"For God so loved the world that he gave his one and only Son,ᵍ that whoever believes in him shall not perish but have eternal lifeᴰ. **17**For God did not send his Son into the world to condemn the world, but to save the world through him. **18**Whoever believes in him is not condemned, but whoever does not believe stands condemned already because he has not believed in the name of God's one and only Son.ʰ **19**This is the verdict: Light has come into the world, but men loved darkness instead of light because their deeds were evil. **20**Everyone who does evil hates the light, and will not come into the light for fear that his deeds will be exposed. **21**But whoever lives by the truth comes into the light, so that it may be seen plainly that what he has done has been done through God."ⁱ

John the Baptist's Testimony About Jesus

22After this, Jesus and his disciplesᴰ went out into the Judean countryside, where he spent some time with them, and baptized. **23**Now John also was baptizing at Aenon near Salim, because there was plenty of water, and

---

Why did Jesus hide his true identity? (2:24)

The people expected the Messiah to be a political and military figure who would lead Israel to independence from Rome. Jesus' purpose was to establish an invisible kingdom, a spiritual movement. He didn't want people thinking of him as a political activist.

What does it mean to be *born again*? (3:3)

To enter God's kingdom requires something that's impossible by human standards—to be reborn. By this, Jesus refers to the work of the Holy Spirit in breathing life into our sinful and dead spiritual nature. When we are *born again*, we become a new person, forgiven of our sins and granted an intimate friendship with God.

Born of water and the Spirit (3:5)

This could refer to physical birth (accompanied by "water breaking") and spiritual birth (the dawning of the spiritual awareness) or to baptism (repentance symbolized by water) and life in the Spirit (awakening to the reality of God's Spirit working in a person's life).

How is the Son like a snake? (3:14)

As Num. 21:8–9 recounts, after poisonous snakes infested the Israelites' camp, Moses made a bronze serpent, attached it to a pole and lifted it up. Those who looked to it with faith were healed. In a similar way, Jesus says he will be lifted up on a cross and those who turn in faith to him will be saved from the poison of sin.

What does it mean to *believe*? (3:16–18)

To *believe* in Christ involves more than just agreeing that Jesus' words are true. It means to trust in Christ alone for your salvation. It is deciding to place your fate in the hands of Jesus, trusting him to be your Lord and his Word to be your command.

What did baptism mean at that time? (3:23–25)

The word *baptism* means to *dip*. The way John the Baptist prepared people for Christ is similar to the Jewish custom of purifying people for worship. To make people ceremonially clean, the Jews would pour water over them or dip them in a pool.

ᵃ23 Or *and believed in him*   ᵇ3 Or *born from above*; also in verse 7
ᶜ6 Or *but spirit*   ᵈ7 The Greek is plural.   ᵉ13 Some manuscripts *Man, who is in heaven*   ᶠ15 Or *believes may have eternal life in him*   ᵍ16 Or *his only begotten Son*   ʰ18 Or *God's only begotten Son*   ⁱ21 Some interpreters end the quotation after verse 15.

people were constantly coming to be baptized. **24**(This was before John was put in prison.) **25**An argument developed between some of John's disciples[D] and a certain Jew[Da] over the matter of ceremonial washing. **26**They came to John and said to him, "Rabbi[D], that man who was with you on the other side of the Jordan—the one you testified about—well, he is baptizing, and everyone is going to him."

27To this John replied, "A man can receive only what is given him from heaven. **28**You yourselves can testify that I said, 'I am not the Christ[b] but am sent ahead of him.' **29**The bride belongs to the bridegroom. The friend who attends the bridegroom waits and listens for him, and is full of joy when he hears the bridegroom's voice. That joy is mine, and it is now complete. **30**He must become greater; I must become less.

31"The one who comes from above is above all; the one who is from the earth belongs to the earth, and speaks as one from the earth. The one who comes from heaven is above all. **32**He testifies to what he has seen and heard, but no one accepts his testimony. **33**The man who has accepted it has certified that God is truthful. **34**For the one whom God has sent speaks the words of God, for God[c] gives the Spirit without limit. **35**The Father loves the Son and has placed everything in his hands. **36**Whoever believes in the Son has eternal life[D], but whoever rejects the Son will not see life, for God's wrath remains on him."[d]

Why didn't John the Baptist become a disciple too? (3:27–30)

John explains that God had called him to point people to the Messiah. That calling never changed. While Jesus called others to *follow him* (1:43) and be his disciples, John's role was to go *ahead of him* (v. 28). See **Why is John the Baptist so important?** (1:6).

Jesus Talks With a Samaritan Woman

4 The Pharisees[D] heard that Jesus was gaining and baptizing more disciples than John, **2**although in fact it was not Jesus who baptized, but his disciples. **3**When the Lord learned of this, he left Judea and went back once more to Galilee.

4Now he had to go through Samaria. **5**So he came to a town in Samaria called Sychar, near the plot of ground Jacob had given to his son Joseph. **6**Jacob's well was there, and Jesus, tired as he was from the journey, sat down by the well. It was about the sixth hour.

7When a Samaritan woman came to draw water, Jesus said to her, "Will you give me a drink?" **8**(His disciples had gone into the town to buy food.)

9The Samaritan woman said to him, "You are a Jew and I am a Samaritan woman. How can you ask me for a drink?" (For Jews do not associate with Samaritans.[e])

10Jesus answered her, "If you knew the gift of God and who it is that asks you for a drink, you would have asked him and he would have given you living water."

11"Sir," the woman said, "you have nothing to draw with and the well is deep. Where can you get this living water? **12**Are you greater than our father Jacob, who gave us the well and drank from it himself, as did also his sons and his flocks and herds?"

13Jesus answered, "Everyone who drinks this water will be thirsty again, **14**but whoever drinks the water I give him will never thirst. Indeed, the water I give him will become in him a spring of water welling up to eternal life."

15The woman said to him, "Sir, give me this water so that I won't get thirsty and have to keep coming here to draw water."

Why did Jesus leave? (4:3)

When Jesus learned that his growing number of followers was arousing the attention of the Pharisees, he left the region, probably to avoid a confrontation with them before he could establish his ministry. Later he would return and face their opposition.

Why were there no other women at the well? (4:7)

Women customarily went to the town well when it was cool, either in the morning or evening. This offered them interaction as well as water. This woman's coming alone in the heat of the day suggests that she was an outcast.

Why the tension between Jews and Samaritans? (4:9)

Racial and religious prejudices separated them. The Samaritans were descendants from foreigners brought to the region centuries earlier to replace the ten tribes of Israel deported by the Assyrians. The foreigners had intermarried with the remaining Israelites, leaving behind a mixed race that worshiped God, but according to their own traditions rather than the Word of God. To Jews, the Samaritans represented the downfall of their nation and also represented forbidden intermarriages between Jews and Gentiles. The Samaritans set up a rival religious system, claiming God should be worshiped on Mount Gerizim (see **Map 9** at the back of this Bible). Also see **What did the priest teach about worship?** (2 Kings 17:28).

a25 Some manuscripts *and certain Jews*   *b28* Or *Messiah*
c34 Greek *he*   *d36* Some interpreters end the quotation after verse 30.   *e9* Or *do not use dishes Samaritans have used*

16He told her, "Go, call your husband and come back."
17"I have no husband," she replied.

Jesus said to her, "You are right when you say you have no husband. 18The fact is, you have had five husbands, and the man you now have is not your husband. What you have just said is quite true."

19"Sir," the woman said, "I can see that you are a prophet.D 20Our fathers worshiped on this mountain, but you JewsD claim that the place where we must worship is in Jerusalem.D"

21Jesus declared, "Believe me, woman, a time is coming when you will worship the Father neither on this mountain nor in Jerusalem. 22You Samaritans worship what you do not know; we worship what we do know, for salvationD is from the Jews. 23Yet a time is coming and has now come when the true worshipers will worship the Father in spirit and truth, for they are the kind of worshipers the Father seeks. 24God is spirit, and his worshipers must worship in spirit and in truth."

25The woman said, "I know that Messiah" (called Christ) "is coming. When he comes, he will explain everything to us."

26Then Jesus declared, "I who speak to you am he."

The Disciples Rejoin Jesus

27Just then his disciplesD returned and were surprised to find him talking with a woman. But no one asked, "What do you want?" or "Why are you talking with her?"

28Then, leaving her water jar, the woman went back to the town and said to the people, 29"Come, see a man who told me everything I ever did. Could this be the Christa?" 30They came out of the town and made their way toward him.

31Meanwhile his disciples urged him, "Rabbi, eat something."

32But he said to them, "I have food to eat that you know nothing about."

33Then his disciples said to each other, "Could someone have brought him food?"

34"My food," said Jesus, "is to do the will of him who sent me and to finish his work. 35Do you not say, 'Four months more and then the harvest'? I tell you, open your eyes and look at the fields! They are ripe for harvest. 36Even now the reaper draws his wages, even now he harvests the crop for eternal life,D so that the sower and the reaper may be glad together. 37Thus the saying 'One sows and another reaps' is true. 38I sent you to reap what you have not worked for. Others have done the hard work, and you have reaped the benefits of their labor."

Many Samaritans Believe

39Many of the Samaritans from that town believed in him because of the woman's testimony, "He told me everything I ever did." 40So when the Samaritans came to him, they urged him to stay with them, and he stayed two days. 41And because of his words many more became believers.

42They said to the woman, "We no longer believe just because of what you said; now we have heard for ourselves, and we know that this man really is the Savior of the world."

a29 Or Messiah

What kind of woman had five husbands? (4:18)

Divorce in the Jewish-Samaritan culture could only be initiated by the husband, who had to state publicly that his wife was unclean, unlovable or incapable of fulfilling her wifely duties. Divorce therefore shamed a woman. Five men had publicly shamed this woman and now she was most likely living with her current partner simply to avoid starvation.

God is spirit (4:24)

God is not limited to one location, nor does he identify with only one nation. The whole universe is his, and he is present everywhere.

Worship in spirit and in truth (4:24)

Genuine worship involves both fact and faith. Truth means we are to worship the right God—the God revealed in the Bible through Jesus Christ. Spirit means that true worship demands more than just outward motions. It is an inner submission of oneself to God (Romans 12:1).

Jesus Heals the Official's Son

43After the two days he left for Galilee. **44**(Now Jesus himself had pointed out that a prophet[D] has no honor in his own country.) **45**When he had arrived in Galilee, the Galileans welcomed him. They had seen all that he had done in Jerusalem[D] at the Passover Feast, for they also had been there.

46Once more he visited Cana in Galilee, where he had turned the water into wine. And there was a certain royal official whose son lay sick at Capernaum. **47**When this man heard that Jesus had arrived in Galilee from Judea, he went to him and begged him to come and heal his son, who was close to death[D].

48"Unless you people see miraculous signs and wonders," Jesus told him, "you will never believe."

49The royal official said, "Sir, come down before my child dies."

50Jesus replied, "You may go. Your son will live."

The man took Jesus at his word and departed. **51**While he was still on the way, his servants met him with the news that his boy was living. **52**When he inquired as to the time when his son got better, they said to him, "The fever left him yesterday at the seventh hour."

53Then the father realized that this was the exact time at which Jesus had said to him, "Your son will live." So he and all his household believed.

54This was the second miraculous sign that Jesus performed, having come from Judea to Galilee.

The Healing at the Pool

5 Some time later, Jesus went up to Jerusalem for a feast of the Jews[D]. **2**Now there is in Jerusalem near the Sheep Gate a pool, which in Aramaic[D] is called Bethesda[a] and which is surrounded by five covered colonnades. **3**Here a great number of disabled people used to lie—the blind, the lame, the paralyzed.[b] **5**One who was there had been an invalid for thirty-eight years. **6**When Jesus saw him lying there and learned that he had been in this condition for a long time, he asked him, "Do you want to get well?"

7"Sir," the invalid replied, "I have no one to help me into the pool when the water is stirred. While I am trying to get in, someone else goes down ahead of me."

8Then Jesus said to him, "Get up! Pick up your mat and walk." **9**At once the man was cured; he picked up his mat and walked.

The day on which this took place was a Sabbath[D], **10**and so the Jews said to the man who had been healed, "It is the Sabbath; the law forbids you to carry your mat."

11But he replied, "The man who made me well said to me, 'Pick up your mat and walk.' "

12So they asked him, "Who is this fellow who told you to pick it up and walk?"

13The man who was healed had no idea who it was, for Jesus had slipped away into the crowd that was there.

14Later Jesus found him at the temple and said to him, "See, you are well again. Stop sinning or something worse

Was Jesus reluctant to perform *signs and wonders*? (4:48)

The *signs and wonders* were intended only to validate Jesus' claims, not to draw attention or gather a following. He was disturbed that people were more interested in sensationalism than they were in a relationship with God. He chose to perform miracles when it would inspire faith, not simply please crowds.

Was this only Jesus' second miracle? (4:54; see 2:23)

No. John was not stating that this is Jesus' second miracle, but that this was the second miracle done in Galilee, the home area of most of his disciples (see **Map 9** at the back of this Bible). While the first part of Jesus' ministry focused here, the second part centered on his activities in Jerusalem. John records only eight specific signs or miracles Jesus performed during three years, though he refers to many others (20:30).

Why did Jesus heal only one of the many who had disabilities? (5:3,5)

Jesus may have healed more than this one man, but John followed only his story. Or perhaps Jesus healed this man because he alone expressed a desire and the faith to be healed. Or perhaps he singled out this man simply to demonstrate God's power.

What happened to verse 4? (5:4)

This verse doesn't appear in the earliest versions of the Bible. It seems to have been added later by scribes and scholars to explain why so many people were there and why they raced to the pool when the water moved. While it explains historical background, most see it more as commentary than part of the original passage. See NIV text note.

Was Jesus threatening the man he healed? (5:14)

While not all physical problems are the result of sin, some are. Perhaps this man was engaging in self-destructive behavior. Some sins have immediate physical, financial and relational consequences. The *something worse* in this case may refer to eternal punishment rather than another illness returning to the man.

---

[a]2 Some manuscripts *Bethzatha*; other manuscripts *Bethsaida*
[b]3 Some less important manuscripts *paralyzed—and they waited for the moving of the waters. 4From time to time an angel of the Lord would come down and stir up the waters. The first one into the pool after each such disturbance would be cured of whatever disease he had.*

may happen to you." **15**The man went away and told the Jews[D] that it was Jesus who had made him well.

Life Through the Son

16So, because Jesus was doing these things on the Sabbath[D], the Jews persecuted him. **17**Jesus said to them, "My Father is always at his work to this very day, and I, too, am working." **18**For this reason the Jews tried all the harder to kill him; not only was he breaking the Sabbath, but he was even calling God his own Father, making himself equal with God.

19Jesus gave them this answer: "I tell you the truth, the Son can do nothing by himself; he can do only what he sees his Father doing, because whatever the Father does the Son also does. **20**For the Father loves the Son and shows him all he does. Yes, to your amazement he will show him even greater things than these. **21**For just as the Father raises the dead and gives them life, even so the Son gives life to whom he is pleased to give it. **22**Moreover, the Father judges no one, but has entrusted all judgment to the Son, **23**that all may honor the Son just as they honor the Father. He who does not honor the Son does not honor the Father, who sent him.

24"I tell you the truth, whoever hears my word and believes him who sent me has eternal life[D] and will not be condemned; he has crossed over from death[D] to life. **25**I tell you the truth, a time is coming and has now come when the dead will hear the voice of the Son of God and those who hear will live. **26**For as the Father has life in himself, so he has granted the Son to have life in himself. **27**And he has given him authority to judge because he is the Son of Man.

28"Do not be amazed at this, for a time is coming when all who are in their graves will hear his voice **29**and come out—those who have done good will rise to live, and those who have done evil will rise to be condemned. **30**By myself I can do nothing; I judge only as I hear, and my judgment is just, for I seek not to please myself but him who sent me.

Testimonies About Jesus

31"If I testify about myself, my testimony is not valid. **32**There is another who testifies in my favor, and I know that his testimony about me is valid.

33"You have sent to John and he has testified to the truth. **34**Not that I accept human testimony; but I mention it that you may be saved. **35**John was a lamp that burned and gave light, and you chose for a time to enjoy his light.

36"I have testimony weightier than that of John. For the very work that the Father has given me to finish, and which I am doing, testifies that the Father has sent me. **37**And the Father who sent me has himself testified concerning me. You have never heard his voice nor seen his form, **38**nor does his word dwell in you, for you do not believe the one he sent. **39**You diligently study[a] the Scriptures because you think that by them you possess eternal life. These are the Scriptures that testify about me, **40**yet you refuse to come to me to have life.

41"I do not accept praise from men, **42**but I know you. I know that you do not have the love of God in your hearts. **43**I have come in my Father's name, and you do not accept me; but if someone else comes in his own

Why the fuss over healing on the Sabbath? (5:16)

The anger came from the Jewish officials, who had developed an elaborate and complicated system of legalistic rules and regulations. Incredibly, healing was forbidden on the Sabbath because it was considered work. Because legalism is the work of pride, when Jesus challenged their system he also challenged their pride. His focus was on the heart, on man's relationship to God and on God's compassion toward human suffering.

Why was Jesus accused of blasphemy? (5:18)

For Jesus to claim he was *always at his work* the way God his Father was, had serious implications. The rabbis believed that while God rested from *creation* the seventh day, his work of sustaining creation always continued. So when Jesus compared his ongoing healing work on the Sabbath with God's perpetual activity, the implications were obvious: Jesus was claiming equality with his Father. For a man to claim equality with God was blasphemy to the Jews, pure and simple.

Eternal life (5:24)

A quality of life which begins when a person believes that Jesus Christ is Lord and that God sent him for our salvation. When physical death occurs, those belonging to Christ will continue to live, because the life that Christ gives us will never end (11:26).

The dead will hear (5:25)

Jesus was referring to the spiritually dead who will receive life as they hear and respond to the gospel.

Why was Jesus concerned about a valid testimony? (5:31–46)

The principles of Old Testament law required two witnesses to establish anything as fact (Deut. 19:15). Jesus pointed to the testimony of John the Baptist and of miracles performed through the Father to validate his claim as Messiah.

---

a 39 Or *Study diligently* (the imperative)

name, you will accept him. **44**How can you believe if you accept praise from one another, yet make no effort to obtain the praise that comes from the only God*a*?

45"But do not think I will accuse you before the Father. Your accuser is Moses, on whom your hopes are set. **46**If you believed Moses, you would believe me, for he wrote about me. **47**But since you do not believe what he wrote, how are you going to believe what I say?"

Jesus Feeds the Five Thousand

6 Some time after this, Jesus crossed to the far shore of the Sea of Galilee (that is, the Sea of Tiberias), **2**and a great crowd of people followed him because they saw the miraculous signs he had performed on the sick. **3**Then Jesus went up on a mountainside and sat down with his disciplesᴰ. **4**The Jewish Passover Feast was near.

5When Jesus looked up and saw a great crowd coming toward him, he said to Philip, "Where shall we buy bread for these people to eat?" **6**He asked this only to test him, for he already had in mind what he was going to do.

7Philip answered him, "Eight months' wages*b* would not buy enough bread for each one to have a bite!"

8Another of his disciples, Andrew, Simon Peter's brother, spoke up, **9**"Here is a boy with five small barley loaves and two small fish, but how far will they go among so many?"

10Jesus said, "Have the people sit down." There was plenty of grass in that place, and the men sat down, about five thousand of them. **11**Jesus then took the loaves, gave thanks, and distributed to those who were seated as much as they wanted. He did the same with the fish.

12When they had all had enough to eat, he said to his disciples, "Gather the pieces that are left over. Let nothing be wasted." **13**So they gathered them and filled twelve baskets with the pieces of the five barley loaves left over by those who had eaten.

14After the people saw the miraculous sign that Jesus did, they began to say, "Surely this is the Prophetᴰ who is to come into the world." **15**Jesus, knowing that they intended to come and make him king by force, withdrew again to a mountain by himself.

Jesus Walks on the Water

16When evening came, his disciples went down to the lake, **17**where they got into a boat and set off across the lake for Capernaum. By now it was dark, and Jesus had not yet joined them. **18**A strong wind was blowing and the waters grew rough. **19**When they had rowed three or three and a half miles,*c* they saw Jesus approaching the boat, walking on the water; and they were terrified. **20**But he said to them, "It is I; don't be afraid." **21**Then they were willing to take him into the boat, and immediately the boat reached the shore where they were heading.

22The next day the crowd that had stayed on the opposite shore of the lake realized that only one boat had been there, and that Jesus had not entered it with his disciples, but that they had gone away alone. **23**Then some boats from Tiberias landed near the place where the people had eaten the bread after the Lord had given thanks. **24**Once the crowd realized that neither Jesus nor his disci-

---

SCRIPTURE LINK (6:1–13)
You can read other accounts of Jesus feeding the five thousand in Matt. 14:13–21; Mark 6:32–44 and Luke 9:10–17.

Why did Jesus test Philip? (6:6; see 2:24–25)
Someone has said, "A test is to reveal the student to the student, not to reveal the student to the teacher." Jesus tested Philip to reveal Philip to Philip, not Philip to Jesus. In doing so, he helped the disciple grow in his faith and understanding of who Jesus was and what he came to accomplish.

SCRIPTURE LINK (6:14)
The Prophet is the one foretold by Moses in Deut. 18:15.

Why did Jesus leave? (6:15)
Too much popularity again caused Jesus to leave. See *Why did Jesus leave?* (4:3). Here the people were ready to make him king. Ruling an earthly kingdom would have sidetracked Jesus from his eternal purpose: to establish the kingdom of God, a spiritual kingdom, throughout the entire world.

SCRIPTURE LINK (6:16–21)
Matthew tells about Jesus walking on water in Matt. 14:22–33. You'll also find it in Mark 6:47–51.

Why did Jesus walk on the water? (6:19)
This incident served to strengthen the disciples' trust in Jesus at a time when they probably felt disappointed and confused by his refusal to be made king the day before (6:14–15). It also provides powerful evidence of Jesus' ability to help us in the storms and troubles we face.

---

a44 Some early manuscripts *the Only One*   *b7* Greek *two hundred denarii*   *c19* Greek *rowed twenty-five or thirty stadia* (about 5 or 6 kilometers)

ples[D] were there, they got into the boats and went to Capernaum in search of Jesus.

Jesus the Bread of Life

25When they found him on the other side of the lake, they asked him, "Rabbi[D], when did you get here?"

26Jesus answered, "I tell you the truth, you are looking for me, not because you saw miraculous signs but because you ate the loaves and had your fill. **27**Do not work for food that spoils, but for food that endures to eternal life[D], which the Son of Man[D] will give you. On him God the Father has placed his seal of approval."

28Then they asked him, "What must we do to do the works God requires?"

29Jesus answered, "The work of God is this: to believe in the one he has sent."

30So they asked him, "What miraculous sign then will you give that we may see it and believe you? What will you do? **31**Our forefathers ate the manna[D] in the desert; as it is written: 'He gave them bread from heaven to eat.'[a]"

32Jesus said to them, "I tell you the truth, it is not Moses who has given you the bread from heaven, but it is my Father who gives you the true bread from heaven. **33**For the bread of God is he who comes down from heaven and gives life to the world."

34"Sir," they said, "from now on give us this bread."

35Then Jesus declared, "I am the bread of life. He who comes to me will never go hungry, and he who believes in me will never be thirsty. **36**But as I told you, you have seen me and still you do not believe. **37**All that the Father gives me will come to me, and whoever comes to me I will never drive away. **38**For I have come down from heaven not to do my will but to do the will of him who sent me. **39**And this is the will of him who sent me, that I shall lose none of all that he has given me, but raise them up at the last day. **40**For my Father's will is that everyone who looks to the Son and believes in him shall have eternal life, and I will raise him up at the last day."

41At this the Jews[D] began to grumble about him because he said, "I am the bread that came down from heaven." **42**They said, "Is this not Jesus, the son of Joseph, whose father and mother we know? How can he now say, 'I came down from heaven'?"

43"Stop grumbling among yourselves," Jesus answered. **44**"No one can come to me unless the Father who sent me draws him, and I will raise him up at the last day. **45**It is written in the Prophets[D]: 'They will all be taught by God.'[b] Everyone who listens to the Father and learns from him comes to me. **46**No one has seen the Father except the one who is from God; only he has seen the Father. **47**I tell you the truth, he who believes has everlasting life. **48**I am the bread of life. **49**Your forefathers ate the manna in the desert, yet they died. **50**But here is the bread that comes down from heaven, which a man may eat and not die. **51**I am the living bread that came down from heaven. If anyone eats of this bread, he will live forever. This bread is my flesh, which I will give for the life of the world."

52Then the Jews began to argue sharply among themselves, "How can this man give us his flesh to eat?"

53Jesus said to them, "I tell you the truth, unless you eat

The work of God is this: to believe (6:29)

The context of this verse (vv. 26–29) suggests that believing, in one sense of the word, can be called *work* because believing is something Jesus was urging the people to do. They were worried about temporary things like food when they needed to invest their efforts in eternal matters. Jesus wanted them to trust in God for who he was, not for the physical conveniences he could offer them. Still, to *believe* is more than work. Faith is a gift of God's grace, prompted by God's mysterious work within us (vv. 44,65).

What is the unique relationship between Jesus and the Father? (6:46,57)

Jesus alone has seen God. He alone has come from God to earth. Therefore he alone can reveal the true character, nature and person of God. We can comprehend God only by comprehending Jesus. But through Jesus we can know God and possess eternal life (see 17:3). He becomes, therefore, the only means by which we can gain eternal life.

Does Jesus literally mean we must eat his flesh and drink his blood? (6:51,53–58)

No. Jesus was not recruiting a cult of cannibals, though Christians were later charged with such atrocities. This is an overstatement, a literary device Jesus often used to communicate a particular truth. In this case, he was making the point that intellectual belief in him is not enough. He called the people to go further than that—to base their entire lives, their very survival, upon him and his words. To *eat and drink* Jesus is to assimilate and allow him into every aspect of our lives. Though these verses may allude to the sacrament of Christian Communion, Jesus did not introduce the Lord's Supper and its symbolism until the night before he was crucified.

---

*a*31 Exodus 16:4; Neh. 9:15; Psalm 78:24,25   *b*45 Isaiah 54:13

the flesh of the Son of Man[D] and drink his blood, you have no life in you. [54]Whoever eats my flesh and drinks my blood has eternal life[D], and I will raise him up at the last day. [55]For my flesh is real food and my blood is real drink. [56]Whoever eats my flesh and drinks my blood remains in me, and I in him. [57]Just as the living Father sent me and I live because of the Father, so the one who feeds on me will live because of me. [58]This is the bread that came down from heaven. Your forefathers ate manna[D] and died, but he who feeds on this bread will live forever." [59]He said this while teaching in the synagogue in Capernaum.

Many Disciples Desert Jesus

[60]On hearing it, many of his disciples[D] said, "This is a hard teaching. Who can accept it?"

[61]Aware that his disciples were grumbling about this, Jesus said to them, "Does this offend you? [62]What if you see the Son of Man ascend to where he was before! [63]The Spirit gives life; the flesh counts for nothing. The words I have spoken to you are spirit[a] and they are life. [64]Yet there are some of you who do not believe." For Jesus had known from the beginning which of them did not believe and who would betray him. [65]He went on to say, "This is why I told you that no one can come to me unless the Father has enabled him."

[66]From this time many of his disciples turned back and no longer followed him.

[67]"You do not want to leave too, do you?" Jesus asked the Twelve.

[68]Simon Peter answered him, "Lord, to whom shall we go? You have the words of eternal life. [69]We believe and know that you are the Holy One of God."

[70]Then Jesus replied, "Have I not chosen you, the Twelve? Yet one of you is a devil!" [71](He meant Judas, the son of Simon Iscariot, who, though one of the Twelve, was later to betray him.)

Jesus Goes to the Feast of Tabernacles

7 After this, Jesus went around in Galilee, purposely staying away from Judea because the Jews[D] there were waiting to take his life. [2]But when the Jewish Feast of Tabernacles was near, [3]Jesus' brothers said to him, "You ought to leave here and go to Judea, so that your disciples may see the miracles you do. [4]No one who wants to become a public figure acts in secret. Since you are doing these things, show yourself to the world." [5]For even his own brothers did not believe in him.

[6]Therefore Jesus told them, "The right time for me has not yet come; for you any time is right. [7]The world cannot hate you, but it hates me because I testify that what it does is evil. [8]You go to the Feast. I am not yet[b] going up to this Feast, because for me the right time has not yet come." [9]Having said this, he stayed in Galilee.

[10]However, after his brothers had left for the Feast, he went also, not publicly, but in secret. [11]Now at the Feast the Jews were watching for him and asking, "Where is that man?"

[12]Among the crowds there was widespread whispering about him. Some said, "He is a good man."

Others replied, "No, he deceives the people." [13]But no

Why did so many disciples abandon Jesus? (6:66)

Some may have been disappointed that he refused to become the conquering king they had anticipated. Others may have found his teachings too hard, his instructions too threatening. Jesus offers eternal life, but he requires acceptance of himself as Savior and Lord. This means his agenda must become his followers' agenda. And that is unacceptable to many would-be disciples.

Feast of Tabernacles (7:2)

The *Feast of Tabernacles* (see Lev. 23:33–43) was a seven-day feast celebrated in September or October. It memorialized the journey from Egypt to Canaan and gave thanks for the rich harvest of the promised land, it was a time of great joy. The feast derived its name from the practice of living in tents or booths made of branches during the celebration.

Did Jesus have physical brothers? (7:5)

Yes, Jesus did have brothers who were sons of Joseph and Mary (see Mark 6:3). Having grown up with Jesus and being so familiar with him, they found it hard to believe he was more than a human being. While they couldn't deny his power, they failed at first to grasp his destiny. They wrongly assumed he wanted recognition and political advancement.

Why did Jesus act secretly? (7:10)

Many influential people hated him and were trying to kill him (v. 1). The more openly Jesus taught, the more intense the opposition would become, and Jesus knew that it was not yet time for him to die (v. 6).

---

[a]63 Or *Spirit*　　[b]8 Some early manuscripts do not have *yet*.

11"No one, sir," she said.

"Then neither do I condemn you," Jesus declared. "Go now and leave your life of sin."

The Validity of Jesus' Testimony

12When Jesus spoke again to the people, he said, "I am the light of the world. Whoever follows me will never walk in darkness, but will have the light of life."

13The Pharisees[D] challenged him, "Here you are, appearing as your own witness; your testimony is not valid."

14Jesus answered, "Even if I testify on my own behalf, my testimony is valid, for I know where I came from and where I am going. But you have no idea where I come from or where I am going. **15**You judge by human standards; I pass judgment on no one. **16**But if I do judge, my decisions are right, because I am not alone. I stand with the Father, who sent me. **17**In your own Law it is written that the testimony of two men is valid. **18**I am one who testifies for myself; my other witness is the Father, who sent me."

19Then they asked him, "Where is your father?"

"You do not know me or my Father," Jesus replied. "If you knew me, you would know my Father also." **20**He spoke these words while teaching in the temple area near the place where the offerings were put. Yet no one seized him, because his time had not yet come.

21Once more Jesus said to them, "I am going away, and you will look for me, and you will die in your sin. Where I go, you cannot come."

22This made the Jews[D] ask, "Will he kill himself? Is that why he says, 'Where I go, you cannot come'?"

23But he continued, "You are from below; I am from above. You are of this world; I am not of this world. **24**I told you that you would die in your sins; if you do not believe that I am ⌊the one I claim to be⌋,[a] you will indeed die in your sins."

25"Who are you?" they asked.

"Just what I have been claiming all along," Jesus replied. **26**"I have much to say in judgment of you. But he who sent me is reliable, and what I have heard from him I tell the world."

27They did not understand that he was telling them about his Father. **28**So Jesus said, "When you have lifted up the Son of Man[D], then you will know that I am ⌊the one I claim to be⌋ and that I do nothing on my own but speak just what the Father has taught me. **29**The one who sent me is with me; he has not left me alone, for I always do what pleases him." **30**Even as he spoke, many put their faith in him.

The Children of Abraham

31To the Jews who had believed him, Jesus said, "If you hold to my teaching, you are really my disciples[D]. **32**Then you will know the truth, and the truth will set you free."

33They answered him, "We are Abraham's descendants[b] and have never been slaves of anyone. How can you say that we shall be set free?"

34Jesus replied, "I tell you the truth, everyone who sins

SCRIPTURE LINK (8:12)

The *light of the world* was also the description of Christ that John used in 1:4–5.

What was Jesus claiming? (8:12–29)

Jesus claimed to be not only on a mission from God, but he claimed to be the unique Son of God who always does what pleases God and who brings light to the entire world. The Pharisees considered this claim preposterous. And indeed, a person who would make such an amazing statement could only be a liar, a lunatic or the authentic Son of God. But none of his listeners could disprove his claim (8:45–46). In fact, *many put their faith in him* (v. 30).

Was Jesus changing his mind about the need for a witness to validate a testimony? (8:14)

In 5:31 Jesus used his miracles and the testimony of John the Baptist to validate his claim as the Messiah. Here, however, his goal was to show a contrast, not to establish a fact. When Jesus said *Even if I testify on my own behalf*, he was not serving as his own witness. Rather, he was drawing a distinction between the Pharisees and himself. The Pharisees lacked the knowledge he had, including who he was and where he was going.

---

a 24 Or *I am he*; also in verse 28   *b* 33 Greek *seed*; also in verse 37

If the Jews believed him why did they want to kill him? (8:37,40; see v. 31)

This is proof that their *belief* fell short of life-changing trust. Perhaps they had formally declared themselves to be his followers, believing in what he could do, not in who he was. They were looking for miracles, political revolution and fulfillment of their personal dreams. But when their expectations for the one they had hoped to be their national savior went unrealized—and when he challenged their religious status quo—their loyalty shifted easily. They were not ready to admit their sinful condition and place their trust in the Lamb of God. Their support for Jesus transformed into opposition.

Is it possible for anyone to keep Christ's word? (8:51)

The phrase doesn't refer to flawless performance, but to belief in Jesus as the Son of God. It is to accept as valid what Jesus has said about himself. Jesus' call to obey his word is a call for people to follow, trust and seek him, allowing his word to dwell in them. The goal is to continually desire God, even if we experience temporary setbacks by not living in perfect obedience.

Was Jesus claiming to be older than Abraham? (8:58–59)

This issue was not age, but the fact that Jesus existed *prior to* Abraham. If Jesus was simply referring to age, he would have said, "Before Abraham was, I was." But for him to say *before Abraham was born—I am!* was a statement of eternal self-existence. To the Jews it was reminiscent of God's own word concerning himself, *I AM WHO I AM* (Exodus 3:14). Jesus was clearly claiming deity, leading to the spontaneous desire to stone him for blasphemy.

SCRIPTURE LINK (8:59)

According to Lev. 24:16, the punishment for blasphemy (insulting God) was death. The Jews clearly understood that Jesus was claiming to be God, which would be blasphemy if claimed by a sinful human being.

is a slave to sin. [35]Now a slave has no permanent place in the family, but a son belongs to it forever. [36]So if the Son sets you free, you will be free indeed. [37]I know you are Abraham's descendants. Yet you are ready to kill me, because you have no room for my word. [38]I am telling you what I have seen in the Father's presence, and you do what you have heard from your father.[a]"

[39]"Abraham is our father," they answered.

"If you were Abraham's children," said Jesus, "then you would[b] do the things Abraham did. [40]As it is, you are determined to kill me, a man who has told you the truth that I heard from God. Abraham did not do such things. [41]You are doing the things your own father does."

"We are not illegitimate children," they protested. "The only Father we have is God himself."

The Children of the Devil

[42]Jesus said to them, "If God were your Father, you would love me, for I came from God and now am here. I have not come on my own; but he sent me. [43]Why is my language not clear to you? Because you are unable to hear what I say. [44]You belong to your father, the devil, and you want to carry out your father's desire. He was a murderer from the beginning, not holding to the truth, for there is no truth in him. When he lies, he speaks his native language, for he is a liar and the father of lies. [45]Yet because I tell the truth, you do not believe me! [46]Can any of you prove me guilty of sin? If I am telling the truth, why don't you believe me? [47]He who belongs to God hears what God says. The reason you do not hear is that you do not belong to God."

The Claims of Jesus About Himself

[48]The Jews[D] answered him, "Aren't we right in saying that you are a Samaritan and demon-possessed?"

[49]"I am not possessed by a demon," said Jesus, "but I honor my Father and you dishonor me. [50]I am not seeking glory[D] for myself; but there is one who seeks it, and he is the judge. [51]I tell you the truth, if anyone keeps my word, he will never see death[D]."

[52]At this the Jews exclaimed, "Now we know that you are demon-possessed! Abraham died and so did the prophets[D], yet you say that if anyone keeps your word, he will never taste death. [53]Are you greater than our father Abraham? He died, and so did the prophets. Who do you think you are?"

[54]Jesus replied, "If I glorify myself, my glory means nothing. My Father, whom you claim as your God, is the one who glorifies me. [55]Though you do not know him, I know him. If I said I did not, I would be a liar like you, but I do know him and keep his word. [56]Your father Abraham rejoiced at the thought of seeing my day; he saw it and was glad."

[57]"You are not yet fifty years old," the Jews said to him, "and you have seen Abraham!"

[58]"I tell you the truth," Jesus answered, "before Abraham was born, I am!" [59]At this, they picked up stones to stone him, but Jesus hid himself, slipping away from the temple grounds.

[a]38 Or presence. Therefore do what you have heard from the Father.
[b]39 Some early manuscripts "If you are Abraham's children," said Jesus, "then"

Jesus Heals a Man Born Blind

9 As he went along, he saw a man blind from birth. **2**His disciples[D] asked him, "Rabbi[D], who sinned, this man or his parents, that he was born blind?"

3"Neither this man nor his parents sinned," said Jesus, "but this happened so that the work of God might be displayed in his life. **4**As long as it is day, we must do the work of him who sent me. Night is coming, when no one can work. **5**While I am in the world, I am the light of the world."

6Having said this, he spit on the ground, made some mud with the saliva, and put it on the man's eyes. **7**"Go," he told him, "wash in the Pool of Siloam" (this word means Sent). So the man went and washed, and came home seeing.

8His neighbors and those who had formerly seen him begging asked, "Isn't this the same man who used to sit and beg?" **9**Some claimed that he was.

Others said, "No, he only looks like him."

But he himself insisted, "I am the man."

10"How then were your eyes opened?" they demanded.

11He replied, "The man they call Jesus made some mud and put it on my eyes. He told me to go to Siloam and wash. So I went and washed, and then I could see."

12"Where is this man?" they asked him.

"I don't know," he said.

The Pharisees Investigate the Healing

13They brought to the Pharisees[D] the man who had been blind. **14**Now the day on which Jesus had made the mud and opened the man's eyes was a Sabbath[D]. **15**Therefore the Pharisees also asked him how he had received his sight. "He put mud on my eyes," the man replied, "and I washed, and now I see."

16Some of the Pharisees said, "This man is not from God, for he does not keep the Sabbath."

But others asked, "How can a sinner do such miraculous signs?" So they were divided.

Why did the disciples assume the man's blindness was the result of his own sin? (9:2)

The rabbis at the time taught, "Bad things happen to evil people." An undue focus on sin and failure led people to believe even a developing infant could somehow incur God's wrath. Jesus refuted this error. In this fallen and sinful world, bad things sometimes happen for no apparent reason. Sometimes they occur simply because we are caught in the crossfire of a sinful world.

Night is coming (9:4)

There are three applications of this passage that deserve our attention: (1) Jesus was referring to his ministry as the light of the world and reminding the disciples he would not always be on earth. (2) Jesus was reminding his followers they also were the light of the world (Matt. 5:16) and needed to do what they could for God in their lives. (3) Jesus was referring to the time between his appearing in Bethlehem and the end of time when all evangelistic opportunities will end.

Did Jesus have to spit and make mud to heal the man's eyes? (9:6)

Jesus was illustrating his ability to use whatever was available to accomplish the impossible. The mud drew the onlookers' attention to the man's eyes and presented a clear demonstration of the power of God. It's also possible that Jesus was allowing time to slip away before the healing was manifested. Still another possibility is that Jesus used this physical act to strengthen the blind man's faith to receive the miracle. See *Why did Jesus spit on the blind man's eyes?* (Mark 8:23).

Does God allow pain in order to display his power? (9:3)

I n a sense, yes. But throughout the Bible we see the heart and mind of God contrasted with the work of Satan. Satan kills, steals and destroys; Jesus, by contrast, gives abundant life (10:10). While Satan's aim is destruction, Jesus came to tear down Satan's work (1 John 3:8). Because God permits Satan room to work, we have to say that pain and suffering occur because God permits it. But the other side of the story is that God can use Satan's evil to accomplish good.

Some of the bad things that happen occur simply because we live in a fallen world. Negative circumstances occur because creation itself was damaged when sin entered the world, opening the door for illness and natural disaster (see Romans 8:19–22). In this case, neither the man nor his parents had done anything to deserve his blind birth. Their suffering came as the result of living in a ruined creation. Nevertheless, God intended to use their terrible experience to accomplish a greater good.

God receives glory when he miraculously intervenes with his healing power. But he also receives glory when people endure their suffering through the power of his grace. See the book of Job and 2 Cor. 12:7–10. In either case God is glorified as the giver of life in an otherwise futile and destructive world.

Why did the disciples assume the man's blindness was the result of his own sin? (9:2)

Why were the man's parents afraid of being put out of the synagogue? (9:22)

The synagogue was the center of Jewish life in all aspects. Socially, spiritually and politically the synagogue stood for all that was Jewish. To be put out of the synagogue was to be cut off from your identity and ostracized from your neighbors. It made you an outcast.

Why did they punish the formerly blind man? (9:34)

The Jewish leaders refused to consider that Jesus might truly be sent from God. They considered him an imposter. When the blind man testified that Jesus had healed him, something only God's power could do, the leaders couldn't refute him. In their exasperation, they banned him from worshiping in the synagogue. Also see previous note.

If you were blind, you would not be guilty of sin (9:41)

All God needs from us to remove our guilt is our recognition that we are guilty and need his forgiveness. John reveals that if we confess our sins we can be forgiven. However, if we say we have no sin, we lie in self-deception (1 John 1:9–10). Claiming we can see—that is, that we can perceive our own spiritual condition when in fact we cannot—keeps us from receiving the healing that is forgiveness.

17Finally they turned again to the blind man, "What have you to say about him? It was your eyes he opened."

The man replied, "He is a prophet[D]."

18The Jews[D] still did not believe that he had been blind and had received his sight until they sent for the man's parents. **19**"Is this your son?" they asked. "Is this the one you say was born blind? How is it that now he can see?"

20"We know he is our son," the parents answered, "and we know he was born blind. **21**But how he can see now, or who opened his eyes, we don't know. Ask him. He is of age; he will speak for himself." **22**His parents said this because they were afraid of the Jews, for already the Jews had decided that anyone who acknowledged that Jesus was the Christ[a] would be put out of the synagogue. **23**That was why his parents said, "He is of age; ask him."

24A second time they summoned the man who had been blind. "Give glory[D] to God,[b]" they said. "We know this man is a sinner."

25He replied, "Whether he is a sinner or not, I don't know. One thing I do know. I was blind but now I see!"

26Then they asked him, "What did he do to you? How did he open your eyes?"

27He answered, "I have told you already and you did not listen. Why do you want to hear it again? Do you want to become his disciples[D], too?"

28Then they hurled insults at him and said, "You are this fellow's disciple! We are disciples of Moses! **29**We know that God spoke to Moses, but as for this fellow, we don't even know where he comes from."

30The man answered, "Now that is remarkable! You don't know where he comes from, yet he opened my eyes. **31**We know that God does not listen to sinners. He listens to the godly man who does his will. **32**Nobody has ever heard of opening the eyes of a man born blind. **33**If this man were not from God, he could do nothing."

34To this they replied, "You were steeped in sin at birth; how dare you lecture us!" And they threw him out.

Spiritual Blindness

35Jesus heard that they had thrown him out, and when he found him, he said, "Do you believe in the Son of Man?"

36"Who is he, sir?" the man asked. "Tell me so that I may believe in him."

37Jesus said, "You have now seen him; in fact, he is the one speaking with you."

38Then the man said, "Lord, I believe," and he worshiped him.

39Jesus said, "For judgment I have come into this world, so that the blind will see and those who see will become blind."

40Some Pharisees[D] who were with him heard him say this and asked, "What? Are we blind too?"

41Jesus said, "If you were blind, you would not be guilty of sin; but now that you claim you can see, your guilt remains.

*a*22 Or *Messiah*   *b*24 A solemn charge to tell the truth (see Joshua 7:19)

The Shepherd and His Flock

10 "I tell you the truth, the man who does not enter the sheep pen by the gate, but climbs in by some other way, is a thief and a robber. ²The man who enters by the gate is the shepherd of his sheep. ³The watchmanᴰ opens the gate for him, and the sheep listen to his voice. He calls his own sheep by name and leads them out. ⁴When he has brought out all his own, he goes on ahead of them, and his sheep follow him because they know his voice. ⁵But they will never follow a stranger; in fact, they will run away from him because they do not recognize a stranger's voice." ⁶Jesus used this figure of speech, but they did not understand what he was telling them.

⁷Therefore Jesus said again, "I tell you the truth, I am the gate for the sheep. ⁸All who ever came before me were thieves and robbers, but the sheep did not listen to them. ⁹I am the gate; whoever enters through me will be saved.ᵃ He will come in and go out, and find pasture. ¹⁰The thief comes only to steal and kill and destroy; I have come that they may have life, and have it to the full.

¹¹"I am the good shepherd. The good shepherd lays down his life for the sheep. ¹²The hired hand is not the shepherd who owns the sheep. So when he sees the wolf coming, he abandons the sheep and runs away. Then the wolf attacks the flock and scatters it. ¹³The man runs away because he is a hired hand and cares nothing for the sheep.

¹⁴"I am the good shepherd; I know my sheep and my sheep know me— ¹⁵just as the Father knows me and I know the Father—and I lay down my life for the sheep. ¹⁶I have other sheep that are not of this sheep pen. I must bring them also. They too will listen to my voice, and there shall be one flock and one shepherd. ¹⁷The reason my Father loves me is that I lay down my life—only to take it up again. ¹⁸No one takes it from me, but I lay it down of my own accord. I have authority to lay it down and authority to take it up again. This command I received from my Father."

¹⁹At these words the Jewsᴰ were again divided. ²⁰Many of them said, "He is demon-possessed and raving mad. Why listen to him?"

²¹But others said, "These are not the sayings of a man possessed by a demon. Can a demon open the eyes of the blind?"

The Unbelief of the Jews

²²Then came the Feast of Dedicationᵇ at Jerusalemᴰ. It was winter, ²³and Jesus was in the temple area walking in Solomon's Colonnade. ²⁴The Jews gathered around him, saying, "How long will you keep us in suspense? If you are the Christ,ᶜ tell us plainly."

²⁵Jesus answered, "I did tell you, but you do not believe. The miracles I do in my Father's name speak for me, ²⁶but you do not believe because you are not my sheep. ²⁷My sheep listen to my voice; I know them, and they follow me. ²⁸I give them eternal lifeᴰ, and they shall never perish; no one can snatch them out of my hand. ²⁹My Father, who has given them to me, is greater than allᵈ; no one

ᵃ9 Or *kept safe*   ᵇ22 That is, Hanukkah   ᶜ24 Or *Messiah*
ᵈ29 Many early manuscripts *What my Father has given me is greater than all*

How is Jesus like a shepherd? (10:1–15)

The shepherd was a figure who represented faithfulness, compassion, guidance and protection. The figure of the shepherd also was a prophetic picture of the Messiah. Jesus not only displayed the characteristics of a good shepherd, he demonstrated the power of the Messiah who would shepherd the people of Israel.

Sheep pen (10:1)

See *Sheep pens* (1 Samuel 24:3).

Who are the other sheep Jesus has? (10:16)

The sheep pen represents Israel, the Jewish people. By saying he has sheep other than the Jews, Jesus is referring to the Gentiles. This is one of Jesus' earliest and clearest references that the Gentiles will be included in his kingdom.

If they were Jews, why weren't they his sheep? (10:26)

Though the Jews were of the lineage of Abraham and ought to have belonged in the "sheep pen" of faith, their unbelief excluded them. Jesus had done miracles before them. He had taught them. He had loved them. Still their hearts were hard toward him.

How had Jesus claimed to be God? (10:33)

Jesus had earlier said, *Before Abraham was born, I am!* See *Was Jesus claiming to be older than Abraham?* (8:58–59). He had also referred to God as his father. See *Why was Jesus accused of blasphemy?* (5:18). Now Jesus becomes even more specific, claiming to be *one* with his Father (v. 30), that is, equal to the Father in the divine essence of his nature.

Why did Jesus call the Psalms the Law? (10:34)

Usually the term was used strictly for the first five books of the Bible, called the Pentateuch. But on occasion, the *Law* referred to the whole collection of Jewish Scriptures, known as the Old Testament to Christians.

In what sense are we all gods? (10:34–35)

Jesus quotes the Jewish Scriptures to show that we all are "gods" in the sense that we all have some sphere of influence over others. He uses the example of human rulers, called "gods" in Psalm 82:6–7. Jesus infers that whenever humans are rulers over others or are in charge of something, they function like little "gods" over those areas. In a far greater way, Jesus, who does the works of God and demonstrates his rule over disease, death and evil, is the Lord God.

Jesus Raises Lazarus (11:1)

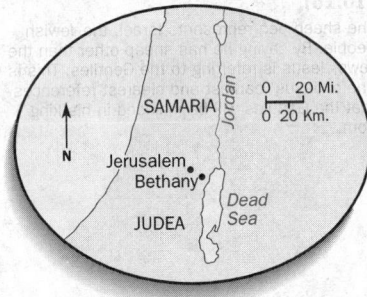

How can sickness bring God glory? (11:4)

By its end result, not by the ordeal itself. There was no glory merely in Lazarus being sick. But when he was raised from the dead, God's glory and power were revealed (v. 45). When sickness is conquered, it brings glory to God—literally, as Jesus did in this case (v. 44), or spiritually, as in the case of those who with God's help live above their physical limitations.

What does daylight have to do with death threats? (11:8–10)

Jesus' disciples were concerned that he might be killed if he went back to Judea. He calmed their fears by using the Jewish day as an analogy. The day was divided into two twelve-hour periods—daylight and darkness. Just as the hours of daylight and darkness were fixed, so the length of his earthly ministry was preordained.

can snatch them out of my Father's hand. **30**I and the Father are one."

31Again the Jews[D] picked up stones to stone him, **32**but Jesus said to them, "I have shown you many great miracles from the Father. For which of these do you stone me?"

33"We are not stoning you for any of these," replied the Jews, "but for blasphemy, because you, a mere man, claim to be God."

34Jesus answered them, "Is it not written in your Law, 'I have said you are gods'[a]? **35**If he called them 'gods,' to whom the word of God came—and the Scripture cannot be broken— **36**what about the one whom the Father set apart as his very own and sent into the world? Why then do you accuse me of blasphemy because I said, 'I am God's Son'? **37**Do not believe me unless I do what my Father does. **38**But if I do it, even though you do not believe me, believe the miracles, that you may know and understand that the Father is in me, and I in the Father." **39**Again they tried to seize him, but he escaped their grasp.

40Then Jesus went back across the Jordan to the place where John had been baptizing in the early days. Here he stayed **41**and many people came to him. They said, "Though John never performed a miraculous sign, all that John said about this man was true." **42**And in that place many believed in Jesus.

The Death of Lazarus

11 Now a man named Lazarus was sick. He was from Bethany, the village of Mary and her sister Martha. **2**This Mary, whose brother Lazarus now lay sick, was the same one who poured perfume on the Lord and wiped his feet with her hair. **3**So the sisters sent word to Jesus, "Lord, the one you love is sick."

4When he heard this, Jesus said, "This sickness will not end in death[D]. No, it is for God's glory[D] so that God's Son may be glorified through it." **5**Jesus loved Martha and her sister and Lazarus. **6**Yet when he heard that Lazarus was sick, he stayed where he was two more days.

7Then he said to his disciples[D], "Let us go back to Judea."

8"But Rabbi[D]," they said, "a short while ago the Jews tried to stone you, and yet you are going back there?"

9Jesus answered, "Are there not twelve hours of daylight? A man who walks by day will not stumble, for he sees by this world's light. **10**It is when he walks by night that he stumbles, for he has no light."

11After he had said this, he went on to tell them, "Our friend Lazarus has fallen asleep; but I am going there to wake him up."

12His disciples replied, "Lord, if he sleeps, he will get better." **13**Jesus had been speaking of his death, but his disciples thought he meant natural sleep.

14So then he told them plainly, "Lazarus is dead, **15**and for your sake I am glad I was not there, so that you may believe. But let us go to him."

16Then Thomas (called Didymus) said to the rest of the disciples, "Let us also go, that we may die with him."

Jesus Comforts the Sisters

17On his arrival, Jesus found that Lazarus had already been in the tomb for four days. **18**Bethany was less than

two miles*a* from Jerusalem*D*, **19**and many Jews*D* had come to Martha and Mary to comfort them in the loss of their brother. **20**When Martha heard that Jesus was coming, she went out to meet him, but Mary stayed at home.

21"Lord," Martha said to Jesus, "if you had been here, my brother would not have died. **22**But I know that even now God will give you whatever you ask."

23Jesus said to her, "Your brother will rise again."

24Martha answered, "I know he will rise again in the resurrection*D* at the last day."

25Jesus said to her, "I am the resurrection and the life. He who believes in me will live, even though he dies; **26**and whoever lives and believes in me will never die. Do you believe this?"

27"Yes, Lord," she told him, "I believe that you are the Christ,*b* the Son of God, who was to come into the world."

28And after she had said this, she went back and called her sister Mary aside. "The Teacher is here," she said, "and is asking for you." **29**When Mary heard this, she got up quickly and went to him. **30**Now Jesus had not yet entered the village, but was still at the place where Martha had met him. **31**When the Jews who had been with Mary in the house, comforting her, noticed how quickly she got up and went out, they followed her, supposing she was going to the tomb to mourn there.

32When Mary reached the place where Jesus was and saw him, she fell at his feet and said, "Lord, if you had been here, my brother would not have died."

33When Jesus saw her weeping, and the Jews who had come along with her also weeping, he was deeply moved in spirit and troubled. **34**"Where have you laid him?" he asked.

"Come and see, Lord," they replied.

35Jesus wept.

36Then the Jews said, "See how he loved him!"

37But some of them said, "Could not he who opened the eyes of the blind man have kept this man from dying?"

Jesus Raises Lazarus From the Dead

38Jesus, once more deeply moved, came to the tomb. It was a cave with a stone laid across the entrance. **39**"Take away the stone," he said.

"But, Lord," said Martha, the sister of the dead man, "by this time there is a bad odor, for he has been there four days."

40Then Jesus said, "Did I not tell you that if you believed, you would see the glory*D* of God?"

41So they took away the stone. Then Jesus looked up and said, "Father, I thank you that you have heard me. **42**I knew that you always hear me, but I said this for the benefit of the people standing here, that they may believe that you sent me."

43When he had said this, Jesus called in a loud voice, "Lazarus, come out!" **44**The dead man came out, his hands and feet wrapped with strips of linen, and a cloth around his face.

Jesus said to them, "Take off the grave clothes and let him go."

How could "doubting Thomas" show such loyalty? (11:16)

Thomas, whom we remember as the doubter (20:24–28), here makes a brave statement. His willingness to follow Jesus back toward Jerusalem, where hostile opponents of Jesus would try to kill him, shows another side of his character.

Why did so many Jews come to Martha and Mary? (11:19)

According to the custom of the day, Jewish sympathizers were expected to make extended calls on the grieving family. For the Jews, comforting the bereaved involved more than paying respects to the deceased. It meant spending a period of mourning (up to 90 days) offering support and sympathy to the family.

Why did Jesus weep if he was going to raise Lazarus? (11:35)

The Jews who had come to comfort Mary and Martha wailed loudly, expressing their grief in the custom of first-century Jewish mourners. *Weeping* (v. 33) conveys this idea, while *wept* (v. 35) in the original language is a completely different word that expresses the idea of quietly shedding tears. Even so, it seems strange that Jesus would weep knowing he was going to raise his friend from the dead. It seems most likely that Jesus cried because of the agonizing impact of Lazarus's death on his family and friends.

What were the Jewish leaders afraid of losing? (11:48)

The leaders were more self-serving than genuinely concerned for the people. They feared that Jesus might incite a rebellion which would result in harsh reprisals by the Romans. The Romans would undoubtedly destroy their temple—place—and dismantle the nation by deporting the population. If that happened, the religious leaders would suffer loss of power and prestige.

Ceremonial cleansing (11:55)

According to the Law of Moses, ceremonial uncleanness disqualified a person from celebrating the Passover (Num. 9:6). The ritual of purification depended on the type of defilement. Some procedures lasted as long as a week and required that the rituals be carried out in the temple. Large numbers of Jewish pilgrims had come early to Jerusalem to purify themselves in preparation for Passover.

SCRIPTURE LINK (12:1–8)

You can find similar accounts of Jesus' anointing in Matt. 26:6–13; Mark 14:3–9 and Luke 7:37–39.

Was pouring perfume on feet a customary ritual? (12:3)

Hospitality in those days called for washing the feet, but not pouring perfume on the feet. Washing travelers' feet after they had walked hot, dusty, dirty roads in sandals soothed and freshened them for their visit. It was also customary to anoint an honored guest's head—not feet—with perfume. Mary (and another woman; see Luke 7:37–38) anointed Jesus' feet because she felt unworthy to anoint his head. In both cases, the women recognized the righteous nature of Christ in contrast to their own sinfulness.

How expensive was the nard? (12:3–5)

Very. It was likely imported from outside the region. John notes that it was *pure nard,* which gave it added value. Judas did some quick calculations and complained about her extravagant waste (v. 5)—equivalent to the annual income of a laborer.

Why was the perfume *intended* for Jesus' burial? (12:7)

It was not uncommon for family or friends to spend enormous sums of money on strong perfumes and spices to mask the odor of a decaying body. Knowing he was facing death soon, Jesus saw a parallel between that custom and what Mary had done. He saw her act of love and devotion as something like a pre-anointing for burial. He defended her actions by reminding them of his approaching death.

Why *not* give to help the poor? (12:8)

Jesus was not being calloused or indifferent toward the needy. He was simply saying that there was little time left for them to express their love for him. They could and should always help the poor, but the worship of God must take priority over all other human endeavors. Also see **Why did Jesus endorse such extravagance?** (Matt. 26:10).

The Plot to Kill Jesus

45Therefore many of the Jews[D] who had come to visit Mary, and had seen what Jesus did, put their faith in him. **46**But some of them went to the Pharisees[D] and told them what Jesus had done. **47**Then the chief priests[D] and the Pharisees called a meeting of the Sanhedrin.

"What are we accomplishing?" they asked. "Here is this man performing many miraculous signs. **48**If we let him go on like this, everyone will believe in him, and then the Romans will come and take away both our place[a] and our nation."

49Then one of them, named Caiaphas, who was high priest that year, spoke up, "You know nothing at all! **50**You do not realize that it is better for you that one man die for the people than that the whole nation perish."

51He did not say this on his own, but as high priest that year he prophesied that Jesus would die for the Jewish nation, **52**and not only for that nation but also for the scattered children of God, to bring them together and make them one. **53**So from that day on they plotted to take his life.

54Therefore Jesus no longer moved about publicly among the Jews. Instead he withdrew to a region near the desert, to a village called Ephraim, where he stayed with his disciples[D].

55When it was almost time for the Jewish Passover, many went up from the country to Jerusalem[D] for their ceremonial cleansing before the Passover. **56**They kept looking for Jesus, and as they stood in the temple area they asked one another, "What do you think? Isn't he coming to the Feast at all?" **57**But the chief priests and Pharisees had given orders that if anyone found out where Jesus was, he should report it so that they might arrest him.

Jesus Anointed at Bethany

12 Six days before the Passover, Jesus arrived at Bethany, where Lazarus lived, whom Jesus had raised from the dead. **2**Here a dinner was given in Jesus' honor. Martha served, while Lazarus was among those reclining at the table with him. **3**Then Mary took about a pint[b] of pure nard, an expensive perfume; she poured it on Jesus' feet and wiped his feet with her hair. And the house was filled with the fragrance of the perfume.

4But one of his disciples, Judas Iscariot, who was later to betray him, objected, **5**"Why wasn't this perfume sold and the money given to the poor? It was worth a year's wages.[c]" **6**He did not say this because he cared about the poor but because he was a thief; as keeper of the money bag, he used to help himself to what was put into it.

7"Leave her alone," Jesus replied. "⌊It was intended⌋ that she should save this perfume for the day of my burial. **8**You will always have the poor among you, but you will not always have me."

9Meanwhile a large crowd of Jews found out that Jesus was there and came, not only because of him but also to see Lazarus, whom he had raised from the dead. **10**So the chief priests made plans to kill Lazarus as well, **11**for on account of him many of the Jews were going over to Jesus and putting their faith in him.

---

*a*48 Or *temple*   *b*3 Greek *a litra* (probably about 0.5 liter)
*c*5 Greek *three hundred denarii*

The Triumphal Entry

12The next day the great crowd that had come for the Feast heard that Jesus was on his way to Jerusalem[D]. **13**They took palm branches and went out to meet him, shouting,

"Hosanna![a]"

"Blessed is he who comes in the name of the Lord!"[b]

"Blessed is the King of Israel!"

14Jesus found a young donkey and sat upon it, as it is written,

15"Do not be afraid, O Daughter of Zion[D];
  see, your king is coming,
  seated on a donkey's colt."[c]

16At first his disciples[D] did not understand all this. Only after Jesus was glorified did they realize that these things had been written about him and that they had done these things to him.

17Now the crowd that was with him when he called Lazarus from the tomb and raised him from the dead continued to spread the word. **18**Many people, because they had heard that he had given this miraculous sign, went out to meet him. **19**So the Pharisees[D] said to one another, "See, this is getting us nowhere. Look how the whole world has gone after him!"

Jesus Predicts His Death

20Now there were some Greeks among those who went up to worship at the Feast. **21**They came to Philip, who was from Bethsaida in Galilee, with a request. "Sir," they said, "we would like to see Jesus." **22**Philip went to tell Andrew; Andrew and Philip in turn told Jesus.

23Jesus replied, "The hour has come for the Son of Man[D] to be glorified. **24**I tell you the truth, unless a kernel of wheat falls to the ground and dies, it remains only a single seed. But if it dies, it produces many seeds. **25**The man who loves his life will lose it, while the man who hates his life in this world will keep it for eternal life[D]. **26**Whoever serves me must follow me; and where I am, my servant also will be. My Father will honor the one who serves me.

27"Now my heart is troubled, and what shall I say? 'Father, save me from this hour'? No, it was for this very reason I came to this hour. **28**Father, glorify your name!"

Then a voice came from heaven, "I have glorified it, and will glorify it again." **29**The crowd that was there and heard it said it had thundered; others said an angel had spoken to him.

30Jesus said, "This voice was for your benefit, not mine. **31**Now is the time for judgment on this world; now the prince of this world will be driven out. **32**But I, when I am lifted up from the earth, will draw all men to myself." **33**He said this to show the kind of death[D] he was going to die.

34The crowd spoke up, "We have heard from the Law that the Christ[d] will remain forever, so how can you say,

SCRIPTURE LINK (12:12–15)

All of the Gospel writers tell of Jesus' triumphal entry into Jerusalem. See Matt. 21:4–9; Mark 11:7–10 and Luke 19:35–38.

Why did Jesus participate in this procession? (12:12–15)

Jesus, at the climax of his ministry, was making a statement. This was an object lesson that proclaimed who he was—the Son of David, the King of kings, the one who conquered sin and sickness. Conquering generals at that time were given a "triumphal entry" upon their return to their home city. Palm branches were often waved during times of celebration and victory (Lev. 23:40; Psalm 118:25–27). The procession caused the city, crowded with people for Passover, to consider Jesus' claims. Also see *Why carpet the road with cloaks?* (Luke 19:36).

Why did Jesus ride a donkey? (12:14)

Donkeys or mules were often associated with leaders (Judges 10:4; 1 Kings 1:33). By riding this young colt, however, Jesus demonstrated his humility and gentleness. He also fulfilled one of the prophecies of the Messiah (Zech. 9:9).

Why wouldn't Jesus meet with the Greeks? (12:20–23)

Why did he seem to evade the issue and begin another teaching discourse? There are two possible explanations: (1) Greeks were known for their interest in exploring novel philosophies and new ideas. It's possible their desire to see Jesus was motivated more by intellectual curiosity than spiritual hunger. (2) More likely, Jesus saw this request from Gentiles as a signal. The *hour* of his greater mission as the Savior of the world was coming to a climax. He would have to devote his full attention to the task ahead—dying for the sins of the world.

Prince of this world (12:31)

A title for Satan that suggests he currently held limited power over the people of this world. Yet, anticipating his death and resurrection, Jesus was preparing to dethrone Satan. In the world to come Satan will be powerless and confined under judgment. Also see *Why was Jesus' time limited if Satan had no hold on him?* (14:30).

---

[a]13 A Hebrew expression meaning "Save!" which became an exclamation of praise   [b]13 Psalm 118:25, 26   [c]15 Zech. 9:9
[d]34 Or *Messiah*

'The Son of Man[D] must be lifted up'? Who is this 'Son of Man'?"

35Then Jesus told them, "You are going to have the light just a little while longer. Walk while you have the light, before darkness overtakes you. The man who walks in the dark does not know where he is going. **36**Put your trust in the light while you have it, so that you may become sons of light." When he had finished speaking, Jesus left and hid himself from them.

The Jews Continue in Their Unbelief

37Even after Jesus had done all these miraculous signs in their presence, they still would not believe in him. **38**This was to fulfill the word of Isaiah the prophet[D]:

> "Lord, who has believed our message
> and to whom has the arm of the Lord been
> revealed?"[a]

39For this reason they could not believe, because, as Isaiah says elsewhere:

> **40**"He has blinded their eyes
> and deadened their hearts,
> so they can neither see with their eyes,
> nor understand with their hearts,
> nor turn—and I would heal them."[b]

41Isaiah said this because he saw Jesus' glory[D] and spoke about him.

42Yet at the same time many even among the leaders believed in him. But because of the Pharisees[D] they would not confess their faith for fear they would be put out of the synagogue; **43**for they loved praise from men more than praise from God.

44Then Jesus cried out, "When a man believes in me, he does not believe in me only, but in the one who sent me. **45**When he looks at me, he sees the one who sent me. **46**I have come into the world as a light, so that no one who believes in me should stay in darkness.

47"As for the person who hears my words but does not keep them, I do not judge him. For I did not come to judge the world, but to save it. **48**There is a judge for the one who rejects me and does not accept my words; that very word which I spoke will condemn him at the last day. **49**For I did not speak of my own accord, but the Father who sent me commanded me what to say and how to say it. **50**I know that his command leads to eternal life[D]. So whatever I say is just what the Father has told me to say."

Jesus Washes His Disciples' Feet

13 It was just before the Passover Feast. Jesus knew that the time had come for him to leave this world and go to the Father. Having loved his own who were in the world, he now showed them the full extent of his love.[c]

2The evening meal was being served, and the devil had already prompted Judas Iscariot, son of Simon, to betray Jesus. **3**Jesus knew that the Father had put all things under his power, and that he had come from God and was returning to God; **4**so he got up from the meal, took off his outer clothing, and wrapped a towel around his waist. **5**After that, he poured water into a basin and began to

Why did Jesus hide? (12:36)
As Jesus' public ministry drew to a close, so did the opportunity for the Jews to accept him as their Messiah. He may have hidden from them to underscore what he had just told them—that soon the light would be taken from them.

If the Jews could not believe, how could they be held accountable? (12:39)
Though we cannot understand everything about the purposes of God, the Bible teaches that his judgments are just. God's actions are consistent with the choices people make. John mentions the people's *inability* to believe after their *unwillingness* to believe (12:37). Because they refused to believe in Jesus, God hardened their hearts.

a38 Isaiah 53:1   b40 Isaiah 6:10   c1 Or he loved them to the last

wash his disciples'ᴰ feet, drying them with the towel that was wrapped around him.

⁶He came to Simon Peter, who said to him, "Lord, are you going to wash my feet?"

⁷Jesus replied, "You do not realize now what I am doing, but later you will understand."

⁸"No," said Peter, "you shall never wash my feet."

Jesus answered, "Unless I wash you, you have no part with me."

⁹"Then, Lord," Simon Peter replied, "not just my feet but my hands and my head as well!"

¹⁰Jesus answered, "A person who has had a bath needs only to wash his feet; his whole body is clean. And you are clean, though not every one of you." ¹¹For he knew who was going to betray him, and that was why he said not every one was clean.

¹²When he had finished washing their feet, he put on his clothes and returned to his place. "Do you understand what I have done for you?" he asked them. ¹³"You call me 'Teacher' and 'Lord,' and rightly so, for that is what I am. ¹⁴Now that I, your Lord and Teacher, have washed your feet, you also should wash one another's feet. ¹⁵I have set you an example that you should do as I have done for you. ¹⁶I tell you the truth, no servant is greater than his master, nor is a messenger greater than the one who sent him. ¹⁷Now that you know these things, you will be blessed if you do them.

Jesus Predicts His Betrayal

¹⁸"I am not referring to all of you; I know those I have chosen. But this is to fulfill the scripture: 'He who shares my bread has lifted up his heel against me.'ᵃ

¹⁹"I am telling you now before it happens, so that when it does happen you will believe that I am He. ²⁰I tell you the truth, whoever accepts anyone I send accepts me; and whoever accepts me accepts the one who sent me."

²¹After he had said this, Jesus was troubled in spirit and testified, "I tell you the truth, one of you is going to betray me."

²²His disciples stared at one another, at a loss to know which of them he meant. ²³One of them, the disciple whom Jesus loved, was reclining next to him. ²⁴Simon Peter motioned to this disciple and said, "Ask him which one he means."

²⁵Leaning back against Jesus, he asked him, "Lord, who is it?"

²⁶Jesus answered, "It is the one to whom I will give this piece of bread when I have dipped it in the dish." Then, dipping the piece of bread, he gave it to Judas Iscariot, son of Simon. ²⁷As soon as Judas took the bread, Satan entered into him.

"What you are about to do, do quickly," Jesus told him, ²⁸but no one at the meal understood why Jesus said this to him. ²⁹Since Judas had charge of the money, some thought Jesus was telling him to buy what was needed for the Feast, or to give something to the poor. ³⁰As soon as Judas had taken the bread, he went out. And it was night.

Jesus Predicts Peter's Denial

³¹When he was gone, Jesus said, "Now is the Son of Manᴰ glorified and God is glorified in him. ³²If God is glo-

ᵃ18 Psalm 41:9

Why was it necessary for Peter to allow Jesus to wash his feet? (13:8)

Peter needed to learn that the Messiah came to serve not to be served (Mark 10:45), ultimately giving himself on the cross. Instead, Peter objected to seeing Jesus perform such a menial task—it was not fitting for the role of the Messiah that Peter had in mind. For more on the custom of footwashing, see *Was pouring perfume on feet a customary ritual?* (12:3).

Should we wash each other's feet? (13:14–15)

Though some Christians practice footwashing, others don't believe Jesus was instituting a church ordinance equal to baptism and the Lord's Supper. This incident is an example of the spirit of humble servanthood that believers are to show one another.

Who was *the disciple . . . Jesus loved?* (13:23)

It was John, the author of this Gospel. Using this phrase does not suggest that John thought he was loved while the others were not. Instead, it probably conveys his amazement that Jesus, the Son of God, loved him.

Satan entered into him (13:27)

It had been predicted that Jesus would be betrayed by one of his close followers (17:12; Acts 1:16–17,20). Nevertheless, Judas, at the start, was chosen on an equal basis along with the other eleven. In time Judas began to give signs of the direction he was taking (6:70). Finally, he rejected Jesus' teaching and began to think only of himself and material gain (12:6). Some think that when Jesus offered bread to Judas, he extended one last gesture of grace and of friendship to his wayward disciple. If so, Judas took the bread but did not repent of the deed he planned to do. From that moment on, he came under the complete control and influence of Satan. Also see *Was the doom of Judas preordained?* (17:12).

rified in him,*a* God will glorify the Son in himself, and will glorify him at once.

33"My children, I will be with you only a little longer. You will look for me, and just as I told the Jews*D*, so I tell you now: Where I am going, you cannot come.

34"A new command I give you: Love one another. As I have loved you, so you must love one another. **35**By this all men will know that you are my disciples*D*, if you love one another."

36Simon Peter asked him, "Lord, where are you going?"

Jesus replied, "Where I am going, you cannot follow now, but you will follow later."

37Peter asked, "Lord, why can't I follow you now? I will lay down my life for you."

38Then Jesus answered, "Will you really lay down your life for me? I tell you the truth, before the rooster crows, you will disown me three times!

What's the test of loving one another? (13:34–35)

God measures love by obedience, not by warm feelings. In his first epistle, John says that believers know that they love one another by obedience to God's commands (1 John 5:2). Love and obedience are so closely connected that John says, *This is love for God: to obey his commands* (1 John 5:3).

SCRIPTURE LINK (13:37–38)

Jesus' prediction of Peter's denial can also be found in Matt. 26:33–35; Mark 14:29–31 and Luke 22:33–34.

What will heaven be like? (14:2)

Jesus described heaven as a house with *many rooms*, a figure of speech for unlimited space. While he did not tell details about heaven or give its location, he assured his followers that wherever he would be, they would be there as well. He was concerned more that they would gain an assurance about heaven than have a full understanding about it.

Jesus Comforts His Disciples

14 "Do not let your hearts be troubled. Trust in God*b*; trust also in me. **2**In my Father's house are many rooms; if it were not so, I would have told you. I am going there to prepare a place for you. **3**And if I go and prepare a place for you, I will come back and take you to be with me that you also may be where I am. **4**You know the way to the place where I am going."

Jesus the Way to the Father

5Thomas said to him, "Lord, we don't know where you are going, so how can we know the way?"

6Jesus answered, "I am the way and the truth and the life. No one comes to the Father except through me. **7**If you really knew me, you would know*c* my Father as well. From now on, you do know him and have seen him."

8Philip said, "Lord, show us the Father and that will be enough for us."

9Jesus answered: "Don't you know me, Philip, even af-

---

a32 Many early manuscripts do not have *If God is glorified in him.*
b1 Or *You trust in God*   *c7* Some early manuscripts *If you really have known me, you will know*

How are Jesus and the Father one? (14:9–28)

Jesus claimed, *Anyone who has seen me has seen the Father.* He was saying that he spoke and acted for God because he was in God and God was in him. He proclaimed that the Father and Son equally possess all the attributes of deity. In other words, Jesus was claiming to be God.

Yet, Jesus also made several distinctions between himself and his Father. His mission as the Son was to *bring glory to the Father* (v. 13). He had come into this world because the Father had sent him (v. 24). And once his mission was complete he was *going to the Father* (v. 28).

The existence of the Father and Son as one God yet two distinct persons baffles the human mind. It's a mystery that cannot be fully explained by logic or reason. Yet, because the Bible teaches the unity of God and the deity of Christ, we must accept the fact that an infinite God cannot be comprehended by finite humans. When we meet Christ face to face, it's possible that some such mysteries will be better understood.

ter I have been among you such a long time? Anyone who has seen me has seen the Father. How can you say, 'Show us the Father'? ¹⁰Don't you believe that I am in the Father, and that the Father is in me? The words I say to you are not just my own. Rather, it is the Father, living in me, who is doing his work. ¹¹Believe me when I say that I am in the Father and the Father is in me; or at least believe on the evidence of the miracles themselves. ¹²I tell you the truth, anyone who has faith in me will do what I have been doing. He will do even greater things than these, because I am going to the Father. ¹³And I will do whatever you ask in my name, so that the Son may bring glory ᴰ to the Father. ¹⁴You may ask me for anything in my name, and I will do it.

Jesus Promises the Holy Spirit

¹⁵"If you love me, you will obey what I command. ¹⁶And I will ask the Father, and he will give you another Counselor to be with you forever— ¹⁷the Spirit of truth. The world cannot accept him, because it neither sees him nor knows him. But you know him, for he lives with you and will be ᵃ in you. ¹⁸I will not leave you as orphans; I will come to you. ¹⁹Before long, the world will not see me anymore, but you will see me. Because I live, you also will live. ²⁰On that day you will realize that I am in my Father, and you are in me, and I am in you. ²¹Whoever has my commands and obeys them, he is the one who loves me. He who loves me will be loved by my Father, and I too will love him and show myself to him."

²²Then Judas (not Judas Iscariot) said, "But, Lord, why do you intend to show yourself to us and not to the world?"

²³Jesus replied, "If anyone loves me, he will obey my teaching. My Father will love him, and we will come to him and make our home with him. ²⁴He who does not love me will not obey my teaching. These words you hear are not my own; they belong to the Father who sent me.

²⁵"All this I have spoken while still with you. ²⁶But the Counselor, the Holy Spirit, whom the Father will send in my name, will teach you all things and will remind you of everything I have said to you. ²⁷Peace ᴰ I leave with you; my peace I give you. I do not give to you as the world gives. Do not let your hearts be troubled and do not be afraid.

²⁸"You heard me say, 'I am going away and I am coming back to you.' If you loved me, you would be glad that I am going to the Father, for the Father is greater than I. ²⁹I have told you now before it happens, so that when it does happen you will believe. ³⁰I will not speak with you much longer, for the prince of this world is coming. He has no hold on me, ³¹but the world must learn that I love the Father and that I do exactly what my Father has commanded me.

"Come now; let us leave.

The Vine and the Branches

15 "I am the true vine, and my Father is the gardener. ²He cuts off every branch in me that bears no fruit, while every branch that does bear fruit he prunes ᵇ so that it will be even more fruitful. ³You are already clean because of the word I have spoken to you. ⁴Remain in me,

ᵃ17 Some early manuscripts *and is* means *cleans.* ᵇ2 The Greek for *prunes* also

---

How can we do greater things than Jesus did? (14:12)

Jesus was not granting his followers sweeping supernatural powers that would out-perform his own miraculous signs. Rather, he was promising the coming of the Holy Spirit and a resulting worldwide ministry. Though the substance of his followers' miracles may be the same as those performed by Jesus, their scope would be greater, multiplied through the growth of the church. As the book of Acts describes, people of the early church fulfilled the prediction that they would do *greater things.*

Counselor (14:16,26)

Means *one who is called alongside.* It conveys the idea of an encourager in the sense of a legal counsel. Just as Jesus had encouraged and assisted his disciples, he assured them the Holy Spirit would be there for them as well.

Prince of this world (14:30)

See *Prince of this world* (12:31).

Why was Jesus' time limited if Satan had no hold on him? (14:30)

Christ knew his time was limited because Satan was working in Judas to betray him. Yet, Satan was not in control of the situation, God was. He allowed Satan's plot to continue because it fit into his own larger plan to redeem the world. God uses even the schemes of the devil to ultimately glorify his name and accomplish his will.

Why did Jesus urge his disciples to remain in him? (15:4)

Because it was the only way they could productively serve him. If they wanted to do the *greater things* he had described earlier (14:12), if they wanted to develop inner characteristics more like Christ (Gal. 5:22–23) and if they wanted to introduce others to Christ (3:15), they could not take matters into their own hands. They would have to rely completely upon him for spiritual life and vitality.

and I will remain in you. No branch can bear fruit by itself; it must remain in the vine. Neither can you bear fruit unless you remain in me.

5"I am the vine; you are the branches. If a man remains in me and I in him, he will bear much fruit; apart from me you can do nothing. **6**If anyone does not remain in me, he is like a branch that is thrown away and withers; such branches are picked up, thrown into the fire and burned. **7**If you remain in me and my words remain in you, ask whatever you wish, and it will be given you. **8**This is to my Father's glory^D, that you bear much fruit, showing yourselves to be my disciples^D.

9"As the Father has loved me, so have I loved you. Now remain in my love. **10**If you obey my commands, you will remain in my love, just as I have obeyed my Father's commands and remain in his love. **11**I have told you this so that my joy may be in you and that your joy may be complete. **12**My command is this: Love each other as I have loved you. **13**Greater love has no one than this, that he lay down his life for his friends. **14**You are my friends if you do what I command. **15**I no longer call you servants, because a servant does not know his master's business. Instead, I have called you friends, for everything that I learned from my Father I have made known to you. **16**You did not choose me, but I chose you and appointed you to go and bear fruit—fruit that will last. Then the Father will give you whatever you ask in my name. **17**This is my command: Love each other.

Can we ask for whatever we want? (15:7)

Jesus was not promising to give us whatever we want. What he did promise was that he would answer the prayers of obedient believers whose requests arise from a healthy relationship with him. As long as we remain in him and his words remain in us, our desires will be consistent with his will. Praying *in his name* (v. 16), then, refers to requests in line with what Christ would want. Such prayers reflect total dependence on him.

What if you don't feel love for someone? (15:12–14,17)

A command to love is not a command to *feel* a certain way. It's a command to *do* loving things. See *What's the test of loving one another?* (13:34–35).

The World Hates the Disciples

18"If the world hates you, keep in mind that it hated me first. **19**If you belonged to the world, it would love you as its own. As it is, you do not belong to the world, but I have chosen you out of the world. That is why the world hates you. **20**Remember the words I spoke to you: 'No servant is greater than his master.'^a If they persecuted me, they will persecute you also. If they obeyed my teaching, they will obey yours also. **21**They will treat you this way because of my name, for they do not know the One who sent me. **22**If I had not come and spoken to them, they would not be guilty of sin. Now, however, they have no excuse for their sin. **23**He who hates me hates my Father as well. **24**If I had not done among them what no one else did, they would not be guilty of sin. But now they have seen these miracles, and yet they have hated both me and my Father. **25**But this is to fulfill what is written in their Law: 'They hated me without reason.'^b

26"When the Counselor comes, whom I will send to you from the Father, the Spirit of truth who goes out from the Father, he will testify about me. **27**And you also must testify, for you have been with me from the beginning.

Does Jesus excuse those who haven't heard of him? (15:22)

Jesus was not offering a blanket pardon to those who have never heard the plan of salvation. He was simply saying that before he came into the world people could plead "not guilty" to rejecting him directly. Still, they had enough spiritual knowledge, which they had ignored and for which they could be condemned (Romans 1:20). Christ has now revealed God so fully and clearly that people are responsible for what they do with their knowledge of him (see v. 23). As for the fate of those who have never had the chance to hear the gospel, see *What happens to good people who never had a chance to hear?* (Romans 2:14–16).

16 "All this I have told you so that you will not go astray. **2**They will put you out of the synagogue; in fact, a time is coming when anyone who kills you will think he is offering a service to God. **3**They will do such things because they have not known the Father or me. **4**I have told you this, so that when the time comes you will remember that I warned you. I did not tell you this at first because I was with you.

---

^a20 John 13:16   ^b25 Psalms 35:19; 69:4

The Work of the Holy Spirit

⁵"Now I am going to him who sent me, yet none of you asks me, 'Where are you going?' ⁶Because I have said these things, you are filled with grief. ⁷But I tell you the truth: It is for your good that I am going away. Unless I go away, the Counselor will not come to you; but if I go, I will send him to you. ⁸When he comes, he will convict the world of guilt*a* in regard to sin and righteousness*D* and judgment: ⁹in regard to sin, because men do not believe in me; ¹⁰in regard to righteousness, because I am going to the Father, where you can see me no longer; ¹¹and in regard to judgment, because the prince of this world now stands condemned.

¹²"I have much more to say to you, more than you can now bear. ¹³But when he, the Spirit of truth, comes, he will guide you into all truth. He will not speak on his own; he will speak only what he hears, and he will tell you what is yet to come. ¹⁴He will bring glory*D* to me by taking from what is mine and making it known to you. ¹⁵All that belongs to the Father is mine. That is why I said the Spirit will take from what is mine and make it known to you.

¹⁶"In a little while you will see me no more, and then after a little while you will see me."

The Disciples' Grief Will Turn to Joy

¹⁷Some of his disciples*D* said to one another, "What does he mean by saying, 'In a little while you will see me no more, and then after a little while you will see me,' and 'Because I am going to the Father'?" ¹⁸They kept asking, "What does he mean by 'a little while'? We don't understand what he is saying."

¹⁹Jesus saw that they wanted to ask him about this, so he said to them, "Are you asking one another what I meant when I said, 'In a little while you will see me no more, and then after a little while you will see me'? ²⁰I tell you the truth, you will weep and mourn while the world rejoices. You will grieve, but your grief will turn to joy. ²¹A woman giving birth to a child has pain because her time has come; but when her baby is born she forgets the anguish because of her joy that a child is born into the world. ²²So with you: Now is your time of grief, but I will see you again and you will rejoice, and no one will take away your joy. ²³In that day you will no longer ask me anything. I tell you the truth, my Father will give you whatever you ask in my name. ²⁴Until now you have not asked for anything in my name. Ask and you will receive, and your joy will be complete.

²⁵"Though I have been speaking figuratively, a time is coming when I will no longer use this kind of language but will tell you plainly about my Father. ²⁶In that day you will ask in my name. I am not saying that I will ask the Father on your behalf. ²⁷No, the Father himself loves you because you have loved me and have believed that I came from God. ²⁸I came from the Father and entered the world; now I am leaving the world and going back to the Father."

²⁹Then Jesus' disciples said, "Now you are speaking clearly and without figures of speech. ³⁰Now we can see

Did Jesus forget Peter's earlier question? (16:5)

Jesus seemed to overlook Peter's earlier question, *Lord, where are you going?* (13:36). Peter, worried about their dilemma if Jesus abandoned them, had asked the right question for the wrong reason. Jesus wanted the disciples to refocus on the direction of his ministry and purpose. Their preoccupation with themselves kept them from getting to the significant spiritual question.

Counselor (16:7)

See *Counselor* (14:16).

How does the Counselor convict the world regarding sin, righteousness and judgment? (16:8)

The Spirit will expose the sin of unbelief (v. 9). The Spirit will also demonstrate that Christ alone is righteous and all others fall short of God's standards (v. 10). Finally, he will show that people who do not repent and believe in Christ will share condemnation with Satan (v. 11).

Prince of this world (16:11)

See *Prince of this world* (12:31).

Is the Holy Spirit still speaking today? (16:13)

Jesus explained that the Spirit would expand the apostles' partial understanding of Christ's life and mission. This aspect of the Spirit's ministry was fulfilled primarily in the writing of the New Testament. That, however, does not prevent the Spirit from continuing to enlighten men and women about what Christ's life and death means. Such personal illumination never contradicts or supersedes the revelation of God in his Word.

Why did Jesus make it so hard to understand what he meant? (16:17–18,25,29)

Jesus did not deliberately try to confuse his disciples. They simply were not prepared to grasp the truth that Jesus came into the world to die, be raised from the dead and then return to his Father (v. 12). Jesus explained as much as they could comprehend at that time. Things would soon become more clear to them after his death and resurrection (v. 25).

---

*a*8 Or *will expose the guilt of the world*

that you know all things and that you do not even need to have anyone ask you questions. This makes us believe that you came from God."

³¹"You believe at last!"ᵃ Jesus answered. ³²"But a time is coming, and has come, when you will be scattered, each to his own home. You will leave me all alone. Yet I am not alone, for my Father is with me.

³³"I have told you these things, so that in me you may have peaceᴰ. In this world you will have trouble. But take heart! I have overcome the world."

Why did Jesus pray to be glorified? (17:1,5)

It wasn't for his own benefit that Jesus asked to be glorified. Rather, he wanted the Father glorified through the coming events of the cross. His prayer was that the work of salvation would be completed, that his death, resurrection and ascension would demonstrate God's love and power to all the world. Such a display would result in God's eternal glory.

Why are so few given to the Son? (17:2,6,9)

Salvation depends upon God's initiative, not ours. First, he sent his Son to fulfill his plan of salvation. He also stirs the human heart to conviction so a person can turn to God. Why then doesn't God stir more hearts to turn to him? Some say the answer is known only to God who predestines certain ones for salvation (Eph. 1:4–5). In this view, God is responsible for who is saved and who is not. Others say that God, who wants everyone to repent (2 Peter 3:9), gives to Christ all who trust in him. They say many have been given spiritual resources to believe, but choose not to. According to this view, anyone who rejects God's offer will be held accountable for that decision.

Glory (17:5,24)

As he finished his work, Jesus prayed that the Father would restore him to the eternal, majestic and exalted position that he once had before he surrendered it to take on human form. His prayer was that he would be glorified to confirm that he had completely fulfilled the will of the Father.

Why didn't Jesus pray for the world? (17:9)

Since he would soon be leaving his followers, he chose here to focus on their needs. Later, he prayed for those who would become believers by hearing the gospel (v. 20). He also prayed that believers would be united as one in Christ so that the world would believe Jesus was sent by the Father (vv. 21,23). It is certain that Jesus had a worldwide vision and wanted all to hear the Good News of God's kingdom (Matt. 28:19; Mark 16:15).

What power exists in the name of the Father? (17:11–12)

In Bible times, a name stood for its owner's essential character. When the Father gave his name to the Son, he commissioned him to act on his behalf and with his authority and power. It's through that authority and power that believers are protected from the evil schemes of Satan.

Was the doom of Judas preordained? (17:12)

Even though God in his divine wisdom knew centuries before exactly what Judas would do (see Psalm 41:9), God was not the author of those actions. Judas made his own choices and was responsible for his own act of treachery. Like all who reject Christ, Judas was therefore doomed to destruction. Still, God could use Judas's deeds to accomplish his own sovereign plan and purpose.

Jesus Prays for Himself

17 After Jesus said this, he looked toward heaven and prayed:

"Father, the time has come. Glorify your Son, that your Son may glorify you. ²For you granted him authority over all people that he might give eternal lifeᴰ to all those you have given him. ³Now this is eternal life: that they may know you, the only true God, and Jesus Christ, whom you have sent. ⁴I have brought you gloryᴰ on earth by completing the work you gave me to do. ⁵And now, Father, glorify me in your presence with the glory I had with you before the world began.

Jesus Prays for His Disciples

⁶"I have revealed youᵇ to those whom you gave me out of the world. They were yours; you gave them to me and they have obeyed your word. ⁷Now they know that everything you have given me comes from you. ⁸For I gave them the words you gave me and they accepted them. They knew with certainty that I came from you, and they believed that you sent me. ⁹I pray for them. I am not praying for the world, but for those you have given me, for they are yours. ¹⁰All I have is yours, and all you have is mine. And glory has come to me through them. ¹¹I will remain in the world no longer, but they are still in the world, and I am coming to you. Holy Father, protect them by the power of your name—the name you gave me—so that they may be one as we are one. ¹²While I was with them, I protected them and kept them safe by that name you gave me. None has been lost except the one doomed to destruction so that Scripture would be fulfilled.

¹³"I am coming to you now, but I say these things while I am still in the world, so that they may have the full measure of my joy within them. ¹⁴I have given them your word and the world has hated them, for they are not of the world any more than I am of the world. ¹⁵My prayer is not that you take them out of the world but that you protect them from the evil one. ¹⁶They are not of the world, even as I am not of it. ¹⁷Sanctifyᴰᶜ them by the truth; your word is truth. ¹⁸As you sent me into the world, I have sent them into the world. ¹⁹For them I sanctify myself, that they too may be truly sanctified.

ᵃ31 Or "Do you now believe?"   ᵇ6 Greek your name; also in verse 26   ᶜ17 Greek hagiazo (set apart for sacred use or make holy); also in verse 19

Jesus Prays for All Believers

20"My prayer is not for them alone. I pray also for those who will believe in me through their message, **21**that all of them may be one, Father, just as you are in me and I am in you. May they also be in us so that the world may believe that you have sent me. **22**I have given them the glory[D] that you gave me, that they may be one as we are one: **23**I in them and you in me. May they be brought to complete unity to let the world know that you sent me and have loved them even as you have loved me.

24"Father, I want those you have given me to be with me where I am, and to see my glory, the glory you have given me because you loved me before the creation of the world.

25"Righteous[D] Father, though the world does not know you, I know you, and they know that you have sent me. **26**I have made you known to them, and will continue to make you known in order that the love you have for me may be in them and that I myself may be in them."

Jesus Arrested

18 When he had finished praying, Jesus left with his disciples[D] and crossed the Kidron Valley[D]. On the other side there was an olive grove, and he and his disciples went into it.

2Now Judas, who betrayed him, knew the place, because Jesus had often met there with his disciples. **3**So Judas came to the grove, guiding a detachment of soldiers and some officials from the chief priests[D] and Pharisees[D]. They were carrying torches, lanterns and weapons.

4Jesus, knowing all that was going to happen to him, went out and asked them, "Who is it you want?"

5"Jesus of Nazareth," they replied.

"I am he," Jesus said. (And Judas the traitor was standing there with them.) **6**When Jesus said, "I am he," they drew back and fell to the ground.

7Again he asked them, "Who is it you want?"

And they said, "Jesus of Nazareth."

8"I told you that I am he," Jesus answered. "If you are looking for me, then let these men go." **9**This happened so that the words he had spoken would be fulfilled: "I have not lost one of those you gave me."[a]

10Then Simon Peter, who had a sword, drew it and struck the high priest's servant, cutting off his right ear. (The servant's name was Malchus.)

11Jesus commanded Peter, "Put your sword away! Shall I not drink the cup the Father has given me?"

Jesus Taken to Annas

12Then the detachment of soldiers with its commander and the Jewish officials arrested Jesus. They bound him **13**and brought him first to Annas, who was the father-in-law of Caiaphas, the high priest that year. **14**Caiaphas was the one who had advised the Jews[D] that it would be good if one man died for the people.

Sanctify (17:17,19)

When Jesus prayed that believers would be sanctified, he was praying that they would be set apart and made righteous by the Word of God. In one sense that has already happened: believers are made righteous the moment they place their faith in Christ. In another sense, however, they enter a process of sanctification: growing in obedience and holiness.

What's the connection between unity and evangelism? (17:21–23)

Jesus did not pray for organizational unity, but for spiritual oneness. He wants all believers to be united in love and grace, just as the Father and Son are one. God desires that the world will see tangible expressions of this unity. As Christians demonstrate God's love in concrete ways, people will be more readily convinced that Jesus himself was the ultimate expression of God's love.

SCRIPTURE LINK (18:3–11)

You can read the other reports of Jesus' arrest in Matt. 26:47–56; Mark 14:43–50 and Luke 22:47–53.

Why did the soldiers fall to the ground? (18:6)

The soldiers, trained to expect violence and physical force, were caught off guard and struck by the power of Jesus' words and courage (see 7:45–46). But that alone doesn't explain their collapse. The divine authority and power of Christ was somehow revealed, causing these armed men to retreat in fear and panic.

SCRIPTURE LINK (18:12–13)

Matthew tells about Jesus' appearance before the high priest in Matt. 26:57.

Why was Jesus brought to the father-in-law of the high priest? (18:13)

This was a preliminary investigation done in preparation for the interrogation Jesus would face before the Sanhedrin. At one time Annas had been the high priest. But after the Romans deposed him, he retained the power behind the office. He was succeeded first by a son, then by his son-in-law, Caiaphas, and still later by three more sons. History tells us that he was wealthy, ambitious and crafty. He was seen by the Jews as the authority alongside his son-in-law (see Luke 3:2).

The other disciple (18:16)

While we cannot know for certain this disciple's identity, most believe it was John making another anonymous reference to himself (13:23). It was a mark of honor and prestige to know the high priest on a personal basis, so this may be a display of humility in his writing.

SCRIPTURE LINK (18:16–18)

See Matt. 26:69–70; Mark 14:66–68 and Luke 22:55–57 for more on Peter's first denial of Jesus.

SCRIPTURE LINK (18:19–24)

Jesus' questioning by the high priest is also documented in Matt. 26:59–68; Mark 14:55–65 and Luke 22:63–71.

SCRIPTURE LINK (18:25–27)

For Peter's second and third denials of Jesus, see also Matt. 26:71–75; Mark 14:69–72 and Luke 22:58–62.

Ceremonial uncleanness (18:28)

The Jews considered Gentile dwellings unclean —even a governor's palace. According to the law, to enter it would defile them for seven days and disqualify them from eating the Passover. See *Ceremonial cleansing* (11:55). Ironically, while they were trying to avoiding ceremonial uncleanness, they were plotting to murder the Son of God.

SCRIPTURE LINK (18:29–40)

You'll find details of Jesus' trial before Pilate in Matt. 27:11–18,20–23; Mark 15:2–15 and Luke 23:2,3,18–25.

Why would the Jews' lack of authority to execute dictate how Jesus would die? (18:31–32)

The Jews apparently were permitted to execute by stoning those guilty of religious laws (see Acts 7:57–59). But the Jewish leaders were unwilling to risk being blamed for Jesus' death by the crowds who supported Jesus. The leaders wanted to avoid stirring up the anger of the many people gathered for the Passover feast, so they sought a Roman conviciton for a political crime, thinking the Roman authorities would then be blamed. They hoped to have the Romans execute Jesus in their own distinct way—by crucifixion. Also see *Why did Jewish leaders seek a Roman judge?* (Mark 15:1).

What did the title *the king of the Jews* mean to Pilate? (18:33)

The Roman government was particularly sensitive to subversive elements in society that would undermine their base of power. Any who claimed to be a leader or a king could be a potential threat. Jesus had been accused of rebelling against Rome and opposing payment of taxes to Caesar (Luke 23:1–2). It was only natural for Pilate to probe Jesus' political aspirations. In Jesus' case, the title carried a deeper spiritual meaning. Since the charge against Jesus carried no real weight, Pilate did not put any stock in it. See *Why wasn't Pilate bothered by Jesus' claim to be king of the Jews?* (Luke 23:3–4).

Peter's First Denial

15Simon Peter and another disciple[D] were following Jesus. Because this disciple was known to the high priest[D], he went with Jesus into the high priest's courtyard, **16**but Peter had to wait outside at the door. The other disciple, who was known to the high priest, came back, spoke to the girl on duty there and brought Peter in.

17"You are not one of his disciples, are you?" the girl at the door asked Peter.

He replied, "I am not."

18It was cold, and the servants and officials stood around a fire they had made to keep warm. Peter also was standing with them, warming himself.

The High Priest Questions Jesus

19Meanwhile, the high priest questioned Jesus about his disciples and his teaching.

20"I have spoken openly to the world," Jesus replied. "I always taught in synagogues or at the temple, where all the Jews[D] come together. I said nothing in secret. **21**Why question me? Ask those who heard me. Surely they know what I said."

22When Jesus said this, one of the officials nearby struck him in the face. "Is this the way you answer the high priest?" he demanded.

23"If I said something wrong," Jesus replied, "testify as to what is wrong. But if I spoke the truth, why did you strike me?" **24**Then Annas sent him, still bound, to Caiaphas the high priest.[a]

Peter's Second and Third Denials

25As Simon Peter stood warming himself, he was asked, "You are not one of his disciples, are you?"

He denied it, saying, "I am not."

26One of the high priest's servants, a relative of the man whose ear Peter had cut off, challenged him, "Didn't I see you with him in the olive grove?" **27**Again Peter denied it, and at that moment a rooster began to crow.

Jesus Before Pilate

28Then the Jews led Jesus from Caiaphas to the palace of the Roman governor. By now it was early morning, and to avoid ceremonial uncleanness[D] the Jews did not enter the palace; they wanted to be able to eat the Passover. **29**So Pilate came out to them and asked, "What charges are you bringing against this man?"

30"If he were not a criminal," they replied, "we would not have handed him over to you."

31Pilate said, "Take him yourselves and judge him by your own law."

"But we have no right to execute anyone," the Jews objected. **32**This happened so that the words Jesus had spoken indicating the kind of death[D] he was going to die would be fulfilled.

33Pilate then went back inside the palace, summoned Jesus and asked him, "Are you the king of the Jews?"

34"Is that your own idea," Jesus asked, "or did others talk to you about me?"

a24 Or (Now Annas had sent him, still bound, to Caiaphas the high priest.)

35"Am I a Jew?" Pilate replied. "It was your people and your chief priests[D] who handed you over to me. What is it you have done?"

36Jesus said, "My kingdom is not of this world. If it were, my servants would fight to prevent my arrest by the Jews[D]. But now my kingdom is from another place."

37"You are a king, then!" said Pilate.

Jesus answered, "You are right in saying I am a king. In fact, for this reason I was born, and for this I came into the world, to testify to the truth. Everyone on the side of truth listens to me."

38"What is truth?" Pilate asked. With this he went out again to the Jews and said, "I find no basis for a charge against him. **39**But it is your custom for me to release to you one prisoner at the time of the Passover. Do you want me to release 'the king of the Jews'?"

40They shouted back, "No, not him! Give us Barabbas!" Now Barabbas had taken part in a rebellion.

Jesus Sentenced to be Crucified

19 Then Pilate took Jesus and had him flogged. **2**The soldiers twisted together a crown of thorns and put it on his head. They clothed him in a purple[D] robe **3**and went up to him again and again, saying, "Hail, king of the Jews!" And they struck him in the face.

4Once more Pilate came out and said to the Jews, "Look, I am bringing him out to you to let you know that I find no basis for a charge against him." **5**When Jesus came out wearing the crown of thorns and the purple robe, Pilate said to them, "Here is the man!"

6As soon as the chief priests and their officials saw him, they shouted, "Crucify! Crucify!"

But Pilate answered, "You take him and crucify him. As for me, I find no basis for a charge against him."

7The Jews insisted, "We have a law, and according to that law he must die, because he claimed to be the Son of God."

8When Pilate heard this, he was even more afraid, **9**and he went back inside the palace. "Where do you come from?" he asked Jesus, but Jesus gave him no answer. **10**"Do you refuse to speak to me?" Pilate said. "Don't you realize I have power either to free you or to crucify you?"

11Jesus answered, "You would have no power over me if it were not given to you from above. Therefore the one who handed me over to you is guilty of a greater sin."

12From then on, Pilate tried to set Jesus free, but the Jews kept shouting, "If you let this man go, you are no friend of Caesar. Anyone who claims to be a king opposes Caesar."

13When Pilate heard this, he brought Jesus out and sat down on the judge's seat at a place known as the Stone Pavement (which in Aramaic[D] is Gabbatha). **14**It was the day of Preparation of Passover Week, about the sixth hour.

"Here is your king," Pilate said to the Jews.

15But they shouted, "Take him away! Take him away! Crucify him!"

"Shall I crucify your king?" Pilate asked.

"We have no king but Caesar," the chief priests answered.

16Finally Pilate handed him over to them to be crucified.

How was Jesus flogged? (19:1)

Flogging was a ruthless punishment that used a leather whip with multiple ends and sharp bits of bone or metal embedded in the ends. It could leave the back raw and bleeding, sometimes exposing bones and organs. Floggings occasionally caused death.

Why was Jesus flogged after being found not guilty? (19:1; see 18:38; 19:4)

This was not a case of following legal channels. Often, Roman rulers made judgment calls according to their own mood—or in response to a bribe. Pilate secretly hoped this vicious beating would satisfy the Jews and cause them to give up their demands that Jesus be crucified (see Luke 23:16,22).

SCRIPTURE LINK (19:1–16)

Matthew talks about Jesus' sentencing in Matt. 27:27–31. Mark covers it in Mark 15:16–20.

Who was most guilty for Christ's death? (19:11)

Pilate was guilty of cowardice and the unjust use of his authority. Caiaphas, who should have been the spiritual leader and thus should have understood how Jesus fulfilled the prophecies of the Messiah, bore even greater guilt. Though he knew about Jesus' miracles and ministry, his hatred and envy caused him to condemn Jesus (see 11:49–50). He saw Jesus' popularity with the people as a threat to the political power that he and other Jewish leaders enjoyed under the Romans (see 11:49–50).

SCRIPTURE LINK (19:17–24)
You can read about Jesus' crucifixion in Matt. 27:33–44; Mark 15:22–32 and Luke 23:33–43.

The Crucifixion

So the soldiers took charge of Jesus. **17**Carrying his own cross, he went out to the place of the Skull (which in Aramaic^D is called Golgotha). **18**Here they crucified him, and with him two others—one on each side and Jesus in the middle.

19Pilate had a notice prepared and fastened to the cross. It read: JESUS OF NAZARETH, THE KING OF THE JEWS. **20**Many of the Jews^D read this sign, for the place where Jesus was crucified was near the city, and the sign was written in Aramaic, Latin and Greek. **21**The chief priests of the Jews protested to Pilate, "Do not write 'The King of the Jews,' but that this man claimed to be king of the Jews."

22Pilate answered, "What I have written, I have written."

23When the soldiers crucified Jesus, they took his clothes, dividing them into four shares, one for each of them, with the undergarment remaining. This garment was seamless, woven in one piece from top to bottom.

24"Let's not tear it," they said to one another. "Let's decide by lot who will get it."

This happened that the scripture might be fulfilled which said,

> "They divided my garments among them
>   and cast lots for my clothing." ^a

So this is what the soldiers did.

25Near the cross of Jesus stood his mother, his mother's sister, Mary the wife of Clopas, and Mary Magdalene. **26**When Jesus saw his mother there, and the disciple^D whom he loved standing nearby, he said to his mother, "Dear woman, here is your son," **27**and to the disciple, "Here is your mother." From that time on, this disciple took her into his home.

The Death of Jesus

28Later, knowing that all was now completed, and so that the Scripture would be fulfilled, Jesus said, "I am thirsty." **29**A jar of wine vinegar was there, so they soaked a sponge in it, put the sponge on a stalk of the hyssop^D plant, and lifted it to Jesus' lips. **30**When he had received the drink, Jesus said, "It is finished." With that, he bowed his head and gave up his spirit.

31Now it was the day of Preparation, and the next day was to be a special Sabbath^D. Because the Jews did not want the bodies left on the crosses during the Sabbath, they asked Pilate to have the legs broken and the bodies taken down. **32**The soldiers therefore came and broke the legs of the first man who had been crucified with Jesus, and then those of the other. **33**But when they came to Jesus and found that he was already dead, they did not break his legs. **34**Instead, one of the soldiers pierced Jesus' side with a spear, bringing a sudden flow of blood and water. **35**The man who saw it has given testimony, and his testimony is true. He knows that he tells the truth, and he testifies so that you also may believe. **36**These things happened so that the scripture would be fulfilled: "Not one of his bones will be broken," ^b **37**and, as another scripture says, "They will look on the one they have pierced." ^c

SCRIPTURE LINK (19:29–30)
Matt. 27:48,50; Mark 15:36–37 and Luke 23:36 tell of Jesus' death.

How did breaking the legs hasten death? (19:31)
The excruciating pain would itself bring the victim closer to death. But even more critical, with his legs broken the victim could not push himself up to catch a breath. Hung on the cross by his arms, the pressure in his chest would cut off his breathing.

Who was the man who saw these things? (19:35)
John was probably referring to himself anonymously again, as he does on several other occasions. See *The other disciple* (18:16). We are not told of any other disciple present at the crucifixion, but we do know John was there (see 19:26–27). He wants us to know he was an eyewitness with a valid testimony.

^a24 Psalm 22:18   ^b36 Exodus 12:46; Num. 9:12; Psalm 34:20   ^c37 Zech. 12:10

The Burial of Jesus

38Later, Joseph of Arimathea asked Pilate for the body of Jesus. Now Joseph was a disciple^D of Jesus, but secretly because he feared the Jews^D. With Pilate's permission, he came and took the body away. **39**He was accompanied by Nicodemus, the man who earlier had visited Jesus at night. Nicodemus brought a mixture of myrrh^D and aloes, about seventy-five pounds.^a **40**Taking Jesus' body, the two of them wrapped it, with the spices, in strips of linen. This was in accordance with Jewish burial customs. **41**At the place where Jesus was crucified, there was a garden, and in the garden a new tomb, in which no one had ever been laid. **42**Because it was the Jewish day of Preparation and since the tomb was nearby, they laid Jesus there.

The Empty Tomb

20 Early on the first day of the week, while it was still dark, Mary Magdalene went to the tomb and saw that the stone had been removed from the entrance. **2**So she came running to Simon Peter and the other disciple, the one Jesus loved, and said, "They have taken the Lord out of the tomb, and we don't know where they have put him!"

3So Peter and the other disciple started for the tomb. **4**Both were running, but the other disciple outran Peter and reached the tomb first. **5**He bent over and looked in at the strips of linen lying there but did not go in. **6**Then Simon Peter, who was behind him, arrived and went into the tomb. He saw the strips of linen lying there, **7**as well as the burial cloth that had been around Jesus' head. The cloth was folded up by itself, separate from the linen. **8**Finally the other disciple, who had reached the tomb first, also went inside. He saw and believed. **9**(They still did not understand from Scripture that Jesus had to rise from the dead.)

Jesus Appears to Mary Magdalene

10Then the disciples went back to their homes, **11**but Mary stood outside the tomb crying. As she wept, she bent over to look into the tomb **12**and saw two angels in white, seated where Jesus' body had been, one at the head and the other at the foot.

13They asked her, "Woman, why are you crying?"

"They have taken my Lord away," she said, "and I don't know where they have put him." **14**At this, she turned around and saw Jesus standing there, but she did not realize that it was Jesus.

15"Woman," he said, "why are you crying? Who is it you are looking for?"

Thinking he was the gardener, she said, "Sir, if you have carried him away, tell me where you have put him, and I will get him."

16Jesus said to her, "Mary."

She turned toward him and cried out in Aramaic^D, "Rabboni!" (which means Teacher).

17Jesus said, "Do not hold on to me, for I have not yet returned to the Father. Go instead to my brothers and tell them, 'I am returning to my Father and your Father, to my God and your God.' "

18Mary Magdalene went to the disciples with the

---

^a39 Greek *a hundred litrai* (about 34 kilograms)

Why did these two secret disciples risk discovery after Jesus was dead? (19:38–39)

During Christ's life, these two apparently kept quiet about their convictions. They probably feared being thrown out of the synagogue (see 7:13; 9:22; 20:19). Now, with Jesus dead, the threat of reprisal seemed remote. Still, to openly ask for the body required tremendous courage. Perhaps the miraculous events accompanying Christ's death on the cross had changed them and given them the boldness to identify with Jesus (see 12:32).

SCRIPTURE LINK (19:38–42)

Accounts of Jesus' burial can be found in Matt. 27:57–61; Mark 15:42–47 and Luke 23:50–56.

SCRIPTURE LINK (20:1–8)

All of the Gospel writers report on the empty tomb. See Matt. 28:1–8; Mark 16:1–8 and Luke 24:1–10.

Who was *the other disciple*? (20:2–4,8)

See *The other disciple* (18:16).

Why did Jesus tell Mary not to hold on to him? (20:17)

Perhaps Jesus wanted Mary to understand the significance of his resurrection. From now on his physical presence would not be so important to his disciples. But his spiritual presence, in the person of the Holy Spirit, would be. It's also possible he wanted her to stop clinging because he was not leaving just yet; she would have opportunity to see him again. For now he wanted her to carry the message of his resurrection to the disciples.

news: "I have seen the Lord!" And she told them that he had said these things to her.

Jesus Appears to His Disciples

19On the evening of that first day of the week, when the disciples[D] were together, with the doors locked for fear of the Jews[D], Jesus came and stood among them and said, "Peace[D] be with you!" **20**After he said this, he showed them his hands and side. The disciples were overjoyed when they saw the Lord.

21Again Jesus said, "Peace be with you! As the Father has sent me, I am sending you." **22**And with that he breathed on them and said, "Receive the Holy Spirit. **23**If you forgive anyone his sins, they are forgiven; if you do not forgive them, they are not forgiven."

Jesus Appears to Thomas

24Now Thomas (called Didymus), one of the Twelve, was not with the disciples when Jesus came. **25**So the other disciples told him, "We have seen the Lord!"

But he said to them, "Unless I see the nail marks in his hands and put my finger where the nails were, and put my hand into his side, I will not believe it."

26A week later his disciples were in the house again, and Thomas was with them. Though the doors were locked, Jesus came and stood among them and said, "Peace be with you!" **27**Then he said to Thomas, "Put your finger here; see my hands. Reach out your hand and put it into my side. Stop doubting and believe."

28Thomas said to him, "My Lord and my God!"

29Then Jesus told him, "Because you have seen me, you have believed; blessed are those who have not seen and yet have believed."

30Jesus did many other miraculous signs in the presence of his disciples, which are not recorded in this book. **31**But these are written that you may[a] believe that Jesus is the Christ, the Son of God, and that by believing you may have life in his name.

a31 Some manuscripts may continue to

Why did Jesus breathe on the disciples? (20:22)

Jesus was giving his disciples the Holy Spirit. In fact, the word for *breath* and *Spirit* are the same. Jesus was preparing them to go into the world as witnesses (v. 21) in the wisdom and power of the Holy Spirit. Apart from such a divine power source, there was no hope of succeeding.

Did the disciples receive the Holy Spirit at this time? (20:22)

In the Old Testament the Holy Spirit came upon believers temporarily for specific tasks. That seems to be the case here. These same disciples would be baptized in the Holy Spirit fifty days later on the day of Pentecost. But in the meantime they needed a temporary infilling to empower them for service until the new ministry of the Spirit began.

Can Christians forgive others' sins? (20:23)

The Scriptures teach that God alone can forgive sins. So Jesus was not giving his followers the authority to pardon sin or pronounce judgment on their own.

What then did Jesus mean? There may be a clue in the Old Testament concept of the things a prophet did. A prophet was said to have accomplished things he actually only reported. When he *declared* something done (see Jer. 1:10), it was as though he had done it himself.

Jesus gave to his disciples, led by the Holy Spirit (v. 22), the authority to declare what God had already done when someone trusts in Christ. *When you forgive anyone's sins,* he seems to be saying, *they have already been forgiven; when you announce they are not forgiven (for failing to trust in Christ), they have not been forgiven.*

Jesus probably did not intend this declaration of forgiveness to be only the work of the apostles or a special class of clergy. Anyone involved in sharing the gospel with others has the authority in Christ's name to announce a person's sins forgiven or not forgiven, depending on their response to the gospel message.

Jesus and the Miraculous Catch of Fish

21 Afterward Jesus appeared again to his disciples[D], by the Sea of Tiberias.[a] It happened this way: **2**Simon Peter, Thomas (called Didymus), Nathanael from Cana in Galilee, the sons of Zebedee, and two other disciples were together. **3**"I'm going out to fish," Simon Peter told them, and they said, "We'll go with you." So they went out and got into the boat, but that night they caught nothing.

4Early in the morning, Jesus stood on the shore, but the disciples did not realize that it was Jesus.

5He called out to them, "Friends, haven't you any fish?"

"No," they answered.

6He said, "Throw your net on the right side of the boat and you will find some." When they did, they were unable to haul the net in because of the large number of fish.

7Then the disciple whom Jesus loved said to Peter, "It is the Lord!" As soon as Simon Peter heard him say, "It is the Lord," he wrapped his outer garment around him (for he had taken it off) and jumped into the water. **8**The other disciples followed in the boat, towing the net full of fish, for they were not far from shore, about a hundred yards.[b] **9**When they landed, they saw a fire of burning coals there with fish on it, and some bread.

10Jesus said to them, "Bring some of the fish you have just caught."

11Simon Peter climbed aboard and dragged the net ashore. It was full of large fish, 153, but even with so many the net was not torn. **12**Jesus said to them, "Come and have breakfast." None of the disciples dared ask him, "Who are you?" They knew it was the Lord. **13**Jesus came, took the bread and gave it to them, and did the same with the fish. **14**This was now the third time Jesus appeared to his disciples after he was raised from the dead.

Jesus Reinstates Peter

15When they had finished eating, Jesus said to Simon Peter, "Simon son of John, do you truly love me more than these?"

"Yes, Lord," he said, "you know that I love you."

Jesus said, "Feed my lambs."

16Again Jesus said, "Simon son of John, do you truly love me?"

He answered, "Yes, Lord, you know that I love you."

Jesus said, "Take care of my sheep."

17The third time he said to him, "Simon son of John, do you love me?"

Peter was hurt because Jesus asked him the third time, "Do you love me?" He said, "Lord, you know all things; you know that I love you."

Jesus said, "Feed my sheep. **18**I tell you the truth, when you were younger you dressed yourself and went where you wanted; but when you are old you will stretch out your hands, and someone else will dress you and lead you where you do not want to go." **19**Jesus said this to indicate the kind of death[D] by which Peter would glorify God. Then he said to him, "Follow me!"

20Peter turned and saw that the disciple whom Jesus loved was following them. (This was the one who had

---

If the disciples knew it was the Lord, why ask? (21:12)
When Jesus invited the disciples to come eat with him, they may have yet been some distance away, making a positive identification difficult. Jesus' post-resurrection body may also have been slightly different in appearance. Neither Mary Magdalene (20:10–18) nor the disciples on the way to Emmaus (Luke 24:13–35) recognized him immediately. In this case as soon as they began talking with him, all doubts were removed from their minds.

Why did Jesus press Peter three times for an answer? (21:15–17)
The repeated questions were for Peter's benefit, not to reassure Jesus of Peter's loyalty. This was particularly important in view of Peter's recent three-fold denial of Jesus (18:15–26). Jesus was helping Peter overcome his own doubts about his love for Christ. Jesus uses two different words for *love*, one higher and nobler than the other. John uses the words interchangeably in his writing, but it's possible Jesus was challenging Peter to consider just how far his love for his Savior would go.

Feed my lambs (21:15–17)
To love Jesus is to love those in the church, which he compares to sheep in a flock. He told Peter to care for them as a shepherd would care for his sheep: feed them (with God's Word); guide and protect them, bring them back if they strayed and help heal them if they were hurt.

SCRIPTURE LINK (21:15–17) *Take care of my sheep*
Peter later echoed this charge to the elders (called shepherds) of churches to which he writes in 1 Peter 5:1–2.

---

*a*1 That is, Sea of Galilee   *b*8 Greek *about two hundred cubits* (about 90 meters)

leaned back against Jesus at the supper and had said, "Lord, who is going to betray you?") **21**When Peter saw him, he asked, "Lord, what about him?"

22Jesus answered, "If I want him to remain alive until I return, what is that to you? You must follow me." **23**Because of this, the rumor spread among the brothers that this disciple[D] would not die. But Jesus did not say that he would not die; he only said, "If I want him to remain alive until I return, what is that to you?"

24This is the disciple who testifies to these things and who wrote them down. We know that his testimony is true.

25Jesus did many other things as well. If every one of them were written down, I suppose that even the whole world would not have room for the books that would be written.

Is the writer defending his own integrity? (21:24)

This brief note was likely added by someone other than John, perhaps the elders or even the entire church at Ephesus where John ministered. They vouch for the integrity of John, who often preached to them about his firsthand experiences with Jesus.

ACTS

Why read this book?

The church today, sometimes persecuted, ridiculed or even ignored, often needs encouragement. The book of Acts reminds us that despite modern challenges the church can be alive and well. Acts shows how revival and church growth comes, not by human effort, but through the power of the Holy Spirit.

Who wrote this book?

Luke, the author of Luke's Gospel. The books of Luke and Acts compose almost one-fourth of the entire New Testament.

Why was it written?

Luke wrote as a historian to tell what happened after the resurrection. Acts is the second volume of the Good News—the sequel to the Gospels. In it Luke explained Christianity's amazing growth, perhaps to legitimize the church to civil authorities, perhaps to confirm the faith of believers. Luke may also have wanted congregations to understand the source of conflict between Jewish and Gentile Christians.

When was it written?

Around A.D. 63 to 70.

To whom was it written?

Luke wrote to Theophilus (a name which meant *lover of God*). This may have been a specific person or perhaps a label for struggling Christians in general. See also the Introduction to Luke.

What to look for in Acts:

As you read what happened *then,* consider its impact *now.* The difficulties faced by the early church can encourage the present-day church. The zeal that took the gospel across ethnic and national boundaries can inspire us today. The Spirit so active in Acts is the same Holy Spirit that currently works in the church.

When did these things happen?

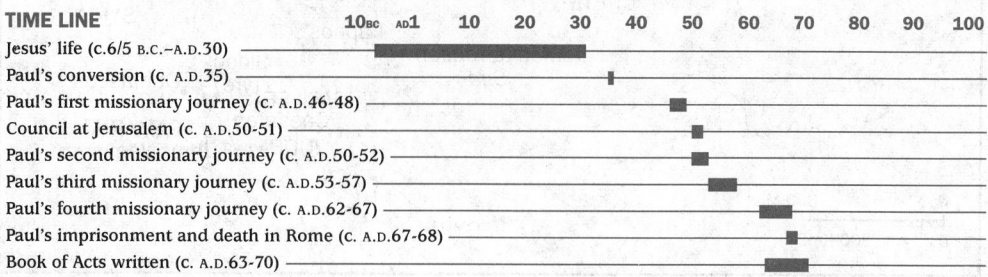

TIME LINE	10 B.C.	A.D. 1	10	20	30	40	50	60	70	80	90	100
Jesus' life (c.6/5 B.C.–A.D.30)												
Paul's conversion (c. A.D.35)												
Paul's first missionary journey (c. A.D.46-48)												
Council at Jerusalem (c. A.D.50-51)												
Paul's second missionary journey (c. A.D.50-52)												
Paul's third missionary journey (c. A.D.53-57)												
Paul's fourth missionary journey (c. A.D.62-67)												
Paul's imprisonment and death in Rome (c. A.D.67-68)												
Book of Acts written (c. A.D.63-70)												

Jesus Taken Up Into Heaven

1 In my former book, Theophilus, I wrote about all that Jesus began to do and to teach ²until the day he was taken up to heaven, after giving instructions through the Holy Spirit to the apostles^D he had chosen. ³After his suffering, he showed himself to these men and gave many convincing proofs that he was alive. He appeared to them over a period of forty days and spoke about the kingdom of God^D. ⁴On one occasion, while he was eating with them, he gave them this command: "Do not leave Jerusalem^D, but wait for the gift my Father promised, which you have heard me speak about. ⁵For John baptized with^a water, but in a few days you will be baptized with the Holy Spirit."

⁶So when they met together, they asked him, "Lord, are you at this time going to restore the kingdom to Israel?"

⁷He said to them: "It is not for you to know the times or dates the Father has set by his own authority. ⁸But you will receive power when the Holy Spirit comes on you; and you will be my witnesses in Jerusalem, and in all Judea and Samaria, and to the ends of the earth."

⁹After he said this, he was taken up before their very eyes, and a cloud hid him from their sight.

¹⁰They were looking intently up into the sky as he was going, when suddenly two men dressed in white stood beside them. ¹¹"Men of Galilee," they said, "why do you stand here looking into the sky? This same Jesus, who has been taken from you into heaven, will come back in the same way you have seen him go into heaven."

^a5 Or in

Does God use a marketing plan? (1:8)

Was the phrase *Judea and Samaria, and to the ends of the earth* a prediction of a scattered church or instructions on how to reach the world? Both. When the disciples obeyed Jesus' instructions to wait for the Holy Spirit, the stage was set for the supernatural events that followed. The church that was scattered by persecution (8:1) was a church that witnessed. The shock waves rippled out from Jerusalem through the known world until Paul reached Rome (ch. 28). Throughout the book Luke shows how the gospel overcame all barriers step by step.

Why the dramatic exit? (1:9)

Christ had prepared his disciples for his eventual departure. But they still had not grasped the significance of all he had taught them (v. 6). Jesus' ascension into the cloud may have been the final lesson for them—a vivid object lesson that he was leaving the physical world and returning to spiritual realms. His extraordinary departure helped the disciples to see Jesus of Nazareth as the Christ of heaven.

How will Christ come? (1:11)

What does it mean that he will come *in the same way* he left? Christ's return will be both unexpected and dramatic, just as his departure was. Scripture clearly states that Jesus will one day return to this earth (see Luke 12:37,40; 1 Thes. 4:15–17; Titus 2:13).

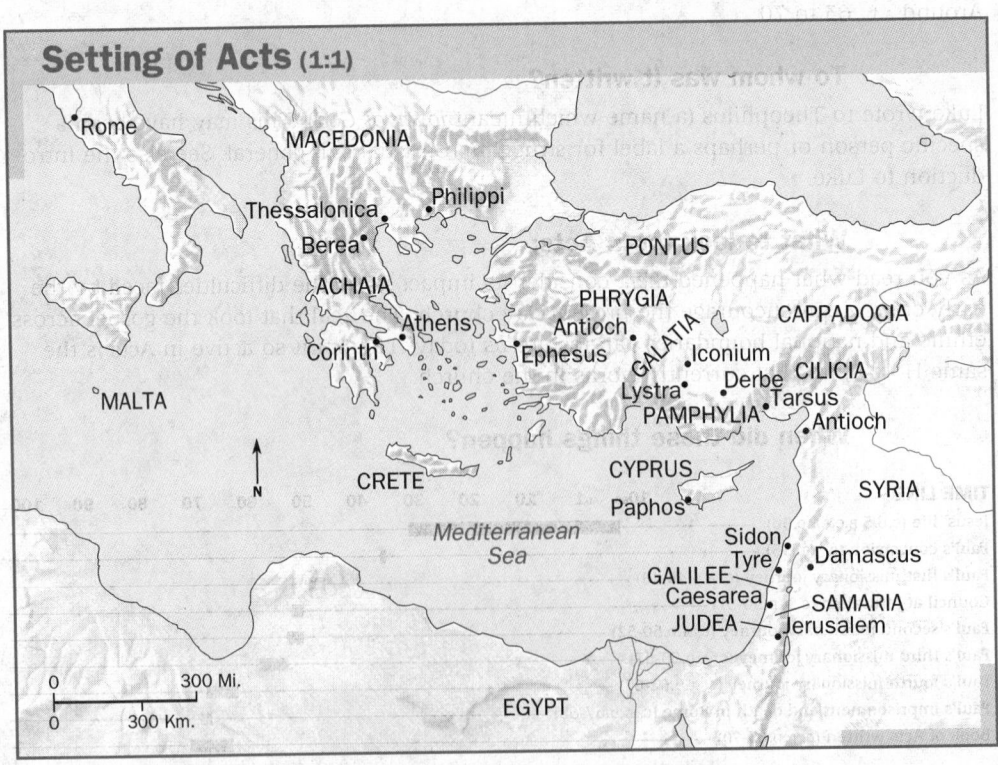

Setting of Acts (1:1)

- Rome
- MACEDONIA
- Thessalonica
- Philippi
- Berea
- ACHAIA
- PONTUS
- PHRYGIA
- Antioch
- Athens
- GALATIA
- CAPPADOCIA
- Corinth
- Ephesus
- Iconium
- Derbe
- CILICIA
- Lystra
- Tarsus
- PAMPHYLIA
- Antioch
- MALTA
- CRETE
- CYPRUS
- SYRIA
- Paphos
- Mediterranean Sea
- Sidon
- Tyre
- Damascus
- GALILEE
- Caesarea
- SAMARIA
- JUDEA
- Jerusalem
- EGYPT
- N
- 0   300 Mi.
- 0   300 Km.

Matthias Chosen to Replace Judas

[12] Then they returned to Jerusalem[D] from the hill called the Mount of Olives, a Sabbath[D] day's walk[a] from the city. [13] When they arrived, they went upstairs to the room where they were staying. Those present were Peter, John, James and Andrew; Philip and Thomas, Bartholomew and Matthew; James son of Alphaeus and Simon the Zealot, and Judas son of James. [14] They all joined together constantly in prayer, along with the women and Mary the mother of Jesus, and with his brothers.

[15] In those days Peter stood up among the believers[b] (a group numbering about a hundred and twenty) [16] and said, "Brothers, the Scripture had to be fulfilled which the Holy Spirit spoke long ago through the mouth of David concerning Judas, who served as guide for those who arrested Jesus— [17] he was one of our number and shared in this ministry."

[18] (With the reward he got for his wickedness, Judas bought a field; there he fell headlong, his body burst open and all his intestines spilled out. [19] Everyone in Jerusalem heard about this, so they called that field in their language Akeldama, that is, Field of Blood.)

[20] "For," said Peter, "it is written in the book of Psalms,

" 'May his place be deserted;
  let there be no one to dwell in it,'[c]

and,

" 'May another take his place of leadership.'[d]

[21] Therefore it is necessary to choose one of the men who have been with us the whole time the Lord Jesus went in and out among us, [22] beginning from John's baptism[D] to the time when Jesus was taken up from us. For one of these must become a witness with us of his resurrection[D]."

[23] So they proposed two men: Joseph called Barsabbas (also known as Justus) and Matthias. [24] Then they prayed, "Lord, you know everyone's heart. Show us which of these two you have chosen [25] to take over this apostolic ministry, which Judas left to go where he belongs." [26] Then they cast lots, and the lot fell to Matthias; so he was added to the eleven apostles[D].

The Holy Spirit Comes at Pentecost

2 When the day of Pentecost came, they were all together in one place. [2] Suddenly a sound like the blowing of a violent wind came from heaven and filled the whole house where they were sitting. [3] They saw what seemed to be tongues of fire that separated and came to rest on each of them. [4] All of them were filled with the Holy Spirit and began to speak in other tongues[e] as the Spirit enabled them.

[5] Now there were staying in Jerusalem God-fearing Jews[D] from every nation under heaven. [6] When they heard this sound, a crowd came together in bewilderment, because each one heard them speaking in his own language. [7] Utterly amazed, they asked: "Are not all these men who are speaking Galileans? [8] Then how is it that each of us hears them in his own native language? [9] Par-

How did Judas die? (1:18–19)

Matthew says he hung himself (Matt. 27:5); Luke says he fell down and burst. The graphic details in Acts may describe what happened sometime after Judas hung himself, when his decomposed body was cut down or disintegrated from decay.

Whatever happened to Matthias? (1:26)

Although we know of no specific accomplishments by Matthias, we should not assume he did nothing. We know nothing about the actions of several of the Twelve. But why all the fuss about choosing a successor to take Judas's place? Apostles, as eyewitnesses to Jesus' ministry (Luke 1:1–4), ensured the accuracy of the gospel during the critical first days of the church. Today we can be confident we have the truth because God planned for men like Matthias to be guardians of the Word.

Why use a lottery to pick an apostle? (1:26)

Jewish people had long believed God used events of random chance to reveal his will, since he controlled all of life (Prov. 16:33). So they used sticks, marked pebbles and the Urim and the Thummim (Exodus 28:30) to cast lots. Not only did God never condemn the practice, he encouraged it in the Old Testament (Lev. 16:8; Prov. 18:18). This incident, however, is the last occasion that lots were cast in the Bible. Following the outpouring of the Holy Spirit, God communicated more directly to his people.

Could this happen again? (2:2–4)

Some believe what happened on the day of Pentecost was unique—it happened only once, they say, and we should not expect it to be repeated. Others claim it can happen again in a personal way to those who surrender to God's Spirit. Specific features of the outpouring of the Holy Spirit never occurred again in Scripture precisely the same as in Acts 2. The gifts of the Spirit, however, are mentioned in some of the New Testament letters (Romans 12:6–8; 1 Cor. 12:1–11; 1 Peter 4:10).

---

[a]12 That is, about 3/4 mile (about 1,100 meters)   [b]15 Greek brothers   [c]20 Psalm 69:25   [d]20 Psalm 109:8   [e]4 Or languages; also in verse 11

thians, Medes and Elamites; residents of Mesopotamia, Judea and Cappadocia, Pontus and Asia, [10]Phrygia and Pamphylia, Egypt and the parts of Libya near Cyrene; visitors from Rome [11](both Jews[D] and converts to Judaism); Cretans and Arabs—we hear them declaring the wonders of God in our own tongues!" [12]Amazed and perplexed, they asked one another, "What does this mean?"

[13]Some, however, made fun of them and said, "They have had too much wine.[a]"

How did some confuse foreign languages with drunken babbling? (2:12–13)

That's the way it often is. What we hear and see often depends upon our point of view. Some of Jesus' early critics charged that he was a glutton and a drunkard who partied with sinners and other undesirables (Luke 7:34). Their bias confused holy joy for public drunkenness. Those same charges were leveled against Jesus' disciples at Pentecost.

Hadn't God's Spirit come to people before this? (2:17)

In the Old Testament God's Spirit was given in a restricted sense—to priests and various selected individuals for special purposes. The uniqueness of Pentecost was that now God's spirit was poured out on all believers—*sons and daughters, young* and *old*. This event was a significant turning point in the history of the early church.

What happened to the moon of blood and the darkened sun? (2:19–20)

As Peter attempted to interpret what was happening, he recalled the prophecy of Joel (Joel 2:28–32). Joel's poetic language described the mysterious and wonderful works of God which defy literal description. His images and symbols predicted cataclysmic changes in heaven and on earth. We should also realize that the *last days* have not yet ended; we may yet see the sun darkened and the moon turned to "blood." See also **When will the moon turn to blood?** (Joel 2:30–32) and **Last days** (2 Tim. 3:1).

Peter Addresses the Crowd

[14]Then Peter stood up with the Eleven, raised his voice and addressed the crowd: "Fellow Jews and all of you who live in Jerusalem[D], let me explain this to you; listen carefully to what I say. [15]These men are not drunk, as you suppose. It's only nine in the morning! [16]No, this is what was spoken by the prophet[D] Joel:

> [17]" 'In the last days, God says,
>   I will pour out my Spirit on all people.
> Your sons and daughters will prophesy,
>   your young men will see visions[D],
>   your old men will dream dreams.
> [18]Even on my servants, both men and women,
>   I will pour out my Spirit in those days,
>   and they will prophesy.
> [19]I will show wonders in the heaven above
>   and signs on the earth below,
>   blood and fire and billows of smoke.
> [20]The sun will be turned to darkness
>   and the moon to blood

[a]13 Or sweet wine

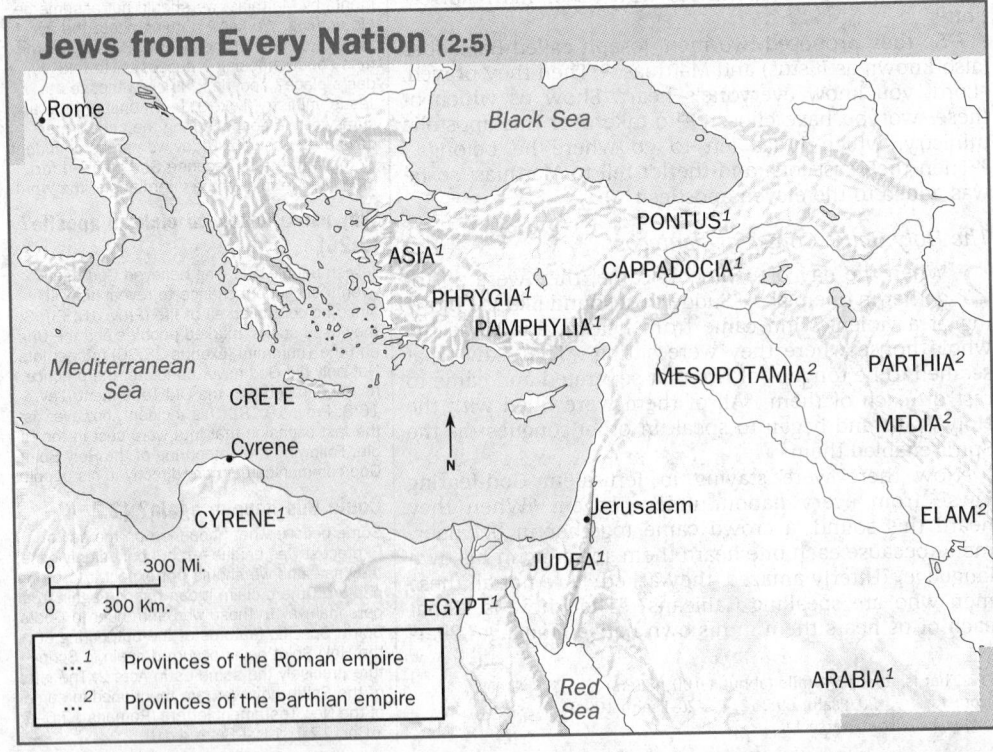

Jews from Every Nation (2:5)

Rome

Black Sea

PONTUS[1]

ASIA[1]

CAPPADOCIA[1]

PHRYGIA[1]

PAMPHYLIA[1]

MESOPOTAMIA[2]

PARTHIA[2]

Mediterranean Sea

CRETE

MEDIA[2]

Cyrene

N

CYRENE[1]

Jerusalem

ELAM[2]

0   300 Mi.

0   300 Km.

JUDEA[1]

EGYPT[1]

Red Sea

ARABIA[1]

...[1]   Provinces of the Roman empire

...[2]   Provinces of the Parthian empire

before the coming of the great and glorious
day of the Lord.^{D}
^{21}And everyone who calls
on the name of the Lord will be saved.'^{a}

^{22}"Men of Israel, listen to this: Jesus of Nazareth was a
man accredited by God to you by miracles, wonders and
signs, which God did among you through him, as you
yourselves know. ^{23}This man was handed over to you by
God's set purpose and foreknowledge; and you, with the
help of wicked men,^{b} put him to death^D by nailing him
to the cross. ^{24}But God raised him from the dead, freeing
him from the agony of death, because it was impossible
for death to keep its hold on him. ^{25}David said about
him:

" 'I saw the Lord always before me.
Because he is at my right hand,
I will not be shaken.
^{26}Therefore my heart is glad and my tongue
rejoices;
my body also will live in hope,
^{27}because you will not abandon me to the grave,
nor will you let your Holy One see decay.
^{28}You have made known to me the paths of life;
you will fill me with joy in your presence.'^{c}

^{29}"Brothers, I can tell you confidently that the patri-
arch^D David died and was buried, and his tomb is here to
this day. ^{30}But he was a prophet^D and knew that God had
promised him on oath that he would place one of his
descendants on his throne. ^{31}Seeing what was ahead, he
spoke of the resurrection^D of the Christ,^{d} that he was
not abandoned to the grave, nor did his body see decay.
^{32}God has raised this Jesus to life, and we are all witnesses
of the fact. ^{33}Exalted to the right hand of God, he has received from the Father the promised Holy Spirit and has
poured out what you now see and hear. ^{34}For David did
not ascend to heaven, and yet he said,

" 'The Lord said to my Lord:
"Sit at my right hand
^{35}until I make your enemies
a footstool^D for your feet." '^{e}

^{36}"Therefore let all Israel be assured of this: God has
made this Jesus, whom you crucified, both Lord and
Christ."

^{37}When the people heard this, they were cut to the
heart and said to Peter and the other apostles^D, "Brothers, what shall we do?"

^{38}Peter replied, "Repent^D and be baptized, every one of
you, in the name of Jesus Christ for the forgiveness of
your sins. And you will receive the gift of the Holy Spirit.
^{39}The promise is for you and your children and for all
who are far off—for all whom the Lord our God will call."

^{40}With many other words he warned them; and he
pleaded with them, "Save yourselves from this corrupt
generation." ^{41}Those who accepted his message were
baptized, and about three thousand were added to their
number that day.

^{a}21 Joel 2:28-32 ^{b}23 Or *of those not having the law* (that is,
Gentiles) ^{c}28 Psalm 16:8-11 ^{d}31 Or *Messiah*. "The Christ"
(Greek) and "the Messiah" (Hebrew) both mean "the Anointed One";
also in verse 36. ^{e}35 Psalm 110:1

Did God cause the crucifixion? (2:23)
In a sense, yes. *God's set purpose* was to save
the world by giving his Son as a sacrifice. Ironically, he used *the help of wicked men*. After the
resurrection the believers discovered that God
had overcome the injustice and cruelty of the
cross by his power and love. God transformed
evil into good; the crucifixion led to our salvation.

The Lord said to my Lord (2:34)
Though this appears confusing at first reading,
its meaning is highly significant. The first *Lord*
refers to God, and the second to another king
that David is recognizing, his Messiah. See *The
LORD says to my Lord* (Psalm 110:1). There are
many New Testament references to this important quotation from David, including several by
Jesus himself. See *Why did Jesus' question
stump the Pharisees?* (Matt. 22:45).

Repent and be baptized (2:38–39)
To *repent* means *to turn from*—to change the
direction of one's life. Turning from sin and
selfishness, a believer follows God with trust
and obedience. Baptism is an act that symbolizes this change. It pictures becoming clean
from sin and emerging a new person in Christ.
Being *baptized* identifies a person with Christ
and his followers.

Did the first Christians live communally? (2:44-45)

See *Did the first Christians live communally?* (4:32-37).

Why would Christians worship in a Jewish temple? (3:1)

Luke shows Jesus' early followers to be faithful Jews as well. Jesus fulfilled God's promises to Israel—showing God's faithfulness, not his rejection. So the temple, the center of Jewish religious life, remained a place of worship for the first Christians. They often met there for what were the later traditional Jewish prayer times, 9:00 a.m., 3:00 p.m. and sunset.

Why did Peter *command* healing rather than pray for it? (3:6)

Peter expected God to heal this man, but he didn't command God to do it. He did, however, tell the man how *he* should respond to God's miracle. Because this man had been crippled all his life, Peter told him what was necessary to make healing a reality for him. Then Peter helped him to his feet. The man would never have received God's healing if he had not responded in faith.

Is ignorance any excuse? (3:14-15,17)

Had the people known Jesus was the Christ, Peter suggested, they might not have helped to kill him. But whether they knew or not, they had committed a terrible sin and needed to repent (v. 19). We are accountable for sin, but the Good News gives us hope of forgiveness. God's mercy can cover all our sins, whether done deliberately or in ignorance.

SCRIPTURE LINK (3:18)

Some of the prophecies foretelling the suffering of the Messiah can be found in Psalm 22 and Isaiah 50:6; 53.

The Fellowship of the Believers

42They devoted themselves to the apostles'ᴰ teaching and to the fellowship, to the breaking of bread and to prayer. **43**Everyone was filled with awe, and many wonders and miraculous signs were done by the apostles. **44**All the believers were together and had everything in common. **45**Selling their possessions and goods, they gave to anyone as he had need. **46**Every day they continued to meet together in the temple courts. They broke bread in their homes and ate together with glad and sincere hearts, **47**praising God and enjoying the favor of all the people. And the Lord added to their number daily those who were being saved.

Peter Heals the Crippled Beggar

3 One day Peter and John were going up to the temple at the time of prayer—at three in the afternoon. **2**Now a man crippled from birth was being carried to the temple gate called Beautiful, where he was put every day to beg from those going into the temple courts. **3**When he saw Peter and John about to enter, he asked them for money. **4**Peter looked straight at him, as did John. Then Peter said, "Look at us!" **5**So the man gave them his attention, expecting to get something from them.

6Then Peter said, "Silver or gold I do not have, but what I have I give you. In the name of Jesus Christ of Nazareth, walk." **7**Taking him by the right hand, he helped him up, and instantly the man's feet and ankles became strong. **8**He jumped to his feet and began to walk. Then he went with them into the temple courts, walking and jumping, and praising God. **9**When all the people saw him walking and praising God, **10**they recognized him as the same man who used to sit begging at the temple gate called Beautiful, and they were filled with wonder and amazement at what had happened to him.

Peter Speaks to the Onlookers

11While the beggar held on to Peter and John, all the people were astonished and came running to them in the place called Solomon's Colonnade. **12**When Peter saw this, he said to them: "Men of Israel, why does this surprise you? Why do you stare at us as if by our own power or godliness we had made this man walk? **13**The God of Abraham, Isaac and Jacob, the God of our fathers, has glorified his servant Jesus. You handed him over to be killed, and you disowned him before Pilate, though he had decided to let him go. **14**You disowned the Holy and Righteousᴰ One and asked that a murderer be released to you. **15**You killed the author of life, but God raised him from the dead. We are witnesses of this. **16**By faith in the name of Jesus, this man whom you see and know was made strong. It is Jesus' name and the faith that comes through him that has given this complete healing to him, as you can all see.

17"Now, brothers, I know that you acted in ignorance, as did your leaders. **18**But this is how God fulfilled what he had foretold through all the prophetsᴰ, saying that his Christᵃ would suffer. **19**Repentᴰ, then, and turn to God, so that your sins may be wiped out, that times of refreshing may come from the Lord, **20**and that he may send the Christ, who has been appointed for you—even Jesus. **21**He

---

ᵃ*18 Or Messiah;* also in verse 20

tles[D] continued to testify to the resurrection[D] of the Lord Jesus, and much grace[D] was upon them all. **34**There were no needy persons among them. For from time to time those who owned lands or houses sold them, brought the money from the sales **35**and put it at the apostles' feet, and it was distributed to anyone as he had need.

36Joseph, a Levite[D] from Cyprus, whom the apostles called Barnabas (which means Son of Encouragement), **37**sold a field he owned and brought the money and put it at the apostles' feet.

Ananias and Sapphira

5 Now a man named Ananias, together with his wife Sapphira, also sold a piece of property. **2**With his wife's full knowledge he kept back part of the money for himself, but brought the rest and put it at the apostles' feet.

3Then Peter said, "Ananias, how is it that Satan has so filled your heart that you have lied to the Holy Spirit and have kept for yourself some of the money you received for the land? **4**Didn't it belong to you before it was sold? And after it was sold, wasn't the money at your disposal? What made you think of doing such a thing? You have not lied to men but to God."

5When Ananias heard this, he fell down and died. And great fear seized all who heard what had happened. **6**Then the young men came forward, wrapped up his body, and carried him out and buried him.

7About three hours later his wife came in, not knowing what had happened. **8**Peter asked her, "Tell me, is this the price you and Ananias got for the land?"

"Yes," she said, "that is the price."

9Peter said to her, "How could you agree to test the Spirit of the Lord? Look! The feet of the men who buried your husband are at the door, and they will carry you out also."

10At that moment she fell down at his feet and died. Then the young men came in and, finding her dead, carried her out and buried her beside her husband. **11**Great fear seized the whole church and all who heard about these events.

The Apostles Heal Many

12The apostles performed many miraculous signs and wonders among the people. And all the believers used to meet together in Solomon's Colonnade. **13**No one else dared join them, even though they were highly regarded by the people. **14**Nevertheless, more and more men and women believed in the Lord and were added to their number. **15**As a result, people brought the sick into the streets and laid them on beds and mats so that at least Peter's shadow might fall on some of them as he passed by. **16**Crowds gathered also from the towns around Jerusalem[D], bringing their sick and those tormented by evil[a] spirits, and all of them were healed.

The Apostles Persecuted

17Then the high priest[D] and all his associates, who were members of the party of the Sadducees[D], were filled with jealousy. **18**They arrested the apostles and

[a]16 Greek *unclean*

Why did Ananias and Sapphira deserve death for one lie? (5:5,10)
If all who lied were struck down as Ananias and Sapphira were, who would be left? Perhaps this happened because their situation was unique. The young church was extremely vulnerable. Unchecked hypocrisy and deception —always destructive in a church—could have undermined the community of the believers. God's swift, severe judgment helped all to maintain a healthy respect for the truth and for God's power in the church (v. 11).

Why would Christians worship in a Jewish temple? (5:12)
See *Why would Christians worship in a Jewish temple?* (3:1).

How could a shadow heal people? (5:15)
God used many means to heal hurting people. The passing shadow of an apostle was just one. God works in different ways at different times. When people respond in faith to God's work, he can respond in various ways to their needs. We may not often see God healing through shadows, but we can see him at work in other ways: a doctor's kindness, a supportive friend, a charitable agency, a supernatural answer to prayer and so on.

put them in the public jail. **19**But during the night an angel of the Lord opened the doors of the jail and brought them out. **20**"Go, stand in the temple courts," he said, "and tell the people the full message of this new life."

21At daybreak they entered the temple courts, as they had been told, and began to teach the people.

When the high priest[D] and his associates arrived, they called together the Sanhedrin[D]—the full assembly of the elders of Israel—and sent to the jail for the apostles[D]. **22**But on arriving at the jail, the officers did not find them there. So they went back and reported, **23**"We found the jail securely locked, with the guards standing at the doors; but when we opened them, we found no one inside." **24**On hearing this report, the captain of the temple guard and the chief priests were puzzled, wondering what would come of this.

25Then someone came and said, "Look! The men you put in jail are standing in the temple courts teaching the people." **26**At that, the captain went with his officers and brought the apostles. They did not use force, because they feared that the people would stone them.

27Having brought the apostles, they made them appear before the Sanhedrin to be questioned by the high priest. **28**"We gave you strict orders not to teach in this name," he said. "Yet you have filled Jerusalem[D] with your teaching and are determined to make us guilty of this man's blood."

29Peter and the other apostles replied: "We must obey God rather than men! **30**The God of our fathers raised Jesus from the dead—whom you had killed by hanging him on a tree. **31**God exalted him to his own right hand as Prince and Savior that he might give repentance[D] and forgiveness of sins to Israel. **32**We are witnesses of these things, and so is the Holy Spirit, whom God has given to those who obey him."

33When they heard this, they were furious and wanted to put them to death[D]. **34**But a Pharisee[D] named Gamaliel, a teacher of the law, who was honored by all the people, stood up in the Sanhedrin and ordered that the men be put outside for a little while. **35**Then he addressed them: "Men of Israel, consider carefully what you intend to do to these men. **36**Some time ago Theudas appeared, claiming to be somebody, and about four hundred men rallied to him. He was killed, all his followers were dispersed, and it all came to nothing. **37**After him, Judas the Galilean appeared in the days of the census and led a band of people in revolt. He too was killed, and all his followers were scattered. **38**Therefore, in the present case I advise you: Leave these men alone! Let them go! For if their purpose or activity is of human origin, it will fail. **39**But if it is from God, you will not be able to stop these men; you will only find yourselves fighting against God."

40His speech persuaded them. They called the apostles in and had them flogged. Then they ordered them not to speak in the name of Jesus, and let them go.

41The apostles left the Sanhedrin, rejoicing because they had been counted worthy of suffering disgrace for the Name. **42**Day after day, in the temple courts and from house to house, they never stopped teaching and proclaiming the good news that Jesus is the Christ.[a]

Who were these revolutionaries? (5:36–38)

They were Jewish patriots who inspired their followers to try overthrowing the Romans by force. Neither succeeded, although some of Judas the Galilean's influence may have persisted among the Jewish Zealots. Gamaliel and the council thought these early Christians were perhaps nothing more than another revolutionary group. Throughout Acts, Christians were often regarded by the authorities as a threat to the political status quo.

How smart was Gamaliel's rule of thumb? (5:38–39)

It depends. Sometimes we are forced to make a decision and take immediate action. Other times we can afford to wait and see what God is doing. Still, success alone does not necessarily indicate God's approval. We may see something that lasts a lifetime as a permanent success; God sees things differently. Faith, patience and insight all can help us grasp God's perspective.

Why rejoice about *suffering disgrace*? (5:41)

The apostles worried less about looking respectable and more about being faithful. Their focus was on eternal things, not temporary, superficial things. The desire to appear respectable to others can hinder a person from effectively pleasing God. To put it another way: it is a great credit if the world discredits someone for an uncompromised commitment to God!

---

*a*42 Or *Messiah*

The Choosing of the Seven

6 In those days when the number of disciples^D was increasing, the Grecian Jews^D among them complained against the Hebraic Jews because their widows were being overlooked in the daily distribution of food. ²So the Twelve gathered all the disciples together and said, "It would not be right for us to neglect the ministry of the word of God in order to wait on tables. ³Brothers, choose seven men from among you who are known to be full of the Spirit and wisdom. We will turn this responsibility over to them ⁴and will give our attention to prayer and the ministry of the word."

⁵This proposal pleased the whole group. They chose Stephen, a man full of faith and of the Holy Spirit; also Philip, Procorus, Nicanor, Timon, Parmenas, and Nicolas from Antioch, a convert to Judaism. ⁶They presented these men to the apostles^D, who prayed and laid their hands on them.

⁷So the word of God spread. The number of disciples in Jerusalem^D increased rapidly, and a large number of priests^D became obedient to the faith.

Stephen Seized

⁸Now Stephen, a man full of God's grace^D and power, did great wonders and miraculous signs among the people. ⁹Opposition arose, however, from members of the Synagogue of the Freedmen (as it was called)—Jews of Cyrene and Alexandria as well as the provinces of Cilicia and Asia. These men began to argue with Stephen, ¹⁰but they could not stand up against his wisdom or the Spirit by whom he spoke.

¹¹Then they secretly persuaded some men to say, "We have heard Stephen speak words of blasphemy^D against Moses and against God."

¹²So they stirred up the people and the elders and the teachers of the law. They seized Stephen and brought him before the Sanhedrin^D. ¹³They produced false witnesses, who testified, "This fellow never stops speaking against this holy place and against the law. ¹⁴For we have heard him say that this Jesus of Nazareth will destroy this place and change the customs Moses handed down to us."

¹⁵All who were sitting in the Sanhedrin looked intently at Stephen, and they saw that his face was like the face of an angel.

Stephen's Speech to the Sanhedrin

7 Then the high priest asked him, "Are these charges true?"

²To this he replied: "Brothers and fathers, listen to me! The God of glory^D appeared to our father Abraham while he was still in Mesopotamia, before he lived in Haran. ³'Leave your country and your people,' God said, 'and go to the land I will show you.'^a

⁴"So he left the land of the Chaldeans and settled in Haran. After the death^D of his father, God sent him to this land where you are now living. ⁵He gave him no inheritance here, not even a foot of ground. But God promised him that he and his descendants after him would possess the land, even though at that time Abraham had no child. ⁶God spoke to him in this way: 'Your descendants will be strangers in a country not their own, and they will be en-

What caused such tension between believers? (6:1)

Conflict between these two groups was likely fueled by raw emotions. The Grecian Jews spoke a different language and had a different cultural background than the Hebraic Jews. The Grecian Jews had no interest in Jewish customs. They had probably lived at one time in Greece or Macedonia and were influenced by that culture (see *Setting of Acts* on page 1504). Some of them may have been Greek converts to Judaism. The church, led by Hebrews, wisely bridged the gap by appointing Greek-speaking leaders to minister to Greek-speaking believers (v. 3).

Why pick on Stephen? (6:9)

A dispute erupted between Stephen and members of the Synagogue of the Freedmen, probably a congregation made up of former slaves. Stephen had apparently insisted that true worship no longer required temple rites. These former slaves, finally back in their ancestral home, did not take kindly to threats against traditional Judaism. So they distorted his words to sound like a direct attack against the law and God (vv. 11,13–14).

What does an angel's face look like? (6:15)

Angels are messengers from God. The Bible frequently describes those who come from God's presence as having shining faces. Stephen brought a message from God when he told the council about Jesus. Little wonder that, for those who heard and understood his testimony that day, Stephen looked like an angel. Perhaps Luke was aware of some irony as he wrote: the one accused of changing the customs of Moses had a face that shined like Moses' (see Exodus 34:29).

Where did Luke get the details of Stephen's speech? (7:2–53)

Luke likely drew from several resources. He may have talked to some who had heard Stephen or perhaps others who heard the story and retold it. Before Scripture was written down, it was carefully passed on as oral tradition. The story of the church's first martyr would have been an important story to the church.

^a3 Gen. 12:1

slaved and mistreated four hundred years. [7]But I will punish the nation they serve as slaves,' God said, 'and afterward they will come out of that country and worship me in this place.'[a] [8]Then he gave Abraham the covenant[D] of circumcision[D]. And Abraham became the father of Isaac and circumcised[D] him eight days after his birth. Later Isaac became the father of Jacob, and Jacob became the father of the twelve patriarchs[D].

[9]"Because the patriarchs were jealous of Joseph, they sold him as a slave into Egypt. But God was with him [10]and rescued him from all his troubles. He gave Joseph wisdom and enabled him to gain the goodwill of Pharaoh king of Egypt; so he made him ruler over Egypt and all his palace.

[11]"Then a famine struck all Egypt and Canaan, bringing great suffering, and our fathers could not find food. [12]When Jacob heard that there was grain in Egypt, he sent our fathers on their first visit. [13]On their second visit, Joseph told his brothers who he was, and Pharaoh learned about Joseph's family. [14]After this, Joseph sent for his father Jacob and his whole family, seventy-five in all. [15]Then Jacob went down to Egypt, where he and our fathers died. [16]Their bodies were brought back to Shechem and placed in the tomb that Abraham had bought from the sons of Hamor at Shechem for a certain sum of money.

[17]"As the time drew near for God to fulfill his promise to Abraham, the number of our people in Egypt greatly increased. [18]Then another king, who knew nothing about Joseph, became ruler of Egypt. [19]He dealt treacherously with our people and oppressed our forefathers by forcing them to throw out their newborn babies so that they would die.

[20]"At that time Moses was born, and he was no ordinary child.[b] For three months he was cared for in his father's house. [21]When he was placed outside, Pharaoh's daughter took him and brought him up as her own son. [22]Moses was educated in all the wisdom of the Egyptians and was powerful in speech and action.

[23]"When Moses was forty years old, he decided to visit his fellow Israelites. [24]He saw one of them being mistreated by an Egyptian, so he went to his defense and avenged[D] him by killing the Egyptian. [25]Moses thought that his own people would realize that God was using him to rescue them, but they did not. [26]The next day Moses came upon two Israelites who were fighting. He tried to reconcile them by saying, 'Men, you are brothers; why do you want to hurt each other?'

[27]"But the man who was mistreating the other pushed Moses aside and said, 'Who made you ruler and judge over us? [28]Do you want to kill me as you killed the Egyptian yesterday?'[c] [29]When Moses heard this, he fled to Midian, where he settled as a foreigner and had two sons.

[30]"After forty years had passed, an angel appeared to Moses in the flames of a burning bush in the desert near Mount Sinai. [31]When he saw this, he was amazed at the sight. As he went over to look more closely, he heard the Lord's voice: [32]'I am the God of your fathers, the God of Abraham, Isaac and Jacob.'[d] Moses trembled with fear and did not dare to look.

[33]"Then the Lord said to him, 'Take off your sandals;

[a]7 Gen. 15:13,14   [b]20 Or *was fair in the sight of God*
[c]28 Exodus 2:14   [d]32 Exodus 3:6

the place where you are standing is holy ground. **34**I have indeed seen the oppression of my people in Egypt. I have heard their groaning and have come down to set them free. Now come, I will send you back to Egypt.'*a*

35"This is the same Moses whom they had rejected with the words, 'Who made you ruler and judge?' He was sent to be their ruler and deliverer by God himself, through the angel who appeared to him in the bush. **36**He led them out of Egypt and did wonders and miraculous signs in Egypt, at the Red Sea*b* and for forty years in the desert.

37"This is that Moses who told the Israelites, 'God will send you a prophet*D* like me from your own people.'*c* **38**He was in the assembly in the desert, with the angel who spoke to him on Mount Sinai, and with our fathers; and he received living words to pass on to us.

39"But our fathers refused to obey him. Instead, they rejected him and in their hearts turned back to Egypt. **40**They told Aaron, 'Make us gods who will go before us. As for this fellow Moses who led us out of Egypt—we don't know what has happened to him!'*d* **41**That was the time they made an idol*D* in the form of a calf. They brought sacrifices*D* to it and held a celebration in honor of what their hands had made. **42**But God turned away and gave them over to the worship of the heavenly bodies. This agrees with what is written in the book of the prophets:

> " 'Did you bring me sacrifices and offerings
>   forty years in the desert, O house of Israel?
> **43**You have lifted up the shrine of Molech*D*
>   and the star of your god Rephan,
>   the idols you made to worship.
> Therefore I will send you into exile*D*'*e* beyond
>   Babylon.

44"Our forefathers had the tabernacle*D* of the Testimony with them in the desert. It had been made as God directed Moses, according to the pattern he had seen. **45**Having received the tabernacle, our fathers under Joshua brought it with them when they took the land from the nations God drove out before them. It remained in the land until the time of David, **46**who enjoyed God's favor and asked that he might provide a dwelling place for the God of Jacob.*f* **47**But it was Solomon who built the house for him.

48"However, the Most High does not live in houses made by men. As the prophet says:

> **49**" 'Heaven is my throne,
>   and the earth is my footstool*D*.
> What kind of house will you build for me?
>   says the Lord.
> Or where will my resting place be?
> **50**Has not my hand made all these things?'*g*

51"You stiff-necked people, with uncircumcised*D* hearts and ears! You are just like your fathers: You always resist the Holy Spirit! **52**Was there ever a prophet your fathers did not persecute? They even killed those who predicted the coming of the Righteous*D* One. And now you have betrayed and murdered him— **53**you who have

a34 Exodus 3:5,7,8,10   *b36* That is, Sea of Reeds
c37 Deut. 18:15   *d40* Exodus 32:1   *e43* Amos 5:25-27
f46 Some early manuscripts *the house of Jacob*   *g50* Isaiah 66:1,2

A prophet (7:37)

Many Jews considered this prophet to be Joshua, but Moses was also describing the coming Messiah (Deut. 18:15), the one sent by God to save and lead his people.

Stiff-necked . . . uncircumcised hearts (7:51)

The prophets characterized Israel as wayward oxen that would stiffen their necks and refuse to be directed. Similar metaphors were *an unruly calf* (Jer. 31:18), *a stubborn heifer* (Hosea 4:16), *breaking one's yoke* (Jer. 2:20) and *uncircumcised hearts* (Jer. 4:4). Stephen used a Scriptural image to show them how they were rejecting the fulfillment of prophecy. Also see *Stiff-necked* (Neh. 9:16); *How does the Spirit circumcise a heart?* (Romans 2:28–29) and *What does it mean to circumcise your hearts?* (Jer. 4:4).

Why wasn't Stephen more diplomatic? (7:51–53)

Perhaps he could have been. But in view of his accusers' prejudice, it's doubtful the outcome would have been any different. Fights within a family can be especially bitter and this was a fight within the family of Israel. Tempers on both sides flared and fierce words were exchanged. Stephen probably felt his message was too important and too urgent to be sugarcoated.

Why did they gnash their teeth? (7:54)

Gnashing one's teeth (that is, grinding them together) was an expression of deep inner distress in that culture. Stephen used the Scriptures to make harsh accusations against Israel. His hearers reacted with great rage, realizing that he had used their own Scriptures to accuse them.

Why could they stone Stephen but not execute Jesus? (7:57–59)

The Sanhedrin handed Jesus over to Pilate for judgment because of the type of accusations they brought against him (John 18:31–35). Yet, they may have been permitted to stone those accused of religious crimes. The charge against Jesus was insurrection against Rome —a political crime that called for crucifixion, the Roman method of execution. Stephen was charged with insurrection against Moses, a religious crime.

Was Saul one of Stephen's killers? (7:58)

Luke introduces Saul as a conspirator in the death of Stephen, though not an active murderer. Saul stood on the sidelines, holding the garments of Stephen's accusers. According to the law, accusers were required to throw the first stones. Some think Saul may have served as a herald, announcing the crime of the accused to passers-by. Later Saul would take a more active role in the persecution of Christians (see 9:1–2).

Why should God forgive those who don't repent? (7:60)

No one is forgiven against his or her own will. But Stephen was following Christ's example, praying that his murderers would find salvation. Stephen's prayer may have contributed to Saul's later conversion, although Saul had to repent and turn to God to receive forgiveness (see ch. 9). Also see **Why did Jesus pray for his captors' forgiveness?** (Luke 23:34).

Why weren't the apostles scattered? (8:1)

The Jewish authorities undoubtedly put pressure on the apostles as well as the whole church. They probably felt that if they could weaken the leaders of this movement, they could affect everyone in it. This perhaps would explain why the apostles chose to remain in Jerusalem despite the obvious danger. Because Jerusalem had long been Israel's leading center, the apostles may have felt compelled to stay where they could have the most influence. They may have gone into hiding since their persecutors would not have intentionally ignored them.

Philip's Journeys (8:5)

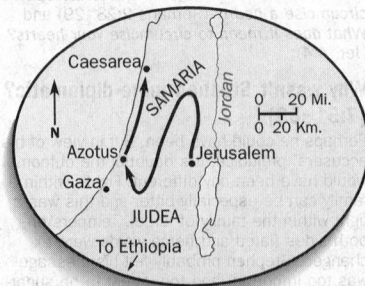

received the law that was put into effect through angels but have not obeyed it."

The Stoning of Stephen

54When they heard this, they were furious and gnashed their teeth at him. **55**But Stephen, full of the Holy Spirit, looked up to heaven and saw the glory[D] of God, and Jesus standing at the right hand of God. **56**"Look," he said, "I see heaven open and the Son of Man[D] standing at the right hand of God."

57At this they covered their ears and, yelling at the top of their voices, they all rushed at him, **58**dragged him out of the city and began to stone him. Meanwhile, the witnesses laid their clothes at the feet of a young man named Saul.

59While they were stoning him, Stephen prayed, "Lord Jesus, receive my spirit." **60**Then he fell on his knees and cried out, "Lord, do not hold this sin against them." When he had said this, he fell asleep.

8 And Saul was there, giving approval to his death[D].

The Church Persecuted and Scattered

On that day a great persecution broke out against the church at Jerusalem[D], and all except the apostles[D] were scattered throughout Judea and Samaria. **2**Godly men buried Stephen and mourned deeply for him. **3**But Saul began to destroy the church. Going from house to house, he dragged off men and women and put them in prison.

Philip in Samaria

4Those who had been scattered preached the word wherever they went. **5**Philip went down to a city in Samaria and proclaimed the Christ[a] there. **6**When the crowds heard Philip and saw the miraculous signs he did, they all paid close attention to what he said. **7**With shrieks, evil[b] spirits came out of many, and many paralytics and cripples were healed. **8**So there was great joy in that city.

Simon the Sorcerer

9Now for some time a man named Simon had practiced sorcery[D] in the city and amazed all the people of Samaria. He boasted that he was someone great, **10**and all the people, both high and low, gave him their attention and exclaimed, "This man is the divine power known as the Great Power." **11**They followed him because he had amazed them for a long time with his magic. **12**But when they believed Philip as he preached the good news of the kingdom of God[D] and the name of Jesus Christ, they were baptized, both men and women. **13**Simon himself believed and was baptized. And he followed Philip everywhere, astonished by the great signs and miracles he saw.

14When the apostles in Jerusalem heard that Samaria had accepted the word of God, they sent Peter and John to them. **15**When they arrived, they prayed for them that they might receive the Holy Spirit, **16**because the Holy Spirit had not yet come upon any of them; they had simply been baptized into[c] the name of the Lord Jesus. **17**Then Peter and John placed their hands on them, and they received the Holy Spirit.

18When Simon saw that the Spirit was given at the lay-

a5 Or Messiah   b7 Greek unclean   c16 Or in

ing on of the apostles'D hands, he offered them money
19and said, "Give me also this ability so that everyone on
whom I lay my hands may receive the Holy Spirit."

20Peter answered: "May your money perish with you,
because you thought you could buy the gift of God with
money! 21You have no part or share in this ministry, because your heart is not right before God. 22RepentD of
this wickedness and pray to the Lord. Perhaps he will forgive you for having such a thought in your heart. 23For I
see that you are full of bitterness and captive to sin."

24Then Simon answered, "Pray to the Lord for me so
that nothing you have said may happen to me."

25When they had testified and proclaimed the word of
the Lord, Peter and John returned to JerusalemD, preaching the gospelD in many Samaritan villages.

Philip and the Ethiopian

26Now an angel of the Lord said to Philip, "Go south to
the road—the desert road—that goes down from Jerusalem to Gaza." 27So he started out, and on his way he met
an Ethiopiana eunuchD, an important official in charge
of all the treasury of Candace, queen of the Ethiopians.
This man had gone to Jerusalem to worship, 28and on
his way home was sitting in his chariot reading the book
of Isaiah the prophetD. 29The Spirit told Philip, "Go to
that chariot and stay near it."

30Then Philip ran up to the chariot and heard the man
reading Isaiah the prophet. "Do you understand what
you are reading?" Philip asked.

31"How can I," he said, "unless someone explains it to
me?" So he invited Philip to come up and sit with him.

32The eunuch was reading this passage of Scripture:

"He was led like a sheep to the slaughter,
    and as a lamb before the shearer is silent,
    so he did not open his mouth.
33In his humiliation he was deprived of justice.
    Who can speak of his descendants?
    For his life was taken from the earth."b

34The eunuch asked Philip, "Tell me, please, who is

a27 That is, from the upper Nile region   b33 Isaiah 53:7,8

Did Simon possess actual power? (8:9–11)

Sorcerers in the first century included a wide
array of spiritualists, con artists, magicians,
astrologers and showmen who earned a living
with their abilities. Whether Simon's powers
were occultic or natural illusions, they were
clearly inferior to the power of the Holy Spirit.
Simon, however, confused the power of the
Spirit with a stronger version of his own kind of
powers. But the Holy Spirit's power—power in
the name of Jesus—was radically different
from his. See the story of another sorcerer
(13:6–12).

How could baptized believers not have the Holy Spirit? (8:14–17)

The Samaritans were apparently baptized with
little or no mention of the Holy Spirit. Some
think this shows that life-changing encounters
with the Holy Spirit can occur even after initial
faith in Christ. Others, however, believe this
merely shows the link between the Spirit and
baptism: the Spirit was given soon after baptism when Peter and John arrived and prayed
over the Samaritans. Also see *Baptize . . .
with the Holy Spirit and with fire* (Matt. 3:11)
and *What is baptism with the Holy Spirit?*
(Luke 3:16).

What did Simon want? (8:18–19)

As a sorcerer, Simon was in the power business. He didn't care what the source of his
power was as long as he could have it. Spiritual, occultic or magical powers were all the
same to Simon—they were a means to earn a
living, commodities to be bought and sold.
When he witnessed the power of the Spirit, unleashed when the apostles placed their hands
on people, Simon wanted to purchase that
power to add to his arsenal. But the Holy Spirit
is a gift, not merchandise to be bought and
sold to the highest bidder, even for the best of
purposes.

Why would a foreigner go to Jerusalem to worship? (8:27)

God-fearing Gentiles sometimes traveled to Jerusalem to worship, even though
they could only enter the outer courts of the temple. Wealthy rulers of foreign
lands sometimes sent gifts to the temple, hoping to gain the favor of Israel's God. Some
even asked that sacrifices be made in their behalf.

Though we don't know how this Ethiopian might have gained possession of a scroll of
Isaiah—a rare and expensive thing in those days—we do know he was intrigued about
Israel's religion (see 13:50). But he was excluded for two reasons: not only was he a foreigner, he was also a eunuch (see Deut. 23:1). He could only stand in the outer court
hoping for a glimpse inside.

However, Isaiah's prophecy offered a way inside. Philip explained about the Suffering
Servant—Jesus. God had already prepared his heart. He quickly accepted the truth of the
gospel and asked to be baptized. Surprisingly, they found water in the desert, and Philip
baptized him (vv. 36–38).

Why did Peter say *perhaps* Simon would be forgiven? (8:22)

Forgiveness, like the Holy Spirit, is a gift of God. The church and church leaders like Peter do not forgive sins, although they can pronounce God's forgiveness of sin. Forgiveness is God's to give, not ours. Peter implied that Simon's forgiveness hinged upon Simon's own attitude. If he would truly repent, he could receive forgiveness as a gift from God. See *Can we set people free from their sin?* (Matt. 18:18) and article: *Can Christians forgive others' sins?* (John 20:23).

What happened when the Spirit suddenly took Philip away? (8:39–40)

The unusual language has led some to think this was a miracle that instantly transported Philip from one place to another. Just as the risen Christ appeared and then suddenly disappeared (1:9; Luke 24:51), perhaps the same mysterious, earth-defying power was also at work in Philip. Others think this was just an elaborate way of saying the Spirit suddenly led Philip away. However it happened, God brought Philip to another place.

How could the Jewish Sanhedrin have any authority in a Gentile city? (9:1–2)

The Sanhedrin governed only religious matters —restricted even in Jerusalem where the Romans maintained control. But the Sanhedrin, as council for all the synagogues throughout the world, could give orders to Jewish congregations even in cities far beyond the borders of Israel. A contemporary analogy might be a decision made by a church denomination that would reach churches in various lands.

Saul in Damascus (9:3)

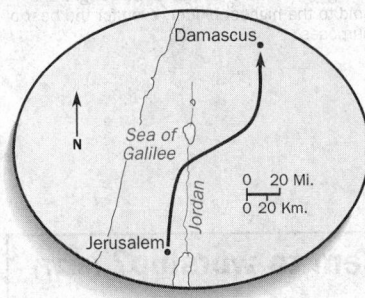

Why would God recruit someone who was fighting against him? (9:5–6)

Why not pick someone who wanted to help? We can only guess why God sovereignly chose to halt Christianity's chief opponent and transform him into its primary proponent (v. 15). God could have used anyone, but it may be that he chose *Saul* as a prime example of what grace could do (1 Tim. 1:16).

the prophet^D talking about, himself or someone else?" **35**Then Philip began with that very passage of Scripture and told him the good news about Jesus.

36As they traveled along the road, they came to some water and the eunuch^D said, "Look, here is water. Why shouldn't I be baptized?"*ᵃ* **38**And he gave orders to stop the chariot. Then both Philip and the eunuch went down into the water and Philip baptized him. **39**When they came up out of the water, the Spirit of the Lord suddenly took Philip away, and the eunuch did not see him again, but went on his way rejoicing. **40**Philip, however, appeared at Azotus and traveled about, preaching the gospel^D in all the towns until he reached Caesarea.

Saul's Conversion

9 Meanwhile, Saul was still breathing out murderous threats against the Lord's disciples^D. He went to the high priest^D **2**and asked him for letters to the synagogues in Damascus, so that if he found any there who belonged to the Way, whether men or women, he might take them as prisoners to Jerusalem^D. **3**As he neared Damascus on his journey, suddenly a light from heaven flashed around him. **4**He fell to the ground and heard a voice say to him, "Saul, Saul, why do you persecute me?"

5"Who are you, Lord?" Saul asked.

"I am Jesus, whom you are persecuting," he replied. **6**"Now get up and go into the city, and you will be told what you must do."

7The men traveling with Saul stood there speechless; they heard the sound but did not see anyone. **8**Saul got up from the ground, but when he opened his eyes he could see nothing. So they led him by the hand into Damascus. **9**For three days he was blind, and did not eat or drink anything.

10In Damascus there was a disciple named Ananias. The Lord called to him in a vision^D, "Ananias!"

"Yes, Lord," he answered.

11The Lord told him, "Go to the house of Judas on Straight Street and ask for a man from Tarsus named Saul, for he is praying. **12**In a vision he has seen a man named Ananias come and place his hands on him to restore his sight."

13"Lord," Ananias answered, "I have heard many reports about this man and all the harm he has done to your saints^D in Jerusalem. **14**And he has come here with authority from the chief priests to arrest all who call on your name."

15But the Lord said to Ananias, "Go! This man is my chosen instrument to carry my name before the Gentiles^D and their kings and before the people of Israel. **16**I will show him how much he must suffer for my name."

17Then Ananias went to the house and entered it. Placing his hands on Saul, he said, "Brother Saul, the Lord— Jesus, who appeared to you on the road as you were coming here—has sent me so that you may see again and be filled with the Holy Spirit." **18**Immediately, something like scales fell from Saul's eyes, and he could see again. He got up and was baptized, **19**and after taking some food, he regained his strength.

---

*ᵃ*36 Some late manuscripts *baptized?" 37Philip said, "If you believe with all your heart, you may." The eunuch answered, "I believe that Jesus Christ is the Son of God."*

Saul in Damascus and Jerusalem

Saul spent several days with the disciples[D] in Damascus. [20]At once he began to preach in the synagogues that Jesus is the Son of God. [21]All those who heard him were astonished and asked, "Isn't he the man who raised havoc in Jerusalem[D] among those who call on this name? And hasn't he come here to take them as prisoners to the chief priests[D]?" [22]Yet Saul grew more and more powerful and baffled the Jews[D] living in Damascus by proving that Jesus is the Christ.[a]

[23]After many days had gone by, the Jews conspired to kill him, [24]but Saul learned of their plan. Day and night they kept close watch on the city gates in order to kill him. [25]But his followers took him by night and lowered him in a basket through an opening in the wall.

[26]When he came to Jerusalem, he tried to join the disciples, but they were all afraid of him, not believing that he really was a disciple. [27]But Barnabas took him and brought him to the apostles[D]. He told them how Saul on his journey had seen the Lord and that the Lord had spoken to him, and how in Damascus he had preached fearlessly in the name of Jesus. [28]So Saul stayed with them and moved about freely in Jerusalem, speaking boldly in the name of the Lord. [29]He talked and debated with the Grecian Jews, but they tried to kill him. [30]When the brothers learned of this, they took him down to Caesarea and sent him off to Tarsus.

[31]Then the church throughout Judea, Galilee and Samaria enjoyed a time of peace[D]. It was strengthened; and encouraged by the Holy Spirit, it grew in numbers, living in the fear of the Lord.

Aeneas and Dorcas

[32]As Peter traveled about the country, he went to visit the saints[D] in Lydda. [33]There he found a man named Aeneas, a paralytic who had been bedridden for eight years. [34]"Aeneas," Peter said to him, "Jesus Christ heals you. Get up and take care of your mat." Immediately Aeneas got up. [35]All those who lived in Lydda and Sharon saw him and turned to the Lord.

[36]In Joppa[D] there was a disciple named Tabitha (which, when translated, is Dorcas[b]), who was always doing good and helping the poor. [37]About that time she became sick and died, and her body was washed and placed in an upstairs room. [38]Lydda was near Joppa; so when the disciples heard that Peter was in Lydda, they sent two men to him and urged him, "Please come at once!"

[39]Peter went with them, and when he arrived he was taken upstairs to the room. All the widows stood around him, crying and showing him the robes and other clothing that Dorcas had made while she was still with them. [40]Peter sent them all out of the room; then he got down on his knees and prayed. Turning toward the dead woman, he said, "Tabitha, get up." She opened her eyes, and seeing Peter she sat up. [41]He took her by the hand and helped her to her feet. Then he called the believers and the widows and presented her to them alive. [42]This became known all over Joppa, and many people believed

If Saul was so convincing, why did they want to kill him? (9:22,29)

Saul was a "turncoat" in their minds. He had been their main weapon against the Christians, but now he had become a Christian himself! His unthinkable act prevented them from seriously considering his words. Overwhelmed by their feelings, they responded irrationally. They refused to listen to logic; all they heard was an enemy.

How dangerous was Saul's escape? (9:25)

Saul's escape was dangerous on two counts. First, he risked getting caught by a murderous mob. To avoid getting caught, Paul escaped under cover of darkness. But that created a second problem. In the darkness Saul could have fallen and been severely injured or even killed. The walls of ancient cities like Damascus were often quite tall, typically built at the top of a hill to protect the city from attack. We don't know how high this wall was, but it could have been several stories.

Saul in Tarsus (9:30)

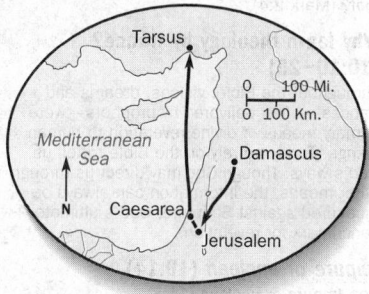

Why did Peter send the people out of the room before doing the miracle? (9:40)

The widows and others whom Dorcas had befriended were probably making such a huge commotion in their great grief that Peter had to send them to another room in order to pray intently.

---

[a]22 Or Messiah   [b]36 Both Tabitha (Aramaic) and Dorcas (Greek) mean gazelle.

A tanner (9:43)

It's significant that Peter stayed with a man whose occupation involved turning animal hides into leather. Contact with dead animals was considered "unclean" by Jewish law. Perhaps God was preparing Peter for his dramatic dream (10:9–23), which helped him understand more clearly what God considers clean and unclean.

What would be a centurion's equivalent rank in today's military? (10:1)

A centurion was a Roman army officer in charge of 100 soldiers, roughly the equivalent of a captain in the United States Army. Cornelius was the centurion in charge of the Roman garrison in Caesarea.

Why go up on a roof to pray? (10:9)

Houses at this time were built with flat roofs, and outside stairways provided easy access to them. It may have been a good place for Peter to go for solitude while the meal was being prepared. Also see *Did these men destroy the roof?* (Mark 2:4).

Why learn theology by trance? (10:10–20)

Throughout the Bible, visions, dreams and trances—often delivered by prophets—were primary means of divine revelation to human beings. Today we rely on the Bible to tell us God's ways. Though God may direct us through other means, the information can always be measured against Scripture, God's ultimate benchmark for revelation.

Impure or unclean (10:14)

See *Impure or unclean* (11:8).

Peter in Caesarea (10:24)

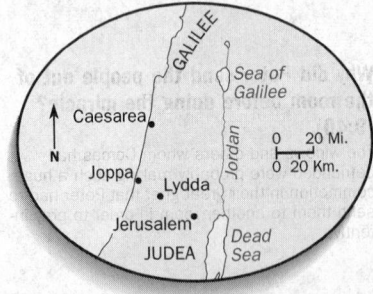

in the Lord. **43**Peter stayed in Joppa[D] for some time with a tanner named Simon.

Cornelius Calls for Peter

10 At Caesarea there was a man named Cornelius, a centurion[D] in what was known as the Italian Regiment. **2**He and all his family were devout and God-fearing; he gave generously to those in need and prayed to God regularly. **3**One day at about three in the afternoon he had a vision[D]. He distinctly saw an angel of God, who came to him and said, "Cornelius!"

4Cornelius stared at him in fear. "What is it, Lord?" he asked.

The angel answered, "Your prayers and gifts to the poor have come up as a memorial offering before God. **5**Now send men to Joppa to bring back a man named Simon who is called Peter. **6**He is staying with Simon the tanner, whose house is by the sea."

7When the angel who spoke to him had gone, Cornelius called two of his servants and a devout soldier who was one of his attendants. **8**He told them everything that had happened and sent them to Joppa.

Peter's Vision

9About noon the following day as they were on their journey and approaching the city, Peter went up on the roof to pray. **10**He became hungry and wanted something to eat, and while the meal was being prepared, he fell into a trance. **11**He saw heaven opened and something like a large sheet being let down to earth by its four corners. **12**It contained all kinds of four-footed animals, as well as reptiles of the earth and birds of the air. **13**Then a voice told him, "Get up, Peter. Kill and eat."

14"Surely not, Lord!" Peter replied. "I have never eaten anything impure or unclean[D]."

15The voice spoke to him a second time, "Do not call anything impure that God has made clean."

16This happened three times, and immediately the sheet was taken back to heaven.

17While Peter was wondering about the meaning of the vision, the men sent by Cornelius found out where Simon's house was and stopped at the gate. **18**They called out, asking if Simon who was known as Peter was staying there.

19While Peter was still thinking about the vision, the Spirit said to him, "Simon, three[a] men are looking for you. **20**So get up and go downstairs. Do not hesitate to go with them, for I have sent them."

21Peter went down and said to the men, "I'm the one you're looking for. Why have you come?"

22The men replied, "We have come from Cornelius the centurion. He is a righteous and God-fearing man, who is respected by all the Jewish people. A holy angel told him to have you come to his house so that he could hear what you have to say." **23**Then Peter invited the men into the house to be his guests.

Peter at Cornelius' House

The next day Peter started out with them, and some of the brothers from Joppa went along. **24**The following day he arrived in Caesarea. Cornelius was expecting them

---

[a]19 One early manuscript *two*; other manuscripts do not have the number.

and had called together his relatives and close friends. **25**As Peter entered the house, Cornelius met him and fell at his feet in reverence^D. **26**But Peter made him get up. "Stand up," he said, "I am only a man myself."

27Talking with him, Peter went inside and found a large gathering of people. **28**He said to them: "You are well aware that it is against our law for a Jew^D to associate with a Gentile^D or visit him. But God has shown me that I should not call any man impure or unclean^D. **29**So when I was sent for, I came without raising any objection. May I ask why you sent for me?"

30Cornelius answered: "Four days ago I was in my house praying at this hour, at three in the afternoon. Suddenly a man in shining clothes stood before me **31**and said, 'Cornelius, God has heard your prayer and remembered your gifts to the poor. **32**Send to Joppa^D for Simon who is called Peter. He is a guest in the home of Simon the tanner, who lives by the sea.' **33**So I sent for you immediately, and it was good of you to come. Now we are all here in the presence of God to listen to everything the Lord has commanded you to tell us."

34Then Peter began to speak: "I now realize how true it is that God does not show favoritism **35**but accepts men from every nation who fear him and do what is right. **36**You know the message God sent to the people of Israel, telling the good news of peace^D through Jesus Christ, who is Lord of all. **37**You know what has happened throughout Judea, beginning in Galilee after the baptism^D that John preached— **38**how God anointed^D Jesus of Nazareth with the Holy Spirit and power, and how he went around doing good and healing all who were under the power of the devil, because God was with him.

39"We are witnesses of everything he did in the country of the Jews and in Jerusalem. They killed him by hanging him on a tree, **40**but God raised him from the dead on the third day and caused him to be seen. **41**He was not seen by all the people, but by witnesses whom God had already chosen—by us who ate and drank with him after he rose from the dead. **42**He commanded us to preach to the people and to testify that he is the one whom God appointed as judge of the living and the dead. **43**All the prophets^D testify about him that everyone who believes in him receives forgiveness of sins through his name."

44While Peter was still speaking these words, the Holy Spirit came on all who heard the message. **45**The circumcised^D believers who had come with Peter were astonished that the gift of the Holy Spirit had been poured out even on the Gentiles. **46**For they heard them speaking in tongues^a and praising God.

Then Peter said, **47**"Can anyone keep these people from being baptized with water? They have received the Holy Spirit just as we have." **48**So he ordered that they be baptized in the name of Jesus Christ. Then they asked Peter to stay with them for a few days.

Peter Explains His Actions

11 The apostles^D and the brothers throughout Judea heard that the Gentiles also had received the word of God. **2**So when Peter went up to Jerusalem, the circumcised believers criticized him **3**and said, "You

^a46 Or other languages

Did the vision eliminate Peter's prejudices? (10:28)

Not completely. Later on, Paul had to confront Peter for some lingering problems in his attitude toward the Gentiles (Gal. 2:11–14). But the vision caused a dramatic change in Peter's attitudes and behavior towards non-Jews.

Why did the risen Jesus appear only to those already convinced? (10:41)

The resurrection was so astounding, mysterious and unexpected that it was not something for the masses. They would not have been able to comprehend what they were seeing, nor would they have been able to respond with believing hearts. Christ appeared especially to these individuals so they might be made witnesses. They received an intimate, face-to-face encounter with the risen Christ so they could then go and tell others.

What was so amazing to Peter's friends? (10:45)

What they saw with their eyes, they could not grasp with their minds. They had always been taught that the promises of Scripture were only for God's chosen people. They could not imagine how Gentiles could be made righteous without first becoming Jews. It confused them to see God take the initiative and give the Holy Spirit to the Gentiles *before* they could earn his favor by following the law.

went into the house of uncircumcised[D] men and ate with them."

[4]Peter began and explained everything to them precisely as it had happened: [5]"I was in the city of Joppa[D] praying, and in a trance I saw a vision[D]. I saw something like a large sheet being let down from heaven by its four corners, and it came down to where I was. [6]I looked into it and saw four-footed animals of the earth, wild beasts, reptiles, and birds of the air. [7]Then I heard a voice telling me, 'Get up, Peter. Kill and eat.'

[8]"I replied, 'Surely not, Lord! Nothing impure or unclean[D] has ever entered my mouth.'

[9]"The voice spoke from heaven a second time, 'Do not call anything impure that God has made clean.' [10]This happened three times, and then it was all pulled up to heaven again.

[11]"Right then three men who had been sent to me from Caesarea stopped at the house where I was staying. [12]The Spirit told me to have no hesitation about going with them. These six brothers also went with me, and we entered the man's house. [13]He told us how he had seen an angel appear in his house and say, 'Send to Joppa for Simon who is called Peter. [14]He will bring you a message through which you and all your household will be saved.'

[15]"As I began to speak, the Holy Spirit came on them as he had come on us at the beginning. [16]Then I remembered what the Lord had said: 'John baptized with[a] water, but you will be baptized with the Holy Spirit.' [17]So if God gave them the same gift as he gave us, who believed in the Lord Jesus Christ, who was I to think that I could oppose God?"

[18]When they heard this, they had no further objections and praised God, saying, "So then, God has granted even the Gentiles[D] repentance[D] unto life."

The Church in Antioch

[19]Now those who had been scattered by the persecution in connection with Stephen traveled as far as Phoenicia, Cyprus and Antioch, telling the message only to Jews[D]. [20]Some of them, however, men from Cyprus and Cyrene, went to Antioch and began to speak to Greeks also, telling them the good news about the Lord Jesus. [21]The Lord's hand was with them, and a great number of people believed and turned to the Lord.

[22]News of this reached the ears of the church at Jerusalem[D], and they sent Barnabas to Antioch. [23]When he arrived and saw the evidence of the grace[D] of God, he was glad and encouraged them all to remain true to the Lord with all their hearts. [24]He was a good man, full of the Holy Spirit and faith, and a great number of people were brought to the Lord.

[25]Then Barnabas went to Tarsus to look for Saul, [26]and when he found him, he brought him to Antioch. So for a whole year Barnabas and Saul met with the church and taught great numbers of people. The disciples[D] were called Christians first at Antioch.

[27]During this time some prophets[D] came down from Jerusalem to Antioch. [28]One of them, named Agabus, stood up and through the Spirit predicted that a severe famine would spread over the entire Roman world. (This happened during the reign of Claudius.) [29]The disciples, each according to his ability, decided to provide help for

Why learn theology by trance? (11:5)
See *Why learn theology by trance*? (10:10–20).

Impure or unclean (11:8)
Unacceptable according to dietary restrictions of the law, thought by some to be for health reasons and by others for religious reasons. The Jews gained insight into God's holiness by visual lessons reinforced in their daily diet. See *Why were some things unclean*? (Lev. 5:2) and article: *Why did God keep some meats off the menu*? (Lev. 11:4–41).

Why up until now had they told the Good News *only* to Jews? (11:19)
Their long history of oppression by others and their own religious vacillations had shaped the Jewish mindset. Their determination to survive as a nation led them to keep their distance from all others. Exception to this rule required Gentiles wishing to join the Jewish community to convert to the faith of Israel by being ritually cleansed and, in the case of men, circumcised. Though Jesus had paved the way for changing this exclusive attitude (Matt. 15:11), the church had not yet discovered that because of Christ, ethnic barriers have been dismantled (Gal. 3:28).

Why the new name? (11:26)
We don't know who first coined the label *Christian*. It simply meant someone who was like Christ or belonged to Christ. Christians previously called themselves disciples, believers, saints and brethren. The Jews apparently called them Nazarenes (24:5; Mark 14:67), a slightly derogatory label based on Jesus' hometown, sometimes scorned because of its insignificance (John 1:46).

Why did those in Judea need more help than others? (11:28–30)
Several factors came into play. First, the church in Jerusalem was notoriously poor. Second, Josephus, the Jewish historian, tells of a famine in Judea around A.D. 46 (Claudius's reign lasted from A.D. 41 to 54). Third, though there was a succession of bad harvests and serious famines in various areas, the resulting shortages were not evenly felt throughout the Roman empire.

[a]16 Or *in*

the brothers living in Judea. **30**This they did, sending their gift to the elders by Barnabas and Saul.

Peter's Miraculous Escape From Prison

12 It was about this time that King Herod arrested some who belonged to the church, intending to persecute them. **2**He had James, the brother of John, put to death**D** with the sword. **3**When he saw that this pleased the Jews**D**, he proceeded to seize Peter also. This happened during the Feast of Unleavened Bread. **4**After arresting him, he put him in prison, handing him over to be guarded by four squads of four soldiers each. Herod intended to bring him out for public trial after the Passover.

5So Peter was kept in prison, but the church was earnestly praying to God for him.

6The night before Herod was to bring him to trial, Peter was sleeping between two soldiers, bound with two chains, and sentries stood guard at the entrance. **7**Suddenly an angel of the Lord appeared and a light shone in the cell. He struck Peter on the side and woke him up. "Quick, get up!" he said, and the chains fell off Peter's wrists.

8Then the angel said to him, "Put on your clothes and sandals." And Peter did so. "Wrap your cloak around you and follow me," the angel told him. **9**Peter followed him out of the prison, but he had no idea that what the angel was doing was really happening; he thought he was seeing a vision**D**. **10**They passed the first and second guards and came to the iron gate leading to the city. It opened for them by itself, and they went through it. When they had walked the length of one street, suddenly the angel left him.

11Then Peter came to himself and said, "Now I know without a doubt that the Lord sent his angel and rescued me from Herod's clutches and from everything the Jewish people were anticipating."

12When this had dawned on him, he went to the house of Mary the mother of John, also called Mark, where many people had gathered and were praying. **13**Peter knocked at the outer entrance, and a servant girl named Rhoda came to answer the door. **14**When she recognized Peter's voice, she was so overjoyed she ran back without opening it and exclaimed, "Peter is at the door!"

15"You're out of your mind," they told her. When she

Why did they think angels might knock on doors? (12:15)

Many Jews believed God assigned angels to protect people (Gen. 48:16; Psalm 34:7; Daniel 3:28; 6:22). Some Jews believed a guardian angel could assume the appearance of the person under its charge. The believers in Mary's home may have been humoring Rhoda, thinking she was confused. Or they may have concluded Peter's guardian angel was indeed outside and were too fearful to immediately open the door.

How common is predictive prophecy? (11:27–30)

This prediction was not an isolated incident. Agabus later predicted a future event in Paul's life (21:10–11). Other portions of the book of Acts show or suggest God revealing the future (18:9–11; 27:21–26).

Some believe miracles and prophecies ceased after the deaths of the apostles. Others say spiritual gifts (for example, 1 Cor. 12:28) all remain in force till Christ returns. Of several purposes of prophecy, foretelling the future is not listed as a major factor (1 Cor. 14:3).

Should Christians today imitate what Christians did in the book of Acts? Not necessarily. Acts *describes* what they did without directly *prescribing* we do the same. Further factors to consider are: (1) what the rest of the New Testament teaches and (2) how the historical circumstances parallel our own.

What caused Herod's dispute with Tyre and Sidon? (12:20)

The shipping and commercial industries of the coastal cities of Tyre and Sidon traded throughout the Mediterranean (see *Map 10* at the back of this Bible). They also traded with Palestine for their food supply. Their quarrel was most likely over commerce. Herod probably believed they had failed to fulfill a contract.

Did worms kill Herod? (12:23)

The word Luke used for *eaten by worms* was a word that medical writers of that period used to describe intestinal tapeworms. The most likely explanation is that when struck by the angel, Herod ruptured an intestinal cyst containing watery fluid and tapeworm larvae. The Jewish historian Josephus wrote that Herod was stricken with pains following his speech and died five days later. So Herod was eaten by worms both before and after his death.

Why was John *also called Mark*? (12:25)

Like others, John used two names depending on whom he was dealing with. See *Why was Saul also called Paul?* (13:9). John was his Jewish name, Mark his Greek. He was the cousin of Barnabas and the son of Mary, a prominent member of the early church who hosted church meetings (12:12). John Mark authored the second Gospel.

Tetrarch (13:1)

A ruler who depended on Rome for his power to govern land conquered by the Romans. A paper king, some would call him king as a courtesy. Manaen may have been raised in the court of Herod the Great (Matt. 2:1), perhaps as the foster-brother of Herod the tetrarch (also called Herod Antipas).

Does fasting make prayer more effective? (13:2–3)

Scripture does not spell out what fasting does or how it works. It does, however, show that some people went without food as a spiritual discipline. These verses suggest two possible results of this discipline: (1) To prepare for ministry. Fasting symbolizes our self-sacrificing dedication to God's purposes. (2) To separate ourselves from worldly concerns so we can better focus on our priorities, values and goals. Fasting helps us become more sensitive to God's voice and direction. Also see *What are the benefits of sincere fasting?* (Matt. 6:18) and *Should Christians fast?* (Luke 5:35).

Why place hands on Saul and Barnabas? (13:3)

The laying on of hands is a basic Christian practice (Heb. 6:1–2), suggesting it is more than mere symbolism. Jesus and his disciples didn't do it for show; they did it for the sake of results, touching to connect people with God's power. The power of the Holy Spirit flowed from Jesus' touch (Luke 6:19). The laying on of hands was an ordained means of granting healing (28:8; Mark 6:5), spiritual gifts (8:17; 2 Tim. 1:6) and of commissioning someone to spiritual office (6:6).

Why was Saul also called Paul? (13:9)

Like many Jews, Paul had two names, one Jewish (Saul) and the other Graeco-Roman (Paul). Just as immigrants today sometimes change their names to assimilate with their new land,

kept insisting that it was so, they said, "It must be his angel."

[16]But Peter kept on knocking, and when they opened the door and saw him, they were astonished. [17]Peter motioned with his hand for them to be quiet and described how the Lord had brought him out of prison. "Tell James and the brothers about this," he said, and then he left for another place.

[18]In the morning, there was no small commotion among the soldiers as to what had become of Peter. [19]After Herod had a thorough search made for him and did not find him, he cross-examined the guards and ordered that they be executed.

Herod's Death

Then Herod went from Judea to Caesarea and stayed there a while. [20]He had been quarreling with the people of Tyre and Sidon; they now joined together and sought an audience with him. Having secured the support of Blastus, a trusted personal servant of the king, they asked for peace[D], because they depended on the king's country for their food supply.

[21]On the appointed day Herod, wearing his royal robes, sat on his throne and delivered a public address to the people. [22]They shouted, "This is the voice of a god, not of a man." [23]Immediately, because Herod did not give praise to God, an angel of the Lord struck him down, and he was eaten by worms and died.

[24]But the word of God continued to increase and spread.

[25]When Barnabas and Saul had finished their mission, they returned from[a] Jerusalem[D], taking with them John, also called Mark.

Barnabas and Saul Sent Off

13 In the church at Antioch there were prophets[D] and teachers: Barnabas, Simeon called Niger, Lucius of Cyrene, Manaen (who had been brought up with Herod the tetrarch[D]) and Saul. [2]While they were worshiping the Lord and fasting, the Holy Spirit said, "Set apart for me Barnabas and Saul for the work to which I have called them." [3]So after they had fasted and prayed, they placed their hands on them and sent them off.

On Cyprus

[4]The two of them, sent on their way by the Holy Spirit, went down to Seleucia and sailed from there to Cyprus. [5]When they arrived at Salamis, they proclaimed the word of God in the Jewish synagogues. John was with them as their helper.

[6]They traveled through the whole island until they came to Paphos. There they met a Jewish sorcerer and false prophet named Bar-Jesus, [7]who was an attendant of the proconsul, Sergius Paulus. The proconsul, an intelligent man, sent for Barnabas and Saul because he wanted to hear the word of God. [8]But Elymas the sorcerer (for that is what his name means) opposed them and tried to turn the proconsul from the faith. [9]Then Saul, who was also called Paul, filled with the Holy Spirit, looked straight at Elymas and said, [10]"You are a child of the devil and an enemy of everything that is right! You are full of all kinds of deceit and trickery. Will you never stop perverting the

a25 Some manuscripts *to*

right ways of the Lord? **11**Now the hand of the Lord is against you. You are going to be blind, and for a time you will be unable to see the light of the sun."

Immediately mist and darkness came over him, and he groped about, seeking someone to lead him by the hand. **12**When the proconsul saw what had happened, he believed, for he was amazed at the teaching about the Lord.

In Pisidian Antioch

13From Paphos, Paul and his companions sailed to Perga in Pamphylia, where John left them to return to JerusalemD. **14**From Perga they went on to Pisidian Antioch. On the SabbathD they entered the synagogue and sat down. **15**After the reading from the Law and the ProphetsD, the synagogue rulers sent word to them, saying, "Brothers, if you have a message of encouragement for the people, please speak."

16Standing up, Paul motioned with his hand and said: "Men of Israel and you GentilesD who worship God, listen to me! **17**The God of the people of Israel chose our fathers; he made the people prosper during their stay in Egypt, with mighty power he led them out of that country, **18**he endured their conducta for about forty years in the desert, **19**he overthrew seven nations in Canaan and gave their land to his people as their inheritance. **20**All this took about 450 years.

"After this, God gave them judges until the time of Samuel the prophet. **21**Then the people asked for a king, and he gave them Saul son of Kish, of the tribe of Benjamin, who ruled forty years. **22**After removing Saul, he made David their king. He testified concerning him: 'I have found David son of Jesse a man after my own heart; he will do everything I want him to do.'

23"From this man's descendants God has brought to Israel the Savior Jesus, as he promised. **24**Before the coming of Jesus, John preached repentanceD and baptismD to all the people of Israel. **25**As John was completing his work, he said: 'Who do you think I am? I am not that one. No, but he is coming after me, whose sandals I am not worthy to untie.'

26"Brothers, children of Abraham, and you God-fearing Gentiles, it is to us that this message of salvation has been sent. **27**The people of Jerusalem and their rulers did not recognize Jesus, yet in condemning him they fulfilled the words of the prophets that are read every Sabbath. **28**Though they found no proper ground for a deathD sentence, they asked Pilate to have him executed. **29**When they had carried out all that was written about him, they took him down from the tree and laid him in a tomb. **30**But God raised him from the dead, **31**and for many days he was seen by those who had traveled with him from Galilee to Jerusalem. They are now his witnesses to our people.

32"We tell you the good news: What God promised our fathers **33**he has fulfilled for us, their children, by raising up Jesus. As it is written in the second Psalm:

" 'You are my Son;
     today I have become your Father.b c

34The fact that God raised him from the dead, never to decay, is stated in these words:

so Paul began to use his Graeco-Roman name as his missionary team moved into Gentile territory. He is called *Paul* through the rest of Acts, which probably was his preference since he spoke often about being God's missionary to the Gentiles.

Is it sometimes right to curse someone? (13:11)

The New Testament never tells us to curse others. Nor was Paul in the habit of cursing his opponents. Directed and empowered by the Holy Spirit (v. 9), however, he made an exception here. Luke describes what Paul did, but he doesn't recommend we adopt this method as an evangelistic tool. Jesus tells us to love our enemies and bless those who persecute us (Matt. 5:44). In this case, however, God led Paul to pronounce judgment on Elymas.

Where does God say this in the Old Testament? (13:22)

This part of Paul's message is more a paraphrase than a direct quote from Scripture, probably alluding to 1 Samuel 13:14. This is an example of an Old Testament concept restated in general terms. Other Old Testament passages referred to in the New Testament may read differently because they were translated from Hebrew to Greek before being translated into English.

---

a18 Some manuscripts *and cared for them*   b33 Or *have begotten you*   c33 Psalm 2:7

" 'I will give you the holy and sure blessings
     promised to David.'ª

35So it is stated elsewhere:

" 'You will not let your Holy One see decay.'ᵇ

36"For when David had served God's purpose in his
own generation, he fell asleep; he was buried with his fathers and his body decayed. 37But the one whom God
raised from the dead did not see decay.
38"Therefore, my brothers, I want you to know that
through Jesus the forgiveness of sins is proclaimed to you.
39Through him everyone who believes is justifiedᴰ from
everything you could not be justified from by the law of
Moses. 40Take care that what the prophetsᴰ have said
does not happen to you:

41" 'Look, you scoffers,
        wonder and perish,
     for I am going to do something in your days
        that you would never believe,
        even if someone told you.'ᶜ"

42As Paul and Barnabas were leaving the synagogue,
the people invited them to speak further about these
things on the next Sabbathᴰ. 43When the congregation
was dismissed, many of the Jewsᴰ and devout converts to
Judaism followed Paul and Barnabas, who talked with
them and urged them to continue in the graceᴰ of God.
44On the next Sabbath almost the whole city gathered
to hear the word of the Lord. 45When the Jews saw the
crowds, they were filled with jealousy and talked abusively against what Paul was saying.
46Then Paul and Barnabas answered them boldly: "We
had to speak the word of God to you first. Since you reject
it and do not consider yourselves worthy of eternal lifeᴰ,
we now turn to the Gentilesᴰ. 47For this is what the Lord
has commanded us:

" 'I have made youᵈ a light for the Gentiles,
     that youᵈ may bring salvationᴰ to the ends
        of the earth.'ᵉ"

48When the Gentiles heard this, they were glad and
honored the word of the Lord; and all who were appointed for eternal life believed.
49The word of the Lord spread through the whole region. 50But the Jews incited the God-fearing women of
high standing and the leading men of the city. They
stirred up persecution against Paul and Barnabas, and expelled them from their region. 51So they shook the dust
from their feet in protest against them and went to Iconium. 52And the disciplesᴰ were filled with joy and with
the Holy Spirit.

In Iconium

14 At Iconium Paul and Barnabas went as usual into
the Jewish synagogue. There they spoke so effectively that a great number of Jews and Gentiles believed. 2But the Jews who refused to believe stirred up
the Gentiles and poisoned their minds against the
brothers. 3So Paul and Barnabas spent considerable time
there, speaking boldly for the Lord, who confirmed the

Why were Paul and Barnabas so com-
bative? (13:46)

The Jews had received more guidance and favor from God than any other people on earth
(Romans 9:4–5), yet they had stubbornly rejected God to cling to hollow religious tradition
(Matt. 15:8–9). Jesus himself expressed anger over their stubborn ways, so we shouldn't
be surprised that Paul and Barnabas were upset. Paul may have hoped to stir the Jews to
envy the Gentiles for their salvation (Romans
11:13–14). Paul's angry rejection was a public
statement that the Jews were in the wrong
(see Mark 6:11). Still, he hoped his own Jewish people would eventually repent (Romans
9:2–4; 11:23).

What does *appointed* mean? (13:48)

People generally interpret *all who were appointed for eternal life* in one of three ways: (1) God
in his sovereign goodness makes the appointments. Some have been predestined from all
eternity for eternal life. (2) People have a free
will but cannot exercise it until God prepares
their hearts. God sovereignly works to open human hearts, who then can choose to respond.
(3) God appoints a standard—belief in Jesus.
People have the freedom to choose or reject
God's standard. In this view, those who are appointed are those who believe in Jesus and
meet the requirement set by God.

How much political clout did the Jews
have? (13:50)

Some, but it was mostly unofficial lobbying by
God-fearing Gentiles. Typically these were
thoughtful women, often wives of city dignitaries, disillusioned with the carnal, all-too-human
characteristics of the many Greek and Roman
gods. They found Judaism with its high moral
standards and worship of one God to be an
appealing alternative. Since wealthy matrons
held more influence in Pisidian Antioch than
elsewhere in the empire, the anti-Paul Jews
recruited their help.

ª34 Isaiah 55:3   ᵇ35 Psalm 16:10   ᶜ41 Hab. 1:5   ᵈ47 The
Greek is singular.   ᵉ47 Isaiah 49:6

message of his graceᴰ by enabling them to do miraculous signs and wonders. **4**The people of the city were divided; some sided with the Jewsᴰ, others with the apostlesᴰ. **5**There was a plot afoot among the Gentilesᴰ and Jews, together with their leaders, to mistreat them and stone them. **6**But they found out about it and fled to the Lycaonian cities of Lystra and Derbe and to the surrounding country, **7**where they continued to preach the good news.

In Lystra and Derbe

8In Lystra there sat a man crippled in his feet, who was lame from birth and had never walked. **9**He listened to Paul as he was speaking. Paul looked directly at him, saw that he had faith to be healed **10**and called out, "Stand up on your feet!" At that, the man jumped up and began to walk.

11When the crowd saw what Paul had done, they shouted in the Lycaonian language, "The gods have come down to us in human form!" **12**Barnabas they called Zeus, and Paul they called Hermes because he was the chief speaker. **13**The priestᴰ of Zeus, whose temple was just outside the city, brought bulls and wreaths to the city gates because he and the crowd wanted to offer sacrificesᴰ to them.

14But when the apostles Barnabas and Paul heard of this, they tore their clothes and rushed out into the crowd, shouting: **15**"Men, why are you doing this? We too are only men, human like you. We are bringing you good news, telling you to turn from these worthless things to the living God, who made heaven and earth and sea and everything in them. **16**In the past, he let all nations go their own way. **17**Yet he has not left himself without testimony: He has shown kindness by giving you rain from heaven and crops in their seasons; he provides you with plenty of food and fills your hearts with joy." **18**Even with these words, they had difficulty keeping the crowd from sacrificing to them.

19Then some Jews came from Antioch and Iconium and won the crowd over. They stoned Paul and dragged him outside the city, thinking he was dead. **20**But after the disciplesᴰ had gathered around him, he got up and went back into the city. The next day he and Barnabas left for Derbe.

The Return to Antioch in Syria

21They preached the good news in that city and won a large number of disciples. Then they returned to Lystra, Iconium and Antioch, **22**strengthening the disciples and encouraging them to remain true to the faith. "We must go through many hardships to enter the kingdom of Godᴰ," they said. **23**Paul and Barnabas appointed eldersᵃ for them in each church and, with prayer and fasting, committed them to the Lord, in whom they had put their trust. **24**After going through Pisidia, they came into Pamphylia, **25**and when they had preached the word in Perga, they went down to Attalia. **26**From Attalia they sailed back to Antioch, where they had been committed to the grace of God for the work they had now completed. **27**On arriving there, they gathered the church together and reported all that God had done through them and how he had opened the door of

ᵃ23 Or Barnabas ordained elders; or Barnabas had elders elected

Why would the people stone someone they had wanted to worship? (14:8-20)

The residents of Lystra (see *Setting of Acts* on page 1504) told a tale: Zeus, the ruler of the gods and Hermes, his spokesman, once visited their town. Disguised as ordinary travelers, dusty and tattered, they walked the streets begging for food. Finally a kindly old couple fed them. Zeus and Hermes rewarded them by granting them a wish. When Paul, the spokesman, and Barnabas, probably taller and more imposing, performed this miracle, the citizens concluded Zeus and Hermes had returned—until Paul convinced them he and Barnabas were mere mortals. The jealous Jews played on the disillusionment of the townspeople.

What do hardships have to do with entering the kingdom? (14:22)

Hardships are not the basis, but the consequence of salvation. Those saved (by grace) will suffer the world's hostility.

How were elders selected? (14:23)

In this case, Paul and Barnabas selected elders themselves. Paul also instructed Titus to appoint elders in new churches (Titus 1:5). The word for *appointed*, however, contains the idea of an election—raising hands in a vote—although some do not believe this necessarily meant an election. In Acts 6:1–7, when a mature Christian church chose deacons (not elders), the congregation made the selection.

How had Paul and Barnabas been committed to the grace of God? (14:26)

The church leaders had placed their hands on Paul and Barnabas in a prayer of dedication (see 13:3). In this way they turned them over to the Lord, trusting God to care for and protect them. They also acknowledged that Paul and Barnabas belonged to the Lord so he could accomplish his purposes through them. More than mere symbol, this commitment was an open declaration of their faith in God; Paul and Barnabas willingly surrendered control of their lives to him. Other examples: 15:40; 20:32; 1 Peter 4:19.

Why did some insist on circumcision? (15:1)

Centuries of religious training caused many to have a well-entrenched interpretation of Old Testament law. Though many Jews accepted Jesus as the Messiah, they still found it difficult to abandon what they had always believed. They saw Jesus' ministry as a supplement, not a completion or fulfillment of Old Testament law (see Matt. 5:17). As a result, they could not casually set aside the core of their beliefs. In their view, circumcision remained essential for a relationship with God. Paul's letter to the Galatians addresses this error.

How should Christians settle heated differences? (15:1–35)

The church in Antioch was divided by a sharp dispute: How many of the Old Testament traditions were New Testament Christians expected to follow? The way the church settled this highly controversial issue proved wise: (1) the church sent representatives to recognized and mature church leaders; (2) all sides were given the opportunity to speak; (3) the apostles and elders (the recognized leaders) discussed the issues and their spokesman, James, summarized their conclusions and presented the decision; (4) everyone agreed to abide by the decision; (5) the council sent a written report back to the church in Antioch along with some delegates to explain the decision.

Can religious councils overturn God-given laws? (15:19–21)

Only God can overturn his laws. The apostles recognized that God had established a new covenant. He had unmistakably spoken through Christ. Leaders today do not have the same authority as the apostles, who were the foundation of the church (Eph. 2:20). However, if church leaders come to realize that their practices or beliefs are only man-made traditions that actually conflict with Scripture, then they not only can, but should overturn them.

Why wasn't faith alone enough? (15:20)

Why did the Gentiles have to follow additional requirements? The council had already settled the issue of salvation: it was by grace through faith alone (15:6–11). The four additional requirements had nothing to do with how the Gentiles would be saved; it had everything to do with how they could live and worship with Jewish believers who were particularly offended by these four types of behavior. These instructions were intended to maintain peace and unity in the church.

Why include sexual immorality with dietary restrictions? (15:20)

The Greek and Roman world was filled with pagan religions. To help the Gentiles break with their past and to ease sensitive Jewish consciences, Gentiles were told to cut themselves off from anything related to pagan worship. They were not to eat food offered to idols. Nor were they to participate in pagan religious festivals—often marked by sensual revelry and sexual immorality. These prohibitions were not intended to cover the whole picture of morality. More specific warnings can be found in later New Testament letters.

faith to the Gentiles[D]. **28**And they stayed there a long time with the disciples[D].

The Council at Jerusalem

15 Some men came down from Judea to Antioch and were teaching the brothers: "Unless you are circumcised[D], according to the custom taught by Moses, you cannot be saved." **2**This brought Paul and Barnabas into sharp dispute and debate with them. So Paul and Barnabas were appointed, along with some other believers, to go up to Jerusalem[D] to see the apostles[D] and elders about this question. **3**The church sent them on their way, and as they traveled through Phoenicia and Samaria, they told how the Gentiles had been converted. This news made all the brothers very glad. **4**When they came to Jerusalem, they were welcomed by the church and the apostles and elders, to whom they reported everything God had done through them.

5Then some of the believers who belonged to the party of the Pharisees[D] stood up and said, "The Gentiles must be circumcised and required to obey the law of Moses."

6The apostles and elders met to consider this question. **7**After much discussion, Peter got up and addressed them: "Brothers, you know that some time ago God made a choice among you that the Gentiles might hear from my lips the message of the gospel[D] and believe. **8**God, who knows the heart, showed that he accepted them by giving the Holy Spirit to them, just as he did to us. **9**He made no distinction between us and them, for he purified[D] their hearts by faith. **10**Now then, why do you try to test God by putting on the necks of the disciples a yoke[D] that neither we nor our fathers have been able to bear? **11**No! We believe it is through the grace[D] of our Lord Jesus that we are saved, just as they are."

12The whole assembly became silent as they listened to Barnabas and Paul telling about the miraculous signs and wonders God had done among the Gentiles through them. **13**When they finished, James spoke up: "Brothers, listen to me. **14**Simon[a] has described to us how God at first showed his concern by taking from the Gentiles a people for himself. **15**The words of the prophets[D] are in agreement with this, as it is written:

16" 'After this I will return
    and rebuild David's fallen tent.
  Its ruins I will rebuild,
    and I will restore it,
17that the remnant[D] of men may seek the Lord,
    and all the Gentiles who bear my name,
  says the Lord, who does these things'[b]
18 that have been known for ages.[c]

19"It is my judgment, therefore, that we should not make it difficult for the Gentiles who are turning to God. **20**Instead we should write to them, telling them to abstain from food polluted by idols[D], from sexual immorality, from the meat of strangled animals and from blood. **21**For Moses has been preached in every city from the earliest times and is read in the synagogues on every Sabbath[D]."

*a*14 Greek *Simeon*, a variant of *Simon*; that is, Peter   *b*17 Amos 9:11,12   *c*17,18 Some manuscripts *things'*— / *18known to the Lord for ages is his work*

The Council's Letter to Gentile Believers

22Then the apostles[D] and elders, with the whole church, decided to choose some of their own men and send them to Antioch with Paul and Barnabas. They chose Judas (called Barsabbas) and Silas, two men who were leaders among the brothers. **23**With them they sent the following letter:

The apostles and elders, your brothers,

To the Gentile[D] believers in Antioch, Syria and Cilicia:

Greetings.

24We have heard that some went out from us without our authorization and disturbed you, troubling your minds by what they said. **25**So we all agreed to choose some men and send them to you with our dear friends Barnabas and Paul— **26**men who have risked their lives for the name of our Lord Jesus Christ. **27**Therefore we are sending Judas and Silas to confirm by word of mouth what we are writing. **28**It seemed good to the Holy Spirit and to us not to burden you with anything beyond the following requirements: **29**You are to abstain from food sacrificed to idols[D], from blood, from the meat of strangled animals and from sexual immorality. You will do well to avoid these things.

Farewell.

30The men were sent off and went down to Antioch, where they gathered the church together and delivered the letter. **31**The people read it and were glad for its encouraging message. **32**Judas and Silas, who themselves were prophets[D], said much to encourage and strengthen the brothers. **33**After spending some time there, they were sent off by the brothers with the blessing of peace[D] to return to those who had sent them.[a] **35**But Paul and Barnabas remained in Antioch, where they and many others taught and preached the word of the Lord.

Disagreement Between Paul and Barnabas

36Some time later Paul said to Barnabas, "Let us go back and visit the brothers in all the towns where we preached the word of the Lord and see how they are doing." **37**Barnabas wanted to take John, also called Mark, with them, **38**but Paul did not think it wise to take him, because he had deserted them in Pamphylia and had not continued with them in the work. **39**They had such a sharp disagreement that they parted company. Barnabas took Mark and sailed for Cyprus, **40**but Paul chose Silas and left, commended by the brothers to the grace[D] of the Lord. **41**He went through Syria and Cilicia, strengthening the churches.

Timothy Joins Paul and Silas

16 He came to Derbe and then to Lystra, where a disciple[D] named Timothy lived, whose mother was a Jewess and a believer, but whose father was a Greek. **2**The brothers at Lystra and Iconium spoke well of him. **3**Paul wanted to take him along on the journey, so he cir-

[a]33 Some manuscripts *them*, *34but Silas decided to remain there*

Why would spiritual leaders argue with each other? (15:39)

Paul and Barnabas quarreled partly because they held such passionate convictions about God's will. For Paul, nothing could eclipse the mission of preaching the gospel and building churches. If John Mark jeopardized that mission, he should minister elsewhere. For Barnabas, nicknamed *the son of encouragement* (4:36), the restoration of one sincere Christian worker justified the risk. In a sense, both Paul and Barnabas were right. Yet in another sense, both were wrong: Although they were spiritually mature, Paul and Barnabas allowed anger to influence them.

cumcised[D] him because of the Jews[D] who lived in that area, for they all knew that his father was a Greek. **4**As they traveled from town to town, they delivered the decisions reached by the apostles[D] and elders in Jerusalem[D] for the people to obey. **5**So the churches were strengthened in the faith and grew daily in numbers.

Paul's Vision of the Man of Macedonia

6Paul and his companions traveled throughout the region of Phrygia and Galatia, having been kept by the Holy Spirit from preaching the word in the province of Asia. **7**When they came to the border of Mysia, they tried to enter Bithynia, but the Spirit of Jesus would not allow them to. **8**So they passed by Mysia and went down to Troas. **9**During the night Paul had a vision[D] of a man of Macedonia standing and begging him, "Come over to Macedonia and help us." **10**After Paul had seen the vision, we got ready at once to leave for Macedonia, concluding that God had called us to preach the gospel[D] to them.

Lydia's Conversion in Philippi

11From Troas we put out to sea and sailed straight for Samothrace, and the next day on to Neapolis. **12**From there we traveled to Philippi, a Roman colony and the leading city of that district of Macedonia. And we stayed there several days.

13On the Sabbath[D] we went outside the city gate to the river, where we expected to find a place of prayer. We sat down and began to speak to the women who had gathered there. **14**One of those listening was a woman named Lydia, a dealer in purple[D] cloth from the city of Thyatira, who was a worshiper of God. The Lord opened her heart to respond to Paul's message. **15**When she and the members of her household were baptized, she invited us to her home. "If you consider me a believer in the Lord," she said, "come and stay at my house." And she persuaded us.

Paul and Silas in Prison

16Once when we were going to the place of prayer, we were met by a slave girl who had a spirit by which she predicted the future. She earned a great deal of money for her owners by fortune-telling. **17**This girl followed Paul and the rest of us, shouting, "These men are servants of

---

Why did God silence Paul's preaching? (16:6–10)

It's possible God prevented Paul from preaching in Asia and Bithynia (see **Map 11** at the back of this Bible) so he'd have a better opportunity with greater results. Luke describes God as the cause of Paul's inability to preach, but Luke doesn't identify the immediate cause. Perhaps it was a dream, an inner voice, a prophecy or something as natural as hindering circumstances (see 18:9–11). God, who knows who will believe, may shut one door only to open another. For another view on preaching in spite of obstacles, see 1 Cor. 16:9.

Why baptize a whole household when only one believed? (16:15)

Luke typically focuses on key people in a story, in this case Lydia. But we don't have to assume that the others did not believe. The members of her household—children, servants and other dependents—*probably* followed her example and believed in the Lord. Since it's possible that some in the household had young babies, some see this verse as a precedent for their practice of baptizing infants. Others insist that wherever Scripture gives details, it is those who believe that are baptized.

Why would an evil spirit advertise the competition? (16:17–18)

Most likely to confuse the issue. Pagan religions of the day commonly referred to a *Most High God,* who was just one of their many gods. So the fortune-teller was not necessarily referring to the true God. In addition, coming from the lips of a diviner, her testimony might suggest one could believe in the God Paul preached and yet continue involvement in idolatry and the occult.

Why did Paul circumcise Timothy (16:3; compare 15:10–12)

Paul circumcised Timothy for the sake of effective ministry, not for salvation. Paul's missionary strategy was to go first to the local synagogue and preach to the Jews. If they knew that his main assistant, Timothy, was uncircumcised, they would scorn Paul and disregard his gospel, rejecting the message because of the messenger. In the eyes of the Jews, an uncircumcised man was a spiritual reject. So Paul circumcised Timothy to avoid unnecessary barriers to the gospel.

Paul would not have circumcised Timothy if it would have compromised the gospel to do so. He wrote to the Galatians to argue that those who were circumcised to make themselves acceptable to God were falling away from grace. Paul had passionate convictions about two things: (1) don't let anything compromise the gospel; (2) don't let anything block the advance of the gospel. See 1 Cor. 9:19–23.

the Most High God, who are telling you the way to be saved." **18**She kept this up for many days. Finally Paul became so troubled that he turned around and said to the spirit, "In the name of Jesus Christ I command you to come out of her!" At that moment the spirit left her.

19When the owners of the slave girl realized that their hope of making money was gone, they seized Paul and Silas and dragged them into the marketplace to face the authorities. **20**They brought them before the magistrates and said, "These men are Jews[D], and are throwing our city into an uproar **21**by advocating customs unlawful for us Romans to accept or practice."

22The crowd joined in the attack against Paul and Silas, and the magistrates ordered them to be stripped and beaten. **23**After they had been severely flogged, they were thrown into prison, and the jailer was commanded to guard them carefully. **24**Upon receiving such orders, he put them in the inner cell and fastened their feet in the stocks.

25About midnight Paul and Silas were praying and singing hymns to God, and the other prisoners were listening to them. **26**Suddenly there was such a violent earthquake that the foundations of the prison were shaken. At once all the prison doors flew open, and everybody's chains came loose. **27**The jailer woke up, and when he saw the prison doors open, he drew his sword and was about to kill himself because he thought the prisoners had escaped. **28**But Paul shouted, "Don't harm yourself! We are all here!"

29The jailer called for lights, rushed in and fell trembling before Paul and Silas. **30**He then brought them out and asked, "Sirs, what must I do to be saved?"

31They replied, "Believe in the Lord Jesus, and you will be saved—you and your household." **32**Then they spoke the word of the Lord to him and to all the others in his house. **33**At that hour of the night the jailer took them and washed their wounds; then immediately he and all his family were baptized. **34**The jailer brought them into his house and set a meal before them; he was filled with joy because he had come to believe in God—he and his whole family.

35When it was daylight, the magistrates sent their officers to the jailer with the order: "Release those men." **36**The jailer told Paul, "The magistrates have ordered that you and Silas be released. Now you can leave. Go in peace[D]."

37But Paul said to the officers: "They beat us publicly without a trial, even though we are Roman citizens, and threw us into prison. And now do they want to get rid of us quietly? No! Let them come themselves and escort us out."

38The officers reported this to the magistrates, and when they heard that Paul and Silas were Roman citizens, they were alarmed. **39**They came to appease them and escorted them from the prison, requesting them to leave the city. **40**After Paul and Silas came out of the prison, they went to Lydia's house, where they met with the brothers and encouraged them. Then they left.

In Thessalonica

17 When they had passed through Amphipolis and Apollonia, they came to Thessalonica, where there was a Jewish synagogue. **2**As his custom was, Paul went into the synagogue, and on three Sabbath[D] days he

Since the evil spirit told the truth, why did Paul cast it out? (16:18)

At first Paul may have seen her as nothing more than a temporary distraction or inconvenience. But as days passed her pronouncements attracted increasing attention. Eventually Paul recognized her as a major hindrance and took decisive action. The truth, coming through the wrong source or delivered inappropriately, can lose its effectiveness.

Did Paul and Silas urge people to break the law? (16:21)

Roman law obligated citizens to worship the emperor and the state. Paul called people to worship and serve God alone. To this extent, they were guilty of threatening the practice of emperor worship through their preaching. But clearly the slave girl's owners used these charges as a pretext to stop Paul from interfering with their business interests.

Was Paul being petty? (16:37)

Why did Paul make the magistrates escort him personally out of prison? His motive may have been to gain respect and some measure of protection from the government officials for the Christians who would remain in the city. Having treated him shamefully the day before, the city officials might be more prone to mistreat the church in the future if they succeeded in hustling Paul out of town. Paul didn't want this kind of menacing precedent to go unchallenged. In addition, Paul may have been setting the stage to return someday.

What alarmed the magistrates so much? (16:38–39)

The Roman empire had three classes of people: slaves, aliens and a relatively small group of citizens. Roman citizens had legal rights which gave them preferential treatment and explicitly protected them from torture. See **Why was the commander alarmed that Paul was a Roman citizen?** (22:29). The magistrates' illegal beating gave Paul a reason to protest to Rome. In a sense he held their political futures in his hands.

reasoned with them from the Scriptures, [3]explaining and proving that the Christ[a] had to suffer and rise from the dead. "This Jesus I am proclaiming to you is the Christ,[a]" he said. [4]Some of the Jews[D] were persuaded and joined Paul and Silas, as did a large number of God-fearing Greeks and not a few prominent women.

[5]But the Jews were jealous; so they rounded up some bad characters from the marketplace, formed a mob and started a riot in the city. They rushed to Jason's house in search of Paul and Silas in order to bring them out to the crowd.[b] [6]But when they did not find them, they dragged Jason and some other brothers before the city officials, shouting: "These men who have caused trouble all over the world have now come here, [7]and Jason has welcomed them into his house. They are all defying Caesar's decrees, saying that there is another king, one called Jesus." [8]When they heard this, the crowd and the city officials were thrown into turmoil. [9]Then they made Jason and the others post bond and let them go.

In Berea

[10]As soon as it was night, the brothers sent Paul and Silas away to Berea. On arriving there, they went to the Jewish synagogue. [11]Now the Bereans were of more noble character than the Thessalonians, for they received the message with great eagerness and examined the Scriptures every day to see if what Paul said was true. [12]Many of the Jews believed, as did also a number of prominent Greek women and many Greek men.

[13]When the Jews in Thessalonica learned that Paul was preaching the word of God at Berea, they went there too, agitating the crowds and stirring them up. [14]The brothers immediately sent Paul to the coast, but Silas and Timothy stayed at Berea. [15]The men who escorted Paul brought him to Athens and then left with instructions for Silas and Timothy to join him as soon as possible.

In Athens

[16]While Paul was waiting for them in Athens, he was greatly distressed to see that the city was full of idols[D]. [17]So he reasoned in the synagogue with the Jews and the God-fearing Greeks, as well as in the marketplace day by day with those who happened to be there. [18]A group of Epicurean and Stoic philosophers began to dispute with him. Some of them asked, "What is this babbler trying to say?" Others remarked, "He seems to be advocating foreign gods." They said this because Paul was preaching the good news about Jesus and the resurrection[D]. [19]Then they took him and brought him to a meeting of the Areopagus, where they said to him, "May we know what this new teaching is that you are presenting? [20]You are bringing some strange ideas to our ears, and we want to know what they mean." [21](All the Athenians and the foreigners who lived there spent their time doing nothing but talking about and listening to the latest ideas.)

[22]Paul then stood up in the meeting of the Areopagus and said: "Men of Athens! I see that in every way you are very religious. [23]For as I walked around and looked carefully at your objects of worship, I even found an altar with this inscription: TO AN UNKNOWN GOD. Now what you worship as something unknown I am going to proclaim to you.

Epicureans (17:18)

Believed the gods were inaccessible and the universe came about by chance, not by God's creation. Consequently they saw no purpose, design or absolute good in life and came to value happiness and pleasure, defined as the absence of pain. They did not actually advocate sensuality, but rather those enjoyments that offered the most permanent satisfaction.

Stoics (17:18)

Believed God is everything—the World Soul, the Absolute Reason—something with which no one could have a personal relationship. Logic and reason were high goals for the Stoics; emotions were irrelevant, if not detrimental. Self-control, morality and duty became their premier character virtues, but caused some to develop spiritual pride.

Why did the philosphers call Paul a babbler? (17:18)

Epicureans and Stoics taught the two chief philosophies of the day. They were proud of their ideas, refined over a 300-year period, and looked down on the less elite teachings, peddled for profit on the streets by itinerants. The philosophers had a slang word for common teachers—babblers (literally, seed-pickers: the word pictures sparrows picking up scraps at the marketplace). In their view Paul had picked up bits and pieces of philosophy to market a second-hand, unsophisticated view of life.

Areopagus (17:19)

A combination board of education, think tank and idea clearing-house. Hundreds of years earlier in classical Greece the Areopagus served as the chief judicial body of Athens. Under Rome it still maintained the pulse of Athenian religion and education. Its members could censor ideas but could not convict Paul of a crime.

Why worship an unknown god? (17:23)

People believed disasters and misfortunes were caused by gods who had become offended. To please their volatile gods, they offered sacrifices. Athens may have had many altars to unknown gods scattered throughout the city. Some six centuries earlier, hoping to stave off a terrible epidemic, the Athenians took a flock of sheep to the Areopagus and released them. Wherever a wandering sheep laid down, it was sacrificed on the nearest altar to appease that god. If no altar was nearby, the people built an altar to an unknown god and sacrificed the sheep on it.

a3 Or Messiah   b5 Or the assembly of the people

24"The God who made the world and everything in it is the Lord of heaven and earth and does not live in temples built by hands. **25**And he is not served by human hands, as if he needed anything, because he himself gives all men life and breath and everything else. **26**From one man he made every nation of men, that they should inhabit the whole earth; and he determined the times set for them and the exact places where they should live. **27**God did this so that men would seek him and perhaps reach out for him and find him, though he is not far from each one of us. **28**'For in him we live and move and have our being.' As some of your own poets have said, 'We are his offspring.'

29"Therefore since we are God's offspring, we should not think that the divine being is like gold or silver or stone—an image made by man's design and skill. **30**In the past God overlooked such ignorance, but now he commands all people everywhere to repent[D]. **31**For he has set a day when he will judge the world with justice by the man he has appointed. He has given proof of this to all men by raising him from the dead."

32When they heard about the resurrection[D] of the dead, some of them sneered, but others said, "We want to hear you again on this subject." **33**At that, Paul left the Council. **34**A few men became followers of Paul and believed. Among them was Dionysius, a member of the Areopagus, also a woman named Damaris, and a number of others.

In Corinth

18 After this, Paul left Athens and went to Corinth. **2**There he met a Jew[D] named Aquila, a native of Pontus, who had recently come from Italy with his wife Priscilla, because Claudius had ordered all the Jews to leave Rome. Paul went to see them, **3**and because he was a tentmaker as they were, he stayed and worked with them. **4**Every Sabbath[D] he reasoned in the synagogue, trying to persuade Jews and Greeks.

5When Silas and Timothy came from Macedonia, Paul devoted himself exclusively to preaching, testifying to the Jews that Jesus was the Christ.[a] **6**But when the Jews opposed Paul and became abusive, he shook out his clothes in protest and said to them, "Your blood be on your own heads! I am clear of my responsibility. From now on I will go to the Gentiles[D]."

7Then Paul left the synagogue and went next door to the house of Titius Justus, a worshiper of God. **8**Crispus, the synagogue ruler, and his entire household believed in the Lord; and many of the Corinthians who heard him believed and were baptized.

9One night the Lord spoke to Paul in a vision[D]: "Do not be afraid; keep on speaking, do not be silent. **10**For I am with you, and no one is going to attack and harm you, because I have many people in this city." **11**So Paul stayed for a year and a half, teaching them the word of God.

12While Gallio was proconsul of Achaia, the Jews made a united attack on Paul and brought him into court. **13**"This man," they charged, "is persuading the people to worship God in ways contrary to the law."

14Just as Paul was about to speak, Gallio said to the Jews, "If you Jews were making a complaint about some misdemeanor or serious crime, it would be reason-

Does God overlook our ignorance? (17:30)
God dealt with people according to the revelation he had given them. Paul spoke here to Gentiles, who had been in the dark about God and his hatred of idols. When God revealed himself to the Jews, he forbade idolatry. The Jews were judged thereafter when they worshiped idols. Now, in Christ, God brought light for all. With further revelation comes further responsibility.

Why had Claudius expelled the Jews from Rome? (18:2)
To maintain public order. The preaching of Christ had apparently caused an uproar in the Jewish community there. One Roman historian wrote, "As the Jews were indulging in constant riots at the instigation of Chrestus, he [Claudius] banished them from Rome." Many think he mistook the name Christus for a common slave name, Chrestus.

Why did Paul work as a tentmaker for a living? (18:3)
Since Jewish rabbis were not supposed to charge for teaching the law, most supported themselves with a trade. Paul, trained as a Pharisee, had learned tent-making, or leather work, in his native Cilicia (see *Setting of Acts* on page 1504). There the chief export was a felted cloth made from goats' hair (called *Cilicium* after the name of the region), which was used in making tents. Since he ministered in cities where there were no churches to care for him, Paul supported himself while preaching the gospel.

Did Crispus's conversion cost him his job as synagogue ruler? (18:8,17)
Originally, a qualified leader apparently could be elected as synagogue ruler. In time, however, the office seems generally to have become hereditary. If this was the case, it seems that Crispus was removed from his position due to his newfound sympathies for Christians and his belief that Jesus was the Christ.

---

a 5 Or *Messiah*; also in verse 28

Why mention Paul's haircut? (18:18)
See *What did purification involve?* (21:24).

What was the baptism of John? (18:25)
A confession of sin and repentance (see Matt. 3:6,11). Apollos came from Alexandria in Egypt, where he had perhaps encountered disciples of John carrying the message of repentance from sin. Another possibility is that he'd been taught by believers in Christ who did not know about or did not practice Christian baptism. With the limited communication of those days, Christianity did not develop uniformly from one area to the next. A person can believe in Christ and receive the Spirit before being baptized (10:44–48).

Why could Priscilla teach when other women were restricted? (18:26)
Although Paul later limited the ministry of women (1 Tim. 2:11–14), some feel he was addressing unique circumstances in Timothy's church. They say Paul's restrictions on women were not intended to be universal, as his esteem for Priscilla demonstrated (Romans 16:3–4). Others see no evidence that Timothy's situation was different; they fear current cultural trends have sidestepped Scriptural standards. They also recognize Paul's enthusiasm for the vital involvement of women in the church (see Romans 16:1–16). For a further discussion, see article: *Why silence the women?* (1 Tim. 2:11).

Why wouldn't real disciples know about the Holy Spirit? (19:2)
Even John had taught about the Holy Spirit. But these disciples, living far from Jerusalem, had evidently heard only portions of John's message from travelers. Later they heard fragments about the gospel of Christ. They believed in Christ but had not received basic instruction.

Why didn't Paul baptize in the way Jesus had instructed? (19:5; see Matt. 28:19)
Luke describes the effect of Christian baptism —the person baptized comes under the authority of Jesus. Luke was not giving a standardized formula to be pronounced at baptism. *In the name of* meant *under the authority or influence of*. More important than the formula pronounced over the person being baptized is that person's own confession of faith in Jesus (22:16; Romans 10:10). Also see 2:38; 8:14–16; 10:48.

able for me to listen to you. **15**But since it involves questions about words and names and your own law—settle the matter yourselves. I will not be a judge of such things." **16**So he had them ejected from the court. **17**Then they all turned on Sosthenes the synagogue ruler and beat him in front of the court. But Gallio showed no concern whatever.

Priscilla, Aquila and Apollos

18Paul stayed on in Corinth for some time. Then he left the brothers and sailed for Syria, accompanied by Priscilla and Aquila. Before he sailed, he had his hair cut off at Cenchrea because of a vow[D] he had taken. **19**They arrived at Ephesus, where Paul left Priscilla and Aquila. He himself went into the synagogue and reasoned with the Jews[D]. **20**When they asked him to spend more time with them, he declined. **21**But as he left, he promised, "I will come back if it is God's will." Then he set sail from Ephesus. **22**When he landed at Caesarea, he went up and greeted the church and then went down to Antioch.

23After spending some time in Antioch, Paul set out from there and traveled from place to place throughout the region of Galatia and Phrygia, strengthening all the disciples[D].

24Meanwhile a Jew named Apollos, a native of Alexandria, came to Ephesus. He was a learned man, with a thorough knowledge of the Scriptures. **25**He had been instructed in the way of the Lord, and he spoke with great fervor[a] and taught about Jesus accurately, though he knew only the baptism[D] of John. **26**He began to speak boldly in the synagogue. When Priscilla and Aquila heard him, they invited him to their home and explained to him the way of God more adequately.

27When Apollos wanted to go to Achaia, the brothers encouraged him and wrote to the disciples there to welcome him. On arriving, he was a great help to those who by grace[D] had believed. **28**For he vigorously refuted the Jews in public debate, proving from the Scriptures that Jesus was the Christ.

Paul in Ephesus

19 While Apollos was at Corinth, Paul took the road through the interior and arrived at Ephesus. There he found some disciples **2**and asked them, "Did you receive the Holy Spirit when[b] you believed?"

They answered, "No, we have not even heard that there is a Holy Spirit."

3So Paul asked, "Then what baptism did you receive?"

"John's baptism," they replied.

4Paul said, "John's baptism was a baptism of repentance[D]. He told the people to believe in the one coming after him, that is, in Jesus." **5**On hearing this, they were baptized into[c] the name of the Lord Jesus. **6**When Paul placed his hands on them, the Holy Spirit came on them, and they spoke in tongues[d] and prophesied. **7**There were about twelve men in all.

8Paul entered the synagogue and spoke boldly there for three months, arguing persuasively about the kingdom of God[D]. **9**But some of them became obstinate; they refused to believe and publicly maligned the Way. So Paul left them. He took the disciples with him and had discus-

a25 Or with fervor in the Spirit   *b2 Or after*   *c5 Or in*
d6 Or other languages

sions daily in the lecture hall of Tyrannus. **10**This went on for two years, so that all the Jews^D and Greeks who lived in the province of Asia heard the word of the Lord.

11God did extraordinary miracles through Paul, **12**so that even handkerchiefs and aprons that had touched him were taken to the sick, and their illnesses were cured and the evil spirits left them.

13Some Jews who went around driving out evil spirits tried to invoke the name of the Lord Jesus over those who were demon-possessed. They would say, "In the name of Jesus, whom Paul preaches, I command you to come out." **14**Seven sons of Sceva, a Jewish chief priest^D, were doing this. **15**One day the evil spirit answered them, "Jesus I know, and I know about Paul, but who are you?" **16**Then the man who had the evil spirit jumped on them and overpowered them all. He gave them such a beating that they ran out of the house naked and bleeding.

17When this became known to the Jews and Greeks living in Ephesus, they were all seized with fear, and the name of the Lord Jesus was held in high honor. **18**Many of those who believed now came and openly confessed their evil deeds. **19**A number who had practiced sorcery^D brought their scrolls together and burned them publicly. When they calculated the value of the scrolls, the total came to fifty thousand drachmas.^a **20**In this way the word of the Lord spread widely and grew in power.

21After all this had happened, Paul decided to go to Jerusalem^D, passing through Macedonia and Achaia. "After I have been there," he said, "I must visit Rome also." **22**He sent two of his helpers, Timothy and Erastus, to Macedonia, while he stayed in the province of Asia a little longer.

The Riot in Ephesus

23About that time there arose a great disturbance about the Way. **24**A silversmith named Demetrius, who made silver shrines of Artemis, brought in no little business for the craftsmen. **25**He called them together, along with the workmen in related trades, and said: "Men, you know we receive a good income from this business. **26**And you see and hear how this fellow Paul has convinced and led astray large numbers of people here in Ephesus and in practically the whole province of Asia. He says that man-made gods are no gods at all. **27**There is danger not only that our trade will lose its good name, but also that the temple of the great goddess Artemis will be discredited, and the goddess herself, who is worshiped throughout the province of Asia and the world, will be robbed of her divine majesty."

28When they heard this, they were furious and began shouting: "Great is Artemis of the Ephesians!" **29**Soon the whole city was in an uproar. The people seized Gaius and Aristarchus, Paul's traveling companions from Macedonia, and rushed as one man into the theater. **30**Paul wanted to appear before the crowd, but the disciples^D would not let him. **31**Even some of the officials of the province, friends of Paul, sent him a message begging him not to venture into the theater.

32The assembly was in confusion: Some were shouting one thing, some another. Most of the people did not even know why they were there. **33**The Jews pushed Alexander to the front, and some of the crowd shouted instructions to him. He motioned for silence in order to make a

---

^a19 A drachma was a silver coin worth about a day's wages.

Why heal with a handkerchief? (19:11–12)

The supernatural signs that accompanied Jesus and the apostles demonstrated their authority. Miracles also showed God's compassion and mercy toward the needy. Perhaps Paul heard of a sick person he could not immediately visit and, recalling Elisha (2 Kings 4:18–29), sent a handkerchief (most likely part of his leatherworking supplies) as a stop-gap measure. Or perhaps God revealed that he should send one of his possessions as an aid to faith for healing. Also see Luke 8:44,48.

How could unbelievers drive out demons? (19:13)

In the ancient world pagan diviners and exorcists were commonplace. When attempting to cast out a demon, they listed the names of many gods, hoping one of them would produce the desired results. Having seen Paul effectively cast out demons in Jesus' name, they added the Lord's name—and for good measure, Paul's—to their catalog. These exorcists had no power over demons, so most likely the demons only deceived people into thinking they had vacated.

Had believers been practicing occultic activities? (19:18)

Only in the past. These new converts became convinced that they should completely destroy all that remained of their former lifestyles. So they cleaned out their bookshelves and burned all their old sorcery material (v. 19).

How much were 50,000 drachmas worth? (19:19)

Since a drachma was approximately a day's wages, this was a multi-million-dollar bonfire in today's currency. The books commanded such a high price because they promised power—over sickness, over people and over circumstances. Power has always been the main allure of the occult, something for which people will pay dearly. Ephesus was renowned in the ancient world as a "shopping center" for occult practices, which explains the large quantity of scrolls.

Why was Artemis called *great*? (19:28)

The Temple of Artemis in Ephesus (see *Setting of Acts* on page 1504) housed an image that supposedly fell from heaven. The temple was considered one of the Seven Wonders of the Ancient World. People from throughout the Roman empire came to see its ornate pillars and imposing structure (large enough to contain a football field). Tourist trade was brisk. Silversmiths molded and sold miniature models of the statue of Artemis and the temple to pilgrims. Paul's preaching, which called people to forsake such idols, threatened the meal ticket of these craftsmen.

defense before the people. **34**But when they realized he was a Jew[D], they all shouted in unison for about two hours: "Great is Artemis of the Ephesians!"

35The city clerk quieted the crowd and said: "Men of Ephesus, doesn't all the world know that the city of Ephesus is the guardian of the temple of the great Artemis and of her image, which fell from heaven? **36**Therefore, since these facts are undeniable, you ought to be quiet and not do anything rash. **37**You have brought these men here, though they have neither robbed temples nor blasphemed[D] our goddess. **38**If, then, Demetrius and his fellow craftsmen have a grievance against anybody, the courts are open and there are proconsuls. They can press charges. **39**If there is anything further you want to bring up, it must be settled in a legal assembly. **40**As it is, we are in danger of being charged with rioting because of today's events. In that case we would not be able to account for this commotion, since there is no reason for it." **41**After he had said this, he dismissed the assembly.

Through Macedonia and Greece

20 When the uproar had ended, Paul sent for the disciples[D] and, after encouraging them, said goodby and set out for Macedonia. **2**He traveled through that area, speaking many words of encouragement to the people, and finally arrived in Greece, **3**where he stayed three months. Because the Jews made a plot against him just as he was about to sail for Syria, he decided to go back through Macedonia. **4**He was accompanied by Sopater son of Pyrrhus from Berea, Aristarchus and Secundus from Thessalonica, Gaius from Derbe, Timothy also, and Tychicus and Trophimus from the province of Asia. **5**These men went on ahead and waited for us at Troas. **6**But we sailed from Philippi after the Feast of Unleavened Bread, and five days later joined the others at Troas, where we stayed seven days.

Eutychus Raised From the Dead at Troas

7On the first day of the week we came together to break bread. Paul spoke to the people and, because he intended to leave the next day, kept on talking until midnight. **8**There were many lamps in the upstairs room where we were meeting. **9**Seated in a window was a young man named Eutychus, who was sinking into a deep sleep as Paul talked on and on. When he was sound asleep, he fell to the ground from the third story and was picked up dead. **10**Paul went down, threw himself on the young man and put his arms around him. "Don't be alarmed," he said. "He's alive!" **11**Then he went upstairs again and broke bread and ate. After talking until daylight, he left. **12**The people took the young man home alive and were greatly comforted.

Paul's Farewell to the Ephesian Elders

13We went on ahead to the ship and sailed for Assos, where we were going to take Paul aboard. He had made this arrangement because he was going there on foot. **14**When he met us at Assos, we took him aboard and went on to Mitylene. **15**The next day we set sail from there and arrived off Kios. The day after that we crossed over to Samos, and on the following day arrived at Miletus. **16**Paul had decided to sail past Ephesus to avoid spending time in the province of Asia, for he was in a hurry to reach Jerusalem[D], if possible, by the day of Pentecost.

Through Macedonia and Greece (20:1)

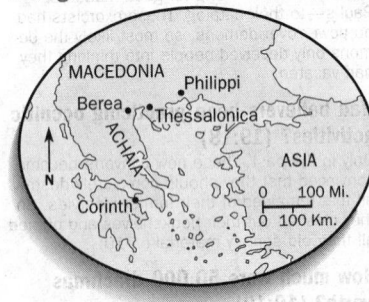

MACEDONIA
Philippi
Berea
Thessalonica
ACHAIA
ASIA
N
Corinth
0   100 Mi.
0 100 Km.

Who were these traveling companions? (20:4)
These men represented churches that Paul had started in Greece and Turkey. Each was carrying a gift from his church to the believers in Jerusalem (see 2 Cor. 8:1–21). The generous gifts and the personal way they were delivered helped strengthen the unity of the young Christian church.

Did the early Christians continue to observe Jewish festivals? (20:6)
Yes, most did. Even Paul observed many Jewish customs (18:18; 21:20–26)—not in order to be righteous before God, but as a cultural tradition and to keep the door of the gospel open to the Jews.

Eutychus (20:9–12)
The young man who died while listening to Paul's long, late-night sermon was probably between eight and 14 years old. His resuscitation by Paul undoubtedly was cause for much relief and joy.

17From Miletus, Paul sent to Ephesus for the elders of the church. **18**When they arrived, he said to them: "You know how I lived the whole time I was with you, from the first day I came into the province of Asia. **19**I served the Lord with great humility and with tears, although I was severely tested by the plots of the JewsD. **20**You know that I have not hesitated to preach anything that would be helpful to you but have taught you publicly and from house to house. **21**I have declared to both Jews and Greeks that they must turn to God in repentanceD and have faith in our Lord Jesus.

22"And now, compelled by the Spirit, I am going to JerusalemD, not knowing what will happen to me there. **23**I only know that in every city the Holy Spirit warns me that prison and hardships are facing me. **24**However, I consider my life worth nothing to me, if only I may finish the race and complete the task the Lord Jesus has given me— the task of testifying to the gospelD of God's graceD.

25"Now I know that none of you among whom I have gone about preaching the kingdom will ever see me again. **26**Therefore, I declare to you today that I am innocent of the blood of all men. **27**For I have not hesitated to proclaim to you the whole will of God. **28**Keep watch over yourselves and all the flock of which the Holy Spirit has made you overseersD,a Be shepherds of the church of God,b which he bought with his own blood. **29**I know that after I leave, savage wolves will come in among you and will not spare the flock. **30**Even from your own number men will arise and distort the truth in order to draw away disciplesD after them. **31**So be on your guard! Remember that for three years I never stopped warning each of you night and day with tears.

32"Now I commit you to God and to the word of his grace, which can build you up and give you an inheritance among all those who are sanctifiedD. **33**I have not coveted anyone's silver or gold or clothing. **34**You yourselves know that these hands of mine have supplied my own needs and the needs of my companions. **35**In everything I did, I showed you that by this kind of hard work we must help the weak, remembering the words the Lord Jesus himself said: 'It is more blessed to give than to receive.' "

36When he had said this, he knelt down with all of them and prayed. **37**They all wept as they embraced him and kissed him. **38**What grieved them most was his statement that they would never see his face again. Then they accompanied him to the ship.

On to Jerusalem

21 After we had torn ourselves away from them, we put out to sea and sailed straight to Cos. The next day we went to Rhodes and from there to Patara. **2**We found a ship crossing over to Phoenicia, went on board and set sail. **3**After sighting Cyprus and passing to the south of it, we sailed on to Syria. We landed at Tyre, where our ship was to unload its cargo. **4**Finding the disciples there, we stayed with them seven days. Through the Spirit they urged Paul not to go on to Jerusalem. **5**But when our time was up, we left and continued on our way. All the disciples and their wives and children accompanied us out of the city, and there on the beach we

a28 Traditionally *bishops*   b28 Many manuscripts *of the Lord*

Did Paul know he was going to die? (20:25)
Paul said the Holy Spirit had warned him of danger in every city he visited, but he seemed to believe this would be his last time to get back to Ephesus. His trip to Jerusalem did result in his arrest and his extradition to Rome, where he was eventually killed, though he may have been released for a time and could have returned to Ephesus. Paul probably didn't know the details, but he knew what faced him, and he willingly went ahead with his mission.

Where did Paul hear these words of Jesus? (20:35)
By this time (approximately A.D. 56; 25 years after the resurrection of Jesus) written and oral collections of the sayings of Jesus had wide circulation. Some became a part of the four Gospels; others did not. The Gospel writers didn't write everything they remembered about Jesus. Rather, the Holy Spirit led them to record only selected sayings and deeds of Christ (John 21:25). Other ancient manuscripts about Jesus have been discovered, but we cannot rely upon them as God-inspired because the early church did not include them in the canon (officially recognized books) of Scripture.

Did Paul disobey the Holy Spirit? (21:4,11–12)
No. Paul was *compelled by the Spirit* to go to Jerusalem (20:22). The people, out of concern for him because of what they had learned *through the Spirit*, urged Paul not to go to Jerusalem. The prophecy, however, did not tell Paul *not* to go; it was simply a warning to let him know what would happen when he did go. All agreed on the meaning of the prophecy, but they disagreed about the correct response.

Prophesied (21:9)

Prophesied (21:9)

Prophesying was done extensively in the early church. It was a spiritual gift, a supernatural empowering to build up God's family. Those with this gift either proclaimed to God's people new truth from God or challenged them with existing Scriptural truths. Both men and women possessed this gift (1 Cor. 11:4–5). Also see article: *How common is predictive prophecy?* (11:27–30).

Why did Jewish believers still follow Old Testament customs? (21:21,24)

The Law of Moses guided Jewish Christians in their social and family lives. They didn't shed their cultural practices when they followed Christ. Looking to the law, then, to order their lives would have been natural, not just to confirm its fulfillment in Christ but to structure society as well. Their Jewish customs were not quickly dismissed.

What did purification involve? (21:24)

Somehow those who had made a Nazirite vow, a self-imposed discipline for special service to God, had defiled their pledge. To correct it, they had to "purify" themselves. This meant waiting seven days, then shaving their heads on the seventh and making offerings—two doves (or pigeons) and a male lamb for each—on day eight. Other sacrifices were required at the conclusion of their Nazirite vows: both a male and female lamb, a ram and a grain and drink offering. See *What was a Nazirite?* (Num. 6:2).

Why did Paul revert to an Old Testament ritual? (21:26; see Gal. 3:25)

Paul's behavior illustrates poignantly one of his ministry's main thrusts: he would do anything, be anything, to win people to Christ. Here that meant accommodating Jewish culture (1 Cor. 9:20). He also hoped to unite Jewish and Gentile Christians, to create a peaceful atmosphere between the two groups. Also see *Is something ever right for one and wrong for another?* (1 Cor. 8:10–11) and *Who would call Paul a "people pleaser"?* (Gal. 1:10).

knelt to pray. **6**After saying good-by to each other, we went aboard the ship, and they returned home.

7We continued our voyage from Tyre and landed at Ptolemais, where we greeted the brothers and stayed with them for a day. **8**Leaving the next day, we reached Caesarea and stayed at the house of Philip the evangelist, one of the Seven. **9**He had four unmarried daughters who prophesied.

10After we had been there a number of days, a prophet^D named Agabus came down from Judea. **11**Coming over to us, he took Paul's belt, tied his own hands and feet with it and said, "The Holy Spirit says, 'In this way the Jews^D of Jerusalem^D will bind the owner of this belt and will hand him over to the Gentiles^D.' "

12When we heard this, we and the people there pleaded with Paul not to go up to Jerusalem. **13**Then Paul answered, "Why are you weeping and breaking my heart? I am ready not only to be bound, but also to die in Jerusalem for the name of the Lord Jesus." **14**When he would not be dissuaded, we gave up and said, "The Lord's will be done."

15After this, we got ready and went up to Jerusalem. **16**Some of the disciples^D from Caesarea accompanied us and brought us to the home of Mnason, where we were to stay. He was a man from Cyprus and one of the early disciples.

Paul's Arrival at Jerusalem

17When we arrived at Jerusalem, the brothers received us warmly. **18**The next day Paul and the rest of us went to see James, and all the elders were present. **19**Paul greeted them and reported in detail what God had done among the Gentiles through his ministry.

20When they heard this, they praised God. Then they said to Paul: "You see, brother, how many thousands of Jews have believed, and all of them are zealous for the law. **21**They have been informed that you teach all the Jews who live among the Gentiles to turn away from Moses, telling them not to circumcise^D their children or live according to our customs. **22**What shall we do? They will certainly hear that you have come, **23**so do what we tell you. There are four men with us who have made a vow^D. **24**Take these men, join in their purification rites and pay their expenses, so that they can have their heads shaved. Then everybody will know there is no truth in these reports about you, but that you yourself are living in obedience to the law. **25**As for the Gentile believers, we have written to them our decision that they should abstain from food sacrificed to idols^D, from blood, from the meat of strangled animals and from sexual immorality."

26The next day Paul took the men and purified^D himself along with them. Then he went to the temple to give notice of the date when the days of purification would end and the offering would be made for each of them.

Paul Arrested

27When the seven days were nearly over, some Jews from the province of Asia saw Paul at the temple. They stirred up the whole crowd and seized him, **28**shouting, "Men of Israel, help us! This is the man who teaches all men everywhere against our people and our law and this place. And besides, he has brought Greeks into the temple area and defiled this holy place." **29**(They had previously seen Trophimus the Ephesian in the city with Paul and

assumed that Paul had brought him into the temple area.)

³⁰The whole city was aroused, and the people came running from all directions. Seizing Paul, they dragged him from the temple, and immediately the gates were shut. ³¹While they were trying to kill him, news reached the commander of the Roman troops that the whole city of Jerusalem ᴰ was in an uproar. ³²He at once took some officers and soldiers and ran down to the crowd. When the rioters saw the commander and his soldiers, they stopped beating Paul.

³³The commander came up and arrested him and ordered him to be bound with two chains. Then he asked who he was and what he had done. ³⁴Some in the crowd shouted one thing and some another, and since the commander could not get at the truth because of the uproar, he ordered that Paul be taken into the barracks. ³⁵When Paul reached the steps, the violence of the mob was so great he had to be carried by the soldiers. ³⁶The crowd that followed kept shouting, "Away with him!"

Paul Speaks to the Crowd

³⁷As the soldiers were about to take Paul into the barracks, he asked the commander, "May I say something to you?"

"Do you speak Greek?" he replied. ³⁸"Aren't you the Egyptian who started a revolt and led four thousand terrorists out into the desert some time ago?"

³⁹Paul answered, "I am a Jew ᴰ, from Tarsus in Cilicia, a citizen of no ordinary city. Please let me speak to the people."

⁴⁰Having received the commander's permission, Paul stood on the steps and motioned to the crowd. When they

22 were all silent, he said to them in Aramaic ᴰᵃ: ¹"Brothers and fathers, listen now to my defense."

²When they heard him speak to them in Aramaic, they became very quiet.

Then Paul said: ³"I am a Jew, born in Tarsus of Cilicia, but brought up in this city. Under Gamaliel I was thoroughly trained in the law of our fathers and was just as zealous for God as any of you are today. ⁴I persecuted the followers of this Way to their death ᴰ, arresting both men and women and throwing them into prison, ⁵as also the high priest ᴰ and all the Council can testify. I even obtained letters from them to their brothers in Damascus, and went there to bring these people as prisoners to Jerusalem to be punished.

⁶"About noon as I came near Damascus, suddenly a bright light from heaven flashed around me. ⁷I fell to the ground and heard a voice say to me, 'Saul! Saul! Why do you persecute me?'

⁸" 'Who are you, Lord?' I asked.

" 'I am Jesus of Nazareth, whom you are persecuting,' he replied. ⁹My companions saw the light, but they did not understand the voice of him who was speaking to me.

¹⁰" 'What shall I do, Lord?' I asked.

" 'Get up,' the Lord said, 'and go into Damascus. There you will be told all that you have been assigned to do.' ¹¹My companions led me by the hand into Damascus, because the brilliance of the light had blinded me.

¹²"A man named Ananias came to see me. He was a devout observer of the law and highly respected by all the Jews living there. ¹³He stood beside me and said, 'Broth-

Who was the Egyptian mistaken for Paul? (21:38)

A Jewish historian during that time reported a story about an ambitious Egyptian posing as a prophet. Along with a large band of ruffians, this man appeared at the Mount of Olives in A.D. 54. He had promised, at his command, the collapse of Jerusalem's walls and the overthrow of Roman power. But when the Roman army marched against him, the crowd scattered and the Egyptian fled.

How many languages did Paul speak? (21:40)

At the very least, Paul knew Hebrew (his native language), Aramaic (a Hebrew dialect popular among Jerusalem Jews) and Greek (the trade language used throughout the Roman world).

Why did the Aramaic language quiet the howling mob? (22:2)

Aramaic was their common language. Hearing Paul speak it caught them by surprise. The unruly crowd immediately identified him as one of their own. That a Jew not from Palestine could speak Aramaic, as well as Greek, impressed them.

Was Paul name-dropping? (22:3)

Gamaliel was highly esteemed as a teacher and religious leader (5:34). Paul mentioned his name to identify further with the volatile crowd and establish credibility. His connection with Gamaliel attested to his early zeal for Judaism.

ᵃ40 Or possibly *Hebrew*; also in 22:2

er Saul, receive your sight!' And at that very moment I was able to see him.

14"Then he said: 'The God of our fathers has chosen you to know his will and to see the Righteous[D] One and to hear words from his mouth. **15**You will be his witness to all men of what you have seen and heard. **16**And now what are you waiting for? Get up, be baptized and wash your sins away, calling on his name.'

17"When I returned to Jerusalem[D] and was praying at the temple, I fell into a trance **18**and saw the Lord speaking. 'Quick!' he said to me. 'Leave Jerusalem immediately, because they will not accept your testimony about me.'

19" 'Lord,' I replied, 'these men know that I went from one synagogue to another to imprison and beat those who believe in you. **20**And when the blood of your martyr[a] Stephen was shed, I stood there giving my approval and guarding the clothes of those who were killing him.'

21"Then the Lord said to me, 'Go; I will send you far away to the Gentiles[D].' "

Why did Paul's mention of the Gentiles inflame the Jews? (22:21–22)

Combined with their original accusation of Paul —*the man who teaches all men everywhere against our people and our law and this place* (21:28)—he implied that Gentiles could approach God directly without going through the nation of Israel. This enraged his Jewish listeners.

Why take off coats and fling dust into the air? (22:23)

Their tantrum expressed their intense anger toward Paul. The cloak removal indicated they were ready to do the dirty work themselves. The throwing of the dust symbolized contempt (2 Samuel 16:13).

Why was the commander alarmed that Paul was a Roman citizen? (22:29)

Roman citizens had certain legal rights: They were exempt from cruel or degrading forms of punishment. If interrogated, they were not to be beaten (16:22–39; 22:25–29). For capital offenses, citizens were beheaded (considered a more humane method of execution) rather than crucified. Citizens had the right of appeal to Rome, which enabled them to bypass the jurisdiction of local magistrates and appointed governors. In this case, the commander realized he had violated Paul's rights by having him beaten and put into chains.

Paul the Roman Citizen

22The crowd listened to Paul until he said this. Then they raised their voices and shouted, "Rid the earth of him! He's not fit to live!"

23As they were shouting and throwing off their cloaks and flinging dust into the air, **24**the commander ordered Paul to be taken into the barracks. He directed that he be flogged and questioned in order to find out why the people were shouting at him like this. **25**As they stretched him out to flog him, Paul said to the centurion[D] standing there, "Is it legal for you to flog a Roman citizen who hasn't even been found guilty?"

26When the centurion heard this, he went to the commander and reported it. "What are you going to do?" he asked. "This man is a Roman citizen."

27The commander went to Paul and asked, "Tell me, are you a Roman citizen?"

"Yes, I am," he answered.

28Then the commander said, "I had to pay a big price for my citizenship."

"But I was born a citizen," Paul replied.

29Those who were about to question him withdrew immediately. The commander himself was alarmed when he realized that he had put Paul, a Roman citizen, in chains.

Before the Sanhedrin

30The next day, since the commander wanted to find out exactly why Paul was being accused by the Jews[D], he released him and ordered the chief priests[D] and all the Sanhedrin[D] to assemble. Then he brought Paul and had him stand before them.

23 Paul looked straight at the Sanhedrin and said, "My brothers, I have fulfilled my duty to God in all good conscience to this day." **2**At this the high priest Ananias ordered those standing near Paul to strike him on the mouth. **3**Then Paul said to him, "God will strike you, you whitewashed wall! You sit there to judge me according to the law, yet you yourself violate the law by commanding that I be struck!"

a20 Or witness

4Those who were standing near Paul said, "You dare to insult God's high priest^D?"

5Paul replied, "Brothers, I did not realize that he was the high priest; for it is written: 'Do not speak evil about the ruler of your people.'^a"

6Then Paul, knowing that some of them were Sadducees^D and the others Pharisees^D, called out in the Sanhedrin^D, "My brothers, I am a Pharisee, the son of a Pharisee. I stand on trial because of my hope in the resurrection^D of the dead." **7**When he said this, a dispute broke out between the Pharisees and the Sadducees, and the assembly was divided. **8**(The Sadducees say that there is no resurrection, and that there are neither angels nor spirits, but the Pharisees acknowledge them all.)

9There was a great uproar, and some of the teachers of the law who were Pharisees stood up and argued vigorously. "We find nothing wrong with this man," they said. "What if a spirit or an angel has spoken to him?" **10**The dispute became so violent that the commander was afraid Paul would be torn to pieces by them. He ordered the troops to go down and take him away from them by force and bring him into the barracks.

11The following night the Lord stood near Paul and said, "Take courage! As you have testified about me in Jerusalem^D, so you must also testify in Rome."

The Plot to Kill Paul

12The next morning the Jews^D formed a conspiracy and bound themselves with an oath not to eat or drink until they had killed Paul. **13**More than forty men were involved in this plot. **14**They went to the chief priests and elders and said, "We have taken a solemn oath not to eat anything until we have killed Paul. **15**Now then, you and the Sanhedrin petition the commander to bring him before you on the pretext of wanting more accurate information about his case. We are ready to kill him before he gets here."

^a5 Exodus 22:28

Was Paul being sarcastic? (23:5)

Some think so. Paul may have been saying in effect, "How could one who ignores God's law —who orders that I be struck—deserve to be high priest? Nevertheless, I will abide by the law." Others, however, feel he was sincerely apologizing for not realizing his harsh words had been directed at the high priest, something prohibited in Scripture.

Did the conspirators die of starvation? (23:14)

Though the plot to kill Paul failed, it's doubtful the oath-takers followed through on their vow. Jewish tradition made exceptions for oaths that could not be fulfilled because of extenuating circumstances. By taking a sacred oath, the plotters demonstrated their serious intentions to kill the apostle. But the oath did not necessarily demonstrate their willingness to die.

Why did the Pharisees rush to Paul's defense? (23:9)

We normally think of Pharisees as opponents of Christians. But here, they were Paul's allies against the Sadducees. Why? The Sadducees, the political rivals of the Pharisees, were the ruling majority of the Sanhedrin. They did not believe in the resurrection of the body after death. The Pharisees, on the other hand, did (23:8). Paul, a former Pharisee, mentioned the resurrection as a diversionary tactic. It caused such discord between the Pharisees and Sadducees that Roman soldiers had to rescue Paul from the resulting melee (23:10).

The Pharisees also supported Paul because they believed that visions (such as the one Paul had on the Damascus road) could be genuine. The influential Sadducees, who represented the wealthier elements of the population, considered visions unbelievable. The uproar in the council was typical of their longstanding disagreements with the Pharisees.

Given the tensions and political rivalry within the council, it is not surprising that the Pharisees were quick to defend Paul's views.

What family did Paul have? (23:16)

This is the only reference to Paul's family relationships. His nephew informed him of a plot against his life. Some people believe that Paul's family disowned him when he converted to Christianity (perhaps what Paul refers to in Phil. 3:8). But his nephew, at least, was willing to help Paul while he was in custody.

Why send Paul to Caesarea? (23:23)

While Jerusalem was the seat of the Jewish government, Caesarea was the Roman headquarters for the region. It was on the coast, and it was a much safer place for Paul while he was in protective custody. See **Map 10** at the back of this Bible.

16But when the son of Paul's sister heard of this plot, he went into the barracks and told Paul.

17Then Paul called one of the centurions^D and said, "Take this young man to the commander; he has something to tell him." **18**So he took him to the commander.

The centurion said, "Paul, the prisoner, sent for me and asked me to bring this young man to you because he has something to tell you."

19The commander took the young man by the hand, drew him aside and asked, "What is it you want to tell me?"

20He said: "The Jews^D have agreed to ask you to bring Paul before the Sanhedrin^D tomorrow on the pretext of wanting more accurate information about him. **21**Don't give in to them, because more than forty of them are waiting in ambush for him. They have taken an oath not to eat or drink until they have killed him. They are ready now, waiting for your consent to their request."

22The commander dismissed the young man and cautioned him, "Don't tell anyone that you have reported this to me."

Paul Transferred to Caesarea

23Then he called two of his centurions and ordered them, "Get ready a detachment of two hundred soldiers, seventy horsemen and two hundred spearmen^a to go to Caesarea at nine tonight. **24**Provide mounts for Paul so that he may be taken safely to Governor Felix."

25He wrote a letter as follows:

26Claudius Lysias,

To His Excellency, Governor Felix:

Greetings.

27This man was seized by the Jews and they were about to kill him, but I came with my troops and rescued him, for I had learned that he is a Roman citizen. **28**I wanted to know why they were accusing him, so I brought him to their Sanhedrin. **29**I found that the accusation had to do with questions about their law, but there was no charge against him that deserved death^D or imprisonment. **30**When I was informed of a plot to be carried out against the man, I sent him to you at once. I also ordered his accusers to present to you their case against him.

31So the soldiers, carrying out their orders, took Paul with them during the night and brought him as far as Antipatris. **32**The next day they let the cavalry go on with him, while they returned to the barracks. **33**When the cavalry arrived in Caesarea, they delivered the letter to the governor and handed Paul over to him. **34**The governor read the letter and asked what province he was from. Learning that he was from Cilicia, **35**he said, "I will hear your case when your accusers get here." Then he ordered that Paul be kept under guard in Herod's palace.

---

a23 The meaning of the Greek for this word is uncertain.

The Trial Before Felix

24 Five days later the high priest[D] Ananias went down to Caesarea with some of the elders and a lawyer named Tertullus, and they brought their charges against Paul before the governor. **2**When Paul was called in, Tertullus presented his case before Felix: "We have enjoyed a long period of peace[D] under you, and your foresight has brought about reforms in this nation. **3**Everywhere and in every way, most excellent Felix, we acknowledge this with profound gratitude. **4**But in order not to weary you further, I would request that you be kind enough to hear us briefly.

5"We have found this man to be a troublemaker, stirring up riots among the Jews[D] all over the world. He is a ringleader of the Nazarene sect **6**and even tried to desecrate[D] the temple; so we seized him. **8**By[a] examining him yourself you will be able to learn the truth about all these charges we are bringing against him."

9The Jews joined in the accusation, asserting that these things were true.

10When the governor motioned for him to speak, Paul replied: "I know that for a number of years you have been a judge over this nation; so I gladly make my defense. **11**You can easily verify that no more than twelve days ago I went up to Jerusalem[D] to worship. **12**My accusers did not find me arguing with anyone at the temple, or stirring up a crowd in the synagogues or anywhere else in the city. **13**And they cannot prove to you the charges they are now making against me. **14**However, I admit that I worship the God of our fathers as a follower of the Way, which they call a sect. I believe everything that agrees with the Law and that is written in the Prophets[D], **15**and I have the same hope in God as these men, that there will be a resurrection[D] of both the righteous[D] and the wicked. **16**So I strive always to keep my conscience clear before God and man.

17"After an absence of several years, I came to Jerusalem to bring my people gifts for the poor and to present offerings. **18**I was ceremonially clean when they found me in the temple courts doing this. There was no crowd with me, nor was I involved in any disturbance. **19**But there are some Jews from the province of Asia, who ought to be here before you and bring charges if they have anything against me. **20**Or these who are here should state what crime they found in me when I stood before the Sanhedrin[D]— **21**unless it was this one thing I shouted as I stood in their presence: 'It is concerning the resurrection of the dead that I am on trial before you today.'"

22Then Felix, who was well acquainted with the Way, adjourned the proceedings. "When Lysias the commander comes," he said, "I will decide your case." **23**He ordered the centurion[D] to keep Paul under guard but to give him some freedom and permit his friends to take care of his needs.

24Several days later Felix came with his wife Drusilla, who was a Jewess. He sent for Paul and listened to him as he spoke about faith in Christ Jesus. **25**As Paul discoursed on righteousness[D], self-control and the judgment to come, Felix was afraid and said, "That's enough for now!

---

a6-8 Some manuscripts him and wanted to judge him according to our law. 7But the commander, Lysias, came and with the use of much force snatched him from our hands 8and ordered his accusers to come before you. By

---

What was the legal process? (24:2)

Those making an accusation would present their charges before a magistrate along with the penalties they desired (see 18:12; John 19:13). Defendants then had opportunity to present their cases. Appeals could be made to the provincial governors, such as Felix. A final appeal could be made to Caesar. See *Could anybody appeal to Caesar?* (25:11–12).

What was the *Nazarene sect*? (24:5)

Tertullus, in an attempt to put Paul in the worst possible light, accused him of belonging to a cult that worshiped a man from Nazareth (see *Map 9* at the back of this Bible). He wanted the governor to view Christians as disturbers of the peace.

The Way (24:14)

The followers of Christ were known as *followers of the Way*. Only later was the term *Christian* commonly used to identify believers.

How had Felix learned about Christianity? (24:22)

He may have heard about it from his wife, Drusilla, a Jewess who would have known about the Messianic movement. King Agrippa II, Drusilla's brother, may have been another possible source of information for Felix. The Romans regarded him as an adviser for Jewish affairs.

What did Paul say that made Felix afraid? (24:25)

Paul's talk of righteousness, self-control and future judgment were touchy issues for a governor noted for his ruthlessness. Tacitus, an ancient Roman writer, said of Felix: "practicing every kind of cruelty and lust, he exercised royal power with the instincts of a slave." Just as Herod Antipas was alarmed by the preaching of John the Baptist (Mark 6:20), Felix may have been conscience-stricken by hearing Paul. However, he put off matters of faith and repentance just as he deferred passing judgment on Paul.

You may leave. When I find it convenient, I will send for you." **26**At the same time he was hoping that Paul would offer him a bribe, so he sent for him frequently and talked with him.

27When two years had passed, Felix was succeeded by Porcius Festus, but because Felix wanted to grant a favor to the JewsD, he left Paul in prison.

The Trial Before Festus

25 Three days after arriving in the province, Festus went up from Caesarea to JerusalemD, **2**where the chief priestsD and Jewish leaders appeared before him and presented the charges against Paul. **3**They urgently requested Festus, as a favor to them, to have Paul transferred to Jerusalem, for they were preparing an ambush to kill him along the way. **4**Festus answered, "Paul is being held at Caesarea, and I myself am going there soon. **5**Let some of your leaders come with me and press charges against the man there, if he has done anything wrong."

6After spending eight or ten days with them, he went down to Caesarea, and the next day he convened the court and ordered that Paul be brought before him. **7**When Paul appeared, the Jews who had come down from Jerusalem stood around him, bringing many serious charges against him, which they could not prove.

8Then Paul made his defense: "I have done nothing wrong against the law of the Jews or against the temple or against Caesar."

9Festus, wishing to do the Jews a favor, said to Paul, "Are you willing to go up to Jerusalem and stand trial before me there on these charges?"

10Paul answered: "I am now standing before Caesar's court, where I ought to be tried. I have not done any wrong to the Jews, as you yourself know very well. **11**If, however, I am guilty of doing anything deserving deathD, I do not refuse to die. But if the charges brought against me by these Jews are not true, no one has the right to hand me over to them. I appeal to Caesar!"

12After Festus had conferred with his council, he declared: "You have appealed to Caesar. To Caesar you will go!"

Festus Consults King Agrippa

13A few days later King Agrippa and Bernice arrived at Caesarea to pay their respects to Festus. **14**Since they were spending many days there, Festus discussed Paul's case with the king. He said: "There is a man here whom Felix left as a prisoner. **15**When I went to Jerusalem, the chief priests and elders of the Jews brought charges against him and asked that he be condemned.

16"I told them that it is not the Roman custom to hand over any man before he has faced his accusers and has had an opportunity to defend himself against their charges. **17**When they came here with me, I did not delay the case, but convened the court the next day and ordered the man to be brought in. **18**When his accusers got up to speak, they did not charge him with any of the crimes I had expected. **19**Instead, they had some points of dispute with him about their own religion and about a dead man named Jesus who Paul claimed was alive. **20**I was at a loss how to investigate such matters; so I asked if he would be willing to go to Jerusalem and stand trial there on these charges. **21**When Paul made his appeal to be held over for

How could Felix jail a man for two years without sentencing? (24:27)
Felix, as governor, held complete authority in sentencing. He could delay indefinitely without making a judgment.

What jurisdiction did Festus have? (25:3)
Festus ruled as governor (or procurator) of Judea from his headquarters in Caesarea (see *Map 9* at the back of this Bible). He was in charge of both military and civil command.

Could anybody appeal to Caesar? (25:11–12)
Only Roman citizens could. See *Why was the commander alarmed that Paul was a Roman citizen?* (22:29). The privilege, however, required that the person making the appeal had the financial means to make a trip to Rome. It was assumed that an appeal to Caesar was allowed only for capital cases. This was the situation for the apostle Paul. An appeal to Caesar could be made after the governor had passed judgment, but evidence indicates that governors did not always honor the right of appeal.

King Agrippa (25:13)
Also called Herod Agrippa II. Though he governed lands to the north, he was appointed by Caesar as custodian of the temple. Agrippa had a poor reputation; rumors persisted that he had an incestuous relationship with his sister, Bernice.

the Emperor's decision, I ordered him held until I could send him to Caesar."

22Then Agrippa said to Festus, "I would like to hear this man myself."

He replied, "Tomorrow you will hear him."

Paul Before Agrippa

23The next day Agrippa and Bernice came with great pomp and entered the audience room with the high ranking officers and the leading men of the city. At the command of Festus, Paul was brought in. **24**Festus said: "King Agrippa, and all who are present with us, you see this man! The whole Jewish community has petitioned me about him in JerusalemD and here in Caesarea, shouting that he ought not to live any longer. **25**I found he had done nothing deserving of deathD, but because he made his appeal to the Emperor I decided to send him to Rome. **26**But I have nothing definite to write to His Majesty about him. Therefore I have brought him before all of you, and especially before you, King Agrippa, so that as a result of this investigation I may have something to write. **27**For I think it is unreasonable to send on a prisoner without specifying the charges against him."

26 Then Agrippa said to Paul, "You have permission to speak for yourself."

So Paul motioned with his hand and began his defense: **2**"King Agrippa, I consider myself fortunate to stand before you today as I make my defense against all the accusations of the JewsD, **3**and especially so because you are well acquainted with all the Jewish customsD and controversies. Therefore, I beg you to listen to me patiently.

4"The Jews all know the way I have lived ever since I was a child, from the beginning of my life in my own country, and also in Jerusalem. **5**They have known me for a long time and can testify, if they are willing, that according to the strictest sect of our religion, I lived as a PhariseeD. **6**And now it is because of my hope in what God has promised our fathers that I am on trial today. **7**This is the promise our twelve tribes are hoping to see fulfilled as they earnestly serve God day and night. O king, it is because of this hope that the Jews are accusing me. **8**Why should any of you consider it incredible that God raises the dead?

9"I too was convinced that I ought to do all that was possible to oppose the name of Jesus of Nazareth. **10**And that is just what I did in Jerusalem. On the authority of the chief priestsD I put many of the saintsD in prison, and when they were put to death, I cast my vote against them. **11**Many a time I went from one synagogue to another to have them punished, and I tried to force them to blasphemeD. In my obsession against them, I even went to foreign cities to persecute them.

12"On one of these journeys I was going to Damascus with the authority and commission of the chief priests. **13**About noon, O king, as I was on the road, I saw a light from heaven, brighter than the sun, blazing around me and my companions. **14**We all fell to the ground, and I heard a voice saying to me in AramaicD,a 'Saul, Saul, why do you persecute me? It is hard for you to kick against the goads.'

15"Then I asked, 'Who are you, Lord?'

" 'I am Jesus, whom you are persecuting,' the Lord re-

Agrippa (25:23)

King Agrippa II ruled over portions of Galilee and Perea (primarily a Gentile area). He was the son of Herod Agrippa I (12:1) and the great-grandson of Herod the Great (Matt. 2:3). When his father died in A.D. 44, Agrippa II was only 17 years old. As a result, Caesar divided his father's territory, putting Judea under the jurisdiction of a governor. Agrippa II was later named king (A.D. 53) and was custodian of the temple with authority to appoint the Jewish high priest.

Emperor (25:25)

A word that appears only twice in the New Testament—here and in v. 21. It was the Greek equivalent of *Augustus* and referred to the way in which the ruler was "augmented," that is, lifted up above other mere mortals. Technically, only the current reigning caesar could be called *Augustus*.

Why was Agrippa so well acquainted with Jewish customs? (26:3)

He served, as his father before him had, as the liaison between the Jewish religious leaders and the Roman government. He was given authority over the Jewish temple and as such had the authority of appointing the Jewish high priest. He would have been familiar with many of the members of the Sanhedrin, the Jewish supreme court.

Why did Paul identify himself so closely with the Jews? (26:5)

Perhaps for two reasons: (1) Paul might have hoped to find a sympathetic ear in Agrippa, a man who was familiar with the Jewish people (see previous note). (2) Paul hoped that Agrippa might see the irony that he—a Jew who believed, as all Pharisees believed, in God's promise of a resurrection—had been charged with preaching about the resurrection. Earlier Paul had used similar tactics when arguing his case before the Pharisees and the Sadducees. See article: *Why did the Pharisees rush to Paul's defense?* (23:9).

Kick against the goads (26:14)

A *goad* was a stick tipped with a pointed piece of iron. Used to direct and guide livestock, a goad annoyed them to pick up the pace if they slowed while plowing. The ancient farmers poked them just enough to steer them in the right direction. Oxen that fought the goad, kicking against it, often injured themselves. The phrase, then, became a proverb describing those who resisted authority: anyone who challenged the gods was like an ox kicking against the goads. Paul, by persecuting Christians, had been challenging God's authority, kicking *against the goads*.

---

a14 Or Hebrew

plied. **16**'Now get up and stand on your feet. I have appeared to you to appoint you as a servant and as a witness of what you have seen of me and what I will show you. **17**I will rescue you from your own people and from the Gentiles[D]. I am sending you to them **18**to open their eyes and turn them from darkness to light, and from the power of Satan to God, so that they may receive forgiveness of sins and a place among those who are sanctified[D] by faith in me.'

19"So then, King Agrippa, I was not disobedient to the vision[D] from heaven. **20**First to those in Damascus, then to those in Jerusalem[D] and in all Judea, and to the Gentiles also, I preached that they should repent and turn to God and prove their repentance[D] by their deeds. **21**That is why the Jews[D] seized me in the temple courts and tried to kill me. **22**But I have had God's help to this very day, and so I stand here and testify to small and great alike. I am saying nothing beyond what the prophets[D] and Moses said would happen— **23**that the Christ[a] would suffer and, as the first to rise from the dead, would proclaim light to his own people and to the Gentiles."

24At this point Festus interrupted Paul's defense. "You are out of your mind, Paul!" he shouted. "Your great learning is driving you insane."

25"I am not insane, most excellent Festus," Paul replied. "What I am saying is true and reasonable. **26**The king is familiar with these things, and I can speak freely to him. I am convinced that none of this has escaped his notice, because it was not done in a corner. **27**King Agrippa, do you believe the prophets? I know you do."

28Then Agrippa said to Paul, "Do you think that in such a short time you can persuade me to be a Christian?"

29Paul replied, "Short time or long—I pray God that not only you but all who are listening to me today may become what I am, except for these chains."

30The king rose, and with him the governor and Bernice and those sitting with them. **31**They left the room, and while talking with one another, they said, "This man is not doing anything that deserves death[D] or imprisonment."

32Agrippa said to Festus, "This man could have been set free if he had not appealed to Caesar."

Paul Sails for Rome

27 When it was decided that we would sail for Italy, Paul and some other prisoners were handed over to a centurion[D] named Julius, who belonged to the Imperial Regiment. **2**We boarded a ship from Adramyttium about to sail for ports along the coast of the province of Asia, and we put out to sea. Aristarchus, a Macedonian from Thessalonica, was with us.

3The next day we landed at Sidon; and Julius, in kindness to Paul, allowed him to go to his friends so they might provide for his needs. **4**From there we put out to sea again and passed to the lee of Cyprus because the winds were against us. **5**When we had sailed across the open sea off the coast of Cilicia and Pamphylia, we landed at Myra in Lycia. **6**There the centurion found an Alexandrian ship sailing for Italy and put us on board. **7**We made slow headway for many days and had difficulty arriving off Cnidus. When the wind did not allow us to hold our course, we sailed to the lee of Crete, opposite Salmone.

Why did Festus berate Paul's education? (26:24)

Much of Paul's defense was based on Old Testament Scripture. To a sensible Roman like Festus, Paul's mention of the resurrection from the dead was absurd. Festus could not believe it. Even if he did believe it privately, a Roman like Festus would not let such a teaching interfere with his daily life. Festus, then, attributed Paul's "bizarre" beliefs, based on the Old Testament, to his Jewish education.

Why did Paul think that King Agrippa believed the prophets? (26:27)

King Agrippa was King Agrippa II, a great-grandson of Herod the Great and one of a long line of Jewish rulers in the Palestine area. As a Jew he was well-schooled in the Old Testament prophets. He may have realized that Jesus had fulfilled predictions made about the Messiah. Agrippa, confronted with the facts drawn from his own religious upbringing, had to make a decision for or against Jesus Christ.

Why couldn't Paul be set free? (26:32)

According to Roman law, a lower court could have dismissed the charges leveled against Paul. Agrippa and Festus found no evidence of wrongdoing. But in 25:11–12, the apostle had asked to stand trial before Caesar himself in Rome. His request protected him from a Jewish ambush (see 25:3) and gave him an opportunity to proclaim the gospel to the Roman emperor.

What was the *Imperial Regiment*? (27:1)

Some believe the *Imperial Regiment* referred to a group of government officials that functioned like special couriers between Rome and its provinces. They escorted food supplies to Rome and performed special police duties. Others think they were a special-forces, military unit trained to handle volatile conflicts.

a 23 Or Messiah

⁸We moved along the coast with difficulty and came to a place called Fair Havens, near the town of Lasea.

⁹Much time had been lost, and sailing had already become dangerous because by now it was after the Fast.ᵃ So Paul warned them, ¹⁰"Men, I can see that our voyage is going to be disastrous and bring great loss to ship and cargo, and to our own lives also." ¹¹But the centurionᴰ, instead of listening to what Paul said, followed the advice of the pilot and of the owner of the ship. ¹²Since the harbor was unsuitable to winter in, the majority decided that we should sail on, hoping to reach Phoenix and winter there. This was a harbor in Crete, facing both southwest and northwest.

The Storm

¹³When a gentle south wind began to blow, they thought they had obtained what they wanted; so they weighed anchor and sailed along the shore of Crete. ¹⁴Before very long, a wind of hurricane force, called the "northeaster," swept down from the island. ¹⁵The ship was caught by the storm and could not head into the wind; so we gave way to it and were driven along. ¹⁶As we passed to the lee of a small island called Cauda, we were hardly able to make the lifeboat secure. ¹⁷When the men had hoisted it aboard, they passed ropes under the ship itself to hold it together. Fearing that they would run aground on the sandbars of Syrtis, they lowered the sea anchor and let the ship be driven along. ¹⁸We took such a violent battering from the storm that the next day they began to throw the cargo overboard. ¹⁹On the third day, they threw the ship's tackle overboard with their own hands. ²⁰When neither sun nor stars appeared for many days and the storm continued raging, we finally gave up all hope of being saved.

²¹After the men had gone a long time without food, Paul stood up before them and said: "Men, you should have taken my advice not to sail from Crete; then you would have spared yourselves this damage and loss. ²²But now I urge you to keep up your courage, because not one of you will be lost; only the ship will be destroyed. ²³Last night an angel of the God whose I am and whom I serve stood beside me ²⁴and said, 'Do not be afraid, Paul. You must stand trial before Caesar; and God has graciously given you the lives of all who sail with you.' ²⁵So keep up your courage, men, for I have faith in God that it will happen just as he told me. ²⁶Nevertheless, we must run aground on some island."

The Shipwreck

²⁷On the fourteenth night we were still being driven across the Adriaticᵇ Sea, when about midnight the sailors sensed they were approaching land. ²⁸They took soundings and found that the water was a hundred and twenty feetᶜ deep. A short time later they took soundings again and found it was ninety feetᵈ deep. ²⁹Fearing that we would be dashed against the rocks, they dropped four anchors from the stern and prayed for daylight. ³⁰In an attempt to escape from the ship, the sailors let the lifeboat down into the sea, pretending they were going to lower

How could ropes hold a ship together? (27:17)

It's likely that the sailors were desperate to reinforce the hull so that it would be less likely to break up. The original language is difficult to interpret and may also have meant that ropes were wrapped around the ship above the water or were stretched between the stern and bow, adding strength that might prevent the ship from cracking in two in the heavy seas. The sailors hoped only that the ropes would keep the ship from complete destruction.

Adriatic Sea (27:27)

Not the Adriatic that appears on modern maps (see NIV text note) but a much larger body of water that extended farther south, at least to Crete and Sicily. Some think that this referred to the *Adrian* or *Hadrian Sea*, meaning the central Mediterranean between Greece, Italy and Africa.

ᵃ9 That is, the Day of Atonement (Yom Kippur)   ᵇ27 In ancient times the name referred to an area extending well south of Italy. ᶜ28 Greek *twenty orguias* (about 37 meters)   ᵈ28 Greek *fifteen orguias* (about 27 meters)

Why cut the ropes to the lifeboat? (27:32)

Paul knew that if the sailors saved themselves in the lifeboat, the soldiers and passengers left on board the ship would be unable to handle the ship. They needed the sailors to handle the rigging and the helm. So it was better to lose the lifeboat than to lose the sailors.

Why would Paul's captors listen to him? (27:36)

Paul's court appearances in Jerusalem and in Caesarea showed him to be a cordial, persuasive personality. His reputation for warmth preceded him. In the course of their journey, Paul had warned the ship's officers not to sail from Crete because of the harsh seasonal storms. Although ignored, his advice was valid. As the journey progressed, then, Paul's credibility climbed.

Why tell how many were on board? (27:37)

Luke records the number of people on the ship in the middle of recounting that they all ate before daylight came. It may be that there was some kind of count made as the food was distributed. The figure does not seem out of line for the larger ships of that day; the historian Josephus tells of a ship that held 600.

What kind of ship was this? (27:38)

Two ships were involved in the first two stages of Paul's journey to Rome (see **Map 11** at the back of this Bible). The first was a smaller, coastal vessel carrying them from Adramyttium to Myra in Lycia (27:2,5). While in Myra the centurion acquired the services of an Alexandrian grain ship. The latter vessel was much larger, carrying more people and cargo than the earlier ship. Its size made it possible to sail into deeper water with stronger winds.

some anchors from the bow. **31**Then Paul said to the centurion^D and the soldiers, "Unless these men stay with the ship, you cannot be saved." **32**So the soldiers cut the ropes that held the lifeboat and let it fall away.

33Just before dawn Paul urged them all to eat. "For the last fourteen days," he said, "you have been in constant suspense and have gone without food—you haven't eaten anything. **34**Now I urge you to take some food. You need it to survive. Not one of you will lose a single hair from his head." **35**After he said this, he took some bread and gave thanks to God in front of them all. Then he broke it and began to eat. **36**They were all encouraged and ate some food themselves. **37**Altogether there were 276 of us on board. **38**When they had eaten as much as they wanted, they lightened the ship by throwing the grain into the sea.

39When daylight came, they did not recognize the land, but they saw a bay with a sandy beach, where they decided to run the ship aground if they could. **40**Cutting loose the anchors, they left them in the sea and at the same time untied the ropes that held the rudders. Then they hoisted the foresail to the wind and made for the beach. **41**But the ship struck a sandbar and ran aground. The bow stuck fast and would not move, and the stern was broken to pieces by the pounding of the surf.

42The soldiers planned to kill the prisoners to prevent any of them from swimming away and escaping. **43**But the centurion wanted to spare Paul's life and kept them from carrying out their plan. He ordered those who could swim to jump overboard first and get to land. **44**The rest were to get there on planks or on pieces of the ship. In this way everyone reached land in safety.

Ashore on Malta

28 Once safely on shore, we found out that the island was called Malta. **2**The islanders showed us unusual kindness. They built a fire and welcomed us all because it was raining and cold. **3**Paul gathered a pile of brushwood and, as he put it on the fire, a viper, driven out by the heat, fastened itself on his hand. **4**When the islanders saw the snake hanging from his hand, they said to each other, "This man must be a murderer; for though he escaped from the sea, Justice has not allowed him to live." **5**But Paul shook the snake off into the fire and suffered no ill effects. **6**The people expected him to swell up or suddenly fall dead, but after waiting a long time and seeing nothing unusual happen to him, they changed their minds and said he was a god.

7There was an estate nearby that belonged to Publius, the chief official of the island. He welcomed us to his home and for three days entertained us hospitably. **8**His father was sick in bed, suffering from fever and dysentery. Paul went in to see him and, after prayer, placed his hands on him and healed him. **9**When this had happened, the rest of the sick on the island came and were cured. **10**They honored us in many ways and when we were ready to sail, they furnished us with the supplies we needed.

Arrival at Rome

11After three months we put out to sea in a ship that had wintered in the island. It was an Alexandrian ship with the figurehead of the twin gods Castor and Pollux. **12**We put in at Syracuse and stayed there three days. **13**From there we set sail and arrived at Rhegium. The next

day the south wind came up, and on the following day we reached Puteoli. **14**There we found some brothers who invited us to spend a week with them. And so we came to Rome. **15**The brothers there had heard that we were coming, and they traveled as far as the Forum of Appius and the Three Taverns to meet us. At the sight of these men Paul thanked God and was encouraged. **16**When we got to Rome, Paul was allowed to live by himself, with a soldier to guard him.

Paul Preaches at Rome Under Guard

17Three days later he called together the leaders of the Jews[D]. When they had assembled, Paul said to them: "My brothers, although I have done nothing against our people or against the customs of our ancestors, I was arrested in Jerusalem[D] and handed over to the Romans. **18**They examined me and wanted to release me, because I was not guilty of any crime deserving death[D]. **19**But when the Jews objected, I was compelled to appeal to Caesar—not that I had any charge to bring against my own people. **20**For this reason I have asked to see you and talk with you. It is because of the hope of Israel that I am bound with this chain."

21They replied, "We have not received any letters from Judea concerning you, and none of the brothers who have come from there has reported or said anything bad about you. **22**But we want to hear what your views are, for we know that people everywhere are talking against this sect."

23They arranged to meet Paul on a certain day, and came in even larger numbers to the place where he was staying. From morning till evening he explained and declared to them the kingdom of God[D] and tried to convince them about Jesus from the Law of Moses and from the Prophets[D]. **24**Some were convinced by what he said, but others would not believe. **25**They disagreed among themselves and began to leave after Paul had made this final statement: "The Holy Spirit spoke the truth to your forefathers when he said through Isaiah the prophet:

26" 'Go to this people and say,
  "You will be ever hearing but never
        understanding;
    you will be ever seeing but never
        perceiving."
27For this people's heart has become calloused;
    they hardly hear with their ears,
    and they have closed their eyes.
  Otherwise they might see with their eyes,
    hear with their ears,
    understand with their hearts
  and turn, and I would heal them.'[a]

28"Therefore I want you to know that God's salvation[D] has been sent to the Gentiles[D], and they will listen!"[b]

30For two whole years Paul stayed there in his own rented house and welcomed all who came to see him. **31**Boldly and without hindrance he preached the kingdom of God and taught about the Lord Jesus Christ.

How restricted was Paul? (28:16)
By the time they arrived in Rome, the apostle had become a trusted prisoner. In the course of the journey, Paul had given counsel (27:9–10), warned against a secret mutiny (27:30–31), encouraged the passengers (27:34), survived a snake bite (28:5–6) and healed a Roman official's father (28:8). Paul arrived as a hero-prisoner. As a result, he was free to live in a rented house with only one soldier guarding him.

When were the Jews let back into Rome? (28:17; 18:2)
During the reign of Emperor Claudius, Jewish people, because of riots in their community, were expelled from Rome. Claudius's edict to expel Jews occurred in A.D. 49 or 50. Some returned after the death of Claudius in A.D. 54. Because of the earlier expulsion, Jews were not inclined to involve themselves with Paul's controversy.

What kind of accusations were made against the Christians? (28:22)
The truthfulness of these leaders is doubtful. Could they have known Christian Jews in the city without also knowing about the Jerusalem tensions between the church and Judaism? The negative press they heard about Christianity can only be speculated. Perhaps like Paul before his conversion, they viewed the church as a threat to Judaism and a denial of Mosaic Law.

How long did Paul have to wait for his appeal? (28:30)
Some Bible experts speculate that since his accusers did not arrive within eighteen months as Roman law required, Paul was released. But during the storm at sea (see 27:23–24), the angel of the Lord assured him that he would stand trial before Caesar. Most likely, then, a case was heard and Paul was released after two years.

Then what happened? (28:30-31)
Luke's purpose was *not* to write a biography of the apostle Paul. His closing comments merely sum up the book: the gospel was proclaimed boldly throughout Jerusalem, Judea, Samaria and into the Roman world (see **Map 11** at the back of this Bible). The rather abrupt ending implies that the story started in the first century would persevere *without hindrance* until Christ's second coming.

---

*a*27 Isaiah 6:9,10   *b*28 Some manuscripts *listen!" 29After he said this, the Jews left, arguing vigorously among themselves.*

ROMANS

Why read this book?

If you've ever struggled to express what it means to follow Christ, Romans can give you the right words to say. It offers one of the clearest expressions of Christian belief, covering major issues—faith and works, law and grace—in lively, practical terms. But be prepared! Reading this book has been a turning point for many. It helped Martin Luther to discover that faith alone justifies—bringing about the Reformation. Luther's comments on Romans later caused John Wesley's heart to be "strangely warmed," sparking another revival. If you desire spiritual renewal, read Romans as a good starting point.

Who wrote this book?

The apostle Paul, who wrote about the grace of God both from experience (Acts 9:1–19) and education (Acts 22:3).

Why was it written?

Paul wrote: (1) To introduce himself to the believers in Rome and enlist their help in spreading the gospel. (2) To develop and defend the truth of the gospel he had been preaching. (3) To encourage the Roman believers to rely solely on God's grace for their salvation (3:24).

When and to whom was it written?

Romans was probably written in A.D. 57 to believers—most of them Gentile—in the capital city of the Roman empire.

What to look for in Romans:

Watch for the major themes of faith, grace, righteousness and justification. You'll find the foundation—vital teaching on faith—in the first eleven chapters. Then, in the last five chapters, you'll discover practical implications of faith—how the teaching works out in everyday life.

When did these things happen?

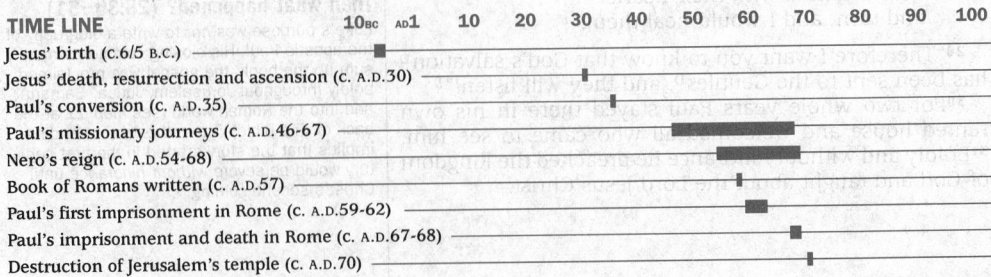

TIME LINE	10BC AD1	10	20	30	40	50	60	70	80	90	100
Jesus' birth (c.6/5 B.C.)											
Jesus' death, resurrection and ascension (c. A.D.30)											
Paul's conversion (c. A.D.35)											
Paul's missionary journeys (c. A.D.46-67)											
Nero's reign (c. A.D.54-68)											
Book of Romans written (c. A.D.57)											
Paul's first imprisonment in Rome (c. A.D.59-62)											
Paul's imprisonment and death in Rome (c. A.D.67-68)											
Destruction of Jerusalem's temple (c. A.D.70)											

1 Paul, a servant of Christ Jesus, called to be an apostle[D] and set apart for the gospel[D] of God— ²the gospel he promised beforehand through his prophets in the Holy Scriptures ³regarding his Son, who as to his human nature was a descendant of David, ⁴and who through the Spirit[a] of holiness was declared with power to be the Son of God[b] by his resurrection[D] from the dead: Jesus Christ our Lord. ⁵Through him and for his name's sake, we received grace[D] and apostleship to call people from among all the Gentiles[D] to the obedience that comes from faith. ⁶And you also are among those who are called to belong to Jesus Christ.

⁷To all in Rome who are loved by God and called to be saints[D]:

Grace and peace to you from God our Father and from the Lord Jesus Christ.

Paul's Longing to Visit Rome

⁸First, I thank my God through Jesus Christ for all of you, because your faith is being reported all over the world. ⁹God, whom I serve with my whole heart in preaching the gospel of his Son, is my witness how constantly I remember you ¹⁰in my prayers at all times; and I pray that now at last by God's will the way may be opened for me to come to you.

¹¹I long to see you so that I may impart to you some spiritual gift to make you strong— ¹²that is, that you and I may be mutually encouraged by each other's faith. ¹³I do not want you to be unaware, brothers, that I planned many times to come to you (but have been prevented from doing so until now) in order that I might have a harvest among you, just as I have had among the other Gentiles.

¹⁴I am obligated both to Greeks and non-Greeks, both to the wise and the foolish. ¹⁵That is why I am so eager to preach the gospel also to you who are at Rome.

¹⁶I am not ashamed of the gospel, because it is the power of God for the salvation[D] of everyone who believes: first for the Jew[D], then for the Gentile. ¹⁷For in the gospel a righteousness from God is revealed, a righteousness that is by faith from first to last,[c] just as it is written: "The righteous[D] will live by faith."[d]

God's Wrath Against Mankind

¹⁸The wrath of God is being revealed from heaven against all the godlessness and wickedness of men who suppress the truth by their wickedness, ¹⁹since what may be known about God is plain to them, because God has made it plain to them. ²⁰For since the creation of the world God's invisible qualities—his eternal power and divine nature—have been clearly seen, being understood from what has been made, so that men are without excuse.

²¹For although they knew God, they neither glorified him as God nor gave thanks to him, but their thinking became futile and their foolish hearts were darkened. ²²Although they claimed to be wise, they became fools ²³and exchanged the glory[D] of the immortal God for images made to look like mortal man and birds and animals and reptiles.

---

a4 Or *who as to his spirit*   *b4* Or *was appointed to be the Son of God with power*   *c17* Or *is from faith to faith*   *d17* Hab. 2:4

What does the resurrection prove? (1:4)

The resurrection proves that Jesus is who he claimed to be. The resurrection also proves that Jesus' promises are reliable: he said he would rise from the dead, and he did. In the resurrection, Jesus defeated death and introduced a whole new order of existence, a brand new creation.

The Spirit of holiness (1:4)

Another way of referring to God's Holy Spirit, showing both God's holiness and his desire that we too should be holy (1 Peter 1:15).

Saints (1:7)

Those who are holy before God, cleansed (sanctified) through salvation and the work of the Holy Spirit (15:16; 1 Cor. 6:11). The word suggests being "set apart," that is, dedicated for God's glory and service.

The Church in Rome (1:7)

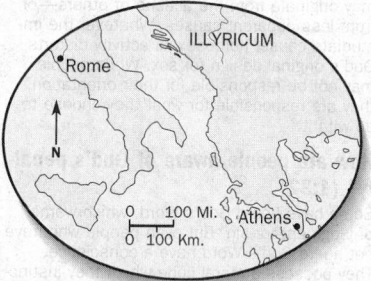

What spiritual gifts can a human being give? (1:11)

None. Only the Holy Spirit can give spiritual gifts (1 Cor. 12:11). But humans can serve to confirm God's work in others—announcing or acknowledging their spiritual gifts (see, for example, 1 Tim. 4:14; 2 Tim. 1:6). Some, however, see Paul wanting to impart something more general, a *gift of grace*—anything from words of insight to deeds of kindness.

Why is the gospel *first for the Jew, then for the Gentile?* (1:16)

The historical fact is that God's plan to save the world began with the Jewish people—but always with the aim that through them, he would bless the rest of the world (Gen. 12:1–3). Jesus came as a human—a Jew—to die on the cross for all, Jew and Gentile alike.

What kinds of righteousness are there besides that *by faith?* (1:17)

See article: *How are we justified?* (5:1).

How is God *clearly seen* in this world? (1:19–20)

Creation offers proof (for those willing to accept it) of a powerful "Someone" behind it all. The astronomical odds against this world happening merely by chance provide insurmountable evidence for a Creator. The intricate beauty and complex design of the creation—from subatomic particles and molecular building blocks of life to galaxies and the expanses of the universe—demonstrate that a "Designer" planned it all.

Why would any thinking person worship carved images? (1:23)

See article: *Why would Israelites be tempted by other gods?* (Joshua 23:7). Also see *Why did people think lifeless idols made by men should be worshiped?* (Psalm 135:15–17).

God gave them over (1:24,26,28)

God let them face the consequences of their own decisions. He withdrew his moderating influence and allowed their sin to run its full course. The natural outgrowth of sin is judgment.

Are all homosexual tendencies the result of sin? (1:26–27)

Some say homosexual tendencies stem from genetics; others say they are developed in certain environments. Still others insist that homosexuality is a spiritual problem. Paul describes the practice of homosexuality as *unnatural*—distorted by the ruinous influence of sin in the world. Homosexual orientation may originate from the actions of others—or from less apparent causes. Whatever the immediate cause, homosexual activity distorts God's original design for sex. While people may not be responsible for their orientation, they are responsible for what they choose to do with it.

How are people aware of God's penalty? (1:32)

Some have heard God's Word, which warns of judgment for sin. But even people who have not heard God's Word have a conscience. They possess a moral code which they instinctively cannot be violated without consequences. Such violations, no matter how small, always lead to some sort of death. Something dies within the human soul.

Why is *doing good* necessary to gain eternal life? (2:7)

Paul is not saying human beings can earn eternal life. It is available only as a gift from God (6:23). What he is saying is that our choices have inevitable consequences: we reap what we sow (Gal. 6:7–8). Choose God's will and discover the life only God can give; go the other way and pay the price. *Doing good* on its own does not gain eternal life; but those who trust God for eternal life will do good.

If God doesn't show favoritism, why were the Jews the chosen people? (2:10–11)

God selected Abraham and his descendants for one purpose: to be a blessing to all peoples on earth (Gen. 12:13). Eventually, the Israelite stream of history flowed to Jesus Christ, *the son of Abraham* (Matt. 1:1), and through him any ethnic group can enter into the blessings of Abraham (Gal. 3:29). Also see *Why is the gospel first for the Jew, then for the Gentile?* (1:16).

24Therefore God gave them over in the sinful desires of their hearts to sexual impurity for the degrading of their bodies with one another. 25They exchanged the truth of God for a lie, and worshiped and served created things rather than the Creator—who is forever praised. Amen.

26Because of this, God gave them over to shameful lusts. Even their women exchanged natural relations for unnatural ones. 27In the same way the men also abandoned natural relations with women and were inflamed with lust for one another. Men committed indecent acts with other men, and received in themselves the due penalty for their perversion.

28Furthermore, since they did not think it worthwhile to retain the knowledge of God, he gave them over to a depraved mind, to do what ought not to be done. 29They have become filled with every kind of wickedness, evil, greed and depravity. They are full of envy, murder, strife, deceit and malice. They are gossips, 30slanderers, God-haters, insolent, arrogant and boastful; they invent ways of doing evil; they disobey their parents; 31they are senseless, faithless, heartless, ruthless. 32Although they know God's righteousD decree that those who do such things deserve deathD, they not only continue to do these very things but also approve of those who practice them.

God's Righteous Judgment

2 You, therefore, have no excuse, you who pass judgment on someone else, for at whatever point you judge the other, you are condemning yourself, because you who pass judgment do the same things. 2Now we know that God's judgment against those who do such things is based on truth. 3So when you, a mere man, pass judgment on them and yet do the same things, do you think you will escape God's judgment? 4Or do you show contempt for the riches of his kindness, tolerance and patience, not realizing that God's kindness leads you toward repentanceD?

5But because of your stubbornness and your unrepentant heart, you are storing up wrath against yourself for the day of God's wrath, when his righteous judgment will be revealed. 6God "will give to each person according to what he has done."a 7To those who by persistence in doing good seek gloryD, honor and immortality, he will give eternal lifeD. 8But for those who are self-seeking and who reject the truth and follow evil, there will be wrath and anger. 9There will be trouble and distress for every human being who does evil: first for the JewD, then for the GentileD; 10but glory, honor and peace for everyone who does good: first for the Jew, then for the Gentile. 11For God does not show favoritism.

12All who sin apart from the law will also perish apart from the law, and all who sin under the law will be judged by the law. 13For it is not those who hear the law who are righteous in God's sight, but it is those who obey the law who will be declared righteous. 14(Indeed, when Gentiles, who do not have the law, do by nature things required by the law, they are a law for themselves, even though they do not have the law, 15since they show that the requirements of the law are written on their hearts, their consciences also bearing witness, and their thoughts now accusing, now even defending them.) 16This will take

a6 Psalm 62:12; Prov. 24:12

place on the day when God will judge men's secrets through Jesus Christ, as my gospel[D] declares.

The Jews and the Law

[17]Now you, if you call yourself a Jew[D]; if you rely on the law and brag about your relationship to God; [18]if you know his will and approve of what is superior because you are instructed by the law; [19]if you are convinced that you are a guide for the blind, a light for those who are in the dark, [20]an instructor of the foolish, a teacher of infants, because you have in the law the embodiment of knowledge and truth— [21]you, then, who teach others, do you not teach yourself? You who preach against stealing, do you steal? [22]You who say that people should not commit adultery, do you commit adultery? You who abhor idols[D], do you rob temples? [23]You who brag about the law, do you dishonor God by breaking the law? [24]As it is written: "God's name is blasphemed[D] among the Gentiles[D] because of you."[a]

[25]Circumcision[D] has value if you observe the law, but if you break the law, you have become as though you had not been circumcised[D]. [26]If those who are not circumcised keep the law's requirements, will they not be regarded as though they were circumcised? [27]The one who is not circumcised physically and yet obeys the law will condemn you who, even though you have the[b] written code and circumcision, are a lawbreaker.

[28]A man is not a Jew if he is only one outwardly, nor is circumcision merely outward and physical. [29]No, a man is a Jew if he is one inwardly; and circumcision is circumcision of the heart, by the Spirit, not by the written code. Such a man's praise is not from men, but from God.

God's Faithfulness

3 What advantage, then, is there in being a Jew, or what value is there in circumcision? [2]Much in every way! First of all, they have been entrusted with the very words of God.

[3]What if some did not have faith? Will their lack of faith nullify God's faithfulness? [4]Not at all! Let God be true, and every man a liar. As it is written:

"So that you may be proved right when you speak
and prevail when you judge."[c]

[5]But if our unrighteousness brings out God's righteousness[D] more clearly, what shall we say? That God is unjust in bringing his wrath on us? (I am using a human argument.) [6]Certainly not! If that were so, how could God judge the world? [7]Someone might argue, "If my falsehood enhances God's truthfulness and so increases his glory[D], why am I still condemned as a sinner?" [8]Why not say—as we are being slanderously reported as saying and as some claim that we say—"Let us do evil that good may result"? Their condemnation is deserved.

No One Is Righteous

[9]What shall we conclude then? Are we any better[d]? Not at all! We have already made the charge that Jews and Gentiles alike are all under sin. [10]As it is written:

[a]24 Isaiah 52:5; Ezek. 36:22   [b]27 Or who, by means of a
[c]4 Psalm 51:4   [d]9 Or worse

What happens to good people who never had a chance to hear? (2:14–16)

It's not as clear as we might wish. Some suggest that since God is inherently fair, he will not hold people accountable for something they never knew. Others insist that because Christ is the only way of salvation, it remains imperative for the church to take the gospel to those who haven't heard. Perhaps both can be true. God knows each individual heart and will judge in a manner consistent with both holiness and love. Still, our mandate is to take the gospel to the world. Also see *Does God overlook our ignorance?* (Acts 17:30) and *What about those who never hear the gospel?* (10:14–15).

Circumcision (2:25)

See article: *Why did God command circumcision?* (Gen. 17:10).

What value does circumcision have? (2:25–27)

Circumcision was a sign of the covenant between God and his people, so it served to remind the Israelites of God's promises and their vows. Under the new covenant, however, circumcision became a symbol of dependence upon human effort and legalism rather than on God's grace. More important than an outward sign is the inward reality (see following note). See *Is circumcision wrong?* (Gal. 5:2). Also see article: *Why did Paul circumcise Timothy?* (Acts 16:3).

How does the Spirit circumcise a heart? (2:28–29)

After we offer ourselves to the Lord, the Spirit can then figuratively *cut around* our hearts, taking away all that keeps our hearts from being wholly dedicated to God. It is this work of grace that makes a person a Jew *inwardly*, someone committed to God alone.

Why did some accuse Paul of promoting evil? (3:8)

Because they thought Paul's preaching about grace would devalue the law, leading people to abandon their moral standards and do whatever they wanted to do. Paul's critics did not understand that grace gives people the power to live holy lives—just as God intended. Grace not only justifies, it transforms. We are made right by grace; by grace we can also live right.

Why did Paul string Old Testament quotes together as if they were one quotation? (3:10–18)

Paul did not suggest that all these quotes were from one source. *It is written* is a general heading covering God's written revelation. It was common in Paul's day to pull together Biblical passages on a single theme. The challenge with such an approach is to avoid pulling verses out of context, something Paul did not do. All these verses speak about the fact that everyone has sinned.

"There is no one righteous[D], not even one;
11   there is no one who understands,
     no one who seeks God.
12All have turned away,
     they have together become worthless;
   there is no one who does good,
     not even one."[a]
13"Their throats are open graves;
     their tongues practice deceit."[b]
"The poison of vipers is on their lips."[c]
14   "Their mouths are full of cursing and
       bitterness."[d]
15"Their feet are swift to shed blood;
16   ruin and misery mark their ways,
17and the way of peace[D] they do not know."[e]
18   "There is no fear of God before their eyes."[f]

19Now we know that whatever the law says, it says to those who are under the law, so that every mouth may be silenced and the whole world held accountable to God. 20Therefore no one will be declared righteous in his sight by observing the law; rather, through the law we become conscious of sin.

Righteousness Through Faith

21But now a righteousness[D] from God, apart from law, has been made known, to which the Law and the Prophets[D] testify. 22This righteousness from God comes through faith in Jesus Christ to all who believe. There is no difference, 23for all have sinned and fall short of the glory[D] of God, 24and are justified[D] freely by his grace[D] through the redemption[D] that came by Christ Jesus. 25God presented him as a sacrifice[D] of atonement,[D,g] through faith in his blood. He did this to demonstrate his justice, because in his forbearance he had left the sins committed beforehand unpunished— 26he did it to demonstrate his justice at the present time, so as to be just and the one who justifies those who have faith in Jesus.

27Where, then, is boasting? It is excluded. On what principle? On that of observing the law? No, but on that of faith. 28For we maintain that a man is justified by faith apart from observing the law. 29Is God the God of Jews[D] only? Is he not the God of Gentiles[D] too? Yes, of Gentiles too, 30since there is only one God, who will justify the circumcised by faith and the uncircumcised through that same faith. 31Do we, then, nullify the law by this faith? Not at all! Rather, we uphold the law.

Abraham Justified by Faith

4 What then shall we say that Abraham, our forefather, discovered in this matter? 2If, in fact, Abraham was justified by works, he had something to boast about— but not before God. 3What does the Scripture say? "Abraham believed God, and it was credited to him as righteousness."[h]

4Now when a man works, his wages are not credited to him as a gift, but as an obligation. 5However, to the man who does not work but trusts God who justifies the wicked, his faith is credited as righteousness. 6David says the same thing when he speaks of the blessedness of

---

Justified (3:24)
See article: How are we justified? (5:1).

Atonement (3:25)
Some define it as at-one-ment. It is the act by which sinners are made one with God—when barriers between God and sinners are removed. Our atonement comes through the crucifixion of Jesus Christ.

Why bring Abraham into the argument? (4:1–3)
Because Abraham is "Exhibit A"—the first person to be called God's "friend" (2 Chron. 20:7). How he became God's friend supports Paul's point: Abraham didn't earn God's friendship through good deeds. Abraham simply took God at his word and believed the promise. His trust is what pleased God, not his works. Paul hoped this strong evidence from Abraham would convince others they could be made righteous simply by believing.

---

a12 Psalms 14:1-3; 53:1-3; Eccles. 7:20   b13 Psalm 5:9
c13 Psalm 140:3   d14 Psalm 10:7   e17 Isaiah 59:7,8
f18 Psalm 36:1   g25 Or as the one who would turn aside his wrath,
taking away sin   h3 Gen. 15:6; also in verse 22

the man to whom God credits righteousness^D apart from works:

⁷"Blessed are they
   whose transgressions are forgiven,
   whose sins are covered.
⁸Blessed is the man
   whose sin the Lord will never count against
      him."^a

⁹Is this blessedness only for the circumcised^D, or also for the uncircumcised^D? We have been saying that Abraham's faith was credited to him as righteousness. ¹⁰Under what circumstances was it credited? Was it after he was circumcised, or before? It was not after, but before! ¹¹And he received the sign of circumcision^D, a seal of the righteousness that he had by faith while he was still uncircumcised. So then, he is the father of all who believe but have not been circumcised, in order that righteousness might be credited to them. ¹²And he is also the father of the circumcised who not only are circumcised but who also walk in the footsteps of the faith that our father Abraham had before he was circumcised.

¹³It was not through law that Abraham and his offspring received the promise that he would be heir of the world, but through the righteousness that comes by faith. ¹⁴For if those who live by law are heirs, faith has no value and the promise is worthless, ¹⁵because law brings wrath. And where there is no law there is no transgression.

¹⁶Therefore, the promise comes by faith, so that it may be by grace^D and may be guaranteed to all Abraham's offspring—not only to those who are of the law but also to those who are of the faith of Abraham. He is the father of us all. ¹⁷As it is written: "I have made you a father of many nations."^b He is our father in the sight of God, in whom he believed—the God who gives life to the dead and calls things that are not as though they were.

¹⁸Against all hope, Abraham in hope believed and so became the father of many nations, just as it had been said to him, "So shall your offspring be."^c ¹⁹Without weakening in his faith, he faced the fact that his body was as good as dead—since he was about a hundred years old—and that Sarah's womb was also dead. ²⁰Yet he did not waver through unbelief regarding the promise of God, but was strengthened in his faith and gave glory^D to God, ²¹being fully persuaded that God had power to do what he had promised. ²²This is why "it was credited to him as righteousness." ²³The words "it was credited to him" were written not for him alone, ²⁴but also for us, to whom God will credit righteousness—for us who believe in him who raised Jesus our Lord from the dead. ²⁵He was delivered over to death^D for our sins and was raised to life for our justification^D.

Peace and Joy

5 Therefore, since we have been justified^D through faith, we^d have peace^D with God through our Lord Jesus Christ, ²through whom we have gained access by faith into this grace in which we now stand. And we^d rejoice in the hope of the glory of God. ³Not only so, but we^d also rejoice in our sufferings, because we know that

^a8 Psalm 32:1,2   ^b17 Gen. 17:5   ^c18 Gen. 15:5   ^d1,2,3 Or let us

---

Is ignorance an excuse? (4:15)
See *Do some get off the hook?* (5:13–14) and *Does God overlook our ignorance?* (Acts 17:30).

How can God say something *is* when it *isn't*? (4:17)
Because he is God—sovereign over all. When he spoke, a new world came into being (Gen. 1). He made the world out of nothing simply by speaking. God is not untruthful or in denial, as humans sometimes are.

How did Christ's *resurrection* accomplish our justification? (4:25)
See article: *How are we justified?* (5:1).

Is all suffering beneficial? (5:3)
Not necessarily. Suffering in itself is not beneficial. Some who dwell only on their suffering never gain its benefits or achieve a higher perspective. But those who focus on what God can do through suffering will be strengthened. They can tap into God's resources, allowing him to make something positive out of the negative. Suffering can yield perseverance, character and hope when we allow God to work in us.

suffering produces perseverance; **4**perseverance, character; and character, hope. **5**And hope does not disappoint us, because God has poured out his love into our hearts by the Holy Spirit, whom he has given us.

6You see, at just the right time, when we were still powerless, Christ died for the ungodly. **7**Very rarely will anyone die for a righteous**D** man, though for a good man someone might possibly dare to die. **8**But God demonstrates his own love for us in this: While we were still sinners, Christ died for us.

9Since we have now been justified**D** by his blood, how much more shall we be saved from God's wrath through him! **10**For if, when we were God's enemies, we were reconciled to him through the death**D** of his Son, how much more, having been reconciled, shall we be saved through his life! **11**Not only is this so, but we also rejoice in God through our Lord Jesus Christ, through whom we have now received reconciliation.

Death Through Adam, Life Through Christ

12Therefore, just as sin entered the world through one man, and death through sin, and in this way death came to all men, because all sinned— **13**for before the law was given, sin was in the world. But sin is not taken into account when there is no law. **14**Nevertheless, death reigned from the time of Adam to the time of Moses, even over those who did not sin by breaking a command, as did Adam, who was a pattern of the one to come.

15But the gift is not like the trespass. For if the many died by the trespass of the one man, how much more did God's grace**D** and the gift that came by the grace of the one man, Jesus Christ, overflow to the many! **16**Again, the gift of God is not like the result of the one man's sin: The judgment followed one sin and brought condemnation, but the gift followed many trespasses and brought justification**D**. **17**For if, by the trespass of the one man, death reigned through that one man, how much more will those who receive God's abundant provision of grace and of

Why was Christ's *blood* necessary to justify us? (5:9)
See article: *How are we justified?* (5:1).

Do some get off the hook? (5:13–14)
Paul is not suggesting that some can escape the consequences of sin by pleading ignorance of the law. His point is that even before the law was given, sin and death exercised power over humanity. Sin resulted in death, even before the commands of the law had defined what sin was. Even when sin goes unrecognized or unacknowledged, it still has an effect.

Trespass (5:15)
One of several synonyms the Bible uses to describe sin. Means *to fall aside* and includes the idea of a false step or a blunder.

How are we justified? (5:1)

To be justified means *to be made right.* Paul's great question was "How is a sinful human being made right with a holy God?" What needs to happen to make this relationship right?

If we could follow the law and live perfectly, we would be right with God. But how can we do that? We are slaves to sin, incapable of obeying God's law!

Yet God wants to have a relationship with us. So he has taken the steps necessary to make the relationship right. In Jesus Christ he does for us what we could never do for ourselves: Jesus lived a wholly righteous life—a perfect life in line with the law, in total relationship with God, the Father. Even more, in Jesus God took upon himself all the punishment our disobedience deserves (3:24). At the cross he fulfilled all that righteousness demanded. His life was given in exchange for ours; his blood paid the price for our justification.

The results of Jesus' sacrifice are personally available to us simply by faith. God has done everything that needs to be done to justify us. All that remains is for us to accept the grace of God shown on the cross. We are justified when we stop trying to justify ourselves and depend completely on the finished work of Jesus Christ.

the gift of righteousness[D] reign in life through the one man, Jesus Christ.

[18]Consequently, just as the result of one trespass was condemnation for all men, so also the result of one act of righteousness was justification that brings life for all men. [19]For just as through the disobedience of the one man the many were made sinners, so also through the obedience of the one man the many will be made righteous[D].

[20]The law was added so that the trespass might increase. But where sin increased, grace[D] increased all the more, [21]so that, just as sin reigned in death[D], so also grace might reign through righteousness to bring eternal life[D] through Jesus Christ our Lord.

Dead to Sin, Alive in Christ

6 What shall we say, then? Shall we go on sinning so that grace may increase? [2]By no means! We died to sin; how can we live in it any longer? [3]Or don't you know that all of us who were baptized into Christ Jesus were baptized into his death? [4]We were therefore buried with him through baptism[D] into death in order that, just as Christ was raised from the dead through the glory[D] of the Father, we too may live a new life.

[5]If we have been united with him like this in his death, we will certainly also be united with him in his resurrection[D]. [6]For we know that our old self was crucified with him so that the body of sin might be done away with,[a] that we should no longer be slaves to sin— [7]because anyone who has died has been freed from sin.

[8]Now if we died with Christ, we believe that we will also live with him. [9]For we know that since Christ was raised from the dead, he cannot die again; death no longer has mastery over him. [10]The death he died, he died to sin once for all; but the life he lives, he lives to God. [11]In the same way, count yourselves dead to sin but alive to God in Christ Jesus. [12]Therefore do not let sin reign in your mortal body so that you obey its evil desires. [13]Do not offer the parts of your body to sin, as instruments of wickedness, but rather offer yourselves to God, as those who have been brought from death to life; and offer the parts of your body to him as instruments of righteousness. [14]For sin shall not be your master, because you are not under law, but under grace.

Slaves to Righteousness

[15]What then? Shall we sin because we are not under law but under grace? By no means! [16]Don't you know that when you offer yourselves to someone to obey him as slaves, you are slaves to the one whom you obey— whether you are slaves to sin, which leads to death, or to obedience, which leads to righteousness? [17]But thanks be to God that, though you used to be slaves to sin, you wholeheartedly obeyed the form of teaching to which you were entrusted. [18]You have been set free from sin and have become slaves to righteousness.

[19]I put this in human terms because you are weak in your natural selves. Just as you used to offer the parts of your body in slavery to impurity and to ever-increasing wickedness, so now offer them in slavery to righteousness leading to holiness. [20]When you were slaves to sin, you were free from the control of righteousness.

[a]6 Or be rendered powerless

How does justification bring *life for all men*? (5:18–19)

This may sound like everyone has been justified because of Christ. But here Paul is not discussing our necessary response to Christ's work on the cross. Instead Paul simply draws a contrast between the two "Adams"—one introducing sin and death into the world, the other bringing righteousness and life. Eternal life is not automatic; it is for those *who receive God's abundant provision of grace* (v. 17).

Why did God want the trespass to *increase*? (5:20)

Increase here does not mean to multiply or grow larger. God merely wanted the trespass to be made more obvious, to be brought out into the open. The law reveals our inability to live up to God's standard, thus preparing us to admit our need for God's grace. God's law highlights our sin so that his grace can be highlighted even more.

What's wrong with sinning and expecting God to forgive? (6:1)

If increasing sin means increasing grace (5:20), why worry about sinning? For three reasons: (1) Sin destroys the moral fabric of our lives. Even when sin has been forgiven, it can leave scars. (2) Sin violates God's purpose for us. He calls us to something infinitely better. (3) Sinning with the intention of asking forgiveness drains all sincerity out of our repentance. Counting on God to forgive deliberate sin offends God's grace and insults the price God paid for sin.

In what sense have we *died to sin*? (6:2–12)

Obviously sin is still around. Few deny that even the most committed Christians are still susceptible to sin. But Paul claims that in a relationship with Jesus Christ, sin loses its authority over us. We are no longer sin's slaves (v. 6). It may still come knocking at our door, threatening us if we refuse to give in, but God's grace makes it possible for us to refuse. Our death to sin, a spiritual reality demonstrated in our baptism (vv. 3–4), can become a physical reality as well.

What does baptism have to do with death? (6:3–5)

When Christ was crucified, he took us with him into death (Gal. 2:20). By his resurrection, he raised us to new life. Baptism symbolizes this dying of the old self and reminds us that we are made new in Christ. Some say immersion is the best way to picture this truth. Others say the spiritual meaning is what matters, not the method of symbolizing it.

How does grace—more than law—free us from sin? (6:14)

The law reveals God's standard but does not provide the spiritual power to measure up to that standard. Grace, on the other hand, cancels out our sin and lets us start over with a clean slate. Grace brings us into a relationship with God and permits us to look to him for the strength necessary to live a righteous life. Knowing God personally—not knowing his law alone—helps us overcome sin.

Who wants to be a slave? (6:18)

Everyone is a slave to someone or something. It's the master who determines whether slavery results in life or death. Apart from the grace of God, we are slaves of sin. And when sin is master, we die. But by grace, we can be slaves of God. When God is master, we live. Slavery does not have to be a negative image: A kite is free to fly only when "a slave" to the string. Cut the string and the kite's freedom to fly is severed as well. Slavery to God frees us to fully be what we were created to be!

How does the law arouse sinful passion? (7:5–8)

When confronted with a *do not,* something within human nature says, "Oh, yeah? Says who?" Though intended to lead us toward a relationship with God (Gal. 3:24), God's law touches our pride. Our rebellious pride says, "Hey, I know what is best . . . " And our spiritual pride says, "Sure, God. I can do that. Watch me." Either way, the law incites our human nature.

Were God's intentions for the law thwarted? (7:10)

No, for two reasons: (1) God intended that the law would make us see just how bad sin is. It shows us that we can't live in our own power; when we try, we die. (2) God intended that the law would lead us to life. It does that by leading us ultimately to Jesus Christ, *the end of the law* (10:4; Gal. 3:24). As the fulfillment of the law, Jesus is the only one who can empower us to live according to God's will (8:3–4). Also see *How is the Law fulfilled?* (Matt. 5:17–18) and *Did Jesus abolish the Old Testament law or fulfill it?* (Eph. 2:15).

Isn't this a cop-out? (7:17,20)

No. Paul was not evading his own responsibility. He was simply trying to get us to take the power of sin more seriously. His graphic terms for sin (*a slave to sin,* v. 14; *waging war,* v. 23) show the respect he had for its power. Paul described the tension we face: we are freed from sin, but not yet fully—just as God's kingdom has come, but is yet coming more fully. He also gives us the keys to dealing with this tension: (1) a renewed mind (v. 25; 8:5–7; 12:2) and (2) the power of the Holy Spirit, infinitely greater than sin and the sinful nature, or flesh (8:4,9–11).

21What benefit did you reap at that time from the things you are now ashamed of? Those things result in death[D]! **22**But now that you have been set free from sin and have become slaves to God, the benefit you reap leads to holiness, and the result is eternal life[D]. **23**For the wages of sin is death, but the gift of God is eternal life in[a] Christ Jesus our Lord.

An Illustration From Marriage

7 Do you not know, brothers—for I am speaking to men who know the law—that the law has authority over a man only as long as he lives? **2**For example, by law a married woman is bound to her husband as long as he is alive, but if her husband dies, she is released from the law of marriage. **3**So then, if she marries another man while her husband is still alive, she is called an adulteress. But if her husband dies, she is released from that law and is not an adulteress, even though she marries another man.

4So, my brothers, you also died to the law through the body of Christ, that you might belong to another, to him who was raised from the dead, in order that we might bear fruit to God. **5**For when we were controlled by the sinful nature,[b] the sinful passions aroused by the law were at work in our bodies, so that we bore fruit for death. **6**But now, by dying to what once bound us, we have been released from the law so that we serve in the new way of the Spirit, and not in the old way of the written code.

Struggling With Sin

7What shall we say, then? Is the law sin? Certainly not! Indeed I would not have known what sin was except through the law. For I would not have known what coveting really was if the law had not said, "Do not covet."[c] **8**But sin, seizing the opportunity afforded by the commandment, produced in me every kind of covetous desire. For apart from law, sin is dead. **9**Once I was alive apart from law; but when the commandment came, sin sprang to life and I died. **10**I found that the very commandment that was intended to bring life actually brought death. **11**For sin, seizing the opportunity afforded by the commandment, deceived me, and through the commandment put me to death. **12**So then, the law is holy, and the commandment is holy, righteous[D] and good.

13Did that which is good, then, become death to me? By no means! But in order that sin might be recognized as sin, it produced death in me through what was good, so that through the commandment sin might become utterly sinful.

14We know that the law is spiritual; but I am unspiritual, sold as a slave to sin. **15**I do not understand what I do. For what I want to do I do not do, but what I hate I do. **16**And if I do what I do not want to do, I agree that the law is good. **17**As it is, it is no longer I myself who do it, but it is sin living in me. **18**I know that nothing good lives in me, that is, in my sinful nature.[d] For I have the desire to do what is good, but I cannot carry it out. **19**For what I do is not the good I want to do; no, the evil I do not want to do—this I keep on doing. **20**Now if I do what I do not want

---

[a]23 Or *through*   [b]5 Or *the flesh*; also in verse 25   [c]7 Exodus
20:17; Deut. 5:21   [d]18 Or *my flesh*

to do, it is no longer I who do it, but it is sin living in me that does it.

²¹So I find this law at work: When I want to do good, evil is right there with me. ²²For in my inner being I delight in God's law; ²³but I see another law at work in the members of my body, waging war against the law of my mind and making me a prisoner of the law of sin at work within my members. ²⁴What a wretched man I am! Who will rescue me from this body of death ᴰ? ²⁵Thanks be to God—through Jesus Christ our Lord!

So then, I myself in my mind am a slave to God's law, but in the sinful nature a slave to the law of sin.

Life Through the Spirit

8 Therefore, there is now no condemnation for those who are in Christ Jesus,ᵃ ²because through Christ Jesus the law of the Spirit of life set me free from the law of sin and death. ³For what the law was powerless to do in that it was weakened by the sinful nature,ᵇ God did by sending his own Son in the likeness of sinful man to be a sin offering ᴰ.ᶜ And so he condemned sin in sinful man,ᵈ ⁴in order that the righteous ᴰ requirements of the law might be fully met in us, who do not live according to the sinful nature but according to the Spirit.

⁵Those who live according to the sinful nature have their minds set on what that nature desires; but those who live in accordance with the Spirit have their minds set on what the Spirit desires. ⁶The mind of sinful manᵉ is death, but the mind controlled by the Spirit is life and peace ᴰ; ⁷the sinful mindᶠ is hostile to God. It does not submit to God's law, nor can it do so. ⁸Those controlled by the sinful nature cannot please God.

⁹You, however, are controlled not by the sinful nature but by the Spirit, if the Spirit of God lives in you. And if anyone does not have the Spirit of Christ, he does not belong to Christ. ¹⁰But if Christ is in you, your body is dead because of sin, yet your spirit is alive because of righ-

Do Spirit-controlled Christians still sin? (8:2-14)

Yes, but not while they are controlled by the Spirit. Having the Spirit of God within does not always mean surrendering to his control. To use Paul's language, we can be *in* the Spirit, but not live *according to* the Spirit. We can live *in* another part of the world, but not live *according to* its customs, patterns and ways. The journey of discipleship involves learning how to let the Spirit have control.

ᵃ1 Some later manuscripts *Jesus, who do not live according to the sinful nature but according to the Spirit,*   ᵇ3 Or *the flesh*; also in verses 4, 5, 8, 9, 12 and 13   ᶜ3 Or *man, for sin*   ᵈ3 Or *in the flesh*   ᵉ6 Or *mind set on the flesh*   ᶠ7 Or *the mind set on the flesh*

Does sin ever quit? (7:14-25)

Not as long as this fallen world exists and our physical bodies remain. No, not until the final coming of God's kingdom. Sin will keep knocking at our door as long as we live in this broken, rebellious, twisted world.

Paul says we have *died to sin* (6:2), that sin's claim upon our lives has been broken. We do not have to give in to it. Jesus Christ breathes his Spirit into us (8:14), giving us the power to resist sin's advances and live a strong, new life. But we must choose to resist sin. Every day. Every moment of every day.

What level of victory over sin can we expect before the day when Christ comes? Less important than the degree of victory is the direction we're going. We can expect, as we learn to yield more of our will to the Holy Spirit, to move more in the direction of obedience. When we fail and do not choose to trust the Spirit to empower us, we can confess our sins, receive forgiveness and keep moving forward. And one day, when we are united with Christ, we will be completely free from sin's influence.

Must we suffer to be heirs? (8:17)

No. That would imply that Christ's suffering on the cross was not enough for our salvation. But the fact is we will suffer as heirs. We can expect suffering in at least two ways: (1) By identifying with Christ in his suffering (Phil. 3:10; 2 Cor. 1:5). If he agonized over the world to reach it, we will face similar struggles. (2) By facing persecution for our faith (Matt. 5:10–12; 2 Tim. 3:12). If the world is hostile to the Lord, we shouldn't be surprised if it is hostile to those who follow him.

Why was creation subjected to frustration? (8:20–21)

Because it suffered from the consequences of human sin. The fall of humankind into sin brought a curse upon the planet: God's order for creation was overturned, leaving the earth to face disasters, disease and death. Paul pictures creation as a woman in childbirth, groaning to be delivered from the condition she is in.

When will our adoption be complete? (8:23)

In Jesus Christ we are already God's children; we have the inner witness of the Holy Spirit crying out in us, *"Abba, Father"* (vv. 14–16). But our adoption into God's family is still in process. We do not yet have our re-created bodies, free from sin, disease and death. See also Phil. 3:20–21.

Why would God intercede with himself? (8:27)

Perhaps this is a picture of God's intense longing for redemption to be complete—almost like he's talking to himself about it. But Paul's main point is that when we groan, we do not groan alone. God cares for us so much that he has come into our world, entered our struggles and sufferings and made them his own—so much so that the Spirit prays for God's will even when we know nothing about it.

Do all bad events have a good purpose? (8:28)

No. There are three important qualifications to notice: (1) It is *in* all things—some good, some bad—that God can be at work. God can redeem things intended for evil, transforming them into good (see, for example, Gen. 50:20). (2) This promise is for *those who love him.* Those who are yet in rebellion cannot depend on everything achieving something good in their lives. (3) The *good* God desires to work is a spiritual, eternal work—preparing us for future glory. Also see **Is all suffering beneficial?** (5:3).

Does God hand-pick his followers? (8:29–30)

Predestined means two things, both intensely practical: (1) It means God is going to fulfill his purpose. Although God allows human beings to make choices, he will bring all humanity and creation to the end he desires. (2) It means that we now know our destiny; it has been preset. God's plan for us is that we should become like Jesus. Some would say this is God's intention and design for the whole human race; others say this destiny is reserved for certain ones. See article: **Does God play favorites?** (9:8–33).

teousness[D]. [11]And if the Spirit of him who raised Jesus from the dead is living in you, he who raised Christ from the dead will also give life to your mortal bodies through his Spirit, who lives in you.

[12]Therefore, brothers, we have an obligation—but it is not to the sinful nature, to live according to it. [13]For if you live according to the sinful nature, you will die; but if by the Spirit you put to death[D] the misdeeds of the body, you will live, [14]because those who are led by the Spirit of God are sons of God. [15]For you did not receive a spirit that makes you a slave again to fear, but you received the Spirit of sonship.[a] And by him we cry, *"Abba*[D],[b] Father."* [16]The Spirit himself testifies with our spirit that we are God's children. [17]Now if we are children, then we are heirs—heirs of God and co-heirs with Christ, if indeed we share in his sufferings in order that we may also share in his glory[D].

Future Glory

[18]I consider that our present sufferings are not worth comparing with the glory that will be revealed in us. [19]The creation waits in eager expectation for the sons of God to be revealed. [20]For the creation was subjected to frustration, not by its own choice, but by the will of the one who subjected it, in hope [21]that[c] the creation itself will be liberated from its bondage to decay and brought into the glorious freedom of the children of God.

[22]We know that the whole creation has been groaning as in the pains of childbirth right up to the present time. [23]Not only so, but we ourselves, who have the firstfruits[D] of the Spirit, groan inwardly as we wait eagerly for our adoption as sons, the redemption[D] of our bodies. [24]For in this hope we were saved. But hope that is seen is no hope at all. Who hopes for what he already has? [25]But if we hope for what we do not yet have, we wait for it patiently.

[26]In the same way, the Spirit helps us in our weakness. We do not know what we ought to pray for, but the Spirit himself intercedes[D] for us with groans that words cannot express. [27]And he who searches our hearts knows the mind of the Spirit, because the Spirit intercedes for the saints[D] in accordance with God's will.

More Than Conquerors

[28]And we know that in all things God works for the good of those who love him,[d] who[e] have been called according to his purpose. [29]For those God foreknew he also predestined to be conformed to the likeness of his Son, that he might be the firstborn[D] among many brothers. [30]And those he predestined, he also called; those he called, he also justified[D]; those he justified, he also glorified.

[31]What, then, shall we say in response to this? If God is for us, who can be against us? [32]He who did not spare his own Son, but gave him up for us all—how will he not also, along with him, graciously give us all things? [33]Who will bring any charge against those whom God has chosen? It is God who justifies. [34]Who is he that condemns? Christ Jesus, who died—more than that, who was raised

---

[a]15 Or *adoption*   [b]15 Aramaic for *Father*   [c]20,21 Or *subjected it in hope.* 21*For*   [d]28 Some manuscripts *And we know that all things work together for good to those who love God*   [e]28 Or *works together with those who love him to bring about what is good—with those who*

to life—is at the right hand of God and is also interced-ing[D] for us. **35**Who shall separate us from the love of Christ? Shall trouble or hardship or persecution or famine or nakedness or danger or sword? **36**As it is written:

> "For your sake we face death[D] all day long;
> we are considered as sheep to be
> slaughtered."[a]

37No, in all these things we are more than conquerors through him who loved us. **38**For I am convinced that nei-ther death nor life, neither angels nor demons,[b] nei-ther the present nor the future, nor any powers, **39**neither height nor depth, nor anything else in all creation, will be able to separate us from the love of God that is in Christ Jesus our Lord.

God's Sovereign Choice

9 I speak the truth in Christ—I am not lying, my con-science confirms it in the Holy Spirit— **2**I have great sorrow and unceasing anguish in my heart. **3**For I could wish that I myself were cursed and cut off from Christ for the sake of my brothers, those of my own race, **4**the peo-ple of Israel. Theirs is the adoption as sons; theirs the di-vine glory[D], the covenants[D], the receiving of the law, the temple worship and the promises. **5**Theirs are the patri-archs[D], and from them is traced the human ancestry of Christ, who is God over all, forever praised![c] Amen.

6It is not as though God's word had failed. For not all who are descended from Israel are Israel. **7**Nor because they are his descendants are they all Abraham's children. On the contrary, "It is through Isaac that your offspring will be reckoned."[d] **8**In other words, it is not the natural children who are God's children, but it is the children of the promise who are regarded as Abraham's offspring. **9**For this was how the promise was stated: "At the ap-pointed time I will return, and Sarah will have a son."[e]

10Not only that, but Rebekah's children had one and the same father, our father Isaac. **11**Yet, before the twins were born or had done anything good or bad—in order that God's purpose in election might stand: **12**not by works but by him who calls—she was told, "The older will serve the younger."[f] **13**Just as it is written: "Jacob I loved, but Esau I hated."[g]

14What then shall we say? Is God unjust? Not at all! **15**For he says to Moses,

> "I will have mercy[D] on whom I have mercy,
> and I will have compassion on whom I have
> compassion."[h]

16It does not, therefore, depend on man's desire or effort, but on God's mercy. **17**For the Scripture says to Phar-aoh: "I raised you up for this very purpose, that I might display my power in you and that my name might be pro-claimed in all the earth."[i] **18**Therefore God has mercy on whom he wants to have mercy, and he hardens whom he wants to harden.

19One of you will say to me: "Then why does God still blame us? For who resists his will?" **20**But who are you, O

In what sense is Christ *the firstborn?* (8:29)

Firstborn was a term related more to position than to order of birth. It was a Hebrew way of saying that someone was especially honored. In another sense, however, Jesus became the first of a brand new kind of humanity, raised from the dead into spiritual life (1 Cor. 15:20). In that sense, Jesus is the firstborn of what we, by grace, are becoming. Also see *Why is Jesus called the firstborn?* (Col. 1:15).

Don't Christians ever lose? (8:37)

We cannot balance physical reality with spiritu-al reality. On the cross, it looked like Jesus was overcome. In reality, he was the overcom-er! The moment he died, he took away the pow-er of the one who held the power of death (Heb. 2:14). He taught his disciples that they would have to lose their lives to really live (Luke 9:24), that they could only be great by becoming slaves (Mark 10:43–44) and that the way to be exalted is to be humbled (Matt. 23:12). Such ideas seem to be contradictions because we see things from the physical realm. But the fact is that even in defeat, in Christ we win.

Did someone call Paul a liar? (9:1)

Probably not. But because some had accused him of turning his back on Israel, Paul used strong language to affirm the truth of what he was saying. He wanted to emphasize that he had not abandoned his own people—that he was still concerned for them. His accusers probably felt that his strong emphasis on grace meant that he was denying the Jews and Scrip-ture.

Was Paul really willing to be *cut off from Christ?* (9:3)

No. This was Paul's dramatic way of express-ing his intense love for the Jews. He was offer-ing to substitute himself in their place, to bear their punishment—much as Christ did for us. Even so, Paul's offer was hypothetical; it's im-possible for one human to do this for another.

How can the people of Israel not be Israel? (9:6)

The first *Israel* refers to the nation—an ethnic category. The second *Israel* refers to individ-uals who genuinely believe in God and come to him through faith in Christ—a spiritual cate-gory. Some who were Israel by the first defini-tion were not by the second. Others, though not Israel in an ethnic sense, had become Isra-el in a spiritual sense (v. 8; Gal. 3:29).

Esau I hated (9:13)

See *How can God hate?* (Mal. 1:2–3).

Why take responsibility for choosing a salvation already decided? (9:16)

The doctrine of election, which we may not fully understand, doesn't rule out human respon-sibility. The Bible is clear that God wants every-one to repent, be saved, come to know the truth and not perish (1 Tim. 2:4). At the same time this verse emphasizes God's sovereignty in the matter. See article: *Does God play favor-ites?* (9:8–33).

---

[a]36 Psalm 44:22   [b]38 Or *nor heavenly rulers*   [c]5 Or *Christ, who is over all. God be forever praised!* Or *Christ. God who is over all be forever praised!*   [d]7 Gen. 21:12   [e]9 Gen. 18:10,14   [f]12 Gen. 25:23   [g]13 Mal. 1:2,3   [h]15 Exodus 33:19   [i]17 Exodus 9:16

man, to talk back to God? "Shall what is formed say to him who formed it, 'Why did you make me like this?' "[a] 21Does not the potter have the right to make out of the same lump of clay some pottery for noble purposes and some for common use?

22What if God, choosing to show his wrath and make his power known, bore with great patience the objects of his wrath—prepared for destruction? 23What if he did this to make the riches of his gloryD known to the objects of his mercyD, whom he prepared in advance for glory— 24even us, whom he also called, not only from the JewsD but also from the GentilesD? 25As he says in Hosea:

> "I will call them 'my people' who are not my
>   people;
>   and I will call her 'my loved one' who is not
>   my loved one,"[b]

26and,

> "It will happen that in the very place where it
>   was said to them,
>   'You are not my people,'
>   they will be called 'sons of the living God.' "[c]

27Isaiah cries out concerning Israel:

> "Though the number of the Israelites be like
>   the sand by the sea,
>   only the remnantD will be saved.

a20 Isaiah 29:16; 45:9   b25 Hosea 2:23   c26 Hosea 1:10

What question is Paul really asking here? (9:22–23)

Paul asks, in essence, how do we respond if God does these things? His hypothetical questions illustrate the sovereign and supreme will of God: If God is like a potter who can mold the clay as he sees fit (v. 21), then he can also work with sinners as he sees fit. He can choose to exercise great patience towards those headed for destruction. At the same time he can use judgment as a means to mold those who are headed for glory. When Paul puts it this way, he shows that God's discipline can actually be a tool of mercy—bringing people to a place of repentance.

Does God play favorites? (9:8–33)

The whole Bible teaches that God is fair and just (Psalm 111:7). It also states that God does not *take pleasure in the death of the wicked* (Ezek. 18:23), but that he wants *all men to be saved* (1 Tim. 2:4).

Therefore, the idea of God's *purpose in election* (v. 11) raises some hard questions, such as "How can God choose some and pass by others?" People have attempted to explain God's election in several ways.

Some hold the view that God elects some to be saved because he knows beforehand that they will choose to accept Christ (8:29). Their election, according to this view, is based on God's foreknowledge (Arminianism).

Others conclude that God, in his wise and sovereign will, chooses some but not others for reasons we cannot understand. His selection may *seem* unfair, but that is simply because we have a limited perspective. Humans, bound in sin, do not naturally seek God (3:11), but when God's grace comes to the *elect,* it frees them to choose God (Calvinism).

Still others emphasize that God elected Jesus, his Son, and that all those who are in Christ by faith share in that corporate election.

What about Pharaoh (vv. 17–18)? While the Bible clearly states that God hardened Pharaoh's heart (v. 18; see Exodus 9:12), it also records Pharaoh's own decision to harden his heart (Exodus 8:15). See article: *Who hardened Pharaoh's heart?* (Exodus 10:1).

The mystery of how God works in *election* is not easily resolved. Difficult questions continue to confound us. In the end we may need to confess that our understanding is limited, that we may be missing some key part of God's plan that would allow us to understand *election* better. For more on the subject, see article: *Why does God harden some people's hearts?* (Exodus 11:3).

28For the Lord will carry out
> his sentence on earth with speed and
>   finality."*a*

29It is just as Isaiah said previously:

> "Unless the Lord Almighty
>   had left us descendants,
> we would have become like Sodom,
>   we would have been like Gomorrah."*b*

Israel's Unbelief

30What then shall we say? That the Gentiles*D*, who did not pursue righteousness*D*, have obtained it, a righteousness that is by faith; **31**but Israel, who pursued a law of righteousness, has not attained it. **32**Why not? Because they pursued it not by faith but as if it were by works. They stumbled over the "stumbling stone." **33**As it is written:

> "See, I lay in Zion*D* a stone that causes men to
>   stumble
> and a rock that makes them fall,
> and the one who trusts in him will never be
>   put to shame."*c*

10 Brothers, my heart's desire and prayer to God for the Israelites is that they may be saved. **2**For I can testify about them that they are zealous for God, but their zeal*D* is not based on knowledge. **3**Since they did not know the righteousness that comes from God and sought to establish their own, they did not submit to God's righteousness. **4**Christ is the end of the law so that there may be righteousness for everyone who believes.

5Moses describes in this way the righteousness that is by the law: "The man who does these things will live by them."*d* **6**But the righteousness that is by faith says: "Do not say in your heart, 'Who will ascend into heaven?'*e*" (that is, to bring Christ down) **7**"or 'Who will descend into the deep?'*f*" (that is, to bring Christ up from the dead). **8**But what does it say? "The word is near you; it is in your mouth and in your heart,"*g* that is, the word of faith we are proclaiming: **9**That if you confess with your mouth, "Jesus is Lord," and believe in your heart that God raised him from the dead, you will be saved. **10**For it is with your heart that you believe and are justified*D*, and it is with your mouth that you confess and are saved. **11**As the Scripture says, "Anyone who trusts in him will never be put to shame."*h* **12**For there is no difference between Jew*D* and Gentile—the same Lord is Lord of all and richly blesses all who call on him, **13**for, "Everyone who calls on the name of the Lord will be saved."*i*

14How, then, can they call on the one they have not believed in? And how can they believe in the one of whom they have not heard? And how can they hear without someone preaching to them? **15**And how can they preach unless they are sent? As it is written, "How beautiful are the feet of those who bring good news!"*j*

16But not all the Israelites accepted the good news. For Isaiah says, "Lord, who has believed our message?"*k* **17**Consequently, faith comes from hearing the message,

What will happen to those who believe in God but not in Christ? (10:3-4)

Those who refuse to accept Christ do not really know God, even if they profess to believe in God. Jesus told the Jews of his day that God could not be their Father because they didn't recognize him as God's Son (John 8:42,47). Also see *What about those who never hear the gospel?* (10:14-15).

Are the Ten Commandments obsolete? (10:4)

No. They express God's standards of righteousness, which remain relevant and contemporary. Christ, however, has completed the law. Certain elements (animal sacrifices, for example) foreshadowed Christ; such things are no longer necessary because Christ has fulfilled the law. The law also made a distinction between holy things and common things (eating certain foods, observing certain days and so on). Christ changed this so that all things have become holy.

How is Christ brought *up* and *down*? (10:6-7)

Paul's Jewish readers would have understood this phrase in light of similar wording found in Deut. 30:11-14. In that passage, Moses assured the Israelites that following the law wasn't too difficult—they wouldn't have to ascend into heaven or cross the sea to follow the law. In the same way, Christians don't have to do heroic deeds to earn salvation. Salvation comes by faith alone.

What does it take to be saved? (10:9-10)

A relationship with God is required for salvation. Even though sin broke this relationship, God provides a way back through Jesus Christ, the mediator who restores the relationship (1 Tim. 2:5). We are saved when we sincerely believe Jesus died and was resurrected, and we trust in him as our only way to eternal life. Such deep convictions will inevitably be confessed by one's words and way of living.

What about those who never hear the gospel? (10:14-15)

Some think God may give special revelations to certain people (as it appears he did at times in the Old Testament). Others suggest that those who accept what little God has given them (for example, the evidence of creation, as in 1:18-20) will find his mercy. Still others, however, see no possibility for such exceptions in the New Testament (John 14:6; Acts 4:12). Even if there were exceptions, they would not undercut Jesus' command to preach the gospel to every person.

---

*a*28 Isaiah 10:22,23   *b*29 Isaiah 1:9   *c*33 Isaiah 8:14; 28:16
*d*5 Lev. 18:5   *e*6 Deut. 30:12   *f*7 Deut. 30:13
*g*8 Deut. 30:14   *h*11 Isaiah 28:16   *i*13 Joel 2:32
*j*15 Isaiah 52:7   *k*16 Isaiah 53:1

and the message is heard through the word of Christ. **18**But I ask: Did they not hear? Of course they did:

> "Their voice has gone out into all the earth,
> their words to the ends of the world."[a]

19Again I ask: Did Israel not understand? First, Moses says,

> "I will make you envious by those who are not
>   a nation;
> I will make you angry by a nation that has
>   no understanding."[b]

20And Isaiah boldly says,

> "I was found by those who did not seek me;
> I revealed myself to those who did not ask
>   for me."[c]

21But concerning Israel he says,

> "All day long I have held out my hands
> to a disobedient and obstinate people."[d]

The Remnant of Israel

11 I ask then: Did God reject his people? By no means! I am an Israelite myself, a descendant of Abraham, from the tribe of Benjamin. **2**God did not reject his people, whom he foreknew. Don't you know what the Scripture says in the passage about Elijah—how he appealed to God against Israel: **3**"Lord, they have killed your prophets[D] and torn down your altars; I am the only one left, and they are trying to kill me"[e]? **4**And what was God's answer to him? "I have reserved for myself seven thousand who have not bowed the knee to Baal[D]."[f] **5**So too, at the present time there is a remnant[D] chosen by grace[D]. **6**And if by grace, then it is no longer by works; if it were, grace would no longer be grace.[g]

7What then? What Israel sought so earnestly it did not obtain, but the elect[D] did. The others were hardened, **8**as it is written:

> "God gave them a spirit of stupor,
>   eyes so that they could not see
>   and ears so that they could not hear,
> to this very day."[h]

9And David says:

> "May their table become a snare and a trap,
>   a stumbling block[D] and a retribution[D] for
>   them.
> **10**May their eyes be darkened so they cannot see,
>   and their backs be bent forever."[i]

Ingrafted Branches

11Again I ask: Did they stumble so as to fall beyond recovery? Not at all! Rather, because of their transgression, salvation[D] has come to the Gentiles[D] to make Israel envious. **12**But if their transgression means riches for the world, and their loss means riches for the Gentiles, how much greater riches will their fullness bring!

13I am talking to you Gentiles. Inasmuch as I am the

Are envy and anger evangelistic techniques? (10:19)

Not techniques, but catalysts. God seems to have provoked Israel's anger and envy to wake them up to what they were missing in Christ. In the same way, a believer's life may first provoke jealousy and resentment in others, but may eventually help them turn to God.

SCRIPTURE LINK (11:2) *Elijah*

See 1 Kings 19.

Remnant (11:5)

Those who remain faithful and escape God's judgment though most of those around them are unfaithful. Although small and insignificant, the *remnant* serves as a symbol of hope pointing toward the vast, innumerable multitude that one day will stand saved before God (Rev. 7:9).

Did Israel—God's chosen people—lose their salvation? (11:7)

No, because God chose Israel as a nation, as an example to other nations of God's earthly ideal. However, he didn't promise eternal salvation to each individual Israelite. Some Israelites chose to reject God's offer (10:21). Much of Israel missed the salvation they *sought so earnestly* because they tried to earn God's favor instead of depending on him for salvation.

Why would God spiritually anesthetize his people? (11:8)

God doesn't want people to have a *spirit of stupor*, but he allows them to reap the consequences of their own choices. The more they follow God's way, the more God will show his way to them. But those who continually resist the things of God will become confused—spiritually deaf and blind.

Will some get a second chance at salvation? (11:11)

This is not about *individuals* cut off from salvation and then grafted in again. Rather, this is about God's dealing with entire "branches" of people—Israel and the Gentiles. Israel has been judged for its unbelief (vv. 5–7). Some of the natural branches, representing unbelieving Israel, have been broken off while the Gentiles, represented by the wild shoot, have been grafted in (v. 17). But this judgment is not permanent, and the people of Israel can yet enjoy salvation by turning in faith to the Messiah (v. 26).

---

a18 Psalm 19:4   *b19* Deut. 32:21   *c20* Isaiah 65:1
d21 Isaiah 65:2   *e3* 1 Kings 19:10,14   *f4* 1 Kings 19:18
g6 Some manuscripts *by grace. But if by works, then it is no longer grace; if it were, work would no longer be work.*   *h8* Deut. 29:4; Isaiah 29:10   *i10* Psalm 69:22,23

apostle[D] to the Gentiles[D], I make much of my ministry [14]in the hope that I may somehow arouse my own people to envy and save some of them. [15]For if their rejection is the reconciliation of the world, what will their acceptance be but life from the dead? [16]If the part of the dough offered as firstfruits[D] is holy, then the whole batch is holy; if the root is holy, so are the branches.

[17]If some of the branches have been broken off, and you, though a wild olive shoot, have been grafted in among the others and now share in the nourishing sap from the olive root, [18]do not boast over those branches. If you do, consider this: You do not support the root, but the root supports you. [19]You will say then, "Branches were broken off so that I could be grafted in." [20]Granted. But they were broken off because of unbelief, and you stand by faith. Do not be arrogant, but be afraid. [21]For if God did not spare the natural branches, he will not spare you either.

[22]Consider therefore the kindness and sternness of God: sternness to those who fell, but kindness to you, provided that you continue in his kindness. Otherwise, you also will be cut off. [23]And if they do not persist in unbelief, they will be grafted in, for God is able to graft them in again. [24]After all, if you were cut out of an olive tree that is wild by nature, and contrary to nature were grafted into a cultivated olive tree, how much more readily will these, the natural branches, be grafted into their own olive tree!

All Israel Will Be Saved

[25]I do not want you to be ignorant of this mystery[D], brothers, so that you may not be conceited: Israel has experienced a hardening in part until the full number of the Gentiles has come in. [26]And so all Israel will be saved, as it is written:

> "The deliverer will come from Zion[D];
> he will turn godlessness away from Jacob.
> [27]And this is[a] my covenant[D] with them
> when I take away their sins."[b]

[28]As far as the gospel[D] is concerned, they are enemies on your account; but as far as election is concerned, they are loved on account of the patriarchs[D], [29]for God's gifts and his call are irrevocable. [30]Just as you who were at one time disobedient to God have now received mercy[D] as a result of their disobedience, [31]so they too have now become disobedient in order that they too may now[c] receive mercy as a result of God's mercy to you. [32]For God has bound all men over to disobedience so that he may have mercy on them all.

Doxology

> [33]Oh, the depth of the riches of the wisdom
> and[d] knowledge of God!
> How unsearchable his judgments,
> and his paths beyond tracing out!
> [34]"Who has known the mind of the Lord?
> Or who has been his counselor?"[e]
> [35]"Who has ever given to God,
> that God should repay him?"[f]

Can we lose our salvation? (11:21–22)

Some say that continuing to sin can result in one's being *cut off* from God in the end. Others believe that once people are genuinely saved, they cannot be lost. They say that those who are cut off only had *appeared* to be saved but were not genuinely saved. We remain in God's grace not by doing good works, but by seeing our salvation solely as the result of God's kindness. Also see article: *Should we fear falling?* (Heb. 6:6).

Are Jews still the chosen people? (11:22–32)

Most understand Paul to be saying that God has planned a special future for Israel, even though he has also now chosen Gentiles as his people. Because historical events have highlighted the Jews' continuous presence as a distinct people (the Holocaust, for instance), many believe that the Jewish people have been preserved so they will come to Christ (v. 26). With Israel's reclamation of its homeland, some also believe there will be a glorious national restoration of Israel under Christ (see Ezek. 36:22—37:28).

[a]27 Or *will be*   [b]27 Isaiah 59:20,21; 27:9; Jer. 31:33,34
[c]31 Some manuscripts do not have *now*.   [d]33 Or *riches and the wisdom and the*   [e]34 Isaiah 40:13   [f]35 Job 41:11

36For from him and through him and to him are
all things.
To him be the glory^D forever! Amen.

Living Sacrifices

How painful is it to be a Christian? (12:1)

Growing, maturing Christians will encounter
some pain. We lose superficial pleasures when
we abandon sinful activities. We may have to
struggle to establish new patterns of living. Becoming *living sacrifices* (that is, giving our lives
totally to God) does not mean endless martyrdom, however. We can find fulfillment and satisfaction in becoming what God created us to
be, no matter what the cost. We will see a
higher purpose in life than simply avoiding
pain.

How can we know God's will? (12:2)

By honoring and obeying him, and by refusing
to be influenced by societal pressures. As we
replace our old way of thinking and adopt an
entirely new perspective—from God's point of
view—we'll begin to recognize God's will more
and more. We'll find it easier to hear his voice
in a variety of situations. God may not dictate
the details of our lives (such as what color
clothes to wear), but he will give us spiritual
principles for everyday decisions. Also see article: *Can we find God's will by putting out a
fleece?* (Judges 6:37–40).

Is Paul against having a positive self-image? (12:3)

Paul urges us to evaluate ourselves honestly.
When we overestimate ourselves, we may try
to do tasks for which we are not equipped.
There are other dangers as well: we may feel
we don't need others to minister to us or we
may despair when we finally realize we can't
live up to the unrealistic expectations we place
on ourselves. True self-worth comes from accepting who we are in Christ and understanding that God loves us as we are. We should
honestly accept how God made and gifted us.

Gifts (12:6)

Abilities given by the Spirit for the purpose of
ministry. *Gifts* are supernatural abilities, above
and beyond natural talent. In some cases,
however, they may spring from a spiritual empowerment of a person's natural abilities.

How much should we give up to live at peace? (12:18)

Our natural response is to surrender little for
the sake of peace. But the Bible teaches that
we are to overlook offenses and work at loving
others, praying for those who attack us (Prov.
19:11; Matt. 5:44). If they continue to attack,
we may confront them or seek protection, but
we do so for their good, hoping to win them
over, not for personal vengeance (Matt.
18:15–17).

Why put *burning coals* on someone? (12:20)

To *heap burning coals* on someone's head has
been understood in several figurative ways.
One view is that our kindness will cause our
enemies' faces to burn with shame and motivate them to change their ways. The Bible never endorses personal revenge or manipulation
of others. To love our enemies means to do
what is ultimately best for them.

12 Therefore, I urge you, brothers, in view of God's
mercy^D, to offer your bodies as living sacrifices^D,
holy and pleasing to God—this is your spiritual^a act of
worship. **2**Do not conform any longer to the pattern of
this world, but be transformed by the renewing of your
mind. Then you will be able to test and approve what
God's will is—his good, pleasing and perfect will.

3For by the grace^D given me I say to every one of you:
Do not think of yourself more highly than you ought, but
rather think of yourself with sober judgment, in accordance with the measure of faith God has given you. **4**Just
as each of us has one body with many members, and
these members do not all have the same function, **5**so in
Christ we who are many form one body, and each member belongs to all the others. **6**We have different gifts, according to the grace given us. If a man's gift is prophesying, let him use it in proportion to his^b faith. **7**If it is
serving, let him serve; if it is teaching, let him teach; **8**if it
is encouraging, let him encourage; if it is contributing to
the needs of others, let him give generously; if it is leadership, let him govern diligently; if it is showing mercy, let
him do it cheerfully.

Love

9Love must be sincere. Hate what is evil; cling to what
is good. **10**Be devoted to one another in brotherly love.
Honor one another above yourselves. **11**Never be lacking
in zeal^D, but keep your spiritual fervor, serving the Lord.
12Be joyful in hope, patient in affliction^D, faithful in
prayer. **13**Share with God's people who are in need. Practice hospitality.

14Bless those who persecute you; bless and do not
curse. **15**Rejoice with those who rejoice; mourn with those
who mourn. **16**Live in harmony with one another. Do not
be proud, but be willing to associate with people of low
position.^c Do not be conceited.

17Do not repay anyone evil for evil. Be careful to do
what is right in the eyes of everybody. **18**If it is possible,
as far as it depends on you, live at peace^D with everyone.
19Do not take revenge, my friends, but leave room for
God's wrath, for it is written: "It is mine to avenge^D; I will
repay,"^d says the Lord. **20**On the contrary:

"If your enemy is hungry, feed him;
if he is thirsty, give him something to drink.
In doing this, you will heap burning coals on
his head."^e

21Do not be overcome by evil, but overcome evil with
good.

Submission to the Authorities

13 Everyone must submit himself to the governing
authorities, for there is no authority except that
which God has established. The authorities that exist have
been established by God. **2**Consequently, he who rebels
against the authority is rebelling against what God has in-

---

^a1 Or *reasonable*   ^b6 Or *in agreement with the*   ^c16 Or *willing*
to do menial work   ^d19 Deut. 32:35   ^e20 Prov. 25:21,22

stituted, and those who do so will bring judgment on themselves. ³For rulers hold no terror for those who do right, but for those who do wrong. Do you want to be free from fear of the one in authority? Then do what is right and he will commend you. ⁴For he is God's servant to do you good. But if you do wrong, be afraid, for he does not bear the sword for nothing. He is God's servant, an agent of wrath to bring punishment on the wrongdoer. ⁵Therefore, it is necessary to submit to the authorities, not only because of possible punishment but also because of conscience.

⁶This is also why you pay taxes, for the authorities are God's servants, who give their full time to governing. ⁷Give everyone what you owe him: If you owe taxes, pay taxes; if revenue, then revenue; if respect, then respect; if honor, then honor.

Love, for the Day Is Near

⁸Let no debt remain outstanding, except the continuing debt to love one another, for he who loves his fellowman has fulfilled the law. ⁹The commandments, "Do not commit adultery," "Do not murder," "Do not steal," "Do not covet,"ᵃ and whatever other commandment there may be, are summed up in this one rule: "Love your neighbor as yourself."ᵇ ¹⁰Love does no harm to its neighbor. Therefore love is the fulfillment of the law.

¹¹And do this, understanding the present time. The hour has come for you to wake up from your slumber, because our salvationᴰ is nearer now than when we first believed. ¹²The night is nearly over; the day is almost here. So let us put aside the deeds of darkness and put on the armor of light. ¹³Let us behave decently, as in the daytime, not in orgies and drunkenness, not in sexual immorality and debauchery, not in dissension and jealousy. ¹⁴Rather, clothe yourselves with the Lord Jesus Christ, and do not think about how to gratify the desires of the sinful nature.ᶜ

ᵃ9 Exodus 20:13-15,17; Deut. 5:17-19,21   ᵇ9 Lev. 19:18
ᶜ14 Or *the flesh*

Why would Paul call Nero *God's servant to do you good?* (13:4)

Nero could hardly be called a servant of God. He persecuted Christians and viciously executed them. See article: *Why were Christians suffering?* (1 Peter 1:6). But in a limited sense, Nero did right when he punished criminals or maintained law and order. Paul urged first-century believers to pray for their rulers so peace would be kept and the gospel could be spread (1 Tim. 2:1–3). Paul probably prayed similarly for Nero.

Is love the only rule? (13:10)

Paul's statement, *love is the fulfillment of the law,* echoes Jesus' teaching that *all the Law and Prophets* hang on two commands: to love God completely and to love others as ourselves (Matt. 22:37–40). All God's commands (in both the Old Testament and New Testament) are practical explanations of how to show love in specific circumstances. Also see *Are the Ten Commandments obsolete?* (10:4).

How close is Christ's return? (13:11–12)

Paul and other New Testament writers taught that Christ would come again "soon." Their language could be understood in terms other than approximate measures of time. Christ's return is "soon" from a prophetic perspective. This perspective isn't concerned with *when* things will happen as much as with *what* will happen. Timing is less important than what is next on the agenda of God's salvation program. From this perspective, the next event is the second coming of Christ.

Does God support bad government? (13:1–7)

God wants rulers—no matter what the system of government or the political ideology—to govern fairly and with justice. God may use human agencies and institutions, such as the ballot box, to promote justice.

In some cases, God permits unjust rulers to seize power. This doesn't mean God participates in their evil activities. Still, he can use human deeds—good or evil—to help accomplish his greater purposes which are always good. For example, God allowed wicked Babylon to discipline the nation of Judah. See article: *Does God use evil to do good?* (Hab. 1:6,13). He permitted brutal rulers to conquer his people in the hopes that his people would turn again to him.

This passage doesn't address the issue of civil disobedience, but other passages do. See article: *Should we not resist oppression?* (Luke 6:29–30). When government intrudes into God's realm of morality and religion, believers *must obey God rather than men* (Acts 5:29; also see Daniel 3, 6).

Also see *Why would Paul call Nero God's servant to do you good?* (13:4).

What does God consider essential? (14:1)

Some instructions are timeless (13:8–10) —essential items on God's list. Other Biblical instructions were intended to address specific situations or times—some having nothing to do with today (2 Tim. 4:13, for example). Instructions for first-century Christians living in a pagan culture—but also containing principles applicable for today—may be interpreted in various ways. One thing is clear, however: such *disputable matters* are not to divide believers. Christians must be non-judgmental, understanding each other's differences (v. 3).

Can we ever criticize? (14:4)

Yes, but not in a condemning manner. Those with wrong motives or negative attitudes who judge others aren't trying to build them up. Instead, they're trying to tear them down. Still, even constructive criticism, given to help the *weak* become *strong*, may require confrontation. But confronting can be done with genuine love and respect. Those who correct others will want to keep in mind their own shortcomings (Gal. 6:1).

Will believers face judgment? (14:10)

Yes. Both believers and unbelievers will appear before God's *judgment seat*, or *great white throne* (2 Cor. 5:10; Rev. 20:11–12). Believers will be pronounced justified by faith in Christ. They will then receive rewards for their faithful deeds (2:6–8; Matt. 16:27; 1 Cor. 3:12–15).

Stumbling block (14:13)

Anything or anyone that causes someone to sin. If your conscience tells you a certain action is sinful, then it is sin for you to do it. If someone else pressures you into this action anyway—perhaps with rationalizations that the thing is not sinful—then that person has become a stumbling block to you (1 Cor. 8:9–13).

Are certain foods off-limits? (14:15)

Certain foods may not always be off-limits, but eating them with those whose faith is weak can be an unloving thing to do. The same thing can be said for other activities (wearing certain clothes or enjoying certain entertainments, for example). It's possible that something can bring glory to God one time and be a stumbling block the next. As an example of how we might behave toward others, consider Jesus: he was tender toward the spiritually weak—but not toward the legalistic critics of his day.

Condemned (14:22–23)

A conviction of the heart for specific sin—not a sentence of exclusion from heaven. Convicted by conscience and God's Spirit, we may confess our sin and find forgiveness from God.

The Weak and the Strong

14 Accept him whose faith is weak, without passing judgment on disputable matters. **2**One man's faith allows him to eat everything, but another man, whose faith is weak, eats only vegetables. **3**The man who eats everything must not look down on him who does not, and the man who does not eat everything must not condemn the man who does, for God has accepted him. **4**Who are you to judge someone else's servant? To his own master he stands or falls. And he will stand, for the Lord is able to make him stand.

5One man considers one day more sacred[D] than another; another man considers every day alike. Each one should be fully convinced in his own mind. **6**He who regards one day as special, does so to the Lord. He who eats meat, eats to the Lord, for he gives thanks to God; and he who abstains, does so to the Lord and gives thanks to God. **7**For none of us lives to himself alone and none of us dies to himself alone. **8**If we live, we live to the Lord; and if we die, we die to the Lord. So, whether we live or die, we belong to the Lord.

9For this very reason, Christ died and returned to life so that he might be the Lord of both the dead and the living. **10**You, then, why do you judge your brother? Or why do you look down on your brother? For we will all stand before God's judgment seat. **11**It is written:

> " 'As surely as I live,' says the Lord,
> 'every knee will bow before me;
>   every tongue will confess to God.' "[a]

12So then, each of us will give an account of himself to God.

13Therefore let us stop passing judgment on one another. Instead, make up your mind not to put any stumbling block[D] or obstacle in your brother's way. **14**As one who is in the Lord Jesus, I am fully convinced that no food[b] is unclean[D] in itself. But if anyone regards something as unclean, then for him it is unclean. **15**If your brother is distressed because of what you eat, you are no longer acting in love. Do not by your eating destroy your brother for whom Christ died. **16**Do not allow what you consider good to be spoken of as evil. **17**For the kingdom of God[D] is not a matter of eating and drinking, but of righteousness[D], peace and joy in the Holy Spirit, **18**because anyone who serves Christ in this way is pleasing to God and approved by men.

19Let us therefore make every effort to do what leads to peace and to mutual edification. **20**Do not destroy the work of God for the sake of food. All food is clean, but it is wrong for a man to eat anything that causes someone else to stumble. **21**It is better not to eat meat or drink wine or to do anything else that will cause your brother to fall.

22So whatever you believe about these things keep between yourself and God. Blessed is the man who does not condemn himself by what he approves. **23**But the man who has doubts is condemned if he eats, because his eating is not from faith; and everything that does not come from faith is sin.

---

a11 Isaiah 45:23   *b14* Or *that nothing*

15

We who are strong ought to bear with the failings of the weak and not to please ourselves. **2**Each of us should please his neighbor for his good, to build him up. **3**For even Christ did not please himself but, as it is written: "The insults of those who insult you have fallen on me."*a* **4**For everything that was written in the past was written to teach us, so that through endurance and the encouragement of the Scriptures we might have hope.

5May the God who gives endurance and encouragement give you a spirit of unity among yourselves as you follow Christ Jesus, **6**so that with one heart and mouth you may glorify the God and Father of our Lord Jesus Christ.

7Accept one another, then, just as Christ accepted you, in order to bring praise to God. **8**For I tell you that Christ has become a servant of the Jews**Db** on behalf of God's truth, to confirm the promises made to the patriarchs**D** **9**so that the Gentiles**D** may glorify God for his mercy**D**, as it is written:

> "Therefore I will praise you among the
> Gentiles;
> I will sing hymns to your name."*c*

10Again, it says,

> "Rejoice, O Gentiles, with his people."*d*

11And again,

> "Praise the Lord, all you Gentiles,
> and sing praises to him, all you peoples."*e*

12And again, Isaiah says,

> "The Root of Jesse will spring up,
> one who will arise to rule over the nations;
> the Gentiles will hope in him."*f*

13May the God of hope fill you with all joy and peace**D** as you trust in him, so that you may overflow with hope by the power of the Holy Spirit.

Paul the Minister to the Gentiles

14I myself am convinced, my brothers, that you yourselves are full of goodness, complete in knowledge and competent to instruct one another. **15**I have written you quite boldly on some points, as if to remind you of them again, because of the grace**D** God gave me **16**to be a minister of Christ Jesus to the Gentiles with the priestly duty of proclaiming the gospel**D** of God, so that the Gentiles might become an offering acceptable to God, sanctified**D** by the Holy Spirit.

17Therefore I glory**D** in Christ Jesus in my service to God. **18**I will not venture to speak of anything except what Christ has accomplished through me in leading the Gentiles to obey God by what I have said and done— **19**by the power of signs and miracles, through the power of the Spirit. So from Jerusalem**D** all the way around to Illyricum, I have fully proclaimed the gospel of Christ. **20**It has always been my ambition to preach the gospel where Christ was not known, so that I would not be building on someone else's foundation. **21**Rather, as it is written:

Strong . . . weak (15:1)

The strong in faith were those who understood that certain foods by themselves were not sinful. With the freedom of that understanding, they could eat those foods in good conscience (14:23). The weak in faith did not have that understanding. Eating such foods would have violated their conscience, causing them to sin (14:23).

How do the Scriptures encourage? (15:4)

They give hope: by revealing God's glorious future for believers; by reminding us of God's grace and power—resources to strengthen believers; by providing examples of those who because of faith persevered, challenging us to do the same.

Can Christians agree on everything? (15:5–7)

No. But the goal is not to think alike or avoid all disagreements. The goal is to glorify God. We can strive for a unity in Christ that supersedes our different preferences and personalities. Our differences need not divide us—in fact, our diversity can enable us to multiply our praise and service for God. Various gifts can combine for greater glory to God. Also see *Does unity mean unanimity?* (Eph. 4:13).

I glory (15:17)

Paul was not bragging about himself. Rather, he was honoring God for what Christ had accomplished through the work he had been given to do (v. 18; 1 Cor. 1:31). When we have this attitude and glory in God's accomplishments through us, we are worshiping God.

---

*a*3 Psalm 69:9   *b*8 Greek *circumcision*   *c*9 2 Samuel 22:50;
Psalm 18:49   *d*10 Deut. 32:43   *e*11 Psalm 117:1
*f*12 Isaiah 11:10

"Those who were not told about him will see,
and those who have not heard will
understand."[a]

22This is why I have often been hindered from coming to you.

Paul's Plan to Visit Rome

23But now that there is no more place for me to work in these regions, and since I have been longing for many years to see you, **24**I plan to do so when I go to Spain. I hope to visit you while passing through and to have you assist me on my journey there, after I have enjoyed your company for a while. **25**Now, however, I am on my way to Jerusalem[D] in the service of the saints[D] there. **26**For Macedonia and Achaia were pleased to make a contribution for the poor among the saints in Jerusalem. **27**They were pleased to do it, and indeed they owe it to them. For if the Gentiles[D] have shared in the Jews'[D] spiritual blessings, they owe it to the Jews to share with them their material blessings. **28**So after I have completed this task and have made sure that they have received this fruit, I will go to Spain and visit you on the way. **29**I know that when I come to you, I will come in the full measure of the blessing of Christ.

30I urge you, brothers, by our Lord Jesus Christ and by the love of the Spirit, to join me in my struggle by praying to God for me. **31**Pray that I may be rescued from the unbelievers in Judea and that my service in Jerusalem may be acceptable to the saints there, **32**so that by God's will I may come to you with joy and together with you be refreshed. **33**The God of peace[D] be with you all. Amen.

Personal Greetings

16 I commend to you our sister Phoebe, a servant[b] of the church in Cenchrea. **2**I ask you to receive her in the Lord in a way worthy of the saints and to give her any help she may need from you, for she has been a great help to many people, including me.

3Greet Priscilla[c] and Aquila, my fellow workers in Christ Jesus. **4**They risked their lives for me. Not only I but all the churches of the Gentiles are grateful to them.

[a]21 Isaiah 52:15   [b]1 Or *deaconess*   [c]3 Greek *Prisca*, a variant of *Priscilla*

Why did Paul need prayer? (15:31)
Even though Paul had healed the sick and raised the dead, he knew that everything he did was possible only because God was working in him. He knew how vital the prayers of others were if he wanted to maintain God's work in his life. Paul suspected correctly that the unbelieving Jews in Jerusalem wanted to harm him. He knew he could benefit by having others pray for him, though circumstances did not turn out the way he might have hoped.

What's important about all these personal greetings? (16:1–16)
It's interesting that Romans, a profound book of doctrine, ends with so many personal greetings. This illustrates the fact that true doctrine leads to loving fellowship among people. It also shows that no matter how admired and significant Paul was as an apostle, he saw himself simply as one of the believers—a fellow worker and friend of those in Christ.

What did women do in the early church? (16:1–2)

Phoebe was a prominent *servant of the church* at Cenchrea (a harbor village serving Corinth; see **Map 11** at the back of this Bible). She probably carried the letter from Paul to the Roman church. Because *servant* is also translated *deacon* in some cases, some believe Phoebe served the church as a deaconess.

Other women (vv. 3,6–7,12–13,15) probably had significant ministry roles including leadership, teaching and evangelism. Many believe *Junias* (v. 7) is feminine and refers to a woman who, along with her husband, was an apostle of the church, serving as a church messenger or missionary (2 Cor. 8:23; Phil. 2:25). For further discussion, see article: *Why silence the women?* (1 Tim. 2:11). Also see *Why can't a woman teach a man?* (1 Tim. 2:12).

5Greet also the church that meets at their house.

Greet my dear friend Epenetus, who was the first convert to Christ in the province of Asia.

6Greet Mary, who worked very hard for you.

7Greet Andronicus and Junias, my relatives who have been in prison with me. They are outstanding among the apostles[D], and they were in Christ before I was.

8Greet Ampliatus, whom I love in the Lord.

9Greet Urbanus, our fellow worker in Christ, and my dear friend Stachys.

10Greet Apelles, tested and approved in Christ.

Greet those who belong to the household of Aristobulus.

11Greet Herodion, my relative.

Greet those in the household of Narcissus who are in the Lord.

12Greet Tryphena and Tryphosa, those women who work hard in the Lord.

Greet my dear friend Persis, another woman who has worked very hard in the Lord.

13Greet Rufus, chosen in the Lord, and his mother, who has been a mother to me, too.

14Greet Asyncritus, Phlegon, Hermes, Patrobas, Hermas and the brothers with them.

15Greet Philologus, Julia, Nereus and his sister, and Olympas and all the saints[D] with them.

16Greet one another with a holy kiss.

All the churches of Christ send greetings.

17I urge you, brothers, to watch out for those who cause divisions and put obstacles in your way that are contrary to the teaching you have learned. Keep away from them. **18**For such people are not serving our Lord Christ, but their own appetites. By smooth talk and flattery they deceive the minds of naive people. **19**Everyone has heard about your obedience, so I am full of joy over you; but I want you to be wise about what is good, and innocent about what is evil.

20The God of peace[D] will soon crush Satan under your feet.

The grace[D] of our Lord Jesus be with you.

21Timothy, my fellow worker, sends his greetings to you, as do Lucius, Jason and Sosipater, my relatives.

22I, Tertius, who wrote down this letter, greet you in the Lord.

23Gaius, whose hospitality I and the whole church here enjoy, sends you his greetings.

Erastus, who is the city's director of public works, and our brother Quartus send you their greetings.[a]

25Now to him who is able to establish you by my gospel[D] and the proclamation of Jesus Christ, according to the revelation[D] of the mystery[D] hidden for long ages past, **26**but now revealed and made known through the prophetic writings by the command of the eternal God, so that all nations might believe and obey him— **27**to the only wise God be glory[D] forever through Jesus Christ! Amen.

Tested and approved (16:10)

That is, mature in the faith. Apelles had probably persevered through many trials, causing others to see him *tested and approved.* God tests us to purify and strengthen us. See *Why does God allow our faith to be tested?* (1 Peter 1:7). We "pass" these "tests" when we persevere and grow in faith because of them.

A holy kiss (16:16)

Kissing the cheek, forehead, beard or hands (but not usually the lips) was frequently used to greet or leave others. Early church writings indicate that, as a rule, men greeted only men while women greeted only women in this way. The principle behind this cultural practice is to express affection for others, although different cultures may choose different methods.

When will Satan be crushed? (16:20)

When Christ returns, Satan will suffer his final defeat (Rev. 20:1–10). Knowing this must have encouraged the Roman church since they were experiencing divisions and obstacles, frustrations instigated by the enemy (vv. 17–19).

Why was salvation a secret for so long? (16:25–26)

It seems unfair that God would hold secret information that could have saved many. But that's not what this verse says. God had revealed himself in various ways through the ages (see, for example, 1:19–20; Heb 1:1–2). Those who trusted in God—even before Christ came—were saved because of their faith. We don't know why God waited until he did to fulfill his promises of the Messiah. Perhaps he delayed so people would realize more fully that they could not save themselves through their own efforts. Also see *The time had fully come* (Gal. 4:4).

---

*a*23 Some manuscripts *their greetings.* *24May the grace of our Lord Jesus Christ be with all of you. Amen.*

1 CORINTHIANS

Why read this book?

Fights. Rumors. Factions. It's all here in 1 Corinthians. Few other passages of Scripture reveal the humanity of Christians as vividly as this book does. Some other topics include: Dealing with a sex-crazed society. Divorce—when is it justified? When Christians can and cannot sue. Get ready! You're about to encounter God's perspective on some hot topics. And in the process you'll see how the church can impact today's world.

Who wrote this book?

Paul, the apostle.

To whom was it written?

Christians in Corinth, an important commercial city in Greece.

Why was it written?

Two or three years after leaving the church he'd started in Corinth, Paul heard disturbing reports: strife and division were seriously threatening the young church. Some had become spiritually arrogant, leading to further problems such as sexual misconduct, wrongs against other believers, abuse of spiritual gifts, and misunderstanding of basic Christian teachings. Paul wrote seeking to restore balance to the church.

When was it written?

Probably in A.D. 54 to 55.

What to look for in 1 Corinthians:

Paul gave the Corinthians what they needed: straightforward advice. Watch for direct, practical information relevant to Christian living and church relationships. You will also encounter great inspiration in these pages. Much of what the Bible has to say about spiritual gifts is found here. It also offers uplifting words about love (ch. 13) and the resurrection (ch. 15).

When did these things happen?

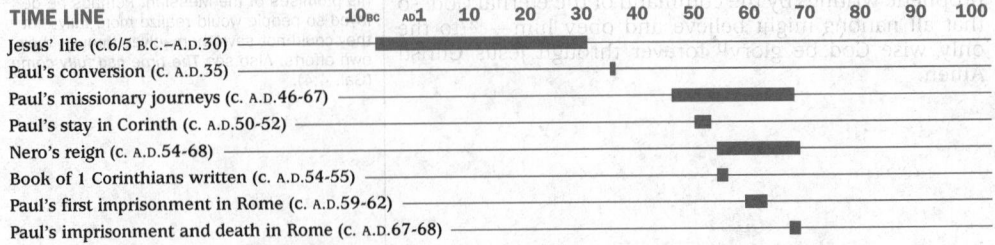

TIME LINE	10 BC	AD 1	10	20	30	40	50	60	70	80	90	100
Jesus' life (c.6/5 B.C.–A.D.30)												
Paul's conversion (C. A.D.35)												
Paul's missionary journeys (C. A.D.46-67)												
Paul's stay in Corinth (C. A.D.50-52)												
Nero's reign (C. A.D.54-68)												
Book of 1 Corinthians written (C. A.D.54-55)												
Paul's first imprisonment in Rome (C. A.D.59-62)												
Paul's imprisonment and death in Rome (C. A.D.67-68)												

1 Paul, called to be an apostle^D of Christ Jesus by the will of God, and our brother Sosthenes,

²To the church of God in Corinth, to those sanctified^D in Christ Jesus and called to be holy, together with all those everywhere who call on the name of our Lord Jesus Christ—their Lord and ours:

³Grace^D and peace^D to you from God our Father and the Lord Jesus Christ.

Thanksgiving

⁴I always thank God for you because of his grace given you in Christ Jesus. ⁵For in him you have been enriched in every way—in all your speaking and in all your knowledge— ⁶because our testimony about Christ was confirmed in you. ⁷Therefore you do not lack any spiritual gift as you eagerly wait for our Lord Jesus Christ to be revealed. ⁸He will keep you strong to the end, so that you will be blameless on the day of our Lord Jesus Christ. ⁹God, who has called you into fellowship with his Son Jesus Christ our Lord, is faithful.

Divisions in the Church

¹⁰I appeal to you, brothers, in the name of our Lord Jesus Christ, that all of you agree with one another so that there may be no divisions among you and that you may be perfectly united in mind and thought. ¹¹My brothers, some from Chloe's household have informed me that there are quarrels among you. ¹²What I mean is this: One of you says, "I follow Paul"; another, "I follow Apollos"; another, "I follow Cephas^a"; still another, "I follow Christ."

¹³Is Christ divided? Was Paul crucified for you? Were you baptized into^b the name of Paul? ¹⁴I am thankful that I did not baptize any of you except Crispus and Gaius, ¹⁵so no one can say that you were baptized into my name. ¹⁶(Yes, I also baptized the household of Stephanas; beyond that, I don't remember if I baptized anyone else.) ¹⁷For Christ did not send me to baptize, but to preach the gospel^D—not with words of human wisdom, lest the cross of Christ be emptied of its power.

Christ the Wisdom and Power of God

¹⁸For the message of the cross is foolishness to those who are perishing, but to us who are being saved it is the power of God. ¹⁹For it is written:

"I will destroy the wisdom of the wise;
    the intelligence of the intelligent I will
        frustrate."^c

²⁰Where is the wise man? Where is the scholar? Where is the philosopher of this age? Has not God made foolish the wisdom of the world? ²¹For since in the wisdom of God the world through its wisdom did not know him, God was pleased through the foolishness of what was preached to save those who believe. ²²Jews^D demand miraculous signs and Greeks look for wisdom, ²³but we preach Christ crucified: a stumbling block^D to Jews and foolishness to Gentiles^D, ²⁴but to those whom God has called, both Jews and Greeks, Christ the power of God and the wisdom of God. ²⁵For the foolishness of God is

---

The Church in Corinth (1:2)

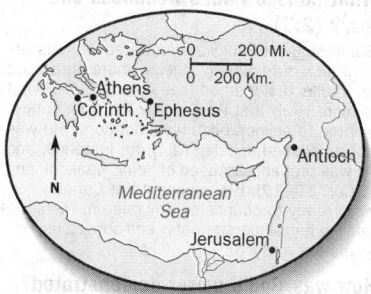

Why call such a flawed church *sanctified*? (1:2)

The word *sanctified* (literally, *made holy*) reflects God's perspective, not necessarily ours. Despite their imperfections, God viewed the Corinthians as forgiven.

Did they actually possess every spiritual gift? (1:7)

Perhaps Paul hoped to disarm his opponents with slight sarcasm and exaggeration. Or, perhaps they did have all the gifts, but weren't using them maturely. Though the Corinthians possessed spiritual gifts, they were plagued with church strife. They fought about being spiritual! Paul writes later that love and unity are better measures of spirituality than gifts (13:1–3). The Corinthians saw themselves as spiritual elites, having all they needed (4:8), but they lacked the evidence of God's grace in their lives.

Can any church be *perfectly united in mind and thought*? (1:10)

Paul wanted to hold out the ideal—the loftiest goal—even if it could never be reached completely. He called on the Corinthians to halt their fighting with one another.

Why did Paul say that Christ did not send him to baptize? (1:17)

Paul was not speaking against baptism. He did baptize a few (1:14,16). However, it's possible some Corinthians believed baptism guaranteed spiritual maturity and security, and Paul seemed to play down such views (also see ch. 10). We, like the Israelites *baptized* in the cloud and sea (10:2), are not guaranteed salvation simply by baptism. More than water is required to be a disciple. See Jesus' full command in Matt. 28:19.

Is Christianity anti-intellectual? (1:18–21)

No. Paul was himself an intellectual. But he meant to drive home a point, that the wisdom and knowledge of *those who are perishing* will not bring them to Christ. In fact, God will destroy that wisdom (v. 19). Paul also may have been thinking of a group in Corinth who opposed him, considering themselves spiritual elites. Later he writes that human knowledge can make people proud and arrogant (8:1). He wanted to show that the work of the cross was a supernatural puzzle far beyond natural thought. It baffled the wisdom of Jewish and Greek systems of thought and, in that sense, was not rational.

---

^a12 That is, Peter   ^b13 Or *in*; also in verse 15
^c19 Isaiah 29:14

What caused Paul's *weakness and fear?* (2:3)

Some suggest Paul was frustrated with his recent lack of results in Athens where he'd used an intellectual method (see Acts 17:17–34). It is more likely that Paul, under fire from critics, wanted to acknowledge his limitations. He was not a polished speaker (2:4), for instance, and he was probably accused of being weak-minded (2 Cor. 10–12). His opponents at Corinth were ready to pounce on any false move—leaving him understandably self-conscious, in *weakness and fear.*

How was God's power demonstrated? (2:4)

By conversions to Christ, but also by signs and wonders such as healings and other supernatural displays of the gifts of the Spirit. Some of Paul's other writings indicate his preaching was accompanied by such things (see Romans 15:18–19; 2 Cor. 12:12; Gal. 3:5).

Why would God keep such vital information secret? (2:7)

Paul wrote from the framework of a Jewish perspective. They believed that God's plan would not be fully revealed until the last days. Paul believed that those last days began with Christ, explaining why God disclosed the long hidden mystery to the saints (Col. 1:26–27). But why would God wait until Jesus' time to unveil his plan? Although Peter linked the delay with God's patience (1 Peter 3:20), Paul only affirmed that God, for whatever reason, has his own timetable and agenda.

Rulers of this age (2:8)

Political and religious rulers clearly were responsible for putting Jesus to death. Some think the phrase may also refer to spiritual powers operating behind the scenes (as in Eph. 6:12).

How does the Spirit teach people? (2:13)

It is a bit vague exactly what Paul meant by *words taught by the Spirit.* His point was that his wisdom originated from God's Spirit, not from human intellect—either his own or that of his teachers. Paul consistently maintained that the Holy Spirit was available to all believers. He lists some of the specific benefits of the Spirit elsewhere (for example, spiritual gifts in 12:1–11 and spiritual fruit in Gal. was 5:22–23).

In what sense does the spiritual person judge all things? (2:15)

Judge is a word that can have many shades of meaning. Here it suggests discernment. The truly spiritual person can determine what is or is not of Christ: how to respond to the immoral (ch. 5), whether or not to eat meat sacrificed to idols (ch. 10), how to behave at the Lord's Supper (ch. 11) and so forth.

Milk . . . solid food (3:2)

Paul saw a parallel between an infant's diet and the Corinthians' spiritual condition. He had first given them *milk*—the basic gospel. But he wanted them to grow beyond that. He wanted them to mature. *Solid food* is not just a matter of having spiritual gifts. It includes using them correctly. Theological knowledge means nothing without the maturity to use it in love (see 8:1).

wiser than man's wisdom, and the weakness of God is stronger than man's strength.

26Brothers, think of what you were when you were called. Not many of you were wise by human standards; not many were influential; not many were of noble birth. **27**But God chose the foolish things of the world to shame the wise; God chose the weak things of the world to shame the strong. **28**He chose the lowly things of this world and the despised things—and the things that are not—to nullify the things that are, **29**so that no one may boast before him. **30**It is because of him that you are in Christ Jesus, who has become for us wisdom from God—that is, our righteousness[D], holiness and redemption[D]. **31**Therefore, as it is written: "Let him who boasts boast in the Lord." [a]

2 When I came to you, brothers, I did not come with eloquence or superior wisdom as I proclaimed to you the testimony about God.[b] **2**For I resolved to know nothing while I was with you except Jesus Christ and him crucified. **3**I came to you in weakness and fear, and with much trembling. **4**My message and my preaching were not with wise and persuasive words, but with a demonstration of the Spirit's power, **5**so that your faith might not rest on men's wisdom, but on God's power.

Wisdom From the Spirit

6We do, however, speak a message of wisdom among the mature, but not the wisdom of this age or of the rulers of this age, who are coming to nothing. **7**No, we speak of God's secret wisdom, a wisdom that has been hidden and that God destined for our glory[D] before time began. **8**None of the rulers of this age understood it, for if they had, they would not have crucified the Lord of glory. **9**However, as it is written:

"No eye has seen,
   no ear has heard,
no mind has conceived
   what God has prepared for those who love
      him"[c]—

10but God has revealed it to us by his Spirit.

The Spirit searches all things, even the deep things of God. **11**For who among men knows the thoughts of a man except the man's spirit within him? In the same way no one knows the thoughts of God except the Spirit of God. **12**We have not received the spirit of the world but the Spirit who is from God, that we may understand what God has freely given us. **13**This is what we speak, not in words taught us by human wisdom but in words taught by the Spirit, expressing spiritual truths in spiritual words.[d] **14**The man without the Spirit does not accept the things that come from the Spirit of God, for they are foolishness to him, and he cannot understand them, because they are spiritually discerned. **15**The spiritual man makes judgments about all things, but he himself is not subject to any man's judgment:

16"For who has known the mind of the Lord
      that he may instruct him?"[e]

But we have the mind of Christ.

[a]31 Jer. 9:24   [b]1 Some manuscripts *as I proclaimed to you God's mystery*   [c]9 Isaiah 64:4   [d]13 Or *Spirit, interpreting spiritual truths to spiritual men*   [e]16 Isaiah 40:13

On Divisions in the Church

3 Brothers, I could not address you as spiritual but as worldly—mere infants in Christ. **2**I gave you milk, not solid food, for you were not yet ready for it. Indeed, you are still not ready. **3**You are still worldly. For since there is jealousy and quarreling among you, are you not worldly? Are you not acting like mere men? **4**For when one says, "I follow Paul," and another, "I follow Apollos," are you not mere men?

5What, after all, is Apollos? And what is Paul? Only servants, through whom you came to believe—as the Lord has assigned to each his task. **6**I planted the seed, Apollos watered it, but God made it grow. **7**So neither he who plants nor he who waters is anything, but only God, who makes things grow. **8**The man who plants and the man who waters have one purpose, and each will be rewarded according to his own labor. **9**For we are God's fellow workers; you are God's field, God's building.

10By the grace**D** God has given me, I laid a foundation as an expert builder, and someone else is building on it. But each one should be careful how he builds. **11**For no one can lay any foundation other than the one already laid, which is Jesus Christ. **12**If any man builds on this foundation using gold, silver, costly stones, wood, hay or straw, **13**his work will be shown for what it is, because the Day will bring it to light. It will be revealed with fire, and the fire will test the quality of each man's work. **14**If what he has built survives, he will receive his reward. **15**If it is burned up, he will suffer loss; he himself will be saved, but only as one escaping through the flames.

16Don't you know that you yourselves are God's temple and that God's Spirit lives in you? **17**If anyone destroys God's temple, God will destroy him; for God's temple is sacred**D**, and you are that temple.

18Do not deceive yourselves. If any one of you thinks he is wise by the standards of this age, he should become a "fool" so that he may become wise. **19**For the wisdom of this world is foolishness in God's sight. As it is written: "He catches the wise in their craftiness"*a*; **20**and again, "The Lord knows that the thoughts of the wise are futile."*b* **21**So then, no more boasting about men! All things are yours, **22**whether Paul or Apollos or Cephas*c* or the world or life or death**D** or the present or the future—all are yours, **23**and you are of Christ, and Christ is of God.

Apostles of Christ

4 So then, men ought to regard us as servants of Christ and as those entrusted with the secret things of God. **2**Now it is required that those who have been given a trust must prove faithful. **3**I care very little if I am judged by you or by any human court; indeed, I do not even judge myself. **4**My conscience is clear, but that does not make me innocent. It is the Lord who judges me. **5**Therefore judge nothing before the appointed time; wait till the Lord comes. He will bring to light what is hidden in darkness and will expose the motives of men's hearts. At that time each will receive his praise from God.

6Now, brothers, I have applied these things to myself and Apollos for your benefit, so that you may learn from us the meaning of the saying, "Do not go beyond what is written." Then you will not take pride in one man over

a19 Job 5:13   *b20* Psalm 94:11   *c22* That is, Peter

How can Christians be worldly? (3:3)

Paul says that being *in Christ* doesn't mean we're necessarily mature. We can be immature believers. Of course, he expects growth. But growth assumes a process—there are always new challenges. In Paul's view, we will not be fully mature before the resurrection (ch. 15).

The Day (3:13)

An Old Testament term for the final judgment and salvation. We will be judged and assigned our eternal destiny on *the Day*.

What is the test of fire? (3:13)

Jewish views about the end times, which heavily influenced Paul, saw fire as an image of testing. Fire burns away impurities in the ore to get to the real essence of the metal. Similarly, the final judgment will test us by burning away worthless impurities in our lives.

What rewards and losses will there be? (3:14–15)

Paul never spells this out. In a general sense, these rewards and losses relate to our obedience. The right we do will endure and bring reward; our wrongs will be destroyed and will demand accountability (see 2 Cor. 5:10).

What *destroys God's temple?* (3:16–17)

The temple here means the people of God—those in whom he lives. Paul was speaking about the disputes and divisions among the Corinthians that threatened to destroy the church, God's dwelling. When the followers of Apollos pitted themselves against the followers of Paul or when arrogant believers scorned others whom they considered to be spiritually inferior, God's temple was being damaged.

All things are yours (3:21)

Paul wanted the Corinthians to see that their factions were robbing them of God's greater work. By cutting out one group or another from their fellowship, they missed what that group could offer.

Why wouldn't Paul be accountable to others? (4:3)

He *was* accountable. The lengths to which he went to explain himself show that. What Paul wanted to emphasize here was that no faction or individual believer could pass *final and ultimate* judgment on him (see 4:5). That decision belonged to God alone.

How reliable are our consciences? (4:4)

The Christian conscience is reasonably reliable. But Paul was certainly not a twentieth-century individualist. So individual conscience was not Paul's primary tool for moral insight. He was much more concerned about relying on the Spirit within the context of the church, the body of believers (see ch. 12).

Why should we *judge nothing before the appointed time?* (4:5)

This refers to the kind of judgment that will take place on the day of the Lord, when eternal destinies will be decided. Though we as believers can (and should) be accountable to each other for our attitudes and behavior, we cannot prejudge the final salvation of another. That is up to God. See *Why wouldn't Paul be accountable to others?* (4:3).

What did it mean to *not go beyond what is written?* (4:6)

The meaning of this phrase has long been debated. It probably refers to Scripture, but if so, what portion? In any event, Paul saw that wisdom and inspiration came from God. He may have been reminding the Corinthians that they were not wiser than God.

Was Paul being sarcastic? (4:7–13)

Yes. Sarcasm was an effective rhetorical device in Paul's day (as it is in ours). Paul used sarcasm to catch his readers off guard, wake them up, shatter their self-righteousness and help them to see the absurdity of their position. Paul challenged the self-proclaimed spiritual elite in Corinth to take a close look at themselves.

Who were the 10,000 guardians? (4:15)

The word for 10,000 can mean a large, indefinite number and is related to our word *myriad*. Paul referred to numerous other leaders and teachers (or potential leaders and teachers). Paul was saying that even if they had countless teachers and caretakers, he would always be their one and only spiritual father.

How far should we go to imitate leaders? (4:16)

A mentor was crucial to discipleship. Leaders are followed as long as they lead with integrity and honor. Paul's point was to say, *Follow my example, as I follow the example of Christ* (11:1). If leaders fail to follow Christ, then they are not to be followed.

Why were the Corinthians proud of immorality? (5:2)

The Corinthians didn't think they were being immoral. They thought they were so spiritually advanced that mundane earthly standards no longer applied to them. They seemed to believe that their level of spirituality permitted them to do what they wanted to do with their bodies.

With you in spirit (5:4)

Not a reference to the Holy Spirit. Paul meant that his thoughts and emotions were with them even if he was not with them physically.

When is the power of the Lord Jesus present? (5:4)

Jesus is always with us. But here Paul wanted to assure the Corinthians that Jesus' power would grant them discernment to properly judge the case of the man who had wed his stepmother.

Why hand a Christian over to Satan? (5:5)

In order to win him back. The abandonment to Satan referred to excommunication not eternal destruction. Paul recommended excommunication with the aim that the man, desperate not to be shut out of the vital church community, would be shocked back to his senses.

What is *old yeast?* (5:7)

Paul said the immoral man in the church was like yeast in bread (v. 6)—a little sin would affect the entire church. He urged them to remove the old yeast from the church.

against another. [7]For who makes you different from anyone else? What do you have that you did not receive? And if you did receive it, why do you boast as though you did not?

[8]Already you have all you want! Already you have become rich! You have become kings—and that without us! How I wish that you really had become kings so that we might be kings with you! [9]For it seems to me that God has put us apostles[D] on display at the end of the procession, like men condemned to die in the arena. We have been made a spectacle to the whole universe, to angels as well as to men. [10]We are fools for Christ, but you are so wise in Christ! We are weak, but you are strong! You are honored, we are dishonored! [11]To this very hour we go hungry and thirsty, we are in rags, we are brutally treated, we are homeless. [12]We work hard with our own hands. When we are cursed, we bless; when we are persecuted, we endure it; [13]when we are slandered, we answer kindly. Up to this moment we have become the scum of the earth, the refuse of the world.

[14]I am not writing this to shame you, but to warn you, as my dear children. [15]Even though you have ten thousand guardians in Christ, you do not have many fathers, for in Christ Jesus I became your father through the gospel[D]. [16]Therefore I urge you to imitate me. [17]For this reason I am sending to you Timothy, my son whom I love, who is faithful in the Lord. He will remind you of my way of life in Christ Jesus, which agrees with what I teach everywhere in every church.

[18]Some of you have become arrogant, as if I were not coming to you. [19]But I will come to you very soon, if the Lord is willing, and then I will find out not only how these arrogant people are talking, but what power they have. [20]For the kingdom of God[D] is not a matter of talk but of power. [21]What do you prefer? Shall I come to you with a whip, or in love and with a gentle spirit?

Expel the Immoral Brother!

5 It is actually reported that there is sexual immorality among you, and of a kind that does not occur even among pagans: A man has his father's wife. [2]And you are proud! Shouldn't you rather have been filled with grief and have put out of your fellowship the man who did this? [3]Even though I am not physically present, I am with you in spirit. And I have already passed judgment on the one who did this, just as if I were present. [4]When you are assembled in the name of our Lord Jesus and I am with you in spirit, and the power of our Lord Jesus is present, [5]hand this man over to Satan, so that the sinful nature[a] may be destroyed and his spirit saved on the day of the Lord.

[6]Your boasting is not good. Don't you know that a little yeast[D] works through the whole batch of dough? [7]Get rid of the old yeast that you may be a new batch without yeast—as you really are. For Christ, our Passover lamb, has been sacrificed. [8]Therefore let us keep the Festival, not with the old yeast, the yeast of malice and wickedness, but with bread without yeast, the bread of sincerity and truth.

[9]I have written you in my letter not to associate with sexually immoral people— [10]not at all meaning the people of this world who are immoral, or the greedy and

a5 Or that his body; or that the flesh

swindlers, or idolaters. In that case you would have to leave this world. **11**But now I am writing you that you must not associate with anyone who calls himself a brother but is sexually immoral or greedy, an idolater or a slanderer, a drunkard or a swindler. With such a man do not even eat.

12What business is it of mine to judge those outside the church? Are you not to judge those inside? **13**God will judge those outside. "Expel the wicked man from among you."[a]

Lawsuits Among Believers

6 If any of you has a dispute with another, dare he take it before the ungodly for judgment instead of before the saints[D]? **2**Do you not know that the saints will judge the world? And if you are to judge the world, are you not competent to judge trivial cases? **3**Do you not know that we will judge angels? How much more the things of this life! **4**Therefore, if you have disputes about such matters, appoint as judges even men of little account in the church![b] **5**I say this to shame you. Is it possible that there is nobody among you wise enough to judge a dispute between believers? **6**But instead, one brother goes to law against another—and this in front of unbelievers!

7The very fact that you have lawsuits among you means you have been completely defeated already. Why not rather be wronged? Why not rather be cheated? **8**Instead, you yourselves cheat and do wrong, and you do this to your brothers.

9Do you not know that the wicked will not inherit the kingdom of God[D]? Do not be deceived: Neither the sexually immoral nor idolaters nor adulterers nor male prostitutes nor homosexual offenders **10**nor thieves nor the greedy nor drunkards nor slanderers nor swindlers will inherit the kingdom of God. **11**And that is what some of you were. But you were washed, you were sanctified[D], you were justified[D] in the name of the Lord Jesus Christ and by the Spirit of our God.

Sexual Immorality

12"Everything is permissible for me"—but not everything is beneficial. "Everything is permissible for me"—but I will not be mastered by anything. **13**"Food for the stomach and the stomach for food"—but God will destroy them both. The body is not meant for sexual immorality, but for the Lord, and the Lord for the body. **14**By his power God raised the Lord from the dead, and he will raise us also. **15**Do you not know that your bodies are members of Christ himself? Shall I then take the members of Christ and unite them with a prostitute? Never! **16**Do you not know that he who unites himself with a prostitute is one with her in body? For it is said, "The two will become one flesh."[c] **17**But he who unites himself with the Lord is one with him in spirit.

18Flee from sexual immorality. All other sins a man commits are outside his body, but he who sins sexually sins against his own body. **19**Do you not know that your body is a temple of the Holy Spirit, who is in you, whom you have received from God? You are not your own; **20**you were bought at a price. Therefore honor God with your body.

How can we win people back by treating them like enemies? (5:11)

By maintaining standards, the church shows concern for its members with the hope that sinners will change their ways.

How are we to judge others in the church? (5:12)

With discernment the church can respond to the behavior of individuals: Do they need an encouraging word, a gentle reprimand or a strong rebuke? See *Why wouldn't Paul be accountable to others?* (4:3) and *Why should we judge nothing before the appointed time?* (4:5).

When will we judge the world and angels? (6:2–3)

Believers will judge on the day of the Lord, at the end of the age. Paul's Jewish frame of reference about the end times shaped the way he wrote. We can only guess what it means to judge angels. Jewish thinking ranked angels in various levels or hierarchies. Perhaps we will judge them according to these hierarchies, deciding where they will be placed. Others point out that there are also fallen angels awaiting judgment (Jude v. 6).

Should Christians never go into court? (6:6)

Paul had nothing to say in favor of one Christian taking another Christian to court. We should take him quite seriously on this. At the same time, we should consider the social setting of his counsel. The worldwide church in Paul's day was extremely small—probably less than one-half of one percent of the Roman empire's population. The Roman court system was clearly pagan, not Christianized in any of its elements. And Paul was concerned with matters internal to the church.

If they'd been *washed* . . . *sanctified* . . . *justified,* why were the Corinthians still so worldly? (6:11)

See *Why call such a flawed church sanctified?* (1:2).

Is *everything* permissible for Christians? (6:12)

Paul was quoting a popular saying that his Corinthian opponents may have used to defend their practices. Paul believed Christians were given great freedom, but he wanted the Corinthians to be more cautious in using it.

Is sexual immorality more serious than other sins? (6:18)

In a spiritual sense, sexual immorality is not worse than other sins, but it does introduce a whole new set of issues. Paul seems to suggest that other sins, *outside* a person's body, do not impact a person's own body as do sexual sins, though other practices (such as substance abuse) also can damage one's body.

How can we honor God with our bodies? (6:20)

By avoiding inappropriate sexual behavior which violates God's plan in two ways: (1) It exposes us to a risk of disease or other bodily harm. (2) It threatens a healthy marital relationship. Faithfulness in marriage parallels the intimate relationship believers have with Christ (see Eph. 5:25–33).

---

a13 Deut. 17:7; 19:19; 21:21; 22:21,24; 24:7　　*b4* Or *matters, do you appoint as judges men of little account in the church?*　　*c16* Gen. 2:24

Why is it good for a man not to marry? (7:1)

Some see this as Paul's specific response to a temporary crisis in Corinth (see v. 26). Others see it as a quote from Paul's opponents. Though some thought themselves so spiritually superior that it didn't matter what they did with their bodies (6:12–16), others thought they were so spiritual they could override normal sexual appetites, abstaining from intercourse even in marriage. Paul may have quoted them simply to state their case before he refuted it (v. 2).

Why did Paul label some instructions his and other instructions the Lord's? (7:10,12)

Sometimes Paul was able to quote Jesus' words directly, probably from a commonly known collection of sayings. The Jews at that time derived their authority from the Torah, God's Word. They made pronouncements with authority because they sat *in Moses' seat* (Matt. 23:2). Paul's rabbinical training may have prompted him to use similar words linking his authority to Christ. He was asserting that his words, too, were authoritative.

How is a non-Christian *sanctified* simply by being married to a Christian? (7:14)

Sanctified here does not mean *saved*. The main concern the Corinthian believers had was whether any children born to a Christian/non-Christian union were legitimate. If such marriages were not recognized by God, then their children would be illegitimate. Paul said such marriages were genuine and that the children from them were not *unclean* but *holy*.

In what sense are a believer's children holy? (7:14)

The believer's family, beyond being merely legitimate (see previous note), has been *set apart for God*. In a sense, it is as if God claims such families for himself, even before they submit to him. Paul does not mean that these children are automatically saved.

How are believers "free" when abandoned by an unbelieving spouse? (7:15)

There are two hotly-debated possibilities: (1) Paul merely affirms that if a believer's spouse leaves, that spouse should be permitted to go. According to this view, the believer still is bound by the marriage covenant should the unbelieving spouse return. (2) The spouse should be permitted to leave, and the abandoned believer should no longer be bound by the marriage covenant. According to this view, the abandoned believer is free to remarry.

Should we always accept our situation as assigned by God? (7:17,20,26)

Paul was more concerned about the *attitudes* of believers than their *circumstances*. A Christian should not need a change in circumstance to find spiritual contentment; trust in God fits all circumstances. Nevertheless, change can be good. If our attitude is right, we should be ready to seize opportunities to improve our circumstances (vv. 21,28).

Marriage

7 Now for the matters you wrote about: It is good for a man not to marry.[a] **2**But since there is so much immorality, each man should have his own wife, and each woman her own husband. **3**The husband should fulfill his marital duty to his wife, and likewise the wife to her husband. **4**The wife's body does not belong to her alone but also to her husband. In the same way, the husband's body does not belong to him alone but also to his wife. **5**Do not deprive each other except by mutual consent and for a time, so that you may devote yourselves to prayer. Then come together again so that Satan will not tempt you because of your lack of self-control. **6**I say this as a concession, not as a command. **7**I wish that all men were as I am. But each man has his own gift from God; one has this gift, another has that.

8Now to the unmarried and the widows I say: It is good for them to stay unmarried, as I am. **9**But if they cannot control themselves, they should marry, for it is better to marry than to burn with passion.

10To the married I give this command (not I, but the Lord): A wife must not separate from her husband. **11**But if she does, she must remain unmarried or else be reconciled to her husband. And a husband must not divorce his wife.

12To the rest I say this (I, not the Lord): If any brother has a wife who is not a believer and she is willing to live with him, he must not divorce her. **13**And if a woman has a husband who is not a believer and he is willing to live with her, she must not divorce him. **14**For the unbelieving husband has been sanctified[D] through his wife, and the unbelieving wife has been sanctified through her believing husband. Otherwise your children would be unclean[D], but as it is, they are holy.

15But if the unbeliever leaves, let him do so. A believing man or woman is not bound in such circumstances; God has called us to live in peace[D]. **16**How do you know, wife, whether you will save your husband? Or, how do you know, husband, whether you will save your wife?

17Nevertheless, each one should retain the place in life that the Lord assigned to him and to which God has called him. This is the rule I lay down in all the churches. **18**Was a man already circumcised[D] when he was called? He should not become uncircumcised[D]. Was a man uncircumcised when he was called? He should not be circumcised. **19**Circumcision is nothing and uncircumcision[D] is nothing. Keeping God's commands is what counts. **20**Each one should remain in the situation which he was in when God called him. **21**Were you a slave when you were called? Don't let it trouble you—although if you can gain your freedom, do so. **22**For he who was a slave when he was called by the Lord is the Lord's freedman; similarly, he who was a free man when he was called is Christ's slave. **23**You were bought at a price; do not become slaves of men. **24**Brothers, each man, as responsible to God, should remain in the situation God called him to.

25Now about virgins: I have no command from the Lord, but I give a judgment as one who by the Lord's mercy[D] is trustworthy. **26**Because of the present crisis, I think that it is good for you to remain as you are. **27**Are you married? Do not seek a divorce. Are you unmarried? Do

a 1 Or "It is good for a man not to have sexual relations with a woman."

not look for a wife. **28**But if you do marry, you have not sinned; and if a virgin marries, she has not sinned. But those who marry will face many troubles in this life, and I want to spare you this.

29What I mean, brothers, is that the time is short. From now on those who have wives should live as if they had none; **30**those who mourn, as if they did not; those who are happy, as if they were not; those who buy something, as if it were not theirs to keep; **31**those who use the things of the world, as if not engrossed in them. For this world in its present form is passing away.

32I would like you to be free from concern. An unmarried man is concerned about the Lord's affairs—how he can please the Lord. **33**But a married man is concerned about the affairs of this world—how he can please his wife— **34**and his interests are divided. An unmarried woman or virgin is concerned about the Lord's affairs: Her aim is to be devoted to the Lord in both body and spirit. But a married woman is concerned about the affairs of this world—how she can please her husband. **35**I am saying this for your own good, not to restrict you, but that you may live in a right way in undivided devotion to the Lord.

36If anyone thinks he is acting improperly toward the virgin he is engaged to, and if she is getting along in years and he feels he ought to marry, he should do as he wants. He is not sinning. They should get married. **37**But the man who has settled the matter in his own mind, who is under no compulsion but has control over his own will, and who has made up his mind not to marry the virgin—this man also does the right thing. **38**So then, he who marries the virgin does right, but he who does not marry her does even better.*a*

39A woman is bound to her husband as long as he lives. But if her husband dies, she is free to marry anyone she wishes, but he must belong to the Lord. **40**In my judgment, she is happier if she stays as she is—and I think that I too have the Spirit of God.

Food Sacrificed to Idols

8 Now about food sacrificed to idols*D*: We know that we all possess knowledge.*b* Knowledge puffs up, but love builds up. **2**The man who thinks he knows something does not yet know as he ought to know. **3**But the man who loves God is known by God.

4So then, about eating food sacrificed to idols: We know that an idol is nothing at all in the world and that there is no God but one. **5**For even if there are so-called gods, whether in heaven or on earth (as indeed there are many "gods" and many "lords"), **6**yet for us there is but one God, the Father, from whom all things came and for whom we live; and there is but one Lord, Jesus Christ, through whom all things came and through whom we live.

7But not everyone knows this. Some people are still so

---

a 36-38 Or 36If anyone thinks he is not treating his daughter properly, and if she is getting along in years, and he feels she ought to marry, he should do as he wants. He is not sinning. He should let her get married. 37But the man who has settled the matter in his own mind, who is under no compulsion but has control over his own will, and who has made up his mind to keep the virgin unmarried—this man also does the right thing. 38So then, he who gives his virgin in marriage does right, but he who does not give her in marriage does even better.   b 1 Or "We all possess knowledge," as you say

---

How could anyone *become uncircumcised?* (7:18)

Surgical procedures existed in the first century that could reverse circumcision. Why? Because some Jews wanted to participate in Greek athletics or the public Roman baths, where men discussed business and politics, trying to advance socially. Though nudity was the style there, the circumcised look was not. It was considered vulgar and uncultured. To avoid humiliation, some were undergoing surgery to reconstruct a foreskin.

Slaves (7:21–24)

Slavery was an unquestioned institution in the Roman empire. Still, Paul saw the slave in a new position, as a spiritual equal to the one who was free (see Gal. 3:28). Also see article: *Why doesn't the Bible condemn slavery?* (1 Peter 2:18–21).

What crisis did the Corinthians face? (7:26)

Paul may simply have seen signs of increasing difficulties and hardships for believers. He knew that until judgment came to the world, the church would remain in tension—living in the world but belonging to the kingdom of God.

Why do married people face more troubles than singles? (7:28)

Paul explains why in vv. 32–35. The unmarried can devote all their time directly to the Lord. Those with spouses have to devote time to their marriages. Since this is a time of crisis and trouble (see previous note), those who are married will find their lives more complicated.

Why did Paul say *the time is short?* (7:29)

Short is a relative term. Paul believed the end of time began when Jesus came to this earth. See *What crisis did the Corinthians face?* (7:26). From his perspective, time was short because Jesus represented the goal and destination of history.

How could a married man live as if he had no wife? (7:29)

Paul makes it clear that married Christians should fulfill their marital obligations (vv. 3–5). But he wants us to be unattached to the things of the world. He wants our attitudes to acknowledge something ultimately more significant than marriage—our final allegiance is to God.

Why should we worry about marriage dividing our commitment to God? (7:34)

Paul is not trying to burden married people. He expects them to affirm and tend to their marriages. Yet he does believe single people can have some advantages with their loyalties to God undivided.

Why did Paul suggest his opinions were shaped by God's Spirit? (7:40)

Paul's Corinthian opponents claimed to speak for God. In the heat of argument Paul insisted his opponents could not claim to have a corner on God's Spirit: *I too have the Spirit of God,* he declared.

How does a conscience become defiled? (8:7)

Through the negative influence of pagan culture. Also see *How reliable are our consciences?* (4:4). A polluted conscience will produce convictions rooted in customs or culture rather than in the Word of God and the work of the Spirit.

Is something ever right for one and wrong for another? (8:10–11)

Sometimes. Those steeped in centuries-old Jewish tradition found it difficult to believe there was nothing wrong with eating meat sacrificed to idols. To do so would have violated their own consciences. Paul, on the other hand, recognized that he could eat such meat without sinning (v. 8). Still, he respected the sensitivities of those who did not feel as he did, knowing that they could be condemned by their consciences. Also see *Stumbling block* (Romans 14:13) and *Strong . . . weak* (Romans 15:1).

What are the consequences when believers *sin against Christ*? (8:12)

Paul doesn't spell them out here. As a whole this letter emphasizes two consequences when believers sin against Christ: (1) members of the church will be damaged, and (2) the unity of the body will be broken.

How can we live up to the expectations of every weak conscience? (8:13)

We can't. But Paul wants us to be sensitive to others. He was frustrated with his Corinthian opponents who trampled on the consciences of the weak. He wants us to be sympathetic to those whose faith might be hindered or destroyed by our freewheeling behavior. But Paul does not expect us to be bound by fear of offending rigid or legalistic Christians.

When did Paul see Jesus? (9:1–2)

Most notably on the Damascus road (Acts 9:1–9). He may also be referring to his experience of being *caught up to paradise* (2 Cor. 12:2–4).

Why wouldn't Paul use his rights as an apostle? (9:15)

Paul wanted to avoid criticism (ch. 4; 2 Cor. 10; 1 Thes. 2). He knew an apostle could abuse his rights. Even if an apostle did not abuse his privileges, some might think that he took advantage of others. So, for the sake of presenting the gospel in the most honorable way possible, he sacrificed his rights. He wanted to avoid even the slightest appearance of impropriety.

accustomed to idols[D] that when they eat such food they think of it as having been sacrificed to an idol, and since their conscience is weak, it is defiled. **8**But food does not bring us near to God; we are no worse if we do not eat, and no better if we do.

9Be careful, however, that the exercise of your freedom does not become a stumbling block[D] to the weak. **10**For if anyone with a weak conscience sees you who have this knowledge eating in an idol's temple, won't he be emboldened to eat what has been sacrificed to idols? **11**So this weak brother, for whom Christ died, is destroyed by your knowledge. **12**When you sin against your brothers in this way and wound their weak conscience, you sin against Christ. **13**Therefore, if what I eat causes my brother to fall into sin, I will never eat meat again, so that I will not cause him to fall.

The Rights of an Apostle

9 Am I not free? Am I not an apostle[D]? Have I not seen Jesus our Lord? Are you not the result of my work in the Lord? **2**Even though I may not be an apostle to others, surely I am to you! For you are the seal of my apostleship in the Lord.

3This is my defense to those who sit in judgment on me. **4**Don't we have the right to food and drink? **5**Don't we have the right to take a believing wife along with us, as do the other apostles and the Lord's brothers and Cephas[a]? **6**Or is it only I and Barnabas who must work for a living?

7Who serves as a soldier at his own expense? Who plants a vineyard and does not eat of its grapes? Who tends a flock and does not drink of the milk? **8**Do I say this merely from a human point of view? Doesn't the Law say the same thing? **9**For it is written in the Law of Moses: "Do not muzzle an ox while it is treading out the grain."[b] Is it about oxen that God is concerned? **10**Surely he says this for us, doesn't he? Yes, this was written for us, because when the plowman plows and the thresher threshes, they ought to do so in the hope of sharing in the harvest. **11**If we have sown spiritual seed among you, is it too much if we reap a material harvest from you? **12**If others have this right of support from you, shouldn't we have it all the more?

But we did not use this right. On the contrary, we put up with anything rather than hinder the gospel[D] of Christ. **13**Don't you know that those who work in the temple get their food from the temple, and those who serve at the altar share in what is offered on the altar? **14**In the same way, the Lord has commanded that those who preach the gospel should receive their living from the gospel.

15But I have not used any of these rights. And I am not writing this in the hope that you will do such things for me. I would rather die than have anyone deprive me of this boast. **16**Yet when I preach the gospel, I cannot boast, for I am compelled to preach. Woe to me if I do not preach the gospel! **17**If I preach voluntarily, I have a reward; if not voluntarily, I am simply discharging the trust committed to me. **18**What then is my reward? Just this: that in preaching the gospel I may offer it free of charge, and so not make use of my rights in preaching it.

19Though I am free and belong to no man, I make my-

*a*5 That is, Peter   *b*9 Deut. 25:4

self a slave to everyone, to win as many as possible. **20**To the Jews[D] I became like a Jew, to win the Jews. To those under the law I became like one under the law (though I myself am not under the law), so as to win those under the law. **21**To those not having the law I became like one not having the law (though I am not free from God's law but am under Christ's law), so as to win those not having the law. **22**To the weak I became weak, to win the weak. I have become all things to all men so that by all possible means I might save some. **23**I do all this for the sake of the gospel[D], that I may share in its blessings.

24Do you not know that in a race all the runners run, but only one gets the prize? Run in such a way as to get the prize. **25**Everyone who competes in the games goes into strict training. They do it to get a crown that will not last; but we do it to get a crown that will last forever. **26**Therefore I do not run like a man running aimlessly; I do not fight like a man beating the air. **27**No, I beat my body and make it my slave so that after I have preached to others, I myself will not be disqualified for the prize.

Warnings From Israel's History

10 For I do not want you to be ignorant of the fact, brothers, that our forefathers were all under the cloud and that they all passed through the sea. **2**They were all baptized into Moses in the cloud and in the sea. **3**They all ate the same spiritual food **4**and drank the same spiritual drink; for they drank from the spiritual rock that accompanied them, and that rock was Christ. **5**Nevertheless, God was not pleased with most of them; their bodies were scattered over the desert.

6Now these things occurred as examples[a] to keep us from setting our hearts on evil things as they did. **7**Do not be idolaters, as some of them were; as it is written: "The people sat down to eat and drink and got up to indulge in pagan revelry."[b] **8**We should not commit sexual immorality, as some of them did—and in one day twenty-three thousand of them died. **9**We should not test the Lord, as some of them did—and were killed by snakes. **10**And do not grumble, as some of them did—and were killed by the destroying angel.

11These things happened to them as examples and were written down as warnings for us, on whom the fulfillment of the ages has come. **12**So, if you think you are standing firm, be careful that you don't fall! **13**No temptation has seized you except what is common to man. And God is faithful; he will not let you be tempted beyond what you can bear. But when you are tempted, he will also provide a way out so that you can stand up under it.

Idol Feasts and the Lord's Supper

14Therefore, my dear friends, flee from idolatry[D]. **15**I speak to sensible people; judge for yourselves what I say. **16**Is not the cup of thanksgiving for which we give thanks a participation in the blood of Christ? And is not the bread that we break a participation in the body of Christ? **17**Because there is one loaf, we, who are many, are one body, for we all partake of the one loaf.

18Consider the people of Israel: Do not those who eat the sacrifices[D] participate in the altar? **19**Do I mean then that a sacrifice offered to an idol is anything, or that an idol is anything? **20**No, but the sacrifices of pagans

Race . . . games . . . crown (9:24–25)

Paul used an athletic metaphor readily understood in Corinth. The most famous Greek games were, of course, the Olympics. But the next most famous were the Isthmian Games, named for the isthmus upon which Corinth was located (see **Map 11** at the back of this Bible). These games were held every two years in a suburb of Corinth. Winners of the various competitions received leafy wreaths which they wore as *crowns*.

Did Paul really beat his own body? (9:27)

There is no evidence Paul literally beat himself. His statement seems to build on the athletic metaphor (vv. 24–26), describing athletic discipline and preparation. Athletes in training have sore and tired bodies, but their bodies are actually strengthened, not abused.

Disqualified (9:27)

This word has been translated in various ways —from the mild *reprimanded* to the severe *reprobate*. Paul continues his athletic metaphor (see above notes) and recalls athletes who, after competing and winning, were stripped of their awards because they had violated the rules. The debate centers on whether the prize lost is salvation itself or reward for faithful ministry. This text alone does not settle the argument. Also see articles: **Can believers fall away?** (Luke 8:13) and **Should we fear falling?** (Heb. 6:6).

SCRIPTURE LINK (10:1–10)

Cloud and sea (Exodus 13:21; 14:22); *food and drink* (Exodus 16:4–35; 17:6; Num. 20:7–11); *bodies in the desert* (Num. 14:29–30); *idolatry* (Exodus 32:4,6); *immorality* (Num. 25:1–9); *testing the Lord* (Num. 21:5–6); *grumbling* (Num. 16:13–14,41–49).

Baptized into Moses (10:2)

Paul recalls the history of Israel and describes Israel's experience as a baptism. *Baptism* means being overwhelmed, covered, submerged—in ancient times, you could be "baptized" by debts. By passing through the Red Sea and by following the pillar of smoke and fire (Exodus 13:21), the Israelites were baptized with the power of God through the ministry of Moses.

How did the Israelites drink *from the spiritual rock that accompanied them?* (10:3–4)

Israel twice received water in the desert from a literal, stationary rock—dramatic miracles that refreshed and sustained the Israelites. In Jewish tradition, however, this miracle was made into an allegory: the rock was interpreted as a symbol of the law—something that was both portable (it *accompanied* them) and spiritual (to sustain them). Paul, however, substituted the law in the allegory with Christ (see also Gal. 3:24–25). With hindsight, he and the early church looked back and saw Christ at work in ancient Israel.

Fulfillment of the ages (10:11)

These are the end times, the last days. See **What crisis did the Corinthians face?** (7:26). Jesus fulfills God's plan for the ages.

*a*6 Or *types*; also in verse 11   *b*7 Exodus 32:6

Why does God allow temptation? (10:13)

Other texts (for example, Romans 8:3–5; James 1:2–4; 1 Peter 1:6–7) address that question. Such passages assure us God is ultimately in control and temptation can make us strong. This text doesn't try to answer the question of why there is temptation. It simply promises believers that no matter what the temptation, God will never abandon them. Also see articles: *Why did testing come to Job?* (Job 23:10), *Why does God test us?* (Psalm 81:7) and *Does the Spirit lead us into temptation?* (Matt. 4:1).

What is permissible? (10:23)

See *Is everything permissible for Christians?* (6:12).

What difference does it make? (10:27–30)

Why can we eat sometimes but not others? Paul makes a distinction between our rights and our obligations to others. Though he's confident we can be thankful for and eat the food God gives us, he's also concerned that we consider the feelings of others. If someone's faith is damaged by seeing us eat something, we should abstain. Also see *How can we live up to the expectations of every weak conscience?* (8:13).

How is man the head of woman? (11:3)

In an age when equal rights are highly valued, this verse raises eyebrows. Some think the word *head* suggests the idea of *ruler*. They understand *head* in the sense of a hierarchy or divine order in which the man directs and leads the woman. Others think *head* means *source*. They see it referring to Adam (the first man) as the source of Eve (the first woman). In their opinion, rather than a hierarchy between men and women, there is an interdependent and equal relationship (v. 12).

What do head coverings signify? (11:4–5,10)

In Paul's Jewish culture, women with uncovered heads were considered sexually loose and insubordinate to men. Men with long hair, on the other hand, were considered beneath their station, since long hair in their culture represented subordination. Some think Paul meant to protect the honor of the church by restraining Corinthian women, newly liberated by the gospel, from rashly abandoning their head coverings. Others, however, think that Paul's instructions point to a permanent relationship —an order established at creation between God and men and women.

How is man God's *glory*? (11:7)

Man is God's glory by being a reflection of the image of God. Left unsaid, however, is the fact that both man *and* woman are created in God's image (Gen. 1:27). Some stress this verse to show that *the woman is the glory of man*. Others stress the interdependence of each sex to the other and the fact that each, ultimately, *comes from God* (vv. 11–12).

are offered to demons, not to God, and I do not want you to be participants with demons. **21**You cannot drink the cup of the Lord and the cup of demons too; you cannot have a part in both the Lord's table and the table of demons. **22**Are we trying to arouse the Lord's jealousy? Are we stronger than he?

The Believer's Freedom

23"Everything is permissible"—but not everything is beneficial. "Everything is permissible"—but not everything is constructive. **24**Nobody should seek his own good, but the good of others.

25Eat anything sold in the meat market without raising questions of conscience, **26**for, "The earth is the Lord's, and everything in it."*a*

27If some unbeliever invites you to a meal and you want to go, eat whatever is put before you without raising questions of conscience. **28**But if anyone says to you, "This has been offered in sacrifice[D]," then do not eat it, both for the sake of the man who told you and for conscience' sake*b*— **29**the other man's conscience, I mean, not yours. For why should my freedom be judged by another's conscience? **30**If I take part in the meal with thankfulness, why am I denounced because of something I thank God for?

31So whether you eat or drink or whatever you do, do it all for the glory[D] of God. **32**Do not cause anyone to stumble, whether Jews[D], Greeks or the church of God— **33**even as I try to please everybody in every way. For I am not seeking my own good but the good of many, so that they may be saved. **1**Follow my example, as I follow the example of Christ.

Propriety in Worship

2I praise you for remembering me in everything and for holding to the teachings,*c* just as I passed them on to you.

3Now I want you to realize that the head of every man is Christ, and the head of the woman is man, and the head of Christ is God. **4**Every man who prays or prophesies with his head covered dishonors his head. **5**And every woman who prays or prophesies with her head uncovered dishonors her head—it is just as though her head were shaved. **6**If a woman does not cover her head, she should have her hair cut off; and if it is a disgrace for a woman to have her hair cut or shaved off, she should cover her head. **7**A man ought not to cover his head,*d* since he is the image and glory of God; but the woman is the glory of man. **8**For man did not come from woman, but woman from man; **9**neither was man created for woman, but woman for man. **10**For this reason, and because of the angels, the woman ought to have a sign of authority on her head. **11**In the Lord, however, woman is not independent of man, nor is man independent of woman. **12**For as woman came from man, so also man is born of woman. But ev-

---

a26 Psalm 24:1   *b28* Some manuscripts *conscience' sake, for "the earth is the Lord's and everything in it"*   *c2* Or *traditions*   *d4-7* Or *4Every man who prays or prophesies with long hair dishonors his head. 5And every woman who prays or prophesies with no covering* ⌊*of hair*⌋ *on her head dishonors her head—she is just like one of the "shorn women." 6If a woman has no covering, let her be for now with short hair, but since it is a disgrace for a woman to have her hair shorn or shaved, she should grow it again. 7A man ought not to have long hair*

erything comes from God. **13**Judge for yourselves: Is it proper for a woman to pray to God with her head uncovered? **14**Does not the very nature of things teach you that if a man has long hair, it is a disgrace to him, **15**but that if a woman has long hair, it is her glory^D? For long hair is given to her as a covering. **16**If anyone wants to be contentious about this, we have no other practice—nor do the churches of God.

The Lord's Supper

17In the following directives I have no praise for you, for your meetings do more harm than good. **18**In the first place, I hear that when you come together as a church, there are divisions among you, and to some extent I believe it. **19**No doubt there have to be differences among you to show which of you have God's approval. **20**When you come together, it is not the Lord's Supper you eat, **21**for as you eat, each of you goes ahead without waiting for anybody else. One remains hungry, another gets drunk. **22**Don't you have homes to eat and drink in? Or do you despise the church of God and humiliate those who have nothing? What shall I say to you? Shall I praise you for this? Certainly not!

23For I received from the Lord what I also passed on to you: The Lord Jesus, on the night he was betrayed, took bread, **24**and when he had given thanks, he broke it and said, "This is my body, which is for you; do this in remembrance of me." **25**In the same way, after supper he took the cup, saying, "This cup is the new covenant^D in my blood; do this, whenever you drink it, in remembrance of me." **26**For whenever you eat this bread and drink this cup, you proclaim the Lord's death^D until he comes.

27Therefore, whoever eats the bread or drinks the cup of the Lord in an unworthy manner will be guilty of sinning against the body and blood of the Lord. **28**A man ought to examine himself before he eats of the bread and drinks of the cup. **29**For anyone who eats and drinks without recognizing the body of the Lord eats and drinks judgment on himself. **30**That is why many among you are weak and sick, and a number of you have fallen asleep. **31**But if we judged ourselves, we would not come under judgment. **32**When we are judged by the Lord, we are being disciplined so that we will not be condemned with the world.

33So then, my brothers, when you come together to eat, wait for each other. **34**If anyone is hungry, he should eat at home, so that when you meet together it may not result in judgment.

And when I come I will give further directions.

Spiritual Gifts

12 Now about spiritual gifts, brothers, I do not want you to be ignorant. **2**You know that when you were pagans, somehow or other you were influenced and led astray to mute idols^D. **3**Therefore I tell you that no one who is speaking by the Spirit of God says, "Jesus be cursed," and no one can say, "Jesus is Lord," except by the Holy Spirit.

4There are different kinds of gifts, but the same Spirit. **5**There are different kinds of service, but the same Lord. **6**There are different kinds of working, but the same God works all of them in all men.

7Now to each one the manifestation of the Spirit is given for the common good. **8**To one there is given through

Why are angels mentioned? (11:10)

The reference to angels here is baffling. One idea is that angels somehow worship with believers on earth. Thus, women should cover their heads when worshiping, especially in the presence of angels, since worship should be done honorably and in order. But there is no clear or certain reading of this allusion.

What is nature's hair length? (11:14–15)

Nature here probably means *inherent in nature,* but that would mean inherent as drawn from the proverbial and cultural wisdom of the time. The study of Roman busts shows that women generally had longer hair than men, but there is enough variation that we can't say exactly what *long* meant to Paul.

What went wrong in church suppers? (11:20–22)

In Corinth, the Lord's Supper was observed along with a larger meal known as the agape or love feast (see Jude 12). Those not getting food to eat probably were poor people—perhaps slaves who didn't have the freedom to arrive at the meal earlier. This created divisions within the church. Paul taught them that the love feast was intended not to satiate hunger, but to draw them together.

What exactly is eating and drinking *in an unworthy manner?* (11:27)

Eating and drinking in such a way that other believers are excluded. To use the church's love feast to divide the church is to use it unworthily (vv. 20–22,33–34).

the Spirit the message of wisdom, to another the message of knowledge by means of the same Spirit, **9**to another faith by the same Spirit, to another gifts of healing by that one Spirit, **10**to another miraculous powers, to another prophecy[D], to another distinguishing between spirits, to another speaking in different kinds of tongues,[a] and to still another the interpretation of tongues.[a] **11**All these are the work of one and the same Spirit, and he gives them to each one, just as he determines.

One Body, Many Parts

12The body is a unit, though it is made up of many parts; and though all its parts are many, they form one body. So it is with Christ. **13**For we were all baptized by[b] one Spirit into one body—whether Jews[D] or Greeks, slave or free—and we were all given the one Spirit to drink.

14Now the body is not made up of one part but of many. **15**If the foot should say, "Because I am not a hand, I do not belong to the body," it would not for that reason cease to be part of the body. **16**And if the ear should say, "Because I am not an eye, I do not belong to the body," it would not for that reason cease to be part of the body. **17**If the whole body were an eye, where would the sense of hearing be? If the whole body were an ear, where would the sense of smell be? **18**But in fact God has arranged the parts in the body, every one of them, just as he wanted them to be. **19**If they were all one part, where would the body be? **20**As it is, there are many parts, but one body.

21The eye cannot say to the hand, "I don't need you!" And the head cannot say to the feet, "I don't need you!" **22**On the contrary, those parts of the body that seem to be weaker are indispensable, **23**and the parts that we think are less honorable we treat with special honor. And the parts that are unpresentable are treated with special modesty, **24**while our presentable parts need no special treatment. But God has combined the members of the body

a10 Or *languages*; also in verse 28   *b13* Or *with*; or *in*

Why are the parts of the church body that seem weaker indispensable? (12:22)

Paul uses the human body as a metaphor. Those parts that don't receive public recognition—the private, covered parts and especially the internal organs—are nonetheless needed for the entire body's health. Likewise, the church needs all its members. Teachers, for instance, may be publicly recognized, but without the work of the janitor, the church would become filthy and all the members would be affected. The *stronger* parts, Paul insists, shouldn't belittle or overlook the *weaker* parts.

What are spiritual gifts? (12:1–31)

Spiritual gifts are known as *spiritual* because they come from the Spirit of God. In his letters, Paul provided three lists of spiritual gifts (also see Romans 12:3–8; Eph. 4:11). Since the lists are not identical, they appear as examples, not comprehensive lists of spiritual gifts.

Though we might ask how spiritual gifts differ from natural talents, Paul was probably unconcerned about distinguishing between physical and spiritual abilities. To him all gifts, "natural" or "supernatural," came from God. The central issue for Paul was people using their abilities to build up and strengthen the church. No wonder he was upset to learn that the Corinthians were misusing their spiritual gifts. Instead of building the church, they were destroying it (3:3,16–17).

Paul probably recognized all abilities that strengthened the church as being spiritual gifts—even those that might be based on "natural" talent and developed by training. He speaks of gifts (teaching and hospitality, for instance) that can be based on innate abilities and can be improved through practice. Nevertheless, Paul also recognized supernatural gifts given extraordinarily and suddenly.

and has given greater honor to the parts that lacked it, **25**so that there should be no division in the body, but that its parts should have equal concern for each other. **26**If one part suffers, every part suffers with it; if one part is honored, every part rejoices with it.

27Now you are the body of Christ, and each one of you is a part of it. **28**And in the church God has appointed first of all apostles^D, second prophets^D, third teachers, then workers of miracles, also those having gifts of healing, those able to help others, those with gifts of administration, and those speaking in different kinds of tongues. **29**Are all apostles? Are all prophets? Are all teachers? Do all work miracles? **30**Do all have gifts of healing? Do all speak in tongues^a? Do all interpret? **31**But eagerly desire^b the greater gifts.

Love

And now I will show you the most excellent way.

13 If I speak in the tongues^c of men and of angels, but have not love, I am only a resounding gong or a clanging cymbal. **2**If I have the gift of prophecy^D and can fathom all mysteries^D and all knowledge, and if I have a faith that can move mountains, but have not love, I am nothing. **3**If I give all I possess to the poor and surrender my body to the flames,^d but have not love, I gain nothing.

4Love is patient, love is kind. It does not envy, it does not boast, it is not proud. **5**It is not rude, it is not self-seeking, it is not easily angered, it keeps no record of wrongs. **6**Love does not delight in evil but rejoices with the truth. **7**It always protects, always trusts, always hopes, always perseveres.

8Love never fails. But where there are prophecies, they will cease; where there are tongues, they will be stilled; where there is knowledge, it will pass away. **9**For we know in part and we prophesy in part, **10**but when perfection comes, the imperfect disappears. **11**When I was a child, I talked like a child, I thought like a child, I reasoned like a child. When I became a man, I put childish ways behind me. **12**Now we see but a poor reflection as in a mirror; then we shall see face to face. Now I know in part; then I shall know fully, even as I am fully known.

13And now these three remain: faith, hope and love. But the greatest of these is love.

Gifts of Prophecy and Tongues

14 Follow the way of love and eagerly desire spiritual gifts, especially the gift of prophecy. **2**For anyone who speaks in a tongue^e does not speak to men but to God. Indeed, no one understands him; he utters mysteries with his spirit.^f **3**But everyone who prophesies speaks to men for their strengthening, encouragement and comfort. **4**He who speaks in a tongue edifies himself, but he who prophesies edifies the church. **5**I would like every one of you to speak in tongues,^g but I would rather have you prophesy. He who prophesies is greater than one who speaks in tongues,^g unless he interprets, so that the church may be edified.

Are apostles and prophets still functioning in the church today? (12:28)

There is agreement that, at the least, the *gifts* of apostles and prophets are present with us today in the form of leadership and teaching. Beyond that, many believe that spiritual gifts and offices—such as prophet and apostle—can still benefit the church today. Others say that certain gifts became unnecessary and ceased when the New Testament was completed.

The greater gifts (12:31)

Probably prophecy (14:1), greater because it does more than many other gifts to build up the church. See *What makes prophecy so important?* (14:1).

What does love have to do with spiritual gifts? (13:1–3)

If we have spiritual gifts but no love, the gifts are useless. Love is a fruit (not a gift) of the Spirit (Gal. 5:22). It is love that unifies the church; the gifts of the Spirit are like tools that accomplish the purpose of love—building up the body. Love controls the use of gifts—they are not to divide the church, nor are they to be used to gain personal recognition. With love, the gifts are of genuine service to the church.

When will knowledge, tongues and prophecy come to an end? (13:8–12)

Only after we have received full revelation: *Now* we see poorly; *then* we will have a complete knowledge (v. 12). Some believe this full knowledge refers to completed text of the New Testament—that when the Bible was finished, the revelation gifts of the Spirit ceased to function. Others say that though we have Scripture, we do not yet know everything completely. They believe Paul was speaking of a time yet to come when everything *imperfect disappears* (v. 10). Paul's conviction that he will *know fully* (v. 12), they say, suggests a time to come when he will be in the presence of God, in heaven. Whether this means at death or when all believers are resurrected is not clear.

When perfection comes, how much will we know? (13:12)

All that can be said is that we will know as much as is possible for redeemed and perfected human beings to know. We will certainly know more than what is possible to know or express now. To *know fully* means to have reached the limits of what it means to be redeemed for eternity in the presence of God.

What makes prophecy so important? (14:1)

Prophecy is a message that edifies, comforts or encourages the church (v. 3). Since Paul places a premium on strengthening the church, he values prophecy highly. Prophecy is understandable to the mind (unlike speaking in tongues). Like Old Testament prophecy, New Testament prophecy was intended to challenge and strengthen the church. People see various expressions of prophecy in preaching, teaching and spontaneous exhortations, among others.

---

^a30 Or *other languages*   ^b31 Or *But you are eagerly desiring*
^c1 Or *languages*   ^d3 Some early manuscripts *body that I may boast*
^e2 Or *another language*; also in verses 4, 13, 14, 19, 26 and 27
^f2 Or *by the Spirit*   ^g5 Or *other languages*; also in verses 6, 18, 22, 23 and 39

How does the gift of tongues help anyone? (14:2–4)

The person speaking in tongues speaks to God. So the speaker edifies himself or herself with this gift of the Holy Spirit, gaining in a supernatural way greater assurance of God's love and power. In a related way, the church can be edified by an utterance in tongues—just as by a prophecy—if it can be interpreted for the congregation (v. 5). Some things that are real are beyond the rational mind. A similar passage, for instance, says that the Spirit communicates our needs to God through groans that cannot be expressed in ordinary speech (Romans 8:26).

Was Paul engaging in spiritual one-upmanship? (14:18)

Yes. Paul was skillful in using rhetoric. Here he was outdoing his Corinthian opponents on their own terms. They bragged about speaking in tongues; Paul (with tongue in cheek) claimed that he spoke in tongues even more. But his emphasis was that it would be even better to prophesy. In a similar manner Paul later confronted boasters with his own boasting—only to conclude that all boasting is futile and beside the point (2 Cor. 11–12).

What do tongues signify to *unbelievers*? (14:20–25)

This is a difficult passage. It hinges on the word *sign*. There is a tendency to read *sign* as something positive, a promising or appealing message. But it also can mean a portent of judgment (Isaiah 20:3, for example). Tongues may be a sign of judgment to unbelievers because only believers have the gift of tongues. Prophecy may be a sign of judgment to believers because the prophet may speak warning or correction to the church.

[6]Now, brothers, if I come to you and speak in tongues, what good will I be to you, unless I bring you some revelation[D] or knowledge or prophecy[D] or word of instruction? [7]Even in the case of lifeless things that make sounds, such as the flute or harp, how will anyone know what tune is being played unless there is a distinction in the notes? [8]Again, if the trumpet does not sound a clear call, who will get ready for battle? [9]So it is with you. Unless you speak intelligible words with your tongue, how will anyone know what you are saying? You will just be speaking into the air. [10]Undoubtedly there are all sorts of languages in the world, yet none of them is without meaning. [11]If then I do not grasp the meaning of what someone is saying, I am a foreigner to the speaker, and he is a foreigner to me. [12]So it is with you. Since you are eager to have spiritual gifts, try to excel in gifts that build up the church.

[13]For this reason anyone who speaks in a tongue should pray that he may interpret what he says. [14]For if I pray in a tongue, my spirit prays, but my mind is unfruitful. [15]So what shall I do? I will pray with my spirit, but I will also pray with my mind; I will sing with my spirit, but I will also sing with my mind. [16]If you are praising God with your spirit, how can one who finds himself among those who do not understand[a] say "Amen" to your thanksgiving, since he does not know what you are saying? [17]You may be giving thanks well enough, but the other man is not edified.

[18]I thank God that I speak in tongues more than all of you. [19]But in the church I would rather speak five intelligible words to instruct others than ten thousand words in a tongue.

[20]Brothers, stop thinking like children. In regard to evil be infants, but in your thinking be adults. [21]In the Law it is written:

> "Through men of strange tongues
>   and through the lips of foreigners
>   I will speak to this people,
>   but even then they will not listen to me,"[b]

says the Lord.

[22]Tongues, then, are a sign, not for believers but for unbelievers; prophecy, however, is for believers, not for unbelievers. [23]So if the whole church comes together and everyone speaks in tongues, and some who do not understand[c] or some unbelievers come in, will they not say that you are out of your mind? [24]But if an unbeliever or someone who does not understand[d] comes in while everybody is prophesying, he will be convinced by all that he is a sinner and will be judged by all, [25]and the secrets of his heart will be laid bare. So he will fall down and worship God, exclaiming, "God is really among you!"

Orderly Worship

[26]What then shall we say, brothers? When you come together, everyone has a hymn, or a word of instruction, a revelation, a tongue or an interpretation. All of these must be done for the strengthening of the church. [27]If anyone speaks in a tongue, two—or at the most three—should speak, one at a time, and someone must interpret.

---

a16 Or *among the inquirers*   *b21* Isaiah 28:11,12   *c23* Or *some inquirers*   *d24* Or *or some inquirer*

28If there is no interpreter, the speaker should keep quiet in the church and speak to himself and God.

29Two or three prophets[D] should speak, and the others should weigh carefully what is said. **30**And if a revelation[D] comes to someone who is sitting down, the first speaker should stop. **31**For you can all prophesy in turn so that everyone may be instructed and encouraged. **32**The spirits of prophets are subject to the control of prophets. **33**For God is not a God of disorder but of peace.

As in all the congregations of the saints[D], **34**women should remain silent in the churches. They are not allowed to speak, but must be in submission, as the Law says. **35**If they want to inquire about something, they should ask their own husbands at home; for it is disgraceful for a woman to speak in the church.

36Did the word of God originate with you? Or are you the only people it has reached? **37**If anybody thinks he is a prophet or spiritually gifted, let him acknowledge that what I am writing to you is the Lord's command. **38**If he ignores this, he himself will be ignored.[a]

39Therefore, my brothers, be eager to prophesy, and do not forbid speaking in tongues. **40**But everything should be done in a fitting and orderly way.

The Resurrection of Christ

15 Now, brothers, I want to remind you of the gospel[D] I preached to you, which you received and on which you have taken your stand. **2**By this gospel you are saved, if you hold firmly to the word I preached to you. Otherwise, you have believed in vain.

3For what I received I passed on to you as of first importance[b]: that Christ died for our sins according to the Scriptures, **4**that he was buried, that he was raised on the third day according to the Scriptures, **5**and that he appeared to Peter,[c] and then to the Twelve. **6**After that, he appeared to more than five hundred of the brothers at the same time, most of whom are still living, though some have fallen asleep. **7**Then he appeared to James, then to all the apostles[D], **8**and last of all he appeared to me also, as to one abnormally born.

9For I am the least of the apostles and do not even deserve to be called an apostle, because I persecuted the church of God. **10**But by the grace[D] of God I am what

---

[a]38 Some manuscripts *If he is ignorant of this, let him be ignorant*
[b]3 Or *you at the first*   [c]5 Greek *Cephas*

Can faith be futile? (15:2)

To have *believed in vain* is part of a rhetorical argument that if Christ was not raised from the dead, our faith is groundless. The resurrection, to Paul's way of thinking, vindicated Jesus and his message. Faith would be futile without it.

When did Jesus appear to 500 people after the resurrection? (15:6)

No one can say exactly. Some think it may have happened when Jesus met his disciples in Galilee (Matt. 28:16–20). Others assume that all those who saw the resurrected Christ would have gathered in Jerusalem as he had instructed. Since only about 120 were there (Acts 1:15), they say Christ must have appeared to the 500 sometime after Pentecost.

Abnormally born (15:8)

This metaphor is ambiguous. The term could refer literally to a miscarriage—suggesting that Paul did not come to be an apostle by conventional means. Or it may refer to a pregnancy going beyond the normal term—thus, Paul would be the last apostle, born past the due date. Some think Paul used the term as a figure of speech meaning an illegitimate birth, perhaps answering critics who charged him with being an "illegitimate" apostle because he was not a part of the original group of apostles.

Why didn't Paul allow women to speak in church? (14:34)

In fact, he did, permitting women even to prophesy (11:5). Various attempts to accommodate these two passages have proposed that: (1) vv. 34–35 were added by a scribe after Paul; (2) women prophesied only outside the meetings; (3) Paul forbade *indiscreet* speech by women; (4) Paul was quoting opponents, but did not endorse their teaching; (5) women (and men) could prophesy, but only men could judge and verify prophecy; (6) women were forbidden to ask disruptive questions in church since they were less educated; (7) Paul urged the church to respect cultural practices regarding women in public, so it could remain effective in reaching people for Christ. Also see article: *Why silence the women?* (1 Tim. 2:11).

I am, and his grace[D] to me was not without effect. No, I worked harder than all of them—yet not I, but the grace of God that was with me. **11**Whether, then, it was I or they, this is what we preach, and this is what you believed.

The Resurrection of the Dead

12But if it is preached that Christ has been raised from the dead, how can some of you say that there is no resurrection[D] of the dead? **13**If there is no resurrection of the dead, then not even Christ has been raised. **14**And if Christ has not been raised, our preaching is useless and so is your faith. **15**More than that, we are then found to be false witnesses about God, for we have testified about God that he raised Christ from the dead. But he did not raise him if in fact the dead are not raised. **16**For if the dead are not raised, then Christ has not been raised either. **17**And if Christ has not been raised, your faith is futile; you are still in your sins. **18**Then those also who have fallen asleep in Christ are lost. **19**If only for this life we have hope in Christ, we are to be pitied more than all men.

20But Christ has indeed been raised from the dead, the firstfruits[D] of those who have fallen asleep. **21**For since death[D] came through a man, the resurrection of the dead comes also through a man. **22**For as in Adam all die, so in Christ all will be made alive. **23**But each in his own turn: Christ, the firstfruits; then, when he comes, those who belong to him. **24**Then the end will come, when he hands over the kingdom to God the Father after he has destroyed all dominion, authority and power. **25**For he must reign until he has put all his enemies under his feet. **26**The last enemy to be destroyed is death. **27**For he "has put everything under his feet."[a] Now when it says that "everything" has been put under him, it is clear that this does not include God himself, who put everything under Christ. **28**When he has done this, then the Son himself will be made subject to him who put everything under him, so that God may be all in all.

29Now if there is no resurrection, what will those do who are baptized for the dead? If the dead are not raised at all, why are people baptized for them? **30**And as for us, why do we endanger ourselves every hour? **31**I die every day—I mean that, brothers—just as surely as I glory[D] over you in Christ Jesus our Lord. **32**If I fought wild beasts in Ephesus for merely human reasons, what have I gained? If the dead are not raised,

> "Let us eat and drink,
> for tomorrow we die."[b]

33Do not be misled: "Bad company corrupts good character." **34**Come back to your senses as you ought, and stop sinning; for there are some who are ignorant of God—I say this to your shame.

The Resurrection Body

35But someone may ask, "How are the dead raised? With what kind of body will they come?" **36**How foolish! What you sow does not come to life unless it dies. **37**When you sow, you do not plant the body that will be, but just a seed, perhaps of wheat or of something else. **38**But God gives it a body as he has determined, and to each kind of seed he gives its own body. **39**All flesh is not the same: Men have one kind of flesh, animals have another, birds

All will be made alive (15:22)

Paul does not suggest a universal salvation here, implying that all will be saved. Though every human being (those *in Adam*) faces physical death because of sin, every believer (those *in Christ*) can anticipate eternal life because of the resurrection.

How will Christ destroy *all dominion, authority and power*? (15:24)

Presumably, this means the same sort of forces that Paul refers to elsewhere (Phil. 2:10; Romans 8:38–39; Eph. 6:12)—spiritual beings and powers over which Christ will assert his Lordship when he comes again. Paul doesn't say exactly how that will happen. His concern is to emphasize that Christ is greater than all the forces of the enemy.

Is Jesus subordinate to the Father? (15:28)

Yes. Writing from the context of the Jews' understanding of God, Paul upholds the uniqueness and singularity of God by pointing to the subordination of Jesus to the Father. Paul speaks of Christ as being both subject to the Father and as having the rights and status of deity (8:6). On the whole, the Bible shows the Father and the Son to be equal in *being* though the Son is subordinate in *function* or *relationship*.

Who was being *baptized for the dead*? (15:29)

One view (among many for this verse) is that some Corinthian believers were worried about the salvation of believers who had died without being baptized, so they were baptized in proxy for the dead. Why did Paul recognize the practice, though, almost appearing to endorse it? It seems he was revealing an inconsistency in their logic. If they didn't believe in the future resurrection, then there was no point in their proxy baptisms. Paul did not sanction the practice; he simply used the behavior of his opponents to make a persuasive point.

How did Paul survive his fight with *wild beasts in Ephesus*? (15:32)

More than likely, *wild beasts* is a metaphor for Paul's human opponents in Ephesus. *Wild beasts* was a label commonly given to wicked people—just the same sort of opponents Paul faced in Corinth. He *survived* such opponents wherever he encountered them by persevering in his confidence in the resurrection.

*a*27 Psalm 8:6   *b*32 Isaiah 22:13

another and fish another. **40**There are also heavenly bodies and there are earthly bodies; but the splendor of the heavenly bodies is one kind, and the splendor of the earthly bodies is another. **41**The sun has one kind of splendor, the moon another and the stars another; and star differs from star in splendor.

42So will it be with the resurrection[D] of the dead. The body that is sown is perishable, it is raised imperishable; **43**it is sown in dishonor, it is raised in glory[D]; it is sown in weakness, it is raised in power; **44**it is sown a natural body, it is raised a spiritual body.

If there is a natural body, there is also a spiritual body. **45**So it is written: "The first man Adam became a living being"[a]; the last Adam, a life-giving spirit. **46**The spiritual did not come first, but the natural, and after that the spiritual. **47**The first man was of the dust of the earth, the second man from heaven. **48**As was the earthly man, so are those who are of the earth; and as is the man from heaven, so also are those who are of heaven. **49**And just as we have borne the likeness of the earthly man, so shall we[b] bear the likeness of the man from heaven.

50I declare to you, brothers, that flesh and blood cannot inherit the kingdom of God[D], nor does the perishable inherit the imperishable. **51**Listen, I tell you a mystery[D]: We will not all sleep, but we will all be changed— **52**in a flash, in the twinkling of an eye, at the last trumpet. For the trumpet will sound, the dead will be raised imperishable, and we will be changed. **53**For the perishable must clothe itself with the imperishable, and the mortal with immortality. **54**When the perishable has been clothed with the imperishable, and the mortal with immortality, then the saying that is written will come true: "Death[D] has been swallowed up in victory."[c]

> **55**"Where, O death, is your victory?
> Where, O death, is your sting?"[d]

56The sting of death is sin, and the power of sin is the law. **57**But thanks be to God! He gives us the victory through our Lord Jesus Christ.

58Therefore, my dear brothers, stand firm. Let nothing move you. Always give yourselves fully to the work of the

a45 Gen. 2:7   *b49* Some early manuscripts *so let us*
c54 Isaiah 25:8   *d55* Hosea 13:14

Last trumpet (15:52)
The *last trumpet* was common imagery in Jewish literature dealing with the end times. It is, figuratively speaking, the trumpet that blows to herald the Lord's return and announce judgment. There are similar references to trumpets in 1 Thes. 4:16; Rev. 8:2; 11:15.

What do we have to look forward to? (15:35–57)

We look forward to Christ's victory, the ultimate defeat of death and sin. Then we will be given imperishable (v. 42), immortal (v. 54) and spiritual (v. 44) bodies. Paul emphasizes bodies, and not just spirits, because bodies are an integral part of personhood. The Hebrew and Jewish tradition esteemed the physical creation and hoped for the renewal of that creation. By Paul's time, this understanding had developed into a strong expectation of a resurrection and of resurrection bodies.

Paul provides no timetable—here or elsewhere—for when that resurrection will occur. Neither does he clearly answer questions about what happens to the soul after death and before the resurrection. What is clear is that he does not expect the resurrection bodies to be given individually, as each person dies. Instead all will be given their resurrection bodies at one time when Christ returns.

Lord, because you know that your labor in the Lord is not in vain.

The Collection for God's People

16 Now about the collection for God's people: Do what I told the Galatian churches to do. **2**On the first day of every week, each one of you should set aside a sum of money in keeping with his income, saving it up, so that when I come no collections will have to be made. **3**Then, when I arrive, I will give letters of introduction to the men you approve and send them with your gift to Jerusalem[D]. **4**If it seems advisable for me to go also, they will accompany me.

Personal Requests

5After I go through Macedonia, I will come to you—for I will be going through Macedonia. **6**Perhaps I will stay with you awhile, or even spend the winter, so that you can help me on my journey, wherever I go. **7**I do not want to see you now and make only a passing visit; I hope to spend some time with you, if the Lord permits. **8**But I will stay on at Ephesus until Pentecost, **9**because a great door for effective work has opened to me, and there are many who oppose me.

10If Timothy comes, see to it that he has nothing to fear while he is with you, for he is carrying on the work of the Lord, just as I am. **11**No one, then, should refuse to accept him. Send him on his way in peace[D] so that he may return to me. I am expecting him along with the brothers.

12Now about our brother Apollos: I strongly urged him to go to you with the brothers. He was quite unwilling to go now, but he will go when he has the opportunity.

13Be on your guard; stand firm in the faith; be men of courage; be strong. **14**Do everything in love.

15You know that the household of Stephanas were the first converts in Achaia, and they have devoted themselves to the service of the saints[D]. I urge you, brothers, **16**to submit to such as these and to everyone who joins in the work, and labors at it. **17**I was glad when Stephanas, Fortunatus and Achaicus arrived, because they have supplied what was lacking from you. **18**For they refreshed my spirit and yours also. Such men deserve recognition.

Final Greetings

19The churches in the province of Asia send you greetings. Aquila and Priscilla[a] greet you warmly in the Lord, and so does the church that meets at their house. **20**All the brothers here send you greetings. Greet one another with a holy kiss.

21I, Paul, write this greeting in my own hand.

22If anyone does not love the Lord—a curse be on him. Come, O Lord[b]!

23The grace[D] of the Lord Jesus be with you.

24My love to all of you in Christ Jesus. Amen.[c]

Why did Paul want the Corinthians to collect gifts for God's people in Jerusalem? (16:1–4)

In several passages Paul makes it clear that Gentiles owe a great debt to Judaism—the debt of their very salvation (2 Cor. 8–9; Romans 15:25–27). So gifts of this sort symbolized gratitude to the "mother church" in Jerusalem. But there is also evidence of a severe famine around Jerusalem at the time, which this collection was intended to help alleviate.

What do Paul's personal words reveal about the early church? (16:10–19)

That God was coming to real people in real-life situations. Paul wrote specific instructions to the Corinthian church about issues of their day. The authenticity they add to Paul's letters increases their drama and impact: because they were written to real people in the real world, they have meaning for us as well.

Why curse those who do not love the Lord? (16:22)

This difficult verse includes a play on words: *anathema* (meaning *be accursed, cut off from God*) is placed immediately beside *maranatha* (*come, Lord!*). Paul does not present a carefully developed theology on salvation and damnation. Still, he sees humanity in the end divided between those who love the Lord and those who don't. These two words express that reality forcefully.

---

a19 Greek *Prisca,* a variant of *Priscilla*   *b22* In Aramaic the expression *Come, O Lord* is *Marana tha.*   *c24* Some manuscripts do not have *Amen.*

2 CORINTHIANS

Why read this book?

You can learn a lot by overhearing a conversation—from a neighboring booth in the restaurant or from kids climbing playground equipment. Even if you don't hear many details, you can often detect emotions that color the conversation. Reading 2 Corinthians is something like that. Though some specifics aren't known, the feelings come through loudly. Paul, the apostle, discusses the joys, sorrows, ambitions, frustrations and assurances he has for the believers at Corinth. Examining his emotions can be helpful in developing our own relationship with God.

Who wrote this book?

Paul, the apostle.

Why was it written?

Inner strife had plagued the church at Corinth. Paul wrote to calm the disagreements, restore unity to the congregation and to reestablish his role as leader.

When was it written?

Around A.D. 55.

What issues does this book raise?

The main issues include handling dissension within the church, false teaching, church leadership and the unique dilemmas of Christians in the world. Other issues include questions of financial support for the church and for the poor.

What to look for in 2 Corinthians:

Watch for practical examples and advice on resolving conflict: personality conflicts between church members, theological conflict over false teachings, cultural conflict between the church and the world.

When did these things happen?

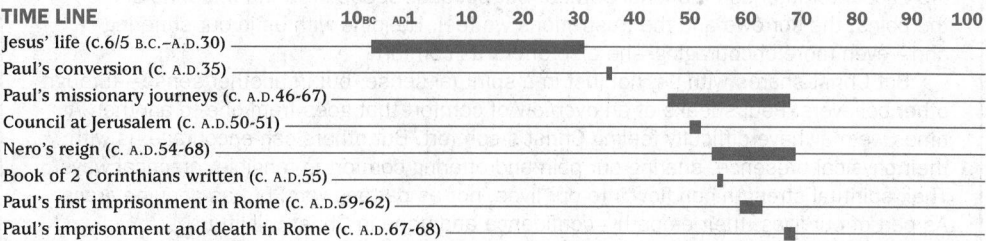

TIME LINE	10BC AD1	10	20	30	40	50	60	70	80	90	100
Jesus' life (c.6/5 B.C.–A.D.30)											
Paul's conversion (c. A.D.35)											
Paul's missionary journeys (c. A.D.46-67)											
Council at Jerusalem (c. A.D.50-51)											
Nero's reign (c. A.D.54-68)											
Book of 2 Corinthians written (c. A.D.55)											
Paul's first imprisonment in Rome (c. A.D.59-62)											
Paul's imprisonment and death in Rome (c. A.D.67-68)											

1 Paul, an apostle[D] of Christ Jesus by the will of God, and Timothy our brother,

To the church of God in Corinth, together with all the saints[D] throughout Achaia:

²Grace[D] and peace[D] to you from God our Father and the Lord Jesus Christ.

The God of All Comfort

³Praise be to the God and Father of our Lord Jesus Christ, the Father of compassion and the God of all comfort, ⁴who comforts us in all our troubles, so that we can comfort those in any trouble with the comfort we ourselves have received from God. ⁵For just as the sufferings of Christ flow over into our lives, so also through Christ our comfort overflows. ⁶If we are distressed, it is for your comfort and salvation[D]; if we are comforted, it is for your comfort, which produces in you patient endurance of the same sufferings we suffer. ⁷And our hope for you is firm, because we know that just as you share in our sufferings, so also you share in our comfort.

⁸We do not want you to be uninformed, brothers, about the hardships we suffered in the province of Asia. We were under great pressure, far beyond our ability to endure, so that we despaired even of life. ⁹Indeed, in our hearts we felt the sentence of death[D]. But this happened that we might not rely on ourselves but on God, who raises the dead. ¹⁰He has delivered us from such a deadly peril, and he will deliver us. On him we have set our hope that he will continue to deliver us, ¹¹as you help us by your prayers. Then many will give thanks on our[a] behalf for the gracious favor granted us in answer to the prayers of many.

[a]11 Many manuscripts *your*

Was Paul complaining? (1:8)

No. The difference between complaining and simply telling the facts depends on our motivation. Complaining implies a selfish motive—we want others to feel sorry for us or to do something for us. Paul made it clear that this was not his motive. He told about his hardships so that God could be glorified. His story witnessed to God's grace and provision.

Was Paul talking about the final resurrection? (1:9)

Only indirectly. He used death as an illustration of one of the central themes in his letter: God can take our weaknesses and turn them into assets. Such a powerful God can do anything —even raise us from death, the ultimate "weakness."

How do Christ's sufferings continue in us? (1:5)

Christians will suffer because of their strong identity with Christ. The Bible says that Christ *learned obedience from what he suffered;* see **Why did Jesus need to learn obedience through suffering?** (Heb. 5:8). Why then should his disciples expect anything less?

Our suffering is, in fact, a link to Jesus Christ. Though he was the Son of God, he endured the frustrations of the flesh while living in a sinful world. We still live in that fallen world and feel the tension caused by its influence. Some face severe physical pain. Others encounter intense emotional battles. But because Jesus lives within us, he shares the pains, the sorrows and the frustrations we feel. He joins with us in our suffering and—even more encouraging—he also offers us comfort.

But Christ shares with us, not just in a spiritual sense, but in another sense—through other believers. Paul speaks of an *overflow* of comfort that goes from one to another. At times we may have difficulty feeling Christ's comfort. But others can encourage us with their physical presence, sharing our pain and offering comfort in tangible, practical ways. Their spiritual strength can flow into our lives, not as pat answers, but as genuine grace. As part of our lives, their empathy, confidence and hope in Christ will lift us.

Christians may go through some tough times. But they should never have to go through them alone.

Paul's Change of Plans

¹²Now this is our boast: Our conscience testifies that we have conducted ourselves in the world, and especially in our relations with you, in the holiness and sincerity that are from God. We have done so not according to worldly wisdom but according to God's grace^D. ¹³For we do not write you anything you cannot read or understand. And I hope that, ¹⁴as you have understood us in part, you will come to understand fully that you can boast of us just as we will boast of you in the day of the Lord^D Jesus.

¹⁵Because I was confident of this, I planned to visit you first so that you might benefit twice. ¹⁶I planned to visit you on my way to Macedonia and to come back to you from Macedonia, and then to have you send me on my way to Judea. ¹⁷When I planned this, did I do it lightly? Or do I make my plans in a worldly manner so that in the same breath I say, "Yes, yes" and "No, no"?

¹⁸But as surely as God is faithful, our message to you is not "Yes" and "No." ¹⁹For the Son of God, Jesus Christ, who was preached among you by me and Silas^a and Timothy, was not "Yes" and "No," but in him it has always been "Yes." ²⁰For no matter how many promises God has made, they are "Yes" in Christ. And so through him the "Amen" is spoken by us to the glory^D of God. ²¹Now it is God who makes both us and you stand firm in Christ. He anointed^D us, ²²set his seal of ownership on us, and put his Spirit in our hearts as a deposit, guaranteeing what is to come.

²³I call God as my witness that it was in order to spare you that I did not return to Corinth. ²⁴Not that we lord it over your faith, but we work with you for your joy, because it is by faith you stand firm. 2 ¹So I made up my mind that I would not make another painful visit to you. ²For if I grieve you, who is left to make me glad but you whom I have grieved? ³I wrote as I did so that when I came I should not be distressed by those who ought to make me rejoice. I had confidence in all of you, that you would all share my joy. ⁴For I wrote you out of great distress and anguish of heart and with many tears, not to grieve you but to let you know the depth of my love for you.

Forgiveness for the Sinner

⁵If anyone has caused grief, he has not so much grieved me as he has grieved all of you, to some extent—not to put it too severely. ⁶The punishment inflicted on him by the majority is sufficient for him. ⁷Now instead, you ought to forgive and comfort him, so that he will not be overwhelmed by excessive sorrow. ⁸I urge you, therefore, to reaffirm your love for him. ⁹The reason I wrote you was to see if you would stand the test and be obedient in everything. ¹⁰If you forgive anyone, I also forgive him. And what I have forgiven—if there was anything to forgive—I have forgiven in the sight of Christ for your sake, ¹¹in order that Satan might not outwit us. For we are not unaware of his schemes.

Ministers of the New Covenant

¹²Now when I went to Troas to preach the gospel^D of Christ and found that the Lord had opened a door for me, ¹³I still had no peace^D of mind, because I did not find my

---

Are Paul's writings as simple as he says? (1:13)

Though they express eternal truths, Paul's writings were aimed at the average church member in Corinth (see *The Church in Corinth* on page 1573). With simplicity and candor he cast the gospel message in such a way that no one would stumble over it (6:3).

Day of the Lord Jesus Christ (1:14)

The day when Jesus Christ will return to judge both the faithful and unfaithful. See *The day of the Lord* (1 Thes. 5:2).

Why was Paul so defensive about his change of plans? (1:17)

Paul's last visit, though brief, had apparently been painful for both him and the Corinthians. His disappointments had prompted him to write a critical letter that, in the short term, threatened their relationship. With his approval rating down, it seems that some of his opponents, probably false teachers in Corinth, had been using Paul's change of plans as evidence that he could not be trusted.

Can we take all God's promises as our own? (1:20)

Paul is *not* saying we can take Biblical promises for ourselves that were given in specific situations to certain people. Paul is, instead, speaking in general terms: the old covenant points to the new; its promises are fulfilled in Christ. Jesus is the reason for and the conclusion of all God's promises.

Why say *Amen* when we pray? (1:20)

Amen is a Hebrew word carried over into English, which means *so be it*. It is used to confirm or endorse—to agree with—what has just been said. It also expresses our humility before God, submitting to his wisdom and will.

Seal of ownership (1:22)

The original word was used in the contracts in Paul's day; it was both the first installment on a loan and the guarantee of its complete payment. Much of what Paul was writing to the Corinthians could only be understood in light of their future hope. The *seal* was their guarantee that the promises would be fulfilled in Christ.

Why was Paul demanding obedience? (2:9)

Paul had likely been testing the faith of his young congregation: Were they willing to name sin for what it was? Willing to discipline one of their own? It would have been more convenient for them to ignore the problem, but Paul had stretched their faith by demanding a response. Here he went on to teach the complementary lesson: it can be as difficult to offer forgiveness and mercy in the face of genuine repentance as it is to discipline.

What was Satan scheming? (2:11)

Paul sensed that Satan was using the false teachers at Corinth to subvert his influence and take over the church. The continued alienation of a repentant member offered Satan an opportunity to create more division in the church. Paul recognized how urgent it was for the church to come together and forgive.

---

^a 19 Greek *Silvanus*, a variant of *Silas*

Triumphal procession (2:14)

Reading these words, the Corinthians undoubtedly thought of a Roman victory celebration. Upon returning home, a victorious general was honored with a parade. He would march with his army through the streets, displaying the spoils and the captives of war. Paul may have meant that believers are Christ's army, sharing in his victory. Or he may have meant that we are Christ's captives, conquered by his love and submitted to his will.

What fragrance indicates both death and life? (2:15–16)

A Roman triumphal procession included spices and incense, burned openly, which sent sweet aromas through the streets. The cheering crowds not only saw and heard the general's exploits, they smelled victory in the air. In the same way, we are witnesses to Christ's victory. Those who respond positively to the news find life and mercy. But those who reject it face death and judgment.

Who peddled the word of God for profit? (2:17)

Paul described the false teachers in the Corinthian church as hucksters of the gospel. Fraudulent ministers focus on their own personal gain instead of the truth of the gospel. If someone alters the message in order to increase "sales," we have reason to be suspicious. Personal profit may be measured in several ways: some may want control over others or fame and recognition as much or more than fortune.

How does the letter kill? (3:6)

Paul means the letter of the law God gave to Moses. Following the law does not kill. But anyone who tries to follow the law falls short of its requirements. In fact, such failure convinces us we are sinners. So the law does a valuable service: though we can't follow it and be saved by it, the law shows us our spiritual need. It puts us in a frame of mind necessary to seek God's help.

Who made their minds dull? (3:14)

When people follow the god of this age (4:4), instead of the God of eternity, God makes their minds dull to the truth. Without God's help, it becomes impossible for them to see the path to salvation brought by Christ. In the sense that God allows people to make their own choices, giving them over in the sinful desires of their hearts, he allows their minds to be made dull. Also see Why would God spiritually anesthetize his people? (Romans 11:8).

What can we see when the veil is removed? (3:16)

There are many things we cannot see even when the veil is removed—many things remain vague, hidden to our understanding (1 Cor. 13:12). But one thing we can clearly see is that the path to righteousness lies through Jesus Christ. With the veil removed we can see that the old covenant has been superseded by the new and that Christ fulfills the law.

When will we be like Christ? (3:18)

Believers are "in process"—looking more like Christ all the time, but not finished until after their earthly life. To express this, Paul borrowed language from two prevailing views of his day: (1) Mystery religions believed a divine revelation would immediately transform a per-

brother Titus there. So I said good-by to them and went on to Macedonia.

¹⁴But thanks be to God, who always leads us in triumphal procession in Christ and through us spreads everywhere the fragrance of the knowledge of him. ¹⁵For we are to God the aroma of Christ among those who are being saved and those who are perishing. ¹⁶To the one we are the smell of death[D]; to the other, the fragrance of life. And who is equal to such a task? ¹⁷Unlike so many, we do not peddle the word of God for profit. On the contrary, in Christ we speak before God with sincerity, like men sent from God.

3 Are we beginning to commend ourselves again? Or do we need, like some people, letters of recommendation to you or from you? ²You yourselves are our letter, written on our hearts, known and read by everybody. ³You show that you are a letter from Christ, the result of our ministry, written not with ink but with the Spirit of the living God, not on tablets of stone but on tablets of human hearts.

⁴Such confidence as this is ours through Christ before God. ⁵Not that we are competent in ourselves to claim anything for ourselves, but our competence comes from God. ⁶He has made us competent as ministers of a new covenant[D]—not of the letter but of the Spirit; for the letter kills, but the Spirit gives life.

The Glory of the New Covenant

⁷Now if the ministry that brought death, which was engraved in letters on stone, came with glory[D], so that the Israelites could not look steadily at the face of Moses because of its glory, fading though it was, ⁸will not the ministry of the Spirit be even more glorious? ⁹If the ministry that condemns men is glorious, how much more glorious is the ministry that brings righteousness[D]! ¹⁰For what was glorious has no glory now in comparison with the surpassing glory. ¹¹And if what was fading away came with glory, how much greater is the glory of that which lasts!

¹²Therefore, since we have such a hope, we are very bold. ¹³We are not like Moses, who would put a veil over his face to keep the Israelites from gazing at it while the radiance was fading away. ¹⁴But their minds were made dull, for to this day the same veil remains when the old covenant is read. It has not been removed, because only in Christ is it taken away. ¹⁵Even to this day when Moses is read, a veil covers their hearts. ¹⁶But whenever anyone turns to the Lord, the veil is taken away. ¹⁷Now the Lord is the Spirit, and where the Spirit of the Lord is, there is freedom. ¹⁸And we, who with unveiled faces all reflect[a] the Lord's glory, are being transformed into his likeness with ever-increasing glory, which comes from the Lord, who is the Spirit.

Treasures in Jars of Clay

4 Therefore, since through God's mercy[D] we have this ministry, we do not lose heart. ²Rather, we have renounced secret and shameful ways; we do not use deception, nor do we distort the word of God. On the contrary, by setting forth the truth plainly we commend ourselves to every man's conscience in the sight of God. ³And even if our gospel[D] is veiled, it is veiled to those who are per-

a18 Or contemplate

ishing. **4**The god of this age has blinded the minds of unbelievers, so that they cannot see the light of the gospelᴰ of the gloryᴰ of Christ, who is the image of God. **5**For we do not preach ourselves, but Jesus Christ as Lord, and ourselves as your servants for Jesus' sake. **6**For God, who said, "Let light shine out of darkness,"ᵃ made his light shine in our hearts to give us the light of the knowledge of the glory of God in the face of Christ.

7But we have this treasure in jars of clay to show that this all-surpassing power is from God and not from us. **8**We are hard pressed on every side, but not crushed; perplexed, but not in despair; **9**persecuted, but not abandoned; struck down, but not destroyed. **10**We always carry around in our body the deathᴰ of Jesus, so that the life of Jesus may also be revealed in our body. **11**For we who are alive are always being given over to death for Jesus' sake, so that his life may be revealed in our mortal body. **12**So then, death is at work in us, but life is at work in you.

13It is written: "I believed; therefore I have spoken."ᵇ With that same spirit of faith we also believe and therefore speak, **14**because we know that the one who raised the Lord Jesus from the dead will also raise us with Jesus and present us with you in his presence. **15**All this is for your benefit, so that the graceᴰ that is reaching more and more people may cause thanksgiving to overflow to the glory of God.

16Therefore we do not lose heart. Though outwardly we are wasting away, yet inwardly we are being renewed day by day. **17**For our light and momentary troubles are achieving for us an eternal glory that far outweighs them all. **18**So we fix our eyes not on what is seen, but on what is unseen. For what is seen is temporary, but what is unseen is eternal.

Our Heavenly Dwelling

5 Now we know that if the earthly tent we live in is destroyed, we have a building from God, an eternal house in heaven, not built by human hands. **2**Meanwhile we groan, longing to be clothed with our heavenly dwelling, **3**because when we are clothed, we will not be found naked. **4**For while we are in this tent, we groan and are burdened, because we do not wish to be unclothed but to be clothed with our heavenly dwelling, so that what is mortal may be swallowed up by life. **5**Now it is God who has made us for this very purpose and has given us the Spirit as a deposit, guaranteeing what is to come.

6Therefore we are always confident and know that as long as we are at home in the body we are away from the Lord. **7**We live by faith, not by sight. **8**We are confident, I say, and would prefer to be away from the body and at home with the Lord. **9**So we make it our goal to please him, whether we are at home in the body or away from it. **10**For we must all appear before the judgment seat of Christ, that each one may receive what is due him for the things done while in the body, whether good or bad.

The Ministry of Reconciliation

11Since, then, we know what it is to fear the Lord, we try to persuade men. What we are is plain to God, and I hope it is also plain to your conscience. **12**We are not trying to commend ourselves to you again, but are giving

ᵃ6 Gen. 1:3   ᵇ13 Psalm 116:10

son. (2) Jewish prophetic teaching taught that personal transformation occurred at the end of time.

Why was Paul so defensive? (4:2)
False teachers were threatening to take over the church at Corinth. Paul had no official position to defend his role in the church. He could only appeal to his personal integrity and the self-evident truth of the gospel. Restating and clarifying the gospel was no problem for him. But defending his own honor was an uncomfortable task causing those unaware of his motives to think he sounded arrogant.

How can we convince the spiritually blind? (4:3–4)
We can't. Believers can, however, preach the good news of Jesus Christ, letting the *Holy Spirit* convince people of their sin and their need for salvation.

How can we carry the death of Jesus in our bodies? (4:10)
Paul links our physical sufferings and hardships to the death of Jesus. See article: **How do Christ's sufferings continue in us?** (1:5). Our sufferings remind us and others of the ultimate suffering, Jesus' death on a cross. Ironically, revealing Christ's sufferings makes it possible for us to reveal his life.

Why does life work in some believers, but death in others? (4:12)
Both life and death are evident in all believers (see previous note). But death or suffering in one believer may be the occasion for life to be produced in others. Paul was probably thinking of his own sufferings. He willingly endured pain so the life-bringing gospel could be made known to others.

What does it mean to waste away? (4:16)
It can mean aging or disease. But it can also refer to a vulnerability to emotional decay—discouragement or depression, for example. Body, mind and spirit are all challenged by the sufferings of this world. But those who are in Christ have an inner core that grows stronger in spite of and in some ways because of, outward suffering.

How do troubles achieve glory? (4:17)
Troubles help us see this world for what it is: imperfect and temporary. That insight leads us to look for the perfect and permanent. It is in that frame of mind that we can begin to see the eternal glory of Christ.

Why talk about a *tent, building or house*? (5:1–5)
Paul used common terms and expressions of his day to help people grasp the significance and enrich their understanding of the gospel. These pictures illustrate the temporary nature of life on earth and the eternal nature of heaven. While we may experience suffering in our earthly bodies, we can look forward to our permanent dwellings in heaven.

Where do we go when we die? (5:8)
Paul uses the imagery of being at home or away from home. But he makes it clear that such language only approximates the real goal —pleasing God (v. 9). Whether at home in the body or at home with the Lord, the important thing is that we glorify God.

Did some think Paul was out of his mind? (5:13)

Paul received all kinds of criticisms. It's entirely possible that some of his opponents used his Damascus road experience as evidence that he was insane and that therefore his message could not be trusted. Others felt such experiences were the measure of spirituality (see 12:12) and criticized Paul for not having enough of them.

What was Christ like from *a worldly point of view?* (5:16)

Paul probably was thinking of his pre-conversion perspective. From that point of view, Christ was a rabble-rousing heretic who incited gullible Jews to give up their traditions; he was a fool for not joining the powerful Jewish political system so he could really accomplish something; he was a poor judge of character who chose common fishermen as his disciples; he associated with sinners; and he was a failure who got himself killed in the end.

What is new when someone is in Christ? (5:17)

Everything. A sinner is changed radically—turned inside out and upside down. Life takes on a whole new direction and purpose. The believer no longer focuses on self but focuses instead on Jesus Christ. But see *When will we be like Christ?* (3:18).

What is the ministry of reconciliation? (5:19)

Ever since sin broke it, God has been reestablishing humankind's relationship with him. God sent Jesus Christ to die for our sin, making it possible for us to be his friends again. In one sense, reconciliation is already done; in another sense, it's necessary to tell people about it. Both are part of the ministry of reconciliation.

How did Jesus become sin? (5:21)

God did not make the sinless Jesus a sinner. But he did cause him to take upon himself all our sin. This was necessary so the ministry of reconciliation could take place. If Jesus had not taken on our sinful condition, the wrongs we have done could never have been made right.

you an opportunity to take pride in us, so that you can answer those who take pride in what is seen rather than in what is in the heart. [13]If we are out of our mind, it is for the sake of God; if we are in our right mind, it is for you. [14]For Christ's love compels us, because we are convinced that one died for all, and therefore all died. [15]And he died for all, that those who live should no longer live for themselves but for him who died for them and was raised again.

[16]So from now on we regard no one from a worldly point of view. Though we once regarded Christ in this way, we do so no longer. [17]Therefore, if anyone is in Christ, he is a new creation; the old has gone, the new has come! [18]All this is from God, who reconciled us to himself through Christ and gave us the ministry of reconciliation: [19]that God was reconciling the world to himself in Christ, not counting men's sins against them. And he has committed to us the message of reconciliation. [20]We are therefore Christ's ambassadors, as though God were making his appeal through us. We implore you on Christ's behalf: Be reconciled to God. [21]God made him who had no sin to be sin[a] for us, so that in him we might become the righteousness[D] of God.

6 As God's fellow workers we urge you not to receive God's grace[D] in vain. [2]For he says,

"In the time of my favor I heard you,
    and in the day of salvation[D] I helped you."[b]

I tell you, now is the time of God's favor, now is the day of salvation.

Paul's Hardships

[3]We put no stumbling block[D] in anyone's path, so that our ministry will not be discredited. [4]Rather, as servants of God we commend ourselves in every way: in great endurance; in troubles, hardships and distresses; [5]in beatings, imprisonments and riots; in hard work, sleepless nights and hunger; [6]in purity, understanding, patience and kindness; in the Holy Spirit and in sincere love; [7]in truthful speech and in the power of God; with weapons of righteousness in the right hand and in the left; [8]through glory[D] and dishonor, bad report and good report; genuine, yet regarded as impostors; [9]known, yet regarded as

[a]21 Or *be a sin offering*   [b]2 Isaiah 49:8

How will believers be judged? (5:10)

S ome wonder how believers can be judged at all, since they are justified by faith and not by works. But this verse simply underscores the responsibility of believers to live according to what they believe. Though salvation is a matter of faith, other eternal rewards depend on faithfulness (1 Cor. 3:8,13–15).

Believers are judged righteous in Christ. But they will also be rewarded according to the things they did *while in the body, whether good or bad.* God expects our actions after salvation to reflect the glory of God within us. It does make a difference what we do. We don't need to know the details of this judgment. We need only to know that the Judge is fair. Only God can fairly balance all the variables: individual gifts, cultural conditions, the uncertainties of life and the opportunities we are given.

unknown; dying, and yet we live on; beaten, and yet not killed; [10]sorrowful, yet always rejoicing; poor, yet making many rich; having nothing, and yet possessing everything.

[11]We have spoken freely to you, Corinthians, and opened wide our hearts to you. [12]We are not withholding our affection from you, but you are withholding yours from us. [13]As a fair exchange—I speak as to my children—open wide your hearts also.

Do Not Be Yoked With Unbelievers

[14]Do not be yoked together with unbelievers. For what do righteousness[D] and wickedness have in common? Or what fellowship can light have with darkness? [15]What harmony is there between Christ and Belial[a]? What does a believer have in common with an unbeliever? [16]What agreement is there between the temple of God and idols[D]? For we are the temple of the living God. As God has said: "I will live with them and walk among them, and I will be their God, and they will be my people."[b]

> [17]"Therefore come out from them
>   and be separate,
>   says the Lord.
>   Touch no unclean[D] thing,
>   and I will receive you."[c]
> [18]"I will be a Father to you,
>   and you will be my sons and daughters,
>   says the Lord Almighty."[d]

7 Since we have these promises, dear friends, let us purify[D] ourselves from everything that contaminates body and spirit, perfecting holiness out of reverence[D] for God.

Paul's Joy

[2]Make room for us in your hearts. We have wronged no one, we have corrupted no one, we have exploited no one. [3]I do not say this to condemn you; I have said before that you have such a place in our hearts that we would live or die with you. [4]I have great confidence in you; I take great pride in you. I am greatly encouraged; in all our troubles my joy knows no bounds.

[5]For when we came into Macedonia, this body of ours had no rest, but we were harassed at every turn—conflicts on the outside, fears within. [6]But God, who comforts the downcast, comforted us by the coming of Titus, [7]and not only by his coming but also by the comfort you had given him. He told us about your longing for me, your deep sorrow, your ardent concern for me, so that my joy was greater than ever.

[8]Even if I caused you sorrow by my letter, I do not regret it. Though I did regret it—I see that my letter hurt you, but only for a little while— [9]yet now I am happy, not because you were made sorry, but because your sorrow led you to repentance[D]. For you became sorrowful as God intended and so were not harmed in any way by us. [10]Godly sorrow brings repentance that leads to salvation[D] and leaves no regret, but worldly sorrow brings death[D]. [11]See what this godly sorrow has produced in you: what earnestness, what eagerness to clear your-

How can God's grace be in vain? (6:1)

God's grace is never futile, but it can be misappropriated. If we claim to believe the gospel but never demonstrate its effects in our lives, what good has it done? If we continue to live for ourselves rather than to fulfill God's purpose, then we have "received" God's grace in vain. The results are the same as if we had never heard the gospel.

Why did Paul feel the need to commend himself? (6:4)

Paul knew the false teachers "commended" themselves, but only for personal gain. Paul wanted the Corinthians to know that not only had he bypassed personal gain, but he had suffered in many ways in order to preach Christ. By commending himself, Paul was devaluing the false teachers and reinforcing his own ministry and message among the Corinthians.

What had damaged the relationship between Paul and the Corinthians? (6:12)

Paul had written a letter of criticism to the Corinthians. The sting of that rebuke opened the door for the false teachers to discredit Paul, with some success. Now, after some time had elapsed, the Corinthians had begun to see the legitimacy of Paul's rebuke.

How much can we associate with unbelievers? (6:14–15,17)

This is not a discussion of Christian ethics but a look at the faith of true believers. Some Corinthians found certain false doctrines appealing and wanted to combine them with the gospel. But there is no room for linking something false with what is true. There can be no middle ground; either we follow Christ alone or we don't follow him at all.

What's required for perfecting holiness? (7:1)

Holiness, as implied in the preceding verses, calls us to recognize that the false must be abandoned for the true; the old covenant must be given up for the new. We must purify—eliminate—anything from our lives that belongs to our old way of life. The motivation and grace for this process stem from a reverence for God, who will simply not allow any halfway efforts, any mixing of old and new.

What was Paul afraid of? (7:5)

Paul was afraid he had lost the faithfulness of the Corinthians, through a combination of his harsh letter and the influence of the false teachers. See *What had damaged the relationship between Paul and the Corinthians?* (6:12).

Why does God want us to be sorrowful? (7:9)

God intends that we feel the full weight of sorrow for sin so we will enjoy the full expression of joy in salvation (v. 10). God wants us to see that living in a fallen world produces sorrow for everyone. He also wants us to see that sorrow is not in line with his purpose since it produces only death.

---

[a]15 Greek *Beliar*, a variant of *Belial*   [b]16 Lev. 26:12; Jer. 32:38; Ezek. 37:27   [c]17 Isaiah 52:11; Ezek. 20:34,41   [d]18 2 Samuel 7:14; 7:8

Had Paul made false accusations? (7:11–12)

No. They proved themselves to be innocent by dealing with the problem, not by presenting evidence to refute Paul's charges. Paul wanted them to discipline the sinner in their church; his accusations were just.

Does the amount we give indicate God's grace in us? (8:1,7)

Yes. Lots of grace leads to lots of giving. Grace is God's free gift to us. With access to unlimited amounts of God's grace, Christians have more than enough. The excess grace overflows to others in a variety of ways, including the giving of gifts.

Was Paul motivating them out of pride? (8:8)

Not exactly. Perhaps *example* is a better word. Paul has just said that because of God's gift of grace in us, we all should want to give. But there are times when the free flow of grace in the lives of some may be blocked for one reason or another, cutting off the source of their generosity. At such times, the example of others who give freely can serve as a model and inspiration to increase the flow of grace.

selves, what indignation, what alarm, what longing, what concern, what readiness to see justice done. At every point you have proved yourselves to be innocent in this matter. [12]So even though I wrote to you, it was not on account of the one who did the wrong or of the injured party, but rather that before God you could see for yourselves how devoted to us you are. [13]By all this we are encouraged.

In addition to our own encouragement, we were especially delighted to see how happy Titus was, because his spirit has been refreshed by all of you. [14]I had boasted to him about you, and you have not embarrassed me. But just as everything we said to you was true, so our boasting about you to Titus has proved to be true as well. [15]And his affection for you is all the greater when he remembers that you were all obedient, receiving him with fear and trembling. [16]I am glad I can have complete confidence in you.

Generosity Encouraged

8 And now, brothers, we want you to know about the grace[D] that God has given the Macedonian churches. [2]Out of the most severe trial, their overflowing joy and their extreme poverty welled up in rich generosity. [3]For I testify that they gave as much as they were able, and even beyond their ability. Entirely on their own, [4]they urgently pleaded with us for the privilege of sharing in this service to the saints[D]. [5]And they did not do as we expected, but they gave themselves first to the Lord and then to us in keeping with God's will. [6]So we urged Titus, since he had earlier made a beginning, to bring also to completion this act of grace on your part. [7]But just as you excel in everything—in faith, in speech, in knowledge, in complete earnestness and in your love for us[a]—see that you also excel in this grace of giving.

[8]I am not commanding you, but I want to test the sincerity of your love by comparing it with the earnestness of others. [9]For you know the grace of our Lord Jesus Christ, that though he was rich, yet for your sakes he became poor, so that you through his poverty might become rich.

[10]And here is my advice about what is best for you in this matter: Last year you were the first not only to give but also to have the desire to do so. [11]Now finish the work, so that your eager willingness to do it may be matched by your completion of it, according to your means. [12]For if the willingness is there, the gift is acceptable according to what one has, not according to what he does not have.

[13]Our desire is not that others might be relieved while you are hard pressed, but that there might be equality. [14]At the present time your plenty will supply what they need, so that in turn their plenty will supply what you need. Then there will be equality, [15]as it is written: "He who gathered much did not have too much, and he who gathered little did not have too little."[b]

Titus Sent to Corinth

[16]I thank God, who put into the heart of Titus the same concern I have for you. [17]For Titus not only welcomed our appeal, but he is coming to you with much enthusiasm and on his own initiative. [18]And we are sending along

[a]7 Some manuscripts *in our love for you*   [b]15 Exodus 16:18

with him the brother who is praised by all the churches for his service to the gospel[D]. **19**What is more, he was chosen by the churches to accompany us as we carry the offering, which we administer in order to honor the Lord himself and to show our eagerness to help. **20**We want to avoid any criticism of the way we administer this liberal gift. **21**For we are taking pains to do what is right, not only in the eyes of the Lord but also in the eyes of men.

22In addition, we are sending with them our brother who has often proved to us in many ways that he is zealous, and now even more so because of his great confidence in you. **23**As for Titus, he is my partner and fellow worker among you; as for our brothers, they are representatives of the churches and an honor to Christ. **24**Therefore show these men the proof of your love and the reason for our pride in you, so that the churches can see it.

9 There is no need for me to write to you about this service to the saints[D]. **2**For I know your eagerness to help, and I have been boasting about it to the Macedonians, telling them that since last year you in Achaia were ready to give; and your enthusiasm has stirred most of them to action. **3**But I am sending the brothers in order that our boasting about you in this matter should not prove hollow, but that you may be ready, as I said you would be. **4**For if any Macedonians come with me and find you unprepared, we—not to say anything about you—would be ashamed of having been so confident. **5**So I thought it necessary to urge the brothers to visit you in advance and finish the arrangements for the generous gift you had promised. Then it will be ready as a generous gift, not as one grudgingly given.

Sowing Generously

6Remember this: Whoever sows sparingly will also reap sparingly, and whoever sows generously will also reap generously. **7**Each man should give what he has decided in his heart to give, not reluctantly or under compulsion, for God loves a cheerful giver. **8**And God is able to make all grace[D] abound to you, so that in all things at all times, having all that you need, you will abound in every good work. **9**As it is written:

> "He has scattered abroad his gifts to the poor;
>   his righteousness[D] endures forever."[a]

10Now he who supplies seed to the sower and bread for food will also supply and increase your store of seed and will enlarge the harvest of your righteousness. **11**You will be made rich in every way so that you can be generous on every occasion, and through us your generosity will result in thanksgiving to God.

12This service that you perform is not only supplying the needs of God's people but is also overflowing in many expressions of thanks to God. **13**Because of the service by which you have proved yourselves, men will praise God for the obedience that accompanies your confession of the gospel of Christ, and for your generosity in sharing with them and with everyone else. **14**And in their prayers for you their hearts will go out to you, because of the surpassing grace God has given you. **15**Thanks be to God for his indescribable gift!

*a*9 Psalm 112:9

Should we flaunt our donations? (8:24)

No. Jesus values secret giving (Matt. 6:3–4), but Paul's concern here is our *motivation* for telling what we do, not the telling itself. Jesus also says we should let others see our good deeds so they will praise God (Matt. 5:16). Paul was not encouraging flaunting. He simply wanted examples of giving to encourage the whole community of believers to give toward this worthwhile project.

Is sowing and reaping an absolute law? (9:6)

It might be better to call it a general principle. And we should realize that only God can define what is to be reaped. Sowing and reaping do not operate according to some inexorable, impersonal law but according to God's sense of justice and mercy. Although we can be confident that the overall effect is fair, the details may often be hidden from us.

What about tithing? (9:7)

If we feel *compelled* to give according to an external standard, the heart is cut out of the gift. Such giving is a matter of works, not grace. See *Does the amount we give indicate God's grace in us?* (8:1). On the other hand, discipline helps us with what we know to be right. Choosing a standard of giving can help us do what we believe in our hearts to be right even if our temporary feelings should waver.

What is the work of grace here? (9:8)

If you don't feel like giving, if you don't want to give, if giving doesn't make sense to you, God, through a work of grace, can turn you around. When his grace floods our lives, we will feel like giving. Suddenly, it will be the sensible thing to do. God gives us the resources and the will to give, abounding *in every good work.*

Rich in every way (9:11)

Paul is not talking about unlimited prosperity. Instead he's saying that God will provide everything we need so we can give without fear. He sparks the desire to give and the wisdom to know how much to give. Afterward he supplies what we need and satisfies us with the contentment of a fulfilling ministry.

Paul's Defense of His Ministry

10 By the meekness and gentleness of Christ, I appeal to you—I, Paul, who am "timid" when face to face with you, but "bold" when away! **2**I beg you that when I come I may not have to be as bold as I expect to be toward some people who think that we live by the standards of this world. **3**For though we live in the world, we do not wage war as the world does. **4**The weapons we fight with are not the weapons of the world. On the contrary, they have divine power to demolish strongholds^D. **5**We demolish arguments and every pretension that sets itself up against the knowledge of God, and we take captive every thought to make it obedient to Christ. **6**And we will be ready to punish every act of disobedience, once your obedience is complete.

7You are looking only on the surface of things.*a* If anyone is confident that he belongs to Christ, he should consider again that we belong to Christ just as much as he. **8**For even if I boast somewhat freely about the authority the Lord gave us for building you up rather than pulling you down, I will not be ashamed of it. **9**I do not want to seem to be trying to frighten you with my letters. **10**For some say, "His letters are weighty and forceful, but in person he is unimpressive and his speaking amounts to nothing." **11**Such people should realize that what we are in our letters when we are absent, we will be in our actions when we are present.

12We do not dare to classify or compare ourselves with some who commend themselves. When they measure themselves by themselves and compare themselves with themselves, they are not wise. **13**We, however, will not boast beyond proper limits, but will confine our boasting to the field God has assigned to us, a field that reaches even to you. **14**We are not going too far in our boasting, as would be the case if we had not come to you, for we did get as far as you with the gospel^D of Christ. **15**Neither do we go beyond our limits by boasting of work done by others.*b* Our hope is that, as your faith continues to grow, our area of activity among you will greatly expand, **16**so that we can preach the gospel in the regions beyond you. For we do not want to boast about work already done in another man's territory. **17**But, "Let him who boasts boast in the Lord."*c* **18**For it is not the one who commends himself who is approved, but the one whom the Lord commends.

Paul and the False Apostles

11 I hope you will put up with a little of my foolishness; but you are already doing that. **2**I am jealous for you with a godly jealousy. I promised you to one husband, to Christ, so that I might present you as a pure virgin to him. **3**But I am afraid that just as Eve was deceived by the serpent's cunning, your minds may somehow be led astray from your sincere and pure devotion to Christ. **4**For if someone comes to you and preaches a Jesus other than the Jesus we preached, or if you receive a different spirit from the one you received, or a different gospel

---

What spiritual weapons do we have? (10:4)

Spiritual weapons can be seen in opposite terms from worldly weapons: physical weakness is a weapon because it can mean spiritual strength in Christ; God-centeredness is a weapon because it produces a supernatural authority that self-centeredness cannot; truth is a weapon because it overcomes cleverness and deceit; even suffering is a weapon because it can be a means of life.

Strongholds (10:4–5)

The walled cities of the Graeco-Roman world. Paul's enemies were using arguments, pretensions and rationalizations as walls against the Christian view. Christians are to counter false teaching—demolishing strongholds.

Did Paul face congregational power plays? (10:10–11)

Some were using Paul's absence as an opportunity to stake their claims as leaders. Apparently they called Paul's authority as an apostle into question. They also raised doubts about his character, his motives, his methods and even his reluctance to confront in person as directly as he did in his letters.

Was Paul commending himself or not? (10:12)

Yes and no. Paul repeatedly protested that he did not want to boast. He admitted his weaknesses and unworthiness to be Christ's minister. But in the face of the serious charges against him, he found that he needed to be loud and clear about the fact that, in spite of his weaknesses, God had indeed called him. Also see *Why did Paul feel the need to commend himself?* (6:4).

Why did Paul speak *as a fool?* (11:1,16,21,23)

Paul was uncomfortable with defending himself. He had already noted that it made him sound as though he were boasting, and he repeatedly digressed to insist that he was not. It made his argument awkward and less direct than his normal style of preaching. That made him feel foolish, but he knew the false teachers had put him in a position where he had to defend himself in spite of his feelings.

Why were the Corinthians so spiritually vulnerable? (11:4)

As a commercial crossroads (see *Map 11* at the back of this Bible), Corinth was exposed to many religions: native pagan gods, philosophy, the many Greek and Roman gods, the Roman imperial cult, mystery religions from the East, the popular Egyptian myth of Osiris, Judaism and now the teachings of Jesus. They may have seen their tolerant views as a healthy thing, but Paul criticized them for being undiscerning.

---

a7 Or Look at the obvious facts   *b13-15 Or 13We, however, will not boast about things that cannot be measured, but we will boast according to the standard of measurement that the God of measure has assigned us—a measurement that relates even to you. 14 . . . . 15Neither do we boast about things that cannot be measured in regard to the work done by others.*   *c17 Jer. 9:24*

from the one you accepted, you put up with it easily enough. **5**But I do not think I am in the least inferior to those "super-apostles^D." **6**I may not be a trained speaker, but I do have knowledge. We have made this perfectly clear to you in every way.

7Was it a sin for me to lower myself in order to elevate you by preaching the gospel^D of God to you free of charge? **8**I robbed other churches by receiving support from them so as to serve you. **9**And when I was with you and needed something, I was not a burden to anyone, for the brothers who came from Macedonia supplied what I needed. I have kept myself from being a burden to you in any way, and will continue to do so. **10**As surely as the truth of Christ is in me, nobody in the regions of Achaia will stop this boasting of mine. **11**Why? Because I do not love you? God knows I do! **12**And I will keep on doing what I am doing in order to cut the ground from under those who want an opportunity to be considered equal with us in the things they boast about.

13For such men are false apostles, deceitful workmen, masquerading as apostles of Christ. **14**And no wonder, for Satan himself masquerades as an angel of light. **15**It is not surprising, then, if his servants masquerade as servants of righteousness^D. Their end will be what their actions deserve.

Paul Boasts About His Sufferings

16I repeat: Let no one take me for a fool. But if you do, then receive me just as you would a fool, so that I may do a little boasting. **17**In this self-confident boasting I am not talking as the Lord would, but as a fool. **18**Since many are boasting in the way the world does, I too will boast. **19**You gladly put up with fools since you are so wise! **20**In fact, you even put up with anyone who enslaves you or exploits you or takes advantage of you or pushes himself forward or slaps you in the face. **21**To my shame I admit that we were too weak for that!

What anyone else dares to boast about—I am speaking as a fool—I also dare to boast about. **22**Are they Hebrews? So am I. Are they Israelites? So am I. Are they Abraham's descendants? So am I. **23**Are they servants of Christ? (I am out of my mind to talk like this.) I am more. I have worked much harder, been in prison more frequently, been flogged more severely, and have been exposed to death^D again and again. **24**Five times I received from the Jews^D the forty lashes minus one. **25**Three times I was beaten with rods, once I was stoned, three times I was shipwrecked, I spent a night and a day in the open sea, **26**I have been constantly on the move. I have been in danger from rivers, in danger from bandits, in danger from my own countrymen, in danger from Gentiles^D; in danger in the city, in danger in the country, in danger at sea; and in danger from false brothers. **27**I have labored and toiled and have often gone without sleep; I have known hunger and thirst and have often gone without food; I have been cold and naked. **28**Besides everything else, I face daily the pressure of my concern for all the churches. **29**Who is weak, and I do not feel weak? Who is led into sin, and I do not inwardly burn?

30If I must boast, I will boast of the things that show my weakness. **31**The God and Father of the Lord Jesus, who is to be praised forever, knows that I am not lying. **32**In Damascus the governor under King Aretas had the city of the Damascenes guarded in order to arrest me. **33**But I was

In what sense did Paul rob churches? (11:8)

Paul wanted to argue his way out of a misunderstanding. In the heat of his argument, to describe his good intentions with the Corinthians, he overstated his case by saying that he had *robbed other churches*. In reality, other churches had voluntarily supported Paul while he refused to take any support from the Corinthians. We can only guess his reasons. Perhaps he didn't want to put himself in obligation to any benefactors in Corinth.

What sort of deception and falsehood had invaded the church? (11:13–15)

The false apostles' list of "accomplishments" was long: in order to gain leadership they told lies about Paul; instead of boasting in the Lord, they boasted about themselves; they preached a false gospel; they accepted money for the same work Paul did for free. Their cumulative deceitfulness qualified them in Paul's book as ministers of Satan.

Was Paul confronting authoritarian cult leaders? (11:20)

They certainly had some of the same features. They used manipulative arguments, attractive half-lies and apparently were willing to use a little physical force (literal slaps in the face) when they thought it necessary.

lowered in a basket from a window in the wall and slipped through his hands.

Paul's Vision and His Thorn

12 I must go on boasting. Although there is nothing to be gained, I will go on to visions^D and revelations from the Lord. ²I know a man in Christ who fourteen years ago was caught up to the third heaven. Whether it was in the body or out of the body I do not know—God knows. ³And I know that this man—whether in the body or apart from the body I do not know, but God knows— ⁴was caught up to paradise. He heard inexpressible things, things that man is not permitted to tell. ⁵I will boast about a man like that, but I will not boast about myself, except about my weaknesses. ⁶Even if I should choose to boast, I would not be a fool, because I would be speaking the truth. But I refrain, so no one will think more of me than is warranted by what I do or say.

⁷To keep me from becoming conceited because of these surpassingly great revelations, there was given me a thorn in my flesh, a messenger of Satan, to torment me. ⁸Three times I pleaded with the Lord to take it away from me. ⁹But he said to me, "My grace^D is sufficient for you, for my power is made perfect in weakness." Therefore I will boast all the more gladly about my weaknesses, so that Christ's power may rest on me. ¹⁰That is why, for Christ's sake, I delight in weaknesses, in insults, in hardships, in persecutions, in difficulties. For when I am weak, then I am strong.

Paul's Concern for the Corinthians

¹¹I have made a fool of myself, but you drove me to it. I ought to have been commended by you, for I am not in the least inferior to the "super-apostles^D," even though I am nothing. ¹²The things that mark an apostle—signs, wonders and miracles—were done among you with great perseverance. ¹³How were you inferior to the other churches, except that I was never a burden to you? Forgive me this wrong!

¹⁴Now I am ready to visit you for the third time, and I will not be a burden to you, because what I want is not your possessions but you. After all, children should not have to save up for their parents, but parents for their children. ¹⁵So I will very gladly spend for you everything I have and expend myself as well. If I love you more, will you love me less? ¹⁶Be that as it may, I have not been a burden to you. Yet, crafty fellow that I am, I caught you by trickery! ¹⁷Did I exploit you through any of the men I sent you? ¹⁸I urged Titus to go to you and I sent our brother with him. Titus did not exploit you, did he? Did we not act in the same spirit and follow the same course?

¹⁹Have you been thinking all along that we have been defending ourselves to you? We have been speaking in the sight of God as those in Christ; and everything we do, dear friends, is for your strengthening. ²⁰For I am afraid that when I come I may not find you as I want you to be, and you may not find me as you want me to be. I fear that there may be quarreling, jealousy, outbursts of anger, factions, slander, gossip, arrogance and disorder. ²¹I am afraid that when I come again my God will humble me before you, and I will be grieved over many who have sinned earlier and have not repented^D of the impurity, sexual sin and debauchery in which they have indulged.

Who was Paul talking about? (12:2)

Himself. In the literary tradition of the day, whenever one talked of a supernatural experience it was common to use oblique references such as this. It was a way of distancing the experience from ordinary experience. It also lent an air of modesty to such descriptions.

What was Paul's thorn in the flesh? (12:7)

Some suggest it was a spiritual problem (anxiety, sexual temptation or perhaps guilt). Others see it as a physical ailment (headaches, epilepsy, malarial fever, a speech impediment or even eye problems). Still others speculate that it referred to Paul's frequent persecutions.

How did miracles qualify Paul as an apostle? (12:12)

The false apostles had probably criticized Paul for not having supernatural experiences and doing miracles as they did. Paul did not want to argue for his apostleship in this way—he wanted to focus on his weaknesses made strong in Jesus Christ—but expectations were so strong that he was forced to. So he reluctantly told about his trip to paradise (vv. 1–6) and recalled that he had done signs, wonders and miracles while he was with them.

Why does Paul sound sarcastic? (12:16)

Paul found himself in the uncomfortable position of being forced to defend his ministry. His frustrations with wasting time and energy to defend himself spilled over into his writing in the form of sarcasm. His caustic comments are best seen as emotional escape valves, the remarks of an energetic, honest, but exasperated man.

Final Warnings

13 This will be my third visit to you. "Every matter must be established by the testimony of two or three witnesses."[a] [2]I already gave you a warning when I was with you the second time. I now repeat it while absent: On my return I will not spare those who sinned earlier or any of the others, [3]since you are demanding proof that Christ is speaking through me. He is not weak in dealing with you, but is powerful among you. [4]For to be sure, he was crucified in weakness, yet he lives by God's power. Likewise, we are weak in him, yet by God's power we will live with him to serve you.

[5]Examine yourselves to see whether you are in the faith; test yourselves. Do you not realize that Christ Jesus is in you—unless, of course, you fail the test? [6]And I trust that you will discover that we have not failed the test. [7]Now we pray to God that you will not do anything wrong. Not that people will see that we have stood the test but that you will do what is right even though we may seem to have failed. [8]For we cannot do anything against the truth, but only for the truth. [9]We are glad whenever we are weak but you are strong; and our prayer is for your perfection. [10]This is why I write these things when I am absent, that when I come I may not have to be harsh in my use of authority—the authority the Lord gave me for building you up, not for tearing you down.

Final Greetings

[11]Finally, brothers, good-by. Aim for perfection, listen to my appeal, be of one mind, live in peace[D]. And the God of love and peace will be with you.

[12]Greet one another with a holy kiss[D]. [13]All the saints[D] send their greetings.

[14]May the grace[D] of the Lord Jesus Christ, and the love of God, and the fellowship of the Holy Spirit be with you all.

How did Paul intend to *not spare* those who had sinned? (13:2)

Paul had already shown that he was a stickler for church discipline. In his previous letter he insisted on discipline for the wayward man (2:5–8). Paul served notice that he would not hesitate to insist on such discipline again. Left unsaid is that he would also insist on mercy for the truly repentant.

What distinguishes true believers from false believers? (13:5)

The test is internal and cannot be standardized to evaluate others. Each one must inspect his or her own heart to see what motivates personal behavior. No one else can evaluate the results. Those who discover they are motivated by Christ living within are true believers. Those who find they are motivated by selfish desires are false believers.

Holy kiss (13:12)

The equivalent of a Western handshake or hug, it was a sign of mutual respect and fellowship. It is still in common usage, especially in Eastern and Russian Orthodox churches.

a1 Deut. 19:15

GALATIANS

Why read this book?

People who care about nutrition often read the labels before buying packaged foods. Why? They're on the lookout for additives and ingredients that may be hazardous to their health. In a similar way, Galatians warns against mixing legalism and human works into the simple gospel. It describes artificial spiritual additives and their toxic effects. This book offers a spiritual health check—a clear explanation of what it means to be saved by faith.

Who wrote this book?

Paul, the apostle.

To whom was it written?

To Christians in Galatia, a Roman province in the central part of what is now called Turkey.

When was it written?

Probably around A.D. 48 to 53, less than 25 years after Jesus Christ's ministry on earth.

Why was it written?

To denounce and correct false teachings that had infiltrated the churches Paul and Barnabas had earlier established. False teachers insisted that Gentile Christians keep the ritual laws of the Jews. Paul, stinging from their personal attacks against him, also wrote to defend his integrity as an apostle and to reassert his love for the Galatians.

What to look for in Galatians:

Galatians will take you back to the basics—what the gospel is, how you receive it and how you can apply it in your daily life. Paul uses several techniques (his own conversion story, an illustration from the life of Abraham and even sarcasm) to persuade the Galatians to return to the pure gospel.

When did these things happen?

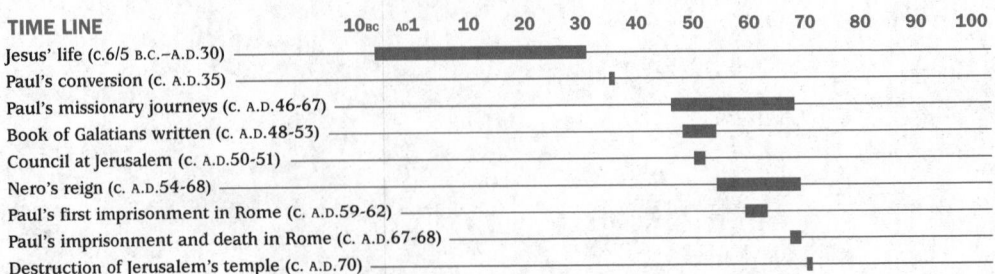

TIME LINE	10 BC	AD 1	10	20	30	40	50	60	70	80	90	100
Jesus' life (c.6/5 B.C.–A.D.30)												
Paul's conversion (c. A.D.35)												
Paul's missionary journeys (c. A.D.46-67)												
Book of Galatians written (c. A.D.48-53)												
Council at Jerusalem (c. A.D.50-51)												
Nero's reign (c. A.D.54-68)												
Paul's first imprisonment in Rome (c. A.D.59-62)												
Paul's imprisonment and death in Rome (c. A.D.67-68)												
Destruction of Jerusalem's temple (c. A.D.70)												

1 Paul, an apostle[D]—sent not from men nor by man, but by Jesus Christ and God the Father, who raised him from the dead— ²and all the brothers with me,

To the churches in Galatia:

³Grace[D] and peace[D] to you from God our Father and the Lord Jesus Christ, ⁴who gave himself for our sins to rescue us from the present evil age, according to the will of our God and Father, ⁵to whom be glory[D] for ever and ever. Amen.

No Other Gospel

⁶I am astonished that you are so quickly deserting the one who called you by the grace of Christ and are turning to a different gospel[D]— ⁷which is really no gospel at all. Evidently some people are throwing you into confusion and are trying to pervert the gospel of Christ. ⁸But even if we or an angel from heaven should preach a gospel other than the one we preached to you, let him be eternally condemned! ⁹As we have already said, so now I say again: If anybody is preaching to you a gospel other than what you accepted, let him be eternally condemned!

¹⁰Am I now trying to win the approval of men, or of God? Or am I trying to please men? If I were still trying to please men, I would not be a servant of Christ.

Paul Called by God

¹¹I want you to know, brothers, that the gospel I preached is not something that man made up. ¹²I did not receive it from any man, nor was I taught it; rather, I received it by revelation[D] from Jesus Christ.

¹³For you have heard of my previous way of life in Judaism, how intensely I persecuted the church of God and tried to destroy it. ¹⁴I was advancing in Judaism beyond many Jews[D] of my own age and was extremely zealous for the traditions of my fathers. ¹⁵But when God, who set me apart from birth[a] and called me by his grace, was pleased ¹⁶to reveal his Son in me so that I might preach him among the Gentiles[D], I did not consult any man, ¹⁷nor did I go up to Jerusalem[D] to see those who were apostles before I was, but I went immediately into Arabia and later returned to Damascus.

¹⁸Then after three years, I went up to Jerusalem to get acquainted with Peter[b] and stayed with him fifteen days. ¹⁹I saw none of the other apostles—only James, the Lord's brother. ²⁰I assure you before God that what I am writing you is no lie. ²¹Later I went to Syria and Cilicia. ²²I was personally unknown to the churches of Judea that are in Christ. ²³They only heard the report: "The man who formerly persecuted us is now preaching the faith he once tried to destroy." ²⁴And they praised God because of me.

Paul Accepted by the Apostles

2 Fourteen years later I went up again to Jerusalem, this time with Barnabas. I took Titus along also. ²I went in response to a revelation and set before them the gospel that I preach among the Gentiles. But I did this privately to those who seemed to be leaders, for fear that I was running or had run my race in vain. ³Yet not even Titus, who was with me, was compelled to be circumcised[D], even though he was a Greek. ⁴This matter

---

ᵃ15 Or *from my mother's womb*   ᵇ18 Greek *Cephas*

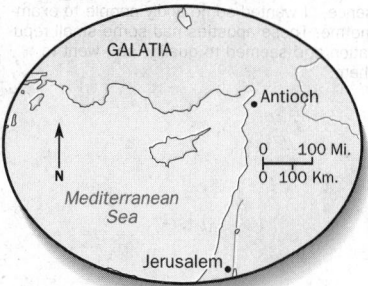

Why seek a human endorsement if you've got God's? (2:2)

Paul's critics had attacked not only the authority of his gospel, but they also said he was a renegade, opposed to and independent from the apostles in Jerusalem. After responding to their first charge with the source of his message, he responded to the second charge by pointing out that the Jerusalem apostles had, in fact, endorsed his message (v. 9).

Was Paul belittling Peter and James? (2:2,6,9)

Why did he say they *seemed to be leaders* and were *reputed to be pillars*? Paul was not trying to put down the other apostles. But perhaps he was emphasizing that Christ is the only head of the church. Paul may also have used the phrases as understatement, saying in essence, "I wanted some godly people to examine me. These apostles had some small reputation and seemed to qualify, so I went to them."

Through the law I died to the law (2:19)

The Old Testament law showed Paul his true condition as a sinner—separated from God. His attempts to follow the law had been an exercise in futility—even the most religiously perfect were guilty. That realization helped Paul see that only by grace through Christ could he know forgiveness. And when he discovered grace was his only hope for salvation, he stopped relying on the law—in a sense, dying to it.

arose, because some false brothers had infiltrated our ranks to spy on the freedom we have in Christ Jesus and to make us slaves. **5**We did not give in to them for a moment, so that the truth of the gospel[D] might remain with you.

6As for those who seemed to be important—whatever they were makes no difference to me; God does not judge by external appearance—those men added nothing to my message. **7**On the contrary, they saw that I had been entrusted with the task of preaching the gospel to the Gentiles[D],[a] just as Peter had been to the Jews[D],[b] **8**For God, who was at work in the ministry of Peter as an apostle[D] to the Jews, was also at work in my ministry as an apostle to the Gentiles. **9**James, Peter[c] and John, those reputed to be pillars, gave me and Barnabas the right hand of fellowship when they recognized the grace[D] given to me. They agreed that we should go to the Gentiles, and they to the Jews. **10**All they asked was that we should continue to remember the poor, the very thing I was eager to do.

Paul Opposes Peter

11When Peter came to Antioch, I opposed him to his face, because he was clearly in the wrong. **12**Before certain men came from James, he used to eat with the Gentiles. But when they arrived, he began to draw back and separate himself from the Gentiles because he was afraid of those who belonged to the circumcision[D] group. **13**The other Jews joined him in his hypocrisy, so that by their hypocrisy even Barnabas was led astray.

14When I saw that they were not acting in line with the truth of the gospel, I said to Peter in front of them all, "You are a Jew, yet you live like a Gentile and not like a Jew. How is it, then, that you force Gentiles to follow Jewish customs?

15"We who are Jews by birth and not 'Gentile sinners' **16**know that a man is not justified[D] by observing the law, but by faith in Jesus Christ. So we, too, have put our faith in Christ Jesus that we may be justified by faith in Christ and not by observing the law, because by observing the law no one will be justified.

17"If, while we seek to be justified in Christ, it becomes evident that we ourselves are sinners, does that mean that Christ promotes sin? Absolutely not! **18**If I rebuild what I destroyed, I prove that I am a lawbreaker. **19**For through the law I died to the law so that I might live for God. **20**I have been crucified with Christ and I no longer live, but Christ lives in me. The life I live in the body, I live by faith in the Son of God, who loved me and gave himself for me. **21**I do not set aside the grace of God, for if righteousness[D] could be gained through the law, Christ died for nothing!"[d]

Faith or Observance of the Law

3 You foolish Galatians! Who has bewitched you? Before your very eyes Jesus Christ was clearly portrayed as crucified. **2**I would like to learn just one thing from you: Did you receive the Spirit by observing the law, or by believing what you heard? **3**Are you so foolish? After beginning with the Spirit, are you now trying to attain your goal

---

[a]7 Greek *uncircumcised*   [b]7 Greek *circumcised*; also in verses 8 and 9   [c]9 Greek *Cephas*; also in verses 11 and 14   [d]21 Some interpreters end the quotation after verse 14.

by human effort? **4**Have you suffered so much for nothing—if it really was for nothing? **5**Does God give you his Spirit and work miracles among you because you observe the law, or because you believe what you heard?

6Consider Abraham: "He believed God, and it was credited to him as righteousness**D**."*a* **7**Understand, then, that those who believe are children of Abraham. **8**The Scripture foresaw that God would justify**D** the Gentiles**D** by faith, and announced the gospel**D** in advance to Abraham: "All nations will be blessed through you."*b* **9**So those who have faith are blessed along with Abraham, the man of faith.

10All who rely on observing the law are under a curse, for it is written: "Cursed is everyone who does not continue to do everything written in the Book of the Law."*c* **11**Clearly no one is justified before God by the law, because, "The righteous**D** will live by faith."*d* **12**The law is not based on faith; on the contrary, "The man who does these things will live by them."*e* **13**Christ redeemed**D** us from the curse of the law by becoming a curse for us, for it is written: "Cursed is everyone who is hung on a tree."*f* **14**He redeemed us in order that the blessing given to Abraham might come to the Gentiles through Christ Jesus, so that by faith we might receive the promise of the Spirit.

The Law and the Promise

15Brothers, let me take an example from everyday life. Just as no one can set aside or add to a human covenant**D** that has been duly established, so it is in this case. **16**The promises were spoken to Abraham and to his seed. The Scripture does not say "and to seeds," meaning many people, but "and to your seed,"*g* meaning one person,

In what sense did Christ become a curse? (3:13)
When God's law is broken, it imposes a curse—the judgment of God. When Christ died on the cross—a tree—not only was that the sign of someone who was cursed (Deut. 21:23), but more than that, it was a sign that Christ received God's punishment for our sin.

*a*6 Gen. 15:6   *b*8 Gen. 12:3; 18:18; 22:18   *c*10 Deut. 27:26   *d*11 Hab. 2:4   *e*12 Lev. 18:5   *f*13 Deut. 21:23   *g*16 Gen. 12:7; 13:15; 24:7

Should we obey or ignore Old Testament law? (3:1–25)

The answer to that question is not cut-and-dried. The law consisted of the commands God gave Moses, some 430 years *after* God established his covenant with Abraham. Paul points out that God had declared Abraham righteous *before* the law existed. Therefore, Paul claims, obeying the law could not be the basis for a relationship with God. Faith is the only basis for that relationship.

The law was never intended to take the place of faith. It was never designed to give the people of Israel a list of rules by which they could earn their salvation. Rather, the law served only to show them how far short of God's standards they fell (v. 19).

The law exposed sin so people would be led to Christ as the only answer to sin. Paul called the law *holy . . . spiritual* (Romans 7:12,14), and *good if one uses it properly* (1 Tim. 1:8). But if the law is used improperly—as a way to try to earn salvation, or to try to impress other people—it serves only to impose *a curse* (v. 10).

However, we should not ignore the Old Testament law. It shows what God considered important. Much of it spells out timeless principles of right living. Parts of the law are still helpful for those who want to live holy lives. But Christians are not bound to obey the Old Testament law to earn God's favor. Christians live a lifestyle of obedience to Christ and to the teachings of the New Testament as an act of gratitude.

What angels and mediator put the law into effect? (3:19)
Jews believed that angels gave the law to Moses, the mediator (Stephen referred to this in Acts 7:38,53).

What Scripture is Paul referring to? (3:22)
This may be a paraphrase—not a direct quote—describing the consequences of Adam and Eve's disobedience (Gen. 3:17-19; also see Romans 8:22). No one, at any time or place, can escape sin's impact.

Has Christ erased ethnic, economic and gender distinctions? (3:28)
Jews are still Jews, Gentiles are still Gentiles and men and women are still men and women. What Christ abolished is discrimination for such differences. Everyone who comes to Christ must come the same way: through faith and repentance.

The time had fully come (4:4)
Jesus didn't arrive late or early. He came right on schedule. Some suggest world conditions were ripe for the rapid spread of the gospel: the ruling Romans had ushered in an era of relative peace through law and order; their network of roads made travel more convenient; the widespread use of the Greek language simplified communication. At the same time the proliferation of empty religions among many people created a spiritual hunger within them for something genuine.

Those who by nature are not gods (4:8)
This is a description of the pagan gods the Galatians had once worshiped, which now are seen to be counterfeit.

Is it wrong to observe holy days? (4:10)
It's not sinful to celebrate a day with special spiritual significance. Today, for example, Christmas and Easter hold special meaning and are cause for celebration. But the Galatians observed Jewish holy days as if they were trying to impress God with their ceremonies and religious busyness. Faith in Christ alone, not ritual or ceremony, makes us right with God. See also Romans 14:5.

How did illness cause Paul to preach? (4:13-15)
There is a lot of speculation about Paul's illness. Malaria was common in the area. Paul had been severely injured in Lystra (Acts 14:19; see *Setting of Acts* on page 1504). He may have suffered from an eye disorder (Gal. 4:15; 6:11). But we don't know with certainty what was wrong. Whatever he suffered from, his point is that it caused him to stay longer than he had planned, resulting in his friendship with the Galatians.

who is Christ. [17]What I mean is this: The law, introduced 430 years later, does not set aside the covenant[D] previously established by God and thus do away with the promise. [18]For if the inheritance depends on the law, then it no longer depends on a promise; but God in his grace[D] gave it to Abraham through a promise.

[19]What, then, was the purpose of the law? It was added because of transgressions until the Seed to whom the promise referred had come. The law was put into effect through angels by a mediator. [20]A mediator, however, does not represent just one party; but God is one.

[21]Is the law, therefore, opposed to the promises of God? Absolutely not! For if a law had been given that could impart life, then righteousness[D] would certainly have come by the law. [22]But the Scripture declares that the whole world is a prisoner of sin, so that what was promised, being given through faith in Jesus Christ, might be given to those who believe.

[23]Before this faith came, we were held prisoners by the law, locked up until faith should be revealed. [24]So the law was put in charge to lead us to Christ[a] that we might be justified[D] by faith. [25]Now that faith has come, we are no longer under the supervision of the law.

Sons of God

[26]You are all sons of God through faith in Christ Jesus, [27]for all of you who were baptized into Christ have clothed yourselves with Christ. [28]There is neither Jew[D] nor Greek, slave nor free, male nor female, for you are all one in Christ Jesus. [29]If you belong to Christ, then you are Abraham's seed, and heirs according to the promise.

4 What I am saying is that as long as the heir is a child, he is no different from a slave, although he owns the whole estate. [2]He is subject to guardians and trustees until the time set by his father. [3]So also, when we were children, we were in slavery under the basic principles of the world. [4]But when the time had fully come, God sent his Son, born of a woman, born under law, [5]to redeem[D] those under law, that we might receive the full rights of sons. [6]Because you are sons, God sent the Spirit of his Son into our hearts, the Spirit who calls out, "Abba,[D,b] Father." [7]So you are no longer a slave, but a son; and since you are a son, God has made you also an heir.

Paul's Concern for the Galatians

[8]Formerly, when you did not know God, you were slaves to those who by nature are not gods. [9]But now that you know God—or rather are known by God—how is it that you are turning back to those weak and miserable principles? Do you wish to be enslaved by them all over again? [10]You are observing special days and months and seasons and years! [11]I fear for you, that somehow I have wasted my efforts on you.

[12]I plead with you, brothers, become like me, for I became like you. You have done me no wrong. [13]As you know, it was because of an illness that I first preached the gospel[D] to you. [14]Even though my illness was a trial to you, you did not treat me with contempt or scorn. Instead, you welcomed me as if I were an angel of God, as if I were Christ Jesus himself. [15]What has happened to all your joy? I can testify that, if you could have done so, you would have torn out your eyes and given them to me.

[a]24 Or *charge until Christ came*   [b]6 Aramaic for *Father*

[16]Have I now become your enemy by telling you the truth?

[17]Those people are zealous to win you over, but for no good. What they want is to alienate you ⌊from us⌋, so that you may be zealous for them. [18]It is fine to be zealous, provided the purpose is good, and to be so always and not just when I am with you. [19]My dear children, for whom I am again in the pains of childbirth until Christ is formed in you, [20]how I wish I could be with you now and change my tone, because I am perplexed about you!

Hagar and Sarah

[21]Tell me, you who want to be under the law, are you not aware of what the law says? [22]For it is written that Abraham had two sons, one by the slave woman and the other by the free woman. [23]His son by the slave woman was born in the ordinary way; but his son by the free woman was born as the result of a promise.

[24]These things may be taken figuratively, for the women represent two covenants[D]. One covenant is from Mount Sinai and bears children who are to be slaves: This is Hagar. [25]Now Hagar stands for Mount Sinai in Arabia and corresponds to the present city of Jerusalem[D], because she is in slavery with her children. [26]But the Jerusalem that is above is free, and she is our mother. [27]For it is written:

"Be glad, O barren woman,
    who bears no children;
break forth and cry aloud,
    you who have no labor pains;
because more are the children of the desolate
        woman
    than of her who has a husband."[a]

[28]Now you, brothers, like Isaac, are children of promise. [29]At that time the son born in the ordinary way persecuted the son born by the power of the Spirit. It is the same now. [30]But what does the Scripture say? "Get rid of the slave woman and her son, for the slave woman's son will never share in the inheritance with the free woman's son."[b] [31]Therefore, brothers, we are not children of the slave woman, but of the free woman.

Freedom in Christ

5 It is for freedom that Christ has set us free. Stand firm, then, and do not let yourselves be burdened again by a yoke[D] of slavery.

[2]Mark my words! I, Paul, tell you that if you let yourselves be circumcised[D], Christ will be of no value to you at all. [3]Again I declare to every man who lets himself be circumcised that he is obligated to obey the whole law. [4]You who are trying to be justified[D] by law have been alienated from Christ; you have fallen away from grace[D]. [5]But by faith we eagerly await through the Spirit the righteousness[D] for which we hope. [6]For in Christ Jesus neither circumcision[D] nor uncircumcision[D] has any value. The only thing that counts is faith expressing itself through love.

[7]You were running a good race. Who cut in on you and kept you from obeying the truth? [8]That kind of persuasion does not come from the one who calls you. [9]"A little yeast[D] works through the whole batch of dough." [10]I am

[a]27 Isaiah 54:1   [b]30 Gen. 21:10

Is this an unusual interpretation of Scripture? (4:24)

It's fair to use a story from one part of the Bible to illustrate a truth clearly stated elsewhere in the Bible. While the story of Hagar and Sarah (Gen. 16,21) is a historic account of two women and their relationship to Abraham, it can also serve to illustrate two different ways God relates to people. In this case Paul uses the story as an allegory to show how the new covenant relationship to God is superior to the old covenant. Thus, Paul's interpretation is valid since it is consistent with the rest of Scripture.

Is circumcision wrong? (5:2)

The actual practice of circumcision didn't disturb Paul (v. 6). He was deeply troubled, however, when people insisted it was necessary to practice it to be right with God. If circumcision, as a cultural practice, allowed for greater opportunity to teach the gospel among the Jews, he had no objection. But if it was done to earn salvation, he was adamantly opposed to it. See article: *Why did Paul circumcise Timothy?* (Acts 16:3).

Do believers have to wait for righteousness? (5:5)

Righteousness can refer to the status of a *right standing* before God, something God immediately bestows on those who are justified by faith in Christ. Or it can also mean *living rightly* before God, something that is a life-long process. Paul refers to the latter use of the word in this case—a righteousness that will only be fully accomplished when we meet the Lord.

Why is the cross offensive? (5:11)

In the first century, the cross was offensive on several counts. It was a humiliation—anyone crucified was branded as a criminal. Furthermore, it was a punishment for the under-privileged; Roman citizens sentenced to die were executed by more humane means. On a deeper level, the cross offends us all because it's a reminder that we are sinful, unacceptable to God. The cross assaults our human pride with a clear statement that we cannot solve sin on our own.

How do we develop the *fruit of the Spirit*? (5:22-26)

Faith and obedience go hand in hand. The *fruit of the Spirit* is something only the Holy Spirit can produce in the life of a believer. As such, it's something we receive by faith—a gift given when we accept Christ as our Savior. At the same time, as we live in obedience to God's commands, the fruit grows and develops in our lives. Our part is seen, for example, in developing love (John 13:34), joy (Phil. 4:4) and peace (Col. 3:15).

Are some believers *not* spiritual? (6:1)

Continuing his thoughts from ch. 5, Paul here refers to those bearing the *fruit of the Spirit*. These are believers whose character traits are evident, who encourage faltering Christians.

Why *watch yourself*? (6:1)

The temptation is to become condescending: "You fell and I didn't." If we take on a "holier-than-thou" attitude, we fall into an equally offensive sin: pride.

Whose burdens should we carry—our own or those of others? (6:2,5)

Paul uses two different words that help us sort out the confusion. *Burdens* (v. 2) are too much for any one person to carry, an overwhelming weight. *Load* (v. 5) means a cargo that is manageable. Christians are required to compassionately assist those who are being crushed by life's unbearable sorrows or troubles. On the other hand, each of us is expected to handle responsibilities within our limits.

Is it okay to be proud? (6:4)

Good pride is legitimate self-esteem, knowing that we have been created in God's image, are redeemed through Christ and are destined for heaven. The only basis for this kind of pride is God's grace. When we forget that, we are headed for illegitimate pride: a smug sense of our significance apart from God. See Romans 12:3.

Why the sudden switch in topics? (6:6)

Paul abruptly raises the subject of sharing as an example of what it means to live by the Spirit. Those who live under the influence of the Spirit will want to take care of those who make their living by teaching God's people.

When can we enjoy the *harvest*? (6:9)

Paul teaches that if we live primarily to please our flesh, we'll find ourselves spiritually impoverished now and bankrupt in heaven later. But if we live by the Spirit we shall see fruit in our present circumstances and also have a rich reward waiting for us in heaven.

---

confident in the Lord that you will take no other view. The one who is throwing you into confusion will pay the penalty, whoever he may be. [11]Brothers, if I am still preaching circumcision[D], why am I still being persecuted? In that case the offense of the cross has been abolished. [12]As for those agitators, I wish they would go the whole way and emasculate themselves!

[13]You, my brothers, were called to be free. But do not use your freedom to indulge the sinful nature[a]; rather, serve one another in love. [14]The entire law is summed up in a single command: "Love your neighbor as yourself."[b] [15]If you keep on biting and devouring each other, watch out or you will be destroyed by each other.

Life by the Spirit

[16]So I say, live by the Spirit, and you will not gratify the desires of the sinful nature. [17]For the sinful nature desires what is contrary to the Spirit, and the Spirit what is contrary to the sinful nature. They are in conflict with each other, so that you do not do what you want. [18]But if you are led by the Spirit, you are not under law.

[19]The acts of the sinful nature are obvious: sexual immorality, impurity and debauchery; [20]idolatry[D] and witchcraft[D]; hatred, discord, jealousy, fits of rage, selfish ambition, dissensions, factions [21]and envy; drunkenness, orgies, and the like. I warn you, as I did before, that those who live like this will not inherit the kingdom of God.

[22]But the fruit of the Spirit is love, joy, peace[D], patience, kindness, goodness, faithfulness, [23]gentleness and self-control. Against such things there is no law. [24]Those who belong to Christ Jesus have crucified the sinful nature with its passions and desires. [25]Since we live by the Spirit, let us keep in step with the Spirit. [26]Let us not become conceited, provoking and envying each other.

Doing Good to All

6 Brothers, if someone is caught in a sin, you who are spiritual should restore him gently. But watch yourself, or you also may be tempted. [2]Carry each other's burdens, and in this way you will fulfill the law of Christ. [3]If anyone thinks he is something when he is nothing, he deceives himself. [4]Each one should test his own actions. Then he can take pride in himself, without comparing himself to somebody else, [5]for each one should carry his own load.

[6]Anyone who receives instruction in the word must share all good things with his instructor.

[7]Do not be deceived: God cannot be mocked. A man reaps what he sows. [8]The one who sows to please his sinful nature, from that nature[c] will reap destruction; the one who sows to please the Spirit, from the Spirit will reap eternal life[D]. [9]Let us not become weary in doing good, for at the proper time we will reap a harvest if we do not give up. [10]Therefore, as we have opportunity, let us do good to all people, especially to those who belong to the family of believers.

Not Circumcision but a New Creation

[11]See what large letters I use as I write to you with my own hand!

[12]Those who want to make a good impression outward-

---

*a*13 Or *the flesh*; also in verses 16, 17, 19 and 24   *b*14 Lev. 19:18
*c*8 Or *his flesh, from the flesh*

ly are trying to compel you to be circumcised[D]. The only reason they do this is to avoid being persecuted for the cross of Christ. **13**Not even those who are circumcised obey the law, yet they want you to be circumcised that they may boast about your flesh. **14**May I never boast except in the cross of our Lord Jesus Christ, through which[a] the world has been crucified to me, and I to the world. **15**Neither circumcision[D] nor uncircumcision[D] means anything; what counts is a new creation. **16**Peace[D] and mercy[D] to all who follow this rule, even to the Israel of God.

17Finally, let no one cause me trouble, for I bear on my body the marks of Jesus.

18The grace[D] of our Lord Jesus Christ be with your spirit, brothers. Amen.

Especially . . . believers (6:10)

Christians of that era often suffered great economic hardship as a result of rejection and persecution. There was no one else to help but other believers. Though Christians should be willing to help anyone in need, caring for believers is still a priority.

Why did he use *large letters*? (6:11)

There are two explanations: If he suffered from an eye disorder (see 4:15), he may have been forced to write in huge letters so he could read them. Or he may have written in larger letters simply to emphasize his authority as an apostle.

The Israel of God (6:16)

Includes those who by faith have received eternal life through the gospel of Jesus Christ. *Abraham's seed* are those who *belong to Christ* and are *heirs according to the promise* (3:29).

What were *the marks of Jesus* on Paul's body? (6:17)

Paul had often been beaten for the sake of Christ—even in Galatia itself (see Acts 14:19). Some of those who would be reading this letter would recall how Paul had nearly died in order to get the message of the gospel to them.

---

[a]14 Or whom

EPHESIANS

Why read this book?

The greatest adventure in life is not an exotic safari, a booming business success or a love relationship with that perfect someone. Rather, it's discovering the purpose for our lives. This letter answers the question men and women have asked throughout all time: "Why am I here?" The answer may startle you, considering the standard talk-show ideas of our age. It has to do with eternity, making peace with God and identifying with Christ. Interested? Read on. The adventure is only beginning.

Who wrote this book?

The apostle Paul.

When was it writtten?

Sometime during Paul's imprisonment in Rome, around A.D. 60 to 62.

To whom was it written and why?

To encourage believers in Ephesus (a city in modern-day Turkey) to think of themselves in a whole new way. Instead of people once involved in idol worship, illicit sex and foolish philosophies, Paul wanted them to think of themselves as people "in Christ"—people with a radically new identity (2:12–13).

What to look for in Ephesians:

In this book you'll learn about God's intentions for his people, and you'll gain insight into the nature of the church. Notice the various word pictures describing the church and how Paul stresses the unity of all believers. The last half of the book offers practical ways to live in unity with God and one another.

When did these things happen?

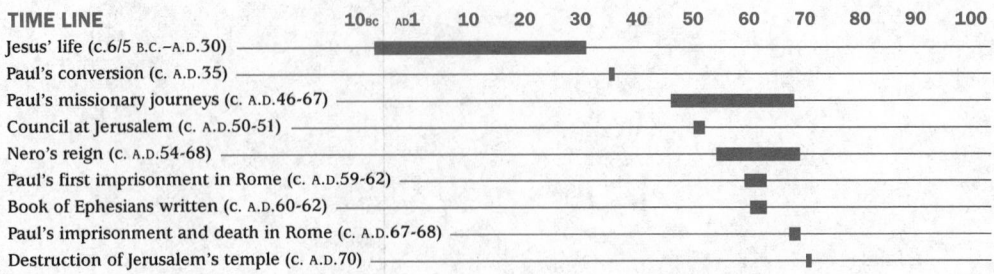

TIME LINE	10 BC	AD 1	10	20	30	40	50	60	70	80	90	100
Jesus' life (c.6/5 B.C.–A.D.30)												
Paul's conversion (c. A.D.35)												
Paul's missionary journeys (c. A.D.46-67)												
Council at Jerusalem (c. A.D.50-51)												
Nero's reign (c. A.D.54-68)												
Paul's first imprisonment in Rome (c. A.D.59-62)												
Book of Ephesians written (c. A.D.60-62)												
Paul's imprisonment and death in Rome (c. A.D.67-68)												
Destruction of Jerusalem's temple (c. A.D.70)												

1 Paul, an apostle[D] of Christ Jesus by the will of God,

To the saints[D] in Ephesus,[a] the faithful[b] in Christ Jesus:

[2]Grace[D] and peace[D] to you from God our Father and the Lord Jesus Christ.

Spiritual Blessings in Christ

[3]Praise be to the God and Father of our Lord Jesus Christ, who has blessed us in the heavenly realms with every spiritual blessing in Christ. [4]For he chose us in him before the creation of the world to be holy and blameless in his sight. In love [5]he[c] predestined us to be adopted as his sons through Jesus Christ, in accordance with his pleasure and will— [6]to the praise of his glorious grace, which he has freely given us in the One he loves. [7]In him we have redemption[D] through his blood, the forgiveness of sins, in accordance with the riches of God's grace [8]that he lavished on us with all wisdom and understanding. [9]And he[d] made known to us the mystery[D] of his will according to his good pleasure, which he purposed in Christ, [10]to be put into effect when the times will have reached their fulfillment—to bring all things in heaven and on earth together under one head, even Christ.

[11]In him we were also chosen,[e] having been predestined according to the plan of him who works out everything in conformity with the purpose of his will, [12]in order that we, who were the first to hope in Christ, might be for the praise of his glory[D]. [13]And you also were included in Christ when you heard the word of truth, the gospel[D] of your salvation[D]. Having believed, you were marked in him with a seal, the promised Holy Spirit, [14]who is a de-

---

a1 Some early manuscripts do not have in Ephesus.   b1 Or believers who are   c4,5 Or sight in love. 5He   d8,9 Or us. With all wisdom and understanding, 9he   e11 Or were made heirs

---

The Church in Ephesus (1:1)

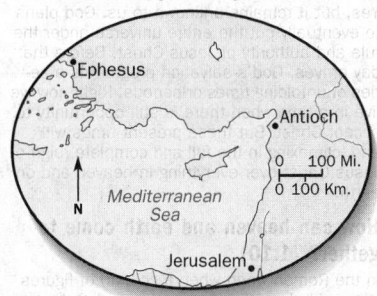

How do *spiritual* blessings affect life on earth? (1:3)

We tend to think of blessings in terms of money, possessions or opportunities. Paul uses the word to refer to the special relationship and position Christ offers: salvation, forgiveness and the hope of eternal life.

How am I adopted into God's family? (1:5)

In the Roman world in which Paul lived, slavery was common. Some slaves were adopted by the family that purchased them and given all the privileges of children. In the same way, believers who were once enslaved to sin and death are purchased by Christ's death and adopted as God's children.

Why is blood necessary to be saved? (1:7)

See *Why did God want blood as payment for sin?* (Heb. 9:22).

What is the *mystery of his will?* (1:9)

See *What's the mystery?* (3:3–4).

If God chooses us, do we have any choice? (1:4–5)

Because we start out spiritually dead, unable to respond to the Lord, only God can give us the gift of life (Eph. 2:1–2). When sin entered the human race, it left everyone helpless. We cannot come to God without his mercy. It is not our own awareness that we're sinful people that *first* turns us to God. Rather, it is God who in his mercy awakens that awareness within us.

Some believe our salvation through Christ is limited completely to God's sovereign choice. The only ones who believe in Christ, they point out, are those whom God appointed for salvation before time began (v. 4). They emphasize that there is no one who seeks God (Romans 3:10–11). However, God in his mercy has chosen to save some (Romans 9:15). Coming to God *does not therefore, depend on man's desire or effort, but on God's mercy* (Romans 9:16).

Others suggest God gives every person the ability to choose—his grace and mercy extend to everyone. These people say that each person has to respond by deciding whether to repent of sin and turn to God. They suggest that God honors people's choices to either refuse or accept Christ's invitation (Luke 13:34).

Also see articles: *How can God appoint someone not yet born?* (Jer. 1:5); *Why does God choose some and reject others?* (Psalm 78:67–68) and *Does God play favorites?* (Romans 9:8–33).

Has God set a deadline? (1:10)

Yes, but it remains unknown to us. God plans to eventually put the entire universe under the rule and authority of Jesus Christ. Before that day arrives, God's salvation program is a series of unfolding *times* or periods. Right now we live in a time when there is still opportunity to accept Christ. But these present times will end, climaxing in the full and complete reign of Jesus Christ over everything in heaven and on earth.

How can heaven and earth come together? (1:10)

In the Roman world when a column of figures were added up, the sum was placed at the top, rather than at the bottom of the column. Paul uses this idea as a picture: at the end of history all spiritual and physical realities will be placed under Christ's authority. Christ will reign as undisputed ruler of the universe.

How are people sealed? (1:13)

In the ancient world a seal was used to signify the genuineness of a document. When goods were being transported, a seal identified their owner and protected them from theft. In government, a seal served as an official emblem of state officials. Paul uses *seal* as a metaphor for the Holy Spirit's supernatural work in a believer's life. It is a sign that we are spiritually genuine, protected and validated as members of God's royal family.

Why the assigned seating? (1:20)

If someone sat at the right hand of a king in Paul's day, everyone knew that person shared in the king's power and authority. Not only did God raise Christ from the dead, but he seated him in a position of dignity and dominion.

How can someone be spiritually dead? (2:1)

Spiritual death is to be separated from God. Unless God intervenes, people without God are headed toward eternal death. People may be physically alive but spiritually dead. Only when God opens their eyes to the truth will people become spiritually alive.

What air space does the devil control? (2:2)

The term *air* was used in the ancient world to refer to spiritual realms where demons operated in the lives of people who refused God's authority. Christ disarmed Satan and his demonic followers on the cross (Col. 2:15), stripping them of their power. Satan still has limited authority, however, over demons in the unseen world, over unbelievers and over the world system (John 12:31). We see the evidences of his influence all around us: hate, war, murder, injustice, racism and moral disintegration. However, Christians can successfully resist Satan's influence and live in obedience to Jesus Christ (6:10–20).

Why doesn't God make everyone alive? (2:5,8)

There are some mysteries the Bible doesn't answer. What Paul describes here is the process by which God makes us alive. He doesn't share with us the reasons why one person is regenerated and another is not. See article: *If God chooses us, do we have any choice?* (1:4–5).

posit guaranteeing our inheritance until the redemption[D] of those who are God's possession—to the praise of his glory[D].

Thanksgiving and Prayer

[15]For this reason, ever since I heard about your faith in the Lord Jesus and your love for all the saints[D], [16]I have not stopped giving thanks for you, remembering you in my prayers. [17]I keep asking that the God of our Lord Jesus Christ, the glorious Father, may give you the Spirit[a] of wisdom and revelation[D], so that you may know him better. [18]I pray also that the eyes of your heart may be enlightened in order that you may know the hope to which he has called you, the riches of his glorious inheritance in the saints, [19]and his incomparably great power for us who believe. That power is like the working of his mighty strength, [20]which he exerted in Christ when he raised him from the dead and seated him at his right hand in the heavenly realms, [21]far above all rule and authority, power and dominion, and every title that can be given, not only in the present age but also in the one to come. [22]And God placed all things under his feet and appointed him to be head over everything for the church, [23]which is his body, the fullness of him who fills everything in every way.

Made Alive in Christ

2 As for you, you were dead in your transgressions and sins, [2]in which you used to live when you followed the ways of this world and of the ruler of the kingdom of the air, the spirit who is now at work in those who are disobedient. [3]All of us also lived among them at one time, gratifying the cravings of our sinful nature[b] and following its desires and thoughts. Like the rest, we were by nature objects of wrath. [4]But because of his great love for us, God, who is rich in mercy[D], [5]made us alive with Christ even when we were dead in transgressions—it is by grace[D] you have been saved. [6]And God raised us up with Christ and seated us with him in the heavenly realms in Christ Jesus, [7]in order that in the coming ages he might show the incomparable riches of his grace, expressed in his kindness to us in Christ Jesus. [8]For it is by grace you have been saved, through faith—and this not from yourselves, it is the gift of God— [9]not by works, so that no one can boast. [10]For we are God's workmanship, created in Christ Jesus to do good works, which God prepared in advance for us to do.

One in Christ

[11]Therefore, remember that formerly you who are Gentiles[D] by birth and called "uncircumcised[D]" by those who call themselves "the circumcision[D]" (that done in the body by the hands of men)— [12]remember that at that time you were separate from Christ, excluded from citizenship in Israel and foreigners to the covenants[D] of the promise, without hope and without God in the world. [13]But now in Christ Jesus you who once were far away have been brought near through the blood of Christ.

[14]For he himself is our peace[D], who has made the two one and has destroyed the barrier, the dividing wall of hostility, [15]by abolishing in his flesh the law with its commandments and regulations. His purpose was to create in himself one new man out of the two, thus making

*a*17 Or *a spirit*   *b*3 Or *our flesh*

peace[D], **16**and in this one body to reconcile both of them to God through the cross, by which he put to death[D] their hostility. **17**He came and preached peace to you who were far away and peace to those who were near. **18**For through him we both have access to the Father by one Spirit.

19Consequently, you are no longer foreigners and aliens[D], but fellow citizens with God's people and members of God's household, **20**built on the foundation of the apostles[D] and prophets[D], with Christ Jesus himself as the chief cornerstone. **21**In him the whole building is joined together and rises to become a holy temple in the Lord. **22**And in him you too are being built together to become a dwelling in which God lives by his Spirit.

Paul the Preacher to the Gentiles

3 For this reason I, Paul, the prisoner of Christ Jesus for the sake of you Gentiles[D]—
2Surely you have heard about the administration of God's grace[D] that was given to me for you, **3**that is, the mystery[D] made known to me by revelation[D], as I have already written briefly. **4**In reading this, then, you will be able to understand my insight into the mystery of Christ, **5**which was not made known to men in other generations as it has now been revealed by the Spirit to God's holy apostles and prophets. **6**This mystery is that through the gospel[D] the Gentiles are heirs together with Israel, members together of one body, and sharers together in the promise in Christ Jesus.

7I became a servant of this gospel by the gift of God's grace given me through the working of his power. **8**Although I am less than the least of all God's people, this grace was given me: to preach to the Gentiles the unsearchable riches of Christ, **9**and to make plain to everyone the administration of this mystery, which for ages past was kept hidden in God, who created all things. **10**His intent was that now, through the church, the manifold wisdom of God should be made known to the rulers and authorities in the heavenly realms, **11**according to his eternal purpose which he accomplished in Christ Jesus our Lord. **12**In him and through faith in him we may approach God with freedom and confidence. **13**I ask you, therefore, not to be discouraged because of my sufferings for you, which are your glory[D].

A Prayer for the Ephesians

14For this reason I kneel before the Father, **15**from whom his whole family[a] in heaven and on earth derives its name. **16**I pray that out of his glorious riches he may strengthen you with power through his Spirit in your inner being, **17**so that Christ may dwell in your hearts through faith. And I pray that you, being rooted and established in love, **18**may have power, together with all the saints[D], to grasp how wide and long and high and deep is the love of Christ, **19**and to know this love that surpasses knowledge—that you may be filled to the measure of all the fullness of God.

20Now to him who is able to do immeasurably more than all we ask or imagine, according to his power that is at work within us, **21**to him be glory in the church and in Christ Jesus throughout all generations, for ever and ever! Amen.

a 15 Or whom all fatherhood

When do we take our seats in heaven? (2:6)

For the present, God sees Christians as spiritually exalted with Jesus Christ. But one day that position will become a physical reality as well.

Why is circumcision significant? (2:11)

See *What value does circumcision have?* (Romans 2:25–27).

Did Jesus abolish the Old Testament law or fulfill it? (2:15)

Christ's life and death met the requirements of Old Testament law. At the same time, Christ's death and resurrection removed the law as a means of coming to God, replacing it with salvation by faith in Christ's finished work. Also see *How is the law fulfilled?* (Matt. 5:17–18).

Am I a spiritual construction project? (2:22)

Prior to the cross, it was believed God's glory could only reside in the temple. But Paul teaches that the church—made up of God's people—is becoming God's new residence. The construction work isn't finished yet. That's why it's described as both a present reality and a future goal.

Does Christ imprison his followers? (3:1)

In a sense, yes. When Paul wrote Ephesians, he was a literal prisoner, probably in Rome. Yet, he wasn't bitter. He had committed himself to serving Christ and preaching the gospel, whatever the cost. In the same way we can, like Paul, identify so closely with Christ that we consider ourselves prisoners to his will.

What's the *mystery?* (3:3–4,6,9)

The term *mystery* does not refer to a riddle or a secret. Rather it refers to a spiritual insight or revelation from God unknown to previous generations. The Old Testament revealed that Gentiles would be saved. But only in the New Testament is the method of salvation made clear and the mystery solved: it is through Jesus Christ, his sacrificial death and his resurrection. Now by faith, both Jews and Gentiles are heirs together of eternal life and will receive the same inheritance in Christ. Also see 1:9; 5:32; 6:19.

Who can receive a special revelation? (3:5)

God's Word has been completed; no revelation can add to it. However, the Holy Spirit can give believers insight to illuminate the Word of God and apply its truths to their individual situations. Many believe spiritual gifts such as wisdom, knowledge and prophecy continue in the church, but we should beware of anyone claiming to have a special knowledge or revelation that supersedes or contradicts the written Word.

How could Paul's sufferings benefit others? (3:13)

Paul was in prison for preaching the gospel to the Ephesians. He put himself at risk for others so they might come to God.

How is grace portioned out? (4:7)

Paul speaks of the grace of God in two ways. First, people are saved by grace, a gift of God (2:8). But grace also means special gifts or abilities given to individuals for ministry—things such as preaching, teaching, helps and so forth. Grace for ministry varies from one individual to the next (Peter mentions *grace in its various forms;* 1 Peter 4:10).

Did Christ descend into hell? (4:9)

See *Who were the spirits in prison?* (1 Peter 3:19–20).

How many heavens are there? (4:10)

The Jews believed there were as many as seven heavens, with God ruling the universe from the highest heaven, his dwelling place. The Bible never says specifically how many heavens exist, but it is clear, however many there are, that Christ is Lord over them all—higher than the highest heaven.

How does Christ *fill the whole universe?* (4:10)

Christ fills the universe by ruling over it. Christ's presence permeates the universe, blessing and filling it everywhere.

Does unity mean unanimity? (4:13)

No. Christ's work on the cross is the basis for spiritual unity (v. 3). Christians are united over essentials of the faith (such as the authority of Scripture, human sinfulness and need for a Savior, the deity of Christ, his death and resurrection, his promised return and so on). But on less crucial matters Christians don't always agree. Believers can differ over non-essentials without being spiritually divided.

What is a mature Christian like? (4:13)

A mature Christian is continually growing in Christ, constantly thinking and acting more like him. Though Christians may never be perfect while living in a sinful world, God's goal still is that we become like Christ (Romans 8:29). Through prayer, Bible study, Christian fellowship and other spiritual disciplines a mature Christian centers his or her life on Christ (2 Peter 3:18). Also see article: *How are Christians sanctified?* (1 Thes. 4:3–12).

Why do believers still sin? (4:22)

Christians are new creatures in Christ (Gal. 2:20; 2 Cor. 5:17). But they are also people who live in the flesh—still vulnerable to the weaknesses and temptations that affect all humans. To live in the flesh is to be influenced by habits and patterns of thinking acquired before coming to Christ. The more we rely on the Spirit, the more we will defeat those inner sinful impulses (Gal. 5:16–17).

When is anger sin? (4:26)

As a natural human emotion, anger is neither right nor wrong. It can be used for either good or evil—just as a knife can be a scalpel or a murder weapon. Anger can be a powerful tool for confronting wrong. Selfish or manipulative anger, however, can cause great harm. Such anger becomes destructive when it controls us rather than us controlling it. *Do not let the sun go down* simply means to deal with anger quickly and appropriately before it leads to sin.

Unity in the Body of Christ

4 As a prisoner for the Lord, then, I urge you to live a life worthy of the calling you have received. **2**Be completely humble and gentle; be patient, bearing with one another in love. **3**Make every effort to keep the unity of the Spirit through the bond of peace[D]. **4**There is one body and one Spirit— just as you were called to one hope when you were called— **5**one Lord, one faith, one baptism[D]; **6**one God and Father of all, who is over all and through all and in all.

7But to each one of us grace[D] has been given as Christ apportioned it. **8**This is why it[a] says:

"When he ascended on high,
    he led captives in his train
    and gave gifts to men."[b]

9(What does "he ascended" mean except that he also descended to the lower, earthly regions[c]? **10**He who descended is the very one who ascended higher than all the heavens, in order to fill the whole universe.) **11**It was he who gave some to be apostles[D], some to be prophets[D], some to be evangelists, and some to be pastors and teachers, **12**to prepare God's people for works of service, so that the body of Christ may be built up **13**until we all reach unity in the faith and in the knowledge of the Son of God and become mature, attaining to the whole measure of the fullness of Christ.

14Then we will no longer be infants, tossed back and forth by the waves, and blown here and there by every wind of teaching and by the cunning and craftiness of men in their deceitful scheming. **15**Instead, speaking the truth in love, we will in all things grow up into him who is the Head, that is, Christ. **16**From him the whole body, joined and held together by every supporting ligament, grows and builds itself up in love, as each part does its work.

Living as Children of Light

17So I tell you this, and insist on it in the Lord, that you must no longer live as the Gentiles[D] do, in the futility of their thinking. **18**They are darkened in their understanding and separated from the life of God because of the ignorance that is in them due to the hardening of their hearts. **19**Having lost all sensitivity, they have given themselves over to sensuality so as to indulge in every kind of impurity, with a continual lust for more.

20You, however, did not come to know Christ that way. **21**Surely you heard of him and were taught in him in accordance with the truth that is in Jesus. **22**You were taught, with regard to your former way of life, to put off your old self, which is being corrupted by its deceitful desires; **23**to be made new in the attitude of your minds; **24**and to put on the new self, created to be like God in true righteousness[D] and holiness.

25Therefore each of you must put off falsehood and speak truthfully to his neighbor, for we are all members of one body. **26**"In your anger do not sin"[d]: Do not let the sun go down while you are still angry, **27**and do not give the devil a foothold. **28**He who has been stealing must steal no longer, but must work, doing something useful

*a*8 Or *God*   *b*8 Psalm 68:18   *c*9 Or *the depths of the earth*
*d*26 Psalm 4:4

with his own hands, that he may have something to share with those in need.

29Do not let any unwholesome talk come out of your mouths, but only what is helpful for building others up according to their needs, that it may benefit those who listen. **30**And do not grieve the Holy Spirit of God, with whom you were sealed for the day of redemption^D. **31**Get rid of all bitterness, rage and anger, brawling and slander, along with every form of malice. **32**Be kind and compassionate to one another, forgiving each other, just as in Christ God forgave you.

5 Be imitators of God, therefore, as dearly loved children **2**and live a life of love, just as Christ loved us and gave himself up for us as a fragrant offering and sacrifice^D to God.

3But among you there must not be even a hint of sexual immorality, or of any kind of impurity, or of greed, because these are improper for God's holy people. **4**Nor should there be obscenity, foolish talk or coarse joking, which are out of place, but rather thanksgiving. **5**For of this you can be sure: No immoral, impure or greedy person—such a man is an idolater—has any inheritance in the kingdom of Christ and of God.^a **6**Let no one deceive you with empty words, for because of such things God's wrath comes on those who are disobedient. **7**Therefore do not be partners with them.

8For you were once darkness, but now you are light in the Lord. Live as children of light **9**(for the fruit of the light consists in all goodness, righteousness^D and truth) **10**and find out what pleases the Lord. **11**Have nothing to do with the fruitless deeds of darkness, but rather expose them. **12**For it is shameful even to mention what the disobedient do in secret. **13**But everything exposed by the light becomes visible, **14**for it is light that makes everything visible. This is why it is said:

> "Wake up, O sleeper,
>   rise from the dead,
> and Christ will shine on you."

15Be very careful, then, how you live—not as unwise but as wise, **16**making the most of every opportunity, because the days are evil. **17**Therefore do not be foolish, but understand what the Lord's will is. **18**Do not get drunk on wine, which leads to debauchery. Instead, be filled with the Spirit. **19**Speak to one another with psalms, hymns and spiritual songs. Sing and make music in your heart to the Lord, **20**always giving thanks to God the Father for everything, in the name of our Lord Jesus Christ.

21Submit to one another out of reverence^D for Christ.

Wives and Husbands

22Wives, submit to your husbands as to the Lord. **23**For the husband is the head of the wife as Christ is the head of the church, his body, of which he is the Savior. **24**Now as the church submits to Christ, so also wives should submit to their husbands in everything.

25Husbands, love your wives, just as Christ loved the church and gave himself up for her **26**to make her holy, cleansing^b her by the washing with water through the word, **27**and to present her to himself as a radiant church, without stain or wrinkle or any other blemish, but holy and blameless. **28**In this same way, husbands ought to

See Jesus' use of anger in Mark 3:5 and John 2:13–17. Also see *When is anger okay?* (James 1:19–20).

What grieves the Holy Spirit? (4:30)
God's Spirit grieves whenever someone in whom he dwells is unfaithful or disloyal. Sin, whether by thought or deed, is an affront to the *Holy* Spirit. Sin drives a wedge between us and God, causing the Spirit great pain and sorrow.

How can I imitate God? (5:1)
Just as a child learns to model the behavior of a parent, believers imitate God when they allow his character to flow through their daily lives. The primary way to imitate our heavenly Father is to follow a pattern of love in all that we do or say (v. 2).

Fruitless deeds of darkness (5:11)
Light and dark are familiar but vivid metaphors for good and evil. Unbelievers live in futility, no more able to do genuine good than a dark cave can produce light. Even if they do what seems to be good, they cannot earn favor with God.

How can I be *filled with the Spirit?* (5:18)
While the Holy Spirit lives in every Christian, Christians are not always *filled* with the Spirit —living continually under the influence and control of the Spirit. When Christians choose out of love to yield completely to the Lord, obeying his commands and asking the Holy Spirit to direct their lives, this filling occurs. This should be an ongoing experience, not something that happens only once.

Can we honestly give thanks for everything? (5:20)
Giving thanks is an act of worship, recognizing that despite difficult circumstances we may face from time to time, God's love and concern are unfailing.

Should we constantly give in to others? (5:21)
In this verse, to submit means to yield in love to another person. Yet there are definite limits involved. Submission should not lead to wrongdoing or questionable behavior. Rather, when we submit by putting our own interests aside, we should see increased unity in the body of Christ and the strengthening of other believers.

Should husbands rule their wives? (5:22)
See article: *Isn't it chauvinistic to teach wives to submit?* (1 Peter 3:5–6).

Should wives submit only to loving husbands? (5:24–33)
Righteous living, for men or women, testifies to the power and grace of God at work in their lives. When wives respect their husbands—even those who don't deserve it—their good character is revealed to others. Through Christ we can live lives of grace rather than lives of grievances. Submission should not, however, mean participating in sinful behavior. Also see article: *Isn't it chauvinistic to teach wives to submit?* (1 Peter 3:5–6).

*a*5 Or *kingdom of the Christ and God*   *b*26 Or *having cleansed*

How does Christ wash the church *with water through the word?* (5:26)

Paul paints a word picture: The truth of Scripture leads to a clean spirit just as water removes dirt from our bodies. As we study and apply God's Word to our daily lives, we grow in holiness and purity.

How does marriage symbolize Christ and the church? (5:32)

Just as the husband and the wife are to be joined together as one (Gen. 2:24), so Christ and the church are united as one. As Christ demonstrates his love for the church and believers respond by showing their love for him, it is similar to the deepening intimacy that exists between a husband and wife.

Do adult children have to obey their parents? (6:1)

Obedience to parents is a fundamental part of preserving an orderly society. Children must obey their parents in order to learn self-discipline and grow in their physical, emotional and spiritual lives. Adult children are obligated to respect and love their parents, but they should not rely on their parents in the same way. Having been raised well, adult children can make wise daily decisions independently.

Can we discipline children without embittering them? (6:4)

Paul warns fathers not to create resentment in their children. This usually occurs when parents impose unreasonable demands without concern for the feelings of the children. Parents are to train their children to distinguish right from wrong in everyday life. But this training should take place within the context of a loving, caring, forgiving relationship (Deut. 6:6–9).

Why didn't Paul tell Christian masters to set their slaves free? (6:9)

See article: *Why doesn't the Bible condemn slavery?* (1 Peter 2:18–21).

Day of evil (6:13)

Not some specific future satanic attack. Nor is it a specific time of spiritual difficulty, such as when death approaches. The phrase refers to spiritual warfare whenever it rages against us.

How do we put on spiritual armor? (6:14–17)

By daily absorbing Scriptural truth, living in obedience, sharing the gospel and trusting Christ. This spiritual armor will protect us from spiritual attack. Only when we overcome temptation in the spiritual realm can we play out that victory in the physical world.

What is praying in the Spirit? (6:18)

When we submit our hearts and minds to the direction and leading of the Holy Spirit and then pray in his power, we are praying in the Spirit. Some believe praying in the Spirit may include the use of certain spiritual gifts such as faith (1 Cor. 12:9) or unknown tongues (1 Cor. 14:2). Also see *What does it mean to pray in the Holy Spirit?* (Jude v. 20).

love their wives as their own bodies. He who loves his wife loves himself. [29]After all, no one ever hated his own body, but he feeds and cares for it, just as Christ does the church— [30]for we are members of his body. [31]"For this reason a man will leave his father and mother and be united to his wife, and the two will become one flesh." [a] [32]This is a profound mystery [D]—but I am talking about Christ and the church. [33]However, each one of you also must love his wife as he loves himself, and the wife must respect her husband.

Children and Parents

6 Children, obey your parents in the Lord, for this is right. [2]"Honor your father and mother"—which is the first commandment with a promise— [3]"that it may go well with you and that you may enjoy long life on the earth." [b]

[4]Fathers, do not exasperate your children; instead, bring them up in the training and instruction of the Lord.

Slaves and Masters

[5]Slaves, obey your earthly masters with respect and fear, and with sincerity of heart, just as you would obey Christ. [6]Obey them not only to win their favor when their eye is on you, but like slaves of Christ, doing the will of God from your heart. [7]Serve wholeheartedly, as if you were serving the Lord, not men, [8]because you know that the Lord will reward everyone for whatever good he does, whether he is slave or free.

[9]And masters, treat your slaves in the same way. Do not threaten them, since you know that he who is both their Master and yours is in heaven, and there is no favoritism with him.

The Armor of God

[10]Finally, be strong in the Lord and in his mighty power. [11]Put on the full armor of God so that you can take your stand against the devil's schemes. [12]For our struggle is not against flesh and blood, but against the rulers, against the authorities, against the powers of this dark world and against the spiritual forces of evil in the heavenly realms. [13]Therefore put on the full armor of God, so that when the day of evil comes, you may be able to stand your ground, and after you have done everything, to stand. [14]Stand firm then, with the belt of truth buckled around your waist, with the breastplate of righteousness [D] in place, [15]and with your feet fitted with the readiness that comes from the gospel [D] of peace. [D] [16]In addition to all this, take up the shield of faith, with which you can extinguish all the flaming arrows of the evil one. [17]Take the helmet of salvation [D] and the sword of the Spirit, which is the word of God. [18]And pray in the Spirit on all occasions with all kinds of prayers and requests. With this in mind, be alert and always keep on praying for all the saints. [D]

[19]Pray also for me, that whenever I open my mouth, words may be given me so that I will fearlessly make known the mystery of the gospel, [20]for which I am an ambassador in chains. Pray that I may declare it fearlessly, as I should.

---

[a]31 Gen. 2:24   [b]3 Deut. 5:16

Final Greetings

²¹Tychicus, the dear brother and faithful servant in the Lord, will tell you everything, so that you also may know how I am and what I am doing. ²²I am sending him to you for this very purpose, that you may know how we are, and that he may encourage you.

²³Peace^D to the brothers, and love with faith from God the Father and the Lord Jesus Christ. ²⁴Grace^D to all who love our Lord Jesus Christ with an undying love.

Tychicus (6:21)
Also mentioned in Acts 20:4; Col. 4:7; 2 Tim. 4:12 and Titus 3:12.

What is spiritual warfare? (6:12)

Paul reminds us that we have spiritual authority and blessings in the unseen or *heavenly realms* (1:3). God wants people to be delivered from the power of Satan and his forces (2:1–2).

The good news is that Satan and his forces have been defeated and disarmed (Col. 2:15). Consequently, there's no need for believers to fear their spiritual enemy. While Satan still has the freedom to tempt and harass Christians, he has no direct authority over them. The armor of God pictures the protection Jesus gives us against demonic attack.

Spiritual warfare for believers, therefore, is fought in the mind, emotions and the will. Scriptural truth is our primary line of defense. That's why Paul frequently urges us to be renewed in our minds (Romans 12:1–2; Col. 3:1–3). The more our minds are filled with the truth of God's Word, the less susceptible we are to Satan's deceptions and temptations.

However, because Satan still rules the unbelieving world, we will, on occasion, have to confront Satan's work in people's lives (for example, Acts 13:9–12). To dislodge Satan's influence in someone's life, a supernatural encounter of God's power and truth may be required.

PHILIPPIANS

Why read this book?

If you've ever had trouble seeing how faith can be dressed in everyday work clothes, Philippians is for you. It puts lofty truths into practical terms. And along the way you'll run a gamut of human experience: joy, bitterness, unity, bickering, arrogance, humiliation. Read Philippians to peek into the heart of its writer—and to be drawn closer to the one who was foremost in his heart, Jesus Christ.

Who wrote this book and to whom was it written?

While under house arrest in Rome, the apostle Paul wrote to believers in the city of Philippi, located in northeastern Greece. It lay ten miles inland from the modern port city of Kavalla.

When was it written?

About A.D. 60 to 62, during the time Paul awaited trial on an appeal to the Roman emperor Nero.

Why was it written?

To thank the Philippians for sending Paul money to help defray his living expenses as he awaited trial (4:10–18). Paul also wanted to warn them against false teachers and urge them to greater unity among themselves.

What is the background of this book?

Philippi, a Roman colony, was where Paul planted the first church on European soil (Acts 16:11–40), probably around A.D. 50. When Paul moved on, the church occasionally sent him aid, one of the few churches in those years to do so (4:15).

What to look for in Philippians:

You'll find one of the Bible's most prominent psalms of praise to Jesus (2:5–11); you'll see the futility of religious activity compared to a relationship with Christ (3:4–11); and you'll gain practical tools to help reshape your thinking according to God's ways (4:4–9).

When did these things happen?

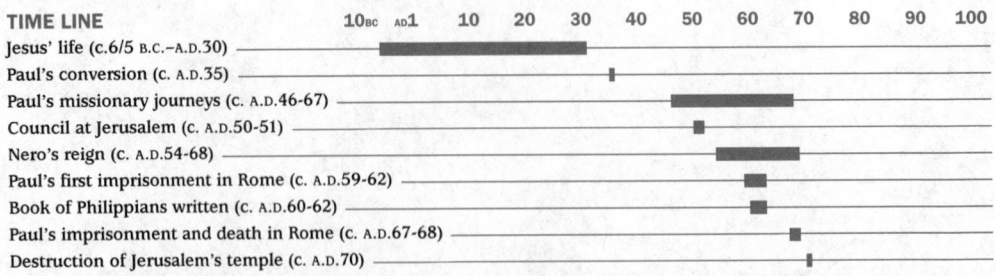

TIME LINE	10BC AD1	10	20	30	40	50	60	70	80	90	100
Jesus' life (c.6/5 B.C.–A.D.30)											
Paul's conversion (c. A.D.35)											
Paul's missionary journeys (c. A.D.46-67)											
Council at Jerusalem (c. A.D.50-51)											
Nero's reign (c. A.D.54-68)											
Paul's first imprisonment in Rome (c. A.D.59-62)											
Book of Philippians written (c. A.D.60-62)											
Paul's imprisonment and death in Rome (c. A.D.67-68)											
Destruction of Jerusalem's temple (c. A.D.70)											

1 Paul and Timothy, servants of Christ Jesus,

To all the saints[D] in Christ Jesus at Philippi, together with the overseers[D][a] and deacons:

[2]Grace[D] and peace[D] to you from God our Father and the Lord Jesus Christ.

Thanksgiving and Prayer

[3]I thank my God every time I remember you. [4]In all my prayers for all of you, I always pray with joy [5]because of your partnership in the gospel[D] from the first day until now, [6]being confident of this, that he who began a good work in you will carry it on to completion until the day of Christ Jesus.

[7]It is right for me to feel this way about all of you, since I have you in my heart; for whether I am in chains or defending and confirming the gospel, all of you share in God's grace with me. [8]God can testify how I long for all of you with the affection of Christ Jesus.

[9]And this is my prayer: that your love may abound more and more in knowledge and depth of insight, [10]so that you may be able to discern what is best and may be pure and blameless until the day of Christ, [11]filled with the fruit of righteousness[D] that comes through Jesus Christ—to the glory[D] and praise of God.

Paul's Chains Advance the Gospel

[12]Now I want you to know, brothers, that what has happened to me has really served to advance the gospel. [13]As a result, it has become clear throughout the whole palace guard[b] and to everyone else that I am in chains for Christ. [14]Because of my chains, most of the brothers in the Lord have been encouraged to speak the word of God more courageously and fearlessly.

[15]It is true that some preach Christ out of envy and rivalry, but others out of goodwill. [16]The latter do so in love, knowing that I am put here for the defense of the gospel. [17]The former preach Christ out of selfish ambition, not sincerely, supposing that they can stir up trouble for me while I am in chains.[c] [18]But what does it matter? The important thing is that in every way, whether from false motives or true, Christ is preached. And because of this I rejoice.

Yes, and I will continue to rejoice, [19]for I know that through your prayers and the help given by the Spirit of Jesus Christ, what has happened to me will turn out for my deliverance.[d] [20]I eagerly expect and hope that I will in no way be ashamed, but will have sufficient courage so that now as always Christ will be exalted in my body, whether by life or by death[D]. [21]For to me, to live is Christ and to die is gain. [22]If I am to go on living in the body, this will mean fruitful labor for me. Yet what shall I choose? I do not know! [23]I am torn between the two: I desire to depart and be with Christ, which is better by far; [24]but it is more necessary for you that I remain in the body. [25]Convinced of this, I know that I will remain, and I will continue with all of you for your progress and joy in the faith, [26]so that through my being with you again your joy in Christ Jesus will overflow on account of me.

[27]Whatever happens, conduct yourselves in a manner

---

[a]1 Traditionally *bishops*   [b]13 Or *whole palace*   [c]16,17 Some late manuscripts have verses 16 and 17 in reverse order.   [d]19 Or *salvation*

The Church in Philippi (1:1)

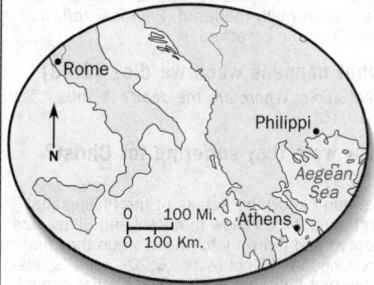

Saints ... overseers ... deacons (1:1)

The word *saints*, meaning those who are dedicated to God, was used for all who believed in Jesus, regardless of their character or spiritual maturity. Also see *What does it take to be an overseer in the church?* (1 Tim. 3:2–7) and *What's the difference between a deacon and an overseer?* (1 Tim. 3:8–12).

What work will God finally complete in us? (1:6)

God will finally complete the work of saving us. If we trust in Christ, we are already fully saved. But God's work in our lives continues *until the day of Christ Jesus*—the time that Christ returns, or until the time when we die and stand before him. Only then shall we *be like him, for we shall see him as he is* (1 John 3:2).

Day of Christ Jesus (1:6,10)

Refers to God's final day of reckoning with mankind. When Christ comes again he will judge those who reject him and receive all who have trusted him (1 Thes. 1:9–10).

Palace guard (1:13)

The Roman military or police who guarded Paul while he awaited trial (Acts 28:16). Paul did not hide his message about Christ from them but rather used the opportunity to plant the gospel in the seat of Roman imperial power.

How did Paul's imprisonment encourage believers to speak out? (1:14)

Courage can be contagious. The world of the early church was not always friendly to the gospel. But, even during great hardship, Paul ignored the potential negative consequences to share the message anyway. His example challenged others to be just as bold in telling others the word of God.

Why were there rival factions among the Christians? (1:15–18)

Rival factions at Rome tried to take advantage of Paul's imprisonment. They were motivated to preach more aggressively, hoping to take over Paul's place of prominence. Perhaps they wanted to prove that their message was somehow better than Paul's. They may have wanted to make Paul, mired in legal difficulties, look bad so that they could look good.

Why did Paul seem to condone insincere preachers? (1:18)

Paul was tolerant toward preachers whose hearts were not entirely pure (v. 15)—but who preached Christ nonetheless. He was not indifferent toward false teaching, nor was he excusing immoral or hateful behavior. But he knew

that Christ could be preached even out of the mixed motives found in imperfect human beings. What really mattered, Paul insisted, was that Christ be preached.

What happens when we die? (1:23)

See article: *Where are the dead?* (1 Thes. 4:14,16).

How were they suffering for Christ? (1:29)

We don't know the details of the Philippians' suffering. We do know that Paul and Silas were beaten and thrown into prison when they first preached in Philippi (Acts 16:20–24). It's possible that believers were facing similar opposition. Paul may also have meant that they faced personal struggles while dealing with the factions and selfishness within their own ranks.

Would *like-minded* Christians have no disagreements? (2:2–5)

No, Christians can have differing opinions and disagree with each other about some things. To be *like-minded* need not suggest a lockstep, cloned behavior. This is instead a call to have attitudes like Christ—loving and accepting one another, even when we're different. In fact, God delights in our diversity; he made every single person unique. But Christ sets a pattern, and the Bible furnishes a standard, for what brings honor to God and promotes love among God's people. We should all be *like-minded* in our obedience to Christ and in our care for others.

What did Jesus give up to come to earth? (2:6–7)

Before his days on earth, Christ enjoyed complete equality with the Father (John 17:24). Even in human form his essential nature remained unchanged; he was still God (John 5:18). Yet so that he might take away the sins of the world, he voluntarily laid aside the privileges and glory of his heavenly authority (v. 8). He surrendered the splendor of his position to identify with sinful humanity.

Will those in hell worship God? (2:10)

Under the earth is the realm of the dead. Heavenly or spiritual beings, the inhabitants of earth and those who have died will all give honor and praise to Jesus. Those *under the earth* will glorify Christ as they submit to the final judgment (Rev. 20:13).

Why does this sound like we have to work to be saved? (2:12–13)

Because, even though God planned for and initiated the work of our salvation, we still must respond to his grace. The work of salvation, though finished on the cross, is still being completed in individuals (1:6). God's grace is fully accomplished in our lives as we cooperate with God, acknowledging his call by our surrender and obedience to him. Because God works within us we are able to work out our salvation.

Drink offering (2:17)

Probably a picture of Old Testament priests pouring wine out on the altar in praise and honor to God (Num. 15:10). Paul would have seen this daily ritual while growing up in Jerusalem (Acts 22:3). While the Philippians offered their *sacrifice and service*, Paul, in prison, offered his very life for the cause of Christ.

worthy of the gospel[D] of Christ. Then, whether I come and see you or only hear about you in my absence, I will know that you stand firm in one spirit, contending as one man for the faith of the gospel [28]without being frightened in any way by those who oppose you. This is a sign to them that they will be destroyed, but that you will be saved—and that by God. [29]For it has been granted to you on behalf of Christ not only to believe on him, but also to suffer for him, [30]since you are going through the same struggle you saw I had, and now hear that I still have.

Imitating Christ's Humility

2 If you have any encouragement from being united with Christ, if any comfort from his love, if any fellowship with the Spirit, if any tenderness and compassion, [2]then make my joy complete by being like-minded, having the same love, being one in spirit and purpose. [3]Do nothing out of selfish ambition or vain conceit, but in humility consider others better than yourselves. [4]Each of you should look not only to your own interests, but also to the interests of others.

[5]Your attitude should be the same as that of Christ Jesus:

> [6]Who, being in very nature[a] God,
> did not consider equality with God something
> to be grasped,
> [7]but made himself nothing,
> taking the very nature[b] of a servant,
> being made in human likeness.
> [8]And being found in appearance as a man,
> he humbled himself
> and became obedient to death[D]—
> even death on a cross!
> [9]Therefore God exalted him to the highest place
> and gave him the name that is above every
> name,
> [10]that at the name of Jesus every knee should
> bow,
> in heaven and on earth and under the earth,
> [11]and every tongue confess that Jesus Christ is
> Lord,
> to the glory[D] of God the Father.

Shining as Stars

[12]Therefore, my dear friends, as you have always obeyed—not only in my presence, but now much more in my absence—continue to work out your salvation[D] with fear and trembling, [13]for it is God who works in you to will and to act according to his good purpose.

[14]Do everything without complaining or arguing, [15]so that you may become blameless and pure, children of God without fault in a crooked and depraved generation, in which you shine like stars in the universe [16]as you hold out[c] the word of life—in order that I may boast on the day of Christ that I did not run or labor for nothing. [17]But even if I am being poured out like a drink offering[D] on the sacrifice[D] and service coming from your faith, I am glad and rejoice with all of you. [18]So you too should be glad and rejoice with me.

---

[a]6 Or *in the form of*   [b]7 Or *the form*   [c]16 Or *hold on to*

Timothy and Epaphroditus

19I hope in the Lord Jesus to send Timothy to you soon, that I also may be cheered when I receive news about you. **20**I have no one else like him, who takes a genuine interest in your welfare. **21**For everyone looks out for his own interests, not those of Jesus Christ. **22**But you know that Timothy has proved himself, because as a son with his father he has served with me in the work of the gospel[D]. **23**I hope, therefore, to send him as soon as I see how things go with me. **24**And I am confident in the Lord that I myself will come soon.

25But I think it is necessary to send back to you Epaphroditus, my brother, fellow worker and fellow soldier, who is also your messenger, whom you sent to take care of my needs. **26**For he longs for all of you and is distressed because you heard he was ill. **27**Indeed he was ill, and almost died. But God had mercy[D] on him, and not on him only but also on me, to spare me sorrow upon sorrow. **28**Therefore I am all the more eager to send him, so that when you see him again you may be glad and I may have less anxiety. **29**Welcome him in the Lord with great joy, and honor men like him, **30**because he almost died for the work of Christ, risking his life to make up for the help you could not give me.

No Confidence in the Flesh

3 Finally, my brothers, rejoice in the Lord! It is no trouble for me to write the same things to you again, and it is a safeguard for you.

2Watch out for those dogs, those men who do evil, those mutilators of the flesh. **3**For it is we who are the circumcision[D], we who worship by the Spirit of God, who glory[D] in Christ Jesus, and who put no confidence in the flesh— **4**though I myself have reasons for such confidence.

If anyone else thinks he has reasons to put confidence in the flesh, I have more: **5**circumcised[D] on the eighth day, of the people of Israel, of the tribe of Benjamin, a Hebrew[D] of Hebrews; in regard to the law, a Pharisee[D]; **6**as for zeal[D], persecuting the church; as for legalistic righteousness[D], faultless.

7But whatever was to my profit I now consider loss for the sake of Christ. **8**What is more, I consider everything a loss compared to the surpassing greatness of knowing Christ Jesus my Lord, for whose sake I have lost all things. I consider them rubbish, that I may gain Christ **9**and be found in him, not having a righteousness of my own that comes from the law, but that which is through faith in Christ—the righteousness that comes from God and is by faith. **10**I want to know Christ and the power of his resurrection[D] and the fellowship of sharing in his sufferings, becoming like him in his death[D], **11**and so, somehow, to attain to the resurrection from the dead.

Pressing on Toward the Goal

12Not that I have already obtained all this, or have already been made perfect, but I press on to take hold of that for which Christ Jesus took hold of me. **13**Brothers, I do not consider myself yet to have taken hold of it. But one thing I do: Forgetting what is behind and straining toward what is ahead, **14**I press on toward the goal to win the prize for which God has called me heavenward in Christ Jesus.

Who were the *dogs* and whom were they mutilating? (3:2)

They were the teachers who insisted that salvation required both trust in Christ and adherence to the Jewish traditions (Acts 15:1). Paul calls them *mutilators* because they compelled Gentile converts to be circumcised, saying that faith in Christ was not enough to have a right relationship with God.

Circumcision (3:3)

See article: *Why did God command circumcision?* (Gen. 17:10).

Why did Paul think it was worthless to be *faultless*? (3:6–8)

At one time, Paul believed he could satisfy God's requirements by keeping religious rules, but he changed his mind after meeting Christ. He came to see that legalism—his list of dos and don'ts—could never achieve genuine righteousness. God makes us righteous when we trust in Christ. We can't make ourselves righteous, no matter how diligent our efforts.

What is *Christ's righteousness,* and how does it become ours? (3:9)

Righteousness refers to a moral aspect of God's nature, his perfect purity and justice. Sinful humans are by nature unrighteous. But when we place our faith in Christ alone, God supernaturally cleanses us from sin and shares with us the *fruit of righteousness* (1:11). God conveys this gift through Christ because of his sacrificial death and resurrection.

Did Paul want to be a martyr? (3:10)

Not necessarily. Paul believed that identifying with the sufferings of Christ was part of trusting in him for salvation. Suffering with Christ in this life precedes the glory we will share with him in the life to come (Romans 8:17). To become like Christ *in his death* means to serve him in costly ways, ways that spell destruction for old habits and patterns.

Why was Paul *straining* to get to heaven? (3:13–14)

Life in Christ involves a tension between two equal but contrasting truths. By faith believers have already *attained* God's full acceptance (v. 16). But in this life no one yet lives out the full measure of Christ's goodness and love. So Paul urges us to *live up to what we have already attained* (v. 16). We are to be fully confident in our salvation, yet at the same time we are to avoid the pride and complacency that could inhibit our continued growth in grace.
See *What work will God finally complete in us?* (1:6) and *Why does this sound like we have to work to be saved?* (2:12–13).

Who were these enemies? (3:18–19)
They were the *dogs* who opposed the cross of Christ by promoting circumcision (3:2). *Their god is their stomach* means that Jewish laws on food had crowded out their personal knowledge of God through faith in Christ. *Glory is in their shame* is likely a blunt way of asserting that these enemies took pride in their circumcision.

Glorious body (3:21)
A new kind of immortal body that will replace our mortal bodies of flesh when God resurrects us to eternal life. See 1 Cor. 15:42–57.

How could a *yokefellow* help feuding women? (4:1–3)
No one knows for sure who this *loyal yokefellow* was. Apparently he (the noun is masculine) was a mature Christian whom Paul could trust to help mediate the dispute, perhaps by bringing them together to reconcile their differences.

How can we think lovely thoughts? (4:8)
Paul is not talking about fleeting impressions that invade our thinking. Thoughts of temptation or discouragement can come unannounced. But we can discipline ourselves, making conscious choices to contemplate good things. Reading uplifting Bible verses, for example, or listing God's attributes can get us on the right track.

Was Paul that good or was he that arrogant? (4:9)
Paul was chosen and equipped to share Christ's blessings with the pagan Gentile world (Acts 9:15; Eph. 3:7). Good role models were rare in pagan centers like Philippi. While Paul knew he was not perfect (3:12), he also knew he had much to offer struggling Gentile believers in the way of instruction and example. He told them to do as he did, not because he was arrogant, but because he led a life of integrity.

What does God give us strength to do? (4:13)
Everything means all that God desires us to do—not absurd, selfish or evil things. In Paul's own example, it meant that God had given him the ability to be content whether he had plenty or overwhelming need. God's grace will sustain us no matter where he leads—even when we lack material things.

Will God meet *needs* like health, food, shelter and long life? (4:19)
God provides many things, including health and basic necessities of life. But when such things are lacking, God still provides what we really need. Jesus tells us to concern ourselves with the kingdom of God—our most important need—and not worry about physical needs (Matt. 6:32–34). *All your needs* must be seen in the light of what the Father gave the Son. In the end, Christ received grace to live—and die—so as to honor God. Whether we face trouble, hardship, persecution or danger, we can always depend on Jesus (Romans 8:35–39). And he is enough.

[15]All of us who are mature should take such a view of things. And if on some point you think differently, that too God will make clear to you. [16]Only let us live up to what we have already attained.

[17]Join with others in following my example, brothers, and take note of those who live according to the pattern we gave you. [18]For, as I have often told you before and now say again even with tears, many live as enemies of the cross of Christ. [19]Their destiny is destruction, their god is their stomach, and their glory[D] is in their shame. Their mind is on earthly things. [20]But our citizenship is in heaven. And we eagerly await a Savior from there, the Lord Jesus Christ, [21]who, by the power that enables him to bring everything under his control, will transform our lowly bodies so that they will be like his glorious body.
4 Therefore, my brothers, you whom I love and long for, my joy and crown, that is how you should stand firm in the Lord, dear friends!

Exhortations

[2]I plead with Euodia and I plead with Syntyche to agree with each other in the Lord. [3]Yes, and I ask you, loyal yokefellow,[a] help these women who have contended at my side in the cause of the gospel[D], along with Clement and the rest of my fellow workers, whose names are in the book of life.

[4]Rejoice in the Lord always. I will say it again: Rejoice! [5]Let your gentleness be evident to all. The Lord is near. [6]Do not be anxious about anything, but in everything, by prayer and petition, with thanksgiving, present your requests to God. [7]And the peace[D] of God, which transcends all understanding, will guard your hearts and your minds in Christ Jesus.

[8]Finally, brothers, whatever is true, whatever is noble, whatever is right, whatever is pure, whatever is lovely, whatever is admirable—if anything is excellent or praiseworthy—think about such things. [9]Whatever you have learned or received or heard from me, or seen in me—put it into practice. And the God of peace will be with you.

Thanks for Their Gifts

[10]I rejoice greatly in the Lord that at last you have renewed your concern for me. Indeed, you have been concerned, but you had no opportunity to show it. [11]I am not saying this because I am in need, for I have learned to be content whatever the circumstances. [12]I know what it is to be in need, and I know what it is to have plenty. I have learned the secret of being content in any and every situation, whether well fed or hungry, whether living in plenty or in want. [13]I can do everything through him who gives me strength.

[14]Yet it was good of you to share in my troubles. [15]Moreover, as you Philippians know, in the early days of your acquaintance with the gospel, when I set out from Macedonia, not one church shared with me in the matter of giving and receiving, except you only; [16]for even when I was in Thessalonica, you sent me aid again and again when I was in need. [17]Not that I am looking for a gift, but I am looking for what may be credited to your account. [18]I have received full payment and even more; I am amply supplied, now that I have received from Epaphroditus the gifts you sent. They are a fragrant offering, an acceptable

a3 Or *loyal Syzygus*

sacrifice[D], pleasing to God. [19]And my God will meet all your needs according to his glorious riches in Christ Jesus.

[20]To our God and Father be glory[D] for ever and ever. Amen.

Final Greetings

[21]Greet all the saints[D] in Christ Jesus. The brothers who are with me send greetings. [22]All the saints send you greetings, especially those who belong to Caesar's household.

[23]The grace[D] of the Lord Jesus Christ be with your spirit. Amen.[a]

What Christians were in *Caesar's household*? (4:22)

Those who belong to Caesar's household refers to employees of the emperor Nero. Those employees had become sympathetic to the gospel—perhaps even converted—as a result of Paul's influence (see 1:13). When Paul wrote to Philippi, Nero (emperor of Rome from A.D. 54 to 68) had not yet become hostile to Christians. It appears Nero's employees could support the Christian cause without incurring the wrath of their employer.

[a]23 Some manuscripts do not have *Amen*.

COLOSSIANS

Why read this book?

Some people have been surprised to discover something new about a friend they thought they knew well. That's one of the exciting things about a relationship with Christ: there's no limit to the things we can learn about him. Reading Colossians is one way we can discover a few more things about Jesus and learn how we can honor him.

Who wrote this book and to whom was it written?

While under house arrest in Rome, the apostle Paul wrote to believers in the small city of Colosse, located in the southwest interior of what is now Turkey.

When was it written?

About A.D. 60 to 62, during the time Paul awaited trial on an appeal to the Roman emperor Nero.

Why was it written?

A group called Gnostics (derived from the word for *knowledge*) claimed that they possessed privileged supernatural knowledge necessary for salvation. Paul wrote to warn about the subtle arguments and false teachings that threatened to undermine the Colossians' faith.

What is the background of this book?

Epaphras, a disciple of Paul, had founded the church at Colosse. Now it was under constant pressure from the numerous religious philosophies abounding in the first-century world. Colosse seems to have become a center for Gnosticism, a hybrid religion and philosophy that mixed Christian, Jewish and possibly pagan beliefs.

What to look for in Colossians:

The supremacy of Christ and what that means for our everyday lives. Look for insights that show specific ways we can develop attitudes and actions to honor the Lord.

When did these things happen?

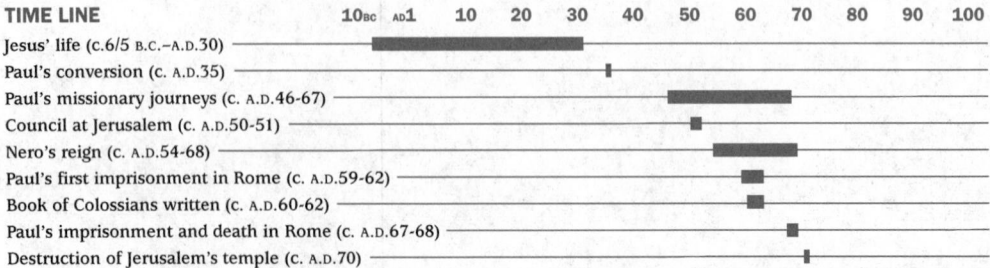

TIME LINE	10 B.C.	A.D. 1	10	20	30	40	50	60	70	80	90	100
Jesus' life (c.6/5 B.C.–A.D.30)												
Paul's conversion (c. A.D.35)												
Paul's missionary journeys (c. A.D.46-67)												
Council at Jerusalem (c. A.D.50-51)												
Nero's reign (c. A.D.54-68)												
Paul's first imprisonment in Rome (c. A.D.59-62)												
Book of Colossians written (c. A.D.60-62)												
Paul's imprisonment and death in Rome (c. A.D.67-68)												
Destruction of Jerusalem's temple (c. A.D.70)												

1 Paul, an apostle[D] of Christ Jesus by the will of God, and Timothy our brother,

2To the holy and faithful[a] brothers in Christ at Colosse:

Grace[D] and peace[D] to you from God our Father.[b]

Thanksgiving and Prayer

3We always thank God, the Father of our Lord Jesus Christ, when we pray for you, **4**because we have heard of your faith in Christ Jesus and of the love you have for all the saints[D]— **5**the faith and love that spring from the hope that is stored up for you in heaven and that you have already heard about in the word of truth, the gospel[D] **6**that has come to you. All over the world this gospel is bearing fruit and growing, just as it has been doing among you since the day you heard it and understood God's grace in all its truth. **7**You learned it from Epaphras, our dear fellow servant, who is a faithful minister of Christ on our[c] behalf, **8**and who also told us of your love in the Spirit.

9For this reason, since the day we heard about you, we have not stopped praying for you and asking God to fill you with the knowledge of his will through all spiritual wisdom and understanding. **10**And we pray this in order that you may live a life worthy of the Lord and may please him in every way: bearing fruit in every good work, growing in the knowledge of God, **11**being strengthened with all power according to his glorious might so that you may have great endurance and patience, and joyfully **12**giving thanks to the Father, who has qualified you[d] to share in the inheritance of the saints in the kingdom of light. **13**For he has rescued us from the dominion of darkness and brought us into the kingdom of the Son he loves, **14**in whom we have redemption,[D,e] the forgiveness of sins.

The Supremacy of Christ

15He is the image of the invisible God, the firstborn[D] over all creation. **16**For by him all things were created: things in heaven and on earth, visible and invisible, whether thrones or powers or rulers or authorities; all things were created by him and for him. **17**He is before all things, and in him all things hold together. **18**And he is the head of the body, the church; he is the beginning and the firstborn from among the dead, so that in everything he might have the supremacy. **19**For God was pleased to have all his fullness dwell in him, **20**and through him to reconcile to himself all things, whether things on earth or things in heaven, by making peace through his blood, shed on the cross.

21Once you were alienated from God and were enemies in your minds because of[f] your evil behavior. **22**But now he has reconciled you by Christ's physical body through death[D] to present you holy in his sight, without blemish and free from accusation— **23**if you continue in your faith, established and firm, not moved from the hope held out in the gospel. This is the gospel that you heard and that has been proclaimed to every creature under heaven, and of which I, Paul, have become a servant.

---

a2 Or *believing*   *b2* Some manuscripts *Father and the Lord Jesus Christ*   *c7* Some manuscripts *your*   *d12* Some manuscripts *us*   *e14* A few late manuscripts *redemption through his blood*   *f21* Or *minds, as shown by*

The Church in Colosse (1:2)

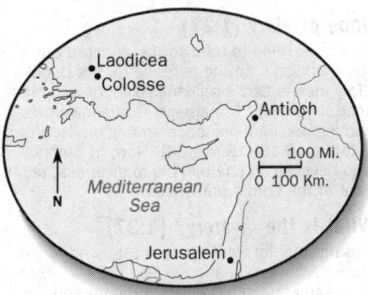

Dominion of darkness (1:13)

The influence and destructive power Satan and sin have over the world, broken only through the authority of Christ. Christians occasionally can fall prey to the darkness, but they don't have to. In Christ we have the resources to overcome Satan.

Why is Jesus called *the firstborn*? (1:15,18)

Paul borrowed this term from his Jewish upbringing: *firstborn* was a Hebrew way of saying someone was *especially honored*. The nation of Israel was called *firstborn* (Exodus 4:22), as was David (Psalm 89:27). The word didn't refer to their physical birth but to their place of honor before God. So Paul is saying that Christ has a place of honor over all creation.

In what way do *all things hold together* in Christ? (1:17)

Science has discovered much about the nature of matter, but many mysteries, especially those related to subatomic particles and the origin of matter, remain unsolved. Still, no matter what human research learns about the *what* of the natural world, the *why* is ultimately found only in God's Son. Christ's creation continues as he sustains the universe. But he also upholds the world in a spiritual sense: his work of redemption brings together sinful people and a holy God.

In what way did all God's fullness dwell in Christ? (1:19)

All believers are to be filled with God's Spirit. Jesus, however, was filled with the *fullness* of God, indicating that he contained the total essence of God's nature and authority. There is nothing of God's character or attributes which are lacking in Christ. *Fullness* was a popular term for the Gnostics (see Introduction: *Why was it written?*), who used it to refer to the combination of all supernatural influences. Paul took their own word to elevate Christ above all other religious ideas and systems. Also see 2:9.

What was *lacking in regard to Christ's afflictions*? (1:24)

Nothing, if we're talking about the price Christ paid for our sins on the cross. No one can, or need, add to his perfect, finished work. But Paul was talking instead about the afflictions that Christ calls his people to bear. Believers must stand, sometimes painfully, against the world and their own wayward hearts to fully love the Lord and others.

Hope of glory (1:27)

Paul uses *hope* to refer to the assured out-come of God's saving purpose for his people. *Glory* means God's brilliant splendor and presence. In the Old Testament, God showed his burning personal presence among the Hebrews (Exodus 19:16–19; 40:34). Now, in Christ, all who believe can share in his forgiveness, confident of the Lord's presence.

What is the *mystery*? (1:27)

The mystery for Paul was a mystery no longer (see his full explanation in Eph. 3:3–4). God chose to bring salvation to Abraham and the Jewish people, though they were rebellious and undeserving. In grace and love he chose them as his own people. But what about non-Jews? Before he met Christ, Paul would have said, "Gentiles have no hope unless they embrace Judaism." But now the mystery has been cleared up: Gentiles and Jews have hope when they embrace Christ.

Why did Paul have to labor so hard if God's power was within? (1:29)

When God works in us, we can work (see 1 Cor. 15:10; Phil. 2:12–13). That was how it was for Jesus, too (John 5:17). Neither Jesus nor Paul were trying to earn favor with the Father by their works. They wanted to honor him with their lives and spared no effort to do so. Paul struggled against temptation from within and opposition from without, using the energy God had placed within him.

What is the *mystery*? (2:2–3)

See *What is the mystery?* (1:27).

What philosophies threatened to captivate the Colossians? (2:8)

Two notions are contained in the idea of the *basic principles of this world*. One is that salvation comes through superior knowledge. Some religious teachers in Paul's day tried to influence the Colossians with this view. The other is that salvation requires superior behavior. As a Pharisee, Paul had once believed this himself, and some at Colosse apparently still did (vv. 20–23).

Circumcision done by Christ (2:11)

In the Old Testament, circumcision was a God-given sign of divine blessing, identifying the people who belonged to God. It was a symbol of how God transforms the sinful heart (Deut. 30:6). That symbol of transformation became reality through Christ. The sinful human nature can be displaced by the personal, life-changing presence of Jesus Christ. The old self is pared away, and the new person in Christ emerges (2 Cor. 5:17).

What did Christ do to the law? (2:13–14)

The term *written code* is a business term. It is a bond, an I.O.U., signed by the debtor himself. Paul uses this metaphor as a way of saying that we, as sinners, are in God's debt: we deserve to pay the penalty of death (Romans 6:23). But how can anyone on earth clear a debt owed to God in heaven? Paul replies that Jesus paid the price by his death, effectively canceling the I.O.U. of sin for all who trust in him.

Paul's Labor for the Church

24Now I rejoice in what was suffered for you, and I fill up in my flesh what is still lacking in regard to Christ's afflictions[D], for the sake of his body, which is the church. **25**I have become its servant by the commission God gave me to present to you the word of God in its fullness— **26**the mystery[D] that has been kept hidden for ages and generations, but is now disclosed to the saints[D]. **27**To them God has chosen to make known among the Gentiles[D] the glorious riches of this mystery, which is Christ in you, the hope of glory[D].

28We proclaim him, admonishing and teaching everyone with all wisdom, so that we may present everyone perfect in Christ. **29**To this end I labor, struggling with all his energy, which so powerfully works in me.

2 I want you to know how much I am struggling for you and for those at Laodicea, and for all who have not met me personally. **2**My purpose is that they may be encouraged in heart and united in love, so that they may have the full riches of complete understanding, in order that they may know the mystery of God, namely, Christ, **3**in whom are hidden all the treasures of wisdom and knowledge. **4**I tell you this so that no one may deceive you by fine-sounding arguments. **5**For though I am absent from you in body, I am present with you in spirit and delight to see how orderly you are and how firm your faith in Christ is.

Freedom From Human Regulations Through Life With Christ

6So then, just as you received Christ Jesus as Lord, continue to live in him, **7**rooted and built up in him, strengthened in the faith as you were taught, and overflowing with thankfulness.

8See to it that no one takes you captive through hollow and deceptive philosophy, which depends on human tradition and the basic principles of this world rather than on Christ.

9For in Christ all the fullness of the Deity lives in bodily form, **10**and you have been given fullness in Christ, who is the head over every power and authority. **11**In him you were also circumcised[D], in the putting off of the sinful nature,[a] not with a circumcision[D] done by the hands of men but with the circumcision done by Christ, **12**having been buried with him in baptism[D] and raised with him through your faith in the power of God, who raised him from the dead.

13When you were dead in your sins and in the uncircumcision[D] of your sinful nature,[b] God made you[c] alive with Christ. He forgave us all our sins, **14**having canceled the written code, with its regulations, that was against us and that stood opposed to us; he took it away, nailing it to the cross. **15**And having disarmed the powers and authorities, he made a public spectacle of them, triumphing over them by the cross.[d]

16Therefore do not let anyone judge you by what you eat or drink, or with regard to a religious festival, a New Moon celebration or a Sabbath[D] day. **17**These are a shadow of the things that were to come; the reality, however, is found in Christ. **18**Do not let anyone who delights in

---

a 11 Or *the flesh*   *b 13* Or *your flesh*   *c 13* Some manuscripts *us*
d 15 Or *them in him*

false humility and the worship of angels disqualify you for the prize. Such a person goes into great detail about what he has seen, and his unspiritual mind puffs him up with idle notions. **19**He has lost connection with the Head, from whom the whole body, supported and held together by its ligaments and sinews, grows as God causes it to grow.

20Since you died with Christ to the basic principles of this world, why, as though you still belonged to it, do you submit to its rules: **21**"Do not handle! Do not taste! Do not touch!"? **22**These are all destined to perish with use, because they are based on human commands and teachings. **23**Such regulations indeed have an appearance of wisdom, with their self-imposed worship, their false humility and their harsh treatment of the body, but they lack any value in restraining sensual indulgence.

Rules for Holy Living

3 Since, then, you have been raised with Christ, set your hearts on things above, where Christ is seated at the right hand of God. **2**Set your minds on things above, not on earthly things. **3**For you died, and your life is now hidden with Christ in God. **4**When Christ, who is your*a* life, appears, then you also will appear with him in glory.D

5Put to death,D therefore, whatever belongs to your earthly nature: sexual immorality, impurity, lust, evil desires and greed, which is idolatry.D **6**Because of these, the wrath of God is coming.*b* **7**You used to walk in these ways, in the life you once lived. **8**But now you must rid yourselves of all such things as these: anger, rage, malice, slander, and filthy language from your lips. **9**Do not lie to each other, since you have taken off your old self with its practices **10**and have put on the new self, which is being renewed in knowledge in the image of its Creator. **11**Here there is no Greek or Jew,D circumcisedD or uncircumcised,D barbarian, Scythian, slave or free, but Christ is all, and is in all.

12Therefore, as God's chosen people, holy and dearly loved, clothe yourselves with compassion, kindness, humility, gentleness and patience. **13**Bear with each other and forgive whatever grievances you may have against one another. Forgive as the Lord forgave you. **14**And over all these virtues put on love, which binds them all together in perfect unity.

15Let the peaceD of Christ rule in your hearts, since as members of one body you were called to peace. And be thankful. **16**Let the word of Christ dwell in you richly as you teach and admonish one another with all wisdom, and as you sing psalms, hymns and spiritual songs with gratitude in your hearts to God. **17**And whatever you do, whether in word or deed, do it all in the name of the Lord Jesus, giving thanks to God the Father through him.

Rules for Christian Households

18Wives, submit to your husbands, as is fitting in the Lord.

19Husbands, love your wives and do not be harsh with them.

20Children, obey your parents in everything, for this pleases the Lord.

What powers and authorities did Jesus disarm? (2:15)

The Bible tells of countless spiritual beings (fallen angels, spirits, demons) that, along with Satan, oppose God and afflict people. Christ disarmed and defeated them by dying on the cross and rising from the dead. By overcoming death, sin's ultimate calling card, Christ publicly defeated the devil and his allies.

What is it that threatens to disconnect people from *the Head?* (2:19)

It is possible to misplace spiritual priorities. Some Colossian believers seem to have moved their focus from Christ to certain dietary rules and religious observances (vv. 16,18). By emphasizing these false rituals and relying on certain religious practices they *lost connection* with the church's *Head,* Jesus Christ. He alone deserves center stage.

In what sense are we *raised with Christ?* (3:1)

We are *raised with Christ* according to God's viewpoint. When Christ was raised, God counted all believers—past, present and future—to have been raised with him.

How can we not think about earthly things? (3:2)

It is impossible not to think of earthly things, at least some of the time. We still have to take care of day to day obligations and activities. But *to set your mind on something* means to "make it your heart's central focus." Paul knew that we would have to tend to earthly affairs. But earthly things must not be permitted to take precedence over the things of God—his word, his service, his praise. This must be the basis from which we pursue jobs, families and other important matters of daily life.

How do we put the *earthly nature* to death? (3:5)

The *earthly nature* and the deeds it typically produces are too strong for mere human willpower to resist. But Christ living within us can overcome the earthly nature. By increasing our trust in Christ, his Spirit increasingly gives us the strength to follow his commands. Over time the *earthly nature* is overshadowed and the *new creation* (2 Cor. 5:17) comes to dominate.

No Greek or Jew (3:11)

Ethnic and class distinctions are part of social life in all times and places. But in the church, the value of individuals does not depend on their race, social status or circumstances of birth. Paul was speaking of our standing before God—we are all sinners who can be forgiven through Christ alone. In that sense all are equal, despite differing backgrounds, abilities and positions. God does not discriminate.

Submission (3:18–4:1)

Those in the Bible (Daniel, Peter, John and others) who engaged in civil disobedience had discerning consciences due to a solid grasp of God's Word. How we submit to (or defy) civil authorities should be guided first by our submission to God. See *Do we always have to submit?* (1 Peter 2:13–17).

---

*a*4 Some manuscripts *our*   *b*6 Some early manuscripts *coming on those who are disobedient*

Will wrong be repaid even if it's forgiven? (3:25)

Repaid for his wrong may refer in part to earthly authorities whom God has appointed to maintain social order (Romans 13:4). It may also suggest the fatherly and sometimes painful discipline God uses to educate and guide his people (Heb. 12:1–11). But it seems Paul may have primarily meant that there will be eternal consequences to be paid by evildoers who refuse to turn to Christ (1 Cor. 6:9–11).

Why didn't Paul tell Christian slave-owners to set their slaves free? (4:1)

See article: *Why doesn't the Bible condemn slavery?* (1 Peter 2:18–21).

What is "salty" conversation for a Christian? (4:5–6)

Salt is a good metaphor for Christian conversation and behavior. Salt improves taste; in the same way, what believers say and do should leave a "good taste" for others. Salt also preserves food; Christians should influence others for eternity with their grace-filled lives. Courteous, honest and compassionate, they should have the *fruit of the Spirit* evident within them.

Why did God include personal notes in Scripture? (4:7–15)

Names like Tychicus, Onesimus and others seem unnecessary in an open letter on Christian doctrine and living. But because they are there, we are reminded that Biblical writers wrote to certain persons in specific places and times. Since Scripture was written for people like us, who faced problems like ours, we know that God's truths are timeless. The Bible can help and guide us because it was, and is, for real people facing real questions.

Why the exchange of letters? (4:16)

Paul and the early church were aware that his teaching and letters bore authority (1 Thes. 2:13; 2 Peter 3:15–16). What he said to Colosse would have importance to Laodicea, only ten miles away and vice versa (see **Map 11** at the back of this Bible). Churches and Christians today rightly study Paul's epistles to discover the insight they provide for growth in Christ. For reasons only God knows, the letter to Laodicea was misplaced early in the history of the church and therefore was not included in the Bible.

What did Paul mean by asking that they remember his chains? (4:18)

Paul never lost his sense of dependence on Christ and on the prayers of other believers. He knew that on his own he would be weak and ineffectual. But through prayer he could find the words and strength needed to do the job he faced (Eph. 6:19–20).

21Fathers, do not embitter your children, or they will become discouraged.

22Slaves, obey your earthly masters in everything; and do it, not only when their eye is on you and to win their favor, but with sincerity of heart and reverence[D] for the Lord. **23**Whatever you do, work at it with all your heart, as working for the Lord, not for men, **24**since you know that you will receive an inheritance from the Lord as a reward. It is the Lord Christ you are serving. **25**Anyone who does wrong will be repaid for his wrong, and there is no favoritism.

4 Masters, provide your slaves with what is right and fair, because you know that you also have a Master in heaven.

Further Instructions

2Devote yourselves to prayer, being watchful and thankful. **3**And pray for us, too, that God may open a door for our message, so that we may proclaim the mystery[D] of Christ, for which I am in chains. **4**Pray that I may proclaim it clearly, as I should. **5**Be wise in the way you act toward outsiders; make the most of every opportunity. **6**Let your conversation be always full of grace[D], seasoned with salt, so that you may know how to answer everyone.

Final Greetings

7Tychicus will tell you all the news about me. He is a dear brother, a faithful minister and fellow servant in the Lord. **8**I am sending him to you for the express purpose that you may know about our[a] circumstances and that he may encourage your hearts. **9**He is coming with Onesimus, our faithful and dear brother, who is one of you. They will tell you everything that is happening here.

10My fellow prisoner Aristarchus sends you his greetings, as does Mark, the cousin of Barnabas. (You have received instructions about him; if he comes to you, welcome him.) **11**Jesus, who is called Justus, also sends greetings. These are the only Jews[D] among my fellow workers for the kingdom of God[D], and they have proved a comfort to me. **12**Epaphras, who is one of you and a servant of Christ Jesus, sends greetings. He is always wrestling in prayer for you, that you may stand firm in all the will of God, mature and fully assured. **13**I vouch for him that he is working hard for you and for those at Laodicea and Hierapolis. **14**Our dear friend Luke, the doctor, and Demas send greetings. **15**Give my greetings to the brothers at Laodicea, and to Nympha and the church in her house.

16After this letter has been read to you, see that it is also read in the church of the Laodiceans and that you in turn read the letter from Laodicea.

17Tell Archippus: "See to it that you complete the work you have received in the Lord."

18I, Paul, write this greeting in my own hand. Remember my chains. Grace be with you.

---

*a*8 Some manuscripts *that he may know about your*

1 THESSALONIANS

Why read this book?

Though centuries old, 1 Thessalonians was written for times like ours. It speaks to a culture filled with seductive images and sexual pressures. It brings eternal perspective to discussions of material things. It questions the secular values that undermine God's ways. If you've ever struggled to maintain a pure life in a free-wheeling society, 1 Thessalonians provides an encouraging word: *The one who calls you is faithful and he will do it* (5:24).

Who wrote this book?

The apostle Paul.

To whom was it written and why?

Paul wrote to the believers in the church at Thessalonica, founded during his second missionary journey. Riots and opposition had forced him to leave them sooner than he desired. But later news of their progress encouraged Paul to write to commend them for growing in the Lord and urge them to correct some misunderstandings.

When was it written?

Possibly as early as A.D. 50 or shortly thereafter.

What to look for in 1 Thessalonians:

As you read, watch for practical ways that Christians can live holy lives in a culture hostile to Christian values. You'll find guidelines on relationships and boundaries for living in an immoral culture. Overshadowing all this is a perspective on life that is shaped by eternity. And you'll find exciting clues about the end times and Jesus' second coming.

When did these things happen?

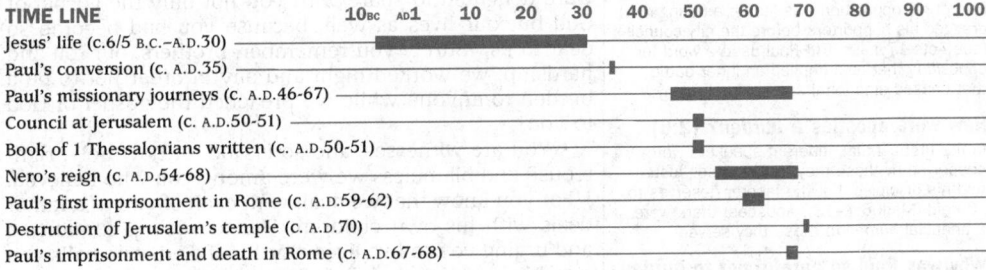

TIME LINE	10BC AD1	10	20	30	40	50	60	70	80	90	100
Jesus' life (c.6/5 B.C.–A.D.30)											
Paul's conversion (c. A.D.35)											
Paul's missionary journeys (c. A.D.46-67)											
Council at Jerusalem (c. A.D.50-51)											
Book of 1 Thessalonians written (c. A.D.50-51)											
Nero's reign (c. A.D.54-68)											
Paul's first imprisonment in Rome (c. A.D.59-62)											
Destruction of Jerusalem's temple (c. A.D.70)											
Paul's imprisonment and death in Rome (c. A.D.67-68)											

The Church in Thessalonica (1:1)

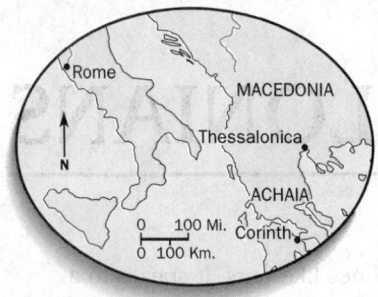

Chosen (1:4)
See *Who are the elect?* (1 Peter 1:1) and article: *If God chooses us, do we have any choice?* (Eph. 1:4–5).

Does the gospel come with more *power* to some than others? (1:5)
Though God's power might be expressed in different ways in different situations, God is always the same. Here, Paul was speaking about the powerful changes that had occurred in the lives of the Thessalonians.

How had the Thessalonians suffered? (1:6)
Jews who were antagonistic to the gospel apparently enlisted the help of some Gentiles who imprisoned and beat those Gentiles who had followed Paul's teachings (see 2:14).

From what idols had the Thessalonians turned? (1:9)
Thessalonians had separate gods for everything—gods of war and love, earth and sea, pleasure and anger, heaven and hell. The ancient Greek religion, adopted by the Romans, was willing to add gods, but it did not want to subtract gods. Yet when they met the one true God through Jesus Christ, the Thessalonians rejected all their former gods.

Coming wrath (1:10)
Divine judgment to be poured out on the wicked and those who refuse to believe (Luke 3:7). Wrath is more than an emotion God feels; it is the just opposition that God has toward sin.

What kind of *opposition* did Paul face in Thessalonica? (2:2)
Part of his opposition was literal: a rioting mob dragged his supporters before the city council (see Acts 17:1–9). But Paul used a word for *opposition* that also implied an inner battle that caused emotional and spiritual agony.

How were apostles a *burden*? (2:6)
In the first century, itinerant speakers were supported by those they taught. Also, Jesus told his disciples that the laborer deserves to be paid (Mark 6:7–13). Apostles, then, were a financial *burden* to those they served.

Why was Paul so careful not to burden them? (2:9)
Though Paul knew his rights, he was determined to avoid wrong. He went beyond the call of duty to avoid being a financial burden to the churches. Perhaps he was influenced by his rabbinical training that forbade him from making religious work a means of income.

1 Paul, Silas[a] and Timothy,

To the church of the Thessalonians in God the Father and the Lord Jesus Christ:

Grace[D] and peace[D] to you.[b]

Thanksgiving for the Thessalonians' Faith

2We always thank God for all of you, mentioning you in our prayers. 3We continually remember before our God and Father your work produced by faith, your labor prompted by love, and your endurance inspired by hope in our Lord Jesus Christ.

4For we know, brothers loved by God, that he has chosen you, 5because our gospel[D] came to you not simply with words, but also with power, with the Holy Spirit and with deep conviction. You know how we lived among you for your sake. 6You became imitators of us and of the Lord; in spite of severe suffering, you welcomed the message with the joy given by the Holy Spirit. 7And so you became a model to all the believers in Macedonia and Achaia. 8The Lord's message rang out from you not only in Macedonia and Achaia—your faith in God has become known everywhere. Therefore we do not need to say anything about it, 9for they themselves report what kind of reception you gave us. They tell how you turned to God from idols[D] to serve the living and true God, 10and to wait for his Son from heaven, whom he raised from the dead—Jesus, who rescues us from the coming wrath.

Paul's Ministry in Thessalonica

2 You know, brothers, that our visit to you was not a failure. 2We had previously suffered and been insulted in Philippi, as you know, but with the help of our God we dared to tell you his gospel in spite of strong opposition. 3For the appeal we make does not spring from error or impure motives, nor are we trying to trick you. 4On the contrary, we speak as men approved by God to be entrusted with the gospel. We are not trying to please men but God, who tests our hearts. 5You know we never used flattery, nor did we put on a mask to cover up greed—God is our witness. 6We were not looking for praise from men, not from you or anyone else.

As apostles[D] of Christ we could have been a burden to you, 7but we were gentle among you, like a mother caring for her little children. 8We loved you so much that we were delighted to share with you not only the gospel of God but our lives as well, because you had become so dear to us. 9Surely you remember, brothers, our toil and hardship; we worked night and day in order not to be a burden to anyone while we preached the gospel of God to you.

10You are witnesses, and so is God, of how holy, righteous[D] and blameless we were among you who believed. 11For you know that we dealt with each of you as a father deals with his own children, 12encouraging, comforting and urging you to live lives worthy of God, who calls you into his kingdom and glory[D].

13And we also thank God continually because, when you received the word of God, which you heard from us, you accepted it not as the word of men, but as it actually

a1 Greek Silvanus, a variant of Silas   *b1 Some early manuscripts you from God our Father and the Lord Jesus Christ*

is, the word of God, which is at work in you who believe. **14**For you, brothers, became imitators of God's churches in Judea, which are in Christ Jesus: You suffered from your own countrymen the same things those churches suffered from the Jews[D], **15**who killed the Lord Jesus and the prophets[D] and also drove us out. They displease God and are hostile to all men **16**in their effort to keep us from speaking to the Gentiles[D] so that they may be saved. In this way they always heap up their sins to the limit. The wrath of God has come upon them at last.[a]

Paul's Longing to See the Thessalonians

17But, brothers, when we were torn away from you for a short time (in person, not in thought), out of our intense longing we made every effort to see you. **18**For we wanted to come to you—certainly I, Paul, did, again and again—but Satan stopped us. **19**For what is our hope, our joy, or the crown in which we will glory[D] in the presence of our Lord Jesus when he comes? Is it not you? **20**Indeed, you are our glory and joy.

3 So when we could stand it no longer, we thought it best to be left by ourselves in Athens. **2**We sent Timothy, who is our brother[D] and God's fellow worker[b] in spreading the gospel[D] of Christ, to strengthen and encourage you in your faith, **3**so that no one would be unsettled by these trials. You know quite well that we were destined for them. **4**In fact, when we were with you, we kept telling you that we would be persecuted. And it turned out that way, as you well know. **5**For this reason, when I could stand it no longer, I sent to find out about your faith. I was afraid that in some way the tempter might have tempted you and our efforts might have been useless.

Timothy's Encouraging Report

6But Timothy has just now come to us from you and has brought good news about your faith and love. He has told us that you always have pleasant memories of us and that you long to see us, just as we also long to see you. **7**Therefore, brothers, in all our distress and persecution we were encouraged about you because of your faith. **8**For now we really live, since you are standing firm in the Lord. **9**How can we thank God enough for you in return for all the joy we have in the presence of our God because of you? **10**Night and day we pray most earnestly that we may see you again and supply what is lacking in your faith.

11Now may our God and Father himself and our Lord Jesus clear the way for us to come to you. **12**May the Lord make your love increase and overflow for each other and for everyone else, just as ours does for you. **13**May he strengthen your hearts so that you will be blameless and holy in the presence of our God and Father when our Lord Jesus comes with all his holy ones.

Living to Please God

4 Finally, brothers, we instructed you how to live in order to please God, as in fact you are living. Now we ask you and urge you in the Lord Jesus to do this more and more. **2**For you know what instructions we gave you by the authority of the Lord Jesus.

What made their words the words of God? (2:13)
God can use humans as instruments to deliver his truth. The radically changed lives of the Thessalonians were proof that the apostles' words were, in fact, God's message. Such supernatural results could come only from the word of God, never the word of a human being. Also see *How can we speak as though speaking the very words of God?* (1 Peter 4:11).

Why did these Jews resent Gentiles hearing the gospel? (2:16)
Racial bigotry caused the Jews to reject the idea of Gentiles worshiping God apart from Judaism. They believed that gatherings of Jews and Gentiles for worship threatened their doctrinal and racial purity. It may also be that they did not want government persecution of Christians to expand to include Jews. Up to that time, Jews enjoyed unique religious privileges throughout the Roman empire.

Heap up their sins to the limit (2:16)
Religious writing of that time suggested there was a limit to God's tolerance of sin. Those who exceeded the limit would provoke his judgment. It's not that God ignores sin, but that he is patient and merciful. He gives even the worst sinners repeated opportunities to repent.

How could Satan thwart the plans of an apostle? (2:18)
Satan could thwart the plans of an apostle, but not the plans of God for an apostle. Paul's plans could be sidetracked only because God permitted Satan to do so. We don't know what specifically went awry, but we can be confident that God even uses setbacks to work out a better result than we had planned.

What trials had they faced? (3:3)
See *How had the Thessalonians suffered?* (1:6).

Why would God destine Christians for trials? (3:3)
God uses our unpleasant experiences to accomplish his higher purposes in us. Suffering for our faith builds character and develops faith within us. Trials can teach what cannot be learned in a classroom. Even Jesus learned obedience by the things he suffered (Heb. 5:8).

What was lacking in their faith? (3:10)
Paul describes something unfinished or perhaps in need of repair. Despite his joy over their spiritual growth, Paul recognized that the Thessalonians' faith was not yet mature. They needed to be encouraged so their faith might be completed. Most likely they needed more teaching, and Paul was writing the letter to help them make up a deficit in their faith.

Who are the *holy ones* who will come with Jesus? (3:13)
The *holy ones* could mean believers. This is its usual meaning. The *holy ones* may also refer to angels (Mark 8:38) or believers who have died and are now with Christ. Some think it could mean both angels and believers.

---

[a]16 Or *them fully*   [b]2 Some manuscripts *brother and fellow worker*; other manuscripts *brother and God's servant*

Does God punish or forgive Christians who sin? (4:6)

Punishment is for those who reject God's ways. It is true that God disciplines those whom he he loves (Heb. 12:6), but discipline is different from punishment. Punishment focuses on justice and the past; discipline focuses on the person and the future. Nevertheless, when someone violates God's principles, there will be consequences even for those who are forgiven. Sexual immorality, for example, can lead to disease and to broken relationships. Also see *How does the Lord discipline?* (Heb. 12:5).

Fall asleep (4:13)

A euphemism for death. Today we might say that someone *passed away* or *went home to be with the Lord.*

Why will Jesus bring the dead when he comes for the living? (4:14)

Those believers in Christ who are dead shall rise first (v. 16). Consequently they can come as resurrected saints with Christ when he returns to the earth. Some suggest that it is their *spirits,* now in the presence of the Lord (2 Cor. 5:8), that will return with Christ and be joined with their resurrected bodies.

The coming of the Lord (4:15)

Refers to the day Jesus returns to the earth to gather believers and judge unbelievers. It may also include some of the dramatic events that precede the actual coming of the Lord: plagues, famines and earthquakes (Matt. 24:7–8,30–31).

Is the meeting in the air literal or figurative? (4:17)

It could be either. Some think this description parallels an ancient custom. When dignitaries would visit a city, the leading citizens would go out of the city and escort them back on the final stage of the journey. The picture here is of the Christians going up to meet Jesus and returning, some say, to earth with him. Others say believers will return with Jesus to heaven. Whether this meeting is literal or figurative, we will unquestionably join him at his return. This event is known as the Rapture.

³It is God's will that you should be sanctified[D]: that you should avoid sexual immorality; ⁴that each of you should learn to control his own body[a] in a way that is holy and honorable, ⁵not in passionate lust like the heathen, who do not know God; ⁶and that in this matter no one should wrong his brother or take advantage of him. The Lord will punish men for all such sins, as we have already told you and warned you. ⁷For God did not call us to be impure, but to live a holy life. ⁸Therefore, he who rejects this instruction does not reject man but God, who gives you his Holy Spirit.

⁹Now about brotherly love we do not need to write to you, for you yourselves have been taught by God to love each other. ¹⁰And in fact, you do love all the brothers throughout Macedonia. Yet we urge you, brothers, to do so more and more.

¹¹Make it your ambition to lead a quiet life, to mind your own business and to work with your hands, just as we told you, ¹²so that your daily life may win the respect of outsiders and so that you will not be dependent on anybody.

The Coming of the Lord

¹³Brothers, we do not want you to be ignorant about those who fall asleep, or to grieve like the rest of men, who have no hope. ¹⁴We believe that Jesus died and rose again and so we believe that God will bring with Jesus those who have fallen asleep in him. ¹⁵According to the Lord's own word, we tell you that we who are still alive, who are left till the coming of the Lord, will certainly not precede those who have fallen asleep. ¹⁶For the Lord himself will come down from heaven, with a loud command, with the voice of the archangel and with the trumpet call of God, and the dead in Christ will rise first. ¹⁷After that, we who are still alive and are left will be caught up together with them in the clouds to meet the Lord in the air. And so we will be with the Lord forever. ¹⁸Therefore encourage each other with these words.

a4 Or learn to live with his own wife; or learn to acquire a wife

---

How are Christians sanctified? (4:3–12)

To be *sanctified* means to be *holy* or to have the quality of *holiness.* It means to become more like Jesus—dedicated and set apart for God's purposes. Some believe sanctification occurs miraculously and instantaneously. Others see it as a process that continues over a lifetime—still a miracle of God. Many combine these views to say that believers are sanctified in Christ and continue to be sanctified as they grow in him.

In this passage Paul lists three areas of life where sanctification can occur: (1) In a relationship with a spouse. Sexual purity cannot be compromised; sexual intimacy is for marriage alone. (2) In relationships between Christians. Trust and love should energize relationships in the church; believers can't live double lives and serve God effectively (vv. 6,9). (3) In relationships with all others. Decent, orderly living according to God's principles should win the respect of those outside the church (vv. 11–12).

With God's help we can choose to obey him, living in line with his will.

5 Now, brothers, about times and dates we do not need to write to you, [2]for you know very well that the day of the Lord[D] will come like a thief in the night. [3]While people are saying, "Peace[D] and safety," destruction will come on them suddenly, as labor pains on a pregnant woman, and they will not escape.

[4]But you, brothers, are not in darkness so that this day should surprise you like a thief. [5]You are all sons of the light and sons of the day. We do not belong to the night or to the darkness. [6]So then, let us not be like others, who are asleep, but let us be alert and self-controlled. [7]For those who sleep, sleep at night, and those who get drunk, get drunk at night. [8]But since we belong to the day, let us be self-controlled, putting on faith and love as a breastplate, and the hope of salvation[D] as a helmet. [9]For God did not appoint us to suffer wrath but to receive salvation through our Lord Jesus Christ. [10]He died for us so that, whether we are awake or asleep, we may live together with him. [11]Therefore encourage one another and build each other up, just as in fact you are doing.

Final Instructions

[12]Now we ask you, brothers, to respect those who work hard among you, who are over you in the Lord and who admonish you. [13]Hold them in the highest regard in love because of their work. Live in peace with each other. [14]And we urge you, brothers, warn those who are idle, encourage the timid, help the weak, be patient with everyone. [15]Make sure that nobody pays back wrong for wrong, but always try to be kind to each other and to everyone else.

[16]Be joyful always; [17]pray continually; [18]give thanks in all circumstances, for this is God's will for you in Christ Jesus.

[19]Do not put out the Spirit's fire; [20]do not treat prophe-

The day of the Lord (5:2)

An Old Testament concept describing the time when God would return to vindicate the righteous and judge the wicked (Isaiah 11:10–11; Amos 5:18). Although it was also used to announce the coming Messiah (Mal. 4:5), the New Testament links it more specifically to Christ's second coming (1 Cor. 1:8; Phil. 1:6; 2 Peter 3:10). *The day of the Lord* is both a time of salvation and also a time of judgment and destruction. See *The day of the LORD* (Zeph. 1:7).

Asleep (5:6)

Earlier Paul used sleep to mean death (4:13–15). Here, *asleep* means being spiritually asleep—unaware of God's will.

Belong to the day (5:8)

This is an extension of the sleep metaphor (see previous note). Because Christians belong to the day, they must have spiritual awareness. Sleep is only appropriate for the night.

Who was *over* the Thessalonians? (5:12)

Church leaders, probably elders who were spiritually mature. Paul usually appointed elders or overseers in the churches (Acts 14:23; 1 Tim. 3:1–7; Titus 1:5–9). Paul called on the people to respect the authority of their elders. They were to obey them unless their authority overstepped Biblical boundaries.

How can people *put out the Spirit's fire?* (5:19)

There are at least two ways individuals can put out the fire of the Spirit: (1) by not giving the Spirit the freedom to act or (2) by attempting to do the Spirit's work in human strength. It is probable that Paul had spiritual gifts in mind, and wanted people to be open to the work of the Spirit. He wanted the Thessalonians to permit the use of spiritual gifts so the church could be built up.

Where are the dead? (4:14,16)

A few take the words *fallen asleep* literally and believe that the dead remain unconscious until the Lord returns. But most see this as a euphemism: that the *body* "sleeps" while the *spirit* remains conscious. When Christians die, their bodies go into the grave while their spirits go to be with Jesus (2 Cor. 5:6–8; Phil. 1:23). When unbelievers die, their bodies go into the grave while their spirits go to a place of torment.

The Old Testament speaks in a limited way about the *grave,* where all go at death. The New Testament uses the Greek word *Hades* for the Old Testament concept (Rev. 20:13), but expands on it considerably. Jesus hinted that *Hades* is divided into two parts—one for the wicked and one for the righteous. For the wicked it is described as torment, agony and fire; for the righteous it is comfort and rest (Luke 16:22–26).

Gehenna is another word for *hell,* the final place of judgment upon the wicked. It was borrowed from the phrase meaning the *Valley of Hinnom,* a place where human sacrifices and pagan worship had occurred (2 Kings 23:10). During New Testament times the place was the Jerusalem city dump where fires burned continually—a graphic image of perpetual torment and judgment (see *Map 8* at the back of this Bible).

When Christ returns, those who have died and are with Jesus will be given new bodies—resurrected, glorified bodies. At the final judgment unbelievers will be thrown into the lake of fire (Rev. 20:11–15).

Why would anyone treat prophecies with contempt? (5:20–21)

Paul's concern is about two opposite errors. On one hand are those that indiscriminately accept everything that claims to be from God. To them Paul says: *Test everything. Hold on to the good.* Prophecy needs to be consistent with Scripture and endorsed by mature leaders (see 1 Cor. 14:29). On the other hand, some have become so skeptical that they are inclined to treat everything with contempt. Rejecting the good along with the bad is an error in the opposite extreme.

Holy kiss (5:26)

In the Jewish synagogues of Paul's time, the kiss was a greeting of respect. Apparently the early Christians adopted this practice, making it a *holy* kiss, intended to show not only Christian love for each other, but love for the Lord.

cies[D] with contempt. **21**Test everything. Hold on to the good. **22**Avoid every kind of evil.

23May God himself, the God of peace[D], sanctify[D] you through and through. May your whole spirit, soul[D] and body be kept blameless at the coming of our Lord Jesus Christ. **24**The one who calls you is faithful and he will do it.

25Brothers, pray for us. **26**Greet all the brothers with a holy kiss[D]. **27**I charge you before the Lord to have this letter read to all the brothers.

28The grace[D] of our Lord Jesus Christ be with you.

2 THESSALONIANS

Why read this book?

Have you ever been puzzled by what's going on in the world around you? This letter provides something stable—an eternal perspective—with which to evaluate society's shifting views. It reminds us that this world is terminal, careening toward its conclusion. But it also reminds us that Christians have a hope for eternity that enables them to live day-to-day in an anti-Christian environment.

Who wrote this book?

The apostle Paul.

To whom was it written and why?

Paul wrote to believers at Thessalonica who, he suspected, needed a stronger dose of the advice he'd given in his first letter.

When was it written?

In the early A.D. 50s, shortly after Paul wrote 1 Thessalonians.

What to look for in 2 Thessalonians:

You'll notice several subjects that parallel those in Paul's first letter to the Thessalonians: suffering (1 Thes. 2:14–16; 2 Thes. 1:3–12); work (1 Thes. 4:9–12; 5:14; 2 Thes. 3:6–15)— and the end times (1 Thes. 4:13—5:11; 2 Thes. 2:1–12). This letter, along with 1 Thessalonians, tells us much of what we know about the end times.

When did these things happen?

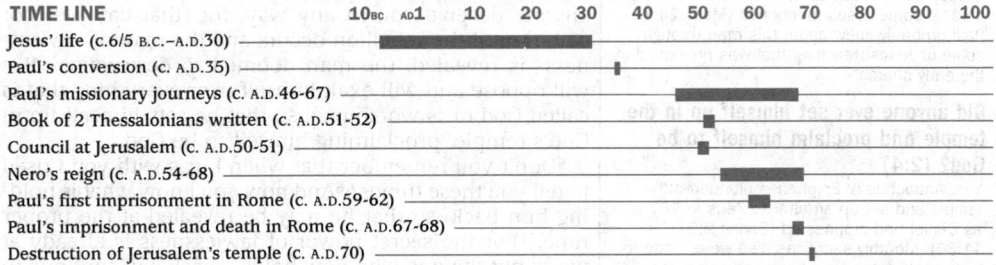

TIME LINE	10 B.C.	A.D.1	10	20	30	40	50	60	70	80	90	100
Jesus' life (c.6/5 B.C.–A.D.30)												
Paul's conversion (c. A.D.35)												
Paul's missionary journeys (c. A.D.46-67)												
Book of 2 Thessalonians written (c. A.D.51-52)												
Council at Jerusalem (c. A.D.50-51)												
Nero's reign (c. A.D.54-68)												
Paul's first imprisonment in Rome (c. A.D.59-62)												
Paul's imprisonment and death in Rome (c. A.D.67-68)												
Destruction of Jerusalem's temple (c. A.D.70)												

What kind of persecutions were the Thessalonians facing? (1:4)

It's possible that secular leaders, thinking that Christians undermined the stability of the political scene, had begun to harass them. Pockets of persecution may have broken out against a family or a leader, and perhaps these had become frequent enough to trouble the church. Some people, no doubt, were beaten, while others may have been imprisoned or robbed of their livelihood.

How did persecution show that God was right? (1:5)

When the righteous suffer, it proves the wickedness of those who persecute. God's judgment yet to come will reward the righteous who suffer, and it will punish the wicked who now inflict pain. The suffering Thessalonians would be rewarded because of their perseverance in suffering.

Blazing fire (1:7)

A metaphor that stresses two things: (1) God will be present. (2) There will be judgment. In the Old Testament fire and judgment are often used together.

Why punish people only because they didn't know God? (1:8)

This expression—borrowed from the Old Testament—was a way of describing those who willfully rejected God, not those who had never heard of him. The phrase *those who do not know God* is another way of saying "those who have no personal relationship with God." Their personal responsibility becomes more clear in the phrase *and do not obey the gospel.* Paul reassured the believers in Thessalonica that justice would eventually come to their persecutors.

Why would anyone think the day of the Lord had already come? (2:2)

Apparently some were genuinely fooled. The false teachers, on the other hand, may have been motivated by a craving for attention and the power to manipulate others.

The man of lawlessness (2:3)

With limited information, there has been much speculation about this man. His deeds (v. 4) parallel some Jesus mentioned (Matt. 24:15). Paul probably knew about this man through some of Jesus' teaching that was preserved in the early church.

Did anyone ever set himself up in the temple and proclaim himself to be God? (2:4)

Yes. Antiochus IV Epiphanes plundered the temple and set up an altar to Zeus in 167 B.C. as Daniel had prophesied (Daniel 9:27; 11:36). Monthly sacrifices also were made to honor Antiochus. Paul borrowed some of the same language here, even though he was speaking of someone yet to come—someone similar to Antiochus, but with a much larger role in history. Paul may have referred to him so people could get a picture of what to look for in this future antichrist. Some understand the false worship to come in the temple in a figurative sense. Others think the temple in Jerusalem will be restored so this can be literally fulfilled.

1 Paul, Silas[a] and Timothy,

To the church of the Thessalonians in God our Father and the Lord Jesus Christ:

2Grace[D] and peace[D] to you from God the Father and the Lord Jesus Christ.

Thanksgiving and Prayer

3We ought always to thank God for you, brothers, and rightly so, because your faith is growing more and more, and the love every one of you has for each other is increasing. **4**Therefore, among God's churches we boast about your perseverance and faith in all the persecutions and trials you are enduring.

5All this is evidence that God's judgment is right, and as a result you will be counted worthy of the kingdom of God[D], for which you are suffering. **6**God is just: He will pay back trouble to those who trouble you **7**and give relief to you who are troubled, and to us as well. This will happen when the Lord Jesus is revealed from heaven in blazing fire with his powerful angels. **8**He will punish those who do not know God and do not obey the gospel[D] of our Lord Jesus. **9**They will be punished with everlasting destruction and shut out from the presence of the Lord and from the majesty of his power **10**on the day he comes to be glorified in his holy people and to be marveled at among all those who have believed. This includes you, because you believed our testimony to you.

11With this in mind, we constantly pray for you, that our God may count you worthy of his calling, and that by his power he may fulfill every good purpose of yours and every act prompted by your faith. **12**We pray this so that the name of our Lord Jesus may be glorified in you, and you in him, according to the grace of our God and the Lord Jesus Christ.[b]

The Man of Lawlessness

2 Concerning the coming of our Lord Jesus Christ and our being gathered to him, we ask you, brothers, **2**not to become easily unsettled or alarmed by some prophecy[D], report or letter supposed to have come from us, saying that the day of the Lord[D] has already come. **3**Don't let anyone deceive you in any way, for ˻that day will not come˼ until the rebellion occurs and the man of lawlessness[c] is revealed, the man doomed to destruction. **4**He will oppose and will exalt himself over everything that is called God or is worshiped, so that he sets himself up in God's temple, proclaiming himself to be God.

5Don't you remember that when I was with you I used to tell you these things? **6**And now you know what is holding him back, so that he may be revealed at the proper time. **7**For the secret power of lawlessness is already at work; but the one who now holds it back will continue to do so till he is taken out of the way. **8**And then the lawless one will be revealed, whom the Lord Jesus will overthrow with the breath of his mouth and destroy by the splendor of his coming. **9**The coming of the lawless one will be in accordance with the work of Satan displayed in all kinds of counterfeit miracles, signs and wonders, **10**and in every sort of evil that deceives those who are perishing. They

---

[a]1 Greek *Silvanus*, a variant of *Silas*   [b]12 Or *God and Lord, Jesus Christ*   [c]3 Some manuscripts *sin*

perish because they refused to love the truth and so be saved. ¹¹For this reason God sends them a powerful delusion so that they will believe the lie ¹²and so that all will be condemned who have not believed the truth but have delighted in wickedness.

Stand Firm

¹³But we ought always to thank God for you, brothers loved by the Lord, because from the beginning God chose you*a* to be saved through the sanctifying^D work of the Spirit and through belief in the truth. ¹⁴He called you to this through our gospel^D, that you might share in the glory^D of our Lord Jesus Christ. ¹⁵So then, brothers, stand firm and hold to the teachings*b* we passed on to you, whether by word of mouth or by letter.

¹⁶May our Lord Jesus Christ himself and God our Father, who loved us and by his grace^D gave us eternal encouragement and good hope, ¹⁷encourage your hearts and strengthen you in every good deed and word.

Request for Prayer

3 Finally, brothers, pray for us that the message of the Lord may spread rapidly and be honored, just as it was with you. ²And pray that we may be delivered from wicked and evil men, for not everyone has faith. ³But the Lord is faithful, and he will strengthen and protect you from the evil one. ⁴We have confidence in the Lord that you are doing and will continue to do the things we command. ⁵May the Lord direct your hearts into God's love and Christ's perseverance.

Warning Against Idleness

⁶In the name of the Lord Jesus Christ, we command you, brothers, to keep away from every brother who is idle and does not live according to the teaching*c* you re-

*a*13 Some manuscripts *because God chose you as his firstfruits*
*b*15 Or *traditions*   *c*6 Or *tradition*

What (or who) is *holding back* the man of lawlessness? (2:6–7)

One view is that Paul in his mission to the Gentiles was holding back this man of lawlessness. Some suggest Paul may have meant the Thessalonian government or the Roman empire. Others think this could mean the church, preventing the rise of the antichrist until it is removed by the Rapture. Still others believe Paul meant that the Holy Spirit would hold back the tide of evil.

Why would God deliberately delude anyone? (2:11)

Those who refuse to believe (v. 10) eventually become incapable of believing. When people resist God, he allows a hardening to develop.

God chose you to be saved (2:13)

See *Who are the elect?* (1 Peter 1:1); also see article: *If God chooses us, do we have any choice?* (Eph. 1:4–5).

Why were idle Christians such a danger? (3:6–13)

For at least three reasons: (1) Their lives were characterized by laziness—a sinful attitude that could spread to others. (2) Other believers felt obligated to provide for the idle Christians, severely draining the church's resources. (3) The idle Christians gave a warped view of Christianity, that those who are most heavenly minded focus only on the return of Christ. Meanwhile, their neglect of practical matters undermined the church's credibility and witness.

What has to happen before Christ returns? (2:3–12)

This passage suggests several things will occur. First, there will be *rebellion*, literally *apostasy*—an abandonment. This will not be a rebellion against the church so much as a defection within the ranks of the church. Second, an individual described as *the man of lawlessness* will come to power, thought by some to be the antichrist (1 John 2:18)—perhaps symbolically portrayed as a beast (Rev. 13:1).

The man of lawlessness will be empowered by Satan to give evidence of his authority with power and signs and false wonders. Many people will be deceived, and they will be judged for believing a lie. After a brief reign on earth, the man of lawlessness will be defeated by Jesus.

There is much speculation over how literally this passage should be interpreted. There have been many throughout history who have been called antichrists. But whether literal or figurative, Paul's words warn about an overall loss of godliness and an increase in rebellion against God. They tell of a man who presumes to put himself in the place of God. Since we know these events will characterize the world before the return of Christ, we must guard against being deceived. We also must live confidently, pleasing Christ, knowing he will be the ultimate victor.

Should this rule be applied today? (3:10)

Any who are unemployed by choice should not receive handouts. In practical terms, however, charity cases are seldom so clear-cut: if a *man* will not work, for example, what should be done for his *children*? Other related issues today (such as welfare, sick-leave and insurance fraud) have become part of the public debate. The Christian response should be one of personal honesty and integrity.

How does it help to withdraw from someone? (3:14)

To *associate with* meant to "mix up together with." Paul's teaching against mixing with the idle seems harsh. But he intended that this practice serve as a warning, not as an excommunication, to one's brothers and sisters in Christ. Other severe forms of church discipline are discussed elsewhere (for example, Titus 3:10).

ceived from us. 7For you yourselves know how you ought to follow our example. We were not idle when we were with you, 8nor did we eat anyone's food without paying for it. On the contrary, we worked night and day, laboring and toiling so that we would not be a burden to any of you. 9We did this, not because we do not have the right to such help, but in order to make ourselves a model for you to follow. 10For even when we were with you, we gave you this rule: "If a man will not work, he shall not eat."

11We hear that some among you are idle. They are not busy; they are busybodies. 12Such people we command and urge in the Lord Jesus Christ to settle down and earn the bread they eat. 13And as for you, brothers, never tire of doing what is right.

14If anyone does not obey our instruction in this letter, take special note of him. Do not associate with him, in order that he may feel ashamed. 15Yet do not regard him as an enemy, but warn him as a brother.

Final Greetings

16Now may the Lord of peace[D] himself give you peace at all times and in every way. The Lord be with all of you.

17I, Paul, write this greeting in my own hand, which is the distinguishing mark in all my letters. This is how I write.

18The grace[D] of our Lord Jesus Christ be with you all.

1 TIMOTHY

Why read this book?

If you learn to play a musical instrument, you'll eventually learn to play that instrument with others. Christians are not solo instruments. They're called to harmonize with others in a group called the church. What you're about to read is like a conductor's handbook. It summarizes guidelines for running a church, offering practical help to believers in their relationships with each other, with church leaders and with the world around them.

Who wrote this book?

Paul, the apostle.

When was it written?

Sometime shortly after Paul was released from imprisonment in Rome, probably around A.D. 63 to 65.

To whom was it written and why?

Paul wrote to Timothy with advice on how to better lead the church at Ephesus (see *The Church in Ephesus* on page 1613). False teachers threatened to undermine Paul's work there and Timothy, one of Paul's dear friends, was in a tough spot.

What to look for in 1 Timothy:

This practical, nitty-gritty wisdom must be understood within the specific situation Paul was addressing. As you read, you might repeatedly ask, "I wonder what conditions in Ephesus prompted Paul to write that?" Look for the underlying principles. You might imagine eavesdropping on the conversation between an older minister and a troubled, younger minister. Though specific problems and answers might never be exactly duplicated, the principles of the gospel never change.

When did these things happen?

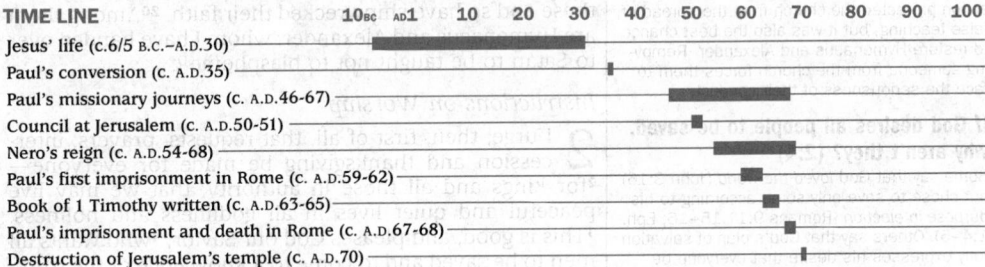

TIME LINE	10 B.C.	A.D.1	10	20	30	40	50	60	70	80	90	100
Jesus' life (c.6/5 B.C.–A.D.30)												
Paul's conversion (c. A.D.35)												
Paul's missionary journeys (c. A.D.46-67)												
Council at Jerusalem (c. A.D.50-51)												
Nero's reign (c. A.D.54-68)												
Paul's first imprisonment in Rome (c. A.D.59-62)												
Book of 1 Timothy written (c. A.D.63-65)												
Paul's imprisonment and death in Rome (c. A.D.67-68)												
Destruction of Jerusalem's temple (c. A.D.70)												

Why did Paul call Timothy a son? (1:2)

Timothy was more than Paul's protégé and co-worker. He was also Paul's special friend and his spiritual son. Paul's ministry had probably led, either directly or indirectly, to Timothy's new life in Christ.

What false teachings were so harmful? (1:3–4)

Paul was concerned about three trends: (1) elitism, an attitude that only a few with special knowledge would be saved; (2) idealism, the teaching that matter was evil; and (3) a fascination with myths and genealogies. These themes ran counter to: (1) salvation based on faith, not knowledge; (2) the goodness of God's creation (and Christ's incarnation); and (3) the sufficiency of Biblical history.

Are the righteous exempt from the law? (1:9)

Not exactly. Because of God's grace and our faith in Jesus Christ, it is possible for us to do what is right. If we did this all the time, we would not need the law. But we don't. No one is 100 percent righteous; we are "works in progress." So we need the law to show us where we fall short.

Is ignorance the basis for mercy? (1:13)

No, ignorance does not earn mercy. The fact is, nothing can earn God's mercy. We still need forgiveness, even if we're unaware that we have sinned. Paul saw that only the mercy and grace of God could reach him in his ignorance. In the same way, we all need God's grace to show us we are sinners in need of salvation (Romans 2:4).

Trustworthy saying (1:15)

This phrase, unique to Paul's pastoral letters to Timothy and Titus, appears four more times (3:1; 4:9; 2 Tim. 2:11; Titus 3:8). It calls attention to an important point.

What prophecies had been made about Timothy? (1:18)

We cannot be sure of the exact prophecies, but it seems likely they were confirmations of Timothy's gifts and call to the ministry. Timothy was someone in whom others saw potential for God's service.

How did Paul hand Hymenaeus and Alexander over to Satan? (1:20)

Paul expelled these men from the body of believers in an attempt to discipline them. Such action protected the church from the spread of false teaching, but it was also the best chance to restore Hymenaeus and Alexander. Removing someone from the church forces them to face the seriousness of their conduct.

If God desires all people to be saved, why aren't they? (2:4)

Some say that God *loved the world* (John 3:16) but chose to save only some according to his *purpose in election* (Romans 9:11,15–16; Eph. 1:4–5). Others say that God's plan of salvation fully expresses his desire that everyone be saved, but requires people to receive or reject him (John 1:11–12). Also see articles: *Does God play favorites?* (Romans 9:8–33) and *If God chooses us, do we have any choice?* (Eph. 1:4–5).

1 Paul, an apostle[D] of Christ Jesus by the command of God our Savior and of Christ Jesus our hope,

2To Timothy my true son in the faith:

Grace[D], mercy[D] and peace[D] from God the Father and Christ Jesus our Lord.

Warning Against False Teachers of the Law

3As I urged you when I went into Macedonia, stay there in Ephesus so that you may command certain men not to teach false doctrines any longer **4**nor to devote themselves to myths and endless genealogies[D]. These promote controversies rather than God's work—which is by faith. **5**The goal of this command is love, which comes from a pure heart and a good conscience and a sincere faith. **6**Some have wandered away from these and turned to meaningless talk. **7**They want to be teachers of the law, but they do not know what they are talking about or what they so confidently affirm.

8We know that the law is good if one uses it properly. **9**We also know that law[a] is made not for the righteous[D] but for lawbreakers and rebels, the ungodly and sinful, the unholy and irreligious; for those who kill their fathers or mothers, for murderers, **10**for adulterers and perverts, for slave traders and liars and perjurers—and for whatever else is contrary to the sound doctrine **11**that conforms to the glorious gospel[D] of the blessed God, which he entrusted to me.

The Lord's Grace to Paul

12I thank Christ Jesus our Lord, who has given me strength, that he considered me faithful, appointing me to his service. **13**Even though I was once a blasphemer and a persecutor and a violent man, I was shown mercy because I acted in ignorance and unbelief. **14**The grace of our Lord was poured out on me abundantly, along with the faith and love that are in Christ Jesus.

15Here is a trustworthy saying that deserves full acceptance: Christ Jesus came into the world to save sinners—of whom I am the worst. **16**But for that very reason I was shown mercy so that in me, the worst of sinners, Christ Jesus might display his unlimited patience as an example for those who would believe on him and receive eternal life[D]. **17**Now to the King eternal, immortal, invisible, the only God, be honor and glory[D] for ever and ever. Amen.

18Timothy, my son, I give you this instruction in keeping with the prophecies[D] once made about you, so that by following them you may fight the good fight, **19**holding on to faith and a good conscience. Some have rejected these and so have shipwrecked their faith. **20**Among them are Hymenaeus and Alexander, whom I have handed over to Satan to be taught not to blaspheme[D].

Instructions on Worship

2 I urge, then, first of all, that requests, prayers, intercession and thanksgiving be made for everyone— **2**for kings and all those in authority, that we may live peaceful and quiet lives in all godliness and holiness. **3**This is good, and pleases God our Savior, **4**who wants all men to be saved and to come to a knowledge of the truth. **5**For there is one God and one mediator between God and men, the man Christ Jesus, **6**who gave himself as a ran-

*a*9 Or *that the law*

som for all men—the testimony given in its proper time. **7**And for this purpose I was appointed a herald and an apostle[D]—I am telling the truth, I am not lying—and a teacher of the true faith to the Gentiles[D].

8I want men everywhere to lift up holy hands in prayer, without anger or disputing.

9I also want women to dress modestly, with decency and propriety, not with braided hair or gold or pearls or expensive clothes, **10**but with good deeds, appropriate for women who profess to worship God.

11A woman should learn in quietness and full submission. **12**I do not permit a woman to teach or to have authority over a man; she must be silent. **13**For Adam was formed first, then Eve. **14**And Adam was not the one deceived; it was the woman who was deceived and became a sinner. **15**But women[a] will be saved[b] through childbearing—if they continue in faith, love and holiness with propriety.

Overseers and Deacons

3 Here is a trustworthy saying: If anyone sets his heart on being an overseer[D],[c] he desires a noble task. **2**Now the overseer must be above reproach, the husband of but one wife, temperate, self-controlled, respectable, hospitable, able to teach, **3**not given to drunkenness, not violent but gentle, not quarrelsome, not a lover of money. **4**He must manage his own family well and see that his children obey him with proper respect. **5**(If anyone does not know how to manage his own family, how can he take care of God's church?) **6**He must not be a recent convert, or he may become conceited and fall under the same judgment as the devil. **7**He must also have a

[a]15 Greek *she*   [b]15 Or *restored*   [c]1 Traditionally *bishop*; also in verse 2

Lift up holy hands (2:8)

The common prayer posture in Judaism and early Christianity. See *Why lift up hands to worship God?* (Psalm 63:4).

What's wrong with hair-dos, jewelry, and fashion? (2:9)

The problem, as most see it, is not the style but the distraction. Apparently, in the Ephesian church, extravagant clothing, hair styles and jewelry were distracting to the worshipers.

Why single out women to talk about modesty? (2:9–10)

In Paul's day modesty was especially important for women because both the Jewish and Hellenistic traditions associated extravagant female styles with sexual license.

Why can't a woman teach a man? (2:12)

Christian women enjoyed more freedom to learn than either Jewish or Greek women of the day. It's possible Paul decided that permitting women to learn was revolutionary enough for that time. Also see article: *Why silence the women?* (2:11).

What does it mean for a woman to be saved through childbearing? (2:15)

Some, because of the phrasing in the original language (literally, *through the childbirth*), take it to mean the birth of Christ which brought salvation. Others suggest that Paul, speaking to the Ephesian situation, felt that the women of the church would be less susceptible to false teachers if they were involved in the care of their families. See article: *Why silence the women?* (2:11).

Trustworthy saying (3:1)

See *Trustworthy saying* (1:15).

Why silence the women? (2:11)

I t's possible Paul means that women in all times and cultures are not to say anything in church or to have authority over men. That would seem to be the conclusion when he says Eve, created second, was first to be deceived (vv. 13–14).

The difficulty with this view, however, is that elsewhere Paul recognizes the authority of women for teaching and evangelizing (Romans 16:1–3; Phil. 4:2–3). To sort out the discrepancy, some think Paul was simply giving advice here on how Christians could accommodate themselves to imperfect cultural conditions—just as he did when he advised slaves without advocating the institution of slavery (6:1–2).

Timothy faced a situation where false teachers (probably church elders) were preying on women—young widows in particular. Restricting their public involvement in church would (1) dramatically undercut the support of the false teachers and (2) gain respect for the church in the Ephesian community at large.

Paul wanted to present the Ephesian church in the best possible light so the gospel would have a better chance of being heard in an essentially hostile environment. He also wanted women to learn (something denied Jewish and Greek women) under calm, peaceful conditions. When we understand Paul's "rules" in this context, we see that he was recommending things to help the church gain integrity in the community. People today disagree about how far those restrictions should be applied.

Overseer (3:1)

A secular Greek term for anyone who had oversight over any project or person. Paul borrows the term for church use.

What does it take to be an overseer in the church? (3:2–7)

Paul probably did not intend this list to be exhaustive. But he wanted to ensure that church leaders would indeed be able to lead. He also wanted to show the culture at large that the church was a respectable institution. He listed qualities that the Greeks admired and used in their own lists of qualifications for leadership positions.

What's the difference between a deacon and an overseer? (3:8–12)

In the language of Paul's day, a deacon was a servant. Whereas overseers led through prayer and the ministry of the word, deacons led by serving in other areas of church life.

How does serving well enhance one's spiritual standing? (3:13)

Some believe Paul means that those who serve well in their assigned duties in the church will be promoted to a higher rank, that of an overseer, for example. Others believe that Paul suggests that those who serve well will gain respect in the eyes of the church and good standing in God's sight.

What's the mystery about godliness? (3:16)

Godliness is somewhat of a paradox: "Trying" to be godly can be dangerous; religious efforts inevitably become too self-centered. Yet, if we don't pay attention to our spiritual side, how can it improve? The solution to this dilemma is to concentrate on Jesus Christ, the subject of this poem. By focusing on him, we can actually move toward inner spiritual maturity. This is the mystery of godliness.

How does the Spirit clearly say things? (4:1)

God speaks to believers in many ways, none of which can be reduced to a formula. Here Paul is probably speaking of a direct revelation that the Spirit gave him. The Spirit also speaks to us through the Bible, in prayer, opportunities and the counsel of godly people.

Later times (4:1)

The time between the first and second comings of Jesus Christ. This admittedly ambiguous term was meant more to describe the general spiritual climate than to pinpoint a date.

What's wrong with abstinence? (4:3–4)

Nothing, unless one abstains out of the mistaken notion (typical of some false teachers known as the Gnostics) that anything material is bad. They claimed that the less contact we have with the evil physical creation, the better. Paul makes the point that God's creation was good. Even though it was marred in the fall, its essential goodness remains.

Trustworthy saying (4:9)

See Trustworthy saying (1:15).

---

good reputation with outsiders, so that he will not fall into disgrace and into the devil's trap.

8Deacons, likewise, are to be men worthy of respect, sincere, not indulging in much wine, and not pursuing dishonest gain. **9**They must keep hold of the deep truths of the faith with a clear conscience. **10**They must first be tested; and then if there is nothing against them, let them serve as deacons.

11In the same way, their wives[a] are to be women worthy of respect, not malicious talkers but temperate and trustworthy in everything.

12A deacon must be the husband of but one wife and must manage his children and his household well. **13**Those who have served well gain an excellent standing and great assurance in their faith in Christ Jesus.

14Although I hope to come to you soon, I am writing you these instructions so that, **15**if I am delayed, you will know how people ought to conduct themselves in God's household, which is the church of the living God, the pillar and foundation of the truth. **16**Beyond all question, the mystery[D] of godliness is great:

> He[b] appeared in a body,[c]
> was vindicated by the Spirit,
> was seen by angels,
> was preached among the nations,
> was believed on in the world,
> was taken up in glory[D].

Instructions to Timothy

4 The Spirit clearly says that in later times some will abandon the faith and follow deceiving spirits and things taught by demons. **2**Such teachings come through hypocritical liars, whose consciences have been seared as with a hot iron. **3**They forbid people to marry and order them to abstain from certain foods, which God created to be received with thanksgiving by those who believe and who know the truth. **4**For everything God created is good, and nothing is to be rejected if it is received with thanksgiving, **5**because it is consecrated[D] by the word of God and prayer.

6If you point these things out to the brothers, you will be a good minister of Christ Jesus, brought up in the truths of the faith and of the good teaching that you have followed. **7**Have nothing to do with godless myths and old wives' tales; rather, train yourself to be godly. **8**For physical training is of some value, but godliness has value for all things, holding promise for both the present life and the life to come.

9This is a trustworthy saying that deserves full acceptance **10**(and for this we labor and strive), that we have put our hope in the living God, who is the Savior of all men, and especially of those who believe.

11Command and teach these things. **12**Don't let anyone look down on you because you are young, but set an example for the believers in speech, in life, in love, in faith and in purity. **13**Until I come, devote yourself to the public reading of Scripture, to preaching and to teaching. **14**Do not neglect your gift, which was given you through a prophetic message when the body of elders laid their hands on you.

---

a 11 Or way, deaconesses   *b 16 Some manuscripts God*   *c 16 Or in the flesh*

15Be diligent in these matters; give yourself wholly to them, so that everyone may see your progress. **16**Watch your life and doctrine closely. Persevere in them, because if you do, you will save both yourself and your hearers.

Advice About Widows, Elders and Slaves

5 Do not rebuke an older man harshly, but exhort him as if he were your father. Treat younger men as brothers, **2**older women as mothers, and younger women as sisters, with absolute purity.

3Give proper recognition to those widows who are really in need. **4**But if a widow has children or grandchildren, these should learn first of all to put their religion into practice by caring for their own family and so repaying their parents and grandparents, for this is pleasing to God. **5**The widow who is really in need and left all alone puts her hope in God and continues night and day to pray and to ask God for help. **6**But the widow who lives for pleasure is dead even while she lives. **7**Give the people these instructions, too, so that no one may be open to blame. **8**If anyone does not provide for his relatives, and especially for his immediate family, he has denied the faith and is worse than an unbeliever.

9No widow may be put on the list of widows unless she is over sixty, has been faithful to her husband,*a* **10**and is well known for her good deeds, such as bringing up children, showing hospitality, washing the feet of the saints**D**, helping those in trouble and devoting herself to all kinds of good deeds.

11As for younger widows, do not put them on such a list. For when their sensual desires overcome their dedication to Christ, they want to marry. **12**Thus they bring judgment on themselves, because they have broken their first pledge. **13**Besides, they get into the habit of being idle and going about from house to house. And not only do they become idlers, but also gossips and busybodies, saying things they ought not to. **14**So I counsel younger widows to marry, to have children, to manage their homes and to give the enemy no opportunity for slander. **15**Some have in fact already turned away to follow Satan.

16If any woman who is a believer has widows in her family, she should help them and not let the church be burdened with them, so that the church can help those widows who are really in need.

17The elders who direct the affairs of the church well are worthy of double honor, especially those whose work is preaching and teaching. **18**For the Scripture says, "Do not muzzle the ox while it is treading out the grain,"*b* and "The worker deserves his wages."*c* **19**Do not entertain an accusation against an elder unless it is brought by two or three witnesses. **20**Those who sin are to be rebuked publicly, so that the others may take warning.

21I charge you, in the sight of God and Christ Jesus and the elect**D** angels, to keep these instructions without partiality, and to do nothing out of favoritism.

22Do not be hasty in the laying on of hands, and do not share in the sins of others. Keep yourself pure.

23Stop drinking only water, and use a little wine because of your stomach and your frequent illnesses.

24The sins of some men are obvious, reaching the place of judgment ahead of them; the sins of others trail behind

What does it mean to neglect one's gift? (4:14)

Having a God-given gift is not enough. Through use and service, both talents and spiritual gifts can be developed and made even more effective. To sidestep opportunities to serve the Lord is to neglect gifts. They can waste away to nothing if left dormant.

Why not help widows under sixty? (5:9)

Paul was dealing with two issues: widows in need and widows being intellectually seduced by false teaching. See article: *Why silence the women?* (2:11). He felt that they would be overwhelmed by their feelings and want to marry (v. 11) and that their idleness would make them more vulnerable spiritually (v. 13). In addition, younger widows could, for the most part, take care of themselves better than older widows. Sixty was probably an arbitrary number —an organizational necessity.

How should elders be honored? (5:17)

Paul wanted to reaffirm elders who taught the truth faithfully. The *double honor* they were to receive included financial support (v. 18).

Why make a special case for elders accused of sin? (5:19–22)

Paul recognized that those who assume ministry responsibilities open themselves up to unwarranted attacks. The false teachers themselves may have led the way in accusing the faithful elders of the church. So Paul reminded Timothy that rumor and innuendo about those in charge were to be dismissed if the stories could not be substantiated by another witness or two.

How do you rebuke an elder? (5:20)

Publicly—to uphold the integrity of the church and warn others of the consequences of sin. However, accusations should not be made public unless and until they are substantiated. Otherwise an innocent leader's reputation could be damaged.

Can a fallen elder be reinstated? (5:20)

Some feel that leaders who abuse their trust have jeopardized their own ministry. Depending on the severity of the offense, it may take longer to regain the confidence of the church. In extreme cases, some say a fallen minister should never be put back in a position of ministry. Others feel that, given enough time to prove one's integrity again, a leader can be restored to a former position like any other fallen believer (Gal. 6:1).

Why did Paul recommend wine? (5:23)

There was widespread medicinal use of wine in both Jewish and Greek circles at the time. Timothy must have had stomachaches and Paul believed wine would calm his stomach. Paul may have had an additional motive: to challenge the asceticism of the false teachers.

a9 Or has had but one husband   *b18 Deut. 25:4*   *c18 Luke 10:7*

How are sins and good deeds revealed? (5:24–25)

Sometimes they are obvious; sometimes it takes time to see them. The elders at Ephesus who were false teachers had hidden sins that would later become evident. So Paul recommended caution—careful "background checks" on those being considered for leadership positions. The most damaging spiritual sins (such as pride and greed) are often the most difficult to detect. In many cases such sins are initially masked as hard work and diligence.

Did Paul favor slavery? (6:1)

See article: *Why doesn't the Bible condemn slavery?* (1 Peter 2:18–21).

What is the difference between concern over doctrine and quarrels about words? (6:4)

See *Which controversies are foolish?* (Titus 3:9).

What is *godliness with contentment?* (6:6–8)

Paul takes a term popular in stoic philosophy at the time, *contentment,* and invests it with Christian meaning. For the Stoics it meant the feeling of being self-sufficient. Paul says it's the feeling that comes from finding sufficiency in Christ. Godliness is profitable, but not in a financial sense. Rather, godliness yields peace of mind—contentment. Contentment is both the sign of true godliness and the reward of true godliness.

Is a desire for money always a root of evil? (6:9–11)

Not always. One can desire money for Christ-centered, not self-centered purposes. Paul assumes some will be rich (vv. 17–18). His counsel to the rich is to be humble, to trust in God rather than money, and to be interested in good deeds, not bank accounts. The key is to focus on the right things.

Is it possible to keep a command like this *without spot or blame?* (6:11–14)

No. But Paul is in the inspirational mode here. Like a coach who gives his team a pep talk, Paul effectively encourages us: "Aim for the best; work to achieve it." With the help of God's grace we can move closer to the goal.

With what false knowledge did Paul contend? (6:20)

See *What false teachings were so harmful?* (1:3–4).

them. [25]In the same way, good deeds are obvious, and even those that are not cannot be hidden.

6 All who are under the yoke[D] of slavery should consider their masters worthy of full respect, so that God's name and our teaching may not be slandered. [2]Those who have believing masters are not to show less respect for them because they are brothers. Instead, they are to serve them even better, because those who benefit from their service are believers, and dear to them. These are the things you are to teach and urge on them.

Love of Money

[3]If anyone teaches false doctrines and does not agree to the sound instruction of our Lord Jesus Christ and to godly teaching, [4]he is conceited and understands nothing. He has an unhealthy interest in controversies and quarrels about words that result in envy, strife, malicious talk, evil suspicions [5]and constant friction between men of corrupt mind, who have been robbed of the truth and who think that godliness is a means to financial gain.

[6]But godliness with contentment is great gain. [7]For we brought nothing into the world, and we can take nothing out of it. [8]But if we have food and clothing, we will be content with that. [9]People who want to get rich fall into temptation and a trap and into many foolish and harmful desires that plunge men into ruin and destruction. [10]For the love of money is a root of all kinds of evil. Some people, eager for money, have wandered from the faith and pierced themselves with many griefs.

Paul's Charge to Timothy

[11]But you, man of God, flee from all this, and pursue righteousness[D], godliness, faith, love, endurance and gentleness. [12]Fight the good fight of the faith. Take hold of the eternal life[D] to which you were called when you made your good confession in the presence of many witnesses. [13]In the sight of God, who gives life to everything, and of Christ Jesus, who while testifying before Pontius Pilate made the good confession, I charge you [14]to keep this command without spot or blame until the appearing of our Lord Jesus Christ, [15]which God will bring about in his own time—God, the blessed and only Ruler, the King of kings and Lord of lords, [16]who alone is immortal and who lives in unapproachable light, whom no one has seen or can see. To him be honor and might forever. Amen.

[17]Command those who are rich in this present world not to be arrogant nor to put their hope in wealth, which is so uncertain, but to put their hope in God, who richly provides us with everything for our enjoyment. [18]Command them to do good, to be rich in good deeds, and to be generous and willing to share. [19]In this way they will lay up treasure for themselves as a firm foundation for the coming age, so that they may take hold of the life that is truly life.

[20]Timothy, guard what has been entrusted to your care. Turn away from godless chatter and the opposing ideas of what is falsely called knowledge, [21]which some have professed and in so doing have wandered from the faith.

Grace[D] be with you.

2 TIMOTHY

Why read this book?

The last words of a dying person often have a significant impact on others. In a sense, 2 Timothy is like that. It's advice from someone who knows he's come to the end of life. Paul, imprisoned in Rome for the second time, realized he would not be released. Facing death as a martyr, he wrote carefully and deliberately to the heart of the gospel. His "dying words" are words for us to live by.

Who wrote this book?

Paul, the apostle.

When was it written?

Probably A.D. 66 to 67, while Paul was held in a Roman prison.

Why was it written?

Many of Paul's supporters, perhaps sensing the hopelessness of his situation, had abandoned him in prison. Time hung heavy for Paul who was suffering both physically and emotionally. His difficult circumstance, concern for the churches he'd begun and, not least of all, his love for Timothy, spurred him to write these words.

What to look for in 2 Timothy:

Look for pithy statements, Paul's attempts to pull together the wisdom of a lifetime of service to God. Watch particularly for the ways he challenged Timothy to a more effective ministry. The nuggets contained in this book were forged in the crucible of life-threatening experiences, but they point to the hope that belongs to all of us in Christ.

When did these things happen?

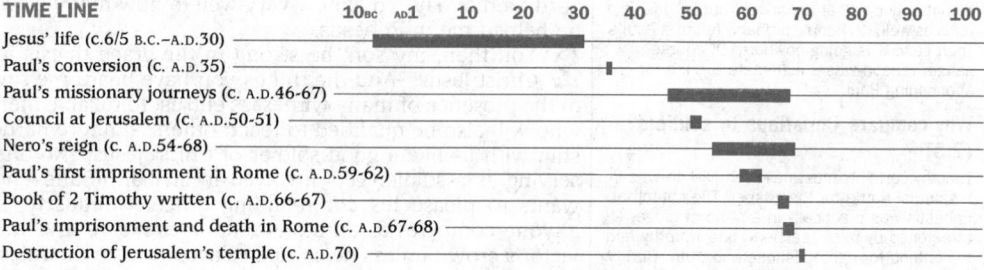

TIME LINE	10 B.C. A.D.1	10	20	30	40	50	60	70	80	90	100
Jesus' life (c.6/5 B.C.–A.D.30)											
Paul's conversion (c. A.D.35)											
Paul's missionary journeys (c. A.D.46-67)											
Council at Jerusalem (c. A.D.50-51)											
Nero's reign (c. A.D.54-68)											
Paul's first imprisonment in Rome (c. A.D.59-62)											
Book of 2 Timothy written (c. A.D.66-67)											
Paul's imprisonment and death in Rome (c. A.D.67-68)											
Destruction of Jerusalem's temple (c. A.D.70)											

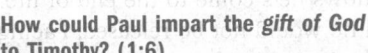

1 Paul, an apostle^D of Christ Jesus by the will of God, according to the promise of life that is in Christ Jesus,

²To Timothy, my dear son:

Grace^D, mercy^D and peace^D from God the Father and Christ Jesus our Lord.

Encouragement to Be Faithful

³I thank God, whom I serve, as my forefathers did, with a clear conscience, as night and day I constantly remember you in my prayers. ⁴Recalling your tears, I long to see you, so that I may be filled with joy. ⁵I have been reminded of your sincere faith, which first lived in your grandmother Lois and in your mother Eunice and, I am persuaded, now lives in you also. ⁶For this reason I remind you to fan into flame the gift of God, which is in you through the laying on of my hands. ⁷For God did not give us a spirit of timidity, but a spirit of power, of love and of self-discipline.

⁸So do not be ashamed to testify about our Lord, or ashamed of me his prisoner. But join with me in suffering for the gospel^D, by the power of God, ⁹who has saved us and called us to a holy life—not because of anything we have done but because of his own purpose and grace. This grace was given us in Christ Jesus before the beginning of time, ¹⁰but it has now been revealed through the appearing of our Savior, Christ Jesus, who has destroyed death^D and has brought life and immortality to light through the gospel. ¹¹And of this gospel I was appointed a herald and an apostle and a teacher. ¹²That is why I am suffering as I am. Yet I am not ashamed, because I know whom I have believed, and am convinced that he is able to guard what I have entrusted to him for that day.

¹³What you heard from me, keep as the pattern of sound teaching, with faith and love in Christ Jesus. ¹⁴Guard the good deposit that was entrusted to you—guard it with the help of the Holy Spirit who lives in us. ¹⁵You know that everyone in the province of Asia has deserted me, including Phygelus and Hermogenes.

¹⁶May the Lord show mercy to the household of Onesiphorus, because he often refreshed me and was not ashamed of my chains. ¹⁷On the contrary, when he was in Rome, he searched hard for me until he found me. ¹⁸May the Lord grant that he will find mercy from the Lord on that day! You know very well in how many ways he helped me in Ephesus.

2 You then, my son, be strong in the grace that is in Christ Jesus. ²And the things you have heard me say in the presence of many witnesses entrust to reliable men who will also be qualified to teach others. ³Endure hardship with us like a good soldier of Christ Jesus. ⁴No one serving as a soldier gets involved in civilian affairs—he wants to please his commanding officer. ⁵Similarly, if anyone competes as an athlete, he does not receive the victor's crown unless he competes according to the rules. ⁶The hardworking farmer should be the first to receive a share of the crops. ⁷Reflect on what I am saying, for the Lord will give you insight into all this.

⁸Remember Jesus Christ, raised from the dead, descended from David. This is my gospel, ⁹for which I am suffering even to the point of being chained like a criminal. But God's word is not chained. ¹⁰Therefore I endure everything for the sake of the elect^D, that they too may

---

How could Paul impart the *gift of God* to Timothy? (1:6)

When he saw Timothy's dedication and abilities, Paul and the church elders set him apart for ministry. Putting their hands on him and praying for him, they prophesied concerning the work he would do (1 Tim. 4:14). God used Paul to help Timothy realize his God-given potential.

What is *a holy life*? (1:9)

A holy life does not necessarily mean one of sinless perfection. First and foremost, it means to be dedicated to the Lord. God wants us to be motivated to faithfully honor and serve him.

Good deposit (1:14)

The gospel. This was especially important in Ephesus, where false teachers were changing and adding to the basic meaning of the message of the gospel.

Why did everyone in Asia abandon Paul? (1:15)

Confined to his prison cell, Paul probably felt even more abandoned than he was. But there are two possible reasons why his former supporters neglected him: (1) It would have been difficult to maintain their contact while separated not only by great distances, but by prison walls as well. (2) People probably felt that Paul's court case was going nowhere. Of course, neither reason was a legitimate excuse for abandoning Paul.

Why compare Christians to soldiers? (2:3)

Timothy certainly must have felt like he was in a spiritual battle for the gospel. The church at Ephesus was practically in a state of siege, threatened by false teachers, and Timothy had to contend for righteousness and truth. But since all analogies have limitations, Paul also compared the Christian's life to that of a farmer and an athlete (vv. 5–6).

Who are *the elect*? (2:10)

There are two possibilities: (1) those whom God has chosen to be saved before time began; (2) those who, through God's grace and power, chose to accept his offer of salvation. See *Who are the elect?* (1 Peter 1:1).

obtain the salvation[D] that is in Christ Jesus, with eternal glory[D]. [11]Here is a trustworthy saying:

> If we died with him,
>   we will also live with him;
> [12]if we endure,
>   we will also reign with him.
> If we disown him,
>   he will also disown us;
> [13]if we are faithless,
>   he will remain faithful,
>   for he cannot disown himself.

A Workman Approved by God

[14]Keep reminding them of these things. Warn them before God against quarreling about words; it is of no value, and only ruins those who listen. [15]Do your best to present yourself to God as one approved, a workman who does not need to be ashamed and who correctly handles the word of truth. [16]Avoid godless chatter, because those who indulge in it will become more and more ungodly. [17]Their teaching will spread like gangrene. Among them are Hymenaeus and Philetus, [18]who have wandered away from the truth. They say that the resurrection[D] has already taken place, and they destroy the faith of some. [19]Nevertheless, God's solid foundation stands firm, sealed with this inscription: "The Lord knows those who are his,"[a] and, "Everyone who confesses the name of the Lord must turn away from wickedness."

[20]In a large house there are articles not only of gold and silver, but also of wood and clay; some are for noble purposes and some for ignoble. [21]If a man cleanses himself from the latter, he will be an instrument for noble purposes, made holy, useful to the Master and prepared to do any good work.

[22]Flee the evil desires of youth, and pursue righteousness[D], faith, love and peace[D], along with those who call on the Lord out of a pure heart. [23]Don't have anything to do with foolish and stupid arguments, because you know they produce quarrels. [24]And the Lord's servant must not quarrel; instead, he must be kind to everyone, able to teach, not resentful. [25]Those who oppose him he must gently instruct, in the hope that God will grant them repentance[D] leading them to a knowledge of the truth, [26]and that they will come to their senses and escape from the trap of the devil, who has taken them captive to do his will.

Godlessness in the Last Days

3 But mark this: There will be terrible times in the last days. [2]People will be lovers of themselves, lovers of money, boastful, proud, abusive, disobedient to their parents, ungrateful, unholy, [3]without love, unforgiving, slanderous, without self-control, brutal, not lovers of the good, [4]treacherous, rash, conceited, lovers of pleasure rather than lovers of God— [5]having a form of godliness but denying its power. Have nothing to do with them.

[6]They are the kind who worm their way into homes and gain control over weak-willed women, who are loaded down with sins and are swayed by all kinds of evil desires, [7]always learning but never able to acknowledge the

[a]19 Num. 16:5 (see Septuagint)

Trustworthy saying (2:11)
See *Trustworthy saying* (1 Tim. 1:15).

Can we earn God's approval? (2:15)
No. But we can do our best to allow God's work to show in our lives. Though we are approved by grace, not works, we demonstrate that we have been approved when the results of his grace in us can be seen. What we are on the inside is recognized by the evidence we produce on the outside (Matt. 7:16).

What does it mean to confess the name of the Lord? (2:19)
To confess his name means that we willingly identify ourselves with him, that we belong to him. Just as a child who is adopted takes the surname of his adoptive parents, so we take on the name of Christ. The counterpart of us confessing his name is that *the Lord knows those who are his.*

What are *foolish and stupid arguments?* (2:23)
See *Which controversies are foolish?* (Titus 3:9).

How can one correct opponents gently? (2:24–25)
Apparently the false teachers at Ephesus thrived on debate. Several times in his letters Paul warned Timothy not to get caught up in such arguments. He was not suggesting, however, that the gospel should be compromised. He wanted the gospel proclaimed with confidence, yet with an attitude of love and respect for the listeners. Even opponents listen better when they are treated with respect. But when opponents insist on antagonistic debate, Paul says it's better to back away.

Last days (3:1)
A Jewish term referring to prophecies of judgment and the end of time. See *Last days* (Isaiah 2:2). Christians used it to refer to those events that would occur just before the second coming of Christ. The term is not too specific, however, since some saw the signs of those events in their first-century society. Also see *How could Peter say the end of all things is near?* (1 Peter 4:7).

A form of godliness (3:5)
Refers to a concentration on the externals of religion—the worship forms, ascetic practices, memorizing religious trivia—without really understanding the basics. True godliness begins only when one submits to God and accepts his Son, Jesus Christ.

What's the difference between *learning and acknowledging truth?* (3:7)
It's possible to know all about God without ever actually knowing God himself. To know about God is to recognize that he exists, creates, rules and even saves. To actually know God, however, means to admit our inadequacy and our need for God and then to give ourselves up to God. To *acknowledge the truth* is the step that brings us into the kingdom.

Jannes and Jambres (3:8)

Although they are not referred to in the Old Testament, Jewish tradition said they were the Egyptian court magicians who opposed Moses (Exodus 7:11).

In what ways are the godly persecuted? (3:12)

Persecution can take many forms—physical, emotional and even spiritual. While some may be tortured and killed for their faith, others may face ridicule and scorn. We should not think we will escape what Jesus and the apostles went through—persecution at the hands of the authorities. Genuine Christianity is unpopular and threatens the vested interests of the world. Being a Christian means to go against the "spirit of the age," for which we can expect to suffer.

God-breathed (3:16)

Paul says that we have God's authoritative Word. God initiated the Bible and inspired its writers. God safeguarded it from error and guided its compilation. The Bible we have is precisely the Word God wanted us to have.

In season and out of season (4:2)

Paul was encouraging Timothy to be persistent. But whether it is persistence in the face of Timothy's mood swings that Paul had in mind, or whether he was referring to the hot and cold reception his teaching received is not clear.

truth. **8**Just as Jannes and Jambres opposed Moses, so also these men oppose the truth—men of depraved minds, who, as far as the faith is concerned, are rejected. **9**But they will not get very far because, as in the case of those men, their folly will be clear to everyone.

Paul's Charge to Timothy

10You, however, know all about my teaching, my way of life, my purpose, faith, patience, love, endurance, **11**persecutions, sufferings—what kinds of things happened to me in Antioch, Iconium and Lystra, the persecutions I endured. Yet the Lord rescued me from all of them. **12**In fact, everyone who wants to live a godly life in Christ Jesus will be persecuted, **13**while evil men and impostors will go from bad to worse, deceiving and being deceived. **14**But as for you, continue in what you have learned and have become convinced of, because you know those from whom you learned it, **15**and how from infancy you have known the holy Scriptures, which are able to make you wise for salvation[D] through faith in Christ Jesus. **16**All Scripture is God-breathed and is useful for teaching, rebuking, correcting and training in righteousness[D], **17**so that the man of God may be thoroughly equipped for every good work.

4 In the presence of God and of Christ Jesus, who will judge the living and the dead, and in view of his appearing and his kingdom, I give you this charge: **2**Preach the Word; be prepared in season and out of season; correct, rebuke and encourage—with great patience and careful instruction. **3**For the time will come when men will not put up with sound doctrine. Instead, to suit their own desires, they will gather around them a great number

How do we know what doctrine is sound? (4:3)

Sound doctrine is the eternal, unchanging truth about God and the gospel. Doctrine that merely scratches "itching ears" cares nothing for the truth; its concern is that it sound good. It focuses on what the listeners want to hear—and on what they will pay for. The distinction is not always so neat, however. Sound doctrine does sound good to some ears. And even the most crass manipulator comes up with bits of truth. Here is a description of the range of approaches to doctrine:

Charlatans. At one end of the scale, charlatans cheat and deceive to sell their ideas. They change their message when it's in their own interest to do so, paying close attention to the likes and dislikes of their audience. Charlatans want the power and profit that goes with a "successful" teaching career. Paul viewed the false teachers in Ephesus as charlatans.

Marketers. In the middle of the scale are marketers—salesmen of religious ideas, experts at whetting people's appetites for their ideas. Sometimes they use tactics that border on the manipulative. Marketers know what they want to communicate, but they're willing to modify it somewhat to help it sell. Marketers are only half-motivated by self-interest. They also have a genuine desire to serve their audience.

Contextualizers. At the other end of the scale are contextualizers—those whose goal is to communicate so people can understand, guarding the integrity of the message as they do. Missionaries, for example, look for the best way to communicate across cultural boundaries. Contextualizers are sincere—concerned about their listeners rather than their own personal gain.

of teachers to say what their itching ears want to hear. [4]They will turn their ears away from the truth and turn aside to myths. [5]But you, keep your head in all situations, endure hardship, do the work of an evangelist, discharge all the duties of your ministry.

[6]For I am already being poured out like a drink offering[D], and the time has come for my departure. [7]I have fought the good fight, I have finished the race, I have kept the faith. [8]Now there is in store for me the crown of righteousness[D], which the Lord, the righteous[D] Judge, will award to me on that day—and not only to me, but also to all who have longed for his appearing.

Personal Remarks

[9]Do your best to come to me quickly, [10]for Demas, because he loved this world, has deserted me and has gone to Thessalonica. Crescens has gone to Galatia, and Titus to Dalmatia. [11]Only Luke is with me. Get Mark and bring him with you, because he is helpful to me in my ministry. [12]I sent Tychicus to Ephesus. [13]When you come, bring the cloak that I left with Carpus at Troas, and my scrolls, especially the parchments.

[14]Alexander the metalworker did me a great deal of harm. The Lord will repay him for what he has done. [15]You too should be on your guard against him, because he strongly opposed our message.

[16]At my first defense, no one came to my support, but everyone deserted me. May it not be held against them. [17]But the Lord stood at my side and gave me strength, so that through me the message might be fully proclaimed and all the Gentiles[D] might hear it. And I was delivered from the lion's mouth. [18]The Lord will rescue me from every evil attack and will bring me safely to his heavenly kingdom. To him be glory[D] for ever and ever. Amen.

Final Greetings

[19]Greet Priscilla[a] and Aquila and the household of Onesiphorus. [20]Erastus stayed in Corinth, and I left Trophimus sick in Miletus. [21]Do your best to get here before winter. Eubulus greets you, and so do Pudens, Linus, Claudia and all the brothers.

[22]The Lord be with your spirit. Grace[D] be with you.

Drink offering (4:6)

In the Old Testament sacrificial system, this was the wine poured out around the base of the altar as an offering to God. As the end of his life approached, Paul saw the drink offering as an analogy for his life—poured out and given to God.

Was Paul discouraged? (4:9–11)

Perhaps. Some of these people were co-workers whom Paul truly loved, and it may have felt to him as though they had abandoned him.

The Lord will repay (4:14)

Paul's attitude toward someone who did him *a great deal of harm* reflects his own teaching in Romans 12:19. *Do not take revenge, my friends, but leave room for God's wrath.*

Did Paul think he would still be released? (4:18)

Probably not. Paul had faced too many of these situations to have any illusions or false hopes. It was not for physical survival that Paul spoke of here, but his spiritual destiny.

---

[a]19 Greek *Prisca*, a variant of *Priscilla*

TITUS

Why read this book?

This short letter shows that it has always been a challenge to develop a good church—even in New Testament days. It tells Titus, a young leader of an argumentative church, to refute false teachers, calm church disunity and find quality leaders. Even with God's Spirit at work, church life means sweat and tears. This letter puts church difficulties into perspective: those who persevere, as Titus did, will discover the power and satisfaction that God gives, then and now.

Who wrote this book?

The apostle Paul, while traveling after his first release from a Roman prison (Acts 27).

To whom was it written and why?

To Titus, a close friend and protégé of Paul (2 Cor. 8:23), who helped Paul organize and lead churches in the eastern half of the Roman empire. Paul wrote these instructions to help Titus lead the troubled church on the island of Crete.

When was it written?

Sometime between A.D. 63 to 65.

What to look for in Titus:

Qualifications of church leaders, guidelines for a godly life—including successful relationships between family, friends and society—and an emphasis on faith that overcomes division and disharmony among believers.

When did these things happen?

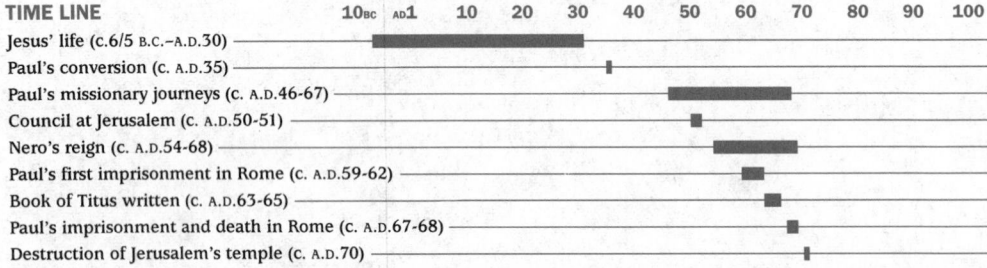

TIME LINE	10BC	AD1	10	20	30	40	50	60	70	80	90	100
Jesus' life (c.6/5 B.C.–A.D.30)												
Paul's conversion (c. A.D.35)												
Paul's missionary journeys (c. A.D.46-67)												
Council at Jerusalem (c. A.D.50-51)												
Nero's reign (c. A.D.54-68)												
Paul's first imprisonment in Rome (c. A.D.59-62)												
Book of Titus written (c. A.D.63-65)												
Paul's imprisonment and death in Rome (c. A.D.67-68)												
Destruction of Jerusalem's temple (c. A.D.70)												

1 Paul, a servant of God and an apostle[D] of Jesus Christ for the faith of God's elect[D] and the knowledge of the truth that leads to godliness— ²a faith and knowledge resting on the hope of eternal life[D], which God, who does not lie, promised before the beginning of time, ³and at his appointed season he brought his word to light through the preaching entrusted to me by the command of God our Savior,

⁴To Titus, my true son in our common faith:

Grace[D] and peace[D] from God the Father and Christ Jesus our Savior.

Titus' Task on Crete

⁵The reason I left you in Crete was that you might straighten out what was left unfinished and appoint[a] elders in every town, as I directed you. ⁶An elder must be blameless, the husband of but one wife, a man whose children believe and are not open to the charge of being wild and disobedient. ⁷Since an overseer[Db] is entrusted with God's work, he must be blameless—not overbearing, not quick-tempered, not given to drunkenness, not violent, not pursuing dishonest gain. ⁸Rather he must be hospitable, one who loves what is good, who is self-controlled, upright, holy and disciplined. ⁹He must hold firmly to the trustworthy message as it has been taught, so that he can encourage others by sound doctrine and refute those who oppose it.

¹⁰For there are many rebellious people, mere talkers and deceivers, especially those of the circumcision[D] group. ¹¹They must be silenced, because they are ruining whole households by teaching things they ought not to teach—and that for the sake of dishonest gain. ¹²Even one of their own prophets[D] has said, "Cretans are always liars, evil brutes, lazy gluttons[D]." ¹³This testimony is true. Therefore, rebuke them sharply, so that they will be sound in the faith ¹⁴and will pay no attention to Jewish myths or to the commands of those who reject the truth. ¹⁵To the pure, all things are pure, but to those who are corrupted and do not believe, nothing is pure. In fact, both their minds and consciences are corrupted. ¹⁶They claim to know God, but by their actions they deny him. They are detestable, disobedient and unfit for doing anything good.

What Must Be Taught to Various Groups

2 You must teach what is in accord with sound doctrine. ²Teach the older men to be temperate, worthy of respect, self-controlled, and sound in faith, in love and in endurance.

³Likewise, teach the older women to be reverent in the way they live, not to be slanderers or addicted to much wine, but to teach what is good. ⁴Then they can train the younger women to love their husbands and children, ⁵to be self-controlled and pure, to be busy at home, to be kind, and to be subject to their husbands, so that no one will malign the word of God.

⁶Similarly, encourage the young men to be self-controlled. ⁷In everything set them an example by doing what is good. In your teaching show integrity, seriousness ⁸and soundness of speech that cannot be condemned, so that

---

ᵃ5 Or *ordain*   ᵇ7 Traditionally *bishop*

Who are the elect? (1:1)

See *If God chooses us, do we have any choice?* (Eph. 1:4–5) and *Who are the elect?* (1 Peter 1:1).

Appointed season (1:3)

Sometimes we understand God's timing; other times we don't (Gal. 4:4; 1 Tim. 6:15). Paul's point is that God always works according to his purpose, inviting us to accept eternal life through Jesus Christ.

What had to be straightened out? (1:5)

Paul left Titus at Crete to organize the churches they had started earlier. These believers needed structure and guidance to withstand the divisive influences of false teachers.

Titus's Task on Crete (1:5)

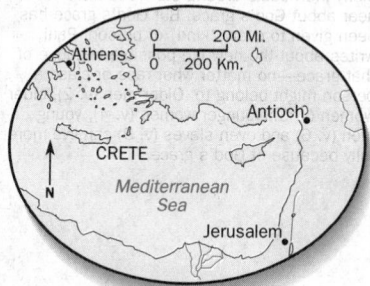

Who can be *blameless*? (1:6)

Paul did not expect church leaders to be sinless in this life. What he probably meant was that a believer's life must be consistently godly and effective to qualify as an elder. Elders must be willing to open every area of their lives to God's scrutiny.

Circumcision group (1:10)

Some so-called believers who demanded that Christians follow a Jewish lifestyle, including the rite of circumcision. They refused to believe that one could be part of God's family without this requirement.

Was Paul slandering Cretans? (1:12–13)

Paul quoted an ancient Cretan poet, Epimenides, to show that Titus's struggles were not his fault. The Cretans were sinful people. Paul's statement should not be interpreted as an ethnic slur because all peoples and cultures have the same faults, not just the Cretans. But by quoting their own poet, Paul made a specific application to give Titus some perspective.

What difference does doctrine make? (2:1)

Some people think doctrine (the right beliefs) doesn't matter. But sound doctrine does not mean just thinking the right thoughts or reading the right books; it means knowing how and why to live the right kind of life. As proper eating and exercise are good for the body, proper teaching is good for the soul.

Self-controlled (2:2)

Paul uses this word, mostly in his letters to Timothy and Titus, to mean resisting temptation. It means emotional control—a disciplined

balance of emotions and will. Self-control means living in gentle strength, able to withstand the influence of passions and environment.

Who was opposing Titus? (2:8)

Titus was confronted more by the existing attitudes in Cretan society than an actual conspiracy against Christianity. These Cretans tended to be argumentative and uncooperative.

Why not free the slaves instead of subjecting them to their masters? (2:9–10)

See article: *Why doesn't the Bible condemn slavery?* (1 Peter 2:18–21).

Has God's grace appeared to *all* people? (2:11)

Many individuals around the world have yet to hear about God's grace. But God's grace has been given to every "kind" of person. Paul writes about the new life possible because of that grace—no matter what race or class a person might belong to. Older men (v. 2), older women (v. 3), younger women (v. 4), young men (v. 6) and even slaves (v. 9) can live more fully because of God's grace.

What is the *washing of rebirth*? (3:5)

The cleansing from sin by the Holy Spirit, a spiritual work that underlies salvation (John 3:5–8). This spiritual rebirth is the event symbolized by baptism.

Which controversies are foolish? (3:9)

Christians have always recognized a common core of beliefs about what is essential for salvation: faith, repentance and submission to the will of God. Paul expected Titus to defend these essentials (vv. 5–8). Anything less significant is not worth fighting about, especially quarreling over who is "more spiritual" due to heritage or lifestyle.

those who oppose you may be ashamed because they have nothing bad to say about us.

9Teach slaves to be subject to their masters in everything, to try to please them, not to talk back to them, **10**and not to steal from them, but to show that they can be fully trusted, so that in every way they will make the teaching about God our Savior attractive. **11**For the grace^D of God that brings salvation^D has appeared to all men. **12**It teaches us to say "No" to ungodliness and worldly passions, and to live self-controlled, upright and godly lives in this present age, **13**while we wait for the blessed hope—the glorious appearing of our great God and Savior, Jesus Christ, **14**who gave himself for us to redeem^D us from all wickedness and to purify^D for himself a people that are his very own, eager to do what is good.

15These, then, are the things you should teach. Encourage and rebuke with all authority. Do not let anyone despise you.

Doing What Is Good

3 Remind the people to be subject to rulers and authorities, to be obedient, to be ready to do whatever is good, **2**to slander no one, to be peaceable and considerate, and to show true humility toward all men.

3At one time we too were foolish, disobedient, deceived and enslaved by all kinds of passions and pleasures. We lived in malice and envy, being hated and hating one another. **4**But when the kindness and love of God our Savior appeared, **5**he saved us, not because of righteous^D things we had done, but because of his mercy^D. He saved us through the washing of rebirth and renewal by the Holy Spirit, **6**whom he poured out on us generously through Jesus Christ our Savior, **7**so that, having been justified^D by his grace, we might become heirs having the hope of eternal life^D. **8**This is a trustworthy saying. And I want you to stress these things, so that those who have trusted in God may be careful to devote themselves to doing what is good. These things are excellent and profitable for everyone.

9But avoid foolish controversies and genealogies^D and

Should we obey bad rulers? (3:1–2)

To submit to rulers and authorities does not mean blind obedience. As he does in Romans 13:1–2, Paul teaches here that government's authority is established by God to keep order on earth. Whether in the home or society, Christians must recognize the authority over them, even if they don't always agree with it. God's authority stands behind every government, right or wrong, but it also stands "over" every human authority, not allowing evil to go unchecked forever.

If government parallels God's law, then Christians are right to obey it. However, if a human law runs counter to God's principles, then it is not wrong to disobey. Even while resisting in those areas where government oversteps its bounds (Acts 5:29), though, Christians must still recognize the authority of government in its other functions. In this way, Christians can obey God with a clear conscience.

Paul doesn't note any exceptions to his general statement because usually in his letters he is combating some imbalance. Apparently, in Crete, many believers were disrespecting authority. So his command here is an unqualified call for obedience.

arguments and quarrels about the law, because these are unprofitable and useless. **10**Warn a divisive person once, and then warn him a second time. After that, have nothing to do with him. **11**You may be sure that such a man is warped and sinful; he is self-condemned.

Final Remarks

12As soon as I send Artemas or Tychicus to you, do your best to come to me at Nicopolis, because I have decided to winter there. **13**Do everything you can to help Zenas the lawyer and Apollos on their way and see that they have everything they need. **14**Our people must learn to devote themselves to doing what is good, in order that they may provide for daily necessities and not live unproductive lives.

15Everyone with me sends you greetings. Greet those who love us in the faith.

Grace D be with you all.

Is there any hope for the *self-condemned*? (3:11)

Can divisive people repent? Yes. Jesus taught that we should repeatedly forgive those who *repent*—even if they stumble and have to repent again and again (Matt. 18:17,21–22). Paul is describing those who continue to be quarrelsome and unrepentant. The church is not condemning them by avoiding them. Their own attitudes and behavior condemn them.

What happened to the Cretan churches? (3:15)

Not much is known. But history as a whole records that they did not prosper, possibly because, being on an island, they were somewhat isolated from the mainstream of church growth. The island was conquered by Islam in the seventh century and it returned to Christianity in the tenth century.

PHILEMON

Why read this book?

C. S. Lewis said "Everyone says that forgiveness is a wonderful idea, until he has something to forgive." Forgiveness is not always easy to ask for or to give. Someone has to swallow the pain of having been hurt. Philemon is a letter that gives us a case study in the cost of asking for forgiveness and of granting it.

Who wrote this book and when was it written?

The apostle Paul, imprisoned in Rome, wrote it between A.D. 60 and 62.

To whom was it written?

Philemon, a wealthy Christian in the church at Colosse (see *The Church in Colosse* on page 1627), who may have become a believer through Paul's ministry (v. 19).

Why was it written?

During Paul's first imprisonment in Rome (A.D. 59 to 62), he met Onesimus, a runaway slave, and led him to faith in Christ (v. 10). Onesimus might have been a great help to him, but Paul chose to send him back to his master, Philemon. Paul wrote this letter to ask Philemon to forgive Onesimus. This letter was likely carried by Tychicus, who was also carrying letters to the Ephesian and Colossian churches (Eph. 6:21-22; Col. 4:7-9). Onesimus traveled with Tychicus.

What to look for in Philemon:

A plea for grace. Most runaway slaves, if caught, faced harsh punishment and sometimes even death. Paul hoped Philemon would become a living illustration of the grace Onesimus had already received through Christ.

When did these things happen?

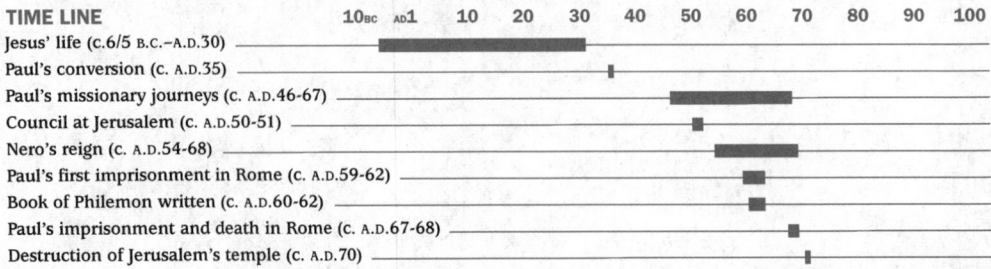

TIME LINE	10BC AD1	10	20	30	40	50	60	70	80	90	100
Jesus' life (c.6/5 B.C.–A.D.30)											
Paul's conversion (c. A.D.35)											
Paul's missionary journeys (c. A.D.46-67)											
Council at Jerusalem (c. A.D.50-51)											
Nero's reign (c. A.D.54-68)											
Paul's first imprisonment in Rome (c. A.D.59-62)											
Book of Philemon written (c. A.D.60-62)											
Paul's imprisonment and death in Rome (c. A.D.67-68)											
Destruction of Jerusalem's temple (c. A.D.70)											

[1]Paul, a prisoner of Christ Jesus, and Timothy our brother,

To Philemon our dear friend and fellow worker, [2]to Apphia our sister, to Archippus our fellow soldier and to the church that meets in your home:

[3]Grace[D] to you and peace[D] from God our Father and the Lord Jesus Christ.

Thanksgiving and Prayer

[4]I always thank my God as I remember you in my prayers, [5]because I hear about your faith in the Lord Jesus and your love for all the saints[D]. [6]I pray that you may be active in sharing your faith, so that you will have a full understanding of every good thing we have in Christ. [7]Your love has given me great joy and encouragement, because you, brother, have refreshed the hearts of the saints.

Paul's Plea for Onesimus

[8]Therefore, although in Christ I could be bold and order you to do what you ought to do, [9]yet I appeal to you on the basis of love. I then, as Paul—an old man and now also a prisoner of Christ Jesus— [10]I appeal to you for my son Onesimus,[a] who became my son while I was in chains. [11]Formerly he was useless to you, but now he has become useful both to you and to me.

[12]I am sending him—who is my very heart—back to you. [13]I would have liked to keep him with me so that he could take your place in helping me while I am in chains for the gospel[D]. [14]But I did not want to do anything without your consent, so that any favor you do will be spontaneous and not forced. [15]Perhaps the reason he was separated from you for a little while was that you might have him back for good— [16]no longer as a slave, but better than a slave, as a dear brother. He is very dear to me but even dearer to you, both as a man and as a brother in the Lord.

[17]So if you consider me a partner, welcome him as you would welcome me. [18]If he has done you any wrong or

[a]10 Onesimus means useful.

Why does Paul call Onesimus his son? (v. 10)

Probably because Paul introduced Onesimus to faith in Christ, thus making him his "spiritual son."

Why did a fugitive go to Paul? (v. 10–12)

Paul may have first met Onesimus during his visit to Philemon's household in Colosse. If so, it's possible that Onesimus, after running away from home, would have looked for Paul in Rome. The renewed acquaintance led to a change of heart for Onesimus, who became a Christian and a devoted helper to Paul.

How had Onesimus been *useless*? (v. 11)

Onesimus probably had not been a model servant. Paul admits that Onesimus may have cheated Philemon or owed him money (v. 18). Paul uses a play on words: *Onesimus*, meaning *useful*, was a common name for a slave. But *Useful* had been useless. Now that he knew Christ, however, he would be true to his name —useful again, both to Philemon and to Paul.

Does Paul want Philemon to set Onesimus free? (v. 16)

It's not clear, but one thing is certain: Paul asks Philemon to do something even more difficult than to simply set Onesimus free. He asks him to love Onesimus as a Christian brother rather than treat him as a slave.

How were runaway slaves usually welcomed? (v. 17)

Slaves in the Roman empire were viewed as property, not people. When runaway slaves were caught, they could legally be tortured to death as a lesson for other would-be runaways. Or they could have the letter *F* (for *Fugitivus*) seared into their foreheads with a hot iron.

Was Paul pressuring Philemon? (vv. 18–19)

Paul wanted Philemon to do him a favor, but he wanted him to do it voluntarily (v. 14). True, he

Why didn't Paul help a runaway slave escape? (v. 12)

Paul sent Onesimus back to his master, possibly back to punishment. Why didn't he let him start life over, in freedom, now that he was *a new creation* in Christ (see 2 Cor. 5:17)?

Paul neither condemned nor condoned slavery. His priority wasn't to challenge the morality of the system. Instead, he wanted to see transformed *people*. He tried to change relationships within the existing system. A master and slave treating one another as brothers was revolutionary. Also see article: *Why doesn't the Bible condemn slavery?* (1 Peter 2:18–21).

In addition, Paul may have been suggesting that true repentance means facing the past, not running away from it. It means trying to reconcile, even when doing so might be risky and costly. Perhaps Paul convinced Onesimus to return to his master because the chance of them being reconciled as Christian brothers was better than the alternative—living a lifetime with unreconciled tension between them.

mentioned the debt Philemon owed him (probably because he played a part in bringing Philemon to Christ). But he did not dwell on it. By offering to pay Onesimus's monetary debt, Paul hoped to remove any reason Philemon might have had for refusing to welcome Onesimus back.

Didn't Paul usually write letters himself? (v. 19)

No. Paul usually dictated his letters to a secretary (see, for example, Romans 16:22). He would then sign his name at the end of his letters to authenticate them as his own (2 Thes. 3:17). In this case, Paul may have written the entire manuscript without the assistance of a secretary. It is possible, however, that Paul here wrote only the promise *I will pay it back*.

owes you anything, charge it to me. **19**I, Paul, am writing this with my own hand. I will pay it back—not to mention that you owe me your very self. **20**I do wish, brother, that I may have some benefit from you in the Lord; refresh my heart in Christ. **21**Confident of your obedience, I write to you, knowing that you will do even more than I ask.

22And one thing more: Prepare a guest room for me, because I hope to be restored to you in answer to your prayers.

23Epaphras, my fellow prisoner in Christ Jesus, sends you greetings. **24**And so do Mark, Aristarchus, Demas and Luke, my fellow workers.

25The grace[D] of the Lord Jesus Christ be with your spirit.

HEBREWS

Why read this book?

We all face frustrations, obstacles and temptations; one's spiritual journey is not always even-paced. But the book of Hebrews offers help for times like these, first by acknowledging the pitfalls and perils, second by encouraging us to never quit. Hebrews is something like a coach's pep talk at halftime: it can help us find the inspiration to keep going in the faith.

Who wrote this book?

The author does not identify himself. Some think it was Paul, but others suggest Barnabas, Luke or Apollos as possible writers.

When was it written?

The letter was written between A.D. 60 and 70.

To whom was it written and why?

Hebrews sounded a warning to early Jewish believers (Hebrews) who, because of persecution and hardship, were pulled strongly toward reverting to their Old Testament way of life.

What to look for in Hebrews:

Look for the vivid Old Testament images used by the writer to illustrate what God has done through Jesus Christ. Notice the strong emotional appeals made to persuade the Jewish believers to stick with the new covenant rather than going back to the old covenant. The writer makes frequent contrasts between Old Testament ritual law and New Testament faith. Along the way, you'll also find strong arguments for the superiority of Jesus Christ.

When did these things happen?

TIME LINE	10 B.C.	A.D. 1	10	20	30	40	50	60	70	80	90	100
Jesus' birth (c.6/5 B.C.)	■											
Jesus' death, resurrection and ascension (c. A.D.30)					■							
Paul's conversion (c. A.D.35)						■						
Council at Jerusalem (c. A.D.50-51)							■					
Nero's reign (c. A.D.54-68)							▬▬▬▬					
Book of Hebrews written (c. A.D.60-70)								▬▬▬				
Paul's imprisonment and death in Rome (c. A.D.67-68)									■			
Destruction of Jerusalem's temple (c. A.D.70)									■			

Last days (1:2)

See *End of the ages* (9:26).

**What is Jesus' relationship to God?
(1:3)**

Jesus Christ is God in the flesh. Although the human mind cannot grasp all of God, this much can be said: Jesus Christ brought the character and majesty of God to a human body, even though God is spirit (John 4:24). At the same time, Jesus willingly stripped himself of the privileges of deity (Phil. 2:1–11). Christ in human form was both God and man—two distinct natures united in one person. Also see *What did Jesus give up to come to earth?* (Phil. 2:6–7).

Where is Jesus? (1:3)

Jesus Christ is with God the Father in heaven. Heaven is the place where God dwells, in the spirit realm, described in human terms as *high . . . above the earth* (Psalm 103:11). At the same time, by the presence of the Holy Spirit within, Jesus also lives in every Christian (John 14:23).

Firstborn **(1:6)**

This term is used here symbolically as a title of position, not an order of birth. In the Old Testament it was used in the same way to describe the privilege and favor God granted to Israel (Exodus 4:22; Jer. 31:9). Some rabbis used this term to describe God himself: the *firstborn* of the world is the Supreme Being.

What do angels do? (1:7)

For the most part they seem to be messengers or servants for God (for example, Luke 1:13,30). Often their messages bring God's guidance to people (Acts 10:3–5). Angels also are assigned to protect God's people (Psalm 34:7), to minister to their needs (1 Kings 19:5–7) and to dispense judgment to the wicked (Acts 12:23). Angels also serve God by giving him honor and praise (Rev. 5:11–12).

How will the earth and heavens perish? (1:10–11)

The Bible hints at some catastrophic event that will destroy the world as we know it. We cannot tell for sure what might cause such total devastation. Peter wrote of the heavens disappearing *with a roar,* the elements being *destroyed by fire* and the earth being *laid bare* (2 Peter 3:10–12). John simply said *the first heaven and the first earth had passed away* (Rev. 21:1).

Who are Christ's enemies? (1:13)

See *Who are Christ's enemies?* (10:13).

**Why show the inferiority of angels?
(1:13–14)**

Some Jews were tempted to honor angels for their part in bringing God's word to them. Some even went so far as to worship angels as supernatural beings (Col. 2:18). Because of this, the writer felt compelled to prove from the Old Testament that the Messiah was superior.

The Son Superior to Angels

1 In the past God spoke to our forefathers through the prophets[D] at many times and in various ways, [2]but in these last days he has spoken to us by his Son, whom he appointed heir of all things, and through whom he made the universe. [3]The Son is the radiance of God's glory[D] and the exact representation of his being, sustaining all things by his powerful word. After he had provided purification for sins, he sat down at the right hand of the Majesty in heaven. [4]So he became as much superior to the angels as the name he has inherited is superior to theirs.

[5]For to which of the angels did God ever say,

"You are my Son;
    today I have become your Father[a]"[b]?

Or again,

"I will be his Father,
    and he will be my Son"[c]?

[6]And again, when God brings his firstborn[D] into the world, he says,

"Let all God's angels worship him."[d]

[7]In speaking of the angels he says,

"He makes his angels winds,
    his servants flames of fire."[e]

[8]But about the Son he says,

"Your throne, O God, will last for ever and
        ever,
    and righteousness[D] will be the scepter[D] of
        your kingdom.
[9]You have loved righteousness and hated
        wickedness;
    therefore God, your God, has set you above
        your companions
    by anointing[D] you with the oil of joy."[f]

[10]He also says,

"In the beginning, O Lord, you laid the
        foundations of the earth,
    and the heavens are the work of your hands.
[11]They will perish, but you remain;
    they will all wear out like a garment.
[12]You will roll them up like a robe;
    like a garment they will be changed.
But you remain the same,
    and your years will never end."[g]

[13]To which of the angels did God ever say,

"Sit at my right hand
until I make your enemies
    a footstool[D] for your feet"[h]?

[14]Are not all angels ministering spirits sent to serve those who will inherit salvation[D]?

a5 Or have begotten you   *b5 Psalm 2:7*   *c5 2 Samuel 7:14;*
1 Chron. 17:13   *d6 Deut. 32:43 (see Dead Sea Scrolls and*
Septuagint)   *e7 Psalm 104:4*   *f9 Psalm 45:6,7*
g12 Psalm 102:25-27   *h13 Psalm 110:1*

Warning to Pay Attention

2 We must pay more careful attention, therefore, to what we have heard, so that we do not drift away. [2]For if the message spoken by angels was binding, and every violation and disobedience received its just punishment, [3]how shall we escape if we ignore such a great salvation[D]? This salvation, which was first announced by the Lord, was confirmed to us by those who heard him. [4]God also testified to it by signs, wonders and various miracles, and gifts of the Holy Spirit distributed according to his will.

Jesus Made Like His Brothers

[5]It is not to angels that he has subjected the world to come, about which we are speaking. [6]But there is a place where someone has testified:

"What is man that you are mindful of him,
    the son of man[D] that you care for him?
[7]You made him a little[a] lower than the angels;
    you crowned him with glory[D] and honor
[8]   and put everything under his feet."[b]

In putting everything under him, God left nothing that is not subject to him. Yet at present we do not see everything subject to him. [9]But we see Jesus, who was made a little lower than the angels, now crowned with glory and honor because he suffered death[D], so that by the grace[D] of God he might taste death for everyone.

[10]In bringing many sons to glory, it was fitting that God, for whom and through whom everything exists, should make the author of their salvation perfect through suffering. [11]Both the one who makes men holy and those who are made holy are of the same family. So Jesus is not ashamed to call them brothers. [12]He says,

"I will declare your name to my brothers;
    in the presence of the congregation I will
        sing your praises."[c]

[13]And again,

"I will put my trust in him."[d]

And again he says,

"Here am I, and the children God has given
    me."[e]

[14]Since the children have flesh and blood, he too shared in their humanity so that by his death he might destroy him who holds the power of death—that is, the devil— [15]and free those who all their lives were held in slavery by their fear of death. [16]For surely it is not angels he helps, but Abraham's descendants. [17]For this reason he had to be made like his brothers in every way, in order that he might become a merciful and faithful high priest[D] in service to God, and that he might make atonement[D] for[f] the sins of the people. [18]Because he himself suffered when he was tempted, he is able to help those who are being tempted.

[a]7 Or him for a little while; also in verse 9   [b]8 Psalm 8:4-6
[c]12 Psalm 22:22   [d]13 Isaiah 8:17   [e]13 Isaiah 8:18   [f]17 Or
and that he might turn aside God's wrath, taking away

What does it mean to drift away? (2:1)
This figurative language pictures a boat that will not stay put without an anchor. It will be carried along by currents or wind. In the same way, if we are not firmly connected to what is spiritually immovable, we cannot be stable and strong in our faith. If we neglect what we have heard, we can drift either intellectually or morally.

What message did angels give? (2:2)
They helped deliver the law to Moses on Mount Sinai (see Map 3 at the back of this Bible). Moses said the Lord came from Sinai with myriads of holy ones (Deut. 33:2). Stephen and Paul said the law was put into effect through angels (Acts 7:53; Gal. 3:19).

Does God still miraculously confirm his Word? (2:3-4)
Many testify that he does—especially in areas where the gospel is newly proclaimed. This fits the pattern of the early days of the church. The truth of God's Word is that God has the power over all that he has created. Signs and wonders, along with gifts of the Spirit, confirm that truth.

Are these words about Jesus? (2:6-8)
Originally, these words spoke of humankind, not Jesus (Psalm 8:4-6). The writer of Hebrews, inspired by the Holy Spirit to go beyond the original meaning of these words, applied them to Jesus, for in him they reach their ultimate fulfillment. Jesus, who called himself the Son of Man, is the true representative of our humanity.

Why did Jesus have to be made perfect? (2:10)
This does not mean there was a time when Jesus wasn't perfect. It simply points to the completion of his assignment. Make . . . perfect means to bring to the rightful or appointed end. By suffering and dying on the cross, the perfect Son of God became our perfect Savior, opening the way to God.

Why did Jesus have to become like us? (2:17)
Jesus became human, not just to die for our sins, but also to be our high priest. To fully communicate God's salvation to us—and identify with our need—Jesus had to become one of us. The qualities of a priest are given in 5:1-3.

Why compare Moses to Christ? (3:2-6)
To the Jews, Moses was the incomparable law giver and mediator. No one in their tradition was greater. But Jewish believers needed to see how much better it was to have Jesus rather than Moses pleading their case before God. Though both were faithful, Moses could not offer the grace of the New Testament as Jesus could.

SCRIPTURE LINK (3:8-11) The rebellion . . . the time of testing in the desert
The climax of the Israelites' numerous complaints in the desert is described in Num. 14.

What is God's *rest*? (3:11,18)

The rest God offered Israel was the promised land of Canaan (see *Setting of Deuteronomy* on page 236). For right now, God's rest means our present enjoyment of his spiritual blessings. There is yet to come, however, a final dimension of God's rest, when believers will be united with Jesus Christ in eternity (4:9–11).

How long is it called *Today*? (3:13)

We don't know how much time is included in *Today*, because we don't know how long we have to live. It is the time of opportunity that we have to hear and obey the gospel. It is also the time set by God for entering his *rest* (4:6–7). For the world as a whole, *Today* continues until Christ comes again.

What is this warning all about? (3:14–19)

Israel's unbelief in the desert (vv. 7–11) serves as a warning to Christians who may be tempted towards apathy or falling away from the faith. Some think death in the desert rather than in the promised land is a warning about losing spiritual blessings in this life, not about losing eternal salvation. Others say it was the judgment in the desert that prevented their entrance into the promised land. For similar warnings, see 2 Cor. 13:5; Phil. 2:12. Also see articles: *Should we fear falling?* (6:6) and *Can believers fall away?* (Luke 8:13).

Can Christians harden their hearts? (3:15)

Yes. This was written to Christians, warning them of that danger. Hardening of the heart is caused by rebelling, complaining, giving up or by being stubborn or unfaithful (vv. 8,15). Christians disagree about the consequences. Some say the price is losing spiritual blessings in this life. Others say the price is missing out on eternal blessings. Hebrews draws from the Old Testament to show that God's people are not exempt from judgment. See previous note.

What does it mean to fall short of God's rest? (4:1)

God's rest is both present and future. See *What is God's rest?* (3:11). Missing God's future rest means missing eternal salvation. Missing God's present rest means living a frustrated life of spiritual frenzy. Those who struggle, striving through their own efforts to gain salvation, have not found rest in Christ.

What gospel did the Old Testament Israelites hear? (4:2)

Gospel means *good news*. The Israelites in the desert heard the good news of a place of peace and rest from their enemies—news about the promised land (Deut. 12:8–10).

What work are we supposed to rest from? (4:10)

We can rest from trying to gain salvation and blessings for ourselves. We can give up our own efforts at being righteous.

Jesus Greater Than Moses

3 Therefore, holy brothers, who share in the heavenly calling, fix your thoughts on Jesus, the apostle[D] and high priest[D] whom we confess. [2]He was faithful to the one who appointed him, just as Moses was faithful in all God's house. [3]Jesus has been found worthy of greater honor than Moses, just as the builder of a house has greater honor than the house itself. [4]For every house is built by someone, but God is the builder of everything. [5]Moses was faithful as a servant in all God's house, testifying to what would be said in the future. [6]But Christ is faithful as a son over God's house. And we are his house, if we hold on to our courage and the hope of which we boast.

Warning Against Unbelief

[7]So, as the Holy Spirit says:

"Today, if you hear his voice,
[8]   do not harden your hearts
   as you did in the rebellion,
     during the time of testing in the desert,
[9]where your fathers tested and tried me
   and for forty years saw what I did.
[10]That is why I was angry with that generation,
   and I said, 'Their hearts are always going astray,
   and they have not known my ways.'
[11]So I declared on oath in my anger,
   'They shall never enter my rest.' "[a]

[12]See to it, brothers, that none of you has a sinful, unbelieving heart that turns away from the living God. [13]But encourage one another daily, as long as it is called Today, so that none of you may be hardened by sin's deceitfulness. [14]We have come to share in Christ if we hold firmly till the end the confidence we had at first. [15]As has just been said:

"Today, if you hear his voice,
   do not harden your hearts
   as you did in the rebellion."[b]

[16]Who were they who heard and rebelled? Were they not all those Moses led out of Egypt? [17]And with whom was he angry for forty years? Was it not with those who sinned, whose bodies fell in the desert? [18]And to whom did God swear that they would never enter his rest if not to those who disobeyed[c]? [19]So we see that they were not able to enter, because of their unbelief.

A Sabbath-Rest for the People of God

4 Therefore, since the promise of entering his rest still stands, let us be careful that none of you be found to have fallen short of it. [2]For we also have had the gospel[D] preached to us, just as they did; but the message they heard was of no value to them, because those who heard did not combine it with faith.[d] [3]Now we who have believed enter that rest, just as God has said,

"So I declared on oath in my anger,
   'They shall never enter my rest.' "[e]

---

[a]11 Psalm 95:7-11   [b]15 Psalm 95:7,8   [c]18 Or *disbelieved*
[d]2 Many manuscripts *because they did not share in the faith of those who obeyed*   [e]3 Psalm 95:11; also in verse 5

And yet his work has been finished since the creation of the world. **4**For somewhere he has spoken about the seventh day in these words: "And on the seventh day God rested from all his work."[a] **5**And again in the passage above he says, "They shall never enter my rest."

6It still remains that some will enter that rest, and those who formerly had the gospel[D] preached to them did not go in, because of their disobedience. **7**Therefore God again set a certain day, calling it Today, when a long time later he spoke through David, as was said before:

"Today, if you hear his voice,
    do not harden your hearts."[b]

8For if Joshua had given them rest, God would not have spoken later about another day. **9**There remains, then, a Sabbath[D]-rest for the people of God; **10**for anyone who enters God's rest also rests from his own work, just as God did from his. **11**Let us, therefore, make every effort to enter that rest, so that no one will fall by following their example of disobedience.

12For the word of God is living and active. Sharper than any double-edged sword, it penetrates even to dividing soul[D] and spirit, joints and marrow; it judges the thoughts and attitudes of the heart. **13**Nothing in all creation is hidden from God's sight. Everything is uncovered and laid bare before the eyes of him to whom we must give account.

Jesus the Great High Priest

14Therefore, since we have a great high priest[D] who has gone through the heavens,[c] Jesus the Son of God, let us hold firmly to the faith we profess. **15**For we do not have a high priest who is unable to sympathize with our weaknesses, but we have one who has been tempted in every way, just as we are—yet was without sin. **16**Let us then approach the throne of grace[D] with confidence, so that we may receive mercy[D] and find grace to help us in our time of need.

5 Every high priest is selected from among men and is appointed to represent them in matters related to God, to offer gifts and sacrifices[D] for sins. **2**He is able to deal gently with those who are ignorant and are going astray, since he himself is subject to weakness. **3**This is why he has to offer sacrifices for his own sins, as well as for the sins of the people.

4No one takes this honor upon himself; he must be called by God, just as Aaron was. **5**So Christ also did not take upon himself the glory[D] of becoming a high priest. But God said to him,

"You are my Son;
    today I have become your Father."[d] [e]

6And he says in another place,

"You are a priest forever,
    in the order of Melchizedek."[f]

7During the days of Jesus' life on earth, he offered up prayers and petitions with loud cries and tears to the one who could save him from death[D], and he was heard because of his reverent submission. **8**Although he was a son,

---

Isn't it a contradiction to *make every effort to enter that rest?* (4:11)

No. This is not a call for human effort to gain salvation. Rather, it's a call to focus our faith on Christ's work, the only means by which we can be saved. The *effort* is directed toward obedience and trust in God, not human works. Christ is the aim of such efforts, not self. Also see *How much effort does the Christian life require?* (2 Peter 1:5).

What does God's sharp word have to do with rest? (4:12–13)

God's word, in this case, is his promise of rest. This refers to a specific word from God (v. 8), not the general Word of God, the Bible. Still, this accurately describes God's Word which, more than letters on a page, is alive with God's Spirit and power. In addition, this word of promise *judges* what's in a person's heart: either a salvation based on trust, resting in God's grace, or a false security based on good works, which results in no rest.

How could Jesus experience every human temptation? (4:15)

Jesus did not have identical circumstances to that of every human being. He wasn't married, never had kids, never hit a midlife crisis and never hobbled through old age. But *tempted in every way* means Jesus faced trials common to the human experience—he dealt with the fundamental issues of life. Jesus felt what it was like to be human, challenged by the same temptations we all face.

Throne of grace (4:16)

God's gracious throne. *The throne of grace* conveys an image of someone petitioning a king for favor. It represents God's presence, the place from which he responds to our prayers.

The order of Melchizedek (5:6,10)

A king-priest during the days of Abraham, long before the Jewish priesthood was established. Since Genesis offers no details about his priesthood, not even his birth and death, he became a symbol of Christ, the eternal high priest. See Gen. 14:18–20; Psalm 110:4.

How did God answer Christ's prayers to be saved from death? (5:7)

Jesus agonized in the Garden of Gethsemane, and God saved him from the power of death through the resurrection. Some suggest he was actually agonizing over *spiritual* death—that is, being separated from his Father when he took on the sin of the world. Still, God gave Jesus peace, even sending an angel to strengthen him (Luke 22:43).

Why did Jesus need to learn obedience through suffering? (5:8)

Jesus' sufferings allowed him to experience obedience in human terms. Suffering was the necessary price of obedience, part of fulfilling the will of God.

Why did Jesus have to be made perfect? (5:9)

See *Why did Jesus have to be made perfect?* (2:10).

---

[a]4 Gen. 2:2   [b]7 Psalm 95:7,8   [c]14 Or *gone into heaven*
[d]5 Or *have begotten you*   [e]5 Psalm 2:7   [f]6 Psalm 110:4

Why were these Christians slow learners? (5:11)

It's possible their minds were hindered by their emotions—that their hearts made it difficult to accept new ideas. Many did not seem ready for the Old Testament priesthood and the sacrificial system to end. Perhaps they felt a nostalgic sense of security in their familiar traditions and rituals of the past.

What are milk-fed Christians like? (5:13)

They're like babies whose development has been stunted. Because they refuse to digest basic spiritual truths, they are unable to stomach "solid food"—more advanced instruction in God's ways.

If these are elementary teachings, what's in the advanced course? (6:1–2)

The writer hints at several things in the context of these verses: (1) *Constant use* (5:14)—we're to put the fundamentals into practice, not just cram information into our heads. (2) *Trained . . . to distinguish good from evil* (5:14) —maturity requires discernment, not just basic understanding of truth. (3) *Land . . . that produces a crop* (v. 7)—simple faith should lead to fruitful lives. (4) *Diligence* (v. 11)—maturity means having a right attitude.

The heavenly gift (6:4)

A picturesque way to describe salvation. Some say that people can taste the gift without really having faith. Others say that those who have tasted are truly believers and must guard against losing their salvation.

The powers of the coming age (6:5)

The spiritual resources of the eternal world (see 2:4).

---

he learned obedience from what he suffered ⁹and, once made perfect, he became the source of eternal salvationᴰ for all who obey him ¹⁰and was designated by God to be high priestᴰ in the order of Melchizedek.

Warning Against Falling Away

¹¹We have much to say about this, but it is hard to explain because you are slow to learn. ¹²In fact, though by this time you ought to be teachers, you need someone to teach you the elementary truths of God's word all over again. You need milk, not solid food! ¹³Anyone who lives on milk, being still an infant, is not acquainted with the teaching about righteousnessᴰ. ¹⁴But solid food is for the mature, who by constant use have trained themselves to distinguish good from evil.

6 Therefore let us leave the elementary teachings about Christ and go on to maturity, not laying again the foundation of repentanceᴰ from acts that lead to deathᴰ,ᵃ and of faith in God, ²instruction about baptismsᴰ, the laying on of hands, the resurrectionᴰ of the dead, and eternal judgment. ³And God permitting, we will do so.

⁴It is impossible for those who have once been enlightened, who have tasted the heavenly gift, who have shared in the Holy Spirit, ⁵who have tasted the goodness of the word of God and the powers of the coming age, ⁶if they fall away, to be brought back to repentance, becauseᵇ to their loss they are crucifying the Son of God all over again and subjecting him to public disgrace.

⁷Land that drinks in the rain often falling on it and that produces a crop useful to those for whom it is farmed receives the blessing of God. ⁸But land that produces thorns and thistles is worthless and is in danger of being cursed. In the end it will be burned.

ᵃ1 Or *from useless rituals*   ᵇ6 Or *repentance while*

Who needs a priest? (5:5,10)

We all do. Since God is an awesome and holy God, sinful humans cannot approach him directly. We need a mediator—a priest—to bring us to God. The writer of Hebrews presented Jesus Christ as the priest his readers needed.

These readers knew their Jewish history and religion: God had appointed Aaron as the first high priest because their ancestors could not come before a holy God and make offerings on their own. As sinners, they benefited spiritually by having an intermediary.

Some Jews apparently had begun to feel a bit insecure about leaving this familiar system. So the writer of Hebrews sought to reassure them by explaining the work of Christ. Building on their understanding of the Old Testament priesthood, the writer asserted that they didn't need to return to the old ways since Jesus is the one true high priest.

The parallels between Christ and the Old Testament high priest are dramatic. Only the high priest could enter the Most Holy Place and he could enter only once a year, on the Day of Atonement. But first he had to offer a blood sacrifice for himself and then for the people. In the same way Christ offered his own blood to make atonement for our sins. Then, on our behalf, he entered *the inner sanctuary behind the curtain* (6:19–20). Hebrews teaches that the only way we can come to God is through our high priest, Jesus Christ.

⁹Even though we speak like this, dear friends, we are confident of better things in your case—things that accompany salvation.D. ¹⁰God is not unjust; he will not forget your work and the love you have shown him as you have helped his people and continue to help them. ¹¹We want each of you to show this same diligence to the very end, in order to make your hope sure. ¹²We do not want you to become lazy, but to imitate those who through faith and patience inherit what has been promised.

The Certainty of God's Promise

¹³When God made his promise to Abraham, since there was no one greater for him to swear by, he swore by himself, ¹⁴saying, "I will surely bless you and give you many descendants."ᵃ ¹⁵And so after waiting patiently, Abraham received what was promised.

¹⁶Men swear by someone greater than themselves, and the oath confirms what is said and puts an end to all argument. ¹⁷Because God wanted to make the unchanging nature of his purpose very clear to the heirs of what was promised, he confirmed it with an oath. ¹⁸God did this so that, by two unchangeable things in which it is impossible for God to lie, we who have fled to take hold of the hope offered to us may be greatly encouraged. ¹⁹We have this hope as an anchor for the soulD, firm and secure. It enters the inner sanctuary behind the curtain, ²⁰where Jesus, who went before us, has entered on our behalf. He has become a high priestD forever, in the order of Melchizedek.

ᵃ14 Gen. 22:17

Why would God have to swear by himself? (6:13)

To reassure Abraham, God swore an oath to show his determination to fulfill his promise (v. 14).

If God swore an oath, should we? (6:13)

Some oaths are wrong because they trivialize the things of God while trying to validate words that may be insincere (Matt. 5:34–37; James 5:12). But some oaths can be good when they demonstrate the intensity of a sincere promise or vow to do something. Also see *Is it wrong to swear to tell the truth in court?* (Matt. 5:34–37).

Two unchangeable things (6:18)

(1) God's promise and (2) his oath (v. 13). They were originally given for Abraham's benefit. But believers in Christ today have experienced the fulfillment of God's promise to Abraham (v. 14)—because people of faith are themselves part of the fulfillment; they are the many descendants of Abraham (Gal. 3:29).

How has Jesus gone before us? (6:19–20)

The writer compresses two word pictures to describe what Jesus did. The more familiar is the Old Testament priest entering the Most Holy Place on behalf of the people. See article: *Who needs a priest?* (5:5). The other image is of a ship nearing port but unable to sail into harbor because of rough seas, thick fog or low tide. A small boat carried an anchor from the ship to the pier so the ship could hold steady or painstakingly winch its way safely through

Should we fear falling? (6:6)

Is falling away from the faith a danger for Christians? Throughout this letter we are warned to be careful, that falling away is a dangerous possibility (see, for example, 10:26–27,36). The words *fall away* suggest a runner dropping out of a race, veering off the track and giving up. The Hebrews would have understood this as a picture of abandoning their faith.

Can people "drop out" to the point where there is no longer any hope for their salvation? Some think so and point out that only God knows when a person's persistent disobedience will bring such judgment. This book's primary example—the Israelites in the desert—shows that judgment came only after God had tolerated many rebellions. The writer's concern for his readers suggests that they were dangerously close to crossing the line where it would be impossible to start over.

Others read these warnings differently, though. They insist that Christians are eternally secure and cannot fall from grace, so these words are intended for those who have merely tasted God's grace but have not truly believed.

Whichever way it's interpreted, those who *fall away* are not those who merely stumble in the race. Christians may have moments of weakness or temporary lapses in their faith; they may stumble and then, by God's grace, return again to the Lord. But those who *fall away* are those who remain unrepentant and persist in their rebellion against God—like those who crucified Jesus.

Also see *What is this warning all about?* (3:14–19) and the articles: *Can believers fall away?* (Luke 8:13) and *Can someone who is saved fall away?* (2 Peter 2:20).

the fog and into the port. Jesus entered the harbor before us, serving as our anchor of hope to lead us into God's presence.

The order of Melchizedek (6:20)
See *The order of Melchizedek* (5:6).

SCRIPTURE LINK (7:1–3) *He met Abraham*
See Gen. 14:18–20. Also see *The order of Melchizedek* (5:6).

How could Melchizedek not have a beginning or end? (7:3)
In actual fact, he did. But since there was no record of his father and mother, because he was *without genealogy,* Melchizedek became a symbol of the coming Christ—a high priest for all eternity. Also see *The order of Melchizedek* (5:6).

If Melchizedek was greater, why did Abraham get the publicity? (7:6–7)
Abraham got the publicity because he had an important role—he was the father of the Jewish nation. He received the promise (6:13–15) and became an example of faith to us (11:11). Melchizedek's role was not as visible because he was primarily an illustration of what was to come—a priesthood with the Messiah as high priest (6:20). The writer was not diminishing Abraham's status, but he did hope to show the Hebrews that the new priesthood was superior to the old.

Perfection (7:11)
The Jewish priesthood was imperfect because it could not bridge the gap between man and God. *Perfection* pointed to the time when Jesus Christ made full and complete access to God possible.

Why couldn't the Messiah have been a priest from the order of Levi? (7:11)
The Levitical priesthood was made up of human priests and was limited to this world. As a result, it could not accomplish God's purposes. Even with sacrifices, sinful humans were limited in how they could approach God; those in this world cannot reach into eternity. But because Jesus as the Son of God was more than human, he could bridge the gap between this world and the heavenly one.

When and how did God swear an oath to Jesus? (7:21–22,28)
We don't really know. The writer quotes Psalm 110:4 to prove that God had intended all along for the Messiah to be a perpetual priest. But that psalm does not tell us when or how God did this. What we can say is that this was part of God's eternal plan, ordered before the foundation of the world.

Melchizedek the Priest

7 This Melchizedek was king of Salem and priest[D] of God Most High. He met Abraham returning from the defeat of the kings and blessed him, [2]and Abraham gave him a tenth of everything. First, his name means "king of righteousness[D]"; then also, "king of Salem" means "king of peace[D]." [3]Without father or mother, without genealogy[D], without beginning of days or end of life, like the Son of God he remains a priest forever.

[4]Just think how great he was: Even the patriarch[D] Abraham gave him a tenth of the plunder[D]! [5]Now the law requires the descendants of Levi who become priests to collect a tenth from the people—that is, their brothers— even though their brothers are descended from Abraham. [6]This man, however, did not trace his descent from Levi, yet he collected a tenth from Abraham and blessed him who had the promises. [7]And without doubt the lesser person is blessed by the greater. [8]In the one case, the tenth is collected by men who die; but in the other case, by him who is declared to be living. [9]One might even say that Levi, who collects the tenth, paid the tenth through Abraham, [10]because when Melchizedek met Abraham, Levi was still in the body of his ancestor.

Jesus Like Melchizedek

[11]If perfection could have been attained through the Levitical priesthood (for on the basis of it the law was given to the people), why was there still need for another priest to come—one in the order of Melchizedek, not in the order of Aaron? [12]For when there is a change of the priesthood, there must also be a change of the law. [13]He of whom these things are said belonged to a different tribe, and no one from that tribe has ever served at the altar. [14]For it is clear that our Lord descended from Judah, and in regard to that tribe Moses said nothing about priests. [15]And what we have said is even more clear if another priest like Melchizedek appears, [16]one who has become a priest not on the basis of a regulation as to his ancestry but on the basis of the power of an indestructible life. [17]For it is declared:

> "You are a priest forever,
>   in the order of Melchizedek."[a]

[18]The former regulation is set aside because it was weak and useless [19](for the law made nothing perfect), and a better hope is introduced, by which we draw near to God.

[20]And it was not without an oath! Others became priests without any oath, [21]but he became a priest with an oath when God said to him:

> "The Lord has sworn
>   and will not change his mind:
>   'You are a priest forever.' "[a]

[22]Because of this oath, Jesus has become the guarantee of a better covenant[D].

[23]Now there have been many of those priests, since death[D] prevented them from continuing in office; [24]but because Jesus lives forever, he has a permanent priesthood. [25]Therefore he is able to save completely[b] those

a17,21 Psalm 110:4   *b25* Or *forever*

who come to God through him, because he always lives to intercede[D] for them.

26Such a high priest[D] meets our need—one who is holy, blameless, pure, set apart from sinners, exalted above the heavens. **27**Unlike the other high priests, he does not need to offer sacrifices[D] day after day, first for his own sins, and then for the sins of the people. He sacrificed for their sins once for all when he offered himself. **28**For the law appoints as high priests men who are weak; but the oath, which came after the law, appointed the Son, who has been made perfect forever.

The High Priest of a New Covenant

8 The point of what we are saying is this: We do have such a high priest, who sat down at the right hand of the throne of the Majesty in heaven, **2**and who serves in the sanctuary, the true tabernacle[D] set up by the Lord, not by man.

3Every high priest is appointed to offer both gifts and sacrifices, and so it was necessary for this one also to have something to offer. **4**If he were on earth, he would not be a priest, for there are already men who offer the gifts prescribed by the law. **5**They serve at a sanctuary that is a copy and shadow of what is in heaven. This is why Moses was warned when he was about to build the tabernacle: "See to it that you make everything according to the pattern shown you on the mountain."[a] **6**But the ministry Jesus has received is as superior to theirs as the covenant[D] of which he is mediator is superior to the old one, and it is founded on better promises.

7For if there had been nothing wrong with that first covenant, no place would have been sought for another. **8**But God found fault with the people and said[b]:

"The time is coming, declares the Lord,
  when I will make a new covenant
with the house of Israel
  and with the house of Judah.
9It will not be like the covenant
  I made with their forefathers
when I took them by the hand
  to lead them out of Egypt,
because they did not remain faithful to my
  covenant,
and I turned away from them,
              declares the Lord.
10This is the covenant I will make with the
  house of Israel
after that time, declares the Lord.
I will put my laws in their minds
  and write them on their hearts.
I will be their God,
  and they will be my people.
11No longer will a man teach his neighbor,
  or a man his brother, saying, 'Know the
    Lord,'
because they will all know me,
  from the least of them to the greatest.
12For I will forgive their wickedness
  and will remember their sins no more."[c]

13By calling this covenant "new," he has made the

In what sanctuary does Jesus serve? (8:2)

Jesus is now at the throne of God, acting as high priest by interceding on behalf of those who trust in him (Romans 8:34). He has not entered an updated version of the old tabernacle; he's entered the very presence of God. The main focus of what Jesus does for us is in heaven, not on earth—in a spiritual place rather than one we can see, in the real sanctuary rather than in a shadow of it (v. 5).

What was wrong with the old covenant? (8:6–7)

First, it was limited. It couldn't accomplish lasting forgiveness, so the sacrifices had to be repeated over and over. Christ's sacrifice, on the other hand, was a permanent solution (7:27). Second, the old covenant had judgment and fear at its core. But the new covenant, based on grace, offered inner peace. Finally, the old covenant could not provide direct access to God; a priest served as a go-between for God and the people. When Christ is our high priest, however, we are in Christ and can enter the presence of God.

What is the new covenant? (8:10–11)

The new covenant (meaning a new agreement or promise) was fulfilled in Christ's death and resurrection. It promises that we can know God through Christ if we trust in his blood as the payment for our sin (9:11–12,18–23). The new covenant provides the means for us to be God's people, making it possible for us to do his will and delight in his company. The new covenant will be expressed most completely, however, when Christ returns to the earth.

---

[a]5 Exodus 25:40   [b]8 Some manuscripts may be translated *fault and said to the people.*   [c]12 Jer. 31:31-34

SCRIPTURE LINK (9:2–4) *Tabernacle*
Read more about the tabernacle in Exodus
25–27.

SCRIPTURE LINK (9:4–5) *Ark of the
covenant*
Read more about the ark in Exodus 25:10–22.

What good were sacrifices that didn't clear the worshiper's conscience? (9:9)

The Old Testament sacrifices had value, even though they could not permanently relieve a person's conscience. First, the loss of life and blood pointed to the awful consequences of sin. Second, the sacrifices underscored the holiness and justice of God. Finally, the sacrifices affirmed the worshiper's faith in the true God. The Israelite's sacrifices helped set them apart from their pagan neighbors as God's people.

Greater and more perfect tabernacle (9:11)

This is the tabernacle in heaven. The difference between the earthly and the heavenly tabernacle is probably like the difference between a picture of a house and the house itself. See *In what sanctuary does Jesus serve?* (8:2).

How does Christ's blood cleanse our consciences? (9:14)

To understand how blood could wash away sin, we have to see things as the first readers of Hebrews did. They were Jews, thoroughly acquainted with Old Testament rituals and sacrifices. They saw blood as part of a divine transaction: life exchanged for death, purity exchanged for sin. This image is, admittedly, an example of spiritual truth limited by the boundaries of human language. See article: *Why was all this blood needed for worship?* (Exodus 29:11–21).

first one obsolete; and what is obsolete and aging will soon disappear.

Worship in the Earthly Tabernacle

9 Now the first covenant[D] had regulations for worship and also an earthly sanctuary. ²A tabernacle[D] was set up. In its first room were the lampstand, the table and the consecrated[D] bread; this was called the Holy Place[D]. ³Behind the second curtain was a room called the Most Holy Place[D], ⁴which had the golden altar of incense[D] and the gold-covered ark of the covenant. This ark contained the gold jar of manna[D], Aaron's staff that had budded, and the stone tablets of the covenant. ⁵Above the ark were the cherubim[D] of the Glory[D], overshadowing the atonement[D] cover.[a] But we cannot discuss these things in detail now.

⁶When everything had been arranged like this, the priests[D] entered regularly into the outer room to carry on their ministry. ⁷But only the high priest entered the inner room, and that only once a year, and never without blood, which he offered for himself and for the sins the people had committed in ignorance. ⁸The Holy Spirit was showing by this that the way into the Most Holy Place had not yet been disclosed as long as the first tabernacle was still standing. ⁹This is an illustration for the present time, indicating that the gifts and sacrifices[D] being offered were not able to clear the conscience of the worshiper. ¹⁰They are only a matter of food and drink and various ceremonial washings—external regulations applying until the time of the new order.

The Blood of Christ

¹¹When Christ came as high priest of the good things that are already here,[b] he went through the greater and more perfect tabernacle that is not man-made, that is to say, not a part of this creation. ¹²He did not enter by means of the blood of goats and calves; but he entered the Most Holy Place once for all by his own blood, having obtained eternal redemption[D]. ¹³The blood of goats and bulls and the ashes of a heifer sprinkled on those who are ceremonially unclean[D] sanctify[D] them so that they are outwardly clean. ¹⁴How much more, then, will the blood of Christ, who through the eternal Spirit offered himself unblemished to God, cleanse our consciences from acts that lead to death[D],[c] so that we may serve the living God!

¹⁵For this reason Christ is the mediator of a new covenant, that those who are called may receive the promised eternal inheritance—now that he has died as a ransom to set them free from the sins committed under the first covenant.

¹⁶In the case of a will,[d] it is necessary to prove the death of the one who made it, ¹⁷because a will is in force only when somebody has died; it never takes effect while the one who made it is living. ¹⁸This is why even the first covenant was not put into effect without blood. ¹⁹When Moses had proclaimed every commandment of the law to all the people, he took the blood of calves, together with water, scarlet wool and branches of hyssop[D], and sprinkled the scroll and all the people. ²⁰He said,

---

[a]5 Traditionally *the mercy seat*   [b]11 Some early manuscripts *are to come*   [c]14 Or *from useless rituals*   [d]16 Same Greek word as *covenant*; also in verse 17

"This is the blood of the covenant[D], which God has commanded you to keep."[a] [21]In the same way, he sprinkled with the blood both the tabernacle[D] and everything used in its ceremonies. [22]In fact, the law requires that nearly everything be cleansed with blood, and without the shedding of blood there is no forgiveness.

[23]It was necessary, then, for the copies of the heavenly things to be purified[D] with these sacrifices[D], but the heavenly things themselves with better sacrifices than these. [24]For Christ did not enter a man-made sanctuary that was only a copy of the true one; he entered heaven itself, now to appear for us in God's presence. [25]Nor did he enter heaven to offer himself again and again, the way the high priest[D] enters the Most Holy Place[D] every year with blood that is not his own. [26]Then Christ would have had to suffer many times since the creation of the world. But now he has appeared once for all at the end of the ages to do away with sin by the sacrifice of himself. [27]Just as man is destined to die once, and after that to face judgment, [28]so Christ was sacrificed once to take away the sins of many people; and he will appear a second time, not to bear sin, but to bring salvation[D] to those who are waiting for him.

Christ's Sacrifice Once for All

10 The law is only a shadow of the good things that are coming—not the realities themselves. For this reason it can never, by the same sacrifices repeated endlessly year after year, make perfect those who draw near to worship. [2]If it could, would they not have stopped being offered? For the worshipers would have been cleansed once for all, and would no longer have felt guilty for their sins. [3]But those sacrifices are an annual reminder of sins, [4]because it is impossible for the blood of bulls and goats to take away sins.

[5]Therefore, when Christ came into the world, he said:

"Sacrifice and offering you did not desire,
    but a body you prepared for me;
[6]with burnt offerings[D] and sin offerings[D]
    you were not pleased.
[7]Then I said, 'Here I am—it is written about me
    in the scroll—
I have come to do your will, O God.' "[b]

[8]First he said, "Sacrifices and offerings, burnt offerings and sin offerings you did not desire, nor were you pleased with them" (although the law required them to be made). [9]Then he said, "Here I am, I have come to do your will." He sets aside the first to establish the second. [10]And by that will, we have been made holy through the sacrifice of the body of Jesus Christ once for all.

[11]Day after day every priest stands and performs his religious duties; again and again he offers the same sacrifices, which can never take away sins. [12]But when this priest had offered for all time one sacrifice for sins, he sat down at the right hand of God. [13]Since that time he waits for his enemies to be made his footstool[D], [14]because by one sacrifice he has made perfect forever those who are being made holy.

[15]The Holy Spirit also testifies to us about this. First he says:

Why did God want blood as payment for sin? (9:22)

Sin was an irreversible affront to God's holiness. The only solution to sin was the death penalty. When blood, signifying life, was poured out, it signified that a life was given up. In the Old Testament the deaths of animals fulfilled this standard of justice. In the New Testament, Jesus' blood fulfilled the requirement of sin, satisfying God's justice so we could be forgiven of our sins.

Copies of the heavenly things (9:23)

See *In what sanctuary does Jesus serve?* (8:2) and *Greater and more perfect tabernacle* (9:11).

Why does Jesus appear for us in God's presence? (9:24)

Like the Old Testament priest who offered blood on behalf of the people, Jesus appears before God to offer his blood as the price for our sins. Other Biblical pictures of what Jesus does for us in God's presence include that of an advocate or defense attorney (1 John 2:1–2) and that of an intercessor (Romans 8:34).

End of the ages (9:26)

This phrase pictures the fulfillment of God's plan for the world. It is similar to *these last days* (1:2). It does not point to a time on the calendar as such, but to the era in which God's eternal plan would be fulfilled in the coming of Christ.

Why is sin still so rampant? (9:26)

Although Jesus has done everything necessary to do away with sin, sinners still must allow his work to take effect in their own lives. Because human nature is infected by sin and because we live in a sinful world, we will have to deal with sin throughout our lives. But the tyranny of sin is broken when we repent and find forgiveness through faith in Jesus (Romans 6:6–7).

Did a lot of bulls and goats die for nothing? (10:4)

No. The sacrifices of the old covenant accomplished a great deal. See *What good were sacrifices that didn't clear the worshiper's conscience?* (9:9).

Why credit Jesus with words from the Old Testament? (10:5–7)

The Old Testament often recognized that God was not content with ritual sacrifice alone (see following note). The writer drew upon one such instance (Psalm 40:6–8) to show his Jewish readers how empty ritual could not put a person right with God. He may have attributed the words to Jesus because they captured the essence of Jesus' teaching (see Mark 12:28–34). It's also possible Jesus may have used these verses while teaching, though we have no record that he did.

What displeased God about sacrifices and offerings? (10:6,8)

Sacrifices, in and of themselves, fell short of what God desired from his people. In a sense, sacrifices were a means to a greater end. What God really wanted was the wholehearted obedience and devotion of his people. So what displeased God about sacrifices was that peo-

---

[a]20 Exodus 24:8   [b]7 Psalm 40:6-8 (see Septuagint)

ple sometimes went no further. They fulfilled the letter but not the spirit of the law. They had the ritual without sincere, heart-felt devotion.

Who are Christ's enemies? (10:13)

Those who reject Christ's words and his sacrifice for their sins. But at the top of the list is Satan, who inspires unbelief and wickedness among all Christ's other enemies. Also, those who oppose the church or persecute Christians are Christ's enemies because, in effect, they persecute him (Acts 9:5).

Made perfect (10:14)

We may struggle for now with imperfection, but we have hope that God's work will be completed in us. See *Who can be as perfect as God?* (Matt. 5:48). Resurrection to immortality will mean perfection, the goal for all Christians. By his sacrifice and his intercession, Jesus guarantees eternal perfection for us.

How are our *hearts sprinkled* and our *bodies washed?* (10:22)

A heart that has been sprinkled means a conscience that has been purified; the guilt has been removed. Jesus Christ does this when he takes away our sin, enters our lives and redirects us toward God. The washing of bodies describes water baptism as a rite connected to this spiritual cleansing (see 1 Peter 3:21–22).

The Day (10:25)

The time when Jesus comes to judge the earth. Unbelievers will be judged for not acknowledging Jesus as Lord and Savior. Christians will be evaluated for the faithfulness of their response to God's work in their lives (1 Cor. 3:10–15).

Is there no forgiveness for sins committed after becoming a Christian? (10:26)

Forgiveness is always available to those who repent and confess their sins (1 John 1:9). This warning is against deliberate, persistent sinning. Those who do sin in this way become spiritually calloused; eventually they may no longer want to be forgiven.

16"This is the covenant[D] I will make with them
  after that time, says the Lord.
I will put my laws in their hearts,
  and I will write them on their minds."[a]

17Then he adds:

"Their sins and lawless acts
  I will remember no more."[b]

18And where these have been forgiven, there is no longer any sacrifice[D] for sin.

A Call to Persevere

19Therefore, brothers, since we have confidence to enter the Most Holy Place[D] by the blood of Jesus, 20by a new and living way opened for us through the curtain, that is, his body, 21and since we have a great priest[D] over the house of God, 22let us draw near to God with a sincere heart in full assurance of faith, having our hearts sprinkled to cleanse us from a guilty conscience and having our bodies washed with pure water. 23Let us hold unswervingly to the hope we profess, for he who promised is faithful. 24And let us consider how we may spur one another on toward love and good deeds. 25Let us not give up meeting together, as some are in the habit of doing, but let us encourage one another—and all the more as you see the Day approaching.

26If we deliberately keep on sinning after we have received the knowledge of the truth, no sacrifice for sins is left, 27but only a fearful expectation of judgment and of raging fire that will consume the enemies of God. 28Anyone who rejected the law of Moses died without mercy[D] on the testimony of two or three witnesses. 29How much more severely do you think a man deserves to be punished who has trampled the Son of God under foot, who has treated as an unholy thing the blood of the covenant that sanctified him, and who has insulted the Spirit of grace[D]? 30For we know him who said, "It is mine to avenge[D]; I will repay,"[c] and again, "The Lord will judge his people."[d] 31It is a dreadful thing to fall into the hands of the living God.

32Remember those earlier days after you had received the light, when you stood your ground in a great contest in the face of suffering. 33Sometimes you were publicly exposed to insult and persecution; at other times you stood side by side with those who were so treated. 34You sympathized with those in prison and joyfully accepted the confiscation of your property, because you knew that you yourselves had better and lasting possessions.

35So do not throw away your confidence; it will be richly rewarded. 36You need to persevere so that when you have done the will of God, you will receive what he has promised. 37For in just a very little while,

"He who is coming will come and will not
    delay.
38 But my righteous[D] one[e] will live by faith.
  And if he shrinks back,
    I will not be pleased with him."[f]

*a*16 Jer. 31:33   *b*17 Jer. 31:34   *c*30 Deut. 32:35   *d*30 Deut. 32:36; Psalm 135:14   *e*38 One early manuscript *But the righteous*   *f*38 Hab. 2:3,4

[39]But we are not of those who shrink back and are destroyed, but of those who believe and are saved.

By Faith

11 Now faith is being sure of what we hope for and certain of what we do not see. [2]This is what the ancients were commended for.

[3]By faith we understand that the universe was formed at God's command, so that what is seen was not made out of what was visible.

[4]By faith Abel offered God a better sacrifice[D] than Cain did. By faith he was commended as a righteous[D] man, when God spoke well of his offerings. And by faith he still speaks, even though he is dead.

[5]By faith Enoch was taken from this life, so that he did not experience death[D]; he could not be found, because God had taken him away. For before he was taken, he was commended as one who pleased God. [6]And without faith it is impossible to please God, because anyone who comes to him must believe that he exists and that he rewards those who earnestly seek him.

[7]By faith Noah, when warned about things not yet seen, in holy fear built an ark to save his family. By his faith he condemned the world and became heir of the righteousness[D] that comes by faith.

[8]By faith Abraham, when called to go to a place he would later receive as his inheritance, obeyed and went, even though he did not know where he was going. [9]By faith he made his home in the promised land like a stranger in a foreign country; he lived in tents, as did Isaac and Jacob, who were heirs with him of the same promise. [10]For he was looking forward to the city with foundations, whose architect and builder is God.

[11]By faith Abraham, even though he was past age—and Sarah herself was barren—was enabled to become a father because he[a] considered him faithful who had made the promise. [12]And so from this one man, and he as good

[a] 11 Or By faith even Sarah, who was past age, was enabled to bear children because she

Who are *those who shrink back and are destroyed*? (10:39)

Some link *those who shrink back* with those who drift away (2:1), harden their hearts (3:8), fall short (4:1), fall away (6:6), throw away their confidence (10:35) or do not persevere (10:36). Some think these words warn Christians about the danger of giving up on their faith or not growing in their faith. Others think they are warnings for pretenders—those who have fooled others and perhaps themselves into thinking they have trusted in Christ. Either way, these warnings should be taken seriously. Instead of drawing back and letting go, we are to draw near and hold fast (vv. 22–23).

Why was Abel's sacrifice better than Cain's? (11:4)

Because it was offered in faith. He responded in faith to the truth he'd heard about God. Some see Abel as a picture of those who recognize their sin and their need of salvation through faith in God's way—that is, by blood sacrifice.

SCRIPTURE LINK (11:5) Enoch . . . *taken from this life*

See Gen. 5:21–24.

How did Noah's faith condemn the world? (11:7)

Noah's faith caused him to act on God's warnings that a flood would cover the world. While Noah believed God, the rest of the people, by contrast, ignored Noah's message of coming judgment. His obedience was an indictment on those who persisted in their disobedience.

What was the promise to Abraham and his descendants? (11:9)

God promised Abraham protection, land, a great reputation and heirs (Gen. 12:1–3; 15:1–6,18; 17:1–10). But the overriding promise was that Abraham would be a blessing to all the families of the earth. This was fulfilled through Jesus, the Messiah, who came from Abraham's descendants.

What is faith like? (11:1)

Faith means abandoning all trust in our own resources, abilities and reasoning—the things we see. It means relying instead on things we cannot see—God's promises, provisions and his concern for us. An inner attitude alone does not define faith, though. For faith to be present, action is required. Faith proves itself by its obedience to the Lord.

The writer of Hebrews expressed faith in two directions: faith toward future things (*what we hope for*) and faith toward invisible things (*what we do not see*). When we are certain God is in control of these areas (and we live like he is in control), that's faith.

The two sides of faith—assurance and expectation—can be seen in the lives of those listed in this chapter. They had strong convictions about unseen present realities. They also had a strong assurance that God's promises would be fulfilled—even in the face of evidence that seemed to suggest otherwise (see, for example, v. 11).

Ultimately, the way we see God will determine the shape of our faith. If we see a big, faithful, all-powerful God, then our faith will rise to those levels. If, on the other hand, we see a smaller God, a distant or less active God, then faith will plateau at those levels.

as dead, came descendants as numerous as the stars in the sky and as countless as the sand on the seashore.

¹³All these people were still living by faith when they died. They did not receive the things promised; they only saw them and welcomed them from a distance. And they admitted that they were aliens[D] and strangers on earth. ¹⁴People who say such things show that they are looking for a country of their own. ¹⁵If they had been thinking of the country they had left, they would have had opportunity to return. ¹⁶Instead, they were longing for a better country—a heavenly one. Therefore God is not ashamed to be called their God, for he has prepared a city for them.

¹⁷By faith Abraham, when God tested him, offered Isaac as a sacrifice[D]. He who had received the promises was about to sacrifice his one and only son, ¹⁸even though God had said to him, "It is through Isaac that your offspring[a] will be reckoned."[b] ¹⁹Abraham reasoned that God could raise the dead, and figuratively speaking, he did receive Isaac back from death[D].

²⁰By faith Isaac blessed Jacob and Esau in regard to their future.

²¹By faith Jacob, when he was dying, blessed each of Joseph's sons, and worshiped as he leaned on the top of his staff.

²²By faith Joseph, when his end was near, spoke about the exodus of the Israelites from Egypt and gave instructions about his bones.

²³By faith Moses' parents hid him for three months after he was born, because they saw he was no ordinary child, and they were not afraid of the king's edict[D].

²⁴By faith Moses, when he had grown up, refused to be known as the son of Pharaoh's daughter. ²⁵He chose to be mistreated along with the people of God rather than to enjoy the pleasures of sin for a short time. ²⁶He regarded disgrace for the sake of Christ as of greater value than the treasures of Egypt, because he was looking ahead to his reward. ²⁷By faith he left Egypt, not fearing the king's anger; he persevered because he saw him who is invisible. ²⁸By faith he kept the Passover and the sprinkling of blood, so that the destroyer of the firstborn[D] would not touch the firstborn of Israel.

²⁹By faith the people passed through the Red Sea[c] as on dry land; but when the Egyptians tried to do so, they were drowned.

³⁰By faith the walls of Jericho[D] fell, after the people had marched around them for seven days.

³¹By faith the prostitute Rahab[D], because she welcomed the spies, was not killed with those who were disobedient.[d]

³²And what more shall I say? I do not have time to tell about Gideon, Barak, Samson, Jephthah, David, Samuel and the prophets[D], ³³who through faith conquered kingdoms, administered justice, and gained what was promised; who shut the mouths of lions, ³⁴quenched the fury of the flames, and escaped the edge of the sword; whose weakness was turned to strength; and who became powerful in battle and routed foreign armies. ³⁵Women received back their dead, raised to life again. Others were tortured and refused to be released, so that they might gain a better resurrection[D]. ³⁶Some faced jeers and flogging, while still others were chained and put in prison.

How did Moses suffer for the sake of Christ? (11:26)

Moses did not suffer on behalf of Christ, but in a Christ-like way. His suffering was seen as an example of the coming Christ, who later suffered on behalf of God's people. Since *Christ* literally means *Anointed One*, the idea could be that Moses accepted the stigma that comes with being chosen by God—just as Jesus did centuries later.

A better resurrection (11:35)

This suggests at least two kinds of resurrection, one being better than the other. The women who *received back their dead* saw a resurrection to this mortal life (1 Kings 17:17–23; 2 Kings 4:32–37). Those who were tortured and died, however, anticipated an eternal resurrection to immortal life. The same word is used for both, although the differences are obvious.

[a]18 Greek *seed*   [b]18 Gen. 21:12   [c]29 That is, Sea of Reeds
[d]31 Or *unbelieving*

37They were stoned[a]; they were sawed in two; they were put to death[D] by the sword. They went about in sheepskins and goatskins, destitute, persecuted and mistreated— **38**the world was not worthy of them. They wandered in deserts and mountains, and in caves and holes in the ground.

39These were all commended for their faith, yet none of them received what had been promised. **40**God had planned something better for us so that only together with us would they be made perfect.

God Disciplines His Sons

12 Therefore, since we are surrounded by such a great cloud of witnesses, let us throw off everything that hinders and the sin that so easily entangles, and let us run with perseverance the race marked out for us. **2**Let us fix our eyes on Jesus, the author and perfecter of our faith, who for the joy set before him endured the cross, scorning its shame, and sat down at the right hand of the throne of God. **3**Consider him who endured such opposition from sinful men, so that you will not grow weary and lose heart.

4In your struggle against sin, you have not yet resisted to the point of shedding your blood. **5**And you have forgotten that word of encouragement that addresses you as sons:

"My son, do not make light of the Lord's
    discipline,
    and do not lose heart when he rebukes you,
6because the Lord disciplines those he loves,
    and he punishes everyone he accepts as a
    son."[b]

7Endure hardship as discipline; God is treating you as sons. For what son is not disciplined by his father? **8**If you are not disciplined (and everyone undergoes discipline), then you are illegitimate children and not true sons. **9**Moreover, we have all had human fathers who disciplined us and we respected them for it. How much more should we submit to the Father of our spirits and live! **10**Our fathers disciplined us for a little while as they thought best; but God disciplines us for our good, that we may share in his holiness. **11**No discipline seems pleasant at the time, but painful. Later on, however, it produces a harvest of righteousness[D] and peace[D] for those who have been trained by it.

12Therefore, strengthen your feeble arms and weak knees. **13**"Make level paths for your feet,"[c] so that the lame may not be disabled, but rather healed.

Warning Against Refusing God

14Make every effort to live in peace with all men and to be holy; without holiness no one will see the Lord. **15**See to it that no one misses the grace[D] of God and that no bitter root grows up to cause trouble and defile many. **16**See that no one is sexually immoral, or is godless like Esau, who for a single meal sold his inheritance rights as the oldest son. **17**Afterward, as you know, when he wanted to inherit this blessing, he was rejected. He could bring about no change of mind, though he sought the blessing with tears.

---

[a]37 Some early manuscripts *stoned; they were put to the test;*
[b]6 Prov. 3:11,12   [c]13 Prov. 4:26

Made perfect (11:40)

Though these Old Testament believers looked to the coming Messiah in faith, their faith was not *perfect*, in the sense of being *complete*, until Christ came. See *Perfection* (7:11) and *Made perfect* (10:14).

Cloud of witnesses (12:1)

Using the analogy of a race, the writer describes earlier heroes of the faith seated in the stadium, as it were, cheering us on to the finish line. The testimony of their lives of faith is their witness. The record they left behind, like cheers from a grandstand, can encourage us to persevere in our faith.

How does the Lord discipline? (12:5)

God disciplines in many ways, sometimes to train or prepare us for his ways, sometimes to punish us for unfaithfulness. He can use sinful people as instruments of discipline (v. 3), our own inner struggles against sin (v. 4) or personal hardships (v. 7). Occasionally discipline may come in the broader context of physical suffering (11:35–38). Israel suffered 40 years in the desert (Num. 14:34); Paul received a "thorn in the flesh" (2 Cor. 12:7).

Can we be more holy by trying harder? (12:14)

To be holy is to be Christ-like, reflecting the glory of God. The Holy Spirit produces within Christians holy characteristics, called the fruit of the Spirit (Gal. 5:22–23). In that sense, we can't produce holiness ourselves. But we are responsible to renounce sins that would otherwise hold us back (v. 1). Also we can focus on Jesus (v. 2) through disciplines such as worship, prayer, service, witness and fellowship.

SCRIPTURE LINK (12:16–17) *Esau ... sold his inheritance*

See Gen. 25:29–34.

SCRIPTURE LINK (12:18-21) *A mountain ... burning with fire*

This describes Mount Sinai and the giving of the law in Exodus 19:12-22.

How does Mount Zion compare to the earlier mountain? (12:22-24)

Mount Sinai (vv. 18-21) stands in contrast to the scene at Mount Zion. Sinai was marked by an awesome display of power causing the people to fear and tremble before God. Zion is a picture of people in joyful worship, freed of condemnation and standing in purity before a holy and righteous God. Sinai represented the law and focused on avoiding sin. Zion reflected God's grace and emphasized righteousness.

Is this warning for believers? (12:25-27)

See Introduction: *Why and for whom was it written?*

What can be shaken ... what cannot be shaken (12:27)

The former refers to the present material universe; the latter, to the abiding, eternal spiritual realm—the kingdom of God to which Christians belong. Eternal things cannot be shaken.

Why this potpourri of advice? (13:1-10)

It appears as though the writer wanted to include more information than he had time or space to cover. He had explored theological concepts quite thoroughly, but he did not want to close without at least touching on several practical concerns, each of which could merit an entire chapter. Still, the impact of all this advice together is strong: those who focus on Jesus (12:2) will be able to accomplish many things for his glory. Personal morality and responsibility should flow from one's persevering faith in Christ.

Does this mean spiritual or physical beings? (13:2)

Strangers may be either humans or angels. The writer here encourages hospitality by recalling the experiences of Abraham and Sarah (Gen. 18:1-15) and of Lot (Gen. 19:1-13). Angels visited them in human form.

What strange teachings were circulating? (13:9-10)

Some were emphasizing visible rituals and routines, showing an inclination toward returning to Old Testament law. Following Jewish legalism, some insisted that *ceremonial foods* (that is, sacrifices prepared by priests at the tabernacle) were the means to approach God. But Christ's sacrifice on the altar of grace left no room for the former rituals.

[18]You have not come to a mountain that can be touched and that is burning with fire; to darkness, gloom and storm; [19]to a trumpet blast or to such a voice speaking words that those who heard it begged that no further word be spoken to them, [20]because they could not bear what was commanded: "If even an animal touches the mountain, it must be stoned."[a] [21]The sight was so terrifying that Moses said, "I am trembling with fear."[b]

[22]But you have come to Mount Zion[D], to the heavenly Jerusalem[D], the city of the living God. You have come to thousands upon thousands of angels in joyful assembly, [23]to the church of the firstborn[D], whose names are written in heaven. You have come to God, the judge of all men, to the spirits of righteous[D] men made perfect, [24]to Jesus the mediator of a new covenant[D], and to the sprinkled blood that speaks a better word than the blood of Abel.

[25]See to it that you do not refuse him who speaks. If they did not escape when they refused him who warned them on earth, how much less will we, if we turn away from him who warns us from heaven? [26]At that time his voice shook the earth, but now he has promised, "Once more I will shake not only the earth but also the heavens."[c] [27]The words "once more" indicate the removing of what can be shaken—that is, created things—so that what cannot be shaken may remain.

[28]Therefore, since we are receiving a kingdom that cannot be shaken, let us be thankful, and so worship God acceptably with reverence[D] and awe, [29]for our "God is a consuming fire."[d]

Concluding Exhortations

13 Keep on loving each other as brothers. [2]Do not forget to entertain strangers, for by so doing some people have entertained angels without knowing it. [3]Remember those in prison as if you were their fellow prisoners, and those who are mistreated as if you yourselves were suffering.

[4]Marriage should be honored by all, and the marriage bed kept pure, for God will judge the adulterer and all the sexually immoral. [5]Keep your lives free from the love of money and be content with what you have, because God has said,

"Never will I leave you;
     never will I forsake you."[e]

[6]So we say with confidence,

"The Lord is my helper; I will not be afraid.
     What can man do to me?"[f]

[7]Remember your leaders, who spoke the word of God to you. Consider the outcome of their way of life and imitate their faith. [8]Jesus Christ is the same yesterday and today and forever.

[9]Do not be carried away by all kinds of strange teachings. It is good for our hearts to be strengthened by grace[D], not by ceremonial foods, which are of no value to those who eat them. [10]We have an altar from which those who minister at the tabernacle[D] have no right to eat.

[11]The high priest[D] carries the blood of animals into the

---

[a]20 Exodus 19:12,13   [b]21 Deut. 9:19   [c]26 Haggai 2:6
[d]29 Deut. 4:24   [e]5 Deut. 31:6   [f]6 Psalm 118:6,7

Most Holy Place[D] as a sin offering[D], but the bodies are burned outside the camp. [12]And so Jesus also suffered outside the city gate to make the people holy through his own blood. [13]Let us, then, go to him outside the camp, bearing the disgrace he bore. [14]For here we do not have an enduring city, but we are looking for the city that is to come.

[15]Through Jesus, therefore, let us continually offer to God a sacrifice[D] of praise—the fruit of lips that confess his name. [16]And do not forget to do good and to share with others, for with such sacrifices God is pleased.

[17]Obey your leaders and submit to their authority. They keep watch over you as men who must give an account. Obey them so that their work will be a joy, not a burden, for that would be of no advantage to you.

[18]Pray for us. We are sure that we have a clear conscience and desire to live honorably in every way. [19]I particularly urge you to pray so that I may be restored to you soon.

[20]May the God of peace[D], who through the blood of the eternal covenant[D] brought back from the dead our Lord Jesus, that great Shepherd of the sheep, [21]equip you with everything good for doing his will, and may he work in us what is pleasing to him, through Jesus Christ, to whom be glory[D] for ever and ever. Amen.

[22]Brothers, I urge you to bear with my word of exhortation, for I have written you only a short letter.

[23]I want you to know that our brother Timothy has been released. If he arrives soon, I will come with him to see you.

[24]Greet all your leaders and all God's people. Those from Italy send you their greetings.

[25]Grace[D] be with you all.

What does it mean to go to Jesus outside the camp? (13:13)

Borrowing another Old Testament image, the writer recalls Israel's camp in the desert which had the tabernacle at its center. To follow Jesus, believers must figuratively leave the old tabernacle system of rules and regulations and go *outside the camp*. It was outside the camp that sin offerings were burned (Exodus 29:14) and where, on the Day of Atonement, a goat was released to symbolically carry away sins (Lev. 16:21–22). In the same way, Jesus took our sins upon himself. To receive his forgiveness, we must *go to him* and confess our sin.

How was blood instrumental in bringing Jesus back from the dead? (13:20)

Technically, his blood did not cause Jesus to be resurrected. Rather, his resurrection confirmed that his blood had been effective in removing our sins. If his blood had not fulfilled the requirements of the new covenant, Jesus would not have been raised from the dead.

JAMES

Why read this book?

If you're looking for practical ways to live as a Christian, you've come to the right book. James shows that it's possible to believe the right things, yet live the wrong way. But this book will also show you how to turn right doctrine into right living.

Who wrote this book?

No one knows for sure which James wrote this letter. Most believe the writer was James, Jesus' brother (Gal. 1:19).

To whom was it written?

The twelve tribes (1:1), meaning either (1) the people of Israel who had become believers in Christ or (2) the church in a symbolic sense—both Jewish and Gentile believers (Gal. 6:16).

Why was it written?

To warn believers of some habits they had fallen into that undermined the essence of what they believed: things such as favoritism, slander, pride, the misuse of wealth and a lack of patience.

When was it written?

James may have been the first New Testament book to be written—between A.D. 40 and 50.

What to look for in James:

This letter takes a no-nonsense approach to hypocrisy. James describes the evil of a tongue out of control, playing favorites with the rich or boasting about plans for tomorrow. Don't look for pious platitudes here, but expect a string of hard-hitting, specific, practical instructions to help you live an authentic Christian life.

When did these things happen?

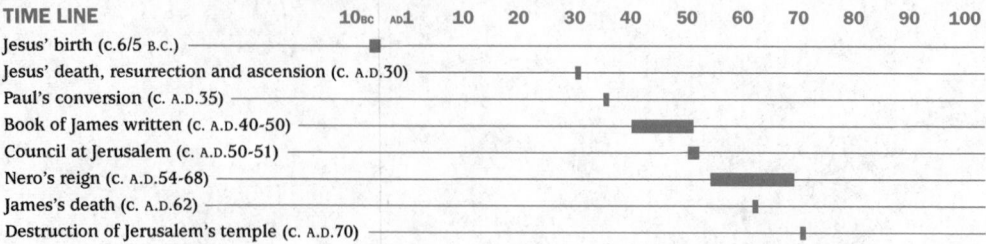

TIME LINE

	10 BC	AD 1	10	20	30	40	50	60	70	80	90	100
Jesus' birth (c.6/5 B.C.)												
Jesus' death, resurrection and ascension (c. A.D.30)												
Paul's conversion (c. A.D.35)												
Book of James written (c. A.D.40-50)												
Council at Jerusalem (c. A.D.50-51)												
Nero's reign (c. A.D.54-68)												
James's death (c. A.D.62)												
Destruction of Jerusalem's temple (c. A.D.70)												

1 James, a servant of God and of the Lord Jesus Christ,

To the twelve tribes scattered among the nations:

Greetings.

Trials and Temptations

2Consider it pure joy, my brothers, whenever you face trials of many kinds, **3**because you know that the testing of your faith develops perseverance. **4**Perseverance must finish its work so that you may be mature and complete, not lacking anything. **5**If any of you lacks wisdom, he should ask God, who gives generously to all without finding fault, and it will be given to him. **6**But when he asks, he must believe and not doubt, because he who doubts is like a wave of the sea, blown and tossed by the wind. **7**That man should not think he will receive anything from the Lord; **8**he is a double-minded man, unstable in all he does.

9The brother in humble circumstances ought to take pride in his high position. **10**But the one who is rich should take pride in his low position, because he will pass away like a wild flower. **11**For the sun rises with scorching heat and withers the plant; its blossom falls and its beauty is destroyed. In the same way, the rich man will fade away even while he goes about his business.

12Blessed is the man who perseveres under trial, because when he has stood the test, he will receive the crown of life that God has promised to those who love him.

13When tempted, no one should say, "God is tempting me." For God cannot be tempted by evil, nor does he tempt anyone; **14**but each one is tempted when, by his own evil desire, he is dragged away and enticed. **15**Then, after desire has conceived, it gives birth to sin; and sin, when it is full-grown, gives birth to death.ᴰ

16Don't be deceived, my dear brothers. **17**Every good and perfect gift is from above, coming down from the Father of the heavenly lights, who does not change like shifting shadows. **18**He chose to give us birth through the word of truth, that we might be a kind of firstfruitsᴰ of all he created.

Listening and Doing

19My dear brothers, take note of this: Everyone should be quick to listen, slow to speak and slow to become angry, **20**for man's anger does not bring about the righteousᴰ life that God desires. **21**Therefore, get rid of all moral filth and the evil that is so prevalent and humbly accept the word planted in you, which can save you.

22Do not merely listen to the word, and so deceive yourselves. Do what it says. **23**Anyone who listens to the word but does not do what it says is like a man who looks at his face in a mirror **24**and, after looking at himself, goes away and immediately forgets what he looks like. **25**But the man who looks intently into the perfect law that gives freedom, and continues to do this, not forgetting what he has heard, but doing it—he will be blessed in what he does.

26If anyone considers himself religious and yet does not keep a tight rein on his tongue, he deceives himself and his religion is worthless. **27**Religion that God our Father accepts as pure and faultless is this: to look after orphans

Twelve tribes (1:1)

This may refer to Jewish descendants of the twelve tribes of Israel (see *Map 4* at the back of this Bible), who now believed in Christ. It also could mean the church, symbolically called the new Israel (Gal. 6:16).

How is joy possible when facing trouble? (1:2)

This doesn't mean we derive pleasure from pain. Instead, this describes a unique kind of joy—the deep sense of well-being that comes from knowing that God is in control of everything in our lives. It's an assurance that he is constantly at work, using both pain and pleasure to develop within us character traits of endurance and patience.

Mature (1:4)

See *What is a mature Christian like?* (Eph. 4:13).

What kind of wisdom can we ask for? (1:5)

We can ask for an understanding of who God is and what he is doing through the trials in our lives (vv. 2–4). Though our grasp of God and his mysterious ways will never be complete, we can gain wisdom we need, enabling us to persevere by giving us "eyes to see" what God wants and helping us face various trials.

Is it a sin to doubt? (1:6–8)

It's not a sin to struggle with questions of who God is and what it means to belong to him. Those are natural questions anyone seeking God must ask. Rather James condemns an attitude that questions whether or not God and his Word can be trusted. A mistrustful, suspicious attitude toward God poisons our spirit, making joy impossible.

Will God ignore our prayers when we waver? (1:7–8)

It's not so much that God withholds answers when our faith is shaky, but that we are not prepared to receive or recognize his answers at such times. To make sense of our sufferings, we must believe that God is somehow going to turn pain, evil and tragedy to eternal good. Without that foundational trust in God, we often don't recognize the answers God sends.

What is acceptable pride? (1:9–10)

See *Is it okay to be proud?* (Gal. 6:4).

Crown of life (1:12)

Drawing from the Greek custom of placing a wreath on the head of a winning athlete, James describes the reward given to believers who cross the finish line: eternal life, victory over death.

How are temptations different from trials? (1:13; see vv. 2–3)

Tempting is trying to get a person to do something wrong. A *trial* is a situation in which God gives a person an opportunity to do something right. God never tries to trip us up. But he does allow tough circumstances to build our character and maturity.

Firstfruits (1:18)

The original readers were the first to trust in Christ as their Savior. So James compared

them to the *firstfruits* of harvest. The term implies worship since the first harvest of a crop was set aside as a gift to the Lord.

When is anger okay? (1:19–20)

Anger is a human emotion and not sinful in itself. Even God and Christ have been angry. In fact, anger at sin, injustice and evil is a sign of godliness and righteousness. But anger that leads to malice, rage and revenge is clearly forbidden and should be handled quickly to prevent damaging attitudes. Also see *When is anger sin?* (Eph. 4:26).

Why was *favoritism* a problem? (2:1–7)

The first-century church, unique in its society, tried to break down class distinctions. In the church, a man of influence could find himself rubbing shoulders with slaves—a slave could be his elder; a slave owner might serve sacraments to a slave. Such unnatural social behavior shocked those who were influenced by the prevailing mindset of the day. Many, caving in to social pressure, felt compelled to give special treatment to those who were esteemed outside the church.

Why are we judged as we judge others? (2:13)

Because the mercy we show indicates the mercy we've received. Those who have tasted God's mercy will naturally be more forgiving toward others. Those who deal harshly with others demonstrate they have not experienced forgiveness personally. Life also seems to prove, as a general rule, the more merciful we are to others, the more we ourselves are treated with compassion.

How could a prostitute be considered righteous? (2:25)

James does not suggest that Rahab's one act of helping the Israelite spies canceled out a lifetime of sexual sin. See Heb. 11:31. Rather, by her actions she demonstrated that she had rejected paganism and put her trust in the God of Israel. Because of her faith, God declared her righteous—even making her part of the lineage of the Messiah (Matt. 1:5).

and widows in their distress and to keep oneself from being polluted by the world.

Favoritism Forbidden

2 My brothers, as believers in our glorious Lord Jesus Christ, don't show favoritism. ²Suppose a man comes into your meeting wearing a gold ring and fine clothes, and a poor man in shabby clothes also comes in. ³If you show special attention to the man wearing fine clothes and say, "Here's a good seat for you," but say to the poor man, "You stand there" or "Sit on the floor by my feet," ⁴have you not discriminated among yourselves and become judges with evil thoughts?

⁵Listen, my dear brothers: Has not God chosen those who are poor in the eyes of the world to be rich in faith and to inherit the kingdom he promised those who love him? ⁶But you have insulted the poor. Is it not the rich who are exploiting you? Are they not the ones who are dragging you into court? ⁷Are they not the ones who are slandering the noble name of him to whom you belong?

⁸If you really keep the royal law found in Scripture, "Love your neighbor as yourself," [a] you are doing right. ⁹But if you show favoritism, you sin and are convicted by the law as lawbreakers. ¹⁰For whoever keeps the whole law and yet stumbles at just one point is guilty of breaking all of it. ¹¹For he who said, "Do not commit adultery," [b] also said, "Do not murder." [c] If you do not commit adultery but do commit murder, you have become a lawbreaker.

¹²Speak and act as those who are going to be judged by the law that gives freedom, ¹³because judgment without mercyᴰ will be shown to anyone who has not been merciful. Mercy triumphs over judgment!

Faith and Deeds

¹⁴What good is it, my brothers, if a man claims to have faith but has no deeds? Can such faith save him? ¹⁵Suppose a brother or sister is without clothes and daily food. ¹⁶If one of you says to him, "Go, I wish you well; keep warm and well fed," but does nothing about his physical needs, what good is it? ¹⁷In the same way, faith by itself, if it is not accompanied by action, is dead.

¹⁸But someone will say, "You have faith; I have deeds." Show me your faith without deeds, and I will show you my faith by what I do. ¹⁹You believe that there is one God. Good! Even the demons believe that—and shudder.

²⁰You foolish man, do you want evidence that faith without deeds is useless [d]? ²¹Was not our ancestor Abraham considered righteousᴰ for what he did when he offered his son Isaac on the altar? ²²You see that his faith and his actions were working together, and his faith was made complete by what he did. ²³And the scripture was fulfilled that says, "Abraham believed God, and it was credited to him as righteousnessᴰ," [e] and he was called God's friend. ²⁴You see that a person is justifiedᴰ by what he does and not by faith alone.

²⁵In the same way, was not even Rahabᴰ the prostitute considered righteous for what she did when she gave lodging to the spies and sent them off in a different direc-

---

[a]8 Lev. 19:18   [b]11 Exodus 20:14; Deut. 5:18   [c]11 Exodus 20:13; Deut. 5:17   [d]20 Some early manuscripts *dead*   [e]23 Gen. 15:6

tion? **26**As the body without the spirit is dead, so faith without deeds is dead.

Taming the Tongue

3 Not many of you should presume to be teachers, my brothers, because you know that we who teach will be judged more strictly. **2**We all stumble in many ways. If anyone is never at fault in what he says, he is a perfect man, able to keep his whole body in check.

3When we put bits into the mouths of horses to make them obey us, we can turn the whole animal. **4**Or take ships as an example. Although they are so large and are driven by strong winds, they are steered by a very small rudder wherever the pilot wants to go. **5**Likewise the tongue is a small part of the body, but it makes great boasts. Consider what a great forest is set on fire by a small spark. **6**The tongue also is a fire, a world of evil among the parts of the body. It corrupts the whole person, sets the whole course of his life on fire, and is itself set on fire by hell**D**.

7All kinds of animals, birds, reptiles and creatures of the sea are being tamed and have been tamed by man, **8**but no man can tame the tongue. It is a restless evil, full of deadly poison.

9With the tongue we praise our Lord and Father, and with it we curse men, who have been made in God's likeness. **10**Out of the same mouth come praise and cursing. My brothers, this should not be. **11**Can both fresh water and salt*a* water flow from the same spring? **12**My broth-

a11 Greek *bitter* (see also verse 14)

Is there a sliding scale of judgment? (3:1)

Those entrusted with greater responsibility will have more to answer for than others. Those in positions of authority will be held accountable for the way they use their influence. One leader with one false teaching, for example, can destroy a whole group of believers. Those who wanted to be teachers to gain prestige were operating out of the wrong motives and were risking spiritual danger.

How can anyone attain perfection? (3:2)

See following note and *Who can be as perfect as God?* (Matt. 5:48).

If the tongue cannot be tamed, why try? (3:8)

Because of human frailties and tendencies to sin, the tongue will never be totally "tamed" in this life. But as believers grow in grace and love, they can use their tongues to build up and bless others, rather than curse or tear them down. The tongue has great potential—for good as well as harm. But the hope for controlling it comes from focusing more on the inner life than on the tongue itself, more on the source than its outflow (vv. 11–12).

Is faith enough? (2:14–24)

A re we saved by grace through faith alone (Eph. 2:8–9) or do we also need works?

James does not argue here for good works as a requirement for salvation. Nor does he say that deeds are more important than beliefs. Rather, he insists that there are two kinds of faith—one legitimate and the other illegitimate; *faith . . . made complete* (v. 22) and *faith without deeds* (v. 20). Both kinds "believe" in one sense of the word. But legitimate faith goes deeper than "right thinking" to "right living."

Confusion may arise, however, when we recall that Paul writes in the Bible that we cannot earn salvation. He uses Abraham as an example of one who received God's promise, not through human effort, but through faith (Gal. 3:6–12).

James also uses Abraham as an example, but his focus is different from Paul's. He skips over the futility of human effort to discuss the futility of deficient faith—faith that stops at the intellectual level. Even demons have that kind of "faith," James thunders (v. 19).

James's point, then, is that Abraham demonstrated legitimate faith—proven by his actions. Abraham's deeds earned him nothing, but they proved his genuine faith: right faith led to right actions. If he had not been able to trust God, Abraham could never have offered his son—the fulfillment of God's promise—on the altar (vv. 21–22). Paul uses Abraham to show that people are justified on the basis of real faith; James shows that Abraham's faith was proven to be real because it worked.

So then, we don't need anything but faith—the right kind of faith—to be saved. And our behavior will show what our faith is made of, whether or not it is legitimate.

ers, can a fig tree bear olives, or a grapevine bear figs? Neither can a salt spring produce fresh water.

Two Kinds of Wisdom

13Who is wise and understanding among you? Let him show it by his good life, by deeds done in the humility that comes from wisdom. **14**But if you harbor bitter envy and selfish ambition in your hearts, do not boast about it or deny the truth. **15**Such "wisdom" does not come down from heaven but is earthly, unspiritual, of the devil. **16**For where you have envy and selfish ambition, there you find disorder and every evil practice.

17But the wisdom that comes from heaven is first of all pure; then peace^D-loving, considerate, submissive, full of mercy^D and good fruit, impartial and sincere. **18**Peacemakers who sow in peace raise a harvest of righteousness^D.

Submit Yourselves to God

4 What causes fights and quarrels among you? Don't they come from your desires that battle within you? **2**You want something but don't get it. You kill and covet, but you cannot have what you want. You quarrel and fight. You do not have, because you do not ask God. **3**When you ask, you do not receive, because you ask with wrong motives, that you may spend what you get on your pleasures.

4You adulterous people, don't you know that friendship with the world is hatred toward God? Anyone who chooses to be a friend of the world becomes an enemy of God. **5**Or do you think Scripture says without reason that the spirit he caused to live in us envies intensely?^a **6**But he gives us more grace^D. That is why Scripture says:

> "God opposes the proud
>   but gives grace to the humble."^b

7Submit yourselves, then, to God. Resist the devil, and he will flee from you. **8**Come near to God and he will come near to you. Wash your hands, you sinners, and purify^D your hearts, you double-minded. **9**Grieve, mourn and wail. Change your laughter to mourning and your joy to gloom. **10**Humble yourselves before the Lord, and he will lift you up.

11Brothers, do not slander one another. Anyone who speaks against his brother or judges him speaks against the law and judges it. When you judge the law, you are not keeping it, but sitting in judgment on it. **12**There is only one Lawgiver and Judge, the one who is able to save and destroy. But you—who are you to judge your neighbor?

Boasting About Tomorrow

13Now listen, you who say, "Today or tomorrow we will go to this or that city, spend a year there, carry on business and make money." **14**Why, you do not even know what will happen tomorrow. What is your life? You are a mist that appears for a little while and then vanishes. **15**Instead, you ought to say, "If it is the Lord's will, we will live and do this or that." **16**As it is, you boast and brag. All such

---

^a5 Or that God jealously longs for the spirit that he made to live in us; or that the Spirit he caused to live in us longs jealously   ^b6 Prov. 3:34

Does God answer prayers if our motives aren't pure? (4:3)

There will always be some selfish elements in our prayers. In spite of this, God graciously hears and answers us when we pray. But if our requests center on ourselves, rather than on God's purposes, God refuses to hear and answer. If he granted such requests, his integrity would be compromised and we would not benefit spiritually.

If God loves the world, why can't we be friends with it? (4:4)

James's strong words seem to contradict John's: *God so loved the world that he gave his one and only Son* (John 3:16). When *world* refers to humanity, we ought to love it as God loves people. But when *world* means the prevailing attitude of hostility toward God and his ways, we should reject it. If we're tolerant about such attitudes against God, we open ourselves to spiritual danger.

What passage was James quoting? (4:5)

James appears to be paraphrasing a verse rather than quoting it directly. This may be a reference to Exodus 20:5.

How do we resist the devil? (4:7)

First we acknowledge that he actually exists. Next, we need to be aware of his activities (see 2 Cor. 2:11) which include temptation, slander and false accusations. Finally, we must stand firmly against his attacks in the name of Jesus Christ. Because of what Christ has already accomplished through his death and resurrection, we can claim spiritual authority over our adversary (1 John 4:4).

How is slandering the same as judging God's law? (4:11)

Jesus said the laws of God are summed up in the commands to love God and to love our neighbor (Matt. 22:34–40). By slandering someone we place ourselves above the law of love, justifying our actions by a standard different from God's.

Is it wrong to plan ahead? (4:13–15)

No. In fact, the Bible encourages us to prepare carefully for the future (Prov. 14:15; 16:3). However, we become presumptuous if our plans ignore God's will. James warns that the sovereign God will eventually prove he has the final say in all matters of our lives.

Do I sin every time I fail to do a good deed? (4:17)

When we realize how much good we leave undone, we realize how far we are from God's standards. It's easy to be overcome with guilt. But the grace of God can reassure those who are in Christ that there is *no condemnation* (Romans 8:1). We fall short, but we fall into the safety net of grace.

boasting is evil. **¹⁷**Anyone, then, who knows the good he ought to do and doesn't do it, sins.

Warning to Rich Oppressors

5 Now listen, you rich people, weep and wail because of the misery that is coming upon you. **²**Your wealth has rotted, and moths have eaten your clothes. **³**Your gold and silver are corroded. Their corrosion will testify against you and eat your flesh like fire. You have hoarded wealth in the last days. **⁴**Look! The wages you failed to pay the workmen who mowed your fields are crying out against you. The cries of the harvesters have reached the ears of the Lord Almighty. **⁵**You have lived on earth in luxury and self-indulgence. You have fattened yourselves in the day of slaughter.ª **⁶**You have condemned and murdered innocent men, who were not opposing you.

Patience in Suffering

⁷Be patient, then, brothers, until the Lord's coming. See how the farmer waits for the land to yield its valuable crop and how patient he is for the autumn and spring rains. **⁸**You too, be patient and stand firm, because the Lord's coming is near. **⁹**Don't grumble against each other, brothers, or you will be judged. The Judge is standing at the door!

¹⁰Brothers, as an example of patience in the face of suffering, take the prophetsᴰ who spoke in the name of the Lord. **¹¹**As you know, we consider blessed those who have persevered. You have heard of Job's perseverance and have seen what the Lord finally brought about. The Lord is full of compassion and mercyᴰ.

¹²Above all, my brothers, do not swear—not by heaven or by earth or by anything else. Let your "Yes" be yes, and your "No," no, or you will be condemned.

The Prayer of Faith

¹³Is any one of you in trouble? He should pray. Is anyone happy? Let him sing songs of praise. **¹⁴**Is any one of you sick? He should call the elders of the church to pray over him and anointᴰ him with oil in the name of the Lord. **¹⁵**And the prayer offered in faith will make the sick person well; the Lord will raise him up. If he has sinned, he will be forgiven. **¹⁶**Therefore confess your sins to each other and pray for each other so that you may be healed. The prayer of a righteousᴰ man is powerful and effective.

¹⁷Elijah was a man just like us. He prayed earnestly that it would not rain, and it did not rain on the land for three and a half years. **¹⁸**Again he prayed, and the heavens gave rain, and the earth produced its crops.

¹⁹My brothers, if one of you should wander from the truth and someone should bring him back, **²⁰**remember this: Whoever turns a sinner from the error of his way will save him from deathᴰ and cover over a multitude of sins.

What will happen to the rich and powerful? (5:1–6)

James sounds like an Old Testament prophet with his severe denunciation (see Amos 6:1–9). But then, Christ could be equally pointed about wealth (Luke 12:13–21), if it's not used for good. The Bible warns of severe consequences for those who live in luxury while the needy suffer. Such behavior violates the law of love—God will punish such injustice.

Why the sudden change from judgment to patience? (5:7–11)

James abruptly shifts to address a different set of people. If he has a warning for the rich, he also has a word for the oppressed. He encourages them to face suffering with patience, waiting for the Lord's return. It's easier to tolerate physical suffering when it's seen in light of Christ's return (2 Cor. 4:16–18).

Will Christians be judged in the next life? (5:9)

See article: *How will believers be judged?* (2 Cor. 5:10).

Is it wrong to take an oath in court? (5:12)

Although some feel it is wrong, James was probably not talking about taking a solemn oath as a legal requirement. Instead, James was saying that believers should not join in society's flippant attitudes toward the truth. Those with no integrity feel compelled to buttress their statements with vows. See *Is it wrong to swear to tell the truth in court?* (Matt. 5:34–37) and *If God swore an oath, should we?* (Heb. 6:13).

Why anoint with oil? (5:14)

Oil was used for medicinal purposes in New Testament times (Luke 10:34). But when administered by church elders in the name of the Lord, it takes on spiritual dimensions. It symbolizes the pouring out of the Holy Spirit upon someone in need of supernatural healing. Christians recognize that all healing comes from God, whether through prayer or medicine.

Is healing guaranteed? (5:15–16)

While James is talking about ministry in a sickroom, it's important to realize he doesn't use the medical term for healing. The word he uses means *made whole* and *forgiven.* When we anoint with oil and pray for healing, we should anticipate God's response. Prayer for healing depends on many factors, but spiritual wholeness should be our highest desire. While God may or may not provide physical healing, he will always offer wholeness and forgiveness.

ª5 Or *yourselves as in a day of feasting*

1 PETER

Why read this book?

Wouldn't it be great to be free of trouble? That's what we sometimes think. But 1 Peter shows us that difficulties and hardships don't have to wear us down. In fact, this letter teaches us that God can use difficulties to strengthen us. Knowing this can bring hope—reassurance that eternal life is God's ultimate purpose. Read 1 Peter to discover how faith, refined by suffering, can help us see the Lord more clearly. This is valuable advice for holding firm in difficult times.

Who wrote this book and why?

Peter, the apostle, saw that increasing hardship and persecution had caused some Christians to wonder if God had abandoned them. He wrote to encourage these believers, offering them hope and meaning in the midst of their suffering.

To whom was it written?

To believers scattered throughout the regions of Asia Minor, in what is now Turkey.

Where and when was it written?

Probably in Rome, sometime between A.D. 60 and 64.

What was the background behind this book?

At first the Roman government had given Christians the same freedom of religion as the Jews. But as the rift between Jews and Christians grew, tolerance for Christianity faded. Roman policy was to ban problem religions, which were perceived as a threat to the stability of the empire. Christians began facing discrimination, acts of violence, arrest and confiscation of property. Some were beginning to waver in their faith. Others feared how much they would have to endure. Peter himself was imprisoned and beaten for his faith; thus he earned the right to address the subject of suffering.

What to look for in 1 Peter:

Reason for hope in the face of trouble and suffering. Take note of the encouraging news Peter sent to his readers.

When did these things happen?

TIME LINE	10 BC	AD 1	10	20	30	40	50	60	70	80	90	100
Jesus' birth (c.6/5 B.C.)												
Peter becomes a disciple (c. A.D.26)												
Jesus' death, resurrection and ascension (c. A.D.30)												
Paul's conversion (c. A.D.35)												
Council at Jerusalem (c. A.D.50-51)												
Nero's reign (c. A.D.54-68)												
Book of 1 Peter written (c. A.D.60-64)												
Destruction of Jerusalem's temple (c. A.D.70)												

1 Peter, an apostle^D of Jesus Christ,

To God's elect^D, strangers in the world, scattered throughout Pontus, Galatia, Cappadocia, Asia and Bithynia, ²who have been chosen according to the foreknowledge of God the Father, through the sanctifying^D work of the Spirit, for obedience to Jesus Christ and sprinkling by his blood:

Grace^D and peace^D be yours in abundance.

Praise to God for a Living Hope

³Praise be to the God and Father of our Lord Jesus Christ! In his great mercy^D he has given us new birth into a living hope through the resurrection^D of Jesus Christ from the dead, ⁴and into an inheritance that can never perish, spoil or fade—kept in heaven for you, ⁵who through faith are shielded by God's power until the coming of the salvation^D that is ready to be revealed in the last time. ⁶In this you greatly rejoice, though now for a little while you may have had to suffer grief in all kinds of trials. ⁷These have come so that your faith—of greater worth than gold, which perishes even though refined by fire—may be proved genuine and may result in praise, glory^D and honor when Jesus Christ is revealed. ⁸Though you have not seen him, you love him; and even though you do not see him now, you believe in him and are filled with an inexpressible and glorious joy, ⁹for you are receiving the goal of your faith, the salvation of your souls^D.

¹⁰Concerning this salvation, the prophets, who spoke of the grace that was to come to you, searched intently and with the greatest care, ¹¹trying to find out the

Who are the *elect*? (1:1)

This is another way of saying "those chosen by God." Some say this means God chooses certain individuals, causing them to turn to him. Others say God chooses those who accept his gift of grace. In either case, it's significant that Peter wrote to people with little influence or affluence in society and that they—who would not have been honored or chosen for anything by society—were chosen by God.

Strangers (1:1)

Christians, some of whom fled Jerusalem to escape persecution (Acts 8:1–4), scattered throughout Pontus and other regions of modern-day Turkey. They were often treated harshly because their ways were different. Also see *Aliens and strangers* (2:11).

Why does God allow our faith to be tested? (1:7)

Not to learn something he doesn't already know. He allows trials so we can discover our own weaknesses and his infinite strength. See article: *Why did testing come to Job?* (Job 23:10).

Proved genuine (1:7)

In Peter's day, potters baked clay pots to give them strength. The process cracked those pots with flaws, but the ones that survived were marked with the same Greek word Peter uses here. We find out what we're made of when our faith is tested.

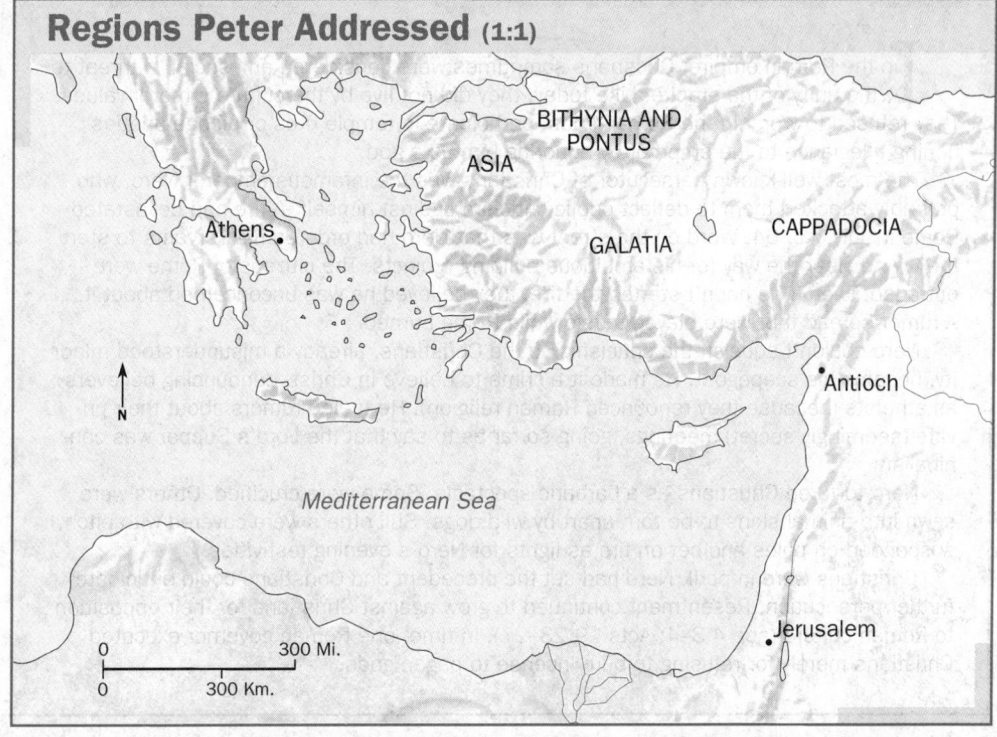

Regions Peter Addressed (1:1)

BITHYNIA AND PONTUS

ASIA

Athens

GALATIA

CAPPADOCIA

Antioch

Mediterranean Sea

N

0   300 Mi.
0   300 Km.

Jerusalem

How much did the Old Testament prophets know? (1:10–11)

Though they could see some details, many things remained a mystery to the prophets. They longed to know more. God used their prophecies, however, to confirm his final revelation in Jesus Christ (Heb. 1:1–2). Knowing Jesus gives us a clearer picture of salvation than the prophets ever knew.

How holy can we get? (1:15)

Some say we're to be morally perfect—that if God commanded something, it's possible for us to reach it. Others say holiness is an ideal we aim for but will not reach until we get to heaven. Still others say to be holy means to be distinctive—living in the Spirit and by the Scriptures, distinguished from non-believers. All these views see holiness as resisting evil and gaining self-control through *the sanctifying work of the Spirit* (1:2,13–17).

time and circumstances to which the Spirit of Christ in them was pointing when he predicted the sufferings of Christ and the glories that would follow. [12]It was revealed to them that they were not serving themselves but you, when they spoke of the things that have now been told you by those who have preached the gospel[D] to you by the Holy Spirit sent from heaven. Even angels long to look into these things.

Be Holy

[13]Therefore, prepare your minds for action; be self-controlled; set your hope fully on the grace[D] to be given you when Jesus Christ is revealed. [14]As obedient children, do not conform to the evil desires you had when you lived in ignorance. [15]But just as he who called you is holy, so be holy in all you do; [16]for it is written: "Be holy, because I am holy." [a]

[17]Since you call on a Father who judges each man's work impartially, live your lives as strangers here in reverent fear. [18]For you know that it was not with perishable things such as silver or gold that you were redeemed[D] from the empty way of life handed down to you from your forefathers, [19]but with the precious blood of Christ, a lamb without blemish or defect. [20]He was chosen before the creation of the world, but was revealed in these last times for your sake. [21]Through him you believe in God, who raised him from the dead and glorified him, and so your faith and hope are in God.

[22]Now that you have purified[D] yourselves by obeying the truth so that you have sincere love for your brothers,

[a]16 Lev. 11:44,45; 19:2; 20:7

Why were Christians suffering? (1:6)

In the Roman empire, Christians sometimes were considered anti-social, a threat to the unity of the empire. Like today, they did not live by the culture's moral values. They refused to worship the Roman gods, participate in temple rites or pledge unquestioning allegiance to the emperor by honoring him as a god.

The most well-known persecutor of Christians was the infamous emperor Nero, who probably attacked them to deflect public criticism against himself. A fire had devastated Rome in July, A.D. 64. Word on the street was that Nero had ordered his servants to start the fire to clear the way for his ambitious building projects. The citizens of Rome were outraged. Even if he hadn't started the fire, they believed he was unconcerned about it. A rumor spread that Nero played music while Rome burned.

Nero couldn't squelch the criticism. So the Christians, already a misunderstood minority, became his scapegoat. He made it a crime to believe in Christ, denouncing believers as atheists (because they renounced Roman religion). He fueled rumors about their private (seemingly secret) meetings, going so far as to say that the Lord's Supper was cannibalism.

Nero tortured Christians as a barbaric spectacle. Some were crucified. Others were sewn into animal skins to be torn apart by wild dogs. Still others were covered with pitch, suspended on poles and set on fire as lights for Nero's evening festivities.

Christians were in peril. Nero had set the precedent and Christians could anticipate further persecution. Resentment continued to grow against Christians for their opposition to Roman culture (see 4:3–4; Acts 19:23–27). In time, one Roman governor executed Christians merely for refusing to burn incense to pagan gods.

love one another deeply, from the heart.ᵃ **²³**For you have been born again, not of perishable seed, but of imperishable, through the living and enduring word of God. **²⁴**For,

> "All men are like grass,
>   and all their gloryᴰ is like the flowers of the
>   field;
> the grass withers and the flowers fall,
> **25**   but the word of the Lord stands forever."ᵇ

And this is the word that was preached to you.

2 Therefore, rid yourselves of all malice and all deceit, hypocrisy, envy, and slander of every kind. **²**Like newborn babies, crave pure spiritual milk, so that by it you may grow up in your salvationᴰ, **³**now that you have tasted that the Lord is good.

The Living Stone and a Chosen People

⁴As you come to him, the living Stone—rejected by men but chosen by God and precious to him— **⁵**you also, like living stones, are being built into a spiritual house to be a holy priesthood, offering spiritual sacrificesᴰ acceptable to God through Jesus Christ. **⁶**For in Scripture it says:

> "See, I lay a stone in Zionᴰ,
>   a chosen and precious cornerstone,
> and the one who trusts in him
>   will never be put to shame."ᶜ

⁷Now to you who believe, this stone is precious. But to those who do not believe,

> "The stone the builders rejected
>   has become the capstoneᴰ,ᵈ"ᵉ

⁸and,

> "A stone that causes men to stumble
>   and a rock that makes them fall."ᶠ

They stumble because they disobey the message—which is also what they were destined for.

⁹But you are a chosen people, a royal priesthood, a holy nation, a people belonging to God, that you may declare the praises of him who called you out of darkness into his wonderful light. **¹⁰**Once you were not a people, but now you are the people of God; once you had not received mercyᴰ, but now you have received mercy.

¹¹Dear friends, I urge you, as aliensᴰ and strangers in the world, to abstain from sinful desires, which war against your soulᴰ. **¹²**Live such good lives among the pagans that, though they accuse you of doing wrong, they may see your good deeds and glorify God on the day he visits us.

Submission to Rulers and Masters

¹³Submit yourselves for the Lord's sake to every authority instituted among men: whether to the king, as the supreme authority, **¹⁴**or to governors, who are sent by him to punish those who do wrong and to commend those who do right. **¹⁵**For it is God's will that by doing good you

ᵃ22 Some early manuscripts *from a pure heart*   ᵇ25 Isaiah 40:6-8
ᶜ6 Isaiah 28:16   ᵈ7 Or *cornerstone*   ᵉ7 Psalm 118:22
ᶠ8 Isaiah 8:14

Perishable . . . imperishable (1:23)
Imperishable seed is a picture of *the enduring word of God* which, when planted within a person's soul, gives birth to spiritual life. *Perishable* seed refers to conception within a mother, leading to the birth of a baby. Physical life, however, comes to an end; those who are *born again* have a spiritual life that is eternal.

Living stones (2:4–5)
An analogy: Believers are like stones that construct a building, but this building is a living spiritual building—the church. *The living Stone* (v. 4) is Christ, the most important building block. See Psalm 118:22; Isaiah 8:14; 28:16.

Should we still offer sacrifices? (2:5)
The Old Testament priests offered animal sacrifices for forgiveness of sin. These are no longer required since Jesus was the final Lamb offered for sin (1:19). But as priests in God's spiritual house, the sacrifice we offer to God is that of ourselves (Romans 12:1). In so doing, we give the Lord gifts of our abilities, our gratitude, our service, our prayers and our praise (see Heb. 13:15).

Cornerstone . . . capstone (2:6–7)
The cornerstone, part of the foundation, set the design and structure of a building. The capstone, literally "head of the corner," could also describe a foundation stone; but here it probably refers to the topmost piece, the finishing touch. From beginning to end, the church is built on Jesus.

Aliens and strangers (2:11)
Typically used to refer to people living in a foreign land, away from their own culture and customs. Many of those to whom Peter wrote were living far from their homeland. See *Strangers* (1:1). Peter uses their experience to picture how believers live on a temporary basis in the world—a place that is not their home. The Christian's homeland is heaven (Phil. 3:20; Heb. 11:13).

Do we *always* have to submit? (2:13–17)
Peter states a principle, not a rigid law. He himself modeled one exception to this principle when the authorities told him to stop speaking about Jesus. "We must obey God rather than men," Peter insisted (Acts 5:29; also see Acts 4:19–20). In similar cases we should submit, *not* to human authorities, but to God's Word and Spirit. Also see article: *Should we obey bad rulers?* (Titus 3:1–2).

should silence the ignorant talk of foolish men. [16]Live as free men, but do not use your freedom as a cover-up for evil; live as servants of God. [17]Show proper respect to everyone: Love the brotherhood of believers, fear God, honor the king.

[18]Slaves, submit yourselves to your masters with all respect, not only to those who are good and considerate, but also to those who are harsh. [19]For it is commendable if a man bears up under the pain of unjust suffering because he is conscious of God. [20]But how is it to your credit if you receive a beating for doing wrong and endure it? But if you suffer for doing good and you endure it, this is commendable before God. [21]To this you were called, because Christ suffered for you, leaving you an example, that you should follow in his steps.

[22]"He committed no sin,
   and no deceit was found in his mouth."[a]

[23]When they hurled their insults at him, he did not retaliate; when he suffered, he made no threats. Instead, he entrusted himself to him who judges justly. [24]He himself bore our sins in his body on the tree, so that we might die to sins and live for righteousness[D]; by his wounds you have been healed. [25]For you were like sheep going astray, but now you have returned to the Shepherd and Overseer[D] of your souls[D].

[a]22 Isaiah 53:9

SCRIPTURE LINK (2:22–25)
Read about the Suffering Servant in Isaiah 53:5–11.

Why call the cross a *tree*? (2:24)
Through the ages people have made public spectacles out of the executions of criminals. Often their bodies were displayed on wooden gallows, poles or even trees. The Old Testament speaks of this shame, which hints at Christ's death on the cross: *Anyone who is hung on a tree is under God's curse* (Deut. 21:22–23). The difference is that the executed criminal bears his own condemnation or curse, whereas Jesus takes our condemnation.

What healing comes from Jesus' wounds? (2:24)
Some believe this verse teaches that Christ's death provides physical healing. Others believe that, while God can indeed heal sick bodies, the purpose of Christ's death was solely to provide healing from the sickness of sin.

Why doesn't the Bible condemn slavery? (2:18–21)

Why didn't Peter tell masters to set their slaves free? Why did he instruct slaves to submit? Part of the answer can be found in Peter's focus. He wanted first to give his readers a Christian perspective—a way to live in an imperfect society where righteous people were persecuted. Peter didn't endorse the system, but he admitted its realities.

It helps to understand first-century slavery. People considered it a fact of life, a position in society, a lower-lower-class. Slaves formed the backbone of the work force in Roman culture—estimated in some areas at more than half the population. Some slaves, ironically, were better off than some free people. Often "professionals" such as teachers, doctors and civil servants were technically slaves. For these reasons and more, slavery was typically viewed as being morally neutral.

We are angered by accounts of the nineteenth-century American slave trade. It tore families apart and robbed people of their freedom and dignity. Many in Peter's day were equally offended by the cruelty of some slave-owners, though they were in the minority.

While the New Testament did not specifically condemn the institution of slavery, it clearly taught that violence and oppression were wrong. Society gave owners the legal right to beat or even kill their slaves for minor infractions. The New Testament, by contrast, revoked the license slave-owners had to mistreat their slaves. Abusive masters would be accountable to God for their actions (see Eph. 6:9; Col. 4:1).

With its emphasis on spiritual freedom, the New Testament planted the seeds that later convicted nineteenth-century society of the oppressiveness of its slave trade. People came to see that Jesus values every person—he died for the master as well as the slave, tyrant as well as oppressed, wealthy as well as poor.

Also see Eph. 6:5–8; Titus 2:9–10 and the book of Philemon.

Wives and Husbands

3 Wives, in the same way be submissive to your husbands so that, if any of them do not believe the word, they may be won over without words by the behavior of their wives, **2**when they see the purity and reverence[D] of your lives. **3**Your beauty should not come from outward adornment, such as braided hair and the wearing of gold jewelry and fine clothes. **4**Instead, it should be that of your inner self, the unfading beauty of a gentle and quiet spirit, which is of great worth in God's sight. **5**For this is the way the holy women of the past who put their hope in God used to make themselves beautiful. They were submissive to their own husbands, **6**like Sarah, who obeyed Abraham and called him her master. You are her daughters if you do what is right and do not give way to fear.

7Husbands, in the same way be considerate as you live with your wives, and treat them with respect as the weaker partner and as heirs with you of the gracious gift of life, so that nothing will hinder your prayers.

Suffering for Doing Good

8Finally, all of you, live in harmony with one another; be sympathetic, love as brothers, be compassionate and humble. **9**Do not repay evil with evil or insult with insult, but with blessing, because to this you were called so that you may inherit a blessing. **10**For,

"Whoever would love life
  and see good days
must keep his tongue from evil
  and his lips from deceitful speech.
11He must turn from evil and do good;
  he must seek peace[D] and pursue it.

What's wrong with being stylish? (3:3–4)

Peter doesn't ban grooming or beauty aids. But he puts them into perspective: if a woman relies on such things to make her beautiful, she will miss the far greater value of inner beauty.

Why call wives *the weaker partner?* (3:7)

Some think Peter may have been referring to physical differences between the sexes. Others think he may have had the vulnerable plight of first-century women in mind. With no public voice and no civil rights, women had only their husbands (or male relatives) as a means of defense. Still others see these words as God's pattern for the home. They point out that prayers become ineffective when these principles are not observed.

How are prayers hindered? (3:7)

When the communication between a husband and wife becomes strained, other relationships can be affected, including communication with God. It's not that God hinders prayers; it's that people can estrange themselves from him. Similar advice on prayer can be found in Matt. 5:23–24; 6:14–15.

Are good works the way to earn a blessing? (3:9–12)

Good works can never be the means to eternal life. However, those who have received God's gift of salvation will demonstrate that God is in their lives by the way they treat those around them. By contrast, those who *repay evil with evil* demonstrate that they have not been truly transformed by God's grace. Also see article: *Is faith enough?* (James 2:14–24).

Isn't it chauvinistic to teach wives to submit? (3:5–6)

Women in the first century had no legal rights and very little public influence. How could they influence their unbelieving husbands to believe in God? Peter explained that in spite of such disadvantages, wives could still have a profound impact on their husbands. They could speak loudly for Christ—not through words, but through their behavior (v. 1) and their Christ-like character (v. 4).

Human logic might suggest that a wife point out her husband's weaknesses or verbalize spiritual principles for him to follow. But Peter sidesteps the flaws of these approaches which tend to put men on the defensive. Instead, Peter recommends that wives disarm their unbelieving husbands and make them more receptive to the gospel by being gentle and quiet.

These verses have sometimes been abused, as have wives. Biblical submission should not be separated from Biblical responsibility (v. 7; Eph. 5:25; Col. 3:19). In this context, Sarah is commended for her submission. However, Abraham, rather than trusting in God, relied on his own schemes, leading to Sarah's mistreatment (see Gen 12:11–13; 20:10–11). See *Why did Abraham lie again about Sarah?* (Gen. 20:2).

Some dismiss these verses in the New Testament as the chauvinistic rhetoric of the first century, but such a view misses the whole servant spirit of Christianity. A submissive spirit runs counter to society's values and it always has (see Mark 10:42–45). However it remains God's standard for all believers—male and female—for all time (see Phil. 2:3–8; Eph. 5:21).

Why be gentle and respectful toward unbelievers? (3:15)

Because arguments don't convince anyone to love God. The gospel will be heard far better when Christians speak *with gentleness and respect*. While Peter writes about speaking respectfully to the malicious, there are times when it is appropriate to resist evil. See *Should evil people never be resisted?* (Matt 5:39) and article: *Does Jesus teach that we should not resist oppression?* (Luke 6:29–30).

Who were the *spirits in prison*? (3:19–20)

Some believe that between his death and resurrection Christ descended to Hades to preach to Old Testament sinners (see Acts 2:27,31; Rev. 1:18); the Apostles' Creed reads, ". . . He descended into hell . . ." Others disagree, saying there can be no salvation after death (Heb. 9:27). Still others see Christ preaching to the fallen angels in prison (Peter says *spirits*), announcing his victory and their impending judgment (see Gen. 6:1–3; 2 Peter 2:4–5; Jude 6).

Does baptism save us? (3:21)

Some say baptism is a necessary element of salvation. Others disagree, pointing to those who received the Holy Spirit before baptism (Acts 10:47). This verse emphasizes that baptism is a *pledge* (the original word was a technical term used to endorse a business contract). It is the sign or outward symbol of our commitment to Jesus Christ.

How does suffering help us be *done with sin*? (4:1)

Physical suffering, harsh as it may be, can equip us with a new outlook on life. Things once thought insignificant take on new meaning; other things lose their value. Sinful desires become less alluring if we have learned to depend on Christ to help us through.

Debauchery (4:3)

Behavior that violates even secular standards of decency.

Those who are now dead (4:6)

Some feel that these died after they heard the gospel (*now* is only implied in the original language). Others take the word *dead* to mean the listeners were spiritually dead—not alive in Christ. See also *Who were the spirits in prison?* (3:19–20).

How could Peter say *the end of all things* is near? (4:7)

Almost everyone agrees that Christ's coming is the next major event for the church. To say the end is near means it could happen at any time—even if centuries roll by while we wait. Peter and other New Testament writers saw that they lived in the final stage of God's dealings with people. So they used terms like *near* and *the last days* in a relative, rather than a precise, sense.

How does love cover sins? (4:8)

This may refer to the way God's love deals with our sins. But the context of this verse speaks of the way love affects our relationships. When we truly love someone, we are much more willing to overlook that person's faults. When we're sinned against, love overrides our reflex for revenge (Prov. 10:12; 1 Cor. 13:5).

[12] For the eyes of the Lord are on the righteous[D]
and his ears are attentive to their prayer,
but the face of the Lord is against those who
do evil."[a]

[13] Who is going to harm you if you are eager to do good? [14] But even if you should suffer for what is right, you are blessed. "Do not fear what they fear[b]; do not be frightened."[c] [15] But in your hearts set apart Christ as Lord. Always be prepared to give an answer to everyone who asks you to give the reason for the hope that you have. But do this with gentleness and respect, [16] keeping a clear conscience, so that those who speak maliciously against your good behavior in Christ may be ashamed of their slander. [17] It is better, if it is God's will, to suffer for doing good than for doing evil. [18] For Christ died for sins once for all, the righteous for the unrighteous, to bring you to God. He was put to death[D] in the body but made alive by the Spirit, [19] through whom[d] also he went and preached to the spirits in prison [20] who disobeyed long ago when God waited patiently in the days of Noah while the ark was being built. In it only a few people, eight in all, were saved through water, [21] and this water symbolizes baptism[D] that now saves you also—not the removal of dirt from the body but the pledge[e] of a good conscience toward God. It saves you by the resurrection[D] of Jesus Christ, [22] who has gone into heaven and is at God's right hand—with angels, authorities and powers in submission to him.

Living for God

4 Therefore, since Christ suffered in his body, arm yourselves also with the same attitude, because he who has suffered in his body is done with sin. [2] As a result, he does not live the rest of his earthly life for evil human desires, but rather for the will of God. [3] For you have spent enough time in the past doing what pagans choose to do—living in debauchery, lust, drunkenness, orgies, carousing and detestable idolatry[D]. [4] They think it strange that you do not plunge with them into the same flood of dissipation[D], and they heap abuse on you. [5] But they will have to give account to him who is ready to judge the living and the dead. [6] For this is the reason the gospel[D] was preached even to those who are now dead, so that they might be judged according to men in regard to the body, but live according to God in regard to the spirit.

[7] The end of all things is near. Therefore be clear minded and self-controlled so that you can pray. [8] Above all, love each other deeply, because love covers over a multitude of sins. [9] Offer hospitality to one another without grumbling. [10] Each one should use whatever gift he has received to serve others, faithfully administering God's grace[D] in its various forms. [11] If anyone speaks, he should do it as one speaking the very words of God. If anyone serves, he should do it with the strength God provides, so that in all things God may be praised through Jesus Christ. To him be the glory[D] and the power for ever and ever. Amen.

---

[a] 12 Psalm 34:12-16   [b] 14 Or *not fear their threats*   [c] 14 Isaiah 8:12   [d] 18,19 Or *alive in the spirit,* 19 *through which*   [e] 21 Or *response*

Suffering for Being a Christian

12Dear friends, do not be surprised at the painful trial you are suffering, as though something strange were happening to you. **13**But rejoice that you participate in the sufferings of Christ, so that you may be overjoyed when his glory^D is revealed. **14**If you are insulted because of the name of Christ, you are blessed, for the Spirit of glory and of God rests on you. **15**If you suffer, it should not be as a murderer or thief or any other kind of criminal, or even as a meddler. **16**However, if you suffer as a Christian, do not be ashamed, but praise God that you bear that name. **17**For it is time for judgment to begin with the family of God; and if it begins with us, what will the outcome be for those who do not obey the gospel^D of God? **18**And,

> "If it is hard for the righteous^D to be saved,
>> what will become of the ungodly and the
>>> sinner?" *a*

19So then, those who suffer according to God's will should commit themselves to their faithful Creator and continue to do good.

To Elders and Young Men

5 To the elders among you, I appeal as a fellow elder, a witness of Christ's sufferings and one who also will share in the glory to be revealed: **2**Be shepherds of God's flock that is under your care, serving as overseers^D—not because you must, but because you are willing, as God wants you to be; not greedy for money, but eager to serve; **3**not lording it over those entrusted to you, but being examples to the flock. **4**And when the Chief Shepherd appears, you will receive the crown of glory that will never fade away.

5Young men, in the same way be submissive to those who are older. All of you, clothe yourselves with humility toward one another, because,

> "God opposes the proud
>> but gives grace^D to the humble." *b*

6Humble yourselves, therefore, under God's mighty hand, that he may lift you up in due time. **7**Cast all your anxiety on him because he cares for you.

8Be self-controlled and alert. Your enemy the devil prowls around like a roaring lion looking for someone to devour. **9**Resist him, standing firm in the faith, because you know that your brothers throughout the world are undergoing the same kind of sufferings.

10And the God of all grace, who called you to his eternal glory in Christ, after you have suffered a little while, will himself restore you and make you strong, firm and steadfast. **11**To him be the power for ever and ever. Amen.

Final Greetings

12With the help of Silas, *c* whom I regard as a faithful brother, I have written to you briefly, encouraging you

---

How can we speak as though *speaking the very words of God*? (4:11)

We can speak with natural ability or with the ability of a spiritual gift (v. 10). Whether preaching, teaching or simply talking with others, we should remember that the Spirit can work through our words. Perhaps Peter was urging preachers to speak God's Word with awe and respect. Or he may have been warning against putting human opinion in place of God's revelation. Also see *What made their words the words of God?* (1 Thes. 2:13).

How can we participate in Christ's sufferings? (4:13)

Perhaps we share in Christ's sufferings by imitating his attitude (see 2:20–21). Some suggest we may share in his sufferings in a symbolic way by suffering *because of righteousness* (Matt. 5:10).

How will the *family of God* be judged? (4:17)

Though believers will be judged for the things they do (2 Cor. 5:10), the *judgment* Peter wrote about more likely relates to the physical sufferings believers were then facing. Christians are not exempt from affliction. Those who persevered through harsh trials proved that their faith was genuine. See article: *How will believers be judged?* (2 Cor. 5:10). Also see *Proved genuine* (1:7).

What is the *crown of glory*? (5:4)

The Greeks of Peter's day awarded champion athletes with a "crown" made of flowers or leaves.

Can the devil devour believers? (5:8)

Believers disagree about whether the devil can destroy our salvation or only our Christian joy and fruitfulness. The Bible repeatedly warns about the power of the devil (2 Cor. 11:14; Eph. 6:11; 1 Tim. 4:1). But Peter reassures us that even though the devil might roar, we can *resist him* (5:9).

Resist him (5:9)

See *How do we resist the devil?* (James 4:7).

How were other believers suffering? (5:9)

The climate of the whole Roman empire was becoming antagonistic toward Christians. They faced public ridicule, beatings, imprisonment and even seizure of their property (Heb. 10:33–34). Also see article: *Why were Christians suffering?* (1:6).

---

a 18 Prov. 11:31   *b 5* Prov. 3:34   *c 12* Greek *Silvanus*, a variant of *Silas*

She who is in Babylon (5:13)

Most think *Babylon* refers to Rome. Because of its material wealth and moral poverty, Rome was called *Babylon* not only by Christian and Jewish writers, but also in Roman literature. Peter was probably in Rome during this time and there is no evidence that he ever traveled east to the actual city of Babylon. A few speculate that *she* could refer to Peter's wife who traveled with him on his missionary journeys (1 Cor. 9:5).

What was the *kiss of love*? (5:14)

In Middle Eastern culture, the kiss was a form of greeting or an expression of friendship and homage. So the kiss was similarly used in synagogues and found its way into Christian gatherings. There among the saints (literally, "holy ones"), the kiss was viewed as *holy* (see Romans 16:16). Peter uses *kiss of love* as an equivalent to a *holy kiss*.

and testifying that this is the true grace of God. Stand fast in it.

¹³She who is in Babylon, chosen together with you, sends you her greetings, and so does my son Mark. ¹⁴Greet one another with a kiss of love.

Peace^D to all of you who are in Christ.

2 PETER

Why read this book?

While the information age we live in has its good points, there can be a downside too. Sometimes we can be swamped with an overload of information. How do we sort it all out? How do we tell which information is important—or true? The danger of receiving false information exists even in the church. That's why the message of 2 Peter is so critical today. This book alerts us to the dangers of wrong teaching and shows us how to spot false teachers.

Who wrote this book and why?

The apostle Peter wrote to warn believers against false teachers who had invaded the Christian community. His hope was that, being forewarned, they would be forearmed, and not taken in by the errors of the false teachers.

To whom was it written?

To the same people who received his first letter: believers scattered throughout the regions of Asia Minor, in what is present-day Turkey.

Where and when was it written?

Probably in Rome, sometime between A.D. 64 and 68.

What was the background behind this book?

The emperor Nero was on the throne in Rome at the time Peter wrote this letter from Rome. Nero was a man without moral principles. His volatile nature created an uncertain and unsteady political climate. As for the church, the Christians in Asia Minor were in danger of being led astray by eloquent but erring teachers.

What to look for in 2 Peter:

Read this as though you had received this letter. You'll find several key themes: (1) the need to develop Christian character (1:1–11); (2) the importance of holding to the truth (1:12–21); (3) warnings against false teachers (2:1–22) and (4) admonitions on how to live in view of the Lord's coming (3:1–18).

When did these things happen?

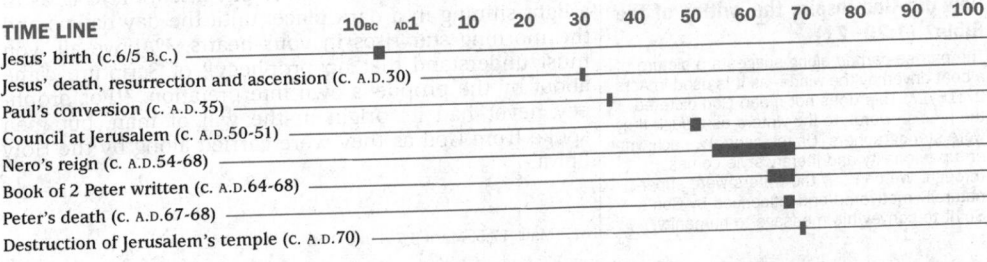

TIME LINE	10 BC	AD 1	10	20	30	40	50	60	70	80	90	100
Jesus' birth (c.6/5 B.C.)												
Jesus' death, resurrection and ascension (c. A.D.30)												
Paul's conversion (c. A.D.35)												
Council at Jerusalem (c. A.D.50-51)												
Nero's reign (c. A.D.54-68)												
Book of 2 Peter written (c. A.D.64-68)												
Peter's death (c. A.D.67-68)												
Destruction of Jerusalem's temple (c. A.D.70)												

1 Simon Peter, a servant and apostleD of Jesus Christ,

To those who through the righteousnessD of our God and Savior Jesus Christ have received a faith as precious as ours:

²GraceD and peaceD be yours in abundance through the knowledge of God and of Jesus our Lord.

Making One's Calling and Election Sure

³His divine power has given us everything we need for life and godliness through our knowledge of him who called us by his own gloryD and goodness. ⁴Through these he has given us his very great and precious promises, so that through them you may participate in the divine nature and escape the corruption in the world caused by evil desires.

⁵For this very reason, make every effort to add to your faith goodness; and to goodness, knowledge; ⁶and to knowledge, self-control; and to self-control, perseverance; and to perseverance, godliness; ⁷and to godliness, brotherly kindness; and to brotherly kindness, love. ⁸For if you possess these qualities in increasing measure, they will keep you from being ineffective and unproductive in your knowledge of our Lord Jesus Christ. ⁹But if anyone does not have them, he is nearsighted and blind, and has forgotten that he has been cleansed from his past sins.

¹⁰Therefore, my brothers, be all the more eager to make your calling and election sure. For if you do these things, you will never fall, ¹¹and you will receive a rich welcome into the eternal kingdom of our Lord and Savior Jesus Christ.

Prophecy of Scripture

¹²So I will always remind you of these things, even though you know them and are firmly established in the truth you now have. ¹³I think it is right to refresh your memory as long as I live in the tent of this body, ¹⁴because I know that I will soon put it aside, as our Lord Jesus Christ has made clear to me. ¹⁵And I will make every effort to see that after my departure you will always be able to remember these things.

¹⁶We did not follow cleverly invented stories when we told you about the power and coming of our Lord Jesus Christ, but we were eyewitnesses of his majesty. ¹⁷For he received honor and glory from God the Father when the voice came to him from the Majestic Glory, saying, "This is my Son, whom I love; with him I am well pleased."ᵃ ¹⁸We ourselves heard this voice that came from heaven when we were with him on the sacredD mountain.

¹⁹And we have the word of the prophetsD made more certain, and you will do well to pay attention to it, as to a light shining in a dark place, until the day dawns and the morning star rises in your hearts. ²⁰Above all, you must understand that no prophecyD of Scripture came about by the prophet's own interpretation. ²¹For prophecy never had its origin in the will of man, but men spoke from God as they were carried along by the Holy Spirit.

How can we *participate* in God's nature? (1:4)
We receive God's nature when we are born again and become *a new creation* (2 Cor. 5:17). But there's a hitch. Our inner being remains housed in a body of flesh which is influenced by sin. As a result, we are not always consistent in living out our new nature. God wants us to mature in our faith, conforming to his will and overcoming temptation. When we act on his promises, then, we participate in his nature.

How much *effort* does the Christian life require? (1:5)
Because of the internal civil war (see previous note) believers need to discipline themselves so they can live more in line with their identity in Christ. Other verses echo this idea of the disciplined life: *continue to work out your salvation* (Phil. 2:12); *strict training* (1 Cor. 9:24–27); *train yourself to be godly* (1 Tim. 4:7). It is important to remember, however, that we cannot be saved by our own efforts. Salvation is God's work, not ours.

What causes such spiritual amnesia? (1:9)
When we reinforce what we've learned, our memories improve. The same thing is true of spiritual memories. Peter urges believers to reinforce what they've learned and experienced. He warns us that if we neglect Christian disciplines, we will forget what God has done and we will live inconsistently.

Isn't God's calling and election sure without our help? (1:10)
Peter tells us that if we see spiritual growth taking place in our lives, we can be confident that we are Christians. Those who encounter God's grace will see evidence of that encounter—both internal and external signs that they have been (and continue to be) changed.

The Majestic Glory (1:17)
Probably a name for God. It is unique, found nowhere else in the Bible. It refers to God's glory revealed on the mountain when Jesus was changed from an earthly appearance to a heavenly appearance (Matt. 17:5).

How did God inspire the writing of the Bible? (1:20–21)
The phrase *carried along* suggests a picture of a boat driven by the wind—as it is used in Acts 27:15,17. This does not mean God dictated the precise words to the writers as though they were stenographers. On the contrary, each writer's personality and literary style comes through. We can say the writers were supernaturally motivated and influenced by God's Spirit to convey his message to humanity.

ᵃ17 Matt. 17:5; Mark 9:7; Luke 9:35

False Teachers and Their Destruction

2 But there were also false prophets[D] among the people, just as there will be false teachers among you. They will secretly introduce destructive heresies, even denying the sovereign Lord who bought them—bringing swift destruction on themselves. [2]Many will follow their shameful ways and will bring the way of truth into disrepute. [3]In their greed these teachers will exploit you with stories they have made up. Their condemnation has long been hanging over them, and their destruction has not been sleeping.

[4]For if God did not spare angels when they sinned, but sent them to hell[D],[a] putting them into gloomy dungeons[b] to be held for judgment; [5]if he did not spare the ancient world when he brought the flood on its ungodly people, but protected Noah, a preacher of righteousness[D], and seven others; [6]if he condemned the cities of Sodom and Gomorrah by burning them to ashes, and made them an example of what is going to happen to the ungodly; [7]and if he rescued Lot, a righteous[D] man, who was distressed by the filthy lives of lawless men [8](for that righteous man, living among them day after day, was tormented in his righteous soul by the lawless deeds he saw and heard)— [9]if this is so, then the Lord knows how to rescue godly men from trials and to hold the unrighteous for the day of judgment, while continuing their punishment.[c] [10]This is especially true of those who follow the corrupt desire of the sinful nature[d] and despise authority.

Bold and arrogant, these men are not afraid to slander celestial beings; [11]yet even angels, although they are stronger and more powerful, do not bring slanderous accusations against such beings in the presence of the Lord. [12]But these men blaspheme[D] in matters they do not understand. They are like brute beasts, creatures of instinct, born only to be caught and destroyed, and like beasts they too will perish.

[13]They will be paid back with harm for the harm they have done. Their idea of pleasure is to carouse in broad daylight. They are blots and blemishes, reveling in their pleasures while they feast with you.[e] [14]With eyes full of adultery, they never stop sinning; they seduce the unstable; they are experts in greed—an accursed brood! [15]They have left the straight way and wandered off to follow the way of Balaam son of Beor, who loved the wages of wickedness. [16]But he was rebuked for his wrongdoing by a donkey—a beast without speech—who spoke with a man's voice and restrained the prophet's madness.

[17]These men are springs without water and mists driven by a storm. Blackest darkness is reserved for them. [18]For they mouth empty, boastful words and, by appealing to the lustful desires of sinful human nature, they entice people who are just escaping from those who live in error. [19]They promise them freedom, while they themselves are slaves of depravity—for a man is a slave to whatever has mastered him. [20]If they have escaped the corruption of the world by knowing our Lord and Savior Jesus Christ and are again entangled in it and overcome, they are worse off at the end than they were at the begin-

a4 Greek *Tartarus*   *b4* Some manuscripts *into chains of darkness*
c9 Or *unrighteous for punishment until the day of judgment*
d10 Or *the flesh*   *e13* Some manuscripts *in their love feasts*

How can you spot a false teacher? (2:1–3)

False teachers often camouflage their lies with truth, making it difficult to catch their errors. Peter tells us: (1) Expect that *there will be false teachers*. We must always be discerning. (2) Watch for those who twist the truth about Christ, *denying the sovereign Lord*. (3) Watch for those with sinful lifestyles, who *follow their shameful ways*. (4) And watch for those with a lust for money or power, who *in their greed . . . will exploit you.*

When did God send fallen angels to hell? (2:4)

We don't know. This may have happened after they joined Satan's rebellion against God, before the creation of man. For reasons unknown to us, however, not all fallen angels were banished to hell. Vast numbers were allowed to influence this world, presumably as *demons* (James 2:19) or *spiritual forces of evil in the heavenly realms* (Eph. 6:12). See article: *Where are the dead?* (1 Thes. 4:14,16). Also see *What angels are chained in darkness?* (Jude v. 6).

How are the unrighteous being continually punished? (2:9)

This speaks of the certainty of judgment that will come upon those who do not repent. But it also suggests that until the time of the final judgment, the wicked still must face the consequences for their sin. Those caught in sinful lifestyles cause themselves pain and destruction in this life as well as the next.

Celestial beings (2:10)

Most likely refers to the fallen angels, Satan's servants (see Jude 8–10). False teachers may have ridiculed them to prove their own authority. Some suggest *celestial beings* may mean church leaders. Also see *How did they slander celestial beings?* (Jude v. 8).

What makes people vulnerable to false teachers? (2:14)

Those most vulnerable and naive are *unstable*, suggesting that they have no foundation in solid Biblical teaching. Those who have stopped growing as Christians are probably even more vulnerable (see 1:5–10). Other contributing factors may be: times of suffering, a reluctance to obey God, an eagerness to please people, or being physically or socially disadvantaged.

What's better about never knowing the right way? (2:20–22)

It appears that there are degrees of punishment for the lost (Matt. 11:20–24). Those who reject the gospel are accountable for more than those who never knew and so never consciously rejected it (Matt. 25:16–28). Still, those who never heard the gospel are judged because they don't live up to what little they know through nature and their own conscience (Romans 1:18–20; 2:12,15). The idea here seems to be that judgment will be less severe if a person rejects God more from ignorance than from rebellion.

ning. **21**It would have been better for them not to have known the way of righteousness[D], than to have known it and then to turn their backs on the sacred[D] command that was passed on to them. **22**Of them the proverbs are true: "A dog returns to its vomit,"[a] and, "A sow that is washed goes back to her wallowing in the mud."

The Day of the Lord

3 Dear friends, this is now my second letter to you. I have written both of them as reminders to stimulate you to wholesome thinking. **2**I want you to recall the words spoken in the past by the holy prophets[D] and the command given by our Lord and Savior through your apostles[D].

3First of all, you must understand that in the last days scoffers will come, scoffing and following their own evil desires. **4**They will say, "Where is this 'coming' he promised? Ever since our fathers died, everything goes on as it has since the beginning of creation." **5**But they deliberately forget that long ago by God's word the heavens existed and the earth was formed out of water and by water. **6**By these waters also the world of that time was deluged and destroyed. **7**By the same word the present heavens and earth are reserved for fire, being kept for the day of judgment and destruction of ungodly men.

8But do not forget this one thing, dear friends: With the Lord a day is like a thousand years, and a thousand years are like a day. **9**The Lord is not slow in keeping his promise, as some understand slowness. He is patient with you, not wanting anyone to perish, but everyone to come to repentance[D].

10But the day of the Lord[D] will come like a thief. The

a22 Prov. 26:11

The earth was formed out of water and by water (3:5)

The land appeared from the water on the third day of creation (Gen. 1:9–10). This is descriptive language, not scientific.

What cataclysmic event does this describe? (3:10,12)

This describes the destruction of the world. It's difficult to say from these verses exactly what will cause this universal meltdown. Some speculate this sounds like a nuclear or cosmic holocaust—a collision with a comet, for example, or a gigantic solar flare. Whatever the method, Christians have no reason to fear the end of the world since, for them, it means a new beginning. When the old is destroyed, God will create a new world, untouched by sin (Rev. 21:1–2).

Can someone who is saved fall away? (2:20–22)

There are basically two positions on this question. Some say the people in these verses were saved, but by falling away, lost their salvation. They support their view from this verse by observing that: (1) these people had a relationship with Christ; (2) they had escaped corruption; (3) they had since become entangled again, worse than before. They also see the tragic results as reasons why the New Testament warnings against falling away are so critical (see, for example, Gal. 5:4; Heb. 6:4–6).

Others disagree and see salvation as an irrevocable gift. They believe people can appear to be saved—that they know *about* Jesus and that their lifestyles *appear* to improve. But this view concludes that such changes are merely superficial and that such people were never truly saved in the first place. Those who hold this position see a distinction between genuine Christians and those who merely dabble in Christianity for a time (see, for example, 1 John 2:19; Romans 8:38–39).

A third view incorporates elements of both of these positions. This view says some people fall away because they were never sincere in their faith while others fall away because they neglected their faith. The dividing line in these various opinions seems to depend on one's view of God's grace: Are God's promises irrevocable or do they depend on our response? Do we have *eternal* security in Christ or do we have *conditional* security in Christ? These questions will probably never be reconciled this side of heaven.

Also see articles: *Can believers fall away?* (Luke 8:13) and *Should we fear falling?* (Heb. 6:6).

heavens will disappear with a roar; the elements will be destroyed by fire, and the earth and everything in it will be laid bare.*a*

11Since everything will be destroyed in this way, what kind of people ought you to be? You ought to live holy and godly lives **12**as you look forward to the day of God and speed its coming.*b* That day will bring about the destruction of the heavens by fire, and the elements will melt in the heat. **13**But in keeping with his promise we are looking forward to a new heaven and a new earth, the home of righteousnessᴰ.

14So then, dear friends, since you are looking forward to this, make every effort to be found spotless, blameless and at peaceᴰ with him. **15**Bear in mind that our Lord's patience means salvationᴰ, just as our dear brother Paul also wrote you with the wisdom that God gave him. **16**He writes the same way in all his letters, speaking in them of these matters. His letters contain some things that are hard to understand, which ignorant and unstable people distort, as they do the other Scriptures, to their own destruction.

17Therefore, dear friends, since you already know this, be on your guard so that you may not be carried away by the error of lawless men and fall from your secure position. **18**But grow in the graceᴰ and knowledge of our Lord and Savior Jesus Christ. To him be gloryᴰ both now and forever! Amen.

How can we cause God's judgment to come more quickly? (3:12)

We are not given enough information to know for sure how we can speed the Lord's return, but we can speculate. Perhaps this relates to doing a better job of evangelizing the world; Jesus said the end would come when the whole world had heard the gospel (Matt. 24:14). Or maybe this refers to our earnest prayers that Christ will return quickly (Rev. 22:20).

New heaven and a new earth (3:13)

The place God has prepared for his people for eternity. Though this language may be somewhat figurative, we know this will be a place without sin where God will live with his saints forever. See Rev. 21:1—22:5.

When were Paul's writings first called Scriptures? (3:16)

This statement of Peter's is the first record we have of Paul's writings being called "Scripture." Since he was recognized as an apostle, however, Paul's writings always had authority (1 Cor. 14:37).

How could they fall from a *secure position*? (3:17)

This seems like a contradiction in terms. An analogy may be the fences at popular lookout points at the Grand Canyon. You're secure, unless you climb over the fence. In the same way, believers are secure as long as they hold to the truth. But if they allow themselves to be led astray by false teachers—if they "climb over the fence"—they could fall into error.

---

*a*10 Some manuscripts *be burned up*   *b*12 Or *as you wait eagerly for the day of God to come*

1 JOHN

Why read this book?

To find out more about the love of God. This book stresses God's love as an example for us to follow in our relationships with each other. But it doesn't stop there. It goes on to encourage us to live right, learning and obeying God's commands. And, in a day when many are being deceived, this short book sounds a clear call for maintaining truth by maintaining fellowship with the Lord.

Who wrote this book?

The apostle John, who also wrote the Gospel of John.

When was it written?

Probably in the A.D. 80s, late in John's life.

To whom was it written and why?

John wrote to encourage and strengthen the believers in a group of churches near Ephesus in the western half of what is today the country of Turkey (see *Map 11* at the back of this Bible).

What was happening at this time?

Many communities were springing up throughout the Roman empire and a loose structure of authority and organization was being recognized. The first great persecution under Nero had come and gone, claiming the lives of thousands of Christians, including Paul and Peter. John is thought to have written as the last surviving apostle, looking back at the gains and setbacks of the early church.

What to look for in 1 John:

Watch for several key definitions. John restores the meanings of words that some false teachers at that time had distorted. You'll also find vivid images with special significance, such as light and darkness or Father and children.

When did these things happen?

TIME LINE	10 BC	AD 1	10	20	30	40	50	60	70	80	90	100
Jesus' birth (c.6/5 B.C.)												
John becomes a disciple (c. A.D.26)												
Jesus' death, resurrection and ascension (c. A.D.30)												
Nero's reign (c. A.D.54-68)												
Destruction of Jerusalem's temple (c. A.D.70)												
Domitian's reign (c. A.D.81-96)												
Book of 1 John written (c. A.D.85-95)												
John's exile on Patmos (c. A.D.90-95)												

The Word of Life

1 That which was from the beginning, which we have heard, which we have seen with our eyes, which we have looked at and our hands have touched—this we proclaim concerning the Word of life. **2**The life appeared; we have seen it and testify to it, and we proclaim to you the eternal life^D, which was with the Father and has appeared to us. **3**We proclaim to you what we have seen and heard, so that you also may have fellowship with us. And our fellowship is with the Father and with his Son, Jesus Christ. **4**We write this to make our^a joy complete.

Walking in the Light

5This is the message we have heard from him and declare to you: God is light; in him there is no darkness at all. **6**If we claim to have fellowship with him yet walk in the darkness, we lie and do not live by the truth. **7**But if we walk in the light, as he is in the light, we have fellowship with one another, and the blood of Jesus, his Son, purifies^D us from all^b sin.

8If we claim to be without sin, we deceive ourselves and the truth is not in us. **9**If we confess our sins, he is faithful and just and will forgive us our sins and purify us from all unrighteousness. **10**If we claim we have not sinned, we make him out to be a liar and his word has no place in our lives.

2 My dear children, I write this to you so that you will not sin. But if anybody does sin, we have one who speaks to the Father in our defense—Jesus Christ, the Righteous^D One. **2**He is the atoning sacrifice^D for our sins, and not only for ours but also for^c the sins of the whole world.

3We know that we have come to know him if we obey his commands. **4**The man who says, "I know him," but does not do what he commands is a liar, and the truth is not in him. **5**But if anyone obeys his word, God's love^d is truly made complete in him. This is how we know we are in him: **6**Whoever claims to live in him must walk as Jesus did.

7Dear friends, I am not writing you a new command but an old one, which you have had since the beginning. This old command is the message you have heard. **8**Yet I am writing you a new command; its truth is seen in him and you, because the darkness is passing and the true light is already shining.

9Anyone who claims to be in the light but hates his brother is still in the darkness. **10**Whoever loves his brother lives in the light, and there is nothing in him^e to make him stumble. **11**But whoever hates his brother is in the darkness and walks around in the darkness; he does not know where he is going, because the darkness has blinded him.

12I write to you, dear children,
  because your sins have been forgiven on
    account of his name.
13I write to you, fathers,
  because you have known him who is from
    the beginning.
I write to you, young men,

---

^a4 Some manuscripts *your*   ^b7 Or *every*   ^c2 Or *He is the one who turns aside God's wrath, taking away our sins, and not only ours but also*   ^d5 Or *word, love for God*   ^e10 Or *it*

What did John proclaim? (1:1)
John presents the basics of Christianity: God is love and life. Through Jesus our lives can be transformed from sin and death to eternal life.

Why would letter writing give John joy? (1:4)
Much more than today, writing required money, time and great effort. But he considered his efforts to be a valuable investment in the spiritual welfare of his readers. Hoping that he could encourage them in their Christian life, he felt great joy. Also see NIV text note.

In what sense is God light? (1:5)
Light suggests the idea that God is open and honest, that he reveals truth. Light also represents goodness and purity in a moral sense. There are no shadows or dark sides to God; he is perfect and free of sin.

How can blood purify? (1:7)
See *How could blood atone for sin?* (Lev. 17:11).

Why can't we be free of sin? (1:8)
Some believe we can live a sinless life of perfection (Romans 6:6). Others say that while perfection is not possible this side of death, a changed life is (2 Cor. 5:17). Some speak of the varying effects of sin, concluding that we *can* be free from the *penalty* and the oppressive *power* of sin. But as long as we remain in a fallen world, they say, we will continue to confront the *presence* of sin.

What does confession do? (1:9)
It frees Christians from self-delusion and frustration. Confession of sin, first to God, then to those who were sinned against, is the first step that allows faith to have its full effect.

How does this letter keep us from sin? (2:1)
John wants Christians to learn from his example and experience. There is a difference between what he says here and in 1:8. While we cannot escape sin totally in this life, it doesn't mean we should give up and give in. We'll never get anywhere if we do so.

Atoning sacrifice (2:2)
John reminds his readers of the Old Testament concept of *atonement* which paid the penalty for sin (death) and thus averted God's wrath. The priest gained atonement by sprinkling the blood of the sacrifice on the *atonement cover* (Lev. 16:14). Just as a lamb or other animal died to pay for sins in the Old Testament, Jesus died for our sins.

What does it mean to *walk as Jesus did*? (2:6)
The word *walk* is a word picture that speaks of one's lifestyle or behavior. Jesus didn't come just to talk, he came to walk with us—show us the way. To *walk as Jesus did* means to follow his example, to live according to his teachings, to trust in him and obey his words.

What new command does John give? (2:8)
The old command had never changed: *Love the LORD your God with all your heart and with all your soul and with all your strength* (Deut. 6:5) and *Love your neighbor as yourself* (Lev. 19:18). But the new command renews and deepens

the old. It calls us to let God's light shine through our lives to a dark world. The new command calls us to live according to the love of God—to live as Jesus lived (vv. 5–6).

Why didn't John address women? (2:12–13)

In the Graeco-Roman culture of his day, John spoke primarily to the men who were leaders of the early church. Our culture today has made us hypersensitive about gender roles and labels, triggering questions about John's language that wouldn't have raised an eyebrow back then. The point is that John's advice was for the whole church, men and women, but that it was conveyed primarily through the male leaders. See articles: *Why didn't Paul allow women to speak in church?* (1 Cor. 14:34) and *Why silence the women?* (1 Tim. 2:11).

What's wrong with loving the world? (2:15)

God loves the world—that is, God loves people who are in the world (John 3:16). There's nothing wrong with loving people. But God hates worldly ways (Zech. 8:17). John uses the word *world* in the second sense here. We dare not love the sinful ways of the world.

Last hour (2:18)

Conveys the idea that the end is close at hand, a theme common among New Testament writers. Also see *Last days* (2 Tim. 3:1).

Antichrist (2:18)

Anyone who opposes and rejects God has the spirit of the antichrist to a certain degree. Dictators like Hitler or Stalin hated Jesus and his gospel, as well as his church. The book of Revelation teaches there will be one final figure on the world scene who will embody the worst of the spirit of the antichrist, but that figure finally will be defeated.

What kind of anointing do Christians have? (2:20)

The anointing of the Holy Spirit here means a sort of certification. Our anointing suggests that we are complete in Christ or that we are commissioned to serve Christ. This anointing also suggests an ongoing presence and ministry of the Spirit within, protecting us from false teachers or leaders and helping us discern between right and wrong.

What does it take to remain in Christ? (2:24)

We need a vital relationship with the Lord, a fellowship (1:3) that sustains life. John explained this more fully in his Gospel when he used the analogy of a branch that remains connected to the vine (John 15:1–8). Some think this warning means that our relationship with Christ (and thus life in Christ) can be lost. Others are confident that once they truly believe, they cannot separate themselves from God's love. See articles: *Can believers fall away?* (Luke 8:13) and *Should we fear falling?* (Heb. 6:6).

Is the Christian's destiny a mystery? (3:2)

No, the Christian's destiny is not a mystery. But the details of what it will be like are not fully understood. We know that we will be in the presence of God (Luke 23:43), with resurrected bodies (1 Cor. 15:42–44). But all that our

because you have overcome the evil one.
I write to you, dear children,
    because you have known the Father.
¹⁴I write to you, fathers,
    because you have known him who is from
        the beginning.
I write to you, young men,
    because you are strong,
    and the word of God lives in you,
    and you have overcome the evil one.

Do Not Love the World

¹⁵Do not love the world or anything in the world. If anyone loves the world, the love of the Father is not in him. ¹⁶For everything in the world—the cravings of sinful man, the lust of his eyes and the boasting of what he has and does—comes not from the Father but from the world. ¹⁷The world and its desires pass away, but the man who does the will of God lives forever.

Warning Against Antichrists

¹⁸Dear children, this is the last hour; and as you have heard that the antichrist[D] is coming, even now many antichrists have come. This is how we know it is the last hour. ¹⁹They went out from us, but they did not really belong to us. For if they had belonged to us, they would have remained with us; but their going showed that none of them belonged to us. ²⁰But you have an anointing[D] from the Holy One, and all of you know the truth.[a] ²¹I do not write to you because you do not know the truth, but because you do know it and because no lie comes from the truth. ²²Who is the liar? It is the man who denies that Jesus is the Christ. Such a man is the antichrist—he denies the Father and the Son. ²³No one who denies the Son has the Father; whoever acknowledges the Son has the Father also.

²⁴See that what you have heard from the beginning remains in you. If it does, you also will remain in the Son and in the Father. ²⁵And this is what he promised us—even eternal life.

²⁶I am writing these things to you about those who are trying to lead you astray. ²⁷As for you, the anointing you received from him remains in you, and you do not need anyone to teach you. But as his anointing teaches you about all things and as that anointing is real, not counterfeit—just as it has taught you, remain in him.

Children of God

²⁸And now, dear children, continue in him, so that when he appears we may be confident and unashamed before him at his coming.

²⁹If you know that he is righteous[D], you know that everyone who does what is right has been born of him.

3 How great is the love the Father has lavished on us, that we should be called children of God! And that is what we are! The reason the world does not know us is that it did not know him. ²Dear friends, now we are children of God, and what we will be has not yet been made known. But we know that when he appears,[b] we shall be like him, for we shall see him as he is. ³Everyone who has this hope in him purifies[D] himself, just as he is pure.

---

a20 Some manuscripts and you know all things   *b2 Or when it is made known*

of God overcomes the world. This is the victory that has overcome the world, even our faith. **5**Who is it that overcomes the world? Only he who believes that Jesus is the Son of God.

6This is the one who came by water and blood—Jesus Christ. He did not come by water only, but by water and blood. And it is the Spirit who testifies, because the Spirit is the truth. **7**For there are three that testify: **8**the*a* Spirit, the water and the blood; and the three are in agreement. **9**We accept man's testimony, but God's testimony is greater because it is the testimony of God, which he has given about his Son. **10**Anyone who believes in the Son of God has this testimony in his heart. Anyone who does not believe God has made him out to be a liar, because he has not believed the testimony God has given about his Son. **11**And this is the testimony: God has given us eternal life**D**, and this life is in his Son. **12**He who has the Son has life; he who does not have the Son of God does not have life.

Concluding Remarks

13I write these things to you who believe in the name of the Son of God so that you may know that you have eternal life. **14**This is the confidence we have in approaching God: that if we ask anything according to his will, he hears us. **15**And if we know that he hears us—whatever we ask—we know that we have what we asked of him.

16If anyone sees his brother commit a sin that does not lead to death**D**, he should pray and God will give him life. I refer to those whose sin does not lead to death. There is a sin that leads to death. I am not saying that he should pray about that. **17**All wrongdoing is sin, and there is sin that does not lead to death.

18We know that anyone born of God does not continue to sin; the one who was born of God keeps him safe, and the evil one cannot harm him. **19**We know that we are children of God, and that the whole world is under the control of the evil one. **20**We know also that the Son of God has come and has given us understanding, so that we may know him who is true. And we are in him who is true—even in his Son Jesus Christ. He is the true God and eternal life.

21Dear children, keep yourselves from idols**D**.

In what sense did Jesus come *by water and blood?* (5:6)

John stressed that Jesus, though God, actually lived a life in a body of flesh and blood. *Water and blood* may refer to Jesus' baptism when he was launched into his work by the Father. Jesus also was granted authority through his death on the cross, where *water and blood* both flowed freely from his side.

Why isn't the text note considered to be Scripture? (5:7–8)

Since the oldest manuscripts do not have these words, they were apparently added centuries after John wrote, perhaps as commentary.

How sure can we be about eternal life? (5:13)

The Holy Spirit is given to all believers and convinces each that they are true children of God (Romans 8:16). Only God can give such internal confirmation; and only he can complete the process that begins when a person becomes a Christian.

Does God close his ears to our misguided requests? (5:14)

In essence, yes. Some prayers he ignores because our hearts desire something that is contrary to his will. He has better things planned than we can ever imagine and is pleased to grant those prayers that are in line with his will. See *Does God answer prayers if our motives aren't pure?* (James 4:3) and *How are prayers hindered?* (1 Peter 3:7).

What sin leads to death? (5:16–17)

Some think the *sin that leads to death* refers to a persistent rebellion to the truth which can only result in spiritual death. Others think it refers to sins that lead to physical death.

One who was born of God keeps him safe (5:18)

Jesus' perfect life and special relationship with the Father allowed him to offer his life for ours to satisfy God's justice. Nothing is too hard for him or too much to do on our behalf.

What can and can't the evil one do? (5:18)

Satan can only do as much as God allows him. Believers can be assured that nothing can separate them from God's love and that nothing can defeat them (Romans 8:35,37–39).

Why bring up a new subject in the last line of the letter? (5:21)

Possibly, like many letter writers, John remembered another point he wanted to make and only had time to jot it down at the end. Whatever the reason, the command is as important as any other he gave in the previous chapters.

---

*a*7,8 Late manuscripts of the Vulgate *testify in heaven: the Father, the Word and the Holy Spirit, and these three are one. 8And there are three that testify on earth: the* (not found in any Greek manuscript before the sixteenth century)

2 JOHN

Why read this book?

To keep on target spiritually. This short book will challenge you to *watch out* (v. 8), to be certain about what you believe and how you live.

Who wrote this book?

The apostle John, who also wrote 1 John and the Gospel of John.

When was it written?

Probably about the same time as 1 John or soon after, in the A.D. 80s.

To whom was it written and why?

John wrote this personal note to Christians who may have felt pressured by false teachers. He wrote it perhaps to accompany his more general letter (1 John). He hoped it would help renew commitment to the truth by further exposing the false teachers.

What was happening at this time?

See Introduction to 1 John.

What to look for in 2 John:

More of the same kinds of things found in 1 John (see Introduction to 1 John), primarily focusing on the truth of the gospel.

When did these things happen?

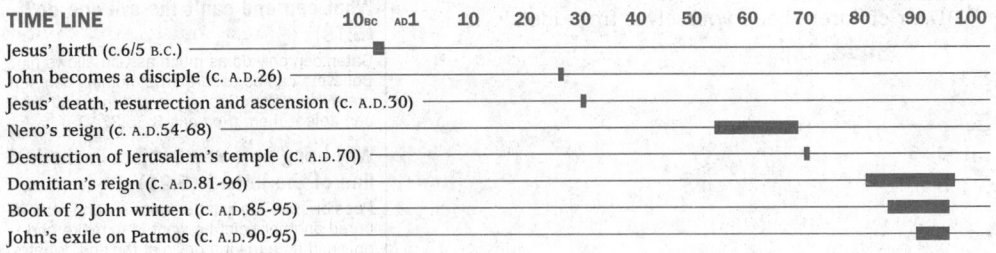

TIME LINE	10BC AD1	10	20	30	40	50	60	70	80	90	100
Jesus' birth (c.6/5 B.C.)											
John becomes a disciple (c. A.D.26)											
Jesus' death, resurrection and ascension (c. A.D.30)											
Nero's reign (c. A.D.54-68)											
Destruction of Jerusalem's temple (c. A.D.70)											
Domitian's reign (c. A.D.81-96)											
Book of 2 John written (c. A.D.85-95)											
John's exile on Patmos (c. A.D.90-95)											

¹The elder,

To the chosen lady and her children, whom I love in the truth—and not I only, but also all who know the truth—²because of the truth, which lives in us and will be with us forever:

³Grace^D, mercy^D and peace^D from God the Father and from Jesus Christ, the Father's Son, will be with us in truth and love.

⁴It has given me great joy to find some of your children walking in the truth, just as the Father commanded us. ⁵And now, dear lady, I am not writing you a new command but one we have had from the beginning. I ask that we love one another. ⁶And this is love: that we walk in obedience to his commands. As you have heard from the beginning, his command is that you walk in love.
⁷Many deceivers, who do not acknowledge Jesus Christ as coming in the flesh, have gone out into the world. Any such person is the deceiver and the antichrist^D. ⁸Watch out that you do not lose what you have worked for, but that you may be rewarded fully. ⁹Anyone who runs ahead and does not continue in the teaching of Christ does not have God; whoever continues in the teaching has both the Father and the Son. ¹⁰If anyone comes to you and does not bring this teaching, do not take him into your house or welcome him. ¹¹Anyone who welcomes him shares in his wicked work.

¹²I have much to write to you, but I do not want to use paper and ink. Instead, I hope to visit you and talk with you face to face, so that our joy may be complete.

¹³The children of your chosen sister send their greetings.

Elder (v. 1)

A title of respect and authority in the early church. His readers should take notice.

The chosen lady (v. 1)

John likely uses a figure of speech to describe the church he is writing to, since this allows him to emphasize that his readers are God's children, who must be cared for and taught. Some, however, think this may have been an actual woman.

Truth (v. 1)

John highlights the reality of the presence of Jesus in this church as *truth*, using the word five times in the first four verses. He is saying that those in fellowship with Christ will have the means to discern right and wrong as well as the power to choose between the two.

Why did some say Jesus did not come in the flesh? (v. 7)

Many people at that time accepted the deity of Jesus but not his humanity. In today's climate of logic and reason, some say the opposite—that he was human, but not God. The truth combines both; Jesus is both God and man at the same time.

What do Christians work for? (v. 8)

The Bible teaches that we cannot work to earn our salvation, but once God's grace has saved us, we can serve God and expect rewards for our work in eternity (1 Cor. 3:11–15; 2 Cor. 5:10). John calls us to keep the faith and to persevere.

How can we tell who is *in the teaching of Christ?* (vv. 9–10)

Any who contradict the teaching of the Bible cannot be in Christ's teaching. Nor can those who live inconsistent lives, disobedient to God's commands in his Word.

3 JOHN

Why read this book?

If you've ever faced conflict in the church, you'll want to read this book. John tells us that while church fights may be unavoidable, there is a correct way to handle them.

Who wrote this book?

The apostle John, who also wrote 1 John and 2 John as well as the Gospel of John.

When was it written?

Probably about the same time as 1 John or soon after, in the A.D. 80s.

To whom was it written and why?

John wrote this brief letter to his friend, Gaius, perhaps to accompany his more general letter (1 John). He wanted to encourage him for his faithful support of legitimate teachers. He also was warning him about the actions of a certain strong-willed leader named Diotrephes.

What was happening at this time?

See Introduction to 1 John.

What to look for in 3 John:

More of the same kinds of things found in 1 John (see Introduction to 1 John), primarily focusing on the truth of the gospel.

When did these things happen?

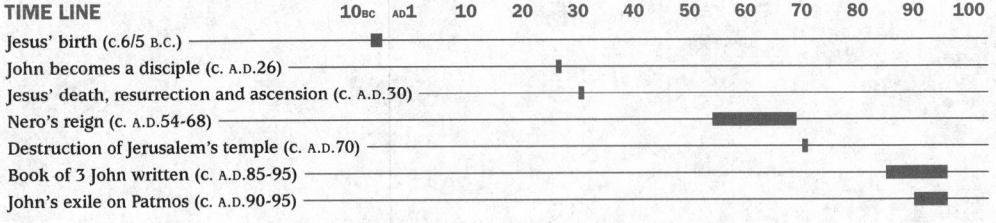

TIME LINE	10 BC	AD 1	10	20	30	40	50	60	70	80	90	100
Jesus' birth (c.6/5 B.C.)												
John becomes a disciple (c. A.D.26)												
Jesus' death, resurrection and ascension (c. A.D.30)												
Nero's reign (c. A.D.54-68)												
Destruction of Jerusalem's temple (c. A.D.70)												
Book of 3 John written (c. A.D.85-95)												
John's exile on Patmos (c. A.D.90-95)												

¹The elder,

To my dear friend Gaius, whom I love in the truth.

²Dear friend, I pray that you may enjoy good health and that all may go well with you, even as your soul^D is getting along well. ³It gave me great joy to have some brothers come and tell about your faithfulness to the truth and how you continue to walk in the truth. ⁴I have no greater joy than to hear that my children are walking in the truth.

⁵Dear friend, you are faithful in what you are doing for the brothers, even though they are strangers to you. ⁶They have told the church about your love. You will do well to send them on their way in a manner worthy of God. ⁷It was for the sake of the Name that they went out, receiving no help from the pagans. ⁸We ought therefore to show hospitality to such men so that we may work together for the truth.

⁹I wrote to the church, but Diotrephes, who loves to be first, will have nothing to do with us. ¹⁰So if I come, I will call attention to what he is doing, gossiping maliciously about us. Not satisfied with that, he refuses to welcome the brothers. He also stops those who want to do so and puts them out of the church.

¹¹Dear friend, do not imitate what is evil but what is good. Anyone who does what is good is from God. Anyone who does what is evil has not seen God. ¹²Demetrius is well spoken of by everyone—and even by the truth itself. We also speak well of him, and you know that our testimony is true.

¹³I have much to write you, but I do not want to do so with pen and ink. ¹⁴I hope to see you soon, and we will talk face to face.

Peace^D to you. The friends here send their greetings. Greet the friends there by name.

Elder (v. 1)
See *Elder* (2 John v. 1).

Truth (v. 1)
See *Truth* (2 John v. 1).

Is it right to pray for health and well-being? (v. 2)
Yes. But there is a danger in assuming that this guarantees physical health and well-being to believers. Our prayers are always answered, though not always in the manner or time we might have hoped. Sometimes the answer is "yes," sometimes it's "not now" and sometimes it's "no." See *Does God close his ears to our misguided requests?* (1 John 5:14).

Who were the traveling brothers? (vv. 3,7)
These brothers may have been teaching elders, chosen by the church like the deacons (Acts 6:3) or possibly by a direct word from God like Paul and Barnabas (Acts 13:2). Their ministry was to travel between churches to encourage various congregations, rather than to minister to one church alone. They may have functioned in several ways—as evangelists, teachers or counselors. They were probably supported by various believers like Gaius (vv. 5–6).

Was Diotrephes a pastor? (v. 9)
We can't be certain. It's clear that he held some authority in the church since he was able to excommunicate some believers from the church (v. 10). But whether his power was based on an official position or from a persuasive personality is not clear.

Do good deeds always indicate service to God? (v. 11)
Good deeds normally reflect a close walk with God. However, this is not always the case. Good can be accomplished by the righteous or the unrighteous, for right reasons or for the wrong. John is speaking, however, of a lifestyle given over to the practice of doing good continually—something that comes only as the result of God's grace.

Demetrius (v. 12)
Probably a lay leader, an example of a Christian who was doing good (v. 11). His deeds were evidence that his life was right with God.

JUDE

Why read this book?

Few enjoy the sound of alarms. Some people disconnect buzzers intended to remind them to buckle their seatbelts—just to avoid irritation. Others unhook smoke detectors that seem to go off too easily. Ignoring such reminders and warnings can be perilous to health. But ignoring spiritual warnings can be worse. That's why we should pay attention to this book. In a few short words, Jude sounds an alarm we dare not disconnect.

Who wrote this book?

Jude, the half-brother of Jesus and full brother of James, who most think also wrote an important letter in the New Testament.

When was it written?

Perhaps just before Peter wrote his second letter, maybe around A.D. 65 or earlier, although some think Jude could have been written later. These two letters seem in part to be interconnected.

Why was it written?

Jude was concerned that Christians might be drawn away from the truth by slippery teachers of false doctrine. He wrote to urge believers *to contend for the faith* (v. 3).

What was happening at this time?

Strange teachings were traveling through some of the churches. Christian imposters had begun assuming roles of leadership. They were teaching that it really didn't matter how people lived if they genuinely had been saved by grace. Sin meant nothing, they reasoned incorrectly, to those who had been forgiven of sin.

What to look for in Jude:

Though this book is brief, don't miss its powerful impact and colorful imagery. Watch for its direct warnings—and God's tremendous promises that accompany them.

¹Jude, a servant of Jesus Christ and a brother of James,

To those who have been called, who are loved by God the Father and kept by*a* Jesus Christ:

²Mercy^D, peace^D and love be yours in abundance.

The Sin and Doom of Godless Men

³Dear friends, although I was very eager to write to you about the salvation^D we share, I felt I had to write and urge you to contend for the faith that was once for all entrusted to the saints^D. ⁴For certain men whose condemnation was written about*b* long ago have secretly slipped in among you. They are godless men, who change the grace^D of our God into a license for immorality and deny Jesus Christ our only Sovereign and Lord.

⁵Though you already know all this, I want to remind you that the Lord*c* delivered his people out of Egypt, but later destroyed those who did not believe. ⁶And the angels who did not keep their positions of authority but abandoned their own home—these he has kept in darkness, bound with everlasting chains for judgment on the great Day. ⁷In a similar way, Sodom and Gomorrah and the surrounding towns gave themselves up to sexual immorality and perversion. They serve as an example of those who suffer the punishment of eternal fire.

⁸In the very same way, these dreamers pollute their own bodies, reject authority and slander celestial beings. ⁹But even the archangel Michael, when he was disputing with the devil about the body of Moses, did not dare to bring a slanderous accusation against him, but said, "The Lord rebuke you!" ¹⁰Yet these men speak abusively against whatever they do not understand; and what things they do understand by instinct, like unreasoning animals—these are the very things that destroy them.

¹¹Woe to them! They have taken the way of Cain; they have rushed for profit into Balaam's error; they have been destroyed in Korah's rebellion.

¹²These men are blemishes at your love feasts, eating

a1 Or *for;* or *in condemnation*   *b4* Or *men who were marked out for*   *c5* Some early manuscripts *Jesus*

Who were these men? (v. 4)

Frauds. Fakes. Perhaps they longed for meaningful relationships like those among believers, but were unwilling to accept Christ on his terms. Or maybe they desired leadership positions so they could control and manipulate others. Some may have been intentionally deceptive while others may have themselves been deceived.

Where was this *written about long ago?* (v. 4)

This may refer in general to Old Testament pronouncements against wickedness. Or it might refer to the words of Enoch quoted later (vv. 14–15).

What angels are chained in darkness? (v. 6)

Angels that rebelled against God. Little is known about these fallen angels, but most think they are now known as demons and evil spirits. Also see *When did God send fallen angels to hell?* (2 Peter 2:4).

Why were these godless men called *dreamers?* (v. 8)

Probably because their so-called god and their counterfeit faith were the products of their own imagination. Or it may be that they relied on dreams and visions to create the impression that they received fresh revelations from God.

How did they *slander celestial beings?* (v. 8)

Apparently, these people ridiculed spiritual powers that they could not understand (v. 10).

Where did this story about Moses' body come from? (v. 9)

Jude quotes from the *Assumption* or *Testament of Moses,* one of many non-Biblical Jewish books. This does not mean that Jude endorsed the book in its entirety or that he thought it to be divinely inspired.

How contentious should we be? (v. 3)

The word *contend* implies that Christians have something worth fighting for. The rest of this book tells us that our battles for the faith sometimes will occur even *inside* the church. When we have a deep love for the truth, our thoughtful convictions must be defended. We cannot afford to settle for an imitation and lose the real thing.

People are not always comfortable with the rigors of firm convictions. But the world and Satan will continually confront our faith, leaving us no choice but to take a stand. If we are not contentious in such situations, all that is left is to retreat.

Tragically, the enemy sometimes dupes people within the church or sends us counterfeit believers. At such times we must contend for the faith within the church itself. Thankfully, we fight these battles with the help of God.

The other side of the coin, however, is that some have elevated matters of personal preference or opinion to the level of an essential doctrine. When believers become contentious over styles, decorating tastes or cultural distinctives, then they've become too contentious. We must contend for the message, not the method.

SCRIPTURE LINK (v. 11) *The way of Cain*

Adam and Eve's first son, Cain, consumed with jealousy and anger, murdered his brother, Abel. See Gen. 4:3–8.

SCRIPTURE LINK (v. 11) *Balaam's error*

Balaam was an ancient pagan sorcerer hired to curse God's people. Though God compelled him to bless Israel instead, his greed apparently motivated him to give advice that proved destructive to the Israelites. See Num. 22–24; 31:16.

SCRIPTURE LINK (v. 11) *Korah's rebellion*

Korah was a Levite who led a rebellion against the authority God had given to Moses and Aaron. See Num. 16:1–3,11.

Love feasts (v. 12)

These were meals that churches held after their worship together, like potluck suppers today. The community of believers gathered in this manner to affirm their love for and their fellowship with each other.

Why did Jude quote Enoch? (vv. 14–15)

Jude wrote during a time when he would have read the Old Testament and non-Biblical Jewish writings such as the book of Enoch. The Bible as a whole contains allusions and quotes from a number of other works of literature.

What does it mean to pray *in the Holy Spirit?* (v. 20)

To pray in the Holy Spirit is to rely on the Spirit to guide our prayers according to God's will and purpose. It means relying on the gifts and power of the Spirit to pray effectively and with faith (Romans 8:26–27). Also see *What is praying in the Spirit?* (Eph. 6:18).

---

with you without the slightest qualm—shepherds who feed only themselves. They are clouds without rain, blown along by the wind; autumn trees, without fruit and uprooted—twice dead. [13]They are wild waves of the sea, foaming up their shame; wandering stars, for whom blackest darkness has been reserved forever.

[14]Enoch, the seventh from Adam, prophesied about these men: "See, the Lord is coming with thousands upon thousands of his holy ones [15]to judge everyone, and to convict all the ungodly of all the ungodly acts they have done in the ungodly way, and of all the harsh words ungodly sinners have spoken against him." [16]These men are grumblers and faultfinders; they follow their own evil desires; they boast about themselves and flatter others for their own advantage.

A Call to Persevere

[17]But, dear friends, remember what the apostles[D] of our Lord Jesus Christ foretold. [18]They said to you, "In the last times there will be scoffers who will follow their own ungodly desires." [19]These are the men who divide you, who follow mere natural instincts and do not have the Spirit.

[20]But you, dear friends, build yourselves up in your most holy faith and pray in the Holy Spirit. [21]Keep yourselves in God's love as you wait for the mercy[D] of our Lord Jesus Christ to bring you to eternal life.

[22]Be merciful to those who doubt; [23]snatch others from the fire and save them; to others show mercy, mixed with fear—hating even the clothing stained by corrupted flesh.

Doxology

[24]To him who is able to keep you from falling and to present you before his glorious presence without fault and with great joy— [25]to the only God our Savior be glory[D], majesty, power and authority, through Jesus Christ our Lord, before all ages, now and forevermore! Amen.

REVELATION

Why read this book?

If it ever seems to you there is more evil in the world than good and that the bad guys are winning, Revelation is for you. It's a book of hope—its central message is that God and good will win over evil, no matter how bad things look now. Revelation tells us that we must live committed, holy lives if we want to participate in God's victorious kingdom.

Who wrote this book?

Probably John, the apostle who also wrote the Gospel of John. Some, however, suggest that a different John may have written it.

When was it written?

Several dates are suggested. The most favored is A.D. 90 to 96, near the end of the reign of the Roman emperor Domitian, about when his persecution of the church began.

To whom was it written and why?

This book went to seven churches in the Roman province of Asia (present-day Turkey) to warn them against falling away from their faith in Christ. It also offered them assurance of ultimate victory for those who remain on God's side.

How does this book differ from other New Testament books?

Revelation is apocalyptic literature. (The Greek word *apocalypse* means *uncovering, unveiling* or *revelation*.) Jewish apocalyptic writing uses figurative language and symbolism to show that evil will be replaced by the goodness and peace of God's kingdom.

What to look for in Revelation:

Look for a combination of warnings and encouragements—alternating challenge and hope. Watch for descriptions of the future as God's kingdom ultimately conquers evil at the end of time. Also notice the picture of the ruling Christ, his divine attributes and his heavenly glory.

When did these things happen?

TIME LINE	10BC AD1	10	20	30	40	50	60	70	80	90	100
Jesus' birth (c.6/5 B.C.)											
John becomes a disciple (c. A.D.26)											
Jesus' death, resurrection and ascension (c. A.D.30)											
Nero's reign (c. A.D.54-68)											
Paul's imprisonment and death in Rome (c. A.D.67-68)											
Destruction of Jerusalem's temple (c. A.D.70)											
Domitian's reign (c. A.D.81-96)											
John's exile on Patmos (c. A.D.90-95)											
Book of Revelation written (c. A.D.90-96)											

How should we understand prophecy in Revelation? (1:1)

Some think this book refers only to events in the first century. Others believe it contains events yet to come at the end of time. Still others see its prophecies both ways—partially fulfilled near the time of writing, but also with a wider fulfillment at the end of time. Some downplay the historical significance of Revelation to emphasize the timeless moral lessons in its visions. Others interpret Revelation primarily as a poetic vision of the triumph of good over evil. Most agree, however, that Revelation is not a puzzle to be solved to tell us when Christ will return.

How *soon* were these things to *take place*? (1:1,3)

Many believe that some of the events outlined in Revelation took place shortly after it was written. Some suggest John felt Christ's resurrection victory guaranteed all future victories, so he could describe them as *present* realities regardless of when they occurred historically. In another sense, *the time is near* for each person. The end of life may come at any time, giving immediacy to what John writes about standing before the throne of God.

How should we understand the numbers in this book? (1:4)

The ancient world often used numbers symbolically as well as literally. (Some of that carries over today when people speak of seven as a lucky number and thirteen as unlucky.) Revelation uses numbers symbolically to communicate something more than quantities. Seven, for instance, suggests completeness, fulfillment and perfection. See *What was so special about the number seven?* (2 Chron. 29:21). As such, seven is often associated with Christ in Revelation.

Seven spirits (1:4)

See *Seven spirits* (4:5).

The Seven Churches (1:4)

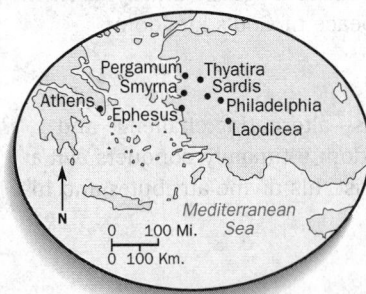

Faithful witness (1:5)

See *Faithful . . . witness* (3:14).

Why are believers called priests? (1:6)

See *Should we still offer sacrifices?* (1 Peter 2:5).

The Alpha and the Omega (1:8)

The first and last letters of the Greek alphabet, a symbolic way of referring to God and his position as Lord over all history, from beginning to end. Also see v. 18.

Prologue

1 The revelation[D] of Jesus Christ, which God gave him to show his servants what must soon take place. He made it known by sending his angel to his servant John, ²who testifies to everything he saw—that is, the word of God and the testimony of Jesus Christ. ³Blessed is the one who reads the words of this prophecy[D], and blessed are those who hear it and take to heart what is written in it, because the time is near.

Greetings and Doxology

⁴John,

To the seven churches in the province of Asia:

Grace[D] and peace[D] to you from him who is, and who was, and who is to come, and from the seven spirits[a] before his throne, ⁵and from Jesus Christ, who is the faithful witness, the firstborn[D] from the dead, and the ruler of the kings of the earth.

To him who loves us and has freed us from our sins by his blood, ⁶and has made us to be a kingdom and priests[D] to serve his God and Father—to him be glory[D] and power for ever and ever! Amen.

⁷Look, he is coming with the clouds,
　　and every eye will see him,
even those who pierced him;
　　and all the peoples of the earth will mourn
　　　　because of him.
　　　　　　　　So shall it be! Amen.

⁸"I am the Alpha and the Omega," says the Lord God, "who is, and who was, and who is to come, the Almighty."

One Like a Son of Man

⁹I, John, your brother and companion in the suffering and kingdom and patient endurance that are ours in Jesus, was on the island of Patmos because of the word of God and the testimony of Jesus. ¹⁰On the Lord's Day I was in the Spirit, and I heard behind me a loud voice like a trumpet, ¹¹which said: "Write on a scroll what you see and send it to the seven churches: to Ephesus, Smyrna, Pergamum, Thyatira, Sardis, Philadelphia and Laodicea."

¹²I turned around to see the voice that was speaking to me. And when I turned I saw seven golden lampstands, ¹³and among the lampstands was someone "like a son of man[D],"[b] dressed in a robe reaching down to his feet and with a golden sash around his chest. ¹⁴His head and hair were white like wool, as white as snow, and his eyes were like blazing fire. ¹⁵His feet were like bronze glowing in a furnace, and his voice was like the sound of rushing waters. ¹⁶In his right hand he held seven stars, and out of his mouth came a sharp double-edged sword. His face was like the sun shining in all its brilliance.

¹⁷When I saw him, I fell at his feet as though dead. Then he placed his right hand on me and said: "Do not be afraid. I am the First and the Last. ¹⁸I am the Living One; I was dead, and behold I am alive for ever and ever! And I hold the keys of death[D] and Hades[D].

¹⁹"Write, therefore, what you have seen, what is now and what will take place later. ²⁰The mystery[D] of the sev-

---

ᵃ4 Or *the sevenfold Spirit*　　ᵇ13 Daniel 7:13

en stars that you saw in my right hand and of the seven golden lampstands is this: The seven stars are the angels*a* of the seven churches, and the seven lampstands are the seven churches.

To the Church in Ephesus

2 "To the angel*b* of the church in Ephesus write:

These are the words of him who holds the seven stars in his right hand and walks among the seven golden lampstands: **2**I know your deeds, your hard work and your perseverance. I know that you cannot tolerate wicked men, that you have tested those who claim to be apostles*D* but are not, and have found them false. **3**You have persevered and have endured hardships for my name, and have not grown weary.

4Yet I hold this against you: You have forsaken your first love. **5**Remember the height from which you have fallen! Repent*D* and do the things you did at first. If you do not repent, I will come to you and remove your lampstand from its place. **6**But you have this in your favor: You hate the practices of the Nicolaitans, which I also hate.

7He who has an ear, let him hear what the Spirit says to the churches. To him who overcomes, I will give the right to eat from the tree of life, which is in the paradise of God.

To the Church in Smyrna

8"To the angel of the church in Smyrna write:

These are the words of him who is the First and the

a20 Or messengers   *b1 Or messenger; also in verses 8, 12 and 18*

In the Spirit (1:10)
See *In the Spirit* (4:2).

Son of man (1:13)
Significantly, John describes Christ *like a son of man*—a link to the book of Daniel (Daniel 7:13–14; 10:5) as well as to the Gospels. *Son of man,* a title for the Messiah, alludes here to the glory and power God the Father assigns to the risen, heavenly Christ.

Did John see real things—or symbols of spiritual things? (1:19–20)
While on the island of Patmos (see **Map 11** at the back of this Bible), John saw *real* things but not necessarily material things. John, *in the Spirit* (v. 10), saw things *more real* than the transient material world. What he saw, however, is often expressed in terms that materialistic minds have difficulty understanding.

Why write to an angel? (2:1)
Some say these were the guardian angels for each of the seven churches. Others say they were human leaders, ministers in these churches serving as *messengers* of God (see NIV text note). Still others see them symbolically, as the spirit of a congregation—the collective personalities of the believers.

In what sense had these believers forsaken their first love? (2:4)
The Ephesians were commended because they resisted false teaching and persevered in the face of opposition. Unfortunately, their firm stand against heresy eroded their sense of compassion. They became better at fighting error than loving one another and, by implication, loving God. The Lord called them back to a sincere love for him, a love demonstrated by their acts of love for one another.

Why such obscure, mysterious language? (1:19–20)

Why write in symbolic language, making it inaccessible to so many? Why not give it to us straight?

While it is true that there are many hidden truths in Revelation, it's also true that the important truths are not inaccessible. Truths that center on the holiness, power and sovereignty of God, his victory over evil and what we need to do to share in that victory do not require special knowledge to be understood. Such truths come through loud and clear even if we can't decipher a single symbol.

God is a God who both reveals and conceals. He makes himself known to us, but only in part. He knows humans with their physical limitations would be completely overwhelmed by a full picture of supernatural realities. Consequently he hides certain things from us.

One way God reveals and conceals himself at the same time is through figurative language and apocalyptic images. Some truths are too profound for pragmatic, rationalistic language. Such truths are best hinted at through the multi-layered language of metaphor and symbol. The description of God as having the appearance of jewels, surrounded by a rainbow of light (4:3), for example, tells something about God beyond mere factual statement.

John's contemporaries were more familiar with this kind of writing than Western readers. We should approach Revelation—indeed the whole Bible—with humility, recognizing our own cultural and personal limitations.

What would it mean to have their lampstand removed? (2:5)

The warning *I will come to you* indicates special judgment against them (see v. 16). Since the lampstand is the symbol of their existence as Christ's church (1:20), its removal would symbolize Christ removing them as his church.

Nicolaitans (2:6)

Apparently followers of Nicolas of Antioch. He taught falsely that Christian freedom and the insignificance of the physical body permitted believers to engage in sexual immorality and other offenses without consequence.

How can believers be poor *and* rich at the same time? (2:9)

Christ guarantees economically poor believers, like those at Smyrna, their spiritual wealth. And he says that those who are smug in their material prosperity, like the Laodiceans, are spiritually impoverished (Matt. 6:19–21).

Why did non-Jews pretend to be Jews? (2:9)

Technically, they were Jews—both by race and by religion. But this is figurative language to say that those who reject Christ forfeit their chance to be God's chosen people.

The second death (2:11)

Eternal punishment in the lake of fire, as opposed to mere physical death (see 20:14–15). This was meant to encourage the believers in Smyrna, some of whom faced physical suffering and death through persecution. They would be spared the more frightening spiritual death.

Who was Antipas? (2:13)

A Christian martyr killed earlier in Pergamum. This was a reminder that the church had held firm during previous times of persecution.

Who were Balaam and Balak? (2:14)

Balak, king of Moab, tried without success to convince Balaam to curse Israel (Num. 22–24). But later, Balaam advised the Moabites to entrap the Israelites in idolatry and immorality (Num. 25:1–2; 31:16).

Hidden manna (2:17)

It was a common expectation among Jews that manna would be provided again when the Messiah came, just as it was with Moses in the desert. This may mean that the new manna would be hidden from all but those who accept Christ as Messiah.

White stone (2:17)

Perhaps a reference to an ancient practice of giving a defendant on trial one of two stones: a white one if found innocent or a black one if found guilty. Or this may have alluded to stones sometimes used as tickets for admission to festivals and royal feasts. Either way, the white stone symbolizes God's favor.

New name (2:17)

The *new name* here may indicate an important change in status for the believer, as when Abram became Abraham. Or it's possible that the name written on the stone is *Christ* or *God*. Either way, this *new name* would be a sign of a unique relationship with God.

Last, who died and came to life again. ⁹I know your afflictions[D] and your poverty—yet you are rich! I know the slander of those who say they are Jews[D] and are not, but are a synagogue of Satan. ¹⁰Do not be afraid of what you are about to suffer. I tell you, the devil will put some of you in prison to test you, and you will suffer persecution for ten days. Be faithful, even to the point of death[D], and I will give you the crown of life.

¹¹He who has an ear, let him hear what the Spirit says to the churches. He who overcomes will not be hurt at all by the second death.

To the Church in Pergamum

¹²"To the angel of the church in Pergamum write:

These are the words of him who has the sharp, double-edged sword. ¹³I know where you live— where Satan has his throne. Yet you remain true to my name. You did not renounce your faith in me, even in the days of Antipas, my faithful witness, who was put to death in your city—where Satan lives. ¹⁴Nevertheless, I have a few things against you: You have people there who hold to the teaching of Balaam, who taught Balak to entice the Israelites to sin by eating food sacrificed to idols[D] and by committing sexual immorality. ¹⁵Likewise you also have those who hold to the teaching of the Nicolaitans. ¹⁶Repent[D] therefore! Otherwise, I will soon come to you and will fight against them with the sword of my mouth.

¹⁷He who has an ear, let him hear what the Spirit says to the churches. To him who overcomes, I will give some of the hidden manna[D]. I will also give him a white stone with a new name written on it, known only to him who receives it.

To the Church in Thyatira

¹⁸"To the angel of the church in Thyatira write:

These are the words of the Son of God, whose eyes are like blazing fire and whose feet are like burnished bronze. ¹⁹I know your deeds, your love and faith, your service and perseverance, and that you are now doing more than you did at first.

²⁰Nevertheless, I have this against you: You tolerate that woman Jezebel, who calls herself a prophetess[D]. By her teaching she misleads my servants into sexual immorality and the eating of food sacrificed to idols. ²¹I have given her time to repent of her immorality, but she is unwilling. ²²So I will cast her on a bed of suffering, and I will make those who commit adultery with her suffer intensely, unless they repent of her ways. ²³I will strike her children dead. Then all the churches will know that I am he who searches hearts and minds, and I will repay each of you according to your deeds. ²⁴Now I say to the rest of you in Thyatira, to you who do not hold to her teaching and have not learned Satan's so-called deep secrets (I will not impose any other burden on you): ²⁵Only hold on to what you have until I come.

²⁶To him who overcomes and does my will to the end, I will give authority over the nations—

²⁷'He will rule them with an iron scepter[D];
   he will dash them to pieces like
     pottery'[a]—

just as I have received authority from my Father. ²⁸I will also give him the morning star. ²⁹He who has an ear, let him hear what the Spirit says to the churches.

To the Church in Sardis

3 "To the angel[b] of the church in Sardis write:

These are the words of him who holds the seven spirits[c] of God and the seven stars. I know your deeds; you have a reputation of being alive, but you are dead. ²Wake up! Strengthen what remains and is about to die, for I have not found your deeds complete in the sight of my God. ³Remember, therefore, what you have received and heard; obey it, and repent[D]. But if you do not wake up, I will come like a thief, and you will not know at what time I will come to you.

⁴Yet you have a few people in Sardis who have not soiled their clothes. They will walk with me, dressed in white, for they are worthy. ⁵He who overcomes will, like them, be dressed in white. I will never blot out his name from the book of life, but will acknowledge his name before my Father and his angels. ⁶He who has an ear, let him hear what the Spirit says to the churches.

To the Church in Philadelphia

⁷"To the angel of the church in Philadelphia write:

These are the words of him who is holy and true, who holds the key of David. What he opens no one can shut, and what he shuts no one can open. ⁸I know your deeds. See, I have placed before you an open door that no one can shut. I know that you have little strength, yet you have kept my word and have not denied my name. ⁹I will make those who are of the synagogue of Satan, who claim to be Jews[D] though they are not, but are liars—I will make them come and fall down at your feet and acknowledge that I have loved you. ¹⁰Since you have kept my command to endure patiently, I will also keep you from the hour of trial that is going to come upon the whole world to test those who live on the earth.

¹¹I am coming soon. Hold on to what you have, so that no one will take your crown. ¹²Him who overcomes I will make a pillar in the temple of my God. Never again will he leave it. I will write on him the name of my God and the name of the city of my God, the new Jerusalem[D], which is coming down out of heaven from my God; and I will also write on him my new name. ¹³He who has an ear, let him hear what the Spirit says to the churches.

To the Church in Laodicea

¹⁴"To the angel of the church in Laodicea write:

These are the words of the Amen, the faithful and

Who was Jezebel? (2:20)
Originally she was a queen of Israel who promoted the immoral cult of Baal (1 Kings 16:31). Her name is used here to categorize a false teacher, a so-called prophetess who misled the believers in Thyatira.

Was it wrong to eat food offered to idols? (2:20)
No. Paul had already shown this act to be morally neutral (1 Cor. 8:4–6,8). But he also warned that, depending on the spiritual maturity of the believer, it could lead to sin (1 Cor. 8:7,12). In this case, the teaching to eat meat offered to idols was part of an insidious doctrine that detracted from holy living.

Who were Jezebel's children? (2:23)
A metaphor indicating those who followed her false teachings. See *Who was Jezebel?* (2:20).

Satan's so-called deep secrets (2:24)
Cults of the time, including Jezebel's, often claimed secret knowledge or wisdom that would be revealed only to those initiated into the cult. These words mock the claims that these "secrets" revealed truth.

The morning star (2:28)
A name for Christ (22:16), perhaps suggesting his rising authority and rule (2:26–27). The more general implication, however, is one of hope—a light to those in darkness.

Why write to an angel? (3:1)
See *Why write to an angel?* (2:1).

Seven spirits (3:1)
See *Seven spirits* (4:5).

Book of life (3:5)
A common Biblical metaphor derived from the ancient practice of keeping a list of citizens. It represents God's records of those who are part of his kingdom. The *book of life* contains a record of all those who accept Jesus Christ as Savior and who will receive eternal life.

Why did non-Jews pretend to be Jews? (3:9)
See *Why did non-Jews pretend to be Jews?* (2:9).

When will *the hour of trial*—the testing of everyone on earth—occur? (3:10)
This trial will occur for unbelievers at the time of Christ's return.

Crown (3:11)
See *What is the crown of glory?* (1 Peter 5:4).

New name (3:12)
See *New name* (2:17).

The Amen (3:14)
A divine title formerly assigned to God. The Hebrew *amen* is translated as the *God of truth* (Isaiah 65:16). Now it is given to Christ, showing that Christ's character itself guarantees the truth of his message. Also see *Why say Amen when we pray?* (2 Cor. 1:20).

Faithful . . . witness (3:14)
A reference to Christ's utter dependability and truthfulness, in contrast to the faithlessness of the church of Laodicea.

---

[a]27 Psalm 2:9   [b]1 Or *messenger*; also in verses 7 and 14
[c]1 Or *the sevenfold Spirit*

Why is being spiritually *cold* better than being *lukewarm*? (3:16)

At least those who are spiritually *cold* cannot pretend that they are all right. Their spiritual needs are obvious. But those who are *lukewarm* may have just enough pretense of religion to cause them to think they are okay. God desires wholehearted, sincere responses. Anything less suggests that other things have a higher priority than a relationship with him. Those who want the "minimum requirement"—just enough of God to get by—risk missing him altogether.

How can believers be poor *and* rich at the same time? (3:17–18).

See *How can believers be poor and rich at the same time?* (2:9).

In the Spirit (4:2)

John uses this phrase to underscore that the source of his vision was God. It came out of a supernatural encounter far beyond the typical indwelling of the Spirit in a believer's life. John was transported into a special, heightened spiritual experience. He repeats the source of his vision here because this chapter opens up a whole new dimension of the revelation.

Why compare God to jewels? (4:3)

Human language cannot contain the splendor of God, so the Bible uses a variety of words to describe him. God is too glorious to be seen directly (Exodus 33:18–23), so here he is described as light shining indirectly through precious jewels. *Jasper . . . carnelian* and *emerald* are used as word pictures to hint at God's brilliant beauty, value and glory. The *rainbow* may have been intended as a reminder of God's covenant with Noah (Gen. 9:12–16), a symbol of God's mercy in the midst of a vision telling of his sovereign judgment.

true witness, the ruler of God's creation. [15]I know your deeds, that you are neither cold nor hot. I wish you were either one or the other! [16]So, because you are lukewarm—neither hot nor cold—I am about to spit you out of my mouth. [17]You say, 'I am rich; I have acquired wealth and do not need a thing.' But you do not realize that you are wretched, pitiful, poor, blind and naked. [18]I counsel you to buy from me gold refined in the fire, so you can become rich; and white clothes to wear, so you can cover your shameful nakedness; and salve to put on your eyes, so you can see.

[19]Those whom I love I rebuke and discipline. So be earnest, and repent[D]. [20]Here I am! I stand at the door and knock. If anyone hears my voice and opens the door, I will come in and eat with him, and he with me.

[21]To him who overcomes, I will give the right to sit with me on my throne, just as I overcame and sat down with my Father on his throne. [22]He who has an ear, let him hear what the Spirit says to the churches."

The Throne in Heaven

4 After this I looked, and there before me was a door standing open in heaven. And the voice I had first heard speaking to me like a trumpet said, "Come up here, and I will show you what must take place after this." [2]At once I was in the Spirit, and there before me was a throne in heaven with someone sitting on it. [3]And the one who sat there had the appearance of jasper and carnelian. A rainbow, resembling an emerald, encircled the throne. [4]Surrounding the throne were twenty-four other thrones, and seated on them were twenty-four elders. They were dressed in white and had crowns of gold on their heads. [5]From the throne came flashes of lightning, rumblings and peals of thunder. Before the throne, seven lamps

What is heaven like? (4:1)

When Revelation speaks of heaven, it does not give us a picture of what heaven will *look like* to the eye. Rather, it conveys images about the nature of God and his relation to his creation.

We can learn bits and pieces about what heaven might be like throughout the Bible, however. For instance, we are told that Christ will gather the elect there (Mark 13:27). We know that he will receive honor (Phil. 2:10), and that his glory will be revealed (John 17:24). We are told that he poured out the Holy Spirit from heaven (Acts 2:33). The Bible also says we will be reunited with loved ones in heaven, an especially appropriate message for the churches in Revelation during this time of martyrdom (2 Samuel 12:23; Luke 20:37–38; 23:43).

Perhaps the primary things we learn about heaven in Revelation are: (1) Heaven is the full and complete expression of God's kingdom. It is a place where God is on his throne (4:1–3). (2) Heaven offers rewards for those who *overcome* in this life (2:7; 3:21). (3) Heaven is God's judgment seat, the place where he pronounces judgment against sinners (8:1—9:21; 16:11). (4) Heaven is full of God's presence and overwhelming glory (4:1–11; 21:1–10). (5) Heaven, because of God's power and holiness, is a place of worship and praise (4:1–11; 19:1–7).

were blazing. These are the seven spirits*a* of God. **6**Also before the throne there was what looked like a sea of glass, clear as crystal.

In the center, around the throne, were four living creatures, and they were covered with eyes, in front and in back. **7**The first living creature was like a lion, the second was like an ox, the third had a face like a man, the fourth was like a flying eagle. **8**Each of the four living creatures had six wings and was covered with eyes all around, even under his wings. Day and night they never stop saying:

> "Holy, holy, holy
> is the Lord God Almighty,
> who was, and is, and is to come."

9Whenever the living creatures give glory*D*, honor and thanks to him who sits on the throne and who lives for ever and ever, **10**the twenty-four elders fall down before him who sits on the throne, and worship him who lives for ever and ever. They lay their crowns before the throne and say:

> **11**"You are worthy, our Lord and God,
> to receive glory and honor and power,
> for you created all things,
> and by your will they were created
> and have their being."

The Scroll and the Lamb

5 Then I saw in the right hand of him who sat on the throne a scroll with writing on both sides and sealed with seven seals. **2**And I saw a mighty angel proclaiming in a loud voice, "Who is worthy to break the seals and open the scroll?" **3**But no one in heaven or on earth or under the earth could open the scroll or even look inside it. **4**I wept and wept because no one was found who was worthy to open the scroll or look inside. **5**Then one of the elders said to me, "Do not weep! See, the Lion of the tribe of Judah, the Root of David, has triumphed. He is able to open the scroll and its seven seals."

6Then I saw a Lamb, looking as if it had been slain,

a5 Or the sevenfold Spirit

Who are the *twenty-four elders?* (4:4)

They seem to be angelic beings whose function is to worship and serve God. One tradition identifies them as representing both Israel (the 12 tribes) and the church (the 12 apostles). Compare, for instance, the description of the new Jerusalem later (21:12–14). They may also call to mind the 24 orders of Levites—the priestly tribe whose job was to lead in worship and serving God.

Seven spirits (4:5)

This may be a reference to the Holy Spirit (see NIV text note). The number *seven* is often used to portray fullness or perfection.

Who are the *four living creatures?* (4:6–8)

They are a second group of angels within the circle of 24 elders (vv. 4–6), modified versions of the creatures seen in the visions of Ezek. 1 and Isaiah 6). They have typically been thought to represent all of creation, with each animal being the strongest of its category. This could symbolize the worship of the Creator by the creation.

Why is it necessary to praise God so much? (4:9–10)

Praise of God, on earth and in heaven, is a spontaneous response to a recognition of the nature and character of God. Just as when we witness a great performance by a musician, athlete or artist, we *want* to express our admiration through shouts and applause, so too, when any created being is truly confronted with the majesty of God, the natural and spontaneous response is praise.

What is this scroll? (5:1)

Many theories have been offered for the particular kind of document being described here. Some say it is a contract, others a certificate of debt, others a deed and still others a will. But what seems clear is that the scroll contains the record of God's judgments, long since made but now to be enacted. Only Christ is worthy to open and enact those judgments.

Why is the *Lion* also a *Lamb?* (5:5–6)

The figurative language here combines numerous images from both the Old and New Testa-

---

What are these objects all about? (chs. 5–10)

The contexts suggest that the scrolls (5:1; 10:2) are concerned with future events. The seals, trumpets and thunders may be seen as part of the scrolls' contents. Each of the sevenfold series seems to lead us to the end of the world.

How do they fit together? John is not a chronologist so, for example, the trumpets do not necessarily follow the seals in strict chronological order. It may help to see John as an artist or musician. If his "musical theme" is the end of the world, then each series (seals, trumpets, thunders) is a "variation" that adds to the composition. Each one heightens and intensifies the final, climactic confrontation between God and the forces of evil.

It is the theological message, not a strict chronology, that really counts. The seals remind us that evil exists only by permission from God. The trumpets call people to repentance. The thunders emphasize God's judgment (8:5).

ments to indicate Christ's ultimate triumph. The *Lion of the tribe of Judah* is taken from Gen. 49:9; the *Root of David* alludes to references in Isaiah 11:10 and the *Lamb* is a frequent symbol as in John 1:29. All are Biblical symbols for the expected Messiah, each capturing a different aspect of his nature and his reign. Though slain, he has gained victory and the seven horns symbolize his strength. The seven eyes symbolize that he sees and knows all (Zech. 4:10).

Seven spirits (5:6)

See *Seven spirits* (4:5).

Why does God need or want so much praise? (5:11–14)

See *Why is it necessary to praise God so much?* (4:9–10).

SCRIPTURE LINK (6:1–17)

See the parallels between this passage and Matt. 24. Both passages mention wars, invasions, famines, earthquakes and persecutions of Christians as *signs* that *the end of the age* is approaching (Matt. 24:3). Both passages assure Christians that Christ is in control of these frightening calamities.

What do the four horsemen symbolize? (6:2,4–5,8; also see Zech. 6:1–8)

The horsemen are thought to symbolize four powerful forces that harm people: brute militarism; war and violence; famine and food shortages; death and hell.

Who is the *conqueror*? (6:2)

Probably a picture of the powerful, destructive force of military conquest. The three riders the *conqueror* is grouped with—violence, famine and death—are evil and brutal in their impact. So it is not likely this conquering rider on a white horse is the same as the one in 19:11–21, which is clearly a reference to Christ.

Why announce the price of food? (6:6)

To show how terrible the famine described here would be. Wheat and barley, staples in the ancient world, would sell at extravagant prices. People would spend an entire day's wages for just enough food to keep them alive.

standing in the center of the throne, encircled by the four living creatures and the elders. He had seven horns and seven eyes, which are the seven spirits[a] of God sent out into all the earth. [7]He came and took the scroll from the right hand of him who sat on the throne. [8]And when he had taken it, the four living creatures and the twenty-four elders fell down before the Lamb. Each one had a harp and they were holding golden bowls full of incense[D], which are the prayers of the saints[D]. [9]And they sang a new song:

> "You are worthy to take the scroll
>   and to open its seals,
> because you were slain,
>   and with your blood you purchased men for
>   God
> from every tribe and language and people
>   and nation.
> [10]You have made them to be a kingdom and
>   priests[D] to serve our God,
>   and they will reign on the earth."

[11]Then I looked and heard the voice of many angels, numbering thousands upon thousands, and ten thousand times ten thousand. They encircled the throne and the living creatures and the elders. [12]In a loud voice they sang:

> "Worthy is the Lamb, who was slain,
> to receive power and wealth and wisdom and
>   strength
> and honor and glory[D] and praise!"

[13]Then I heard every creature in heaven and on earth and under the earth and on the sea, and all that is in them, singing:

> "To him who sits on the throne and to the
>   Lamb
> be praise and honor and glory and power,
>   for ever and ever!"

[14]The four living creatures said, "Amen," and the elders fell down and worshiped.

The Seals

6 I watched as the Lamb opened the first of the seven seals. Then I heard one of the four living creatures say in a voice like thunder, "Come!" [2]I looked, and there before me was a white horse! Its rider held a bow, and he was given a crown, and he rode out as a conqueror bent on conquest.

[3]When the Lamb opened the second seal, I heard the second living creature say, "Come!" [4]Then another horse came out, a fiery red one. Its rider was given power to take peace[D] from the earth and to make men slay each other. To him was given a large sword.

[5]When the Lamb opened the third seal, I heard the third living creature say, "Come!" I looked, and there before me was a black horse! Its rider was holding a pair of scales in his hand. [6]Then I heard what sounded like a voice among the four living creatures, saying, "A quart[b] of wheat for a day's wages,[c] and three quarts of barley for a day's wages,[c] and do not damage the oil and the wine!"

[7]When the Lamb opened the fourth seal, I heard the

[a]6 Or *the sevenfold Spirit*   [b]6 Greek *a choinix* (probably about a liter)   [c]6 Greek *a denarius*

voice of the fourth living creature say, "Come!" **8**I looked, and there before me was a pale horse! Its rider was named Death[D], and Hades[D] was following close behind him. They were given power over a fourth of the earth to kill by sword, famine and plague, and by the wild beasts of the earth.

9When he opened the fifth seal, I saw under the altar the souls[D] of those who had been slain because of the word of God and the testimony they had maintained. **10**They called out in a loud voice, "How long, Sovereign Lord, holy and true, until you judge the inhabitants of the earth and avenge[D] our blood?" **11**Then each of them was given a white robe, and they were told to wait a little longer, until the number of their fellow servants and brothers who were to be killed as they had been was completed.

12I watched as he opened the sixth seal. There was a great earthquake. The sun turned black like sackcloth[D] made of goat hair, the whole moon turned blood red, **13**and the stars in the sky fell to earth, as late figs drop from a fig tree when shaken by a strong wind. **14**The sky receded like a scroll, rolling up, and every mountain and island was removed from its place.

15Then the kings of the earth, the princes, the generals, the rich, the mighty, and every slave and every free man hid in caves and among the rocks of the mountains. **16**They called to the mountains and the rocks, "Fall on us and hide us from the face of him who sits on the throne and from the wrath of the Lamb! **17**For the great day of their wrath has come, and who can stand?"

144,000 Sealed

7 After this I saw four angels standing at the four corners of the earth, holding back the four winds of the earth to prevent any wind from blowing on the land or on the sea or on any tree. **2**Then I saw another angel coming up from the east, having the seal of the living God. He called out in a loud voice to the four angels who had been given power to harm the land and the sea: **3**"Do not harm the land or the sea or the trees until we put a seal on the foreheads of the servants of our God." **4**Then I heard the number of those who were sealed: 144,000 from all the tribes of Israel.

5From the tribe of Judah 12,000 were sealed,
  from the tribe of Reuben 12,000,
  from the tribe of Gad 12,000,
6from the tribe of Asher 12,000,
  from the tribe of Naphtali 12,000,

What *altar* has souls beneath it? (6:9)

In the book of Revelation the *altar* usually represents being near God (8:3,5). The imagery is reminiscent of the altar of sacrifice (Exodus 29:12), which stood in the temple's outer court. That altar had a trough under it to catch the blood of the sacrificed animals. However, the victims here whose souls (that is, lives) are poured out under the altar are Christians who were killed because of their witness.

Why would God set a certain number who had to die for their faith? (6:11)

God allows certain things to occur, including the deaths of his servants, which further his ultimate purposes. One early Christian wrote, "The blood of the martyrs is the seed of the Church," meaning that non-Christians see the faith and courage of martyrs and then decide to convert, causing the church to grow. The fact that there is a *number . . . to be killed* emphasizes that ultimately God is in control.

Is this shaking of earth and heaven literal or symbolic? (6:12–17)

People disagree. Some see a literal reading (see 2 Peter 3:10) and note that other poetic descriptions in this chapter describe literal calamities such as war and famine. Other people, however, say this symbolizes God's final judgment using images familiar in Old Testament prophecies (Isaiah 2:10; 34:4; Joel 2:31).

Day of their wrath (6:17)

The time of judgment at Christ's final coming (Zeph. 1:14–15; Nahum 1:6). It will bring wrath on the wicked and reward to the faithful. All of ch. 7 focuses on those who are spared God's wrath.

Four winds of the earth (7:1)

In the Old Testament, wind often denotes judgment from God (Jer. 4:11–12). To have wind blowing from all four *corners* (like our four compass points) of the earth, shows that God's judgment will be complete and come to the entire earth.

When will these terrifying events happen? (6:1–17)

Prior to and on *the great day of their wrath* (that is, the wrath of God and Christ; v. 17). The six *seals* opened in this chapter, though, represent ever-present atrocities: military invasions, wars, famines, deaths, martyrdoms of Christians, earthquakes. Newspaper headlines and news telecasts bombard us with images of these threats which have always existed. It seems likely, though, that these horrors will increase greatly as the end nears.

This passage reminds us, however, that evil powers work only by divine permission. The riders *were given* certain powers by God (vv. 2,4,8).

What is the seal of God? (7:2)

In Ezek. 9:3–4, a mark (perhaps an "x" or "+")
is placed on the foreheads of the faithful to
protect them from judgment. Similarly, these
servants of our God (v. 3) are promised protection from God's wrath (6:12–17), though not
necessarily from all physical danger. Interestingly, later in Revelation a similar marking indicates the followers of the beast (13:16–18),
who will be singled out to receive *God's fury*
(14:9–10).

Why is no one sealed except Jews? (7:4)

In Revelation, vocabulary originally applied to
the Jews is often used for all Christians. For
example, Christians are called *a kingdom and
priests* (1:6), a phrase previously applied only
to the Jews (Exodus 19:5–6). So the 144,000
people from the various *tribes of Israel*
(vv. 4–8) may symbolize all Christians whether
Jews or Gentiles.

Why did an elder ask John a question he couldn't answer? (7:13–14)

As a rhetorical device. It ensures no one mis-
understands the identity of those clothed in
white: the faithful who have been saved by *the
blood of the Lamb.* This vision answers the
question posed by John in 6:17: only the faithful will stand before God and the Lamb (7:9)
and be rewarded (7:15–17).

from the tribe of Manasseh 12,000,
[7]from the tribe of Simeon 12,000,
from the tribe of Levi 12,000,
from the tribe of Issachar 12,000,
[8]from the tribe of Zebulun 12,000,
from the tribe of Joseph 12,000,
from the tribe of Benjamin 12,000.

The Great Multitude in White Robes

[9]After this I looked and there before me was a great
multitude that no one could count, from every nation,
tribe, people and language, standing before the throne
and in front of the Lamb. They were wearing white robes
and were holding palm branches in their hands. [10]And
they cried out in a loud voice:

> "Salvation[D] belongs to our God,
>   who sits on the throne,
>   and to the Lamb."

[11]All the angels were standing around the throne and
around the elders and the four living creatures. They fell
down on their faces before the throne and worshiped
God, [12]saying:

> "Amen!
> Praise and glory[D]
>   and wisdom and thanks and honor
>   and power and strength
> be to our God for ever and ever.
> Amen!"

[13]Then one of the elders asked me, "These in white
robes—who are they, and where did they come from?"
[14]I answered, "Sir, you know."
    And he said, "These are they who have come out of the
great tribulation; they have washed their robes and made
them white in the blood of the Lamb. [15]Therefore,

> "they are before the throne of God
>   and serve him day and night in his temple;

What is the *great tribulation*? (7:14)

Some think this may refer to the suffering generally endured by Christians throughout history—already begun when John wrote his revelation. Others believe it will
be a unique and especially intense period of trouble that will come at the end of time.
Among those who believe the great tribulation will occur at the end of time, there are
three main views that relate the tribulation to the Rapture, when the church will be taken
to meet the Lord in the air (1 Thes. 4:17). They are: (1) The tribulation will occur before
the Rapture. This view is called *post-tribulationalism.* (2) The Rapture will occur before the
tribulation, a view called *pre-tribulationalism.* (3) The Rapture will occur during the tribulation. This view is called *mid-tribulationalism.*
    Jesus taught his disciples that they should expect difficulties and troubles in this
world (John 16:33). In fact, many in the early church suffered severely for their faith (Acts
5:40–41; Heb. 10:32–33). Revelation hints that believers could expect tribulation (2:10;
12:17), and the apostle Paul said that Christians who remain faithful will be persecuted
(2 Tim. 3:12).
    Regardless of when the *great tribulation* takes place—today or in the future—
countless people (v. 9) will come out of it victorious.

and he who sits on the throne will spread his
tent over them.
¹⁶Never again will they hunger;
    never again will they thirst.
The sun will not beat upon them,
    nor any scorching heat.
¹⁷For the Lamb at the center of the throne will
    be their shepherd;
he will lead them to springs of living water.
And God will wipe away every tear from their
    eyes."

The Seventh Seal and the Golden Censer

8 When he opened the seventh seal, there was silence
in heaven for about half an hour.

²And I saw the seven angels who stand before God, and
to them were given seven trumpets.

³Another angel, who had a golden censer^D, came and
stood at the altar. He was given much incense^D to offer,
with the prayers of all the saints^D, on the golden altar before the throne. ⁴The smoke of the incense, together
with the prayers of the saints, went up before God from
the angel's hand. ⁵Then the angel took the censer, filled
it with fire from the altar, and hurled it on the earth; and
there came peals of thunder, rumblings, flashes of lightning and an earthquake.

The Trumpets

⁶Then the seven angels who had the seven trumpets
prepared to sound them.

⁷The first angel sounded his trumpet, and there came
hail and fire mixed with blood, and it was hurled down
upon the earth. A third of the earth was burned up, a third
of the trees were burned up, and all the green grass was
burned up.

⁸The second angel sounded his trumpet, and something
like a huge mountain, all ablaze, was thrown into the sea.
A third of the sea turned into blood, ⁹a third of the living
creatures in the sea died, and a third of the ships were
destroyed.

¹⁰The third angel sounded his trumpet, and a great star,
blazing like a torch, fell from the sky on a third of the rivers and on the springs of water— ¹¹the name of the star
is Wormwood.^a A third of the waters turned bitter, and
many people died from the waters that had become bitter.

¹²The fourth angel sounded his trumpet, and a third of
the sun was struck, a third of the moon, and a third of the
stars, so that a third of them turned dark. A third of the
day was without light, and also a third of the night.

¹³As I watched, I heard an eagle that was flying in midair call out in a loud voice: "Woe! Woe! Woe to the inhabitants of the earth, because of the trumpet blasts about to
be sounded by the other three angels!"

9 The fifth angel sounded his trumpet, and I saw a star
that had fallen from the sky to the earth. The star was
given the key to the shaft of the Abyss^D. ²When he
opened the Abyss, smoke rose from it like the smoke
from a gigantic furnace. The sun and sky were darkened
by the smoke from the Abyss. ³And out of the smoke
locusts^D came down upon the earth and were given power like that of scorpions of the earth. ⁴They were told not

^a11 That is, Bitterness

How is time measured in heaven? (8:1)

Saying the *silence in heaven* lasted *about half
an hour* is a poetic way of saying this was a
long silence. In the Bible, silence often comes
before or with God's judgments (Hab. 2:20;
Zech. 2:13). Thus, this long, dramatic pause
signals that the judgment to come is going to
be just as long and dramatic. The silence prepares people to hear the seven trumpets of
judgment (8:6).

Censer (8:3)

A container for burning incense. Both this passage (v. 4) and the Psalms (141:2) link prayer
with burning incense, since both ascend heavenward. This image of prayer as incense appears before both the seals (5:8) and the trumpets (8:3–6), emphasizing the power of prayer
to bring God's intervention.

Why announce judgment with a trum-pet fanfare? (8:7)

In Bible times and well beyond, trumpets were
used to warn people and gather them before a
battle or national emergency (Num. 10:2–3).
Thus, trumpets came to symbolize warning,
judgment and a call to repentance (Joshua 6:5;
Joel 2:1). Paul links a trumpet and Christ's return (1 Thes. 4:16). The trumpets sounded in
8:6—9:16 warn of coming judgment and call
people to repentance (9:20–21).

Could this be a meteor shower? (8:7–11)

Probably not. The falling *hail, fire, mountain*
and *star* depicted here picture God's judgment
on the physical world: the earth (v. 7), the sea
(vv. 8–9), the fresh water (vv. 10–11) and the
stars and planets (v. 12). In other words, there
will be massive (though limited) destruction of
creation, a severe warning to sinful people.

How could *a third* of the sun's light be shut off? (8:12)

The frequent use of *a third* (vv. 7–12) shows
that the destruction of Creation will be enormous, yet also limited by God. Perhaps this
could mean that some sort of atmospheric
condition or global pollution will reduce visibili-
ty by one-third.

Woe! Woe! Woe . . . ! (8:13)

In this transitional verse the eagle, symbolizing
wrath (Deut. 28:49), announces that with the
final three trumpets things are going to get
worse. The first four trumpets affected the
physical world, but these last three will hurt
people directly. These woes will befall *the inhabitants of the earth*, a phrase used in Revelation (see 6:10) to describe people who are not
followers of God and who will fall under judgment.

What kind of star is this? (9:1–2)

Perhaps an angel who carries out God's will, or
perhaps Satan or one of his agents. Either
way, it is no doubt God who gives the key
(v. 1); he is permitting the terrifying events to
occur.

The Abyss (9:2)

A bottomless pit; in the Bible the Abyss means
the dwelling place of the dead (Romans 10:7)
or demons (Luke 8:31).

What kind of locusts are these? (9:3)

They represent a powerful force that will torture people who do not follow God. In the ancient world locusts were abhorred. They wreaked utter devastation on crops and were unstoppable (Exodus 10:14–15; Joel 1:4). These locust-like scorpions torture people *for five months* (v. 5)—the life cycle of a locust, a symbol for a short period of time.

Who is *Abaddon*? (9:11)

Abaddon means Destroyer, so perhaps *destruction* is being personified. Or, if this *angel of the Abyss* is the same as the *star* (9:1), *Abaddon* may refer to Satan.

Four angels . . . bound at the great river Euphrates (9:14)

Revelation frequently presents angels as carrying out God's will (7:1–3). Beyond the Euphrates River lay Israel's enemies, Babylonia and Assyria (see *Map 7* at the back of this Bible). This picture stands for God allowing a huge, destructive "army" to set out.

What are these horses and riders? (9:17–19)

The words describing them—*plagues of fire, smoke and sulfur . . . snakes*—emphasize how horribly evil these *mounted troops* (v. 16) are. They may stand for revolting, ferocious and powerful demonic forces. They may stand for a literal army. Or perhaps they symbolize brutal military power which has caused untold bloodshed over the centuries.

Why would people whose lives were spared not repent? (9:20–21)

Ten devastating plagues did not soften Pharaoh's heart either (Exodus 11:10). Great suffering tends to intensify whatever is in a person's character. If someone is already God-fearing and tender, suffering may make him or her more so. But if a person mocks God and is rebellious, suffering may increase those qualities.

What's so bad about magic? (9:21)

In the ancient world, magic often involved drugs and the casting of spells on people (Isaiah 47:12–15). This kind of magic touches evil spiritual forces opposed to God. Such magic is far different from the sleight-of-hand entertainment with which we are most familiar.

Why keep parts of the vision secret? (10:4)

We do not know. But such hidden visions (Daniel 8:26) remind us that we do not know everything about the future—only God does. *It is the glory of God to conceal a matter* (Prov. 25:2), because that forces us to acknowledge that God alone is all-knowing. However, if the content were vital to our understanding of the message, God would have permitted John to record what was revealed.

to harm the grass of the earth or any plant or tree, but only those people who did not have the seal of God on their foreheads. **5**They were not given power to kill them, but only to torture them for five months. And the agony they suffered was like that of the sting of a scorpion when it strikes a man. **6**During those days men will seek death[D], but will not find it; they will long to die, but death will elude them.

7The locusts[D] looked like horses prepared for battle. On their heads they wore something like crowns of gold, and their faces resembled human faces. **8**Their hair was like women's hair, and their teeth were like lions' teeth. **9**They had breastplates like breastplates of iron, and the sound of their wings was like the thundering of many horses and chariots rushing into battle. **10**They had tails and stings like scorpions, and in their tails they had power to torment people for five months. **11**They had as king over them the angel of the Abyss[D], whose name in Hebrew[D] is Abaddon, and in Greek, Apollyon.[a]

12The first woe is past; two other woes are yet to come.

13The sixth angel sounded his trumpet, and I heard a voice coming from the horns[b] of the golden altar that is before God. **14**It said to the sixth angel who had the trumpet, "Release the four angels who are bound at the great river Euphrates." **15**And the four angels who had been kept ready for this very hour and day and month and year were released to kill a third of mankind. **16**The number of the mounted troops was two hundred million. I heard their number.

17The horses and riders I saw in my vision[D] looked like this: Their breastplates were fiery red, dark blue, and yellow as sulfur. The heads of the horses resembled the heads of lions, and out of their mouths came fire, smoke and sulfur. **18**A third of mankind was killed by the three plagues of fire, smoke and sulfur that came out of their mouths. **19**The power of the horses was in their mouths and in their tails; for their tails were like snakes, having heads with which they inflict injury.

20The rest of mankind that were not killed by these plagues still did not repent[D] of the work of their hands; they did not stop worshiping demons, and idols[D] of gold, silver, bronze, stone and wood—idols that cannot see or hear or walk. **21**Nor did they repent of their murders, their magic arts, their sexual immorality or their thefts.

The Angel and the Little Scroll

10 Then I saw another mighty angel coming down from heaven. He was robed in a cloud, with a rainbow above his head; his face was like the sun, and his legs were like fiery pillars. **2**He was holding a little scroll, which lay open in his hand. He planted his right foot on the sea and his left foot on the land, **3**and he gave a loud shout like the roar of a lion. When he shouted, the voices of the seven thunders spoke. **4**And when the seven thunders spoke, I was about to write; but I heard a voice from heaven say, "Seal up what the seven thunders have said and do not write it down."

5Then the angel I had seen standing on the sea and on the land raised his right hand to heaven. **6**And he swore by him who lives for ever and ever, who created the heavens and all that is in them, the earth and all that is in it,

*a*11 *Abaddon* and *Apollyon* mean *Destroyer*.   *b*13 That is, projections

and the sea and all that is in it, and said, "There will be no more delay! **7**But in the days when the seventh angel is about to sound his trumpet, the mystery^D of God will be accomplished, just as he announced to his servants the prophets^D."

8Then the voice that I had heard from heaven spoke to me once more: "Go, take the scroll that lies open in the hand of the angel who is standing on the sea and on the land."

9So I went to the angel and asked him to give me the little scroll. He said to me, "Take it and eat it. It will turn your stomach sour, but in your mouth it will be as sweet as honey." **10**I took the little scroll from the angel's hand and ate it. It tasted as sweet as honey in my mouth, but when I had eaten it, my stomach turned sour. **11**Then I was told, "You must prophesy again about many peoples, nations, languages and kings."

The Two Witnesses

11 I was given a reed like a measuring rod and was told, "Go and measure the temple of God and the altar, and count the worshipers there. **2**But exclude the outer court; do not measure it, because it has been given to the Gentiles^D. They will trample on the holy city for 42 months. **3**And I will give power to my two witnesses, and they will prophesy for 1,260 days, clothed in sackcloth^D." **4**These are the two olive trees and the two lampstands that stand before the Lord of the earth. **5**If anyone tries to harm them, fire comes from their mouths and devours their enemies. This is how anyone who wants to harm them must die. **6**These men have power to shut up the sky so that it will not rain during the time they are prophesying; and they have power to turn the waters into blood and to strike the earth with every kind of plague as often as they want.

7Now when they have finished their testimony, the beast that comes up from the Abyss^D will attack them, and overpower and kill them. **8**Their bodies will lie in the street of the great city, which is figuratively called Sodom and Egypt, where also their Lord was crucified. **9**For three and a half days men from every people, tribe, language and nation will gaze on their bodies and refuse them burial. **10**The inhabitants of the earth will gloat over them and will celebrate by sending each other gifts, because these two prophets had tormented those who live on the earth.

11But after the three and a half days a breath of life from God entered them, and they stood on their feet, and terror struck those who saw them. **12**Then they heard a loud voice from heaven saying to them, "Come up here." And they went up to heaven in a cloud, while their enemies looked on.

13At that very hour there was a severe earthquake and a tenth of the city collapsed. Seven thousand people were killed in the earthquake, and the survivors were terrified and gave glory^D to the God of heaven.

14The second woe has passed; the third woe is coming soon.

The Seventh Trumpet

15The seventh angel sounded his trumpet, and there were loud voices in heaven, which said:

Mystery of God (10:7)
In Paul's writings, *mystery* refers to God's strategy to redeem people through Christ (Eph. 3:9). Here, the context suggests that the *mystery* means God's purpose in history, namely that *the kingdom of the world* will become *the kingdom of our Lord and of his Christ* (11:15).

Why eat a scroll? (10:9)
The prophet Ezekiel (2:8—3:3) swallowed a scroll and pronounced woe upon Israel. Eating a scroll symbolizes accepting the scroll's message, taking it in. That message is sweet, because it comes from God, and bitter because it proclaims harsh judgments.

What temple is being measured? (11:1)
Not the temple in Jerusalem, which had been destroyed years before John received this revelation. Instead, the *temple* probably symbolizes the church (1 Cor. 3:16). Measuring that temple possibly means, in light of Zech. 2:1–5, that the church is set apart from all that is unholy. God will protect it and *be its glory within* (Zech. 2:5).

42 months . . . 1,260 days (11:2–3)
These numbers and the phrase *time, times and half a time* (12:14), all refer to 3 ½ years. They stem from prophecies in Daniel 7:25 and 9:27, prophecies initially fulfilled when Antiochus IV (Epiphanes), king of Syria, subdued Jerusalem for 3 ½ years beginning in 168 B.C. During this period the temple was desecrated and the Jewish people were ordered to abandon their faith. Thus, John uses these numbers to symbolize a coming time of intense distress for the church.

Two witnesses (11:3)
The *two witnesses* bring to mind Moses and Elijah, who were able to *turn the waters into blood* (v. 6; see Exodus 7:17), call fire that *devours their enemies* (v. 5; see 2 Kings 1:10) and *shut up the sky so that it will not rain* (v. 6; see 1 Kings 17:1). Moses and Elijah may represent the Law and prophecy, both of which give *testimony* to Christ (Matt. 17:2–3). The Hebrew people held that at least two witnesses were needed to establish the truth of legal testimony (Deut. 19:15; John 8:17).

Why is the beast permitted to kill God's servants? (11:7)
God protected them (v. 5), but now, in his sovereign plan, permits them to die, perhaps to reveal starkly the people's wickedness who *gloat over them* (v. 10). Various attempts to silence God's witnesses have occurred over the years —imprisonment, banishment, ridicule and even capital punishment. In spite of such terrible opposition by God's adversaries, Christians are encouraged to remain faithful because they will have the ultimate victory (vv. 11–12).

The great city (11:8)
Symbol for corrupt and evil worldly power. A collage of images describes this godless culture as being like wicked Sodom (Gen. 19:1–13), oppressive Egypt (Exodus 1–15) and hard-hearted Jerusalem, the city that rejected and crucified Christ (Matt. 23:37–39).

How will these prophets torment people? (11:10)
By prophesying against people's wicked lifestyles and by performing various painful proofs (vv. 5–6) that they are telling the truth.

Why are they visibly taken into heaven? (11:12)

The two witnesses, like Elijah (2 Kings 2:11), receive vindication. Some say this depicts the witnessing church which, though opposed, eventually triumphs. The fate of the two witnesses parallels Christ's fate: witness, opposition, death, resurrection, ascension.

Do these survivors repent? (11:13)

This is the first time in Revelation that evil people acknowledge God (9:20–21). However, saying they *gave glory to the God of heaven* may not mean they repented; it may mean only that in extreme terror they acknowledged a powerful God.

Ark of his covenant (11:19)

In Solomon's temple the ark, a symbol of God's presence, had been closed off from view and kept in the Most Holy Place (2 Chron. 5:7). Later, the temple was pillaged and burned by the Babylonians (2 Kings 25:8–27). To have the ark reappear symbolizes the complete establishment of God's kingdom (v. 15). The relationship between God and God's servants will be fully realized (21:3).

Who is the *woman clothed with the sun*? (12:1)

Since the woman gives birth to a son *who will rule all the nations with an iron scepter* (12:5; Psalm 2:9), she has been seen as Mary, mother of Jesus. Since the woman has other *offspring—those who obey God's commandments and hold to the testimony of Jesus* (12:17), she has been seen as the church. It seems better to view the woman as "all the people of God."

Who or what is the *red dragon*? (12:3)

The devil, or Satan (v. 9). He is portrayed as violent (red), clever (seven heads), strong (horns) and controlling (crowns).

When was there war in heaven? (12:7)

When Christ overcame Satan through his death, resurrection and ascension. Now Satan has no right to accuse Christians (v. 10), because their sins have been paid for. And he cannot conquer people who no longer fear death (v. 11; Heb. 2:14–15). Thus, vv. 7–9 contain the heavenly counterpart to the action described in vv. 1–6.

SCRIPTURE LINK (12:9) *The great dragon was hurled down*

Some see parallels in Old Testament prophecies in Isaiah 14:12–15 and Ezek. 28:11–19.

The accuser (12:10)

Satan. In Hebrew, *Satan* means *accuser* or *adversary*.

How can believers use the *blood of the Lamb* against Satan? (12:11)

Through Christ's sacrificial death Christians are forgiven by God, so Satan can no longer accuse them of guilt. The blood of Christ is the only hope of escaping the deadly power and guilt of sin.

> "The kingdom of the world has become the
>   kingdom of our Lord and of his Christ,
>   and he will reign for ever and ever."

16And the twenty-four elders, who were seated on their thrones before God, fell on their faces and worshiped God, **17**saying:

> "We give thanks to you, Lord God Almighty,
>   the One who is and who was,
>   because you have taken your great power
>   and have begun to reign.
> **18**The nations were angry;
>   and your wrath has come.
>   The time has come for judging the dead,
>   and for rewarding your servants the
>   prophetsᴰ
>   and your saintsᴰ and those who reverenceᴰ
>   your name,
>   both small and great—
>   and for destroying those who destroy the
>   earth."

19Then God's temple in heaven was opened, and within his temple was seen the ark of his covenantᴰ. And there came flashes of lightning, rumblings, peals of thunder, an earthquake and a great hailstorm.

The Woman and the Dragon

12 A great and wondrous sign appeared in heaven: a woman clothed with the sun, with the moon under her feet and a crown of twelve stars on her head. **2**She was pregnant and cried out in pain as she was about to give birth. **3**Then another sign appeared in heaven: an enormous red dragon with seven heads and ten horns and seven crowns on his heads. **4**His tail swept a third of the stars out of the sky and flung them to the earth. The dragon stood in front of the woman who was about to give birth, so that he might devour her child the moment it was born. **5**She gave birth to a son, a male child, who will rule all the nations with an iron scepterᴰ. And her child was snatched up to God and to his throne. **6**The woman fled into the desert to a place prepared for her by God, where she might be taken care of for 1,260 days.

7And there was war in heaven. Michael and his angels fought against the dragon, and the dragon and his angels fought back. **8**But he was not strong enough, and they lost their place in heaven. **9**The great dragon was hurled down—that ancient serpent called the devil, or Satan, who leads the whole world astray. He was hurled to the earth, and his angels with him.

10Then I heard a loud voice in heaven say:

> "Now have come the salvationᴰ and the power
>   and the kingdom of our God,
>   and the authority of his Christ.
> For the accuser of our brothers,
>   who accuses them before our God day and
>   night,
>   has been hurled down.
> **11**They overcame him
>   by the blood of the Lamb
>   and by the word of their testimony;
>   they did not love their lives so much
>   as to shrink from deathᴰ.
> **12**Therefore rejoice, you heavens

and you who dwell in them!
But woe to the earth and the sea,
  because the devil has gone down to you!
He is filled with fury,
  because he knows that his time is short."

¹³When the dragon saw that he had been hurled to the earth, he pursued the woman who had given birth to the male child. ¹⁴The woman was given the two wings of a great eagle, so that she might fly to the place prepared for her in the desert, where she would be taken care of for a time, times and half a time, out of the serpent's reach. ¹⁵Then from his mouth the serpent spewed water like a river, to overtake the woman and sweep her away with the torrent. ¹⁶But the earth helped the woman by opening its mouth and swallowing the river that the dragon had spewed out of his mouth. ¹⁷Then the dragon was enraged at the woman and went off to make war against the rest of her offspring—those who obey God's commandments and hold to the testimony of Jesus. ¹And the drag-

13 on^a stood on the shore of the sea.

The Beast out of the Sea

And I saw a beast coming out of the sea. He had ten horns and seven heads, with ten crowns on his horns, and on each head a blasphemous name. ²The beast I saw resembled a leopard, but had feet like those of a bear and a mouth like that of a lion. The dragon gave the beast his power and his throne and great authority. ³One of the heads of the beast seemed to have had a fatal wound, but the fatal wound had been healed. The whole world was astonished and followed the beast. ⁴Men worshiped the dragon because he had given authority to the beast, and they also worshiped the beast and asked, "Who is like the beast? Who can make war against him?"

⁵The beast was given a mouth to utter proud words and blasphemies^D and to exercise his authority for forty-two months. ⁶He opened his mouth to blaspheme^D God, and to slander his name and his dwelling place and those who live in heaven. ⁷He was given power to make war against the saints^D and to conquer them. And he was given authority over every tribe, people, language and nation. ⁸All inhabitants of the earth will worship the beast—all whose names have not been written in the book of life belonging to the Lamb that was slain from the creation of the world.^b

⁹He who has an ear, let him hear.

¹⁰If anyone is to go into captivity,
  into captivity he will go.
If anyone is to be killed^c with the sword,
  with the sword he will be killed.

This calls for patient endurance and faithfulness on the part of the saints.

The Beast out of the Earth

¹¹Then I saw another beast, coming out of the earth. He had two horns like a lamb, but he spoke like a dragon. ¹²He exercised all the authority of the first beast on his behalf, and made the earth and its inhabitants worship

---

Time, times and half a time (12:14)

See *42 months . . . 1,260 days* (11:2–3).

Who or what is the beast from the sea? (13:1–2)

The beast from the sea (Job 41; Daniel 7:2–7) is an ally or agent of Satan who wars against the saints. Probably John's readers would have seen the beast as the oppressive Roman government, which was becoming increasingly hostile toward Christians. Today the beast could symbolize any world power that opposes God's servants.

Why does the beast have a fatal wound? (13:3)

Possibly to show that Satan tries to steal the authority of Christ, who rules because of his death and resurrection. The image also suggests that the beast is not easily killed; when one evil empire falls, another appears.

Why does God allow the beast to conquer the saints? (13:7)

At times God permits (note the verb *was given* vv. 5,7) defeat and suffering. It looked like Christ was defeated on the cross, and at times throughout history it has seemed as if God's people have been defeated. But ultimately, Christians will prevail because God in Christ has prevailed for us.

The book of life (13:8)

The book of life was a familiar Jewish image (Exodus 32:32–33; Psalm 69:28; Daniel 12:1; Phil. 4:3). It contains the names of citizens in God's kingdom. Also see *Book of life* (3:5).

How was the Lamb *slain from the creation of the world*? (13:8)

God planned to save the world through Christ's death long before the world was even created (1 Peter 1:18–20). Jesus' death was no afterthought or accident but the direct plan of God.

Who is destined for captivity or execution? (13:10)

Certain *saints*. Christians can expect persecution, and God allows some to be captured or killed. Christians are called to accept what God allows. That requires *patient endurance and faithfulness*.

Who or what is the beast that comes out of the earth? (13:11–12)

If John's readers saw oppressive political power in the first beast (vv. 1–10), probably they saw the second beast as the seductive religious power of the emperor's cult. At that time, Roman law required all people to worship the emperor as a god. Today, the two beasts remind us that both government and religion can become Satan's arenas; he can use them to coerce or deceive.

---

^a1 Some late manuscripts *And I*   ^b8 Or *written from the creation of the world in the book of life belonging to the Lamb that was slain*   ^c10 Some manuscripts *anyone kills*

Why a breathing, speaking image of the first beast? (13:15)

The first beast used violent measures to oppress Christians; the second beast religiously deceives people. Giving breath to the first beast probably shows that false religion (in John's day, emperor worship) will use political power to enforce commitment.

What mark could restrict free enterprise? (13:17)

Just as Christians are sealed, non-Christians are marked. See *What is the seal of God?* (7:2). Both images convey the idea of allegiance. Unless John's readers worshiped the emperor to prove their allegiance, they would be socially and economically cut off. Throughout history, Christians have lost jobs and opportunities because they stood for Christ.

What does 666 mean? (13:18)

Some have seen in this number a reference to Nero, the first emperor to persecute Christians. Others have seen a reference to some evil person of their day, such as Adolf Hitler, but efforts to identify a specific person have been unsatisfactory. If the number seven symbolizes the fullness of God (3:1; 5:6), perhaps six is associated with evil, falling one short of completeness. The threefold six, then, would emphasize how completely evil this beast is. Essentially, John exhorts all Christians to discern evil.

Are only 144,000 redeemed? (14:3)

The 144,000 probably refers symbolically to all of God's servants. See *Why is no one sealed except Jews?* (7:4).

Defiled themselves (14:4)

This may refer to sexual purity. It more likely means that the redeemed have not committed spiritual adultery (v. 8)—they have not given themselves to this world's evil.

Babylon the Great (14:8)

Ancient Babylon (see *Map 7* at the back of this Bible) was noted for its decadence, lust, idolatry and oppression of God's people (Isaiah 47). Here it serves as a symbol for Rome (1 Peter 5:13). John proclaims that the anti-Christian empire of Rome (and any anti-Christian power) is doomed.

Is this hell? (14:10-11)

Burning sulfur is commonly associated with the torments of hell. These verses describe the unending suffering of all those who give allegiance to worldly evil. In vv. 9–12 an angel announces the doom of those who submit to the beast. They are condemned to experience God's fury eternally. The passage thus exhorts Christians to remain faithful no matter what the cost.

Like a son of man (14:14)

The Son of Man is a title for the Messiah, clearly associated with Jesus Christ (Daniel 7:13; Matt. 24:30). The crown and the sickle indicate that Christ is both victor and judge.

---

the first beast, whose fatal wound had been healed. ¹³And he performed great and miraculous signs, even causing fire to come down from heaven to earth in full view of men. ¹⁴Because of the signs he was given power to do on behalf of the first beast, he deceived the inhabitants of the earth. He ordered them to set up an image in honor of the beast who was wounded by the sword and yet lived. ¹⁵He was given power to give breath to the image of the first beast, so that it could speak and cause all who refused to worship the image to be killed. ¹⁶He also forced everyone, small and great, rich and poor, free and slave, to receive a mark on his right hand or on his forehead, ¹⁷so that no one could buy or sell unless he had the mark, which is the name of the beast or the number of his name.

¹⁸This calls for wisdom. If anyone has insight, let him calculate the number of the beast, for it is man's number. His number is 666.

The Lamb and the 144,000

14 Then I looked, and there before me was the Lamb, standing on Mount Zion^D, and with him 144,000 who had his name and his Father's name written on their foreheads. ²And I heard a sound from heaven like the roar of rushing waters and like a loud peal of thunder. The sound I heard was like that of harpists playing their harps. ³And they sang a new song before the throne and before the four living creatures and the elders. No one could learn the song except the 144,000 who had been redeemed^D from the earth. ⁴These are those who did not defile themselves with women, for they kept themselves pure. They follow the Lamb wherever he goes. They were purchased from among men and offered as firstfruits^D to God and the Lamb. ⁵No lie was found in their mouths; they are blameless.

The Three Angels

⁶Then I saw another angel flying in midair, and he had the eternal gospel^D to proclaim to those who live on the earth—to every nation, tribe, language and people. ⁷He said in a loud voice, "Fear God and give him glory^D, because the hour of his judgment has come. Worship him who made the heavens, the earth, the sea and the springs of water."

⁸A second angel followed and said, "Fallen! Fallen is Babylon the Great, which made all the nations drink the maddening wine of her adulteries."

⁹A third angel followed them and said in a loud voice: "If anyone worships the beast and his image and receives his mark on the forehead or on the hand, ¹⁰he, too, will drink of the wine of God's fury, which has been poured full strength into the cup of his wrath. He will be tormented with burning sulfur in the presence of the holy angels and of the Lamb. ¹¹And the smoke of their torment rises for ever and ever. There is no rest day or night for those who worship the beast and his image, or for anyone who receives the mark of his name." ¹²This calls for patient endurance on the part of the saints^D who obey God's commandments and remain faithful to Jesus.

¹³Then I heard a voice from heaven say, "Write: Blessed are the dead who die in the Lord from now on."

"Yes," says the Spirit, "they will rest from their labor, for their deeds will follow them."

The Harvest of the Earth

14I looked, and there before me was a white cloud, and seated on the cloud was one "like a son of man[D]"[a] with a crown of gold on his head and a sharp sickle in his hand. **15**Then another angel came out of the temple and called in a loud voice to him who was sitting on the cloud, "Take your sickle and reap, because the time to reap has come, for the harvest of the earth is ripe." **16**So he who was seated on the cloud swung his sickle over the earth, and the earth was harvested.

17Another angel came out of the temple in heaven, and he too had a sharp sickle. **18**Still another angel, who had charge of the fire, came from the altar and called in a loud voice to him who had the sharp sickle, "Take your sharp sickle and gather the clusters of grapes from the earth's vine, because its grapes are ripe." **19**The angel swung his sickle on the earth, gathered its grapes and threw them into the great winepress[D] of God's wrath. **20**They were trampled in the winepress outside the city, and blood flowed out of the press, rising as high as the horses' bridles for a distance of 1,600 stadia.[b]

Seven Angels With Seven Plagues

15 I saw in heaven another great and marvelous sign: seven angels with the seven last plagues—last, because with them God's wrath is completed. **2**And I saw what looked like a sea of glass mixed with fire and, standing beside the sea, those who had been victorious over the beast and his image and over the number of his name. They held harps given them by God **3**and sang the song of Moses the servant of God and the song of the Lamb:

> "Great and marvelous are your deeds,
>   Lord God Almighty.
> Just and true are your ways,
>   King of the ages.
> **4**Who will not fear you, O Lord,
>   and bring glory[D] to your name?
> For you alone are holy.
> All nations will come
>   and worship before you,
> for your righteous[D] acts have been revealed."

5After this I looked and in heaven the temple, that is, the tabernacle[D] of the Testimony, was opened. **6**Out of the temple came the seven angels with the seven plagues. They were dressed in clean, shining linen and wore golden sashes around their chests. **7**Then one of the four living creatures gave to the seven angels seven golden bowls filled with the wrath of God, who lives for ever and ever. **8**And the temple was filled with smoke from the glory of God and from his power, and no one could enter the temple until the seven plagues of the seven angels were completed.

The Seven Bowls of God's Wrath

16 Then I heard a loud voice from the temple saying to the seven angels, "Go, pour out the seven bowls of God's wrath on the earth."

2The first angel went and poured out his bowl on the land, and ugly and painful sores broke out on the people

What is this first *harvest of the earth?* (14:15–16)

In the New Testament, harvest is used to depict the gathering of God's people (Matt. 9:37–38). Perhaps the first harvest means the saints will be protected from God's wrath, which is released at the second harvest (v. 19).

What are these grapes of wrath? (14:19–20)

A winepress relentlessly crushes grapes; this symbolizes the relentless force of God's wrath on those who rebel against him. Also see *What does it mean to tread a winepress?* (19:15).

Seven angels . . . seven last plagues (15:1)

See *How should we understand the numbers in this book?* (1:4).

Why is God so angry? (15:1)

God's wrath is against those who reject Christ as Savior and those who persecute believers. God is angry because he is just and must judge evil.

When will God's wrath be completed? (15:1)

Some think these three sets of seven judgments—seals, trumpets and bowls (chs. 6–19)—were executed during the early years of the church. Others think they represent judgments during the time between Christ's first and second comings. Still others think they are predictions of God's wrath just prior to Christ's return.

Who conquers the beast? (15:2)

Though the beast initially persecutes and conquers believers (13:7), his success is short-lived. Through Jesus Christ, who wins the final battle and guarantees the beast's defeat (19:20), believers are able to stand against the beast.

The song of Moses . . . song of the Lamb (15:3)

The song of Moses is usually thought to be the one in Exodus 15. Or it may have been the song in Deut. 32, written and taught by Moses (see Deut. 31:22). The song of the Lamb, then, is the one listed here (vv. 3–4).

What temple is in heaven? (15:5)

See *Ark of his covenant* (11:19).

Seven angels . . . seven bowls (16:1)

See *How should we understand the numbers in this book?* (1:4).

God's wrath (16:1)

Those who see God only as a God of love may be surprised to learn that he is also a God of wrath. God has righteous anger against sin and the sinner who refuses to repent and accept God's salvation. Also see *Why is God so angry?* (15:1).

What did God want the plagues to accomplish? (16:2–4)

God's purpose is to bring sinners to repentance and faith. But their resistance and rebellion (vv. 9,11) prevent God's purposes from being accomplished. The secondary purpose of the plagues, however, is fulfilled; for those who refuse to repent, the plagues become horrendous punishment.

[a]14 Daniel 7:13   [b]20 That is, about 180 miles (about 300 kilometers)

When does hostility against God turn to bloodshed? (16:6)

As if ignoring or disobeying God were not enough, some escalate their opposition to God until it becomes an obsession. When they can't get at God directly, they strike out at those who represent him—his messengers and those who obey him.

How can an altar talk? (16:7)

This may be figurative language in which an altar is personified so it can speak. Or this may mean that a voice is heard from between the horns of the altar (see 9:13).

In what sense will the beast's kingdom be *plunged into darkness*? (16:10)

This could be literal darkness, similar to the plague in Egypt (Exodus 10:21–22) or the darkness when Christ died (Matt. 27:45). The larger picture, however, may more likely describe a kingdom plagued with confusion and chaos—symbolized by darkness.

Kings from the East (16:12)

Some think these are the Parthians, enemies of Rome from just south of the Caspian Sea in what is now Iran (see **Jews from Every Nation** on page 1506). Others think they symbolize the forces of evil or, in contrast, the armies of God. Still others see them as Asian kings from the Far East who will take part in the final battle at Armageddon (v. 16).

Why describe the appearance of evil spirits? (16:13)

Perhaps the image of frogs illustrates the deeds of these evil spirits as something from a dark, spiritual swamp.

Who is the *false prophet*? (16:13)

Some think the *false prophet* is the second beast (13:11–17). It has been suggested that the *false prophet*, the dragon and the first beast (13:1–8) make up a counterfeit trinity.

What would entice world leaders to this battle? (16:14)

Two things may be involved in bringing the world leaders into the battle: (1) Something quite natural—the kings are easily enticed because of their hatred for God and the truth. (2) Something quite extraordinary and supernatural—miracles and signs convince the kings they cannot lose if they join the side of the beast.

who had the mark of the beast and worshiped his image.

³The second angel poured out his bowl on the sea, and it turned into blood like that of a dead man, and every living thing in the sea died.

⁴The third angel poured out his bowl on the rivers and springs of water, and they became blood. ⁵Then I heard the angel in charge of the waters say:

> "You are just in these judgments,
>   you who are and who were, the Holy One,
>   because you have so judged;
> ⁶for they have shed the blood of your saints^D
>   and prophets^D,
> and you have given them blood to drink as
>   they deserve."

⁷And I heard the altar respond:

> "Yes, Lord God Almighty,
>   true and just are your judgments."

⁸The fourth angel poured out his bowl on the sun, and the sun was given power to scorch people with fire. ⁹They were seared by the intense heat and they cursed the name of God, who had control over these plagues, but they refused to repent^D and glorify him.

¹⁰The fifth angel poured out his bowl on the throne of the beast, and his kingdom was plunged into darkness. Men gnawed their tongues in agony ¹¹and cursed the God of heaven because of their pains and their sores, but they refused to repent of what they had done.

¹²The sixth angel poured out his bowl on the great river Euphrates, and its water was dried up to prepare the way for the kings from the East. ¹³Then I saw three evil^a spirits that looked like frogs; they came out of the mouth of the dragon, out of the mouth of the beast and out of the mouth of the false prophet. ¹⁴They are spirits of demons performing miraculous signs, and they go out to the kings of the whole world, to gather them for the battle on the great day of God Almighty.

¹⁵"Behold, I come like a thief! Blessed is he who stays awake and keeps his clothes with him, so that he may not go naked and be shamefully exposed."

¹⁶Then they gathered the kings together to the place that in Hebrew^D is called Armageddon.

¹⁷The seventh angel poured out his bowl into the air,

^a 13 Greek *unclean*

Armageddon (16:16)

Armageddon comes from two Hebrew words: *mount* and *Megiddo*. The mountain of the city of Megiddo stands at the head of the Plain of Esdraelon, south and east of Mount Carmel where Elijah challenged the prophets of Baal (see **Map 6** at the back of this Bible). This plain was the site of many Old Testament battles.

Many think *Armageddon* refers to a battle that will occur before the return of Christ on the great day of God Almighty (16:14). Some think this battle will be more like a war with a number of battles in various locations: Egypt (Daniel 11:40–45), Jerusalem (Zech. 14:2) as well as the plain of Esdraelon (Megiddo). Whether understood literally or symbolically, most see it as God's final defeat of evil.

and out of the temple came a loud voice from the throne, saying, "It is done!" **18**Then there came flashes of lightning, rumblings, peals of thunder and a severe earthquake. No earthquake like it has ever occurred since man has been on earth, so tremendous was the quake. **19**The great city split into three parts, and the cities of the nations collapsed. God remembered Babylon the Great and gave her the cup filled with the wine of the fury of his wrath. **20**Every island fled away and the mountains could not be found. **21**From the sky huge hailstones of about a hundred pounds each fell upon men. And they cursed God on account of the plague of hail, because the plague was so terrible.

The Woman on the Beast

17 One of the seven angels who had the seven bowls came and said to me, "Come, I will show you the punishment of the great prostitute, who sits on many waters. **2**With her the kings of the earth committed adultery and the inhabitants of the earth were intoxicated with the wine of her adulteries."

3Then the angel carried me away in the Spirit into a desert. There I saw a woman sitting on a scarlet beast that was covered with blasphemous names and had seven heads and ten horns. **4**The woman was dressed in purple^D and scarlet, and was glittering with gold, precious stones and pearls. She held a golden cup in her hand, filled with abominable things and the filth of her adulteries. **5**This title was written on her forehead:

MYSTERY
BABYLON THE GREAT
THE MOTHER OF PROSTITUTES
AND OF THE ABOMINATIONS OF THE EARTH.

6I saw that the woman was drunk with the blood of the saints^D, the blood of those who bore testimony to Jesus.

When I saw her, I was greatly astonished. **7**Then the angel said to me: "Why are you astonished? I will explain to you the mystery^D of the woman and of the beast she rides, which has the seven heads and ten horns. **8**The beast, which you saw, once was, now is not, and will come up out of the Abyss^D and go to his destruction. The inhabitants of the earth whose names have not been written in the book of life from the creation of the world will be astonished when they see the beast, because he once was, now is not, and yet will come.

9"This calls for a mind with wisdom. The seven heads are seven hills on which the woman sits. **10**They are also seven kings. Five have fallen, one is, the other has not yet come; but when he does come, he must remain for a little while. **11**The beast who once was, and now is not, is an eighth king. He belongs to the seven and is going to his destruction.

12"The ten horns you saw are ten kings who have not yet received a kingdom, but who for one hour will receive authority as kings along with the beast. **13**They have one purpose and will give their power and authority to the beast. **14**They will make war against the Lamb, but the Lamb will overcome them because he is Lord of lords and King of kings—and with him will be his called, chosen and faithful followers."

15Then the angel said to me, "The waters you saw, where the prostitute sits, are peoples, multitudes, nations and languages. **16**The beast and the ten horns you saw will

How do we know these are Jesus' words? (16:15)
Because these words are similar to earlier words Jesus speaks to the churches (see 3:3,18). Similar warnings to be prepared for Christ's coming are found in the Gospels (Matt. 25:1–13, for example). Also, it's clear that these words are not John's. Throughout the book he speaks as an observer to these events, not as a participant.

Babylon the Great (16:19)
See *Babylon the Great* (14:8).

Seven angels . . . seven bowls (17:1)
See *How should we understand the numbers in this book?* (1:4).

The great prostitute (17:1)
Not easy to identify, *the great prostitute* has been linked to Babylon, Rome and Jerusalem (see v. 18). It may be that she symbolizes all cultures that are unfaithful to God (their actions here are represented by *adultery*).

Scarlet beast (17:3)
Scarlet is most likely used to symbolize blasphemy in contrast to the purity and faithfulness symbolized by the color *white* (19:8,11,14). This beast is most likely the first beast (13:1).

Blasphemous names (17:3)
Blasphemy seems to be the primary feature of the beast's character (13:1,5–6). *Covered with blasphemous names* suggests that the beast is completely and irrevocably opposed to God.

In the Spirit (17:3)
See *In the Spirit* (4:2).

Why keep things a mystery? (17:5)
See article: *Why such obscure, mysterious language?* (1:19–20).

Babylon the Great (17:5)
See *Babylon the Great* (14:8).

Why is the beast in the past and future but not the present? (17:8)
The three stages represent the beast's rise to power, its mortal wound, and its miraculous recovery (13:3). John does not write from his own time but from the perspective of the prophesied events, quoting the angel (v. 7).

Can these events be linked in an understandable way to history? (17:9–14)
The symbolism of these verses is difficult. One view links these kings to the Roman emperors: Augustus, Tiberius, Caligula, Claudius and Nero are the *five* [who] *have fallen*, Vespasian is the *one* [who] *is*, and Titus is *the other* [who] *has not yet come*. Another view sees these kings as nations: from the past—Old Babylon, Assyria, New Babylon, Medo-Persia and Graeco-Macedonia; from the present—Rome; from the future—the kingdom of the antichrist.

Will Christians be part of this war? (17:14)

The *called, chosen and faithful followers* are with the Lord, although it's not clear whether they are part of this war or simply spectators to it. Some say these are believers who decide for Christ *after* the church is raptured and so are still in the world. Others say the raptured church will return to earth to be with the Lord at this time. Still others believe that Christ will not come for his church until after this battle.

Why are two evils—the beast and the prostitute—at odds with each other? (17:16)

The wicked act selfishly and with hatred toward each other as well as toward the righteous. Both the beast and the prostitute want power over the whole world, so their selfish goals conflict.

Babylon the Great (18:2)

See *Babylon the Great* (14:8).

What had the nations done? (18:3)

They were guilty of adulteries with Babylon (that is, Rome), the *great prostitute* (17:1). Their adulteries most likely included cultic prostitution in pagan religions. But they also included excessive materialism—accumulating wealth by any means, illegal or otherwise.

At what point should God's people separate from the world? (18:4)

God's people are *in* but not *of* the world. Some feel they should isolate themselves from society, but they find it difficult to penetrate society with the gospel. Others strive to communicate well, but they find identifying with the culture weakens their distinctive counter-culture message. The line is difficult to draw. In any case, there is a point for a decision: let go of the world or let go of your convictions.

What kind of *glory and luxury* did Babylon have? (18:7)

The Bible uses the *glory and luxury* of Babylon to symbolize selfish excess and sin. Babylon's decadent lifestyle included idolatry, prostitution, pride, and an unrestrained appetite for luxury and wealth.

Woe! (18:10)

See *Woe! Woe! Woe . . . !* (8:13).

hate the prostitute. They will bring her to ruin and leave her naked; they will eat her flesh and burn her with fire. **17**For God has put it into their hearts to accomplish his purpose by agreeing to give the beast their power to rule, until God's words are fulfilled. **18**The woman you saw is the great city that rules over the kings of the earth."

The Fall of Babylon

18 After this I saw another angel coming down from heaven. He had great authority, and the earth was illuminated by his splendor. **2**With a mighty voice he shouted:

> "Fallen! Fallen is Babylon the Great!
>   She has become a home for demons
> and a haunt for every evil[a] spirit,
>   a haunt for every unclean[D] and detestable
>   bird.
> **3**For all the nations have drunk
>   the maddening wine of her adulteries.
> The kings of the earth committed adultery with
>   her,
>   and the merchants of the earth grew rich
>   from her excessive luxuries."

4Then I heard another voice from heaven say:

> "Come out of her, my people,
>   so that you will not share in her sins,
>   so that you will not receive any of her
>   plagues;
> **5**for her sins are piled up to heaven,
>   and God has remembered her crimes.
> **6**Give back to her as she has given;
>   pay her back double for what she has done.
>   Mix her a double portion from her own cup.
> **7**Give her as much torture and grief
>   as the glory[D] and luxury she gave herself.
> In her heart she boasts,
>   'I sit as queen; I am not a widow,
>   and I will never mourn.'
> **8**Therefore in one day her plagues will overtake
>   her:
>   death[D], mourning and famine.
> She will be consumed by fire,
>   for mighty is the Lord God who judges her.

9"When the kings of the earth who committed adultery with her and shared her luxury see the smoke of her burning, they will weep and mourn over her. **10**Terrified at her torment, they will stand far off and cry:

> " 'Woe! Woe, O great city,
>   O Babylon, city of power!
> In one hour your doom has come!'

11"The merchants of the earth will weep and mourn over her because no one buys their cargoes any more— **12**cargoes of gold, silver, precious stones and pearls; fine linen, purple[D], silk and scarlet cloth; every sort of citron wood, and articles of every kind made of ivory, costly wood, bronze, iron and marble; **13**cargoes of cinnamon and spice, of incense[D], myrrh[D] and frankincense, of wine and olive oil, of fine flour and wheat; cattle and

a2 Greek unclean

sheep; horses and carriages; and bodies and souls[D] of men.

¹⁴"They will say, 'The fruit you longed for is gone from you. All your riches and splendor have vanished, never to be recovered.' ¹⁵The merchants who sold these things and gained their wealth from her will stand far off, terrified at her torment. They will weep and mourn ¹⁶and cry out:

" 'Woe! Woe, O great city,
    dressed in fine linen, purple[D] and scarlet,
    and glittering with gold, precious stones and
        pearls!
¹⁷In one hour such great wealth has been
        brought to ruin!'

"Every sea captain, and all who travel by ship, the sailors, and all who earn their living from the sea, will stand far off. ¹⁸When they see the smoke of her burning, they will exclaim, 'Was there ever a city like this great city?' ¹⁹They will throw dust on their heads, and with weeping and mourning cry out:

" 'Woe! Woe, O great city,
    where all who had ships on the sea
        became rich through her wealth!
In one hour she has been brought to ruin!
²⁰Rejoice over her, O heaven!
    Rejoice, saints[D] and apostles[D] and
        prophets[D]!
God has judged her for the way she treated
    you.' "

²¹Then a mighty angel picked up a boulder the size of a large millstone[D] and threw it into the sea, and said:

"With such violence
    the great city of Babylon will be thrown
        down,
    never to be found again.
²²The music of harpists and musicians, flute
        players and trumpeters,
    will never be heard in you again.
No workman of any trade
    will ever be found in you again.
The sound of a millstone
    will never be heard in you again.
²³The light of a lamp
    will never shine in you again.
The voice of bridegroom and bride
    will never be heard in you again.
Your merchants were the world's great men.
    By your magic spell all the nations were led
        astray.
²⁴In her was found the blood of prophets and
        of the saints,
    and of all who have been killed on the
        earth."

Hallelujah!

19

After this I heard what sounded like the roar of a great multitude in heaven shouting:

"Hallelujah[D]!
Salvation[D] and glory[D] and power belong to
    our God,
²   for true and just are his judgments.
He has condemned the great prostitute

Hallelujah (19:1)
Comes from two Hebrew words that mean
praise the Lord or *praise Yah[weh]*.

The great prostitute (19:2)
See *The great prostitute* (17:1).

Twenty-four elders (19:4)
See *Who are the twenty-four elders?* (4:4).

Four living creatures (19:4)
See *Who are the four living creatures?* (4:6–8).

Who is the *bride* of the Lamb? (19:7)
The church of Christ, the people of God. The
bride is a frequent Biblical picture for God's
people. Ancient Jewish customs called for the
groom to go to his fiancée's house, and take
her to his own house to be his bride. The wedding would then be followed by festive celebrations lasting up to seven days. The early
church saw this as a vivid image of the relationship we have with Christ. We are cleansed
from sin, *bright and clean* (v. 8), and therefore
can expect him to come to take us to his home
where we will celebrate. See Matt. 25:1–13;
Eph. 5:25–27.

Why one brief note explaining symbolism? (19:8)

John helps his readers with this parenthetical note. He apparently didn't feel more explanations were necessary since most of his symbols probably were well known to his readers.

Why does the angel announce that these words are true? (19:9)

The other words that John wrote down were just as true. But the angel wanted to offer further assurance to John and his readers, emphasizing the certainty of the great prostitute's demise and the *wedding supper of the Lamb.* Such assurances are common throughout Revelation (see 1:2; 17:17; 21:5; 22:6).

In what sense is *the testimony of Jesus* the *spirit of prophecy?* (19:10)

This may mean that what Jesus said about himself and the Father is really the essence of the prophetic message. Or this may refer to what has been testified about Jesus—that the true spirit of prophecy bears witness to Jesus.

What is heaven? (19:11)

See articles: *What is heaven like?* (4:1) and *What will eternal life be like?* (21:22–27).

Why does the rider have so many names? (19:11–13,16)

In Biblical times, names not only identified people—they described or expressed their character. It is possible that Jesus also has a name *no one knows* (v. 12) because his character can not be exhaustively revealed. Compare *New name* (2:17).

Why would a sword come out of his mouth? (19:15)

The sword symbolizes the word of Christ coming from his mouth—a word of judgment that will *strike down the nations.*

What does it mean to tread a winepress? (19:15)

The treading of the grapes is a common Biblical metaphor to picture the execution of God's wrath upon his enemies. Also see *Winepress* (Isaiah 63:2) and *What are these grapes of wrath?* (14:19–20).

who corrupted the earth by her adulteries. He has avenged[D] on her the blood of his servants."

3And again they shouted:

"Hallelujah[D]!
The smoke from her goes up for ever and ever."

4The twenty-four elders and the four living creatures fell down and worshiped God, who was seated on the throne. And they cried:

"Amen, Hallelujah!"

5Then a voice came from the throne, saying:

"Praise our God,
    all you his servants,
you who fear him,
    both small and great!"

6Then I heard what sounded like a great multitude, like the roar of rushing waters and like loud peals of thunder, shouting:

"Hallelujah!
    For our Lord God Almighty reigns.
7Let us rejoice and be glad
    and give him glory[D]!
For the wedding of the Lamb has come,
    and his bride has made herself ready.
8Fine linen, bright and clean,
    was given her to wear."
(Fine linen stands for the righteous[D] acts of the saints[D].)

9Then the angel said to me, "Write: 'Blessed are those who are invited to the wedding supper of the Lamb!' " And he added, "These are the true words of God." **10**At this I fell at his feet to worship him. But he said to me, "Do not do it! I am a fellow servant with you and with your brothers who hold to the testimony of Jesus. Worship God! For the testimony of Jesus is the spirit of prophecy[D]."

What does *the wedding of the Lamb* represent? (19:7)

Throughout the Bible weddings and marriages are used to picture larger truths. In the Old Testament Israel is the bride and wife of the Lord (Isaiah 54:5). In the New Testament that imagery is applied to the church (Eph. 5:22–32). Christ's deep love for the church and his commitment to it are symbolized by the marriage covenant. Just as a husband and wife are one, Christ and the church are also united as one.

There were two important steps to a Jewish marriage: the betrothal (the promised agreement to marry) and the actual wedding ceremony. These two events were often separated by an extended period of time during which the couple remained faithful to one another though the wedding ceremony was not yet finalized.

Our betrothal to Christ takes place at the point of salvation. But the wedding ceremony occurs when Christ, the bridegroom, comes to take his bride. In this verse the church is finally ready to enter into the long-awaited union with the Lord Jesus Christ.

The Rider on the White Horse

11I saw heaven standing open and there before me was a white horse, whose rider is called Faithful and True. With justice he judges and makes war. **12**His eyes are like blazing fire, and on his head are many crowns. He has a name written on him that no one knows but he himself. **13**He is dressed in a robe dipped in blood, and his name is the Word of God. **14**The armies of heaven were following him, riding on white horses and dressed in fine linen, white and clean. **15**Out of his mouth comes a sharp sword with which to strike down the nations. "He will rule them with an iron scepter^D."^a He treads the winepress^D of the fury of the wrath of God Almighty. **16**On his robe and on his thigh he has this name written:

KING OF KINGS AND LORD OF LORDS.

17And I saw an angel standing in the sun, who cried in a loud voice to all the birds flying in midair, "Come, gather together for the great supper of God, **18**so that you may eat the flesh of kings, generals, and mighty men, of horses and their riders, and the flesh of all people, free and slave, small and great."

19Then I saw the beast and the kings of the earth and their armies gathered together to make war against the rider on the horse and his army. **20**But the beast was captured, and with him the false prophet^D who had performed the miraculous signs on his behalf. With these signs he had deluded those who had received the mark of the beast and worshiped his image. The two of them were thrown alive into the fiery lake of burning sulfur. **21**The rest of them were killed with the sword that came out of the mouth of the rider on the horse, and all the birds gorged themselves on their flesh.

The Thousand Years

20 And I saw an angel coming down out of heaven, having the key to the Abyss^D and holding in his hand a great chain. **2**He seized the dragon, that ancient serpent, who is the devil, or Satan, and bound him for a

^a 15 Psalm 2:9

Is this Armageddon? (19:19)

Probably so. The preparation for Armageddon occurred earlier (16:12–16): the river Euphrates was dried up, and unclean spirits from the mouths of the dragon, the beast and the false prophet were released to go out and stir up the kings of the world to bring them to battle against God. Here their task is accomplished, and the armies of the world are now allied against God and his armies.

Beast (19:20)

See *Who or what is the beast from the sea?* (13:1–2).

The false prophet (19:20)

See *Who is the false prophet?* (16:13).

Fiery lake of burning sulfur (19:20)

The place of final torment for the wicked— John's description of what is elsewhere referred to in the New Testament as *gehenna*, which is translated as *hell*. This was the name of the valley south and west of Jerusalem where human sacrifices had occurred, giving it an unholy reputation. Later it was a place where garbage was burned—its continual flames becoming a picture for eternal judgment. Also see *Hell* (Matt. 5:22).

Abyss (20:1)

See *The Abyss* (9:2).

Why do believers who died of natural causes have to wait for their resurrection? (20:4–5)

They don't—if you understand that the martyrs mentioned in v. 4 represent all those who stood firm for Christ, as many commentators do. In this view, all believers are resurrected at the same time. Some think this means that there are two resurrections, the first for the righteous and the second for the wicked with the earthly reign of Christ in between. Others believe the Bible teaches a single, general resurrection of both the righteous and the wicked when Christ returns.

Why bind Satan for only a thousand years? (20:2)

There are different opinions about this 1,000-year period called the Millennium (from the Latin word for *thousand*). Some think it is a symbolic period of time (not a literal 1,000 years) when Satan's power is restrained as the church fulfills the work of the kingdom (*amillennialism*).

Others understand the Millennium in the literal sense of a 1,000-year period. Some of them believe Christ will come to take believers out of this world and then return to rule from Jerusalem over the whole earth (*premillennialism*). During his 1,000-year reign, according to this view, Satan will be held captive. At the end of the time, Satan will be released for one final onslaught against God (vv. 7–10), probably to bring a final resolution to the ongoing struggle between good and evil.

Others who view the Millennium in the sense of a literal 1,000-year period see the ideal reign of Christ coming about through the increasing impact of the church upon the world (*postmillennialism*). According to them, Christ will return after the Millennium.

Gog and Magog (20:8)

Magog is one of Noah's grandsons (Gen. 10:2). Gog and Magog, people from *the far north* (Ezek. 38:1; 39:2), are enemies of Israel. These names may symbolize those from anywhere who band together to oppose God and his people. Also see **Who were all these nations?** (Ezek. 38:2–6).

What kind of eternal torment must the devil endure? (20:10)

The *lake of burning sulfur* describes unimaginable and never ending pain. Even this extreme picture, though, is limited in its ability to describe the intensity of pain in the spiritual realm.

What are the books that will be opened? (20:12)

The books—like a ledger—contain an exhaustive record of every evil act, word and thought of the unrighteous. Some think they may also include the deeds of the righteous that will be rewarded (2 Cor. 5:10). The *book of life*, however, contains only names, not deeds. Those forgiven by God's grace through Christ will have their names listed in it.

Book of life (20:12)

See *Book of life* (3:5).

Sea ... death ... Hades (20:13)

The three terms are used to describe the universal scope of judgment. No one will escape; all will be raised to face judgment. *Death* and *Hades* probably mean the same thing. Each portrays the idea that the dead await final judgment. When the judgment is complete, *death and Hades* will be thrown into the lake of fire (v. 14), no longer to be feared.

Second death (20:14)

Eternal separation from God, the destiny of the wicked. Those sentenced to the *lake of fire* forever experience this *second death*.

What happens to the earth, sea and heaven? (21:1)

The word *new* indicates new in quality, not necessarily in time and space (Isaiah 65:17). The world of sin, suffering and rebellion against God is destroyed (2 Peter 3:10). A new earth and heaven where God dwells with his people comes as *the home of righteousness* (2 Peter 3:13).

The new Jerusalem (21:2)

John's vision includes not only a new earth and heaven but a *new Jerusalem*. There is some disagreement over whether the *new Jerusalem* is an actual city or a symbolic representation of the church in its perfected and eternal state. Either way, it is eternal and comes from heaven. Like the original Jerusalem, it is to be the place where God lives with his people.

What will be different when the old order of things ends? (21:4)

The *old order* is characterized by the debilitating effects of sin: suffering, sorrow, death, mourning and pain. These will be gone and past forever. God will wipe away all tears and death will be no more!

Alpha and the Omega, the Beginning and the End (21:6)

See *The Alpha and the Omega* (1:8).

thousand years. ³He threw him into the Abyss^D, and locked and sealed it over him, to keep him from deceiving the nations anymore until the thousand years were ended. After that, he must be set free for a short time.

⁴I saw thrones on which were seated those who had been given authority to judge. And I saw the souls^D of those who had been beheaded because of their testimony for Jesus and because of the word of God. They had not worshiped the beast or his image and had not received his mark on their foreheads or their hands. They came to life and reigned with Christ a thousand years. ⁵(The rest of the dead did not come to life until the thousand years were ended.) This is the first resurrection^D. ⁶Blessed and holy are those who have part in the first resurrection. The second death^D has no power over them, but they will be priests^D of God and of Christ and will reign with him for a thousand years.

Satan's Doom

⁷When the thousand years are over, Satan will be released from his prison ⁸and will go out to deceive the nations in the four corners of the earth—Gog and Magog—to gather them for battle. In number they are like the sand on the seashore. ⁹They marched across the breadth of the earth and surrounded the camp of God's people, the city he loves. But fire came down from heaven and devoured them. ¹⁰And the devil, who deceived them, was thrown into the lake of burning sulfur, where the beast and the false prophet^D had been thrown. They will be tormented day and night for ever and ever.

The Dead Are Judged

¹¹Then I saw a great white throne and him who was seated on it. Earth and sky fled from his presence, and there was no place for them. ¹²And I saw the dead, great and small, standing before the throne, and books were opened. Another book was opened, which is the book of life. The dead were judged according to what they had done as recorded in the books. ¹³The sea gave up the dead that were in it, and death and Hades gave up the dead that were in them, and each person was judged according to what he had done. ¹⁴Then death and Hades were thrown into the lake of fire. The lake of fire is the second death. ¹⁵If anyone's name was not found written in the book of life, he was thrown into the lake of fire.

The New Jerusalem

21 Then I saw a new heaven and a new earth, for the first heaven and the first earth had passed away, and there was no longer any sea. ²I saw the Holy City, the new Jerusalem^D, coming down out of heaven from God, prepared as a bride beautifully dressed for her husband. ³And I heard a loud voice from the throne saying, "Now the dwelling of God is with men, and he will live with them. They will be his people, and God himself will be with them and be their God. ⁴He will wipe every tear from their eyes. There will be no more death or mourning or crying or pain, for the old order of things has passed away."

⁵He who was seated on the throne said, "I am making everything new!" Then he said, "Write this down, for these words are trustworthy and true."

⁶He said to me: "It is done. I am the Alpha and the Omega, the Beginning and the End. To him who is thirsty I will

give to drink without cost from the spring of the water of life. **7**He who overcomes will inherit all this, and I will be his God and he will be my son. **8**But the cowardly, the unbelieving, the vile, the murderers, the sexually immoral, those who practice magic arts, the idolaters and all liars— their place will be in the fiery lake of burning sulfur. This is the second death.ᴰ"

9One of the seven angels who had the seven bowls full of the seven last plagues came and said to me, "Come, I will show you the bride, the wife of the Lamb." **10**And he carried me away in the Spirit to a mountain great and high, and showed me the Holy City, Jerusalemᴰ, coming down out of heaven from God. **11**It shone with the gloryᴰ of God, and its brilliance was like that of a very precious jewel, like a jasper, clear as crystal. **12**It had a great, high wall with twelve gates, and with twelve angels at the gates. On the gates were written the names of the twelve tribes of Israel. **13**There were three gates on the east, three on the north, three on the south and three on the west. **14**The wall of the city had twelve foundations, and on them were the names of the twelve apostlesᴰ of the Lamb.

15The angel who talked with me had a measuring rod of gold to measure the city, its gates and its walls. **16**The city was laid out like a square, as long as it was wide. He measured the city with the rod and found it to be 12,000 stadiaᵃ in length, and as wide and high as it is long. **17**He measured its wall and it was 144 cubitsᴰᵇ thick,ᶜ by man's measurement, which the angel was using. **18**The wall was made of jasper, and the city of pure gold, as pure as glass. **19**The foundations of the city walls were decorated with every kind of precious stone. The first foundation was jasper, the second sapphire, the third chalcedony, the fourth emerald, **20**the fifth sardonyx, the sixth carnelian, the seventh chrysolite, the eighth beryl, the ninth topaz, the tenth chrysoprase, the eleventh jacinth, and the twelfth amethyst.ᵈ **21**The twelve gates were twelve pearls, each gate made of a single pearl. The great street of the city was of pure gold, like transparent glass.

22I did not see a temple in the city, because the Lord God Almighty and the Lamb are its temple. **23**The city does not need the sun or the moon to shine on it, for the glory of God gives it light, and the Lamb is its lamp. **24**The nations will walk by its light, and the kings of the earth will bring their splendor into it. **25**On no day will its gates ever be shut, for there will be no night there. **26**The glory and honor of the nations will be brought into it. **27**Nothing impure will ever enter it, nor will anyone who does what is shameful or deceitful, but only those whose names are written in the Lamb's book of life.

The River of Life

22 Then the angel showed me the river of the water of life, as clear as crystal, flowing from the throne of God and of the Lamb **2**down the middle of the great street of the city. On each side of the river stood the tree of life, bearing twelve crops of fruit, yielding its fruit every month. And the leaves of the tree are for the healing of the nations. **3**No longer will there be any curse. The throne of God and of the Lamb will be in the city, and his

ᵃ16 That is, about 1,400 miles (about 2,200 kilometers)   ᵇ17 That is, about 200 feet (about 65 meters)   ᶜ17 Or high   ᵈ20 The precise identification of some of these precious stones is uncertain.

Are cowards and murderers in the same league? (21:8)
Some suggest that each group mentioned here at one time had professed faith in Christ as Savior. But then, under varying circumstances, they demonstrated they were not believers. This would put them all in the same league. Their fear is not normal apprehension (which is not sin), but a lack of commitment.

Magic (21:8)
See *What's so bad about magic?* (9:21).

Second death (21:8)
See *Second death* (20:14).

The bride (21:9–10)
Some say that *the bride, the wife of the Lamb* refers to the new Jerusalem. Others, however, believe this means the church, now "married" to Christ and living in the new Jerusalem. See *Who is the bride of the Lamb?* (19:7). Also see article: *What does the wedding of the Lamb represent?* (19:7).

In the Spirit (21:10)
See *In the Spirit* (4:2).

Twelve gates . . . twelve angels . . . twelve tribes . . . twelve foundations . . . twelve apostles (21:12–14)
The number twelve is both literal and symbolic. There certainly were twelve tribes and twelve apostles. However, the number twelve also symbolizes fullness and completeness.

Why is heaven depicted as a cube? (21:16)
This shape would immediately remind the Jewish reader of the inner sanctuary of the temple, the Most Holy Place, where God's presence dwelt. It was a perfect cube: 20 cubits high, 20 cubits wide and 20 cubits long (1 Kings 6:20). Here again is a perfect place where God takes up his residence with his people.

Book of life (21:27)
See *Book of life* (3:5).

What does the water flowing from the throne of God symbolize? (22:1)
Some think the flowing water refers to the Holy Spirit, others to the promise of eternal life and still others to the abundant life that God gives to his people. Probably all these ideas are included in this symbol.

Twelve crops of fruit (22:2)
See *How should we understand the numbers in this book?* (1:4).

The healing of the nations (22:2)
The tree of life will produce abundant fruit for eating. It will also have medicinal leaves for the final healing of the nations—those included in the new Jerusalem. This symbolizes the completeness of Christ's death in overcoming the effects of sin. So powerful is the death of Christ that it completely and for all time removes the consequences of sin.

What curse comes to an end? (22:3)

This may mean that the curse placed on creation and humanity because of Adam's sin has finally come to an end (Gen. 3:8–24), though the curse's effects will be greatly curtailed during the earthly reign of Christ.

Why does the angel announce that these words are true? (22:6)

See *Why does the angel announce that these words are true?* (19:9).

Soon . . . the time is near (22:6,10)

There are those who think John was mistaken to believe that Jesus would return quickly. But probably the words underscore the *immediacy*, not the *timing*, of Christ's return. He can come at any time; every generation should expect his coming. Also see *How could Peter say the end of all things is near?* (1 Peter 4:7).

Why does the angel give up on wrongdoers and the vile? (22:11)

Some see the angel's words as an exhortation to repent. The return of Christ will be swift and at an unexpected time; there won't be time to seek forgiveness then. Others see these words as a warning that repeated actions form character: do something long enough and there comes a point when character has been firmly set and cannot be changed.

The Alpha and the Omega . . . First and the Last . . . Beginning and the End (22:13)

See *The Alpha and the Omega* (1:8).

Dogs (22:15)

This is a term used in the Bible to picture wickedness; traitors (Psalm 59:5–6), the heathen (Matt. 15:26–27) and Judaizers (Phil. 3:2) are called *dogs*.

Magic (22:15)

See *What's so bad about magic?* (9:21).

Root and the Offspring of David (22:16)

Jesus is identified with the prophecy of Isaiah that the Messiah would come forth as *a shoot . . . from the stump of Jesse* (Isaiah 11:1,10).

servants will serve him. [4]They will see his face, and his name will be on their foreheads. [5]There will be no more night. They will not need the light of a lamp or the light of the sun, for the Lord God will give them light. And they will reign for ever and ever.

[6]The angel said to me, "These words are trustworthy and true. The Lord, the God of the spirits of the prophets[D], sent his angel to show his servants the things that must soon take place."

Jesus Is Coming

[7]"Behold, I am coming soon! Blessed is he who keeps the words of the prophecy[D] in this book."

[8]I, John, am the one who heard and saw these things. And when I had heard and seen them, I fell down to worship at the feet of the angel who had been showing them to me. [9]But he said to me, "Do not do it! I am a fellow servant with you and with your brothers the prophets and of all who keep the words of this book. Worship God!"

[10]Then he told me, "Do not seal up the words of the prophecy of this book, because the time is near. [11]Let him who does wrong continue to do wrong; let him who is vile continue to be vile; let him who does right continue to do right; and let him who is holy continue to be holy."

[12]"Behold, I am coming soon! My reward is with me, and I will give to everyone according to what he has done. [13]I am the Alpha and the Omega, the First and the Last, the Beginning and the End.

[14]"Blessed are those who wash their robes, that they may have the right to the tree of life and may go through the gates into the city. [15]Outside are the dogs, those who practice magic arts, the sexually immoral, the murderers, the idolaters and everyone who loves and practices falsehood.

[16]"I, Jesus, have sent my angel to give you[a] this testimony for the churches. I am the Root and the Offspring of David, and the bright Morning Star."

[17]The Spirit and the bride say, "Come!" And let him

[a]16 The Greek is plural.

What will eternal life be like? (21:22–27)

Some think the new Jerusalem is an actual city, while others think it is a symbolic representation of the church triumphant. Some think it will hover over the earth during the Millennium and throughout eternity; others think it pictures the eternal state only.

Whatever the details, the picture is one of indescribable beauty and glory. Eternal life means a whole new dimension of living: there will be people with new life, purpose and action. God is the focus of this city, the source of light (and everything else). God's spectacular glory illuminates the city as is illustrated by the lack of night. His presence fills the whole city, making the need for a temple obsolete—the new Jerusalem itself is a temple filled with the glory of God.

Eternal life will be pure, untainted by anything evil. In the new Jerusalem we can escape not only the power and penalty of sin, but also its presence.

who hears say, "Come!" Whoever is thirsty, let him come; and whoever wishes, let him take the free gift of the water of life.

18I warn everyone who hears the words of the prophecy[D] of this book: If anyone adds anything to them, God will add to him the plagues described in this book. **19**And if anyone takes words away from this book of prophecy, God will take away from him his share in the tree of life and in the holy city, which are described in this book.

20He who testifies to these things says, "Yes, I am coming soon."

Amen. Come, Lord Jesus.

21The grace[D] of the Lord Jesus be with God's people. Amen.

Morning Star (22:16)

As the light of dawn approaches, the morning star announces the start of a new day—the dark night is past. Jesus is the hope of the world for the end of sin and tribulation, foretold as *A star* [that] *will come out of Jacob* (Num. 24:17). Also see *The morning star* (2:28).

Who would want to add to or subtract from this book? (22:18–19)

John didn't want anyone to distort its message given by a revelation from Christ. There are other similar warnings in the Bible (Deut. 4:2; Prov. 30:5–6; Gal. 1:6–7).

Table of Weights and Measures

	Biblical Unit		Approximate American Equivalent	Approximate Metric Equivalent
WEIGHTS	talent	(60 minas)	75 pounds	34 kilograms
	mina	(50 shekels)	1¼ pounds	0.6 kilogram
	shekel	(2 bekas)	⅖ ounce	11.5 grams
	pim	(⅔ shekel)	⅓ ounce	7.6 grams
	beka	(10 gerahs)	⅕ ounce	5.5 grams
	gerah		¹⁄₅₀ ounce	0.6 gram
LENGTH	cubit		18 inches	0.5 meter
	span		9 inches	23 centimeters
	handbreadth		3 inches	8 centimeters
CAPACITY				
Dry Measure	cor [homer]	(10 ephahs)	6 bushels	220 liters
	lethek	(5 ephahs)	3 bushels	110 liters
	ephah	(10 omers)	⅗ bushel	22 liters
	seah	(⅓ ephah)	7 quarts	7.3 liters
	omer	(¹⁄₁₀ ephah)	2 quarts	2 liters
	cab	(¹⁄₁₀ ephah)	1 quart	1 liter
Liquid Measure	bath	(1 ephah)	6 gallons	22 liters
	hin	(⅙ bath)	4 quarts	4 liters
	log	(¹⁄₇₂ bath)	⅓ quart	0.3 liter

The figures of the table are calculated on the basis of a shekel equaling 11.5 grams, a cubit equaling 18 inches and an ephah equaling 22 liters. The quart referred to is either a dry quart (slightly smaller than a liter) or a liquid quart (slightly larger than a liter), whichever is applicable. The ton referred to in the footnotes is the American ton of 2,000 pounds.

This table is based upon the best available information, but it is not intended to be mathematically precise; like the measurement equivalents in the footnotes, it merely gives approximate amounts and distances. Weights and measures differed somewhat at various times and places in the ancient world. There is uncertainty particularly about the ephah and the bath; further discoveries may shed more light on these units of capacity.

This dictionary contains definitions of some of the names, words, phrases and place names found in the Scripture text of the New International Version. As you read the Bible, you will find these dictionary words marked in the Scripture text with a small "D"—alerting you that a definition of that word or phrase can be found in the dictionary.

A

Abba
An Aramaic word best translated *Daddy* (Mark 14:36). *Abba* was a deeply personal and affectionate word, that most of Jesus' contemporaries would have considered disrespectful to use in addressing God.

Abomination
That which is repugnant or detestable to God or his people, such as idolatry or immorality (Isaiah 66:3).

Abyss
A bottomless pit where, at the end of the age, Satan will be banished for a time (Rev. 20:3). The Greeks used this word to describe the underworld of spirits, suggesting a place so deep it is unfathomable (Luke 8:31).

Acacia
A durable wood readily available in the Sinai Desert and used in the Old Testament tabernacle. Today the gum of the acacia tree is used for commercial and medicinal uses.

Afflict
See *Affliction*.

Affliction
Hardships, calamities and suffering, often lasting a long time. Sometimes imposed by others, sometimes self-imposed and at other times divinely imposed.

Alien
In the Old Testament, a non-Israelite living in Israel, typically in poverty. Later, a stranger away from home.

Anoint
The symbolic act of pouring oil on objects or individuals as a sign of consecration. The name *Messiah* means *the Anointed One*.

Antichrist
Anyone who opposes or rejects God has, to some degree, the spirit of antichrist (1 John 2:18). Also, at the end of the age, the figure who will embody the worst of the spirit of antichrist but who will finally be defeated.

Apostle
Someone sent to represent another; in the New Testament someone who had seen Jesus and been commissioned by him to teach others about him.

Aramaic
The common language in Palestine at the time of Jesus and the early church.

Asherah poles
See *Poles, Asherah*.

Ashtoreth
Female consort of the chief Canaanite god, Baal. The goddess of love, fertility and war. Also known as Ishtar to Babylonians, Aphrodite to Greeks and Venus to Romans. Also called Asherah.

Assembly, Sacred
The gathering of the entire Israelite community for common worship, celebration or repentance. See *Old Testament Feasts* on page 168.

Atonement
Act by which sinners are made "at one" with God—when barriers of sin between God and sinners are removed. The Day of Atonement was an Old Testament annual fast when the high priest entered the Most Holy Place to atone for the sins of the people (Lev. 16). Sacrifices on the Day of Atonement cleansed the whole nation of sin—even unknown transgressions. Later Christ's death made the final atonement for believers, making further sacrifices unnecessary (Heb. 9:23-28).

Avenge
To get back at or punish someone who has done wrong.

B

Baal
The Canaanite fertility god believed to be responsible for germinating crops, increasing flocks and adding children to the community. Best known of the Canaanite gods.

Backsliding
To turn or move away from a relationship with God.

Baptism
A Christian rite symbolizing cleansing from sin and identification with Jesus. Sprinkling, immersion and pouring are three ways Christians today practice water baptism.

Beelzebub
Satan, the prince of demons. In the Old Testament, Baal was a Canaanite deity, whose name was expanded to Beelzebul (meaning *Exalted* or *Prince Baal*).

Birthright
In the Old Testament, special rights given to the firstborn son, including the authority as leader of the family.

Blaspheme
To speak about God or holy things in a careless, false or insulting way.

Blasphemy
See *Blaspheme*.

Block, Stumbling
Anything or anyone that causes someone to sin.

Bloodguilt
The verdict on a person for crimes deserving death.

Breastpiece
A colorful pouch nine inches square, attached to the attire of the Old Testament high priest. Twelve precious stones on the pouch represented the 12 tribes of Israel—so when it hung around the priest's neck, the people could be close to his heart. Inside the breastpiece were the Urim and Thummim (Exodus 28:15,30; See *Urim;* See *Thummim*).

Burnt offering
See *Offering, Burnt*.

Byword
An object of scorn and ridicule, a term of verbal abuse (Job 17:6).

C

Calamus
An aromatic spice cane; its juice was an ingredient in incense offerings (Isaiah 43:24).

Capstone
Either the bottom corner of a building (a foundation stone) or the keystone of an archway (Mark 12:10). It can cause a person to stumble (1 Peter 2:8), or it can fall on someone (Matt. 21:44).

Censer
A container used for burning incense (Rev. 8:3).

Centurion
A Roman army officer in charge of 100 soldiers.

Chaff
(1) After wheat was harvested, the chaff (the seed covering, straw and dust) was blown away from the grain in a process called winnowing. See *Fork, Winnowing.* (2) A word used to describe the wicked who would be separated from the righteous at judgment (Psalm 1:4).

Cherub
A winged, angelic being who exists primarily to glorify God and to vindicate God's holiness against the presumptuous pride of fallen humans. Symbolic attendant marking the place of God's enthronement in his earthly kingdom (Exodus 25:18). The plural of *cherub* is *cherubim*.

Circumcise
See *Circumcision*.

Circumcision
Cutting off the foreskin of the penis—usually on the eighth day after birth (Gen. 17:10-14). It was a

physical reminder of the special, spiritual relationship between God and his chosen people.

Cistern
Covered pits cut into rock or clay to catch and store rainwater (Jer. 14:3). Critical to life in an arid climate, cisterns symbolize security.

Citadel
A tower or building equipped for war, especially one in a city, often thought of as the city's final defense unit.

Collectors, Tax
Those employed by Roman authorities to collect taxes for them. They were notorious for imposing more taxes than were required, skimming off the top to line their own pockets. They were despised by the Jews for collaborating with the Roman government that ruled over them.

Concubine
A woman who belonged to a man in a relationship inferior to that of a wife. Commonly found in ancient cultures where polygamy was practiced, a concubine was often one of the spoils of war—with the primary purpose of bearing children for the man.

Consecrate
To set aside or dedicate for God's use (Exodus 13:2).

Covenant
A mutually binding agreement between two parties. In the Old Testament, God entered into a covenant with Israel. But God alone set the conditions to the agreement. In return for their loyalty and obedience, God promised to protect and love Israel and to give them his presence. The *new covenant* (Heb. 8:7) brought salvation to God's people through the shedding of Jesus' blood.

Cows, Sea
Dugongs (see NIV text note on Exodus 25:5)—marine animals abounding on the coral banks of the Red Sea and in other tropical waters. A dugong can grow to be 11 feet long, with a round head, fish-like tail and flippers for forelimbs. Their appearance is similar to seals.

Cubit
A unit of measurement 18 to 21 inches in length—from the elbow to the tip of the middle finger.

Cyrus
The founder of the Persian empire, Cyrus the Great ruled Persia from 559 to 530 B.C.

D

Day of the Lord
An Old Testament concept describing the time when God would intervene to vindicate the righteous and judge the wicked (Isaiah 2:12). The New Testament links it more specifically to Jesus' second coming (1 Cor. 1:8). The *Day of the Lord* was both a time of salvation and of judgment.

Death
The end of physical life. Spiritual death means separation from God (Eph. 2:1-5). Other uses of the word include: the end of a sinful way of life

(Romans 6:4-8) and the final and irreversible separation from God after judgment (Rev. 20:11-15).

Decapolis
The name of the confederation of ten Gentile cities wrenched from Jewish control by the Roman general Pompey in 63 B.C. All but one were east of the Jordan River. See *Map 9* at the back of this Bible.

Desecrate
To treat without respect or reverence (Lev. 21:12).

Disciple
A student or follower; an adherent to the teachings of a particular teacher or school of thought. In the New Testament, *disciple* usually refers to a follower of Jesus.

Dissipation
Living only for your own pleasure; wasting your life on foolish or evil pleasures.

Divination
Using a human intermediary or inanimate objects, such as the examination of animal entrails, to receive messages from the spirit world.

Dregs
Sediment that forms during the fermentation of wine. When not separated from the wine, dregs caused bitter tasting wine. Used as a picture of undesirable characteristics and the bitterness of God's wrath on the wicked (Psalm 75:8).

Drink offering
See *Offering, Drink*.

Dross
The worthless by-product left over and thrown out after refining precious metals like gold or silver ore. A picture of how those who stray are treated (Psalm 119:119).

E

Edict
An order made by someone with power to enforce it.

Edom
The nation of descendants of Esau, the twin brother of Jacob (Gen. 25:23-28). Located south of the Dead Sea amid the reddish sandstone of the Rift Valley (see *Map 6* at the back of this Bible), Edom was often hostile to Israel (Obad. v. 1).

Elect
Those chosen for a particular relationship or function. The people of God chosen in Christ before the foundation of the world (Eph. 1:4).

Ephod
One of six articles of clothing specified for Israelite priests' uniforms (Exodus 28:4-8), the ephod consisted of a sleeveless garment made of finely twisted linen. In some instances in the Old Testament, the word is used to describe an object of worship (Judges 8:27).

Eternal life
See *Life, Eternal*.

Eunuch
A castrated male who in the ancient Near East was often employed in a governmental position. The term came to designate an officer, whether physically a eunuch or not.

Exile
One who is banished from his or her own country and taken captive to a foreign land. One of the means God used in the Old Testament to punish his people, purging them of their sinful ways.

Extol
To praise highly, to glorify, to laud (Psalm 34:1).

Extortion
Gaining something from someone by force or by some other illegal means.

F

Fear of the Lord
See *Lord, Fear of the*.

Fellowship offering
See *Offering, Fellowship*.

Festival, New Moon
Both a religious and a civil Old Testament festival (1 Samuel 20:5), the New Moon festival was celebrated at the beginning of each month and is often mentioned in the Old Testament together with the Sabbath (Isaiah 1:13).

Firstborn
Oldest son and the possessor of special privileges. In the Old Testament the term often described the privilege and favor God granted to Israel (Exodus 4:22). In the New Testament, Jesus is called the *firstborn* of the Father, the one who rules over all (Heb. 1:6).

Firstfruits
The first ripe crops of the season. The offering of the firstfruits was a gift of the first and best part of the harvest, signifying that all of Israel's sustenance came from God (Exodus 23:19). In the New Testament, the term is applied to Jesus (1 Cor. 15:20) and to believers (James 1:18).

Footstool
A stool for supporting the feet of someone sitting on a throne (2 Chron. 9:18). The Bible depicts God's *footstool* as (1) the earth (Isaiah 66:1), (2) the ark of the covenant (which in the Old Testament represented God's presence among the Israelites (1 Chron. 28:2), (3) the temple (Psalm 99:5) and (4) the defeated enemies of the Messiah (Psalm 110:1).

Fork, Winnowing
A large, wooden fork used in Bible times to toss the threshed grain into the air so the wind would blow away the lighter chaff while the heavier grain dropped back to the ground.

G

Gabriel
An angel whose name means *man of God* or *God is powerful*. He heralded the coming births of John the Baptist (Luke 1:11-20) and Jesus (Luke 1:26).

Genealogy
A list of a person's ancestors or descendants.

Gentile

A term for anyone who is not an Israelite. Jews and Gentiles have been reconciled to God and to each other through Christ (Eph. 2:11-22).

Glory

An essential quality of God's character (Psalm 63:2), his glory is his worthiness. Everything about him testifies that he is worthy to receive praise, honor and respect. In the New Testament, Jesus is revealed to be the *Lord of glory* (1 Cor. 2:8). In the Bible, glory is often associated with brightness or splendor (Luke 2:9).

Glutton

A person who habitually eats too much.

God, Kingdom of

God's rule on earth. Both present and still future. Began with the arrival of Christ and will be consummated when Christ comes back to earth for the second time.

Gospel

Good news—specifically, the good news of salvation through Jesus Christ, who died for our sins and rose again. *Gospel* describes the message of Christianity, as well as the first four books of the New Testament (Matthew, Mark, Luke and John) in which the record of Jesus' life and teaching is found.

Grace

Unmerited favor, unearned benefit, undeserved kindness. God's amazing gift of forgiveness of sins and power to live with dignity in the present and with hope for the future.

Grain offering

See *Offering, Grain*.

Guilt offering

See *Offering, Guilt*.

H

Hades

Greek word referring to the place of the dead, akin to the Hebrew *Sheol*.

Hallelujah

Occurring only four times in the New Testament, *hallelujah* comes from two Hebrew words that mean *praise the Lord* (Rev. 19:1).

Hebrew

(1) The language in which most of the Old Testament was written. (2) Another name for an Israelite; a descendant of Abraham. (3) Sometimes refers to a broader group, including non-Israelites descended from Eber (Gen. 10:21-32)—such as Arameans (descendants of Nahor) and Moabites and Ammonites (descendants of Lot).

Hell

Place of final punishment for the wicked. In the New Testament, the word *hell* typically translates the Greek word *ge[h]enna.* and is used as a metaphor to picture hell. *Ge[h]enna* comes from a Hebrew expression meaning *the Valley of Ben Hinnom,* a deep ravine outside Jerusalem where human sacrifices had at one time been offered to the pagan god, Molech (2 Kings 23:10). See *Topheth.*

Herodians

A group of Jews who opposed Jesus and supported the Herods, a line of Judean kings during Jesus' lifetime. They were supporters of Rome, from which the Herods received their authority.

High places

See *Places, High*.

Holy kiss

See *Kiss, Holy*.

Holy Place

See *Place, Holy*.

Hosts, Starry

The stars and other heavenly bodies, the worship of which is warned against in the Bible (Deut. 4:19).

Hyssop

A plant used in a ritual cleansing ceremony. Its hairy branches were dipped in sacrificial blood, which was then brushed or sprinkled on the object or person being cleansed (Exodus 12:22), symbolizing spiritual cleansing from sin.

I

Idol

Image of a god (Exodus 20:3-4). Anything that takes the place of God or steals our affections from him—often things like our relationships, work or hobbies.

Idolatry

The worship of false gods, sometimes by means of images. Anything that takes us away from the worship of the one true God (Romans 1:18-25).

Incense

Aromatic substances such as frankincense and myrrh burned to make a fragrant smoke. Used as an offering in worship. Can symbolize either prayers (Psalm 141:2) or the presence of God (Exodus 30:1-10).

Intercede

To pray for another person, usually to obtain God's help.

J

Jericho

An ancient city situated several miles west of the Jordan River and north of the Dead Sea. See *Map 4* at the back of this Bible.

Jerusalem

(1) The capital of Israel before it split into two kingdoms in 930 B.C. After the split, it was the capital of the southern kingdom of Judah. (2) The place where Solomon built the temple. (3) Captured by the Babylonians in 597 B.C. and then destroyed by them in 586 B.C., Jerusalem was rebuilt between 538 and 445 B.C. (4) Jewish center of worship during the time of Jesus. See *Zion.*

Jew

Derived from *Judah,* the term originally denoted one belonging to the tribe of Judah and later was applied to all the descendants of Abraham. Other names: Israelites and Hebrews.

Joppa
A seaport located about 35 miles northwest of Jerusalem, known today as Jaffa. See *Map 6* at the back of this Bible.

Jubilee
An Old Testament celebration held every 50 years (Lev. 25:10). During the 49th and 50th years, the land would have lain idle for two consecutive years (Isaiah 37:30), enslaved Israelites were freed and property was returned to its original owners.

Justification
That act of God whereby he places us in a right relationship with him (Romans 5:16); a declaration of innocence or righteousness, a freeing from guilt or blame.

Justify
To erase someone's sins; to declare righteous.

K

Kidron Valley
See *Valley, Kidron*.

Kingdom of God
See *God, Kingdom of*.

Kiss, Holy
A sign of mutual respect and trust; the equivalent of a handshake or hug (2 Cor. 13:12).

L

Lament
A musical or poetic dirge—a song of sorrow, a cry of grief (often a recognition of judgment). The Bible book of Lamentations is composed of five laments.

Legion
A very large number (Mark 5:9). The name of a Roman army division of 6,000 soldiers.

Leprosy
Known today as "Hansen's disease," although the Biblical term included other types of skin diseases as well. Can cause paralysis, deformity and gangrene.

Leviathan
(1) A great marine mammal—possibly a crocodile (see NIV text note on Job 41:1) or a sea serpent. (2) Thought by some to be an ancient mythological dragon that caused eclipses by twisting itself around the sun (Job 3:8). (3) A creature said by ancient mythology to represent the chaotic waters overcome by God at creation (Psalm 74:14; 89:10; See *Rahab*).

Levite
The name given to the descendants of Levi. Given a place of privilege and responsibility among God's people in overseeing worship and in caring for the tabernacle. Only Levites could become priests, but not all Levites were priests.

Life, Eternal
A quality of life that begins the moment someone trusts in Jesus for salvation (John 3:36) and continues after physical death through fellowship with God in life that will never end (Jude v. 21).

Line, Measuring
(1) A rope, string or cord of a specific length used for measuring. (2) Sometimes used to picture God's thorough and calculated punishment of Judah and other nations (2 Kings 21:13), but also used as a symbol of restoration (Zech. 1:16).

Locust
An insect similar to the grasshopper but more aggressive. An army of these insects can devastate entire fields of crops within minutes.

Lord, Fear of the
An attitude of reverence or worship in the presence of God—an attitude of humility and awe more than dread and fright (Prov. 1:7).

Lyre
A harplike instrument made of wood and distinguished by its number of strings (historians say the lyre had about ten strings). Lyres typically had a sound board over which the vibrating strings could resonate.

M

Magicians
Ancient wise men who were expected to foretell the future and influence such events as harvests, droughts and battles (Daniel 2:2). Many claimed to possess occult knowledge.

Man, Son of
An expression found in the Old Testament and used as a self-description of Jesus in the New Testament. Over 90 times Ezekiel is called *son of man* to emphasize his humanity in the presence of Almighty God (Ezek. 2:1). Jesus used this name to show he was the Messiah prophesied by Daniel (Daniel 7:13).

Mandrake
A fragrant flowering plant that grew wild in desert areas. Thought by ancients to possess magical powers, it was used for medicinal purposes and as a charm against evil spirits; it was also credited with aphrodisiac qualities.

Manna
The food God miraculously supplied during the Israelites' 40 years of wilderness wandering (the manna stopped at the time of their first Passover in Canaan). Israelites described its appearance as *white like coriander seed* and its taste as *wafers made with honey* (Exodus 16:31).

Measuring line
See *Line, Measuring*.

Medium
Someone believed to be able to consult with ghosts or spirits; a person through whom the spirit of a dead person would communicate with the living (Isaiah 8:19). The practice was condemned and prohibited in the Old Testament (Deut. 18:10-11).

Meeting, Tent of
Another name for the tabernacle, for it was the place where God showed his presence and met with his people.

Mercy
Compassion or kindness shown to someone instead of severity, especially to someone who doesn't deserve it.

Midwife
A person who helps with the birth of a baby (Gen. 35:17).

Millstone
One of a pair of stones used to crush grain for flour.

Molech
Traditionally understood as the name of a pagan god to whom children were burned in sacrifice (Lev. 18:21).

Most Holy Place
See *Place, Most Holy*.

Myrrh
A fragrant gum extracted from a small tree growing in certain areas of the Middle East. Its oil was used as a spice, as a medicine and as a cosmetic; myrrh was applied to Jesus' body after his burial (John 19:39-40). One of the gifts of the Magi to Jesus after his birth (Matt. 2:11).

Mystery
Among the Greeks, a secret imparted only to the initiated. For Paul in the New Testament, a divine truth once hidden but now revealed in the gospel. The Christian mystery is God's strategy to redeem people through Christ (Eph. 3:2-9)—Jews and Gentiles united in Christ.

N

Nazirite
One who demonstrated total consecration to the Lord by taking a vow of separation and abstinence for the purpose of some special service; the three standard prohibitions were abstaining from grape products, from haircuts and from contact with dead bodies (Num. 6:2-8).

Negev
The area stretching southward from Beersheba in southern Palestine (see *Map 2* at the back of this Bible). It is usually desertlike, but at times there are seasons of rain that leave pools of water (Psalm 126:4).

New Moon festival
See *Festival, New Moon*.

New wine
See *Wine, New*.

O

Offal
The entrails of an animal burned as part of a sin offering (Exodus 29:14).

Offering, Burnt
The most frequent of the sacrifices at the Old Testament sanctuary—offered morning and evening of every day. To make payment for sins, a worshiper voluntarily brought an unblemished animal to the priest and laid his hand on the animal's head to express identification. The priest then killed it and burned it up completely, symbolizing the person's total devotion to God (Lev. 1). See *Old Testament Sacrifices* on page 138.

Offering, Drink
Usually a wine or oil poured out as a sacrifice of dedication to God—part of the regular offerings made every day in connection with the grain offering (Exodus 29:38-41). In the New Testament, it is a picture of expending one's life for the cause of Christ (Phil. 2:17).

Offering, Fellowship
To express gratitude to God, a worshiper sacrificed an unblemished animal on the altar. Part of it was burned, and a portion of it was eaten by the worshiper, symbolizing peace and fellowship with God (Lev. 3). Traditionally called *peace offerings*. See *Old Testament Sacrifices* on page 138.

Offering, Grain
An offering presented as an act of worship (Lev. 2). It was intended simply to remember God's favor and, by remembering, to please him. The worshiper who offered the sacrifice brought prepared loaves of bread, wafers or small cakes to the sanctuary; a portion was consumed by fire and the rest of the offering was eaten by the priests. See *Old Testament Sacrifices* on page 138.

Offering, Guilt
An offering that absolved the worshiper in instances where restitution was required—in cases of theft or cheating, for example. A ram was offered (no substitutes allowed), and complete restitution plus 20 percent was to be paid, satisfying both God and the person wronged. Only guilt offerings eased guilty consciences with restitution for sin. See *Old Testament Sacrifices* on page 138.

Offering, Sin
The Old Testament blood sacrifice required for unintentional sins (Lev. 4:1-35). Sin offerings were made for the whole congregation on all feast days and especially on the Day of Atonement, and they were prescribed for individuals in a number of instances that demanded payment of the penalty for sins. See *Old Testament Sacrifices* on page 138.

Offering, Thank
A type of fellowship offering, the thank offering expressed gratitude to God for deliverance from trouble, healing of sickness, answers to prayer or some other blessing received (Lev. 7:12).

Offering, Wave
A ceremony whereby offerings are dedicated to the Lord—most likely by lifting the object up before the Lord. A number of objects could be the subject of the wave offering, including the breast portion of the fellowship offering (Lev. 7:30).

Oracle
An announcement or message from God. The word often suggests unwelcome news or judgment.

Ordination
An Old Testament ritual signifying the responsibilities and privileges of the Levitical priesthood (Lev. 8:22). The Hebrew word translated *ordination* literally meant *to fill the hand* and probably referred to offerings placed in their hands. Ordination of ministers today has its roots in this Old Testament practice.

P

Parable

A saying or story that drives home a point using illustrations from everyday life; a comparison of two objects for the purpose of teaching. Jesus told many parables during the course of his life on earth.

Patriarch

The father of a family or head of a tribe or race; a forefather of the Israelites (Heb. 7:4).

Peace

The Biblical concept of peace has at its root the meaning of "totality," or "completeness." Important nuances of meaning include such things as "fulfillment," "maturity," "soundness," "wholeness," "harmony," "security," "well-being" and "prosperity." Also connotes absence of war and freedom from disturbance.

Pharisees

A powerful branch of the Jewish religious community during Jesus' time. Considered to be religious experts, this group believed that the oral law of the Jewish faith was as equally authoritative and inspired by God as the Torah, or written law. Consequently, they obeyed very strictly God's laws and all the tradition of interpretation they had established. Jesus reserved some of his harshest criticism for them (Matt. 23).

Place, Holy

Part of the Israelite sanctuaries (tabernacle and temple), located just outside the Most Holy Place. Contained the altar of incense, the table for the bread of the Presence and the lampstand (see *Tabernacle Furnishings* on page 110 and *Temple Furnishings* on page 453).

Place, Most Holy

The inner sanctuary of both the Old Testament tabernacle and the temple, containing the ark of the covenant, the symbol of God's presence. The high priest alone was allowed to enter it once each year on the Day of Atonement (Lev. 16).

Places, High

Places of worship often associated with pagan religious practices, immorality and human sacrifice. Religious objects were placed on the tops of hills to appease pagan gods (Num. 33:52). Generally, Israelites were forbidden to worship God there, and God commanded them to destroy these areas.

Plunder

To rob or loot as an act of war. Used as a noun, plunder refers to the spoils gained through the act of looting.

Poles, Asherah

Wooden poles, perhaps carved in the image of Asherah, Canaanite goddess of love and war, set up in her honor and placed near the altars in Canaanite worship.

Precepts

Commands, usually divine injunctions setting forth human obligations.

Priest

The person appointed to act on behalf of men and women in relation to God. The Old Testament group of male leaders descended from Aaron, who performed religious duties in the temple. The New Testament calls Jesus the great high priest (Heb. 4:14) and the body of Christ a holy priesthood (1 Peter 2:5).

Profane

To make a holy thing impure or defiled by treating it with disrespect or irreverence.

Prophecy

The message of a prophet. Also, a spiritual gift, a supernatural empowering to build up God's family. Those with this gift either proclaimed to God's people new truth from God or challenged them with existing Scriptural truths (1 Cor. 14:1–5).

Prophet

A mouthpiece for God, one who receives a message from God and proclaims it to a specific audience.

Prophetess

A female prophet (Exodus 15:20).

Prostitute, Shrine

A special class of ancient Middle Eastern prostitutes (male and female) used in the fertility cults. They performed sexual acts in the temple of their god as acts of religious devotion (Deut. 23:17).

Purify

To make clean or pure. To be ceremonially pure means to be free from defects that would disqualify someone or something from holy uses or holy acts. To be ethically pure means to show oneself, in thought and conduct, to be a person chosen by God.

Purple

A symbol of wealth and royalty. The most highly prized dye in the ancient world, purple dye was obtained from various shellfish common to Phoenicia (a name that means *land of purple*).

Q

Quail

A small spotted bird similar to the partridge; quail migrated from North Africa through Egypt, Sinai and Palestine. God provided quail along with manna (see *Manna*) as food to sustain the Israelites in their desert wanderings (Exodus 16:13).

R

Rabbi

A title of respect meaning *my master* or *my teacher*, given to teachers of the law (Matt. 23:2–7). Jesus was also addressed as *Rabbi* (Mark 9:5).

Rahab

(1) Old Testament prostitute from Jericho who hid two Hebrew spies and helped them escape danger (Joshua 2:1). (2) A name symbolizing a mythical sea monster that allegedly ruled over the chaos at the time of creation (Psalm 89:10; Isaiah 51:9). See *Leviathan*. (3) A nickname for Egypt (Psalm 87:4; Isaiah 30:7). (4) A symbol of hostility toward God's people.

Redeem

To obtain release by paying a price, to buy back.

Redeemer

One who delivers from bondage or trouble. Applied to family situations where a *kinsman-redeemer* was responsible to protect the interests of needy members of the extended family (Ruth 3:9). Applied to God as the protector and deliverer of Israel (Isaiah 41:14). Though Jesus is not specifically called "Redeemer" in the New Testament, he is the one in whom believers have redemption (Eph. 1:7).

Redemption

Deliverance and freedom—described in the New Testament as freedom from the penalty of sin by payment of a ransom. Through his death on the cross Jesus paid the ransom for us (Romans 3:24) and set us free.

Remnant

(1) The remaining part or group after destruction or dispersal (2 Kings 19:30–31). (2) Those who escape God's judgment because of God's grace (Romans 11:5). (3) A symbol of hope pointing toward the great multitude that one day will stand saved before God (Rev. 7).

Repent

To consciously turn from sin to God; to be sorry for what you have done and to resolve not to do it again.

Repentance

A profound change of mind from sin-centeredness to God-centeredness. Though repentance may represent only regret or remorse over a past thought or action, in its fullest sense it connotes a change of orientation involving a deliberate redirection for the future (Acts 26:20).

Reproach

To rebuke or chide, to blame or accuse. Used as a noun, a source of disgrace or shame, an expression of disapproval or rebuke (Psalm 79:4).

Resurrection

The act of coming back to life after being dead. Described as applying to both the righteous and the wicked (Daniel 12:2). Jesus' resurrection (Matt. 28:1–10), along with his death, is considered essential to the salvation of believers (Romans 4:25) and guarantees our resurrection (1 Cor. 15:12–19).

Retribution

Deserved punishment for doing wrong, but also deserved reward for doing good.

Revelation

The act of disclosure or making known; more particularly, God's self-unveiling, his deliberate disclosure of true knowledge of himself and his purposes and actions on our behalf (Eph. 1:17).

Revere

See *Reverence*.

Reverence

An attitude of deep respect, honor and deference. Our worthy response to God's majesty and holiness. From an attitude of reverence naturally flow obedient actions (2 Cor. 7:1). See *Lord, Fear of the*.

Righteous

See *Righteousness*.

Righteousness

The fulfillment of the demands of a relationship. God brings believers into a right relation with him, erasing their guilt and crediting righteousness to them (Romans 3:21–22) and helping them to be devoted to the service of what God says is right (Romans 6:11–13).

Ring, Signet

A ring containing a design or a name of someone in authority and used to make an impression in soft clay or wax. Used to authorize official documents. A symbol of authority (Gen. 41:42).

S

Sabbath

The Hebrew weekly day of rest and worship observed on the seventh day of the week. It began at sunset on Friday and ended at sunset on Saturday.

Sackcloth

A coarse material, dark in color, usually made of goat's hair. Worn especially during times of mourning or social protest. A symbol of grief and mourning.

Sacred assembly

See *Assembly, Sacred*.

Sacred stones

See *Stones, Sacred*.

Sacrifice

A gift or offering to God (Exodus 12:27). See *Old Testament Sacrifices* on page 138. Something offered to God to atone for sin. Jesus is the ultimate sacrifice, which satisfies God's wrath toward humankind (1 John 4:10). Believers are to live in such a way that they offer themselves to God as *living sacrifices* (Romans 12:1).

Sadducees

A group of leaders in the Jewish religious community opposed to both the teachings of the Pharisees and Jesus. During the first century A.D. they held considerable political power and controlled the highest Jewish court in the land, the Sanhedrin. They denied the doctrine of the resurrection of the body (Mark 12:18) and the existence of angels and spirits (Acts 23:8).

Saints

Those dedicated to God and set apart for his service (Phil. 1:1). All who believe in Jesus, regardless of their character or spiritual maturity.

Salvation

Deliverance from danger or death; especially deliverance from all that separates people from God (Titus 2:12).

Sanctification

Act of God by which believers become more and more conformed to Christ's image (1 Thessalonians 4:3).

Sanctify

To make holy; to set apart (John 17:17).

Sanhedrin

The highest Jewish authority in Palestine prior to A.D. 70. This court, composed of 70 members and the high priest as president, had complete control

over the religious affairs of Israel and had the final say-so in the interpretation of Mosaic Law. It also governed civil affairs and tried certain criminal cases under the authority of the Romans; it could not, however, impose capital punishment (John 18:31).

Satrap
An official who ruled over a major division of the Persian empire (Ezra 8:36).

Scepter
A staff or pole the king held as a symbol of his royal authority.

Sea Cows
See Cows, Sea.

Seer
A person who prophesies future events. A prophet. One who speaks the word of God (1 Samuel 9:9). See Prophet.

Selah
Generally believed to be a musical cue or instruction for the performer. Some think it may have been a call for a pause or interlude or for a brief liturgical response by the congregation.

Shekel
The basic weight used in ancient Semitic systems of measurement. The exact weight of a shekel is not known. Some estimate it weighed between 11.3 and 11.47 grams. See Table of Weights and Measures on page 1739.

Shrine prostitute
See Prostitute, Shrine.

Siege works
See Works, Siege.

Signet ring
See Ring, Signet.

Sin offering
See Offering, Sin.

Son of man
See Man, Son of.

Sorcery
The use of means believed to have supernatural power to produce or prevent a particular result; the craft of controlling or using such means of supernatural powers. Included in the list of magical arts condemned and prohibited in the Old Testament (Deut. 18:10).

Soul
Represents primarily the life force of the person; also the inner life, encompassing desires and emotions. The part of a person that does not die (Rev. 6:9).

Starry hosts
See Hosts, starry.

Stones, Sacred
Stone monuments used in idol worship, often engraved with writing and likely intended to be representations of the pagan deity (2 Kings 3:2). Explicitly forbidden to the Israelites (Lev. 26:1-2).

Stronghold
A place of refuge or defense, such as a tower, fortress or fortified hilltop from which an enemy could be resisted. A metaphor for refuge and security (Psalm 27:1).

Stumbling block
See Block, Stumbling.

T

Tabernacle
A tent used by the Israelites as a place of worship while they were on the move in the desert (Exodus 25:9). Its basic structure was 15 feet wide by 45 feet long by 15 feet high, a space about half the size of a football field. The holy place of God's presence among his people, the tabernacle was also called the Tent of Meeting (see Meeting, Tent of). Also see Tabernacle Furnishings on page 110.

Tax collectors
See Collectors, Tax.

Tent of Meeting
See Meeting, Tent of.

Tetrarch
Originally a ruler over a fourth of a region; later used of a number of rulers (lower in rank than kings) who depended on Rome for power to govern land conquered by the Romans.

Thank offering
See Offering, Thank.

Thummim
Together with Urim, some sort of devices by which an Old Testament priest could discern God's will (Exodus 28:30). They were possibly sacred lots or stones cast like dice to determine a yes or no answer from God.

Tithe
One-tenth of one's income. The dedication of a tenth of agricultural products, livestock or other goods to the worship of a deity or to the persons who served in the worship of the deity. In the Old Testament, the Israelites devoted a tithe to support the Levites (Num. 18:21), freeing them to serve the Lord. Some suggest that the New Testament standard for giving for the Lord's work is an amount proportionate to one's income (1 Cor. 16:2).

Topheth
A place in the Valley of Ben Hinnom just outside Jerusalem, where apostate Israelites sacrificed children to the pagan god, Molech (Jer. 7:31). Used as a trash dump with perpetual fires that symbolized judgment. Topheth may derive from the Aramaic word for fireplace. See Hell.

U

Uncircumcised
(1) Males who have not had a circle of skin cut off at the front end of the penis (Gen. 17:14). See Circumcision. (2) Figuratively, a heart that is unresponsive is said to be uncircumcised (Acts 7:51), that is, not consecrated to the Lord. (3) Gentiles were called uncircumcised (Eph. 2:11), but Paul said real circumcision is circumcision of the heart (Romans 2:29).

Unclean
Ritually defiled or polluted, for which various rituals of cleansing were prescribed (Lev. 5:2). By the

blood of Jesus, *unclean* sinners are cleansed (Heb. 10:22) and enabled to live a fruitful Christian life (2 Peter 1:5-9).

Uncleanness
See *Unclean*.

Urim
Together with Thummim, some sort of devices by which an Old Testament priest could discern God's will (Exodus 28:30). They were possibly sacred lots or stones cast like dice to determine a yes or no answer from God.

Usury
Interest, often excessive, charged on money lent (Psalm 15:5).

V

Valley, Kidron
Just east of Jerusalem, between the city and the Mount of Olives (see *Map 8* at the back of this Bible). Pagan relics were destroyed there under Asa, Hezekiah and Josiah (2 Kings 23:4–6).

Vision
A supernatural revelation, message or insight communicated through images seen only within a person's mind or spirit. The pictures seen in a vision may illustrate spiritual truths or future events (Isaiah 1:1).

Vow
A solemn, voluntary promise made to God to perform some action or refrain from performing some action in return for some hoped-for benefits (Judges 11:30–31).

W

Watchman
Someone on a tower or a high point entrusted to watch for approaching messengers or enemies (Ezek. 3:17).

Watchtower
A tower where guards could watch for danger or where a group of people could find protection from invaders.

Wave offering
See *Offering, Wave*.

Wine, New
The newly pressed juice of the grape. It contains less flavor and less alcohol because of the short aging process.

Winepress
A large vat or trough where several people could work together stomping on grapes to squeeze out the juice so it could be drained off and collected.

Wineskin
A leather container used to store wine (Matt. 9:17).

Winnowing fork
See *Fork, Winnowing*.

Witchcraft
A title linked with the practice of predicting the future by interpreting omens, examining livers of sacrificed animals, and contacting the dead—among other techniques. The Old Testament law prohibited these occultic and magical practices (Deut. 18:9-12).

Works, Siege
Military equipment used in capturing a walled city. Assyrian art shows wheeled battering rams and huge, wheeled towers packed with archers. Soldiers pushed these towers against the wall and used them as protected ladders.

Y

Yeast
(1) A substance that causes bread to rise—often by putting a bit of dough from an earlier batch in the flour, which fermented the entire loaf of bread. (2) A symbol of the pervasiveness of the kingdom of heaven (Matt. 13:33). (3) A symbol of undesirable teaching (Matt. 16:6). (4) A symbol of the pervasiveness of evil (1 Cor. 5:6–7).

Yoke
(1) A piece of timber or a heavy wooden pole formed to fit over the necks of animals (often two oxen) and connected to a plow or cart. (2) A figurative description of slavery and oppression (1 Kings 12:4); in contrast to the heavy "yoke" of the law (Gal. 5:1), the *yoke* of Jesus is easy to bear (Matt. 11:29–30).

Z

Zeal
Impassioned devotion to a person or a cause.

Zion
One of the hills on which Jerusalem stood. Often used to refer to the temple or Jerusalem as a whole (Psalm 48).

The index to subjects will help you find information on a variety of subjects covered in the notes of *The Quest Study Bible*. References to articles are indicated by **A**. References to book introductions are indicated by **I**. References to Scripture Links are indicated by **SL**.

A

AIDS, 2 Samuel 12:14–15 (p. 417 **A**)

Abandonment, Ezra 10:3 (p. 641 **A**)

Abortion, Exodus 21:22–23 (p. 105); Psalms 139:13–16 (p. 855 **A**); Jeremiah 20:17 (p. 1071)

Abuse (physical), Genesis 16:9 (p. 21); Exodus 20:4–5 (p. 102); Isaiah 50:4–6 (p. 1011)

Addiction, Proverbs 5:22–23 (p. 871); Jeremiah 13:23 (p. 1061); Mark 9:43–47 (p. 1396)

Adoption, Genesis 15:2 (p. 19); 41:51–52 (p. 61); 48:5 (p. 70); 50:23 (p. 75); Exodus 2:10 (p. 78); Deuteronomy 21:17 (p. 263); Ephesians 1:5 (p. 1613)
  Spiritual, Genesis 6:2 (p. 9); Psalms 2:7 (p. 730)

Adultery, Genesis 35:22 (p. 50); Numbers 5:31 (p. 186); Proverbs 2:22 (p. 867); 5:3–10 (p. 871 **A**); 5:22–23 (p. 871); 23:27 (p. 898); 31:3 (p. 909); Ezekiel 23:25 (p. 1169); Matthew 19:1–9 (p. 1361); Mark 10:1–12 (p. 1397)
  Spiritual, Ezekiel 6:9 (p. 1145); Hosea 4:12 (p. 1237 **A**)

Advice, 1 Chronicles 21:3–4 (p. 564); Proverbs (p. 864 **I**); 15:22 (p. 886); Daniel 6:2 (p. 1220)

Alcohol use, Genesis 9:22–24 (p. 13); 9:25 (p. 13); Leviticus 10:9 (p. 147); Esther 1:8 (p. 666); Psalms 104:14–15 (p. 823); 116:13 (p. 836); Proverbs 20:1 (p. 893); 23:29–35 (p. 898); Hosea 4:11 (p. 1237); Joel 1:5 (p. 1250); Luke 1:15 (p. 1414); 1 Timothy 5:23 (p. 1645)

Altars, Genesis 12:7–8 (p. 17); 33:20 (p. 48); Joshua 8:31 (p. 295); 2 Kings 16:10 (p. 510); Amos 3:14 (p. 1260); Revelation 6:9 (p. 1717); 16:7 (p. 1726)

Ambition, Genesis 11:4 (p. 15); Numbers 16:3 (p. 203); Judges 18:20 (p. 346); Jeremiah 45:5 (p. 1107); Matthew 20:20–21 (p. 1362); 1 Corinthians 7:17,20,26 (p. 1578)

Angel of the Lord, Judges 2:1,4 (p. 321); 6:11,14 (p. 327); Psalms 34:7 (p. 756); Isaiah 31:8–9 (p. 980); Ezekiel 40:3 (p. 1195); Zechariah 12:8 (p. 1319)

Angels, Exodus 23:20–23 (p. 107); 2 Chronicles 32:21 (p. 620); Job 33:23–24 (p. 715); Psalms 29:1 (p. 751); Daniel 8:16 (p. 1225); 10:12 (p. 1228); Luke 1:19 (p. 1414); Acts 6:15 (p. 1513); 1 Corinthians 6:2–3 (p. 1577); Hebrews 1:7 (p. 1660); 2 Peter 2:4 (p. 1693); Jude v. 6 (p. 1707)
  Guardian, Psalms 91:11 (p. 813); Ezekiel 9:1–2 (p. 1148); Matthew 18:8 (p. 1359); Acts 12:15 (p. 1523)

Anger, 1 Chronicles 13:11 (p. 555); Job 15:13 (p. 694 **A**); 32:2–5 (p. 713); 32:19 (p. 714); Proverbs 14:29 (p. 885 **A**); Daniel 2:5 (p. 1212); Nahum (p. 1287 **I**); Acts 15:39 (p. 1529); Ephesians 4:26 (p. 1616); James 1:19–20 (p. 1678)

Antichrist, 2 Thessalonians 2:3–12 (p. 1639 **A**); 1 John 2:18 (p. 1698)

Apostles, Luke 6:13 (p. 1425); Acts 1:26 (p. 1505); 8:1 (p. 1516); 15:19–21 (p. 1528); 1 Corinthians 9:15 (p. 1580); 12:28 (p. 1585); 15:8 (p. 1587); 2 Corinthians 12:12 (p. 1602); Galatians 1:1 (p. 1605)

Arguments, Job 18:2 (p. 697); Acts 15:39 (p. 1529)

Ark of the covenant, Exodus 16:34 (p. 99); 25:10–22 (p. 109); Numbers 4:5 (p. 183); 7:89 (p. 191); Joshua 6:9 (p. 291); 1 Samuel 4:5,7,10 (p. 363); 2 Samuel 6:7 (p. 409 **A**); 1 Kings 8:1–6 (p. 455); 8:9 (p. 455); 1 Chronicles 13:9–10 (p. 555); 13:10,14 (p. 555 **A**); 15:2 (p. 556); 2 Chronicles 35:3 (p. 624)

Armageddon, Zechariah 12:3 (p. 1318); Revelation 16:16 (p. 1726 **A**); 19:19 (p. 1731)

Assassination, Judges 3:21 (p. 323); 1 Kings 2:32 (p. 445)

Atonement, Isaiah 27:8–9 (p. 973); 53:5 (p. 1015); Ezekiel 16:63 (p. 1157); John 1:29 (p. 1467); Romans 3:25 (p. 1554)

Attitude, Genesis 4:5–7 (p. 7); Psalms 73:3–5 (p. 793 **A**); 77:12 (p. 797 **A**); 81:11 (p. 804); 86:11 (p. 807 **A**); Ecclesiastes 11:10 (p. 924); Isaiah 1:11–14 (p. 938); Jeremiah 17:10 (p. 1067); Joel 2:13 (p. 1252)

B

Baptism, Matthew 3:6 (p. 1335); 3:11 (p. 1335); Mark 1:4 (p. 1382); 1:8 (p. 1382); Luke 12:50 (p. 1442); John 3:23–25 (p. 1469); Acts 8:14–17 (p. 1517); 19:5 (p. 1534); Romans 6:3–5 (p. 1557); 1 Corinthians 10:2 (p. 1581); Hebrews 10:22 (p. 1670); 1 Peter 3:21 (p. 1688)

Becoming Christ's disciples, Matthew 4:20 (p. 1337); 8:20 (p. 1343); 16:24 (p. 1358); 28:19 (p. 1379); Mark 1:16–17 (p. 1383); 8:34 (p. 1395); 10:21 (p. 1398); Luke 6:13 (p. 1425); 9:23 (p. 1434); 9:57–62 (p. 1435); John 1:40–42 (p. 1467); 8:51 (p. 1480); Ro-

D

Kingdom of heaven, Matthew 4:17 (p. 1337); 13:24 (p. 1352)

Kings, Deuteronomy 17:15 (p. 259); 1 Samuel 8:5–9 (p. 367**A**); 10:24 (p. 370); 1 Kings 12:16 (p. 465); 2 Kings 11:12 (p. 503); 23:34 (p. 523); 25:30 (p. 527-530**A**); 2 Chronicles 25:2 (p. 609**A**); Ezekiel 28:2 (p. 1177); Daniel 3:13–14 (p. 1215)

Kings' income, 2 Chronicles 9:13–14 (p. 591)

Kosher, Genesis 7:2–3 (p. 10); 9:4 (p. 12); 32:32 (p. 47); Leviticus 11:4–41 (p. 148**A**); Deuteronomy 14:3 (p. 255); Daniel 1:8,12 (p. 1211)

L

Languages, Genesis 10:25 (p. 14); 11:1 (p. 15); Acts 21:40 (p. 1539)

Last days, Isaiah 2:2 (p. 939); 24:18–20 (p. 970); Joel 2:30–32 (p. 1254); Micah 4:1 (p. 1280); Acts 2:19–20 (p. 1506); 1 Corinthians 7:29 (p. 1579); 2 Thessalonians 2:2 (p. 1638); 2 Timothy 3:1 (p. 1649); Hebrews 9:26 (p. 1669); 1 Peter 4:7 (p. 1688)

Lawlessness, Deuteronomy 7:22 (p. 247); Judges (p. 319**I**); 21:10–11 (p. 351); Proverbs 29:18 (p. 907)

Laws, Exodus 18:15–16 (p. 100); Numbers 27:5–11 (p. 221); Daniel 6:8 (p. 1221)

Laying on of hands, Acts 13:3 (p. 1524); 2 Timothy 1:6 (p. 1648)

Laziness, Proverbs 6:6–11 (p. 872**A**); 2 Thessalonians 3:6–13 (p. 1639)

Leaders

Ability, Judges 6:25 (p. 328); 12:8,11,13 (p. 339); 13:25 (p. 340); 14:6 (p. 340); 1 Samuel 10:9–11 (p. 370); 11:6 (p. 371); 2 Kings 2:9 (p. 487); Isaiah 45:1 (p. 1002)

Choosing, Genesis 49:10–12 (p. 72); Exodus 6:14–27 (p. 83); Deuteronomy 16:18 (p. 258); 31:3 (p. 276); Judges 11:4–6 (p. 336); 1 Chronicles 5:2 (p. 540); 12:2 (p. 553); Isaiah 3:6 (p. 941); Hosea 8:4 (p. 1241); 1 Timothy 3:2–7 (p. 1644); 5:24–25 (p. 1646)

Preparation, Exodus 17:9 (p. 99); Deuteronomy 34:9 (p. 284); 1 Kings 3:7 (p. 447); 19:19 (p. 478); Proverbs 30:21–23 (p. 909)

Responsibility, Jeremiah 23:1 (p. 1074); Ezekiel 44:20–23 (p. 1203); Malachi 2:3 (p. 1324); James 3:1 (p. 1679)

Wicked, Job 34:29–30 (p. 717); Ezekiel 11:3 (p. 1149); Hosea (p. 1233**I**); Zephaniah (p. 1299**I**)

Leadership, Nehemiah 3:1–32 (p. 647**A**); Proverbs 30:29–31 (p. 909); Ecclesiastes 10:16–17 (p. 923); Matthew 20:26–28 (p. 1363); Luke 22:24–26 (p. 1458)

Life

After death (Old Testament), Numbers 20:24 (p. 209); 1 Samuel 28:19 (p. 397); 2 Samuel 12:23 (p. 417); Psalms 6:5 (p. 733); 17:15 (p. 741); 30:9 (p. 752); 49:15 (p. 771); Proverbs 2:18 (p. 867);

Ecclesiastes 9:10 (p. 922); 12:7 (p. 925)

Principles, Proverbs 3:1–4 (p. 868**A**)

Source, Genesis 2:7 (p. 4); Job 27:3 (p. 707); Psalms 104:30 (p. 823); Ecclesiastes 12:7 (p. 925)

Unfair, Genesis 18:25 (p. 24); 2 Samuel 21:6,9,14 (p. 432**A**); Job 1:13–19 (p. 679**A**); 34:19 (p. 716**A**); Psalms 73:3–5 (p. 793**A**); Ecclesiastes 2:26 (p. 914); 4:13–16 (p. 916)

Value of, 2 Kings 11:1–2 (p. 502); Job 3:10–16 (p. 681); Ecclesiastes 12:6 (p. 925)

Without God, Ecclesiastes 1:2 (p. 912**A**); 6:12 (p. 918)

Lifespan, Genesis 5:5 (p. 8); 6:3 (p. 9); Numbers 33:39 (p. 230); 2 Kings 20:2–3 (p. 517); Job 7:6 (p. 685); Psalms 90:5–6 (p. 812); 91:16 (p. 813); Ecclesiastes 11:9 (p. 924); Isaiah 38:10–14 (p. 991); 65:20 (p. 1033); Jeremiah 25:11–12 (p. 1078); Luke 13:6–9 (p. 1442)

Lifestyle, Job 2:11–13 (p. 680); 4:1 (p. 682**A**); Psalms 101:4 (p. 819); Proverbs 10:16 (p. 877); 21:17 (p. 895); 23:15 (p. 898**A**); Ezekiel 18:24 (p. 1160**A**); Mark 8:15 (p. 1394); Romans 14:1 (p. 1568); 1 John 2:6 (p. 1697); Revelation 18:4 (p. 1728)

Light, Genesis 1:14–16 (p. 2); Psalms 13:3 (p. 738); 112:4 (p. 833); 119:105 (p. 842); Isaiah 42:6 (p. 997); 58:8,10 (p. 1023); 60:3 (p. 1025); 1 John 1:5 (p. 1697)

Loans, Exodus 22:25 (p. 106); Leviticus 25:36–37 (p. 171); Deuteronomy 23:19 (p. 266); 24:10–13 (p. 266); Nehemiah 5:10–11 (p. 650); Proverbs 6:1–5 (p. 871); 22:7 (p. 896); 22:26 (p. 897)

Loneliness, Psalms 42:3–4 (p. 765); 102:6–7 (p. 820); 102:16–18 (p. 821)

Looking back, Ecclesiastes 7:10 (p. 918)

Looting, Joshua 8:2 (p. 294); 2 Samuel 8:11–12 (p. 413); 2 Kings 14:8 (p. 506); 2 Chronicles 25:10 (p. 610); Esther 9:10,15 (p. 675)

Lord's Supper, Luke 22:19–20 (p. 1458); 1 Corinthians 11:20–22 (p. 1583)

Love

For God, Numbers 30:2 (p. 224); Deuteronomy (p. 235**I**); Psalms 37:4 (p. 759); 69:9 (p. 788); 112:2–8 (p. 833**A**); 130:5–6 (p. 849); Luke 14:26 (p. 1445**A**); John 21:15–17 (p. 1501); Romans 13:10 (p. 1567); Hebrews 10:6,8 (p. 1669); Revelation 2:4 (p. 1711)

For others, Matthew 5:48 (p. 1340); John 13:34–35 (p. 1490); 15:12–14,17 (p. 1492); Romans 12:18 (p. 1566); 12:20 (p. 1566); 13:10 (p. 1567); 1 Corinthians 1:7 (p. 1573); 3:2 (p. 1574); 13:1–3 (p. 1585); 1 John 4:16 (p. 1700)

Loyalty, Deuteronomy (p. 235**I**); 1 Kings 11:17–19 (p. 463); 2 Chronicles 11:13–14 (p. 594); 11:16 (p. 594); Psalms 16:4 (p. 740); 84:11 (p. 806); Proverbs 17:17 (p. 889**A**)

Luck, Ecclesiastes 9:11–12 (p. 922)

Lust, 2 Samuel 13:15 (p. 419)

Lying, Exodus 1:19–20 (p. 77); 1 Samuel 21:2

INDEX TO IN-TEXT MAPS

The NIV Concordance, created by Edward W. Goodrick and John R. Kohlenberger III, has been developed specifically for use with the New International Version. Like all concordances, it is a special index which contains an alphabetical listing of words used in the Bible text. By looking up key words, readers can find verses and passages for which they remember a word or two but not their location.

This concordance contains 2,000 word entries, with some 13,000 Scripture references. Each word entry is followed by the Scripture references in which that particular word is found, as well as by a brief excerpt from the surrounding context. The first letter of the entry word is italicized to conserve space and to allow for a longer context excerpt. Variant spellings due to number and tense and compound forms follow the entry in parentheses, and direct the reader to check other forms of that word in locating a passage.

This concordance contains a number of "block entries," which highlight some of the key events and characteristics in the lives of certain Bible figures. The descriptive phrases replace the brief context surrounding each occurrence of the name. In those instances where more than one Bible character has the same name, that name is placed under one block entry, and each person is given a number (1), (2), etc. Insignificant names are not included.

Word or block entries marked with an asterisk (*) list every verse in the Bible in which the word appears.

This concordance is a valuable tool for Bible study. While one of its key purposes is to help the reader find forgotten references to verses, it can also be used to do word studies and to locate and trace biblical themes. Be sure to use this concordance as more than just a verse finder. Whenever you look up a verse, aim to discover the intended meaning of the verse in context. Give special attention to the flow of thought from the beginning of the passage to the end.

GENESIS	Ge	NAHUM	Na
EXODUS	Ex	HABAKKUK	Hab
LEVITICUS	Lev	ZEPHANIAH	Zep
NUMBERS	Nu	HAGGAI	Hag
DEUTERONOMY	Dt	ZECHARIAH	Zec
JOSHUA	Jos	MALACHI	Mal
JUDGES	Jdg	MATTHEW	Mt
RUTH	Ru	MARK	Mk
1 SAMUEL	1Sa	LUKE	Lk
2 SAMUEL	2Sa	JOHN	Jn
1 KINGS	1Ki	ACTS	Ac
2 KINGS	2Ki	ROMANS	Ro
1 CHRONICLES	1Ch	1 CORINTHIANS	1Co
2 CHRONICLES	2Ch	2 CORINTHIANS	2Co
EZRA	Ezr	GALATIANS	Gal
NEHEMIAH	Ne	EPHESIANS	Eph
ESTHER	Est	PHILIPPIANS	Php
JOB	Job	COLOSSIANS	Col
PSALMS	Ps	1 THESSALONIANS	1Th
PROVERBS	Pr	2 THESSALONIANS	2Th
ECCLESIASTES	Ecc	1 TIMOTHY	1Ti
SONG OF SONGS	SS	2 TIMOTHY	2Ti
ISAIAH	Isa	TITUS	Tit
JEREMIAH	Jer	PHILEMON	Phm
LAMENTATIONS	La	HEBREWS	Heb
EZEKIEL	Eze	JAMES	Jas
DANIEL	Da	1 PETER	1Pe
HOSEA	Hos	2 PETER	2Pe
JOEL	Joel	1 JOHN	1Jn
AMOS	Am	2 JOHN	2Jn
OBADIAH	Ob	3 JOHN	3Jn
JONAH	Jnh	JUDE	Jude
MICAH	Mic	REVELATION	Rev

AARON
Priesthood of (Ex 28:1; Nu 17; Heb 5:1-4; 7), garments (Ex 28; 39), consecration (Ex 29), ordination (Lev 8).

Spokesman for Moses (Ex 4:14-16, 27-31; 7:1-2). Supported Moses' hands in battle (Ex 17:8-13). Built golden calf (Ex 32; Dt 9:20). Talked against Moses (Nu 12). Priesthood opposed (Nu 16); staff budded (Nu 17). Forbidden to enter land (Nu 20:1-12). Death (Nu 20:22-29; 33:38-39).

ABANDON
Dt   4:31 he will not a or destroy you
1Ti   4: 1 in later times some will a the faith

ABBA
Ro   8:15 And by him we cry, "A, Father."
Gal   4: 6 the Spirit who calls out, "A, Father

ABEL
Second son of Adam (Ge 4:2). Offered proper sacrifice (Ge 4:4; Heb 11:4). Murdered by Cain (Ge 4:8; Mt 23:35; Lk 11:51; 1Jn 3:12).

ABHORS
Pr   11: 1 The Lord a dishonest scales,

ABIGAIL
Wife of Nabal (1Sa 25:30); pled for his life with David (1Sa 25:14-35). Became David's wife (1Sa 25:36-42).

ABIJAH
Son of Rehoboam; king of Judah (1Ki 14:31-15:8; 2Ch 12:16-14:1).

ABILITY (ABLE)
Ezr   2:69 According to their a they gave
2Co   1: 8 far beyond our a to endure,
          8: 3 were able, and even beyond their a.

ABIMELECH
1. King of Gerar who took Abraham's wife Sarah, believing her to be his sister (Ge 20). Later made a covenant with Abraham (Ge 21:22-33).

2. King of Gerar who took Isaac's wife Rebekah, believing her to be his sister (Ge 26:1-11). Later made a covenant with Isaac (Ge 26:12-31).

ABLE (ABILITY ENABLE ENABLED ENABLES)
Eze   7:19 and gold will not be a to save them
Da   3:17 the God we serve is a to save us
Ro   8:39 will be a to separate us
        14: 4 for the Lord is a to make him stand
      16:25 to him who is a to establish you
2Co   9: 8 God is a to make all grace abound
Eph   3:20 him who is a to do immeasurably
2Ti   1:12 and am convinced that he is a
       3:15 which are a to make you wise
Heb   7:25 he is a to save completely
Jude   :24 To him who is a to keep you
Rev   5: 5 He is a to open the scroll

ABOLISH
Mt   5:17 that I have come to a the Law

ABOMINATION
Da   11:31 set up the a that causes desolation.

ABOUND (ABOUNDING)
2Co   9: 8 able to make all grace a to you,
Php   1: 9 that your love may a more

ABOUNDING (ABOUND)
Ex   34: 6 slow to anger, a in love
Ps   86: 5 a in love to all who call to you.

ABRAHAM
Covenant relation with the Lord (Ge 12:1-3; 13:14-17; 15; 17; 22:15-18; Ex 2:24; Ne 9:8; Ps 105; Mic 7:20; Lk 1:68-75; Ro 4; Heb 6:13-15).

Called from Ur, via Haran, to Canaan (Ge 12:1; Ac 7:2-4; Heb 11:8-10). Moved to Egypt, nearly lost Sarah to Pharaoh (Ge 12:10-20). Divided the land with Lot (Ge 13). Saved Lot from four kings (Ge 14:1-16); blessed by Melchizedek (Ge 14:17-20; Heb 7:1-20). Declared righteous by faith (Ge 15:6; Ro 4:3; Gal 3:6-9). Fathered Ishmael by Hagar (Ge 16).

Name changed from Abram (Ge 17:5; Ne 9:7). Circumcised (Ge 17; Ro 4:9-12). Entertained three visitors (Ge 18); promised a son by Sarah (Ge 18:9-15; 17:16). Moved to Gerar; nearly lost Sarah to Abimelech (Ge 20). Fathered Isaac by Sarah (Ge 21:1-7; Ac 7:8; Heb 11:11-12); sent away Hagar and Ishmael (Ge 21:8-21; Gal 4:22-30). Tested by offering Isaac (Ge 22; Heb 11:17-19; Jas 2:21-24). Sarah died; bought field of Ephron for burial (Ge 23). Secured wife for Isaac (Ge 24). Death (Ge 25:7-11).

ABSALOM
Son of David by Maacah (2Sa 3:3; 1Ch 3:2). Killed Amnon for rape of his sister Tamar; banished by David (2Sa 13). Returned to Jerusalem; received by David (2Sa 14). Rebelled against David; seized kingdom (2Sa 15-17). Killed (2Sa 18).

ABSTAIN (ABSTAINS)
1Pe   2:11 to a from sinful desires,

ABSTAINS* (ABSTAIN)
Ro   14: 6 thanks to God; and he who a,

ABUNDANCE (ABUNDANT)
Lk   12:15 consist in the a of his possessions."
Jude   : 2 peace and love be yours in a.

ABUNDANT (ABUNDANCE)
Dt   28:11 will grant you a prosperity—
Ps 145:   7 will celebrate your a goodness
Pr   28:19 works his land will have a food,
Ro   5:17 who receive God's a provision

ACCEPT (ACCEPTED ACCEPTS)
Ex   23: 8 "Do not a a bribe,
Pr   10: 8 The wise in heart a commands,
     19:20 Listen to advice and a instruction,
Ro   15: 7 A one another, then, just
Jas   1:21 humbly a the word planted in you,

ACCEPTED (ACCEPT)
Lk   4:24 "no prophet is a in his hometown.

ACCEPTS (ACCEPT)
Ps   6: 9 the Lord a my prayer.
Jn   13:20 whoever a anyone I send a me;

ACCOMPANY
Mk   16:17 these signs will a those who believe
Heb   6: 9 your case—things that a salvation.

ACCOMPLISH
Isa   55:11 but will a what I desire

ACCORD
Nu   24:13 not do anything of my own a,
Jn   10:18 but I lay it down of my own a.
     12:49 For I did not speak of my own a,

ACCOUNT (ACCOUNTABLE)
Mt   12:36 to give a on the day of judgment
Ro   14:12 each of us will give an a of himself
Heb   4:13 of him to whom we must give a.

ACCOUNTABLE (ACCOUNT)
Eze 33: 6 but I will hold the watchman a
Ro   3:19 and the whole world held a to God.

ACCUSATION (ACCUSE)
1Ti   5:19 Do not entertain an a

ACCUSATIONS (ACCUSE)
2Pe   2:11 do not bring slanderous a

ACCUSE (ACCUSATION ACCUSATIONS)
Pr   3:30 Do not a a man for no reason—
Lk   3:14 and don't a people falsely—

ACHAN*
Sin at Jericho caused defeat at Ai; stoned (Jos 7; 22:20; 1Ch 2:7).

ACHE*
Pr   14:13 Even in laughter the heart may a,

ACKNOWLEDGE
Mt   10:32 a him before my Father in heaven.
1Jn   4: 3 spirit that does not a Jesus is not

ACQUIT
Ex   23: 7 to death, for I will not a the guilty.

ACTION (ACTIONS ACTIVE ACTS)
Jas   2:17 if it is not accompanied by a,
1Pe   1:13 minds for a; be self-controlled;

ACTIONS (ACTION)
Mt   11:19 wisdom is proved right by her a."
Gal   6: 4 Each one should test his own a.
Tit   1:16 but by their a they deny him.

ACTIVE (ACTION)
Heb   4:12 For the word of God is living and a

ACTS (ACTION)
Ps 145: 12 all men may know of your mighty a
     150: 2 Praise him for his a of power;
Isa   64: 6 all our righteous a are like filthy
Mt   6: 1 not to do your 'a of righteousness'

ADAM
First man (Ge 1:26-2:25; Ro 5:14; 1Ti 2:13). Sin of (Ge 3; Hos 6:7; Ro 5:12-21). Children of (Ge 4:1-5:5). Death of (Ge 5:5; Ro 5:12-21; 1Co 15:22).

ADD

Dt 12:32 do not a to it or take away from it.
Pr 30: 6 Do not a to his words,
Lk 12:25 by worrying can a a single hour
Rev 22:18 God will a to him the plagues

ADMIRABLE*

Php 4: 8 whatever is lovely, whatever is a—

ADMONISH

Col 3:16 and a one another with all wisdom,

ADOPTED (ADOPTION)

Eph 1: 5 In love he predestined us to be a

ADOPTION (ADOPTED)

Ro 8:23 as we wait eagerly for our a as sons,

ADORE*

SS 1: 4 How right they are to a you!

ADORNMENT* (ADORNS)

1Pe 3: 3 should not come from outward a,

ADORNS (ADORNMENT)

Ps 93: 5 holiness a your house

ADULTERY

Ex 20:14 "You shall not commit a.
Mt 5:27 that it was said, 'Do not commit a.'
5:28 lustfully has already committed a
5:32 the divorced woman commits a.
15:19 murder, a, sexual immorality, theft

ADULTS*

1Co 14:20 but in your thinking be a.

ADVANCED

Job 32: 7 a years should teach wisdom.'

ADVANTAGE

Ex 22:22 "Do not take a of a widow
Dt 24:14 Do not take a of a hired man who is
1Th 4: 6 should wrong his brother or take a

ADVERSITY

Pr 17:17 and a brother is born for a.

ADVICE

1Ki 12: 8 rejected the a the elders
12:14 he followed the a of the young men
Pr 12: 5 but the a of the wicked is deceitful.
12:15 but a wise man listens to a.
19:20 Listen to a and accept instruction,
20:18 Make plans by seeking a;

AFFLICTION

Ro 12:12 patient in a, faithful in prayer.

AFRAID (FEAR)

Ge 26:24 Do not be a, for I am with you;
Ex 3: 6 because he was a to look at God.
Ps 27: 1 of whom shall I be a?
56: 3 When I am a, / I will trust in you.
Pr 3:24 lie down, you will not be a;
Jer 1: 8 Do not be a of them, for I am
Mt 8:26 You of little faith, why are you so a
10:28 be a of the One who can destroy
10:31 So don't be a; you are worth more
Mk 5:36 "Don't be a; just believe."
Jn 14:27 hearts be troubled and do not be a.
Heb 13: 6 Lord is my helper; I will not be a.

AGED

Job 12:12 Is not wisdom found among the a?
Pr 17: 6 children are a crown to the a,

AGREE

Mt 18:19 on earth a about anything you ask
Ro 7:16 want to do, I a that the law is good.
Php 4: 2 with Syntyche to a with each other

AHAB

Son of Omri; king of Israel (1Ki 16:28-22:40), husband of Jezebel (1Ki 16:31). Promoted Baal worship (1Ki 16:31-33); opposed by Elijah (1Ki 17:1; 18; 21), a prophet (1Ki 20:35-43), Micaiah (1Ki 22:1-28). Defeated Ben-Hadad (1Ki 20). Killed for failing to kill Ben-Hadad and for murder of Naboth (1Ki 20:35-21:40).

AHAZ

Son of Jotham; king of Judah, (2Ki 16; 2Ch 28; Isa 7).

AHAZIAH

1. Son of Ahab; king of Israel (1Ki 22:51-2Ki 1:18; 2Ch 20:35-37).
2. Son of Jehoram; king of Judah (2Ki 8:25-29; 9:14-29), also called Jehoahaz (2Ch 21:17-22:9; 25:23).

AIM

1Co 7:34 Her a is to be devoted to the Lord
2Co 13:11 A for perfection, listen

AIR

Mt 8:20 and birds of the a have nests,
1Co 9:26 not fight like a man beating the a.
Eph 2: 2 of the ruler of the kingdom of the a,
1Th 4:17 clouds to meet the Lord in the a.

ALABASTER

Mt 26: 7 came to him with an a jar

ALERT

Jos 8: 4 All of you be on the a.
Mk 13:33 Be a! You do not know
Eph 6:18 be a and always keep on praying
1Th 5: 6 but let us be a and self-controlled.

ALIEN (ALIENATED)

Ex 22:21 "Do not mistreat an a

ALIENATED (ALIEN)

Gal 5: 4 by law have been a from Christ;

ALIVE (LIVE)

Ac 1: 3 convincing proofs that he was a.
Ro 6:11 but a to God in Christ Jesus.
1Co 15:22 so in Christ all will be made a.

ALMIGHTY (MIGHT)

Ge 17: 1 "I am God A; walk before me
Job 11: 7 Can you probe the limits of the A?
33: 4 the breath of the A gives me life.
Ps 91: 1 will rest in the shadow of the A.
Isa 6: 3 "Holy, holy, holy is the LORD A;

ALTAR

Ge 22: 9 his son Isaac and laid him on the a,
Ex 27: 1 "Build an a of acacia wood,
1Ki 18:30 and he repaired the a of the LORD
2Ch 4: 1 made a bronze a twenty cubits
4:19 the golden a; the tables

ALWAYS

Ps 16: 8 I have set the LORD a before me.
51: 3 and my sin is a before me.
Mt 26:11 The poor you will a have with you,

Mt

Mt 28:20 And surely I will be with you a,
1Co 13: 7 a protects, a trusts, a hopes, a
Php 4: 4 Rejoice in the Lord a.
1Pe 3:15 A be prepared to give an answer

AMAZIAH

Son of Joash; king of Judah (2Ki 14; 2Ch 25).

AMBASSADORS

2Co 5:20 We are therefore Christ's a,

AMBITION

Ro 15:20 It has always been my a
1Th 4:11 Make it your a to lead a quiet life,

AMON

Son of Manasseh; king of Judah (2Ki 21:18-26; 1Ch 3:14; 2Ch 33:21-25).

ANANIAS

1. Husband of Sapphira; died for lying to God (Ac 5:1-11).
2. Disciple who baptized Saul (Ac 9:10-19).
3. High priest at Paul's arrest (Ac 22:30-24:1).

ANCHOR

Heb 6:19 We have this hope as an a

ANCIENT

Da 7: 9 and the A of Days took his seat.

ANDREW*

Apostle; brother of Simon Peter (Mt 4:18; 10:2; Mk 1:16-18, 29; 3:18; 13:3; Lk 6:14; Jn 1:35-44; 6:8-9; 12:22; Ac 1:13).

ANGEL (ANGELS ARCHANGEL)

Ps 34: 7 The a of the LORD encamps
Ac 6:15 his face was like the face of an a.
2Co 11:14 Satan himself masquerades as an a
Gal 1: 8 or an a from heaven should preach

ANGELS (ANGEL)

Ps 91:11 command his a concerning you
Mt 18:10 For I tell you that their a
25:41 prepared for the devil and his a.
Lk 20:36 for they are like the a.
1Co 6: 3 you not know that we will judge a?
Heb 1: 4 as much superior to the a
1:14 Are not all a ministering spirits
2: 7 made him a little lower than the a;
13: 2 some people have entertained a
1Pe 1:12 Even a long to look
2Pe 2: 4 For if God did not spare a

ANGER (ANGERED ANGRY)

Ex 32:10 alone so that my a may burn
34: 6 slow to a, abounding in love
Dt 29:28 In furious a and in great wrath
2Ki 22:13 Great is the LORD's a that burns
Ps 30: 5 For his a lasts only a moment,
Pr 15: 1 but a harsh word stirs up a.
29:11 A fool gives full vent to his a,

ANGERED (ANGER)

Pr 22:24 do not associate with one easily a,
1Co 13: 5 it is not easily a, it keeps no record

ANGRY (ANGER)

Ps 2:12 Kiss the Son, lest he be a
Pr 29:22 An a man stirs up dissension,
Jas 1:19 slow to speak and slow to become a

ANGUISH

Ps 118: 5 In my a I cried to the LORD.

ANOINT

Ps 23: 5 You a my head with oil;
Jas 5:14 and a him with oil in the name

ANT*
Pr 6: 6 Go to the *a*, you sluggard;

ANTICHRIST
1Jn 2:18 have heard that the *a* is coming,
2Jn : 7 person is the deceiver and the *a*.

ANTIOCH
Ac 11:26 were called Christians first at *A*.

ANXIETY (ANXIOUS)
1Pe 5: 7 Cast all your *a* on him

ANXIOUS (ANXIETY)
Pr 12:25 An *a* heart weighs a man down,
Php 4: 6 Do not be *a* about anything,

APOLLOS*
Christian from Alexandria, learned in the Scriptures; instructed by Aquila and Priscilla (Ac 18:24-28). Ministered at Corinth (Ac 19:1; 1Co 1:12; 3; Tit 3:13).

APOSTLES
See also Andrew, Bartholomew, James, John, Judas, Matthew, Nathanael, Paul, Peter, Philip, Simon, Thaddaeus, Thomas.
Mk 3:14 twelve—designating them *a*—
Ac 1:26 so he was added to the eleven *a*.
2:43 signs were done by the *a*.
1Co 12:28 God has appointed first of all *a*,
15: 9 For I am the least of the *a*
2Co 11:13 masquerading as *a* of Christ.
Eph 2:20 built on the foundation of the *a*

APPEAR (APPEARANCE APPEARING)
Mk 13:22 false prophets will a and perform
2Co 5:10 we must all *a* before the judgment
Col 3: 4 also will *a* with him in glory.
Heb 9:24 now to *a* for us in God's presence.
9:28 and he will *a* a second time,

APPEARANCE (APPEAR)
1Sa 16: 7 Man looks at the outward *a*,
Gal 2: 6 God does not judge by external *a*—

APPEARING (APPEAR)
2Ti 4: 8 to all who have longed for his *a*.
Tit 2:13 the glorious *a* of our great God

APPLY
Pr 22:17 *a* your heart to what I teach,
23:12 A your heart to instruction

APPROACH
Eph 3:12 in him we may *a* God with freedom
Heb 4:16 Let us then *a* the throne of grace

APPROVED
2Ti 2:15 to present yourself to God as one *a*,

AQUILA*
Husband of Priscilla; co-worker with Paul, instructor of Apollos (Ac 18; Ro 16:3; 1Co 16:19; 2Ti 4:19).

ARARAT
Ge 8: 4 came to rest on the mountains of *A*.

ARCHANGEL* (ANGEL)
1Th 4:16 with the voice of the *a*
Jude : 9 a Michael, when he was disputing

ARCHITECT*
Heb 11:10 whose *a* and builder is God.

ARK
Ge 6:14 So make yourself an *a*
Dt 10: 5 put the tablets in the *a* I had made,

2Ch 35: 3 "Put the sacred *a* in the temple that
Heb 9: 4 This *a* contained the gold jar

ARM (ARMY)
Nu 11:23 "Is the LORD's *a* too short?
1Pe 4: 1 a yourselves also with the same

ARMAGEDDON*
Rev 16:16 that in Hebrew is called *A*.

ARMOR (ARMY)
1Ki 20:11 on his *a* should not boast like one
Eph 6:11 Put on the full *a* of God
6:13 Therefore put on the full *a* of God,

ARMS (ARMY)
Dt 33:27 underneath are the everlasting *a*.
Ps 18:32 It is God who *a* me with strength
Pr 31:20 She opens her *a* to the poor
Isa 40:11 He gathers the lambs in his *a*
Mk 10:16 And he took the children in his *a*,

ARMY (ARM ARMOR ARMS)
Ps 33:16 No king is saved by the size of his *a*
Rev 19:19 the rider on the horse and his *a*.

AROMA
2Co 2:15 For we are to God the *a* of Christ

ARRAYED*
Ps 110: 3 A in holy majesty,
Isa 61:10 and *a* me in a robe of righteousness

ARROGANT
Ro 11:20 Do not be *a*, but be afraid.

ARROWS
Eph 6:16 you can extinguish all the flaming *a*

ASA
King of Judah (1Ki 15:8-24; 1Ch 3:10; 2Ch 14-16).

ASCENDED
Eph 4: 8 "When he *a* on high,

ASCRIBE
1Ch 16:28 *a* to the LORD glory and strength,
Job 36: 3 I will *a* justice to my Maker.
Ps 29: 2 A to the LORD the glory due his

ASHAMED (SHAME)
Lk 9:26 If anyone is *a* of me and my words,
Ro 1:16 I am not *a* of the gospel,
2Ti 1: 8 So do not be *a* to testify about our
2:15 who does not need to be *a*

ASSIGNED
Mk 13:34 with his *a* task, and tells the one
1Co 3: 5 as the Lord has *a* to each his task.
7:17 place in life that the Lord *a* to him

ASSOCIATE
Pr 22:24 do not *a* with one easily angered,
Ro 12:16 but be willing to *a* with people
1Co 5:11 am writing you that you must not *a*
2Th 3:14 Do not *a* with him,

ASSURANCE
Heb 10:22 with a sincere heart in full *a* of faith

ASTRAY
Pr 10:17 ignores correction leads others *a*.
Isa 53: 6 We all, like sheep, have gone *a*,

Jer 50: 6 their shepherds have led them *a*
Jn 16: 1 you so that you will not go *a*.
1Pe 2:25 For you were like sheep going *a*,
1Jn 3: 7 do not let anyone lead you *a*.

ATHALIAH
Evil queen of Judah (2Ki 11; 2Ch 23).

ATHLETE*
2Ti 2: 5 if anyone competes as an *a*,

ATONEMENT
Ex 25:17 "Make a cover of pure gold—
30:10 Once a year Aaron shall make *a*
Lev 17:11 it is the blood that makes *a*
23:27 this seventh month is the Day of *A*.
Nu 25:13 and made *a* for the Israelites."
Ro 3:25 presented him as a sacrifice of *a*,
Heb 2:17 that he might make *a* for the sins

ATTENTION
Pr 4: 1 pay *a* and gain understanding.
5: 1 My son, pay *a* to my wisdom,
22:17 Pay *a* and listen to the sayings
Tit 1:14 and will pay no *a* to Jewish myths

ATTITUDE (ATTITUDES)
Eph 4:23 new in the *a* of your minds;
Php 2: 5 Your *a* should be the same
1Pe 4: 1 yourselves also with the same *a*,

ATTITUDES (ATTITUDE)
Heb 4:12 it judges the thoughts and *a*

ATTRACTIVE
Tit 2:10 teaching about God our Savior *a*.

AUTHORITIES (AUTHORITY)
Ro 13: 5 it is necessary to submit to the *a*,
13: 6 for the *a* are God's servants,
Tit 3: 1 people to be subject to rulers and *a*,
1Pe 3:22 *a* and powers in submission to him.

AUTHORITY (AUTHORITIES)
Mt 7:29 because he taught as one who had *a*
9: 6 the Son of Man has *a* on earth
28:18 "All *a* in heaven and on earth has
Ro 13: 1 for there is no *a* except that which
13: 2 rebels against the *a* is rebelling
1Co 11:10 to have a sign of *a* on her head.
1Ti 2: 2 for kings and all those in *a*,
2:12 to teach or to have *a* over a man;
Heb 13:17 your leaders and submit to their *a*.

AVENGE (VENGEANCE)
Dt 32:35 It is mine to *a*; I will repay.

AVOID
Pr 20: 3 It is to a man's honor to *a* strife,
20:19 so *a* a man who talks too much.
1Th 4: 3 you should *a* sexual immorality;
5:22 A every kind of evil.
2Ti 2:16 A godless chatter, because those
Tit 3: 9 But *a* foolish controversies

AWAKE
Ps 17:15 when I *a*, I will be satisfied

AWE (AWESOME)
Job 25: 2 "Dominion and *a* belong to God;
Ps 119:120 I stand in *a* of your laws.
Ecc 5: 7 Therefore stand in *a* of God.
Isa 29:23 will stand in *a* of the God of Israel.
Jer 33: 9 they will be in *a* and will tremble
Hab 3: 2 I stand in *a* of your deeds,
Mal 2: 5 and stood in *a* of my name.
Mt 9: 8 they were filled with *a*;

Lk   7:16 They were all filled with *a*
Ac   2:43 Everyone was filled with *a*,
Heb 12:28 acceptably with reverence and *a*,

AWESOME (AWE)
Ge   28:17 and said, "How *a* is this place!
Ex   15:11 *a* in glory,
Dt   7:21 is among you, is a great and *a*
             God.
      10:17 the great God, mighty and *a*,
      28:58 revere this glorious and *a*
             name—
Jdg 13: 6 like an angel of God, very *a*.
Ne   1: 5 of heaven, the great and *a* God,
      9:32 the great, mighty and *a* God,
Job 10:16 again display your *a* power
      37:22 God comes in *a* majesty.
Ps   45: 4 let your right hand display *a*
             deeds.
      47: 2 How *a* is the LORD Most High,
      66: 5 how *a* his works in man's
             behalf!
      68:35 You are *a*, O God,
      89: 7 he is more *a* than all who
             surround
      99: 3 praise your great and *a* name—
      111: 9 holy and *a* is his name.
      145: 6 of the power of your *a* works,
Da   9: 4 "O Lord, the great and *a* God,

BAAL
1Ki 18:25 Elijah said to the prophets of *B*,

BAASHA
      King of Israel (1Ki 15:16-16:7; 2Ch 16:1-6).

BABIES (BABY)
Lk   18:15 also bringing *b* to Jesus
1Pe   2: 2 Like newborn *b*, crave pure

BABY (BABIES)
Isa 49:15 "Can a mother forget the *b*
Lk   1:44 the *b* in my womb leaped for joy.
      2:12 You will find a *b* wrapped in
             strips
Jn   16:21 but when her *b* is born she
             forgets

BABYLON
Ps 137: 1 By the rivers of *B* we sat and
             wept

BACKSLIDING
Jer   3:22 I will cure you of *b*."
      14: 7 For our *b* is great;
Eze 37:23 them from all their sinful *b*,

BALAAM
      Prophet who attempted to curse Israel (Nu 22-24; Dt 23:4-5; 2Pe 2:15; Jude 11). Killed (Nu 31:8; Jos 13:22).

BALM
Jer   8:22 Is there no *b* in Gilead?

BANISH
Jer 25:10 I will *b* from them the sounds of
             joy

BANQUET
SS   2: 4 He has taken me to the *b* hall,
Lk   14:13 when you give a *b*, invite the
             poor,

BAPTIZE (BAPTIZED)
Mt   3:11 He will *b* you with the Holy Spirit
Mk   1: 8 he will *b* you with the Holy
             Spirit."
1Co   1:17 For Christ did not send me to *b*,

BAPTIZED (BAPTIZE)
Mt   3: 6 they were *b* by him in the Jordan
Mk   1: 9 and was *b* by John in the
             Jordan.
      10:38 or be *b* with the baptism I am
      16:16 believes and is *b* will be saved,
Jn   4: 2 in fact it was not Jesus who *b*,
Ac   1: 5 but in a few days you will be *b*

BARABBAS
Mt   27:26 Then he released *B* to them.

BARBS*
Nu   33:55 allow to remain will become *b*

BARE
Heb   4:13 and laid *b* before the eyes of
             him

BARNABAS*
      Disciple, originally Joseph (Ac 4:36), prophet (Ac 13:1), apostle (Ac 14:14). Brought Paul to apostles (Ac 9:27), Antioch (Ac 11:22-29; Gal 2:1-13), on the first missionary journey (Ac 13-14). Together at Jerusalem Council, they separated over John Mark (Ac 15). Later co-workers (1Co 9:6; Col 4:10).

BARREN
Ps 113: 9 He settles the *b* woman

BARTHOLOMEW*
      Apostle (Mt 10:3; Mk 3:18; Lk 6:14; Ac 1:13). Possibly also known as Nathanael (Jn 1:45-49; 21:2).

BATH
Jn   13:10 person who has had a *b* needs
             only

BATHSHEBA
      Wife of Uriah who committed adultery with and became wife of David (2Sa 11), mother of Solomon (2Sa 12:24; 1Ki 1-2; 1Ch 3:5).

BATTLE
2Ch 20:15 For the *b* is not yours, but
             God's.
Ps   24: 8 the LORD mighty in *b*.
Ecc   9:11 or the *b* to the strong,

BEAR (BEARING BIRTH BIRTHRIGHT BORN FIRSTBORN NEWBORN)
Ge   4:13 punishment is more than I
             can *b*.
Ps   38: 4 like a burden too heavy to *b*.
Isa 53:11 and he will *b* their iniquities.
Da   7: 5 beast, which looked like a *b*.
Mt   7:18 A good tree cannot *b* bad fruit,
Jn   15: 2 branch that does *b* fruit he
             prunes
      15:16 and appointed you to go and *b*
             fruit—
Ro   15: 1 ought to *b* with the failings
1Co 10:13 tempted beyond what you can *b*.
Col   3:13 *B* with each other and forgive

BEARING (BEAR)
Eph   4: 2 *b* with one another in love.
Col   1:10 *b* fruit in every good work,

BEAST
Rev 13:18 him calculate the number of
             the *b*,

BEAT (BEATING)
Isa   2: 4 They will *b* their swords
Joel 3:10 *B* your plowshares into swords
1Co   9:27 I *b* my body and make it my
             slave

BEATING (BEAT)
1Co   9:26 I do not fight like a man *b* the
             air.
1Pe   2:20 if you receive a *b* for doing
             wrong

BEAUTIFUL (BEAUTY)
Ge   6: 2 that the daughters of men
             were *b*,
      12:11 "I know what a *b* woman you
             are.
      12:14 saw that she was a very *b*
             woman.
      24:16 The girl was very *b*, a virgin;
      26: 7 of Rebekah, because she is *b*."
      29:17 Rachel was lovely in form,
Job 38:31 "Can you bind the *b* Pleiades?
Pr   11:22 is a *b* woman who shows no
Ecc   3:11 He has made everything *b*
Isa   4: 2 of the LORD will be *b*
      52: 7 How *b* on the mountains

Eze 20: 6 and honey, the most *b* of all
             lands.
Zec   9:17 How attractive and *b* they will
             be!
Mt   23:27 which look *b* on the outside
      26:10 She has done a *b* thing to me.
Ro   10:15 "How *b* are the feet
1Pe   3: 5 in God used to make
             themselves *b*.

BEAUTY (BEAUTIFUL)
Ps   27: 4 to gaze upon the *b* of the LORD
      45:11 The king is enthralled by your *b*;
Pr   31:30 is deceptive, and *b* is fleeting;
Isa 33:17 Your eyes will see the king in
             his *b*
      53: 2 He had no *b* or majesty
      61: 3 to bestow on them a crown of *b*
Eze 28:12 full of wisdom and perfect in *b*.
1Pe   3: 4 the unfading *b* of a gentle

BED
Heb 13: 4 and the marriage *b* kept pure,

BEELZEBUB
Lk   11:15 "By *B*, the prince of demons,

BEER
Pr   20: 1 Wine is a mocker and *b* a
             brawler;

BEERSHEBA
Jdg 20: 1 all the Israelites from Dan to *B*

BEGINNING
Ge   1: 1 In the *b* God created the
             heavens
Ps 102: 25 In the *b* you laid the foundations
     111: 10 of the LORD is the *b* of wisdom;
Pr   1: 7 of the LORD is the *b* of
             knowledge
Jn   1: 1 In the *b* was the Word,
1Jn   1: 1 That which was from the *b*,
Rev 21: 6 and the Omega, the *B* and the
             End.

BEHAVE
Ro   13:13 Let us *b* decently, as in the
             daytime

BELIEVE (BELIEVED BELIEVER BELIEVERS BELIEVES BELIEVING)
Mt   18: 6 one of these little ones who *b* in
             me
      21:22 If you *b*, you will receive
             whatever
Mk   1:15 Repent and *b* the good news!"
      9:24 "I do *b*; help me overcome my
      16:17 signs will accompany those
             who *b*:
Lk   8:50 just *b*, and she will be healed."
      24:25 to *b* all that the prophets have
Jn   1: 7 that through him all men
             might *b*.
      3:18 does not *b* stands condemned
      6:29 to *b* in the one he has sent."
      10:38 you do not *b* me, *b* the miracles.
      11:27 "I *b* that you are the Christ,
      14:11 *B* me when I say that I am
      16:30 This makes us *b* that you came
      16:31 "You *b* at last!" Jesus
             answered.
      17:21 that the world may *b* that you
             have
      20:27 Stop doubting and *b*."
      20:31 written that you may *b* that
             Jesus is
Ac   16:31 They replied, "*B* in the Lord
             Jesus,
      24:14 I *b* everything that agrees
Ro   3:22 faith in Jesus Christ to all
             who *b*.
      4:11 he is the father of all who *b*
      10: 9 *b* in your heart that God raised
             him
      10:14 And how can they *b* in the one
      10:26 so that all nations might *b*
1Th   4:14 We *b* that Jesus died and rose
             again
2Th   2:11 delusion so that they will *b* the
             lie
1Ti   4:10 and especially of those who *b*.

Tit   1: 6 a man whose children *b*
Heb 11: 6 comes to him must *b* that he
     exists
Jas   2:19 Even the demons *b* that—
1Jn   4: 1 Dear friends, do not *b* every
     spirit,

BELIEVED (BELIEVE)

Ge   15: 6 Abram *b* the LORD, and he
Jnh   3: 5 The Ninevites *b* God.
Jn   1:12 to those who *b* in his name,
     2:22 Then they *b* the Scripture
     3:18 because he has not *b* in the
     name
     20: 8 He saw and *b.*
     20:29 who have not seen and yet
     have *b.*"
Ac   13:48 were appointed for eternal life *b.*
Ro   4: 3 Scripture say? "Abraham *b* God,
     10:14 call on the one they have not *b*
     in?
1Co 15: 2 Otherwise, you have *b* in vain.
Gal   3: 6 Consider Abraham: "He *b* God,
2Ti   1:12 because I know whom I have *b,*
Jas   2:23 that says, "Abraham *b* God,

BELIEVER (BELIEVE)

1Co   7:12 brother has a wife who is not
     a *b*
2Co   6:15 What does a *b* have in common

BELIEVERS (BELIEVE)

Ac   4:32 All the *b* were one in heart
     5:12 And all the *b* used to meet
     together
1Co   6: 5 to judge a dispute between *b?*
1Ti   4:12 set an example for the *b* in
     speech,
1Pe   2:17 Love the brotherhood of *b,*

BELIEVES (BELIEVE)

Pr   14:15 A simple man *b* anything,
Mk   9:23 is possible for him who *b.*"
     11:23 *b* that what he says will happen,
     16:16 Whoever *b* and is baptized will
     be
Jn   3:16 that whoever *b* in him shall not
     3:36 Whoever *b* in the Son has
     eternal
     5:24 *b* him who sent me has eternal
     life
     6:35 and he who *b* in me will never
     be
     6:40 and *b* in him shall have eternal
     life,
     6:47 he who *b* has everlasting life.
     7:38 Whoever *b* in me, as the
     Scripture
     11:26 and *b* in me will never die.
Ro   1:16 for the salvation of everyone
     who *b*
     10: 4 righteousness for everyone
     who *b.*
1Jn   5: 1 Everyone who *b* that Jesus is
     5: 5 Only he who *b* that Jesus is the
     Son

BELIEVING (BELIEVE)

Jn   20:31 and that by *b* you may have life

BELONG (BELONGS)

Dt   29:29 The secret things *b*
Job 25: 2 "Dominion and awe *b* to God;
Ps   47: 9 for the kings of the earth *b* to
     God;
     95: 4 and the mountain peaks *b* to
     him.
Jn   8:44 You *b* to your father, the devil,
     15:19 As it is, you do not *b* to the
     world,
Ro   1: 6 called to *b* to Jesus Christ.
     7: 4 that you might *b* to another,
     14: 8 we live or die, we *b* to the Lord.
Gal   5:24 Those who *b* to Christ Jesus
     have
1Th   5: 8 But since we *b* to the day, let us
     be

BELONGS (BELONG)

Job 41:11 Everything under heaven *b* to
     me.
Ps 111: 10 To him *b* eternal praise.

Eze 18: 4 For every living soul *b* to me,
Jn   8:47 He who *b* to God hears what
     God
Ro   12: 5 each member *b* to all the
     others.

BELOVED (LOVE)

Dt   33:12 "Let the *b* of the LORD rest
     secure

BELT

Isa   11: 5 Righteousness will be his *b*
Eph   6:14 with the *b* of truth buckled

BENEFIT (BENEFITS)

Ro   6:22 the *b* you reap leads to
     holiness,
2Co   4:15 All this is for your *b,*

BENEFITS (BENEFIT)

Ps 103: 2 and forget not all his *b.*
Jn   4:38 you have reaped the *b* of their
     labor

BENJAMIN

   Twelfth son of Jacob by Rachel (Ge 35:16-24; 46:19-21; 1Ch 2:2). Jacob refused to send him to Egypt, but relented (Ge 42-45).

BEREANS*

Ac   17:11 the *B* were of more noble
     character

BESTOWS

Ps   84:11 the LORD *b* favor and honor;

BETHLEHEM

Mt   2: 1 After Jesus was born in *B* in
     Judea,

BETRAY

Pr   25: 9 do not *b* another man's
     confidence,

BIND (BINDS)

Dt   6: 8 and *b* them on your foreheads.
Pr   6:21 *B* them upon your heart forever;
Isa 61: 1 me to *b* up the brokenhearted,
Mt   16:19 whatever you *b* on earth will be

BINDS (BIND)

Ps 147: 3 and *b* up their wounds.
Isa 30:26 when the LORD *b* up the bruises

BIRDS

Mt   8:20 and *b* of the air have nests,

BIRTH (BEAR)

Ps   58: 3 Even from *b* the wicked go
     astray;
Mt   1:18 This is how the *b* of Jesus Christ
1Pe   1: 3 great mercy he has given us
     new *b*

BIRTHRIGHT (BEAR)

Ge   25:34 So Esau despised his *b.*

BLAMELESS

Ge   17: 1 walk before me and be *b.*
Job   1: 1 This man was *b* and upright;
Ps   84:11 from those whose walk is *b.*
   119: 1 Blessed are they whose ways
     are *b,*
Pr   19: 1 Better a poor man whose walk
     is *b*
1Co   1: 8 so that you will be *b* on the day
Eph   5:27 any other blemish, but holy
     and *b.*
Php   2:15 so that you may become *b* and
     pure
1Th   3:13 hearts so that you will be *b*
     5:23 and body be kept *b* at the
     coming
Tit   1: 6 An elder must be *b,* the husband
     of
Heb   7:26 *b,* pure, set apart from sinners,
2Pe   3:14 effort to be found spotless, *b*

BLASPHEMES

Mk   3:29 whoever *b* against the Holy
     Spirit

BLEMISH

1Pe   1:19 a lamb without *b* or defect.

BLESS (BLESSED BLESSING BLESSINGS)

Ge   12: 3 I will *b* those who *b* you,
Ro   12:14 Bless those who persecute
     you; *b*

BLESSED (BLESS)

Ge   1:22 God *b* them and said, "Be
     fruitful
     2: 3 And God *b* the seventh day
     22:18 nations on earth will be *b,*
Ps   1: 1 *B* is the man
     2:12 *B* are all who take refuge in him.
     33:12 *B* is the nation whose God is
     41: 1 *B* is he who has regard for the
     weak
     84: 5 *B* are those whose strength is
   106: 3 *B* are they who maintain justice,
   112: 1 *B* is the man who fears the
     LORD.
   118: 26 *B* is he who comes in the name
Pr   29:18 but *b* is he who keeps the law.
     31:28 Her children arise and call her *b;*
Mt   5: 3 saying: "*B* are the poor in spirit,
     5: 4 *B* are those who mourn,
     5: 5 *B* are the meek,
     5: 6 *B* are those who hunger
     5: 7 *B* are the merciful,
     5: 8 *B* are the pure in heart,
     5: 9 *B* are the peacemakers,
     5:10 *B* are those who are persecuted
     5:11 "*B* are you when people insult
     you,
Lk   1:48 on all generations will call me *b,*
Jn   12:13 "*B* is he who comes in the name
Ac   20:35 'It is more *b* to give than to
     receive
Tit   2:13 while we wait for the *b* hope—
Jas   1:12 *B* is the man who perseveres
Rev   1: 3 *B* is the one who reads the
     words
     22:14 "*B* are those who wash their
     robes,

BLESSING (BLESS)

Eze 34:26 there will be showers of *b.*

BLESSINGS (BLESS)

Pr   10: 6 *B* crown the head of the
     righteous,

BLIND

Mt   15:14 a *b* man leads a *b* man, both
     will fall
     23:16 "Woe to you, *b* guides! You say,
Jn   9:25 I was *b* but now I see!"

BLOOD

Ge   9: 6 "Whoever sheds the *b* of man,
Ex   12:13 and when I see the *b,* I will pass
     24: 8 "This is the *b* of the covenant
     that
Lev 17:11 For the life of a creature is in
     the *b,*
Ps   72:14 for precious is their *b* in his
     sight.
Pr   6:17 hands that shed innocent *b,*
Mt   26:28 This is my *b* of the covenant,
Ro   3:25 of atonement, through faith in
     his *b*
     5: 9 have now been justified by his *b,*
1Co 11:25 cup is the new covenant in
     my *b;*
Eph   1: 7 we have redemption through
     his *b,*
     2:13 near through the *b* of Christ.
Col   1:20 by making peace through his *b,*
Heb   9:12 once for all by his own *b,*
     9:22 of there is no forgiveness.
1Pe   1:19 but with the precious *b* of
     Christ,
1Jn   1: 7 and the *b* of Jesus, his Son,
Rev   1: 5 has freed us from our sins by
     his *b,*
     5: 9 with your *b* you purchased men
     7:14 white in the *b* of the Lamb.
     12:11 him by the *b* of the Lamb

BLOT (BLOTS)
Ex   32:32 then *b* me out of the book you
            have
Ps   51: 1 *b* out my transgressions.
Rev   3: 5 I will never *b* out his name

BLOTS (BLOT)
Isa   43:25 "I, even I, am he who *b* out

BLOWN
Eph   4:14 and *b* here and there by every
            wind
Jas   1: 6 doubts is like a wave of the
            sea, *b*

BOAST
1Ki   20:11 armor should not *b* like one who
Ps   34: 2 My soul will *b* in the LORD;
      44: 8 In God we make our *b* all day
            long,
Pr   27: 1 Do not *b* about tomorrow,
1Co   1:31 Let him who boasts *b* in the
            Lord."
Gal   6:14 May I never *b* except in the
            cross
Eph   2: 9 not by works, so that no one
            can *b*.

BOAZ
Wealthy Bethlehemite who showed favor to
Ruth (Ru 2), married her (Ru 4). Ancestor of
David (Ru 4:18-22; 1Ch 2:12-15), Jesus (Mt
1:5-16; Lk 3:23-32).

BODIES (BODY)
Ro   12: 1 to offer your *b* as living
            sacrifices,
1Co   6:15 not know that your *b* are
            members
Eph   5:28 to love their wives as their
            own *b*.

BODY (BODIES)
Zec   13: 6 What are these wounds on
            your *b*?'
Mt   10:28 afraid of those who kill the *b*
      26:26 saying, "Take and eat; this is
            my *b*
      26:41 spirit is willing, but the *b* is
            weak."
Jn   13:10 wash his feet; his whole *b* is
            clean.
Ro   6:13 Do not offer the parts of your *b*
      12: 4 us has one *b* with many
            members,
1Co   6:19 not know that your *b* is a temple
      11:24 "This is my *b*, which is for you;
      12:12 The *b* is a unit, though it is
            made up
Eph   5:30 for we are members of his *b*.

BOLD (BOLDNESS)
Ps138: 3 you made me *b* and
            stouthearted.
Pr   21:29 A wicked man puts up a *b* front,
      28: 1 but the righteous are as *b* as a
            lion.

BOLDNESS* (BOLD)
Ac   4:29 to speak your word with great *b*.

BONDAGE
Ezr   9: 9 God has not deserted us in
            our *b*.

BOOK (BOOKS)
Jos   1: 8 Do not let this *B* of the Law
            depart
Ne   8: 8 They read from the *B* of the Law
Jn   20:30 which are not recorded in this *b*.
Php   4: 3 whose names are in the *b* of
            life.
Rev   21:27 written in the Lamb's *b* of life.

BOOKS (BOOK)
Ecc   12:12 Of making many *b* there is no
            end,

BORN (BEAR)
Isa   9: 6 For to us a child is *b*,
Jn   3: 7 at my saying, 'You must be *b*
            again

1Pe   1:23 For you have been *b* again,
1Jn   4: 7 Everyone who loves has been *b*
       5: 1 believes that Jesus is the Christ
            is *b*

BORROWER
Pr   22: 7 and the *b* is servant to the
            lender.

BOUGHT
Ac   20:28 which he *b* with his own blood.
1Co   6:20 You are not your own; you
            were *b*
       7:23 You were *b* at a price; do not
2Pe   2: 1 the sovereign Lord who *b*
            them—

BOW
Ps   95: 6 Come, let us *b* down in worship,
Isa   45:23 Before me every knee will *b*;
Ro   14:11 'every knee will *b* before me;
Php   2:10 name of Jesus every knee
            should *b*,

BRANCH (BRANCHES)
Isa   4: 2 In that day the *B* of the LORD will
Jer   33:15 I will make a righteous *B* sprout

BRANCHES (BRANCH)
Jn   15: 5 "I am the vine; you are the *b*.

BRAVE
2Sa   2: 7 Now then, be strong and *b*,

BREAD
Dt   8: 3 that man does not live on *b*
            alone
Pr   30: 8 but give me only my daily *b*.
Ecc   11: 1 Cast your *b* upon the waters,
Isa   55: 2 Why spend money on what is
            not *b*
Mt   4: 4 'Man does not live on *b* alone,
       6:11 Give us today our daily *b*.
Jn   6:35 Jesus declared, "I am the *b* of
            life.
      21:13 took the *b* and gave it to them,
1Co   11:23 took *b*, and when he had given

BREAK (BREAKING BROKEN)
Nu   30: 2 he must not *b* his word
Jdg   2: 1 'I will never *b* my covenant
Isa   42: 3 A bruised reed he will not *b*,
Mt   12:20 A bruised reed he will not *b*,

BREAKING (BREAK)
Jas   2:10 at just one point is guilty of *b* all

BREASTPIECE (BREASTPLATE)
Ex   28:15 Fashion a *b* for making
            decisions—

BREASTPLATE* (BREASTPIECE)
Isa   59:17 He put on righteousness as
            his *b*,
Eph   6:14 with the *b* of righteousness in
            place
1Th   5: 8 putting on faith and love as a *b*,

BREATHED (GOD-BREATHED)
Ge   2: 7 *b* into his nostrils the breath of
            life,
Jn   20:22 And with that he *b* on them

BREEDS*
Pr   13:10 Pride only *b* quarrels,

BRIBE
Ex   23: 8 "Do not accept a *b*,
Pr   6:35 will refuse the *b*, however great
            it

BRIDE
Rev   19: 7 and his *b* has made herself
            ready,

BRIGHTER (BRIGHTNESS)
Pr   4:18 shining ever *b* till the full light

BRIGHTNESS (BRIGHTER)
2Sa   22:13 Out of the *b* of his presence
Da   12: 3 who are wise will shine like
            the *b*

BROAD
Mt   7:13 and *b* is the road that leads

BROKEN (BREAK)
Ps   51:17 The sacrifices of God are a *b*
            spirit;
Ecc   4:12 of three strands is not quickly *b*.
Jn   10:35 and the Scripture cannot be *b*—

BROKENHEARTED* (HEART)
Ps   34:18 The LORD is close to the *b*
      109: 16 and the needy and the *b*.
      147: 3 He heals the *b*
Isa   61: 1 He has sent me to bind up
            the *b*,

BROTHER (BROTHER'S BROTHERS)
Pr   17:17 and a *b* is born for adversity.
      18:24 a friend who sticks closer than
            a *b*.
      27:10 neighbor nearby than a *b* far
            away.
Mt   5:24 and be reconciled to your *b*;
      18:15 "If your *b* sins against you,
Mk   3:35 Whoever does God's will is my *b*
Lk   17: 3 "If your *b* sins, rebuke him,
1Co   8:13 if what I eat causes my *b* to fall
1Jn   2:10 Whoever loves his *b* lives
       4:21 loves God must also love his *b*.

BROTHER'S (BROTHER)
Ge   4: 9 "Am I my *b* keeper?" The LORD

BROTHERS (BROTHER)
Ps133: 1 is when *b* live together in unity!
Pr   6:19 who stirs up dissension
            among *b*.
Mt   25:40 one of the least of these *b* of
            mine,
Mk   10:29 or *b* or sisters or mother or
            father
Heb   13: 1 Keep on loving each other as *b*.
1Pe   3: 8 be sympathetic, love as *b*,
1Jn   3:14 death to life, because we love
            our *b*.

BUILD (BUILDING BUILDS BUILT)
Mt   16:18 and on this rock I will *b* my
            church,
Ac   20:32 which can *b* you up and give you
1Co   14:12 excel in gifts that *b* up the
            church.
1Th   5:11 one another and *b* each other
            up,

BUILDING (BUILD)
1Co   3: 9 you are God's field, God's *b*.
2Co   10: 8 us for *b* you up rather
Eph   4:29 helpful for *b* others up according

BUILDS (BUILD)
Ps127: 1 Unless the LORD *b* the house,
1Co   3:10 one should be careful how he *b*.
       8: 1 Knowledge puffs up, but love *b*
            up.

BUILT (BUILD)
Mt   7:24 is like a wise man who *b* his
            house
Eph   2:20 *b* on the foundation of the
            apostles
       4:12 the body of Christ may be *b* up

BURDEN (BURDENED BURDENS)
Ps   38: 4 like a *b* too heavy to bear.
Mt   11:30 my yoke is easy and my *b* is
            light."

BURDENED (BURDEN)
Gal   5: 1 do not let yourselves be *b* again

BURDENS (BURDEN)
Ps   68:19 who daily bears our *b*.
Gal   6: 2 Carry each other's *b*,

BURIED
Ro   6: 4 *b* with him through baptism
1Co   15: 4 that he was *b*, that he was
            raised

BURNING
Lev 6: 9 the fire must be kept *b* on the altar.
Ro 12:20 you will heap *b* coals on his head."

BUSINESS
Da 8:27 and went about the king's *b*.
1Th 4:11 to mind your own *b* and to work

BUSY
1Ki 20:40 While your servant was *b* here
2Th 3:11 They are not *b*; they are
Tit 2: 5 to be *b* at home, to be kind,

CAESAR
Mt 22:21 "Give to *C* what is Caesar's,

CAIN
Firstborn of Adam (Ge 4:1), murdered brother Abel (Ge 4:1-16; 1Jn 3:12).

CALEB
Judahite who spied out Canaan (Nu 13:6); allowed to enter land because of faith (Nu 13:30-14:38; Dt 1:36). Possessed Hebron (Jos 14:6-15:19).

CALF
Ex 32: 4 into an idol cast in the shape of a *c*,
Lk 15:23 Bring the fattened *c* and kill it.

CALL (CALLED CALLING CALLS)
Ps 105: 1 to the LORD, *c* on his name;
      145: 18 near to all who *c* on him,
Pr 31:28 children arise and *c* her blessed;
Isa 5:20 Woe to those who *c* evil good
      55: 6 *c* on him while he is near.
      65:24 Before they *c* I will answer;
Jer 33: 3 '*C* to me and I will answer you
Mt 9:13 come to *c* the righteous,
Ro 10:12 and richly blesses all who *c* on him,
      11:29 gifts and his *c* are irrevocable.
1Th 4: 7 For God did not *c* us to be impure,

CALLED (CALL)
1Sa 3: 5 and said, "Here I am; you *c* me."
2Ch 7:14 if my people, who are *c*
Ps 34: 6 This poor man *c*, and the LORD
Mt 21:13 " 'My house will be *c* a house
Ro 8:30 And those he predestined, he also *c*
1Co 7:15 God has *c* us to live in peace.
Gal 5:13 You, my brothers, were *c* to be free
1Pe 2: 9 of him who *c* you out of darkness

CALLING (CALL)
Jn 1:23 I am the voice of one *c* in the desert
Ac 22:16 wash your sins away, *c* on his name
Eph 4: 1 worthy of the *c* you have received.
2Pe 1:10 all the more eager to make your *c*

CALLS (CALL)
Joel 2:32 And everyone who *c*
Jn 10: 3 He *c* his own sheep by name
Ro 10:13 "Everyone who *c* on the name

CAMEL
Mt 19:24 it is easier for a *c* to go
      23:24 strain out a gnat but swallow a *c*.

CANAAN
1Ch 16:18 "To you I will give the land of *C*

CANCELED
Lk 7:42 so he *c* the debts of both.
Col 2:14 having *c* the written code,

CAPITAL
Dt 21:22 guilty of a *c* offense is put to death

CAPSTONE (STONE)
Ps 118: 22 has become the *c*;
1Pe 2: 7 has become the *c*,"

CARE (CAREFUL CARES CARING)
Ps 8: 4 the son of man that you *c* for him?
Pr 29: 7 The righteous *c* about justice
Lk 10:34 him to an inn and took *c* of him.
Jn 21:16 Jesus said, "Take *c* of my sheep.
Heb 2: 6 the son of man that you *c* for him?
1Pe 5: 2 of God's flock that is under your *c*,

CAREFUL (CARE)
Ex 23:13 "Be *c* to do everything I have said
Dt 6: 3 be *c* to obey so that it may go well
Jos 23: 6 be *c* to obey all that is written
      23:11 be very *c* to love the LORD your
Pr 13:24 he who loves him is *c*
Mt 6: 1 "Be *c* not to do your 'acts
Ro 12:17 Be *c* to do what is right in the eyes
1Co 3:10 each one should be *c* how he builds
      8: 9 Be *c*, however, that the exercise
Eph 5:15 Be very *c*, then, how you live—

CARELESS
Mt 12:36 for every *c* word they have spoken.

CARES (CARE)
Ps 55:22 Cast your *c* on the LORD
Na 1: 7 He *c* for those who trust in him,
Eph 5:29 but he feeds and *c* for it, just
1Pe 5: 7 on him because he *c* for you.

CARING* (CARE)
1Th 2: 7 like a mother *c* for her little
1Ti 5: 4 practice by *c* for their own family

CARRIED (CARRY)
Ex 19: 4 and how I *c* you on eagles' wings
Isa 53: 4 and *c* our sorrows,
Heb 13: 9 Do not be *c* away by all kinds
2Pe 1:21 as they were *c* along by the Holy

CARRIES (CARRY)
Dt 32:11 and *c* them on its pinions.
Isa 40:11 and *c* them close to his heart;

CARRY (CARRIED CARRIES)
Lk 14:27 anyone who does not *c* his cross
Gal 6: 2 *C* each other's burdens,
      6: 5 for each one should *c* his own load.

CAST
Ps 22:18 and *c* lots for my clothing.
      55:22 *C* your cares on the LORD
Ecc 11: 1 *C* your bread upon the waters,
Jn 19:24 and *c* lots for my clothing."
1Pe 5: 7 *C* all your anxiety on him

CATCH (CAUGHT)
Lk 5:10 from now on you will *c* men."

CATTLE
Ps 50:10 and the *c* on a thousand hills.

CAUGHT (CATCH)
1Th 4:17 and are left will be *c* up together

CAUSE (CAUSES)
Pr 24:28 against your neighbor without *c*,
Ecc 8: 3 Do not stand up for a bad *c*,
Mt 18: 7 of the things that *c* people to sin!
Ro 14:21 else that will *c* your brother
1Co 10:32 Do not *c* anyone to stumble,

CAUSES (CAUSE)
Isa 8:14 a stone that *c* men to stumble
Mt 18: 6 if anyone *c* one of these little ones

CAUTIOUS*
Pr 12:26 A righteous man is *c* in friendship,

CEASE
Ps 46: 9 He makes wars *c* to the ends

CENSER
Lev 16:12 is to take a *c* full of burning coals

CENTURION
Mt 8: 5 had entered Capernaum, a *c* came

CERTAIN (CERTAINTY)
2Pe 1:19 word of the prophets made more *c*,

CERTAINTY* (CERTAIN)
Lk 1: 4 so that you may know the *c*
Jn 17: 8 They knew with *c* that I came

CHAFF
Ps 1: 4 They are like *c*

CHAINED
2Ti 2: 9 But God's word is not *c*.

CHAMPION
Ps 19: 5 like a *c* rejoicing to run his course.

CHANGE (CHANGED)
1Sa 15:29 of Israel does not lie or *c* his mind;
Ps 110: 4 and will not *c* his mind:
Jer 7: 5 If you really *c* your ways
Mal 3: 6 "I the LORD do not *c*.
Mt 18: 3 unless you *c* and become like little
Heb 7:21 and will not *c* his mind:
Jas 1:17 who does not *c* like shifting

CHANGED (CHANGE)
1Co 15:51 but we will all be *c*— in a flash,

CHARACTER
Ru 3:11 that you are a woman of noble *c*.
Pr 31:10 A wife of noble *c* who can find?
Ro 5: 4 perseverance, *c*; and *c*, hope.
1Co 15:33 "Bad company corrupts good *c*."

CHARGE
Ro 8:33 Who will bring any *c*
2Co 11: 7 the gospel of God to you free of *c*?
2Ti 4: 1 I give you this *c*: Preach the Word;

CHARIOTS
2Ki 6:17 and *c* of fire all around Elisha.
Ps 20: 7 Some trust in *c* and some in horses,

CHARM
Pr 31:30 *C* is deceptive, and beauty is

CHASES
Pr 12:11 he who *c* fantasies lacks judgment.

CHATTER* (CHATTERING)
1Ti 6:20 Turn away from godless *c*
2Ti 2:16 Avoid godless *c*, because those

CHATTERING* (CHATTER)
Pr 10: 8 but a *c* fool comes to ruin.
      10:10 and a *c* fool comes to ruin.

CHEAT* (CHEATED)
Mal 1:14 "Cursed is the *c* who has
1Co 6: 8 you yourselves *c* and do wrong,

CHEATED (CHEAT)
Lk 19: 8 if I have *c* anybody out of anything,
1Co 6: 7 Why not rather be *c*? Instead,

CHEEK
Mt   5:39 someone strikes you on the right c,

CHEERFUL* (CHEERS)
Pr   15:13 A happy heart makes the face c,
     15:15 but the c heart has a continual feast
     15:30 A c look brings joy to the heart,
     17:22 A c heart is good medicine,
2Co   9: 7 for God loves a c giver.

CHEERS (CHEERFUL)
Pr   12:25 but a kind word c him up.

CHILD (CHILDISH CHILDREN)
Pr   20:11 Even a c is known by his actions,
     22: 6 Train a c in the way he should go,
     22:15 Folly is bound up in the heart of a c
     23:13 not withhold discipline from a c;
     29:15 c left to himself disgraces his mother.
Isa   7:14 The virgin will be with c
     9: 6 For to us a c is born,
     11: 6 and a little c will lead them.
     66:13 As a mother comforts her c,
Mt   1:23 "The virgin will be with c
     18: 2 He called a little c and had him
Lk   1:42 and blessed is the c you will bear!
     1:80 And the c grew and became strong
1Co 13:11 When I was a c, I talked like a c,
1Jn   5: 1 who loves the father loves his c

CHILDISH* (CHILD)
1Co 13:11 When I became a man, I put c ways

CHILDREN (CHILD)
Dt   4: 9 Teach them to your c
     11:19 them to your c, talking about them
Ps   8: 2 From the lips of c and infants
Pr   17: 6 Children's c are a crown
     31:28 Her c arise and call her blessed;
Mt   7:11 how to give good gifts to your c,
     11:25 and revealed them to little c.
     18: 3 you change and become like little c
     19:14 "Let the little c come to me,
     21:16 " 'From the lips of c and infants
Mk   9:37 one of these little c in my name
     10:14 "Let the little c come to me,
     10:16 And he took the c in his arms,
     13:12 c will rebel against their parents
Lk   10:21 and revealed them to little c.
     18:16 "Let the little c come to me,
Ro   8:16 with our spirit that we are God's c.
2Co 12:14 parents, but parents for their c.
Eph   6: 1 C, obey your parents in the Lord,
     6: 4 do not exasperate your c; instead,
Col   3:20 C, obey your parents in everything,
     3:21 Fathers, do not embitter your c,
1Ti   3: 4 and see that his c obey him
     3:12 and must manage his c and his
     5:10 bringing up c, showing hospitality,
1Jn   3: 1 that we should be called c of God!

CHOOSE (CHOOSES CHOSE CHOSEN)
Dt   30:19 Now c life, so that you
Jos 24:15 then c for yourselves this day
Pr   8:10 C my instruction instead of silver,
     16:16 to c understanding rather
Jn   15:16 You did not c me, but I chose you

CHOOSES (CHOOSE)
Jn   7:17 If anyone c to do God's will,

CHOSE (CHOOSE)
Ge   13:11 So Lot c for himself the whole plain

Ps   33:12 the people he c for his inheritance.
Jn   15:16 but I c you and appointed you to go
1Co   1:27 But God c the foolish things
Eph   1: 4 he c us in him before the creation
2Th   2:13 from the beginning God c you

CHOSEN (CHOOSE)
Isa 41: 8 Jacob, whom I have c,
Mt   22:14 For many are invited, but few are c
Lk   10:42 Mary has c what is better,
     23:35 the Christ of God, the C One."
Jn   15:19 but I have c you out of the world.
1Pe   1:20 He was c before the creation
     2: 9 But you are a c people, a royal

CHRIST (CHRIST'S CHRISTIAN CHRISTS)
Mt   1:16 was born Jesus, who is called C.
     16:16 Peter answered, "You are the C,
     22:42 "What do you think about the C?
Jn   1:41 found the Messiah" (that is, the C).
     20:31 you may believe that Jesus is the C,
Ac   2:36 you crucified, both Lord and C."
     5:42 the good news that Jesus is the C.
     9:22 by proving that Jesus is the C.
     17: 3 proving that the C had to suffer
     18:28 the Scriptures that Jesus was the C.
     26:23 that the C would suffer and,
Ro   3:22 comes through faith in Jesus C
     5: 6 we were still powerless, C died
     5: 8 While we were still sinners, C died
     5:17 life through the one man, Jesus C.
     6: 4 as C was raised from the dead
     8: 1 for those who are in C Jesus,
     8: 9 Spirit of C, he does not belong to C.
     8:35 us from the love of C?
     10: 4 C is the end of the law
     14: 9 C died and returned to life
     15: 3 For even C did not please himself
1Co   1:23 but we preach C crucified:
     2: 2 except Jesus C and him crucified.
     3:11 one already laid, which is Jesus C.
     5: 7 For C, our Passover lamb,
     8: 6 and there is but one Lord, Jesus C,
     10: 4 them, and that rock was C.
     11: 1 as I follow the example of C.
     11: 3 the head of every man is C,
     12:27 Now you are the body of C,
     15: 3 that C died for our sins according
     15:14 And if C has not been raised,
     15:22 so in C all will be made alive.
     15:57 victory through our Lord Jesus C.
2Co   3: 3 show that you are a letter from C,
     4: 5 not preach ourselves, but Jesus C
     5:10 before the judgment seat of C,
     5:17 Therefore, if anyone is in C,
     11: 2 you to one husband, to C,
Gal   2:20 I have been crucified with C
     3:13 C redeemed us from the curse
     6:14 in the cross of our Lord Jesus C,
Eph   1: 3 with every spiritual blessing in C.
     3: 8 the unsearchable riches of C,
     4:13 measure of the fullness of C.
     5: 2 as C loved us and gave himself up
     5:23 as C is the head of the church,
     5:25 just as C loved the church
Php   1:21 to live is C and to die is gain.
     1:27 worthy of the gospel of C.
     4:19 to his glorious riches in C Jesus.
Col   1:27 which is C in you, the hope of glory

Col   1:28 may present everyone perfect in C.
     2: 6 as you received C Jesus as Lord,
     2:17 the reality, however, is found in C.
     3:15 Let the peace of C rule
2Th   2: 1 the coming of our Lord Jesus C
1Ti   1:15 C Jesus came into the world
     2: 5 the man C Jesus, who gave himself
2Ti   2: 3 us like a good soldier of C Jesus.
     3:15 salvation through faith in C Jesus.
Tit   2:13 our great God and Savior, Jesus C,
Heb   3:14 to share in C if we hold firmly
     9:14 more, then, will the blood of C,
     9:15 For this reason C is the mediator
     9:28 so C was sacrificed once
     10:10 of the body of Jesus C once for all.
     13: 8 Jesus C is the same yesterday
1Pe   1:19 but with the precious blood of C,
     2:21 because C suffered for you,
     3:18 For C died for sins once for all,
     4:14 insulted because of the name of C,
1Jn   2:22 man who denies that Jesus is the C.
     3:16 Jesus C laid down his life for us.
     5: 1 believes that Jesus is the C is born
Rev 20: 4 reigned with C a thousand years.

CHRIST'S (CHRIST)
2Co   5:14 For C love compels us,
     5:20 We are therefore C ambassadors,
     12: 9 so that C power may rest on me.

CHRISTIAN (CHRIST)
1Pe   4:16 as a C, do not be ashamed,

CHRISTS (CHRIST)
Mt   24:24 For false C and false prophets will

CHURCH
Mt   16:18 and on this rock I will build my c,
     18:17 if he refuses to listen even to the c,
Ac   20:28 Be shepherds of the c of God,
1Co   5:12 of mine to judge those outside the c
     14: 4 but he who prophesies edifies the c.
     14:12 to excel in gifts that build up the c.
     14:26 done for the strengthening of the c.
Eph   5:23 as Christ is the head of the c,
Col   1:24 the sake of his body, which is the c.

CIRCUMCISED
Ge   17:10 Every male among you shall be c.

CIRCUMSTANCES
Php   4:11 to be content whatever the c.
1Th   5:18 continually; give thanks in all c,

CITIZENS (CITIZENSHIP)
Eph   2:19 but fellow c with God's people

CITIZENSHIP (CITIZENS)
Php   3:20 But our c is in heaven.

CITY
Mt   5:14 A c on a hill cannot be hidden.
Heb 13:14 here we do not have an enduring c,

CIVILIAN*
2Ti   2: 4 a soldier gets involved in c affairs—

CLAIM (CLAIMS)
Pr 25: 6 do not *c* a place among great men;
1Jn 1: 6 If we *c* to have fellowship
   1: 8 If we *c* to be without sin, we
   1:10 If we *c* we have not sinned,

CLAIMS (CLAIM)
Jas 2:14 if a man *c* to have faith
1Jn 2: 6 Whoever *c* to live in him must walk
   2: 9 Anyone who *c* to be in the light

CLAP
Ps 47: 1 *C* your hands, all you nations;
Isa 55:12 will *c* their hands.

CLAY
Isa 45: 9 Does the *c* say to the potter,
   64: 8 We are the *c*, you are the potter;
Jer 18: 6 "Like *c* in the hand of the potter,
La 4: 2 are now considered as pots of *c*,
Da 2:33 partly of iron and partly of baked *c*.
Ro 9:21 of the same lump of *c* some pottery
2Co 4: 7 we have this treasure in jars of *c*
2Ti 2:20 and *c*; some are for noble purposes

CLEAN
Lev 16:30 you will be *c* from all your sins.
Ps 24: 4 He who has *c* hands and a pure
Mt 12:44 the house unoccupied, swept *c*
   23:25 You *c* the outside of the cup
Mk 7:19 Jesus declared all foods "*c*.")
Jn 13:10 to wash his feet; his whole body is *c*
   15: 3 are already *c* because of the word
Ac 10:15 impure that God has made *c*."
Ro 14:20 All food is *c*, but it is wrong

CLING (CLINGS)
Ro 12: 9 Hate what is evil; *c* to what is good.

CLINGS (CLING)
Ps 63: 8 My soul *c* to you;

CLOAK
2Ki 4:29 "Tuck your *c* into your belt,

CLOSE (CLOSER)
Ps 34:18 LORD is *c* to the brokenhearted
Isa 40:11 and carries them *c* to his heart;
Jer 30:21 himself to be *c* to me?'

CLOSER (CLOSE)
Ex 3: 5 "Do not come any *c*," God said.
Pr 18:24 there is a friend who sticks *c*

CLOTHE (CLOTHED CLOTHES CLOTHING)
Ps 45: 3 *c* yourself with splendor
Isa 52: 1 *c* yourself with strength.
Ro 13:14 *c* yourselves with the Lord Jesus
Col 3:12 *c* yourselves with compassion,
1Pe 5: 5 *c* yourselves with humility

CLOTHED (CLOTHE)
Ps 30:11 removed my sackcloth and *c* me
Pr 31:25 She is *c* with strength and dignity;
Lk 24:49 until you have been *c* with power

CLOTHES (CLOTHE)
Mt 6:25 the body more important than *c*?
   6:28 "And why do you worry about *c*?
Jn 11:44 Take off the grave *c* and let him go

CLOTHING (CLOTHE)
Dt 22: 5 A woman must not wear men's *c*,
Mt 7:15 They come to you in sheep's *c*,

CLOUD (CLOUDS)
Ex 13:21 them in a pillar of *c* to guide them
Isa 19: 1 See, the LORD rides on a swift *c*

Lk 21:27 of Man coming in a *c* with power
Heb 12: 1 by such a great *c* of witnesses,

CLOUDS (CLOUD)
Ps 104: 3 He makes the *c* his chariot
Da 7:13 coming with the *c* of heaven.
Mk 13:26 coming in *c* with great power
1Th 4:17 with them in the *c* to meet the Lord

CO-HEIRS* (INHERIT)
Ro 8:17 heirs of God and *c* with Christ,

COALS
Pr 25:22 you will heap burning *c* on his head
Ro 12:20 you will heap burning *c* on his head

COLD
Pr 25:25 Like *c* water to a weary soul
Mt 10:42 if anyone gives even a cup of *c* water
   24:12 the love of most will grow *c*,

COMFORT (COMFORTED COMFORTS)
Ps 23: 4 rod and your staff, they *c* me.
  119: 52 and I find *c* in them.
  119: 76 May your unfailing love be my *c*,
Zec 1:17 and the LORD will again *c* Zion
1Co 14: 3 encouragement and *c*.
2Co 1: 4 so that we can *c* those
   2: 7 you ought to forgive and *c* him,

COMFORTED (COMFORT)
Mt 5: 4 for they will be *c*.

COMFORTS* (COMFORT)
Job 29:25 I was like one who *c* mourners.
Isa 49:13 For the LORD *c* his people
   51:12 "I, even I, am he who *c* you.
   66:13 As a mother *c* her child,
2Co 1: 4 who *c* us in all our troubles,
   7: 6 But God, who *c* the downcast,

COMMAND (COMMANDED COMMANDING COMMANDMENT COMMANDMENTS COMMANDS)
Ex 7: 2 You are to say everything I *c* you,
Nu 24:13 to go beyond the *c* of the LORD—
Dt 4: 2 Do not add to what I *c* you
   30:16 For I *c* you today to love
   32:46 so that you may *c* your children
Ps 91:11 For he will *c* his angels concerning
Pr 13:13 but he who respects a *c* is rewarded
Ecc 8: 2 Obey the king's *c*, I say,
Joel 2:11 mighty are those who obey his *c*.
Jn 14:15 love me, you will obey what I *c*.
   15:12 My *c* is this: Love each other
1Co 14:37 writing to you is the Lord's *c*.
Gal 5:14 law is summed up in a single *c*:
1Ti 1: 5 goal of this *c* is love, which comes
Heb 11: 3 universe was formed at God's *c*,
1Jn 3:23 this is his *c*: to believe in the name
2Jn : 6 his *c* is that you walk in love.

COMMANDED (COMMAND)
Ps 33: 9 he *c*, and it stood firm.
  148: 5 for he *c* and they were created.
Mt 28:20 to obey everything I have *c* you.
1Co 9:14 Lord has *c* that those who preach
1Jn 3:23 and to love one another as he *c* us.

COMMANDING (COMMAND)
2Ti 2: 4 he wants to please his *c* officer.

COMMANDMENT (COMMAND)
Jos 22: 5 But be very careful to keep the *c*
Mt 22:38 This is the first and greatest *c*.
Jn 13:34 "A new *c* I give you: Love one
Ro 7:12 and the *c* is holy, righteous
Eph 6: 2 which is the first *c* with a promise

COMMANDMENTS (COMMAND)
Ex 20: 6 who love me and keep my *c*.
   34:28 of the covenant—the Ten *C*.
Ecc 12:13 Fear God and keep his *c*,
Mt 5:19 one of the least of these *c*
   22:40 the Prophets hang on these two *c*."

COMMANDS (COMMAND)
Dt 7: 9 those who love him and keep his *c*.
   11:27 the blessing if you obey the *c*
Ps 112: 1 who finds great delight in his *c*.
  119: 47 for I delight in your *c*
  119: 86 All your *c* are trustworthy;
  119: 98 Your *c* make me wiser
  119:127 Because I love your *c*
  119:143 but your *c* are my delight.
  119:172 for all your *c* are righteous.
Pr 3: 1 but keep my *c* in your heart,
   6:23 For these *c* are a lamp,
   10: 8 The wise in heart accept *c*,
Da 9: 4 all who love him and obey his *c*,
Mt 5:19 teaches these *c* will be called great
Jn 14:21 Whoever has my *c* and obeys
Ac 17:30 but now he *c* all people everywhere
1Co 7:19 Keeping God's *c* is what counts.
1Jn 5: 3 And his *c* are not burdensome,
   5: 3 This is love for God: to obey his *c*.

COMMEND (COMMENDED COMMENDS)
Ecc 8:15 So I *c* the enjoyment of life,
Ro 13: 3 do what is right and he will *c* you.
1Pe 2:14 and to *c* those who do right.

COMMENDED (COMMEND)
Heb 11:39 These were all *c* for their faith,

COMMENDS (COMMEND)
2Co 10:18 not the one who *c* himself who is

COMMIT (COMMITS COMMITTED)
Ex 20:14 "You shall not *c* adultery.
Ps 37: 5 *C* your way to the LORD;
Mt 5:27 that it was said, 'Do not *c* adultery.'
Lk 23:46 into your hands I *c* my spirit."
Ac 20:32 I *c* you to God and to the word
1Co 10: 8 We should not *c* sexual immorality,
1Pe 4:19 to God's will should *c* themselves

COMMITS (COMMIT)
Pr 6:32 man who *c* adultery lacks
   29:22 a hot-tempered one *c* many sins.
Mt 19: 9 marries another woman *c* adultery

COMMITTED (COMMIT)
Nu 5: 7 and must confess the sin he has *c*.
1Ki 8:61 But your hearts must be fully *c*
2Ch 16: 9 those whose hearts are fully *c*
Mt 5:28 lustfully has already *c* adultery
2Co 5:19 And he has *c* to us the message
1Pe 2:22 "He *c* no sin,

COMMON
Pr 22: 2 Rich and poor have this in *c*:
1Co 10:13 has seized you except what is *c*
2Co 6:14 and wickedness have in *c*?

COMPANION (COMPANIONS)
Pr 13:20 but a *c* of fools suffers harm.
   28: 7 a *c* of gluttons disgraces his father.
   29: 3 *c* of prostitutes squanders his

COMPANIONS (COMPANION)
Pr 18:24 A man of many *c* may come to ruin

COMPANY
Pr   24: 1 do not desire their *c*;
Jer   15:17 I never sat in the *c* of revelers,
1Co   15:33 "Bad *c* corrupts good character."

COMPARED (COMPARING)
Eze   31: 2 Who can be *c* with you in majesty?
Php   3: 8 I consider everything a loss *c*

COMPARING* (COMPARED)
Ro   8:18 present sufferings are not worth *c*
2Co   8: 8 the sincerity of your love by *c* it
Gal   6: 4 without *c* himself to somebody else

COMPASSION (COMPASSIONATE COMPASSIONS)
Ex   33:19 I will have *c* on whom I will have *c*.
Ne   9:19 of your great *c* you did not
   9:28 in your *c* you delivered them time
Ps   51: 1 according to your great *c*
  103:   4 and crowns you with love and *c*.
  103: 13 As a father has *c* on his children,
  145:   9 he has *c* on all he has made.
Isa   49:13 and will have *c* on his afflicted ones
  49:15 and have no *c* on the child she has
Hos   2:19 in love and *c*.
   11: 8 all my *c* is aroused.
Jnh   3: 9 with *c* turn from his fierce anger
Mt   9:36 When he saw the crowds, he had *c*
Mk   8: 2 "I have *c* for these people;
Ro   9:15 and I will have *c* on whom I have *c*
Col   3:12 clothe yourselves with *c*, kindness,
Jas   5:11 The Lord is full of *c* and mercy.

COMPASSIONATE (COMPASSION)
Ne   9:17 gracious and *c*, slow to anger
Ps 103:   8 The LORD is *c* and gracious,
  112:   4 the gracious and *c* and righteous
Eph   4:32 Be kind and *c* to one another,
1Pe   3: 8 love as brothers, be *c* and humble.

COMPASSIONS* (COMPASSION)
La   3:22 for his *c* never fail.

COMPELLED (COMPELS)
Ac   20:22 "And now, *c* by the Spirit,
1Co   9:16 I cannot boast, for I am *c* to preach.

COMPELS (COMPELLED)
2Co   5:14 For Christ's love *c* us, because we

COMPETENCE* (COMPETENT)
2Co   3: 5 but our *c* comes from God.

COMPETENT* (COMPETENCE)
Ro   15:14 and *c* to instruct one another.
1Co   6: 2 are you not *c* to judge trivial cases?
2Co   3: 5 Not that we are *c* in ourselves
   3: 6 He has made us *c* as ministers

COMPETES*
1Co   9:25 Everyone who *c* in the games goes
2Ti   2: 5 Similarly, if anyone *c* as an athlete,
   2: 5 unless he *c* according to the rules.

COMPLACENT
Am   6: 1 Woe to you who are *c* in Zion,

COMPLAINING*
Php   2:14 Do everything without *c* or arguing

COMPLETE
Jn   15:11 and that your joy may be *c*.
  16:24 will receive, and your joy will be *c*.
  17:23 May they be brought to *c* unity
Ac   20:24 *c* the task the Lord Jesus has given
Php   2: 2 then make my joy *c*
Col   4:17 to it that you *c* the work you have
Jas   1: 4 so that you may be mature and *c*,
   2:22 his faith was made *c* by what he did

CONCEAL (CONCEALED CONCEALS)
Ps   40:10 I do not *c* your love and your truth
Pr   25: 2 It is the glory of God to *c* a matter;

CONCEALED (CONCEAL)
Jer   16:17 nor is their sin *c* from my eyes.
Mt   10:26 There is nothing *c* that will not be
Mk   4:22 and whatever is *c* is meant

CONCEALS (CONCEAL)
Pr   28:13 He who *c* his sins does not prosper,

CONCEITED
Ro   12:16 Do not be *c*.
Gal   5:26 Let us not become *c*, provoking
1Ti   6: 4 he is *c* and understands nothing.

CONCEIVED
Mt   1:20 what is *c* in her is from the Holy
1Co   2: .9 no mind has *c*

CONCERN (CONCERNED)
Eze   36:21 I had *c* for my holy name, which
1Co   7:32 I would like you to be free from *c*.
  12:25 that its parts should have equal *c*
2Co   11:28 of my *c* for all the churches.

CONCERNED (CONCERN)
Jnh   4:10 "You have been *c* about this vine,
1Co   7:32 An unmarried man is *c* about

CONDEMN (CONDEMNATION CONDEMNED CONDEMNING CONDEMNS)
Job   40: 8 Would you *c* me to justify yourself?
Isa   50: 9 Who is he that will *c* me?
Lk   6:37 Do not *c*, and you will not be
Jn   3:17 Son into the world to *c* the world,
  12:48 very word which I spoke will *c* him
Ro   2:27 yet obeys the law will *c* you who,
1Jn   3:20 presence whenever our hearts *c* us.

CONDEMNATION (CONDEMN)
Ro   5:18 of one trespass was *c* for all men,
   8: 1 there is now no *c* for those who are

CONDEMNED (CONDEMN)
Ps   34:22 no one will be *c* who takes refuge
Mt   12:37 and by your words you will be *c*."
  23:33 How will you escape being *c* to hell
Jn   3:18 Whoever believes in him is not *c*,
   5:24 has eternal life and will not be *c*;
  16:11 prince of this world now stands *c*.
Ro   14:23 But the man who has doubts is *c*
1Co   11:32 disciplined so that we will not be *c*
Heb   11: 7 By his faith he *c* the world

CONDEMNING (CONDEMN)
Pr   17:15 the guilty and *c* the innocent—
Ro   2: 1 judge the other, you are *c* yourself,

CONDEMNS (CONDEMN)
Ro   8:34 Who is he that *c*? Christ Jesus,
2Co   3: 9 the ministry that *c* men is glorious,

CONDUCT
Pr   10:23 A fool finds pleasure in evil *c*,
  20:11 by whether his *c* is pure and right.
  21: 8 but the *c* of the innocent is upright.
Ecc   6: 8 how to *c* himself before others?
Jer   4:18 "Your own *c* and actions
  17:10 to reward a man according to his *c*,
Eze   7: 3 I will judge you according to your *c*
Php   1:27 *c* yourselves in a manner worthy
1Ti   3:15 to *c* themselves in God's household

CONFESS (CONFESSION)
Lev   16:21 and *c* over it all the wickedness
  26:40 " 'But if they will *c* their sins
Nu   5: 7 must *c* the sin he has committed.
Ps   38:18 I *c* my iniquity;
Ro   10: 9 That if you *c* with your mouth,
Php   2:11 every tongue *c* that Jesus Christ is
Jas   5:16 Therefore *c* your sins to each other
1Jn   1: 9 If we *c* our sins, he is faithful

CONFESSION (CONFESS)
Ezr   10:11 Now make *c* to the LORD.
2Co   9:13 obedience that accompanies your *c*

CONFIDENCE
Ps   71: 5 my *c* since my youth.
Pr   3:26 for the LORD will be your *c*
  11:13 A gossip betrays a *c*,
  25: 9 do not betray another man's *c*,
  31:11 Her husband has full *c* in her
Isa   32:17 will be quietness and *c* forever.
Jer   17: 7 whose *c* is in him.
Php   3: 3 and who put no *c* in the flesh—
Heb   3:14 till the end the *c* we had at first.
   4:16 the throne of grace with *c*,
  10:19 since we have *c* to enter the Most
  10:35 So do not throw away your *c*;
1Jn   5:14 This is the *c* we have

CONFORM* (CONFORMED)
Ro   12: 2 Do not *c* any longer to the pattern
1Pe   1:14 do not *c* to the evil desires you had

CONFORMED (CONFORM)
Ro   8:29 predestined to be *c* to the likeness

CONQUERORS
Ro   8:37 than *c* through him who loved us.

CONSCIENCE (CONSCIENCES)
Ro   13: 5 punishment but also because of *c*.
1Co   8: 7 since their *c* is weak, it is defiled.
   8:12 in this way and wound their weak *c*
  10:25 without raising questions of *c*,
  10:29 freedom be judged by another's *c*?
Heb   10:22 to cleanse us from a guilty *c*
1Pe   3:16 and respect, keeping a clear *c*,

CONSCIENCES* (CONSCIENCE)
Ro   2:15 their *c* also bearing witness,
1Ti   4: 2 whose *c* have been seared
Tit   1:15 their minds and *c* are corrupted.

Heb 9:14 cleanse our *c* from acts that lead

CONSCIOUS*
Ro 3:20 through the law we become *c* of sin
1Pe 2:19 of unjust suffering because he is *c*

CONSECRATE (CONSECRATED)
Ex 13: 2 "*C* to me every firstborn male.
Lev 20: 7 " '*C* yourselves and be holy,

CONSECRATED (CONSECRATE)
Ex 29:43 and the place will be *c* by my glory.
1Ti 4: 5 because it is *c* by the word of God

CONSIDER (CONSIDERATE CONSIDERED CONSIDERS)
1Sa 12:24 *c* what great things he has done
Job 37:14 stop and *c* God's wonders.
Ps 8: 3 When I *c* your heavens,
107: 43 and *c* the great love of the LORD.
143: 5 and *c* what your hands have done.
Lk 12:24 *C* the ravens: They do not sow
12:27 about the rest? "*C* how the lilies
Php 2: 3 but in humility *c* others better
3: 8 I *c* everything a loss compared
Heb 10:24 And let us *c* how we may spur one
Jas 1: 2 *C* it pure joy, my brothers,

CONSIDERATE* (CONSIDER)
Tit 3: 2 to be peaceable and *c*,
Jas 3:17 then peace-loving, *c*, submissive,
1Pe 2:18 only to those who are good and *c*,
3: 7 in the same way be *c* as you live

CONSIDERED (CONSIDER)
Job 1: 8 "Have you *c* my servant Job?
2: 3 "Have you *c* my servant Job?
Ps 44:22 we are *c* as sheep to be slaughtered.
Isa 53: 4 yet we *c* him stricken by God,
Ro 8:36 we are *c* as sheep to be slaughtered

CONSIDERS (CONSIDER)
Pr 31:16 She *c* a field and buys it;
Ro 14: 5 One man *c* one day more sacred
Jas 1:26 If anyone *c* himself religious

CONSIST
Lk 12:15 a man's life does not *c*

CONSOLATION
Ps 94:19 your *c* brought joy to my soul.

CONSTRUCTIVE*
1Co 10:23 but not everything is *c*.

CONSUME (CONSUMING)
Jn 2:17 "Zeal for your house will *c* me."

CONSUMING (CONSUME)
Dt 4:24 For the LORD your God is a *c* fire,
Heb 12:29 and awe, for our "God is a *c* fire."

CONTAIN
1Ki 8:27 the highest heaven, cannot *c* you.
2Pe 3:16 His letters *c* some things that are

CONTAMINATES*
2Co 7: 1 from everything that *c* body

CONTEMPT
Pr 14:31 He who oppresses the poor shows *c*
17: 5 He who mocks the poor shows *c*
18: 3 When wickedness comes, so does *c*
Da 12: 2 others to shame and everlasting *c*.
Ro 2: 4 Or do you show *c* for the riches

Gal 4:14 you did not treat me with *c*
1Th 5:20 do not treat prophecies with *c*.

CONTEND (CONTENDING)
Jude : 3 you to *c* for the faith that was once

CONTENDING* (CONTEND)
Php 1:27 *c* as one man for the faith

CONTENT (CONTENTMENT)
Pr 13:25 The righteous eat to their hearts' *c*,
Php 4:11 to be *c* whatever the circumstances
4:12 I have learned the secret of being *c*
1Ti 6: 8 and clothing, we will be *c* with that.
Heb 13: 5 and be *c* with what you have,

CONTENTMENT (CONTENT)
1Ti 6: 6 But godliness with *c* is great gain.

CONTINUAL (CONTINUE)
Pr 15:15 but the cheerful heart has a *c* feast.

CONTINUE (CONTINUAL)
Php 2:12 *c* to work out your salvation
2Ti 3:14 *c* in what you have learned
1Jn 5:18 born of God does not *c* to sin;
Rev 22:11 and let him who is holy *c* to be holy
22:11 let him who does right *c* to do right;

CONTRITE*
Ps 51:17 a broken and *c* heart,
Isa 57:15 also with him who is *c* and lowly
57:15 and to revive the heart of the *c*.
66: 2 he who is humble and *c* in spirit,

CONTROL (CONTROLLED SELF-CONTROL SELF-CONTROLLED)
Pr 29:11 a wise man keeps himself under *c*.
1Co 7: 9 But if they cannot *c* themselves,
7:37 but has *c* over his own will,
1Th 4: 4 you should learn to *c* his own body

CONTROLLED (CONTROL)
Ps 32: 9 but must be *c* by bit and bridle
Ro 8: 6 but the mind *c* by the Spirit is life
8: 8 Those *c* by the sinful nature cannot

CONTROVERSIES
Tit 3: 9 But avoid foolish *c* and genealogies

CONVERSATION
Col 4: 6 Let your *c* be always full of grace,

CONVERT
1Ti 3: 6 He must not be a recent *c*,

CONVICT
Jn 16: 8 he will *c* the world of guilt in regard

CONVINCED (CONVINCING)
Ro 8:38 For I am *c* that neither death
2Ti 1:12 and am *c* that he is able
3:14 have learned and have become *c*

CONVINCING* (CONVINCED)
Ac 1: 3 and gave many *c* proofs that he was

CORNELIUS*
Roman to whom Peter preached; first Gentile Christian (Ac 10).

CORNERSTONE (STONE)
Isa 28:16 a precious *c* for a sure foundation;

Eph 2:20 Christ Jesus himself as the chief *c*.
1Pe 2: 6 a chosen and precious *c*,

CORRECT (CORRECTING CORRECTION CORRECTS)
2Ti 4: 2 *c*, rebuke and encourage—

CORRECTING* (CORRECT)
2Ti 3:16 *c* and training in righteousness,

CORRECTION (CORRECT)
Pr 10:17 whoever ignores *c* leads others
12: 1 but he who hates *c* is stupid.
15: 5 whoever heeds *c* shows prudence.
15:10 he who hates *c* will die.
29:15 The rod of *c* imparts wisdom,

CORRECTS* (CORRECT)
Job 5:17 "Blessed is the man whom God *c*;
Pr 9: 7 Whoever *c* a mocker invites insult;

CORRUPT (CORRUPTS)
Ge 6:11 Now the earth was *c* in God's sight

CORRUPTS* (CORRUPT)
Ecc 7: 7 and a bribe *c* the heart.
1Co 15:33 "Bad company *c* good character."
Jas 3: 6 It *c* the whole person, sets

COST
Pr 4: 7 Though it *c* all you have, get
Isa 55: 1 milk without money and without *c*.
Rev 21: 6 to drink without *c* from the spring

COUNSEL (COUNSELOR)
1Ki 22: 5 "First seek the *c* of the LORD."
Pr 15:22 Plans fail for lack of *c*,
Rev 3:18 I *c* you to buy from me gold refined

COUNSELOR (COUNSEL)
Isa 9: 6 Wonderful *C*, Mighty God,
Jn 14:16 he will give you another *C* to be
14:26 But the *C*, the Holy Spirit,

COUNT (COUNTING COUNTS)
Ro 4: 8 whose sin the Lord will never *c*
6:11 *c* yourselves dead to sin

COUNTING (COUNT)
2Co 5:19 not *c* men's sins against them.

COUNTRY
Jn 4:44 prophet has no honor in his own *c*.)

COUNTS (COUNT)
Jn 6:63 The Spirit gives life; the flesh *c*
1Co 7:19 God's commands is what *c*.
Gal 5: 6 only thing that *c* is faith expressing

COURAGE (COURAGEOUS)
Ac 23:11 "Take *c*! As you have testified
1Co 16:13 stand firm in the faith; be men of *c*;

COURAGEOUS (COURAGE)
Dt 31: 6 Be strong and *c*.
Jos 1: 6 and *c*, because you will lead these

COURSE
Ps 19: 5 a champion rejoicing to run his *c*.
Pr 15:21 of understanding keeps a straight *c*.

COURTS
Ps 84:10 Better is one day in your *c*
100: 4 and his *c* with praise;

COVENANT (COVENANTS)
Ge 9: 9 "I now establish my *c* with you

Ex 19: 5 if you obey me fully and keep
my c,
1Ch 16:15 He remembers his c forever,
Job 31: 1 "I made a c with my eyes
Jer 31:31 "when I will make a new c
1Co 11:25 "This cup is the new c in my
blood;
Gal 4:24 One c is from Mount Sinai
Heb 9:15 Christ is the mediator of a
new c,

COVENANTS (COVENANT)
Ro 9: 4 theirs the divine glory, the c,
Gal 4:24 for the women represent two c.

COVER (COVER-UP COVERED COVERS)
Ps 91: 4 He will c you with his feathers,
Jas 5:20 and c over a multitude of sins.

COVER-UP (COVER)
1Pe 2:16 but do not use your freedom as
a c

COVERED (COVER)
Ps 32: 1 whose sins are c.
Isa 6: 2 With two wings they c their
faces,
Ro 4: 7 whose sins are c.
1Co 11: 4 with his head c dishonors his
head.

COVERS (COVER)
Pr 10:12 but love c over all wrongs.
1Pe 4: 8 love c over a multitude of sins.

COVET
Ex 20:17 You shall not c your neighbor's
Ro 13: 9 "Do not steal," "Do not c,"

COWARDLY*
Rev 21: 8 But the c, the unbelieving, the
vile,

CRAFTINESS (CRAFTY)
1Co 3:19 "He catches the wise in their c";

CRAFTY (CRAFTINESS)
Ge 3: 1 the serpent was more c than
any
2Co 12:16 c fellow that I am, I caught you

CRAVE
Pr 23: 3 Do not c his delicacies,
1Pe 2: 2 newborn babies, c pure spiritual

CREATE (CREATED CREATION CREATOR)
Ps 51:10 C in me a pure heart, O God,
Isa 45:18 he did not c it to be empty,

CREATED (CREATE)
Ge 1: 1 In the beginning God c the
heavens
1:21 God c the great creatures of the
sea
1:27 So God c man in his own image,
Ps 148: 5 for he commanded and they
were c
Isa 42: 5 he who c the heavens and
stretched
Ro 1:25 and served c things rather
1Co 11: 9 neither was man c for woman,
Col 1:16 For by him all things were c:
1Ti 4: 4 For everything God c is good,
Rev 10: 6 who c the heavens and all that
is

CREATION (CREATE)
Mk 16:15 and preach the good news to
all c.
Jn 17:24 me before the c of the world.
Ro 8:19 The c waits in eager expectation
8:39 depth, nor anything else in all c,
2Co 5:17 he is a new c; the old has gone,
Col 1:15 God, the firstborn over all c.
1Pe 1:20 chosen before the c of the
world,
Rev 13: 8 slain from the c of the world.

CREATOR (CREATE)
Ge 14:22 God Most High, C of heaven

Ro 1:25 created things rather than
the C—

CREATURE (CREATURES)
Lev 17:11 For the life of a c is in the
blood,

CREATURES (CREATURE)
Ge 6:19 bring into the ark two of all
living c,
Ps 104: 24 the earth is full of your c.

CREDIT (CREDITED)
Ro 4:24 to whom God will c
righteousness
1Pe 2:20 it to your c if you receive a
beating

CREDITED (CREDIT)
Ge 15: 6 and he c it to him as
righteousness.
Ro 4: 5 his faith is c as righteousness.
Gal 3: 6 and it was c to him as
righteousness
Jas 2:23 and it was c to him as
righteousness

CRIED (CRY)
Ps 18: 6 I c to my God for help.

CRIMSON
Isa 1:18 though they are red as c,

CRIPPLED
Mk 9:45 better for you to enter life c

CRITICISM
2Co 8:20 We want to avoid any c

CROOKED
Pr 10: 9 he who takes c paths will be
found
Php 2:15 children of God without fault in
a c

CROSS
Mt 10:38 and anyone who does not take
his c
Lk 9:23 take up his c daily and follow
me.
Ac 2:23 to death by nailing him to the c.
1Co 1:17 lest the c of Christ be emptied
Gal 6:14 in the c of our Lord Jesus Christ,
Php 2: 8 even death on a c!
Col 1:20 through his blood, shed on
the c.
2:14 he took it away, nailing it to
the c.
2:15 triumphing over them by the c.
Heb 12: 2 set before him endured the c,

CROWD
Ex 23: 2 Do not follow the c in doing
wrong.

CROWN (CROWNED CROWNS)
Pr 4: 9 present you with a c of
splendor."
10: 6 Blessings c the head
12: 4 noble character is her
husband's c,
17: 6 Children's children are a c
Isa 61: 3 to bestow on them a c of beauty
Zec 9:16 like jewels in a c.
Mt 27:29 then twisted together a c of
thorns
1Co 9:25 it to get a c that will last forever.
2Ti 4: 8 store for me the c of
righteousness,
Rev 2:10 and I will give you the c of life.

CROWNED (CROWN)
Ps 8: 5 and c him with glory and honor.
Pr 14:18 the prudent are c with
knowledge.
Heb 2: 7 you c him with glory and honor

CROWNS (CROWN)
Rev 4:10 They lay their c before the
throne
19:12 and on his head are many c.

CRUCIFIED (CRUCIFY)
Mt 20:19 to be mocked and flogged and c.
27:38 Two robbers were c with him,
Lk 24: 7 be c and on the third day be
raised
Jn 19:18 Here they c him, and with him
two
Ac 2:36 whom you c, both Lord and
Christ
Ro 6: 6 For we know that our old self
was c
1Co 1:23 but we preach Christ c: a
stumbling
2: 2 except Jesus Christ and him c.
Gal 2:20 I have been c with Christ
5:24 Christ Jesus have c the sinful

CRUCIFY (CRUCIFIED CRUCIFYING)
Mt 27:22 They all answered, "C him!"
"Why
27:31 Then they led him away to c
him.

CRUCIFYING* (CRUCIFY)
Heb 6: 6 to their loss they are c the Son

CRUSH (CRUSHED)
Ge 3:15 he will c your head,
Isa 53:10 it was the LORD's will to c him
Ro 16:20 The God of peace will soon c
Satan

CRUSHED (CRUSH)
Ps 34:18 and saves those who are c in
spirit.
Isa 53: 5 he was c for our iniquities;
2Co 4: 8 not c; perplexed, but not in
despair;

CRY (CRIED)
Ps 34:15 and his ears are attentive to
their c;
40: 1 he turned to me and heard my c.
130: 1 Out of the depths I c to you,

CUP
Ps 23: 5 my c overflows.
Mt 10:42 if anyone gives even a c of cold
water
23:25 You clean the outside of the c
26:39 may this c be taken from me.
1Co 11:25 after supper he took the c,
saying,

CURSE (CURSED)
Dt 11:26 before you today a blessing and
a c
21:23 hung on a tree is under God's c.
Lk 6:28 bless those who c you, pray
Gal 3:13 of the law by becoming a c for
us,
Rev 22: 3 No longer will there be any c.

CURSED (CURSE)
Ge 3:17 "C is the ground because of you;
Dt 27:15 "C is the man who carves an
image
27:16 "C is the man who dishonors his
27:17 "C is the man who moves his
27:18 "C is the man who leads the
blind
27:19 C is the man who withholds
justice
27:20 "C is the man who sleeps
27:21 "C is the man who has sexual
27:22 "C is the man who sleeps
27:23 "C is the man who sleeps
27:24 "C is the man who kills his
27:25 "C is the man who accepts a
bribe
27:26 "C is the man who does not
uphold
Ro 9: 3 I could wish that I myself were c
Gal 3:10 "C is everyone who does not

CURTAIN
Ex 26:33 The c will separate the Holy
Place
Lk 23:45 the c of the temple was torn in
two.
Heb 10:20 opened for us through the c,

CYMBAL*

1Co 13: 1 a resounding gong or a clanging c.

DANCE (DANCING)

Ecc 3: 4 a time to mourn and a time to d,
Mt 11:17 and you did not d;

DANCING (DANCE)

Ps 30:11 You turned my wailing into d;
149: 3 Let them praise his name with d

DANGER

Pr 27:12 The prudent see d and take refuge,
Ro 8:35 famine or nakedness or d or sword?

DANIEL

Hebrew exile to Babylon, name changed to Belteshazzar (Da 1:6-7). Refused to eat unclean food (Da 1:8-21). Interpreted Nebuchadnezzar's dreams (Da 2; 4), writing on the wall (Da 5). Thrown into lion's den (Da 6). Visions of (Da 7-12).

DARK (DARKNESS)

Job 34:22 There is no d place, no deep
Pr 31:15 She gets up while it is still d;
Ro 2:19 a light for those who are in the d,
2Pe 1:19 as to a light shining in a d place,

DARKNESS (DARK)

Ge 1: 4 he separated the light from the d.
2Sa 22:29 the LORD turns my d into light.
Jn 3:19 but men loved d instead of light
2Co 6:14 fellowship can light have with d?
Eph 5: 8 For you were once d, but now you
1Pe 2: 9 out of d into his wonderful light.
1Jn 1: 5 in him there is no d at all.
2: 9 but hates his brother is still in the d.

DAUGHTERS

Joel 2:28 sons and d will prophesy,

DAVID

Son of Jesse (Ru 4:17-22; 1Ch 2:13-15), ancestor of Jesus (Mt 1:1-17; Lk 3:31). Anointed king by Samuel (1Sa 16:1-13). Musician to Saul (1Sa 16:14-23; 18:10). Killed Goliath (1Sa 17). Relation with Jonathan (1Sa 18:1-4; 19-20; 23:16-18; 2Sa 1). Disfavor of Saul (1Sa 18:6-23:29). Spared Saul's life (1Sa 24; 26). Among Philistines (1Sa 21:10-14; 27-30). Lament for Saul and Jonathan (2Sa 1). Anointed king of Judah (2Sa 2:1-11); of Israel (2Sa 5:1-4; 1Ch 11:1-3). Promised eternal dynasty (2Sa 7; 1Ch 17; Ps 132). Adultery with Bathsheba (2Sa 11-12). Absalom's revolt (2Sa 14-18). Last words (2Sa 23:1-7). Death (1Ki 2:10-12; 1Ch 29:28).

DAWN

Ps 37: 6 your righteousness shine like the d,
Pr 4:18 is like the first gleam of d,

DAY (DAYS)

Ge 1: 5 God called the light "d,"
Ex 20: 8 "Remember the Sabbath d
Lev 23:28 because it is the D of Atonement,
Nu 14:14 before them in a pillar of cloud by d,
Jos 1: 8 meditate on it d and night,
Ps 84:10 Better is one d in your courts
96: 2 proclaim his salvation d after d.
118: 24 This is the d the LORD has made;
Pr 27: 1 not know what a d may bring forth.
Joel 2:31 and dreadful d of the LORD.
Ob : 15 The d of the LORD is near
Lk 11: 3 Give us each d our daily bread.
Ac 17:11 examined the Scriptures every d
2Co 4:16 we are being renewed d by d.

1Th 5: 2 for you know very well that the d
2Pe 3: 8 With the Lord a d is like

DAYS (DAY)

Dt 17:19 he is to read it all the d, of his life
Ps 23: 6 all the d of my life,
90:10 The length of our d is seventy years
Ecc 12: 1 Creator in the d of your youth,
Joel 2:29 I will pour out my Spirit in those d.
Mic 4: 1 In the last d
Heb 1: 2 in these last d he has spoken to us
2Pe 3: 3 that in the last d scoffers will come,

DEACONS

1Ti 3: 8 D, likewise, are to be men worthy

DEAD (DIE)

Dt 18:11 or spiritist or who consults the d.
Mt 28: 7 'He has risen from the d
Ro 6:11 count yourselves d to sin
Eph 2: 1 you were d in your transgressions
1Th 4:16 and the d in Christ will rise first.
Jas 2:17 is not accompanied by action, is d.
2:26 so faith without deeds is d.

DEATH (DIE)

Nu 35:16 the murderer shall be put to d.
Ps 23: 4 the valley of the shadow of d,
116: 15 is the d of his saints.
Pr 8:36 all who hate me love d."
14:12 but in the end it leads to d.
Ecc 7: 2 for d is the destiny of every man;
Isa 25: 8 he will swallow up d forever.
53:12 he poured out his life unto d,
Jn 5:24 he has crossed over from d to life.
Ro 5:12 and in this way d came to all men,
6:23 For the wages of sin is d,
8:13 put to d the misdeeds of the body,
1Co 15:21 For since d came through a man,
15:55 Where, O d, is your sting?"
Rev 1:18 And I hold the keys of d and Hades
20: 6 The second d has no power
20:14 The lake of fire is the second d.
21: 4 There will be no more d

DEBAUCHERY

Ro 13:13 not in sexual immorality and d,
Eph 5:18 drunk on wine, which leads to d.

DEBORAH

Prophetess who led Israel to victory over Canaanites (Jdg 4-5).

DEBT (DEBTORS DEBTS)

Ro 13: 8 Let no d remain outstanding,
13: 8 continuing d to love one another,

DEBTORS (DEBT)

Mt 6:12 as we also have forgiven our d.

DEBTS (DEBT)

Dt 15: 1 seven years you must cancel d.
Mt 6:12 Forgive us our d,

DECAY

Ps 16:10 will you let your Holy One see d.
Ac 2:27 will you let your Holy One see d.

DECEIT (DECEIVE)

Mk 7:22 greed, malice, d, lewdness, envy,
1Pe 2: 1 yourselves of all malice and all d,
2:22 and no d was found in his mouth."

DECEITFUL (DECEIVE)

Jer 17: 9 The heart is d above all things
2Co 11:13 men are false apostles, d workmen,

DECEITFULNESS (DECEIVE)

Mk 4:19 the d of wealth and the desires
Heb 3:13 of you may be hardened by sin's d.

DECEIVE (DECEIT DECEITFUL DECEITFULNESS DECEIVED DECEIVES DECEPTIVE)

Lev 19:11 " 'Do not d one another.
Pr 14: 5 A truthful witness does not d,
Mt 24: 5 'I am the Christ,' and will d many.
Ro 16:18 and flattery they d the minds
1Co 3:18 Do not d yourselves.
Eph 5: 6 Let no one d you with empty words
Jas 1:22 to the word, and so d yourselves.
1Jn 1: 8 we d ourselves and the truth is not

DECEIVED (DECEIVE)

Ge 3:13 "The serpent d me, and I ate."
Gal 6: 7 Do not be d: God cannot be
1Ti 2:14 And Adam was not the one d;
2Ti 3:13 to worse, deceiving and being d.
Jas 1:16 Don't be d, my dear brothers.

DECEIVES (DECEIVE)

Gal 6: 3 when he is nothing, he d himself.
Jas 1:26 he d himself and his religion is

DECENCY*

1Ti 2: 9 women to dress modestly, with d

DECEPTIVE (DECEIVE)

Pr 31:30 Charm is d, and beauty is fleeting;
Col 2: 8 through hollow and d philosophy,

DECLARE (DECLARED DECLARING)

1Ch 16:24 D his glory among the nations,
Ps 19: 1 The heavens d the glory of God;
96: 3 his glory among the nations,
Isa 42: 9 and new things I d;

DECLARED (DECLARE)

Mk 7:19 Jesus d all foods "clean.")
Ro 2:13 the law who will be d righteous.
3:20 no one will be d righteous

DECLARING (DECLARE)

Ps 71: 8 d your splendor all day long.
Ac 2:11 we hear them d the wonders

DECREED (DECREES)

La 3:37 happen if the Lord has not d it?
Lk 22:22 Son of Man will go as it has been d,

DECREES (DECREED)

Lev 10:11 Israelites all the d the LORD has
Ps 119:112 My heart is set on keeping your d

DEDICATE (DEDICATION)

Nu 6:12 He must d himself to the LORD
Pr 20:25 for a man to d something rashly

DEDICATION (DEDICATE)

1Ti 5:11 sensual desires overcome their d

DEED (DEEDS)

Col 3:17 you do, whether in word or d,

DEEDS (DEED)

1Sa 2: 3 and by him d are weighed.
Ps 65: 5 with awesome d of righteousness,
66: 3 "How awesome are your d!
78: 4 the praiseworthy d of the LORD,

DEEP
Ps　86:10 you are great and do
　　　　　marvelous *d*;
　　92: 4 For you make me glad by your *d*,
　111: 3 Glorious and majestic are his *d*,
Hab　3: 2 I stand in awe of your *d*, O LORD.
Mt　 5:16 that they may see your good *d*
Ac　26:20 prove their repentance by
　　　　　their *d*.
Jas　 2:14 claims to have faith but has
　　　　　no *d*?
　　　2:20 faith without *d* is useless?
1Pe　2:12 they may see your good *d*

DEEP (DEPTH)
1Co　2:10 all things, even the *d* things
1Ti　3: 9 hold of the *d* truths of the faith

DEER
Ps　42: 1 As the *d* pants for streams of
　　　　　water,

DEFEND (DEFENSE)
Ps　74:22 Rise up, O God, and *d* your
　　　　　cause;
Pr　31: 9 *d* the rights of the poor and
　　　　　needy
Jer　50:34 He will vigorously *d* their cause

DEFENSE (DEFEND)
Ps　35:23 Awake, and rise to my *d*!
Php　1:16 here for the *d* of the gospel.
1Jn　2: 1 speaks to the Father in our *d*—

DEFERRED*
Pr　13:12 Hope *d* makes the heart sick,

DEFILE (DEFILED)
Da　1: 8 Daniel resolved not to *d* himself

DEFILED (DEFILE)
Isa　24: 5 The earth is *d* by its people;

DEFRAUD
Lev　19:13 Do not *d* your neighbor or rob
　　　　　him.

DEITY*
Col　2: 9 of the *D* lives in bodily form,

DELIGHT (DELIGHTS)
1Sa　15:22 "Does the LORD *d*
Ps　1: 2 But his *d* is in the law of the
　　　　　LORD
　　16: 3 in whom is all my *d*.
　　35: 9 and *d* in his salvation.
　　37: 4 *D* yourself in the LORD
　　43: 4 to God, my joy and my *d*.
　　51:16 You do not *d* in sacrifice,
　119:77 for your law is my *d*.
Pr　29:17 he will bring *d* to your soul.
Isa　42: 1 my chosen one in whom I *d*;
　　55: 2 and your soul will *d* in the
　　　　　richest
　　61:10 I *d* greatly in the LORD;
Jer　9:24 for in these I *d*,"
　　15:16 they were my joy and my
　　　　　heart's *d*,
Mic　7:18 but *d* to show mercy.
Zep　3:17 He will take great *d* in you,
Mt　12:18 the one I love, in whom I *d*;
1Co　13: 6 Love does not *d* in evil
2Co　12:10 for Christ's sake, I *d* in
　　　　　weaknesses,

DELIGHTS (DELIGHT)
Ps　22: 8 since he *d* in him."
　　35:27 who *d* in the well-being
　　36: 8 from your river of *d*.
　　37:23 if the LORD *d* in a man's way,
Pr　3:12 as a father the son he *d* in.
　　12:22 but he *d* in men who are
　　　　　truthful.
　　23:24 he who has a wise son *d* in him.

DELILAH*
　Woman who betrayed Samson (Jdg 16:4-
　22).

**DELIVER (DELIVERANCE DELIVERED
DELIVERER DELIVERS)**
Ps　72:12 For he will *d* the needy who cry
　　　　　out

Ps　79: 9 *d* us and forgive our sins
Mt　6:13 but *d* us from the evil one.'
2Co　1:10 hope that he will continue to *d*
　　　　　us,

DELIVERANCE (DELIVER)
Ps　3: 8 From the LORD comes *d*.
　　32: 7 and surround me with songs
　　　　　of *d*.
　　33:17 A horse is a vain hope for *d*;

DELIVERED (DELIVER)
Ps　34: 4 he *d* me from all my fears.
Ro　4:25 He was *d* over to death for our
　　　　　sins

DELIVERER (DELIVER)
Ps　18: 2 is my rock, my fortress and
　　　　　my *d*;
　　40:17 You are my help and my *d*;
　140: 7 O Sovereign LORD, my strong *d*,
　144: 2 my stronghold and my *d*,

DELIVERS (DELIVER)
Ps　34:17 he *d* them from all their
　　　　　troubles.
　　34:19 but the LORD *d* him from them all
　　37:40 The LORD helps them and *d*
　　　　　them
　　37:40 he *d* them from the wicked

DEMANDED
Lk　12:20 This very night your life will be *d*
　　12:48 been given much, much will
　　　　　be *d*;

DEMONS
Mt　12:27 And if I drive out *d* by
　　　　　Beelzebub,
Mk　5:15 possessed by the legion of *d*,
Ro　8:38 neither angels nor *d*, neither
Jas　2:19 Good! Even the *d* believe that—

DEMONSTRATE (DEMONSTRATES)
Ro　3:26 he did it to *d* his justice

DEMONSTRATES* (DEMONSTRATE)
Ro　5: 8 God *d* his own love for us in
　　　　　this:

DEN
Da　6:16 and threw him into the lions' *d*.
Mt　21:13 you are making it a '*d* of
　　　　　robbers.' "

DENARIUS
Mk　12:15 Bring me a *d* and let me look at
　　　　　it."

DENIED (DENY)
1Ti　5: 8 he has *d* the faith and is worse

DENIES (DENY)
1Jn　2:23 No one who *d* the Son has

DENY (DENIED DENIES DENYING)
Ex　23: 6 "Do not *d* justice to your poor
Job　27: 5 till I die, I will not *d* my integrity.
La　3:35 to *d* a man his rights
Lk　9:23 he must *d* himself and take up
　　　　　his
Tit　1:16 but by their actions they *d* him.

DENYING* (DENY)
Eze　22:29 mistreat the alien, *d* them
　　　　　justice.
2Ti　3: 5 a form of godliness but *d* its
　　　　　power.
2Pe　2: 1 the sovereign Lord who bought

DEPART (DEPARTED)
Ge　49:10 The scepter will not *d* from
　　　　　Judah,
Job　1:21 and naked I will *d*.
Mt　25:41 '*D* from me, you who are cursed,
Php　1:23 I desire to *d* and be with Christ,

DEPARTED (DEPART)
1Sa　4:21 "The glory has *d* from Israel"—
Ps 119:102 I have not *d* from your laws,

DEPOSIT
2Co　1:22 put his Spirit in our hearts as
　　　　　a *d*,
　　　5: 5 and has given us the Spirit as
　　　　　a *d*,
Eph　1:14 who is a *d* guaranteeing our
2Ti　1:14 Guard the good *d* that was

DEPRAVED (DEPRAVITY)
Ro　1:28 he gave them over to a *d* mind,
Php　2:15 fault in a crooked and *d*
　　　　　generation,

DEPRAVITY (DEPRAVED)
Ro　1:29 of wickedness, evil, greed and *d*.

DEPRIVE
Dt　24:17 Do not *d* the alien or the
　　　　　fatherless
Pr　18: 5 or to *d* the innocent of justice.
Isa　10: 2 to *d* the poor of their rights
　　29:21 with false testimony *d* the
　　　　　innocent
1Co　7: 5 Do not *d* each other

DEPTH (DEEP)
Ro　8:39 any powers, neither height nor *d*,
　　11:33 the *d* of the riches of the
　　　　　wisdom

DESERT
Nu　32:13 wander in the *d* forty years,
Ne　9:19 you did not abandon them in
　　　　　the *d*.
Ps　78:19 "Can God spread a table in
　　　　　the *d*?
　　78:52 led them like sheep through
　　　　　the *d*.
Mk　1:13 and he was in the *d* forty days,

DESERTED (DESERTS)
Ezr　9: 9 our God has not *d* us
Mt　26:56 all the disciples *d* him and fled.
2Ti　1:15 in the province of Asia has *d*
　　　　　me,

DESERTING (DESERTS)
Gal　1: 6 are so quickly *d* the one who
　　　　　called

DESERTS (DESERTED DESERTING)
Zec　11:17 who *d* the flock!

DESERVE (DESERVES)
Ps 103:10 he does not treat us as our
　　　　　sins *d*
Jer　21:14 I will punish you as your
　　　　　deeds *d*,
Mt　22: 8 those I invited did not *d* to
　　　　　come.
Ro　1:32 those who do such things *d*
　　　　　death,

DESERVES (DESERVE)
2Sa　12: 5 the man who did this *d* to die!
Lk　10: 7 for the worker *d* his wages.
1Ti　5:18 and "The worker *d* his wages."

DESIRABLE (DESIRE)
Pr　22: 1 A good name is more *d*

DESIRE (DESIRABLE DESIRES)
Ge　3:16 Your *d* will be for your husband,
Dt　5:21 You shall not set your *d*
1Ch 29:18 keep this *d* in the hearts
Ps　40: 6 Sacrifice and offering you did
　　　　　not *d*
　　40: 8 I *d* to do your will, O my God;
　　73:25 earth has nothing I *d* besides
　　　　　you
Pr　3:15 nothing you *d* can compare
　　10:24 what the righteous *d* will be
　　11:23 The *d* of the righteous ends only
Isa　26: 8 are the *d* of our hearts.
　　53: 2 appearance that we should *d*
　　　　　him.
　　55:11 but will accomplish what I *d*
Hos　6: 6 For I *d* mercy, not sacrifice,
Mt　9:13 learn what this means: 'I *d*
　　　　　mercy,
Ro　7:18 For I have the *d* to do what is
　　　　　good,

1Co 12:31 But eagerly *d* the greater gifts.
 14: 1 and eagerly *d* spiritual gifts,
Php 1:23 I *d* to depart and be with Christ,
Heb 13:18 *d* to live honorably in every way.
Jas 1:15 Then, after *d* has conceived,

DESIRES (DESIRE)
Ge 4: 7 at your door; it *d* to have you,
Ps 34:12 and *d* to see many good days,
 37: 4 he will give you the *d* of your heart.
 103: 5 satisfies your *d* with good things,
 145: 19 He fulfills the *d* of those who fear
Pr 11: 6 the unfaithful are trapped by evil *d*.
 19:22 What a man *d* is unfailing love;
Mk 4:19 and the *d* for other things come in
Ro 8: 5 set on what that nature *d*;
 13:14 to gratify the *d* of the sinful nature.
Gal 5:16 and you will not gratify the *d*
 5:17 the sinful nature *d* what is contrary
1Ti 3: 1 an overseer, he *d* a noble task.
 6: 9 and harmful *d* that plunge men
2Ti 2:22 Flee the evil *d* of youth,
Jas 1:20 about the righteous life that God *d*.
 4: 1 from your *d* that battle within you?
1Pe 2:11 to abstain from sinful *d,* which war
1Jn 2:17 The world and its *d* pass away,

DESOLATE
Isa 54: 1 are the children of the *d* woman

DESPAIR
Isa 61: 3 instead of a spirit of *d.*
2Co 4: 8 perplexed, but not in *d;* persecuted,

DESPISE (DESPISED DESPISES)
Job 42: 6 Therefore I *d* myself
Pr 1: 7 but fools *d* wisdom and discipline.
 3:11 do not *d* the LORD's discipline
 23:22 do not *d* your mother
Lk 16:13 devoted to the one and *d* the other.
Tit 2:15 Do not let anyone *d* you.

DESPISED (DESPISE)
Ge 25:34 So Esau *d* his birthright.
Isa 53: 3 He was *d* and rejected by men,
1Co 1:28 of this world and the *d* things—

DESPISES (DESPISE)
Pr 14:21 He who *d* his neighbor sins,
 15:20 but a foolish man *d* his mother.
 15:32 who ignores discipline *d* himself,
Zec 4:10 "Who *d* the day of small things?

DESTINED (DESTINY)
Lk 2:34 "This child is *d* to cause the falling

DESTINY (DESTINED PREDESTINED)
Ps 73:17 then I understood their final *d.*
Ecc 7: 2 for death is the *d* of every man;

DESTITUTE
Pr 31: 8 for the rights of all who are *d.*
Heb 11:37 *d,* persecuted and mistreated—

DESTROY (DESTROYED DESTROYS DESTRUCTION)
Pr 1:32 complacency of fools will *d* them;
Mt 10:28 of the One who can *d* both soul

DESTROYED (DESTROY)
Job 19:26 And after my skin has been *d,*
Isa 55:13 which will not be *d.*"
1Co 8:11 for whom Christ died, is *d*
 15:26 The last enemy to be *d* is death.
2Co 5: 1 if the earthly tent we live in is *d,*
Heb 10:39 of those who shrink back and are *d,*

2Pe 3:10 the elements will be *d* by fire,

DESTROYS (DESTROY)
Pr 6:32 whoever does so *d* himself.
 11: 9 mouth the godless *d* his neighbor,
 18: 9 is brother to one who *d.*
 28:24 he is partner to him who *d.*
Ecc 9:18 but one sinner *d* much good.
1Co 3:17 If anyone *d* God's temple,

DESTRUCTION (DESTROY)
Pr 16:18 Pride goes before *d,*
Hos 13:14 Where, O grave, is your *d?*
Mt 7:13 broad is the road that leads to *d.*
Gal 6: 8 from that nature will reap *d;*
2Th 1: 9 punished with everlasting *d*
1Ti 6: 9 that plunge men into ruin and *d.*
2Pe 2: 1 bringing swift *d* on themselves.
 3:16 other Scriptures, to their own *d.*

DETERMINED (DETERMINES)
Job 14: 5 Man's days are *d;*
Isa 14:26 This is the plan *d* for the whole
Da 11:36 for what has been *d* must take place
Ac 17:26 and he *d* the times set for them

DETERMINES* (DETERMINED)
Ps 147: 4 He *d* the number of the stars
Pr 16: 9 but the LORD *d* his steps.
1Co 12:11 them to each one, just as he *d.*

DETESTABLE (DETESTS)
Pr 21:27 The sacrifice of the wicked is *d*—
 28: 9 even his prayers are *d.*
Isa 1:13 Your incense is *d* to me.
Lk 16:15 among men is *d* in God's sight.
Tit 1:16 They are *d,* disobedient

DETESTS (DETESTABLE)
Dt 22: 5 LORD your God *d* anyone who
 23:18 LORD your God *d* them both.
 25:16 LORD your God *d* anyone who
Pr 12:22 The LORD *d* lying lips,
 15: 8 The LORD *d* the sacrifice
 15: 9 The LORD *d* the way
 15:26 The LORD *d* the thoughts
 16: 5 The LORD *d* all the proud of heart
 17:15 the LORD *d* them both.
 20:23 The LORD *d* differing weights,

DEVIL (DEVIL'S)
Mt 13:39 the enemy who sows them is the *d.*
 25:41 the eternal fire prepared for the *d*
Lk 4: 2 forty days he was tempted by the *d.*
 8:12 then the *d* comes and takes away
Eph 4:27 and do not give the *d* a foothold.
2Ti 2:26 and escape from the trap of the *d,*
Jas 4: 7 Resist the *d,* and he will flee
1Pe 5: 8 Your enemy the *d* prowls
1Jn 3: 8 who does what is sinful is of the *d,*
Rev 12: 9 that ancient serpent called the *d*

DEVIL'S* (DEVIL)
Eph 6:11 stand against the *d* schemes.
1Ti 3: 7 into disgrace and into the *d* trap.
1Jn 3: 8 was to destroy the *d* work.

DEVOTE (DEVOTED DEVOTING DEVOTION DEVOUT)
Job 11:13 "Yet if you *d* your heart to him
Jer 30:21 for who is he who will *d* himself
Col 4: 2 *D* yourselves to prayer, being
1Ti 4:13 *d* yourself to the public reading
Tit 3: 8 may be careful to *d* themselves

DEVOTED (DEVOTE)
Ezr 7:10 For Ezra had *d* himself to the study
Ac 2:42 They *d* themselves
Ro 12:10 Be *d* to one another
1Co 7:34 Her aim is to be *d* to the Lord

DEVOTING (DEVOTE)
1Ti 5:10 *d* herself to all kinds of good deeds.

DEVOTION (DEVOTE)
1Ch 28: 9 and serve him with wholehearted *d*
Eze 33:31 With their mouths they express *d,*
1Co 7:35 way in undivided *d* to the Lord.
2Co 11: 3 from your sincere and pure *d*

DEVOUR
2Sa 2:26 "Must the sword *d* forever?
Mk 12:40 They *d* widows' houses
1Pe 5: 8 lion looking for someone to *d.*

DEVOUT (DEVOTE)
Lk 2:25 Simeon, who was righteous and *d.*

DIE (DEAD DEATH DIED DIES)
Ge 2:17 when you eat of it you will surely *d*
Ex 11: 5 Every firstborn son in Egypt will *d,*
Ru 1:17 Where you *d* I will *d,* and there I
2Ki 14: 6 each is to *d* for his own sins."
Pr 5:23 He will *d* for lack of discipline,
 10:21 but fools *d* for lack of judgment.
 15:10 he who hates correction will *d.*
 23:13 with the rod, he will not *d.*
Ecc 3: 2 a time to be born and a time to *d,*
Isa 66:24 their worm will not *d,* nor will their
Eze 3:18 that wicked man will *d* for his sin,
 18: 4 soul who sins is the one who will *d.*
 33: 8 'O wicked man, you will surely *d,'*
Mt 26:52 "for all who draw the sword will *d*
Jn 11:26 and believes in me will never *d.*
Ro 5: 7 Very rarely will anyone *d*
 14: 8 and if we *d,* we *d* to the Lord.
1Co 15:22 in Adam all *d,* so in Christ all will
 15:31 I *d* every day—I mean that,
Php 1:21 to live is Christ and to *d* is gain.
Heb 9:27 Just as man is destined to *d*
Rev 14:13 Blessed are the dead who *d*

DIED (DIE)
Ro 5: 6 we were still powerless, Christ *d*
 6: 2 By no means! We *d* to sin;
 6: 8 if we *d* with Christ, we believe that
 14:15 brother for whom Christ *d.*
1Co 8:11 for whom Christ *d,* is destroyed
 15: 3 that Christ *d* for our sins according
2Co 5:14 *d* for all, and therefore all *d.*
Col 3: 3 For you *d,* and your life is now
1Th 5:10 He *d* for us so that, whether we are
2Ti 2:11 If we *d* with him,
Heb 9:15 now that he has *d* as a ransom
1Pe 3:18 For Christ *d* for sins once for all,
Rev 2: 8 who *d* and came to life again.

DIES (DIE)
Job 14:14 If a man *d,* will he live again?
Pr 11: 7 a wicked man *d,* his hope perishes;
Jn 11:25 in me will live, even though he *d,*
1Co 15:36 does not come to life unless it *d.*

DIFFERENCE (DIFFERENT)
Ro 10:12 For there is no *d* between Jew

DIFFERENT (DIFFERENCE)
1Co 12: 4 There are *d* kinds of gifts,
2Co 11: 4 or a *d* gospel from the one you

DIGNITY
Pr 31:25 She is clothed with strength and *d;*

DIGS
Pr   26:27 If a man *d* a pit, he will fall into it;

DILIGENCE (DILIGENT)
Heb   6:11 to show this same *d* to the very end

DILIGENT (DILIGENCE)
Pr   21: 5 The plans of the *d* lead to profit
1Ti   4:15 Be *d* in these matters; give yourself

DIRECT (DIRECTS)
Ps 119: 35 *D* me in the path of your
     119:133 *D* my footsteps according
Jer   10:23 it is not for man to *d* his steps.
2Th   3: 5 May the Lord *d* your hearts

DIRECTS (DIRECT)
Ps   42: 8 By day the Lord *d* his love,
Isa   48:17 who *d* you in the way you should

DIRGE
Mt   11:17 we sang a *d*,

DISAPPEAR
Mt   5:18 will by any means *d* from the Law
Lk   16:17 earth to *d* than for the least stroke

DISAPPOINT* (DISAPPOINTED)
Ro   5: 5 And hope does not *d* us,

DISAPPOINTED (DISAPPOINT)
Ps   22: 5 in you they trusted and were not *d*.

DISASTER
Ps   57: 1 wings until the *d* has passed.
Pr   3:25 Have no fear of sudden *d*
     17: 5 over *d* will not go unpunished.
Isa   45: 7 I bring prosperity and create *d*;
Eze   7: 5 An unheard-of *d* is coming.

DISCERN (DISCERNING DISCERNMENT)
Ps   19:12 Who can *d* his errors?
     139: 3 You *d* my going out and my lying
Php   1:10 you may be able to *d* what is best

DISCERNING (DISCERN)
Pr   14: 6 knowledge comes easily to the *d*.
     15:14 The *d* heart seeks knowledge,
     17:24 A *d* man keeps wisdom in view,
     17:28 and *d* if he holds his tongue.
     19:25 rebuke a *d* man, and he will gain

DISCERNMENT (DISCERN)
Pr   17:10 A rebuke impresses a man of *d*
     28:11 a poor man who has *d* sees

DISCIPLE (DISCIPLES)
Mt   10:42 these little ones because he is my *d*,
Lk   14:27 and follow me cannot be my *d*.

DISCIPLES (DISCIPLE)
Mt   28:19 Therefore go and make *d*
Jn   8:31 to my teaching, you are really my *d*
     13:35 men will know that you are my *d*
Ac   11:26 The *d* were called Christians first

DISCIPLINE (DISCIPLINED DISCIPLINES)
Ps   38: 1 or *d* me in your wrath.
     39:11 You rebuke and *d* men for their sin;
     94:12 Blessed is the man you *d*, O Lord
Pr   1: 7 but fools despise wisdom and *d*.
     3:11 do not despise the Lord's *d*
     5:12 You will say, "How I hated *d*!
     5:23 He will die for lack of *d*,
     6:23 and the corrections of *d*
     10:17 He who heeds *d* shows the way

Pr   12: 1 Whoever loves *d* loves knowledge,
     13:18 He who ignores *d* comes to poverty
     13:24 who loves him is careful to *d* him.
     15: 5 A fool spurns his father's *d*,
     15:32 He who ignores *d* despises himself.
     19:18 *D* your son, for in that there is hope
     22:15 the rod of *d* will drive it far
     23:13 Do not withhold *d* from a child;
     29:17 *D* your son, and he will give you
Heb   12: 5 do not make light of the Lord's *d*,
     12: 7 as *d*; God is treating you
     12:11 No *d* seems pleasant at the time,
Rev   3:19 Those whom I love I rebuke and *d*.

DISCIPLINED (DISCIPLINE)
Pr   1: 3 for acquiring a *d* and prudent life,
Jer   31:18 'You *d* me like an unruly calf,
1Co   11:32 we are being *d* so that we will not
Tit   1: 8 upright, holy and *d*.
Heb   12: 7 For what son is not *d* by his father?

DISCIPLINES (DISCIPLINE)
Dt   8: 5 your heart that as a man *d* his son,
Pr   3:12 the Lord *d* those he loves,
Heb   12: 6 because the Lord *d* those he loves,
     12:10 but God *d* us for our good,

DISCLOSED
Lk   8:17 is nothing hidden that will not be *d*,

DISCOURAGED
Jos   1: 9 Do not be terrified; do not be *d*,
     10:25 "Do not be afraid; do not be *d*.
1Ch   28:20 or *d*, for the Lord God,
Isa   42: 4 he will not falter or be *d*
Col   3:21 children, or they will become *d*.

DISCREDITED
2Co   6: 3 so that our ministry will not be *d*.

DISCRETION*
1Ch   22:12 May the Lord give you *d*
Pr   1: 4 knowledge and *d* to the young—
     2:11 *D* will protect you,
     5: 2 that you may maintain *d*
     8:12 I possess knowledge and *d*.
     11:22 a beautiful woman who shows no *d*.

DISCRIMINATED*
Jas   2: 4 have you not *d* among yourselves

DISFIGURED
Isa   52:14 his appearance was so *d*

DISGRACE (DISGRACEFUL DISGRACES)
Pr   11: 2 When pride comes, then comes *d*,
     14:34 but sin is a *d* to any people.
     19:26 is a son who brings shame and *d*.
Ac   5:41 of suffering *d* for the Name.
Heb   13:13 the camp, bearing the *d* he bore.

DISGRACEFUL (DISGRACE)
Pr   10: 5 during harvest is a *d* son.
     17: 2 wise servant will rule over a *d* son,

DISGRACES (DISGRACE)
Pr   28: 7 of gluttons *d* his father.
     29:15 but a child left to itself *d* his mother

DISHONEST
Pr   11: 1 The Lord abhors *d* scales,
     29:27 The righteous detest the *d*;
Lk   16:10 whoever is *d* with very little will
1Ti   3: 8 wine, and not pursuing *d* gain.

DISHONOR (DISHONORS)
Lev   18: 7 " 'Do not *d* your father
Pr   30: 9 and so *d* the name of my God.
1Co   15:43 it is sown in *d*, it is raised in glory;

DISHONORS (DISHONOR)
Dt   27:16 Cursed is the man who *d* his father

DISMAYED
Isa   28:16 the one who trusts will never be *d*.
     41:10 do not be *d*, for I am your God.

DISOBEDIENCE (DISOBEY)
Ro   5:19 as through the *d* of the one man
     11:32 to *d* so that he may have mercy
Heb   2: 2 and *d* received its just punishment,
     4: 6 go in, because of their *d*.
     4:11 fall by following their example of *d*.

DISOBEDIENT (DISOBEY)
2Ti   3: 2 proud, abusive, *d* to their parents,
Tit   1: 6 to the charge of being wild and *d*.
     1:16 *d* and unfit for doing anything

DISOBEY (DISOBEDIENCE DISOBEDIENT)
Dt   11:28 the curse if you *d* the commands
2Ch   24:20 'Why do you *d* the Lord's
Ro   1:30 they *d* their parents; they are

DISORDER
1Co   14:33 For God is not a God of *d*
2Co   12:20 slander, gossip, arrogance and *d*.
Jas   3:16 there you find *d* and every evil

DISOWN
Pr   30: 9 I may have too much and *d* you
Mt   10:33 I will *d* him before my Father
     26:35 to die with you, I will never *d* you."
2Ti   2:12 If we *d* him,

DISPLAY (DISPLAYS)
Eze   39:21 I will *d* my glory among the nations
1Ti   1:16 Christ Jesus might *d* his unlimited

DISPLAYS (DISPLAY)
Isa   44:23 he *d* his glory in Israel.

DISPUTE (DISPUTES)
Pr   17:14 before a *d* breaks out.
1Co   6: 1 If any of you has a *d* with another,

DISPUTES (DISPUTE)
Pr   18:18 Casting the lot settles *d*

DISQUALIFIED
1Co   9:27 I myself will not be *d* for the prize.

DISREPUTE*
2Pe   2: 2 will bring the way of truth into *d*.

DISSENSION*
Pr   6:14 he always stirs up *d*.
     6:19 and a man who stirs up *d*
     10:12 Hatred stirs up *d*,
     15:18 A hot-tempered man stirs up *d*,
     16:28 A perverse man stirs up *d*,
     28:25 A greedy man stirs up *d*,
     29:22 An angry man stirs up *d*,
Ro   13:13 debauchery, not in *d* and jealousy.

DISSIPATION*
Lk 21:34 will be weighed down with d,
1Pe 4: 4 with them into the same flood of d,

DISTINGUISH
1Ki 3: 9 and to d between right and wrong.
Heb 5:14 themselves to d good from evil.

DISTORT
2Co 4: 2 nor do we d the word of God.
2Pe 3:16 ignorant and unstable people d,

DISTRESS (DISTRESSED)
Ps 18: 6 In my d I called to the LORD;
Jnh 2: 2 "In my d I called to the LORD,
Jas 1:27 after orphans and widows in their d

DISTRESSED (DISTRESS)
Ro 14:15 If your brother is d

DIVIDED (DIVISION)
Mt 12:25 household d against itself will not
Lk 23:34 they d up his clothes by casting lots
1Co 1:13 Is Christ d? Was Paul crucified

DIVINATION
Lev 19:26 " 'Do not practice d or sorcery.

DIVINE
Ro 1:20 his eternal power and d nature—
2Co 10: 4 they have d power
2Pe 1: 4 you may participate in the d nature

DIVISION (DIVIDED DIVISIONS DIVISIVE)
Lk 12:51 on earth? No, I tell you, but d.
1Co 12:25 so that there should be no d

DIVISIONS (DIVISION)
Ro 16:17 to watch out for those who cause d
1Co 1:10 another so that there may be no d
11:18 there are d among you,

DIVISIVE* (DIVISION)
Tit 3:10 Warn a d person once,

DIVORCE
Mal 2:16 "I hate d," says the LORD God
Mt 19: 3 for a man to d his wife for any
1Co 7:11 And a husband must not d his wife.
7:27 Are you married? Do not seek a d.

DOCTOR
Mt 9:12 "It is not the healthy who need a d,

DOCTRINE
1Ti 4:16 Watch your life and d closely.
Tit 2: 1 is in accord with sound d.

DOMINION
Ps 22:28 for d belongs to the LORD

DOOR
Ps 141: 3 keep watch over the d of my lips.
Mt 6: 6 close the d and pray to your Father
7: 7 and the d will be opened to you.
Rev 3:20 I stand at the d and knock.

DOORKEEPER
Ps 84:10 I would rather be a d in the house

DOUBLE-EDGED
Heb 4:12 Sharper than any d sword,
Rev 1:16 of his mouth came a sharp d sword.
2:12 of him who has the sharp, d sword.

DOUBLE-MINDED (MIND)
Ps 119:113 I hate d men,
Jas 1: 8 he is a d man, unstable

DOUBT
Mt 14:31 he said, "why did you d?"
21:21 if you have faith and do not d,
Mk 11:23 and does not d in his heart
Jas 1: 6 he must believe and not d,
Jude :22 Be merciful to those who d;

DOWNCAST
Ps 42: 5 Why are you d, O my soul?
2Co 7: 6 But God, who comforts the d,

DRAW (DRAWING DRAWS)
Mt 26:52 "for all who d the sword will die
Jn 12:32 up from the earth, will d all men
Heb 10:22 let us d near to God

DRAWING (DRAW)
Lk 21:28 because your redemption is d near

DRAWS (DRAW)
Jn 6:44 the Father who sent me d him,

DREADFUL
Heb 10:31 It is a d thing to fall into the hands

DRESS
1Ti 2: 9 I also want women to d modestly,

DRINK (DRUNK DRUNKARDS DRUNKENNESS)
Pr 5:15 D water from your own cistern,
Lk 12:19 Take life easy; eat, d and be merry
Jn 7:37 let him come to me and d.
1Co 12:13 were all given the one Spirit to d.
Rev 21: 6 to d without cost from the spring

DRIVES
1Jn 4:18 But perfect love d out fear,

DROP
Pr 17:14 so d the matter before a dispute
Isa 40:15 Surely the nations are like a d

DRUNK (DRINK)
Eph 5:18 Do not get d on wine, which leads

DRUNKARDS (DRINK)
Pr 23:21 for d and gluttons become poor,
1Co 6:10 nor the greedy nor d nor slanderers

DRUNKENNESS (DRINK)
Lk 21:34 weighed down with dissipation, d
Ro 13:13 and d, not in sexual immorality
Gal 5:21 factions and envy; d, orgies,
1Pe 4: 3 living in debauchery, lust, d, orgies,

DRY
Isa 53: 2 and like a root out of d ground.
Eze 37: 4 'D bones, hear the word

DUST
Ge 2: 7 man from the d of the ground
Ps 103:14 he remembers that we are d.
Ecc 3:20 all come from d, and to d all return.

DUTY
Ecc 12:13 for this is the whole d of man.
Ac 23: 1 I have fulfilled my d to God
1Co 7: 3 husband should fulfill his marital d

DWELL (DWELLING)
1Ki 8:27 "But will God really d on earth?
Ps 23: 6 I will d in the house of the LORD
Isa 43:18 do not d on the past.
Eph 3:17 so that Christ may d in your hearts
Col 1:19 to have all his fullness d in him,
Col 3:16 the word of Christ d in you richly

DWELLING (DWELL)
Eph 2:22 to become a d in which God lives

EAGER
Pr 31:13 and works with e hands.
1Pe 5: 2 greedy for money, but e to serve;

EAGLE'S (EAGLES)
Ps 103: 5 your youth is renewed like the e.

EAGLES (EAGLE'S)
Isa 40:31 They will soar on wings like e;

EAR (EARS)
1Co 2: 9 no has heard,
12:16 if the e should say, "Because I am

EARNED
Pr 31:31 Give her the reward she has e,

EARS (EAR)
Job 42: 5 My e had heard of you
Ps 34:15 and his e are attentive to their cry;
Pr 21:13 If a man shuts his e to the cry
2Ti 4: 3 to say what their itching e want

EARTH (EARTHLY)
Ge 1: 1 God created the heavens and the e.
Ps 24: 1 e is the LORD's, and everything
108: 5 and let your glory be over all the e.
Isa 6: 3 the whole e is full of his glory."
51: 6 the e will wear out like a garment
55: 9 the heavens are higher than the e,
66: 1 and the e is my footstool.
Jer 23:24 "Do not I fill heaven and e?"
Hab 2:20 let all the e be silent before him."
Mt 6:10 done on e as it is in heaven.
16:19 bind on e will be bound
24:35 Heaven and e will pass away,
28:18 and on e has been given to me.
Lk 2:14 on e peace to men
1Co 10:26 The e is the Lord's, and everything
Php 2:10 in heaven and on e and under the e,
2Pe 3:13 to a new heaven and a new e,

EARTHLY (EARTH)
Php 3:19 Their mind is on e things.
Col 3: 2 on things above, not on e things.

EAST
Ps 103: 12 as far as the e is from the west,

EASY
Mt 11:30 For my yoke is e and my burden is

EAT (EATING)
Ge 2:17 but you must not e from the tree
Isa 55: 1 come, buy and e!
65:25 and the lion will e straw like the ox,
Mt 26:26 "Take and e; this is my body."
Ro 14: 2 faith allows him to e everything,
1Co 8:13 if what I e causes my brother to fall
10:31 So whether you e or drink
2Th 3:10 man will not work, he shall not e."

EATING (EAT)
Ro 14:17 kingdom of God is not a matter of e

EDICT
Heb 11:23 they were not afraid of the king's e.

EDIFIES
1Co 14: 4 but he who prophesies e the
church

EFFECT
Isa 32:17 e of righteousness will be
quietness
Heb 9:18 put into e without blood.

EFFORT
Lk 13:24 "Make every e to enter
Ro   9:16 depend on man's desire or e,
    14:19 make every e to do what leads
Eph 4: 3 Make every e to keep the unity
Heb 4:11 make every e to enter that rest,
    12:14 make every e to live in peace
2Pe 1: 5 make every e to add
     3:14 make every e to be found
spotless,

ELAH
Son of Baasha; king of Israel (1Ki 16:6-14).

ELDERLY* (ELDERS)
Lev 19:32 show respect for the e

ELDERS (ELDERLY)
1Ti 5:17 The e who direct the affairs

ELECTION
Ro   9:11 God's purpose in e might stand:
2Pe 1:10 to make your calling and e sure.

ELI
High priest in youth of Samuel (1Sa 1-4).
Blessed Hannah (1Sa 1:12-18); raised Sam-
uel (1Sa 2:11-26).

ELIJAH
Prophet; predicted famine in Israel (1Ki
17:1; Jas 5:17). Fed by ravens (1Ki 17:2-6).
Raised Sidonian widow's son (1Ki 17:7-24).
Defeated prophets of Baal at Carmel (1Ki
18:16-46). Ran from Jezebel (1Ki 19:1-9).
Prophesied death of Azariah (2Ki 1). Succeeded by Elishah (1Ki 19:19-21; 2Ki 2:1-
18). Taken to heaven in whirlwind (2Ki 2:11-
12).
Return prophesied (Mal 4:5-6); equated
with John the Baptist (Mt 17:9-13; Mk 9:9-13;
Lk 1:17). Appeared with Moses in transfiguration of Jesus (Mt 17:1-8; Mk 9:1-8).

ELISHA
Prophet; successor of Elijah (1Ki 19:16-
21); inherited his cloak (2Ki 2:1-18). Miracles
of (2Ki 2-6).

ELIZABETH*
Mother of John the Baptist, relative of Mary
(Lk 1:5-58).

EMBITTER*
Col 3:21 Fathers, do not e your children,

EMPTY
Eph 5: 6 no one deceive you with e
words,
1Pe 1:18 from the e way of life handed

ENABLE (ABLE)
Lk   1:74 to e us to serve him without fear
Ac   4:29 e your servants to speak your
word

ENABLED (ABLE)
Lev 26:13 e you to walk with heads held
high.
Jn   6:65 unless the Father has e him."

ENABLES (ABLE)
Php 3:21 by the power that e him

ENCAMPS*
Ps 34: 7 The angel of the Lord e

ENCOURAGE (ENCOURAGEMENT)
Ps 10:17 you e them, and you listen
Isa 1:17 e the oppressed.
Ac 15:32 to e and strengthen the
brothers.
Ro 12: 8 if it is encouraging, let him e;

1Th 4:18 Therefore e each other
2Ti 4: 2 rebuke and e— with great
patience
Tit 2: 6 e the young men to be
Heb 3:13 But e one another daily, as long
    10:25 but let us e one another—

ENCOURAGEMENT (ENCOURAGE)
Ac   4:36 Barnabas (which means Son
of E),
Ro 15: 4 e of the Scriptures we might
have
    15: 5 and e give you a spirit of unity
1Co 14: 3 to men for their strengthening, e
Heb 12: 5 word of e that addresses you

END
Ps 119: 33 then I will keep them to the e.
Pr 14:12 but in the e it leads to death.
    19:20 and in the e you will be wise.
    23:32 In the e it bites like a snake
Ecc 12:12 making many books there is
no e,
Mt 10:22 firm to the e will be saved.
Lk 21: 9 but the e will not come right
away
Ro 10: 4 Christ is the e of the law
1Co 15:24 the e will come, when he hands

ENDURANCE (ENDURE)
Ro 15: 4 through e and the
encouragement
    15: 5 May the God who gives e
2Co 1: 6 which produces in you patient e
Col 1:11 might so that you may have
great e
1Ti 6:11 faith, love, e and gentleness.
Tit 2: 2 and sound in faith, in love and
in e.

ENDURE (ENDURANCE ENDURES)
Ps 72:17 May his name e forever;
Pr 12:19 Truthful lips e forever,
    27:24 for riches do not e forever,
Ecc 3:14 everything God does will e
forever;
Mal 3: 2 who can e the day of his
coming?
2Ti 3: 3 E hardship with us like a good
     2:12 if we e, / we will also reign
Heb 12: 7 E hardship as discipline; God is
Rev 3:10 kept my command to e patiently,

ENDURES (ENDURE)
Ps 112: 9 his righteousness e forever;
    136: 1 His love e forever.
Da   9:15 made for yourself a name that e

ENEMIES (ENEMY)
Ps 23: 5 in the presence of my e.
Mic 7: 6 a man's e are the members
Mt   5:44 Love your e and pray
Lk 20:43 hand until I make your e

ENEMY (ENEMIES ENMITY)
Pr 24:17 Do not gloat when your e falls;
    25:21 If your e is hungry, give him food
    27: 6 but an e multiplies kisses.
1Co 15:26 The last e to be destroyed is
death.
1Ti 5:14 and to give the e no opportunity

ENJOY (JOY)
Dt   6: 2 and so that you may e long life.
Eph 6: 3 and that you may e long life
Heb 11:25 rather than to e the pleasures of
sin

ENJOYMENT (JOY)
Ecc 4: 8 and why am I depriving myself
of e
1Ti 6:17 us with everything for our e.

ENLIGHTENED* (LIGHT)
Eph 1:18 that the eyes of your heart may
be e
Heb 6: 4 for those who have once been e,

ENMITY* (ENEMY)
Ge   3:15 And I will put e

ENOCH
Walked with God and taken by him (Ge
5:18-24; Heb 11:5). Prophet (Jude 14).

ENTANGLED (ENTANGLES)
2Pe 2:20 and are again e in it and
overcome,

ENTANGLES* (ENTANGLED)
Heb 12: 1 and the sin that so easily e,

ENTER (ENTERED ENTERS
ENTRANCE)
Ps 100: 4 E his gates with thanksgiving
Mt   5:20 will certainly not e the kingdom
     7:13 "E through the narrow gate.
    18: 8 It is better for you to e life
maimed
Mk 10:15 like a little child will never e it."
    10:23 is for the rich to e the kingdom

ENTERED (ENTER)
Ro   5:12 as sin e the world through one
man,
Heb 9:12 but he e the Most Holy Place
once

ENTERS (ENTER)
Mk   7:18 you see that nothing that e a
man
Jn 10: 2 The man who e by the gate is

ENTERTAIN
1Ti 5:19 Do not e an accusation
Heb 13: 2 Do not forget to e strangers,

ENTHRALLED*
Ps 45:11 The king is e by your beauty;

ENTHRONED (THRONE)
1Sa 4: 4 who is e between the cherubim.
Ps   2: 4 The One e in heaven laughs;
    102: 12 But you, O Lord, sit e forever;
Isa 40:22 He sits e above the circle

ENTICE
Pr   1:10 My son, if sinners e you,
2Pe 2:18 they e people who are just
escaping

ENTIRE
Gal 5:14 The e law is summed up

ENTRUSTED (TRUST)
1Ti 6:20 guard what has been e to your
care.
2Ti 1:12 able to guard what I have e to
him
    1:14 Guard the good deposit that
was e
Jude : 3 once for all e to the saints.

ENVY
Pr   3:31 Do not e a violent man
    14:30 but e rots the bones.
1Co 13: 4 It does not e, it does not boast,

EPHRAIM
1. Second son of Joseph (Ge 41:52;
46:20). Blessed as firstborn by Jacob (Ge
48).
2. Synonymous with Northern Kingdom (Isa
7:17; Hos 5).

EQUAL
Isa 40:25 who is my e?" says the Holy
One.
Jn   5:18 making himself e with God.
1Co 12:25 that its parts should have e
concern

EQUIP* (EQUIPPED)
Heb 13:21 e you with everything good

EQUIPPED (EQUIP)
2Ti 3:17 man of God may be thoroughly e

ERROR
Jas 5:20 Whoever turns a sinner from
the e

ESAU

Firstborn of Isaac, twin of Jacob (Ge 25:21-26). Also called Edom (Ge 25:30). Sold Jacob his birthright (Ge 25:29-34); lost blessing (Ge 27). Reconciled to Jacob (Gen 33).

ESCAPE (ESCAPING)

Ro   2:   3 think you will e God's judgment?
Heb   2:   3 how shall we e if we ignore such

ESCAPING (ESCAPE)

1Co   3:15 only as one e through the flames.

ESTABLISH

Ge   6:18 But I will e my covenant with you,
1Ch 28:   7 I will e his kingdom forever
Ro   10:   3 God and sought to e their own,

ESTEEMED

Pr   22:   1 to be e is better than silver or gold.
Isa   53:   3 he was despised, and we e him not.

ESTHER

Jewess who lived in Persia; cousin of Mordecai (Est 2:7). Chosen queen of Xerxes (Est 2:8-18). Foiled Haman's plan to exterminate the Jews (Est 3-4; 7-9).

ETERNAL (ETERNALLY ETERNITY)

Ps   16:11 with e pleasures at your right hand.
   111: 10 To him belongs e praise.
   119: 89 Your word, O LORD, is e;
Isa   26:   4 LORD, the LORD, is the Rock e.
Mt   19:16 good thing must I do to get e life?"
   25:41 into the e fire prepared for the devil
   25:46 they will go away to e punishment,
Jn   3:15 believes in him may have e life.
   3:16 him shall not perish but have e life.
   3:36 believes in the Son has e life,
   4:14 spring of water welling up to e life."
   5:24 believes him who sent me has e life
   6:68 You have the words of e life.
   10:28 I give them e life, and they shall
   17:   3 this is e life: that they may know
Ro   1:20 his e power and divine nature—
   6:23 but the gift of God is e life
2Co   4:17 for us an e glory that far outweighs
   4:18 temporary, but what is unseen is e.
1Ti   1:16 believe on him and receive e life.
   1:17 Now to the King e, immortal,
Heb   9:12 having obtained e redemption.
1Jn   5:11 God has given us e life,
   5:13 you may know that you have e life.

ETERNALLY (ETERNAL)

Gal   1:   8 let him be e condemned! As we

ETERNITY (ETERNAL)

Ps   93:   2 you are from all e.
Ecc   3:11 also set e in the hearts of men;

ETHIOPIAN

Jer   13:23 Can the E change his skin

EUNUCHS

Mt   19:12 For some are e because they were

EVANGELIST (EVANGELISTS)

2Ti   4:   5 hardship, do the work of an e,

EVANGELISTS* (EVANGELIST)

Eph   4:11 some to be prophets, some to be e,

EVE

2Co   11:   3 as E was deceived by the serpent's
1Ti   2:13 For Adam was formed first, then E

EVEN-TEMPERED*

Pr   17:27 and a man of understanding is e.

EVER (EVERLASTING FOREVER)

Ex   15:18 LORD will reign for e and e."
Dt   8:19 If you e forget the LORD your
Ps   5:11 let them e sing for joy.
   10:16 The LORD is King for e and e;
   25:   3 will e be put to shame,
   26:   3 for your love is e before me,
   45:   6 O God, will last for e and e;
   52:   8 God's unfailing love for e and e.
   89:33 nor will I e betray my faithfulness.
   145:   1 I will praise your name for e and e.
Pr   4:18 shining e brighter till the full light
   5:19 may you e be captivated
Isa   66:   8 Who has e heard of such a thing?
Jer   31:36 the descendants of Israel e cease
Da   7:18 it forever—yes, for e and e.'
   12:   3 like the stars for e and e.
Mk   4:12 e hearing but never understanding;
Jn   1:18 No one has e seen God,
Rev   1:18 and behold I am alive for e and e!
   22:   5 And they will reign for e and e.

EVER-INCREASING* (INCREASE)

Ro   6:19 to impurity and to e wickedness,
2Co   3:18 into his likeness with e glory,

EVERLASTING (EVER)

Dt   33:27 and underneath are the e arms.
Ne   9:   5 your God, who is from e to e."
Ps   90:   2 from e to e you are God.
   139: 24 and lead me in the way e.
Isa   9:   6 E Father, Prince of Peace.
   33:14 Who of us can dwell with e burning
   35:10 e joy will crown their heads.
   45:17 the LORD with an e salvation;
   54:   8 but with e kindness
   55:   3 I will make an e covenant with you,
   63:12 to gain for himself e renown,
Jer   31:   3 "I have loved you with an e love;
Da   9:24 to bring in e righteousness,
   12:   2 some to e life, others to shame
Jn   6:47 the truth, he who believes has e life.
2Th   1:   9 punished with e destruction
Jude   :   6 bound with e chains for judgment

EVER-PRESENT*

Ps   46:   1 an e help in trouble

EVIDENCE (EVIDENT)

Jn   14:11 on the e of the miracles themselves.

EVIDENT (EVIDENCE)

Php   4:   5 Let your gentleness be e to all.

EVIL

Ge   2:   9 of the knowledge of good and e.
Job   1:   1 he feared God and shunned e.
   1:   8 a man who fears God and shuns e."
   34:10 Far be it from God to do e,
Ps   23:   4 I will fear no e,
   34:14 Turn from e and do good;
   51:   4 and done what is e in your sight,
   97:10 those who love the LORD hate e,
   101:   1 I will have nothing to do with e.
Pr   8:13 To fear the LORD is to hate e;
   10:23 A fool finds pleasure in e conduct,
   11:27 e comes to him who searches for it.

EXACT

Heb   1:   3 the e representation of his being,

EXALT (EXALTED EXALTS)

Ps   30:   1 I will e you, O LORD,
   34:   3 let us e his name together.
   118: 28 you are my God, and I will e you.
Isa   24:15 e the name of the LORD, the God

EXALTED (EXALT)

2Sa   22:47 E be God, the Rock, my Savior!
1Ch   29:11 you are e as head over all.
Ne   9:   5 and may it be e above all blessing
Ps   21:13 Be e, O LORD, in your strength;
   46:10 I will be e among the nations,
   57:   5 Be e, O God, above the heavens;
   97:   9 you are far above all gods.
   99:   2 he is e over all the nations.
   108:   5 Be e, O God, above the heavens,
   148: 13 for his name alone is e;
Isa   6:   1 e, and the train of his robe filled
   12:   4 and proclaim that his name is e.
   33:   5 The LORD is e, for he dwells
Eze   21:26 The lowly will be e and the e will be
Mt   23:12 whoever humbles himself will be e.
Php   1:20 always Christ will be e in my body,
   2:   9 Therefore God e him

EXALTS (EXALT)

Ps   75:   7 He brings one down, he e another.
Pr   14:34 Righteousness e a nation,
Mt   23:12 For whoever e himself will be

EXAMINE (EXAMINED)

Ps   26:   2 e my heart and my mind;
Jer   17:10 and the mind,
La   3:40 Let us e our ways and test them,
1Co   11:28 A man ought to e himself
2Co   13:   5 E yourselves to see whether you

EXAMINED (EXAMINE)

Ac   17:11 e the Scriptures every day to see

EXAMPLE (EXAMPLES)

Jn   13:15 have set you an e that you should
1Co   11:   1 Follow my e, as I follow

Pr   24:19 Do not fret because of e men
   24:20 for the e man has no future hope,
Isa   5:20 Woe to those who call e good
   13:11 I will punish the world for its e,
   55:   7 and the e man his thoughts.
Hab   1:13 Your eyes are too pure to look on e;
Mt   5:45 He causes his sun to rise on the e
   6:13 but deliver us from the e one.'
   7:11 If you, then, though you are e,
   12:35 and the e man brings e things out
Jn   17:15 you protect them from the e one.
Ro   2:   9 for every human being who does e:
   12:   9 Hate what is e; cling
   12:17 Do not repay anyone e for e.
   16:19 and innocent about what is e.
1Co   13:   6 Love does not delight in e
   14:20 In regard to e be infants,
Eph   6:16 all the flaming arrows of the e one.
1Th   5:22 Avoid every kind of e.
1Ti   6:10 of money is a root of all kinds of e.
2Ti   2:22 Flee the e desires of youth,
Jas   1:13 For God cannot be tempted by e,
1Pe   2:16 your freedom as a cover-up for e;
   3:   9 Do not repay e with e or insult

1Ti 4:12 set an *e* for the believers in speech,
Tit 2: 7 In everything set them an *e*
1Pe 2:21 leaving you an *e*, that you should

EXAMPLES* (EXAMPLE)
1Co 10: 6 Now these things occurred as *e*
10:11 as *e* and were written down
1Pe 5: 3 to you, but being *e* to the flock.

EXASPERATE*
Eph 6: 4 Fathers, do not *e* your children;

EXCEL (EXCELLENT)
1Co 14:12 to *e* in gifts that build up the church
2Co 8: 7 But just as you *e* in everything—

EXCELLENT (EXCEL)
1Co 12:31 now I will show you the most *e* way
Php 4: 8 if anything is *e* or praiseworthy—
1Ti 3:13 have served well gain an *e* standing
Tit 3: 8 These things are *e* and profitable

EXCHANGED
Ro 1:23 *e* the glory of the immortal God
1:25 They *e* the truth of God for a lie,

EXCUSE (EXCUSES)
Jn 15:22 they have no *e* for their sin,
Ro 1:20 so that men are without *e*.

EXCUSES* (EXCUSE)
Lk 14:18 "But they all alike began to make *e*.

EXISTS
Heb 2:10 and through whom everything *e*,
11: 6 to him must believe that he *e*

EXPECT (EXPECTATION)
Mt 24:44 at an hour when you do not *e* him.

EXPECTATION (EXPECT)
Ro 8:19 waits in eager *e* for the sons
Heb 10:27 but only a fearful *e* of judgment

EXPEL*
1Co 5:13 *E* the wicked man from among you

EXPENSIVE
1Ti 2: 9 or gold or pearls or *e* clothes,

EXPLOIT
Pr 22:22 Do not *e* the poor because they are
2Co 12:17 Did I *e* you through any

EXPOSE
1Co 4: 5 will *e* the motives of men's hearts.
Eph 5:11 of darkness, but rather *e* them.

EXTENDS
Pr 31:20 and *e* her hands to the needy.
Lk 1:50 His mercy *e* to those who fear him,

EXTINGUISHED
2Sa 21:17 the lamp of Israel will not be *e*."

EXTOL*
Job 36:24 Remember to *e* his work,
Ps 34: 1 I will *e* the LORD at all times;
68: 4 *e* him who rides on the clouds—
95: 2 and *e* him with music and song.
109: 30 mouth I will greatly *e* the LORD;
111: 1 I will *e* the LORD with all my heart
115: 18 it is we who *e* the LORD,
117: 1 *e* him, all you peoples.
145: 2 and *e* your name for ever and ever.
145: 10 your saints will *e* you.
147: 12 *E* the LORD, O Jerusalem;

EXTORT*
Lk 3:14 "Don't *e* money and don't accuse

EYE (EYES)
Ex 21:24 you are to take life for life, *e* for *e*,
Ps 94: 9 Does he who formed the *e* not see?
Mt 5:29 If your right *e* causes you to sin,
5:38 '*E* for *e*, and tooth for tooth.'
7: 3 of sawdust in your brother's *e*
1Co 2: 9 "No *e* has seen,
Col 3:22 not only when their *e* is on you
Rev 1: 7 and every *e* will see him,

EYES (EYE)
Nu 33:55 remain will become barbs in your *e*
Jos 23:13 on your backs and thorns in your *e*,
2Ch 16: 9 For the *e* of the LORD range
Job 31: 1 "I made a covenant with my *e*
36: 7 He does not take his *e*
Ps 119: 18 Open my *e* that I may see
121: 1 I lift up my *e* to the hills—
141: 8 But my *e* are fixed on you,
Pr 3: 7 Do not be wise in your own *e*;
4:25 Let your *e* look straight ahead,
15: 3 The *e* of the LORD are everywhere
Isa 6: 5 and my *e* have seen the King,
Hab 1:13 Your *e* are too pure to look on evil;
Jn 4:35 open your *e* and look at the fields!
2Co 4:18 So we fix our *e* not on what is seen,
Heb 12: 2 Let us fix our *e* on Jesus, the author
Jas 2: 5 poor in the *e* of the world to be rich
1Pe 3:12 For the *e* of the Lord are
Rev 7:17 wipe away every tear from their *e*.
21: 4 He will wipe every tear from their *e*

EZEKIEL
Priest called to be prophet to the exiles (Eze 1-3).

EZRA
Priest and teacher of the Law who led a return of exiles to Israel to reestablish temple and worship (Ezr 7-8). Corrected intermarriage of priests (Ezr 9-10). Read Law at celebration of Feast of Tabernacles (Neh 8).

FACE (FACES)
Ge 32:30 "It is because I saw God *f* to *f*,
Ex 34:29 was not aware that his *f* was radiant
Nu 6:25 the LORD make his *f* shine
1Ch 16:11 seek his *f* always.
2Ch 7:14 and seek my *f* and turn
Ps 4: 6 Let the light of your *f* shine upon us
27: 8 Your *f*, LORD, I will seek.
31:16 Let your *f* shine on your servant;
105: 4 seek his *f* always.
119:135 Make your *f* shine
Isa 50: 7 Therefore have I set my *f* like flint,
Mt 17: 2 His *f* shone like the sun,
1Co 13:12 mirror; then we shall see *f* to *f*.
2Co 4: 6 the glory of God in the *f* of Christ.
1Pe 3:12 but the *f* of the Lord is
Rev 1:16 His *f* was like the sun shining

FACES (FACE)
2Co 3:18 who with unveiled *f* all reflect

FACTIONS
Gal 5:20 selfish ambition, dissensions, *f*

FADE
1Pe 5: 4 of glory that will never *f* away.

FAIL (FAILING FAILINGS FAILS)
1Ch 28:20 He will not *f* you or forsake you

2Ch 34:33 they did not *f* to follow the LORD.
Ps 89:28 my covenant with him will never *f*.
Pr 15:22 Plans *f* for lack of counsel,
Isa 51: 6 my righteousness will never *f*.
La 3:22 for his compassions never *f*.
2Co 13: 5 unless, of course, you *f* the test?

FAILING (FAIL)
1Sa 12:23 sin against the LORD by *f* to pray

FAILINGS (FAIL)
Ro 15: 1 ought to bear with the *f* of the weak

FAILS (FAIL)
1Co 13: 8 Love never *f*.

FAINT
Isa 40:31 they will walk and not be *f*.

FAIR
Pr 1: 3 doing what is right and just and *f*;
Col 4: 1 slaves with what is right and *f*,

FAITH (FAITHFUL FAITHFULLY FAITHFULNESS FAITHLESS)
2Ch 20:20 Have *f* in the LORD your God
Hab 2: 4 but the righteous will live by his *f*—
Mt 9:29 According to your *f* will it be done
17:20 if you have *f* as small as a mustard
24:10 many will turn away from the *f*
Mk 11:22 "Have *f* in God," Jesus answered.
Lk 7: 9 I have not found such great *f*
12:28 will he clothe you, O you of little *f*!
17: 5 "Increase our *f*!" He replied,
18: 8 will he find *f* on the earth?"
Ac 14: 9 saw that he had *f* to be healed
14:27 the door of *f* to the Gentiles.
Ro 1:12 encouraged by each other's *f*.
1:17 is by *f* from first to last,
1:17 "The righteous will live by *f*."
3: 3 What if some did not have *f*?
3:22 comes through *f* in Jesus Christ
3:25 a sacrifice of atonement, through *f*
4: 5 his *f* is credited as righteousness.
5: 1 we have been justified through *f*,
10:17 *f* comes from hearing the message,
14: 1 Accept him whose *f* is weak,
14:23 that does not come from *f* is sin.
1Co 13: 2 and if I have a *f* that can move
13:13 And now these three remain: *f*,
16:13 stand firm in the *f*; be men
2Co 5: 7 We live by *f*, not by sight.
13: 5 to see whether you are in the *f*;
Gal 2:16 Jesus that we may be justified by *f*
2:20 I live by *f* in the Son of God,
3:11 "The righteous will live by *f*."
3:24 that we might be justified by *f*.
Eph 2: 8 through *f*— and this not
4: 5 one Lord, one *f*, one baptism;
6:16 to all this, take up the shield of *f*,
Col 1:23 continue in your *f*, established
1Th 5: 8 on *f* and love as a breastplate,
1Ti 2:15 if they continue in *f*, love
4: 1 later times some will abandon the *f*
5: 8 he has denied the *f* and is worse
6:12 Fight the good fight of the *f*.
2Ti 3:15 wise for salvation through *f*
4: 7 finished the race, I have kept the *f*.
Phm : 6 may be active in sharing your *f*,
Heb 10:38 But my righteous one will live by *f*.
11: 1 *f* is being sure of what we hope for
11: 3 By *f* we understand that

Heb 11: 5 By *f* Enoch was taken from this
life
11: 6 And without *f* it is impossible
11: 7 By *f* Noah, when warned about
11: 8 By *f* Abraham, when called to go
11:17 By *f* Abraham, when God tested
11:20 By *f* Isaac blessed Jacob
11:21 By *f* Jacob, when he was dying,
11:22 By *f* Joseph, when his end was
near
11:24 By *f* Moses, when he had grown
up
11:31 By *f* the prostitute Rahab,
12: 2 the author and perfecter of our *f*,
Jas 2:14 if a man claims to have *f*
2:17 In the same way, *f* by itself,
2:26 so *f* without deeds is dead.
2Pe 1: 5 effort to add to your *f* goodness;
1Jn 5: 4 overcome the world, even our *f*.
Jude : 3 to contend for the *f* that was
once

FAITHFUL (FAITH)

Nu 12: 7 he is *f* in all my house.
Dt 7: 9 your God is God; he is the *f*
God,
32: 4 A *f* God who does no wrong,
2Sa 22:26 "To the *f* you show yourself *f*,
Ps 25:10 of the LORD are loving and *f*
31:23 The LORD preserves the *f*,
33: 4 he is *f* in all he does.
37:28 and will not forsake his *f* ones.
97:10 for he guards the lives of his *f*
ones
145: 13 The LORD is *f* to all his promises
146: 6 the LORD, who remains *f* forever.
Pr 31:26 and *f* instruction is on her
tongue.
Mt 25:21 'Well done, good and *f* servant!
Ro 12:12 patient in affliction, *f* in prayer.
1Co 4: 2 been given a trust must prove *f*.
10:13 And God is *f*; he will not let you
be
1Th 5:24 The one who calls you is *f*
2Ti 2:13 he will remain *f*,
Heb 3: 6 But Christ is *f* as a son
10:23 for he who promised is *f*.
1Pe 4:19 themselves to their *f* Creator
1Jn 1: 9 he is *f* and just and will forgive
us
Rev 1: 5 who is the *f* witness, the
firstborn
2:10 Be *f*, to the point of death,
19:11 whose rider is called *F* and True.

FAITHFULLY (FAITH)

Dt 11:13 if you *f* obey the commands I
am
1Sa 12:24 and serve him *f* with all your
heart;
1Ki 2: 4 and if they walk *f* before me
1Pe 4:10 *f* administering God's grace

FAITHFULNESS (FAITH)

Ps 57:10 your *f* reaches to the skies.
85:10 Love and *f* meet together;
86:15 to anger, abounding in love
and *f*.
89: 1 mouth I will make your *f* known
89:14 love and *f* go before you.
91: 4 his *f* will be your shield
117: 2 the *f* of the LORD endures
forever.
119: 75 and in *f* you have afflicted me.
Pr 3: 3 Let love and *f* never leave you;
Isa 11: 5 and *f* the sash around his waist.
La 3:23 great is your *f*.
Ro 3: 3 lack of faith nullify God's *f*?
Gal 5:22 patience, kindness, goodness, *f*,

FAITHLESS (FAITH)

Ps 119:158 I look on the *f* with loathing,
Jer 3:22 "Return, *f* people;
Ro 1:31 they are senseless, *f*, heartless,
2Ti 2:13 if we are *f*,

FALL (FALLEN FALLING FALLS)

Ps 37:24 though he stumble, he will not *f*,
55:22 he will never let the righteous *f*.
69: 9 of those who insult you *f* on me.
Pr 11:28 Whoever trusts in his riches
will *f*,

Lk 11:17 a house divided against itself
will *f*.
Ro 3:23 and *f* short of the glory of God,
Heb 6: 6 if they *f* away, to be brought
back

FALLEN (FALL)

2Sa 1:19 How the mighty have *f*!
Isa 14:12 How you have *f* from heaven,
1Co 15:20 of those who have *f* asleep.
Gal 5: 4 you have *f* away from grace.
1Th 4:15 precede those who have *f*
asleep.

FALLING (FALL)

Jude : 24 able to keep you from *f*

FALLS (FALL)

Pr 24:17 Do not gloat when your enemy *f*;
Jn 12:24 a kernel of wheat *f* to the
ground
Ro 14: 4 To his own master he stands
or *f*.

FALSE (FALSEHOOD FALSELY)

Ex 20:16 "You shall not give *f* testimony
23: 1 "Do not spread *f* reports.
Pr 13: 5 The righteous hate what is *f*,
19: 5 A *f* witness will not go
unpunished,
Mt 7:15 "Watch out for *f* prophets.
19:18 not steal, do not give *f*
testimony,
24:11 and many *f* prophets will appear
Php 1:18 whether from *f* motives or true,
1Ti 1: 3 not to teach *f* doctrines any
longer
2Pe 2: 1 there will be *f* teachers among
you.

FALSEHOOD (FALSE)

Ps 119:163 I hate and abhor *f*
Pr 30: 8 Keep *f* and lies far from me;
Eph 4:25 each of you must put off *f*

FALSELY (FALSE)

Lev 19:12 " 'Do not swear *f* by my name
Lk 3:14 and don't accuse people *f*—
1Ti 6:20 ideas of what is *f* called
knowledge,

FALTER*

Pr 24:10 If you *f* in times of trouble,
Isa 42: 4 he will not *f* or be discouraged

FAMILIES (FAMILY)

Ps 68: 6 God sets the lonely in *f*,

FAMILY (FAMILIES)

Pr 15:27 greedy man brings trouble to
his *f*,
31:15 she provides food for her *f*
Lk 9:61 go back and say good-by to
my *f*."
12:52 in one *f* divided against each
other,
1Ti 3: 4 He must manage his own *f* well
3: 5 how to manage his own *f*,
5: 4 practice by caring for their own *f*
5: 8 and especially for his
immediate *f*,

FAMINE

Ge 41:30 seven years of *f* will follow them.
Am 8:11 but a *f* of hearing the words
Ro 8:35 or persecution or *f* or nakedness

FAN*

2Ti 1: 6 you to *f* into flame the gift of
God,

FAST

Dt 13: 4 serve him and hold *f* to him.
Jos 22: 5 to hold *f* to him and to serve
him
23: 8 to hold *f* to the LORD your God,
Ps 119: 31 I hold *f* to your statutes, O LORD;
139: 10 your right hand will hold me *f*.
Mt 6:16 "When you *f*, do not look
somber
1Pe 5:12 Stand *f* in it.

FATHER (FATHER'S FATHERLESS FATHERS FOREFATHERS)

Ge 2:24 this reason a man will leave
his *f*
17: 4 You will be the *f* of many
nations.
Ex 20:12 "Honor your *f* and your mother,
21:15 "Anyone who attacks his *f*
21:17 "Anyone who curses his *f*
Lev 18: 7 " 'Do not dishonor your *f*
19: 3 you must respect his mother
and *f*,
Dt 5:16 "Honor your *f* and your mother,
21:18 son who does not obey his *f*
Ps 27:10 Though my *f* and mother forsake
68: 5 A *f* to the fatherless, a defender
Pr 10: 1 A wise son brings joy to his *f*,
17:21 there is no joy for the *f* of a fool.
23:22 Listen to your *f*, who gave you
life,
23:24 *f* of a righteous man has great
joy;
28: 7 of gluttons disgraces his *f*.
29: 3 loves wisdom brings joy to his *f*,
Isa 9: 6 Everlasting *F*, Prince of Peace.
Mt 6: 9 " 'Our *F* in heaven,
10:37 "Anyone who loves his *f*
15: 4 'Honor your *f* and mother'
19: 5 this reason a man will leave
his *f*
Lk 12:53 *f* against son and son against *f*,
23:34 Jesus said, "*F*, forgive them,
Jn 6:44 the *F* who sent me draws him,
6:46 No one has seen the *F*
8:44 You belong to your *f*, the devil,
10:30 I and the *F* are one."
14: 6 No one comes to the *F*
14: 9 who has seen me has seen
the *F*.
Ro 4:11 he is the *f* of all who believe
2Co 6:18 "I will be a *F* to you,
Eph 6: 2 "Honor your *f* and mother"—
Heb 12: 7 what son is not disciplined by
his *f*?

FATHER'S (FATHER)

Pr 13: 1 A wise son heeds his *f*
instruction,
15: 5 A fool spurns his *f* discipline,
19:13 A foolish son is his *f* ruin,
Lk 2:49 had to be in my *F* house?"
Jn 2:16 How dare you turn my *F* house
10:29 can snatch them out of my *F*
hand.
14: 2 In my *F* house are many rooms;

FATHERLESS (FATHER)

Dt 10:18 He defends the cause of the *f*
24:17 Do not deprive the alien or the *f*
24:19 Leave it for the alien, the *f*
Ps 68: 5 A father to the *f*, a defender
Pr 23:10 or encroach on the fields of
the *f*,

FATHERS (FATHER)

Ex 20: 5 for the sin of the *f* to the third
Lk 11:11 "Which of you *f*, if your son asks
Eph 6: 4 *F*, do not exasperate your
children;
Col 3:21 *F*, do not embitter your children,

FATHOM*

Job 11: 7 "Can you *f* the mysteries of
God?
Ps 145: 3 his greatness no one can *f*.
Ecc 3:11 yet they cannot *f* what God has
Isa 40:28 and his understanding no one
can *f*
1Co 13: 2 and can *f* all mysteries and all

FAULT (FAULTS)

Mt 18:15 and show him his *f*, just
Php 2:15 of God without *f* in a crooked
Jas 1: 5 generously to all without
finding *f*,
Jude : 24 his glorious presence without *f*

FAULTFINDERS*

Jude : 16 These men are grumblers and *f*;

FAULTS (FAULT)

Ps 19:12 Forgive my hidden *f*.

FAVORITISM*

Ex   23: 3 and do not show *f* to a poor man
Lev 19:15 to the poor or *f* to the great,
Ac   10:34 true it is that God does not show *f*
Ro   2:11 For God does not show *f*.
Eph   6: 9 and there is no *f* with him.
Col   3:25 for his wrong, and there is no *f*.
1Ti   5:21 and to do nothing out of *f*.
Jas   2: 1 Lord Jesus Christ, don't show *f*.
      2: 9 But if you show *f*, you sin

FEAR (AFRAID FEARS)

Dt   6:13 *F* the LORD your God, serve him
      10:12 but to *f* the LORD your God,
      31:12 and learn to *f* the LORD your God
Ps   19: 9 The *f* of the LORD is pure,
      23: 4 I will *f* no evil,
      27: 1 whom shall I *f*?
      91: 5 You will not *f* the terror of night,
      111:10 *f* of the LORD is the beginning
Pr   8:13 To *f* the LORD is to hate evil;
      9:10 *f* of the LORD is the beginning
      10:27 The *f* of the LORD adds length
      14:27 The *f* of the LORD is a fountain
      15:33 *f* of the LORD teaches a man
      16: 6 through the *f* of the LORD a man
      19:23 The *f* of the LORD leads to life:
      29:25 *F* of man will prove to be a snare,
Isa 11: 3 delight in the *f* of the LORD.
      41:10 So do not *f*, for I am with you;
Lk   12: 5 I will show you whom you should *f*:
Php   2:12 to work out your salvation with *f*
1Jn   4:18 But perfect love drives out *f*,

FEARS (FEAR)

Job   1: 8 a man who *f* God and shuns evil."
Ps   34: 4 he delivered me from all my *f*.
Pr   31:30 a woman who *f* the LORD is
1Jn   4:18 The one who *f* is not made perfect

FEED

Jn   21:15 Jesus said, "*F* my lambs."
      21:17 Jesus said, "*F* my sheep.
Ro   12:20 "If your enemy is hungry, *f* him;
Jude   :12 shepherds who *f* only themselves.

FEET (FOOT)

Ps   8: 6 you put everything under his *f*:
      22:16 have pierced my hands and my *f*.
      40: 2 he set my *f* on a rock
      110: 1 a footstool for your *f*."
      119:105 Your word is a lamp to my *f*
Ro   10:15 "How beautiful are the *f*
1Co   12:21 And the head cannot say to the *f*,
      15:25 has put all his enemies under his *f*.
Heb 12:13 "Make level paths for your *f*,"

FELLOWSHIP

2Co   6:14 what *f* can light have with darkness
      13:14 and the *f* of the Holy Spirit
Php   3:10 the *f* of sharing in his sufferings,
1Jn   1: 6 claim to have *f* with him yet walk
      1: 7 we have *f* with one another,

FEMALE

Ge   1:27 male and *f* he created them.
Gal   3:28 *f*, for you are all one in Christ Jesus

FERVOR

Ro   12:11 but keep your spiritual *f*, serving

FIELD (FIELDS)

Mt   6:28 See how the lilies of the *f* grow.
      13:38 *f* is the world, and the good
1Co   3: 9 you are God's *f*, God's building.

FIELDS (FIELD)

Lk   2: 8 were shepherds living out in the *f*

Jn   4:35 open your eyes and look at the *f*!

FIG (FIGS)

Ge   3: 7 so they sewed *f* leaves together

FIGHT (FOUGHT)

Ex   14:14 The LORD will *f* for you; you need
Dt   1:30 going before you, will *f* for you,
      3:22 The LORD your God himself will *f*
Ne   4:20 Our God will *f* for us!"
Ps   35: 1 *f* against those who *f* against me.
Jn   18:36 my servants would *f*
1Co   9:26 I do not *f* like a man beating the air.
2Co 10: 4 The weapons we *f*
1Ti   1:18 them you may *f* the good *f*,
      6:12 Fight the good *f* of the faith.
2Ti   4: 7 fought the good *f*, I have finished

FIGS (FIG)

Lk   6:44 People do not pick *f*

FILL (FILLED FILLS FULL FULLNESS FULLY)

Ge   1:28 and increase in number; *f* the earth
Ps   16:11 you will *f* me with joy
      81:10 wide your mouth and I will *f* it.
Pr   28:19 who chases fantasies will have his *f*
Hag   2: 7 and I will *f* this house with glory,"
Jn   6:26 you ate the loaves and had your *f*.
Ac   2:28 you will *f* me with joy
Ro   15:13 the God of hope *f* you with all joy

FILLED (FILL)

Ps   72:19 may the whole earth be *f*
      119: 64 The earth is *f* with your love,
Eze 43: 5 the glory of the LORD *f* the temple
Hab   2:14 For the earth will be *f*
Lk   1:15 and he will be *f* with the Holy Spirit
      1:41 and Elizabeth was *f* with the Holy
Jn   12: 3 the house was *f* with the fragrance
Ac   2: 4 All of them were *f*
      4: 8 Then Peter, *f* with the Holy Spirit,
      9:17 and be *f* with the Holy Spirit."
      13: 9 called Paul, *f* with the Holy Spirit,
Eph   5:18 Instead, be *f* with the Spirit.
Php   1:11 *f* with the fruit of righteousness

FILLS (FILL)

Nu   14:21 of the LORD *f* the whole earth,
Ps 107: 9 and *f* the hungry with good things.
Eph   1:23 fullness of him who *f* everything

FILTHY

Isa 64: 6 all our righteous acts are like *f* rags;
Col   3: 8 and *f* language from your lips.
2Pe   2: 7 by the *f* lives of lawless men

FIND (FINDS FOUND)

Nu   32:23 be sure that your sin will *f* you out.
Dt   4:29 you will *f* him if you look for him
1Sa 23:16 and helped him *f* strength in God.
Ps   36: 7 *f* refuge in the shadow
      91: 4 under his wings you will *f* refuge;
Pr   14:22 those who plan what is good *f* love
      31:10 A wife of noble character who can *f*
Jer   6:16 and you will *f* rest for your souls.
Mt   7: 7 seek and you will *f*; knock
      11:29 and you will *f* rest for your souls.
      16:25 loses his life for me will *f* it.
Lk   18: 8 will he *f* faith on the earth?"

Jn   10: 9 come in and go out, and *f* pasture.

FINDS (FIND)

Ps   62: 1 My soul *f* rest in God alone;
      112: 1 who *f* great delight
      119:162 like one who *f* great spoil.
Pr   18:22 He who *f* a wife *f* what is good
Mt   7: 8 he who seeks *f*; and to him who
      10:39 Whoever *f* his life will lose it,
Lk   12:37 whose master *f* them watching
      15: 4 go after the lost sheep until he *f* it?

FINISH (FINISHED)

Jn   4:34 him who sent me and to *f* his work.
      5:36 that the Father has given me to *f*,
Ac   20:24 if only I may *f* the race
2Co 8:11 Now *f* the work, so that your eager
Jas   1: 4 Perseverance must *f* its work

FINISHED (FINISH)

Ge   2: 2 seventh day God had *f* the work he
Jn   19:30 the drink, Jesus said, "It is *f*."
2Ti   4: 7 I have *f* the race, I have kept

FIRE

Ex   13:21 in a pillar of *f* to give them light,
Lev   6:12 *f* on the altar must be kept burning;
Isa 30:27 and his tongue is a consuming *f*.
Jer   23:29 my word like *f*," declares
Mt   3:11 you with the Holy Spirit and with *f*.
      5:22 will be in danger of the *f* of hell.
      25:41 into the eternal *f* prepared
Mk   9:43 where the *f* never goes out.
Ac   2: 3 to be tongues of *f* that separated
1Co   3:13 It will be revealed with *f*,
1Th   5:19 Do not put out the Spirit's *f*;
Heb 12:29 for our "God is a consuming *f*."
Jas   3: 5 set on *f* by a small spark.
2Pe   3:10 the elements will be destroyed by *f*,
Jude   :23 snatch others from the *f*
Rev 20:14 The lake of *f* is the second death.

FIRM

Ex   14:13 Stand *f* and you will see
2Ch 20:17 stand *f* and see the deliverance
Ps   33:11 of the LORD stand *f* forever,
      37:23 he makes his steps *f*;
      40: 2 and gave me a *f* place to stand.
      89: 2 that your love stands *f* forever,
      119: 89 it stands *f* in the heavens.
Pr   4:26 and take only ways that are *f*.
Zec   8:23 nations will take *f* hold of one Jew
Mk   13:13 he who stands *f* to the end will be
1Co   16:13 on your guard; stand *f* in the faith;
2Co 1:24 because it is by faith you stand *f*.
Eph   6:14 Stand *f* then, with the belt
Col   4:12 that you may stand *f* in all the will
2Th   2:15 stand *f* and hold to the teachings
2Ti   2:19 God's solid foundation stands *f*,
Heb   6:19 an anchor for the soul, *f* and secure
1Pe   5: 9 Resist him, standing *f* in the faith,

FIRST

Isa 44: 6 I am the *f* and I am the last;
      48:12 I am the *f* and I am the last.
Mt   5:24 *F* go and be reconciled
      6:33 But seek *f* his kingdom
      7: 5 *f* take the plank out
      20:27 wants to be *f* must be your slave—
      22:38 This is the *f* and greatest
      23:26 *F* clean the inside of the cup

Mk 13:10 And the gospel must *f* be preached
Ac 11:26 disciples were called Christians *f*
Ro 1:16 *f* for the Jew, then for the Gentile.
1Co 12:28 in the church God has appointed *f*
2Co 8: 5 they gave themselves *f* to the Lord
1Ti 2:13 For Adam was formed *f*, then Eve.
Jas 3:17 comes from heaven is *f* of all pure;
1Jn 4:19 We love because he *f* loved us.
3Jn :9 but Diotrephes, who loves to be *f*,
Rev 1:17 I am the *F* and the Last.
2: 4 You have forsaken your *f* love.

FIRSTBORN (BEAR)
Ex 11: 5 Every *f* son in Egypt will die,

FIRSTFRUITS
Ex 23:19 "Bring the best of the *f* of your soil

FISHERS
Mk 1:17 "and I will make you *f* of men."

FITTING*
Ps 33: 1 it is *f* for the upright to praise him.
147: 1 how pleasant and *f* to praise him!
Pr 10:32 of the righteous know what is *f*,
19:10 It is not *f* for a fool to live in luxury
26: 1 honor is not *f* for a fool.
1Co 14:40 everything should be done in a *f*
Col 3:18 to your husbands, as is *f* in the Lord
Heb 2:10 sons to glory, it was *f* that God,

FIX
Dt 11:18 *F* these words of mine
Pr 4:25 *f* your gaze directly before you.
2Co 4:18 we *f* our eyes not on what is seen,
Heb 3: 1 heavenly calling, *f* your thoughts
12: 2 Let us *f* our eyes on Jesus,

FLAME (FLAMES FLAMING)
2Ti 1: 6 you to fan into *f* the gift of God,

FLAMES (FLAME)
1Co 3:15 only as one escaping through the *f*.
13: 3 and surrender my body to the *f*,

FLAMING (FLAME)
Eph 6:16 you can extinguish all the *f* arrows

FLASH
1Co 15:52 in a *f*, in the twinkling of an eye,

FLATTER (FLATTERING FLATTERY)
Job 32:21 nor will I *f* any man;
Jude :16 *f* others for their own advantage.

FLATTERING (FLATTER)
Ps 12: 2 their *f* lips speak with deception.
12: 3 May the LORD cut off all *f* lips
Pr 26:28 and a *f* mouth works ruin.

FLATTERY (FLATTER)
Ro 16:18 and *f* they deceive the minds
1Th 2: 5 You know we never used *f*,

FLAWLESS*
2Sa 22:31 the word of the LORD is *f*.
Job 11: 4 You say to God, 'My beliefs are *f*
Ps 12: 6 And the words of the LORD are *f*,
18:30 the word of the LORD is *f*.
Pr 30: 5 "Every word of God is *f*;
SS 5: 2 my dove, my *f* one.

FLEE
Ps 139: 7 Where can I *f* from your presence?

1Co 6:18 *F* from sexual immorality.
10:14 my dear friends, *f* from idolatry.
1Ti 6:11 But you, man of God, *f* from all this
2Ti 2:22 *F* the evil desires of youth,
Jas 4: 7 Resist the devil, and he will *f*

FLEETING
Ps 89:47 Remember how *f* is my life.
Pr 31:30 Charm is deceptive, and beauty is *f*

FLESH
Ge 2:23 and *f* of my *f*;
2:24 and they will become one *f*.
Job 19:26 yet in my *f* I will see God;
Eze 11:19 of stone and give them a heart of *f*.
36:26 of stone and give you a heart of *f*.
Mk 10: 8 and the two will become one *f*.'
Jn 1:14 The Word became *f* and made his
6:51 This bread is my *f*, which I will give
1Co 6:16 "The two will become one *f*."
Eph 5:31 and the two will become one *f*."
6:12 For our struggle is not against *f*

FLOCK (FLOCKS)
Isa 40:11 He tends his *f* like a shepherd:
Eze 34: 2 not shepherds take care of the *f*?
Zec 11:17 who deserts the *f*!
Mt 26:31 the sheep of the *f* will be scattered.'
Ac 20:28 all the *f* of which the Holy Spirit
1Pe 5: 2 Be shepherds of God's *f* that is

FLOCKS (FLOCK)
Lk 2: 8 keeping watch over their *f* at night.

FLOG
Ac 22:25 to *f* a Roman citizen who hasn't

FLOODGATES
Mal 3:10 see if I will not throw open the *f*

FLOURISHING
Ps 52: 8 *f* in the house of God;

FLOW (FLOWING)
Nu 13:27 and it does *f* with milk and honey!
Jn 7:38 streams of living water will *f*

FLOWERS
Isa 40: 7 The grass withers and the *f* fall,

FLOWING (FLOW)
Ex 3: 8 a land *f* with milk and honey—

FOLDING
Pr 6:10 a little *f* of the hands to rest—

FOLLOW (FOLLOWING FOLLOWS)
Ex 23: 2 Do not *f* the crowd in doing wrong.
Lev 18: 4 and be careful to *f* my decrees.
Dt 5: 1 Learn them and be sure to *f* them.
Ps 23: 6 Surely goodness and love will *f* me
Mt 16:24 and take up his cross and *f* me.
Jn 10: 4 his sheep *f* him because they know
1Co 14: 1 *F* the way of love and eagerly
Rev 14: 4 They *f* the Lamb wherever he goes.

FOLLOWING (FOLLOW)
1Ti 1:18 by *f* them you may fight the good

FOLLOWS (FOLLOW)
Jn 8:12 Whoever *f* me will never walk

FOOD (FOODS)
Pr 20:13 you will have *f* to spare.
22: 9 for he shares his *f* with the poor.

Pr 25:21 If your enemy is hungry, give him *f*
31:15 she provides *f* for her family
Da 1: 8 to defile himself with the royal *f*
Jn 6:27 Do not work for *f* that spoils,
Ro 14:14 fully convinced that no *f* is unclean
1Co 8: 8 But *f* does not bring us near to God
1Ti 6: 8 But if we have *f* and clothing,
Jas 2:15 sister is without clothes and daily *f*.

FOODS (FOOD)
Mk 7:19 Jesus declared all *f* "clean.")

FOOL (FOOLISH FOOLISHNESS FOOLS)
Ps 14: 1 The *f* says in his heart,
Pr 15: 5 A *f* spurns his father's discipline.
17:28 Even a *f* is thought wise
18: 2 A *f* finds no pleasure
26: 5 Answer a *f* according to his folly,
28:26 He who trusts in himself is a *f*,
Mt 5:22 But anyone who says, 'You *f*!'

FOOLISH (FOOL)
Pr 10: 1 but a *f* son grief to his mother.
17:25 A *f* son brings grief to his father
Mt 7:26 practice is like a *f* man who built
25: 2 of them were *f* and five were wise.
1Co 1:27 God chose the *f* things of the world

FOOLISHNESS (FOOL)
1Co 1:18 of the cross is *f* to those who are
1:25 For the *f* of God is wiser
2:14 for they are *f* to him, and he cannot
3:19 of this world is *f* in God's sight.

FOOLS (FOOL)
Pr 14: 9 *F* mock at making amends for sin,
1Co 4:10 We are *f* for Christ, but you are

FOOT (FEET FOOTHOLD)
Jos 1: 3 every place where you set your *f*,
Isa 1: 6 From the sole of your *f* to the top
1Co 12:15 If the *f* should say, "Because I am

FOOTHOLD (FOOT)
Eph 4:27 and do not give the devil a *f*.

FORBEARANCE*
Ro 3:25 because in his *f* he had left the sins

FORBID
1Co 14:39 and do not *f* speaking in tongues.

FOREFATHERS (FATHER)
Heb 1: 1 spoke to our *f* through the prophets

FOREKNEW* (KNOW)
Ro 8:29 For those God *f* he
11: 2 not reject his people, whom he *f*.

FOREVER (EVER)
1Ch 16:15 He remembers his covenant *f*,
16:34 his love endures *f*.
Ps 9: 7 The LORD reigns *f*;
23: 6 dwell in the house of the LORD *f*.
33:11 the plans of the LORD stand firm *f*
86:12 I will glorify your name *f*.
92: 8 But you, O LORD, are exalted *f*.
110: 4 "You are a priest *f*,
119:111 Your statutes are my heritage *f*;
Jn 6:51 eats of this bread, he will live *f*.
14:16 Counselor to be with you *f*—
1Co 9:25 it to get a crown that will last *f*.
1Th 4:17 And so we will be with the Lord *f*.

Heb 13: 8 same yesterday and today and *f*.
1Pe 1:25 but the word of the Lord
stands *f*."
1Jn 2:17 who does the will of God lives *f*.

FORFEIT
Lk 9:25 and yet lose or *f* his very self?

FORGAVE (FORGIVE)
Ps 32: 5 and you *f*
Eph 4:32 just as in Christ God *f* you.
Col 2:13 He *f* us all our sins, having
3:13 Forgive as the Lord *f* you.

FORGET (FORGETS FORGETTING)
Dt 6:12 that you do not *f* the LORD,
Ps 103: 2 and *f* not all his benefits.
137: 5 may my right hand *f* its skill.
Isa 49:15 "Can a mother *f* the baby
Heb 6:10 he will not *f* your work

FORGETS (FORGET)
Jn 16:21 her baby is born she *f* the
anguish
Jas 1:24 immediately *f* what he looks
like.

FORGETTING (FORGET)
Php 3:13 *F* what is behind and straining

FORGIVE (FORGAVE FORGIVENESS FORGIVING)
2Ch 7:14 will *f* their sin and will heal their
Ps 19:12 *F* my hidden faults.
Mt 6:12 *F* us our debts,
6:14 For if you *f* men when they sin
18:21 many times shall I *f* my brother
Mk 11:25 in heaven may *f* you your sins."
Lk 11: 4 *F* us our sins,
23:34 Jesus said, "Father, *f* them,
Col 3:13 *F* as the Lord forgave you.
1Jn 1: 9 and just and will *f* us our sins

FORGIVENESS (FORGIVE)
Ps 130: 4 But with you there is *f*;
Ac 10:43 believes in him receives *f* of
sins
Eph 1: 7 through his blood, the *f* of sins,
Col 1:14 in whom we have redemption,
the *f*
Heb 9:22 the shedding of blood there is
no *f*.

FORGIVING (FORGIVE)
Ne 9:17 But you are a *f* God, gracious
Eph 4:32 to one another, *f* each other,

FORMED
Ge 2: 7 And the LORD God *f* man
Ps 103: 14 for he knows how we are *f*,
Isa 45:18 but *f* it to be inhabited—
Ro 9:20 "Shall what is *f* say to him who *f*
it,
1Ti 2:13 For Adam was *f* first, then Eve.
Heb 11: 3 understand that the universe
was *f*

FORSAKE (FORSAKEN)
Jos 1: 5 I will never leave you nor *f* you.
24:16 "Far be it from us to *f* the LORD
2Ch 15: 2 but if you *f* him, he will *f* you.
Ps 27:10 Though my father and mother *f*
me
Isa 55: 7 Let the wicked *f* his way
Heb 13: 5 never will I *f* you."

FORSAKEN (FORSAKE)
Ps 22: 1 my God, why have you *f* me?
37:25 I have never seen the
righteous
Mt 27:46 my God, why have you *f* me?"
Rev 2: 4 You have *f* your first love.

FORTRESS
Ps 18: 2 The LORD is my rock, my *f*
71: 3 for you are my rock and my *f*.

FOUGHT (FIGHT)
2Ti 4: 7 I have *f* the good fight, I have

FOUND (FIND)
1Ch 28: 9 If you seek him, he will be *f* by
you;
Isa 55: 6 Seek the LORD while he may
be *f*;
Da 5:27 on the scales and *f* wanting.
Lk 15: 6 with me; I have *f* my lost
sheep.'
15: 9 with me; I have *f* my lost coin.'
Ac 4:12 Salvation is *f* in no one else,

FOUNDATION
Isa 28:16 a precious cornerstone for a
sure *f*;
1Co 3:11 For no one can lay any *f* other
Eph 2:20 built on the *f* of the apostles
2Ti 2:19 God's solid *f* stands firm,

FOXES
Mt 8:20 "*F* have holes and birds

FRAGRANCE
2Co 2:16 of death; to the other, the *f* of
life.

FREE (FREED FREEDOM FREELY)
Ps 146: 7 The LORD sets prisoners *f*,
Jn 8:32 and the truth will set you *f*."
Ro 6:18 You have been set *f* from sin
Gal 3:28 slave nor *f*, male nor female,
1Pe 2:16 *f* men, but do not use your
freedom

FREED (FREE)
Rev 1: 5 has *f* us from our sins by his
blood,

FREEDOM (FREE)
Ro 8:21 into the glorious *f* of the children
2Co 3:17 the Spirit of the Lord is, there
is *f*.
Gal 5:13 But do not use your *f* to indulge
1Pe 2:16 but do not use your *f* as a cover-
up

FREELY (FREE)
Isa 55: 7 and to our God, for he will *f*
pardon
Mt 10: 8 Freely you have received, *f* give.
Ro 3:24 and are justified *f* by his grace
Eph 1: 6 which he has *f* given us

FRIEND (FRIENDS)
Ex 33:11 as a man speaks with his *f*.
Pr 17:17 A *f* loves at all times,
18:24 there is a *f* who sticks closer
27: 6 Wounds from a *f* can be trusted,
27:10 Do not forsake your *f* and the *f*
Jas 4: 4 Anyone who chooses to be a *f*

FRIENDS (FRIEND)
Pr 16:28 and a gossip separates close *f*.
Zec 13: 6 given at the house of my *f*.'
Jn 15:13 that he lay down his life for
his *f*.

FRUIT (FRUITFUL)
Ps 1: 3 which yields its *f* in season
Pr 11:30 The *f* of the righteous is a tree
Mt 7:16 By their *f* you will recognize
Jn 15: 2 branch in me that bears no *f*,
Gal 5:22 But the *f* of the Spirit is love,
joy,
Rev 22: 2 of *f*, yielding its *f* every month.

FRUITFUL (FRUIT)
Ge 1:22 "Be *f* and increase in number
Ps 128: 3 Your wife will be like a *f* vine
Jn 15: 2 prunes so that it will be even
more *f*.

FULFILL (FULFILLED FULFILLMENT)
Ps 116: 14 I will *f* my vows to the LORD
Mt 5:17 come to abolish them but to *f*
them.
1Co 7: 3 husband should *f* his marital
duty

FULFILLED (FULFILL)
Pr 13:19 A longing *f* is sweet to the soul,
Mk 14:49 But the Scriptures must be *f*."

Ro 13: 8 loves his fellowman has *f* the
law.

FULFILLMENT (FULFILL)
Ro 13:10 Therefore love is the *f* of the
law.

FULL (FILL)
Ps 127: 5 whose quiver is *f* of them.
Pr 31:11 Her husband has *f* confidence
Isa 6: 3 the whole earth is *f* of his glory."
11: 9 for the earth will be *f*
Jn 10:10 may have life, and have it to
the *f*.
Ac 6: 3 known to be *f* of the Spirit

FULLNESS (FILL)
Col 1:19 to have all his *f* dwell in him,
2: 9 in Christ all the *f* of the Deity
lives

FULLY (FILL)
1Ki 8:61 your hearts must be *f* committed
2Ch 16: 9 whose hearts are *f* committed
Ps 119: 4 that are to be *f* obeyed.
119:138 they are *f* trustworthy.
1Co 15:58 Always give yourselves *f*

FUTURE
Ps 37:37 there is a *f* for the man of
peace.
Pr 23:18 There is surely a *f* hope for you,
Ro 8:38 neither the present nor the *f*,

GABRIEL*
Angel who interpreted Daniel's visions (Da
8:16-26; 9:20-27); announced births of John
(Lk 1:11-20), Jesus (Lk 1:26-38).

GAIN (GAINED)
Ps 60:12 With God we will *g* the victory,
Mk 8:36 it for a man to *g* the whole
world,
1Co 13: 3 but have not love, I *g* nothing.
Php 1:21 to live is Christ and to die is *g*.
3: 8 that I may *g* Christ and be found
1Ti 6: 6 with contentment is great *g*.

GAINED (GAIN)
Ro 5: 2 through whom we have *g* access

GALILEE
Isa 9: 1 but in the future he will honor *G*

GALL
Mt 27:34 mixed with *g*; but after tasting it,

GAP
Eze 22:30 stand before me in the *g* on
behalf

GARDENER
Jn 15: 1 true vine, and my Father is
the *g*.

GARMENT (GARMENTS)
Ps 102: 26 they will all wear out like a *g*.
Mt 9:16 of unshrunk cloth on an old *g*,
Jn 19:23 This *g* was seamless, woven

GARMENTS (GARMENT)
Ge 3:21 The LORD God made *g* of skin
Isa 61:10 me with *g* of salvation
63: 1 with his *g* stained crimson?"
Jn 19:24 "They divided my *g* among them

GATE (GATES)
Mt 7:13 For wide is the *g* and broad is
Jn 10: 9 I am the *g*; whoever enters

GATES (GATE)
Ps 100: 4 Enter his *g* with thanksgiving
Mt 16:18 the *g* of Hades will not
overcome it

GATHER (GATHERS)
Zec 14: 2 I will *g* all the nations to
Jerusalem
Mt 12:30 he who does not *g* with me
scatters
23:37 longed to *g* your children
together,

GATHERS (GATHER)
Isa   40:11 He *g* the lambs in his arms
Mt   23:37 a hen *g* her chicks under her wings,

GAVE (GIVE)
Ezr   2:69 According to their ability they *g*
Job   1:21 LORD *g* and the LORD has taken
Jn   3:16 so loved the world that he *g* his one
2Co   8: 5 they *g* themselves first to the Lord
Gal   2:20 who loved me and *g* himself for me
1Ti   2: 6 who *g* himself as a ransom

GAZE
Ps   27: 4 to *g* upon the beauty of the LORD
Pr   4:25 fix your *g* directly before you.

GENEALOGIES
1Ti   1: 4 themselves to myths and endless *g.*

GENERATIONS
Ps   22:30 future *g* will be told about the Lord
  102: 12 your renown endures through all *g.*
  145: 13 dominion endures through all *g.*
Lk   1:48 now on all *g* will call me blessed,
Eph   3: 5 not made known to men in other *g*

GENEROUS
Ps112: 5 Good will come to him who is *g*
Pr   22: 9 A *g* man will himself be blessed,
2Co   9: 5 Then it will be ready as a *g* gift,
1Ti   6:18 and to be *g* and willing to share.

GENTILE (GENTILES)
Ro   1:16 first for the Jew, then for the G.
  10:12 difference between Jew and G—

GENTILES (GENTILE)
Isa   42: 6 and a light for the G,
Ro   3: 9 and G alike are all under sin.
  11:13 as I am the apostle to the G,
1Co   1:23 block to Jews and foolishness to G,

GENTLE (GENTLENESS)
Pr   15: 1 A *g* answer turns away wrath,
Zec   9: 9 *g* and riding on a donkey,
Mt   11:29 for I am *g* and humble in heart,
  21: 5 *g* and riding on a donkey,
1Co   4:21 or in love and with a *g* spirit?
1Pe   3: 4 the unfading beauty of a *g*

GENTLENESS* (GENTLE)
2Co   10: 1 By the meekness and *g* of Christ,
Gal   5:23 faithfulness, *g* and self-control.
Php   4: 5 Let your *g* be evident to all.
Col   3:12 kindness, humility, *g* and patience.
1Ti   6:11 faith, love, endurance and *g.*
1Pe   3:15 But do this with *g* and respect,

GETHSEMANE
Mt   26:36 disciples to a place called G,

GIDEON*
  Judge, also called Jerub-Baal; freed Israel from Midianites (Jdg 6-8; Heb 11:32). Given sign of fleece (Jdg 8:36-40).

GIFT (GIFTS)
Pr   21:14 A *g* given in secret soothes anger,
Mt   5:23 if you are offering your *g*
Ac   2:38 And you will receive the *g*
Ro   6:23 but the *g* of God is eternal life
1Co   7: 7 each man has his own *g* from God;
2Co   8:12 the *g* is acceptable according
  9:15 be to God for his indescribable *g!*
Eph   2: 8 it is the *g* of God—not by works,
1Ti   4:14 not neglect your *g,* which was

2Ti   1: 6 you to fan into flame the *g* of God,
Jas   1:17 and perfect *g* is from above,
1Pe   4:10 should use whatever *g* he has

GIFTS (GIFT)
Ro   11:29 for God's *g* and his call are
  12: 6 We have different *g,* according
1Co   12: 4 There are different kinds of *g,*
  12:31 But eagerly desire the greater *g.*
  14: 1 and eagerly desire spiritual *g,*
  14:12 excel in *g* that build up the church.

GILEAD
Jer   8:22 Is there no balm in G?

GIVE (GAVE GIVEN GIVER GIVES GIVING)
Nu   6:26 and *g* you peace." '
1Sa   1:11 then I will *g* him to the LORD
2Ch   15: 7 be strong and do not *g* up,
Pr   21:26 but the righteous *g* without sparing
  23:26 My son, *g* me your heart.
  30: 8 but *g* me only my daily bread.
  31:31 G her the reward she has earned,
Isa   42: 8 I will not *g* my glory to another
Eze   36:26 I will *g* you a new heart
Mt   6:11 G us today our daily bread.
  10: 8 Freely you have received, freely *g.*
  22:21 "G to Caesar what is Caesar's,
Mk   8:37 Or what can a man *g* in exchange
Lk   6:38 G, and it will be given to you.
  11:13 Father in heaven *g* the Holy Spirit
Jn   10:28 I *g* them eternal life, and they shall
  13:34 "A new commandment I *g* you:
Ac   20:35 blessed to *g* than to receive.' "
Ro   12: 8 let him *g* generously;
  13: 7 G everyone what you owe him:
  14:12 each of us will *g* an account
2Co   9: 7 Each man should *g* what he has
Rev   14: 7 "Fear God and *g* him glory,

GIVEN (GIVE)
Nu   8:16 are to be *g* wholly to me.
Ps115: 16 but the earth he has *g* to man.
Isa   9: 6 to us a son is *g,*
Mt   6:33 and all these things will be *g* to you
  7: 7 "Ask and it will be *g* to you;
Lk   22:19 saying, "This is my body *g* for you;
Jn   3:27 man can receive only what is *g* him
Ro   5: 5 the Holy Spirit, whom he has *g* us.
1Co   4: 2 those who have been *g* a trust must
  12:13 we were all *g* the one Spirit to drink
Eph   4: 7 to each one of us grace has been *g*

GIVER* (GIVE)
Pr   18:16 A gift opens the way for the *g*
2Co   9: 7 for God loves a cheerful *g.*

GIVES (GIVE)
Ps119:130 The unfolding of your words *g* light;
Pr   14:30 A heart at peace *g* life to the body,
  15:30 good news *g* health to the bones.
  28:27 He who *g* to the poor will lack
Isa   40:29 He *g* strength to the weary
Mt   10:42 if anyone *g* even a cup of cold water
Jn   6:63 The Spirit *g* life; the flesh counts
1Co   15:57 He *g* us the victory
2Co   3: 6 the letter kills, but the Spirit *g* life.

GIVING (GIVE)
Ne   8: 8 *g* the meaning so that the people

Ps   19: 8 *g* joy to the heart.
Mt   6: 4 so that your *g* may be in secret.
2Co   8: 7 also excel in this grace of *g.*

GLAD (GLADNESS)
Ps   31: 7 I will be *g* and rejoice in your love,
  46: 4 whose streams make *g* the city
  97: 1 LORD reigns, let the earth be *g;*
  118: 24 let us rejoice and be *g* in it.
Pr   23:25 May your father and mother be *g;*
Zec   2:10 and be *g,* O Daughter of Zion.
Mt   5:12 be *g,* because great is your reward

GLADNESS (GLAD)
Ps   45:15 They are led in with joy and *g;*
  51: 8 Let me hear joy and *g;*
  100: 2 Serve the LORD with *g;*
Jer   31:13 I will turn their mourning into *g;*

GLORIFIED (GLORY)
Jn   13:31 Son of Man *g* and God is *g* in him.
Ro   8:30 those he justified, he also *g.*
2Th   1:10 comes to be *g* in his holy people

GLORIFY (GLORY)
Ps   34: 3 G the LORD with me;
  86:12 I will *g* your name forever.
Jn   13:32 God will *g* the Son in himself,
  17: 1 G your Son, that your Son may

GLORIOUS (GLORY)
Ps   45:13 All *g* is the princess
  111: 3 G and majestic are his deeds,
  145: 5 of the *g* splendor of your majesty,
Isa   4: 2 the LORD will be beautiful and *g,*
  12: 5 for he has done *g* things;
  42:21 to make his law great and *g.*
  63:15 from your lofty throne, holy and *g.*
Mt   19:28 the Son of Man sits on his *g* throne,
Lk   9:31 appeared in *g* splendor, talking
Ac   2:20 of the great and *g* day of the Lord.
2Co   3: 8 of the Spirit be even more *g?*
Php   3:21 so that they will be like his *g* body.
  4:19 to his riches in Christ Jesus.
Tit   2:13 the *g* appearing of our great God
Jude   :24 before his *g* presence without fault

GLORY (GLORIFIED GLORIFY GLORIOUS)
Ex   15:11 awesome in *g,*
  33:18 Moses said, "Now show me your *g*
1Sa   4:21 "The *g* has departed from Israel"—
1Ch   16:24 Declare his *g* among the nations,
  16:28 ascribe to the LORD *g*
  29:11 and the *g* and the majesty
Ps   8: 5 and crowned him with *g* and honor
  19: 1 The heavens declare the *g* of God;
  24: 7 that the King of *g* may come in.
  29: 1 ascribe to the LORD *g*
  72:19 the whole earth be filled with his *g.*
  96: 3 Declare his *g* among the nations,
Pr   19:11 it is to his *g* to overlook an offense.
  25: 2 It is the *g* of God to conceal
Isa   6: 3 the whole earth is full of his *g.*"
  48:11 I will not yield my *g* to another.
Eze   43: 2 and the land was radiant with *g*
Mt   24:30 of the sky, with power and great *g.*
  25:31 the Son of Man comes in his *g,*
Mk   8:38 in his Father's *g* with the holy
  13:26 in clouds with great power and *g,*
Lk   2: 9 and the *g* of the Lord shone

Lk   2:14 saying, "G to God in the highest,
Jn   1:14 We have seen his g, the g of the
           One
     17: 5 presence with the g I had with
           you
     17:24 to see my g, the g you have
           given
Ac   7: 2 The God of g appeared
Ro   1:23 exchanged the g of the immortal
      3:23 and fall short of the g of God,
      8:18 with the g that will be revealed
      9: 4 theirs the divine g, the
           covenants,
1Co 10:31 whatever you do, do it all for
           the g
     11: 7 but the woman is the g of man.
     15:43 it is raised in g; it is sown
2Co   3:10 comparison with the
           surpassing g,
      3:18 faces all reflect the Lord's g,
      4:17 us an eternal g that far
           outweighs
Col   1:27 Christ in you, the hope of g.
      3: 4 also will appear with him in g.
1Ti   3:16 was taken up in g.
Heb   1: 3 The Son is the radiance of
           God's g,
      2: 7 you crowned him with g and
           honor
1Pe   1:24 and all their g is like the flowers
Rev   4:11 to receive g and honor and
           power,
     21:23 for the g of God gives it light,

GLUTTONS
Tit   1:12 always liars, evil brutes, lazy g."

GNASHING
Mt   8:12 where there will be weeping
           and g

GNAT*
Mt   23:24 You strain out a g but swallow

GOAL
2Co   5: 9 So we make it our g to please
           him,
Gal   3: 3 to attain your g by human effort?
Php   3:14 on toward the g to win the prize

GOAT (GOATS SCAPEGOAT)
Isa 11: 6 the leopard will lie down with
           the g

GOATS (GOAT)
Nu   7:17 five male g and five male lambs

GOD (GOD'S GODLINESS GODLY GODS)
Ge   1: 1 In the beginning G created
      1: 2 and the Spirit of G was hovering
      1:26 Then G said, "Let us make man
      1:27 So G created man in his own
           image
      1:31 G saw all that he had made,
      2: 3 And G blessed the seventh day
      2:22 Then the Lord G made a woman
      3:21 The Lord G made garments
      3:23 So the Lord G banished him
      5:22 Enoch walked with G 300 years
      6: 2 sons of G saw that the
           daughters
      9:16 everlasting covenant between G
     17: 1 "I am G Almighty; walk before
           me
     21:33 name of the Lord, the Eternal G.
     22: 8 "G himself will provide the lamb
     28:12 and the angels of G were
           ascending
     32:28 because you have struggled
           with G
     32:30 "It is because I saw G face to
           face,
     35:10 G said to him, "Your name is
           Jacob
     41:51 G has made me forget all my
     50:20 but G intended it for good
Ex   2:24 G heard their groaning
      3: 6 because he was afraid to look
           at G.
      6: 7 own people, and I will be your G.
      8:10 is no one like the Lord our G.

Ex   13:18 So G led the people
     15: 2 He is my G, and I will praise
           him,
     17: 9 with the staff of G in my hands."
     19: 3 Then Moses went up to G,
     20: 2 the Lord your G, who brought
     20: 5 the Lord your G, am a jealous G,
     20:19 But do not have G speak to us
     22:28 "Do not blaspheme G
     31:18 inscribed by the finger of G.
     34: 6 the compassionate and
           gracious G,
     34:14 name is Jealous, is a jealous G.
Lev 18:21 not profane the name of your G.
     19: 2 the Lord your G, am holy.
     26:12 walk among you and be your G,
Nu   22:38 I must speak only what G puts
     23:19 G is not a man, that he should
           lie,
Dt   1:17 for judgment belongs to G.
      3:22 Lord your G himself will fight
      3:24 For what g is there in heaven
      4:24 is a consuming fire, a jealous G.
      4:31 the Lord your G is a merciful G,
      4:39 heart this day that the Lord is G
      5:11 the name of the Lord your G,
      5:14 a Sabbath to the Lord your G.
      5:26 of the living G speaking out of
           fire,
      6: 4 Lord our G, the Lord is one.
      6: 5 Love the Lord your G
      6:13 the Lord your G, serve him only
      6:16 Do not test the Lord your G
      7: 9 your G is G; he is the faithful G,
      7:12 the Lord your G will keep his
      7:21 is a great and awesome G.
      8: 5 the Lord your G disciplines you.
     10:12 but to fear the Lord your G,
     10:14 the Lord your G belong
     10:17 For the Lord your G is G of gods
     11:13 to love the Lord your G
     13: 3 The Lord your G is testing you
     13: 4 the Lord your G you must
     15: 6 the Lord your G will bless you
     19: 9 to love the Lord your G
     25:16 the Lord your G detests anyone
     29:29 belong to the Lord our G,
     30: 2 return to the Lord your G
     30:16 today to love the Lord your G,
     30:20 you may love the Lord your G,
     31: 6 for the Lord your G goes
     32: 3 Oh, praise the greatness of
           our G!
     32: 4 A faithful G who does no wrong,
     33:27 The eternal G is your refuge,
Jos   1: 9 for the Lord your G will be
     14: 8 the Lord my G wholeheartedly.
     22: 5 to love the Lord your G,
     22:34 Between Us that the Lord is G.
     23:11 careful to love the Lord your G.
     23:14 the Lord your G gave you has
Jdg 16:28 O G, please strengthen me just
Ru   1:16 be my people and your G my G.
1Sa   2: 2 there is no Rock like our G.
      2: 3 for the Lord is a G who knows,
      2:25 another man, G may mediate
     10:26 men whose hearts G had
           touched.
     12:12 the Lord your G was your king.
     17:26 defy the armies of the living G?"
     17:46 world will know that there is a G
     30: 6 strength in the Lord his G.
2Sa 14:14 But G does not take away life;
     22: 3 my G is my rock, in whom I take
     22:31 "As for G, his way is perfect;
1Ki   4:29 G gave Solomon wisdom
      8:23 there is no G like you in heaven
      8:27 "But will G really dwell on earth?
      8:61 committed to the Lord our G,
     18:21 If the Lord is G, follow him;
     18:37 are G, and that you are turning
     20:28 a g of the hills and not a g
2Ki 19:15 G of Israel, enthroned
1Ch 16:35 Cry out, "Save us, O G our
           Savior;
     28: 2 for the footstool of our G,
     28: 9 acknowledge the G of your
           father,
     29:10 G of our father Israel,
     29:17 my G, that you test the heart
2Ch   2: 4 for the Name of the Lord my G

2Ch   5:14 of the Lord filled the temple
           of G
      6:18 "But will G really dwell on earth
     18:13 I can tell him only what my G
           says
     20: 6 are you not the G who is in
           heaven?
     25: 8 for G has the power to help
     30: 9 for the Lord your G is gracious
     33:12 the favor of the Lord his G
Ezr   8:22 "The good hand of our G is
      9: 6 "O my G, I am too ashamed
      9:13 our G, you have punished us
           less
Ne   1: 5 the great and awesome G,
      8: 8 from the Book of the Law of G,
      9:17 But you are a forgiving G,
      9:32 the great, mighty and
           awesome G,
Job   1: 1 he feared G and shunned evil.
      2:10 Shall we accept good from G,
      4:17 a mortal be more righteous
           than G?
      5:17 is the man whom G corrects;
     11: 7 Can you fathom the mysteries
           of G
     19:26 yet in my flesh I will see G;
     22:13 Yet you say, 'What does G
           know?
     25: 4 can a man be righteous
           before G?
     33:14 For G does speak—now one
           way,
     34:12 is unthinkable that G would do
     36:26 is G— beyond our understanding!
     37:22 G comes in awesome majesty.
Ps   18: 2 my G is my rock, in whom I take
     18:28 my G turns my darkness into
           light.
     19: 1 The heavens declare the glory
           of G;
     22: 1 G, my G, why have you forsaken
     29: 3 the G of glory thunders,
     31:14 I say, "You are my G."
     40: 3 a hymn of praise to our G.
     40: 8 I desire to do your will, O my G;
     42: 2 thirsts for G, for the living G.
     42:11 Put your hope in G,
     45: 6 O G, will last for ever and ever;
     46: 1 G is our refuge and strength,
     46:10 "Be still, and know that I am G;
     47: 7 For G is the King of all the
           earth;
     50: 3 Our G comes and will not be
           silent;
     51: 1 Have mercy on me, O G,
     51:10 Create in me a pure heart, O G,
     51:17 O G, you will not despise.
     62: 7 my honor depend on G;
     65: 5 O G our Savior,
     66: 1 Shout with joy to G, all the
           earth!
     66:16 listen, all you who fear G;
     68: 6 G sets the lonely in families,
     71:17 my youth, O G, you have taught
     71:19 reaches to the skies, O G,
     71:22 harp for your faithfulness, O
           my G;
     73:26 but G is the strength of my heart
     77:13 What g is so great as our God?
     78:19 Can G spread a table in the
           desert?
     81: 1 Sing for joy to G our strength;
     84: 2 out for the living G.
     84:10 a doorkeeper in the house of
           my G
     86:12 O Lord my G, with all my heart;
     89: 7 of the holy ones G is greatly
           feared;
     90: 2 to everlasting you are G.
     91: 2 my G, in whom I trust."
     95: 7 for he is our G
    100: 3 Know that the Lord is G.
    108: 1 My heart is steadfast, O G;
    113: 5 Who is like the Lord our G,
    139:23 Search me, O G, and know my
Pr   3: 4 in the sight of G and man.
     25: 2 of G to conceal a matter;
     30: 5 "Every word of G is flawless;
Ecc 11: 5 cannot fathom what G has done
     11: 5 cannot understand the work
           of G,

Ecc　12:13 Fear G and keep his
Isa　　9: 6 Wonderful Counselor, Mighty G,
　　37:16 you alone are G over all
　　40: 3 a highway for our G.
　　40: 8 the word of our G stands
　　　　　forever."
　　40:28 The LORD is the everlasting G,
　　41:10 not be dismayed, for I am
　　　　　your G.
　　44: 6 apart from me there is no G.
　　52: 7 "Your G reigns!"
　　55: 7 to our G, for he will freely
　　　　　pardon.
　　57:21 says my G, "for the wicked."
　　59: 2 you from your G;
　　61:10 my soul rejoices in my G.
　　62: 5 so will your G rejoice over you.
Jer　23:23 "Am I only a G nearby,"
　　31:33 I will be their G,
　　32:27 "I am the LORD, the G
Eze　28:13 the garden of G;
Da　　3:17 the G we serve is able to save
　　　　　us
　　　9: 4 O Lord, the great and
　　　　　awesome G,
Hos 12: 6 and wait for your G always.
Joel　2:13 Return to the LORD your G,
Am　　4:12 prepare to meet your G, O
　　　　　Israel."
Mic　6: 8 and to walk humbly with your G.
Na　　1: 2 LORD is a jealous and
　　　　　avenging G;
Zec 14: 5 Then the LORD my G will come,
Mal　3: 8 Will a man rob G? Yet you rob
　　　　　me.
Mt　　1:23 which means, "G with us."
　　　5: 8 for they will see G.
　　　6:24 You cannot serve both G
　　19: 6 Therefore what G has joined
　　19:26 but with G all things are
　　　　　possible."
　　22:21 and to G what is God's."
　　22:37 " 'Love the Lord your G
　　27:46 which means, "My G, my G,
Mk　12:29 the Lord our G, the Lord is one.
　　16:19 and he sat at the right hand
　　　　　of G.
Lk　　1:37 For nothing is impossible
　　　　　with G."
　　　1:47 my spirit rejoices in G my Savior,
　　10: 9 'The kingdom of G is near you.'
　　10:27 " 'Love the Lord your G
　　18:19 "No one is good—except G
　　　　　alone.
Jn　　1: 1 was with G, and the Word
　　　　　was G.
　　　1:18 seen G, but G the One and Only,
　　　3:16 "For G so loved the world that
　　　　　he
　　　4:24 G is spirit, and his worshipers
　　　　　must
　　14: 1 Trust in G; trust also in me.
　　20:28 "My Lord and my G!"
Ac　　2:24 But G raised him from the dead,
　　　5: 4 You have not lied to men but
　　　　　to G
　　　5:29 "We must obey G rather than
　　　　　men!
　　　7:55 to heaven and saw the glory
　　　　　of G,
　　17:23 TO AN UNKNOWN G.
　　20:27 to you the whole will of G.
　　20:32 "Now I commit you to G
Ro　　1:17 a righteousness from G is
　　　　　revealed,
　　　2:11 For G does not show favoritism.
　　　3: 4 Let G be true, and every man a
　　　　　liar.
　　　3:23 and fall short of the glory of G,
　　　4:24 to whom G will credit
　　　5: 8 G demonstrates his own love for
　　　　　us
　　　6:23 but the gift of G is eternal life
　　　8:28 in all things G works for the
　　　　　good
　　11:22 the kindness and sternness
　　　　　of G:
　　14:12 give an account of himself to G.
1Co　1:20 Has not G made foolish
　　　2: 9 what G has prepared
　　　3: 6 watered it, but G made it grow.

1Co　6:20 Therefore honor G with your
　　　　　body.
　　　7:24 each man, as responsible to G,
　　　8: 8 food does not bring us near
　　　　　to G;
　　10:13 G is faithful; he will not let you
　　　　　be
　　10:31 do it all for the glory of G.
　　14:33 For G is not a G of disorder
　　15:28 so that G may be all in all.
2Co　1: 9 rely on ourselves but on G,
　　　2:14 be to G, who always leads us
　　　3: 5 but our competence comes
　　　　　from G.
　　　4: 7 this all-surpassing power is
　　　　　from G
　　　5:19 that G was reconciling the world
　　　5:21 G made him who had no sin
　　　6:16 we are the temple of the
　　　　　living G.
　　　9: 7 for G loves a cheerful giver.
　　　9: 8 G is able to make all grace
　　　　　abound
Gal　　2: 6 G does not judge by external
　　　6: 7 not be deceived: G cannot be
Eph　2:10 which G prepared in advance for
　　　　　us
　　　4: 6 one baptism; one G and Father
　　　5: 1 Be imitators of G, therefore,
Php　2: 6 Who, being in very nature G,
　　　4:19 And my G will meet all your
　　　　　needs
1Th　2: 4 trying to please men but G,
　　　4: 7 For G did not call us to be
　　　　　impure,
　　　4: 9 taught by G to love each other.
　　　5: 9 For G did not appoint us
1Ti　　2: 5 one mediator between G and
　　　　　men,
　　　4: 4 For everything G created is
　　　　　good,
　　　4: 5 for this is pleasing to G.
Tit　　2:13 glorious appearing of our
　　　　　great G
Heb　1: 1 In the past G spoke
　　　4:12 For the word of G is living
　　　6:10 G is not unjust; he will not forget
　　10:31 to fall into the hands of the
　　　　　living G
　　11: 6 faith it is impossible to
　　　　　please G,
　　12:10 but G disciplines us for our
　　　　　good,
　　12:29 for our "G is a consuming fire."
　　13:15 offer to G a sacrifice of praise—
Jas　　1:13 For G cannot be tempted by evil,
　　　2:19 You believe that there is one G.
　　　2:23 "Abraham believed G,
　　　4: 4 the world becomes an enemy
　　　　　of G.
　　　4: 8 Come near to G and he will
　　　　　come
1Pe　4:11 it with the strength G provides,
2Pe　1:21 but men spoke from G
1Jn　1: 5 G is light; in him there is no
　　　3:20 For G is greater than our hearts,
　　　4: 7 for love comes from G.
　　　4: 9 This is how G showed his love
　　　4:11 Dear friends, since G so loved
　　　　　us,
　　　4:12 No one has ever seen G;
　　　4:16 G is love.
Rev　4: 8 holy is the Lord G Almighty,
　　　7:17 G will wipe away every tear
　　19: 6 For our Lord G Almighty reigns.

GOD-BREATHED* (BREATHED)
2Ti　　3:16 All Scripture is G and is useful

GOD'S (GOD)
2Ch 20:15 For the battle is not yours,
　　　　　but G.
Job 37:14 stop and consider G wonders.
Ps　　52: 8 I trust in G unfailing love
　　69:30 I will praise G name in song
Mk　　3:35 Whoever does G will is my
　　　　　brother
Jn　　7:17 If anyone chooses to do G will,
　　10:36 'I am G Son'? Do not believe me
Ro　　2: 3 think you will escape G
　　　　　judgment?

Ro　　2: 4 not realizing that G kindness
　　　　　leads
　　　3: 3 lack of faith nullify G
　　　　　faithfulness?
　　　7:22 in my inner being I delight in G
　　　　　law
　　　9:16 or effort, but on G mercy.
　　11:29 for G gifts and his call are
　　12: 2 and approve what G will is—
　　12:13 Share with G people who are
　　13: 6 for the authorities are G
　　　　　servants,
1Co　7:19 Keeping G commands is what
2Co　6: 2 now is the time of G favor,
Eph　1: 7 riches of G grace that he
　　　　　lavished
1Th　4: 3 It is G will that you should be
　　　5:18 for this is G will for you
1Ti　　6: 1 so that G name and our
　　　　　teaching
2Ti　　2:19 G solid foundation stands firm,
Tit　　1: 7 overseer is entrusted with G
　　　　　work,
Heb　1: 3 The Son is the radiance of G
　　　　　glory
　　　9:24 now to appear for us in G
　　　　　presence.
　　11: 3 was formed at G command,
1Pe　2:15 For it is G will that
　　　3: 4 which is of great worth in G
　　　　　sight.
1Jn　2: 5 G love is truly made complete

GODLINESS (GOD)
1Ti　　2: 2 and quiet lives in all g and
　　　　　holiness.
　　　4: 8 but g has value for all things,
　　　6: 6 g with contentment is great
　　　　　gain.
　　　6:11 and pursue righteousness, g,
　　　　　faith,

GODLY (GOD)
Ps　　4: 3 that the LORD has set apart
　　　　　the g
2Co　7:10 G sorrow brings repentance that
　　11: 2 jealous for you with a g jealousy.
2Ti　　3:12 everyone who wants to live a g
　　　　　life
2Pe　3:11 You ought to live holy and g
　　　　　lives

GODS (GOD)
Ex　20: 3 "You shall have no other g
Ac　19:26 He says that man-made g are
　　　　　no g

GOLD
Job 23:10 tested me, I will come forth
　　　　　as g.
Ps　19:10 They are more precious than g,
　119:127 more than g, more than pure g,
Pr　22: 1 esteemed is better than silver
　　　　　or g.

GOLGOTHA
Jn　19:17 (which in Aramaic is called G).

GOLIATH
Philistine giant killed by David (1Sa 17;
21:9).

GOOD
Ge　　1: 4 God saw that the light was g,
　　　1:31 he had made, and it was very g.
　　　2:18 "It is not g for the man to be
　　　　　alone.
　　50:20 but God intended it for g
Job　2:10 Shall we accept g from God,
Ps　14: 1 there is no one who does g.
　　34: 8 Taste and see that the LORD
　　　　　is g;
　　37: 3 Trust in the LORD and do g;
　　84:11 no g thing does he withhold
　　86: 5 You are forgiving and g, O Lord
　103: 5 satisfies your desires with g
　　　　　things,
　119: 68 You are g, and what you do is g;
　133: 1 How g and pleasant it is
　147: 1 How g it is to sing praises
Pr　　3: 4 you will win favor and a g name
　　11:27 He who seeks g finds g will,

Pr 17:22 A cheerful heart is *g* medicine,
18:22 He who finds a wife finds what is *g*
22: 1 A *g* name is more desirable
31:12 She brings him *g*, not harm,
Isa 5:20 Woe to those who call evil *g*
52: 7 the feet of those who bring *g* news,
Jer 6:16 ask where the *g* way is,
32:39 the *g* of their children after them.
Mic 6: 8 has showed you, O man, what is *g*.
Mt 5:45 sun to rise on the evil and the *g*,
7:17 Likewise every *g* tree bears *g* fruit,
12:35 The *g* man brings *g* things out
19:17 "There is only One who is *g*.
25:21 'Well done, *g* and faithful servant!
Mk 3: 4 lawful on the Sabbath: to do *g*
8:36 What *g* is it for a man
Lk 6:27 do *g* to those who hate you,
Jn 10:11 "I am the *g* shepherd.
Ro 8:28 for the *g* of those who love him,
10:15 feet of those who bring *g* news!"
12: 9 Hate what is evil; cling to what is *g*.
1Co 10:24 should seek his own *g*, but the *g*
15:33 Bad company corrupts *g* character
2Co 9: 8 you will abound in every *g* work.
Gal 6: 9 us not become weary in doing *g*,
6:10 as we have opportunity, let us do *g*
Eph 2:10 in Christ Jesus to do *g* works,
Php 1: 6 that he who began a *g* work
1Th 5:21 Hold on to the *g*.
1Ti 3: 7 have a *g* reputation with outsiders,
4: 4 For everything God created is *g*,
6:12 Fight the *g* fight of the faith.
6:18 them to do *g*, to be rich in *g* deeds,
2Ti 3:17 equipped for every *g* work.
4: 7 I have fought the *g* fight, I have
Heb 12:10 but God disciplines us for our *g*,
1Pe 2: 3 you have tasted that the Lord is *g*.
2:12 Live such *g* lives among the pagans

GOSPEL

Ro 1:16 I am not ashamed of the *g*,
15:16 duty of proclaiming the *g* of God,
1Co 1:17 to preach the *g*— not with words
9:16 Woe to me if I do not preach the *g*!
15: 1 you of the *g* I preached to you,
Gal 1: 7 a different *g*— which is really
Php 1:27 in a manner worthy of the *g*

GOSSIP

Pr 11:13 A *g* betrays a confidence,
16:28 and a *g* separates close friends.
18: 8 of a *g* are like choice morsels;
26:20 without *g* a quarrel dies down.
2Co 12:20 slander, *g*, arrogance and disorder.

GRACE (GRACIOUS)

Ps 45: 2 lips have been anointed with *g*,
Jn 1:17 and truth came through Jesus
Ac 20:32 to God and to the word of his *g*,
Ro 3:24 and are justified freely by his *g*
5:15 came by the *g* of the one man,
5:17 God's abundant provision of *g*
5:20 where sin increased, *g* increased all
6:14 you are not under law, but under *g*.
11: 6 if by *g*, then it is no longer by works
2Co 6: 1 not to receive God's *g* in vain.
8: 9 For you know the *g*
9: 8 able to make all *g* abound to you,
12: 9 "My *g* is sufficient for you,
Gal 2:21 I do not set aside the *g* of God,
5: 4 you have fallen away from *g*.

Eph 1: 7 riches of God's *g* that he lavished
2: 5 it is by *g* you have been saved.
2: 7 the incomparable riches of his *g*,
2: 8 For it is by *g* you have been saved,
Php 1: 7 all of you share in God's *g* with me.
Col 4: 6 conversation be always full of *g*,
2Th 2:16 and by his *g* gave us eternal
2Ti 2: 1 be strong in the *g* that is
Tit 2:11 For the *g* of God that brings
3: 7 having been justified by his *g*,
Heb 2: 9 that by the *g* of God he might taste
4:16 find *g* to help us in our time of need
4:16 the throne of *g* with confidence,
Jas 4: 6 but gives *g* to the humble."
2Pe 3:18 But grow in the *g* and knowledge

GRACIOUS (GRACE)

Nu 6:25 and be *g* to you;
Pr 22:11 a pure heart and whose speech is *g*
Isa 30:18 Yet the LORD longs to be *g* to you

GRAIN

1Co 9: 9 ox while it is treading out the *g*."

GRANTED

Php 1:29 For it has been *g* to you on behalf

GRASS

Ps103: 15 As for man, his days are like *g*,
1Pe 1:24 "All men are like *g*,

GRAVE (GRAVES)

Pr 7:27 Her house is a highway to the *g*,
Hos 13:14 Where, O *g*, is your destruction?

GRAVES (GRAVE)

Jn 5:28 are in their *g* will hear his voice
Ro 3:13 "Their throats are open *g*;

GREAT (GREATER GREATEST GREATNESS)

Ge 12: 2 "I will make you into a *g* nation
Dt 10:17 the *g* God, mighty and awesome,
2Sa 22:36 you stoop down to make me *g*.
Ps 19:11 in keeping them there is *g* reward.
89: 1 of the LORD's *g* love forever;
103: 11 so *g* is his love for those who fear
107: 43 consider the *g* love of the LORD.
108: 4 For *g* is your love, higher
119:165 G peace have they who love your
145: 3 G is the LORD and most worthy
Pr 23:24 of a righteous man has *g* joy;
Isa 42:21 to make his law *g* and glorious.
La 3:23 *g* is your faithfulness.
Mk 10:43 whoever wants to become *g*
Lk 21:27 in a cloud with power and *g* glory.
1Ti 6: 6 with contentment is *g* gain.
Tit 2:13 glorious appearing of our *g* God
Heb 2: 3 if we ignore such a *g* salvation?
1Jn 3: 1 How *g* is the love the Father has

GREATER (GREAT)

Mk 12:31 There is no commandment *g*
Jn 1:50 You shall see *g* things than that."
15:13 G love has no one than this,
1Co 12:31 But eagerly desire the *g* gifts.
Heb 11:26 as of *g* value than the treasures
1Jn 3:20 For God is *g* than our hearts,
4: 4 is in you is *g* than the one who is

GREATEST (GREAT)

Mt 22:38 is the first and *g* commandment.
Lk 9:48 least among you all—he is the *g*."
1Co 13:13 But the *g* of these is love.

GREATNESS (GREAT)

Ps145: 3 his *g* no one can fathom.

150: 2 praise him for his surpassing *g*.
Isa 63: 1 forward in the *g* of his strength?
Php 3: 8 compared to the surpassing *g*

GREED (GREEDY)

Lk 12:15 on your guard against all kinds of *g*
Ro 1:29 kind of wickedness, evil, *g*
Eph 5: 3 or of any kind of impurity, or of *g*,
Col 3: 5 evil desires and *g*, which is idolatry
2Pe 2:14 experts in *g*— an accursed brood!

GREEDY (GREED)

Pr 15:27 A *g* man brings trouble
1Co 6:10 nor thieves nor the *g* nor drunkards
Eph 5: 5 No immoral, impure or *g* person—
1Pe 5: 2 not *g* for money, but eager to serve;

GREEN

Ps 23: 2 makes me lie down in *g* pastures,

GREW (GROW)

Lk 2:52 And Jesus *g* in wisdom and stature,
Ac 16: 5 in the faith and *g* daily in numbers.

GRIEF (GRIEVE)

Ps 10:14 O God, do see trouble and *g*;
Pr 14:13 and joy may end in *g*.
La 3:32 Though he brings *g*, he will show
Jn 16:20 but your *g* will turn to joy.
1Pe 1: 6 had to suffer *g* in all kinds of trials.

GRIEVE (GRIEF)

Eph 4:30 do not *g* the Holy Spirit of God,
1Th 4:13 or to *g* like the rest of men,

GROUND

Ge 3:17 "Cursed is the *g* because of you;
Ex 3: 5 where you are standing is holy *g*."
Eph 6:13 you may be able to stand your *g*,

GROW (GREW)

Pr 13:11 by little makes it *g*.
1Co 3: 6 watered it, but God made it *g*.
2Pe 3:18 But *g* in the grace and knowledge

GRUMBLE (GRUMBLING)

1Co 10:10 And do not *g*, as some of them did
Jas 5: 9 Don't *g* against each other,

GRUMBLING (GRUMBLE)

Jn 6:43 "Stop *g* among yourselves,"
1Pe 4: 9 to one another without *g*.

GUARANTEE (GUARANTEEING)

Heb 7:22 Jesus has become the *g*

GUARANTEEING (GUARANTEE)

2Co 1:22 as a deposit, *g* what is to come.
Eph 1:14 who is a deposit *g* our inheritance

GUARD (GUARDS)

Ps141: 3 Set a *g* over my mouth, O LORD;
Pr 4:23 Above all else, *g* your heart,
Isa 52:12 the God of Israel will be your rear *g*.
Mk 13:33 Be on *g*! Be alert! You do not know
1Co 16:13 Be on your *g*; stand firm in the faith
Php 4: 7 will *g* your hearts and your minds
1Ti 6:20 *g* what has been entrusted

GUARDS (GUARD)

Pr 13: 3 He who *g* his lips *g* his life,
19:16 who obeys instructions *g* his life,

Pr 21:23 He who *g* his mouth and his tongue
22: 5 he who *g* his soul stays far

GUIDE

Ex 13:21 of cloud to *g* them on their way
15:13 In your strength you will *g* them
Ne 9:19 cease to *g* them on their path,
Ps 25: 5 *g* me in your truth and teach me,
43: 3 let them *g* me;
48:14 he will be our *g* even to the end.
67: 4 and *g* the nations of the earth.
73:24 You *g* me with your counsel,
139: 10 even there your hand will *g* me,
Pr 4:11 I *g* you in the way of wisdom
6:22 When you walk, they will *g* you;
Isa 58:11 The Lord will *g* you always;
Jn 16:13 comes, he will *g* you into all truth.

GUILTY

Ex 34: 7 does not leave the *g* unpunished;
Jn 8:46 Can any of you prove me *g* of sin?
Heb 10:22 to cleanse us from a *g* conscience
Jas 2:10 at just one point is *g* of breaking all

HADES

Mt 16:18 the gates of *H* will not overcome it.

HAGAR

Servant of Sarah, wife of Abraham, mother of Ishmael (Ge 16:1-6; 25:12). Driven away by Sarah while pregnant (Ge 16:5-16); after birth of Isaac (Ge 21:9-21; Gal 4:21-31).

HAGGAI*

Post-exilic prophet who encouraged rebuilding of the temple (Ezr 5:1; 6:14; Hag 1-2).

HAIR (HAIRS)

Lk 21:18 But not a *h* of your head will perish
1Co 11: 6 for a woman to have her *h* cut

HAIRS (HAIR)

Mt 10:30 even the very *h* of your head are all

HALLELUJAH*

Rev 19: 1

HALLOWED (HOLY)

Mt 6: 9 *h* be your name,

HAND (HANDS)

Ps 16: 8 Because he is at my right *h*,
37:24 the Lord upholds him with his *h*.
139: 10 even there your hand will *g* me,
Ecc 9:10 Whatever your *h* finds to do,
Mt 6: 3 know what your right *h* is doing,
Jn 10:28 one can snatch them out of my *h*.
1Co 12:15 I am not a *h*, I do not belong

HANDS (HAND)

Ps 22:16 they have pierced my *h*
24: 4 He who has clean *h* and a pure
31: 5 Into your *h* I commit my spirit;
31:15 My times are in your *h;*
Pr 10: 4 Lazy *h* make a man poor,
31:20 and extends her *h* to the needy.
Isa 55:12 will clap their *h*.
65: 2 All day long I have held out my *h*
Lk 23:46 into your *h* I commit my spirit."
1Th 4:11 and to work with your *h,*
1Ti 2: 8 to lift up holy *h* in prayer,
5:22 hasty in the laying on of *h,*

HANNAH*

Wife of Elkanah, mother of Samuel (1Sa 1). Prayer at dedication of Samuel (1Sa 2:1-10). Blessed (1Sa 2:18-21).

HAPPY

Ps 68: 3 may they be *h* and joyful.

Pr 15:13 A *h* heart makes the face cheerful.
Ecc 3:12 better for men than to be *h*
Jas 5:13 Is anyone *h?* Let him sing songs

HARD (HARDEN HARDSHIP)

Ge 18:14 Is anything too *h* for the Lord?
Mt 19:23 it is *h* for a rich man
1Co 4:12 We work *h* with our own hands.
1Th 5:12 to respect those who work *h*

HARDEN (HARD)

Ro 9:18 he hardens whom he wants to *h.*
Heb 3: 8 do not *h* your hearts

HARDHEARTED* (HEART)

Dt 15: 7 do not be *h* or tightfisted

HARDSHIP (HARD)

Ro 8:35 Shall trouble or *h* or persecution
2Ti 2: 3 Endure *h* with us like a good
4: 5 endure *h*, do the work
Heb 12: 7 Endure *h* as discipline; God is

HARM

Ps 121: 6 the sun will not *h* you by day,
Pr 3:29 not plot *h* against your neighbor,
31:12 She brings him good, not *h,*
Ro 13:10 Love does no *h* to its neighbor.
1Jn 5:18 and the evil one cannot *h* him.

HARMONY

Ro 12:16 Live in *h* with one another.
2Co 6:15 What *h* is there between Christ
1Pe 3: 8 live in *h* with one another;

HARVEST

Mt 9:37 *h* is plentiful but the workers are
Jn 4:35 at the fields! They are ripe for *h.*
Gal 6: 9 at the proper time we will reap a *h*
Heb 12:11 it produces a *h* of righteousness

HASTE (HASTY)

Pr 21: 5 as surely as *h* leads to poverty.
29:20 Do you see a man who speaks in *h?*

HASTY* (HASTE)

Pr 19: 2 nor to be *h* and miss the way.
Ecc 5: 2 do not be *h* in your heart
1Ti 5:22 Do not be *h* in the laying

HATE (HATED HATES HATRED)

Lev 19:17 " 'Do not *h* your brother
Ps 5: 5 you *h* all who do wrong.
45: 7 righteousness and *h* wickedness;
97:10 those who love the Lord *h* evil,
139: 21 Do I not *h* those who *h* you,
Pr 8:13 To fear the Lord is to *h* evil;
Am 5:15 *H* evil, love good;
Mal 2:16 "I *h* divorce," says the Lord God
Mt 5:43 your neighbor and *h* your enemy."
10:22 All men will *h* you because of me,
Lk 6:27 do good to those who *h* you,
Ro 12: 9 *H* what is evil; cling to what is good

HATED (HATE)

Ro 9:13 "Jacob I loved, but Esau I *h.*"
Eph 5:29 no one ever *h* his own body,
Heb 1: 9 righteousness and *h* wickedness;

HATES (HATE)

Pr 6:16 There are six things the Lord *h,*
13:24 He who spares the rod *h* his son,
Jn 3:20 Everyone who does evil *h* the light,
1Jn 2: 9 *h* his brother is still in the darkness.

HATRED (HATE)

Pr 10:12 *H* stirs up dissension,
Jas 4: 4 with the world is *h* toward God?

HAUGHTY

Pr 16:18 a *h* spirit before a fall.

HAY

1Co 3:12 costly stones, wood, *h* or straw,

HEAD (HEADS HOTHEADED)

Ge 3:15 he will crush your *h,*
Ps 23: 5 You anoint my *h* with oil;
Pr 25:22 will heap burning coals on his *h,*
Isa 59:17 and the helmet of salvation on his *h*
Mt 8:20 of Man has no place to lay his *h.*"
Ro 12:20 will heap burning coals on his *h.*"
1Co 11: 3 and the *h* of Christ is God.
12:21 And the *h* cannot say to the feet,
Eph 5:23 For the husband is the *h* of the wife
2Ti 4: 5 keep your *h* in all situations,
Rev 19:12 and on his *h* are many crowns.

HEADS (HEAD)

Lev 26:13 you to walk with *h* held high.
Isa 35:10 everlasting joy will crown their *h.*

HEAL (HEALED HEALING HEALS)

2Ch 7:14 their sin and will *h* their land.
Ps 41: 4 *h* me, for I have sinned against you
Mt 10: 8 *H* the sick, raise the dead,
Lk 4:23 to me: 'Physician, *h* yourself!
5:17 present for him to *h* the sick.

HEALED (HEAL)

Isa 53: 5 and by his wounds we are *h.*
Mt 9:22 he said, "your faith has *h* you."
14:36 and all who touched him were *h.*
Ac 4:10 this man stands before you *h.*
14: 9 saw that he had faith to be *h*
Jas 5:16 for each other so that you may be *h*
1Pe 2:24 by his wounds you have been *h.*

HEALING (HEAL)

Eze 47:12 for food and their leaves for *h.*"
Mal 4: 2 rise with *h* in its wings.
1Co 12: 9 to another gifts of *h*
12:30 Do all have gifts of *h?* Do all speak
Rev 22: 2 are for the *h* of the nations.

HEALS (HEAL)

Ex 15:26 for I am the Lord, who *h* you."
Ps 103: 3 and *h* all your diseases;
147: 3 He *h* the brokenhearted

HEALTH (HEALTHY)

Pr 3: 8 This will bring *h* to your body
15:30 and good news gives *h* to the bones

HEALTHY (HEALTH)

Mk 2:17 "It is not the *h* who need a doctor,

HEAR (HEARD HEARING HEARS)

Dt 6: 4 *H,* O Israel: The Lord our God,
31:13 must *h* it and learn
2Ch 7:14 then will I *h* from heaven
Ps 94: 9 he who implanted the ear not *h?*
Isa 29:18 that day the deaf will *h* the words
65:24 while they are still speaking I will *h*
Mt 11:15 He who has ears, let him *h.*
Jn 8:47 reason you do not *h* is that you do
2Ti 4: 3 what their itching ears want to *h.*

HEARD (HEAR)

Job 42: 5 My ears had *h* of you
Isa 66: 8 Who has ever *h* of such a thing?
Mt 5:21 "You have *h* that it was said
5:27 "You have *h* that it was said
5:33 you have *h* that it was said
5:38 "You have *h* that it was said,
5:43 "You have *h* that it was said,
1Co 2: 9 no ear has *h,*
1Th 2:13 word of God, which you *h* from us,
2Ti 1:13 What you *h* from me, keep

Jas　　1:25 not forgetting what he has *h*,

HEARING (HEAR)
Ro　10:17 faith comes from *h* the message,

HEARS (HEAR)
Jn　　5:24 whoever *h* my word and believes
1Jn　5:14 according to his will, he *h* us.
Rev　3:20 If anyone *h* my voice and opens

HEART (BROKENHEARTED HARDHEARTED HEARTS WHOLEHEARTEDLY)
Ex　25: 2 each man whose *h* prompts him
Lev　19:17 Do not hate your brother in your *h*.
Dt　　4:29 if you look for him with all your *h*
　　　6: 5 Lord your God with all your *h*
　　10:12 Lord your God with all your *h*
　　15:10 and do so without a grudging *h*;
　　30: 6 you may love him with all your *h*
　　30:10 Lord your God with all your *h*
Jos　22: 5 and to serve him with all your *h*
1Sa　13:14 sought out a man after his own *h*,
　　16: 7 but the Lord looks at the *h*."
2Ki　23: 3 with all his *h* and all his soul,
1Ch　28: 9 for the Lord searches every *h*
2Ch　7:16 and my *h* will always be there.
Job　22:22 and lay up his words in your *h*.
　　37: 1 "At this my *h* pounds
Ps　　14: 1 The fool says in his *h*,
　　19:14 and the meditation of my *h*
　　37: 4 will give you the desires of your *h*.
　　45: 1 My *h* is stirred by a noble theme
　　51:10 Create in me a pure *h*, O God,
　　51:17 a broken and contrite *h*,
　　66:18 If I had cherished sin in my *h*,
　　86:11 give me an undivided *h*,
　119:11 I have hidden your word in my *h*
　119: 32 for you have set my *h* free.
　139: 23 Search me, O God, and know my *h*
Pr　　3: 5 Trust in the Lord with all your *h*
　　4:21 keep them within your *h*;
　　4:23 Above all else, guard your *h*,
　　7: 3 write them on the tablet of your *h*.
　　13:12 Hope deferred makes the *h* sick,
　　14:13 Even in laughter the *h* may ache,
　　15:30 A cheerful look brings joy to the *h*,
　　17:22 A cheerful *h* is good medicine,
　　24:17 stumbles, do not let your *h* rejoice,
　　27:19 so a man's *h* reflects the man.
Ecc　8: 5 wise *h* will know the proper time
SS　　4: 9 You have stolen my *h*, my sister,
Isa　40:11 and carries them close to his *h*;
　　57:15 and to revive the *h* of the contrite.
Jer　17: 9 The *h* is deceitful above all things
　　29:13 when you seek me with all your *h*.
Eze　36:26 I will give you a new *h*
Mt　　5: 8 Blessed are the pure in *h*,
　　6:21 treasure is, there your *h* will be
　　12:34 of the *h* the mouth speaks.
　　22:37 the Lord your God with all your *h*
Lk　　6:45 overflow of his *h* his mouth speaks.
Ro　　2:29 is circumcision of the *h*,
　　10:10 is with your *h* that you believe
1Co　14:25 the secrets of his *h* will be laid bare.
Eph　5:19 make music in your *h* to the Lord,
　　6: 6 doing the will of God from your *h*.
Col　3:23 work at it with all your *h*,
1Pe　1:22 one another deeply, from the *h*.

HEARTS (HEART)
Dt　　11:18 Fix these words of mine in your *h*
1Ki　8:39 for you alone know the *h* of all men
　　8:61 your *h* must be fully committed

Ps　　62: 8 pour out your *h* to him,
Ecc　3:11 also set eternity in the *h* of men;
Jer　31:33 and write it on their *h*.
Lk　16:15 of men, but God knows your *h*.
　　24:32 "Were not our *h* burning within us
Jn　14: 1 "Do not let your *h* be troubled.
Ac　15: 9 for he purified their *h* by faith.
Ro　2:15 of the law are written on their *h*,
2Co　3: 2 written on our *h*, known
　　3: 3 but on tablets of human *h*.
　　4: 6 shine in our *h* to give us the light
Eph　3:17 dwell in your *h* through faith.
Col　3: 1 set your *h* on things above,
Heb　3: 8 do not harden your *h*
　　10:16 I will put my laws in their *h*,
1Jn　3:20 For God is greater than our *h*,

HEAT
2Pe　3:12 and the elements will melt in the *h*.

HEAVEN (HEAVENLY HEAVENS)
Ge　14:19 Creator of *h* and earth.
1Ki　8:27 the highest *h*, cannot contain you.
2Ki　2: 1 up to *h* in a whirlwind,
2Ch　7:14 then will I hear from *h*
Isa　14:12 How you have fallen from *h*,
　　66: 1 "*H* is my throne,
Da　7:13 coming with the clouds of *h*.
Mt　　6: 9 "'Our Father in *h*,
　　6:20 up for yourselves treasures in *h*,
　　16:19 bind on earth will be bound in *h*,
　　19:23 man to enter the kingdom of *h*.
　　24:35 *H* and earth will pass away,
　　26:64 and coming on the clouds of *h*."
　　28:18 "All authority in *h*
Mk　16:19 he was taken up into *h*
Lk　15: 7 in over one sinner who repents
　　18:22 and you will have treasure in *h*.
Ro　10: 6 'Who will ascend into *h*?'" (that is,
2Co　5: 1 an eternal house in *h*, not built
　　12: 2 ago was caught up to the third *h*.
Php　2:10 *h* and on earth and under the earth,
　　3:20 But our citizenship is in *h*.
1Th　1:10 and to wait for his Son from *h*,
Heb　8: 5 and shadow of what is in *h*.
　　9:24 he entered *h* itself, now to appear
2Pe　3:13 we are looking forward to a new *h*
Rev　21: 1 Then I saw a new *h* and a new earth

HEAVENLY (HEAVEN)
Ps　　8: 5 him a little lower than the *h* beings
2Co　5: 2 to be clothed with our *h* dwelling,
Eph　1: 3 in the *h* realms with every spiritual
　　1:20 at his right hand in the *h* realms,
2Ti　4:18 bring me safely to his *h* kingdom.
Heb　12:22 to the *h* Jerusalem, the city

HEAVENS (HEAVEN)
Ge　　1: 1 In the beginning God created the *h*
1Ki　8:27 The *h*, even the highest heaven,
2Ch　2: 6 since the *h*, even the highest
Ps　　8: 3 When I consider your *h*,
　　19: 1 The *h* declare the glory of God;
　　102: 25 the *h* are the work of your hands.
　　108: 4 is your love, higher than the *h*;
　　119: 89 it stands firm in the *h*.
　　139: 8 If I go up to the *h*, you are there;
Isa　51: 6 Lift up your eyes to the *h*,
　　55: 9 "As the *h* are higher than the earth,
　　65:17 new *h* and a new earth.
Joel　2:30 I will show wonders in the *h*

Eph　4:10 who ascended higher than all the *h*,
2Pe　3:10 The *h* will disappear with a roar;

HEBREW
Ge　14:13 and reported this to Abram the *H*.

HEEDS
Pr　13: 1 wise son *h* his father's instruction,
　　13:18 whoever *h* correction is honored.
　　15: 5 whoever *h* correction shows
　　15:32 whoever *h* correction gains

HEEL
Ge　　3:15 and you will strike his *h*."

HEIRS (INHERIT)
Ro　　8:17 then we are *h*– *h* of God
Gal　3:29 and *h* according to the promise.
Eph　3: 6 gospel the Gentiles are *h* together
1Pe　3: 7 as *h* with you of the gracious gift

HELL
Mt　　5:22 will be in danger of the fire of *h*.
Lk　16:23 In *h*, where he was in torment,
2Pe　2: 4 but sent them to *h*, putting them

HELMET
Isa　59:17 and the *h* of salvation on his head;
Eph　6:17 Take the *h* of salvation
1Th　5: 8 and the hope of salvation as a *h*.

HELP (HELPED HELPER HELPING HELPS)
Ps　18: 6 I cried to my God for *h*.
　　30: 2 my God, I called to you for *h*
　　46: 1 an ever-present *h* in trouble.
　　79: 9 *H* us, O God our Savior,
　　121: 1 where does my *h* come from?
Isa　41:10 I will strengthen you and *h* you;
Jnh　2: 2 depths of the grave I called for *h*,
Mk　9:24 *h* me overcome my unbelief!"
Ac　16: 9 Come over to Macedonia and *h* us
1Co　12:28 those able to *h* others, those

HELPED (HELP)
1Sa　7:12 "Thus far has the Lord *h* us."

HELPER (HELP)
Ge　　2:18 I will make a *h* suitable for him."
Ps　10:14 you are the *h* of the fatherless.
Heb　13: 6 Lord is my *h*; I will not be afraid.

HELPING (HELP)
Ac　9:36 always doing good and *h* the poor.
1Ti　5:10 *h* those in trouble and devoting

HELPS (HELP)
Ro　8:26 the Spirit *h* us in our weakness.

HEN
Mt　23:37 as a *h* gathers her chicks

HERITAGE (INHERIT)
Ps 127: 3 Sons are a *h* from the Lord.

HEROD
1. King of Judea who tried to kill Jesus (Mt 2; Lk 1:5).
2. Son of 1. Tetrarch of Galilee who arrested and beheaded John the Baptist (Mt 14:1-12; Mk 6:14-29; Lk 3:1, 19-20; 9:7-9); tried Jesus (Lk 23:6-15).
3. Grandson of 1. King of Judea who killed James (Ac 12:2); arrested Peter (Ac 12:3-19). Death (Ac 12:19-23).

HERODIAS
Wife of Herod the Tetrarch who persuaded her daughter to ask for John the Baptist's head (Mt 14:1-12; Mk 6:14-29).

HEZEKIAH

King of Judah. Restored the temple and worship (2Ch 29-31). Sought the Lord for help against Assyria (2Ki 18-19; 2Ch 32:1-23; Isa 36-37). Illness healed (2Ki 20:1-11; 2Ch 32:24-26; Isa 38). Judged for showing Babylonians his treasures (2Ki 20:12-21; 2Ch 32:31; Isa 39).

HID (HIDE)

Ge   3: 8 and they *h* from the Lord God
Ex   2: 2 she *h* him for three months.
Jos   6:17 because she *h* the spies we sent.
Heb 11:23 By faith Moses' parents *h* him

HIDDEN (HIDE)

Ps   19:12 Forgive my *h* faults.
  119: 11 I have *h* your word in my heart
Pr   2: 4 and search for it as for *h* treasure,
Isa   59: 2 your sins have *h* his face from you,
Mt   5:14 A city on a hill cannot be *h*.
  13:44 of heaven is like treasure *h*
Col   1:26 the mystery that has been kept *h*
  2: 3 in whom are *h* all the treasures
  3: 3 and your life is now *h* with Christ

HIDE (HID HIDDEN)

Ps   17: 8 *h* me in the shadow of your wings
  143: 9 for I *h* myself in you.

HILL (HILLS)

Mt   5:14 A city on a *h* cannot be hidden.

HILLS (HILL)

Ps   50:10 and the cattle on a thousand *h*.
  121: 1 I lift up my eyes to the *h*—

HINDER (HINDERS)

1Sa 14: 6 Nothing can *h* the Lord
Mt   19:14 come to me, and do not *h* them,
1Co   9:12 anything rather than *h* the gospel
1Pe   3: 7 so that nothing will *h* your prayers.

HINDERS (HINDER)

Heb 12: 1 let us throw off everything that *h*

HINT*

Eph   5: 3 even a *h* of sexual immorality,

HOLD

Ex   20: 7 Lord will not *h* anyone guiltless
Lev   19:13 " 'Do not *h* back the wages
Jos   22: 5 to *h* fast to him and to serve him
Ps   73:23 you *h* me by my right hand.
Pr   4: 4 "Lay *h* of my words
Isa   54: 2 do not *h* back;
Mk   11:25 if you *h* anything against anyone,
Php   2:16 as you *h* out the word of life—
  3:12 but I press on to take *h* of that
Col   1:17 and in him all things *h* together.
1Th   5:21 *H* on to the good.
1Ti   6:12 Take *h* of the eternal life
Heb 10:23 Let us *h* unswervingly

HOLINESS (HOLY)

Ex   15:11 majestic in *h*,
Ps   29: 2 in the splendor of his *h*.
  96: 9 in the splendor of his *h*;
Ro   6:19 to righteousness leading to *h*.
2Co   7: 1 perfecting *h* out of reverence
Eph   4:24 God in true righteousness and *h*.
Heb 12:10 that we may share in his *h*.
  12:14 without *h* no one will see the Lord.

HOLY (HALLOWED HOLINESS)

Ex   19: 6 kingdom of priests and a *h* nation.'
  20: 8 the Sabbath day by keeping it *h*.
Lev   11:44 and be *h*, because I am *h*.
  20: 7 " 'Consecrate yourselves and be *h*,

Lev   20:26 You are to be *h* to me because I,
  21: 8 Consider them *h*, because I
  22:32 Do not profane my *h* name.
Ps   16:10 will you let your *H* One see decay.
  24: 3 Who may stand in his *h* place?
  77:13 Your ways, O God, are *h*.
  99: 3 he is *h*.
  99: 5 he is *h*.
  99: 9 for the Lord our God is *h*.
  111: 9 *h* and awesome is his name.
Isa   5:16 the *h* God will show himself *h*
  6: 3 *H, h, h* is the Lord Almighty;
  40:25 who is my equal?" says the *H* One.
  57:15 who lives forever, whose name is *h*:
Eze 28:25 I will show myself *h* among them
Da   9:24 prophecy and to anoint the most *h*.
Hab   2:20 But the Lord is in his *h* temple;
Ac   2:27 will you let your *H* One see decay.
Ro   7:12 and the commandment is *h*,
  12: 1 as living sacrifices, *h* and pleasing
Eph   5: 3 improper for God's *h* people.
2Th   1:10 to be glorified in his *h* people
2Ti   1: 9 saved us and called us to a *h* life—
  3:15 you have known the *h* Scriptures,
Tit   1: 8 upright, *h* and disciplined.
1Pe   1:15 But just as he who called you is *h*,
  1:16 is written: "Be *h*, because I am *h*."
  2: 9 a royal priesthood, a *h* nation,
2Pe   3:11 You ought to live *h* and godly lives
Rev   4: 8 *"H, h, h* is the Lord God

HOME (HOMES)

Dt   6: 7 Talk about them when you sit at *h*
Ps   84: 3 Even the sparrow has found a *h*,
Pr   3:33 but he blesses the *h* of the righteous
Mk   10:29 "no one who has left *h* or brothers
Jn   14:23 to him and make our *h* with him.
Tit   2: 5 to be busy at *h*, to be kind,

HOMES (HOME)

Ne   4:14 daughters, your wives and your *h*."
1Ti   5:14 to manage their *h* and to give

HOMOSEXUAL*

1Co   6: 9 male prostitutes nor *h* offenders

HONEST

Lev   19:36 Use *h* scales and *h* weights.
Dt   25:15 and *h* weights and measures,
Job   31: 6 let God weigh me in *h* scales
Pr   12:17 truthful witness gives *h* testimony,

HONEY

Ex   3: 8 a land flowing with milk and *h*—
Ps   19:10 than *h* from the comb.
  119:103 sweeter than *h* to my mouth!

HONOR (HONORABLE HONORABLY HONORED HONORS)

Ex   20:12 *"H* your father and your mother,
Nu   25:13 he was zealous for the *h* of his God
Dt   5:16 *"H* your father and your mother,
1Sa   2:30 Those who *h* me I will *h*,
Ps   8: 5 and crowned him with glory and *h*.
Pr   3: 9 *H* the Lord with your wealth,
  15:33 and humility comes before *h*.
  20: 3 It is to a man's *h* to avoid strife,
Mt   15: 4 *'H* your father and mother'
Ro   12:10 *H* one another above yourselves.
1Co   6:20 Therefore *h* God with your body.
Eph   6: 2 *"H* your father and mother"—
1Ti   5:17 well are worthy of double *h*,

Heb   2: 7 you crowned him with glory and *h*
Rev   4: 9 *h* and thanks to him who sits

HONORABLE (HONOR)

1Th   4: 4 body in a way that is holy and *h*,

HONORABLY (HONOR)

Heb 13:18 and desire to live *h* in every way.

HONORED (HONOR)

Ps   12: 8 when what is vile is *h* among men.
Pr   13:18 but whoever heeds correction is *h*.
1Co 12:26 if one part is *h*, every part rejoices
Heb 13: 4 Marriage should be *h* by all,

HONORS (HONOR)

Ps   15: 4 but *h* those who fear the Lord.
Pr   14:31 to the needy *h* God.

HOOKS

Isa   2: 4 and their spears into pruning *h*.
Joel   3:10 and your pruning *h* into spears.

HOPE (HOPES)

Job   13:15 Though he slay me, yet will I *h*
Ps   42: 5 Put your *h* in God,
  62: 5 my *h* comes from him.
  119: 74 for I have put my *h* in your word.
  130: 7 O Israel, put your *h* in the Lord,
  147: 11 who put their *h* in his unfailing love
Pr   13:12 *H* deferred makes the heart sick,
Isa   40:31 but those who *h* in the Lord
Ro   5: 4 character; and character, *h*.
  8:24 But *h* that is seen is no *h* at all.
  12:12 Be joyful in *h*, patient in affliction,
  15: 4 of the Scriptures we might have *h*.
1Co 13:13 now these three remain: faith, *h*
  15:19 for this life we have *h* in Christ,
Col   1:27 Christ in you, the *h* of glory.
1Th   5: 8 and the *h* of salvation as a helmet.
1Ti   6:17 but to put their *h* in God,
Tit   2:13 while we wait for the blessed *h*—
Heb   6:19 We have this *h* as an anchor
  11: 1 faith is being sure of what we *h* for
1Jn   3: 3 Everyone who has this *h*

HOPES (HOPE)

1Co 13: 7 always *h*, always perseveres.

HORSE

Ps 147: 10 not in the strength of the *h*,
Pr   26: 3 A whip for the *h*, a halter
Zec   1: 8 before me was a man riding a red *h*
Rev   6: 2 and there before me was a white *h*!
  6: 4 Come!" Then another *h* came out,
  6: 5 and there before me was a black *h*!
  6: 8 and there before me was a pale *h*!
  19:11 and there before me was a white *h*,

HOSANNA

Mt   21: 9 *"H* in the highest!"

HOSHEA

Last king of Israel (2Ki 15:30; 17:1-6).

HOSPITABLE* (HOSPITALITY)

1Ti   3: 2 self-controlled, respectable, *h*,
Tit   1: 8 Rather he must be *h*, one who loves

HOSPITALITY (HOSPITABLE)

Ro   12:13 Practice *h*.
1Ti   5:10 as bringing up children, showing *h*,
1Pe   4: 9 Offer *h* to one another

HOSTILE
Ro   8: 7 the sinful mind is *h* to God.

HOT
1Ti   4: 2 have been seared as with a *h* iron.
Rev   3:15 that you are neither cold nor *h*.

HOT-TEMPERED
Pr   15:18 A *h* man stirs up dissension,
       19:19 A *h* man must pay the penalty;
       22:24 Do not make friends with a *h* man,
       29:22 and a *h* one commits many sins.

HOTHEADED (HEAD)
Pr   14:16 but a fool is *h* and reckless.

HOUR
Ecc   9:12 knows when his *h* will come:
Mt   6:27 you by worrying can add a single *h*
Lk   12:40 the Son of Man will come at an *h*
Jn   12:23 The *h* has come for the Son of Man
       12:27 for this very reason I came to this *h*

HOUSE (HOUSEHOLD STOREHOUSE)
Ex   20:17 shall not covet your neighbor's *h*.
Ps   23: 6 I will dwell in the *h* of the LORD
       84:10 a doorkeeper in the *h* of my God
      122: 1 "Let us go to the *h* of the LORD."
      127: 1 Unless the LORD builds the *h*,
Pr   7:27 Her *h* is a highway to the grave,
       21: 9 than share a *h* with a quarrelsome
Isa   56: 7 a *h* of prayer for all nations."
Zec   13: 6 given at the *h* of my friends.'
Mt   7:24 is like a wise man who built his *h*
       12:29 can anyone enter a strong man's *h*
       21:13 My *h* will be called a *h* of prayer,'
Mk   3:25 If a *h* is divided against itself,
Lk   11:17 a *h* divided against itself will fall.
Jn   2:16 How dare you turn my Father's *h*
         2:17 the *h* was filled with the fragrance
       14: 2 In my Father's *h* are many rooms;
Heb   3: 3 the builder of a *h* has greater honor

HOUSEHOLD (HOUSE)
Jos   24:15 my *h*, we will serve the LORD."
Mic   7: 6 are the members of his own *h*.
Mt   10:36 will be the members of his own *h*.'
       12:25 or *h* divided against itself will not
1Ti   3:12 manage his children and his *h* well.
         3:15 to conduct themselves in God's *h*,

HUMAN (HUMANITY)
Gal   3: 3 to attain your goal by *h* effort?

HUMANITY* (HUMAN)
Heb   2:14 he too shared in their *h* so that

HUMBLE (HUMBLED HUMBLES HUMILIATE HUMILITY)
2Ch   7:14 will *h* themselves and pray
Ps   25: 9 He guides the *h* in what is right
Pr   3:34 but gives grace to the *h*.
Isa   66: 2 he who is *h* and contrite in spirit,
Mt   11:29 for I am gentle and *h* in heart,
Eph   4: 2 Be completely *h* and gentle;
Jas   4:10 *H* yourselves before the Lord,
1Pe   5: 6 *H* yourselves,

HUMBLED (HUMBLE)
Mt   23:12 whoever exalts himself will be *h*,
Php   2: 8 he *h* himself

HUMBLES (HUMBLE)
Mt   18: 4 whoever *h* himself like this child is
       23:12 whoever *h* himself will be exalted.

HUMILIATE* (HUMBLE)
Pr   25: 7 than for him to *h* you
1Co   11:22 and *h* those who have nothing?

HUMILITY (HUMBLE)
Pr   11: 2 but with *h* comes wisdom.
       15:33 and *h* comes before honor.
Php   2: 3 but in *h* consider others better
Tit   3: 2 and to show true *h* toward all men.
1Pe   5: 5 clothe yourselves with *h*

HUNGRY
Ps   107: 9 and fills the *h* with good things.
      146: 7 and gives food to the *h*.
Pr   25:21 If your enemy is *h*, give him food
Eze   18: 7 but gives his food to the *h*
Mt   25:35 For I was *h* and you gave me
Lk   1:53 He has filled the *h* with good things
Jn   6:35 comes to me will never go *h*,
Ro   12:20 "If your enemy is *h*, feed him;

HURT (HURTS)
Ecc   8: 9 it over others to his own *h*.
Mk   16:18 deadly poison, it will not *h* them
Rev   2:11 He who overcomes will not be *h*

HURTS* (HURT)
Ps   15: 4 even when it *h*,
Pr   26:28 A lying tongue hates those it *h*,

HUSBAND (HUSBAND'S HUSBANDS)
1Co   7: 3 The *h* should fulfill his marital duty
         7:10 wife must not separate from her *h*.
         7:11 And a *h* must not divorce his wife.
         7:13 And if a woman has a *h* who is not
         7:39 A woman is bound to her *h* as long
2Co   11: 2 I promised you to one *h*, to Christ,
Eph   5:23 For the *h* is the head of the wife
         5:33 and the wife must respect her *h*.
1Ti   3: 2 the *h* of but one wife, temperate,

HUSBAND'S (HUSBAND)
Pr   12: 4 of noble character is her *h* crown,
1Co   7: 4 the *h* body does not belong

HUSBANDS (HUSBAND)
Eph   5:22 submit to your *h* as to the Lord.
         5:25 *H*, love your wives, just
Tit   2: 4 the younger women to love their *h*
1Pe   3: 1 same way be submissive to your *h*
         3: 7 *H*, in the same way be considerate

HYMN
1Co   14:26 everyone has a *h*, or a word

HYPOCRISY (HYPOCRITE HYPOCRITES)
Mt   23:28 but on the inside you are full of *h*
1Pe   2: 1 *h*, envy, and slander of every kind.

HYPOCRITE (HYPOCRISY)
Mt   7: 5 You *h*, first take the plank out

HYPOCRITES (HYPOCRISY)
Ps   26: 4 nor do I consort with *h*;
Mt   6: 5 when you pray, do not be like the *h*

HYSSOP
Ps   51: 7 with *h*, and I will be clean;

IDLE (IDLENESS)
1Th   5:14 those who are *i*, encourage
2Th   3: 6 away from every brother who is *i*
1Ti   5:13 they get into the habit of being *i*

IDLENESS* (IDLE)
Pr   31:27 and does not eat the bread of *i*.

IDOL (IDOLATRY IDOLS)
Isa   44:17 From the rest he makes a god, his *i*;
1Co   8: 4 We know that an *i* is nothing at all

IDOLATRY (IDOL)
Col   3: 5 evil desires and greed, which is *i*.

IDOLS (IDOL)
1Co   8: 1 Now about food sacrificed to *i*:

IGNORANT (IGNORE)
1Co   15:34 for there are some who are *i* of God
Heb   5: 2 to deal gently with those who are *i*
1Pe   2:15 good you should silence the *i* talk
2Pe   3:16 which *i* and unstable people distort

IGNORE (IGNORANT IGNORES)
Dt   22: 1 do not *i* it but be sure
Ps   9:12 he does not *i* the cry of the afflicted
Heb   2: 3 if we *i* such a great salvation?

IGNORES (IGNORE)
Pr   10:17 whoever *i* correction leads others
       15:32 He who *i* discipline despises

ILLUMINATED*
Rev   18: 1 and the earth was *i* by his splendor.

IMAGE
Ge   1:26 "Let us make man in our *i*,
         1:27 So God created man in his own *i*,
1Co   11: 7 since he is the *i* and glory of God;
Col   1:15 He is the *i* of the invisible God,
         3:10 in knowledge in the *i* of its Creator.

IMAGINE
Eph   3:20 more than all we ask or *i*,

IMITATE (IMITATORS)
1Co   4:16 Therefore I urge you to *i* me.
Heb   6:12 but to *i* those who through faith
       13: 7 of their way of life and *i* their faith.
3Jn   :11 do not *i* what is evil but what is

IMITATORS* (IMITATE)
Eph   5: 1 Be *i* of God, therefore,
1Th   1: 6 You became *i* of us and of the Lord
         2:14 became *i* of God's churches

IMMANUEL
Isa   7:14 birth to a son, and will call him *I*.
Mt   1:23 and they will call him *I*"—

IMMORAL* (IMMORALITY)
Pr   6:24 keeping you from the *i* woman,
1Co   5: 9 to associate with sexually *i* people
         5:10 the people of this world who are *i*,
         5:11 but is sexually *i* or greedy,
         6: 9 Neither the sexually *i* nor idolaters
Eph   5: 5 No *i*, impure or greedy person—
Heb   12:16 See that no one is sexually *i*,
       13: 4 the adulterer and all the sexually *i*.
Rev   21: 8 the murderers, the sexually *i*,
       22:15 the sexually *i*, the murderers,

IMMORALITY (IMMORAL)

1Co 6:13 The body is not meant for sexual *i*,
6:18 Flee from sexual *i*.
10: 8 We should not commit sexual *i*,
Gal 5:19 sexual *i*, impurity and debauchery;
Eph 5: 3 must not be even a hint of sexual *i*,
1Th 4: 3 that you should avoid sexual *i*;
Jude : 4 grace of our God into a license for *i*

IMMORTAL* (IMMORTALITY)

Ro 1:23 glory of the *i* God for images made
1Ti 1:17 Now to the King eternal, *i*,
6:16 who alone is *i* and who lives

IMMORTALITY (IMMORTAL)

Ro 2: 7 honor and *i*, he will give eternal life
1Co 15:53 and the mortal with *i*.
2Ti 1:10 and *i* to light through the gospel.

IMPERISHABLE

1Pe 1:23 not of perishable seed, but of *i*,

IMPORTANCE* (IMPORTANT)

1Co 15: 3 passed on to you as of first *i*:

IMPORTANT (IMPORTANCE)

Mt 6:25 Is not life more *i* than food,
23:23 have neglected the more *i* matters
Mk 12:29 "The most *i* one," answered Jesus,
12:33 as yourself is more *i* than all burnt
Php 1:18 The *i* thing is that in every way,

IMPOSSIBLE

Mt 17:20 Nothing will be *i* for you."
Lk 1:37 For nothing is *i* with God."
18:27 "What is *i* with men is possible
Heb 6:18 things in which it is *i* for God to lie,
11: 6 without faith it is *i* to please God,

IMPROPER*

Eph 5: 3 these are *i* for God's holy people.

IMPURE (IMPURITY)

Ac 10:15 not call anything *i* that God has
Eph 5: 5 No immoral, *i* or greedy person—
1Th 4: 7 For God did not call us to be *i*,
Rev 21:27 Nothing *i* will ever enter it,

IMPURITY (IMPURE)

Ro 1:24 hearts to sexual *i* for the degrading
Eph 5: 3 or of any kind of *i*, or of greed,

INCENSE

Ex 40: 5 Place the gold altar of *i* in front
Ps 141: 2 my prayer be set before you like *i*;
Mt 2:11 him with gifts of gold and of *i*

INCOME

Ecc 5:10 wealth is never satisfied with his *i*.
1Co 16: 2 sum of money in keeping with his *i*,

INCOMPARABLE*

Eph 2: 7 ages he might show the *i* riches

INCREASE (EVER-INCREASING INCREASED INCREASES INCREASING)

Ge 1:22 "Be fruitful and *i* in number
Ps 62:10 though your riches *i*,
Isa 9: 7 Of the *i* of his government
Lk 17: 5 said to the Lord, "*I* our faith!"
1Th 3:12 May the Lord make your love *i*

INCREASED (INCREASE)

Ac 6: 7 of disciples in Jerusalem *i* rapidly,
Ro 5:20 But where sin *i*, grace *i* all the more

INCREASES (INCREASE)

Pr 24: 5 and a man of knowledge *i* strength;

INCREASING (INCREASE)

Ac 6: 1 when the number of disciples was *i*,
2Th 1: 3 one of you has for each other is *i*.
2Pe 1: 8 these qualities in *i* measure,

INDEPENDENT*

1Co 11:11 however, woman is not *i* of man,
11:11 of man, nor is man *i* of woman.

INDESCRIBABLE*

2Co 9:15 Thanks be to God for his *i* gift!

INDISPENSABLE*

1Co 12:22 seem to be weaker are *i*,

INEFFECTIVE*

2Pe 1: 8 they will keep you from being *i*

INEXPRESSIBLE*

2Co 12: 4 He heard *i* things, things that man
1Pe 1: 8 are filled with an *i* and glorious joy,

INFANTS

Mt 21:16 " 'From the lips of children and *i*
1Co 14:20 In regard to evil be *i*,

INFIRMITIES

Isa 53: 4 Surely he took up our *i*

INHERIT (CO-HEIRS HEIRS HERITAGE INHERITANCE)

Ps 37:11 But the meek will *i* the land
37:29 the righteous will *i* the land
Mt 5: 5 for they will *i* the earth.
Mk 10:17 "what must I do to *i* eternal life?"
1Co 15:50 blood cannot *i* the kingdom of God

INHERITANCE (INHERIT)

Dt 4:20 to be the people of his *i*,
Pr 13:22 A good man leaves an *i*
Eph 1:14 who is a deposit guaranteeing our *i*
5: 5 has any *i* in the kingdom of Christ
Heb 9:15 receive the promised eternal *i*—
1Pe 1: 4 and into an *i* that can never perish,

INIQUITIES (INIQUITY)

Ps 78:38 he forgave their *i*
103: 10 or repay us according to our *i*.
Isa 59: 2 But your *i* have separated
Mic 7:19 and hurl all our *i* into the depths

INIQUITY (INIQUITIES)

Ps 51: 2 Wash away all my *i*
Isa 53: 6 the *i* of us all.

INJUSTICE

2Ch 19: 7 the LORD our God there is no *i*

INNOCENT

Pr 17:26 It is not good to punish an *i* man,
Mt 10:16 shrewd as snakes and as *i* as doves.
27: 4 "for I have betrayed *i* blood."
1Co 4: 4 but that does not make me *i*.

INSCRIPTION

Mt 22:20 And whose *i*?" "Caesar's,"

INSOLENT

Ro 1:30 God-haters, *i*, arrogant

INSTITUTED

Ro 13: 2 rebelling against what God has *i*,
1Pe 2:13 to every authority *i* among men:

INSTRUCT (INSTRUCTION)

Ps 32: 8 I will *i* you and teach you
Pr 9: 9 *I* a wise man and he will be wiser
Ro 15:14 and competent to *i* one another.
2Ti 2:25 who oppose him must gently *i*,

INSTRUCTION (INSTRUCT)

Pr 1: 8 Listen, my son, to your father's *i*
4: 1 Listen, my sons, to a father's *i*;
4:13 Hold on to *i*, do not let it go;
8:10 Choose my *i* instead of silver,
8:33 Listen to my *i* and be wise;
13: 1 A wise son heeds his father's *i*,
13:13 He who scorns *i* will pay for it,
16:20 Whoever gives heed to *i* prospers,
16:21 and pleasant words promote *i*.
19:20 Listen to advice and accept *i*,
23:12 Apply your heart to *i*
1Co 14: 6 or prophecy or word of *i*?
14:26 or a word of *i*, a revelation,
Eph 6: 4 up in the training and *i* of the Lord.
1Th 4: 8 he who rejects this *i* does not reject
2Th 3:14 If anyone does not obey our *i*
1Ti 1:18 I give you this *i* in keeping
6: 3 to the sound of our Lord Jesus
2Ti 2: 2 with great patience and careful *i*.

INSULT

Pr 9: 7 corrects a mocker invites *i*;
12:16 but a prudent man overlooks an *i*.
Mt 5:11 Blessed are you when people *i* you,
Lk 6:22 when they exclude you and *i* you
1Pe 3: 9 evil with evil or *i* with *i*,

INTEGRITY

1Ki 9: 4 if you walk before me in *i* of heart
Job 2: 3 And he still maintains his *i*,
27: 5 till I die, I will not deny my *i*.
Pr 10: 9 The man of *i* walks securely,
11: 3 The *i* of the upright guides them,
29:10 Bloodthirsty men hate a man of *i*
Tit 2: 7 your teaching show *i*, seriousness

INTELLIGENCE

Isa 29:14 the *i* of the intelligent will vanish."
1Co 1:19 *i* of the intelligent I will frustrate."

INTELLIGIBLE

1Co 14:19 I would rather speak five *i* words

INTERCEDE (INTERCEDES INTERCESSION)

Heb 7:25 he always lives to *i* for them.

INTERCEDES (INTERCEDE)

Ro 8:26 but the Spirit himself *i* for us

INTERCESSION* (INTERCEDE)

Isa 53:12 and made *i* for the transgressors.
1Ti 2: 1 and thanksgiving be made

INTERESTS

1Co 7:34 his wife—and his *i* are divided.
Php 2: 4 only to your own *i*, but also to the
2:21 everyone looks out for his own *i*,

INTERMARRY (MARRY)

Dt 7: 3 Do not *i* with them.

INVENTED*

2Pe 1:16 We did not follow cleverly *i* stories

INVESTIGATED
Lk 1: 3 I myself have carefully *i* everything

INVISIBLE
Ro 1: 20 of the world God's *i* qualities—
Col 1: 15 He is the image of the *i* God,
1Ti 1: 17 immortal, *i*, the only God,

INVITE (INVITED INVITES)
Lk 14: 13 you give a banquet, *i* the poor,

INVITED (INVITE)
Mt 22: 14 For many are *i*, but few are chosen
25: 35 I was a stranger and you *i* me in,

INVITES (INVITE)
1Co 10: 27 If some unbeliever *i* you to a meal

INVOLVED
2Ti 2: 4 a soldier gets *i* in civilian affairs—

IRON
1Ti 4: 2 have been seared as with a hot *i*.
Rev 2: 27 He will rule them with an *i* scepter;

IRREVOCABLE*
Ro 11: 29 for God's gifts and his call are *i*.

ISAAC
Son of Abraham by Sarah (Ge 17:19; 21:1-7; 1Ch 1:28). Offered up by Abraham (Ge 22; Heb 11:17-19). Rebekah taken as wife (Ge 24). Fathered Esau and Jacob (Ge 25:19-26; 1Ch 1:34). Tricked into blessing Jacob (Ge 27). Father of Israel (Ex 3:6; Dt 29:13; Ro 9:10).

ISAIAH
Prophet to Judah (Isa 1:1). Called by the LORD (Isa 6).

ISHMAEL
Son of Abraham by Hagar (Ge 16; 1Ch 1:28). Blessed, but not son of covenant (Ge 17:18-21; Gal 4:21-31). Sent away by Sarah (Ge 21:8-21).

ISRAEL (ISRAELITES)
1. Name given to Jacob (see JACOB).
2. Corporate name of Jacob's descendants; often specifically Northern Kingdom.
Dt 6: 4 Hear, O *I*: The LORD our God,
1Sa 4: 21 "The glory has departed from *I*"—
Isa 27: 6 *I* will bud and blossom
Jer 31: 10 'He who scattered *I* will gather
Eze 39: 23 of *I* went into exile for their sin,
Mk 12: 29 'Hear, O *I*, the Lord our God,
Lk 22: 30 judging the twelve tribes of *I*.
Ro 9: 6 all who are descended from *I* are *I*.
11: 26 And so all *I* will be saved,
Eph 3: 6 Gentiles are heirs together with *I*,

ISRAELITES (ISRAEL)
Ex 14: 22 and the *I* went through the sea
16: 35 The *I* ate manna forty years,
Hos 1: 10 "Yet the *I* will be like the sand
Ro 9: 27 the number of the *I* be like the sand

ITCHING*
2Ti 4: 3 to say what their *i* ears want to hear

JACOB
Second son of Isaac, twin of Esau (Ge 26:21-26; 1Ch 1:34). Bought Esau's birthright (Ge 26:29-34); tricked Isaac into blessing him (Ge 27:1-37). Abrahamic covenant perpetuated through (Ge 28:13-15; Mal 1:2). Vision at Bethel (Ge 28:10-22). Wives and children (Ge 29:1-30:24; 35:16-26; 1Ch 2-9). Wrestled with God; name changed to Israel (Ge 32:22-32). Sent sons to Egypt during

famine (Ge 42-43). Settled in Egypt (Ge 46). Blessed Ephraim and Manasseh (Ge 48). Blessed sons (Ge 49:1-28; Heb 11:21). Death (Ge 49:29-33). Burial (Ge 50:1-14).

JAMES
1. Apostle; brother of John (Mt 4:21-22; 10:2; Mk 3:17; Lk 5:1-10). At transfiguration (Mt 17:1-13; Mk 9:1-13; Lk 9:28-36). Killed by Herod (Ac 12:2).
2. Apostle; son of Alphaeus (Mt 10:3; Mk 3:18; Lk 6:15).
3. Brother of Jesus (Mt 13:55; Mk 6:3; Lk 24:10; Gal 1:19) and Judas (Jude 1). With believers before Pentecost (Ac 1:13). Leader of church at Jerusalem (Ac 12:17; 15; 21:18; Gal 2:9, 12). Author of epistle (Jas 1:1).

JAPHETH
Son of Noah (Ge 5:32; 1Ch 1:4-5). Blessed (Ge 9:18-28).

JARS
2Co 4: 7 we have this treasure in *j* of clay

JEALOUS (JEALOUSY)
Ex 20: 5 the LORD your God, am a *j* God,
34: 14 whose name is Jealous, is a *j* God.
Dt 4: 24 God is a consuming fire, a *j* God.
Joel 2: 18 the LORD will be *j* for his land
Zec 1: 14 I am very *j* for Jerusalem and Zion,
2Co 11: 2 I am *j* for you with a godly jealousy

JEALOUSY (JEALOUS)
1Co 3: 3 For since there is *j* and quarreling
2Co 11: 2 I am jealous for you with a godly *j*.
Gal 5: 20 hatred, discord, *j*, fits of rage,

JEHOAHAZ
1. Son of Jehu; king of Israel (2Ki 13:1-9).
2. Son of Josiah; king of Judah (2Ki 23:31-34; 2Ch 36:1-4).

JEHOASH
Son of Jehoahaz; king of Israel (2Ki 13-14; 2Ch 25).

JEHOIACHIN
Son of Jehoiakim; king of Judah exiled by Nebuchadnezzar (2Ki 24:8-17; 2Ch 36:8-10; Jer 22:24-30; 24:1). Raised from prisoner status (2Ki 25:27-30; Jer 52:31-34).

JEHOIAKIM
Son of Josiah; king of Judah (2Ki 23:34-24:6; 2Ch 36:4-8; Jer 22:18-23; 36).

JEHORAM
Son of Jehoshaphat; king of Judah (2Ki 8:16-24).

JEHOSHAPHAT
Son of Asa; king of Judah (1Ki 22:41-50; 2Ki 3; 2Ch 17-20).

JEHU
King of Israel (1Ki 19:16-19; 2Ki 9-10).

JEPHTHAH
Judge from Gilead who delivered Israel from Ammon (Jdg 10:6-12:7). Made rash vow concerning his daughter (Jdg 11:30-40).

JEREMIAH
Prophet to Judah (Jer 1:1-3). Called by the LORD (Jer 1). Put in stocks (Jer 20:1-3). Threatened for prophesying (Jer 11:18-23; 26). Opposed by Hananiah (Jer 28). Scroll burned (Jer 36). Imprisoned (Jer 37). Thrown into cistern (Jer 38). Forced to Egypt with those fleeing Babylonians (Jer 43).

JEROBOAM
1. Official of Solomon; rebelled to become first king of Israel (1Ki 11:26-40; 12:1-20;

2Ch 10). Idolatry (1Ki 12:25-33); judgment for (1Ki 13-14; 2Ch 13).
2. Son of Jehoash; king of Israel (1Ki 14:23-29).

JERUSALEM
2Ki 23: 27 and I will reject *J*, the city I chose,
2Ch 6: 6 now I have chosen *J* for my Name
Ne 2: 17 Come, let us rebuild the wall of *J*,
Ps 122: 6 Pray for the peace of *J*:
125: 2 As the mountains surround *J*,
137: 5 If I forget you, O *J*,
Isa 40: 9 You who bring good tidings to *J*,
65: 18 for I will create *J* to be a delight
Joel 3: 17 *J* will be holy;
Zep 3: 16 On that day they will say to *J*,
Zec 2: 4 '*J* will be a city without walls
8: 8 I will bring them back to live in *J*;
14: 8 living water will flow out from *J*,
Mt 23: 37 "O *J*, *J*, you who kill the prophets
Lk 13: 34 die outside *J*! "O *J*, *J*,
21: 24 *J* will be trampled
Jn 4: 20 where we must worship is in *J*."
Ac 1: 8 and you will be my witnesses in *J*,
Gal 4: 25 corresponds to the present city of *J*
Rev 21: 2 I saw the Holy City, the new *J*,

JESUS
LIFE: Genealogy (Mt 1:1-17; Lk 3:21-37). Birth announced (Mt 1:18-25; Lk 1:26-45). Birth (Mt 2:1-12; Lk 2:1-40). Escape to Egypt (Mt 2:13-23). As a boy in the temple (Lk 2:41-52). Baptism (Mt 3:13-17; Mk 1:9-11; Lk 3:21-22; Jn 1:32-34). Temptation (Mt 4:1-11; Mk 1:12-13; Lk 4:1-13). Ministry in Galilee (Mt 4:12-18:35; Mk 1:14-9:50; Lk 4:14-13:9; Jn 1:35-2:11; 4; 6), Transfiguration (Mt 17:1-8; Mk 9:2-8; Lk 9:28-36), on the way to Jerusalem (Mt 19-20; Mk 10; Lk 13:10-19:27), in Jerusalem (Mt 21-25; Mk 11-13; Lk 19:28-21:38; Jn 2:12-3:36; 5; 7-12). Last supper (Mt 26:17-35; Mk 14:12-31; Lk 22:1-38; Jn 13-17). Arrest and trial (Mt 26:36-27:31; Mk 14:43-15:20; Lk 22:39-23:25; Jn 18:1-19:16). Crucifixion (Mt 27:32-66; Mk 15:21-47; Lk 23:26-55; Jn 19:28-42). Resurrection and appearances (Mt 28; Mk 16; Lk 24; Jn 20-21; Ac 1:1-11; 7:56; 9:3-6; 1Co 15:1-8; Rev 1:1-20).
MIRACLES. Healings: official's son (Jn 4:43-54), demoniac in Capernaum (Mk 1:23-26; Lk 4:33-35), Peter's mother-in-law (Mt 8:14-17; Mk 1:29-31; Lk 4:38-39), leper (Mt 8:2-4; Mk 1:40-45; Lk 5:12-16), paralytic (Mt 9:1-8; Mk 2:1-12; Lk 5:17-26), cripple (Jn 5:1-9), shriveled hand (Mt 12:10-13; Mk 3:1-5; Lk 6:6-11), centurion's servant (Mt 8:5-13; Lk 7:1-10), widow's son raised (Lk 7:11-17), demoniac (Mt 12:22-23; Lk 11:14), Gadarene demoniacs (Mt 8:28-34; Mk 5:1-20; Lk 8:26-39), woman's bleeding and Jairus' daughter (Mt 9:18-26; Mk 5:21-43; Lk 8:40-56), blind man (Mt 9:27-31), mute man (Mt 9:32-33), Canaanite woman's daughter (Mt 15:21-28; Mk 7:24-30), deaf man (Mk 7:31-37), blind man (Mk 8:22-26), demoniac boy (Mt 17:14-18; Mk 9:14-29; Lk 9:37-43), ten lepers (Lk 17:11-19), man born blind (Jn 9:1-7), Lazarus raised (Jn 11), crippled woman (Lk 13:11-17), man with dropsy (Lk 14:1-6), two blind men (Mt 20:29-34; Mk 10:46-52; Lk 18:35-43), Malchus' ear (Lk 22:50-51). Other Miracles: water to wine (Jn 2:1-11), catch of fish (Lk 5:1-11), storm stilled (Mt 8:23-27; Mk 4:37-41; Lk 8:22-25), 5,000 fed (Mt 14:15-21; Mk 6:35-44; Lk 9:10-17; Jn 6:1-14), walking on water (Mt 14:25-33; Mk 6:48-52; Jn 6:15-21), 4,000 fed (Mt 15:32-39; Mk 8:1-9), money from fish (Mt 17:24-27), fig tree cursed (Mt 21:18-22; Mk 11:12-14), catch of fish (Jn 21:1-14).
MAJOR TEACHING: Sermon on the Mount (Mt 5-7; Lk 6:17-49), to Nicodemus (Jn 3), to Samaritan woman (Jn 4), Bread of Life (Jn 6:22-59), at Feast of Tabernacles (Jn 7-8), woes to Pharisees (Mt 23; Lk 11:37-54), Good Shepherd (Jn 10:1-18), Olivet Dis-

course (Mt 24-25; Mk 13; Lk 21:5-36), Upper Room Discourse (Jn 13-16).

PARABLES: Sower (Mt 13:3-23; Mk 4:3-25; Lk 8:5-18), seed's growth (Mk 4:26-29), wheat and weeds (Mt 13:24-30, 36-43), mustard seed (Mt 13:31-32; Mk 4:30-32), yeast (Mt 13:33; Lk 13:20-21), hidden treasure (Mt 13:44), valuable pearl (Mt 13:45-46), net (Mt 13:47-51), house owner (Mt 13:52), good Samaritan (Lk 10:25-37), unmerciful servant (Mt 18:15-35), lost sheep (Mt 18:10-14; Lk 15:4-7), lost coin (Lk 15:8-10), prodigal son (Lk 15:11-32), dishonest manager (Lk 16:1-13), rich man and Lazarus (Lk 16:19-31), persistent widow (Lk 18:1-8), Pharisee and tax collector (Lk 18:9-14), payment of workers (Mt 20:1-16), tenants and the vineyard (Mt 21:28-46; Mk 12:1-12; Lk 20:9-19), wedding banquet (Mt 22:1-14), faithful servant (Mt 24:45-51), ten virgins (Mt 25:1-13), talents (Mt 25:14-30; Lk 19:12-27).

DISCIPLES see APOSTLES. Call of (Jn 1:35-51; Mt 4:18-22; 9:9; Mk 1:16-20; 2:13-14; Lk 5:1-11, 27-28). Named Apostles (Mk 3:13-19; Lk 6:12-16). Twelve sent out (Mt 10; Mk 6:7-11; Lk 9:1-5). Seventy sent out (Lk 10:1-24). Defection of (Jn 6:60-71; Mt 26:56; Mk 14:50-52). Final commission (Mt 28:16-20; Jn 21:15-23; Ac 1:3-8).

Ac	2: 32	God has raised this J to life,
	9: 5	"I am J, whom you are persecuting
	15: 11	of our Lord J that we are saved,
	16: 31	"Believe in the Lord J,
Ro	3: 24	redemption that came by Christ J.
	5: 17	life through the one man, J Christ.
	8: 1	for those who are in Christ J,
1Co	2: 2	except J Christ and him crucified.
	8: 6	and there is but one Lord, J Christ,
	12: 3	and no one can say, "J is Lord,"
2Co	4: 5	not preach ourselves, but J Christ
Gal	2: 16	but by faith in J Christ.
	3: 28	for you are all one in Christ J.
	5: 6	in Christ J neither circumcision
Eph	2: 10	created in Christ J
	2: 20	with Christ J himself as the chief
Php	1: 6	until the day of Christ J.
	2: 5	be the same as that of Christ J:
	2: 10	name of J every knee should bow,
Col	3: 17	do it all in the name of the Lord J,
2Th	2: 1	the coming of our Lord J Christ
1Ti	1: 15	Christ J came into the world
2Ti	3: 12	life in Christ J will be persecuted,
Tit	2: 13	our great God and Savior, J Christ,
Heb	2: 9	But we see J, who was made a little
	3: 1	fix your thoughts on J, the apostle
	4: 14	through the heavens, J the Son
	7: 22	J has become the guarantee
	7: 24	but because J lives forever,
	12: 2	Let us fix our eyes on J, the author
2Pe	1: 16	and coming of our Lord J Christ,
1Jn	1: 7	and the blood of J, his Son,
	2: 1	J Christ, the Righteous One.
	2: 6	to live in him must walk as J did.
	4: 15	anyone acknowledges that J is
Rev	22: 20	Come, Lord J.

JEW (JEWS JUDAISM)

Zec	8: 23	of one J by the edge of his robe
Ro	1: 16	first for the J, then for the Gentile.
	10: 12	there is no difference between J
1Co	9: 20	To the Jews I became like a J,
Gal	3: 28	There is neither J nor Greek,

JEWELRY (JEWELS)

1Pe	3: 3	wearing of gold j and fine clothes.

JEWELS (JEWELRY)

Isa	61: 10	as a bride adorns herself with her j.
Zec	9: 16	like j in a crown.

JEWS (JEW)

Mt	2: 2	who has been born king of the J?
	27: 11	"Are you the king of the J?" "Yes,
Jn	4: 22	for salvation is from the J.
Ro	3: 29	Is God the God of J only?
1Co	1: 22	J demand miraculous signs
	9: 20	To the J I became like a Jew,
	12: 13	whether J or Greeks, slave or free
Gal	2: 8	of Peter as an apostle to the J,
Rev	3: 9	claim to be J though they are not,

JEZEBEL

Sidonian wife of Ahab (1Ki 16:31). Promoted Baal worship (1Ki 16:32-33). Killed prophets of the LORD (1Ki 18:4, 13). Opposed Elijah (1Ki 19:1-2). Had Naboth killed (1Ki 21). Death prophesied (1Ki 21:17-24). Killed by Jehu (2Ki 9:30-37).

JOASH

Son of Ahaziah; king of Judah. Sheltered from Athaliah by Jehoiada (2Ki 11; 2Ch 22:10-23:21). Repaired temple (2Ki 12; 2Ch 24).

JOB

Wealthy man from Uz; feared God (Job 1:1-5). Righteousness tested by disaster (Job 1:6-22), personal affliction (Job 2). Maintained innocence in debate with three friends (Job 3-31), Elihu (Job 32-37). Rebuked by the LORD (Job 38-41). Vindicated and restored to greater stature by the LORD (Job 42). Example of righteousness (Eze 14:14, 20).

JOHN

1. Son of Zechariah and Elizabeth (Lk 1). Called the Baptist (Mt 3:1-12; Mk 1:2-8). Witness to Jesus (Mt 3:11-12; Mk 1:7-8; Lk 3:15-18; Jn 1:6-35; 3:27-30; 5:33-36). Doubts about Jesus (Mt 11:2-6; Lk 7:18-23). Arrest (Mt 4:12; Mk 1:14). Execution (Mt 14:1-12; Mk 6:14-29; Lk 9:7-9). Ministry compared to Elijah (Mt 11:7-19; Mk 9:11-13; Lk 7:24-35).

2. Apostle; brother of James (Mt 4:21-22; 10:2; Mk 3:17; Lk 5:1-10). At transfiguration (Mt 17:1-13; Mk 9:1-13; Lk 9:28-36). Desire to be greatest (Mk 10:35-45). Leader of church at Jerusalem (Ac 4:1-3; Gal 2:9). Elder who wrote epistles (2Jn 1; 3Jn 1). Prophet who wrote Revelation (Rev 1:1; 22:8).

3. Cousin of Barnabas, co-worker with Paul, (Ac 12:12-13:13; 15:37), see MARK.

JOIN (JOINED)

Pr	23: 20	Do not j those who drink too much
	24: 21	and do not j with the rebellious,
Ro	15: 30	to j me in my struggle by praying
2Ti	1: 8	j with me in suffering for the gospel

JOINED (JOIN)

Mt	19: 6	Therefore what God has j together,
Mk	10: 9	Therefore what God has j together,
Eph	2: 21	him the whole building is j together
	4: 16	j and held together

JOINTS

Heb	4: 12	even to dividing soul and spirit, j

JOKING

Eph	5: 4	or coarse j, which are out of place,

JONAH

Prophet in days of Jeroboam II (2Ki 14:25). Called to Nineveh; fled to Tarshish (Jnh 1:1-3). Cause of storm; thrown into sea (Jnh 1:4-

16). Swallowed by fish (Jnh 1:17). Prayer (Jnh 2). Preached to Nineveh (Jnh 3). Attitude reproved by the LORD (Jnh 4). Sign of (Mt 12:39-41; Lk 11:29-32).

JONATHAN

Son of Saul (1Sa 13:16; 1Ch 8:33). Valiant warrior (1Sa 13-14). Relation to David (1Sa 18:1-4; 19-20; 23:16-18). Killed at Gilboa (1Sa 31). Mourned by David (2Sa 1).

JORAM

1. Son of Ahab; king of Israel (2Ki 3; 8-9; 2Ch 22).

JORDAN

Nu	34: 12	boundary will go down along the J
Jos	4: 22	Israel crossed the J on dry ground.'
Mt	3: 6	baptized by him in the J River.

JOSEPH

1. Son of Jacob by Rachel (Ge 30:24; 1Ch 2:2). Favored by Jacob, hated by brothers (Ge 37:3-4). Dreams (Ge 37:5-11). Sold by brothers (Ge 37:12-36). Served Potiphar; imprisoned by false accusation (Ge 39). Interpreted dreams of Pharaoh's servants (Ge 40), of Pharaoh (Ge 41:1-40). Made greatest in Egypt (Ge 41:41-57). Sold grain to brothers (Ge 42-45). Brought Jacob and sons to Egypt (Ge 46-47). Sons Ephraim and Manasseh blessed (Ge 48). Blessed (Ge 49:22-26; Dt 33:13-17). Death (Ge 50:22-26; Ex 13:19; Heb 11:22). 12,000 from (Rev 7:8).

2. Husband of Mary, mother of Jesus (Mt 1:16-24; 2:13-19; Lk 1:27; 2; Jn 1:45).

3. Disciple from Arimathea, who gave his tomb for Jesus' burial (Mt 27:57-61; Mk 15:43-47; Lk 24:50-52).

4. Original name of Barnabas (Ac 4:36).

JOSHUA

1. Son of Nun; name changed from Hoshea (Nu 13:8, 16; 1Ch 7:27). Fought Amalekites under Moses (Ex 17:9-14). Servant of Moses on Sinai (Ex 24:13; 32:17). Spied Canaan (Nu 13). With Caleb, allowed to enter land (Nu 14:6, 30). Succeeded Moses (Dt 1:38; 31:1-8; 34:9).

Charged Israel to conquer Canaan (Jos 1). Crossed Jordan (Jos 3-4). Circumcised sons of wilderness wanderings (Jos 5). Conquered Jericho (Jos 6), Ai (Jos 7-8), five kings at Gibeon (Jos 10:1-28), southern Canaan (Jos 10:29-43), northern Canaan (Jos 11-12). Defeated at Ai (Jos 7). Deceived by Gibeonites (Jos 9). Renewed covenant (Jos 8:30-35; 24:1-27). Divided land among tribes (Jos 13-22). Last words (Jos 23). Death (Jos 24:28-31).

2. High priest during rebuilding of temple (Hag 1-2; Zec 3:1-9; 6:11).

JOSIAH

Son of Amon; king of Judah (2Ki 22-23; 2Ch 34-35).

JOTHAM

Son of Azariah (Uzziah); king of Judah (2Ki 15:32-38; 2Ch 26:21-27:9).

JOY (ENJOY ENJOYMENT JOYFUL OVERJOYED REJOICE REJOICES REJOICING)

Dt	16: 15	and your j will be complete.
1Ch	16: 27	strength and j in his dwelling place.
Ne	8: 10	for the j of the LORD is your
Est	9: 22	their sorrow was turned into j
Job	38: 7	and all the angels shouted for j?
Ps	4: 7	have filled my heart with greater j
	21: 6	with the j of your presence.
	30: 11	sackcloth and clothed me with j,
	43: 4	to God, my j and my delight.
	51: 12	to me the j of your salvation
	66: 1	Shout with j to God, all the earth!
	96: 12	the trees of the forest will sing for j;

Ps 107: 22 and tell of his works with songs of *j*
119:111 they are the *j* of my heart.
Pr 10: 1 A wise son brings *j* to his father,
10:28 The prospect of the righteous is *j*,
12:20 but *j* for those who promote peace.
Isa 35:10 everlasting *j* will crown their heads
51:11 Gladness and *j* will overtake them,
55:12 You will go out in *j*
Lk 1:44 the baby in my womb leaped for *j*.
2:10 news of great *j* that will be
Jn 15:11 and that your *j* may be complete.
16:20 but your grief will turn to *j*.
2Co 8: 2 their overflowing *j* and their
Php 2: 2 then make my *j* complete
4: 1 and long for, my *j* and crown,
1Th 2:19 For what is our hope, our *j*,
Phm : 7 Your love has given me great *j*
Heb 12: 2 for the *j* set before him endured
Jas 1: 2 Consider it pure *j*, my brothers,
1Pe 1: 8 with an inexpressible and glorious *j*,
2Jn : 4 It has given me great *j* to find some
3Jn : 4 I have no greater *j*

JOYFUL (JOY)
Ps 100: 2 come before him with *j* songs.
Hab 3:18 I will be *j* in God my Savior.
1Th 5:16 Be *j* always; pray continually;

JUDAH
1. Son of Jacob by Leah (Ge 29:35; 35:23; 1Ch 2:1). Tribe of blessed as ruling tribe (Ge 49:8-12; Dt 33:7).
2. Name used for people and land of Southern Kingdom.
Jer 13:19 All *J* will be carried into exile,
Zec 10: 4 From *J* will come the cornerstone,
Heb 7:14 that our Lord descended from *J*,

JUDAISM (JEW)
Gal 1:13 of my previous way of life in *J*,

JUDAS
1. Apostle (Lk 6:16; Jn 14:22; Ac 1:13). Probably also called Thaddaeus (Mt 10:3; Mk 3:18).
2. Brother of James and Jesus (Mt 13:55; Mk 6:3), also called Jude (Jude 1).
3. Apostle, also called Iscariot, who betrayed Jesus (Mt 10:4; 26:14-56; Mk 3:19; 14:10-50; Lk 6:16; 22:3-53; Jn 6:71; 12:4; 13:2-30; 18:2-11). Suicide of (Mt 27:3-5; Ac 1:16-25).

JUDGE (JUDGED JUDGES JUDGING JUDGMENT)
Ge 18:25 Will not the *J* of all the earth do
1Ch 16:33 for he comes to *j* the earth.
Ps 9: 8 He will *j* the world in righteousness
Joel 3:12 sit to *j* all the nations on every side.
Mt 7: 1 Do not *j*, or you too will be judged.
Jn 12:47 For I did not come to *j* the world,
Ac 17:31 a day when he will *j* the world
Ro 2:16 day when God will *j* men's secrets
1Co 4: 3 indeed, I do not even *j* myself.
6: 2 that the saints will *j* the world?
Gal 2: 6 not *j* by external appearance—
2Ti 4: 1 who will *j* the living and the dead,
4: 8 which the Lord, the righteous *J*,
Jas 4:12 There is only one Lawgiver and *J*,
4:12 who are you to *j* your neighbor?
Rev 20: 4 who had been given authority to *j*.

JUDGED (JUDGE)
Mt 7: 1 "Do not judge, or you too will be *j*.

1Co 11:31 But if we *j* ourselves, we would not
Jas 3: 1 who teach will be *j* more strictly.
Rev 20:12 The dead were *j* according

JUDGES (JUDGE)
Jdg 2:16 Then the LORD raised up *j*,
Ps 58:11 there is a God who *j* the earth."
Heb 4:12 it *j* the thoughts and attitudes
Rev 19:11 With justice he *j* and makes war.

JUDGING (JUDGE)
Mt 19:28 *j* the twelve tribes of Israel.
Jn 7:24 Stop *j* by mere appearances,

JUDGMENT (JUDGE)
Dt 1:17 of any man, for *j* belongs to God.
Ps 1: 5 the wicked will not stand in the *j*,
119: 66 Teach me knowledge and good *j*,
Pr 6:32 man who commits adultery lacks *j*;
12:11 but he who chases fantasies lacks *j*.
Ecc 12:14 God will bring every deed into *j*,
Isa 66:16 the LORD will execute *j*,
Mt 5:21 who murders will be subject to *j*.'
10:15 on the day of *j* than for that town.
12:36 have to give account on the day of *j*
Jn 5:22 but has entrusted all *j* to the Son,
7:24 appearances, and make a right *j*."
16: 8 to sin and righteousness and *j*:
Ro 14:10 stand before God's *j* seat.
14:13 Therefore let us stop passing *j*
1Co 11:29 body of the Lord eats and drinks *j*
2Co 5:10 appear before the *j* seat of Christ,
Heb 9:27 to die once, and after that to face *j*,
10:27 but only a fearful expectation of *j*
1Pe 4:17 For it is time for *j* to begin
Jude : 6 bound with everlasting chains for *j*

JUST (JUSTICE JUSTIFICATION JUSTIFIED JUSTIFY JUSTLY)
Dt 32: 4 and all his ways are *j*.
Ps 37:28 For the LORD loves the *j*
111: 7 of his hands are faithful and *j*;
Pr 1: 3 doing what is right and *j* and fair;
2: 8 for he guards the course of the *j*
Da 4:37 does is right and all his ways *j*.
Ro 3:26 as to be *j* and the one who justifies
Heb 2: 2 received its *j* punishment,
1Jn 1: 9 and *j* and will forgive us our sins
Rev 16: 7 true and *j* are your judgments."

JUSTICE (JUST)
Ex 23: 2 do not pervert *j* by siding
23: 6 "Do not deny *j* to your poor people
Job 37:23 in his *j* and great righteousness,
Ps 9: 8 he will govern the peoples with *j*.
9:16 The LORD is known by his *j*;
11: 7 he loves *j*;
45: 6 a scepter of *j* will be the scepter
101: 1 I will sing of your love and *j*;
106: 3 Blessed are they who maintain *j*,
Pr 21:15 When *j* is done, it brings joy
28: 5 Evil men do not understand *j*,
29: 4 By *j* a king gives a country stability
29:26 from the LORD that man gets *j*.
Isa 9: 7 it with *j* and righteousness
28:17 I will make *j* the measuring line
30:18 For the LORD is a God of *j*.
42: 1 and he will bring *j* to the nations.
42: 4 till he establishes *j* on earth.
56: 1 "Maintain *j*
61: 8 "For I, the LORD, love *j*;

Jer 30:11 I will discipline you but only with *j*;
Eze 34:16 I will shepherd the flock with *j*.
Am 5:15 maintain *j* in the courts.
5:24 But let *j* roll on like a river,
Zec 7: 9 'Administer true *j*; show mercy
Lk 11:42 you neglect *j* and the love of God.
Ro 3:25 He did this to demonstrate his *j*,

JUSTIFICATION (JUST)
Ro 4:25 and was raised to life for our *j*.
5:18 of righteousness was *j* that brings

JUSTIFIED (JUST)
Ac 13:39 him everyone who believes is *j*
Ro 3:24 and are *j* freely by his grace
3:28 For we maintain that a man is *j*
5: 1 since we have been *j* through faith,
5: 9 Since we have now been *j*
8:30 those he called, he also *j*; those he *j*,
1Co 6:11 you were *j* in the name
Gal 2:16 observing the law no one will be *j*.
3:11 Clearly no one is *j* before God
3:24 to Christ that we might be *j* by faith
Jas 2:24 You see that a person is *j*

JUSTIFY (JUST)
Gal 3: 8 that God would *j* the Gentiles

JUSTLY (JUST)
Mic 6: 8 To act *j* and to love mercy

KEEP (KEEPER KEEPING KEEPS KEPT)
Ge 31:49 "May the LORD *k* watch
Ex 20: 6 and *k* my commandments.
Nu 6:24 and *k* you;
Ps 18:28 You, O LORD, *k* my lamp burning
19:13 *K* your servant also from willful
119: 9 can a young man *k* his way pure?
121: 7 The LORD will *k* you
141: 3 *k* watch over the door of my lips.
Pr 4:24 *k* corrupt talk far from your lips.
Isa 26: 3 You will *k* in perfect peace
Mt 10:10 for the worker is worth his *k*.
Lk 12:35 and *k* your lamps burning,
Gal 5:25 let us *k* in step with the Spirit.
Eph 4: 3 Make every effort to *k* the unity
1Ti 5:22 *K* yourself pure.
2Ti 4: 5 *k* your head in all situations,
Heb 13: 5 *K* your lives free from the love
Jas 1:26 and yet does not *k* a tight rein
2: 8 If you really *k* the royal law found
Jude :24 able to *k* you from falling

KEEPER (KEEP)
Ge 4: 9 I my brother's *k*?" The LORD

KEEPING (KEEP)
Ex 20: 8 the Sabbath day by *k* it holy.
Ps 19:11 in them there is great reward.
Mt 3: 8 Produce fruit in *k* with repentance.
Lk 2: 8 *k* watch over their flocks at night.
1Co 7:19 *K* God's commands is what counts.
2Pe 3: 9 Lord is not slow in *k* his promise,

KEEPS (KEEP)
Pr 17:28 a fool is thought wise if he *k* silent,
Am 5:13 Therefore the prudent man *k* quiet
1Co 13: 5 is not easily angered, it *k* no record
Jas 2:10 For whoever *k* the whole law

KEPT (KEEP)
Ps 130: 3 If you, O LORD, *k* a record of sins,
2Ti 4: 7 finished the race, I have *k* the faith.

1Pe 1: 4 spoil or fade—*k* in heaven for you,

KEYS

Mt 16:19 I will give you the *k* of the kingdom

KILL (KILLS)

Mt 17:23 They will *k* him, and on the third

KILLS (KILL)

Lev 24:21 but whoever *k* a man must be put
2Co 3: 6 for the letter *k*, but the Spirit gives

KIND (KINDNESS KINDS)

Ge 1:24 animals, each according to its *k*,"
2Ch 10: 7 "If you will be *k* to these people
Pr 11:17 A *k* man benefits himself,
    12:25 but a *k* word cheers him up.
    14:21 blessed is he who is *k* to the needy.
    14:31 whoever is *k* to the needy honors
    19:17 He who is *k* to the poor lends
Da 4:27 by being *k* to the oppressed.
Lk 6:35 because he is *k* to the ungrateful
1Co 13: 4 Love is patient, love is *k*.
    15:35 With what *k* of body will they
Eph 4:32 Be *k* and compassionate
1Th 5:15 but always try to be *k* to each other
2Ti 2:24 instead, he must be *k* to everyone,
Tit 2: 5 to be busy at home, to be *k*,

KINDNESS (KIND)

Ac 14:17 He has shown *k* by giving you rain
Ro 11:22 Consider therefore the *k*
Gal 5:22 peace, patience, *k*, goodness,
Eph 2: 7 expressed in his *k* to us
2Pe 1: 7 brotherly *k*; and to brotherly *k*,

KINDS (KIND)

1Co 12: 4 There are different *k* of gifts,
1Ti 6:10 of money is a root of all *k* of evil.

KING (KINGDOM KINGS)

1. Kings of Judah and Israel: see Saul, David, Solomon.

2. Kings of Judah: see Rehoboam, Abijah, Asa, Jehoshaphat, Jehoram, Ahaziah, Athaliah (Queen), Joash, Amaziah, Uzziah, Jotham, Ahaz, Hezekiah, Manasseh, Amon, Josiah, Jehoahaz, Jehoiakim, Jehoiachin, Zedekiah.

3. Kings of Israel: see Jeroboam I, Nadab, Baasha, Elah, Zimri, Tibni, Omri, Ahab, Ahaziah, Joram, Jehu, Jehoahaz, Jehoash, Jeroboam II, Zechariah, Shallum, Menahem, Pekah, Pekahiah, Hoshea.

Jdg 17: 6 In those days Israel had no *k*;
1Sa 12:12 the Lord your God was your *k*.
Ps 24: 7 that the *K* of glory may come in.
Isa 32: 1 See, a *k* will reign in righteousness
Zec 9: 9 See, your *k* comes to you,
1Ti 6:15 the *K* of kings and Lord of lords,
1Pe 2:17 of believers, fear God, honor the *k*.
Rev 19:16 K OF KINGS AND LORD

KINGDOM (KING)

Ex 19: 6 you will be for me a *k* of priests
1Ch 29:11 Yours, O Lord, is the *k*;
Ps 45: 6 justice will be the scepter of your *k*.
Da 4: 3 His *k* is an eternal *k*;
Mt 3: 2 Repent, for the *k* of heaven is near
    5: 3 for theirs is the *k* of heaven.
    6:10 your *k* come,
    6:33 But seek first his *k* and his
    7:21 Lord,' will enter the *k* of heaven,
    11:11 least in the *k* of heaven is greater

Mt 13:24 "The *k* of heaven is like a man who
    13:31 *k* of heaven is like a mustard seed,
    13:33 "The *k* of heaven is like yeast that
    13:44 *k* of heaven is like treasure hidden
    13:45 the *k* of heaven is like a merchant
    13:47 *k* of heaven is like a net that was let
    16:19 the keys of the *k* of heaven;
    18:23 the *k* of heaven is like a king who
    19:24 for a rich man to enter the *k* of God
    24: 7 rise against nation, and *k* against *k*.
    24:14 gospel of the *k* will be preached
    25:34 the *k* prepared for you
Mk 9:47 better for you to enter the *k* of God
    10:14 for the *k* of God belongs to such
    10:23 for the rich to enter the *k* of God!"
Lk 10: 9 'The *k* of God is near you.'
    12:31 seek his *k*, and these things will be
    17:21 because the *k* of God is within you
Jn 3: 5 no one can enter the *k* of God
    18:36 "My *k* is not of this world.
1Co 6: 9 the wicked will not inherit the *k*
    15:24 hands over the *k* to God the Father
Rev 1: 6 has made us to be a *k* and priests
    11:15 of the world has become the *k*

KINGS (KING)

Ps 2: 2 The *k* of the earth take their stand
    72:11 All *k* will bow down to him
Da 7:24 ten horns are ten *k* who will come
1Ti 2: 2 for *k* and all those in authority,
Rev 1: 5 and the ruler of the *k* of the earth.

KINSMAN-REDEEMER (REDEEM)

Ru 3: 9 over me, since you are a *k*."

KISS

Ps 2:12 K the Son, lest he be angry
Pr 24:26 is like a *k* on the lips.
Lk 22:48 the Son of Man with a *k*?"

KNEE (KNEES)

Isa 45:23 Before me every *k* will bow;
Ro 14:11 'every *k* will bow before me;
Php 2:10 name of Jesus every *k* should bow,

KNEES (KNEE)

Isa 35: 3 steady the *k* that give way;
Heb 12:12 your feeble arms and weak *k*.

KNEW (KNOW)

Job 23: 3 If only I *k* where to find him;
Jnh 4: 2 I *k* that you are a gracious
Mt 7:23 tell them plainly, 'I never *k* you.

KNOCK

Mt 7: 7 *k* and the door will be opened
Rev 3:20 I am! I stand at the door and *k*.

KNOW (FOREKNEW KNEW KNOWING KNOWLEDGE KNOWN KNOWS)

Dt 18:21 "How can we *k* when a message
Job 19:25 I *k* that my Redeemer lives,
    42: 3 things too wonderful for me to *k*.
Ps 46:10 "Be still, and *k* that I am God;
    139: 1 and you *k* me.
    139:23 Search me, O God, and *k* my heart;
Pr 27: 1 for you do not *k* what a day may
Jer 24: 7 I will give them a heart to *k* me,
    31:34 his brother, saying, 'K the Lord,'
Mt 6: 3 let your left hand *k* what your right
    24:42 you do not *k* on what day your

Lk 1: 4 so that you may *k* the certainty
Jn 3:11 we speak of what we *k*,
    4:22 we worship what we do *k*,
    9:25 One thing I do *k*.
    10:14 I *k* my sheep and my sheep *k* me—
    17: 3 that they may *k* you, the only true
    21:24 We *k* that his testimony is true.
Ac 1: 7 "It is not for you to *k* the times
Ro 6: 6 For we *k* that our old self was
    7:18 I *k* that nothing good lives in me,
    8:28 we *k* that in all things God works
1Co 2: 2 For I resolved to *k* nothing
    6:15 Do you not *k* that your bodies are
    6:19 Do you not *k* that your body is
    13:12 Now I *k* in part; then I shall *k* fully,
    15:58 because you *k* that your labor
Php 3:10 I want to *k* Christ and the power
2Ti 1:12 because I *k* whom I have believed,
Jas 4:14 *k* what will happen tomorrow.
1Jn 2: 4 The man who says, "I *k* him,"
    3:14 We *k* that we have passed
    3:16 This is how we *k* what love is:
    5: 2 This is how we *k* that we love
    5:13 so that you may *k* that you have

KNOWING (KNOW)

Ge 3: 5 and you will be like God, *k* good
Php 3: 8 of *k* Christ Jesus my Lord,

KNOWLEDGE (KNOW)

Ge 2: 9 the tree of the *k* of good and evil.
Job 42: 3 obscures my counsel without *k*?'
Ps 19: 2 night after night they display *k*.
    73:11 Does the Most High have *k*?"
    139: 6 Such *k* is too wonderful for me,
Pr 1: 7 of the Lord is the beginning of *k*,
    10:14 Wise men store up *k*,
    12: 1 Whoever loves discipline loves *k*,
    13:16 Every prudent man acts out of *k*,
    19: 2 to have zeal without *k*,
Isa 11: 9 full of the *k* of the Lord
Hab 2:14 filled with the *k* of the glory
Ro 11:33 riches of the wisdom and *k* of God!
1Co 8: 1 K puffs up, but love builds up.
    8:11 Christ died, is destroyed by your *k*.
    13: 2 can fathom all mysteries and all *k*,
2Co 2:14 everywhere the fragrance of the *k*
    4: 6 light of the *k* of the glory of God
Eph 3:19 to know this love that surpasses *k*
Col 2: 3 all the treasures of wisdom and *k*.
1Ti 6:20 ideas of what is falsely called *k*,
2Pe 3:18 grow in the grace and *k* of our Lord

KNOWN (KNOW)

Ps 16:11 You have made *k* to me the path
    105: 1 make *k* among the nations what he
Isa 46:10 *k* the end from the beginning,
Mt 10:26 or hidden that will not be made *k*.
Ro 1:19 since what may be *k* about God is
    11:34 "Who has *k* the mind of the Lord?
    15:20 the gospel where Christ was not *k*,
2Co 3: 2 written on our hearts, *k*
2Pe 2:21 than to have *k* it and then

KNOWS (KNOW)

1Sa 2: 3 for the Lord is a God who *k*,
Job 23:10 But he *k* the way that I take;
Ps 44:21 since he *k* the secrets of the heart?
    94:11 The Lord *k* the thoughts of man;
Ecc 8: 7 Since no man *k* the future,
Mt 6: 8 for your Father *k* what you need

Mt   24:36 "No one *k* about that day or hour,
Ro   8:27 who searches our hearts *k* the mind
1Co   8: 2 who thinks he *k* something does
2Ti   2:19 The Lord *k* those who are his," and

LABAN

Brother of Rebekah (Ge 24:29-51), father of Rachel and Leah (Ge 29-31).

LABOR

Ex   20: 9 Six days you shall *l* and do all your
Isa   55: 2 and your *l* on what does not satisfy
Mt   6:28 They do not *l* or spin.
1Co   3: 8 rewarded according to his own *l*.
     15:58 because you know that your *l*

LACK (LACKING LACKS)

Pr   15:22 Plans fail for *l* of counsel,
Ro   3: 3 Will their *l* of faith nullify God's
Col   2:23 *l* any value in restraining sensual

LACKING (LACK)

Ro   12:11 Never be *l* in zeal, but keep your
Jas   1: 4 and complete, not *l* anything.

LACKS (LACK)

Pr   6:32 who commits adultery *l* judgment;
     12:11 he who chases fantasies *l* judgment
Jas   1: 5 any of you *l* wisdom, he should ask

LAID (LAY)

Isa   53: 6 and the Lord has *l* on him
1Co   3:11 other than the one already *l*,
1Jn   3:16 Jesus Christ *l* down his life for us.

LAKE

Rev   19:20 into the fiery *l* of burning sulfur.
     20:14 The *l* of fire is the second death.

LAMB (LAMB'S LAMBS)

Ge   22: 8 "God himself will provide the *l*
Ex   12:21 and slaughter the Passover *l*.
Isa   11: 6 The wolf will live with the *l*,
     53: 7 he was led like a *l* to the slaughter,
Jn   1:29 *L* of God, who takes away the sin
1Co   5: 7 our Passover *l*, has been sacrificed.
1Pe   1:19 a *l* without blemish or defect.
Rev   5: 6 Then I saw a *L*, looking
     5:12 "Worthy is the *L*, who was slain,
     14: 4 They follow the *L* wherever he

LAMB'S (LAMB)

Rev   21:27 written in the *L* book of life.

LAMBS (LAMB)

Lk   10: 3 I am sending you out like *l*
Jn   21:15 Jesus said, "Feed my *l*."

LAMENT

2Sa   1:17 took up this *l* concerning Saul

LAMP (LAMPS)

2Sa   22:29 You are my *l*, O Lord;
Ps   18:28 You, O Lord, keep my *l* burning;
     119:105 Your word is a *l* to my feet
Pr   31:18 and her *l* does not go out at night.
Lk   8:16 "No one lights a *l* and hides it
Rev   21:23 gives it light, and the Lamb is its *l*.

LAMPS (LAMP)

Mt   25: 1 be like ten virgins who took their *l*
Lk   12:35 for service and keep your *l* burning,

LAND

Ge   1:10 God called the dry ground "*l*,"
     1:11 "Let the *l* produce vegetation:
     12: 7 To your offspring I will give this *l*."
Ex   3: 8 a *l* flowing with milk and honey—
Nu   35:33 Do not pollute the *l* where you are.
Dt   34: 1 Lord showed him the whole *l*—
Jos   13: 2 "This is the *l* that remains:
     14: 4 Levites received no share of the *l*
2Ch   7:14 their sin and will heal their *l*.
     7:20 then I will uproot Israel from my *l*,
Eze   36:24 and bring you back into your own *l*.

LANGUAGE

Ge   11: 1 Now the whole world had one *l*
Ps   19: 3 There is no speech or *l*
Jn   8:44 When he lies, he speaks his native *l*
Ac   2: 6 heard them speaking in his own *l*.
Col   3: 8 slander, and filthy *l* from your lips.
Rev   5: 9 from every tribe and *l* and people

LAST (LASTING LASTS LATTER)

2Sa   23: 1 These are the *l* words of David:
Isa   44: 6 I am the first and I am the *l*;
Mt   19:30 But many who are first will be *l*,
Mk   10:31 are first will be *l*, and the *l* first."
Jn   15:16 and bear fruit—fruit that will *l*.
Ro   1:17 is by faith from first to *l*,
2Ti   3: 1 will be terrible times in the *l* days.
2Pe   3: 3 in the *l* days scoffers will come,
Rev   1:17 I am the First and the *L*.
     22:13 the First and the *L*, the Beginning

LASTING (LAST)

Ex   12:14 to the Lord—a *l* ordinance.
Lev   24: 8 of the Israelites, as a *l* covenant.
Nu   25:13 have a covenant of a *l* priesthood,
Heb   10:34 had better and *l* possessions.

LASTS (LAST)

Ps   30: 5 For his anger *l* only a moment,
2Co   3:11 greater is the glory of that which *l*!

LATTER (LAST)

Job   42:12 The Lord blessed the *l* part

LAUGH (LAUGHS)

Ecc   3: 4 a time to weep and a time to *l*,

LAUGHS (LAUGH)

Ps   2: 4 The One enthroned in heaven *l*;
     37:13 but the Lord *l* at the wicked,

LAVISHED

Eph   1: 8 of God's grace that he *l* on us
1Jn   3: 1 great is the love the Father has *l*

LAW (LAWS)

Dt   31:11 you shall read this *l* before them
     31:26 "Take this Book of the *L*
Jos   1: 8 of the *L* depart from your mouth;
Ne   8: 8 from the Book of the *L* of God,
Ps   1: 2 and on his *l* he meditates day
     19: 7 The *l* of the Lord is perfect,
     119: 18 wonderful things in your *l*.
     119: 72 *l* from your mouth is more precious
     119: 97 Oh, how I love your *l*!
     119:165 peace have they who love your *l*,
Isa   8:20 To the *l* and to the testimony!
Jer   31:33 "I will put my *l* in their minds
Mt   5:17 that I have come to abolish the *L*
     7:12 sums up the *L* and the Prophets.
     22:40 All the *L* and the Prophets hang
Lk   16:17 stroke of a pen to drop out of the *L*.

Jn   1:17 For the *l* was given through Moses;
Ro   2:12 All who sin apart from the *l* will
     2:15 of the *l* are written on their hearts,
     5:13 for before the *l* was given,
     5:20 *l* was added so that the trespass
     6:14 because you are not under *l*,
     7: 6 released from the *l* so that we serve
     7:12 *l* is holy, and the commandment is
     8: 3 For what the *l* was powerless to do
     10: 4 Christ is the end of the *l*
     13:10 love is the fulfillment of the *l*.
Gal   3:13 curse of the *l* by becoming a curse
     3:24 So the *l* was put in charge to lead us
     5: 3 obligated to obey the whole *l*.
     5: 4 justified by *l* have been alienated
     5:14 The entire *l* is summed up
Heb   7:19 (for the *l* made nothing perfect),
     10: 1 The *l* is only a shadow
Jas   1:25 intently into the perfect *l* that gives
     2:10 For whoever keeps the whole *l*

LAWLESSNESS*

2Th   2: 3 and the man of *l* is revealed,
     2: 7 power of *l* is already at work;
1Jn   3: 4 sins breaks the law; in fact, sin is *l*.

LAWS (LAW)

Lev   25:18 and be careful to obey my *l*,
Ps   119: 30 I have set my heart on your *l*.
     119:120 I stand in awe of your *l*.
Heb   8:10 I will put my *l* in their minds
     10:16 I will put my *l* in their hearts,

LAY (LAID LAYING)

Job   22:22 and *l* up his words in your heart.
Isa   28:16 "See, I *l* a stone in Zion,
Mt   8:20 of Man has no place to *l* his head."
Jn   10:15 and I *l* down my life for the sheep.
     15:13 that he *l* down his life
1Co   3:11 no one can *l* any foundation other
1Jn   3:16 And we ought to *l* down our lives
Rev   4:10 They *l* their crowns

LAYING (LAY)

1Ti   5:22 Do not be hasty in the *l* on of hands
Heb   6: 1 not *l* again the foundation

LAZARUS

1. Poor man in Jesus' parable (Lk 16:19-31).
2. Brother of Mary and Martha whom Jesus raised from the dead (Jn 11:1-12:19).

LAZY

Pr   10: 4 *L* hands make a man poor,
Heb   6:12 We do not want you to become *l*,

LEAD (LEADERS LEADERSHIP LEADS LED)

Ex   15:13 "In your unfailing love you will *l*
Ps   27:11 *l* me in a straight path
     61: 2 *l* me to the rock that is higher
     139: 24 and *l* me in the way everlasting.
     143: 10 *l* me on level ground.
Ecc   5: 6 Do not let your mouth *l* you
Isa   11: 6 and a little child will *l* them.
Da   12: 3 those who *l* many to righteousness,
Mt   6:13 And *l* us not into temptation,
1Jn   3: 7 do not let anyone *l* you astray.

LEADERS (LEAD)

Heb   13: 7 Remember your *l*, who spoke
     13:17 Obey your *l* and submit

LEADERSHIP (LEAD)
Ro 12: 8 if it is *l*, let him govern diligently;

LEADS (LEAD)
Ps 23: 2 he *l* me beside quiet waters,
Pr 19:23 The fear of the LORD *l* to life:
Isa 40:11 he gently *l* those that have
young.
Mt 7:13 and broad is the road that *l*
15:14 If a blind man *l* a blind man,
Jn 10: 3 sheep by name and *l* them out.
Ro 14:19 effort to do what *l* to peace
2Co 2:14 always *l* us in triumphal
procession

LEAH
Wife of Jacob (Ge 29:16-30); bore six sons
and one daughter (Ge 29:31-30:21; 34:1;
35:23).

LEAN
Pr 3: 5 *l* not on your own understanding;

LEARN (LEARNED LEARNING)
Isa 1:17 *l* to do right!
Mt 11:29 yoke upon you and *l* from me,

LEARNED (LEARN)
Php 4:11 for I have *l* to be content
whatever
2Ti 3:14 continue in what you have *l*

LEARNING (LEARN)
Pr 1: 5 let the wise listen and add to
their *l*,
2Ti 3: 7 always *l* but never able

LED (LEAD)
Ps 68:18 you *l* captives in your train;
Isa 53: 7 he was *l* like a lamb to the
slaughter
Am 2:10 and I *l* you forty years in the
desert
Ro 8:14 those who are *l* by the Spirit
Eph 4: 8 he *l* captives in his train

LEFT
Jos 1: 7 turn from it to the right or to
the *l*,
Pr 4:27 Do not swerve to the right or
the *l*;
Mt 6: 3 do not let your *l* hand know what
25:33 on his right and the goats on
his *l*.

LEGION
Mk 5: 9 "My name is *L*," he replied,

LEND (LENDS)
Dt 15: 8 freely *l* him whatever he needs.
Ps 37:26 are always generous and *l*
freely;
Lk 6:34 if you *l* to those from whom you

LENDS (LEND)
Pr 19:17 to the poor *l* to the LORD.

LENGTH (LONG)
Ps 90:10 The *l* of our days is seventy
years—
Pr 10:27 The fear of the LORD adds *l* to
life

LEPROSY
2Ki 7: 3 men with *l* at the entrance

LETTER (LETTERS)
Mt 5:18 not the smallest *l*, not the least
2Co 3: 2 You yourselves are our *l*, written
3: 6 for the *l* kills, but the Spirit gives
2Th 3:14 not obey our instruction in this *l*,

LETTERS (LETTER)
2Co 3: 7 which was engraved in *l* on
stone,
10:10 "His *l* are weighty and forceful,
2Pe 3:16 His *l* contain some things that
are

LEVEL
Ps 143:10 lead me on *l* ground.
Pr 4:26 Make *l* paths for your feet

Isa 26: 7 The path of the righteous is *l*;
Heb 12:13 "Make *l* paths for your feet,"

LEVI (LEVITES)
1. Son of Jacob by Leah (Ge 29:34; 46:11;
1Ch 2:1). Tribe of blessed (Ge 49:5-7; Dt
33:8-11), chosen as priests (Nu 3-4), numbered (Nu 3:39; 26:62), allotted cities, but
not land (Nu 18; 35; Dt 10:9; Jos 13:14; 21),
land (Eze 48:8-22), 12,000 from (Rev 7:7).
2. See MATTHEW.

LEVITES (LEVI)
Nu 1:53 The *L* are to be responsible
8: 6 "Take the *L* from among the
other
18:21 I give to the *L* all the tithes in
Israel

LEWDNESS
Mk 7:22 malice, deceit, *l*, envy, slander,

LIAR (LIE)
Pr 19:22 better to be poor than a *l*.
Jn 8:44 for he is a *l* and the father of
lies.
Ro 3: 4 Let God be true, and every man
a *l*.

LIBERATED*
Ro 8:21 that the creation itself will be *l*

LIE (LIAR LIED LIES LYING)
Lev 19:11 " 'Do not *l*.
Nu 23:19 God is not a man, that he
should *l*,
Dt 6: 7 when you *l* down and when you
get
Ps 23: 2 me *l* down in green pastures,
Isa 11: 6 leopard will *l* down with the goat,
Eze 34:14 they will *l* down in good grazing
Ro 1:25 exchanged the truth of God for
a *l*,
Col 3: 9 Do not *l* to each other,
Heb 6:18 which it is impossible for God
to *l*,

LIED (LIE)
Ac 5: 4 You have not *l* to men but to
God."

LIES (LIE)
Ps 34:13 and your lips from speaking *l*.
Jn 8:44 for he is a liar and the father
of *l*.

LIFE (LIVE)
Ge 2: 7 into his nostrils the breath of *l*,
2: 9 of the garden were the tree of *l*
9:11 Never again will all *l* be cut
Ex 21:23 you are to take *l* for *l*, eye for
eye,
Lev 17:14 the *l* of every creature is its
blood.
24:18 must make restitution—*l* for *l*.
Dt 30:19 Now choose *l*, so that you
Ps 16:11 known to me the path of *l*;
23: 6 all the days of my *l*,
34:12 Whoever of you loves *l*
39: 4 let me know how fleeting is my *l*.
49: 7 No man can redeem the *l*
104: 33 I will sing to the LORD all my *l*;
Pr 1: 3 a disciplined and prudent *l*,
6:23 are the way to *l*,
7:23 little knowing it will cost him
his *l*.
8:35 For whoever finds me finds *l*
11:30 of the righteous is a tree of *l*,
21:21 finds *l*, prosperity and honor.
Jer 10:23 that a man's *l* is not his own;
Eze 37: 5 enter you, and you will come
to *l*.
Da 12: 2 some to everlasting *l*, others
Mt 6:25 Is not *l* more important than
food,
7:14 and narrow the road that leads
to *l*,
10:39 Whoever finds his *l* will lose it,
16:25 wants to save his *l* will lose it,
20:28 to give his *l* as a ransom for
many."

Mk 10:45 to give his *l* as a ransom for
many."
Lk 12:15 a man's *l* does not consist
12:22 do not worry about your *l*,
14:26 even his own *l*— he cannot be
my
Jn 1: 4 In him was *l*, and that *l* was
3:15 believes in him may have
eternal *l*.
3:36 believes in the Son has
eternal *l*,
4:14 of water welling up to eternal *l*."
5:24 him who sent me has eternal *l*
6:35 Jesus declared, "I am the bread
of *l*
6:47 he who believes has
everlasting *l*.
6:68 You have the words of eternal *l*.
10:10 I have come that they may
have *l*,
10:15 and I lay down my *l* for the
sheep.
10:28 I give them eternal *l*, and they
shall
11:25 "I am the resurrection and the *l*.
14: 6 am the way and the truth and
the *l*.
15:13 lay down his *l* for his friends.
20:31 that by believing you may have *l*
Ac 13:48 appointed for eternal *l* believed.
Ro 4:25 was raised to *l* for our
justification.
6:13 have been brought from death
to *l*;
6:23 but the gift of God is eternal *l*
8:38 convinced that neither death
nor *l*,
1Co 15:19 If only for this *l* we have hope
2Co 3: 6 letter kills, but the Spirit gives *l*.
Gal 2:20 The *l* I live in the body, I live
Eph 4: 1 I urge you to live a *l* worthy
Php 2:16 as you hold out the word of *l*—
Col 1:10 order that you may live a *l*
worthy
1Th 4:12 so that your daily *l* may win
1Ti 4: 8 for both the present *l* and the *l*
4:16 Watch your *l* and doctrine
closely.
6:19 hold of the *l* that is truly *l*.
2Ti 3:12 to live a godly *l* in Christ Jesus
will
Jas 1:12 crown of *l* that God has
promised
3:13 Let him show it by his good *l*,
1Pe 3:10 "Whoever would love *l*
2Pe 1: 3 given us everything we need for *l*
1Jn 3:14 we have passed from death to *l*,
5:11 has given us eternal *l*, and this *l*
is
Rev 13: 8 written in the book of *l* belonging
20:12 was opened, which is the book
of *l*.
21:27 written in the Lamb's book of *l*.
22: 2 side of the river stood the tree
of *l*,

LIFT (LIFTED)
Ps 121: 1 I *l* up my eyes to the hills—
134: 2 *L* up your hands in the sanctuary
La 3:41 Let us *l* up our hearts and our
1Ti 2: 8 everywhere to *l* up holy hands

LIFTED (LIFT)
Ps 40: 2 He *l* me out of the slimy pit,
Jn 3:14 Moses *l* up the snake in the
desert,
12:32 when I am *l* up from the earth,

LIGHT (ENLIGHTENED)
Ge 1: 3 "Let there be *l*," and there was *l*.
2Sa 22:29 LORD turns my darkness into *l*.
Job 38:19 "What is the way to the abode
of *l*?
Ps 4: 6 Let the *l* of your face shine upon
us
19: 8 giving *l* to the eyes.
27: 1 LORD is my *l* and my salvation—
56:13 God in the *l* of life.
76: 4 You are resplendent with *l*,
104: 2 He wraps himself in *l*
119:105 and a *l* for my path.

Ps 119:130 The unfolding of your words gives *l*;
Isa 2: 5 let us walk in the *l* of the LORD.
    9: 2 have seen a great *l*;
   49: 6 also make you a *l* for the Gentiles,
Mt 4:16 have seen a great *l*;
    5:16 let your *l* shine before men,
   11:30 yoke is easy and my burden is *l*."
Jn 3:19 but men loved darkness instead of *l*
    8:12 he said, "I am the *l* of the world.
2Co 4: 6 made his *l* shine in our hearts
    6:14 Or what fellowship can *l* have
   11:14 masquerades as an angel of *l*.
1Ti 6:16 and who lives in unapproachable *l*,
1Pe 2: 9 of darkness into his wonderful *l*.
1Jn 1: 5 God is *l*; in him there is no
    1: 7 But if we walk in the *l*,
Rev 21:23 for the glory of God gives it *l*,

LIGHTNING
Da 10: 6 his face like *l*, his eyes like flaming
Mt 24:27 For as the *l* that comes from the east
   28: 3 His appearance was like *l*,

LIKENESS
Ge 1:26 man in our image, in our *l*,
Ps 17:15 I will be satisfied with seeing your *l*
Isa 52:14 his form marred beyond human *l*—
Ro 8: 3 Son in the *l* of sinful man
    8:29 to be conformed to the *l* of his Son,
2Co 3:18 his *l* with ever-increasing glory,
Php 2: 7 being made in human *l*.
Jas 3: 9 who have been made in God's *l*.

LILIES
Lk 12:27 "Consider how the *l* grow.

LION
Isa 11: 7 and the *l* will eat straw like the ox.
1Pe 5: 8 around like a roaring *l* looking
Rev 5: 5 See, the *L* of the tribe of Judah,

LIPS
Ps 8: 2 From the *l* of children and infants
   34: 1 his praise will always be on my *l*.
  119:171 May my *l* overflow with praise,
Pr 13: 3 He who guards his *l* guards his life,
   27: 2 someone else, and not your own *l*.
Isa 6: 5 For I am a man of unclean *l*,
Mt 21:16 " 'From the *l* of children
Col 3: 8 and filthy language from your *l*.

LISTEN (LISTENING LISTENS)
Dt 30:20 *l* to his voice, and hold fast to him.
Pr 1: 5 let the wise *l* and add
Jn 10:27 My sheep *l* to my voice; I know
Jas 1:19 Everyone should be quick to *l*,
    1:22 Do not merely *l* to the word,

LISTENING (LISTEN)
1Sa 3: 9 Speak, LORD, for your servant is *l*
Pr 18:13 He who answers before *l*—

LISTENS (LISTEN)
Pr 12:15 but a wise man *l* to advice.

LIVE (ALIVE LIFE LIVES LIVING)
Ex 20:12 so that you may *l* long
   33:20 for no one may see me and *l*."
Dt 8: 3 to teach you that man does not *l*
Job 14:14 If a man dies, will he *l* again?
Ps 119:175 Let me *l* that I may praise you,
Isa 55: 3 hear me, that your soul may *l*.
Eze 37: 3 can these bones *l*?" I said,
Hab 2: 4 but the righteous will *l* by his faith
Mt 4: 4 'Man does not *l* on bread alone,

Ac 17:24 does not *l* in temples built by hands
   17:28 'For in him we *l* and move
Ro 1:17 "The righteous will *l* by faith."
2Co 5: 7 We *l* by faith, not by sight.
Gal 2:20 The life *l* *l* in the body, I *l* by faith
    5:25 Since we *l* by the Spirit, let us keep
Php 1:21 to *l* is Christ and to die is gain.
1Th 5:13 *l* in peace with each other.
2Ti 3:12 who wants to *l* a godly life
Heb 12:14 Make every effort to *l* in peace
1Pe 1:17 *l* your lives as strangers here

LIVES (LIVE)
Job 19:25 I know that my Redeemer *l*,
Isa 57:15 he who *l* forever, whose name is
Da 3:28 to give up their *l* rather than serve
Jn 14:17 for he *l* with you and will be in you.
Ro 7:18 I know that nothing good *l* in me,
   14: 7 For none of us *l* to himself alone
1Co 3:16 and that God's Spirit *l* in you?
Gal 2:20 I no longer live, but Christ *l* in me.
Heb 13: 5 Keep your *l* free from the love
2Pe 3:11 You ought to live holy and godly *l*
1Jn 3:16 to lay down our *l* for our brothers.
    4:16 Whoever *l* in love *l* in God,

LIVING (LIVE)
Ge 2: 7 and man became a *l* being.
Jer 2:13 the spring of *l* water,
Mt 22:32 the God of the dead but of the *l*."
Jn 7:38 streams of *l* water will flow
Ro 12: 1 to offer your bodies as *l* sacrifices,
Heb 4:12 For the word of God is *l* and active.
   10:31 to fall into the hands of the *l* God.
Rev 1:18 I am the *L* One; I was dead,

LOAD
Gal 6: 5 for each one should carry his own *l*.

LOCUSTS
Mt 3: 4 His food was *l* and wild honey.

LOFTY
Ps 139: 6 too *l* for me to attain.
Isa 57:15 is what the high and *l* One says—

LONELY
Ps 68: 6 God sets the *l* in families,

LONG (LENGTH LONGED LONGING LONGS)
1Ki 18:21 "How *l* will you waver
Jn 9: 4 As *l* as it is day, we must do
Eph 3:18 to grasp how wide and *l* and high
1Pe 1:12 Even angels *l* to look

LONGED (LONG)
Mt 13:17 righteous men *l* to see what you see
   23:37 how often I have *l*
2Ti 4: 8 to all who have *l* for his appearing.

LONGING (LONG)
Pr 13:19 A *l* fulfilled is sweet to the soul,
2Co 5: 2 *l* to be clothed with our heavenly

LONGS (LONG)
Isa 30:18 Yet the LORD *l* to be gracious

LOOK (LOOKING LOOKS)
Dt 4:29 you will find him if you *l* for him
Job 31: 1 not to *l* lustfully at a girl.
Ps 34: 5 Those who *l* to him are radiant;
Pr 4:25 Let your eyes *l* straight ahead,
Isa 60: 5 Then you will *l* and be radiant,

Hab 1:13 Your eyes are too pure to *l* on evil;
Zec 12:10 They will *l* on me, the one they
Mk 13:21 'L, here is the Christ!' or, 'L,
Lk 24:39 *L* at my hands and my feet.
Jn 1:36 he said, "L, the Lamb of God!"
    4:35 open your eyes and *l* at the fields!
   19:37 "They will *l* on the one they have
Jas 1:27 to *l* after orphans and widows
1Pe 1:12 long to *l* into these things.

LOOKING (LOOK)
2Co 10: 7 You are *l* only on the surface
Rev 5: 6 I saw a Lamb, *l* as if it had been

LOOKS (LOOK)
1Sa 16: 7 Man *l* at the outward appearance,
Lk 9:62 and *l* back is fit for service
Php 2:21 For everyone *l* out

LORD† (LORD'S† LORDING)
Ne 4:14 Remember the *L*, who is great
Job 28:28 'The fear of the *L*— that is wisdom,
Ps 54: 4 the *L* is the one who sustains me.
   62:12 and that you, O *L*, are loving.
   86: 5 You are forgiving and good, O *L*,
  110: 1 The LORD says to my *L*:
  147: 5 Great is our *L* and mighty in power
Isa 6: 1 I saw the *L* seated on a throne,
Da 9: 4 "O *L*, the great and awesome God,
Mt 3: 3 'Prepare the way for the *L*,
    4: 7 'Do not put the *L* your God
    7:21 "Not everyone who says to me, 'L,
   22:37 " 'Love the *L* your God
   22:44 For he says, " 'The *L* said to my *L*:
Mk 12:11 the *L* has done this,
   12:29 the *L* our God, the *L* is one.
Lk 2: 9 glory of the *L* shone around them,
    6:46 "Why do you call me, 'L, L,'
   10:27 " 'Love the *L* your God
Ac 2:21 on the name of the *L* will be saved.'
   16:31 replied, "Believe in the *L* Jesus,
Ro 10: 9 with your mouth, "Jesus is *L*,"
   10:13 on the name of the *L* will be saved
   12:11 your spiritual fervor, serving the *L*.
   14: 8 we live to the *L*; and if we die,
1Co 1:31 Let him who boasts boast in the *L*."
    3: 5 the *L* has assigned to each his task.
    7:34 to be devoted to the *L* in both body
   10: 9 We should not test the *L*,
   11:23 For I received from the *L* what I
   12: 3 "Jesus is *L*," except by the Holy
   15:57 victory through our *L* Jesus Christ.
   16:22 If anyone does not love the *L*—
2Co 3:17 Now the *L* is the Spirit,
    8: 5 they gave themselves first to the *L*
   10:17 Let him who boasts boast in the *L*."
Gal 6:14 in the cross of our *L* Jesus Christ,
Eph 4: 5 one *L*, one faith, one baptism;
    5:10 and find out what pleases the *L*.
    5:19 make music in your heart to the *L*,
Php 2:11 confess that Jesus Christ is *L*,
    3: 1 my brothers, rejoice in the *L*!
    4: 4 Rejoice in the *L* always.
Col 2: 6 as you received Christ Jesus as *L*,
    3:17 do it all in the name of the *L* Jesus,
    3:23 as working for the *L*, not for men,
    4:17 work you have received in the *L*."

1Th 3:12 May the *L* make your love increase
     5: 2 day of the *L* will come like a thief
     5:23 at the coming of our *L* Jesus Christ.
2Th 2: 1 the coming of our *L* Jesus Christ
2Ti 2:19 "The *L* knows those who are his,"
Heb 12:14 holiness no one will see the *L*.
    13: 6 *L* is my helper; I will not be afraid.
Jas 4:10 Humble yourselves before the *L*,
1Pe 1:25 the word of the *L* stands forever."
     2: 3 you have tasted that the *L* is good.
     3:15 in your hearts set apart Christ as *L*.
2Pe 1:16 and coming of our *L* Jesus Christ,
     2: 1 the sovereign *L* who bought
     3: 9 The *L* is not slow in keeping his
Jude :14 the *L* is coming with thousands
Rev 4: 8 holy, holy is the *L* God Almighty,
     4:11 You are worthy, our *L* and God,
    17:14 he is *L* of lords and King of kings—
    22:20 Come, *L* Jesus.

LORD'S† (LORD†)
Ac 21:14 and said, "The *L* will be done."
1Co 10:26 "The earth is the *L*, and everything
    11:26 you proclaim the *L* death
2Co 3:18 faces all reflect the *L* glory,
2Ti 2:24 And the *L* servant must not quarrel
Jas 4:15 you ought to say, "If it is the *L* will,

LORDING* (LORD†)
1Pe 5: 3 not *I* it over those entrusted to you,

LORD‡ (LORD'S‡)
Ge 2: 4 When the *L* God made the earth
     2: 7 the *L* God formed the man
     3:21 The *L* God made garments of skin
     7:16 Then the *L* shut him in.
    15: 6 Abram believed the *L*,
    18:14 Is anything too hard for the *L*?
    31:49 "May the *L* keep watch
Ex   3: 2 the angel of the *L* appeared to him
     9:12 the *L* hardened Pharaoh's heart
    14:30 That day the *L* saved Israel
    20: 2 "I am the *L* your God, who
    33:11 The *L* would speak to Moses face
    40:34 glory of the *L* filled the tabernacle.
Lev 19: 2 'Be holy because I, the *L* your God,
Nu   8: 5 *L* said to Moses: "Take the Levites
    14:21 glory of the *L* fills the whole earth,
Dt   2: 7 forty years the *L* your God has
     5: 9 the *L* your God, am a jealous God,
     6: 4 The *L* our God, the *L* is one.
     6: 5 Love the *L* your God
     6:16 Do not test the *L* your God
    10:14 To the *L* your God belong
    10:17 For the *L* your God is God of gods
    11: 1 Love the *L* your God and keep his
    28: 1 If you fully obey the *L* your God
    30:16 today to love the *L* your God,
    30:20 For the *L* is your life, and he will
    31: 6 for the *L* your God goes with you;
Jos 22: 5 to love the *L* your God, to walk
    24:15 my household, we will serve the *L*

1Sa 1:28 So now I give him to the *L*.
     2: 2 "There is no one holy like the *L*;
     7:12 "Thus far has the *L* helped us."
    12:22 his great name the *L* will not reject
    15:22 "Does the *L* delight
2Sa 22: 2 "The *L* is my rock, my fortress
1Ki 2: 3 and observe what the *L* your God
     8:11 the glory of the *L* filled his temple.
     8:61 fully committed to the *L* our God,
    18:21 If the *L* is God, follow him;
2Ki 13:23 But the *L* was gracious to them
1Ch 16: 8 Give thanks to the *L*, call
    16:23 Sing to the *L*, all the earth;
    28: 9 for the *L* searches every heart
    29:11 O *L*, is the greatness and the power
2Ch 5:14 the glory of the *L* filled the temple
    16: 9 of the *L* range throughout the earth
    19: 6 judging for man but for the *L*,
    30: 9 for the *L* your God is gracious
Ne   1: 5 Then I said: "O *L*, God of heaven,
Job 1:21 *L* gave and the *L* has taken away;
    38: 1 the *L* answered Job out
    42: 9 and the *L* accepted Job's prayer.
Ps   1: 2 But his delight is in the law of the *L*
     9: 9 The *L* is a refuge for the oppressed,
    12: 6 And the words of the *L* are flawless
    16: 8 I have set the *L* always before me.
    18:30 the word of the *L* is flawless.
    19: 7 The law of the *L* is perfect,
    19:14 O *L*, my Rock and my Redeemer.
    23: 1 The *L* is my shepherd, I shall not be
    23: 6 I will dwell in the house of the *L*
    27: 1 The *L* is my light and my salvation
    27: 4 to gaze upon the beauty of the *L*
    29: 1 Ascribe to the *L*, O mighty ones,
    32: 2 whose sin the *L* does not count
    33:12 is the nation whose God is the *L*,
    33:18 But the eyes of the *L* are
    34: 3 Glorify the *L* with me;
    34: 7 The angel of the *L* encamps
    34: 8 Taste and see that the *L* is good;
    34:18 The *L* is close to the brokenhearted
    37: 4 Delight yourself in the *L*
    40: 1 I waited patiently for the *L*;
    47: 2 How awesome is the *L* Most High,
    48: 1 Great is the *L*, and most worthy
    55:22 Cast your cares on the *L*
    75: 8 In the hand of the *L* is a cup
    84:11 For the *L* God is a sun and shield;
    86:11 Teach me your way, O *L*,
    89: 5 heavens praise your wonders, O *L*,
    91: 2 I will say of the *L*, "He is my refuge
    95: 1 Come, let us sing for joy to the *L*;
    96: 1 Sing to the *L* a new song;
    98: 4 Shout for joy to the *L*, all the earth,
   100: 1 Shout for joy to the *L*, all the earth.
   103: 1 Praise the *L*, O my soul;
   103: 8 The *L* is compassionate
   104: 1 O *L* my God, you are very great!
   107: 8 to the *L* for his unfailing love
   110: 1 The *L* says to my Lord:
   113: 4 *L* is exalted over all the nations,
   115: 1 Not to us, O *L*, not to us

Ps 116: 15 Precious in the sight of the *L*
   118: 1 Give thanks to the *L*, for he is good
   118: 24 This is the day the *L* has made;
   121: 2 My help comes from the *L*,
   121: 5 The *L* watches over you—
   125: 2 so the *L* surrounds his people
   127: 1 Unless the *L* builds the house,
   127: 3 Sons are a heritage from the *L*,
   130: 3 If you, O *L*, kept a record of sins,
   135: 6 The *L* does whatever pleases him,
   136: 1 Give thanks to the *L*, for he is good
   139: 1 O *L*, you have searched me
   144: 3 O *L*, what is man that you care
   145: 3 Great is the *L* and most worthy
   145: 18 The *L* is near to all who call on him
Pr   1: 7 The fear of the *L* is the beginning
     3: 5 Trust in the *L* with all your heart
     3: 9 Honor the *L* with your wealth,
     3:12 the *L* disciplines those he loves,
     3:19 By wisdom the *L* laid the earth's
     5:21 are in full view of the *L*,
     6:16 There are six things the *L* hates,
    10:27 The fear of the *L* adds length to life
    11: 1 The *L* abhors dishonest scales,
    12:22 The *L* detests lying lips,
    14:26 He who fears the *L* has a secure
    15: 3 The eyes of the *L* are everywhere,
    16: 2 but motives are weighed by the *L*.
    16: 4 The *L* works out everything
    16: 9 but the *L* determines his steps.
    16:33 but its every decision is from the *L*.
    18:10 The name of the *L* is a strong tower
    18:22 and receives favor from the *L*.
    19:14 but a prudent wife is from the *L*.
    19:17 to the poor lends to the *L*,
    21: 3 to the *L* than sacrifice.
    21:30 that can succeed against the *L*.
    21:31 but victory rests with the *L*.
    22: 2 The *L* is the Maker of them all.
    24:18 or the *L* will see and disapprove
    31:30 a woman who fears the *L* is
Isa 6: 3 holy, holy is the *L* Almighty;
    11: 2 The Spirit of the *L* will rest on him
    11: 9 full of the knowledge of the *L*
    12: 2 The *L*, the *L*, is my strength
    24: 1 the *L* is going to lay waste the earth
    25: 8 The Sovereign *L* will wipe away
    29:15 to hide their plans from the *L*,
    33: 6 the fear of the *L* is the key
    35:10 the ransomed of the *L* will return.
    40: 5 the glory of the *L* will be revealed,
    40: 7 the breath of the *L* blows on them.
    40:10 the Sovereign *L* comes with power,
    40:28 The *L* is the everlasting God,
    40:31 but those who hope in the *L*
    42: 8 "I am the *L*; that is my name!
    43:11 I, even I, am the *L*,
    44:24 I am the *L*,
    45: 5 I am the *L*, and there is no other;
    45:21 Was it not I, the *L*?
    51:11 The ransomed of the *L* will return.
    53: 6 and the *L* has laid on him
    53:10 and the will of the *L* will prosper
    55: 6 Seek the *L* while he may be found;
    58: 8 of the *L* will be your rear guard.
    58:11 The *L* will guide you always;
    59: 1 the arm of the *L* is not too short
    61: 3 a planting of the *L*

---

†This entry represents the translation of the Hebrew name for God, *Yahweh,* always indicated in the NIV by Lord. For Lord, see the concordance entries **LORD**† and **LORD'S**†.

Isa   61:10 I delight greatly in the *L*;
Jer   1: 9 Then the *L* reached out his hand
      9:24 I am the *L*, who exercises kindness,
     16:19 O *L*, my strength and my fortress,
      17: 7 is the man who trusts in the *L*,
La   3:40 and let us return to the *L*.
Eze   1:28 of the likeness of the glory of the *L*.
Hos   1: 7 horsemen, but by the *L* their God."
      3: 5 They will come trembling to the *L*
      6: 1 "Come, let us return to the *L*.
Joel   2: 1 for the day of the *L* is coming.
      2:11 The day of the *L* is great;
      3:14 For the day of the *L* is near
Am   5:18 long for the day of the *L*?
Jnh   1: 3 But Jonah ran away from the *L*
Mic   4: 2 up to the mountain of the *L*,
      6: 8 And what does the *L* require of you
Na   1: 2 The *L* takes vengeance on his foes
      1: 3 The *L* is slow to anger
Hab   2:14 knowledge of the glory of the *L*,
      2:20 But the *L* is in his holy temple;
Zep   3:17 The *L* your God is with you,
Zec   1:17 and the *L* will again comfort Zion
      9:16 The *L* their God will save them
     14: 5 Then the *L* my God will come,
     14: 9 The *L* will be king
Mal   4: 5 and dreadful day of the *L* comes.

LORD'S† (LORD†)

Ex   34:34 he entered the *L* presence
Nu   14:41 you disobeying the *L* command?
Dt   6:18 is right and good in the *L* sight,
     32: 9 For the *L* portion is his people,
Jos   21:45 Not one of all the *L* good promises
Ps   24: 1 The earth is the *L*, and everything
     32:10 but the *L* unfailing love
     89: 1 of the *L* great love forever;
   103: 17 *L* love is with those who fear him,
Pr   3:11 do not despise the *L* discipline
Isa   24:14 west they acclaim the *L* majesty.
     62: 3 of splendor in the *L* hand,
Jer   48:10 lax in doing the *L* work!
La   3:22 of the *L* great love we are not
Mic   4: 1 of the *L* temple will be established

LOSE (LOSES LOSS LOST)

1Sa   17:32 "Let no one *l* heart on account
Mt   10:39 Whoever finds his life will *l* it,
Lk   9:25 and yet *l* or forfeit his very self?
Jn   6:39 that I shall *l* none of all that he has
Heb   12: 3 will not grow weary and *l* heart.
     12: 5 do not *l* heart when he rebukes you

LOSES (LOSE)

Mt   5:13 But if the salt *l* its saltiness,
Lk   15: 4 you has a hundred sheep and *l* one
     15: 8 has ten silver coins and *l* one.

LOSS (LOSE)

Ro   11:12 and their *l* means riches
1Co   3:15 he will suffer *l*; he himself will be
Php   3: 8 *l* consider everything a *l* compared

LOST (LOSE)

Ps   73: 2 I had nearly *l* my foothold.
Jer   50: 6 "My people have been *l* sheep;
Eze   34: 4 the strays or searched for the *l*.
     34:16 for the *l* and bring back the strays.
Mt   18:14 any of these little ones should be *l*.
Lk   15: 4 go after the *l* sheep until he finds it?
     15: 6 with me; I have found my *l* sheep.'

Lk   15: 9 with me; I have found my *l* coin.'
     15:24 is alive again; he was *l* and is found
     19:10 to seek and to save what was *l*."
Php   3: 8 for whose sake I have *l* all things.

LOT (LOTS)

Nephew of Abraham (Ge 11:27; 12:5). Chose to live in Sodom (Ge 13). Rescued from four kings (Ge 14). Rescued from Sodom (Ge 19:1-29; 2Pe 2:7). Fathered Moab and Ammon by his daughters (Ge 19:30-38).

Est   3: 7 the *l*) in the presence of Haman
     9:24 the *l*) for their ruin and destruction.
Pr   16:33 The *l* is cast into the lap,
     18:18 Casting the *l* settles disputes
Ecc   3:22 his work, because that is his *l*.
Ac   1:26 Then they drew lots, and the *l* fell

LOTS (LOT)

Ps   22:18 and cast *l* for my clothing.
Mt   27:35 divided up his clothes by casting *l*.

LOVE (BELOVED LOVED LOVELY LOVER LOVERS LOVES LOVING)

Ge   22: 2 your only son, Isaac, whom you *l*,
Ex   15:13 "In your unfailing *l* you will lead
     20: 6 showing *l* to a thousand generations
     20: 6 of those who *l* me
     34: 6 abounding in *l* and faithfulness,
Lev   19:18 but *l* your neighbor as yourself.
     19:34 *l* him as yourself,
Nu   14:18 abounding in *l* and forgiving sin
Dt   5:10 showing *l* to a thousand generations
     5:10 of those who *l* me
     6: 5 *L* the Lord your God
     7:13 He will *l* you and bless you
   10:12 to walk in all his ways, to *l* him,
   11:13 to *l* the Lord your God
     13: 6 wife you *l*, or your closest friend
     30: 6 so that you may *l* him
Jos   22: 5 to *l* the Lord your God, to walk
1Ki   3: 3 Solomon showed his *l*
     8:23 you who keep your covenant of *l*
2Ch   5:13 his *l* endures forever."
Ne   1: 5 covenant of *l* with those who *l* him
Ps   18: 1 I *l* you, O Lord, my strength.
     23: 6 Surely goodness and *l* will follow
     25: 6 O Lord, your great mercy and *l*,
     31:16 save me in your unfailing *l*.
     32:10 but the Lord's unfailing *l*
     33: 5 the earth is full of his unfailing *l*.
     33:18 whose hope is in his unfailing *l*,
     36: 5 Your *l*, O Lord, reaches
     36: 7 How priceless is your unfailing *l*!
     45: 7 You *l* righteousness and hate
     51: 1 according to your unfailing *l*;
     57:10 For great is your *l*, reaching
     63: 3 Because your *l* is better than life,
     66:20 or withheld his *l* from me!
     70: 4 may those who *l* your salvation
     77: 8 Has his unfailing *l* vanished forever
     85: 7 Show us your unfailing *l*, O Lord
     85:10 *L* and faithfulness meet together;
     86:13 For great is your *l* toward me;
     89: 1 of the Lord's great *l* forever;
     89:33 but I will not take my *l* from him,
     92: 2 to proclaim your *l* in the morning
     94:18 your *l*, O Lord, supported me.
   100: 5 is good and his *l* endures forever;
   101: 1 I will sing of your *l* and justice;
   103: 4 crowns you with *l* and compassion.
   103: 8 slow to anger, abounding in *l*.
   103: 11 so great is his *l* for those who fear
   107: 8 to the Lord for his unfailing *l*
   108: 4 For great is your *l*, higher
   116: 1 I *l* the Lord, for he heard my

Ps   118: 1 his *l* endures forever.
   119: 47 because I *l* them.
   119: 64 The earth is filled with your *l*,
   119: 76 May your unfailing *l* be my
   119: 97 Oh, how I *l* your law!
   119:119 therefore I *l* your statutes.
   119:124 your servant according to your *l*
   119:132 to those who *l* your name.
   119:159 O Lord, according to your *l*.
   119:163 but I *l* your law.
   119:165 peace have they who *l* your law,
   122: 6 "May those who *l* you be secure.
   130: 7 for with the Lord is unfailing *l*
   136: 1 -26 His *l* endures forever.
   143: 8 of your unfailing *l*,
   145: 8 slow to anger and rich in *l*.
   145: 20 over all who *l* him,
   147: 11 who put their hope in his unfailing *l*
Pr   3: 3 Let *l* and faithfulness never leave
     4: 6 *l* her, and she will watch over you.
     5:19 you ever be captivated by her *l*.
     8:17 I *l* those who *l* me,
     9: 8 rebuke a wise man and he will *l* you
   10:12 but *l* covers over all wrongs.
   14:22 those who plan what is good find *l*
   15:17 of vegetables where there is *l*
   17: 9 over an offense promotes *l*,
   19:22 What a man desires is unfailing *l*,
   20: 6 claims to have unfailing *l*,
   20:13 Do not *l* sleep or you will grow
   20:28 through *l* his throne is made secure
   21:21 who pursues righteousness and *l*
   27: 5 rebuke than hidden *l*.
Ecc   9: 6 Their *l*, their hate
     9: 9 life with your wife, whom you *l*,
SS   2: 4 and his banner over me is *l*.
     8: 6 for *l* is as strong as death,
     8: 7 Many waters cannot quench *l*;
     8: 7 all the wealth of his house for *l*,
Isa   5: 1 I will sing for the one I *l*
   16: 5 In *l* a throne will be established;
   38:17 In your *l* you kept me
   54:10 yet my unfailing *l* for you will not
   55: 3 my faithful *l* promised to David.
   61: 8 "For I, the Lord, *l* justice;
   63: 9 In his *l* and mercy he redeemed
Jer   5:31 and my people *l* it this way.
   31: 3 you with an everlasting *l*;
   32:18 You show *l* to thousands
   33:11 his *l* endures forever."
La   3:22 of the Lord's great *l* we are not
     3:32 so great is his unfailing *l*,
Eze   33:32 more than one who sings *l* songs
Da   9: 4 covenant of *l* with all who *l* him
Hos   2:19 in *l* and compassion.
     3: 1 Go, show your *l* to your wife again,
   11: 4 with ties of *l*;
   12: 6 maintain *l* and justice,
Joel   2:13 slow to anger and abounding in *l*,
Am   5:15 Hate evil, *l* good;
Mic   3: 2 you who hate good and *l* evil;
     6: 8 To act justly and to *l* mercy
Zep   3:17 he will quiet you with his *l*,
Zec   8:19 Therefore *l* truth and peace."
Mt   3:17 "This is my Son, whom I *l*;
     5:44 *L* your enemies and pray
     6:24 he will hate the one and *l* the other,
     17: 5 "This is my Son, whom I *l*;
     19:19 and '*l* your neighbor as yourself.' "
     22:37 " '*L* the Lord your God
Lk   6:32 Even 'sinners' *l* those who *l* them.
     7:42 which of them will *l* him more?"
   20:13 whom I *l*; perhaps they will respect
Jn   13:34 I give you: *L* one another.
   13:35 disciples, if you *l* one another."
   14:15 "If you *l* me, you will obey what I
   15:13 Greater *l* has no one than this,

Jn 15:17 This is my command: L each other.
21:15 do you truly l me more than these
Ro 5: 5 because God has poured out his l
5: 8 God demonstrates his own l for us
8:28 for the good of those who l him,
8:35 us from the l of Christ?
8:39 us from the l of God that is
12: 9 L must be sincere.
12:10 to one another in brotherly l
13: 8 continuing debt to l one another,
13: 9 "L your neighbor as yourself."
13:10 Therefore l is the fulfillment
13:10 L does no harm to its neighbor.
1Co 2: 9 prepared for those who l him"—
8: 1 Knowledge puffs up, but l builds up
13: 1 have not l, I am only a resounding
13: 2 but have not l, I am nothing.
13: 3 but have not l, I gain nothing.
13: 4 Love is patient, l is kind.
13: 4 L is patient, love is kind.
13: 6 L does not delight in evil
13: 8 L never fails.
13:13 But the greatest of these is l.
13:13 three remain: faith, hope and l.
14: 1 way of l and eagerly desire spiritual
16:14 Do everything in l.
2Co 5:14 For Christ's l compels us,
8: 8 sincerity of your l by comparing it
8:24 show these men the proof of your l
Gal 5: 6 is faith expressing itself through l.
5:13 rather, serve one another in l.
5:22 But the fruit of the Spirit is l, joy,
Eph 1: 4 In l he predestined us
2: 4 But because of his great l for us,
3:17 being rooted and established in l,
3:18 and high and deep is the l of Christ,
3:19 and to know this l that surpasses
4: 2 bearing with one another in l.
4:15 Instead, speaking the truth in l,
5: 2 loved children and live a life of l,
5:25 l your wives, just as Christ loved
5:28 husbands ought to l their wives
5:33 each one of you also must l his wife
Php 1: 9 that your l may abound more
2: 2 having the same l, being one
Col 1: 5 l that spring from the hope that is
2: 2 in heart and united in l,
3:14 And over all these virtues put on l,
3:19 l your wives and do not be harsh
1Th 1: 3 your labor prompted by l,
4: 9 taught by God to l each other.
5: 8 on faith and l as a breastplate,
2Th 3: 5 direct your hearts into God's l
1Ti 1: 5 The goal of this command is l,
2:15 l and holiness with propriety.
4:12 in life, in l, in faith and in purity.
6:10 For the l of money is a root
6:11 faith, l, endurance and gentleness.
2Ti 1: 7 of power, of l and of self-discipline.
2:22 and pursue righteousness, faith, l,
3:10 faith, patience, l, endurance,
Tit 2: 4 women to l their husbands
Phm : 9 yet I appeal to you on the basis of l.
Heb 6:10 and the l you have shown him
10:24 may spur one another on toward l
13: 5 free from the l of money
Jas 1:12 promised to those who l him.
2: 5 he promised those who l him?
2: 8 "L your neighbor as yourself,"

1Pe 1:22 the truth so that you have sincere l
1:22 l one another deeply,
2:17 L the brotherhood of believers,
3: 8 be sympathetic, l as brothers,
3:10 "Whoever would l life
4: 8 Above all, l each other deeply,
4: 8 l covers over a multitude of sins.
5:14 Greet one another with a kiss of l.
2Pe 1: 7 and to brotherly kindness, l.
1:17 "This is my Son, whom I l;
1Jn 2: 5 God's l is truly made complete
2:15 Do not l the world or anything
3: 1 How great is the l the Father has
3:10 anyone who does not l his brother.
3:11 We should l one another.
3:14 Anyone who does not l remains
3:16 This is how we know what l is:
3:18 let us not l with words or tongue
3:23 to l one another as he commanded
4: 7 Dear friends, let us l one another,
4: 7 for l comes from God.
4: 8 Whoever does not l does not know
4: 9 This is how God showed his l
4:10 This is l: not that we loved God,
4:11 we also ought to l one another.
4:12 and his l is made complete in us.
4:16 God is l.
4:16 Whoever lives in l lives in God,
4:17 l is made complete among us
4:18 But perfect l drives out fear,
4:19 l because he first loved us.
4:20 If anyone says, "I l God,"
4:21 loves God must also l his brother.
5: 2 we know that we l the children
5: 3 This is l for God: to obey his
2Jn : 5 I ask that we l one another.
: 6 his command is that you walk in l.
: 6 this is l: that we walk in obedience
Jude :12 men are blemishes at your l feasts,
:21 Keep yourselves in God's l
Rev 2: 4 You have forsaken your first l.
3:19 Those whom I l I rebuke
12:11 they did not l their lives so much

LOVED (LOVE)
Ge 24:67 she became his wife, and he l her;
29:30 and he l Rachel more than Leah.
37: 3 Now Israel l Joseph more than any
Dt 7: 8 But it was because the LORD l you
1Sa 1: 5 a double portion because he l her,
20:17 because he l him as he l himself.
Ps 44: 3 light of your face, for you l them.
Jer 2: 2 how as a bride you l me
31: 3 "I have l you with an everlasting
Hos 2:23 to the one I called 'Not my l one.'
3: 1 though she is l by another
9:10 became as vile as the thing they l.
11: 1 "When Israel was a child, I l him,
Mal 1: 2 "But you ask, 'How have you l us?'
Mk 12: 6 left to send, a son, whom he l.
Jn 3:16 so l the world that he gave his one
3:19 but men l darkness instead of light
11: 5 Jesus l Martha and her sister
12:43 for they l praise from men more
13: 1 Having l his own who were
13:23 the disciple whom Jesus l,
13:34 As I have l you, so you must love
14:21 He who loves me will be l

Jn 15: 9 the Father has l me, so have I l you.
15:12 Love each other as I have l you.
19:26 the disciple whom he l standing
Ro 8:37 conquerors through him who l us.
9:13 "Jacob I l, but Esau I hated."
9:25 her 'my l one' who is not my l one,"
11:28 they are l on account
Gal 2:20 who l me and gave himself for me.
Eph 5: 2 as Christ l us and gave himself up
5:25 just as Christ l the church
2Th 2:16 who l us and by his grace gave us
2Ti 4:10 for Demas, because he l this world,
Heb 1: 9 You have l righteousness
1Jn 4:10 This is love: not that we l God,
4:11 Dear friends, since God so l us,
4:19 We love because he first l us.

LOVELY (LOVE)
Ps 84: 1 How l is your dwelling place,
SS 2:14 and your face is l.
5:16 he is altogether l.
Php 4: 8 whatever is l, whatever is

LOVER (LOVE)
SS 2:16 Beloved My l is mine and I am his;
7:10 I belong to my l,
1Ti 3: 3 not quarrelsome, not a l of money.

LOVERS (LOVE)
2Ti 3: 2 People will be l of themselves,
3: 3 without self-control, brutal, not l
3: 4 l of pleasure rather than l of God—

LOVES (LOVE)
Ps 11: 7 he l justice;
33: 5 The LORD l righteousness
34:12 Whoever of you l life
91:14 Because he l me," says the LORD.
127: 2 for he grants sleep to those he l.
Pr 3:12 the LORD disciplines those he l,
12: 1 Whoever l discipline l knowledge,
13:24 he who l him is careful
17:17 A friend l at all times,
17:19 He who l a quarrel l sin;
22:11 He who l a pure heart and whose
Ecc 5:10 whoever l wealth is never satisfied
Mt 10:37 anyone who l his son or daughter
Lk 7:47 has been forgiven little l little."
Jn 3:35 Father l the Son and has placed
10:17 reason my Father l me is that I lay
12:25 The man who l his life will lose it,
14:21 obeys them, he is the one who l me.
14:23 Jesus replied, "If anyone l me,
Ro 13: 8 for he who l his fellowman has
2Co 9: 7 for God l a cheerful giver.
Eph 5:28 He who l his wife l himself.
5:33 must love his wife as he l himself,
Heb 12: 6 the Lord disciplines those he l,
1Jn 2:10 Whoever l his brother lives
2:15 If anyone l the world, the love
4: 7 Everyone who l has been born
4:21 Whoever l God must also love his
5: 1 who l the father l his child
3Jn : 9 but Diotrephes, who l to be first,
Rev 1: 5 To him who l us and has freed us

LOVING (LOVE)
Ps 25:10 All the ways of the LORD are l
62:12 and that you, O Lord, are l.
145:17 and l toward all he has made.

Heb 13: 1 Keep on *l* each other as
brothers.
1Jn 5: 2 by *l* God and carrying out his

LOWLY
Job 5:11 The *l* he sets on high,
Pr 29:23 but a man of *l* spirit gains
honor.
Isa 57:15 also with him who is contrite
and *l*
Eze 21:26 *l* will be exalted and the exalted
1Co 1:28 He chose the *l* things of this
world

LUKE*
Co-worker with Paul (Col 4:14; 2Ti 4:11;
Phm 24).

LUKEWARM*
Rev 3:16 So, because you are *l*— neither
hot

LUST
Pr 6:25 Do not *l* in your heart
Col 3: 5 sexual immorality, impurity, *l,*
1Th 4: 5 not in passionate *l* like the
heathen,
1Jn 2:16 the *l* of his eyes and the
boasting

LYING (LIE)
Pr 6:17 a *l* tongue,
26:28 A *l* tongue hates those it hurts,

MACEDONIA
Ac 16: 9 "Come over to *M* and help us."

MADE (MAKE)
Ge 1:16 He also *m* the stars.
1:25 God *m* the wild animals
according
2:22 Then the LORD God *m* a woman
2Ki 19:15 You have *m* heaven and earth.
Ps 95: 5 The sea is his, for he *m* it,
100: 3 It is he who *m* us, and we are
his;
118: 24 This is the day the LORD has *m;*
139: 14 I am fearfully and wonderfully *m;*
Ecc 3:11 He has *m* everything beautiful
Mk 2:27 "The Sabbath was *m* for man,
Jn 1: 3 Through him all things were *m;*
Ac 17:24 "The God who *m* the world
Heb 1: 2 through whom he *m* the
universe.
Rev 14: 7 Worship him who *m* the
heavens,

MAGI
Mt 2: 1 *M* from the east came to
Jerusalem

MAGOG
Eze 38: 2 of the land of *M,* the chief prince
39: 6 I will send fire on *M*
Rev 20: 8 and *M*— to gather them for
battle.

MAIDEN
Pr 30:19 and the way of a man with a *m.*
Isa 62: 5 As a young man marries a *m,*
Jer 2:32 Does a *m* forget her jewelry,

MAIMED
Mt 18: 8 It is better for you to enter life *m*

MAJESTIC (MAJESTY)
Ex 15: 6 was *m* in power.
15:11 *m* in holiness,
Ps 8: 1 how *m* is your name in all the
earth
29: 4 the voice of the LORD is *m.*
111: 3 Glorious and *m* are his deeds,
SS 6:10 *m* as the stars in procession?
2Pe 1:17 came to him from the *M* Glory,

MAJESTY (MAJESTIC)
Ex 15: 7 In the greatness of your *m*
Dt 33:26 and on the clouds in his *m.*
1Ch 16:27 Splendor and *m* are before him;
Est 1: 4 the splendor and glory of his *m.*
Job 37:22 God comes in awesome *m.*

Job 40:10 and clothe yourself in honor
and *m*
Ps 45: 4 In your *m* ride forth victoriously
93: 1 The LORD reigns, he is robed
in *m*
110: 3 Arrayed in holy *m,*
145: 5 of the glorious splendor of
your *m,*
Isa 53: 2 or *m* to attract us to him,
Eze 31: 2 can be compared with you in *m?*
2Pe 1:16 but we were eyewitnesses of
his *m.*
Jude :25 only God our Savior be glory, *m,*

MAKE (MADE MAKER MAKES MAKING)
Ge 1:26 "Let us *m* man in our image,
2:18 I will *m* a helper suitable for
him."
12: 2 "I will *m* you into a great nation
Ex 22: 3 thief must certainly *m*
restitution,
Nu 6:25 the LORD *m* his face shine
Ps 108: 1 *m* music with all my soul.
Isa 14:14 I will *m* myself like the Most
High
29:16 "He did not *m* me"?
Jer 31:31 "when I will *m* a new covenant
Mt 3: 3 *m* straight paths for him.' "
28:19 and *m* disciples of all nations,
Mk 1:17 "and I will *m* you fishers of
men."
Lk 13:24 "*M* every effort to enter
14:23 country lanes and *m* them come
in,
Ro 14:19 *m* every effort to do what leads
2Co 5: 9 So we *m* it our goal to please
him,
Eph 4: 3 *M* every effort to keep the unity
Col 4: 5 *m* the most of every opportunity.
1Th 4:11 *M* it your ambition
Heb 4:11 *m* every effort to enter that rest,
12:14 *M* every effort to live in peace
2Pe 1: 5 *m* every effort to add
3:14 *m* every effort to be found
spotless,

MAKER (MAKE)
Job 4:17 Can a man be more pure than
his *M*
36: 3 I will ascribe justice to my *M.*
Ps 95: 6 kneel before the LORD our *M;*
Pr 22: 2 The LORD is the *M* of them all.
Isa 45: 9 to him who quarrels with his *M,*
54: 5 For your *M* is your husband—
Jer 10:16 for he is the *M* of all things,

MAKES (MAKE)
1Co 3: 7 but only God, who *m* things
grow.

MAKING (MAKE)
Ps 19: 7 *m* wise the simple.
Ecc 12:12 Of *m* many books there is no
end,
Jn 5:18 himself equal with God.
Eph 5:16 *m* the most of every opportunity,

MALE
Ge 1:27 *m* and female he created them.
Gal 3:28 slave nor free, *m* nor female,

MALICE (MALICIOUS)
Ro 1:29 murder, strife, deceit and *m.*
Col 3: 8 *m,* slander, and filthy language
1Pe 2: 1 rid yourselves of all *m*

MALICIOUS (MALICE)
Pr 26:24 A *m* man disguises himself
1Ti 3:11 not *m* talkers but temperate
6: 4 *m* talk, evil suspicions

MAN (MEN WOMAN WOMEN)
Ge 1:26 "Let us make *m* in our image,
2: 7 God formed the *m* from the dust
2:18 for the *m* to be alone
2:23 she was taken out of *m.*
9: 6 Whoever sheds the blood of *m,*
Dt 8: 3 *m* does not live on bread
1Sa 13:14 a *m* after his own heart
15:29 he is not a *m* that he
Job 14: 1 *M* born of woman is of few

Job 14:14 If a *m* dies, will he live
Ps 1: 1 Blessed is the *m* who does
8: 4 what is *m* that you are
119: 9 can a young *m* keep his
127: 5 Blessed is the *m* whose quiver
Pr 14:12 that seems right to a *m,*
30:19 way of a *m* with a maiden.
Isa 53: 3 a *m* of sorrows,
Mt 19: 5 a *m* will leave his father
Mk 8:36 What good is it for a *m*
Lk 4: 4 'M does not live on bread
Ro 5:12 entered the world through one *m*
1Co 11: 3 each *m* should have his own
11: 3 head of every *m* is Christ,
11: 3 head of woman is *m*
13:11 When I became a *m,*
Php 2: 8 found in appearance as a *m,*
1Ti 2: 5 the *m* Christ Jesus,
2:11 have authority over a *m;*
Heb 9:27 as *m* is destined to die

MANAGE
Jer 12: 5 how will you *m* in the thickets
1Ti 3: 4 He must *m* his own family well
3:12 one wife and must *m* his
children
5:14 to *m* their homes and to give

MANASSEH
1. Firstborn of Joseph (Ge 41:51; 46:20).
Blessed (Ge 48).
2. Son of Hezekiah; king of Judah (2Ki
21:1-18; 2Ch 33:1-20).

MANGER
Lk 2:12 in strips of cloth and lying in
a *m.*"

MANNA
Ex 16:31 people of Israel called the
bread *m.*
Dt 8:16 He gave you *m* to eat in the
desert,
Jn 6:49 Your forefathers ate the *m*
Rev 2:17 I will give some of the hidden *m.*

MANNER
1Co 11:27 in an unworthy *m* will be guilty
Php 1:27 conduct yourselves in a *m*
worthy

MARITAL* (MARRY)
Ex 21:10 of her food, clothing and *m*
rights.
Mt 5:32 except for *m* unfaithfulness,
19: 9 except for *m* unfaithfulness,
1Co 7: 3 husband should fulfill his *m* duty

MARK (MARKS)
Cousin of Barnabas (Col 4:10; 2Ti 4:11;
Phm 24; 1Pe 5:13), see JOHN.
Ge 4:15 Then the LORD put a *m* on Cain
Rev 13:16 to receive a *m* on his right hand

MARKS (MARK)
Jn 20:25 Unless I see the nail *m* in his
hands
Gal 6:17 bear on my body the *m* of
Jesus.

MARRED
Isa 52:14 his form *m* beyond human
likeness

MARRIAGE (MARRY)
Mt 22:30 neither marry nor be given in *m;*
24:38 marrying and giving in *m,*
Ro 7: 2 she is released from the law
of *m.*
Heb 13: 4 by all, and the *m* bed kept pure,

MARRIED (MARRY)
Ro 7: 2 by law a *m* woman is bound
1Co 7:27 Are you *m?* Do not seek a
divorce.
7:33 But a *m* man is concerned about
7:36 They should get *m.*

MARRIES (MARRY)
Mt 5:32 and anyone who *m* the divorced
19: 9 and *m* another woman commits

Lk   16:18 the man who *m* a divorced
            woman

MARRY (INTERMARRY MARITAL MARRIAGE MARRIED MARRIES)
Mt   22:30 resurrection people will
            neither *m*
1Co   7: 1 It is good for a man not to *m*.
       7: 9 control themselves, they
            should *m*,
1Ti   5:14 So I counsel younger widows
            to *m*,

MARTHA*
    Sister of Mary and Lazarus (Lk 10:38-42;
Jn 11; 12:2).

MARVELED
Lk   2:33 mother *m* at what was said
            about

MARY
    1. Mother of Jesus (Mt 1:16-25; Lk 1:27-
56; 2:1-40). With Jesus at temple (Lk 2:41-
52), at the wedding in Cana (Jn 2:1-5), questioning his sanity (Mk 3:21), at the cross (Jn
19:25-27). Among disciples after Ascension
(Ac 1:14).
    2. Magdalene; former demoniac (Lk 8:2).
Helped support Jesus' ministry (Lk 8:1-3). At
the cross (Mt 27:56; Mk 15:40; Jn 19:25),
burial (Mt 27:61; Mk 15:47). Saw angel after
resurrection (Mt 28:1-10; Mk 16:1-9; Lk 24:1-
12); also Jesus (Jn 20:1-18).
    3. Sister of Martha and Lazarus (Jn 11).
Washed Jesus' feet (Jn 12:1-8).

MASQUERADES*
2Co   11:14 for Satan himself *m* as an angel

MASTER (MASTERED MASTERS)
Mt   10:24 nor a servant above his *m*.
      23: 8 for you have only one *M*
      24:46 that servant whose *m* finds him
      25:21 "His *m* replied, 'Well done,
Ro   6:14 For sin shall not be your *m*,
      14: 4 To his own *m* he stands or falls.
2Ti   2:21 useful to the *M* and prepared

MASTERED* (MASTER)
1Co   6:12 but I will not be *m* by anything.
2Pe   2:19 a slave to whatever has *m* him.

MASTERS (MASTER)
Mt   6:24 "No one can serve two *m*.
Eph   6: 5 obey your earthly *m* with respect
       6: 9 And *m*, treat your slaves
Tit   2: 9 subject to their *m* in everything,

MATTHEW*
    Apostle; former tax collector (Mt 9:9-13;
10:3; Mk 3:18; Lk 6:15; Ac 1:13). Also called
Levi (Mk 2:14-17; Lk 5:27-32).

MATURE (MATURITY)
Eph   4:13 of the Son of God and
            become *m*,
Php   3:15 of us who are *m* should take
            such
Heb   5:14 But solid food is for the *m*,
Jas   1: 4 work so that you may be *m*

MATURITY* (MATURE)
Heb   6: 1 about Christ and go on to *m*,

MEAL
Pr   15:17 Better a *m* of vegetables where
1Co   10:27 some unbeliever invites you to
            a *m*
Heb   12:16 for a single *m* sold his
            inheritance

MEANING
Ne   8: 8 and giving the *m* so that the
            people

MEANS
1Co   9:22 by all possible *m* I might save
            some

MEAT
Ro   14: 6 He who eats *m*, eats to the
            Lord,
      14:21 It is better not to eat *m*

MEDIATOR
1Ti   2: 5 and one *m* between God and
            men,
Heb   8: 6 of which he is *m* is superior
       9:15 For this reason Christ is the *m*
      12:24 to Jesus the *m* of a new
            covenant,

MEDICINE*
Pr   17:22 A cheerful heart is good *m*,

MEDITATE (MEDITATES MEDITATION)
Jos   1: 8 from your mouth; *m* on it day
Ps 119:15 I *m* on your precepts.
      119:78 but I will *m* on your precepts.
      119:97 I *m* on it all day long.
      145: 5 I will *m* on your wonderful works.

MEDITATES* (MEDITATE)
Ps   1: 2 and on his law he *m* day and
            night.

MEDITATION* (MEDITATE)
Ps   19:14 of my mouth and the *m* of my
            heart
      104:34 May my *m* be pleasing to him,

MEDIUM
Lev   20:27 " 'A man or woman who is a *m*

MEEK (MEEKNESS)
Ps   37:11 But the *m* will inherit the land
Mt   5: 5 Blessed are the *m*,

MEEKNESS* (MEEK)
2Co   10: 1 By the *m* and gentleness of
            Christ,

MEET (MEETING)
Ps   85:10 Love and faithfulness *m*
            together;
Am   4:12 prepare to *m* your God, O
            Israel."
1Th   4:17 them in the clouds to *m* the
            Lord

MEETING (MEET)
Heb   10:25 Let us not give up *m* together,

MELCHIZEDEK
Ge   14:18 *M* king of Salem brought out
            bread
Ps 110: 4 in the order of *M*."
Heb   7:11 in the order of *M*, not in the
            order

MELT
2Pe   3:12 and the elements will *m* in the
            heat.

MEMBERS
Mic   7: 6 a man's enemies are the *m*
Ro   7:23 law at work in the *m* of my body,
      12: 4 of us has one body with
            many *m*,
1Co   6:15 not know that your bodies are *m*
      12:24 But God has combined the *m*
Eph   4:25 for we are all *m* of one body.
Col   3:15 as *m* of one body you were
            called

MEN (MAN)
Mt   4:19 will make you fishers of *m*
       5:16 your light shine before *m*
      12:36 *m* will have to give account
Jn   12:32 will draw all *m* to myself
Ac   5:29 obey God rather than *m*!
Ro   1:27 indecent acts with other *m*,
       5:12 death came to all *m*,
1Co   9:22 all things to all *m*
2Co   5:11 we try to persuade *m*.
1Ti   2: 4 wants all *m* to be saved
2Ti   2: 2 entrust to reliable *m*
2Pe   1:21 but *m* spoke from God

MENAHEM
    King of Israel (2Ki 15:17-22).

MERCIFUL (MERCY)
Dt   4:31 the LORD your God is a *m* God;
Ne   9:31 for you are a gracious and *m*
            God.
Mt   5: 7 Blessed are the *m*,
Lk   6:36 Be *m*, just as your Father is *m*.
Heb   2:17 in order that he might become
            a *m*
Jude   :22 Be *m* to those who doubt;
            snatch

MERCY (MERCIFUL)
Ex   33:19 *m* on whom I will have *m*,
Ps   25: 6 O LORD, your great *m* and love,
Isa   63: 9 and *m* he redeemed them;
Hos   6: 6 For I desire *m*, not sacrifice,
Mic   6: 8 To act justly and to love *m*
Hab   3: 2 in wrath remember *m*.
Mt   12: 7 'I desire *m*, not sacrifice,' you
      23:23 justice, *m* and faithfulness.
Ro   9:15 "I will have *m* on whom I
            have *m*,
Eph   2: 4 who is rich in *m*, made us alive
Jas   2:13 *M* triumphs over judgment!
1Pe   1: 3 In his great *m* he has given us
            new

MESSAGE
Isa   53: 1 Who has believed our *m*
Jn   12:38 "Lord, who has believed our *m*
Ro   10:17 faith comes from hearing the *m*,
1Co   1:18 For the *m* of the cross is
2Co   5:19 to us the *m* of reconciliation.

MESSIAH*
Jn   1:41 "We have found the *M*" (that is,
       4:25 I know that *M*" (called Christ)
            "is

METHUSELAH
Ge   5:27 Altogether, *M* lived 969 years,

MICHAEL
    Archangel (Jude 9); warrior in angelic
realm, protector of Israel (Da 10:13, 21;
12:1; Rev 12:7).

MIDWIVES
Ex   1:17 The *m*, however, feared God

MIGHT (ALMIGHTY MIGHTY)
Jdg   16:30 Then he pushed with all his *m*,
2Sa   6:14 before the LORD with all his *m*,
Ps   21:13 we will sing and praise your *m*.
Zec   4: 6 'Not by *m* nor by power,
1Ti   6:16 To him be honor and *m* forever.

MIGHTY (MIGHT)
Ex   6: 1 of my *m* hand he will drive them
Dt   7: 8 he brought you out with a *m*
            hand
2Sa   1:19 How the *m* have fallen!
      23: 8 the names of David's *m* men:
Ps   24: 8 The LORD strong and *m*,
      50: 1 The *M* One, God, the LORD,
      89: 8 You are *m*, O LORD,
      136:12 with a *m* hand and outstretched
      147: 5 Great is our Lord and *m* in
            power;
Isa   9: 6 Wonderful Counselor, *M* God,
Zep   3:17 he is *m* to save.
Eph   6:10 in the Lord and in his *m* power.

MILE*
Mt   5:41 If someone forces you to go
            one *m*,

MILK
Ex   3: 8 a land flowing with *m* and
            honey—
Isa   55: 1 Come, buy wine and *m*
1Co   3: 2 I gave you *m*, not solid food,
Heb   5:12 You need *m*, not solid food!
1Pe   2: 2 babies, crave pure spiritual *m*,

MILLSTONE (STONE)
Lk   17: 2 sea with a *m* tied around his
            neck

MIND (DOUBLE-MINDED MINDFUL MINDS)

1Sa 15:29 Israel does not lie or change his m;
1Ch 28: 9 devotion and with a willing m,
Ps 26: 2 examine my heart and my m;
Isa 26: 3 him whose m is steadfast,
Mt 22:37 all your soul and with all your m.'
Ac   4:32 believers were one in heart and m.
Ro   7:25 I myself in my m am a slave
     8: 7 the sinful m is hostile to God.
    12: 2 by the renewing of your m.
1Co 2: 9 no m has conceived
    14:14 spirit prays, but my m is unfruitful.
2Co 13:11 be of one m, live in peace.
Php 3:19 Their m is on earthly things.
1Th 4:11 to m your own business
Heb 7:21 and will not change his m:

MINDFUL* (MIND)

Ps   8: 4 what is man that you are m of him,
Lk   1:48 God my Savior, for he has been m
Heb 2: 6 What is man that you are m of him,

MINDS (MIND)

Ps   7: 9 who searches m and hearts,
Jer 31:33 "I will put my law in their m
Eph 4:23 new in the attitude of your m;
Col 3: 2 Set your m on things above,
Heb 8:10 I will put my laws in their m
Rev 2:23 I am he who searches hearts and m,

MINISTERING (MINISTRY)

Heb 1:14 Are not all angels m spirits sent

MINISTRY (MINISTERING)

Ac   6: 4 to prayer and the m of the word."
2Co 5:18 gave us the m of reconciliation:
2Ti 4: 5 discharge all the duties of your m.

MIRACLES (MIRACULOUS)

1Ch 16:12 his m, and the judgments he
Ps 77:14 You are the God who performs m;
Mt 11:20 most of his m had been performed,
    11:21 If the m that were performed
    24:24 and perform great signs and m
Mk   6: 2 does m! Isn't this the carpenter?
Jn 10:32 "I have shown you many great m
    14:11 the evidence of the m themselves.
Ac   2:22 accredited by God to you by m,
    19:11 God did extraordinary m
1Co 12:28 third teachers, then workers of m,
Heb 2: 4 it by signs, wonders and various m,

MIRACULOUS (MIRACLES)

Jn   3: 2 could perform the m signs you are
     9:16 "How can a sinner do such m signs
    20:30 Jesus did many other m signs
1Co 1:22 Jews demand m signs and Greeks

MIRE

Ps 40: 2 out of the mud and m;
Isa 57:20 whose waves cast up m and mud.

MIRIAM

Sister of Moses and Aaron (Nu 26:59). Led dancing at Red Sea (Ex 15:20-21). Struck with leprosy for criticizing Moses (Nu 12). Death (Nu 20:1).

MIRROR

Jas 1:23 a man who looks at his face in a m

MISERY

Ex   3: 7 "I have indeed seen the m
Jdg 10:16 he could bear Israel's m no longer.
Hos 5:15 in their m they will earnestly seek
Ro   3:16 ruin and m mark their ways,
Jas 5: 1 of the m that is coming upon you.

MISLED

1Co 15:33 Do not be m: "Bad company

MISS

Pr 19: 2 nor to be hasty and m the way.

MIST

Hos 6: 4 Your love is like the morning m,
Jas 4:14 You are a m that appears for a little

MISUSE*

Ex 20: 7 "You shall not m the name
Dt   5:11 "You shall not m the name
Ps 139:20 your adversaries m your name.

MOCK (MOCKED MOCKER MOCKERS MOCKING)

Ps 22: 7 All who see me m me;
Pr 14: 9 Fools m at making amends for sin,
Mk 10:34 who will m him and spit on him,

MOCKED (MOCK)

Mt 27:29 knelt in front of him and m him.
    27:41 of the law and the elders m him.
Gal 6: 7 not be deceived: God cannot be m.

MOCKER (MOCK)

Pr   9: 7 corrects a m invites insult;
     9:12 if you are a m, you alone will suffer
    20: 1 Wine is a m and beer a brawler;
    22:10 Drive out the m, and out goes strife

MOCKERS (MOCK)

Ps   1: 1 or sit in the seat of m.

MOCKING (MOCK)

Isa 50: 6 face from m and spitting.

MODEL*

Eze 28:12 " 'You were the m of perfection,
1Th 1: 7 And so you became a m
2Th 3: 9 to make ourselves a m for you

MOMENT

Job 20: 5 the joy of the godless lasts but a m.
Ps 30: 5 For his anger lasts only a m,
Isa 66: 8 or a nation be brought forth in a m?
Gal 2: 5 We did not give in to them for a m,

MONEY

Ecc 5:10 Whoever loves m never has m
Isa 55: 1 and you who have no m,
Mt   6:24 You cannot serve both God and M.
Lk   9: 3 no bread, no m, no extra tunic.
1Co 16: 2 set aside a sum of m in keeping
1Ti 3: 3 not quarrelsome, not a lover of m.
     6:10 For the love of m is a root
2Ti 3: 2 lovers of m, boastful, proud,
Heb 13: 5 free from the love of m
1Pe 5: 2 not greedy for m, but eager to serve

MOON

Ps 121: 6 nor the m by night.
Joel 2:31 and the m to blood
1Co 15:41 m another and the stars another;

MORNING

Ge   1: 5 and there was m-- the first day.
Dt 28:67 In the m you will say, "If only it
Ps   5: 3 In the m, O LORD,

2Pe 1:19 and the m star rises in your hearts.
Rev 22:16 of David, and the bright M Star."

MORTAL

1Co 15:53 and the m with immortality.

MOSES

Levite; brother of Aaron (Ex 6:20; 1Ch 6:3). Put in basket into Nile; discovered and raised by Pharaoh's daughter (Ex 2:1-10). Fled to Midian after killing Egyptian (Ex 2:11-15). Married to Zipporah, fathered Gershom (Ex 2:16-22).

Called by the LORD to deliver Israel (Ex 3-4). Pharaoh's resistance (Ex 5-11). Passover and Exodus (Ex 12-13). Led Israel through Red Sea (Ex 14). Song of deliverance (Ex 15:1-21). Brought water from rock (Ex 17:1-7). Raised hands to defeat Amalekites (Ex 17:8-16). Delegated judges (Ex 18; Dt 1:9-18).

Received Law at Sinai (Ex 19-23; 25-31; Jn 1:17). Announced Law to Israel (Ex 19:7-8; 24; 35). Broke tablets because of golden calf (Ex 32; Dt 9). Saw glory of the LORD (Ex 33-34). Supervised building of tabernacle (Ex 36-40). Set apart Aaron and priests (Lev 8-9). Numbered tribes (Nu 1-4; 26). Opposed by Aaron and Miriam (Nu 12). Sent spies into Canaan (Nu 13). Announced forty years of wandering for failure to enter land (Nu 14). Opposed by Korah (Nu 16). Forbidden to enter land for striking rock (Nu 20:1-13; Dt 1:37). Lifted bronze snake for healing (Nu 21:4-9; Jn 3:14). Final address to Israel (Dt 1-33). Succeeded by Joshua (Nu 27:12-23; Dt 34). Death (Dt 34:5-12).

"Law of Moses" (1Ki 2:3; Ezr 3:2; Mk 12:26; Lk 24:44). "Book of Moses" (2Ch 25:12; Ne 13:1). "Song of Moses" (Ex 15:1-21; Rev 15:3). "Prayer of Moses" (Ps 90).

MOTH

Mt   6:19 where m and rust destroy,

MOTHER (MOTHER'S)

Ge   2:24 and m and be united to his wife,
     3:20 because she would become the m
Ex 20:12 "Honor your father and your m,
Lev 20: 9 " 'If anyone curses his father or m,
Dt   5:16 "Honor your father and your m,
    21:18 who does not obey his father and m
    27:16 who dishonors his father or his m."
1Sa 2:19 Each year his m made him a little
Ps 113: 9 as a happy m of children.
Pr 23:25 May your father and m be glad;
    29:15 child left to himself disgraces his m.
    31: 1 an oracle his m taught him:
Isa 49:15 "Can a m forget the baby
    66:13 As a m comforts her child,
Mt 10:37 or m more than me is not worthy
    15: 4 'Honor your father and m'
    19: 5 and m and be united to his wife,
Mk   7:10 'Honor your father and your m,'
    10:19 honor your father and m.' "
Jn 19:27 to the disciple, "Here is your m."

MOTHER'S (MOTHER)

Job 1:21 "Naked I came from my m womb,
Pr   1: 8 and do not forsake your m teaching

MOTIVES*

Pr 16: 2 but m are weighed by the LORD.
1Co 4: 5 will expose the m of men's hearts.
Php 1:18 whether from false m or true,
1Th 2: 3 spring from error or impure m,
Jas 4: 3 because you ask with wrong m,

MOUNTAIN (MOUNTAINS)

Mic 4: 2 let us go up to the m of the LORD,
Mt 17:20 say to this m, 'Move from here

MOUNTAINS (MOUNTAIN)
Isa 52: 7 How beautiful on the *m*
    55:12 the *m* and hills
1Co 13: 2 if I have a faith that can move *m*,

MOURN (MOURNING)
Ecc 3: 4 a time to *m* and a time to dance,
Isa 61: 2 to comfort all who *m*,
Mt 5: 4 Blessed are those who *m*,
Ro 12:15 *m* with those who *m*.

MOURNING (MOURN)
Jer 31:13 I will turn their *m* into gladness;
Rev 21: 4 There will be no more death or *m*

MOUTH
Jos 1: 8 of the Law depart from your *m*;
Ps 19:14 May the words of my *m*
    40: 3 He put a new song in my *m*,
  119:103 sweeter than honey to my *m*!
Pr 16:23 A wise man's heart guides his *m*,
    27: 2 praise you, and not your own *m*;
Isa 51:16 I have put my words in your *m*
Mt 12:34 overflow of the heart the *m* speaks.
    15:11 into a man's *m* does not make him
Ro 10: 9 That if you confess with your *m*,

MUD
Ps 40: 2 out of the *m* and mire;
Isa 57:20 whose waves cast up mire and *m*.
2Pe 2:22 back to her wallowing in the *m*."

MULTITUDE (MULTITUDES)
Isa 31: 1 who trust in the *m* of their chariots
1Pe 4: 8 love covers over a *m* of sins.
Rev 7: 9 me was a great *m* that no one could

MULTITUDES (MULTITUDE)
Joel 3:14 *M*, *m* in the valley of decision!

MURDER (MURDERER MURDERERS)
Ex 20:13 "You shall not *m*.
Mt 15:19 *m*, adultery, sexual immorality,
Ro 13: 9 "Do not *m*," "Do not steal,"
Jas 2:11 adultery," also said, "Do not *m*."

MURDERER (MURDER)
Nu 35:16 he is a *m*; the *m* shall be put
Jn 8:44 He was a *m* from the beginning,
1Jn 3:15 who hates his brother is a *m*,

MURDERERS (MURDER)
1Ti 1: 9 for *m*, for adulterers and perverts,
Rev 21: 8 the *m*, the sexually immoral,

MUSIC
Jdg 5: 3 I will make *m* to the LORD.
Ps 27: 6 and make *m* to the LORD.
    95: 2 and extol him with *m* and song.
    98: 4 burst into jubilant song with *m*;
  108: 1 make *m* with all my soul.
Eph 5:19 make *m* in your heart to the Lord,

MUSTARD
Mt 13:31 kingdom of heaven is like a *m* seed,
    17:20 you have faith as small as a *m* seed,

MUZZLE
Dt 25: 4 Do not *m* an ox while it is treading
Ps 39: 1 I will put a *m* on my mouth
1Co 9: 9 "Do not *m* an ox while it is

MYRRH
Mt 2:11 of gold and of incense and of *m*.
Mk 15:23 offered him wine mixed with *m*,

MYSTERY
Ro 16:25 to the revelation of the *m* hidden
1Co 15:51 I tell you a *m*: We will not all sleep,
Eph 5:32 This is a profound *m*—
Col 1:26 the *m* that has been kept hidden
1Ti 3:16 the *m* of godliness is great:

MYTHS
1Ti 4: 7 Have nothing to do with godless *m*

NADAB
    Son of Jeroboam I; king of Israel (1Ki 15:25-32).

NAIL* (NAILING)
Jn 20:25 "Unless I see the *n* marks

NAILING* (NAIL)
Ac 2:23 him to death by *n* him to the cross.
Col 2:14 he took it away, *n* it to the cross.

NAKED
Ge 2:25 The man and his wife were both *n*,
Job 1:21 *N* I came from my mother's womb,
Isa 58: 7 when you see the *n*, to clothe him,
2Co 5: 3 are clothed, we will not be found *n*.

NAME
Ex 3:15 This is my *n* forever, the *n*
    20: 7 "You shall not misuse the *n*
Dt 5:11 "You shall not misuse the *n*
    28:58 this glorious and awesome *n*—
1Ki 5: 5 will build the temple for my *N*.'
2Ch 7:14 my people, who are called by my *n*,
Ps 34: 3 let us exalt his *n* together.
  103: 1 my inmost being, praise his holy *n*.
  147: 4 and calls them each by *n*.
Pr 22: 1 A good *n* is more desirable
    30: 4 What is his *n*, and the *n* of his son?
Isa 40:26 and calls them each by *n*.
    57:15 who lives forever, whose *n* is holy:
Jer 14: 7 do something for the sake of your *n*
Da 12: 1 everyone whose *n* is found written
Joel 2:32 on the *n* of the LORD will be saved
Zec 14: 9 one LORD, and his *n* the only *n*.
Mt 1:21 and you are to give him the *n* Jesus,
    6: 9 hallowed be your *n*,
    18:20 or three come together in my *n*,
Jn 10: 3 He calls his own sheep by *n*
    16:24 asked for anything in my *n*.
Ac 4:12 for there is no other *n*
Ro 10:13 "Everyone who calls on the *n*
Php 2: 9 him the *n* that is above every *n*,
Col 3:17 do it all in the *n* of the Lord Jesus,
Heb 1: 4 as the *n* he has inherited is superior
Rev 20:15 If anyone's *n* was not found written

NAOMI
    Mother-in-law of Ruth (Ru 1). Advised Ruth to seek marriage with Boaz (Ru 2-4).

NARROW
Mt 7:13 "Enter through the *n* gate.

NATHANAEL
    Apostle (Jn 1:45-49; 21:2). Probably also called Bartholomew (Mt 10:3).

NATION (NATIONS)
Ge 12: 2 "I will make you into a great *n*
Ps 33:12 Blessed is the *n* whose God is

Pr 14:34 Righteousness exalts a *n*,
Isa 65: 1 To a *n* that did not call on my name
1Pe 2: 9 a royal priesthood, a holy *n*,
Rev 7: 9 from every *n*, tribe, people

NATIONS (NATION)
Ge 17: 4 You will be the father of many *n*.
    18:18 and all *n* on earth will be blessed
Ex 19: 5 of all *n* you will be my treasured
Ne 1: 8 I will scatter you among the *n*,
Ps 96: 3 Declare his glory among the *n*,
Isa 40:15 Surely the *n* are like a drop
Eze 36:23 *n* will know that I am the LORD.
Hag 2: 7 and the desired of all *n* will come,
Zec 8:23 *n* will take firm hold of one Jew
    14: 2 I will gather all the *n* to Jerusalem
Mt 28:19 and make disciples of all *n*,
Rev 21:24 The *n* will walk by its light,

NATURAL (NATURE)
Ro 6:19 you are weak in your *n* selves.
1Co 15:44 If there is a *n* body, there is

NATURE (NATURAL)
Ro 8: 4 do not live according to the sinful *n*
    8: 8 by the sinful *n* cannot please God.
Gal 5:19 The acts of the sinful *n* are obvious:
    5:24 Jesus have crucified the sinful *n*
Php 2: 6 Who, being in very *n* God,

NAZARENE
Mt 2:23 prophets: "He will be called a *N*."

NAZIRITE
Jdg 13: 7 because the boy will be a *N* of God

NECESSARY
Ro 13: 5 it is *n* to submit to the authorities,

NEED (NEEDS NEEDY)
Ps 116: 6 when I was in great *n*, he saved me.
Mt 6: 8 for your Father knows what you *n*
Ro 12:13 with God's people who are in *n*.
1Co 12:21 say to the hand, "I don't *n* you!"
1Jn 3:17 sees his brother in *n* but has no pity

NEEDLE
Mt 19:24 go through the eye of a *n*

NEEDS (NEED)
Isa 58:11 he will satisfy your *n*
Php 4:19 God will meet all your *n* according

NEEDY (NEED)
Pr 14:21 blessed is he who is kind to the *n*.
    14:31 to the *n* honors God.
    31:20 and extends her hands to the *n*.
Mt 6: 2 "So when you give to the *n*,

NEGLECT (NEGLECTED)
Ne 10:39 We will not *n* the house of our God
Ps 119: 16 I will not *n* your word.
Ac 6: 2 for us to *n* the ministry of the word
1Ti 4:14 Do not *n* your gift, which was

NEGLECTED (NEGLECT)
Mt 23:23 But you have *n* the more important

NEHEMIAH
    Cupbearer of Artaxerxes (Ne 2:1); governor of Israel (Ne 8:9). Returned to Jerusalem to rebuild walls (Ne 2-6). With Ezra, reestablished worship (Ne 8). Prayer confessing nation's sin (Ne 9). Dedicated wall (Ne 12).

NEIGHBOR (NEIGHBOR'S)
Ex   20:16 give false testimony against
         your *n*.
Lev   19:13 Do not defraud your *n* or rob
         him.
      19:18 but love your *n* as yourself.
Pr   27:10 better a *n* nearby than a brother
         far
Mt   19:19 and 'love your *n* as yourself.' "
Lk   10:29 who is my *n*?" In reply Jesus
         said:
Ro   13:10 Love does no harm to its *n*.

NEIGHBOR'S (NEIGHBOR)
Ex   20:17 You shall not covet your *n* wife,
Dt   5:21 not set your desire on your *n*
         house
      19:14 not move your *n* boundary stone
Pr   25:17 Seldom set foot in your *n*
         house—

NEW
Ps   40: 3 He put a *n* song in my mouth,
Ecc   1: 9 there is nothing *n* under the
         sun.
Isa   65:17 *n* heavens and a *n* earth.
Jer   31:31 "when I will make a *n* covenant
Eze   36:26 give you a *n* heart and put a *n*
         spirit
Mt   9:17 Neither do men pour *n* wine
Lk   22:20 "This cup is the *n* covenant
2Co   5:17 he is a *n* creation; the old has
         gone,
Eph   4:24 and to put on the *n* self, created
2Pe   3:13 to a *n* heaven and a *n* earth,
1Jn   2: 8 Yet I am writing you a *n*
         command;

NEWBORN (BEAR)
1Pe   2: 2 Like *n* babies, crave pure
         spiritual

NEWS
Isa   52: 7 the feet of those who bring
         good *n*,
Mk   1:15 Repent and believe the good *n!*"
      16:15 preach the good *n* to all
         creation.
Lk   2:10 I bring you good *n*
Ac   5:42 proclaiming the good *n* that
         Jesus
      17:18 preaching the good *n* about
         Jesus
Ro   10:15 feet of those who bring good *n!*"

NICODEMUS*
   Pharisee who visted Jesus at night (Jn 3).
Argued fair treatment of Jesus (Jn 7:50-52).
With Joseph, prepared Jesus for burial (Jn
19:38-42).

NIGHT
Job   35:10 who gives songs in the *n*,
Ps   1: 2 on his law he meditates day
         and *n*.
      91: 5 You will not fear the terror of *n*,
Jn   3: 2 He came to Jesus at *n* and said,
1Th   5: 2 Lord will come like a thief in
         the *n*.
       5: 5 We do not belong to the *n*
Rev   21:25 for there will be no *n* there.

NOAH
   Righteous man (Eze 14:14, 20) called to
build ark (Ge 6-8; Heb 11:7; 1Pe 3:20; 2Pe
2:5). God's covenant with (Ge 9:1-17). Drunkenness of (Ge 9:18-23). Blessed sons,
cursed Canaan (Ge 9:24-27).

NOBLE
Ru   3:11 you are a woman of *n* character.
Ps   45: 1 My heart is stirred by a *n* theme
Pr   12: 4 of *n* character is her husband's
      31:10 A wife of *n* character who can
         find?
      31:29 "Many women do *n* things,
Isa   32: 8 But the *n* man makes *n* plans,
Lk   8:15 good soil stands for those with
         a *n*.
Ro   9:21 of clay some pottery for *n*
         purposes
Php   4: 8 whatever is *n*, whatever is right,

2Ti   2:20 some are for *n* purposes

NOTHING
Ne   9:21 in the desert; they lacked *n*,
Jer   32:17 N is too hard for you
Jn   15: 5 apart from me you can do *n*.

NULLIFY
Ro   3:31 Do we, then, *n* the law by this
         faith

OATH
Dt   7: 8 and kept the *o* he swore

OBEDIENCE (OBEY)
2Ch   31:21 in *o* to the law and the
         commands,
Pr   30:17 that scorns *o* to a mother,
Ro   1: 5 to the *o* that comes from faith.
       6:16 to *o*, which leads to
         righteousness?
2Jn   : 6 that we walk in *o* to his
         commands.

OBEDIENT (OBEY)
Lk   2:51 with them and was *o* to them.
Php   2: 8 and became *o* to death—
1Pe   1:14 As *o* children, do not conform

OBEY (OBEDIENCE OBEDIENT OBEYED)
Ex   12:24 "O these instructions as a
         lasting
Dt   6: 3 careful to *o* so that it may go
         well
      13: 4 Keep his commands and *o* him;
      21:18 son who does not *o* his father
      30: 2 and *o* him with all your heart
      32:46 children to *o* carefully all the
         words
1Sa   15:22 To *o* is better than sacrifice,
Ps   119: 34 and *o* it with all my heart.
Mt   28:20 to *o* everything I have
         commanded
Jn   14:23 loves me, he will *o* my teaching.
Ac   5:29 "We must *o* God rather than
         men!
Ro   6:16 slaves to the one whom you *o*—
Gal   5: 3 obligated to *o* the whole law.
Eph   6: 1 *o* your parents in the Lord,
       6: 5 *o* your earthly masters with
         respect
Col   3:20 *o* your parents in everything,
1Ti   3: 4 and see that his children *o* him
Heb   13:17 O your leaders and submit
1Jn   5: 3 love for God: to *o* his
         commands.

OBEYED (OBEY)
Ps   119: 4 that are to be fully *o*.
Jnh   3: 3 Jonah *o* the word of the LORD
Jn   17: 6 and they have *o* your word.
Ro   6:17 you wholeheartedly *o* the form
Heb   11: 8 *o* and went, even though he did
         not
1Pe   3: 6 who *o* Abraham and called him
         her

OBLIGATED
Ro   1:14 I am *o* both to Greeks
Gal   5: 3 himself be circumcised that he
         is *o*

OBSCENITY
Eph   5: 4 Nor should there be *o*, foolish
         talk

OBSOLETE
Heb   8:13 he has made the first one *o*;

OBTAINED
Ro   9:30 not pursue righteousness,
         have *o* it,
Php   3:12 Not that I have already *o* all this,
Heb   9:12 having *o* eternal redemption.

OFFENDED (OFFENSE)
Pr   18:19 An *o* brother is more unyielding

OFFENSE (OFFENDED OFFENSIVE)
Pr   17: 9 over an *o* promotes love,

Pr   19:11 it is to his glory to overlook
         an *o*.

OFFENSIVE (OFFENSE)
Ps   139: 24 See if there is any *o* way in me,

OFFER (OFFERED OFFERING OFFERINGS)
Ro   12: 1 to *o* your bodies as living
         sacrifices,
Heb   13:15 therefore, let us continually *o*

OFFERED (OFFER)
Heb   7:27 once for all when he *o* himself.
      11: 4 By faith Abel *o* God a better

OFFERING (OFFER)
Ge   22: 8 provide the lamb for the burnt *o*,
Ps   40: 6 Sacrifice and *o* you did not
         desire,
Isa   53:10 the LORD makes his life a guilt *o*,
Mt   5:23 if you are *o* your gift at the altar
Eph   5: 2 as a fragrant *o* and sacrifice to
         God.
Heb   10: 5 "Sacrifice and *o* you did not
         desire,

OFFERINGS (OFFER)
Mal   3: 8 do we rob you?' "In tithes and *o*.
Mk   12:33 is more important than all
         burnt *o*

OFFICER
2Ti   2: 4 wants to please his
         commanding *o*.

OFFSPRING
Ge   3:15 and between your *o* and hers;
      12: 7 "To your *o* I will give this land."

OIL
Ps   23: 5 You anoint my head with *o*;
Isa   61: 3 the *o* of gladness
Heb   1: 9 by anointing you with the *o* of
         joy."

OLIVE (OLIVES)
Zec   4: 3 Also there are two *o* trees by it,
Ro   11:17 and you, though a wild *o* shoot,
Rev   11: 4 These are the two *o* trees

OLIVES (OLIVE)
Jas   3:12 a fig tree bear *o*, or a grapevine
         bear

OMEGA
Rev   1: 8 "I am the Alpha and the *O*,"

OMRI
   King of Israel (1Ki 16:21-26).

OPINIONS*
1Ki   18:21 will you waver between two *o*?
Pr   18: 2 but delights in airing his own *o*.

OPPORTUNITY
Ro   7:11 seizing the *o* afforded
Gal   6:10 as we have *o*, let us do good
Eph   5:16 making the most of every *o*,
Col   4: 5 make the most of every *o*.
1Ti   5:14 to give the enemy no *o* for
         slander.

OPPOSES
Jas   4: 6 "God *o* the proud
1Pe   5: 5 because, "God *o* the proud

OPPRESS (OPPRESSED)
Ex   22:21 "Do not mistreat an alien or *o*
         him,
Zec   7:10 Do not *o* the widow

OPPRESSED (OPPRESS)
Ps   9: 9 The LORD is a refuge for the *o*,
Isa   53: 7 He was *o* and afflicted,
Zec   10: 2 *o* for lack of a shepherd.

ORDAINED
Ps   8: 2 you have *o* praise

ORDERLY
1Co   14:40 done in a fitting and *o* way.

Col   2: 5 and delight to see how *o* you are

ORGIES*
Ro   13:13 not in *o* and drunkenness,
Gal   5:21 drunkenness, *o*, and the like.
1Pe   4: 3 *o*, carousing and detestable

ORIGIN
2Pe   1:21 For prophecy never had its *o*

ORPHANS
Jn   14:18 will not leave you as *o*; I will come
Jas   1:27 to look after *o* and widows

OUTCOME
Heb 13: 7 Consider the *o* of their way of life
1Pe   4:17 what will the *o* be for those who do

OUTSIDERS*
Col   4: 5 wise in the way you act toward *o*;
1Th   4:12 daily life may win the respect of *o*
1Ti   3: 7 also have a good reputation with *o*,

OUTSTANDING
SS   5:10 *o* among ten thousand.
Ro   13: 8 no debt remain *o*,

OUTSTRETCHED
Ex   6: 6 and will redeem you with an *o* arm
Jer   27: 5 and *o* arm I made the earth
Eze   20:33 an *o* arm and with outpoured wrath

OUTWEIGHS
2Co   4:17 an eternal glory that far *o* them all.

OVERCOME (OVERCOMES)
Mt   16:18 and the gates of Hades will not *o* it.
Mk   9:24 I do believe; help me *o* my unbelief
Jn   16:33 But take heart! I have *o* the world."
Ro   12:21 Do not be *o* by evil, but *o* evil
1Jn   5: 4 is the victory that has *o* the world,
Rev 17:14 but the Lamb will *o* them

OVERCOMES* (OVERCOME)
1Jn   5: 4 born of God *o* the world.
       5: 5 Who is it that *o* the world?
Rev   2: 7 To him who *o*, I will give the right
       2:11 He who *o* will not be hurt at all
       2:17 To him who *o*, I will give some
       2:26 To him who *o* and does my will
       3: 5 He who *o* will, like them, be
       3:12 Him who *o* I will make a pillar
       3:21 To him who *o*, I will give the right
      21: 7 He who *o* will inherit all this,

OVERFLOW (OVERFLOWS)
Ps 119:171 May my lips *o* with praise,
Lk   6:45 out of the *o* of his heart his mouth
Ro   15:13 so that you may *o* with hope
2Co   4:15 to *o* to the glory of God.
1Th   3:12 *o* for each other and for everyone

OVERFLOWS* (OVERFLOW)
Ps   23: 5 my cup *o*.
2Co   1: 5 also through Christ our comfort *o*.

OVERJOYED* (JOY)
Da   6:23 The king was *o* and gave orders
Mt   2:10 they saw the star, they were *o*.
Jn   20:20 The disciples were *o*
Ac   12:14 she was so *o* she ran back
1Pe   4:13 so that you may be *o*

OVERSEER (OVERSEERS)
1Ti   3: 1 anyone sets his heart on being an *o*,

1Ti   3: 2 Now the *o* must be above reproach,
Tit   1: 7 Since an *o* is entrusted

OVERSEERS* (OVERSEER)
Ac   20:28 the Holy Spirit has made you *o*.
Php   1: 1 together with the *o* and deacons:
1Pe   5: 2 as *o*— not because you must,

OVERWHELMED
Ps   38: 4 My guilt has *o* me
      65: 3 When we were *o* by sins,
Mt   26:38 "My soul is *o* with sorrow
Mk   7:37 People were *o* with amazement.

OWE
Ro   13: 7 If you *o* taxes, pay taxes; if revenue
Phm   :19 to mention that you *o* me your very

OX
Dt   25: 4 Do not muzzle an *o*
Isa   11: 7 and the lion will eat straw like the *o*
1Co   9: 9 "Do not muzzle an *o*

PAGANS
Mt   5:47 Do not even *p* do that? Be perfect,
1Pe   2:12 such good lives among the *p* that,

PAIN (PAINFUL)
Ge   3:16 with *p* you will give birth
Job   33:19 may be chastened on a bed of *p*
Jn   16:21 woman giving birth to a child has *p*

PAINFUL (PAIN)
Ge   3:17 through *p* toil you will eat of it
Heb 12:11 seems pleasant at the time, but *p*.
1Pe   4:12 at the *p* trial you are suffering,

PALMS
Isa   49:16 you on the *p* of my hands;

PANTS
Ps   42: 1 As the deer *p* for streams of water,

PARADISE*
Lk   23:43 today you will be with me in *p*."
2Co   12: 4 God knows—was caught up to *p*.
Rev   2: 7 of life, which is in the *p* of God.

PARALYTIC
Mk   2: 3 bringing to him a *p*, carried by four

PARDON (PARDONS)
Isa   55: 7 and to our God, for he will freely *p*.

PARDONS* (PARDON)
Mic   7:18 who *p* sin and forgives

PARENTS
Pr   17: 6 and *p* are the pride of their children
Lk   18:29 left home or wife or brothers or *p*
      21:16 You will be betrayed even by *p*,
Ro   1:30 they disobey their *p*; they are
2Co   12:14 for their *p*, but *p* for their children.
Eph   6: 1 Children, obey your *p* in the Lord,
Col   3:20 obey your *p* in everything,
2Ti   3: 2 disobedient to their *p*, ungrateful,

PARTIALITY
Dt   10:17 who shows no *p* and accepts no
2Ch 19: 7 our God there is no injustice or *p*
Lk   20:21 and that you do not show *p*

PARTICIPATION
1Co 10:16 is not the bread that we break a *p*

PASS
Ex   12:13 and when I see the blood, I will *p*
La   1:12 to you, all you who *p* by?
Lk   21:33 Heaven and earth will *p* away,
1Co 13: 8 there is knowledge, it will *p* away.

PASSION (PASSIONS)
1Co   7: 9 better to marry than to burn with *p*.

PASSIONS (PASSION)
Gal   5:24 crucified the sinful nature with its *p*
Tit   2:12 to ungodliness and worldly *p*,

PASSOVER
Ex   12:11 Eat it in haste; it is the LORD's *P*.
Dt   16: 1 celebrate the *P* of the LORD your
1Co   5: 7 our *P* lamb, has been sacrificed.

PAST
Isa   43:18 do not dwell on the *p*.
Ro   15: 4 in the *p* was written to teach us,
Heb   1: 1 In the *p* God spoke

PASTORS*
Eph   4:11 and some to be *p* and teachers,

PASTURE (PASTURES)
Ps   37: 3 dwell in the land and enjoy safe *p*.
     100: 3 we are his people, the sheep of his *p*
Jer   50: 7 against the LORD, their true *p*,
Eze   34:13 I will *p* them on the mountains
Jn   10: 9 come in and go out, and find *p*.

PASTURES (PASTURE)
Ps   23: 2 He makes me lie down in green *p*,

PATCH
Mt   9:16 No one sews a *p* of unshrunk cloth

PATH (PATHS)
Ps   27:11 lead me in a straight *p*
   119:105 and a light for my *p*.
Pr   15:19 the *p* of the upright is a highway.
      15:24 The *p* of life leads upward
Isa   26: 7 The *p* of the righteous is level;
Lk   1:79 to guide our feet into the *p* of peace
2Co   6: 3 no stumbling block in anyone's *p*,

PATHS (PATH)
Ps   23: 3 He guides me in *p* of righteousness
      25: 4 teach me your *p*;
Pr   3: 6 and he will make your *p* straight.
Ro   11:33 and his *p* beyond tracing out!
Heb 12:13 "Make level *p* for your feet,"

PATIENCE (PATIENT)
Pr   19:11 A man's wisdom gives him *p*;
2Co   6: 6 understanding, *p* and kindness;
Gal   5:22 joy, peace, *p*, kindness, goodness,
Col   1:11 may have great endurance and *p*,
      3:12 humility, gentleness and *p*.

PATIENT (PATIENCE PATIENTLY)
Pr   15:18 but a *p* man calms a quarrel.
Ro   12:12 Be joyful in hope, *p* in affliction,
1Co 13: 4 Love is *p*, love is kind.
Eph   4: 2 humble and gentle; be *p*,
1Th   5:14 help the weak, be *p* with everyone.

PATIENTLY (PATIENT)
Ps   40: 1 I waited *p* for the LORD;

Ro   8:25 we do not yet have, we wait for
           it p.

PATTERN

Ro   5:14 who was a p of the one to
           come.
      12: 2 longer to the p of this world,
2Ti   1:13 keep as the p of sound
           teaching,

PAUL

Also called Saul (Ac 13:9). Pharisee from Tarsus (Ac 9:11; Php 3:5). Apostle (Gal 1). At stoning of Stephen (Ac 8:1). Persecuted Church (Ac 9:1-2; Gal 1:13). Vision of Jesus on road to Damascus (Ac 9:4-9; 26:12-18). In Arabia (Gal 1:17). Preached in Damascus; escaped death through the wall in a basket (Ac 9:19-25). In Jerusalem; sent back to Tarsus (Ac 9:26-30).

Brought to Antioch by Barnabas (Ac 11:22-26). First missionary journey to Cyprus and Galatia (Ac 13-14). Stoned at Lystra (Ac 14:19-20). At Jerusalem council (Ac 15). Split with Barnabas over Mark (Ac 15:36-41).

Second missionary journey with Silas (Ac 16-20). Called to Macedonia (Ac 16:6-10). Freed from prison in Philippi (Ac 16:16-40). In Thessalonica (Ac 17:1-9). Speech in Athens (Ac 17:16-33). In Corinth (Ac 18). In Ephesus (Ac 19). Return to Jerusalem (Ac 20). Farewell to Ephesian elders (Ac 20:13-38). Arrival in Jerusalem (Ac 21:1-26). Arrested (Ac 21:27-36). Addressed crowds (Ac 22), Sanhedrin (Ac 23:1-11). Transferred to Caesarea (Ac 23:12-35). Trial before Felix (Ac 24), Festus (Ac 25:1-12). Before Agrippa (Ac 25:13-26:32). Voyage to Rome; shipwreck (Ac 27). Arrival in Rome (Ac 28).

PAY (REPAID REPAY)

Lev 26:43 They will p for their sins
Pr   22:17 P attention and listen
Mt   22:17 Is it right to p taxes to Caesar
Ro   13: 6 This is also why you p taxes,
2Pe   1:19 you will do well to p attention to
           it,

PEACE (PEACEMAKERS)

Nu   6:26 and give you p."
Ps   34:14 seek p and pursue it.
     85:10 righteousness and p kiss each
           other
    119:165 Great p have they who love your
    122: 6 Pray for the p of Jerusalem:
Pr   14:30 A heart at p gives life to the
           body,
     17: 1 Better a dry crust with p and
           quiet
Isa   9: 6 Everlasting Father, Prince of P.
     26: 3 You will keep in perfect p
     48:22 "There is no p," says the LORD,
Zec   9:10 He will proclaim p to the
           nations.
Mt   10:34 I did not come to bring p,
Lk   2:14 on earth p to men on whom his
Jn   14:27 P I leave with you; my p
     16:33 so that in me you may have p.
Ro   5: 1 we have p with God
1Co   7:15 God has called us to live in p.
     14:33 a God of disorder but of p.
Gal   5:22 joy, p, patience, kindness,
Eph   2:14 he himself is our p, who has
           made
Php   4: 7 the p of God, which transcends
           all
Col   1:20 by making p through his blood,
      3:15 Let the p of Christ rule
1Th   5: 3 While people are saying, "P
2Th   3:16 the Lord of p himself give you p
2Ti   2:22 righteousness, faith, love and p,
1Pe   3:11 he must seek p and pursue it.
Rev   6: 4 power to take p from the earth

PEACEMAKERS* (PEACE)

Mt   5: 9 Blessed are the p,
Jas   3:18 P who sow in peace raise a
           harvest

PEARL* (PEARLS)

Rev 21:21 each gate made of a single p.

PEARLS (PEARL)

Mt   7: 6 do not throw your p to pigs.
     13:45 like a merchant looking for
           fine p.
1Ti   2: 9 or gold or p or expensive
           clothes,
Rev 21:21 The twelve gates were twelve p,

PEKAH

King of Israel (2Ki 15:25-31; Isa 7:1).

PEKAHIAH*

Son of Menahem; king of Israel (2Ki 15:22-26).

PEN

Mt   5:18 letter, not the least stroke of
           a p,

PENTECOST

Ac   2: 1 of P came, they were all
           together

PEOPLE (PEOPLES)

Dt   32: 9 the LORD's portion is his p,
Ru   1:16 Your p will be my p
2Ch   7:14 if my p, who are called
Jer 24: 7 They will be my p,
Zec   2:11 and will become my p.
Lk   2:10 joy that will be for all the p.
Ac   15:14 from the Gentiles a p.
2Co   6:16 and they will be my p."
Tit   2:14 a p that are his very own,
1Pe   2: 9 you are a chosen p,
Rev 21: 3 They will be his p,

PEOPLES (PEOPLE)

Da   7:14 all p, nations and men
Mic   4: 1 and p will stream to it.

PERCEIVING

Isa   6: 9 be ever seeing, but never p.'

PERFECT (PERFECTER PERFECTION)

SS   6: 9 but my dove, my p one, is
           unique,
Isa 26: 3 You will keep in p peace
Mt   5:48 as your heavenly Father is p.
Ro   12: 2 his good, pleasing and p will.
2Co 12: 9 for my power is made p
Col   1:28 so that we may present
           everyone p
      3:14 binds them all together in p
           unity.
Heb   9:11 and more p tabernacle that is
           not
     10:14 he has made p forever those
           who
Jas   1:17 Every good and p gift is from
           above
      1:25 into the p law that gives
           freedom,
      3: 2 he is a p man, able
1Jn   4:18 But p love drives out fear,

PERFECTER* (PERFECT)

Heb 12: 2 the author and p of our faith,

PERFECTION (PERFECT)

Ps 119: 96 To all p I see a limit;
2Co 13:11 Aim for p, listen to my appeal,
Heb   7:11 If p could have been attained

PERFORMS

Ps   77:14 You are the God who p miracles;

PERISH (PERISHABLE)

Ps   1: 6 but the way of the wicked will p.
    102: 26 They will p, but you remain;
Lk   13: 3 unless you repent, you too will
           all p
Jn   10:28 eternal life, and they shall
           never p;
Col   2:22 These are all destined to p with
           use,
Heb   1:11 They will p, but you remain;
2Pe   3: 9 not wanting anyone to p,

PERISHABLE (PERISH)

1Co 15:42 The body that is sown is p,

PERJURERS

1Ti   1:10 for slave traders and liars
           and p—

PERMISSIBLE (PERMIT)

1Co 10:23 "Everything is p"— but not

PERMIT (PERMISSIBLE)

1Ti   2:12 I do not p a woman to teach

PERSECUTE (PERSECUTED PERSECUTION)

Mt   5:11 p you and falsely say all kinds
Jn   15:20 they persecuted me, they will p
           you
Ac   9: 4 why do you p me?" "Who are
           you,
Ro   12:14 Bless those who p you; bless

PERSECUTED (PERSECUTE)

1Co   4:12 when we are p, we endure it;
2Ti   3:12 life in Christ Jesus will be p,

PERSECUTION (PERSECUTE)

Ro   8:35 or hardship or p or famine

PERSEVERANCE (PERSEVERE)

Ro   5: 3 we know that suffering
           produces p;
      5: 4 p, character; and character,
           hope.
Heb 12: 1 run with p the race marked out
Jas   1: 3 the testing of your faith
           develops p.
2Pe   1: 6 p; and to p, godliness;

PERSEVERE* (PERSEVERANCE PERSEVERED PERSEVERES)

1Ti   4:16 P in them, because if you do,
Heb 10:36 You need to p so that

PERSEVERED* (PERSEVERE)

Heb 11:27 he p because he saw him who
           is
Jas   5:11 consider blessed those who
           have p.
Rev   2: 3 You have p and have endured

PERSEVERES* (PERSEVERE)

1Co 13: 7 trusts, always hopes, always p.
Jas   1:12 Blessed is the man who p

PERSUADE

2Co   5:11 is to fear the Lord, we try to p
           men.

PERVERSION (PERVERT)

Lev 18:23 sexual relations with it; that is
           a p.
Jude   : 7 up to sexual immorality and p.

PERVERT (PERVERSION PERVERTS)

Gal   1: 7 are trying to p the gospel of
           Christ.

PERVERTS* (PERVERT)

1Ti   1:10 for murderers, for adulterers
           and p,

PESTILENCE

Ps   91: 6 nor the p that stalks in the
           darkness

PETER

Apostle, brother of Andrew, also called Simon (Mt 10:2; Mk 3:16; Lk 6:14; Ac 1:13), and Cephas (Jn 1:42). Confession of Christ (Mt 16:13-20; Mk 8:27-30; Lk 9:18-27). At transfiguration (Mt 17:1-8; Mk 9:2-8; Lk 9:28-36; 2Pe 1:16-18). Caught fish with coin (Mt 17:24-27). Denial of Jesus predicted (Mt 26:31-35; Mk 14:27-31; Lk 22:31-34; Jn 13:31-38). Denied Jesus (Mt 26:69-75; Mk 14:66-72; Lk 22:54-62; Jn 18:15-27). Commissioned by Jesus to shepherd his flock (Jn 21:15-23).

Speech at Pentecost (Ac 2). Healed beggar (Ac 3:1-10). Speech at temple (Ac 3:11-26), before Sanhedrin (Ac 4:1-22). In Samaria (Ac 8:14-25). Sent by vision to Cornelius (Ac 10). Announced salvation of Gentiles in Jerusalem

(Ac 11; 15). Freed from prison (Ac 12). Inconsistency at Antioch (Gal 2:11-21). At Jerusalem Council (Ac 15).

PHARISEES
Mt 5:20 surpasses that of the P

PHILIP
1. Apostle (Mt 10:3; Mk 3:18; Lk 6:14; Jn 1:43-48; 14:8; Ac 1:13).
2. Deacon (Ac 6:1-7); evangelist in Samaria (Ac 8:4-25), to Ethiopian (Ac 8:26-40).

PHILOSOPHY*
Col 2: 8 through hollow and deceptive p,

PHYLACTERIES*
Mt 23: 5 They make their p wide

PHYSICAL
1Ti 4: 8 For p training is of some value,
Jas 2:16 but does nothing about his p needs,

PIECES
Ge 15:17 and passed between the p.
Jer 34:18 and then walked between its p.

PIERCED
Ps 22:16 they have p my hands and my feet.
Isa 53: 5 But he was p for our transgressions,
Zec 12:10 look on me, the one they have p,
Jn 19:37 look on the one they have p."

PIGS
Mt 7: 6 do not throw your pearls to p.

PILATE
Governor of Judea. Questioned Jesus (Mt 27:1-26; Mk 15:15; Lk 22:66-23:25; Jn 18:28-19:16); sent him to Herod (Lk 23:6-12); consented to his crucifixion when crowds chose Barabbas (Mt 27:15-26; Mk 15:6-15; Lk 23:13-25; Jn 19:1-10).

PILLAR
Ge 19:26 and she became a p of salt.
Ex 13:21 ahead of them in a p of cloud
1Ti 3:15 the p and foundation of the truth.

PIT
Ps 40: 2 He lifted me out of the slimy p,
103: 4 who redeems your life from the p
Mt 15:14 a blind man, both will fall into a p."

PITIED
1Co 15:19 we are to be p more than all men.

PLAGUE
2Ch 6:28 "When famine or p comes

PLAIN
Ro 1:19 what may be known about God is p

PLAN (PLANNED PLANS)
Job 42: 2 no p of yours can be thwarted.
Pr 14:22 those who p what is good find love
Eph 1:11 predestined according to the p

PLANK
Mt 7: 3 attention to the p in your own eye?
Lk 6:41 attention to the p in your own eye?

PLANNED (PLAN)
Ps 40: 5 The things you p for us
Isa 46:11 what I have p, that will I do.
Heb 11:40 God had p something better for us

PLANS (PLAN)
Ps 20: 4 and make all your p succeed.

Ps 33:11 p of the LORD stand firm forever,
Pr 20:18 Make p by seeking advice;
Isa 32: 8 But the noble man makes noble p,

PLANTED (PLANTS)
Ps 1: 3 He is like a tree p by streams
Mt 15:13 Father has not p will be pulled
1Co 3: 6 I p the seed, Apollos watered it,

PLANTS (PLANTED)
1Co 3: 7 So neither he who p nor he who
9: 7 Who p a vineyard and does not eat

PLATTER
Mk 6:25 head of John the Baptist on a p."

PLAYED
Lk 7:32 " 'We p the flute for you,
1Co 14: 7 anyone know what tune is being p

PLEADED
2Co 12: 8 Three times I p with the Lord

PLEASANT (PLEASE)
Ps 16: 6 for me in p places;
133: 1 How good and p it is
147: 1 how p and fitting to praise him!
Heb 12:11 No discipline seems p at the time,

PLEASE (PLEASANT PLEASED PLEASES PLEASING PLEASURE PLEASURES)
Pr 20:23 and dishonest scales do not p him.
Jer 6:20 your sacrifices do not p me."
Jn 5:30 for I seek not to p myself
Ro 8: 8 by the sinful nature cannot p God.
15: 2 Each of us should p his neighbor
1Co 7:32 affairs—how he can p the Lord.
10:33 I try to p everybody in every way.
2Co 5: 9 So we make it our goal to p him,
Gal 1:10 or of God? Or am I trying to p men
1Th 4: 1 how to live in order to p God,
2Ti 2: 4 wants to p his commanding officer.
Heb 11: 6 faith it is impossible to p God,

PLEASED (PLEASE)
Mt 3:17 whom I love; with him I am well p
1Co 1:21 God was p through the foolishness
Col 1:19 For God was p to have all his
Heb 11: 5 commended as one who p God.
2Pe 1:17 whom I love; with him I am well p

PLEASES (PLEASE)
Ps 135: 6 The LORD does whatever p him,
Pr 15: 8 but the prayer of the upright p him.
Jn 3: 8 The wind blows wherever it p.
8:29 for I always do what p him."
Col 3:20 in everything, for this p the Lord.
1Ti 2: 3 This is good, and p God our Savior,
1Jn 3:22 his commands and do what p him.

PLEASING (PLEASE)
Ps 104: 34 May my meditation be p to him,
Ro 12: 1 p to God—which is your spiritual
Php 4:18 an acceptable sacrifice, p to God.
Heb 13:21 may he work in us what is p to him,

PLEASURE (PLEASE)
Ps 5: 4 You are not a God who takes p
147: 10 His p is not in the strength
Pr 21:17 He who loves p will become poor;
Eze 18:32 For I take no p in the death

Eph 1: 5 in accordance with his p and will—
1: 9 of his will according to his good p,
2Ti 3: 4 lovers of p rather than lovers

PLEASURES (PLEASE)
Ps 16:11 with eternal p at your right hand.
Heb 11:25 rather than to enjoy the p of sin
2Pe 2:13 reveling in their p while they feast

PLENTIFUL
Mt 9:37 harvest is p but the workers are

PLOW (PLOWSHARES)
Lk 9:62 "No one who puts his hand to the p

PLOWSHARES (PLOW)
Isa 2: 4 They will beat their swords into p
Joel 3:10 Beat your p into swords

PLUNDER
Ex 3:22 And so you will p the Egyptians."

POINT
Jas 2:10 yet stumbles at just one p is guilty

POISON
Mk 16:18 and when they drink deadly p,
Jas 3: 8 It is a restless evil, full of deadly p.

POLLUTE* (POLLUTED)
Nu 35:33 " 'Do not p the land where you are.
Jude : 8 these dreamers p their own bodies,

POLLUTED* (POLLUTE)
Ezr 9:11 entering to possess is a land p
Pr 25:26 Like a muddied spring or a p well
Ac 15:20 to abstain from food p by idols,
Jas 1:27 oneself from being p by the world.

PONDER
Ps 64: 9 and p what he has done.
119: 95 but I will p your statutes.

POOR (POVERTY)
Dt 15: 4 there should be no p among you,
15:11 There will always be p people
Ps 34: 6 This p man called, and the LORD
82: 3 maintain the rights of the p
112: 9 scattered abroad his gifts to the p,
Pr 10: 4 Lazy hands make a man p,
13: 7 to be p, yet has great wealth.
14:31 oppresses the p shows contempt
19: 1 Better a p man whose walk is
19:17 to the p lends to the LORD,
22: 2 Rich and p have this in common:
22: 9 for he shares his food with the p
28: 6 Better a p man whose walk is
31:20 She opens her arms to the p
Isa 61: 1 me to preach good news to the p.
Mt 5: 3 saying: "Blessed are the p in spirit,
11: 5 the good news is preached to the p.
19:21 your possessions and give to the p,
26:11 The p you will always have
Mk 12:42 But a p widow came and put
Ac 10: 4 and gifts to the p have come up
1Co 13: 3 If I give all I possess to the p
2Co 8: 9 yet for your sakes he became p,
Jas 2: 2 and a p man in shabby clothes

PORTION
Dt 32: 9 For the LORD's p is his people,
2Ki 2: 9 "Let me inherit a double p

La   3:24 to myself, "The LORD is my *p*;

POSSESS (POSSESSING POSSESSION POSSESSIONS)

Nu   33:53 for I have given you the land to *p*.
Jn   5:39 that by them you *p* eternal life.

POSSESSING* (POSSESS)

2Co   6:10 nothing, and yet *p* everything.

POSSESSION (POSSESS)

Ge   15: 7 to give you this land to take *p* of it
Nu   13:30 "We should go up and take *p*
Eph   1:14 of those who are God's *p*—

POSSESSIONS (POSSESS)

Lk   12:15 consist in the abundance of his *p*."
2Co 12:14 what I want is not your *p* but you.
1Jn   3:17 If anyone has material *p*

POSSIBLE

Mt   19:26 but with God all things are *p*."
Mk   9:23 "Everything is *p* for him who
       10:27 all things are *p* with God."
Ro   12:18 If it is *p*, as far as it depends on you,
1Co   9:22 by all means I might save some.

POT (POTSHERD POTTER POTTERY)

2Ki   4:40 there is death in the *p*!"
Jer   18: 4 But the *p* he was shaping

POTSHERD (POT)

Isa   45: 9 a *p* among the potsherds

POTTER (POT)

Isa   29:16 Can the pot say of the *p*,
       45: 9 Does the clay say to the *p*,
       64: 8 We are the clay, you are the *p*;
Jer   18: 6 "Like clay in the hand of the *p*,
Ro   9:21 Does not the *p* have the right

POTTERY (POT)

Ro   9:21 of clay some *p* for noble purposes

POUR (POURED)

Ps   62: 8 *p* out your hearts to him,
Joel 2:28 I will *p* out my Spirit on all people.
Mal   3:10 *p* out so much blessing that you
Ac   2:17 I will *p* out my Spirit on all people.

POURED (POUR)

Ac   10:45 of the Holy Spirit had been *p* out
Ro   5: 5 because God has *p* out his love

POVERTY (POOR)

Pr   14:23 but mere talk leads only to *p*.
       21: 5 as surely as haste leads to *p*.
       30: 8 give me neither *p* nor riches,
Mk   12:44 out of her *p*, put in everything—
2Co   8: 2 and their extreme *p* welled up
       8: 9 through his *p* might become rich.

POWER (POWERFUL POWERS)

1Ch 29:11 LORD, is the greatness and the *p*
2Ch 32: 7 for there is a greater *p* with us
Job 36:22 "God is exalted in his *p*.
Ps   63: 2 and beheld your *p* and your glory.
       68:34 Proclaim the *p* of God,
      147: 5 Great is our Lord and mighty in *p*;
Pr   24: 5 A wise man has great *p*,
Isa 40:10 the Sovereign LORD comes with *p*
Zec   4: 6 nor by *p*, but by my Spirit,'
Mt   22:29 do not know the Scriptures or the *p*
      24:30 on the clouds of the sky, with *p*
Ac   1: 8 you will receive *p* when the Holy
       4:33 With great *p* the apostles
      10:38 with the Holy Spirit and *p*,

Ro   1:16 it is the *p* of God for the salvation
1Co   1:18 to us who are being saved it is the *p*
      15:56 of death is sin, and the *p*
2Co 12: 9 for my *p* is made perfect
Eph   1:19 and his incomparably great *p*
Php   3:10 and the *p* of his resurrection
Col   1:11 strengthened with all *p* according
2Ti   1: 7 but a spirit of *p*, of love
Heb   7:16 of the *p* of an indestructible life.
Rev   4:11 to receive glory and honor and *p*,
      19: 1 and glory and *p* belong to our God,
      20: 6 The second death has no *p*

POWERFUL (POWER)

Ps   29: 4 The voice of the LORD is *p*;
Lk   24:19 *p* in word and deed before God
2Th   1: 7 in blazing fire with his *p* angels.
Heb   1: 3 sustaining all things by his *p* word.
Jas   5:16 The prayer of a righteous man is *p*

POWERLESS

Ro   5: 6 when we were still *p*, Christ died
       8: 3 For what the law was *p* to do

POWERS (POWER)

Ro   8:38 nor any *p*, neither height nor depth
1Co 12:10 to another miraculous *p*,
Col   1:16 whether thrones or *p* or rulers
       2:15 And having disarmed the *p*

PRACTICE

Lev 19:26 " 'Do not *p* divination or sorcery.
Mt   23: 3 for they do not *p* what they preach.
Lk   8:21 hear God's word and put it into *p*."
Ro   12:13 *P* hospitality.
1Ti   5: 4 to put their religion into *p* by caring

PRAISE (PRAISED PRAISES PRAISING)

Ex   15: 2 He is my God, and I will *p* him,
Dt   32: 3 Oh, *p* the greatness of our God!
Ru   4:14 said to Naomi: "*P* be to the LORD.
2Sa 22:47 The LORD lives! *P* be to my Rock
1Ch 16:25 is the LORD and most worthy of *p*;
2Ch 20:21 and to *p* him for the splendor
Ps   8: 2 you have ordained *p*
       33: 1 it is fitting for the upright to *p* him.
       34: 1 his *p* will always be on my lips.
       40: 3 a hymn of *p* to our God.
       48: 1 the LORD, and most worthy of *p*,
       68:19 *P* be to the Lord, to God our Savior
       89: 5 The heavens *p* your wonders,
      100: 4 and his courts with *p*;
      105: 2 Sing to him, sing *p* to him;
      106: 1 *P* the LORD.
      119:175 Let me live that I may *p* you,
      139: 14 I *p* you because I am fearfully
      145: 21 Let every creature *p* his holy name
      146: 1 *P* the LORD, O my soul.
      150: 2 *p* him for his surpassing greatness.
      150: 6 that has breath *p* the LORD.
Pr   27: 2 Let another *p* you, and not your
      27:21 man is tested by the *p* he receives.
      31:31 let her works bring her *p*
Mt   5:16 and *p* your Father in heaven.
      21:16 you have ordained *p*'?"
Jn   12:43 for they loved *p* from men more
Eph   1: 6 to the *p* of his glorious grace,
       1:12 might be for the *p* of his glory.
       1:14 to the *p* of his glory.
Heb 13:15 offer to God a sacrifice of *p*—
Jas   5:13 happy? Let him sing songs of *p*.

PRAISED (PRAISE)

1Ch 29:10 David *p* the LORD in the presence
Ne   8: 6 Ezra *p* the LORD, the great God;
Da   2:19 Then Daniel *p* the God of heaven
Ro   9: 5 who is God over all, forever *p*!
1Pe   4:11 that in all things God may be *p*

PRAISES (PRAISE)

2Sa 22:50 I will sing *p* to your name.
Ps   47: 6 Sing *p* to God, sing *p*;
      147: 1 How good it is to sing *p* to our God,
Pr   31:28 her husband also, and he *p* her:

PRAISING (PRAISE)

Ac   10:46 speaking in tongues and *p* God.
1Co 14:16 If you are *p* God with your spirit,

PRAY (PRAYED PRAYER PRAYERS PRAYING)

Dt   4: 7 is near us whenever we *p* to him?
1Sa 12:23 the LORD by failing to *p* for you.
2Ch   7:14 will humble themselves and *p*
Job 42: 8 My servant Job will *p* for you,
Ps 122: 6 *P* for the peace of Jerusalem:
Mt   5:44 and *p* for those who persecute you,
       6: 5 "And when you *p*, do not be like
       6: 9 "This, then, is how you should *p*:
      26:36 Sit here while I go over there and *p*
Lk   6:28 *p* for those who mistreat you.
      18: 1 them that they should always *p*
      22:40 "*P* that you will not fall
Ro   8:26 do not know what we ought to *p*,
1Co 14:13 in a tongue should *p* that he may
1Th   5:17 Be joyful always; *p* continually;
Jas   5:13 one of you in trouble? He should *p*.
       5:16 *p* for each other so that you may be

PRAYED (PRAY)

1Sa   1:27 I *p* for this child, and the LORD
Jnh   2: 1 From inside the fish Jonah *p*
Mk   14:35 *p* that if possible the hour might

PRAYER (PRAY)

2Ch 30:27 for their *p* reached heaven,
Ezr   8:23 about this, and he answered our *p*.
Ps   6: 9 the LORD accepts my *p*.
       86: 6 Hear my *p*, O LORD;
Pr   15: 8 but the *p* of the upright pleases him
Isa 56: 7 a house of *p* for all nations."
Mt   21:13 house will be called a house of *p*,'
Mk   11:24 whatever you ask for in *p*,
Jn   17:15 My *p* is not that you take them out
Ac   6: 4 and will give our attention to *p*
Php   4: 6 but in everything, by *p* and petition
Jas   5:15 *p* offered in faith will make the sick
1Pe   3:12 and his ears are attentive to their *p*,

PRAYERS (PRAY)

1Ch   5:20 He answered their *p*, because they
Mk   12:40 and for a show make lengthy *p*.
1Pe   3: 7 so that nothing will hinder your *p*.
Rev   5: 8 which are the *p* of the saints.

PRAYING (PRAY)

Mk   11:25 And when you stand *p*,
Jn   17: 9 I am not *p* for the world,
Ac   16:25 and Silas were *p* and singing hymns
Eph   6:18 always keep on *p* for all the saints.

PREACH (PREACHED PREACHING)

Mt   23: 3 they do not practice what they *p*.

Mk 16:15 and *p* the good news to all
creation.
Ac 9:20 At once he began to *p*
Ro 10:15 how can they *p* unless they are
sent
15:20 to *p* the gospel where Christ
was
1Co 1:17 to *p* the gospel—not with words
1:23 wisdom, but we *p* Christ
crucified:
9:14 that those who *p* the gospel
should
9:16 Woe to me if I do not *p* the
gospel!
2Co 10:16 so that we can *p* the gospel
Gal 1: 8 from heaven should *p* a gospel
2Ti 4: 2 I give you this charge: P the
Word;

PREACHED (PREACH)
Mk 13:10 And the gospel must first be *p*
Ac 8: 4 had been scattered *p* the word
1Co 9:27 so that after I have *p* to others,
15: 1 you of the gospel I *p* to you,
2Co 11: 4 other than the Jesus we *p*,
Gal 1: 8 other than the one we *p* to you,
Php 1:18 false motives or true, Christ
is *p*.
1Ti 3:16 was *p* among the nations,

PREACHING (PREACH)
Ro 10:14 hear without someone *p* to
them?
1Co 9:18 in *p* the gospel I may offer it
free
1Ti 4:13 the public reading of Scripture,
to *p*
5:17 especially those whose work
is *p*

PRECEPTS
Ps 19: 8 The *p* of the LORD are right,
111: 7 all his *p* are trustworthy.
111:10 who follow his *p* have good
119: 40 How I long for your *p!*
119: 69 I keep your *p* with all my heart.
119:104 I gain understanding from
your *p;*
119:159 See how I love your *p;*

PRECIOUS
Ps 19:10 They are more *p* than gold,
116: 15 in the sight of the LORD
Pr 8:11 for wisdom is more *p* than
rubies,
Isa 28:16 a *p* cornerstone for a sure
1Pe 1:19 but with the *p* blood of Christ,
2: 6 a chosen and *p* cornerstone,
2Pe 1: 4 us his very great and *p*
promises,

PREDESTINED* (DESTINY)
Ro 8:29 *p* to be conformed to the
likeness
8:30 And those he *p*, he also called;
Eph 1: 5 In love he *p* us to be adopted
1:11 having been *p* according

PREDICTION*
Jer 28: 9 only if his *p* comes true."

PREPARE (PREPARED)
Ps 23: 5 You *p* a table before me
Am 4:12 *p* to meet your God, O Israel."
Jn 14: 2 there to *p* a place for you.
Eph 4:12 to *p* God's people for works

PREPARED (PREPARE)
Mt 25:34 the kingdom *p* for you
1Co 2: 9 what God has *p* for those who
love
Eph 2:10 which God in advance for us
2Ti 4: 2 be *p* in season and out of
season;
1Pe 3:15 Always be *p* to give an answer

PRESENCE (PRESENT)
Ex 25:30 Put the bread of the P on this
table
Ezr 9:15 one of us can stand in your *p.*"
Ps 31:20 the shelter of your *p* you hide
them

Ps 89:15 who walk in the light of your *p,*
90: 8 our secret sins in the light of
your *p*
139: 7 Where can I flee from your *p?*
Jer 5:22 "Should you not tremble in
my *p?*
Heb 9:24 now to appear for us in God's *p.*
Jude :24 before his glorious *p* without
fault

PRESENT (PRESENCE)
2Co 11: 2 so that I might *p* you as a pure
Eph 5:27 and to *p* her to himself
2Ti 2:15 Do your best to *p* yourself to
God

PRESERVES
Ps 119:50 Your promise *p* my life.

PRESS (PRESSED PRESSURE)
Php 3:14 I *p* on toward the goal

PRESSED (PRESS)
Lk 6:38 *p* down, shaken together

PRESSURE (PRESS)
2Co 1: 8 We were under great *p,* far
11:28 I face daily the *p* of my concern

PREVAILS
1Sa 2: 9 "It is not by strength that one *p;*

PRICE
Job 28:18 the *p* of wisdom is beyond
rubies.
1Co 6:20 your own; you were bought at
a *p.*
7:23 bought at a *p;* do not become
slaves

PRIDE (PROUD)
Pr 8:13 I hate *p* and arrogance,
16:18 P goes before destruction,
Da 4:37 And those who walk in *p* he is
able
Gal 6: 4 Then he can take *p* in himself,
Jas 1: 9 ought to take *p* in his high
position.

PRIEST (PRIESTHOOD PRIESTS)
Heb 4:14 have a great high *p* who has
gone
4:15 do not have a high *p* who is
unable
7:26 Such a high *p* meets our need—
8: 1 We do have such a high *p,*

PRIESTHOOD (PRIEST)
Heb 7:24 lives forever, he has a
permanent *p.*
1Pe 2: 5 into a spiritual house to be a
holy *p,*
2: 9 you are a chosen people, a
royal *p,*

PRIESTS (PRIEST)
Ex 19: 6 you will be for me a kingdom
of *p*
Rev 5:10 to be a kingdom and *p*

PRINCE
Isa 9: 6 Everlasting Father, P of Peace.
Jn 12:31 now the *p* of this world will be
Ac 5:31 as P and Savior that he might
give

PRISON (PRISONER)
Isa 42: 7 to free captives from *p*
Mt 25:36 I was in *p* and you came to visit
me
1Pe 3:19 spirits in *p* who disobeyed long
ago
Rev 20: 7 Satan will be released from
his *p*

PRISONER (PRISON)
Ro 7:23 and making me a *p* of the law of
sin
Gal 3:22 declares that the whole world is
a *p*
Eph 3: 1 the *p* of Christ Jesus for the
sake

PRIVILEGE*
2Co 8: 4 pleaded with us for the *p* of
sharing

PRIZE
1Co 9:24 Run in such a way as to get
the *p.*
Php 3:14 on toward the goal to win the *p*

**PROCLAIM (PROCLAIMED
PROCLAIMING)**
1Ch 16:23 *p* his salvation day after day.
Ps 19: 1 the skies *p* the work of his
hands.
50: 6 the heavens *p* his
righteousness,
68:34 P the power of God,
118: 17 will *p* what the LORD has done.
Zec 9:10 He will *p* peace to the nations.
Ac 20:27 hesitated to *p* to you the whole
will
1Co 11:26 you *p* the Lord's death

PROCLAIMED (PROCLAIM)
Ro 15:19 I have fully *p* the gospel of
Christ.
Col 1:23 that has been *p* to every
creature

PROCLAIMING (PROCLAIM)
Ro 10: 8 the word of faith we are *p:*

PRODUCE (PRODUCES)
Mt 3: 8 P fruit in keeping with
repentance.
3:10 tree that does not *p* good fruit
will

PRODUCES (PRODUCE)
Pr 30:33 so stirring up anger *p* strife."
Ro 5: 3 that suffering *p* perseverance;
Heb 12:11 it *p* a harvest of righteousness

PROFANE
Lev 22:32 Do not *p* my holy name.

PROFESS*
1Ti 2:10 for women who *p* to worship
God.
Heb 4:14 let us hold firmly to the faith
we *p.*
10:23 unswervingly to the hope we *p,*

PROMISE (PROMISED PROMISES)
1Ki 8:20 The LORD has kept the *p* he
made
Ac 2:39 The *p* is for you and your
children
Gal 3:14 that by faith we might receive
the *p*
1Ti 4: 8 holding *p* for both the present
life
2Pe 3: 9 Lord is not slow in keeping
his *p,*

PROMISED (PROMISE)
Ex 3:17 And I have *p* to bring you up out
Dt 26:18 his treasured possession as
he *p,*
Ps 119: 57 I have *p* to obey your words.
Ro 4:21 power to do what he had *p.*
Heb 10:23 for he who *p* is faithful.
2Pe 3: 4 "Where is this 'coming' he *p?*

PROMISES (PROMISE)
Jos 21:45 one of all the LORD's good *p*
Ro 9: 4 the temple worship and the *p.*
2Pe 1: 4 us his very great and precious *p,*

PROMPTED
1Th 1: 3 your labor *p* by love, and your
2Th 1:11 and every act *p* by your faith.

PROPHECIES (PROPHECY)
1Co 13: 8 where there are *p,* they will
cease;
1Th 5:20 do not treat *p* with contempt.

PROPHECY (PROPHESY)
1Co 14: 1 gifts, especially the gift of *p.*
2Pe 1:20 you must understand that no *p*

PROPHESY (PROPHECIES PROPHECY PROPHESYING PROPHET PROPHETS)
Joel 2:28 Your sons and daughters will *p*,
Mt   7:22 Lord, did we not *p* in your name,
1Co 14:39 my brothers, be eager to *p*,

PROPHESYING (PROPHESY)
Ro   12: 6 If a man's gift is *p*, let him use it

PROPHET (PROPHESY)
Dt   18:18 up for them a *p* like you
Am   7:14 "I was neither a *p* nor a prophet's
Mt   10:41 Anyone who receives a *p*
Lk   4:24 "no *p* is accepted in his hometown.

PROPHETS (PROPHESY)
Ps 105: 15 do my *p* no harm."
Mt   5:17 come to abolish the Law or the *P*;
      7:12 for this sums up the Law and the *P*.
     24:24 false Christs and false *p* will appear
Lk   24:25 believe all that the *p* have spoken!
Ac   10:43 All the *p* testify about him that
1Co 12:28 second *p*, third teachers, then
     14:32 The spirits of *p* are subject
Eph   2:20 foundation of the apostles and *p*,
Heb   1: 1 through the *p* at many times
1Pe   1:10 Concerning this salvation, the *p*,
2Pe   1:19 word of the *p* made more certain,

PROSPER (PROSPERITY PROSPERS)
Pr   28:25 he who trusts in the LORD will *p*.

PROSPERITY (PROSPER)
Ps   73: 3 when I saw the *p* of the wicked.
Pr   13:21 but *p* is the reward of the righteous.

PROSPERS (PROSPER)
Ps   1: 3 Whatever he does *p*.

PROSTITUTE (PROSTITUTES)
1Co   6:15 of Christ and unite them with a *p*?

PROSTITUTES (PROSTITUTE)
Lk   15:30 property with *p* comes home,
1Co   6: 9 male *p* nor homosexual offenders

PROSTRATE
Dt   9:18 again I fell *p* before the LORD

PROTECT (PROTECTS)
Ps   32: 7 you will *p* me from trouble
Pr   2:11 Discretion will *p* you,
Jn   17:11 *p* them by the power of your name

PROTECTS (PROTECT)
1Co 13: 7 It always *p*, always trusts,

PROUD (PRIDE)
Pr   16: 5 The LORD detests all the *p*
Ro   12:16 Do not be *p*, but be willing
1Co 13: 4 it does not boast, it is not *p*.

PROVE
Ac   26:20 *p* their repentance by their deeds.
1Co   4: 2 been given a trust must *p* faithful.

PROVIDE (PROVIDED PROVIDES)
Ge   22: 8 "God himself will *p* the lamb
Isa 43:20 because I *p* water in the desert
1Ti   5: 8 If anyone does not *p*

PROVIDED (PROVIDE)
Jnh   1:17 But the LORD *p* a great fish
      4: 6 Then the LORD God *p* a vine
      4: 7 dawn the next day God *p* a worm,
      4: 8 God *p* a scorching east wind,

PROVIDES (PROVIDE)
1Ti   6:17 who richly *p* us with everything
1Pe   4:11 it with the strength God *p*,

PROVOKED
Ecc   7: 9 Do not be quickly *p* in your spirit,

PRUDENT
Pr   14:15 a *p* man gives thought to his steps.
     19:14 but a *p* wife is from the LORD.
Am   5:13 Therefore the *p* man keeps quiet

PRUNING
Isa   2: 4 and their spears into *p* hooks.
Joel 3:10 and your *p* hooks into spears.

PSALMS
Eph   5:19 Speak to one another with *p*,
Col   3:16 and as you sing *p*, hymns

PUBLICLY
Ac   20:20 have taught you *p* and from house
1Ti   5:20 Those who sin are to be rebuked *p*,

PUFFS
1Co   8: 1 Knowledge *p* up, but love builds up

PULLING
2Co 10: 8 building you up rather than *p* you

PUNISH (PUNISHED PUNISHES)
Ex   32:34 I will *p* them for their sin."
Pr   23:13 if you *p* him with the rod, he will
Isa 13:11 I will *p* the world for its evil,
1Pe   2:14 by him to *p* those who do wrong

PUNISHED (PUNISH)
La   3:39 complain when *p* for his sins?
2Th   1: 9 be *p* with everlasting destruction
Heb 10:29 to be *p* who has trampled the Son

PUNISHES (PUNISH)
Heb 12: 6 and he *p* everyone he accepts

PURE (PURIFIES PURIFY PURITY)
2Sa 22:27 to the *p* you show yourself *p*,
Ps   24: 4 who has clean hands and a *p* heart,
     51:10 Create in me a *p* heart, O God,
    119: 9 can a young man keep his way *p*?
Pr   20: 9 can say, "I have kept my heart *p*;
Isa 52:11 Come out from it and be *p*,
Hab   1:13 Your eyes are too *p* to look on evil;
Mt   5: 8 Blessed are the *p* in heart,
2Co 11: 2 I might present you as a *p* virgin
Php   4: 8 whatever is *p*, whatever is lovely,
1Ti   5:22 Keep yourself *p*.
Tit   1:15 To the *p*, all things are *p*,
      2: 5 to be self-controlled and *p*,
Heb 13: 4 and the marriage bed kept *p*,
1Jn   3: 3 him purifies himself, just as he is *p*.

PURGE
Pr   20:30 and beatings *p* the inmost being.

PURIFIES* (PURE)
1Jn   1: 7 of Jesus, his Son, *p* us from all sin.
      3: 3 who has this hope in him *p* himself,

PURIFY (PURE)
Tit   2:14 to *p* for himself a people that are
1Jn   1: 9 and *p* us from all unrighteousness.

PURITY (PURE)
2Co   6: 6 in *p*, understanding, patience
1Ti   4:12 in life, in love, in faith and in *p*.

PURPOSE
Pr   19:21 but it is the LORD's *p* that prevails
Isa 55:11 and achieve the *p* for which I sent it
Ro   8:28 have been called according to his *p*.
Php   2: 2 love, being one in spirit and *p*.

PURSES
Lk   12:33 Provide *p* for yourselves that will

PURSUE
Ps   34:14 seek peace and *p* it.
2Ti   2:22 and *p* righteousness, faith,
1Pe   3:11 he must seek peace and *p* it.

QUALITIES (QUALITY)
2Pe   1: 8 For if you possess these *q*

QUALITY (QUALITIES)
1Co   3:13 and the fire will test the *q*

QUARREL (QUARRELSOME)
Pr   15:18 but a patient man calms a *q*.
     17:14 Starting a *q* is like breaching a dam;
     17:19 He who loves a *q* loves sin;
2Ti   2:24 And the Lord's servant must not *q*;

QUARRELSOME (QUARREL)
Pr   19:13 a *q* wife is like a constant dripping.
1Ti   3: 3 not violent but gentle, not *q*,

QUICK-TEMPERED
Tit   1: 7 not *q*, not given to drunkenness,

QUIET (QUIETNESS)
Ps   23: 2 he leads me beside *q* waters,
Zep   3:17 he will *q* you with his love,
Lk   19:40 he replied, "if they keep *q*,
1Ti   2: 2 we may live peaceful and *q* lives
1Pe   3: 4 beauty of a gentle and *q* spirit,

QUIETNESS (QUIET)
Isa 30:15 in *q* and trust is your strength,
     32:17 the effect of righteousness will be *q*
1Ti   2:11 A woman should learn in *q*

QUIVER
Ps 127: 5 whose *q* is full of them.

RACE
Ecc   9:11 The *r* is not to the swift
1Co   9:24 that in a *r* all the runners run,
2Ti   4: 7 I have finished the *r*, I have kept
Heb 12: 1 perseverance the *r* marked out

RACHEL
Daughter of Laban (Ge 29:16); wife of Jacob (Ge 29:28); bore two sons (Ge 30:22-24; 35:16-24; 46:19).

RADIANCE (RADIANT)
Heb   1: 3 The Son is the *r* of God's glory

RADIANT (RADIANCE)
Ex   34:29 he was not aware that his face was *r*
Ps   34: 5 Those who look to him are *r*;
SS   5:10 *Beloved* My lover is *r* and ruddy,
Isa 60: 5 Then you will look and be *r*,
Eph   5:27 her to himself as a *r* church,

RAIN (RAINBOW)
Mt   5:45 and sends *r* on the righteous

RAINBOW (RAIN)
Ge   9:13 I have set my *r* in the clouds,

RAISED (RISE)
Ro   4:25 was *r* to life for our justification.
     10: 9 in your heart that God *r* him
1Co 15: 4 that he was *r* on the third day

RAN (RUN)
Jnh   1: 3 But Jonah *r* away from the LORD

RANSOM

Mt   20:28 and to give his life as a *r* for many."
Heb   9:15 as a *r* to set them free

RAVENS

1Ki   17: 6 The *r* brought him bread
Lk   12:24 Consider the *r*: They do not sow

READ (READS)

Jos   8:34 Joshua *r* all the words of the law—
Ne   8: 8 They *r* from the Book of the Law
2Co   3: 2 known and *r* by everybody.

READS (READ)

Rev   1: 3 Blessed is the one who *r* the words

REAL (REALITY)

Jn   6:55 is *r* food and my blood is *r* drink.

REALITY* (REAL)

Col   2:17 the *r*, however, is found in Christ.

REAP (REAPS)

Job   4: 8 and those who sow trouble *r* it.
2Co   9: 6 generously will also *r* generously.

REAPS (REAP)

Gal   6: 7 A man *r* what he sows.

REASON

Isa   1:18 "Come now, let us *r* together,"
1Pe   3:15 to give the *r* for the hope that you

REBEKAH

Sister of Laban, secured as bride for Isaac (Ge 24). Mother of Esau and Jacob (Ge 25:19-26). Taken by Abimelech as sister of Isaac; returned (Ge 26:1-11). Encouraged Jacob to trick Isaac out of blessing (Ge 27:1-17).

REBEL

Mt   10:21 children will *r* against their parents

REBUKE (REBUKED REBUKING)

Pr   9: 8 *r* a wise man and he will love you.
    27: 5 Better is open *r*
Lk   17: 3 "If your brother sins, *r* him,
2Ti   4: 2 correct, *r* and encourage—
Rev   3:19 Those whom I love I *r*

REBUKED (REBUKE)

1Ti   5:20 Those who sin are to be *r* publicly,

REBUKING (REBUKE)

2Ti   3:16 *r*, correcting and training

RECEIVE (RECEIVED RECEIVES)

Ac   1: 8 you will *r* power when the Holy
    20:35 'It is more blessed to give than to *r*
2Co   6:17 and I will *r* you."
Rev   4:11 to *r* glory and honor and power,

RECEIVED (RECEIVE)

Mt   6: 2 they have *r* their reward in full.
    10: 8 Freely you have *r*, freely give.
1Co   11:23 For I *r* from the Lord what I
Col   2: 6 just as you *r* Christ Jesus as Lord,
1Pe   4:10 should use whatever gift he has *r*

RECEIVES (RECEIVE)

Mt   7: 8 everyone who asks *r*; he who seeks
    10:40 he who *r* me *r* the one who sent me.
Ac   10:43 believes in him *r* forgiveness of sins

RECKONING

Isa   10: 3 What will you do on the day of *r*,

RECOGNIZE (RECOGNIZED)

Mt   7:16 By their fruit you will *r* them.

RECOGNIZED (RECOGNIZE)

Mt   12:33 for a tree is *r* by its fruit.
Ro   7:13 in order that sin might be *r* as sin,

RECOMPENSE

Isa   40:10 and his *r* accompanies him.

RECONCILE (RECONCILED RECONCILIATION)

Eph   2:16 in this one body to *r* both of them

RECONCILED (RECONCILE)

Mt   5:24 First go and be *r* to your brother;
Ro   5:10 we were *r* to him through the death
2Co   5:18 who *r* us to himself through Christ

RECONCILIATION* (RECONCILE)

Ro   5:11 whom we have now received *r*.
    11:15 For if their rejection is the *r*
2Co   5:18 and gave us the ministry of *r*:
    5:19 committed to us the message of *r*.

RECORD

Ps   130: 3 If you, O LORD, kept a *r* of sins,

RED

Isa   1:18 though they are *r* as crimson,

REDEEM (KINSMAN-REDEEMER REDEEMED REDEEMER REDEMPTION)

2Sa   7:23 on earth that God went out to *r*
Ps   49: 7 No man can *r* the life of another
Gal   4: 5 under law, to *r* those under law,

REDEEMED (REDEEM)

Gal   3:13 Christ *r* us from the curse
1Pe   1:18 or gold that you were *r*

REDEEMER (REDEEM)

Job   19:25 I know that my *R* lives,

REDEMPTION (REDEEM)

Ps   130: 7 and with him is full *r*.
Lk   21:28 because your *r* is drawing near."
Ro   8:23 as sons, the *r* of our bodies.
Eph   1: 7 In him we have *r* through his blood
Col   1:14 in whom we have *r*, the forgiveness
Heb   9:12 having obtained eternal *r*.

REFLECT

2Co   3:18 unveiled faces all *r* the Lord's

REFUGE

Nu   35:11 towns to be your cities of *r*,
Dt   33:27 The eternal God is your *r*,
Ru   2:12 wings you have come to take *r*."
Ps   46: 1 God is our *r* and strength,
    91: 2 "He is my *r* and my fortress,

REHOBOAM

Son of Solomon (1Ki 11:43; 1Ch 3:10). Harsh treatment of subjects caused divided kingdom (1Ki 12:1-24; 14:21-31; 2Ch 10-12).

REIGN

Ex   15:18 The LORD will *r*
Ro   6:12 Therefore do not let sin *r*
1Co   15:25 For he must *r* until he has put all
2Ti   2:12 we will also *r* with him.
Rev   20: 6 will *r* with him for a thousand years

REJECTED (REJECTS)

Ps   118: 22 The stone the builders *r*
Isa   53: 3 He was despised and *r* by men,
1Ti   4: 4 nothing is to be *r* if it is received
1Pe   2: 4 by men but chosen by God
    2: 7 "The stone the builders *r*

REJECTS (REJECTED)

Lk   10:16 but he who *r* me *r* him who sent me
Jn   3:36 whoever *r* the Son will not see life,

REJOICE (JOY)

Ps   2:11 and *r* with trembling.
    66: 6 come, let us *r* in him.
    118: 24 let us *r* and be glad in it.
Pr   5:18 may you *r* in the wife of your youth
Lk   10:20 but *r* that your names are written
    15: 6 'R with me; I have found my lost
Ro   12:15 Rejoice with those who *r*; mourn
Php   4: 4 *R* in the Lord always.

REJOICES (JOY)

Isa   61:10 my soul *r* in my God.
Lk   1:47 and my spirit *r* in God my Savior,
1Co   12:26 if one part is honored, every part *r*
    13: 6 delight in evil but *r* with the truth.

REJOICING (JOY)

Ps   30: 5 but *r* comes in the morning.
Lk   15: 7 in the same way there will be more *r*
Ac   5:41 *r* because they had been counted

RELIABLE

2Ti   2: 2 witnesses entrust to *r* men who will

RELIGION

1Ti   5: 4 all to put their *r* into practice
Jas   1:27 *R* that God our Father accepts

REMAIN (REMAINS)

Nu   33:55 allow to *r* will become barbs
Jn   15: 7 If you *r* in me and my words
Ro   13: 8 Let no debt *r* outstanding,
1Co   13:13 And now these three *r*: faith,
2Ti   2:13 he will *r* faithful,

REMAINS (REMAIN)

Ps   146: 6 the LORD, who *r* faithful forever.
Heb   7: 3 Son of God he *r* a priest forever.

REMEMBER (REMEMBERS REMEMBRANCE)

Ex   20: 8 "R the Sabbath day
1Ch   16:12 *R* the wonders he has done,
Ecc   12: 1 *R* your Creator
Jer   31:34 and will *r* their sins no more."
Gal   2:10 we should continue to *r* the poor,
Php   1: 3 I thank my God every time I *r* you.
Heb   8:12 and will *r* their sins no more."

REMEMBERS (REMEMBER)

Ps   103: 14 he *r* that we are dust.
    111: 5 he *r* his covenant forever.
Isa   43:25 and *r* your sins no more.

REMEMBRANCE (REMEMBER)

1Co   11:24 which is for you; do this in *r* of me

REMIND

Jn   14:26 will *r* you of everything I have said

REMOVED

Ps   30:11 you *r* my sackcloth and clothed me
    103: 12 so far has he *r* our transgressions
Jn   20: 1 and saw that the stone had been *r*

RENEW (RENEWED RENEWING)

Ps   51:10 and *r* a steadfast spirit within me.
Isa   40:31 will *r* their strength.

RENEWED (RENEW)
Ps 103: 5 that your youth is *r* like the eagle's.
2Co 4: 16 yet inwardly we are being *r* day

RENEWING (RENEW)
Ro 12: 2 transformed by the *r* of your mind.

RENOUNCE (RENOUNCES)
Da 4: 27 *R* your sins by doing what is right,

RENOUNCES (RENOUNCE)
Pr 28: 13 confesses and *r* them finds

RENOWN
Isa 63: 12 to gain for himself everlasting *r*,
Jer 32: 20 have gained the *r* that is still yours.

REPAID (PAY)
Lk 14: 14 you will be *r* at the resurrection
Col 3: 25 Anyone who does wrong will be *r*

REPAY (PAY)
Dt 32: 35 It is mine to avenge; I will *r*.
Ru 2: 12 May the LORD *r* you
Ps 116: 12 How can I *r* the LORD
Ro 12: 19 "It is mine to avenge; I will *r*,"
1Pe 3: 9 Do not *r* evil with evil

REPENT (REPENTANCE REPENTS)
Job 42: 6 and *r* in dust and ashes."
Jer 15: 19 "If you *r*, I will restore you
Mt 4: 17 "*R*, for the kingdom of heaven is
Lk 13: 3 unless you *r*, you too will all perish.
Ac 2: 38 Peter replied, "*R* and be baptized,
  17: 30 all people everywhere to *r*.

REPENTANCE (REPENT)
Lk 3: 8 Produce fruit in keeping with *r*.
  5: 32 call the righteous, but sinners to *r*."
Ac 26: 20 and prove their *r* by their deeds.
2Co 7: 10 Godly sorrow brings *r* that leads

REPENTS (REPENT)
Lk 15: 10 of God over one sinner who *r*."
  17: 3 rebuke him, and if he *r*, forgive him

REPROACH
1Ti 3: 2 Now the overseer must be above *r*,

REPUTATION
1Ti 3: 7 also have a good *r* with outsiders,

REQUESTS
Ps 20: 5 May the LORD grant all your *r*.
Php 4: 6 with thanksgiving, present your *r*

REQUIRE
Mic 6: 8 And what does the LORD *r* of you

RESCUE (RESCUES)
Da 6: 20 been able to *r* you from the lions?"
2Pe 2: 9 how to *r* godly men from trials

RESCUES (RESCUE)
1Th 1: 10 who *r* us from the coming wrath.

RESIST
Jas 4: 7 *R* the devil, and he will flee
1Pe 5: 9 *R* him, standing firm in the faith,

RESOLVED
Ps 17: 3 I have *r* that my mouth will not sin.
Da 1: 8 But Daniel *r* not to defile himself
1Co 2: 2 For I *r* to know nothing while I was

RESPECT (RESPECTABLE)
Lev 19: 3 " 'Each of you must *r* his mother
  19: 32 show *r* for the elderly and revere
Pr 11: 16 A kindhearted woman gains *r*,

Mal 1: 6 where is the *r* due me?" says
1Th 4: 12 so that your daily life may win the *r*
  5: 12 to *r* those who work hard
1Ti 3: 4 children obey him with proper *r*.
1Pe 2: 17 Show proper *r* to everyone:
  3: 7 them with *r* as the weaker partner

RESPECTABLE* (RESPECT)
1Ti 3: 2 self-controlled, *r*, hospitable,

REST
Ex 31: 15 the seventh day is a Sabbath of *r*,
Ps 91: 1 will *r* in the shadow
Jer 6: 16 and you will find *r* for your souls.
Mt 11: 28 and burdened, and I will give you *r*.

RESTITUTION
Ex 22: 3 "A thief must certainly make *r*,
Lev 6: 5 He must make *r* in full, add a fifth

RESTORE (RESTORES)
Ps 51: 12 *R* to me the joy of your salvation
Gal 6: 1 are spiritual should *r* him gently.

RESTORES (RESTORE)
Ps 23: 3 he *r* my soul.

RESURRECTION
Mt 22: 30 At the *r* people will neither marry
Lk 14: 14 repaid at the *r* of the righteous."
Jn 11: 25 Jesus said to her, "I am the *r*
Ro 1: 4 Son of God by his *r* from the dead:
1Co 15: 12 some of you say that there is no *r*
Php 3: 10 power of his *r* and the fellowship
Rev 20: 5 This is the first *r*.

RETRIBUTION
Jer 51: 56 For the LORD is a God of *r*;

RETURN
2Ch 30: 9 If you *r* to the LORD, then your
Ne 1: 9 but if you *r* to me and obey my
Isa 55: 11 It will not *r* to me empty,
Hos 6: 1 "Come, let us *r* to the LORD.
Joel 2: 12 "*r* to me with all your heart,

REVEALED (REVELATION)
Dt 29: 29 but the things *r* belong to us
Isa 40: 5 the glory of the LORD will be *r*,
Mt 11: 25 and *r* them to little children.
Ro 1: 17 a righteousness from God is *r*,
  8: 18 with the glory that will be *r* in us.

REVELATION (REVEALED)
Gal 1: 12 I received it by *r* from Jesus Christ.
Rev 1: 1 *r* of Jesus Christ, which God gave

REVENGE (VENGEANCE)
Lev 19: 18 " 'Do not seek *r* or bear a grudge
Ro 12: 19 Do not take *r*, my friends,

REVERE (REVERENCE)
Ps 33: 8 let all the people of the world *r* him

REVERENCE (REVERE)
Lev 19: 30 and have *r* for my sanctuary.
Ps 5: 7 in *r* will I bow down
Col 3: 22 of heart and *r* for the Lord.
1Pe 3: 2 when they see the purity and *r*

REVIVE (REVIVING)
Ps 85: 6 Will you not *r* us again,
Isa 57: 15 to *r* the spirit of the lowly

REVIVING (REVIVE)
Ps 19: 7 the soul.

REWARD (REWARDED)
Ps 19: 11 in keeping them there is great *r*.
  127: 3 children a *r* from him.

Pr 19: 17 he will *r* him for what he has done.
  25: 22 and the LORD will *r* you.
  31: 31 Give her the *r* she has earned,
Jer 17: 10 to *r* a man according to his conduct
Mt 5: 12 because great is your *r* in heaven,
  6: 5 they have received their *r* in full.
  16: 27 and then he will *r* each person
1Co 3: 14 built survives, he will receive his *r*.
Rev 22: 12 I am coming soon! My *r* is with me

REWARDED (REWARD)
Ru 2: 12 May you be richly *r* by the LORD,
Ps 18: 24 The LORD has *r* me according
Pr 14: 14 and the good man *r* for his.
1Co 3: 8 and each will be *r* according

RICH (RICHES)
Pr 23: 4 Do not wear yourself out to get *r*;
Jer 9: 23 or the *r* man boast of his riches,
Mt 19: 23 it is hard for a *r* man
2Co 6: 10 yet making many *r*; having nothing
  8: 9 he was *r*, yet for your sakes he
1Ti 6: 17 Command those who are *r*

RICHES (RICH)
Ps 119: 14 as one rejoices in great *r*.
Pr 30: 8 give me neither poverty nor *r*,
Isa 10: 3 Where will you leave your *r*?
Ro 9: 23 to make the *r* of his glory known
  11: 33 the depth of the *r* of the wisdom
Eph 2: 7 he might show the incomparable *r*
  3: 8 to the Gentiles the unsearchable *r*
Col 1: 27 among the Gentiles the glorious *r*

RID
Ge 21: 10 "Get *r* of that slave woman
1Co 5: 7 Get *r* of the old yeast that you may
Gal 4: 30 "Get *r* of the slave woman

RIGHT (RIGHTS)
Ge 18: 25 the Judge of all the earth do *r*?"
Ex 15: 26 and do what is *r* in his eyes,
Dt 5: 32 do not turn aside to the *r*
Ps 16: 8 Because he is at my *r* hand,
  19: 8 The precepts of the LORD are *r*,
  63: 8 your *r* hand upholds me.
  110: 1 "Sit at my *r* hand
Pr 4: 27 Do not swerve to the *r* or the left;
  14: 12 There is a way that seems *r*
Isa 1: 17 learn to do *r*!
Jer 23: 5 and do what is just and *r* in the land
Hos 14: 9 The ways of the LORD are *r*;
Mt 6: 3 know what your *r* hand is doing,
Jn 1: 12 he gave the *r* to become children
Ro 9: 21 Does not the potter have the *r*
  12: 17 careful to do what is *r* in the eyes
Eph 1: 20 and seated him at his *r* hand
Php 4: 8 whatever is *r*, whatever is pure,
2Th 3: 13 never tire of doing what is *r*.

RIGHTEOUS (RIGHTEOUSNESS)
Ps 34: 15 The eyes of the LORD are on the *r*
  37: 25 yet I have never seen the *r* forsaken
  119:137 *R* are you, O LORD,
  143: 2 for no one living is *r* before you.
Pr 3: 33 but he blesses the home of the *r*.
  11: 30 The fruit of the *r* is a tree of life,
  18: 10 the *r* run to it and are safe.
Isa 64: 6 and all our *r* acts are like filthy rags
Hab 2: 4 but the *r* will live by his faith—
Mt 5: 45 rain on the *r* and the unrighteous.
  9: 13 For I have not come to call the *r*,

Mt   13:49 and separate the wicked from
                the r
        25:46 to eternal punishment, but the r
Ro   1:17 as it is written: "The r will live
         3:10 "There is no one r, not even
                one;
1Ti   1: 9 that law is made not for the r
1Pe   3:18 the r for the unrighteous,
1Jn   3: 7 does what is right is r, just as
                he is r.
Rev   19: 8 stands for the r acts of the
                saints.)

RIGHTEOUSNESS (RIGHTEOUS)
Ge   15: 6 and he credited it to him as r.
1Sa   26:23 Lord rewards every man for his r
Ps   9: 8 He will judge the world in r;
        23: 3 He guides me in paths of r
        45: 7 You love r and hate wickedness;
        85:10 r and peace kiss each other.
        89:14 R and justice are the foundation
       111: 3 and his r endures forever.
Pr   14:34 R exalts a nation,
        21:21 He who pursues r and love
Isa   5:16 will show himself holy by his r.
        59:17 He put on r as his breastplate,
Eze   18:20 The r of the righteous man will
                be
Da   9:24 to bring in everlasting r,
        12: 3 and those who lead many to r,
Mal   4: 2 the sun of r will rise with healing
Mt   5: 6 those who hunger and thirst
                for r,
         5:20 unless your r surpasses that
         6:33 But seek first his kingdom and
                his r
Ro   4: 3 and it was credited to him as r."
         4: 9 faith was credited to him as r.
         6:13 body to him as instruments of r.
2Co   5:21 that in him we might become
                the r
Gal   2:21 for if r could be gained
         3: 6 and it was credited to him as r."
Eph   6:14 with the breastplate of r in
                place,
Php   3: 9 not having a r of my own that
2Ti   3:16 correcting and training in r,
         4: 8 is in store for me the crown of r,
Heb   11: 7 became heir of the r that comes
2Pe   2:21 not to have known the way of r,

RIGHTS (RIGHT)
La   3:35 to deny a man his r
Gal   4: 5 that we might receive the full r

RISE (RAISED)
Isa   26:19 their bodies will r.
Mt   27:63 'After three days I will r again.'
Jn   5:29 those who have done good will r
1Th   4:16 and the dead in Christ will r
                first.

ROAD
Mt   7:13 and broad is the r that leads

ROBBERS
Jer   7:11 become a den of r to you?
Mk   15:27 They crucified two r with him,
Lk   19:46 but you have made it 'a den
                of r.' "
Jn   10: 8 came before me were thieves
                and r,

ROCK
Ps   18: 2 The Lord is my r, my fortress
        40: 1 he set my feet on a r
Mt   7:24 man who built his house on
                the r.
        16:18 and on this r I will build my
                church
Ro   9:33 and a r that makes them fall,
1Co   10: 4 the spiritual r that accompanied

ROD
Ps   23: 4 your r and your staff,
Pr   13:24 He who spares the r hates his
                son,
        23:13 if you punish him with the r,

ROOM (ROOMS)
Mt   6: 6 But when you pray, go into
                your r,

Lk   2: 7 there was no r for them in the
                inn.
Jn   21:25 the whole world would not
                have r

ROOMS (ROOM)
Jn   14: 2 In my Father's house are
                many r;

ROOT
Isa   53: 2 and like a r out of dry ground.
1Ti   6:10 of money is a r of all kinds of
                evil.

ROYAL
Jas   2: 8 If you really keep the r law found
1Pe   2: 9 a r priesthood, a holy nation,

RUBBISH*
Php   3: 8 I consider them r, that I may
                gain

RUDE*
1Co   13: 5 It is not r, it is not self-seeking,

RUIN (RUINS)
Pr   18:24 many companions may come
                to r,
1Ti   6: 9 desires that plunge men into r

RUINS (RUIN)
Pr   19: 3 A man's own folly r his life,
2Ti   2:14 and only r those who listen.

RULE (RULER RULERS RULES)
1Sa   12:12 'No, we want a king to r over
                us'—
Ps   2: 9 You will r them with an iron
       119:133 let no sin r over me.
Zec   9:10 His r will extend from sea to sea
Col   3:15 the peace of Christ r in your
                hearts,
Rev   2:27 He will r them with an iron
                scepter;

RULER (RULE)
Ps   8: 6 You made him r over the works
Eph   2: 2 of the r of the kingdom of the
                air,
1Ti   6:15 God, the blessed and only R,

RULERS (RULE)
Ps   2: 2 and the r gather together
Col   1:16 or powers or r or authorities;

RULES (RULE)
Ps   103: 19 and his kingdom r over all.
Lk   22:26 one who r like the one who
                serves.
2Ti   2: 5 he competes according to the r.

RUMORS
Mt   24: 6 You will hear of wars and r of
                wars,

RUN (RAN)
Isa   40:31 they will r and not grow weary,
1Co   9:24 R in such a way as to get the
                prize.
Heb   12: 1 let us r with perseverance the
                race

RUST
Mt   6:19 where moth and r destroy,

RUTH*
Moabitess; widow who went to Bethlehem
with mother-in-law Naomi (Ru 1). Gleaned in
field of Boaz; shown favor (Ru 2). Proposed
marriage to Boaz (Ru 3). Married (Ru 4:1-12);
bore Obed, ancestor of David (Ru 4:13-22);
Jesus (Mt 1:5).

SABBATH
Ex   20: 8 "Remember the S day
Dt   5:12 "Observe the S day
Col   2:16 a New Moon celebration or a S
                day

SACKCLOTH
Mt   11:21 would have repented long ago
                in s

SACRED
Mt   7: 6 "Do not give dogs what is s;
1Co   3:17 for God's temple is s, and you

SACRIFICE (SACRIFICED SACRIFICES)
Ge   22: 2 S him there as a burnt offering
Ex   12:27 'It is the Passover s to the Lord.
1Sa   15:22 To obey is better than s,
Hos   6: 6 For I desire mercy, not s,
Mt   9:13 this means: 'I desire mercy,
                not s.'
Heb   9:26 away with sin by the s of
                himself.
        13:15 offer to God a s of praise—
1Jn   2: 2 He is the atoning s for our sins,

SACRIFICED (SACRIFICE)
1Co   5: 7 our Passover lamb, has been s.
         8: 1 Now about food s to idols:
Heb   9:28 so Christ was once

SACRIFICES (SACRIFICE)
Ps   51:17 The s of God are a broken spirit;
Ro   12: 1 to offer your bodies as living s,

SADDUCEES
Mk   12:18 S, who say there is no
                resurrection,

SAFE (SAVE)
Ps   37: 3 in the land and enjoy s pasture.
Pr   18:10 the righteous run to it and are s.

SAFETY (SAVE)
Ps   4: 8 make me dwell in s.
1Th   5: 3 people are saying, "Peace
                and s,"

SAINTS
Ps   116: 15 is the death of his s.
Ro   8:27 intercedes for the s in
                accordance
Eph   1:18 of his glorious inheritance in
                the s,
         6:18 always keep on praying for all
                the s
Rev   5: 8 which are the prayers of the s.
        19: 8 for the righteous acts of the s.)

SAKE
Ps   44:22 Yet for your s we face death all
                day
Php   3: 7 loss for the s of Christ.
Heb   11:26 He regarded disgrace for the s

SALT
Ge   19:26 and she became a pillar of s.
Mt   5:13 "You are the s of the earth.

SALVATION (SAVE)
Ex   15: 2 he has become my s.
1Ch   16:23 proclaim his s day after day.
Ps   27: 1 The Lord is my light and my s—
        51:12 Restore to me the joy of your s
        62: 2 He alone is my rock and my s;
        85: 9 Surely his s is near those who
                fear
        96: 2 proclaim his s day after day.
Isa   25: 9 let us rejoice and be glad in
                his s."
        45:17 the Lord with an everlasting s;
        51: 6 But my s will last forever,
        59:17 and the helmet of s on his head;
        61:10 me with garments of s
Jnh   2: 9 S comes from the Lord."
Zec   9: 9 righteous and having s,
Lk   2:30 For my eyes have seen your s,
Jn   4:22 for s is from the Jews.
Ac   4:12 S is found in no one else,
        13:47 that you may bring s to the ends
Ro   11:11 s has come to the Gentiles
2Co   7:10 brings repentance that leads
                to s
Eph   6:17 Take the helmet of s and the
                sword
Php   2:12 to work out your s with fear
1Th   5: 8 and the hope of s as a helmet.
2Ti   3:15 wise for s through faith
Heb   2: 3 escape if we ignore such a
                great s?

Heb 6: 9 case—things that accompany s.
1Pe 1:10 Concerning this s, the prophets,
2: 2 by it you may grow up in your s,

SAMARITAN
Lk 10:33 But a S, as he traveled, came where

SAMSON
Danite judge. Birth promised (Jdg 13). Married to Philistine (Jdg 14). Vengeance on Philistines (Jdg 15). Betrayed by Delilah (Jdg 16:1-22). Death (Jdg 16:23-31). Feats of strength: killed lion (Jdg 14:6), 30 Philistines (Jdg 14:19), 1,000 Philistines with jawbone (Jdg 15:13-17), carried off gates of Gaza (Jdg 16:3), pushed down temple of Dagon (Jdg 16:25-30).

SAMUEL
Ephraimite judge and prophet (Heb 11:32). Birth prayed for (1Sa 1:10-18). Dedicated to temple by Hannah (1Sa 1:21-28). Raised by Eli (1Sa 2:11, 18-26). Called as prophet (1Sa 3). Led Israel to victory over Philistines (1Sa 7). Asked by Israel for a king (1Sa 8). Anointed Saul as king (1Sa 9-10). Farewell speech (1Sa 12). Rebuked Saul for sacrifice (1Sa 13). Announced rejection of Saul (1Sa 15). Anointed David as king (1Sa 16). Protected David from Saul (1Sa 19:18-24). Death (1Sa 25:1). Returned from dead to condemn Saul (1Sa 28).

SANCTIFIED (SANCTIFY)
Ac 20:32 among all those who are s.
Ro 15:16 to God, s by the Holy Spirit.
1Co 6:11 But you were washed, you were s,
7:14 and the unbelieving wife has been s
Heb 10:29 blood of the covenant that s him,

SANCTIFY (SANCTIFIED SANCTIFYING)
1Th 5:23 s you through and through.

SANCTIFYING (SANCTIFY)
2Th 2:13 through the s work of the Spirit

SANCTUARY
Ex 25: 8 "Then have them make a s for me,

SAND
Ge 22:17 and as the s on the seashore.
Mt 7:26 man who built his house on s.

SANDALS
Ex 3: 5 off your s, for the place where you
Jos 5:15 off your s, for the place where you

SANG (SING)
Job 38: 7 while the morning stars s together
Rev 5: 9 And they s a new song:

SARAH
Wife of Abraham, originally named Sarai; barren (Ge 11:29-31; 1Pe 3:6). Taken by Pharaoh as Abraham's sister; returned (Ge 12:10-20). Gave Hagar to Abraham; sent her away in pregnancy (Ge 16). Name changed; Isaac promised (Ge 17:15-21; 18:10-15; Heb 11:11). Taken by Abimelech as Abraham's sister; returned (Ge 20). Isaac born; Hagar and Ishmael sent away (Ge 21:1-21; Gal 4:21-31). Death (Ge 23).

SATAN
Job 1: 6 and S also came with them.
Zec 3: 2 said to S, "The LORD rebuke you,
Mk 4:15 S comes and takes away the word
2Co 11:14 for S himself masquerades
12: 7 a messenger of S, to torment me.
Rev 12: 9 serpent called the devil, or S,

Rev 20: 2 or S, and bound him for a thousand
20: 7 S will be released from his prison

SATISFIED (SATISFY)
Isa 53:11 he will see the light ⌐of life⌐ and be s

SATISFIES (SATISFY)
Ps 103: 5 who s your desires with good things,

SATISFY (SATISFIED SATISFIES)
Isa 55: 2 and your labor on what does not s?

SAUL
1. Benjamite; anointed by Samuel as first king of Israel (1Sa 9-10). Defeated Ammonites (1Sa 11). Rebuked for offering sacrifice (1Sa 13:1-15). Defeated Philistines (1Sa 14). Rejected as king for failing to annihilate Amalekites (1Sa 15). Soothed from evil spirit by David (1Sa 16:14-23). Sent David against Goliath (1Sa 17). Jealousy and attempted murder of David (1Sa 18:1-11). Gave David Michal as wife (1Sa 18:12-30). Second attempt to kill David (1Sa 19). Anger at Jonathan (1Sa 20:26-34). Pursued David: killed priests at Nob (1Sa 22), went to Keilah and Ziph (1Sa 23), life spared by David at En Gedi (1Sa 24) and in his tent (1Sa 26). Rebuked by Samuel's spirit for consulting witch at Endor (1Sa 28). Wounded by Philistines; took his own life (1Sa 31; 1Ch 10).
2. See PAUL

SAVE (SAFE SAFETY SALVATION SAVED SAVIOR)
Isa 63: 1 mighty to s."
Da 3:17 the God we serve is able to s us
Zep 3:17 he is mighty to s.
Mt 1:21 he will s his people from their sins
16:25 wants to s his life will lose it,
Lk 19:10 to seek and to s what was lost."
Jn 3:17 but to s the world through him.
1Ti 1:15 came into the world to s sinners—
Jas 5:20 of his way will s him from death

SAVED (SAVE)
Ps 34: 6 he s him out of all his troubles.
Isa 45:22 "Turn to me and be s,
Joel 2:32 on the name of the LORD will be s;
Mk 13:13 firm to the end will be s.
16:16 believes and is baptized will be s,
Jn 10: 9 enters through me will be s.
Ac 4:12 to men by which we must be s."
16:30 do to be s?" They replied,
Ro 9:27 only the remnant will be s.
10: 9 him from the dead, you will be s.
1Co 3:15 will suffer loss; he himself will be s,
15: 2 By this gospel you are s,
Eph 2: 5 it is by grace you have been s—
2: 8 For it is by grace you have been s,
1Ti 2: 4 who wants all men to be s

SAVIOR (SAVE)
Ps 89:26 my God, the Rock my S.'
Isa 43:11 and apart from me there is no s.
Hos 13: 4 no S except me.
Lk 1:47 and my spirit rejoices in God my S,
2:11 of David a S has been born to you;
Jn 4:42 know that this man really is the S
Eph 5:23 his body, of which he is the S.
1Ti 4:10 who is the S of all men,
Tit 2:10 about God our S attractive.
2:13 appearing of our great God and S,
3: 4 and love of God our S appeared,
1Jn 4:14 Son to be the S of the world.
Jude :25 to the only God our S be glory,

SCALES
Lev 19:36 Use honest s and honest weights,
Da 5:27 You have been weighed on the s

SCAPEGOAT (GOAT)
Lev 16:10 by sending it into the desert as a s.

SCARLET
Isa 1:18 "Though your sins are like s,

SCATTERED
Jer 31:10 'He who s Israel will gather them
Ac 8: 4 who had been s preached the word

SCEPTER
Rev 19:15 "He will rule them with an iron s."

SCHEMES
2Co 2:11 For we are not unaware of his s.
Eph 6:11 stand against the devil's s.

SCOFFERS
2Pe 3: 3 that in the last days s will come,

SCORPION
Rev 9: 5 sting of a s when it strikes a man.

SCRIPTURE (SCRIPTURES)
Jn 10:35 and the S cannot be broken—
1Ti 4:13 yourself to the public reading of S,
2Ti 3:16 All S is God-breathed
2Pe 1:20 that no prophecy of S came about

SCRIPTURES (SCRIPTURE)
Lk 24:27 said in all the S concerning himself.
Jn 5:39 These are the S that testify about
Ac 17:11 examined the S every day to see

SCROLL
Eze 3: 1 eat what is before you, eat this s;

SEA
Ex 14:16 go through the s on dry ground.
Isa 57:20 the wicked are like the tossing s,
Mic 7:19 iniquities into the depths of the s.
Jas 1: 6 who doubts is like a wave of the s,
Rev 13: 1 I saw a beast coming out of the s.

SEAL (SEALS)
Jn 6:27 God the Father has placed his s
2Co 1:22 set his s of ownership on us,
Eph 1:13 you were marked in him with a s,

SEALS (SEAL)
Rev 5: 2 "Who is worthy to break the s
6: 1 opened the first of the seven s.

SEARCH (SEARCHED SEARCHES SEARCHING)
Ps 4: 4 s your hearts and be silent.
139: 23 S me, O God, and know my heart;
Pr 2: 4 and s for it as for hidden treasure,
Jer 17:10 "I the LORD s the heart
Eze 34:16 I will s for the lost and bring back
Lk 15: 8 and s carefully until she finds it?

SEARCHED (SEARCH)
Ps 139: 1 O LORD, you have s me

SEARCHES (SEARCH)
Ro 8:27 And he who s our hearts knows
1Co 2:10 The Spirit s all things,

SEARCHING (SEARCH)
Am 8:12 s for the word of the LORD,

SEARED
1Ti 4: 2 whose consciences have been s

SEASON
2Ti 4: 2 be prepared in s and out of s;

SEAT (SEATED SEATS)
Ps 1: 1 or sit in the s of mockers.
Da 7: 9 and the Ancient of Days took his s.
2Co 5:10 before the judgment s of Christ,

SEATED (SEAT)
Ps 47: 8 God is on his holy throne.
Isa 6: 1 I saw the Lord s on a throne,
Col 3: 1 where Christ is s at the right hand

SEATS (SEAT)
Lk 11:43 you love the most important s

SECRET (SECRETS)
Dt 29:29 The s things belong
Jdg 16: 6 Tell me the s of your great strength
Ps 90: 8 our s sins in the light
Pr 11:13 but a trustworthy man keeps a s.
Mt 6: 4 so that your giving may be in s.
2Co 4: 2 we have renounced s and shameful
Php 4:12 I have learned the s

SECRETS (SECRET)
Ps 44:21 since he knows the s of the heart?
1Co 14:25 the s of his heart will be laid bare.

SECURE (SECURITY)
Ps 112: 8 His heart is s, he will have no fear;
Heb 6:19 an anchor for the soul, firm and s.

SECURITY (SECURE)
Job 31:24 or said to pure gold, 'You are my s,'

SEED (SEEDS)
Lk 8:11 of the parable: The s is the word
1Co 3: 6 I planted the s, Apollos watered it,
2Co 9:10 he who supplies s to the sower
Gal 3:29 then you are Abraham's s,
1Pe 1:23 not of perishable s,

SEEDS (SEED)
Jn 12:24 But if it dies, it produces many s.
Gal 3:16 Scripture does not say "and to s,"

SEEK (SEEKS SELF-SEEKING)
Dt 4:29 if from there you s the LORD your
1Ch 28: 9 If you s him, he will be found
2Ch 7:14 themselves and pray and s my face
Ps 119: 2 s you with all my heart;
Isa 55: 6 S the LORD while he may be
65: 1 found by those who did not s me.
Mt 6:33 But s first his kingdom
Lk 19:10 For the Son of Man came to s
Ro 10:20 found by those who did not s me;
1Co 7:27 you married? Do not s a divorce.

SEEKS (SEEK)
Jn 4:23 the kind of worshipers the Father s.

SEER
1Sa 9: 9 of today used to be called a s.)

SELF-CONTROL (CONTROL)
1Co 7: 5 you because of your lack of s.
Gal 5:23 faithfulness, gentleness and s.
2Pe 1: 6 and to knowledge, s; and to s,

SELF-CONTROLLED* (CONTROL)
1Th 5: 6 are asleep, but let us be alert and s.
5: 8 let us be s, putting on faith and love
1Ti 3: 2 s, respectable, hospitable,
Tit 1: 8 who is s, upright, holy
2: 2 worthy of respect, s, and sound
2: 5 to be s and pure, to be busy at home
2: 6 encourage the young men to be s.
2:12 to live s, upright and godly lives
1Pe 1:13 prepare your minds for action; be s;
4: 7 and s so that you can pray.
5: 8 Be s and alert.

SELF-INDULGENCE
Mt 23:25 inside they are full of greed and s.

SELF-SEEKING (SEEK)
1Co 13: 5 it is not s, it is not easily angered,

SELFISH*
Ps 119: 36 and not toward s gain.
Pr 18: 1 An unfriendly man pursues s ends;
Gal 5:20 fits of rage, s ambition, dissensions,
Php 1:17 preach Christ out of s ambition,
2: 3 Do nothing out of s ambition
Jas 3:14 and s ambition in your hearts,
3:16 you have envy and s ambition,

SEND (SENDING SENT)
Isa 6: 8 S me!" He said, "Go and tell this
Mt 9:38 to s out workers into his harvest
Jn 16: 7 but if I go, I will s him to you.

SENDING (SEND)
Jn 20:21 Father has sent me, I am s you."

SENSES*
Lk 15:17 "When he came to his s, he said,
1Co 15:34 Come back to your s as you ought,
2Ti 2:26 and that they will come to their s

SENSUAL
Col 2:23 value in restraining s indulgence.

SENT (SEND)
Isa 55:11 achieve the purpose for which I s it.
Mt 10:40 me receives the one who s me.
Jn 4:34 "is to do the will of him who s me
Ro 10:15 can they preach unless they are s?
1Jn 4:10 but that he loved us and s his Son

SEPARATE (SEPARATED SEPARATES)
Mt 19: 6 has joined together, let man not s."
Ro 8:35 Who shall s us from the love
1Co 7:10 wife must not s from her husband.
2Co 6:17 and be s, says the Lord.

SEPARATED (SEPARATE)
Isa 59: 2 But your iniquities have s

SEPARATES (SEPARATE)
Pr 16:28 and a gossip s close friends.

SERPENT
Ge 3: 1 the s was more crafty than any
Rev 12: 9 that ancient s called the devil

SERVANT (SERVANTS)
1Sa 3:10 "Speak, for your s is listening."
Mt 20:26 great among you must be your s,
25:21 'Well done, good and faithful s!

SERVANTS (SERVANT)
Lk 17:10 should say, 'We are unworthy s;
Jn 15:15 longer call you s, because a servant

SERVE (SERVICE SERVING)
Dt 10:12 to s the LORD your God
Jos 22: 5 and to s him with all your heart
24:15 this day whom you will s,
Mt 4:10 Lord your God, and s him only.' "
6:24 "No one can s two masters.
20:28 but to s, and to give his life
Eph 6: 7 S wholeheartedly,

SERVICE (SERVE)
1Co 12: 5 There are different kinds of s,
Eph 4:12 God's people for works of s,

SERVING (SERVE)
Ro 12:11 your spiritual fervor, s the Lord.
Eph 6: 7 as if you were s the Lord, not men,
Col 3:24 It is the Lord Christ you are s.
2Ti 2: 4 No one s as a soldier gets involved

SEVEN (SEVENTH)
Ge 7: 2 Take with you s of every kind
Jos 6: 4 march around the city s times,
1Ki 19:18 Yet I reserve s thousand in Israel—
Pr 6:16 s that are detestable to him:
24:16 a righteous man falls s times,
Isa 4: 1 In that day s women
Da 9:25 comes, there will be s 'sevens,'
Mt 18:21 Up to s times?" Jesus answered,
Lk 11:26 takes s other spirits more wicked
Ro 11: 4 for myself s thousand who have not
Rev 1: 4 To the s churches in the province
6: 1 opened the first of the s seals.
8: 2 and to them were given s trumpets.
10: 4 And when the s thunders spoke,
15: 7 to the s angels s golden bowls filled

SEVENTH (SEVEN)
Ge 2: 2 By the s day God had finished
Ex 23:12 but on the s day do not work,

SEXUAL (SEXUALLY)
1Co 6:13 body is not meant for s immorality,
6:18 Flee from s immorality.
10: 8 should not commit s immorality,
Eph 5: 3 even a hint of s immorality,
1Th 4: 3 that you should avoid s immorality

SEXUALLY (SEXUAL)
1Co 5: 9 to associate with s immoral people
6:18 he who sins s sins against his own

SHADOW
Ps 23: 4 through the valley of the s of death,
36: 7 find refuge in the s of your wings.
Heb 10: 1 The law is only a s

SHALLUM
King of Israel (2Ki 15:10-16).

SHAME (ASHAMED)
Ps 34: 5 their faces are never covered with s
Pr 13:18 discipline comes to poverty and s,
Heb 12: 2 endured the cross, scorning its s,

Lk 16:13 "No s can serve two masters.
Php 2: 7 taking the very nature of a s,
2Ti 2:24 And the Lord's s must not quarrel;

SHARE (SHARED)
Ge   21:10 that slave woman's son will never s
Lk   3:11 "The man with two tunics should s
Gal   4:30 the slave woman's son will never s
    6: 6 in the word must s all good things
Eph   4:28 something to s with those in need.
1Ti   6:18 and to be generous and willing to s.
Heb 12:10 that we may s in his holiness.
    13:16 to do good and to s with others,

SHARED (SHARE)
Heb   2:14 he too s in their humanity so that

SHARON
SS   2: 1 I am a rose of S,

SHARPER*
Heb   4:12 S than any double-edged sword,

SHED (SHEDDING)
Ge   9: 6 by man shall his blood be s;
Col   1:20 through his blood, s on the cross.

SHEDDING (SHED)
Heb   9:22 without the s of blood there is no

SHEEP
Ps 100: 3 we are his people, the s
    119:176 I have strayed like a lost s.
Isa 53: 6 We all, like s, have gone astray,
Jer 50: 6 "My people have been lost s;
Eze 34:11 I myself will search for my s
Mt   9:36 helpless, like s without a shepherd.
Jn   10: 3 He calls his own s by name
    10:15 and I lay down my life for the s.
    10:27 My s listen to my voice; I know
    21:17 Jesus said, "Feed my s.
1Pe   2:25 For you were like s going astray,

SHELTER
Ps   61: 4 take refuge in the s of your wings.
    91: 1 in the s of the Most High

SHEM
   Son of Noah (Ge 5:32; 6:10). Blessed (Ge 9:26). Descendants (Ge 10:21-31; 11:10-32).

SHEPHERD (SHEPHERDS)
Ps   23: 1 LORD is my s, I shall not be in want.
Isa 40:11 He tends his flock like a s:
Jer 31:10 will watch over his flock like a s.'
Eze 34:12 As a s looks after his scattered
Zec 11:17 "Woe to the worthless s,
Mt   9:36 and helpless, like sheep without a s.
Jn   10:11 The good s lays down his life
    10:16 there shall be one flock and one s.
1Pe   5: 4 And when the Chief S appears,

SHEPHERDS (SHEPHERD)
Jer 23: 1 "Woe to the s who are destroying
Lk   2: 8 there were s living out in the fields
Ac   20:28 Be s of the church of God,
1Pe   5: 2 Be s of God's flock that is

SHIELD
Ps   28: 7 LORD is my strength and my s;
Eph   6:16 to all this, take up the s of faith,

SHINE (SHONE)
Ps   4: 6 Let the light of your face s upon us,
    80: 1 between the cherubim, s forth
Isa 60: 1 "Arise, s, for your light has come,

Da   12: 3 are wise will s like the brightness
Mt   5:16 let your light s before men,
    13:43 the righteous will s like the sun
2Co   4: 6 made his light s in our hearts
Eph   5:14 and Christ will s on you."

SHIPWRECKED*
2Co 11:25 I was stoned, three times I was s,
1Ti   1:19 and so have s their faith.

SHONE (SHINE)
Mt   17: 2 His face s like the sun,
Lk   2: 9 glory of the Lord s around them,
Rev 21:11 It s with the glory of God,

SHORT
Isa 59: 1 of the LORD is not too s to save,
Ro   3:23 and fall s of the glory of God,

SHOULDERS
Isa   9: 6 and the government will be on his s
Lk   15: 5 he joyfully puts it on his s

SHOWED
1Jn   4: 9 This is how God s his love

SHREWD
Mt   10:16 Therefore be as s as snakes and

SHUN*
Job 28:28 and to s evil is understanding.' "
Pr   3: 7 fear the LORD and s evil.

SICK
Pr   13:12 Hope deferred makes the heart s,
Mt   9:12 who need a doctor, but the s.
    25:36 I was s and you looked after me,
Jas   5:14 of you s? He should call the elders

SICKLE
Joel   3:13 Swing the s,

SIDE
Ps   91: 7 A thousand may fall at your s,
    124: 1 If the LORD had not been on our s
2Ti   4:17 But the Lord stood at my s

SIGHT
Ps   90: 4 For a thousand years in your s
    116: 15 Precious in the s of the LORD
2Co   5: 7 We live by faith, not by s.
1Pe   3: 4 which is of great worth in God's s.

SIGN (SIGNS)
Isa   7:14 the Lord himself will give you a s:

SIGNS (SIGN)
Mk   16:17 these s will accompany those who
Jn   20:30 Jesus did many other miraculous s

SILENT
Pr   17:28 a fool is thought wise if he keeps s,
Isa 53: 7 as a sheep before her shearers is s,
Hab   2:20 let all the earth be s before him.'
1Co 14:34 women should remain s
1Ti   2:12 over a man; she must be s.

SILVER
Pr   25:11 is like apples of gold in settings of s.
Hag   2: 8 'The s is mine and the gold is mine,'
1Co   3:12 s, costly stones, wood, hay or straw

SIMON
  1. See PETER.

  2. Apostle, called the Zealot (Mt 10:4; Mk 3:18; Lk 6:15; Ac 1:13).
  3. Samaritan sorcerer (Ac 8:9-24).

SIN (SINFUL SINNED SINNER SINNERS SINNING SINS)
Nu   5: 7 and must confess the s he has
    32:23 be sure that your s will find you
Dt   24:16 each is to die for his own s.
1Ki   8:46 for there is no one who does not s
2Ch   7:14 and will forgive their s and will heal
Ps   4: 4 In your anger do not s;
    32: 2 whose s the LORD does not count
    32: 5 Then I acknowledged my s to you
    51: 2 and cleanse me from my s.
    66:18 If I had cherished s in my heart,
    119: 11 that I might not s against you.
    119:133 let no s rule over me.
Isa   6: 7 is taken away and your s atoned
Mic   7:18 who pardons s and forgives
Mt   18: 6 little ones who believe in me to s,
Jn   1:29 who takes away the s of the world!
    8:34 everyone who sins is a slave to s.
Ro   5:12 as s entered the world
    5:20 where s increased, grace increased
    6:11 count yourselves dead to s
    6:23 For the wages of s is death,
    14:23 that does not come from faith is s.
2Co   5:21 God made him who had no s to be s
Gal   6: 1 if someone is caught in a s,
Heb   9:26 to do away with s by the sacrifice
    11:25 the pleasures of s for a short time.
    12: 1 and the s that so easily entangles,
1Pe   2:22 "He committed no s,
1Jn   1: 8 If we claim to be without s,
    3: 4 in fact, s is lawlessness.
    3: 5 And in him is no s.
    3: 9 born of God will continue to s,
    5:18 born of God does not continue to s;

SINCERE
Ro   12: 9 Love must be s.
Heb 10:22 near to God with a s heart

SINFUL (SIN)
Ps   51: 5 Surely I was s at birth
    51: 5 s from the time my mother
Ro   7: 5 we were controlled by the s nature,
    8: 4 not live according to the s nature
    8: 9 are controlled not by the s nature
Gal   5:19 The acts of the s nature are obvious
    5:24 Jesus have crucified the s nature
1Pe   2:11 abstain from s desires, which war

SING (SANG SINGING SONG SONGS)
Ps   30: 4 S to the LORD, you saints of his;
    47: 6 S praises to God, s praises;
    59:16 But I will s of your strength,
    89: 1 I will s of the LORD's great love
    101: 1 I will s of your love and justice;
Eph   5:19 S and make music in your heart

SINGING (SING)
Ps   63: 5 with s lips my mouth will praise
Ac   16:25 Silas were praying and s hymns

SINNED (SIN)
2Sa 12:13 "I have s against the LORD."
Job   1: 5 "Perhaps my children have s
Ps   51: 4 Against you, you only, have I s
Da   9: 5 we have s and done wrong.
Mic   7: 9 Because I have s against him,

Lk   15:18 I have s against heaven
Ro   3:23 for all have s and fall short
1Jn   1:10 claim we have not s, we make him

SINNER (SIN)

Ecc   9:18 but one s destroys much good.
Lk   15: 7 in heaven over one s who repents
     18:13 'God, have mercy on me, a s.'
1Co   14:24 convinced by all that he is a s
Jas   5:20 Whoever turns a s from the error
1Pe   4:18 become of the ungodly and the s?"

SINNERS (SIN)

Ps   1: 1 or stand in the way of s
Pr   23:17 Do not let your heart envy s,
Mt   9:13 come to call the righteous, but s."
Ro   5: 8 While we were still s, Christ died
1Ti   1:15 came into the world to save s—

SINNING (SIN)

Ex   20:20 be with you to keep you from s.
1Co   15:34 stop s; for there are some who are
Heb   10:26 If we deliberately keep on s
1Jn   3: 6 No one who lives in him keeps on s
     3: 9 go on s, because he has been born

SINS (SIN)

2Ki   14: 6 each is to die for his own s."
Ezr   9: 6 our s are higher than our heads
Ps   19:13 your servant also from willful s;
     32: 1 whose s are covered.
     103: 3 who forgives all your s
     130: 3 O Lord, kept a record of s,
Pr   28:13 who conceals his s does not
Isa   1:18 "Though your s are like scarlet,
     43:25 and remembers your s no more.
     59: 2 your s have hidden his face
Eze   18: 4 soul who s is the one who will die.
Mt   1:21 he will save his people from their s
     18:15 "If your brother s against you,
Lk   11: 4 Forgive us our s,
     17: 3 "If your brother s, rebuke him,
Ac   22:16 be baptized and wash your s away,
1Co   15: 3 died for our s according
Eph   2: 1 dead in your transgressions and s,
Col   2:13 us all our s, having canceled
Heb   1: 3 he had provided purification for s,
     7:27 He sacrificed for their s once for all
     8:12 and will remember their s no more
     10:12 for all time one sacrifice for s,
Jas   4:17 ought to do and doesn't do it, s.
     5:16 Therefore confess your s
     5:20 and cover over a multitude of s.
1Pe   2:24 He himself bore our s in his body
     3:18 For Christ died for s once for all,
1Jn   1: 9 If we confess our s, he is faithful
Rev   1: 5 has freed us from our s by his blood

SITS

Ps   99: 1 s enthroned between the cherubim,
Isa   40:22 He s enthroned above the circle
Mt   19:28 of Man s on his glorious throne,
Rev   4: 9 thanks to him who s on the throne

SKIN

Job   19:20 with only the s of my teeth.
     19:26 And after my s has been destroyed,
Jer   13:23 Can the Ethiopian change his s

SLAIN (SLAY)

Rev   5:12 "Worthy is the Lamb, who was s,

SLANDER (SLANDERED SLANDERERS)

Lev   19:16 " 'Do not go about spreading s
1Ti   5:14 the enemy no opportunity for s.
Tit   3: 2 to s no one, to be peaceable

SLANDERED (SLANDER)

1Co   4:13 when we are s, we answer kindly.

SLANDERERS (SLANDER)

Ro   1:30 They are gossips, s, God-haters,
1Co   6:10 nor the greedy nor drunkards nor s
Tit   2: 3 not to be s or addicted

SLAUGHTER

Isa   53: 7 he was led like a lamb to the s,

SLAVE (SLAVERY SLAVES)

Ge   21:10 "Get rid of that s woman
Mt   20:27 wants to be first must be your s—
Jn   8:34 everyone who sins is a s to sin.
1Co   12:13 whether Jews or Greeks, s or free
Gal   3:28 s nor free, male nor female,
     4:30 Get rid of the s woman and her son
2Pe   2:19 a man is a s to whatever has

SLAVERY (SLAVE)

Ro   6:19 parts of your body in s to impurity
Gal   4: 3 were in s under the basic principles

SLAVES (SLAVE)

Ro   6: 6 that we should no longer be s to sin
     6:22 and have become s to God,

SLAY (SLAIN)

Job   13:15 Though he s me, yet will I hope

SLEEP (SLEEPING)

Ps   121: 4 will neither slumber nor s.
1Co   15:51 We will not all s, but we will all be

SLEEPING (SLEEP)

Mk   13:36 suddenly, do not let him find you s.

SLOW

Ex   34: 6 and gracious God, s to anger,
Jas   1:19 s to speak and s to become angry,
2Pe   3: 9 The Lord is not s in keeping his

SLUGGARD

Pr   6: 6 Go to the ant, you s;
     20: 4 A s does not plow in season;

SLUMBER

Ps   121: 3 he who watches over you will not s;
Pr   6:10 A little sleep, a little s,
Ro   13:11 for you to wake up from your s,

SNAKE (SNAKES)

Nu   21: 8 "Make a s and put it up on a pole;
Pr   23:32 In the end it bites like a s
Jn   3:14 Moses lifted up the s in the desert,

SNAKES (SNAKE)

Mt   10:16 as shrewd as s and as innocent
Mk   16:18 they will pick up s with their hands;

SNATCH

Jn   10:28 no one can s them out of my hand.
Jude   :23 s others from the fire and save

SNOW

Ps   51: 7 and I will be whiter than s.

SOAR

Isa   40:31 They will s on wings like eagles;

SODOM

Ge   19:24 rained down burning sulfur on S
Ro   9:29 we would have become like S,

SOIL

Ge   4: 2 kept flocks, and Cain worked the s.
Mt   13:23 on good s is the man who hears

SOLDIER

1Co   9: 7 as a s at his own expense?
2Ti   2: 3 with us like a good s of Christ Jesus

SOLE

Dt   28:65 place for the s of your foot.
Isa   1: 6 From the s of your foot to the top

SOLID

2Ti   2:19 God's s foundation stands firm,
Heb   5:12 You need milk, not s food!

SOLOMON

Son of David by Bathsheba; king of Judah (2Sa 12:24; 1Ch 3:5, 10). Appointed king by David (1Ki 1); adversaries Adonijah, Joab, Shimei killed by Benaiah (1Ki 2). Asked for wisdom (1Ki 3; 2Ch 1). Judged between two prostitutes (1Ki 3:16-28). Built temple (1Ki 5-7; 2Ch 2-5); prayer of dedication (1Ki 8; 2Ch 6). Visited by Queen of Sheba (1Ki 10; 2Ch 9). Wives turned his heart from God (1Ki 11:1-13). Jeroboam rebelled against (1Ki 11:26-40). Death (1Ki 11:41-43; 2Ch 9:29-31).

Proverbs of (1Ki 4:32; Pr 1:1; 10:1; 25:1); psalms of (Ps 72; 127); song of (SS 1:1).

SON (SONS)

Ge   22: 2 "Take your s, your only s, Isaac,
Ex   11: 5 Every firstborn s in Egypt will die,
Dt   21:18 rebellious s who does not obey his
Ps   2: 7 He said to me, "You are my S;
     2:12 Kiss the S, lest he be angry
Pr   10: 1 A wise s brings joy to his father,
     13:24 He who spares the rod hates his s,
     29:17 Discipline your s, and he will give
Isa   7:14 with child and will give birth to a s,
Hos   11: 1 and out of Egypt I called my s.
Mt   2:15 "Out of Egypt I called my s."
     3:17 "This is my S, whom I love;
     11:27 one knows the S except the Father,
     16:16 "You are the Christ, the S
     17: 5 "This is my S, whom I love;
     20:18 and the S of Man will be betrayed
     24:30 They will see the S of Man coming
     24:44 the S of Man will come at an hour
     27:54 "Surely he was the S of God!"
     28:19 and of the S and of the Holy Spirit,
Mk   10:45 even the S of Man did not come
     14:62 you will see the S of Man sitting
Lk   9:58 but the S of Man has no place
     18: 8 when the S of Man comes,
     19:10 For the S of Man came to seek
Jn   3:14 so the S of Man must be lifted up,
     3:16 that he gave his one and only S,
     17: 1 Glorify your S, that your S may
Ro   8:29 conformed to the likeness of his S,
     8:32 He who did not spare his own S,
1Co   15:28 then the S himself will be made
Gal   4:30 rid of the slave woman and her s,
1Th   1:10 and to wait for his S from heaven,
Heb   1: 2 days he has spoken to us by his S,
     10:29 punished who has trampled the S
1Jn   1: 7 his S, purifies us from all sin.

1Jn   4: 9 only S into the world that we might
    5: 5 he who believes that Jesus is the S
    5:11 eternal life, and this life is in his S.

SONG (SING)
Ps   40: 3 He put a new s in my mouth,
   96: 1 Sing to the LORD a new s;
  149: 1 Sing to the LORD a new s,
Isa   49:13 burst into s, O mountains!
   55:12 will burst into s before you,
Rev   5: 9 And they sang a new s:
   15: 3 and sang the s of Moses the servant

SONGS (SING)
Job   35:10 who gives s in the night,
Ps 100: 2 come before him with joyful s.
Eph   5:19 with psalms, hymns and spiritual s.
Jas   5:13 Is anyone happy? Let him sing s

SONS (SON)
Joel   2:28 Your s and daughters will prophesy
Jn   12:36 so that you may become s of light."
Ro   8:14 by the Spirit of God are s of God.
2Co   6:18 and you will be my s and daughters
Gal   4: 5 we might receive the full rights of s.
Heb 12: 7 discipline; God is treating you as s.

SORROW (SORROWS)
Jer   31:12 and they will s no more.
Ro   9: 2 I have great s and unceasing
2Co   7:10 Godly s brings repentance that

SORROWS (SORROW)
Isa   53: 3 a man of s, and familiar

SOUL (SOULS)
Dt   6: 5 with all your s and with all your
   10:12 all your heart and with all your s,
Jos   22: 5 with all your heart and all your s."
Ps   23: 3 he restores my s.
   42: 1 so my s pants for you, O God.
   42:11 Why are you downcast, O my s?
  103: 1 Praise the LORD, O my s;
Pr   13:19 A longing fulfilled is sweet to the s,
Isa   55: 2 your s will delight in the richest
Mt   10:28 kill the body but cannot kill the s.
   16:26 yet forfeits his s? Or what can
   22:37 with all your s and with all your
Heb   4:12 even to dividing s and spirit,

SOULS (SOUL)
Pr   11:30 and he who wins s is wise.
Jer   6:16 and you will find rest for your s.
Mt   11:29 and you will find rest for your s.

SOUND
1Co 14: 8 if the trumpet does not s a clear call
   15:52 the trumpet will s, the dead will
2Ti   4: 3 men will not put up with s doctrine.

SOVEREIGN
Da   4:25 that the Most High is s

SOW (SOWS)
Job   4: 8 and those who s trouble reap it.
Mt   6:26 they do not s or reap or store away
2Pe   2:22 and, "A s that is washed goes back

SOWS (SOW)
Pr   11:18 he who s righteousness reaps a sure
   22: 8 He who s wickedness reaps trouble
2Co   9: 6 Whoever s sparingly will

Gal   6: 7 A man reaps what he s.

SPARE (SPARES)
Ro   8:32 He who did not s his own Son,
   11:21 natural branches, he will not s you

SPARES (SPARE)
Pr   13:24 He who s the rod hates his son,

SPEARS
Isa   2: 4 and their s into pruning hooks.
Joel   3:10 and your pruning hooks into s.
Mic   4: 3 and their s into pruning hooks.

SPECTACLE
1Co   4: 9 We have been made a s
Col   2:15 he made a public s of them,

SPIN
Mt   6:28 They do not labor or s.

SPIRIT (SPIRIT'S SPIRITS SPIRITUAL SPIRITUALLY)
Ge   1: 2 and the S of God was hovering
   6: 3 "My S will not contend
2Ki   2: 9 inherit a double portion of your s,"
Job 33: 4 The S of God has made me;
Ps   31: 5 Into your hands I commit my s;
   51:10 and renew a steadfast s within me.
   51:11 or take your Holy S from me.
   51:17 sacrifices of God are a broken s;
  139: 7 Where can I go from your S?
Isa   57:15 him who is contrite and lowly in s,
   63:10 and grieved his Holy S.
Eze   11:19 an undivided heart and put a new s
   36:26 you a new heart and put a new s
Joel   2:28 I will pour out my S on all people.
Zec   4: 6 but by my S,' says the LORD
Mt   1:18 to be with child through the Holy S
   3:11 will baptize you with the Holy S
   3:16 he saw the S of God descending
   4: 1 led by the S into the desert
   5: 3 saying: "Blessed are the poor in s,
   26:41 s is willing, but the body is weak."
   28:19 and of the Son and of the Holy S,
Lk   1:80 child grew and became strong in s;
   11:13 Father in heaven give the Holy S
Jn   4:24 God is s, and his worshipers must
   7:39 Up to that time the S had not been
   14:26 But the Counselor, the Holy S,
   16:13 But when he, the S of truth, comes,
   20:22 and said, "Receive the Holy S.
Ac   1: 5 will be baptized with the Holy S."
   2: 4 of them were filled with the Holy S
   2:38 will receive the gift of the Holy S.
   6: 3 who are known to be full of the S
   19: 2 "Did you receive the Holy S
Ro   8: 9 And if anyone does not have the S
   8:26 the S helps us in our weakness.
1Co   2:10 God has revealed it to us by his S.
   2:14 man without the S does not accept
   6:19 body is a temple of the Holy S,
   12:13 baptized by one S into one body—
2Co   3: 6 the letter kills, but the S gives life.
   5: 5 and has given us the S as a deposit.
Gal   5:16 by the S, and you will not gratify
   5:22 But the fruit of the S is love, joy,
   5:25 let us keep in step with the S.
Eph   1:13 with a seal, the promised Holy S,

Eph   4:30 do not grieve the Holy S of God,
   5:18 Instead, be filled with the S.
   6:17 of salvation and the sword of the S,
2Th   2:13 the sanctifying work of the S
Heb   4:12 even to dividing soul and s,
1Pe   3: 4 beauty of a gentle and quiet s,
2Pe   1:21 carried along by the Holy S.
1Jn   4: 1 Dear friends, do not believe every s

SPIRIT'S (SPIRIT)
1Th   5:19 not put out the S fire; do not treat

SPIRITS (SPIRIT)
1Co 12:10 to another distinguishing between s,
   14:32 The s of prophets are subject
1Jn   4: 1 test the s to see whether they are

SPIRITUAL (SPIRIT)
Ro   12: 1 this is your s act of worship.
   12:11 but keep your s fervor, serving
1Co   2:13 expressing s truths in s words.
   3: 1 I could not address you as s but
   12: 1 Now about s gifts, brothers,
   14: 1 of love and eagerly desire s gifts,
   15:44 a natural body, it is raised a s body.
Gal   6: 1 you who are s should restore him
Eph   1: 3 with every s blessing in Christ.
   5:19 with psalms, hymns and s songs.
   6:12 and against the s forces of evil
1Pe   2: 2 newborn babies, crave pure s milk,
   2: 5 are being built into a s house

SPIRITUALLY (SPIRIT)
1Co   2:14 because they are s discerned.

SPLENDOR
1Ch 16:29 the LORD in the s of his holiness.
   29:11 the glory and the majesty and the s,
Job 37:22 of the north he comes in golden s;
Ps   29: 2 in the s of his holiness.
   45: 3 clothe yourself with s and majesty.
   96: 6 S and majesty are before him;
   96: 9 in the s of his holiness;
  104: 1 you are clothed with s and majesty.
  145: 5 of the glorious s of your majesty,
Isa   61: 3 the LORD for the display of his s.
   63: 1 Who is this, robed in s,
Lk   9:31 appeared in glorious s, talking
2Th   2: 8 and destroy by the s of his coming.

SPOIL
Ps 119:162 like one who finds great s.

SPOTLESS
2Pe   3:14 make every effort to be found s,

SPREAD (SPREADING)
Ac   12:24 of God continued to increase and s.
   19:20 the word of the Lord s widely

SPREADING (SPREAD)
1Th   3: 2 God's fellow worker in s the gospel

SPRING
Jer   2:13 the s of living water,
Jn   4:14 in him a s of water welling up
Jas   3:12 can a salt s produce fresh water.

SPUR*
Heb 10:24 how we may s one another

SPURNS*
Pr   15: 5 A fool s his father's discipline,

STAFF
Ps   23: 4 your rod and your s,

STAKES
Isa 54: 2 strengthen your s.

STAND (STANDING STANDS)
Ex   14:13 S firm and you will see
2Ch 20:17 s firm and see the deliverance
Ps   1: 5 Therefore the wicked will not s
      40: 2 and gave me a firm place to s.
   119:120 I s in awe of your laws.
Eze 22:30 s before me in the gap on behalf
Zec 14: 4 On that day his feet will s
Mt   12:25 divided against itself will not s.
Ro   14:10 we will all s before God's
           judgment
1Co 10:13 out so that you can s up under
           it.
    15:58 Therefore, my dear brothers, s
           firm
Eph   6:14 S firm then, with the belt
2Th   2:15 s firm and hold to the teachings
           we
Jas   5: 8 You too, be patient and s firm,
Rev   3:20 Here I am! I s at the door

STANDING (STAND)
Ex   3: 5 where you are s is holy ground."
Jos   5:15 the place where you are s is
           holy."
1Pe   5: 9 Resist him, s firm in the faith,

STANDS (STAND)
Ps   89: 2 that your love s firm forever,
   119: 89 it s firm in the heavens.
Mt   10:22 but he who s firm to the end will
           be
2Ti   2:19 God's solid foundation s firm,
1Pe   1:25 but the word of the Lord s
           forever

STAR (STARS)
Nu   24:17 A s will come out of Jacob;
Rev 22:16 and the bright Morning S."

STARS (STAR)
Da   12: 3 like the s for ever and ever.
Php 2:15 in which you shine like s

STATURE
Lk   2:52 And Jesus grew in wisdom
           and s,

STEADFAST
Ps   51:10 and renew a s spirit within me.
Isa 26: 3 him whose mind is s,
1Pe   5:10 and make you strong, firm
           and s.

STEAL
Ex   20:15 "You shall not s.
Mt   19:18 do not s, do not give false
Eph   4:28 has been stealing must s no
           longer,

STEP (STEPS)
Gal   5:25 let us keep in s with the Spirit.

STEPS (STEP)
Pr   16: 9 but the LORD determines his s.
Jer 10:23 it is not for man to direct his s.
1Pe   2:21 that you should follow in his s.

STICKS
Pr   18:24 there is a friend who s closer

STIFF-NECKED
Ex   34: 9 Although this is a s people,

STILL
Ps   46:10 "Be s, and know that I am God;
Zec   2:13 Be s before the LORD, all
           mankind

STIRS
Pr   6:19 and a man who s up dissension
   10:12 Hatred s up dissension,
   15: 1 but a harsh word s up anger.
   15:18 hot-tempered man s up
           dissension,
   16:28 A perverse man s up dissension,
   28:25 A greedy man s up dissension,
   29:22 An angry man s up dissension,

STONE (CAPSTONE CORNERSTONE MILLSTONE)
1Sa 17:50 the Philistine with a sling and
           a s;
Isa   8:14 a s that causes men to stumble
Eze 11:19 remove from them their heart
           of s
Mk   16: 3 "Who will roll the s away
Lk   4: 3 tell this s to become bread."
Jn   8: 7 the first to throw a s at her."
2Co 3: 3 not on tablets of s but on
           tablets

STOOP
2Sa 22:36 you s down to make me great.

STORE
Pr   10:14 Wise men s up knowledge,
Mt   6:19 not s up for yourselves
           treasures

STOREHOUSE (HOUSE)
Mal 3:10 Bring the whole tithe into the s,

STRAIGHT
Pr   3: 6 and he will make your paths s.
    4:25 Let your eyes look s ahead,
   15:21 of understanding keeps a s
           course.
Jn   1:23 'Make s the way for the Lord.' "

STRAIN
Mt   23:24 You s out a gnat but swallow

STRANGER (STRANGERS)
Mt   25:35 I was a s and you invited me in,
Jn   10: 5 But they will never follow a s;

STRANGERS (STRANGER)
1Pe   2:11 as aliens and s in the world,

STREAMS
Ps   1: 3 He is like a tree planted by s
   46: 4 is a river whose s make glad
Ecc   1: 7 All s flow into the sea,
Jn   7:38 s of living water will flow

STRENGTH (STRONG)
Ex   15: 2 The LORD is my s and my song;
Dt   6: 5 all your soul and with all your s.
2Sa 22:33 It is God who arms me with s
Ne   8:10 for the joy of the LORD is your s."
Ps   28: 7 The LORD is my s and my shield;
    46: 1 God is our refuge and s,
    96: 7 ascribe to the LORD glory and s.
   118: 14 The LORD is my s and my song;
   147: 10 not in the s of the horse,
Isa 40:31 will renew their s.
Mk 12:30 all your mind and with all your s.'
1Co 1:25 of God is stronger than man's s.
Php 4:13 through him who gives me s.
1Pe 4:11 it with the s God provides,

STRENGTHEN (STRONG)
2Ch 16: 9 to s those whose hearts are fully
Ps 119: 28 s me according to your word.
Isa 35: 3 S the feeble hands,
   41:10 I will s you and help you;
Eph   3:16 of his glorious riches he may s
           you
2Th 2:17 and s you in every good deed
Heb 12:12 s your feeble arms and weak
           knees.

STRENGTHENING (STRONG)
1Co 14:26 done for the s of the church.

STRIFE
Pr   20: 3 It is to a man's honor to avoid s,
   22:10 out the mocker, and out goes s;

STRIKE (STRIKES)
Ge   3:15 and you will s his heel."
Zec 13: 7 "S the shepherd,
Mt   26:31 " 'I will s the shepherd,

STRIKES (STRIKE)
Mt   5:39 If someone s you on the right

STRONG (STRENGTH STRENGTHEN STRENGTHENING)
Dt   31: 6 Be s and courageous.
1Ki   2: 2 "So be s, show yourself a man,
Pr   18:10 The name of the LORD is a s
           tower
   31:17 her arms are s for her tasks.
SS   8: 6 for love is as s as death,
Lk   2:40 And the child grew and
           became s;
Ro   15: 1 We who are s ought to bear
1Co 1:27 things of the world to shame
           the s.
   16:13 in the faith; be men of courage;
           be s
2Co 12:10 For when I am weak, then I
           am s.
Eph   6:10 be s in the Lord and in his
           mighty

STRUGGLE
Ro   15:30 me in my s by praying to God
Eph   6:12 For our s is not against flesh
Heb 12: 4 In your s against sin, you have
           not

STUDY
Ezr   7:10 Ezra had devoted himself to
           the s
Ecc 12:12 and much s wearies the body.
Jn   5:39 You diligently s the Scriptures

STUMBLE (STUMBLING)
Ps   37:24 though he s, he will not fall,
   119:165 and nothing can make them s.
Isa   8:14 a stone that causes men to s
Jer 31: 9 a level path where they will
           not s,
Eze   7:19 for it has made them s into sin.
1Co 10:32 Do not cause anyone to s,
1Pe   2: 8 and, "A stone that causes men
           to s

STUMBLING (STUMBLE)
Ro   14:13 up your mind not to put any s
           block
1Co 8: 9 freedom does not become a s
           block
2Co 6: 3 We put no s block in anyone's
           path,

SUBDUE
Ge   1:28 in number; fill the earth and s it.

SUBJECT (SUBJECTED)
1Co 14:32 of prophets are s to the control
   15:28 then the Son himself will be
           made s
Tit   2: 5 and to be s to their husbands,
    2: 9 slaves to be s to their masters
    3: 1 Remind the people to be s to
           rulers

SUBJECTED (SUBJECT)
Ro   8:20 For the creation was s

SUBMISSION (SUBMIT)
1Co 14:34 but must be in s, as the Law
           says.
1Ti   2:11 learn in quietness and full s.

SUBMISSIVE (SUBMIT)
Jas   3:17 then peace-loving,
           considerate,
1Pe   3: 1 in the same way be s
    5: 5 in the same way be s

SUBMIT (SUBMISSION SUBMISSIVE SUBMITS)
Ro   13: 1 Everyone must s himself
   13: 5 necessary to s to the
           authorities,
1Co 16:16 to s to such as these
Eph   5:21 S to one another out of
           reverence
Col   3:18 Wives, s to your husbands,
Heb 12: 9 How much more should we s
   13:17 Obey your leaders and s
Jas   4: 7 S yourselves, then, to God.
1Pe   2:18 s yourselves to your masters

SUBMITS* (SUBMIT)
Eph   5:24 Now as the church s to Christ,

SUCCESSFUL
Jos   1: 7 that you may be s wherever you
             go.
2Ki   18: 7 he was s in whatever he
             undertook.
2Ch 20:20 in his prophets and you will
             be s."

SUFFER (SUFFERED SUFFERING SUFFERINGS SUFFERS)
Isa   53:10 to crush him and cause him
             to s,
Mk   8:31 the Son of Man must s many
             things
Lk   24:26 the Christ have to s these things
    24:46 The Christ will s and rise
Php   1:29 to s for him, since you are going
1Pe   4:16 However, if you s as a Christian,

SUFFERED (SUFFER)
Heb   2: 9 and honor because he s death,
       2:18 Because he himself s
1Pe   2:21 Christ s for you, leaving you

SUFFERING (SUFFER)
Isa   53: 3 of sorrows, and familiar with s.
Ac   5:41 worthy of s disgrace for the
             Name.
2Ti   1: 8 But join with me in s for the
             gospel,
Heb   2:10 of their salvation perfect
             through s.

SUFFERINGS (SUFFER)
Ro   8:17 share in his s in order that we
             may
       8:18 that our present s are not worth
2Co   1: 5 as the s of Christ flow
Php   3:10 the fellowship of sharing in
             his s,

SUFFERS (SUFFER)
Pr   13:20 but a companion of fools s
             harm.
1Co 12:26 If one part s, every part s with it;

SUFFICIENT
2Co   12: 9 said to me, "My grace is s for
             you,

SUITABLE
Ge   2:18 I will make a helper s for him."

SUN
Ecc   1: 9 there is nothing new under
             the s.
Mal   4: 2 the s of righteousness will rise
Mt   5:45 He causes his s to rise on the
             evil
     17: 2 His face shone like the s,
Rev   1:16 His face was like the s shining
    21:23 The city does not need the s

SUPERIOR
Heb   1: 4 he became as much s to the
             angels
       8: 6 ministry Jesus has received is
             as s

SUPERVISION
Gal   3:25 longer under the s of the law.

SUPREMACY* (SUPREME)
Col   1:18 in everything he might have
             the s.

SUPREME (SUPREMACY)
Pr   4: 7 Wisdom is s; therefore get
             wisdom.

SURE
Nu   32:23 you may be s that your sin will
             find
Dt   6:17 Be s to keep the commands
    14:22 Be s to set aside a tenth
Isa   28:16 cornerstone for a s foundation;
Heb 11: 1 faith is being s of what we hope
             for

2Pe   1:10 to make your calling and
             election s.

SURPASS* (SURPASSES SURPASSING)
Pr   31:29 but you s them all."

SURPASSES (SURPASS)
Mt   5:20 unless your righteousness s that
Eph   3:19 to know this love that s
             knowledge

SURPASSING* (SURPASS)
Ps 150: 2 praise him for his s greatness.
2Co   3:10 in comparison with the s glory.
       9:14 of the s grace God has given
             you.
Php   3: 8 the s greatness of knowing
             Christ

SURROUNDED
Heb   12: 1 since we are s by such a great
             cloud

SUSPENDS*
Job   26: 7 he s the earth over nothing.

SUSTAINING* (SUSTAINS)
Heb   1: 3 s all things by his powerful word.

SUSTAINS (SUSTAINING)
Ps   18:35 and your right hand s me;
   146:   9 and s the fatherless and the
             widow,
   147:   6 The LORD s the humble
Isa   50: 4 to know the word that s the
             weary.

SWALLOWED
1Co 15:54 "Death has been s up in
             victory."
2Co   5: 4 so that what is mortal may be s
             up

SWEAR
Mt   5:34 Do not s at all: either by heaven,

SWORD (SWORDS)
Ps   45: 3 Gird your s upon your side,
Pr   12:18 Reckless words pierce like a s,
Mt   10:34 come to bring peace, but a s.
   26:52 all who draw the s will die by
             the s.
Lk   2:35 a s will pierce your own soul
             too."
Ro   13: 4 for he does not bear the s
Eph   6:17 of salvation and the s of the
             Spirit,
Heb   4:12 Sharper than any double-
             edged s,
Rev   1:16 came a sharp double-edged s.

SWORDS (SWORD)
Isa   2: 4 They will beat their s
Joel   3:10 Beat your plowshares into s

SYMPATHETIC*
1Pe   3: 8 in harmony with one another;
             be s,

SYNAGOGUE
Lk   4:16 the Sabbath day he went into
Ac   17: 2 custom was, Paul went into
             the s,

TABERNACLE
Ex   40:34 the glory of the LORD filled the t.

TABLE (TABLES)
Ps   23: 5 You prepare a t before me

TABLES (TABLE)
Ac   6: 2 word of God in order to wait
             on t.

TABLET (TABLETS)
Pr   3: 3 write them on the t of your
             heart.
       7: 3 write them on the t of your
             heart.

TABLETS (TABLET)
Ex   31:18 he gave him the two t
Dt   10: 5 and put the t in the ark I had
             made,
2Co   3: 3 not on t of stone but on t

TAKE (TAKEN TAKES TAKING TOOK)
Dt   12:32 do not add to it or t away from
             it.
    31:26 "T this Book of the Law
Job   23:10 But he knows the way that I t;
Ps   49:17 for he will t nothing with him
    51:11 or t your Holy Spirit from me.
Mt   10:38 anyone who does not t his cross
    11:29 T my yoke upon you and learn
    16:24 deny himself and t up his cross

TAKEN (TAKE)
Lev   6: 4 must return what he has stolen
             or t
Isa   6: 7 your guilt is t away and your sin
Mt   24:40 one will be t and the other left.
Mk   16:19 he was t up into heaven
1Ti   3:16 was t up in glory.

TAKES (TAKE)
1Ki   20:11 should not boast like one who t
             it
Ps   5: 4 You are not a God who t
             pleasure
Jn   1:29 who t away the sin of the world!
Rev 22:19 And if anyone t words away

TAKING (TAKE)
Ac   15:14 by t from the Gentiles a people
Php   2: 7 t the very nature of a servant,

TALENT
Mt   25:15 to another one t, each according

TAME*
Jas   3: 8 but no man can t the tongue.

TASK
Mk   13:34 each with his assigned t,
Ac   20:24 complete the t the Lord Jesus
             has
1Co   3: 5 the Lord has assigned to each
             his t.
2Co   2:16 And who is equal to such a t?

TASTE (TASTED)
Ps   34: 8 T and see that the LORD is good;
Col   2:21 Do not t! Do not touch!"?
Heb   2: 9 the grace of God he might t
             death

TASTED (TASTE)
1Pe   2: 3 now that you have t that the
             Lord

TAUGHT (TEACH)
Mt   7:29 he t as one who had authority,
1Co   2:13 but in words t by the Spirit,
Gal   1:12 nor was I t it; rather, I received
             it

TAXES
Mt   22:17 Is it right to pay t to Caesar or
             not
Ro   13: 7 If you owe t, pay t; if revenue,

TEACH (TAUGHT TEACHER TEACHERS TEACHES TEACHING)
Ex   33:13 t me your ways so I may know
             you
Dt   4: 9 t them to your children
       8: 3 to t you that man does not live
    11:19 T them to your children, talking
1Sa 12:23 I will t you the way that is good
Ps   32: 8 t you in the way you should go;
    51:13 I will t transgressors your ways,
    90:12 T us to number our days aright,
   143: 10 T me to do your will,
Jer   31:34 No longer will a man t his
             neighbor
Lk   11: 1 said to him, "Lord, t us to pray,
Jn   14:26 will t you all things and will
             remind
1Ti   2:12 I do not permit a woman to t
       3: 2 respectable, hospitable, able
             to t,

Tit   2: 1 You must *t* what is in accord
Heb 8:11 No longer will a man *t* his
           neighbor
Jas   3: 1 know that we who *t* will be
           judged
1Jn 2:27 you do not need anyone to *t*
           you.

TEACHER (TEACH)
Mt 10:24 "A student is not above his *t,*
Jn 13:14 and *T,* have washed your feet,

TEACHERS (TEACH)
1Co 12:28 third *t,* then workers of miracles,
Eph 4:11 and some to be pastors and *t,*
Heb 5:12 by this time you ought to be *t,*

TEACHES (TEACH)
1Ti   6: 3 If anyone *t* false doctrines

TEACHING (TEACH)
Pr   1: 8 and do not forsake your
           mother's *t.*
Mt 28:20 *t* them to obey everything I have
Jn   7:17 whether my *t* comes from God or
   14:23 loves me, he will obey my *t.*
1Ti   4:13 of Scripture, to preaching and
           to *t.*
2Ti   3:16 is God-breathed and is useful
           for *t,*
Tit   2: 7 In your *t* show integrity,

TEAR (TEARS)
Rev 7:17 God will wipe away every *t*

TEARS (TEAR)
Ps 126: 5 Those who sow in *t*
Php 3:18 and now say again even with *t,*

TEETH (TOOTH)
Mt   8:12 will be weeping and gnashing
           of *t.*

TEMPERATE*
1Ti   3: 2 *t,* self-controlled, respectable,
    3:11 not malicious talkers but *t*
Tit   2: 2 Teach the older men to be *t,*

TEMPEST
Ps 55: 8 far from the *t* and storm."

TEMPLE (TEMPLES)
1Ki   8:27 How much less this *t* I have
           built!
Hab 2:20 But the LORD is in his holy *t;*
1Co   3:16 that you yourselves are God's *t*
      6:19 you not know that your body is
           a *t*
2Co   6:16 For we are the *t* of the living
           God.

TEMPLES (TEMPLE)
Ac 17:24 does not live in *t* built by hands.

TEMPT (TEMPTATION TEMPTED)
1Co   7: 5 again so that Satan will not *t*
           you

TEMPTATION (TEMPT)
Mt   6:13 And lead us not into *t,*
   26:41 pray so that you will not fall
           into *t.*
1Co 10:13 No *t* has seized you except what
           is

TEMPTED (TEMPT)
Mt   4: 1 into the desert to be *t* by the
           devil.
1Co 10:13 he will not let you be *t*
Heb 2:18 he himself suffered when he
           was *t,*
    4:15 but we have one who has been *t*
Jas   1:13 For God cannot be *t* by evil,

TEN (TENTH TITHE TITHES)
Ex 34:28 covenant—the *T*
           Commandments.
Ps 91: 7 *t* thousand at your right hand,
Mt 25:28 it to the one who has the *t*
           talents.
Lk   15: 8 suppose a woman has *t* silver
           coins

TENTH (TEN)
Dt 14:22 Be sure to set aside a *t*

TERRIBLE (TERROR)
2Ti   3: 1 There will be *t* times

TERROR (TERRIBLE)
Ps 91: 5 You will not fear the *t* of night,
Lk 21:26 Men will faint from *t,*
           apprehensive
Ro 13: 3 For rulers hold no *t*

TEST (TESTED TESTS)
Dt   6:16 Do not *t* the LORD your God
Ps 139: 23 *t* me and know my anxious
Ro   12: 2 Then you will be able to *t*
1Co   3:13 and the fire will *t* the quality
1Jn   4: 1 *t* the spirits to see whether they
           are

TESTED (TEST)
Ge 22: 1 Some time later God *t* Abraham.
Job 23:10 when he has *t* me, I will come
           forth
Pr   27:21 man is *t* by the praise he
           receives.
1Ti   3:10 They must first be *t;* and then

TESTIFY (TESTIMONY)
Jn   5:39 are the Scriptures that *t* about
           me,
2Ti   1: 8 ashamed to *t* about our Lord,

TESTIMONY (TESTIFY)
Isa   8:20 and to the *t!* If they do not
           speak
Lk   18:20 not give false *t,* honor your
           father

TESTS (TEST)
Pr   17: 3 but the LORD *t* the heart.
1Th   2: 4 but God, who *t* our hearts.

THADDAEUS
  Apostle (Mt 10:3; Mk 3:18); probably also
known as Judas son of James (Lk 6:16; Ac
1:13).

THANKFUL (THANKS)
Heb 12:28 let us be *t,* and so worship God

THANKS (THANKFUL THANKSGIVING)
1Ch 16: 8 Give *t* to the LORD, call
Ne   12:31 assigned two large choirs to
           give *t.*
Ps 100: 4 give *t* to him and praise his
           name.
1Co 15:57 *t* be to God! He gives us the
           victory
2Co   2:14 *t* be to God, who always leads
           us
     9:15 *T* be to God for his indescribable
1Th   5:18 give *t* in all circumstances,

THANKSGIVING (THANKS)
Ps 95: 2 Let us come before him with *t*
   100: 4 Enter his gates with *t*
Php 4: 6 by prayer and petition, with *t,*
1Ti   4: 3 created to be received with *t*

THIEF (THIEVES)
Ex   22: 3 A *t* must certainly make
           restitution
1Th   5: 2 day of the Lord will come like a *t*
Rev 16:15 I come like a *t!* Blessed is he
           who

THIEVES (THIEF)
1Co   6:10 nor homosexual offenders nor *t*

THINK (THOUGHT THOUGHTS)
Ro   12: 3 Do not *t* of yourself more highly
Php 4: 8 praiseworthy—*t* about such
           things

THIRST (THIRSTY)
Ps 69:21 and gave me vinegar for my *t.*
Mt   5: 6 Blessed are those who hunger
           and *t*
Jn   4:14 the water I give him will never *t.*

THIRSTY (THIRST)
Isa 55: 1 "Come, all you who are *t,*
Jn   7:37 "If anyone is *t,* let him come to
           me
Rev 22:17 Whoever is *t,* let him come;

THOMAS
  Apostle (Mt 10:3; Mk 3:18; Lk 6:15; Jn
11:16; 14:5; 21:2; Ac 1:13). Doubted resurrection (Jn 20:24-28).

THONGS
Mk   1: 7 *t* of whose sandals I am not
           worthy

THORN (THORNS)
2Co 12: 7 there was given me a *t* in my
           flesh,

THORNS (THORN)
Nu 33:55 in your eyes and *t* in your sides.
Mt 27:29 then twisted together a crown
           of *t*
Heb 6: 8 But land that produces *t*

THOUGHT (THINK)
Pr   14:15 a prudent man gives *t* to his
           steps.
1Co 13:11 I talked like a child, I *t* like a
           child,

THOUGHTS (THINK)
Ps 94:11 The LORD knows the *t* of man;
   139: 23 test me and know my anxious *t.*
Isa 55: 8 "For my *t* are not your *t,*
Heb 4:12 it judges the *t* and attitudes

THREE
Ecc 4:12 of *t* strands is not quickly
           broken.
Mt 12:40 *t* nights in the belly of a huge
           fish,
   18:20 or *t* come together in my name,
   27:63 'After *t* days I will rise again.'
1Co 13:13 And now these *t* remain: faith,
   14:27 or at the most *t*— should speak,
2Co 13: 1 testimony of two or *t*
           witnesses."

THRESHING
2Sa 24:18 an altar to the LORD on the *t*
           floor

THRONE (ENTHRONED)
2Sa   7:16 your *t* will be established forever
Ps 45: 6 Your *t,* O God, will last for ever
    47: 8 God is seated on his holy *t.*
Isa   6: 1 I saw the Lord seated on a *t,*
    66: 1 "Heaven is my *t*
Heb 4:16 Let us then approach the *t* of
           grace
    12: 2 at the right hand of the *t* of God.
Rev 4:10 They lay their crowns before
           the *t*
   20:11 Then I saw a great white *t*
   22: 3 *t* of God and of the Lamb will be

THROW
Jn   8: 7 the first to *t* a stone at her."
Heb 10:35 So do not *t* away your
           confidence;
    12: 1 let us *t* off everything that
           hinders

THWART*
Isa 14:27 has purposed, and who can *t*
           him?

TIBNI
  King of Israel (1Ki 16:21-22).

TIME (TIMES)
Est   4:14 come to royal position for such
           a *t*
Da   7:25 to him for a *t,* times and half a *t*
Hos 10:12 for it is *t* to seek the LORD.
Ro   9: 9 "At the appointed *t* I will return,
Heb 9:28 and he will appear a second *t,*
   10:12 for all *t* one sacrifice for sins,
1Pe   4:17 For it is *t* for judgment to begin

TIMES (TIME)
Ps	9: 9 a stronghold in *t* of trouble.
	31:15 My *t* are in your hands;
	62: 8 Trust in him at all *t*, O people;
Pr	17:17 A friend loves at all *t*,
Am	5:13 for the *t* are evil.
Mt	18:21 how many *t* shall I forgive my
Ac	1: 7 "It is not for you to know the *t*
Rev	12:14 *t* and half a time, out

TIMIDITY*
2Ti 1: 7 For God did not give us a spirit of *t*

TIMOTHY
Believer from Lystra (Ac 16:1). Joined Paul on second missionary journey (Ac 16-20). Sent to settle problems at Corinth (1Co 4:17; 16:10). Led church at Ephesus (1Ti 1:3). Co-writer with Paul (1Th 1:1; 2Th 1:1; Phm 1).

TIRE (TIRED)
2Th 3:13 never *t* of doing what is right.

TIRED (TIRE)
Ex	17:12 When Moses' hands grew *t*,
Isa	40:28 He will not grow *t* or weary,

TITHE (TEN)
Lev	27:30 " 'A *t* of everything from the land,
Dt	12:17 eat in your own towns the *t*
Mal	3:10 the whole *t* into the storehouse,

TITHES (TEN)
Mal 3: 8 'How do we rob you?' "In *t*

TITUS
Gentile co-worker of Paul (Gal 2:1-3; 2Ti 4:10); sent to Corinth (2Co 2:13; 7-8; 12:18), Crete (Tit 1:4-5).

TODAY
Mt	6:11 Give us *t* our daily bread.
Lk	23:43 *t* you will be with me in paradise."
Heb	3:13 daily, as long as it is called *T*,
	13: 8 Christ is the same yesterday and *t*

TOIL
Ge 3:17 through painful *t* you will eat of it

TOLERATE
Hab	1:13 you cannot *t* wrong.
Rev	2: 2 that you cannot *t* wicked men,

TOMB
Mt	27:65 make the *t* as secure as you know
Lk	24: 2 the stone rolled away from the *t*,

TOMORROW
Pr	27: 1 Do not boast about *t*,
Isa	22:13 "for *t* we die!"
Mt	6:34 Therefore do not worry about *t*,
Jas	4:13 "Today or *t* we will go to this

TONGUE (TONGUES)
Ps	39: 1 and keep my *t* from sin;
Pr	12:18 but the *t* of the wise brings healing.
1Co	14: 2 speaks in a *t* does not speak to men
	14: 4 He who speaks in a *t* edifies himself
	14:13 in a *t* should pray that he may
	14:19 than ten thousand words in a *t*.
Php	2:11 every *t* confess that Jesus Christ is
Jas	1:26 does not keep a tight rein on his *t*,
	3: 8 but no man can tame the *t*.

TONGUES (TONGUE)
Isa	28:11 with foreign lips and strange *t*
	66:18 and gather all nations and *t*,
Mk	16:17 in new *t*; they will pick up snakes
Ac	2: 4 and began to speak in other *t*

Ac	10:46 For they heard them speaking in *t*
	19: 6 and they spoke in *t* and prophesied
1Co	12:30 Do all speak in *t*? Do all interpret?
	14:18 speak in *t* more than all of you.
	14:39 and do not forbid speaking in *t*.

TOOK (TAKE)
1Co	11:23 the night he was betrayed, *t* bread,
Php	3:12 for which Christ Jesus *t* hold of me.

TOOTH (TEETH)
Ex	21:24 eye for eye, *t* for *t*, hand for hand,
Mt	5:38 'Eye for eye, and *t* for *t*.'

TORMENTED
Rev 20:10 They will be *t* day and night

TORN
Gal	4:15 you would have *t* out your eyes
Php	1:23 I do not know! I am *t*

TOUCH (TOUCHED)
Ps 105:	15 "Do not *t* my anointed ones;
Lk	24:39 It is I myself! *T* me and see;
2Co	6:17 *T* no unclean thing,
Col	2:21 Do not taste! Do not *t*!"?

TOUCHED (TOUCH)
1Sa	10:26 men whose hearts God had *t*.
Mt	14:36 and all who *t* him were healed.

TOWER
Ge	11: 4 with a *t* that reaches to the heavens
Pr	18:10 of the LORD is a strong *t*;

TOWNS
Nu	35: 2 to give the Levites *t* to live
	35:15 These six *t* will be a place of refuge

TRACING*
Ro 11:33 and his paths beyond *t* out!

TRADITION
Mt	15: 6 word of God for the sake of your *t*.
Col	2: 8 which depends on human *t*

TRAIN (TRAINING)
Pr	22: 6 *T* a child in the way he should go,
Eph	4: 8 he led captives in his *t*

TRAINING (TRAIN)
1Co	9:25 in the games goes into strict *t*.
2Ti	3:16 correcting and *t* in righteousness,

TRAMPLED
Lk	21:24 Jerusalem will be *t*
Heb	10:29 to be punished who has *t* the Son

TRANCE
Ac 10:10 was being prepared, he fell into a *t*.

TRANSCENDS*
Php 4: 7 which *t* all understanding,

TRANSFIGURED
Mt 17: 2 There he was *t* before them.

TRANSFORM* (TRANSFORMED)
Php 3:21 will *t* our lowly bodies

TRANSFORMED (TRANSFORM)
Ro	12: 2 be *t* by the renewing of your mind.
2Co	3:18 are being *t* into his likeness

TRANSGRESSION (TRANSGRESSIONS TRANSGRESSORS)
Isa 53: 8 for the *t* of my people he was

Ro	4:15 where there is no law there is no *t*.

TRANSGRESSIONS (TRANSGRESSION)
Ps	32: 1 whose *t* are forgiven,
	51: 1 blot out my *t*.
	103: 12 so far as he has removed our *t* from us
Isa	53: 5 But he was pierced for our *t*,
Eph	2: 1 you were dead in your *t* and sins,

TRANSGRESSORS (TRANSGRESSION)
Ps	51:13 Then I will teach *t* your ways,
Isa	53:12 and made intercession for the *t*.
	53:12 and was numbered with the *t*.

TREADING
Dt	25: 4 an ox while it is *t* out the grain.
1Co	9: 9 an ox while it is *t* out the grain."

TREASURE (TREASURED TREASURES)
Isa	33: 6 of the LORD is the key to this *t*.
Mt	6:21 For where your *t* is, there your
2Co	4: 7 But we have this *t* in jars of clay

TREASURED (TREASURE)
Dt	7: 6 to be his people, his *t* possession.
Lk	2:19 But Mary *t* up all these things

TREASURES (TREASURE)
Mt	6:19 up for yourselves *t* on earth,
Col	2: 3 in whom are hidden all the *t*
Heb	11:26 of greater value than the *t* of Egypt,

TREAT
Lev	22: 2 sons to *t* with respect the sacred
1Ti	5: 1 *T* younger men as brothers,
1Pe	3: 7 and *t* them with respect

TREATY
Dt 7: 2 Make no *t* with them, and show

TREE
Ge	2: 9 and the *t* of the knowledge of good
	2: 9 of the garden were the *t* of life
Dt	21:23 hung on a *t* is under God's curse.
Ps	1: 3 He is like a *t* planted by streams
Mt	3:10 every *t* that does not produce good
	12:33 for a *t* is recognized by its fruit.
Gal	3:13 is everyone who is hung on a *t*."
Rev	22:14 they may have the right to the *t*

TREMBLE (TREMBLING)
1Ch	16:30 *T* before him, all the earth!
Ps 114:	7 *T*, O earth, at the presence

TREMBLING (TREMBLE)
Ps	2:11 and rejoice with *t*.
Php	2:12 out your salvation with fear and *t*,

TRESPASS
Ro 5:17 For if, by the *t* of the one man,

TRIALS
1Th	3: 3 one would be unsettled by these *t*.
Jas	1: 2 whenever you face *t* of many kinds,
2Pe	2: 9 how to rescue godly men from *t*

TRIBES
Ge	49:28 All these are the twelve *t* of Israel,
Mt	19:28 judging the twelve *t* of Israel.

TRIBULATION*
Rev 7:14 who have come out of the great *t*;

TRIUMPHAL* (TRIUMPHING)
Isa	60:11 their kings led in *t* procession.
2Co	2:14 us in *t* procession in Christ

TRIUMPHING* (TRIUMPHAL)
Col   2:15 of them, *t* over them by the cross.

TROUBLE (TROUBLED TROUBLES)
Job   14: 1 is of few days and full of *t*.
Ps   46: 1 an ever-present help in *t*.
    107: 13 they cried to the LORD in their *t*,
Pr   11:29 He who brings *t* on his family will
    24:10 If you falter in times of *t*,
Mt   6:34 Each day has enough *t* of its own.
Jn   16:33 In this world you will have *t*.
Ro   8:35 Shall *t* or hardship or persecution

TROUBLED (TROUBLE)
Jn   14: 1 "Do not let your hearts be *t*.
    14:27 Do not let your hearts be *t*

TROUBLES (TROUBLE)
1Co   7:28 those who marry will face many *t*
2Co   1: 4 who comforts us in all our *t*,
    4:17 and momentary *t* are achieving

TRUE (TRUTH)
Dt   18:22 does not take place or come *t*,
1Sa   9: 6 and everything he says comes *t*.
Ps 119:160 All your words are *t*;
Jn   17: 3 the only *t* God, and Jesus Christ,
Ro   3: 4 Let God be *t*, and every man a liar.
Php   4: 8 whatever is *t*, whatever is noble,
Rev 22: 6 These words are trustworthy and *t*.

TRUMPET
1Co   14: 8 if the *t* does not sound a clear call,
    15:52 For the *t* will sound, the dead will

TRUST (ENTRUSTED TRUSTED TRUSTS TRUSTWORTHY)
Ps   20: 7 we *t* in the name of the LORD our
    37: 3 *T* in the LORD and do good;
    56: 4 in God I *t*; I will not be afraid.
   119: 42 for I *t* in your word.
Pr   3: 5 *T* in the LORD with all your heart
Isa   30:15 in quietness and *t* is your strength,
Jn   14: 1 *T* in God; *t* also in me.
1Co   4: 2 been given a *t* must prove faithful.

TRUSTED (TRUST)
Ps   26: 1 I have *t* in the LORD
Isa   25: 9 we *t* in him, and he saved us.
Da   3:28 *t* in him and defied the king's
Lk   16:10 *t* with very little can also be *t*

TRUSTS (TRUST)
Ps   32:10 surrounds the man who *t* in him.
Pr   11:28 Whoever *t* in his riches will fall,
    28:26 He who *t* in himself is a fool,
Ro   9:33 one who *t* in him will never be put

TRUSTWORTHY (TRUST)
Ps 119:138 they are fully *t*.
Pr   11:13 but a *t* man keeps a secret.
Rev 22: 6 "These words are *t* and true.

TRUTH (TRUE TRUTHFUL TRUTHS)
Ps   51: 6 Surely you desire *t*
Isa   45:19 I, the LORD, speak the *t*;
Zec   8:16 are to do: Speak the *t* to each other,
Jn   4:23 worship the Father in spirit and *t*,
    8:32 Then you will know the *t*,
    8:32 and the *t* will set you free."
    14: 6 I am the way and the *t* and the life.
    16:13 comes, he will guide you into all *t*.
    18:38 "What is *t*?" Pilate asked.
Ro   1:25 They exchanged the *t* of God
1Co   13: 6 in evil but rejoices with the *t*.
2Co   13: 8 against the *t*, but only for the *t*.

Eph   4:15 Instead, speaking the *t* in love,
    6:14 with the belt of *t* buckled
2Th   2:10 because they refused to love the *t*
1Ti   2: 4 to come to a knowledge of the *t*.
    3:15 the pillar and foundation of the *t*.
2Ti   2:15 correctly handles the word of *t*.
    3: 7 never able to acknowledge the *t*.
Heb 10:26 received the knowledge of the *t*,
1Pe   1:22 by obeying the *t* so that you have
2Pe   2: 2 the way of *t* into disrepute.
1Jn   1: 6 we lie and do not live by the *t*.
    1: 8 deceive ourselves and the *t* is not

TRUTHFUL (TRUTH)
Pr   12:22 but he delights in men who are *t*.
Jn   3:33 it has certified that God is *t*.

TRUTHS (TRUTH)
1Co   2:13 expressing spiritual *t*
1Ti   3: 9 hold of the deep *t* of the faith
Heb   5:12 to teach you the elementary *t*

TRY (TRYING)
Ps   26: 2 Test me, O LORD, and *t* me,
Isa   7:13 enough to *t* the patience of men?
1Co 14:12 *t* to excel in gifts that build up
2Co   5:11 is to fear the Lord, we *t*
1Th   5:15 always *t* to be kind to each other

TRYING (TRY)
2Co   5:12 We are not *t* to commend ourselves
1Th   2: 4 We are not *t* to please men but God

TUNIC
Lk   6:29 do not stop him from taking your *t*.

TURN (TURNED TURNS)
Ex   32:12 *T* from your fierce anger; relent
Dt   5:32 do not *t* aside to the right
    28:14 Do not *t* aside from any
Jos   1: 7 do not *t* from it to the right
2Ch   7:14 and *t* from their wicked ways,
    30: 9 He will not *t* his face from you
Ps   78: 6 they in *t* would tell their children.
Pr   22: 6 when he is old he will not *t* from it.
Isa   29:16 You *t* things upside down,
    30:21 Whether you *t* to the right
    45:22 "*T* to me and be saved,
    55: 7 Let him *t* to the LORD.
Eze   33:11 *T*! *T* from your evil ways!
Mal   4: 6 He will *t* the hearts of the fathers
Mt   5:39 you on the right cheek, *t*
    10:35 For I have come to *t*
Jn   12:40 nor *t*— and I would heal them."
Ac   3:19 Repent, then, and *t* to God,
    26:18 and *t* them from darkness to light,
1Ti   6:20 *T* away from godless chatter
1Pe   3:11 He must *t* from evil and do good;

TURNED (TURN)
Ps   30:11 You *t* my wailing into dancing;
    40: 1 he *t* to me and heard my cry.
Isa   53: 6 each of us has *t* to his own way;
Hos   7: 8 Ephraim is a flat cake not *t* over.
Joel   2:31 The sun will be *t* to darkness
Ro   3:12 All have *t* away,

TURNS (TURN)
2Sa 22:29 the LORD *t* my darkness into light
Pr   15: 1 A gentle answer *t* away wrath,
Isa   44:25 and *t* it into nonsense,
Jas   5:20 Whoever *t* a sinner from the error

TWELVE
Ge   49:28 All these are the *t* tribes of Israel,
Mt   10: 1 He called his *t* disciples to him

TWINKLING*
1Co   15:52 in a flash, in the *t* of an eye,

UNAPPROACHABLE*
1Ti   6:16 immortal and who lives in *u* light,

UNBELIEF (UNBELIEVER UNBELIEVERS UNBELIEVING)
Mk   9:24 help me overcome my *u*!"
Ro   11:20 they were broken off because of *u*,
Heb   3:19 able to enter, because of their *u*.

UNBELIEVER* (UNBELIEF)
1Co   7:15 But if the *u* leaves, let him do so.
    10:27 If some *u* invites you to a meal
    14:24 if an *u* or someone who does not
2Co   6:15 have in common with an *u*?
1Ti   5: 8 the faith and is worse than an *u*.

UNBELIEVERS (UNBELIEF)
1Co   6: 6 another—and this in front of *u*!
2Co   6:14 Do not be yoked together with *u*.

UNBELIEVING (UNBELIEF)
1Co   7:14 For the *u* husband has been
Rev 21: 8 But the cowardly, the *u*, the vile,

UNCERTAIN*
1Ti   6:17 which is so *u*, but to put their hope

UNCHANGEABLE*
Heb   6:18 by two *u* things in which it is

UNCIRCUMCISED
1Sa   17:26 Who is this *u* Philistine that he
Col   3:11 circumcised or *u*, barbarian,

UNCIRCUMCISION
1Co   7:19 is nothing and *u* is nothing.
Gal   5: 6 neither circumcision nor *u* has any

UNCLEAN
Isa   6: 5 ruined! For I am a man of *u* lips,
Ro   14:14 fully convinced that no food is *u*
2Co   6:17 Touch no *u* thing,

UNCONCERNED*
Eze 16:49 were arrogant, overfed and *u*;

UNCOVERED
Heb   4:13 Everything is *u* and laid bare

UNDERSTAND (UNDERSTANDING UNDERSTANDS)
Job 42: 3 Surely I spoke of things I did not *u*,
Ps   73:16 When I tried to *u* all this,
   119:125 that I may *u* your statutes.
Lk   24:45 so they could *u* the Scriptures.
Ac   8:30 "Do you *u* what you are reading?"
Ro   7:15 I do not *u* what I do.
1Co   2:14 and he cannot *u* them,
Eph   5:17 but *u* what the Lord's will is.
2Pe   3:16 some things that are hard to *u*,

UNDERSTANDING (UNDERSTAND)
Ps 119:104 I gain *u* from your precepts;
   147: 5 his *u* has no limit.
Pr   3: 5 and lean not on your own *u*;
    4: 7 Though it cost all you have, get *u*.
    10:23 but a man of *u* delights in wisdom.
    11:12 but a man of *u* holds his tongue.
    15:21 a man of *u* keeps a straight course.
    15:32 whoever heeds correction gains *u*.
    23:23 get wisdom, discipline and *u*.
Isa   40:28 and his *u* no one can fathom.
Da   5:12 a keen mind and knowledge and *u*,

Mk 4:12 and ever hearing but never *u*;
12:33 with all your *u* and with all your
Php 4: 7 of God, which transcends all *u*,

UNDERSTANDS (UNDERSTAND)
1Ch 28: 9 and *u* every motive
1Ti 6: 4 he is conceited and *u* nothing.

UNDIVIDED*
1Ch 12:33 to help David with *u* loyalty—
Ps 86:11 give me an *u* heart,
Eze 11:19 I will give them an *u* heart
1Co 7:35 way in *u* devotion to the Lord.

UNDOING
Pr 18: 7 A fool's mouth is his *u*,

UNDYING*
Eph 6:24 Lord Jesus Christ with an *u* love.

UNFADING*
1Pe 3: 4 the *u* beauty of a gentle

UNFAILING
Ps 33: 5 the earth is full of his *u* love.
119: 76 May your *u* love be my comfort,
143: 8 bring me word of your *u* love,
Pr 19:22 What a man desires is *u* love;
La 3:32 so great is his *u* love.

UNFAITHFUL (UNFAITHFULNESS)
Lev 6: 2 is *u* to the LORD by deceiving his
1Ch 10:13 because he was *u* to the LORD;
Pr 13:15 but the way of the *u* is hard.

UNFAITHFULNESS (UNFAITHFUL)
Mt 5:32 except for marital *u*, causes her
19: 9 for marital *u*, and marries
another

UNFOLDING
Ps 119:130 the *u* of your words gives light;

UNGODLINESS
Tit 2:12 It teaches us to say "No" to *u*

UNIT
1Co 12:12 body is a *u*, though it is made
up

UNITED (UNITY)
Ro 6: 5 If we have been *u* with him
Php 2: 1 from being *u* with Christ,
Col 2: 2 encouraged in heart and *u* in
love,

UNITY (UNITED)
Ps 133: 1 is when brothers live together
in *u*!
Ro 15: 5 a spirit of *u* among yourselves
Eph 4: 3 effort to keep the *u* of the Spirit
4:13 up until we all reach *u* in the
faith
Col 3:14 them all together in perfect *u*.

UNIVERSE
Php 2:15 which you shine like stars in
the *u*
Heb 1: 2 and through whom he made
the *u*.

UNKNOWN
Ac 17:23 TO AN *U* GOD.

UNLEAVENED
Ex 12:17 "Celebrate the Feast of *U* Bread,

UNPROFITABLE
Tit 3: 9 because these are *u* and
useless.

UNPUNISHED
Ex 34: 7 Yet he does not leave the
guilty *u*;
Pr 19: 5 A false witness will not go *u*,

UNREPENTANT*
Ro 2: 5 stubbornness and your *u* heart,

UNRIGHTEOUS*
Zep 3: 5 yet the *u* know no shame.
Mt 5:45 rain on the righteous and the *u*.

1Pe 3:18 the righteous for the *u*, to bring
you
2Pe 2: 9 and to hold the *u* for the day

UNSEARCHABLE
Ro 11:33 How *u* his judgments,
Eph 3: 8 preach to the Gentiles the *u*
riches

UNSEEN
2Co 4:18 on what is seen, but on what
is *u*.
4:18 temporary, but what is *u* is
eternal.

UNSTABLE*
Jas 1: 8 he is a double-minded man, *u*
2Pe 2:14 they seduce the *u*; they are
experts
3:16 ignorant and *u* people distort,

UNTHINKABLE*
Job 34:12 It is *u* that God would do wrong,

UNVEILED*
2Co 3:18 with *u* faces all reflect the
Lord's

UNWORTHY
Job 40: 4 "I am *u*— how can I reply to you?
Lk 17:10 should say, 'We are *u* servants;

UPRIGHT
Job 1: 1 This man was blameless and *u*;
Pr 2: 7 He holds victory in store for
the *u*,
15: 8 but the prayer of the *u* pleases
him.
Tit 1: 8 who is self-controlled, *u*, holy
2:12 *u* and godly lives in this present

UPROOTED
Jude :12 without fruit and *u*— twice dead.

USEFUL
2Ti 2:21 *u* to the Master and prepared
3:16 Scripture is God-breathed and
is *u*

USELESS
1Co 15:14 our preaching is *u*
Jas 2:20 faith without deeds is *u*?

USURY
Ne 5:10 But let the exacting of *u* stop!

UTTER
Ps 78: 2 I will *u* hidden things, things
from of

UZZIAH
Son of Amaziah; king of Judah also known
as Azariah (2Ki 15:1-7; 1Ch 6:24; 2Ch 26).

VAIN
Ps 33:17 A horse is a *v* hope for
deliverance;
Isa 65:23 They will not toil in *v*
1Co 15: 2 Otherwise, you have believed
in *v*.
15:58 labor in the Lord is not in *v*.
2Co 6: 1 not to receive God's grace in *v*.

VALLEY
Ps 23: 4 walk through the *v* of the
shadow
Isa 40: 4 Every *v* shall be raised up,
Joel 3:14 multitudes in the *v* of decision!

VALUABLE (VALUE)
Lk 12:24 And how much more *v* you are

VALUE (VALUABLE)
Mt 13:46 When he found one of great *v*,
1Ti 4: 8 For physical training is of
some *v*,
Heb 11:26 as of greater *v* than the
treasures

VEIL
Ex 34:33 to them, he put a *v* over his
face.

2Co 3:14 for to this day the same *v*
remains

VENGEANCE (AVENGE REVENGE)
Isa 34: 8 For the LORD has a day of *v*,

VICTORIES (VICTORY)
Ps 18:50 He gives his king great *v*;
21: 1 great is his joy in the *v* you give!

VICTORIOUSLY* (VICTORY)
Ps 45: 4 In your majesty ride forth *v*

VICTORY (VICTORIES VICTORIOUSLY)
Ps 60:12 With God we will gain the *v*,
1Co 15:54 "Death has been swallowed up
in *v*
15:57 He gives us the *v* through our
Lord
1Jn 5: 4 This is the *v* that has overcome

VINDICATED
1Ti 3:16 was *v* by the Spirit,

VINE
Jn 15: 1 "I am the true *v*, and my Father
is

VINEGAR
Mk 15:36 filled a sponge with wine *v*,

VIOLATION
Heb 2: 2 every *v* and disobedience
received

VIOLENCE
Isa 60:18 No longer will *v* be heard
Eze 45: 9 Give up your *v* and oppression

VIPERS
Ro 3:13 "The poison of *v* is on their
lips."

VIRGIN
Isa 7:14 The *v* will be with child
Mt 1:23 "The *v* will be with child
2Co 11: 2 that I might present you as a
pure *v*

VIRTUES*
Col 3:14 And over all these *v* put on love,

VISION
Ac 26:19 disobedient to the *v* from
heaven.

VOICE
Ps 95: 7 Today, if you hear his *v*,
Isa 30:21 your ears will hear a *v* behind
you,
Jn 5:28 are in their graves will hear his *v*
10: 3 and the sheep listen to his *v*.
Heb 3: 7 "Today, if you hear his *v*,
Rev 3:20 If anyone hears my *v* and opens

VOMIT
Pr 26:11 As a dog returns to its *v*,
2Pe 2:22 "A dog returns to its *v*," and,

VOW
Nu 30: 2 When a man makes a *v*

WAGES
Lk 10: 7 for the worker deserves his *w*.
Ro 4: 4 his *w* are not credited to him
6:23 For the *w* of sin is death,

WAILING
Ps 30:11 You turned my *w* into dancing;

WAIST
2Ki 1: 8 with a leather belt around
his *w*."
Mt 3: 4 he had a leather belt around
his *w*.

WAIT (WAITED WAITS)
Ps 27:14 *W* for the LORD;
130: 5 I *w* for the LORD, my soul waits,
Isa 30:18 Blessed are all who *w* for him!
Ac 1: 4 *w* for the gift my Father
promised,

Ro   8:23 as we *w* eagerly for our adoption
1Th 1:10 and to *w* for his Son from heaven,
Tit   2:13 while we *w* for the blessed hope—

WAITED (WAIT)
Ps   40: 1 I *w* patiently for the LORD;

WAITS (WAIT)
Ro   8:19 creation *w* in eager expectation

WALK (WALKED WALKS)
Dt   11:19 and when you *w* along the road,
Ps   1: 1 who does not *w* in the counsel
       23: 4 Even though I *w*
      89:15 who *w* in the light of your presence
Isa   2: 5 let us *w* in the light of the LORD.
      30:21 saying, "This is the way; *w* in it."
      40:31 they will *w* and not be faint.
Jer   6:16 ask where the good way is, and *w*
Da   4:37 And those who *w* in pride he is able
Am   3: 3 Do two *w* together
Mic 6: 8 and to *w* humbly with your God.
Mk   2: 9 'Get up, take your mat and *w*'?
Jn   8:12 Whoever follows me will never *w*
1Jn 1: 7 But if we *w* in the light,
2Jn   : 6 his command is that you *w* in love.

WALKED (WALK)
Ge   5:24 Enoch *w* with God; then he was no
Jos 14: 9 which your feet have *w* will be your
Mt 14:29 *w* on the water and came toward

WALKS (WALK)
Pr   13:20 He who *w* with the wise grows wise

WALL
Jos 6:20 *w* collapsed; so every man charged
Ne   2:17 let us rebuild the *w* of Jerusalem,
Rev 21:12 It had a great, high *w*

WALLOWING
2Pe 2:22 back to her *w* in the mud."

WANT (WANTED WANTING WANTS)
1Sa 8:19 "We *w* a king over us.
Ps   23: 1 is my shepherd, I shall not be in *w*.
Lk   19:14 'We don't *w* this man to be our king
Ro   7:15 For what I *w* to do I do not do,
Php 3:10 I *w* to know Christ and the power

WANTED (WANT)
1Co 12:18 of them, just as he *w* them to be.

WANTING (WANT)
Da   5:27 weighed on the scales and found *w*
2Pe 3: 9 with you, not *w* anyone to perish,

WANTS (WANT)
Mt 20:26 whoever *w* to become great
Mk   8:35 For whoever *w* to save his life will
Ro   9:18 he hardens whom he *w* to harden.
1Ti   2: 4 who *w* all men to be saved

WAR (WARS)
Isa   2: 4 nor will they train for *w* anymore.
Da   9:26 *W* will continue until the end,
2Co 10: 3 we do not wage *w* as the world does
Rev 19:11 With justice he judges and makes *w*

WARN (WARNED WARNINGS)
Eze 3:19 But if you do *w* the wicked man

Eze 33: 9 if you do *w* the wicked man to turn

WARNED (WARN)
Ps   19:11 By them is your servant *w*;

WARNINGS (WARN)
1Co 10:11 and were written down as *w* for us,

WARS (WAR)
Ps   46: 9 He makes *w* cease to the ends
Mt 24: 6 You will hear of *w* and rumors of *w*,

WASH (WASHED WASHING)
Ps   51: 7 *w* me, and I will be whiter
Jn   13: 5 and began to *w* his disciples' feet,
Ac 22:16 be baptized and *w* your sins away,
Rev 22:14 Blessed are those who *w* their robes

WASHED (WASH)
1Co 6:11 you were *w*, you were sanctified,
Rev 7:14 they have *w* their robes

WASHING (WASH)
Eph 5:26 cleansing her by the *w* with water
Tit   3: 5 us through the *w* of rebirth

WATCH (WATCHES WATCHING WATCHMAN)
Ge   31:49 "May the LORD keep *w*
Jer 31:10 will *w* over his flock like a shepherd
Mt 24:42 "Therefore keep *w*, because you do
      26:41 *W* and pray so that you will not fall
Lk   2: 8 keeping *w* over their flocks at night
1Ti   4:16 *W* your life and doctrine closely.

WATCHES (WATCH)
Ps   1: 6 For the LORD *w* over the way
   121: 3 he who *w* over you will not slumber

WATCHING (WATCH)
Lk   12:37 whose master finds them *w*

WATCHMAN (WATCH)
Eze 3:17 I have made you a *w* for the house

WATER (WATERED WATERS)
Ps   1: 3 like a tree planted by streams of *w*,
      22:14 I am poured out like *w*,
Pr   25:21 if he is thirsty, give him *w* to drink.
Isa 49:10 and lead them beside springs of *w*.
Jer   2:13 broken cisterns that cannot hold *w*.
Zec 14: 8 On that day living *w* will flow out
Mk   9:41 anyone who gives you a cup of *w*
Jn   4:10 he would have given you living *w*."
      7:38 streams of living *w* will flow
Eph 5:26 washing with *w* through the word,
1Pe 3:21 this *w* symbolizes baptism that now
Rev 21: 6 cost from the spring of the *w* of life.

WATERED (WATER)
1Co 3: 6 I planted the seed, Apollos *w* it,

WATERS (WATER)
Ps   23: 2 he leads me beside quiet *w*,
Ecc 11: 1 Cast your bread upon the *w*,
Isa 58:11 like a spring whose *w* never fail.
1Co 3: 7 plants nor he who *w* is anything,

WAVE (WAVES)
Jas   1: 6 he who doubts is like a *w* of the sea,

WAVES (WAVE)
Isa 57:20 whose *w* cast up mire and mud.
Mt   8:27 Even the winds and the *w* obey him
Eph 4:14 tossed back and forth by the *w*,

WAY (WAYS)
Dt   1:33 to show you the *w* you should go.
2Sa 22:31 "As for God, his *w* is perfect;
Job 23:10 But he knows the *w* that I take;
Ps   1: 1 or stand in the *w* of sinners
      37: 5 Commit your *w* to the LORD;
   119: 9 can a young man keep his *w* pure?
   139:24 See if there is any offensive *w* in me
Pr   14:12 There is a *w* that seems right
      16:17 he who guards his *w* guards his life.
      22: 6 Train a child in the *w* he should go,
Isa 30:21 saying, "This is the *w*; walk in it."
      53: 6 each of us has turned to his own *w*;
      55: 7 Let the wicked forsake his *w*
Mt   3: 3 'Prepare the *w* for the Lord,
Jn   14: 6 "I am the *w* and the truth
1Co 10:13 also provide a *w* out so that you can
      12:31 will show you the most excellent *w*.
Heb 4:15 who has been tempted in every *w*,
      9: 8 was showing by this that the *w*
     10:20 and living *w* opened for us

WAYS (WAY)
Ex 33:13 teach me your *w* so I may know
Ps   25:10 All the *w* of the LORD are loving
      51:13 I will teach transgressors your *w*,
Pr   3: 6 in all your *w* acknowledge him,
Isa 55: 8 neither are your *w* my *w*,"
Jas   3: 2 We all stumble in many *w*.

WEAK (WEAKER WEAKNESS)
Mt 26:41 spirit is willing, but the body is *w*."
Ro 14: 1 Accept him whose faith is *w*,
1Co 1:27 God chose the *w* things
      8: 9 become a stumbling block to the *w*.
      9:22 To the *w* I became *w*, to win the *w*.
2Co 12:10 For when I am *w*, then I am strong.
Heb 12:12 your feeble arms and *w* knees.

WEAKER (WEAK)
1Co 12:22 seem to be *w* are indispensable,
1Pe 3: 7 them with respect as the *w* partner

WEAKNESS (WEAK)
Ro   8:26 the Spirit helps us in our *w*.
1Co 1:25 and the *w* of God is stronger
2Co 12: 9 for my power is made perfect in *w*
Heb 5: 2 since he himself is subject to *w*.

WEALTH
Pr   3: 9 Honor the LORD with your *w*,
Mk 10:22 away sad, because he had great *w*.
Lk   15:13 and there squandered his *w*

WEAPONS
2Co 10: 4 The *w* we fight with are not

WEARIES (WEARY)
Ecc 12:12 and much study *w* the body.

WEARY (WEARIES)
Isa 40:31 they will run and not grow *w*,
Mt 11:28 all you who are *w* and burdened,
Gal 6: 9 Let us not become *w* in doing good,

WEDDING

Mt 22:11 who was not wearing w clothes.
Rev 19: 7 For the w of the Lamb has come,

WEEP (WEEPING WEPT)

Ecc 3: 4 a time to w and a time to laugh,
Lk 6:21 Blessed are you who w now,

WEEPING (WEEP)

Ps 30: 5 w may remain for a night,
126: 6 He who goes out w,
Mt 8:12 where there will be w and gnashing

WELCOMES

Mt 18: 5 whoever w a little child like this
2Jn :11 Anyone who w him shares

WELL

Lk 17:19 your faith has made you w."
Jas 5:15 in faith will make the sick person w

WEPT (WEEP)

Ps 137: 1 of Babylon we sat and w
Jn 11:35 Jesus w.

WEST

Ps 103: 12 as far as the east is from the w,

WHIRLWIND (WIND)

2Ki 2: 1 to take Elijah up to heaven in a w,
Hos 8: 7 and reap the w.
Na 1: 3 His way is in the w and the storm,

WHITE (WHITER)

Isa 1:18 they shall be as w as snow;
Da 7: 9 His clothing was as w as snow;
Rev 1:14 hair were w like wool, as w as snow,
3: 4 dressed in w, for they are worthy.
20:11 Then I saw a great w throne

WHITER (WHITE)

Ps 51: 7 and I will be w than snow.

WHOLE

Mt 16:26 for a man if he gains the w world,
24:14 will be preached in the w world
Jn 13:10 to wash his feet; his w body is clean
21:25 the w world would not have room
Ac 20:27 proclaim to you the w will of God.
Ro 3:19 and the w world held accountable
8:22 know that the w creation has been
Gal 3:22 declares that the w world is
5: 3 obligated to obey the w law.
Eph 4:13 attaining to the w measure
Jas 2:10 For whoever keeps the w law
1Jn 2: 2 but also for the sins of the w world.

WHOLEHEARTEDLY (HEART)

Dt 1:36 because he followed the LORD w
Eph 6: 7 Serve w, as if you were serving

WICKED (WICKEDNESS)

Ps 1: 1 walk in the counsel of the w
1: 5 Therefore the w will not stand
73: 3 when I saw the prosperity of the w.
Pr 10:20 the heart of the w is of little value.
11:21 The w will not go unpunished,
Isa 53: 9 He was assigned a grave with the w
55: 7 Let the w forsake his way
57:20 But the w are like the tossing sea,
Eze 3:18 that w man will die for his sin,
18:23 pleasure in the death of the w?
33:14 to the w man, 'You will surely die,'

WICKEDNESS (WICKED)

Eze 28:15 created till w was found in you.

WIDE

Isa 54: 2 stretch your tent curtains w,
Mt 7:13 For w is the gate and broad is
Eph 3:18 to grasp how w and long and high

WIDOW (WIDOWS)

Dt 10:18 cause of the fatherless and the w,
Lk 21: 2 saw a poor w put in two very small

WIDOWS (WIDOW)

Jas 1:27 look after orphans and w

WIFE (WIVES)

Ge 2:24 and mother and be united to his w,
24:67 she became his w, and he loved her;
Ex 20:17 shall not covet your neighbor's w,
Dt 5:21 shall not covet your neighbor's w.
Pr 5:18 in the w of your youth.
12: 4 w of noble character is her
18:22 He who finds a w finds what is
19:13 quarrelsome w is like a constant
31:10 w of noble character who can find?
Mt 19: 3 for a man to divorce his w for any
1Co 7: 2 each man should have his own w,
7:33 how he can please his w—
Eph 5:23 the husband is the head of the w
5:33 must love his w as he loves himself,
1Ti 3: 2 husband of but one w, temperate,
Rev 21: 9 I will show you the bride, the w

WILD

Lk 15:13 squandered his wealth in w living.
Ro 11:17 and you, though a w olive shoot,

WILL (WILLING WILLINGNESS)

Ps 40: 8 I desire to do your w, O my God;
143: 10 Teach me to do your w,
Isa 53:10 Yet it was the LORD's w
Mt 6:10 your w be done
26:39 Yet not as I w, but as you w."
Jn 7:17 If anyone chooses to do God's w,
Ac 20:27 to you the whole w of God.
Ro 12: 2 and approve what God's w is—
1Co 7:37 but has control over his own w,
Eph 5:17 understand what the Lord's w is.
Php 2:13 for it is God who works in you to w
1Th 4: 3 God's w that you should be
5:18 for this is God's w for you
Heb 9:16 In the case of a w, it is necessary
10: 7 I have come to do your w, O God
Jas 4:15 "If it is the Lord's w,
1Jn 5:14 we ask anything according to his w,
Rev 4:11 and by your w they were created

WILLING (WILL)

Ps 51:12 grant me a w spirit, to sustain me.
Da 3:28 were w to give up their lives rather
Mt 18:14 Father in heaven is not w that any
23:37 her wings, but you were not w.
26:41 The spirit is w, but the body is weak

WILLINGNESS (WILL)

2Co 8:12 For if the w is there, the gift is

WIN (WINS)

Php 3:14 on toward the goal to w the prize
1Th 4:12 your daily life may w the respect

WIND (WHIRLWIND)

Jas 1: 6 blown and tossed by the w.

WINE

Pr 20: 1 W is a mocker and beer a brawler;
Isa 55: 1 Come, buy w and milk
Mt 9:17 Neither do men pour new w
Lk 23:36 They offered him w vinegar
Ro 14:21 not to eat meat or drink w
Eph 5:18 on w, which leads to debauchery.

WINESKINS

Mt 9:17 do men pour new wine into old w.

WINGS

Ru 2:12 under whose w you have come
Ps 17: 8 hide me in the shadow of your w
Isa 40:31 They will soar on w like eagles;
Mal 4: 2 rise with healing in its w.
Lk 13:34 hen gathers her chicks under her w,

WINS (WIN)

Pr 11:30 and he who w souls is wise.

WIPE

Rev 7:17 God will w away every tear

WISDOM (WISE)

1Ki 4:29 God gave Solomon w and very
Ps 111: 10 of the LORD is the beginning of w;
Pr 31:26 She speaks with w,
Jer 10:12 he founded the world by his w
Mt 11:19 But w is proved right by her actions
Lk 2:52 And Jesus grew in w and stature,
Ro 11:33 the depth of the riches of the w
Col 2: 3 are hidden all the treasures of w
Jas 1: 5 of you lacks w, he should ask God,

WISE (WISDOM WISER)

1Ki 3:12 give you a w and discerning heart,
Job 5:13 He catches the w in their craftiness
Ps 19: 7 making w the simple.
Pr 3: 7 Do not be w in your own eyes;
9: 8 rebuke a w man and he will love
10: 1 A w son brings joy to his father,
11:30 and he who wins souls is w.
13:20 He who walks with the w grows w,
17:28 Even a fool is thought w
Da 12: 3 Those who are w will shine like
Mt 11:25 hidden these things from the w
1Co 1:27 things of the world to shame the w;
2Ti 3:15 able to make you w for salvation

WISER (WISE)

1Co 1:25 of God is w than man's wisdom,

WITHER (WITHERS)

Ps 1: 3 and whose leaf does not w.

WITHERS (WITHER)

Isa 40: 7 The grass w and the flowers fall,
1Pe 1:24 the grass w and the flowers fall,

WITHHOLD

Ps 84:11 no good thing does he w
Pr 23:13 Do not w discipline from a child;

WITNESS (WITNESSES)

Jn 1: 8 he came only as a w to the light.

WITNESSES (WITNESS)

Dt 19:15 by the testimony of two or three w.

Ac   1: 8 and you will be my *w* in Jerusalem,

WIVES (WIFE)
Eph   5:22 *W*, submit to your husbands
       5:25 love your *w*, just as Christ loved
1Pe   3: 1 words by the behavior of their *w*,

WOE
Isa   6: 5 "*W* to me!" I cried.

WOLF
Isa   65:25 *w* and the lamb will feed together,

WOMAN (MAN)
Ge   2:22 God made a *w* from
       3:15 between you and the *w*,
Lev   20:13 as one lies with a *w*,
Dt   22: 5 *w* must not wear men's
Ru   3:11 a *w* of noble character
Pr   31:30 a *w* who fears the Lord
Mt   5:28 looks at a *w* lustfully
Jn   8: 3 a *w* caught in adultery.
Ro   7: 2 a married *w* is bound to
1Co   11: 3 the head of the *w* is man,
     11:13 a *w* to pray to God with
1Ti   2:11 A *w* should learn in

WOMEN (MAN)
Lk   1:42 Blessed are you among *w*,
1Co   14:34 *w* should remain silent in
1Ti   2: 9 want *w* to dress modestly
Tit   2: 3 teach the older *w* to be
1Pe   3: 5 the holy *w* of the past

WOMB
Job   1:21 Naked I came from my mother's *w*,
Jer   1: 5 you in the I knew you,
Lk   1:44 the baby in my *w* leaped for joy.

WONDER (WONDERFUL WONDERS)
Ps   17: 7 Show the *w* of your great love,

WONDERFUL (WONDER)
Job   42: 3 things too *w* for me to know.
Ps   31:21 for he showed his *w* love to me
     119: 18 *w* things in your law.
     119:129 Your statutes are *w*;
     139: 6 Such knowledge is too *w* for me,
Isa   9: 6 *W* Counselor, Mighty God,
1Pe   2: 9 out of darkness into his *w* light.

WONDERS (WONDER)
Job   37:14 stop and consider God's *w*.
Ps 119: 27 then I will meditate on your *w*.
Joel   2:30 I will show *w* in the heavens
Ac   2:19 I will show *w* in the heaven above

WOOD
Isa   44:19 Shall I bow down to a block of *w*?"
1Co   3:12 costly stones, *w*, hay or straw,

WORD (WORDS)
Dt   8: 3 but on every *w* that comes
2Sa   22:31 the *w* of the Lord is flawless.
Ps 119: 9 By living according to your *w*.
     119: 11 I have hidden your *w* in my heart
     119:105 Your *w* is a lamp to my feet
Pr   12:25 but a kind *w* cheers him up.
     25:11 A *w* aptly spoken
     30: 5 "Every *w* of God is flawless;
Isa   55:11 so is my *w* that goes out
Jn   1: 1 was the *W*, and the *W* was
     1:14 The *W* became flesh and made his
2Co   2:17 we do not peddle the *w* of God
     4: 2 nor do we distort the *w* of God
Eph   6:17 of the Spirit, which is the *w* of God.
Php   2:16 as you hold out the *w* of life—
Col   3:16 Let the *w* of Christ dwell
2Ti   2:15 and who correctly handles the *w*
Heb   4:12 For the *w* of God is living
Jas   1:22 Do not merely listen to the *w*,
2Pe   1:19 And we have the *w* of the prophets

WORDS (WORD)
Dt   11:18 Fix these *w* of mine in your hearts
Ps 119:103 How sweet are your *w* to my taste
    119:130 The unfolding of your *w* gives light;
    119:160 All your *w* are true;
Pr   30: 6 Do not add to his *w*,
Jer   15:16 When your *w* came, I ate them;
Mt   24:35 but my *w* will never pass away.
Jn   6:68 You have the *w* of eternal life.
     15: 7 in me and my *w* remain in you,
1Co   14:19 rather speak five intelligible *w*
Rev   22:19 And if anyone takes *w* away

WORK (WORKER WORKERS WORKING WORKMAN WORKMANSHIP WORKS)
Ex   23:12 "Six days do your *w*,
Nu   8:11 ready to do the *w* of the Lord.
Dt   5:14 On it you shall not do any *w*,
Ecc   5:19 his lot and be happy in his *w*—
Jer   48:10 lax in doing the Lord's *w*!
Jn   6:27 Do not *w* for food that spoils,
     9: 4 we must do the *w* of him who sent
1Co   3:13 test the quality of each man's *w*.
Php   1: 6 that he who began a good *w*
     2:12 continue to *w* out your salvation
Col   3:23 Whatever you do, *w* at it
1Th   5:12 to respect those who *w* hard
2Th   3:10 If a man will not *w*, he shall not eat
2Ti   3:17 equipped for every good *w*.
Heb   6:10 he will not forget your *w*

WORKER (WORK)
Lk   10: 7 for the *w* deserves his wages.
1Ti   5:18 and "The *w* deserves his wages."

WORKERS (WORK)
Mt   9:37 is plentiful but the *w* are few.
1Co   3: 9 For we are God's fellow *w*;

WORKING (WORK)
Col   3:23 as *w* for the Lord, not for men,

WORKMAN (WORK)
2Ti   2:15 a *w* who does not need

WORKMANSHIP* (WORK)
Eph   2:10 For we are God's *w*, created

WORKS (WORK)
Pr   31:31 let her *w* bring her praise
Ro   8:28 in all things God *w* for the good
Eph   2: 9 not by *w*, so that no one can boast.
     4:12 to prepare God's people for *w*

WORLD (WORLDLY)
Ps   50:12 for the *w* is mine, and all that is in it
Isa   13:11 I will punish the *w* for its evil,
Mt   5:14 "You are the light of the *w*.
     16:26 for a man if he gains the whole *w*,
Mk   16:15 into all the *w* and preach the good
Jn   1:29 who takes away the sin of the *w*!
     3:16 so loved the *w* that he gave his one
     8:12 he said, "I am the light of the *w*.
     15:19 As it is, you do not belong to the *w*,
     16:33 In this *w* you will have trouble.
     18:36 "My kingdom is not of this *w*.
Ro   3:19 and the whole *w* held accountable
1Co   3:19 the wisdom of this *w* is foolishness
2Co   5:19 that God was reconciling the *w*
     10: 3 For though we live in the *w*,
1Ti   6: 7 For we brought nothing into the *w*,
1Jn   2: 2 but also for the sins of the whole *w*.

1Jn   2:15 not love the *w* or anything in the *w*.
Rev   13: 8 slain from the creation of the *w*.

WORLDLY (WORLD)
Tit   2:12 to ungodliness and *w* passions,

WORM
Mk   9:48 " 'their *w* does not die,

WORRY (WORRYING)
Mt   6:25 I tell you, do not *w* about your life,
     10:19 do not *w* about what to say

WORRYING (WORRY)
Mt   6:27 of you by *w* can add a single hour

WORSHIP
1Ch   16:29 *w* the Lord in the splendor
Ps   95: 6 Come, let us bow down in *w*,
Mt   2: 2 and have come to *w* him."
Jn   4:24 and his worshipers must *w* in spirit
Ro   12: 1 this is your spiritual act of *w*.

WORTH (WORTHY)
Job   28:13 Man does not comprehend its *w*;
Pr   31:10 She is *w* far more than rubies.
Mt   10:31 are *w* more than many sparrows.
Ro   8:18 sufferings are not *w* comparing
1Pe   1: 7 of greater *w* than gold,
     3: 4 which is of great *w* in God's sight.

WORTHLESS
Pr   11: 4 Wealth is *w* in the day of wrath,
Jas   1:26 himself and his religion is *w*.

WORTHY (WORTH)
1Ch   16:25 For great is the Lord and most *w*
Eph   4: 1 to live a life *w* of the calling you
Php   1:27 in a manner *w* of the gospel
3Jn   : 6 on their way in a manner *w* of God.
Rev   5: 2 "Who is *w* to break the seals

WOUNDS
Pr   27: 6 *W* from a friend can be trusted,
Isa   53: 5 and by his *w* we are healed.
Zec   13: 6 'What are these *w* on your body?'
1Pe   2:24 by his *w* you have been healed.

WRATH
2Ch   36:16 scoffed at his prophets until the *w*
Ps   2: 5 and terrifies them in his *w*, saying,
     76:10 Surely your *w* against men brings
Pr   15: 1 A gentle answer turns away *w*,
Jer   25:15 filled with the wine of my *w*
Ro   1:18 The *w* of God is being revealed
     5: 9 saved from God's *w* through him!
1Th   5: 9 God did not appoint us to suffer *w*
Rev   6:16 and from the *w* of the Lamb!

WRESTLED
Ge   32:24 and a man *w* with him till daybreak

WRITE (WRITING WRITTEN)
Dt   6: 9 *W* them on the doorframes
Pr   7: 3 *w* them on the tablet of your heart.
Heb   8:10 and *w* them on their hearts.

WRITING (WRITE)
1Co   14:37 him acknowledge that what I am *w*

WRITTEN (WRITE)
Jos   1: 8 careful to do everything *w* in it.
Da   12: 1 everyone whose name is found *w*

Lk   10:20 but rejoice that your names
are w
Jn   20:31 these are w that you may
believe
1Co   4: 6 "Do not go beyond what is w."
2Co   3: 3 w not with ink but with the Spirit
Col   2:14 having canceled the w code,
Heb 12:23 whose names are w in heaven.

WRONG (WRONGDOING WRONGED WRONGS)

Ex   23: 2 Do not follow the crowd in
doing w
Nu   5: 7 must make full restitution for
his w,
Job 34:12 unthinkable that God would
do w,
1Th   5:15 that nobody pays back w for w,

WRONGDOING (WRONG)

Job   1:22 sin by charging God with w.

WRONGED (WRONG)

1Co   6: 7 not rather be w? Why not rather

WRONGS (WRONG)

Pr   10:12 but love covers over all w.
1Co 13: 5 angered, it keeps no record
of w.

YEARS

Ps   90: 4 For a thousand y in your sight
90:10 The length of our days is
seventy y
2Pe   3: 8 the Lord a day is like a
thousand y,
Rev 20: 2 and bound him for a thousand y.

YESTERDAY

Heb 13: 8 Jesus Christ is the same y

YOKE (YOKED)

Mt   11:29 Take my y upon you and learn

YOKED (YOKE)

2Co   6:14 Do not be y together

YOUNG (YOUTH)

Ps 119: 9 How can a y man keep his way
1Ti   4:12 down on you because you are y,

YOUTH (YOUNG)

Ps 103: 5 so that your y is renewed like
Ecc 12: 1 Creator in the days of your y,
2Ti   2:22 Flee the evil desires of y,

ZEAL

Pr   19: 2 to have z without knowledge,
Ro   12:11 Never be lacking in z,

ZECHARIAH

1. Son of Jeroboam II; king of Israel (2Ki
15:8-12).
2. Post-exilic prophet who encouraged rebuilding of temple (Ezr 5:1; 6:14; Zec 1:1).
3. Father of John the Baptist (Lk 1:13; 3:2).

ZEDEKIAH

Mattaniah, son of Josiah (1Ch 3:15), made
king of Judah by Nebuchadnezzar (2Ki 24:17-
25:7; 2Ch 36:10-14; Jer 37-39; 52:1-11).

ZERUBBABEL

Descendant of David (1Ch 3:19; Mt 1:3).
Led return from exile (Ezr 2-3; Ne 7:7; Hag
1-2; Zec 4).

ZIMRI

King of Israel (1Ki 16:9-20).

ZION

Ps 137: 3 "Sing us one of the songs of Z!"
Jer   50: 5 They will ask the way to Z
Ro   9:33 I lay in Z r stone that causes
men
11:26 "The de   r will come from Z;

COURSE 1: INTRODUCTION TO THE BIBLE

TIME COMMITMENT:
Two weeks

GOAL:
To survey basic Biblical foundations

Course 1 is a place to begin reading the Bible. Three two-week reading courses take you quickly into passages of the Bible every Christian should know. These were selected with two concerns in mind: first, they are frequently quoted or referred to. Second, they are relatively easy to read and understand. Course 1 is a sampler, designed to whet your appetite for more.

1. Two Weeks on the Life and Teachings of Jesus

- ☐ Day 1   LUKE 1: Preparing for Jesus' arrival
- ☐ Day 2   LUKE 2: The story of Jesus' birth
- ☐ Day 3   MARK 1: The beginning of Jesus' ministry
- ☐ Day 4   MARK 9: A day in the life of Jesus
- ☐ Day 5   MATTHEW 5: The Sermon on the Mount
- ☐ Day 6   MATTHEW 6: The Sermon on the Mount
- ☐ Day 7   LUKE 15: Parables of Jesus
- ☐ Day 8   JOHN 3: A conversation with Jesus
- ☐ Day 9   JOHN 14: Jesus' final instructions
- ☐ Day 10   JOHN 17: Jesus' prayer for his disciples
- ☐ Day 11   MATTHEW 26: Betrayal and arrest
- ☐ Day 12   MATTHEW 27: Jesus' execution on a cross
- ☐ Day 13   JOHN 20: Resurrection
- ☐ Day 14   LUKE 24: Jesus' appearance after resurrection

2. Two Weeks on the Life and Teachings of Paul

- ☐ Day 1   ACTS 9: The conversion of Saul
- ☐ Day 2   ACTS 16: Paul's Macedonian call and a jailbreak
- ☐ Day 3   ACTS 17: Scenes from Paul's missionary journey
- ☐ Day 4   ACTS 26: Paul tells his life story to a king
- ☐ Day 5   ACTS 27: Shipwreck on the way to Rome
- ☐ Day 6   ACTS 28: Paul's arrival in Rome
- ☐ Day 7   ROMANS 3: Paul's theology in a nutshell
- ☐ Day 8   ROMANS 7: Struggle with sin
- ☐ Day 9   ROMANS 8: Life in the Spirit
- ☐ Day 10   1 CORINTHIANS 13: Paul's description of love
- ☐ Day 11   1 CORINTHIANS 15: Thoughts on the afterlife
- ☐ Day 12   GALATIANS 5: Freedom in Christ
- ☐ Day 13   EPHESIANS 3: Paul's summary of his mission
- ☐ Day 14   PHILIPPIANS 2: Imitating Christ

3. Two Weeks on the Old Testament

- ☐ Day 1   GENESIS 1: The story of creation
- ☐ Day 2   GENESIS 3: The origin of sin
- ☐ Day 3   GENESIS 22: Abraham and Isaac
- ☐ Day 4   EXODUS 3: Moses' encounter with God
- ☐ Day 5   EXODUS 20: The gift of the Ten Commandments
- ☐ Day 6   1 SAMUEL 17: David and Goliath
- ☐ Day 7   2 SAMUEL 11: David and Bathsheba
- ☐ Day 8   2 SAMUEL 12: Nathan's rebuke of the king
- ☐ Day 9   1 KINGS 18: Elijah and the prophets of Baal
- ☐ Day 10   JOB 38: God's answer to Job
- ☐ Day 11   PSALM 51: A classic confession
- ☐ Day 12   ISAIAH 40: Words of comfort from God
- ☐ Day 13   DANIEL 6: Daniel and the lions
- ☐ Day 14   AMOS 4: A prophet's stern warning

COURSE 2: EVERY BOOK IN THE BIBLE

TIME COMMITMENT: **GOAL:**
Six months   **To gain an overview of the entire Bible**

Course 2 includes 186 of the 1,189 chapters in the Bible. Many well-known parts of the Bible are not represented, and from some books (Leviticus, for example), you will read only a single chapter. These 186 chapters have been selected because they are understandable to the average reader without commentary. Taken together, they provide a good foundation of Bible understanding.

If you miss a few days, don't worry. Just resume reading when you can, about a chapter a day. In 180 total days, you will get an overview that includes something from every book in the Bible.

GENESIS □1 □2 □3 □4 □7 □8 □15 □19 □22 □27 □28 □37 □41 □45
EXODUS □3 □10-11 □14 □20 □32
LEVITICUS □26
NUMBERS □11 □14
DEUTERONOMY □4 □8 □28
JOSHUA □2 □6 □7 □24
JUDGES □6 □7 □16
RUTH □1
1 SAMUEL □3 □16 □17 □20
2 SAMUEL □6 □11 □12
1 KINGS □3 □8 □17 □18
2 KINGS □5 □17 □22
1 CHRONICLES □17
2 CHRONICLES □20 □30 □32
EZRA □3
NEHEMIAH □2 □8
ESTHER □4
JOB □1-2 □38 □42
PSALMS □19 □23 □27 □51 □84 □103 □139
PROVERBS □4 □10
ECCLESIASTES □3
SONG OF SONGS □2
ISAIAH □6 □25 □40 □52 □53 □55
JEREMIAH □2 □15 □31 □38
LAMENTATIONS □3
EZEKIEL □1 □2-3 □4 □37
DANIEL □1 □3 □5 □6
HOSEA □2-3 □11
JOEL □2
AMOS □4
OBADIAH □Obadiah
JONAH □3-4
MICAH □6
NAHUM □1

HABAKKUK □1
ZEPHANIAH □3
HAGGAI □1
ZECHARIAH □8
MALACHI □3
MATTHEW □5 □6 □13 □19 □26 □27 □28
MARK □1 □2 □3 □4 □5 □6 □7 □8 □9 □10 □11 □12 □13 □14 □15-16
LUKE □1 □2 □10 □12 □15 □16 □18 □24
JOHN □3 □6 □10 □14 □15 □16 □17 □20
ACTS □1 □2 □5 □9 □16 □17 □26 □27 □28
ROMANS □3 □7 □8 □12
1 CORINTHIANS □13 □15
2 CORINTHIANS □4 □12
GALATIANS □3
EPHESIANS □2 □3
PHILIPPIANS □2
COLOSSIANS □1
1 THESSALONIANS □3-4
2 THESSALONIANS □2
1 TIMOTHY □1
2 TIMOTHY □2
TITUS □2
PHILEMON □Philemon
HEBREWS □2 □11 □12
JAMES □1
1 PETER □1
2 PETER □1
1 JOHN □3
2 and 3 JOHN □2, 3 John
JUDE □Jude
REVELATION □1 □12 □21

COURSE 3: EVERY WORD OF THE BIBLE

TIME COMMITMENT: **GOAL:**
Three years   **To read all the way through the Bible with understanding**

Course 3 takes you through every word of the Bible, alternating between Old Testament readings and New Testament readings. Other Bible-reading plans allot only a year for this project, requiring that at least 3 chapters be read each day. But many readers find such a pace to be unrealistic and discouraging. For this reason, Course 3 assigns usually only one chapter a day. (Some short chapters have been combined, so occasionally you will read two brief chapters in a day.) The reading plan works out evenly to a three-year total.

GENESIS □1 □2 □3 □4 □5 □6 □7 □8 □9 □10-11 □12 □13 □14 □15 □16 □17 □18 □19 □20 □21 □22 □23 □24 □25 □26 □27 □28 □29 □30 □31 □32 □33

□34 □35 □36 □37 □38 □39 □40 □41 □42 □43 □44 □45 □46 □47 □48 □49 □50

MATTHEW 1-9 □1 □2 □3 □4 □5 □6 □7 □8 □9

EXODUS □1 □2 □3 □4 □5 □6 □7 □8 □9 □10-11 □12 □13 □14 □15 □16 □17 □18 □19 □20 □21 □22 □23 □24 □25 □26 □27 □28 □29 □30 □31 □32 □33 □34 □35 □36 □37 □38 □39 □40

MATTHEW 10-20 □10 □11 □12 □13 □14 □15 □16 □17 □18 □19 □20

LEVITICUS 1-14 □1 □2 □3 □4 □5 □6 □7 □8 □9 □10 □11-12 □13 □14

MATTHEW 21-28 □21 □22 □23 □24 □25 □26 □27 □28

LEVITICUS 15-27 □15 □16 □17 □18 □19 □20 □21 □22 □23 □24 □25 □26 □27

MARK 1-8 □1 □2 □3 □4 □5 □6 □7 □8

NUMBERS □1-2 □3 □4 □5 □6 □7 □8 □9 □10 □11 □12 □13 □14 □15 □16 □17 □18 □19 □20 □21 □22 □23 □24 □25 □26 □27 □28 □29 □30 □31 □32 □33 □34 □35 □36

MARK 9-16 □9 □10 □11 □12 □13 □14 □15-16

DEUTERONOMY 1-17 □1 □2 □3 □4 □5 □6 □7 □8 □9 □10 □11 □12 □13 □14 □15 □16 □17

LUKE 1-8 □1 □2 □3 □4 □5 □6 □7 □8

DEUTERONOMY 18-34 □18 □19 □20 □21 □22 □23 □24 □25 □26 □27 □28 □29 □30 □31 □32 □33 □34

LUKE 9-16 □9 □10 □11 □12 □13 □14 □15 □16

JOSHUA □1 □2 □3 □4 □5 □6 □7 □8 □9 □10 □11 □12-13 □14-15 □16-17 □18 □19 □20 □21 □22 □23 □24

LUKE 17-24 □17 □18 □19 □20 □21 □22 □23 □24

JUDGES □1 □2 □3 □4 □5 □6 □7 □8 □9 □10 □11 □12 □13 □14 □15 □16 □17 □18 □19 □20 □21

JOHN 1-7 □1 □2 □3 □4 □5 □6 □7

RUTH □1 □2 □3 □4

1 SAMUEL 1-15 □1 □2 □3 □4 □5 □6 □7 □8 □9 □10 □11 □12 □13 □14 □15

JOHN 8-14 □8 □9 □10 □11 □12 □13 □14

1 SAMUEL 16-31 □16 □17 □18 □19 □20 □21 □22 □23 □24 □25 □26 □27 □28 □29 □30 □31

JOHN 15-21 □15 □16 □17 □18 □19 □20 □21

2 SAMUEL □1 □2 □3 □4 □5 □6 □7 □8 □9 □10 □11 □12 □13 □14 □15 □16 □17 □18 □19 □20 □21 □22 □23 □24

ACTS 1-7 □1 □2 □3 □4 □5 □6 □7

1 KINGS 1-11 □1 □2 □3 □4-5 □6 □7 □8 □9 □10 □11

ACTS 8-14 □8 □9 □10 □11 □12 □13 □14

1 KINGS 12-22 □12 □13 □14 □15 □16 □17 □18 □19 □20 □21 □22

ACTS 15-21 □15 □16 □17 □18 □19 □20 □21

2 KINGS □1 □2 □3 □4 □5 □6 □7 □8 □9 □10 □11 □12 □13 □14 □15 □16 □17 □18 □19 □20 □21 □22 □23 □24 □25

ACTS 22-28 □22 □23 □24 □25 □26 □27 □28

1 CHRONICLES 1-14 □1-9 □10 □11 □12 □13 □14

ROMANS 1-8 □1 □2 □3 □4 □5 □6 □7 □8

1 CHRONICLES 15-29 □15 □16 □17 □18 □19 □20 □21 □22 □23-27 □28 □29

ROMANS 9-16 □9 □10 □11 □12-13 □14 □15-16

2 CHRONICLES 1-18 □1 □2 □3 □4 □5 □6 □7 □8 □9 □10 □11 □12 □13 □14 □15 □16-17 □18

1 CORINTHIANS 1-9 □1 □2 □3 □4-5 □6 □7 □8-9

2 CHRONICLES 19-36 □19 □20 □21 □22 □23 □24 □25 □26-27 □28 □29 □30 □31 □32 □33 □34 □35 □36

1 CORINTHIANS 10-16 □10 □11 □12 □13 □14 □15 □16

EZRA □1-2 □3 □4 □5 □6 □7 □8 □9 □10

NEHEMIAH □1 □2-3 □4 □5 □6 □7 □8 □9 □10 □11 □12 □13

2 CORINTHIANS □1 □2-3 □4 □5 □6 □7 □8-9 □10 □11 □12-13

ESTHER □1 □2 □3 □4 □5 □6-7 □8 □9-10

JOB 1-21 □1 □2 □3 □4 □5 □6 □7 □8 □9 □10 □11 □12 □13 □14 □15 □16 □17 □18 □19 □20 □21

GALATIANS □1 □2 □3 □4 □5-6

JOB 22-42 □22 □23 □24 □25-26 □27 □28 □29 □30 □31 □32 □33 □34 □35 □36 □37 □38 □39 □40 □41 □42

EPHESIANS □1 □2 □3 □4 □5 □6

PSALMS 1-40 □1-2 □3-4 □5 □6 □7 □8 □9 □10 □11-12 □13-14 □15-16 □17 □18 □19 □20-21 □22 □23-24 □25 □26 □27 □28-29 □30 □31 □32 □33 □34 □35 □36 □37 □38 □39 □40

PHILIPPIANS □1 □2 □3 □4

PSALMS 41-80 □41 □42-43 □44 □45 □46-47 □48 □49 □50 □51 □52 □53-54 □55 □56 □57 □58 □59 □60-61 □62 □63-64 □65 □66 □67 □68 □69 □70 □71 □72 □73 □74 □75 □76 □77 □78 □79 □80

COLOSSIANS □1 □2 □3 □4

PSALMS 81-121 □81 □82 □83 □84 □85 □86 □87 □88 □89 □90 □91 □92-93 □94 □95 □96 □97 □98-99 □100-101 □102 □103 □104 □105 □106 □107 □108 □109

□110-111 □112 □113 □114 □115 □116-117 □118 □119:1-48 □119:49-96 □119:97-144 □119:145-176 □120-121

1 THESSALONIANS □1-2 □3-4 □5

2 THESSALONIANS □1-2 □3

PSALMS 122-150 □122-123 □124-125 □126-128 □129-130 □131-132 □133-134 □135 □135 □137-138 □139 □140 □141-142 □143 □144 □145 □146 □147 □148 □149-150

PROVERBS □1 □2 □3 □4 □5 □6 □7 □8 □9 □10 □11 □12 □13 □14 □15 □16 □17 □18 □19 □20 □21 □22 □23 □24 □25 □26 □27 □28 □29 □30 □31

1 TIMOTHY □1-2 □3-4 □5 □6

ECCLESIASTES □1 □2 □3 □4 □5 □6 □7 □8 □9 □10 □11 □12

SONG OF SONGS □1 □2 □3 □4 □5 □6 □7 □8

2 TIMOTHY □1 □2 □3 □4

ISAIAH 1-36 □1 □2 □3 □4-5 □6 □7 □8 □9 □10 □11 □12 □13 □14 □15 □16 □17 □18 □19-20 □21 □22 □23 □24 □25 □26 □27 □28 □29 □30 □31 □32 □33 □34 □35 □36

TITUS □1 □2-3

ISAIAH 37-66 □37 □38-39 □40 □41 □42 □43 □44 □45 □46 □47 □48 □49 □50 □51 □52 □53 □54 □55 □56 □57 □58 □59 □60 □61 □62 □63 □64 □65 □66

PHILEMON □Philemon

JEREMIAH 1-26 □1 □2 □3 □4 □5 □6 □7 □8 □9 □10 □11 □12 □13 □14 □15 □16 □17 □18 □19 □20 □21 □22 □23 □24 □25 □26

HEBREWS 1-7 □1 □2 □3-4 □5-6 □7

JEREMIAH 27-52 □27 □28 □29 □30 □31 □32 □33 □34 □35 □36 □37 □38 □39 □40 □41 □42 □43 □44-45 □46 □47 □48 □49 □50 □51 □52

HEBREWS 8-13 □8 □9 □10 □11 □12 □13

LAMENTATIONS □1 □2 □3 □4 □5

EZEKIEL 1-24 □1 □2-3 □4 □5 □6 □7 □8 □9 □10 □11 □12 □13 □14 □15 □16 □17 □18 □19 □20 □21 □22 □23 □24

JAMES □1 □2 □3-4 □5

EZEKIEL 25-48 □25 □26 □27 □28 □29 □30 □31 □32 □33 □34 □35 □36 □37 □38 □39 □40 □41 □42 □43 □44 □45 □46 □47 □48

1 PETER □1 □2 □3 □4-5

DANIEL □1 □2 □3 □4 □5 □6 □7 □8 □9 □10 □11 □12

2 PETER □1 □2 □3

HOSEA □1 □2-3 □4 □5 □6-7 □8 □9 □10 □11-12 □13-14

1 JOHN □1-2 □3 □4 □5

JOEL □1 □2 □3

AMOS □1 □2 □3 □4 □5 □6 □7 □8 □9

OBADIAH □Obadiah

JONAH □1-2 □3-4

2 and 3 JOHN □2 John, 3 John

MICAH □1 □2 □3 □4 □5 □6 □7

NAHUM □1 □2 □3

JUDE □Jude

HABAKKUK □1 □2 □3

ZEPHANIAH □1 □2 □3

REVELATION 1-7 □1 □2 □3 □4-5 □6 □7

HAGGAI □1 □2

REVELATION 8-14 □8 □9 □10-11 □12 □13 □14

ZECHARIAH □1 □2-3 □4-5 □6 □7 □8 □9 □10 □11 □12-13 □14

MALACHI □1 □2 □3-4

REVELATION □15-22 □15-16 □17 □18 □19

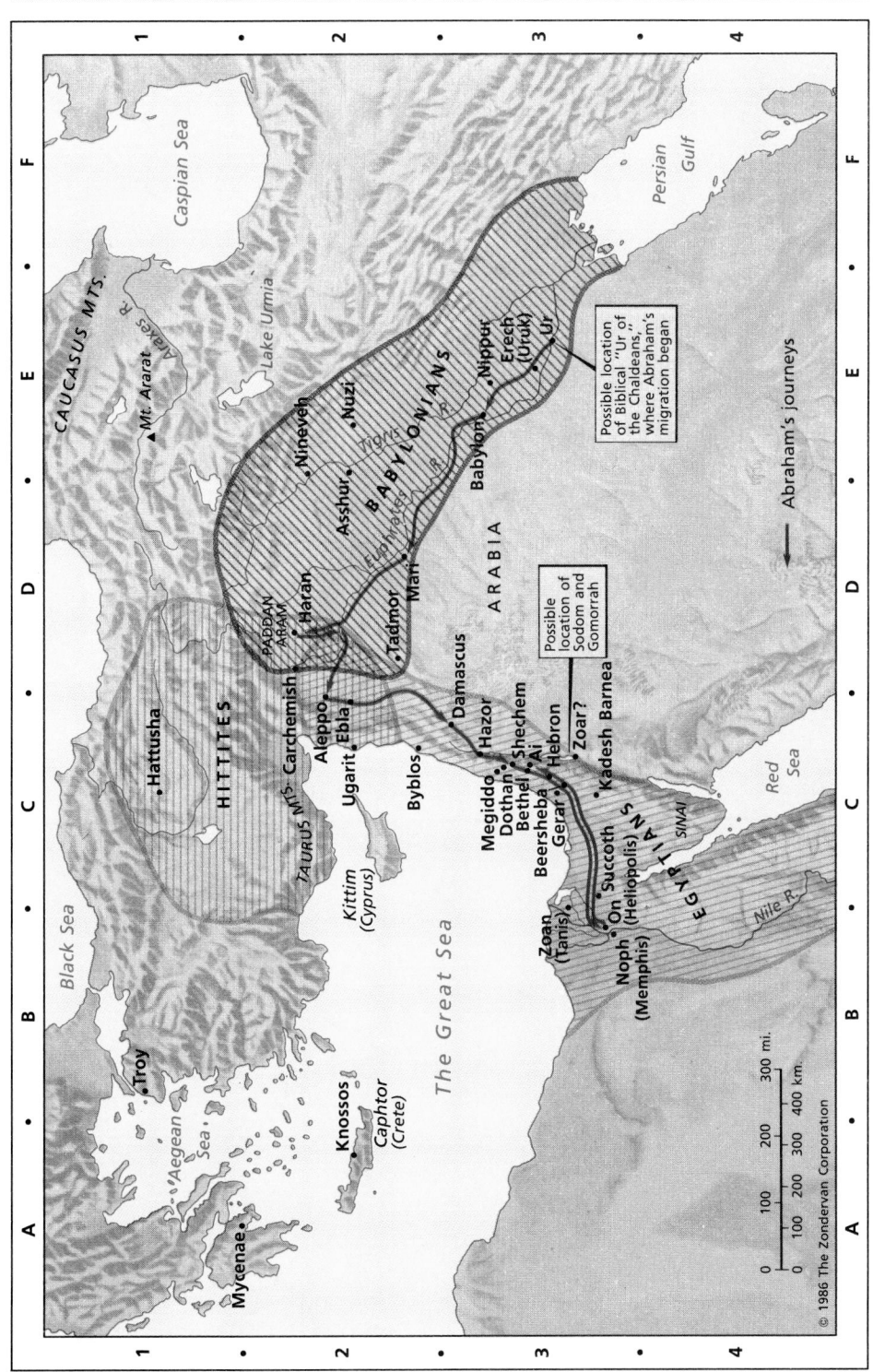

© 1986 The Zondervan Corporation

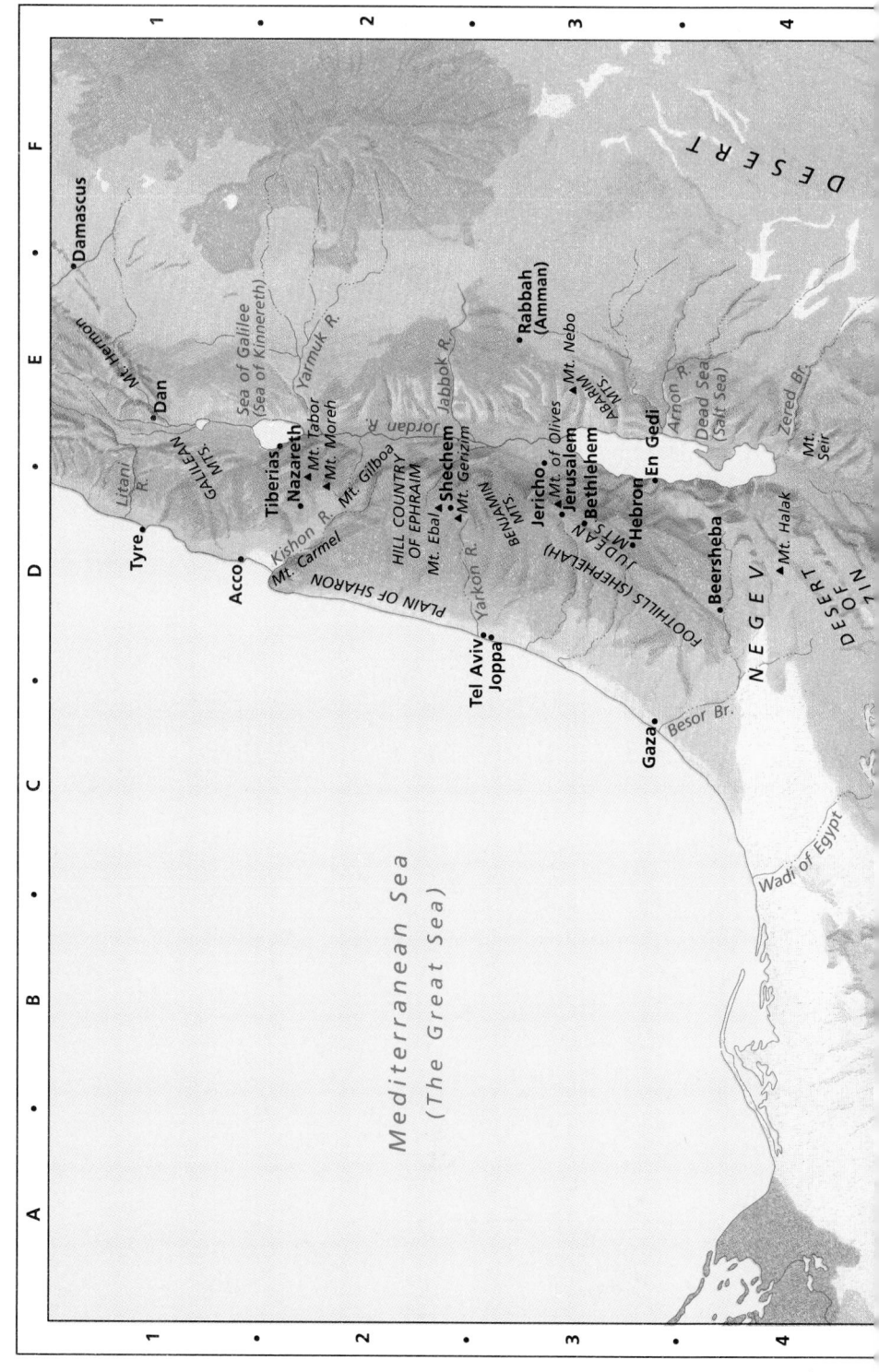

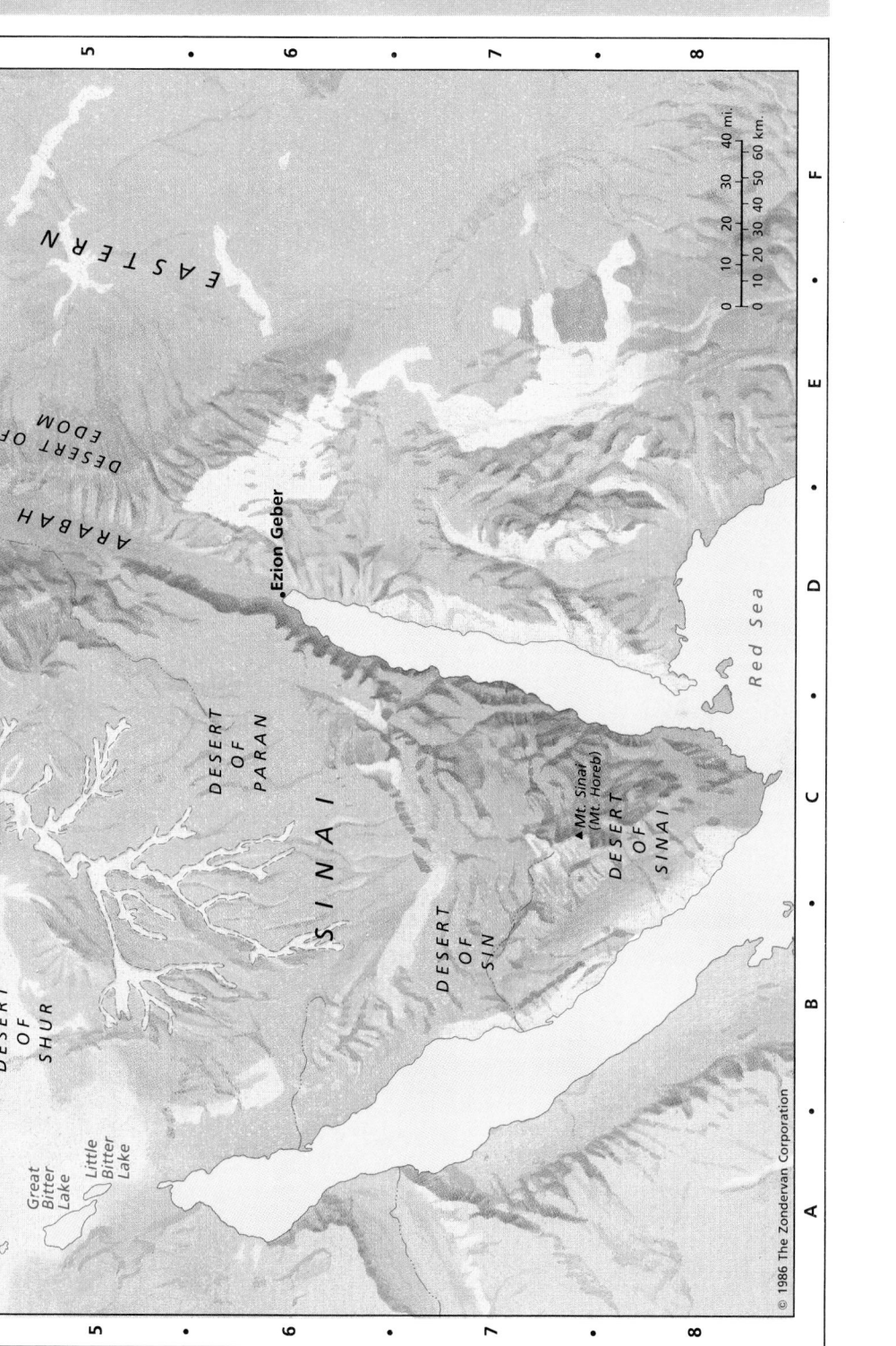

Great Bitter Lake

Little Bitter Lake

DESERT OF SHUR

DESERT OF PARAN

S I N A I

DESERT OF SIN

▲Mt. Sinai (Mt. Horeb)

DESERT OF SINAI

•Ezion Geber

ARABAH

DESERT OF EDOM

E A S T E R N

Red Sea

0   10   20   30   40 mi.
0 10 20 30 40 50 60 km.

© 1986 The Zondervan Corporation

Map 3: EXODUS AND CONQUEST OF CANAAN

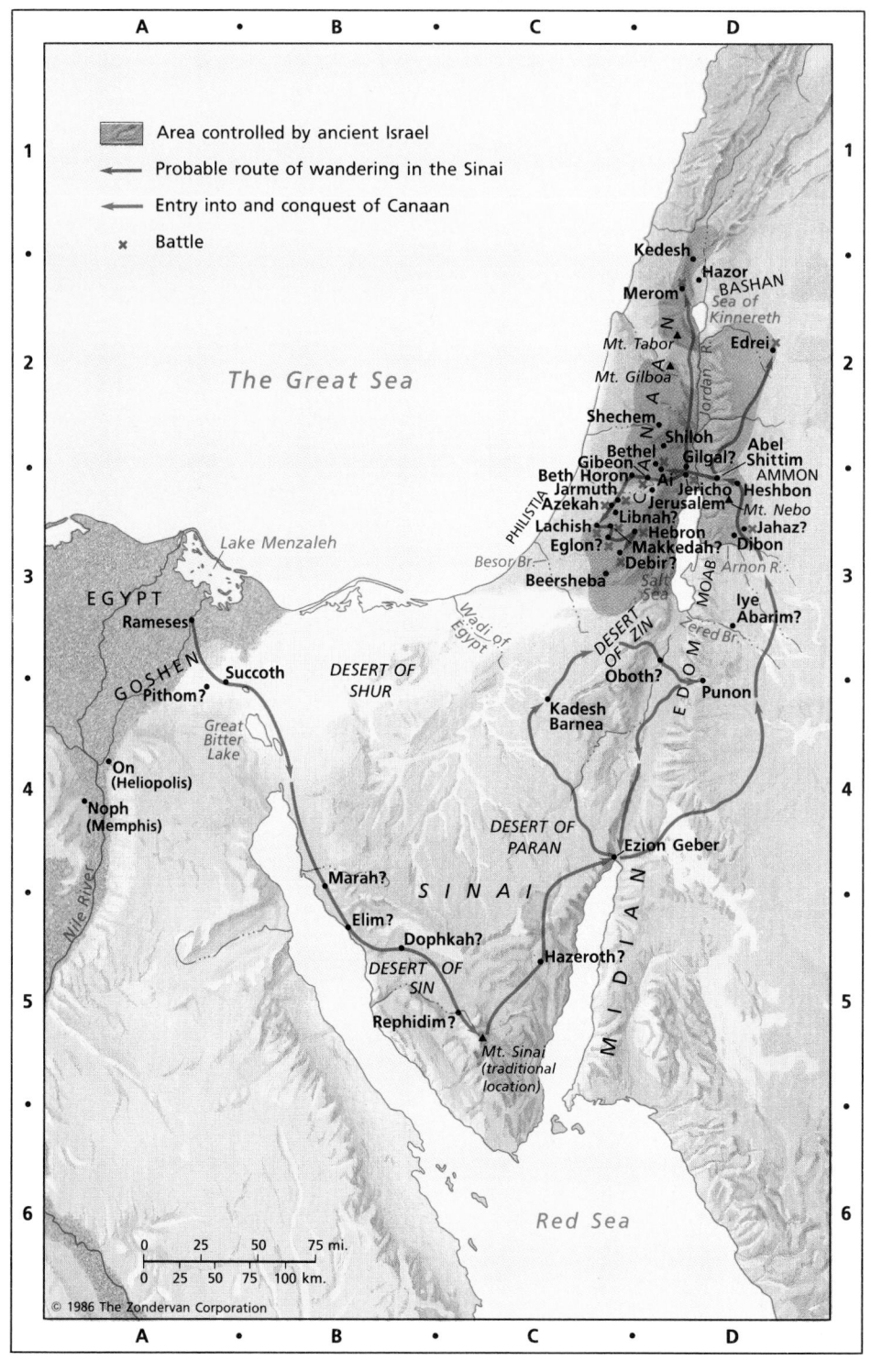

Area controlled by ancient Israel

Probable route of wandering in the Sinai

Entry into and conquest of Canaan

× Battle

The Great Sea

Kedesh
Hazor
Merom
BASHAN
Sea of Kinnereth
Mt. Tabor
Mt. Gilboa
Edrei
Shechem
Shiloh
Bethel
Gibeon
Gilgal?
Abel Shittim
AMMON
Beth Horon
Ai
Jericho
Heshbon
Jarmuth
Jerusalem
Mt. Nebo
Azekah
Libnah?
Jahaz?
Lachish
Hebron
Dibon
Eglon?
Makkedah?
Debir?
Beersheba
Salt Sea
Arnon R.
MOAB
Iye Abarim?
Besor Br.
PHILISTIA

EGYPT
Rameses
Wadi of Egypt
DESERT OF ZIN
Zered Br.
EDOM
GOSHEN
Pithom?
Succoth
DESERT OF SHUR
Oboth?
Punon
Great Bitter Lake
Kadesh Barnea
On (Heliopolis)
Noph (Memphis)
DESERT OF PARAN
Ezion Geber
Nile River
Marah?
SINAI
Elim?
MIDIAN
Dophkah?
Hazeroth?
DESERT OF SIN
Rephidim?
Mt. Sinai (traditional location)
Red Sea
Lake Menzaleh

0   25   50   75 mi.
0   25 50 75 100 km.

© 1986 The Zondervan Corporation

A   B   C   D

Map 4: LAND OF THE TWELVE TRIBES

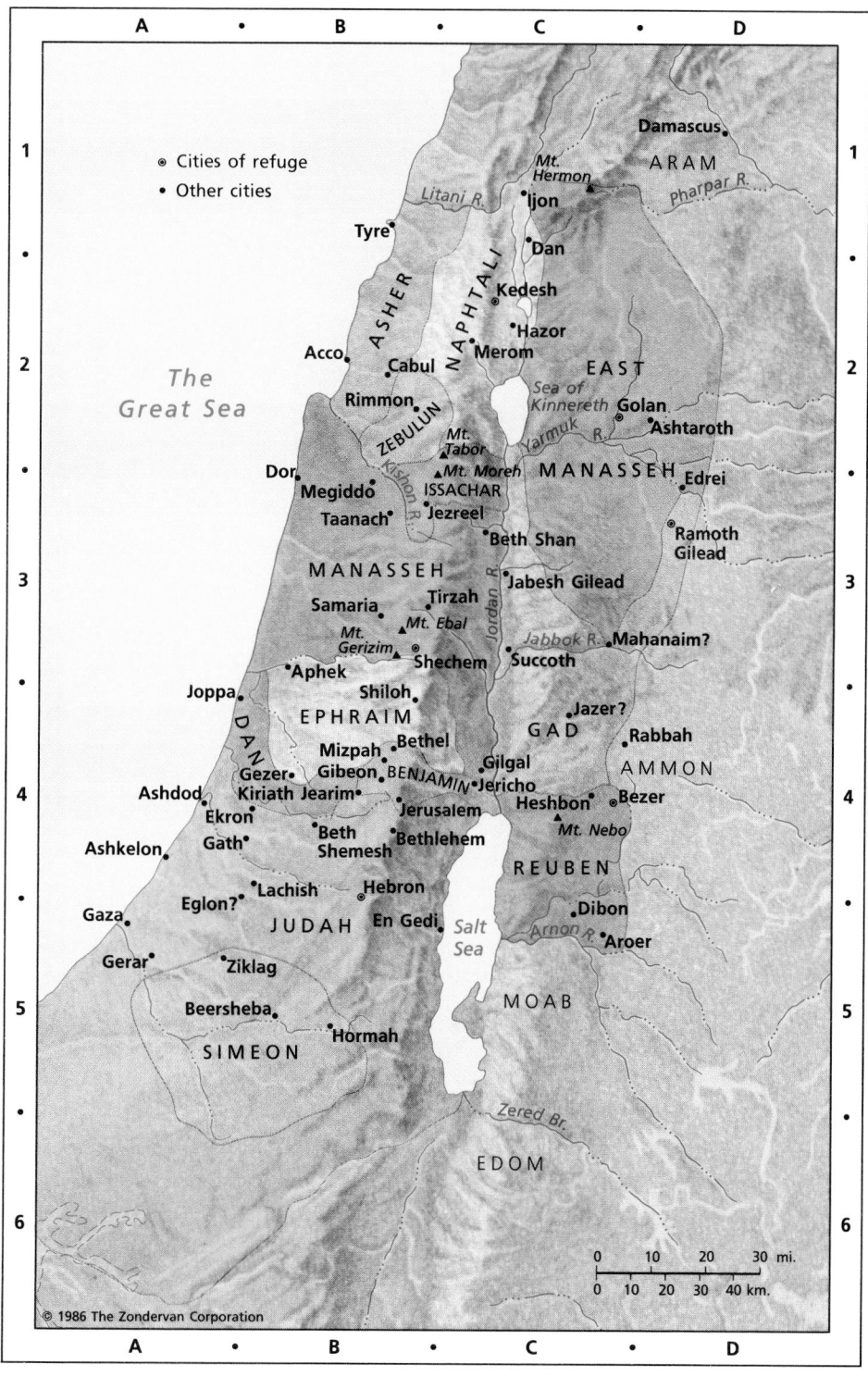

Cities of refuge
Other cities

Damascus

ARAM

Mt. Hermon
Litani R.
Ijon
Pharpar R.

Tyre
Dan

A S H E R
Kedesh

Hazor

Acco
Cabul
Merom
EAST

N A P H T A L I

Rimmon
ZEBULUN
Sea of Kinnereth
Golan
Ashtaroth

The Great Sea

Mt. Tabor
Yarmuk R.

Dor
Kishon R.
Mt. Moreh
M A N A S S E H
Edrei

Megiddo
ISSACHAR

Taanach
Jezreel
Ramoth Gilead

Beth Shan

M A N A S S E H
Jabesh Gilead

Jordan R.

Samaria
Tirzah
Mt. Ebal
Jabbok R.
Mahanaim?

Mt. Gerizim
Shechem
Succoth

Aphek
Joppa
Shiloh
Jazer?

E P H R A I M
G A D
Rabbah

D A N
Mizpah
Bethel
AMMON

Gezer
Gibeon
BENJAMIN
Gilgal
Jericho

Ashdod
Kiriath Jearim
Heshbon
Bezer

Ekron
Jerusalem
Mt. Nebo

Gath
Beth Shemesh
Bethlehem

Ashkelon

R E U B E N

Lachish
Hebron
Salt Sea
Dibon

Gaza
Eglon?
En Gedi
Arnon R.
Aroer

Gerar
J U D A H

Ziklag

Beersheba
M O A B

Hormah
S I M E O N

Zered Br.

E D O M

0   10   20   30 mi.
0   10   20   30   40 km.

© 1986 The Zondervan Corporation

Map 5: KINGDOM OF DAVID AND SOLOMON

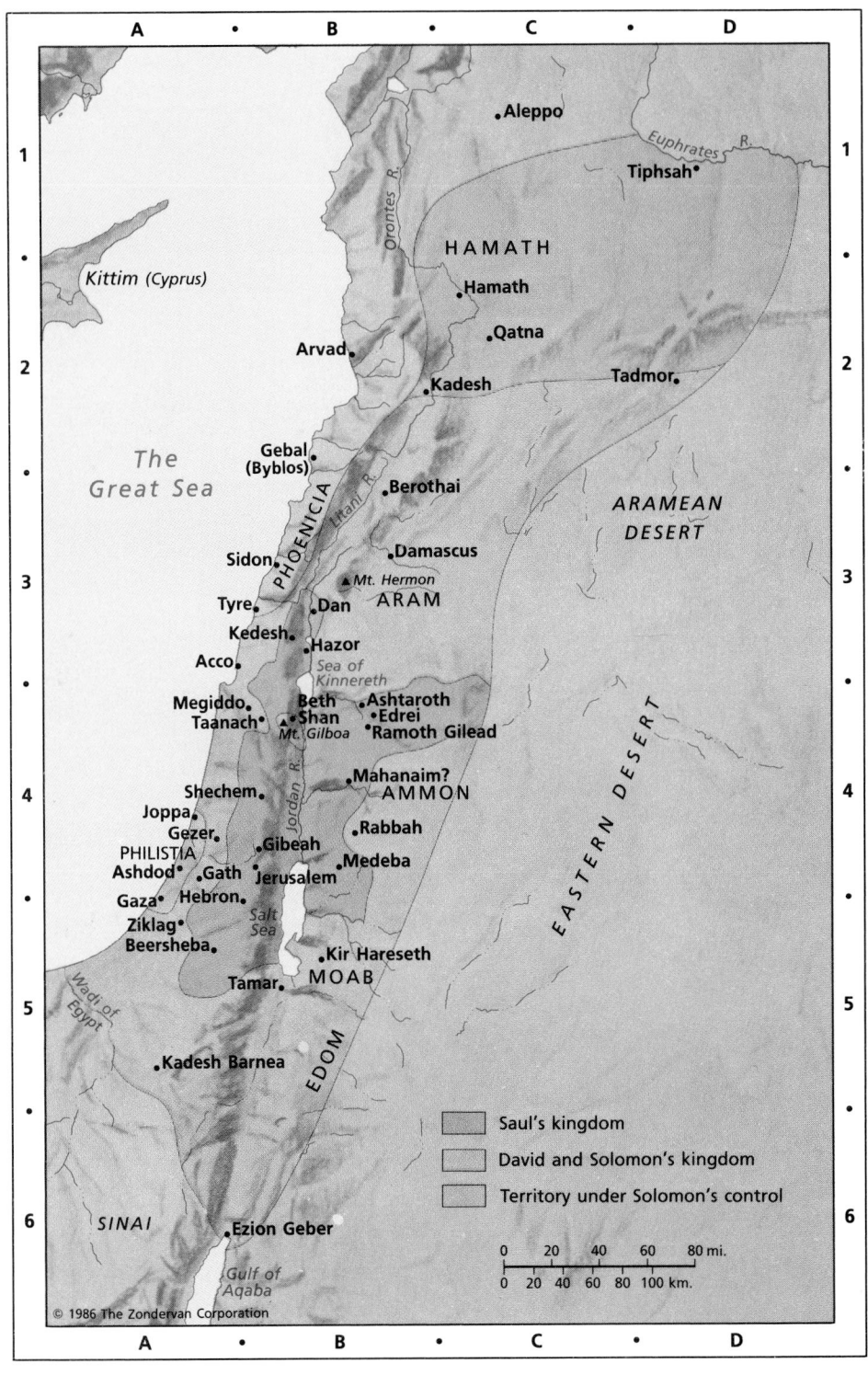

Aleppo

Euphrates R.

Tiphsah

HAMATH

Kittim (Cyprus)

Hamath

Qatna

Arvad

Kadesh

Tadmor

The
Great Sea

Gebal
(Byblos)

Berothai

ARAMEAN
DESERT

Sidon

Damascus

Mt. Hermon

Tyre

Dan

ARAM

Kedesh

Hazor

Acco

Sea of
Kinnereth

Megiddo

Beth
Shan

Ashtaroth

Taanach

Mt. Gilboa

Edrei

Ramoth Gilead

Mahanaim?

AMMON

Shechem

Joppa

Rabbah

Gezer

PHILISTIA

Gibeah

Ashdod

Gath

Jerusalem

Medeba

Gaza

Hebron

Ziklag

Salt
Sea

Beersheba

EASTERN DESERT

Kir Hareseth

Tamar

MOAB

Kadesh Barnea

EDOM

Saul's kingdom

David and Solomon's kingdom

Territory under Solomon's control

SINAI

Ezion Geber

0   20   40   60   80 mi.

0 20 40 60 80 100 km.

Gulf of
Aqaba

© 1986 The Zondervan Corporation

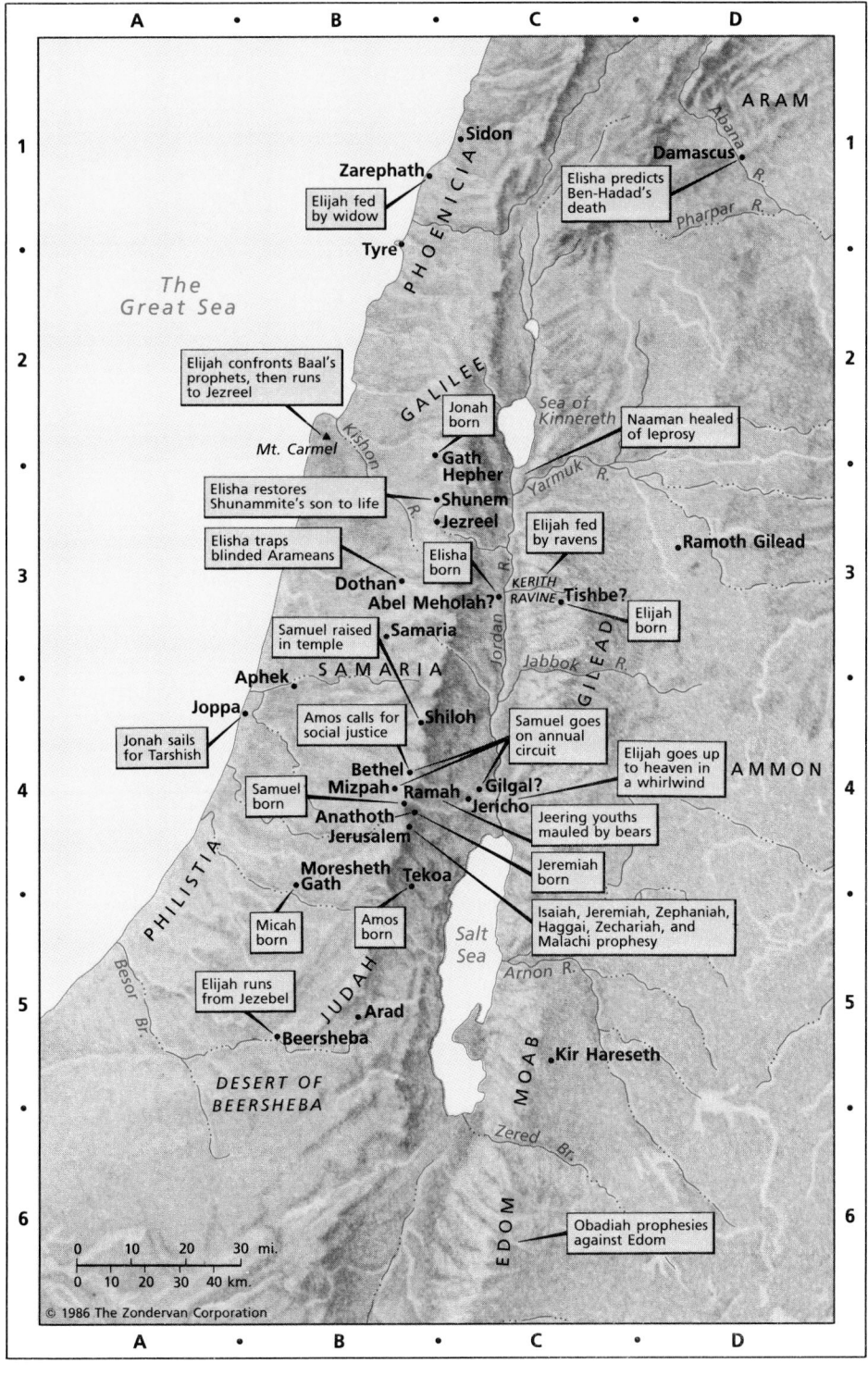

A • **B** • **C** • **D**

ARAM

1

•Sidon

Zarephath•

| Elijah fed by widow |

Damascus•

| Elisha predicts Ben-Hadad's death |

Tyre•

PHOENICIA

Abana R.

Pharpar R.

The Great Sea

2

| Elijah confronts Baal's prophets, then runs to Jezreel |

GALILEE

Jonah born

Sea of Kinnereth

| Naaman healed of leprosy |

Mt. Carmel

Kishon R.

•Gath Hepher

•Shunem

•Jezreel

Yarmuk R.

| Elisha restores Shunammite's son to life |

Elisha born

| Elijah fed by ravens |

•Ramoth Gilead

| Elisha traps blinded Arameans |

Dothan•

Abel Meholah?•

KERITH RAVINE

•Tishbe?

Jordan R.

| Elijah born |

3

| Samuel raised in temple |

•Samaria

SAMARIA

GILEAD

Jabbok R.

Aphek•

Joppa•

Shiloh•

| Jonah sails for Tarshish |

| Amos calls for social justice |

| Samuel goes on annual circuit |

| Elijah goes up to heaven in a whirlwind |

AMMON

4

Bethel•

Mizpah•

Ramah•

•Gilgal?

•Jericho

| Samuel born |

Anathoth•

Jerusalem•

| Jeering youths mauled by bears |

| Jeremiah born |

Moresheth•

•Gath

•Tekoa

| Isaiah, Jeremiah, Zephaniah, Haggai, Zechariah, and Malachi prophesy |

| Micah born |

| Amos born |

Salt Sea

PHILISTIA

JUDAH

Arnon R.

| Elijah runs from Jezebel |

•Arad

•Beersheba

Besor Br.

MOAB

•Kir Hareseth

5

DESERT OF BEERSHEBA

Zered Br.

EDOM

6

| Obadiah prophesies against Edom |

0   10   20   30 mi.

0 10 20 30 40 km.

© 1986 The Zondervan Corporation

A • **B** • **C** • **D**

Map 7: ASSYRIAN AND BABYLONIAN EMPIRES

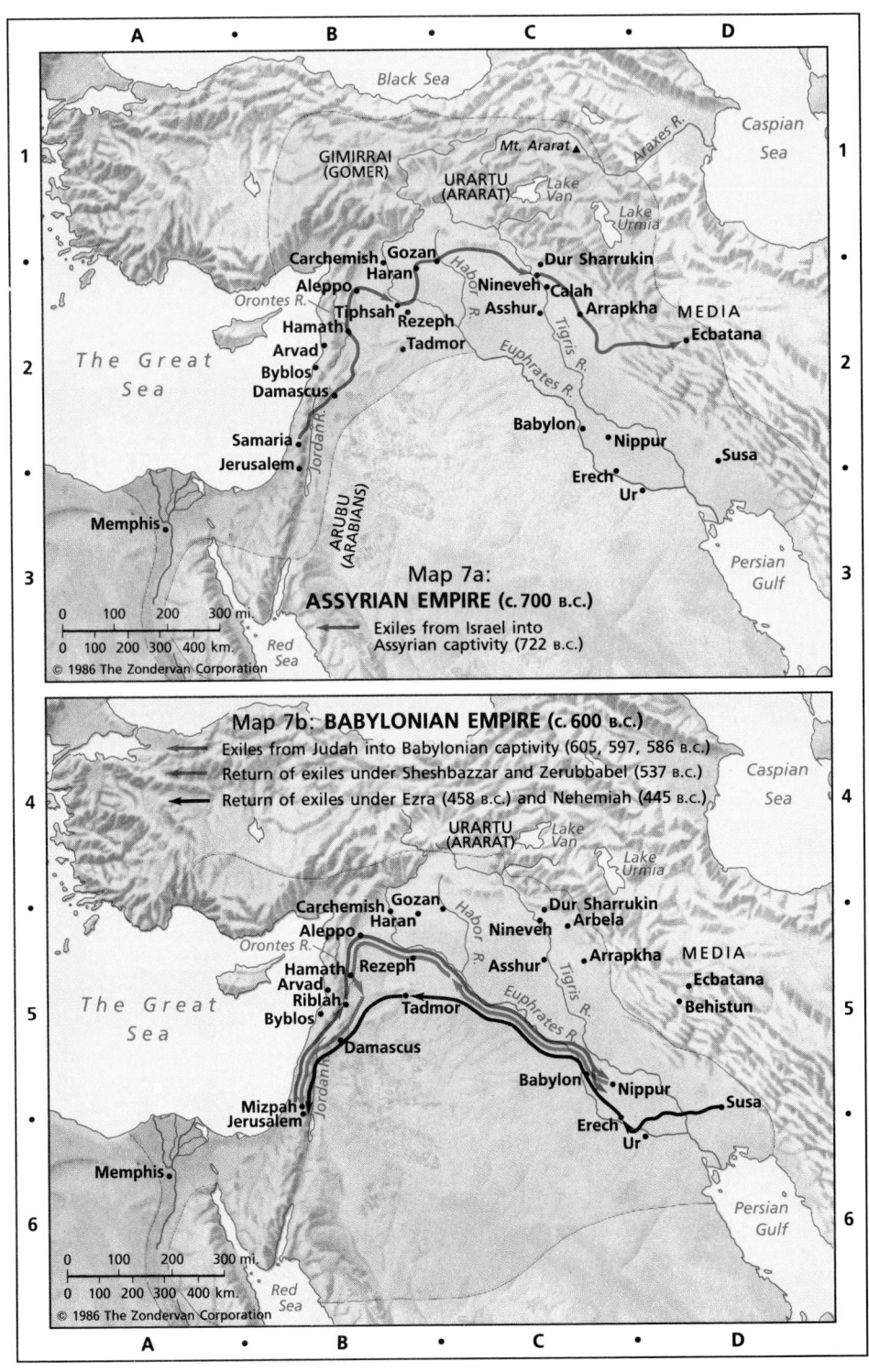

Map 7a:
ASSYRIAN EMPIRE (c. 700 B.C.)

→ Exiles from Israel into Assyrian captivity (722 B.C.)

© 1986 The Zondervan Corporation

Map 7b: BABYLONIAN EMPIRE (c. 600 B.C.)

→ Exiles from Judah into Babylonian captivity (605, 597, 586 B.C.)
→ Return of exiles under Sheshbazzar and Zerubbabel (537 B.C.)
→ Return of exiles under Ezra (458 B.C.) and Nehemiah (445 B.C.)

© 1986 The Zondervan Corporation

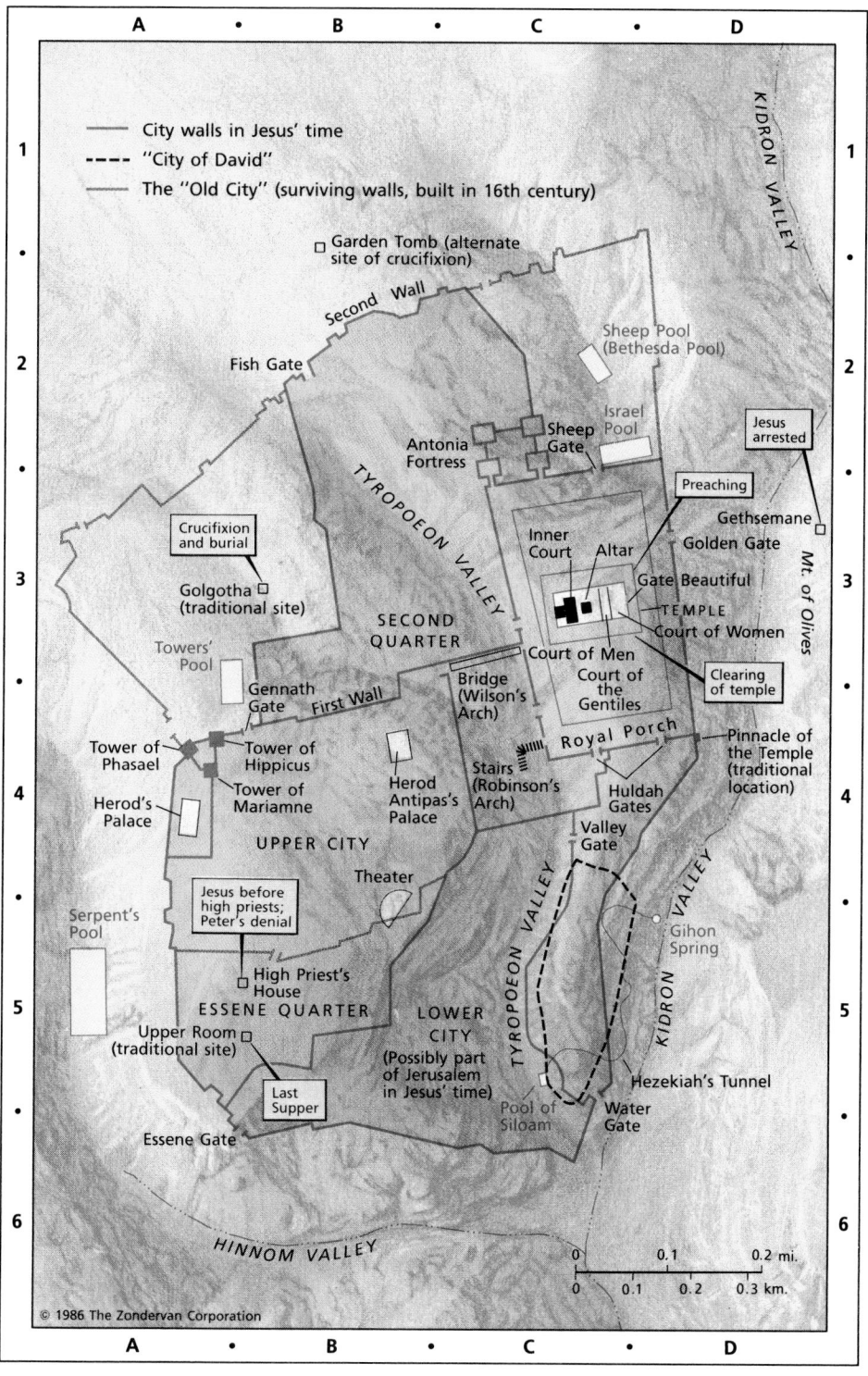

A • B • C • D

City walls in Jesus' time
"City of David"
The "Old City" (surviving walls, built in 16th century)

KIDRON VALLEY

Garden Tomb (alternate site of crucifixion)

Second Wall

Sheep Pool (Bethesda Pool)

Fish Gate

Israel Pool

Antonia Fortress

Sheep Gate

Jesus arrested

Preaching

Gethsemane

Golden Gate

TYROPOEON VALLEY

Crucifixion and burial

Inner Court

Altar

Gate Beautiful

Golgotha (traditional site)

TEMPLE

Court of Women

SECOND QUARTER

Towers' Pool

Gennath Gate

First Wall

Bridge (Wilson's Arch)

Court of Men

Court of the Gentiles

Clearing of temple

Royal Porch

Tower of Phasael

Tower of Hippicus

Tower of Mariamne

Herod's Palace

Herod Antipas's Palace

Stairs (Robinson's Arch)

Huldah Gates

Pinnacle of the Temple (traditional location)

Valley Gate

UPPER CITY

Theater

TYROPOEON VALLEY

KIDRON VALLEY

Serpent's Pool

Jesus before high priests; Peter's denial

Gihon Spring

High Priest's House

ESSENE QUARTER

LOWER CITY (Possibly part of Jerusalem in Jesus' time)

Upper Room (traditional site)

Last Supper

Pool of Siloam

Water Gate

Hezekiah's Tunnel

Essene Gate

HINNOM VALLEY

Mt. of Olives

0   0.1   0.2 mi.
0   0.1   0.2   0.3 km.

© 1986 The Zondervan Corporation

A • B • C • D

1 2 3 4 5 6

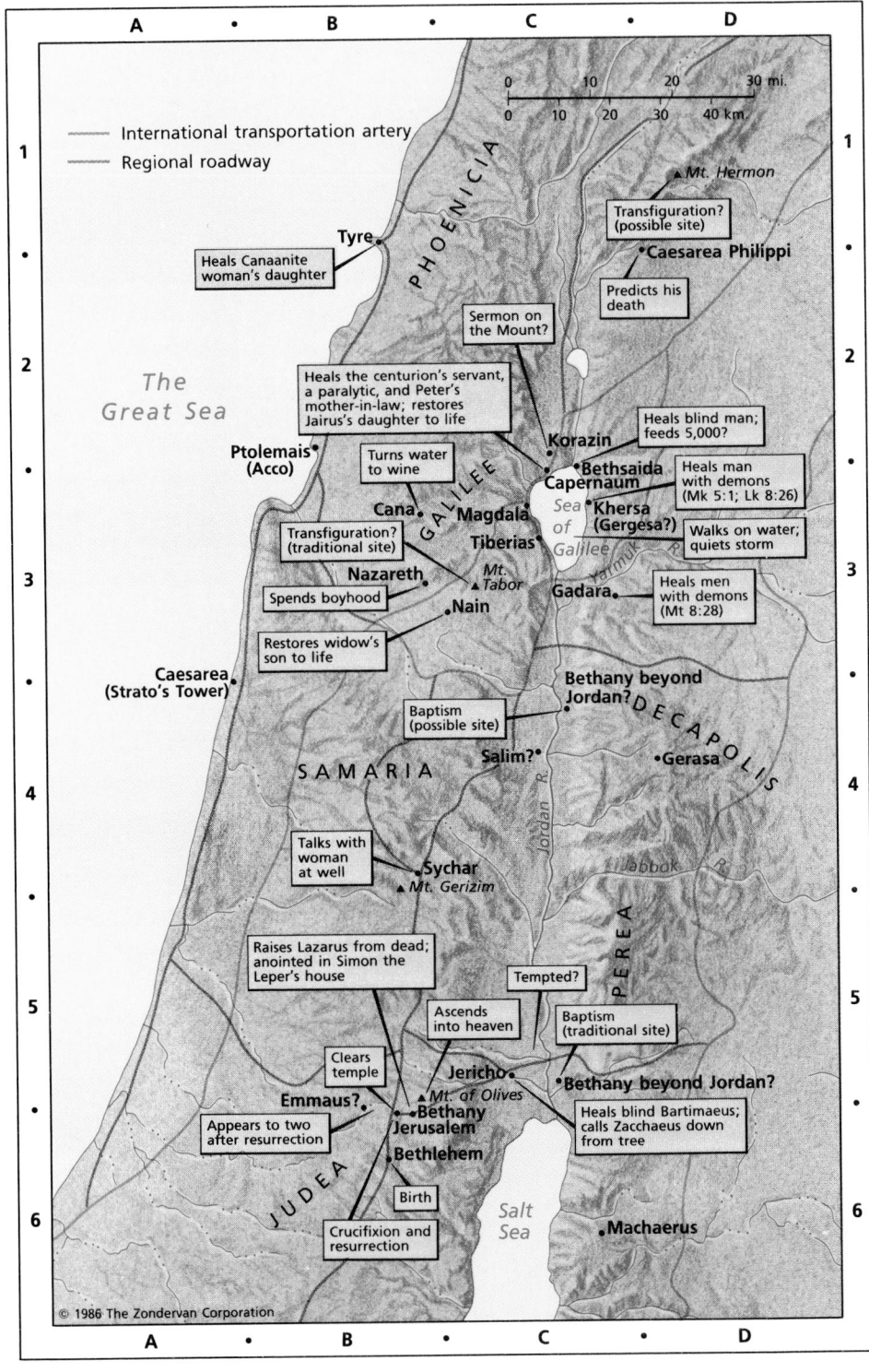

International transportation artery
Regional roadway

PHOENICIA

Mt. Hermon

Transfiguration?
(possible site)

Caesarea Philippi

Tyre

Heals Canaanite
woman's daughter

Predicts his
death

Sermon on
the Mount?

The
Great Sea

Heals the centurion's servant,
a paralytic, and Peter's
mother-in-law; restores
Jairus's daughter to life

Heals blind man;
feeds 5,000?

Ptolemais
(Acco)

Turns water
to wine

Korazin

Bethsaida
Capernaum

Heals man
with demons
(Mk 5:1; Lk 8:26)

Cana

Magdala

GALILEE

Sea
of
Galilee

Khersa
(Gergesa?)

Walks on water;
quiets storm

Transfiguration?
(traditional site)

Tiberias

Yarmuk R.

Nazareth

Mt.
Tabor

Gadara

Heals men
with demons
(Mt 8:28)

Spends boyhood

Nain

Restores widow's
son to life

Caesarea
(Strato's Tower)

Bethany beyond
Jordan?

DECAPOLIS

Baptism
(possible site)

Salim?

Gerasa

SAMARIA

Jordan R.

Jabbok R.

Talks with
woman
at well

Sychar

Mt. Gerizim

PEREA

Raises Lazarus from dead;
anointed in Simon the
Leper's house

Tempted?

Ascends
into heaven

Baptism
(traditional site)

Clears
temple

Jericho

Bethany beyond Jordan?

Emmaus?

Mt. of Olives

Bethany

Heals blind Bartimaeus;
calls Zacchaeus down
from tree

Appears to two
after resurrection

Jerusalem

Bethlehem

JUDEA

Birth

Salt
Sea

Crucifixion and
resurrection

Machaerus

© 1986 The Zondervan Corporation

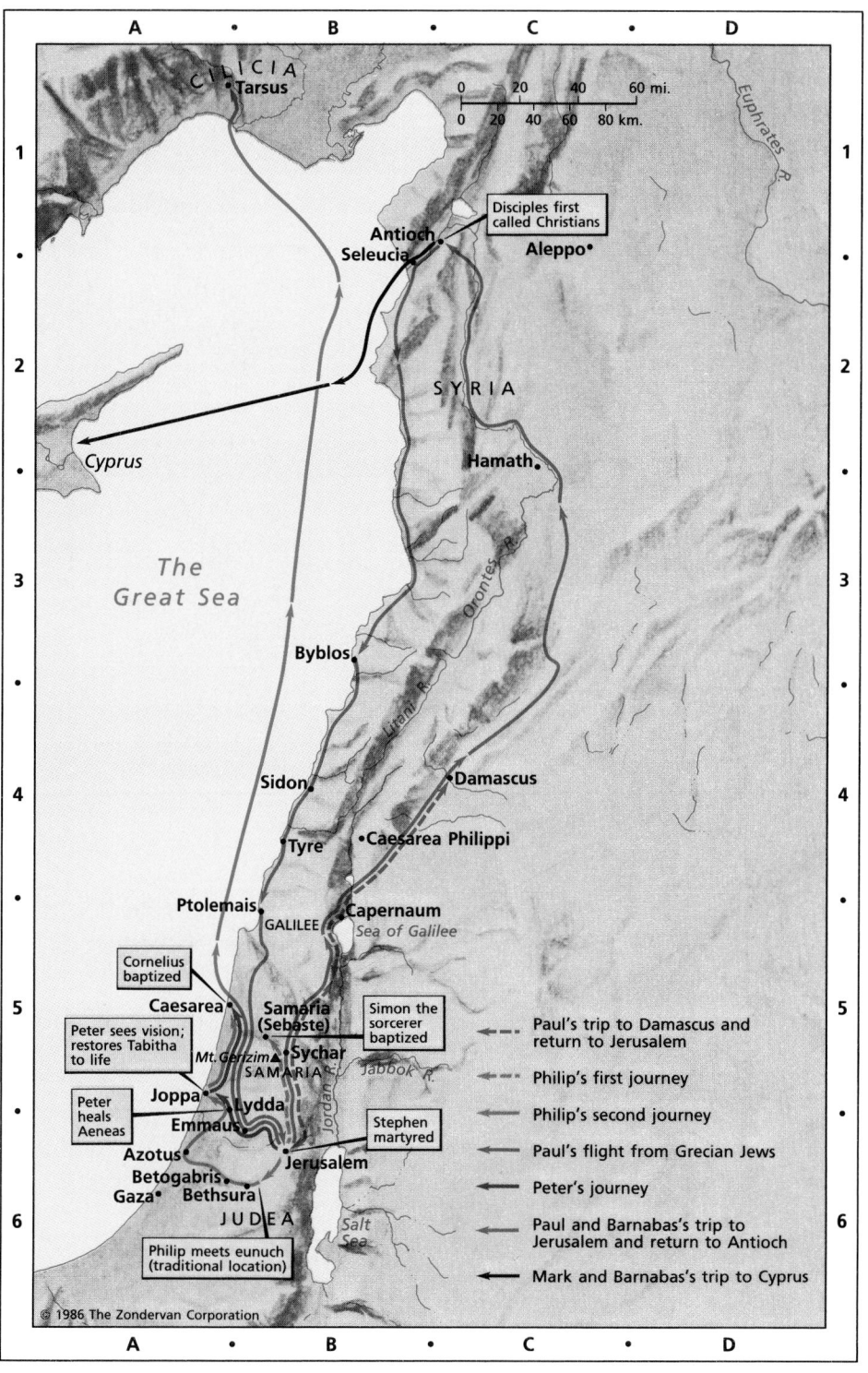

Map 10: **APOSTLES' EARLY TRAVELS**

CILICIA
•Tarsus

0   20   40   60 mi.
0   20 40 60 80 km.

Disciples first
called Christians

Antioch•
Seleucia

Aleppo•

S Y R I A

Hamath•

Cyprus

*The
Great Sea*

Orontes R.

Byblos•

Litani R.

Sidon•

Damascus•

Tyre•

•**Caesarea Philippi**

Ptolemais•
GALILEE

Capernaum
Sea of Galilee

Cornelius
baptized

Caesarea•

Samaria
(Sebaste)

Simon the
sorcerer
baptized

Peter sees vision;
restores Tabitha
to life

Mt. Gerizim▲
SAMARIA

Sychar•

Jabbok R.

Peter
heals
Aeneas

Joppa•
Lydda•
Emmaus•

Jordan

Stephen
martyred

Azotus•
Betogabris•
Gaza• **Bethsura**•

Jerusalem•

J U D E A

*Salt
Sea*

Philip meets eunuch
(traditional location)

Euphrates R.

- - - Paul's trip to Damascus and
return to Jerusalem

- - - Philip's first journey

——— Philip's second journey

——— Paul's flight from Grecian Jews

——— Peter's journey

——— Paul and Barnabas's trip to
Jerusalem and return to Antioch

——— Mark and Barnabas's trip to Cyprus

© 1986 The Zondervan Corporation

Map 11: PAUL'S MISSIONARY JOURNEYS

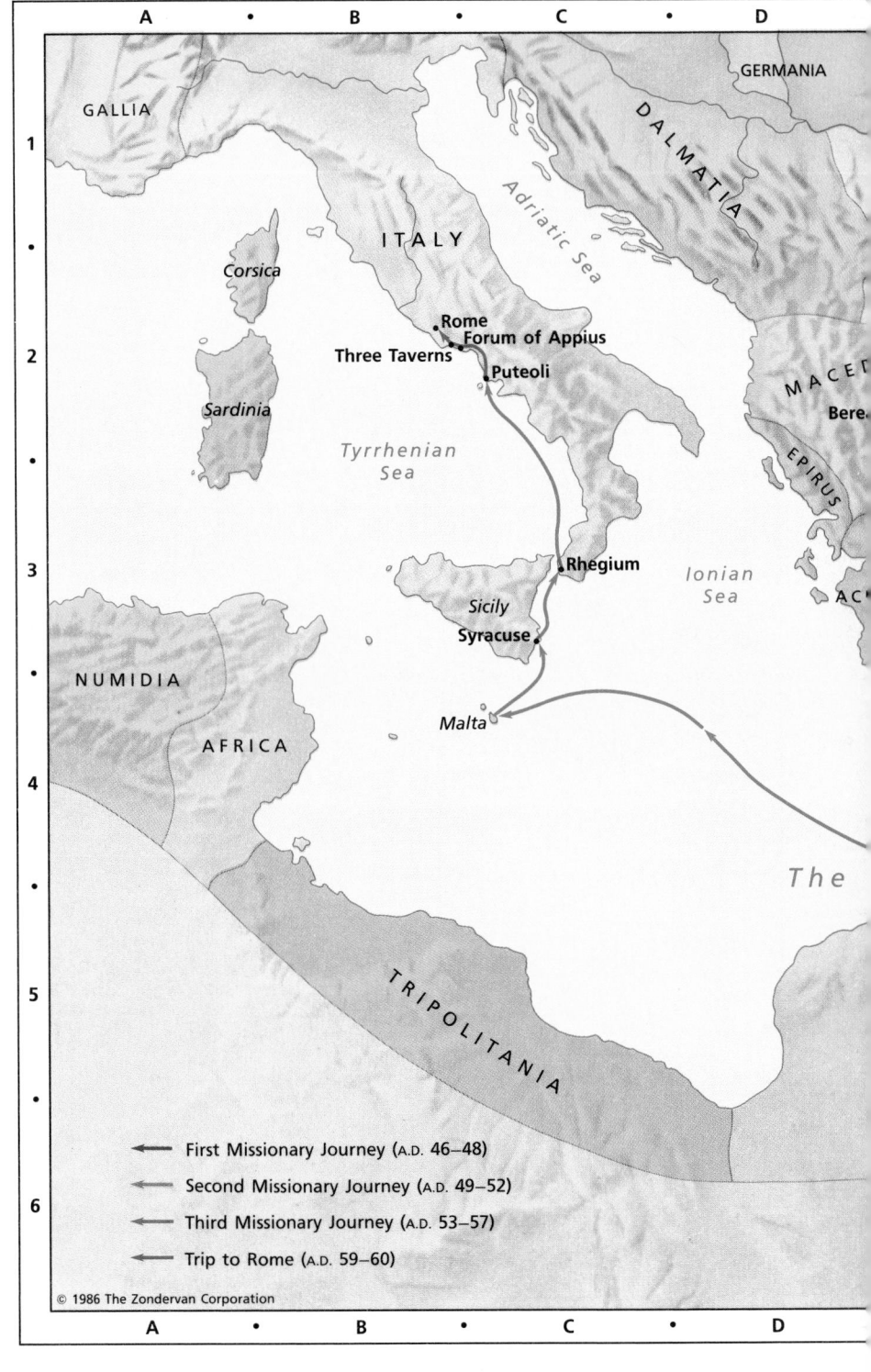

GERMANIA

GALLIA

DALMATIA

ITALY

Adriatic Sea

Corsica

Rome
Forum of Appius
Three Taverns
Puteoli

MACED

Bere

EPIRUS

Sardinia

Tyrrhenian
Sea

Rhegium

Ionian
Sea

AC

NUMIDIA

Sicily

Syracuse

AFRICA

Malta

The

TRIPOLITANIA

First Missionary Journey (A.D. 46–48)

Second Missionary Journey (A.D. 49–52)

Third Missionary Journey (A.D. 53–57)

Trip to Rome (A.D. 59–60)

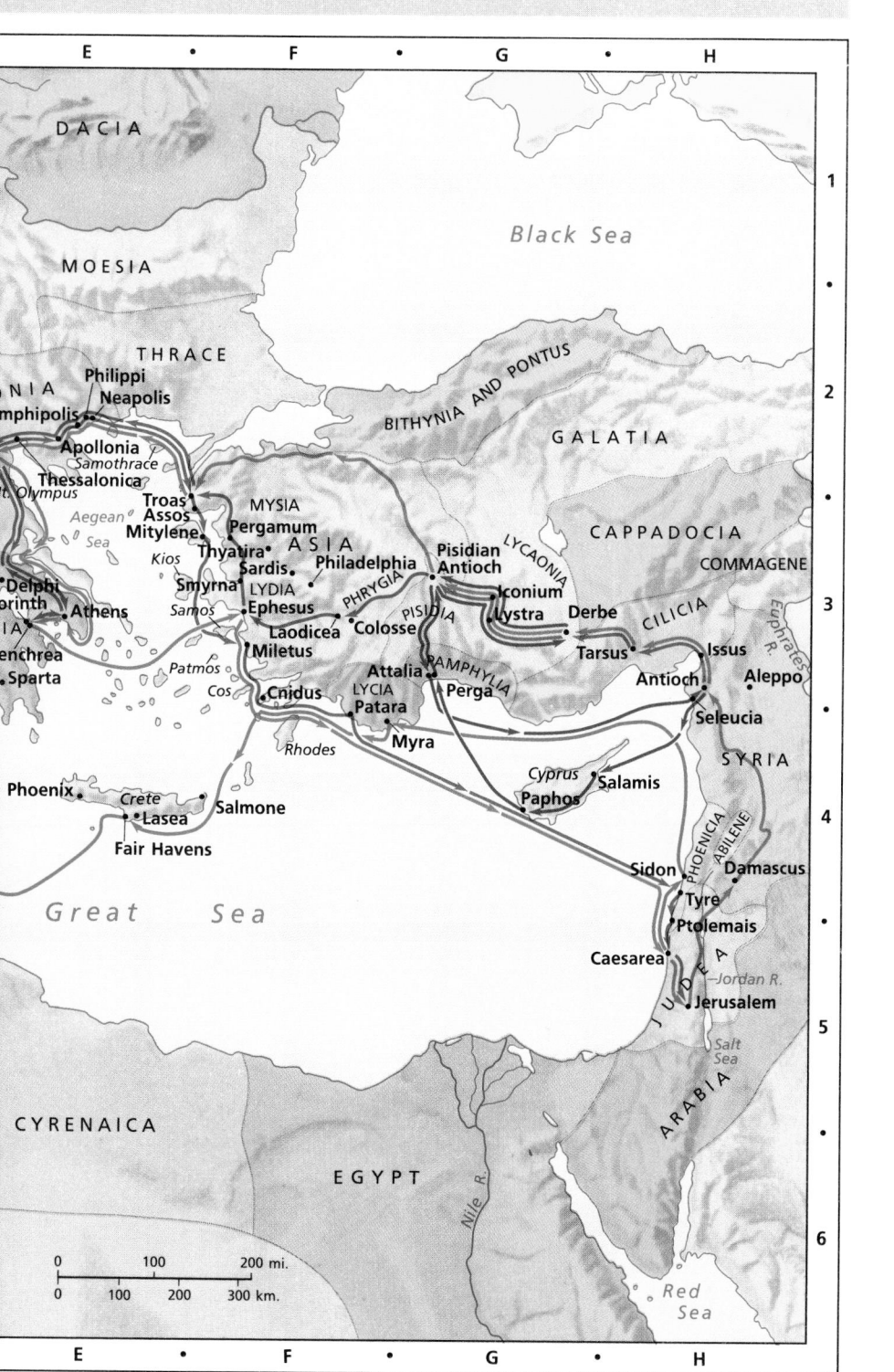

E • F • G • H

1

DACIA

Black Sea

MOESIA

2

THRACE

NIA
Philippi
mphipolis Neapolis
Apollonia
Samothrace
Thessalonica
Mt. Olympus
Aegean
Sea
Troas
Assos
Mitylene
Pergamum
Thyatira
Sardis
Smyrna
Ephesus
Laodicea
Miletus
Delphi
orinth
Athens
IA
enchrea
Sparta
Kios
Samos
Patmos
Cos
Cnidus
Patara
Rhodes

BITHYNIA AND PONTUS

GALATIA

CAPPADOCIA

COMMAGENE

MYSIA

ASIA

Philadelphia
PHRYGIA
Colosse
PISIDIA
Pisidian
Antioch
Iconium
Lystra
Derbe
Tarsus
Issus
Antioch
Aleppo
Seleucia

LYCAONIA

CILICIA

Euphrates R.

3

Attalia
PAMPHYLIA
LYCIA
Perga
Patara
Myra

Cyprus
Salamis
Paphos

SYRIA

Phoenix
Crete
Lasea
Fair Havens
Salmone

Sidon
Tyre
Ptolemais
Caesarea
Jerusalem

PHOENICIA
ABILENE
Damascus

4

Great   Sea

JUDEA
Jordan R.
Salt
Sea

5

CYRENAICA

ARABIA

EGYPT

Nile R.

6

0   100   200 mi.
0   100   200   300 km.

Red
Sea

E • F • G • H

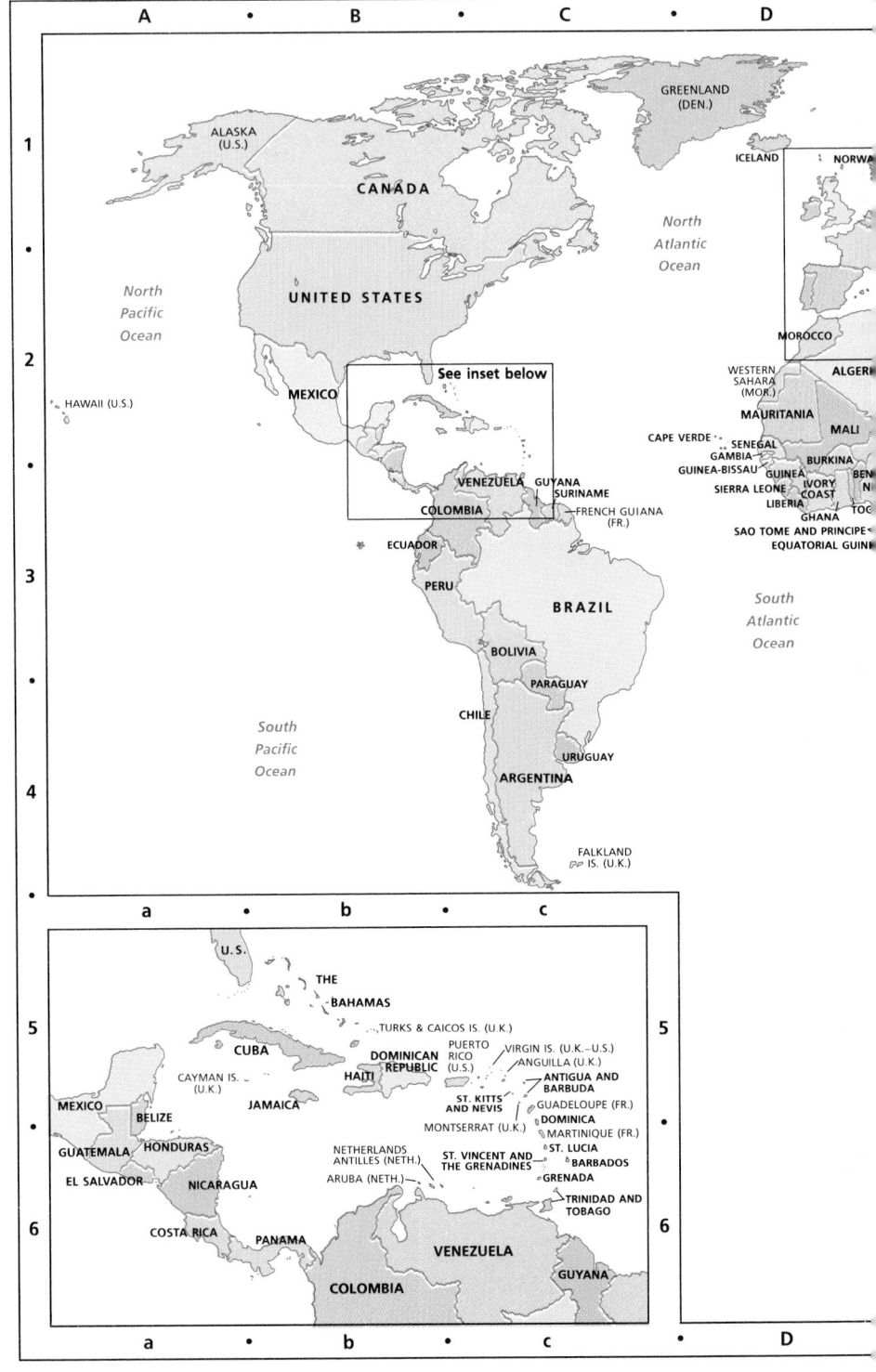

A • B • C • D

1

North
Atlantic
Ocean

GREENLAND
(DEN.)

ALASKA
(U.S.)

ICELAND | NORWA

CANADA

MOROCCO

North
Pacific
Ocean

UNITED STATES

WESTERN
SAHARA
(MOR.)

ALGER

MAURITANIA

MALI

HAWAII (U.S.)

MEXICO

CAPE VERDE

SENEGAL
GAMBIA
GUINEA-BISSAU GUINEA

BURKINA

IVORY
COAST

BEN
N

SIERRA LEONE
LIBERIA

TOG

VENEZUELA GUYANA
SURINAME

FRENCH GUIANA
(FR.)

GHANA

SAO TOME AND PRINCIPE

EQUATORIAL GUIN

COLOMBIA

See inset below

2

ECUADOR

PERU

BRAZIL

South
Atlantic
Ocean

3

BOLIVIA

PARAGUAY

CHILE

South
Pacific
Ocean

URUGUAY

ARGENTINA

4

FALKLAND
IS. (U.K.)

a • b • c

U.S.

THE
BAHAMAS

TURKS & CAICOS IS. (U.K.)

CUBA

DOMINICAN
REPUBLIC

PUERTO
RICO
(U.S.)

VIRGIN IS. (U.K.–U.S.)
ANGUILLA (U.K.)

5

CAYMAN IS.
(U.K.)

HAITI

ANTIGUA AND
BARBUDA

MEXICO

BELIZE

JAMAICA

ST. KITTS
AND NEVIS

GUADELOUPE (FR.)
DOMINICA

GUATEMALA HONDURAS

MONTSERRAT (U.K.)

MARTINIQUE (FR.)
ST. LUCIA

EL SALVADOR

NICARAGUA

NETHERLANDS
ANTILLES (NETH.)

ARUBA (NETH.)

ST. VINCENT AND
THE GRENADINES

BARBADOS

GRENADA

COSTA RICA

PANAMA

TRINIDAD AND
TOBAGO

6

VENEZUELA

GUYANA

COLOMBIA

a • b • c • D

E   •   F   •   G   •   H

SVALBARD
(NOR.)

FINLAND   See inset below   RUSSIA   **1**
SWEDEN

North
Pacific
Ocean

KAZAKSTAN   MONGOLIA

UZBEKISTAN KYRGYZSTAN
TURKMENISTAN TAJIKISTAN   NORTH
KOREA   JAPAN
TURKEY   AFGHANISTAN   CHINA   SOUTH
KOREA
TUNISIA   IRAQ   IRAN
PAKISTAN
QATAR   NEPAL BHUTAN   **2**
LIBYA EGYPT SAUDI
ARABIA   BANGLADESH   TAIWAN
UNITED ARAB   INDIA   BURMA   LAOS
EMIRATES   OMAN   (MYANMAR)
NIGER   ERITREA YEMEN   THAILAND
CHAD   SUDAN   CAMBODIA   PHILIPPINES
DJIBOUTI   VIETNAM
CENTRAL   ETHIOPIA   SRI LANKA
RIA   AFRICAN   BRUNEI
REPUBLIC   UGANDA   SOMALIA   MALDIVES   MALAYSIA
CAMEROON   SINGAPORE
CONGO   RWANDA KENYA
ABON   BURUNDI   SEYCHELLES   INDONESIA   PAPUA
NEW   **3**
ZAIRE   TANZANIA   Indian Ocean   GUINEA
COMOROS   SOLOMON
ANGOLA   ISLANDS
MALAWI   VANUATU
ZAMBIA   MOZAMBIQUE
NAMIBIA ZIMBABWE   MAURITIUS   NEW
BOTSWANA   MADAGASCAR RÉUNION (FR.)   AUSTRALIA   CALEDONIA
(FR.)
SWAZILAND
SOUTH LESOTHO   NEW
AFRICA   ZEALAND   **4**

f   •   g   •   h

FAEROE IS.
(DEN.)   NORWAY   FINLAND
SWEDEN   EST.
LATVIA
UNITED   DENMARK   LITH.   RUSSIA   **5**
5   KINGDOM
IRELAND   NETHERLANDS   BELARUS
BELGIUM   GERMANY   POLAND
CZECH   KAZAKSTAN
LUXEMBOURG   REPUBLIC SLOVAKIA   UKRAINE
SWITZERLAND   AUSTRIA HUNGARY   MOLDOVA
LIECH. SLOV.
FRANCE   CROATIA BOS.&   ROMANIA
MONACO   SAN   HERZ.
MARINO   YUGO. BULGARIA   GEORGIA
ANDORRA   ITALY   ALBANIA   F.Y.R.   ARMENIA
PORTUGAL   MACED.
SPAIN   GREECE   TURKEY   AZERBAIJAN
6   GIBRALTAR (U.K.)   CYPRUS   SYRIA   **6**
MALTA   LEBANON
MOROCCO   TUNISIA   WEST BANK   IRAQ
ISRAEL
ALGERIA   LIBYA   JORDAN KUWAIT
EGYPT

E   •   f   •   g   •   h

Map 13: ROMAN EMPIRE

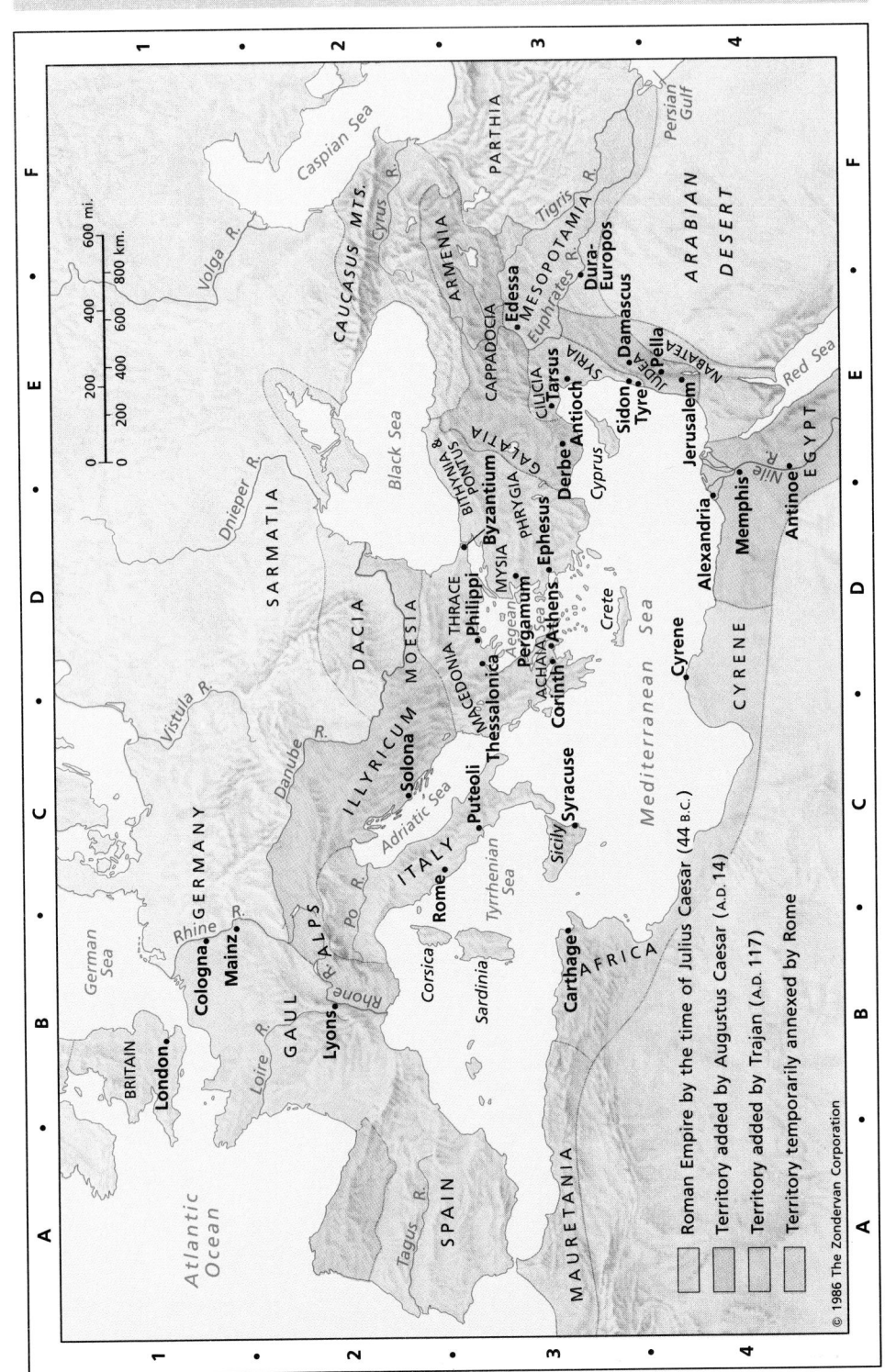

Roman Empire by the time of Julius Caesar (44 B.C.)

Territory added by Augustus Caesar (A.D. 14)

Territory added by Trajan (A.D. 117)

Territory temporarily annexed by Rome

© 1986 The Zondervan Corporation

600 mi.

800 km.

0   200   400   600

0   200   400

Atlantic Ocean

German Sea

BRITAIN

London

GAUL

Cologna

Mainz

Rhine R.

Lyons

Loire R.

Rhone R.

ALPS

SPAIN

Tagus R.

Corsica

Sardinia

Rome

Puteoli

ITALY

Tyrrhenian Sea

Sicily

Syracuse

MAURETANIA

Carthage

AFRICA

GERMANY

Vistula R.

SARMATIA

Dnieper R.

DACIA

MOESIA

ILLYRICUM

Solona

Adriatic Sea

Danube R.

Po R.

MACEDONIA

THRACE

Philippi

Thessalonica

ACHAIA

Corinth

Athens

Aegean Sea

MYSIA

Pergamum

PHRYGIA

Ephesus

Crete

BITHYNIA & PONTUS

Byzantium

GALATIA

Derbe

Mediterranean Sea

Black Sea

Caspian Sea

Volga R.

CAUCASUS MTS.

Cyrus R.

ARMENIA

CAPPADOCIA

CILICIA

Tarsus

Antioch

SYRIA

Sidon

Tyre

Damascus

Pella

JUDEA

Jerusalem

NABATEA

Red Sea

PARTHIA

Persian Gulf

Edessa

MESOPOTAMIA

Euphrates R.

Tigris R.

Dura-Europos

ARABIAN DESERT

Cyprus

Cyrene

CYRENE

Alexandria

Memphis

EGYPT

Nile R.

Antinoe